the university desk encyclopedia

the university desk encyclopedia

Elsevier

Wentworth

ISBN: 0–525–93001–9

Library of Congress Catalog Card Number: 76–51902

Trade edition published by E. P. Dutton, Inc., New York.

Letter from the Chief Editors

If this encyclopedia could tell you about itself, it would say: "I answer your questions." After thousands of years of civilization the bulk of human knowledge almost defies condensation. That's why it has taken more than five years of dedicated effort by a staff of experts that at one period or another has included 34 editors, 172 writers, 12 production people and 39 consultants and advisors, to create a book that can make good this claim in just over 1000 pages. Their work has condensed for you the vital facts from every field of knowledge with special emphasis on relevance for today and therefore a lot of space on science and technology.

But our aim has always been clear. We didn't want to be annoyingly telegraphic or unrecognizably abbreviated. Rather, we set out to give you the facts you want – when and where you want them. To make the kind of reference book you would have wanted to make for yourself. A book to answer questions from your family, your business, your classroom. Questions on subjects ranging from everyday things such as houseplants and US geography to the complexities of bacteriology and nuclear fusion.

To satisfy today's need for answers, condensation and selection are vital. But to make a book that satisfies a hunger for knowledge, condensation isn't enough. We wanted a book that would enlarge your knowledge, a book so attractive you'd want to browse. So, we filled the U.D.E. with pictures – pictures that are not only beautiful to look at but also informative. Where a chart, a table or a diagram could tell you at a glance what it takes some other books a thousand words to explain, we included it. Wherever a map could pinpoint a place for you, we used this too. We were not simply embellishing an attractive volume, but attempting to break through the communication barrier which encyclopedias often maintain, and so to bring the subjects to life.

And, having invited you to browse, we added page-long articles on special subjects to unlock doors and allow a glimpse of what lies behind. Some 46 times throughout the encyclopedia, we have thought it right to depart from our normally brief formula, to create full-scale articles that treat particularly interesting subjects in depth. These subjects have been chosen for their timeliness, and for their timelessness. The topics range from *Biological Clocks* to the newly-revealed *Archaeological Treasures of China*. You'll find Isaac Asimov on *Science Fiction*, John McHale on *Futurology* – and much, much more.

So, you see, when the U.D.E. answers your questions, it answers them quickly and concisely, as a good desk encyclopedia should. But it doesn't turn you off, doesn't begrudge you fuller knowledge if you want it. It's really a kind of combined microscope and telescope. Look hastily through the microscope and there's a quick answer to any reference question you are likely to ask in the course of a day. But take a moment to adjust your focus – study the pictures, follow the fascinating cross-references, browse among the special features – and it becomes a telescope. You'll find yourself scanning a vast field of knowledge reaching as far back as the origins of history and as far forward as the outer reaches of the universe.

Herman Friedhoff

Ben Lenthall

The Editors of the University Desk Encyclopedia

Senior Editors

Courtlandt Canby BA

Philip Gardner MA

Michael Scott Rohan BA

John-David Yule MA PhD

Jonathan Lamède
Andrew McNeillie BA

Science Editors

Paul Barnett

Graham Bateman BSc PhD

Peter Hutchinson BSc PhD

Bridget Gibbs BSc

Associate Editors

Bernard Dod MA BLitt

Juliet Grindle MA DPhil

Howard Loxton

Bill MacKeith MA

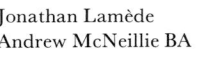

Penelope Marcus BA

Lydia Segrave

Ann Currah BA

Margaret Histed BA

Robert MacDonald BA

John Niespolo BA MA SJ

Michael O'Connell BA BLitt

Elaine Paintin BA

Research and Administration

Mel Cooper BA MA

Dennis Friedhoff

Wendy Johnson BA

Betty Yao Lin BA

Liz Digby-Firth

Denise Ford

Carmen Foulsham

Andrew Ivett BA

John Sanders

Jerome D. Umansko MA

Chief Editors

Herman Friedhoff

Ben Lenthall BA

The Advisory Board of the University Desk Encyclopedia

Dr. Frederick G. Armstrong
Chairman, Educational Consultant, formerly Vice-President, Aspen Institute for Humanistic Studies.

Dr. Noel J. Brown
Director, New York Liaison Office, United Nations Environment Programme.

Lord Alan Bullock
Formerly Vice-Chancellor, Oxford University; Master of St. Catherine's College, Oxford; author of such notable historical works as *Hitler – A Study in Tyranny*, *The Liberal Tradition*, and others.

Dr. Frederick Burkhardt
President Emeritus, American Council of Learned Societies. Former President of Bennington College; former Chairman, National Committee on Libraries and Information Sciences.

Betty Friedan
Founder and first President, National Organization for Women; organized National Women's political caucus; author, *The Feminine Mystique* and *It Changed My Life*.

Dr. Dorothy Gregg
Vice-President Communications, Celanese Corporation.

Professor Anthony Hallam
Lapworth Professor of Geology, University of Birmingham, England.

Professor Vernon Heywood
Head of the Department of Plant Sciences, University of Reading, England.

Professor Emrys Jones
Head of the Department of Geography, London School of Economics, University of London.

Eric Larabee
Author and editor. Former Director of the N.Y. State Council on the Arts; associate editor, *Harpers Magazine*; executive editor, *American Heritage*; managing editor, *Horizon*.

Harold D. Lasswell
Professor Emeritus of Political Science, Yale University; fellow, Center of Advanced Studies in Behavioral Sciences, Stanford University; fellow of the World Academy of Arts and Sciences.

Dr. Lloyd Motz
Professor of Astronomy and Physics, Columbia University. Recipient of the Gravity Research Foundation's first prize for theory of the structure of fundamental particles.

Harriet Fleischl Pilpel
Senior New York attorney; director of Planned Parenthood–World Population; author and lecturer on marriage law and women's rights.

Special Features

Polar Regions by Dr. Frederick G. Armstrong, consultant on the Alaska pipeline project.

Science Fiction by Isaac Asimov, BA, MA, PhD, associate professor of biochemistry, Boston University School of Medicine.

Civil War, US by Courtlandt Canby, BA (Harvard).

Fusion Power by David R. Langford, BA (Oxford), physicist, H.M. Ministry of Defence.

Futurology by Dr. John McHale, director, Center for Integrative Studies, School of Advanced Technology, New York State University.

Archaeology by Elaine Paintin, BA (Oxford), assistant keeper at the British Museum, London.

The Presidency by Larry Sabato, BA (University of Philadelphia).

Life by Professor P. C. Sylvester-Bradley, head of the geology department at the University of Leicester.

Medicine by David Turk, DM (Oxford), MRCP, FRC Path, consultant bacteriologist at the Radcliffe Infirmary, Oxford.

Racial Minorities by William J. Wilson, professor of sociology at the University of Chicago.

Other features contributed by:

Sally Adams MA
Paul Barnett
Graham Bateman PhD
Linda Burke D Phil
Martin Cantor D Phil
Jim Drummond D Phil
Peter R Finch MA
Rory Forsyth
Peter M. Goodwin
Juliet Grindle D Phil
Peter Hanley MD
Peter Hutchinson PhD
Jocelyn Kynch D Phil
Paul Levy BA, MA
Tony Loftas MSc, MI Biol
Michael Maguire MA, B Litt
Penelope Marcus BA
Michael Skelding BA
John Thorp B Phil
Michael Worthington MA, MSc, PhD, ANU
John-David Yule MA, PhD

Board of Consultants

How to get the most from this encyclopedia

Entries and how they are listed.

All entries are listed in alphabetical order. To find the entry you want, just look up its keyword, the word that appears in **bold type** at the beginning of each entry. The overall order is determined by everything that forms the main part of the keyword, whether one word or more; this part is—with a few exceptions—in bold capitals. **ALEXANDER SEVERUS**, therefore, comes before **ALEXANDER THE GREAT**. Sometimes the main part of the keyword is the same in two or more entries. In this case the entries are usually distinguished by a subsidiary part (not in capitals) after a comma: the initial letters *after* the comma will decide the order they come in.

ALEXANDER, name of three Russian Tsars. **Alexander I**
ALEXANDER I (1888–1934), king of Yugoslavia from
ALEXANDER, Grover Cleveland (1887–1950), one of
ALEXANDER ARCHIPELAGO, group of some 1 100
ALEXANDER CITY, city in E Ala., 45mi NE of
ALEXANDER NEVSKY (1220–1263), Russian national
ALEXANDER OF HALES (c1170–1245), English Schol-
ALEXANDER OF TUNIS, Harold (Rupert Leofric George), 1st Earl (1891–1969), British field marshal and
ALEXANDER SARCOPHAGUS, monumental stone
ALEXANDER SEVERUS (208–235 AD), proclaimed
ALEXANDER THE GREAT (356–323 BC), king of

WASHINGTON, industrial city in SW Ind., seat of
WASHINGTON, Booker Taliaferro (1856–1915), black
WASHINGTON, George (1732–1799), first president of
WASHINGTON, Lake, 20mi-long lake in W central
WASHINGTON, Martha Custis (1731–1802), wife of
WASHINGTON, Mount, highest peak of the PRESI-
WASHINGTON, Treaty of (1871), agreement by the
WASHINGTON CONFERENCE, post-WWI meetings

Keywords for places.

We have kept similar entries as close together as possible. In cases where many entries have no subsidiary keyword part to distinguish them, places—countries, states and cities, in that order—come before everything else. Places of the same name but in different countries appear in the alphabetical order of the country. For example, **BRISTOL** in England comes before all the towns called **BRISTOL** in the US. When there is more than one place of the same name in a country, these appear in the alphabetical order of their state.

BRISTOL, port and university city in SW England. It was
BRISTOL, industrial city in central Conn. on the
BRISTOL, industrial borough in SE Pa. on the Delaware
BRISTOL, port in E R.I. on Narragansett Bay, seat of

Keywords for people.

In entries with the same keyword, people come after places. Saints come before popes, followed by emperors and then kings. Kings with the same name are placed in the alphabetical order of their countries. In other cases we have followed normal order of precedence.

Keywords appear in the form most familiar to the majority of readers. Well-known people are given the commonest form of their names; the full name is repeated in the following brackets with birth and death dates. Where the keyword is a pseudonym the real name will appear either in this way or in the text if less well known. We have tried to be sensible about nicknames, preferring in most cases to include them in quotes after the forenames. "Bix" Beiderbecke, for example, is easy to find under **BEIDERBECKE, Leon Bismarck "Bix"**, because there are no other **BEIDERBECKE** entries to confuse it with. In some cases, however, people are so well known by their nicknames that they would be hard to find without them, especially among other similar names; in such cases we have included the nickname in the keyword, and placed the actual name in brackets following, with dates.

JOHN, Saint (d. c30 AD), called John the Baptist, the
JOHN, name of 22 popes and 2 antipopes. **Saint John I** (d.
JOHN, name of eight Byzantine emperors. **John I**
JOHN, name of two kings of France. **John I the**
JOHN, name of two kings of Hungary. **John I Zapolya**
JOHN, name of three kings of Poland. **John I Albert**
JOHN, name of six kings of Portugal. **John I the Great**

LEWIS, C.S. (Clive Staples Lewis; 1898–1963), British author, literary scholar and Christian apologist. Of more

BEIDERBECKE, Leon Bismarck "Bix" (1903–1931), US jazz musician. An accomplished pianist and brilliant

RUTH, Babe (George Herman Ruth; 1895–1948), famous US baseball player. Sold to the New York Yankees in 1920

Finding names with prefixes or titles.

Names with prefixes such as De, Van, Von, etc. appear in the commonest form; for major figures other forms of the name have been cross-referred. Mc is always treated as alphabetically equivalent to Mac. Titles such as Saint, Sir or Lord appear before the forenames but have been disregarded in establishing the alphabetical order.

VAN GOGH, Vincent Willem (1853–1890), Dutch painter and POSTIMPRESSIONIST. His early work in Holland

GOGH, Vincent van. See VAN GOGH, VINCENT.

JOSQUIN DES PRÉS (c1450–1521), major Flemish composer. He traveled widely in Europe; much of his work

DES PRÉS, Josquin. See JOSQUIN DES PRÉS.

Abbreviations that are spelled out.

On page 12 you will find listed the full meaning of the abbreviations used in the University Desk Encyclopedia. Common abbreviations, you will find, are rarely used as keywords. Instead, the full name is given, with the abbreviation in brackets following. For instance, you won't find **CIA** listed. Rather, you'll find **CENTRAL INTELLIGENCE AGENCY (CIA)**.

Subheadings.

Bold type is used not only for keywords but also for subheadings. These normally indicate the divisions of longer entries, breaking them up to make the information easier to find. They also give alternative names for the keywords, or titles of subsidiary entries. Sometimes, so you can spot them at a glance, subheadings are used for important people, members of a family forming the subject of an entry, or concepts within entries—that is, subjects that might otherwise appear as entries in their own right in a larger encyclopedia. Subheadings are also used in particular to indicate the section in an entry to which a one-line cross-reference entry elsewhere refers. Occasionally "sub" subheadings have been used: these are in *italic type*.

Cross-references.

A sophisticated system of cross-references has been used, so that each entry (like a building block) combines with others to enable you to follow up lines of interest and to gain a vision of the true dimensions of any particular subject. These cross-references, indicated by SMALL CAPITALS, reduce the amount of overlapping in different entries, so that we have been able to give as much information as possible in the space. Cross-references indicate entries which provide further relevant information, or which explain an unfamiliar term. They have been used selectively to enable the reader who follows them to glean the maximum information, thus making an index unnecessary. One-line cross-references guide you to where the information has been placed. Those at the end of an article (after "see" or "see also") lead on to related topics. Common sense has determined the form of cross-references in the text, so that, for example, "in the treaty of PARIS" cross-refers to **PARIS, Treaty of,** and a plural keyword may occasionally be cross-referred to in a singular form.

Chemical elements and compounds.

After the keyword for each chemical element its chemical symbol appears in parentheses. Its atomic weight, melting point, boiling point and specific gravity (where known) appear at the end. Similarly chemical compounds have their chemical formula given, and their melting point and boiling point.

CENTRAL INTELLIGENCE AGENCY (CIA), established in 1947 by the National Security Act to coordinate,

MARX BROTHERS, Groucho, Harpo and Chico, famous US film and radio comedy team. The original team consisted of **Chico** (Leonard; 1891–1961), **Groucho** (Julius; 1895–), **Gummo** (Milton; 1894–), **Harpo** (Arthur; 1893–1964), and **Zeppo** (Herbert; 1901–). In films such as *Animal Crackers* (1930), *Duck Soup* (1933) and *A Night at the Opera* (1935) they established their blend of wisecracking verbal routines and frenetic slapstick.

PALEONTOLOGY, or **paleobiology**, study of the remains of living organisms of past eras. The two branches are *paleobotany* and *paleozoology*, dealing with plants and animals respectively. Such studies are essential to STRATIGRAPHY, and provide important evidence for EVOLUTION and CONTINENTAL DRIFT theories. (See also FOSSILS; PALEOCLIMATOLOGY; RADIOCARBON DATING.)

PALEOZOIC, the earliest era of the PHANEROZOIC, comprising two sub-eras: the **Lower Paleozoic**, 570–400 million years ago, containing the CAMBRIAN, ORDOVICIAN and SILURIAN periods; and the **Upper Paleozoic**, 400–225 million years ago, containing the DEVONIAN, MISSISSIPPIAN, PENNSYLVANIAN and PERMIAN periods. (See GEOLOGY.)

MERCURY (Hg), or **quicksilver**, silvery-white liquid metal in Group IIB of the PERIODIC TABLE; an anomalous TRANSITION ELEMENT. It occurs as CINNABAR, calomel and rarely as the metal, which has been known from ancient times. It is extracted by roasting cinnabar in air and condensing the mercury vapor. Mercury is fairly inert, tarnishing only slowly in moist air, and soluble in oxidizing acids only; it is readily attacked by the HALOGENS and sulfur. It forms Hg^{2+} and some Hg_2^{2+} compounds, and many important ORGANOMETALLIC COMPOUNDS. Mercury and its compounds are highly toxic. The metal is used to form AMALGAMS; for electrodes, and in barometers, thermometers, diffusion PUMPS, and mercury-vapor lamps (see LIGHTING, ARTIFICIAL). Various mercury compounds are used as pharmaceuticals. AW 200.6, mp −39°C, bp 357°C, sg 13.546 (20°C). **Mercury(II) cyanate** ($Hg[ONC]_2$), or **mercury fulminate**, is a white crystalline solid, sensitive to percussion, and used as a detonator. **Mercury(II) chloride** ($HgCl_2$), or **corrosive sublimate**, is a colorless crystalline solid prepared by direct synthesis. Although highly toxic, it is used in dilute solution as an ANTISEPTIC, and also as a fungicide and a polymerization catalyst. mp 276°C, bp 302°C. **Mercury(I) chloride** (Hg_2Cl_2), or **calomel**, is a white rhombic crystalline solid, found in nature. It is used in ointments and formerly found use as a LAXATIVE. A calomel/mercury cell with potassium chloride electrolyte (the Weston cell) is used to provide a standard ELECTROMOTIVE FORCE. mp 303°C, bp 384°C.

Foreign words.

If a keyword has an interesting derivation, or is a foreign word needing translation, this is indicated in parentheses. So, occasionally, is an obscure pronunciation, or an alternative name for a place.

Populations.

Populations – the latest available census figures – are given at the end of articles on towns and cities.

MACRAMÉ (from Turkish *maqrama*, towel fringing), the craft of knotting cord or rope. It spread from the Middle

MESSINA, historic seaport city in NE Sicily opposite mainland Italy. Sicily's third largest city and capital of Messina Province, Messina's industries include chemical and food manufacturing. It was founded as a Greek colony c700 BC. Pop 261 500.

MESTA (Turkish: *Kara Su*, Greek: *Nestos*), river in SW Bulgaria and NE Greece. Rising in the W Rhodope Mts, it

MESTIZO (Spanish: mixture), person of mixed racial ancestry, especially one of mixed Spanish and Amerind

Tables

Some information, though essential, would take up too much space if given as part of the main text. We have therefore provided tables where they would give ready access to a set of data.

Countries, states and provinces.

The major entries on countries of the world are accompanied by country panels showing a location map, the national flag, and standard information on languages, religion, currency and so on. Similarly, the entries on American states and Canadian provinces are accompanied by state panels.

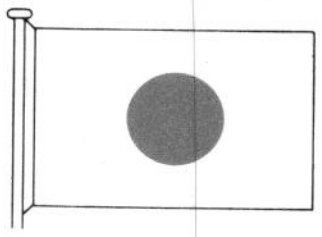

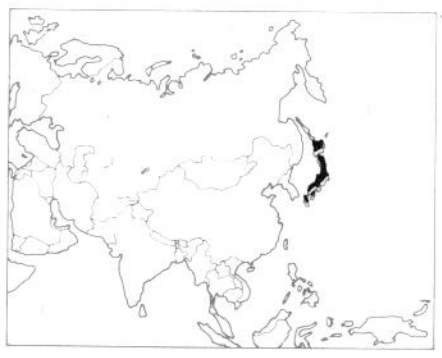

Official Name: Japan
Capital: Tokyo
Area: 142 726.5sq mi
Population: 108 430 000
Languages: Japanese
Religions: Shinto, Buddhism
Monetary Unit(s): 1 Yen = 100 sen = 1000 rin

US Presidents.

Each President of the United States has a full-length entry together with a presidential panel giving his portrait and details of his birth and death dates, term of office and political party.

Warren Gamaliel HARDING

29th US President

Born: November 2, 1865
Died: August 2, 1923
Term of office: March 4, 1921—August 2, 1923
Political party: Republican

Abbreviations

A – ampere
A – mass number
Å – angstrom unit
a – are, atto-
ABA – American Bar Association
ABC – American Broadcasting Company
AC – alternating current
AD – *anno domini* (in the year of our Lord)
a.d.c. – aide-de-camp
ad lib., ad libit. – *ad libitum* (at one's pleasure)
ae., aet., aetat. – *aetatis* (aged)
AF – audio frequency
AFC – automatic frequency control
AFL–CIO – American Federation of Labor–Congress of Industrial Organizations
Ala. – Alabama
AM – amplitude modulation
a.m. – *ante meridiem* (in the morning)
AMA – American Medical Association
ANZAC – Australian and New Zealand Army Corps
AP – Associated Press
ARC – American Red Cross
Ariz. – Arizona
Ark. – Arkansas
asb – apostilb
ASPCA – American Society for the Prevention of Cruelty to Animals
atm – atmosphere
AU – astronomical unit
AV – Authorized Version (Bible)
AW – atomic weight
AWOL – absent without leave

b – barn
b. – born
BC – before Christ
bhp – brake horse power
bp – boiling point
Btu – British thermal unit

C – coulomb
c – circa, centi-
c – electromagnetic constant (speed of light)
C° – centigrade degree
°C – degrees Celsius
Cal – SEE kcal
Cal. – California
cal – calorie
CBC – Canadian Broadcasting Corporation
CBS – Columbia Broadcasting System
ccp – cubic close-packed
cd – candela
CENTO – Central Treaty Organization
CGS – centimetre-gram-second (system)
Ci – curie
CIA – Central Intelligence Agency
c.o.d. – cash, or collect, on delivery
Col. – Colorado
COMECON – Council for Mutual Economic Assistance
Conn. – Connecticut
cos – cosine
cosec – SEE csc
cosech – SEE csch
cosh – hyperbolic cosine
cot – cotangent
coth – hyperbolic cotangent
CSA – Confederate States of America
csc – cosecant
csch – hyperbolic cosecant
CST – Central Standard Time
cu ft – cubic foot
cwt – hundredweight

d – day, deci-
d. – died
da – deka-
DAR – Daughters of the American Revolution
DAV – Disabled American Veterans
dB – decibel
DC – direct current
Del. – Delaware
DIN – Deutsche Industrie Norm
dp – decimal place
dr – dram
DST – Daylight Saving Time
dyn – dyne

e – electron charge, base of natural logarithms
ECG – electrocardiogram
EDT – Eastern Daylight Time
EEC – European Economic Community
EEG – electroencephalogram
e.g. – *exempli gratia* (for example)
EHF – extremely high frequency
emf – electromotive force
emu – electromagnetic unit
esr – electron spin resonance
EST – Eastern Standard Time
esu – electrostatic unit
et al. – *et alii* (and others—persons)
etc. – *et cetera* (and others—things)
eV – electron volt

F – farad
f – femto-
f/ – aperture ratio
°F – degrees Fahrenheit
FAO – Food and Agriculture Organization
FBI – Federal Bureau of Investigation
fcc – face-centered cubic
Fla. – Florida
FM – frequency modulation
ft – foot

G – universal constant of gravitation, giga-
g – gram
g – acceleration due to gravity
Ga. – Georgia
gal – gallon
GATT – General Agreement on Tariffs and Trade
Gb – gilbert
GI – general, or government, issue (US Army)
GMT – Greenwich Mean Time
GNP – gross national product
gr – grain
Gs – gauss

H – henry
h – hour, hecto-
h – Planck constant
ha – hectare
hcf – highest common factor
hcp – hexagonal close-packed
HF – high frequency
HMS – His/Her Majesty's Ship
hp – horse power
Hz – hertz

i – imaginary operator
Ia. – Iowa
id. – *idem* (the same)
Ida. – Idaho
i.e. – *id est* (that is)
IF – intermediate frequency
iff – if and only if
Ill. – Illinois
IMF – International Monetary Fund
in – inch
Ind. – Indiana
IQ – intelligence quotient
ir – infrared
IRA – Irish Republican Army
ITU – International Telecommunications Union

J – joule

K – kelvin
k – kilo-
k – Boltzmann constant
Kan. – Kansas
kcal – kilocalorie
kg – kilogram
KGB – *Komitet Gosudarstvennoye Bezopastnosti* (Committee for State Security)
kgf – kilogram-force
KKK – Ku Klux Klan
kn – knot
Ky. – Kentucky

L – lambert
l – litre
La. – Louisiana
lb – pound
lbf – pound-force
lcm – lowest common multiple
LF – low frequency
lm – lumen
ln – natural logarithm
log – common logarithm
LST – Landing Ship Tank
LW – long wave
lx – lux
ly – light year

M – mega-
m – metre, milli-
Mass. – Massachusetts
mbar – millibar
Md. – Maryland
Me. – Maine
MF – medium frequency
mi – mile
Mich. – Michigan
min – minute (time)
Minn. – Minnesota
MIT – Massachusetts Institute of Technology
MKSA – metre-kilogram-second-ampere (system)
mmHg – millimetres of mercury
Mo. – Missouri
Mont. – Montana
MP – military police
mp – melting point
mph – miles per hour
MST – Mountain Standard Time
MW – medium wave, molecular weight
Mx – maxwell

N – newton
N – Avogadro number, neutron number
n – nano-
NAACP – National Association for the Advancement of Colored People
NASA – National Aeronautics and Space Administration
NATO – North Atlantic Treaty Organization
N.B. – *nota bene* (note, mark well)
NBC – National Broadcasting Company
NBS – National Bureau of Standards
N.C. – North Carolina
N.D. – North Dakota
Neb. – Nebraska
Nev. – Nevada
N.H. – New Hampshire
N.J. – New Jersey
N.M. – New Mexico
nmr – nuclear magnetic resonance
NTP – SEE STP
N.Y. – New York

Oe – oersted
OECD – Organization for Economic Cooperation and Development
Okla. – Oklahoma
O.N. – oxidation number
op. cit. – *opere citato* (in the work cited)
Ore. – Oregon
O.S. – Old Style (calendar)
oz – ounce

P – poise
p – pico-
Pa – pascal
Pa. – Pennsylvania
pc – parsec
PGA – Professional Golfers Association
pH – hydrogen ion concentration
ph – phot
Pl – poiseuille
p.m. – *post meridiem* (after noon)
pop – population
POW – prisoner of war
ppm – parts per million
PRO – public relations officer
pro tem. – *pro tempore* (for the time being)
P.S. – *post scriptum* (postscript)
psi – pounds per square inch
PST – Pacific Standard Time
pt – pint
PTA – Parent-Teacher Association

Q.E.D. – *quod erat demonstrandum* (which was to be proved)
qt – quart

R – röntgen
R – universal gas constant
°R – degrees Rankine (or Réaumur)
rad – radian, SEE ALSO rd
RAF – Royal Air Force
RCAF – Royal Canadian Air Force
RCMP – Royal Canadian Mounted Police
rd – rad (dose)
RF – radio frequency
R.I. – Rhode Island
R.I.P. – *requiescat in pace* (let him/her rest in peace)
rms – root-mean-square
rpm – revolutions per minute
RSFSR – Russian Soviet Federated Socialist Republic
RSV – Revised Standard Version (Bible)
R.S.V.P. – *répondez s'il vous plaît* (please reply)

s – second
sb – stilb
S.C. – South Carolina
S.D. – South Dakota
SEATO – Southeast Asia Treaty Organization
sec – secant
sech – hyperbolic secant
seq. – *sequentia* (following)
sf – significant figure
sg – specific gravity
SHAPE – Supreme Headquarters Allied Powers (Europe)
SHF – superhigh frequency
sin – sine
sinh – hyperbolic sine
SJ – Society of Jesus
SOS – (international distress signal—an arbitrary code)
sp(p) – species
sq mi – square mile
sr – steradian
SSR – Soviet Socialist Republic
St – stokes
St. – Saint
STP – standard temperature and pressure
subl – sublimation point
SW – short wave

T – tesla, tera-
t – tonne
tan – tangent
tanh – hyperbolic tangent
TASS – *Telegraphnoye Agentstvo Sovyetskovo Soyuza* (the Soviet News Agency)
Tenn. – Tennessee
Tex. – Texas
TVA – Tennessee Valley Authority

U. – University
u – atomic mass unit
UFO – unidentified flying object
UHF – ultrahigh frequency
UK – United Kingdom
UN – United Nations
UNESCO – United Nations Educational, Scientific and Cultural Organization
UNICEF – United Nations Children's Fund
US – United States
USAF – United States Air Force
USCG – United States Coast Guard
USN – United States Navy
USS – United States Ship
USSR – Union of Soviet Socialist Republics
Ut. – Utah
uv – ultraviolet

V – volt
v. – *versus* (against)
VA – Veterans Administration
Va. – Virginia
VD – venereal disease
VHF – very high frequency
VIP – very important person
Vt. – Vermont
VTOL – vertical takeoff and landing

W – watt
Wash. – Washington
Wb – weber
WHO – World Health Organization
Wis. – Wisconsin
WMO – World Meteorological Organization
W.Va. – West Virginia
WWI – World War I
WWII – World War II
Wyo. – Wyoming

yd – yard
YMCA – Young Men's Christian Association
yr – year
YWCA – Young Women's Christian Association

Z – atomic number

/ – (virgule) per
% – percent
‰ – per mille (per thousand)
° – degree (angle)
′ – minute (angle)
″ – second (angle)
ε_0 – permittivity of free space
μ – micron, micro-
μ_0 – permeability of free space
Ω – ohm

A

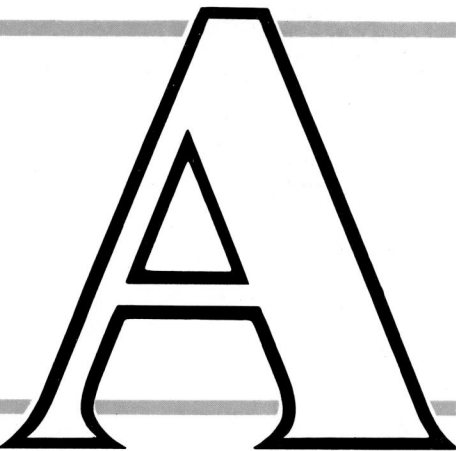

A, first letter of the English and of many other alphabets, derived from the Latin, Etruscan and Greek alphabets. The capital letter "A" is from the Greek *alpha*, which in turn came from an ancient North Semitic symbol. The small letter "a" came from the Roman. (See also ALPHABET.)
AA, (pronounced *ah-ah*), block lava. (See LAVA.)
AACHEN (French: Aix-la-Chapelle), important West German industrial city in a coal region near the Belgian and Dutch borders. A spa since Roman times, it was the capital of the Frankish Emperor CHARLEMAGNE, who was founder of its famous cathedral which holds his tomb. Aachen was the coronation seat of the German Emperors until 1531, and site of two major European peace conferences (see AIX-LA-CHAPELLE, TREATIES OF). Pop 176 800.
AALAND ISLANDS. See ALAND ISLANDS.
AALBORG, historic city of northern Denmark, founded 1342; now an important industrial center and port (on Lim Fjord near the North Sea). Pop 99 815.
AALESUND. See ALESUND.
AALTO, Alvar (1898–1976), Finnish architect and designer. His early buildings were functionalist (e.g., Toppila Mill at Oulu, 1930), as was his famous plywood furniture. But his later work, such as the dormitory at MASSACHUSETTS INSTITUTE OF TECHNOLOGY (MIT), Cambridge, Mass., 1947, emphasized natural materials and free forms.
AARDVARK (Afrikaans: earth pig), southern African burrowing mammal (*Orycteropus afer*) of the family Orycteropidae. A nocturnal animal, up to 2m (6ft) in length and weighing up to 70kg (150lb), the aardvark has a stout body with a plump, ratlike tail, elongated piglike snout, large ears and powerful limbs. It feeds on TERMITES, picking them out of their nests with its long, sticky tongue.
AARDWOLF (Afrikaans: earth wolf), hyena-like mammal (*Proteles cristatus*) native to S and E central Africa. The aardwolf is the size of a large FOX and has a black-striped, yellowish coat with a mane of long hair. Solitary and nocturnal, it spends the day in deserted AARDVARK or other burrows, feeding at night mainly on insects. It defends itself by excreting an obnoxious fluid from its anal glands. Family: Protelidae.
AARHUS, second-largest and second-oldest city in Denmark, a seaport and industrial center on Aarhus Bay on the E coast of Jutland. Pop 237 514.
AARON, first high priest of the Israelites. The elder brother of MOSES, he helped lead the Exodus from Egypt and ruled the Israelites while Moses was on Mt. Sinai. However, he angered God by making a golden calf for the tribes to worship and was not allowed to enter the Promised Land.
ABA, industrial city on the Aba R in east-central Nigeria. Its chief industry is processing the region's palm oil. Pop 157 923.
ABACA. See MANILA HEMP.
ABACO ISLANDS, two narrow islands in the northernmost BAHAMAS, Great Abaco (about 100mi long) and Little Abaco (about 30mi long), settled by Loyalists after the American Revolution. Pop 6 500.
ABACUS, in architecture, the flat upper member of the capital of a column. It is found in the CLASSICAL ORDERS and also in Romanesque and Gothic architecture.
ABACUS, or counting frame, a simple calculating instrument still widely used in Asia. It comprises a wooden frame containing a series of parallel rods divided into upper and lower portions. The rods represent the powers of 10, with each of the five beads on their lower portion counting 1 and the two on their upper portion each counting 5. In the hands of a skilled operator it allows addition, subtraction, multiplication and division problems to be solved with great rapidity.
ABADAN, port in SW Iran, on Abadan Island in the Shatt-al-Arab delta, at the head of the Persian Gulf. A most important oil-refining center and a petroleum pipeline terminus since 1909. Pop 302 189.
ABALONE, or earshell, any large saltwater mollusk of the genus *Haliotis*, native to warm seas throughout the world. The fleshy "body" of the abalone is edible and the MOTHER-OF-PEARL on the inside of the single flattened oval shell is commercially important. Family: Fissurellidae.
ABAMPERE, the unit of current in the CGS electromagnetic system of units (emu—see CGS UNITS). Other **ab-units** include the abcoulomb, abohm and abvolt. They derive from equations in which the PERMEABILITY of free space is set dimensionless (see DIMENSIONS) and equal to UNITY.

Ab-units

Quantity	CGS emu system	SI units
Charge	1 abcoulomb	10 coulomb (10C)
Current	1 abampere	10 ampere (10A)
Potential	1 abvolt	10 nanovolt (10^{-8}V)
Resistance	1 abohm	1 nanoohm ($10^{-9}\Omega$)
Capacitance	1 abfarad	1 gigafarad (10^{9}F)
Inductance	1 abhenry	1 nanohenry (10^{-9}H)

The Aardvark is the only living creature to have hollow tubes (*left*) radiating through its teeth, providing continuous new growth to make up for the wear caused by constant chewing. It also has powerful foreclaws (*upper left*) which enable it to break into termite nests for food and dig the burrows in which it sleeps.

ABBASIDS, dynasty of Arab caliphs descended from Abbas, uncle of the Prophet MOHAMMED. They ruled the Islamic Arab empire, following the OMAYYADS, from 750 until overthrown by the Mongol HULAGU KHAN (grandson of Genghis Khan) in 1258. The Abbasids founded Baghdad (c762) as their capital and made it a center for the arts and sciences. The dynasty was at its most magnificent during the reigns of HARUN AL-RASHID (786–809) and his son al-Ma'mun (813–833).

ABBE, Cleveland (1838–1916), nicknamed "Old Probabilities," US astronomer and meteorologist. In 1869, as director of the Cincinnati Observatory, he published the first daily weather forecasts in the US, becoming in 1871 the first chief meteorologist of the US Weather Service.

ABBE, Ernst (1840–1905), German physicist, research director of and partner in the optical firm of Carl ZEISS and founder of the Carl Zeiss Foundation (1891). He invented an apochromatic condenser LENS for use in a MICROSCOPE.

ABBEVILLE, city in S La., seat of Vermilion Parish, located about 65mi SE of Baton Rouge; founded 1843. Pop 10996.

ABBEVILLIAN, term for prehistoric cultural stage characterized by crude stone handaxes made c540000–480000 BC in the Pleistocene Ice Age and discovered near Abbeville in the Somme Valley, France. The term is rarely used today.

ABBEY, monastic community of 12 or more, led by an abbot or abbess. The first abbey in Western Europe was built in France c360 AD, but most later abbeys were inspired by the example of St. BENEDICT OF NURSIA, who founded Monte Cassino Abbey in S Italy in the 6th century and laid down the monastic rules of celibacy, poverty, obedience, work and prayer. The typical Benedictine abbey was built in a quadrangle with the church on the northern side, and with workshops, dormitories, kitchens and library opening onto it. Later abbeys, such as those of the CISTERCIANS, became more elaborate. Abbeys were important centers of learning in medieval Europe. (See also MONASTERY.)

ABBEY THEATRE, Irish repertory theater founded by W. B. YEATS and Lady GREGORY in 1904, during the Irish literary revival. It fostered playwrights and actors such as J. M. SYNGE, Sean O'CASEY, Barry Fitzgerald and Siobhan McKenna. In 1924 it became the first state-subsidized, English-speaking theater.

ABBOT, Charles Greeley (1872–1973), US astrophysicist, noted for his studies of solar radiation, and director of the Smithsonian Astrophysical Observatory from 1907 to 1944.

ABBOTT, George (1889-   ), US playwright and director of comedies and musicals including *The Boys from Syracuse*, *Room Service*, *Pal Joey*, *Damn Yankees* and *Pajama Game*. He won a Pulitzer Prize (1960) for the musical *Fiorello!*

ABBOTT, Grace (1878–1939), US social worker who administered the first federal Child Labor Act (1917) and US Children's Bureau (1921–34).

ABBOTT, Sir John Joseph Caldwell (1821–1893), prime minister of Canada 1891–92. A lawyer by profession, he served in the Canadian legislature until 1887, when he was appointed to the Senate. As adviser to shipping magnate Sir Hugh Allan, he was involved in the PACIFIC SCANDAL over election contributions, and was out of public office between 1874 and 1880.

ABBOTT, Lyman (1835–1922), US Congregationalist clergyman and author. He advocated the Social Gospel and the harmonization of modern scientific knowledge with orthodox religion.

ABBREVIATIONS, shortened forms of words or phrases achieved by (1) deletion of last letters—Maj., Major; (2) internal contraction—ft, foot; (3) use of initial letters—R.C., Roman Catholic; or (4) substitution—e.g., for example. One type, the acronym, is formed from the initial and other letters of a phrase—AWOL, absent without leave. The sources of abbreviations are often Latin or French.

The use of the period is variable, in some countries replacing omitted letters within a word rather than being placed at the end. In scientific use, it should be omitted to avoid confusion with the multiplication or decimal point.

The fine Gothic-style gate of St. Edmund's Abbey in the English town of Bury St. Edmunds in East Anglia, which dates from the 11th century. England once had many magnificent abbeys built in the Gothic style but, sadly, a great number of them were destroyed during the Reformation, when Henry VIII sought to weaken the power of the church.

A.B.C. POWERS, a loose entente between Argentina, Brazil and Chile, initiated about 1906 and taking its name from the countries' initials. The entente's mediation averted a US–Mexican war in 1914. Its aims were cooperation and mutual nonaggression, though a treaty signed by the three countries in May 1915 had little real effect.

ABD-EL-KRIM (1882–1963), Riff leader of Moroccan resistance to the Franco-Spanish protectorates. In 1921, after routing a Spanish army, he set up his own state. He surrendered to the French in 1926.

ABDOMEN, in VERTEBRATES, the part of the body between the CHEST and the PELVIS. In man, it contains most of the GASTROINTESTINAL TRACT (from the stomach to the colon) together with the LIVER, GALL BLADDER and SPLEEN in a potential cavity lined by PERITONEUM, while the KIDNEYS, ADRENAL GLANDS and PANCREAS lie behind this cavity, with the abdominal AORTA and inferior VENA CAVA. It is surrounded and protected by a muscular abdominal wall attached to the spine, ribs and pelvic bones and is separated from the chest by the DIAPHRAGM. In ARTHROPODS, the abdomen is the rear division of the body.

ABDUL AZIZ (1830–1876), Turkish sultan from 1861 to 1876. His reign saw provincial revolt and extravagant modernization which led, through inefficiency, to the country's bankruptcy (1874).

ABDUL BAHA (1844–1921), leader of the BAHA'I FAITH, founded by his father Baha'u'llah. His 1911–13 tour of the West won many converts.

ABDUL HAMID, name of two Turkish sultans. **Abdul Hamid I** (1725–1789), succeeded in 1774. Turkey was weakened by the Treaty of Kuchuk Kainarji (1774) with Russia, by the forced cession of Bukovina to Austria (1775), and by continued foreign wars and internal revolt. **Abdul Hamid II** (1842–1918), succeeded in 1876. His war with Russia in 1877 resulted in Turkey's loss of control over many of her European territories. He was notorious for the bloody massacres of Armenians in 1894–96. In 1908, the Young Turks forced him to restore a parliamentary constitution, and he was deposed in 1909.

ABDULLAH IBN HUSSEIN (1882–1951), emir of

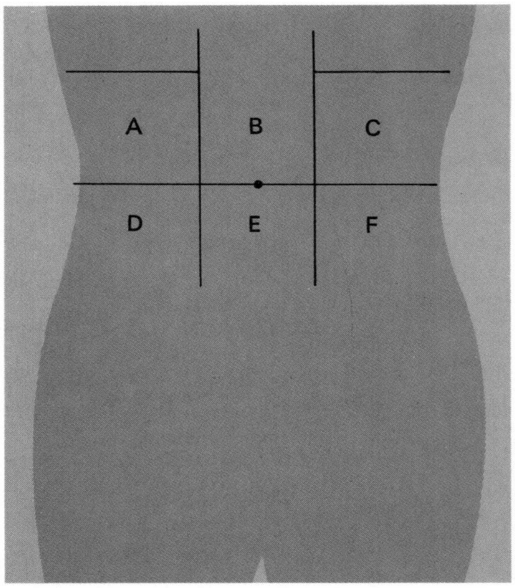

The precise area of the abdomen where stomach-ache is felt is generally an important indication as to what is wrong. For this purpose the surface of the abdomen has been divided into six areas—A. Upper right abdomen, B. Upper middle abdomen, C. Upper left abdomen, D. Lower right abdomen, E. Lower middle abdomen, F. Lower left abdomen. Pain in the *upper right abdomen* is an indicator of an infected gall bladder or of gall stones, an infection of the pancreas, hernia of the esophagus, a stomach ulcer or an abscess in the liver. Pain in the *upper middle abdomen* indicates a damaged stomach wall, an infected gall bladder or pancreas, a stomach ulcer or an ulcer in the duodenal duct, hernia of the esophagus or an infection in the lining of the stomach wall. Pain in the *lower right abdomen* indicates ailments of the ovaries, appendicitis, stone in the ureter, infection of the mucous membrane in the large intestine, infection of the tissue around the womb or ailments of the kidneys. Pain in the *upper left abdomen* indicates ailments of the spleen, infection in the pancreas, irritation of the diaphragm, damaged stomach wall, inflammation of the lungs or malignant growths in the pancreas. Pain in the *lower middle abdomen* indicates pregnancy, formation of stones in the ureter, or disturbances in the muscular mechanisms of the stomach. Pain in the *lower left abdomen* indicates formation of stones in the ureter, ailments of the ovaries, ailments of the S-shaped part of the large intestine, kidney complaints or infection of the tissue around the womb.

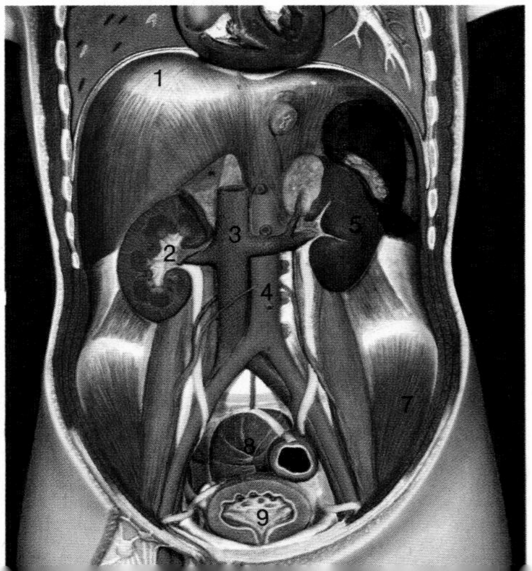

Back wall of the stomach:
1. Diaphragm.
2. Right Kidney.
3. Rena Cava.
4. Aorta.
5. Left Kidney.
6. Spleen.
7. Pelvic Muscle.
8. S-shaped Intestine.
9. Bladder.

Transjordan from 1921; king of Jordan from its independence in 1946. After the creation of Israel in 1948, he annexed most of the remainder of Palestine. He was assassinated by Arab extremists in 1951.

ABDUL MEJID (1823–1861), Turkish sultan from 1839. Made peace with rebellious Egypt and instituted a new liberal era, which helped secure British and French support in the Crimean War.

À BECKET, Thomas. See BECKET, THOMAS À.

ABEL, second son of Adam and Eve, killed by his elder brother Cain. The story is told in the Koran as well as the Old Testament (Genesis 4). The Christian Church considers him the prototype of the faithful innocent.

ABEL, John Jacob (1857–1938), US pharmacologist who first isolated the hormone ADRENALINE (1897) and prepared INSULIN in crystalline form (1926).

ABEL, Niels Henrik (1802–1829), Norwegian mathematician who proved (1824) that the general EQUATION of the fifth degree cannot be solved algebraically. A pioneering memoir on transcendental functions (1826) was published posthumously in 1841.

ABELARD, Peter (1079–1142), leading French Scholastic philosopher and teacher. His career was marked by controversy and by a famous love affair with Héloïse, one of his pupils. Following the birth of a child,Héloïse and Abelard married secretly, and in revenge Héloïse's uncle had Abelard castrated. After separating to take up monastic life, the couple exchanged a series of moving love letters. The church condemned Abelard's original teachings as heretical.

ABELIAN GROUP, a GROUP in which, for every pair of elements a and b under an operation *, the commutative law (see ALGEBRA) holds: a*b = b*a. For example, the set of all integers under multiplication is an infinite abelian group. The name commemorates the work of Niels ABEL.

ABENAKI INDIANS. See ABNAKI INDIANS.

ABEOKUTA, town on the Ogun R in SW Nigeria, 48mi N of Lagos. Main industries are cotton weaving and dyeing. Pop 226 000.

ABERDEEN, Scotland's third city and major fishing port, between the rivers Don and Dee. It is the county seat of Aberdeenshire. The chief industries apart from fishing are those relating to oil, papermaking and granite dressing. Its first royal charter was granted in 1178. Pop 182 000.

ABERDEEN, town in NE Md. settled in about 1800. It has canneries and a furniture plant. Aberdeen Proving Ground, the US Army Ordnance test center, is nearby. Pop 12 375.

ABERDEEN, seat of Brown Co., S.D. Marketing center of a rich agricultural area based on livestock and cereals. Pop 26 476.

ABERDEEN, city in SW Wash., a principal urban center and seaport. It has lumber, dairy and canning industries. Pop 18 741.

ABERDEEN, George Hamilton Gordon, 4th Earl of (1784–1860), British statesman. As British foreign secretary he negotiated the WEBSTER-ASHBURTON TREATY (1842) and the Oregon Treaty (1846) with the US. In 1852–55 he was prime minister of a coalition government that fell due to mishandling of the CRIMEAN WAR.

ABERDEEN AND TEMAIR, John Campbell Gordon, 1st Marquis of (1847–1934), lord lieutenant of Ireland (1886; 1906–15) and governor general of Canada (1893–98). During his term in Canada he governed an unsettled political scene, marked by sectional disputes, with considerable skill.

ABERHART, William (1878–1943), political leader and founder of the Canadian Social Credit Party. He was premier of Alberta from 1935 to 1943. His radical monetary policies were squashed by the federal government.

ABERNATHY, Rev. Ralph David (1926–), American Negro civil rights leader and Baptist minister. After the murder of Martin Luther KING in 1968 he became president of the Southern Christian Leadership Conference and led the "Poor People's March" on Washington, D.C., that year.

ABERRATION OF LIGHT, in astronomy, a displacement between a star's observed and true position caused by the earth's motion about the sun and the finite nature of the velocity of light. The effect is similar to that observed by a man walking in the rain: though the rain is in fact falling vertically, because of his motion it appears to be falling at an angle. The maximum aberrational displacement is 20.5″ of arc; stars on the ECLIPTIC appear to move to and fro along a line of 41″; stars 90° from the ecliptic appear to trace out a circle of radius 20.5″; and stars in intermediate positions ellipses of major axis 41″.

ABERRATION, Optical, the failure of a lens to form a perfect image of an object. The commonest types are chromatic aberration, where DISPERSION causes colored fringes to appear around the image; and spherical aberration, where blurring occurs because light from the outer parts of the lens is brought to a focus at a shorter distance from the lens than that passing through the center. Chromatic aberration can be reduced by using an ACHROMATIC LENS and spherical aberration by separating the elements of a compound lens.

ABERYSTWYTH, city and seaside resort in Dyfed, Wales, at the mouth of the Ystwyth and Rheidol rivers. Home of the National Library of Wales. Pop 10 688.

ABIDJAN, capital and chief port of Ivory Coast, W Africa. A major communications center, its main industries are canning, shipping, the export of coffee, rubber and cocoa. Pop 510 000.

ABILENE, agricultural city in central Kan., seat of Dickinson Co. Its main industries are grain milling and the processing of dairy products. A famous 19th-century "cowtown," it was the boyhood home of former President Dwight D. Eisenhower, is now the site of his grave and a memorial museum. Pop 6 746.

ABILENE, city in W central Texas, seat of Taylor Co. A commercial, financial and educational center, the city manufactures oilfield equipment and processes agricultural products. Pop 90 571.

ABINGTON, town in Mass., 19mi SE of Boston. A major Abolitionist center (1846–65), it is mainly residential. Pop 12 334.

ABIOGENESIS. See SPONTANEOUS GENERATION.

ABITIBI RIVER, flows 340mi northwards through E Ontario, Canada. Its power is harnessed at Abitibi Canyon near Fraserdale and used for mining gypsum and lignite in the area.

ABLATION, in aerospace technology, the FUSION and EVAPORATION of the surface layers of an object heated by frictional contact with air (e.g. a spacecraft on reentry into the atmosphere). HEAT SHIELDS incorporate outer layers which ablate, thus preventing overheating of the spacecraft's interior.

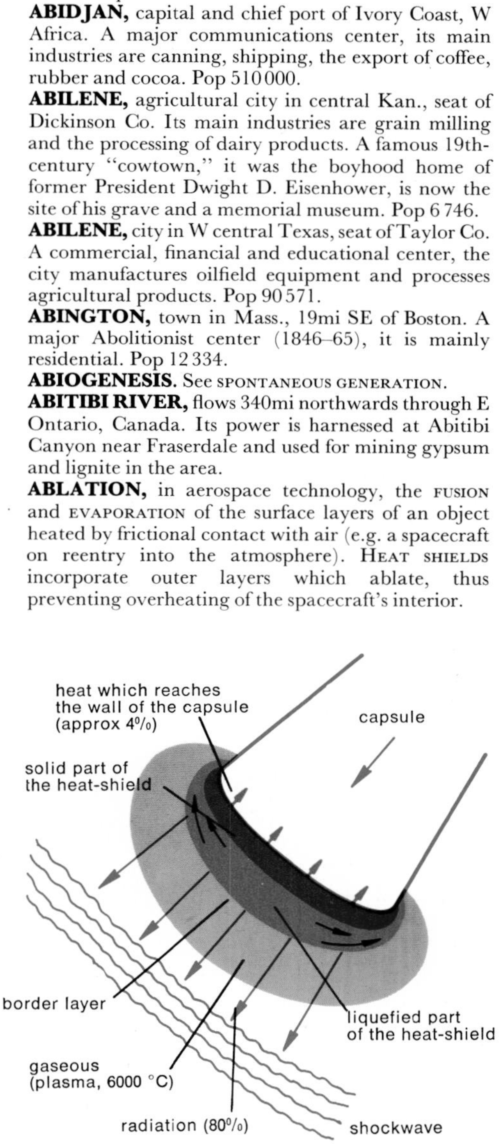

The Ablation Shield (Heat Shield) of a spacecraft is made of a material which burns with difficulty and is a poor conductor of heat. It is reinforced with quartz fibers which toughen the material when it is molten. Friction with the air causes the outer layer of the shield to become gaseous and the border layer between gas and liquid reflects about 80% of the friction heat into the surrounding air in the form of radiation.

ABLATION, in glaciology, the loss of snow and ice from the surface of a GLACIER by melting, EVAPORATION OR SUBLIMATION; also, the quantity so lost.

ABNAKI INDIANS, confederation of North American Algonquian-speaking tribes. Many were Christianized by Jesuits and were allies of the French against the British. After the destruction of their center, Norridgewock (1724), they moved to Quebec.

ABO. See TURKU.

ABOLITIONISM, movement in the US and other countries which aimed at the abolition of slavery. The *Liberator*, an antislavery paper edited by William Lloyd GARRISON, began publication in 1831, and in 1833 the American Anti-Slavery Society was founded in Philadelphia. Some abolitionists used their homes as "stations" for fugitive slaves on the UNDERGROUND RAILROAD, and the movement produced much literature, such as Harriet Beecher STOWE's novel *Uncle Tom's Cabin.* But in 1840 the abolitionists split over the formation of a political party, and John BROWN's single-handed effort to free the slaves in 1859 was a failure. The matter remained a crucial political issue and was a major factor in the outbreak of the Civil War. Lincoln's Emancipation Proclamation (1863) and the 13th Amendment (1865) completed the abolition of slavery in the US.

ABOMINABLE SNOWMAN. See YETI.

ABORIGINES, a mythical Italian tribe held to have been the first inhabitants of that country (Latin: *ab origine*). The term is now applied to the earliest known occupants of any region; hence its application to the AUSTRALIAN ABORIGINES, although it appears that the TASMANIANS were Australia's first inhabitants.

ABORTION, ending of PREGNANCY before the fetus is able to survive outside the womb. It can occur spontaneously (in which case it is often termed **miscarriage**) or it can be artificially induced. Spontaneous abortion may occur as a result of maternal or fetal disease and faulty implantation in the WOMB. Induction may be mechanical, chemical or using HORMONES, the maternal risk varying with fetal age, the method used and the skill of the physician. In most countries, and until recently throughout the US, the practice was considered criminal unless the mother's life was at risk. In recent years, despite continuing moral controversy, abortion has become widely regarded as a means of BIRTH CONTROL.

ABOUKIR (also Abukir), Egyptian village on the Mediterranean coast between Alexandria and the Rosetta mouth of the Nile, on the site of ancient Canopus. The Battle of Aboukir Bay in 1798 saw the defeat of Napoleon's fleet by Nelson and marked the beginning of an Anglo-French rivalry in Egypt lasting until 1904. Pop 8 000.

ABRABANEL, Isaac (1437–1508), Jewish theologian and statesman, born in Lisbon. Forced out of Portugal after King ALFONSO V's death and out of Spain when the Jews were expelled (1492), he became a minister of state in Venice. His best known works are commentaries on the Bible.

ABRAHAM, biblical father of the Hebrew race, first of the patriarchs and regarded as the founder of JUDAISM. The Book of Genesis describes him as a descendant of Shem, and son of Terah, being born in UR of the Chaldees. He vowed to worship God and was promised that his people should inherit Canaan through his son Isaac. However, as a test of faith and obedience, God commanded Abraham to slay Isaac. Abraham unquestioningly obeyed, and Isaac was spared. Through Abraham's faith a covenant of plenty and fecundity was established between God and the Israelite race.

ABRAHAM, Karl (1877–1925), German psychoanalyst whose most important work concerned the development of the LIBIDO, particularly in infancy. He suggested that various PSYCHOSES should be interpreted in terms of the interruption of this development.

ABRAHAM, Plains of, site of the decisive battle in the Canadian theater during the FRENCH AND INDIAN WARS when WOLFE defeated the French at Quebec (1759).

ABRAMS, General Creighton Williams (1914–1974), US Chief of Staff in Vietnam (1972).

Formerly commanding general of US armed forces in Vietnam (1968–72).

ABRASION, the wearing down of a surface when a harder surface rubs over it. Abrasion results from small chips of the softer material being sheared off when they obstruct the passage of irregularities in the surface of the harder material. Unwanted abrasion in BEARINGS can be prevented by LUBRICATION.

ABRASIVE, any material used to cut, grind or polish a softer material by ABRASION. Mild abrasives such as CHALK are incorporated in toothpaste, and others, SILICA, PUMICE or ALUMINUM oxide, are used in household cleansers; but various industrial applications demand even harder abrasives (see HARDNESS) such as CARBORUNDUM, BORAZON or DIAMOND. Some abrasives are used in solid blocks (as with knife-grinding stones), but **coated abrasives** such as sandpaper in which abrasive granules are stuck onto a carrier make more economic use of the material. **Sandblasting** exemplifies a third technique in which abrasive particles are thrown against the workpiece in a stream of compressed air or steam. Sandblasting is used for cleaning buildings and engraving glass.

ABREACTION. See CATHARSIS.

ABRUZZI E MOLISE, central Italian region bordering the Adriatic Sea. It consists of five provinces named after their chief cities: L'Aquila, Chieti, Pescara and Teramo which make up the Abruzzi, and Campobasso which since 1965 constitutes the separate Molise region. It contains some of the highest APENNINE peaks but is generally poor in resources.

ABSALOM, third son of King DAVID of Israel. He fled his father's court after committing fratricide. He later returned and was pardoned, but revolted against David, proclaiming himself king, and was killed, against David's wishes, after the subsequent battle.

ABSAROKA INDIANS. See CROW INDIANS.

ABSAROKA RANGE, part of the Rocky Mts, in S Mont. and NW Wyo. between the Yellowstone R and the Bighorn Basin. Franks Peak (13 140ft) is the highest point.

ABSCESS, a localized accumulation of PUS, usually representing one response of the body to bacterial infection. Abscesses, which may occur in any tissue or organ of the body, often show themselves in pain, redness and swelling. They may drain spontaneously, otherwise they should be incised.

ABSCISIC ACID, formerly known as abscisin II or dormin, a plant HORMONE that inhibits plant growth, induces bud DORMANCY and promotes leaf ABSCISSION (shedding).

ABSCISSA, in CARTESIAN COORDINATES, the distance (measured parallel to the *x*-axis) of a point from the *y*-axis, positive in sign to the right of the *y*-axis, negative to its left. The abscissa of the point (a, b) is thus a.

ABSCISSION, in botany, the process whereby plants shed leaves, flowers and fruits. Controlled by plant HORMONES (abscisins) such as ABSCISIC ACID, leaf drop occurs in many plants through the formation of an intermediate **abscission layer** of cells which constricts sap flow to the leaf and is then broken.

ABSINTHE, a bitter, green, distilled liqueur principally flavored with an aromatic oil (also used in vermouth) obtained from the **wormwood** *Artemisia absinthium*, itself also known as absinthe. Allegations that absinthe is poisonous led to the drink's prohibition in many countries, including the US and Canada.

ABSOLUTE, an adjective frequently encountered in scientific terminology, used to imply a fundamental theoretic or physical significance, as opposed to one merely empirical or practical (as in absolute SPACE-TIME, TEMPERATURE scale, UNITS); to define an actual, as opposed to an apparent, relative or comparative, measurement (as in absolute HUMIDITY; MAGNITUDE), or to describe a limiting case (as in ABSOLUTE ZERO or, for an aircraft, absolute ceiling). In philosophy the term refers to what is unconditional, noncontingent, self-existent or even arbitrary. In 19th-century IDEALISM, the Absolute (Idea) came to refer to the ultimate cosmic totality.

ABSOLUTE ZERO, the TEMPERATURE at which all substances have zero thermal ENERGY and thus, it is believed, the lowest possible temperature. Although

The style of Abstract Expressionism is shown in *Woman in a Landscape* (1970) by De Kooning, whose main preoccupation is the female form; in the chaos of his brushstrokes we see a reflection of the violence and fear of our time.

Kline was one of the pioneers of Abstract Expressionism and his paintings, all on a large scale, show an obsession with the force of the actual brushstroke, much influenced by oriental calligraphy.

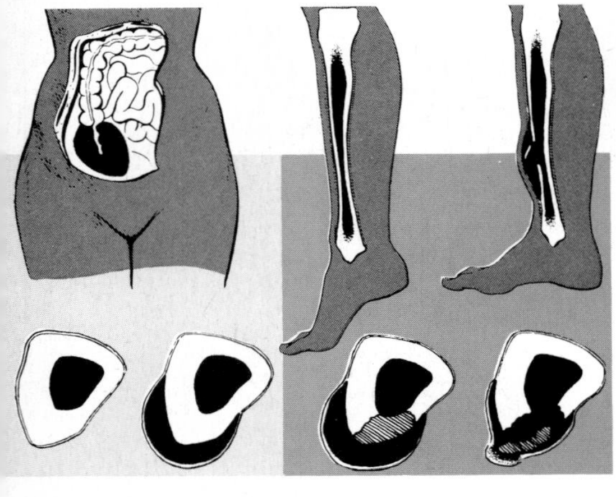

Examples of suppuration spreading (abscesses). *Upper left:* Formation of an abscess around an infected, suppurating appendix. The other illustrations show a suppurating infection of the bone marrow in which a quantity of pus collects in the bone hollow under the periosteum causing some of the bone to perish and be rejected.

A pioneer work of Abstract Art is *Circular Form* (1912–13) by Robert Delauney, one of a series of disk paintings exploring the simultaneous contrasts of colors, though retaining elements of symbolism.

An outstanding example of Abstract Art is Mondrian's *Composition in Red, Yellow and Blue* (1921). In his mature work Mondrian sought to express the harmony and logic that govern both art and the universe.

many substances retain some nonthermal ZERO-POINT ENERGY at absolute zero, this cannot be eliminated and so the temperature cannot be reduced further. Originally conceived as the temperature at which an ideal GAS at constant pressure would contract to zero volume, absolute zero is of great significance in THERMODYNAMICS, and is used as the fixed point for ABSOLUTE temperature scales. In practice the absolute zero of temperature is unattainable, although temperatures within a few millionths of a KELVIN of it have been achieved in CRYOGENICS laboratories.

$$0\,K = -273.16^\circ C = -459.69^\circ F$$

ABSOLUTION, theological term for the act of setting free from guilt, sin or ecclesiastical penalty. In Roman Catholic usage the priest, acting as Christ's intermediary, grants this remission through the oral confession of the penitent. Two of the acknowledged conditions for absolution are sincere contrition and a firm intention of personal amendment.

ABSOLUTISM, form of government in which all power is held by an unchecked ruler. Monarchies in the ancient world were usually absolute, but with the rise of FEUDALISM, the nobility often limited royal power. With the destruction of feudal rights opportunities for absolutism reappeared. In England the STUART attempt to rule by DIVINE RIGHT failed but in Europe, and especially France, absolutism flourished until the early 19th century. More sophisticated 20th-century forms such as NAZISM and COMMUNISM are better termed TOTALITARIANISM.

ABSORPTION, any process by which a substance incorporates another substance into itself, or takes in radiant or sound ENERGY. In chemistry it is distinguished from ADSORPTION in which the adsorbed substance merely adheres to the surface of the adsorbent. In AIR-POLLUTION control and the chemical industries gas absorption is a key process, while the varying extent to which different surfaces absorb SOUND is an important factor in ACOUSTIC design. According to QUANTUM THEORY, an atom or MOLECULE can absorb a PHOTON of ELECTROMAGNETIC RADIATION only if the quantum of energy so received raises it exactly from its present ENERGY LEVEL to a higher one, a fact of great significance for SPECTROSCOPY and for the theory of DYES and COLOR vision.

ABSTRACT ART, term applied to 20th-century paintings and sculptures which have no representational function. The precursors were CÉZANNE, SEURAT and GAUGUIN who believed that the formal elements of painting—color, line and composition—could be used expressively. FAUVISM and CUBISM developed these ideas. The first completely abstract works were painted by KANDINSKY and MONDRIAN in 1912. By 1914 Kandinsky's pictures were composed of regular non-representational forms, and color was used freely. In Paris, DELAUNAY, Kupka, and Morgan Russell developed the Orphist movement which influenced the German painter MARC. Mondrian and van DOESBURG launched DE STIJL in Holland in 1917, which applied abstract theories to architecture and design, and affected British art. In Russia MALEVICH led the movement of SUPREMATISM and El LISSITZKY and Tatlin were involved in CONSTRUCTIVISM. Many abstract artists went to the US before WWII, where they developed the tradition.

ABSTRACT EXPRESSIONISM, American movement of ABSTRACT ART which explored the emotional, expressive power of non-figurative painting. The "action painter" Jackson POLLOCK stressed the creative act and dripped and spattered paint on the canvas. KLINE and DE KOONING are in the same tradition.

ABU BAKR (c573–634), the first Muslim caliph of Arabia in 632, following MOHAMMED's death. He ordered incursions into Syria and Iraq, thus beginning the Muslim conquests. He was Mohammed's closest companion and adviser.

ABU DHABI, an Arab state, member of the UNITED ARAB EMIRATES, located on the southern side of the Persian Gulf; mostly desert, it has extensive oil deposits. Ruled by Sheikh Zayed bin Sultan al Nayahan, it joined with other Arab states in the oil embargo of the 1972 Arab–Israeli war.

ABUNDANCE RATIO. See ISOTOPES.

AB-UNITS. See ABAMPERE.

ABU SIMBEL, archaeological site of two temples commissioned by RAMSES II (13th century BC) on the west bank of the Nile 762mi south of Cairo. The Aswan High Dam construction threatened to submerge the site, but a UNESCO project, supported internationally, saved the temples by removing them and reconstructing them above the future waterline.

ABYDOS, Greek name for a religious center in Middle Egypt inhabited since the early dynastic period (3100–2686 BC) and connected with the god OSIRIS. It is noted for its tombs of early dynastic kings and its 19th-dynasty temple (c1300 BC).

ABYDOS, colony of Miletus in Asia Minor, on the HELLESPONT shore. Here in 480 BC XERXES built a bridge of ships to invade Greece. The city was conquered by Philip V of Macedonia in 200 BC.

ABYSSAL FAUNA, the animals inhabiting the oceans at depths greater than 1km. Here, temperatures range between 5°C and 1°C, the pressure approaches 600atm (at 6km depth) and daylight is absent. Abyssal animals are all highly specialized, some being parasites, others scavengers or predators. Some of these animals are blind; some sport bioluminescent (see LUMINESCENCE) lures and body panels.

ABYSSAL HILLS, small hills on the OCEAN floor, commonly flanking or projecting through the ABYSSAL

The great temple at Abu Simbel was built facing east and so orientated that the early morning sun shone through two great halls into the sacred inner chamber (210ft within the cliff) illuminating the figures of Ramses and the sun gods Amon-Re and Re-Horakhte. On October 21, the day of Heb Sed, the sun rises exactly opposite the entrance in a depression of the hills on the other side of the Nile and shines down the corridor on Ramses II himself. This astonishing natural phenomenon of lighting, ingeniously plotted by Egyptian builders in about 1260 BC, still occurs twice a year although its schedule has been advanced several days by the transfer of the temple to its new location.

PLAINS. They are thought to represent once volcanic seamounts now largely buried by sediment.

ABYSSAL PLAIN, a large flat area of the OCEAN floor, lying usually between 4km and 6km below the surface. These plains, which together cover some 40% of the earth's surface, are formed of thick layers of mud and other sediments.

ABYSSINIA. See ETHIOPIA.

ABYSSINIAN CAT, slender breed of "foreign" type with long tail, almond-shaped eyes and pointed ears. Recognized in two colors: ruddy and red, both having a lighter belly. The Ruddy has a brick-red nose and black paw pads, in the Red both are pink. Each hair of the Abyssinian's coat has two or three distinct bands of black or dark brown on the ground color (known as "agouti" ricking). It has been claimed that the breed descends from cats of ancient Egypt but this has no basis in fact. The breed is intelligent and affectionate but may be unhappy if confined to an apartment.

ACACIA, a genus comprising about 800 species of mainly tropical and subtropical trees and shrubs. Feathery foliage and a mass of fragrant, golden-yellow flowers make many acacias popular garden plants. Other species yield gum arabic, TANNIN and wood. Family: Leguminosae.

ACADEMIC FREEDOM, the right of members of the academic community to freedom of thought and expression. Historically, it dates back to the Greek philosopher Socrates' attempt in 399 BC to have taught his pupils "to follow the argument wherever it may lead." In this century in the US the American Association of University Professors' code of conduct proposes complete freedom of research, but restricts classroom freedom to open discussion of the teacher's own subject. Despite this stand, scholastic immunity has been affected by Boards of Trustees, government agencies which fund some university projects, and student rebels who object to the politics or theories of certain professors.

ACADÉMIE FRANÇAISE (French Academy), a literary, linguistic society officially recognized in 1635. Membership is limited to 40, the so-called "Immortals," and includes prominent public men as well as literary figures. It has been criticized for electing men with personal influence, while often ignoring those with real merit. MOLIÈRE and ZOLA were never elected. Over the centuries, the Academy has produced the *Dictionnaire*, considered the official arbiter of the French language.

ACADEMY, name given to various institutions and societies of learning. The name originated from the Greek olive groves dedicated to the demigod Academos, where PLATO and his successors taught. Notable modern academies are the ACADÉMIE FRANÇAISE and the Academy of Sciences of the USSR. The two leading US academies are the American Academy of Arts and Sciences and the AMERICAN ACADEMY OF ARTS AND LETTERS. The term applies also to special schools such as military academies.

ACADEMY AWARDS, the annual awards ("Oscars") given by the Academy of Motion Picture Arts and Sciences for outstanding achievement in various branches of film-making. The major awards are for best leading and supporting actor and actress, best direction, best screenplay and best film.

ACADIA, the name given to Nova Scotia and neighboring regions of New Brunswick, Prince Edward Island and parts of Quebec and Maine, by the French colonists who settled there starting in 1604. All but Prince Edward Island and Cape Breton passed under British control by the TREATY OF UTRECHT (1713). The French colonists, dispersed by the British in 1755, are the subject of LONGFELLOW's poem *Evangeline.* Those who went to Louisiana are the ancestors of the present-day CAJUNS.

ACADIA NATIONAL PARK covers 65.1sq mi in Me., centered on the Mount Desert Island area. Its mountains, forests and lakes make it an important wildlife reserve.

ACANTHOCEPHALA, or spiny-headed worms, a phylum of worms parasitic (see PARASITE) on vertebrates such as fish and birds. Named for the proboscis, which bears tiny hooks that anchor them to the intestinal walls of their hosts, these worms are so degenerate that most have little more than a reproductive system and simple brain. They often cause fatal infections.

ACANTHUS, a genus of shrubs and herbs native to the Mediterranean region. The deeply-lobed leaves have been much used as motifs in art, notably as decoration on Corinthian columns; in Christian art they symbolize heaven. Family: Acanthaceae.

ACAPULCO DE JUÁREZ, tourist center in SW Mexico, 190mi from Mexico City in the state of Guerrero. Founded c1550, it was once a major trading port with a fine natural harbor but is now famous for its climate and beaches. Pop 234 866.

ACARINA, subclass including MITES and TICKS.

ACCELERATION, the rate at which the VELOCITY of a moving body changes. Since velocity, a VECTOR quantity, is speed in a given direction, a body can accelerate both by changing its speed and by changing its direction. The units of acceleration, itself a vector quantity, are those of velocity per unit time—e.g., metres per second, per second (m/s^2). In calculus notation, acceleration **a** is the first differential of velocity **v** with respect to time *t*:

$$\mathbf{a} = \frac{d\mathbf{v}}{dt}$$

According to NEWTON's second law of MOTION, acceleration is always the result of a force acting on a body; the acceleration **a** produced in a body of mass *m* by a force **F** is given by $\mathbf{a} = \mathbf{F}/m$. The **acceleration due to gravity** (g) of a body falling freely near the earth's surface is about $9.81 m/s^2$. In the aerospace industry the accelerations experienced by men and machines are often expressed as multiples of g. Headward (vertical) accelerations of as little as $3g$ can cause pilots to black out (see SPACE MEDICINE).

ACCELERATORS, Particle, atomic research tools used to accelerate SUBATOMIC PARTICLES to high velocities. Their power is rated according to the kinetic energy they impart, measured in ELECTRON VOLTS (eV). Linear accelerators use electrostatic and electromagnetic fields to accelerate particles in a straight line, but greater energies are obtained by leading the particles around a spiral or circular path (see BETATRON; BEVATRON; CYCLOTRON; SYNCHROCYCLOTRON; SYNCHROTRON).

ACCELEROMETER, a device used to measure ACCELERATION, usually consisting of a heavy body of known mass free to move in only one dimension, in which it is supported by springs. Any acceleration experienced along that line is computed from electrical measurements of the resulting distortion in the springs. Three such instruments set at mutual right angles are needed to measure accelerations in three dimensions.

ACCESSORY. See ACCOMPLICE.

ACCLIMATIZATION, the process of adjustment that allows an individual organism to survive under changed conditions. In a hot, sunny climate man acclimatizes by eating less, drinking more and wearing lighter clothes; furthermore, his skin may darken. At higher altitudes he can adjust to the diminished oxygen by increased production of red blood corpuscles. (See also ADAPTATION.)

ACCOMPLICE, in criminal law, a person who helps commit a crime. An accessory to a crime is considered a type of accomplice, and COMMON LAW distinguishes between accessories before the fact, who encourage others to commit a crime, and accessories after the fact, who obstruct the arrest of the fugitive. The tendency of modern US law is to hold that an accomplice or an accessory before the fact participates in a crime to the same degree as does the principal offender.

ACCORDION, small portable reed organ, used for jazz as well as folk music. Tuned metal reeds are set in vibration by air directed at them from the central bellows through valves operated by piano-type keys on the instrument's right. Buttons on the left produce chords. Although they were known in ancient China, the first modern accordions were built in the 1820s.

ACCOUNTING, the recording and analysis of financial transactions in order to reveal the financial position of an individual or firm. While the bookkeeper merely records transactions and makes no attempt at analysis, it is the accountant who analyses the data thus collected and produces balance sheets and income (or profit-and-loss) statements. On a balance sheet assets must balance liabilities. An income statement balances income against expenditure over a given period, recording any difference between them as a profit or loss, and is used to assess the performance of a firm. All such financial statements are audited, that is, checked for accuracy and fairness by independent accountants. The US professional body for accountants is the American Institute of Accountants, founded in 1916.

ACCRA, W African seaport on the Gulf of Guinea, capital of Ghana. The center of a rich cacao-producing district, it is now a major export harbor. The city grew up around several 17th century European forts and later became the terminus of a railroad into the interior. Pop 564 194.

ACCUMULATOR, or storage battery. See BATTERY.

ACETALDEHYDE (CH_3CHO), or ethanal, a colorless, flammable liquid, an ALDEHYDE, made by catalytic oxidation of ETHANOL. An important reagent, it is used in the manufacture of dyes, plastics and many other organic chemicals. In the presence of acids it forms the cyclic polymers paraldehyde, $(CH_3CHO)_3$, and metaldehyde, $(CH_3CHO)_4$. The former is used as a hypnotic, and the latter as a solid fuel for portable stoves and as a poison for snails and slugs.

ACETATES, compounds in which the acid hydrogen atom in ACETIC ACID is replaced either by a metal (forming soluble acetate SALTS containing the ion CH_3COO^-) or by an organic radical (giving a covalent ESTER such as ethyl acetate, $CH_3COOC_2H_5$). Acetate esters are of great commercial importance, being used as solvents and for the manufacture of plastics and fibers. The various cellulose acetates are used in sheet form as a base for photographic films and also as the well-known fibers, Celanese and Arnel.

ACETIC ACID, or ethanoic acid (CH_3COOH), most important of the CARBOXYLIC ACIDS, is a pungent, colorless liquid used to make ACETATES. It is important in BIOSYNTHESIS. Acetic acid is produced by bacterial action on alcohol in air (yielding VINEGAR), and industrially by the oxidation of ACETALDEHYDE or ETHANOL. Pure ("glacial") acetic acid solidifies to ice-like crystals at 17°C; it is corrosive. MW 60.85, bp 118°C.

ACETONE (CH_3COCH_3), or 2-propanone, the simplest KETONE, a fragrant, colorless liquid used in industry as a solvent and for organic synthesis. It is prepared by fermentation of starch or dehydrogenation of 2-propanol (see ALCOHOLS). Large amounts of acetone occur in diabetics (see DIABETES; ACIDOSIS). MW 58.08, mp −95°C, bp 56°C.

ACETYLCHOLINE (ACh), a substance playing an important role in the transmission of nerve impulses within the NERVOUS SYSTEM. On release from the end of one nerve fiber, it stimulates the adjoining one before being rapidly broken down by the enzyme cholinesterase to choline and ACETIC ACID, of which it is the ester.

ACETYLENE, or ethyne (CHCH), the simplest ALKYNE; a colorless, flammable gas prepared by reaction of water and calcium carbide (or acetylide; see CARBON); it is a very weak ACID. Acetylene may explode when under pressure, so is stored dissolved in acetone. It is used in the oxyacetylene torch for cutting and WELDING metals, in lamps, and in the synthesis of ACETALDEHYDE, VINYL compounds, neoprene rubbers and various solvents and insecticides. MW 26.04, subl −84°C.

ACETYLSALICYLIC ACID. See ASPIRIN.

ACHAEANS, one of the four main ethnic groups of ancient Greece and traditionally victors in the TROJAN WAR (in HOMER synonymous with all Greeks). They may have entered northern Greece about 2000 BC and, moving south, created the Bronze Age civilization of MYCENAE. Other authorities believe they came to Greece only shortly before the DORIANS in the 12th century BC, dominating Mycenae only briefly before being displaced by the Dorians.

ACHAEMENIANS, Persian dynasty dominating much of W Asia (6th–4th centuries BC). The outstanding rulers were CYRUS THE GREAT (founder, reigned 559–529), DARIUS I and XERXES I. It ended when ALEXANDER THE GREAT defeated DARIUS III in 330.

ACHENE, dry indehiscent FRUIT with one seed, as in the BUTTERCUP.

ACHERON, river in Epirus (Greece) some parts of which flow underground. In mythology it was one of the five rivers of HADES across which the ferryman, CHARON, carried the shades of the dead.

ACHESON, Dean Gooderham (1893–1971), US statesman who helped rebuild Europe's economic and military strength after WWII. He served Roosevelt and Truman in the State Department (1941–53), becoming secretary of state in 1949. After the war he promoted the recovery of Europe and worked to curb Soviet expansion by helping to formulate the TRUMAN DOCTRINE, MARSHALL PLAN and NATO.

ACHESON, Edward Goodrich (1856–1931), US inventor who discovered the powerful abrasive, CARBORUNDUM, and devised a method for producing high-quality GRAPHITE. Earlier he had assisted EDISON in developing the incandescent filament lamp.

ACHEULIAN, a lower Paleolithic (see STONE AGE) culture, prevalent about 430 000–130 000 years ago, whose remains were first discovered near St. Acheul (France). The type-tool is a flint hand ax.

ACHILLES, legendary Greek warrior of the TROJAN WAR, celebrated by HOMER. He was dipped in the STYX by his mother Thetis and made invulnerable except at the point on his heel by which she had held him. Joining in the Greek attack on Troy, he killed many men including the Trojan hero HECTOR (in revenge for the death of Achilles' friend Patroclus). Achilles was himself killed when the god APOLLO guided an arrow from the Trojan prince PARIS into his heel.

ACHILLES TENDON, the TENDON from the calf muscles to the heel bone, important in standing, walking and running. In the ACHILLES myth, it was the warrior's only vulnerable part.

ACHROMATIC LENS, or achromat, a compound LENS designed to minimize the effects of chromatic ABERRATION, which is due to the dispersion of light in REFRACTION. This is done by employing lens elements made of glasses of different dispersive powers, traditionally crown glass and flint glass. In practice a given lens can be correctly balanced only for a few wavelengths.

ACID, a substance capable of providing HYDROGEN ions (H^+) for chemical reaction. In an important class of chemical reactions (acid-base reactions) a hydrogen ION (identical to the physicist's PROTON) is transferred from an acid to a BASE, this being defined as any substance which can accept hydrogen ions. The strength of an acid is a function of the availability of its acid protons (see PH). Free hydrogen ions are available only in SOLUTION where the minute proton is stabilized by association with a solvent molecule. In aqueous solution it exists as the hydronium ion (H_3O^+).

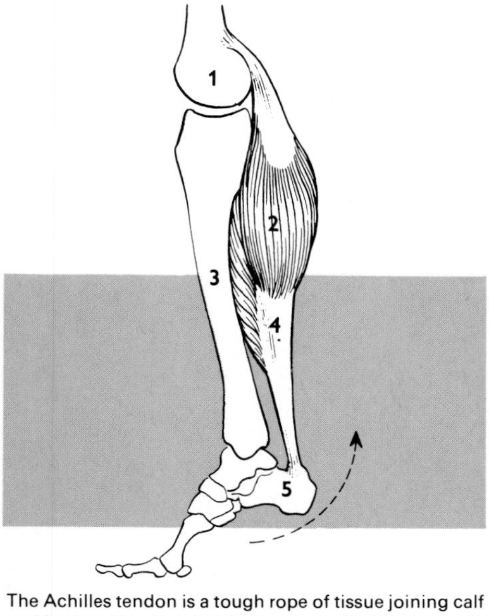

The Achilles tendon is a tough rope of tissue joining calf and heel: 1. Knee joint; 2. Calf muscle; 3. Shin-bone; 4. Achilles tendon; 5. Heelbone.

The Acropolis; the elevated sacred precinct of Athens with the Parthenon in the foreground.

Chemists use several different definitions of acids and bases simultaneously. In the Lewis theory, an alternative to the Brönsted-Lowry theory outlined above, species which can accept ELECTRON pairs from bases are defined as acids.

Many chemical reactions are speeded up in acid solution, giving rise to important industrial applications (acid-base CATALYSIS). Mineral acids including SULFURIC ACID, NITRIC ACID and HYDROCHLORIC ACID find widespread use in industry. Organic acids, which occur widely in nature, tend to be weaker. CARBOXYLIC ACIDS (including ACETIC ACID and OXALIC ACID) contain the acidic group –COOH; aromatic systems with attached hydroxyl group (PHENOLS) are often also acidic. AMINO ACIDS, constitutive of proteins, are essential components of all living systems.

ACID ANHYDRIDES, class of organic compounds derived formally (but not in practice) from CARBOXYLIC ACIDS by elimination of water, of general formula RCOOCOR′; prepared by reaction of an ACID CHLORIDE with a carboxylate. Chemically they resemble acid chlorides, but are less violently reactive. They are used in the FRIEDEL-CRAFTS and DIELS-ALDER reactions, and to make ESTERS.

ACID CHLORIDES, or acyl chlorides, class of organic compounds of general formula RCOCl; prepared by reacting CARBOXYLIC ACIDS with phosphorus (III or V) chloride or thionyl chloride ($SOCl_2$). They are volatile, fuming, pungent liquids, corrosive and very reactive. They react with ALCOHOLS to give ESTERS, with AMMONIA and AMINES to give AMIDES, and with water to give carboxylic acids. They are reduced to KETONES by GRIGNARD REAGENTS and in the FRIEDEL-CRAFTS REACTION. Other acid HALIDES are similar. (See also ALDEHYDES; ACID ANHYDRIDES.)

ACIDOSIS, medical condition in which the acid-base balance in the blood PLASMA is disturbed in the direction of excess acidity, the pH falling below 7.35. It may cause deep sighing breathing and drowsiness or coma. Respiratory acidosis, associated with lung disease, heart failure and central respiratory depression, results from underbreathing and a consequent buildup of plasma CARBON dioxide. Alternative metabolic causes include the ingestion of excess acids (as in ASPIRIN overdose), KETOSIS (resulting from malnutrition or diabetes), heavy alkali loss (as from a FISTULA) and the inability to excrete acid which occurs in some KIDNEY disorders. (See also ALKALOSIS.)

ACNE, a common pustular SKIN disease of the face and upper trunk, most prominent in ADOLESCENCE. BLACKHEADS become secondarily inflamed due either to local production of irritant FATTY ACIDS by BACTERIA or to bacterial infection itself. In severe cases, with secondary infection and picking of spots, scarring may occur. Acne may be aggravated by diet (chocolate and nuts being worst offenders), by HORMONE imbalance, by greasy skin or by poor hygiene. Methods of treatment include degreasing the skin, removing the blackheads, controlling diet or hormones, and exposure to ULTRAVIOLET RADIATION. TETRACYCLINES may be used to decrease fatty acid formation.

ACOMA, Indian pueblo (village) in N.M., 60mi SW of Albuquerque. Founded by Acoma Indians c1100 AD, the original village crowns a 350ft high sandstone mesa. It remains a center for traditional Indian ceremonies.

ACONCAGUA, snowcapped peak in the ANDES (22 834ft), the highest in the W Hemisphere. The summit is in NW Argentina, the W slopes in Chile. It was first climbed by E. A. Fitzgerald's expedition in 1897.

ACONITES, also known as monkshood or **wolfsbane**, a genus (*Aconitum*) of herbaceous PERENNIAL plants widespread in the N hemisphere. Many are cultivated for their showy racemes (see INFLORESCENCE) of purplish-blue, yellow or white hood-shaped flowers. Aconite roots are a source of the poisonous ALKALOID aconitine, at one time used extensively in medicine. Family: Ranunculaceae.

ACORN WORM (Enteropneusta), a class of worm-like marine animals with an acorn-shaped proboscis. They burrow in the intertidal zone on sandy or muddy shores, feeding on nutrients in the sand. Most are about 0.1m (4in) in length. Phylum: Chordata.

ACOUSTICS, the science of SOUND, dealing with its production, transmission and effects. Engineering acoustics deals with the design of sound-systems and their components, such as MICROPHONES, headphones and LOUDSPEAKERS; musical acoustics is concerned with the construction of musical instruments, and ULTRASONICS studies sounds having frequencies too high for men to hear them. Architectural acoustics gives design principles of rooms and buildings having optimum acoustic properties. This is particularly important for auditoriums, where the whole audience must be able to hear the speaker or performers clearly and without ECHOES. Also, the **reverberation time** (the time taken for the sound to decay to one millionth of its original intensity) must be matched to the intended uses of the hall; for speech it should be less than 1s; for chamber music between 1s and 2s; for larger scale works, from 2s to 3.5s. All this is achieved by attending to the geometry and furnishings of the hall and incorporating the appropriate sound-absorbing, diffusing and reflecting surfaces. **Anechoic chambers,** used for testing acoustic equipment, are completely surfaced with diffusing and absorbing

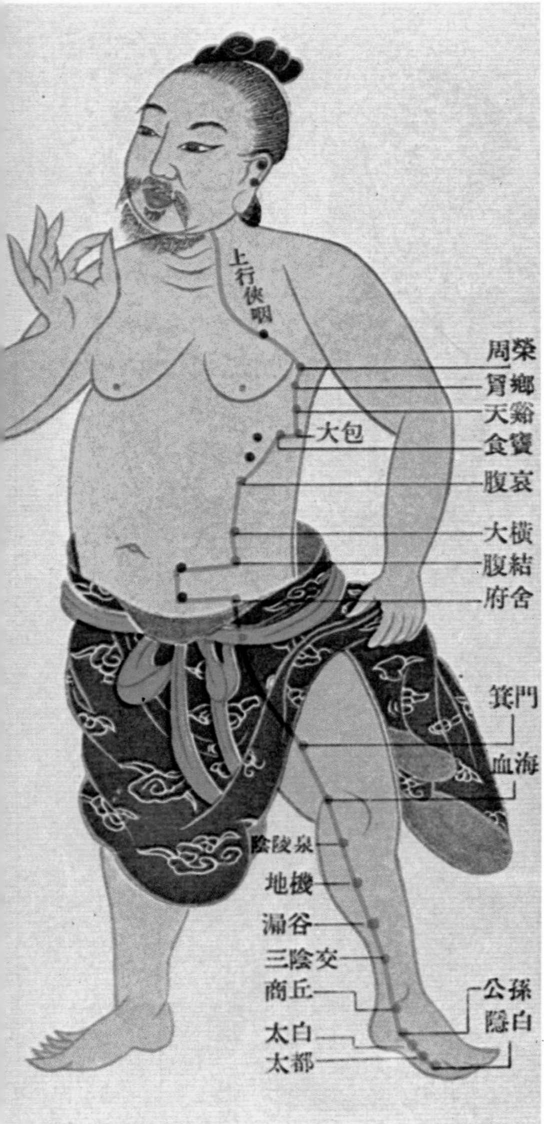

One of the main acupuncture channels, shown in a Chinese illustration from the Ming dynasty (1368–1644). The major areas and their functions are linked with the acupuncture treatment of ailments connected with them.

materials so that reverberation is eliminated. **Noise insulation engineering** is a further increasingly important branch of acoustics.

ACQUIRED CHARACTERISTICS, modifications in an organism resulting from interaction with its environment. In 1801 LAMARCK proposed an evolutionary theory in which the assumption that acquired characteristics could be inherited provided the mechanism for species divergence. In later editions of *The Origin of Species*, DARWIN moved towards accepting this explanation in parallel to that of NATURAL SELECTION, but eventually the Lamarckian mechanism was entirely discounted. It is now thought, however, that organisms which reproduce asexually (see REPRODUCTION) can pass on acquired characteristics. (See also ADAPTATION; EVOLUTION.)

ACRE (AKKO), historic seaport in NW Israel on the Mediterranean Sea. It was the Old Testament Akko and the New Testament Ptolemais. Under Christian crusaders (1104–1291) it was a door to Asia for Europe's pilgrims and traders. Pop 33 900.

ACROPHOBIA, a morbid fear of heights, sometimes associated with physical symptoms; often an isolated PHOBIA in otherwise normal people.

ACROPOLIS (Greek: high city), the fortified hilltop site of an ancient Greek city. Such places eventually became sanctuaries for city gods and centers of religious ceremonies. Remains of their defenses and temples are known from the sites of many ancient Greek cities. The most famous is the Acropolis of ATHENS, with its Parthenon.

ACROSTIC, written composition where the initial or final letters (sometimes both) in successive lines spell a word or phrase. A popular verse form among the rhetoricians of antiquity, it appears now in literary puzzles.

ACTAEON, in Greek mythology, a hunter who chanced to see the goddess Artemis bathing. For this she changed him into a stag, and his own dogs tore him to pieces.

ACTH (Adrenocorticotrophic Hormone), or corticotropin, a HORMONE secreted by the PITUITARY GLAND which stimulates the secretion of various STEROID hormones from the cortex of the ADRENAL GLANDS. ACTH has been used in the treatment of a number of diseases including MULTIPLE SCLEROSIS.

ACTING. See MIME; MOTION PICTURES; STANISLAVSKY, CONSTANTIN; THEATER AND DRAMA.

ACTINIDES, the 15 elements with atomic numbers (see ATOM) 89–103, beginning with ACTINIUM, analogous to the LANTHANUM SERIES, though rather more diverse in properties. They are separated by ion-exchange CHROMATOGRAPHY. The elements through uranium occur in nature; except actinium, they show higher valencies than +3. The TRANSURANIUM ELEMENTS are synthetic; the +3 valence state becomes progressively more stable, and higher valencies less stable. (See also PERIODIC TABLE.)

ACTINIUM (Ac), radioactive TRANSITION ELEMENT in Group IIIB of the PERIODIC TABLE, resembling LANTHANUM; it occurs in URANIUM ores, and Ac^{227} (half-life 22yr) is formed by irradiation of RADIUM. It is the prototypical member of the ACTINIDES. (For the **Actinium Series**, see RADIOACTIVITY.) AW 227, mp 1050°C, sg 10.

ACTINOMYCETES, a large group of filamentous mold-like bacteria found in all types of soil. They help maintain soil fertility by their action in breaking down organic matter, and they are valuable as a source of ANTIBIOTICS such as STREPTOMYCIN.

ACTINOZOA. See ANTHOZOA.

ACTION FRANÇAISE, French nationalist and anti-republican movement, formed in 1898 and led by Charles MAURRAS. Its newspaper *Action Française* (1908–44) advocated extreme rightwing monarchism. Although banned in 1936, the movement revived to make a pro-VICHY stand in WWII.

ACTION PAINTING. See ABSTRACT EXPRESSIONISM.

ACTIUM (now Akra Nikolaos), promontory on the W coast of Greece. A great sea battle was fought near it in 31 BC when Octavian's naval forces crushed those of Mark ANTONY and CLEOPATRA. Victory gave mastery of the Roman world to Octavian, later the first Roman emperor AUGUSTUS.

ACTIVATION ENERGY, the ENERGY which must be supplied to molecules to enable them to react together, usually obtained from their kinetic (thermal) energy. It represents the energy above the ground state of a transient activation complex which decomposes to give the products. (See also KINETICS, CHEMICAL.)

ACT OF GOD, an unforeseeable and disruptive natural event such as an earthquake, flood or storm. Acts of God may figure in insurance policies as causes of damage for which insurance companies disclaim liability.

ACT OF SETTLEMENT, British parliamentary act of 1701 securing the succession of the Hanoverian line. It increased parliamentary control over the monarch, who was also required to belong to the Protestant CHURCH OF ENGLAND.

ACT OF UNION, four acts of the British parliament uniting England with Wales (1536), Scotland (1707) and Ireland (1801), and uniting Upper and Lower Canada (1840).

ACTON, town in NE Mass., 13mi S of Lowell. Pop 14 770.

ACTON, John Emerich Edward Dalberg Acton, 1st Baron (1834–1902), English Catholic historian and moralist, proponent of the Christian liberal ethic. He attacked nationalism, racism and authoritarianism and made the famous remark: "All power tends to corrupt, and absolute power corrupts absolutely." Lord Acton introduced German research methods into English history and launched the monumental *Cambridge Modern History*.

ACTORS STUDIO, the professional workshop for actors, established in New York City in 1947; Lee STRASBERG became director in 1948. The school's training, often called "the Method," is based on the teachings of Constantin STANISLAVSKI and stresses an actor's psychological interpretation of his role and emotional identification with the personality of the character he plays.

ACTS OF THE APOSTLES, fifth book of the New Testament, a unique history of the early Christian Church. Probably written between 60 and 90 AD by the Evangelist Luke, it is a continuation of St. Luke's Gospel and deals mainly with the deeds of the apostles Peter and Paul. Events described include the descent of the Holy Spirit at PENTECOST, St. Stephen's martyrdom, and St. Paul's conversion, journeys and missionary work.

ACTUARY, a person who calculates insurance risks and premiums. Actuaries working for insurance organizations use statistics and mathematical probability to calculate policyholders' premiums and the cash reserves needed by insurers to meet possible claims.

ACUPUNCTURE, an ancient Chinese medical practice in which fine needles are inserted into the body at specified points, used for relieving pain and in treating a variety of conditions including MALARIA and RHEUMATISM. It was formerly believed that this would correct the imbalance between the opposing forces of YIN AND YANG in the body which lay behind the symptoms of sickness. Although it is not yet understood how acupuncture works, it is still widely practiced in China and increasingly in the West, mainly as a form of ANESTHESIA.

ACUTE, term descriptive of an ANGLE of less than 90°.

ADA, agricultural center in S central Okla., seat of Pontotoc Co. It has oil refineries and brick, cement and glass industries. Pop 14 859.

ADAGIO, musical term meaning slow or a slow movement. An *adagio* piece should be played faster than *largo* but slower than *andante*.

ADAM, first man and father of the human race, according to the Old Testament Book of Genesis. This tells how God made Adam (Hebrew for "man") from *adamah* (Hebrew for "dust") and Adam's wife Eve from one of his ribs. The tale of their temptation, fall and expulsion from Paradise is the basis of such Judaic and Christian concepts as grace, sin and divine retribution.

ADAM, Adolphe-Charles (1803–1856), French composer, best remembered for his ballet *Giselle* (1841). He also wrote operatic, religious and choral works.

ADAM, Robert (1728–1792) and **James** (1730–1794), Scottish architect brothers who developed the neoclassical "Adam style" in England. Robert's studies of ancient Roman architecture in Italy helped to inspire their joint designs of graceful and sumptuous buildings, interiors and furnishings which brought a new elegance to many town and country houses in Britain, the Continent and America.

ADAMOV, Arthur (1908–1970), French-Russian writer and leading figure in the avant-garde theater since the mid-1940s. He is best known for his plays *Ping-Pong* (1955) and *Paolo Paoli* (1957).

ADAMS, manufacturing town in W Mass., 14mi NE of Pittsfield. It produces chemicals, textiles and paper. Pop 11 772.

ADAMS, Abigail (1744–1818), wife of President John ADAMS and mother of President John Quincy ADAMS. Largely self-educated but highly intelligent, she wrote letters giving a lively account of contemporary American life.

ADAMS, Brooks (1848–1927), US historian, son of Charles Francis ADAMS, who saw economic history as a series of growth cycles. In 1900 he predicted that the US and Russia would be the only world powers in 1950, but that America's wealth would decline and

Abigail Adams, wife of John Adams.

her democratic tradition would be destroyed by uncontrolled private business.

ADAMS, Charles Francis (1807–1886), US diplomat and son of John Quincy ADAMS. He supported the new Republican Party after 1856 and, as minister to Britain (1861–68), helped to keep Britain neutral during the American Civil War. In 1871–72 he represented the US in the ALABAMA CLAIMS settlement.

ADAMS, Henry (Brooks) (1838–1918), major US historian, brother of Brooks ADAMS, whose history of the Jefferson and Madison administrations is a classic work. His other works include *Mont-Saint-Michel and Chartres* (1913), on the social and religious background of medieval culture, and his autobiography, *The Education of Henry Adams*, in which he attempted to show how ill-prepared his generation was for the technological society of the 20th century.

ADAMS, John (1735–1826), one of the leaders in America's struggle for independence and second president of the US (1797–1801).

Born at Braintree (now Quincy), Mass., he gained political prominence as one of the chief protesters against the STAMP ACT (1765). At the First Continental Congress called to protest against the INTOLERABLE ACTS of 1774 he helped draft a declaration of rights and a petition to the king. Adams was now a major figure in colonial politics. At the Second Continental Congress he urged the creation of a Continental Army headed by George Washington, and later helped draft the DECLARATION OF INDEPENDENCE. In and after the REVOLUTIONARY WAR he served abroad as a diplomat (1778–88), gaining American support from France and Holland and helping to forge peace with Britain, to which he became the first American minister (1785–88).

Adams now began an active political career at home. As runner-up to Washington in the first two presidential elections he automatically became the nation's first vice-president (1789–96). When Washington retired, Adams was elected president in 1796, heading the new FEDERALIST PARTY favoring strong central government in opposition to the Republicans (later renamed Democrats) under Thomas Jefferson.

Adams soon faced major problems. His moderate federalism antagonized extreme Federalists including Alexander HAMILTON, who intrigued against him, especially when Adams refused to fight France over French seizures of American shipping in the Anglo-French conflict following the French Revolution. Instead, Adams sought peace with France, and (after the fiasco of the XYZ AFFAIR) secured a Franco-US treaty (1800)—but alienated Federalist supporters by not consulting Congress. He had already angered the pro-French Republicans by a seemingly autocratic distrust of popular democracy, and his (reluctant) involvement in the ALIEN AND SEDITION ACTS (1798) curbing criticism of Congress's military preparations against France.

Unpopularity lost Adams the election of 1800, but his policy of non-involvement had saved the country from what could have been a costly war. Adams was the first president to live in the White House in Washington.

John ADAMS
2nd US President

Born: October 30, 1735
Died: July 4, 1826
Term of Office: March 4, 1797–March 3, 1801
Political Party: Federalist

ADAMS, John Couch (1819–1892), British astronomer who, independently of LEVERRIER, inferred the existence of the planet NEPTUNE from the PERTURBATIONS it induced in the orbit of URANUS.

ADAMS, John Quincy (1767–1848), sixth president of the US (1825–29) and sole example of a son following his father (John ADAMS) to the presidency. However, his main achievement, promoting national expansion, came while he was secretary of state.

Trained in law and educated in international affairs by his father, he held diplomatic posts abroad under George Washington, John Adams and James Monroe, becoming the first American ambassador to Russia (1809–14) and helping to negotiate the Treaty of GHENT (1814).

As Monroe's secretary of state (1817–25), he helped formulate the MONROE DOCTRINE, declaring US opposition to European involvement in the Americas (a cornerstone of future US foreign policy), and urged recognition of the emergent Latin American states. He negotiated the ADAMS-ONÍS TREATY with Spain (1819) for the purchase of Florida and fixed a border with Mexico to the Pacific Ocean, prerequisites for national expansion. He also helped to restrict British influence to N of the 49th parallel as far W as the Rockies.

Elected president in 1824, Adams had been an unpopular compromise choice and faced a hostile congressional coalition headed by Andrew JACKSON. Congressional opposition largely blocked Adams' ambitious schemes for national improvements including a national bank and university, new roads and canals, and protective tariffs. His main presidential achievement, completion of the ERIE CANAL, was offset by the passing of the unpopular "Tariff of Abominations" (1828).

Adams lost the 1828 election but went on (1831–48) to be the only ex-president to sit in the House of Representatives, where he spoke eloquently in defense of civil liberties.

John Quincy ADAMS
6th US President

Born: July 11, 1767
Died: February 23, 1848
Term of Office: March 4, 1925–March 3, 1829
Political Party: Democratic Republican

ADAMS, Maude (1872–1953), US actress famous around the turn of the century. She is best remembered for her leading roles in plays by James BARRIE, Edmond ROSTAND and Shakespeare.

ADAMS, Samuel (1722–1803), American revolutionary leader and signer of the Declaration of Independence. His forceful oratory and inflammatory writings increased colonial discontent with British rule. Adams opposed the sugar and stamp acts, helped organize the BOSTON TEA PARTY, pioneered the COMMITTEES OF CORRESPONDENCE and urged independence at the First Continental Congress (1774). He served as governor of Mass. (1794–97).

ADAMS, Sherman (1899–), US politician, President Eisenhower's assistant 1953–58. He resigned on being widely criticized for taking gifts from an industrialist whose affairs were under government investigation.

ADAMS BRIDGE, line of shoals between Sri Lanka (Ceylon) and SE India; the reputed remains of a causeway by which the legendary hero RĀMA reached Ceylon to rescue his wife Sītā.

ADAMS-ONÍS TREATY, also called the **Transcontinental Treaty**, US-Spanish agreement (1819) defining the western boundary of the US, negotiated by J. Q. ADAMS and the Spanish minister Onís. Spain ceded Florida to the US in return for the abandonment of the US claims to Texas.

ADAMS PEAK, mountain in SW Sri Lanka (Ceylon), 7360ft high. A 5ft long depression in its summit, variously called the footprint of Adam, Buddha and Siva, attracts Muslim, Buddhist and Hindu pilgrims.

ADANA, fourth-largest city in Turkey, strategically located at the foot of the Taurus Mts in the S. A major agricultural market center, it produces machinery, textiles and tobacco. Pop 529926.

ADAPAZARI, city in NW Turkey, 80mi E of Istanbul. It produces textiles and tobacco. Pop 152171.

ADAPTATION, the process of modification of the form or functions of a part of an organism, to fit it for its environment and so to achieve efficiency in life and reproduction. Adaptation of individual organisms is called ACCLIMATIZATION, and is temporary since it involves ACQUIRED CHARACTERISTICS; the permanent adaptation of species arises from transmitted genetic variations preserved by NATURAL SELECTION (see also EVOLUTION). Successful and versatile adaptation in an organism usually leads to widespread distribution and long-term survival. Examples include the development of lungs in amphibians, and of wings in birds and insects. The term is sometimes also used for the modified forms of the organism.

ADAPTIVE RADIATION, a sequence of EVOLUTION in which an unspecialized group of organisms gives rise to various differentiated types adapted to specific modes of life. Early placental

Adaptive radiation

"Fresh woods, and pastures new" Milton...

The effects of adaptive radiation are visible all around us, but are not immediately obvious; it seems usual and natural that some animals should burrow, some swim, some fly. And yet they are the result of a long and complex process. Technically, adaptive radiation is a term used to describe a comparatively rapid evolution of certain animals and plants into widely divergent species and genera. Imagine an animal with four legs of about equal length. To move about quickly, to search for food or escape from enemies, it can either increase the length of all four legs to give speed in running, or it can grow long hindlegs only to bound along. It is then known as a cursorial or running animal. There are other lines it or its descendants can follow, however. It may burrow in the ground, so becoming fossorial (from the Latin *fossor*: digger). It may take to the trees and become arboreal or tree-dwelling. It may take to the air and become aerial, or flying, or it may take to water and become aquatic.

In fact, it has happened many times that the descendants of one species or type of animal have taken these radiating paths of development, some to remain terrestrial, others to become fossorial, arboreal, aerial or aquatic. They have become adapted, each to its own mode of life, by changes in structure, by growing long claws (fossorial), sharp claws for climbing (arboreal), wings (aerial) or flippers (aquatic).

This diversification is caused by one or more of several factors. Geographical isolation is one of them and it forced marsupials in Australia to radiate, because there was no competition from other mammals. Marsupials such as the kangaroo, the bandicoot, the marsupial squirrel, "badger," "cat," "tiger," "mouse," are mammals which give birth to living, but very incompletely developed, young of minute size which continue development while attached to the mother's teats in a second womb – the pouch. Physiological improvement in efficiency is another reason for diversification. Improvement in bodily functions enabled true mammals to develop greater efficiency in colonizing their environment and, as a result, they eclipsed or made extinct previously dominant groups such as reptiles or marsupials and were themselves able to radiate.

Finally and most important of all, some animals achieved a breakthrough into a new kind of environment in which the ecological niches were numerous and vacant. The ecological niche of a species, one of the most fundamental concepts in modern biology, is the environment most favorable for a particular organism which is better adapted to that environment than any other organism. Briefly, a species requires two things from its environment. First there must be enough space for its members to live in, to build nests or dig holes, to provide shelter. Secondly, there must be enough food. Thus the power of flight in insects and in birds threw open the possibilities and opportunities of life in the air, where unutilized space and food were to be found.

Throughout the fossil record there has been a succession of adaptive radiations, of plants as well as of animals, belonging to groups each with more efficient powers of adaptation to their environment than the preceding group. The invasion of land and of fresh waters, after life in the sea, enabled innumerable ecological niches which had never been occupied before to be colonized.

Adaptive radiation is the modern equivalent of the "Principle of Divergence" put forward by Darwin in answer to his question, "How does the lesser difference between varieties become augmented into the greater difference between species?" The solution is "the more diversified the descendants from any one species become in structure, constitution and habits, by so much will they be better enabled to seize on many and widely diversified places in the polity of nature." In other words, divergence is related to the existence of a multiplicity of ecological niches to which organisms, provided that they are capable of producing inheritable variation through crossing, may become progressively adapted.

The opposite of adaptive radiation is seen in "persistent types" in which groups of organisms show in their lineages that they have undergone scarcely any evolution at all during very long periods of time, and show very little diversification, their genera, families and orders having very few species, and sometimes only one. Examples of persistent types are the lampshell *Lingula*, almost unchanged since Ordovician times (180 million years ago). It may be noticed that all these animals are marine and that life in the sea is characterized by a constancy of conditions with few new ecological niches.

It was because of the adaptive radiations of successive groups of animals during the past 500 million years or so, that the Carboniferous (Mississippian and Pennsylvanian) and Permian periods have been called the Age of Amphibia; from the Permian to the Cretaceous: the Age of Reptiles; and the Tertiary Era: the Age of Mammals. The Jurassic period was also that of the adaptive radiation of insects and flowering plants. They were ecologically connected because the insects served to promote cross-pollination and hence inheritable variation in the plants, while the latter provided the insects with habitats and food. This is reflected in the great number of surviving species belonging to these complementary classes of organisms; 850,000 insects and 250,000 flowering plants.

The adaptive radiation of reptiles during the Mesozoic period, between 225 and 65 million years ago. Seven of the forms shown here evolved from a common ancestral type called a thecodont of which *Euparkeria* is an example. These forms were each characterized by different ways of life. The plesiosaurs became aquatic and lived on a diet of fish. The pterosaurs were able to fly, but were also fish-feeders. The remaining forms, the dinosaurs, were terrestrial but lived in different habitats and had differing food preferences. Allosaurs were carnivorous and powerful enough to attack even the largest of their contemporaries. Cetiosaurs were herbivorous and probably lived in swamp regions, feeding on aquatic vegetation. *Iguanodon* was a carnivore, and both *Protoceratops* and the Ankylosaurs were herbivores. The adaptive radiation of reptiles has a long history. The first reptiles are known from fossils preserved in Upper Carboniferous (Pennsylvanian) rocks. These specimens come from coal-swamp deposits and it is not known if other forms existed at the same time, living in upland regions where preservation is less likely to occur. From these early forms, the radiation began and reached its climax during the Cretaceous period 65 to 136 million years ago. The reptiles shown here are a sample of representatives of many groups. Most of these groups became extinct rather suddenly at the end of the Cretaceous for reasons that are not entirely understood, and only the snakes, lizards, turtles and crocodiles survive as important groups today.

Similar radiations are well-known in other groups of animals. The Mammals began their radiation after the end of the Cretaceous and are still an important element in the faunas of today, although there was some reduction of their numbers during the Ice Ages. In a similar way, birds are undergoing an extensive adaptive radiation at the present time, and there is much evidence that new species are evolving, particularly on islands and in equatorial forest regions.

mammals, for example, gave rise to modern burrowing, climbing, flying, running and swimming forms.

ADDAMS, Jane (1860–1935), American social reformer who pioneered the settlement house movement in the US. (See SOCIAL SETTLEMENTS.) With Ellen Gates Starr she founded Chicago's Hull House (1889) which provided social and cultural activities for poor European immigrants. An ardent pacifist, she became first president of the Women's International League for Peace and Freedom, and was co-winner, with Nicholas Murray BUTLER, of the 1931 Nobel Peace Prize.

ADDAX, species of large antelope (*Addax nasomaculatus*), once widespread in the Sahara desert but now scarce. It is well adapted to desert life, with big, splayed hoofs, the ability to conserve water, and a coat that is mainly sandy-colored in summer, becoming duller brown in winter. It stands about 1 m (40in) tall. Family: Bovidae.

ADDEND, in ALGEBRA, one of two or more terms undergoing ADDITION. For example, in the expression $x+y+z$, each of x, y, z is an addend.

ADDER, the European or Northern VIPER (*Vipera berus*), with a short, thick, brownish body and a dark zigzag pattern along its back. Its venom is dangerously toxic. The harmless HOGNOSE SNAKES of North America are sometimes called "blowing adders". Family: Viperidae.

ADDICTION. See DRUG ADDICTION.

ADDIS ABABA, capital of Ethiopia, standing on an 8000ft central plateau. It has the former imperial palace and government buildings, and since the 1950s hospitals, theaters and factories have been built. It is the headquarters of the Organization of African Unity. Pop 958 700.

ADDISON, town in NE Ill., a suburb of Chicago. It has metal foundries and factories producing heating equipment. Pop 24 482.

ADDISON, Joseph (1672–1719), English man of letters and public servant, whose witty, elegant style had a lasting effect on English prose. He wrote plays, poems, and above all essays dealing with the literature, life and manners of the day in *The Tatler* and *The Spectator* (which he founded with Sir Richard STEELE). He was secretary of state 1717–18.

ADDISON'S DISEASE, failure of STEROID production by the ADRENAL GLAND cortex, first described by English physician **Thomas Addison** (1793–1860). Its features include brownish skin pigmentation, loss of appetite, nausea and vomiting, weakness, and malaise and faintness on standing. The stress associated with an infection or an operation can lead to sudden collapse. Autoimmune disease (see IMMUNITY), TUBERCULOSIS and disseminated CANCER may damage the adrenals and long-term steroid therapy may suppress normal production. Treatment is normally by steroid replacement.

ADDITION, one of the basic operations of ALGEBRA and ARITHMETIC, denoted by the sign "+". The addition of positive numbers can best be defined in terms of SET THEORY: if one considers set A to contain 4 elements, set B to contain 5 elements, then $A \cup B$

contains 9 elements; i.e., 4+5=9. The addition of negative numbers is equivalent to SUBTRACTION in that $a+(-b)\equiv a-b$.

ADE, George (1866–1944), American newspaper humorist and playwright whose *Fables in Slang* (1899) used colloquialisms and down-to-earth characters to poke fun at society.

ADELAIDE, capital of South Australia state, founded in 1836 and named for Queen Adelaide of Great Britain. It is a manufacturing and marketing center with about two-thirds of South Australia's population. Nearby Port Adelaide is the state's main shipping center. Met pop 809 466.

ADELARD OF BATH, 12th-century English Scholastic philosopher and traveler who helped introduce Arabic scientific learning into Christian Europe. He translated Euclid from an Arabic text into Latin, and wrote about the abacus and astrolabe.

ADÉLIE COAST, coastal Antarctica between latitudes 66°–70°S and longitudes 136°–142°E. Discovered by France's Dumont D'Urville in 1840, it was claimed by France in 1938.

ADEN, seaport of the People's Democratic Republic of Yemen (Southern Yemen), on the Gulf of Aden. Under British rule (1839–1967) it became a coaling station for ships sailing between Europe and India via the Suez Canal.

ADEN, Gulf of, 920mi long W arm of the Arabian Sea between Somalia and Southern Yemen, linked to the Red Sea by the narrow BAB EL-MANDEB. It is part of the Suez Canal–Indian Ocean sea route.

ADENA CULTURE, Amerindian culture (c1000 BC–800 AD) which flourished in the middle Ohio R valley. Adena Indians grew corn, built circular houses and earthen burial mounds, made pottery, shaped stone and copper ornaments and traded widely.

ADENAUER, Konrad (1876–1967), first chancellor of West Germany (1949–63), who headed its spectacular postwar economic and financial recovery. A politician since before WWI, he was twice imprisoned by the Nazis. He became leader of the Christian Democratic Union party in 1947, and as chancellor made West Germany an integral part of W Europe, taking it into NATO and the European Common Market.

ADENOIDS, lymphoid tissue (see LYMPH) draining the nose, situated at the back of the throat. They are normally largest in the first five years and by adult life have undergone ATROPHY. Excessive size resulting from repeated nasal infection may lead to mouthbreathing, middle-ear diseases, sinusitis and chest infection. If these are prominent or persistent complications, surgical removal of the adenoids may be needed.

ADENOSINE TRIPHOSPHATE (ATP). See NUCLEOTIDES.

ADEODATUS, name of two popes. **Saint Adeodatus I**, pope 615–18, a Roman, succeeded BONIFACE IV in 615. **Adeodatus II**, pope 672–76, was a Benedictine monk noted for his mild nature.

ADHESION, the force of attraction between contacting surfaces of unlike substances, such as glue and wood or water and glass. Adhesion is due to

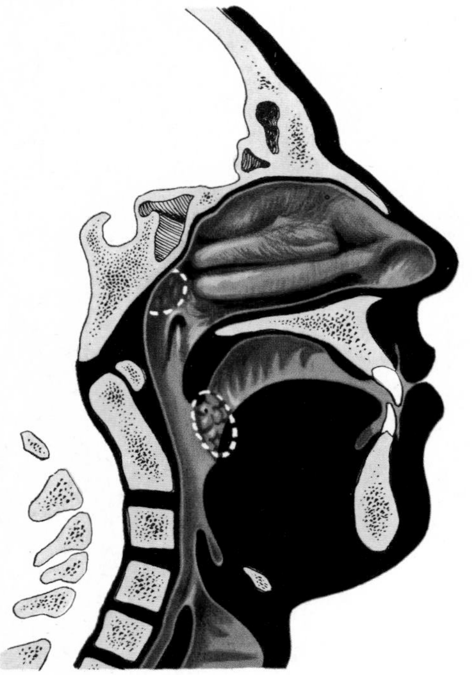

Infected adenoids are a frequent source of disease in the body, particularly in young children; failure to treat or remove the source of infection may, in some cases, affect the body's entire system.

intermolecular forces of the same kind as those causing COHESION. Thus the force depends on the nature of the materials, temperature and the pressure between the surfaces. A liquid in contact with a solid surface will "wet" it if the adhesive force is greater than the cohesive force within the liquid. (See also ADHESIVES; SOLDERING; SOLUTION.)

ADHESIVES, substances that bond surfaces to each other by mechanical ADHESION (the adhesive filling the pores of the substrate) and in some cases by chemical reaction. Thermoplastic adhesives (including most animal and vegetable glues) set on cooling or evaporation of the solvent. Thermosetting adhesives (including the epoxy resins) set on heating or when mixed with a catalyst. There are now many strong, long-lasting adhesives designed for use in such varied fields as electronics, medicine, house-building and bookbinding, and for bonding plastics, wood and rubber. (See also CEMENT, GLUE, SOLDERING.)

ADIABATIC PROCESS, in THERMODYNAMICS, a change in a system without transfer of HEAT to or from the environment. An example of an adiabatic process is the vertical flow of air in the atmosphere; air expands and cools as it rises, and contracts and grows warmer as it descends. The generation of heat when a gas is rapidly compressed, as in a piston engine or SOUND waves, is approximately adiabatic.

ADIGE, river in N Italy, the most important after the Po. Rising in South Tyrol and flowing through Trent and Verona, it enters the Adriatic Sea N of the Po Delta. About 220mi long, it is navigable for 170mi.

ADIPOSE TISSUE, specialized fat-containing connective TISSUE, mainly lying under the skin and within the ABDOMEN, whose functions include FAT storage, energy release and insulation. In individuals its distribution varies with age, sex and OBESITY.

ADIRONDACK MOUNTAINS, range in NE N.Y., in Hamilton, Essex, Franklin and Clinton Counties, source of the Hudson R. Although often taken as part of the Appalachians, they are in fact related to the Laurentian Hills of Canada. Mt Marcy (5 344ft) is the highest peak. The 200 lakes and millions of acres of woodland (largely included in the Adirondack Forest Preserve) make the region a tourist and sportsman's paradise. Important resources include lumber, iron ore and graphite.

ADJUTANT STORKS. See STORKS; MARABOU.

ADLER, Alfred (1870–1937), Austrian psychiatrist who broke away from FREUD to found his own psychoanalytic school, "individual psychology," which saw AGGRESSION as the basic drive. Adler emphasized the importance of feelings of inferiority in individual maladjustments to society.

ADLER, Dankmar (1844–1900), German-born US architect and engineer, whose partnership with Louis SULLIVAN from 1881 helped to create the famous Chicago School of architecture. His first important work was the Chicago Central Music Hall (1879).

ADLER, Felix (1851–1933), German-born American educator and social reformer, founder of the ETHICAL CULTURE MOVEMENT. He held professorships in Semitic literature and in social and political ethics, and championed educational, housing and child-labor reforms.

ADMETUS. See ALCESTIS.

ADMINISTRATIVE LAW, the law regulating the powers and activities of governmental bodies and officials. In the US, where the wide functions of administrative agencies make them almost a fourth branch of government, their operations are ultimately subject to judicial review. In many European countries special administrative courts exist.

ADMIRALTY ISLANDS, group of 40 volcanic and coral islands in the SW Pacific, in the W Bismarck Archipelago, part of the Territory of New Guinea. Discovered in 1616 by the Dutch navigator Schouten, they were claimed by Germany in 1884 and were under Australian administration from 1914. Principal export is copra.

ADOBE (from Spanish *adobar*, to plaster), sun-dried brick made from clay soil mixed with grass or straw. The earliest building material of Egypt and Assyria, it is still used in China, Japan and particularly Mexico, Central America and the SW states of the US.

ADOLESCENCE, in humans, the transitional period between childhood and adulthood. The term has no precise biological meaning, but adolescence is generally considered to start with the onset of PUBERTY and to end at the age of about 20. In primitive societies the period is marked by RITES OF PASSAGE such as that at puberty and that on MARRIAGE. These formal rites are reflected less overtly in more sophisticated societies, and this lack of formalization, where the individual is expected to adjust to standards which he does not fully appreciate, is believed to be responsible, as much as physiological (see PHYSIOLOGY) and hormonal (see HORMONES) changes, for adolescent emotional stresses. The frustration by society, through parental or other disapproval, of the adolescent's sex drive, which during this period is exceptionally strong, causes further stresses. Partial outlets are found through masturbation (sexual stimulation by oneself), diary-writing, artistic creativity, political militancy and, frequently, vandalism. These emotional stresses, coupled with those caused by differences in the ages at which physical developments take place in different individuals (see INFERIORITY COMPLEX), create enormous educational and social problems that are often underestimated.

ADONIJAH, in the Old Testament, son and heir to King David. Denied the throne, he was put to death following the accession of his half-brother Solomon.

ADONIS, asteroid about one mile in diameter with a highly eccentric ORBIT. Its perihelion is within the orbit of Venus, its aphelion beyond that of Mars. It was discovered in 1936.

ADONIS, in Greek myth, a beautiful youth fought over by APHRODITE and PERSEPHONE. ZEUS decreed that he should spend the summer on earth with Aphrodite and the winter in the underworld with Persephone, thus symbolizing the cycle of the seasons. He is identified with the Middle Eastern vegetation god Tammuz.

ADOPTION, creates a parent-child relationship where no such natural or legal relationship exists. Legislation varies from country to country and state to state, but the suitability of prospective parents is always the major consideration. The US adoption rate is high, with many government and private agencies involved in placing homeless children. Finding sufficient adopters is, however, growing more difficult, particularly in urban areas.

ADOPTIONISM, 8th-century Christian heresy which maintained that Christ was divine only through adoption by God at his baptism. It was preached most actively by the Spanish bishop Felix and opposed by ALCUIN. Felix finally recanted at the Synod of Aix-la-Chapelle (799).

ADOPTIVE EMPERORS, Roman emperors (NERVA, TRAJAN, HADRIAN, ANTONINUS PIUS) who adopted as son the man best qualified to rule after them. The practice was broken by MARCUS AURELIUS, who in 180 AD appointed his own son COMMODUS.

ADOWA. See ADWA.

ADRENAL GLANDS, or **Suprarenal Glands,** two ENDOCRINE GLANDS, one above each kidney. The inner portion (medulla) produces the hormones ADRENALINE and noradrenaline and is part of the autonomic NERVOUS SYSTEM. The outer portion (cortex), which is regulated by ACTH, produces a number of STEROID HORMONES which control sexual development and function, glucose metabolism and electrolyte balance. Adrenal cortex damage causes ADDISON'S DISEASE.

ADRENALINE, or **Epinephrine,** a HORMONE secreted by the ADRENAL GLANDS, together with smaller quantities of **Noradrenaline.** The nerve endings of the sympathetic NERVOUS SYSTEM also secrete both hormones, noradrenaline in greater quantities. They are similar chemically and in their pharmacological effects. These constitute the "fight or flight" response to stress situations: blood pressure is raised, smaller blood-vessels are constricted, heart rate is increased, METABOLISM is accelerated, and levels of blood glucose and FATTY ACIDS are raised. Adrenaline is used as a heart stimulant, and to treat serious acute ALLERGIES.

ADRIAN, city in SE Mich., seat of Lenawee Co., on Raisin R, 59mi SW of Detroit. Center of a truck farming region. Pop 20 382.

ADRIAN, name of six popes. **Adrian I** (d.795) was pope 772–95. He enlisted Charlemagne's help in crushing the Lombards and enlarging papal territories, condemned ADOPTIONISM and, through his legates at the second Council of NICAEA (787), joined in the condemnation of Iconoclasm. **Adrian II** (792–872) was pope 867–72. **Saint Adrian III** (d.885) was pope 884–85. **Adrian IV** (c1100–1159), born Nicholas Breakspear, was the only English pope (1154–59). He died while preparing to lead a coalition of Italian forces against the Holy Roman Emperor Frederick I. **Adrian V** (d.1276) was pope for five weeks in 1276. **Adrian VI** (1459–1523) was the last non-Italian (and only Dutch) pope. After his election in 1522 he attempted to correct abuses within the Church, but during his 20-month reign failed to check the advance of the Reformation.

ADRIAN, Edgar Douglas. 1st Baron Adrian of Cambridge (1889–), English physiologist who shared the 1932 Nobel Prize for Physiology or Medicine with Charles SHERRINGTON for work elucidating the functioning of the neurons of the NERVOUS SYSTEM.

ADRIANOPLE. See EDIRNE.

ADRIANOPLE, Battle of, decisive victory of the VISIGOTHS and their allies, led by FRITIGERN, over the Romans in 378 AD. The Emperor VALENS and two-thirds of his army perished. THEODOSIUS I had to allow the Visigoth army to settle within the empire, opening the way for future barbarian inroads.

ADRIANOPLE, Treaty of, concluded the Russo-Turkish War of 1828–29. It gave Russia control of the Danube estuary and part of the Black Sea.

ADRIATIC SEA, arm of the Mediterranean, between Italy, and Yugoslavia and Albania. Along the Italian coast, which is straight and flat with shallow lagoons and marshes in the N, the chief ports include Venice, Ancona and Brindisi. At the head of the Adriatic on the Italian-Yugoslav border lies the port of Trieste. The indented Yugoslav coast is lined by the steep limestone cliffs and numerous islands of Dalmatia. Among the major ports are Rijeka, Split and Dubrovnik. On the marshy Albanian coast the main port is Durrës. The Adriatic coast extends for about 500mi with an average width of 110mi. The Straits of Otranto link it to the Ionian Sea to the S.

ADSORPTION, the ADHESION of molecules of a fluid (the adsorbate) to a solid surface (the adsorbent); the degree of adsorption depends on temperature, pressure and the surface area—porous solids such as CHARCOAL being especially suitable. The forces binding the adsorbate may be physical or chemical; chemical adsorption is specific, and is used to separate mixtures (see CHROMATOGRAPHY). Adsorption is used in GAS MASKS and to purify and decolorize liquids. (See also ABSORPTION.)

ADULT EDUCATION, learning undertaken by adults. It was at first an attempt to give people opportunities missed in youth. While this remains a major aim, adult education is now seen more as part of a continuing process. With improvements in formal education, the demand for adult education has increased. In America it started with the LYCEUM MOVEMENT, early in the 19th century. After the Civil War important advances were made by the CHAUTAUQUA MOVEMENT and in various federal AGRICULTURAL EDUCATION acts. During the Depression the WORKS PROJECTS ADMINISTRATION provided education programs for 2000000 adults, and after WWII came the G.I. BILL OF RIGHTS. In the 1960s federal funds provided for basic literacy programs under the Economic Opportunity Act.

ADVENT from Latin *adventus*, coming or arrival), in the CHURCH YEAR, the season before Christmas. It includes four Sundays, starting from the Sunday nearest St. Andrew's Day (Nov. 30), and marks the beginning of the church year. Advent has been observed since the 6th century as a season of meditative preparation for Christmas and Christ's birth and second coming.

ADVENTISTS, Christian sects, mainly in the US, who believe in the imminent advent (SECOND COMING) of Christ. Adventism grew from the teachings of William MILLER, who announced the end of the world would come in 1843. After the failure of Miller's predictions new Adventist churches arose. The largest is the Seventh-day Adventists, formally organized in 1863. Its members observe Saturday as the Sabbath and support an extensive missionary program.

ADVERTISING, paid publicity designed to persuade people to buy a product or service or to adopt a viewpoint. Advertising started with storekeeper's signs, but modern advertisers include manufacturers, as well as political candidates and governments—using media ranging from billboards to magazines, newspapers, radio and television. In the US advertising provides these media with most of their income and is very big business, accounting for no less than $20 billion a year, involving some 5000 advertising offices and employing some 100000 specialists backed by as many clerical and administrative personnel.

Most advertising material comes from advertising agencies which formulate advertising campaigns, buy the necessary time or space in the media chosen, and produce the actual advertisements. Large agencies also offer specialized market research and other facilities. Most agency earnings come from commissions deducted from the payments that clients make for the space or time bought.

Key agency staff include the agency chief in overall charge; account executives providing liaison between the agency and its clients; copywriters writing the texts of advertisements and working with artists and layout men handling illustrations and typography; the space-buyer; the research department assessing market potential; and the traffic department supervising work flow.

ADVOCATUS DIABOLI (Latin: devil's advocate), common name for the promoter of the faith, a Roman Catholic official appointed by a bishop to discover defects in arguments brought forward to support a beatification or canonization.

ADWA (Adowa), town in Tigre province, N Ethiopia, about 80mi S of Asmara. The humiliating defeat of Italian forces here in 1896 by Emperor Menelik II was followed by recognition of Ethiopia's independence. Pop 15712.

AEDES, a genus of MOSQUITO; the carriers of YELLOW FEVER. Family: Culicidae.

AECHMEA, a genus of BROMELIADS, several of which are cultivated as house plants. The variety "Silver King" produces broad silver and green leaves and short-lived blue flowers surrounded by persistent pink bracts. Family: Bromeliaceae.

AEDUI, Celtic tribe living in what is now Burgundy. In 121 BC they supported Rome against their neighbors in Gaul and in 48 AD became the first people of Gaul to send senators to Rome. Their main settlements were at the sites of modern Autun and Nevers.

AEGADIAN ISLANDS (or Egadi Islands), group of small islands off W Sicily. Here the Romans destroyed the Carthaginian Fleet in 241 BC, to end the first PUNIC WAR. Fishing is the main activity.

AEGEAN CIVILIZATION, a collective term for the BRONZE AGE civilizations surrounding the Aegean Sea, usually extended to include the preceding STONE AGE cultures there. Early archaeological work in the area was performed by Heinrich SCHLIEMANN in the 1870s–80s, whose successes included the location of

One of the principal sites of the Aegean Civilization is the palace at Knossos on the island of Crete. Named the palace of Minos for the legendary king, it was built about 1900 BC. The northern entrance passage (*above*) leads straight into the Central Court.

Sir Arthur Evans began excavating the Minoan palace in 1899 and the far-reaching importance of his discoveries was soon evident. This is a reconstruction of the West wing seen from the central court, executed by Evans' draftsman. The remains preserved today give the ground-floor plans only, although it is reasonable to assume that the splendid staircase led to major rooms above.

The Aegean Civilization produced rich frescoes. This detail of a mural depicting children boxing is in a house on the volcanic island of Thera. Ash and pumice from an eruption in 1500 BC effectively sealed contemporary buildings, which have only recently been completely excavated.

Troy, and early in this century by Sir Arthur EVANS. The Bronze Age cultures of the Aegean have been identified as follows: **Helladic**, the cultures of the Greek mainland, including subdivisions such as Macedonian; **Cycladic**, the cultures not only of the Cyclades but of all the Aegean Islands except Crete; and **Minoan**, the cultures of Crete, so named by Evans for MINOS, in legend the most powerful of Cretan kings. The Late Helladic cultures are often termed **Mycenaean**.

Around 3000 BC the region was invaded by Chalcolithic (i.e. bronze- and stone-using) peoples, displacing the previous Neolithic inhabitants. This population appears to have remained static until around 2000 BC, when the Greek tribes arrived on the mainland, overpowering and submerging the previous cultures. Around the same time Crete established a powerful seafaring empire, and throughout the area there were rapid and substantial advances in the arts, technology and social organization. Around 1550 BC it would appear that the Mycenaeans occupied Crete, and certainly by this time the Greeks were established as the dominant culture in the area. The Cretan civilization seems to have been eclipsed about 1400 BC. During the 17th century BC there emerged on the mainland a wealthy and powerful aristocracy, whose riches have been discovered in many of their tombs. It would appear that for several hundred years there was a period of stability, since fortifications were not added to the aristocrats' palaces until the 13th century BC. The artistry of this era is exquisite, as evidenced by archaeological discoveries in the tombs: gold cups superbly wrought, small sculptures, jewelry, dagger blades inlaid with precious metals, and delicate frescoes. During the 13th century BC there probably was a war with Troy, ending with the destruction of that city around 1260 BC and a general decline of the civilizations as a whole into the so-called Dark Ages. (See also MINOAN CIVILIZATION; MINOAN LINEAR SCRIPT.)

AEGEAN SEA, arm of the Mediterranean Sea between mainland Greece and Turkey. It is about 400mi long and 200mi wide and has 2500 islands: among them the N and S SPORADES (including the DODECANESE) and CYCLADES groups; EUBOEA, LESBOS and SAMOTHRACE. Many of the islands are the peaks of submerged mountains. Almost all are Greek. Islanders live by farming, fishing and tourism. The Aegean civilization was the first in Europe, and the area became the heart of the Classical Greek world.

AEGEUS, legendary king of Athens, annually forced to sacrifice youths and girls to the Cretan MINOTAUR because he had killed King MINOS' son. Aegeus' son Theseus killed the beast but forgetfully sailed home under black sails, a sign of mourning. Believing Theseus dead, Aegeus drowned himself in the sea—hence its name, "Aegean."

AEGINA, Greek island in the Saronic Gulf, 17mi SW of Athens. By the 5th century BC it was one of the richest commercial states in Greece, with a famous temple of Aphaia, but Athens expelled its inhabitants in 431 BC. Modern Aegina depends on farming, fishing and tourism. Pop 9850.

AEGIR, in Norse mythology, a giant and sea god featured in the EDDAS. His wife Rán reigned over those who had drowned.

AEGIS, the fear-inspiring attribute of ZEUS and his daughter ATHENA. Depicted as a goatskin either worn as a cloak or carried as a shield, it was adorned with serpents, scales and a MEDUSA's head.

AEGISTHUS. See CLYTEMNESTRA.

AEGOSPOTAMI (or Aegospotamos), river and town in ancient Thrace, scene of the last and decisive battle of the PELOPONNESIAN WAR. In 405 BC the Spartans under Lysander destroyed the Athenian fleet while it was beached at the river mouth.

AEHRENTHAL, Count Alois Lexa von (1854–1912), Austro-Hungarian foreign minister (1906–12) who formally annexed BOSNIA AND HERZEGOVINA in 1908. This inflamed Slav opinion, eventually precipitating WWI.

AELFRIC (c955–1010 AD), Anglo-Saxon homilist, grammarian and translator, abbot of Eynsham; the greatest writer of Old English prose. His *Catholic Homilies, Saints' Lives* and other works helped spread the monastic revival.

AENEAS, in Greek and Roman myth, a Trojan hero, son of APHRODITE and ANCHISES. He escaped from the fall of Troy to Carthage, where he lived with DIDO. At the gods' command he deserted her and went to Italy, where he founded Lavinium, legendary parent city of Rome. VERGIL's *Aeneid* tells Aeneas' story to glorify the Emperor AUGUSTUS, reputedly his descendant.

AENEID. See AENEAS; VERGIL.

AEOLIAN HARP, stringed musical instrument played by the wind. Named for Aeolus, Greek god of the winds, it usually comprises 8–15 catgut strings stretched above a long, narrow wooden sound box and tuned in unison.

AEOLIAN ISLANDS. See LIPARI ISLANDS.

AEOLIS, NE coast of Asia Minor and nearby islands, once peopled by the Aeolians, a Greek tribe which founded cities there c1000 BC.

AEOLUS, in Classical mythology, guardian and god of the winds. He kept them in a cavern on his island of Aeolia, releasing them at will.

AEPYORNIS. See ELEPHANT BIRDS.

AERIAL PHOTOGRAPHY. See PHOTOGRAMMETRY.

AEROBE, an organism that needs oxygen for its survival. The term is usually applied to certain kinds of BACTERIA. (See also ANAEROBE.)

AERODYNAMIC EFFICIENCY, the EFFICIENCY with which an AIRFOIL uses the AERODYNAMIC forces acting on it: in particular the ratio of lift to drag.

AERODYNAMICS, the branch of physics dealing with the flow of air or other gas around a body in motion relative to it. Aerodynamic forces depend on the body's size, shape and velocity; and on the density, compressibility, VISCOSITY, temperature and pressure of the gas. At low velocities, flow around the body is streamlined or laminar, and causes low drag; at higher velocities TURBULENCE occurs, with fluctuating eddies, and drag is much greater. "Streamlined" objects, such as AIRFOILS, are designed to maintain laminar flow even at relatively high velocities. Pressure impulses radiate at the speed of SOUND ahead of a moving body; at SUPERSONIC velocities these impulses pile up, producing a shock wave—the "sonic boom" (see DOPPLER EFFECT). In AIRPLANE design all of these factors must be considered. In normal cruising flight all the forces acting on an airplane must balance. The lift provided by the wings must equal the aircraft's weight; the forward thrust of the engine must balance the forces of drag. Lift occurs because the wing's upper surface is more convex, and therefore longer, than the lower surface. Air must therefore travel faster past the upper surface than past the lower, which leads to reduced pressure above the wing. (See also WIND TUNNEL; REYNOLDS NUMBER.)

AEROEMBOLISM, presence of air in the blood circulation. Direct entry of air into veins may occur through trauma, cannulation or surgery, and a large air embolus reaching the HEART may cause death. In acute decompression (as with flying to high altitude or sudden surfacing after deep diving) bubbles of air come out of solution. These may block small blood vessels causing severe muscle pains ("**bends**"), tingling and choking sensations and occasionally PARALYSIS or COMA. Recompression and slow decompression is the correct treatment.

AERONAUTICS, the technology of aircraft design, manufacture and performance. See AERODYNAMICS; AIR-CUSHION VEHICLE; AIRPLANE; AIRSHIP; BALLOON; FLIGHT, HISTORY OF; GLIDER; HELICOPTER.

AEROSOL, a suspension of small liquid or solid particles (0.1–100μm diameter) in a gas. Examples include smoke (solid particles in air), FOG and CLOUDS. Aerosol particles can remain in suspension for hours, or even indefinitely. Commercial aerosol sprays are widely used for insecticides, air fresheners, paints, cosmetics, etc. (See also COLLOID; ATMOSPHERE.)

AEROSPACE MEDICINE. See SPACE MEDICINE.

AERTSEN, Pieter (c1508–1575), Dutch painter of

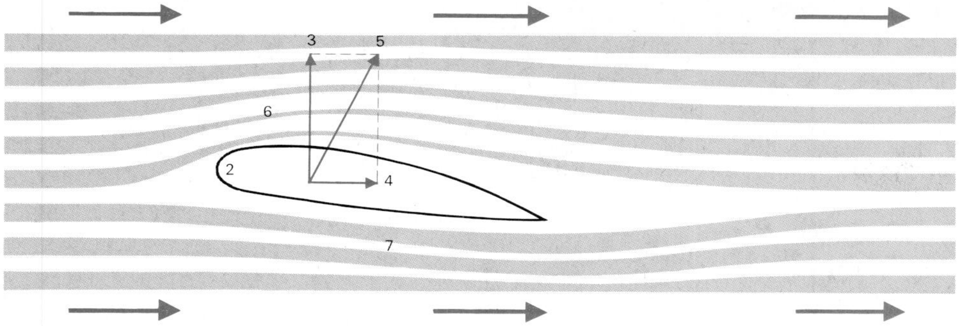

Of fundamental significance in aerodynamics is the air-foil shape. The arrows (1) show the relative motion of the air through which the airfoil (2) is moving. Air travels past the upper edge faster than past the lower edge, so that there is a region of low pressure (6) above the airfoil and one of high pressure (7) below. This results in the airfoil experiencing vertical *lift* (3) at right angles to the *drag* force (4). The resultant of the lift and the drag forces is the *aerodynamic force* (5).

finely-detailed still lifes and domestic interiors. He is regarded as one of the founders of GENRE painting in the Netherlands.

AESCHINES (389–314 BC), Athenian orator whose policy of appeasing Philip II of Macedonia aroused DEMOSTHENES' opposition. Demosthenes eventually forced Aeschines into exile.

AESCHYLUS (c525–456 BC), earliest of the three great dramatists of ancient Greece, regarded as the "father of tragedy." Only 7 of at least 80 plays survive, including *The Persians*, *Prometheus Bound* and the *Oresteia*. The latter is a trilogy based on the murder of Agamemnon by his wife Clytemnestra, and the subsequent revenge by their son Orestes. Aeschylus elaborated Greek dramatic form by adding a second actor and exploiting the dramatic possibilities of dialogue. His tragedies develop a belief that worldly success may lead to pride, incurring the punishment of providence. His style is marked by a unique grandeur and richness.

AESCULAPIUS, the Roman god of healing and medicine. In Greek myth he was known as Asclepius (or Asklepios), the son of APOLLO and Coronis, and learned the art of healing from CHIRON the centaur. His symbol was a snake entwined around a staff.

AESOP, traditional Greek author of animal fables, said to have been a slave on 6th-century BC Samos. He may be a wholly legendary figure. Rooted in folklore, Aesop's fables acquired literary additions and influenced writers such as LA FONTAINE.

AESTHETICS, the study of the nature of art as a whole. The term, from the Greek *aisthesis* ("sense perception"), was coined in the 18th century, though philosophers have discussed art and beauty since PLATO and ARISTOTLE. Modern aesthetics, however, recognizes that not all art is necessarily beautiful in the classic sense.

Philosophers have differed as to whether there are objective formal criteria of artistic value, or whether these criteria are entirely subjective. KANT tried to reconcile the two approaches by arguing that subjective aesthetic judgments involve universal attributes of imagination and understanding. Particularly influential in modern times have been CROCE, who saw aesthetics as a matter of intuitive knowledge, and SANTAYANA, who argued that beauty lay in the pleasure experienced by the observer. Various attempts have also been made to analyze art and its experience in terms of the psychology of perception.

AESTIVATION. See HIBERNATION.

AETHELBALD. See ETHELBALD.

AETHELBERT. See ETHELBERT.

AETHELRED. See ETHELRED.

AETHELSTAN. See ATHELSTAN.

AETHELWULF. See ETHELWULF.

AETIUS, Flavius (c396–454), Roman general who, under VALENTINIAN III, held effective power in the Western Empire from c433. With the help of the Visigoths, he defeated ATTILA at the Battle of Châlons in 451. Valentinian, fearful of Aetius' ambitions, murdered him with his own hand.

AETOLIA, region of ancient Greece N of the Gulf of Corinth. In the 3rd century BC it was the home of the powerful Aetolian League. The League supported Rome against Philip V of Macedon (212–197 BC), but later allied with Antiochus III of Syria and was finally subjugated by Rome in 189 BC.

AFARS AND ISSAS. See FRENCH TERRITORY OF AFARS AND ISSAS.

AFFECT, in psychology. See EMOTION.

AFFENPINSCHER, toy dog breed of uncertain origin known in Europe since the 17th century. Its wiry stiff coat is red, gray or black; it weighs a maximum of 8lb and has a moustache, bushy eyebrows and black mask.

AFFIDAVIT, a formal written statement sworn before a court bailiff, notary public or other person qualified to administer an oath. It may be admissible evidence in legal proceedings, but has little weight as opposed to oral testimony.

AFGHAN HOUND, ancient breed of dog, introduced into the US in 1926. It is tall (25–27in; weight 50–60lb), has a long-haired silky coat, curved tail, and great speed and endurance. It was originally used for hunting.

AFGHANISTAN, republic in Central Asia. It is a mountainous and rugged country, bisected by the mountains of the Hindu Kush, which form a major watershed. The main rivers are the Amu Darya (Oxus), Hari Rud, Kabul, Farah Rud and Helmand. The climate can range from 0°F in winter to 113°F in summer.

Economy and People. The economy is mainly pastoral and agricultural, and the chief exports are agricultural products. Though industrialization may be facilitated by further exploitation of natural gas deposits, the emphasis is still on craft industries. Manufactured goods, including machinery and petroleum products, are imported. There are no railways and few good roads. Strategically placed between the USSR, China, Kashmir, Pakistan and Iran, Afghanistan has received substantial development aid from the US and USSR.

The main cities are Kabul (the capital), Kandahar, Baghlan and Herat. Most Afghans live a traditional, rural life; about 2.5 million are nomadic. Though elementary education is compulsory, 90% of the people are illiterate.

History. Conquered by Alexander the Great in 330 BC, Afghanistan retained elements of Greek culture as the kingdom of BACTRIA (c250–150 BC). After a brief period of Buddhist culture, the country fell to the Arabs in the 7th century AD, and Islam became the dominant culture. Afghanistan was subsequently overwhelmed by Genghis Khan and Tamerlane, and from his base in Kabul, Babur (1483–1530) established the MOGUL EMPIRE in India.

Afghanistan became a united state in 1747 under AHMED SHAH, founder of the Durani dynasty. During the 19th century Britain and Russia contested influence over the country, but later Amanullah (ruled 1919–29) succeeded in wresting control of foreign policy from the British. He began modernizing Afghanistan, and proclaimed a monarchy in 1926. The last king, Mohammed Zahir Shah, ruled from 1933 to 1973, when he was overthrown in a coup led by Lt. Gen. Sardar Mohammed Daud Khan. The latter became president and prime minister of the new republic.

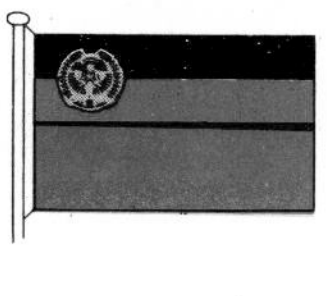

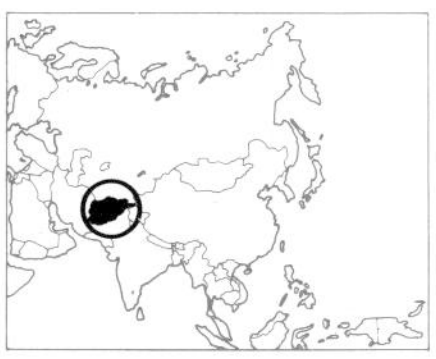

Official name: Republic of Afghanistan
Capital: Kabul
Area: 250 000sq mi
Population: 17 087 000
Languages: Pushtu: Dari Persian
Religions: Muslim (Sunni)
Monetary Unit(s): 1 Afghani = 100 puls

The Afghan hound was first bred by the Egyptians several thousand years before Christ, though it was later, in Afghanistan, that it was developed into a good hunting dog.

AFONSO, name of six kings of Portugal. **Afonso I Henriques** (c1109–1185), count of Portugal from 1112, became the first Portuguese king in 1139 AD. His mother, Countess Teresa, ruled as regent until 1128. He fought León, Castile and the Moors, and took Santarém and Lisbon from the Moors in 1147. **Afonso II the Fat** (1185–1223), reigned from 1211. Conflict with the Church led to his excommunication in 1219. **Afonso III of Boulogne** (1210–1279) reigned from 1248. He took the rest of the ALGARVE from the Moors, and allowed the first representation of commoners in the cortes (legislative assembly). **Afonso IV the Brave** (1290–1357), reigned from 1325. He provoked his son Pedro's rebellion by sanctioning the murder of Pedro's mistress, Inés de Castro. **Afonso V the African** (1432–1481), king from 1438, campaigned in N Africa and unsuccessfully tried to seize the throne of Castile. **Afonso VI the Victorious** (1643–1683), reigned 1656–67. A dissolute ruler, he was deposed by his brother Pedro.

AFRICA, the world's second-largest continent—a land of tropical forests, grasslands and deserts, famous for big game. It was perhaps man's first home, and was the cradle of the Negro peoples. Since the 1950s the new nations of Africa have seen great social and

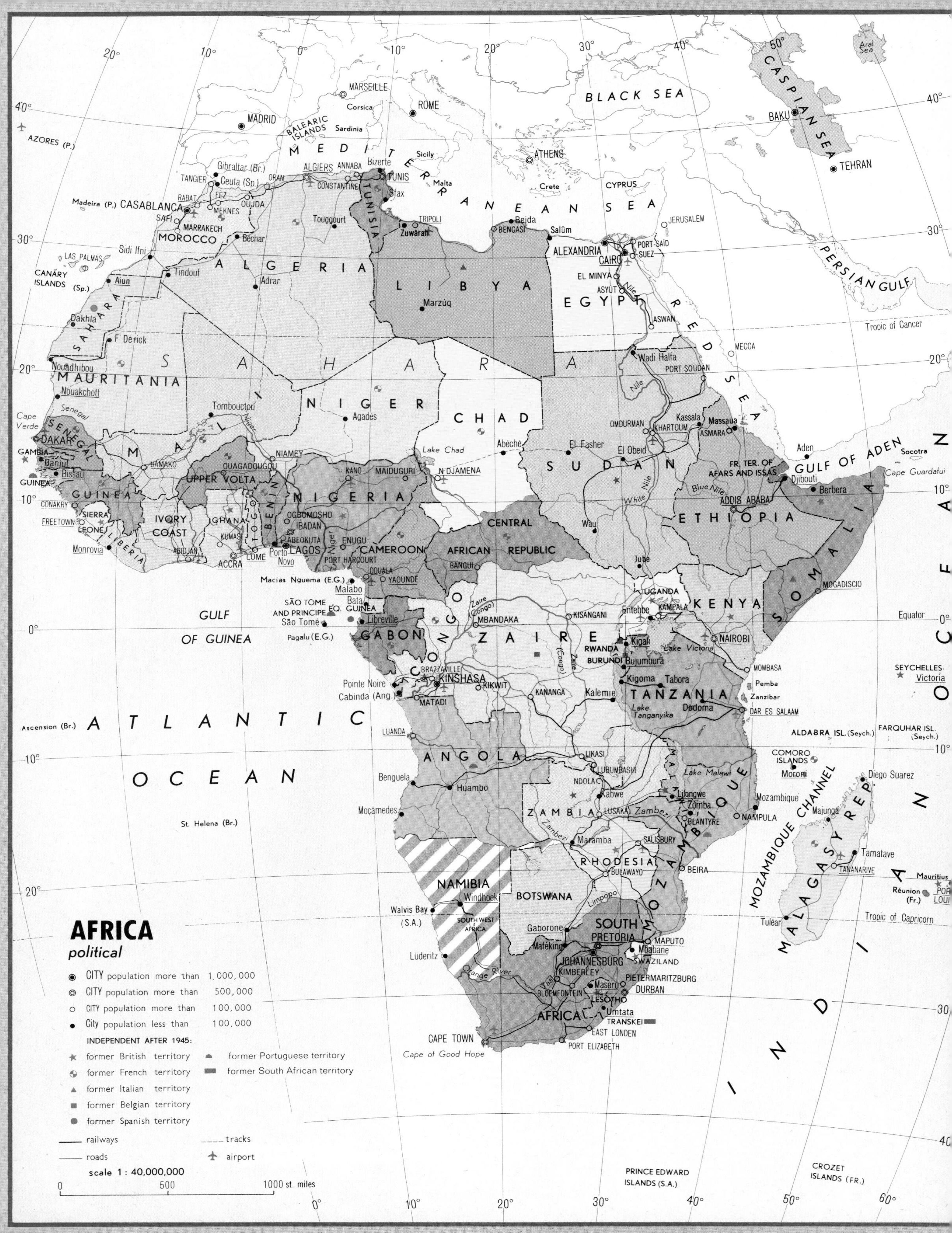

AFRICA
political
CITY population more than 1,000,000
CITY population more than 500,000
CITY population more than 100,000
City population less than 100,000
INDEPENDENT AFTER 1945:
former British territory
former French territory
former Italian territory
former Belgian territory
former Spanish territory
former Portuguese territory
former South African territory
railways
roads
tracks
airport
scale 1 : 40,000,000
0
500
1000 st. miles
ATLANTIC OCEAN
INDIAN OCEAN
MEDITERRANEAN SEA
BLACK SEA
CASPIAN SEA
Aral Sea
RED SEA
PERSIAN GULF
GULF OF ADEN
GULF OF GUINEA
MOZAMBIQUE CHANNEL
SAHARA
Tropic of Cancer
Tropic of Capricorn
Equator
MOROCCO
ALGERIA
TUNISIA
LIBYA
EGYPT
SAHARA
MAURITANIA
MALI
NIGER
CHAD
SUDAN
SENEGAL
GAMBIA
GUINEA-BISSAU
GUINEA
SIERRA LEONE
LIBERIA
IVORY COAST
GHANA
TOGO
BENIN
UPPER VOLTA
NIGERIA
CAMEROON
CENTRAL AFRICAN REPUBLIC
ETHIOPIA
FR. TER. OF AFARS AND ISSAS
SOMALIA
EQ. GUINEA
GABON
CONGO
ZAIRE
UGANDA
KENYA
RWANDA
BURUNDI
TANZANIA
ANGOLA
ZAMBIA
MALAWI
MOZAMBIQUE
RHODESIA
NAMIBIA
SOUTH WEST AFRICA
BOTSWANA
SOUTH AFRICA
SWAZILAND
LESOTHO
TRANSKEI
MALAGASY REP.
MARSEILLE
Corsica
ROME
MADRID
BALEARIC ISLANDS
Sardinia
Sicily
Malta
ATHENS
Crete
CYPRUS
JERUSALEM
BAKU
TEHRAN
AZORES (P.)
Gibraltar (Br.)
TANGIER
Ceuta (Sp.)
ORAN
ALGIERS
ANNABA
CONSTANTINE
Bizerte
TUNIS
Sfax
Madeira (P.)
CASABLANCA
RABAT
FEZ
OUJDA
MEKNES
SAFI
MARRAKECH
Touggourt
TRIPOLI
Zuwārah
Beida
BENGASI
Salûm
ALEXANDRIA
PORT-SAID
CAIRO
SUEZ
Sidi Ifni
Bechar
LAS PALMAS
CANARY ISLANDS (Sp.)
Aiun
Tindouf
Adrar
EL MINYA
ASYUT
Nile
Marzūq
ASWAN
Dakhla
F Dérick
MECCA
Wadi Halfa
PORT SOUDAN
Nouadhibou
Nouakchott
Senegal
Tombouctou
Niger
Agades
Cape Verde
DAKAR
Banjul
Bissau
BAMAKO
OUAGADOUGOU
NIAMEY
Lake Chad
Abéché
N'DJAMENA
KANO
MAIDUGURI
OMDURMAN
KHARTOUM
Kassala
Massaua
ASMARA
El Fasher
El Obeid
White Nile
Blue Nile
Aden
Socotra
Cape Guardafui
Djibouti
Berbera
ADDIS ABABA
CONAKRY
FREETOWN
Monrovia
KUMASI
ABIDJAN
ACCRA
LOMÉ
OGBOMOSHO
IBADAN
ABEOKUTA
LAGOS
Porto Novo
ENUGU
PORT HARCOURT
DOUALA
YAOUNDÉ
BANGUI
Wau
Juba
Macias Nguema (E.G.)
Malabo
Bata
SÃO TOME AND PRINCIPE
São Tomé
Libreville
Pagalu (E.G.)
Zaire (Congo)
MBANDAKA
KISANGANI
Entebbe
KAMPALA
MOGADISCIO
NAIROBI
Kigali
Bujumbura
Lake Victoria
BRAZZAVILLE
KINSHASA
Pointe Noire
Cabinda (Ang.)
MATADI
KIKWIT
KANANGA
Kalemie
Kigoma
Tabora
MOMBASA
Pemba
Zanzibar
Dodoma
DAR ES SALAAM
Lake Tanganyika
SEYCHELLES
Victoria
Ascension (Br.)
LUANDA
ALDABRA ISL. (Seych.)
FARQUHAR ISL. (Seych.)
COMORO ISLANDS
Moroni
LIKASI
LUBUMBASHI
Benguela
Huambo
NDOLA
Kabwe
Lake Malawi
Diego Suarez
Lilongwe
Zomba
Moçâmedes
Mozambique
BLANTYRE
NAMPULA
Majunga
LUSAKA
Zambezi
St. Helena (Br.)
Maramba
SALISBURY
Tamatave
BULAWAYO
BEIRA
TANANARIVE
Mauritius
Réunion (Fr.)
Windhoek
Walvis Bay (S.A.)
Limpopo
Tuléar
Gaborone
PRETORIA
MAPUTO
Mbabane
Lüderitz
Mafeking
JOHANNESBURG
Orange River
KIMBERLEY
Vaal
PIETERMARITZBURG
BLOEMFONTEIN
Maseru
DURBAN
Umtata
EAST LONDEN
CAPE TOWN
PORT ELIZABETH
Cape of Good Hope
PRINCE EDWARD ISLANDS (S.A.)
CROZET ISLANDS (FR.)

1

2

3

4

Africa is a continent of strong contrasts. (1) in Morocco one can still find castles and fortresses, such as this one in Ovarzazate, which date back to the time of feudal rulers. (2) An example of the rich and varied flora. The extraordinary Baobab or Monkey-bread tree looks, when its leaves fall, as though the roots rather than the branches are pointing to the sky. (3) No less extraordinary, but perhaps more familiar, are these elephants in the Tsavo National Park in South-east Kenya, one of many large nature reserves. (4) Masai warriors from Tanzania standing in front of a typical native dwelling. The man on the left holds the symbols of his office as chief of the settlement.

political change and have formed a new force in world politics. But most are too poor to profit much from their often rich resources.

Land. Africa is a vast landmass straddling the equator and extending almost 5000mi from N to S and 4600mi from E to W. Only at the Suez Isthmus does it touch another landmass (Asia). Much of Africa is an ancient plateau, broken by the Congo Basin in the W, the Atlas and Ahaggar Mts in the NW, and other mountains in the E, ranging S from Ethiopia to South Africa. Africa's highest peak, Mt Kilimanjaro (19340ft) is in E central Africa. E Africa's GREAT RIFT VALLEY contains the world's second largest area of lakes. The Nile, Niger, Congo and Zambezi are major rivers. Coasts are smooth, lacking natural harbors.

W equatorial Africa is uniformly hot and rainy and supports dense rainforest, the home of gorillas, chimpanzees, monkeys and okapis. N, S and E of these forests are tropical areas with one annual rainy season. Their savanna grasslands are roamed by lions, giraffes, antelopes and zebras. N of the northern savannas and SW of the southern savannas lie great deserts including the SAHARA and KALAHARI. Here drought-resistant scrub and desert foxes survive. Extreme N and S Africa have a Mediterranean-type climate with mild wet winters and warm dry summers. Tough-leaved olives, cork oaks etc. survive the summer drought, and animals include porcupines in the N and the Cape buffalo in the S. Grasslands cover Africa's high mountain slopes, scoured by birds of prey. Crocodiles and hippopotamuses live in lakes and rivers, where water birds include storks and flamingoes.

People. Some 70% of Africa's 390 million people are Negroes, but whites predominate N of the Sahara and include fair-skinned Atlas Mts Berbers and olive-skinned Egyptian Arabs. Whites and Negroes intermingle in Ethiopia and the Sahara. S of the Sahara live various Negro groups, Congo Forest pygmies, and (in the SW) the dwindling HOTTENTOTS and BUSHMEN. The S and SE also have 5 million Europeans (mainly of Dutch and British origin) and Asians.

Africa has around 1 000 languages, excluding those established by Europeans. Islam, Christianity and animism are major religious forces. Colonial and national divisions and urbanization have partly disrupted tribal village life. Workers flock to mines and towns, absorbing Western skills and culture, yet most Africans remain poor and many endure debilitating diseases.

Economy. Outside the S and parts of the N, Africa is economically undeveloped. Agriculture mainly involves subsistence raising of millet, sorghum, maize (corn), cassava, etc.; or nomadic cattle herding. But colonization established locally commercial tea, coffee, cocoa and citrus plantations geared to world markets. Africa provides one-twentieth of the world's minerals. These include gold and diamonds from South Africa, chrome and copper from Rhodesia, uranium and copper from Zaire, oil from Libya and Algeria. Except in South Africa and the Mediterranean states, manufacturing industry lags—mainly through insufficient capital, skilled labor and home markets. Africa lacks a comprehensive rail or surfaced road network and transportation problems hinder international trade. The continent mainly exports tropical crops and minerals, importing machinery and manufactured goods. South Africa alone handles 45% of all exports and 20% of all imports.

History. Fossil finds 2.6 million years old suggest that man may have evolved in E Africa. But the later rise and spread of Negroes S of the Sahara remains largely unrecorded. The north's history is better known. By 3000 BC Egypt had one of the world's first civilizations and from the 9th century BC Phoenicians founded coastal colonies, later seized by Rome. In the 7th century AD Arabs overran N Africa (Arab traders also influenced the E). Powerful medieval states arose S of the Sahara, but southern Africa remained unknown to Europe until the 1400s when Portugal explored and colonized its coasts, pioneering the slave trade that decimated populations in W Africa. In the 19th century European explorers probed interior Africa, and by 1900 almost all Africa lay divided among colonial European powers (Great Britain, France, Belgium, Portugal, Spain, Italy and Germany). Since then most colonies have given rise to independent states that seek to strengthen black Africa's place in world affairs.

AFRICAN METHODIST EPISCOPAL CHURCH, Negro Protestant denomination akin to but separate from white Methodist denominations. Founded in Philadelphia (1816) by the Rev. Richard Allen, it is the largest Negro Methodist body, with 6 105 churches and 1 166 000 members.

AFRICAN METHODIST EPISCOPAL ZION CHURCH (the AME Zion Church), independent Negro Methodist denomination founded in New York City by Negroes disaffected by white prejudices. They built a church in 1800 and formed the denomination in 1821. It has 940 000 members.

AFRICAN NATIONAL CONGRESS, black South African organization devoted to creating a "united democratic South Africa" and founded in 1912. Leaders like Albert LUTHULI encouraged passive resistance to APARTHEID, and the South African government banned the ANC in 1961.

AFRICAN VIOLET, any of the genus *Saintpaulia* of hairy PERENNIAL herbs with velvety heart-shaped leaves and purple, pink or white violet-like flowers. The African violet is native to tropical E Africa, but the species *S. ionantha* is widely cultivated as a houseplant. Indoors, they should be placed in a sunny east or south window in winter, but moved to avoid direct sunlight in the summer. They grow well between 10°C and 27°C (60°F and 80°F) and should be regularly watered to keep the soil evenly moist. Propagation is by seeds, leaf cuttings and dividing the plants. Family: Gesneriaceae.

AFRIKAANS, an official language of South Africa. It evolved from the South Holland form of Dutch spoken by 17th-century BOER settlers, but incorporated Bantu, Hottentot, Malayo-Portuguese and English words.

AFRIKA KORPS, mechanized German force that fought brilliantly in N Africa in WWII (1941–43). Led by Field Marshal Erwin ROMMEL, it stiffened

AFRICA

Geological structure

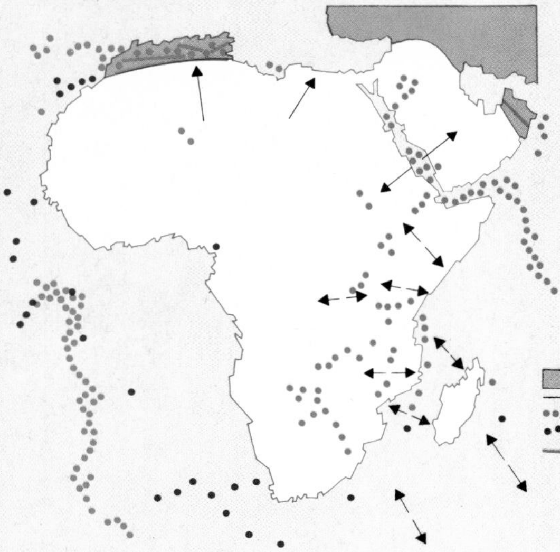

Regions of Tertiary mountain folding
Direction of movement of continental plates
Earthquake centers
Volcanoes
Mountain belts

Geology

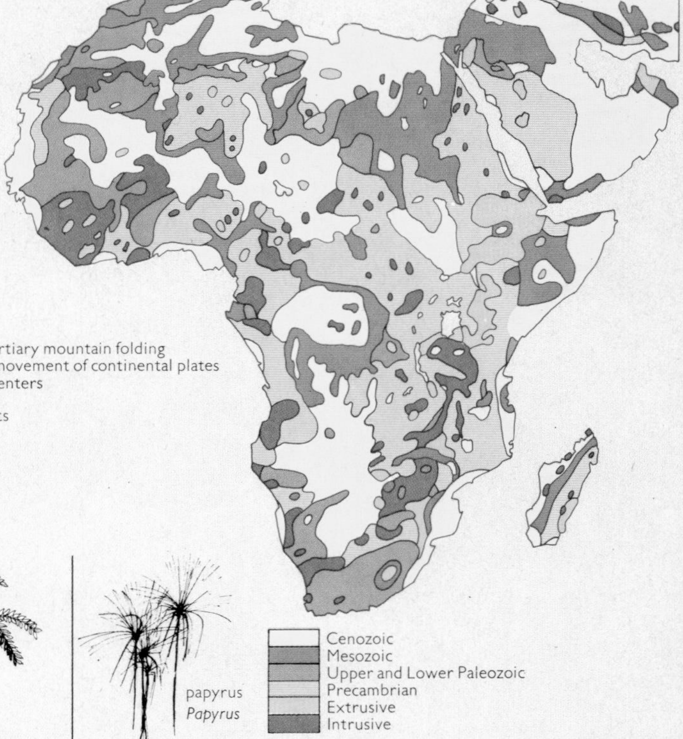

Cenozoic
Mesozoic
Upper and Lower Paleozoic
Precambrian
Extrusive
Intrusive

Flora and fauna

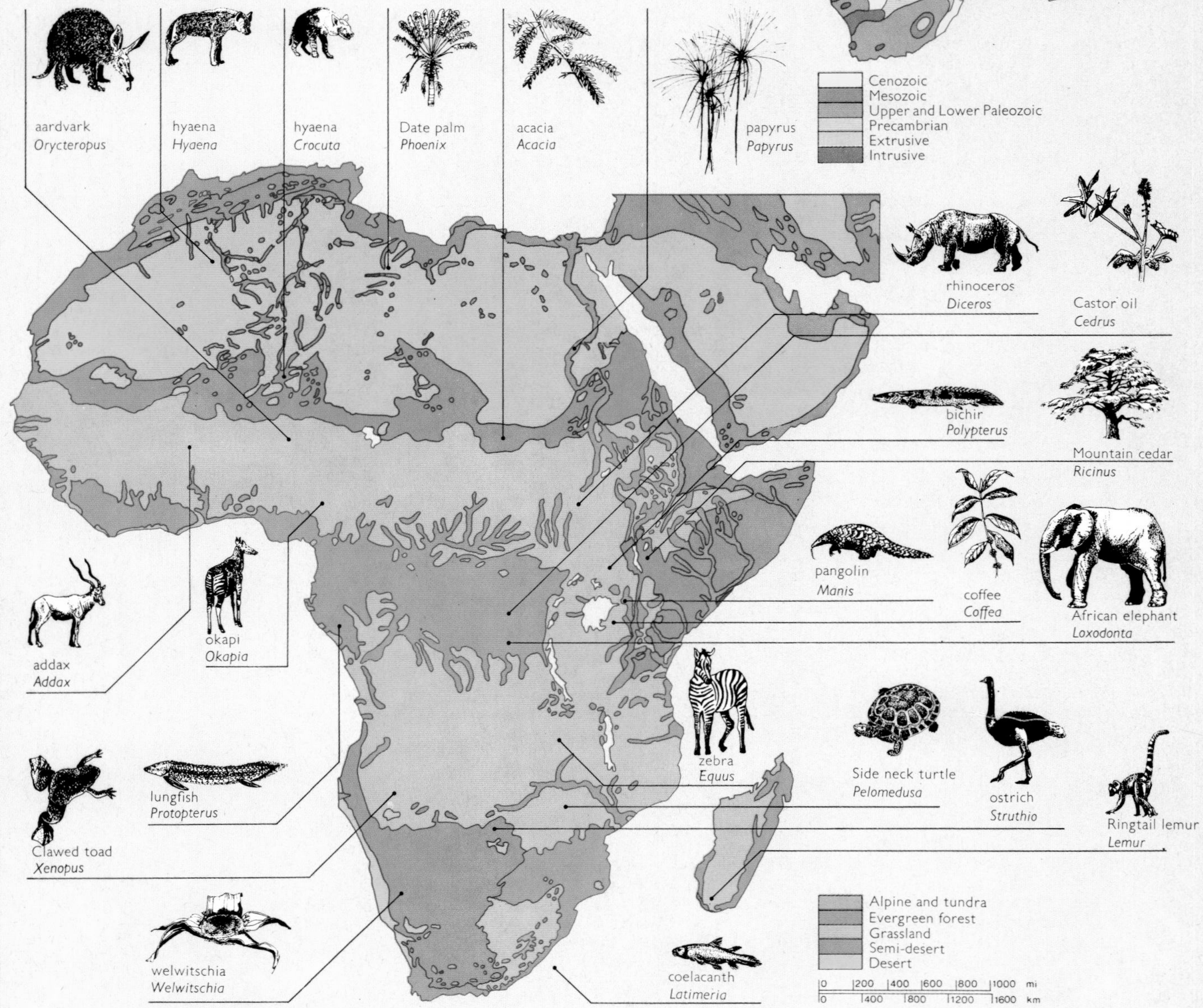

aardvark
Orycteropus
hyaena
Hyaena
hyaena
Crocuta
Date palm
Phoenix
acacia
Acacia
papyrus
Papyrus
rhinoceros
Diceros
Castor oil
Cedrus
bichir
Polypterus
Mountain cedar
Ricinus
addax
Addax
okapi
Okapia
pangolin
Manis
coffee
Coffea
African elephant
Loxodonta
zebra
Equus
Side neck turtle
Pelomedusa
ostrich
Struthio
Ringtail lemur
Lemur
lungfish
Protopterus
Clawed toad
Xenopus
welwitschia
Welwitschia
coelacanth
Latimeria
Alpine and tundra
Evergreen forest
Grassland
Semi-desert
Desert
0 200 400 600 800 1000 mi
0 400 800 1200 1600 km

Italian resistance, making huge advances before its decisive defeat at EL-ALAMEIN.

AFRIKANERS. See BOERS.

AFTERBIRTH, the material, primarily the PLACENTA, expelled from the mother's body after child delivery.

AFTERBURNER, device used in AIRPLANE turbojet engines (see JET PROPULSION) during periods of takeoff, climb or dash to increase thrust by as much as 100% or more by the burning of additional fuel.

AFTERGLOW, the radiant coloration of the western sky following sunset. It arises from the SCATTERING of sunlight by dust particles (see COLLOID) in the upper atmosphere. The term is also used as an alternative name for phosphorescence (see LUMINESCENCE).

AFTERIMAGE, the persistence of a visual image after the original image has gone. It may be positive (the same COLOR or shade as the original) or negative (the complementary color) depending on the background color. It is a perceptual illusion due to the differential stimulation of the EYE's retinal receptors.

AGADIR, Atlantic seaport in SW Morocco, occupied by the Portuguese 1505–41. It was the scene of the Franco-German confrontation over Morocco (1911) which almost led to war. In 1960, Agadir was devastated by earthquakes and a tidal wave. Pop 61 192.

AGA KHAN, spiritual leader of the Ismaili sect of SHI'ITE Muslims, an hereditary title. His millions of followers are dispersed through the Near East, India, Pakistan and parts of Africa, and are descended from 14th-century Hindus converted by Persian Ismailis. **Aga Khan I** (1800–1881), a Persian provincial governor who emigrated to India in 1840, was invested as leader of the sect in 1866. **Aga Khan II**, Ali Shah, held the title from 1881 until his death in 1885. **Aga Khan III**, Sultan Sir Mohammed Shah (1877–1957), spent much time in Europe and took an active part in international affairs. He represented British India at numerous conferences and as first president of the All-Indian Muslim League worked for Indian independence. **Aga Khan IV**, Prince Karim (1936–), inherited the title in 1957.

AGAMEMNON, in Greek legend, a son of ATREUS and king of Mycenae who organized the expedition against Troy recounted in Homer's ILIAD. Before setting sail he was forced to sacrifice his daughter IPHIGENIA, and was murdered on his return by his wife CLYTEMNESTRA and her lover, his cousin Aegisthus. His death was avenged by his son ORESTES and his daughter ELECTRA. These events are the subject of AESCHYLUS' trilogy, the *Oresteia*.

AGAMIDS, a family of Old World LIZARDS (Agamidae) containing about 300 species. Agamids live on the ground, in rocks or in trees, and most feed on insects. They are often spiny and their skin changes color according to their emotional state and the temperature.

AGANA, capital of Guam, US island territory in the W Pacific. Bombed heavily in WWII, it has been rebuilt with US aid. Pop 2 131.

AGAPE, Greek word for "love" that occurs frequently in the New Testament, where it signifies both God's love for men and Christian love and charity, as distinct from *philia* (love between friends) and *eros* (sexual love). In its charitable sense *agape* was used to describe a meal held by early Christians to promote fellowship and benefit the poor, and was a prototype of the Eucharist.

AGAPETUS, name of two popes. **Saint Agapetus I**, pope from 545 to 536. On behalf of the Ostrogoth King Theodahad, he unsuccessfully begged the Emperor Justinian not to reconquer Italy. He died in Constantinople. **Agapetus II**, pope from 946 to 955, was a gifted administrator who attempted to restore discipline in the Church.

AGAR, or agar-agar, gelatinous product prepared from the ALGAE *Gracilaria* and *Gelidium*. It dissolves in hot water, the solution gelling on cooling (see COLLOID). Its main use is as a thickener in bacteria culture mediums and in cooking.

AGARICS, FUNGI of the family Agaricaceae. Agarics, better known as MUSHROOMS or toadstools, have umbrella-shaped fruiting bodies, which bear spores on gills that radiate below a fleshy cap. There are both poisonous and edible species. Class: Basidiomycetes.

AGASIAS, name of two Greek sculptors of the 1st century BC, both from Ephesus. The *Borghese Warrior* in the Louvre, Paris, is attributed to Agasias, son of Dositheus.

AGASSIZ, Jean Louis Rodolphe (1807–1873), Swiss-American naturalist, geologist and educator, who first proposed (1840) that large areas of the northern continents had been covered by ice sheets (see ICE AGE) in the geologically recent past. He is also noted for his studies of fishes. Becoming natural history professor at Harvard in 1848, he founded the Museum of Comparative Zoology there in 1859. On his death he was succeeded as its curator by his son, **Alexander Agassiz** (1835–1910).

AGASSIZ, Lake, a large prehistoric lake which covered parts of N.D., Minn., Manitoba, Ontario and Saskatchewan in the PLEISTOCENE epoch, named for Louis AGASSIZ. It was formed by the melting ice sheet as it retreated (see ICE AGE). When all the ice had melted, the lake drained northward, leaving fertile silt.

AGATE, a gemstone, a variety of CHALCEDONY streaked with bands of color, formed by intermittent depositions of mineral or organic matter, usually SILICA, on the walls of cavities in volcanic rock. It is often used in jewelry and ornamental work, usually after having been dyed.

AGAVE, a genus of economically important, fleshy rosette plants of the family Agavaceae. There are about 300 species, growing mostly in arid regions of America. Some species, notably *A. americana*, are given the name century plant because they take as long as 50 or 60 years to produce the massive panicles of flowers. Useful fibers such as SISAL are obtained from the leaves of certain agaves, and the sap of several species is fermented to make the popular Mexican drink pulque. Several small species are grown as house plants where they should be placed in a sunny south window, avoiding temperatures below 7°C (45°F). They should be watered weekly in the spring and summer, but in other seasons should only be watered when the soil becomes dry. Agaves are easily propagated by removing offsets.

AGAWAM, name of the original settlement on the site of what became IPSWICH, Mass.

AGAWAM, town in Mass., on the Connecticut R below SW Springfield, settled in 1636. Pop 21 717.

AGEE, James (1909–1955), US writer remarkable for his sensitive character studies and polished prose style. *Let Us Now Praise Famous Men* (1941) portrayed the life of the Alabama sharecropper. From 1943 to 1948 Agee was film critic of *The Nation*, after which he wrote several screenplays, including *The Quiet One* (1949) and *The African Queen* (1951). His partly autobiographical novel, *A Death in the Family* (1957), won a Pulitzer Prize in 1958.

AGELADAS (c540–460 BC), Greek sculptor of Argos famed for statues of gods and athletes, and by popular tradition held to be teacher of MYRON, PHIDIAS and POLYCLITUS.

AGENCE FRANCE-PRESSE, French news service founded in 1943, financially dependent on the French government. Its reporting of events in South America and the Far East is considered to be particularly authoritative.

AGENCY, in law, the relationship between two parties, one of whom (the *agent*) has the authority to act for the other (the *principal*). Authority may be either *express* (stated explicitly by the principal) or *implied* (that which the agent would normally require to carry out his task). Employees are agents of their employers. Lawyers, brokers, auctioneers, builders and the like are also agents for their clients. An agent acting within the scope of his real or apparent authority binds the principal precisely as if he had acted himself.

AGENCY FOR INTERNATIONAL DEVELOPMENT (AID), US government agency formed in 1962 to administer foreign economic aid. It promotes long-range economic programs in developing countries by securing loans from private industry, guaranteeing investment abroad, and supporting certain international organizations. Its best-known program is the ALLIANCE FOR PROGRESS.

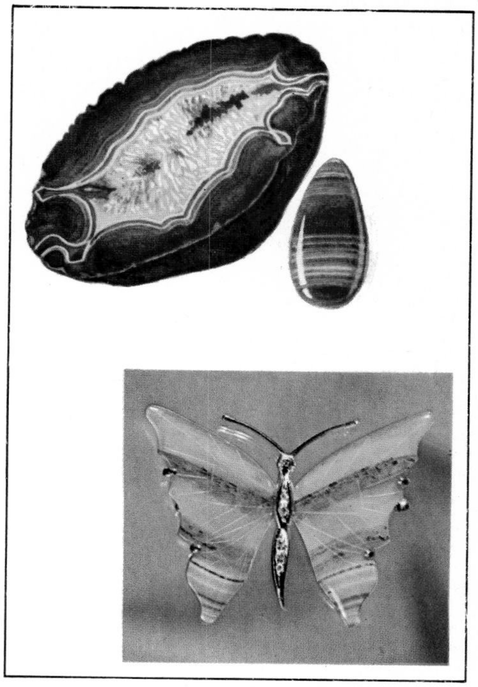

A smoothly polished piece of agate; a decorative piece cut in cabochon, and a piece made into an ornament.

AGENDA. See PARLIAMENTARY PROCEDURE.

AGENOR, in Greek legend, king of Phoenician Tyre and father of Europa, Phoenix, Cilix and Cadmus. When Europa was kidnapped by Zeus, Agenor sent his sons after her. They never returned, each founding a colony along the Aegean.

AGE OF CONSENT, age at which one becomes legally responsible for one's actions, usually 18 or 21. One may marry without parental consent, and be party to and contract and incur debts and civil liabilities. It is also the age, usually 14 or 15, below which sexual intercourse is deemed statutory rape, even if voluntary.

The tall, flower-bearing stalks of the agave, native to tropical America. The leaves of this useful plant produce fibers such as sisal, pita and hemp.

AGE OF REASON. See ENLIGHTENMENT, THE.

AGERATUM, a genus of popular garden annuals of the family Compositae. The plants bear clusters of tiny, tube-shaped flowers, usually white, blue or pink in color. Normally under 600mm (2ft) high, they are cultivated as border plants.

AGE SET, a compulsory grouping by age practiced by certain peoples of N and NE Africa. Each male of the TRIBE is enlisted either at birth or at a particular age in an age set, in which he will remain for the rest of his life. As he and the rest of his set grow older, the set adopts different functions within the tribe. The number of sets within a tribe is limited, their names recurring in cycles.

AGESILAUS II (c444–360 BC), king of Sparta from 399. In 394 he twice defeated a coalition of Thebes, Athens, Argos and Corinth. Sparta's war with the coalition was ended in 386 by the King's Peace, though Agesilaus provoked a renewal of the war with Thebes in which Sparta's defeat at LEUCTRA (371) ended its supremacy in Greece.

AGES OF MAN, ancient Greek and Roman concept of history as divisible into five distinct ages: the Golden Age of peace and plenty; the Silver Age, when man became sinful and abandoned religion; the Brazen Age of warfare; the Heroic Age of noble deeds by demigods; and the Iron Age, when sin and shame triumphed. For the pessimistic ancients, the last represented the present and future of mankind.

AGGADAH (Aramaic: telling), that portion of the TALMUD (about 30%) which is non-legal and comprises, among many other topics, legends, allegorical interpretations of the Bible, moral tales and aphorisms.

AGGLOMERATE, rock made up of angular fragments of lava in a matrix of smaller, often ashy, particles. It is a result of volcanic activity (see VOLCANO). (See also CONGLOMERATE.)

AGGLUTINATIVE LANGUAGES (from Latin *gluten*, glue), LANGUAGES (e.g. Turkish) in which words are formed by joining together groups of MORPHEMES (individual meaning elements), so that a single word may convey the sense of a complete English clause. Their words do not undergo INFLECTION.

AGGLUTININS, ANTIBODIES found in BLOOD plasma which cause the agglutination (sticking together) of ANTIGENS such as foreign red blood cells and bacteria. Each agglutinin acts on a specific antigen, removing it from the blood. An agglutinin is produced in large quantities after immunization with its particular antigen. Agglutinins which agglutinate red blood cells are called isohemagglutinins, and the blood group of an individual is determined by which of these are present in his blood. Group O blood contains isohemagglutinins anti-A and anti-B; group A contains anti-B; group B contains anti-A, and group AB contains neither.

AGGREGATE, building material which is mixed with an adhesive such as CEMENT to make CONCRETE and MORTAR. Fine aggregate, usually sand or crushed stone, is used for smaller structural members where a smooth surface is required; coarse aggregate, such as pebbles, for larger members.

AGGREGATE DEMAND, total demand for goods and services in an economy. The total *supply* of goods and services in an economy is called aggregate supply. Because aggregate demand ultimately determines the overall level of production and employment, the analysis of its make-up is of key importance in economic planning.

AGGREGATES, Theory of. See SET THEORY.

AGGREGATION, in ECOLOGY, the grouping together of plants or animals in response to environmental as opposed to behavioral stimuli.

AGGREGATION, in physics, the clustering of particles into larger groups or aggregates such as those forming rigid bodies.

AGGRESSION, behavior adopted by animals, especially vertebrates, in the defense of their territories and in the establishment of social hierarchies. An animal's aggressive behavior is usually directed towards members of its own species, but it is possible that the behavior of predators, although not generally regarded as aggression, may be controlled by the same mechanism. Aggressive behavior is commonly ritualized, the combatants rarely inflicting serious wounds upon one another. Ritual fighting has become established by the evolution of a language of signs, such as the threat posture, by which animals make known their intentions. Equally as important are submission or appeasement postures, which signal that one combatant acknowledges defeat.

It has been claimed in recent years that such signs are particularly well developed in man, and that he is unique in having aggressive tendencies which have led to the extermination of large numbers of his own species. Detractors from such claims point out that comparisons between social and political situations and those occurring in animal populations are invalid or, at best, misleading.

AGGRESSION, in international law, an unprovoked act of force by one state against another. The UN Charter calls for all members to refrain from "the threat or use of force," but permits collective or individual self-defense against "armed attack." Problems arise, as they did for the LEAGUE OF NATIONS, in distinguishing an armed attack from a preventative strike against an enemy, and in dealing with direct aggression through subversion, economic pressure and propaganda.

AGINCOURT, village in NW France, scene of a decisive battle in the HUNDRED YEARS' WAR. On Oct. 25, 1415, English forces under HENRY V routed the French under Claude d'Albret, demonstrating the power of the English longbow over a heavily armored enemy. The French lost over 7000 men, the English only a few hundred.

AGING, the process of progressive degeneration that occurs in an organism by which it becomes more liable to die. The rate of aging is more or less constant for a given species so that the life span of any individual is determined within limits.

AGIS II (d. c398 BC), king of Sparta c427 and commander in the PELOPONNESIAN WAR (431–04). On the advice of ALCIBIADES he occupied Decelea in Attica (413), from which the Spartans dominated the lands around Athens, forcing the Athenians to import their food.

AGITPROP (*agit*ation and *prop*aganda), term describing any art form, but particularly theater, having an explicit political message and aiming at stirring the audience to action. Agitprop originated in Russia after the Bolshevik Revolution, when mobile troupes of actors toured the country using theater as a "weapon".

Saint Agnes, the patron saint of young girls, carries the martyr's crown she won for choosing death rather than marriage to a pagan. On her feast day, January 21, the pope blesses two lambs in the church of Saint Agnes and their wool is used to weave ceremonial *pallia* for archbishops.

AGLAIA. See GRACES.

AGLIPAY, Gregorio (1860–1940), Philippine religious leader, founder of the Philippine Independent Church, a national Catholic Church independent of the jurisdiction of Rome.

AGNATHA, a primitive class of fish-like vertebrates which lack jaws. Fossil forms lived 450–350 million years ago. Their evolutionary relationship with the living forms, HAGFISHES and LAMPREYS, remains a subject of controversy.

AGNES, Saint (b. c304), virgin martyr of the early Christian church, executed for refusing to marry the son of a Roman prefect. She is the patron saint of young girls and her feast is observed on January 21.

AGNEW, Spiro Theodore (1918–), elected vice-president of the US in 1968 and 1972. Born in Baltimore, Md., the son of a Greek immigrant, Agnew received a law degree from Baltimore U. in 1947. He was elected county executive of Baltimore (1962), and governor of Md. (1966–68), and gained a reputation as a moderate liberal, though he later took a conservative stand towards civil rights demonstrations and urban unrest. As vice-president, he was regarded as the Nixon administration's conservative spokesman on domestic issues. Agnew's resignation from the vice-presidency in 1973 followed a federal income tax charge on which, pleading no contest, he was fined $10000 and given a suspended prison sentence.

AGNON, Shmuel Yosef (1888–1970), Israeli writer remembered for his penetrating and often introspective novels and stories of Jewish life in his native Galicia and in Palestine. In 1966 he shared the Nobel Prize for Literature for works which include *Bridal Canopy* (1937), *A Guest for the Night* (1938) and his greatest novel *The Day Before Yesterday* (1945).

AGNOSTICISM, doctrine that man cannot know about things beyond the realm of his experience, in particular about God. It is a skeptical reservation of judgment in the absence of proof rather than an explicit rejection of any divine order.

AGNUS DEI (Latin: Lamb of God), the representation of a lamb as an emblem of Christ, usually within a nimbus with a cross above its head. Based on a biblical reference to Jesus as the sacrificial "Lamb of God," it is also a supplication intoned by Roman Catholics before Communion.

AGONISTIC BEHAVIOR, behavior resulting from conflict between an animal's instinct to fight and its instinct to flee when it is confronted by a member of its own species at the border of its territory. Agonistic behavior often results in would-be combatants presenting their flanks to one another, thus avoiding both threat and submissive postures.

AGORA, the public square and marketplace of ancient Greek towns where civic and commercial meetings were held. Surrounded by colonnades and public buildings, it sometimes contained temples and statues of heroes. The famed Agora of Athens has been extensively excavated and reconstructed.

AGORAPHOBIA, a morbid fear of public places, a pathological PHOBIA for the unfamiliar. The sufferers, commonly young women, may be unable to leave the home. Behavior therapy may be successful.

AGOSTINO DI DUCCIO (1418–1481?), Florentine sculptor famed for his subtle and delicate handling of marble. His finest works are the reliefs in ALBERTI's Tempio Malatestiano in Rimini and on the façade of S. Bernardino in Perugia.

AGOULT, Marie Comtesse d' (1805–1876), author and famed Parisian society hostess in the 1840s. She was the mistress of Franz LISZT for 10 years. Under the pseudonym Daniel Stern, she wrote novels, social and political tracts and memoirs.

AGOUTI, several species of rodents of the genus *Dasyprocta* found mainly in forests in Central and South America and the West Indies. The common agouti, a rabbit-sized burrowing animal, feeds on

1

2

3

4

5

Rudimentary forms of agriculture are still practiced in large areas of the world. Primitive people, using only the crudest implements, grow limited crops on small clearings carved out of the midst of virgin forests (1). But because most people are tied to one place, more intensive cultivation has become necessary. A primitive wooden plough (2) may be used, but since nearly all other tasks are done by hand (3), the number of workers required per acre is extremely high. At least a third of the world's population is dependent on this kind of intensive primitive agriculture, cultivating one staple crop such as rice (4). In many tropical regions large plantations (5) specialize in a single main export crop.

leaves and fruit. It is hunted for its white tasty flesh. Family: Dasyproctidae.

AGRA, historic city of NE India, on the Yamuna R 110mi SE of New Delhi. It is the capital of the division and district of Agra in Uttar Pradesh state and an important military and commercial center. During the late 16th and early 17th centuries, Agra was the capital of the MOGUL EMPIRE; it still has several magnificent Mogul buildings, including the world-famous tomb, the TAJ MAHAL. Pop 594 858.

AGRAMONTE, Aristides (1869–1931), Cuban physician and bacteriologist, a member of the US Army Yellow Fever Commission headed by Walter REED which in 1900 proved that YELLOW FEVER can be transmitted only by certain mosquitos.

AGRANULOCYTOSIS, a BLOOD condition in which there are inadequate numbers of granulocytes, white cells that eliminate BACTERIA. It is a rare complication of certain drugs and systemic diseases. Severe throat infections and SEPTICEMIA are common; ANTIBIOTICS are the mainstay of treatment.

AGRAPHA OF JESUS, (the "unwritten" of Jesus), name given to utterances ascribed to Jesus but documented in sources other than the Gospels.

AGRARIAN REVOLUTION, advances in farming methods in 18th-century England and Western Europe in which three English agriculturists played an important part. Robert BAKEWELL sponsored scientific breeding of animals. Jethro TULL invented new agricultural machinery and imported root crops and clover from Europe. Charles, Viscount TOWNSHEND used these crops and another new arrival, artificial grasses, in his new "four-course" system of crop rotation. This eliminated the fallow year and supplied more fodder for the animals, which no longer had to be slaughtered in quantity before winter, leaving more meat and more manure for cereal crops. Higher profits motivated renewed enclosure of land, thus encouraging the urban drift of peasant farmers.

AGRICOLA, Georgius, Georg Bauer (1494–1555), German physician and scholar, "the father of mineralogy." His pioneering studies in geology, metallurgy and mining feature in his *De natura fossilium* (1546) and *De re metallica* (1556).

AGRICOLA, Gnaeus Julius (40–93 AD), Roman general. As proconsul of Britain (77–84) he defeated the Caledonians and extended Roman rule into Scotland. His son-in-law, the historian TACITUS, wrote the famous biography of Agricola.

AGRICOLA, Johann (or Johann Schneider; 1494–1566), German Lutheran reformer. He studied under LUTHER but later embraced ANTINOMIANISM, leading to vigorous controversy with Luther and MELANCHTHON. He recanted in 1540 and was made court preacher at Brandenburg.

AGRICOLA, Rodolphus (Roelof Huysman; 1443–1485), Dutch scholar whose work was important in the dissemination of humanist learning. His writings include a life of PETRARCH (1477) and the great *De formando studio* (1484) which outlined his views on education.

AGRICULTURAL ADJUSTMENT ADMINISTRATION (AAA), US NEW DEAL agency established in 1933 to reduce the output of staple crops and so raise prices. In 1936 the Supreme Court ruled as unconstitutional the AAA processing tax for regulating production, seeing it as an infringement on the power of the states. But a second Agricultural Adjustment Act (1938) virtually reestablished, with improvements, the old AAA program, and formulated the principle of the "ever-normal granary." (See also PARITY.)

AGRICULTURAL EDUCATION, in organized form, began at the end of the 18th century with a few agricultural societies in the US and Britain. In America the government first became involved when the Morrill Act (1862) established the LAND GRANT COLLEGES. Direct education of farmers came with the Smith-Lever Agricultural Act (1914), which provided for demonstration work by agents in cooperation with agricultural colleges and experimental stations. In 1917 the federal government began to sponsor agricultural education in secondary schools. Subsequent expansion has included the Future Farmers of America and Four-H clubs, which encourage interest among young people.

AGRICULTURAL PARITY. See PARITY.

AGRICULTURE, the science and practice of farming in the widest sense, including the production of crops of all types, the rearing of livestock and the care of the soil. Man's settled agricultural activities probably date back about 10 000 years. But the essential characteristic of true agriculture, the storing and sowing of seeds, did not develop until the Neolithic period (see STONE AGE). The practice probably originated in the highlands of the Near East and spread to the river valleys of Mesopotamia, Egypt and China. By the 4th or 5th millennium BC men were growing grain and keeping livestock, and using stone tools for chopping and digging the ground. Much of the agriculture was practiced by nomadic tribes, who moved from one place to another as soon as they had exhausted the fertility of the soil. As the density of population grew, and nomadic life became more difficult, more clearly defined agricultural systems arose. On these were based the great civilizations of antiquity.

Ancient Egypt possessed a highly productive agriculture owing to the fertility of the Nile valley, whose soil was perpetually replenished by the annual flooding of the river. The Egyptians were familiar with the principles of irrigation, crop rotation and livestock breeding. The Romans too were good farmers and several of their agricultural treatises

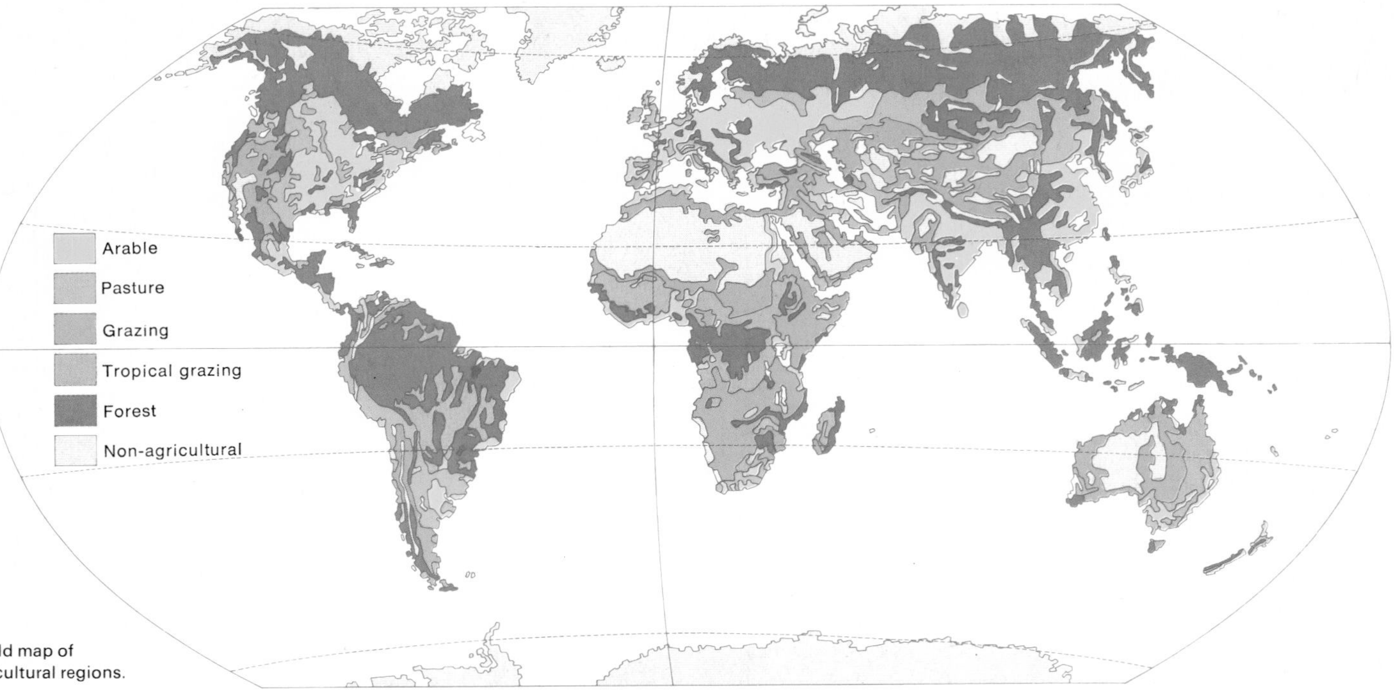

World map of agricultural regions.

make interesting reading. The medieval European farm economy rested on the MANORIAL SYSTEM. The usual method adopted was a three-field crop rotation, one field being sown with wheat or rye, the second with a combination of barley, oats, beans and peas, and the third being left fallow to recover its fertility. With the coming of the industrial revolution, farming underwent radical changes. The AGRARIAN REVOLUTION of the 18th and 19th centuries replaced the old village communities with individual farms and estates. Farming therefore became concentrated in fewer hands, and its output was geared to supplying food for the urban population and raw materials for the manufacturers.

The Indians of North America were agriculturalists long before the Europeans arrived. The first colonists inherited methods already established for growing corn, beans, pumpkins, tobacco and many other crops. The great expansion of farming to the west of the Appalachians began after the Revolution. A new type of agriculture developed, combining large tracts of land with relatively small amounts of labor and capital. During the 19th century America led the world in agricultural development. Many factors played a part in this: the transportation revolution, the invention of such new machines as MCCORMICK's reaper, which opened up the prairies to wheat farmers, the introduction of artificial FERTILIZERS and the increase of specialization were all instrumental in raising the productivity of the farms.

Agriculture in most advanced countries is today marked by increasing specialization, with farmers tending to concentrate more and more on a particular line of production. This factor, together with the fall in the number of farm laborers, has led to a high degree of mechanization and produced great sophistication in agricultural techniques. Milking machinery, automated poultry farms, harvesting by combines, grain drying, and automatic potato planting and manure spreading are almost universal. Artificial insemination is commonly used as a means of improving cattle stock. Crops are selectively bred to improve yields and increase resistance to disease. Livestock are fattened in feedlots, weeds and pests are controlled by chemicals, and antibiotics are fed to farm animals to speed their growth.

AGRICULTURE, US Department of, executive department of the US government concerned with the promotion and regulation of agriculture. Established in 1862, the department today operates through research, credit extension, conservation, crop control, distribution and other programs.

AGRIGENTO, capital of Agrigento province in SW Sicily. Once the most powerful city in Sicily after Syracuse (6th century BC), it is today the site of a remarkably well-preserved group of Doric temples. Agrigento is the center for a wine and olive producing region; it also exports sulfur. Pop 51 682.

AGRIMONY, any plant of a genus (*Agrimonia*) of perennial herbs with spikes of yellow flowers. The underground part of the stem is used as an astringent and contains tannin. Family: Rosaceae.

AGRIPPA, Marcus Vipsanius (63–12 BC), Roman military leader and statesman. He was a trusted friend of the Emperor AUGUSTUS, whom he served loyally in many military campaigns and as governor of several important provinces. Married to the emperor's daughter Julia, he became heir designate of Augustus. Agrippa supervised many large-scale public works projects in Rome, including the original PANTHEON.

AGRIPPINA THE ELDER (c14 BC–33 AD), granddaughter of Augustus, wife of Germanicus Caesar, and mother of Agrippina the Younger and the Emperor CALIGULA. Exiled by TIBERIUS, against whom she may have conspired, she starved herself to death.

AGRIPPINA THE YOUNGER (15–59 AD), mother (by her first husband) of NERO. She later married the Emperor CLAUDIUS and had Nero made heir designate. It is thought that Agrippina, in 54, may have been responsible for poisoning Claudius. During the first few years of Nero's reign she dominated him completely, until he finally had her murdered.

AGRONOMY, the branch of agricultural science dealing with production of field crops and management of the SOIL. The agronomist studies crop diseases, selective breeding, crop rotation and climatic factors. He also tests and analyzes the soil, investigates SOIL EROSION and designs LAND RECLAMATION and IRRIGATION schemes.

AGUADILLA, port in NW Puerto Rico, on the Mona Passage. It is a trading center for a region producing sugar cane, fruit and coconuts. The town was founded in 1775; Columbus possibly visited the site in 1493. Pop 21 031.

AGUASCALIENTES, capital city of the state of Aguascalientes in central Mexico. It stands at over 6 000ft above sea level, and has mineral springs and a mild climate which make it a popular tourist center and spa. The city is a marketing and manufacturing center for the state and an important rail junction. Pop 181 277.

AGUINALDO, Emilio (1869–1964), leader of the Philippine independence movement against both Spain (1896–99) and the US (1899–1901). Used by the US to help capture the Philippines during the Spanish–American War (1898), he later led Filipino guerrilla warfare against US occupation and was finally captured in 1901. He withdrew from public life until WWII when, in 1942, he supported the Japanese occupation of the Philippines. Imprisoned by the US in 1945, he was granted an amnesty at the end of the war.

AGULHAS, Cape, southernmost point of Africa, about 100mi E of the Cape of Good Hope. The lighthouse at its tip marks the geographical divide between the Indian and Atlantic oceans. Seaward of the Cape lies the dangerous Agulhas Bank.

AGULHAS CURRENT, part of the South EQUATORIAL CURRENT. It flows S down the E coast of Africa, then E towards Australia. It is also fed by the MOZAMBIQUE CURRENT.

AHAB, king of Israel from c874 to 853 BC. Urged by his wife JEZEBEL, he abandoned the worship of Jehovah and introduced the cult of BAAL, thus provoking the wrath of the Hebrew prophets. Elijah foretold his death. In 853 he was killed fighting the Syrians.

AHAD HA'AM (1856–1927), Hebrew pen name, meaning "one of the people," of Asher Ginzberg, Russian Hebrew writer and proponent of "spiritual Zionism." Opposed to political Zionism, he believed that a Jewish nation in Palestine was to be achieved through spiritual rebirth.

AHAGGAR (or HOGGAR) MOUNTAINS, rugged plateau and mountain region in the Sahara Desert of SE Algeria. These barren and unpopulated highlands are composed of three massifs: Kudia, Tefest and Muidir. Mount Tahat (9 852ft) is the region's highest peak.

AHASUERUS, name of three kings in the Bible. The Ahasuerus in the Book of ESTHER is probably XERXES I of Persia. The two others are CYAXARES I of Media and the father of Darius the Mede, king of the Chaldeans.

AHAZ, king of Judah c731–727 BC who alienated the prophet Isaiah by worshiping Syrian idols. When Syria and Israel tried to make him their ally against Assyria he sought help from the Assyrian king and was forced to become his vassal.

AHAZIAH, name of two biblical kings. **Ahaziah**, king of Israel, son of Ahab, reigned from c853–852 BC. **Ahaziah**, king of Judah for one year (c846 BC), was killed by JEHU while visiting King Jehoram of Israel.

AHIDJO, Ahmadou (1924–   ), President of the

Republic of Cameroun, which achieved independence from France under his leadership in 1960.

AHIMELECH, in the Old Testament, the priest of Nob suspected by King SAUL of being in league with DAVID by giving him food and a sword. At the king's order, Ahimelech and the other priests were murdered.

AHIMSA, doctrine of the Jains of India which opposes the killing or injuring of living things. It is a prominent ethical principle of both HINDUISM and BUDDHISM.

AHITOPHEL, in the Old Testament, a trusted counselor of David who defected to help lead ABSALOM's revolt. When Absalom ignored his advice, Ahitophel foresaw disaster and hanged himself.

AHMADABAD, city in NW India, capital of Gujarat state, on the Sabarmati R about 290mi N of Bombay. One of the largest and most important cities of Mogul India, it is today a railroad junction and a major trade center, particularly for cotton textiles. Pop 1 588 378.

AHMED, name of three Ottoman sultans. **Ahmed I** (1590–1617), reigned from 1603. He ended a war in Hungary by the Treaty of Zsitvatörök (1606), from which Transylvania gained independence. **Ahmed II** (1642–1695), became Sultan in 1691. Later that year the Turks were badly defeated by the Austrians and expelled from Hungary. **Ahmed III** (1673–1736), ruled from 1703. He gave asylum to CHARLES XII of Sweden after the latter's defeat by PETER the Great (1709) which resulted in a war between Russia and Turkey (1711–13). There followed a war with Austria (1715–1718). Another, this time disastrous, war with Persia led to a revolt (1730) in which Ahmed was deposed; he died in prison.

AHMED SHAH (c1723–1773), Afghan ruler who founded the Durani dynasty. Through several successful invasions of India he acquired a huge empire. Although unable to hold his empire together, he succeeded in strengthening and uniting Afghanistan, and is thus often thought of as founder of the modern nation.

AHMOSE, name of two Egyptian pharaohs. **Ahmose I** (reigned c1570–1546 BC), rid Egypt of its HYKSOS conquerors. **Ahmose II** (reigned 569–526 BC), generally known by his Greek name, Amasis, survived NEBUCHADNEZZAR's invasion, strengthened ties with the Greek states and conquered Cyprus. He was the last powerful pharaoh before Egypt fell to Persia.

AHRIMAN AND AHURA MAZDA, spirits of darkness and light in the ancient Persian religion, ZOROASTRIANISM. Ahriman, the spirit of evil, was constantly engaged in a struggle for the souls of men with Ahura Mazda, creator of heaven and earth and the embodiment of wisdom and good.

AHVENANMAA ISLANDS. See ÅLAND ISLANDS.

AHWAZ (or Ahvāz), city in SW Iran, 70mi NE of the port of Abadan, and capital of Khūzestān Province. An important oil center, it is a junction on the Trans-Iranian railroad and stands on the navigable reaches of the Karu R. Pop 260 000.

AI. See SLOTH.

AID, a type of tax in the Middle Ages paid to lords and kings. In Carolingian times aids raised money for wars and other emergencies. Later feudal lords could demand aid only on the knighting of their eldest son or the marriage of their eldest daughter or to raise ransom money.

AIDAN, Saint (d. 651), Irish monk from Iona who became first bishop of Lindisfarne. Under Oswald, king of Northumbria, he was instrumental in firmly establishing Christianity in northern England.

AIDE-DE-CAMP, officer who acts as the confidential personal assistant of a high-ranking military commander. The aide's principal duties are to deal with appointments, messages, correspondence and travel arrangements.

AID TO DEPENDENT CHILDREN (ADC), program of federal and state aid to needy children and the families on which they are dependent. Aid varies from state to state, but the federal government contributes well over half the amount. Some 5 500 000 recipients are given a monthly average of about $56 each.

AIEA, residential city in Hawaii, NW of Honolulu on the island of Oahu. It stands on the E shore of Pearl Harbor and is also a sugar refining center. Pop 12 560.

AIKEN, city in S.C., seat of Aiken Co., 120mi NW of Charleston. It was founded in 1835, and has long been a popular winter resort. Its industries include textile manufacture and kaolin mining. Pop 13 436.

AIKEN, Conrad Potter (1889–1973), US writer, whose *Selected Poems* (1929) won a Pulitzer Prize. His often incisive critiques and essays on poetry were published in *A Reviewer's ABC* (1958). Other prose works include the novel *Great Circle* (1933) and his sensitive autobiography *Ushant* (1952).

AILANTHUS, a genus of tropical-looking deciduous trees native to Asia and Australia but now widely cultivated in Europe and N America. The best known species *A. altissima* grows rapidly to heights of up to 15m (50ft), and produces greenish, malodorous flowers. It thrives in polluted urban conditions in almost any kind of substrate. Family Simaroubaceae.

AILERONS, the control surfaces on the outer trailing edges of an AIRPLANE's wings, moved in opposite senses (one up, the other down) to cause or correct roll, particularly in banking (tilting the plane into a turn). When combined with the ELEVATORS (as in *Concorde*) they become "elevons."

AINU, the primitive hunting and fishing AUSTRALOID Japanese ABORIGINES. They are distinguished by stockiness, pale skins and profuse body hair, hence their frequent description as "the Hairy Ainu." Ainu speech, little used now, bears no relation to any other language. They are now few in numbers, many having been absorbed into ordinary Japanese society.

AIR. See ATMOSPHERE.

AIR BLADDER, or swim bladder, organ found in modern bony fishes that has evolved from the lungs of earlier forms. Control of the gas pressure inside the bladder enables the fish to remain buoyant in water at any depth.

AIR BRAKE, on trains, the fail-safe brake patented by George WESTINGHOUSE in 1872, which is released when the engineer allows compressed air to enter the train air line and applied when the pressure is released. On many trucks and buses, the air brake is applied, using compressed air, on depressing the brake pedal.

AIR-BREATHING FISHES, a group of unrelated fishes that can breathe atmospheric air directly. The group includes the LUNGFISHES, MUDSKIPPERS and some CATFISHES. Their ability is achieved in a variety of ways and is a response to living in water with low concentrations of OXYGEN. Their distribution is mainly limited to equatorial regions.

AIR COMPRESSOR. See JET PROPULSION; PUMP.

AIR CONDITIONING, the regulation of the temperature, humidity, circulation and composition of the air in a building, room or vehicle. In warm weather an air-conditioning plant, working like a refrigerator (see REFRIGERATION), cools, dehumidifies (see also DEHYDRATION) and filters the air. In colder weather it may be reversed to run as a HEAT PUMP.

The first commercial air-conditioning installation dates from 1902, when W. H. CARRIER designed a cooling and humidifying system for a New York printing plant. During the 1920s, motion-picture theaters and then office buildings, department stores and hospitals began to install air-conditioning equipment. After WWII, home units became available, resulting in the rapid growth of the industry manufacturing the equipment. Room air conditioners (window units) are the most widely used domestic equipment, though the installation of the more versatile central air-conditioning equipment (unitary equipment) is becoming more widespread.

AIR-COOLED ENGINE. See INTERNAL COMBUSTION ENGINE.

AIRCRAFT CARRIER, the largest type of warship in the world. While early carriers had straight flight decks, modern vessels use angled decks for simultaneous takeoffs and landings. Planes are launched by steam catapults, and arresting cables are used to bring landing aircraft to a halt. Each carrier is equipped with anti-aircraft guns and missiles, and is protected by its own planes and sister ships. The US Navy's Forrestal class carriers are over 1 000ft long, weigh up to 75 000 tons when loaded, and can carry over 100 airplanes. The largest built so far is the US nuclear-powered carrier *Enterprise* (1 101ft), displacing about 85 000 tons and able to run five years without refueling.

The first successful takeoff from a ship's deck was made in 1910, and aircraft carriers played a limited role in WWI. They emerged fully in WWII as a decisive factor in the Pacific campaign. Despite the development of long-range aircraft and vulnerability to nuclear attack, they remain a vital part of the US fleet.

AIR-CUSHION VEHICLE (ACV), or **Hovercraft,** a versatile marine, land or amphibious vehicle which supports its weight on a high-pressure air cushion maintained by a system of fans. Because this minimizes the friction between the craft and the ground, the auxiliary propulsion equipment can maintain speeds up to 100 knots, even over difficult surfaces. Although the air-cushion principle was rediscovered by the UK engineer Christopher Cockerell in the early 1950s, technical difficulties have so far limited the use of ACVs to military applications and ferry services on a few short sea crossings. **Ground-effect machines** (GEMs) are sometimes distinguished from ACVs as, like AIRPLANES, they

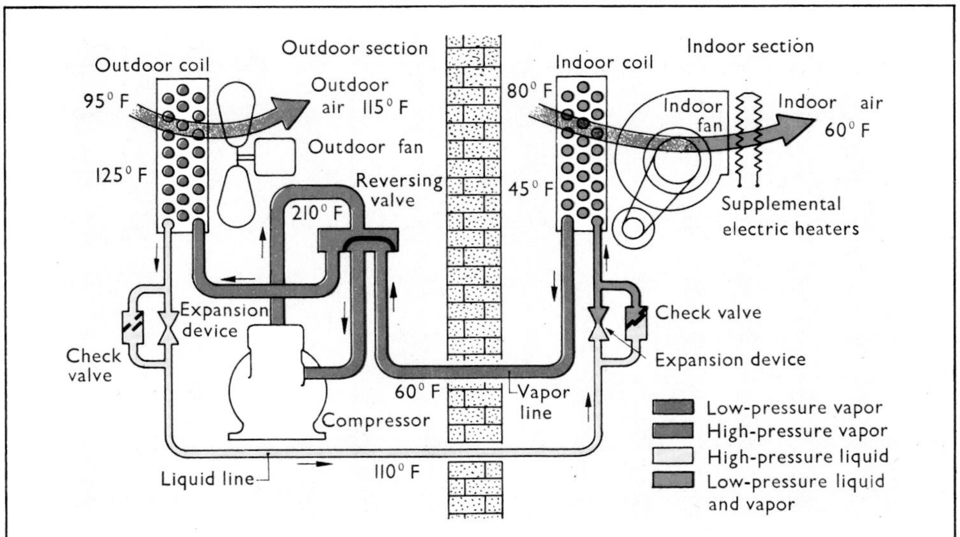

Basically, air conditioners are heat pumps. When liquid evaporates or expands to form a gas it absorbs heat from its surroundings. Here refrigerant vaporizes in the indoor coil, thereby absorbing heat and cooling the room. Next, vapor is circulated through a compressor to an outdoor coil, where it is condensed into a liquid. Since this process is the reverse of evaporation, heat is given off into the surrounding air.

MAJOR AIR FORCES OF EAST AND WEST

NATO Forces	Military Personnel	Combat Aircraft	Warsaw Pact Forces	Military Personnel	Combat Aircraft
USA	830 000	6 000	USSR	550 000	9 000
UK	109 000	500	Poland	55 000	700
W. Germany	104 000	460	Czechoslovakia	40 000	505
Italy	76 000	325	East Germany	25 000	325
Turkey	55 000	290	Bulgaria	22 000	250

derive most of their lift from their aerodynamic design and forward motion (see also GROUND EFFECT).

AIR DEFENSE, the means of detecting and intercepting enemy aircraft or missiles entering a country's airspace. The US Air Defense Command (ADC) relies on a chain of radar systems around the world including the Ballistic Missile Early Warning Systems (BMEWS), Distant Early Warning Line (DEW), Semi-Automatic Ground Environment (SAGE) and Over-the-Horizon radar (OTH). Their range will be significantly expanded by the Airborne Warning and Control System (AWACS) now being tested, and the newly developed Over-the-Horizon Backscatter radar (OTHB). The Space Defense Center, located in the North American Air Defense Command (NORAD) in Cheyenne, Wyo., coordinates optical and electronic information about man-made satellites. But at present the only defense against an attack launched from space is a viable deterrent.

AIREDALE TERRIER, variety of dog originally bred for otter hunting in the Aire valley, Yorkshire, England. Airedales are large terriers, weighing 40–50lb, with short black and tan coats.

The Airedale terrier, nicknamed the "king of terriers," is intelligent, powerful and affectionate. It has been used as a wartime dispatch carrier, police-dog, guard and big-game hunter.

AIRFOIL, any surface designed to have a mechanical interaction with the air through which it passes. In particular the term refers to the cross-sectional shape of an AIRPLANE wing, though the tailfin and propeller blades are also airfoils.

AIR FORCE, Royal Canadian (RCAF), the aeronautical division of the Canadian military establishment until all the armed forces were merged into a single service in January 1968.

The new unified Armed Forces of Canada include important air elements. The Mobile Command maintains land and tactical air forces that can be rapidly deployed in other parts of the world. Ground support aircraft, including six helicopter squadrons, are an important component of this command. The new Maritime Command includes former RCAF Maritime Air Command. Its two primary tasks are antisubmarine warfare (utilizing the aircraft carrier *Bonaventure* and helicopter-carrying destroyers), and surveillance operations along the extensive Canadian coastline. Air Transport Command (eight squadrons) provides strategic air lift capability. Its functions also include tactical air support and search and rescue missions. Total personnel numbers about 36 000. Though the air elements now have both nuclear and conventional bombing capability, it is likely that nuclear strike weapons will disappear as Canadian contributions to NATO are reduced.

AIR FORCE, United States, a highly complex and sophisticated branch of the Department of Defense, which controls one of the largest accumulations of destructive power ever known. The United States Air Force employs 830 000 men on active duty, flies some 126 000 aircraft, has total assets and equipment worth about 100 billion dollars and an annual budget of from 25 to 30 billion dollars. It deploys some of the most advanced aircraft in the world. It has over 500 strategic bombers among which are the eight-engined B-52s that may be armed with missiles or nuclear bombs, or carry more than fifty 750lb bombs. The USAF also operates over 2 300 fighter attack planes, many of which, like the F-4 Phantoms, are capable of supersonic speeds. For reconnaissance purposes there are planes such as the SR-71, which can reach three times the speed of sound at 80 000ft. The Air Force operates over 6 000 fighter aircraft all told. The huge C-5A transport plane can carry 700 men, 16 trucks, or two battle tanks 5 000mi without refueling. But the most powerful items of equipment, at least in terms of pure destructive potential, are nuclear missiles.

Air Force personnel are organized into several different "commands." Three combat commands are responsible for the actual fighting. They are the Strategic Air Command (SAC), which is the long range bombardment and reconnaissance force, the Tactical Air Command (TAC), which supports land and sea forces in action, and the Air Defense Command (ADC), which warns against attacks from a hostile force, and provides the first line of defense. Other commands are devoted to transport, communications and intelligence. There are also several training commands, such as the AIR FORCE ACADEMY, which ensure a steady flow of trained recruits.

AIR FORCE, US Department of the, division of the US Department of Defense controlling military aviation, including missile and aerospace programs.

AIR FORCE ACADEMY, US, national center which trains men to become officers in the US Air Force. Established in 1954, it is located at Colorado Springs, Col. Studies include basic and military sciences, aeronautic theory and airmanship, in addition to liberal arts. Graduates are awarded a BS degree and are commissioned as second-lieutenants in the Air Force.

AIRGLOW, a faint reddish or greenish light, of similar nature to the AURORA, visible in night skies at low and middle latitudes. It is caused by the reforming of molecules split by the sun's ultraviolet light.

AIR GUN, a weapon using compressed air to fire a dart or pellet with a maximum range of about 90m. The charge of air released on pressing the trigger is produced either by prior compression or instantaneously by releasing a spring-loaded piston. In the similar **gas gun,** a replaceable carbon dioxide reservoir provides several hundred charges.

AIR LAW, the law governing the use and status of air space. A body of international rules was first formulated at the Paris Convention of 1919 which established that all nations have the right to control their air space. The Chicago Convention of 1944 (Convention on International Civil Aviation) recognized the right of civil aircraft of the signatory states to fly across or land in each other's territories for non-commercial purposes (subject to certain limitations). Commercial scheduled air services are arranged bilaterally. The Convention established the International Civil Aviation Organization (ICAO), which formulates technical standards and codifies the law with respect to liability, property rights and criminal acts, including HIJACKING.

AIR LOCK, an airtight chamber with two doors used to allow men and materials to pass between environments having different air pressures. Air locks are used on caissons facilitating underwater excavation, on spacecraft, as submarine escape hatches and in industrial high-vacuum installations.

AIR MASS. See METEOROLOGY.

AIR NATIONAL GUARD, reserve force of the US Air Force numbering some 60 000 men in all the states and territories. Enlistment is voluntary, and the men are given short periods of paid training throughout the year, under the supervision of the Continental Air Command. Normally under state command, the guard may be activated by the federal government.

AIRPLANE, a powered heavier-than-air craft which obtains lift from the aerodynamic effect of the air rushing over its wings (see AERODYNAMICS). The typical airplane has a cigar-shaped fuselage which carries the pilot and payload; wings to provide lift; a power unit to provide forward thrust; stabilizers and a tail fin for controlling the plane in flight, and landing gear for supporting it on the ground. The plane is piloted using the throttle and the three basic control surfaces: the ELEVATORS on the stabilizers which determine "pitch" (whether the plane is climbing, diving or flying horizontally); the rudder on the tail fin which governs "yaw" (the rotation of the plane about a vertical axis), and the AILERONS on the wings which control "roll" (the rotation of the plane about the long axis through the fuselage). In turning the plane, both the rudder and the ailerons must be used to "bank" the plane into the turn. The airplane's control surfaces are operated by moving a control stick or steering column (elevators and ailerons) in conjunction with a pair of footpedals (rudder).

The pilot has many instruments to guide him. Chief among these are the air-speed indicator, altimeter, compass, fuel gauge and engine-monitoring instruments. Large modern aircraft also have flight directors, artificial horizons, course indicators, slip and turn indicators, instruments which interact with ground-based navigation systems and radar. In case any individual instrument fails, most are duplicated. (See also AIR TRANSPORTATION; FLIGHT, HISTORY OF.)

AIR PLANT. See EPIPHYTE.

AIR POLLUTION, the contamination of the atmosphere by harmful vapors, AEROSOLS and dust particles, resulting principally from the activities of man but to a lesser extent from natural processes. Natural pollutants include pollen particles, salt-water spray, wind-blown dust and fine debris from volcanic eruptions. Most man-made pollution involves the products of COMBUSTION—smoke (from burning wood, coal, and oil in municipal, industrial and domestic furnaces); carbon monoxide and lead (from automobiles), and oxides of nitrogen and sulfur dioxide (mainly from burning coal)—though other industrial processes, crop-spraying and atmospheric nuclear explosions also contribute. Most air pollution arises in the urban environment, with a large portion of that coming from the AUTOMOBILE. **Pollution control** involves identifying the sources of contamination; developing improved or alternative technologies and sources of raw materials, and persuading industries and individuals to adopt these, if need be under the sanction of legislation. Automobile emission control is a key area for current research, exploring avenues such as the RECYCLING and thorough OXIDATION of exhaust gases; the production of lead-free GASOLINE, and the

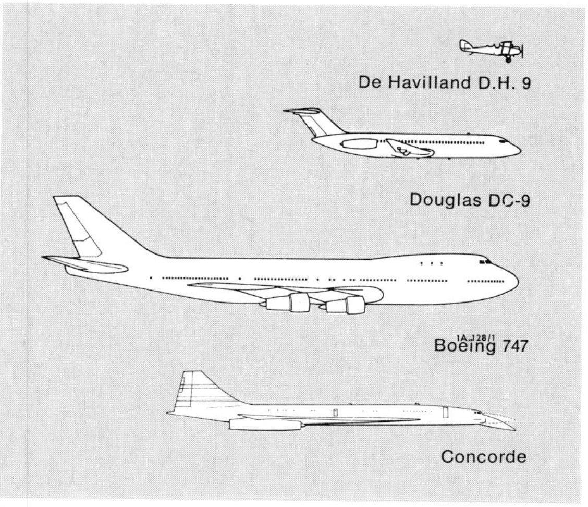

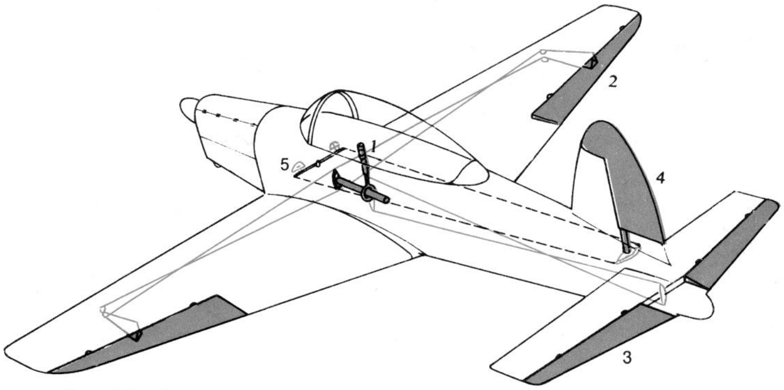

Left: The growth and development of passenger airplanes.
Above: controls of a typical light plane. The control column (1) moves both the ailerons (2) and the elevators (3); the rudder (4) is moved by pedals (5).
Below: the American Boeing 747 "Jumbo," one of the world's largest passenger aircraft, and the Anglo-French *Concorde*, first supersonic passenger airplane.

Air transportation

Higher, faster, bigger, cheaper

The increasing pace of modern life is forcing us to develop even faster and more far-ranging techniques of air transportation. Against this, however, must now be set the demands of the fuel crisis and the environment, and much controversy has raged over the latest advance in passenger transport, the supersonic airliner. The speed of sound at sea level in the "International Standard Atmosphere" is 762mph. At altitudes between 36000ft and 65000ft it is about 658mph, the decrease being caused by the lower air temperature (−56.5°C) at these altitudes. Concorde, the only supersonic airliner already flying for which comprehensive information is available, cruises at nearly twice the speed of sound, a speed often referred to as "Mach 2." This speed was carefully chosen, taking into consideration efficiency, economy and relative improvement over currently-used subsonic aircraft. It is no coincidence that the Russian supersonic airliner, the Tu-144, is also designed to cruise at Mach 2. The American SST project for a Mach 3 airliner, now in doubt, looked further into the future than the Anglo-French and Russian aircraft, because the attainment of Mach 3 cruising speed is disproportionately more expensive to achieve, requiring new and relatively untried construction materials and a new scale of aerodynamic performance which has not yet been fully tested by operational aircraft.

At Mach 2 the outer surface of the aircraft's skin is frictionally heated to 120°C, which approaches the limit for the use of aluminum alloys; at Mach 3 the skin temperature is around 250°C, requiring the use of steel-based alloys, rather than aluminum.

The airframe efficiency is of prime importance in deciding on the feasibility of supersonic cruising. It is measured in the terms of lift to drag (L/D) ratio and is typically about 16 for today's subsonic jets, cruising at around Mach 0.8. The L/D ratio falls sharply to around 9 in the transonic region of speed, but then falls more slowly to around 7.0 in the Mach 2 to Mach 3 region. Fortunately, the fuel and power efficiency of turbojet engines increases from around 25% at subsonic speeds to around 40% between Mach 2.0 and 3.0, so a supersonic transport which rivals the efficiency of present-day subsonic aircraft is theoretically possible.

One of the most controversial environmental issues has been the expansion of airports, both in terms of the land they occupy and the nuisance they create. One answer to this might be the development of the vertical takeoff airliner. Vertical takeoff and landing (VTOL) aircraft have two important advantages: they can travel from city center to city center, and by rising vertically their noise "footprint" on the ground is kept to a minimum, thus causing the least possible annoyance to people living close to the airport. But they are expensive. Most designs for inter-city airliners require the use of as many as 12 downwards-pointing "lift" engines which serve no useful purpose from the moment takeoff has been achieved until it is time to land. This means the aircraft has to carry the dead weight of 12 engines during the journey. In addition, the power-to-weight ratio of VTOL aircraft has to be greater than 1.0, a ratio not required for conventional aircraft because it is not necessary to have one pound of engine thrust for every pound of aircraft weight, the lift being provided by the airflow over the wings. A vertical takeoff airliner, however, uses pure engine power for lift at takeoff, and so needs very light, powerful engines. These can be built, but at present are not economically feasible. Another reason why VTOL airliners are not likely within the next decade or two is that entirely new airports will have to be built, close to the city centers they serve, and as this requires international cooperation and agreement, and very considerable expenditure, it is unlikely to happen all at once. Perhaps by the end of the 20th century economic and environmental priorities may favor the VTOL. Until this happens, air transport for very short distances will not be competitive with land transportation.

The short takeoff and landing (STOL) airliner is the practical compromise between conventional aircraft requiring runways of several miles in length, and vertical takeoff aircraft. STOL aircraft require anything up to about $\frac{1}{2}$-mile runways, which means they can operate very close to city centers, on relatively modest airstrips. They have larger wings than conventional aircraft of the same seating capacity, and are capable of climbing rapidly because of the greater lift achieved by these larger wings. This reduces the duration of noise heard on the ground. But the penalty for this is that STOL aircraft are not as fast as conventional planes. Calculations show, however, that they have an important role to fill in city center to city center transportation. Because of the high lifting ability of the wings, they are relatively cheap transporters of cargo. At long distances, however, they do not compare favorably with conventional aircraft.

Most STOL aircraft are still on the drawing board at present because aircraft manufacturers are waiting to see what official government policies are going to be. But some examples actually flying are the Canadian De Havilland Twin Otter, a 14-passenger STOL aircraft and the 9-seater Fairy Britten Norman Islander. There will undoubtedly be a swing towards quiet STOL aircraft in the next decade or so, particularly as existing airports become congested with conventional traffic, but at present the demand is not sufficient to force the issue.

In the meantime the prevailing problem of aircraft noise remains. It is usually considered in three ways: the quantity or power of the noise, the quality of the noise (the proportion of power in different frequency or pitch ranges) and the overall nuisance value of an airport measured in terms of the number of aircraft movements per hour and the volume of noise.

Modern turbojets give two main types of noise: the deep thunderous roar of the engine, caused by the "scrubbing" action of the high-speed exhaust gases on the surrounding atmosphere, and the high-pitched whistle caused by turbine blades as they cut through the lines of airflow within the engines. Traditional turbojet designs paid no heed to the noise production and had high-speed exhausts and whistling turbine blades, the whistle often being aggravated by the use of guide vanes at the air intake of the engine. Modern "quiet" engines, such as those used in the Douglas DC 10 and the Lockheed Tristar, use high-bypass-ratio turbojets. These pass as much as five times the volume of air used for fuel burning around the outside of the combustion chambers, to mix with the burned gases in the tailpipe and reduce the overall speed of the exhaust. The lower exhaust speeds cause a reduction in the low-frequency thunderous roar of the engines. The limit to what can be done is reached when the bypass fan needed to produce high bypass ratios gets so large that the tips of its blades reach the speed of sound, causing an additional noise problem.

The high-pitched whistle is being reduced in modern engines by eliminating inlet guide vanes altogether; by designing the turbine blades themselves to cope with the flow of air; and in some instances by giving the blades variable pitch, not unlike the swiveling airscrews used for piston-engined and jet-prop aircraft.

Existing engines can be quieted by the addition of "hush kits." These consist of a tail pipe extension, which improves the mixing of the jet exhaust with the surrounding air, and acoustic lining of the engine consisting of "honeycomb" metal, to absorb noise in the places where it is being created.

Some measure of the progress already achieved is gained by considering the fact that aircraft are now bigger and quieter—the Boeing 747 "Jumbo Jet" and the Lockheed Tristar are examples of this. The result is that despite the huge increase of passengers, the additional noise pollution is likely to be very small over the next decade, and should eventually be reduced when all available engineering techniques have been applied to the problem. In a decade, individual noisy aircraft should have disappeared, and the general level of noise from an airport could be reduced to a low-pitched background rumble.

Beyond the environmental issues the cultural impact of increased air travel has both good and bad aspects. The modern turbojet, forming the basis of mass long-distance transport, is one of the powerful factors responsible for creating a more uniform world culture. The tourist industry has paralleled the explosive growth of jet transport, with much of the huge increase in numbers of passengers being those traveling for leisure. Ironically, wherever tourism succeeds on a large scale, the demands of the tourists for material comfort, as well as the culture and languages they bring with them, erode local traditions and help change social and economic relations. Eventually, tourism affects the physical appearance of cities and towns; if they become economically dependent on tourism they will build to cater for vacation needs. Underdeveloped countries accessible to jet travel are thus changing more rapidly both culturally and materially than they would otherwise have. It may be that within a few decades only the inhabitants of very remote places will still provide the picturesque contrast with modern life that tourists go out of their way to see.

Jet transport has also made us vulnerable to sudden outbreaks of infectious diseases by making it possible for an infected person to fly to another country before the disease becomes evident. Immigration health controls are quite powerless to detect a disease in the incubation period, and the populations in countries free of particular diseases are more susceptible year by year to each disease which is absent, because the body often "forgets" how to fight any germ it has not encountered for many years.

Freight-carrying, too, has had a dramatic effect on society. Very few aircraft are now designed purely to carry passengers, or, for that matter, purely for freight. The versatile design of most aircraft results from the need to transport both passengers and freight at the lowest possible price. Freight is normally used by the airlines to fill up any available payload capacity in the aircraft to ensure that it is flying at all times with a full load. Normally, this means that cargo is not kept waiting for a plane leaving with few enough passengers, but is distributed in the most efficient and economical way between the available aircraft. The result is that many commodities can now be carried by air which have traditionally been transported by sea. Fresh foods, for example, are now exported by air when the demand is strong enough, and the resulting increase in the price of food is not more than people in industrial countries can afford to pay. The tiny Sheikhdom of Abu Dhabi in the Persian Gulf depends entirely on air transport for its supply of fresh vegetables, because there are no indigenous crops. And by the year 2000 we may see entire landlocked countries dependent on air transport for almost every import—provided they can afford the high price.

Air transport has the principal advantage of speed and the secondary advantage of being able to deliver the goods reasonably close to their ultimate destination, thus reducing some of the overall costs. There are already systems in operation, such as at London's Heathrow airport, where all cargo is under computer control.

Every item is entered into the computer's electronic memory as soon as it enters the airport, and all information concerning the status of a particular cargo can be obtained instantly. Nevertheless, the current boom in air freight cannot go on indefinitely. Aircraft remain the least economical form of transport in terms of fuel costs, and the oil crisis greatly increased the price of aviation fuel, thus upsetting the delicate balance which enables air transport, despite its cost, to have the advantage over its surface competitors. And this is a serious handicap for the growth of air transportation as a whole.

It is now clear that for both political and environmental reasons a greater economy of energy consumption will have to be imposed on all aspects of life. We cannot go on consuming more and more energy unless we find new alternative sources for it. And aircraft now depend on the fuel most limited both by political situations and the draining of natural reserves—oil. It is neither convenient nor completely safe to contemplate using nuclear power for air propulsion, which means that aircraft will continue to use liquid fuels. One type of fuel is likely to be rather similar to the fuels used today, but manufactured from vegetable products—inevitably a costly procedure. Another type of fuel is hydrogen, which can be manufactured by passing an electric current through water. But large amounts of this fuel would only be available if there were a plentiful supply of electricity. If cheap alternative sources of energy for power generation do not emerge by the next century, air transport would be one of the first casualties, being the least energy-economical means of transport. In the 1970s a trend has developed towards fewer and larger aircraft, the so-called "Jumbo Jets." In a sense these are more economical, but the extra space they require and their general complexity of operation leave them still highly controversial. The search for new solutions to the problems of air transportation continues—and one new solution may turn out in fact to be a very old one indeed.

Despite the great advances the modern airplane has made in all respects, including economy, it still remains the most costly means of transport. The great cost handicap is caused by the fact that since it is heavier than air it needs continuous power in large quantities to keep it flying. The airship, on the other hand, needs no power at all to keep it in the air. It needs only a small engine to stop it drifting in the wind and to push it along. In theory, airships could be as cheap as marine ships for transporting cargo over long distances, and would be particularly useful for landlocked countries, though passengers would probably continue to fly in heavier-than-air machines at far greater speeds than an airship would be capable of. But since airships can be huge, they might one day compete with ocean liners for passengers who want luxury accommodation and are in no hurry.

The progress of the airship has been held up by two factors: a continuing concern dating back to the 1930s that airships are not safe, and lack of sufficiently strong environmental pressure for such a clean, quiet and economical form of transport. In the 1930s airships were discredited to some extent when the British R-101 and the German *Hindenburg* airships crashed, and structural engineering was not so advanced as it is today. But airships can now be built which are as safe as any airplane. A recent design, of which large models are already flying, uses a ducted fan in a "flying saucer" body, giving unprecedented control over maneuverability. The future of air transportation may lie, not with the aircraft, but with its slower but less costly cousin, the airship.

Air transportation is expanding just as fast as road transportation; airports seem to be increasing as fast as highways. The map below shows the maze of landing approaches to airfields in the New York area, especially John F. Kennedy International Airport (*right*).

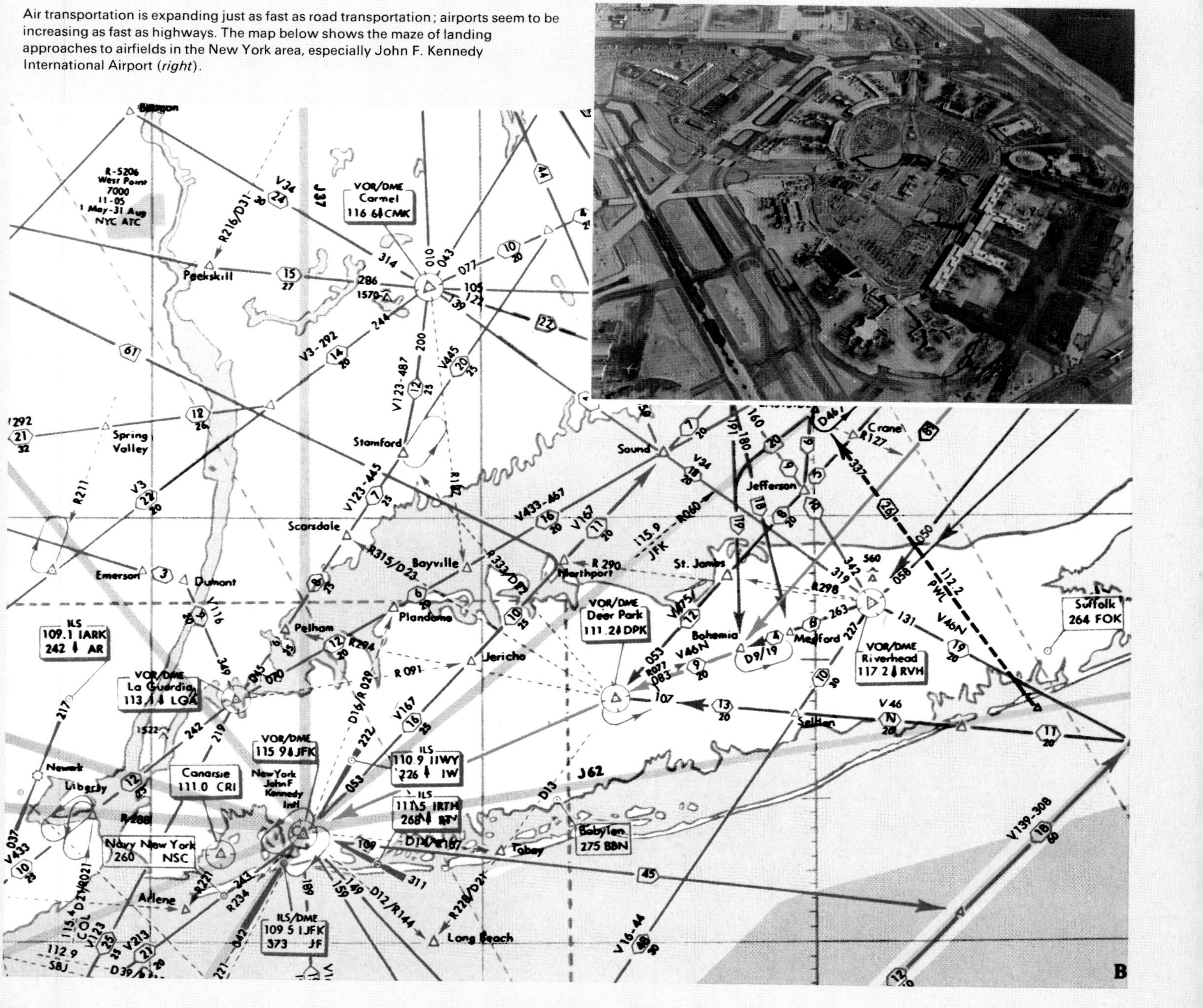

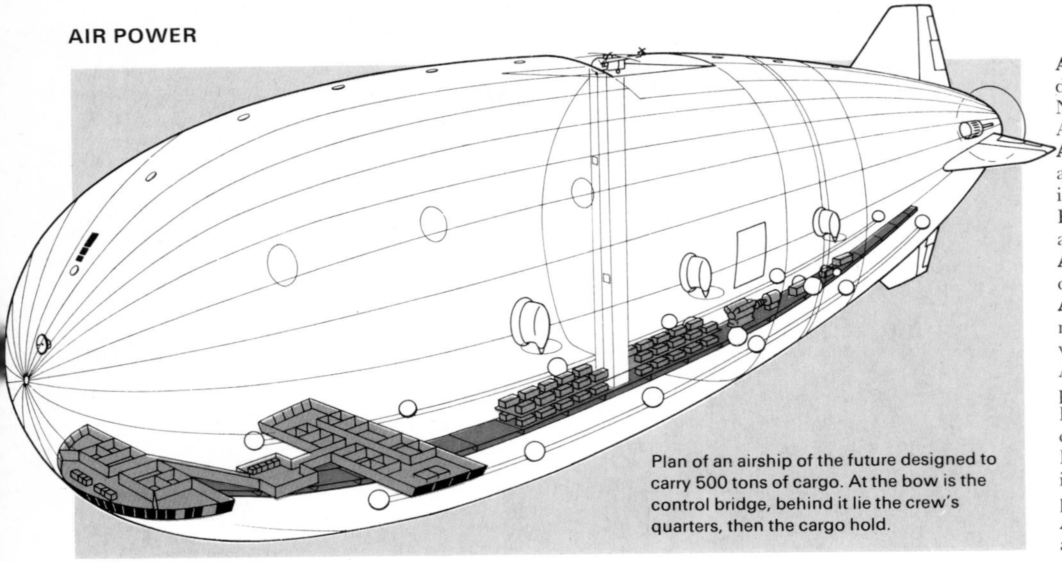

Plan of an airship of the future designed to carry 500 tons of cargo. At the bow is the control bridge, behind it lie the crew's quarters, then the cargo hold.

development of alternatives to the conventional INTERNAL COMBUSTION ENGINE. On the industrial front, flue-gas cleansing using catalytic conversion (see CATALYSIS) or centrifugal, water-spray or electrostatic precipitators is becoming increasingly widespread. The matching of smokestack design to local meteorological and topographic conditions is important for the efficient dispersal of remaining pollutants. Domestic pollution can be reduced by restricting the use of high-pollution fuels as in the UK's "smokeless zones." In the short term, the community must be prepared to pay the often high prices of such pollution-control measures, but bearing in mind the continuing economic rewards ensuing and the vital necessity of preserving the purity of the air we breathe, the sacrifice must be worthwhile. (See also POLLUTION).

AIR POWER, the military potential of aircraft and airborne weapons. The reality of air power has changed the basic concepts of strategy. In the past, armies were obliged to base their tactics not only on the time it took them to move forward against the enemy, but on the limitations imposed by natural barriers such as rivers, canals and mountain chains. Vulnerable points were bound to be strongly protected. Air power, operating almost unrestricted in three dimensions, with little concern for natural barriers, has made defense much more difficult. Between the two world wars, theorists such as the Italian Giulio Douhet and the US General William ("Billy") MITCHELL postulated that victory in a future war would be achieved only by using strategic bombing to destroy an enemy's industries, and possibly morale, before he had a chance to strike back. This strategy was employed too late in WWII to provide a real test of its effectiveness. Fear of escalation limited the use of air power in the Korean War, but the Vietnam War showed that bombing alone could not defeat unconventional forces operating in dense cover.

The aircraft used in these engagements were nonetheless terrifying weapons, even when compared with the already sophisticated planes of WWII. Some bombers can now fly 11 000mi from a base on one continent, bomb a target on another, and return to base. Modern fighters fly at supersonic speeds, have tremendous maneuverability and can carry missiles, either of an air-to-ground or air-to-air type. New laser-guided "smart" bombs have proved deadly accurate for strategic bombing. Reconnaissance aircraft equipped with high-resolution cameras are able to distinguish objects one foot apart from a height of 50 000ft. Helicopters have proved essential for transporting troops over dangerous or rugged terrain as well as for combat missions.

While manned aircraft still form the basis of air power, it is the intercontinental ballistic missile (ICBM) that now provides the principal means of carrying on strategic nuclear war. Orbiting weapons are technically possible and may be developed in the absence of an arms-limitation agreement. Thus air power has now become aerospace power. (See also MISSILE.)

AIR PRESSURE. See ATMOSPHERE.

AIR PUMP. See PUMP.

AIR-RAID SHELTER. See FALLOUT SHELTER.

AIR RIGHTS, rights to use of building space, especially over railroad tracks, highways, bridge and tunnel approaches and so on. Air rights were used in New York City over the New York Central track as early as 1910. As urban land grew scarcer in all big cities, such rights became increasingly valuable for housing developments and office construction.

AIR SACS, small respiratory cavities: in birds, leading off the lungs and often entering into the bones; in many insects, expansions in the TRACHEAE.

AIRSCREW. See PROPELLER.

AIRSHIP, or dirigible, a lighter-than-air, self-propelled aircraft whose buoyancy is provided by gasbags containing hydrogen or helium. The first successful airship was designed by Henri Giffard, a French engineer, and flew over Paris in 1852, though it was only with the development of the INTERNAL COMBUSTION ENGINE that the airship became truly practical. From 1900 Germany led the world in airship design, as Count Ferdinand von ZEPPELIN began to construct his famous "Zeppelins." Most of the large airships built during the next 40 years were of the "rigid" type, with a metal-lattice frame, and used hydrogen as the lifting gas. Their vulnerability in storms and a series of spectacular fire disasters brought an abrupt end to their use in about 1937. During WWII much use was made of small "nonrigid" patrol airships ("blimps") in which the gasbag formed the outer skin and altitude was controlled by inflating and venting air "ballonets" inside the main gas bag. Most existing craft are of this type, with engines slung beneath the gasbag either on the cabin or in separate "nacelles." "Semi-rigid" airships are similar to blimps but, being larger, usually have a longitudinal metal keel. Airship enthusiasts envisage a great future for airships filled with nonflammable helium, noiselessly transporting freight right into the heart of large cities.

AIRSICKNESS. See MOTION SICKNESS.

AIR SPACE. See AIR LAW.

AIR TURBULENCE, irregular eddying in the ATMOSPHERE, such as that encountered in gusts of wind. Turbulence disperses water vapor, dust, smoke and other pollutants through the atmosphere, and is important in transferring heat energy upward from the ground. There is little turbulence in the upper atmosphere except in developing thunderclouds. **Clear-air turbulence** (CAT), which is often found around the margins of JET STREAMS, can be hazardous to high-flying jet aircraft.

AIR UNIVERSITY, school established in 1946 at Maxwell Air Force Base near Montgomery, Ala., which provides advanced scientific and technical training for US Air Force officers. The Air Force ROTC program is also supervised by the Air University.

AISNE RIVER, of N France, rising in Meuse department, flows 175mi from the Argonne Forest NW and W to join the Oise R near Compiègne. The Aisne valley was the scene of heavy fighting in WWI.

AIX-EN-PROVENCE (or Aix), city of S France, about 19mi N of Marseille. Colonized by the Romans in 123 BC, it became the capital of medieval Provence. Industries produce foodstuffs, textiles, flour and olive oil. Pop 79 948.

AIX-LA-CHAPELLE, French name for the German city of AACHEN.

AIX-LA-CHAPELLE, Congress of (1818), meeting at Aachen (Aix-la-Chapelle) at which the victors in the Napoleonic Wars—Great Britain, Austria, Prussia and Russia—agreed to preserve the political arrangements they had established for Europe at the Congress of Vienna (1815). But it also confirmed the withdrawal of occupying troops from France, which was to be restored to the status of an independent major power and was to join the other powers in the Quintuple Alliance.

AIX-LA-CHAPELLE, Treaties of, name of two agreements. The first treaty (1668) ended the War of DEVOLUTION between France and the TRIPLE ALLIANCE of England, Holland and Sweden over France's claim to the Spanish Netherlands. It allowed France to retain most of the Flanders towns captured the previous year. The second treaty (1748) concluded the War of the AUSTRIAN SUCCESSION, in which several nations, led by France and Prussia, had tried to annex the vast territories held by the Empress Maria Theresa of Austria. By the terms of the treaty the empress' right to the Hapsburg throne was recognized, and Prussia gained the important region of Silesia.

AIX-LES-BAINS, spa and resort in Savoy, E France, with warm sulfur springs visited since Roman times. A gateway to the French Alps and a winter sports center. Pop 20 594.

AJACCIO, capital of the French island of Corsica in the Mediterranean, a port on the W coast. Celebrated as the birthplace of Napoleon, it is today a commercial center and popular resort. Industries include fishing and shipbuilding. Pop 38 776.

AJANTA, village in Maharashtra, India, famous for some 29 richly decorated caves in the side of a nearby steep ravine. Rediscovered in1819 by British troops, the caves are Buddhist monastic dwellings and shrines containing elaborate carvings, statues and frescoes, some dating from the 2nd century BC.

AJAX, name of two legendary Greek kings in the TROJAN WAR. **Ajax the Greater**, king of Salamis, was renowned for his size and strength. He defeated HECTOR and helped rescue ACHILLES' body from the Trojans. Driven mad with anger when AGAMEMNON awarded Achilles' armor to ODYSSEUS, he killed himself. **Ajax the Lesser**, son of the king of Locris, arrogant though brave and swift-footed, raped CASSANDRA and was destroyed by Poseidon for offending the gods.

AJMER, city in Rajasthan state, NW India, 220mi SW of New Delhi. A rail and cotton textile center, once an important Mogul capital. Pop 262 480.

AKASHI, historic city on the S coast of Honshu Island, Japan, 12mi W of Kobe on Akashi Strait. Industries include chemicals, textiles and machinery. Pop 206 525.

AKBAR (1542–1605), greatest of the MOGUL emperors, who extended Mogul power over most of Afghanistan and India. An excellent administrator, he pursued a policy of religious toleration and took an active interest in the study of religious sects. He also improved social laws, commerce and transportation.

AKELEY, Carl Ethan (1864–1926), American naturalist and sculptor of animals who pioneered large-scale museum displays of stuffed animals, especially African big game, in their natural habitats.

AKHENATON (or Ikhnaton), title taken by Amenhotep IV, king of Egypt c1379–1362 BC. Married to NEFERTITI, he started the cult of the sun-god ATON, despite the opposition of the priesthood of Amon-Ra. Changing his name to Akhenaton ("he who serves Aton"), he moved the capital from Thebes, city of Amon, to Akhetatón (now Tell el-Amarna), where he fostered a naturalistic school of art and literature. After his death the old religion was reestablished and Akhenaton's name was erased from his monuments.

AKHMATOVA, Anna, pseudonym of Anna Andreyevna Gorenko (1889–1966), Russian poet who joined the reaction against Symbolist vagueness and obscurity. Her own poems, often confessional lyrics, are notable for clarity and formal precision.

AKIBA BEN JOSEPH (c40–135), famous Jewish rabbi, one of the greatest compilers of Hebrew law, whose work later formed the basis of the MISHNAH. After supporting a revolt against the Romans, he was executed as a rebel.

AKIHITO (1933–), crown prince of Japan, elder son of Emperor Hirohito and Empress Nagako Kuni. His marriage to a commoner, Michiko Shodo, in 1959 was followed in 1960 by the birth of a son and heir.

AKITA, port on the W coast of the Japanese island of Honshu, N of Tokyo, and capital of Akita prefecture. It is an important industrial city, and nearby are Japan's largest oil fields. Pop 235 873.

AKKAD, Semitic kingdom in Lower Mesopotamia, N of Sumer, founded by Sargon c2360 BC. Its center was the strongly fortified city of Akkad (Agade), N of Nippur. The Akkadian dynasty overthrew the Sumerian Kish and ruled Mesopotamia from c2360 to 2180 BC.

AKLAVIK, fur trading settlement on the Mackenzie R Delta in the Northwest Territory, Canada. Ground conditions forced transfer of the district administrative center to Inuvik in 1955. Pop 611.

AKRON, industrial city in NE Ohio on the Cuyahoga R, seat of Summit Co., 36mi S of Cleveland. Akron is famed as the rubber and tire manufacturing capital of the world: B. F. Goodrich founded his pioneer rubber factory here in 1871. Other industries produce transportation equipment, metal products and plastics. Pop 275 425.

AKSAKOV, Sergei Timofeyevich (1791–1859), Russian writer, whose *Family Chronicle* (1846–56) and *Years of Childhood* (1858) combine the novel and memoir forms. He was a prominent member of the Slavophile movement, as were his writer sons Konstantin (1817–1860) and Ivan (1823–1886).

AKSUM (or Axum), town in Tigre province, N Ethiopia, capital of an ancient Ethiopian kingdom, the Aksumite Empire, from about the 1st to the 7th centuries AD. Aksum is Ethiopia's most sacred city: the biblical Ark of the Covenant is said to be kept in the Church of St. Mary Zion. Gigantic carved stelae, as large as the obelisks of Egypt, stand as the most impressive achievements of Aksumite art. Pop 12 804.

AKUREYRI, third-largest city of Iceland, a leading fishing port situated on the N coast at the head of Eyja Fjord 60mi S of the Arctic Circle. Pop 10 755.

AKUTAGAWA RYUNOSUKE (1892–1927), Japanese writer of short stories, poetry and plays. From medieval themes he turned to autobiographical subjects. His work's fantastic and morbid nature reveals susceptibilities which led to his suicide. His most famous story is *Rashomon* (1915).

ALABAMA, southern state, whose traditionally agricultural economy, once based on cotton, has greatly changed since the 1930s. Economic diversification, aided by the exploitation of hydroelectricity, has led to marked industrial growth, particularly in iron and steel production.

NE Alabama runs into the SW end of the Appalachians. It includes the Cumberland Plateau, a series of forested mineral-rich ridges, and a section of the Piedmont region. The Black Belt, a narrow strip of prairie land, crosses the East Gulf Coastal Plain (drained by the Alabama, Tombigbee and other rivers), which occupies most of the southern two-thirds of the state. SW Alabama touches the Gulf of Mexico at Mobile Bay. Climate is mild and moist.

About half the people now live in six urban areas, including the steel center of Birmingham in the N central part of the state, and Alabama's only Gulf port, Mobile. Coal, iron ore, limestone, bauxite, timber and oil provide raw materials for the state's industries, which are now the chief source of income. Cotton now accounts for only 5% of farm income; livestock and poultry for nearly 75%. In the N,

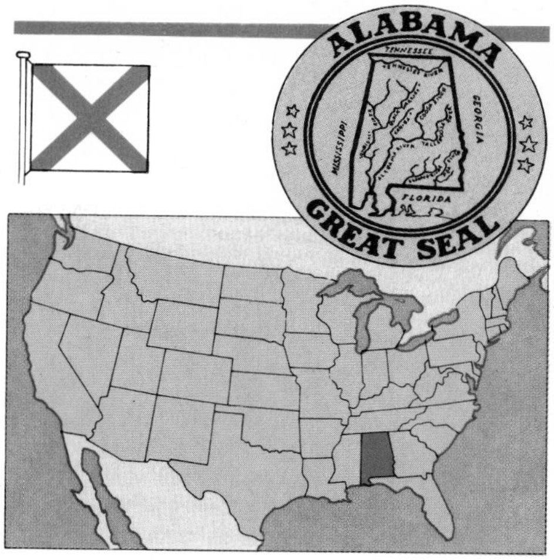

Name of state: Alabama
Capital: Montgomery
Statehood: Dec. 14, 1819 (22nd state)
Familiar name: Cotton or Yellowhammer State
Area: 51 609sq mi;
Population: 3 444 165
Elevation: Highest—2 407ft, Cheaha Mountain.
Motto: Audemus jura nostra defendere ("We dare defend our rights.")
State flower: Camellia
State bird: Yellowhammer
State tree: Southern pine
State song: "Alabama"

Tennessee Valley Authority dams provide low-cost hydroelectricity.

Choctaws, Creeks and other members of the FIVE CIVILIZED TRIBES originally peopled Alabama (the state is named for a Choctaw tribe). Spain's Hernando DE SOTO explored the region in 1540, and France's Sieur de BIENVILLE founded the first lasting European settlement in the Mobile area in 1702. France ceded the region to Britain (1763), which lost it to the US (1783), but Spain held the Mobile area until 1812. The defeat of the Creeks at the Battle of HORSESHOE BEND (1814) opened S Alabama to settlers, who developed a slave-based plantation economy. At the outbreak of the Civil War Montgomery became the first Confederate capital, but in the Battle of MOBILE BAY (1864), Admiral David Farragut closed one of the last remaining Confederate ports. Industry began to develop towards the end of the century, but one-crop farming and the sharecropping system brought widespread agricultural depression and poverty, accentuated from 1915 by the depredations of the boll weevil. TVA projects and WWII boosted industry, and despite racial tension in the 1950s and 1960s, Alabama has become a leader in the South in basing its economy firmly on manufacturing.

ALABAMA CLAIMS, compensation claimed by the US from Britain for property seized and destroyed by the *Alabama* and other Confederate vessels during the Civil War. Britain was charged with violating its neutrality by allowing the Confederate warships to be built or equipped in its shipyards. In 1871 the dispute was submitted to an international tribunal, which found Britain liable and awarded the US $15 500 000 in gold.

ALABAMA RIVER, formed by the junction of the Tallapoosa and Coosa rivers near Montgomery, Ala., flows W and SW 315mi to join the Tombigbee about 40mi N of Mobile, forming the Mobile and Tensaw rivers. Navigable throughout its course, its headwaters are harnessed to produce hydroelectricity.

ALABASTER, fine-grained, massive form of GYPSUM, usually translucent and white; used ornamentally for centuries, being easily carved. Ancient oriental alabaster was a yellowish MARBLE.

ALADDIN, hero of a story in the *Arabian Nights* who,

The classical elegance of the Alabama State Capitol in Montgomery. The city was capital of the confederacy during the Civil War.

as the son of a poor widow, comes into possession of a magic lamp with which he gains great riches and power. The story, set in China, originated in Muslim Persia, but the magic lamp also occurs as a theme in European and Oriental folklore.

ALAGOAS, agricultural state in NE Brazil. Its capital is the port of Maceió. Increasing industrialization is aided by hydroelectric power from the São Francisco R to the S. The chief industry is sugar refining. Pop 1 606 174.

ALAIN-FOURNIER, pseudonym of Henri Alban Fournier (1886–1914), French writer whose one novel, *Le Grand Meaulnes* (1913), is the haunting tale of a boy's attempt to rediscover the dreamlike setting of his meeting with a beautiful girl.

ALAMANCE, Battle of, victory of colonial North Carolina militia over 2 000 poorly organized REGULATORS at Alamance Creek near Burlington, May 16, 1771. Defeat led many of these upcountry farmers to migrate to Tenn.

ALAMANNI, confederation of Germanic tribes, first described in 213 AD, when they lived in the Main R region. The Alamanni dialect and other cultural vestiges survive in parts of Switzerland, S Germany and Alsace-Lorraine.

ALAMEDA, city in W Calif., on two islands and a peninsula in San Francisco Bay. Connected to the mainland by a tunnel and bridges, it is an important shipbuilding and steel center. Pop 70 968.

ALAMEIN, El. See EL ALAMEIN.

ALAMO, Spanish mission-fortress in San Antonio, Texas, the site of a heroic defense in 1836 by less than 200 Texans in the struggle for independence from Mexico. All the defenders, including such heroes as Davy CROCKETT and Jim BOWIE, died in a lengthy siege by 4 000 Mexicans under General SANTA ANNA.

ALAMOGORDO, town in S central N.M., seat of Otero Co. and the center of an agricultural, timber and recreation area which includes White Sands National Monument. The first atomic bomb was exploded near Alamogordo in a test on July 16, 1945. Pop 23 035.

ALANBROOKE, Alan Francis Brooke, 1st Viscount (1888–1963), British field marshal, one of the leading military strategists of WWII. Chief of the Imperial General Staff 1941–46, he participated in important wartime conferences of the Allies.

ÅLAND ISLANDS, archipelago in the Baltic Sea between Sweden and Finland. Originally Swedish, they today form the Finnish province of Ahvenanaa, though some 96% of the population speaks Swedish. Fishing, shipping, tourism and farming are principal occupations. Pop 20 789.

ALANI, a warlike tribe of Asia Minor who resembled the Mongols and spoke an Iranian language. Around the 1st century AD they made several attacks on the eastern Roman Empire. The Alani eventually migrated westward across S Europe and were absorbed by the Huns and Vandals.

ALARCÓN, Hernando de (c1466–1540), Spanish explorer of Mexico and the American Southwest, who proved that Baja California was a peninsula and not an island and discovered the mouth of the Colorado R.

ALARCÓN, Pedro Antonio de (1833–1891),

Spanish regional writer best known for his novel *The Three-Cornered Hat* (1874). His work is distinguished by sharp realistic observation and picturesque effects.

ALARCÓN Y MENDOZA, Juan Ruiz de (c1580–1639). Spanish playwright of the Golden Age who wrote brilliant moralizing comedies. The best-known, *The Suspicious Truth*, influenced the great French dramatist, CORNEILLE.

ALARIC, name of two Visigoth kings. **Alaric I** (c370–410) was commander of the Visigoth auxiliaries under the Roman Emperor Theodosius until the latter's death, when Alaric was proclaimed king by his countrymen. After invading Greece and N Italy, he captured and sacked Rome in 410. **Alaric II** (d. 507), ruled Spain and S Gaul from 484, and issued the Breviary of Alaric, a Visigoth code of Roman law, in 506. His army was defeated and he was slain by Clovis I, king of the Franks.

ALASKA, largest of the 50 states, and potentially one of the richest, America's "Last Frontier." It occupies the extreme NW corner of North America, bounded N by the Arctic Ocean, W by the Bering Sea, S by the Pacific Ocean, and E by the Yukon and British Columbia. Alaska lies only 51mi E of the Siberian mainland across the Bering Strait. Including the coasts of thousands of offshore islands (notably the 1200mi long Aleutian Islands, the Alexander Archipelago and the Pribilof Islands), Alaska's coastline exceeds those of all the other states combined. Major mountain chains are the Brooks Range in the N and the Alaska Range in the S (with Mt McKinley reaching 20320ft), separated by the Central Plateau through which the 1800mi long Yukon R flows. In the far N, the lowland North Slope faces the Arctic Ocean. The climate is cold in the N and the interior, but during the long daylight hours of the brief interior summer temperatures can be extremely high. Warm ocean currents and sheltering mountains make the climate of the S mild and moist.

Alaska is still the least populated of the 50 states, though its population grew by a third in the 1960s. Most people live in Anchorage (the largest city), Fairbanks and smaller centers in the Panhandle. Minerals (especially oil from the Kenai Peninsula; also gravel, coal and copper) are the state's chief source of income. Hunting fur seals is also important, and Alaska has the largest commercial fisheries of any state. Processing of the fish catch and production of pulp and lumber are the largest industries. Farms are few and most food must be imported, which adds to the high cost of living. Transportation is difficult in this remote, rugged state where long winters hamper road construction and maintenance. The 1523mi ALASKA HIGHWAY links Fairbanks with Canada and the US, and roads and a railroad join some southern centers, but much travel is by sea or air.

Russia claimed Alaska after Vitus BERING and Alexander CHIRIKOV sighted it (1741), Grigori SHELEKHOV founded the first lasting settlement, on Kodiak Island (1784), and in 1799 Alexander BARANOV founded Sitka. Secretary of State William H. SEWARD bought Alaska for the US in 1867 for $7.2 million (about 2 cents an acre). Economic growth remained slow until the 1896 Klondike gold rush in the neighboring Yukon and then in Alaska. Gold supplies dwindled, and the period of continuous growth only began when WWII revealed Alaska's great strategic importance. Since Alaska gained statehood in 1959, the discovery of North Slope oil and gas fields (among the world's largest) has opened prospects of huge expansion. But much depends on a trans-Alaskan oil pipeline from Prudhoe Bay to Valdez on the ice-free Gulf of Alaska. Its cost is estimated to exceed $7.7 billion, and in July 1973 the Senate approved a bill opening the way for its construction.

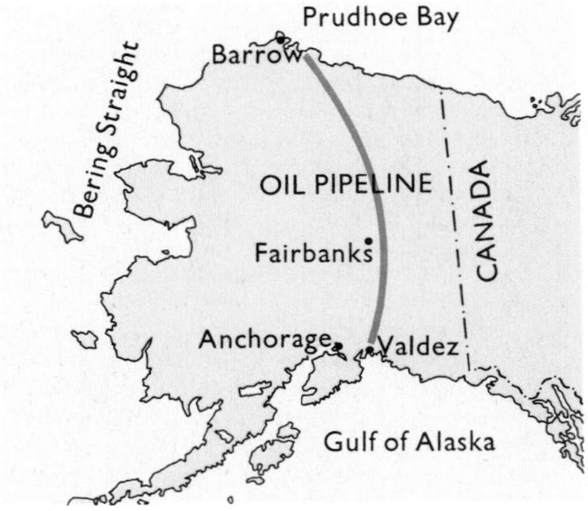

Oil pipeline in Alaska stretching from Barrow in the Prudhoe Bay to Valdez in the Gulf of Alaska.

Name of state: Alaska
Capital: Juneau
Statehood: Jan. 3, 1959 (49th state)
Familiar name: Last frontier; Land of the Midnight Sun; Great Land
Area: 586,400sq mi
Population: 302,173
Elevation: Highest—20,320ft, Mt. McKinley. Lowest—sea level, Pacific coast
Motto: "North to the future"
State flower: Forget-me-not
State Bird: Willow ptarmigan
State tree: Sitka spruce
State song: "Alaska's Flag"

ALASKA, Gulf of, broad inlet of the Pacific off the S coast of Alaska, bounded E by the Alexander Archipelago, W by the Alaska Peninsula.

ALASKA BOUNDARY DISPUTE, disagreement concerning the demarcation of the border between the Alaska Panhandle and Canada, which arose in 1898 during the Klondike gold rush. Skagway and the head of the LYNN CANAL, through which supplies reached the Yukon, were claimed to be in Canadian territory. The question was settled in favor of America by a joint US–British commission in 1903.

ALASKA CURRENT, warm current of the N Pacific Ocean flowing N then W along the coast of the Gulf of Alaska. (See OCEAN CURRENTS.)

ALASKA HIGHWAY, road extending 1523mi between Fairbanks, Alaska, and Dawson Creek, British Columbia; the sole overland link between Alaska and the road systems of Canada and the 48 states. It was built by the US as a strategic all-weather military route in 1942, and in 1946 Canada took over control of the 1221mi passing through its territory.

ALASKAN BROWN BEAR, subspecies of BROWN BEAR (*Ursus arctos*), the largest surviving land carnivore, measuring up to 3m (10ft) in length and weighing perhaps 780kg (1700lb). The largest variety, found mainly on Kodiak Island, is known as the Kodiak Bear.

ALASKAN MALAMUTE, wolflike Arctic sled dog, developed by the Mahlemut Eskimos of NW Alaska. It has a heavy coat, gray or white and black, and a great bushy tail, and possesses great strength and endurance. Average height, 24in at the shoulder; weight, 75–85lb.

ALASKA PENINSULA, 500mi long peninsula extending SW from the Alaskan mainland, between the Bering Sea and the Pacific. The rugged, volcanic ALEUTIAN RANGE forms its backbone. Sparsely populated, it includes the KATMAI NATIONAL MONUMENT near its N end.

ALASKA RANGE, mountain chain of S Alaska, extending E in a broad arc from the base of the Alaska Peninsula. Among its many towering peaks is Mt McKinley (20320ft), highest in North America.

ALAVA, Cape, westernmost point of the US excluding Alaska and Hawaii, located in the Ozette Lake region, Callam Co, NW Wash.

AL-AZHAR UNIVERSITY, mosque-university in Cairo, oldest in the Middle East, founded by the FATIMIDS in 970. Reforms in 1961 modernized its medieval religious curriculum. It has more than 8000 students from throughout the Muslim world.

ALBA, Duke of. See ALVA (OR ALBA), FERNANDO ALVAREZ DE TOLEDO, DUKE OF.

ALBACETE, city in SE Spain, 135mi SE of Madrid, capital of Albacete province (5737sq mi). It lies on the high irrigated plain of La Mancha. Knives made in Albacete are renowned throughout Spain, and large crops of saffron are grown nearby. Pop 93233.

ALBACORE *(Thunnus alalunga)*, a white-fleshed species of TUNA, widely distributed in warm seas. Up to 1m (3ft) long and 35kg (77lb) in weight, large quantities are caught each year in the Pacific Ocean for canning.

ALBA LONGA, ancient city SE of Rome, on the W shore of Lake Albano. According to tradition it was founded by ASCANIUS in 1152 BC and was the birthplace of ROMULUS AND REMUS. Reputedly the oldest Latin city and the progenitor of Rome, it was destroyed by the Romans c600 BC.

ALBAN, Saint (c3rd century), the first Christian martyr in Britain. Thought to have served in the Roman army, he returned to Britain in the late 3rd or early 4th century and was martyred during the persecutions of the Emperor Diocletian.

ALBANEL, Charles (1613–1696), French Jesuit missionary and explorer in Canada, who led an expedition overland from Quebec to Hudson Bay (1671–72) and claimed that region for France. He was captured by the British in 1674, but returned in 1676 to serve in missions in W Canada.

ALBANIA, communist nation in SE Europe, the smallest Balkan State. Albania is bounded on the N and NE by Yugoslavia, S and SE by Greece, W by the Adriatic Sea. Barren mountains (reaching 9026ft in the North Albanian Alps), with wooded lower slopes, dominate all inland Albania. They are pierced by the Drin, Vijosë and other rivers flowing W to the narrow fertile plain which flanks the N and central coast. Summers are hot and dry; winters mild and moist.

Albanians (mainly descendants of ancient Balkan hill tribes) are officially atheists; but traditionally Muslims outnumber Christians. Two Albanian

The terminus of the Alaska Highway is marked by this modern "milestone" at Fairbanks, Alaska.

A group of Albanian students setting off for a compulsory period of work on one of the country's many collective farms.

dialects are spoken: Gheg in the N, Tosk in the S. Most people live on the coast or in the fertile mountain basins linked by poor roads. Agricultural products include corn, wheat, sugar beets, tobacco and cotton. Industries are small but under rapid development. Copper, chromium, nickel, coal, naphtha and oil are being exploited, and Chinese aid is helping

Official name: The People's Republic of Albania
Capital: Tiranë
Area: 11 101sq mi
Population: 2 135 600
Languages: Albanian
Religions: No official religion
Monetary unit(s): 1 Lek = 100 qintars

hydroelectric schemes and farm mechanization. But agriculture remains the basis of the economy.

About 300 BC Albania was part of the region known as ILLYRIA, which came under Greek, Roman and then Byzantine influence and control. Between 300 AD and 1100 AD it was successively invaded by Goths, Bulgars, Slavs and Normans. Later, the national hero SCANDERBEG (d. 1468) delayed, but failed to stop, Ottoman Turkish conquest. Turkish rule Islamized Albania and suppressed nationalist aspirations until the First Balkan War (1912). Occupied in WWI, ruled by self-proclaimed King Zog I (1928–39), then annexed by Italy and occupied in WWII, Albania regained independence under Enver HOXHA's communist regime in 1945. By the early 1960s friction with the West and Russia left distant Communist China as Albania's only major ally. In spite of gradual diplomatic rapprochements in the early 1970s and limited industrial growth, Albania remains probably Europe's poorest and most isolated country.

ALBANIAN, Indo-European language developed from ancient Albanian. It is a separate branch of the Indo-European family. Though spoken in an area nearer to Greece than to Rome, it shows the influence of Latin rather than Greek.

ALBANO, Lake, lake occupying an ancient volcanic crater in the Alban Hills SE of Rome, 6mi in circumference. CASTEL GANDOLFO lies on its W bank.

ALBANY, residential city of W Cal., located on San Francisco Bay N of Berkeley. Settled in 1853. Pop 14 672

ALBANY, commercial and industrial city of SW Ga., seat of Dougherty Co., 170mi S of Atlanta on the Flint R. Founded in 1836, Albany is a transportation hub and center of a rich agricultural region. Pop 72 623.

ALBANY, capital of N.Y. State and seat of Albany Co. on the W bank of the Hudson R about 145mi N of New York City. An important industrial and shipping center, Albany can be reached by ocean-going vessels sailing up the Hudson and is also a major railroad junction. Its industries produce chemicals, paper, felt and textiles. Established in 1614 as Fort Nassau, a Dutch fur-trading post, it was renamed Albany in honor of the Duke of York and Albany when the British assumed control of New Netherlands in 1664. The site of the ALBANY CONGRESS of 1754, the city became the capital of N.Y. State in 1797. The opening of the Erie and Champlain canals in the 1820s and the first railroad connection with Schenectady in 1831 established Albany's position as a commercial and shipping center. Pop 115 781.

ALBANY, industrial city of W Ore., seat of Linn Co., on the Willamette R 24mi S of Salem. Pop 18 181.

ALBANY, Fort, trading post at the mouth of the Albany R on James Bay in Ontario, Canada. Founded by the Hudson's Bay Company in the 1680s, it was the only trading post in the region remaining in English hands during QUEEN ANNE' WAR (1701–13).

ALBANY CONGRESS (1754), a meeting of 25 representatives from seven British colonies at Albany, N.Y., aimed at conciliating the Iroquois and improving the common defense of the colonies against the French. The congress adopted a plan, chiefly designed by Benjamin FRANKLIN, providing for greater colonial unity, one of the first significant attempts at colonial cooperation. The colonial governments later rejected the plan.

ALBANY REGENCY, group of politicians in the N.Y. state capital who controlled the state Democratic Party (1820–48) with the first political machine in the US. The "spoils system" was its guiding principle, and it sought to encourage popular participation in politics by rewarding the party faithful with government jobs.

ALBANY RIVER, flows 610mi through Ontario, Canada, E and NE from Lake St. Joseph to James Bay. Once an important fur trader's route, four Hudson Bay trading posts still lie along its course.

ALBATEGNIUS, or **Albatenius** or **al-Battani.** See BATTANI, ABU-ABDULLAH MUHAMMAD IBN-JABIR AL-.

ALBATROSSES, the 14 species of large, long-winged, gliding, hook-billed seabirds forming the family Diomedeidae in the tubenose order, Procellariiformes. Two species form the genus *Phoebetria* (sooty albatrosses), the other 12 the *Diomedea*. Most albatrosses are white with darker markings on the back, wings and tail. The wandering albatross (*D. exulans*) has the broadest wingspan of any living bird—up to 3.5m (11.5ft). Living mainly over the southern oceans, albatrosses have wings uniquely adapted for gliding flight.

ALBEDO, the ratio between the amount of light reflected from a surface and the amount of light incident upon it. The term is usually applied to celestial objects within the SOLAR SYSTEM: the moon reflects about 7% of the sunlight falling upon it, and hence has an albedo of 0.07.

ALBEE, Edward Franklin (1928–), US playwright who gained international fame with his play *Who's Afraid of Virginia Woolf?* (1962), a penetrating commentary on contemporary American marriage. His other plays include *The Zoo Story* (1958) and *The American Dream* (1961), both one-act plays, *Tiny Alice* (1964) and *A Delicate Balance* (1966), which won a Pulitzer Prize.

ALBEMARLE, industrial and commercial city in the Piedmont region of N.C., 40mi NE of Charlotte, seat of Stanly Co. It manufactures textiles, hosiery and lumber. Pop 11 126.

ALBEMARLE, Duke of. See MONCK, GEORGE.

ALBEMARLE SOUND, shallow arm of the Atlantic, extending 52mi into NE N.C., protected from the open sea by a long barrier beach.

ALBENIZ, Isaac (1860–1909), Spanish composer and pianist. A child prodigy, he wrote operas and songs, but is best remembered for his later piano works, including the suite *Iberia* (1906–9), based on Spanish folk themes and popular music forms.

ALBERS, Josef (1888–1976), German-American painter, graphic artist and art teacher, whose style of geometrical abstraction and theories of art have influenced many modern artists. A teacher at the BAUHAUS in Germany (1923–33), he emigrated to the US (1933) and headed the department of design at Yale (1950–58).

ALBERT, name of two German emperors. **Albert I** (c1255–1308), son of Rudolf I of the House of HAPSBURG, deposed his predecessor and rival Adolf of Nassau to gain the throne in 1298. He was murdered by his nephew John the Parricide. **Albert II** (1397–1429), became German emperor and king of Bohemia and Hungary in 1438. Son-in-law of Emperor Sigismund, he began the period of virtually unbroken Hapsburg rule over the Holy Roman Empire that lasted until 1806.

ALBERT (1490–1568), last grand master of the TEUTONIC KNIGHTS (elected 1511) and first duke of Prussia. He became a Protestant and in 1525 secularized the domains of the Teutonic Order, creating the secular and hereditary duchy of Prussia. On his son's death without a successor in 1618 Prussia passed to the Elector of Brandenburg, member of the senior HOHENZOLLERN line.

ALBERT I (1875–1934), King of Belgium (1909–34). Nephew and successor of LEOPOLD II, he did much to improve conditions in the Belgian Congo. In Belgium he strengthened national defense and the merchant fleet, and introduced various social reforms. During WWI he personally commanded the armed forces.

ALBERT, Lake, 2064sq mi lake between Uganda and Zaire, also known as Albert Nyanza, now Lake Mobuto Seso. The source of the Albert Nile, it is fed by the Semliki R, draining Lake Edward (or Lake Idi Amin Dada) and by the Victoria Nile. It was discovered 1864 by Sir Samuel Baker.

ALBERT, Prince (Francis Charles Augustus Albert Emmanuel; 1819–1861), Prince Consort of England, husband of Queen Victoria. German-born son of the Duke of Saxe-Coburg-Gotha, he married Victoria in 1840, and as her trusted adviser worked to establish the nonpartisan influence of the crown in government. A man of irreproachable character, he was deeply mourned by Victoria after his early death.

ALBERTA, Canada's westernmost prairie province, the country's leading petroleum producer and a rich agricultural region. The S and E was originally covered by prairie grasslands, fertile but dry and rising towards the Rocky Mountains in the SW. The rugged Rockies (containing BANFF, JASPER and other national parks) dominate the W; dense forests and swamp cover the N. The Peace, Athabasca and other rivers drain the province, and the Athabasca and Lesser Slave are the largest of many lakes. Long cold winters alternate with hot, sunny summers.

About 45% of all Albertans are of British origin; others are of German, Ukrainian, Scandinavian and French descent. Most of the 30 000 Indians live on reserves. Nearly half the rapidly growing population lives in the Edmonton and Calgary metropolitan areas, and the rural population has declined to less than a third of the total. Alberta is responsible for Canada's third-largest farm output, producing wheat, barley, sugar beets, sheep and cattle. Flour mills and sugar refineries are among food-processing industries. The province is also rich in lumber, fur and fish. But since the 1950s Alberta's mineral wealth and manufacturing have become the chief source of income. The province produces 66% of Canada's crude oil and 80% of its natural gas, as well as coal from Canada's largest deposits. Full exploitation of the immensely rich Athabasca oil sands still remains in the future. Oil refining and petrochemical production are major industries.

In 1670 unexplored Alberta became part of RUPERT'S LAND, granted to the Hudson's Bay Company. Anthony Henday was its earliest European visitor (1754), and Fort Chipewyan (1788) was among the first of the settlements founded by fur traders and missionaries. But few white settlers arrived until after 1869, when the Canadian Government bought Rupert's Land. The arrival of the Mounties (1874), completion of the Canadian Pacific Railway (1885) and peace treaties handing most Indian lands to the Canadian government by 1899, encouraged immigrants. Alberta became a province in 1905. Depressed farm income during the 1920s and 1930s led to the victory of the SOCIAL CREDIT PARTY (1935), which stayed in power until 1971. Discovery of oil and natural gas at Leduc, near Edmonton, in 1947 opened a new era in the province's history. Petroleum has made Alberta one of Canada's richest provinces, and although 1970 saw production outstrip the increase in known reserves for the first time, Alberta's mineral wealth is still phenomenal. It is forecast that by 1977 exports of high-grade coking coal to Japan will exceed 23 million tons a year.

Name of province: Alberta
Joined confederation: Sept. 1, 1905
Capital: Edmonton
Area: 255 285sq mi
Population: 1 627 674

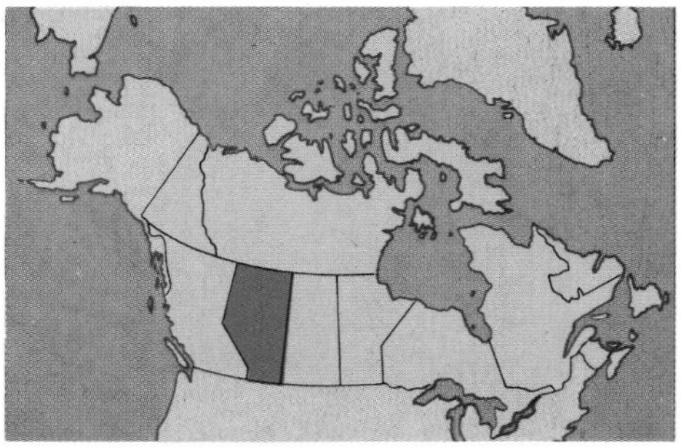

Albinism is a congenital condition with a 25% chance of transmission. The diagram shows: 1. The two parents (a. the father, b. the mother); the chromosomes are represented by symbols, albinism is shown by the black band. 2. The sexual cells of the father (*left*) and the mother (*right*). 3. The next generation: the symptoms of albinism are only found in (a) one out of four of them.

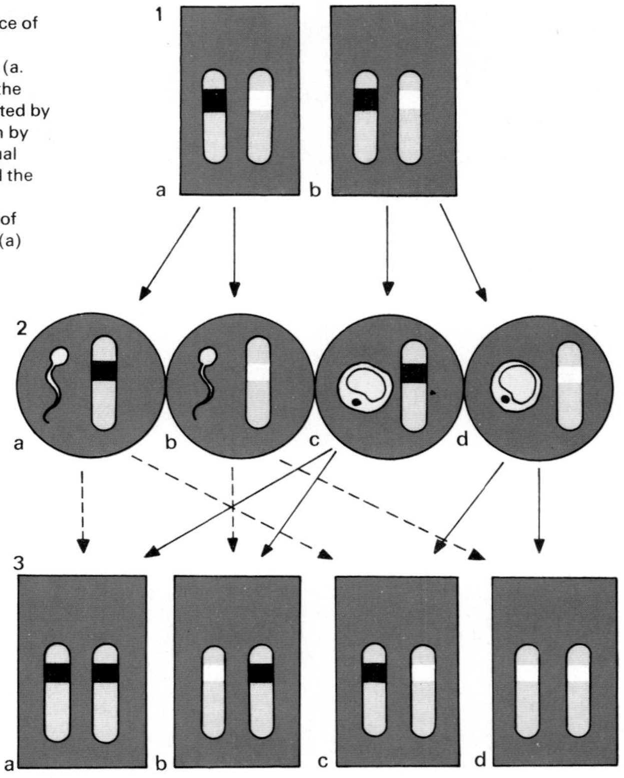

ALBERT CANAL, 81mi Belgian ship canal linking the industrial city of Liège, on the Meuse, with the port of Antwerp on the Scheldt. Completed 1939.

ALBERTI, Domenico (c1710–1740), Venetian composer who gave his name to a style of accompaniment where the left hand plays broken chords, the "Alberti Bass."

ALBERTI, Leon Battista (1404–1472), Florentine Renaissance scholar, architect and art theorist whose contributions in the arts and sciences make him typical of the Renaissance "Universal Man." Architectural works include the Palazzo Rucellai in Florence and the Tempio Malatestiano (S. Francesco) in Rimini.

ALBERT LEA, city in S Minn., seat of Freeborn Co., an agricultural marketing center with farm-related industries. Pop 19 418.

ALBERT NYANZA. See ALBERT, LAKE.

ALBERT THE BEAR (c1100–1170), first margrave of Brandenburg, important figure in Germany's eastward expansion into Slavic and pagan territory beyond the Elbe. Granted the North March in 1134, by war and skillful diplomacy he acquired the lands of the Slavic Wends, including Brandenburg.

ALBERTUS MAGNUS, Saint (c1200–1280), German scholastic philosopher and scientist; the teacher of St. Thomas AQUINAS. Albert's main significance was in promoting the study of ARISTOTLE and in helping to establish Aristotelianism and the study of the natural sciences within Christian thought. In science he did important work in botany and was possibly the first to isolate ARSENIC.

ALBI (Gallo-Roman Albiga), city in S France, on the Tarn R about 40mi NE of Toulouse, which gave its name to the ALBIGENSES. Several medieval buildings remain, including the brick Cathedral of Ste. Cécile. Pop 42 930.

ALBIGENSES, members of a heretical sect of the 12th- and 13th-century CATHARI who took their name from the city of ALBI in S France. Believing that worldly things represented the forces of evil and that the human spirit was good, they attacked the Church as the instrument of the devil, condemning many of the sacraments. Pope Innocent III broke the power of the sect in 1208. See also: DUALISM and MANICHAEISM.

ALBINO, an organism lacking the pigmentation normal to its kind. The skin and hair of albino animals (including man) is uncolored while the irises of their eyes appear pink. Albinism, which may be total or only partial, is generally inherited. Albino plants contain no CHLOROPHYLL and thus, being unable to perform PHOTOSYNTHESIS, rapidly die.

ALBINONI, Tomaso (1671–1750), Italian composer. A famous violinist, he also wrote over 50 operas. BACH, his contemporary, made use of several of Albinoni's themes in his own compositions.

ALBION, industrial city in S Mich., on the Kalamazoo R, 40mi SW of Lansing. Pop 12 112.

ALBITE, common mineral occurring in igneous rocks, consisting of sodium aluminum silicate ($NaAlSi_3O_8$); often forms vitreous crystals of various colors. It is one of the three end-members (pure compounds) of the FELDSPAR group.

ALBOIN (d. 572), king of the LOMBARDS, conqueror of N Italy (568–572), made Pavia his capital. According to legend, he was slain by order of his wife Rosamund, whose father he had murdered.

ÅLBORG. See AALBORG.

ALBRIGHT, Ivan le Lorraine (1897–), US painter of microscopically detailed realistic works whose mood and symbolism are largely sinister. His works include *That Which I Should Have Done I Did Not Do* (1941), which took ten years to paint.

ALBUMIN, group of PROTEINS soluble in water and in 50% saturated sulfate solution; present in animals and plants. Ovalbumin is the chief protein in egg white; serum albumin occurs in blood PLASMA, where it controls osmotic pressure.

ALBUQUERQUE, largest city in N.M., seat of Bernalillo Co., on the Rio Grande R. Founded in 1706 on the old Chihuahua Trail, it is today an important commercial and industrial city with defense and atomic energy installations, as well as a transportation and tourist center. Pop 243 751.

ALBUQUERQUE, Afonso de (1453–1515), Portuguese admiral and second viceroy of Portuguese India, who extended Portuguese influence in the Far East (1503–15), and secured the Far Eastern trade routes from foreign intervention. He died at sea after having been deposed by rivals.

ALCAEUS, Greek lyric poet of c600 BC. Like his contemporary, Sappho, he came from the island of Lesbos and wrote in the Aeolic dialect. He is best remembered for poetry about his fondness for wine. The four-line Alcaic stanza, named for him, was widely used in Greek lyric poetry, and was adopted by the Latin poet Horace and by English poets such as Tennyson.

ALCAMENES (460–400 BC), Greek sculptor, somewhat younger than PHIDIAS. After Phidias' death he became the leading sculptor in Athens. Apart from a famous Roman copy of his statue of Hermes, few examples of his work survive.

ALCAN HIGHWAY. See ALASKA HIGHWAY.

ALCATRAZ, rocky island in San Francisco Bay, famous as the site (1933–63) of a federal prison for dangerous criminals, nicknamed "the Rock." In 1970 the island was occupied for a time by a group of American Indians.

ALCAZAR, name for the massive fortified palaces built in Spain under Muslim rule. The ALHAMBRA in Granada is a well-known and beautiful example. The Alcazar of Toledo withstood a famous siege in 1936 during the Spanish Civil War.

ALCAZARQUIVIR (Ksar el-Kebir), city in N Morocco, site of the famous "Battle of the Three Kings" (1578) in which the Moors destroyed the Portuguese army led by King Sebastian, who was killed. Two years later Portugal passed under the rule of King Philip II of Spain.

ALCESTIS, in Greek legend, wife of Admetus, king of Pherae in Thessaly, who made a pact with Apollo to die in her husband's place. A classic example of love and conjugal fidelity, she is the subject of a tragedy by EURIPIDES and an opera by GLUCK.

ALCHEMY, a blend of philosophy, mysticism and chemical technology, originating before the Christian era, seeking variously the conversion of base metals into gold, the prolongation of life and the secret of immortality. In the Classical world alchemy began in Hellenistic Egypt and passed through the writings of the great Arab alchemists such as Al-Razi (RHAZES) to the Latin West. The late medieval period saw the discovery of NITRIC, SULFURIC and HYDROCHLORIC acids and ETHANOL (*aqua vitae*, the water of life) in the alchemists' pursuit of the "philosopher's stone" or *elixir* which would transmute base metals into gold.

In the early 16th century PARACELSUS set alchemy on a new course, towards a chemical pharmacy (IATROCHEMISTRY), although other alchemists—including John DEE and even Isaac NEWTON—continued to work along mystical, quasireligious lines. Having strong ties with ASTROLOGY, interest in alchemy, particularly in the Hermetic writings (see HERMES TRISMEGISTUS), has never quite died out, though without any further benefit to medical or chemical science. (See also CHEMISTRY.)

ALCIBIADES (c450–404 BC), Athenian statesman and general, nephew of PERICLES and a favorite student of SOCRATES. Always a disturbing influence, during the Peloponnesian War he temporarily fell out of favor. Escaping to Sparta, he betrayed Athens, but later rejoined his fleet, which he led successfully against Sparta. Once more out of favor, he was assassinated in exile.

ALCINOÜS, in Greek legend, king of Phaeacia and grandson of POSEIDON. He entertained Odysseus after the mariner had been shipwrecked and rescued by Alcinoüs' daughter Nausicaä.

ALCMAEONIDAE, Athenian family of great political influence between 7th and 5th centuries BC. Among its members were CLEISTHENES, PERICLES and ALCIBIADES.

ALCMENE, in Greek legend, daughter of Electryon, king of Mycenae, and the wife of Amphitryon. She became mother of Heracles by Zeus, who had assumed her husband's form.

ALCOCK, Sir John William (1892–1919) and **Brown, Sir Arthur Whitten** (1886–1948), British airmen who in 1919 made the first nonstop Atlantic flight, from St. John's, Newfoundland to Clifden, Ireland.

ALCOHOLIC BEVERAGES, drinks containing ETHANOL, the only variety of ALCOHOL that may be consumed in moderation without damaging effects. Popular alcoholic beverages include BEER, WINE, WHISKEY, BRANDY, RUM and compounded liquors such as liqueurs and GIN. They vary widely in alcoholic content, ranging from 2% or 3% in light beers to more than 60% in some VODKAS and distilled fruit brandy. (See also DISTILLED LIQUOR.)

Intoxicating beverages were known to the ancient Egyptians and Babylonians, and in the past many people used them instead of impure water. Today their use is general for conviviality; excessive drinking may be due to ALCOHOLISM. (See also INTOXICATION.) Many governments strictly control the sale of alcoholic beverages, and they are an important source of revenue.

ALCOHOLICS ANONYMOUS (A.A.), world-wide organization numbering over 400000 anonymous members, in which former alcoholics aid those suffering from ALCOHOLISM. It stresses self-help, and all involved pool their experiences for mutual encouragement.

ALCOHOLISM, compulsive drinking of alcohol in excess, one of the most serious problems in modern society. Many people drink for relaxation and can stop drinking without ill effects; the alcoholic cannot give up drinking without great discomfort: he is dependent on alcohol, physically and psychologically.

Alcohol is a DEPRESSANT that acts initially by reducing activity in the higher centers of the BRAIN. The drinker loses judgment and inhibitions; he feels free of his responsibilities and anxieties. This is the basis for initial psychological dependence. With further alcohol intake, thought and body control are impaired (see also INTOXICATION). The alcoholic starts by drinking more and longer than his fellows. He then finds that the unpleasant symptoms of withdrawal—

Alcazar in Segovia, Spain, built in the 11th century during the period of Moorish rule. These impressive fortresses were the palaces of Moorish kings.

"hangover," tremor, weakness and hallucinations—are relieved by alcohol. In this way his drinking extends through the greater part of the day and physical dependence is established. The alcoholic often has a reduced tolerance to the effects of alcohol and may suffer from AMNESIA after a few drinks. Social pressures soon lead to secretive drinking, work is neglected and financial difficulties add to the disintegration of personality; denial and pathological jealousy hasten social isolation. Alcohol depresses the appetite and the alcoholic may stop or reduce eating. Many of the diseases associated with alcoholism are in part due to MALNUTRITION and VITAMIN deficiency: CIRRHOSIS, NEURITIS, dementia, and KORSAKOV'S PSYCHOSIS. Prolonged alcohol withdrawal leads to DELIRIUM TREMENS. Treatment of alcoholism is very difficult. SEDATIVES and ANTABUSE may help to counteract dependence. Reconciliation of the patient to society is crucial; he must understand the reasons for his drinking and learn to approach his problems and fears realistically. Psychotherapy and ALCOHOLICS ANONYMOUS are valuable in this. Total abstinence is essential to avoid relapse.

ALCOHOLS, class of ALIPHATIC COMPOUNDS, of general formula ROH, containing a hydroxyl group bonded to a carbon atom. They are classified as monohydric, dihydric, etc., according to the number of hydroxyl groups; and as primary, secondary or tertiary according to the number of hydrogen atoms adjacent to the hydroxyl group. Alcohols occur widely in nature, and are used as solvents and antifreezes and in chemical manufacture. They are obtained by fermentation, oxidation or hydration of ALKENES from petroleum and natural gas, and by reduction of fats and oils.

Alcoholic Beverages

Alcohol content

Brandy	45–55%
Whiskey	40–54%
Vodka	40–70%
Rum	40–70%
Gin	40%
Port, Sherry, Muscatel	up to 21%
Vermouth	15–20%
Wines	14% or less
Beers	2–6%

Alcohols of lower molecular weight are colorless, flammable liquids, miscible with water; those of higher molecular weight are waxy solids, decreasingly soluble in water. They are weak acids, and form salts (alkoxides RO^-) with the alkali metals. With carboxylic acids (and sulfuric acid catalyst) they react to give ESTERS; on dehydration alcohols give ALKENES and ETHERS. Primary alcohols may readily be oxidized to ALDEHYDES or further to CARBOXYLIC ACIDS; secondary alcohols may be oxidized to KETONES. The hydroxyl group may be replaced by HALOGENS or PSEUDOHALOGENS to give ALKYL HALIDES, NITRILES, etc. The simplest alcohols are METHANOL and ETHANOL (the intoxicating constituent of ALCOHOLIC BEVERAGES); others include BENZYL ALCOHOL, ETHYLENE GLYCOL and GLYCEROL. (See also CARBOHYDRATES; STEROLS; PHENOLS; HYDROXIDES.)

ALCOTT, (Amos) Bronson (1799–1888), US educator, philosopher and author. As a teacher in several Conn. schools, his progressive methods were too advanced to be popular. In 1840 he retired to Concord, Mass., where he was closely associated with the TRANSCENDENTALISM of Emerson, Hawthorne, Thoreau and Channing. His writings include *Concord Days* (1872) and *Table Talk* (1877).

ALCOTT, Louisa May (1832–1888), US author of *Little Women* (1869) and other autobiographical books for children. Daughter of Amos Bronson ALCOTT, she began by publishing stories in magazines like the *Atlantic Monthly*. *Hospital Sketches* (1863) was based on her experiences as a Union nurse in the Civil War.

ALCUIN (735–804 AD), English prelate and scholar whose classical and humanist scholarship influenced medieval teaching of the liberal arts. In 781 he became master of the palace school of CHARLEMAGNE and supervised Charlemagne's program of ecclesiastical and educational reform among the Franks in the Carolingian empire.

ALCYONARIANS, colonial CORALS of the subclass Alcyonaria (or Octocorallia) commonly having eight feathered tentacles. They include the soft corals (Alcyonacea) such as dead man's fingers (*Alcyonium digitatum*) and blue coral (*Heliopora*—which alone among the alcyonarians is strong enough to form coral reefs); the horny corals (Gorgonacea) such as precious coral (*Corallium rubrum*) and the sea fan (*Gorgonia*); and the sea pens (Pennatulacea). Phylum: Cnidaria. Class: Anthozoa.

ALDABRA ISLANDS, group of four coral islets constituting a small oval atoll enclosing a lagoon, 265mi NW of Madagascar. Part of the BRITISH INDIAN OCEAN TERRITORY, they are famed for rare fauna, which include tortoises and sea turtles. South Island has been made a nature reserve.

ALDANOV, Mark (1889–1957), pseudonym of Mark Alexandrovich Landau, Russian emigré writer of novels about the French Revolution and later ideological conflicts. After 1919 he lived in France and the US.

ALDAN RIVER, second-largest tributary of the Lena R of E Siberia. Navigable for 800 of its 1400mi length.

ALDEBARAN (Alpha Tauri), the 14th brightest star in the night sky and the brightest star in TAURUS. At a distance of 21pc, it has an absolute magnitude varying about −0.8.

ALDEGREVER, Heinrich (1502–c1555), German painter and engraver. One of the "little masters," his work was influenced by DÜRER'S assimilation of Italian Renaissance discoveries in classical art.

ALDEHYDES, class of organic compounds of general formula RCHO, containing a carbonyl group (see also KETONES). They are highly reactive, and find many uses in industry in the preparation of solvents, dyes, resins and other compounds. Many aldehydes occur in nature and are often responsible for the flavor and scent of animals and plants. The simplest aldehydes are FORMALDEHYDE and ACETALDEHYDE. Aromatic aldehydes, such as BENZALDEHYDE and vanillin, are used in dyes and as perfumes and food flavorings. Aldehydes can be prepared by dehydrogenation or oxidation of primary ALCOHOLS, or by reduction of ACID CHLORIDES. Aldehydes may be reduced to primary alcohols, or oxidized to

CARBOXYLIC ACIDS (if ammoniacal silver nitrate is used, a silver MIRROR is formed). They undergo addition reactions with BASES such as AMMONIA and CYANIDES; and condensation reactions with HYDRAZINE, alcohols, ACID ANHYDRIDES and other reactive compounds.

ALDEN, John (c1599–1687), a MAYFLOWER Pilgrim Father, an able assistant to the governor of Plymouth Colony. He is best known through LONGFELLOW's poem *The Courtship of Miles Standish,* based on the legend that he courted Priscilla Mullens on behalf of Miles Standish, but married her himself.

ALDER, any of 30 species of deciduous trees and shrubs of the genus *Alnus* found throughout North America, Europe and Asia. Most common in the eastern US is the speckled alder *A. incana*, which grows as a large shrub to medium-sized tree (up to 25m (82ft)). The alders of the Pacific coast, such as the red alder *A. rubra*, are larger, and may reach heights of up to 40m (130ft). Most alder wood is used to make charcoal, except that of the red alder which is important in furniture making. Alder bark is used for dyeing and tanning. Family: Betulaceae.

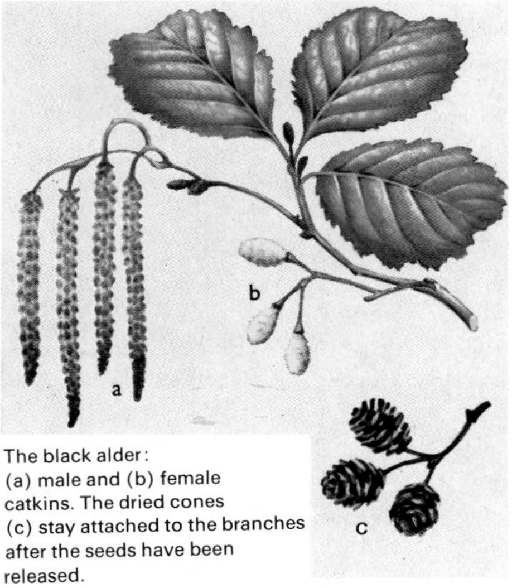

The black alder: (a) male and (b) female catkins. The dried cones (c) stay attached to the branches after the seeds have been released.

ALDER, Kurt (1902–1958), German organic chemist who shared the 1950 Nobel Prize for Chemistry with Otto DIELS for demonstrating the usefulness of the diene synthesis (DIELS–ALDER REACTION) in forming ALICYCLIC COMPOUNDS.

ALDER DAM, multiple-arch dam built in 1944 across the Nisqually R near the town of Alder, Wash. It is 330ft high and 1 600ft long. The dam reservoir is used for generating hydroelectric power.

ALDERFLIES (Sialidae), a family of insects in the suborder Negaloptera of the order Neuroptera. They have two pairs of wings and live near the ponds and streams inhabited by their larvae. Related families include the American DOBSON FLIES and the SNAKE FLIES.

ALDERMEN, elected municipal officers in US, now usually identical with councilmen. Aldermen represent a ward or district. In colonial times they were chosen by the councilmen and functioned also as magistrates. Some retain the role of justice of the peace.

ALDERNEY. See CHANNEL ISLANDS.

ALDINGTON, Richard (1892–1962), English novelist, critic, biographer and pre-WWI IMAGIST poet, who wrote a controversial biography of T. E. LAWRENCE.

ALDRICH, Nelson Wilmarth (1841–1915), US senator from R.I. (1881–1911), powerful Republican spokesman for conservative Eastern financial and business interests. A protectionist, he was also concerned with banking reforms and was co-sponsor of the **Aldrich Vreeland Currency Act** (1908), which provided for emergency bank note issues and created the National Monetary Commission, of which he was chairman. Its proposals were influential in the establishment of the FEDERAL RESERVE SYSTEM.

ALDRICH, Thomas Bailey (1836–1907). US editor and writer of poems, stories, novels and essays. He was editor of the *Atlantic Monthly* (1881–90). *The Story of a Bad Boy* (1870), his best-known book, tells of his youth in Portsmouth, N.H.

ALDRIDGE, Ira Frederick (1805–1867), first US Negro to achieve fame as an actor. Known in Britain and on the Continent for his bold interpretations of such Shakespearean roles as Lear, Othello and Macbeth, he eventually became a British citizen.

ALDRIN, Edwin Eugene, Jr. (1930–), US Air Force colonel and astronaut; 2nd man to walk on the moon during the Apollo II space flight (1969). On the Gemini 12 flight (1966), his only previous space mission, he made a record 5½-hr space walk.

ALDUS MANUTIUS (1450–1515), Venetian founder of the *Aldine Press* whose scrupulous editions of Greek and Roman classics (including Aristotle) advanced Renaissance scholarship. He was the first man to use italic type (1501) especially cut in order to produce cheap, pocket-sized editions of the Latin classics.

ALE, in the US, a light-colored, top-fermented beer with an alcohol content of about 5%. It excludes bottom-fermented or continental-type beers. Malt liquors such as ale are generally called beer in England.

ALEATORY MUSIC (from Latin *alea*, dice), music dependent on chance; applied to the post-1950 tendency of composers to leave some elements in their work to be settled by the performer's decision or by random chance. John CAGE's work is perhaps the best-known example.

ALEICHEM, Sholem. See SHOLEM ALEICHEM.

ALEKHINE, Alexander (1892–1946), Moscow-born world champion chess player, naturalized in France. He defeated Capablanca in the world championship at Buenos Aires, 1927, lost to Max Euwe 1935 but regained the title in 1937 and held it until his death.

ALEKSEYEV, Mikhail Vasilievich (1857–1918), Russian general during WWI, commander-in-chief after the tsar's abdication in 1917. An opponent of the Bolsheviks in the civil war, he acted as head of the counterrevolutionary government with General KORNILOV's forces in the S.

ALEMÁN, Mateo (1547–1614), Spanish writer of picaresque novels reflecting his own colorful life. *Guzman de Alfarache* (1599) was widely translated.

ALEMÁN VALDÉS, Miguel (1902–), President of Mexico (1946–1952), a successful lawyer, son of a revolutionary general. He initiated a vigorous program of economic development.

ALEMANNI. See ALAMANNI.

ALEMBERT, Jean Le Rond d' (1717–1783), French philosopher, physicist and mathematician, a leading figure in the French ENLIGHTENMENT and coeditor with DIDEROT of the renowned *Encyclopedia.* His early fame rested on his formulation of D'ALEMBERT'S PRINCIPLE in mechanics (1743). His other works treat calculus, music, philosophy and astronomy.

ALEMBIC, an early type of still, popularly associated with the experiments of alchemists (see ALCHEMY); the term strictly refers only to a particular form of DISTILLATION head.

ALENÇON, city in NW France, on the Sarthe R, capital of Orne department, famous for lace-making. It was captured by William the Conqueror in 1048, and later became the seat of a powerful countship and dukedom. Pop 31 656.

ALENTEJO, former province of SE Portugal, 10428sq mi, capital Evora. It is a rich agricultural region, once known as the "Granary of Portugal." Pop 687 000.

ALEPH NULL ($\aleph_0$). See TRANSFINITE CARDINAL NUMBER.

ALEPPO (Halab), second-largest city of Syria, located in the N, at the junction of ancient caravan routes. An important city since Hittite times more than 3 000 years ago, it was long one of the greatest emporiums of the Middle East. Today Aleppo is a leading manufacturing center, with a population including many Armenian and Syrian Christians. Pop 639 000.

ALESSANDRIA, city on Tanaro R, Piedmont region, NW Italy. Rail and business center 35mi SE of Turin. Founded 1168, once a stronghold commanding Alpine passes. Pop 104 977.

ÅLESUND, Norway's largest fishing port, located on islands at the mouth of the Stor Fjord 180mi NE of Bergen. Pop 40 000.

ALEURITES, a genus (*Aleurites*) of tropical and subtropical trees containing five species. All bear large fruits which contain nuts rich in oil. Among them are the tungoil and candlenut trees. Family: Euphorbiaceae.

ALEUT, native of the Aleutian and Pribilof islands and W Alaska Peninsula, closely related to the Eskimo, and speaking a broadly similar language. When the first Russians arrived at the Aleutians there were about 25 000 Aleuts, able hunters (especially of the sea otter) and fishermen, with a well-developed material culture. They came from the Alaska mainland about 2000 BC. Today possibly as few as 1 000 Aleuts live on the Aleutians and nearby territories.

ALEUTIAN CURRENT, or Subarctic Current, eastward-flowing ocean current of the N Pacific, skirting the ALEUTIAN ISLANDS. It divides to form the ALASKA CURRENT and the CALIFORNIA CURRENT, a third branch entering the Bering Sea.

ALEUTIAN ISLANDS, chain of some 150 Alaskan islands of volcanic origin, extending 1 200mi SW and then NW from the Alaska Peninsula in a wide arc, and separating the Bering Sea from the Pacific. These treeless, rugged and foggy islands support a population of 6 000; fishing is the chief occupation. In 1942 the Japanese occupied Agattu, Attu and Kiska, the westernmost islands of this strategic chain, and bombed the naval base at Dutch Harbor.

ALEUTIAN RANGE, mountain chain forming the backbone of the Alaska Peninsula. The peaks of its submerged westward continuation rise above the sea as the arc of the Aleutian Islands. Many peaks are active volcanoes.

ALEWIFE, or branch herring (*Alosa*—or *Pomolobus*—*pseudoharengus*), a fish of the HERRING and SHAD family (Clupeidae) caught in large numbers along the Atlantic coast of North America. Growing up to 300mm (12in) long, adult fish return to coastal rivers to spawn, though one variety spends its whole life in the fresh water of the Great Lakes.

ALEXANDER, name of eight popes. **Saint Alexander I**, 5th pope after St. Peter, 105–115. **Alexander II** (Anselm of Lucca; d. 1073), pope 1061–73, laid the foundations of the reform movement that reached fruition under GREGORY VII. His deposition of the bishop of Milan for simony led to the INVESTITURE CONTROVERSY. **Alexander III** (Orlando Bandinelli; d. 1181), pope 1159–81, continued the long battle against the Emperor FREDERICK I Barbarossa. Opposed by three antipopes, he was victor over Frederick at the Battle of Legano (1176). He convened the Third Lateran Council (1179) and forced King Henry II of England to recognize papal supremacy. He canonized Thomas à BECKET. **Alexander IV** (Rinaldo Segni; d. 1261), pope 1254–61, continued papal opposition to the HOHENSTAUFENS. **Alexander V** (Pietro di Candia; c1339–1410), Greek-born antipope (1409–10) elected unanimously by the Council of PISA. **Alexander VI** (Rodrigo Borgia; 1431–1503), pope from 1492, most notorious of the Renaissance popes. Born in Valencia, Spain, he was deeply involved in the political turmoil of the Italy of his day. His efforts were directed at increasing the temporal power of the papacy and creating great hereditary domains for his children, among them Cesare and Lucrezia BORGIA. He was a keen patron of the great artists of his day. **Alexander VII** (Fabio Chigi; 1599–1667), pope from 1655. He ruled at a time when the papacy was losing temporal power, and was worsted in controversy with Louis XIV of France. **Alexander VIII** (Pietro Ottoboni; 1610–1691), pope from 1689; he sought a solution for the quarrel with Louis XIV.

ALEXANDER, name of three Russian Tsars. **Alexander I** (1777–1825) succeeded his father, Paul

The infamous Pope Alexander VI portrayed in a detail from a fresco by Pinturicchio and his school in the Borgia apartments of the Vatican. One of the greatest patrons of Renaissance art, his interest in religious matters was minimal.

I, in 1801, with a reforming program which he later abandoned. In 1805 he joined England and Austria against Napoleon. After French victories at Austerlitz and Friedland, however, Napoleon proposed joint Franco-Russian domination of Europe. But mutual mistrust came to a head when Alexander encouraged British, not French, trade. Napoleon invaded Russia in 1812. Almost the whole French army was destroyed in the freezing Russian winter, and in 1814 Alexander entered Paris. In 1815 he formed a coalition with Austria and Prussia, the HOLY ALLIANCE. At his death, internal repression was abetted by a corrupt Church and enforced by the secret police, and the country itself faced economic ruin and rebellion. **Alexander II** (1818–1881), succeeded his father, Nicholas I, in 1855. Russian defeat in the CRIMEAN WAR and peasant unrest forced on him limited reforms, most importantly the emancipation of the serfs in 1861. But this did not satisfy revolutionary groups, and fear of their activities inspired him at first to more reactionary policies. He finally relented, but on the very day he signed a decree for moderate reform he was killed by nihilist bombs. In foreign policies he was a moderate, making peace in the Crimea and keeping out of the FRANCO-PRUSSIAN WAR (1870–71), though extending Russian power in the Far East as well as in Central Asia. **Alexander III** (1845–1894) succeeded his father Alexander II in 1881. He discarded the latter's proposals for moderate reform in favor of rigid repression and persecution of minorities. But industrial development prospered and construction of the TRANS-SIBERIAN RAILROAD began. In Europe his policies were peaceful.

ALEXANDER I (1888–1934), king of Yugoslavia from 1921 until his assassination by a Croatian terrorist at Marseille. He became prince-regent of Serbia in 1914 and commanded the Serbian forces in WWI. An autocratic ruler, he earned the enmity of separatist minorities.

ALEXANDER, Grover Cleveland (1887–1950), one of the greatest right-handed pitchers of all times, playing with the Phillies, Cubs and Cardinals from 1911 to 1930. He gained the major league record for shutouts in a season (16) and the National League career record in complete games and shutouts.

ALEXANDER ARCHIPELAGO, group of some 1 100 islands lying along the rugged coast of the Alaska Panhandle. The most important are Prince of Wales, home of the Haida Indians, Admiralty, Chicagof and Baranof, site of Sitka, once capital of Russian North America.

ALEXANDER CITY, city in E Ala., 45mi NE of Montgomery, handles textiles and lumber. Pop 12 358.

ALEXANDER NEVSKY (1220–1263), Russian national hero and saint. His victories over the Swedes the Neva R (1240) and over the Teutonic Knights on the ice of Lake Peipus (1242) made him preeminent among Russian princes.

ALEXANDER OF HALES (c1170–1245), English Scholastic who was the first Franciscan professor at Paris, where he founded the school of Friars Minor. A student of AUGUSTINE, he laid the foundations of Franciscan theology.

ALEXANDER OF TUNIS, Harold (Rupert Leofric George), 1st Earl (1891–1969), British field marshal and statesman, in charge of the evacuation from DUNKERQUE (1940), later commander of British forces in the Middle East (under whom MONTGOMERY won the victory at EL ALAMEIN), and eventually Supreme Allied Commander in the Mediterranean. Governor-General of Canada (1946–52) and British minister of defense (1952–54).

ALEXANDER SARCOPHAGUS, monumental stone coffin, dating from c315 BC, one of the great achievements of HELLENISTIC CULTURE. Carved in high relief are friezes showing Alexander the Great fighting the Persians and hunting lions.

ALEXANDER SEVERUS (208–235 AD), proclaimed Roman Emperor by the Praetorian Guards in 222 after the murder of his cousin HELIOGABALUS. Unsuccessful against the Persians, he was slain by mutineers while campaigning in Gaul.

ALEXANDER THE GREAT (356–323 BC), king of Macedonia (336–323 BC) and conqueror of the Persian Empire. The son of PHILIP II of Macedonia, he was born in Pella and educated by ARISTOTLE, the great philosopher. In 338 Philip's defeat of the Thebans and Athenians at CHAERONEA brought all the Greek city-states but Sparta under Macedonian rule. At the age of 20 Alexander succeeded his father and went on to execute Philip's plans for freeing the Greeks of Asia Minor from Persian rule. He invaded the Persian Empire with 30 000 infantry and 5 000 cavalry, but military victory was not his only concern; he also took with him a team of scholars, with the aim of bringing the blessings of Greek culture to Asia. After his defeat of the Persian King DARIUS III at ISSUS in 333, he pressed on to subdue Phoenicia and Egypt, founding Alexandria. As his dominions in the East spread, he thought of himself more and more as an Eastern prince, thus alienating much of his Macedonian army. In 331 Alexander again defeated Darius in the decisive battle of GAUGAMELA, after which the principal cities of the Persian Empire, Babylon, Susa and Persepolis, fell easily to his attack. He was proclaimed king of Asia, and then moved on eastward through Bactria and along the Indus Valley to the Indian Ocean. He had intended to go on to conquer India, but his men refused. On his return to Babylon he began planning further conquests, but did not have time to realize in detail his plans for consolidating the union he had achieved between the East and the West. With no legitimate succession, the empire was pulled apart after his death by rival generals, known collectively as the DIADOCHI. But though he lived to be only 33, he had conquered the greatest empire civilization had yet known, and he prepared the way for the penetration of HELLENISTIC CULTURE into all parts of the known world.

ALEXANDRA FYODOROVNA (1872–1918), Russian tsarina (1894–1917), consort of NICHOLAS II. She was unpopular because of her relations with the unscrupulous monk RASPUTIN and her alleged pro-German sympathies during WWI. Shot with the tsar and their family by the Bolsheviks at Ekaterinburg.

ALEXANDRIA, chief port and second-largest city of Egypt, at the NW corner of the Nile delta, 130mi from Cairo. Alexandria was founded by Alexander the Great in 331 BC; it was the capital of Ptolemaic Egypt and a great center of trade and learning in the Hellenistic and Roman world. Among its ancient landmarks were the greatest library of antiquity, a renowned museum and school, and the famous PHAROS. The city entered a long period of decline after the Arab conquest of 642, but since the time of MEHMET ALI it has grown into Egypt's principal channel for foreign trade, a cosmopolitan city with many of the country's industries. Pop 2 032 000.

ALEXANDRIA, city in central La., 200mi NW of New Orleans on the Red R. It was burned by Union troops in 1864. Chief industries are food processing and lumber. Pop 41 557.

ALEXANDRIA, historic city in Va., on the Potomac R 6mi S of Washington, D.C., settled late 17th century by Scottish merchants, laid out 1749 and part of D.C. from 1791 to 1847. A residential town rich in colonial architecture and historic associations, it was once the home of George WASHINGTON and Robert E. LEE. Pop 110 938.

ALEXANDRIA CONFERENCE, meeting between representatives of Md. and Va., concerning navigation and commerce. It was originally planned for Alexandria, Va., but held primarily at Mount Vernon in 1785. From this meeting came the call for the ANNAPOLIS CONVENTION.

ALEXANDRIAN LIBRARY, the greatest collection of books in antiquity, containing perhaps 400 000 manuscripts, in Alexandria, Egypt. Commenced under PTOLEMY Soter, it came to be housed mainly in the Museum (see ALEXANDRIAN SCHOOL). Portions were destroyed by fires between 47 BC and the final fall of the city to the Arabs in 646 AD.

ALEXANDRIAN SCHOOL, or *Museum* (place dedicated to the MUSES), founded c300 BC, the foremost center of learning in the ancient world during the HELLENISTIC AGE, and which housed the ALEXANDRIAN LIBRARY. The school was renowned from the first, its teachers including the mathematicians APOLLONIUS OF PERGA, EUCLID and HERO; the physicians ERASISTRATUS, EUDEMUS and HEROPHILUS; the geographer ERATOSTHENES and the astronomer HIPPARCHUS. The last great Alexandrian scientist was Claudius PTOLEMY, who worked in the city between 127 AD and 151 AD. With the decline of Hellenistic culture, activity in the school turned away from original research towards compilation and criticism, the study of mystical philosophy and theology assuming an increasingly significant role.

ALEXANDRINE. See HEXAMETER.

ALEXANDRITE, rare variety of the mineral CHRYSOBERYL, found in the Urals. A valuable GEM, it has a brilliant luster, and appears dark green in daylight but red in artificial or transmitted light.

ALEXIA, a disorder of language, the complete inability to comprehend the written word. (See SPEECH AND SPEECH DISORDERS; DYSLEXIA.)

ALEXIS (1629–1676), second ROMANOV tsar of Russia, ascended the throne 1645. He conquered much of Ukraine from Poland (1667), and also fought Sweden. With such able reformers as the Patriarch NIKON, who was later disgraced, he slowly began the westernization of Russia afterwards carried much further by his son Peter the Great.

ALEXIUS, name of five Byzantine emperors. **Alexius I Comnenus** (1048–1118), emperor from 1081 after the overthrow of Emperor Nicephorus III. A talented general, he defended the empire against Normans (led by Robert GUISCARD) and Scythians. He used members of the First Crusade to reconquer territory lost to the Turks. His life, the *Alexiad*, was written by his daughter Anna Comnena. **Alexius II Comnenus** (1168–1183), son of Manuel I, became emperor 1180, and was deposed and murdered by his uncle Andronicus. **Alexius III Angelus** (d. 1210) became emperor in 1195 when he deposed and blinded his brother Isaac II. This served as the pretext for the attack by members of the Fourth Crusade on Constantinople in 1203. He fled and died in exile. **Alexius IV Angelus** (d. 1204), son of Isaac II, arranged for the crusaders to depose his uncle Alexius III in 1203. He ruled as co-emperor with his father, but was put to death by Alexius V after only six months. **Alexius V** (d. 1204), known as Ducas Mourtzuphlos, overthrew Alexius IV and Isaac II. This led to the sack of Constantinople by the crusaders. He was executed and BALDWIN I made first Latin emperor.

ALFALFA, or **lucerne,** important forage plant, *Medicago sativa*, widely grown for pasture, hay and silage. The high protein content of this PERENNIAL makes it an excellent food for livestock, and the nitrogen-fixing BACTERIA in the nodules on its roots are important in enriching depleted soil. Alfalfa is of particular value in arid countries as its extremely long taproot enables it to survive severe drought. Alfalfa has trifoliate leaves and dense clusters of small purple, blue or yellow flowers. Family: Leguminosae.

ALFALFA CATERPILLAR, larva of the alfalfa

butterfly (*Colias eurytheme*) which, feeding on ALFALFA and other LEGUMINOUS PLANTS, is a major pest in the southwestern US. Family: Pieridae.

ALFIERI, Count Vittorio (1749–1803), Italian dramatist and poet, founder of modern Italian tragic drama. Among his works are *Saul*, *Maria Stuarda* and *Oreste* (1787–89). Hatred of tyranny and a passionate republicanism marked his impetuous and stormy life.

ALFONSO, name of five kings of Aragon. **Alfonso I** (d. 1134), known as "the Battler," was king of Navarre and Aragon from 1104. He defeated the ALMORAVIDS and conquered Saragossa (1118). **Alfonso II** (1152–1196), king from 1162, through inheritance added the countship of Barcelona to the Aragonese crown, and also ruled Provence and Roussillon. **Alfonso III** (1265–1291), king from 1285, lost a power struggle with his nobles and was forced to cede many royal prerogatives. **Alfonso IV** (1299–1336), became king 1327. **Alfonso V** (1396–1458), called "the Magnanimous," became king of Aragon and Sicily 1416, and defeated rival claims of René of Anjou to become king of Naples 1443. He made Naples the site of his brilliant and cultured court.

ALFONSO, name of 11 kings of Asturias, León and Castile. **Alfonso I** (d. 757), king of Asturias from 739. **Alfonso II** (d. 842) king of Asturias from 791, moved the capital to Oviedo and made SANTIAGO DE COMPOSTELLA a Christian shrine. **Alfonso III** (c839–910), called "the Great," king of Asturias from 866, extended the kingdom against the Moors. **Alfonso IV** (d. 933), was king of León and Asturias 926–931. **Alfonso V** (994–1028), king of León from 999, recovered territory lost to the Moors. **Alfonso VI** (c1042–1109) king of León from 1065, became king of Castile 1072 and took Toledo 1085, becoming the most powerful Christian ruler in Spain. After 1086 he was at war with the ALMORAVIDS. His reign is noted for the exploits of the CID. **Alfonso VII** (c1104–1157), king of León and Castile from 1126. His early victories were eclipsed by the ALMOHAD invasion (1146). He divided his realm between his sons. **Alfonso VIII** (1155–1214), king of Castile from 1158, established its predominance over León. His victory at Las Navas de Tolosa (1212) broke Almohad power in Spain. **Alfonso IX** (1171–1230), king of León from 1188, failed to recover lands lost to Castile, but defeated the Almohads at Merida (1230). **Alfonso X** (1221–1284), king of León and Castile from 1252, took Cartagena and Cádiz from the Moors. He was a patron of learning and a legal reformer. **Alfonso XI** (1311–1350), king of León and Castile from 1312, restored order to the kingdom, and recaptured Algeciras (1344).

ALFONSO, Spanish form of the Portuguese AFONSO, name of six kings of Portugal.

ALFONSO XII (1857–1885), king of Spain from the fall of the first republic in 1874, son of Isabella II. He was generally popular, and his reign marked a move towards constitutional monarchy.

ALFONSO XIII (1886–1941), king of Spain, posthumous son of Alfonso XII, became king at birth and began personal rule in 1902. His intervention in politics brought instability and unpopularity and he associated himself with the dictatorship of PRIMO DE RIVERA. After a republican landslide in municipal elections he was forced to leave the country in 1931, though he refused to abdicate. His grandson JUAN CARLOS became head of state on General Franco's death.

ALFRED THE GREAT (c848–899), king of the West Saxons from 871. He halted the Danish invasions, making his kingdom of Wessex the nucleus of a unified England. Already a noted general, he came to the throne in the middle of a Danish invasion which he had to buy off despite spirited resistance. He used the truce period to consolidate his army and navy, and won a conclusive victory at Edington (878). He occupied London in 886 and was recognized as overlord of all England not in the extensive DANELAW. A pious ruler, he had many writers, such as BOETHIUS and BEDE, translated for his subjects' benefit, and introduced educational and legal reforms.

ALFVÉN, Hannes Olof Gösta (1908–   ), Swedish physicist who shared the 1970 Nobel Prize for Physics with Louis NÉEL for contributing to the development of PLASMA physics. Alfvén himself introduced the study of MAGNETOHYDRODYNAMICS.

ALGAE, a large and extremely diverse group of plants, including some of the simplest organisms known to man. They are mostly aquatic, and range in size from microscopic single-celled organisms living on trees, in snow, ponds and the surface waters of oceans to strands of seaweed several metres long in the deep oceans. Some algae are free-floating, some are motile (see LOCOMOTION) and some grow attached to a substrate.

Algae are separated into seven major divisions, primarily on the basis of pigmentation. Blue-green algae have also been grouped in the algae by some authorities but differ from other algae in that they are prokaryotic organisms (see PROKARYOTE). Green algae (division Chlorophyta) are found mainly in freshwater and may be single-celled, form long filaments (like *Spirogyra*) or a flat leaf-like mass of cells called a thallus (like the sea lettuce, *Ulva lactuca*). Golden-brown algae (division Chrysophyta) also include the DIATOMS. Brown algae (division Phaeophyta) include the familiar seaweeds found on rocky shores. The largest, the KELPS, can grow to enormous lengths. Red algae (division Rhodophyta) are found mostly in warmer seas and include several species of economic importance. Desmids and dinoflagellates (both in division Pyrrophyta) are single-celled algae and are important constituents of marine PLANKTON. Yellow-green algae and chloromonads (division Xanthophyta) are mainly freshwater forms, mostly unicellular and nonmotile. Motile unicellular algae such as *Euglena* (division Euglenophyta) are classified by some biologists as PROTOZOA, but most contain CHLOROPHYLL and can synthesize their own food.

Algae in both marine and freshwater plankton are important as the basis of food chains (see ECOLOGY). Many of the larger algae are important to man; for example, the red algae *Porphyra* and *Chondrus crispus* are used as foodstuffs. *Gelidium*, another red alga, is a source of AGAR, and the kelps (such as the giant kelp *Macrocystis*) produce alginates, one use of which is in the manufacture of ice cream. Other uses of algae are in medicine and as manure. (See also PLANT KINGDOM.)

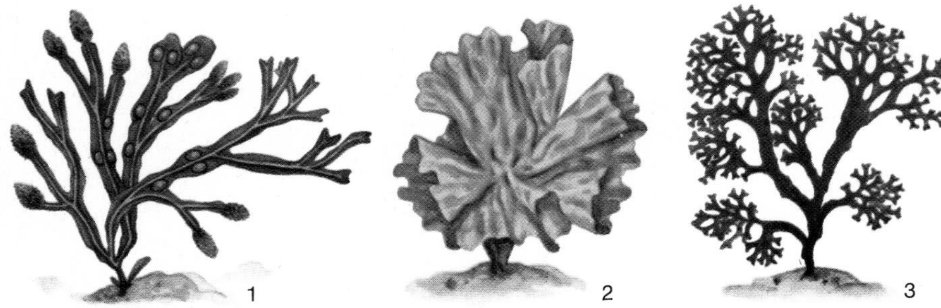

Fucus vesiculosus (1), species of brown algae measuring up to 0·9m (3ft) in length and growing along nontropical coasts. *Ulva lactuca* (2), largest of the green algae 1m (3·3ft across), is called the sea lettuce. *Chondrus crispus*, or Irish moss (3), species of red algae found in northern seas.

ALGARDI, Alessandro (1595–1654), Italian baroque sculptor, pupil of Lodovico CARRACCI, contemporary and more conservative rival of BERNINI. His masterpieces include the tomb of Pope Leo XI (1642) and a great relief of St. Leo and Attila the Hun (1646–50), both in St. Peter's, Rome.

ALGARVE, ancient Moorish kingdom (8th–13th centuries) in S Portugal, later a province under the Portuguese crown. Coextensive with a modern administrative district named for Faro, its capital, it is 1 958sq mi in area and a tourist center.

ALGEBRA, that part of mathematics dealing with the relationships and properties of number systems by use of general symbols (such as a, b, x, y) to represent mathematical quantities. These are combined by addition $(x+y)$, subtraction $(x-y)$, multiplication $(x \times y,\ x.y$ or most usually $xy)$ and division $(x \div y,\ x/y$ or most usually $\frac{x}{y})$. The relationships between them are expressed by symbols such as $=$ ("is equal to"), $\neq$ ("is not equal to") $\simeq$ (is approximately equal to"), $>$ ("is greater than"), and $<$ ("is less than"). These

Terms Used in Algebra

Function:	combination of symbols standing for quantities e.g. ax^2+bx+c
Variable:	quantity able to take a range of values e.g. x, above
Constant:	quantity that is fixed, e.g. a, b above
Equation:	function put equal to a constant, in particular zero e.g. $ax^2+bx+c=0$
Root:	value of the variable that will satisfy an equation e.g. $x = -\frac{b}{2a} \pm \frac{\sqrt{b^2-4ac}}{2a}$ for the above
Identity:	an equation that holds for all values of the variable e.g. $(x+1)(x-1)-(x^2-1)=0$
Coefficient:	part of a product, usually a constant before a variable e.g. a, b above
Polynomial:	a finite sum of integral powers of a variable, with coefficients e.g. the function above
Algebraic number:	one that can be the root of a polynomial with integral coefficients, e.g. the roots of $3x^2+5x-2=0$

symbols are also used in ARITHMETIC. Should a number be multiplied by itself one or more times it is said to be raised to a power:

$$x.x = x^2,$$
$$x.x.x = x^3, \text{ etc.}$$

x^2 is termed "x to the power of two" or more usually "x squared"; x^3 is termed "x to the power of three" or more often "x cubed." From this emerges the concept of the ROOT: if $x^2 = y$ then x is the square root of y or $\sqrt[2]{y}$ (or $\sqrt{y}$).

Algebraic operations are described by the Associative, Commutative and Distributive Laws (see table).

Statements such as $x+y=z$ or $x^2=y$ are termed identities. Should one of the terms in such an identity be of unknown value, then we may discover its value through examination of the identity: if in the first example $x=3$, y is unknown and $z=7$, then $3+y=7$ and $y+4$. This is known as solution of an EQUATION.

Expressions containing two or more terms, such as $x+y+z$, are called polynomials. A special case is an expression containing two terms, such as $x+y$, which is termed a binomial.

Not all quantities combine in the ways described above. In vector algebra (see VECTOR ANALYSIS), for example, the operation equivalent to multiplication is not commutative: $\mathbf{a} \times \mathbf{b} = -\mathbf{b} \times \mathbf{a}$. There are thus different algebras to cope with different types of quantities. A special example of this is the application of algebraic techniques to LOGIC.

In higher algebra, a set of items combinable by an operation "x" is called a group if, for any a and b, $a\,x\,b$ is a unique element of the set (if, say, $a=3$ and $b=\sqrt{4}$, $a\,x\,b$ would not be unique if x implied multiplication, since $\sqrt{4}=+2$ or -2, and hence $a \times b$ equals $+6$ or -6), if $a\,x\,y=b$ and $z\,x\,b=a$ have unique solutions, and if the operation $a\,x\,b\,x\,c$ is associative. If the operation is commutative the group is called a commutative group: the set of all INTEGERS, for example, is commutative with respect to addition; the set of all RATIONAL NUMBERS is commutative with respect to multiplication. Should the set of mathematical quantities be distributive for, say, the two operations "$\times$" and "$+$" the set is called a ring; and should the multiplication be commutative the set is a commutative ring: the set of all integers is an example. If for any non-zero element a, there is an element a', known as its inverse, such that $a.a'=1$, the set is termed a field: the set of all rational numbers is such a field.

Algebraic methods are used throughout mathematics. (See also ALGEBRAIC GEOMETRY; BINOMIAL THEOREM; CALCULUS; GROUPS; MATHEMATICS; SET THEORY.)

Commutation, Association and Distribution

Addition and multiplication in the field of real numbers are said to be *commutative* since

$$a+b=b+a$$

and $$a.b=b.a.$$

Division and subtraction are not commutative since

$$\frac{a}{b} \neq \frac{b}{a}$$

and $$a-b \neq b-a.$$

Addition and multiplication are also *associative*, since

$$a+(b+c)=(a+b)+c$$

and $$a.(b.c)=(a.b).c,$$

but division and subtraction are not associative, since

$$a \div (b \div c) \neq (a \div b) \div c$$

[since $a \div (b \div c) = (a.c) \div b$,
$(a \div b) \div c = a \div (b.c)$],

and $$a-(b-c) \neq (a-b)-c$$

[since $a-(b-c)=a-b+c$,
$(a-b)-c=a-b-c$].

Addition and multiplication are together *distributive* since

$$a.(b+c)=a.b+a.c$$

and this is commutative since

$$(b+c).a=b.a+c.a=a.b+a.c.$$

ALGEBRAIC GEOMETRY, that branch of ALGEBRA concerned with the visual realization of algebraic FUNCTIONS, whether such realization is practically possible or not. An extension of ANALYTIC GEOMETRY, it is now used primarily as an intuitive aid in discovering or understanding THEOREMS.

ALGECIRAS, seaport on the Bay of Algeciras in Cadiz province, S Spain, 6mi W of Gibraltar. Originally Moorish, it was resettled by Spain in 1704. Its main industries are shipping, fishing and tourism. Pop 81 662.

ALGECIRAS CONFERENCE, meeting of the great powers, including the US, at Algeciras, Spain, to settle the Moroccan crisis of 1906. French demands for a protectorate over Morocco had brought strong German protests. The conference guaranteed German trade and investments, but allowed Spain and France policing and other powers that paved the way for complete control.

ALGER, Horatio (1834–1899), US author of more than 100 boys' books, in which the heroes rise from rags to riches through virtue and hard work. Among his books were *Ragged Dick* (1867), *Luck and Pluck* (1869) and *Sink or Swim* (1870).

ALGER, Russell Alexander (1836–1907), US secretary of war (1897–99) under William McKinley, widely criticized for inefficiency and mismanagement in the War Department during the SPANISH–AMERICAN WAR. From 1902 until his death he was a US senator from Mich.

ALGERIA, socialist republic in North Africa extending from the Mediterranean deep into the Sahara Desert. The Atlas Mountains, running E–W, divide the country into three regions: the rugged coastal zone in the N, clothed with evergreen trees; the steppe, covered with scrub and grass, pocked by salt lakes and flanked by the Atlas ranges; and the stony and sandy Sahara Desert in the S, with the sharply fretted Ahaggar Mountains reaching 9 852ft in the SE. Apart from the Tafna and Chéliff (in the NW), most rivers are intermittent and useless for irrigation or hydroelectricity. The climate is marked by mild winters and warm, dry summers in the N, and by greater extremes on the steppe; the Sahara varies between roasting days and frosty nights.

Some 75% of Algerians (chiefly Muslim Arabs and Berbers, but still including some Christian Europeans) live in the fertile coastal area. The ports of Algiers, Oran and Annaba, and northern trading centers (Constantine, Sidi-bel-Abbes, Blida) provide urban employment, but most Algerians still live on the land; their distribution reflects the mainly agricultural economy. Northern farms produce citrus fruits, grapes, grain and vegetables. Nomads tend sheep, goats and cattle on the steppe; and desert oases yield dates. Iron ore, coal, zinc, phosphates and, recently, Saharan oil and natural gas (now exported to the US) are the basis of industrial growth, assisted by extensive road and rail systems.

Phoenicians settled N Algeria c1200 BC. It became part of Carthage but after the victory of Rome in 201 BC became the Roman province of Numidia. Vandals (by 440 AD), Byzantines (in 534) and Arabs (in the 17th century) all conquered the area. Moors expelled from Spain became the Algerian-based BARBARY PIRATES (from 1518 under nominal Ottoman Turkish control). They ravaged Mediterranean shipping until defeated by US warships. The French then absorbed all Algeria (1830–1909), and French colonists largely governed it until a nationalist revolt (1954–62) forced France to grant Algeria independence. An exodus of skilled French followed, and Algeria is still recovering from the consequent economic damage, largely by harnessing foreign capital and expertise to a program of state-controlled growth.

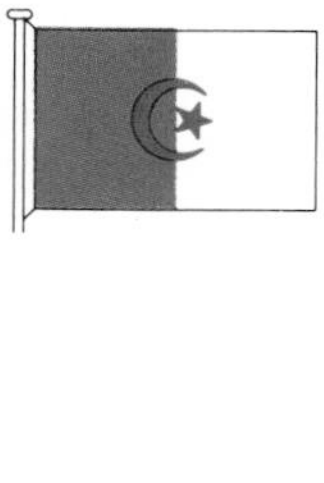

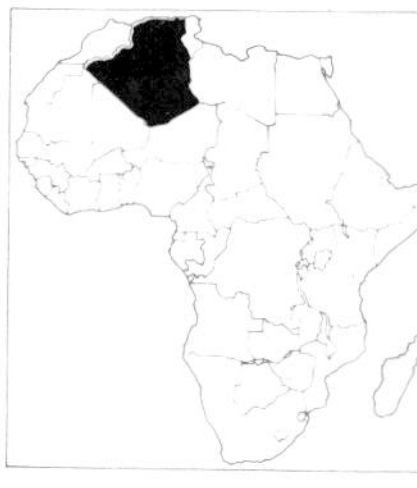

Official Name: The People's Republic of Algeria
Capital: Algiers
Area: 952 198sq mi
Population: 1 769 000
Languages: Arabic, Berber, French
Religions: Muslim
Monetary Unit(s): 1 Algerian dinar = 100 centimes

ALGIERS, capital, major port and largest city of Algeria. Founded by Berbers in 935 on the site of the Roman settlement of Icosium, it was taken by the French in 1830. The modern city lies at the base of a hill overlooking the Bay of Algiers; higher up the slope is the old Moorish city, dominated by the Casbah, a citadel built by the Turks. Pop 903 530.

ALGIN, polysaccharide (see CARBOHYDRATES) extracted from brown seaweeds. A derivative, sodium alginate, is a thickening agent and emulsion stabilizer used in the food industry, especially ice cream manufacture, and as sizing in paper and textiles.

ALGOL, Beta Persei, second-brightest star in the constellation PERSEUS. It is a multiple star of at least three but probably four components, two of which form an eclipsing binary (see VARIABLE STAR) causing a 10h diminution of brightness every 59h.

ALGOL (*Algo*rithmic *L*anguage, sometimes given as *Alg*ebraic *O*riented *L*anguage), universal COMPUTER language devised 1958, adapted 1960. Similar to FORTRAN, but with several important advantages, it is used more in Europe than in the US.

ALGONQUIAN (or Algonkian), largest North American Indian linguistic family, including languages spoken from Newfoundland to the Great Plains and from the Churchill R to Cape Hatteras. In parts of New York occupied by the Iroquois, and elsewhere, there were breaks in this continuity, but isolated Algonquian tribes were also found in California and the Gulf states. (See INDIANS, NORTH AMERICAN.)

ALGONQUIN (or ALGONKIN) INDIANS, North American Indian tribe. Among the first with whom the French made an alliance, they were driven out of their territory along the St. Lawrence and Ottawa rivers by the Iroquois in the 17th and 18th centuries. Some united with the Ottawa Indians; a few remain in Ontario and Quebec. Originally the name "Algonquin" was applied only to the Weskarini of the Gatineau valley, but it was widened to include other closely related tribes such as the Nipissing and Abitibi. It gave its name to the ALGONQUIAN linguistic division.

ALGORITHM, a set of simple mathematical operations which together, in the right order, constitute a complex mathematical operation. Algorithms are used extensively in COMPUTER science (see ALGOL).

A simple algorithm

The object is to find the square root of 9 using only simple arithmetical operations. An initial "guess" is made—in this case 4—and the calculator then proceeds:

(try out guess)	$9 \div 4 = 2.25$
(find the mean of guess and result	$2.25 + 4 = 6.25$ $6.25 \div 2 = 3.125$
(try this result)	$9 \div 3.125 = 2.88$
(find the mean of this result and previous one)	$2.88 + 3.125 = 6.005$ $6.005 \div 2 = 3.0025$

and so on. Already the calculator is close to the right answer—3—and he will know that it has been attained when two successive averaging operations yield the same result to the accuracy that he requires.

ALGREN, Nelson (1909–), US naturalistic novelist, best known for his fiction describing Chicago slum life; author of *The Man with a Golden Arm* (1949) and *A Walk on the Wild Side* (1956).

The Alhambra in Granada, Spain, combines all the grace and beauty of Moorish architecture. The picture shows the Court of Myrtles with its elegant marble pool and symmetrical arcade.

ALHAMBRA, 13th-century citadel and palace dominating the city of Granada, the finest large-scale example of Moorish architecture in Spain. The name is Arabic for "the red castle." It is decorated in an elaborate but delicate style.

ALHAMBRA, city in S. Cal., in the San Gabriel Valley ENE of Los Angeles. Its industries include steel products, plastics and machinery. Pop 62 125.

ALI (c600–661), fourth Arab caliph (from 656), cousin and son-in-law of the prophet MUHAMMAD. Assassinated by a fanatic and succeeded by the OMAYYAD caliphs, he is especially venerated by the SHI'ITE sect of Islam. (See also CALIPHATE.)

ALI, Muhammad (1942–), US heavyweight boxer. Born Cassius Marcellus Clay in Louisville, Ky., he fought his way to the world heavyweight championship, dethroning Sonny LISTON in 1964. Ali was stripped of his title in 1967 by the World Boxing Association while he was appealing against conviction for draft evasion, later overturned. He returned to the ring in 1971 only to be defeated by Joe FRAZIER, but beat him in a return match in 1974.

ALI BABA, in the *Arabian Nights*, a poor woodcutter who discovers the magic words, "Open Sesame," which open the doors to the Forty Thieves' treasure-cave. He outwits the thieves and takes the hoard.

ALIBI, in criminal law, evidence that an accused person was not present at the time and place of the alleged offense. A proven alibi is said to be "established."

ALICANTE, Mediterranean seaport capital of Alicante province, SE Spain. A popular resort, busy fishing port and shipping center for regional produce, its industries include papermaking, tilemaking and cigarette manufacture. Pop 184 716.

ALICE, city, seat of Jim Wells Co., S Tex., 45mi W of Corpus Christi; an oil refinery and agricultural processing center. Pop 20 121.

ALICE SPRINGS, town in the Northern Territory, Australia, lying in the center of the continent at an altitude of 1 900ft. It is a major shipping center for livestock and for minerals, some mined locally. Pop 11 118.

ALICYLIC COMPOUNDS, class of organic compounds in which carbon atoms are linked to form one or more rings. AROMATIC COMPOUNDS are excluded because of their special properties. In general, alicyclic compounds resemble analogous ALIPHATIC COMPOUNDS. However, strain occurs in small rings (with three, four or five members) because the angles between adjacent bonds are less than the preferred angle of 109° 28′, and these compounds are less stable and more reactive. Larger rings are nonplanar and unstrained. Many TERPENES, such as MENTHOL, are alicyclic. (See also HETEROCYCLIC COMPOUNDS.)

ALIEN, any person who is not a citizen of the country in which he is living or traveling. An alien is generally subject to the laws of the host country and, except for the vote, a resident alien has most of the same rights and duties as a citizen. At present over 3 000 000 aliens are resident or studying in the US. (See also NATURALIZATION.)

ALIEN AND SEDITION ACTS, four unpopular laws passed by the US Congress in 1798. Two empowered the president to expel or imprison aliens; one made naturalization more difficult; another, the Sedition Act, punished those who wrote or spoke "with intent to defame" the government. Enacted by the Federalists to prepare for a possible war with France (see XYZ AFFAIR), and to silence Jeffersonian criticism, the Alien Acts were not put into force. But several Jeffersonian newspaper editors were convicted under the Sedition Act. This led to the KENTUCKY AND VIRGINIA RESOLUTIONS.

ALIENATION, or estrangement, a term first used in philosophy by HEGEL in the early 19th century to express awareness of the gulf that exists between man the conscious agent and man the victim of the actions of others. The notion was adopted by Karl MARX to describe the situation of men working under institutions which rule them rather than serve them, or under conditions in which repetitive toil replaces creative craftsmanship.

ALIENATION OF AFFECTION, in US law, a conduct that intentionally interferes with a marriage relationship. Historically, most such suits have been brought by wives against the woman who has helped break up the marriage. A number of states have abolished such suits.

ALIGARH, city in Uttar Pradesh, N India, 70mi SE of Delhi, encompassing the ancient Hindu town of Koil and fortress of Aligarh; an industrial and market center. It is the site of Aligarh Muslim University, the fruit of the Aligarh Movement—whose goal was to bring Western ideas to the Muslims of British India and which was the precursor of the MUSLIM LEAGUE. Pop 254 008.

ALIGHIERI, Dante. See DANTE.

ALI KHAN, Liaquat (1895–1951), prime minister of Pakistan from independence in 1947 until his assassination by an Afghan fanatic. Chief aide of Muhammad Ali JINNAH, he became secretary of the MUSLIM LEAGUE in 1937.

ALIMENTARY CANAL. See GASTROINTESTINAL TRACT.

ALIMONY, payment made under court order after legal separation and divorce, usually for the support of a wife; in some cases it may be awarded to the husband. It can be paid in one lump sum or at regular intervals, with the amount depending on the husband's means, the wife's ability to earn, the length of the marriage and the conduct of the parties leading to separation. Payments cease after either party dies or the wife remarries.

ALINSKY, Saul (1909–1972, US pioneer in community organization, known for his early community action work in the Chicago stockyards area (1939). Creator of the Woodlawn Organization on Chicago's South Side (1960), he founded a school in community organization there in 1969.

ALI PASHA (1741–1822), called "the Lion of Yannina," Ottoman pasha of Yannina (now Ioannina, NW Greece). After regaining his father's Albanian territories, in 1787 he crushed a rebellion at Scutari for the Turks, who appointed him pasha. With alternate British and French support he held Epirus, Albania and Thessaly until the Turks, fearing his power, had him murdered.

ALIPHATIC COMPOUNDS, major class of organic compounds that includes all those with carbon atoms linked in straight or branched open chains. The other classes are ALICYCLIC, HETEROCYCLIC and AROMATIC compounds.

ALIQUIPPA, steelmaking borough on the Ohio R in W Penn., 18mi NW of Pittsburgh. Pop 22 277.

ALIZARIN, 1,2-dihydroxyanthraquinone, a once-important orange-red DYE, originally extracted from the root of the MADDER (*Rubia tinctorum*) but after 1871 made synthetically from ANTHRAQUINONE by a process developed by PERKIN (1869). An earlier German synthesis (1868) was the first laboratory preparation of a natural dyestuff. Alizarin is now little used.

ALJUBARROTA, village in W central Portugal, scene of a great battle in 1385, in which the Portuguese, led by Nuno Álvares Pereira and aided by English archers, defeated much larger Castilian forces. Victory ensured the independence of Portugal, opening up a brilliant period in its history.

ALKALI, a water-soluble compound of the ALKALI METALS (or ammonia) which acts as a strong BASE producing a high concentration of hydroxyl ions in aqueous solution. Alkalis neutralize acids to form salts and turn red litmus paper blue. Common alkalis are sodium hydroxide ($NaOH$), ammonia (NH_3), sodium carbonate (Na_2CO_3) and potassium carbonate (K_2CO_3). They have important industrial applications in the manufacture of glass, soap, paper and textiles. Caustic alkalis are corrosive and can cause severe burns.

ALKALI FLATS, level, barren areas in dry regions covered with EVAPORITES, mainly salts of the ALKALI METALS and ALKALINE–EARTH METALS. Alkali flats are formed by the repeated periodic evaporation of shallow lakes lacking outlets.

ALKALI METALS, highly reactive metals in Group IA of the PERIODIC TABLE, comprising LITHIUM, SODIUM, POTASSIUM, RUBIDIUM, CESIUM and FRANCIUM. They are soft and silvery-white with low melting points. Alkali metals react with water to give off hydrogen, and so much heat is generated (except by lithium and sodium) that spontaneous combustion may occur. Because of this extreme reactivity they never occur naturally as the metals, but are always found as monovalent ionic salts.

ALKALINE-EARTH METALS, gray-white metals in Group IIA of the PERIODIC TABLE, comprising BERYLLIUM, MAGNESIUM, CALCIUM, STRONTIUM, BARIUM and RADIUM. They never occur in an uncombined state, but are usually found as carbonates or sulfates. Except for beryllium, they are highly reactive and inflammable, readily dissolving in acids to form divalent ionic salts. The hydroxides of the four heaviest elements are alkalis.

ALKALOIDS, narcotic poisons found in certain plants and fungi. They have complex molecular

ALKALOIDS

Name	Source	Uses and effects
Morphine	Asiatic poppy	Relieves pain and depresses the nervous system
Quinine	Cinchone bark	Effective in the treatment of malaria
Atropine	Belladonna	Used to dilate the pupils of the eye during surgery and to relax the smooth muscles
Strychnine	Nux vomica seeds	Muscle stimulant
Reserpine	Snakeroot	Reduces anxiety and tension
Ephedrine	*Ephedra* plants	Decongestant for colds, hay fever and asthma
Nicotine	Tobacco	Used as an insecticide
Curare	Various plants	Relaxes voluntary muscles
Mescaline	Peyote cactus	Hallucinogenic
Cocaine	Coca leaves	Local anaesthetic

structures and are usually heterocyclic nitrogen-containing BASES. Many, such as coniine (from hemlock) or atropine (deadly nightshade), are extremely poisonous. Others, such as morphine, nicotine and cocaine, can be highly addictive, and some, such as mescaline, are psychedelics. But in small doses alkaloids are often powerful medicines, and are used as analgesics, tranquilizers, and cardiac and respiratory stimulants. Other examples are quinine, reserpine and ephedrine. Caffeine (found in coffee and tea) is a stimulant. Although alkaloids may be found in any part of the plant, they are usually contained in the seeds, seed capsules, bark or roots. One plant, the opium poppy, contains about 30 alkaloids. Alkaloids are extracted from plants and separated by chromatography; synthetic alkaloids are seldom economically competitive.

ALKALOSIS, medical condition in which the blood PLASMA becomes excessively alkaline (i.e., the PH rises above 7.45) with resulting nausea, anorexia or TETANY. Respiratory alkalosis is due to over-ventilation with loss of plasma CARBON dioxide. Metabolic causes can include the consumption of excess ALKALI or the large acid loss involved in severe vomiting. (See also ACIDOSIS.)

ALKANES, or **Paraffins,** the homologous series of saturated HYDROCARBONS of general formula C_nH_{2n+2}. The lowest members, which are gases, are METHANE, ETHANE, PROPANE and BUTANE; higher members are named for the number of carbon atoms in the molecule. From pentane (C_5H_{12}) to heptadecane ($C_{17}H_{36}$) they are liquids, and above that waxy solids. Alkanes with four or more carbon atoms have several ISOMERS, the straight-chain isomers being called normal alkanes (*n*-alkanes). Branched alkanes are named as derivatives of the longest straight chain in the molecule. Alkanes are obtained from petroleum and natural gas; they may be synthesized by hydrogenation of ALKENES or from carbon monoxide and hydrogen. They are soluble in most organic solvents, but not in water. The lower alkanes are less reactive than the higher alkanes. Typical reactions include combustion in air, decomposition and rearrangement on heating, isomerization and condensation with alkenes (with acid catalyst), nitration, sulfonation, and halogenation by fluorine, chlorine and bromine (with heat or light). The monovalent radicals C_nH_{2n+1} derived from alkanes by loss of one hydrogen atom are called alkyl groups (methyl, ethyl, etc.), usually denoted by the symbol R. (See also OCTANE.)

ALKENES, or **Olefins,** the homologous series of unsaturated HYDROCARBONS having one or more double bonds (see BOND, CHEMICAL) between adjacent carbon atoms. The monoalkenes (one double bond) have general formula C_nH_{2n}; their systematic names are derived from those of the corresponding ALKANES by replacing the suffix -ane by -ene. They are prepared by thermal cracking of alkanes (from petroleum or natural gas), dehydration of ALCOHOLS, or base-catalyzed elimination of hydrogen halides from ALKYL HALIDES. Alkenes physically resemble the corresponding alkanes, but chemically their properties are due mainly to the double bond. Many reagents add across the double bond: hydrogen (with nickel or platinum catalyst), halogens, hydrogen halides, and sulfuric acid. Alkenes are oxidized by permanganate or hypochlorite to GLYCOLS, and by OZONE to ozonides which readily decompose to ALDEHYDES and KETONES. Alkenes may readily be polymerized (by catalysts) to give plastics and resins. (See also ETHYLENE; BUTADIENE; ISOPRENE.)

AL-KHWARIZMI. See KHWARIZMI, MUHAMMAD IBN-MUSA AL-.

ALKMAAR, town in the province of North Holland, the Netherlands, N of Amsterdam. A major agricultural center, it is famed for its weekly cheese market. Pop 51 643.

ALKYLATION, the introduction of an alkyl group (see ALKANES) into a compound by substitution or addition, usually done by reacting the compound with an ALKENE or an ALKYL HALIDE. (See FRIEDEL-CRAFTS REACTION.) Specifically in petroleum refining, alkylation refers to the thermal or catalytic process in which branched alkanes are reacted with alkenes to yield highly branched products of high OCTANE rating.

ALKYL HALIDES, organic compounds consisting of an alkyl group (see ALKANES) bonded to a HALOGEN atom; polyhalogen derivatives of alkanes are similar. They are prepared by direct halogenation of alkanes (except for the iodides), addition of hydrogen halides to ALKENES, or halogenation of ALCOHOLS by hydrogen halides, phosphorus (III) halides, etc. Alkyl halides are used as solvents and as intermediates in chemical manufacture. The halogen atom is readily replaced by other NUCLEOPHILES such as hydroxide or cyanide. Elimination of hydrogen halides (base-catalyzed) yields alkenes.

ALKYNES, or acetylenes, the homologous series of unsaturated HYDROCARBONS having one or more triple bonds (see BOND, CHEMICAL) between adjacent carbon atoms. The monoalkynes (one triple bond) have general formula C_nH_{2n-2}; their systematic names are derived from those of the corresponding ALKANES by replacing the suffix -ane by -yne. They are prepared by elimination of two hydrogen halide molecules from a dihaloalkane. Alkynes physically resemble the corresponding alkanes, but chemically their properties are due mainly to the triple bond, and are similar to those of the ALKENES. Addition reactions take place in two stages, forming first a substituted alkene and then a substituted alkane. The triple bond being nucleophilic (see NUCLEOPHILES), alkynes add to unsaturated compounds such as aldehydes or ketones. Alkynes readily polymerize to various products, including AROMATIC and ALICYCLIC compounds.

ALLAH, Arabic name (*al-ilah*) for the supreme being, used by the prophet Mohammed to designate the God of ISLAM.

ALLAHABAD, capital of Uttar Pradesh state, N India, at the confluence of the sacred Ganges and Jumna rivers. The goal of Hindu pilgrims, the city was given its present name (meaning "city of God") by the Mogul emperor AKBAR, who built a fort and palace there. The famous Pillar of ASOKA (240 BC) is also in the city. Site of one of India's oldest universities, Allahabad is an important administrative, cultural and commercial center. Pop 491 702.

ALL-AMERICAN CANAL, completed 1940, brings water 80mi from the Colorado R to irrigate 500 000 acres of the Imperial Valley, Cal. A branch delivering an equal amount of water to the Coachella Valley was opened in 1958.

ALLAN, Sir Hugh (1810–1882), Scottish-born Canadian businessman and shipowner. He was awarded the charter for construction of the Canadian Pacific Railway, but revelation of the PACIFIC SCANDAL (1873) led to its cancellation and the dissolution of his rail company.

ALLEGHENY MOUNTAINS, range of the central Appalachians extending from SW Va. through Md. into N central Pa. The Alleghenies run parallel to and W of the Blue Ridge Mountains, with average heights of 2 000ft in the N and more than 4 500ft in the S. The steep E slope is called the Allegheny Front. The upland region between the Cumberland Plateau and Mohawk Valley is known as the Allegheny Plateau.

ALLEGHENY RIVER, important headstream of the Ohio R. Rising in Potter Co., N central Pa., it crosses the SW corner of N.Y., then flows S through Pa. to Pittsburgh, where it joins the Monongahela to form the Ohio R.

ALLEGORY, term applicable in any of the arts where the literal content of the work is subsidiary to its symbolic meaning. Concrete and material images are used to represent more abstract notions; thus death might be personified as a reaper. BUNYAN'S *Pilgrim's Progress* is a classic example of allegory in literature; many modern writers also use allegory. It is common in the visual arts, perhaps most notably those of the Renaissance and Baroque periods, as for example in BOTTICELLI'S *Primavera*.

ALLEGRETTO, musical term meaning rather lively; less lively than allegro.

ALLEGRO (Italian, from Latin *alacer*: lively, eager), musical term meaning in lively tempo, rather fast.

ALLELE, or allelomorph, one of the two or more genes that can and do occupy particular loci on homologous chromosomes. Different alleles are responsible for the different though similar effects of genetic variation (e.g., whether an individual has brown, green or blue eyes) and are interconvertible by mutation. (See HEREDITY.)

ALLEMANDE, stately dance, generally in duple time, originating in Germany; one version, in 3/4 time, was a forerunner of the waltz. After 1620 the term also denoted the movement opening a suite.

ALLEN, Ethan (1738–1789), American revolution-

Allegory in medieval art is beautifully exemplified in the series of tapestries entitled *The Lady with the Unicorn*, woven in about 1500 at Bruges, Flanders. The lion and the unicorn symbolise the soul's duality, and are pictured here as guardians of the lady, who represents the human spirit beguiled by earthly treasures, yet capable of attaining divine status.

Allentown became the guardian of the original Liberty Bell when the British occupied Philadelphia in 1777. The bell was returned after the Revolution, but there is still a replica on the site where it was kept.

ary hero, leader of the GREEN MOUNTAIN BOYS of Vermont. In May 1775 he took the British garrison at TICONDEROGA, together with its valuable cannon, but in Sept. was captured in a reckless attack on Montreal. Released after almost three years, he was unsuccessful in petitioning Congress for Vt.'s statehood; he then attempted to negotiate the annexation of Vt. by British Canada.

ALLEN, Fred (stage name of John Florence Sullivan, 1894–1956), US comedian who achieved enormous success with his radio show, broadcast 1932–50. The wry humor and nasal delivery of his *Allen's Alley* sketches won him national popularity.

ALLEN, Frederick Lewis (1890–1954), US journalist and social historian. After teaching at Harvard he entered journalism, becoming chief editor of *Harper's Magazine* (1941–54). His historical works, including *Only Yesterday* (1932), were readable and popular.

ALLEN, Hervey (1889–1949), US novelist and poet, co-founder of the Poetry Society of S.C. His best-known work is a long historical novel set in Napoleonic times, *Anthony Adverse* (1933), which was an international success.

ALLEN, Horatio (1802–1890), US railroad engineer who purchased from England the first full-sized locomotive in America, George STEPHENSON's *Stourbridge Lion*, for the Delaware and Hudson Company (1829). He later became president of the Erie Railroad.

ALLEN, Ira (1751–1814), younger brother of Ethan Allen, one of the GREEN MOUNTAIN BOYS. A member of the convention that declared Vermont's independence in 1777, he held various posts in its government.

ALLEN, Richard (1760–1831), US Negro clergyman, founder and first bishop of the AFRICAN METHODIST EPISCOPAL CHURCH (1816), previously the first Negro to be ordained as a minister in the Methodist Church.

ALLEN, William (1532–1594), English cardinal, founder of the Roman Catholic college at DOUAI in Belgium, which produced the DOUAY BIBLE and trained priests for undercover missionary work in Elizabethan England. He was made cardinal in 1587.

ALLENBY, Edmund Henry Hynman Allenby, 1st Viscount (1861–1936), British field marshal who directed the brilliant campaign that won Palestine and Syria from the Turks in WWI. From 1919–25 he was British High Commissioner in Egypt.

ALLENDE, Salvador (1908–1973), Marxist founder of the Chilean Socialist Party, elected president of Chile in 1970, having won the largest minority vote. He subsequently failed to win a majority in the 1972 elections. His radical reform program disrupted the economy; strikes and widespread famine led to a military coup and his suicide.

ALLEN PARK, city in SE Mich., 10mi SW of Detroit, of which it is a residential suburb. Pop 40 747.

ALLENSTEIN. See OLSZTYN.

ALLENTOWN, commercial and industrial city in E Pa., seat of Lehigh Co., on the Lehigh R 50mi NW of Philadelphia. Founded in 1762, it possesses many Revolutionary War associations. Its factories produce trucks, buses, electronic equipment, cement and textiles. Pop 109 527.

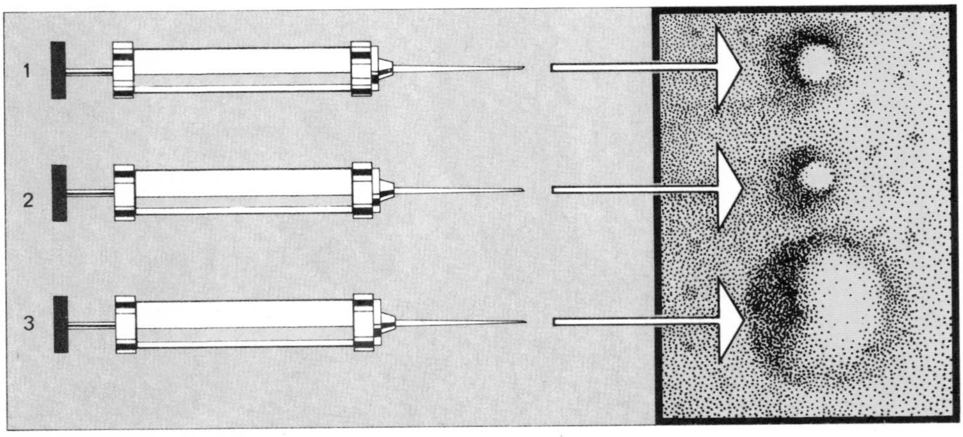

Allergy in an individual can be determined by a simple test:
1. An injection of Histamine produces a slight positive reaction.
2. A small amount of the allergy-producing substance also results in a slight positive reaction.
3. A second injection of this substance results in a strong positive reaction.

ALLEPPEY, seaport in Kerala state, SW India, on the Arabian sea. Its economy is largely based on coconut products. Pop 163 977.

ALLERGY, a state of abnormal sensitivity to foreign material (allergen) in susceptible individuals. It is essentially the inappropriate reaction of ANTIBODY AND ANTIGEN defense responses to environmental substances. Susceptibility is often inherited but manifestations vary with age. Exposure to allergen induces the formation of antibodies; when, at a later date, the material is again encountered, it reacts with the antibodies causing release of HISTAMINE from mast cells in the tissues. INFLAMMATION follows, with local irritation, redness and swelling, which in skin appear as ECZEMA or urticaria (see HIVES). In the nose and eyes HAY FEVER results, and in the GASTROINTESTINAL tract diarrhea may occur. In the LUNGS a specific effect leads to spasm of bronchi, which gives rise to the wheeze and breathlessness of ASTHMA. In most cases, the route of entry determines the site of the response; but skin rashes may occur regardless of route and asthma may follow eating allergenic material. If the allergen is injected, ANAPHYLAXIS may occur. Localized allergic reactions in skin following chronic exposure to chemicals (e.g., nickel, poison ivy) are the basis of contact dermatitis. Common allergens include drugs (PENICILLIN, ASPIRIN), foods (shellfish), plant pollens, animal furs or feathers, insect stings and the house dust mite. Treatment includes ANTIHISTAMINES, cromoglycate, STEROIDS and desensitizing INJECTIONS; ADRENALINE may be life-saving in severe allergic reactions. (See also IMMUNITY.)

ALLERTON, Isaac (c1586–1659), Mayflower Pilgrim and settler in Plymouth Colony, who frequently acted as negotiator and agent for the colony in England. After exceeding his authority he was dismissed and eventually settled in New Haven.

ALLIANCE usually takes the form of a treaty, binding two or more states together for mutual defense or interests. European history has produced many instances in which one nation's predominance has provoked the formation of alliances against it. Examples are the GRAND ALLIANCE which faced Louis XIV, and the QUADRUPLE ALLIANCE, which defeated Napoleon. On the eve of WWI the major European powers were divided into two alliances, the TRIPLE ALLIANCE and the TRIPLE ENTENTE, and the clash between two opposing powers drew all into a worldwide conflagration. The LEAGUE OF NATIONS, and the ideal of collective security, could not prevent the acts of aggression that led ultimately to WWII, and despite the UN, the Cold War produced a new series of alliances, with long-range military planning. Among these are the NORTH ATLANTIC TREATY ORGANIZATION, the SOUTH-EAST ASIA TREATY ORGANIZATION and the CENTRAL TREATY ORGANIZATION. Russia and the Eastern European countries have formed the WARSAW PACT.

ALLIANCE, industrial city in NE Ohio, on the Mahoning R, 50mi SE of Cleveland. The site was settled by Quakers in 1805 and the town formed by the union of four neighboring villages in 1854. It manufactures and distributes a wide variety of steel products, machinery and other industrial goods. Pop 26 547.

ALLIANCE FOR PROGRESS, program designed to aid the economic and social development of Latin America, instituted by President John F. Kennedy in 1961 and brought into being when 22 nations and the US signed the Charter of Punta del Este. The Latin American countries draw up development plans and guarantee the larger part of capital costs, the US meeting the remainder. Most US funds are administered by the AGENCY FOR INTERNATIONAL DEVELOPMENT, and since 1970 the ORGANIZATION OF AMERICAN STATES has also reviewed and coordinated programs.

ALLIES, two or more nations bound by treaty or alliance to act together against a common enemy in case of war. In WWI the "Allies" were the members of the TRIPLE ENTENTE, together with Serbia, Belgium, Japan, Italy and, as an "associated power," the US. In WWII "Allies" was the popular term for some 25 nations that opposed the Axis powers. The major nations among the Allies were the US, Britain, Russia, China and, later, the Free French. These five became the permanent members of the UN Security Council, established in 1945.

ALLIGATOR GAR (*Lepisosteus spatula*), a species of GAR found in the southern US. Often exceeding 3m (10ft) in length, it is one of the largest of freshwater fishes.

ALLIGATOR LIZARDS (*Gerrhonotus*), a genus of ANGUID LIZARDS comprising about 30 species found in North and Central America. Unlike some other anguids all alligator lizards have well-formed legs. They are ground-dwellers and insectivores, some species giving birth to live young. Family: Anguidae.

ALLIGATOR PEAR. See AVOCADO.

ALLIGATORS, two species of large aquatic, carnivorous lizard-like REPTILES comprising the genus *Alligator*. With the CAIMANS, they form the family Alligatoridae of the order Crocodilia. They differ from the true CROCODILES in the arrangement of their teeth and in their generally broader snout. The American alligator (*A. mississippiensis*), now largely restricted to Fla. and La. through over-hunting, has been known to attain 6m (20ft) in length, but the rare Chinese alligator (*A. sinensis*), which inhabits the upper Yangtze valley, rarely exceeds 1.8m (6ft). Alligators can live up to 75 years.

ALLIGATOR SNAPPER, or alligator (snapping) turtle (*Macroclemys*—or *Macrochelys*—*temmincki*), the largest freshwater TURTLE of the US, attaining a weight of over 90kg (200lb). It lives at the bottom of lakes and streams, and feeds on fish which are attracted by a lure that grows from the floor of its mouth. Family: Chelydridae. (See also SNAPPING TURTLE.)

ALLILUYEVA, Svetlana (1927–), daughter of Stalin, who emigrated to the US in 1967. Her *Twenty Letters to a Friend* (1968) gives a fascinating description of Stalin and life in the Kremlin. *Only One Year* (1969) tells of America's impact upon her.

ALLISON, William Boyd (1829–1908), US Senator from Iowa (1873–1908). Spokesman for midwestern farming interests and one of the most influential Republican politicians of the period, he was co-sponsor of the BLAND–ALLISON SILVER PURCHASE ACT.

ALLITERATION, device in poetry of repeating a sound, usually a consonant, at the beginning of neighboring words; in the line from TENNYSON's *Lotos Eaters*, "Surely, surely, slumber is more sweet than toil," the "s" and "l" sounds are alliterative. Early Germanic, Old Norse and Old English verse is characterized by subtle accented alliterative measures, and it is often found in Gaelic and Welsh poetry. LANGLAND's *Piers Plowman* exemplifies a school of alliterative verse which survived in W England until the late 14th century.

ALLIUM, genus of bulbous plants of the family Liliaceae, including ONIONS, GARLIC, CHIVES, LEEKS and SHALLOTS. They are hardy PERENNIAL (occasionally BIENNIAL) plants, most with the typical onion smell. The erect stems have basal leaves and terminate in more or less globular clusters of white, yellow, red or purple flowers. Many species are cultivated as garden plants.

ALLOBROGES, ancient Celtic tribe of E Gaul in the Rhône R Geneva area. Subjugated by Rome in 121 BC, their appeal to Julius Caesar for aid against the attacking Helvetii in 58 BC brought about the GALLIC WARS.

ALLOMORPH. See MORPHEME.

ALLON, Yigal (1918–), Israeli politician, a commander of the Hagana in the 1947–48 Arab–Israeli War. He first entered the cabinet as minister of labor (1961), became deputy prime minister (1968) and foreign minister in 1974.

ALLOPATHY (from German *Allopathie*, term coined 1842 by HAHNEMANN), the cure of a disease by the induction of symptoms differing from those of the disease; the opposite of HOMEOPATHY. A variation, **enantiopathy**, the countering of an overabundance of one HUMOR by the overabundance of another, was used in medieval times.

ALLOPHONE. See PHONEME.

ALLOSAURUS, or Antrodemus, large carnivorous DINOSAUR of the late JURASSIC and early CRETACEOUS periods, up to 11m (36ft) in length and weighing about two tonnes. Family: Megalosauridae (see MEGALOSAURUS).

Alligators are slower-moving and less aggressive than crocodiles, except in danger or when seizing prey. They also live twice as long.

ALLOTROPY, the occurrence of some elements in more than one form (known as allotropes) which differ in their crystalline or molecular structure. Allotropes may have strikingly different physical or chemical properties. Allotropy in which the various forms are stable under different conditions and are reversibly interconvertible at certain temperatures and pressures, is called enantiotropy. Notable examples of allotropy include DIAMOND and GRAPHITE, OXYGEN and OZONE, and SULFUR. (See also POLYMORPHISM.)

ALLOUEZ, Claude Jean (1622–1689), French Jesuit missionary in New France. A colleague of Père MARQUETTE, he traveled widely and founded many missions, chiefly in the region SW of the Great Lakes. He died at Fort St. Jean, near modern Niles, Mich.

ALLOY, a combination of metals with each other or with nonmetals such as carbon or phosphorus. They are useful because their properties can be adjusted as desired by varying the proportions of the constituents. Very few metals are used today in a pure state. Alloys are formed by mixing their molten components. The structures of alloys consisting mainly of one component may be substitutional or interstitial, depending on the relative sizes of the atoms. The study of alloy structures in general is complex. (See also PHASE EQUILIBRIA.)

The commonest alloys are the different forms of STEEL, which all contain a large proportion of iron and small amounts of carbon and other elements. BRASS and BRONZE, two well-known and ancient metals, are alloys of copper, while PEWTER is an alloy of tin and lead. The very light but strong alloys used in aircraft construction are frequently alloys of aluminum with magnesium, copper or silicon. SOLDERS contain tin with lead and bismuth; type metal is an alloy of lead, tin and antimony. Among familiar alloys are those used in coins: modern "silver" coinage in most countries is an alloy of nickel and copper. Special alloys are used for such purposes as die-casting, dentistry, high-temperature use, and for making thermocouples, magnets and low-expansion materials. (See also AMALGAM; BABBITT METAL; GERMAN SILVER; GUN METAL; INVAR; MONEL METAL.)

ALLPORT, Gordon Willard (1897–1967). US psychologist, important figure in the study of personality, who stressed the "functional autonomy of motives." Among his many works, *The Nature of Prejudice* (1954) has become a classic in its field.

ALL SAINTS' DAY, religious feast day celebrating all Christian saints, observed by most Christian churches on Nov. 1. Its present form dates from the reign of Pope Gregory III (731–741).

ALL SOULS' DAY, Roman Catholic holy day when people offer prayers and masses for souls believed to be in PURGATORY. It is held on Nov. 2 (or Nov. 3 if Nov. 2 is a Sunday).

ALLSPICE, aromatic spice prepared from dried berries of the pimento or allspice tree, *Pimenta dioica* (family: Myrtaceae), of the W Indies and Central America. The spice is named for its flavor, reminiscent of cloves, cinnamon and nutmeg. It is used in baking, flavoring mincemeat and pickling. The name allspice has been given to other aromatic shrubs, notably the Carolina allspice.

Some Common Alloys

Name	Normal or typical composition	Uses or properties
Alnico-4	55% Fe, 28% Ni, 12% Al, 5% Co	Magnets
Babbitt metal	91% Sn, 4.5% Sb, 4.5% Cu	Bearings
Brass	60% Cu, 40% Zn	General engineering and decorative uses
Bronze	92% Cu, 8% Sn	General engineering and decorative uses
Coinage metal	95% Cu, 4% Sn, 1% Zn	"Copper" coins
Coinage metal	75% Cu, 25% Ni	"Silver" coins
Constantan	55% Cu, 45% Ni	Thermocouples
Dental amalgam	52% Hg, 33% Ag, 12.5% Sn, 2% Cu, 0.5% Zn	Dental fillings
Elektron	86.5% Mg, 11% Al, 1.5% Zn, 1% Mn	Very light aircraft parts
German silver	56% Cu, 24% Zn, 20% Ni	Base for electroplating
Gun metal	88% Cu, 10% Sn, 2% Zn	Strong and tough
Invar	64% Fe, 36% Ni	Zero temperature coefficient of expansion
Monel metal	67% Ni, 33% Cu	Corrosion-resistant
Nichrome	60% Ni, 25% Fe, 15% Cr	Electrical heating elements
Pewter	65% Sn, 30% Pb, 5% Sb	Drinking vessels
Solder	60% Pb, 35% Sn, 5% Bi	Electrical connections
Stainless steel	73% Fe, 18% Cr, 8% Ni, 1% C	Corrosion-resistant
Wood's metal	50% Bi, 25% Pb, 12.5% Sn, 12.5% Cd	Low mp

ALLSTON, Washington (1779–1843), first major US landscape painter. He painted large dramatic canvases of biblical and Classical scenes, but this early Italianate style gave way to romanticism influenced by TURNER.

ALLUVIUM, material such as GRAVEL, SILT and SAND deposited, mainly near their mouths, by streams and rivers. Alluvium makes rich agricultural soil, and the earliest civilizations originated as farming communities centered on alluvial flood plains.

ALMA, Canadian paper-milling city in S Quebec. It stands on the Saguenay R near Lake St. John. Pop 22 353.

ALMA, small river in SW Crimea. Here the first battle of the CRIMEAN WAR occurred (Sept. 1854) when Franco-British troops under St.-Arnaud and Lord RAGLAN defeated Prince Menshikov's Russians.

ALMA-ATA, capital of the Kazakh Soviet Socialist Republic, in Central Asia. It makes heavy machinery, garments, footwear, processed food, etc., and is a cultural center with a university, opera house and research institutes. Pop 730 000.

ALMADÉN, historic mining town in S central Spain, in the Sierra Morena. Its mercuric ores have been worked since Roman times. Pop 10 774.

ALMAGEST. See PTOLEMY, CLAUDIUS.

ALMAGRO, Diego de (1475–1538), Spanish conquistador who helped to capture Peru. He joined Francisco PIZARRO in the conquest (1533), then fruitlessly sought gold in Chile. Returning to Peru, he claimed and seized Cuzco, then was defeated and executed by Pizarro's brother.

ALMANAC, originally a calendar giving the positions of the planets, the phases of the moon, etc., particularly as used by navigators (nautical almanacs), but now any yearbook of miscellaneous information, often containing abstracts of annual statistics.

ALMANACH DE GOTHA, handbook of the genealogies of Europe's royal and noble families, founded in Germany (1763) and later annually produced at Gotha. Publication stopped in 1944 but was resumed in 1959.

AL-MANSŪRA, Egyptian commercial and manufacturing city in the Nile Delta, on the Nile's Damietta branch. It is the capital of Daqahlīya governorate. Pop 212 300.

ALMEIDA, Francisco de (c1450–1510), first viceroy of Portuguese India (1505–09). His conquests, forts and trading posts strengthened Portuguese influence in coastal India and E Africa and spread it E to Sumatra.

ALMERÍA, seaport capital of Almería province in SE Spain. Founded by Phoenicians, it flourished under the Romans and Moors. An export center, it has various industries, including chemicals and fish canning. Pop 114 510.

ALMOHAD and ALMORAVID, two medieval Muslim sects and dynasties originating among N African Berbers. First the Almoravids built an empire covering most of NW Africa and much of Spain (1063–1142). The Almohads conquered and enlarged the territory (1144–58), but their empire broke up after 1212 when the combined forces of the Christian kings of Aragon, Castile and Navarre defeated them at Las Navas de Tolosa in the south of Spain.

ALMOND, nut or seed of the almond tree, *Prunus amygdalus,* native to SW Asia, but also grown commercially in the Mediterranean region and California. There are two types of nuts, sweet and bitter. Sweet almonds, much used in confectionery, are edible; the inedible bitter almonds yield oil used in the manufacture of flavoring extracts and in cosmetics. The tree is grown in temperate regions for its beautiful pink blossom.

ALMQUIST, Carl Jonas Love (1793–1866), Swedish writer of romantic and increasingly realistic stories and plays, some unconventionally advocating free love. His best-known works appear in a massive collection, *The Book of the Briar Rose* (1832–50).

ALOE, genus of succulent perennials resembling the AGAVE and mostly native to S Africa. Most have a basal rosette of stiff, pointed, fleshy leaves usually edged with spines and sometimes mottled or striped. Tubular red or yellow flowers are borne in racemes (see INFLORESCENCE) on tall stems. Aloes are important medicinally for the purgative, aloes, obtained from the juice of their leaves. Many are grown as ornamental plants in warm regions. Family: Liliaceae.

ALOPECIA. See BALDNESS.

ALPACA, S American herbivore (*Lama pacos*) closely related to the LLAMA. It has a long body and neck, and is about 1m (3ft) high at the shoulder. Its long thick coat of black, brown or yellowish hair provides valuable wool. All alpacas are now domesticated, living mainly in the Andes above 13 000ft. Family: Camelidae.

ALPENA, seat of Alpena Co., NE Mich., on Thunder Bay, Lake Huron. It is a resort and major producer of cement. Pop 13 805.

ALPHABET (from Greek *alpha* and *beta*), a set of characters intended to represent the sounds of spoken language. Because of this intention (which in practice is never realized) written languages employing alphabets are quite distinct from those using characters which represent whole words (see IDEOGRAM; HIEROGLYPHICS). The word alphabet is, however, usually extended to describe syllabaries, languages in which characters represent syllables. The chief alphabets of the world are Roman (Latin), Greek, Hebrew, Cyrillic (Slavic), Arabic and Devanagari.

Alphabets probably originated around 2000 BC. Hebrew, Arabic and other written languages sprang from a linear alphabet which had appeared c1500 BC. From the Phoenician alphabet, which appeared around 1700 BC, was derived the Greek. Roman letters were derived from Greek and from the rather similar Etruscan, also a descendant of the Greek. Most of the letters we now use are from the Latin alphabet, U and W being distinguished from V, and J from I, in the early Middle Ages. The Cyrillic alphabet, used with the Slavic languages, derives from the Greek. It is thought that Devanagari was possibly invented to represent Sanskrit.

The alpaca is a haughty-looking animal, which spits when annoyed. It was first domesticated by the Incas, who wove its fine, light wool into robes.

Major Alphabets of the World

Cyprian Phoenician	Hebrew letter	Hebrew name	Greek Ancient corresponding forms	Greek Modern letter	Greek Modern name	Early Anglo-Saxon Runes		Arabic solitary form of letter	Arabic name	Russian (Cyrillic) letter	Russian transliteration	Sanskrit letter	transliteration	letter	transliteration	Modern European (Latin-based)
𐤀	א	aleph	𐤀	Α α	alpha	ᚠ	f	ا	alif	А а	a	अ	a	ञ	ñ	A
𐤁	ב	beth	𐤁	Β β	beta	ᚢ	u	ب	bā'	Б б	b	आ	ā	ट	ṭ	B
	ג	gimel	𐤂	Γ γ	gamma	ᚦ	th	ت	tā'	В в	v	इ	i	ठ	ṭh	C
𐤃	ד	daleth	Δ	Δ δ	delta	ᚩ	o	ث	thā'	Г г	g	ई	ī	ड	ḍ	D
	ה	he	𐤄	Ε ε	epsilon	ᚱ	r	ج	jīm	Д д	d	उ	u	ढ	ḍh	E
	ו	waw	𐤆	Ζ ζ	zeta	ᚳ	k	ح	hā'	Е е	e	ऊ	ū	ण	ṇ	F
‡	ז	zayin	𐤇	Η η	eta	ᚷ	zh	خ	khā'	Ж ж	zh	ऋ	ṛ	त	t	G
𐤇	ח	heth	⊕	Θ θ	theta	ᚹ	w	د	dāl	З з	z	ॠ	ṝ	थ	th	H
𐤈	ט	teth	𐤉	Ι ι	iota	ᚻ	h	ذ	dhāl	И и Й й	i, ĭ	ऌ	ḷ	द	d	I
𐤉	י	yod	𐤊	Κ κ	kappa	ᚾ	n	ر	rā'	К к	k	ॡ	ḹ	ध	dh	J
𐤊	כ ך	kaph	𐤋	Λ λ	lambda	ᛁ	i	ز	zā'	Л л	l	ए	e	न	n	K
𐤋	ל	lamed	𐤌	Μ μ	mu	ᛄ	j	س	sīn	М м	m	ऐ	ai	प	p	L
𐤌	מ ם	mem	𐤍	Ν ν	nu	ᛇ	rh	ش	shīn	Н н	n	ओ	o	फ	ph	M
𐤍	נ ן	nun		Ξ ξ	xi	ᛈ	p	ص	sād	О о	o	औ	au	ब	b	N
𐤎	ס	samekh	O	Ο ο	omicron	ᛉ	r	ض	dād	П п	p	•	ṁ	भ	bh	O
𐤏	ע	ayin	𐤐	Π π	pi	ᛋ	s	ط	tā'	Р р	r	:	ḥ	म	m	P
	פ ף	pe	𐤓	Ρ ρ	rho	ᛏ	t	ظ	zā'	С с	s	क	k	य	y	Q
𐤑	צ ץ	sadhe	ϟ	Σ σ	sigma	ᛒ	b	ع	'ayn	Т т	t	ख	kh	र	r	R
𐤒	ק	qoph	X	Τ τ	tau	ᛖ	e	غ	ghayn	У у	u	ग	g	ल	l	S
𐤓	ר	resh		Υ υ	upsilon	ᛗ	m	ف	fā'	Ф ф	f	घ	gh	व	v	T
𐤔	שׂ	sin		Φ φ	phi	ᛚ	l	ق	qāf	Х х	kh	ङ	ṅ	श	ś	U
𐤕	שׁ	shin		Χ χ	chi	ᛝ	ng	ك	kāf	Ц ц	ts	च	c	ष	ṣ	V
	ת	taw		Ψ ψ	psi	ᛞ	d	ل	lām	Ч ч	ch	छ	ch	स	s	W
				Ω ω	omega	ᛟ	œ	م	mīm	Ш ш	sh	ज	j	ह	h	X
						ᚪ	a	ن	nūn	Щ щ	shch	झ	jh			Y
			Ϝ			ᚫ	æ	ه	hā'	Ъ ъ	″					Z
			Ϻ			ᛠ	ea	و	wāw	Ы ы	y					
			Ϙ			ᚣ	y	ي	yā'	Ь ь	′					
								ء	hamzah	Э э	e					
										Ю ю	yu					
										Я я	ya					

Chinese and Japanese are the only major languages that function without alphabets, although Japanese has syllabary elements. (See also CUNEIFORM and WRITING, HISTORY OF; and, for the evolution of the letters of our alphabet, the headings to each alphabetical section.)

ALPHA CENTAURI, multiple star in the constellation CENTAURUS, comprising a DOUBLE STAR around which orbits at a distance of 10000AU a red dwarf, Proxima Centauri, which is the nearest star to the solar system, being 1.33parsecs distant.

ALPHA PARTICLES, HELIUM nuclei ($_2He^4$) emitted at velocities of about 1.6Mm/s from radioactive materials undergoing alpha disintegration (see RADIOACTIVITY). Alpha particles, discovered by RUTHERFORD in 1899, carry a double positive charge and are strongly absorbed by air, thin paper and metal foils.

ALPHEUS, main river of the Peloponnesus in S Greece; 75mi long. In Greek mythology the frequent disappearances of its headwaters underground represented the river god Alpheus pursuing the maiden ARETHUSA beneath the Ionian Sea to emerge at Syracuse in Sicily.

ALPHONSO. See AFONSO; ALFONSO.

ALPHONSUS LIGUORI, Saint (1696–1787), Italian priest who founded the Congregation of the Most Holy Redeemer (Redemptorist Order), a society of missionary preachers working with the rural poor. He was canonized in 1839.

ALPS, Europe's largest mountain range, 650mi long and 30–180mi wide. Its fold mountains result from earth movements in Tertiary times (15–70 million years ago). There are three main divisions. The Western Alps, with the highest peak, Mont Blanc (15782ft), run along the French-Italian border. The Central Alps run NE and E through Switzerland. The Eastern Alps extend through S Germany, Austria and NE Italy into Yugoslavia. Peaks are snowy and etched by ice action. Valleys were glacially deepened, and many glaciers remain.

ALSACE-LORRAINE, region in NE France occupying 5608sq mi W of the Rhine. It produces grains and grapes; timber, coal, potash and salt (from the Vosges Mts); iron ore and textiles. Metz, Nancy, Strasbourg and Verdun are the chief cities.

The people are part French, part German in origin. France and Germany have long disputed control of the area. In medieval times it was in the Holy Roman Empire. France took Alsace after 1648 and Lorraine in 1766. Germany seized most of both in 1871, lost them to France after WWI, regained control in WWII, then lost it again.

ALSIP, village in NW Ill., 15mi SSW of Chicago. Pop 11141.

ALTADENA, unincorporated urban community in Cal., NE of Pasadena. Pop 42380.

ALTAIC LANGUAGES, group of languages comprising three subgroups: Mongol, Manchu-Tungus and principally the TURKIC LANGUAGES. The Altaic languages are spoken in the USSR, Turkey, Iran, Afghanistan, China and the Mongolian People's Republic.

ALTAI MOUNTAINS, mountain system in Central Asia, occupying part of the USSR and Mongolia. Its parallel ranges geologically resemble the Alps, but cover a larger area. The highest peak is Mt Belukha (15157ft).

ALTAIR, brightest star in the constellation AQUILA and the eleventh brightest in the night sky (apparent magnitude +0.89). It has an extremely rapid rotation and is 4.9 parsecs from the earth.

ALTAMIRA, cave near Santander, N Spain, inhabited during the Aurignacian, upper Solutrean and Magdalenian periods. In 1879 the daughter of an amateur archaeologist discovered the striking cave paintings, believed to date from the Magdalenian period. They depict such animals as bison, boars, horses.

ALTAMONT, unincorporated urban community in S Ore. It lies E of Klamath Falls. Pop 15746.

ALTAR, surface (usually raised) where a sacrifice or other religious ceremony is performed. Early civilizations used earth mounds or rocks. Greek and Roman altars were carved marble pedestals. Jews had ornate metal-covered wooden altars. In Christian churches the term altar describes the Communion Table, where the eucharistic elements are consecrated.

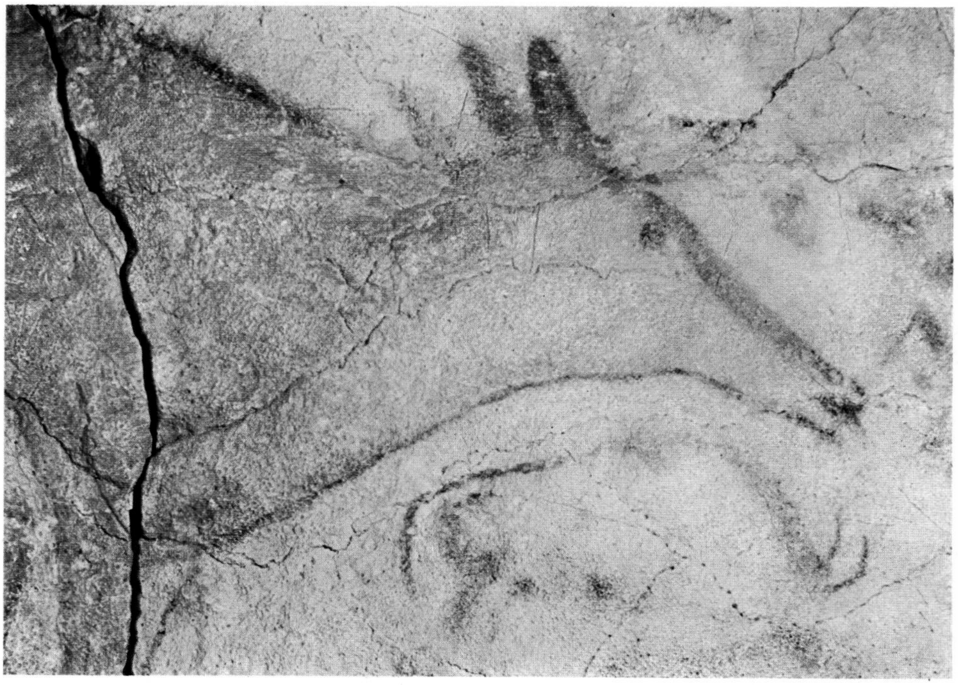

The Altamira caves contain supreme examples of Paleolithic art. This powerfully lifelike drawing of a deer was executed between 14000 and 10000 BC.

ALTARPIECE, decorated panel or screen, movable or fixed, used for backing an altar. Altarpieces are especially linked with Roman Catholic and Orthodox ritual. They may feature paintings, stone or wood carvings, metal castings, gilding, embroidery, mosaics or ceramics. Baroque examples are often magnificently elaborate.

ALTDORFER, Albrecht (1480–1538), German painter and engraver. Most of his paintings had religious subjects, but because of the prominence of forest and mountain settings he is often held to be the first German landscape painter.

ALTED(V). See DEL.

ALTERNATING CURRENT (AC). See ELECTRICITY.

ALTERNATION OF GENERATIONS, a feature of the life cycle of most plants and many lower animals by which successive generations reproduce alternately sexually and asexually. In animals the feature is exhibited by FLUKES, TAPEWORMS and some Cnidaria including the common JELLYFISH (*Aurelia aurita*) and the sea fir *Obelia*. In plants the sexually reproducing or **gametophyte** generation gives rise to HAPLOID male and female sex cells (GAMETES) which, on FERTILIZATION, produce a DIPLOID ZYGOTE which in turn germinates into the asexually reproducing **sporophyte** generation. This reproduces by forming SPORES which germinate to give the gametophyte generation again. In lower plants such as the LIVERWORTS and MOSSES, the gametophyte generation is dominant but in flowering plants the gametophytes are reduced to microscopic proportions, the plant itself being the sporophyte generation. (See also REPRODUCTION.)

ALTGELD, John Peter (1847–1902), US political leader and jurist who sought to defend the individual against abuses of governmental power and vested interests. As a Cook Co., Ill., superior court judge he argued that legal practice was weighted against the poor. Elected Democratic governor of Illinois (1892), he backed labor and championed reform, arousing controversy by freeing three anarchists imprisoned for Chicago's HAYMARKET AFFAIR riot (1886) and by opposing President Cleveland's use of troops to crush the PULLMAN STRIKE of 1894.

ALTICHIERO (active 1369–90), Italian painter, founder of the Verona school. His few surviving works are mainly in Padua, in the form of frescoes showing the influence of GIOTTO.

ALTIMETER, an instrument used for estimating the height of an aircraft above sea level. Most are modified aneroid BAROMETERS and work on the principle that air pressure decreases with increased altitude, but these must be constantly recalibrated throughout the flight to take account of changing meteorological conditions (local ground temperature and air pressure reduced to sea level). **Radar altimeters,** which compute ABSOLUTE altitudes (the height of the aircraft above the ground surface immediately below) from the time taken for RADAR waves to be reflected to the aircraft from the ground, although essential for blind landings, are as yet too expensive for general installation.

ALTIPLANO, a high plateau region in S America between the W and E cordilleras of the Andes. Its bleak grasslands lie at 12000ft and run S from Peru through Bolivia and into Argentina. It contains lakes Titicaca and Poopó.

ALTITUDE SICKNESS, a condition of OXYGEN lack in blood and tissues due to low atmospheric PRESSURE. Night vision is impaired, followed by breathlessness, headache, and faintness. At 5000m mental changes include indifference, euphoria and faulty judgment but complete ACCLIMATIZATION is possible up to those heights. At very high altitude (6000m to 7000m), CYANOSIS, COMA and death rapidly supervene. Treatment is by oxygen and descent. The use of pressurized cabins prevents the occurrence of the condition.

ALTO ADIGE, mountainous region of Alpine N Italy, long disputed by German and Italian states. It is part of the autonomous region of Trentino-Alto Adige. The area became a Hapsburg holding in the 14th century; passed to Italy after WWI; was briefly held by Germany in WWII and in 1966 gained a measure of autonomy after Austria backed demands by its German-speaking majority. It produces hydroelectric power and chemicals.

ALTOCUMULUS. See CLOUDS.

ALTON, city in SW Ill. on the Mississippi R bluffs. Part of the St. Louis metropolitan area, it is a transportation and commercial center in a heavily industrialized region. Alton refines oil and makes explosives, machinery, bricks, flour, glass, shoes and textiles. It was incorporated in 1837. Pop 39700.

ALTOONA, industrial city in S central Pa. at the foot of the Allegheny Mts, 90mi E of Pittsburgh. One of the world's largest manufacturers and repairers of railroad rolling stock, it makes automobile and machine parts, clothing and electrical goods. It was incorporated in 1868. Pop 63 115.

ALTOSTRATUS. See CLOUDS.

ALTRUISM, devotion to the good of others. A term coined by Auguste COMTE (1798–1857) for a moral attitude the opposite of egoism.

ALTUS, seat of Jackson Co., SW Okla. It is a food-processing center and the home of Altus Junior College. Pop 23 302.

ALUM, a double salt comprising sulfates of two metals (one monovalent, one trivalent) combined with 12 molecules of water of crystallization: $M^{I}M^{III}(SO_4)_2.12H_2O$. The monovalent metal is commonly potassium, sodium or ammonium; the trivalent metal may be aluminum, chromium or ferric iron. Alums are soluble in water and are usually acid. They are used as astringents (styptic pencils), as a mordant in dyes, and in the manufacture of baking powder, antiperspirants and fire extinguishers. Potash alum (potassium aluminum sulfate, $KAl(SO_4)_2.12H_2O$) is used in the sizing of paper and in water purification.

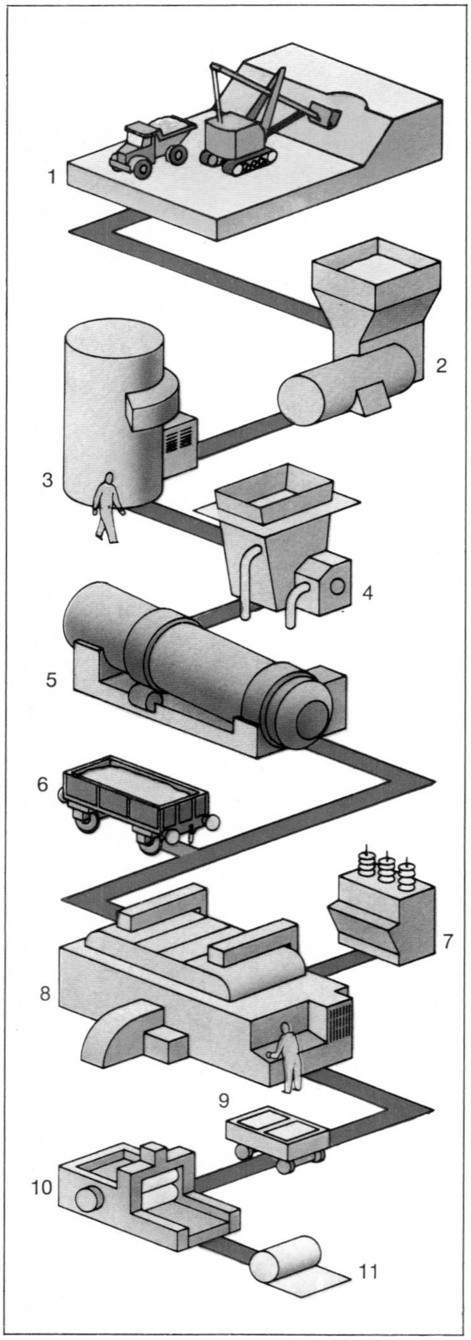

The extraction of aluminum from bauxite:
1. Mining bauxite; 2. The bauxite is broken up, dried and ground; 3. It is converted to sodium aluminate by the addition of a solution of sodium hydroxide; 4. Other elements are removed by filtration; 5. The residue is heated at very high temperature in a tubular furnace; 6. Cryolite is added; 7–9. Molten aluminum is released by electrolysis. 10–11. The aluminum is rolled into sheets.

ALUMINA, or aluminum oxide. See ALUMINUM.

ALUMINUM (Al), silvery-white metal in Group IIIA of the PERIODIC TABLE, the most abundant metal, comprising 8% of the earth's crust. It occurs naturally as BAUXITE, CRYOLITE, FELDSPAR, clay and many other minerals, and is smelted by the HALL-HÉROULT PROCESS, chiefly in the US, USSR and Canada. It is a reactive metal, but in air is covered with a protective layer of the oxide. Aluminum is light and strong when alloyed, so that aluminum ALLOYS are used very widely in the construction of machinery, and domestic appliances. It is also a good conductor of electricity and is often used in overhead transmission cables where lightness is crucial. AW 27.0, mp 660°C, bp 2467°C, sg 2.6989 (20°C).

Aluminum compounds are trivalent and mainly cationic (see CATION), though with strong bases aluminates are formed. (See also ALUM.) **Aluminum Oxide** (Al_2O_3), or **Alumina,** is a colorless or white solid occurring in several crystalline forms, and is found naturally as CORUNDUM, EMERY and BAUXITE. Solubility in acid and alkali increases with hydration. mp 2045°C, bp 2980°C. **Aluminum Chloride** ($AlCl_3$) is a colorless crystalline solid, used as a catalyst (see FRIEDEL-CRAFTS REACTION).The hexahydrate is used in deodorants and as an astringent.

ALUM ROCK, unincorporated urban community in Cal., NE of San Jose. Pop 18 355.

ALVA (or ALBA), Fernando Álvarez de Toledo, Duke of (1507–1582), Spanish general who tyrannized the Netherlands. During his brutal campaign against rebellious Dutch Protestants (1567–73), he executed some 18 000 people, including the counts of Horn and EGMONT. Hated for his atrocities and harsh taxes, and harassed by WILLIAM THE SILENT's liberating army, Alva was recalled to Spain in 1573. In 1580 he conquered Portugal for Spain.

ALVARADO, Pedro de (c1485–1541), Spanish colonizer of Guatemala. He was CORTES' chief lieutenant in the conquest of Mexico (1519–21), then (1523–24) led the force that seized what is now Guatemala and El Salvador. As governor of Guatemala he instituted forced Indian labor and founded many cities.

ALVAREZ, Luis Walter (1911–), US physicist awarded the 1968 Nobel Prize for Physics for work on SUBATOMIC PARTICLES, including the discovery of the transient resonance particles. He helped develop much of the hardware of NUCLEAR PHYSICS.

ALVIN, city in SE Tex., 25mi S of Houston in an agricultural and oilfield area. It is the home of Alvin Junior College. Pop 10 671.

ALYSSUM, genus of Old World herbaceous plants of the family Brassicaceae. Sweet alyssum (*A. maritimum*), a hardy annual, is a border plant with narrow gray-green leaves and clusters of white, lilac or pink, fragrant flowers. Many other species have yellow blooms, and many are perennials.

AM (Amplitude Modulation). See RADIO.

AMADEO I (1845–1890), king of Spain. A son of Italy's Victor Emmanuel II, he was chosen king by the Cortes (Spanish parliament) in 1870 after the fall of the Bourbons. Unrest forced his abdication in 1873, and he retired to Italy.

AMAGASAKI, Japanese city on Honshu Island. Part of the fast-growing Osaka-Kobe industrial complex, it is a center of heavy industry, producing iron and steel, chemicals, machinery and glass. Pop 553,696.

AMALEKITES, nomadic desert tribe south of Palestine, recorded in the Old Testament as ancient enemies of the Hebrews. Joshua repulsed them and they were later fought by kings Saul and David, but were not finally crushed until the time of Hezekiah, king of Judah.

Hippeastrum, a member of the Amaryllis family

AMALFI, seaport in Italy SE of Naples. A picturesque town on a steep headland, it is a popular tourist center on a spectacularly mountainous coast. Amalfi was an important maritime republic in the Middle Ages. Pop 7 162.

AMALGAM, an ALLOY of MERCURY with other metals. Most metals except iron will form amalgams; those with high mercury content are liquid, but most are solid. Amalgams of some NOBLE METALS occur naturally: SILVER and GOLD are extracted from their ores by forming amalgams. Dental amalgam, containing silver, copper, zinc and tin, is used to fill TEETH. Various amalgams may be used as ELECTRODES. (See also MIRROR.)

AMANA SOCIETY, religious community comprising Amana and associated villages, founded in Ia. in the mid-19th century. Originating in a German Pietist sect which stressed the divine inspiration of the Bible, the society farmed 25 000 acres of prairie and practiced self-sufficiency based on communal labor and property sharing. In 1932 it became a cooperative corporation.

AMANITA, genus of mainly poisonous MUSHROOMS found in woods and forests. They have white spores and gills, a ring of tissue (annulus) surrounding the stem just below the cap, and a sac or cup (volva) around the swollen base of the stalk. The volva is the remains of the membrane that completely enclosed the young mushroom. The commonest species, the fly agaric (*A. muscaria*), is poisonous but not usually fatal; it has a distinctive scarlet cap. Family: Agaricaceae.

AMARANTH, any of a large genus (*Amaranthus*) of herbaceous annuals of the family Amaranthaceae, mainly of tropical origin. Amaranths are named from the Greek for "unfading" because dried specimens keep their color. Many are weeds, but those cultivated include love-lies-bleeding, *A. caudatus,* a handsome plant with long tassels of crimson flowers.

AMARILLO, city in N Tex., seat of Potter Co. and the Panhandle's main manufacturing and transportation center. It processes meat, wheat, oil and zinc, and makes synthetic rubber and farm and oilfield equipment. Large helium processing plants are nearby. Pop 127 010.

AMARYLLIS, genus containing a single species, *A. belladonna,* native to S Africa but widely grown as an ornamental. Also called belladonna lily, it has a long stem bearing a terminal cluster of showy, lilylike flowers. Straplike leaves develop after the flowers. The name amaryllis is often applied to any member of the family. Amaryllidaceae. Amaryllis is a popular house plant requiring a light position in a sunny east, south or west window and a temperature between 17°C and 24°C (62°F and 75°F). After blooming the stem should be cut off at soil level. Propagation is by means of offsets.

AMASIS. See AHMOSE.

AMATI, Italian family of violin makers in Cremona (16th–17th centuries). Noted members were Andrea, his sons Antonio and Girolamo, and Girolamo's son Nicolò (1596–1684), the most famous of all. His superb instruments became models for those of Andrea GUARNERI and Antonio STRADIVARI.

AMAZONAS, state in NW Brazil straddling the Amazon R and occupying 604000sq mi, mainly of equatorial forest. Products: rubber, jute, cattle. Capital: Manaus.

AMAZON RIVER, world's largest river in volume and drainage area, and second-longest, at 3900mi. Its basin drains 40% of South America. The Amazon rises in Andean Peru near the Pacific Ocean and flows E through the world's largest equatorial forest to the Atlantic Ocean. It is a broad sluggish stream up to 30mi wide in flood, with hundreds of tributaries, 17 of which are more than 1000mi long.

Fed by annual runoff from 70–120in of rain, the river pours an estimated one-fifth of all water falling on earth into the Atlantic Ocean, where its current extends 200mi out to sea. Tides are felt 600mi upstream and oceangoing vessels can travel 2300mi to Iquitos in Peru. Other parts are Belém and Manaus, handling river commerce in hardwoods and other forest products of sparsely peopled Amazonia. Spain's Vicente Pinzón discovered the river mouth in 1500; Francisco de OREILANA was first to travel downriver from the Andes to the Atlantic (1541).

St. Ambrose asserted the supremacy of spiritual over temporal power when he excommunicated Theodosus I for his massacre of the Thessalonians. This mosaic is in the San Saliro church in Milan.

AMAZONS, in Greek legend, a race of warrior women living in the Black Sea area. Their name derives from the Greek word for "breastless," due to their alleged practice of removing the right breast to aid archery. One myth relates how HERCULES, as his ninth labor, took the girdle of the Amazonian queen Hippolyta. Later tales associate Amazons with Brazil and with Dahomey in West Africa.

AMBASSADOR, highest rank in the diplomatic service. An ambassador is usually the chief representative of his government in a foreign country.

AMBEDKAR, Bhimrao Ramji (1893–1956), Indian politician who championed his fellow "untouchables," members of the lowest Hindu caste in India. He helped ensure that India's constitution of 1949 banned discrimination against them but failed to eliminate the untouchable castes from Hinduism.

AMBER, fossilized RESIN from prehistoric EVERGREENS. Brownish-yellow and translucent, it is highly valued and can be easily cut and polished for ornamental purposes. Its chief importance is that FOSSIL insects up to 20 million years old have been found embedded in it. The main source of amber is along the shores of the Baltic Sea.

AMBERGRIS, waxy solid formed in the intestines of SPERM WHALES, perhaps to protect them from the bony parts of their squid diet. When obtained from dead whales, it is soft, black and evil-smelling, but on weathering (as when found as flotsam) it becomes hard, gray and fragrant, and is used as a perfume fixative and in the East as a spice.

AMBERJACKS (or **Amberfish**), voracious seafish, principally important for food and sport; the genus *Seriola* of the family Carangidae. They have deep, compressed bodies, slender and crescentic tailfins, and grow to over 45kg (100lb) in weight.

AMBIDEXTERITY. See HANDEDNESS.

AMBIVALENCE, contrasting and alternating EMOTIONS toward a person or object, typified by the "love–hate" relationship. FREUD suggested that ambivalence was basic to many NEUROSES.

AMBO, early Christian form of church pulpit comprising a stand raised on steps, from which the Epistle and the Gospel were read.

AMBON (Amboina), historically valuable spice island of Indonesia's Moluccas, 314sq mi in area. It is partly volcanic, and produces sago, copra and cloves (once providing much of the world's supplies). Discovered by the Portuguese in 1512, it was mainly held by the Dutch from 1599 until independence in 1949 within Indonesia, from which it tried to secede in 1950. Pop 72679.

AMBRIDGE, borough in W Pa., with the world's biggest bridge-building company and largest structural steel plant. It is 17mi WNW of Pittsburgh. Pop 11342.

AMBROSE, Saint (c340–397), an important Father of the Latin Church. A Roman governor who became the influential bishop of Milan, he attacked imperial moral standards and strengthened the position of the Church amid the ruins of the Roman Empire by his preaching and writing. St. AUGUSTINE was one of his converts.

AMBROSIA, in Greek mythology, the food or drink of the gods. Eating it gained perpetual youth and beauty for the gods and goddesses, who rubbed it into their skins to preserve their immortality. (See also NECTAR.)

AMBULANCE, vehicle designed to carry sick or wounded people to hospital. Modern ambulances contain first-aid appliances, and warning lights and sirens help rapid travel through traffic. Most military ambulances bear a red cross on a white ground, and are theoretically protected from attack in war by the Geneva Convention.

AMEBAS. See AMOEBAS.

AMEN, old Hebrew word, roughly meaning "it is so," used in Jewish and Christian worship. In the Bible it is a positive response to a blessing or curse, and in Christian churches it is the congregation's answer to a minister's prayer.

An ambo in the Basilica of Septimus Severus at Leptis Magna in North Africa. Serving as a pulpit, the ambo was often made of marble and decorated with carvings or mosaics.

AMENDMENT, in legislation, a change in a bill or motion under discussion, or in an existing law or constitution. In the US CONGRESS a bill passed by one house may be condemned by the other and a joint conference committee may work out a compromise or amendment. (See also UNITED STATES CONSTITUTION.)

AMENEMHET (or Amenemmes), name of various pharaohs, notably three of the 12th dynasty (Middle Kingdom), who ruled Egypt at a time of relative peace and of artistic creation. **Amenemhet I** reigned c1991–1962 BC) founded the dynasty, restored government after civil strife and moved the capital from Thebes to It-towe (El-Lisht). **Amenemhet II** (reigned c1929–1895 BC) developed agriculture and trade with Punt (Somalia). **Amenemhet III** (reigned c1842–1797 BC) reclaimed thousands of acres for agriculture in the FAYUM oasis by drainage.

AMENHOTEP (or Amenophis—"Amon is satisfied"), name of four pharaohs of the 18th dynasty (New Kingdom), who ruled Egypt during a period of prosperous imperialism. **Amenhotep I** (reigned c1546–1526 BC) extended Egypt's power W into Libya and S into Nubia, reorganized government and built temples. **Amenhotep II** (reigned c1450–1425 BC) pursued an aggressive policy in Asia. **Amenhotep III** (reigned c1417–1379 BC) used diplomacy to preserve an empire ranging from Mesopotamia to Ethiopia, and indulged in lavish royal building programs. **Amenhotep IV** (reigned c1379–1362 BC) changed his name to AKHENATON.

AMERICA, the two major continents of the Western Hemisphere, North and South America, or only the United States. The term was coined in 1507 by the German geographer Martin Waldseemüller in honor of the Italian navigator Amerigo Vespucci, who supposedly discovered much of South America—the area to which the term was originally confined.

AMERICA FIRST COMMITTEE, isolationist organization that opposed US involvement in WWII. It was founded by R. Douglas Stuart, Jr., in September 1940. Its supporters numbered 800000 and included the HEARST newspapers and Charles LINDBERGH, but the Committee collapsed after Japan attacked Pearl Harbor.

AMERICAN ACADEMY IN ROME, institute for US students engaged in advanced studies in fine arts and Classical subjects in Rome, Italy. Annual fellowships offer a fixed stipend, travel allowances and residence facilities.

AMERICAN ACADEMY OF ARTS AND LETTERS, organization to promote literature and the fine arts in the US, founded in 1904. Based in New

American literature

A tradition develops

One can no longer deny the ambition and sophistication of America's serious literature: William Faulkner's cycle of novels about Yoknapatawpha County is comparable to Balzac's *Comédie Humaine* cycle in conception and aim; Eugene O'Neill wrote over 40 plays exploring relentlessly not only the passions of his characters but the technical limitations of the modern theater; Herman Melville's *Moby Dick* is one of the great epic novels of world literature. America's most successful and admired literature has always had a democratic flavor; though there is a split in the imagination between "popular" and "literary" production, it is not as self-conscious or deeply divisive as in Europe. Popular writers on themes of contemporary concern such as Pearl S. Buck who won the Nobel Prize for Literature in 1936 have often, in their day, had literary reputations which seemed exaggerated to later readers, but the more "literary" writers have been accessible to a wide audience, and the energy and colloquialism of American prose, poetry and drama have been among the nation's most striking characteristics.

Early American literature was heavily influenced by European models, but a native element soon emerged. Notable expressions of the Colonial, Puritan and Revolutionary experiences include Cotton Mather's *Magnalia Christi Americana* (1702), the poetry of Ann Bradstreet (d.1672), and Benjamin Franklin's *Poor Richard's Almanac* (begun 1732) which, along with his autobiography, has been accepted as a classic of the country's literature. An egalitarian ideal is profoundly ingrained in the imaginative experience of Americans. It has been expressed in literature throughout America's history, particularly in the major political writings of the Revolution, including the *Declaration of Independence* (1776). Washington Irving (1783–1859), the first American writer to achieve—in his *Sketchbook* (1820)—a literary style which his compatriots recognized as definably American, was also among the first to complain of American Philistinism and to become an expatriate. American perspective was present in the awkward yet powerful historical novels of James Fenimore Cooper (1789–1851) and was a much more important distinguishing feature of the work of the Transcendentalists of Concord, Massachusetts (led by Emerson and Thoreau) than the often-noted influence of German romanticism. This New England school of writers dominated the achievement of the mid-19th century in American letters. Ralph Waldo Emerson (1803–1882) was a founder of the Transcendental Club and a man who encouraged and supported younger talents than himself much as Ezra Pound was to do in the next century. In such works as his Harvard address, *The American Scholar* (1837), he was a major force for independence of thought and confidence in American art. His friend Henry David Thoreau (1817–1862) turned personal and political crises in his life into works of wide impact such as his pungent essay *On the Duty of Civil Disobedience* (1849) and his book *Walden* (1854). Both men were also in the vanguard of establishing a serious body of American poetry. Contemporaneously, the idiosyncratic imagination that Edgar Allen Poe (1809–1849) displayed in feverish poetry and prose was much less popular, though his work influenced the French poet Charles Baudelaire and the Symbolists later in the century, and he is now accepted as one of America's most original artists.

Though Henry Wadsworth Longfellow (1807–1882) exceeded him in popularity, Walt Whitman (1819–1892) is arguably the first considerable American poet of this period (Emerson and Poe being more distinguished for their prose). His *Leaves of Grass* (1855–1892) presents his sincere concern for democracy, his appreciation of the wound inflicted on the nation by the Civil War, and his awareness of the plight of the individual buffeted by America's historical and social demands, seen through a prism of optimistic rhetoric which owes some of its technical audacity to William Blake. Emily Dickinson (1830–1886), the other considerable poet of the period, only published five poems in her lifetime, though she is now much admired. Her obscure life has been seen as typifying the introspective poet's fate in colorful, competitive and gregarious America.

In the decade of the 1850s Nathaniel Hawthorne (1804–1864) and Herman Melville (1819–1891) established the novel in America as a mature and complex mode of expression. Hawthorne's *The Scarlet Letter* (1850) is not only concerned with the guilt and need for secrecy felt by the individual living in a Puritan culture, but like *The House of the Seven Gables* (1851) and *The Marble Faun* (1860, set in Rome) with the need of the individual to question accepted moral standards. Melville, initially a highly successful writer of semi-autobiographical and romantic travel books in which the larger metaphysical concerns went unnoticed, later touched on the undertow of madness or perversion in the human mind, particularly in the epic *Moby Dick* (1851). His stories, however, are disciplined by an awareness of mental balance and an implicit optimism. Two of the most popular succeeding writers were the humorists Bret Harte (1836–1902) and Mark Twain (1835–1910). Their fiction, of California and Mississippi respectively, confirmed the public in a taste for and confidence in native literature with native backgrounds. Twain's pioneering breakthroughs in form and style have been particularly influential on later American writers.

Two American novelists in the past century produced major bodies of internationally acclaimed work—Henry James (1843–1916) and William Faulkner (1897–1962). James was one of the many American writers to go into voluntary exile in Europe (Eliot, Pound, Santayana; for lesser periods Hemingway, Fitzgerald, James Baldwin; more recently Mary McCarthy, Gore Vidal and Robert Lowell), and his place as an "American" writer is problematic because of his place in the European tradition of the novel and his development of a self-conscious and highly-wrought style which is at odds with the characteristic American genius for the direct and colloquial. Faulkner's subject matter and settings, by contrast, are totally American, almost defiantly regional, and he was among the first to study the legacy of the Civil War (1861–1865) to the South. Although his experimental prose and construction verge, at times, on the incoherent, the power of his work makes it consistently gripping. Other American novelists have produced impressive individual works, though their complete output varies widely in quality and most of them never fulfilled early promise with later development. One might mention Edith Wharton (1862–1937) whose society novels were heavily influenced by James; Willa Cather (1876–1947) and her restrained, elegiac novels of the West; Theodore Dreiser (1871–1945) and Sherwood Anderson (1876–1941), both mainly interested in the naturalistic novel; John Dos Passos (1896–1970), James T. Farrell (1904—), John Steinbeck (1902–1968) and Thomas Wolfe (1900–1938), all of whom produced novels respected for their serious craftsmanship and their honest attempts to portray aspects of life with which the individual writers were personally familiar, from small-town living to itinerant labor during the Depression. Sinclair Lewis (1885–1951) wrote satirical novels of protest against social hypocrisy which earned him the first Nobel Prize for Literature awarded to an American (1930). F. Scott Fitzgerald (1896–1940) and Ernest Hemingway (1899–1961) were two of the most spectacularly famous writers after World War I. Hemingway's terse style, itself influenced by the experiments of Gertrude Stein (1874–1946), was highly influential and fashionable; and Fitzgerald's *The Great Gatsby* (1924) and many of his short stories vividly convey the atmosphere of the so-called Roaring Twenties. Since World War II, Norman Mailer (1923—) and Mary McCarthy (1912—), in the tradition of Steinbeck, excel both as journalists and novelists, and Mailer particularly has attempted to mix journalism and fiction to produce a new genre. Saul Bellow (1915—) is among the most respected contemporary novelists; every new work confirms his skills. The Beat novelist Jack Kerouac (1922–1969) and writers such as William Burroughs (*Naked Lunch*, 1959), and Hubert Selby, Jr. (*Last Exit to Brooklyn*, 1946) followed Henry Miller (1891—) in writing harsh, deliberately provocative books using frankly realistic details and language. Individual novels such as Joseph Heller's *Catch-22* (1961) and Ken Kesey's *One Flew Over the Cuckoo's Nest* (1962) have been outstanding successes and indicate that Mark Twain's brand of satiric humor has its direct descendants.

One cannot trace traditions in the genres of American literature over the past hundred years as fruitfully as one can in other national literatures. In the drama, for instance, Eugene O'Neill (1888–1953) stands alone as the greatest playwright the country has produced. Having grown up in a period when plays consisted entirely of ephemeral melodramas, O'Neill appeared when American drama was striving towards more complex effects and he helped pioneer both social and psychological protest on Broadway. Though one could discuss influences on him and the impetus his stature and integrity still give to American theater, he is typical of American prose writers and dramatists in being more easily appreciated for his idiosyncratic contribution than for his part in a school or era. The lively theatrical activity of O'Neill's era produced writers as different as the radical Clifford Odets (1906–1963), the farceurs Kaufmann and Hart, and included the WPA experiments; audiences applauded talents as diverse as those of Thornton Wilder (1897–1975), a highly successful novelist who turned to writing humane and nostalgic plays, and the strongminded Lillian Hellman (1905—). After WWII Tennessee Williams (1914—), Arthur Miller (1915—) and Edward Albee (1929—) emerged as strikingly original dramatists, while the American theater as a whole continued in a restless and exploratory phase.

Poetry has rarely been a popular or challenging form of literature in America. The most academically respected figures, such as T. S. Eliot (1888–1965), Ezra Pound (1885–1973), William Carlos Williams (1883–1963) and Wallace Stevens (1879–1955), often seem the most obscure to American readers. The relatively conventional works of Carl Sandburg (1878–1967) and Robert Frost (1874–1963) have been popular, however, perhaps because their idiom is more immediately recognizable as native (even though Frost, in particular, was heavily influenced by foreign literature and had his first success in England). Alan Ginsberg (1926—) is the foremost name among the Beat poets; his iconoclastic and declamatory poems, especially *Howl* (1955), were among the most intense and shared experiences of a generation of American youth. Robert Lowell (1917—), now living abroad, continues to produce important work; the reputation of John Berryman (1914–1972) has been growing; and one of the most famous writers of the recent past is the American-born poet Sylvia Plath (1932–1963).

American literature contributed much to other national literatures, but its own liveliest and most important tradition is that of individuals bearing unique witness in an unselfconsciously colloquial voice. Its most vigorous success has arguably been its prose tradition, whether fiction or journalism or *belles lettres*, but it has produced masterpieces in every genre and continues to do so.

York City, it has 50 members outstanding in literature, art and music. It makes awards to writers, artists and musicians and sponsors exhibitions.

AMERICAN ANTISLAVERY SOCIETY, body devoted to abolishing slavery in the US. Founded in 1833 on principles stated by William Lloyd GARRISON, it became a strong abolitionist force, persisting until 1870.

AMERICAN ASSOCIATION FOR THE ADVANCEMENT OF SCIENCE (AAS), the largest US organization for the promotion of scientific understanding. Founded in Boston in 1848 but now centered in Washington, it has over 100000 individual and 300 corporate members. Its publications include the weekly, *Science*.

AMERICAN BAR ASSOCIATION (ABA), voluntary organization for members of the US legal profession, founded in 1878. It promotes the study of law and the administration of justice, and upholds professional standards.

AMERICAN BROADCASTING COMPANIES, INC. (ABC). See BROADCASTING NETWORKS, US.

AMERICAN CIVIL LIBERTIES UNION (ACLU), organization dedicated to defending constitutional freedoms in the US, founded in 1920. Its work includes providing legal aid in cases of violated civil liberties, including those of minorities.

AMERICAN COLONIZATION SOCIETY, US body formed in 1822 to found an overseas home for free Negroes. Some abolitionists thought it secretly pro-slavery. Its West African colony, established in 1816, became Africa's first black republic, LIBERIA, in 1847.

AMERICAN EXPEDITIONARY FORCE (AEF), US force serving in Europe in WWI, under General John PERSHING. The first troops arrived in June 1917 and the first major action was in May 1918. The AEF fought in 13 battles (including BELLEAU WOOD). The war ended with 1993000 US troops holding one-quarter of the Allied line on the Western Front. The AEF lost 50000 killed in action and more than 50000 by disease. Some 200000 men were wounded.

AMERICAN FARM BUREAU FEDERATION. See FARM FEDERATION, AMERICAN.

AMERICAN FEDERATION OF LABOR AND CONGRESS OF INDUSTRIAL ORGANIZATIONS (AFL-CIO), powerful US federation of labor unions created in 1955 by the merger of the AFL and CIO. Its 125 constituent unions represent over 15 million members. A national president, secretary-treasurer and 27 vice-presidents make up the executive council. This enforces policy decisions made at biennial conventions attended by several thousand delegates.

The organization's main objectives are more pay, fewer working hours and better working conditions for employees, obtained by union–management agreements that preserve industrial harmony and prosperity. Each affiliated union conducts its own collective bargaining and determines much of its own policy. The AFL-CIO takes influential stands on such issues as social welfare, conservation, education and international problems. It has recently backed Democratic presidential candidates.

The AFL originated in 1886 in the reorganized Federation of Organized Trade and Labor Unions. Initially led by Samuel GOMPERS, it comprised only craft unions, excluding unskilled and semiskilled workers, whose numbers multiplied as mass production increased in the early 1900s. To cater for these workers, AFL dissidents in 1935 formed the Committee for Industrial Organization, later the CIO, led by John L. LEWIS. In the 1950s laws hostile to organized labor encouraged union cooperation and in 1955 the AFL and CIO merged, with George MEANY (head of AFL) as president. Friction has persisted between craft (AFL) and industrial (CIO) elements.

AMERICAN FRIENDS SERVICE COMMITTEE, US Quaker philanthropic organization founded in Philadelphia, Pa., in 1917 to help in post-WWI relief and reconstruction abroad. With its British counterpart, it gained the 1947 Nobel Peace Prize for helping to build schools, orphanages and hospitals in war-ravaged parts of Europe. It has often helped in international relief operations after great disasters.

AMERICAN FUR COMPANY, the earliest US trading monopoly, founded 1808 by John Jacob Astor. With his Pacific Fur Co., it controlled the fur trade from the Great Lakes W to the Pacific and monopolized trade in the Mississippi valley.

AMERICAN GEOGRAPHICAL SOCIETY, organization, originating in New York, that became internationally famous under Isaiah Bowman (director 1915–35) for its studies of polar areas and pioneer settlements, and for mapping the whole of South America.

AMERICAN INDEPENDENT PARTY, US political party formed in the 1960s. George WALLACE was its unsuccessful presidential candidate in 1968. In the 1972 national elections 65 party candidates ran for Congress or for governorships in 20 states, but none was elected.

AMERICAN JEWISH COMMITTEE, organization founded in 1906 by a group of Jewish Americans, led by Jacob Schiff, to protect the civil and religious liberties of Jews throughout the world. It publishes a journal and yearbook.

AMERICAN JEWISH CONGRESS, human rights organization founded in 1918. It aims to defend religious freedom and Jewish culture, and maintains close links between US Jewry and Israel.

AMERICAN JEWISH JOINT DISTRIBUTION COMMITTEE, American Jewish body, founded in 1914 to help stricken Jewish communities abroad, notably in WWI. After WWII it helped develop schools, hospitals and synagogues in war-torn Europe.

AMERICAN LABOR PARTY, N.Y. State left-wing political party (1936–56). Founded by labor leaders, it helped elect its member Fiorello LA GUARDIA mayor of New York (1937–1941) and Herbert LEHMAN governor (1938). In WWII it split over attitudes to Russia: the right under David DUBINSKY accused Sidney HILLMAN's left of being communist-controlled. The party disbanded in 1956.

AMERICAN LEGION, organization of US war veterans, founded in 1919. Its 2600000 members are survivors of WWI and WWII and the Korean and Vietnam wars. The legion publicizes national defense needs, cares for needy veterans and their families and influences legislation.

AMERICAN LIBRARY ASSOCIATION (ALA), organization of librarians which aims to improve library services throughout the world. Founded in Philadelphia, Pa., in 1876 by Melvin DEWEY, it is the world's oldest and largest library association, influencing library development in many parts of the world.

AMERICAN MEDICAL ASSOCIATION (AMA), organization of US physicians mainly from state medical associations. It was founded in 1847 to advance medical knowledge, raise medical standards, improve public health and support the medical profession. It holds conferences, issues periodicals and investigates standards in pharmacy, foods, medical education and hospitals, and has influenced national and state legislation.

AMERICAN MUSEUM OF NATURAL HISTORY, an institution in New York City founded in 1869 and dedicated to research and popular education in anthropology, astronomy, mineralogy and natural history. Its public museums include the Hayden Planetarium and it publishes several technical and popular periodicals.

AMERICAN PARTY. See KNOW-NOTHINGS.

AMERICAN PHILOSOPHICAL SOCIETY, the oldest surviving US learned society, based in Philadelphia where it was founded by Benjamin FRANKLIN in 1743. The US counterpart of the ROYAL SOCIETY OF LONDON (1660), it currently has approaching 600 US and foreign members. It has an extensive library, much relating to early American science, its own regular publications commencing in 1769 with its *Transactions*.

AMERICAN PROTECTIVE ASSOCIATION (APA), anti-Roman Catholic secret society founded in 1887. Its members blamed Catholic immigrants for unemployment during the depression of the 1890s. It collapsed after 1896, split by national election issues.

AMERICAN REVOLUTION. See REVOLUTIONARY WAR, AMERICAN.

AMERICAN RIVER, small river in N central Cal. It rises in the Sierra Nevada and flows SW for almost 30mi to Sacramento, where it joins the Sacramento R.

AMERICAN SAMOA. See SAMOA.

AMERICAN SHORTHAIR, breed of cat developed in US, also known as Domestic Shorthair. A well-built cat with medium to large body, it has a longer nose than the European type from which it descends and a squarer muzzle and firm chin. Its thick coat has an even, hard texture and may be a wide range of solid, tabby or shaded colors.

AMERICAN'S CREED, William Tyler Page's prize-winning "summary of American political faith." Drawing upon the Constitution and the Declaration of Independence, it stressed that the United States was a democratic federal republic based upon freedom, equality, justice and humanity, and proclaimed its citizens' duty "to love it; to support its Constitution; to obey its laws; to respect its flag, and to defend it against all enemies."

AMERICAN SOCIETY FOR THE PREVENTION OF CRUELTY TO ANIMALS (ASPCA), oldest US humane organization, founded in 1866 by Henry BERGH. Limited to N.Y. State and based in New York City, it works to prevent maltreatment of animals by publicizing abuses, enforcing protective laws and providing veterinary aid.

AMERICAN SYSTEM, Senator Henry Clay's name for his national economic plan featuring protective tariffs to help industry, reestablish a national bank, finance new roads and canals to open the West and broaden agricultural markets. Under President Monroe tariffs were indeed raised and a national bank reestablished. But the more extreme schemes of President John Quincy Adams alienated sectional interests, and after 1829 Andrew Jackson let American System provisions lapse.

AMERICAN VETERANS' COMMITTEE, US organization of WWII veterans concerned with broad domestic issues, such as civil rights, unemployment, education, the cost of living and public housing. It now has over 25000 members.

AMERICA'S CUP, the most famous international yachting trophy, held continuously by the US since 1851, when the New York Yacht Club's *America* outraced 14 British sailing craft. Yacht clubs of any country may challenge the US holders in US waters, 12-meter yachts competing for the best four out of seven races. The race takes place about once every six years. (See YACHTS AND YACHTING.)

AMERICA THE BEAUTIFUL, popular patriotic

The American Museum of Natural History owes some items in its world-famous collections to Theodore Roosevelt, who was highly regarded as a natural historian. His statue is seen outside the Roosevelt Memorial Building, one of 19 buildings housing 50 exhibition halls.

song, with words written in 1893 by Katherine Lee Bates and music by Samuel A. Ward.

AMERICIUM (Am), silvery-white radioactive TRANSURANIUM ELEMENT, one of the ACTINIDES. It is prepared by NEUTRON irradiation of PLUTONIUM. Am^{241}, the most readily available ISOTOPE (half-life 458yr), emits GAMMA RAYS and is used in industrial density and thickness gauges.

AMERICUS, industrial city in SW central Ga., seat of Sumter Co. Its industries include canning, lumber-milling and shirt-making. Pop 16091.

AMERINDS, term coined (1897–98) by John Wesley POWELL to denote the American INDIANS. It is believed that the Amerinds originated in NE Asia, having crossed the Bering Strait (perhaps by land bridge) before the 10th millennium BC. However, there are marked blood-type differences between them and the Asian Mongoloid peoples.

AMES, city in central Ia., 28mi N of Des Moines. It is the home of the Iowa State University of Science and Technology. Pop 39505.

AMES, Fisher (1758–1808), US congressman from Mass., who worked for a strong federal government led by moral men of wealth; he tended to distrust full democracy. In the House of Representatives (1789–97) he backed HAMILTON's Federalist policies and opposed commercial action against Britain.

AMES, Oakes (1804–1873), US industrialist, who bribed congressmen to prevent government scrutiny of his CRÉDIT MOBILIER COMPANY, which had made vast profits by overspending government grants in building the Union Pacific Railroad. His exposure in 1872 brought government censure upon himself and other major public figures.

AMES, William (1576–1633), English Puritan theologian, exiled in Holland, who attacked Church ceremonial and championed strict CALVINISM against the more liberal stance of Arminianism.

AMESBURY, manufacturing town in NE Mass. on the Merrimack R. It was once a major shipbuilding center. Pop 11388.

AMETHYST, transparent violet or purple variety of QUARTZ, colored by iron or manganese impurities. The color changes to yellow on heating. Amethysts are semiprecious GEMS. The best come from Brazil, Uruguay, Ariz. and the USSR.

AMHARIC, official language of Ethiopia, spoken by some six million people. It is a Semitic tongue evolved mostly from ancient Ge'ez or Ethiopic. Its alphabet has 33 characters, each with seven forms that represent a consonant and different vowels.

AMHERST, town in W Mass., N of Springfield. It has the U. of Massachusetts (founded 1863) and Amherst College (opened 1821), a major independent liberal arts college. Emily DICKINSON and Robert FROST lived there. Pop 26331.

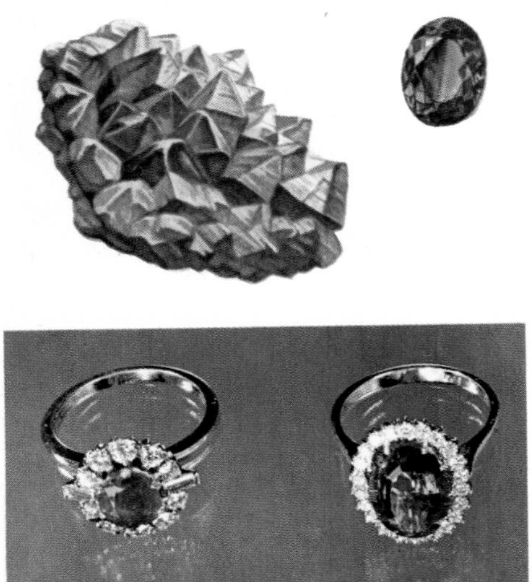

Amethyst shown in crystal formation, as a cut gem and set into rings. This crystal was much prized by the Egyptians for its supposed healing properties.

AMHERST, Jeffrey Amherst, 1st Baron (1717–1797), British major-general who helped take Canada from the French. He captured Louisburg fortress on Cape Breton Island (1758), then Ticonderoga and Crown Point (1759) and lastly Montreal (1760). While governor-general of British North America (1760–63) he crushed a pro-French Indian rising led by PONTIAC. He later became commander-in-chief of the British army (1772–95).

AMICUS CURIAE, or friend of the court, legal term for a stranger to the case assisting the court on factual or legal points. Though an infrequent practice, the US Supreme Court permits federal, state and local governments to present their views in any case that concerns them.

AMIDES, class of ALIPHATIC COMPOUNDS, of general formula $RCONH_2$, derived from CARBOXYLIC ACIDS and AMMONIA by replacing the acid hydroxyl group by the amino group (NH_2). N-substituted amides are derived from primary or secondary AMINES instead of ammonia. Other amides are derived analogously from inorganic OXY-ACIDS or from SULFONIC ACIDS (see also SULFA DRUGS). Amides are prepared by reaction of ACID CHLORIDES, ACID ANHYDRIDES or ESTERS with AMMONIA or AMINES, or by partial HYDROLYSIS of NITRILES. Most simple amides are low-melting solids with strong HYDROGEN BONDING, soluble in water. Formamide and N-substituted amides are liquids widely used as solvents. Amides are both weak ACIDS and weak BASES. They may be hydrolyzed to CARBOXYLIC ACIDS, and dehydrated to NITRILES. Metallic HYDRIDES convert them to AMINES, and treatment with bromine and sodium hydroxide (the Hofmann degradation) yields amines with one fewer carbon atom. Polymeric amides (such as NYLON) are used as SYNTHETIC FIBERS, and similar amide linkages join AMINO ACIDS in PROTEINS and PEPTIDES. (See also UREA; IMIDES.)

AMIENS, city in N France and capital of the Somme department. A trade center since Roman times, it makes cotton, silk, wool and other textiles, also machinery and chemicals; and trades in farm produce. It has France's largest cathedral and a university. Pop 117888.

AMIENS, Peace of (1802), short-lived Franco-British truce ending the FRENCH REVOLUTIONARY WARS. Britain returned to France or its allies all conquests except Trinidad and Ceylon. France recognized the Republic of the Seven Ionian Islands and Malta was to return to the Knights of Malta.

AMIN DADA, Idi (c1925–   ), Ugandan field marshal who became president in 1971, deposing Milton Obote. A flamboyant and dictatorial ruler, he expelled Uganda's Asian middle class in 1972 and purged many opponents. In 1975 he became president of the ORGANIZATION OF AFRICAN UNITY.

AMINES, class of organic compounds derived from AMMONIA by replacing one or more hydrogen atoms by alkyl groups (see ALKANES) or aryl groups (see AROMATIC COMPOUNDS). Primary amines have general formula RNH_2; secondary R_2NH; and tertiary R_3N. HETEROCYCLIC nitrogen bases (including the ALKALOIDS and PYRIDINE) are tertiary amines. Amines may be formed by reduction of AMIDES, NITRILES or NITRO COMPOUNDS, or by reaction of ammonia with organic HALIDES, ALCOHOLS or SULFONIC ACIDS. Simple amines are pungent liquids which are strong BASES and LIGANDS; many occur naturally in decaying organic matter. They give AMIDES with acid derivatives. Amines have many uses, including the manufacture of dyes, drugs and SYNTHETIC FIBERS. (See also ANILINE; AMINO ACIDS.)

AMINO ACIDS, an important class of CARBOXYLIC ACIDS containing one or more amino ($-NH_2$) groups (see AMINES). Twenty or so α-amino acids ($RCH[NH_2]COOH$) are the building blocks of the PROTEINS found in all living matter. They are also found and synthesized in cells. Amino acids are white, crystalline solids, soluble in water; they can act as ACIDS or BASES depending on the chemical environment (see PH). In neutral solution they exist as ZWITTERIONS. An amino acid mixture may be analyzed by CHROMATOGRAPHY. All α-amino acids (except glycine) contain at least one asymmetric carbon atom to which are attached the carboxyl group, the amino group, a hydrogen atom and a fourth group (R) that differs for each amino acid and determines its character. Thus amino acids can exist in two mirror-image forms (see STEREOISOMERS). Generally only L-isomers occur in nature, but a few bacteria contain D-isomers. Humans synthesize most of the amino acids needed for NUTRITION, but depend on protein foods for eight "essential amino acids" which they cannot produce. Inside the body, amino acids derived from food are metabolized (see METABOLISM) in various ways. As each amino acid contains both an acid and an amino group, they can form a long chain of amino acids bridged by AMIDE links and called PEPTIDES. Peptide synthesis from constituent amino acids is a stage in PROTEIN SYNTHESIS. Thus some are converted into HORMONES, ENZYMES and NUCLEIC ACIDS. Proteins may be broken down again by HYDROLYSIS into their constituent amino acids, as in DIGESTION. When amino acids are deaminated (the amino group removed), the nitrogen passes out as UREA. The remainder of the molecule enters the CITRIC ACID CYCLE, being broken down to provide energy.

Scientists have produced amino acids and simple peptide chains by combining carbon dioxide, ammonia and water vapor under the sort of conditions (including electric discharges) thought to exist on earth millions of years ago. This may provide a clue to the origin of LIFE.

AMIS, Kingsley (1922–   ), English novelist, poet and critic. He emerged as one of the ANGRY YOUNG MEN in *Lucky Jim* (1954), an amusing attack on social and academic pretensions. Among his later works are *New Maps of Hell* (1960), *One Fat Englishman* (1963), and *The Green Man* (1969).

AMISH, conservative group of the MENNONITE sect, founded by Jakob AMMANN in Switzerland in the 1690s. In the 18th century members settled in what are now Ind., Ohio and Pa., and today they live in 23 states. Literal interpretation of the Bible leads their farm communities to reject modern life (including electricity and cars). Amish wear old-style clothes, plow with horses and observe the Sabbath strictly. (See also PENNSYLVANIA DUTCH.)

AMISTAD CASE, US legal case of 1841, involving Negro slaves who mutinied aboard the Spanish slaveship *Amistad* and sought asylum as free men in the US. John Quincy ADAMS successfully defended them in the Supreme Court against the Van Buren administration's decision to return the Negroes to their Spanish masters.

AMMAN, capital and largest city of Jordan, 25mi NE of the Dead Sea. Jordan's main industrial and trading center, it has food and tobacco processing and produces textiles, leatherware and cement. Some historic buildings predate the Hellenistic period. In biblical times it was the capital of the AMMONITES. Much damage was caused by the fighting between government troops and Palestinian guerrillas in 1970. Pop 570000.

AMMANATI, Bartolomeo (1511–1592), Florentine sculptor and architect, influenced by MICHELANGELO. He designed Florence's Trinitá bridges (1567–69) and Fountain of Neptune (1576).

AMMANN, Jakob, 17th-century Swiss MENNONITE bishop who, in 1693–97, broke with the Mennonite Church in Switzerland and Alsace, founding the AMISH group which spread to North America.

AMMANN, Othmar Hermann (1897–1965), US engineer. He designed the George Washington Bridge in New York City (1931), the San Francisco Golden Gate Bridge (1935) and the Verrazano-Narrows Bridge in New York (1964).

AMMETER, an instrument used to measure electric currents greater than 1 μA. Most direct-current ammeters are similar in design to the moving-coil GALVANOMETERS used for smaller currents, though they differ in passing most of the test current through a low "shunt" RESISTANCE (thus bypassing the coil) and in using a pointer fixed to the coil assembly to indicate the reading on the linearly calibrated scale. For alternating currents either a rectifier can be used with a moving-coil instrument or the less sensitive hot-wire or moving-iron instruments can be used. (See also ELECTRICITY; VOLTMETER.)

AMMONIA (NH_3), colorless acrid gas, made by the HABER PROCESS; a covalent HYDRIDE. The pyramidal molecule turns inside out very rapidly, which is the basis of the ammonia clock (see ATOMIC CLOCK). Ammonia's properties have typical anomalies due to HYDROGEN BONDING; liquid ammonia is a good solvent. Ammonia is a BASE; its aqueous solution contains ammonium hydroxide, and is used as a household cleaning fluid. It forms ammine (NH_3) LIGAND complexes with transition metal ions, and yields AMIDES and AMINES with many organic compounds. Ammonia is used as a fertilizer, a refrigerant, in the OSTWALD PROCESS, and to make ammonium salts, UREA, and many drugs, dyes and plastics. mp −78°C, bp −33°C.

On reaction with acids, ammonia gives ammonium salts, containing the NH_4^+ ion, which resemble ALKALI METAL salts. They are mainly used as fertilizers. The analogous quaternary ammonium salts, NR_4^+, are made by alkylation of tertiary AMINES and are used as ANTISEPTICS. **Ammonium Chloride** (NH_4Cl), or **Sal Ammoniac,** a colorless crystalline solid used in dry cells and as a flux, formed as a by-product in the SOLVAY PROCESS. subl 340°C. **Ammonium Nitrate** (NH_4NO_3), a colorless crystalline solid, used as a fertilizer and in explosives. mp 170°C. (See also HYDRAZINE.)

AMMONITES, extinct order of MOLLUSKS (Class: CEPHALOPODA), extant between 200 and 70 million years ago. Typically spiral-shelled, of diameter 0.01–2m (0.4in–6.6ft), (though helical—see HELIX—shells have been found), they evolved rapidly and their FOSSILS are thus of use in dating geological strata.

AMMONITES, pastoral Semitic people recorded in the Old Testament as enemies of the Israelites. Reputedly descended from Lot, they lived E of the Jordan and Dead Sea and N of Moab, with Rabbath Ammon (now AMMAN) as their chief city.

AMMUNITION, any material designed to be used with destructive effect against a target or an enemy. It includes mines, self-propelled missiles, BOMBS, TORPEDOES and grenades, together with gun ammunition. Sufficient materials to operate a weapon a single time constitute a round of ammunition. **Gun ammunition** usually comprises a bullet, shell or shot, a propellant charge and a primer which fires the propellant. High-explosive shells also include a fuse which detonates the charge either upon impact or a fixed time after firing. All this is usually supplied as a single unit (fixed ammunition) although large artillery often uses separate-loading ammunition for ease of handling. The propellant is usually a mixture of relatively slow burning explosives which liberates a large volume of gas on firing, thus propelling the projectile up the gun barrel. The size of ammunition depends on the **caliber** of gun used. This is the diameter of the barrel, usually expressed in mm or in decimal fractions of an inch. (See also BALLISTICS.)

AMNESIA, the total loss of MEMORY for a period of time or for events. In cases of CONCUSSION, **retrograde amnesia** is the permanent loss of memory for events just preceding a head injury while **post-traumatic** amnesia applies to a period after injury during which the patient may be conscious but incapable of recall, both at the time and later. Similar behavior to the latter, termed **fugue**, occurs as a psychiatric phenomenon.

AMNESTY, a pardon granted by a government to a large group of people accused of political or other offenses. It is usually designed to promote goodwill and reconciliation, as in the US Amnesty Act of 1865 which pardoned most men who had fought in the Confederate forces.

AMNION, a tough membrane surrounding the EMBRYO of reptiles, birds and mammals and containing the AMNIOTIC FLUID. All land-laid EGGS contain amnions; those of fishes and amphibians do not, and thus must be laid in moist surroundings or water. (See also AMNIOTES; PLACENTA.)

AMNIOTES, those VERTEBRATES (mammals, reptiles, birds) characterized by the development of an AMNION to protect the EMBRYO.

AMNIOTIC FLUID, the fluid contained within the AMNION of AMNIOTES which provides a moist, aquatic environment for the EMBRYO. (See also PLACENTA.)

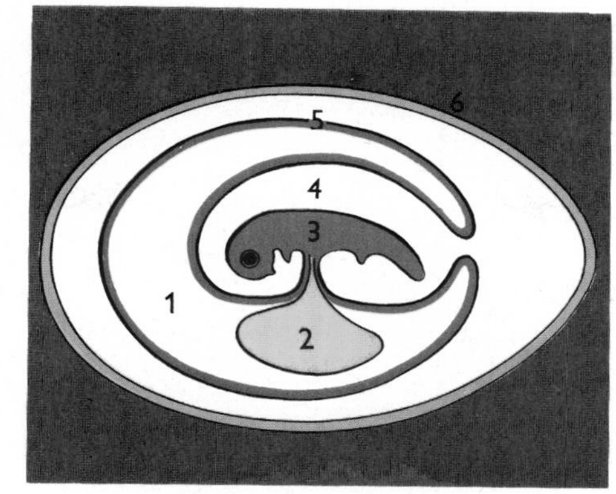

Amniotic egg with parts shown diagrammatically: 1. allantoic cavity, 2. yolk sacs, 3. embryo, 4. fluid-filled amniotic cavity, 5. amnion, 6. shell.

AMOEBAS, a large order (Amoebida) of the class Sarcodina (Rhizopodea) of PROTOZOA. They are unicellular (see CELL), a relatively rigid outer layer of ectoplasm surrounding a more fluid mass of endoplasm, in which lie one or more nuclei. They move by extending PSEUDOPODIA, into which they flow; and feed by surrounding and absorbing organic particles. REPRODUCTION is almost always asexual, generally by binary FISSION, though sometimes by multiple fission of the nucleus; a tough wall of CYTOPLASM forms about each of these small nuclei to create cysts. These can survive considerable rigors, returning to normal amoeboid form when circumstances are more clement. (Some species of amoeba may form a single cyst to survive adversity.) Certain amoebas can reproduce sexually. Amoebas are found wherever there is moisture, some parasitic (see PARASITE) forms living within other animals: *Entamoeba histolytica,* for example, causes amoebic DYSENTERY in man. The type-species is *Amoeba proteus,* which has a single nucleus and can form only one pseudopodium at a time.

AMON (also Ammon or Amen), ancient Egyptian deity who became associated with the sun-god Ra and, as Amon-Ra, embodied the universal animating force. His cult evolved at Thebes after 2100 BC, and 18th-dynasty pharaohs, crediting him with their conquests, made his priesthood rich and powerful. Amon lost importance after Assyria sacked Thebes (663 BC), but the Greeks identified him with Zeus.

AMORITES, biblical term for Canaanites. More generally, an ancient seminomadic W Semitic tribe of Arabia, Palestine and Syria (3rd millennium BC). They ruled BABYLON (c1830–1531 BC) but were displaced by the MITANNI and crushed by the HITTITES (16th–13th centuries BC).

AMORTIZATION, reduction of a loan by a series of payments, usually spread out over the period for which the loan was made. Bank loans and mortgages are often paid off in this way.

AMOS (8th century BC), Hebrew prophet, the first to proclaim clearly that there was one God for all peoples. A shepherd from Judah, he preached in neighboring Israel, denouncing its corruption until expelled by the king. The probably posthumous biblical Book of Amos is the earliest record of a prophet's sayings and life.

AMOY (Hsia-men), seaport in SE China, on Amoy Island. It produces food and paper products, wine and chemicals. Its fine natural harbor has good dock facilities and trades in sugar, lumber and tobacco. Amoy was the first Chinese port to trade with NW Europe. Pop 400 000.

AMPERE (A), the SI base unit of electric current, named for A.M. AMPÈRE and defined as the constant current which, if maintained in two straight parallel conductors of infinite length, of negligible circular cross-section, and placed 1 metre apart in vacuum, would produce between these conductors a force equal to 2×10^{-7} newton per metre of length. (See ELECTRICITY; SI UNITS.)

AMPÈRE, André Marie (1775–1836), French mathematician, physicist and philosopher best remembered for many discoveries in electrodynamics and electromagnetism. In the early 1820s he developed OERSTED's experiments on the interaction between magnets and electric currents and investigated the forces set up between current-carrying conductors.

AMPHETAMINES, a group of STIMULANT drugs, including **benzedrine** and **methedrine,** now in medical disfavor following widespread abuse and addiction. They counteract fatigue, suppress appetite, speed up performance (hence **"Speed"**) and give confidence, but pronounced DEPRESSION often follows; thus psychological and then physical addiction are encouraged. A paranoid PSYCHOSIS (resembling SCHIZOPHRENIA) may result from prolonged use, although it may be that amphetamine abuse is rather an early symptom of the psychosis. While no longer acceptable in treatment of OBESITY, they are useful in **narcolepsy**, a rare condition of abnormal sleepiness.

AMPHIBIA, a class of vertebrates, including FROGS, TOADS, NEWTS, SALAMANDERS and CAECILIANS. Typically they spend part of their life in water, part on land. They are distinct from REPTILES in that their EGGS lack AMNIONS, and must hence be laid in moist conditions, and that their soft, moist skins have no scales. They are of the subphylum VERTEBRATA, of the phylum CHORDATA. It is thought that amphibia were the first vertebrates to venture from the aquatic environment on to the land, and that they were the ancestors of all other vertebrates (see EVOLUTION). They are cold-blooded, and therefore many species hibernate (see HIBERNATION) during winter. Their development is in two stages: the egg develops into a larval form (see LARVA), which is usually solely aquatic, then the larva into an adult. Adult amphibia are carnivorous. (See also illustration p. 62.)

AMPHIBIOUS WARFARE, coordinated use of naval, air and landing forces to seize a beachhead. Such warfare reached full development in WWII in N Africa, W Europe and the Pacific. Naval and air bombardment softened up defenses, then special landing craft moved inshore to land the infantry and artillery.

AMPHIBOLES, a class of SILICATE minerals found in igneous rocks and metamorphic SCHISTS and GNEISSES. They contain infinite double-chains of SiO_4 tetrahedra, and have a cleavage of about 56°. Amphiboles include HORNBLENDE, JADE and certain ASBESTOS minerals.

AMPHICTYONY, in Classical Greece, an association of neighboring states based on a common religious center. The amphictyonic council administered the religious and temporal affairs of the major shrines concerned. The most important such body was the Delphic Amphictyony, linked with temples at Delphi and Thermopylae, which could declare a sacred war against violators or arbitrate in a dispute.

AMPHIOXUS, the genus *Branchiostoma* which, with the genus *Asymmetron*, comprises the subphylum Cephalochordata, the **lancelets**. Worm-like marine CHORDATES, 40–75mm (1.6–3.0in) long and inhabiting shallow coastal waters, they are important because of their probable resemblance to early ancestors of the VERTEBRATES (see also EVOLUTION).

AMPHIPODA, one of the largest orders of CRUSTACEA (phylum ARTHROPODA) with over 3600 species, found in both fresh and salt water. Typical amphipods include freshwater SHRIMPS and sandhoppers.

AMPHITHEATER, originally a round or elliptical theater with tiers of seats surrounding a central arena; now any stadium with a central stage. Roman amphitheaters were first of wood, then of stone. The most famous is Rome's COLOSSEUM (seating 50 000, and the largest of all).

AMPHITRYON. See ALCMENE.

AMPHORA, a two-handled pot with a narrower neck than body, one of the main vessel shapes in classical Greek pottery. In one-piece amphorae neck and body form a continuous curve; in neck amphorae

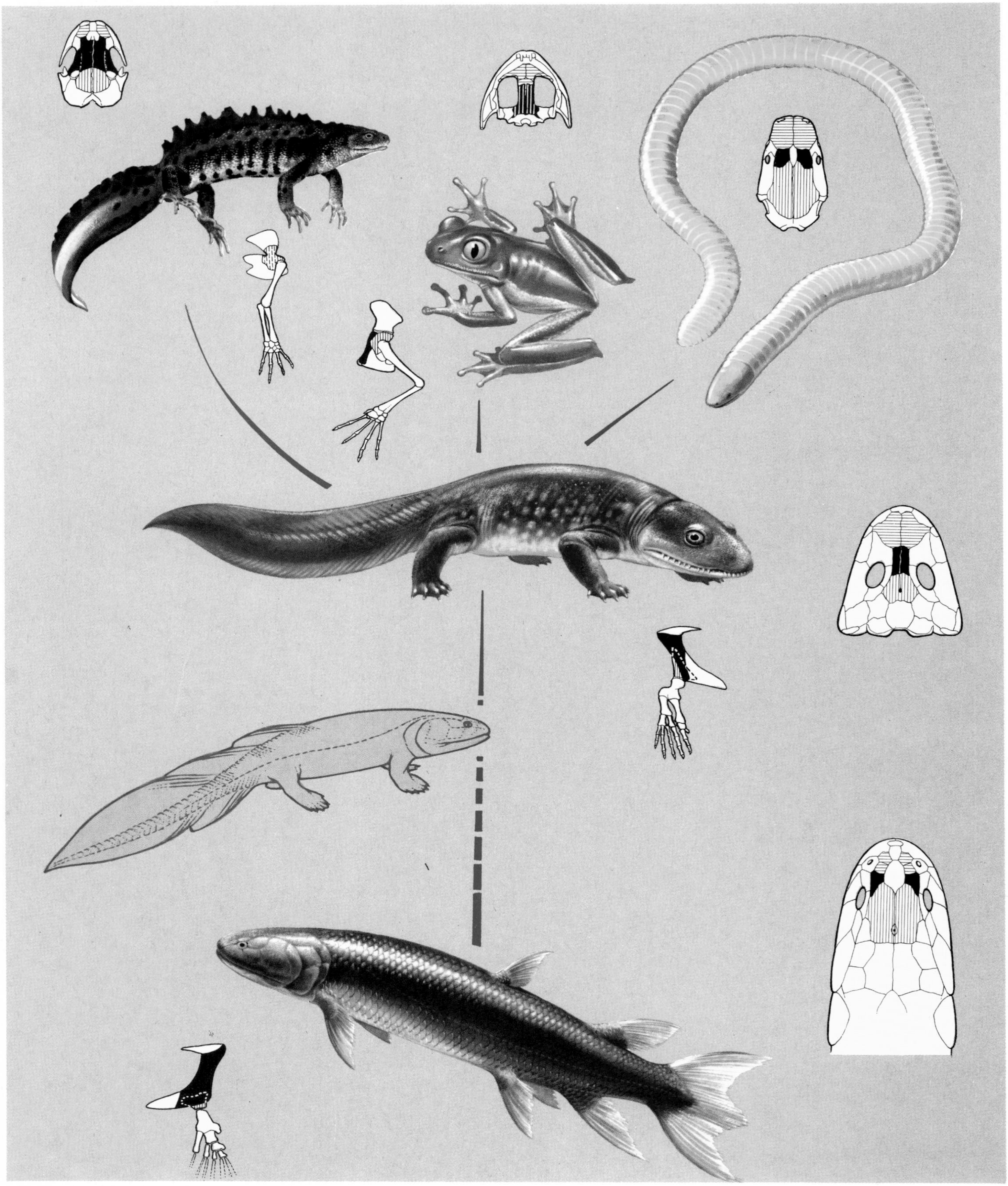

During the evolution of Amphibia there have been two major events. (1.) From rhipidistian fish (*bottom*) evolved a form *Ichthyostega* (*center*), able to walk on land. A hypothetical stage between the two is shown in blue. (2.) From *Ichthyostega* three separate groups evolved: Urodela (amphibians with tails, *top left*); Anura (amphibians which lose their tails in adulthood and are adapted for jumping, *top center*); and Apoda (legless amphibians, *top right*). The main structural changes in the skull and forelimb which accompanied these events are shown.

there is a sharp angle between neck and body. The smallest amphorae are called **amphoriskoi**.

AMPLIFIER, any device which increases the strength of an input signal. Amplifiers play a vital role in most electronic devices: RADIO and TELEVISION receivers, PHONOGRAPHS, TAPE-RECORDERS and COMPUTERS: but nonelectronic devices such as the horn of a windup phonograph or the PANTOGRAPH used for enlarging drawings are also amplifiers of a kind. Electronic amplifiers, usually based on TRANSISTORS or ELECTRON TUBES, can be thought of as a sort of variable switch in which the output from a power source is controlled (modulated) by a weak input signal. An important factor is the fidelity (see HIGH-FIDELITY) with which the waveform of the output signal reproduces that of the input over the desired BANDWIDTH.

AMPLITUDE, in WAVE MOTIONS, the maximum displacement from its MEAN value of the oscillating property; thus for a PENDULUM, half the extent of its swing. **Amplitude modulation** (AM) is a common method of encoding a carrier wave in RADIO.

AMPUTATION, the surgical or traumatic removal of a part or the whole of a limb or other structure. It is necessary for severe limb damage, infective GANGRENE, loss of BLOOD supply and certain types of CANCER. Healthy tissue is molded to form a stump as a base for artificial limb prosthesis (see PROSTHETICS).

AMRAVATI, university town and marketing center of W central India, in Maharashtra state. It processes and markets the cotton grown in the surrounding Amravati district. Pop 193 636.

AMRITSAR, principal and largest city in Punjab state, N India. It has important chemical and textile industries and rolling mills, and also produces electrical equipment, bicycles and carpets. The city is the center of the Sikh faith and has the Sikhs' main place of worship, the Golden Temple or Darbar Sahib ("court divine"). There are several colleges of higher education. The city is in the Amritsar district, a prosperous agricultural region. Pop 432 663.

AMSTERDAM, capital and largest city of the Netherlands, and one of Europe's great commercial, financial and cultural centers. It stands in N Holland at the S of man-made Lake IJssel. This "Venice of the North" is centered on a series of concentric semicircular canals. Other canals linked to the Rhine and North Sea make Amsterdam one of Europe's major transshipment ports. It is also a major rail center and has an international airport.

Amsterdam is world-famous for diamond cutting and polishing and produces chemicals, machinery, bicycles, beer and textiles. It has an important stock exchange, two universities and about 40 museums. Amsterdam grew from a medieval fishing village, and had become a major city by the 17th century. Pop 807 742.

AMSTERDAM, manufacturing city in E central N.Y. State, on the Mohawk R. It produces textiles, plastics and electronics equipment. Pop 25 524.

AMU DARYA (ancient Oxus), the major river of Soviet Central Asia. Rising in the Pamir Mts, it flows 1 578mi, NW between the USSR and Afghanistan, then W and NW to enter the Aral Sea through a delta. The lower 900mi are navigable, and this stretch also irrigates large arid areas.

AMULET, a natural or artificial object believed to bring good luck (in which case it may be termed a **talisman**) or ward off evil. It is either placed at the focus of its desired sphere of influence (e.g., over a doorway) or carried or worn.

AMUNDSEN, Roald (1872–1928), Norwegian polar explorer who was the first man to reach the S Pole (Dec 14, 1911). His party beat the ill-fated Robert F. SCOTT expedition by one month. In the Arctic he was the first to navigate the Northwest Passage (1903–06), later crossing the N Pole in the dirigible *Norge* (1926). He was lost over the Barents Sea in an air search for the Italian explorer Umberto NOBILE.

AMUR RIVER, river in NE Asia. Rising in Mongolia, it flows 2 700mi NE through the USSR, then SE, dividing the USSR from China, then NE through the USSR into the Tatar Strait. Navigable for the six months it is not frozen, it carries oil, grain and lumber. The Amur has fisheries and hydroelectric installations.

AMYL COMPOUNDS, organic compounds containing the amyl group C_5H_{11} (see ALKANES), which has eight ISOMERS. They include the amyl ALCOHOLS, synthesized from HYDROCARBONS or extracted from FUSEL OIL, and used as a solvent. **Isoamyl nitrite** ($C_5H_{11}ONO$) is a VASODILATOR used to give relief in ANGINA PECTORIS. **Amyl acetate** (which has a pleasant, fruity smell and is known as banana oil) is used as a solvent for NITROCELLULOSE and as a flavoring for candy.

ANABAPTISTS ("rebaptizers"), radical Protestant sects of the REFORMATION that sought a return to primitive Christianity. The first group was formed in 1523 at Zurich by dissatisfied followers of Ulrich ZWINGLI. Denying the validity of infant baptism, they rebaptized adult converts. Most stressed the dictates of individual conscience, and urged nonviolence and separation of church and state. Despite widespread persecution (notably at Münster) their doctrines spread, inspiring the MENNONITES in the Netherlands and the HUTTERITES in Moravia.

ANABASIS. See XENOPHON.

ANABLEPS. See FOUR-EYED FISHES.

ANACLETUS, name of a pope and an antipope. **Saint Anacletus** (or Cletus), the third pope (76–88 or 79–91), was probably martyred. **Anacletus II** (d. 1138) was antipope (1130–38) in rivalry to INNOCENT II, and held Rome until his death.

ANACONDA, city in SW Mont., seat of Deer Lodge Co., ranking among the world's biggest producers of nonferrous metal. It produces copper, zinc and phosphates, and was founded in 1883. Pop 9 771.

ANACONDAS, two species, subfamily Boidae, of South American BOA. *Eunectes notaeus* is found in Paraguay and *E. murinus*, probably the largest SNAKE in the world with a length up to about 15m (50ft) though more usually 3–6m (10–20ft), throughout Brazil. Anacondas do not have a poisonous bite, killing prey by constriction. In general they shun human beings.

ANACOSTIA RIVER, 12mi long tributary entering the Potomac R SE of central Washington, D.C.

ANACREON (c582–c485BC), Greek lyric poet who celebrated wine and love in mellow, simple verses. These were later copied in the so-called Anacreontics; fashionable in 18th-century Europe. His main patrons were the "tyrants" (absolute rulers) of Samos and Athens.

ANAEROBE, any organism whose RESPIRATION does not make use of OXYGEN. Many BACTERIA and PARASITES are **facultative anaerobes** (that is, they can survive without oxygen for short or long periods), and a few are **obligate anaerobes** (unable to use oxygen in respiration). (See also AEROBE.)

ANAGRAM, the letters of a word or phrase rearranged to form another word or phrase. Stemming perhaps from ancient beliefs in the magical efficacy of letters, anagrams have been used as occult formulas, as a form of code and as pseudonyms. Today they feature in crossword puzzles.

ANAHEIM, industrial city in S Cal. Over 300 industries produce aircraft parts, canned fruit, chemicals, electronic equipment and hardware. DISNEYLAND draws 5 million visitors annually. German settlers founded Anaheim as a cooperative community in 1857. Pop 166 408.

ANALGESICS, drugs used for relief of pain. They mainly impair perception of or emotional response to pain by action on the higher BRAIN centers. ASPIRIN and paracetamol are mild but effective. Phenylbutazone, indomethacin and ibuprofen are, like aspirin, useful in treating RHEUMATOID ARTHRITIS by reducing INFLAMMATION as well as relieving pain. NARCOTIC analgesics derived from OPIUM ALKALOIDS range from the milder CODEINE and dextropropoxyphene, suitable for general use, to the highly effective euphoriant and addictive MORPHINE and HEROIN. These are reserved for severe acute pain and terminal disease, where addiction is either unlikely or unimportant. Pethidine (demerol) is an intermediate narcotic.

ANALOGUE, in a plant or animal, an organ performing the same function as one in another species but which differs from it in origin and structure (i.e., is not a HOMOLOGUE). Thus a bird's wing and a bee's wing are in this sense merely analogous.

Anacondas are semiaquatic, often lying in muddy water with only the eyes and top of the head protruding. Their prey is usually small animals which come to the water to drink.

ANALYSIS, the branch of MATHEMATICS concerned particularly with the concepts of FUNCTION and LIMIT. Its important divisions are CALCULUS, ANALYTIC GEOMETRY and the study of DIFFERENTIAL EQUATIONS.

ANALYSIS, in psychology, determination of the individual components of a complex experience or mental process: often also used for PSYCHOANALYSIS.

ANALYSIS, Chemical, determination of the compounds or elements comprising a chemical substance. Qualitative analysis deals with what a sample contains; quantitative analysis finds the amounts. The methods available depend on the size of the sample: macro (>100mg), semimicro (1–100mg), micro (1μg–1mg), or submicro (<1μg). Chemical analysis is valuable in chemical research, industry, archaeology, medicine and many other fields. A representative sample must first be taken (see STATISTICS) and prepared for analysis. Preliminary separation is often carried out by CHROMATOGRAPHY, ION-EXCHANGE, DISTILLATION or precipitation.

In qualitative analysis, classical methods involve characteristic reactions of substances. After preliminary tests—inspection, heating, and FLAME TESTS—systematic schemes are followed which separate the various IONS into groups according to their reactions with standard reagents, and which then identify them individually. Cations and anions are analyzed separately. For organic compounds, carbon and hydrogen are identified by heating with copper (II) oxide, carbon dioxide and water being formed; nitrogen, halogens and sulfur are identified by heating with molten sodium and testing the residue for CYANIDE, HALIDES and SULFIDE respectively. Classical quantitative analysis is performed by GRAVIMETRIC ANALYSIS and VOLUMETRIC ANALYSIS.

Modern chemical analysis employs instrumental methods to give faster, more accurate assessments than do classical methods. Many modern methods have the additional advantage of being nondestructive. They include COLORIMETRY, SPECTROPHOTOMETRY, POLAROGRAPHY, MASS SPECTROSCOPY, DIFFERENTIAL THERMAL ANALYSIS, potentiometric titration (see POTENTIOMETER), and methods for determining MOLECULAR WEIGHT. Neutron activation analysis subjects a sample to NEUTRON irradiation and measures the strength of induced radioactivity and its rate of decay. In X-ray analysis, a sample is irradiated with X RAYS and emits X rays of different, characteristic wavelengths (see also X-RAY DIFFRACTION.

ANALYTIC GEOMETRY, that branch of GEOMETRY based on the idea that a POINT may be defined relative to another point or to AXES by a set of numbers. In plane geometry, there are usually two axes, commonly designated the x- and y-axes, at right ANGLES. The position of a point in the plane of the axes may then be defined by a pair of numbers (x, y), its coordinates, which give its distance in units in the x- and y-direction from the **origin** (the point of INTERSECTION of the two axes). In three dimensions

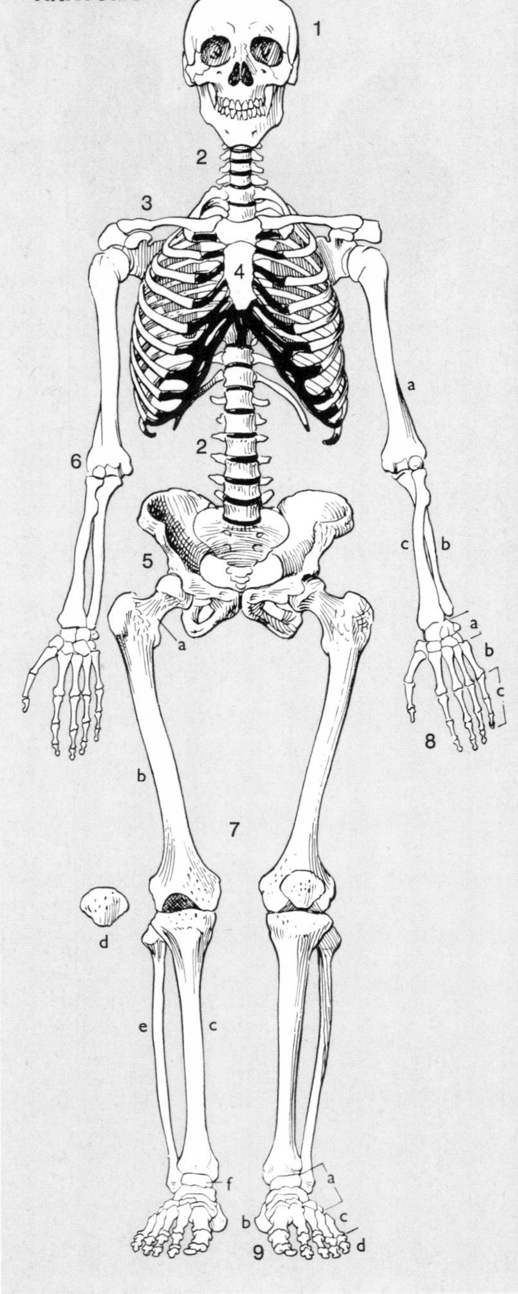

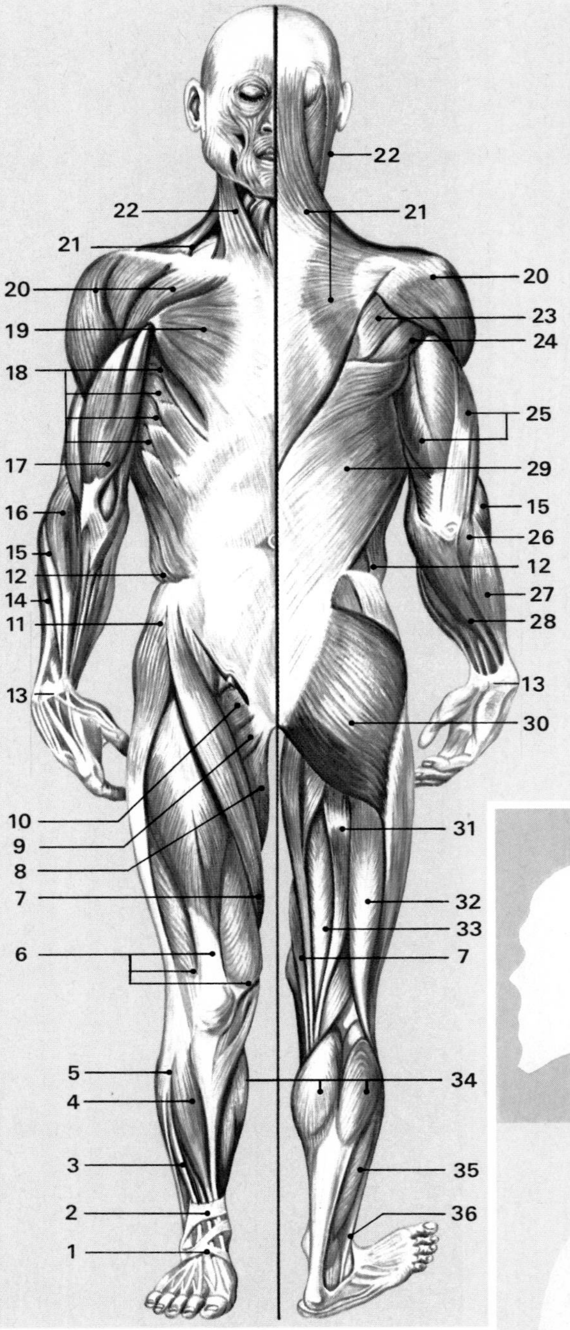

1. Inferior extensor retinaculum
2. Superior extensor retinaculum
3. Extensor digitorum longus
4. Tibialis anterior
5. Peroneus longus
6. Quadriceps femoris
7. Sartorius
8. Gracilis
9. Adductor longus
10. Pectineus
11. Tensor fasciae latae
12. External oblique
13. Flexor retinaculum
14. Extensor carpi radialis brevis
15. Extensor carpi radialis longus
16. Brachioradialis
17. Biceps
18. Serratus anterior
19. Pectoralis major
20. Deltoid
21. Trapezius
22. Sternomastoid
23. Infraspinatus
24. Teres major
25. Triceps
26. Extensor carpi ulnaris
27. Extensor digitorum
28. Flexor carpi ulnaris
29. Latissimus dorsi
30. Gluteus maximus
31. Semitendinosus
32. Biceps femoris
33. Semimembranosus
34. Gastrocnemius
35. Soleus
36. Peroneus brevis

Above left: Parts of the skeleton. (1) skull; (2) spinal column; (3) clavicle; (4) sternum; (5) pelvis; (6) arm—(a) humerus, (b) ulna, (c) radius; (7) legs—(a) neck of the femur, (b) femur, (c) tibia, (d) patella, (e) fibula, (f) talus; (8) hand—(a) carpus, (b) hand-bones (metacarpels), (c) fingers; (9) foot—(a) tarsals, (b) calcaneum, (c) metatarsals, (d) toes.

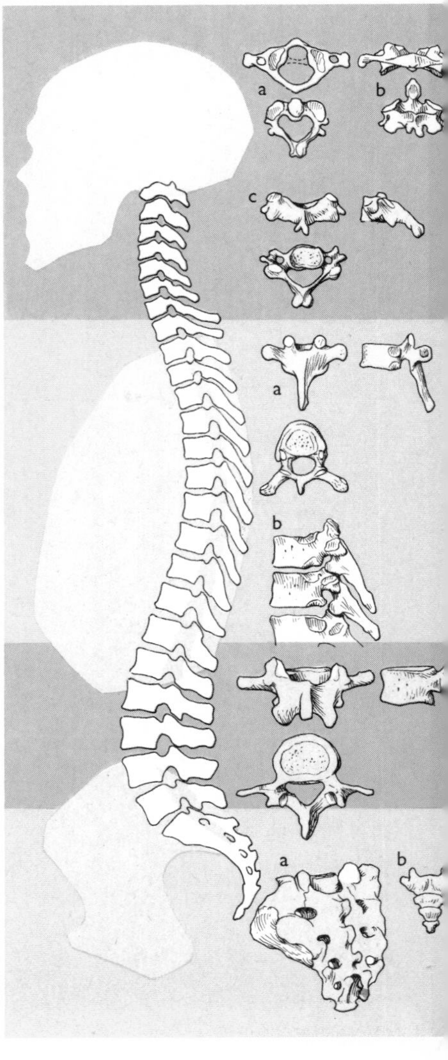

Right: (1) The vertebrae of the neck. Atlas and axis seen from above (a) and behind (b). There are two vertebral surfaces on the atlas on which the head can swivel backward and forward. The hole in the vertebra is divided in two by a tendon (indicated by a dotted line) which separates the neural spine of the axis from the spinal cord. The atlas and the head can turn horizontally around this spine. The other neck vertebrae (c) are characterized by two pierced transverse processes and the spinous process which is divided at the end. (2) The thoracic vertebrae—(a) *left:* from behind; *right:* side view, and *below:* from above—have three extra vertebra surfaces on either side for articulation with the ribs. As a result there are two turning points—shown in white in (b)—which form an axis around which the rib can turn. (3) The lumbar vertebrae stick straight out at the back, allowing considerable backward bending. (4) The sacral vertebrae (a) are fused into one, and have vertebral surfaces on the side for articulation with the hipbones. The tail vertebrae or coccyx (b) consists of three or four fused vertebrae. Sometimes the joint with the sacral vertebrae is movable; sometimes the sacral vertebrae and coccyx are completely fused into one bony structure.

there are three axes, usually at mutual right angles, commonly designated the x-, y- and z-axes. (See also ABSCISSA; ORDINATE; and CARTESIAN COORDINATES.) In the coordinates (x, y, z), consider the situation when two of these have fixed values: there is a set of points, called a coordinate LINE, corresponding to all values of the third coordinate. Repeating this for each of the three coordinates, it can be seen that through each point defined by this coordinate system there are three coordinate lines. For all points, all three of these are straight (the system is rectilinear) and at mutual right angles (the system is rectangular). In plane polar coordinates there are two coordinated lines through each point: these are at right angles and one is curved (the system is rectangular and curvilinear).

Equation of a curve. A CURVE may be defined as a set of points. A relationship may be established between the coordinates of every point of the set, and this relationship is known as the EQUATION of the curve. The simplest form of plane curve is the straight LINE, which in the system we have described has an equation of the form $y=ax+b$, where a and b are CONSTANTS. Set $a=2$ and $b=3$: then, if $x=1$, $y=2+3=5$, if $x=2$, $y=4+3=7$, and so on; and conversely if $y=1$, $x=(1-3)/2=-1$, and so on. All points whose coordinates satisfy the relationship $y=2x+3$ will lie on this line. Equations of curves may involve higher POWERS of x or y: a parabola (see CONIC SECTIONS) may be expressed as $y=ax^2+b$. Since $x^2=(-x)^2$ for all values of x, the curve is symmetrical (see SYMMETRY) about the y-axis. Similarly, the curve $x=ay^2+b$ is symmetrical about the x-axis.

These principles may be applied to different coordinate systems, and to figures in more than two dimensions.

(See also ALGEBRAIC GEOMETRY; ANALYSIS; CALCULUS; CYLINDRICAL COORDINATES; FUNCTION; SPHERICAL COORDINATES.)

ANANIAS, name of several people mentioned in the New Testament. The most notable was a member of the earliest Christian community who, with his wife Sapphira, was struck dead at Peter's rebuke for lying. They had pretended to give the Church all their wealth, but kept some back.

ANAPHYLAXIS, a severe allergic reaction (see ALLERGY) due to injection of foreign material, mediated by HISTAMINE and KININS. In man, sudden severe breathlessness—due to spasm in bronchi and larynx—and circulatory collapse (SHOCK) occur. ADRENALINE and ANTIHISTAMINES should be given.

ANARCHISM, political belief that government should be abolished and the state replaced by the voluntary cooperation of individuals and groups. Like socialists, anarchists believe that existing governments tend to defend injustice, and they would do away with the institution of private property. But, unlike socialists, they believe that government is unnecessary and intrinsically harmful.

Pioneers of modern anarchism included England's William GODWIN (1756–1836), France's Pierre Joseph PROUDHON (1809–1865) and the Russian propagandist of violence, Mikhail BAKUNIN (1814–1876). Political leaders, such as President William McKinley (1901), have been assassinated by individual anarchists, and the SACCO–VANZETTI CASE strengthened the popular idea that anarchism meant terrorism. Outside SYNDICALISM, once strong in Spain, anarchism has had little political influence, but has recently become linked with student radicalism in Europe and America.

ANASAZI (Navaho: ancient ones), a prehistoric culture of the American Southwest, whose modern manifestation is the PUEBLO INDIANS. The earliest Anasazi remains are dated c50 AD. They were skilled basket weavers, in later times farmers and outstanding potters. Between about 1000 and 1300 AD they built the famous cliff dwellings.

ANASTASIA (1901–1918?), Russian grand duchess. Daughter of the last tsar, Nicholas II, she was probably murdered with her family during the Revolution. Several women later claimed to be Anastasia but none could prove her identity.

ANASTASIUS, name of four popes. **Saint Anastasius I** (d. 401) condemned the works of ORIGEN; was later canonized. **Anastasius II** (d. 498) caused a schism at Rome by his support of Acacius, an Eastern patriarch deposed by an earlier pope. **Anastasius III** (d. 913) lacked power, since Rome was under the Theophylact family. **Anastasius IV** (1073–1154) ended a controversy with FREDERICK BARBAROSSA over the see of Magdeburg and restored the see of York to St. William.

ANASTASIUS I (c430–518), East Roman emperor (491–518) whose sound administration enriched the Byzantine Empire and so helped to make possible the great reign of JUSTINIAN.

ANATHEMA, solemn ritual curse or ban pronounced upon a person or thing by an ecclesiastical authority. It involves banishment from the Church or religious community. The ancient Christian Church used it on incorrigible offenders, especially heretics.

ANATOLIA, large mountainous plateau in Asian Turkey, now more or less identical with the peninsula of ASIA MINOR.

ANATOMY, the structure and form of biological organisms (see BIOLOGY) and its study (MORPHOLOGY). The subject has three main divisions: gross anatomy, dealing with components visible to the naked eye; microscopic anatomy, dealing with microstructures seen only with the aid of an optical MICROSCOPE, and submicroscopic anatomy, dealing with still smaller ultrastructures. Since structure is closely related to function, anatomy is related to PHYSIOLOGY. (See also HUMAN BODY; EMBRYOLOGY.)

The study of anatomy is as old as that of MEDICINE, though for many centuries physicians' knowledge of anatomy left much to be desired. ANAXAGORAS had studied the anatomy of animals and anatomical observations can be found in the Hippocratic writings (see HIPPOCRATES), but it was ARISTOTLE who was the true father of comparative anatomy, and human dissection (the basis of all systematic human anatomy) was rarely practiced before the era of the ALEXANDRIAN SCHOOL and the work of HEROPHILUS and ERASISTRATUS. The last great experimental anatomist of antiquity was GALEN. His theories, as transmitted through the writings of the Arab scholars RHAZES and AVICENNA, held sway throughout the medieval period. Further progress had to await the revival of the practice of human dissection by SERVETUS and VESALIUS in the 16th century. The latter founded the famous Paduan school of anatomy which also included FALLOPIUS and FABRICIUS, whose pupil William HARVEY reunited the studies of anatomy and physiology in postulating the circulation of the BLOOD in *de Motu Cordis* (1628). This theory was confirmed some years later when MALPIGHI discovered the capillaries linking the arteries with the veins. Since the 17th century many important anatomical schools have been founded and the study of anatomy has become an essential part of medical training. Important developments in the late 18th century included the foundation of HISTOLOGY by BICHAT and that of modern comparative anatomy by CUVIER.

The rise of microscopic anatomy has of course depended on the development of the microscope; it found its greatest success in the announcement of SCHWANN's cell theory in 1839.

ANAXAGORAS (c500–c428 BC), Greek philosopher of the Ionian school, resident in Athens, who taught that the elements were infinite in number and that every thing contained a portion of every other thing. He also discovered the true cause of ECLIPSES, thought of the sun as a blazing rock and showed that air has substance.

ANAXIMANDER (c610–c545 BC), Greek philosopher of the Ionian school who taught that the cosmos was all derived from one primordial substance by a process of the separating out of opposites. He was probably the first Greek to attempt a map of the whole known world and thought of the earth as a stubby cylinder situated at the center of all things. Animal life, he thought, had begun in the sea.

ANAXIMENES OF MILETUS (6th century BC), Greek philosopher of the Ionian school who held that all things were derived from air; this becoming, for instance, fire on rarefaction, water, and finally earth on condensation.

ANCESTOR WORSHIP, ritual propitiation and veneration of dead kin in the belief that their spirits influence the fortunes of the living. It has figured strongly in Asian faiths, notably Confucianism in China, Shintoism in Japan and Hinduism in India, and also occurs in Africa and Melanesia.

ANCHISES, in Greek mythology, a shepherd seduced by APHRODITE, who bore him a son, the Trojan hero AENEAS. When Troy fell, Aeneas carried his blind father from the burning city on his shoulders and took him to Sicily.

ANCHOR, heavy object attached to a rope, chain or cable and used for mooring a ship, buoy or other floating object to the seabed. Modern anchors are usually of forged steel, with arms ending in broad tapered flukes that dig into the seabed to help prevent dragging. Ocean liners may have anchors of 20 000lb or more.

ANCHORAGE, largest city in Alaska and its main commercial and transportation center, located in S Alaska on Cook Inlet. It is a seaport with road and rail communications with the mining and farming interior and with an international airport. Anchorage has a major petroleum industry, canneries, sawmills and railroad shops, and is an important air defense center. Pop 48 029.

ANCHORITES, religious recluses and ascetics. In early Christian times many such hermits lived in the Middle East, especially in Egypt.

ANCHOVIES, family (Engraulidae) of small, shoal-forming fishes allied to the HERRING, usually inhabiting salt water. They are most often 100–150mm (4–6in), sometimes up to 300mm (1ft) long. About 100 species are known. They have a pointed snout and a long lower jaw extending behind the eye. (Order: Clupeiformes).

ANCIEN RÉGIME ("old order"), the political and social system of France overthrown by the Revolution of 1789. It was based on an absolute monarchy and on privileged social classes.

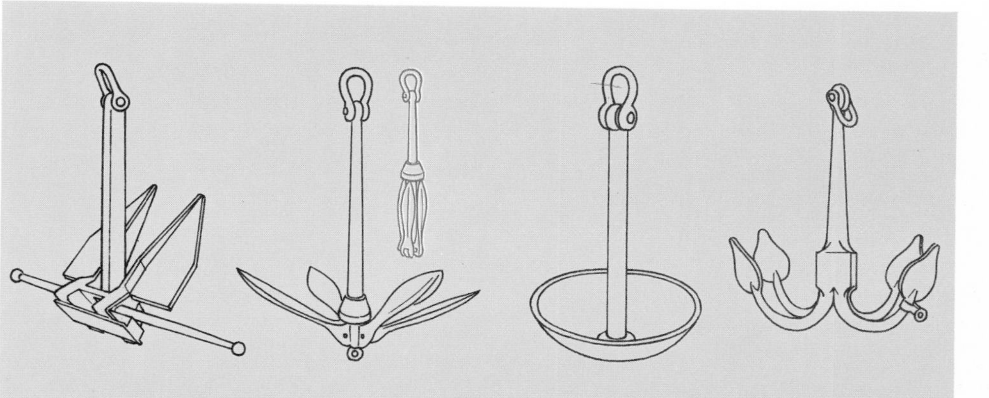

Different types of anchor: (*from left to right*) Danforth anchor, kedge, mushroom anchor, grapnel.

ANCONA, capital of Ancona province in E central Italy. An important fishing and commercial port on the Adriatic and a popular seaside resort, Ancona was founded by the Greeks c390 BC and became a Roman naval base. Pop 112 881.

ANDALUSIA, populous region of S Spain, extending to the Atlantic and Mediterranean and embracing eight provinces. It includes the Sierra Morena and Sierra Nevada Mts, and the warm fertile Guadalquivir River Valley—"the garden of Spain." There is metal mining, food processing and tourism along the Costa del Sol. Phoenicians first settled the area; later came Greeks, Romans and Vandals. Arabs and Berbers built a rich medieval culture. Today there is much rural poverty.

ANDALUSIA, city in S Ala., seat of Covington Co. It lies 65mi W of Dothan. Pop 10 092.

ANDAMAN AND NICOBAR ISLANDS, two island groups in the Bay of Bengal, forming a territory of India (area 3 200sq mi). The islands produce copra, coconut oil, rubber, coffee, rice, wood and wood products. Port Blair is the capital. Andamanese include the shy primitive Negrito aborigines.

ANDAMAN SEA, the Bay of Bengal E of the Andaman and Nicobar Islands. Area: 218 000sq mi.

ANDANTE, musical term meaning moderately slow (between ADAGIO and ALLEGRETTO). Also a musical piece to be played at that tempo.

ANDERS, William Alison (1933–), US astronaut and administrator. He was a member of the Apollo 8 crew which made the first manned moon orbit in 1968. In 1975 he became chairman of the newly-formed NUCLEAR REGULATORY COMMISSION.

ANDERS, Wladislaw (1892–1970), Polish general whose Polish army-in-exile helped the Allies win Italy in WWII. In England after 1945 he was a leader of exiled anticommunist Poles.

ANDERSEN, Hans Christian (1805–1875), Danish writer, best remembered for his 168 fairy tales. Based on folklore and observation of people and events in Andersen's life, they have a deceptively simple, slyly humorous style and often carry a moral message for adults as well as children.

ANDERSON, seat of Madison Co., Ind. and site of prehistoric mounds. Its products include automobile equipment. Pop 70 787.

ANDERSON, city in NW S.C., seat of Anderson Co., an industrial center set in and serving a farming region. Pop 27 556.

ANDERSON, Carl David (1905–), US physicist who shared the 1936 Nobel Prize for Physics for his discovery of the positron (1932). Later he was codiscoverer of the first meson (see SUBATOMIC PARTICLES).

ANDERSON, Elizabeth Garrett (1836–1917), one of the first Englishwomen to become a doctor (1865). She helped establish the place of women in the professions and founded a women's hospital and a medical school for women.

ANDERSON, Dame Judith (1898–), Australian-born actress who worked in the US. She is best known for her tragic roles in the plays of Eugene O'NEILL and Shakespeare and in Robinson JEFFERS' version of *Medea* (1947).

ANDERSON, Marian (1902–), US Negro contralto. Overcoming the handicaps of poverty and discrimination, she became an international opera star in the 1930s, and in 1955 was the first Negro to sing a leading role at the Metropolitan Opera, New York.

ANDERSON, Maxwell (1888–1959), US playwright. After early realistic plays, he concentrated on the revival of verse drama, achieving some success with such plays as *Elizabeth the Queen* (1930), *Winterset* (1935) and *High Tor* (1936).

ANDERSON, Robert (1805–1871), US army major, born in Ky. He defended Fort Sumter, Charleston, S.C. in 1861 against the Confederate attack which brought on the Civil War.

ANDERSON, Sherwood (1876–1941), US writer. His novels and short stories deal largely with men rebelling against contemporary industrial society. He is best remembered for *Winesburg, Ohio* (1919), stories of the frustrations of small-town Midwestern life.

ANDERSONVILLE, village in W Ga. where some 13 000 Union troops died of disease or wounds in a Confederate prison (1864–65). Its dreadful conditions provoked Union propaganda and reprisals. The site is now a federal park.

ANDES, South America's largest mountain range, 4 500mi long and averaging 200–250mi wide, running close to the entire W coast of the continent. Only the Himalayas exceed its average height of 12 500ft, and ACONCAGUA (22 835ft) is the highest peak in the W Hemisphere.

The Andes rose largely in the Cenozoic era (the last 70 million years), and volcanic eruptions and earthquakes suggest continuing uplift. There are three main sections. The S Andes form a single range (cordillera) dividing Chile and Argentina, with peaks ranging from 20 000ft in the N to 7 000ft in the S. The central Andes form two ranges flanking the high Bolivian plateau (the ALTIPLANO). The N Andes divide in Colombia and form four ranges ending in the Caribbean area. Many high Andean peaks are jagged and snowy, and glaciers fill some southern valleys.

ANDHRA PRADESH, state in SE India on the Bay of Bengal, formed in 1953 and enlarged in 1956 to include most of the Telugu-speaking population. Area: 106 272sq mi. Capital: Hyderabad. Products: rice, millet, wheat, peanuts, cotton, tobacco, coal and manganese.

ANDIZHAN, city in the USSR, capital of Andizhan Oblast (region) of the Uzbek SSR of Central Asia. It is a railroad center on the Syr Darya R in the fertile Fergana Valley. Cotton and machine-making factories serve neighboring cotton-growing and oil-producing areas. Pop 188 000.

ANDORRA, tiny semi-independent European state in the E Pyrenees between France and Spain. It is a land of mountains and mountain valleys, averaging over 6 000ft and ringed by peaks up to 10 000ft.

The Andorrans are mainly Catalan-speaking Roman Catholics. Most live in six municipalities, Andorra la Vella (pop 14 038) being the largest. Tourism is the economic mainstay. But the people also grow tobacco, rye, barley, grapes and potatoes; raise sheep and cattle, and exploit local lead and iron. Smuggling is a common pursuit. Since 1278 Andorra has been a co-principality, now under the bishop of Urgel in Spain and the French head of state.

Official Name: Andorra
Capital: La Vella
Area: 190sq mi
Population: 23 094
Languages: Catalan; French; Spanish
Religions: Roman Catholic
Monetary unit(s): French franc; Spanish peseta

ANDOVER, town in NE Mass., famous for the nation's oldest incorporated school (Phillips Academy, boys' secondary school, founded 1778) and New England's oldest incorporated girls' school (Abbot Academy, founded 1829). Pop 23 695.

ANDRADA E SILVA, José Bonifácio de (1763–1838), Brazilian geologist and statesman, father of Brazilian independence. He helped create an independent monarchy under PEDRO I, whom he served as prime minister (1822–23) until exiled for his democratic views. He was later tutor to Pedro II.

ANDRASSY, Count Gyula (1823–1890), first prime minister of Hungary within Austria–Hungary (1867) and Austro-Hungarian foreign minister (1871–79). As foreign minister and supporter of Hungarian independence he forged close ties with Germany to counter Russian and Slav ambitions.

ANDRÉ, John (1750–1780), British army officer, hanged as a spy by the Americans during the Revolutionary War. He secretly met Benedict ARNOLD behind American lines to arrange Arnold's surrender of West Point fort, but was caught in civilian clothes, with incriminating papers.

ANDREA DEL SARTO (1486–1530), leading 16th-century Florentine painter, influenced by Michelangelo and Dürer and renowned for delicately-colored church frescoes. He rivalled Raphael's classicism but foreshadowed MANNERISM through his pupils PONTORMO, ROSSO and VASARI.

ANDRÉE, Salomon August (1854–1897), Swedish Arctic explorer and balloonist. In 1897 he and two others tried to reach the N Pole from Spitsbergen by balloon, but were forced down after only 300mi. Their bodies were found in 1930.

ANDREW, Saint (1st century AD), one of Christ's 12 Apostles, formerly a fisherman and disciple of John the Baptist. He reputedly preached in what is now Russia and was martyred in Patras, Greece, on an X-shaped ("St. Andrew's") cross. He is the patron saint of Russia and of Scotland.

ANDREW II (1175–1235), king of Hungary (1205–35) who was forced by his nobles to issue the Golden Bull (1222), a national charter curbing royal power and extending the rights and privileges of the nobles and lesser landowners.

ANDREW, John Albion (1818–1867), US abolitionist and pioneer Republican politician. He helped found the Republican party in Mass. (1854), defended John BROWN (1859) and as governor of Mass. (1861–66) energetically recruited Union troops for the Civil War.

ANDREWES, Lancelot (1555–1626), English High Church bishop who developed the liturgy and molded ANGLICANISM by his copious writings. A royal chaplain, he helped produce the King James version of the Bible.

ANDREWS, Charles McLean (1863–1943), US historian. He stressed colonial America's dependence upon Britain in works like *The Colonial Period of American History* (1934–38), the first volume of which won him a Pulitzer Prize.

ANDREWS, Roy Chapman (1884–1960), US naturalist, explorer and author. From 1906 he worked for the AMERICAN MUSEUM OF NATURAL HISTORY (later becoming its director, 1935–41) and made important expeditions to Alaska, the Far East and Central Asia. Among many important discoveries he made in Mongolia were the first known fossil dinosaur eggs.

ANDREWS AIR FORCE BASE, Md., serves Washington, D.C., and is the USAF Systems Command headquarters.

ANDREYEV, Leonid Nikolayevich (1871–1919), Russian novelist, short-story writer and playwright. Ranging from earlier realistic social protest to later symbolism, his work (e.g., *The Seven That Were Hanged*, 1908) reflects a basic pessimism and preoccupation with death.

ANDRIA, city in the province of Bari, SE Italy. An agricultural center with Roman remains and a medieval cathedral. A vast castle built by Frederick II (1240) lies 9mi S. Pop 79 980.

ANDRIĆ, Ivo (1892–1975), Yugoslav novelist who won the Nobel Prize for Literature in 1961, largely for the epic quality of *The Bridge on the Drina*. His themes are man's insecurity and isolation in face of change and death.

ANDROCLES, fugitive Roman slave whose story was told in the 1st century AD. He won a lion's friendship by removing a thorn from its paw, and the lion later recognized him in the arena and spared him. George Bernard SHAW used the tale in his comedy *Androcles and the Lion*.

ANDROECIUM. See FLOWER.

ANDROGENS, STEROID HORMONES which produce secondary male characteristics such as facial and body hair and a deep voice. They also develop the male reproductive organs. The main androgen is TESTOSTERONE, produced in the TESTES; others are produced in small quantities in the cortex of the ADRENAL GLANDS. Small amounts occur in women in addition to the ESTROGENS and may produce some male characteristics. (See also ENDOCRINE GLANDS; PUBERTY.)

ANDROMACHE, in Greek legend, Hector's noble wife, whose relatives all died in the Trojan War. HOMER's *Iliad* movingly records her farewell to Hector and her mourning for his death. She later married Achilles' son Neoptolemus and subsequently Hector's brother Helenus.

ANDROMEDA, in Greek mythology, an Ethiopian princess chained to a rock as sacrifice to a sea monster, to appease the angry sea god, POSEIDON. Perseus killed the monster and married her.

ANDROMEDA, constellation in the N Hemisphere. The Great Andromeda Nebula (M31), seen near the DOUBLE STAR Gamma Andromedae, is the most distant object visible to the naked eye in N skies. It is the nearest external GALAXY to our own, like it a spiral but larger (49kpc across), and about 600kpc from earth.

ANDROMEDA, genus of low evergreen shrubs with small drooping pink flowers. It includes bog rosemary, *A. glaucophylla*. Family: Ericaceae.

ANDROS, largest island (1 600sq mi) of the BAHAMAS.

ANDROS, mountainous Greek island in the Aegean Cyclades group, producing wine, fruit and tobacco.

ANDROS, Sir Edmund (1637–1714), British governor of the Dominion of New England, 1686–89. His attempt to curb the colonists' rights caused a rebellion. Imprisoned and sent to England for trial, he was acquitted and became governor of Virginia 1692–98 and Maryland 1693–94.

ANDROSCOGGIN, river rising in NE N.H. and flowing 157mi S and SE to the Kennebec R in S Maine. It provides power and water for papermaking and other industries.

ANECHOIC CHAMBER. See ACOUSTICS.

ANEMIA, condition in which the amount of HEMOGLOBIN in the BLOOD is abnormally low, thus reducing the blood's oxygen-carrying capacity. Anemic people may feel weak, tired, faint and breathless, have a rapid pulse and appear pale.

Of the many types of anemia, five groups can be described. In **iron-deficiency anemia**, the red blood cells are smaller and paler than normal. Usual causes include inadequate diet (especially in PREGNANCY), failure of iron absorption, and chronic blood loss (as from heavy MENSTRUATION HEMORRHAGE or disease of the GASTROINTESTINAL TRACT). Iron replacement is essential and in severe cases blood transfusion may be needed. In **megaloblastic anemia**, the red cells are larger than normal. This may be due to nutritional lack of VITAMIN B_{12} or folate, but the most important cause is **pernicious anemia**. B_{12} is needed for red-cell formation and patients with pernicious anemia cannot absorb B_{12} because they lack a factor in the stomach essential for absorbtion. Regular B_{12} injections are needed for life. In **aplastic anemia**, inadequate numbers of red cells are produced by the bone MARROW owing to damage by certain poisons, drugs or irradiation. Treatment includes transfusions and androgens. In **hemolytic anemia**, the normal life span of red cells is reduced, either because of ANTIBODY reactions or because they are abnormally fragile. A form of the latter is **sickle-cell anemia**, a hereditary disease, common among NEGROIDS in which abnormal hemoglobin is made. Finally, many chronic diseases including RHEUMATOID ARTHRITIS, chronic infection and UREMIA suppress red-cell formation and thus cause anemia.

ANEMOMETER, any instrument for measuring wind speed. The rotation type, which estimates wind speed from the rotation of cups mounted on a vertical shaft, is the most common of mechanical anemometers. The pressure-tube instrument utilizes the PITOT-TUBE effect, while the sonic or acoustic anemometer depends on the velocity of sound in the wind. For laboratory work a hot-wire instrument is used: here air flow is estimated from the change in RESISTANCE it causes by cooling an electrically heated wire.

ANEMONE, genus of mainly N temperate perennial herbs of the buttercup family (Ranunculaceae). Up to 3ft high, anemones have deeply cut, whorled leaves and white, pink, red, blue or, rarely, yellow flowers.

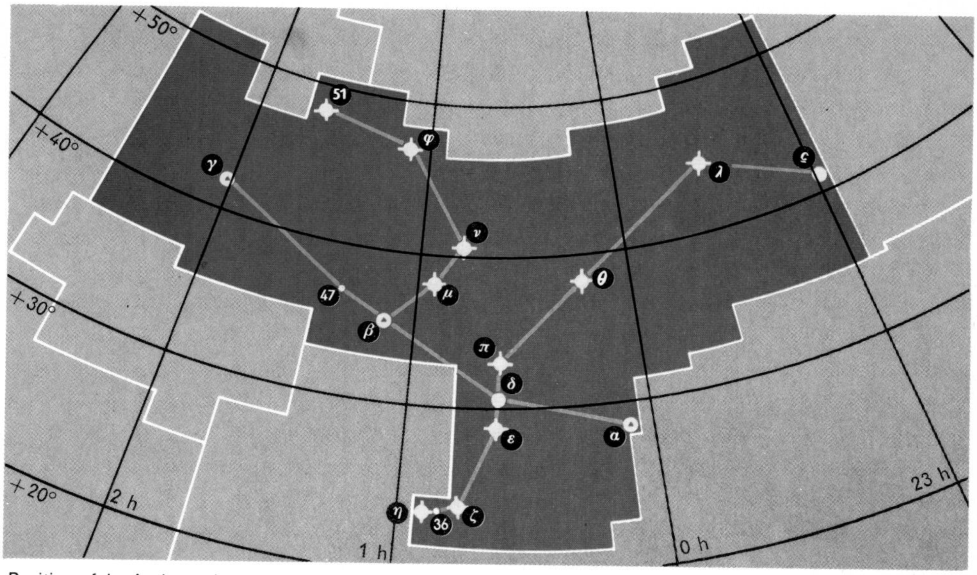

Position of the Andromeda constellation in the Northern Hemisphere. The numbers and the letters of the Greek alphabet refer to the names of the individual stars, according to the international standard. The Great Andromeda Nebula has a nucleus of bright red stars of the type called Population II, while the spiral arms consist of blue stars (Population I) and clouds of gas and dust.

Many are cultivated, but some, such as the wood anemone and PASQUE FLOWER, grow wild.

ANESTHESIA, or absence of sensation, may be of three types: general, local or pathological. **General anesthesia** is a reversible state of drug-induced unconsciousness with muscle relaxation and suppression of REFLEXES; this facilitates many surgical procedures and avoids distress. An anesthesiologist attends to ensure stable anesthesia and to protect vital functions. While ETHANOL and NARCOTICS have been used for their anesthetic properties for centuries, modern anesthesia dates from the use of diethyl ETHER by William MORTON in 1846, and of CHLOROFORM by Sir James SIMPSON in 1847. Nowadays injections of short-acting BARBITURATES, such as SODIUM PENTOTHAL, are frequently used to induce anesthesia rapidly; inhaled agents, including halothane, ether, nitrous oxide, trichlorethylene and cyclopropane, are used for induction and maintenance. **Local** and **regional anesthesia** are the reversible blocking of pain impulses by chemical action of COCAINE derivatives (e.g., PROCAINE, lignocaine). Nerve trunks are blocked for minor SURGERY and DENTISTRY, and more widespread anesthesia may be achieved by blocking spinal nerve roots, useful in obstetrics and patients unfit for general anesthesia. **Pathological anesthesia** describes loss of sensation following trauma or disease.

ANEURYSM, a pathological enlargement of, or defect in, a blood vessel. These may occur in the HEART after CORONARY THROMBOSIS, or in the AORTA and ARTERIES due to ARTERIOSCLEROSIS, high blood pressure, congenital defect, trauma or infection (specifically syphilis). They may rupture, causing HEMORRHAGE, which in the heart or aorta is rapidly fatal. Again, their enlargement may cause pain, swelling or pressure on nearby organs; these complications are most serious in the arteries of the BRAIN. SURGERY for aneurysm includes tying off and removal; larger vessels may be repaired by synthetic grafts.

ANFINSEN, Christian Boehmer (1916–), US

Anemia can only be correctly diagnosed on the basis of detailed laboratory blood tests. After the blood has been taken from a vein in the arm: 1. the blood is transferred to a sterile tube. 2. The liquid part of the blood is separated from the cells by a centrifuge. 3. The cells can now be analysed for hemoglobin content. Anemia caused by iron deficiency can be diagnosed by this method.

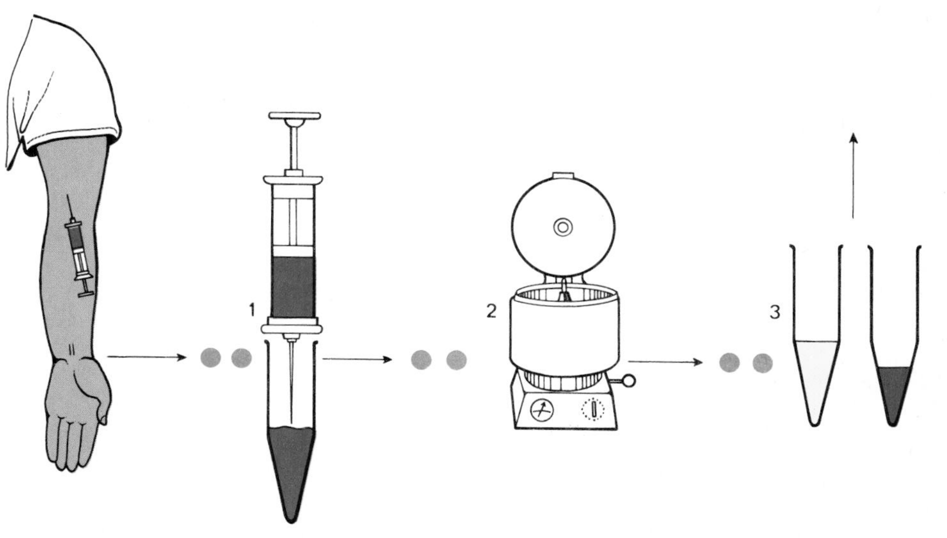

biochemist, corecipient of the 1972 Nobel Prize for Chemistry for research into the structure of the ENZYME ribonuclease (see also NUCLEIC ACIDS).

ANGARA RIVER, a major navigable river of the USSR, in Siberia. From Lake Baikal it flows 1 150mi (N then W to the Yenisei R), draining 400 000sq mi and, at Bratsk, driving one of the world's largest hydroelectric power plants. In its middle reaches navigation is hindered by many rapids.

ANGARSK, rapidly-growing industrial city of the USSR, on the Angara R in central Siberia. It has major petroleum and electro-metallurgical industries, and produces mining equipment, chemicals, cement and furniture. Pop 204 000.

ANGEL, supernatural messenger and servant of the deity. Angels figure in Christianity, Judaism, Islam and Zoroastrianism. In Christianity, angels traditionally serve and praise God, but guardian angels may protect the faithful against the devil (the fallen angel Lucifer). The hierarchy of angels was said to have nine orders: CHERUBIM, Seraphim, Thrones; Dominions, Virtues, Powers; Principalities, ARCHANGELS, Angels.

ANGEL FALLS, world's highest known waterfall (3 212ft), on the Churún R in SE Venezuela. US aviator Jimmy Angel discovered it in 1935.

ANGEL FISHES, name applied to the BUTTERFLY FISHES, the monkfish or angel shark, and the genus *Pterophyllum*. MONKFISHES are of the family Squatinidae (Order: Pleurotremata). Their prominent pectoral fins (see FISHES) make them appear like a hybrid of SHARK and RAY. They have no anal fins, two dorsal fins, and their nostrils have two BARBELS that extend to form a mouth. The largest, *Squatina squatina*, can be as long as 2.5m (8ft). The genus PTEROPHYLLUM are freshwater fishes with deep bodies and slender, filamentous pelvic rays. The flanks are light brown, marked with four darker vertical bars which are of use in camouflage. There are three generally recognized species: *P. eimeki*, *P. altum* and *P. scalare*. (Family: CICHLIDAE.)

ANGELICA, genus of tall aromatic herbs of the family Umbelliferae. Native to the N Hemisphere, they have ridged stems, deeply dissected leaves and umbels (see INFLORESCENCE) of white or greenish flowers. Most important is *A. archangelica*, which yields an oil used in perfumes and to flavor liqueurs. Its shoots are used in making sweetmeats.

ANGELICO, Fra (c1400–1455), Italian painter and Dominican friar, a major figure in Renaissance art. His church frescoes and altarpieces, using religious figures, combined traditionally bright, clear colors with the new use of perspective settings. His Tuscan backgrounds are among the first great Renaissance landscapes.

ANGELL, Sir Norman (1874–1967), British economist and internationalist, awarded the Nobel Peace Prize in 1933. A journalist most of his life, he argued in his book *The Great Illusion* (1910) that war was futile and best prevented by the mutual economic interest of nations.

ANGELUS, Roman Catholic prayer in honor of the Incarnation, consisting of three verses, each followed by a response and an *Ave Maria*, accompanied by bells. It is recited thrice daily except during Easter. The name comes from the first prayer, which begins, "The Angel of the Lord declared unto Mary. . . ."

ANGERS, capital of the department of Maine-et-Loire in W France, a historic city on the Maine R, with a medieval cathedral and castle. It makes cables, textiles, shoes, electrical equipment and liqueurs. Pop 128 533.

ANGEVIN, name of two medieval royal dynasties originating in the Anjou region of W France. The earliest ruled in parts of France, Jerusalem, and in England after Henry II, son of Geoffrey of Anjou, became England's first Angevin (or Plantagenet) ruler in 1154. His descendants held power in England until 1485. The younger branch began in 1266 when Charles, brother of Louis IX of France, became king of Naples and Sicily. This dynasty ruled in Italy, Hungary and Poland until the end of the 15th century.

ANGINA PECTORIS, severe, short-lasting CHEST pain caused by inadequate blood supply to the myocardium (see HEART), often due to coronary artery disease such as ARTERIOSCLEROSIS. It is precipitated by exertion or other stresses which demand increased heart work. Pain may spread to nearby areas, often the arms; sweating and breathlessness may occur. It is rapidly relieved or prevented by sucking NITROGLYCERIN tablets or inhaling AMYL nitrite.

ANGIOSPERMS, or **flowering plants,** large and very important class of seed-bearing plants, characterized by having seeds that develop completely enclosed in the tissue of the parent plant, rather than unprotected as in the only other seed-bearing group, the GYMNOSPERMS. Containing about 250 000 species distributed throughout the world, and ranging in size from tiny herbs to huge trees, angiosperms are the dominant land flora of the present day. They have sophisticated mechanisms to ensure that pollination and fertilization take place and that the resulting seeds are readily dispersed and able to germinate. There are two subclasses: MONOCOTYLEDONS (with one leaf) and DICOTYLEDONS (with two).

ANGKOR, extensive ruins in NW Cambodia from the ancient KHMER EMPIRE, noted for the city Angkor Thom and the Angkor Wat temple complex. Covering 40sq mi and dating from the 9th–13th centuries, the remains were found in 1861. Angkor Thom with its temples and palace is intersected by a canal system and has a perimeter wall 8mi long. Angkor Wat is a massive complex of carved Hindu temples with a 2.5mi perimeter, and is the foremost example of Khmer art and architecture.

ANGLE, in plane GEOMETRY, the figure formed by the intersection of two straight lines. The point of intersection is known as the vertex.

Consider the two lines to be radii of a CIRCLE of unit radius. There is then a direct way of defining the magnitudes of angles in terms of the proportion of the circle's circumference cut off by their two sides: as the length of the circle's circumference is given by $2\pi r$, and $r=1$, the **radian** (rad) is defined as the magnitude of an angle whose two sides cut off $1/2\pi$ of the circumference. A **degree** (°) is defined as an angle whose two sides cut off 1/360 of the circumference.

An angle of $\pi/2$ rad (90°), whose sides cut off one quarter of the circumference, is a **right angle,** the two lines being said to be PERPENDICULAR. Should the two sides cut off one half of the circumference (πrad or 180°), the angle is a straight angle or straight line. Angles less than $\pi/2$ rad are termed acute; those greater than $\pi/2$ but less than πrad, obtuse; and those greater than πrad but less than 2πrad, reflex. Pairs of angles that add up to $\pi/2$ rad are termed complementary; those that add up to πrad, supplementary. Further properties of angles lie in the province of TRIGONOMETRY.

In SPHERICAL GEOMETRY a **spherical angle** is that formed by intersecting arcs of two great circles: its magnitude is equal to that of the angle between the PLANES (see DIHEDRAL ANGLE) of the great circles.

A **solid angle** is formed by a conical surface (see CONE). Considering its vertex to lie at the center of a SPHERE, then a measure of its magnitude may be obtained from the ratio between the area (L^2) of the surface of the sphere cut off by the angle, and the square (R^2) of the sphere's radius. Solid angles are measured in steradians (sr), an angle of one steradian subtending an area of R^2 at distance R.

ANGLERFISHES, the order Lophiiformes, a highly specialized group of marine FISHES found in all oceans and at all depths. There are three suborders: Lophioidea, Antennarioidea and Ceratioidea. All three are typified by a long dorsal fin ending in a lure (luminescent in Ceratioidea) with which prey are attracted toward the anglerfish's mouth.

ANGLES, Germanic tribe from which England derives its name. Coming from the Schleswig-Holstein area of N Germany, the Angles, with the SAXONS and JUTES, invaded England from the 5th century and founded kingdoms including East Anglia, Mercia and Northumbria. (See also ANGLO-SAXONS.)

ANGLESEY, island separated from NW Wales by the Menai Strait, linked by causeway to Holyhead Island. The chief occupations are farming and stock raising. Pop 59 705.

ANGLICANISM, the body of doctrines originally developed by the CHURCH OF ENGLAND and now broadly followed by the other members of the Anglican Communion. These include the Anglican Church of Canada, the EPISCOPAL CHURCH in the US, and other episcopal churches in former British colonies and elsewhere.

ANGLO-SAXON CHRONICLE, historical record of England from early Christian times until after the Norman Conquest. Various versions were made between 890 and 1155, based on monastic annals, genealogies and episcopal records. They constitute the oldest W European history written in the vernacular, and the chief source for Anglo-Saxon history.

ANGLO-SAXONS, collective name for the Germanic peoples who dominated England from the 5th to the 11th centuries. They originated as tribes of ANGLES, SAXONS and JUTES who invaded England after Roman rule collapsed, creating kingdoms that eventually united to form the English nation. In modern usage, Anglo-Saxons are the English or their emigrant descendants in other parts of the world.

ANGOLA, independent state in SW Africa, formerly a Portuguese overseas province. Angola is bounded on the N and NE by Zaire; on the SE by Zambia; on the S by SW Africa; and on the W by the Atlantic Ocean. Beyond the coastal plain is a dominant central plateau 5 000ft high. Main rivers include the Congo, Zambezi, Cuanza and Cunene. The warm wet N has tropical rain forest; the cooler, seasonally dry plateau supports savanna. There is abundant savanna wildlife.

Over 90% of Angolans are African (mostly Bantu with a few Bushmen). Bantu tongues and animist beliefs predominate among the largely illiterate majority. The capital, Luanda (pop 224 540), and most towns lie in the W, but population is scattered and depends mainly on farming (coffee, sugarcane, corn, cotton, sisal) and mining (diamonds, iron ore, oil). Industry (alcohol, cotton goods, fisheries) is limited.

The Bantu Bakongo kingdom held NW Angola when the Portuguese navigator Diogo CAM arrived in 1482. Portugal exerted control over Angola from 1576 onwards, and the export of Negro slaves to Brazil caused severe depopulation. Portuguese colonization and economic development grew in the early 20th century. Nationalist guerrillas were active from 1961 and war among the three major groups broke out upon independence (1975). With support from Cuba and the USSR, the left-wing group MPLA soon gained virtual control of the country.

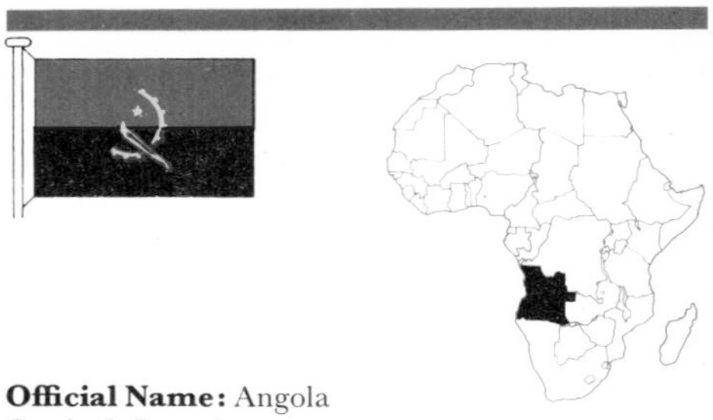

Official Name: Angola
Capital: Luanda
Area: 481 351sq mi
Population: c5 673 046
Languages: Bantu; Portuguese
Religions: Roman Catholic; Protestant; animist
Monetary unit(s): 1 Angolan escudo = 100 centavos

ANGORA, term used for long-haired varieties of goats, cats and rabbits. Originally it referred to goats bred in the Angora (now Ankara) region of Turkey. The silky white hair of Angora goats has long been used for fine yarns and fabrics, especially for making mohair cloth.

ANGOSTURA BARK, the aromatic bitter bark of two South American trees, *Galipea officinalis* and *Cusparia febrifuga* (family: Rutaceae), used for the flavoring, angostura bitters. Named for Angostura (now Ciudad Bolivar), Venezuela, it was once used as a fever-reducing agent.

Angora cats are tough enough to take care of themselves in fights with other cats, although they tend to be slower and heavier.

ANGOULÊME, historic city in SW France, capital of Charente department. It produces paper, textiles, brandy and ceramics. Historic buildings include a Romanesque cathedral. Pop 47 822.

ANGRY YOUNG MEN, post-WWII generation of British writers whose works reflected a mood scathingly critical of established social values, as in John OSBORNE's play *Look Back in Anger* (1956). Most had lower middle-class or working-class backgrounds and leftist political sympathies. They included Kingsley AMIS, Arnold WESKER, John Braine, John Wain, Alan Sillitoe and Doris Lessing.

ANGST, German word meaning dread or anxiety. It implies modern man's unease, frustration and sense of insignificance in face of an inexplicable universe, and reflects a loss of faith in God and of man's belief in himself. It appears in the literature of EXISTENTIALISM and in works by Franz KAFKA, T. S. ELIOT, W. H. AUDEN and others.

ÅNGSTRÖM, Anders Jonas (1814–1874), Swedish physicist who was one of the founders of SPECTROSCOPY and was the first to identify hydrogen in the solar spectrum (1862). The ANGSTROM UNIT is named in his honor.

ANGSTROM UNIT (Å), the CGS UNIT used to express optical wavelengths (see LIGHT), and equal to 0.1nm.

ANGUID LIZARDS (Anguidae), a family of small LIZARDS comprising seven genera with about 75 species. They include the North and Central American ALLIGATOR LIZARDS (*Gerrhonotus*) and the Eurasian and North African **blindworm** or **slowworm** (*Anguis fragilis*), a limbless, smooth-scaled lizard, harmless to man and able to shed its tail when in danger. Order: Squamata.

ANGUILLA, small self-governing island in the West Indies (area 35sq mi), 150mi E of Puerto Rico. Its mainly Negro people fish and produce salt, boats and livestock. Britain supervises external affairs. Anguilla's union with St. Christopher-Nevis was dissolved in 1971. Pop 5 000.

ANGWANTIBO (*Arctocebus calabarensis*), small W African PRIMATE related to the LORISES and MONKEYS. Arboreal, golden brown with large, forward-directed eyes and a total length of some 300mm (12in), it is rarely seen and little is known about its behavior.

ANHALT-DESSAU, Leopold I, Prince of (1676–1747), Prussian field marshal whose reorganization of the Prussian army laid the foundations for the military triumphs of FREDERICK II. He streamlined infantry training, enforced rigid discipline and introduced a system of fire control.

ANHINGA (*Anhinga anhinga*), sole species of the family Anhingidae, order Pelecaniformes; aquatic birds akin to the CORMORANTS. They swim with only head and neck above water, spearing fish with their long bills. They are found in tropical and warm temperate regions (but not in Europe). They are also known as darters or snakebirds.

ANHYDRIDES, compounds derived from others by reversible DEHYDRATION. Most inorganic anhydrides are soluble OXIDES which dissolve in water to give ALKALIS or OXYACIDS. (See also ACID ANHYDRIDES.)

ANHYDRITE, mineral form of anhydrous calcium sulfate (see CALCIUM), occurring worldwide as white-gray masses of orthorhombic CRYSTALS. Thick beds of anhydrite are formed where old seawater lagoons have evaporated. It is used in producing sulfuric acid and ammonium sulfate and as a drying agent.

ANIAKCHAK, dormant volcano on the Alaskan Peninsula which has one of the world's largest craters (6.75mi in diameter). Discovered in the Aleutian range in 1922, it last erupted in 1931.

ANILINE, or aminobenzene ($C_6H_5NH_2$), a primary aromatic AMINE. It is a toxic, oily, colorless liquid, readily oxidized to various products, and a weak BASE. It is made by the reduction of nitrobenzene or by reaction of chlorobenzene with AMMONIA. Aniline is used in making synthetic dyes, rubber, pharmaceuticals, explosives and resins. (See also AROMATIC COMPOUNDS; DIAZONIUM COMPOUNDS.)

ANIMA AND ANIMUS, terms used by JUNG to denote, respectively, the unconscious female part of the male personality and the unconscious male part of the female personality. (See also PERSONA.)

ANIMAL, any organism that is classified in the ANIMAL KINGDOM. There is no single criterion that defines an animal, and it is not possible to distinguish all animals from all plants by simply listing characters found in one group and not the other. This is because animals and plants have evolved from a common ancestor, and organisms that have changed little since the separation of these two groups display intermediate characteristics. Apart from such intermediate forms, the vast majority of animals are able to respond to stimulation by rapid, controlled movement; they are composed of cells contained within a membrane; and they are unable to manufacture foodstuffs from inorganic chemicals such as are found in soil and water.

Animals are unable to manufacture foodstuffs because they do not possess a chemical called CHLOROPHYLL which is found in almost all plants. For this reason, animals are ultimately dependent on plants for their food.

The ability to move in response to external stimulae has led to the evolution of increasingly refined sense organs with which to monitor the surrounding environment, of muscles that make movement possible, and a nervous system that links them together. The development of a co-ordinating center, the brain, makes possible a greater variety of responses in "higher" animals. (See also ANIMAL BEHAVIOR; ECOLOGY; EVOLUTION; FOSSIL; TAXONOMY; ZOOLOGY.)

ANIMAL BEHAVIOR, the responses of animals to internal and external stimuli. Study of these responses can enable advances to be made in our understanding of human PSYCHOLOGY and behavior. Animal responses may be learned by the animal during its lifetime or may be instinctive or inherited (see HEREDITY; INSTINCT).

Even the simplest animals are capable of learning—to associate a particular stimulus with pain or pleasure, to negotiate mazes, etc. Moreover, there are critical periods in an animal's life when it is capable of learning a great deal in a very short time. Thus baby geese hatched in the absence of the mother will follow the first moving object they see, another animal or a human being. If, later, they must choose between this other animal and the mother, they prefer the other animal. This rapid early learning is called **imprinting.**

Among even the most intelligent animals much behavior is instinctive: the shape of a baby's head, for example, evokes an instinctive parental response in man. The complicated dance of the BEES, by which they inform the hive of the whereabouts of food, each species of bee having its own dance "dialect," is an example of more complex instinctive behavior. Instinctive ritual, too, plays its part (see APPEASEMENT BEHAVIOR; MATING RITUALS). Instinct can determine the behavior of a single animal, or of a whole animal society (see HIBERNATION; MIGRATION). (See also AGGRESSION; ETHOLOGY; TERRITORIALITY.)

ANIMAL HUSBANDRY, branch of agriculture dealing with the care and breeding of livestock, often making profitable use of land unsuitable for arable farming. Though scientific husbandry dates from only the 18th century, many special skills have been evolved to deal with various animals. Man, however, may have first domesticated an animal—the sheep—about 8 000 years ago. (See also AGRICULTURE.)

ANIMAL KINGDOM, Animalia, one of the two kingdoms into which all living organisms are classified (see PLANT KINGDOM). In practice, the borderline between the two is not clearly defined (see ANIMAL; PLANT) but for most general purposes the difference is clear. More than a million distinct species of animals have been identified, and these are divided into various groups, groups within groups, etc. (see TAXONOMY).

Animalia has two main subkingdoms: the PROTOZOA, or unicellular animals such as AMOEBAS; and the METAZOA, or multicellular organisms. Sometimes there is considered to be a third subkingdom, the Parazoa, loosely organized multicellular organisms, the SPONGES, but these are more generally considered to be a part of the Metazoa. Each subkingdom is divided into phyla (singular, phylum): there is only one phylum, Protozoa, in the subkingdom Protozoa; but around 25 (depending upon one's system of classification) in the Metazoa. Within these phyla, animals are further divided into classes, based primarily on their bodily structure but also (though the two are usually equivalent) on their evolutionary history (see EVOLUTION); classes may be grouped into subphyla. Thus the phylum CHORDATA has, amongst others, the subphylum VERTEBRATA which includes classes such as AMPHIBIA, Pisces (FISHES), Reptilia (REPTILES), Aves (BIRDS) and Mammalia (MAMMALS). In the same way, classes contain (in descending order of magnitude) orders, families, genera, species and subspecies.

MAN is a vertebrate of the order PRIMATES, suborder Anthropoidea (see ANTHROPOID APES), family Hominidae, genus *Homo* and species *sapiens* (see also PREHISTORIC MAN).

ANIMATION, cinematographic technique creating the illusion of movement by projecting a series of drawings or photographs showing successive views of an action. The first animated cartoons were made by Émile Cohl in France in 1907. Walt DISNEY pioneered sound and color in films such as the *Mickey Mouse* cartoons and the full-length *Fantasia,* which became world famous. In modern cartoon making, drawings on transparent celluloid ("cells") are superimposed to form each picture and only cells showing motion need changing from frame to frame.

ANIMISM, a term first used by E. B. TYLOR to designate a general belief in spiritual beings, which belief he held to be the origin of all religions. A common corruption of Tylor's sense is to refer to a belief that all natural objects possess spirits as animism. PIAGET has proposed that the growing child characteristically passes through an animistic phase.

ANIMUS. See ANIMA AND ANIMUS.

ANION, a negatively-charged ION which moves to the ANODE in ELECTROLYSIS; often a BASE.

ANIS, three species (genus *Crotophaga*) of the CUCKOO or Cuculidae family, found in warmer areas of the Americas. Insectivorous, they are sociable, usually building communal nests and grouping within territories (see TERRITORIALITY). They are around 400mm (16in) long, with mainly black plumage.

ANISE, an E Mediterranean herb (*Pimpinella anisum*) widely cultivated for its licorice-flavored seedlike fruits called anise seed. The fruits yield spice and oil used to flavor foods, candy and liqueurs such as OUZO. Family: Umbelliferae.

ANJOU, former province of W France, now a wine-growing area in the department of Maine-et-Loire. Its name derives from the Celtic Andes tribe, which occupied the area before the Romans. Anjou was a county in the 9th century, later a powerful feudal state, and a duchy in 1360; it became part of the French monarchy in 1480.

ANJOU, town in S Quebec, Canada. It lies 5mi N of Montreal. Pop 33 842.

ANKARA, capital of Turkey and of Ankara province in Asia Minor. It produces textiles, cement, flour and beer, and trades in local Angora wool and grain. Landmarks: the university, ATATURK's mausoleum and the old fortress. Ankara (formerly Ancyra or Angora) may be pre-Hittite in origin. It replaced ISTANBUL as Turkey's capital in 1923. Pop 1 208 791.

SOME OF THE FORMS OF ANIMAL LIFE

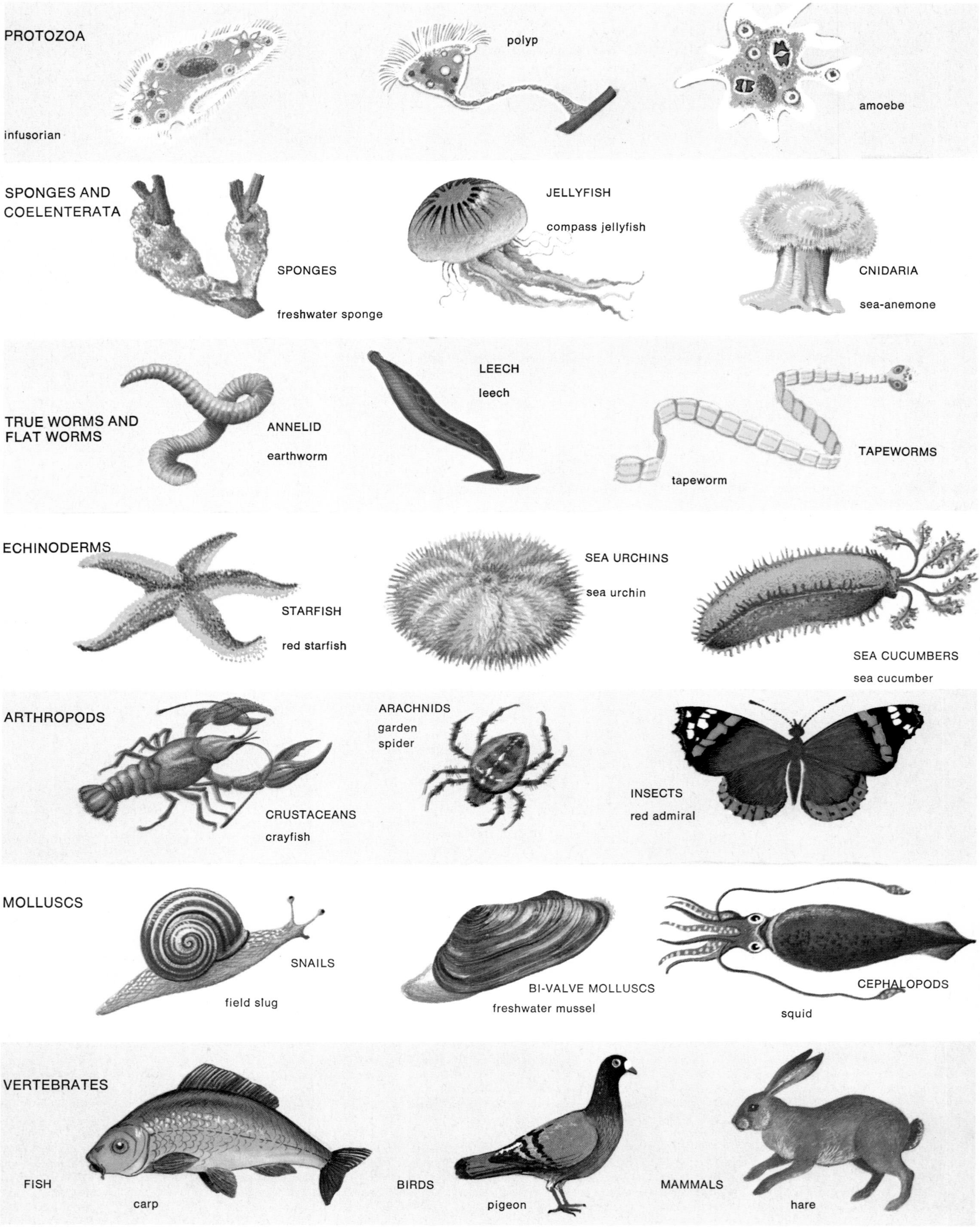
PROTOZOA
infusorian
polyp
amoebe
SPONGES AND COELENTERATA
SPONGES
freshwater sponge
JELLYFISH
compass jellyfish
CNIDARIA
sea-anemone
TRUE WORMS AND FLAT WORMS
ANNELID
earthworm
LEECH
leech
TAPEWORMS
tapeworm
ECHINODERMS
STARFISH
red starfish
SEA URCHINS
sea urchin
SEA CUCUMBERS
sea cucumber
ARTHROPODS
CRUSTACEANS
crayfish
ARACHNIDS
garden spider
INSECTS
red admiral
MOLLUSCS
SNAILS
field slug
BI-VALVE MOLLUSCS
freshwater mussel
CEPHALOPODS
squid
VERTEBRATES
FISH
carp
BIRDS
pigeon
MAMMALS
hare

ANKH, ancient Egyptian hieroglyphic symbol of life comprising a cross with a loop instead of a vertical upper arm. It was adopted by Coptic Christians, who used it on their monuments.

ANKYLOSIS, fusion or stiffness of a JOINT, restricting movement. It may be caused by injury, SURGERY, inflammatory ARTHRITIS and TUBERCULOSIS.

ANN, Cape, E peninsula of Essex Co., Mass.; 30mi N of Boston. It is noted for old fishing villages, resorts and artists' colonies. Gloucester and Rockport are its main towns.

ANNA, Jewish prophetess; daughter of Phanuel of the tribe of Asher. Widowed at an early age, she then served in the Temple by continual prayer and fasting. At the age of 84 she witnessed the presentation of JESUS CHRIST.

ANNABA (formerly Bone), seaport in NE Algeria. It was originally a 12th-century BC Phoenician port, and later the port of Roman Hippo Regius. Industries: iron and steel, chemicals and transport equipment. Exports: mineral grain and wine. Pop 150161.

ANNA COMNENA (1083-d. after c1148), Byzantine princess and historian. Her *Alexiad* dealt mainly with the life of her father, Emperor ALEXIUS I COMNENUS, and gave a Byzantine viewpoint of the confrontation of East and West during the First Crusade.

ANNA IVANOVNA (1693–1740), empress of Russia from 1730, who stopped the decline of royal power. Elected "puppet" empress by the nobles' supreme privy council, she overthrew it and, with German advisers, waged costly wars against the Poles and Turks, and opened Russia's way to Central Asia.

ANNAM, ancient SE Asian Kingdom (now the republic of VIETNAM). Under Chinese domination from the 2nd century BC, Annam first became independent in 1428. It expanded S, was split in two in the 16th century, but was reunited with French help in 1802. By the later 1800s Annam was divided into French-dominated Tonkin, Annam and Cochin-China. From WWII to the division in 1954, the whole region, nominally ruled by Emperor Bao Dai, was known as Vietnam.

ANNAPOLIS, capital city of Md., seat of Anne Arundel Co. on the Severn R near Chesapeake Bay. A historic and beautiful city, it was settled in 1649 by Puritans from Va. and was given its present name in 1694. It was the site of the ANNAPOLIS CONVENTION of 1786. It has many historic buildings, including the statehouse (1772). It is the site of St. John's College (founded 1696) and the US Naval Academy (established 1845). There are a number of local industries, including seafood. Pop 150161.

ANNAPOLIS BASIN, sea inlet in W Nova Scotia. It is located in the Bay of Fundy, at the mouth of the Annapolis R.

ANNAPOLIS CONVENTION (1786), meeting which foreshadowed the US Constitutional Convention. It was held at ANNAPOLIS, Md., to discuss problems of interstate commerce. Alexander HAMILTON and James MADISON wanted its scope broadened to discuss revision of the ARTICLES OF CONFEDERATION. But only five of the 13 states were represented and thus a full-scale meeting was called for, which led to the Constitutional Convention at Philadelphia.

ANNAPOLIS ROYAL, seat of Annapolis Co. on the W Coast of Nova Scotia, Canada. It is one of North America's oldest settlements N of the Gulf of Mexico. The town originated nearby on Annapolis Basin in the French town of Port Royal (1605), moving to the present site in 1636. After nearly a century of fighting, the British finally captured it in 1710 and renamed it for Queen Anne. It is now a summer resort with national historic parks, and serves a farming area. Pop 723.

ANNAPURNA, Himalayan mountain in Nepal with the world's 11th-highest peak (26391ft). Its conquest in 1950 by Maurice Herzog's team was the first such success involving any great Himalayan peak.

ANN ARBOR, city in SE Mich. and seat of Washtenaw Co. It is on the Huron R in a farming region 36mi W of Detroit. The city has light precision industries and is the home of the U of Michigan. Pop 99797.

ANNAS (1st century AD), Jewish high priest who conducted the first interrogation of Jesus after his arrest. He held office jointly with his son-in-law Caiaphas and is named in Luke 3 and John 18.

ANNATES, medieval Church practice by which certain new church office-holders paid the first year's income to their bishop or to the pope. The practice was not uniform, aroused protest and gradually fell into disuse after the Middle Ages.

ANNE (1665–1714), queen of Great Britain and Ireland 1702–14 and last of the Stuart monarchs. A devout Anglican Protestant of Whig persuasion, she was influenced in political and religious affairs by the Duke of MARLBOROUGH and his wife, Sarah. Her reign was dominated by the War of the SPANISH SUCCESSION (1701–14). It also saw the ACT OF UNION (1707) uniting England and Scotland to form the kingdom of Great Britain.

ANNE OF AUSTRIA (1601–1666), queen consort (1615–43) and regent (1643–51) of France. She was the daughter of PHILIP III of Spain. Anne married LOUIS XIII and on his death effectively ruled for her young son LOUIS XIV through Cardinal MAZARIN, until the latter died and Louis assumed power.

ANNE OF BOHEMIA (1366–1394), queen consort of England (1382–94) as the wife of RICHARD II. She was the daughter of the Emperor CHARLES IV.

ANNE OF BRITTANY (1477–1514), queen consort of France's CHARLES VIII and his successor LOUIS XII, and duchess of Brittany (from 1488). Her daughter's marriage to the future FRANCIS I led to the union of France with Brittany, the last great feudal territory in the land.

ANNE OF CLEVES (1515–1557), queen consort and fourth wife of England's HENRY VIII. She was the daughter of a powerful German noble, and Henry married her (1540) on Thomas CROMWELL's advice to forge international bonds. But he disliked her and six months later had Parliament annul the marriage.

ANNE OF DENMARK (1574–1619), first queen of England and Scotland through marrying (1589) Scotland's James VI (later England's JAMES I). Daughter of Frederick II of Denmark and Norway.

ANNEALING, the slow heating and cooling of METALS and GLASS to remove stresses which have arisen in CASTING, cold working or machining (see MACHINE TOOLS). The annealed material is tougher and easier to process further. (See also METALLURGY.)

ANNECY, capital of the Haute-Savoie department in E France. A tourist center located on Lake Annecy in the Savoy Alps, it has textile, paper and precision industries. There are picturesque canals, arcaded streets and a historic castle and cathedral. Pop 54484.

ANNELIDA, an INVERTEBRATE phylum of around 9000 species, the segmented worms. It includes marine WORMS, EARTHWORMS and LEECHES.

ANNEXATION, assertion of sovereignty by a state over territory previously outside its rule. It may occur by force or by peaceful occupation, purchase, referendum, etc. An annexed territory becomes part of the annexing country and its peoples become citizens of that country.

ANNISTON, industrial city and seat of Calhoun Co. in NE Ala. It produces chemicals, pipes and textiles. Anniston originated in 1872 as a private company town. Pop 31533.

ANNOBON, tiny volcanic mountainous island (7sq mi) in the Gulf of Guinea. It is part of Equatorial Guinea and exports cocoa, coffee, copra and palm kernels. Pop 1436.

ANNUAL, plant that completes its life cycle in one growing season and then dies. Annuals propagate themselves only by seeds. They include such garden flowers and food plants as MARIGOLDS, CORNFLOWERS, CEREALS, PEAS and TOMATOES. Preventing seeding may convert an annual, e.g. MIGNONETTE, to a biennial or a perennial.

ANNUAL RINGS, concentric rings each representing one year's growth, visible in cross sections of woody plants. Each ring is usually composed of two growth layers, a broad, large-celled layer representing spring growth and a narrow, denser layer showing summer growth. The relative amounts of these layers are affected by the environment, a fact that forms the basis of the science of DENDROCHRONOLOGY.

The statehouse of Annapolis is the oldest still in general use in the United States. The Treaty of Paris ending the Revolutionary War was ratified here in 1784.

ANNUITY, an annual, monthly or other regular payment, usually for a predetermined period. Common examples include legacies payable as annuities instead of as lump sums, and pensions paid to individuals by insurance companies in return for previous contributions.

ANNULMENT, decree to the effect that a marriage was invalid when contracted. Grounds for annulment include fraud, force and close blood links between the parties. The Roman Catholic Church recognizes annulment but not DIVORCE.

ANNUNCIATION, in Christian belief, the archangel GABRIEL's announcement to the Virgin MARY that she would give birth to the Messiah. The Roman Catholic Church celebrates the annunciation as Lady Day, March 25. The annunciation appears in many Christian paintings.

ANNUNZIO, Gabriele D'. See D'ANNUNZIO, GABRIELE.

ANOA, a subgenus of the genus *Bubalus* (family BOVIDAE) containing two species of small, slender straight-horned BUFFALO of Sulawesi (Celebes).

ANODE, the positive ELECTRODE of a BATTERY, electric CELL or ELECTRON TUBE. ELECTRONS, which conventionally carry negative charge, enter the device at the CATHODE and leave by the anode.

ANODIZING, a process for building up a corrosion-resistant or decorative oxide layer on the surface of metal (usually ALUMINUM) objects. The item to be coated is made the ANODE in a CELL containing an aqueous solution of sulfuric, chromic or oxalic acid as electrolyte. The desired oxide coating is formed when a current is passed through the cell (see ELECTROLYSIS). Further treatment can render this oxide layer waterproof, electrically insulating or brightly colored.

ANOINTMENT, application of oil to an object or person, usually as part of a ritual of CONSECRATION, healing, BAPTISM, or ORDINATION. The Old Testament records anointing as a coronation rite. Roman Catholic priests perform anointing of the sick (see EXTREME UNCTION) as a sacrament. (See also MESSIAH.)

ANOKA, city in E Minn., seat of Anoka Co. It is on the Mississippi R NNW of Minneapolis and serves a farming area. Pop 13489.

ANOLE, any of about 175 species of LIZARDS of the genus *Anolis*, family Iguanidae. They can change color and hence are sometimes erroneously called CHAMELEONS. Found in Central America and the West Indies, they are 125–475mm (5–19in) long and good climbers. Territorial defence (see TERRITORIALITY) in

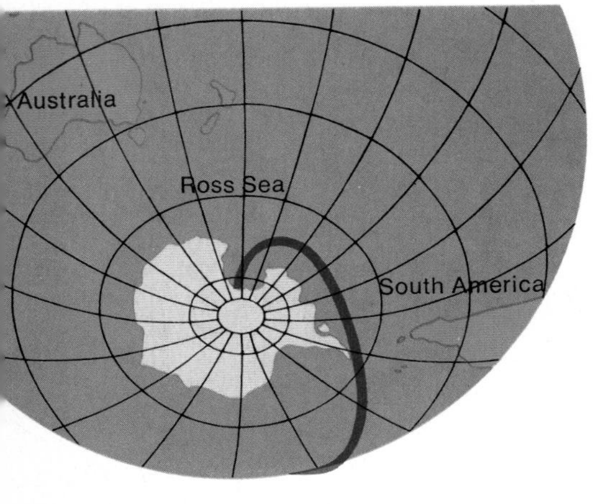

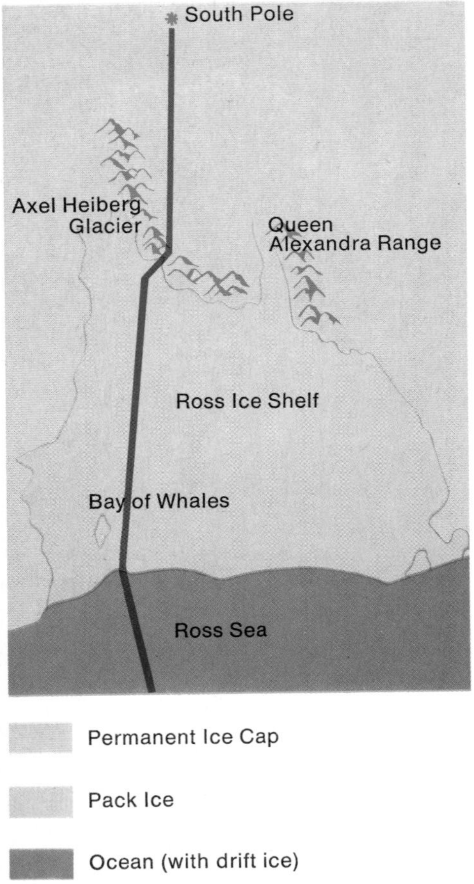

Antarctica was the last and most formidable continent to be explored by man. The red line on the map shows the successful route of Roald Amundsen who was the first to reach the South Pole. Amundsen's prize was hard won, as there had been expeditions since the 1890s. A Belgian party under De Gerlache de Gomery had discovered the Palmer Islands in 1898 and there had been a German expedition in the same year. Erich von Drygalski led a German South Pole attempt in 1901 and Nordenskjöld discovered Graham Land, Louis Philippe Land and King Oscar II Land in 1902 to 1903. Scott and Bruce were in the Antarctic in 1904 and in 1909 Shackleton reached the magnetic South Pole. Even after Amundsen's success, Scott arrived at the Pole just over a month later on January 18, 1912. Many expeditions have since been made to consolidate man's conquest of the continent.

the males is by expansion of a brightly colored throat sac.

ANOPHELES, a genus of MOSQUITOES. The only known MALARIA carrier, it also transmits ENCEPHALITIS and FILARIASIS.

ANOREXIA NERVOSA, pathological loss of appetite with secondary MALNUTRITION and HORMONE changes. It often affects young women with diet obsession and may reflect underlying psychiatric disease.

ANORTHITE, mineral occurring in igneous rocks, consisting of calcium aluminum silicate ($CaAl_2Si_2O_8$); vitreous white or gray crystals. It is one of the three end-members (pure compounds) of the FELDSPAR group.

ANOUILH, Jean (1910–), French playwright of polished, highly theatrical dramas which emphasize the dilemma of modern man who must compromise in order to achieve happiness. His works include *Antigone* (1944), *The Lark* (1953) and *Beckett* (1959).

ANOXIA, or hypoxia, lack of oxygen in BLOOD and body TISSUES. ASPHYXIA, LUNG disease, PARALYSIS of respiratory muscles and some forms of COMA prevent enough oxygen reaching the blood. Disease of HEART or circulation may also lead to tissue anoxia. Irreversible BRAIN damage follows prolonged anoxia.

ANSCHLUSS, the union of Austria with Germany, effected (in violation of the VERSAILLES TREATY) when the Nazi army entered Austria on March 12, 1938. It had a logical basis in a common Austro-German language and culture, but was forced by Adolf Hitler for Nazi aggrandizement.

ANSELM, Saint (1033–1109), archbishop of Canterbury (from 1093) who upheld Church authority and became the first scholastic philosopher. He endured repeated exile for challenging the right of English kings to influence Church affairs. Anselm saw reason as the servant of faith and probably invented the ontological "proof" of God's existence: that our idea of a perfect being implies the existence of such a being.

ANSERMET, Ernest (1883–1969), Swiss conductor who directed many STRAVINSKY ballet premieres. He founded the *Orchestre de la Suisse Romande* in 1918, conducting it until his death.

ANSGAR, Saint (801–865), Frankish missionary and apostle of Scandinavia. He became first archbishop of Hamburg in 832, and he worked to bring Christianity to Denmark and Sweden.

ANSHAN, industrial city in Liaoning province, NE China; a major center of iron and steel production. After extensive damage in WWII, the Chinese rebuilt and expanded its industries, which now include chemicals and cement. Pop 1 050 000.

ANSKY, Shloime (pen name of Solomon Samuel Rapaport, 1863–1920), Russian Yiddish author and playwright, best known for *The Dybbuk* (1916), an arresting tragedy of demonic possession. He was active in Russian Jewish socialism, but left Russia after the Revolution, and died in Poland.

ANSON, Adrian Constantine (known as "Cap" or "Pop" Anson; 1851–1922), great US baseball player. In 1939 he was elected to baseball's Hall of Fame as "the greatest hitter and greatest National League player-manager of the 19th century."

ANSON, George Anson, 1st Baron (1697–1762), English admiral, known as "father of the navy" for his Admiralty reforms—which contributed to British naval success in the SEVEN YEARS' WAR (1756–63). He was made a baron after his victory over the French off Cape Finisterre (1747).

ANSONIA, industrial city in SW Conn. near New Haven. It manufactures brass and copper goods, and sundry products. The area was settled in 1651. Pop 21 160.

ANTABUSE, or disulfiram (tetraethylthiuram disulfide), drug used in the treatment of ALCOHOLISM. Though nontoxic, it prevents the breakdown of ACETALDEHYDE, a highly toxic product of ETHANOL metabolism. Thus if alcohol is drunk after Antabuse has been taken, unpleasant symptoms occur, including palpitations and vomiting.

ANTACIDS, mild ALKALIS or BASES taken by mouth to neutralize excess STOMACH acidity for relief of DYSPEPSIA, including peptic ULCER and HEARTBURN. MILK OF MAGNESIA, aluminum hydroxide and sodium bicarbonate are common antacids.

ANTAEUS, in Greek mythology, giant son of POSEIDON and GAEA (Earth). A wrestler who killed all challengers, he renewed his strength by touching the earth. HERCULES slew him by raising him into the air and crushing him.

ANTAKYA. See ANTIOCH.

ANTALYA, ancient city in S Turkey, capital of Antalya province. Founded in the 2nd century BC, it was fortified in Roman times and used as a camp by the crusaders. A seaport and market center for fruit and grain, and a vacation center. Pop 71 833.

ANTARCTICA, a continental landmass of almost 6 000 000sq mi, covered by an icecap between 6000 and 14 000ft thick, except where mountain peaks, such as the 16 900ft Vinson Massif, break through the ice. The general shape of the continent is circular, indented by the arc-shaped Weddell Sea (S of the Atlantic Ocean) and the rectangular Ross Sea (S of New Zealand). The Antarctic Peninsula and other areas facing Tierra del Fuego are structurally similar to the adjacent South American coast while the rest of the continent resembles Australia and South Africa. Such facts provide evidence for the theory of CONTINENTAL DRIFT, also supported by recent fossil discoveries.

No warm ocean currents or winds reach the mainland, so the climate is intensely cold. All precipitation falls as snow, and in winter temperatures as low as −80°F and winds up to 100mph occur frequently. Few animals other than mites, microscopic rotifers and tiny wingless insects can survive inland; but the coasts and offshore waters support seabirds, including penguins, skuas, petrels and fulmars, and marine mammals (whales and seals). Vegetation is limited to lichen, mosses and fungi S of the 62nd parallel, though it is richer in the N offshore islands.

Captain James COOK was the first to attempt a scientific exploration of the Antarctic region (1773), but he believed that the whole area was a frozen ocean. The mainland was probably first sighted in 1820 by the American sea captain, Nathaniel PALMER. Expeditions to the area were led by the Englishmen Weddell (1823) and Biscoe (1832) and the American Charles WILKES (1838–40). James Clark ROSS discovered the sea later named for him, and charted much of the Antarctic coast between 1840 and 1842, taking his English team as far as latitude 78°9′S. About the turn of the century a series of Belgian, Norwegian, German, British and French expeditions gathered much valuable data, and on Dec. 14, 1911, the Norwegian Roald AMUNDSEN reached the S Pole, a month before Captain Robert SCOTT. Sir Ernest SHACKLETON had come within 100mi of the Pole in 1909, and later led other expeditions (1914 and 1921). Admiral Richard Evelyn BYRD was responsible for many Antarctic expeditions, including "Operation Highjump" (1946–47), the largest to date.

Since the International Geophysical Year (1957–58), international cooperation in Antarctica has increased. On Dec. 1, 1959, 12 nations signed the 30-year Antarctic Treaty, temporarily setting aside various territorial claims and reserving the area S of 60°S for peaceful scientific investigation. There are now over 30 permanent stations belonging to 10 countries on the continent itself, the largest being McMurdo Station on the Ross Ice Shelf, equipped with Antarctica's first nuclear reactor. Seven other stations on the nearby islands are used for meteorological research.

ANTARES, Alpha Scorpii, a DOUBLE STAR comprising a red supergiant 480 times larger than the sun and a blue star of unknown type 3 times larger than the sun (apparent magnitudes +1.23 and +5.5). It is 52pc from the earth.

ANTEATERS, four species of MAMMALS, family Myrmecophagidae, order EDENTATA, including the Giant Anteater (*Myrmecophaga tridactyla*) and the TAMANDUA, among others. They have long snouts, tubular mouths and long, sticky tongues with which they catch their food, chiefly ANTS and TERMITES. Other animals with the same adaptations and feeding-habits, and thus also sometimes called anteaters, are the AARDVARK, ECHIDNA, NUMBAT and PANGOLIN.

ANTELOPES, slenderly built, graceful, swift-

Antelopes include the graceful impala, a member of the hartebeest-gnu tribe.

moving hollow-horned RUMINANTS of the family BOVIDAE, order ARTIODACTYLA. The term generally includes the American PRONGHORN, *Antilocapra americana,* the sole living member of the Antilocapridae family. Common features include a hairy muzzle, narrow cheek-teeth and permanent, backward-pointing HORNS. Distribution is throughout Africa and Asia (except for the Pronghorn) in widely varying habitats. They range in size from the Royal Antelope, probably the smallest hoofed mammal, standing about 250mm (10in) high at the shoulders, to the Giant ELAND, which may be as tall as 2m (6.6ft) at the shoulders. Other examples include the ADDAX, GAZELLE, GNU, HARTEBEEST, IMPALA, ORYX, SAIGA and WATER BUCK.

ANTENNA, or aerial, a component in an electrical circuit which radiates or receives RADIO waves. In essence a transmitting antenna is a combination of conductors which converts AC electrical ENERGY into ELECTROMAGNETIC RADIATION. The simple **dipole** consists of two straight conductors aligned end on and energized at the small gap which separates them. The length of the dipole determines the frequency for which this configuration is most efficient. It can be made directional by adding electrically isolated director and reflector conductors in front and behind. Other configurations include the folded dipole, the highly-directional loop antenna and the dish type used for MICROWAVE links. Receiving antennas can consist merely of a short DIELECTRIC rod or a length of wire for low-frequency signals. For VHF and microwave signals, complex antenna configurations similar to those used for transmissions must be used. (See also RADIO TELESCOPE.)

ANTHEIL, George (1900–1959), noted US pianist and composer. He studied under Ernest BLOCH and brought popular motifs into serious music in works such as *Jazz Symphony* (1925). In 1936 he began writing music for motion pictures, and after WWII developed a neoclassical style influenced by STRAVINSKY.

ANTHEMIUS OF TRALLES (d. 543 AD), Byzantine mathematician and physicist, who with Isidorus of Miletus designed the great church of HAGIA SOPHIA built in Constantinople between 532 and 537 AD.

ANTHER. See FLOWER.

ANTHOCYANINS, pigments producing most red, purple and blue colors in higher plants. Their main function is to provide flowers and fruit with bright colors to attract insects and other animals for purposes of POLLINATION and seed dispersal.

ANTHOLOGY, a collection of literary compositions illustrating a theme, demonstrating a kind of writing, or displaying the works of a single author. Anthologies were common in classical times, and widespread in Arabian, Persian, Chinese and Indian literature. The first printed anthology of English verse was *Tottel's Miscellany* (1557). There are now many anthologies covering a broad range of literary periods and forms. Verse anthologies are widely used in American colleges and universities.

ANTHONY, Susan Brownell (1820–1906), major US leader of the fight for women's rights. She was a N.Y. schoolteacher who backed the temperance and abolitionist movements, but devoted herself to female suffrage after befriending Elizabeth Cady STANTON. She co-founded the National Woman Suffrage Association (1869), and served as president of the National American Woman Suffrage Association (1892–1900). She also helped to write *The History of Woman Suffrage.*

ANTHONY OF PADUA, Saint (1195–1231), Franciscan friar, theologian and preacher. He was born near Lisbon, but taught and preached in France and Italy. Canonized a year after his death, he is the patron saint of the poor, and his feast day is June 13. He is invoked to aid the discovery of lost objects.

ANTHOZOA, or Actinozoa, class of marine INVERTEBRATES including SEA ANEMONES and CORALS. They are radially-arranged sedentary POLYPS, often flowerlike and brightly colored. Anemones are single soft polyps; corals are polyp colonies with strong skeletons. Phylum: CNIDARIA.

ANTHRACITE. See COAL.

ANTHRAQUINONE, a yellow, crystalline KETONE made from anthracene or by condensation of BENZENE and phthalic anhydride (see ACID ANHYDRIDES). It is the parent of numerous DYES of all colors, which are bright, fast and suitable for natural and synthetic fibers: they include ALIZARIN and COCHINEAL.

ANTHRAX, a rare BACTERIAL DISEASE causing characteristic SKIN pustules and LUNG disease; it may progress to SEPTICEMIA and death. Anthrax spores, which can survive for years, may be picked up from infected animals (such as sheep or cattle), or bone meal. Treatment is with PENICILLIN and people at risk are VACCINATED; the isolation of animal cases and DISINFECTION of spore-bearing material is essential. It was the first disease in which bacteria were shown (by KOCH) to be causative and it had one of the earliest effective vaccines, developed by PASTEUR.

ANTHROPOID APES, the animals (genus *Pan*) most closely resembling MAN (genus *Homo*) and probably sharing with him a common evolutionary ancestor (see EVOLUTION). Together the genera *Pan* and *Homo* form the family Hominidae in the suborder Anthropoidea (order PRIMATES). The apes concerned, the GORILLA and CHIMPANZEE, have a far higher intelligence than the other primates and greater manual dexterity. The term "anthropoid apes" is often also used to embrace the ORANG-UTAN (family Pongidae) and GIBBON (family Hylobatidae), the other members of the superfamily Hominoidea. (See also MONKEYS.)

ANTHROPOLOGY, the study of man from biological, cultural and social viewpoints. HERODOTUS may perhaps be called the father of anthropology, but it was not until the 14th and 15th centuries AD, with the mercantilist expansion of the Old World into new regions, that contact with other peoples kindled a scientific interest in the subject. In the modern age there are two main disciplines, physical anthropology and cultural anthropology, the latter embracing social anthropology. **Physical anthropology** is the study of man as a biological species, his past EVOLUTION and his contemporary physical characteristics. In its study of PREHISTORIC MAN it has many links with ARCHAEOLOGY, the difference being that anthropology is concerned with the remains or fossils of man himself while archaeology is concerned with the remains of his material culture. The physical anthropologist studies also the difference between RACES and groups, relying to a great extent on techniques of ANTHROPOMETRY and, more recently, genetic studies. **Cultural anthropology** is divided into several classes. ETHNOGRAPHY is the study of the culture of a single group, either primitive (see PRIMITIVE MAN) or civilized. Fieldwork is the key to ethnographical studies, which are themselves the key to cultural anthropology. ETHNOLOGY is the comparative study of the cultures of two or more groups. Cultural anthropology is also concerned with cultures of the past, and the borderline in this case between it and archaeology is vague. **Social anthropology** is concerned primarily with social relationships and their significance and consequences in primitive societies. In recent years its field has been extended to cover more civilized societies, though these are still more generally considered the domain of SOCIOLOGY.

Though it might appear that anthropology could amplify the differences between races or groups, its results in fact indicate the opposite: physical anthropology has shown that divisions between races are at best dubious; and, with cultural anthropology, that tensions between races are of cultural, rather than biological, origin. (See also CEPHALIC INDEX; CLAN; ENDOGAMY AND EXOGAMY; FAMILY; MARRIAGE; TRIBE.)

ANTHROPOMETRY, the anthropological study of the physical characteristics of man; originally restricted to measurements of parts of the body, it now includes blood-typing, biostatistics, etc.

Anthropoid apes are the animals closest to man in anatomy, social organization and intelligence. They have been widely studied, both in captivity and in their natural habitat, for the light they may shed on human behavior. Three of the most common anthropoid apes are shown here: (1) the orang-utan, (2) the gorilla and (3) the chimpanzee.

Lincoln meets McClellan after the battle of Antietam. Historic photograph by Matthew B. Brady.

Anthropometry has contributed considerably to modern ideas of human evolution.

ANTHROPOMORPHISM, the attribution of human characteristics to that which is not human. It occurs in mythology, religion, literature (especially in fables where animals are credited with human feelings) and in common phrases such as "the cruel sea" and "the angry sky."

ANTHROPOSOPHY, a spiritual movement developed under Rudolf STEINER, who founded the Anthroposophical Society in 1912. It aims at higher spiritual experience and knowledge, through man's inner powers independent of the senses. Steiner claimed his "spiritual science" had practical applications, especially in education, and some schools are based on his ideas.

ANTIAIRCRAFT DEFENSE. See ARTILLERY; MISSILE.

ANTIBALLISTIC MISSILE. See MISSILE.

ANTIBES, port on the French Riviera in the Alpes-Maritimes department, containing Roman and medieval remains. It is a tourist resort, and produces perfumes, flowers, fruit and olives. Pop 47 547.

ANTIBIOTICS, substances produced by microorganisms that kill or prevent growth of other microorganisms; their properties are made use of in the treatment of bacterial and fungal infection. PASTEUR noted the effect and Alexander FLEMING in 1929 first showed that the mold *Penicillium notatum* produced PENICILLIN, a substance able to destroy certain bacteria. It was not until 1940 that FLOREY and CHAIN were able to manufacture sufficient penicillin for clinical use. The isolation of STREPTOMYCIN by WAKSMAN, of Gramicidin (from tyrothricin) by DUBOS, and of the Cephalosporins were among early discoveries of antibiotics useful in human infection. Numerous varieties of antibiotics now exist and the search continues for new ones. Semi-synthetic antibiotics, in which the basic molecule is chemically modified, have increased the range of naturally occurring substances.

Each antibiotic is effective against a wider or narrower range of bacteria at a given dosage; their mode of action ranges from preventing cell-wall synthesis to interference with PROTEIN and NUCLEIC ACID metabolism. Bacteria resistant to antibiotics either inherently lack susceptibility to their mode of action or have acquired resistance by ADAPTATION (e.g., by learning to make substances which inactivate an antibiotic). Among the more important antibiotics are the PENICILLINS, Cephalosporins, TETRACYCLINES, STREPTOMYCIN, Gentamicin and Rifampicin. Each group has its own particular value and side effect, and antibiotics may induce ALLERGY. Many antibiotics are effective by mouth but INJECTION may be more suitable; topical application can also be used.

ANTIBODIES AND ANTIGENS. As one of the body's defense mechanisms, PROTEINS called antibodies are made by specialized white cells to counter foreign proteins known as antigens. Common antigens are VIRUSES, bacterial products (including TOXINS) and allergens (see ALLERGY). A specific antibody is made for each antigen. Antibody reacts with antigen in the body, leading to a number of effects including enhanced phagocytosis by white cells, activation of complement (a substance capable of damaging cell membranes) and HISTAMINE release. Antibodies are produced faster and in greater numbers if the body has previously encountered the particular antigen. IMMUNITY to second attacks of diseases such as MEASLES and CHICKENPOX, and VACCINATION against diseases not yet contracted are based on this principle. Antibody detection in blood samples may show AGGLUTININS, precipitins or complement fixation, according to the technique used and the antibody involved.

ANTICHRIST, the opponent of Christ. The name is given to enemies of the Church and to impersonal evil forces. The concept can be traced to Jewish tradition and is mentioned by name in the Epistles of St. John. Christian writers commonly associate the idea of the coming of Antichrist with the approach of the end of the world.

ANTICLERICALISM, hostility towards Church influence on secular affairs. The movement began in REFORMATION Europe as an attack on clerical abuses. Later, it centered on the belief that Church dogma was opposed to scientific progress. In some countries it has led to the suppression of religious activity.

ANTICOAGULANTS, drugs that interfere with blood CLOTTING, used to treat or prevent THROMBOSIS and clot EMBOLISM. The two main types are heparin, which is injected and has an immediate but short-lived effect, and the coumarins (including WARFARIN) which are taken by mouth and are longer-lasting. They affect different parts of the clotting mechanism, coumarins depleting factors made in the LIVER.

ANTI-COMINTERN PACT, an agreement between Germany and Japan (1936), ostensibly to counter the influence of a Russian-inspired anti-capitalist organization, the COMINTERN (Communist International). The pact was later joined by Italy, Spain, Bulgaria, Rumania, Hungary, Denmark and Finland, countries that directly or indirectly aided the German war effort in WWII.

ANTICOSTI, Canadian island (3043sq mi) in the Gulf of St. Lawrence. The terrain is rocky and forested; main activities are lumbering and fishing. Pop c500.

ANTIDEPRESSANTS, drugs used in the treatment of DEPRESSION; they are of two types: tricyclic compounds and monoamine oxidase inhibitors. Although their mode of action is obscure, they have revolutionized the treatment of depression.

ANTIETAM, Battle of, a bloody encounter which repulsed Confederate General Robert E. LEE's first northward thrust during the Civil War. It was fought in Sept. 1862 when 40 000 men under Lee met 70 000 Union troops under McCLELLAN at Antietam Creek, Md. McClellan used only two-thirds of his army and sustained 12 000 casualties, while Lee used his total force, losing almost a quarter of it. Halted before he could reach Washington, Lee was forced to retreat over the Potomac.

ANTIFEDERALISTS, name given in the US to those who opposed the ratification of the Federal Constitution of 1787. They feared that centralized power would become despotic. After the new government's inauguration, the Antifederalist group joined the Republicans to form the DEMOCRATIC-REPUBLICAN PARTY under Jefferson.

ANTIFREEZE, a substance added to water, particularly that in AUTOMOBILE cooling systems, to prevent ice forming in cold weather. The additive most commonly used is ETHYLENE GLYCOL; METHANOL and ETHANOL, although cheaper alternatives, tend to need more frequent replacement, being much more volatile.

ANTIGENS. See ANTIBODIES AND ANTIGENS.

ANTIGONE, in Greek myth, the daughter of OEDIPUS, noted for her fidelity and courage. She followed her father into exile. Later she buried her brother Polynices against the orders of King CREON. Creon imprisoned Antigone who killed herself, provoking the suicide of Creon's son Haemon to whom she was betrothed. Antigone is the heroine of plays by SOPHOCLES, EURIPIDES and ANOUILH.

ANTIGONUS, name of three Macedonian kings. **Antigonus I Cyclops** (382–301 BC), general under ALEXANDER THE GREAT, and king 306–301 BC, was a skilled statesman who tried but failed to unite Alexander's former lands in Asia under his own rule. **Antigonus II Gonatas** (c320–239 BC), king of Macedon 283–239 BC. He had to fight fiercely to defend his title from his enemy Pyrrhus. **Antigonus III Doson** (c263–221 BC), king of Macedon 227–221 BC. He established a confederacy of the Greek states which he used as a weapon against Sparta.

ANTIGUA, island in the E Caribbean Sea, one of Britain's West Indies Associated States. Britain handles only defense and external affairs. Tourism and the production of sugar, cotton and molasses are the major industries. Antigua was discovered by Columbus in 1493. Pop 73 000.

ANTIGUA, former capital of Guatemala, in S central Guatemala. It is an old Spanish city (1542) noted for its colonial architecture. Antigua was largely destroyed by an earthquake in 1773 and the capital was moved to Guatemala City. Pop 21 984.

ANTIHISTAMINES, drugs that counteract HISTAMINE action; they are useful in HAY FEVER and HIVES (in which ALLERGY causes histamine release) and in some insect bites. They also act as SEDATIVES and may relieve MOTION SICKNESS.

ANTIKNOCK ADDITIVES, substances added to GASOLINE to slow the burning of the fuel and thus prevent "knocking," the premature ignition of the combustion mixture in the cylinder head. Most widely used is LEAD tetraethyl [$Pb(C_2H_5)_4$]. This is usually mixed with 1,2-dibromo- and 1,2-dichloroethane, which prevent the formation of lead deposits in the engine.

ANTILLES. See WEST INDIES.

ANTILOGARITHM. See LOGARITHMS.

ANTI-MASONIC PARTY, US political faction active from 1827 to 1836. It emerged after the disappearance in 1826 of William Morgan, author of a book revealing the secrets of FREEMASONRY. The Masons were accused of murdering him and public outrage was exploited politically against Masons in office, first by Thurlow WEED and William H. SEWARD in New York state against Martin VAN BUREN and the ALBANY REGENCY, then by a national campaign to defeat President Andrew Jackson, himself a Mason, which won a number of congressional seats.

ANTIMATTER, a variety of MATTER differing from the matter which predominates in our part of the UNIVERSE in that it is composed of antiparticles rather than particles. Individual antiparticles, many of which have been found in COSMIC RAY showers or produced using particle ACCELERATORS, differ from their particle counterparts in that they are oppositely charged (as with the antiproton-PROTON pair) or in that their magnetic moment is orientated in the opposite sense with respect to their SPIN (as with the antineutrino and neutrino). In our part of the universe antiparticles are very short-lived, being rapidly annihilated in collisions with their corresponding particles, their mass-energy reappearing as a gamma-ray PHOTON. (The reverse is also true; a high-energy GAMMA RAY sometimes spontaneously forms itself into a positron-ELECTRON pair.) However, it is by no means inconceivable that regions of the universe exist in which all the matter is antimatter, composed of what are to us antiparticles. The first antiparticle, the positron (i.e., the antielectron), was discovered by C. D. ANDERSON in 1932, only four years after DIRAC had theoretically predicted the existence of antiparticles. (See also SUBATOMIC PARTICLES.)

ANTIMONY (Sb), brittle, silver-white metal in Group VA of the PERIODIC TABLE, occurring mainly as STIBNITE, which is roasted to give antimony (III) oxide. Its ALLOTROPY resembles that of ARSENIC. Antimony, though rather unreactive, forms trivalent and pentavalent oxides, halides and oxyanions. It is used in SEMICONDUCTORS and in lead ALLOYS, chiefly BABBITT METAL, PEWTER, type metal and in lead storage batteries. Certain antimony compounds are used in the manufacture of medicines, paints, matches, explosives and fireproofing materials. AW 121.75, mp 631°C, bp 1750°C, sg 6.691 (20°C).

ANTIN, Mary (1881–1949), Russian-born US writer noted for her autobiography *The Promised Land* (1912) and her book on immigrants *They Who Knock at Our Gates* (1914).

ANTINOMIANISM, heretical doctrine that Christians are set free by grace from the obligation to obey the moral law, especially the TEN COMMANDMENTS. In the patristic period it was held by many gnostics (see GNOSTICISM) and the followers of MARCION and MONTANUS. At the Reformation it was revived by Johann AGRICOLA and the ANABAPTISTS, though opposed by the Reformers, and was later held by radical sects during the COMMONWEALTH, Anne HUTCHINSON in New England and many METHODISTS and dispensationalists (see DISPENSATIONALISM). Antinomians have often been accused of licentiousness, in some cases justly.

ANTIOCH (now Antakya), ancient city in Asia Minor on the Orontes R. Founded c300 BC by Seleucus Nicator, it became the capital of the SELEUCID Empire and, in 64 BC, the Asian capital of the Roman Empire. Antioch was an important center of early Christianity. Antakya, the modern commercial city, became part of French-administered Syria after WWI and joined Turkey in 1939. Pop 57855.

There were four antipopes in succession in Avignon (France) after the Great Schism in 1378. Seen here is the magnificent palace which was built for them.

ANTIOCH, coastal town in W Cal., settled in 1849. It processes and handles a wide range of local farm produce. Pop 28060.

ANTIOCHUS, name of 13 kings of the SELEUCID dynasty. **Antiochus I Soter** (c324–261 BC), king 280–261. He crushed the Gauls in Asia Minor but lost parts of the Seleucid Empire to Egypt. **Antiochus II Theos** (c287–247 BC), king 261–247. **Antiochus III the Great** (c242–187 BC), king 223–187. He regained Parthia and Bactria, defeated Egypt and conquered Palestine and S Syria. **Antiochus IV Epiphanes** (c215–163 BC), king 175–163. His hellenization policy provoked a Jewish revolt. **Antiochus V Eupator** (173–162 BC), king 163–162. **Antiochus VI Theos** (d. 142 BC), king 145–142. **Antiochus VII Euergetes** (c158–129? BC), king c138–129? He destroyed Jerusalem. **Antiochus VIII Philometor** (d. 96 BC), king 125–96; from 115 sharing his realm with **Antiochus IX Philopator** (d. 95 BC), king 115–95. **Antiochus X Eusebes** (d. 92 BC), king 95–93. **Antiochus XI Epiphanes Philadelphus** (d. 92 BC), king 92. **Antiochus XII Dionysus** (d. 85 BC). **Antiochus XIII Asiaticus,** king 69–64, deposed by Rome.

ANTIPARTICLES. See ANTIMATTER; SUBATOMIC PARTICLES.

ANTIPATER (c397–319 BC), Macedonian general and regent of Macedonia during Alexander the Great's Asian campaigns (334–23). He put down the rebellion of several Greek cities at the Battle of Crannon.

ANTIPOPE, a pretender to the papal throne, elected by a faction in the Roman Catholic Church or by a secular ruler. The first antipope was Hippolytus (3rd century); the last was Felix V (abdicated 1449). In the GREAT SCHISM (1378) Italy elected Urban VI while France set up court for Clement VII in Avignon. Their successors were deposed by the Council of CONSTANCE (1415).

ANTIPRISM, a right PRISM, one of whose regular (see POLYGON) bases has been rotated parallel to the PLANE in which it lies through an ANGLE equal to half that subtended by each of the sides of the base at its center. The faces of an antiprism are congruent isosceles TRIANGLES.

ANTIQUES, objects valued for their age, rarity, craftsmanship and historic interest. Originally applied to Greek and Roman art, the term is now often used for articles over 100 years old, although it sometimes includes early 20th-century items. Antique furniture, household objects, jewelry, china, coins and books are all sought by the collector. Antique collecting began its serious vogue in the 18th century.

ANTI-RENT WAR, 19th-century dispute in which tenant farmers in N.Y. claimed land owned by hereditary landowners. Violence erupted in 1839 when tenants refused to pay back rents of $400000. Anti-renters gained political support, the N.Y. constitution was amended and in 1847 the farms were granted to the tenants.

ANTI-SALOON LEAGUE, temperance organization established in 1893 to curb the sale of liquor. It played an important part in the campaign to achieve national PROHIBITION.

ANTI-SEMITISM, hostility towards Jews, ranging from social prejudice to genocide. Common motives for anti-Semitism include religious opposition to Judaism, national resentment of a people who remain in some ways apart from the life of the country they live in and simple jealousy of the Jews' material success. Anti-Semitism has often been justified by the notion that the Jews' exile and persecution were punishment for their part in Christ's crucifixion. Segregation, expulsion and massacres have dogged Europe's Jewish communities, notably in the Middle Ages, and later in Tsarist Russia and in Nazi Germany before and during WWII, when some 6000000 Jews were put to death in concentration camps at AUSCHWITZ, BELSEN, BUCHENWALD and elsewhere. Despite the decline of avowed anti-Semitism since WWII, anti-Jewish feeling has increased in Arab lands hostile to the young Jewish state of Israel. Jews are still persecuted in the USSR.

ANTISEPTICS, or germicides, substances that kill or prevent the growth of microorganisms (particularly BACTERIA and FUNGI); they are used to avoid SEPSIS from contamination of body surfaces and surgical instruments. Some antiseptics are used as disinfectants to make places or objects GERM-free. VINEGAR and cedar oil have been used from earliest times to treat wounds and for EMBALMING. Modern antisepsis was pioneered by SEMMELWEIS, LISTER and KOCH, and dramatically reduced deaths from childbirth and surgery. Commonly used antiseptics and disinfectants include IODINE, CHLORINE, hypochlorous acid, ETHANOL, isopropanol (see ALCOHOLS), PHENOLS (including hexachlorophene), quaternary ammonium salts (see AMMONIA), FORMALDEHYDE, hydrogen PEROXIDE, potassium permanganate, and acriflavine (an acridine dye). Heat, ULTRAVIOLET and ionizing radiations also have antiseptic effects. (See also STERILIZATION; ASEPSIS.)

ANTITOXINS, antibodies produced in the body against the TOXINS of some bacteria. They are also formed after INOCULATION of toxoid, chemically inactivated toxin that can still confer IMMUNITY.

ANTITRUST LEGISLATION, laws passed by Congress to prevent trade restraint or unfair competition by large corporations. (See also MONOPOLY.)

ANTLERITE, green mineral consisting of basic copper sulfate ($Cu_3[OH]_4SO_4$). A minor COPPER ore of widespread occurrence, it is formed by oxidation of primary copper minerals.

ANTLERS, the horns of DEER. Unlike other animal HORNS, they are made of BONE rather than modified EPIDERMIS.

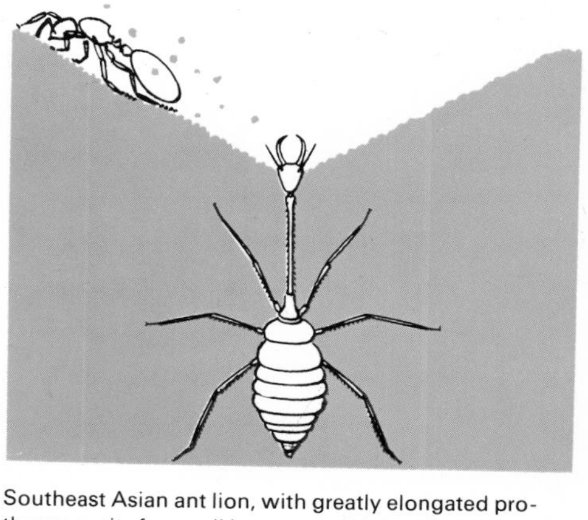

Southeast Asian ant lion, with greatly elongated prothorax, waits for small insects to slide into its conical pit.

ANT LIONS (or doodlebugs), carnivorous LARVAE of the Myrmeleontidae (Order: NEUROPTERA). Most dig pits, using their ABDOMENS as plows, and bury themselves at the bottom, seizing any insect that falls into the pit and sucking it dry. As the adult form cannot feed, the larva must eat enough to sustain it.

ANTOFAGASTA, a major Pacific seaport city in N Chile, capital of Antofagasta Province. An important industrial center, it processes and exports copper, nitrates and sulfur mined nearby. It was ceded to Chile by Bolivia in 1883. Pop 133000.

ANTOINETTE, Marie. See MARIE ANTOINETTE.

ANTONELLO DA MESSINA (c1430–1479), allegedly the first Italian to paint in oils. He was influenced by Dutch and Flemish painters and excelled in spatial composition. The S. Cassiano altarpiece in Venice and a *St. Sebastian* in Dresden are among his major works.

ANTONESCU, Ion (1882–1946), Rumanian general and pro-Nazi right-wing leader. Becoming prime minister in 1940, he persuaded King Carol to abdicate and established a military dictatorship favoring the AXIS POWERS. He was executed as a war criminal.

ANTONINUS PIUS (86–161 AD), Roman emperor, the last to achieve relative stability in the empire. Chosen consul in 120 AD, he adopted MARCUS AURELIUS and Lucius Verus as successors. He was a prudent and economical ruler, tolerant of Christians. (See also ADOPTIVE EMPERORS.)

ANTONIONI, Michelangelo (1912–), Italian film director of international renown. His motion pictures include *L'Avventura* (1959), *La Notte* (1961), *Eclipse* (1962), *The Red Desert* (1964), *Blow Up* (1966) and *Zabriskie Point* (1969).

ANTONY, Mark (or Marcus Antonius; c82–30 BC), Roman general who became one of three joint rulers of the Roman state. He fought notably in Gaul and became a tribune in 50 BC and a consul in 44 BC. After Caesar's murder, Antony, his brother-in-law Octavian (see AUGUSTUS) and Lepidus formed a Triumvirate (43 BC), dividing the empire into three. Antony controlled the E from the Adriatic to the Euphrates, but alienated Octavian by falling in love with the Egyptian queen, CLEOPATRA, and combining forces with her. Attacked by Octavian, Antony committed suicide after his naval defeat at ACTIUM.

ANTONY OF THEBES, Saint (c251–356), Egyptian hermit, considered the founder of Christian MONASTICISM. He founded a desert community of ascetics near Fayum, then lived alone in a mountain cave near the Red Sea and died aged over 100. He supported St. ATHANASIUS in the Arian controversy.

ANTS, social INSECTS of the family Formicidae of the order HYMENOPTERA, recognizable through the petiole or "waist" between abdomen and THORAX. There are some 3500 species of ant, each species containing three distinct castes: male, female and worker. **Males** can be found only at certain times of year: winged, they are not readmitted to the nest after the mating flight. The **queen** is likewise winged, but she rubs her wings off after mating; she may survive for as long as 15 years, still laying eggs fertilized during the original mating flight. The **workers** are sterile females, sometimes falling into two distinct size categories, the larger ones (soldiers) defending the nest and assisting with heavier work. The most primitive ants (*Ponerinae*) may form nests with only a few individuals; nests of wood ants (*Formica rufa*), however, may contain more than 100000 individuals. *Dorylinae*, the so-called Army Ants, do not build nests at all but are nomadic, traveling in "armies" up to 150000 strong: like *Ponerinae* (but unlike the more sophisticated species, which are vegetarian) they are carnivorous. Nesting ants welcome some insects, mainly BEETLES, to their nests, and often "farm" APHIDS for honeydew.

ANTUNG (Tan-tung), city in NE China in Liaoning province. It is a port on the Yalu R, which carries lumber down to the city for processing and provides hydroelectric power for Antung's heavy industries. There are also food processing and textile plants. Pop 450000.

Ants live in a great variety of structures. This cross-section shows the nest of wood ants with (*top right*) eggs, (*underneath*) an intruder, (*middle left*) small larvae, (*middle right*) big larvae, (*bottom*) pupae.

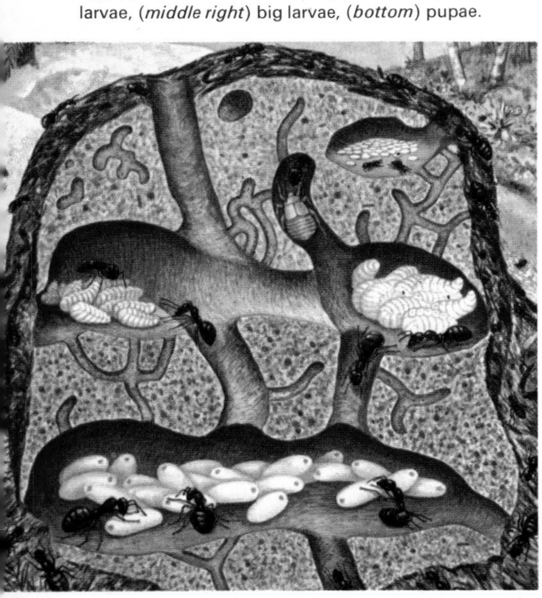

ANTWERP, Belgium's second-largest city and leading port, on the Scheldt R 60mi from the North Sea. It is the capital of Antwerp province, the commercial and cultural center of Flemish Belgium (with a large university) and an important manufacturing city, with oil, metal, automobile and diamond industries. Around 1560 it was the leading port of Europe, and the center of the great Flemish school of painting: artists like BREUGHEL, RUBENS and VAN DYCK worked there.

ANUBIS, Egyptian god of the dead, usually shown with the head of a dog or jackal. He conducted the dead to the underworld and there weighed their hearts on the scales of justice.

ANURADHAPURA, capital of the North-Central province of Sri Lanka, former capital of the Sinhalese kings and site of Buddhist ruins. Its ancient Bo tree reputedly sprang from a branch of the tree under which the Buddha attained enlightenment. Restoration of the ruins has attracted tourists and pilgrims. Pop 30000.

ANVIL, smooth-faced block of iron on which malleable heated metals are hammered into shape. One end, the "beak" or "bick," is usually cone-shaped to allow the forging of curved pieces of metal. The shape, size and weight of an anvil vary according to its specific purpose.

ANXIETY, one of two reactions of the EGO to outside threat. **Signal anxiety** warns the ego of impending threat so that **primary anxiety,** the EMOTION connected with dissolution of the ego, may be avoided (see DEFENSE MECHANISM). Primary anxiety, however, does occur in nightmares (see DREAMS).

ANYANG (Chang-Te), city in NE China in N Honan province between Chengchow and Peking. An important trade and manufacturing center in a coal mining area, it is the site of ruins dating back to the Shang dynasty (c1500–1100 BC), the earliest documented historical culture in China. Pop 225000.

ANZA, Juan Bautista de (1735–1788), Spanish explorer who founded San Francisco in 1776. He made one of the longest journeys in the history of North American exploration, probing N from the deserts of S Cal. via San Gabriel (Los Angeles) and Monterey.

ANZIO, Italian fishing port and seaside resort about 30mi S of Rome. As the ancient Roman Antium, the town was the birthplace of the emperors CALIGULA and NERO. A busy port and a famous resort, Anzio was badly damaged when the Allies landed there in Jan. 1944, and a force of 50000 men was pinned down at the beachhead by German counteroffensives. Pop 22108.

ANZUS PACT, treaty signed on Sept. 1, 1951, by Australia, New Zealand and the US for mutual defense in the Pacific. The name consists of the initials of the participating countries.

AOMORI, capital and largest city of Aomori prefecture, Japan. It is the chief seaport of N Honshu Island. Pop 240063.

AORTA, the chief systemic ARTERY, distributing oxygenated blood to the whole body except the LUNGS via its branches. (See also BLOOD CIRCULATION; HEART.)

AOSTA, town in NW Italy strategically sited near Alpine passes to France and Switzerland. Aosta has extensive Roman remains, including an amphitheater. It is the capital of Valle d'Aosta province and produces chemicals, textiles and steel. Pop 35257.

AOUDAD (*Ammotragus lervia*), or **Barbary sheep,** large wild SHEEP found in the mountains of NW Africa. The males have sharp-pointed, backward-curving HORNS of length 500–750mm (20–30in) and long manes.

APACHE INDIANS, North American Indians of the Athabaskan linguistic family. The major tribes were the Jicarilla, Lipan, Mescalero, Airavaipa, Coyotero, Pinaleno, Kiowa and Chiricahua. Apaches lived in SW North America, maintaining a nomadic hunting culture that depended on free movement over a large area. The arrival of white settlers thus threatened their survival, and many Apaches rejected repeated federal government attempts to confine the tribes to reservations. Bloody conflicts followed, and Apache numbers were greatly decimated by 1896, when the last great Apache chief, GERONIMO, was captured. Most present-day Apaches live on federal reservations in Okla., N.M. and Ariz.

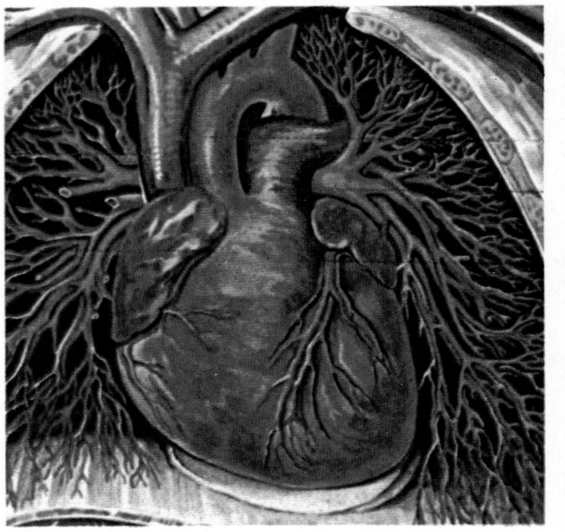

The aorta, the principal body artery, arises from the left ventricle of the heart, and curves upward into the chest to supply blood for the head, neck, shoulders and arms, before descending to the abdominal cavity where branches supply the digestive organs, the kidneys, the adrenal and reproductive glands, and the legs. The coronary arteries, which supply the heart itself, divide from the aorta just after it leaves the left ventricle.

APALACHEE INDIANS, tribe of North American Indians that once lived around Apalachee Bay in N Fla. Spanish Franciscans converted many to Christianity (c1600), but in the early 1700s British forces crushed the tribe and its survivors were enslaved.

APALACHICOLA RIVER, navigable river in SW Ga. and N Fla. It flows S for 90mi, entering the Gulf of Mexico at Apalachicola Bay in Fla.

APARTHEID, policy of strict racial segregation practiced in the Republic of South Africa in order to maintain the domination of the white minority. Segregation and discrimination against non-white peoples is observed in housing, employment, education and public services, and enforced by legislation punishing dissent or resistance with imprisonment, exile or house arrest. The policy also involves the "separate development" of eight Bantu homelands, where black people have a measure of self-government. Organizations suppressed for opposing apartheid have included the AFRICAN NATIONAL CONGRESS, the Pan-African Congress and Alan PATON's Liberal Party. Apartheid is almost universally condemned outside South Africa.

APATITE, the chief PHOSPHATE mineral, found in the Kola peninsula, USSR, N Africa, Mont. and Fla., and mined for FERTILIZER and as the major ore of PHOSPHORUS. Its chemical composition is $Ca_5(PO_4)_3X$, where $X = F$ (fluorapatite, the most common), Cl (chlorapatite), OH (hydroxyapatite) or a mixture of all three; it forms hexagonal crystals.

APES. See ANTHROPOID APES.

APELLES (4th century BC), Greek artist reputed to be the greatest painter of the ancient world. He worked as court painter of Macedonia and his portraits of Alexander the Great were particularly famous. None of Apelles' paintings have survived.

APENNINES, mountain chain forming the backbone of the Italian peninsula. It is about 800mi long and 25–80mi wide. The highest peak is Monte Corno (9560ft). The predominant rocks are limestone and dolomite; sulfur and cinnabar (sulfide of mercury) are mined in the volcanic area near Vesuvius. Olives, grapes and grains are widely grown; lack of fertile topsoil prevents intensive agriculture.

APEX, that ANGLE of a POLYGON or POLYHEDRON farthest from the side or plane designated the base of the figure. The apex of a CONE is its vertex.

APHASIA, a speech defect resulting from injury to certain areas of the brain and causing inability to use or comprehend words; it may be partial (dysphasia) or total. Common causes are cerebral THROMBOSIS, HEMORRHAGE and brain TUMORS. (See SPEECH DISORDERS AND SPEECH THERAPY.)

APHELION. See ORBIT.

APHIDS (or greenflies or plant-lice), some 4000 species of sap-feeding insects, comprising the family Aphididae of the order HOMOPTERA. They have needle-like mouthparts with which they pierce the plant tissue, the pressure within this forcing the sap into the insect's gut. Because of the damage caused by their feeding and because many species carry harmful VIRUSES, aphids are one of the world's greatest crop pests. The life cycle is a complex one, so that within a species there may at any one time be a diversity of forms; winged and wingless, reproducing sexually or parthenogenetically (see PARTHENOGENESIS; REPRODUCTION; also ALTERNATION OF GENERATIONS). Aphids excrete (see EXCRETION) a substance known as honeydew, a major food source for ANTS and other insects.

APHRODISIAC, anything contributing to sexual excitement. Aphrodisiacs may be external (touch, sight, etc.) or internal (foods, drugs, etc.), the latter working usually by SUGGESTION or, like alcohol (see ETHANOL) and MARIJUANA, by lowering INHIBITIONS. Most foods traditionally regarded as aphrodisiac depend for their efficacy merely on their chance genital shape.

APHRODITE, the Greek goddess of love, fertility and beauty. She was supposedly the daughter of ZEUS and Dione, or alternatively rose from the sea near Cyprus. Her intensely sensual beauty aroused jealousy among other goddesses, particularly after PARIS chose her as the most beautiful goddess over HERA and ATHENA. Aphrodite was the wife of HEPHAESTUS (but took divine and mortal lovers). Aeneas and Eros were her sons. The Greeks honored her with major shrines at Athens, Corinth, Sparta, Cos, Cnidus and Cyprus, and the Romans identified her with Venus.

APIA, capital, main port and commercial center of Western Samoa, sited on the N coast of Upolu Island. Robert Louis STEVENSON died there in 1894 and is buried nearby. Pop 30593.

APICULTURE. See BEEKEEPING.

APIS, a bull-god of ancient Egypt. He was regarded as the reincarnation of OSIRIS and worshiped at MEMPHIS in the form of a living bull with distinctive markings (replaced at death by a similar animal). Enormous sarcophagi containing the mummified bodies of such bulls were found at Memphis in 1850. (See also SERAPIS.)

APOCALYPSE, a prophetic revelation, usually about the end of the world and the ensuing establishment of a heavenly kingdom. Jewish and Christian apocalyptic writings appeared in Palestine between 200 BC and 150 AD and offered hope of liberation to a people under alien rule. (See also MESSIAH; REVELATION, BOOK OF.)

APOCRYPHA, writings not accepted by Jews or all Christians as canonical (that is, as part of Holy Scripture). Protestants use the term mainly for books written in the two centuries before Christ and included in the SEPTUAGINT and the VULGATE, but not in the Hebrew Bible. These include Esdras I and II, Tobit, Judith, additions to Esther, the Wisdom of Solomon, Ecclesiasticus, Baruch, the Song of the Three Children, Susanna and the Elders, Bel and the Dragon, the Prayer of Manasses and Maccabees I and II. (See also BIBLE; PSEUDEPIGRAPHA.)

APODA. See CAECILIANS.

APOGEE. See ORBIT.

APOLLINAIRE, Guillaume (real name: Wilhelm Apollinaris de Kostrowitzki; 1880–1918), influential French avant-garde poet and critic. The friend of DERAIN, DUFY and PICASSO, he helped to publicize Cubist and primitive art. His poetry, as in the collections *Alcools* (1913) and *Calligrammes* (1918), often anticipated SURREALISM with its use of startling associations and juxtapositions.

APOLLO, major deity in Greek and Roman mythology. In the Greek myths, Apollo was the son of ZEUS and Leto, and twin of ARTEMIS. Second only to Zeus, he had the power of the sun as giver of light and life. He was the god of justice and masculine beauty, and the purifier of those stained by crime. He was the divine patron of the arts, leader of the MUSES, and god of music and poetry. Apollo was a healer, but could also send disease, and from his foreknowledge he spoke through the ORACLE at DELPHI. The Romans adopted Apollo, honoring him as healer and as god of the sun.

APOLLONIUS OF PERGA (b. c262 BC), the "Great Geometer," who, building on the foundation of EUCLID, went on to investigate the properties of CONIC SECTIONS, introducing the terms ellipse, hyperbola and parabola and exploring the properties of tangents.

APOLLONIUS OF RHODES (b. c295 BC) Greek epic poet who was a pupil of CALLIMACHUS and later head of the ALEXANDRIAN LIBRARY. His best-known work is the epic poem *Argonautica*, the story of JASON and the ARGONAUTS written in a style and meter owing much to Homer.

APOLLO PROJECT. See SPACE EXPLORATION.

APOPLEXY, obsolete term for STROKE due to cerebral HEMORRHAGE.

APOSTILB (asb), in PHOTOMETRY, a unit of LUMINANCE, being that of a uniformly diffusing surface reflecting or emitting one lumen per square metre.

APOSTLEBIRD, E Australian species, *Struthidea cinerea*, of sociable birds. Fluffy and grey, with short thick bills, they run clumsily and fly poorly. Family: Grallinidae.

APOSTLE ISLANDS, group of 20 islands in Wis., located in SW Lake Superior. The largest island, Madeline, has the group's only settlement, La Pointe. The islands attract many tourists.

APOSTLES, the 12 disciples closest to Jesus, whom he chose to proclaim his teaching. They were Andrew, John, Bartholomew, Judas, Jude, the two Jameses, Matthew, Peter, Philip, Simon and Thomas. When Judas died, Matthias replaced him. Paul and Barnabas became known as apostles for their work in spreading the Gospel.

APOSTLES' CREED, a CREED ascribed to Christ's apostles and maintained in its present form since the early Middle Ages. The Roman Catholic Church uses it in the sacraments of baptism and confirmation. It is also used by various Protestant denominations.

APOSTOLIC FATHERS, early Christian writers of the first two centuries after Christ, regarded by tradition as the disciples of the 12 apostles. They include Paul's assistant Barnabas; Hermas, a 2nd-century Roman; St. Clement of Rome, a disciple of Peter; Polycarp and Papias, followers of John; and Ignatius, bishop of Antioch.

APOSTOLIC SEE, the see of the bishop of Rome, the highest office in the hierarchy of the Roman Catholic Church. The first bishop of Rome was St. Peter, and the pope (see PAPACY) is his successor.

APOSTOLIC SUCCESSION, a doctrine held by several Christian churches. They believe that Christ's apostles ordained the first bishops and other priests, that these ordained their successors, and so on, forging an unbroken chain of succession reaching to the present day. Many Protestants reject the doctrine as unproven and unnecessary.

APOTHECARIES' WEIGHTS, a system of weights formerly used by pharmacists in preparing medicines.

Apothecaries' weights

Unit	Symbol	Equivalent in same system	Approximate SI equivalent
Pound	lb (lb ap)	12 ounces	0.373 242 kg
ounce	℥ (oz ap)	8 drams†	31.103 g
dram†	ʒ (dr ap)	3 scruples	3.888 g
scruple	℈ (s ap)	20 grains	1.296 g
grain	gr	–	*64.798 91 mg

†drachm in UK *exact equivalent

1oz ap = 1oz troy = 1.0971oz avoirdupois = 31.103g (See also PHARMACY; WEIGHTS AND MEASURES.)

APPALACHIA, the economically poor S part of the Appalachian Mts. It includes parts of 13 states, covers 355 counties and has 16 million inhabitants. In 1965 Congress voted $1.2 billion towards rebuilding the region's declining economy and improving social conditions.

APPALACHIAN MOUNTAINS, group of mountain ranges in E North America about 1800mi long and 120–375mi wide, stretching south from Newfoundland to central Ala. The system's ancient sandstone, limestone, slate and other rocks have been folded, eroded, uplifted and again eroded. Major ranges of the N include the Notre Dame, Green, White and Adirondack Mts. The central area has the Allegheny Mts and part of the Blue Ridge Mts. The S contains the S Blue Ridge, Cumberland, Black and Great Smoky Mts. The highest peak is Mt Mitchell (6684ft) in N.C.

Appalachian forests yield much timber, and rich deposits of coal and iron have stimulated the growth of such industrial areas as Birmingham and Pittsburgh. The Connecticut, Hudson, Delaware, Susquehanna, Potomac, Kanawha, Tennessee and other rivers have cut deep gaps in the ranges. But in the early years of the US the Appalachians were a barrier to westward expansion.

APPALACHIAN TRAIL, the longest marked footpath in the world, stretching 2000mi along the crest of the Appalachian Mts from Mt Katahdin in N Me. to Springer Mountain and Mt Oglethorpe in N Ga.

APPEAL, in law, the transfer of a case decided in a lower court for review by a higher court. If the higher court finds the lower court made legal errors, the appeal may be allowed. If the decision of the lower court is upheld, appeal to a higher appeals court may still be possible. The highest appeals court in the US is the SUPREME COURT. But this only considers cases involving important federal or constitutional matters. The right to appeal is fundamental to the legal system, since it allows errors to be rectified and may establish principles which contribute to the progress of the law.

APPEASEMENT, conciliatory policy adopted by a government to avoid conflict with a potentially hostile body. A noted example is the Franco-British appeasement of Nazi Germany that resulted in the hollow MUNICH PACT (1938).

APPEASEMENT BEHAVIOR, action (usually ritual) taken by one animal to allay AGGRESSION toward it by another member of its species. There are a vast number of appeasement (or submission) rituals, the most common among mammals being the adoption of the submissive sexual posture, even by one male towards another. (See also MATING RITUALS; TERRITORIALITY.)

APPEL, Karel (1921–), Dutch expressionist and action painter, a founder of the international experimental art group Cobra. His work is marked by colorful yet aggressive sensuality.

APPENDICITIS, inflammation of the APPENDIX, often caused by obstruction to its narrow opening,

Appendicitis pain is felt at various points (*red circles*), depending on the position of the appendix.

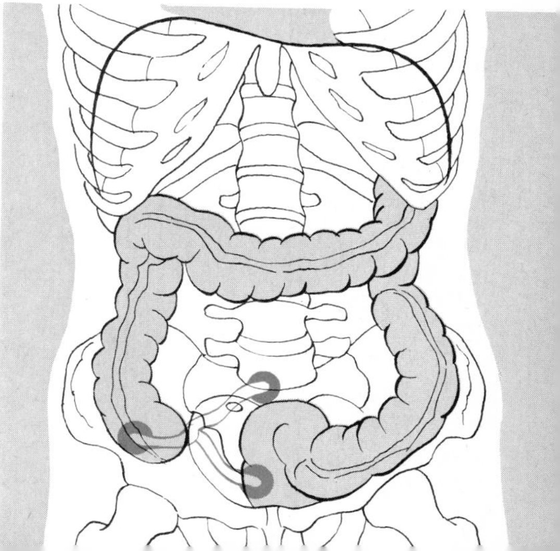

followed by swelling and bacterial infection. Acute appendicitis may lead to rupture of the organ, formation of an ABSCESS or PERITONITIS. Symptoms include abdominal pain, usually in the right lower ABDOMEN, nausea, vomiting and FEVER. Early surgical removal of the appendix is essential; any abscess requires drainage of PUS and delayed excision.

APPENDIX, Vermiform, narrow tubular structure opening into the cecum (see GASTROINTESTINAL TRACT) found in some vertebrates, including man. The human appendix contains lymphoid tissue (see LYMPH) and is probably vestigial. (See APPENDICITIS.)

APPIA, Adolphe (1862–1928), Swiss stage designer whose ideas revolutionized early 20th-century theater. He stressed the use of three-dimensional settings and of mobile lighting with controlled intensity and color.

APPIAN WAY, the oldest and most famous Roman road. Built by Appius Claudius Caecus in 312 BC to link Rome and Capua, it was later extended to Brindisi, covering in all about 350mi. Sections near Rome are still largely intact.

APPLE, popular edible fruit of the apple tree, *Malus sylvestris* (family Rosaceae), widely cultivated in temperate climates. Over 7 000 varieties are known but only about 40 are commercially important, the most popular US variety being Delicious. Some 15%–20% of the world's crop is produced in the US, mostly in the states of Wash., N.Y., Cal., Mich., and Va. There are three main types of apples: cooking, dessert, and those used in making CIDER.

APPLE MAGGOT, or railroad worm, wormlike larva of the apple fly, *Rhagoletis pomonella*. The larva causes serious damage to apple crops by burrowing through the fruit after hatching from eggs laid under the skin. Family: Trypetidae.

APPLESEED, Johnny (1774–1845), US folk hero, a mild eccentric whose real name was John Chapman. As a pioneer in the Ohio river region he wandered around for some 40 years, planting and tending apple orchards and preaching religion.

APPLETON, city in E Wis. on the Fox R, seat of Outagamie Co. and a major center for the processing of agricultural and dairy products and the manufacture of paper goods. Site of the first US hydroelectric station (1882) and of Lawrence University (1847). Pop 57 143.

APPLETON, Sir Edward Victor (1892–1965), English physicist who discovered the Appleton layer (since resolved as two layers termed F_1 and F_2) of ionized gas molecules in the IONOSPHERE. His work in atmospheric physics won him the 1947 Nobel Prize for Physics and contributed to the development of RADAR. During WWII he helped develop the ATOMIC BOMB.

APPOMATTOX COURT HOUSE, US historical site in central Va., where the Civil War was ended with Lee's surrender to Grant on April 9, 1865. The McLean House (where the surrender took place) and other buildings have been reconstructed as part of the 972-acre Appomattox Court House National Historical Park.

APPORTIONMENT, Legislative, the distribution of voters' representation in the lawmaking bodies. Although each state, whatever its size, elects two senators only, members of the US House of Representatives are elected from districts with equal populations, and the federal census results in a reapportionment of seats each decade. Since the 1970 census, each congressman represents about 460 000 voters.

In the past, state legislature district boundaries were often erratically drawn to give voting advantage to one political party (see GERRYMANDER). Also, most counties had equal representation in state senates; thus, one vote in a rural county might be worth 30 times that in a city, due to lower population. But in 1962 the Supreme Court ruled that unfair districting may be brought before federal courts, and later rulings established that one man's vote should be "worth as much as another's," or, "one man, one vote." This principle is slowly shifting political power from rural to urban areas.

APPRENTICE, person working under the experienced guidance of another to learn a craft, trade or business. Modern labor unions often insist on an

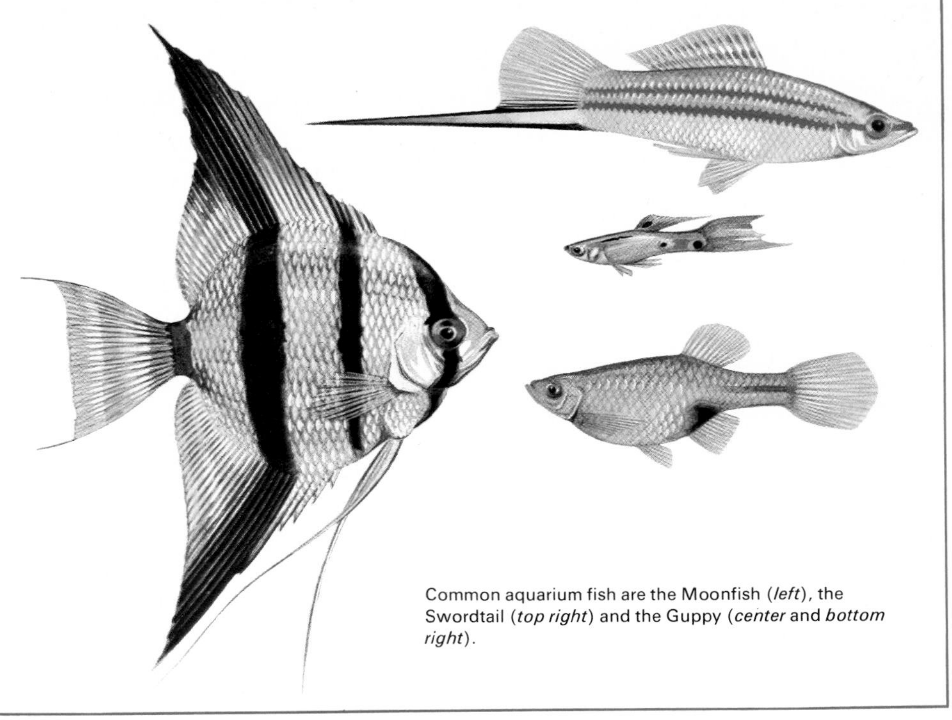

Common aquarium fish are the Moonfish (*left*), the Swordtail (*top right*) and the Guppy (*center* and *bottom right*).

apprenticeship before full membership is granted. In medieval Europe, apprenticeship was part of the GUILD system and constituted a legal obligation.

APPROPRIATION, the authorization to spend public money for a specific purpose; usually controlled by the legislature. In the US the President submits the annual federal budget to Congress, which then votes suitable appropriations.

APPROXIMATION, the setting of an approximate value V_a in place of a true but imprecisely known value V where $V - V_a$ lies within known limits. There are several different ways of expressing approximations and their limits of accuracy.

If we approximate 2.365 420 2 by 2.365 420 we say that this is correct to 6 decimal places, in that the six figures after the decimal point are correct (see also DECIMAL SYSTEM). It is common practice, when approximating to $(n-1)$ decimal places a number that has *n* decimal places, to round *up* if the *n*th figure after the point is 5 or greater, *down* if it is less than 5. Thus 3.65 can be written as 3.7 to 1 decimal place; 3.64 as 3.6.

Similarly, 2.365 420 2 can be expressed as 2.365 420 to 7 significant figures, since the first 7 figures are correct, rounding down.

An alternative way of writing approximations is by use of the sign ± (read "plus or minus"). Thus $2.365\,420 \pm 0.000\,000\,4$ is an approximation stating that the correct value lies between 2.365 419 6 and 2.365 420 4. This can be expressed as a percentage (see PERCENT): $2.365\,420 \pm 0.000\,016\,9\%$.

Approximation is required in almost all computations, due either to inherent inaccuracies in the calculating device or to the technique of calculation, or because greater accuracy is unnecessary. The techniques of approximation to a FUNCTION are of paramount importance in CALCULUS.

APRICOT, orange-colored fruit of the apricot tree, *Prunus armeniaca* (family Rosaceae), native to China but grown throughout temperate regions. Commercial production is mainly in central and SE Asia, Europe and the US; over 90% of the US crop comes from California. Apricots are eaten fresh, or preserved by drying or canning; the kernels are used to make a liqueur. Apricot trees are often grown as ornamentals.

APRIL, fourth month of the year in the Gregorian calendar; first full spring month in the Northern Hemisphere. The Christian EASTER and Jewish PASSOVER usually fall in April. The month is probably named from *aperire* (Latin: to open), referring to the opening spring buds. Birthstone: diamond. Astrological signs: Aries and Taurus.

APRIL FOOLS' DAY, or All Fools' Day, April 1, the traditional day for practical jokes. The custom probably began in France in 1564, when New Year's Day was changed from April 1 to Jan. 1. Those continuing to observe April 1 were ridiculed.

A PRIORI AND A POSTERIORI, terms descriptive of knowledge or reasoning reflecting whether or not it is the result of our experience of the real world. Alleged knowledge attained solely through reasoning from arbitrary principles is *a priori* (Latin: from earlier things); that gained empirically, from observation or experience, is *a posteriori* (Latin: from later things). This modern usage of the terms derives from the philosopher KANT.

APSE, semicircular or polygonal recess or area at the end of a building, covered with a half-dome or hemispherical vault; usually placed at the sanctuary end of a church. In Latin and Byzantine Christian churches apses were often elaborately decorated. The apse was also a characteristic feature of the ancient Roman BASILICA; the magistrate's seat was placed in it.

APSIDES, Line of, the imaginary straight line connecting the two points of an elliptical ORBIT which represent the orbiting body's greatest (higher apsis) and least (lower apsis) distances from the body around which it is revolving.

APTERYX. See KIWI.

APTITUDE TESTS, tests designed to measure a person's potential ability. Although satisfactory in dealing with well-defined skills such as problem-solving, they are less successful in the artistic fields. Widely used in vocational guidance and college entry, they are also used for staff selection by some companies.

APULEIUS, Lucius (c125–185 AD), Roman author of *Metamorphoses* or *The Golden Ass*. The hero of this story is turned into an ass, whose humorous adventures provide a fascinating insight into contemporary Roman society.

APULIA (Italian: *Puglia*), SE region forming the "heel" of the "boot" of Italy. It is composed of the provinces of Bari, Brindisi, Foggia, Lecce and Taranto. Its principal town and main port is Bari; it also contains the important naval base and steel industry of Taranto.

AQABA, Gulf of, NE arm of the Red Sea, between the Sinai Peninsula and Saudi Arabia. Geologically part of the Rift Valley of Africa and Asia, it is some 110mi long and 5–17mi wide. At the N end of the Gulf stand the ports of Aqaba (Jordan) and Eilat (Israel). The Egyptian blockade of Eilat sparked off the 1967 Arab-Israeli Six Days' War.

AQUALUNG or **SCUBA** (*s*elf-*c*ontained *u*nderwater *b*reathing *a*pparatus), a device allowing divers to breath and move about freely underwater. It comprises a mouthpiece, a connecting tube, a valve and at least one compressed-air cylinder. The key component is the "demand valve" which allows the diver to breathe air at the PRESSURE prevailing in the surrounding water however great the pressure in his supply cylinder. Used air is vented into the water.

AQUAMARINE, transparent pale blue or blue-green semiprecious GEM stone; a variety of BERYL.

AQUA REGIA, caustic mixture of one part NITRIC ACID and three parts HYDROCHLORIC ACID, which dissolves gold and platinum. It is used in analysis of minerals and alloys, and as a powerful cleaning agent.

AQUARIUM (or aquavivarium), tank or tanks for the display of fish and marine plants and animals. Aquaria provide an environment as close to the original habitat as possible: they may be fresh- or salt-water, tropical or cold. Although pet fish were kept as long ago as 2500 BC, it was not until 1853 that the first public aquarium was established (London), the first in the US in 1856 (New York). Today there are many public and private aquaria.

AQUARIUS (the Water Bearer), a large but faint constellation on the ECLIPTIC; the 11th sign of the ZODIAC.

AQUATINT, an ENGRAVING process used with particular success by GOYA, in which the plate is repeatedly etched through a porous (usually resin) ground. What are to produce the white areas of the finished print are stopped out with acid-resisting varnish before the first ETCHING, the other areas being stopped out in order of increasing darkness between subsequent etchings. The color-wash effect of aquatint is particularly striking when used in combination with drypoint.

AQUAVIT (or Akvavit), colorless spirits distilled from grain or potatoes and flavored with caraway seeds. It is popular in Scandinavia.

AQUEDUCT, man-made conduit for water. The Babylonians and Egyptians built large-scale underground aqueducts, but the Romans preferred a row of arches supporting the channels along which water flowed downhill from mountains to cities. Rome itself was supplied by nine aqueducts, but the most famous Roman ones are at Segovia and Tarragona, Spain, and near Nîmes, France (the *Pont du Gard*).

This modern aqueduct carries water from Colorado to the dry regions of southern California to irrigate them. Many segments of the canal run through desert areas.

AQUEOUS HUMOR, the clear, watery fluid between the cornea and the lens of the EYE.

AQUIFER, an underground rock formation through which GROUNDWATER can easily percolate. SANDSTONES, GRAVEL beds and jointed LIMESTONES make good aquifers.

AQUILA (the Eagle), large autumn constellation in the Northern Hemisphere, lying in the plane of the Milky Way. (See also ALTAIR.)

AQUILEIA, Italian city at the head of the Adriatic near Trieste. An important Roman commercial city, it was destroyed by ATTILA in 452. It later became well-known as a medieval theological center. Pop 3150.

AQUINAS, St. Thomas (c1225–1274 AD), known as the "angelic doctor," major Christian theologian and philosopher who attempted to reconcile faith with reason. In his *Summa Theologica* he uses Aristotelian logic to examine the existence of God: he finds God the logical uncaused cause, the prime reason for order in the universe. He sees man as a rational social animal gaining knowledge from sensory experience. His morality is based on the principle of man's harmony with himself, with other men and with God. Thomism, the philosophy of St. Thomas, has been very influential, and his teachings are basic to Roman Catholic theology.

AQUITAINE, historic French region, between the rivers Garonne and Loire, extending to the Pyrenees. Henry II of England's marriage to Eleanor of Aquitaine in 1152 resulted in centuries of Anglo-French territorial conflicts. The French crown regained control of Aquitaine in 1453, at the end of the HUNDRED YEARS' WAR.

ARAB, one whose language is Arabic and who identifies with Arab culture. Arabic belongs to the Semitic group of languages, which also includes Hebrew. Besides the countries of the Arabian Peninsula, the Arab world includes Algeria, Egypt, Iraq, Jordan, Lebanon, Libya, Morocco, Sudan, Syria and Tunisia. Arab culture spread after the coming of MOHAMMED (c570 AD). In the 7th century the Arabs extended their hegemony from NW Africa and Spain to Afghanistan and N India and many people were converted to the religion of ISLAM, adopting Arabic language and culture. Although Arab political control crumbled in the 10th and 11th centuries, the culture remained.

The precepts of Islam, as set out in the KORAN, still govern much of Arab life and social institutions. There are, however, non-Muslim peoples also considered Arabs, and many Arabs had adopted Christianity before and retained it after the rise of Islam. In the 20th century, reaction to the creation of the state of Israel has strengthened growing Pan-Arab nationalism and led to four ARAB–ISRAELI WARS.

ARABESQUE, elaborate decorative style characterized by curved or intertwining shapes with grotesque, animal, human or symbolic forms and delicate foliage. Arab culture introduced the use of geometric rather than figurative forms.

ARABIA (Arabic: *Jazirat al-Arab*, the "island of the Arabs"), Asian peninsula bounded by the Red Sea, Indian Ocean and Persian Gulf. It comprises Saudi Arabia, the Republic of Yemen, the Southern Yemen People's Republic, the Sultanate of Oman and the Persian Gulf States, including the Bahrain Islands, Qatar and the United Arab Emirates. The world's richest reserves of petroleum were discovered in the peninsula in the 1930s and have since flooded wealth into an almost feudal seminomadic society, creating large income-differentials within it. In 1973, Saudi Arabia and other Arab countries cut back oil supplies to the West, thus adding an important new economic weapon to the continuing Arab–Israeli conflict.

Between the birth of Christ and the emergence of MOHAMMED (c570 AD), various foreign powers influenced or controlled the area. Mecca, on a busy caravan route, was a prosperous trading center, but other towns remained little more than small oasis farming settlements. When Mohammed first achieved prominence, Arabia was divided between continually

In Arabia the contrast of old and new is striking. Here are seen an ancient watchtower and a modern oil refining plant near Abu Dhabi, one of the United Arab Emirates.

warring tribes. His founding of ISLAM resulted in a partial unification of the Arab tribes and rapid political and territorial expansion. By 800 Muslims controlled almost half the civilized world. But this power crumbled by the 11th century, when Turkey began its domination of the area. In the 18th and 19th centuries the Islamic Wahhabi movement weakened this power. In the 19th century Britain gained considerable footholds in Aden and on the Persian Gulf. After the Turks joined the Central Powers at the start of WWI, the British successfully encouraged the Arabs to revolt (1916). But it was only with the discovery of oil that the West developed interests in the region, primarily economic ones.

ARABIAN NIGHTS, or *The Thousand and One Nights*, a collection of 8th–16th century Arabic stories, probably of Indian origin with Persian and Arab additions. The stories, which include *Aladdin, Ali Baba* and *Sinbad*, are linked by Scheherazade who, sentenced to die at dawn, tells her husband the king one story per night, leaving the ending till the next day. She is reprieved after 1001 nights.

ARABIAN SEA, NW Indian Ocean, between India and Arabia. Connected with the Persian Gulf by the Gulf of Oman, and with the Red Sea by the Gulf of Aden. Its ports include Bombay and Karachi. It has always been important as a trade route between Europe and the Far East.

ARABIC, one of the SEMITIC LANGUAGES. The Arabic ALPHABET comprises 28 letters, all consonants, vowels being expressed either by positioned points or, in some cases, by insertion of the letters *alif*, *waw* and *ya* in positions where they would not otherwise occur, thereby representing the long *a*, *u* and *i* respectively. Arabic is written from right to left. Classical Arabic, the language of the Koran, is today used occasionally in writing, rarely in speech; a standardized modern Arabic being used for newspapers, etc. Arabic played a large part in the dissemination of knowledge through medieval Europe as many ancient Greek and Roman texts were available solely in Arabic translation.

ARAB-ISRAELI WARS, the results of persistent conflicts between Israel and the Arabs since the BALFOUR DECLARATION (1917) pronounced British Palestine a Jewish national home. When Britain's mandate ended, the Jews declared an independent state of Israel (May 14, 1948). The next day, Egypt, Iraq, Transjordan (Jordan), Lebanon and Syria attacked, but within a month Israel had occupied the greater part of Palestine. By July 1949, separate cease-fires had been concluded with the Arab states, where hundreds of thousands of Palestinian Arabs now sought refuge.

On Oct. 29, 1956, with the Suez Canal and Gulf of Aqaba closed to her ships, Israel invaded Egypt, which had nationalized the canal in July. British and French supporting troops occupied the canal banks, but were replaced by a UN force after international furore. By March 1957 all Israeli forces had left Egypt

Archaeology

The new China reveals its ancient treasures

Chinese history has long held a fascination for people in the West and for centuries Chinese art has been highly prized. But the communist takeover in China in 1949 severed all cultural links with the Western world and the flow of art and archaeological material out of China dried up completely. It was generally believed abroad that Chinese culture would inevitably suffer, particularly as in 1948 the Kuomintang government had shipped to Taiwan the bulk of the Palace Museum collection from Peking.

The Cultural Revolution of the 1960s, during which contingents of the People's Liberation Army (the Red Guards) roamed the Chinese countryside urging on peasants and workers a return to revolutionary fervor, and many universities and museums were closed, increased Western fears that the study of China's past had been destroyed by the new regime. However, in 1971 news first reached the outside world that in the previous 15 years or so, and more especially during the Cultural Revolution itself, sensational new discoveries had been made during widespread excavations all over China. Far from destroying her heritage, the new China was bent on preserving it, and was encouraging the study of her ancient past to an extent unknown before.

It was not until 1973 that the West got its first glimpse of some of the archaeological material which had been unearthed, mainly from tombs, since 1949. Two exhibitions of the finest treasures were mounted simultaneously in Paris and Tokyo. The exhibits sent to Paris were later shown in London, Vienna and Toronto, reaching Washington in December 1974.

In fact the communist regime had never discouraged interest in China's past. Mao Tse-tung always believed that China's democratic essence could be distilled from her feudal past. An appreciation of their historic struggles and sufferings would inspire the Chinese people to build the new socialist society. What the peasants and workers had created with their own sweat and toil for their feudal masters was now to be returned to them. Mao had always been a nationalist in the broadest sense, even collaborating intermittently with the Kuomintang of Chiang Kai-shek, particularly against Japanese aggression. He even used, in the final stages of the 1948–49 campaign, a strategic plan devised at the beginning of the Han Dynasty. Thus, after 1949, a scheme for reconstruction was initiated—the decaying Peking palaces were restored, the Palace Museum was reestablished and new museums opened in the provinces. A national archaeological service was created with networks in each province. And for the first time since Europe had made contact with China the export of works of art and archaeological material was prohibited.

It was the Cultural Revolution that played the most astonishing part in the new excavations. From 1966 onwards the Red Guards were heeding Mao's exhortation "Ku wei chin yung"—make the past serve the present. Apart from many chance finds—such as the hoard of T'ang Dynasty (618–906 AD) silver, jade and gold found in the southern suburbs of Sian in 1970—the People's Liberation Army itself conducted excavations of many tomb sites, with the aid of experts. The most sensational of these tombs both date from the Western Han Dynasty (206 BC–8 AD)—located at Man-ch'eng (Hopei province) and Changsha (Hunan province). It was from the tombs at Man-ch'eng that the startling jade funeral suits came, which had encased the bodies of Prince Liu Sheng and his wife, Princess Tou Wan. Jade was thought to be the congealed semen of the dragon and to possess powers of preservation that would prevent bodily decay, but the dust found inside the two suits sadly belied this belief. Fragments of jade suits, which were constructed from hundreds of small pieces of jade held together with specially knotted loops of gold or silver wire, had been found previously. But none had ever been recovered sufficiently complete to be reconstituted until the Man-ch'eng tombs were excavated in 1968.

The recent exhibitions of archaeological finds have shed a great deal of light on China's past, from the Palaeolithic period (c600 000–7000 BC) right down to the Yüan Dynasty (1271–1368 AD). Jaw and skull fragments found in 1963–64 at Lan-t'ien near Sian proved to be from the earliest hominid yet found in China, predating even the famous Peking Man. Some remarkable pieces of pottery from the Neolithic period (7th to 2nd millennium BC) attest the technological achievements of China's first farmers. Exhibits from Pan-p'o, excavated in 1954–57, representing the Yang-shao Neolithic culture of central China, reveal the use of high-temperature firing of pottery in kilns of advanced design, and a variety of decorative techniques (e.g. stamping, burnishing and painting). Later people developed the use of the potter's wheel.

The exhibitions were particularly rich in bronze ware representative of the skills and expertise of a people who came late to metalworking compared with the West. The Shang Dynasty (c1550–c1027 BC)—the first historical dynasty and a period of inward-looking theocratic rule—was the Chinese age of bronze. More than 20 bronze objects in the Washington exhibition—especially weapons, tools and wine vessels—witnessed the emergence of Chinese society, during the Shang period, from its Neolithic stage. The Shang developed a form of ideographic writing (sometimes preserved on oracle bones), white kaolin pottery, chariots, city walls and a knowledge of metallurgy that befitted China's attainment of a high level of civilization. Shang bronzes were cast, using piece molds, and were often decorated with distinctive animal motifs, frequently the dragon, a creature particularly characteristic of the Shang. So far no evidence of contact with civilization outside China has been shown for this period; the Chinese appear to have developed their bronze technology independently of outside influence.

But perhaps the most fascinating phenomenon illustrated in the Washington exhibition is the cult of the horse which swept China during the Later, or Eastern Han Dynasty (24–220 AD). Until the 1st century AD the Chinese had possessed only their own native horses—slow, small and ineffective in battle—similar to the steppe ponies still found in Central Asia and possibly related to Przhevalsky's Horse. But a nation's might depended on the quality of its horseflesh, and during the later Han period, when contacts with the northwest were renewed, the Chinese acquired a new breed of horse—according to legend the "Heavenly Horses" that sweated blood—from the Kingdom of Fergana (now in Soviet Central Asia) but more probably from the Persian province of Sogdiana (now Bokhara). These western horses, probably an Arab breed, became the objects of an almost religious veneration in China, the emperor even believing that one of these mysterious creatures would finally carry him up to heaven. It became the custom to make images of the horses, so different in appearance and temperament from their placid and docile predecessors. The tomb excavations of the 1950s and 1960s furnished ample proof of this veneration. Bronze and pottery representations of horses were prolific in the Washington exhibition, which was dominated by the magnificent bronze figure of the "flying horse" from Wu-wei in Kansu province. Suspended in space, with one hoof delicately resting on the back of a swallow in flight, it embodies the ideal of the "celestial" horse, combining power and majesty in its limbs with the ethereal grace of its pose.

The Han Dynasty saw other examples of contact with the world outside China. Art and commerce flourished while the first Buddhist influences reached China

---

in exchange for access to the Gulf of Aqaba.

In 1967 Egypt closed the gulf to Israel and on June 5, at the start of the Six-Day War, Israeli air strikes destroyed Arab air forces on the ground. Israel won the west bank of the Jordan R, the Golan Heights, the Gaza Strip, the Sinai Peninsula and the Old City of Jerusalem. A ceasefire was accepted by June 10. In the following years, worldwide Arab anti-Jewish terrorism became common, reaching a climax in the 1972 Munich Olympic massacre of Israeli sportsmen.

On Oct. 6, 1973, Yom Kippur (the Jewish Day of Atonement), Egypt and Syria attacked Israel to regain the lost territories. A ceasefire was signed on Nov. 11, 1973. Although Israeli troops penetrated deep into Syria and crossed onto the W bank of the Suez Canal, initial Arab success restored confidence and encouraged oil-rich Arab states to use economic measures against Israel's Western sympathizers. (See also MIDDLE EAST.)

ARAB LEAGUE, an organization to promote economic, cultural and political cooperation between Arab states, set up on March 22, 1945. Although quite successful in its first two aims, it has only achieved real political unity of action in 1956 (Suez Crisis), 1961 (Franco–Tunisian conflict) and 1973 (cutback of oil to the West). The league originally comprised Egypt, Iraq, Lebanon, Saudi Arabia, Syria, Transjordan (Jordan) and Yemen. These were joined by Libya (1953), Sudan (1956), Tunisia and Morocco (1958), Kuwait (1961), Algeria (1962) and the People's Democratic Republic of Yemen (1968). The Republic of Somalia became the League's twentieth member in 1974. (See also MIDDLE EAST.)

ARACAJU, capital of Sergipe state on the Cotinguiba R in NE Brazil. It serves as port and industrial center to the surrounding cotton and sugar producing area. Pop 182 000.

ARACHNE, maiden in Greek myth who beat the goddess Athena in a weaving contest. Provoked by Athena, she hanged herself, but the goddess changed the rope into a cobweb and Arachne into a spider.

ARACHNIDA, class of ARTHROPODS whose most important members are SPIDERS; SCORPIONS; HARVESTMEN; MITES and TICKS. Most of the 60 000 species are harmless to man, but a few have poisonous bites (e.g., the BLACK WIDOW spider). With a cephalothorax (a fused head and THORAX), four pairs of legs and two pairs of other appendages, they are quite unlike INSECTS. Most are land-dwelling, some parasitic (see PARASITE). Their size ranges from almost invisibly small to about 150mm (6in) in length.

ARAD, Israeli town in the Negev Desert, 15mi W of the Dead Sea. Established in 1962, near the site of biblical Arad, it manufactures textiles and chemical products. Pop 4 500.

ARAD, city in W Romania on the Mureşul R. Its products include machine tools, textiles, railroad cars, grain and wine. In 1849 it served briefly as the headquarters of the Hungarian rebellion; the city has a large Hungarian minority. Pop 139 000.

ARAFAT, Yassir (1929–   ), Palestinian leader of the anti-Israel Al Fatah guerrillas, and chairman of the PALESTINE LIBERATION ORGANIZATION since 1968.

1

2

4

3

5

These archaeological finds span 1 600 years of Chinese history and display a mastery in art of richness, color, movement, dignity and superlative grace. (1) Jade funeral suit of the princess Tou Wan from the Western Han dynasty, 2nd century BC. (2) and (3) Porcelain vases from the Yüan dynasty, 14th century AD. (4) White glazed spittoon from the T'ang dynasty, 9th century AD. (5) Bronze horse from the Eastern Han dynasty, 2nd century AD.

from India in the 1st century BC. Tao Buddhism quickly took root in China and deeply affected Chinese religious practice, reflected in changing art styles. Objects of Buddhist religious art were few in the exhibition but one striking example was the Buddhist altar, dating from the T'ang Dynasty, carved from white marble, which represents the Buddha seated under śala trees between disciples and Bodhisattvas. It was excavated at Lin-chang (Hopei province) in 1959.

The two Han tombs at Man-ch'eng and Ma-wang-tui, both excavated during the Cultural Revolution, have provided the two exhibitions with some of their richest treasures. Certainly the most astonishing tomb is that of Ma-wang-tui, at Changsha in southern China. Excavated in 1971, many of its contents were exhibited in Tokyo soon after their discovery. The tomb was most unusual in that it had never been robbed and contained the body of a woman (probably the wife of Li Tsang, a nobleman of Ta) perfectly preserved from decay by the protective layers of charcoal, plaster and wood lining her burial chamber. It was even possible to determine that she had died of tuberculosis. An inventory, left in the tomb, listed 312 articles buried with the dead woman. Most of these are perfectly preserved; the silk in particular has maintained its original magnificent appearance. The coffin was covered with a silk pall colorfully embroidered with birds' feathers included in the design, and the body was wrapped in 20 layers of silk. The most precious object in the tomb is a silk hanging scroll, depicting scenes from the world of man and from the heavens and nether regions. Before this discovery no authentic hanging scroll earlier than the Buddhist banners of the T'ang Dynasty had been known, but the recent find indicates that these scrolls were being made 1 000 years earlier.

Western connoisseurs of Chinese art have for centuries valued the possession of Chinese porcelain. Although the exhibitions concentrated on the less well-known technological achievements of Chinese art, they also included some magnificent specimens of porcelain. The exotic impact of the Mongol court during the Yüan Dynasty is particularly evident in the porcelain of that period. Underglaze painting in blue was introduced from Persia in the 14th century and was the beginning of China's famous blue-and-white porcelain, later so popular in Europe. One typical Yüan vase was featured in the Washington exhibition: it is eight-faceted in underglaze blue and decorated with dragons in a popular wave pattern. The combination of space-filling techniques with the more traditional Chinese floral motifs is very characteristic of Yüan porcelain, for which three underglazes were used—blue (cobalt), red (probably iron) and green (copper). Most of this new Yüan porcelain was found during the excavation within the city of Peking of the original Mongol capital of Kublai Khan, founded in 1267. A cache of some of the earliest blue-and-white pieces known was found there in an excavated mansion of a nobleman.

The recent exhibitions of Chinese art and archaeology mounted outside China show the pride the Chinese have retained in their past, heeding Mao's words—don't destroy old things, only old attitudes of mind. But they have also exemplified a professional and scientific approach to excavation not associated with pre-Revolutionary Chinese archaeology. Not least, the exhibitions have revealed a hopeful spirit of friendship and cooperation between China and the rest of the world and a generous desire on her part to share the magnificent cultural achievements of the Chinese people.

In Nov. 1974 Arafat opened a debate on Palestine at the UN, where he led the first non-governmental delegation to take part in a General Assembly plenary session.

ARAFURA SEA, part of the Pacific Ocean, covering 250 000sq mi between N Australia, Indonesia and W New Guinea.

ARAGO, Dominique François Jean (1786–1853), French physicist and mathematician whose work helped establish the wave theory of LIGHT. He discovered the polarization of light in quartz crystals (1811) and was awarded the Royal Society's Copley Medal in 1825 for demonstrating the magnetic effect of a rotating copper disk.

ARAGON, historic region of NE Spain, stretching from the central Pyrenees to S of the Ebro R. The medieval kingdom of Aragon comprised what are now Huesca, Teruel and Saragossa provinces though the influence of the kings of Aragon was more extensive. King Ferdinand II of Aragon's marriage to Isabella of Castile (1469) laid the foundations of a unified Spain. Aragon's sovereignty was ended 1707–09 by Philip V during the war of SPANISH SUCCESSION (1701–14).

ARAGON, Louis (1897–), French novelist, poet and journalist, a leading figure in the dadaist and surrealist movements of the 1920s and 1930s, as is reflected in his early poetry. He joined the Communist Party in the 1930s, and thereafter turned to social realism. After WWII he edited the left-wing weekly *Les Lettres Françaises.*

ARAGUAIA RIVER, main tributary of the Tocantins R in central Brazil. It is 1 632mi long and divides to form the 200mi long island of Bananal in NW Goiás state.

ARAKCHEYEV, Count Aleksei Andreyevich (1769–1834), powerful Russian general and statesman under Tsars Paul I and Alexander I. He was notorious for the harsh disciplinary methods of his reorganization of Paul I's army. (In Russian, *arakcheyevchina* means callous, inhuman behavior.)

ARALIA, *Fatsia japonica,* an evergreen shrub native to Japan and Formosa, which produces glossy, dark-green palmate leaves and panicles of white flowers. It is a popular house plant favoring temperatures between 16°C and 21°C (60°F and 70°F). Aralia requires little watering and is propagated by means of seeds, rooted side shoots and cuttings. The closely related false aralia (*Dizygotheca elegantissima*) is native to the New Hebrides and differs from the true aralia in that its palmate leaves are divided into linear leaflets and it requires more watering. Family: Araliaceae.

ARAL SEA, saltwater lake covering 24 749sq mi in the Kazakh and Uzbek republics of the USSR. It is the fourth-largest inland lake in the world and is fed by the AMU DARYA and SYR DARYA rivers. The sea is commercially important for its bass, carp, perch and sturgeon.

ARAMAEANS, nomadic Semites of the N Syrian desert in the 11th to 8th centuries BC. They assimilated features of earlier FERTILE CRESCENT civilizations. Most of the smaller Aramaean tribes were subjugated by the Assyrians 740–720 BC. But the Chaldean tribe, which settled near the Tigris and

Euphrates estuary, extended its control over all Mesopotamia, succeeding the Assyrians. (See also BABYLONIA AND ASSYRIA.)

ARAMAIC, the Semitic language of the ARAMAEANS. Its use spread throughout Syria and Mesopotamia from the 8th century BC onwards and it became the official language of the Persian Empire. Aramaic was probably spoken by Jesus and the apostles, being by then the everyday language of Palestine. Parts of the Old Testament are in Aramaic. It survives only in isolated Lebanese villages and among some NESTORIANS of N Iraq and E Turkey.

ARAN ISLANDS, three small islands at the mouth of Galway Bay, Ireland: Inishmore (Big Island); Inishmaan (Middle Island); and Inisheer (East Island), Tourism is increasingly replacing the traditional subsistence occupations of fishing and farming. The islands have many pre-Christian and early Christian ruins. Pop 1 648.

ARANJUEZ, town in central Spain on the Tagus R. Standing on the site of a Roman settlement, Aranjuez was rebuilt in the 18th century by King Ferdinand VI and is today a popular tourist attraction. Pop 29 548.

ARANY, János (1817–1882), Hungarian nationalist epic poet who sprang to fame with the publication of the first part of his epic trilogy *Toldi* (1847). Other important works include *The Death of King Buda* (1864) and Hungarian translations of Shakespeare, Goethe and Aristophanes.

ARAPAHO, North American Indian tribe of the ALGONQUIAN family. They lived as nomadic buffalo hunters on the Great Plains in two groups — the N and S Arapaho. Fierce enemies of white settlement, they were forced into reservations at the end of the 19th century. By the 1970s, only 5000 remained, mostly on reservations in Okla. and Wyo.

ARARAT, Mount, dormant volcanic mountain in E Turkey with two peaks (16950ft and 13000ft) 7mi apart. Genesis 8:4 says that Noah's Ark landed "upon the mountains of Ararat." The Armenians venerate the mountain as the Mother of the World. The last eruption was in 1840.

ARAS RIVER (Russian: *Araks*), the ancient river of Araxes, flows some 570mi from S of Erzurum in Turkish Armenia to the Caspian Sea, partly forming the border between the USSR in the north and Turkey and Iran in the south.

ARAUCANIAN INDIANS, South American tribes famous for their resistance to the 16th-century Spanish invasion of what is now central Chile. Many Araucanians crossed the Andes into Argentina. During the 19th century the Araucanians were settled on Chilean and Argentinian reservations where they have since maintained much of their traditional culture.

ARAWAK INDIANS, linguistic group of often culturally distinct South American tribes, now living mostly in Brazil, the Guianas and Peru. They also inhabited the Caribbean islands at the time Columbus landed there in 1492, but were later exterminated by the CARIB INDIANS.

ARBELA. See GAUGAMELA.

ARBITRAGE, the buying of commodities in one market by a speculator who immediately sells for a higher price in another market. Such opportunities exist only momentarily, as arbitrage tends to equalize price discrepancies between markets by equalizing the forces of supply and demand. The practice is common in stocks and shares, and in precious-metal and foreign-exchange markets.

ARBITRATION, process for settling disputes by submitting the issues involved to the judgment of an impartial third party or arbitrator. In the recent past, most US industrial collective bargaining agreements have allowed for an arbitrator to act in cases where problems of interpretation arise. An arbitration service, providing panels for commercial and industrial disputes, has been established by the American Arbitration Association. Several state and federal laws ensure the enforcement of agreements to submit disputes to arbitration. The Taft-Hartley Act (1947) provides for emergency fact-finding boards if serious strikes loom but, as their decisions are not binding, they lack the power of arbitrating bodies. (See also FEDERAL MEDIATION AND CONCILIATION SERVICES; INTERNATIONAL COURT OF JUSTICE; INTERNATIONAL LAW.)

ARBOR DAY, annual tree-planting day in some US states. In northern areas it is normally held in the spring and in southern areas in winter. It was first held in Neb. on April 10, 1872.

ARBORETUM (from Latin *arbor*, tree), a collection of clearly labeled trees and shrubs kept for educational, scientific and ornamental purposes. Notable examples are the US National Arboretum, Wash., D.C.; the Arnold Arboretum, Harvard; and in the Royal Botanic Gardens, Kew, England.

ARBORVITAE (Latin: **tree of life**), any of five species of the genus *Thuja* of aromatic evergreen trees native to North America and E Asia. Best known are the northern white cedar or eastern arborvitae (*T. occidentalis*) and the western red cedar or giant arborvitae (*T. plicata*). Family: Cupressaceae. (See also CEDAR).

ARBUTHNOT, John (1667–1735), Scots-born mathematician, physician to Queen Anne and eminent satirist. Arbuthnot belonged to the famous Scriblerus Club, together with Alexander POPE, Jonathan SWIFT, and John GAY. He is noted for *The History of John Bull* (1712) and his contribution to *The Memoirs of Martinus Scriblerus* (1741).

ARBUTHNOT AND AMBRISTER, Case of, the court-martial and execution of two British traders, Alexander Arbuthnot and Robert Ambrister, during Gen. Andrew Jackson's unauthorized raid into Spanish Fla. in 1818. The incident speeded the cession of E Fla. under the ADAMS–ONÍS TREATY (1819).

ARBUTUS, genus of broadleaved evergreen shrubs or trees native to S Europe, S Asia and western North America. Best known are the madroña tree (*A. menziesii*) and the strawberry tree (*A. unedo*), cultivated as ornamentals in warm regions for their white or pink flowers and bright orange-red berries. The **trailing arbutus** is an unrelated species belonging to the genus *Epigaea*. Family: Ericaceae.

ARBUTUS-HALETHORPE-RELAY, an unincorporated town of three villages. It is a residential and industrial suburb of Baltimore, Md. Pop 22 402.

ARC. See CIRCLE.

ARCADE, a row of arches supported by piers or columns, as in the COLOSSEUM and in the Roman aqueduct near Nîmes, France. In Gothic cathedrals, the rows of arches separating the side aisles from the nave are known as arcades. The term can also refer to a narrow roofed-in street lined with shops.

ARCADIA, ancient Greek region in central PELOPONNESUS, enclosed by mountains. The simple life of its rustic inhabitants amid its idyllic pastures and fertile valleys was used by Classical pastoral poets and later writers, such as SANNAZZARO and Sir Philip SIDNEY, as the ideal of innocent, virtuous living.

ARCADIA, mainly residential city in SW Cal. The Santa Anita racetrack is located here. Pop 42 868.

ARCADIUS (c377–408), first emperor of the Eastern Roman Empire, jointly with his father Theodosius I until the latter's death in 395. In 402, he shared his rule with his son Theodosius II. A weak ruler, Arcadius was dominated by his wife and ministers.

ARCARO, Eddie (George Edward Arcaro; 1916–), by the mid-1970s the only US jockey to have won the triple crown twice (1941 and 1948). Arcaro was also the world's third-greatest race-winner (4 779 wins) and the second-greatest money-winner (more than $30 million).

ARC DE TRIOMPHE, Napoleon I's triumphal arch in the Place Charles de Gaulle at the end of the Champs Elysées, Paris. It was built 1806–36 and is 162ft high and 147ft wide. Inspired by Roman triumphal arches, it bears reliefs celebrating Napoleon's victories. The arch is also the site of the tomb of France's Unknown Soldier.

ARCE, Manuel José (c1783–1847), the Central American Federation's first president (1825–29). He had been a leader of the Central American revolt against Spain and the opposition to Mexico's territorial ambitions but, as president, his popularity waned and he was eventually deposed.

ARCH, structural device to span openings and support loads. In ARCHITECTURE the simplest form of arch is the round (semicircular): here, as in most arches, wedge-shaped stones (**voussoirs**) are fitted together so that stresses in the arch exert outward forces on them; downward forces from the load combine with these to produce a diagonal resultant termed the THRUST. The voussoirs at each end of the arch are termed **springers**; that in the center, usually the last to be inserted, is the **keystone**. Although the arch was known in Ancient Egypt and Greece, it was not until Roman times that its use became popular.

ARCHAEOLOGY, the study of the past through identification and interpretation of the material remains of human cultures. A comparatively new science, involving many academic and scientific disciplines, including ANTHROPOLOGY, history, PALEOGRAPHY and PHILOLOGY, it makes use of numerous scientific techniques. Its keystone is fieldwork.

Archaeology was born in the early 18th century. There were some excavations of Roman and other sites, and the famous ROSETTA STONE, which provided the key to Egyptian HIEROGLYPHICS, was discovered in 1799 and deciphered in 1818. In 1832 archaeological time was classified into three divisions: STONE AGE, BRONZE AGE and IRON AGE; though this system is now more commonly used to describe cultures of PRIMITIVE MAN.

However, it was not until the 19th century that archaeology graduated from its amateur status to become a systematized science. SCHLIEMANN, Arthur EVANS, WOOLLEY, CARTER and others adopted an increasingly scientific approach in their researches.

Excavation is a painstaking procedure, as great care must be taken not to damage any object or fragment of an object, and each of the different levels of excavation must be carefully documented and photographed. The location of suitable sites for excavation is assisted by historical accounts, topographical surveys and aerial photography.

Dating is accomplished in several ways. First, of course, is comparison of the relative depths of objects that are discovered. Analysis of the types of pollen in an object can provide an indication of its date. The most widespread dating technique is RADIOCARBON DATING, incorporating the corrections formulated through discoveries in DENDROCHRONOLOGY.

(See also ABU SIMBEL; AURIGNACIAN; BARROW; CAIRN; CARNAC; CELTS; DOLMEN; EPIGRAPHY; GRAFFITO; KITCHEN MIDDEN; LAKE DWELLING; LA TÈNE; MEGALITHIC MONUMENTS; MOUNDS; PREHISTORIC MAN; PYRAMIDS OF EGYPT; STONEHENGE.)

ARCHAEOPTERYX, or *Archaeopteryx lithographica*, pigeon-sized FOSSIL animal displaying both BIRD and REPTILE characteristics. The toothed head and long tail were clearly reptilian, but the FEATHERS with which the animal was covered are thought to have

The mound at Tell es-Sa'idiyeh in the Jordan valley, an ancient settlement which is being investigated by an American expedition led by J. B. Pritchard. This is slow and meticulous work since the smallest shard of pottery can be essential in identifying and dating the various levels of habitation of the site.

1

2

3

4

5

6

Some of man's greatest achievements in architecture: (1) The great pyramid of King Khufu (Cheops) is over 4500 years old and covers 13 acres. (2) The Parthenon on the Acropolis in Athens, a model for neo-classical buildings the world over. (3) The Basilica of Saint Peter in Rome, the world's largest Christian church. Built between 1492 and 1612, its architects included Michelangelo and Bernini. (4) The impressive Colosseum or Flavian Amphitheater in Rome, built between 70 and 82 AD. (5) French Gothic at its finest, the imposing nave of Rheims cathedral seen from the choir. (6) Time will judge this strikingly modern office building on 42nd Street, New York.

been almost identical with those of modern birds. *Archaeopteryx*, although aerial, probably could not fly actively, only glide.

ARCHANGEL, a prince of angels, or chief angel, often entrusted with God's messages and counsel to men. The most prominent are Gabriel (Daniel 8:16; 9:21; Luke 1:19, 26), Michael (Daniel 10:13, 21; 12:1; Jude 9; Revelation 12:7) and Raphael (Tobit). Later writings refer to the archangels Phanuel, Raguel, Remiel, Uriel and Saraquael.

ARCHANGEL. See ARKHANGELSK.

ARCHBISHOP, a metropolitan BISHOP of the Roman Catholic, Anglican and Eastern churches, and the Lutheran churches of Finland and Sweden, having jurisdiction over the bishops of a church province, or archdiocese, within which he consecrates bishops and presides over synods. Archbishops do not form a separate order of MINISTRY. The term may be applied to the bishops of distinguished sees, or PATRIARCHS.

ARCHEAN, synonym for ARCHEOZOIC.

ARCHEOZOIC, the portion of the PRECAMBRIAN prior to about 2390 million years ago. (See also GEOLOGY; PROTEROZOIC.)

ARCHER FISHES, several species, particularly *Toxotes jaculatrix*, comprising the family Toxotidae (order Perciformes), named for their ability to "shoot down" insects by squirting droplets of water from their mouths, with 100% accuracy over distances of 1m (3ft) or more. Generally less than 200mm (8in) long, they usually have silvery bodies with three or four dark bars on the flanks.

ARCHERY, shooting with bow and arrow, used in warfare by primitive peoples in the Americas, Africa and Asia, and in ancient Greece and the Near East. It was vital in medieval European warfare. The English longbow's superiority over the French crossbow won the Battle of AGINCOURT (1415). Between the 14th and 15th centuries, the bow's use in W Europe declined with the development of firearms. But in late 18th-century England archery was revived as a sport. The US National Archery Association was formed in 1879 and, since 1900, archery has been part of the Olympic Games. The sport involves shooting at a standard circular target marked with colored concentric circles.

ARCHES NATIONAL PARK, 82950 acres in E Utah containing natural rock arches formed by weathering and erosion.

ARCHETYPE, term used by JUNG to refer to the COLLECTIVE UNCONSCIOUS.

ARCHIMEDES (c287–212 BC), Greek mathematician and physicist who spent most of his life at his birthplace, Syracuse (Sicily). In mathematics he worked on the areas and volumes associated with CONIC SECTIONS, fixed the value of PI (π) between $3\frac{10}{70}$ and $3\frac{10}{71}$ and defined the **Archimedean Spiral** ($r = a\theta$). He founded the science of HYDROSTATICS with his enunciation of **Archimedes' Principle**. This states that the force acting to buoy up a body partially or totally immersed in a fluid is equal to the weight of the fluid displaced. In MECHANICS he studied the properties of the LEVER and applied his experience in the construction of military catapults and grappling irons. He is also said to have invented the **Archimedes Screw**, a machine for raising water still used to irrigate fields in Egypt. This consists of a helical tube or a cylindrical tube containing a close-fitting screw with the lower end dipping in the water. When the tube (or screw) is rotated, water is moved up the tube and is discharged from the top.

ARCHIPENKO, Alexander (1887–1964), Ukrainian-born US sculptor, famous for nude female torsos in which naturalistic forms are reduced to elegant geometric shapes.

ARCHITECTURE has usually been defined as the art of building. The architect today is both an artist and an engineer who must combine a knowledge of design and construction, and of the available resources in labor, techniques and materials, to produce a harmonious, durable and functional whole. His building must be fitted to its environment and must satisfy the social needs for which it is required—whether it is a church, dwelling, factory or office building. In the past all this was accomplished in a traditional manner by largely anonymous builders; today the architect plans both the aesthetics and the construction of his building in a highly conscious manner, often deliberately attempting to communicate artistic concepts and abstract ideas through the structure itself.

The architect designs buildings for human activities; and most such buildings spring directly out of the culture of their time. Hence architecture in any period is one of the most visible and significant expressions of the culture that produced it. The

Egyptian pyramid, for instance, as a royal tomb, translated the pharaoh's hope for an eternal afterlife into huge, long-lasting piles of masonry, while the awesome, columned halls of the royal palace at Persepolis were built to display the majesty of the ancient kings of Persia. The Islamic mosque and the Gothic cathedral, one open to sunny skies, the other closed and vaulted against northern weather, provided equally generous spaces for communal worship. Rome and the modern city both produced apartment houses for urban living; the Pueblo Indians built them for agricultural communities. The English stately home expressed the power and aspirations of a remarkable ruling class, while the modern glass skyscraper fulfills the needs of our industrial and business society.

Architecture has always been limited by the materials and techniques at its command; conversely, architectural advances and the development of new styles have been marked by the adoption of new materials or the discovery of new techniques. Traditionally the materials have been stone, earth, brick, wood, glass, concrete, iron and steel—with plastics and new metals added today. With its great compressive strength, stone has been the material of most major buildings in the past. It gave rise to the common post and lintel type of construction, and to the arch, the latter culminating in the soaring lightness of the Gothic cathedrals. The acme of the ancient post and lintel construction was reached in the classic simplicity of the Greek temple, notably in the PARTHENON. To these elements the Romans added daring experiments in vaulting, made possible by the use of concrete, as in the PANTHEON (2nd century AD), carried still further in Byzantine, Romanesque and Islamic architecture. But the tensile strength of stone is poor, while wood and steel have tensile as well as compressive strength. This made frame construction possible, as in the wooden buildings of Japan or the steel-framed modern building. Geodesic and stressed-frame methods of construction, with reinforced concrete, have further extended the range of the modern architect.

Not only new materials and techniques, but also developments in social and institutional needs, the exigencies of climate and the need to express new aspirations and ideals in differing cultures have brought about changing styles in architecture. Often new architectures have repeated and elaborated older styles, as in the Renaissance and the Greek and Roman revivals. The use of ornamentation or decoration in architecture—as in the intricate surface decoration of Islamic buildings or the elaborations of the Rococo—has varied in response to changing tastes. Today we are emerging from a period of intense reaction against surface decoration embodied in the plain and functional International style of recent modern architecture. Styles change, but at all times and in all places the architect has attempted to manipulate space, mass, light and color to produce the optimum proportion and scale called for by the human mind. Thus the importance of architecture in civilization is three-fold: it is an art, it is made for people, and it is always a major expression of culture.

ARCHIVES, documents of a public body preserved in an organized fashion. Systematic collection and supervision by a central government agency began in 1789 with the French *Archives Nationales.* The US National Archives and Records Service (originating in 1934) houses records in the National Archives Building, Washington, D.C. It has the originals of the DECLARATION OF INDEPENDENCE and the CONSTITUTION. Corporations, foundations, universities and cities also keep archives, which now include tape recordings and space-saving microfilms.

ARCHON (Greek: ruler), title held by chief magistrates in ancient Greek city states. After 683 BC nine elected archons ruled Athens.

ARC LAMP, an intensely bright and comparatively efficient form of LIGHTING used for lighthouses, floodlights and spotlights, invented by DAVY in 1809. An arc discharge is set up when two carbon ELECTRODES at a moderate POTENTIAL difference (typically 40V) are "struck" (touched together then drawn apart). The light is emitted from vaporized carbon IONS in the discharge. In modern lamps the arc is enclosed in an atmosphere of high-pressure XENON.

ARCTIC REGIONS, regions N of the Arctic Circle (66°30′ N); alternatively regions N of the tree line. The Arctic comprises the Arctic Ocean, Greenland, Spitsbergen and other islands, extreme N Europe, N Siberia, Alaska and N Canada. The central feature is the Arctic Ocean, opening S into the N Atlantic Ocean and joined with the N Pacific Ocean by the Bering Strait. The Arctic Ocean comprises two main basins and has a shallow rim floored by the continental shelves of Eurasia and North America. Much of the ocean surface is always covered by ice.

The Arctic climate is cold. In midwinter the sun never rises and the mean Jan. temperature is −33°F, far lower in interior Canada and Siberia. Snow and ice never melt in high altitudes and latitudes, but elsewhere the short mild summer with 24 hours' sunlight a day thaws the sea and the topsoil. In spring, melting icebergs floating south from the Arctic Ocean endanger N Atlantic shipping. Vegetation is varied but confined mainly to shrubs, flowering herbaceous plants, mosses and lichens. Wild mammals include polar bears, reindeer, musk oxen, moose, wolves, weasels, foxes and lemmings. Geese, ducks, gulls, cranes, falcons, auks and ptarmigan all nest in the Arctic, and its seas harbor whales, seals, cod, salmon and shrimp. Eskimos, Lapps, Russians and others make up a human population of several million. Eskimos have lived in the Arctic for at least 9000 years, and total 60000 or more. Once exclusively hunters and fishermen, Eskimos now work in towns and on oil fields. The USSR has agricultural, mining and fishing industries in Siberia; and the US, Canada and USSR man air bases and meteorological stations.

Vikings were the first recorded Arctic explorers: Norwegians visited the Russian Arctic in the 9th century and the Icelander ERIC THE RED established a Greenland settlement c982 AD. In the 16th and 17th centuries search for a "Northwest Passage" and a "Northeast Passage" to the Orient encouraged exploration. In the 16th century Martin FROBISHER reached Baffin Island and Willem BARENTS explored Novaya Zemlya and saw Spitsbergen. Henry HUDSON probed E Greenland and the Hudson Strait in the early 17th century. But the longed-for passages remained undiscovered, and interest in Arctic exploration declined until Canadian and Russian fur traders revived it late in the 18th century. Early in the 19th century the British naval officers John and James ROSS, W. E. PARRY, John RAE and Sir John FRANKLIN traveled to unexplored areas, James Ross discovering the north magnetic pole. N. A. E. Nordenskjöld of Sweden navigated the Northeast Passage (1878–79) and R. AMUNDSEN the Northwest Passage (1906) and in 1909 Robert E. PEARY reached the North Pole. Richard E. BYRD and Floyd BENNETT overflew the Pole in 1926, pioneering polar air exploration and transpolar air travel. In 1958 the US nuclear submarine *Nautilus* reached the Pole under the ice-cap.

Modern technologists are learning to exploit the Arctic's considerable economic resources, which include metals, fluorides, phosphates and mineral fuels. To supply oil to the US, an 800mi pipeline is being thrown across oil-rich Alaska.

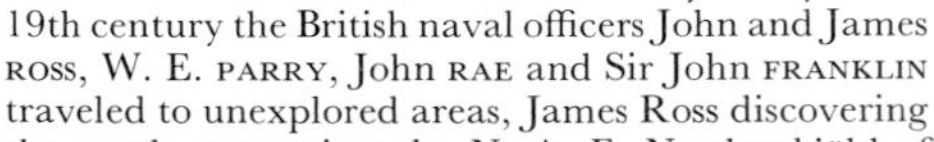

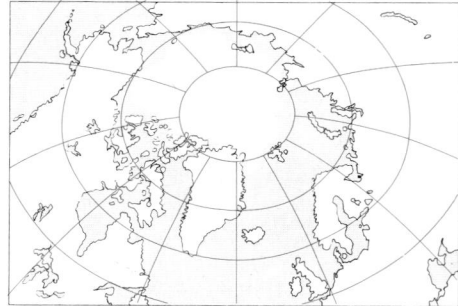

ARCTIC TERN. See TERNS.

ARCTURUS, Alpha Boötis, a red giant star 11pc distant. It has a very high PROPER MOTION and an apparent magnitude of −0.04.

ARDASHIR I (reigned c224–c240 AD), king of Persia (Iran) who founded its Sassanid dynasty (see SASSANIANS). Crowned at Ctesiphon after defeating Artabanus V, the last Parthian king, he reunited Persia and seized lands E into Central Asia. He established ZOROASTRIANISM as the state religion.

ARDENNES, tract of oak and beech forest in SE Belgium, N Luxembourg and around the Meuse valley of N France. The area is a sparsely populated plateau with some agriculture and quarrying. It was a battleground in WWI and WWII (see BATTLE OF THE BULGE).

ARDMORE, city in S Okla. It is the seat of Carter Co., and an agricultural and manufacturing center processing zinc and oil. Pop 20881.

AREA, in plane GEOMETRY, the measure of the extent of an enclosed surface or region in terms of the number of squares with sides of unit length, or fractions of those squares, that could be fitted exactly into it. Areas are usually measured in square metres (m^2). The area of an enclosed region on a curved surface is given by the area it would cover if spread out on a PLANE surface.

ARECIBO, seaport town in N Puerto Rico, 50mi W of the capital San Juan. It is a commercial and industrial center in an agricultural area. Pop 73283.

ARENDT, Hannah (1906–1975), German-born US political philosopher. She was the first woman to become a full professor at Princeton U. In *Origins of Totalitarianism* (1951) she traced nazism and communism back to 19th-century anti-Semitism and imperialism.

AREOPAGUS, hill NW of the Acropolis of Athens; also the name of the supreme city council which once met there to pass judgment on matters of state, religion and morality.

AREQUIPA, city in S Peru, located at 8000ft between the Pacific Ocean and the Andes. It is the capital of Arequipa Department and Peru's third largest city, producing textiles, shoes and foodstuffs and trading in wool. The Spanish founded Arequipa in 1540 on the site of an Inca city. Pop 194700.

ARES, the Greek god of war. See MARS.

ARETHUSA, in Greek mythology, a nymph changed by the goddess ARTEMIS into a fountain and underground stream to save her from pursuit by the amorous river god ALPHEUS.

ARETINO, Pietro (1492–1556), Italian satirist and playwright who wrote coarse, sensual and lively political satires. His works include *I Ragionamenti* (1534–36), dialogues between prostitutes describing the escapades of contemporary notables.

AREZZO, city in N central Italy on the Arno R. It was founded by the Etruscans, and has medieval and Renaissance buildings and paintings (notably church frescoes by PIERO DELLA FRANCESCA). Arezzo is the capital of Arezzo Province and center of an agricultural area, with textile and leather industries. The work of its goldsmiths is world famous. Pop 84839.

ARGALI, *Ovis ammon*, the largest living wild SHEEP (family BOVIDAE), found in China, Nepal and E and Central USSR. They weigh 75–200kg (170–440lb) and are 1.2–1.8m (4–6ft) long. Males have large spiral HORNS, females smaller, curved ones.

ARGALL, Sir Samuel (d. 1626), daring English navigator and soldier in North America. He pioneered a N sea route to Va. (1609), captured POCAHONTAS (1612), crushed French colonies in Me. and Nova Scotia and became deputy governor of Va. (1617–19).

ARGAND BURNER, an improved oil lamp invented in 1784 by the Genevan physicist, Amié Argand. A hollow wick and cylindrical glass chimney increased the supply of air to the flame, thus improving light output and reducing the smell, smoke and flickering that were characteristic of earlier forms of oil LIGHTING.

ARGAND DIAGRAM, a way of representing complex numbers graphically (see IMAGINARY NUMBERS), named for the French mathematician Jean Robert Argand (1768–1822) by whom it was devised.

ARGENTEUIL, industrial suburb of Paris, on the N bank of the Seine R. It is dominated by the electrical and metal industries. Pop 90480.

ARGENTINA, second largest country in Latin America, economically one of its most advanced nations.

The Land. Argentina occupies most of South America E of the Andes. There are four main areas: W, N, Central and S. The W comprises the Andes Mts which exceed 20 000ft in parts of the N but are low in the S. The N consists largely of the forests of the Gran Chaco, and the swampy Mesopotamia region in the NE. Central Argentina comprises great grassy plains or *pampas*, a temperate region and economically the most important area, with two-thirds of the population. In the S lie the barren and cold plateaus of Patagonia.

People. About 90% of the people are descended from S European immigrants. Less than 1% are native Indians. The national language is Spanish and about 90% of the population are Roman Catholic. Over 70% live in urban areas. Argentina has a better educational system and a higher proportion of literate people than most Latin American states. Grain growing and cattle raising dominate the pampas, the S is a big sheep raising region, and sugarcane, grapes, citrus fruits, tobacco, rice and cotton all grow in the subtropical N. Oil and other minerals come from the N and the S. But over 40% of the labor force works in industry, notably in food processing, chemicals, plastics, machine tools and automobiles. Much of this industry is located in and around the capital, Buenos Aires.

History. Argentina's first Spanish settlers arrived in the 16th century. After nearly 300 years of Spanish rule, independence followed the war of 1816. The 19th century was a period of increasing European immigration and economic progress. Argentina's development during the 20th century has suffered from political uncertainties and social unrest. The reformist but dictatorial government of Juan PERON (1946–55) ended with a military uprising and was followed by several military and civilian governments. Widespread violence broke out in the early 1970s and in 1973 popular demand restored the ageing Peron to power. He died in 1974, however, and was succeeded by his wife Isabel PERON. She was unable to solve Argentina's problems, and after a brief lull unrest culminated in her overthrow in 1976. The commanders of the bloodless armed-forces coup were sworn in as a ruling junta; Gen. Jorge Videla was named president. Mme. Peron was held for trial on corruption charges. The government introduced stern measures to cope with increasing instability.

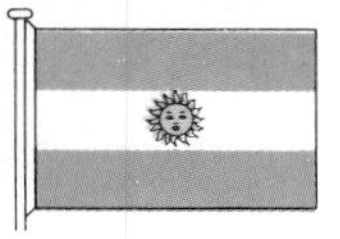

Official Name: The Republic of Argentina
Capital: Buenos Aires
Area: 1 072 163sq mi
Population: 23 539 000
Languages: Spanish
Religions: Roman Catholic
Monetary unit(s): 1 Argentine peso = 100 centavos

ARGENTITE, a soft, dark SULFIDE ore of SILVER (Ag_2S), related to CHALCOCITE. It occurs in Norway, Czechoslovakia, South America, Mexico and Nev.

ARGINUSAE, ancient name for a group of islands in the Aegean Sea, SE of Lesbos. A naval battle fought there in 406 BC resulted in the last Athenian victory of the Peloponnesian War.

ARGOL. See TARTARIC ACID.

ARGON (Ar), the commonest of the NOBLE GASES, comprising 0.934% of the ATMOSPHERE. It is used as an inert shield for arc welding and for the production of silicon and germanium crystals, to fill electric light bulbs and fluorescent lamps, and in argon–ion LASERS. AW 39.9, mp −189°C, bp −186°C.

ARGONAUT (*Argonauta argo*), sole species of the genus *Argonauta* of the class CEPHALOPODA; often called paper NAUTILUS because the female secretes a papery shell-like structure resembling that of the PEARLY NAUTILUS.

ARGONAUTS, heroes of Greek mythology who set sail under JASON to find the GOLDEN FLEECE. They reputedly included such illustrious figures as ORPHEUS, HERCULES, CASTOR AND POLLUX and THESEUS. The Argonauts set forth in the ship *Argo* for Colchis E of the Black Sea, where the fleece was guarded by a dragon. After many perils they obtained the fleece and returned to mainland Greece.

ARGONNE FOREST, a wooded hilly region south of the Ardennes, in NE France. In 1792 it was the site of the French victory over the Prussians at Valmy. The Meuse-Argonne offensive of late 1918 was one of the major US actions fought in WWI.

ARGONNE NATIONAL LABORATORY, a nuclear power research center 25mi S of Chicago. The University of Chicago operates it for the US ENERGY RESEARCH AND DEVELOPMENT ADMINISTRATION.

ARGOS, city-state of ancient Greece on the plain of Argolis in the NE Peloponnesus. After the destruction of Corinth (146 BC) Argos became the leading member of the Achaean League.

ARIA, formal solo song in opera and oratorio. It was developed in 17th-century opera and given its formalized pattern by SCARLATTI. GLUCK and MOZART turned it from a singer's display piece into an integral part of the drama. WAGNER and most modern composers tend to avoid the aria form.

ARIADNE, in Greek mythology, daughter of the Cretan King MINOS and Queen Pasiphaë. She helped THESEUS escape from the labyrinth and both fled from Crete, but Theseus abandoned her at Naxos. The god DIONYSUS found her there and later married her.

ARIANISM, 4th-century Christian heresy founded in Alexandria by the priest Arius. He taught that Christ was not coequal and coeternal with God the Father, for the Father had created him. To curb Arianism, the Emperor Constantine called the first Council of NICAEA (325), and the first Nicene Creed declared that God the Father and Christ the Son were of the same substance. Arianism later almost triumphed, but most of the church returned to orthodoxy by the end of the century (see TRINITY).

ARICA, city in N Chile, a Pacific port and terminus of the La Paz railroad. Peru lost it to Chile in the War of the Pacific (1880), but in 1929 Peru and Bolivia were granted its use as a free port for the shipment of mineral exports. Pop 63 160.

ARIES (the Ram), second constellation of the ZODIAC. In N skies it is a winter constellation.

ARIES, First Point of, the vernal equinox, a point of intersection of the EQUATOR and the ECLIPTIC used as the zero of celestial longitude. Owing to PRECESSION, the First Point of Aries is currently in PISCES.

ARIKARA INDIANS, North American Caddoan-speaking tribe now in Fort Berthold Reservation, N.D. They originally lived in villages along the upper Missouri R.

AROSTO, Ludovico (1474–1533), Italian poet best remembered for the epic *Orlando Furioso*. This continued the Roland legend, depicting the hero as a love-torn knight. The work greatly influenced later poets, such as SPENSER and BYRON.

ARISTARCHUS OF SAMOS (c310–230 BC), Alexandrian Greek astronomer who realized that the sun is larger than the earth and who is reported by ARCHIMEDES to have taught that the earth orbited a motionless sun.

ARISTIDES (c530–468 BC), Athenian statesman and general, a founder of the DELIAN LEAGUE. He fought at the battle of MARATHON, and was elected archon for 489 BC. Ostracized in 482 BC, he was recalled in 480 BC and helped repulse the Persians. Later he fixed Greek cities' contributions to the Delian League.

ARISTOCRACY (from Greek *aristos*, the best, and *kratos*, rule), originally meaning the ruling of a state by its best citizens in the interest of all. It was used by both PLATO and ARISTOTLE in this sense. Gradually the term came to mean a form of government ruled by a small privileged class. Today, the term refers to members of a family which traditionally has hereditary privileges and rank.

ARISTOPHANES (c450–385 BC), comic dramatist of ancient Greece. Political, social and literary satire, witty dialogue, vigorous ribaldry, cleverly contrived comic situations and fine choral lyrics all feature in his works. Eleven of his 40 plays survive, notably *The Frogs* (satirizing Euripides), *The Clouds* (satirizing Socrates), *Lysistrata* (a plea for pacifism) and *The Birds* (a fantasy about a sky city).

ARISTOTLE (384–322 BC), Greek philosopher, one of the most influential thinkers of the ancient world. He was the son of the Macedonian court physician, and studied at PLATO's academy in Athens. In 343 BC he became tutor to the young ALEXANDER THE GREAT. In 335 BC Aristotle set up his own school at the Lyceum in Athens (see PERIPATETIC SCHOOL). Many of Aristotle's teachings survive as lecture notes. His work covered a vast range, including *Physics*, *Metaphysics*, *On the Soul*, *On the Heavens*, and several works on LOGIC and BIOLOGY, in both of which subjects he was a pioneer.

In studying such diverse topics as nature, man or the soul, Aristotle considered how things became what they were and what function they performed. In doing this he introduced his fourfold analysis of causes (formal, material, efficient and final), and such important notions as form and matter, substance and accident, actual and potential—all of which became philosophical commonplaces. In logic he invented the SYLLOGISM. The *Nicomachean Ethics* argues that virtue is a "mean" between extremes. *Politics* considers civic participation a natural outgrowth of human instinct. *Poetics* argues that a tragic drama brings emotional CATHARSIS through "pity and fear" evoked by the stage action. Aristotle's writings reached the West through Latin translations in the 11th and 13th centuries and had a prevailing influence on medieval and later thought.

ARITHMETIC (from Greek *arithmos*, number), the science of NUMBER. Until the 16th century arithmetic was viewed as the study of all the properties and relations of all numbers; in modern times, the term usually denotes the study of the positive REAL NUMBERS and ZERO under the operations of ADDITION, SUBTRACTION, MULTIPLICATION and DIVISION. Arithmetic can therefore be viewed as merely a special case of ALGEBRA, although it is of importance in considerations of the history of MATHEMATICS.

ARIUS. See ARIANISM.

ARIZONA, state of the SW US. Once a largely worthless desert area, Ariz. has developed rapidly and in population is now one of the fastest growing states in the Union.

The Colorado Plateau to the N contains such spectacular features as the Grand Canyon, the Painted Desert, the Petrified Forest and Monument Valley, all of which have helped to make tourism an important part of the economy. A mountain chain, heavily forested and rich in minerals, extends NW to SE, while desert occupies the SW.

Population is predominantly urban, about half being concentrated in the Phoenix metropolitan area. More Indians live in Ariz. than in any other state, the majority on the 19 reservations which cover almost 25% of the total land area. The Navaho, Hopi and Apache are the largest of the 15 tribes.

With the aid of irrigation and of a long growing season, Ariz. has developed a varied and intensive agricultural economy. About 60% of farm income comes from livestock products. More than 1 000 000 beef cattle and 500 000 sheep are raised on ranches and grazing land. Cotton is the principal cash crop, while truck farming is so extensive it has earned the state a reputation as the "Salad Bowl of the Nation."

Ariz. is also rich in minerals, supplying half the nation's copper as well as mining gold, silver, tungsten, molybdenum, zinc and vanadium. Manufacturing began with the smelting of copper and

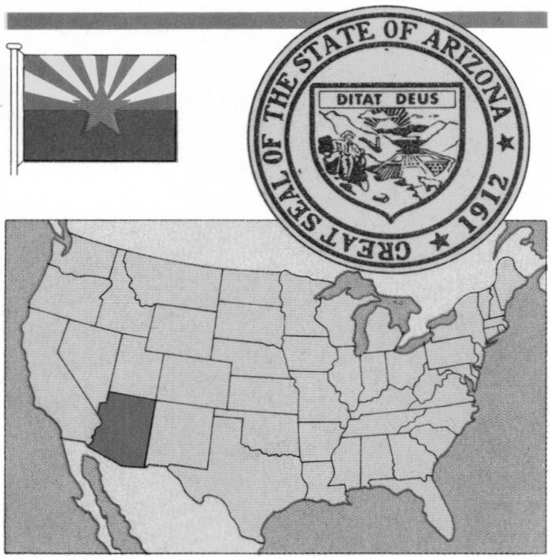

Name of state: Arizona
Capital: Phoenix
Statehood: Feb. 14, 1912 (48th state)
Familiar name: Grand Canyon State
Area: 113 909sq mi
Population: 1 752 122
Elevation: Highest—12 670ft, Humphrey's Peak. Lowest—100ft, Colorado River at the Mexican border
Motto: Didat Deus ("God Enriches")
State flower: Saguaro (Giant Cactus)
State bird: Cactus wren
State tree: Paloverde
State song: "Arizona"

other ores and the establishment of sawmills.

Since WWII, industrial growth has been rapid and manufacturing now contributes more than agriculture or mining to the state's wealth. The electronics and electrical industry centered in Phoenix employs the largest number of workers engaged in manufacturing. Other industries include food processing and aircraft construction.

Ariz. was under Spanish influence from 1539, when it was first explored by Friar Marcos de Niza, until the Treaty of GUADALUPE HIDALGO (1848) which granted it to the US. Movement for statehood began after the defeat of the Navahos—by Kit CARSON (1863)—and the Apache (1886), and in 1912 Ariz. became the nation's 48th state.

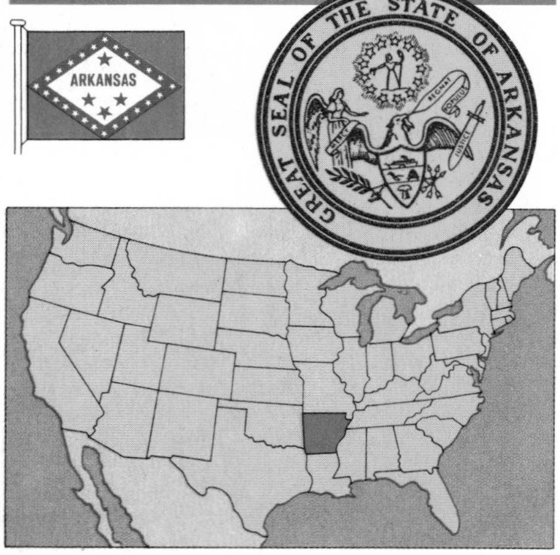

Name of state: Arkansas
Capital: Little Rock
Statehood: June 15, 1836 (25th state)
Familiar name: Land of Opportunity; Wonder State
Area: 53 104sq mi
Population: 1 886 210
Elevation: Highest—2 823ft, Magazine Mountain. Lowest—55ft, Ouachita River at the Louisiana border
Motto: Regnat Populus ("The People Rule")
State flower: Apple Blossom
State bird: Mockingbird
State tree: Pine
State song: "Arkansas"

ARKANSAS, state of the S central US on the W bank of the Mississippi R. Ark. has suffered in the past from over-dependence on the cotton crop and from low per capita income, but industrial growth has accelerated since the mid-1950s. Now income from manufacturing exceeds that from agriculture and, after two decades of decline, recent figures show an increase in population.

In addition to the Mississippi, Ark. has several major rivers, including the Arkansas, Red, Ouachita, White and St. Francis rivers. To the N and W are the rugged Ozark and Ouachita Mts, while the alluvial plain in the E is the chief agricultural region. More than half the state is forested. Three national forests—in the Ozarks, the Ouachitas and the Gulf Coastal Plain—have been established to protect valuable timberlands. Climate is mild and rainy, though tornadoes are frequent.

Cotton and soybeans are the most important cash crops. Ark. supplies about 10% of the national cotton total while Mississippi Co. is the country's leading soybean producer. Rice, introduced in the 1920s, is now the state's third most important crop. In the W, however, livestock and poultry provide the major farm income.

Ark. has important mineral deposits, producing more than 95% of the bauxite mined in the US. There are also valuable oil and natural gas fields, as well as deposits of barite, manganese, bromine and coal. The only diamond field in the US (no longer in industrial use) is the Murfreesboro in SE Ark. Arkansas' forests provide timber and pulp for lumber, paper and other wood products, which account for a major share of the state's industry.

First explored by Hernando DE SOTTO (1541), Ark. passed from Spanish to French hands, and then to the US as part of the LOUISIANA PURCHASE (1803). It first entered the Union as a slave state in 1836 and was readmitted after the Civil War in 1868 over President Andrew Johnson's veto. The Reconstruction period was marked by controversy and discontent. Racism brought Ark. into the headlines in 1957 when federal troops were called in to enforce integration at a Little Rock school.

ARKANSAS CITY, city in S Kan. at the junction of the Arkansas and Walnut rivers. It mills flour and refines oil. Pop 13 216.

ARKANSAS POST, village in SE Ark. on the Arkansas R. The state's oldest white settlement (founded as a trading post in 1686), it was the first capital of Arkansas Territory.

ARKANSAS RIVER, longest tributary of the Mississippi–Missouri R system. It rises in the Rocky Mts of central Col. and flows 1 450mi through Kan., Okla., and Ark. to the Mississippi R. It is the main water source for Ark. state, and is controlled by dams and locks to curb flooding.

ARKHANGELSK (Archangel), city and major port in NW USSR, the administrative center for Arkhangelsk oblast. It stands on the Northern Dvina R and although icebound for six months is of considerable economic importance, specializing in furs, timber, paper-making and shipbuilding. Archangel was Russia's leading port until the founding of St. Petersburg (1703).Pop 343 000.

ARK OF THE COVENANT, in the Old Testament, the chest containing the tablets bearing the Ten Commandments received by Moses. The most sacred object of ancient Israel, before it was deposited in the Temple it used to be carried into battle.

ARKWRIGHT, Sir Richard (1732–1792), English industrialist and inventor of cotton carding and SPINNING machinery. In 1769 he patented a spinning frame which was the first machine able to produce cotton thread strong enough to use in the warp. He was a pioneer of the factory system of production,

Arlington National Cemetery in N Va. contains the grave of President John F. Kennedy, marked by an "eternal flame." Thousands pay their respects every year.

building several water- and later steam-powered mills. (See also CROMPTON, SAMUEL; HARGREAVES, JAMES.)

ARLES, city in SE France, on the Rhone R, a river port and center for chemical and metal industries. Its Roman ruins include an amphitheater still in use. Arles became capital of the kingdom of Arles (Burgundy) in the 10th century, passing to the French crown in the 14th century. Pop 45 774.

ARLINGTON, residential town in NE Mass., a NW suburb of Boston. It manufactures wood products and leather goods. Pop 53 524.

ARLINGTON, unincorporated residential community in SE N.Y. near Poughkeepsie. It is the site of Vassar College. Pop 11 203.

ARLINGTON, city in N Tex., 13mi E of Fort Worth. It assembles automobiles, produces chemicals and has the University of Texas at Arlington. Pop 89 723.

ARLINGTON, county in N Va., forming a residential suburb of Washington, D.C., W of the Potomac R. It is the site of Arlington National Cemetery and of the Pentagon. Pop 174 284.

ARLINGTON HEIGHTS, village in NE Ill., 25mi NW of Chicago. It makes electrical equipment and has Arlington Park racetrack. Pop 64 884.

ARLINGTON NATIONAL CEMETERY, famous US national cemetery in N Va. It was established in 1864 on land once owned by George Washington CUSTIS and Robert E. LEE. Over 160 000 American war dead and public figures are buried here. Monuments include the Curtis–Lee Mansion, the mast of the battleship *Maine*, the Tomb of the Unknown Soldier and the grave of John F. Kennedy with its eternal flame.

ARLISS, George (1868–1946), British actor who became popular in the US while touring with Mrs Patrick Campbell (1901). He won an Academy Award for the title role in the film *Disraeli* (1930).

ARM, the part of the human forelimb between WRIST and SHOULDER. The upper arm bone (humerus) is attached at the shoulder by a ball and socket JOINT and to the lower arm by a hinge joint at the elbow. The lower arm consists of the ulna and the radius, which rotates over the ulna to turn the wrist. The chief arm muscles are the BICEPS and TRICEPS and the strong hand muscles.

ARMADA, fleet of armed ships, in particular Spain's "Invincible Armada," 130 ships carrying 27 000 men sent by PHILIP II in 1588 to seize control of the English Channel for an invasion of England. After a running fight with Howard, DRAKE, HAWKINS and FROBISHER, the Spaniards took refuge in Calais Roads. Driven out by fire-ships, the surviving vessels nearly all perished in storms as they attempted to return to Čadiz via N Scotland and W Ireland.

ARMADILLOS, the sole armored MAMMALS, 20 species (family Dasypodidae) of the order ENDENTATA, which also contains ANTEATERS and SLOTHS. They range in length from about 120mm (5in) to about

1.5m (5ft). They are usually nocturnal, sometimes diurnal, and live in burrows either excavated by themselves or deserted by other animals. Polyembryony (production of several identical offspring from a single fertilized EGG) is general amongst armadillos.

ARMAGEDDON, biblical site of the world's last great battle, in which the powers of good will destroy the forces of evil (Revelation 16:16). The name may refer to biblical MEGIDDO.

ARMAGNAC, hilly farming area of SW France noted for its brandy. Count Bernard VII of Armagnac was virtual ruler of France in 1413–18. Armagnac passed to the French crown in 1607. The chief city, Auch, is a commercial center.

ARMATURE, the part of an electric MOTOR or GENERATOR which includes the principal current-carrying windings. In small motors it usually comprises several coils of wire wound on a soft iron core and mounted on the drive shaft, though on larger AC motors the armature is often the stationary component. When the current flows in the armature winding of a motor, it interacts with the magnetic field produced by the field windings giving rise to a TORQUE between the rotor and stator. In the generator the armature is rotated in a magnetic field giving rise to an ELECTROMOTIVE FORCE in the windings.

ARMENIA, historic country in SW Asia S of the Caucasus Mts, now mainly divided between the Armenian Soviet Socialist Republic (pop 2493000) and NE Turkey. Primarily a tableland, the entire region averages some 6000–7000ft above sea level. A range of mountains cuts across it from E to W; the highest point being Mt Ararat (16945ft) in Turkey. The Tigris, Euphrates, Kyros and Araxes rivers all have their source in the highlands.

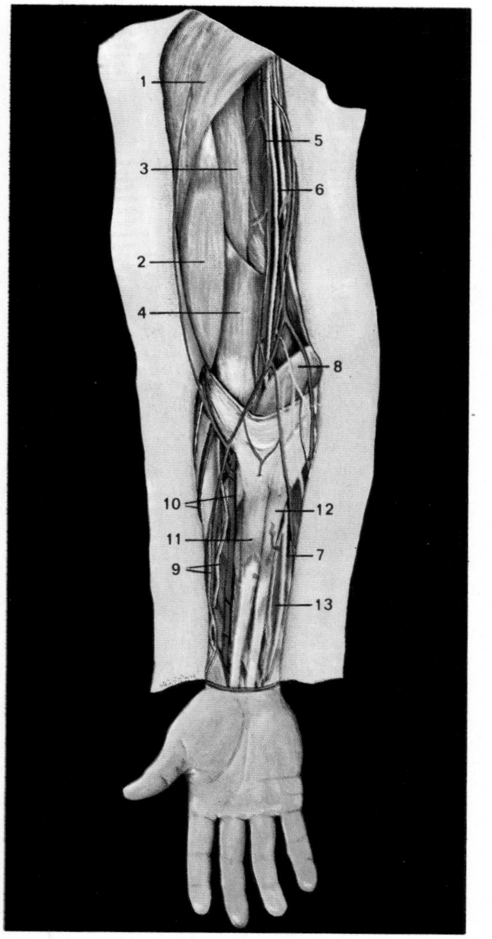

The muscles and nerves of the arm. 1 Deltoid. 2 Biceps. 3 Coracobrachialis. 4 Brachialis. 5 Brachial artery. 6 Median nerve. 7 Ulnar nerve. 8 Pronator teres. 9 Branches of the radial nerve. 10 Radial artery and vein. 11 Flexor carpi radialis. 12 Palmaris longus. 13 Ulnar artery.

Armenia's landscape extends from subtropical lowland to snow-covered peaks. Small mountain pastures provide rich grazing for sheep and cattle, while the valleys are fertile when irrigated. The main crops are green vegetables, barley, potatoes, wheat, sugar beat and grapes. Pomegranates, figs, peaches and apricots are also grown.

Mining is the chief industry, the mountains yielding small but useful quantities of copper, iron, manganese, nepheline and molybdenum. Transportation facilities are limited, but industrialization is increasing. Hydroelectric schemes, particularly on Lake Sevan, have been a prime factor in Soviet Armenia's economic growth.

Armenia was conquered in 328 BC by Alexander the Great and in 66 BC by Rome. In 303 AD it became the first country to make Christianity its state religion. Later it was successively under Byzantine, Persian, Arab, Seljuk, Mongol and Ottoman Turkish control. Russian influence grew in the 19th century. A short-lived Armenian republic emerged after WWI but was swiftly absorbed by the USSR and Turkey.

ARMENIA, industrial city in W central Colombia. It serves as the transportation center for a rich coffee-producing district. Pop 142191.

ARMENIAN, an Indo-European language related to Indo-Iranian and Greek. It evolved in the mountainous region of Armenia.

ARMENIAN CHURCH, the national church of Armenia. It evolved as part of the EASTERN CHURCH and adopted a form of MONOPHYSITISM.

ARMILLARY SPHERE, a model displaying the mutual dispositions of the imaginary circles of classical astronomy in which metal circles were used to represent the celestial EQUATOR, the ECLIPTIC, the TROPICS, the arctic and antarctic circles, the hours of the day, the HORIZON and a MERIDIAN. Derived from ancient astronomical instruments, armillary spheres became particularly popular in the 17th and 18th centuries.

ARMINIANS (or Remonstrants), group of Protestant congregations inspired by the Dutch theologian Jacobus Arminius (1560–1609). Arminianism attempted to show that, contrary to John CALVIN's doctrine of PREDESTINATION, man's free will and God's sovereignty were not incompatible. The Arminians, though persecuted initially, were legally tolerated in the Netherlands from 1630. Arminian theology greatly influenced John WESLEY, founder of Methodism.

ARMINIUS (or Hermann, c18 BC–19 AD), military leader and chief of a Germanic tribe, the Cherusci, who defeated Quintus Varus (9 AD). Although defeated in his turn by Germanicus (16 AD), he forced Rome to abandon plans of conquering what is now Germany. The Roman historian TACITUS called Arminius the "undoubted liberator of Germany." Arminius died in a tribal feud.

ARMOR, protective clothing or covering used in armed combat. The earliest armor consisted of boiled and hardened animal skins but, with the coming of organized military campaigns, armor became more sophisticated. Roman soldiers wore standardized armor made of iron. Later, chain mail, a fabric of interlocking metal rings, was developed. By the end of the 11th century it was the standard form of armor. It provided poor protection against heavy blows, however, and thus the Middle Ages saw the development of full suits of metal plates with chain mail joints for flexibility. Later, as these suits were used more for tournaments and state occasions, certain cities, notably Milan and Augsburg, became renowned for their armorial artistry. Full armor was used in Europe only until the 16th century. Modern armor employs nylon, fiberglass and other synthetic materials.

ARMORPLATE, metal protective covering consisting usually, but not always, of several layers of differently heat-treated metals (see METALLURGY) whose combined properties provide the best possible protection. Case-hardened (see CASE-HARDENING) body armor appeared as early as the 15th century; but it was not until the 19th century that armorplate was applied to ships, playing an important part in the Crimean War. Since the 19th century, armorplate has been made either of several laminae, typically carbon STEEL with a backing of WROUGHT IRON, or as a single thick layer of metal. Modern armorplate is applied to land vehicles such as tanks as well as to sea-going craft.

ARMORY SHOW, officially the International Exhibition of Modern Art, the first show of its kind to be held in the US at the 69th Regiment Armory, New York City, Feb.–March 1913. Comprising over 1300 works it included a large section of paintings by contemporary Americans, and works by such modern European artists as BRANCUSI, BRAQUE, CÉZANNE, DUCHAMP, MATISSE and PICASSO. The avant-garde paintings caused much controversy but also the acceptance of modern art in the US.

ARMOUR, Philip Danforth (1832–1901), US meatpacking pioneer and philanthropist. He made his fortune supplying pork to Union forces in the Civil War, and in 1870 established Armour & Co. which soon made Chicago the meatpacking center of the US. He founded the Armour Institute of Technology in 1892.

ARMSTRONG, Edwin Howard (1890–1954), US electronics engineer who developed the FEEDBACK concept for AMPLIFIERS (1912), invented the superheterodyne circuit used in radio receivers (1918) and perfected FM RADIO (1925–39).

ARMSTRONG, Louis Daniel (1900–1971), US jazz musician renowned as a virtuoso trumpeter and master of improvization. "Satchmo" grew up in the back streets of New Orleans, moved to Chicago in 1922 and by the 1930s was internationally famous. In later life he played at concerts around the world as "goodwill ambassador" for the State Department.

ARMSTRONG, Neil Alden (1930–), first man to set foot on the moon. Born in Wapakoneta, Ohio, he studied aeronautical engineering at Purdue U. (1947–55) with time out on active service in the Korean War. He joined NASA in 1962, commanding Gemini 8 (1966), and landing the Apollo II module on the moon on July 20, 1969.

ARMSTRONG, Samuel Chapman (1839–1893), US educator and philanthropist. He was colonel of a Negro regiment in the Civil War and agent of the FREEDMAN'S BUREAU (Va.). Armstrong founded the Hampton Institute (1868), an industrial school for Negroes and Red Indians.

ARMY, traditionally the land fighting force of a nation. By a narrower definition an army is also a large unit of ground forces under a single commander (e.g. the US Fifth Army).

The 20th century has shown how far the modern army depends upon technology and industry. Germany was defeated in WWII not by superior military power but by superior machine power. However, the constant development of weapons and detection systems makes any land force extremely vulnerable. Modern armies must, therefore, be highly mobile, a need which has led to a blurring of the traditional distinctions between army, navy and air force. Cooperation among the services is essential for the successful application of advanced technology. Canada, for example, has combined all three branches of her armed forces.

Primitive armies perhaps consisted of raiding parties mainly engaged in individual combat, using rudimentary weapons such as stones and clubs. Later, skills in handling horses and chariots increased the complexity and mobility of armies, while the development of artillery, which had its origins in catapult machines, and the revolutionary invention of gunpowder in China, extended their range of effectiveness. Formation tactics evolved through the Macedonian *phalanx* and Roman *legion.*

It might be said that the modern army has brought all these developments to a very high level of sophistication. Rapid mobility, first made practicable by the construction of rail networks in the 19th century, has been increased in the 20th century by the development of air transportation. Nuclear weaponry has taken the effective range of firepower virtually to its limits and the value of tactical formations has largely been eliminated by radar detection equipment, making unconventional military units (e.g. guerrillas, paratroops) increasingly important in warfare.

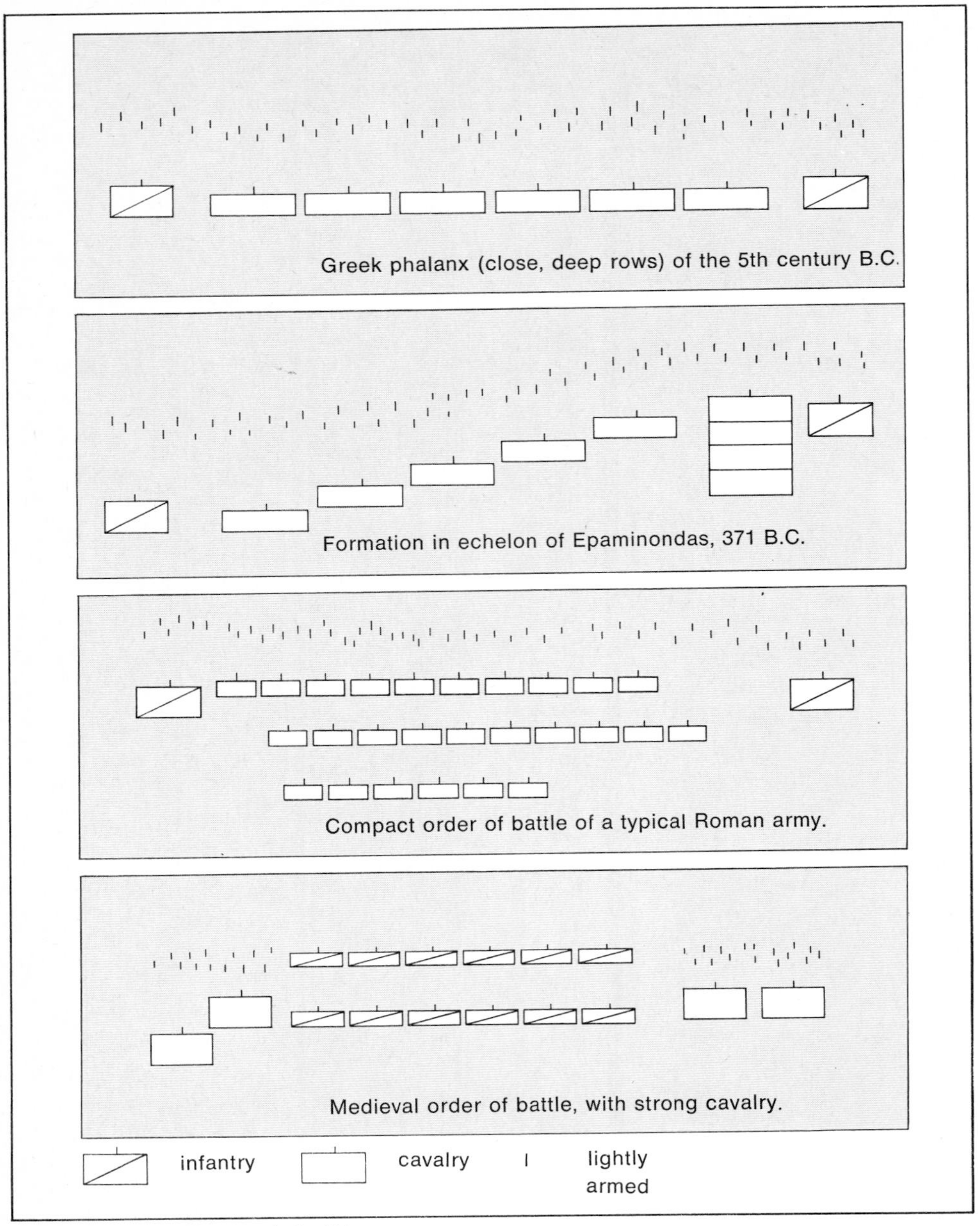

Army formations in different periods of history.

In peacetime, too, a modern army performs an important function, acting both as a deterrent and as an emergency aid and control force. Its highly developed technology involves a large number of civilians in a variety of servicing roles.

ARMY, Canadian, since 1967, part of the integrated Canadian Armed Forces. It is a volunteer body, 45 000 strong with 40 000 reserves. Troops are mainly involved in international military cooperation, through NATO and UN peacekeeping operations. Formed in 1871, the Canadian Army fought for the British in the BOER WAR, and against Germany in WWI at such historic battles as Vimy Ridge (1917). In WWII, Canadian troops distinguished themselves at Dieppe (1942), and as part of 21 Army Group took part in D-Day and helped to liberate Holland. The present army has modern though not nuclear equipment.

ARMY, United States, though not the world's largest army, certainly one of the best equiped and most powerful land forces the world has ever known, organized to fight any war, local or global, conventional or atomic.

The highest ranking officer is the chief of staff, answerable to the secretary of the army, a civilian who in turn is responsible to the secretary of defense and the president. Under the chief of staff come several major commands: the *Continental Army Command*, responsible for US ground defense; the *Air Defense Command*; the *Army Matériel Command*, charged with procuring equipment, weapons, etc. for army units; the *Army Combat Developments Command*, which equips and organizes army units, plus various other commands.

The US Army originated in the colonial forces who fought in the 18th-century FRENCH AND INDIAN WARS. Its main role, until well into the 19th century, was the protection of settlers against Indians. However, it fought successfully in the MEXICAN WAR (1846–48) and during the Civil War its strength rose to about 3 000 000 men.

In 1903 the army was radically reorganized, gaining a General Staff Corps and chief of staff. Numbers increased to 4 000 000 by 1918. WWII brought conscription, raising the number of men on active duty from 200 000 in 1939 to over 8 000 000 in 1945. In the Korean War the US Army contingent formed the core of the UN forces. In the Vietnam War the army faced new tactics of infiltration and guerrilla warfare. Conscription ended with US participation in that war in Jan. 1973 and the estimated strength of the army in June 1973 was 825 000, after the major withdrawal from SE Asia.

In peacetime, the US Army comprises the Regular Army (professional career soldiers), members of the reserves and National Guard on active duty and female personnel (notably the WOMEN'S ARMY CORPS). The army's peacetime work includes helping to train military forces of friendly powers and performing various civilian assistance tasks and emergency measures.

ARMY, US Department of the, branch of the US Department of Defense, responsible for the US Army. It was established in 1947 and succeeded the cabinet-level War Department, created by Congress in 1789.

ARMY WORM, the CATERPILLARS of *Leucania unipuncta*, one of the species of owlet MOTHS (family Noctuidae, order LEPIDOPTERA, so named for their habit of travelling in large groups, feeding on corn, cotton and other crops. The name is also applied to the LARVAE of other Lepidopteran species which travel in groups from one feeding ground to another.

ARNAUD, Antoine (1612–1694), French priest who succeeded the Abbé de Saint-Cyran as Jansenist leader. Opposed by the Jesuits he fled to Brussels in 1679, where he continued to promulgate JANSENISM. Arnaud collaborated with PASCAL in writing the so-called *Port-Royal Logic*.

ARNAUD, Henri (1641–1721), Protestant pastor and leader of the WALDENSES. In 1689 Arnaud led 1 000 Waldenses from Swiss exile back into Piedmont, where their fortunes at the hands of Victor Amadeus II of Savoy varied according to whether Savoy was at war and in need of an ally or not. In the latter event, the Waldenses suffered considerable persecution.

ARNDT, Ernst Moritz (1769–1860), German patriot and poet. His writings persuaded the Swedish king to end serfdom, but he is best known for pamphlets, poems and songs rallying Prussia against Napoleon I and domination by the French.

ARNE, Thomas Augustine (1710–1778), English composer whose settings of Shakespeare's *Blow, Blow, Thou Winter Wind* and *Where The Bee Sucks* became perennial favorites. He also composed the air *Rule Britannia*.

ARNHEM, capital of the Dutch province of Gelderland, on the N bank of the Rhine about 60mi E of Rotterdam. Its industries include shipbuilding and synthetic fiber manufacture. A major but ill-fated Allied paratroop drop occurred here in 1944 during WWII. Pop 132 330.

ARNHEM LAND, area on the NE coast of Australia's Northern Territory, discovered by the Dutch explorer Carstenz in 1623 and named for his ship *Arnhem*. It is the site of an aboriginal reserve.

ARNICA, large genus of N hemisphere herbs with yellow flowers, found mainly in NW America. The European mountain arnica (*A. montana*) yields arnicin, once used in liniments. Family: Compositae.

ARNIM, Bettina von (1785–1859), German authoress best known for her correspondence with GOETHE. She was the sister of Clemens BRENTANO and wife of Ludwig Joachim von Arnim.

ARNIM, Ludwig Joachim von (1781–1831), German Romantic poet. With Clemens BRENTANO he edited a famous collection of German folk poetry, *Des Knaben Wunderhorn* (1806).

ARNOLD, Benedict (1741–1801), American general and traitor in the Revolutionary War. He fought outstandingly for the American cause at Ticonderoga (1775) and Saratoga (1777) and in 1778 received command of Philadelphia. But, in 1780 Arnold was reprimanded for abusing his authority. That year, however, he assumed the important command of West Point and with John ANDRÉ plotted its surrender to the British in revenge for past criticisms. André's capture forced Arnold to flee to the British side, and in 1781 he went into exile in London.

ARNOLD, Henry Harley (1886–1950), pioneer aviator and US Air Force general who helped build US air power and develop the air force as a unified separate service. "Hap" Arnold held several early flying records, became chief of the Air Corps (1938), headed the Army Air Forces in WWII and was made general of the Army (1944), being later retitled general of the Air Force.

ARNOLD, Matthew (1822–1888), English poet and literary critic. His poetry, perhaps best represented by the collections *Empedocles on Etna, and other Poems*

(1852) and *New Poems* (1867), is characteristically introspective, though Arnold could equally achieve a classical impersonsality. Both in his poetry and his criticism (*Culture and Anarchy* 1869; *Literature and Dogma* 1873) Arnold showed a keen awareness of the changing cultural climate of his time. He worked as a schools inspector (1851–86) and was Professor of Poetry at Oxford (1857–67).

ARNOLD, Thomas (1795–1842), English headmaster of Rugby School whose approach to teaching, with its stress on character development, radically influenced English public school education. He was the father of Matthew ARNOLD.

ARNOLD, Thurman Wesley (1891–), prominent US lawyer. As assistant attorney general (1939–43), he passed 320 antitrust suits against industrial monopoly. Arnold wrote *The Folklore of Capitalism* (1937), a satire on American society.

ARNOLD OF BRESCIA (c1100–1155), Italian religious reformer and political activist. Strongly opposed to the temporal power of the pope, Arnold joined and soon led a revolutionary republican movement which replaced papal authority in Rome (1148). When the republic fell he was hanged as a heretic.

ARNOLDSON, Klas Pontus (1844–1916), Swedish pacifist writer and politician who advocated permanent Swedish neutrality. In 1908 he shared the Nobel Peace Prize with Fredrik BAJER.

ARNOLFO DI CAMBIO (c1245–1302?), Florentine Gothic sculptor and architect. He designed Florence Cathedral and worked on the Palazzo Vecchio. He is also renowned for the funerary monuments he sculpted.

ARNO RIVER, river in central Italy, about 150mi long. It rises in the Apennine Mts and flows via Florence into the Ligurian Sea, 7mi W of Pisa. In 1966 it flooded and destroyed many art treasures and manuscripts in Florence.

AROMATIC COMPOUNDS, major class of organic compounds containing one or more planar rings of atoms having special stability due to their electronic structure. This includes TORUS-shaped ORBITALS above and below the plane of the ring, known as a 1-electron system, containing (4n+2) electrons (i.e. 6, 10, 14 and so on). Such systems can be represented by RESONANCE structures of alternate single and double bonds (see BOND, CHEMICAL) round the ring. Typical properties of aromatic compounds include ease of formation, tendency to react by substitution rather than addition, and modification of the properties of attached groups. The most important aromatic compounds are BENZENE and its derivatives, including PHENOLS, TOLUENE, BENZALDEHYDE, BENZOIC ACID, BENZYL ALCOHOL, ANILINE and SALICYLIC ACID. Compounds with more than one benzene ring (polycyclic) include NAPHTHALENE and anthracene. Non-benzenoid aromatics include cyclopentadienyl and cycloheptatrienylium ions (see FERROCENE) and azulene. Many HETEROCYCLIC COMPOUNDS are aromatic.

AROOSTOOK RIVER, river about 140mi long, rising in N Me. and running E to enter the St. John R in New Brunswick, Canada. It lends its name to the fertile Aroostook Co.

AROOSTOOK WAR, boundary dispute of 1839 between settlers of Me. and New Brunswick, Canada. Both sides claimed lands along the Aroostook R. War between the US and Britain was averted by a truce and the appointment of a boundary commission. Its findings were incorporated into the WEBSTER-ASHBURTON TREATY of 1842.

ÁRPÁD, first dynasty of Hungarian rulers, founded by Árpád (c840–907). As chief of the MAGYARS he overran Hungary in c896. Árpád founded a centralized state and his successors replaced the nomadic Magyar culture with one based on settled agriculture. St. Stephen (1001–38) strengthened his crown by establishing Christianity, but invasions and internal strife weakened the monarchy and on the death of Andrew III (1301) the crown passed to the House of Anjou.

ARP, Jean or **Hans** (1887–1966), Franco-Swiss sculptor, painter and poet. Briefly associated with the BLAUE REITER, he was a cofounder of DADA in Zurich (1916) and later a Surrealist. From the 1930s he created sculptures and reliefs remarkable for their elemental purity and strength.

ARRAIGNMENT, legal term denoting the calling of a person to a court of law to answer an indictment, to plead guilty or not guilty. He may enter various motions, on which the judge must rule before setting the time, place and manner of the trial. Between ARREST and arraignment, a preliminary hearing may be held at which BAIL is set or withheld.

ARRAS, French industrial city, capital of the Pas-de-Calais department. Once famous for fine tapestries, to which it gave its name, it is now a marketing and processing center for agricultural products. Arras suffered extensive damage in both world wars. Pop 48 494.

ARRAU, Claudio (1903–), famous Chilean pianist. A child prodigy, he became noted throughout his long career mainly for his performances of the Romantic composers such as BRAHMS.

ARREST, the taking into custody of a person suspected of a crime. Usually, an arrest is made by police following the issue of a court warrant, backed by evidence implicating the named person. Generally, an arrest may be made without a warrant only when the arresting officer has witnessed the crime, or on the strength of suspicious behavior. Sometimes a "citizen's arrest" may be made by a private person.

ARRHENIUS, Svante August (1859–1927), Swedish physical chemist whose theory concerning the DISSOCIATION of SALTS in solution (see CONDUCTIVITY) earned him the 1903 Nobel Prize for Chemistry and laid the foundations for the study of ELECTROCHEMISTRY.

ARRIAN (c96–180 AD), Greek philosopher and historian from Bithynia, Asia Minor. He was governor of Cappadocia under HADRIAN, and wrote an important history of ALEXANDER THE GREAT.

ARROW, Kenneth (1921–),US economist, a professor at Harvard and former adviser on economic affairs to the US government. In 1972 he won the Nobel Prize for Economic Science.

ARROWHEAD, any of the genus *Sagittaria* of perennial aquatics with large arrow-shaped leaves and small white flowers, that grow erect in shallow water in temperate and tropical regions. The common arrowhead (*S. sagittifolia*), widespread in Europe and Asia, is cultivated in China for its edible TUBERS. Family: Alismataceae.

ARROWROOT, a form of edible starch obtained from the RHIZOMES of various tropical plants. True arrowroot is the West Indian arrowroot (*Maranta arundinacea*). Easily digestible, it is used in feeding invalids and children, and also as a thickening agent in sauces.

ARROW-WORMS, worm-like animal PLANKTON (mainly of the genus *Sagitta*) whose 50 or so species constitute the phylum Chaetognatha. They are torpedo-shaped, 3–100mm (0.1–4in) long, and HERMAPHRODITE. They drift with the sea around them and have low environmental tolerance: hence examination of those species present in a seawater sample can tell much of OCEAN CURRENTS and other sea movements.

ARSACIDS, dynasty of kings who ruled PARTHIA (present-day N Iran) between 247 BC and 227 AD. It is named for its founder, Arsaces, a chief of the Parni tribe, which originated E of the Caspian. At its height, the Arsacid empire stretched from the Euphrates to Afghanistan.

ARSENIC (As), metalloid in Group VA of the PERIODIC TABLE. Its chief ore is ARSENOPYRITE, which is roasted to give arsenic (III) oxide, or white arsenic, used as a poison. Arsenic has two main allotropes (see ALLOTROPY): yellow arsenic, As_4, resembling white PHOSPHORUS; and gray (metallic) arsenic. It burns in air and reacts with most other elements, forming trivalent and pentavalent compounds, all highly toxic. It is used as a doping agent in TRANSISTORS; gallium arsenide is used in LASERS. AW 74.9, subl 613°C, sg 1.97 (yellow), 5.73 (gray).

ARSENOPYRITE, or mispickel, silvery-white mineral with metallic luster, crystallizing in the monoclinic system, iron sulfarsenide (FeAsS). It is the chief ore of ARSENIC, and is found in the US, Canada, Germany, England and Scandinavia.

ARSON, a crime involving the deliberate firing of a building or other property owned by another person. In the US arson is now a statutory crime in most jurisdictions.

ART. See COMMERCIAL ART; PAINTING; SCULPTURE. Also entries under various styles and periods, for example ABSTRACT ART; BAROQUE; CUBISM; IMPRESSIONISM.

ARTAGNAN, Charles de Batz, Seigneur d' (c1611–1673), brilliant French soldier killed at the siege of Maastricht. His alleged memoirs were published in 1700. Alexandre DUMAS used his name for the hero of his *The Three Musketeers* and its sequels.

ARTAUD, Antonin (1896–1948), French author, actor and director. His theories of a "Theater of Cruelty," where the elemental forces of the psyche would be spectacularly exposed, have had a strong influence on modern theater.

ARTAXERXES, the name of three Persian kings. **Artaxerxes I,** Longimanus, became king in 465 BC after the murder of his father XERXES. He suppressed several revolts, made peace with Athens and allowed the Jews to return to Judea. He died in 424 BC. **Artaxerxes II,** Memnon, who ruled 404–358 BC, suffered a succession of revolts. **Artaxerxes III,** Ochus, ruled 358–338 BC. Ruthless in his attempts to restore his empire, he was murdered by his favorite minister, Bagoas.

ARTEMIS, in Greek mythology, goddess of chastity and of the hunt, counterpart of the Roman DIANA. Daughter of ZEUS and twin to APOLLO, she was also said to protect childbirth and wild animals and was sometimes linked with the moon. Grain and animals were sacrificed to her at harvest time. One of her most famous temples was at Ephesus in Asia Minor.

ARTEMISIA, name of two queens of Caria, Asia Minor. The first was queen of Halicarnassus c480 BC. She assisted XERXES against the Greeks at Salamis. The second ruled c353–350 BC. Sister and wife of Mausolus, she built the famous MAUSOLEUM for him.

ARTERIOSCLEROSIS, disease of arteries in which the wall becomes thickened and rigid, and blood flow is hindered. **Atherosclerosis** is the formation of fatty deposits (containing CHOLESTEROL) in the inner lining of an ARTERY, followed by scarring and calcification. It is commoner in older age groups, but in DIABETES, disorders of fat METABOLISM and high-blood pressure, its appearance may be earlier. Excess saturated fats in the blood may play a role in its formation. A rarer form, **medial sclerosis,** is caused by degeneration and calcification of the middle muscular layer of the artery. Narrowing or obstruction of cerebral arteries may lead to STROKE, while that of coronary arteries causes ANGINA PECTORIS and CORONARY THROMBOSIS. Reduced blood flow to the limbs may cause CRAMP on exertion, ULCERS and GANGRENE. Established arteriosclerosis cannot be reversed, but a low fat diet, exercise and the avoidance of smoking help in prevention. Surgery by artery-replacement or removal of deposits is occasionally indicated.

ARTERY, blood vessel which carries BLOOD from the HEART to the TISSUES (see BLOOD CIRCULATION). The arteries are elastic and expand with each PULSE. In most vertebrates, the two main arteries leaving the heart are the pulmonary artery, which carries blood from the body to the LUNGS to be reoxygenated, and the AORTA which supplies the body with oxygenated blood. Major arteries supply each limb and organ and within each they divide repeatedly until arterioles and CAPILLARIES are reached. Fish have only one arterial system, which leads from the heart via the GILLS to the body. (See also ARTERIOSCLEROSIS.)

ARTESIA, residential city in Cal., NE of Long Beach. Pop 14 757.

ARTESIA, city in N.M., 36mi N of Carlsbad. The local industries are oil refining and agriculture. Pop 10 315.

ARTESIAN WELL, a well in which water rises under hydrostatic pressure above the level of the AQUIFER in which it has been confined by overlying impervious strata. Often pumping is necessary to bring the water to the surface, but true artesian wells (named for the

French province of Artois where they were first constructed) flow without assistance.

ARTEVELDE, Jacob van (c1290–1345), Flemish leader who formed a federation of towns to protect their common textile industry. At the start of the Hundred Years' War (1337), Bruges, Ypres, Ghent and other towns dependent on English wool supplies decided to maintain an armed neutrality under Artevelde as captain-general. Artevelde's dictatorial methods and his later proposal to accept the authority of the English led to a riot in which he was killed.

ART GALLERY. See MUSEUM.

ARTHRITIS, INFLAMMATION, with pain and swelling, of JOINTS. **Osteoarthritis** is most common, though there is no true inflammation; it is a wear-and-tear arthritis, causing pain and limitation of movement. OBESITY, previous trauma and inflammatory arthritis predispose. Bacterial infection (e.g., by STAPHYLOCOCCI or TUBERCULOSIS), with PUS in the joint, and GOUT, due to deposition of crystals in SYNOVIAL FLUID, may lead to serious joint destruction. **Rheumatoid arthritis** is a systemic disease manifested mainly in joints, with inflammation of synovial membranes and secondary destruction. In the hands, tendons may be disrupted and extreme deformity can result. Arthritis also occurs in many other systemic diseases including RHEUMATIC FEVER, LUPUS erythematosus, PSORIASIS and some VENEREAL DISEASES. Treatment of arthritis includes anti-inflammatory ANALGESICS (e.g., ASPIRIN), rest, local heat and PHYSIOTHERAPY. STEROIDS are sometimes helpful but their long-term use is now discouraged. Badly damaged joints may need surgical treatment or replacement.

ARTHROPODA, largest and most diverse phylum of the ANIMAL KINGDOM, containing, amongst others, INSECTS, MILLIPEDES, CENTIPEDES, CRUSTACEA, ARACHNIDA, and KING CRABS. They are characterized by a segmented EXOSKELETON with jointed limbs. This is shed at intervals, the arthropod emerging in a new, soft exoskeleton which has developed beneath: often this molting is followed by rapid growth. Molting may cease on attainment of adulthood, but many crustacea molt periodically throughout their lives. FOSSIL arthropods include the TRILOBITES.

ARTHUR, legendary British king and folk hero. In origin he was possibly a 6th-century military leader whose activities, much embroidered, became the basis of the ARTHURIAN LEGENDS.

ARTHUR, Chester Alan (1830–1886), 21st president of the US. Arthur was vice-president to James A. Garfield and became president on the latter's assassination in 1881. Born in Fairfield, Vt., he was the son of a teacher from N Ireland. He entered a New York City law office in 1853 and soon after won a reputation as a progressive attorney in two important civil rights cases. During the Civil War he became quartermaster-general of the N.Y. Militia.

Returning to the law after the war, Arthur became active in city politics as a Republican, and President Grant appointed him customs collector for the port of New York in 1871. In this post, Arthur's name became linked with the "spoils system" and, although his personal integrity was not openly doubted, he was eventually removed from office in 1878 following an inquiry instigated by President Hayes. Arthur attended the Republican National Convention of 1880 and was chosen to make up the ticket under Garfield. On Garfield's death, he supported demands for the reform of the civil service, and the important PENDLETON ACT was passed in 1883. His attempts to cut taxes and tariff duties failed to gain the backing of Congress.

Arthur's stand against narrow party interests won the approval of many of his critics but alienated his own party, and cost him the renomination in 1884. He retired to his law practice.

Chester Alan ARTHUR
21st US President

Born: October 5, 1830
Died: November 18, 1886
Term of Office: September 20, 1881–March 3, 1885
Political Party: Republican

ARTHURIAN LEGENDS, the literature relating the feats of King ARTHUR and his knights. Arthur himself is mentioned in a 9th-century chronicle, but the basis of the legends is found in GEOFFREY OF MONMOUTH (1137). From then until the 16th century a cycle of romances of chivalry developed, mainly written in French and in both prose and verse, drawing upon Celtic folklore (probably from Brittany) and incorporating the life and death of Arthur himself, the loves of LANCELOT and GUINEVERE and of Tristan and Yseult, the story of Merlin and the quest for the HOLY GRAIL. From them Sir Thomas MALORY distilled his *Morte d'Arthur* (1485), which inspired Lord TENNYSON'S *Idylls of the King* (1859) and T. H. White's *The Once and Future King* (1958).

ARTICHOKE, perennial plant, often called the globe artichoke (*Cynara scolymus*), cultivated for the immature flower heads, which are eaten as a vegetable. The so-called Jerusalem artichoke (*Helianthus tuberosus*) is a perennial American sunflower with edible tuberous roots. Both are in the family Compositae.

ARTICLES OF CONFEDERATION, the first written framework of government for the US. They were drafted in 1776–77 after the Declaration of Independence, but it was 1781 before all 13 states ratified them. The states were wary of a centralized and remote government because of their experience of the English Parliament, and the national government they set up had limited powers. It was to operate through Congress, at which each state had one vote, and to control foreign affairs, war and peace, coinage, the post office and some other matters. But "sovereignty, freedom and independence" remained with the separate states. Congress had no way of enforcing its decrees, and there were no federal courts. The shortcomings of the Articles were evident, particularly with reference to interstate trade, and the Constitutional Convention of 1787 abandoned them in favor of the present UNITED STATES CONSTITUTION which took effect in 1789.

ARTIFICIAL INSEMINATION, introduction of SPERM into the vagina by means other than copulation. The technique is widely used for breeding livestock as it produces many offspring from one selected male (see HEREDITY). It has a limited use in treating human IMPOTENCE and STERILITY.

ARTIFICIAL LIMBS. See PROSTHETICS.

ARTIFICIAL ORGANS, mechanical devices that can perform the functions of bodily organs. The **heart-lung machine** can maintain BLOOD CIRCULATION and oxygenation and has enabled much new cardiac SURGERY. **Artificial kidneys** clear waste products from the blood (see UREMIA) by DIALYSIS and may take over KIDNEY function for life. Both machines require ANTICOAGULANTS during use.

ARTIFICIAL RESPIRATION, the means of inducing RESPIRATION when it has ceased, as after DROWNING, ASPHYXIA, in COMA or respiratory PARALYSIS. It must be continued until natural breathing returns and ensuring a clear airway via the mouth to the lungs is essential. The most common first aid methods are: "mouth-to-mouth", in which air is breathed via the mouth into the lungs and is then allowed to escape, and the less effective Holger Nielsen technique where rhythmic movements of the CHEST force air out and encourage its entry alternately. If prolonged artificial respiration is needed, mechanical pumps are used and these may support respiration for months or even years.

ARTIFICIAL SELECTION, the method by which man has determined the evolution of certain animals and plants by selecting for breeding those individuals which display desired characters. These include fast growth rates in cattle, heavy crop yields and disease resistance in plants. (See also DOMESTICATION.)

ARTIGAS, José Gervasio (1764–1850), Uruguayan hero who fought for national independence from Spain. At one time protector of 350 000sq mi of country, he was defeated by the Portuguese in 1820, dying in exile before independence was won.

ARTILLERY, once the term for all military machinery, it now refers to guns too heavy to be carried by one or two men. The branch of the army involved is also known as the artillery. Modern artillery may be said to have its origins in the 14th century when weapons that used gunpowder were first developed. The importance of artillery in battle increased as it became more mobile, and scientific advances improved its accuracy and effectiveness. WWII saw the development of specialized antitank and antiaircraft guns, and the first really effective use of rockets. Since then the guided MISSILE has been produced, with its long ranges and high accuracy. It is so effective that it may obviate the need for much conventional artillery.

ART INSTITUTE OF CHICAGO, art museum and school, founded in 1879. It contains works from many periods but is noted especially for its collections of French 19th and 20th century art and of Japanese prints.

ARTIODACTYLA, one of the largest orders of MAMMALS, the cloven-hoofed UNGULATES (e.g., CATTLE, DEER, PIGS, SHEEP, GOATS, GIRAFFES, HIPPOPOTAMUSES, CAMELS). They have two or four toes on each foot (except PECCARIES, which have four toes on each forefoot, three on each hind-): in four-toed Artiodactyls the weight on each limb is borne by the center two toes. (See also PERISSODACTYLA.)

ART NOUVEAU, late 19th-century art movement which influenced decorative styles throughout the West. Its themes were exotic or decadent and its characteristic line sinuous and highly ornamental. The movement aimed to reunite art and life, and so to produce everyday objects of beauty. It was of importance in the applied arts, some notable architecture, furniture, jewelry and book designs being produced in this style. Graphic art too was much affected by Art Nouveau, as seen in the work of Aubrey BEARDSLEY. Other notable artists of the movement were the painter Gustav KLIMT and the architects Antonio GAUDI and Victor HORTA, and in the applied arts TIFFANY, Lalique and Charpentier.

ART STUDENTS LEAGUE, art school in New York City, set up by students in 1875 as a self-governing institution. Artists of worldwide reputation often occupy teaching posts at the school.

ARTZYBASHEFF, Boris (1899–1965), Russian-born US illustrator and writer. He illustrated his own books and those of others, and designed many covers for *Time* magazine.

ARUBA, small island off the Venezuelan coast, 45mi W of Curaçao, part of the NETHERLANDS ANTILLES. It is about 19mi long and 4mi wide, and is inhabited by people of Indian and Negro descent who speak a hybrid language called *Papiamento.* The chief industry is the refining of crude oil imported from Venezuela. Pop 59 813.

ARUM, popular name for many herbaceous perennial plants of the family Araceae. The plants have characteristic small flowers that are clustered on a swollen axis (the spadix) which is surrounded by a large showy bract (the spathe). Most species grow in swampy habitats in tropical and subtropical regions. In Britain the family is represented by the cuckoo-pint (*Arum maculatum*) and in the US by JACK-IN-THE-PULPIT (*Arisaema triphyllum*). All arums have a poisonous and acrid juice.

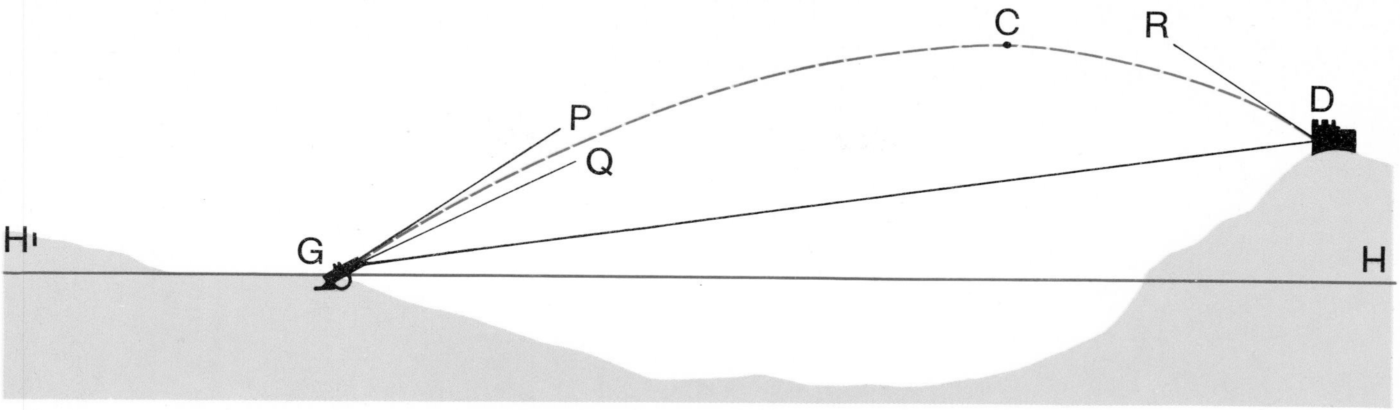

The first forms of artillery were the great stone-throwing machines of the Greeks and Romans. The study of modern ballistics deals with the path (trajectory) of a projectile from the time of firing until it hits the target area. In this diagram H'-H is a horizontal line through the location of the gun (G). GD shows the line of sight to the target (D), GQ is the line of sight before firing and GP is the actual exit line (due to movement of the gun on firing). C is the peak of the trajectory and RD the direction of impact.

ARUSHA, town in N Tanzania, 45mi SW of Mt Kilimanjaro. It is a center for coffee-growing and for big-game hunting. The Arusha Declaration, made by President NYERERE in 1967, outlined policies of socialism for Tanzania. Pop 32 452.

ARVADA, town in N central Col., near Denver. An agricultural center, it also manufactures wood and metal products. Pop 46 814.

ARVERNI, a Gallic tribe which dominated the area of present-day Auvergne. Their territory was greatly reduced by the Romans in 121 BC. In 52 BC the Arverni together with the rest of Gaul revolted under the leadership of VERCINGETORIX, but were defeated by Julius Caesar in the GALLIC WARS.

ARYAN (Sanskrit: noble), name once used for the family of languages now known as Indo-European. The word acquired political connotations in Nazi Germany, being interpreted as "Nordic" or non-Jewish in race, and has thus been discredited in modern usage.

The European ash (*Fraxinus excelsior*) is found in both Europe and Asia Minor, while the very similar white ash (*F. americana*) is the most common species in the United States. This picture shows a branch of the European ash with leaves (a) and fruit (b); c. shows the flowering branch; d. shows the female and e. the male inflorescence; f. is the winged seed that is dispersed by wind.

ASA (d. 870 BC), king of Judah, c911–870 BC. The Bible records that he spent much of his reign in conflict with King Baasha of Israel, against whom he enlisted Aramaean aid. Asa was a zealous campaigner against worship. He was succeeded by his son JEHOSHAPHAT.

ASAFETIDA, a pungent-smelling gum resin obtained from an Asian herb (*Ferula assafoetida*) of the parsley family. It is used in Asia as a condiment and in Europe as a flavoring agent. It has some medicinal properties as a sedative.

ASAHIKAWA, city on Hokkaido Island, Japan, which manufactures textiles and wood products. Pop 288 492.

ASBESTOS, name of various fibrous minerals, chiefly CHRYSOTILE and AMPHIBOLE. Canada and the USSR are the chief producers. It is a valuable industrial material because it is refractory, alkali-and acid-resistant and an electrical insulator. It can be spun to make fireproof fabrics for protective clothing and safety curtains, or molded to make tiles, bricks and automobile brake linings. Asbestos particles may cause PNEUMOCONIOSIS and lung CANCER if inhaled.

ASBURY, Francis (1745–1816), first Methodist bishop in the US. Born in England, he came to the US in 1771 as a Methodist missionary. With his energetic guidance, and despite his ill-health, Methodism in the US became widely established. Asbury was elected bishop in 1784.

ASBURY PARK, Atlantic coast resort in N.J. The city was incorporated in 1897, and is now a popular convention center as well as a summer resort, second in N.J. only to Atlantic City. Pop 16 533.

ASCANIUS, according to VERGIL, the son of AENEAS and Creusa, who escaped from Troy with his father. LIVY, however, made his mother the Italian princess Lavinia. He succeeded his father as king of Lavinium from which he migrated to found ALBA LONGA. He was also known as Iulus from whom Julius Caesar's family claimed descent.

ASCENSION, The, the bodily ascent into heaven of Jesus Christ on the 40th day after his resurrection. The event, described in the New Testament, signifies Christ's entry into glory and thus promises believers a heavenly life. Ascension Day is a major Christian festival. (See CHURCH YEAR.)

ASCENSION ISLAND, small volcanic island in the S Atlantic, 750mi NW of the British colony of St. Helena, of which it is a dependency. During WWII US forces built an airstrip there and it now has an important missile and satellite tracking station. Most of the population centers on Georgetown. The island is 34sq mi in area. Pop 1 363.

ASCETICISM, the practice of acts of self-denial or self-mortification as a religious exercise. The underlying belief is that bodily deprivation benefits spiritual progress. Asceticism is common to almost all religions and may take many forms. At one extreme are acts such as self-flagellation, sleeping on beds of nails and exposure to heat or cold. More frequent are acts of fasting and the rejection of material comforts.

ASCH, Sholem (1880–1957), leading Yiddish novelist and playwright. Born in Poland, he spent most of his life in the US. His many books deal with Jewish life both in Europe and the US, and with the relationship between Judaism and Christianity, as in *The Nazarene* (1939).

ASCHAM, Roger (1516–1568), English writer and scholar, noted for his prose style, his humanist learning and his love of Greek literature. He was tutor to the future Queen Elizabeth and a diplomat of the Tudor court. He wrote two books, *Toxophilus* (1545) and *The Schoolmaster* (1570).

ASCLEPIUS. See AESCULAPIUS.

ASCORBIC ACID, or Vitamin C. See VITAMIN.

ASCOT, English town near Windsor. It is the site of the famous June horse race meeting, Royal Ascot, traditionally attended by British royalty.

ASEPSIS, the principle in modern SURGERY of excluding GERMS. Means include the STERILIZATION of instruments, dressings, gowns and gloves, and the use of ANTISEPTICS for cleaning the skin of patient and surgeon.

ASGARD, in Norse mythology, the realm of the gods. It contained many halls and palaces; chief of these was VALHALLA, where ODIN entertained warriors killed in battle. The only entry to Asgard was by the rainbow bridge called BIFROST.

ASH, the inorganic residue left after organic substances are burned. Some ash is commercially useful: plant ash is a FERTILIZER and seaweed ash yields IODINE. Conglomerated ash may be called clinker.

ASH, trees and shrubs of the genus *Fraxinus*, a member of the olive family, native to the N hemisphere. Ashes have compound leaves with the leaflets arranged in opposite pairs and single-winged keys of fruit. The main US species is the white ash (*Fraxinus americana*), which is the tallest ash (up to 40m (130ft)) and produces timber used for tool handles and baseball bats. Several species of the genus *Sorbus* are also given the name ash e.g. the rowan or MOUNTAIN ASH, but these are not true ashes.

ASHANTI, a region of S Ghana, and the name of the people who live there. From the 17th century to 1902, when Britain annexed the region, the powerful Ashanti Confederacy linked several small kingdoms under one chief. The symbol of their unity was the sacred GOLDEN STOOL which, in their religion of ancestor-worship, represents the departed spirits of the Ashanti. The present-day Ashanti are a thriving agrarian people numbering about one million.

ASHCAN SCHOOL, or "The Eight," name given to a New York City group of painters, formed in 1908. They were so called because they chose to paint everyday aspects of city life. The Eight— Arthur DAVIES, William GLACKENS, Ernest LAWSON, George

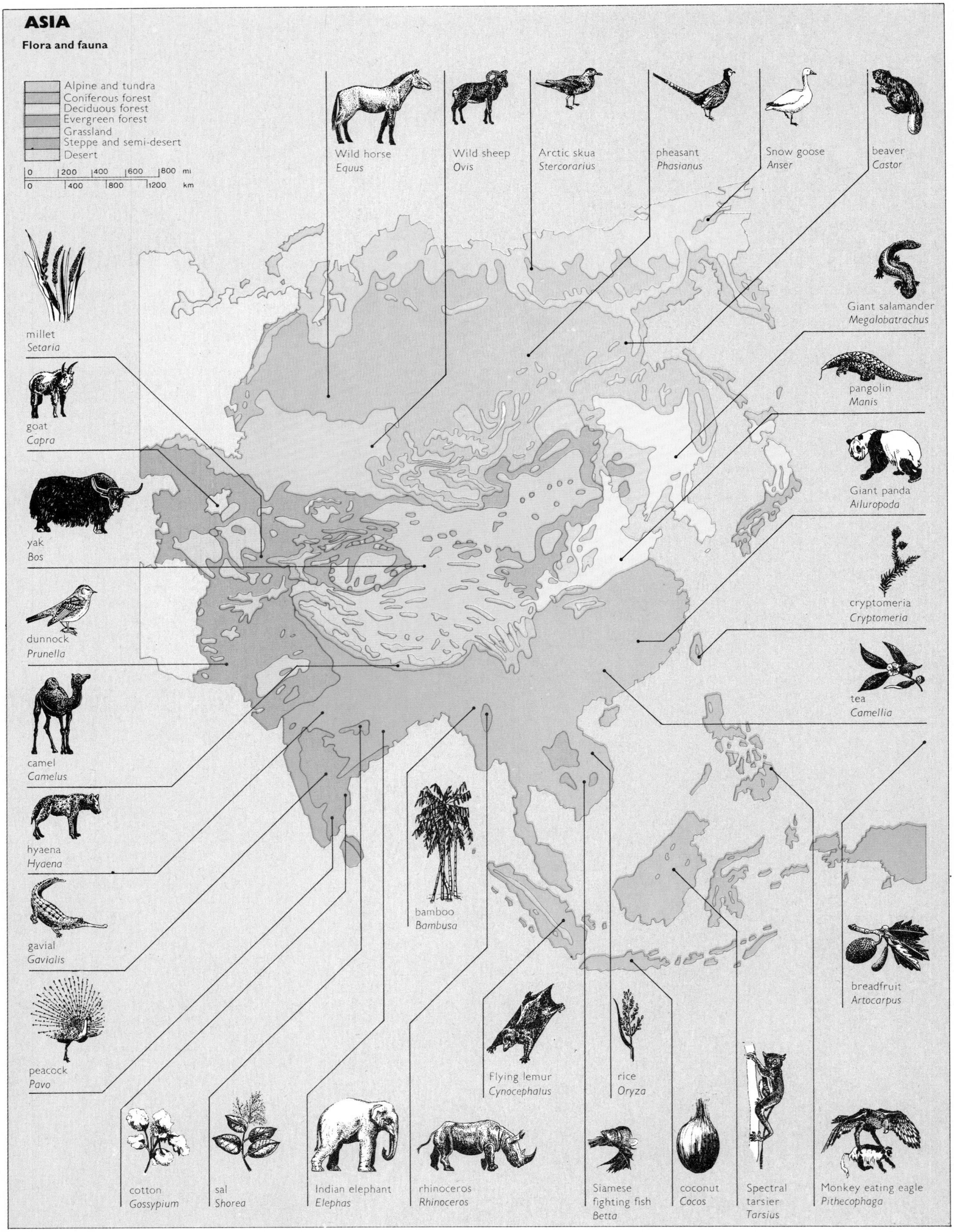
ASIA
Flora and fauna
Alpine and tundra
Coniferous forest
Deciduous forest
Evergreen forest
Grassland
Steppe and semi-desert
Desert
0 200 400 600 800 mi
0 400 800 1200 km
Wild horse
Equus
Wild sheep
Ovis
Arctic skua
Stercorarius
pheasant
Phasianus
Snow goose
Anser
beaver
Castor
millet
Setaria
goat
Capra
yak
Bos
dunnock
Prunella
camel
Camelus
hyaena
Hyaena
gavial
Gavialis
peacock
Pavo
Giant salamander
Megalobatrachus
pangolin
Manis
Giant panda
Ailuropoda
cryptomeria
Cryptomeria
tea
Camellia
breadfruit
Artocarpus
bamboo
Bambusa
Flying lemur
Cynocephalus
rice
Oryza
cotton
Gossypium
sal
Shorea
Indian elephant
Elephas
rhinoceros
Rhinoceros
Siamese
fighting fish
Betta
coconut
Cocos
Spectral
tarsier
Tarsius
Monkey eating eagle
Pithecophaga

A glimpse of Asia's infinite variety: (*top left*) an Islamic mosque in Lahore, West Pakistan; (*middle*) the timeless atmosphere of a fruit and vegetable market in Surabaya, the center of a rich agricultural region; (*bottom left*) terraced rice paddies in Java which provide the population with its staple diet; (*right*) Tokyo, capital of Japan and probably the world's largest city. The monorail was introduced in 1964 when the Olympic Games were held here; the building in the background is the city's highest structure, the Tokyo Tower (1 092ft), built in a mere 15 months from 1957–58.

LUKS, Maurice PRENDERGAST, Everett SHINN, Robert HENRI and John SLOAN—differed in many ways but were united in their dislike of academicism. They were instrumental in bringing the ARMORY SHOW to New York in 1913; it was the first major exhibition in the US of the work of PICASSO and other important European artists.

ASHDOD, ancient city in Israel, 20mi S of Tel Aviv, now a rapidly expanding deep water port and development town. It was once a major Philistine city and a center of the cult of Dagon. Pop 37 600.

ASHE, Arthur (1943–), US tennis player. In 1975 he became the first Negro to win the Wimbledon men's singles. In 1968 he won the US Men's National Singles title, the first Negro and first US player since 1955 to do so.

ASHEBORO, seat of Randolph Co., N.C., 25mi S of Greensboro. It is an industrial town whose chief manufactures are hosiery and wood products. Pop 10 797.

ASHER, a tribe of Israel named for the son of Jacob and Leah's maid, Zilpah. It occupied the NW part of Palestine, S of Dan.

ASHEVILLE, city and mountain resort, seat of Buncombe Co., N.C. Its industries include the manufacture of textiles and paper, and the processing of agricultural products. It is the site of Biltmore House, the palatial former home of George Vanderbilt. Pop 57 681.

ASHIKAGA, Japanese city 50mi N of Tokyo. The city, an old silk-weaving center, was the ancestral home of a dynasty of SHOGUNS who ruled from 1338 to 1573. Pop 156 004.

ASHKENAZIM, those Jews whose medieval ancestors lived in Germany. Persecution drove them to spread throughout central and E Europe, and in the 19th and 20th centuries overseas, notably to the US. Their ritual and Hebrew pronunciation differ from those of the SEPHARDIM (Jews of Oriental countries). Up to the beginning of the 20th century most Ashkenazim spoke Yiddish. Most Jews in the US and the majority of the world's Jews are Ashkenazim. (See also JEWS.)

ASHKENAZY, Vladimir (1937–), celebrated Russian pianist, now living in Iceland. In 1955 he won the Chopin Competition in Warsaw, and was joint winner of the Tchaikovsky Competition in Moscow in 1962.

ASHKHABAD, capital of the Turkmen SSR, USSR, 25mi from the Iranian border. It is an important center for light industry, notably textiles and leather goods. The city was extensively rebuilt after serious earthquake damage in 1948. Pop 253 000.

ASHLAND, city in E Ky. on the Ohio R, in a region of clay, coal and oil deposits. It is a center for the iron, steel and petroleum industries. Pop 29 245.

ASHLAND, city in Ohio, 60mi SW of Cleveland. It manufactures pumps, automobile parts and rubber goods. Pop 19 872.

ASHLAND, city in S Ore. on Bear Creek. Nearby are gold mines, marble and granite quarries and mineral springs. Pop 12 342.

ASHLEY, William Henry (c1778–1838), US fur-trader and politician. He explored the area W of Missouri as far as the Great Salt Lake and helped to make known the OREGON TRAIL.

ASHMUN, Jehudi (1794–1828), US missionary. A Congregationalist minister, he was sent by the American Colonization Society to the settlement of freed slaves in Liberia. His efforts saved the settlement from extinction.

ASHOKA. See ASOKA.

ASHTABULA, city in NE Ohio on Lake Erie. It is an important railroad terminus and a center for industry, commerce and shipping. Pop 24 313.

ASHTON, Sir Frederick (1906–), British dancer and choreographer. His work, which included such new productions as *Façade* (1931) and *La Fille Mal Gardée* (1960), has had great influence on British ballet. He was director of the Royal Ballet 1963–70.

ASHUR, ancient capital of Assyria, on the W bank of the Tigris, at Qal'at Sharqat in N Iraq. It was first settled by Sumerians in the 3rd millennium BC.

ASHUR, warlike god of the Assyrians, whose symbol, a winged solar disk, suggests he was in fact a sun-god. Ashur headed the Assyrian pantheon, and came to be identified with the Sumerian Enlil and the Babylonian MARDUK.

ASHURBANIPAL, last of the great kings of Assyria, ruled from c669–630 BC over a huge empire which included Babylonia, Syria and Palestine. His reign was prosperous, though troubled by numerous revolts. He established the library of cuneiform tablets in Nineveh, discovered in the 1840s.

ASHURNASIRPAL, name of two kings of Assyria. **Ashurnasirpal I,** ruled c1049–1031 BC. **Ashurnasirpal II** ruled 884–859 BC and laid the basis for the organization and growth of the Assyrian Empire.

ASH WEDNESDAY, first of the 40 days of the Christian fast of LENT. The name derives from the early practice of sprinkling penitents with ashes. Today the ash of burnt palms is used to mark the sign of the cross on the foreheads of believers.

ASIA, the world's largest continent, covers more than 16 980 000sq mi (nearly one-third of the earth's land surface) and has about 2 600 000 000 people (nearly 60% of the total world population). It extends from the Arctic Ocean in the N to the Indian Ocean in the S, and from the Pacific Ocean in the E to the Mediterranean in the W. Its border with Europe is formed by the Black Sea, the Caucasus Mts, the Caspian Sea, the Ural R and the Ural Mts. In the SW, Asia is separated from Africa by the Red Sea and the Suez Canal. The combined land mass of Europe and Asia is sometimes treated as a single continent, Eurasia.

Land. Asia is a continent of infinite diversity, with

ATLANTIC OCEAN
ARCTIC
NORTH SEA
BALTIC SEA
DUBLIN
EDINBURGH
LONDON
LISBON
MADRID
PARIS
AMSTERDAM
BERLIN
OSLO
STOCKHOLM
HELSINKI
PRAGUE
WARSAW
VIENNA
BUDAPEST
BUCHAREST
SOFIA
ROME
ALGIERS
ATHENS
ISTANBUL
IZMIR
ANKARA
ADANA
EUROPE
MEDITERRANEAN SEA
BLACK SEA
AFRICA
Spitsbergen
Franz Josef Land
North Cape
Novaya Zemlya
Dickson
Dudinka
MURMANSK
ARKHANGELSK
TALLINN
RIGA
VILNIUS
MINSK
LENINGRAD
YAROSLAVL
Volga
Dnepr
LVOV
DNEPROPETROVSK
KRIVOY ROG
ODESSA
KIEV
MOSCOW
GORKIY
KAZAN
PERM
VORONEZH
KHARKOV
DONETSK
ZAPOROZHYE
Don
ROSTOV
SARATOV
VOLGOGRAD
KUJBYSJEV
UFA
URALSK
ASTRAKHAN
SVERDLOVSK
CHELYABINSK
MAGNITOGORSK
KURGAN
TYUMEN
Tobolsk
Vorkuta
Salekhard
Ob
Irtysh
OMSK
NOVOSIBIRSK
KEMEROVO
NOVOKUZNETSK
KARAGANDA
SEMIPALATINSK
UNION OF SOVIET
Aral Sea
Lake Balkhash
ALMA ATA
FRUNZE
TASHKENT
SAMARKAND
DUSHANBE
KASHGAR
URUMCHI
ASHKHABAD
MASHHAD
TBILISI
YEREVAN
BAKU
CASPIAN SEA
TABRIZ
RASHT
TEHRAN
QOM
ESFAHAN
SHIRAZ
IRAN
TURKEY
CYPRUS
NICOSIA
BEIRUT
LEBANON
SYRIA
ALEPPO
DAMASCUS
JERUSALEM
ISRAEL
AMMAN
JORDAN
CAIRO
BENGASI
MOSUL
BAGHDAD
IRAQ
AL BASRAH
ABADAN
KUWAIT
SAUDI ARABIA
Medina
JIDDAH
MECCA
RIYADH
Manama
BAHRAIN
Doha
QATAR
UNITED ARAB EMIRATES
Dubayy
Muscat
OMAN
YEMEN (ARAB REP.)
Sana
YEMEN (PEOPLE'S DEM. REP.)
Madinet al-Shaab
Aden
KURIA-MURIA ISLANDS
Socotra (P.D.R.)
RED SEA
KHARTOUM
ADDIS ABABA
NAIROBI
MOGADISCIO
MOMBASA
DAR ES SALAAM
AFGHANISTAN
KABUL
KANDAHAR
Islamabad
RAWALPINDI
JAMMU AND KASHMIR
Indus
PAKISTAN
LAHORE
MULTAN
KARACHI
HYDERABAD
DELHI
NEW DELHI
JAIPUR
AGRA
NEPAL
KATMANDU
Brahmaputra
LUCKNOW
KANPUR
ALLAHABAD
VARANASI
AHMADABAD
INDORE
INDIA
CALCUTTA
NAGPUR
BOMBAY
PUNE
HYDERABAD
BHUBANESWAR
BAY OF BENGAL
BANGALORE
MADRAS
KOZHIKODE
MADURAI
LACCADIVE ISLANDS (INDIA)
SRI LANKA (CEYLON)
COLOMBO
MALDIVE ISLANDS
Male
ARABIAN SEA
INDIAN OCEAN

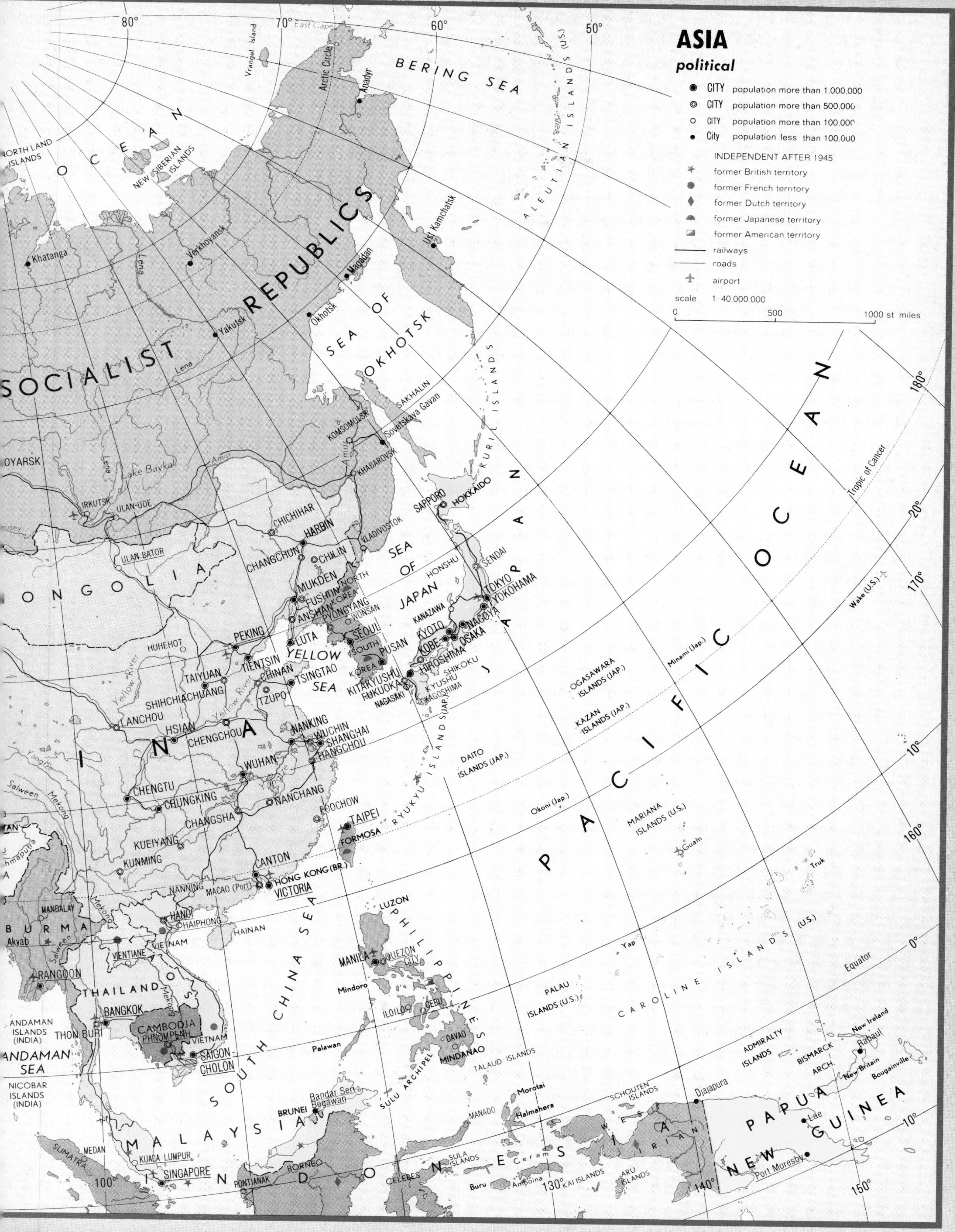
ASIA
political
CITY population more than 1,000,000
CITY population more than 500,000
CITY population more than 100,000
City population less than 100,000
INDEPENDENT AFTER 1945
former British territory
former French territory
former Dutch territory
former Japanese territory
former American territory
railways
roads
airport
scale 1:40,000,000
0
500
1000 st. miles
BERING SEA
ALEUTIAN ISLANDS (U.S.)
East Cape
Vrangel Island
Arctic Circle
Anadyr
NEW SIBERIAN ISLANDS
NORTH LAND ISLANDS
OCEAN
SOCIALIST REPUBLICS
Khatanga
Verkhoyansk
Ust Kamchatsk
Magadan
Okhotsk
Yakutsk
Lena
SEA OF OKHOTSK
SAKHALIN
Sovetskaya Gavan
KOMSOMOLSK
KHABAROVSK
Amur
KURIL ISLANDS
Lake Baykal
IRKUTSK
ULAN-UDE
OYARSK
ULAN BATOR
MONGOLIA
CHICHIHAR
HARBIN
CHANGCHUN
CHILIN
VLADIVOSTOK
MUKDEN
FUSHUN
ANSHAN
NORTH KOREA
PYONGYANG
WONSAN
SEOUL
SOUTH KOREA
PUSAN
LUTA
PEKING
TIENTSIN
HUHEHOT
TAIYUAN
SHIHCHIACHUANG
CHINAN
TSINGTAO
TZUPO
YELLOW SEA
Yellow River
LANCHOU
HSIAN
CHENGCHOU
NANKING
WUCHIN
SHANGHAI
HANGCHOU
WUHAN
CHENGTU
CHUNGKING
NANCHANG
CHANGSHA
KUEIYANG
KUNMING
FOOCHOW
TAIPEI
FORMOSA
CANTON
HONG KONG (BR.)
VICTORIA
MACAO (Port)
NANNING
Yangtze
Salween
Mekong
CHINA
SEA OF JAPAN
HOKKAIDO
SAPPORO
SENDAI
HONSHU
TOKYO
YOKOHAMA
KANAZAWA
KYOTO
NAGOYA
KOBE
OSAKA
HIROSHIMA
SHIKOKU
KYUSHU
KITAKYUSHU
FUKUOKA
NAGASAKI
KAGOSHIMA
JAPAN
RYUKYU ISLANDS (JAP.)
DAITO ISLANDS (JAP.)
OGASAWARA ISLANDS (JAP.)
KAZAN ISLANDS (JAP.)
Minami (Jap.)
Okoni (Jap.)
MARIANA ISLANDS (U.S.)
Guam
Truk
Wake (U.S.)
PACIFIC OCEAN
Tropic of Cancer
Equator
CAROLINE ISLANDS (U.S.)
Yap
PALAU ISLANDS (U.S.)
LUZON
PHILIPPINES
MANILA
QUEZON CITY
Mindoro
ILOILO
CEBU
DAVAO
MINDANAO
Palawan
SULU ARCHIPEL
TALAUD ISLANDS
SOUTH CHINA SEA
HAINAN
HANOI
HAIPHONG
VIETNAM
VIENTIANE
LAOS
BURMA
MANDALAY
Akyab
RANGOON
THAILAND
BANGKOK
THON BURI
CAMBODJA
PHNOMPENH
SAIGON-CHOLON
ANDAMAN ISLANDS (INDIA)
ANDAMAN SEA
NICOBAR ISLANDS (INDIA)
MALAYSIA
KUALA LUMPUR
SINGAPORE
MEDAN
SUMATRA
BRUNEI
Bandar Seri Bagawan
BORNEO
PONTIANAK
CELEBES
MANADO
Morotai
Halmahera
SULA ISLANDS
Ceram
Buru
Amboina
KAI ISLANDS
ARU ISLANDS
INDONESIA
WEST IRIAN
SCHOUTEN ISLANDS
Djajapura
ADMIRALTY ISLANDS
BISMARCK ARCH.
New Ireland
Rabaul
New Britain
Bougainville
PAPUA NEW GUINEA
Lae
Port Moresby
80°
70°
60°
50°
180°
20°
170°
10°
160°
0°
10°
150°
140°
130°
100°

extremes of every kind, the ultimate physical contrast being between Mt Everest (29 028ft), the world's highest mountain, and the Dead Sea (1 294ft below sea level). At its heart is the great system of mountain chains and high plateaus focused on the Pamir Knot. Among these huge mountain chains are the Karakoram Range, Himalayas, Kunlun Shan, Tien Shan, Altai Mountains, Hindu Kush and Sulaiman Range. Extensions include the lesser ranges of Asia Minor and, E of India, the Arakan Yoma range (Assam and Burma) which reappears in Indonesia. Another system of ranges stretches from E Siberia to Japan and the Philippines. The major plateaus include the plateau of Tibet, the Tarim basin and the great plateau of Mongolia. The triangular lowland region N of the mountains embraces the Turanian basin, the W Siberian lowlands and the low plateau of central Siberia. Weaknesses in the earth's crust are reflected in the active volcanoes of Indonesia, the Philippines, Japan and the Kamchatka peninsula. Earthquakes and tremors are frequent in Japan and also occur in Turkey, Iran and Pakistan.

The major rivers include the Ob and its tributary, the Irtysh, and the Yenisey and Lena, all flowing to the Arctic Ocean; the Indus (Pakistan), Ganges (India and Bangladesh) and Brahmaputra (China and India); and the Yellow and Yangtze rivers in China. Lake Baikal is the largest freshwater lake in Eurasia. There are many semiarid or arid regions such as the Gobi Desert in Mongolia and the Great Sandy Desert of Arabia.

Climate and Vegetation. Asia has every known type of climate, from the polar to the tropical. The heart of the continent has extremes of temperature in winter and summer; rainfall (May–Oct.) averages less than 10in annually. Much of Asia is monsoonal, however, and annual rainfall in Assam and Burma may reach 400in. Vegetation ranges from the tundra of the far north to the *taiga* (coniferous forest) of Siberia, the treeless grasslands of the steppes and the tropical rain forests of India and SE Asia.

People. The product of thousands of years of migrations, invasions, conquests and intermingling, the people of Asia belong mainly to three ethnic groups: Mongoloid (including Chinese, Japanese and Koreans), Caucasoid (including Arabs, Afghans, Iranians, Pakistanis and most Indian people) and Negroid (in parts of the Philippines and SE Asia). Racial mixtures are frequent in SE Asia, where the Malays are the largest group. The population is unevenly distributed, almost uninhabited areas like "High Asia" (the heart of the continent) and the deserts contrasting with the densely populated Ganges valley and the great cities of Japan and China. About one in every three Asians is urban-dwelling.

A multitude of languages and dialects is spoken, derived from Indo-European, Altaic, Semitic, Sino-Tibetan and other language families. Asia was the birthplace of several religions. Hinduism claims the largest following, but there are also millions of Buddhists and Muslims. Only about 4% of Asians are Christians.

Economic Development. About 66% of the population depend on agriculture, vital to a continent whose population is increasing at a rate of about 100 000 every 24 hours. The considerable mineral resources are not yet fully developed. Industrialization has been most rapid in Japan, third only to the US and the USSR as an industrial superpower.

History. Man has lived in Asia for about 500 000 years. The earliest-known civilizations—Sumerian, Babylonian and Assyrian—evolved in Mesopotamia. In S Asia the Indus valley civilization flowered in the 3rd millennium BC, while China's remarkable culture began in the Yellow R valley about 4 000–5 000 years ago.

ASIA MINOR, peninsula in SW Asia comprising most of modern Turkey. Mountainous and surrounded on three sides by sea, it is bounded on the E by the upper Euphrates R. Civilizations such as that of Troy flourished here from the Bronze Age onwards. After the destruction of the Hittite empire in 1200 BC, the land belonged successively to the Medes, Persians, Greeks and Romans. In the 5th century AD it passed to the Byzantine Emperors and remained among their last possessions, constantly eroded as their power declined until in the 15th century it became part of the OTTOMAN EMPIRE and remained so until the Republic of Turkey was founded (1923).

ASIATIC BLACK BEAR, or Himalayan Bear, *Selenarctos thibetanus*, a large BEAR (family Ursidae) inhabiting the high-altitude forests of central Asia. It has a black coat with a white chevron on the chest.

ASIMOV, Isaac (1920–   ), prolific US author and educator, best known for his science fiction books such as the *Foundation* trilogy (1951–53) and *The Gods Themselves* (1972), and for his many science books for laymen. He was associate professor of biochemistry at Boston U. from 1955.

ASKENASE, Stefan (1896–   ), Belgian pianist, born in Poland, who has gained a worldwide reputation for his performances of CHOPIN.

ASMARA, second-largest city in Ethiopia, capital of the province of Eritrea, about 40mi from the Red Sea on a plateau 7 500ft above sea level. It is a road and rail link between the inland and coast and a center for light industry. Pop 218 360.

ASOKA (d. 232 BC), third emperor of the Maurya dynasty of India, whose acceptance of BUDDHISM as the official religion of his vast empire had a major effect on that faith's predominance in Asia. He was said to have been so repelled by a particularly bloody victory of his troops over what is now Orissa that he turned to nonviolence and the Buddhist way of righteousness, and sent missionaries into Burma, Ceylon, Syria, Greece and Egypt.

ASP, the Egyptian COBRA *Naja haje* (family: Elapidae), an extremely poisonous snake up to 2m (6.6ft) in length. Sacred in ancient Egypt, it was legendarily the cause of Cleopatra's death. The name is also applied to the horned and asp VIPERS.

ASPARAGUS, genus of perennial plants belonging to the lily family and native to many parts of the world from Siberia to S Africa. *Asparagus officinalis* is the common garden asparagus cultivated for its edible shoots. Some species (*A. setaceus* and *A. densiflorus sprengeri*) are grown for their attractive foliage which consists of conspicuous leaf-like branches (cladodes) that arise from tuberous or fibrous roots. Indoors they should be grown in a sunny east or west window during the winter, but moved to avoid direct sun in the summer. They grow best between 16°C and 21°C (60°F and 70°F) and should be watered often enough to keep the soil evenly moist. Propagation is by seeds or division of plants.

ASPASIA (5th century BC), mistress of the Athenian statesman PERICLES. A well educated woman from Miletus, she became the mother of his successor, PERICLES THE YOUNGER. She was the friend of SOCRATES.

ASPEN, city in W central Col. on the Roaring Fork R, seat of Pitkin Co. The city was founded by prospectors c1878. After a decline it became a ski resort and cultural center, site of the Aspen Music Festival. Pop 2 437.

ASPEN, name given to several species of the genus *Populus*, which also contains the POPLARS and the COTTONWOODS. Aspens are fast-growing but short-lived trees native to Europe and N America. Examples are, the common European aspen (*P. tremula*) and the American or quaking aspen (*P. tremuloides*), so-called because of the fluttering motion produced in its branches by the wind. Aspen wood is light but tough and used for furniture, matches and wood pulp. (See also WILLOW.)

ASPHALT, a tough black material used in road paving, roofing and canal and reservoir lining. Now obtained mainly from PETROLEUM refinery residues (although natural deposits are still worked), it consists mainly of heavy HYDROCARBONS.

ASPHODEL, common name for several species of the genus *Asphodelus*, which are hardy herbaceous plants with white flowers, native to the Mediterranean region and India. Also yellow-flowered plants of the genus *Asphodeline*, which the Greeks planted in graveyards and which are linked by Homer with the underworld of the dead.

ASPHYXIA, the complex of symptoms due to inability to take oxygen into or excrete carbon dioxide from the LUNGS. The commonest causes are DROWNING, suffocation or strangling; inhalation of toxic gases, obstruction of LARYNX, TRACHEA or BRONCHI (which can occur in severe cases of CROUP, ASTHMA and DIPHTHERIA). Early ARTIFICIAL RESPIRATION is essential.

ASPIDISTRA, small genus of plants native to China and Japan. They have long been popular as houseplants because their attractive foliage is resistant to dirt, soot, lack of light and noxious fumes. *Aspidistra elatior* is a commonly cultivated species, which has a variegated form with striped foliage. Indoors, they should be grown in a bright north window or any similar light and grow best between 10°C and 21°C (50°F and 70°F). They should be watered weekly, enough to keep the soil evenly moist. They are propagated by leaf cuttings or by dividing the plant. Family: Liliaceae.

ASPIRIN, or **acetylsalicylic acid,** an effective analgesic, which also reduces FEVER and INFLAMMATION and also affects BLOOD platelets. It is useful in HEADACHE, minor feverish illness, MENSTRUATION pain, RHEUMATIC FEVER, inflammatory ARTHRITIS, and may also be used to prevent THROMBOSIS. Aspirin may cause gastrointestinal irritation and HEMORRHAGE, and should be avoided in cases of peptic ULCER.

ASQUITH, Herbert Henry (1852–1928), prime minister of Britain 1908–16, 1st Earl of Oxford and Asquith. His term as head of the British LIBERAL PARTY was one of great activity and political reform, but his leadership foundered in Dec. 1916 over his conduct of WWI, coupled with the chaos brought about by the EASTER REBELLION in Ireland. He resigned in favor of the rival Liberal leader David LLOYD GEORGE.

ASS. See DONKEY.

ASSAM, state in the far NE of India, lying around the Brahmaputra R beneath the Himalayas and separated from most of India by Bangladesh. The area, surrounded by Burma, China, Tibet and Bengal, became an Indian state in 1950. Its capital is Shillong. The climate is subtropical. E Himalayas lie along its N border, and the terrain becomes hilly beyond the S Brahmaputra plain. Its principal crop is tea. Textiles and oil are also important.

ASSASSIN, perpetrator of a political murder. The term derives from the name given to members of a fanatical sect of Islam founded by Hasan ibn-al-Sabbah, who refused to recognize the SELJUK regime in Persia at the end of the 11th century. His followers hid in the mountains and made periodic murderous raids on their enemies after smoking HASHISH; hence "hashshasin," which became "assassin."

ASSASSINATION, murder of a prominent person for broadly political reasons. Although there has been a modern tendency to assassination by a lone individual, it has usually been practiced by rivals for power or their representatives. There have been instances of assassination throughout recorded history. In the last 100 years US presidents Garfield and Kennedy, Prime Minister Verwoerd of South Africa, Mahatma Gandhi, Martin Luther King and many other public figures have been assassinated.

ASSASSIN BUGS, around 3 000 species of blood-sucking bugs of the family Reduviidae, order HEMIPTERA. They usually feed on insect blood but also attack higher animals. Their mouthparts are tubular, adapted for piercing and sucking. They are important carriers and transmitters of CHAGAS' DISEASE.

ASSATEAGUE ISLAND, 32mi long barrier island off the Atlantic coast of Md. and Va. It is a natural wildlife reserve, and was made part of the US National Seashore in 1965.

ASSAULT, in law, refers to the expressed threat of attack, while BATTERY refers to the attack itself. Aggravated assault implies an added threat or offence, such as "assault with a deadly weapon." Assault can constitute a MISDEMEANOR or a FELONY.

ASSAYING, a method of chemical ANALYSIS for determining NOBLE METALS in ores or alloys, used since the 2nd millennium BC. The sample is fused with a flux containing LEAD (II) oxide. This produces a lead button containing the noble metals, which is heated in oxygen to oxidize the lead and other impurities, leaving a bead of the noble metals which is weighed and separated chemically.

ASSEMBLIES OF GOD, largest of the Protestant PENTECOSTAL denominations in the US. They were organized as a separate entity in 1914, and later established their headquarters in Springfield, Mo. They now have over 1 million members.
ASSEMBLY LINE. See MASS PRODUCTION.
ASSER, Tobias Michael Carel (1838–1913), Dutch jurist who, together with Alfred H. FRIED, was awarded the Nobel Peace Prize in 1911 for his contributions to INTERNATIONAL LAW.
ASSESSMENT, a levy made by organizations such as governments, corporations and clubs on their citizens, stockholders or members; and sometimes the means by which it is apportioned. The term is commonly used in property taxation, when it includes valuation.
ASSIGNAT, paper currency issued by the revolutionary governments of France 1790–96. It was redeemable at only $\frac{1}{30}$ of its original value by 1796, when it was replaced by *mandats territoriaux*.
ASSIGNMENT, in law, usually the transfer of rights in tangible or, especially, intangible property or prospects, such as insurance policies, business contracts, certificates of corporate shares, and rights to monies due or to become due.
ASSINIBOIA, once the name of two separate districts of Canada. One was formed by the HUDSON'S BAY COMPANY around the Red River in 1835 and the other was in the NORTHWEST TERRITORY (in present-day S Saskatchewan and Manitoba).
ASSINIBOINE RIVER, runs about 450mi through S Saskatchewan and Manitoba. Discovered in 1736, it served as a major route for explorers and settlers of the Canadian plains.
ASSINIBOIN INDIANS, Sioux tribe of the North American plains who left the Yanktonai Sioux to spread out from Canada across the NW US. A nomadic people, they lived primarily by hunting. Like other Sioux, they took quickly to the use of horses and guns. They were easily defeated by the white settlers, because of the extinction of the buffalo, and were placed on reservations in 1884. (See also PLAINS INDIANS.)
ASSISI, town about 15mi SE of Perugia in Italy, situated on Mt Subasio above the plains of Umbria. The birthplace of St. FRANCIS and St. CLARE, it is also noted for its medieval buildings, particularly the Gothic Basilica of St. Francis and the Church of St. Clare. Pop 24 755.
ASSISI, Saint Francis of. See FRANCIS OF ASSISI, SAINT.
ASSIUT. See ASYUT.
ASSOCIATED PRESS (AP), the oldest and largest US news agency, founded in 1848 by six New York City newspapers, now with offices sending and receiving throughout the world. It is a non-profit organization financed by subscriptions from member newspapers, periodicals and broadcasting stations.
ASSOCIATION, in PSYCHOLOGY, the mental linking of one item with others: e.g., black and white, Tom with Dick and Harry, etc. The connections are described by the primary (similarity and contiguity) and secondary (frequency, recency, vividness and primacy) laws of association. In **association tests,** subjects are presented with one word and asked to respond either with a specifically related word, such as a rhyme or antonym, or merely with the first word that comes to mind.
ASSOCIATION FOOTBALL. See SOCCER.
ASSOCIATIONISM, a psychological school which held that the sole mechanism of human learning consisted in the permanent association in the intellect of impressions which had been repeatedly presented to the senses. Originating in the philosophy of John LOCKE and developed through the work of John Gay, David HARTLEY, James and John Stuart MILL and Alexander Bain, the "association of ideas" was the dominant theme in British PSYCHOLOGY for 200 years.
ASSOCIATIVE LAW. See ALGEBRA.
ASSONANCE, repetition of the vowel sounds of words (m*oo*d, m*oo*n), as compared with standard RHYME, which matches the sounds of terminal syllables (moon, June). The technique was popular in Classical writing and in medieval poetry in Romance languages, as well as in traditional Celtic verse.
ASSUMPTION OF THE VIRGIN, official dogma

Some Important Assassinations in History

Name	*Position*	*Date of Assassination*
Hipparchus	Tyrant of Athens	514 BC
Philip II	King of Macedon	336 BC
Julius Caesar	Roman general and statesman	44 BC
Thomas à Becket	Archbishop of Canterbury	1170
William the Silent	Prince of Orange	1584
Henry III	King of France	1589
Henry IV	King of France	1610
Jean Paul Marat	French revolutionary	1793
Paul I	Czar of Russia	1801
Spencer Perceval	British Prime Minister	1812
Abraham Lincoln	US President	1865
Alexander II	Czar of Russia	1881
James Garfield	US President	1881
M. F. S. Carnot	President of France	1894
Elizabeth	Empress of Austria	1898
Umberto I	King of Italy	1900
William McKinley	US President	1901
Alexander	King of Serbia	1903
Carlos I	King of Portugal	1908
Francisco Madero	President of Mexico	1913
George I	King of Greece	1913
Franz Ferdinand	Heir to the throne of Austria	1914
Jean Jaurès	French socialist philosopher and politician	1914
Rasputin	Russian monk and courtier	1916
Kurt Eisner	Bavarian statesman	1919
Venustiano Carranza	President of Mexico	1920
Matthias Erzberger	German statesman	1922
Walter Rathenau	German statesman	1922
Giacomo Matteotti	Italian socialist	1924
Alvaro Obregon	President-elect of Mexico	1928
Hamaguchi Osaci	Prime Minister of Japan	1930
Paul Doumer	President of France	1932
Engelbert Dollfuss	Chancellor of Austria	1934
Alexander I	King of Yugoslavia	1934
Louis Barthou	French statesman	1934
Huey P. Long	US Senator	1935
Leon Trotsky	Exiled Russian revolutionary	1940
Mohandas K. Gandhi	Indian nationalist leader	1948
Count Folke Bernadette	UN mediator in Palestine	1948
Abdullah Ibn Hussein	King of Jordan	1951
Faisal II	King of Iraq	1958
Stefan Bandera	Ukrainian nationalist leader	1959
John F. Kennedy	US President	1963
Hendrik Verwoerd	South African Prime Minister	1966
Martin Luther King	US civil rights leader	1968
Robert F. Kennedy	US Senator	1968
Tom Mboya	Kenyan minister	1969
Faisal	King of Saudi Arabia	1975

Astrology: the signs of the zodiac.

1. Aries	Mar. 21–Apr. 19	Ram	7. Libra	Sep. 23–Oct. 23	Scales
2. Taurus	Apr. 20–May 20	Bull	8. Scorpio	Oct. 24–Nov. 21	Scorpion
3. Gemini	May 21–June 21	Twins	9. Sagittarius	Nov. 22–Dec. 21	Archer
4. Cancer	June 22–July 22	Crab	10. Capricorn	Dec. 22–Jan. 19	Goat
5. Leo	July 23–Aug. 22	Lion	11. Aquarius	Jan. 20–Feb. 18	Water bearer
6. Virgo	Aug. 23–Sep. 22	Virgin	12. Pisces	Feb. 19–Mar. 20	Fish

of the Roman Catholic Church (declared by Pope PIUS XII in 1950) that the Virgin Mary was "assumed into heaven body and soul" at the end of her life. The feast day of the Assumption is August 15.

ASSUR. See ASHUR.

ASSYRIA. See BABYLONIA AND ASSYRIA.

ASSYRIAN CHURCH. See NESTORIANS.

ASTAIRE, Fred (1899–   ), US dancer and actor, born Frederick Austerlitz. First in partnership with his sister Adele and later with Ginger ROGERS, he became one of the most popular and imitated US musical comedy stars on stage and in motion pictures.

ASTARTE, Phoenician goddess of fertility, love and war. Her cult was widespread in the Near East. She is mentioned in the Old Testament as Ashtoreth. There were shrines to her at Hierapolis, Tyre and Sidon.

ASTATINE (At), radioactive HALOGEN, occurring naturally in minute quantities, and prepared by bombarding BISMUTH with ALPHA PARTICLES. The most stable isotope, At^{210}, has half-life 8.3h. Tracer studies show that astatine closely resembles IODINE. AW 210, mp 302°C, bp 337°C.

ASTER, genus of mainly perennial plants with nearly 600 species, native mainly to North America but also found in Asia, Europe and South America. Asters are widely cultivated for their colorful daisy-like flowers that are in shades of red, white and mauve. Many cultivated varieties are available

ASTEROIDS, the thousands of planetoids or minor planets, ranging in diameter from a few metres to 760km (CERES), most of whose orbits lie in the Asteroid Belt between the orbits of Mars and Jupiter. Vesta is the only asteroid visible to the naked eye, though Ceres was the first to be discovered (1801 by PIAZZI). Their total mass is estimated to be 0.001 that of the earth. A second asteroid belt beyond the orbit of Pluto has been postulated. (See also METEORITE; SOLAR SYSTEM.)

ASTHMA, chronic respiratory disease marked by recurrent attacks of wheezing and acute breathlessness. It is due to abnormal bronchial sensitivity and is usually associated with ALLERGY to house dust mite, pollen, FUNGI, furs and other substances which may precipitate an attack. Chest infection, exercise or emotional upset may also provoke an attack. The symptoms are caused by spasm of bronchioles (see BRONCHI) and the accumulation of thick MUCUS. Cyanosis may occur in severe attacks. Desensitization INJECTIONS, cromoglycate, STEROIDS and drugs that dilate bronchi are used in prevention; acute attacks may require OXYGEN, aminophylline or ADRENALINE, and steroids.

ASTI, ancient city in the Piedmont region of NW Italy on the Tanaro R, 28mi SW of Turin. Capital of Asti province, the city is the center of an important agricultural region where Asti Spumante sparkling wine is produced.

ASTIGMATISM, a defect of VISION in which the LENS of the EYE exhibits different curvatures in different planes, corrected using cylindrical lenses. Also, an ABERRATION occurring with lenses having spherical surfaces.

ASTON, Francis William (1877–1945), British physicist who designed the first mass spectrograph (see MASS SPECTROSCOPY) and used it to identify and separate the ISOTOPES of the nonradioactive elements. This work earned him the Nobel Prize for Chemistry in 1922 and led to the formulation of the whole-number rule for isotopic weights (see ATOMIC WEIGHT).

ASTORIA, city in NW Ore., on the Columbia R; seat of Clatsop Co. Founded in 1814 as a trading post for J. J. Astor's Pacific Fur Company, it was an outpost of Northwest development. Pop 10 244.

ASTRAKHAN, city in the USSR, capital of Astrakhan Oblast in the Russian Soviet Federal Socialist Republic, on the delta of the Volga R about 60mi from the Caspian Sea. Once a TARTAR capital, it is now a major port and rail center near the Baku oil fields and in a rich agricultural region. Pop 411 000.

ASTRINGENT, agent used to shrink mucous membranes and to dry up secretions or wet lesions. They may act by vasoconstriction, dehydration (as with ETHANOL) or by denaturing proteins (as with TANNIN).

ASTROLABE, an astronomical instrument dating from the Hellenic Period, used to measure the altitude of celestial bodies and, before the introduction of the SEXTANT, as a navigational aid. It consisted of a vertical disk with an engraved scale across which was mounted a sighting rule or "alidade" pivoted at its center.

ASTROLOGY, the art and science of divining the future from the study of the heavens. Originating in ancient Mesopotamia as a means for predicting the fate of states and their rulers, the astrology which found its way into Hellenistic culture applied itself also to the destinies of individuals. Together with the desire to devise accurate CALENDARS, astrology provided a key incentive leading to the earliest systematic ASTRONOMY and was a continuing spur to the development of astronomical techniques until the 17th century. The majority of classical and medieval astronomers, PTOLEMY and KEPLER among them, practiced astrology, often earning their livelihoods thus. Astrology exercised its greatest influence in the Graeco-Roman world and again in renaissance Europe (despite the opposition of the Church) and, although generally abandoned after the 17th century, it has continued to excite a fluctuating interest down to the present. The key datum in Western astrology is the position of the stars and planets, described relative to the 12 divisions of the ZODIAC, at the moment of an individual's birth.

ASTRONAUT, name given to US test pilots and scientists chosen by the NATIONAL AERONAUTICS AND SPACE ADMINISTRATION to man US space flights. The first seven astronauts were chosen in 1959. The first manned flight was made by Commander Alan B. SHEPARD in 1961. Lt. Col. John GLENN, Jr., became the first American to orbit the earth in 1962, and astronauts Edwin Eugene ALDRIN, Jr., and Neil Alden ARMSTRONG became the first men on the moon in 1969. (See also SPACE EXPLORATION.)

ASTRONOMICAL UNIT (AU), a unit of distance equal to 149.6Gm—approximately the mean distance of the earth from the sun—used for describing distances within the solar system. (See SI UNITS.)

ASTRONOMY, the study of the heavens. Born at the crossroads of agriculture and religion, astronomy, the earliest of the sciences, was of great practical importance in ancient civilization. Before 2000 BC, Babylonians, Chinese and Egyptians all sowed their crops according to calendars computed from the regular motions of the sun and moon.

Although early Greek philosophers were more concerned with the physical nature of the heavens than with precise observation, later Greek scientists (see ARISTARCHUS; HIPPARCHUS) returned to the problems of positional astronomy. The vast achievement of Greek astronomy was epitomized in the writings of Claudius PTOLEMY. His *Almagest*, passing through Arabic translations, was eventually transmitted to medieval Europe and remained the chief authority among astronomers for over 1 400 years.

Throughout this period the main purpose of positional astronomy had been to assist in the casting of

A Moorish astrolabe made in Toledo, Spain in 1068 AD. As well as degree scales and alidade, it has six plates, five of which bear the names of various cities, their latitude and the duration of their longest day.

accurate horoscopes, the twin sciences of astronomy and ASTROLOGY having not yet parted company. The structure of the universe meanwhile remained the preserve of (Aristotelian) physics. The work of COPERNICUS represented an early attempt to harmonize an improved positional astronomy with a true physical theory of planetary motion. Against the judgment of antiquity that sun, moon and planets circled the earth as lanterns set in a series of concentric transparent shells, in his *de Revolutionibus* (1543) Copernicus argued that the sun lay motionless at the center of the planetary system.

Although the Copernican (or heliocentric) hypothesis proved to be a sound basis for the computation of navigators' tables (the needs for which were stimulating renewed interest in astronomy), it did not become unassailably established in astronomical theory until NEWTON published his mathematical derivation of KEPLER'S LAWS in 1687. In the meanwhile KEPLER, working on the superb observational data of Tycho BRAHE, had shown the orbit of Mars to be elliptical and not circular and GALILEO had used the newly invented TELESCOPE to discover SUNSPOTS, the phases of Venus and four moons of Jupiter.

Since the 17th century the development of astronomy has followed on successive improvements in the design of telescopes. In 1781 William HERSCHEL discovered Uranus, the first discovery of a new PLANET to be made in historical times. Measurement of the PARALLAX of a few stars in 1838 first allowed the estimation of interstellar distances. Analysis of the FRAUNHOFER LINES in the spectrum of the sun gave scientists their first indication of the chemical composition of the STARS.

In the present century the scope of observational astronomy has extended as radio and X-ray telescopes (see X-RAY ASTRONOMY) have come into use, leading to the discovery of QUASARS, PULSARS and neutron stars. In their turn these discoveries have enabled cosmologists to develop ever more self-consistent models of the UNIVERSE. (See also COSMOLOGY; OBSERVATORY.)

ASTROPHOTOGRAPHY, photography of celestial objects, usually by focusing a TELESCOPE onto a photographic plate. Of paramount importance in, e.g., measurement of stellar PARALLAX, astrophotography has almost entirely replaced direct observation.

ASTROPHYSICS, deals with the physical and chemical nature of celestial objects and events, using data produced by RADIO ASTRONOMY and SPECTROSCOPY. By investigating the laws of the universe as they currently operate, astronomers can formulate theories of stellar evolution and behavior (see COSMOLOGY).

ASTURIAS, historic region of Spain, now part of the modern province of Oviedo. Originally a Visigothic refuge from the Moorish invasions, it became a powerful and independent Christian kingdom from the 8th to the 10th centuries. From 1388 until 1931 the heir to the Spanish throne was called Prince of Asturias. Today this mountainous region is a major mining center for coal and other minerals.

ASTURIAS, Miguel Angel (1899–), Guatemalan writer and diplomat. He won the Lenin Peace Prize in 1966 and the Nobel Prize for Literature in 1967. His books *The Cyclone* (1950) and *The Green Pope* (1954) attacked the exploitation of Guatemalan Indians.

ASUNCIÓN, capital, main port and industrial center of Paraguay. Founded in 1537 by Spanish explorers, it rivaled Buenos Aires until the 18th century. A large part of the city was destroyed in the War of the Triple Alliance (1865–70), but much colonial architecture remains. Modern industries include sugar refining, textiles, distilling and ship-building. Pop 387 676.

ASWAN, capital of the Aswan governorate, upper Egypt, on the Nile 555mi S of Cairo. Granite from Aswan's quarries was used by the pharaohs to build temples and pyramids. Hydroelectric schemes serve the local iron-mining, fertilizer and quarrying industries. Tourism is also important. Pop 206 300.

ASWAN HIGH DAM, dam built on the Nile 1960–70, located 4mi above the 1902 Nile dam. Having created the vast Lake Nasser, stretching some 300mi along the course of the Nile, the dam's waters have brought over 1 million acres under irrigation.

ASYLUM, Right of, a state's right to grant protection to a refugee from another country. Asylum is granted by most countries only to political fugitives; ordinary criminals are not usually given asylum, though political crimes are loosely defined. The right to asylum is recognized by signatories to the UN Universal Declaration of Human Rights (1948).

ASYMPTOTE, term used in ANALYTIC GEOMETRY. If a CURVE is such that a straight LINE may be drawn which the curve approaches ever more closely (but never meets) with increasing distance from the origin, then the straight line is termed an asymptote and the curve asymptotic. Consider the curve with equation $y = 1/x$, where x is always greater than zero. As x tends to infinity, y tends to, but never equals, zero. One asymptote of the curve is therefore the x-axis. In the same way, as x tends to zero, y tends to infinity; and therefore the other asymptote of the curve is the y-axis. All hyperbolas (see CONIC SECTIONS) are asymptotic.

ASYUT, city in Upper Egypt on the Nile about 250mi S of Cairo. A commercial and educational center, it produces textiles, pottery, ivory and wood carvings. Pop 181 200.

ATABRINE (quinacrine hydrochloride), a synthetic ALKALOID drug for treating MALARIA and TAPEWORM, introduced in WWII when the Japanese captured natural QUININE supplies, and now rarely used.

ATACAMA DESERT, extremely arid plateau in N Chile, 600mi long with an average width of 90mi. Rich in borax and saline deposits, it is a major source of natural nitrates, copper and other minerals.

ATAHUALPA (c1500–1533), last Inca emperor of Peru. He was the eldest son of Huayna Capac, who died in 1525, leaving the kingdom to his younger son Huascar. Atahualpa inherited the Quito region and a large army. In 1530 he attacked Huascar, deposing him in 1532, just before the arrival of the CONQUISTADORS under PIZARRO. Atahualpa refused to accept Christianity and Spanish suzerainty; the Spaniards kidnapped him, extorted a vast ransom and murdered him after a show trial.

ATALANTA, in Greek myth, a huntress whose suitors had to run a foot race with her. She was to marry the first to defeat her, but the losers' lives were forfeit. She was beaten by Hippomenes: on APHRODITE's advice, he threw in her path golden apples which she stopped to pick up.

ATASCADERO, unincorporated urban community in Cal., shopping center for a large agricultural area. Pop 10 290.

ATATURK, Kemal (originally: Mustafa Kemal; 1881–1938), first president (1923–38) of the modern Turkish state he helped to found. Born in Salonika, he received a military education and, as a member of the Young Turk movement, helped depose the Ottoman Sultan Abdul Hamid II in 1909. After distinguished service in the Second Balkan War (1913) and WWI, he led the Turkish war of independence as the head of a provisional government in Ankara (1919–23), repulsing a Greek invasion of ANATOLIA. Heading the new republic, Kemal reduced the power of Islam, abolishing the caliphate and the DERVISH sects, substituted Roman for Arabic lettering, rid TURKISH of Arabic words and modernized Turkey's economy. In 1934 he passed a law requiring all Turks to use surnames in the Western style and himself took the name Ataturk— "Father of the Turks."

ATAVISM, the inheritance (see HEREDITY) by an individual organism of characteristics not shown by its parental generation. Once thought to be throwbacks to an ancestral form, atavisms are now known to be primarily the result of the random reappearance of recessive traits (see GENETICS), though they may result also from aberrations in the development of the embryo or from disease.

ATAXIA, impaired coordination of body movements resulting in unsteady gait, difficulty in fine movements and speech disorder. Caused by disease of the cerebellum or spinal cord, ataxia occurs with MULTIPLE SCLEROSIS, certain hereditary conditions and in the late stages of syphilis (see VENEREAL DISEASES).

ATCHAFALAYA RIVER, 225mi river rising in central La., flowing S to Atchafalaya Bay. It serves as a distributary for the Red and Mississippi rivers.

ATCHISON, city on the Missouri R, seat of Atchison Co., NE Kan. Settled in 1854, it became a railroad terminus for opening the West; it is now a processing center for grain and livestock, with flour-milling and other light industries. Pop 12 565.

The Aswan High Dam was opened in January 1971 and stores water from the Nile in an artificial lake, enabling large areas of previously parched, infertile land to be irrigated. Unfortunately the building of the dam necessitated flooding the ancient temples on the island of Philae.

ATCHISON, David Rice (1807–1886), US proslavery Democrat senator. Appointed to represent Mo. in 1843, he was reelected in 1849, but defeated in 1855. He later led raids against free-soil settlers in Kan.

ATHABASCA, river and lake in N Alberta and Saskatchewan, Canada. The river rises in Jasper National Park and flows 765mi to the 3 000sq mi lake. The Athabascan tar sands between Fort McMurray and Fort Chipewyan are rich in crude oil. Uranium mining and fur trapping are the region's main industries.

ATHABASCAN, subgroup of the Na-Dené languages, spoken by many North American Indians. The Chipewyan, Slave and Sarsi Indians of the NW speak the Athabascan language, as do many lesser-known tribes along the Pacific coast from Ore. to Cal. The Navaho and Apache languages in Ariz., N.M. and Tex. belong to the same linguistic group.

ATHALIAH, in the Bible, queen of Judah c842–36 BC. Usurping the throne on the death of her son Ahaziah, she massacred all the males of the royal house of Judah except Jehoash. She is the subject of a play by Racine.

ATHANASIAN CREED (sometimes called *Quicumque Vult*, from its opening words), Latin CREED expounding chiefly the doctrines of the Trinity and the Incarnation, regarded as authoritative by the Roman Catholic and Anglican churches, and also by some Protestant churches. Modern scholars believe it was composed in the 5th century.

ATHANASIUS, Saint (c293–373), Egyptian ecclesiastical statesman of the early Church. A devout adherent of the Orthodox faith and opponent of ARIANISM, he took an active part in the religious and political controversies of his time, suffering many banishments as a result.

ATHEISM, denial of the existence of any divine being and hence of the validity of religion. It must be distinguished from AGNOSTICISM, which regards the question as insoluble. Theoretical atheism may be put forward as a philosophical possibility; practical atheism treats the non-existence of divinity as an everyday world view.

ATHELSTAN (895–939), grandson of Alfred the Great, first Saxon king effectively to rule all England (924–39). A strong but benevolent king, he crushed a northern invasion at Brunanburh in 937.

ATHENA (Pallas Athene), Greek goddess of wisdom and war who sprang fully-grown from ZEUS' head. She bore a helmet, lance and the AEGIS. The patroness of Athens, she protected legendary heroes such as ODYSSEUS. In peacetime she taught men agriculture, law, shipbuilding and all the crafts of civilization. The Romans identified her with Minerva.

ATHENAEUM, ancient Greek word for buildings

Astronomy

Black holes

Unless the physical laws that man has formulated are hopelessly inaccurate, there exist within the universe black holes, phenomena that are more horrifying than any product of the fantasy-writer's pen. They are areas of such high gravitation that anything which comes too close is sucked into them and can never escape. Even light itself is unable to leave these regions, and because of this they are invisible. We call them black holes. The consequences of the black hole hypothesis, if indeed it is correct, necessitate a revision or extension of known physical laws, and may even provide us with an explanation of the "Big Bang," the primordial explosion in which the universe was formed. But black holes have more than theoretical importance. Matter falling into a black hole could be transformed into energy with considerable efficiency, and might someday provide the ultimate source of energy.

How do they come about? In order to understand this, we have to review what we know of stellar evolution. Stars are probably born out of eddies in the interstellar gas and dust which form such a large part of our universe. A typical star starts life as a huge amorphous cloud of gas, slowly spinning about a point somewhere within it. Because of the effects of gravity, the cloud slowly shrinks and, as it does so, two interesting effects emerge. The first is that the cloud of gas begins to spin faster and faster in order to conserve overall angular momentum. The second comes about through the release of the potential energy of the particles of gas as they move closer to the cloud's center of gravity: heat is generated. In time, the temperature becomes high enough for nuclear reactions to begin, hydrogen being converted into helium, this process being accompanied by further release of heat, light and a whole range of other forms of energy radiation. After a period of extreme instability, the star—for that is what it is by now—settles down to millions of years of comparatively uneventful existence.

Not all stars are the same size. Our sun is rather below average in terms of both mass and brightness. In general, the bigger and brighter a new star is, the shorter will be its lifespan: our sun is already some 4 000–5 000 million years old, and can be expected to continue shining very much as it does now for approximately as long again. A star very much more massive than the sun, however, may enjoy this period of stability for no more than a million years or so. On the other hand, stars much smaller than the sun never become hot enough for nuclear reactions to begin, and so they rapidly become smaller and fainter until they are what we call White Dwarfs.

The Crab Nebula in the constellation Taurus is the remnant of an exploded star, or supernova. The light from the explosion reach the earth in 1054 AD, according to contemporary Chinese records. At the center of the expanding shell of luminous gases is a pulsar, believed to be a rapidly rotating neutron star, which emits pulses of electromagnetic radiation at both optical and radio wavelengths.

The sun gives light and warmth because of the conversion of hydrogen, the lightest and commonest element of the universe, into helium. As far as we can tell, this is the way that most normal stars shine. However, there comes a time when the hydrogen runs out.

There are two forces working to change the size of a star. One is gravity, which tends to make it smaller; the other is energy production in the star's core, which tends to make the star as a whole larger. Toward the end of the star's hydrogen-burning period, there is a conflict between these two forces. Nuclear reactions are still going on in the core, and this forces the outer layers of the star outwards. The core itself contracts under gravity until the temperature within it is great enough for the conversion of helium into heavier elements—with the release of vast amounts of energy—to begin. This is known as the Red Giant stage of the star's existence. To give some idea of the size of the star during this period: if the Red Giant Betelgeuse were placed where the sun is now, the earth would be within its outer layers. But these outer layers are extraordinarily diffuse—they approximate to a laboratory vacuum.

Obviously a star cannot survive for long as a Red Giant. The situation is just too precariously unstable. After a (cosmically) short elapse of time, one of three things happens. If the star is of comparable mass to the sun, it will begin to fall in upon itself rapidly, and end its life as a White Dwarf. If the star has a mass more than about twice that of the sun, however, the collapse will be far too rapid for any kind of stability to be achieved. The star will explode, throwing much of itself off into space and leaving behind a swiftly shrinking remnant. This is a supernova, and we can see through comparatively small telescopes the remains of one. This is the gas cloud known as the Crab Nebula, the remains of a supernova observed by the Chinese in 1054 AD. At its center can be detected a very small, very faint celestial object—the remnant of the original star, shrunk to the point where the protons and electrons of its atoms have run together to form neutrons. It is so densely packed that a thimbleful of its material would weigh something like a thousand million tons. It is called a neutron star.

But if a star is even more massive than this, its contraction at the end of its Red Giant stage is too rapid for even a neutron star to be left after the supernova explosion. Once it has started to contract, there is literally nothing that can stop it. Eventually it passes a point of no return known as the Schwartzschild Radius to create a gravitational field so intense that not even light can escape from it. The star goes on collapsing even beyond this, until the matter of which it was formed is crushed right out of existence by infinite gravitational forces. The star has gone, but it leaves behind it a black hole.

Black holes are so far beyond the bounds of our everyday experience that it is hard for human language to describe them. We cannot call them celestial objects since, unlike stars and planets, they probably contain no matter at all—though they do have mass. We can think of them as being regions of space that once contained bodies: in essence, they are self-perpetuating gravitational fields. Obviously the words at our disposal are incapable of dealing with such events, and we have had to invent new ones while discovering afresh new significances for some old ones.

It was in 1917 that the German physicist Karl Schwartzschild investigated the circumstances that would surround a spherical object of colossal density. He proposed that an object could be so dense that spacetime around it would be distorted to the extent that even light would be unable to escape from it. Consider an object of mass *m*. If it is compressed into a smaller and smaller radius without any loss of mass, light will eventually begin to have difficulty escaping from it. Finally, when its radius has achieved some critical value, it will be too dense for the light to leave at all. This critical value for the object's radius is called the Schwartzschild Radius, and it can be calculated very easily from the formula

$$r_S = \frac{2Gm}{c^2},$$

where r_S stands for the Schwartzschild Radius, G for the universal constant of gravitation, *m* for the mass of the object and c for the velocity of light. To see how this formula works, we can calculate the Schwartzschild Radius for the earth—though there is no reason to believe that the earth will ever become a black hole (and yet it may very well one day be swallowed up by one). Working in SI Units, we have a value for G of 6.7×10^{-11} and a value for c of 3×10^8 metres per second. The mass of the earth is 6×10^{24} kilograms. For the earth, then,

$$r_S = \frac{2 \times 6.7 \times 10^{-11} \times 6 \times 10^{24}}{(3 \times 10^8)^2} \text{ metres}$$

$$= \frac{80.4 \times 10^{13}}{9 \times 10^{16}} \text{ metres}$$

$$= 9 \times 10^{-3} \text{ metres (approximately).}$$

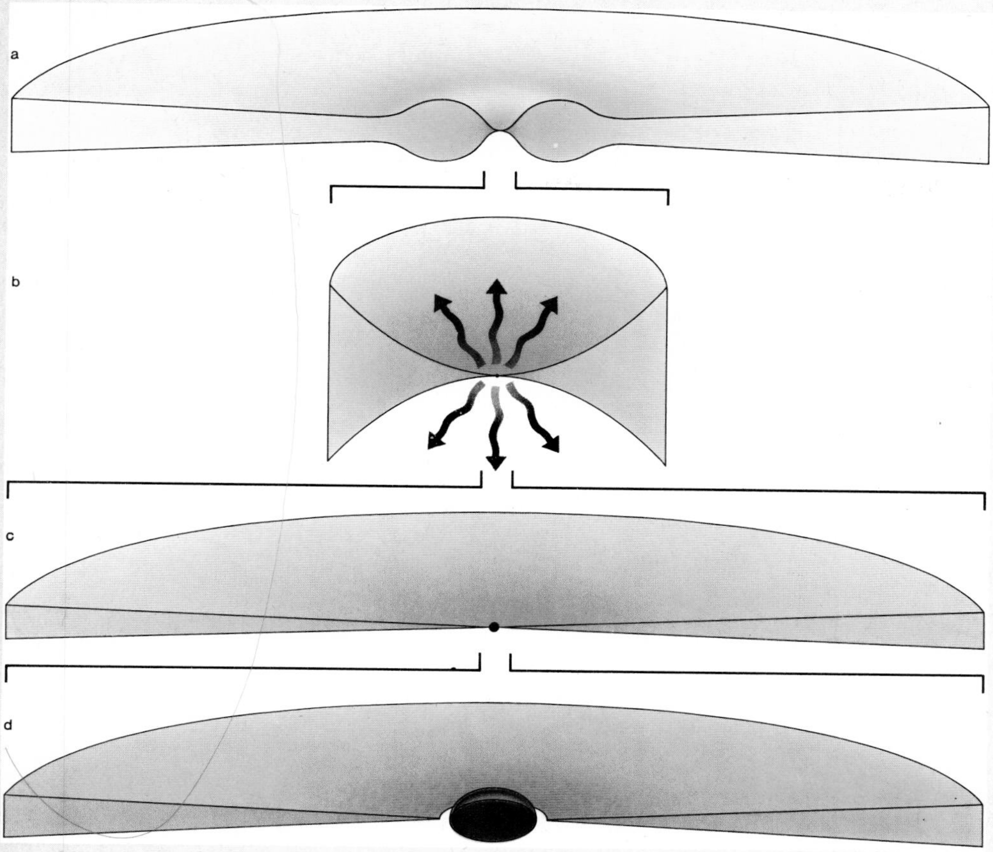

A model of the black hole Cygnus X-1. (A) shows the accretion disk surrounding the black hole composed of gases from the primary star which are orbiting the black hole and gradually being sucked in. The shape of the disk, which is a few million kilometres across and a few tens of thousands of kilometres thick, results from the competition between gravity and the tendency of the hot gases to expand. Near the black hole (B) X-rays are emitted, the heat thus generated locally affecting the shape of the disk. Still closer to the black hole (C) gravity triumphs. Very close to the black hole (D), which is perhaps a few kilometres across, the disk terminates as gravitational forces become so strong that the gases are sucked directly into the black hole.

In other words, for the earth ever to become a black hole, it would somehow have to be compressed until it had a radius of only nine millimetres. For the sake of comparison, the value of the Schwartzschild Radius for the sun is of the order of three kilometres.

Because light cannot pass outward further than the Schwartzschild Radius, we will never be able to see anything that happens inside a spherical black hole. We therefore call this boundary of the black hole, which is at a distance from the center equal to the Schwartzschild Radius, the event horizon. We can detect things that happen on this side of the event horizon, but we can detect nothing beyond it. Most of all—and in a way it is a pity—we cannot observe what is going on at the very center of the black hole, where matter is being crushed out of existence through the action of infinite gravitational forces. We call this center point the singularity.

The Schwartzschild Radius, the event horizon, the singularity; these are the three unfamiliar items of terminology that we must use when talking of black holes.

If we were to go and look at a black hole, we would find things there very odd indeed. To begin with, we would have to be careful not to go too close in case we were sucked in—in fact, we would have to keep using the rockets of our spacecraft in order not to drift closer to the black hole than our chosen observation position. If we dropped something—say a very powerful torch—into the black hole, we would soon begin to notice something very strange indeed about its fall. This is because, according to predictions of relativity theory, objects in a strong gravitational field experience time dilation. That is to say, an observer traveling with our torch would think that time was passing just as normal, would be able to look at the seconds ticking away on his watch, but we who were observing him from the spaceship above would see the torch falling more and more slowly. Moreover, its light would become redder, again because of the effects of gravity; until eventually the light would have moved so far into the infrared that we would no longer be able to see anything at all. The torch would eventually reach the event horizon, where its time dilation would be infinite. If we could detect it at all from outside—which we could not, since the red shift would also be infinite—its image would apparently be frozen at the event horizon of the black hole, there to remain forever.

We could, if we were adventurous and if our spacecraft were a very powerful one indeed, use this effect in order to travel into the future. If we spent a few months skipping backwards and forwards close to a black hole, traveling past it fast enough to avoid being sucked in, we could return to earth to find that thousands of years had passed. The expense would be enormous, the risks unbelievably high; but it could in theory be done.

One must obviously ask oneself, "How can we detect black holes?" As they are such dangerous things to have around, the sooner we confirm our theories, the better. But the task is not an easy one. To begin with, they are invisible, even to the radio telescope, since all forms of radiation, including light, are unable to escape from them. One way of approaching the problem is to consider the effects of a black hole's gravitational field on the celestial objects near to it.

Many of the stars we can see are in fact binaries. Very much in the same way as the earth and the moon form a double planet, these stars are double stars: one of the stars closest to us, Sirius, consists of a bright star some 26 times more luminous than the sun, and a White Dwarf star, known affectionately to astronomers as the Pup, only one ten-thousandth as bright as this. We can detect other binaries where it appears that one of the components is a neutron star. Naturally, as soon as the black hole hypothesis came into vogue, astronomers began to wonder if a binary could be detected with a black hole as one of its components.

This is not as difficult as it sounds—assuming, of course, that such binaries are there to be found. Although only a few, nearby binaries can be seen telescopically as such, many more distant ones can be detected by use of the spectroscope. If two stars are in orbit around each other, we can expect to see manifestations of the Doppler Effect in their spectra. Examination of these spectra can reveal the masses of the two stars involved. The problem, then, is to find a star whose spectrum varies in such a way that we can tell that it is a binary, though we can see only the spectrum of a single component, and whose invisible component has a mass more than a few times that of the sun. There are several candidates, but the most notable is the star HDE 226868 in the constellation Cygnus.

The other approach to the problem of detecting black holes is by consideration of radiation emitted by matter falling into the black hole. There is good reason to believe that matter being sucked in in this way will be a prolific emitter of X rays.

One of the X-ray sources found by the X-ray satellite UHURU displayed the remarkable characteristic of rapid fluctuation in strength. The rapid fluctuation showed that the source, named Cygnus X-1, was comparatively small—no more than about 30 000 kilometres across. Then it was realized that Cygnus X-1 and the star HDE 226868 were the same. Soon new spectroscopic evidence made it seem probable that matter was flowing from the visible component of the binary into the invisible component. This invisible component fits our picture of a black hole perfectly.

Recently, it has been suggested that there may exist phenomena which are the reverse of black holes; that is to say, areas where there is a negative gravitational field and matter is being created. Although there is no evidence that these phenomena (termed, naturally enough, white holes) exist, there are certain galaxies which we can observe that seem to be exploding, very much as if there were an emormous outpouring of matter within them. Possibly evidence for white holes? Just possibly.

Black holes are indeed a terrifying prospect, and their existence seems strongly probable. Perhaps even more terrifying is the realization that, if some of our cosmological ideas are correct, then the ultimate end of our universe *must* be its becoming a vast black hole.

But then, perhaps the original cosmic egg from which our universe came was also a black hole which for some reason exploded, and perhaps we are witnessing only one stage in the infinite cycle of an oscillating universe. Until we find—and perhaps even visit—a black hole we can speculate forever.

Athens seen from the Acropolis, the ancient sacred precinct around which the modern city with its wide streets and skyscrapers has been built.

dedicated to ATHENA. It has since been applied to Hadrian's academy in Rome (c135 AD), to certain European schools and literary magazines and to some libraries in the US.

ATHENS, capital of Greece, on the SW side of the Attica peninsula. Athens lies on a plain near the Saronic Gulf, with mountains to the W, N and E. The city was already important by c1500 BC, but reached its political peak after the PERSIAN WARS (490–479 BC) when it led the DELIAN LEAGUE. In the 5th century PERICLES used the League's funds to rebuild the ACROPOLIS. Athens became a major center of art, architecture, philosophy and drama, the home of SOPHOCLES and EURIPEDES. Athens lost her supremacy to SPARTA in the PELOPONNESIAN WAR (431–404 BC), and later became a subject of Macedon and Rome.

Greater Athens (covering 167sq mi) is today the country's administrative, political, cultural and economic center. Tourism is a major source of income, but Athens is also an industrial center. Among its products are carpets, ships, petroleum, chemicals, textiles, electrical goods and canned foods. Exports handled at the city's port, Piraeus, include tobacco, oil, wine, aluminum and marble. Pop 862 133.

ATHENS, city in Ala., seat of Limestone Co. The center of an agricultural area, it also has some light industry. Pop 14 360.

ATHENS, city in NE Ga., seat of Clarke Co. Founded in 1801, Athens is the site of Georgia U., the oldest state university in the US. Cotton processing, lumber and electrical equipment are the main local industries. Pop 44 342.

ATHENS, seat of Athens Co., Ohio. The site of Ohio U., it has flourishing steel and machinery industries. Pop 23 310.

ATHENS, seat of McMinn Co., Tenn., the site of Tennessee Wesleyan College (1866). Flour-milling and farm implement manufacture are the main local industries. Pop 11 790.

ATHEROSCLEROSIS. See ARTERIOSCLEROSIS.

ATHLETE'S FOOT, a common form of RINGWORM, a contagious fungal infection of the feet, causing inflammation and scaling or maceration of the skin, especially between the toes. It may be contracted in swimming pools or from shared towels or footwear. Treatment consists in foot hygiene, dusting powder, certain CARBOXYLIC ACIDS and antifungal ANTIBIOTICS.

ATHLETICS. See TRACK AND FIELD.

ATHOL, industrial town in central Mass. It manufactures wood and leather goods. Pop 11 185.

ATHOS, Mount, mountain in NE Greece, since the Middle Ages the site of a famous monastic community. It was formerly a great seat of learning, but fewer than 2 000 monks of the Eastern Orthodox Church live there today. The peninsula of Athos, however, contains numerous associated monasteries, ruled from Karyai.

ATKINSON, Joseph E. (1865–1948), Canadian newspaper publisher and philanthropist. Manager of the *Toronto Star* from 1899 to 1948, he vastly increased its circulation. He also founded a major charitable institution in Ontario.

ATLANTA, capital and largest city of Ga., seat of Fulton Co. Founded 1837 as the terminus of the Western and Atlantic Railroad, Atlanta was a major supply center during the Civil War and was burned to the ground by Union forces in 1864. It was rapidly rebuilt, and is today the major commercial and financial center of the S Atlantic states. The town has more than 20 colleges and universities. Pop 496 973.

ATLANTA CAMPAIGN, a Union offensive in the Civil War, against the Confederacy's major rail center, begun in May 1864 at Chattanooga, Tenn. Gen. Sherman's 100 000 Union troops forced the retreat of 60 000 Confederate troops and captured Atlanta in September. His army set the city ablaze before it left (Nov. 16) on "its march to the sea," ending in the capture of Savannah and the splitting of the Confederacy.

ATLANTIC CABLES, the telegraph and telephone cables on the bed of the North Atlantic Ocean linking North America with Europe. The first successful cable was laid by promoter Cyrus West Field (1819–1892) under the direction of William Thomson (later Lord KELVIN) at the third attempt, in 1858, but this soon failed and was replaced by a more permanent one in 1866. The first Atlantic telephone cable was not laid until 1956 and the method is at present suffering strong competition from communications SATELLITES.

ATLANTIC CHARTER, declaration of common objectives signed by F. D. Roosevelt and Churchill on Aug. 14, 1941, before America entered WWII. It

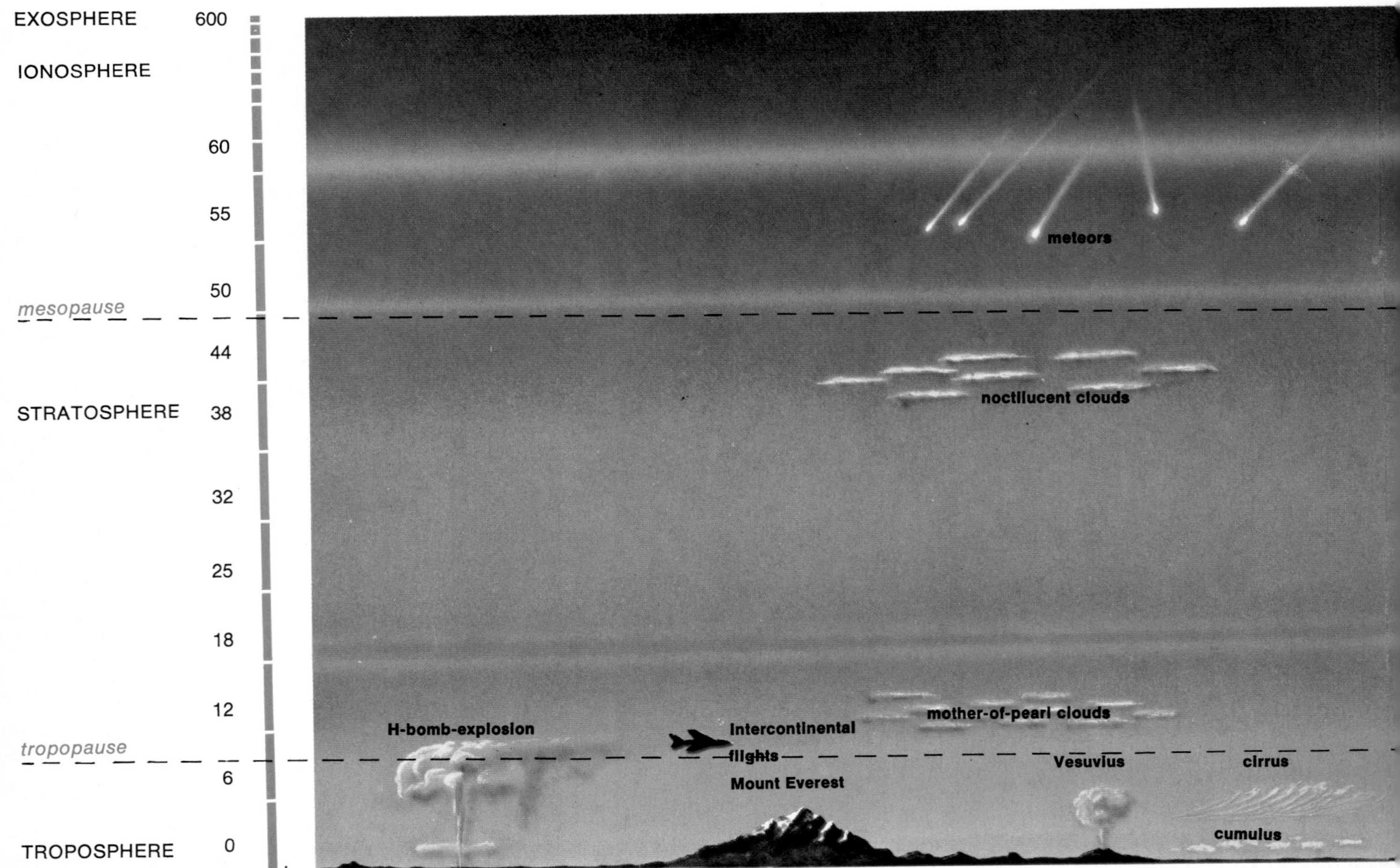

Schematic representation of the atmosphere.

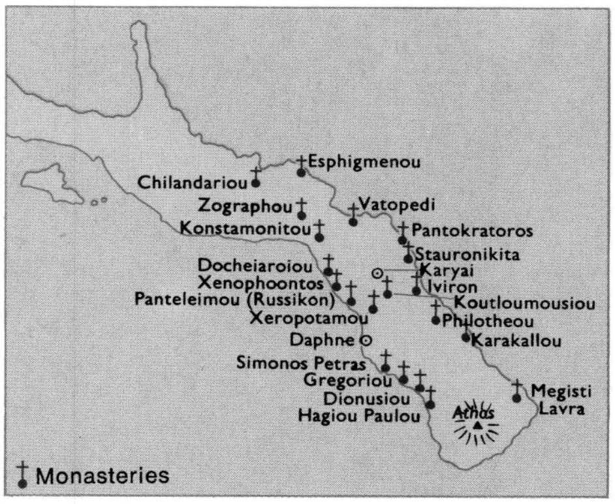

The southern part of the peninsula of Athos in Greece comprises the virtually independent state of the monks of Mount Athos, also known as the Holy Mountain. It supports 20 monasteries of the Order of Saint Basil of the Orthodox church. No female, either human or animal, is allowed to enter the territory.

affirmed the determination of the American and British governments not to extend their territories and to promote every people's right to independence and self-determination.

ATLANTIC CITY, seaside resort and convention center in SE N.J., home of the Miss America Pageant. Its famous Boardwalk (1870) is lined by hotels and restaurants and has the Convention Hall, one of the world's largest auditoriums. Pop 47 859.

ATLANTIC INTRACOASTAL WATERWAY, a shallow sheltered water route extending 1 134mi along the Atlantic seaboard from Norfolk, Va., to Key West, Fla., and serving pleasure craft and light shipping. The Atlantic route and the GULF INTRACOASTAL WATERWAY together make up the INTRACOASTAL WATERWAY.

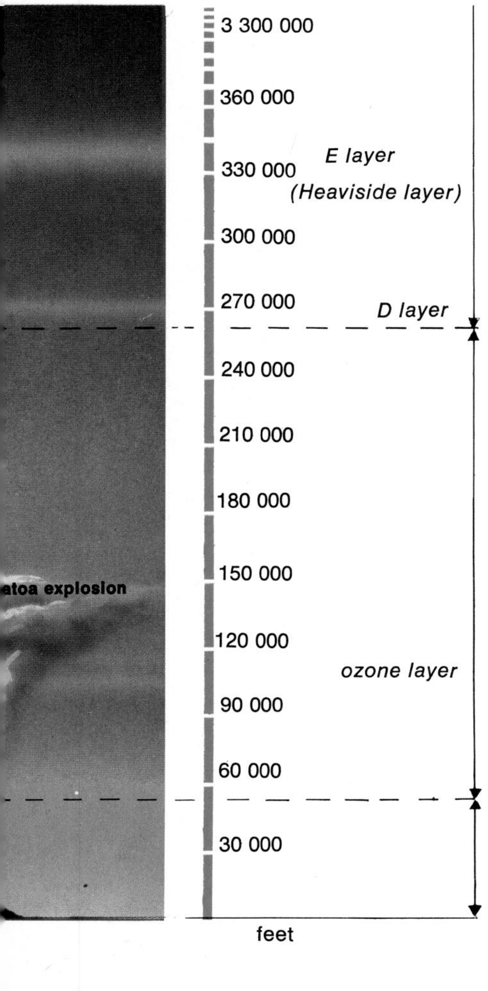

ATLANTIC OCEAN, ocean separating North and South America from Europe and Africa and creating by its currents the GULF STREAM which moderates the climate of NW Europe. It is the second largest of the world's oceans. A continental shelf extending from all coasts drops to at least 10 000ft. The Mid-Atlantic Ridge extends from Iceland south to Bouvet island, SSW of Cape Horn. Lying between highly industrialized continents, the N Atlantic carries the greatest proportion of the world's shipping. About half the world's fish comes from the area, 60% from the GRAND BANKS; some Atlantic fish species are verging on extinction due to the rapid development of modern fishing techniques and increasing pollution.

ATLANTIS, a mythical continent from which the Atlantic takes its name. Atlantis, as described by PLATO in the *Timaeus* and *Critias*, is situated just beyond the PILLARS OF HERCULES. He presents it as an advanced civilization that was destroyed by volcanic eruptions and earthquakes, sinking into the sea. The legend has fascinated men since antiquity, and many searches for the lost continent have been made.

ATLAS, one of the TITANS in Greek legend. He took part in the revolt against the gods and was condemned by ZEUS to hold up the heavens; he is usually represented as carrying the world on his shoulders.

ATLAS, a collection of maps and geographical information. Special subject atlases may deal with a variety of topics such as climate, resources, industry, languages and population.

ATLAS, the uppermost VERTEBRA of the spinal column, supporting the skull, and forming a pivot joint with the **axis** vertebra below it, thus allowing the head to turn. (See also SKELETON.)

ATLAS MOUNTAINS, an extension of the Alpine system into Morocco and Tunisia, the highest peak being Mt Toubkal (13 660ft). Between their barren, parallel ranges, where there are deposits of coal and other minerals, including oil, lie inhabitable valleys and plateaus. Olive and citrus crops are cultivated on some of the moister N slopes.

ATLAS ROCKET. See SPACE EXPLORATION.

ATMOSPHERE, the roughly spheroidal envelope of GAS, VAPOR and AEROSOL particles surrounding the EARTH, retained by gravity and forming a major constituent in the environment of most forms of terrestrial life, protecting it from the impact of METEORS, COSMIC RAY particles and harmful solar radiation. The composition of the atmosphere and most of its physical properties vary with ALTITUDE, certain key properties being used to divide the whole into several zones, the upper and lower boundaries of which change with LATITUDE, the time of day and the season of the year. About 75% of the total MASS of atmosphere and 90% of its water vapor and aerosols are contained in the **troposphere,** the lowest zone. Excluding water vapor,the **air** of the troposphere contains 78% NITROGEN; 20% OXYGEN; 0.9% ARGON; and 0.03% CARBON dioxide, together with traces of the other NOBLE GASES; and METHANE, HYDROGEN and nitrous oxide. The water vapor content fluctuates within wide margins as water is evaporated from the OCEANS, carried in CLOUDS and precipitated upon the continents. The air flows in meandering currents, transferring ENERGY from the warm equatorial regions to the colder poles (see also GREENHOUSE EFFECT). The troposphere is thus the zone in which weather occurs (see METEOROLOGY), as well as that in which most air-dependent life exists. Apart from occasional INVERSIONS, the TEMPERATURE falls with increasing altitude through the troposphere until at the tropopause (altitude 7km at the poles; 16km on the equator) it becomes constant (about 217K), and then slowly increases again into the **stratosphere** (up to about 48km). The upper stratosphere contains the OZONE layer which filters out the dangerous ULTRAVIOLET RADIATION incident from the SUN. Above the stratosphere, the **mesosphere** merges into the IONOSPHERE, a region containing various layers of charged particles (IONS) of immense importance in the propagation of RADIO waves, being used to reflect signals between distant ground stations. At greater altitudes still, the ionosphere passes into the **exosphere,** a region of rarefied HELIUM and hydrogen gases, in turn merging into the interplanetary medium. In all, the atmosphere has a mass of about 5.2×10^{18}kg, its DENSITY being about 1.23kg/m^3 at sea level. Its WEIGHT results in its exerting an average **air pressure** of 101.3kPa (1 013mbar) near the surface, this fluctuating greatly with the weather and falling off rapidly with height (see also PRESSURE). The other PLANETS of the SOLAR SYSTEM (with the possible exception of PLUTO), though only two of their SATELLITES, all have distinctive atmospheres, though none of these contains as much life-supporting oxygen as does that of the earth.

ATMOSPHERE (atm), CGS UNIT of PRESSURE. See BAR.

ATMOSPHERIC REFRACTION, the REFRACTION of light rays passing through the ATMOSPHERE, due to variations in its density and temperature which produce corresponding variations in its refractive index. Under standard conditions, slight curvature results in the case of rays with a horizontal component, and thus the apparent position of celestial bodies is altered. Unusual density variations may produce MIRAGES, shimmer and other deceptive effects.

ATOLL, a typically circular CORAL reef enclosing a LAGOON. Many atolls, often supporting low arcuate islands, are found in the Pacific Ocean.

The formation of an atoll: 1. Fringe reefs are created on mountain slopes rising up out of the sea at the point where land and water meet, so that they are submerged at high tide. 2. The surface of the sea rises in relation to the mountain range. The coral now continues to grow as a barrier reef on the foundation provided by the fringe reef in the last stage. 3. As the sea level continues to rise only the top of the mountain remains visible in the middle of a circle of reefs. 4. The mountain top has completely disappeared below the water leaving a lagoon surrounded by coral reefs. An atoll has come into being.

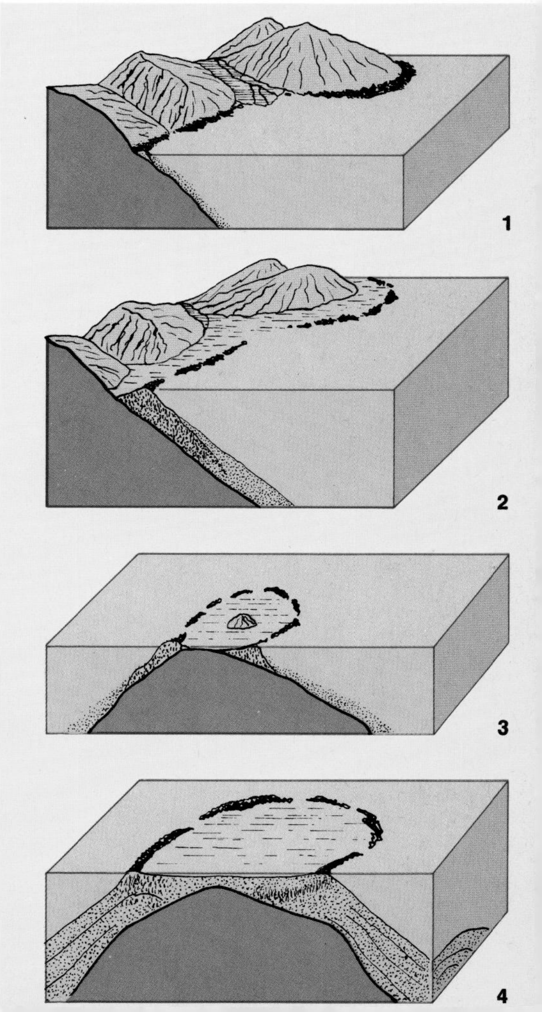

ATOM, classically one of the minute, indivisible, homogeneous material particles of which material objects are composed (see ATOMISM), and in 20th-century science the name given to a relatively stable package of MATTER, typically about 0.1nm across, and itself made up of at least two SUBATOMIC PARTICLES. Every atom consists of a tiny nucleus (containing positively charged PROTONS and electrically neutral NEUTRONS) with which is associated a number of negatively charged ELECTRONS. These, although individually much smaller than the nucleus, occupy a hierarchy of ORBITALS which represent the atom's electronic ENERGY LEVELS, and fill most of the space taken up by the atom. The number of protons in the nucleus of an atom (the atomic number, Z) defines of which chemical ELEMENT the atom is an example. In an isolated neutral atom the number of electrons equals the atomic number, but in an electrically charged ION of the same atom there is either a surfeit or a deficit of electrons. The number of neutrons in the nucleus (the neutron number, N) can vary between different atoms of the same element, the resulting species being called the ISOTOPES of the element. Most stable isotopes have slightly more neutrons than protons. Although the nucleus is very small, it contains nearly all the MASS of the atom—protons and neutrons having very similar masses, and the mass of the electron (about 0.05% of the proton mass) being almost negligible. Counting the proton mass as one, this means that the mass of the atom is roughly equal to the total number of its protons and neutrons. This number $Z+N$, is known as the mass number of the atom, A. In equations representing nuclear reactions the atomic number of an atom is often written as a subscript preceding the chemical symbol for the element and the mass number as a superscript following it. Thus an atomic nucleus with mass number 16 and containing 8 protons belongs to an atom of "oxygen-16", written $_8O^{16}$. The average of the mass numbers of the various naturally occurring isotopes of an element, weighted according to their relative abundance, gives the chemical ATOMIC WEIGHT of the element. Subatomic particles fired into atomic nuclei can cause nuclear reactions giving rise either to new isotopes of the original element or to atoms of a different element, and emitting ALPHA PARTICLES, BETA RAYS or GAMMA RAYS.

The earliest atomistic concept, regarding the atom as that which could not be subdivided, was implicit in the first modern, chemical atomic theory, that of John DALTON (1808). Although it survives in the once-common chemical definition of atom—the smallest fragment of a chemical element which retains the properties of that element and can take part in chemical reactions—chemists now recognize that it is the MOLECULE and not the atom which is the natural chemical unit of matter. The atomic nuclei form the vertebra of the molecules; but it is the interaction of the VALENCE electrons associated with these nuclei, rather than the properties of the individual component atoms, which is responsible for the chemical behavior of matter.

ATOMIC BOMB, a weapon of mass destruction deriving its energy from nuclear FISSION. The first atomic bomb was exploded at Alamogordo, N.M., on July 16, 1945. As in the bomb dropped over Hiroshima, Japan a few weeks later (August 6), the fissionable material was uranium-235, but when Nagasaki was destroyed by another bomb three days after that, plutonium-239 was used. Together the Hiroshima and Nagasaki bombs killed more than 100 000 people. Since the early 1950s, the power of the fission bomb (equivalent to some 20 000 tons of TNT in the case of the Hiroshima bomb) has been vastly exceeded by that of the HYDROGEN BOMB which depends on nuclear FUSION. (See also NUCLEAR WARFARE.)

ATOMIC CLOCK, a device which utilizes the exceptional constancy of the FREQUENCIES associated with certain electron SPIN reversals (as in the CESIUM clock) or the inversion of AMMONIA molecules (the ammonia clock) to define an accurately reproducible TIME scale.

ATOMIC ENERGY. See NUCLEAR ENERGY.

ATOMIC ENERGY COMMISSION. See ENERGY RESEARCH AND DEVELOPMENT ADMINISTRATION; NUCLEAR REGULATORY COMMISSION.

ATOMIC NUMBER, (Z). See ATOM.

ATOMIC REACTOR. See NUCLEAR REACTOR.

ATOMIC WASTE DISPOSAL. See NUCLEAR ENERGY.

ATOMIC WEIGHT, the MEAN MASS of the ATOMS of an ELEMENT weighted according to the relative abundance of its naturally occurring ISOTOPES and measured relative to some standard. Since 1961 this standard has been provided by the CARBON isotope C^{12} whose atomic mass is defined to be exactly 12. On this scale atomic weights for the naturally occurring elements range from 1.008 (HYDROGEN) to 238.03 (URANIUM).

ATOMISM, the theory that all matter consists of atoms—minute indestructible particles, homogeneous in substance but varied in shape. Developed in the 5th century BC by LEUCIPPUS and DEMOCRITUS and adopted by EPICURUS, it was expounded in detail by the Roman poet LUCRETIUS.

ATOMS-FOR-PEACE, a plan for promoting international cooperation in the development of atomic power for non-military purposes, proposed to the UN by President Eisenhower in 1953. Although not adopted, it led to the establishment in 1957 of the International Atomic Energy Agency (IAEA) to which both Soviet-bloc and Western nations belong.

ATOM SMASHER. See ACCELERATORS, PARTICLE.

ATON, Egyptian sun god, represented as a solar disk extending into a human hand, holding out the gift of life. During the religious revolution of the pharaoh AKHENATON, the monotheistic worship of Aton was the state religion of Egypt. After the pharaoh's death the cult was eradicated, and POLYTHEISM restored.

ATONALITY, systematic departure in music from established tonal centers. The notion of tonality was increasingly blurred in the 19th century by the fluid chromaticism of WAGNER, Richard STRAUSS and MAHLER, foreshadowing DEBUSSY's "whole-tone" scale. SCHÖNBERG and his disciples BERG and WEBERN went one stage further, abandoning tonal structure altogether and substituting the TWELVE-TONE system. Schönberg's *Moses and Aaron* and Berg's *Wozzeck* are leading examples of atonal composition.

ATONEMENT ("at-one-ment"), in most religions, the reconciliation of sinful man to the Holy by rituals of sacrifice, expiation and penance. In Christian theology, the atonement is made on man's behalf by JESUS CHRIST, who, in his death, offered himself to God as a sacrifice. Various complementary theories of the atonement have been held. (See also COMMUNION; JUSTIFICATION BY FAITH.)

ATONEMENT, Day of, Jewish sacred day of YOM KIPPUR.

ATP (adenosine triphosphate). See NUCLEOTIDES.

ATREUS, grandson of TANTALUS and legendary king of Mycenae. In order to obtain the throne he served the flesh of two of his brother Thyestes' three sons to him at a banquet. The survivor, Aegisthus, revenged their deaths on Atreus' son, AGAMEMNON.

ATRIUM, the part of an early Roman house used as a reception room and as the center of family life. Later the term referred to an entrance hall, and, in consecrated buildings, a large colonnaded courtyard preceding the main portal of the church.

ATROPHY, wasting away of bodily TISSUES or organs because of disease, MALNUTRITION, disuse or old age. (See also MUSCULAR DYSTROPHY.)

ATROPINE, an ALKALOID derived from HYOSCYAMINE obtained from Belladonna. It decreases the effects of the parasympathetic NERVOUS SYSTEM, and is used to dilate the pupils of the eyes, to increase heart-rate, to reduce the secretion of mucus and saliva, and to relax SPASM.

ATSINA INDIANS (Gros Ventres), warlike branch of the ARAPAHO tribe, now greatly reduced in numbers, who hunted buffalo on the Great Plains and now live on a Mont. reservation.

ATTACHÉ, diplomatic official attached to an embassy or other foreign post, generally one who is expert in a specialized field. American diplomatic attachés may be recruited from the various government departments, industry or other civilian walks of life.

ATTACHMENT, legal seizure of property. Its purpose is to prevent a defendant from disposing of disputed property before trial, or to guarantee that he will pay any judgment against him.

ATTAINDER, loss of civil rights (including rights of ownership and disposition of property) by someone outlawed or sentenced to death. Although attainder has been more or less abolished, US citizens convicted of treason still lose most of their rights.

ATTALUS, name of three kings of PERGAMUM. **Attalus I Soter** (269–197 BC), declared himself king after defeating the Galatians in 230 BC. He supported Rome against Philip V of Macedon, and thus, with Roman assistance, was able to make Pergamum one of the most important Hellenistic kingdoms. **Attalus II Philadelphus** (c220–138 BC), succeeded his brother Eumenes II, the eldest son of Attalus I, c160 BC. He maintained the Attalids' pro-Roman policies and their patronage of the arts. **Attalus III Philometor** (c170–133 BC), succeeded his uncle and at his death bequeathed his kingdom to Rome.

ATTENTION, the process of mental selection in which the individual concentrates on certain elements by considering them apart their environment. Active attention is a voluntary focusing of the mind; passive attention is involuntary reaction to outside stimuli. ELECTROENCEPHALOGRAPHS show that attention is characterized by fast, low-amplitude BRAIN waves.

ATTERBURY, Francis (1663–1732), English prelate, writer and politician. He was chaplain to Queen Anne, and swore allegiance to George I, but subsequently turned JACOBITE and was convicted of treason and sentenced to exile in 1723.

ATTICA, name of an ancient province in E central Greece and also the modern department of which Athens is capital. A fertile area, it produces wine, olives, grain and vegetables.

ATTILA (c406–453), king of the Huns, who claimed dominion from the Alps and the Baltic to the Caspian. From 441–50 he ravaged the Eastern Roman Empire as far as Constantinople and invaded Gaul in 451, this expedition earning him the title of "Scourge of God." The following year he invaded Italy, but retired without attacking Rome. He died of overindulgence at his wedding feast.

ATTIS (or Atys), a nature deity worshiped in Asia Minor and Greece. The myth of Attis, said to have been driven to madness by CYBELE after he had rejected her advances, includes his selfemasculation and his transformation into a fir tree by ZEUS.

ATTLEBORO, city in SE Mass. Its industries include the manufacture of jewelry, silverware, precision instruments, textiles and paper products. The city's museum contains Indian artifacts. Pop 32 226.

ATTLEE, Clement Richard Attlee, 1st Earl (1883–1967), British statesman and prime minister (1945–51). Attlee led the Labour party from 1935 and served in Winston CHURCHILL's wartime coalition cabinet. During his administration he instituted a broad program of social reform and nationalization.

ATTORNEY. See LEGAL PROFESSION.

ATTORNEY GENERAL, chief law officer in the US federal and state governments. The US attorney general is a member of the president's cabinet and heads the Department of Justice. He advises the president on legal questions and enforces federal law. State attorneys general have similar functions.

ATTU, westernmost island of the Aleutians, in the N Pacific. Mountainous and rugged, it covers 388sq mi and has no permanent population. The Japanese held Attu briefly during WWII.

ATTUCKS, Crispus (c1723–1770), black American who was the first of five men to die in the BOSTON MASSACRE. He has been remembered as the first colonial shot by British troops.

ATWATER, city in Cal. It is an agricultural trading and manufacturing center. Pop 11 640.

AUBER, Daniel François Esprit (1782–1871), French composer whose operas, with librettos by dramatist Eugène SCRIBE, influenced 19th-century *opéra comique* and, later, the development of romantic opera.

AUBREY, John (1626–1697), English natural philosopher and antiquary, better known for his *Brief Lives,* vivid biographical sketches, mainly of his contemporaries, first published in 1813.

AUBURN, city in E Ala., home of Auburn U. and a cotton-processing center. Pop 22767.

AUBURN, town in central Mass., a residential suburb 5mi S of Worcester. Pop 15347.

AUBURN, industrial city in SW Me., seat of Androscoggin Co., on the Androscoggin R opposite Lewiston. It is a shoe-manufacturing center. Pop 24151.

AUBURN, industrial city in the Finger Lakes region, seat of Cayuga Co., N.Y. It produces diesel engines, electronic equipment, shoes, foodstuffs and plastics. Pop 34599.

AUBURN, city in W central Wash., 11mi NE of Tacoma. It manufactures metal goods, pottery and timber products. Pop 21817.

AUBUSSON, town in the Creuse department, in central France. It is famed for its handmade Savonnerie carpets and Gobelins and Beauvais tapestries. Pop 5669.

AUBUSSON, Pierre d' (1423–1503), cardinal and grand master of the order of St. John of Jerusalem. He defended Rhodes against the Turkish sultan Mohammed II in 1480. Dissent within his own ranks led to the failure of his expedition against the Turks in 1501.

AUCHINCLOSS, Louis Stanton (1917–), US novelist whose work, noted for its character analysis, often deals with East Coast upper-class life. His best known books include *The Rector of St. Justin* (1964) and *A World of Profit* (1969).

AUCKLAND, second largest city, chief port and commercial and manufacturing center of New Zealand, between Waitemata and Manukau harbors on North Island. It has a shipbuilding industry and produces textiles, foodstuffs, vehicles, chemicals and plastics. Founded in 1840, it was New Zealand's capital until 1865. Pop 151508.

AUCKLAND ISLANDS, six uninhabited volcanic islands covering 234sq mi in the S Pacific. They lie 200mi S of New Zealand, to whom they belong.

AUCTION, method of selling goods in which prospective buyers bid against each other, and the highest bidder receives the goods. It is illegal to form an "auction ring," whereby buyers agree not to bid against each other, in order to obtain articles at low prices.

AUDEN, W. H. (1907–1973), Wystan Hugh Auden, English poet and a major influence on modern poetry, particularly during the 1930s when his highly energetic, often witty verse probed and laid bare Europe's ailing culture in the years that were to lead to WWII. Auden went to the US in 1939, becoming an American citizen in 1946. From this point his work reflects his growing religious concern (*The Double Man*, 1941). Some of Auden's best mature writing appeared in *Nones* (1951) and *The Shield of Achilles* (1955). He also collaborated on drama and opera librettos, and wrote literary criticism.

AUDIOVISUAL EDUCATION, the use of visual material and recorded sound as teaching aids. Blackboards, maps and diagrams are early examples. Now, films, radio, tape recordings and television are in widespread use. Audiovisual techniques are an integral part of school courses, and can help pupils to a better grasp of study material. Industry and government agencies also make use of these techniques.

AUDITING, official examination of accounts, usually carried out by a certified public accountant. (See ACCOUNTING; BOOKKEEPING.)

AUDUBON, borough in SW N.J., a suburb 4mi SSE of Camden. It was named for J. J. AUDUBON. Pop 10802.

AUDUBON, John James (1785–1851), US artist and naturalist famous for his bird paintings, born in Santo Domingo (Haiti) of French parents and brought up in France. Some years after emigrating to the US in 1803, he embarked on what was to become his major achievement: the painting of all the then-known birds of North America. His *Birds of America* (London: 1827–38), was followed by a US edition (1840–44) and other illustrated works on American natural history.

AUDUBON SOCIETY, National, US nature conservancy organization, named for J. J. AUDUBON. Itself running many nature sanctuaries, it works closely with government departments in the fight to preserve American wildlife.

AUER, Leopold (1845–1930), Hungarian-born violinist, a famous teacher of the instrument. He taught in Russia, Germany and England before emigrating in 1918 to the US, where he worked in New York and Philadelphia.

AUGEAN STABLES, in Classical mythology, the vast filthy stables of King Augeias. They were cleaned by HERCULES in one day as his fifth labor by diverting the rivers Alpheus and Peneius through them.

AUGSBURG, West German industrial city on the Lech R, 30mi WNW of Munich. A free city until 1806, when it became part of Bavaria, Augsburg was a flourishing artistic and trading center during the Renaissance. Today it is a major commercial and railroad center for S Germany. Pop 214400.

AUGSBURG, Peace of (1555), agreement between Ferdinand—future Holy Roman Emperor, acting for his brother Emperor Charles V—and the German princes to end the religious wars of the REFORMATION. It legalized the coexistence of Lutheranism (as the sole recognized form of Protestantism) and Roman Catholicism in the empire. Each territory was to adhere to the denomination of its ruling prince.

AUGSBURG, War of the League of (1689–97), war between Louis XIV of France and the Grand Alliance, comprising the League of Augsburg (Emperor Leopold I and Saxony, Bavaria, the Palatinate, Savoy, Sweden and Spain), the Netherlands and England. The immediate cause was French devastation of the Palatinate in 1688. By the Treaty of RYSWICK which ended the war, Louis returned Luxembourg and Lorraine, but kept Strasbourg, and recognized William III as king of England.

AUGSBURG CONFESSION, statement of Lutheran beliefs presented to the Diet of Augsburg on June 25, 1530. The Confession was largely the work of Philip MELANCHTHON, and was an attempt to reconcile LUTHER's reforms with Roman Catholicism. Emperor Charles V rejected the document, sealing the break between the Lutherans and Rome.

AUGURY, ancient Roman ritual divination of the future by natural phenomena or signs. Seers, or augurs, were always consulted before any important matter of state was initiated, and thus augury was often very influential.

AUGUST, eighth month of the Gregorian CALENDAR, named in honor of Emperor Augustus in 8 BC. It was previously called *Sextilis*, since (until 153 BC) it had been the sixth month. It was made the same length as July (named for Julius Caesar) by taking a day from February.

AUGUSTA, city in E Ga., seat of Richmond Co. A river port on the Savannah R, it is one of the world's largest cotton manufacturing centers. It is also a winter resort and the home of the U. of Georgia School of Medicine. Augusta was founded as a trading post in 1735, and in the 18th century was briefly state capital. Pop 59864.

AUGUSTA, capital of Me. and seat of Kennebec Co., at the head of navigation on Kennebec R. The city produces textiles, shoes, paper and foodstuffs. The site was first occupied by a Plymouth Colony trading post in 1628. Pop 21945.

AUGUSTAN AGE, the high point of Roman culture, marked by the reign of Emperor Augustus (27 BC–14 AD) and the literary works of Livy, Horace, Ovid and Vergil. In the first half of the 18th century, English neoclassicists sought to emulate such writers and the term Augustan denoted all that was admirable in art and politics, though, in a manner typical of the period's liking for paradox and representative of its political divisions, it was often used ironically.

AUGUSTINE, Saint (354–430), Christian theologian and writer, the most prominent of the Latin Fathers of the Church. During his early years in Carthage, N Africa, he embraced MANICHAEISM, but in Rome (where he arrived in 383) he was much influenced by NEOPLATONISM. Moving to Milan, he met and was greatly impressed by St. Ambrose, bishop of Milan, and became a baptized Christian in 387.

Ordained a priest in 391, he became bishop of Hippo in N Africa in 396. There followed many famous books, including the autobiographical *Confessions* (397–401) and *De Civitate Dei* (413–26), the great Christian philosophy of history.

Augusta, Maine, has an imposing State House which was originally designed in 1829 by Bulfinch.

AUGUSTINE, Saint (d. c604–07), first archbishop of Canterbury (from 601). A Benedictine monk, he was sent to England by Pope Gregory the Great to convert the pagans and bring the Celtic Church under the control of Rome. Arriving in 597, he was given support by King ETHELBERT of Kent.

AUGUSTINIAN FATHERS, common name for the Order of the Hermit Friars of St. Augustine, a Roman Catholic order dedicated to the advancement of learning and to missionary work. It was created in 1256 by Pope Alexander IV from a number of Italian hermit groups and adopted the Rule of St. Augustine of Hippo. The order now has some 4000 members.

AUGUSTUS (63 BC–14 AD), the honorific title given in 27 BC to Gaius Julius Caesar Octavius, great-nephew and heir of Julius Caesar. With Marcus Aemilius LEPIDUS and Mark ANTONY he formed a triumvirate which avenged his great-uncle's murder by the defeat and death of the main conspirators at Philippi (42 BC). The deposition of Lepidus (36 BC) and the suicide of Antony after his defeat at ACTIUM (31 BC) left Augustus sole master of the Roman World. He proceeded to make good the ravages of 50 years of civil war, instituting religious, legal and administrative reforms and patronizing literature and the arts. While nominally restoring the Republic, his control of the state's finances and armed forces made him the sole ruler and he is accounted first Roman Emperor, a title deriving from the Latin word for commander-in-chief, *imperator*. He was succeeded by his stepson TIBERIUS. (See also ROME, ANCIENT.)

AUKS, 22 species (including the extinct GREAT AUK) of marine diving birds of the family Alcidae (order Charadriiformes), including RAZORBILLS, PUFFINS, GUILLEMOTS and MURRES. Lengths vary between about 150mm (6in) and about 750mm (30in): the smallest is the dovekie, or Little Auk (*Plautus alle*), which is about the size of a ROBIN. They usually breed in colonies, sometimes of millions of individuals, and nest on high ledges or in burrows.

AULD LANG SYNE, Scottish song traditionally sung on Hogmanay (New Year's Eve). Written by Robert Burns c1788, its title means "old long since," or old times.

AULIS, ancient Greek seaport in Boeotia. The Greek expedition against Troy sailed from Aulis after AGAMEMNON had sacrificed IPHIGENIA in order to propitiate the goddess Artemis.

AUNG SAN, U (c1916–1947), Burmese statesman and national hero. A leader of the Burmese independence movement in the 1940s, he negotiated an agreement with Britain in 1947. But later that year he and six of his colleagues were assassinated.

AURANGZEB (or Alamgir; 1618–1707), sixth Mogul emperor of India (from 1658). He enlarged the empire to its greatest extent, but his costly military campaigns and his religious persecution of Hindus and others hastened the empire's downfall.

AURELIAN (Lucius Domitius Aurelianus; c212–275), Roman emperor (270–75) who consolidated the imperial territories. He repulsed the barbarians, began construction of a wall—the Aurelian wall—around Rome and recovered the western provinces, Gaul, Spain and Britain. He was murdered by some of his officers.

AURELIUS, Marcus. See MARCUS AURELIUS.

AUREOMYCIN. See TETRACYCLINES; ANTIBIOTICS.

AURIC, Georges (1899–), French composer, especially of ballet and film music. The youngest member of the group of composers known as *Les Six*, he was administrator of the two Paris opera houses 1962–68.

AURIGA (the Charioteer), winter constellation of N skies, containing CAPELLA, Alpha Aurigae, the fifth brightest star in the night sky.

AURIGNACIAN, an Upper Paleolithic (see STONE AGE) European culture named for Aurignac in S France. It is marked by fine cave paintings, sculptures, and bone, horn and stone-flake toolmaking.

AURIOL, Vincent (1884–1966), first president of the Fourth Republic of France (1947–54). An active socialist, he was finance minister in Léon BLUM's government. He opposed the Vichy regime in 1940 and in 1943 managed to escape to England, where he worked with General DE GAULLE.

AUROCHS, species (*Bos primigenius*) or sub-species (*Bos taurus primigenius*) of wild CATTLE, extinct since 1627, probably the ancestors of our domestic breeds. The bulls, some 2m (6.6ft) tall at the shoulder, were black with forward-curving horns. (Family: Bovidae.)

AURORA, city in NE central Col. A residential suburb 5mi E of Denver, it also produces aircraft parts and sports equipment. Pop 74 974.

AURORA, industrial city and important trading center in NE Ill., 37mi W of Chicago. It produces machinery, transportation equipment, tools, chemicals and glass. Pop 74 182.

AURORA, in Classical myth, goddess of the dawn (called Eos by the Greeks). She rose in the east, drawn in a chariot, and brought the morning dew.

AURORA, or **polar lights,** striking display of lights seen in night skies near the earth's geomagnetic poles. The *aurora borealis* (northern lights) is seen in Canada, Alaska and N Scandinavia; the *aurora australis* (southern lights) is seen in Antarctic regions. The auroras are caused by the collision of air molecules in the upper atmosphere with charged particles from the sun that have been accelerated and "funneled" by the earth's magnetic field. Particularly intense auroras are associated with high solar activity. Nighttime AIRGLOW is termed the permanent aurora.

AUSABLE CHASM, spectacular gorge in the Adirondacks, NE N.Y. This popular tourist attraction consists of a 2mi long series of waterfalls and rapids in the Ausable R flowing beneath sheer cliff faces.

AUSCHWITZ, present-day Oświęcim in Poland, site of a notorious Nazi concentration camp in WWII. Some 4 million inmates, mostly Jews, were murdered there. The town is now a transportation center with a chemical industry. Pop 39 600.

AUSTEN, Jane (1775–1817), English novelist. Daughter of a clergyman, in novels like *Sense and Sensibility* (1811), *Pride and Prejudice* (1813) and *Emma* (1815–16), she portrayed the provincial middle-class of her time with great subtlety and ironic insight. Her novels are admired as among the finest in the English language.

AUSTERLITZ, town in what is now S Czechoslovakia where, on Dec. 2, 1805, Napoleon's army defeated the combined forces of Emperor Francis I of Austria and Tsar Alexander I of Russia. This "Battle of the Three Emperors" was among the French emperor's most brilliant campaigns and marked the beginning of his rise to mastery in Europe.

AUSTIN, city in S Minn., seat of Mower Co., on the Cedar R. It is an agricultural trading center with food-processing industries. Pop 25 074.

AUSTIN, capital of Tex. and seat of Travis Co. It manufactures machinery, furniture and foodstuffs and is the home of the U. of Texas and St. Edward's U. Founded in 1838, the city was originally named Waterloo, but on becoming state capital in 1839 it was renamed in honor of Stephen Austin. Pop 251 808.

AUSTIN, Moses (1761–1821), US merchant who laid the basis for American colonization of Texas. In 1821 he was given permission to settle 300 families in Texas (then part of Mexico). His son, Stephen AUSTIN, implemented the plan after his death.

AUSTIN, Stephen Fuller (1793–1836), US pioneer statesman who helped create the state of Texas, son of Moses Austin. In 1821 he brought 300 families to Tex. and was made the settlement's administrator. Between 1822 and 1830 he presented Texan demands for autonomy to the Mexican government; the negotiations proved difficult, and the Mexicans went so far as to imprison Austin. On his release in 1835, he joined the Texan rebellion and led the volunteer army against Mexico. In 1836, Sam HOUSTON appointed Austin secretary of state of the Republic of Tex.

AUSTRALASIA, term sometimes used to indicate an area of the S Pacific that includes Australia, New Zealand, Tasmania and adjacent islands. In a wider sense, it has been used to include OCEANIA. The term's lack of adequate definition has led to a decline in its use and importance.

AUSTRALIA, island continent entirely occupied by a single nation, the Commonwealth of Australia, a federation of six states (NEW SOUTH WALES, VICTORIA, QUEENSLAND, SOUTH AUSTRALIA, WESTERN AUSTRALIA and TASMANIA) and two territories (NORTHERN TERRITORY, and AUSTRALIAN CAPITAL TERRITORY containing Canberra, the federal capital).

Australia led Papua New Guinea, self-governing from 1973, toward full independence and controls Norfolk Island, the Cocos (Keeling) Islands, Christmas Island (Indian Ocean) and about 5 000 000sq mi of Antarctica.

Land. The flat Western Plateau or Australian Shield extends from the NE coast across nearly half of the continent, sloping eastward with Lake Eyre, 43ft below sea level, as its lowest point. In the desert-like "Red Heart" of the continent are the rugged Macdonnell and Musgrave ranges. Plains stretch from the Gulf of Carpentaria to the S coast. Parallel to the E coast is the Great Dividing Range, running from N Queensland to Tasmania (Mt Kosciusko, 7 316ft, is Australia's highest peak). Along the Queensland coast is the Great Barrier Reef, the world's largest coral reef. Major rivers include the Murray (1 600mi) and its tributaries the Darling and Murrumbidgee.

Climate. Australia enjoys a mainly warm, dry and sunny climate. Summer maximum shade temperatures are well above 100°F in most areas. Annual rainfall sometimes exceeds 117in in E Queensland, but only a small part of Australia has plentiful rainfall and evaporation is high. Basically the N is a monsoon zone of dry winters and wet summers, separated by a transitional zone from the S, where summer drought and winter rains prevail.

A striking display of *aurora borealis*.

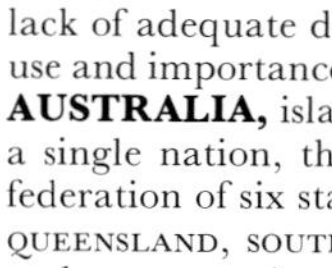

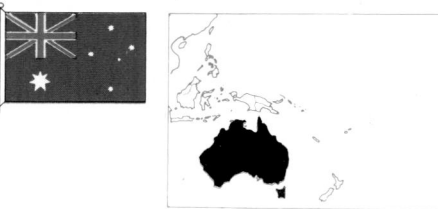

Official Name: Australia
Capital: Canberra
Area: 2 967 909sq mi
Population: 13 131 300
Languages: English
Religions: No official religion; Protestant
Monetary unit(s): 1 Australian dollar = 100 cents

Gum trees (eucalyptus) and wattles (acacia) are the continent's typical vegetation. The unique wildlife includes the platypus and spiny anteater, the most primitive surviving mammals; the koala bear, kangaroo, wallaby and wombat; the dingo, a wild dog; the emu, kookaburra and other colorful birds; and the deadly tiger-snake and other reptiles.

People and Economy. The people are mainly of British origin but there are some 106 000 Aborigines, now mostly detribalized, and many immigrants from Italy, Yugoslavia, Greece, Germany, the Netherlands and the US. Most of the population is concentrated in the coastal cities, of which the largest is Sydney.

Australia provides about 30% of the world's wool and is a major producer of wheat and meat. The rich mineral resources include iron ore, gold, copper, silver, lead, zinc, bauxite, uranium and some oil and natural gas. Australia is highly industrialized and products range from aircraft, ships and automobiles to textiles, chemicals, electrical equipment and metal goods.

History. Discovered by the Dutch in the early 1600s, Australia was claimed for Britain by Capt James COOK (1770). New South Wales, the first area settled, began as a penal colony with the arrival of the "First Fleet" under Capt. Arthur Phillip (1788). But free settlement began in 1816 and no convicts were sent to Australia after 1840. The gold rushes (1851, 1892) brought more people to Australia, and in 1901 the six self-governing colonies formed the independent Commonwealth of Australia.

AUSTRALIAN ABORIGINES, aboriginal population (see ABORIGINES) of AUSTRALIA. They have dark wavy hair (except in childhood), medium stance, broad noses and narrow heads—typical AUSTRALOID features. Before white encroachment in the 18th and 19th centuries they lived by well-organized nomadic food-gathering and hunting and numbered about 300 000. Since the enfranchisement of the remaining 40 000 full-blooded aborigines in 1962, varyingly successful attempts at integration have been made. (See also TASMANIANS.) Recent researches have suggested that they may be the result of interbreeding between an original population of *Homo erectus* and the insurgent earliest members of *Homo sapiens* (see PREHISTORIC MAN).

AUSTRALIA

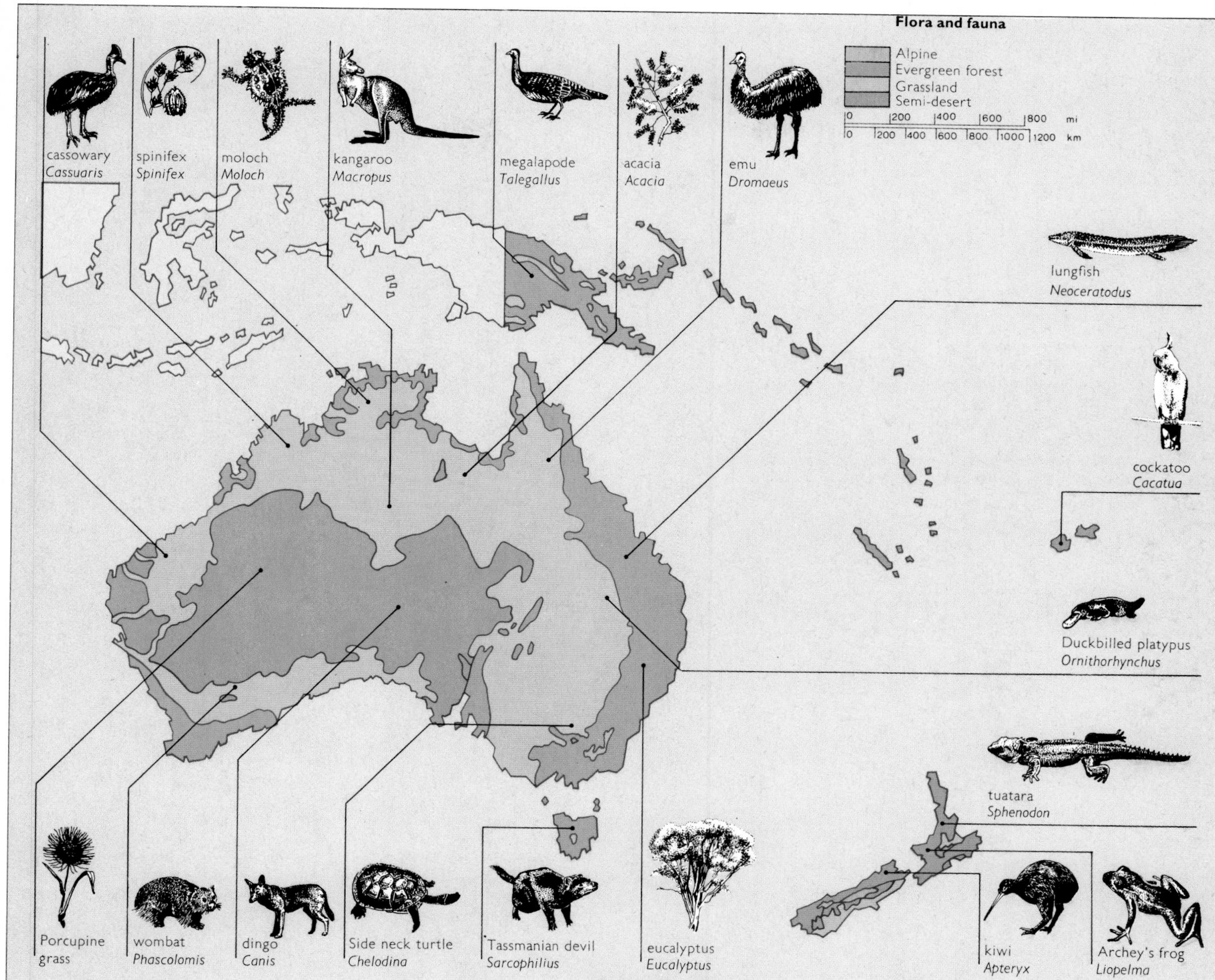

Flora and fauna
Alpine
Evergreen forest
Grassland
Semi-desert
0 200 400 600 800 mi
0 200 400 600 800 1000 1200 km
cassowary Cassuaris
spinifex Spinifex
moloch Moloch
kangaroo Macropus
megalapode Talegallus
acacia Acacia
emu Dromaeus
lungfish Neoceratodus
cockatoo Cacatua
Duckbilled platypus Ornithorhynchus
tuatara Sphenodon
Porcupine grass
wombat Phascolomis
dingo Canis
Side neck turtle Chelodina
Tassmanian devil Sarcophilius
eucalyptus Eucalyptus
kiwi Apteryx
Archey's frog Liopelma

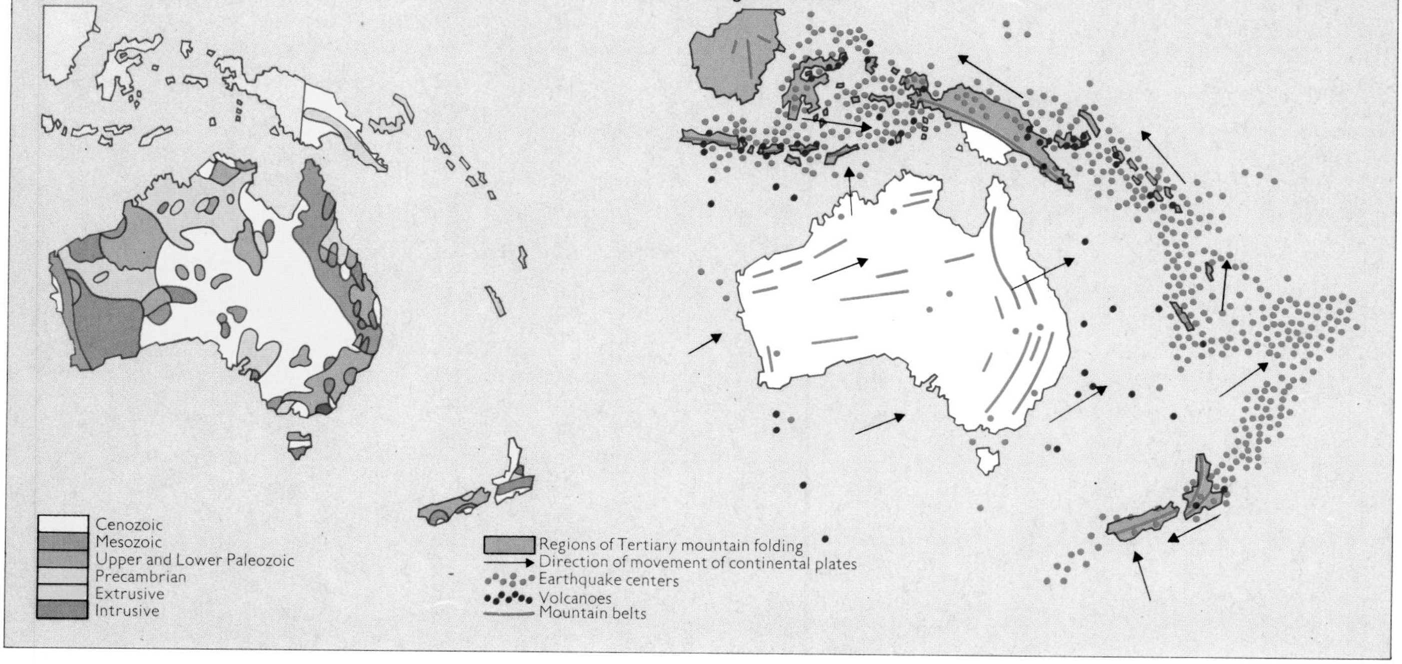

Geological structure
Cenozoic
Mesozoic
Upper and Lower Paleozoic
Precambrian
Extrusive
Intrusive
Regions of Tertiary mountain folding
Direction of movement of continental plates
Earthquake centers
Volcanoes
Mountain belts

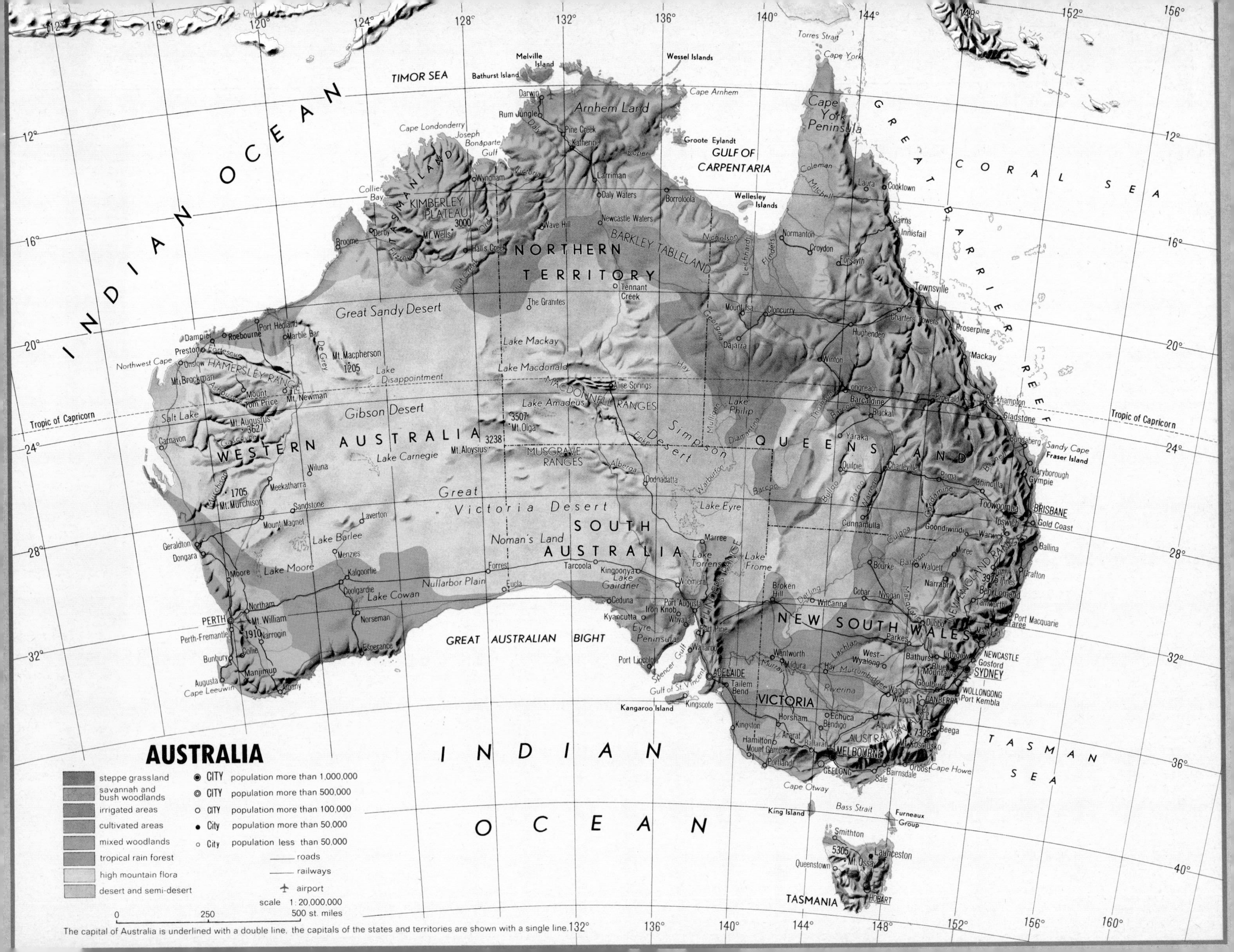
AUSTRALIA
steppe grassland
savannah and bush woodlands
irrigated areas
cultivated areas
mixed woodlands
tropical rain forest
high mountain flora
desert and semi-desert
CITY population more than 1,000,000
CITY population more than 500,000
CITY population more than 100,000
City population more than 50,000
City population less than 50,000
roads
railways
airport
scale 1: 20,000,000
0 250 500 st. miles
The capital of Australia is underlined with a double line, the capitals of the states and territories are shown with a single line.
INDIAN OCEAN
TIMOR SEA
CORAL SEA
GREAT BARRIER REEF
TASMAN SEA
GREAT AUSTRALIAN BIGHT
GULF OF CARPENTARIA
Tropic of Capricorn
WESTERN AUSTRALIA
NORTHERN TERRITORY
QUEENSLAND
SOUTH AUSTRALIA
NEW SOUTH WALES
VICTORIA
TASMANIA
AUSTRALIAN ALPS
KIMBERLEY PLATEAU
BARKLEY TABLELAND
HAMERSLEY RANGE
MACDONNELL RANGES
MUSGRAVE RANGES
FLINDERS RANGE
NEW ENGLAND RANGE
Great Sandy Desert
Gibson Desert
Great Victoria Desert
Simpson Desert
Nullarbor Plain
Noman's Land
Arnhem Land
Cape York Peninsula
Eyre Peninsula
Lake Mackay
Lake Macdonald
Lake Disappointment
Lake Amadeus
Lake Carnegie
Lake Eyre
Lake Torrens
Lake Frome
Lake Gairdner
Lake Barlee
Lake Moore
Lake Cowan
Lake Philip
Darwin
Alice Springs
Tennant Creek
PERTH
ADELAIDE
MELBOURNE
CANBERRA
SYDNEY
BRISBANE
HOBART
NEWCASTLE
WOLLONGONG
GEELONG
Townsville
Cairns
Rockhampton
Launceston
Kalgoorlie
Broken Hill
Mount Isa
Mt. Ossa 5305
Mt. Kosciusko 7328
Mt. Olga 3507
Mt. Aloysius 3238
Bass Strait
Torres Strait
Kangaroo Island
King Island
Melville Island
Bathurst Island
Groote Eylandt
Wessel Islands
Wellesley Islands
Furneaux Group
Fraser Island

Australia exhibits striking contrasts between the urban and the rural. (*Below*): In Canberra, the federal capital a clock tower at least 150ft high commemorates the foundation of the city. The carillon was presented by the British Government. (*Top left*): One of the most important industries is sheep breeding—there are on an average 15 sheep for every inhabitant of the country. (*Bottom left*): Koala bears, one of the best-known marsupials, feeding on the leaves of the eucalyptus tree.

AUSTRALIAN ALPS, mountain ranges in SE Australia which form the S part of the Great Dividing Range. They include the highest peak in Australia, Mt Kosciusko (7316ft). The important Kiewa and Snowy mountains hydroelectric projects are located in the alps region.

AUSTRALIAN ANTARCTIC TERRITORY, area claimed by Australia in 1933. It includes the islands and territory (except Adélie Land) between long. 45°E and 160°E, and below lat. 60°S.

AUSTRALIAN CAPITAL TERRITORY, an area in SE New South Wales chosen in 1908 as the seat of the federal government. It contains the capital, CANBERRA. Pop 144000.

AUSTRALIAN TERRIER, breed of dog created in Australia from Yorkshire, Cairn and other terriers. Smallest of the working terrier breeds it has a short, straight coat in blue and tan or sandy red with a soft top knot and stands 10in high, weighing 10–11lb.

AUSTRALOIDS, an ethnic group including the AUSTRALIAN ABORIGINES, the AINU, the DRAVIDIANS, the population of the Vedda of SRI LANKA and, debatably, Melanesians, Negritos and Papuans.

AUSTRALOPITHECUS. See PREHISTORIC MAN.

AUSTRASIA, E part of the Kingdom of the Merovingian Franks (6th–8th centuries), including areas of France, Germany and the Netherlands. Originating in 511 as part of the realm of Clovis I, it finally became part of Charlemagne's empire.

AUSTRIA, a federal republic in central Europe divided into nine provinces: Vienna, Lower Austria, Burgenland, Upper Austria, Salzburg, Styria, Carinthia, Tyrol and Vorarlberg. There are four physical regions: the Austrian Alps to the W, including the highest mountain in Austria, Grossglockner (12457ft); the N Alpine foreland, a plateau cut by fertile valleys between the Danube and the Alps; the Austrian granite plateau, N of the Danube; and the E lowlands, where the capital, Vienna, stands. Most rivers drain north from the mountains into the Danube and its tributaries. Climate varies widely: in general, summers are warm, winters fairly severe, with moderate rainfall throughout the year.

Economy. Austria's economy is chiefly agricultural, but the farms are small, and the only crops the country is self-sufficient in are sugar beet and potatoes. Other important crops include grains, grapes, fruits, tobacco, flax and hemp; wines and beers are produced in quantity. Almost 40% of the country is forested: wood and paper products account for 9% of the national income. Iron ore is the most important mineral resource, but there are also deposits of lead, magnesium, copper, salt, zinc, aluminum, silver and gypsum. There is oil near Zisterdorf, but production has decreased in favor of natural gas. The areas around Vienna, Graz and Linz are the chief industrial centers. Tourism has also helped to stimulate economic growth in recent years.

History. Inhabited from prehistoric times, settled by the CELTS and subsequently part of the Roman Empire, in the 3rd century AD Austria was devastated by invading VANDALS, GOTHS, ALAMANNI, HUNS and AVARS. Early in the 9th century CHARLEMAGNE made Austria the East March, which the Babenberg family inherited in 967 and retained as a duchy until their extinction in 1246. In 1276 the HAPSBURGS acquired these lands and when from 1438 they became hereditary emperors, being Archdukes of Austria already, they made VIENNA the political and cultural capital of the HOLY ROMAN EMPIRE. Until their fall in 1918, the history of Austria is the history of the Hapsburg lands. (See AUSTRIA-HUNGARY; AUSTRIAN SUCCESSION, WAR OF; AUSTRO-PRUSSIAN WAR; FRENCH REVOLUTIONARY WARS; NAPOLEONIC WARS; SEVEN YEARS' WAR; SPANISH SUCCESSION, WAR OF; THIRTY YEARS' WAR.) By the Treaty of VERSAILLES, independent states (Czechoslovakia, Hungary, Yugoslavia) were created from what had wholly or partially been within the old empire, while Austria herself, the Hapsburg patrimony, became a republic. Following the ANSCHLUSS in 1938, Austria became part of HITLER's Third Reich, regaining nominal independence following the Allied victory in 1945, although the COLD WAR prevented her achieving real autonomy until 1955.

Austria's contributions to culture, especially in

music, have been large: MOZART, HAYDN, SCHUBERT, BRUCKNER and MAHLER were all Austrians, while BEETHOVEN, Johann STRAUSS, and Franz LEHAR spent most of their lives in Vienna. Vienna is also considered the home of Freudian analysis.

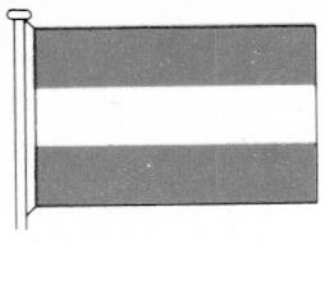

Official Name: The Republic of Austria
Capital: Vienna
Area: 32 366sq mi
Population: 7 456 403
Languages: German, Slovenian, Croatian
Religions: Roman Catholic
Monetary unit(s): 1 Schilling = 100 groschen

AUSTRIA-HUNGARY, name given to the empire formed by the union of the Kingdom of Hungary and the Austrian Empire in 1867. It ceased to exist at the end of WWI, and its lands were divided among the East European nations.

AUSTRIAN SUCCESSION, War of the (1740–1748), war fought between the Austrian Empire and European powers disputing the right of MARIA THERESA to Austrian territories inherited from her father. It was called KING GEORGE'S WAR by Americans because of the involvement of Britain's George II. The treaty of AIX-LA-CHAPELLE, ending the war, guaranteed Maria Theresa's right to the throne on condition that she ceded Silesia to Prussia.

AUSTRO-PRUSSIAN WAR (or "Seven Weeks' War"), war fought in 1866 by Austria against Prussia and Italy. Count Otto von BISMARCK, the Prussian premier, involved Austria in a dispute over the joint Austro-Prussian rule of SCHLESWIG-HOLSTEIN which forced her to declare war on June 14. By keeping the French neutral, he left Austria politically isolated. Despite the collapse of his Italian allies, the Prussian General MÖLTKE broke the Austrians at the battle of Königgrätz on July 3. The Peace of Prague (signed Aug. 23) excluded Austria from the new German confederation and ceded Venice to Italy, a major step towards Bismarck's dream of German unification under Prussia.

AUTISM, withdrawal from reality and relations with others. Pathological autism occurs in various psychoses, especially SCHIZOPHRENIA. Certain children who fail to establish normal communication with others or social responses are termed autistic; it may represent a juvenile form of schizophrenia.

AUTOBIOGRAPHY, biography written by the subject himself. St. Augustine's *Confessions* (5th century AD) is generally regarded as the first, and the modern form of autobiography is believed to have grown out of the Christian tendency towards self-examination. Today the influence of psychoanalysis and the need to assert individuality may have a similar influence. Some notable autobiographies include those written by CELLINI, Jean Jacques ROUSSEAU, Benjamin FRANKLIN, George SAND, Cardinal NEWMAN and HITLER.

AUTOCLAVE, a strong-walled pressure vessel suitable for heating liquids above their BOILING POINTS, used in the study of high-pressure chemical reactions, for sterilizing and cooking and for impregnating wood. The industrial autoclave derives from Denis Papin's "steam digester" of 1679, the prototype for the modern PRESSURE COOKER.

AUTOCRACY, government by an individual (such as the Russian Tsars or Louis XIV of France) or by a group (such as the Nazis or Fascists), having absolute power without reference to the wish of the people. (See also ABSOLUTISM; DICTATORSHIP; TOTALITARIANISM.)

AUTOGIRO, a short-takeoff, heavier-than-air flying machine that derives its lift from a rotating wing which turns in response to the aerodynamic forces (see AERODYNAMICS) acting on it as the aircraft is driven forward through the air by a conventional PROPELLER. It is potentially faster and mechanically far simpler than the HELICOPTER, capable of flying more slowly than the AIRPLANE, and impossible to stall.

AUTOGRAPH, original manuscript of words or music in the writer's own hand, or any specimen of a person's handwriting, particularly his signature. The collection of autographs first became popular in the 17th century.

AUTOMATIC PILOT. See GYROPILOT.

AUTOMATIC TRANSMISSION. See TRANSMISSION.

AUTOMATION, the detailed control of a production process without recourse to human decision-making at every point, typically involving a negative-FEEDBACK system. (See MECHANIZATION AND AUTOMATION.)

AUTOMOBILE, or passenger car, a small self-propelled passenger-carrying vehicle designed to operate on ordinary HIGHWAYS and usually supported on four wheels. Power is provided in most modern automobiles by an INTERNAL COMBUSTION ENGINE which uses GASOLINE (vaporized and premixed with a suitable quantity of air in the CARBURETOR) as FUEL. This is ignited in the (usually 4, 6 or 8) cylinders of the engine by SPARK PLUGS, fired from the DISTRIBUTOR in the appropriate sequence. The gas supply and thus the engine speed is controlled from the accelerator pedal. The driving power is communicated to the road wheels through the TRANSMISSION which includes a clutch (enabling the driver to disengage the engine without stopping it), a gearbox (allowing the most efficient use to be made of the engine power), various drive-shafts (with universal joints), and a DIFFERENTIAL which allows the driving wheels to turn at marginally different rates in cornering. Steering is controlled from a hand wheel which moves a transverse tie rod mounted between the independently-pivoted front wheels. Service BRAKES of various types are mounted on all wheels, an additional parking-brake mechanism being used when stationary. In modern automobiles service brakes and steering may be power-assisted and the transmission automatic rather than manually controlled with a gearshift. Although the first propelled steam vehicles were built by the French army officer Nicholas-Joseph Cugnot in the 1760s, it was not until Karl BENZ and Gottlieb DAIMLER began to build gasoline-powered carriages in the mid-1880s that the day of the modern automobile dawned. The DURYEA brothers built the first US automobile in 1893 and within a few years several automobile manufacturers, including Henry FORD, had started into business. The Ford Motor Company itself was founded in 1903, pioneering the cheap mass-market auto with the Model T of 1908. The AUTOMOBILE INDUSTRY expanded fitfully until the 1960s, improving automobile performance, comfort and styling, but more recently has been forced by economic considerations and the activity of consumer groups (led by Ralph NADER) to pay more attention to safety and environmental factors. (See also AUTOMOBILE EMISSION CONTROL; AUTOMOBILE RACING; DRIVING; HIGHWAY SAFETY.)

AUTOMOBILE EMISSION CONTROL, the reduction of the AIR POLLUTION caused by AUTOMOBILES by modification of the fuel and careful design. The principal pollutants are unburnt HYDROCARBONS, CARBON monoxide, oxides of NITROGEN and LEAD halide particles. The last can be eliminated if alternatives to lead-based ANTIKNOCK ADDITIVES in the GASOLINE are used but the others require redesigned cylinder heads, recycling and afterburning of exhaust gases and better metering of the GASOLINE supply through FUEL INJECTION. An alternative approach investigates alternatives to the conventional INTERNAL COMBUSTION ENGINE—BATTERY- and FUEL-CELL-powered vehicles, GAS-TURBINE and even steam-powered units.

AUTOMOBILE INSURANCE. See INSURANCE.

AUTOMOBILE RACING, a variety of forms of competition using specially designed or adapted motor vehicles. The drivers of Formula One cars compete under FIA (Federation Internationale de l'Automobile) rules for the title of world champion, won by scoring the highest points in nine out of eleven Grand Prix events. Sports car competition is more between the manufacturers, involving such races as the LE MANS 24 hours. Attempts on the land speed record are carefully scrutinized by the FIA; following the approval of jet-powered cars the record now stands at over 425mph. Stock car racing is controlled in the US by the National Association for Stock Car Racing.

AUTONOMIC NERVOUS SYSTEM. See NERVOUS SYSTEM.

AUTOPSY, or postmortem examination, the dissection of a corpse to determine the cause of death and the nature and progress of the prior disease by the

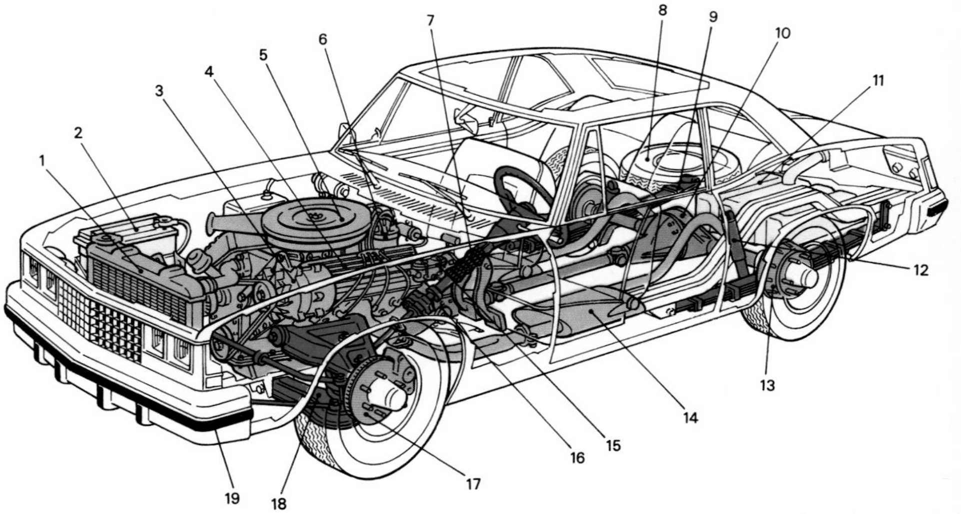

Layout of a typical modern automobile with automatic transmission. The engine, radiator and exhaust system are shown in brown, the transmission in green, the braking system in red, the steering and the suspension in blue, and the storage battery and fuel tank in yellow. 1. radiator; 2. battery; 3. AC generator; 4. V8 engine; 5. air cleaner and carburetor; 6. distributor; 7. telescopic steering column; 8. spare wheel; 9, rear spring; 10. differential and rear axle; 11. fuel tank; 12. shock absorber; 13. drum brake (rear); 14. exhaust system; 15. brake master cylinder; 16. automatic transmission; 17. disk brake (front); 18. front suspension; 19. energy absorbing bumpers.

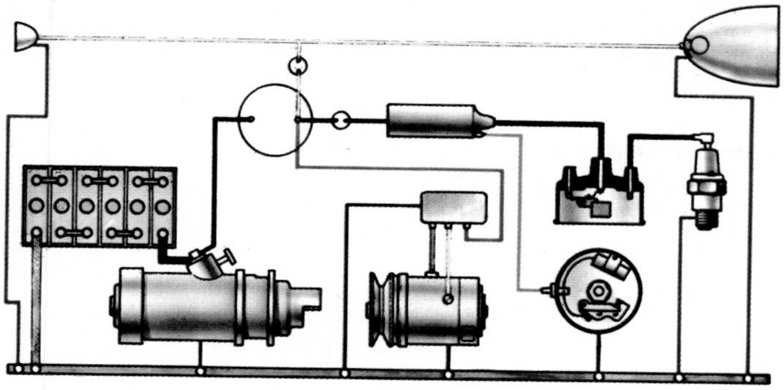

Electrical system with a battery as power store, an AC generator run from the engine to recharge the battery and the major power consumers themselves.

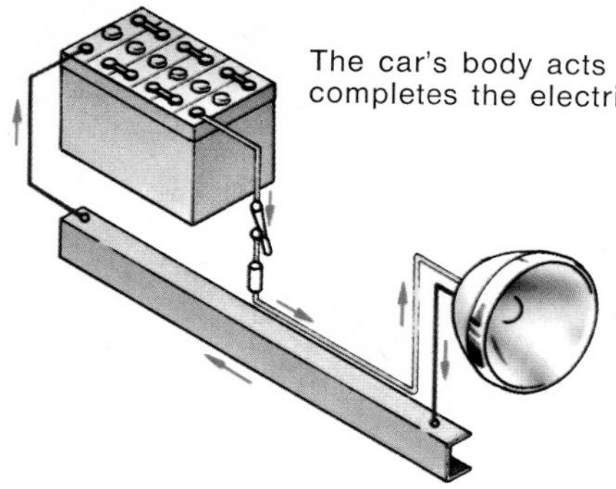

The car's body acts as the return and so completes the electrical circuit.

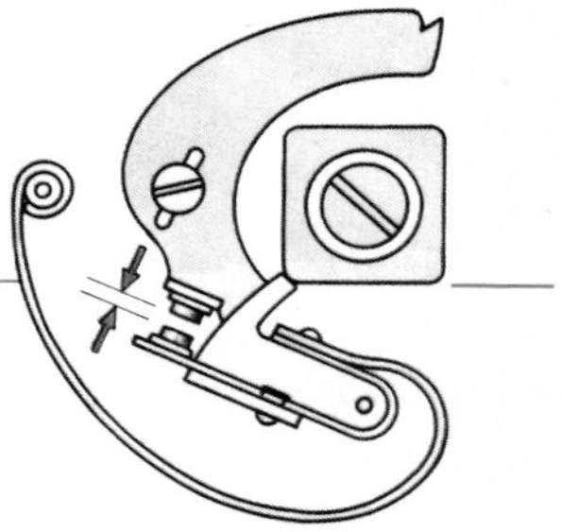

Breaker points are separated by the breaker cam (center) which periodically separates the points.

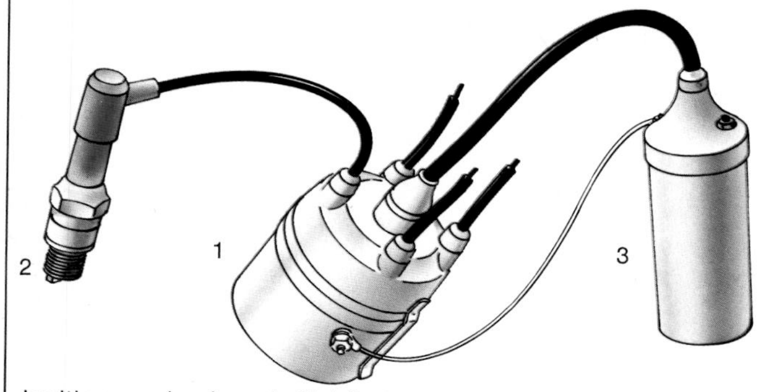

Ignition mechanism. 1. Distributor cap. 2. Sparkplug. 3. Coil.

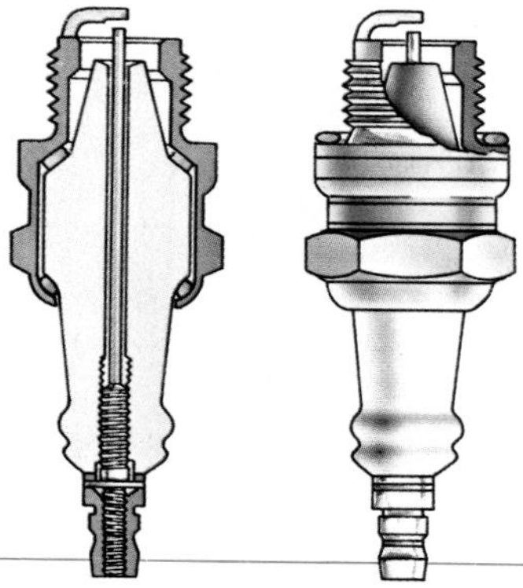

Spark plug with connector nut, insulator and body.

The liquid in the cooling system conducts the heat from the cylinders, transferring it to the radiator, a water pump (a) assists the natural convection.

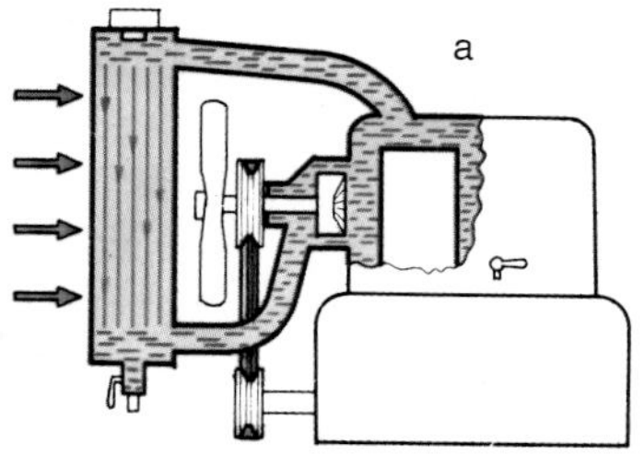

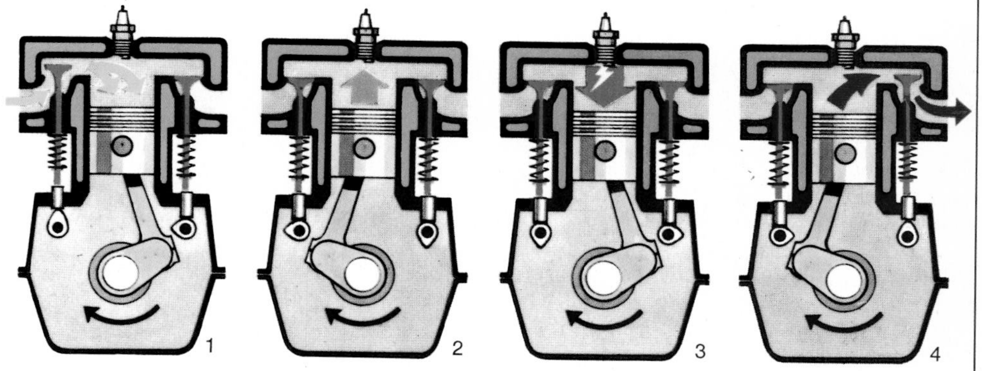

The movement of a piston. 1. The piston descends, sucking an air-gasoline mixture. 2. The piston rises, compressing the mixture. 3. The mixture explodes, forcing the piston down. 4. As the piston rises again he burnt gases are driven out as exhaust.

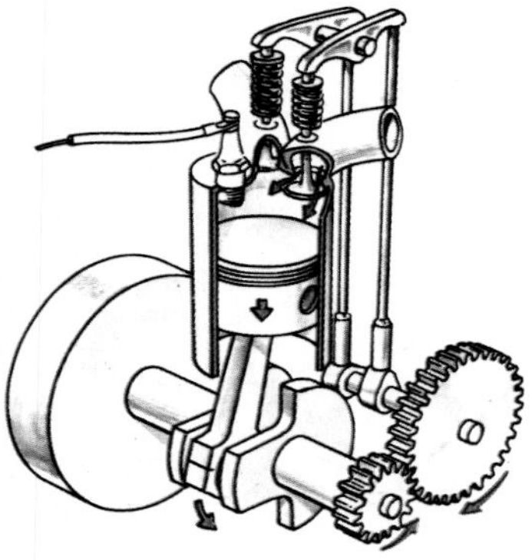

Valve in operation via timing cogs, camshaft and rockers.

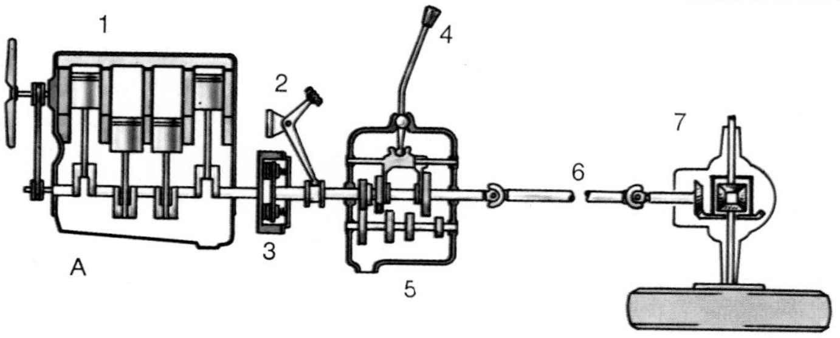

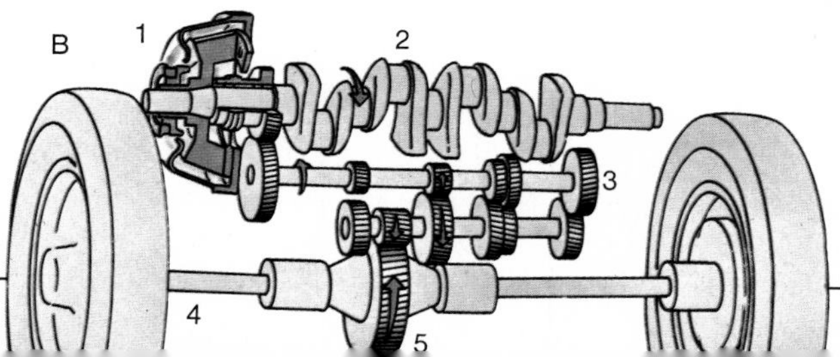

A. Engine power is usually transmitted via the clutch, gearbox, propeller shaft and conical gearwheels to the rear axles which drive the rear wheels. 1. Engine. 2. Clutch pedal. 3. Clutch. 4. Gearshift. 5. Gearbox. 6. Shaft. 7. Differential. B. Compact construction of a transverse-mounted front engine. 1. Clutch. 2. Crankshaft. 3. Gearbox. 4. Drive shafts. 5. Differential.

recognition of abnormal ANATOMY (see PATHOLOGY). It enables assessment of diagnosis and treatment; in FORENSIC MEDICINE, it may determine identity and the manner and time of death.

AUTO-SUGGESTION. See SUGGESTION.

AUTOTROPH, an organism which requires only inorganic compounds and solar energy (see PHOTOSYNTHESIS). Green plants and some bacteria are autotrophs; animals, fungi and most bacteria are **heterotrophs,** requiring also organic compounds. Autotrophs form the primary link in the food chain (see ECOLOGY).

AUTUMN. See SEASONS.

AUVERGNE, former province of S central France in the Massif Central now divided between three departments. Its principal city is Clermont-Ferrand. It was once the home of the Arverni, whose chief, VERCINGETORIX, rebelled against Julius Caesar.

AUXERRE, city of NE France and capital of the Yonne department, producing metal goods, paints and wine (notably CHABLIS), and containing some remarkable medieval building. Pop 33 700.

AUXINS, HORMONES which promote lengthwise plant growth, and control ABSCISSION and the plant's responses to light and gravity (see TROPISMS). Natural auxins are derivatives of indole (see HETEROCYCLIC COMPOUNDS). Synthetic auxins are used for crop control and as WEEDKILLERS.

AVALANCHE, mass of snow, ice and mixed rubble moving down a mountainside or over a precipice, usually caused by loud noises or other shock waves acting on snow already unstable from subsurface thawing. They can be major factors in EROSION.

AVALON, in Celtic mythology and ARTHURIAN LEGEND the land of the blessed, an earthly paradise lying westwards over the sea where heroes such as King Arthur and Ogier the Dane were taken after death.

AVARS, peoples, possibly of Mongol origin, who built an Eastern European Empire c500–800 AD threatening the Byzantine and Carolingian empires. They were crushed by CHARLEMAGNE.

AVATAR (Sanskrit *avatara*, to descend), the descent of a god to earth in human or other form. It is used especially of the various forms in which the god VISHNU visited the world.

AVDAT, archaeological site in the Negev Desert of S Israel including a 1st-century BC rain storage system and Byzantine ruins.

AVELLANEDA, city in Argentina, part of greater Buenos Aires. It is an important industrial center, notably for meat packing. Pop 337 538.

AVENTINE HILL. See SEVEN HILLS OF ROME.

AVERAGE. See MEAN, MEDIAN AND MODE.

AVERNUS (or Averno), lake in Italy 10mi W of Naples. About 2mi wide and 118ft deep, it has no natural outlet. The sinister sulfurous fumes that rise from the lake led the ancients to regard it as an entrance to the underworld.

AVERROËS, Latin name of abu-al-Walid Muhammad ibn-Ahmad **ibn-Rushd** (1126–1198), Spanish/N African Arab philosopher, a commentator on Aristotle and Plato who exerted a great influence on the development of the later Latin scholastic philosophy.

AVESTA. See ZEND AVESTA.

AVE MARIA (Hail Mary), opening words of a Roman Catholic prayer to the Virgin Mary. It is based on the words of the angel Gabriel concerning the Incarnation, and Elizabeth's greeting (Luke 1:28–42).

AVIARY, large cage or glassed enclosure for housing birds, either indoors or outdoors according to the climate and the species. The best aviaries try to reproduce the bird's natural environment, sometimes including trees and streams.

AVIATION. See AERODYNAMICS; FLIGHT, HISTORY OF.

AVICENNA, Latin name of abu-Ali al-Husayn **ibn-Sina** (980–1037), the greatest of the Arab scientists of the medieval period. His *Canon of Medicine* remained a standard medical text in Europe until the Renaissance.

AVIGNON, French city on the E bank of the Rhone, capital of the Vaucluse department; its industries include the production of metals and textiles and food processing. It was a Roman outpost, and the home of the popes during the BABYLONIAN CAPTIVITY (1309–1378). Pop 78 871.

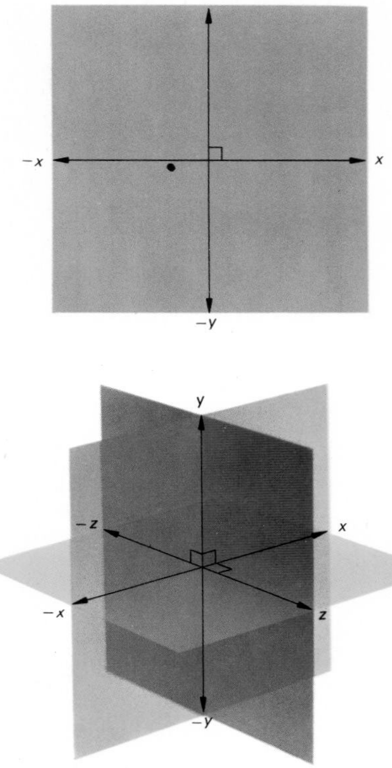

Axes used in rectangular coordinate systems. Those on the left are used in plane geometry, the *x*-axis being at right angles to the *y*-axis. Those on the right are for use in three dimensions, the *x*-, *y*- and *z*-axes being at mutual right angles.

AVILA, capital of Avila Province in central Spain, about 50mi W of Madrid. Captured from the Moors in 1088, it was the birthplace of St. TERESA OF AVILA, the mystic. The city's imposing medieval remains attract many tourists. Pop 30 983.

AVILA CAMACHO, Manuel (1897–1955), Mexican soldier and statesman. As Mexico's president during WWII he supported the US and promoted Latin American opposition to the Axis powers.

AVOCADO, *Persea americana*. tree native to middle America, Mexico and the West Indies. The fruit, the avocado or **"alligator" pear** is green or purple with pale yellow flesh rich in protein, vitamins, iron and oil and a large central seed. Avocado is also grown as a foliage house plant requiring a few hours of sunlight each day, although direct summer sun should be avoided. They grow well at average house temperatures, but fail to thrive above 24°C (75°F) and should be watered regularly to keep the soil evenly moist. They are propagated by means of the pits (hard seeds). Family: Agavaceae.

AVOCETS, wading birds of the genus *Recurvirostrata*, family Recurvirostridae and order Charadriiformes. The four species are typified by black-and-white plumage, long legs and a long, slender up-curving bill. Distribution is world-wide.

AVOGADRO, Count Amedeo (1776–1856), Italian physicist who first realized that gaseous ELEMENTS might exist as MOLECULES which contain more than one ATOM, thus distinguishing molecules from atoms. In 1811 he published **Avogadro's hypothesis**—that equal volumes of all GASES under the same conditions of TEMPERATURE and PRESSURE contain the same number of molecules—but his work in this area was ignored by chemists for over 50 years. The **Avogadro Number** ($\mathcal{N}$), the number of molecules in one MOLE of substance, 6.02×10^{23}, is named for him.

AVOIRDUPOIS (corruption of French: property of weight), the system of weights customarily used in the US (and formerly in the UK) for most goods except gems and drugs for which are employed respectively TROY WEIGHTS and APOTHECARIES WEIGHTS. There are 7 000 grains or 16 ounces in the pound avoirdupois (see WEIGHTS AND MEASURES).

AVON, name of several British rivers. The longest, the Warwickshire or "Shakespeare" Avon flows 96mi from Northamptonshire to join the Severn at Tewkesbury.

AVON, Earl of. See EDEN, ANTONY.

AVON LAKE, residential village in N. Ohio, situated on Lake Erie, 18mi W of Cleveland.. Pop 12 261.

AVVAKUM PETROVICH (1621–1682), Russian archpriest of the OLD BELIEVERS who broke away from the Orthodox Church. Rejecting the liturgical reforms of Patriarch NIKON, Avvakum was excommunicated, banished to Siberia and finally burnt at the stake. His autobiography, *Zhitie* (*Life*), is among the classics of early Russian literature.

AWOL, abbreviation for "Absent Without Leave," an offence against military regulations, differing from desertion in the assumption that the offender intended to return.

AX, tool used for chopping. Prehistoric axes were made of chipped stone fastened to a wooden handle. Modern ax-heads are of steel. The ax was once both a tool and a weapon, as with the Indian tomahawk.

AXELROD, Julius (1912–   ), US biochemist who shared the 1970 Nobel Prize for Medicine or Physiology with Bernard KATZ and Ulf von EULER for their independent contributions toward elucidating the chemistry of the transmission of nerve impulses (see NERVOUS SYSTEM). Axelrod identified a key ENZYME in this mechanism.

AXES, in mathematics, straight lines used as reference lines. In plane ANALYTIC GEOMETRY (and GRAPHS) two axes, usually at right angles, are most commonly used. In three-dimensional geometry, three axes, usually at mutual right angles, are most common. Their point of INTERSECTION is the **origin.**

AXIOM, one of the fundamental propositions which must be assumed true without proof in the compilation of a logical system (see LOGIC). An axiom need not be self-evident but should be consistent with the other axioms of the system. Closely related is the **postulate** which is a less arbitrary or basic assumption, provisionally accepted for some particular purpose but more freely open to substitution.

AXIS. See ATLAS; VERTEBRAE.

AXIS OF SYMMETRY, a LINE drawn through a geometric figure such that the figure is symmetrical (see SYMMETRY) about it. The line may be considered as an axis of rotation: if the figure is rotated about it, there will be two or more positions which are indistinguishable from each other. If the letter Z, for example, is rotated about an axis drawn perpendicularly into the paper through the center of the diagonal stroke, there will be two correspondent positions: the letter has 2-fold rotational symmetry about that axis. In general, if a figure has n correspondent positions on rotation about an axis, it is said to have n-fold symmetry about that axis. (See also PLANE OF SYMMETRY.)

AXIS POWERS, countries that fought against the Allies in WWII. The Rome-Berlin Axis, a diplomatic agreement between Hitler and Mussolini, was reinforced by an Italian-German military pact in 1939. In 1940 Japan joined the pact, then Hungary, Bulgaria, Romania, Slovakia and Croatia.

AXOLOTL, neotenic LARVA (see NEOTENY) of the SALAMANDER *Ambystoma mexicanum*. Perhaps owing to iodine deficiency in the lakes near Mexico City where they are found, they usually never become adult; but in a controlled environment they may develop into normal adult salamanders. They are 100–175mm (4–7in) in length. The term is also applied to neotenic larvae of other salamanders.

AXON, the fiber of a nerve cell that conducts impulses away from the cell body. (See NERVOUS SYSTEM.)

AXUM. See AKSUM.

AYACUCHO, Battle of, encounter that led to Peruvian independence. In 1824 South American revolutionaries under Antonio José de Sucre defeated Spanish forces under Viceroy José de la Serna on the plains of Ayacucho, Peru, bringing the end of Spanish rule in South America.

AYE-AYE (*Daubentonia madagascariensis*), nearly extinct cat-sized nocturnal LEMUR of Madagascar, where it is regarded as an evil omen. Its jaw has no canines (see TEETH), but has two continuously-growing incisors separated by a gap from the premolars. It feeds on plants and insects, digging out wood-boring LARVAE with its teeth and the long thin middle finger of each hand.

AYER, Sir Alfred Jules (1910–), English philosopher whose *Language, Truth and Logic* (1936) was influential in founding the "Oxford school" of philosophy, with its emphasis on the careful analysis of the use of words. The LOGICAL POSITIVISM of the Vienna Circle was an important formative influence in his philosophy.

AYMARA, Amerindian group numbering some 500 000, in the central Andes, Bolivia and Peru. Mainly herdsmen, they lead a meager existence under harsh climatic conditions.

AYMÉ, Marcel (1902–1967), French author noted for his humorous novels, *The Green Mare* (1933) and *The Conscience of Love* (1960). He also wrote children's stories and several plays, including *Clérambard* (1949).

AYOCK, Charles Brantlay (1859–1912), governor of N.C. 1901–05, noted for his educational reforms. He campaigned for the establishment of rural high schools and against child labor.

AYR, port on Scotland's W coast at the mouth of the Ayr R, capital of Ayrshire. It is the center of a farming region known for Ayrshire cattle.

AYUB KHAN, Mohammad (1907–1974), president of Pakistan 1958–69. He won office by a military coup, introduced land, education and local government reforms and created a new constitution.

AZALEA, a number of species of the genus RHODODENDRON, cultivated principally for ornamental purposes. Best known in the US are the pinxter, *R. nudiflorum*; the flame azalea, *R. calendulaceum*; and the rhodora, *R. canadense*. Azaleas have funnel-shaped, usually fragrant flowers with 5–10 STAMENS. As house plants they will bloom for weeks if kept in a sunny position at temperatures between 15°C and 21°C (60°F and 70°F) and watered often enough to keep the soil moist. They are propagated by shoot cuttings taken in the spring. Family: Ericaceae.

AZAZEL, evil spirit thought by the early Hebrews to inhabit the wilderness. On the Day of Atonement (see YOM KIPPUR) he was sent a goat, laden with the people's cast-off sins: hence the term scapegoat.

AZEOTROPIC MIXTURE, or constant-boiling-point mixture, a SOLUTION of two or more liquids which on DISTILLATION behaves as a pure liquid: its boiling-point is invariable at a given pressure, and the composition of the vapor phase is the same as that of the liquid. (See also PHASE EQUILIBRIA.)

AZERBAIDZHAN (Azerbaijan), mountainous region E of the Caspian Sea divided between Iran and the USSR by the Araks R. Settled by MEDES as part of the Persian Empire, it was periodically dominated by Romans, Arabs, Mongols and Turks, returning to Persia in the 16th century. The Russian Tsar Alexander I annexed N Azerbaidzhan in 1813. An independent republic was formed there in 1918 but was conquered by the Soviets in 1920. Now a Transcaucasian socialist republic, its subtropical plain produces cotton, wheat and tobacco. It is rich in minerals, especially oil, and its capital Baku is an industrial and refining city. Iranian Azerbaidzhan was made an autonomous republic by a communist revolt in 1945 but Iran regained it in 1946. Its eastern province (capital Tabriz) grows grain, its western (capital Rezaiyeh) tobacco and fruit.

AZIMUTH, in navigation and astronomy, the angular distance measured from 0–360° along the horizon eastward from an observer's north point to the point of intersection of the horizon and a great circle (see CELESTIAL SPHERE; SPHERICAL GEOMETRY) passing through the observer's ZENITH and a star or planet.

AZO COMPOUNDS, class of organic compounds of general formula R—N—N—R′. The most important azo compounds have AROMATIC groups for R and R′, and are made by coupling of DIAZONIUM COMPOUNDS with NUCLEOPHILES such as PHENOLS or aromatic AMINES. They comprise more than half the DYES commercially available.

AZOIC, the portion of geological time prior to the CRYPTOZOIC. (See also GEOLOGY; PRECAMBRIAN.)

AZORES, nine mountainous islands in the N Atlantic 800mi W of Portugal. Santa Maria and São Miguel to the E have the largest population concentrations. Their economy is agricultural, producing fruits and grain. Colonized in the mid-15th century, the islands have been under Portuguese rule ever since. Pop 336 100.

AZOV, Sea of, shallow 200mi long sea in SW USSR. Joined to the Black Sea by the Kerch Strait, it is fed at its E end by the Don R. A busy fishing industry is centered on the ports of Taganrog, Rostov and Zhdanov.

AZTEC RUINS NATIONAL MONUMENT, area of 27 acres near Aztec, N.M. It contains the ruins of a 12th-century Pueblo Indian town.

AZTECS, pre-Columbian Indians of central Mexico, traditionally thought to have migrated from Aztlán in the N to the Valley of Mexico. A warrior tribe, they took over the cities of the Toltecs, from whom they also derived part of their culture. The Aztec empire consisted of a confederation of three city states, Tenochtitlán (the capital, site of present-day Mexico City), Tlacopan and Texcoco. Religious belief contributed greatly to Aztec political and social structure. The two chief gods were Huitzilopochtli, god of war and the sun, and QUETZALCOATL, god of learning. Hundreds of human victims were sacrificed to these and other gods. The Aztecs were superb artisans, working in gold, silver and copper, and creating fine pottery and mosaics. They are famed for their lavishly decorated temples, such as those at Tenochtitlán, Tula, Cuicuilco, Xochicalco and Cholula. The arrival of the conquistador Hernán CORTÉS (1519) heralded the collapse of the Aztec empire. (See also MONTEZUMA.)

AZUAY, province of S Ecuador in the Andes Mts., 3 211sq mi in area. Its capital, Cuenca, lies in a fertile basin. Its development aided by the Andean Mission, the province produces sugarcane, coffee, cotton, cereals and dairy products.

AZURITE, blue mineral consisting of basic COPPER carbonate ($Cu_3[OH]_2[CO_3]_2$), occurring with MALACHITE, notably in France, SW Africa and Ariz. It forms monoclinic crystals used as GEMS, and was formerly used as a pigment.

AZUSA, city in SW Cal., 18mi ENE of Los Angeles. A shipping center for citrus fruits, it manufactures chemicals, fiberglass and rockets. Pop 25 217.

AZ-ZAQAZIG. See ZAGAZIG.

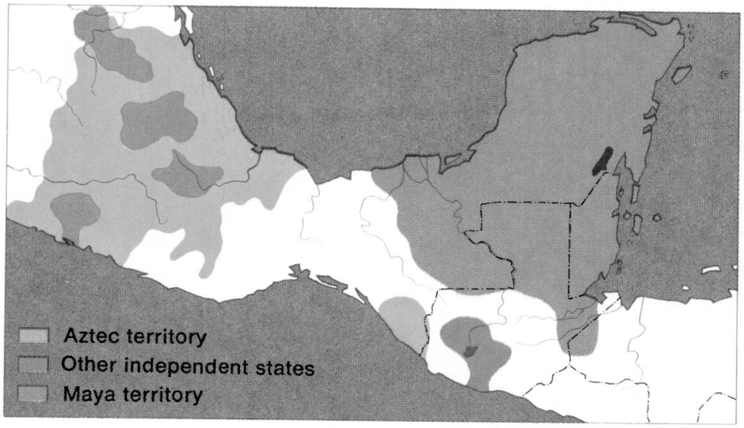

A major center of Aztec religion was at Teotihuacan, near Mexico City, where this gigantic Sun Pyramid is found. The other main pyramid is dedicated to the moon, and there are also many smaller shrines.

B

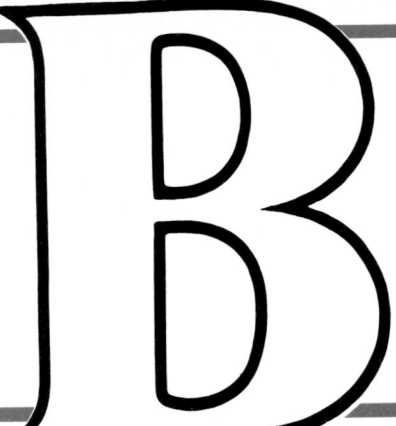

B, second letter of the alphabet. It can be traced back to an ancient Semitic character, the origin of both the Hebrew *beth* ("house") and Greek *beta* (*β*). The lower-case "b" developed in late Roman times.

BAAL, Semitic word meaning "lord" or "owner," name of an ancient Near East fertility deity. Canaanite tablets dating from c2500 BC represent him combating Mot, god of drought and sterility. There were many local variants: in Babylonia, Baal was known as Bel, and in Phoenicia, as Melkart.

BAALBEK, ancient Heliopolis (city of the sun), a town in Lebanon 53mi NE of Beirut, noted for its Roman remains. The Romans made it an important religious center, building the magnificent temples of Jupiter and Bacchus, the ruins of which still stand. The modern town is an agricultural center for the rich Bekaa region. Pop 11 700.

BAAL SHEM TOV (Hebrew: Master of the Good Name; c1700–1760), born Israel ben Eliezer, in the Ukraine, founder of the Jewish sect of HASIDISM. He stressed joy and simple piety against the formalistic aridity of orthodox Judaism.

BAATH, socialist party in Syria and Iraq dedicated to pan-Arab nationalism and social reform. The 1963 coup in Iraq was engineered by Baath supporters. In both countries its appeal to the educated officer class has kept it close to power.

BAB, The. See BAHA'I FAITH.

BABAR. See BABUR.

BABBAGE, Charles (1792–1871), English mathematician and inventor who devoted much labor and expense to an unsuccessful attempt to devise mechanical calculating engines (see CALCULATING MACHINE). More significant was the part he played with J. HERSCHEL and G. Peacock in introducing the Leibnizian "d" notation for CALCULUS into British mathematical use in place of the less flexible "dot" notation devised by NEWTON.

BABBITT, Irving (1865–1933), US scholar and noted opponent of Romanticism. He led the New Humanism, a movement in literary criticism which stressed classical reason and restraint. His works include *The New Laokoön* (1910) and *On Being Creative* (1932).

BABBITT METAL, an ALLOY containing 89% TIN, 9% ANTIMONY and 2% COPPER, devised in 1839 by US inventor **Isaac Babbitt** (1799–1862) for lining BEARINGS. Today the term babbitt metal is also applied to other high-tin and high-LEAD bearing alloys.

BABCOCK, Stephen Moulton (1843–1931), US agricultural chemist who devised the **Babcock test** for determining the butterfat content of milk (1890).

BABEL, Isaac Emanuilovich (1894–1941?), Russian short-story writer. The famous collection of stories *Red Cavalry* (1926) is based on his service with the Red Cossacks. His other works are often about Jewish life in Russia before and after the Revolution. Arrested c1938, he died in a Siberian prison camp.

BABEL, Tower of, in the Old Testament, a tower begun by Noah's descendants to try to reach heaven. Jehovah frustrated the builders by making them speak many languages. The story may refer to the ZIGGURAT of Babylon.

BAB EL-MANDEB (Arabic: Gate of Tears), 20mi-wide strait at the S tip of the Arabian peninsula, linking the Red Sea with the Gulf of Aden and the Indian Ocean.

BABENBERG, the first Austrian dynasty (976–1246). Under it, territory was extended and rulers' power strengthened. It was succeeded by the HAPSBURGS, who built the Austrian Empire.

BABEUF, François Noel (1760–1797), French revolutionary agitator, also known as Gracchus. His "Manifesto of Equals" advocated common ownership of property and the right of all to work. He was executed for plotting to overthrow the DIRECTORY.

BABIES' BREATH, herb of the pink family, Caryophyllaceae, found in Europe, Asia and North America. It is 0.6–0.9m (2–3ft) high and has delicate white or pink flowers.

BABIRUSA, *Babyrossa babyrossa*, a large, almost hairless HOG of the Suidae family, limited to the Celebes (Sulawesi) and Molucca islands. It stands roughly 0.6–0.8m (2–2.5ft) at the shoulders, and has a rough, brownish-grey skin. In the males, the upper tusks are slightly backward-curving, the lower tusks extending outward. (Order: ARTIODACTYLA.)

BABOONS, social MONKEYS of the African SAVANNAS, distinguished by their long muzzles (particularly in the males) and large size. They move in troops containing as few as 20 individuals or as many as 150 or more. They are highly aggressive (see AGGRESSION) and dangerous omnivores. There is generally a hierarchical structure within each troop, though the nature of this may change with differing circumstances: females are always subordinate to males, though females with infants are treated with great consideration. Appeasement (see APPEASEMENT BEHAVIOR) is usually by "presentation," the adoption even by males of a subservient sexual posture. Their bodies are covered with unusually long hair, except for parts of the face, and the buttocks, which may be brightly colored. They belong to the PRIMATE order and the family Cercopithedidae. (See also DRILL; MANDRILL.)

BABSON, Roger Ward (1875–1967), US statistician and economist, founder of the Babson Business Statistical Organization (1904) and of three schools of business administration.

BABUR (also Baber or Babar; born Zahir ud-Din Muhammad; 1483–1530), founder of the MOGUL EMPIRE in India, a descendant of Tamerlane and Genghis Khan. Losing Fergana, which he had inherited, and failing in his ambition to win Samarkand, Babur made his reputation by conquests over Afghan rulers in N India 1522–29, providing territory that his grandson AKBAR was to build into a great empire.

BABY. See BIRTH; OBSTETRICS; PEDIATRICS.

BABYLON, capital of the ancient kingdom of Babylonia, between the Tigris and Euphrates rivers 55mi S of modern Baghdad. Prosperous under HAMMURABI (reigned c1729–1686 BC) and his successors, it was later conquered by Hittites, Kassites and Assyrians. The reign (605–561 BC) of NEBUCHADNEZZAR II was marked by the building of its great walls, temples, ZIGGURAT and Hanging Gardens. Cyrus of Persia took Babylon in 539 BC. Alexander the Great died at Babylon in 323 BC, his plans to rebuild part of the city coming to nothing. (See also BABYLONIA AND ASSYRIA.)

BABYLON, residential and resort village on the S shore of Long Island, N.Y. Pop 12 588.

BABYLONIA AND ASSYRIA, ancient kingdoms of the Near East. Both lay in MESOPOTAMIA, the fertile area between the rivers Tigris and Euphrates. Around 3200 BC the SUMERIANS migrated westwards into S Babylonia and established what is generally considered to be the first major civilization, based on CITY-STATES such as UR. Clay tablets from SUMER, inscribed in CUNEIFORM script, have preserved king-lists, historical records and even some literature from this period, including the Epic of GILGAMESH.

Babylonia. In the 24th century BC N Babylonia was conquered by a Semitic people who established the kingdom of AKKAD. Its founder, SARGON the Great (c2360–2305 BC), conquered Sumer, but after two centuries Akkadian culture was shattered in the north by an invasion of Gutians from Iran. In the south a Sumerian renaissance flowered in the creation of such monuments as the ZIGGURATS.

In the first centuries of the 2nd millennium BC invading Semitic AMORITES established Babylon as the center of power in Mesopotamia. HAMMURABI (c1728–1686 BC), the sixth king of the Amorite

Many remains of the Babylonian-Assyrian civilization were discovered in the royal cemetery at Ur, including a lyre decorated with this magnificent golden bull's head.

dynasty, drew up a remarkable code of laws, but his S Babylonian Empire did not long survive his death. In about 1531 BC Babylon was sacked by a HITTITE army, leaving Babylonia wide open to an invasion of KASSITES, who ruled there until about 1150 BC. Despite flourishing trade and a strong alliance with Egypt, the Kassites were weakened by a series of internal conflicts and wars with neighboring nations.

Assyria. The Assyrians took their name from Ashur, their first capital, on the banks of the Tigris. Conquered by Sargon of Akkad, they later came under Sumerian rule, and around 1475 BC the Hurrian king of MITANNI made Assyria a vassal state. Assyria only became a great military power after the decline of the Hurrian kingdom. King Adadnirari I (1308–1276 BC) captured CARCHEMISH, defeated the Hittites and the Kassites, and reached the Euphrates. Under King TIGLATH-PILESER I (1116–1078 BC) this Middle Assyrian Empire spread across Syria and Phoenicia into Anatolia and overwhelmed Babylon.

After a period of decline, Assyria rose to new power under such warrior kings as Shalmaneser III (859–825 BC), Tiglath-Pileser III (745–727 BC) and Sargon II (722–705 BC). In addition to Babylonia, Syria, Israel, Carchemish and Tyre, even Egypt became subject to Assyrian rule. Sargon's son SENNACHERIB (705–681 BC) made his capital, NINEVEH, into one of the most magnificent cities of its time. It is to ASHURBANIPAL (c669–630 BC) that we owe much of our knowledge of the literature of ancient Mesopotamia: some 25 000 tablets from his library are now in the British Museum, London. The kingdom collapsed after his death, in the face of an alliance of CHALDEA with the SCYTHIANS and MEDES.

Neo-Babylonian Empire. Under the Chaldean King NABOPOLASSAR (626–605 BC) Babylonia recovered its independence. The new empire was consolidated by his son NEBUCHADNEZZAR II (605–562 BC), who continued his father's war with Egypt and put down revolts in Tyre and Judah, destroying Jerusalem in 586 BC. He also built the famous HANGING GARDENS OF BABYLON. The internal power struggle following his death was settled by the accession of the usurper Nabonidus to the throne in 555 BC. Nabonidus' son Belshazzar held power in Babylon when CYRUS THE GREAT, king of the Medes and Persians, captured the city in 539 BC. Babylonia then became a province of the Persian Empire.

BABYLONIAN CAPTIVITY, exile of the Jews to Babylon after the conquest of Jerusalem by NEBUCHADNEZZAR II in 597 BC and 586 BC. In 538 BC CYRUS THE GREAT, who had taken Babylon, allowed them to return to Judea. The term is also used in European history for the period from 1309 to 1377 when, under French domination, the popes resided at Avignon in S France. Pope Gregory XI returned to Rome in 1377, but after his death the papacy was split by the GREAT SCHISM.

BABY'S TEARS, *Helxine solierolii*, a half-hardy, creeping perennial plant native to Corsica, which is widely cultivated outdoors for ground cover and as a house plant for its attractive densely-set pale or mid-green foliage. Indoors, the plants should be grown in a sunny position, watered every three days and can tolerate a temperature range of 4°C to 24°C (40°F to 75°F). Propagation is achieved by removing rooted stems or by taking cuttings. Family: Urticaceae.

BACCALAUREATE. See DEGREE, ACADEMIC.

BACCARAT, card game, probably of French origin, played in casinos. Players bet against the bank, and the winner is the one who, in a two-card deal and optional one-card draw, gains a point total whose last digit is nearest to nine. Picture cards count as nothing.

BACCHUS, Roman god of wine and fertility, counterpart of the Greek DIONYSUS. The *bacchanalia* held in his honor became increasingly licentious, and the Senate banned them in 186 BC.

BACH, name of a family of musicians originating in Thuringia, Germany. **Johann Sebastian Bach** (1685–1750) was one of the greatest composers of all time. His music is a culmination and enrichment of the polyphonic tradition of BAROQUE music, but also reflects the harmonic innovations which were supplanting polyphony. Bach held posts at the courts of the Duke of Weimar and Prince Leopold of Köthen, and was musical director of St. Thomas' School, Leipzig.

Bach first excelled as an organist, and his works include many organ compositions. Other keyboard works include *The Well-Tempered Clavier* and the *Goldberg Variations*. Among his instrumental masterpieces are the works for solo violin and cello and the six *Brandenburg Concertos*. The bulk of Bach's work is religious in inspiration, as seen particularly in his choral works. In addition to more than 200 cantatas, these include the famous *St. Matthew Passion*, *St. John Passion*, *B Minor Mass* and *Christmas Oratorio*.

Of Bach's 20 children, some became composers in their own right. **Wilhelm Friedemann Bach** (1710–1784) was organist at Dresden and Halle, and left some undistinguished compositions. **Carl Philipp Emanuel Bach** (1714–1788) was an outstanding composer and keyboard musician, whose development of symphonic, concerto and sonata forms influenced Haydn, Mozart and Beethoven. His *Essay on the True Art of Playing Keyboard Instruments* remains an essential manual of 18th-century techniques. He was court musician to Frederick the Great and musical director at Hamburg. **Johann Christoph Friedrich Bach** (1732–1794) was chamber musician and *Konzertmeister* to Count Wilhelm of Bückeburg and a prolific composer. **Johann Christian Bach** (1735–1782) wrote numerous graceful orchestral and chamber works and several operas. He was particularly successful in England, where he spent the last 20 years of his life.

BACHELOR'S BUTTON. See CORNFLOWER.

BACILLUS, genus of rod-shaped BACTERIA of the family Bacillaceae.

BACKBONE. In animals, see VERTEBRATES; INVERTEBRATES; in man, see SKELETON; VERTEBRAE.

BACKGAMMON, game for two people. Each player has 15 pieces arranged on a board marked with 24 triangular points. The object is to move all the pieces, by casting dice, to the inner table and remove them from the board before the other player does so. The game dates back to ancient Babylon, Greece and Rome.

BACK RIVER, Canadian river, flowing 605mi NE from the Mackenzie district of the Northwest Territories of the Arctic Ocean.

BACKSWIMMERS, aquatic BUGS (family Notonectidae) similar to the WATER BOATMEN but differing from them in that they swim on their backs. They are vicious predators and often attack fish and other animals larger than themselves. They can inflict painful though not usually dangerous bites.

BACKUS, Isaac (1724–1806), American clergyman, leader of the New England Baptists. He helped found the First Baptist Church at Middleborough, Mass., in 1756. His history of New England (1777–96) is a source of religious history for the period.

BACON, meat from the sides of pigs. In the US it comes from the fatty side between the 4th or 5th rib and the hipbone. It is cured, preserved with salt, sugar and sodium nitrate or sodium nitrite, and smoked over a hardwood fire.

BACON, Francis; Lord Verulam, Viscount St. Albans (1561–1626), English philosopher and statesman who rose to become Lord Chancellor (1618–21) to JAMES I but is chiefly remembered for the stimulus he gave to scientific research in England. Although his name is indelibly associated with the method of INDUCTION and the rejection of A PRIORI reasoning in science, the painstaking collection of miscellaneous facts without any recourse to prior theory which he advocated in the *Novum Organum* (1620) has never been adopted as a practical method of research. The application of the Baconian method was, however, an important object in the foundation of the ROYAL SOCIETY OF LONDON some 40 years later.

BACON, Francis (1909–), British painter. A self-taught artist, he developed a unique style which expresses the isolation and horror of the human condition, concentrating on distorted figures which manage to convey both panic and menace.

BACON, Nathaniel. See BACON'S REBELLION.

BACON, Roger (c1214–1292?), English scholar renowned in his own day for his great knowledge of science and remembered today for allegedly prophesying many of the inventions of later centuries: aircraft; telescopes; steam engines; microscopes. In fact he was a wealthy lecturer in the schools of Oxford and Paris with a passion for alchemical and other experiments, whose later life was overshadowed by disputes with the Franciscan Order, of which he had become a member in 1257. His principal writings (in aid of an encyclopedia of knowledge) were the *Opus Majus*, *Opus Minor* and *Opus Tertium*.

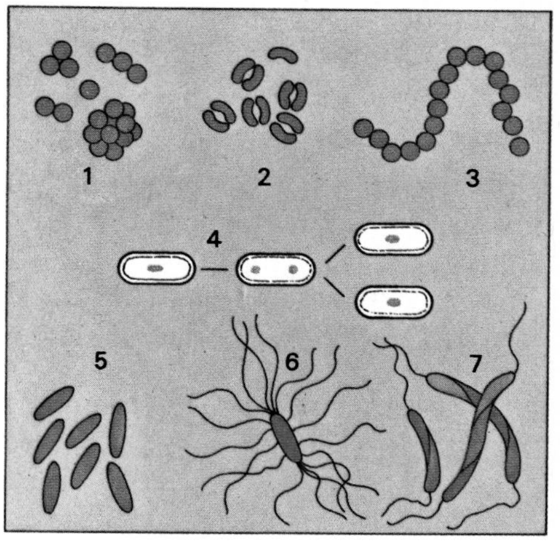

Different types of bacteria: (1) cocci, (2) diplococci, (3) streptococci, (5) bacilli. Some bacteria possess hairlike flagella; for example, (6) flagellate rods or (7) flagellate spirilla. At (4) a bacillus is shown undergoing reproduction by binary fission.

BACON'S REBELLION, a rising in colonial America led by planter Nathaniel Bacon (1647–1676) against the governor of Va., Sir William BERKELEY. When Berkeley failed to defend the frontier against Indians, Bacon claimed the right of frontiersmen to form their own militia and led unauthorized forces against the Indians in 1676. Proclaimed traitor, he marched on Jamestown and briefly controlled the colony, instituting legal reforms. The subsequent civil war against forces raised by Berkeley ended shortly after Bacon's death.

BACTERIA, unicellular microorganisms between 0.3 and 2 μm in diameter. They differ from plant and animal cells in that their nucleus is not a distinct organelle surrounded by a membrane: they are usually placed in a separate kingdom, the Protista.

The majority of bacteria are saprophytic: they exist independently of living hosts and are involved in processes of decomposition of dead animal and plant material. As such they are essential to the natural economy of living things.

Some bacteria are parasitic, and their survival depends on their presence in or on other living cells. They may be commensals (see COMMENSALISM), which coexist harmlessly with host cells, or pathogens, which damage the host organism by producing toxins, which may cause tissue damage (see BACTERIAL DISEASES). This distinction is not absolute: *Escherichia coli* is a commensal in the human intestine, but may cause infection in the urinary tract.

Bacteria are like plant cells in that they are surrounded by a rigid cell wall. Most species are incapable of movement, but certain types can swim using hairlike flagella (see FLAGELLATES). Bacteria vary in their food requirements: AUTOTROPHS can obtain energy by oxidizing substances which they have built up from simple inorganic matter; heterotrophs need organic substances for nutrition. Aerobic (see AEROBE) bacteria need oxygen to survive, whereas anaerobic (see ANAEROBE) species do not. Included in the latter group are the putrefactive bacteria, which aid decomposition. Bacteria generally reproduce asexually by binary FISSION, but some species reproduce sexually. Some can survive adverse conditions by forming highly resistant spores.

Bacteria are important to man in many ways. Commensal bacteria in the human intestine aid digestion of food; industrially they are used in the manufacture of, for example, acetone, citric acid and butyl alcohol and in many dairy products. Some bacteria, especially the ACTINOMYCETES, produce ANTIBIOTICS, used in destroying pathogenic bacteria. **Classification.** There is no standard way of classifying bacteria. The higher bacteria are filamentous and the cells may be interdependent—they include the family ACTINOMYCETES. The lower bacteria are subdivided according to shape: COCCI (round), BACILLI (cylindrical), VIBRIOS (curved), and SPIRILLA (spiral). Cocci live singly, in pairs (DIPLOCOCCI), in clusters (STAPHYLOCOCCI) or in chains (STREPTOCOCCI)—as a group they are of great medical importance. SPIROCHETES form a separate group from the above: although spiral they are able to move. Bacteria are also classified medically in terms of their response to GRAM'S STAIN: those absorbing it are termed Gram-positive, those not, Gram-negative. (See also BACTERIOLOGY; MICROBIOLOGY.)

BACTERIAL DISEASES, diseases caused by BACTERIA or their products. Many bacteria have no effect and some are beneficial, while only a small number lead to disease. This may be a result of bacterial growth, the INFLAMMATION in response to it or of TOXINS (e.g., TETANUS, BOTULISM and CHOLERA). Bacteria may be contracted from the environment, other animals or humans, or from other parts of a single individual. Infection of SKIN and soft tissues with STAPHYLOCOCCUS or STREPTOCOCCUS leads to BOILS, CARBUNCLES, IMPETIGO, CELLULITIS, SCARLET FEVER and ERYSIPELAS. ABSCESS represents the localization of bacteria, while SEPTICEMIA is infection circulating in the BLOOD. Sometimes a specific bacteria causes a specific disease (e.g., ANTHRAX, DIPHTHERIA, TYPHOID FEVER), but any bacteria in some organs cause a similar disease: in LUNGS, PNEUMONIA occurs; in urinary tract, CYSTITIS or pyelonephritis, and in the BRAIN coverings, MENINGITIS. Many VENEREAL DISEASES are due to bacteria. In some diseases (e.g., TUBERCULOSIS, LEPROSY, RHEUMATIC FEVER), many manifestations are due to hypersensitivity (see IMMUNITY) to the bacteria. While ANTIBIOTICS have greatly reduced death and ill-health from bacteria, and VACCINATION against specific diseases (e.g., WHOOPING COUGH) has limited the number of cases, bacteria remain an important factor in disease.

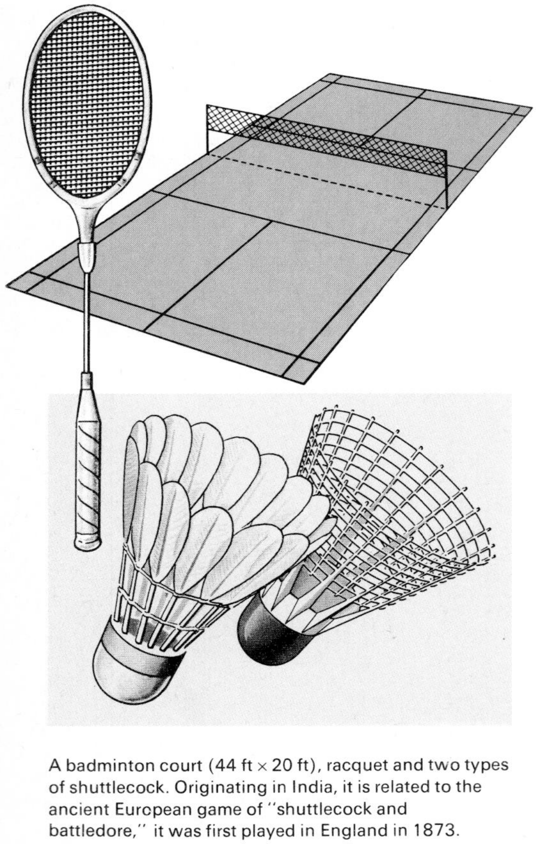

A badminton court (44 ft × 20 ft), racquet and two types of shuttlecock. Originating in India, it is related to the ancient European game of "shuttlecock and battledore," it was first played in England in 1873.

BACTERIOLOGICAL WARFARE. See CHEMICAL AND BIOLOGICAL WARFARE.

BACTERIOLOGY, the science that deals with BACTERIA, their characteristics and their activities as related to medicine, industry and agriculture. Bacteria were discovered in 1676 by Anton von LEEUWENHOEK. Modern techniques of study originate from about 1870 with the use of stains and the discovery of culture methods using plates of nutrient AGAR media. Much pioneering work was done by Louis PASTEUR and Robert KOCH. (See also BACTERIAL DISEASES; NITROGEN FIXATION; SPONTANEOUS GENERATION.)

BACTERIOPHAGE, or **phage**, a VIRUS which attacks BACTERIA. They have a thin PROTEIN coat surrounding a central core of DNA (or occasionally RNA), and a small protein tail. The phage attaches itself to the bacterium and injects the NUCLEIC ACID into the cell. This genetic material (see GENETICS) alters the metabolism of the bacterium, and several hundred phages develop inside it: eventually the cell bursts, releasing the new, mature phages. Study of phages has revealed much about PROTEIN SYNTHESIS and nucleic acids.

BACTRIA, ancient country of central Asia between the Amu Darya R and the Hindu Kush Mts. The area is now part of Afghanistan and the Tadzhik and Uzbek soviet socialist republics. From the mid-6th century BC it was successively ruled by the Persian Empire, ALEXANDER THE GREAT and the SELEUCIDS. Bactria played an important part in the dissemination of Hellenistic culture through central Asia.

BADAJOZ, city in SW Spain near the Portuguese border. Formerly the capital of a Moorish kingdom, it is now the capital of Badajoz province and a center for food processing and transit trade with Portugal. Pop 101 710.

BADALONA, suburb of Barcelona in NE Spain. A port with shipyards, it manufactures glass, textiles and chemicals. Pop 162 888.

BAD AXE, Battle of. See BLACK HAWK WAR.

BADEN (Baden-Baden), city and spa in SW West Germany, located in the Rhine Valley near the Black Forest. Its springs annually attract some 60 000 tourists. Pop 39 074.

BADEN-POWELL, Robert, 1st Baron Baden-Powell of Gilwell (1857–1941), British army officer, founder in 1907 of the BOY SCOUTS and in 1910, with his sister Agnes Baden-Powell, of the Girl Guides. (See also GIRL SCOUTS AND GIRL GUIDES.)

BADEN-WÜRTTEMBERG, state in SW West Germany formed in 1952 from three postwar provinces. It is a tourist area, containing the Black Forest, Lake Constance, Swabian Jura Mts, Neckar R and the university city of Heidelberg. Cereals, fruit and cattle are raised but the economy depends largely on the industrial cities of Mannheim, Karlsruhe and the capital, Stuttgart.

BADGERS, medium-sized omnivorous burrowing MAMMALS of the WEASEL family Mustelidae. There are six genera (seven including the RATEL) distributed throughout Eurasia, North America and parts of Indonesia. They have potent anal scent GLANDS especially effective in the Oriental Stink Badgers *Mydaus* and *Suillotaxus*. Three genera, *Meles*, *Taxidea* (which includes the American Badger, *T. Taxus*) and *Melogale*, have distinctive black and white facial masks. Badgers are almost always nocturnal.

BADLANDS, arid to semiarid areas of pinnacles, ridges and gullies, usually lacking in vegetation, formed by heavy EROSION of non-uniform rock. The Big Badlands of S.D. are particularly notable.

BADLANDS NATIONAL MONUMENT, some 243 508 acres of badlands in SW S.D. It comprises barren ravines and ridges of multicolored shale; its sandstone layers are famous for fossils.

BADMINTON, game similar to tennis, originating in India. Two or four players use lightweight rackets to hit a small feather-flighted hemisphere of cork known as a shuttlecock or "bird" over a net. The object is to return the ball before it hits the ground.

BADOGLIO, Pietro (1871–1956), Italian field marshal and statesman, instrumental in Italy's seizure of Ethiopia (1935) and in MUSSOLINI's overthrow (1943). He became prime minister and surrendered Italy to the Allies on Sept. 3, 1943.

BAECK, Leo (1873–1956), German rabbi, a leader of Reform Judaism. He braved Nazi persecution rather than emigrate and was one of the few to survive the Theresienstadt concentration camp. His major work, *Essence of Judaism* (1905), stresses the ethical importance of Judaism.

BAEDEKER, Karl (1801–1859), German publisher who developed the tourist guidebooks which bear his name. "Baedekers" now cover most European and many non-European countries.

BAEKELAND, Leo Hendrik (1863–1944), Belgian-born chemist who, after emigrating to the US in 1889, devised Velox photographic printing paper (selling the process to EASTMAN in 1899) and went on to discover BAKELITE, the first modern synthetic PLASTIC.

BAER, Karl Ernst von (1792–1876), Estonian-born German embryologist who discovered the mammalian egg (see REPRODUCTION) and the NOTOCHORD of the vertebrate embryo. He is considered to have been one of the founders of comparative EMBRYOLOGY.

BAER, Max (1909–1969), US prizefighter, world heavyweight champion 1934–35. Baer beat Primo Carnera for the world title. He retired in 1941 having won 65 out of 79 fights.

BAEYER, Johann Friedrich Wilhelm Adolf von (1835–1917), German organic chemist who proposed a "strain theory" to account for the relative stabilities of ring compounds (see ALICYCLIC COMPOUNDS). He was awarded the 1905 Nobel Prize for Chemistry for his research on dyestuffs: in 1878 he had become the first to synthesize INDIGO.

BAEZ, Joan (1941–), US folk singer noted for the purity of her voice and simple, direct style. She sings traditional ballads, and pacifist and protest songs, many of which she composes herself.

BAFFIN, William (c1584–1622), English navigator and Arctic explorer. As pilot on a vessel seeking the Northwest Passage, he discovered Baffin Bay (1616) and reached 77°45′N—setting a record that stood for more than 200 years.

BAFFIN BAY, branch of the Atlantic Ocean N of Davis Strait, between Baffin Island and Greenland. The bay, which is frozen for most of the year, reaches a depth of some 1500 fathoms. It was named for the explorer William Baffin.

BAFFIN ISLAND, island between Greenland and Canada, part of Canada's Northwest Territories. It is a rugged, glaciated tract of some 183 810sq mi with an impressive 7000ft high mountain range along its E coast. The largely Eskimo population lives by fishing, fur-trading and whaling. There is also some coal mining. Pop 3 387.

BAGEHOT, Walter (1826–1877), English social scientist, editor and literary critic, a man of great originality and influence. Among his most important works are *The English Constitution* (1867), *Physics and Politics* (1872) and *Lombard Street* (1873). Bagehot, who came from a banking family, edited *The Economist* from 1861 until his death.

BAGHDAD, capital of Iraq, situated on the Tigris R, some 330mi inland from the Persian Gulf. It is Iraq's main communications, trading and industrial center, and manufactures petroleum products and textiles. Founded in 762 AD, it was a center of Muslim culture until 1258 when it was sacked and largely destroyed by the Mongols. Baghdad was ruled by Turkey from 1638, captured by Britain in WWI and finally made capital of the new nation of Iraq in 1921. Pop 2 183 760.

BAGHDAD PACT. See CENTRAL TREATY ORGANIZATION.

BAGNELL DAM, power dam on the Osage R in central Mo., completed 1931. It forms the 130mi-long Lake of the Ozarks and supplies electricity to E Mo.

BAGOT, Sir Charles (1781–1843), British diplomat who, as minister to the US, negotiated the RUSH-BAGOT CONVENTION (1817) restricting fortification on the Great Lakes. Bagot was governor-general of Canada from 1841 until his death.

BAGPIPE, wind instrument in which air is blown into a leather bag and forced out through musical pipes. The melody is played on one or two pipes (the chanters) while one or more drone pipes sound bass tones. The bagpipe originated in Asia, but is best known as Scotland's national instrument.

BAHADUR SHAH II (1775–1862), titular emperor of India, last of the Mogul emperors. He became a reluctant figurehead in the SEPOY REBELLION after which the British exiled him to Burma.

BAHA'I FAITH, religion founded by the Persian Mirza Husain Ali, known as Baha'u'llah ("glory of god"), in the second half of the 19th century. It developed from the teaching of the prophet Bab (1820–1850) who preached in Persia until Islamic leaders had him executed. Mirza Husain Ali (1817–1892) succeeded him and founded Baha'i, proclaiming himself a manifestation of God. The Baha'i faith is based on belief in human brotherhood and promotes peace and racial justice. It has a world-wide following.

BAHAMAS, a nation of some 700 subtropical islands and more than 2 000 islets or *cays* extending about 760mi from the SE coast of Fla. to the N coast of Haiti. The most important island is New Providence, where the capital, Nassau, is situated. Among the largest islands in the chain are Andros, Great Abaco, Grand Bahama and Inagua.

About 85% of the population is Negro. Most people live in Nassau or elsewhere on New Providence. The economy is based on tourism and fishing and on the export of wood products, cement, salt and crayfish.

Columbus probably made his first New World landfall on Watling Island (San Salvador). English settlement began in the 1640s, and British rule was almost unbroken until internal self-government in 1964. Full independence came in 1973.

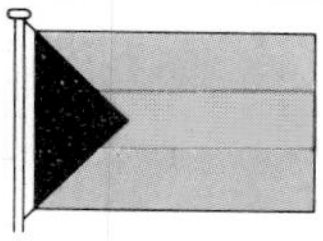

Official Name: The Commonwealth of the Bahamas
Capital: Nassau
Area: 5 386.25sq mi
Population: 168 812 (total for all islands)
Languages: English
Religions: No official religion
Monetary Unit(s): 1 Bahamian dollar = 100 cents

Lack of labor and good roads prevents the Bahamas fully exploiting the few natural resources to be found there; the economy has come to depend on tourists heading for sunny beaches.

BAHA'U'LLAH. See BAHA'I FAITH.

BAHIA, Brazilian state on the Atlantic coast. The population is concentrated in the moist, fertile coastal belt which produces sugar, cacao, rubber and lumber. Mining and cattle raising are carried out on the dry inland plateau.

BAHIA, city in Brazil. See SALVADOR.

BAHIA BLANCA, city in E Argentina, about 340mi SW of Buenos Aires. A major port, exporting oil, cattle, wheat and wool, it is also the main base of the Argentinian navy. Pop 161 745.

BAHRAIN, independent Arab sheikhdom, an archipelago in the Persian Gulf between the Saudi Arabian coast and the Qatar peninsula. The economy is based on oil drilling and refining, pearl fishing being now relatively unimportant. The main population centers are Manama and Muharraq. Bahrain was a British protectorate 1882–1971.

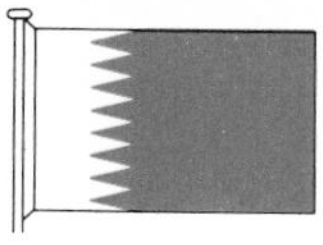

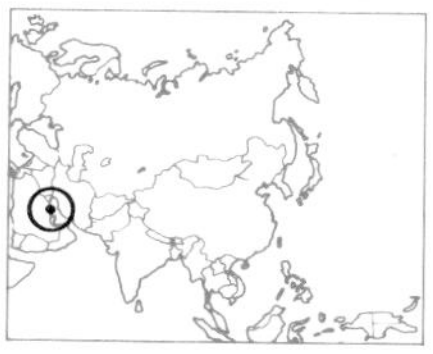

Official Name: Bahrain
Capital: Manama
Area: 255sq mi
Population: 216 815
Languages: Arabic, English
Religions: Muslim
Monetary Unit(s): 1 Bahrain dinar = 1 000 fils

BAIKAL, Lake, Russia's third-largest lake, situated in E Siberia. It covers 11 780sq mi and has a maximum depth of 5 715ft, which makes it the world's deepest lake. Lake Baikal is fed by more than 300 rivers and is used for transporting lumber and for salmon fishing. Much of its flora and fauna is unique.

BAIL, the release of a prisoner from custody pending a court appearance, against a financial security. Procedures vary, but in the US the amount is fixed by the judge; under the Bail Reform Act (1966) it must generally be granted, except in cases where the prisoner is likely to flee or be a danger to the community. Where bail is refused, credit is given against sentence for time spent in jail.

BAILE ÁTHA CLIATH, Irish name of DUBLIN.

BAILEY, James Anthony (1847–1906), US circus owner. In 1881 his circus merged with that of Phineas T. BARNUM, to form the famous Barnum & Bailey Circus. Bailey owned it after Barnum died.

BAILEY, Liberty Hyde (1858–1954), US horticulturalist and botanist who, as professor of HORTICULTURE at Cornell U. (1888–1913), did much to put US horticulture on a scientific footing.

BAILEY, Mildred (real name Mildred Rinker; 1907–1951), US jazz singer. She joined Paul Whiteman's band in 1929, becoming one of the first female singers to appear regularly with a leading band.

BAILEY, Pearl (1918–), US jazz singer and actress. She sang with Count BASIE and Cootie Williams and acted in stage and motion-picture musicals, including *Porgy and Bess* and *Hello Dolly*.

BAILEY BRIDGE, a strong temporary bridge built to a design devised in 1941 for military use by British engineer **Sir Donald Coleman Bailey** (1901–). The design, a variant of which, resting on plywood floats called "pontoons", is used for crossing broad rivers, has proved of lasting value in peacetime emergencies.

BAILLY, Jean Sylvain (1736–1793), French astronomer and politician. After studying the satellites of Jupiter and writing a five-volume history of astronomy (1775–87), he turned to politics, becoming mayor of Paris 1789–91; he was executed in the Terror.

BAILY'S BEADS, named for Francis Baily (1774–1844), the apparent fragmentation of the thin crescent of the sun just before totality in a solar ECLIPSE, caused by sunlight shining through mountains at the edge of the lunar disk.

BAINBRIDGE, city in SW Ga., seat of Decatur Co. It is a barge terminal on the Flint R and a rural trading center. Pop 10 887.

BAINBRIDGE, William (1774–1833), US naval officer. He commanded the *Philadelphia* in the BARBARY WARS and was captured, with his crew, at Tripoli (1803). In the War of 1812 his ship, the *Constitution*, took the British frigate *Java*.

BAIRAM (Turkish: festival), two Islamic festivals. The Lesser Bairam (after RAMADAN) involves visiting friends and gift-giving. At the Sacrifice Bairam (near the year's end) an animal is sacrificed and eaten or given to the poor.

BAIRD, John Logie (1888–1946), Scottish inventor who, by first transmitting moving pictorial images (1925), inaugurated the TELEVISION era. Although the Baird system was tested when the British public television service began in 1936, it was dropped in favor of a rival which used electronic rather than mechanical scanning.

BAJA CALIFORNIA (Lower California), peninsula in NW Mexico W of the Gulf of California. A dry mountainous area, it extends for 760mi and is 25–150mi wide. To the N the state of Baja California forms the boundary with the US, while in the S is the territory of Baja California Sur. The main border cities, Mexicali and Tijuana, benefit from nearby US markets, but the region is generally undeveloped with agriculture limited by poor water supply. The peninsula is of great archaeological interest, settlement there probably dating back to around 21000 BC. The Spanish landed here in 1533.

BAJAZET. See BAYAZID.

BAJER, Fredrik (1837–1922), Danish politician and campaigner for world peace and women's emancipation. He helped found the International Peace Bureau at Bern (1891) and in 1908 was joint winner of the Nobel Peace Prize.

BAKELITE, synthetic RESIN discovered by Leo BAEKELAND, made by chemical reaction of FORMALDEHYDE and PHENOL. It is a thermosetting PLASTIC (see also POLYMERS). A hard, strong material, it is used as an electrical insulator, an adhesive and a paint binder.

BAKER, George Pierce (1866–1935), influential US teacher of dramatic composition. He was professor at Harvard (1905–24), and at Yale (1925–33), where he founded the experimental Yale drama school. His students included Eugene O'NEILL.

BAKER, Josephine (1906–1975), US-born, naturalized-French singer and dancer of international fame. Film and stage artist, philanthropist and social campaigner, Miss Baker, a Negro, won a special place in the hearts of the French people.

BAKER, Newton Diehl (1871–1937), US lawyer and politician, secretary of war (1916–21). He advocated US membership of the LEAGUE OF NATIONS.

BAKER, Ray Stannard (1870–1946), US journalist and author, awarded a Pulitzer prize for his *Woodrow Wilson—Life and Letters* (1927–39). At the request of President Wilson, Baker led the American Press Bureau at the Paris Peace Conference (1919). He also wrote homely philosophical essays under the pseudonym David Grayson.

BAKER, Sir Samuel White (1821–1893), English explorer who discovered the sources of the Nile (1861–64), an achievement shared by John Hanning SPEKE. Baker explored and named Lake Albert.

BAKER ISLAND, tiny, uninhabited US atoll in the central Pacific Ocean, E of the Gilbert Islands. It was claimed as US territory in 1936.

BAKERSFIELD, city in S central Cal., seat of Kern Co. It is an oil-producing and refining center and manufactures electrical goods. Pop 69 515.

BAKER VS. CARR. See APPORTIONMENT; LEGISLATIVE.

BAKEWELL, Robert (1725–1795), English agriculturalist who pioneered the selective BREEDING of sheep and cattle for meat and introduced the technique of repeated INBREEDING.

BAKING. See BREAD.

BAKING POWDER, white YEAST substitute which causes dough to rise by giving off carbon dioxide bubbles when moistened. It is composed of SODIUM bicarbonate; an acid (usually TARTARIC ACID or ALUM) which reacts with sodium bicarbonate in water to release carbon dioxide; and an inert substance such as starch to retard the reaction while the powder is dry.

BAKING SODA, or sodium bicarbonate. See SODIUM.

BAKST, Léon Nikolaevich (Lev Samuilovich Rosenberg; 1866–1924), Russian painter and theater designer. He designed sets and costumes for DIAGHILEV's ballets. Bakst later settled in Paris.

BAKU, capital of the SSR of Azerbaidzhan, on the Caspian Sea's west coast. It is an important port and railhead and one of Russia's major oil-refining centers. There are also electrical, shipbuilding, textile and other industries. Pop 1 261 000.

BAKUNIN, Mikhail Alexandrovich (1814–1876), Russian revolutionary, a founder of political ANARCHISM. He was involved in uprisings in Paris (1848) and Dresden (1849). Exiled to Siberia (1857), he escaped to England (1861). Bakunin founded anarchist groups in W Europe and joined the First INTERNATIONAL, but clashed bitterly with MARX and was expelled from the movement with his followers.

BALAAM, Old Testament non-Israelite prophet. Balak, king of Moab, asked him to curse the Israelites, but at Jehovah's command he blessed them instead.

BALAKIREV, Mili Alekseyevich (1837–1910), Russian nationalist composer, leader of "The Five." His works include two symphonies; the symphonic poem *Tamara* (1867–82); piano pieces, notably a sonata and *Islamey* (1869), and many songs.

BALAKLAVA, seaport village in the Crimean region, SW USSR, and site of a CRIMEAN WAR battle (Oct. 25, 1854), commemorated by Tennyson's *The Charge of the Light Brigade* (1854).

BALALAIKA, plucked, usually three-stringed instrument of ancient Slavic origin used in Russian and E European folk music. It has a triangular body and long fretted neck. Its six sizes may be combined in ensemble playing.

BALANCE, instrument used for measuring the WEIGHT of an object, typically by comparison with objects of known weight. The equal-arm balance, known to ancient Egyptians and Mesopotamians, consists of two identical pans hung from either end of a centrally suspended beam. When objects of equal weight are placed in each pan, the beam swings level because the MOMENTS of the gravitational FORCES acting on each object and pan about the central pivot or fulcrum are equal in magnitude and opposite in sense. Other types of beam balance involve fixed weights sliding along or hung below unequal beam arms, but the principle of the balancing of equal and opposite gravitational moments remains the same. The relatively inaccurate spring balance utilizes HOOKE's law to determine the weight of the specimen from the extension it produces in a coiled spring, and the much finer TORSION balance utilizes the resistance of a wire to being twisted. Modern chemical microbalances can measure weights as small as 1μg.

BALANCE OF NATURE, late 19th-and early 20th-century concept of Nature existing in an EQUILIBRIUM maintained by interdependencies between different animals and plants. In fact, this balance is unstable, since many factors (e.g., climate, POLLUTION) may cause dynamic change in large or small natural populations. (See also ECOLOGY.)

BALANCE OF PAYMENTS, the balance between what a country pays out abroad and what it receives. Factors involved are trade, invisible earnings (as from insurance and banking) and the movement of capital between countries. A country receiving more than it pays out has a balance of payment surplus; a country paying out more than it receives has a balance of payment deficit. A persistent deficit may call for DEVALUATION.

BALANCE OF POWER, situation in which a nation or group of nations match the power of another nation or group of nations. After WWII the concept became global with the confrontation of two superpowers, the US and USSR, and their supporters. But this pattern has been affected by national changes in economic or military power, for instance in China.

BALANCHINE, George (real name: Georgy Melitonovich Balanchivadze; 1904–), Russian-born choreographer, founder of an American ballet style. He worked for DIAGHILEV, and in 1934, with Lincoln Kerstein, founded the School of American Ballet. He was artistic director of the Ballet Society, which in 1948 became the New York City Ballet.

The bald eagle at Grant's Tomb in New York City.

BALATON, Lake, largest lake (232sq mi) in central Europe, in W Hungary SW of Budapest. About 48mi long, 9mi wide, and up to 35ft deep, it is frozen in winter, but its shores have many summer resorts.

BALBO, Italo (1896–1940), Italian aviator, Fascist leader and first air minister (1929–33), who built up Italian air power. Distrusted by Mussolini, he was made governor of Libya, dying there when Italian troops shot down his plane, allegedly in error.

BALBOA, Vasco Núñez de (c1475–1519), Spanish conquistador who discovered the Pacific Ocean. In 1510 he cofounded and became leader of the first lasting European settlement on the American mainland, Antigua in Darién (Panama). Encouraged by Indian tales of a wealthy kingdom on "the other sea," in 1513 Balboa led an expedition across the isthmus, saw the Pacific, and claimed it and all its coasts for Spain. Pedrarias DÁVILA succeeded Balboa in Darién and jealously had him executed on a false charge of treason.

BALCH, Emily Greene (1867–1961), US sociologist, economist and humanitarian, joint winner of the 1946 Nobel Peace Prize. Secretary of the Women's International League for Peace and Freedom 1919–22 and 1934–35, she was its honorary president from 1936.

BALCHEN, Bernt (1899–), Norwegian-born US aviator, Richard E. BYRD's pilot in the first plane to fly over the South Pole (1929). Earlier he flew with Roald AMUNDSEN in the Arctic.

BALCH SPRINGS, town in NE Tex., an E suburb of Dallas. It was incorporated in 1953. Pop 10 464.

BALD CYPRESS, or swamp cypress, *Taxodium distichum*, long-lived deciduous trees growing to 36m (120ft), native to the southern US and used as ornamentals. The roots are buttressed and near water produce woody humps called "cypress knees."

BALD EAGLE, *Haliaetus leucocephalus*, only North American native EAGLE, the national bird of the US since 1782. About 1m (3.2ft) long with a wingspan around 2m (6.6ft), it is black, with white feathers on neck, tail and head giving it a bald appearance. It preys on fish and is protected in all states. Family: Accipitridae.

BALDER (or Baldur), Norse god of light, called "the beautiful," son of FRIGG and ODIN. Frigg made all earthly things promise not to harm Balder but omitted mistletoe. LOKI, the jealous fire god, tricked the blind god Hödr into throwing a stick of mistletoe at Balder and so killed him.

BALDNESS, or **alopecia,** loss of hair, usually from the scalp, due to disease of hair FOLLICLES. **Male-pattern baldness** is an inherited tendency, often starting in the twenties. **Alopecia areata** is a disease of unknown cause producing patchy baldness, though it may be total. Prolonged FEVER, LUPUS erythematosus and RINGWORM may lead to temporary baldness, as may certain drugs and poisons.

BALDUNG GRIEN, Hans (c1484–1545), German painter and engraver. He was at first influenced by DÜRER. His masterpiece is the Freiburg cathedral altarpiece containing the *Coronation of the Virgin* (1516). His morbid allegorical paintings include a dramatic "Death and the Maiden" series.

BALDWIN, unincorporated community in SE N.Y. on Long Island's Baldwin Bay. A resort, with fisheries and light manufacturing. Pop 34 525.

BALDWIN, name of the first and last Latin emperors of Constantinople. **Baldwin I** (1172–1205) reigned 1204–05. A leader in the Fourth Crusade, he instituted a feudal form of government. He was killed by Bulgarian invaders. **Baldwin II** (1217–1273) reigned 1228–61. A poor and largely powerless ruler, he was deposed by Michael VIII Palaeologus.

BALDWIN, name of five crusader kings of Jerusalem. **Baldwin I** (1058–1118) reigned 1100–18. He founded the kingdom, captured Acre, Beirut and Sidon and encouraged Christian immigration. **Baldwin II** (d. 1131) reigned 1118–31. He defined Church rights and regulated the nobility. **Baldwin III** (1132–1162) reigned 1143–62, taking part in the Second Crusade. **Baldwin IV** (1161–1185) reigned 1174–85. Despite his leprosy, he ably defended the kingdom against SALADIN. **Baldwin V** (1177–1186) was nominal ruler 1185–86.

BALDWIN, James (1924–), black US novelist, essayist and playwright, dealing with racial themes. *Go Tell It On The Mountain* (1953) reflects his Harlem adolescence; *Another Country* (1962) deals with sexual and racial identity. His nonfiction includes *The Fire, Next Time* (1963), on racial oppression.

BALDWIN, Matthias William (1795–1866), US industrialist who built the locomotive *Old Ironsides* for the Philadelphia and Germantown Railway in 1832 and went on to found the Baldwin Locomotive Works. His generous support of abolitionism later led to a Southern boycott of his locomotives.

BALDWIN, Robert (1804–1858), Canadian statesman, leader, with Louis LAFONTAINE, of the first responsible Canadian administration: the "Great Ministry" (1848–51). He later worked for improved relations between English and French Canadians.

BALDWIN, Stanley, Earl Baldwin of Bewdley (1867–1947) British Conservative statesman, prime minister 1923–24, 1924–29, 1935–37. He maintained stable government, but provoked labor hostility (before and after the General Strike of 1926) and failed to curb unemployment or to rearm against Nazi Germany. He handled the crisis of EDWARD VIII's abdication. He became Earl Baldwin of Bewdley on his retirement.

BALDWIN PARK, city in S Cal., in San Gabriel Valley. It was incorporated in 1956. Pop 47 285.

BALEARIC ISLANDS, group of Mediterranean islands off E Spain, under Spanish rule since 1349. The largest are Majorca, Minorca and Ibiza. Products include grapes, olives and citrus fruit. Tourism is important.

BALEEN, material found as fibrous plates hanging in rows from the roof of the mouth in whalebone WHALES and often known as whalebone. Its function is to strain PLANKTON, on which these whales feed, from the water. Strong and elastic, it was used for many purposes before the advent of PLASTIC and spring STEEL.

BALEWA, Sir Abubakar Tafawa (1912–1966), first prime minister of Nigeria (1957–66), murdered in a military coup. He founded and led a major political party, the Northern People's Congress.

BALFOUR, Arthur James Balfour, 1st Earl of (1848–1930), English statesman best known for the BALFOUR DECLARATION. He was an influential Conservative member of parliament 1874–1911; prime minister 1902–05; and foreign secretary 1916–19.

BALFOUR DECLARATION, statement of British policy issued in 1917 by Foreign Secretary Arthur BALFOUR. It guaranteed a Jewish national home in Palestine without prejudice to the rights of non-Jews there, but did not mention a separate Jewish state. In 1922 the League of Nations approved a British mandate in Palestine based on the Balfour Declaration. (See also PALESTINE; WEIZMANN, CHAIM; ZIONISM.)

BALI, volcanic island (2171sq mi) of the Lesser Sunda group, Indonesia, E of Java. Freed from Japanese occupation after WWII, it became an Indonesian province in 1950. Rice is the main crop. The largely Hindu Balinese are famous for dancing, GAMELAN music and decorative arts.

BALINESE CAT, recently developed breed of Siamese conformation but with long fur. The coat should be fine and silky with the darker points of the Siamese (seal, blue, chocolate or lilac). There must be no tendency to Persian body or head shape.

BALIOL, John de (1249–1315), Anglo-Norman king of Scotland 1292–96. Edward I of England granted him the kingdom in 1292 against the claim of Robert the Bruce. When Scottish nobles rejected English domination, Edward invaded Scotland, imprisoned Baliol (1296–99), then exiled him to Normandy.

BALKAN PENINSULA, SE Europe S of the Danube and Sava rivers and abutting the Adriatic, Ionian, Mediterranean, Aegean and Black seas. It comprises Bulgaria, Albania, Greece, European Turkey and most of Yugoslavia. The region is mountainous and limited in natural resources. Its SLAVS, Turks' and Greeks live mainly in small communities, raising sheep, goats, vines and cereals. Little industry exists outside big cities like Belgrade, Athens and Istanbul.

The area was influenced by Greece; ruled by Rome (c148 BC-mid-5th century AD); then partly controlled by the Byzantine Empire. Invading Slavs and others founded ancient Bulgaria and Serbia, and crusaders seized the S early in the 13th century. But by 1500 the Ottoman Turks held almost all the Balkans. New nations emerged through 19th-century nationalist movements, which also sparked off the BALKAN WARS and WORLD WAR I. After WWII Albania, Bulgaria and Yugoslavia became communist; Turkey and Greece joined NATO.

BALKAN WARS, two wars in which the Ottoman Empire lost almost all its European territory. In the First Balkan War (1912–13) Serbia, Bulgaria, Greece and Montenegro conquered all Turkey's European possessions except Constantinople. But Bulgaria, Serbia and Greece disputed control in Macedonia. In the Second Balkan War (1913) Bulgaria attacked Serbia, but was itself attacked by Romania, Greece and Turkey. In the ensuing Treaty of Bucharest (Aug. 1913) Bulgaria lost territory to each of her enemies.

BALKHASH, Lake, shallow lake in the USSR in SE Kazakh republic. About 376mi long and 46mi wide; frozen Nov.–March. There are shipyards, shipping services, fisheries and a copper refinery.

BALL, George Wildman (1909–   ), US diplomat who influenced US foreign policy in the 1960s. He was undersecretary of state under Johnson and Kennedy, and for a brief period US ambassador to the UN.

BALLA, Giacomo (1871–1958), Italian painter, a leading exponent of FUTURISM. His works include attempts to show objects in motion and pioneer abstract paintings.

BALLAD, simple verse narrative, often meant to be sung, originally anonymous and orally transmitted. Many ballads comprise rhymed four-line stanzas each followed by a refrain. Traditionally, ballads celebrated folk heroes or related popular romances, and were developed by European minstrels of the Middle Ages. Romantic writers, such as Sir Walter SCOTT, WORDSWORTH and COLERIDGE adapted the form. The US has a rich tradition of ballads, from the anonymous *Frankie and Johnny* to the work of Bob Dylan.

BALLARAT, city in SE Australia, in S central Victoria. Founded in the 1851 gold rush, it is now a manufacturing center producing iron and steel and processed agricultural products. Pop 39 606.

BALLET, form of theatrical dance that tells a story or expresses a theme, mood or idea. It originated in Renaissance Italian court entertainments introduced into France in 1581 by Catherine de Médicis. Louis XIV in 1661 established the first ballet school, whose ballet master, Pierre Beauchamp, originated the five basic foot positions of ballet.

Early 18th-century ballet was part of opera, and dancers were hampered by heavy costumes; but by the mid-18th century pantomime ballet, in which all meaning was conveyed by movement, had evolved. The French choreographer Jean-Georges Noverre made ballet an independent art uniting plot, music, decor and movement. The 19th century emphasized lightness and grace: dancing *sur les pointes* (on the tips of the toes) and the short tutu appeared. Russia became the world ballet center with the appointment of Marius PETIPA to the Imperial Ballet in 1862. He inspired the originals of *Swan Lake*, *The Nutcracker Suite* and *The Sleeping Beauty*.

Early in the 1900s, in Paris, the Russian Ballet of Sergei DIAGHILEV, with NIJINSKY, PAVLOVA, MASSINE and FOKINE, revitalized dance drama. In 1933 Ninette de Valois formed England's first permanent company, now the Royal Ballet, noted for ASHTON's choreography. BALANCHINE established American ballet in the 1930s, his New York City Ballet fusing classical tradition with modern dance as developed by Isadora DUNCAN, Ruth ST. DENIS, Martha GRAHAM and Jerome ROBBINS. (See also CHOREOGRAPHY; DANCE.)

BALLINGER, Richard Achilles (1858–1922), US secretary of the interior 1909–11, accused by PINCHOT of abandoning Theodore Roosevelt's land conservation policy and illegally selling Alaskan coal deposits. Though cleared by investigation, Ballinger resigned. The affair split the Republican Party.

BALLISTIC MISSILE. See MISSILE.

BALLISTICS, the science concerned with the behavior of projectiles, traditionally divided into three parts. **Interior ballistics** is concerned with the progress of the projectile before it is released from the launching device. In the case of a gun this involves determining the propellant charge, barrel design and firing mechanism needed to give the desired muzzle velocity and stabilizing spin to the projectile. **External ballistics** is concerned with the free flight of the projectile. At the beginning of the 17th century GALILEO determined that the trajectory (flight path) of a projectile should be parabolic (see CONIC SECTIONS), as indeed it would be if the effects of air resistance, the rotation and curvature of the earth, the variation of air density and gravity with height, and the rotational INERTIA of the projectile could be ignored. The shockwaves accompanying projectiles moving faster than the speed of sound (see SUPERSONICS) are also the concern of this branch.

Terminal or **penetration ballistics** deals with the behavior of projectiles on impacting at the end of their trajectory. The velocity-to-mass ratio of the impact particle is an important factor and results are of equal interest to the designers of AMMUNITION and of ARMORPLATE. A relatively recent development in the science is **forensic ballistics**, which now plays an important role in the investigation of gun crimes.

BALLOON, a nonpowered, nonrigid lighter-than-air craft comprising a bulbous envelope containing the lifting medium and a payload-carrying basket or "gondola" suspended below. Balloons may be captive (secured to the ground by a cable, as in the barrage balloons used during WWII to protect key installations and cities from low-level air bombing) or free-flying (blown along and steered at the mercy of the WIND). Lift may be provided either by GAS (usually HYDROGEN or noninflammable HELIUM) or by heating the air in the envelope. A balloon rises or descends through the air until it reaches a level at which it is in EQUILIBRIUM in accordance with ARCHIMEDES' principle. In this situation the total WEIGHT of the balloon and payload is equal to that of the volume of air which it is displacing.

If the pilot of a gas balloon wishes to ascend, he throws ballast (usually sand) over the side, thus reducing the overall DENSITY of the craft; to descend he releases some of the lifting gas through a small valve in the envelope. The ALTITUDE of a hot-air balloon is controlled using the PROPANE burner which heats the air; increased heat causes the craft to rise; turning off the burner gives a period of level flight followed by a slow descent as the trapped air cools.

The MONTGOLFIER brothers' hot-air balloon became the first manned aircraft in 1783, and in the same year the first gas balloon was flown by Jacques CHARLES. In 1785 Jean BLANCHARD piloted a balloon across the English Channel. In due time the powered balloon, or AIRSHIP, was developed, though free balloons have remained popular for sporting, military and scientific purposes. The upper atmosphere is explored using unmanned gas balloons, and RADIOSONDE balloons are in regular meteorological use. In 1931 Auguste PICCARD pioneered high-altitude manned flights. Many modern sporting balloons are built on the hot-air principle.

A Bali-Hindu temple, where many festivals are celebrated with colorful dances in thanksgiving for a good rice-harvest and other benefits. Such temples are the focal point of this distinctively Balinese religion—basically Hindu but with many ancient native beliefs—which plays a major role in family and village life.

BALLOT. See VOTING.

BALLOU, Hosea (1771–1852), US clergyman, a

Diagram of a modern gas balloon. 1. landing-run line; 2. valve cord; 3. rip cord; 4. equator; 5. rip panel; 6. safety device; 7. valve; 8 & 9. net; 10. rain deflector; 11. appendix; 12. load ring; 13. basket ropes; 14. anchor cable.

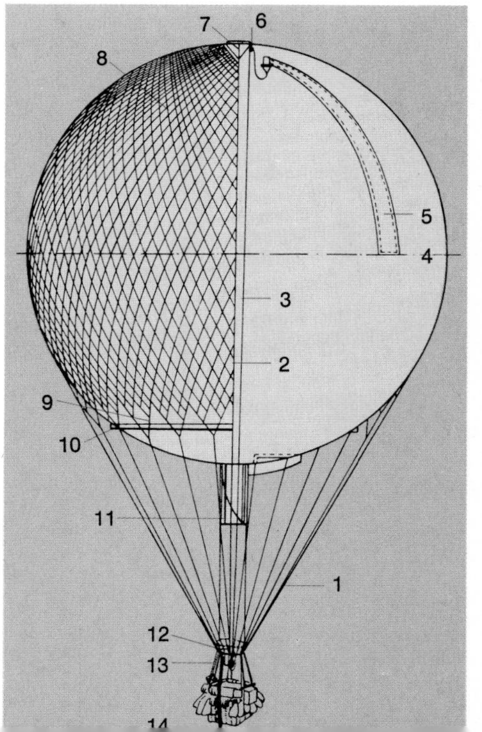

leading exponent of UNIVERSALISM. Ballou separated Universalist doctrine from Calvinist influence and introduced aspects of UNITARIANISM. He was pastor of the Second Universalist Church in Boston 1817–52, and founder-editor of *The Universalist Magazine* 1819–28.

BALLPOINT PEN, pen designed to minimize ink leakage. At one end of a narrow, cylindrical ink reservoir a freely-rotating metal ball is held in a socket. The viscous (see VISCOSITY) ink is drawn through internal ducts in the socket by capillary action (see CAPILLARITY). Ballpoint pens came into general use in the late 1930s.

BALLROOM DANCING. See DANCE.

BALLWIN, city in E Mo., a residential suburb of St. Louis. It was founded in 1837. Pop 10656.

BALM, herb (*Melissa officinalis*) with lemon-scented leaves used for seasoning, in liqueurs and for medical purposes. Native to Europe, but cultivated in North America. Flowers are white and yellow, and tubular.

BALMONT, Konstantin Dmitriyevich (1867–1943), Russian symbolist poet and translator. He supported the revolutionary movements, and his early verse extolled liberty. After 1918 he lived in Paris.

BALMORAL CASTLE, private residence of the British monarch, near Braemar, in Grampian, Scotland. It was built 1853–56 by Prince ALBERT, who bequeathed it to Queen VICTORIA.

BALSA, West Indian and South American tree (*Ochroma lagopus*) producing a very light wood twice as buoyant as cork. Balsa is used for rafts, life preservers, small boats, gliders and model airplanes.

BALSAM, term often used for any aromatic substance from trees or shrubs but strictly confined to resins and oleoresins (such as Peru balsam used in perfume or Tolu balsam used in cough medicines) containing benzoic or cinnamic acid. Also, a garden herb (*Impatiens balsamina*) with pale green lanceolate leaves and pink flowers, although some varieties have white, crimson and purple flowers.

BALSAM FIR, evergreen tree (*Abies balsamea*) that grows to 25m (82ft), and is native to Canada and the northeastern US. They are grown for Christmas trees and are the source of Canada balsam, a cement used for glass in optical instruments.

BALTIC LANGUAGES, group of INDO-EUROPEAN LANGUAGES, closely related to the Slavonic languages, spoken in the area SE of the Baltic Sea. They include Lithuanian, Lettish and the now extinct Old Prussian.

BALTIC SEA, an arm of the Atlantic Ocean, bounded by Sweden, Finland, the USSR, Poland, Germany and Denmark. It is linked to the North Sea by the SKAGERRAK, KATTEGAT and ØRESUND. Its 163000sq mi of weakly saline water freeze over in winter. There is a limited fishing industry based on herring, cod and salmon. Baltic trade flourished in the 14th century through the HANSEATIC LEAGUE, but declined in competition with Atlantic ports. Copenhagen. Stockholm, Helsinki, Leningrad and Kiev are the main ports. (See also BOTHNIA, GULF OF; FINLAND, GULF OF.)

BALTIC STATES, the former Baltic coast republics of Estonia, Latvia and Lithuania. They became independent in 1918 but were annexed by the USSR in 1940.

BALTIMORE, largest city in Md., on the Patapsco R near Chesapeake Bay. It is the seventh-largest city in the US, one of the nation's busiest ports and an important road, rail and air transportation hub. Since WWI it has become a leading manufacturing center with metallurgical, electronic and food-processing industries. Baltimore is the educational center of Md., with Johns Hopkins U. and many other institutions. Established in 1729 and named for Lord Baltimore, the city grew as a grain-exporting port. It suffered economic disruption as a Civil War "border city," and was largely rebuilt after the great fire of 1904. Pop 905759.

BALTIMORE, David (1938–   ), US virologist who shared the 1975 Nobel Prize for Physiology or Medicine with R. DULBECCO and H. M. TEMIN in recognition of their work linking VIRUSES with the development of some cancerous tumors.

BALTIMORE, Lord. See CALVERT.

BALTIMORE ORIOLE, *Icterus galbula*, North American songbird of the family Icteridae (not Oriolidae, as are true ORIOLES). About 200mm (8in) long, it has a wingspan of about 300mm (12in). Males are black and bright orange; females and young are olive, yellow and brownish.

BALUCHISTAN, mountainous, largely barren area of W Asia comprising SE Iran and, as Baluchistan province, W Pakistan (capital: Quetta). The people are largely pastoral nomads and, increasingly, arable farmers, renowned for their handwoven carpets.

BALUCHITHERIUM, extinct genus of RHINOCEROS known from FOSSILS of the late OLIGOCENE and early MIOCENE found in Asia. Probably the world's largest land MAMMAL, it stood some 6m (20ft) at the shoulders.

BALZAC, Honoré de (1799–1850), French novelist noted for his acute social observation and sweeping vision. In the nearly 100 works forming *La Comédie Humaine*, he attempted to portray all levels of contemporary French society, their interdependence and the influence of the environment upon them. The most famous such novels include *Eugénie Grandet* (1833), *Le Père Goriot* (1834) and *La Cousine Bette* (1846). Balzac had a great capacity for hard work, but was also known for his debts and love affairs.

BAMAKO, capital and largest town of Mali, a trade and transportation center on the Niger R. It exports oil products, cement, livestock and nuts. Pop 201300.

BAMBERG, cathedral city in Bavaria, West Germany, on the Regnitz R. Sovereign bishopric 1007–1802, it is now a commercial and shipping center for machinery, textiles and beer. Pop 70581.

Baltimore's excellent harbor and location near Chesapeake Bay, with over 100 miles of waterfront, have made the city a leading port, handling over 40000000 tons of cargo a year.

Bananas growing in Jamaica. There are over 100 varieties in cultivation.

BAMBOO, woody grasses with hollow stems found in Asia, Africa, Australia and the southern US. Some species grow to 36m (120ft). In Asia the young shoots are a major foodstuff, while mature stems are used in building houses and furniture. Amorphous SILICA from stems is used as a catalyst in some chemical processes.

BAMIAN, valley in Afghanistan, WNW of Kabul. A former Buddhist center, it has hundreds of man-made caves and two massive carved Buddha figures—all from the 7th century AD.

BANANA, edible fruit of a large (9m—30ft) perennial stooling herb that reaches maturity within 15 months from planting. Cultivated clones evolved in SE Asia from two wild species, *Musa acuminata* and *M. balbisiana*, and spread across the Pacific, Africa and the New World. Main areas of commercial cultivation are in tropical and South America and the West Indies, a major part of the crop being exported to the US and Europe; but bananas are of great importance locally in many tropical diets.

BANARAS. See VARANASI.

BANCROFT, George (1800–1891), US historian and statesman whose 10-volume *History of the United States* (1834–74) was the first attempt fully to cover US history. As secretary of the navy (1845–46), he helped develop the US Naval Academy, Annapolis. His *History* became the standard work, though it was later criticized for its strong nationalistic bias.

BANCROFT, Hubert Howe (1832–1918), US historian and publisher. The 39-volume history of western North America, the *West American Historical Series*, which he edited and partly wrote, remains a useful source for the history of the West.

BAND, a musical ensemble generally of wind and percussion instruments, though sometimes devoted to a particular type of instrument. Bands accompany military and civil parades and other ceremonies, and play dance music. Famous US bands have included those founded by John Philip SOUSA and Glen MILLER.

BANDA, Hastings Kamuzu (1906–   ), African nationalist leader, first prime minister (1964–66) and president of Malawi (from 1966). As leader of the Nyasaland nationalists, and head of the Malawi Congress Party from 1960, he sought dissolution of the Federation of Rhodesia and Nyasaland. He later had a moderating influence on African affairs.

BANDAGE, piece of material used to bind up wounds, hold dressings in place, or support injured limbs (see FRACTURES). Variously shaped pieces of sterilized crepe, muslin, gauze, cotton, linen or elastic fabric are used. (See also FIRST AID.)

BANDA ISLANDS, volcanic islands in E Indonesia, in the S Moluccas. Banda, Bandanaira and Gunung Api are the largest. Produce: spices, fruit and coconuts.

BANDARANAIKE, Sirimavo Ratwatte Dias (1916–   ), prime minister of Sri Lanka and the world's first woman premier. After the assassination of her husband, Prime Minister Solomon Bandaranaike,

in 1959, she led his Sri Lanka Freedom Party to victory in 1960, continuing his pro-Buddhist and pro-Sinhalese policies. She lost office in 1965 but was returned in 1970 with a landslide victory for her left-oriented coalition.

BANDA SEA, sea in the E Malay archipelago, part of the Pacific Ocean. It covers about 285 000sq mi and lies between the Sulawesi, Ceram and Timor islands.

BANDED ANTEATER. See NUMBAT.

BANDELIER NATIONAL MONUMENT, area of 46sq mi in N central N.M. near Santa Fe, noted for its many remains of CLIFF DWELLER homes. It was established in 1916 and named for archaeologist Adolph Bandelier.

BANDELLO, Matteo (1485–1561), Italian writer, diplomat and monk. His 214 stories or *novelle* greatly influenced European literature, and provided the bases of plots used by Shakespeare (*Romeo and Juliet*) and John WEBSTER (*The Duchess of Malfi*).

BANDICOOTS, several genera of the family Peramelidae. They are roughly rabbit-sized MARSUPIALS, probably most closely related to the DASYURES. They have tapering snouts, varying in length from species to species. There are considerable reproductive differences from other marsupials: though GESTATION is for only 12 days, the newborn young are comparatively large; while in the UTERUS, the EMBRYOS are nourished by a complex PLACENTA quite unlike those of other marsupials. Their FOSSIL history is problematic, so that their relationship to other marsupials is not fully understood.

BANDIERA, Attilo (1810–1844) and **Emilio** (1819–1844), Italian patriots who rebelled against Austrian rule. While in the Austrian navy, they were influenced by MAZZINI and founded the secret society *Esperia* (1841). Betrayal of their plans to seize a warship and attack Messina forced them to flee to Corfu (1844). They raided Calabria, but were betrayed and executed.

BANDINELLI, Baccio (c1493–1560), Italian sculptor, a leading artist at Cosimo I de' Medici's court in Florence. His famous marble statue of Hercules and Cacus (1534) stands in the Piazza della Signoria, Florence.

BANDJARMASIN, capital of South Kalimantan province, Indonesia, in a marshy plain on the S coast of Borneo. Its harbor handles rubber, timber and pepper exports. Pop 281 000.

BANDUNG, capital of West Java province, Indonesia, 75mi SE of Djakarta. It is a cultural, educational, tourist, transportation and manufacturing (textiles and machinery) center. Pop 1 202 000.

BANDUNG CONFERENCE, first major conference on world affairs by (29) independent African and Asian nations, held in Bandung, April 1955. It condemned colonialism and urged world peace and economic and cultural cooperation.

BANDWIDTH, in telecommunications, the difference (expressed in HERTZ) between the upper and lower limits of the band range of FREQUENCIES either needed or available to transmit a given signal, or which can be adequately passed by a component device.

BANEBERRY, popular name for several species of the genus *Acteae*, family Ranunculaceae. Herbaceous plants with poisonous red (*A. rubra*) white (*A. alba*) or black (*A. spicata*) berries, their berries and rootstocks act as emetics and cathartics.

BANERJEA, Sir Surendranath (1848–1925). Indian nationalist leader who opposed GANDHI's methods of civil disobedience, preferring constitutional means of achieving self-government.

BANFF, resort in Alberta, Canada, in the Bow R Valley of the Rocky Mts. It is the center for Banff National Park. Pop 3 530.

BANFF NATIONAL PARK, Canada's first national park, founded 1885. Situated in SW Alberta, it covers 2 564sq mi of spectacular mountain scenery, and is also noted for sulfur springs and rich wildlife.

BANGALORE, capital of Karnataka State, S India. A major industrial, transportation and educational center with a university and research laboratories. Products include electrical equipment, chemicals and textiles. Pop 1 648 000.

BANGKOK, capital of Thailand, on the Chao

Within Bangkok's palace walls, Wat Phra Keo or the Chapel of the Emerald Buddha is the city's most interesting temple. Built in 1785 it was the king's place of worship and is more elaborate than any other Thai temple. Its central feature is a huge image of the Buddha made of jasper. The great king Mongkut claimed that it was made at least 500 years ago and was moved from Chiengrai to Lampang, to Lau, to Vien Chan, to Dhanapuri and finally to Bangkok in 1784. Images of the Buddha which also represent two kings of the present dynasty flank the main image which is covered in golden ornaments and jewels.

Phraya R near the Gulf of Siam. It is Thailand's chief port, manufacturing center and university city, with many picturesque Buddhist temples. Also SEATO headquarters and regional headquarters for the World Health Organization and UNESCO. Pop 2 840 000.

BANGLADESH (Bengal Nation), republic in the NE of the Indian subcontinent, on the Bay of Bengal; formerly East PAKISTAN. It is a low-lying tropical land centered on the alluvial Ganges-Brahmaputra Delta, and subject to heavy rains, flooding and severe cyclones. Overpopulation accentuates periodic famines and epidemics among the mainly Muslim Bengalis. Bangladesh produces 80% of the world's jute, also rice, wheat, sugarcane, tea, fish and lumber.

As East Pakistan (Pakistan's eastern province), the area sought greater independence under Sheikh Mujibur RAHMAN, whose Awami League won a majority in the 1970 Pakistan election. West Pakistan refused autonomy and troops crushed large-scale opposition in the ensuing civil war (March–Dec. 1971). But guerrilla fighting continued, Bengalis exiled in India proclaimed a Bengali republic, and Indian invasion forces overran the West Pakistani forces. A Bangladesh government was established in Dacca in Dec. 1971, and Mujibur Rahman became prime minister in Jan. 1972. But the war had left the country with severe economic and political problems, and in 1975 Mujibur Rahman established a presidential, one-party regime. In Aug. 1975 he and his family were assassinated in a coup; two military counter-coups and martial law followed in Nov. 1975 with promises of eventual elections.

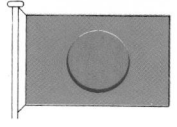

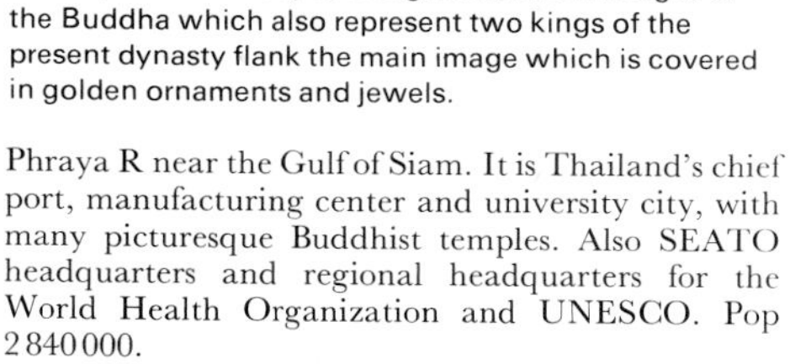

Official Name: Bangladesh
Capital: Dacca
Area: 5 126sq mi
Population: 75 000 000
Languages: Bengali, Bihari, Hindi
Religions: Muslim; Hindu
Monetary Unit(s): 1 Taka = 100 paisa

BANG'S DISEASE. See BRUCELLOSIS.

BANGUI, largest city, capital and chief port of the Central African Republic, on the Ubangi R. Pop 302 000.

BANJO, stringed musical instrument with a circular skin soundboard and a long fretted neck. Its 4–9 strings are played by plucking. The banjo originated among Negro slaves in North America, and may have derived from W African instruments. It became popular in 19th-century minstrel shows and early jazz bands and for some folk music.

BANJUL (formerly Bathurst), capital and largest city of Gambia; a port on Africa's Atlantic coast. The country's commercial and transportation center, it was founded by the British in 1816. Pop 36 570.

BANKHEAD, Tallulah Brockman (1903–1968), US actress, famous for her colorful performances in plays such as *The Little Foxes* (1939) and *The Skin of Our Teeth* (1942). Among her films was *Lifeboat* (1943).

BANKHEAD, William Brockman (1874–1940), US politician, speaker of the House of Representatives 1936–40. A Democratic Congressman for Ala. from 1917, he was the father of actress Tallulah Bankhead. His brother, **John Hollis Bankhead** (1872–1946), was a Democratic senator from Ala. from 1931.

BANK HOLIDAY, period when all banks are legally closed. In particular, four days in March 1933 when President F. D. Roosevelt closed all banks to stem panicky withdrawals by depositors. Britain's regular bank holidays are public holidays.

BANKING, the business dealing with money and credit transactions. It can be traced back beyond 2500 BC, but modern banking originated in medieval Italy (taking its name from *banca*, the money-lender's bench). Banking grew among traders needing to exchange one country's coins for those of another, to buy and sell without handling bulky gold or silver, and to borrow cash to bridge the period between buying goods and selling them. Thus major trading cities such as Venice, Antwerp, Hamburg and London also became great banking centers.

Banking in the US. The first BANK OF THE UNITED STATES (1791–1811) was promoted by Alexander HAMILTON to finance industrial and commercial expansion. But politicians prejudiced against national banks closed the bank and its successor (1816–36). For 30 years, before the Civil War, WILDCAT BANKS incorporated in western border states profited from selling largely worthless notes in east coast cities. The 1863 National Bank Act forced banks to pledge US government bonds with the treasury to back their note issues, but bank insolvencies continued in times of depression.

In 1913 the FEDERAL RESERVE SYSTEM was set up to strengthen the US banking system. Bank failures in 1933 led to a BANK HOLIDAY (after which only solvent banks were allowed to reopen) and to the setting up of the FEDERAL DEPOSIT INSURANCE CORPORATION. Today, some states do not allow banks to maintain branches. There are restrictions, too, on the number and type of subsidiary companies a bank may own.

Banking services. Banks offer four main services: safe storage, interest payments on deposits, money transfer and loans. Deposits are now in checks and banknotes rather than in gold and silver, therefore customers use individual safe-storage facilities mainly for valuables. Deposits are in effect loans to a bank, thus banks pay interest on cash deposits.

Money transfer involves the use of checks and credit cards to transfer cash from the customer's bank account to someone else's or to himself. Against receipt of securities, banks lend money to customers at specified rates of interest over specified periods. By offering special services they compete for customers, whose deposits provide the basis for the banks' profits.

Banks as creators of money. Banks "create"

A typical village of the Sotho (Basuto), a Bantu tribe living in Lesotho, an enclave in South Africa.

money by lending sums banked by depositors. For instance, a $5000 bank deposit may engender a $4000 bank loan, which raises the money supply from $5000 to $9000. (The $1000 not lent forms "liquid" assets which the bank keeps to cover depositors' claims for immediate repayments.) The money supply deeply affects a nation's economy, for money is the means of measuring the relative value of all commodities. (See also CHECK; CREDIT; ECONOMICS; MINT, UNITED STATES BUREAU OF THE; MONEY.)

BANK OF CANADA, government-owned central bank of Canada, in Ottawa, founded 1934. It issues all Canadian banknotes and controls the supply of money to all Canadian banks, thereby helping to keep the economy stable.

BANK OF ENGLAND, central bank of the British government, founded 1694, nationalized 1946. It acts as banker for the government and the country's commercial banks; advises the government on finance; influences the money supply; finances the government deficit; issues banknotes; and administers the foreign exchange reserve.

BANK OF THE UNITED STATES, name of two central banks set up in the early years of the US. In 1791 Alexander HAMILTON created the First Bank of the US, chartered by Congress for 20 years, with a central office in Philadelphia. It held government deposits and was able to extend some control over the issue of paper currency and the extension of credit. However, its constitutionality was questioned, and it was so strongly opposed by agrarian interests and by the state banks that its charter was not renewed.

The nation's chaotic financial system after the War of 1812 led Congress to charter the Second Bank of the US in 1816 for another 20-year period. However, opposition continued, especially in the West, and in 1832 President JACKSON refused to extend the charter. In the "Bank War" which followed, Nicholas BIDDLE, the bank's president, restricted national credit, and Jackson retaliated by withdrawing government deposits from the bank. The bank's charter was allowed to expire in 1836 without renewal. Only with the creation of the FEDERAL RESERVE SYSTEM in 1913 were the first real steps taken towards a central US banking system.

BANKRUPTCY, legal status of a person whom the courts have declared unable to pay his debts. Its purpose is to give the bankrupt a new start, and to secure a fair distribution of his remaining assets among creditors. Under the US Federal Bankruptcy Act, wages of the bankrupt's employees have priority in this distribution. The debtor is not relieved of alimony or taxes.

BANKS, Sir Joseph (1743–1820), British botanist and president of the ROYAL SOCIETY OF LONDON (1778–1820), the foremost British man of science of his time. He accompanied COOK as naturalist on his first expedition (1768–71) and was a key figure in the establishment of the Botanic Gardens at Kew, London.

BANKS ISLAND, island in the Arctic archipelago, Northwest Territories, Canada. The Amundsen Gulf separates it from the mainland. Its area of 26 400sq mi is mostly hilly terrain.

BANKS ISLANDS, five small volcanic islands in the S Pacific, NE of the New Hebrides; jointly administered by France and Great Britain. Pop 3 720.

BANNEKER, Benjamin (1731–1806), American mathematician and astronomer, notable as the first American Negro to gain distinction in science and the author of celebrated ALMANACS (1791–1802).

BANNING, city in SE Cal. A fruit-farming center, it also produces electronic components. Pop 12 034.

BANNISTER, Roger Gilbert (1929–), British athlete, first man to run a mile in under four minutes. On May 6, 1954, at Oxford, his time was 3 minutes 59.4 seconds.

BANNOCKBURN, battlefield named for a village in Stirlingshire, Scotland. Here, in 1314, Scottish forces under Robert BRUCE routed the numerically superior English army of King EDWARD II assuring the throne of Scotland for Bruce and securing Scottish independence until the 18th century.

BANNOCK INDIANS, tribe of hunters who lived in E Ida. and W Wyo. After they were forced onto reservations, conditions there drove them in 1878 to join the last Indian uprising in the Northwest. They were defeated by General O. O. HOWARD.

BANNS OF MARRIAGE, public announcements of an impending marriage, with the object that persons aware of any impediment to the marriage may make their objections known. In the US there is no legal requirement for banns: only the Roman Catholic Church requires them.

BANSHEE, in Irish legend, a supernatural spirit, usually attached to a particular family, whose mournful wails foretell a death in the family.

BANTAM, any miniature CHICKEN, bred mostly for ornament. They are usually about 25% the weight of their full-size counterparts.

BANTENG, wild ox (*Bos banteng* or *javanicus*, family BOVIDAE) of SE Asia, similar to, but rather smaller than, the GAUR, to which it is closely related. Distribution is wide but discontinuous. They usually live in herds of 10–30, but many bulls live solitarily except in the rutting season, which differs from place to place.

BANTING, Sir Frederick Grant (1891–1941), Canadian physiologist who, with C. H. BEST, first isolated the hormone INSULIN from the pancreases of dogs (1922). For this he shared the 1923 Nobel Prize for Physiology or Medicine with J. J. R. MACLEOD who had provided the experimental facilities.

BANTU, outmoded collective term for a group of tribes in central, E and S Africa possessing a common group of languages. The term may also be used in South Africa to denote black Africans as distinct from Afrikaners.

BANTUSTANS, or "Homelands," in South Africa, nine areas in which black Africans may have a large degree of economic and political independence to secure their own development. The largest is the Transkei, self-governing since 1963. In practice, Bantustans are often poverty-stricken areas due to the poor land and frequent lack of state aid, and many men have to leave their families to find work elsewhere. Provision for self-government in all the Bantustans was made in the Bantu Homelands Constitution Bill of 1971; around 46% of the black population now live on them, and they are coming to represent a significant political force.

BANYAN TREE, *Ficus bengalensis*, a tree sacred to Hindus in India. Many hanging aerial roots are produced from branches which take root in the soil and form new trunks. In time one tree may become a tangled mass of additional trunks that cover a wide area.

BAOBAB, *Adansonia digitata*, a tree native to tropical Africa characterized by a barrel-like trunk up to 9m (30ft) in diameter. It produces gourd-like edible woody fruit and the bark fibers are used to make rope and cloth. The trunks are sometimes excavated to form houses.

BAO DAI (1913–), Vietnamese emperor during the French colonial period. He was the last emperor of ANNAM (1932–45), until overthrown by the Viet Minh. He was later made head of state of a unified Vietnam (1949–55) created by the French in a final bid to retain Indochina, but was forced into exile.

BAPTISM, Christian SACRAMENT which constitutes an initiation into the Church. The ceremony involves the application of water by sprinkling, pouring or immersion according to the denomination. Baptism has its origins in pagan and Jewish ceremony, and was commanded by Christ (Matthew 28:19). (See also JOHN THE BAPTIST.)

BAPTISTERY, place in a church where the ceremony of BAPTISM is performed, or a separate building erected near the church for that purpose. Many of the Renaissance baptisteries were beautifully decorated buildings; Protestant baptisteries tend to be more simple.

BAPTISTS, members of the many independent branches of the Baptist Church, one of the most diverse of Protestant denominations. There are more than 31 000 000 Baptists in the world, most of whom live in America. In general, Baptist churches are lay churches having no elaborate priesthood, and are known for their evangelistic and revivalist traditions. The strongest unifying principle among all Baptist churches is the method of baptism by total immersion in water when a person who has reached the age of reason professes faith in Christ.

The history of the Baptists can be traced to religious dissension in Europe in the early 17th century, particularly in the Puritan movement. Baptist churches were established in the English colonies after the Restoration (1660), but it was only with America's 18th-century religious revival, the GREAT AWAKENING, that the Baptist tradition spread, notably in the Midwest and the South, where it is still most influential. The Baptists have always had a great interest in higher education and have founded many colleges and universities throughout the US.

BAR, a unit of pressure in the CGS system equal to 100kPa. The **millibar** (mbar or mb) — 100Pa — is commonly used in meteorology. The standard **atmosphere** is 1013.25mbar.

BAR, name for a professional association of lawyers, deriving from the rail that enclosed the judge in court. To be eligible to speak in court a lawyer had to be "called to the bar," hence the English term "barrister." The largest and most important association in the US is the AMERICAN BAR ASSOCIATION. Most states also have their own bar associations.

BARA, Theda (1890–1955), US film star, born Theodosia Goodman. The word "vamp" (short for vampire) was coined to describe the evil but enticing women she portrayed between 1915 and 1920.

BARABBAS, a murderer released by PILATE in place of Jesus. According to Luke 23:18–25, Pilate asked the mob to choose between the two. They chose Barabbas, and Pilate "washed his hands" of the matter.

BARABOO, city in S central Wis., seat of Sauk Co. It is the home of the Circus World Museum. Pop 7 931.

BARANOF ISLAND, island in SE Alaska, in the W Alexander Archipelago. The former Russian capital of Alaska, Sitka, is on the island.

BARANOV, Alexander (1746–1819), manager of the Russian-American Fur Company and once virtual governor of Alaska. Under him Russian influence in North America reached its height.

BÁRÁNY, Robert (1876–1936), Austrian-born physiologist who received the 1914 Nobel Prize for Physiology or Medicine for research on the functioning of the organs of the inner EAR. From 1916 he continued his research in Sweden.

BARATARIA BAY, small bay in SE La., W of the Mississipi Delta. Now a shrimping center, it was the headquarters of the pirates Jean and Pierre LAFITTE, who led a band of privateers and smugglers c1810–15.

BARBADOS, small island nation in the Caribbean; a parliamentary state, part of the British Commonwealth. Nearly 90% of the population is of African descent. Barbados has a warm climate with fertile soil, and sugarcane remains the main crop. Efforts are being made to diversify agriculture, however, and to establish light industry and encourage tourism. Barbados, claimed by the British in 1605, remained a colony for over 300 years. Independence was granted in 1966.

BARBADOS CHERRY, *Malphigia glabra*, a West Indian shrub which produces crimson flowers and deep-red fruit that are a rich source of VITAMIN C. The fruit is used in jams and preserves.

BARBARA, Saint, 4th-century Christian martyr, protectress against lightning and patroness of fireworks-makers, artillerymen and miners. According to legend her pagan father, enraged at her avowal of Christianity, beheaded her and was struck dead by lightning. She is no longer listed in the Church calendar.

BARBARIANS, term originally used by the Greeks to describe all non-Greek-speaking peoples. The Romans used it to refer to peoples living beyond the borders of Roman civilization, particularly those such as the GOTHS, HUNS and VANDALS, who invaded the declining Roman Empire in the 5th century AD. (See DARK AGES.)

BARBAROSSA, European name for Khair ed-Din (d. 1546), one of a family of Turkish Barbary pirates active in the W Mediterranean. He took Algiers (1518) and Tunis (1534) for the Turks, and commanded the Turkish fleet from 1533.

BARBAROSSA, Frederick. See FREDERICK I (Holy Roman Emperor).

BARBARY APE, small tailless MACAQUES of Algeria, Morocco and Gibraltar; the species *Macaca sylvana* of the Cercopithecidae family. Legend has it that the British will lose the Rock of Gibraltar should its small colony of Barbary apes depart.

BARBARY SHEEP. See AOUDAD.

BARBARY STATES, countries along the Mediterranean coast of N Africa, the region of present-day ALGERIA, TUNISIA, LIBYA and MOROCCO. Named for the Berber tribes who lived there, the Barbary states were known from the 16th to the 19th centuries as centers of piracy. The area was ruled earlier by Carthage, Rome and Byzantium, then conquered by the Arabs in the 8th century. After centuries of relative autonomy, the states were taken over, largely by France, in the 19th century.

BARBARY WARS, two wars waged by the US against the BARBARY STATES of N Africa. By the late 18th century brigandage by the Barbary states had become a highly organized and lucrative trade. The first Barbary War, or Tripolitan War, broke out in May 1801. For 15 years the US had been forced to pay tribute to protect its shipping. The war was sparked by new, exorbitant demands by the pasha of Tripoli. The US blockaded Tripoli, and subjected it to naval bombardment. But the war was not won until 1805, when Capt. William Eaton marched his forces 500mi across the desert from Alexandria to take Derna and threaten Tripoli itself. The second Barbary War was fought in 1815 with Algiers. Commodore Stephen DECATUR was despatched to suppress an upsurge of piracy. Forcing his way into the harbor of Algiers, he compelled the dey of Algiers to sign a treaty ending piracy and freeing all US captives. Decatur went on to exact similar treaties from Tunis and Tripoli.

BARBED WIRE, fencing material comprising a single or double strand of steel or aluminum WIRE with sharply-pointed wire "barbs" twisted round it at short intervals. The introduction of barbed-wire fencing in the American West (following the invention of an efficient manufacturing technique by Joseph E. Glidden in 1873) marked an important epoch in the development of US agriculture.

Official Name: Barbados
Capital: Bridgetown
Area: 166sq mi
Population: 241 296
Languages: English
Religions: Anglican, Methodist, Moravian, Roman Catholic
Monetary Unit(s): 1 East Caribbean dollar = 100 cents

BARBELS, the genus *Barbus* of freshwater fish (family Cyprinidae) rather like CARP. One of the commonest species is the European Barbel, *B. barbus* (or *vulgarus*), which feeds on small fishes or burrows with its snout for worms. The name comes from the four slender tactile (see TOUCH) organs, called barbels, which protrude around the mouth.

BARBER, Samuel (1910–   ), US composer. His works include two symphonies (1936; 1944), the ballet *Medea* (1946) and the operas *Vanessa* (1958) and *Antony and Cleopatra* (1966). Barber won the 1958 and 1963 Pulitzer music prizes.

BARBERINI, aristocratic Italian family prominent in the 16th and 17th centuries. The power and wealth of the family was established by Maffeo Barberini (1568–1644) who, as Pope URBAN VIII, used his position to enrich his brothers and nephews. The Barberini were generous patrons of the arts.

BARBERRY, evergreen ornamental shrubs of the genus *Berberis*. Flowers are yellowish, frequently hanging in clusters, producing red or yellow fruits. The fruits are used in preserves and the bark yields a yellow dye used in leather manufacture.

BARBERTON, city in NE Ohio, a suburb of Akron. It produces tires, chemicals and insulation materials. Pop 33 052.

BARBETS, brightly-colored, powerfully-built birds with, usually, relatively large, heavy beaks showing serrations along the cutting edges of the upper mandible, members of the Capitonidae family (order Piciformes). Found pan-tropically, they are closely related to the HONEYGUIDES.

BARBIROLLI, Sir John (1899–1970), English conductor, famous for his interpretations of SIBELIUS and other late classics. After conducting the New York Philharmonic Orchestra (1937–42), he began a lifelong association with the Hallé Orchestra in Manchester, and conducted the Houston Symphony Orchestra (1961–67).

BARBITURATES, a class of drugs acting on the central NERVOUS SYSTEM which may be SEDATIVES, anesthetics or anticonvulsants. They depress nerve cell activity, the degree of depression and thus clinical effect varying in different members of the class. Although widely used in the past for insomnia, their use is now discouraged in view of high rates of addiction and their danger in over-dosage; safer alternatives are now available. Short-acting barbiturates are useful in ANESTHESIA; phenobarbitone is used in treatment of CONVULSIONS, often in combination with other drugs.

BARBIZON SCHOOL, group of French painters of natural and rural subjects, active 1830–70, who frequented the village of Barbizon, near Paris. It included Théodore ROUSSEAU, Diaz de la Peña, COROT, MILLET, Dupré, Troyon, Daubigny and Jacque.

BARBUDA, coral island in the Leeward Islands, West Indies. It is a dependency of ANTIGUA, and its main product is sea-island cotton. Barbuda's only settlement is Codrington. Pop 1000.

BARBUSSE, Henri (1873–1935), French author best known for his bitter WWI novel, *Le Feu* (*Under Fire,* 1916). *Clarté* (*Light,* 1919), his next novel, expressed Barbusse's ideas for the achievement of world peace. It inspired a short-lived international movement.

BARCAROLE, musical composition in the style of the songs of Venetian *barcaiuoli* or gondoliers. Typified by a gently rocking rhythm in $\frac{6}{8}$ or $\frac{12}{8}$ time, barcaroles were written by many composers, including Chopin, Mendelssohn and Offenbach.

BARCELONA, Spain's second-largest city and chief port, and its greatest industrial and commercial center. Located in NE Spain on the Mediterranean, it is the historic capital of Catalonia. Barcelona was reputedly founded by Hamilcar Barca c230 BC. The countship of Barcelona was united with Aragon in 1137, and during the Middle Ages Barcelona became one of the Mediterranean's great maritime and commercial cities. The center of Catalan nationalism in modern times, it was the stronghold of left-wing politics and Republican allegiance in the Spanish Civil War. Pop 1 745 142.

BARCLAY, Robert (1648–1690), Scottish Quaker, whose greatest work, *Apology for the True Christian Divinity* (in Latin, 1676), is an early and important systematic statement of Quaker belief. Barclay, William Penn and 10 other Quakers were granted the proprietorship of East Jersey, of which Barclay was nominal governor 1682–88.

BAR COCHBA, Simon (d. 135 AD), leader of the last Jewish revolt against Roman rule in Palestine (132–35 AD), during the reign of Hadrian. Hailed as the Messiah by Rabbi AKIBA, he was at first successful and captured Jerusalem, but the revolt was finally put down and Bar Cochba slain.

BARD, Celtic poet-musician of ancient and medieval times, most notably in Ireland and Wales. The bards were highly esteemed figures, and bardic poetry reached a high level of sophistication. In Wales the tradition has been revived in the EISTEDDFODS.

BARDEEN, John (1908–   ), US physicist who shared the 1956 Nobel Prize for Physics with SHOCKLEY and BRATTAIN for their development of the TRANSISTOR. In 1972 he became the first person to win the physics prize a second time, sharing the award with COOPER and SCHRIEFFER for their development of a comprehensive theory of SUPERCONDUCTIVITY.

BARDOT, Brigitte (1934–   ), French film actress who first rose to fame in *And God Created Woman* (1956), and became a leading sex-symbol of the 1950s and 1960s.

BAREILLY, city on the Ramganga R, Uttar Pradesh State, N India. Products include cotton and sugar. Founded by the Moguls 1537. Pop 326 127.

BARENTS, Willem (c1550–1597), Dutch navigator, for whom the Barents Sea is named. He made three voyages to the Arctic in search of a NE passage to Asia. After discovering Spitsbergen on his third voyage and wintering in the Arctic, he died before reaching home.

BARENTS SEA, shallow arm of the Arctic Ocean N of Norway and European Russia, bounded by Svalbard (Spitsbergen) to the NW, Franz Josef Land to the N and Novaya Zemlya to the E. The SW portion is warmed by the North Atlantic Drift and remains ice-free in winter; on its coast lies the strategic port of Murmansk.

BARGE, a flat-bottomed freight vessel which may be pushed, towed or self-propelled and is used mainly on inland waterways. The term is also applied to small vessels used to convey important personages.

BARGELLO, national museum of art in Florence, Italy, housed in a 13th–14th-century palace which was once an official residence and later a prison. It houses a world-famous collection of Renaissance sculpture.

BARI, port in SE Italy on the Adriatic, capital of the region of Apulia (Puglia). It is the center of a rich agricultural region, and has a famous basilica of St. Nicholas, its patron saint. Pop 364 852.

BARING, Evelyn. See CROMER, EVELYN BARING, 1ST EARL OF.

BARITE, commonest barium mineral, consisting of barium sulfate (see BARIUM); white or yellow orthorhombic crystals. It is very dense and is mined for use in oil-well drilling muds and as the chief source of barium compounds. Largest US deposits are in Mo. and Ark.

BARIUM (Ba), silvery-white ALKALINE-EARTH METAL resembling CALCIUM; chief ores BARITE and witherite ($BaCO_3$). Barium is used to remove traces of gases from vacuum tubes; its compounds are used in making flares, fireworks, paint pigments and poisons. AW 137.3, mp 725°C, bp 1640°C, sg 3.5 (20°C). **Barium Sulfate** ($BaSO_4$), highly insoluble and opaque to X-rays, can be safely ingested for X-ray examination of the GASTROINTESTINAL TRACT.

BARIUM ENEMA; Barium Meal. See GASTROINTESTINAL TRACT.

BARK, general term for the covering of stems of woody plants, comprising the secondary phloem, cork cambium and CORK. The bark is impervious to water and protects the stem from excessive evaporation; it also protects the more delicate tissues within. Extracts

of bark may have medicinal uses, e.g., QUININE from CHINCHONA bark. (See TREE.)
BARK BEETLE. See ENGRAVER BEETLE.
BARKLA, Charles Glover (1877–1944), British physicist who was awarded the 1917 Nobel Prize for Physics for research on the scattering of X RAYS by GASES, in particular for his discovery of the "characteristic radiation" scattered by different elements.
BARKLEY, Alben William (1877–1956), 35th vice-president of the US (1949–53), under Truman. A Democrat from Ky., Barkley served in the US House of Representatives (1913–27) and the Senate (1927–49), including 10 years (beginning 1937) as majority leader. He returned to the Senate in 1954.
BAR KOKHBA, Simon. See BAR COCHBA, SIMON.
BARLAAM AND JOSAPHAT, one of the most widespread religious romances of the Middle Ages. It tells of the conversion to Christianity of the Indian prince, Josaphat, by the hermit Barlaam. A Christianized version of the BUDDHA legend, its earliest versions may date from the 7th century.
BARLACH, Ernst (1870–1938), German Expressionist sculptor, graphic artist and playwright, whose powerful figures in bronze or wood owe much to a very personal combination of Gothic and cubist influences. Barlach also produced many woodcuts and lithographs, some of them to illustrate his own dramas.
BARLEY, *Hordeum vulgare* and *H. distichon*, remarkably adaptable and hardy cereal, cultivated since ancient times. The USSR is the world's largest producer, with Canada and the US following. Over half of the world crop is used for animal feed and 10% (more in the US and W Europe) is turned into MALT. For human consumption barley, is ground into a flour used to make porridge or flatbread, or, in the US and elsewhere, polished to produce "pearl barley," commonly used in soup. Six-rowed and two-rowed barleys are the commonest varieties.
BARLOW, Joel (1754–1812), American man of letters and diplomat, one of the HARTFORD WITS. Barlow was author of the mock-pastoral *The Hasty Pudding* (1796) and a long epic about the promise of the New World, *The Vision of Columbus* (1787), revised as *The Columbiad* (1807). A friend of liberals in France and Britain, he was US consul to Algiers (1795–96) and an envoy to France (1811–12).
BARMECIDES, or Barmakids, Persian family whose members attained positions of great wealth and power under the early ABBASID caliphs of Baghdad. In 803 AD, however, Caliph HARUN AL-RASHID brutally eliminated the family. The term Barmecide Feast, referring to an illusory magnificence, comes from a tale in the ARABIAN NIGHTS.
BAR MITZVAH (Hebrew: son of the commandment), Jewish religious ceremony marking a boy's coming of age at his 13th birthday. The event is usually celebrated in the synagogue by calling on the boy to read the weekly portion of the Law (Torah) or the Prophets. Some congregations have a ceremony for girls, the "Bath Mitzvah." Reform Judaism often has a joint confirmation ceremony at 15 or 16.
BARN (b), unit of nuclear CROSS-SECTION (area) equal to 10^{-28} m^2.
BARNABAS, Saint (1st century AD), early Christian apostle, a Jew from a Cypriot family who joined the early church in Jerusalem. He introduced PAUL to the other apostles and apparently accompanied him on his first missionary journey.
BARNACLE GOOSE, *Branta leucopsis* (family Anatidae), small GOOSE resembling the CANADA GOOSE *Branta canadensis*. It winters around the North Sea and breeds in TUNDRA regions of the W Palearctic (see ZOOGEOGRAPHY). In the Middle Ages both it and the BRANT GOOSE (sometimes also called Barnacle Goose) were thought to be hatched from GOOSE BARNACLES, and hence eaten on Fridays as fish.
BARNACLES, marine CRUSTACEA of the subclass Cirripedia, whose free-swimming LARVAE are an important part of the PLANKTON. Most adults are HERMAPHRODITE. Their SHELLS consist primarily of CALCIUM carbonate (see also LIMESTONE). Adults attach themselves to solid surfaces (even the bodies of other sea animals) and trap plankton by means of feathery organs known as cirri. There are some 1000 species.
BARNARD, Christiaan Neethling (1922–), South African surgeon who performed the first successful human heart TRANSPLANT operation in 1967.
BARNARD, Edward Emerson (1857–1923), US astronomer who discovered the fifth satellite of JUPITER (1892). In 1916 he discovered **Barnard's star**, a red dwarf STAR only 6ly from the earth and which has the largest known stellar PROPER MOTION.
BARNARD, Frederick Augustus Porter (1809–1889), president of Columbia College (1864–89), which he helped transform into a great university. He was an advocate of higher education for women; Barnard College (founded 1889) bears his name.
BARNARD, Henry (1811–1900), US educator, pioneer in the improvement and better supervision of public education in the US. He was instrumental in the creation of the US Office of Education and was the first US commissioner of education (1867–70).
BARNAUL, city of SW Siberia, USSR, on the Ob R, capital of Altai territory. An important transportation hub with cotton mills and heavy industry. Pop 439000.
BARNBURNERS, radical, antislavery faction of the N.Y. State Democratic Party in the 1840s, opponents of the HUNKERS. Breaking away from the party in 1847–48, they joined the FREE-SOIL PARTY in supporting Martin Van Buren for the presidency. This threw the state's electoral votes, and victory, to the Whig candidate Zachary Taylor. The Barnburners disbanded, but many later joined the new Republican Party.
BARNEGAT BAY, 30mi-long arm of the Atlantic, parallel to the coast of Ocean Co., N.J.
BARNES, Djuna (1892–), US poet, playwright and novelist. Her works include a collection of stories and poems entitled *A Book* (1923), and the novels *Ryder* (1928) and *Nightwood* (1936).
BARNETT, Samuel Augustus (1844–1913), English social reformer and clergyman, vicar of St. Jude's, Whitechapel, in one of London's worst slums. He became warden of Toynbee Hall (1884), the world's first settlement house and the inspiration for hundreds of similar projects in England and the US.
BARNEVELDT, Jan van Olden. See OLDENBARNEVELT, JOHAN VAN.
BARNEY, Joshua (1759–1818), American naval officer. He served with distinction in the American Revolution, and later commanded in the French navy (1796–1802). In the War of 1812 he led the naval defense of Chesapeake Bay (1814) and fought heroically at the head of 500 sailors at BLADENSBURG.
BARN OWLS, several species of nocturnal OWLS of the genus *Tyto* (family Tytonidae). The common Barn Owl *Tyto alba* is found almost worldwide; it is about 450mm (17.7in) long, and has a pale face with smaller eyes than most owls.
BARNSTABLE, town on Cape Cod, SE Mass., seat of Barnstable Co. Settled about 1638 and once a flourishing port, it is now a popular summer resort. The town includes the villages of Hyannis and Hyannis Port. Pop 19842.
BARNSTORMERS, pilots who took their planes on the US country fair circuits of the 1920s and 1930s to perform stunt aerobatics. Some became test pilots and pioneers in commercial aviation; among famous barnstormers was Charles A. LINDBERGH.
BARN SWALLOWS, two species of the genus *Hirundo*, *H. rustica* (the European swallow) and *H. erythrogaster*, which together are the best-known and most widespread SWALLOWS (Hirundinidae).
BARNUM, Phineas Taylor (1810–1891), US impresario, showman and publicist. The hoaxes, freaks and curiosities exhibited in his American Museum (founded 1841) in New York included the original Siamese twins and General Tom Thumb. He toured Europe, and in 1850 engaged soprano Jenny LIND for a US tour. In 1871 he opened his famous traveling circus show, which merged in 1881 with James A. BAILEY's show to become the Barnum and Bailey "Greatest Show on Earth."

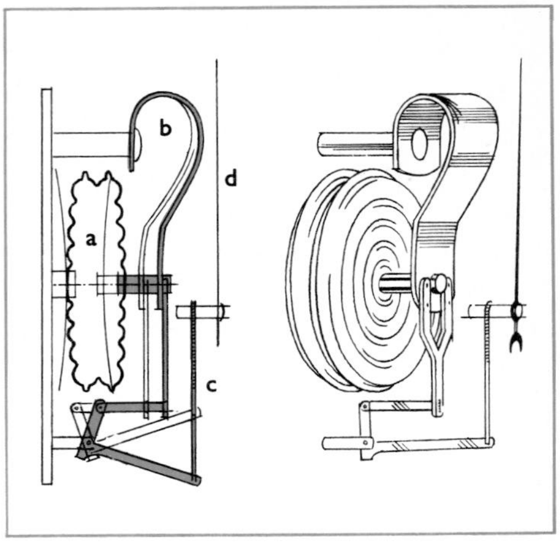

The aneroid barometer comprises a partially evacuated corrugated metal box (a), prevented from collapsing by a spring (b). The strain in this spring, proportional to the difference in pressures between the air inside and that outside the box, is amplified by a train of levers that operate a pointer (d) that moves over a calibrated scale. Aneroid barometers are convenient to use but require regular calibration against an accurate mercury barometer.

BARODA, city in Gujara State, W India. Situated in a rich agricultural region, textiles are its main industry. It was formerly capital of the powerful princely state of Baroda (1734–1947). Pop 467422.
BAROMETER, an instrument for measuring air pressure (see ATMOSPHERE), used in WEATHER FORECASTING and for determining ALTITUDE. Most commonly encountered is the **aneroid barometer** in which the effect of the air in compressing an evacuated thin cylindrical corrugated metal box is amplified mechanically and read off on a scale or, in the **barograph**, used to draw a trace on a slowly rotating drum, thus giving a continuous record of the barometric pressure. The aneroid instrument is that used for aircraft ALTIMETERS. The earliest barometers, as invented by TORRICELLI in 1643, consisted simply of a glass tube about 800mm long closed at one end and filled with MERCURY before being inverted over a pool of mercury. Air pressure acting on the surface of the pool held up a column of mercury about 760mm tall in the tube, a "Torricellian" vacuum appearing in the closed end of the tube. The height of the column was read as a measure of the pressure. In the **Fortin barometer**, devised by Jean Fortin (1750–1831) and still used for accurate scientific work, the lower mercury level can be finely adjusted and the column height is read off with the aid of a VERNIER SCALE.
BARON, European title of nobility. The word originally referred to any individual holding land directly from the crown. The English hereditary barons, as they first appeared in the 14th century, were summoned individually to parliament. Today barons constitute the lowest rank of the English peerage.
BARONET, British hereditary title, first instituted in 1611 ostensibly to support troops in Ulster, in fact to raise money. The title ranks between those of baron and knight; the holder is not a member of the peerage and is addressed as *Sir*.
BARONS' WAR (1263–67), English civil war between a baronial faction led by Simon de MONTFORT, Earl of Leicester, and the supporters of King HENRY III. The war was the result of Henry's refusal to abide by the reforms of the Provisions of Oxford (1258). Henry was defeated at the Battle of Lewes (1264) and taken prisoner; de Montfort consolidated his own power and summoned a parliament. In 1265 Henry's son, the future EDWARD I, killed de Montfort at the Battle of Evesham and restored the monarchy.
BAROQUE, dynamic and expressive style that dominated European art c1600–1750. The term has been used to describe not only the painting, sculpture and architecture of the period, but also, by analogy,

its music. Baroque was born in a rejection of the balance of Renaissance Classicism and the uncertainty of Mannerism. Much Baroque art is characterized by its emotional appeal, and by the energy and fluidity of its forms. From the works of CARAVAGGIO and, above all, BERNINI in Rome, the dramatic and illusionistic style of the High Baroque spread throughout Europe, glorifying faith in the Counter-Reformation Church and the absolutist state. In N Europe as well as in Italy, through painters as diverse as RUBENS and REMBRANDT, the Baroque created a new vocabulary of artistic expression.

BAROQUE MUSIC, that period of music c1600–1750 which began with the development of OPERA, CANTATA, ORATORIO and RECITATIVE, and ended with the death of its two greatest composers, HANDEL and J. S. BACH. Baroque music shared with the visual arts of its time dynamism, exuberance and forceful emotional expression. Musically, this was shown by ornamented melodies and by a striking use of harmonies and strong rhythms. The idea of stylistic contrast between instruments developed the CONCERTO form. In addition, both the SONATA and FUGUE forms developed, because of the increased attention paid to counterpoint.

BARQUISIMETO, city in NW Venezuela, 165mi WSW of Caracas, founded 1552. It is the country's third-largest city, the commercial, agricultural and communications center of a large region. Pop 334 333.

BARRACUDAS, the family Sphyraenidae (order Perciformes), tropical marine fishes renowned for their ferocity. The smallest is *Sphyraena borealis*, about 0.5m (20in) long; the largest the Great Barracuda, *S. barracuda*, which attains lengths around 2.5m (8.2ft). The latter frequently attacks swimmers but, oddly, has a reputation in some areas for harmlessness. Related to the more peaceable family Mugilidae (the grey MULLETS), it is in many areas more feared than the SHARK.

BARRANQUILLA, chief Caribbean port and fourth-largest city of Colombia, 15mi above the mouth of the Magdalena R. A growing industrial city since the 1930s, its products include textiles and cement. Pop 693 900.

One of the most beautiful examples of the Baroque style is the church in Vierzehnheiligen in Bavaria (Germany), which is a famous place of pilgrimage.

BARRAS, Paul François Jean Nicolas, Vicomte de (1755–1829), French revolutionary. At first a JACOBIN, in favor of Louis XVI's execution, he turned against ROBESPIERRE and commanded the troops that arrested him (1794). Barras became the most powerful member of the DIRECTORY, and aided Napoleon's rise to power. But after Napoleon's coup d'etat of 18 Brumaire (1799), Barras was exiled.

BARRAULT, Jean-Louis (1910–), French actor, director, producer and mime. A member of the Comédie Française 1940–46, and director of the Théâtre de France 1959–68. His most famous film role was as the mime in *Les Enfants du Paradis* (1944).

BARRE, city in central Vt., famed for its enormous granite quarries. It also has a machine and tool-making industry. Pop 10 209.

BARREL, cylindrical container made of wooden staves, bound by metal hoops. The ancient art of barrel-making—cooperage—is still practiced. Staves of well-dried wood are set into a head truss ring, then softened by steam and curved into shape. The staves are held in position by metal hoops, the ends trimmed and circular headpieces fitted. The barrel is also a unit of dry and liquid capacity (see WEIGHTS AND MEASURES).

BARREL ORGAN, mechanical musical instrument which plays a tune when a pinned barrel, activating a series of organ pipes, is turned. It was once used both in churches and by street musicians.

BARREN GROUNDS, sparsely inhabited, treeless plains of N Canada, extending N and W from the 59th parallel at Hudson Bay to Great Slave and Great Bear lakes and the Arctic Ocean. It is a bare, poorly drained region with extensive rocky outcrops and a permanently frozen subsoil. There are many lakes and rivers and, in summer, vast swampy areas. Wildlife includes herds of musk ox and barren-ground caribou.

BARRÈS, (Auguste) Maurice (1862–1923), French man of letters and political figure, best known for his intransigent nationalism and emphasis on regional ties. Among his many influential novels, *The Uprooted* (1897) stands preeminent.

BARRIE, city and summer resort in SE Ontario, on Lake Simcoe at the head of Kempenfelt Bay; seat of Simcoe Co. Pop 26 985.

BARRIE, Sir James Matthew (1860–1937), Scottish playwright and novelist. His plays—including *The Admirable Crichton* (1902), *Peter Pan* (1904) and *Dear Brutus* (1917)—are marked by charm and ingenuity, and range in tone from whimsy and sentimentality to satire and pathos.

BARRIER REEF, CORAL REEF, lying roughly parallel to a shore. (See GREAT BARRIER REEF; LAGOON).

BARRINGTON, town and resort center in E R.I. on Narragansett Bay, 8mi SE of Providence; included in Mass. until 1746. Pop 17 554.

BARRIOS, Eduardo (1884–1963), Chilean novelist, known for the psychological insight of such powerful novels as *The Love-Crazed Boy* (1915) and *Brother Ass* (1922).

BARRIOS, Justo Rufino (1835–1885), dictator of Guatemala. He became commander of the army in 1871 and assumed the presidency in 1873. Barrios brought the country economic progress and social reform, but his forcible attempts to revive Central American unity ended with his death during an invasion of El Salvador.

BARRISTER, in England, Wales and some Commonwealth countries, a lawyer who acts as an advocate in the superior courts, as distinct from a solicitor, who handles most legal matters but cannot appear in higher courts. (See LEGAL PROFESSION.)

BARRON, James (1769–1851), US naval commodore, who was commander of the frigate CHESAPEAKE in its disastrous engagement with the British warship *Leopard* in 1807. He surrendered and allowed the removal of four sailors the British claimed as deserters. Barron was court-martialed and temporarily suspended from duty. Blaming Commodore DECATUR for being refused a further sea command, he killed him in a duel in 1820.

BARROW, also termed a tumulus or MOUND (in the US), a large mound of earth and stones containing or covering an ancient burial place. Long barrows are generally Neolithic, round ones Early Bronze Age.

BARROW, Isaac (1630–1677), English mathematician and theologian. The first Lucasian professor of mathematics in the University of Cambridge (1663), Barrow resigned in favor of his pupil Isaac NEWTON in 1669. His work on tangents and areas was influential in Newton's development of the CALCULUS.

BARROW, Sir John (1764–1848), English traveler and government official, an important promoter and patron of Arctic exploration and chief founder of the Royal Geographical Society. As second secretary of the Admiralty (1804–06, 1807–48), he was responsible for the voyages of Sir John ROSS, W. E. PARRY and others in search of the NW Passage.

BARROW, Point, northernmost point on the North American continent (71°23′N), at the tip of Point Barrow Peninsula on the Arctic coast of Alaska. Named for Sir John Barrow. The city of Barrow (pop 2 104) lies some 12mi S.

BARRY, Sir Charles (1795–1860), English architect who, with his assistant A. W. Pugin, designed the Houses of Parliament in London (1840–60), a masterpiece of the Gothic Revival. Among his other buildings was the Reform Club in London (1837).

BARRY, John (1745–1803), Irish-born naval hero famed for many brilliant exploits in the Revolutionary War, often called the "Father of the American navy." As ranking captain of the navy (from 1794) he commanded the frigate *United States* and saw action in the undeclared naval war with France (1798–1800).

BARRY, Philip (1896–1949), US playwright, best known for popular drawing-room comedies such as *Holiday* (1928) and *The Philadelphia Story* (1939).

BARRYMORE, name of a noted American theatrical family. The father was the British actor Herbert Blythe (1847–1905), who adopted the stage name **Maurice Barrymore**. He came to the US in 1875 and married actress Georgina Drew. **Lionel Barrymore** (1878–1954), their eldest child, became an outstanding character actor on stage and radio and in many films—continuing to act even after arthritis had confined him to a wheelchair. **Ethel Barrymore** (1879–1959), famous for her beauty, style and wit, gave many distinctive performances on stage and screen. She won an Academy Award for her supporting role in *None But the Lonely Heart* (1944). **John Barrymore** (1882–1942) was a distinguished interpreter of Shakespearean roles, particularly *Richard III* (1920) and *Hamlet* (1922). Later he became a popular and flamboyant film actor, nicknamed "the great profile." His children, **Diana Barrymore** (1921–1960) and **John Barrymore, Jr** (1932–), also became actors.

BARSTOW, railroad city and tourist center in S Cal., in the Mojave Desert, San Bernardino Co. Pop 17 442.

BARTER, trade by direct exchange of commodities—or services—without the use of currency. Many primitive economies are based on barter, but barter agreements also feature in modern international trade. Barter can reappear at times of acute inflation.

BARTH, Heinrich (1821–1865), German geographer and explorer. After traveling in the lands fringing the Mediterranean, he made a series of journeys in Africa (1850–55), recorded in the classic *Travels and Discoveries in North and Central Africa* (1857–58).

BARTH, John (1930–), US novelist known for his ironic style and use of comic and elaborate allegory. His best-known works include *The Sot-Weed Factor* (1960) and *Giles Goat-Boy* (1966).

BARTH, Karl (1886–1968), Swiss theologian, one of the most influential voices of 20th-century Protestantism. He taught in Germany 1921–35, was expelled by the Nazis and spent the rest of his life in Basel. In his "crisis theology," Barth stressed revelation and grace and reemphasized the principles of the Reformation, initiating a movement away from theological "liberalism" (see NEO-ORTHODOXY).

BARTHOLDI, Frédéric Auguste (1834–1904), French sculptor, creator of the Statue of Liberty (see LIBERTY, STATUE OF). His other monumental works include the *Lion of Belfort* at Belfort, France.

Fra Bartolommeo's coloring for *The Vision of St Bernard of Clairvaux* (1504–07) was influenced by Leonardo da Vinci's famous cartoon for the *Holy Family with St Anne* (c.1501).

BARTHOLIN (Latin: Bartholinus), family of Danish physicians. **Caspar Berthelsen Bartholin** (1585–1629) was author of the much-used *Institutiones Anatomicae* (1611). This was enlarged by his son, **Thomas Bartholin** (1616–1680), noted also for his study of the human lymphatic system (1652). **Erasmus Bartholin** (1625–1698), brother of Thomas, in 1669 discovered the phenomenon of DOUBLE REFRACTION in Iceland spar crystals. **Caspar Bartholin** (1655–1738), son of Thomas, was the discoverer of Bartholin's vaginal glands.

BARTHOLOMEW, Saint, one of the 12 Apostles, sometimes identified with NATHANAEL. He was said to have preached in the Middle East, Asia Minor and India, and to have been martyred in Armenia by being flayed alive. His feast day in the West is Aug 24.

BARTHOLOMEW'S DAY MASSACRE. See SAINT BARTHOLOMEW'S DAY MASSACRE.

BARTLESVILLE, city on the Caney R in NE Okla., seat of Washington Co. and a major center for the petroleum and natural gas industries. Pop 29 683.

BARTLETT, John (1820–1905), US editor and publisher, best known for his famous *Familiar Quotations*, which has gone through more than a dozen editions since its first appearance in 1855.

BARTLETT, Josiah (1729–1795), American patriot and physician, delegate to the Continental Congress (1775–76, 1778–79) and signer of the Declaration of Independence. He was chief executive (1790–92) and first governor (1793–94) of N.H.

BARTLETT, Robert Abram (1875–1946), Newfoundland-born US Arctic explorer. He served on Robert E. PEARY's Arctic expeditions between and 1909, and subsequently conducted annual voyages to the Far North (1925–41).

BARTLETT DAM, on the Verde R 35mi NE of Phoenix, Ariz., one of the highest multiple-arch dams in the US (287ft). It was completed in 1939 as the final unit of the Salt River Reclamation Project.

BARTÓK, Béla (1881–1945), Hungarian composer, one of the major figures of 20th-century music. He was also a virtuoso concert pianist, and taught piano at the Budapest Academy of Music (1907–34). In 1940 he emigrated to the US. His work owes much to the rhythmic and melodic vitality of E European folk music, on which he was an authority. Bartók's works include such masterpieces as his six string quartets (1908–39), *Music for Strings, Percussion and Celesta* (1936) and *Concerto for Orchestra* (1943).

BARTOLOMMEO, Fra (c1472–1517), Florentine painter of the High Renaissance, born Baccio della Porta. A Dominican monk, he painted religious subjects (largely altarpieces) with telling grandeur and simplicity.

BARTON, Clara (1821–1912), founder of the American Red Cross (1881) and its first president. She began a lifetime of relief work by organizing care and supplies for the wounded in the Civil War. On a trip to Europe (1869–73) she became involved in the activities of the International Red Cross and was later influential in extending the range of its relief work.

BARTON, Sir Derek Harold Richard (1918–　　), British organic chemist who shared the 1969 Nobel Prize for Chemistry with Odd HASSEL for the development of CONFORMATIONAL ANALYSIS.

BARTON, Sir Edmund (1849–1920), Australian statesman, leader of the successful movement to create an Australian federal government. Active in politics from 1879, he was the first prime minister of the new Commonwealth of Australia (1901–03).

BARTOW, city in central Fla., seat of Polk Co., in a region of citrus groves and phosphate mining. Pop 12 891.

BARTRAM, name of two American naturalists, father and son. **John Bartram** (1699–1777) began planting America's first botanical garden at Kingsessing, Pa., in 1728. **William Bartram** (1739–1823), became famous for his book *Travels* (1791), based on his travels with his father in the SE US, said to have inspired Wordsworth and Coleridge.

BARUCH, Bernard Mannes (1870–1965), US financier and public official, who made a fortune on Wall Street and became an influential adviser to US presidents. He served Woodrow Wilson as chairman of the War Industries Board in WWI and at the Versailles peace talks; was adviser to F. D. Roosevelt in WWII; and under Truman was US delegate to the UN Atomic Energy Commission, where he proposed the "Baruch Plan" for the international control of atomic energy.

BARUCH, Book of, a biblical work attributed to Baruch, the prophet Jeremiah's secretary. Relegated to the APOCRYPHA by Protestants, it is included in the Old Testament by Roman Catholics. The book survives in a Greek version, and is probably the work of several authors of Hellenistic times.

BARYONS, in particle physics, a class of SUBATOMIC PARTICLES (comprising the nucleons and hyperons) distinct from the mesons.

BARZANI, Mullah Mustafa (1903–　　), Kurdish nationalist leader in Iraq, member of an ancient ruling family. He led a long, sporadic rebellion against the Iraqi government in the 1960s and 1970s, seeking Kurdish autonomy within Iraq, which led to final Kurdish defeat in 1975.

BARZUN, Jacques (1907–　　), US historian and educator, born in France. He taught at Columbia U. from 1929, and has written numerous works on education and on the arts.

BASAL METABOLIC RATE (BMR), a measure of the rate at which an animal at rest uses energy. Human BMR is a measure of the heat output per unit time from a given area of body surface, the subject being at rest under certain standard conditions. It is usually estimated from the amounts of oxygen and carbon dioxide exchanged in a certain time. (See METABOLISM.)

BASALT, a dense igneous rock, mainly plagioclase FELDSPAR, fine-grained and dark gray to black in color; volcanic in origin, it is widespread as lava flows or intrusions. Basalt can assume a striking columnar structure, as exhibited in the Palisades along the Hudson R, or in Devils Postpile in Cal., and it can also form vast plateaus, such as the 200 000sq mi Deccan of India. Most oceanic islands of volcanic origin, such as Hawaii, are basaltic.

BASE, in chemistry, the complement of an acid. Bases used to be defined as substances which react with acids to form SALTS, or as substances which give rise to hydroxyl ions (see HYDROXIDE) in aqueous solution. Some such inorganic strong bases are known as ALKALIS. In modern terms, bases are species which can accept a HYDROGEN ion from an acid, or which can donate an electron-pair to a Lewis ACID.

BASEBALL, America's national sport, had its beginnings more than a century ago. Its true origins are obscure, and the supposed role of Abner DOUBLEDAY has been hotly disputed. It is generally thought that the sport is a hybrid, loosely developed from the English games of cricket and rounders. Many of its rules were first set down by Alexander Cartwright of the New York Knickerbocker Baseball Club, founded in 1845. The National Association of Baseball Players was organized in 1858; the game became popular among Union troops in the Civil War, and in 1865 a convention of 91 amateur clubs met in New York. **The major leagues.** In 1869 the Cincinnati Red Stockings became the first fully professional baseball team. The National Association of Professional Baseball Players was formed in 1871; it was replaced by a new National League of Professional Baseball Clubs in 1876. Attempts at creating a rival league failed until the turn of the century, when the American League had become sufficiently established to match the National League.

The first World Series between the leading teams in each league was played in 1903. In 1933 the first "All-Star" exhibition game was played, followed in 1939 by the establishment of a Baseball Hall of Fame in Cooperstown, N.Y. In 1953 the major leagues started shifting franchises to new cities and a great expansion began. By 1969, each league had grown to 12 clubs, divided into two six-team divisions, with playoffs for the league pennant and the right to play in a final World Series.

BASEL, second-largest city in Switzerland, capital of (and virtually coextensive with) the half-canton of Basel-Stadt. A port on the Rhine near the junction of the French and German borders, it is a major center of industry, commerce and international finance. It joined the Swiss confederation in 1501 and figured prominently in the Reformation. Pop 212 857.

BASEL, Council of, general Church council opened

in Basel, Switzerland, in 1431, concerned with the heresy of Jan HUS and the continuing struggle over papal supremacy. Pope Eugene IV tried to dissolve the council, but it denied his right to do so, claiming that as an ecumenical council it, rather than the pope, held ultimate authority. Eugene relented, but in 1437 ordered it to move to Ferrara, Italy, to consider reunion with the Eastern Church. Most bishops complied, but a small number remained in Basel, deposing Eugene and electing the antipope Felix V in 1439, and continuing to meet until 1449.

BASENJI, ancient breed of African hound with a short silky coat, curled tail and erect ears, weighing 20–25lb. Known as the "barkless dog," it is a tireless runner.

BASIC ENGLISH, selected vocabulary of 850 English words, meant for use as an auxiliary or international language. Developed by English scholar C. K. OGDEN between 1926 and 1930, it was the first attempt to create a usable, simpler language system out of an existing one.

BASIE, William "Count" (1904–   ), US jazz pianist, composer and bandleader. Count Basie's big band, which included some of the outstanding jazz musicians of the time, brought the ragged rhythm and improvisational verve of jazz into the smooth swing era of the late 1930s and 1940s. He continues to be an active jazz player.

BASIL, *Ocimum basilicum*, aromatic annual herb of the mint family, native to Asia. The leaves are used fresh or dried in cooking and in the preparation of Chartreuse liqueur.

BASIL, name of two Byzantine emperors. **Basil I** (d.886), known as the Macedonian, came of peasant origin and founded a brilliant dynasty. He took power in 867, having the Emperor Michael III, whose favorite he was, assassinated. He reformed the legal system, beat off the Arabs, and extended the empire to the upper Euphrates. **Basil II** (c954–1025), *Bulgaroctonus* (Bulgar-slayer), reigned as co-emperor with real power from 976. He ruthlessly subjugated Bulgaria and annexed most of Armenia. His reign marked a zenith of Byzantine power unequaled since JUSTINIAN I.

BASILAN, island group in the S Philippines, including Basilan Island and some 50 tiny islets, S of Mindanao. In 1948 it was made a chartered city. Pop 222 600.

BASILICA, in its earliest usage, a type of large public building of ancient Rome. The term came to refer to a building of characteristic rectangular layout, with a central area (nave) separated by rows of columns from two flanking side aisles with high windows. At one or both ends was a semicircular or polygonal apse. This design was adopted as a basic pattern for Christian churches from the time of Constantine. The term "basilica" is also a canonical title for certain important Roman Catholic churches.

BASILISKS, the genus *Basiliscus* (family Iguanidae), LIZARDS of Central America. Their chief means of catching prey and evading enemies is speed, and they are well known for their ability to dash across the surface of still water: this they can do only until their speed begins to slacken, at which point they must start to swim. One species, the Banded Basilisk *Basiliscus vittatus*, shows the ability to change color according to its environment. The name is also applied to the cockatrice, born of a cockerel and a serpent, a legendary beast whose glance was fatal.

BASIL THE GREAT, Saint (c330–379), one of the great Fathers of the Eastern Church, a founder of Greek monasticism and author of the *Longer* and *Shorter Rules* for monastic life. As Bishop of Caesarea, he also played a role in subduing ARIANISM. His brother was St. GREGORY OF NYSSA.

BASIN AND RANGE PROVINCE, geological region of the SW US extending into NW Mexico, bounded by the Columbia Plateau, the Sierra Nevada, the Wasatch Mts and the Colorado Plateau. It is a semidesert region with parallel mountain ranges and valley basins running N to S. Many sections have no outlet to the sea; the Great Salt Lake is one remnant of much larger lakes that once existed.

BASIN STREET, nightclub district of New Orleans, which became a famous center for blues and early jazz, commemorated in many popular songs.

BASKERVILLE, John (1706–1775), English printer and type designer, whose elegant Baskerville type was the ancestor and inspiration of the "modern" group of typefaces. He took great care in all aspects of his craft and produced many handsome editions. This book's text is set in a modern Baskerville.

BASKETBALL, the most popular indoor sport in the US. Its object is to score points by propelling a ball through a hoop and net construction, the "basket," 18in in diameter and 10ft from the floor. It is played on a court with maximum dimensions of 94 × 50ft by two teams, each consisting of 12 players and a coach, with five players on the court at any one time. The ball may be moved by "passing" from one player to another, or by "dribbling," in which case the ball must not be kicked, or held for more than one pace. Rules vary in detail between organizations.

Conceived by Dr. James A. NAISMITH in 1891, the game quickly became popular. In 1898, teams from New York, Brooklyn, Philadelphia and southern New Jersey formed the first professional league, but these early leagues lasted only a few seasons. International interest was fostered by an exhibition game played at the 1904 Olympics in St. Louis, Mo. In America, the game's early history was dominated by teams such as the New York Celtics and the Harlem Globetrotters, and in 1938 the first National Invitation Tournament was held at Madison Square Garden. The union of the National Basketball League, the Basketball Association of America and the American Basketball Association has created a strong league of great popularity.

Basketball is a sport where it is a great advantage to be tall. Here a player tries to net the ball.

BASKET MAKERS, a prehistoric Indian culture of the American Southwest, earliest members of the ANASAZI group. From about 700 AD all Anasazi are called PUEBLO INDIANS, after their multistoried adobe dwellings, or *pueblos*. (See also CLIFF DWELLERS.)

BASKET WEAVING, the technique which normally preceded the invention of ceramics in primitive cultures, though evidence is rare except in pictorial and written records. The Romans, for example, relied on imported basketware, and in the SW of the US the BASKET MAKERS produced some of the finest examples of early basketry (1st and 2nd centuries AD). Basket weaving was also prominent in Japan, China, the Philippines and Indonesia. Recently, craft societies have revived the art.

BASKIN, Leonard (1922–   ), American graphic artist and sculptor. He studied art at New York and Yale universities, and in Paris and Florence. After winning a Guggenheim Fellowship for graphics in 1953, he taught at Smith College, Mass., where he founded the Gehenna Press.

BASKING SHARK, *Cetorhinus maximum*, second largest of the SHARKS, attaining lengths of up to 15m (50ft) and weights of over 4 tonnes. Found chiefly in temperate waters, it is, unusually for a shark, not carnivorous but feeds on PLANKTON. It is fished commercially in many parts of the world. It is the sole member of the Cetorhinidae family.

BASOV, Nikolai Gennadievich (1922–   ), Soviet physicist who shared the 1964 Nobel Prize for Physics with TOWNES and PROKHOROV for research in quantum physics which led to the development of LASERS and MASERS.

BASQUES, a people of unknown origin living mainly in the vicinity of the Pyrenees Mts (about 100 000 in France and 600 000 in NE Spain). Ethnically they seem to belong to the Caucasoid group, but research

Baseball: batter and catcher await the pitch. Often a great batter will have a characteristic stance.

into their blood groups indicates a long separation from other Europeans; their language is remarkably conservative and quite unlike the Indo-European tongues. Basques were living along the Ebro valley in N Spain in the 3rd century BC, and have preserved many features of their ancient culture despite incursions by Romans, Visigoths, Moors and Franks, and eventual Spanish rule. After the Spanish Civil War, in which many Basques fought against General Franco, an effort was made to subdue the region. A surge of Basque nationalism in recent years was marked by the assassination of Admiral Luis Blanco by the Basque resistance movement ETA in Dec. 1973 and the execution of five terrorists shortly before Franco's death.

BASRA, city in Iraq, major port situated on the Shatt-el-Arab about 75mi from the Persian Gulf. Main products include petroleum and dates. Basra was a noted center of Arab culture from the 8th to the 13th centuries. Pop 311 000.

BAS RELIEF, or low relief. See RELIEF.

BASS, term used for two species, *Dicentrarchus labrax* and *D. punctatus*, of the Serranidae family (order Perciformes). Coastal fish, they usually weigh 1–3kg (2–7lb) though sometimes up to 8kg (18lb). In America the term Black Bass is applied to the freshwater fishes (genus *Micropterus* and family Centrarchidae) *M. salmoides* and *M. dolomieu*. They are nest-builders and predatory, occasionally playing with their prey rather as a cat does with a mouse.

BASS, or double bass, largest instrument of the violin family. Usually it stands about 6ft high, and has four, or sometimes five, 42.5in strings of copper or steel. It is played with a bow, or the strings may be plucked.

BASS, Sam (1851–1878), US outlaw. He rode the West, first with the Joel Collins gang and then with one of his own. Called the "Robin Hood of Texas," he died of gunshot wounds.

BASSAE, in S Greece, site of a temple of Apollo built at the end of the 5th century BC, possibly by Ictinus, builder of the PARTHENON. The splendid 101ft-long temple frieze is now in the British Museum, London.

BASSANO, Jacopo (Jacopo da Ponte; c1510–1592), leading member of a family of Italian painters. Arriving in Venice c1534, he was at first influenced by TITIAN, TINTORETTO and others. With its use of everyday scenes in religious subjects, his work tended towards GENRE painting, a tradition continued by his three sons.

BASSET HOUND, a hunting dog 11–15in high at the shoulder, weighing 25–45lb. It has a long, bulky body, with a large head, a long nose and long ears. It is used to hunt foxes, rabbits and pheasants and is also popular as a pet.

The short-legged Basset Hound's name is derived from the French word "bas," meaning low; it was once widely used for unearthing foxes and badgers during a hunt.

BASS ISLANDS, three islands in W Lake Erie, about 55mi W of Cleveland, Ohio. The battle of Lake Erie was fought off the largest island, South Bass (3.5mi long) on Sept. 10, 1813. (See ERIE, BATTLE OF LAKE.)

BASSOON, the bass of the woodwind family, an 8ft conical tube bent double, with a double reed mouthpiece, 8 holes, and 20–22 keys. It has a range of 3.5 octaves (B-flat bass to E-flat alto) but irrational key placing and an unstable pitch make it difficult to play. The contrabassoon is 6ft long and sounds an octave lower.

BASS STRAIT, 75–150mi wide channel separating Australia and Tasmania. It contains King Island and the Hunter and Furneaux islands.

BASSWOOD. See LINDEN.

BASTILLE, fortress in Paris built in 1370, destroyed during the French Revolution. It was first used to house political prisoners by Cardinal Richelieu, in the 17th century, but was almost empty by the time of the Revolution. It remained a symbol of oppression, however, and its capture on July 14, 1789, was the first act of the Revolution. Today, July 14 is a French national holiday.

BASTOGNE, small town on the Ardennes plateau in SE Belgium. During the German counter-offensive of 1944, the BATTLE OF THE BULGE, an American division under Gen. Anthony McAuliffe was surrounded here for some weeks before the Germans were driven back. Pop 6694.

BASTROP, city in La., 165mi N of Baton Rouge. Its industries include lumber, chemicals and natural gas. Pop 14 713.

BASUTOLAND. See LESOTHO.

BATAAN, 30mi-long peninsula of S Luzon Island, Philippines, on the W side of Manila Bay. In WWII US-Filipino troops under Gen. WAINWRIGHT defended Bataan against the Japanese until forced to surrender on April 9, 1942. Out of 600 000 prisoners made to march 70mi to prison camps, over 100 000 died of starvation or maltreatment. Bataan was retaken by US forces in Feb. 1945.

BATAVI, ancient Germanic people who inhabited part of what is now the Netherlands. Subjected to Rome by Germanicus in c13 BC, they were conquered by the Salian Franks in the 3rd century AD.

BATAVIA, city in W N.Y., seat of Genesee Co. An agricultural trade center making electronic products and paper. Pop 17 338.

BATAVIAN REPUBLIC, republic formed by the United Provinces of the Netherlands after the French occupation of 1795. It lasted until 1806, when NAPOLEON made his brother, Louis BONAPARTE, king of Holland. (See also NETHERLANDS, THE.)

BATES, Henry Walter (1825–1892), English entomologist who first drew attention to the phenomenon of mimicry. One form, **Batesian mimicry**, is named for him.

BATES, Katharine Lee (1859–1929), US author, best known for writing the lyrics of AMERICA THE BEAUTIFUL. She was professor of English at Wellesley College and wrote much children's literature.

BATESON, William (1861–1926), English biologist, known as the "father of GENETICS." In 1900 he translated MENDEL's classic HEREDITY paper into English and thereafter his work did much to promote general acceptance of the Mendelian theory.

BATFISHES, name applied sometimes to the Ogcocephalidae family of ANGLERFISHES, but more correctly to members of the family Platacidae, order Perciformes. They have highly compressed, almost circular bodies, and large, winglike FINS. They are found in the Indo-Pacific region.

BATH, famous resort city in the county of Avon, England, on the Avon R about 12mi from Bristol. Noted for its mineral springs since Roman times, it is distinguished for its elegant Georgian architecture. Its industries include bookbinding, printing and weaving. Pop 84 760.

BATH, city in Me., on the Kennebec R, seat of Sagadahoc Co., famous for its shipbuilding since Colonial times. Pop 4674.

BATH, Order of the, British honor, established by George I in 1725 (supposedly based on an order founded in 1399). There are two divisions, military and civil, with three classes in each: knight grand cross (G.C.B.), knight commander (K.C.B.) and companion (C.B.).

BATH MITZVAH. See BAR MITZVAH.

BATHOLITH, large subterranean mass of IGNEOUS ROCK formed by the intrusion of MAGMA across the enclosing rock beds, and its subsequent cooling. Batholiths have an extent of over 100km², and frequently form the cores of mountain ranges.

BÁTHORY, name of an aristocratic Hungarian family of the 16th century. **Stephen Báthory** (1477–1534) governed Transylvania from 1529 and supported John I Zápolya of Hungary against the Hapsburgs. **Stephen Báthory** (1533–1586), his son, was elected prince of Transylvania in 1571 and king of Poland in 1575, becoming one of Poland's greatest rulers. He reformed the judiciary and army, defeated Ivan the Terrible of Russia, and formed an alliance with Turkey to stave off Austrian domination. **Sigismund Báthory** (1572–1613), Stephen's nephew, ruled Transylvania 1581–99, adopting an anti-Turkish policy and espousing the Counter-Reformation. **Elizabeth Báthory,** who died in prison in 1614, was said to have murdered 600 virgins to bathe in their blood which she believed would rejuvenate her.

BATHS AND BATHING. In the past baths have served a primarily religious, social or pleasurable function far more often than a hygienic one. The Egyptians, Assyrians and Greeks all used baths, but the Romans developed bathing as a central social habit, constructing elaborate public buildings, often ornately decorated and of enormous size, with several rooms for disrobing, exercise, and entertainment, as well as bathing. Men and women bathed at separate times, except for one brief period in the 1st century AD. The baths were tended by slaves. After the fall of the Roman Empire bathing declined in popularity in Europe, though it did survive as a part of monastic routine and in Muslim countries. In Russia and Turkey the steam bath became popular. The crusaders brought steam bathing back with them from the Middle East, but an association with immorality caused it to fall into disrepute.

In the 18th century, it became fashionable to spend a season at a watering-place, such as BATH in England, but only 19th-century research into hygiene made a virtue of bathing, often with primitive and usually portable cold baths at schools and institutions. Only after WWI did plumbing and bathtub production allow the bath to become a permanent installation in the home.

BATHSHEBA, in the Bible, wife of Uriah the Hittite, one of King DAVID's captains. David placed Uriah in the front line of battle, where he was killed. The king then married Bathsheba. She bore him SOLOMON, who was proclaimed successor to the throne in place of Adonijah, David's eldest son.

BATHURST. See BANJUL.

BATHYSCAPHE, submersible deep-sea research vessel, invented by Auguste PICCARD in the late 1940s, comprising a small, spherical, pressurized passenger cabin suspended beneath a cigar-shaped flotation hull. On the surface most of the flotation tanks in the hull are filled with GASOLINE, the rest, sufficient to float the vessel, with air. To dive the air is vented and seawater takes its place. During descent, sea water is allowed to enter the gasoline-filled tanks from the bottom, compressing the gasoline and thus increasing the DENSITY of the vessel. The rate of descent is checked by releasing iron ballast. To begin ascent, the remaining ballast is jettisoned. As the vessel rises, the gasoline expands, expelling water from the flotation tanks, thus lightening the vessel further and accelerating the ascent. Battery-powered motors provide the vessel with a degree of submarine mobility.

BATHYSPHERE, a hollow steel sphere suspended by cables from a surface ship and used for deep-sea research before the development of the BATHYSCAPHE. The first bathysphere was built and used by engineer Otis Barton and naturalist William BEEBE in 1930.

BATIK, a dyeing technique. Before the fabric is dipped into the dye the portions which are to remain uncolored are covered with wax. When the dye is dry, the wax is removed by boiling. The technique was introduced into Europe from Indonesia by Dutch traders.

BATISTA Y ZALDÍVAR, Fulgencio (1901–1973), Cuban military dictator. Becoming army chief of staff after the overthrow of the Machado government in 1933, he appointed and deposed presidents at will. He was himself president 1940–44, and took the title permanently in 1952. After his overthrow by CASTRO in 1959 he lived in exile in Spain.

BATON ROUGE, capital of La. since 1849, situated on the Mississippi R W of New Orleans. It is an important trade and communications center producing oil, chemicals and aluminum. Pop 165 963.

BATS, the order Chiroptera, the flying MAMMALS. Since they are all nocturnal, and many tropical, it is not generally realized that bats account for about one-seventh of mammalian species. There are two suborders: the Megachiroptera ("big bats"), with weights from 25g (0.9oz) to 1kg (2.2lb) and wingspans of about 250–1500mm (10in–5ft); and the Microchiroptera ("little bats"), weights of about 3–200g (0.1–7oz) and wingspans of 150–900mm (6–35in). The former usually have large eyes adapted for night vision, but the latter navigate by use of echolocation (see ECHO; SONAR). Most are insectivorous, but some are vegetarian and yet others carnivorous—the three species of the family Desmodontidae (the VAMPIRE BATS) are blood suckers, preying on birds and mammals.

BATTANI, abu-Abdullah Muhammad ibn-Jabir, al-, or Latin **Albategnius** or **Albatenius** (c858–929), Arab mathematician and astronomer who improved on the results of Claudius PTOLEMY by applying TRIGONOMETRY to astronomical computations. He had a powerful influence on medieval European ASTRONOMY.

BATTERING RAM, a heavy beam, sometimes strengthened at one end with a mass of metal shaped like a ram's head; used in warfare until the end of the Middle Ages to weaken or break down enemy walls and gates with repeated, rhythmic blows.

BATTERY, a device for converting internally-stored chemical ENERGY into direct-current ELECTRICITY. The term is also applied to various other electricity sources, including the SOLAR CELL and the nuclear cell, but is usually taken to exclude the FUEL CELL, which requires the continuous input of a chemical fuel for its operation. Chemical batteries consist of one or more electrochemical (voltaic) cells (comprising two ELECTRODES immersed in a conducting electrolyte) in which a chemical reaction occurs when an external circuit is completed between the electrodes. Most of the energy liberated in this reaction can be tapped if a suitable load is placed in the external circuit, impeding the flow of ELECTRONS from CATHODE to ANODE. (The conventional current, of course, flows in the opposite sense.) Batteries are classified in two main divisions. In **primary cells**, the chemical reaction is ordinarily irreversible and the battery can yield only a finite quantity of electricity. Single primary-cell batteries are used in flashlights, shavers, LIGHT METERS, etc. The most common type is the dry **Leclanché cell,** which has a ZINC cathode, a CARBON anode and uses ammonium chloride paste as electrolyte. MANGANESE dioxide "depolarizer" is distributed around the anode (mixed with powdered GRAPHITE) to prevent the accumulation of the HYDROGEN gas which would otherwise stop the

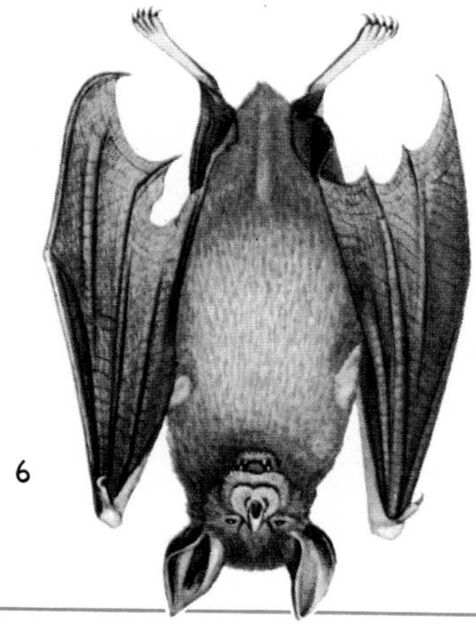

Bats are more dependent on flying than other animals for, unlike birds and insects, their legs are not well-adapted to walking.

The small bats (Microchiroptera) include 1. *Myotis myotis,* 3in long with a 2in tail and 14–17in wingspan (from central and southern Europe and as far east as China); 2. *Eptesicus serotinus*, moves on all fours: length 3in, tail 2in, wingspan 13–14in (Europe, North Africa and Asia); 3. *Plecotus auritus* hanging from branch, length 2in, 2in tail, 9–10in wingspan (native to Europe, North Africa and Asia); 4. blood-sucking vampire bat (*Desmodus rotundus*), moves on all fours and is tailless, length 3in, 14in wingspan (Central and South America); 5. *Vampyrus spectrum,* length 6in (tailless), 14in wingspan (Guyana and northern Brazil); 6. *Rhinolophus hipposideros,* length 1½in, tail 1in, 9in wingspan.

A standard lead-acid auto battery. The electrodes consist of alternate plates of lead (*green*) and lead coated with lead dioxide (*red*) separated by sulfuric acid electrolyte (*yellow*). The specific gravity of the acid decreases in use from cl.3 to cl.14, at which value the battery needs recharging.

operation of the cell. The dry Leclanché cell gives a nominal 1.54V. For the higher voltages necessary to power transistor radios, batteries containing several thin laminar cells are used. **Secondary cells**, known also as storage batteries or **accumulators**, can be recharged and reused at will provided too much electricity has not been abstracted from them. The most common type, as used in AUTOMOBILES, is the lead-acid type, in which both electrodes are made of LEAD (the positive covered with lead (IV) oxide when charged) and the electrolyte is dilute SULFURIC ACID. Its voltage is about 2V, depending on the state of charge. The robust yet light nickel-iron battery (having a POTASSIUM hydroxide solution electrolyte) is widely used in telephone exchanges and other heavy-duty situations but is being partly displaced by the nickel-cadmium type. They give about 1.3V.

The first battery was the voltaic pile invented c1800 by VOLTA. This comprised a stack of pairs of silver and zinc disks, each pair separated by a brine-soaked board. For many years from 1836 the standard form of battery was the **Daniell cell**, with a zinc cathode, a copper cathode and a porous-pot barrier separating the anode electrolyte (copper(II) sulfate) from the cathode electrolyte (sulfuric acid). The lead-acid storage battery was invented by Gaston Planté in 1859 and the wet Leclanché cell, the prototype for the modern dry cell, by Georges Leclanché in 1865.

BATTERY, in law. See ASSAULT.

BATTERY, The, a park at the S end of Manhattan Island, New York City, containing Castle Clinton, a fort built 1808–11 to defend New York harbor.

BATTLE CREEK, city in S Mich., located where Battle Creek joins the Kalamazoo R. Famous as the home of the cereal industry created by W. K. Kellogg, it also produces electrical equipment and machinery. Pop 38 931.

BATTLE HYMN OF THE REPUBLIC, American patriotic song, unofficial hymn of Union troops in the Civil War. Written in 1861 by Julia Ward HOWE and sung to the tune of *John Brown's Body*, it later became a Protestant hymn and a protest marching song.

BATTLE OF BRITAIN, air battle in WWII from Aug. 8 to Oct. 31, 1940, between the British Royal Air Force (RAF) and the German Luftwaffe. The Germans intended to weaken British defenses and morale before invading the country. The Luftwaffe forces were much greater than those of the RAF, but the latter proved to be technically and tactically superior. The Germans first bombed shipping and ports, then airfields and Midland industries and, finally, in Sept., London. Daylight raids proving too costly, the Germans turned to night attacks. At the end the RAF had lost some 900 planes, the Germans over 2300, and Hitler had postponed his projected invasion indefinitely, thus tacitly admitting failure.

BATTLE OF THE ATLANTIC, the WWII air and sea effort of the Axis powers to stop US supplies coming to Britain and the USSR. Allied convoys, guarded by British, Canadian and later US destroyers and escort carriers, ran the gauntlet of German U-boats and surface raiders. Through antisubmarine devices, air patrols and bombing of submarine pens and factories the Allies gradually overcame the Axis threat at sea.

BATTLE OF THE BULGE, last major western counteroffensive by the Germans in WWII. They planned to capture Liège and Antwerp, thus dividing the Allied armies. The German assault in the Ardennes began on Dec. 16, 1944, and created a huge "bulge" into the Allied lines. Although suffering about 77000 casualties, the Allies stopped the German advance by Jan. 16, 1945.

BATTLESHIP, historically the largest of conventionally-armed warships. Though some battleships are still kept in reserve, aircraft carriers superseded them during WWII as the largest fighting ships afloat. The first US battleships were the *Indiana*, *Massachusetts* and *Oregon*, completed in 1895–96. Since 1946 no more have been built. (See also DREADNOUGHT; NAVY.)

BATU KHAN (d. 1255 AD), Mongol conqueror of Russia, grandson of GENGHIS KHAN. He ruled the westernmost part of the MONGOL EMPIRE and threatened eastern Europe from 1235 to 1242. He founded the khanate of the GOLDEN HORDE which ruled southern Russian for 200 years, isolating it from western European developments.

BAUCIS AND PHILEMON, in Greek mythology, an old man and his wife who gave hospitality to ZEUS and HERMES. The two gods, disguised as travelers, had been refused hospitality by all others in Phrygia. In reward, the aged couple were spared from a flood, their house became a temple and after death they were turned into trees. Their names are associated with faithful marriage.

BAUDELAIRE, Charles Pierre (1821–1867), French poet and critic, forerunner of SYMBOLISM. The poems in *Les Fleurs du Mal* (1857), with their sensitive probing of even the mos bizarre sensations, outraged public opinion and led to the poet being tried for obscenity. His later prose poems were posthumously published in *Le Spleen de Paris* (1869). He was also a brilliant critic of music and fine art, and was renowned for his translations of Edgar Allan POE.

BAUDOUIN I (1930–), fifth king of the Belgians. He spent WWII with his family in Nazi internment, and succeeded his father, King Leopold III, who abdicated in 1951. In 1960 Baudouin proclaimed Congolese independence. He married a Spanish noblewoman, now Queen Fabiola.

BAUER, George. See AGRICOLA, GEORGIUS.

BAUHAUS, the most influential school of design and architecture in the 20th century. Walter GROPIUS founded it in 1919 at Weimar, Germany, and its teachers included some of the leading artists of the time. Gropius' ideal of uniting form with function is now a universal canon of design, and the dictum "less is more" has influenced much US design. The Bauhaus left Weimar in 1925 and was installed in new premises designed by Gropius in Dessau in 1927. The school was closed by the Nazis in 1933. Bauhaus teachers Gropius, FEININGER and MIES VAN DER ROHE later moved to the US.

BAUM, Lyman Frank (1856–1919), US children's writer, author of the famous *Wonderful Wizard of Oz* (1900), a tale of a girl carried by a cyclone to a land of adventure. The 1939 film adaptation became a motion-picture classic.

BAUMÉ, Antoine (1728–1804), French chemist, inventor of the Baumé HYDROMETER and remembered in the Baumé hydrometer scales, used to describe the DENSITIES of liquids.

BAUXITE, the main ore of ALUMINUM, consisting of hydrated aluminum oxide, usually with iron oxide impurity. It is a claylike, amorphous material formed by the weathering of silicate rocks, especially under tropical conditions. High-grade bauxite, being highly refractory, is used as a lining for furnaces. Synthetic corundum is made from it, and it is an ingredient in some quick-setting cements. Leading bauxite-producing countries include Jamaica, Australia, the USSR, Surinam, Guyana, France, Guinea and the US (especially Ark.).

BAVARIA (German: Bayern), largest state in West Germany. Its area is 27239sq mi and its population 10.5 million. MUNICH is the capital and administrative center. Bavaria manufactures machinery, precision instruments, textiles and toys. Brewing is also important and the annual Munich beer festival is a European occasion. Bavaria is also famous as a cultural center, with three universities, a technical institute, academies of arts and sciences, two leading museums and the BAYREUTH festival. The Christian Social Union (CSU), Bavaria's own distinctive political party, has played a vital part in national politics since WWII.

BAXTER, Richard (1615–1691), leading Puritan minister. He was ordained into the Church of England (1638), but later adopted a moderate Puritan stance and favored limited toleration of dissent. He was famous for his powerful sermons and his stirring autobiography.

BAY, popular name for the LAUREL tree (*Laurus nobilis*), also known as the sweet bay or bay laurel, native to the Mediterranean countries. Dried leaves are used to season foods. Bay trees are planted as ornamentals and their leaves were used in Classical Greece to crown heroes.

BAYAMÓN, industrial town in NE central Puerto Rico, close to SAN JUAN. The oldest Spanish settlement in Puerto Rico, Caparra, stood nearby. Pop 146552.

BAYAR, Mahmud Cêlal (1883–), president of Turkey 1950–60. He was prominent in ATATURK's nationalist movement after WWI, and later became economics minister (1932–37) and prime minister (1937–38) of the Turkish republic. He founded the opposition Democratic Party in 1946.

BAYARD, name of a family of US politicians and statesmen from Del. **James Asheton Bayard** (1767–1815) was a senator 1805–13, and helped negotiate the Treaty of GHENT, ending the War of 1812. His sons, **James Asheton Bayard** (1799–1880) and **Richard Henry Bayard** (1796–1868) also represented Del. in the Senate. **Thomas Francis Bayard** (1828–1898) was US secretary of state 1885–89 and US ambassador to Britain 1893–97.

BAYARD, Pierre Terrail, Seigneur de (c1473–1524), French commander famous for his bravery, who became the epitome of French chivalry. He first distinguished himself in French campaigns in Italy. Later at Mézières in 1521, with only 1000 men against 35000, he held off an invasion of central France by the emperor Charles V.

BAYAZID, name of two Ottoman sultans. **Bayazid I** (1354–1403), reigned 1389–1402. He waged successful campaigns in Anatolia and SE Europe, and defeated an allied Christian force at Nicopolis in 1396. He was defeated and captured at Angora (Ankara) in 1402 by TAMERLANE, who had invaded Anatolia in 1399, and died in captivity. **Bayazid II** (1447–1512), reigned 1481–1512 and was noted for his devotion to Islam and his cultural interests. He fought the Poles in the Crimea (1484), the Mamelukes of Syria and Egypt (1485–91), and the Venetians in the Levant and the Balkans (1499–1503). His victories made possible the expansion of the Ottoman Empire, but in 1511 his rule was menaced by the Persian Safavids and he finally abdicated in favor of his son Selim.

BAYBERRY, or candleberry, small aromatic West Indian tree (*Pimenta racemosa*), whose leathery leaves are used to make bay rum, a cosmetics ingredient. Also, the name of North American shrubs, *Myrica cerifera* and *M. pensylvanica*, related to the WAX MYRTLE.

BAY CITY, port in Mich., on Lake Huron, about 108mi NW of Detroit. Its products include boats, automobile parts, electrical equipment and machinery. Pop 49449.

BAY CITY, city in SE Tex., seat of Matagorda Co. A shipping and industrial center, with sulfur mines and oil wells nearby. Pop 11733.

BAYEUX TAPESTRY, embroidered linen wall-hanging of the early Middle Ages, depicting the Norman Conquest of England in 1066. It is 231ft long and 19.5in wide, and contains over 70 scenes. It is believed to have been commissioned by Bishop Odo, half-brother of WILLIAM the Conqueror, for Bayeux Cathedral in NW France.

BAYLE, Pierre (1647–1706), French philosopher, whose great *Historical and Critical Dictionary* (1697) embodied his skeptical critique of Christian orthodoxy. His rationalistic approach to belief strongly influenced 18th-century thinkers.

BAYLISS, Sir William Maddock (1860–1924), English physiologist who, in collaboration with **Ernest Henry Starling** (1866–1927), introduced the term HORMONE to describe substances which, when secreted from one part of the body, have a specific effect on another. In 1902 they discovered SECRETIN, one of the first hormones to be identified. Bayliss also introduced the saline injection for cases of surgical SHOCK during WWI.

BAYLOR, Elgin (1934–), US basketball star, named "Rookie of the Year" in 1959. In 1960, while playing for the Los Angeles Lakers, he broke all existing NBA records by scoring 71 points in one game.

BAY OF PIGS, English name for Bahia de Cochinos, SW Cuba, scene of an abortive invasion of Cuba on April 17, 1961. The invaders were Cubans who had

The Bayeux Tapestry is not in fact a tapestry. As can be seen here, the pattern is embroidered on a linen background and not woven into the material. Formerly displayed at festivals, its age has made it too fragile, and it is now preserved in the Bayeux museum. The portion shown here depicts William of Normandy's fleet enjoying a last meal before crossing the English Channel. The tapestry is a valuable record of life at the time of the Norman Conquest.

fled to the US after Fidel CASTRO seized power. Although Americans were not directly involved, the CIA had helped plan the invasion.

BAYONET, blade fitted at the muzzle of a rifle to turn it into a stabbing or thrusting weapon. Early models (devised for 17th-century muskets) plugged into the barrel; modern ones fit below it.

BAYONNE, city and port in N.J., about 8mi SW of New York City. It has oil refineries, produces chemicals, paint, electric motors and boats and is the site of a naval supply depot. Pop 72 743.

BAYOU (from Choctaw *bayuk*, a creek), a minor creek or river tributary to a larger body of water, especially in La. By extension, the term is applied to muddy or sluggish bodies of water in general.

BAY PSALM BOOK, name commonly given to the first book printed in Colonial America. *The Whole Booke of Psalmes Faithfully Translated into English Metre* was published in Cambridge, Mass., in 1640 as a hymnal for the Massachusetts Bay Colony. It was the work of Richard MATHER, John ELIOT and Thomas Weld and was printed by Stephen DAY.

BAYREUTH, industrial city in NE Bavaria, in West Germany. It is famous as the last home of Richard WAGNER and as the site of his opera house, the *Festspielhaus*, where the annual Wagnerian festival (begun in 1876) is now run by Wagner's grandson Wolfgang. Pop 63 530.

BAY SHORE, unincorporated town and resort in SE N.Y., on the S shore of Long Island, on Great South Bay. Pop 11 119.

BAYTOWN, city in SE Tex., 22mi ESE of Houston. It produces, refines and ships oil, and manufactures petrochemicals. Pop 43 980.

BAY VILLAGE, residential city in N Ohio on Lake Erie, a W suburb of Cleveland. There is a wildlife reserve nearby. Pop 18 163.

BAZOOKA, portable rocket launcher first used in WWII, constructed from a 5ft-long, smoothbore tube. One man rests it on his shoulder, aims and fires the weapon, while another loads the rockets. Originally capable of penetrating 5in armorplate at 300yd, it is being constantly improved and developed.

BCG VACCINE (*B*acillus *C*almette-*G*uérin), anti-TUBERCULOSIS vaccine (see VACCINATION) developed by CALMETTE and GUÉRIN.

BEA, Augustin (1881–1968), German cardinal. An adviser to Pius XI and Pius XII, he encouraged ecumenism at the Second VATICAN COUNCIL, and headed the Secretariat for Promoting Christian Unity.

BEACH, stretch of SAND, shingle, GRAVEL and other material along the shore of a lake, river or sea. Caused by erosion and deposition of sediment by waves, it usually extends from the furthest point reached by waves out to a water depth of around 10m.

BEACH GRASS, common name for sand-binding grasses (*Ammophila*) found on sandy coasts of Europe and North America. These perennials with creeping root stocks are used notably in the Netherlands, on Cape Cod, Mass., and around San Francisco to hold down protective coastal dunes.

BEACH PLUM, *Prunus maritima*, a beach species of the genus *Prunus*, native to the North American coasts from Nova Scotia to Va., and frequently planted as ornamentals.

BEACON, a city in SE N.Y., located at the foot of Mt Beacon on the Hudson R, site of signal fires during the Revolution. It produces baking machinery, bricks, hats and clothing. Pop 13 255.

BEACON, originally a warning signal, for example, a fire kindled at a prominent point on the coast to warn or guide shipping. The word came to denote any coastal sign for guiding sea vessels. By analogy, "beacon" is also used to describe certain radio aids to navigation.

BEACON HILL, most famous of three hills in Boston, Mass. A beacon stood there in the Colonial period. The state capitol was constructed on it in 1795, and its streets are lined with elegant, early red-brick houses.

BEACONSFIELD, Lord. See DISRAELI, BENJAMIN.

BEADED LIZARD, the species *Heloderma horridum* which, with the Gila Monster *H. suspectum*, comprises the family Helodermatidae (suborder Sauria). These two LIZARDS are found in the southwestern US and Mexico; and are the only venomous lizards known. They bite only when severely provoked, and their poison apparatus is so primitive and inefficient that the bite is rarely serious, and hardly ever lethal to man. Carnivorous, they can fast for months because of their ability to store fat in their tails.

BEADLE, Erastus Flavel (1821–1894), US publisher who issued his first DIME NOVEL in 1860. It was immediately popular. He later published mostly western stories, especially about Kit CARSON.

BEADLE, George Wells (1903–   ), US geneticist who shared part of the 1958 Nobel Prize for Physiology or Medicine with E. L. TATUM (and J. LEDERBERG) for work showing that individual GENES controlled the production of particular ENZYMES (1937–40).

BEADS, a term derived from the Saxon word *biddan*, meaning to pray. The 165 rosary beads used by Roman Catholics to keep count of prayers are beads in this original sense. Beads were used by prehistoric man, who ascribed magical properties to them: these have gradually become mixed with or superseded by their ornamental use. Styles and materials have often changed, but beads have never gone out of fashion.

BEAGLE, the smallest trailing hound, often used for hare hunts. Its short coat shows black, white and brown coloring. It stands 13–15in high at the shoulder.

The beagle is the smallest of the English hounds and the one most commonly seen at a hunt. It is generally used for hare hunting, with the field following on foot.

BEAGLE, H.M.S., British survey ship which, under the command of **Captain Robert Fitzroy** (1805–1865), and carrying Charles DARWIN as naturalist, sailed around the world between 1831 and 1836. Darwin's observations on this voyage, particularly those of the fauna of the Galápagos Islands, helped bring him to his theory of EVOLUTION.

BEAK, or **bill,** general term for a rigid, projecting oral structure. All MONOTREMES, BIRDS (for both of which the term "bill" is preferred) and TURTLES, as well as some FISH, CEPHALOPODA and INSECTS, are beaked, as were many DINOSAURS. Beak shapes and sizes are usually highly specialized.

BEAKED WHALES, several genera of toothed WHALES which, with the BOTTLENOSED WHALES, make up the family Ziphiidae (order CETACEA). Some species are well known, but a number are known only from isolated bodies or even skulls: it is not certain that this infrequency of discovery is due to genuine rarity. Typically, the males have two large TEETH at the tip of the lower jaw, the number of further teeth (if any) varying from species to species.

BEAN, common name given to a number of species of the family Leguminosae, cultivated for the food value of their seeds, immature pods and shoots. Important species include: the SOYBEAN (*Glycine max*), the fruit of which has a high protein content and is a dietary staple in Asia and is now grown in the US; the common garden bean or French bean (*Phaseolus vulgaris*), grown extensively in Europe and the US; the Scarlet Runner bean (*P. multiflorus*), which may be grown as an ornamental plant as well as for its pods; the Lima bean (*P. lunatus*), originating from South America; the Broad bean (*Vicia fabo*), grown mainly in Europe; and the Mung bean, the source of bean sprouts popular in Chinese cuisine and staple in Asia. Bean plants in general are of great value in replenishing nitrogen-deficient soils, using, in association with BACTERIA, a process known as NITROGEN FIXATION. (See LEGUMINOUS PLANTS.)

BEAN, Judge Roy (c1825–1903), US justice of the peace who called himself "the only law west of the Pecos." After an adventurous early life which included arrest, jail break and proprietorship of tent saloons, he settled at what later became Langtry in W Tex. He built a combination store, saloon and pool hall, and held court as justice and coroner. His decisions were more notable for six-gun drama and humor than legal sagacity.

BEAN BEETLE, or Mexican Bean Beetle, *Epilachna varivestis*, a species of BEETLE important as a crop pest since it eats the leaves of LEGUMES. It is of the family Coccinellidae (the LADYBUGS). Resistant to DDT, it is controlled by use of the rather less toxic Methoxychlor.

BEAR FLAG REPUBLIC, republic declared in 1846 by a group of American settlers in Sacramento Valley, Cal., who rejected Mexican rule. Their flag, with a grizzly bear, a single star and the words "California Republic," was raised at Sonoma in June 1846. The explorer John C. FRÉMONT aided the insurgents, but the Republic collapsed after the outbreak of the Mexican War in May 1846; this ended in Feb. 1848 with Cal. ceded to the US. The Cal. state flag is still modeled on the "Bear Flag."

BEARD, growth of hair on a man's chin, cheeks and neck, regarded by many races as a symbol of strength and virility. Among the ancient Egyptians, Assyrians and Chinese the beard had a ritual significance. The religious cult of the beard is still prevalent in Eastern cultures. Indian Sikhs are forbidden to remove a hair from their bodies; Hindus are usually clean-shaven. The Western habit of shaving became common with the Romans.

BEARD, Charles Austin (1874–1948), controversial US historian, author of *An Economic Interpretation of the Constitution* (1913), and co-author, with his wife **Mary Ritter Beard** (1876–1958), of *The Rise of American Civilization* (1927), a popular survey. Beard's iconoclastic analysis of the origins of the Constitution in terms of the economic self-interest of its authors was a landmark in US historiography. He later became a bitter critic of the ROOSEVELT administration and the circumstances of US entry into WWII.

BEARD, Daniel Carter (1850–1941), organizer of the BOY SCOUTS of America. As National Scout Commissioner (1910–41), he gave the movement its distinctly American character, based on Indian and pioneer lore.

BEARDED LIZARD, or bearded dragon, large LIZARD of the family Agamidae (see AGAMIDS), *Amphibolurus barbatus*, found in Australia. It grows to about 600mm (2ft) long, is insectivorous, and changes color according to emotional state. It frequently runs on its hind legs only, not for greater speed but as a form of temperature control. It derives its name from the "beard" of pointed scales under its throat which it puffs out when in danger or for territorial defense (see TERRITORIALITY).

BEARDSLEY, Aubrey Vincent (1872–1898), English illustrator and author. By 1894 Beardsley had become art editor of the *Yellow Book* magazine and a prolific artist. His graphic style was one of sharp black-and-white contrasts, with flowing lines and detailed patterning; his subject matter tended towards the decadent or erotic, for instance, Oscar WILDE's *Salomé*, or ARISTOPHANES' *Lysistrata*.

BEARINGS, components of MACHINES which support and direct loads while reducing FRICTION where moving parts are in contact. The simplest type is the journal bearing in which a rotating shaft is supported in a hole in a fixed frame. The inner surface of the hole is usually lined with a bearing metal such as BABBITT METAL to reduce wear. Friction and wear are also reduced by suitable LUBRICATION. Lubricants, which include greases, oils, water and even air, form a thin FLUID film between the moving parts of the bearing. Usually the motion itself is sufficient to form the film (hydrodynamic bearings) but sometimes the lubricant must be applied under PRESSURE (hydrostatic bearings) as in air-lubricated dental drills. For many applications roller bearings and ball bearings are used. In these a separator holds a series of short cylinders or balls between the inner and outer

A black bear (*Ursus americanus*) in the Great Smoky Mountains National Park. This bear is a familiar sight in US national parks, although where it is not protected it is hunted for its valuable fur.

rings of the bearing. In recent years dry (unlubricated) plastic bearings and self-lubricating bearings have been developed for applications where lubrication is difficult or undesirable.

BEAR MOUNTAIN, a peak (1 305ft), also a recreational park N of New York City, overlooking the Hudson R. It is popular all year around, with good hiking trails and a river steamer service.

BEARS, the world's largest extant terrestrial carnivores, characterized by their heavy build, thick limbs, diminutive tail and small ears and included in a single mammalian family, Ursidae. The differences between the seven species are small and are mainly limited to details of the skeleton. All have coarse thick hair which is, with the exception of the POLAR BEAR, dark in color. The varieties of the BROWN BEAR have the widest distribution. Other species are the NORTH AMERICAN BLACK BEAR, the SPECTACLED BEAR, the ASIATIC BLACK BEAR, the SUN BEAR and the SLOTH BEAR.

BEARS AND BULLS. See STOCKS AND THE STOCK MARKET.

BEAT GENERATION, literary movement of the 1950s, which burst onto the American scene in 1956 with Jack KEROUAC's *On the Road* (the adventures of the original social dropout), Allen GINSBERG's *Howl and Other Poems* and work by such poets as Lawrence Ferlinghetti and Gregory Corso, and later by the novelist William S. BURROUGHS. The movement was a protest against complacent middle-class values and, though shortlived, influenced artistic experiments for the next 15 years.

BEATIFICATION, act or decree by which the pope directs the public veneration of a deceased person whose life manifested unusual Christian virtue. The honor bestows the title "Blessed" on the person and is usually a preliminary for CANONIZATION. It is preceded by a thorough investigation of the candidate's life.

BEATING, a phenomenon of importance in RADIO and ACOUSTICS resulting from the INTERFERENCE of two wave-trains of similar frequency (see WAVE MOTION) in which a new periodicity is set up in the aggregate AMPLITUDE having frequency equal to the difference of the two constituent frequencies. Beats between two musical notes of similar pitch can often be heard as an unpleasant throbbing; beating between two ULTRASONIC tones may result in an audible tone.

BEATITUDES, eight blessings pronounced by Christ as a prologue to the Sermon on the Mount (Matthew 5:3–10). Jesus calls "Blessed" those who are poor in spirit, the meek, those who mourn, those who seek after holiness, the merciful, the pure in heart, the peacemakers and those who suffer persecution for righteousness' sake.

BEATLES, The, British vocal and instrumental group that inspired and dominated popular music in the 1960s. The group comprised **George Harrison** (1943–), **John Lennon** (1940–), **Paul McCartney** (1942–) and **Ringo Starr** (1940–). From the clubs of Liverpool the Beatles became international stars in 1963 with *She Loves You*. They separated at the beginning of the 1970s.

BEATON, Sir Cecil Walter Hardy (1904–), English photographer and designer, well known for his royal portraits, collections such as *Cecil Beaton's Scrapbook* (1937) and for set and costume designs for shows and films such as *My Fair Lady* (1956). He was knighted in 1972.

BEATON (or **Bethune), David** (1494–1546), Scottish churchman, archbishop of St. Andrews and primate of Scotland (1539). He crowned MARY QUEEN OF SCOTS in 1543 and became chancellor of Scotland. His persecution of Reformers led to his murder.

BEATRICE, city in SE Neb. Situated in a grain and livestock-raising area, it produces farm machinery and dairy produce. Pop 12 389.

BEATRICE, name given by the Italian poet DANTE ALIGHIERI to his ideal woman, signifying "bearer of blessings." She was based on the real Beatrice Portinari (d. 1290). Her main function in the *Divine Comedy* is as the intercessor who sends VIRGIL to Dante's aid, meets him in Purgatory and guides him through Paradise.

BEATTY, David, 1st Earl Beatty of the North Sea and of Brooksby (1871–1936), British admiral famous for his part in the Battle of JUTLAND (1916). He served in Egypt and Sudan and in China during the BOXER REBELLION. A rear admiral in 1910, he was made first sea lord and given an earldom in 1919.

BEAUFORT, second oldest city in S.C., on Port Royal Island, 50mi SW of Charleston. A yachting center and resort, Beaufort also has fishing and canning industries. Pop 9434.

BEAUFORT SCALE, method of measuring wind force, developed in 1806 by the British Admiral Sir Francis Beaufort. Wind strength is measured on a scale ranging from 0–12 (0–17 in Britain and the US). Internationally, the scale has now been superseded by measurement in knots. (See WIND.)

BEAUFORT SEA, part of the Arctic Ocean, N of Alaska and W of BANKS ISLAND. It reaches a maximum depth of about 15 000ft.

BEAUHARNAIS, Hortense de (1783–1837), daughter of Alexandre and of Joséphine de BEAUHARNAIS. As the wife of Louis BONAPARTE, she was Queen of Holland (1806–10) and mother of NAPOLEON III.

BEAUHARNAIS, Joséphine de (1763–1814), first wife of NAPOLEON I and empress of the French. Before her marriage to Napoleon in 1796 (annulled in 1809) she had been the wife of Alexandre, vicomte de Beauharnais (1760–94). Their son, **Eugène de Beauharnais** (1781–1824), was made viceroy of Italy by Napoleon. He distinguished himself in campaigns against Austria and Russia.

BEAUJOLAIS, hilly region in E France, producing red wines, mainly from vineyards on the Saône R.

BEAUMARCHAIS, Pierre Augustin Caron de (1732–1799), French dramatist and variously an artist, litigant and political agent. His best-known plays, *The Barber of Seville* (1775) and *The Marriage of Figaro* (1784; the basis of MOZART's opera) ridiculed the established order and the nobility. He was instrumental in furnishing the Americans with arms and money at the outbreak of the Revolution.

BEAUMONT, second-ranking port of Tex., at the head of navigation of the Neches R. It has some of the world's largest oil refineries and several lumber mills. Pop 115 919.

BEAUMONT, Francis (c1584–1616), and **FLETCHER, John** (1579–1625), English Jacobean playwrights. Their many plays, both as individuals and in collaboration, strongly influenced English drama. Their best-known collaborations are *Philaster* (c1608), *The Maid's Tragedy* (c1609) and *A King and No King* (1611).

BEAUMONT, William (1785–1853), US army physician noted for his researches into the human DIGESTIVE SYSTEM. While on assignment in northern Mich. in 1822 he treated a trapper with a serious stomach wound; when the wound healed, an opening (or FISTULA) into the victim's stomach remained, through which Beaumont was able to extract gastric juices for analysis.

BEAUREGARD, Pierre Gustave Toutant de (1818–1893), Confederate general during the American Civil War. In 1861 Beauregard commanded the attack on FORT SUMTER, S.C., which opened the war. He distinguished himself at the First Battle of BULL RUN, shared command at SHILOH and held off Union naval attacks on Charleston. Joining General Joseph E. JOHNSTON, he fell back to the Carolinas in the face of Sherman's Georgia campaign, and remained there until the end of the war.

BEAUVOIR, Simone de (1908–), French writer, friend of Jean-Paul SARTRE and a leading exponent of EXISTENTIALISM and the rôle of women in politics and intellectual life. Her best-known works are *The Second Sex* (1953) and *The Mandarins* (1956). She has also written an autobiographical trilogy, and a moving account of her mother's death, *A Very Easy Death* (1966).

BEAVERBROOK, William Maxwell Aitken, 1st Baron (1879–1964), Canadian-born British newspaper owner and Conservative cabinet minister. His government posts included minister of aircraft production 1940–42, and lord privy seal 1943–45. Among his mass-circulation newspapers are the *Daily Express*, *Sunday Express* and *Evening Standard*.

BEAVER DAM, city in SE central Wis. Various manufactures include outboard motors, shoes and foundry products. Pop 14 265.

BEAVER FALLS, city in W Pa., on Beaver R. Industries include coal and clay mining. Pop 14 375.

BEAVERS, large RODENTS (family Castoridae), weighing up to 40kg (90lb) or over, of northern lands. They have thick, furry waterproof coats, powerful, webfooted hindlegs and small forelimbs with dexterous, sensitive paws. They are lissencephalic (smooth-brained), but nevertheless by far the most intelligent rodents: their technical constructive skill, exemplified by their building, from logs and mud, dams and lodges (domes up to 7m (23ft) in diameter in which they live), is surpassed only by that of man. The dominant features of their SKULLS are the powerful incisors (see TEETH), with which they fell trees and gnaw logs into shape. Their large, heavy tails are used on land for balance and in the water as rudders. Their respiratory system (see RESPIRATION) enables them to remain underwater for up to 15 minutes.

BEAVERTON, city in NW Ore., near Portland, at the center of an agricultural region. Pop 18 577.

BEBEL, August (1840–1913), leading German socialist and co-founder of the Social Democratic party (1869). A strong anti-militarist and fighter for women's rights, his *Women and Socialism* was published in 1879.

BEBOP. See BOP.

BEC, Benedictine abbey in Normandy, France, founded in 1034. The abbey gained eminence under the medieval abbots ANSELM and LANFRANC.

BECCARIA, Cesare Bonesana, Marchese di (1738–1794), Italian criminologist and economist, instrumental in many major reforms in the treatment of criminals. His *Essay on Crimes and Punishments* (1764) recommended the abolition of capital punishment and torture.

BECHER, Johann Joachim (1635–1682), German chemist, physician and economist whose conception of an active principle of combustion was developed by his pupil STAHL into the PHLOGISTON theory.

BECHET, Sidney (1897–1959), US jazz clarinet and soprano saxophone player, who performed with such leading jazz artists as Bunk Johnson, King Oliver and Clarence Williams. After many tours in Europe, he settled in France in 1947.

BECHUANALAND. See BOTSWANA.

BECK, Jozef (1894–1944), Polish politician, foreign

minister in 1932. His friendly relations with the German Nazi party enabled Poland to gain border territory from Czechoslovakia. However, when Hitler threatened Poland, Beck was forced to take refuge in Romania, where he remained until his death.

BECK, Ludwig (1880–1944), German general and chief of general staff, 1935. He resigned in protest from the Nazi party in 1938, and was then involved in the attempt to assassinate Hitler in 1944. When the plot failed, he was shot.

BECKER, Carl Lotus (1873–1945), US historian of Cornell University, Ithaca, N.Y., who brought an elegant style and original insights to such subjects as *The Declaration of Independence* (1922) and *The Heavenly City of the Eighteenth-Century Philosophers* (1932).

BECKET, Thomas à, Saint (1118–1170), martyr and archbishop of Canterbury. He first served as chancellor under HENRY II, becoming a close friend, but in 1162 was appointed archbishop of Canterbury. Thereafter he supported the Church against the monarchy, and soon he and the king were at odds. The rift culminated in Becket's refusal to approve the royal "Constitutions of Clarendon," which sought to limit Church authority. A threatened papal interdict brought a temporary reconciliation, but in 1170 the intransigent Becket was murdered in the cathedral at Canterbury by four knights inspired by some rash words of the king's. Becket was canonized in 1173.

BECKETT, Samuel Barclay (1906–   ), Irish dramatist and novelist, resident in France since 1937. His work, much of it written in French, deals with habit, boredom and suffering, and is deeply pessimistic. His novels include *Murphy* (1938) and the trilogy, *Molloy*, *Malone Dies*, and *The Unnamable* (1951–53). Among his plays are *Waiting for Godot* (1952) and *Happy Days* (1961). Beckett won the 1969 Nobel Prize for Literature.

BECKLEY, city in SW Va., seat of Raleigh Co., in a coal-mining area. Pop 19 884.

BECKMANN, Max (1884–1950), German expressionist painter and graphic artist. In 1933 his work was declared degenerate by the Nazis and he took refuge in Holland (1937–47) and then in the US.

BECKMANN THERMOMETER, a mercury-in-glass THERMOMETER used in CALORIMETRY which offers an accuracy of up to ± 0.001K but which has a range of only 5K. This is achieved through its having a large bulb and fine bore. It was devised by the German organic chemist **Ernst Otto Beckmann** (1853–1923), who is also remembered for his discovery (1886) of the Beckmann rearrangement of ketoximes (see OXIMES) into AMIDES under acid CATALYSIS.

BECKWORTH, James Pierson (c1798–1867), US fur trader, explorer and army scout, born a Negro slave. His discovery in the 1850s of the lowest pass over the N Sierra Nevada (now named for him) opened a major trail to the Sacramento Valley, Cal.

BECQUEREL, Antoine Henri (1852–1908), French physicist who, having discovered natural RADIOACTIVITY in a URANIUM salt in 1896, shared the 1903 Nobel physics prize with Pierre and Marie CURIE.

BEDBUGS, a number of BUGS of the family Cimicidae, order HEMIPTERA, bloodsuckers parasitic (see PARASITES) on man and other animals. The common bed-bug, *Cimex lectularius*, found throughout most of the world, is about 5mm (0.2in) long and 3mm (0.12in) broad, and colored usually mahogany brown, though it may appear reddish if it has recently fed or purplish if an older meal is still in its gut. Adults may survive for up to a year without feeding. Very occasionally they transmit dangerous diseases such as CHAGAS' DISEASE and PLAGUE, but this is most uncommon.

BEDDOES, Thomas (1760–1808), English chemist and physician, who pioneered the inhalation of various gases in medicine. While in Bristol (from 1792) he gathered around him an important group of scientists and men of letters, including DAVY, WATT, S. T. COLERIDGE, SOUTHEY and WORDSWORTH.

BEDDOES, Thomas Lovell (1803–1849), English poet, best known for the dark drama *Death's Jest Book* (1850). Like much of his work, it is more a meditation on death than a play. He studied at Oxford and in Germany, but his radical politics forced him to flee to Switzerland, where he committed suicide.

BEDE, Saint (c673–735), known as "The Venerable," an Anglo-Saxon monk and scholar whose work embraced most of contemporary learning. His *Ecclesiastical History of the English Nation* is indispensable for the early history of England.

BEDFORD, city in S Ind., seat of Lawrence Co. It has famous limestone quarries. Pop 13 087.

BEDFORD, town in E Mass., 15mi NW of Boston. It is the center of a poultry, dairying and truck farming region. Pop 13 513.

BEDFORD, city in NE Ohio, a residential suburb of Cleveland, which lies 11mi to the NW. Pop 17 552.

BEDFORD, city in N Tex., 15mi ENE of Fort Worth. Pop 10 049.

BEDFORD HEIGHTS, residential village in N Ohio, a suburb of Cleveland. Pop 13 063.

BEDLAM, familiar name for London's oldest insane asylum. It is a corruption of the name St. Mary of Bethlehem, founded in 1247 as a priory and made a hospital for the insane (1547). The term is now used for a madhouse or any uproar or chaos.

BEDLINGTON TERRIER, a breed of terrier dog, first bred in Northumberland, England. A sporting dog, it weights 18–24lb and stands about 13in high, with long legs and powerful muzzle. Bedlingtons are dark blue, liver or tan in color.

BEDLOE'S ISLAND. See LIBERTY ISLAND.

BEDOUIN, nomadic herdsmen of the Syrian, Arabian and Sahara deserts. Although Muslim, Bedouin society retains pre-Islamic beliefs. It is comprised of rigidly hierarchical tribal groups, some of which still practice slavery. Such values as obedience, generosity, honor, cunning, vengefulness and forgiveness are emphasized. (See ARAB; NOMAD.)

BEDSORES, sores and ULCERS occurring in bedridden patients when pressure and friction restrict skin blood supply. They may be prevented by frequent change of position and bathing; treatment includes ASTRINGENTS SILICONE creams and ultraviolet light.

BEDSTRAW, herbs of the madder family (Rubiaceae), genus GALIUM, once used in Europe for stuffing mattresses. They are low-growing, with weak stems and lacy flowers. North American species total about 20, and include the goosegrass of the eastern states.

BEE, superfamily (Apoidea) of insects which convert nectar and pollen into HONEY for use as food. There are about 20 000 species. Bees and flowering plants are largely interdependent; plants are pollinated (or fertilized) as the bees gather their pollen. Many farmers keep bees specially for this purpose.

Most bees are solitary and each female builds her own nest, although many bees may occupy a single site. Eggs are laid in cells provided with enough pollen-nectar paste to feed the larva until it becomes a flying, adult bee. Social bees (honeybees and bumblebees) live in a complex society of 10 000–50 000 members. Headed by the queen, whose function is to lay eggs (up to 2 000 a day), the community comprises female workers which collect pollen and build cells, and male bees, or drones, which fertilize the few young queens that appear each fall. Parasitic bees, not equipped to build hives, develop in the cells of the host working bees.

BEEBE, Charles William (1877–1962), US naturalist remembered for the descents into the ocean depths he made with Otis Barton in their BATHYSPHERE. Diving off Bermuda in 1934 they reached a then-record depth of 3 028ft (923m).

BEECH, deciduous trees of the family Fagaceae, native in the N Hemisphere. Of 10 known species the main ones are the European beech (*Fagus sylvatica*) and the American beech (*F. grandifolia*). The beech grows up to 30m (100ft) high, has smooth gray bark and dark green, oval leaves. In Europe, several varieties— the Copper, Purple and Fern-leaved—are used ornamentally. Wood from the American beech is

Schematic view of a beaver dam and lodge. Of all the mammals the beaver's technical skill is rivalled only by that of man. The dams are built to increase the depth of the small streams in which the beaver colony lives and to prevent the streams freezing solid in winter. The mud packed around the lodges freezes hard and prevents wolves and other enemies from entering.

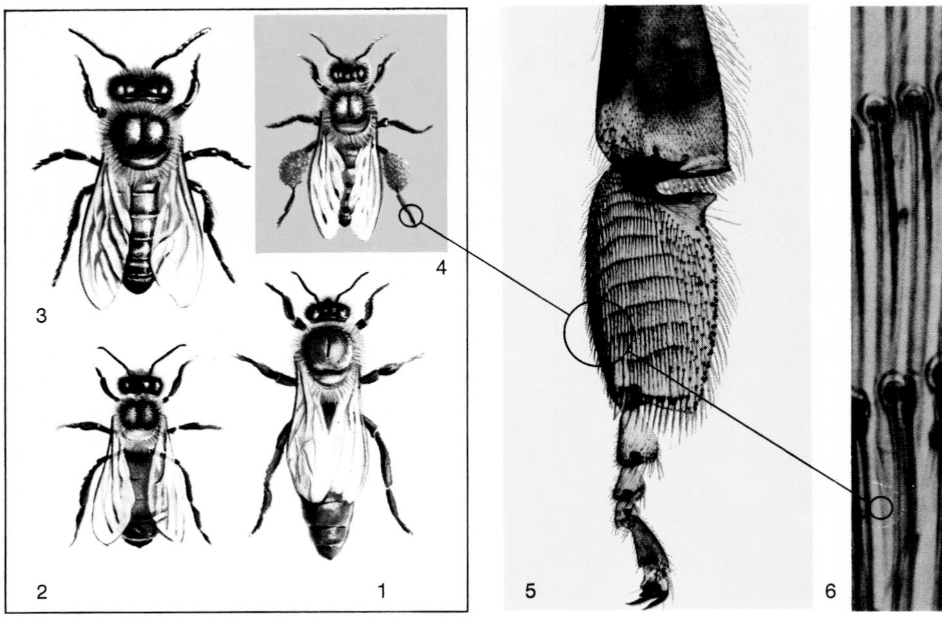

The bees in a hive are of three kinds: the queen (1), the male drone (2) and the female worker (3). Pollen is the stuff of life to all of them; it is gathered by the worker, in "baskets" on each hindleg (4). Part of the hindleg, enlarged 26 times (5), shows fine hairs and the pollen "basket". When enlarged 165 times (6) the pollen-bearing cells become clearly visible.

used in furniture, plywood composition and gunstocks.

BEECHAM, Sir Thomas (1879–1961), English conductor. He introduced many operas to England, notably Richard STRAUSS' *Der Rosenkavalier*, and was an eloquent advocate of the music of his friend DELIUS. Beecham founded two orchestras, the London Philharmonic and the Royal Philharmonic.

BEECHER, Henry Ward (1813–1887), US clergyman, lecturer, preacher and author; minister of Plymouth Congregational Church (1847–87), who was the subject of a notorious and sensational lawsuit for adultery. Like his father, Lyman BEECHER, he was renowned as an orator. He was a staunch advocate of ABSOLITIONISM.

BEECHER, Lyman (1775–1863), US clergyman and liberal theologian who helped found the American Bible Society (1816). Beecher's sermons against slavery and intemperance made him one of the most influential orators of his time. His daughter was Harriet Beecher STOWE.

Characteristic aspects of the beech tree: a. leaf of the common beech tree, b. leaf of the colorful copper beech, c. male inflorescence, d. female inflorescence (the beech has both organs), e. open cupule with two tetrahedral oil-containing seeds.

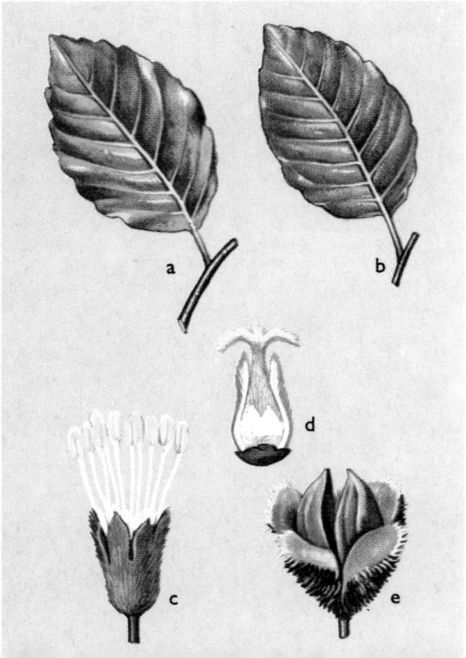

BEECH GROVE, city in central Ind., 7mi SE of Indianapolis. It produces electrical goods and is a dairy-farming center. Pop 13832.

BEE-EATERS, the family Meropidae of the order Coraciiformes, insect-eating birds found mainly in tropical and subtropical areas. There are 24 species in 3 genera, the most important, *Merops*, containing 21 species including the best known, *M. apiaster*. All nest in holes burrowed in soft earth or sand, excavating oval chambers some 150–250mm (6–10in) long at the end of tunnels up to 2.5m (8.2ft) in length.

BEEF, the flesh of CATTLE. Beef cattle, bred to produce high quality meat, are heavily built with short necks and legs. They are usually slaughtered at the age of about three years, although modern techniques can fatten animals up within a year. About 12 cuts (e.g. brisket, sirloin, rump) are taken from a carcass. For the best flavor and texture, beef must be cooled and matured under controlled conditions.

BEEFEATER, obscure nickname given to the costumed warders of the Tower of London and sometimes to the YEOMEN OF THE GUARD. A great tourist attraction, Beefeaters' costumes date back to Tudor times.

BEEFLIES, the family Bombyliidae (order Diptera) of insects, many of which resemble BEES. Most have a long PROBOSCIS used to obtain NECTAR, and most are found in tropical or subtropical areas. Many beefly LARVAE are parasitic (see PARASITE).

BEEKEEPING, or **apiculture**, the husbandry (see ANIMAL HUSBANDRY) of BEES. The chief purpose of apiculture is the POLLINATION of crops, but commercial products of the hive include BEESWAX and of course HONEY: some 120000 tonnes of honey are produced annually both in the USA and in the USSR.

BEELZEBUB, or Baalsebub ("Lord of flies"), god worshiped by the Philistines of Palestine. Being a pagan deity, he appears in the New Testament as the chief demon (Matthew 12:24). He is among the fallen angels in MILTON's *Paradise Lost*.

BEER, an ALCOHOLIC BEVERAGE made by fermenting cereals (see BREWING). Known since ancient times, beer became common where the climate was unsuited to WINE production. Beer includes all the malt liquors variously called ale, stout, porter (drunk in the UK and Ireland) and lager. The alcohol content is 3–7%.

BEERBOHM, Sir Max (1872–1956), English satirical writer and caricaturist, educated at Merton College, Oxford. He is best known for the caustic yet benign wit of his caricatures of eminent Victorian and Edwardian figures, and for his satirical novel about Oxford, *Zuleika Dobson* (1911).

BEERNAERT, Auguste Marie François (1829–1912), Belgian statesman, co-winner of the 1909 Nobel Peace Prize. A liberal member of the Catholic party, he served as premier 1884–94, introducing electoral and labor reforms.

BEERS, Clifford Whittingham (1876–1943), founder of the US mental hygiene movement. After three years as a mental patient, he wrote *A Mind that Found Itself* (1908), an exposé of the abuse of the mentally ill. He helped found the National Commission for Mental Hygiene (1909).

BEERSHEBA, chief city in southern Israel (the Negev), about 45mi SW of Jerusalem. Home of the Biblical patriarchs ISAAC and ABRAHAM and once the southernmost town of JUDAH, it is now a major industrial and trading center. Pop 77400.

BEESWAX, substance secreted by worker BEES and used to build the cell walls of the honeycomb. It contains cerotic acid, myricin and long-chain ALKANES, and melts at around 65°C. The purified wax is used for candles and in furniture waxes, cosmetics, some printing inks and elsewhere.

BEET, *Beta vulgaris*, biennial plant with a fleshy taproot. The most extensively grown variety is SUGAR BEET, which provides 33% of the world's SUGAR. Also cultivated are the garden (or red) beet, eaten, either boiled or pickled, the MANGELWURZEL, used as forage, and the leaf beet (SWISS CHARD), used as a potherb.

BEETHOVEN, Ludwig van (1770–1827), German composer, born in Bonn. His prodigious talent was soon recognized: HAYDN singled him out and offered to take the young musician on as a pupil in Vienna. There Beethoven's remarkable piano playing attracted attention, as did his eccentric behavior. When aged about 30, Beethoven started to go deaf. From then on normal life was impossible, and he died without having been able to hear much of his mature work.

Beethoven's creative life is commonly divided into three periods. The *Pathétique* piano sonata and the First Symphony belong to the period when he was still influenced by Haydn and MOZART. To the middle period belong works in his own individual style, such as the Third (*Eroica*) and Fifth Symphonies, Fifth Piano Concerto (*Emperor*), the *Kreutzer* Violin Sonata and the opera *Fidelio*. His later, more intense, highly individual works include the Ninth (Choral) Symphony, the *Missa Solemnis* (Mass in D) and the innovating late string quartets, including the *Grosse Fuge*.

BEETLES, common name for all insects of the order Coleoptera, the largest in the animal kingdom. Beetles occur in diverse forms, colors and habitats and range from 0.4mm to over 150mm in length. They are distinguished by hard protective wing cases which enclose a more fragile pair of wings. Some, however, such as the ground beetles and weevils, are flightless. All beetles develop from eggs into LARVAE and then pupate (see PUPA) before becoming adults. The life cycle can range from the usual three larval stages to as many as 12 or more and may last for as little as 2–3 weeks or as much as 5 years. Beetles and their larvae eat animal, vegetable and even inorganic matter; some eat carrion, others live off dung and a number prey on other beetles. Among the economically harmful beetles are the potato-destroying COLORADO BEETLE, and the woodworm and DEATHWATCH BEETLES which attack and destroy furniture and woodwork.

BEEVILLE, city in S Tex., seat of Bee Co., It is a trade center for a county producing livestock, dairy products and oil. Pop 13811.

BEGONIA, a genus of perennial plants with about 900 species. Mostly succulent herbs, native to tropical regions, they are cultivated in house and garden for their colorful foliage, for example *Begonia diadema*, *B. rex* (silver leaf) and *B. masoniana* (iron cross), or for their attractive large flowers, for example *B.* × *tuberhybrida* and the Reiger begonias. They have tuberous, rhizomatous or fibrous roots. Indoors, begonias grow best in a sunny east or west window during the winter, but the degree of direct summer sunlight that individual varieties can tolerate varies. They grow best within the temperature range 16°C to 21°C (60°F to 70°F) and hot dry air must be avoided. The soil should be kept evenly moist, avoiding extreme dryness or wetness. They can be propagated from seed, tuber and rhizome cuttings, leaf cuttings or division of the tubers. Family: Begoniaceae.

BEGUINES, religious communities of women established in Europe in the 12th century. Devoted to charitable works, Beguines were not, however, bound by any religious oath. From 1200 the movement spread from Belgium across W Europe. After a decline, it revived in the 1700s and a few communities still exist in Belgium and the Netherlands.

BEHAIM, Martin (d. 1507), German traveler and geographer who made the earliest extant globe (1492). He accompanied the Portuguese explorer Diogo CAM's expedition along the W African coast to the mouth of the Congo R (1484).

BEHAN, Brendan (1923–1964), Irish playwright and author, noted for his vivid ribaldry and satire. His best-known works, *The Quare Fellow* (1956), *The Hostage* (1959) and the autobiographical *Borstal Boy* (1958), deal largely with his experiences in the Irish Republican Army and subsequent imprisonment.

BEHAVIORAL SCIENCES, those sciences dealing with human activity, individually or socially. The term, which is sometimes treated synonymously with SOCIAL SCIENCES, embraces such fields as physical and, in particular, cultural and social ANTHROPOLOGY, PSYCHOLOGY and SOCIOLOGY.

BEHAVIORISM, school of PSYCHOLOGY based on the proposal that behavior should be studied empirically—by objective observations of reactions—(see EMPIRICISM) rather than speculatively. It had its roots in ANIMAL BEHAVIOR studies, defining behavior as the actions and reactions of a living organism (and, by extension, man) in its environment; and more specifically in the work of PAVLOV in such fields as conditioned REFLEXES. Behaviorism developed as an effective factor in US psychology following the work of J. B. WATSON just before WWI; and since then it has influenced most schools of psychological thought.

BEHISTUN ROCK, a massive rock near the village of Behistun, Iran. On it are carved reliefs and cuneiform inscriptions in old Persian, Susian and Assyrian. In 1835 Sir Henry RAWLINSON scaled the rock and copied the inscriptions. Once deciphered, they provided a key to the interpretation of ancient Mesopotamian and all other cuneiform texts.

BEHN, Aphra (1640–1689), English dramatist, novelist and poet, the first professional English woman writer. Her many works, including the novel *Oronako* and the plays *The Forced Marriage* and *The Rover*, show technical ingenuity, wit and vivacity.

BEHRENS, Peter (1868–1940), German architect who pioneered a mode of functional design suited to industrial technology. His most influential work was the AEG turbine factory in Berlin (1908–09). He influenced LE CORBUSIER and GROPIUS.

BEHRING, Emil Adolf von (1854–1917), German bacteriologist who was awarded the first Nobel Prize for Physiology or Medicine (1901) in recognition of his part in the development of an ANTITOXIN giving protection against DIPHTHERIA.

BEHRMAN, Samuel Nathaniel (1893–   ), US dramatist noted for his comedies of manners (*Biography*, 1932; *No Time for Comedy*, 1939). He has also written film scripts and a biography of satirist Max BEERBOHM (1960).

BEIDERBECKE, Leon Bismarck "Bix" (1903–1931), US jazz musician. An accomplished pianist and brilliant trumpet player, he joined the renowned Paul WHITEMAN band in 1928. Despite his early death through alcoholism and general ill health, he greatly influenced the development of jazz.

BEIRA, city in Mozambique, SE Africa, and a major port on the Indian Ocean, serving Rhodesia, Zambia and Malawi. The main exports are copper, cotton, chromium and tea. The city also serves as a Rhodesian holiday resort. Pop 113 770.

BEIRUT, capital and chief port of Lebanon on the E Mediterranean coast. It stands on a triangular peninsula at the foot of the Lebanon Mts. Beirut is an important commercial center and a major hub for international airways and railroads. Pop 710 000.

BÉKÉSY, Georg von (1899–   ), Hungarian-born US physicist who was awarded the 1961 Nobel Prize for Physiology or Medicine for his development of a new theory of the physical mechanism of hearing (see EAR).

BEL, a unit used to express power level relative to an arbitrary reference level defined as the common LOGARITHM of the ratio of the powers. Named for Alexander Graham BELL, the bel is seldom used, the DECIBEL (1dB = 0.1 bel) and NEPER being preferred by acoustics and telecommunications engineers.

BELAFONTE, Harry (1927–   ), US singer and actor, born in New York City. Famous originally for his West Indian calypso music, he has since worked as a film, TV and theater producer. Belafonte has also been active in civil rights.

BELASCO, David (1853–1931), US playwright and theatrical producer. In New York after 1880 he became famous for mounting spectacular productions, with lavishly detailed sets, to promote newly-discovered stars.

BEL CANTO, style of singing in 19th-century Italian opera, characterized by the singer's extravagant ornamentation of the music in order to heighten the emotional content and display versatility. Two great modern exponents are Maria CALLAS and Joan SUTHERLAND.

BELÉM, capital of Pará state, N Brazil, and chief port on the Amazon R basin, about 90mi from the Atlantic. Founded in 1616 by the Portuguese, Belém now handles rubber, Brazil nuts and timber exports. Pop 642 514.

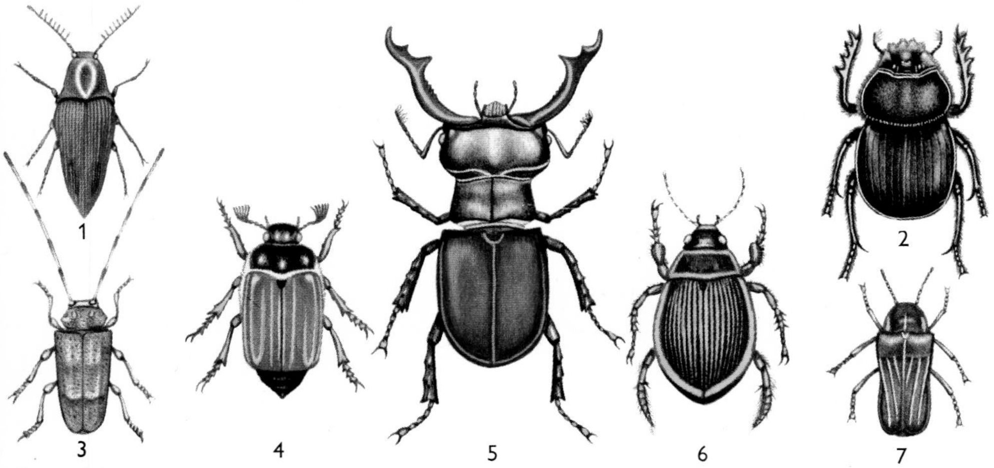

Some of the nearly 300 000 species of beetle include: 1. click or snapping beetle *Corymbites virens*. 2. scarab beetle *Scarabaeus sacer* (1 in long). 3. *Acanthocinus aedilis*. 4. cockchafer *Melolontha melolontha* (1–1¼ in). 5. stag beetle *Lucanus cervanus* (male 2½ in, female 1½ in). 6. diving beetle *Dytiscus marginalis* (1⅜ in). 7. glowworm *Lampyris noctiluca* (⅝ in).

BELFAST, seaport and capital of Northern Ireland (Ulster). Despite major shipbuilding and other industries, the area remains the most depressed in Britain. Since 1969 Belfast has seen violent clashes between the dominant Protestants and the Roman Catholic minority. Pop 360 150.

BELGAE, name given by Julius CAESAR to the most northerly group of Gallic tribes, inhabiting very roughly what is now Belgium. They formed a coalition against Caesar in 58 BC, but were subdued and virtually wiped out in 53 BC. Earlier they had crossed to Britain and established Belgic centers at Colchester and St. Albans, where they also opposed Caesar's invasion of 55–54 BC.

BELGIAN SHEEPDOG (Groenendael), robust dog noted for intelligence and working ability. Standing 24in high and weighing 54lb, it looks like a shaggy black German Shepherd dog.

Official Name: Belgium
Capital: Brussels
Area: 11 778sq mi
Population: 9 726 850
Languages: French, Flemish, German
Religions: Roman Catholic
Monetary Unit(s): 1 Belgian franc = 100 centimes

BELGIUM, kingdom of NW Europe, bordered to the W by France, to the E by Luxembourg and West Germany and to the N by the Netherlands. It has a short North Sea coastline. Belgium is one of Europe's most densely populated countries. There are nine regions: Antwerp, Brabant, E Flanders, W Flanders, Hainault, Liège, Limburg, Namur and Luxembourg.

Flanders borders the sea and consists mostly of a flat plain with sandy beaches; further inland, the region is intensively cultivated and drained by the Leie, Scheldt and Dender rivers. Central Belgium consists of a low plateau (300–600ft) which is also a rich agricultural area. The southern edge of this plateau is bounded by the Sambre-Meuse valley, the main industrial and coal-mining region of Belgium. About 25% of all Belgians live in this area of only 800sq mi. In SE Belgium lies the ARDENNES plateau, a mainly uncultivated area of peat bogs and woodlands, about 1000–1 500ft high. The country has a generally temperate climate.

Belgium has long been politically and culturally divided for the reason that it has never been linguistically united. A line running East-West, just S of Brussels, divides the Flemish-speaking Flemings in the north and the French-speaking Walloons in the south. Both languages are in official use. The predominant religion in Belgium as a whole is Roman Catholicism.

The kingdom of Belgium emerged only in the 1830s, when it seceded from the Netherlands. A revolutionary government proclaimed independence, and in 1839 Belgium was recognized as a perpetually neutral sovereign state. The country was led to prosperity under Kings LEOPOLD I and II.

Belgian neutrality was violated by Germany in 1914 and 1940, and massive destruction was caused before its liberation by Allied and resistance forces in 1944. Belgium recovered rapidly, economically and industrially, under King BAUDOUIN, and is now a prosperous member of the European COMMON MARKET, thanks to successful manufacturing industries and transportation systems.

BELGRADE, capital of Yugoslavia, a busy port and industrial center at the junction of the Danube and Sava rivers. Important products include machine tools, tractors, furniture and foodstuffs. Pop 741 613.

BELGRANO, Manuel (1770–1820), leading figure in the Argentine Revolution (1810). He won decisive victories over the royalists at Tucumán (1812) and Salta (1813), and was a member of the governing junta. He was superseded by SAN MARTÍN in 1814.

BELINSKY, Vissarion Grigoryevich (1811–1848), Russian literary critic who founded the socially conscious school of criticism dominant in Russia until the end of the 19th century. He championed what he saw as the social realism of GOGOL, LERMONTOV and PUSHKIN.

BELISARIUS (c505–565 AD), famous Byzantine general under Justinian I. He crushed the VANDALS in N Africa (533) and the OSTROGOTHS in Italy, taking Rome in 536. His later Italian campaigns (544–48) were largely unsuccessful. In 559 Belisarius was called from retirement to repel the Huns and Slavs from the gates of Constantinople.

BELIZE (formerly British Honduras), a self-governing British crown colony, on the subtropical Caribbean coast of Central America. About 70mi wide and 174mi long, it is bordered to the N and NW by Mexico and to the S and W by Guatemala, whose territorial claims over Belize have complicated and delayed moves towards full independence. In the N the region is drained by the Belize, Hondo and New rivers, and along the coast are swamp and tropical jungle. The people are of mixed European, African and native Mayan origin. Lumber, chicle, tropical fruit and sugar are the main products.

BELKNAP, William Worth (1829–1890), US lawyer and Civil War general. In 1869 he was made secretary of war by President U. S. Grant, but resigned in 1876 when impeached for alleged acceptance of bribes. The Senate failed to reach the two-thirds majority needed to convict.

BELL, residential city in Cal., 5mi S of Los Angeles. It manufactures automobile parts and paint products. Pop 21 836.

Alexander Graham Bell, the inventor of the telephone, making the first call from New York to Chicago in 1892.

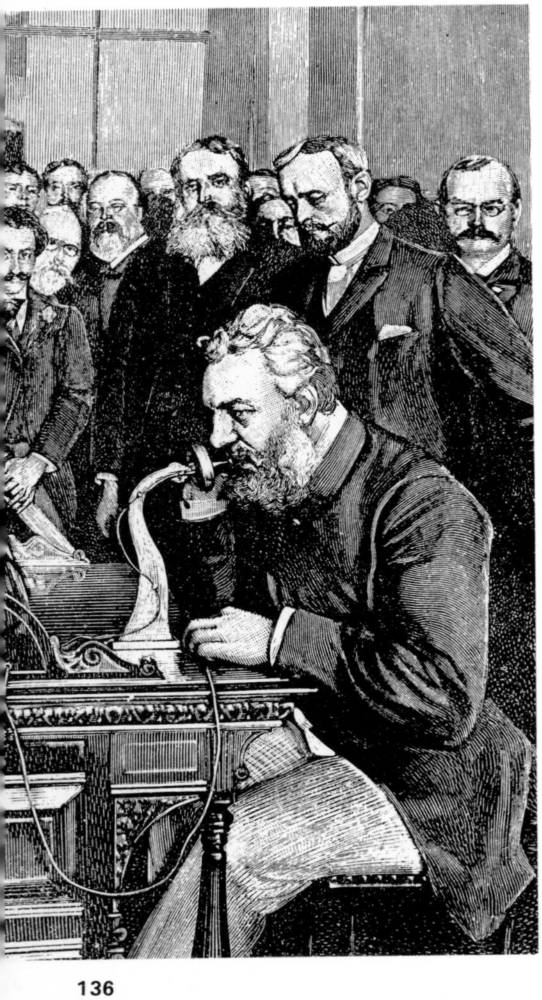

BELL, a resonant metal object in the form of a cup hung from its closed end (the head), which rings when struck with a "clapper" near its rim. It is used ritually, to give audible time signals and as a warning device. Modern bells are cast in BELL METAL to carefully computed designs so that the correct mix of fundamentals and overtones is produced when the bell is rung. As well as large bells hung in peals (tuned sets) in church towers and CAMPANILES (freestanding bell towers), there are also the smaller handbells and tubular chimes, which are musical instruments of increasing popularity. (See also CAMPANOLOGY.)

BELL, Alexander Graham (1847–1922), Scottish-born US scientist and educator who invented the TELEPHONE (1876), founded the Bell Telephone Company and devised the wax-cylinder PHONOGRAPH and various aids for teaching the deaf. In later life he helped perfect the AILERON for airplanes.

BELL, Alexander Melville (1819–1905), Scots educationalist, father of A. G. BELL. He moved to the US in 1881, where he devised and pioneered "visible speech" to aid deaf mutes.

BELL, Sir Charles (1774–1842), Scottish anatomist, a pioneer investigator of the working of the NERVOUS SYSTEM, whose most important discovery was to distinguish the functions of sensory and motor nerves.

BELL, Clive (1881–1964), English art and literary critic and member of the BLOOMSBURY GROUP. He married Virginia WOOLF's sister, Vanessa Stephen (1907). Some of his best criticism is to be found in his books *Art* (1914) and *Since Cézanne* (1922).

BELL, Electric, audible warning device in which a small clapper is made to vibrate rapidly against a resonant metal gong. This is usually achieved by using a direct-current ELECTROMAGNET to attract the clapper arm toward the gong, while a make-and-break contact cuts off the current just before the clapper strikes, so that the spring-loaded clapper arm recoils—remaking the circuit and commencing another cycle. In the single-action bell, there is no repeater mechanism.

BELL, James Madison (1826–1902), US Negro poet and abolitionist. A freed man, he helped recruit men for the pre-Civil War raid on HARPERS FERRY and dedicated his poem *The Day and The War* to his friend John BROWN.

BELL, John (1797–1869), "Tennessee Bell," presidential candidate of the CONSTITUTIONAL UNION PARTY (1860) who lost to Lincoln on the eve of the American Civil War. As congressman 1827–41 and senator 1847–59, he was leader of a conservative group of anti-secessionist southerners. He held Tenn. in the Union until President Lincoln's call to arms, when he openly, but not actively, espoused the rebel cause.

BELLADONNA, or **deadly nightshade,** *Atropa belladonna*, poisonous bushy herb, native to Europe and parts of Asia. Its dried leaves and roots provide the belladonna drug from which medicinal ALKALOIDS such as ATROPINE are produced. Modern synthetic drugs are more reliable and are superseding belladonna alkaloids. (See also BITTERSWEET.)

BELLAIRE, city in Tex., a suburb within Houston. Pop 19 009.

BELLAMY, Edward (1850–1898), US author. His Utopian *Looking Backward: 2000–1877* (1888) pictured a benevolent state socialism with worker-ownership. Following its success, "Bellamy Clubs" and a "Nationalist" movement to promote his ideas attracted a nationwide following.

BELLAY, Du. See DU BELLAY.

BELLBIRD, name used for a number of birds whose calls sound bell-like. In South America the name is applied to the genus *Procnias* (family Cotingidae), several species around the size of a THRUSH. In Australia are the Crested bellbird, *Oreoica guttaralis* (family Pachycephalinae), and the Bell miner, *Manorina melanophrys* (family Meliphagidae). This latter is related to the New Zealand bellbird, *Anthornis melanura*, which eats honey, insects and fruit, and is found in and around forests.

BELLEAU WOOD, Battle of (June 6–25, 1918), part of the WWI second battle of the Marne in which a brigade of US Marines, with French support, halted five German divisions. In 1923 the battlefield was dedicated as a memorial to the American dead.

BELLEFONTAINE-NEIGHBORS, residential city in Mo., N of St. Louis. Pop 13 987.

BELLE GLADE, city in Fla., on the SE shore of Lake Okeechobee, It was completely rebuilt in 1928 after severe hurricane damage. Pop 15 949.

BELLE ISLE, Strait of, channel between N Newfoundland and SE Labrador, Canada. About 90mi long and 10–20mi wide, it links the Gulf of St. Lawrence with the Atlantic.

BELLEROPHON, legendary Greek hero, in the ILIAD the son of Glaucus. King Proetus of Argos, told by his wife that Bellerophon had seduced her, sent him to King Iobates of Lycia to have him killed. Iobates set him against various enemies, including the CHIMERA, which he overcame with the aid of the winged horse, PEGASUS. Proud of his success, he tried to fly to Olympus, but was thrown to earth and became a melancholy wanderer.

BELLEVILLE, industrial city in SE Ontario, Canada, seat of Hastings Co. Pop 34 498.

BELLEVILLE, industrial city in SW Ill., situated in a coal-mining region. It is the seat of St. Clair Co. and Scott Air Force Base is close by. Pop 41 699.

BELLEVILLE, manufacturing town in NE N.J., on the Passaic R near Newark. It was settled by the Dutch in the 17th century. Pop 37 629.

BELLEVUE, city in E Neb., on the Missouri R near Omaha. A trading post in the early 19th century, it is the oldest town in Neb. Pop 21 953.

BELLEVUE, borough in Pa., residential suburb of Pittsburgh. Pop 11 586.

BELLEVUE, city in Wash., the site of Bellevue Community College. Pop 61 102.

BELLFLOWER, city in Cal., NE of Long Beach. A truck-farming center. Pop 51 454.

BELLFLOWER, genus (*Campanula*) of annuals, biennials and herbaceous perennials with bell-shaped flowers, native to N temperate zones, though some are found on tropical mountainsides. Examples are *Campanula rotundifolia*, the harebell or Scots bluebell, and *C. medium*, the Canterbury bell. (See also BLUEBELL.)

BELL GARDENS, city in Cal., suburb of Los Angeles. It adjoins the cities of Downey and Bell. Pop 29 308.

BELLIGERENCY. See WAR.

BELLINGHAM, town in E Mass., 19mi SE of Worcester. Pop 13 967.

BELLINGHAM, commercial and industrial port in Wash., on Bellingham Bay. The seat of Whatcom Co., it was previously named Whatcom (1852–90) and Fairhaven (1890–1903). Pop 39 375.

BELLINGSHAUSEN SEA, inlet of the S Pacific on the Antarctic coast between Alexander Island and Thurston Island.

BELLINI, family of Early Renaissance Venetian artists. **Jacopo** (c1400–c1470) evolved a much-imitated compositional technique of depicting small figures in vast, precisely detailed architectural settings. Few of his paintings survive, but he influenced others directly and through his sons and son-in-law, Andrea MANTEGNA. **Gentile** (c1429–1507), his elder son, is noted for his strong, realistic portraits as well as for his use of PERSPECTIVE to give a sense of true spatial depth. **Giovanni** (c1430–1516), the younger son, was the greatest Early Renaissance Venetian painter. His early works were influenced by Mantegna, but he later developed the poetic use of light and color for which he is famous. His pupils, TITIAN and GIORGIONE, continued and developed his style.

BELLINI, Vincenzo (1801–1835), Italian opera composer of the BEL CANTO school. His most popular works today are his last three: *La Sonnambula* (1831) *Norma* (1831) and *I Puritani* (1835).

BELLMAWR, mainly residential borough in N.J., 5mi S of Camden, formerly named Heddings. Pop 15 618.

BELL METAL, a BRONZE with a high tin content (15–25%), used for casting bells because of its sonority.

BELLMORE, urban community in N.Y. on the S shore of Long Island. Pop 18 431.

BELLOC, (Joseph Pierre) Hilaire (1870–1953), French-born English poet, essayist and historian. An ardent Roman Catholic polemicist and close friend of G. K. CHESTERTON, his first well-known work was *The Bad Child's Book of Beasts* (1896).

BELLOTTO, Bernardo (1720–1780), Italian painter and etcher of city scenes. Until recently, many of his best works were attributed to his uncle and teacher, CANALETTO.

BELLOW, Saul (1915–), Canadian-born US novelist noted for his narrative skill and for his studies of Jewish American life. His best-known books are *Herzog* (1964) and *The Adventures of Augie March* (1953). Other novels include *Dangling Man* (1944), *Henderson the Rain King* (1959), *Mr. Sammler's Planet* (1970) and *Humboldt's Gift* (1975).

BELLOWS, device used to produce a blast of air to speed the burning of a fire, or for musical instruments (accordions and organs). Bellows usually consist of two variously-shaped boards hinged at the nozzle end, and elsewhere joined by pleated leather sides. As the boards are opened, air is drawn in through a valve; as they are shut it is forced out through the nozzle. A blacksmith's bellows has two such chambers working out-of-phase, thus ensuring a continuous flow of air.

BELLOWS, George Wesley (1882–1925), US painter and lithographer; one of the most interesting early 20th-century "realists." Bellows, who remained aloof from modern European influences, was also influential in reviving US lithography.

BELL TELEPHONE LABORATORIES, research organization set up in 1925 by the American Telephone and Telegraph Company. The Bell Laboratories have been responsible for many important developments in telecommunications technology, notably the TRANSISTOR.

BELLWOOD, village in Ill, 13mi W of Chicago. It produces hardware, iron castings and light trucks. Pop 22 096.

BELMONT, city in Cal., near San Francisco. It is the site of the College of Notre Dame. Pop 23 667.

BELMONT, residential town in NE Mass., suburb of Boston. Pop 28 285.

BELMOPAN, capital of Belize (formerly British Honduras) since 1970. It is situated 41mi SW of the former capital Belize City. Pop 1000.

BELO HORIZONTE, fast-growing city and capital of Minas Gerais state in E Brazil. It is linked by super-highways to Rio de Janeiro and São Paulo. Situated in an important cotton and cattle region, it has chemical, furniture and iron and steel industries. Pop 1 235 001.

BELOIT, industrial city in S Wis., in Rock Co., situated on Rock R on the Ill. border. It is the seat of Beloit College. Pop 35 729.

BELORUSSIAN SOVIET SOCIALIST REPUBLIC, also Byelorussia or White Russia, a constituent republic of the USSR on Poland's E border. A quarter of this region of plains and marshes, with some hilly outcrops, is valuable forest land. Other resources are peat, rock salt and limited deposits of phosphorite, limestone and iron ore. The Dnieper, Pripet, Berezina and Western Dvina rivers form an extensive waterway network. Agriculture is the principal occupation, with flax, potatoes, hemp, sugar beet and livestock (dairy cattle and pigs) the main products. Manufactures, at Minsk, Vitebsk, Comel, Mogilëv, Grodno and Brest, include agricultural machinery, trucks, wood products and textiles. By 1795 Belorussia had been absorbed into the Russian Empire. Eastern Belorussia was made part of the USSR in 1921. The W region, a part of Poland from 1921, was annexed by the USSR in 1945.

BELSEN, German village in Lower Saxony, former site of the infamous Nazi concentration camp where over 115 000 people, mostly Jews, were killed.

BELSHAZZAR, co-regent with (c550–540 BC), and son of, Nabonidus of Babylon. The Old Testament Book of Daniel relates that, during a feast epitomizing Babylon's decadence, an Aramaic inscription appeared on the wall, predicting Belshazzar's doom and Babylon's downfall. That night CYRUS THE GREAT captured Babylon and slew Belshazzar.

BELTON, city in Mo., 12mi S of Kansas City. Pop 12 179.

BELUGA, *Huso huso*, the largest STURGEON, found in seas and rivers of the USSR, and achieving lengths of nearly 9m (30ft); also, *Delphinapterus leucas*, a small DOLPHIN, sometimes known as the White Whale, related to the NARWHAL and found in northern seas at lengths up to 5.5m (18ft).

BELVIDERE, industrial city in Ill., seat of Boone Co., situated on the Kishwaukee R near Rockford. It has an automobile assembly plant. Pop 14 061.

BELZONI, Giovanni Battista (1778–1823), Italian Egyptologist and one-time circus strongman. He shipped the colossal bust of Rameses II from Egypt to the British Museum (1816). He is also famed for having opened the ABU SIMBEL temple (1817), discovering the entrance to the pyramid of Chephren (1818) and later the emerald mines of Zubara and the ruins of the city of Berenice.

BEMBO, Pietro (1470–1547), Italian humanist, scholar, writer and cardinal. He played an important part in the Renaissance language debate, writing one of the first Italian grammars, and advocating a literary language modelled on the examples of BOCCACCIO and PETRARCH.

BEMELMANS, Ludwig (1898–1962), Italian-American writer and illustrator of *Hansi* (1934), *Madeline* (1939), *My War with the United States* (1937) and other satiric and children's stories.

BEMIDJI, city in Minn., seat of Beltrami Co. It is a summer resort and produces cement, bricks and lumber. Pop 11 490.

BENARES. See VARANASI.

BEN BELLA, Ahmed (1918–), Algerian revolutionary who helped plan the 1954 anti-French revolt. After the post-independence power struggle of 1963, Ben Bella became president but was ousted by Col. BOUMEDIENNE's coup of June 19, 1965.

BENCHLEY, Robert Charles (1889–1945), US writer, drama critic of *Life,* 1920–29, and the *New Yorker,* 1929–40. He is best known for his short humorous pieces, published in several collections, and his satirical short films.

BEND, industrial city in Ore., seat of Deschutes Co. It is situated on the Deschutes R, in the E foothills of the Cascade Range. Pop 13 710.

BENDIX, Vincent (1882–1945), US inventor and industrialist who devised the Bendix self-starter for AUTOMOBILES and developed a four-wheeled brake system.

BENDS. See AEROEMBOLISM.

BENEDICT, name of 15 popes and 2 antipopes. **Benedict I** (d. 579), pope c574–79 during the Lombard invasion of Italy. **Saint Benedict II** (d. 685), pope c684–85, persuaded Emperor Constantine IV to abolish imperial confirmation of a pope-elect. **Benedict III** (d. 858), pope 855–58, restored Rome, after it had been devastated by the Saracens in 846. **Benedict IV** (d. 903), pope 900–03. He crowned the Emperor Louis III (the Blind) and granted privileges to the German Fulda monastery. **Benedict V** (d. c966), pope or antipope from May to June 964. Elected by the Romans, he was deposed and imprisoned by Emperor Otto I who had given the papacy to Leo VIII. **Benedict VI** (d. 974), pope 973–74. Following the death of Otto I, who had given him office, he was deposed and killed by a group of Roman nobles led by Crescentius. **Benedict VII** (d. 983), pope 974–83. He replaced the antipope Boniface VII, under Emperor Otto II. His quiet reign strengthened the papacy and advanced monasticism. **Benedict VIII** (d. 1024), pope 1012–24. First of the Tusculan popes. He crowned his ally Henry II of Germany emperor (1014), restored papal authority in the Italian feudal states and allied with the Normans against the Saracens. **Benedict IX** (c1011–c1055), pope 1032–45. Overthrown in 1045, he regained power in the same year but then sold the papacy to Gregory VI. A later attempt to recover the papacy was unsuccessful. **Benedict X** (d. c1080), antipope 1058–59. He was named pope by a faction who opposed the future Pope Gregory VII. **Blessed Benedict XI** (1240–1304), pope 1303–04. He improved relations with France. **Benedict XII** (1285–1342), pope 1334–42. His attempted reformation of religious orders and intervention in politics failed because the papacy lacked prestige.

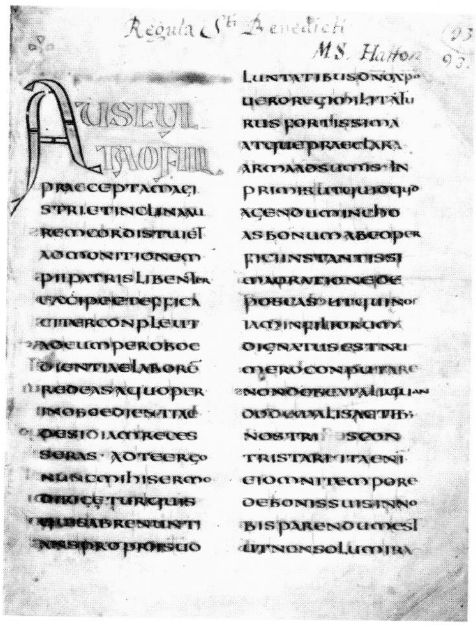

Page of the oldest extant manuscript of the Rule of St. Benedict, a series of conditions and precepts for monastic life. Written at Canterbury *c* 700, the rules it sets out are perhaps less austere than they might seem to modern eyes.

Benedict XIII (c1328–c1423), antipope 1394–1423. Expected to abdicate and end the GREAT SCHISM, he refused, fleeing to Spain in 1417. Another **Benedict XIII** (1649–1730), was pope 1724–30. He attempted church reform, but unwisely left political matters to the corrupt Cardinal Coscia. **Benedict XIV**, antipope, claimed rule c1425–30. Also **Benedict XIV** (1675–1758), pope 1740–58. Elected after six months and 255 ballots, he was inflexible in spiritual matters, but compromised on the political front. He made territorial concessions to Spain, Naples, Portugal and Sardinia. **Benedict XV** (1854–1922), pope 1914–22. He maintained strict neutrality during WWI, condemned immoral acts on both sides and attempted to reestablish peace.

BENEDICT, Ruth (née Fulton; 1887–1948), US cultural anthropologist, whose extensive fieldwork helped illustrate the theory of cultural relativism—that what is deemed deviant in one culture may be normal in another. (See ANTHROPOLOGY.)

BÉNÉDICTINE, popular French liqueur, first prepared in the early 16th century at the Benedictine monastery at Fécamp, Normandy. It contains herbs, brandy, honey and sugar; its exact recipe is a secret.

BENEDICTINE ORDERS, the "Black Monks," order of monks and nuns following the rule of St. Benedict of Nursia. Their motto is "Pray and work." Stress is laid on a combination of prayer, choral office, study and manual labor under an abbot's supervision. There has been a great revival of the Benedictine rule since 1830 in Europe and the US.

BENEDICTION, a formal blessing of the people at the end of a church service. Also, a Roman Catholic devotion venerating the Blessed Sacrament.

BENEDICT OF NURSIA, Saint (c480–547), father of Western monasticism, whose "rule" set the pattern of monastic life from the mid-7th century. For three years he lived as a hermit near Subiaco, Italy. His piety attracted many followers, some of whom he later grouped in 12 monasteries. Benedict also founded the monastery of MONTE CASSINO.

BENEFICE (from Latin *beneficium*, a kindness or benefit), church office providing a living or income in return for spiritual duties, usually those of a parish priest or vicar. The term originally referred to the life tenure of land granted by Frankish kings.

BENEFIT OF CLERGY, 12th-century English law enabling clergy accused of felony to be tried by the more lenient ecclesiastical courts. From 1576 clergy were tried by the secular courts, the usual punishment being a year's imprisonment. The privilege was next extended to laymen who could read, or in effect memorize, the first verse of Psalm 51. By 1707 it could be claimed by any first-time offender although most serious crimes were excluded. The law was abolished in 1827.

BENE ISRAEL, or Beni Israel (Hebrew: Sons of Israel), Jewish community in and around Bombay, India. According to tradition, its members arrived in India as early as the 2nd century AD and underwent a religious revival c900. They observe Jewish ritual but also some Hindu customs. Many now live in Israel.

BENELUX, a custom union between Belgium, the Netherlands and Luxembourg, established in 1944 and revised by the Hague protocol of 1947. Benelux is often used collectively for the countries themselves.

BENEŠ, Eduard (1884–1948), cofounder, with Tomáš MASARYK, of the Czechoslovak Republic. He was foreign minister 1918–35, prime minister 1921–22 and president 1935–38 and 1940–48. His appeals to Britain and France in 1938 failed to prevent Hitler's occupation of the Sudetenland. He died after the 1948 communist coup.

BENÉT, Stephen Vincent (1898–1943), US poet, novelist and short story writer, whose works center on US history and tradition. His epic poems *John Brown's Body* (1928) and *Western Star* (1943) won Pulitzer prizes. Among his most famous short stories is *The Devil and Daniel Webster* (1937).

BENEZET, Anthony (1713–1784), French-born American Quaker author and educator. He fought against slavery, wrote several antislavery tracts, and established schools for Negro education.

BENGAL, region including Bangladesh and NE India on the Bay of Bengal. Its chief city, Calcutta, was capital of British India 1833–1912, and it was an autonomous province from 1935 until the partition of India in 1947. The W became West Bengal State and the E was included in Pakistan until Bangladesh's 1971 declaration of independence. Most of the S is occupied by the Ganges-Brahmaputra delta.

BENGAL, Bay of, arm of the Indian Ocean between India on the W and Burma on the E. Large amounts of silt deposited by the rivers Ganges, Brahmaputra, Mahanadi, Godavari and Krishna make its N and W reaches very shallow. Surface currents in the bay alter direction with the change from NE to SW monsoon.

BENGALI, Indo-Aryan language, related to Assamese, Bihari and Oriya. One of the principal languages of the Indian subcontinent, it has a rich literary heritage and is spoken by some 40 million people in Bangladesh and 25 million in West Bengal.

BENGHÁZI, second-largest city of Libya and one of the two official capitals (the other is Tripoli). It is a port on the Gulf of Sidra and the marketing center for a rich agricultural region. It was the scene of heavy fighting in WWII. Pop 170 000.

BENGUELA CURRENT, cool ocean current, with a high PLANKTON content, flowing northward in the S Atlantic along the W coast of South Africa to merge with the S EQUATORIAL CURRENT.

BEN-GURION, David (1886–1973), Polish-born founder and first prime minister of Israel. After WWI he cofounded the *Haganah* underground Jewish army and the *Histadrut*, the General Federation of Jewish Labor (1920). He became leader of the *Mapai* labor party (1930) and the World Zionist Organization (1935). As prime minister and defense minister, 1949–53 and 1955–63, he, more than any other leader, molded modern Israel.

BENIN, historic W African kingdom, on the Guinea Coast. It flourished between the 14th and 17th centuries, later enjoying a lively trade in pepper and ivory. Its culture was highly sophisticated: Benin bronze sculpture is now world-famous. By the 19th century the slave trade had decimated its male population. It became part of British Nigeria in 1897.

BENIN, Peoples Republic of, African republic, bounded by Togo, Upper Volta, Niger, Nigeria and the Atlantic; until 1975 known as Dahomey. The population is concentrated in the S coastal region where Cotonou, the capital, major port and commercial center, is located. There are four major tribes: the Fon, Adja and YORUBA in the S and the Bariba in the NE and central regions. Some Europeans, mostly French, inhabit the country. There are some technical schools and one university, but illiteracy is high. Animism survives alongside Islam and Christianity.

The climate is equatorial, supporting Benin's agriculturally-based economy. Coconuts and cotton supplement the more important palm-oil, produced mainly in the S and accounting for about 67% of the total value of the country's exports. Excessive dependence on palm-oil, on foreign aid and on inadequate transportation have made Benin economically unstable, and have given it a chronic trade imbalance. French subsidies have improved road and rail services but Benin is hampered by lack of natural and financial resources. There is little scope for industrialization beyond the few existing food processing plants.

Dahomey came under French influence in 1851, after taking a profitable part in the slave trading which earned the region the title of the Slave Coast. It became part of French West Africa in 1904 but gained independence in 1960 and joined the UN. Since then it has suffered from political turmoil, including a series of coups in the 1960s. A three-man Presidential Council was established in 1970. Each member was to serve as president for two-year periods, but the council was overthrown by the army in 1972 and a military government established.

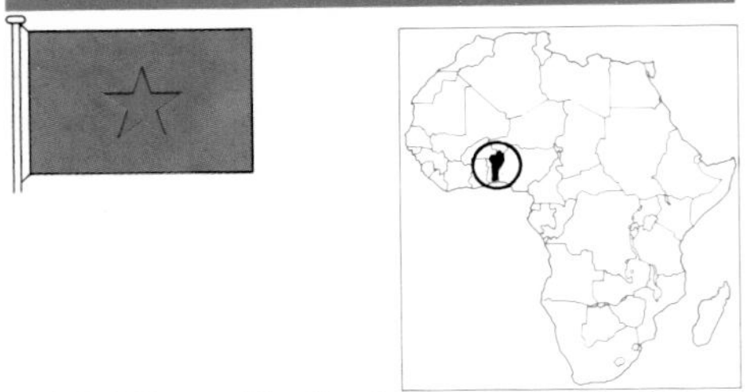

Official Name: The People's Republic of Benin
Capital: Cotonou
Seat of Government: Porto Novo
Area: 43 480sq mi **Population:** 2 760 000
Languages: French; Fon, Mina, Yoruba, Dendi
Religions: Animist; Muslim, Roman Catholic, Protestant
Monetary Unit(s): 1 CFA franc = 100 centimes

BENIN CITY, capital and chief commercial center of Mid-West State, Nigeria, in the delta of the Niger R. Pop 121 699.

BENJAMIN, in the Old Testament, youngest son of JACOB and RACHEL, and JOSEPH's only full brother. The tribe of Benjamin derived its name from him.

BENJAMIN, Judah Philip (1811–1884), West Indian-born US politician and lawyer, called the "brains of the Confederacy." As US senator from La. (1852–61), he proved an able advocate of the Southern cause. After secession, Jefferson DAVIS, his personal friend, appointed him successively attorney general, secretary of war, and finally secretary of state (1862–65) in the Confederate government. On the collapse of the Confederacy Benjamin fled to England, where he became a highly successful barrister.

BENNETT, (Enoch) Arnold (1867–1931), English novelist, journalist and playwright. He is famous for his novels set in the Potteries of Staffordshire: *Anna of the Five Towns* (1902), *The Old Wives' Tale* (1908), *Clayhanger* (1910), *Hilda Lessways* (1911) and *These Twain* (1916).

BENNETT, Floyd (1890–1928), US aviator who piloted Richard BYRD on the first flight over the N Pole (May 9, 1926). He was awarded the Congressional Medal of Honor.

BENNETT, James Gordon (1795–1872), Scottish-born US newspaper publisher and editor, pioneer of modern news reporting. In 1835 he launched the popular, sensationalist *New York Herald*, becoming the first to print stock market items and use the telegraph as a news source. His son, **James Gordon Bennett** (1841–1918), sent H. M. STANLEY to find David LIVINGSTONE (1869), and founded the *New York Evening Telegram* (1869) and the *Paris Herald* (1887).

BENNETT, Richard Bedford, Viscount (1870–1947), Canadian premier 1930–35. He presided over the 1932 Ottawa Conference which created preferential tariffs within the British Commonwealth. He was leader of the Conservative Party (1927–38) and was created a viscount in 1941.

BENNETT, William Andrew Cecil (1900–), Canadian politician; leader of the Social Credit Party and premier of British Columbia 1952–73.

BENNINGTON, town in SW Vt., seat of Bennington Co. On Aug. 16, 1777, during the Revolutionary War, the GREEN MOUNTAIN BOYS defeated a British raiding force nearby. The present small manufacturing town includes the first Vt. schoolhouse, several colonial buildings and W. L. GARRISON's printing shop. Pop 14 536.

BENNY, Jack (1894–1973), US comedian, born Benjamin Kubelsky. He had his own radio and TV shows, and appeared in movies, including *Broadway Melody* (1936), *Charley's Aunt* (1941) and *The Horn Blows at Midnight* (1946).

BENSENVILLE, industrial and residential village in NE Ill., 18mi NW of Chicago. Close by is O'Hare Airport. Pop 12 956.

BENSON, Ezra Taft (1899–), US agricultural economist and leader of the farmers' cooperative movement. He was a member of the National Agricultural Advisory Commission in WWII and US secretary of agriculture 1953–61.

BENT, William (1809–1869), US fur trader and pioneer, the first permanent white resident in Col. He formed Bent, St. Vrain & Company in the upper Arkansas valley and ran BENT'S FORT.

BENT GRASS, common name for species of grass from the genus *Agrostis*, native to North America, Europe and N Africa. Redtop (*Agrostis alba*) is much used for pastures, while creeping bent (*A. palustris*) is used for lawns and golf greens.

BENTHAM, Jeremy (1748–1843), English philosopher, economist and jurist. He propounded UTILITARIANISM, the aim of which was to achieve "the greatest happiness of the greatest number," and argued that legislation should be governed by that aim. These ideas were expressed in *An Introduction to the Principles of Morals and Legislation* (1789). He had a major influence on prison and law reform in the 19th century, and on the thinking of J. S. MILL and D. RICARDO. His head and skeleton, dressed in his own suit, sit in University College, London.

BENTHOS, plants and animals living on the sea bottom, as distinct from NEKTON (creatures which swim freely) and PLANKTON (creatures which drift with the current). Benthos include sea anemones and sea cucumbers. (See also OCEAN.)

BENTLEY, Eric (1916–), British-born US drama critic and university teacher. Through his translations and theater work he was instrumental in introducing the plays and ideas of BRECHT to the English-speaking world.

BENTON, industrial city in Ark., seat of Saline Co. It is situated in a bauxite-mining district near Little Rock. Pop 16 499.

BENTON, Thomas Hart (1782–1858), US statesman. He represented Mo. in the US Senate for 30 years (1821–51), championing the development of the West and the interests of the common man. Benton was a leader in the fight against the Second Bank of the United States, earning the nickname "Old Bullion Benton" for his advocacy of hard money. His principles led him to oppose the Mexican War, and his opposition to the spread of slavery lost him his Senate seat and brought his brief career in the House (1853–55) to an end.

BENTON, Thomas Hart (1889–1975), US painter, grandnephew of Senator T. H. Benton. He was a leader of the influential 1930s Regionalist school of painting, devoted to depicting the life of rural America. He was particularly well known for his vivid murals of the mid-western scene.

BENTON HARBOR, industrial and commerical city in SW Mich., on Lake Michigan. It is the home of the religious colony of the House of David. Pop 16 481.

BENTONITE, fine-grained CLAY formed from volcanic ASH (see VOLCANISM; VOLCANO) by the hydration (formation of HYDRATES or ABSORPTION of water) of, and loss of BASES and perhaps SILICA from, tiny particles of volcanic GLASS present in the ash. SODIUM bentonites, which expand considerably when saturated with water, are used diversely, as in the making of PAPER and sealing of DAMS. CALCIUM bentonites are used in the making of FULLER'S EARTH.

BENT'S FORT, famous fortified fur-trading post. It was built in 1833–34 by Bent, St. Vrain & Company on the Arkansas R, by the main Santa Fe trail, in present-day SE Col. It could garrison 200 men and hold 300 horses. (See also BENT, WILLIAM.)

BENUE RIVER, chief tributary of the Niger R in W Africa. It rises in N Cameroon and flows W across E central Nigeria for about 870mi.

BENZ, Karl (1844–1929), German engineer who built the first commercially successful AUTOMOBILE (1885). His earliest autos were tricycle carriages powered by a small INTERNAL-COMBUSTION ENGINE.

BENZALDEHYDE (C_6H_5CHO), colorless liquid with a smell of almonds. It is an aromatic ALDEHYDE, found in bitter almonds but synthesized from TOLUENE, and is used as a flavoring and in chemical synthesis. It is oxidized to BENZOIC ACID. mp −26°C, bp 179°C.

BENZEDRINE, or **amphetamine,** the prototypical member of the AMPHETAMINES.

BENZENE (C_6H_6), colorless toxic liquid HYDROCARBON produced from PETROLEUM by reforming, and from COAL GAS and COAL TAR. It is the prototypical AROMATIC COMPOUND: its molecular structure, first proposed by KEKULÉ, is based on a regular planar hexagon of carbon atoms. Stable and not very reactive, benzene forms many substitution products, and also reacts with the HALOGENS to give addition products—including γ-benzene hexachloride, a powerful insecticide. It is used as a solvent, in motor fuel, and as the starting material for the manufacture of a vast variety of other aromatic compounds, especially PHENOL, STYRENE, ANILINE and maleic anhydride. mp 5°C, bp 80°C.

BENZINE, volatile, inflammable liquid obtained from PETROLEUM. It is a mixture of aliphatic HYDROCARBONS, used as a solvent in DRY CLEANING.

BENZOIC ACID (C_6H_5COOH), white crystalline solid, an aromatic CARBOXYLIC ACID. It occurs naturally in many plants, and is made by oxidation of TOLUENE. It is mainly used as a food preservative. mp 122°C, bp 249°C. Compounds containing the benzoyl group (C_6H_5CO-) were studied by von LIEBIG and WÖHLER.

BEN-ZVI, Itzhak (1884–1963), Russian-born second president of Israel (1952–63). He was active in Jewish pioneer and self-defense groups in Palestine from 1907, and in 1929 was a founder of the VAAD LEUMI (National Council of Palestine Jews).

BENZYL ALCOHOL ($C_6H_5CH_2OH$), or phenylcarbinol, colorless liquid, an aromatic ALCOHOL whose esters are found in flowers and used in perfumes. It is used in color-film developing and in dyeing. mp −15°C, bp 205°C.

BEOWULF, anonymous heroic epic poem, c8th century, the greatest extant poem in Old English. The poem uses elements of Germanic legend and is set in Scandinavia. It tells of the hero Beowulf's victories over the monster Grendel and Grendel's mother, his battle with a dragon and his death and burial. The only manuscript (c1000) is in the British Museum.

BERBERS, several culturally separate N African tribes who speak the Hamitic Berber language or any of its many dialects. Almost all the tribes are Muslim. They live mainly in Algeria, Libya, Morocco and Tunisia. Most are farmers or nomadic herders, but some are oasis-dwellers. They include the Jerbans, Kabyles, Mzabites, Riffians, Beraber, Shluh, Shawia and TUAREGS.

BERCEUSE (French: lullaby), a musical composition, often in 6/8 time, with a rocking bass line similar to a lullaby. The German term is *Wiegenlied.*

BERCHTESGADEN, small SE Bavarian resort town in the Bavarian Alps, West Germany. Nearby, Hitler built the Berghof, his fortified chalet retreat, with its deep mountainside bunkers. Pop 4 500.

BERCHTOLD, Count Leopold von (1863–1942), Austro-Hungarian foreign minister 1912–15. His ultimatum to Serbia (July 23, 1914), following the assassination of Archduke FRANZ FERDINAND, was the spark that ignited WORLD WAR I.

BERDYAEV, Nikolai Aleksandrovich (1874–1948), Russian religious philosopher. A Marxist in his youth, he later turned to Christianity and created a highly individual Christian existentialism. Expelled from the USSR in 1922, he settled in Paris.

BEREA, city in NE Ohio, near Cleveland, packing and shipping center for the vegetable-growing area to its west. Pop 22 396.

BERENSON, Bernard (1865–1959), Lithuanian-born US art historian. An expert on Italian Renaissance painting, he wrote the definitive study *Italian Painters of the Renaissance* (1894–1907). Berenson bequeathed his Italian villa, art collection and library to Harvard.

BEREZINA RIVER, river in the Belorussian SSR, (USSR), a 365mi-long tributary of the Dnieper. Battles were fought there during Napoleon's retreat from Moscow (Nov. 26–28, 1812) and during the German advance on Smolensk (July 3–8, 1941).

BERG, Alban (1885–1935), Austrian composer of expressive TWELVE-TONE MUSIC. A pupil of SCHOENBERG, he adopted his technique in such works as the opera *Wozzeck* (1925). (See also ATONALITY.)

BERGAMO, industrial city in N Italy, provincial capital of Lombardy. It was ruled by the Visconti family (1296–1428), Venice (1428–1797) and Austria (1814–59). Pop 124 626.

BERGAMOT, *Citrus aurantium, C. bergamia,* citrus tree with pale yellow or green pear-shaped fruit, grown in the southern US and Italy. The rind is used in perfumes and essences.

BERGEN, seaport city in SW Norway, on the By Fjord, Norway's third-largest city and second most important port, a major manufacturing center. It was a member of the medieval HANSEATIC LEAGUE. Pop 115 590.

BERGEN, Edgar John (1903–   ), US ventriloquist-comedian, famous for his radio and motion-picture appearances with his dummies Charlie McCarthy and Mortimer Snerd.

BERGENFIELD, borough in NE N.J. A residential suburb of New York City, it has light industries. Pop 29 000.

BERGER, Victor Louis (1860–1929), the first US Socialist congressman (1911–13, 1918, 1919, 1923–29). Born in Austria, Berger was a founder and leader of the American Socialist Party. In WWI he was sentenced to 20 years' imprisonment for aiding the enemy, but was freed on appeal.

BERGERAC, Cyrano de. See CYRANO DE BERGERAC.

BERGH, Henry (1811–1888), founder and first president of the American Society for the Prevention of Cruelty to Animals (1866). He also helped to found the Society for the Prevention of Cruelty to Children (1875).

BERGIUS, Friedrich (1884–1949), German industrial chemist who, during WWI, developed a process for making GASOLINE by the high-pressure HYDROGENATION of COAL. He shared the 1931 Nobel chemistry prize with Karl BOSCH for work on high-pressure reactions.

BERGMAN, (Ernst) Ingmar (1918–   ), Swedish film and stage director, producer and writer. He combines realism with imaginative symbolism to explore themes such as good and evil, love, old age and death. Famous motion pictures include *The Seventh Seal* (1956), *Wild Strawberries* (1957), *Persona* (1966) and *Cries and Whispers* (1971).

BERGMAN, Ingrid (1915–   ), Swedish stage and screen actress. She went to Hollywood in 1939 and became an internationally admired film star, winning Academy Awards for *Gaslight* (1944), *Anastasia* (1956) and *Murder on the Orient Express* (1974). She has made several notable stage appearances in Paris, London and New York.

BERGSON, Henri Louis (1859–1941), French philosopher, the first exponent of PROCESS PHILOSOPHY. Reacting against the physicists' definition of TIME and substituting a notion of experienced duration; rejecting the psychophysical parallelism of the day and asserting the independence of mind, and viewing EVOLUTION not as a mechanistic but as a creative process energized by an *élan vital* (vital impulse), Bergson was perhaps the most original philosopher of the early 20th century. He was awarded the Nobel Prize for Literature in 1927.

BERIA, Lavrenti Pavlovich (1899–1953), head of the Soviet secret police (1938–53). As commissar for internal affairs he was responsible for thousands of political executions. Shortly after Stalin's death he was secretly executed for treason.

BERIBERI, deficiency disease caused by lack of VITAMIN B_1 (thiamine); it may occur in MALNUTRITION, ALCOHOLISM or as an isolated deficiency. NEURITIS leading to sensory changes, and foot or wrist drop, palpitations, EDEMA and HEART failure are features; there may be associated dementia. Onset may be insidious or acute. Treatment is thiamine replacement; thiamine enrichment of common foods prevents beriberi.

BERING, Vitus Jonassen (1681–1741), Danish explorer. Sailing in the service of Russia, he probed N through the Bering Sea and discovered BERING STRAIT (1728) and Alaska (1741). He died of scurvy on Bering Island.

BERING SEA, the extreme N arm of the N Pacific Ocean, 885 000sq mi in area, bounded by E Siberia, Alaska and the Aleutian Islands. It contains Nunivak Island, St. Lawrence Island, the Pribilof Islands (all US) and the Komandorskiye Islands (USSR). The international dateline crosses it diagonally.

BERING SEA CONTROVERSY, Anglo-American dispute in the late 19th century. When indiscriminate slaughter by various nations threatened the valuable seal herds of the US-owned Pribilof Islands in the Bering Sea, the US seized three Canadian ships (1886) and claimed dominion over the Bering Sea (1889). Britain objected, and in 1893 an arbitration tribunal declared the Bering Sea international.

BERING STRAIT, linking the Arctic and Pacific oceans and separating Asia (the USSR) from America (Alaska). It contains the Diomede Islands and is ice-bound from Nov. to June.

BERKELEY, city in W Cal., on San Francisco Bay, opposite the Golden Gate bridge. A residential suburb of San Francisco, it has the main campus of the U. of Cal. and research laboratories. Pop 116 716.

BERKELEY, city in E Mo., on the Coldwater R. It is a NW residential suburb of St. Louis. Pop 19 743.

BERKELEY, George (1685–1753), Irish philosopher and bishop who, rejecting the views of LOCKE as to the nature of material substance, substituted the *esse-percipi* principle: to be is to be perceived (or to be capable of perception). His visit to Rhode Island (1728–31) is commemorated in the name of Berkeley, Cal.

BERKELEY, John Berkeley, 1st Baron (d. 1678), a Royalist commander in the English Civil War. He became one of the first co-proprietors of Carolina (1663) and New Jersey (1664), but never visited North America.

BERKELEY, Sir William (1606–1677), royal governor of Virginia (1642–52 and 1660–77). His autocratic rule in his second term and an inability or unwillingness to deal with Indian frontier attacks caused BACON'S REBELLION (1676). Berkeley's harsh treatment of the rebels led to his recall to England.

BERKELIUM (Bk), a TRANSURANIUM ELEMENT in the ACTINIDE series. Bk^{249} is prepared by bombarding curium-244 with neutrons.

BERKLEY, residential city in SE Mich., just N of Detroit. Pop 21 879.

BERKMAN, Alexander (1870–1936), Polish-born US anarchist. During a steel strike, he tried to assassinate the Carnegie Steel Co. head, Henry C. Frick (1892). He served 14 years' imprisonment. In 1917 he was imprisoned for draft obstruction, then deported to Russia in 1919.

BERKSHIRE HILLS (the Berkshires), scenic highlands of W Mass., in Berkshire Co. They are part of the Appalachians and are an all-year-round resort area. The highest peak is the 3 491ft Mt Greylock.

BERLAGE, Hendrik Petrus (1856–1934), a Dutch pioneer of modern architecture. His buildings include the massively severe Stock Exchange (1898–1903) and Diamond Exchange (1899–1900) in Amsterdam. Berlage favored functional design and was much influenced by Frank Lloyd WRIGHT.

A grim view from the French sector of West Berlin, showing part of the infamous Wall and the desolate rows of empty houses in the Eastern sector behind.

BERLE, Adolf Augustus, Jr. (1895–1971), US public servant and diplomat. Original "brain truster" and Latin American adviser to F. D. Roosevelt, he was assistant secretary of state (1938–44) and later ambassador to Brazil (1945–46) and chairman of President Kennedy's Latin American Task Force (1961–63).

BERLE, Milton (1908–), US comedian, born Milton Berlinger. He played in vaudeville and BURLESQUE and became a star in early television.

BERLICHINGEN, Goetz von (c1481–1562), German robber knight and mercenary commander. He lost his left hand in battle and replaced it with one of iron, for which he was nicknamed "Goetz Ironhand." Goethe wrote a play based on his life (1773).

BERLIN, major city located in the E central part of East Germany, with a corridor to West Germany. It covers 341sq mi and stands on a sandy plain at the center of a network of roads, railroads and waterways.

Berlin was the capital of Germany, 1871–1945. Since WWII it has been divided into East Berlin (formerly the Russian zone, now capital of communist East Germany) and West Berlin (a state of West Germany, though not constitutionally part of it). West Berlin contains 12 districts of the original city and is divided into British, French and US zones. East Berlin contains 8 districts of the old city. The BERLIN WALL separates both halves of the city; East Germany and the USSR have restricted movement between them and at times between West Berlin and West Germany (see BERLIN AIRLIFT). The Four Power Agreement of June 1972 guaranteed freer access to West Berlin and allowed its citizens to visit the East.

Berlin emerged in the Middle Ages, became the capital of Prussia in 1701 and grew into one of Europe's greatest political, commercial and cultural centers. The city was shattered in WWII, but has been rebuilt and revitalized. Pop: East Berlin 1 085 400; West Berlin 2 131 900.

BERLIN, industrial town in central Conn., SSW of Hartford. It includes the villages of East Berlin and Kensington. Pop 14 149.

BERLIN, city in N N.H. It lies in the White Mts, on the Androscoggin and Dead rivers, and makes paper and wood products.

BERLIN, Conference of, held in Berlin (1884–85) by 14 countries to discuss colonial rivalries in Africa. It established the principle that occupation of African territory had to be effective to be legal, recognized the Congo Free State set up by Leopold of Belgium and discussed the control of the Congo and Niger rivers.

BERLIN, Congress of, international meeting held in June–July 1878 to settle problems created by the 1877–78 Russo-Turkish war, notably Russian claims to Balkan territory. The resultant Treaty of Berlin was signed on Aug. 24. Romania, Bulgaria, Serbia and Montenegro became independent; Romania gained N Dobrudja and ceded Bessarabia to Russia; Russian possession of the Caucasus was confirmed; the UK gained Cyprus, and Austria-Hungary was to administer Bosnia-Hercegovina. The congress was chaired by BISMARCK, acting as "honest broker."

BERLIN, Irving (1888–), US song writer, born in Russia as Israel Baline. He wrote over 900 popular songs, including *Alexander's Ragtime Band* (1911) and the more recent *God Bless America* and *White Christmas* (1942); also musicals, including *Annie Get Your Gun* (1946) and *Call Me Madam* (1950). He won a Congressional gold medal (1954) for his patriotic songs.

BERLIN, Sir Isaiah (1909–), Latvian-born British philosopher and social historian. His books include *The Inevitability of History* (1954), *The Age of Enlightenment* (1956) and *Two Concepts of Liberty* (1959). He was knighted in 1957.

BERLIN AIRLIFT, operation by the UK and US to fly essential supplies into West Berlin during the Russian blockade of Allied land and water routes to the city (June 28, 1948–May 12, 1949). It continued until Sept. 30, 1949, involving 250 000 flights, 2 million tons of supplies and a cost of $224 million.

BERLIN DECREE, a proclamation by Napoleon I (Nov. 21, 1806) formally closing Europe to British trade. By thus starting his CONTINENTAL SYSTEM, Napoleon hoped to force peace on his terms. (See also MILAN DECREE.)

BERLIN WALL, 27mi-long wall built in Aug. 1961 by the East Germans to separate East and West Berlin. Made of concrete, steel and barbed wire, it is floodlit and constantly patrolled by armed guards. There are 12 official crossing points.

BERLIOZ, Louis Hector (1803–1869), French Romantic composer of dramatic, descriptive works, some for immense orchestras. Major works include his *Symphonie Fantastique* (1830), *Requiem* (1837), the choral symphony *Romeo and Juliet* (1838–39), the oratorio *The Childhood of Christ* (1850–54) and the operas *Benvenuto Cellini* (1838) and *The Trojans* (1856–59). Throughout his career, Berlioz had to support himself by journalism, although he was much in demand as a conductor.

BERMAN, Shelley (1926–), US comedian whose album *Inside Shelley Berman* (1959) sparked off a new trend in low-key "stand-up" comedy. He later turned to straight acting.

BERMUDA, British colony comprising over 300 coral islands of which 20 are inhabited. It lies in the N Atlantic Ocean, 580mi E of N.C. The main island is Bermuda Island, with the capital, Hamilton. The climate is warm and the vegetation lush and tropical. Bermuda's first British colonists arrived in 1609. Some 60% of present inhabitants are descendants of Negro slaves, and the rest mainly British. The economy depends on tourism and two US bases. Pop 53 000.

BERMUDA GRASS (also called Bahama, scutch or wire grass), a grass used in pastures, lawns and golf greens, particularly in the S US and other countries with warm climates. It grows 50mm (2in) long and has a ring of white hairs on part of the leaf sheath. (See also GRASSES.)

BERN (Berne), capital city of Switzerland and of Bern canton. It lies on the Aare R in the German-speaking area. It is an important commercial, industrial and cultural center and the headquarters of some major international communications organizations. Bern was founded in 1191 and retains many old buildings. Pop 162 405.

BERNADETTE, Saint (1844–1879), born Marie-Bernarde Soubirous. French peasant girl who claimed to have had 18 visions of the Virgin Mary in a LOURDES grotto in 1858. The grotto became a shrine, and she was beatified (1925) and canonized (1933) Her feast day is Feb. 18 in France, April 16 elsewhere.

BERNADOTTE, Count Folke (1895–1948), Swedish UN mediator in the 1948 Arab–Israeli war. In spring 1945 he was the go-between for HIMMLER's offer to the Allies of a conditional Nazi surrender. It was rejected. On Sept. 17, 1948, he was assassinated in Jerusalem by the Zionist Stern gang.

BERNADOTTE, Jean Baptiste Jules (1763–1844), French general who founded Sweden's present royal dynasty. He became one of Napoleon's marshals (1804), and was elected Swedish crown prince in 1810. He fought Napoleon at Leipzig (1813) and ruled Sweden and Norway as Charles XIV (1818–44).

BERNANOS, Georges (1888–1948), French novelist whose theme was the struggle of good and evil forces for man's soul. His masterpiece was *Journal d'un Curé de Campagne* (Diary of a Country Priest).

BERNARD, Claude (1813–1887), French physiologist regarded as the father of experimental medicine. Following the work of BEAUMONT he opened artificial FISTULAS in animals to study their DIGESTIVE SYSTEMS. He demonstrated the role of the PANCREAS in digestion, discussed the presence and function of GLYCOGEN in the LIVER (1856) and in 1851 reported the existence of the vasomotor nerves (see VASOMOTION).

BERNARD OF CLAIRVAUX, Saint (1090–1153), French theologian and mystic who reinvigorated the CISTERCIANS and inspired the Second Crusade. The founder abbot of Clairvaux Abbey (1115–53), he established 68 religious houses. He was adviser to popes, kings and bishops and was instrumental in ABELARD's condemnation (1140). Bernard was canonized in 1174. His feast day is Aug. 20. (See also CRUSADES.)

BERNARD OF MENTHON, Saint (923–1008), French priest and benefactor of travelers. About 962 AD he founded hospices in two Alpine passes, named in his honor the Great and Little St. Bernard passes. He was canonized in 1681 and made the patron saint of mountain climbers in 1923. His feast day is June 15.

BERNAYS, Edward L. (1891–), Austrian-born US originator of professional public relations. He opened the first US public relations firm (1919) and later lectured on public relations. He was a nephew of Sigmund Freud.

BERNE CONVENTION, international copyright protection agreement signed in 1886 by over 40 countries and periodically revised. It now has 59 members. It covers literary publications, drama, motion pictures, artwork, music, records and photographs. The US did not sign but subscribed to the similar Universal Copyright Convention (1952).

BERNESE MOUNTAIN DOG, sturdy (26in high) and handsome long-haired Swiss breed of dog, originally used by the basket makers of Bern to pull wagons. It is black and tan with a white chest, tail tip, feet and blaze on the head.

BERNHARDT, Sarah (1844–1923), French actress of great emotional power, born Henriette Rosine Bernard. She achieved great successes in classic French plays, created many roles for Victorien Sardou and ROSTAND, and made several triumphant worldwide tours.

BERNINI, Giovanni Lorenzo (1598–1680), Italian sculptor and architect who gave Rome many of its characteristic BAROQUE features. He designed the tomb of Urban VIII, the canopy over the high altar in St. Peter's, the Piazza S. Pietro, the *Four Rivers* fountain in the Piazza Navona and the statue *St. Teresa in Ecstasy*.

BERNOULLI, family of Swiss mathematicians important in establishing CALCULUS as a mathematical tool of widespread application. **Jacques (Jakob) Bernoulli** (1654–1705), who applied calculus to many geometrical problems, is best remembered in the Bernoulli numbers and the Theorem of Bernoulli that appeared in a posthumous work on PROBABILITY. **Jean (Johann) Bernoulli** (1667–1748), brother of Jacques, also a propagandist on behalf of the Leibnitzian calculus, assisted his brother in founding the calculus of variations. **Daniel Bernoulli** (1700–1782), son of Jean, anatomist, botanist and mathematician—perhaps the family's most famous member—published his *Hydrodynamics* in 1738, applying calculus to that science. In it he proposed **Bernoulli's principle,** which states that in any small volume of space through which a fluid is flowing steadily, the total ENERGY, comprising the pressure, potential and kinetic energies, is constant. This means that the PRESSURE is inversely related to the VELOCITY.

This principle is applied in the design of the AIRFOIL, the key component in making possible all heavier-than-air craft, where the faster flow of air over the longer upper surface results in reduction of pressure there and hence a lifting force acting on the airfoil (see also AERODYNAMICS).

BERNSTEIN, Eduard (1850–1932), German political theorist and historian. He lived and worked in London (1888–1901), formulating a non-violent program of social reform for the German Social Democratic Party. He was influenced by MARX, ENGELS and the FABIAN SOCIETY.

BERNSTEIN, Leonard (1918–), US conductor–composer, best known for his score for the musical film *West Side Story* (1957). He rose to fame as conductor of the New York Philharmonic Orchestra (1958–69). His varied works include the symphony *The Age of Anxiety* and the scores for the musical *On the Town* (1944) and the film *On the Waterfront* (1954).

BERRA, Lawrence Peter "Yogi" (1925–), US baseball player for the New York Yankees, 1946–63. He gained the record for world series played (75) and the greatest number of series hits (71). He won the American League's "Most Valuable Player Award" in 1951, 1954 and 1955.

BERRIGAN, Daniel (1922–) and **Philip** (1924–), Roman Catholic priests in the pacifist "Catonsville Nine" group. In 1969, as a Vietnam War protest, the nine broke into the Selective Service Office at Catonsville, Md., and poured ox-blood over records and files. The Berrigans were convicted and given three years; in 1972 Philip was tried on conspiracy charges but acquitted.

BERRY, a fleshy FRUIT normally with many seeds, although occasionally only one, as in the date. The TOMATO, MELON, ORANGE and GRAPE are examples of berries. The name is often given to "false fruits" such as the STRAWBERRY, and aggregate fruits such as the RASPBERRY. (See also DRUPE.)

BERRYMAN, John (1914–1972), US poet, active from the 1930s. His reputation was confirmed by the long poem *Homage to Mistress Bradstreet* (1956). Berryman's later work, distinguished by its black ironies and linguistic innovation, includes *His Toy, His Dream, His Rest* (1968) and *Dream Songs* (1969). He committed suicide, throwing himself off a bridge in Minneapolis.

BERTHELOT, Pierre Eugène Marcel(l)in (1827–1907), French chemist and statesman, who pioneered the synthesis of organic compounds not found in nature and later introduced the terms exothermic and endothermic (descriptive of chemical reactions) to THERMOCHEMISTRY. His public career was crowned in 1895 when he became foreign secretary.

BERTHOLLET, Claude Louis, Count (1748–1822), Savoyard-born French chemist noted for his work on CHLORINE (first using it in BLEACHING) but best remembered for his generally erroneous belief that the components in a chemical compound might be present in any of a continuous range of proportions (see COMPOSITION, CHEMICAL).

BERTILLON, Alphonse (1853–1914), French criminologist who devised a system (*Bertillonage*) for identifying criminals based on anthropometric measurements (see ANTHROPOMETRY), adopted by the French police in 1888 and used until the adoption of fingerprinting (see FINGERPRINTS).

BERWICK, industrial borough in E central Pa., on the Susquehanna R. It makes rolling stock, metal products and clothing. Pop 12 274.

BERWYN, residential city in NE Ill., 10mi W of Chicago. The Cook Co. Forest Reserve and Brookfield Zoo are nearby. Pop 52 502.

BERYL, aluminum beryllium silicate ($Al_2[Be_3(SiO_3)_6]$), the commonest ore of BERYLLIUM, mainly found as hexagonal crystals in granite throughout the world. EMERALD is a deep-green beryl with some chromium; AQUAMARINE is a pale-blue beryl. mp 1400°C.

BERYLLIUM (Be), a gray ALKALINE-EARTH METAL, found mainly as BERYL, prepared by reducing beryllium fluoride with magnesium. It is strong, hard and very light, and has a high melting point and high heat absorption—all useful properties. Combined with copper it makes a very hard alloy resistant to corrosion and fatigue. It is also used in NUCLEAR REACTOR construction to moderate neutrons, and in X-RAY tube windows. Beryllium is relatively unreactive; it forms divalent, tetracoordinate compounds which are poisonous, causing the disease berylliosis. The refractory **Beryllium Oxide** (BeO) is used in ceramics and in electronics. AW 9.01, mp 1278°C, bp 2970°C, sg 1.848 (20°C).

BERZELIUS, Jöns Jakob, Baron (1779–1848), Swedish chemist who determined the ATOMIC WEIGHTS of nearly 40 elements before 1818, discovered CERIUM (1803), SELENIUM (1818) and THORIUM (1829), introduced the terms PROTEIN, ISOMERISM and CATALYSIS and devised the modern method of writing empirical formulas (1813).

BESANT, Annie (1847–1933), British theosophist and social reformer, born Annie Wood. Mrs. Besant joined the FABIAN SOCIETY and was an early advocate of birth control. Madame BLAVATSKY's writings converted her to THEOSOPHY and she joined the Theosophical Society (1889) and became international president (1907–33). She also championed independence for India, becoming president of the Indian National Congress (1917).

BESSARABIA, historic region of SE Europe, NW of the Black Sea, between the Dniester and Danube rivers. After various Russo–Turkish conflicts it was ceded to Russia in 1812. After the CRIMEAN WAR it passed to Moldavia (1856) but was regained by Russia (1878). Romania controlled it almost continuously from 1918 to 1944, when it joined the USSR as part of the Moldavian and Ukrainian SSR.

BESSARION, John (c1410–1472), Byzantine humanist scholar and churchman. As a Byzantine archbishop at the councils of Ferrara and Florence he tried to reunite the divided Greek and Latin churches. He stayed in Italy, becoming a cardinal and helping to spread Greek classical learning.

BESSEL, Friedrich Wilhelm (1784–1846), German astronomer who first observed stellar PARALLAX (1838) and set new standards of accuracy for positional astronomers. From the parallax observation, which was of 61 Cygni, he calculated the star to be about 6 ly distant, setting a new lower limit for the scale of the universe. In applied mathematics he was the first to employ **Bessel functions** in a systematic way.

BESSEMER, city in N central Ala., SW of Birmingham. It produces steel, railroad rolling stock and lumber. Pop 33 428.

BESSEMER, Sir Henry (1813–1898), British inventor of the BESSEMER PROCESS for the manufacture of steel, patented in 1856.

BESSEMER PROCESS, the first cheap, large-scale method of making STEEL from PIG IRON, invented in the 1850s by Henry BESSEMER. The Bessemer converter is a pivoting, pear-shaped BLAST FURNACE lined with refractory bricks. The furnace is tilted, loaded with molten pig iron, then righted. Compressed air blown through the tuyeres burns off most of the carbon and converts silicon and manganese to slag as the temperature rises. If lime is added, an afterblow removes phosphorus. The process is largely superseded by the OPEN-HEARTH PROCESS.

BEST, Charles Herbert (1899–), US–Canadian physiologist who assisted F. G. BANTING in the isolation of INSULIN but, to Banting's annoyance, did not share in the Nobel prize that Banting shared with J. J. R. MACLEOD.

BESTIARY, medieval or other collection of prose or poetry detailing characteristics and habits of real or imagined animals and drawing morals therefrom. The earliest such compilation, *Physiologus* (The Naturalist), appeared in Greek before 200 AD.

BETANCOURT, Rómulo (1908–), Venezuelan politician and founder of the left-wing Acción Democrática party (1941). Provisional president 1945–47 and president 1958–63, he spent 1948–58 in exile after a military coup, and survived an assassination attempt in 1960.

BETA RAY, a stream of beta particles (i.e., ELECTRONS or POSITRONS) emitted from radioactive nuclei undergoing beta disintegration (see RADIOACTIVITY). Beta particles are emitted with velocities approaching that of light and can penetrate up to 1mm of lead. Positive beta rays are not emitted from any naturally occurring material.

The fountain of the Four Rivers in Rome, by Bernini and his pupils, was a triumph of the fantastic Baroque imagination. Dramatic effect is paramount; the free composition, the expressive postures of the figures and the swirling drapery contribute to the impression of vitality.

BETATRON, an electron ACCELERATOR in which the particles are accelerated in a circular path of constant radius by a steadily increasing magnetic field produced by an alternating-current ELECTROMAGNET. The maximum energy attained by the ELECTRONS is about 300MeV.

BETELGEUSE, Alpha Orionis, second brightest star in ORION. An irregularly variable red supergiant (see VARIABLE STAR) with a variable radius some 300 times that of the sun, it is over 150pc from earth.

BETEL NUT, fruit of the betel palm (*Areca catechu*), native to tropical Asia. It is boiled, sliced, dried and chewed as a stimulant with betel pepper vine leaves (*Piper betle*) and coral lime. Chewing produces red saliva which may temporarily stain the mouth orange–brown.

BETHANY (Al-Ayzariyah), village in Israeli-occupied Jordan, on the Mt of Olives, 2mi E of Jerusalem. Here Christ raised LAZARUS from the dead.

BETHANY, residential city in central Okla., a suburb of Oklahoma City. Pop 21 785.

BETHE, Hans Albrecht (1906–), German-born US theoretical physicist who proposed the nuclear CARBON CYCLE to account for the sun's energy output (1938). During WWII he worked on the Manhattan Project. He was awarded the 1967 Nobel physics prize for his work on the source of stellar energy.

BETHEL (Baytin), village in Israeli-occupied Jordan, 11mi E of Jerusalem. In Old Testament times the place was held to be holy. Here ABRAHAM raised an altar (Gen. 12:8) and JACOB dreamed of a heavenly ladder (Gen. 28:10–22).

BETHEL, town in SW Conn., producing tools, chemicals and electronic components. Pop 10 945.

BETHEL PARK, residential borough in SW Pa., a S suburb of Pittsburgh. It was the center of the 1791 WHISKEY REBELLION against a federal liquor tax. Pop 34 791.

BETHESDA, residential district in central Md., a NW suburb of Washington, D.C., and site of the US Navy Medical Center, National Cancer Institute and other medical centers. Pop 71 621.

BETHLEHEM (Bayt Lahm), town in Israeli-occupied Jordan SSW of Jerusalem, traditional birthplace of Christ. A basilica built by the Emperor CONSTANTINE over the Grotto of the Nativity (326–33) and rebuilt by JUSTINIAN I now forms the Church of the

The low entrance to the Church of the Nativity forces pilgrims to bow their heads. The church was rebuilt by the Emperor Justinian in the 6th century, on the spot where Christ's birthplace is supposed to have been.

Nativity, a major attraction for tourists and pilgrims. Pop 16 313.

BETHLEHEM, city in E Pa., on the Lehigh R, 5mi E of Allentown, a major US producer of steel and cement. Home of the Bach Choir and annual Bach Festival, it is also the chief US center of the Moravian Church. Pop 72 686.

BETHMANN-HOLLWEG, Theobald von (1856–1921), German chancellor (1909–17) who was opposed to WWI but defended Germany's role during it. His calling the international guarantee of Belgian neutrality "a scrap of paper" was considered typical German cynicism.

BETHPAGE, unincorporated urban community in SE N.Y., in central Long Island. Pop 18 555.

BETHUNE, Mary McLeod (1875–1955), black US educator and civil rights activist. She founded the Daytona Normal and Industrial School for Negro Girls (1904), now Bethune–Cookman College, and was Director of Negro Affairs in the National Youth Administration (1936–44) and President F. D. ROOSEVELT's adviser on minority problems.

BETJEMAN, Sir John (1906–), English poet laureate and architectural conservationist, often called a lyrical satirist. His books include *New Bats in Old Belfries* (1940), *Selected Poems* (1948), *Collected Poems* (1958), *Victorian and Edwardian Architecture in London* (1969).

BETTA. See FIGHTING FISH.

BETTELHEIM, Bruno (1903–), Austrian-born US psychologist who drew on his prewar experience as an inmate of Nazi concentration camps to describe men's behavior in extreme situations (1943). His subsequent work has mainly concerned the treatment of autistic (see AUTISM) and disturbed children.

BETTENDORF, industrial city in E Ia., 5mi E of Davenport. It is the upper-Mississippi terminal for oil tankers. Pop 22 126.

BETTER BUSINESS BUREAU, a US non-profit-making corporation designed to protect consumers from unfair or illegal business practices. It handles offending businesses by persuasion or referral to a government agency. The bureau has over 100 000 members and annually handles some 4 million inquiries.

BETTI, Ugo (1892–1953), Italian playwright and poet, once a judge. His plays, deeply concerned with guilt and evil, are often shaped as judicial enquiries. His works include *La Padrona* (1927) and *Il Giocatore* (1951).

BETTING. See GAMBLING.

BEVAN, Aneurin "Nye" (1897–1960), British labor leader and major left-wing socialist politician. As minister of health (1945–50) under ATTLEE, he introduced and administered the 1946 National Health Act which established a vast national health program.

BEVATRON, contraction for *b*illion *e*lectron-*v*olt synchro*tron*, a name used to describe several high-energy particle ACCELERATORS, first applied to a 6-GeV proton SYNCHROTRON at the U. of Cal., Berkeley.

BEVERIDGE, Albert Jeremiah (1862–1927), US historian and republican senator (1899–1911). In 1912 he joined the insurgent Progressive Party and thereafter gained no major political post. He won a 1920 Pulitzer Prize for *The Life of John Marshall* (4 vols., 1916–19).

BEVERIDGE, William Henry, 1st Baron of Tuggal (1879–1963), British economist and social planner whose report on social insurance (1942) revolutionized the British welfare system. It became law under the 1945–51 Labour government. Beveridge became a knight in 1919 and a baron in 1946.

BEVERLY, residential and manufacturing city in Mass., 16mi NE of Boston. The first US navy ship, *Hannah*, sailed from there Sept. 5, 1775. Pop 38 348.

BEVERLY HILLS, residential city in SW Cal. It is a W suburb of Los Angeles, famous as the home of many movie stars. Pop 33 416.

BEVERLY HILLS, village in SE Mich., S of Pontiac. It was called Westwood Village from 1958 to 1959. Pop 13 598.

BEVIN, Ernest (1881–1951), British labor leader and statesman. He formed the Transport and General Workers' Union (1922), the nation's largest union. He was minister of labor in WWII and as foreign minister in 1945–51 took a tough pro-European, anti-Soviet stand.

BEWICK, Thomas (1753–1828), English reviver of the art of wood engraving. His masterpieces are the *Chillingham Bull* (1789) and his plates for Beilby's *History of British Birds* (1797–1804).

BEXLEY, residential city in central Ohio, on the Scioto R. Surrounded by Columbus, it is politically independent. Pop 14 888.

BEZA, Theodore, or de Bèze (1519–1605), French Calvinist theologian, CALVIN's successor in Geneva (1564). His Latin translation of the New Testament was a source for the King James version.

BHAGALPUR, city in NE India, in the state of Bihar. It lies on the Ganges R. Bhagalpur makes textiles and has four colleges. Pop 178 216.

BHAGAVAD-GĪTĀ (song of the Lord), anonymous SANSKRIT poem of about 200 BC, embedded in the Mahābhārata epic, a world-famous religious discourse. It consists of a dialogue (700 verses), covering many aspects of Hindu religious thought, between Prince Arjuna and the god KRISHNA on a field of battle.

BHARAL (or Blue Sheep; burrhel; burhal; nahur), a mountain GOAT of Asia, *Pseudois nayaur.* There are three races, the smallest being a dwarf Chinese variety. In general, bharals rarely exceed 70kg (154lb) in weight, but have disproportionately large HORNS, up to 0.9m (3ft) in length. (Family: BOVIDAE.)

BHATPARA, city in NE India in the state of West Bengal. It is a jute center on the Hooghly R near Calcutta. Bhatpara was an ancient center of Sanskrit culture. Pop 160 607.

BHAVE, Vinoba (1895–), Indian religious leader who founded the *Bhoodan Yajna* (land-gift movement) in 1951. He persuaded landlords to give land for the landless; 5.5 million acres were redistributed thus.

BHAVNAGAR, or Bhaunagar, seaport city in W India, 200mi N of Bombay. It produces iron, bricks and textiles and has several colleges. Pop 222 462.

BHOPAL, capital of the state of Madhya Pradesh in central India. It makes electrical equipment. Its Taj-ul-Masjid mosque is said to be India's largest. Pop 325 721.

BHUMIBOL, Adulyadej (1927–), US-born constitutional monarch of Thailand from 1946, after the assassination of his brother Ananda Mahidol. He was formally crowned in 1950.

BHUTAN (or Drukyul), kingdom in the E Himalayas between Tibet and India. It is a mountainous land with fertile subtropical valleys. Rice, tea and other farm products dominate its mainly subsistence economy. Poor communications have hampered development. Some 65% of the people are Bhutias of Tibetan–Himalayan origin. There are also many Nepalese. Dzongkha is the official language and LAMAISM the major faith. Bhutan is ruled by the hereditary king (Druk Gyalpo) with a council of ministers and national assembly. China has claimed Bhutanese territory since the 1950s but India controls Bhutan's external affairs.

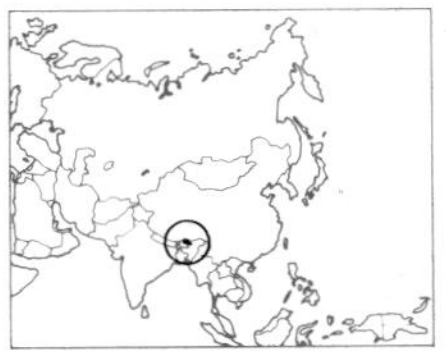

Official Name: Bhutan
Capital: Thimbu
Area: 18 000sq mi
Population: 1 010 000
Languages: Dzongkha
Religions: Buddhist, Hindu
Monetary Unit(s): 1 Indian rupee = 2 tikchung = 100 paise

BHUTTO, Zulfikar Ali (1928–), president of Pakistan from Dec. 1971, after the Bangladesh succession. He succeeded Yahya Khan. Bhutto, a lawyer, was educated at the U. of Cal., and in Britain at Oxford and Lincoln's Inn.

BIAFRA, name assumed by Nigeria's Eastern Region during its attempted secession (1967–70). Under the leadership of Colonel Ojukwu, the IBO people of the Eastern Region declared their independence in May, 1967, and the civil war, for which both sides had been preparing for some time, broke out. Outnumbered and outgunned, the Biafrans suffered heavy losses, with large numbers dying from starvation, before their final surrender. The former breakaway region was divided to form the East-Central Rivers and South-Eastern states.

BIALIK, Haim Nahman (1873–1934), one of the greatest of modern Hebrew poets. Born in the Ukraine, he settled in Palestine in 1924. Firmly rooted in tradition, his poetry gave fiery expression to Jewish national aspirations, making Bialik his people's national poet.

BIALYSTOK, capital city of Bialystok province in NE Poland. An industrial center, it also processes local agricultural products and lumber. During WWII it was occupied first by German and then by Russian troops. Pop 166 600.

BIARRITZ, famous resort in SW France. It stands on the Bay of Biscay near Bayonne, in the department of Basses Pyrénées. Pop 26 750.

BIBLE, collection of sacred books of JUDAISM and CHRISTIANITY, often called the Holy Scriptures. Being inspired (that is, given by God), they form the basis for belief and practice (see CANON). Modern theologians generally regard the Bible as the record and vehicle of divine revelation: equally the word of God and the word of man. Major biblical themes center in God, his creation and care of the world, his righteousness, love, and saving activity (see COVENANT; JESUS CHRIST; CHURCH). The Bible has had an incalculable influence on the thought, attitudes, beliefs, art, science and politics of Western society.

The Christian Bible comprises the OLD TESTAMENT and the NEW TESTAMENT. The Hebrew Bible is essentially the Old Testament. Its 39 books, plus the 27 of the New Testament, make up the Protestant Bible. Most of the books of disputed authority, known as the APOCRYPHA, are included in the Old Testament by the Eastern and Roman Catholic Churches while in Protestant editions they are excluded or placed between the two Testaments.

There have been many versions and many translations of the Bible. The original Old Testament, written almost entirely in Hebrew, was translated into Aramaic (the TARGUMS) and later into Greek (see SEPTUAGINT) and Latin. The VULGATE is still the standard Latin version in the Roman Catholic Church. It was the basis of the first major English version, named for John WYCLIFFE, and completed in 1388. The REFORMATION aimed to give the Bible to the common people, and Martin LUTHER's German version pioneered much translation work. Several scholarly English translations, including those by William TYNDALE and Miles COVERDALE, appeared in the 16th century. A significant Roman Catholic translation by the English colleges in exile of Rheims and Douai appeared in 1582 and 1610. Still supreme among English versions is the King James or Authorized Version (1611), a major work of English literature. This remains perhaps the most popular translation, although outmoded by later, more accurate versions, notably the Revised Version (1881 and 1885) and the Revised Standard Version (1952). The Roman Catholic Church has produced the Jerusalem Bible (1966), and Ronald Knox's version (1945 and 1949). The New English Bible (1962 and 1970), produced by an interdenominational committee, is another major modern translation.

The Bible has now been translated into more than 1400 languages, and millions of copies are sold annually throughout the world. (See also BIBLE SOCIETIES.)

BIBLE SOCIETIES, societies first founded by Protestants in the early 18th century to make the Bible available cheaply to as many people as possible. Major foundations include the British and Foreign Bible Society formed in 1804, and the American Bible Society founded in 1816. In 1946 US and other groups cooperated to create the United Bible Societies. Similar societies exist within the Roman Catholic Church. In addition there are independent bodies, such as the Gideons International Organization, founded in Wis. in 1899, which distributes free Bibles to prisons, hospitals and hotels.

BIBLIOTHÈQUE NATIONALE, the French national library in Paris. Developed from early royal collections, some of which date back to the 14th century, it now has over 6 million books, and the legal right to receive any book published in France.

BICAMERAL SYSTEM, division of a legislature into two chambers, or houses. The US Congress, for example, is divided into the Senate and the House of Representatives; the British parliament comprises the House of Lords and the House of Commons.

BICARBONATE OF SODA, or sodium bicarbonate. See SODIUM.

Bible: One of the oldest manuscripts of the Pentateuch, the so-called Scroll of Akisha supposedly written by the great-grandson of Aaron. It is held by the small Samaritan community in Nablus (the Biblical Shechem) on the West bank of Jordan; they have never allowed it to be examined by scholars.

The Books of the Old Testament

Roman Catholic Canon	Protestant Canon	Jewish Scripture
Genesis	Genesis	*Law*
Exodus	Exodus	Genesis
Leviticus	Leviticus	Exodus
Numbers	Numbers	Leviticus
Deuteronomy	Deuteronomy	Numbers
Josue	Joshua	Deuteronomy
Judges	Judges	
Ruth	Ruth	*Prophets*
1 & 2 Kings	1 & 2 Samuel	Joshua
3 & 4 Kings	1 & 2 Kings	Judges
1 & 2 Paralipomenon	1 & 2 Chronicles	1 & 2 Samuel
1 Esdras	Ezra	1 & 2 Kings
2 Esdras	Nehemiah	Isaiah
Tobias		Jeremiah
Judith		Ezekiel
Esther	Esther	Hosea
Job	Job	Joel
Psalms	Psalms	Amos
Proverbs	Proverbs	Obadiah
Ecclesiastes	Ecclesiastes	Jonah
Canticles of Canticles	Song of Solomon	Micah
Wisdom of Solomon		Nahum
Ecclesiasticus		Habakkuk
Isaias	Isaiah	Zephaniah
Jeremias	Jeremiah	Haggai
Lamentations	Lamentations	Zechariah
Baruch		Malachi
Ezechiel	Ezekiel	
Daniel	Daniel	*Hagiographa*
Osee	Hosea	Psalms
Joel	Joel	Proverbs
Amos	Amos	Job
Abdias	Obadiah	Song of Solomon
Jonas	Jonah	Ruth
Michaes	Micah	Lamentations
Nahum	Nahum	Ecclesiastes
Habacuc	Habakkuk	Esther
Sophonias	Zephaniah	Daniel
Aggeus	Haggai	Ezra
Zacharias	Zechariah	Nehemiah
Malachias	Malachi	1 & 2 Chronicles
1 & 2 Machabees		

Protestant Apocrypha

- 1 & 2 Esdras
- Tobit
- Judith
- Additions to Esther
- Wisdom of Solomon
- Ecclesiasticus or the Wisdom of Jesus Son of Sirach
- Baruch
- Prayer of Azariah and the Song of the Three Holy Children
- Susanna
- Bel and the Dragon
- The Prayer of Manasses
- 1 & 2 Maccabees

The Books of the New Testament

Gospels: Matthew, Mark, Luke, John

Acts of the Apostles

Epistles: Pauline — Romans, 1 & 2 Corinthians, Galatians, Ephesians, Philippians, Colossians, 1 & 2 Thessalonians, 1 & 2 Timothy, Titus, Philemon.
Non-Pauline — Hebrews, James, 1 & 2 Peter, 1, 2, & 3 John, Jude.

Revelation (Roman Catholic Canon: Apocalypse)

BICARBONATES, or hydrogen carbonates, acid salts of carbonic acid (see CARBON), containing the ion HCO_3^-. Bicarbonates are formed by the action of carbon dioxide on carbonates in aqueous solution; this reaction is reversed on heating. Dissolved calcium and magnesium bicarbonates give rise to HARD WATER.

BICEPS, either of two MUSCLES that are split in two in their upper part to form a Y-shape. *Biceps brachii* is the chief upper ARM muscle, attached to the shoulder blade and the radius. *Biceps femoris* is a thigh muscle (see LEG), attached to the PELVIS, the FEMUR and the FIBULA.

BICHAT, Marie François Xavier (1771–1802), French anatomist and pathologist, the founder of HISTOLOGY. Although working without the MICROSCOPE, Bichat distinguished 21 types of elementary TISSUES from which the organs of the body are composed.

BICHIRS, the genus *Polypterus* (family Polypteridae) containing some ten species of primitive African freshwater fishes. They may be descended from the order Crossopterygii, which contains the COELACANTH, but FOSSIL evidence for this is lacking.

BICHONS FRISES, small breed of lapdog, akin to a miniature poodle, standing 11–12in high. Its long (3–5in), white, curly coat is sometimes lion-clipped.

BICKERDYKE, Mary Ann Bell (1817–1901), US Civil War nurse. She organized hospital and welfare services for Federal armies campaigning under generals Grant and Sherman, greatly raising standards of hygiene and general medical care.

BIDAULT, George (1899–   ), French statesman, opponent of France's decolonization policies, now living in exile in Brazil. He was prime minister (1946; 1949–50) and foreign secretary (1944; 1947–48; 1953–54). In 1962 he was exiled by President de Gaulle for backing militant opposition to Algerian independence.

BIDDEFORD, industrial city in SW Me., first settled in 1630. It makes shoes and automotive products. Pop 19983.

BIDDLE, Francis Beverley (1886–1968), US lawyer who became US solicitor-general in 1940 and attorney general in WWII (1941–45). After the war he served on the war crimes tribunal at Nuremberg.

BIDDLE, James (1783–1848), US naval officer. In an adventurous life, he was shipwrecked, imprisoned by Barbary pirates and captured by the British during the War of 1812. He later claimed the Oregon territory for the US (1817) and negotiated the first treaty between the US and China (1846).

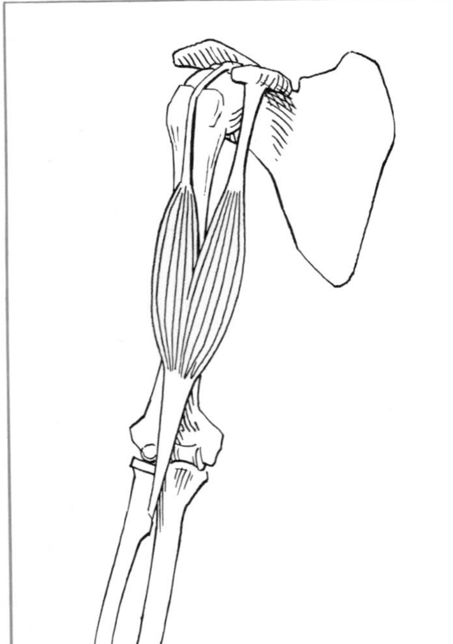

The biceps of the arm (*colored area*) has two heads (origins), one of which is attached to the shoulder blade and the other to the shoulder joint. The elbow is bent by contracting the biceps.

BIDDLE, Nicholas (1786–1844), president of the second BANK OF THE UNITED STATES (1823–36). He made it the nation's first authoritative central bank. Renewal of the bank's charter was vetoed by President Jackson after Biddle had unwisely made rechartering a major presidential election issue.

BIEDERMEIER, utilitarian bourgeois style of furniture prevailing in Germany between about 1810 and 1850. The term derived from the caricature bourgeois figure "Papa Biedermeier" who featured in a popular magazine of the 1850s, and came to apply disparagingly to German bourgeois taste of the period.

BIEL, or Bienne, city in Switzerland, 17mi NNW of Bern. It is a railroad junction and manufactures watches, machinery, paper and pottery. Pop 64333.

BIELEFELD, West German industrial city, 38mi E of Münster. It makes machine tools, chemicals, bicycles and textiles. Pop 168695.

BIENNIAL, plant that completes its LIFE CYCLE in two years. During the first year leaves are produced and food is stored (as in the CARROT and CABBAGE) for use in the second year when the plant bears flowers and fruit, then dies. (See ANNUAL; PERENNIAL.)

BIENVILLE, Jean Baptiste le Moyne, Sieur de (1680–1768), French naval office who founded New Orleans. Born in Canada, he helped to colonize French Louisiana, which he governed at various periods between 1701 and 1743.

BIERCE, Ambrose (Gwinett) (1842–1914?), US short-story writer and satirical journalist. His works include the gloomy tales of *Can Such Things Be?* (1893) and the cynical definitions of *The Devil's Dictionary* (1906). He disappeared without trace during the Mexican Revolution of 1913–14.

BIERSTADT, Albert (1830–1902), German-born US la landscape painter. He is famous for his massive, realistic Western scenes.

BIFROST, in Norse mythology, the rainbow bridge linking *Midgard* (the earth) with ASGARD (the home of the gods).

BIGAMY, the crime of being married to two persons simultaneously. A person remarrying without knowing that his or her first marriage remains valid is still held by most courts to be guilty of bigamy. The second spouse is innocent of bigamy though, in some parts of the US, technically punishable.

BIG BANG THEORY. See COSMOLOGY; HUBBLE; LEMAÎTRE.

BIG BEN, the bell in the clock tower of the Houses of Parliament, London, and commonly the clock itself. It weighs 13 tons and is named for Sir Benjamin Hall, commissioner of works in 1856 when the bell was installed.

BIG BEND NATIONAL PARK, vast tract of mountains and desert on the Texan border with Mexico, in the Big Bend of the Rio Grande. The park, which covers some 708221 acres, was established in 1944 and is the last great expanse of truly wild land left in Tex.

BIG BERTHA, any of several types of massive artillery developed by the Germans in WWI and nicknamed for Bertha von Bohlen, head of the powerful KRUPP family of munition-makers.

BIG BROTHERS OF AMERICA, a social welfare organization in the US and Canada. Its professionally supervised male volunteers help boys who are either fatherless or in need of parental care.

BIG DIPPER. See GREAT BEAR.

BIGELOW, John (1817–1911), US journalist, author and diplomat. As US consul in Paris (1861–64), he prevented the Confederate states gaining French-built warships. Bigelow also served as minister to France (1865–66). He was co-editor of the New York *Evening Post* (1848–61).

BIGGS, E(dward) Power (1906–   ), English-born US concert organist. He is a master of old and modern music, and has edited various organ works.

BIGHORN, *Ovis canadensis*, wild SHEEP of North America, particularly Canada. There are several races, males of the smallest (Nelson's bighorn) weighing around 80lb; those of the largest (Rocky Mountain and California bighorn) as much as 270lb. They are very aggressive, the males commonly breaking off their large, curving horns in fight. (Family: BOVIDAE.)

BIGHORN MOUNTAINS, part of the eastern Rocky Mountains, ranging from N Wyo. to Mont. Cloud Peak (13175ft) is the highest point.

BIGHORN RIVER, river flowing 336mi, largely through canyons, from Wind R canyon, Wyo., to Yellowstone R in Mont.

BIGNONIA, several hundred species of creeping and climbing plants, native to the warmer regions of the New World. Best known in the US is the cross vine. The common trumpet creeper of the eastern US produces numerous aerial roots.

BIGOT, François (1703–c1777), French administrator, intendant (1748–60) of New France (French Canada). He used his position to perpetuate massive frauds, weakening French influence and playing directly into the hands of the British. On his return to France he was imprisoned, then banished.

BIG RAPIDS, city in central Mich., seat of Mecasta Co. It is a summer resort and a center for natural gas and oil wells. Pop 11995.

BIG SISTERS ASSOCIATION, US Protestant social welfare agency, counseling girls of under 16 and boys of under 10. It was founded in 1908.

BIHAR, state in E India, in the Ganges Basin, bordering Nepal and Bangladesh. Most of its inhabitants are Hindu and speak Bihari. The agricultural N grows rice, jute and sugar. The mineral-rich S yields 50% of India's coal, 25% of its iron and most of its mica and copper.

BIKANER, capital of the former Indian state of Bikaner, in NW India. It is known for its blankets and carpets. Pop 190868.

BIKINI, an atoll in the Marshall Islands in the central Pacific Ocean. It was the site of US nuclear bomb tests in the 1940s and 1950s.

BILBAO, a major seaport in N Spain, capital of Vizcaya province. It is important for heavy industry, including shipbuilding and metallurgy, and for its fishing fleet. Pop 410490.

BILBO, Theodore Gilmore (1877–1947), US politician and Southern champion of white supremacy and state sovereignty. He was senator from Miss. 1935–47. Bilbo, a Democrat, died while Republican senators were seeking his expulsion from the senate after allegations of corruption.

BILE, a yellow-brown fluid secreted by the liver and containing salts derived from CHOLESTEROL. Stored and concentrated in the GALL BLADDER and released into the DUODENUM after a meal, the bile emulsifies fats and aids absorption of fat-soluble vitamins A, D, E and K. Other constituents of bile are in fact waste products. Yellow bile and black bile were two of the HUMORS of Hippocratic medicine.

BILHARZIA, chronic PARASITIC DISEASE of the BLADDER, intestine or LIVER, caused by *Schistosoma* species; often contracted by swimming in infected water.

BILINGUALISM, proficiency in two languages, acquired by study or resulting from the interaction of different linguistic groups. In the political sense the term refers to the coexistence of such groups in a particular country. Among bilingual countries are Canada (English and French) and Belgium (French and Flemish).

BILL. See BEAK.

BILLERICA, town in NE Mass., S of Lowell. Pop 31648.

BILLIARDS, name for several indoor games in which balls set on a felt-covered rectangular table are struck by the end of a long tapering stick (the cue). Obscure in origin, billiards was popular in France and England as early as the 14th century. The name came from the French *billard* which meant "a cue." Until the 19th century billiard balls were made of ivory, but now compressed plastic composition balls are most common. The cue has a rubber cushion tip. The table usually has a slate bed in a wooden frame and must be plumb level. In most forms of the game, the table has six pockets: one in each corner and one midway along each of the longer sides. The object is to sink balls into the pockets by playing one ball off another or, in games played without pockets, to hit the balls against each other successively. **Carom billiards** and **English billiards** feature two white cue balls and one red ball. **Snooker** has one white cue ball, 15 red balls and six balls of other colors. **Pool** has one white cue ball, and 15 numbered colored balls.

BILLINGS, city in S Mont., seat of Yellowstone Co. It manufactures farm machinery, processes agricultural produce and has oil wells and refineries. Pop 61 581.

BILLINGS, Josh, pen name of Henry Wheeler Shaw (1818–1885), US dialect humorist. His books include *Josh Billings' Farmers Allminax* (1870) and *Josh Billings Struggling with Things* (1881).

BILLINGS, William (1746–1800), American church music composer. He published the first of his six collections, *The New England Psalm Singers*, in 1770.

BILL OF ATTAINDER. See ATTAINDER.

BILL OF EXCHANGE, or draft, a commercial document by which one party directs another to pay the person or organization named on the bill a certain sum of money at a certain time. Banks and businesses often transfer money in this way.

BILL OF LADING, a shipper's written contract specifying goods accepted for transport, and undertaking their delivery. In order to secure delivery, the receiver must usually present a copy of this bill forwarded to him by the vendor.

BILL OF RIGHTS, a constitutional document which defines the rights of a people, safeguarding them against undue governmental interference. In the US these rights and safeguards are embodied in the first 10 amendments to the Constitution. After the Revolutionary War there was great popular demand for constitutionally defined rights to limit the power of the new government. Bills of rights were drafted in eight states between 1776 and 1781, but when the Constitution was drawn up in 1787 no such bill was included; because of this several states refused to ratify it. Two years after the Constitution had been passed, James Madison presented a bill of rights to Congress, basing it closely on his own state of Va.'s bill of 1776. Twelve amendments to the Constitution were proposed in the debate on Madison's bill, 10 of which were accepted, and on Dec. 15, 1791, Secretary of State Thomas Jefferson proclaimed the Federal Bill of Rights in full force. The bill guarantees freedom of speech, of the press and of religion. It protects against arbitrary searches and gives everyone the right to bear arms. It sets out proper procedures for trials, giving to all the right to trial by jury and to cross-examine witnesses. The core of the bill is in the 5th Amendment which states that no person shall "be deprived of life, liberty, or property, without due process of law."

Originally the bill only limited the power of the federal government, but in 1868 the 14th Amendment was ratified, extending the powers of the bill to cover state as well as federal government. The Supreme Court interpreted the 14th Amendment as guaranteeing only the first 8 of the 10 clauses in the Bill of Rights, as they are "of the very essence of a scheme of ordered liberty." However, in recent years the tendency has been to interpret the 14th Amendment as making all the protections of the Bill of Rights applicable to both state and federal governments.

BILL OF RIGHTS, English, an act passed by the English parliament in 1689 to consolidate constitutional government after the GLORIOUS REVOLUTION. It abolished the royal power to suspend laws, established free parliamentary elections and defined citizens' rights.

BILLROTH, Albert Christian Theodor (1829–1894), German surgeon and founder of modern abdominal SURGERY. A keen pianist, he is also remembered for his friendship with BRAHMS.

BILLY THE KID (1859–1881), nickname of the US outlaw, born William H. Bonney. Notorious in the Southwest as a cattle thief and murderer, he was eventually captured and sentenced to hang. He escaped from jail by killing two guards but was soon tracked down and killed by Sheriff Pat Garrett.

BILOXI, city in SE Miss. The first white settlement in the Miss. valley, it was founded in 1719, and named for the Biloxi Indians. It is now a resort with

The Bill of Rights

ARTICLES IN ADDITION TO, AND AMENDMENT OF, THE CONSTITUTION OF THE UNITED STATES OF AMERICA, PROPOSED BY CONGRESS, AND RATIFIED BY THE SEVERAL STATES, PURSUANT TO THE FIFTH ARTICLE OF THE ORIGINAL CONSTITUTION

AMENDMENT [I]

Congress shall make no law respecting an establishment of religion, or prohibiting the free exercise thereof; or abridging the freedom of speech, or of the press; or the right of the people peaceably to assemble, and to petition the Government for a redress of grievances.

AMENDMENT [II]

A well regulated Militia, being necessary to the security of a free State, the right of the people to keep and bear Arms, shall not be infringed.

AMENDMENT [III]

No soldier shall, in time of peace be quartered in any house, without the consent of the Owner, nor in time of war, but in a manner to be prescribed by law.

AMENDMENT [IV]

The right of the people to be secure in their persons, houses, papers, and effects, against unreasonable searches and seizures, shall not be violated, and no Warrants shall issue, but upon probable cause, supported by Oath or affirmation, and particularly describing the place to be searched, and the persons or things to be seized.

AMENDMENT [V]

No person shall be held to answer for a capital, or otherwise infamous crime, unless on a presentment or indictment of a Grand Jury, except in cases arising in the land or naval forces, or in the Militia, when in actual service in time of War or public danger; nor shall any person be subject for the same offence to be twice put in jeopardy of life or limb; nor shall be compelled in any criminal case to be a witness against himself, nor be deprived of life, liberty, or property, without due process of law; nor shall private property be taken for public use, without just compensation.

AMENDMENT [VI]

In all criminal prosecutions, the accused shall enjoy the right to a speedy and public trial, by an impartial jury of the State and district wherein the crime shall have been committed, which district shall have been previously ascertained by law, and to be informed of the nature and cause of the accusation; to be confronted with the witnesses against him; to have compulsory process of obtaining witnesses in his favor, and to have the Assistance of Counsel for his defence.

AMENDMENT [VII]

In Suits at common law, where the value in controversy shall exceed twenty dollars, the right of trial by jury shall be preserved, and no fact tried by a jury, shall be otherwise reexamined in any Court of the United States, than according to the rules of the common law.

AMENDMENT [VIII]

Excessive bail shall not be required, nor excessive fines imposed, nor cruel and unusual punishments inflicted.

AMENDMENT [IX]

The enumeration in the Constitution, of certain rights, shall not be construed to deny or disparage others retained by the people.

AMENDMENT [X]

The powers not delegated to the United States by the Constitution, nor prohibited by it to the States, are reserved to the States respectively, or to the people.

boatbuilding and fish canning industries, and oyster and shrimp fisheries. Pop 48 486.

BIMETALLIC STRIP. See THERMOSTAT.

BIMETALLISM, use of two metals, usually gold and silver, to back a currency. It was widespread until the late 19th century, when most countries adopted the monometallic gold standard to reduce speculation encouraged by the different relative values of gold and silver in different countries. (See also FREE SILVER; GRESHAM'S LAW.)

BIMINI ISLANDS, islands in the W Bahamas, 50mi E of Miami and 110mi WNW of Nassau. Alice Town and Bailey Town are the main centers, with tourism the chief industry.

BINARY NUMBER SYSTEM, a number system which uses the POWERS of 2. Thus the number which in our everyday system, the DECIMAL SYSTEM, would be represented as 25 $(=(2\times10^1)+(5\times10^0))$ is in binary notation 11001 $(=(1\times2^4)+(1\times2^3)+(0\times2^2)+(0\times2^1)+(1\times2^0))$, which is equivalent to $(1\times16)+(1\times8)+(1\times1)$ or $(16+8+1)$.
The system is of particular note since digital COMPUTERS use binary numbers for calculation.

BINARY OPERATION, for any ordered pair of elements (a, b) in a set S (see SET THEORY), an operation * such that $a*b$ is a unique element of S. Examples of binary operations in the FIELD of REAL NUMBERS include ADDITION, MULTIPLICATION and SUBTRACTION. (See also ALGEBRA.)

BINARY STAR. See DOUBLE STAR.

BINDWEEDS, common name for trailing and climbing plants of the genus CONVOLVULUS.

BINET, Alfred (1857–1911), French psychologist who pioneered methods of mental testing. He collaborated with Théodore Simon in devising the Binet-Simon tests, widely used to estimate INTELLIGENCE.

BINGHAM, George Caleb (1811–1879), US genre painter noted for his Midwestern river scenes, for example, *The Jolly Flatboatmen* (1846). He also treated political subjects, for example, *Canvassing for a Vote* (1851), one of an electioneering series.

BINGHAM, Hiram (1875–1956), US explorer and statesman. He discovered the INCA cities of Vitcos and Machu Picchu (1911–1912). Bingham headed the US Air Personnel Division in WWI, and was governor of Conn. 1925 and US senator 1925–33.

BINGHAMTON, city in S N.Y., seat of Broome Co., on the Susquehanna and Chenango rivers. An industrial city founded in 1788, together with Endicott and Johnson City it forms the "Triple Cities." Pop 64 123.

BINOCULARS, an optical instrument comprising two compact TELESCOPES mounted parallel, used to obtain magnified stereoscopic views of distant scenes.

The prism system used in most binoculars was invented by Ignazo Porro of Italy in 1851. Light enters the objective lens (*left*) and is reflected through two prisms to the eyepiece (*right*). This makes the binoculars shorter and enhances the stereoscopic effect by separating the objective lenses.

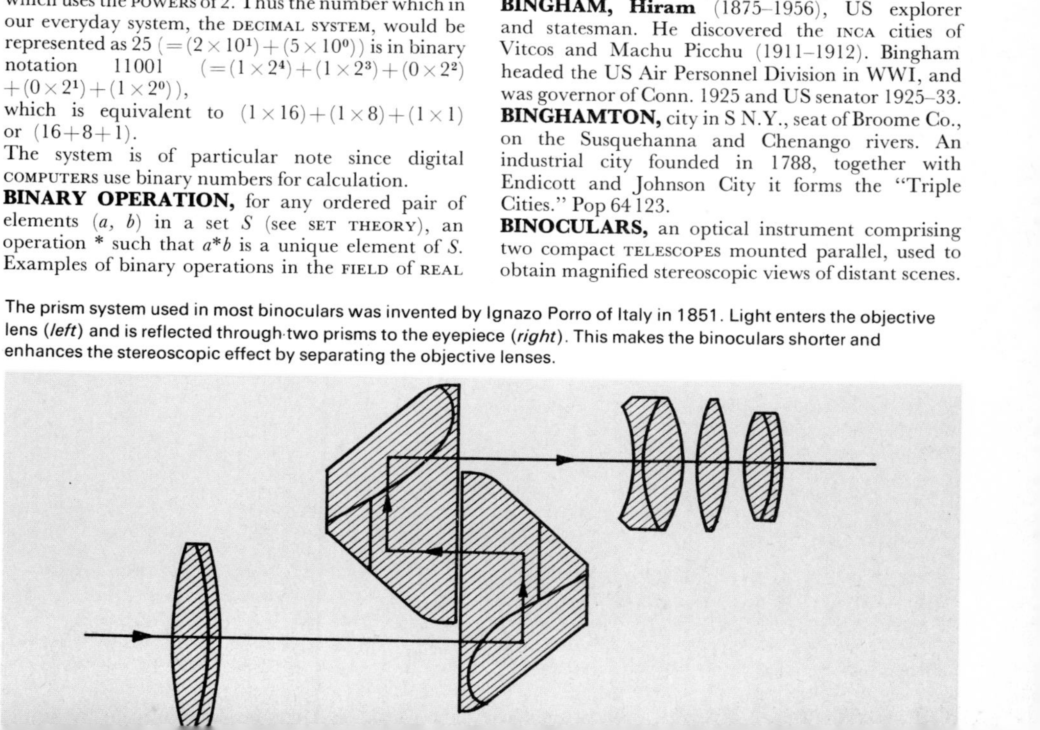

The opera glass employs Galilean telescopes and the field glass uses low-power nautical telescopes, but for greater magnifications, reflecting PRISMS must be used to allow an objective lens of long focal length to be incorporated without making the instrument too elongate to be convenient in use. The arrangement of the prisms in the prismatic binocular also allows the objectives to be set farther apart than the eyes of the user, thus allowing the stereoscopic effect to be enhanced. The separation of the eyepiece mountings and the focusing of the individual eyepieces is adjustable in most models.

BINOCULAR VISION, the use of two EYES, set a small distance apart in the head and aligned approximately parallel, to view a single object. Owing to PARALLAX, the images in the two eyes are slightly different, which enables the observer to perceive what is seen in three dimensions and so to judge distance, size and shape. Only man and some higher animals possess binocular vision. (See also STEREOSCOPE.)

BINOMIAL. See POLYNOMIAL.

BINOMIAL COEFFICIENTS, in the expansion (see BINOMIAL THEOREM) of $(a+b)^n$, the CO-EFFICIENTS of the POWERS of a and b. The coefficient of a typical term, $a^{(n-r)}b^r$, may be written $\binom{n}{r}$.

BINOMIAL THEOREM, the theorem that a binomial (see POLYNOMIAL) $(a+b)$ may be raised to the POWER n by application of the formula

$$(a+b)^n = a^n + na^{(n-1)}b + \frac{(n-1).n}{2}\cdot a^{(n-2)}b^2 + \ldots + an.b^{(n-1)} + b^n$$

(for evaluation of COEFFICIENTS see PASCAL'S TRIANGLE). Thus, for example,

$$(a+b)^4 = a^4 + 4a^3b + 6a^2b^2 + 4ab^3 + b^4.$$

Expansion of $(a-b)^n$ is equivalent to expansion of $(a+(-b))^n$. Thus, for example,

$$(a-b)^4 = a^4 + 4a^3(-b) + 6a^2(-b)^2 + 4a(-b)^3 + (-b)^4$$
$$= a^4 - 4a^3b + 6a^2b^2 - 4ab^3 + b^4.$$

Note that the expansion of $(a+b)^n$ has $(n+1)$ terms.

BINTURONG, *Arctictis binturong*, a medium-sized carnivorous mammal of the family Viverridae, related to civets. It has tufted ears, a long prehensile tail and shaggy, grey-black fur. It is nocturnal, living in forests of SE Asia.

BIOCHEMISTRY, study of the substances occurring in living organisms and the reactions in which they are involved. It is a science on the border between BIOLOGY and ORGANIC CHEMISTRY. The main constituents of living matter are water, CARBOHYDRATES, LIPIDS and PROTEINS. The total chemical activity of the organism is known as its METABOLISM. Plants use sunlight as an energy source to produce carbohydrates from carbon dioxide and water (see PHOTOSYNTHESIS). The carbohydrates are then stored as starch; used for structural purposes, as in the CELLULOSE of plant cell walls; or oxidized through a series of reactions including the CITRIC ACID CYCLE, the energy released being stored as adenosine triphosphate (see NUCLEOTIDES). In animals energy is stored mainly as lipids, which as well as forming fat deposits are components of all cell membranes. Proteins have many functions, of which metabolic regulation is perhaps the most important. ENZYMES, which control almost all biochemical reactions, and some HORMONES are proteins. Plants synthesize proteins using simpler nitrogenous compounds from the soil. Animals obtain proteins from food and break them down by HYDROLYSIS to AMINO ACIDS. New proteins are made according to the pattern determined by the sequence of NUCLEIC ACIDS in the GENES. Many reactions occur in all CELLS and may be studied in simple systems. Methods used by biochemists and chemists are similar and include labelling with radioactive ISOTOPES and separation techniques such as CHROMATOGRAPHY, used to analyze very small amounts of substances, and the high-speed CENTRIFUGE. Molecular structures may be determined by X-RAY DIFFRACTION. Landmarks in biochemistry include the synthesis of urea by WÖHLER (1828), the pioneering research of VON LIEBIG, PASTEUR and BERNARD, and more recently the elucidation of the structure of DNA by James WATSON and Francis CRICK in 1953.

BIOGENESIS, theory that all living organisms are derived from other living organisms. It is the opposite of the theory of SPONTANEOUS GENERATION. (See also LIFE.)

BIOLOGICAL CLOCKS, the mechanisms which control the rhythm of various activities of plants and animals. Some activities, such as mating, migration and hibernation, have a yearly cycle; others, chiefly reproductive functions (including human menstruation) follow the lunar month. The majority, however, have a period of roughly 24 hours, called a **circadian rhythm**. As well as obvious rhythms such as the patterns of leaf movement in plants and the activity/sleep cycle in animals, many other features such as body temperature and cell growth oscillate daily. Although related to the day/night cycle, circadian rhythms are not directly controlled by it. Organisms in unvarying environments will continue to show 24-hr rhythms, but the pattern can be changed—the clock reset. Scientists in the Arctic, with 6 months of daylight, used watches which kept a 21-hr day, and gradually their body rhythms changed to a 21-hr period. The delay in adjustment is important in modern travel. After moving from one time zone to another, it takes some time for the body to adjust to the newly imposed cycle. Biological clocks are important in animal navigation. Many animals, such as migrating birds or bees returning to the hive, navigate using the sun. They can only do this if they have some means of knowing what time of day it is. (See also MIGRATION.) Biological clocks are apparently inborn, not learned, but need to be triggered. An animal kept in the light from birth shows no circadian rhythms, but if placed in the dark for an hour or so immediately starts rhythms based on a 24-hr cycle. Once started, the cycles are almost independent of external changes, indicating that they cannot be based on a simple rhythm of chemical reactions, which would be affected by temperature. The biological clock may be somehow linked to external rhythms in geophysical forces, or may be an independent and slightly adjustable biochemical oscillator. In either case the mechanism is unknown. Not all biological rhythms are controlled by a "clock": in many cases they are determined simply by the time taken to complete a certain sequence of actions. For example, the heart rate depends on the time taken for the heart muscles to contract and relax. Unlike those controlled by biological clocks, such rhythms are easily influenced by drugs and temperature.

BIOLOGICAL CONTROL, the control of pests by the introduction of natural predators, parasites or disease, or by modifying the environment so as to encourage those already present. This first took place in Cal. in 1888, when Australian Ladybird beetles were introduced to eliminate the damage to citrus trees by the cottony-cushion scale insect. Another example is the introduction of MYXOMATOSIS to combat crop damage by rabbits. The "sterile male" technique is used to control many insect pests. Large numbers of males are bred, sterilized with X-rays and released. Since the females mate only once, many of them with the sterile males, the population rapidly decreases.

BIOLOGICAL WARFARE. See CHEMICAL AND BIOLOGICAL WARFARE.

BIOLOGY, the study of living things, i.e. the science of plants and animals, including humans. Broadly speaking there are two main branches of biology, the study of ANIMALS (ZOOLOGY) and the study of PLANTS (BOTANY). Within each of these main branches are a number of traditional divisions dealing with structure (ANATOMY, CYTOLOGY), development and function PHYSIOLOGY, EMBRYOLOGY), inheritance GENETICS, EVOLUTION), classification (TAXONOMY) and interrelations of organisms with each other and with their environment (ECOLOGY). These branches are also split into a number of specialist fields, such as MYCOLOGY, ENTOMOLOGY, HERPETOLOGY.

However, the traditional division into zoology and botany no longer applies since groups of biosciences have developed which span their limits, e.g. MICROBIOLOGY, BACTERIOLOGY, VIROLOGY, OCEANOGRAPHY, MARINE BIOLOGY, LIMNOLOGY. There are also biosciences that bridge the gap between the physical sciences of chemistry, physics and geology, e.g., BIOCHEMISTRY, BIOPHYSICS and PALEONTOLOGY. Similarly there are those that relate to areas of human behavior, e.g., PSYCHOLOGY and SOCIOLOGY.

Disciplines such as MEDICINE, VETERINARY MEDICINE, AGRONOMY and HORTICULTURE also have a strong basis in biology.

To a large extent the history of biology is the history of its constituent sciences. Since the impetus to investigate the living world generally arose in a desire to improve the techniques of medicine or of agriculture, most early biologists were in the first instance physicians or landowners. An exception is provided by ARISTOTLE, the earliest systematist of biological knowledge and himself an outstanding biologist—he founded the science of comparative anatomy—but most other classical authors, as GALEN, CELSUS and the members of the Hippocratic school, were primarily physicians. In the medieval period much biological knowledge became entangled in legend and allegory. The classical texts continued to be the principal sources of knowledge although new compilations, such as AVICENNA's *Canon* of medicine, were produced by Muslim philosophers. In 16th-century Europe interest revived in descriptive natural history, the work of GESNER being notable; physicians such as PARACELSUS began to develop a chemical pharmacology (see IATROCHEMISTRY) and experimental anatomy revived in the work of VESALIUS, FABRICIUS and FALLOPIUS. The discoveries of SERVETUS, HARVEY and MALPIGHI followed. Quantitative plant physiology began with the work of van HELMONT and was taken to spectacular ends in the work of Stephen HALES. In the 17th century, microscopic investigations began with the work of HOOKE and van LEEUWENHOEK; GREW advanced the study of plant organs and RAY laid the foundation for LINNAEUS' classic 18th-century formulation of the classification of plants. This same era saw BUFFON devise a systematic classification of animals and von HALLER lay the groundwork for the modern study of physiology.

The 17th century had seen controversies over the role of mechanism in biological explanation—LA METTRIE had even developed the theories of DESCARTES to embrace the mind of man; the 19th century saw similar disputes, now couched in the form of the mechanist-vitalist controversy concerning the possible chemical nature of life (see BICHAT; MAGENDIE; Claude BERNARD). Development biology, foreshadowed by LAMARCK, was thoroughly established following the work of DARWIN; in anatomy, SCHWANN and others developed the cell concept; in histology Bichat's pioneering work was continued; in physiology, organic and even physical chemists began to play a greater role, and medical theory was revolutionized by the advent of bacteriology (see PASTEUR; KOCH). The impact of MENDEL's discoveries in genetics was not felt until the early 1900s. Possibly the high point of 20th-century biology came with the proposal of the double-helix model for DNA (see NUCLEIC ACIDS), the chemical carrier of genetic information, by CRICK and WATSON in 1953.

BIOLUMINESCENCE, the production of nonthermal light by living organisms such as fireflies, many marine animals, bacteria and fungi. The effect is an example of CHEMILUMINESCENCE. In some cases its utility to the organism is not apparent, though in others its use is clear. Thus, in the firefly, the ABDOMEN of the female glows, enabling the male to find her. Similarly, LUMINESCENCE enables many deep-sea fish to locate each other or to attract their prey. The glow in a ship's wake at night is due to luminescent microorganisms.

BIOME, ecological region characterized by the predominant vegetation type, such as savanna. The biome is the largest biogeographical unit. (See ECOLOGY.)

BIOMEDICAL ENGINEERING, development and application of mechanical electrical, electronic and nuclear devices in medicine. The many recent

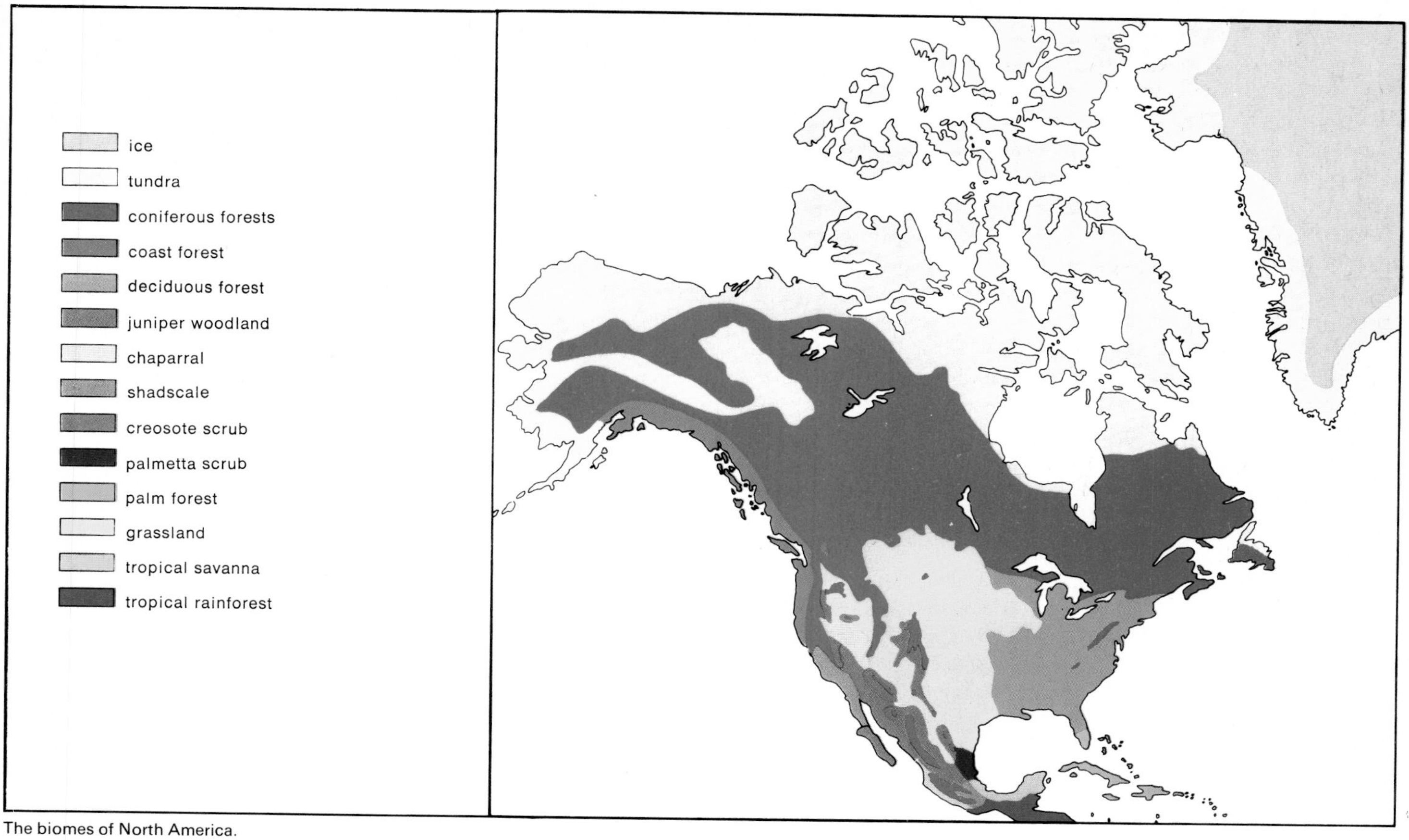

The biomes of North America.

advances in biomedical engineering have occurred in four main areas: ARTIFICIAL ORGANS; new surgical techniques involving the use of LASERS, cryosurgery and ULTRASONICS; diagnosis and monitoring using thermography and computers; and PROSTHETICS.

BIONICS, the science of designing artificial systems which have the desirable characteristics of living organisms. These may be simply imitations of nature, such as military vehicles with jointed legs, or, more profitably, systems which embody a principle learned from nature. Examples of the latter include RADAR, inspired by the echolocation system of bats, or the development of associative memories in COMPUTERS as in the human brain.

BIOPHYSICS, a branch of BIOLOGY in which the methods and principles of PHYSICS are applied to the study of living things. It has grown up in the 20th century alongside the development of ELECTRONICS. Its tools include the ELECTROENCEPHALOGRAPH and the ELECTRON MICROSCOPE, its techniques those of SPECTROSCOPY and X-RAY DIFFRACTION and its problems the study of nerve transmission, BIOLUMINESCENCE and materials transfer in RESPIRATION and secretion.

BIOPSY, removal and microscopic examination of tissue from a living patient for purposes of diagnosis. The tissue is removed by needle, suction, swabbing, scraping or excision.

BIOSPHERE, the region inhabited by living things. It forms a thin layer around the earth, including the surface of the LITHOSPHERE, the HYDROSPHERE and the lower ATMOSPHERE. The importance of the concept was first pointed out by LAMARCK.

BIOSYNTHESIS, or **anabolism,** the biochemical reactions by which living cells build up simple molecules into complex ones. These reactions require energy, which is obtained from light (see PHOTOSYNTHESIS) or from ATP which is produced in degradation reactions. (See also METABOLISM; PROTEIN SYNTHESIS.)

BIOT, Jean Baptiste (1774–1862), French physicist who first demonstrated the extraterrestrial origin of and hence the actual existence of METEORITES (1803); who accompanied GAY-LUSSAC on his pioneering BALLOON ascent to collect data concerning the upper ATMOSPHERE (1804); and who, having shown that some organic substances show OPTICAL ACTIVITY (1815), first developed the methods of POLARIMETRY—despite his rejection of the wave theory of LIGHT.

BIOTIN. See VITAMINS.

BIOTITE, a range of iron-rich varieties of MICA, grading into PHLOGOPITE. It is a constituent of most igneous and many metamorphic rocks.

The birch is a common tree throughout the Northern Hemisphere and an important source of lumber for furniture and veneering and bark for tanning and thatching. Birch tree: a. male and female inflorescence, b. the fruit and seeds, c. a birch leaf.

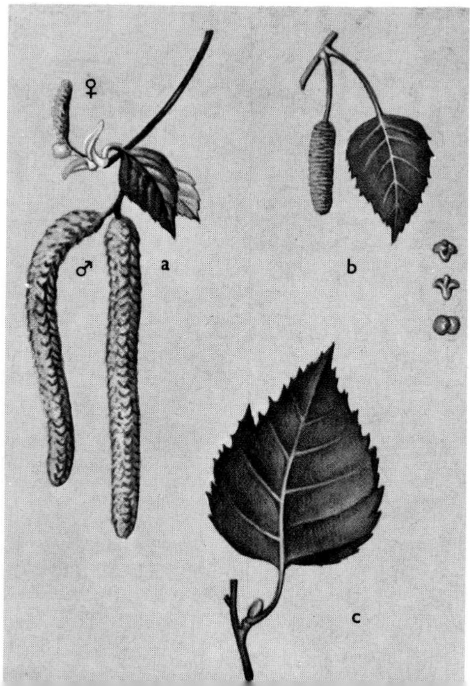

BIRCH, deciduous trees and shrubs of the genus *Betula*, native to the higher northern latitudes. The bark is normally smooth, white and peeling, and the leaves are oval, pointed and toothed, turning yellow in autumn. The male and female flowers are borne in separate catkins and seeds form in cone-like clusters. The close-grained wood is used for furniture and veneers, the bark for tanning and thatching. Best-known species are the North American paper birch (*Betula papyrifera*), the yellow birch (*B. lutea*) and the European or silver birch (*B. pendula*).

BIRCH, John. See JOHN BIRCH SOCIETY.

BIRD, type of animal adapted for flight and unique in its body covering of feathers. Birds are the largest group of VERTEBRATES, with over 8 500 extant species. They are descended from the group of prehistoric reptiles which took to living in trees (see ARCHAEOPTERYX). Their most striking anatomical features are those associated with flight. The forelimbs are modified as wings and are associated with enormous breast muscles which make powered flight possible. Even in FLIGHTLESS BIRDS such as the PENGUIN and OSTRICH it is clear that the forelimbs were once used as wings. The rest of the skeleton is constructed of thin, light bones. A further weight reduction resulted from the replacement of the teeth by a horny beak or bill early in the evolutionary history of birds. Feathers, developed from scales (still present on the legs), streamline the body, and provide flight surfaces.

Flightless birds are mainly adapted for running or swimming. Runners such as the ostrich have strong legs and swimmers have their wings modified as flippers as in the penguin. Birds have been able to adapt to diverse ways of life, ranging from that of the Emperor penguin of the Antarctic to Egyptian plovers of equatorial desert regions, because, being warm-blooded, they can function independently of the surrounding temperature. Different groups of birds have evolved a variety of shapes and sizes of bill to take advantage of different food sources. The majority of birds are active by day. Owls, the prominent nocturnal group, have highly developed night vision

Biology

Biological clocks

For over two hundred years, it has been known that animals and plants display rhythmic activities that are not directly associated with environmental changes. To explain such activity, the concept of the biological clock was formulated and this has been the subject of observation, experiment and debate ever since.

Rhythmic activity in plants was first noticed two centuries ago by de Mairan. He placed plants in a cave, so providing constant conditions, and discovered that for many weeks they bent their leaves daily as if towards the sun. Later, Darwin, Hofmeister and Pfeffer made more observations of rhythmic activity in animals and plants, but it was not until this century that such scientists as Bunning recognized that these rhythms were generated internally; they became known as endogenous rhythms.

In 1959 Franz Halberg coined a new word, *circadian*, from the Latin *circa*, about, and *dies*, a day. The word is important because endogenous rhythms only approximate to 24 hour periods. A rhythm which did have an exact twenty-four hour period would be attributed to a daily geophysical stimulus.

Rhythms that are the result of activity of a biological clock have, by definition, three characteristics: they do not correspond exactly to the length of a day; they do not change with external changes of temperature; and they do not change with any other changes in the external environment.

It is in this last area that a nice distinction has to be drawn, for it is known that the phasing of circadian rhythms is determined by external factors, usually light and dark, serving to entrain these endogenous oscillators. The crucial test is to discover what happens to the rhythms under constant conditions. De Coursey tried this by keeping Flying squirrels—normally only active at night—in the dark for two and a half years. Each Flying squirrel was in fact active for the same proportion of time each day, and the period of the rhythm was 24 hours 21 minutes, plus or minus six minutes. Each squirrel had its own period and none was exactly 24 hours.

This and other comparable experiments with other organisms showed that, under constant conditions, and therefore in the absence of a natural external synchronizer, the rhythm becomes what is known as "free running." That is, without any environmental synchronizer, the true phasing of the rhythm becomes apparent. The environmental cue for these rhythms is known as the *zeitgeber*.

Clues to the possible causes of gastric ulcers have been provided by the work of Halberg on biochemical rhythms in mice. Effectively, he considered variables such as the level of stored glycogen in the liver, the rate of liver-cell division and the secretion of enzymes from the stomach during the day. He found that each of these followed a circadian rhythm. It seems that it is important for these rhythms to remain in phase with each other for the stomach and liver to function correctly. If mice are put into constant light, their rhythms run freely and have a different period. The animals fall ill as a result.

Certain animals (known as sun-oriented) move at a definite angle to the sun's direction. Ants of various species have been shown to do this; if they are trapped beneath a box when returning to their nest, they will take up a new direction on release. This is at an angle to their former direction, approximately equal to the angle through which the sun moved during their imprisonment. This behavior seems to be shown only by relatively inexperienced ants which are not foraging far afield. As the ants mature, they use other methods of orientation, and allow for the sun's movement, so that they run in the same compass direction even after imprisonment. The biological usefulness of this rhythm in orientation is obvious, since the ants forage for food some distance from the nest, and need to know direction. Such an allowance for the sun's movement occurs in many animals, including bees, sand-hoppers and birds.

The pond skater at certain times heads consistently south using sun-orientation. If kept in a room where the only light-source is a lamp, at 6 a.m. it will head at an angle of about 90° to the right of the fixed lamp. This angle is found to reduce throughout the day, until at midday the insect heads toward the light. During the afternoon the angle increases again, the insect heading to the left of the light. With a moving sun, this behavior would ensure that the insect always headed south. Evidence received from studies where attempts were made to reset the phases further substantiates the belief that such sun-orientation is governed by an endogenous clock. Starlings were kept in conditions identical except for lighting. Group A was kept under natural conditions: at that time of year 12 hours light and 12 hours dark. Group B was kept under artificial conditions, again of 12 hours light and 12 hours dark, but with a six-hour delay, so that "dawn" was six hours later for group B. When these birds were released eight hours after dawn, the birds from group A oriented themselves at an angle of 120° to the sun, and the birds from group B oriented themselves at 30° to the sun, because they thought it was only two hours after dawn. This shows that the clock is set or synchronized by the dawn, and measurement of time from dawn governs their orientation to the sun.

The evidence of a daily clock led to speculation about the possibility of the existence of other endogenous rhythms, particularly an annual rhythm. This seemed feasible since certain animals display yearly behavior patterns such as migration, hibernation, molting and breeding. It is obviously much more difficult to demonstrate the existence of an endogenous annual clock, since this necessitates long-term study. The first clear indication of the existence of an annual clock was discovered by Fisher when studying hibernation. He used Golden-mantled ground squirrels, inhabitants of the Rocky Mountains which normally remain active, steadily gaining weight, throughout the summer, and then in October stop eating and drinking, finding a secure place in which to stay until more favorable weather conditions prevail. During this time of hibernation the body temperature drops to about freezing point (0°C). If hibernation is an endogenous rhythm, then even when placed in a constant environment the squirrel should hibernate for some part of the year. To test this idea, in late August, the squirrel was housed in a windowless room at a constant temperature of 0°C with 12 hours light each day. It was given an unlimited amount of food and water. The squirrel ate, drank and behaved normally; it was active and maintained its body temperature at a normal 37°C, despite the freezing conditions of its room, as expected for a warm-blooded animal. In October, the squirrel stopped eating and drinking and went into hibernation, its body temperature dropping to 0°C. It remained in this condition except for occasional awakening until April, when it resumed its eating and drinking, and its body temperature rose to 37°C again. Throughout the months of April to August, it was active and gained the weight it had lost during hibernation.

The experiment was repeated with many ground squirrels at temperatures of 0°C and 25°C, and similar results were obtained. That is, regardless of temperature, the animals were active for a few months and then went into hibernation. The period of the cycle was 11 months when it was free-running. It thus fulfilled the three criteria of an endogenous clock—the rhythm was not exactly a year, not synchronous with any periodic external signal, and not appreciably affected by ambient temperature. Following Halberg's terminology,

estimated to be up to 100 times more sensitive than that of man. All birds lay eggs, sometimes in quite elaborate nests. Incubation is by one or both parents, dependent on species.

Many bird species have become extinct, and others are threatened, despite the efforts of conservationists. (See also BIRDSONG; FEATHER; FLIGHT; MIGRATION; NEST.) See illustration page 150.

BIRD BANDING, placing numbered metal or plastic bands on the legs, wings or necks of birds for identification. Birds are banded as nestlings or when trapped in nets. All relevant data is recorded at a national agency whose address is on the band. Birds found can then be reported, an important aid to studies of migration and distribution.

BIRD LICE, small, wingless insects of the genus *Mallophaga*, parasitic on birds and mammals. Sometimes called "biting lice," they differ from sucking lice in having tooth-like mandibles adapted for feeding on feathers, hair and scales.

BIRD MIGRATION. See MIGRATION.

BIRD OF PARADISE, perennial flowers of the genus *Strelitzia*, particularly *S. reginae*, so named for the resemblance of the orange and purple flowers to the colorful BIRDS OF PARADISE. They are native to South Africa, but are now extensively grown as a florist's flower in the US.

BIRD OF PARADISE. See BIRDS OF PARADISE.

BIRD SANCTUARIES, areas set aside for the protection of birds, either as reserves or as "hostels" for the injured. Reserves can help to preserve rare species. The first US official state sanctuary was established at Lake Merritt, Cal., in 1870.

BIRDSEYE, Clarence (1886–1956), US inventor and industrialist who, having observed during fur-trading expeditions to Labrador (1912–16) that many foods keep indefinitely if frozen, developed a process for the rapid commercial freezing of foodstuffs. In 1924 he organized the company later known as General Foods to market frozen produce.

BIRD'S NEST SOUP, Chinese soup made mainly from the nests of cave-dwelling swifts of the genus *Collocalia*. The nests themselves are made from the birds' saliva.

BIRDS OF PARADISE, members of the family Paradisaeidae, found in forests of Australia and New Guinea. The males have colorful and elaborately-shaped tail feathers designed to attract females and used in courtship displays. There are 43 species, many of which are rare due to their slaughter by collectors, a practice made illegal in 1924.

BIRDSONG, the pattern of notes, often musical and complex, with which birds attract a mate and proclaim their territory. Ornithologists call all such sounds songs, though those that are harsh and unmusical are often referred to simply as the "voice."

BIRD WATCHING, observation of birds in their natural surroundings. Observers may study such things as courtship and nesting, migration patterns, and the occurrence of rare or threatened species. Bird-watching societies in the US include the Nuttall Ornithological Club and the American Ornithologists' Union.

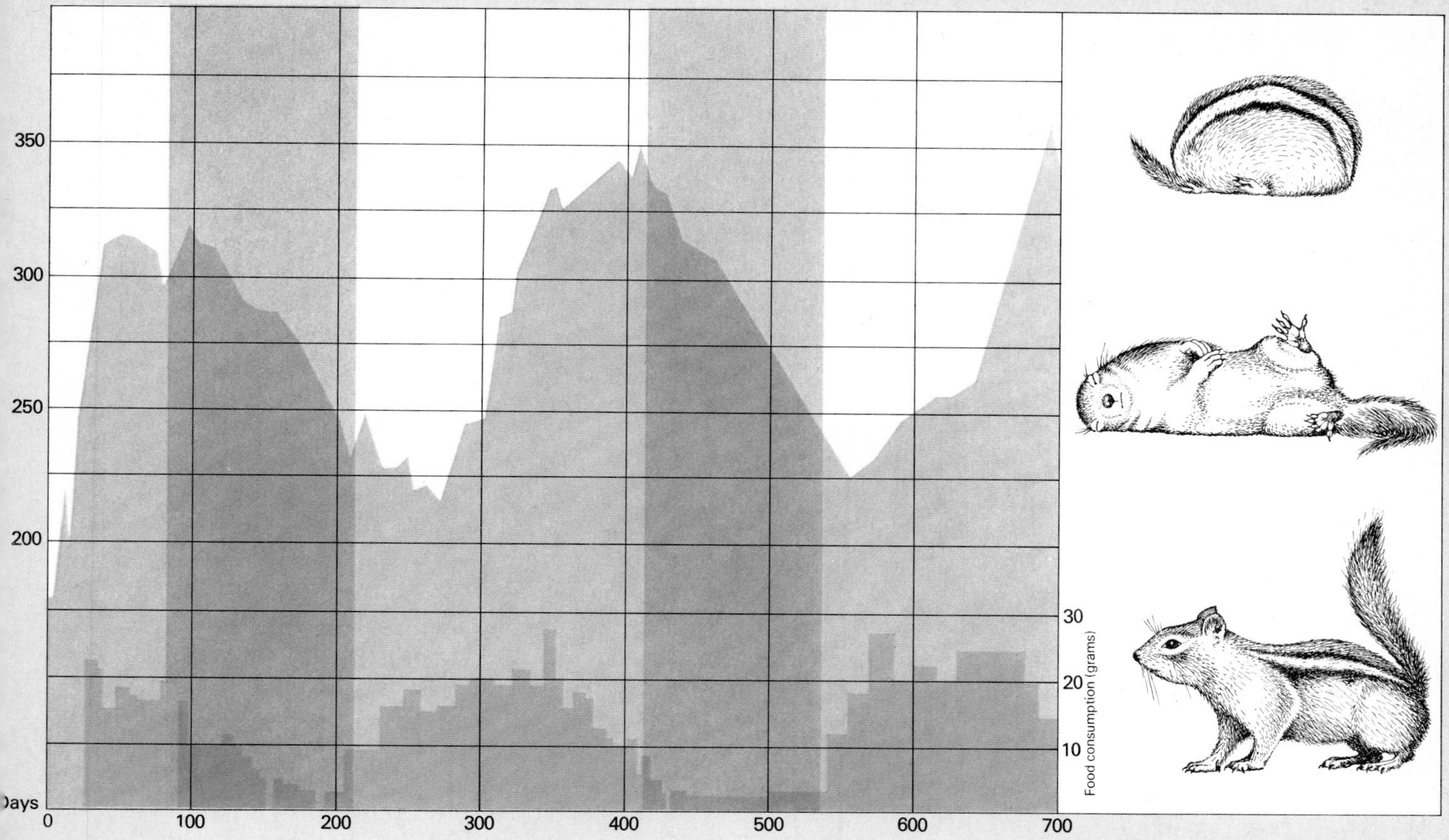

Left: The ground squirrel hibernates for a period of about 130 days in each year. This particular animal was kept for two years in a room at constant temperature (22°C) and 12 hours light each day. Despite the lack of external stimuli, it hibernated regularly (gray bands) under the control of its own biological clock. Body weight (light brown) and food consumption (darker brown) fluctuated likewise.

Right: The arousal of a ground squirrel from hibernation. In this case its body temperature rose from 1.7°C (just above freezing point, the ambient temperature) to the normal 37°C in only two hours.

this rhythm has been called circannual.

Another interesting yearly cycle is the annual growth and shedding of antlers by deer in the northern hemisphere. Ordinarily they shed their antlers in winter, and are in velvet (that is, growing a replacement set of antlers) from spring to fall. Tropical deer transported to zoos in the temperate zone persist in the same kind of annual cycle that they showed in their natural habitat. By experiments using artificial-light regimes, Goss has shown conclusively that antler-shedding is another phenomenon under the control of a biological clock.

Care must be taken not to attribute all daily and annual occurrences to circadian and circannual endogenous rhythms. In mammals, and other animals, activities such as mating tend to happen at a particular time of year. This is usually linked to the gestation period, and ensures that the young are born in favorable conditions when food supply is greatest. Sheep tend to come "on heat" (estrous) during the autumn, when they conceive, thus giving birth to lambs in the spring.

If sheep are subjected experimentally to shortening day-lengths imitating autumn conditions, they come into estrous. Reproductive cycles in birds, mammals, fishes, reptiles and amphibia tend to be regulated by light, an effect known as photo-periodism.

Despite study of circadian and circannual rhythms, and the exogenous phenomena like photo-periodism, no theory to explain the endogenous clock has emerged. In fact, it has so far defied explanation, particularly since it is independent of temperature, whereas chemical reactions are speeded up by an increase in temperature.

Two general models to explain the working of the clock have been proposed. The first assumes control from the nucleus, present in each cell, which does indeed control many of the cell's activities. However, circadian rhythms persist in cells which have lost their nuclei, and in cells in which the nucleic acids have been inhibited.

The second model has been proposed by Hastings, who has implicated the cell membrane—the outer boundary of the cell. Membranes are complex entities whose functions depend on the interaction of many cooperating components, and which are therefore likely to respond much more slowly than a simple on-off switch to changes in their biochemical environment. This could perhaps account for the slow period of circadian rhythms.

BIRD WOMAN. See SACAJAWEA.

BIREFRINGENCE. See DOUBLE REFRACTION.

BIRGITTA, Saint. See BRIDGET OF SWEDEN, SAINT.

BIRKENHEAD, 1st Earl of. See SMITH, FREDERICK.

BIRKHOFF, George David (1884–1944), US mathematician who made important contributions to the analysis of dynamical systems.

BIRLING, or logrolling, sport originating among North American lumberjacks during the late 19th century. Two contestants balanced on a floating log spin the log with their feet in an attempt to dislodge each other.

BIRMAN, breed of cat first recognized in France but said to have been introduced from Cambodia. It has a long, low body and longish tail on short legs. In the US it should have a Roman nose with low-set nostrils. The coat has points like those of the Siamese, which may be seal, blue, chocolate (champagne) or frost (lilac) in color, but its paws are white as though it had walked in a pail of milk.

BIRMINGHAM, second-largest city in Britain, about 110mi NW of London. A source of metal products since medieval times, it is now an industrial city of world status making vehicles, machine tools, armaments, electrical equipment and toys. It has two universities. Pop 1008000.

BIRMINGHAM, city of N central Ala., seat of Jefferson Co. The largest city in Ala., it is the South's chief iron and steel producer and a major rail and air terminus with a port linked to the Gulf of Mexico. It is also an educational center. Pop 300910.

BIRMINGHAM, city in SE Mich., a residential center 17mi NW of Detroit. Pop 26170.

BIRNEY, James Gillespie (1792–1857), leading US abolitionist. Birney, who came from an old slave-owning family, freed his slaves in 1834. He launched the abolitionist newspaper the *Philanthropist* in 1836, became executive secretary of the AMERICAN ANTI-SLAVERY SOCIETY in 1837 and founded the LIBERTY PARTY, standing as its presidential candidate in 1840 and 1844.

BIROBIDZHAN, or Jewish Autonomous Oblast, subdivision of the USSR in SE Siberia, allocated to Jewish immigrants in 1928. Other settlers now outnumber Jews. Occupations include agriculture, lumbering, iron and tin mining and marble and limestone quarrying.

BIRTH, emergence from the mother's WOMB, or, in the case of most lower animals, from the EGG, marking the beginning of an independent life. The birth process is triggered by HORMONE changes in the mother's bloodstream. Birth may be induced, if required, by oxytocin. Mild labor pains (contractions of the womb) are the first sign that a woman is about to give birth. Initially occurring about every 20 minutes, in a few hours they become stronger and occur every few minutes. This is the first stage of labor, usually lasting about 14 hours. The contractions push the baby downward, usually head first, which breaks the membranes surrounding the baby, and the AMNIOTIC FLUID escapes.

In the second stage of labor, stronger contractions push the baby through the cervix and vagina. This is

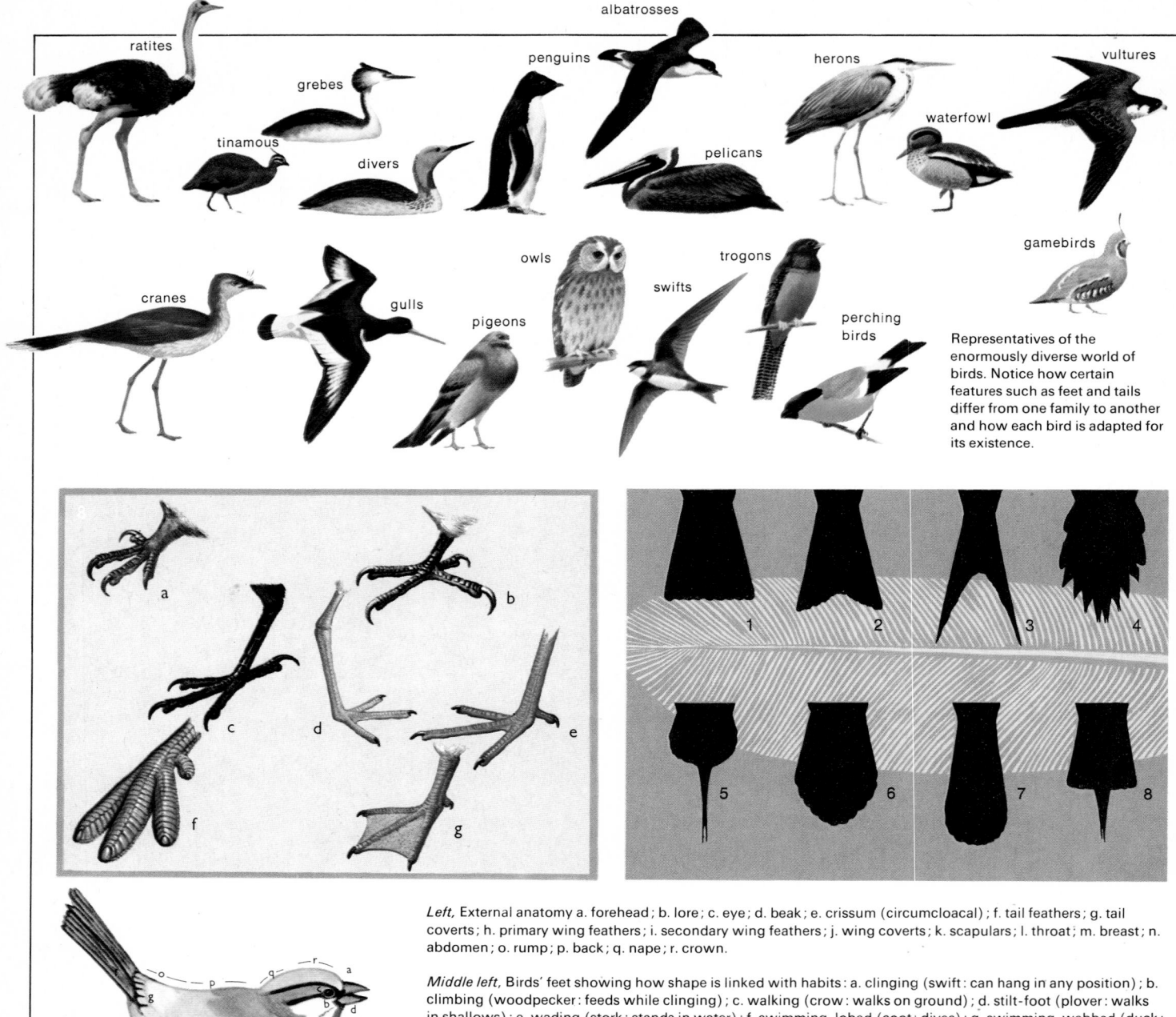

Representatives of the enormously diverse world of birds. Notice how certain features such as feet and tails differ from one family to another and how each bird is adapted for its existence.

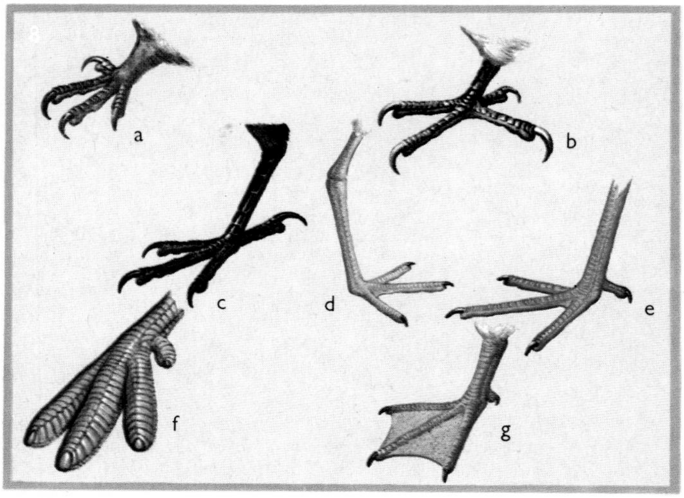

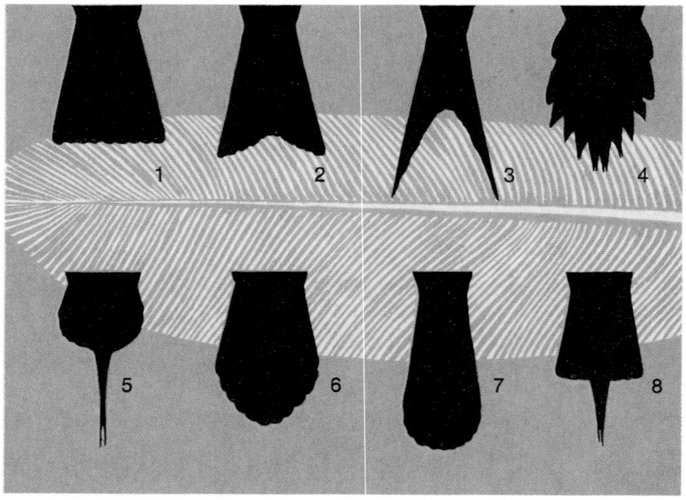

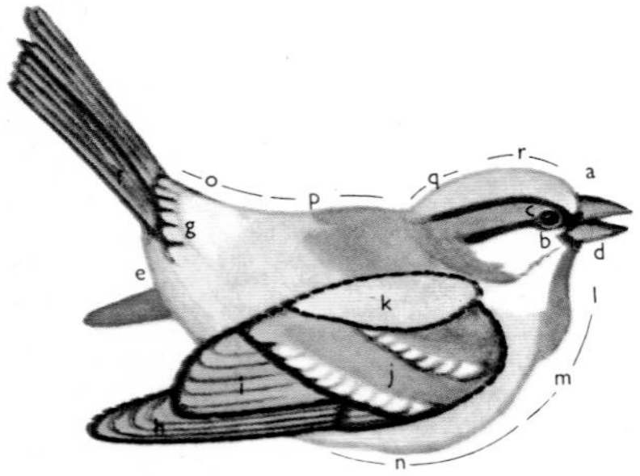

Left, External anatomy a. forehead; b. lore; c. eye; d. beak; e. crissum (circumcloacal); f. tail feathers; g. tail coverts; h. primary wing feathers; i. secondary wing feathers; j. wing coverts; k. scapulars; l. throat; m. breast; n. abdomen; o. rump; p. back; q. nape; r. crown.

Middle left, Birds' feet showing how shape is linked with habits: a. clinging (swift: can hang in any position); b. climbing (woodpecker: feeds while clinging); c. walking (crow: walks on ground); d. stilt-foot (plover: walks in shallows); e. wading (stork: stands in water); f. swimming, lobed (coot: dives); g. swimming, webbed (duck: swims on surface).

Middle right, Eight types of bird tails: 1. square-ended (starling), 2. cleft (linnet), 3. deeply forked (swallow), 4. with spiky feathers (woodpecker), 5. pintail (duck), 6. graduated tail (raven), 7. fantail (cuckoo), 8. elongated central rectrices (bee-eater).

the most painful part and lasts less than 2 hours. Anesthetics (see ANESTHESIA) or ANALGESICS are usually given, and delivery aided by hand or obstetric forceps. A CESARIAN SECTION may be performed if great difficulty occurs. Some women choose "natural childbirth," in which no anesthetic is used, but pain is minimized by prior relaxation exercises.

As soon as the baby is born, its nose and mouth are cleared of fluid and breathing starts, whereupon the UMBILICAL CORD is cut and tied. In the third stage of labor the PLACENTA is expelled from the womb and bleeding is stopped by further contractions. Birth normally occurs 38 weeks after conception. Premature births are those occurring after less than 35 weeks. Most premature babies develop normally with medical care, but if born before 28 weeks the chances of survival are poor. (See also EMBRYO; GESTATION; OBSTETRICS; PREGNANCY.)

BIRTH CONTROL, prevention of unwanted births, by means of CONTRACEPTION, ABORTION, STERILIZATION and formerly infanticide. It is medically advisable if the child would be likely to be defective. At family level, birth control can help to prevent poverty, while globally it could help prevent mass starvation.

Certain forms of birth control have been used from ancient times, but modern methods have been available only since the late 19th century. Arising out of the early WOMEN'S RIGHTS movement, the first birth control clinics were opened in 1916 in the US by Margaret SANGER, and in 1921 in Britain by Marie STOPES. The need for worldwide birth control intensified from the 1920s onwards as the world population "exploded," with modern medicine cutting the death rate while the BIRTH RATE stayed high. In 1952 international groups formed the International Planned Parenthood Federation. In the 1960s the UN urged the universal adoption of voluntary birth control. The chief hindrances are apathy, ignorance and social pressure for large families. Ethical and religious objections to artificial forms of birth control derive from the view that procreation is the primary purpose of marriage and of coitus, and (in the case of abortion) from the sanctity of life. The most influential proponent of this view is the Roman Catholic Church. (See also PLANNED PARENTHOOD–WORLD POPULATION.)

BIRTHMARKS, skin blemishes, usually congenital. There are two main types: pigmented nevuses, or moles, which are usually brown or black and may be raised or flat; and vascular nevuses, local growths of small blood vessels, such as the "strawberry mark" and the "port-wine stain." Although harmless, they are sometimes removed for cosmetic reasons or if they show malignant tendencies. (See also TUMOR.)

BIRTH RATE, ratio of the annual number of births in a population to the total midyear population, usually expressed in births per 1000 persons. Being uncorrected for sex and age distribution, it is a crude measure of fertility. Birth rates range from around 50 per 1000 in some developing countries to under 20 per 1000 in advanced nations. (See also DEMOGRAPHY.)

BIRTHSTONES, gemstones associated with the months of the year. Each supposedly imparts a particular quality to people born in the month to which it belongs.

BISCAY, Bay of, part of the Atlantic Ocean bordering W France and N Spain, renowned for sudden and violent storms. Principal ports are Nantes, Bordeaux (France), Bilbao and Santander (Spain).

BISCAYNE BAY, inlet of the Atlantic Ocean off SE Fla., part of the intracoastal waterway. Miami is situated on its NW shore; Miami Beach, Key Biscayne and other islands lie to the E.

BISCAYNE NATIONAL MONUMENT, a coastal area of some 96 300 acres in SE Fla. It is noted for its coral reefs and great variety of marine life.

BISHOP, highest order in the ministry of the Roman Catholic, Anglican, Eastern and some Lutheran Churches. As head of his diocese, a bishop administers its affairs, supervises its clergy and administers CONFIRMATION and ORDINATION. Roman Catholic bishops are appointed by the pope, Anglican bishops by the sovereign. In the US, Protestant Episcopal bishops are elected by both clergy and laity. (See also APOSTOLIC SUCCESSION; ARCHBISHOP; MINISTRY).

BISHOP, Elizabeth (1911–), US poet, now living in Brazil, widely acclaimed for her succinct and lyrical style. Her books include the Pulitzer prizewinning *North and South–A Cold Spring* (1955) and *Questions of Travel* (1965).

BISHOP, William Avery (1894–1956), Canadian air ace of WWI, winner of the Victoria Cross and the Distinguished Service Medal. He is credited with having shot down 72 enemy aircraft, 25 in one 10-day period in 1918.

BISK, town and port in E Altai Krai, USSR, near the junction of the Biya and Katun rivers. Terminus of a branch of the Turkistan–Siberia railroad, it produces textiles and food-processing machinery. Pop 194 000.

BISMARCK, city in N.D., seat of Burleigh Co. The city, which overlooks the Missouri R, was a busy river port in the 19th century. It is now a grain and livestock-trading center. There are rich lignite and petroleum deposits nearby. Pop 34 703.

BISMARCK, German battleship (over 45 000 tons) famous for one of the most dramatic chases in naval history (May 23–26, 1941). Pursued through the Denmark Strait, she sank the British battle cruiser *Hood*, was later torpedoed by aircraft from the *Ark Royal* and finally sunk 400mi off the French coast.

BISMARCK, Prince Otto von (1815–1898), the "Iron Chancellor," who was largely responsible for creating a unified Germany. Born of Prussian gentry, he entered politics in 1847. From the first he was intent on increasing German power. He served as ambassador to Russia and France, then as chancellor (prime minister). He defeated Austria in the AUSTRO–PRUSSIAN WAR and annexed or coerced neighboring states into the North German Federation. Following his defeat of Napoleon III in the FRANCO–PRUSSIAN WAR, the German Empire was created and Bismarck made imperial chancellor and prince in 1871. He was forced to resign in 1890 after the accession of Kaiser William II.

BISMARCK ARCHIPELAGO, more than 300 mountainous, volcanic islands in the SW Pacific. Captured by Japan in WWII and used as a defense center, the islands were returned to Australia and are now administered by her as part of New Guinea.

BISMARCK SEA, between New Guinea's NE coast and the Bismarck archipelago in the SW Pacific. It is about 500mi from E to W. Allied aircraft destroyed a Japanese convoy here in 1943.

BISMUTH (Bi), metal in Group VA of the PERIODIC TABLE, brittle and silvery-gray with a red tinge. It occurs naturally as the metal, and as the sulfide and oxide, from which it is obtained by roasting and reduction with carbon. In the US it is obtained as a byproduct of the refining of copper and lead ores. Bismuth is rather unreactive; it forms trivalent and some pentavalent compounds. Physically and chemically it is similar to LEAD and ANTIMONY. Bismuth is used in low-melting-point alloys in fire-detection safety devices. Since bismuth expands on solidification, it is used in alloys for casting dies and type metal. Bismuth (III) oxide is used in GLASS and CERAMICS; various bismuth salts are used in medicine. AW 209.0, mp 271°C, bp 1560°C, sg 9.747 (20°C).

BISON, ox-like animals, of the family Bovidae, which may weigh over a tonne and stand 1.8m (6ft) tall. Their forequarters are covered by a shaggy mane. The American bison, often miscalled the buffalo, once grazed the plains and valleys from Mexico to W Canada in herds of millions and was economically vital to the Plains Indians. Hunted ruthlessly by the white man, it was almost extinct by 1900. There are still a few herds in US and Canadian national parks. The European bison is wild in parts of E Europe.

BISULFATES. See SULFATES.

BIT, abbreviation for *bi*nary digi*t*, in computer technology and information theory, the smallest conceivable unit of information, representing a choice between only two possible states: the presence or absence of a signal pulse; + or −; 0 or 1; a switch being off or on. The capacity of an information storage or handling device is measured in bits.

BIT, originally a small silver US coin, the term now applies to a sum equivalent to one-eighth of a dollar. A short bit is a 10 cent piece.

BITHYNIA, ancient region of Asia Minor occupied at an early date by Thracian tribes. A Roman province from 74 BC, it later became part of the BYZANTINE EMPIRE.

In winter the bison is covered with a thick coat of fur which molts in the spring, leaving it looking somewhat ragged. There are two sorts of bison, the European (shown here) and the American bison.

BITTERLING, *Rhodeus sericeus*, a fish of the family Cyprinidae which grows to 75mm (3in) and which inhabits fresh waters of Europe and Asia Minor. It is noted for its interdependence with the freshwater mussel in which the female deposits her eggs. The male sheds his milt nearby, and this is sucked through the mussel's siphon, so that the eggs are fertilized in safety. The mussel benefits because its larvae are distributed by the female bitterling, which carries them away on her skin.

BITTERNS, wading birds, related to the HERONS, which live in marshes. Bitterns have plumage usually streaked with brown, which provides camouflage when the bird stands motionless with neck and bill turned upward against a background of reeds. Bitterns are well known for the distinctive mating calls produced by the males.

BITTERROOT, *Lewisia rediva*, hardy, herbaceous perennial plant native to the Rocky Mts. Each plant has a thick rootstock, crowned by a rosette of fleshy leaves, and bears a large cactus-like, rose-red flower. The bitter-tasting root is used as food by the Indians.

BITTERROOT RANGE, mountain range, an outlying part of the Rocky Mts system. With a maximum altitude of 9000–10 000ft, it forms part of the boundary between Ida. and Mont.

BITTERS, liquids extracted from bitter herbs, barks and flowers. Sometimes used medicinally, they are better known for their use in flavoring alcoholic drinks. The most common types are angostura, cinchona and camomile.

BITTERSWEET, or woody nightshade (*Solanum dulcamara*), a climbing shrub, native to Europe and Asia and naturalized in the US. Found in hedges and brushwood, it has a small purple flower. Although poisonous, the leaves and berries are an old remedy used for skin diseases and rheumatism. (See also BELLADONNA.)

BITUMEN, any naturally-occurring HYDROCARBON, including PETROLEUM, but referring especially to the solid hydrocarbons such as WAX, PITCH, ASPHALT and GILSONITE. These are fusible and soluble in organic solvents, unlike the **pyrobitumens**.

BITUMINOUS COAL. See COAL.

BITUMINOUS SANDS, sands which contain natural BITUMEN. The largest deposit is in the Athabasca region of N Alberta, and there are substantial deposits in Cal. and Ut. The heavy tar is extracted and synthetic crude oil produced.

BIVALVE, name for some 7000 species of shellfish, including the OYSTER, CLAM and MUSSEL, that have two shells (valves) joined together by a muscular hinge. Most live in the sea, though there are some freshwater species. They range in size from the Giant clam (almost 1.2m (4ft) long) to the Turton clam (only 1mm (0.01in) long). The valves, open except when the animal is disturbed, contain the fleshy body. This consists of a foot, by which the animal moves, and the viscera. There is no head, only a mouth towards which food is directed by moving hairs known as cilia. Most

The first and last stages of the birth process: at the beginning the baby's head is just above the opening of the cervix; it then turns to the side so that it passes down the birth canal. During the last stage of birth the shoulders turn while the doctor supports the head.

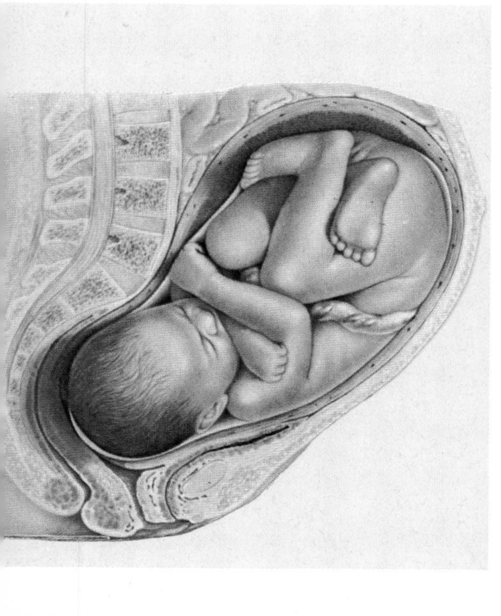

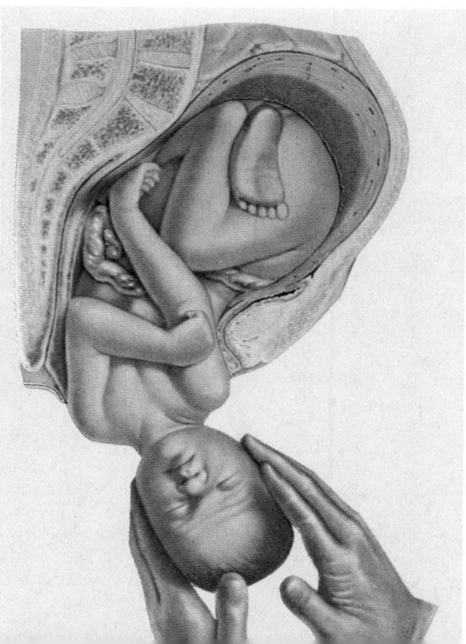

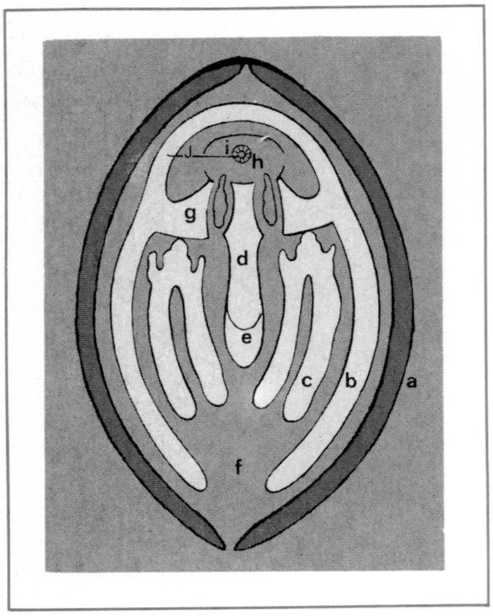

Bivalves include about 7000 species of shellfish and the mussel (shown in cross-section) is one of the most common: a. shell; b. mantle; c. gill; d. viscera; e. foot; f. mantle cavity; g. kidney; h. heart; i. pericardium; j. intestine.

bivalves feed on PLANKTON, though the "boring" bivalve feeds on wood. Bivalves are prey to whelks, birds, fish and aquatic mammals. They are also commercially important. (See also MOLLUSK.)

BIWA, Lake, Japan's largest lake (about 260sq mi), situated in W Honshu, and so named because it is shaped like the "biwa," a Japanese musical instrument. It is drained by the Yodo R.

BIZERTE, Tunisian port on the Mediterranean, capital of Bizerte province. It became a French military base in 1895, and was of great strategic importance in WWII. France withdrew in 1963. Industries include oil refining, fishing and phosphate production. Pop 51 708.

BIZET, Georges (1838–1875), French composer. The works for which he is now famous—the piano suite *Jeux d'Enfants* (1871), the incidental music for DAUDET's *L'Arlésienne* (1872), and the operas *Les Pêcheurs de Perles* (1863), and *Carmen* (1875)—were mostly ignored or vilified when first performed. The failure of *Carmen* fatally affected his health, but it has survived to become one of the most popular operas.

BJÖRLING, Jussi (1911–1960), internationally famous Swedish operatic tenor. He specialized in Italian opera, especially works by VERDI and PUCCINI.

BJØRNSON, Bjørnstjerne Martinius (1832–1910), major Norwegian poet, critic, novelist, dramatist and politician; winner of the Nobel Prize for Literature (1903). Concerned at first with Norwegian history, he later wrote about modern social problems.

BLACK, Davidson (1884–1934), Canadian anthropologist who inferred the existence of "Peking Man," an early species of hominid, from the discovery of a single tooth (1927), but later reinterpreted his discovery as representing a variety of *Pithecanthropus erectus* (see PREHISTORIC MAN).

BLACK, Eugene Robert (1898–), 3rd president of the International Bank for Reconstruction and Development (WORLD BANK), 1949–62. He helped build the bank into a major instrument for world economic development.

BLACK, Hugo Lafayette (1886–1971), US politician and jurist, Supreme Court associate justice 1937–71, senator from Ala. 1927–37. He backed NEW DEAL legislation and, although an ex-Ku Klux Klan member, was a noted campaigner for civil rights.

BLACK, Joseph (1728–1799), Scottish physician and chemist who investigated the properties of CARBON DIOXIDE, discovered the phenomena of LATENT and SPECIFIC HEATS, distinguished HEAT from TEMPERATURE and pioneered the techniques used in the quantitative study of CHEMISTRY.

BLACK AND TANS, name for recruits to the Royal Irish constabulary and also to the "Auxis" or Auxiliary Division, made up of demobilized British officers, introduced into Ireland in 1920 to maintain order during the struggle for Home Rule. They wore black berets and khaki or tan uniforms. Their repressive measures earned "the Tans" lasting hatred in Ireland and did much to discredit British rule there.

BLACKBEARD (d. 1718), nickname of Edward Teach, an English pirate proverbial for his extreme savagery. A privateer in the War of the Spanish Succession, he turned to piracy in the West Indies and along the Atlantic coast. Blackbeard was killed when his ship was taken by a British force.

BLACKBELT, name once commonly used for a broad belt of rich black soil across S.C., Ga., Ala. and Miss., used for cotton planting. The black belt is also the highest JUDO award.

BLACKBERRY, a BRAMBLE, (hardy, thorny shrub of the genus *Rubus*) producing soft, edible fruit. Native to north temperate regions, it has become a pest in Australia, New Zealand and Chile. Originally about 20 species, these are now represented by many thousands of cultivated hybrids and varieties.

BLACKBIRD, name for several dark-colored birds, including the Red-winged blackbird, Yellow-headed blackbird and the GRACKLE. Their song is loud and monotonous; they eat fruit, insects and worms. The European blackbird is a member of the THRUSH family Turdidae; the New World blackbird a member of the ORIOLE family Icteridae.

BLACK BODY, in theoretical physics, an object which absorbs all the ELECTROMAGNETIC RADIATION which falls on it. In practice, no object acts as a perfect black body, though a closed box admitting radiation only through a small hole is a good approximation. Black bodies are also ideal thermal radiators.

BLACKBODY RADIATION, the ELECTROMAGNETIC RADIATION emitted from a BLACK BODY in virtue of its thermal energy. The derivation of its properties by PLANCK in 1901 was the occasion of the proposal and first success of QUANTUM THEORY. The energy emitted from a black body is proportional to the fourth power of its (absolute) temperature (Stefan-BOLTZMANN Law). The intensity SPECTRUM of radiation from a black body takes the form of a skew hump which tails off in its longer-wavelength branch. Its precise shape is described in WIEN's laws, the first of which (Wien's displacement law) states that the greatest emission occurs at a wavelength which is inversely proportional to the absolute temperature.

BLACK BUCK, *Antilope cervicapra*, a species of Asian antelope that was once common but is now limited to a few thousand survivors. Black buck live in herds in plains and woodlands. The doe and young are yellow-fawn with white eye-rings; the buck is dark brown with spiral horns up to 0.6m (2ft) long.

BLACK CANYON OF THE GUNNISON, a national monument in Col., established in 1933. It centers on a 10mi section of the Black Canyon, a deep 50mi-long gorge of the Gunnison R. In places it reaches a depth of 3 000ft.

BLACK CODES, laws enacted by the Southern states after the Civil War. Allegedly intended to facilitate the transition from slavery to freedom, they were in fact a veiled device to deny real equality to newly-freed blacks. In 1866 the Civil Rights Act provided full rights to Negroes and further amendments were made during the next four years. However, some codes persisted into the 20th century.

BLACK DEATH, name for an epidemic of bubonic PLAGUE which swept through Asia and Europe in the mid-14th century, annihilating whole communities and perhaps halving the population of Europe. Originating in China, it was carried by flea-infested rats on vessels trading to the West. Its economic effects were far-reaching. It also fanned the flames of superstition and religious prejudice. European Jews, accused of poisoning wells, were massacred, and the idea that the plague was punishment for sin led to a wave of fanatical penance. (See also PLAGUE.)

BLACK EARTH. See CHERNOZEM.

BLACKETT, Patrick Maynard Stuart, Baron (1897–1974), British physicist who, having developed the Wilson CLOUD CHAMBER into an instrument for observing COSMIC RAYS, won the 1948 Nobel physics prize for the results he obtained using it.

BLACK-EYED PEA. See COWPEA.

BLACK-EYED SUSAN, or yellow daisy (*Rudbeckia hirta*), a hardy annual or biennial coneflower, the state flower of Md. Native to North America, it grows 0.3–0.6m (1–2ft) high and bears from 20–40 orange-yellow ray flowers around a group of brown florets. (See also COMPOSITAE.)

BLACKFISH, name for two species of fish. The freshwater type, the Alaska blackfish (*Dallia pectoralis*), found in Canada, Alaska and Siberia, eats mosquito and midge larvae and grows to 200mm (8in). They are reputed to be able to survive even when frozen solid. The marine blackfish (*Centrolophus niger*) is found in European waters and grows to 0.9m (3ft). The name is also given to the pilot whale *Globicephala melaena*.

BLACK FLIES, small two-winged biting flies of the family Simuliidae, common throughout the world. The LARVAE live in fresh water and the adults feed on mammalian blood. One central European species can cause death from blood loss and debilitation.

BLACKFOOT INDIANS, tribes of the ALGONQUIAN linguistic family, chiefly the Siksika, Piegan and Blood. Originally hunters and trappers, they adopted firearms and kept vast herds of horses, giving them power in Mont., Alberta and Saskatchewan. The disappearance of the bison, a smallpox epidemic and "incidents" with the white man led to a great reduction in their numbers. There are now under 8 000 Blackfoot on reservations in Mont. and Alberta.

BLACK FOREST, wooded mountain range in the province of Baden-Württemberg, SW West Germany An area of great scenic beauty, it is an important tourist attraction, with lumbering, clock and toy industries.

BLACK FRIDAY, term referring to disasters, particularly financial, occurring on Fridays. The most famous American Black Friday was Sept. 24, 1869, when the speculators Jay GOULD and James FISK tried to corner the gold market with the connivance of government officials. Government gold sales were stopped and prices rose rapidly until the plot was discovered and sales resumed. The market collapsed, and many were ruined.

BLACK HAND. See MAFIA.

BLACK HAWK WAR, revolt by Sauk and Fox Indians (1832), following their removal in 1831 from fertile lands owned by the Indians in the Illinois country. Refusing to recognize government claims to the lands, a group of Sauk and Fox Indians, led by Black Hawk, returned to plant corn the following spring but were once more driven out, pursued, and finally almost completely annihilated at the Massacre of Bad Axe River.

BLACKHEAD, or **comedo**, a plug of dried sebum in the duct of a SEBACEOUS GLAND, often obstructing flow of sebum, so producing a small pimple. (See ACNE.)

BLACK HILLS, mountain range in S.D. and Wyo., famous for the Mt Rushmore Memorial. Here, the heads of past US presidents are carved out of the mountainside. The Black Hills are rich in minerals, including gold. Highest point is Harney Peak (7 242ft).

BLACK HOLE, the final stage of evolution for very massive stars, following total gravitational collapse. At the center of the black hole are the infinitely densely packed remains of the star, perhaps only a few km across, if not crushed entirely out of existence. The gravitational field of a black hole is so intense that nothing, not even ELECTROMAGNETIC RADIATION (including light), can escape. For this reason black holes can only be detected through their gravitational effects on other bodies and through the emission of X- and gamma-rays by matter falling into them. It has been suggested that the end of the universe will be its becoming a single black hole. (See also ASTRONOMY, Special Feature.)

BLACK HOLE OF CALCUTTA, prison cell where 146 British captives were incarcerated on the night of June 20, 1756, during which all but 23 were suffocated. They were held by the Nawab of Bengal, who opposed the monopoly of the EAST INDIA COMPANY.

BLACKJACK, popular card game, the object of which is to obtain a score higher than the dealer (banker) without exceeding 21. Ace counts as 1 or 11, and a picture card is 10. The best hand is ace and picture card.
BLACK LUNG DISEASE, a lay term for PNEUMOCONIOSIS, which affects coal miners.
BLACKMAIL. See EXTORTION.
BLACKMORE, Richard Doddridge (1825–1900), English author of 14 novels, notably *Lorna Doone* (1869), a romance set in the English west country during the 17th century.
BLACK MOUNTAINS, in W N.C., highest range of the Appalachians, and an extension of the Blue Ridge Mts. The highest point is Mt Mitchell (6 684ft).
BLACKMUN, Harry (1908–), US lawyer, elevated to the US Court of Appeals (Eighth Circuit) in 1959, and in 1970 appointed Supreme Court justice by President Nixon.
BLACKMUR, Richard Palmer (1904–1965), US critic, editor and poet. His criticism, for which he is best known, is closely analytical. Among his books are *The Expense of Greatness* (1940) and *Language and Gesture* (1952). He taught at Princeton U. (1940–43; 1946–65).
BLACK MUSLIMS, the chief US black nationalist movement, founded in 1930 by Wali Farad. He rejected racial integration, taught thrift, hard work and cleanliness, and foretold an Armageddon where Black would crush White. Under Elijah MUHAMMAD, the Muslims proclaimed black supremacy and demanded a nation within the US.
BLACK PANTHER PARTY, US black revolutionary party, founded in 1966, advocating "armed self-defense" by black people. Though small in numbers, it enjoyed considerable influence until weakened by disputes in the early 1970s. Under the leadership of Eldridge CLEAVER and Huey P. Newton, the party opened community centers and bookshops and fought legal battles with the authorities, frequently securing the release of members held on violence charges.
BLACKPOOL, large seaside town in Lancashire, NW England. It is a popular vacation and conference center. Pop 151 311.
BLACK POWER, slogan coined in the mid-1960s by US black activists. It stands primarily for pride in "blackness" and a belief in the superiority of black culture. It is also associated with the advocacy of physical force to achieve social justice for blacks.
BLACK POWDER. See GUNPOWDER.
BLACK SEA, tideless inland sea between Europe and Asia, bordered by Turkey, Bulgaria, Romania and the USSR, and linked to the Sea of Azov and (via the Bosporus) to the Mediterranean. It covers 180 000sq mi and is up to 7 250ft deep. The Danube, Dniester, Bug, Don and Dnieper rivers all flow into the sea, which is vital to Soviet shipping. The chief ports are Odessa, Sevastopol, Batumi, Constanta and Varna. Russia's Black Sea coast is an important resort area.
BLACK SHIRTS. See FASCISM.
BLACKSNAKE, *Constrictor constrictor*, one of the largest nonvenomous North American SNAKES, varying in length from 1.2m to 2.1m (4–6.9ft) and slate black in color as an adult. Very agile, known as the "racer," it can move as fast as a running man.
BLACK SOX SCANDAL, ironic term for the scandal which shook the world of baseball 1919–20 and led to radical reorganization in the administration of the sport. It involved members of the Chicago White Sox and broke out when Edward Cicotte confessed to accepting a bribe to influence the outcome of the 1919 World Series. He named seven other players allegedly involved. All eight were suspended for a season but were cleared of fraud.
BLACKSTONE, Sir William (1723–1780), English jurist whose *Commentaries on the Laws of England* (1765–69) deeply influenced jurisprudence and the growth of COMMON LAW. He was the first professor of English Law at Oxford 1758–63, became a member of parliament 1761 and was a judge in the Court of Common Pleas 1770–80.
BLACKTHORN, wild European plum (*Prunus spinosa*), also known as the SLOE. (See also HAWTHORNS.)
BLACK TUPELO, also known as black-gum, sour gum (*Nyssa sylvatica*), deciduous tree native to eastern North American woods and swamps. It bears bluish-black fruits, has a tough useful wood, and is noted for the red tints of the leaves produced in the autumn.
BLACK WARRIOR AFFAIR, incident in 1854 which came near to provoking war between the US and Spain. It occurred when the Spanish seized the US merchant vessel *Black Warrior* at Havana and attempted to impose a $6 000 fine for violation of customs regulations. The South were all for war but the North opposed the idea. The release of the *Black Warrior* took the heat out of the situation.
BLACK WATCH (Royal Highland Regiment), prestigious Scottish regiment with a sober blue and green TARTAN. It originated in 1725 as a number of independent peacekeeping companies formed to watch over rival Highland clans. In 1740 it became part of the British army.
BLACKWELL, Elizabeth (1821–1910), English-born first woman doctor of medicine. Rebuffed at first by the authorities and later ostracized by her fellow students, she went on to gain her degree, with the highest grades for her year, at Geneva, N.Y., in 1849. After study in Europe, she returned to the US in 1857 and opened a hospital run by women (later also a medical school for women) in New York City.
BLACK WIDOW, *Latroclectas matans*, a common US name for the only SPIDER whose bite is dangerous to man. The female has a rounded shiny abdomen and a scarlet hourglass-shaped mark on the underside; the male is smaller and harmless.
BLADDER, a hollow muscular sac; especially the urinary bladder (see also AIR BLADDER; GALL BLADDER), found in most vertebrates except birds. In humans it lies in the front of the PELVIS. URINE trickles continually into the bladder from the KIDNEYS through two tubes called ureters, and the bladder stretches until it contains about 500ml, causing desire to urinate. The bladder empties through the urethra, a tube which issues from its base, being normally closed by the external sphincter muscle. The female urethra is about 30mm long: the male urethra, which runs through the PROSTATE GLAND and the PENIS , is about 200mm long. The bladder is liable to CYSTITIS and to the formation of CALCULI.
BLADDERWORT, INSECTIVOROUS PLANTS of the genus *Utricularia*, native in tropical and temperate regions, occurring in ponds and slow-flowing streams. Leaves are normally finely dissected and bear small bladders. Small insects are trapped in the bladders and their decomposed bodies are used as a supplementary source of nitrogen.
BLADENSBURG, Battle of, fought at Bladensburg, a town in S central Md., 7mi ENE of Washington. On Aug. 21, 1814, outnumbered British troops defeated American forces and went on to sack and burn many public buildings in Washington.
BLAINE, city in Minn., 12mi NW of Minneapolis. It is a center for agriculture and tourism. Pop 20 640.
BLAINE, James Gillespie (1830–1893), US statesman and post-Civil War Republican leader. His career was marked by an intense rivalry with fellow-Republican Roscoe CONKLING and also by allegations of corruption. Blaine served as congressman 1863–76 (speaker 1869–75) and US senator 1876–81; he was secretary of state 1881, 1889–92, and presidential candidate 1884. He backed RECONSTRUCTION and protective tariffs but fostered PAN AMERICANISM as an extension of the MONROE DOCTRINE.
BLAIR, US family influential in 19th-century politics. **Francis Preston Blair** (1791–1876), politician and journalist, a member of Andrew Jackson's "kitchen cabinet." Blair played an important part in forming the new Republican Party and also in organizing the unsuccessful HAMPTON ROADS PEACE CONFERENCE. He lived at the famous BLAIR HOUSE. His eldest son, **Montgomery Blair** (1813–1883), an eminent lawyer, defended Scott in the DRED SCOTT CASE, and served as postmaster general under Lincoln 1861–64. After the Civil War he backed Andrew Johnson's moderate policies and became a Democrat. His brother, **Francis Preston Blair, Jr.** (1821–1875), was a soldier and an ardent abolitionist. As a Republican congressman he helped keep Mo. in the Union during the Civil War. He was Democratic vice-presidential candidate in 1868.
BLAIR, Henry, 19th-century US slave and inventor who became the first negro to hold a patent when he obtained patents for a corn harvester (1835) and a cotton planter (1836). In 1858, however, it was ruled that slaves could not hold federal patents; this situation prevailed until after the Civil War.
BLAIR HOUSE, official guest house of the US government, on Pennsylvania Ave. in Washington, D.C. It was used as a temporary White House by President Truman 1948–52. The house, built in 1824, was named for its second owner, Francis Preston BLAIR, whose family sold it to the government 1942.
BLAISE, Saint, 4th-century Christian martyr, an Armenian bishop reputed to have saved the life of a boy who had swallowed a fishbone. He was invoked in medieval times as a cure for sore throats.
BLAKE, Edward (1833–1912), Irish–Canadian lawyer and politician. He was premier of Ontario 1871–72 and minister of justice 1875–77 in Alexander MACKENZIE's federal Liberal government. Blake resigned as Liberal leader (1880–87) after two general election defeats. But he went on to serve in the British parliament as an Irish nationalist 1892–1907.

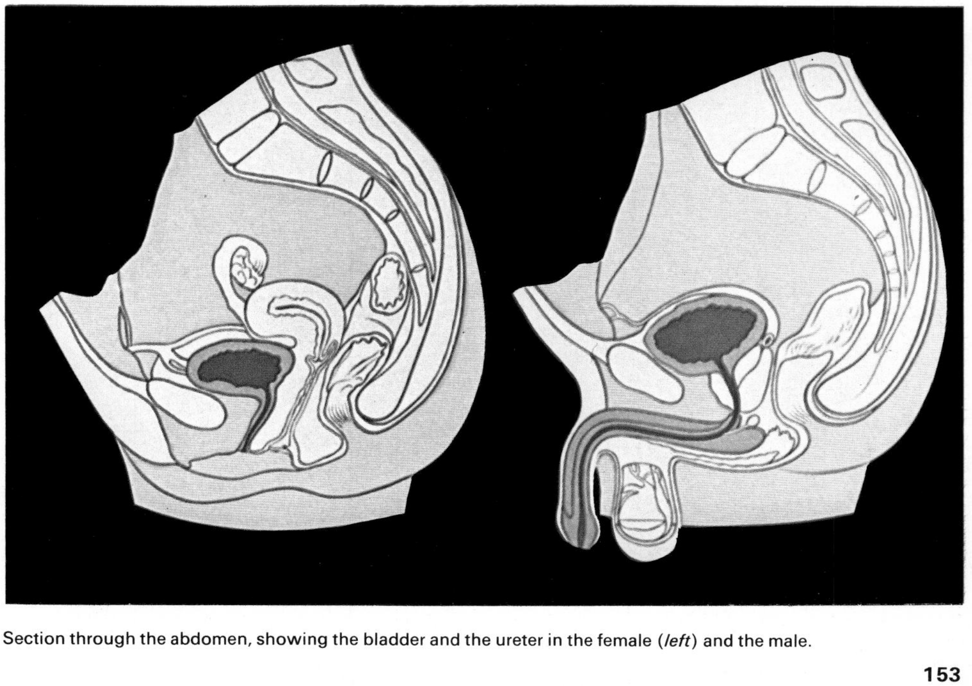

Section through the abdomen, showing the bladder and the ureter in the female (*left*) and the male.

BLAKE, Robert (1599–1657), English admiral who fought for the parliamentarians in the English Civil War. He made an important contribution to the organization of the Commonwealth navy, which he was to command decisively against the Dutch in 1652–53, ending for the time being their naval supremacy.

BLAKE, William (1757–1827), English poet, painter and prophet. He was apprenticed to an engraver 1772–79 and developed his own technique of engraving plates with both text and illustrations which were then colored by hand. In this manner he reproduced his *Songs of Innocence* (1789) and *Songs of Experience* (1794), collections of lyrics that contrast natural beauty and energy with the ugliness of man's material world. Blake was a revolutionary in both politics and religion and this is reflected in his art, particularly in the powerful though often opaque "Prophetic Books" which form the bulk of his work. Among perhaps the most impressive of these are *The Marriage of Heaven and Hell* (1793) and the epic *Jerusalem* (begun c1804). Blake's work was little understood by his contemporaries.

BLAKEY, Art (1919–), US jazz drummer who joined the Fletcher Henderson band in 1939 and has played with most of the big names in modern jazz. He formed the Jazz Messengers in 1955.

BLANC, (Jean Joseph Charles) Louis (1811–1882), French politician whose egalitarian ideas influenced modern socialism. He was a member of the provisional government in the 1848 Revolution, after which he was driven into exile in England. On his return to France he reentered politics but followed a less radical line.

BLANC, Mont, highest peak (15771ft) in the European Alps, in SE France on the border with Italy. The world's longest road tunnel (7.5mi) runs through its base.

BLANCHARD, Jean Pierre François, (1783–1809), French balloonist and inventor who made the first aeronautical crossing of the English Channel (1785) and the first BALLOON ascent in America (1793). He also invented the PARACHUTE (1785).

BLAND, James A. (1854–1911), US Negro songwriter and banjo player in Negro minstrel shows. His *Carry Me Back to Old Virginny* is the Va. state song.

BLAND, Richard Parks (1835–1899), American politician known as "Silver Dick" for his support of FREE SILVER. Bland was a Democratic member of Congress from Mo. 1872–95, 1897–99, and coauthor of the BLAND-ALLISON SILVER PURCHASE ACT. He was defeated as a Democratic presidential nominee by William Jennings BRYAN in 1896.

BLAND-ALLISON SILVER PURCHASE ACT, legislation of 1878 authorizing the US treasury to coin specific amounts of silver each month. It was a sop to the FREE SILVER lobby and helped to restore the value of silver, which had diminished after 1873 when most modern nations, including the US, adopted the gold standard. (See also BIMETALLISM; SHERMAN SILVER PURCHASE ACT.)

BLANK VERSE, unrhymed verse in iambic lines of five stresses. It is basically 10-syllabled but not rigidly so. The form originated in Italy. It was introduced into England by the Earl of SURREY, used to great effect by MARLOWE and by SHAKESPEARE, whose innovations made it a vehicle for natural speech rhythms. MILTON's *Paradise Lost* is written in highly distinctive and flexible blank verse.

BLANQUI, (Louis) Auguste (1805–1881), French revolutionary thinker and activist, an advocate of class struggle as a means to achieving COMMUNISM. He was involved in the revolutions of 1830, 1848 and 1870, and spent some 40 years in prison or exile. The Blanquist party became part of the French Socialist party in 1905.

BLANTYRE, city in S Malawi, in the Shire Highlands. It is the largest town and major commercial center of Malawi, with textiles, cement, canning, distilling and tobacco-processing industries. Pop 169000.

BLARNEY STONE, stone at Blarney Castle, SW Ireland. People who kiss this stone are said to acquire the gift of *blarney*, or skillful flattery.

BLASCO IBAÑEZ, Vicente (1867–1928), Spanish politician and novelist. He is best known for *Blood and Sand* (1909) and *The Four Horsemen of the Apocalypse* (1916), but his true literary worth is to be found in his earlier naturalistic novels, such as *The Cabin* (1899) and *Reeds and Mud* (1902).

BLASIUS, Saint. See BLAISE, SAINT.

BLASPHEMY, act of insult, contempt or irreverance directed against God or something held sacred. In the Old Testament it is a sin punishable by stoning to death. Many US states have antiblasphemy laws.

BLAST FURNACE, furnace in which a blast of hot, high-pressure air is used to force combustion; used mainly to reduce IRON ore to PIG IRON, and also for lead, tin and copper. It consists of a vertical, cylindrical stack surmounting the bosh (the combustion zone) and the hearth from which the molten iron and slag are tapped off. Modern blast furnaces are about 30m high and 10m in diameter, and can produce more than 1800 tonnes per day. Layers of iron oxide ore, COKE and LIMESTONE are loaded alternately into the top of the stack. The burning coke heats the mass and produces CARBON monoxide, which reduces the ore to iron; the limestone decomposes and combines with ash and impurities to form a SLAG, which floats on the molten iron. The hot gases from the top of the stack are burned to preheat the air blast.

BLASTOMYCOSIS, rare FUNGAL DISEASE caused by infection of lungs, skin and viscera by *Blastomyces* fungi. Characteristic SKIN lesions, ABSCESSES and FEVER occur. Treatment is with ANTIBIOTICS.

BLASTULA, a hollow sphere composed of a single layer of cells, formed by cleavage of a fertilized OVUM; the first stage in the development of the EMBRYO. In mammals a similar cluster, the blastocyst, is formed, with an inner cell mass and a spherical envelope that develops into the PLACENTA. (See also EMBRYOLOGY.)

BLAUE REITER (Blue Rider), group of Expressionist painters formed by KANDINSKY and MARC in Germany 1911–14. They issued an almanac, *Der Blaue Reiter*, containing the artists' essays and pictures, and essays by SCHOENBERG, BERG and WEBERN. KLEE and ARP were invited to show at the exhibitions they organized in Germany. (See EXPRESSIONISM.)

BLAVATSKY, Helena Petrovna (1831–1891), Russian occultist, founder of the Theosophical Society (1875). She expounded her theory of human and religious evolution in *Isis Unveiled* (1877). (See also THEOSOPHY.)

BLEACHING, process of whitening materials by sunlight, ULTRAVIOLET RADIATION or chemicals that reduce or oxidize DYES into a colorless form. Hydrogen PEROXIDE is used to bleach wool, silk and cotton; HYPOCHLORITES, including BLEACHING POWDER, are used for cotton; and sodium chlorite for synthetic fibers. Sulfur dioxide bleaches are impermanent. Careful control of pH is essential.

BLEACHING POWDER, white powder consisting of calcium HYPOCHLORITE and basic calcium chloride, made by reacting CALCIUM hydroxide with CHLORINE. It is used for BLEACHING and as a DISINFECTANT, but in time loses its strength.

BLEEDING. See HEMORRHAGE.

BLEEDING HEART, *Dicentra spectabilis*, garden plant native to China and Japan, with rose-red, hanging, heart-shaped flowers and gray-green leaves.

BLENDE. See SPHALERITE.

BLENHEIM, Battle of, battle in the War of the SPANISH SUCCESSION. On Aug. 13, 1704, an English army under the Duke of MARLBOROUGH, with Austrian troops under EUGENE OF SAVOY, defeated a superior French–Bavarian force near Blenheim, Bavaria. The battle ended Louis XIV's hopes of mastering Europe.

BLENNERHASSETT, Harman (1765–1831), American conspirator suspected of plotting with Aaron BURR to create an independent southwestern nation by seizing lands from the US and Mexico. He emigrated from Britain in 1796, purchasing and settling on the Ohio R island that still bears his name. He was cleared of treason in 1807 but lost much of his fortune in the process.

BLENNY, any blennoid fish, the wolf fish, the viviparous blenny or the Giant kelpfish, *Heterostichus rostratus*, which can grow to 0.6m (2ft). Their fins are spiny and their scales are covered in mucus.

BLÉRIOT, Louis (1872–1936), French pioneer aviator and airplane manufacturer. In 1909 he became the first person to fly a heavier-than-air machine across the English Channel.

BLESSING, act of invoking divine favor. In the Christian religion the blessing, usually set words and an appropriate gesture, is given by a minister. The Jewish religion has many blessings for different occasions: these are uttered as a religious duty by the observant Jew.

BLEULER, Eugen (1857–1939), Swiss psychiatrist who introduced the term SCHIZOPHRENIA (1908) as a generic term for a group of mental illnesses which he had learned to differentiate in a classic research project. He was an early supporter of FREUD but later criticized his dogmatism.

BLIGH, William (1754–1817), English admiral, captain of HMS BOUNTY at the time of the famous mutiny (1789). Master of the *Resolution* on COOK's last voyage to the Pacific, he later fought at Camperdown and Copenhagen. In 1805 he became governor of New South Wales, where his overbearing behavior caused another revolt.

BLIGHT. See PLANT DISEASES.

BLIMP. See AIRSHIP.

BLINDFISH, species of fish living in cave or deep-sea environments, and which have reduced vision or lost their eyes. Not all are blind, especially deep-sea forms which possess light organs. Blindfish have well developed LATERAL-LINE systems and are often colorless.

BLINDNESS, severe loss or absence of VISION, caused by injury to the EYES, congenital defects, or diseases including CATARACT, DIABETES, GLAUCOMA, LEPROSY, TRACHOMA and VASCULAR disease. MALNUTRITION (especially VITAMIN A deficiency) may cause blindness in children. Infant blindness can result if the mother had GERMAN MEASLES early in PREGNANCY; it was also formerly caused by gonorrheal infection of eyes at birth, but routine use of silver nitrate reduced this risk. Transient blindness may occur if one is exposed to a vertical ACCELERATION of more than 5*g*. Cortical blindness is a disease of the higher perceptive centers in the BRAIN concerned with vision: the patient may even deny blindness despite severe disability. Blindness due to cataract may be relieved by removal of the eye lens and the use of GLASSES. Prevention or early recognition and treatment of predisposing conditions is essential to save sight, as established blindness is rarely recoverable.

Many special books (using BRAILLE), instruments, utensils and games have been designed for the blind. With the help of guide dogs or long canes, many blind persons can move about freely. They can detect obstacles around them by the change of pitch of high-frequency sound from the feet or a cane, a skill acquired by training, and by using other senses.

BLIND SNAKES, members of two snake families, the Typhlopidae and Leptolyphlopidae. They are harmless, burrowing snakes with blunt tails, numerous rows of glossy scales and dry skins. Their eyes are hidden beneath head scales.

BLIND SPOT, the area of the retina of each EYE where the optic nerve and blood vessels enter, about 2mm in diameter. It has no light-sensitive receptors. In binocular vision the two spots do not receive corresponding images, and so are not noticeable.

BLINDWORM (*Anguis fragilis*). See ANGUID LIZARDS.

BLINK COMPARATOR, or Blink Microscope, astronomical instrument used to detect differences between apparently similar star pictures, viewed as in a STEREOSCOPE, by rapidly obscuring each alternately. Anything that has moved flickers. The planet PLUTO was discovered this way. It can also detect variable stars and those of large PROPER MOTION.

BLISS, Sir Arthur (1891–1975), English composer and Master of the Queen's Music. He is best known for his ballet *Checkmate* (1937), his *Colour Symphony* (1922), cinema scores such as *Things to Come* (1935), and the less successful opera, *The Olympians* (1949).

BLISS, Tasker H. (1853–1930), US soldier and diplomat. A graduate of West Point, he served with distinction in the Spanish–American War. American chief of staff 1917–18, he became a delegate to the Paris Peace Conference after WWI.

BLISTER, a swelling filled with serum or BLOOD formed between two layers of skin following BURNS, friction or contact with certain corrosive chemicals (vesicants). Blisters also occur in certain skin diseases.

BLISTER BEETLES, long-legged beetles of the family Meloidae, found throughout the world. Their bodies contain cantharidin, a blistering agent. They feed on honey and can be crop pests.

BLISTER RUST, fungus disease of white pines in North America, causing a large annual loss of trees. The causal fungus (*Cronartium ribicola*) requires as a secondary host members of the genus *Ribes* (currants and gooseberries) to complete its LIFE CYCLE. Control measures include removal of *Ribes* species from the vicinity of white-pine forests. (See also PLANT DISEASES.)

BLITZKRIEG, a German word meaning "lightning war." Originally used to describe German tactics in WWII, it is now applied to any fast military advance, such as the 1944 sweep through France by the US 3rd Army under PATTON.

BLITZSTEIN, Marc (1905–1964), US composer and concert pianist. He wrote operas, ballets, symphonies and film music; his best-known work is the *Airborne Symphony* (1944–46), a tribute to the history of flight.

BLIXEN, Karen. See DINESEN, ISAK.

BLIZZARD, snowstorm in which wind velocity reaches 32mph (14m/s) or more, the temperature is below freezing and visibility poor. Blizzards are common in polar regions.

BLOCH, Ernest (1880–1959), Jewish American–Swiss composer. He made great use of traditional Jewish music, particularly in his *Sacred Service* (1930–33) and *Three Jewish Poems* (1913).

BLOCH, Felix (1905–), Swiss-born US physicist who shared the 1952 Nobel Prize for Physics with E. M. PURCELL for developing a method for determining the magnetic fields of NEUTRONS in atomic nuclei (see ATOM). This was developed into the nuclear magnetic resonance (nmr) method of determining chemical structures (see SPECTROSCOPY).

BLOCH, Konrad Emil (1912–), German-born US biochemist who shared the 1964 Nobel Prize for Physiology or Medicine with F. LYNEN for developing an isotopic labeling technique (see ISOTOPES), which he used to elucidate the path by which CHOLESTEROL is synthesized in the body.

BLOCH, Markus Elieser (1723–1799), German ichthyologist whose 12-volume *General Natural History of Fishes* (1782–95) remained for many years a standard work in the field.

BLOCK, Adriaen, 17th-century Dutch mariner, after whom BLOCK ISLAND is named. He made a detailed survey of the New England coast (1614–16), and the first real map of the area was drawn according to his observations.

BLOCK, Herbert L. (1909–), US political cartoonist. His dry and witty cartoons have been appearing under the signature *Herblock* in the *Washington Post* since 1943. He was awarded Pulitzer prizes in 1942 and 1954.

BLOCKADE, a war maneuver designed to cut an enemy's supply routes by obstructing outside access to his territory. Napoleon introduced the CONTINENTAL SYSTEM in order to strangle British trade; in the CIVIL WAR, the Federal navy's command of waterways weakened the Confederates. In WWI the British navy blockaded Germany; in WWII German U-boats cut off much of Britain's food supply. In 1948 a Soviet blockade of West Berlin was broken by the BERLIN AIRLIFT.

BLOCKHOUSE, small fortified building, often used at military sites and missile and atomic testing areas. Early blockhouses were crude wooden forts used by American settlers as protection against Indians.

BLOCK ISLAND, a small island off R.I., part of Washington Co., and coextensive with New Shoreham, a resort town. On the coasts there are important lighthouses.

BLOEMFONTEIN, city in South Africa. Capital of Orange Free State, it is an important industrial and transportation center. Michigan U. maintains an astronomical observatory here. Pop 180 179.

BLOK, Alexander Alexandrovich (1880–1921), Russian dramatist and poet. He rose to fame as a symbolist poet before the 1917 Revolution but later adopted revolutionary ideas, with which he eventually became disillusioned.

BLONDEL, a little-used photometric unit for describing the helios of a source, numerically equivalent to the APOSTILB. It was named for the French physicist André Eugène Blondel (1863–1938).

BLONDIN, Charles (1842–1897), French acrobat. As a crowning point in his career he crossed Niagara Falls four times between 1855 and 1860 on a tightrope in progressively more hazardous ways.

BLOOD, the body fluid pumped by the heart through the vessels of those animals (all vertebrates and many invertebrates) in which diffusion alone is not adequate for transport of materials, and which therefore require BLOOD CIRCULATION systems. Blood plays a part in every major bodily activity. As the body's main transport medium it carries a variety of materials: oxygen and nutrients (such as glucose) to the tissues for growth and repair (see METABOLISM); carbon dioxide and wastes from the tissues for excretion; HORMONES to various tissues and organs for chemical signaling; digested food from the gut to the LIVER; immune bodies for prevention of infection and clotting factors to help stop bleeding to all parts of the body. Blood also plays a major role in HOMEOSTASIS, as it contains BUFFERS which keep the acidity (pH) of the body fluids constant and, by carrying heat from one part of the body to another, tends to equalize body temperature.

The adult human has about 5 litres of blood, half PLASMA and half blood cells (erythrocytes or red cells, leukocytes or white cells, and thrombocytes or platelets). The formation of blood cells (hemopoiesis) occurs in bone MARROW, lymphoid tissue and the RETICULOENDOTHELIAL SYSTEM. Red cells (about 5 million per mm^3) are produced at a rate of over 100 million per minute and live only about 120 days. They have no nucleus, but contain a large amount of the red pigment HEMOGLOBIN, responsible for oxygen transfer from lungs to tissues and carbon dioxide transfer from tissues to lungs. (Some lower animals employ copper-based HEMOCYANINS instead of hemoglobin. Others, e.g., cockroaches, have no respiratory pigments.) White cells (about 6000 per mm^3) are concerned with defense against infection and poisons. There are three types of white cells: granulocytes (about 70%), which digest bacteria and greatly increase in number during acute infection; lymphocytes (20–25%), which participate in immune reactions (see IMMUNITY; ANTIBODIES); and monocytes (3–8%), which digest nonbacterial particles, usually during chronic infection. (See also HODGKIN'S DISEASE; LEUKEMIA.) Platelets, which live for about 8 days and which are much smaller than white cells and about 40 times as numerous, assist in the initial stages of blood CLOTTING together with at least 12 plasma clotting factors and fibrinogen. This occurs when blood vessels are damaged, causing THROMBOSIS, and when HEMORRHAGE occurs (see also HEMOPHILIA).

Blood from different individuals may differ in the type of antigen on the surface of its red cells and the type of ANTIBODY in its plasma. Consequently, in a blood TRANSFUSION, if the blood groups of the donor and recipient are incompatible with respect to antigens and antibodies present, a dangerous reaction occurs, involving aggregation or clumping of the red cells of the donor in the recipient's circulation. Many blood group systems have been discovered, the first and most important being the ABO system by Karl LANDSTEINER in 1900. In this system, blood is classified by whether the red cells have antigens A (blood group A), B (group B), A and B (group AB), or neither A nor B antigens (group O). Another important antigen is the Rhesus antigen (or Rh factor). People who have the Rh factor (84%) are designated Rh+, those who do not, Rh−. Rhesus antibodies do not occur naturally but may develop in unusual circumstances. In a few cases, where Rh− women are pregnant with Rh+ babies, blood leakage from baby to mother causes production of antibodies by the mother which may progressively destroy the blood of any subsequent baby. (See also EDEMA; POLYCYTHEMIA; SEPTICEMIA; SERUM; TOXEMIA.)

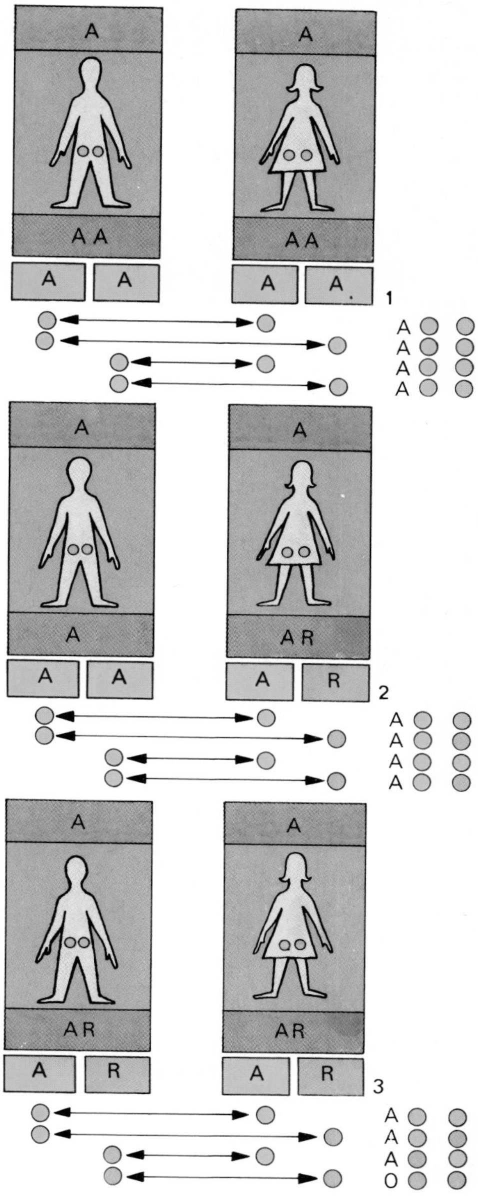

The genetic determination of blood groups. The genes A and B, giving rise to the antigens A and B, are dominant, but are often paired with a recessive gene R which gives rise neither to antigens A nor B. In 1, both parents have genes AA and thus belong to group A. All their children (*right*) thus have genes AA and are of group A. In 2, the mother has a recessive gene R; however, both parents and all their children are still of group A, although 50% of the children also carry R. In 3, both parents have the genes AR, thus although both are still group A, 25% of their children have two R genes and thus belong to group O. All the other children are group A, although two-thirds are heterozygous (AR) and one-third homozygous with AA.

BLOOD, Council of, the nickname of the Council of Troubles, a tribunal set up by Philip II of Spain to subdue the Protestant Dutch. It had EGMONT and other Dutch patriots executed.

BLOOD AND IRON, from the German *Blut und Eisen*, a cliché indicating the use of military force to impose one's will. It was first used by BISMARCK in 1886 to describe his foreign policy.

BLOOD CIRCULATION, the movement of BLOOD from the HEART through the ARTERIES, CAPILLARIES and VEINS and back to the heart. The circulatory system has two distinct parts in animals with lungs: the pulmonary circulation, in which blood is pumped from the right ventricle to the left atrium via the blood vessels of the lungs (where the blood is oxygenated and

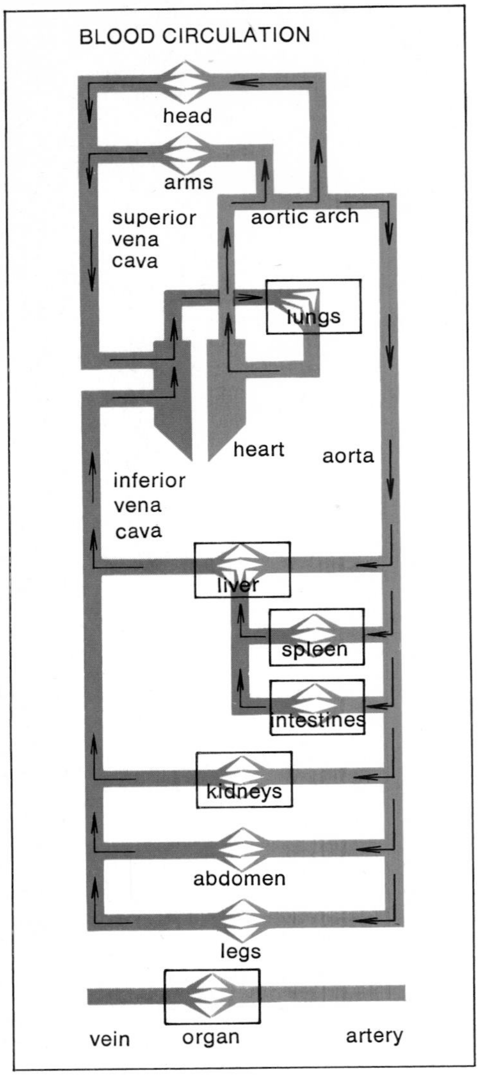

carbon dioxide is eliminated); and the systemic circulation, in which the oxygenated blood is pumped from the left ventricle to the right atrium via the blood vessels of the body tissues (where—in the capillaries—the blood is deoxygenated and carbon dioxide is taken up). As it leaves the heart, the blood is under considerable pressure—about 120mmHg maximum (systolic pressure) and 80mmHg minimum (diastolic pressure). Sustained high blood pressure, or **hypertension**, occurs in kidney and hormone diseases and in old age, but generally its cause is unknown. It may lead to ARTERIOSCLEROSIS and heart, brain and kidney damage. Low blood pressure occurs in SHOCK, TRAUMA and ADDISON'S DISEASE.

The bloodhound originates from Europe; it is one of the main breeds traditionally used for tracking because of its extremely sensitive nose.

BLOOD FEUD. See VENDETTA.

BLOODHOUND, a breed of dog famous for its ability to track by scent. Its coat is generally either tan or black, or both, and when fully grown it reaches from 23in to 27in in height. It has a characteristically heavy-jowled face.

BLOOD POISONING. See SEPTICEMIA.

BLOODROOT, *Sanguinaria canadensis*, a North American member of the poppy family with white or pinkish flowers, also called red puccoon. An acrid, orange-red juice is produced from the rootstock. The plant is a source of the medicinal ALKALOID sanguinarine.

BLOODSTONE, a dark-green variety of CHALCEDONY containing nodules of red JASPER, used in medieval sculptures of martyrdom or flagellation.

BLOODY MARY. See MARY (Tudor).

BLOODY SHIRT, from the phrase "waving the bloody shirt." It was first applied to American politicians who referred to Civil War casualties in their speeches in order to arouse feeling on RECONSTRUCTION issues.

BLOOMER, Amelia Jenks (1818–1894), US feminist reformer. A famous lecturer, she also edited *The Lily*, a journal which campaigned for temperance and women's rights. In a search for more practical clothes for women she unsuccessfully tried to introduce the baggy pantaloons which were derisively nicknamed "bloomers."

BLOOMINGTON, city in Ill., SW of Chicago. It is a railroad center, with coal mining, iron production, dairying and agriculture in the area. It is the home of Ill. Wesleyan U. Pop 39 393.

BLOOMINGTON, town in Ind., seat of Monroe County, 50mi SW of Indianapolis. Set in an agricultural and quarrying area, the town has a flourishing electronics industry. It is also the home of Indiana U. Pop 42 890.

BLOOMINGTON, a town in Minn., SW of Chicago. In recent years it has become a center for light industry. Pop 81 970.

BLOOMSBURG, town in Pa., seat of Columbia Co., on Fishing Creek. Its principal industries are textiles and frozen foods. Pop 11 652.

BLOOMSBURY GROUP, name applied to a coterie of writers and artists who met in Bloomsbury, London, in the early 20th century. Influenced by G. E. MOORE, they gathered about Virginia and Leonard WOOLF, and Virginia's sister, Vanessa Bell. The group included Clive BELL, E. M. FORSTER, Roger FRY, Duncan GRANT, J. M. KEYNES and Lytton STRACHEY.

BLOUNT, William (1749–1800), one of the signers of the Constitution. He became a senator from Tenn. but was expelled from the Senate when he became involved in a plot to invade Spanish Florida with Indian aid.

BLOW, John (1649–1708), English composer, the teacher of Henry PURCELL. His *Venus and Adonis* (1680–85), written for the court, is considered to be the first true English opera.

BLOWFLY, also known as the bluebottle or greenbottle. It is a large fly of the family Calliphoridae, that lays eggs in carrion, excrement or open wounds where it may be beneficial because it eats infectious bacteria. It attacks livestock and because of its breeding habits spreads dysentery and perhaps jaundice and anthrax.

BLOWGUN, weapon used by some Pacific and South American tribes. It consists of a long tube from which a small dart is blown; it may be accurate up to 40yd or more. The dart is made most effective by being smeared with a poison such as CURARE or the sap of the UPAS tree.

BLOWPIPE, narrow tapered tube through which air is blown into a flame to increase the temperature and to direct part of the flame—the oxidizing or reducing zone—onto a substance undergoing chemical ANALYSIS. (See FLAME TEST.)

BLOWTORCH, portable burner used for melting solder and removing paint. The fuel—liquid or pressurized gas—is mixed with compressed air in order to obtain a hot flame.

BLUBBER, the layer of fat below the skin of the WHALE and some other marine mammals; it is several inches thick and provides buoyancy, insulation and energy reserves. It yields oil which was once used for lighting, and more recently for making soap and margarine. A blue whale can yield more than 20 tonnes of oil.

BLÜCHER, Gebhard Leverecht von (1742–1819), Prussian commander, a fierce opponent of Napoleon. After distinguished service at Jena (1806), he was made a field marshal for his part in the Battle of Leipzig (1813). He led Prussian troops into Paris a year later. In 1815 the timely intervention of the Prussian army under Blücher made conclusive victory at Waterloo possible.

BLUE BABY, infant born with a HEART defect (a hole between the right and left sides, or malformation of the arteries) that permits much of the BLOOD to bypass the LUNGS. The resulting lack of oxygen causes CYANOSIS. These conditions used to be fatal but can now often be corrected by surgery.

BLUEBEARD, villain of a traditional tale in which a rich man, who has had several wives, marries a young girl. He forbids her to enter a particular room in his castle; she disobeys him, and finds there the bodies of former wives he has murdered. In some versions he threatens to kill her also, but she is saved by her brothers. MAETERLINCK based a play on the legend. BARTOK's opera *Duke Bluebeard's Castle* (1911) is a more modern symbolic treatment of the story.

BLUEBELL, name given to several unrelated species of plants with bell-shaped flowers: in England, the wild hyacinth (*Scilla nonscripta*), in Scotland the harebell (*Campanula rotundifolia*), and in the US the Virginia cowslip (*Mertensia virginica*) and the Californian bluebell (*Phacelia*). (See also BELLFLOWER.)

BLUEBERRY, common name used for woody shrubs of the genus *Vaccinium*. They bear sweet, edible, blue fruit that are used in jams and pastry fillings. In Britain, the common species (*Vaccinium myrtillus*) is known as the bilberry. Many cultivated varieties have been developed.

BLUEBIRD, songbird which visits the US as a summer bird of passage. A member of the family Turdidae, it often nests near human habitations. Its upper part is sky-blue in color and its breast is chestnut. Its song is mellow and sweet. The female lays four or five eggs.

BLUEBONNET, *Lupinus subcarnosus*, the state flower of Tex. which in spring transforms the Tex. plains into a sea of blue. (See also LUPIN.)

BLUEBOTTLE. See BLOWFLY.

BLUE CRAB, the name for several crabs common on the Atlantic coast of the US. They belong to the genus *Callinectes* and are edible. In Australia it is the name of another edible crab, *Portunus pelagicus*.

BLUE EAGLE, emblem of the US NATIONAL RECOVERY ADMINISTRATION (1933–36). It had to be displayed on all goods manufactured under the administration's codes; householders were encouraged to display it as a sign that in the national interest they would buy only goods so marked.

BLUEFIELD, city in W Va. A rail center for the locality, its main industry is mineral mining, especially coal. Pop 15 921.

BLUEFIELDS, port in E Nicaragua, 175mi E of Managua. It is an export center for local wood, fruit and sea produce. Pop 25 953.

BLUEFISH, voracious fish of the family Pomatomidae found in the Atlantic Ocean off Africa. It can grow to a length of about 1.2m (4ft) and attain a weight of 5.5–9kg (12–20lb). Large shoals of bluefish pursue and kill enormous numbers of small fish. They are caught commercially and are a popular game fish.

BLUEGRASS, general name for several hundred species of grass of the genus *Poa*. Most common is the Kentucky bluegrass (*Poa pratensis*), which is used as a pasture and lawn grass throughout North America.

BLUE GRASS, a style of folk music which originated in the Blue Grass country of Ky.

BLUE-GREEN ALGAE, widely distributed photosynthetic prokaryotic (see CELL), microrganisms forming the class Schizophyceae of the division Schizophyta of the PLANT KINGDOM. An important property of blue-green algae is NITROGEN FIXATION.

The Blue Ridge Parkway has been designed to affect the area's beautiful scenery as little as possible.

BLUE ISLAND, a city in NE Ill., part of a dairying and farming region. Pop 22 598.
BLUEJAY. See JAY.
BLUE LAW, term for any US law strictly regulating morality and social behavior. The name was first given to puritanical laws made by the New Haven Colony. After the Revolutionary War their use declined, though there are still a few such laws controlling Sabbath observance and sexual practices. An extreme blue law was the PROHIBITION constitutional amendment of 1917–20.
BLUE MOUNTAINS, part of the Great Dividing Range of Australia, in New South Wales. They form a dissected plateau, covering an area of 545sq mi and reaching a height of 4 000ft.
BLUE MOUNTAINS, well-wooded range of mountains reaching from NE Ore. to SE Wash. and rising to a height of nearly 9 000ft.
BLUE NILE, a river in Sudan which joins the White Nile at Khartoum to form the NILE.
BLUEPRINT, a process used for copying architectural and engineering plans. Paper sensitized with iron (III) ammonium citrate and potassium ferricyanide is exposed to ULTRAVIOLET LIGHT through a transparent original. Where the light strikes the paper, a blue coloration results, which is often intensified with potassium dichromate solution. The result is a white copy of the original on a blue background. The OZALID PROCESS is now more widely used.
BLUE RIDER. See BLAUE REITER.
BLUE RIDGE MOUNTAINS, a range lying E of the Appalachians and stretching through Md., W. Va., Va., N.C. and Ga. for 615mi. Shenandoah National Park is sited here and part of the Appalachian Trail follows the crest of the range.
BLUES, type of US Negro music, often sad and slow, characterized by the use of flattened "blue notes." It derived from the work songs, spirituals and "field hollers" of the Negroes of the South and became a principal basis of the JAZZ idiom. The characteristic pattern of the blues is a 12-bar structure with certain distinctive harmonies, but the form is flexible and has undergone many adaptations. At first a song, usually with guitar, harmonica or piano accompaniment, the blues have since also become an instrumental form, and their influence has pervaded many types of modern music. They were first popularized by W. C. HANDY's *Memphis Blues* and *St. Louis Blues*.
BLUE SKY LAWS, name given to laws passed in most US states, regulating the sale of stocks and bonds for the protection of the investor. The first blue sky law was enacted in Kansas in 1911, and many states soon followed this example. The name derived from a politician's assertion that a corrupt promoter would offer to sell shares in the blue sky itself.
BLUESTOCKING, belittling term for a woman of intellectual pretensions. The nickname was given to a group of English society ladies c1780 because their literary meetings were attended by a certain Benjamin Stillingfleet, wearing blue (ordinary) stockings.
BLUET, popular name for perennial flowers of the genus *Houstonia*, native to North America. In particular, *Houstonia caerulea*, also known as Innocence or Quaker-ladies, which grows in grassy regions and produces small light-blue flowers that fade to white with age.
BLUE VITRIOL, or copper (II) sulfate. See COPPER.
BLUE WHALE, *Balaenoptera musculus*, the largest species of whale and the largest known animal. It may reach 30m (100ft) in length and weigh 130 tonnes. A member of the RORQUAL family, it has a small dorsal fin on its blue-colored back and a series of ridges running down its chest. It feeds on PLANKTON, straining its food through the BALEEN which hangs from its upper jaw. The Blue whale lives mainly in the Antarctic Ocean, moving to warmer waters to breed. Like other whales it is a mammal (family Balaenopteridae), being warm-blooded and suckling its young. In the 20th century the number of Blue whales has been severely reduced by whaling and it is now a protected species.
BLUING, process used in laundering to brighten white fabrics. The fabric is immersed briefly in a dilute blue dye solution at about 45°C, to counteract the yellowish tint which washing generally produces. A blue dye is often added to detergents.
BLUM, Léon (1872–1950), creator of the modern French Socialist Party, and the first socialist and the first Jew to become premier of France. As premier in 1936 and 1938 he led the Popular Front, a coalition of Socialists and Radicals opposed to fascism. He carried out major domestic reforms and was greatly concerned with defense against the Rome-Berlin axis.
BLUMENBACH, Johann Friedrich (1752–1840), German physiologist generally regarded as the father of physical ANTHROPOLOGY. As a result of careful measurement of a large collection of skulls, he divided mankind into five racial groups: Caucasian,

The wild boar (Sus scrofa) is found in central and southern Europe, North Africa and eastern Asia; it is a favorite target of huntsmen because of its strength and speed as well as its ferocity when cornered.

Mongolian, Malayan, Ethiopian and American.
BLUNDERBUSS, a muzzle-loading FLINTLOCK gun with a large bore and a short flared barrel. Originating in Holland, it was popular in the 17th and 18th centuries. It was an inaccurate weapon, though deadly at short range.
BLY, Nellie, pen name of Elizabeth Cochrane (1867–1922), US woman reporter. Her most famous exploit was her successful attempt in 1889 to beat the record of Jules Verne's Phileas Fogg (*Around the World in Eighty Days*): it took her 72 days, 6 hours, 11 minutes and 14 seconds.
BLYTHEVILLE, city in NE Ark., seat of Mississippi Co., 5mi S of the Mo. border. It is the trade and industrial center for a rich agricultural region. Pop 24 752.
BMEWS (BALLISTIC MISSILE EARLY WARNING SYSTEM). See AIR DEFENSE.
B'NAI B'RITH (Hebrew: Sons of the Covenant), Jewish service and cultural organization. Founded in New York City in 1843, B'nai B'rith was first concerned with social work and the establishment of community centers for Jewish students. It has greatly expanded and now has branches in 33 countries.
BOADICEA (BOUDICCA), British queen of the Iceni in Norfolk. In 60 AD she led a revolt against Roman ill-treatment, and sacked Camulodunum (Colchester), Londinium (London) and Verulamium (St. Albans) before being defeated in 61. She reportedly took poison to avoid capture.
BOAR, the wild pig, *Sus scrofa*, smaller than the domestic pig, dark gray or brown in color with large upward-pointing tusks. It inhabits many parts of Europe, N Africa and Asia. Its favorite habitat is marshy ground and deciduous woods, where it feeds on roots and grain and sometimes small animals. Boars have long been hunted for sport. The male domestic pig is also called a boar.
BOAS, nonpoisonous snakes that kill their prey by squeezing and suffocating it. Boas range from 2.5m to 9m (8–30ft) in length and feed on birds and

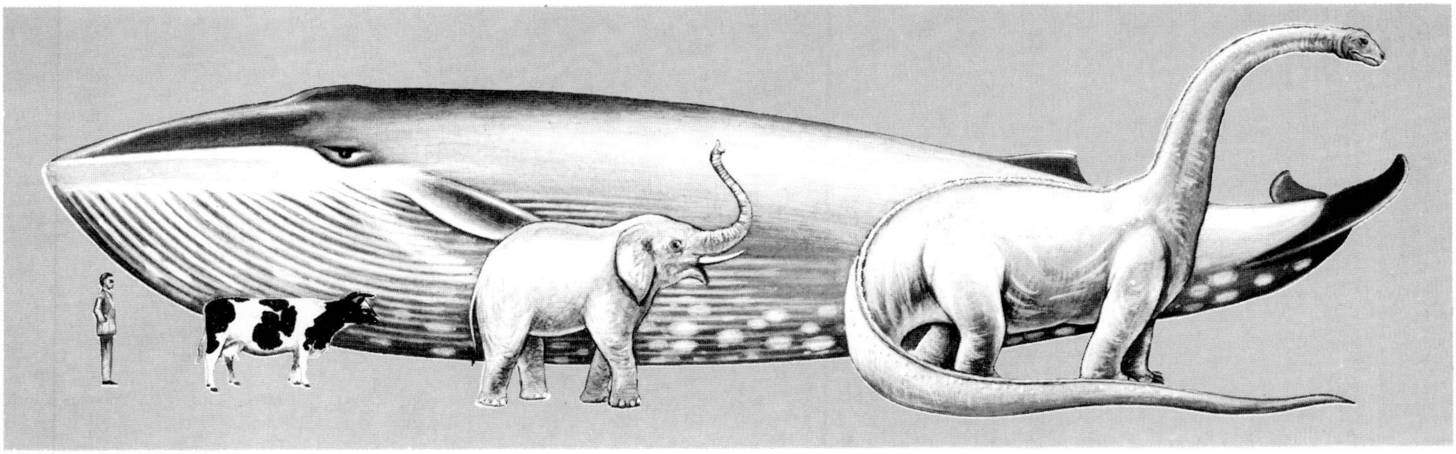

The Blue Whale, probably the largest animal ever, compared with a man, cow, elephant and the extinct brontosaurus.

Head of a python, a member of the boa family.

mammals. They are found mostly in tropical America and the West Indies, and live on the ground or in trees. Boas give birth to live young and have vestigial hind limbs and a rudimentary pelvis. There are 35 species, including the ANACONDA.

BOAS, Franz (1858–1942), German-born US anthropologist who played a leading part in the establishment of the cultural-relativist school of ANTHROPOLOGY in the English-speaking world.

BOATS AND BOATING. Boats are nautical craft, smaller in size than a SHIP. They may be propelled by sail, motor, paddle, oars or pole. The first boats were rafts and dugout CANOES. Many early boats were made from skins stretched over a framework. They were used for fishing and transport, and similar craft are still built. Today boats are used in LIFESAVING, as auxiliary craft, for pleasure or in sports such as sailing, ROWING, WATER SKIING or SKIN DIVING, all of which are widely popular in the US. Small-boat sailing, with numerous organized classes of boat and national and international competition, is now a popular sport all over the world. (See also CATAMARAN; DINGHY; HYDROFOIL; MOTORBOATING; YACHTS AND YACHTING.)

BOBCAT, a wild cat, *Lynx rufus*, closely related to the LYNX, named for its short (150mm—6in) tail. It grows to a length of about 0.9m (3ft) and has a brown and white coat with black spots and stripes. It is nocturnal, feeding on rodents and occasionally on livestock. The bobcat is found in most parts of North and Central America.

BOBOLINK, *Dolichonyx oryzivorus*, a North American migratory songbird named for its distinctive song. Also called ricebird or reedbird, it is 150–200mm (6–8in) long with a dull plumage—except in spring, when the male is black and yellow. The bobolink breeds in the US and S Canada, migrating to South America for the winter.

BOBSLED, a heavy sled used on packed snow or ice runs, having four runners and carrying two or four people. The bobsled derived from the toboggan in Switzerland and became popular in the early 20th century. Bobsledding has been included in the winter Olympic Games since 1928, but with its steep runs and speeds up to 100mph it is very dangerous and is not widely practiced.

BOBWHITE, *Colinus virginiarus*, North American gamebird related to the QUAIL and PARTRIDGE. It is about 250mm (10in) long and reddish-brown in color. Bobwhites feed on insects and seeds and keep within a group or covey.

BOCA RATON, resort city in SE Fla., 17mi N of Fort Lauderdale. It is a radar training center for the USAF. Pop 28 506.

BOCCACCIO, Giovanni (1313–1375), great Italian writer and humanist of the early Renaissance whose work had a lasting influence on European literature. A classical scholar and a friend and admirer of PETRARCH, his works include *Filostrato*, *Teseida* and the famous DECAMERON tales—the first literary expression of Renaissance humanist realism.

BOCCHERINI, Luigi (1743–1805), Italian composer and cellist, noted for his chamber music. His numerous charming and elegant works have been compared to those of HAYDN, his contemporary.

BOCCIONI, Umberto (1882–1916), Italian painter and sculptor. A pioneer of Italian FUTURISM, he was a signer of the "Manifesto of Futurist Painters" (1910). He tried to capture movement and the speed and sensations of modern life by using dynamic forms.

BOCHUM, industrial city in the Ruhr area of West Germany. Once an important mining center, the city has a unique mining museum. It was badly bombed during WWII. Pop 346 010.

BÖCKLIN, Arnold (1827–1901), major Swiss painter. Primarily a landscape painter, he drew inspiration from Italy, often using mythological subjects, and strongly influenced German Romantic painting.

BODAWPAYA (1745–1819), king of Burma from 1782 to 1819. In 1784 he conquered the kingdom of Arakan and extended his territory into British India, an action which eventually led to the first Burmese War.

BODENSEE. See CONSTANCE, LAKE.

BODE, Johann Elert (1747–1826), German astronomer remembered for promoting **Bode's Law**, a numerical relationship which was found to hold between the radii of the ORBITS of the then-known PLANETS. Bode started from the sequence 0, 3, 6, 12, 24, 48, 96, 192, . . . and added 4 to each member: 4, 7, 10, 16, 28, 52, 100, 196, . . . ; then, if the radius of the orbit of the earth was taken to be 10, he found that MERCURY fell into place at 4, VENUS at ~ 7, MARS at 16, JUPITER at 52 and SATURN at ~ 100. The discovery of URANUS at ~ 196 initiated a hunt for a missing planet at 28, which was supplied by the asteroid CERES but when NEPTUNE was discovered in 1846, it failed to satisfy the "law," which immediately declined in importance.

BODHISATTVA, in Mahayana (a form of BUDDHISM), a gentle spiritual being, a potential Buddha who, through generosity and compassion, postpones his entry to NIRVANA to help mankind. Buddhist legend has many instances of the lives and good works of the many bodhisattvas.

BODIN, Jean (c1530–1596), French political philosopher who argued that stable government lay in a moderate absolutism founded on divine right, but subject to divine and natural law. Tolerant in religion, he also tried to show that religious differences could be settled by adherence to the Ten Commandments.

BODLEIAN LIBRARY, the library of Oxford University. Originally established in the 14th century, it was restored 1598–1602 by the English diplomat Sir Thomas Bodley (1545–1613). Its collection has grown from 2 000 to 2.5 million books, including many oriental and other MSS.

BODONI, Giambattista (1740–1813), Italian printer and type-designer. The Bodoni typeface, with its sharp contrast between thick and thin strokes, has been widely used in modern printing.

BODY. See HUMAN BODY; SOMATOTYPES.

BODY-BUILDING, development of the muscles to increase strength or improve the physique. Body-building is undertaken by athletes and sportsmen to strengthen particular parts of the body within the context of its overall development. The chief method uses training with weights, gradually increasing the heaviness of the weights and the number of times an exercise is done. This results in hypertrophy or an increase in size of the muscles exercised.

BOEOTIA, E central Greece, ancient region and department (modern capital: Lebadea). In the 5th and 4th centuries BC the Boeotian League, led by the city of Thebes, was an important military power rivaling Athens and Sparta. Boeotia was the home of the poets Hesiod and Pindar.

BOERHAAVE, Hermann (1668–1738), Dutch chemist and physician, renowned in his day as a leading man of science, although he made no discoveries of lasting importance. His teaching did much to establish Leiden as a medical center of international repute.

BOERS (Dutch: farmers), in South Africa, term once used for people of Dutch, German and Huguenot descent who settled in the Cape of Good Hope from 1652. The British annexed the Cape in 1806, and in 1835–43 the Boers left on the Great Trek to found the new republics of the Transvaal and the Orange Free State. Now called Afrikaners, they speak their own language (AFRIKAANS) and belong to the Dutch Reformed Church. Their racial attitudes resulted in the notorious APARTHEID policy.

BOER WAR, or South African War, fought between the British and the Boers from 1899 to 1902. The Boers resented British territorial ambitions, while the British aimed at a united South Africa and complained of the harsh treatment the Boers, under Paul KRUGER, gave to immigrant gold prospectors. In 1895 tension was increased by the Jameson Raid, aimed at supporting an anti-Boer rebellion in the Transvaal. Believing they would win foreign support, the Boers took the offensive in 1899. In the early part of the war the Boers besieged Ladysmith and Mafeking, but by late 1900 they had to resort to guerrilla tactics, and their resistance steadily weakened. The war ended with the treaty of Vereeniging in 1902. The British victory was marred by incompetence and much loss of life, and by the use of insanitary internee camps.

BOETHIUS, Anicius Manlius Severinus (c480–525), Roman philosopher, statesman and Christian theologian whose works were a major source of Classical thought for medieval Scholastic philosophers. A high official under THEODORIC THE GREAT, he was accused of treason and executed. While in prison, he wrote his influential work *On the Consolation of Philosophy*.

BOG, commonly, any marsh or SWAMP; specifically, a low-lying area, usually formed by the action of GLACIERS, which is poorly drained, perhaps containing shallow water, and in which organic matter is accumulating.

BOGALUSA, city in E La., 60mi NE of New Orleans. The local industries make paper, furniture and tung oil. Pop 21 423.

BOGART, Humphrey DeForest (1899–1957), US film actor, famous for his screen image as the cool, tough anti-hero. Some of his most notable films were *The Maltese Falcon* (1942), *Casablanca* (1942) and *The African Queen* (1951)—for which he won an Academy Award.

BOĞAZKÖY, village in N central Turkey, 125mi E of Ankara, site of Hattusas, capital of the HITTITE Empire. King Labarnas II made it his capital in the 17th century BC. It was destroyed in 1190 BC and reinhabited in the 8th century BC. In 1906–07 excavations uncovered thousands of Hittite cuneiform tablets at Boğazköy.

BOGOMILS, religious sect founded in Bulgaria in the 10th century by the priest Bogomil. Its members held that all material things were created by the devil and that therefore all close contact with matter, even the Eucharist, must be rejected. The sect flourished in the Balkans until the 14th century. (See also CATHARI.)

BOGOR, city in W Java, Indonesia, 36mi S of Djakarta. The city contains a noted botanical garden. Pop 196 000.

BOGOTÁ, capital and largest city of Colombia. First settled by the Spanish in 1538, it is today a commercial and cultural center, the site of the National University. Its climate is mild because of its altitude of over 8 500ft, at the edge of an Andean plateau. Pop 2 818 000.

BOHEMIA, historic region in central Europe. It was once part of the Austro-Hungarian Empire. In 1918, after a war-torn history, it became a province in the republic of Czechoslovakia, of which its chief city, Prague, became the capital. In 1949 it lost its separate provincial status. The area is rich in minerals and in fine agricultural land.

BOHEMIAN, term describing a carefree unconventional mode of life, derived from a French name for gypsies. It was applied to the life led by artists in 19th-century Paris, romanticized by novelist Henri Murger in a book which became the basis for PUCCINI's opera, *La Bohème* (1896).

BOHLEN, Charles Eustis (1904–), US diplomat and adviser on Soviet affairs. He served as adviser and interpreter at Russian conferences for presidents Roosevelt and Truman, and was US ambassador to the USSR (1953–57), the Philippines (1957–59) and France (1962–68).

BÖHME, Jakob (1575–1624), German mystic and religious philosopher. Claiming divine revelation, he argued that all opposites, including good and evil, are reconciled in God. His ideas influenced many late philosophers and theologians.

BOHR, Niels Henrik David (1885–1962), Danish

physicist who proposed the Bohr model of the ATOM while working with RUTHERFORD in Manchester, England, in 1913. Bohr suggested that a HYDROGEN atom consisted of a single electron performing a circular orbit around a central PROTON (the nucleus), the energy of the ELECTRON being quantized (i.e., the electron could only carry certain well-defined quantities of energy—see QUANTUM THEORY). At one stroke this accounted both for the properties of the atom and for the nature of its characteristic radiation (a SPECTRUM comprising several series of discrete sharp lines). In 1927 Bohr proposed the COMPLEMENTARITY PRINCIPLE to account for the apparent paradoxes which arose on comparing the wave and particle approaches to describing SUBATOMIC PARTICLES. After escaping from Copenhagen in 1943 he went to the UK and then to the USA, where he helped develop the ATOMIC BOMB, but he was always deeply concerned about the graver implications for humanity of this development. In 1922 he received the Nobel Prize for Physics in recognition of his contributions to atomic theory. His son, **Aage Niels Bohr** (1922–), shared the 1975 Nobel Prize for Physics with B. MOTTELSON and J. RAINWATER for contributions made to the physics of the atomic nucleus.

BOIL, an ABSCESS in a hair FOLLICLE, usually caused by infection with STAPHYLOCOCCUS. A **sty** is a boil on the eyelid; a **carbuncle** is a group of contiguous boils. Small boils may heal spontaneously, but most cannot until PUS has escaped, by thinning and rupture of overlying SKIN. This is hastened by local application of heat. In severe cases lancing and ANTIBIOTICS may be required.

BOILEAU (-DESPRÉAUX), Nicolas (1636–1711), French poet, satirist and literary critic. His insistence on classical standards, notably in the didactic poem *L'Art poétique* (1674), greatly influenced literary taste both in France and England in the 18th century.

BOILER, device used to convert WATER into STEAM by the action of HEAT (see also BOILING POINT), usually to drive a STEAM ENGINE. A boiler requires a heat source (i.e., a FURNACE), a surface whereby the heat may be conveyed to the water, and enough space for steam to form. The two main types of boiler are the fire-tube, where the hot gases are passed through tubes surrounded by water; and the water-tube, where the water is passed through tubes surrounded by hot gases. Fuels include COAL, OIL and fuel GAS; NUCLEAR ENERGY is also used. HERO designed boilers, but used them only in toys. Steam power proper was barely considered until the 17th century, and little used before the 18th.

BOILING POINT, the temperature at which the VAPOR PRESSURE of a liquid becomes equal to the external pressure, so that boiling occurs; the temperature at which a liquid and its vapor are at equilibrium. Measurement of boiling point is important in chemical ANALYSIS and the determination of MOLECULAR WEIGHTS. (See also EVAPORATION; PHASE EQUILIBRIUM; PRESSURE COOKER.)

The Idaho state capitol in Boise. The city is situated in an attractive wooded region and has a mild, pleasant climate, making it a popular vacation area.

BOISE, capital city of Ida., founded in 1863. It is a center for wool and agricultural products and manufactures steel, furniture and electrical goods. Pop 74 990.

BOITO, Arrigo (1842–1918), Italian poet and composer. His own operas include *Mefistofele* (1868; revised 1875) and *Nerone* (1918), though he is best known as the librettist of VERDI's *Otello* and *Falstaff* and of PONCHELLI's *La Gioconda*.

BOK, Edward William (1863–1930), US editor, writer and philanthropist. In 1889 he became editor of *The Ladies' Home Journal* and used the magazine to campaign for good causes. In his retirement he wrote the Pulitzer prize-winning *The Americanization of Edward Bok* (1920).

BOKHARA. See BUKHARA.

BOLAS (from the Spanish *boleadoras*), a hunting weapon used by South American Indians. It is made up of one, two or three balls of stone or iron attached by cords to a common center. The bolas is thrown, usually from horseback, so that it winds round the legs of an animal and prevents its escape.

BOLERO, a Spanish national dance for one or two people. The steps are intricate and are performed to a clear rhythm usually marked by castanets. Many composers, such as RAVEL in *Bolero*, employ this rhythm.

BOLETUS, a common MUSHROOM of the class BASIDIOMYCETES. Most species grow in the ground in woodland areas, the fruiting bodies appearing in the autumn. They may be brown, red or yellow in color. Some species are edible (e.g. *Boletus edulis*), while a few are poisonous.

BOLEYN, Anne (c1507–1536), second wife of HENRY VIII and mother of Elizabeth I. When he met her, Henry was already tiring of his first queen, who had failed to produce a son, and he married Anne in 1533 as soon as he was divorced. Their daughter Elizabeth was born later that year, but Anne too bore no living son. She was beheaded, having been convicted, on dubious evidence, of adultery and incest.

BOLGER, Ray (1904–), US comedian, dancer and actor. He appeared on stage in musical comedy, in films and on television. His successes include *On Your Toes* (1936), *The Wizard of Oz* (1939) and *Where's Charley?* (1948).

BOLINGBROKE, Henry of. See HENRY IV (King of England).

BOLINGBROKE, Henry St. John, 1st Viscount (1678–1751), English statesman. A member of the Tory party, as secretary of state he successfully handled the negotiations for the treaty of UTRECHT (1713). He lost office on the death of Queen Anne, and in 1715 was forced to seek exile in France, where he remained for the next 10 years. Out of the mainstream of affairs, Bolingbroke devoted his time to political journalism and the study of history.

BOLÍVAR, Simón (1783–1830), South American soldier, statesman and liberator. Born of a wealthy Venezuelan family, he studied in Europe, where he was influenced by the work of the 18th-century rationalists, particularly by ROUSSEAU. Bolívar returned to South America in 1807, convinced that the Spanish colonies were ready to fight for independence. After two abortive attempts, he successfully liberated Venezuela in 1821. His country united with New Granada and Quito to form the state of Gran Colombia, with Bolívar as president. He went on to liberate Peru (1824) and to form, from Upper Peru, the republic of Bolivia (1825). Bolívar envisaged a united South America, but Peru and Bolivia turned against him in 1826. Venezuela seceded from Gran Colombia in 1829, and in the following year Bolívar resigned as president. He died of tuberculosis.

BOLIVIA, landlocked South American republic, bordered by Brazil to the N and E, Paraguay to the SE, Argentina to the S, and in the W by Peru and Chile. Bolivia has an unhappy history of recurring military coups and, though not lacking in potential, is the poorest country in South America.

Land. There are three main regions: the Oriente lowlands in the E, consisting largely of tropical rainforest and swamps; the Montanas, a central zone of mountains and fertile valleys; and in the W, the Altiplano, a bleak Andean plain of coarse grassland, the home of most of the people. At its northern end, shared with Peru, is Lake Titicaca, South America's largest lake and at 12 500ft the world's highest navigable stretch of water.

People. About 75% of the population is concentrated within Andean Bolivia. The Oriente, in contrast, averages less than 2 persons per sq mi. As much as 70% of the population consists of pure Amerindians.

The Bolivian constitution of 1967 vests executive power in the president, elected for a four-year term by direct popular vote, and his cabinet, and provides for a National Congress, consisting of an elected senate and chamber of deputies.

Economy. Minerals, particularly tin, but also, increasingly, petroleum and natural gas, dominate Bolivia's economy and form more than 90% of her exports. Antimony, lead, tungsten, bismuth and zinc are also important, while there are also large, but as yet unexploited, deposits of iron and manganese. Inadequate transportation has considerably hampered Bolivia's growth. Some 80% of the population still depends on the land for a livelihood. On the Altiplano the main crops are potatoes, barley, quinoa and beans. Sheep, llamas and alpacas are the chief livestock. Corn, wheat, barley, tobacco, dairy cattle and a wide variety of fruits and vegetables are raised in the Montana region.

History. Bolivia, formerly Upper Peru, was freed from Spanish rule by Simón BOLÍVAR. Its subsequent history has been one of repeated upheaval, both internal and external, involving disputes with neighboring Chile, Brazil and Paraguay.

Official Name: The Republic of Bolivia
Capital: La Paz
Area: 424 160sq mi
Population: 5 062 500
Languages: Spanish
Religions: Roman Catholic
Monetary Unit(s): 1 Peso Bolivian = 100 centavos

The peaks of the Bolivian Andes, in the middle of the Nevado Condoriri range, are at least 5 600m above sea level.

BÖLL, Heinrich (1917–), German author and winner of the Nobel Prize for Literature in 1972. His books are bitterly satiric, exploring themes of despair and love in post-WWII Europe. Important among his works are *Billiards at Half Past Nine* (1961) and *The Clown* (1965).

BOLLINGEN PRIZE, a prize of $5000 awarded to US poets by the Yale University Library. The prize was originally given by the Library of Congress and was first awarded, amid great controversy, to Ezra POUND (1969) who, at the time, stood accused of treason during WWII. Other winners have been e. e. CUMMINGS and Robert FROST.

BOLL WEEVIL, *Anthonomus grandis*, the most damaging cotton pest in the US. The beetle, which is 6mm (0.24in) long, lays eggs in cotton buds and fruit and feeds on the bolls and blossoms, causing an estimated loss of $203000000 every year. It first appeared in the US in the 1890s from Middle America. Modern methods of combating it include soil improvement, cleansing its hibernating places and the use of insecticides.

BOLLWORMS, the name once given to a number of cotton pests. The cotton bollworm, also known as the corn ear-worm, is the LARVA of a gelechid MOTH, found in the US mainly near the Mexican border. Bollworms cause millions of dollars worth of damage to cotton crops each year.

BOLOGNA, Italian city 51mi N of Florence at the foot of the Apennines. It is an ancient Etruscan and Roman city, with a university founded c1088, many medieval buildings and some fine Renaissance paintings and sculptures. Capital of the Emilia-Romagna region, it is an agricultural and industrial center, producing farm machinery and chemicals. Pop 502421.

BOLOMETER, an instrument used to measure radiant ENERGY, usually in the infrared and microwave regions of the spectrum of ELECTROMAGNETIC RADIATION. It comprises a lens or stop system which focuses the test radiation on a thermoconductive device (usually a THERMISTOR), which is set in a WHEATSTONE BRIDGE circuit with another nonilluminated reference thermistor. Sensitive bolometers are used in conjunction with spectroscopes to measure the intensities of spectral lines (see SPECTROSCOPY).

BOLSHEVISM, name given to the policy of the majority group (Russian *bolsheviki*) at the 1903 congress of the Russian Social Democratic Workers' party, as opposed to the minority or *mensheviki*. The bolsheviks, under the leadership of LENIN, formed a radical left-wing group in 1917 and took over the leadership of the Russian Revolution. Their doctrines derived from the work of MARX and ENGELS and upheld a revolution led by workers and peasants. (See COMMUNISM.)

BOLSHOI THEATER, Russian theater, ballet and opera house. The Bolshoi, which possesses one of the largest stages in the world, is the home of the famous ballet school. Its classical ballet and opera productions have a worldwide reputation.

BOLTON, industrial city in Lancashire, N England, noted for its textiles. Iron, chemicals and paper are also important products. Pop 153977.

BOLTS AND SCREWS, devices in which the principle of the screw thread, which may be traced back as far as ARCHIMEDES, is applied to the fastening together of objects. A screw is essentially conical, with a sharp point and widening toward the head—which is usually shaped to take a screwdriver—with a helical ridge (see CONE; HELIX). If the point is pressed into the material (usually wood) and the screw longitudinally rotated by means of a screwdriver, the screw will be driven into the wood and will be held in place by FRICTION. A bolt is essentially cylindrical, again with a helical ridge (see CYLINDER), and has a broad head usually shaped to take a spanner or wrench. It is used in conjunction with a nut, a member containing a prethreaded hole into which the bolt fits. The objects to be fastened are held together by the pressure of the bolthead on one side, the nut on the other. The distance between consecutive turns of a screw thread is termed the **pitch** of the thread.

BOLTZMANN, Ludwig (1844–1906), Austrian physicist who made fundamental contributions to THERMODYNAMICS, classical statistical mechanics and KINETIC THEORY. The **Boltzmann constant** (k), the quotient of the universal gas constant R and the AVOGADRO number ($\mathcal{N}$), is used in statistical mechanics.

BOLYAI FARKAS (1775–1856), Hungarian mathematician who expended much effort in trying to prove the Euclidean parallel lines postulate. His son, **Bolyai János** (1802–1860), renowned as a duelist and violinist, was a codiscoverer of NON-EUCLIDEAN GEOMETRY, having worked out his theory before 1823, thus preceding Lobachevski.

BOLZANO, city in N Italy, 58mi S of the Brenner Pass. Part of the Tyrol until 1918, much of the city is bilingual. It is the center of a fruit and wine region, and its proximity to the pass encourages commerce and tourism. Its industries include steel and textiles. Pop 103479.

BOMB, device designed to explode, with the aim of destroying property or killing and maiming human beings. A bomb may be dropped from an aircraft, incorporated in a warhead, or "planted" in position. Essential to all bombs is a fuze (see AMMUNITION), in effect a miniature bomb whose explosion precipitates the explosion of the bomb proper. In particular, fuzes of **timebombs** incorporate devices such that the fuze, and hence the bomb, may be set to explode after a determined elapse of time. Types of conventional bombs include **fragmentation bombs**, with cases designed to disintegrate into shrapnel; **fire bombs** and **incendiary bombs**, whose purpose is to destroy by fire (see NAPALM); **gas bombs**, whose explosion distributes poisonous gas (see CHEMICAL AND BIOLOGICAL WARFARE); **smoke bombs**, which create a smokescreen; and **photoflash bombs**, used in night photography. Underwater bombs, designed to explode at a specific depth, are usually termed **depth charges**. (See also ATOMIC BOMB; EXPLOSIVES; HYDROGEN BOMB; GRENADE.)

BOMBAY, large seaport in W India and capital of Maharashtra State. Bombay was built on several small islands, now joined to each other and to the mainland, forming an area of 25sq mi. Its large harbor deals with the bulk of India's imports, notably wheat and machinery, and many exports such as cotton, rice and manganese. Local industries include textiles, leather goods and printing. Bombay is an important cultural center, with a university founded in 1857. The city is overcrowded, with a fast growing, mainly Hindu, population. Pop 5700358.

BOMBER, aircraft used to carry and drop bombs. Early in WWI bombs were simply dropped over the side of an airplane. Later bombsights, dropping devices and heavy planes capable of carrying great loads were developed; these were hard to maneuver under attack. Modern NUCLEAR WEAPONS are smaller and lighter than conventional bombs and the modern jet-powered bomber is light and fast, with a range greatly increased by midair refueling techniques.

BONAIRE, island in the Netherlands Antilles, off the coast of Venezuela and 30mi E of Curaçao. The island has an important petroleum industry. Pop 8099.

BOND, Chemical, the links which hold ATOMS together in compounds. In the 19th century it was found that many substances, known as **covalent compounds**, could be represented by structural FORMULAS in which lines represented bonds. By using double and triple bonds, most organic compounds could be formulated with constant VALENCES of the constituent atoms. STEREOISOMERISM showed that the bonds must be localized in fixed directions in space. **Electrovalent compounds** (see ELECTROCHEMISTRY) consist of oppositely charged IONS arranged in a lattice; here the bonds are nondirectional electrostatic interactions. The theory that atoms consists of electrons orbiting in shells around the nucleus (see PERIODIC TABLE) led to a simple explanation of both kinds of bonding: atoms combine to achieve highly-stable filled outer shells containing 2, 8 or 18 electrons, either by transfer of electrons from one atom to the other **(ionic bond)**, or by the sharing of one electron from each atom so that both electrons orbit around both nuclei **(covalent bond)**. In the **coordinate bond**, a variant of the covalent bond, both shared electrons are provided by one atom. QUANTUM THEORY has now shown that electrons occupy ORBITALS having certain shapes and energies, and that, when atoms combine, the outer atomic orbitals are mixed to form molecular orbitals. The energy difference constitutes the bond energy—the energy required to break the bond by separating the atoms. Molecular orbitals are classified as σ if symmetric when rotated through 180° about the line joining the nuclei, or π if antisymmetric. The energy and length of chemical bonds, and the angles between them, may be investigated by SPECTROSCOPY and X-RAY DIFFRACTION. (See also HYDROGEN BONDING.)

A Japanese black pine (*Pinus thunbergii*) that has undergone bonsai treatment. In its natural habitat this species grows at the rate of about 0.75m (2.5ft) each year, but this miniature specimen has yet to achieve this height even after 85 years of loving care and attention.

BOND, William Cranch (1789–1859), US astronomer, first director of the Harvard Observatory and a pioneer of ASTROPHOTOGRAPHY. In 1850 he made the first DAGUERREOTYPE of a celestial object and discovered the third, "crape," ring of SATURN.

BONDERIZING, chemical process to help prevent CORROSION of iron, steel and other metals. The surface is sprayed with or immersed in a hot PHOSPHATE solution, and a superficial insoluble phosphate layer is formed. The metal is then usually painted or lacquered.

BONDI, Sir Hermann (1919–), Austrian-born British cosmologist who with T. GOLD in 1948 formulated the steady-state theory (see COSMOLOGY).

BONDING, undertaking by bond to make good a third party's debt or potential liability if the third party fails to do so. Fidelity bonding, for example, protects the employer's interests with respect to his employees. In a contract, a surety bond may be required to protect against loss incurred by one party defaulting.

BONE, the hard tissue that forms the SKELETON of vertebrates. Bones support the body, protect its organs, act as anchors for MUSCLES and as levers for the movement of limbs, and are the main reserve of calcium and phosphate in the body. Bone consists of living cells (osteocytes) embedded in a matrix of COLLAGEN fibers with calcium salts similar in composition to hydroxyapatite (see APATITE) deposited between them. Some carbonates are also present. All bones have a shell of compact bone in concentric layers (lamellae) around the blood vessels, which run in small channels (Haversian canals). Within this shell is porous or spongy bone, and in the case of "long" bones (see below) there is a hollow cavity containing MARROW. The bone is enveloped by a fibrous membrane, the periosteum, which is sensitive to pain, unlike the bone itself, and which has a network of nerves and blood vessels which penetrate the bone surface. After primary growth has ended, bone formation (ossification) occurs where the periosteum joins the bone, where there are many bone-forming cells (osteoblasts). Ossification begins in the embryo at the end of the second month, mostly by transformation of CARTILAGE: some cartilage cells become osteoblasts and secrete collagen and a hormone which causes calcium salts to be deposited. Vitamin D makes calcium available from the food to the blood, and its deficiency leads to RICKETS. The two ends of a "long" bone (the epiphyses) ossify separately from the shaft, and are attached to it by cartilaginous plates, at which lengthwise growth takes place. Radical growth is controlled by the periosteum, and at the same time the core of the bone is eroded by osteoclast cells to make it hollow. Primary growth is stimulated by the PITUITARY and SEX HORMONES; it is completed in adolescence, when the epiphyses fuse to the shaft. Bones are classified anatomically as "long," cylindrical and usually hollow, with a knob at each end; "short," spongy blocks with a thin shell; and "flat" two parallel layers of compact bone with a spongy layer in between. Some hand and foot bones are short; the ribs, sternum, skull and shoulder-blades are flat; and most other bones are long. The shape and structure of bones are quickly modified if the forces on them alter. Disorders of bone include OSTEOMYELITIS and various TUMORS and CANCER. Dead bone is not readily absorbed and can be a focus of infection. In old age thinning and weakening of the bones by loss of calcium (osteoporosis) is common.

BÔNE. See ANNABA.

BONE CHINA, fine PORCELAIN first introduced c1800 (see SPODE). It is made of china clay mixed with bone-ash and china stone, and is similar to hard porcelain but more workable and less easily chipped.

BONE FISH, herring-like fish with unusual ribbon larvae and a large number of fine bones. A popular game fish, one species is found in all warm seas, the other only in the West Indies and off Mexico.

BONE MEAL, ground BONE used as fertilizer, providing essential nitrogen, phosphorus and calcium. Sterilized, it is used as an animal feed.

BONESET, *Eupatorium perfoliatum*, a perennial herb, 0.6–1.8m (2–6ft) high, with white tubular flowers borne in clusters and lanceolate, toothed and wrinkled leaves. It is native to wet areas of North America, where it is also known as agueweed or Indian sage.

BONGO, *Boocerus euryceros*, a large chestnut-colored ANTELOPE with vertical white stripes and spiraled horns, a member of the mammalian family Bovidae. They roam in herds in the dense riverside areas of W and Central Africa, feeding at night on herbs and young shoots.

BONHEUR, Rosa (1822–1899), French artist famous for her animal paintings. She made her reputation with *The Horse Fair* (1853), a scene full of vigor and grace, representative of her most accomplished work.

BONHOEFFER, Dietrich (1906–1945), German Lutheran pastor and theologian. He was the author of many radical books on ecumenism and Christianity in a secular world. A prominent anti-Nazi, he was arrested in 1943 and executed at Flossenbürg concentration camp two years later.

BONHOMME RICHARD, French vessel commanded by the American naval hero, John Paul JONES. Sailing off the English coast on the evening of Sept. 25, 1779, the *Bonhomme Richard* engaged the British frigate *Serapis* in one of the classic single-ship actions. After prolonged fighting, the English surrendered; their vessel was boarded and the badly holed *Bonhomme Richard* left to sink.

BONIFACE, Saint (c672–754), English missionary, the apostle of Germany. Backed by CHARLES MARTEL and later by PEPIN THE SHORT, he organized the German Church, reformed the Frankish clergy and advanced the conversion of the Saxons. He was martyred by the Frisians.

BONIFACE, name of nine popes. **Saint Boniface I** (d. 422), pope 418–22. He is remembered as a foe of PELAGIANISM. **Boniface II** (d. 532), pope 530–32. A Goth by descent, he was nominated by his predecessor, FELIX IV, and, in turn, tried to nominate his own successor, but the clergy of Rome forced him to abandon the idea. **Boniface III** (d. 607) was pope from Feb. to Nov. 607. **Saint Boniface IV** (d. 615), pope 608–15. He resolved a dispute between the newly-founded Anglo-Saxon Church and the Irish St. Columban. **Boniface V** (d. 625), pope 619–25. He did much to help establish Christianity in England, particularly in Northumbria. **Boniface VI** (d. 896) was pope for 15 days in April 896. **Boniface VII** (d. 985), pope June–July 974 and 984–85. He was substituted by the Roman barons for the assassinated BENEDICT VI. Ejected by Emperor Otto II he fled to Constantinople, but returned on Otto's death, imprisoned Pope JOHN XV and reinstated himself. **Boniface VIII** (c1235–1303), pope 1294–1303. He steadfastly asserted papal authority over the political leaders of Europe and involved the papacy in a series of conflicts with leading powers. His bull "Unam Sanctam," which called for the subjugation of temporal to spiritual authority, led to a clash with Philip IV of France. In 1303 the king's emissaries attacked Benedict in his palace at Anagni, where he was about to excommunicate Philip; the populace intervened, but Boniface collapsed and died three weeks later in Rome. **Boniface IX** (1355–1404), pope 1389–1404, during the GREAT SCHISM. He restored papal authority in Rome and in the major part of the papal states.

BONINGTON, Richard Parkes (1801–1828), English artist noted for his watercolor landscapes and GENRE subjects. He spent most of his brief career in France; among those he influenced there were DELACROIX and COROT.

BONIN ISLANDS, group of volcanic islands about 500mi SE of Japan. In all there are 27 islands with some 200 inhabitants. They were administered by the US 1945–68, when they were returned to Japan.

BONITO, three species of fish of the family Scombridae, resembling the blue-fin TUNA. Rarely more than 750mm (30in) long, they weigh about 3kg (6.6lb) and are a valuable food source. The Striped bonito is found in warmer oceanic waters, the other two species in the Atlantic and Pacific.

BONN, capital of West Germany since the partition of the country after WWII (1949). This historic city is situated on the Rhine, in North Rhine-Westphalia. The birthplace of Beethoven, it has a museum and hall devoted to the composer. Much of the city has been rebuilt since WWII. It is now West Germany's administrative center and has attracted many modern industries. Pop 274 518.

BONNARD, Pierre (1867–1947), French artist and leader of the *Intimiste* school. His works are characterized by the use of bright colors and simplified forms. He painted mostly interiors with nudes, and landscapes. While at the Académie Julian he met Maurice Denis and Jean VUILLARD, with whom he formed the group known as the NABIS.

The bongo antelope, with its unmistakable spiralling horns and white vertical stripes.

BONNEVILLE, Benjamin Louis Eulalie de (1796–1878), French–American soldier and frontiersman. He explored the far west (1832–35) and distinguished himself in the Mexican War (1846–48). But he is remembered largely because of Washington IRVING's romanticized biography, *The Adventures of Captain Bonneville, U.S.A.* (1837).

BONNEVILLE DAM, large hydroelectric dam spanning the Columbia R in NW Ore., about 40mi E of Portland. It is 170ft high and 1 250ft wide and was built 1933–43 as part of the New Deal program.

BONNEVILLE FLATS, an extremely level stretch of arid salt desert W of the Great Salt Lake in Ut. It is a favorite location for land speed trials and one where many world records have been established.

BONNEY, William. See BILLY THE KID.

BONNIE PRINCE CHARLIE. See CHARLES, EDWARD STUART.

BONSAI, the ancient oriental art of growing trees in dwarf form. The modern enthusiast may spend three years cultivating the "miniature" trees, mainly by root pruning and shoot trimming. Plants that can be "dwarfed" include the cedars, myrtles, junipers, oaks, cypresses, pyracanthas and pines. Bonsai has spread worldwide, and is a fast-growing hobby in North America, where there are many "bonsai" clubs.

BONUS MARCH, a demonstration, in 1932, in Washington, D.C. by some 15 000 jobless veterans of WWI. They hoped to persuade Congress to enable them to cash bonus certificates issued in 1924 in recognition of their war service. President Hoover worsened his reputation by ordering the military to drive the "Bonus Army" from the city. In 1936 Congress finally passed a law, against a presidential veto, allowing the exchange of the certificates.

BOOBIES, large fish-eating birds (of the family Sulidae), so named because they are not afraid of man and are easily captured. They live mainly by tropical and subtropical waters and are excellent fliers. They have long wings, long, wedge-shaped tails, straight, sharp bills and short legs.

BOOKBINDING, the craft of joining up leaves or folios into a volume with a protective cover. It began, as we know it, after rolls of PAPYRUS gave way to sheets of PARCHMENT as the commonly used writing material. Leather bindings, often richly tooled, were used for many centuries but are now reserved for special editions. Today the entire process, from folding the paper into sections to fitting the cover or case, can be mechanized. Cover materials include cloth, heavy paper, molded plastic paper and imitation leather.

BOOKKEEPING, the systematic recording of financial transactions. The single-entry system consists of a single account which shows the debts owed to and by the firm in question. The double-entry system is more detailed; the debit and credit items are entered in a journal; they are then classified in a ledger. From this information a comprehensive balance sheet can be drawn up. The monthly system was developed to meet the needs of a complex commercial society. There are a number of separate daybooks and the monthly totals are posted to the ledger accounts. ACCOUNTING differs in that it also includes the analysis of financial data.

BOOK LOUSE, a minute winged or wingless insect attracted to the paste used in bookbinding. It has chisel-like mandibles which can gnaw through leather bindings and riddle the leaves with small holes.

BOOK OF COMMON PRAYER, the official LITURGY of the CHURCH OF ENGLAND, including (among others) the services of Morning and Evening Prayer and Holy COMMUNION, and the Psalter, Gospels and Epistles. The first Prayer Book was written by CRANMER (1549); a more reformed version (see ANGLICANISM; REFORMATION) was published in 1552 and, with minor revisions, 1559 and 1662. The 1662 Prayer Book has been used ever since, and has been a major formative influence on the English language. Since 1966, various modern experimental services have also legally been in use.

BOOK OF HOURS, books of prayers to be said at the canonical hours, widely used by laymen during the late Middle Ages. These were often masterpieces of the miniaturist's art; among the most famous are the Rohan and the de Berry Hours.

BOOK OF KELLS, a copy of the Gospels from the late 8th century, completed by the monks of Kells in County Meath, Ireland. Its richly elaborate decoration makes it one of the finest examples of medieval illuminated manuscripts. It is now in the library of Trinity College, Dublin.

BOOK OF MORMON. See MORMONS.

BOOK OF THE DEAD, collections of prayers and incantations entombed with the dead in ancient Egypt: they were intended to assist the spirit in the after-life. Written on papyrus in simplified HIEROGLYPHICS, often with supplementary illustration, the books vary greatly in length and content.

BOOLE, George (1815–1864), British mathematician and logician, chiefly remembered for devising **Boolean algebra**, which allowed mathematical methods to be applied to nonquantifiable entities such as logical propositions. In the 20th century Boolean algebra has become important in the design of telecommunications systems and electronic logic circuits, and hence in COMPUTER technology. An example of a Boolean algebra is the algebra of sets (see SET THEORY). (See also LOGIC.)

BOOMERANG, Australian aboriginal term for a curved or angled throwing stick used in hunting and in warfare. The famous returning boomerang serves no practical purpose and is used for sporting purposes.

BOOMSLANG, *Dispholidus typus*, large green to brown treesnake of Southern Africa with venomous fangs at the back of the upper jaw. The most venomous of back-fanged snakes, it feeds on small animals.

BOONE, a city in Ia., seat of Boone Co. Rich in coal and clay, it is an important industrial center surrounded by fertile farmland. Pop 12468.

BOONE, Daniel (1734–1820), American pioneer and hunter. In 1767 he made his first trip into what is now Ky. and built a fort there, called Boonesboro. In 1778 he was captured by the Shawnee, who were allied with the British against the American revolutionaries. Boone escaped to warn settlers at Boonesboro of a planned attack, which they successfully resisted. Traditionally, he is hailed as the founder of Ky., which he was not, and more justly as a great frontiersman.

Page 29 recto from the Book of Kells, the introduction to Matthew 1.1.

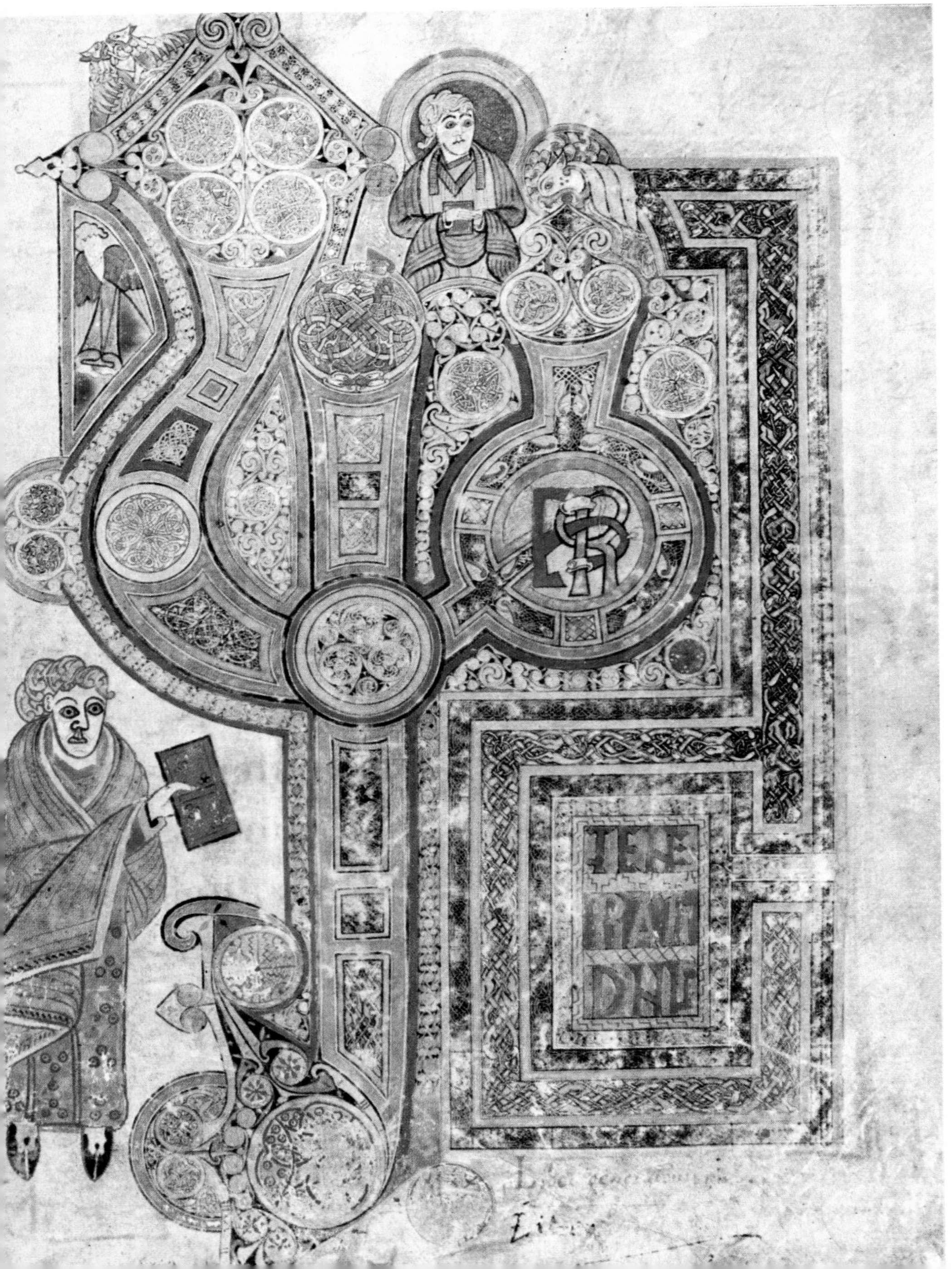

BOÖTES (the Herdsman), a constellation of the N Hemisphere, containing the star ARCTURUS.

BOOTH, an English family, founders and leaders of the SALVATION ARMY. **William Booth** (1829–1912) started his career as a Methodist minister, but left the church in 1861 to work among the poor in the slums of London. In 1878 he founded the Salvation Army, assisted by his wife **Catherine Booth** (1829–1890), a noted orator who did valuable work for women's rights. **William Bramwell Booth** (1856–1929), the eldest son of William Booth, served as second general of the Salvation Army. **Ballington Booth** (1859–1940), second son, brought the Salvation Army to the US in 1887. With his wife Maud, he instituted the VOLUNTEERS OF AMERICA, a similar organization. **Catherine Booth-Clibborn** (1859–1905), the eldest daughter of William Booth, founded the Salvation Army in France and Switzerland. **Emma Moss Booth-Tucker** (1860–1903) helped to establish the Salvation Army in India in 1881. **Herbert Henry Booth** (1862–1926), the youngest son of William Booth, founded the Salvation Army in Australia and New Zealand. **Evangeline Cory Booth** (1865–1950), daughter of William Booth, was the Salvation Army's first woman general, with international command of the organization (1934–39). She also commanded the US Salvation Army (1904–34) and wrote popular evangelical songs.

BOOTH, Charles (1840–1916), British merchant and sociologist, who applied statistical research methods to sociology. The 17-volume *Life and Labour of the People in London* (1903) is his major work. A member of the royal commission on the poor law (1905–09), Booth also wrote *Poor Law Reform* (1910).

BOOTH, Edwin Thomas (1833–1892), US actor, famous on both the New York and London stages. His Shakespearean roles, particularly Hamlet, were considered theatrical landmarks. The son of Junius Brutus BOOTH, he was the brother of Lincoln's assassin, John Wilkes BOOTH.

BOOTH, John Wilkes (1838–1865), US actor who assassinated Abraham Lincoln, a son of the actor Junius Brutus BOOTH. He was a Confederate sympathizer; eager to avenge the South's defeat, he shot President Lincoln during a performance at Ford's Theater, Washington, D.C., on April 14th, 1865. Booth, breaking a leg, escaped but was finally trapped in a barn near Bowling Green, Va., where he was either shot or shot himself.

BOOTH, Junius Brutus (1796–1852), English-born actor, founder of a famous American family of actors. Emigrating to the US in 1821, he achieved great success, particularly in Shakespeare. He was the father of Edwin and John Wilkes BOOTH.

BOOTHIA PENINSULA, the extreme N tip of Canada, in the Northwest Territories. Named for Sir Felix Booth, who financed exploration by Sir John ROSS, it is about 170mi long. The N magnetic pole was first located on its west coast (1831).

BOOTLEGGING. See PROHIBITION.

BOP, or Bebop, seminal style of modern JAZZ, named for its basic rhythmic feature. Inspired by musicians like Dizzy GILLESPIE and Charlie PARKER, Bop emerged in the 1940s to break with the Blues tradition and explore new harmonic and rhythmic fields. It added greater sophistication and complexity to jazz, deepening and reinvigorating it.

BORAGE, *Borago officinalis*, hardy annual culinary herb, native to the E Mediterranean region, but naturalized in many parts of Europe and North America. It is used in salads and in drinks, to which it gives a cucumber-like flavor.

BORAH, William Edgar (1865–1940), Republican senator from Ida. 1907–40, a vigorous and independent champion of progressive reforms. He opposed US membership of the League of Nations and was a prominent isolationist on the eve of WWII, but was also a farsighted chairman of the Senate Foreign Relations Committee (1924–33).

BORANES, covalent HYDRIDES of boron, of unusual molecular structure: they have hydrogen-bridge bonding, and the boron atoms form the vertices of polyhedra. Boranes are volatile, reactive and often flammable in air. They may be used as high-energy fuels for rockets and jet planes.

BORAX, mineral name for sodium tetraborate, $Na_2B_4O_7.10H_2O$, found mainly in Cal. (For sodium borates see SODIUM; KERNITE.)

BORAZON, cubic form of boron nitride (BN), resembling DIAMOND in structure and properties. It is made by heating hexagonal boron nitride (a white powder resembling GRAPHITE) to 1500°C at 65 000atm pressure. Borazon is as hard as diamond, and more useful industrially because it is more resistant to oxidation and heat.

BORCHERT, Wolfgang (1921–1947), German poet, playwright and short-story teller. His works, written in a uniquely vivid poetic style, reflect German despair just after WWII. His best-known work is the play *The Man Outside* (1947).

BORCHGREVINK, Carsten Egeberg (1864–1934), Norwegian naturalist and Antarctic explorer. In 1895 he was among the first group to land on Antarctica, and in 1899 his (British) expedition was the first to winter there.

BORDEAUX, city in SW France and capital of Gironde department, on the Garonne R. It is France's third-largest port and chief center for the French wine trade. Bordeaux also has canning and shipbuilding industries. The city dates from Roman times. Pop 270 996.

BORDEAUX MIXTURE, FUNGICIDE made from COPPER sulfate, CALCIUM hydroxide and water. It was once widely used on crops, but has generally been replaced by fungicides less harmful to fruit and foliage.

BORDEN, Gail (1801–1874), US inventor of the first process for making condensed milk by evaporation. He also influenced the development of Tex.: he helped to write its first state constitution, prepared the first topographical map of Tex. and laid out the city of Houston.

BORDEN, Lizzie Andrew (1860–1927), US woman accused of murdering her father and stepmother with an ax on Aug. 4, 1892. She was acquitted but remained popularly condemned. The murder became part of American folklore.

BORDEN, Sir Robert Laird (1854–1937), Canadian prime minister (1911–20) who gave his country a new and more independent voice in world affairs. Borden became Conservative leader in 1901. He was a vigorous WWI prime minister, forming a Union party government with pro-conscription Liberals in 1917, and securing separate representation for Canada at the peace conference and in the League of Nations.

BORDER STATES, slave states along the border between the Deep South and the North, marked by their divided sympathies in the Civil War. Va. (except the future W.Va.) seceded. But though Ky., Md. and Mo. provided the Confederacy with some soldiers, like loyal Del., their governments remained faithful to the Union cause.

BORDER TERRIER, courageous working dog from the borders of England and Scotland which can run with horses and dig a fox or badger out of its earth. Its harsh, weatherproof coat should be red, wheaten, grizzle and tan or blue and tan, height about 12in and weight 13–15½lb.

BORDER WAR (1854–59), conflict on the Kan.–Mo. border in the area known as "Bleeding Kansas." After the KANSAS–NEBRASKA ACT, proslavery "Border Ruffians" from Mo. infiltrated Kan. and, by fraud and intimidation in the 1855 elections, made Kan. a slave state, beginning four years of skirmishing, murder and pillage by opposing proslavery and antislavery Free-State bands. Violence was intensified by the proslavery attack on Lawrence, Kan., and John BROWN's antislavery raid on Pottawatomie in 1856.

BORDET, Jules Jean-Baptiste Vincent (1870–1961), Belgian bacteriologist and immunologist awarded the 1919 Nobel Prize for Physiology or Medicine for his discovery of the substances later named "complement" and the process of complement fixation (see ANTIBODIES AND ANTIGENS). He also discovered the BACILLUS responsible for WHOOPING-COUGH.

BORE, or **eagre**, tidal phenomenon of rivers that widen gradually toward broad mouths, and that are subject to high TIDES. During spring flood, larger quantities of water from the sea than can normally flow upriver are driven into the rivermouth, resulting in a high wave that travels upriver at great speed. Perhaps the best-known bores are those of the Ganges, the Severn and the Bay of FUNDY.

BOREAS, the north wind as personified in Greek mythology. The god reputedly lived in Thrace, and saved Athens by wrecking the fleet of Xerxes of Persia.

BORELLI, Giovanni Alfonso (1608–1679), Italian astronomer, physicist and physiologist, the founder of iatrophysics. After making contributions to astronomy, including the proposal that COMETS travel along elliptical paths, he turned his attention to the working of the living body and successfully explained MUSCLE action on mechanical principles.

BORGER, city in NW Tex., with a petroleum industry based on nearby oil and gas fields. It is the home of Frank Phillips College. Pop 20 911.

BORGES, Jorge Luis (1899–   ), Argentinian poet and prose writer. At first influenced by the metaphorical style of Spanish *Ultráismo*, he later developed a unique form between short story and essay, the "fiction." Some of the best examples are in his *Ficciones* (1944) and *El Aleph* (1949).

BORGHESE, aristocratic Roman family, originally from Siena. Camillo Borghese (1552–1621) became Pope PAUL V. The many Borghese cardinals included the noted art collector, **Scipione Borghese** (1576–1633), patron of Giovanni Lorenzo BERNINI. He commissioned the Borghese Palace and Villa Borghese, two of Rome's finest Baroque buildings. **Prince Camillo Filippo Ludovico Borghese** (1775–1832) married Napoleon's sister Marie Pauline and became duke of Guastalla. Borghese family power declined with falling land values in the 1890s.

BORGIA, powerful Italian family descended from the Borjas of Valencia in Spain. **Alfonso de Borja** (1378–1458) became Pope CALIXTUS III. By bribery, his nephew **Rodrigo Borgia** (1431–1503) became Pope ALEXANDER VI in 1492 and worked to enrich his family by crushing the Italian princes. His son, **Cesare Borgia** (c1476–1507), used war, duplicity and murder to seize much of central Italy. Alexander's notorious daughter, **Lucrezia Borgia** (1480–1519), was probably a pawn in her family's schemes. As duchess of Ferrara (from 1501), she generously patronized the arts and learning.

BORGLUM, Gutzon (1867–1941), US sculptor best remembered for Mt Rushmore N.D. National Memorial, with its enormous portrait heads of Washington, Jefferson, Lincoln and Theodore Roosevelt. After Borglum's death the project was completed by his son. (See RUSHMORE, MOUNT.)

BORGNE, Lake, inlet of the Gulf of Mexico, forming the E boundary of New Orleans. It links the Gulf with Lake Ponchartrain through the Rigolets channel. On Dec. 14, 1814, as a prelude to the Battle of New Orleans, the British navy suffered heavy losses defeating the Americans here.

BORIC ACID (H_3BO_3), or boracic acid, colorless crystalline solid, a weak inorganic acid. It gives boric oxide (B_2O_3) when strongly heated; SODIUM borate typifies its salts. Boric acid is used as an external antiseptic, in the production of glass and as a welding flux.

BORIS III (1894–1943), king of Bulgaria 1918–43. During a reign fraught with political upheavals, he strengthened the monarchy, assuming dictatorial powers in 1935. Taking sides with Germany in WWII, he died under mysterious circumstances.

BORIS GODUNOV. See GODUNOV, BORIS FEDOROVICH.

BORLAUG, Norman Ernest (1914–   ), US agricultural scientist who was awarded the 1970 Nobel Peace Prize for his part in the development of improved varieties of CEREAL CROPS, important in the GREEN REVOLUTION.

The temples at Borobudur were built around 800 AD when the Buddhist Saliendra dynasty ruled the island of Jawa, Indonesia. They contain over three miles of stone carvings of Buddhist legends.

BORMAN, Frank (1928–   ), US astronaut. In 1965 he commanded *Gemini 7*, whose 14 days in earth orbit set a new endurance record. In 1968 he led James LOVELL and William ANDERS in the *Apollo 8* flight, the first manned voyage around the moon. Borman retired from NASA in 1970.

BORMANN, Martin Ludwig (1900–1945?), German Nazi politician who wielded brutal power as Hitler's deputy from 1941. Though he vanished in 1945, he was sentenced to death for war crimes at the NUREMBERG TRIALS in 1946. It is now thought he was probably killed as Berlin fell.

BORN, Max (1872–1970), German theoretical physicist active in the development of quantum physics, whose particular contribution was the probabilistic interpretation of the SCHRÖDINGER wave equation, thus providing a link between WAVE MECHANICS and the QUANTUM THEORY. Sharing the Nobel physics prize with BOTHE in 1954, he devoted his later years to the philosophy of physics.

BORNEO, largest island of the Malay Archipelago and third largest in the world (290 320sq mi). It contains the Indonesian provinces of Central, E, W, and S KALIMANTAN, with the sultanate of BRUNEI and the Malaysian states of SABAH and SARAWAK to the N and NW. Borneo is a mountainous equatorial island largely clad in tropical rain forest, and drained by several major rivers. Its highest point is Mt Kinabalu (13 455ft). Its peoples include Dayak, Malays, Arabs and Chinese. Products include copra, rubber, rice, timber, oil, bauxite and coal. The Portuguese reached Borneo in the 1500s, followed by the Dutch and the British, who had most influence in the 19th century.

BORNHOLM, Danish island (227sq mi) in the Baltic Sea 95mi ESE of Copenhagen. Bornholm is a vacation resort and exports fish, granite and kaolin.

BORNITE, reddish-brown SULFIDE mineral of iron and copper (Cu_5FeS_4); a COPPER ore, called "peacock ore" because of its tarnish when fractured. Its occurrence is widespread, especially in Chile, Peru and Tasmania. It alters to CHALCOCITE.

BORNU, a province of NE Nigeria, W of Lake Chad. From about the 13th century it was part of the powerful Muslim empire of Kanem-Bornu. The center of power shifted to Bornu, where the empire reached its height c1600. Bornu became part of the British protectorate of Northern Nigeria in 1902.

BOROBUDUR, Jawanese temple of c800 AD, one of the world's greatest Buddhist monuments. It is a stone pyramid capping a low hill near Jogjakarta, Indonesia, with 2mi of carved terraces crowned by a huge pinnacled dome or stupa.

BORODIN, Alexander Porfirevich (1833–1887), Russian composer and chemist, one of the group known as the FIVE. Though music came second to his

Bosch's *Temptation of St. Anthony* (c. 1490). Unlike many other treatments of this subject the saint is not shown assailed by conventional demons; his temptations are depicted in Bosch's characteristic hallucinatory symbolism, to which St. Anthony's stoical calm is well contrasted.

scientific work in St. Petersburg, he wrote some notable works, including the opera *Prince Igor* (1869–87) and three symphonies.

BORODINO, Russian village 70mi WSW of Moscow, where Napoleon gained a Pyrrhic victory over General KUTUZOV's Russian forces on Sept. 7, 1812.

BORON (B), nonmetallic element in Group IIIA of the PERIODIC TABLE, occurring as KERNITE and BORAX in Cal. and Turkey. Boron has three black crystalline allotropes and an amorphous form, and is best prepared by reduction of the halides with hydrogen. Normally inert, it becomes reactive at high temperatures; it is trivalent. Boron is a trace element vital to plant growth; it is used to produce heat-resistant alloy steels, and boron fibers are used as a high-strength construction material. Boron-steel rods absorb neutrons in nuclear reactors. The borates are salts of BORIC ACID; the SODIUM salts are the most important. AW 10.8, mp 2 300°C, bp 2 550°C, sg 2.34 (See also BORANES; BORAZON.)

BOROUGH, a unit of local government originating with medieval English towns which had been granted autonomy. In the US today a borough can be an administrative division of a big city, an incorporated town (in several E states), or the equivalent of a county (in Alaska).

BORROMEO, Saint Charles (1538–1584), Italian Roman Catholic religious reformer. As secretary of state to Pope Pius IV he influenced the Council of TRENT. As archbishop of Milan he developed popular children's "Sunday Schools" and priests' seminaries, and set a high personal standard of clerical selflessness.

BORROMINI, Francesco (1599–1667), major Italian Baroque architect, renowned for his dramatic use of space and light. Among his best-known works are the Roman churches of Sant'Ivo alla Sapienza and San Carlo alle Quattro Fontane.

BORROW, George Henry (1803–1881), English writer, linguist and traveler. In books like *The Bible in Spain* (1843) and *Lavengro* (1851) he romanticized his travels in Britain and Europe, and gave lively accounts of gypsies and other colorful people.

BORZOI, or Russian wolfhound, breed of tall, lean, longhaired dogs developed in Russia for hunting wolves. Borzois may be white or dark, with black, gray or tan spots. Similar to greyhounds and are swift runners.

BOSCH, Hieronymous (c1450–1516), Dutch painter, from 's Hertogenbosch in North Brabant, whose work is unique in its grotesque fantasy. In paintings such as *Haywain* and *Garden of Delights* he uses an array of part-human, part-animal, part-vegetable figures to express an obscure, obsessive symbolism stressing the forces of evil.

BOSCH, Juan (1909–), Dominican writer and political leader. He founded the *Las Cuevas* literary group and, in exile (1937–61), the Dominican Revolutionary Party. He was elected president of the Dominican Republic in 1963, but was deposed the same year.

BOSCH, Karl (1874–1940), German industrial chemist who adapted the HABER PROCESS for AMMONIA manufacture for large-scale industrial use. In 1931 he shared the Nobel chemistry prize with F. BERGIUS for their work on high-pressure synthesis.

BOSCO, Saint John (1815–1888), Italian priest, a pioneer in education for the poor. In Turin he founded a school for poor boys and the now international Salesian Order. Later he cofounded a society of nuns to help poor girls.

BOSE, Sir Jagadis Chandra (1858–1937), Indian biologist who devised and used sensitive instruments for measuring the growth and response to stimuli of plants.

BOSE-EINSTEIN STATISTICS, in QUANTUM MECHANICS, the statistical behavior of a system of indistinguishable particles with a number of discrete states, each of which may be occupied at any one time by any number of particles. SUBATOMIC PARTICLES that show this behavior are termed bosons. (See also FERMI-DIRAC STATISTICS.)

BOSNIA AND HERZEGOVINA, a constituent republic of Yugoslavia. Most of its 19 741sq mi are mountainous, with barren limestone in the SW (the Dinaric Alps), forests in the E and arable land in the N. The population of over 3 700 000 consists of Serbs (Orthodox), Croats (Roman Catholics) and Muslims. The capital is Sarajevo. Once independent states, they were held by the Ottoman Empire from the late 15th century until occupied (1878) and annexed (1908) by Austria–Hungary.

BOSON. See SUBATOMIC PARTICLES.

BOSPORUS, Turkish strait 19mi long and about 0.5mi to 2.25mi wide connecting the Black Sea and Sea of Marmara. Historically important as the sole sea link between the Black Sea and the Mediterranean, it was bridged in 1973.

BOSSIER CITY, industrial town in NW La. It is a suburb of Shreveport, and has timber yards and oil refineries. Pop 41 595.

BOSSUET, Jacques Bénigne (1627–1704), French prelate and historian who was renowned for his eloquence as an orator, especially in his funeral orations. He was bishop of Condom (1669–71) and of Meaux (from 1681). He wrote the famous *Discourse on Universal History* (1681).

BOSTON, capital and largest city of Mass., a seaport on Massachusetts Bay. It is the most populous state capital, New England's leading city and the nearest major US seaport to Europe. It is also a major commercial, financial, manufacturing, cultural and educational center. Boston's industries include shipbuilding, electronics, chemicals, plastics, rubber products and printing. The city's wool market is the nation's largest. Historic buildings include the Old State House, Paul Revere House, Christ Church and Faneuil Hall. Boston itself has many notable educational institutions, and nearby Cambridge has Harvard University and the Massachusetts Institute of Technology. Settled by English Puritans in 1630, Boston became the capital of Massachusetts Bay Colony and—in the BOSTON MASSACRE and BOSTON TEA PARTY—led colonial unrest that erupted into the REVOLUTIONARY WAR. Modern Boston shares the acute urban problems of most large US cities. Pop 641 017.

BOSTON, Siege of (1775–76), the landward encirclement of British-held Boston by American forces in the Revolutionary War. The British had won a costly victory at BUNKER HILL, but Washington eventually took Dorchester Heights, which commanded the town, and mounted his artillery (captured at TICONDEROGA) there. As a result, on March 17, 1776, the British evacuated Boston.

BOSTON MARATHON, annual marathon race held since 1897 from Hopkinton, Mass. to Boston.

BOSTON MASSACRE, an incident which strengthened anti-British feeling in America preceding the REVOLUTIONARY WAR. On March 5, 1770, some 60 Bostonians, enraged by the presence of British soldiers in Boston, harassed a British sentry. Troops came to his aid and fired on the mob, killing three and wounding eight (two died later).

BOSTON POLICE STRIKE, stoppage called on Sept. 9, 1919, when Mass. authorities had failed to recognize a police labor union or to offer better working conditions. Gangs terrorized Boston for two nights until Governor Calvin Coolidge's firm action in calling out the state militia and ending the strike catapulted him to the vice-presidency in 1920.

BOSTON PORT ACT, a British law of 1774, largely a reprisal for the BOSTON TEA PARTY. It ordered the closure of Boston port from June 1, 1774, until restitution had been made for the lost tea and the colonists had proved their loyalty to the Crown. The act was one of the INTOLERABLE ACTS that helped provoke the Revolutionary War.

BOSTON TEA PARTY, American revolutionary incident at Boston on Dec. 16, 1773. In protest against the tea tax and British import restrictions, a party of colonial patriots disguised in Indian dress boarded three British East India Company ships and dumped their cargo of tea into the harbor.

BOSTON TERRIER, US breed of dog, developed in Boston after 1870. It is small, with a square head, short muzzle and dark, smooth coat with white markings. The Boston terrier is a popular pet and show dog.

The Boston terrier, bred from the English bulldog and the white English terrier, is one of the relatively few breeds originated in the United States.

BOSWELL, James (1740–1795), Scottish writer and advocate, most famous for his *Life of Johnson* (1791), one of the greatest of English biographies. In his private journals he recorded his life and times with great zest. From them he culled the accounts of his travels in Corsica and elsewhere, and the brilliant conversations which distinguish the portrait of his friend Samuel JOHNSON.

BOSWORTH FIELD, site of a battle near Leicester, England. There, on Aug. 22, 1485, Richard III was defeated and killed by Lancastrians under Henry Tudor (Henry VII)—who thus ended the Wars of the ROSES and founded the Tudor dynasty.

BOTANICAL GARDENS, collections of living plants made for scientific and educational purposes, often also providing recreation. They may contain flower beds, greenhouses, pools, herbaria and laboratories. Among their principal functions are the preservation of rare plants and the development of new varieties.

BOTANY, the study of plant life. Botany and ZOOLOGY are the major divisions of BIOLOGY. There are many specialized disciplines within botany, the classical ones being morphology, physiology, GENETICS, ECOLOGY and TAXONOMY. Although the presentday botanist often specializes in a single discipline, he frequently draws upon techniques and information obtained from others.

The plant morphologist studies the form and structure of plants, perhaps the whole plant and its major components, while the plant anatomist concentrates upon the cellular and subcellular structure, perhaps using the ELECTRON MICROSCOPE. The behavior and functioning of plants is studied by the plant physiologist, though since he frequently uses biochemical techniques, he is often called a plant biochemist. A plant geneticist uses biochemical and biophysical techniques to study the mechanism of inheritance and may relate this to the EVOLUTION of an individual. An important practical branch of genetics is plant BREEDING. The plant ecologist relates the form (morphology and anatomy), function (physiology) and evolution of plants to their environment. The plant taxonomist or systematic botanist specializes in the science of classification, which involves cataloging, indentifying and naming plants using their morphological, physiological and genetic characters. CYTOLOGY, the study of the individual cell, necessarily involves techniques used in morphology, physiology and genetics.

Within these broad divisions there are many specialist fields of research. The plant physiologist may, for instance, be particularly interested in PHOTOSYNTHESIS or RESPIRATION. Similarly, the systematic botanist may specialize in the study of ALGAE (algology), FUNGI (mycology) or MOSSES (bryology). Other specialists study the plant in relation to its uses (economic botany), PLANT DISEASES (plant pathology) or the agricultural importance of plants (agricultural botany). BACTERIOLOGY is often considered to be a division of botany since bacteria are often classified as plants. (See also AGRONOMY; BIOCHEMISTRY; BIOPHYSICS; HORTICULTURE; PLANT; PLANT KINGDOM.)

The forerunners of the botanists were men who collected herbs for medical use long before philosophers turned to the scientific study of nature. However, the title of "father of botany" goes to THEOPHRASTUS, a pupil of ARISTOTLE, whose *Inquiry into Plants* sought to classify the types, parts and uses of the members of the plant kingdom. Passing over the work of the elder Pliny and that of his contemporary, Dioscorides, botany received few further lasting contributions until the Renaissance, the intervening period making do with the more or less fabulous "herbals" of the medical herbalists. The most famous pre-Darwinian classification of the plant kingdom was that of LINNAEUS, in which modern binomial names first appeared (1753). While Nehemiah GREW and John RAY had laid the foundations for plant anatomy and physiology in the 17th and 18th centuries, and HOOKE had even identified the cell (1665) with the aid of the MICROSCOPE, these subjects were not actively pursued until the 19th century when R. BROWN identified the nucleus and SCHWANN proposed his comprehensive cell theory. The work of DARWIN revolutionized the theory of classification, while that of MENDEL pointed the way to a true science of plant breeding.

British soldiers firing on the citizens of Boston—an engraving of the so-called Boston Massacre an effective piece of anti-British propaganda.

BOTANY BAY, inlet S of Sydney, New South Wales, Australia. It was named for its shores' varied plants by Captain COOK, who landed there in 1770. Australia's first penal colony was planned for the site in 1788, but was soon transferred N to Port Jackson.

BOTFLY, any member of three families of flies (Cuterebridae, Gasterophilidae and Oestridae) whose larvae are parasitic on mammals. They include horse botflies, the human botfly and warble flies. Bots infest stomach linings, nasal passages or subcutaneous muscle. In tropical America, some cause much damage to the hides of cattle.

BOTHA, Louis (1862–1919), Boer politician and general, first prime minister of the Union of South Africa (1910–19). He led guerrilla fighting in the BOER WARS (1899–1902), but as premier worked to reconcile Boers and British.

BOTHE, Walter Wilhelm Georg Franz (1891–1957), German experimental physicist who devised the coincidence method for the detection of COSMIC RAY showers (1929). This work won him a share (with BORN) in the 1954 Nobel physics prize.

BOTHNIA, Gulf of, N arm of the Baltic Sea, E of Sweden and W of Finland, about 400mi long and 50–150mi wide. It has low salinity and is frozen for 3–7 months of the year.

BOTHWELL, James Hepburn, 4th Earl of (c1536–1578), powerful Scottish noble who married MARY QUEEN OF SCOTS in May 1567, after helping to murder her husband, Lord Darnley. In June he fled Scotland, and later died in a Danish prison.

BO TREE, *Ficus religiosa*, the sacred fig or pipal (peepul) tree, under which traditionally BUDDHA gained enlightenment at Buddha Gaya. A cutting reputedly survives at Anuradhapura, Sri Lanka.

BOTSWANA (formerly Bechuanaland Protectorate), landlocked republic in South Africa bounded by South Africa, SW Africa and Rhodesia. It is mainly plateau (at 3 300ft), with the Okavango Swamp in the N, the Kalahari Desert in the S and SW, and mountains in the E. Rivers include the Limpopo and Zambezi. The climate is broadly subtropical, with one rainy season (averaging 18in of rain), supporting savanna vegetation except in the Kalahari Desert.

A few Bushmen survive in the desert and elsewhere, but Bantu-speaking Negroes form the majority. They live chiefly in the SE around Gaborone, the capital. Cattle raising and export dominate the economy. Products include corn, peanuts, sorghum, asbestos and manganese. Copper and diamond finds made since 1969 may transform the backward economy.

Immigrant Negro tribes largely ousted the aboriginal Bushmen after 1600. In 1885 the area was placed under British supervision and became known as the Bechuanaland Protectorate. As Botswana, it became an independent member of the Commonwealth of Nations in 1966.

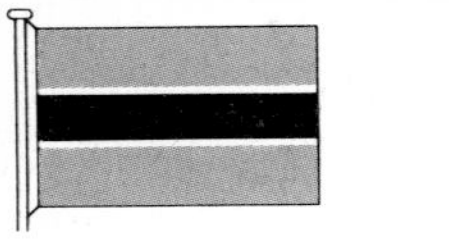

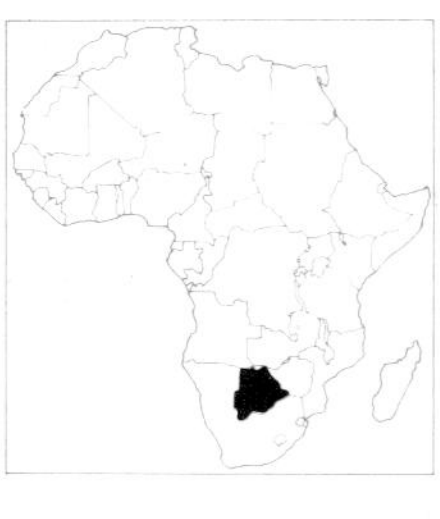

Official Name: Botswana
Capital: Gaborone
Area: 222 000sq mi
Population: 630 379
Languages: English; Tswana, Khoisan
Religions: Christian (15%); and tribal religions
Monetary Unit(s): 1 Rand = 100 cents

BOTTICELLI, Sandro (c1444–1510), one of the greatest painters of the Italian Renaissance, born Alessandro di Mariano Filipepi in Florence. His work is noted for superb draftsmanship, a use of sharp yet graceful and rhythmic line, and exquisite coloring. Among his most famous works are the allegorical tableaux on mythological subjects, *Primavera* and *The Birth of Venus*.

BOTTLED GAS, liquefied PETROLEUM gas (LPG) kept under pressure in steel cylinders and used for fuel by campers etc., and for tractors and buses. It is PROPANE, BUTANE or a mixture of the two.

BOTTLE-NOSED WHALE, two species of whales, *Hyperoodon rostratus* and *H. planifrons*, with a projecting snout, like a bottle-neck or beak, and a domed forehead containing an oil reservoir. They feed mainly on cuttlefish and are quite widespread. Individuals may reach 9m (30ft) in length.

BOTTLE TREE, any of several Australian trees of the genus *Brachychiton* with bulging bottle-shaped trunks (a water storage device) and bright red or yellow flowers. They are also grown as ornamentals in Cal. and Fla.

BOTULISM, usually fatal type of FOOD POISONING caused by a toxin produced by the anaerobic bacteria *Clostridium botulinum* and *C. parabotulinum*, which normally live in soil but may infect badly canned food. The toxin paralyzes the nervous system. Thorough cooking destroys both bacteria and toxin.

BOTVINNIK, Mikhail (1911–   ), Russian world chess champion (1948–56, 1958–60, 1961–63). His 1948 victory was the first secured under World Chess Federation auspices.

BOUCHER, François (1703–1770), French painter whose work epitomizes the ROCOCO taste of 18th-century France. Influenced by TIEPOLO, he painted airy, delicately-colored portraits and mythological scenes. He also designed Gobelin tapestries and decorated interiors.

BOUCICAULT, Dion (c1822–1890), Irish-born actor and playwright active in London and New York. The 150 plays that he wrote or adapted, such as *London Assurance* (1841) and *The Shaughraun* (1874), ranged from light social drama to melodrama.

BOUDICCA. See BOADICEA.

BOUGAINVILLE, largest of the Solomon Islands (3 880sq mi) and site of copper deposits found in 1964. Previously agricultural and part of a UN Trust Territory administered by Australia from 1947, it unsuccessfully attempted secession from Papua New Guinea upon independence (1975). Pop 77 800.

BOUGAINVILLE, Louis Antoine de (1729–1811), French officer and navigator who led the first French voyage around the world (1766–69), discovering Bougainville and visiting Tahiti, Samoa and the New Hebrides.

BOUGAINVILLEA, genus of tropical South American shrubs, including climbers which have large gaudy purple or red bracts (modified leaves) enclosing tiny flowers. It is a popular decorative plant in Fla., S Cal. and along the coast of the Gulf of Mexico.

BOUILLON, Godfrey of. See GODFREY OF BOUILLON.

BOULANGER, Georges Ernest Jean Marie (1837–1891), French general, leader of an anti-republican movement which threatened the government in the late 1880s. War minister 1886–87 and a member of the Chamber of Deputies 1888 and 1889, he was convicted of treason in 1889, but had by then fled to Brussels. He later committed suicide.

BOULANGER, Nadia (1887–   ), enormously influential French teacher of musical composition. Her pupils included US composers Aaron Copland, Roy Harris and Virgil Thomson, as well as Darius Milhaud. She is also renowned as an instrumentalist and conductor.

BOULDER, city in central Col. 25mi NW of Denver. Seat of Boulder Co., home of the University of Colorado, and a resort and space research center. Pop 66 870.

BOULDER DAM. See HOOVER DAM.

BOULEZ, Pierre (1925–   ), versatile French composer and conductor, noted for his extension of 12-tone techniques in *Le Marteau sans maître* (1951) and *Pli selon Pli* (1960). He has conducted many of the world's leading orchestras.

BOULLE, André Charles (1642–1732), French cabinetmaker to Louis XIV who devised the style called, in a corruption of his name, "buhl": ebony or other wood inlaid with metal, mother-of-pearl or tortoiseshell.

BOULOGNE, French seaport in the Pas-de-Calais department, on the English Channel. The French terminus for a boat and hovercraft service to England, and France's chief fishing port, it has foundries, canning factories, ceramic works, cement factories and wine depots. Pop 49 276.

BOULT, Sir Adrian Cedric (1889–   ), English conductor. He was founder and first director of the BBC Symphony Orchestra (1930–49) and became noted for his interpretations of English composers, especially ELGAR and VAUGHAN WILLIAMS.

BOULTON, Matthew (1728–1809), English industrial innovator and a founder member of the LUNAR SOCIETY OF BIRMINGHAM. In 1775 he went into partnership with James WATT to manufacture the latter's improved STEAM ENGINE. Boulton became England's foremost manufacturer and it is often said that his engines powered the INDUSTRIAL REVOLUTION.

BOUMÉDIENNE, Houari (real name: Mohammed Boukharouba; 1927–   ), president of Algeria. A teacher, he became active in the Algerian rebellion against France in 1955. After independence (1962), he was defense minister and vice-premier. In 1965 he overthrew President BEN BELLA and assumed power.

Cluster of bougainvillea flowers; the spectacularly brilliant bracts which surround the creamy flowers can be shades of purple or crimson, and range through the palest pinks and yellows to pure white.

Bourges contains many masterpieces of Gothic architecture such as the Palais Jacques Coeur, shown here. The buildings grouped around the Cour d'Honneur bear witness to the city's prosperity in the 15th century.

BOUNDARY LAYER, the portion of a FLUID near to a surface in motion relative to it: specifically, the layers of air nearest to the wing of an aircraft in flight (see AERODYNAMICS). Because of the air's VISCOSITY, these layers are subject to SHEARING, which reduces their velocity relative to the wing; thus lift is reduced and drag increased. Turbulence may also occur. (See also REYNOLDS NUMBER.)

BOUND BROOK, borough in N central N.J., 7mi NW of New Brunswick. It makes chemicals and roofing products. Pop 10 263.

BOUNTIES, Military, in US history, cash or land grants awarded to recruits to encourage enlistment. The practice was used by the colonists and continued in the Revolutionary War and afterwards. In the Civil War Congress and the states competed in offering bounties, giving rise to bounty jumping and reenlistment, and leading to much exploitation of the system.

BOUNTIFUL, city in N Ut., 8mi N of Salt Lake City. It serves an area noted for its truck farming and cherry orchards. Pop 27 956.

BOUNTY, Mutiny on the, uprising on *H.M.S. Bounty* in the S Pacific Ocean in 1789. Mutineers under master's mate Fletcher Christian cast their overbearing commander, Lt. William BLIGH, and 18 others adrift in a longboat. Bligh brought his party 3 618mi to Timor. Some of the mutineers founded a colony on Pitcairn Island.

BOUQUET, Henry (1719–1765), British colonel who fought the French and the Indians in North America. During PONTIAC's Rebellion he decisively defeated the Indians at Bushy Run (1763), and in 1764 he pacified the Shawnee and Delaware in Ohio.

BOURASSA, Henri (1868–1952), French Canadian journalist and politician who championed French Canadians and fought for Canadian independence from Britain. He was several times a member of the Canadian House of Commons, and was founder and editor of the Montreal daily *Le Devoir* (1910–32).

BOURBAKI, Nicolas, pen-name adopted by a group of French mathematicians under which (since 1939) they have published a momentous survey of mathematics along original but strictly formal lines. The work of the Bourbaki authors has been of considerable importance in the development of 20th-century mathematics.

BOURBON, whiskey produced from corn mash, and especially from at least 51% mashed corn mixed with malt and rye and aged in containers of newly charred oak. First made in the 1780s, it is named for Bourbon Co., Ky.

BOURBONS, powerful French family which for generations ruled France, Naples and Sicily (the Two Sicilies), Parma and Spain, named for the castle of Bourbon NW of Moulins. The family is popularly remembered for its love of luxury and its obdurate resistance to political progress.

Bourbons became part of the French ruling house when a Bourbon heiress married Duke Robert, Louis IX's sixth son, in 1272. In 1589 their descendant, Henry of Navarre, founded France's Bourbon dynasty (as HENRY IV). Bourbon rule in France was interrupted with Louis XVI's execution in 1793, was restored in 1814 under Louis XVIII, and finally ended with Louis Philippe's overthrow in 1848.

Meanwhile, Louis XIV's grandson came to the Spanish throne in 1700 as Philip V. In Italy, cadet branches of his family ruled Parma 1748–1860 and Naples and Sicily (the TWO SICILIES) 1759–1861. Bourbons ruled Spain to 1931, when Alfonso XIII abdicated. In 1947 Spain was again declared a monarchy, and in 1975 Prince Juan Carlos of Bourbon succeeded the head of state, General Franco.

BOURGEOIS, Léon Victor Auguste (1851–1925), French statesman who won the 1920 Nobel Peace Prize for peace-keeping work, which included helping to found the League of Nations. He was France's prime minister 1895–96.

BOURGES, city in central France, capital of Cher department. It is an agricultural market and major transport junction, producing aircraft, textiles and chemicals. It has a famous 13th-century cathedral. Pop 70 814.

BOURGOGNE. See BURGUNDY.

BOURGUIBA, Habib Ben Ali (1903–), Tunisian nationalist politician who became Tunisia's first president in 1957. He led the campaign for independence from the 1930s onwards and was imprisoned by the French several times. He was made president for life in 1976.

BOURKE-WHITE, Margaret (1906–1971), US photographer and war correspondent who covered WWII and the Korean War for Time-Life Inc.

BOURNE, summer resort town in SE Mass., on Cape Cod Canal, 14mi W of Barnstable. Pop 14 000.

BOURNE, Randolph Silliman (1886–1918), US writer. A noted social critic, he wrote many essays expressing radical criticism of American education and its way of life. He was an ardent pacifist, and opposed US entry into WWI.

BOURNEMOUTH, town on Poole Bay in Hampshire, S England. It is a popular year-round seaside resort, with fine beaches, public parks and entertainment facilities. Pop 153 425.

BOUSSINGAULT, Jean-Baptiste Joseph Dieudonné (1802–1887), French agricultural chemist who studied the GERMINATION of SEEDS and promoted the use of inorganic fertilizers containing NITROGEN and PHOSPHORUS compounds.

BOUTS, Dirk (also Dierick or Thierry; c1420–1475), Netherlandish painter whose sober work conveys intense emotion. His backgrounds (especially landscapes) are vivid and lifelike, his figures dignified. His masterpiece is the Louvain altarpiece, *The Last Supper*.

BOUTWELL, George Sewall (1818–1905), US politician, a radical Republican prominent in urging President Andrew Johnson's impeachment. He served as governor of Mass. (1851–52) and (after helping to found the state Republican Party) in the House of Representatives (1863–69), as US secretary of the treasury (1869–73) and as a US senator (1873–77).

BOUVIERS DES FLANDRES, dog breed, originally a cattle-droving dog of Belgium and N France, which responds well to training and was extensively used as an ambulance and messenger dog in WWI. In Belgium all champions must first qualify in working trials. Rugged and with a slightly shaggy coat that ranges from drab yellow to black, gray and brindle, it stands 26in high and weighs 77–88lb.

BOVET, Daniel (1907–), Swiss-born Italian pharmacologist who discovered the first ANTIHISTAMINE and later developed CURARE and curare-like compounds for use as muscle-relaxants during surgery. He was awarded the 1957 Nobel Prize for Physiology or Medicine.

BOVIDAE, a mammal family of hoofed, even-toed ruminants with permanent, unbranched horns. It comprises the ANTELOPES, CATTLE, GOATS and SHEEP and originated over 20 million years ago somewhere in Eurasia. Order: ARTIODACTYLA.

BOW, in music, a device used to play instruments of the VIOLIN family. It consists of a resinated horsehair band stretched between the ends of a curved wooden stick. When the bow is drawn across a violin string the string vibrates, producing a sound.

BOW, Clara (1905–1965), US silent-screen actress famous in the 1920s (notably in *It* and *Wings*) as the "It" girl, personifying the post-WWI era of "flaming youth" and flappers.

BOW AND ARROW. See ARCHERY; CROSSBOW.

BOWDITCH, Nathaniel (1773–1838), self-taught US mathematician and astronomer remembered for his *New American Practical Navigator* (1802), "the seaman's bible," later made standard in the US navy. He was the first to describe the LISSAJOUS' FIGURES (Bowditch curves), later studied in detail by Lissajous.

BOWDLER, Thomas (1754–1825), Scottish editor and doctor, whose popular *Family Shakespeare* expunged all supposedly blasphemous or indecent passages from Shakespeare's plays. The term "bowdlerize" came to mean any such misguided attempt to "clean up" a text.

BOWDOIN, James (1726–1790), American revolutionary leader and scientist. Bowdoin served in the Mass. legislature (1753–76) and supported the patriots' cause. As governor of Mass. (1785–87), he suppressed SHAYS' REBELLION. He was first president of the American Academy of Arts and Sciences.

BOWELL, Sir Mackenzie (1823–1917), Canadian Conservative statesman. He served as a cabinet minister, was prime minister (1894–96) until forced to resign by a government split, then led the Conservative opposition (1896–1906).

BOWEN, Elizabeth (1899–1973), English-Irish novelist, born in Dublin, whose works are distinguished by their meticulous style and fine emotional sensitivity. They include *The Death of the Heart* (1938), *The Heat of the Day* (1949) and *Eva Trout* (1969).

BOWERBIRD, any of a family of thrush-sized birds (Ptilonorhynchidae) of Australia and New Guinea that build courtship bowers of sticks decorated with bones, shells and flowers. The males tend to be brightly colored.

BOWERY, The, notorious district in lower Manhattan, New York City. Its pawnshops, saloons and cheap hotels traditionally attracted derelicts, alcoholics and the unemployed.

BOWFIN, *Amia calva*, voracious freshwater fish of North America. It is up to 750mm (30in) long with a cylindrical body and a long dorsal fin. Bowfins are the sole survivors of a fish family 130 million years old.

BOWIE, James (c1796–1836), Texan frontier hero who reputedly invented the Bowie hunting knife. He grew rich by land speculation and slave trading, moving W from Ga. to Ala., Miss., La., and eventually Tex. Bowie joined the Texan fight for independence from Mexico and was one of the leaders at the ALAMO, where he died.

BOWLES, Chester Bliss (1901–), US government official under four Democratic presidents (F. D. Roosevelt to Johnson). As director of the OFFICE OF PRICE ADMINISTRATION (OPA) he helped curb WWII inflation. He was governor of Connecticut (1949–51), ambassador to India (1951–53; 1963–69) and special presidential adviser on African, Asian and Latin-American affairs.

BOWLES, Samuel (1826–1878), US newspaper editor who transformed the Mass. *Springfield Republican* (founded by his father) into one of the nation's most influential papers. He became an opponent of slavery, and his paper's concise hard-hitting prose set a new standard of journalism.

BOWLING, popular indoor sport which involves rolling a ball to knock down wooden pins. In tenpin bowling, the most popular form in the US, players aim a large heavy ball down a long wooden lane at 10 pins set in a triangle. The number of pins felled determines the score. Bowling became popular in 14th-century Europe, and was brought to America by the Dutch in the 17th century. Tenpin bowling was standardized by the American Bowling Congress, founded in 1895.

BOWLING GREEN, city in S Ky., seat of Warren Co. It trades in tobacco and produces chemicals and automobile parts. Pop 36 253.

BOWLING GREEN, city in NW Ohio, seat of Wood Co. Home of Bowling Green State U., it is an educational and residential center. Pop 21 760.

BOWLS, Lawn, game played on a level grass green, where large bowls are rolled as close as possible to a small white ball, the jack. The game dates back to 13th-century England and France, and became very popular in colonial America.

BOX ELDER, or ash-leaf maple, *Acer negundo*, a deciduous North American tree unlike other maples in having several leaflets on a single petiole. It grows rapidly to reach up to 22m (72ft) and is sometimes grown as a shade tree.

BOXER, breed of medium-sized dog with broad chest, square head with a black mask, and short brownish coat. Boxers do sometimes playfully hit out with their forelegs.

The courageous, intelligent Boxer dog, often used in police work, was named for its manner of "boxing" with its paws before beginning to fight. The breed includes strains of bulldog and terrier.

BOXER REBELLION, violent uprising in China in 1900 directed against foreigners and instigated by the secret society "Harmonious Fists" (called Boxers by the Europeans). Encouraged by the Dowager Empress TZ'U HSI, the Boxers showed their dislike of growing European influence and commercial exploitation in China, attacking missionaries and Chinese converts to Christianity. When the European powers sent troops to protect their nationals at Peking they were repulsed (June 10–26, 1900). The German minister in Peking was murdered and foreign legations were besieged for nearly two months until

Bowling, an old sport that in its modern commercialized form has become very popular. The picture shows the action of bowling, the ball being swept down and along in a smooth curve.

Basic boxing techniques: 1. The boxer's stance, front and side views with the left foot forward and the left fist extended (a left-handed boxer may reverse the position); 2. right hook to the head; 3. uppercut; 4. infighting; after having been ordered to "break" by the referee; 5. defense: covering the front of the body with both arms while bending the knees; 6. pulling the stomach back to avoid an attack in that area.

relieved by an international force. Boxer violence was the pretext for Russian occupation of S Manchuria. On Sept 7, 1901, China was forced to sign the humiliating Boxer Protocol, in which it promised to pay a huge indemnity to the US and the European powers concerned.

BOXING, the sport of skilled fist-fighting. Two contestants wearing padded gloves attack each other by punching prescribed parts of the body, and defend themselves by avoiding or blocking their opponent's punches. Boxing contests are arranged between opponents in the same weight division or class: there are 10 classes ranging from flyweight to heavyweight. Fights take place in a square roped-off ring and consist of a number of two- or three-minute rounds separated by rests. Scoring is usually made by a referee and two judges.

If a contest goes its full length, the contestant awarded the most points or rounds wins by a *decision*. But a win can occur earlier by a *knockout*, if a boxer legitimately knocks down his opponent and the man cannot regain his feet in 10 seconds. A fight may also end in a *technical knockout* if the referee decides that a boxer is physically unfit to go on fighting. Boxing rules are slightly different for amateurs and professionals, and interstate and international practices vary in some respects.

Boxing can be traced back to the Olympic Games of ancient Greece, and to Roman gladiatorial contests where fighters' hands were encased in an iron-studded guard called a *cestus*. Modern boxing has its roots in 18th-century English fairground fights between bare-knuckled pugilists, who battered each other for bets until one could no longer continue. James Figg (1696–1734) opened one of the first boxing arenas in London in 1719, and champion fighter John Broughton (1704–1789) designed the first boxing gloves and in 1743 introduced some rules of fair play.

Modern rules date from those introduced for glove fighting by the Marquis of Queensberry in 1867. Glove fighting became firmly established after 1892, when James J. CORBETT beat John L. SULLIVAN in New Orleans in the first acknowledged gloved heavyweight world championship contest. The National Sporting Club in England laid down weight ratings that helped to internationalize boxing. World heavyweight contests promoted by men like Tex Rickard (who set up the first million-dollar gate) continue to dominate public interest. Since 1900, the US has often held the heavyweight title, through holders like Jack Dempsey, 1919–26, Gene Tunney, 1926–28, Joe Louis, 1937–49, Rocky Marciano, 1952–56, Cassius Clay (MOHAMMED ALI), 1964–67 and from 1973 and Joe Frazier, 1970–73. (See also the names listed.)

BOXING DAY, official holiday in Great Britain and parts of the Commonwealth of Nations, observed on the first weekday after Christmas Day.

BOX TURTLE, genus *Terrapene*, land or freshwater turtles about 125mm (5in) long with a hinged lower shell which can be raised to seal the whole shell. Land species include the US, eastern and ornate box turtles.

BOXWOOD, or box, several species of genus *Buxus*, which are slow-growing evergreen shrubs or trees that have small glossy leaves. Native to Eurasia and N Africa and found in eastern North America, the box is much valued for hedging. Boxwood is used for making some wind instruments.

BOYAR, member of the Russian aristocracy that dominated government and army from the 10th century. In the 15th and 16th centuries the boyars (through the tsar's boyar council) virtually ran Russia. Their power later declined, until the title was abolished by Peter the Great in 1711.

BOYCE, William (1710–1779), English composer, organist and compiler of English church music. His works included church and theater music and eight remarkable symphonies.

BOYCOTT, the refusal to deal with a person or organization as a sign of disapproval or as a means of forcing them to meet certain demands. The word comes from **Captain Charles Boycott** (1832–1897), an English estate manager in Ireland who refused demands to lower rents and was isolated by the tenants who worked for him.

BOYD, Belle (1843–1900), Confederate spy in the American Civil War. An actress, she lived in Va., and passed military information to the South. Caught in 1862, she was released for lack of evidence in 1863.

BOYD-ORR, John, Baron (1880–1971), British agricultural scientist and nutritionist who was awarded the 1949 Nobel Peace Prize for his services to the FOOD AND AGRICULTURE ORGANIZATION (FAO) of which he was director 1945–48.

BOYER, Charles (1899–), French-born US stage and screen actor famous as a romantic matinee idol. In his later years he showed his skill in character roles.

BOYER, Jean Pierre (c1773–1850), dictatorial mulatto president of Haiti (1818–43). He conquered Santo Domingo in 1822, establishing his rule over the whole island of Hispaniola, but was ousted in 1843 and died an exile in Paris.

BOYLE, Robert (1627–1691), British natural philosopher often called the father of modern CHEMISTRY for his rejection of the theories of the alchemists and his espousal of ATOMISM. A founder member of the ROYAL SOCIETY OF LONDON, he was noted for his pneumatic experiments.

BOYLE'S LAW, or Mariotte's Law, an empirical relation reported by BOYLE (1662) and MARIOTTE (1676) but actually discovered by Boyle's assistant R. Townely, which states that given a fixed MASS of GAS at constant TEMPERATURE, its VOLUME is inversely proportional to its PRESSURE. Real gases deviate considerably from this law.

BOYNE, Battle of the, battle on the R Boyne in E Ireland on July 1, 1690, which ended JAMES II's attempt to regain the English throne. WILLIAM III's 35000 troops decisively defeated the Catholic JACOBITES' 21000. Northern Ireland's Protestants celebrate (July 12) the victory to this day.

BOYNTON BEACH, resort city in SE Fla., on the Atlantic coast 52mi N of Miami. Pop 18115.

BOYS' CLUBS OF AMERICA, national federation of boys' clubs chartered by Congress, with headquarters in New York City. It presides over 600 clubs devoted to recreation and social, mental and vocational development for more than 600000 boys aged 7–18.

BOY SCOUTS, international boys' organization founded in 1907 by Sir Robert BADEN-POWELL to develop character, initiative and good citizenship. It stresses outdoor skills in woodcraft and nature lore. There are some 8000000 scouts in about 100 countries. Members of the Boy Scouts of America include Cubs (aged 8–10), Scouts (11–17) and Explorers (14 plus). Senior scouts include Sea Scouts and Air Scouts.

BOYSENBERRY, variety of tender trailing blackberry, prized for its large, reddish-black, sharp-tasting fruit. It is widely grown in the southern US.

BOYS TOWN, incorporated village in Neb. 10mi W of Omaha. Founded in 1917 by Father Edward J. Flanagan as a national center for homeless boys, it is self-governing, managed by representatives of the 1000 boys who live there.

BOZEMAN, city in S Mont., seat of Gallatin Co. An agricultural trade center, it is the home of Mont. State U. Pop 18670.

BOZEMAN, John M. (1835–1867), US explorer and gold prospector, who pioneered in 1862–63 a new direct route linking Mont. and Col. through what became known as the Bozeman Pass. He was later killed by Indians. Bozeman, Mont., was founded by him.

BRABANT, province of Belgium. A rich agricultural and industrial region, it is also, with the capital Brussels, the country's cultural center. Together with Antwerp province and the Dutch province of North Brabant, it formed the Duchy of Brabant in the 13th and 14th centuries.

BRACHIOSAURUS, largest of the amphibious DINOSAURS. This reptile measured 25m (82ft), including its long neck and tail, weighed about 50 tonnes and probably browsed in water. It lived in North America and E Africa about 140 million years ago.

BRACKEN, or brake, genus of ferns (*Pteridium*) found in many parts of the world. They grow very close together on poor soils in temperate climates. The RHIZOME produces plume-shaped fronds, which die in the autumn, but often remain standing during the winter. (See also PTERIDOPHYTES.)

BRACKENRIDGE, Hugh Henry (1748–1816), US writer and jurist, best remembered for his vast picaresque novel, *Modern Chivalry* (1792–1815), which satirizes American notions of democracy. He served in the Pa. assembly (1786–87), and in 1799 was appointed to the Pa. Supreme Court.

BRACKET FUNGI, so-called from the shape of the semicircular reproductive bodies produced on the surface of infected wood. Brackets may persist for several years. Bracket fungi belong to the order Polyporales of the class BASIDIOMYCETES. (See also FUNGI.)

BRACTON, Henry de (d. 1268), English judge, whose *Laws and Customs of England* was the first systematic work on English law. His *Note Book* of important legal decisions embodied the trend towards case law, which still deeply influences English common law today.

BRADBURY, Ray (1920–), leading US short-story writer. His style is characteristically delicate and colorful. Among his best-known science-fiction works are *The Martian Chronicles* (1950) and *Fahrenheit 451* (1953).

BRADDOCK, Edward (1695–1755), commander-in-chief of British forces in North America, who was disastrously defeated in the FRENCH AND INDIAN WARS. Unused to frontier conditions, in 1755 he led a cumbersome expedition against Fort Duquesne (on the site of present-day Pittsburgh), which ran into a French and Indian ambush. Braddock was fatally wounded and his men were routed. Among the survivors was a Virginian officer, George Washington.

BRADDOCK'S ROAD, a road across the Allegheny Mts, made in 1755 by General Edward Braddock's army to move supplies from Cumberland, Md., to Fort Duquesne (now Pittsburgh, Pa.). A section of the route later became part of the NATIONAL ROAD.

BRADENTON, city of W Fla., S of Tampa Bay. It is the seat of Manatee Co., a winter resort, and center of a rich farming region. Pop 21 040.

BRADFORD, city in W Yorkshire, England, a major center of the worsted, wool and other textile industries, and an international wool-trading center. It is the home of Bradford U. Pop 462 000.

BRADFORD, city in NW Pa. It has oil refineries and produces chemicals and explosives. Pop 15 061.

BRADFORD, William (1590–1657), Pilgrim Father, who helped to establish PLYMOUTH COLONY and governed it most of his life (reelected 30 times from 1621). He described the *Mayflower*'s voyage and the colony's first years in his *History of Plymouth Plantation*.

BRADLAUGH, Charles (1833–1891), English radical who was the first professed atheist to enter parliament. He championed secularism, women's rights, birth control and labor unions.

BRADLEY, James (1693–1762), English astronomer who discovered the ABERRATION OF LIGHT (1728) and the earth's nutation (see NUTATION, ASTRONOMICAL).

BRADLEY, Omar Nelson (1893–), US general. In 1944–45 he led the 12th Army Group (1 000 000 men in four armies) in Europe. He was chief of staff of the US Army (1948–49) and first chairman of the joint chiefs of staff (1949–53).

BRADSTREET, Anne Dudley (c1612–1672), English–American colonial poet. She began writing after her emigration to Mass. in 1630. Her poems deal with personal reflections on the Puritan ethic and her coming to spiritual terms with it. Her collection, *The Tenth Muse Lately Sprung Up in America*, was published in England in 1650.

BRADSTREET, John (1711–1774), British colonel in the FRENCH AND INDIAN WARS. By astute use of waterways, he moved his forces up to take Fort Frontenac (1758), thus badly damaging French communications in Canada. Later, during PONTIAC's Rebellion, he commanded the forces at Detroit (1764).

BRADY, James Buchanan ("Diamond Jim"; 1856–1917), US railroad tycoon and philanthropist. He acquired his fortune through the selling of railroad equipment, and the establishing of two steel railroad car manufacturing firms. He is noted as a legendary spender on both entertainments and charities.

BRADY, Mathew B. (c1823–1896), US photographer of eminent people and historic events. He photographed 18 US presidents and spent his fortune in hiring 20 teams of photographers to take over 3 500 shots covering almost every big battle of the Civil War. The project bankrupted him. His most famous photographs are those of Lincoln and of the battles at Bull Run and Gettysburg.

BRAGG, Braxton (1817–1876), Confederate general. He led the Army of Tennessee that defeated William S. ROSECRANS at Chickamauga (1863), but soon afterwards lost to Ulysses S. GRANT at Chattanooga and forfeited his command.

BRAGG, Sir William Henry (1862–1942), British physicist who shared the 1915 Nobel Prize for Physics with his son, **Sir William Lawrence Bragg** (1890–1971), for learning how to deduce the atomic structure of CRYSTALS from their X-RAY DIFFRACTION patterns (1912).

BRAHE, Tycho (1546–1601), Danish astronomer, the greatest exponent of naked-eye positional ASTRONOMY. KEPLER became his assistant in 1601 and was driven to postulate an elliptical orbit for MARS only because of his absolute confidence in the accuracy of Tycho's data. Brahe is also remembered for the "Tychonic system," in which the planets circled the sun, which in turn orbited a stationary earth, this being the principal 17th-century rival of the Copernican hypothesis.

BRAHMA, in HINDUISM, together with VISHNU and SHIVA part of the Trimurti. Traditionally the creator of the universe and personification of the Absolute, he is represented in Hindu art as having four arms and four faces.

BRAHMAGUPTA (c598–660), Hindu mathematician and astronomer whose writings influenced Arab and hence medieval European scholars.

BRAHMAN or Brahmin, member of the highest-ranking Hindu priestly caste. Only Brahmans may interpret the VEDAS, the sacred scriptures of HINDUISM; they may enter other professions without losing caste, however, and may marry women of other castes. (See also BRAHMANISM.)

BRAHMANISM, Indian religion based on belief in

Four-headed statue of Brahma from 13th- or 14th-century temple ruins in Jawa.

BRAHMA. It developed c500 BC from old Dravidian and Aryan beliefs. Its ritual, symbolism and theosophy came from the *Brahmanas*, sacred writings of the priestly caste, and from the UPANISHADS. It developed the "divinely ordered" caste system and gave rise to modern HINDUISM.

BRAHMAN OX. See ZEBU.

BRAHMAPUTRA RIVER, rises in the Himalayas and flows about 1800mi through Tibet, Assam, Bangladesh and S to the Ganges, forming the Ganges-Brahmaputra delta on the Bay of Bengal. A holy river to the Indians, its name means "son of Brahma."

BRAHMS, Johannes (1833–1897), major German Romantic composer. Though strongly influenced by Beethoven and the Romantic movement, he developed his own rhythmic originality and emotional intensity, while using classical forms. He lived largely in Vienna from 1863. His major works include four symphonies, two piano concertos, a violin concerto, a double concerto for violin and cello, piano and chamber works, songs, part-songs and choral works—notably *A German Requiem* (1868) and the *Alto Rhapsody* (1869).

BRĂILA, city in SE Romania on the Danube R, the country's second-largest port. It ships grain and manufactures metal products, processed foods and textiles. Pop 154 000.

BRAILLE, system of writing devised for the blind by Louis BRAILLE. It employs patterns of raised dots that can be read by touch. Braille typewriters and printing presses have been devised for the mass-production of books for the blind.

BRAILLE, Louis (1809–1852), French inventor of

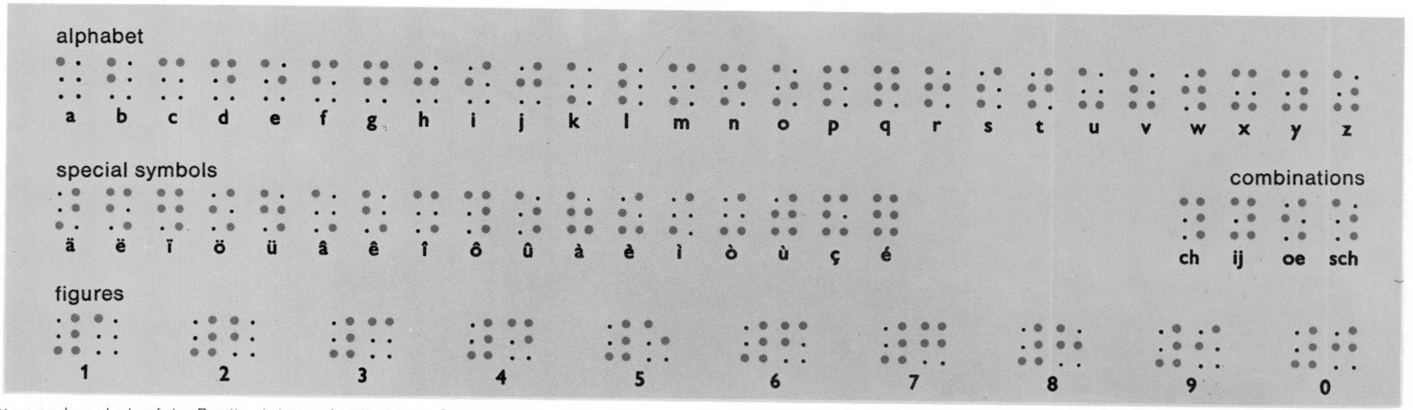

Letters and symbols of the Braille alphabet for the blind. Symbols in the second row accommodate foreign languages.

Brain

The brain and nervous system

All the bodily systems are necessary to the support of life, but the nervous system is the most important among them for it governs and coordinates their operations. The beating of the heart, the secretion of glands, breathing, the processes of digestion, for example, are all triggered, monitored and adjusted by nervous impulses. And the nervous system is of primary importance, too, in another way: it is the physical basis of all the mental activities and properties without which human life would be of no interest: consciousness, sensation, thought, speech, memory, emotion, character and skill.

The nervous system has a certain gross similarity to a telephone system: it works electrically, it carries information in the form of electrical pulses, and all the nervous pathways of the body converge upon the brain and spinal cord, just as all the telephone lines in an area converge upon a central exchange. The "central exchange," the brain and spinal cord, is known as the Central Nervous System (CNS); the remaining, outlying nervous pathways constitute the Peripheral Nervous System. The analogy with a telephone system must not, however, be pressed too far: for one thing, nervous pathways are not continuous like wires, but are made up of discrete units, nerve cells. For another thing, the speed of propagation of a charge in a wire is about one million times faster than it is in a nerve pathway. Thirdly, whereas a telephone system has one central power supply, the power supply of the nervous system is spread throughout: each nerve cell is, in effect, its own booster battery. Fourthly, although a line connecting one telephone to the exchange is able to carry information in both directions, nerve fibers conduct in one direction only; those which carry stimulus information from the sensory organs to the CNS are called afferent or sensory pathways; those which carry pulses outwards from the CNS to the muscles which they activate are called efferent or motor pathways.

At birth, the human body contains some 10 billion nerve cells or neurones, the structural unit out of which the nervous system is built. Thereafter many die, and although existing cells may grow in size, new ones are not produced. The main parts of the nerve cells are the cell body or soma, containing the nucleus; the axon; and the dendrites. The axon and dendrites are known as cell processes; dendrites carry an impulse toward the cell body, and the axon carries it away from the cell body to communicate it to another cell.

A nerve cell has only one axon but many dendrites, and the dendrites are in general more branched than the axon. The ends of the axon lie adjacent to, but not quite touching, the dendrites or cell bodies of other neurones; the region where the two nearly touch is called a synapse, and the small space separating them the synaptic cleft. Across the synaptic cleft the impulse from one cell is communicated to another cell. The synaptic cleft, however, is a sort of resistor, and one pulse crossing it may not be enough to trigger an impulse in the next cell. But if several impulses enter a cell simultaneously at different synapses, they may together suffice to trigger that cell. (The more often a synapse is crossed, the less resistant it

The brain in longitudinal section. The most striking feature of the human brain is the cerebrum; this large convoluted area, accounting for about two-thirds of the brain by weight, governs sensation and motor action in the body as well as higher functions such as thought and speech. The semicircular area in the middle of the diagram, the corpus callosum, consists of millions of tiny nerve fibers running from one side of the brain to the other. The cerebellum, at the base of the brain, governs motor "feedback"; it tells the brain how a motor action is progressing, so that any necessary modifying action may be initiated by the cerebrum. The pituitary gland regulates the body's hormone balance; other areas are concerned with lower responses such as reflexes, and also the conduction of nerve messages.

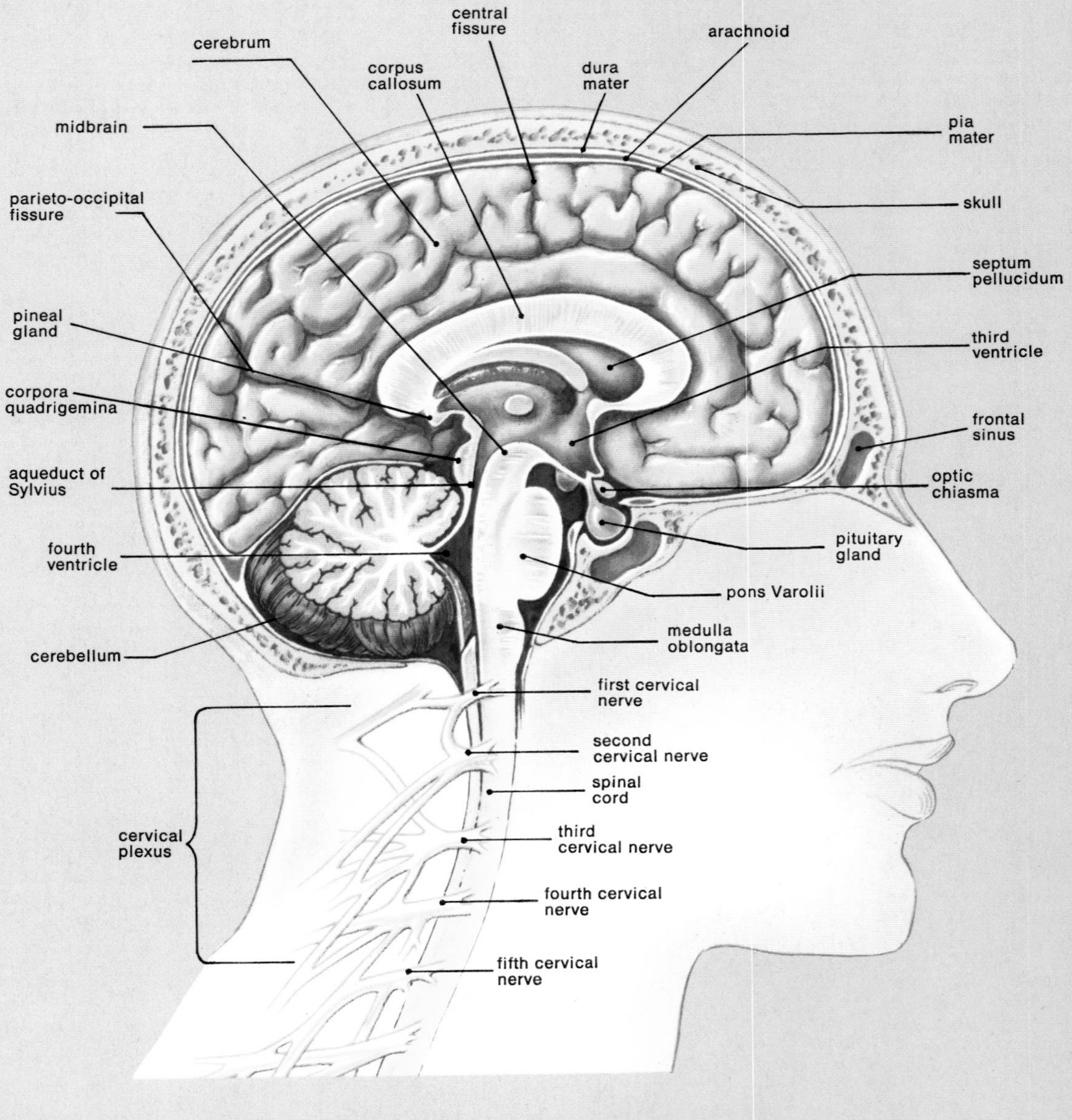

is thought to become; this lessening of resistance could explain both the phenomenon of memory and that of the entrenching of habits in the human character.)

Some axons are surrounded by a segmented white substance known as myelin, rather like the insulation round a wire. These myelin sheaths give a white color to parts of the brain—"white matter;" "gray matter" consists of agglomerations of nerve cells and processes which are not sheathed in myelin.

At the outer ends of the sensory pathways are structures known as sensory receptors. These have the capacity to translate stimulation of various types into electrical energy, which is then carried by the sensory pathways to the brain. Touch-receptors convert mechanical energy, heat-receptors convert thermal energy, the rods and cones of the retina convert light energy, the receptors of the inner ear convert sound energy, and the tastebuds of the tongue and olfactory cells of the nasal cavities convert chemical energy. Not all these receptors are on the surface of the body: there are touch receptors at all bone joints and in most muscles and in the gut. Thus we can tell the position of our body without looking, we can feel whether or not our muscles are tensed, and we have various visceral sensations. There are, curiously, no touch receptors in the brain itself, so that if a metal probe were to be pressed solely into the brain, it would not be felt. The motor or efferent pathways all end in muscles to which they communicate their electrical impulses, thereby causing them to flex or to relax. The mechanism of the muscle is not well understood.

For convenience of description the brain can be divided into three parts: the brain stem, the cerebellum and the cerebrum. The brain stem is, in the main, a relay station for nervous pathways between the higher parts of the brain and the rest of the body; consequently, if it is damaged sensory and motor functions are greatly impaired. But the brain stem is also responsible for some "sub-voluntary" activities, for example, respiration and digestion. Both the cerebellum and the cerebrum are divided by pieces of hard matter into two hemispheres each, one on either side of the head. The cerebellum is responsible for the coordination of voluntary muscular movements and for posture. The cerebrum is the highest center of the brain, and the latest in evolutionary development. It is responsible for sensation, thought and the initiation of voluntary motor activity. Each of the cerebral hemispheres consists of two main parts: the basal ganglia, a complicated collection of bunches of gray matter which cluster about the top of the brain stem, and, arching over these ganglia like a big, deeply wrinkled umbrella, the cortex. (*Cortex* is the Latin word for the bark of a tree.) The cortex, also of gray matter, is separated from the basal ganglia by tracts of white matter. It is conventional to divide the cerebral cortex into lobes: frontal, parietal, temporal and occipital. Each cerebral hemisphere is in communication with the opposite side of the body; the cerebellar hemispheres, on the other hand, control the movement of the same side of the body.

In the last few decades a great deal of progress has been made in matching up areas of the cortex (and of the basal ganglia) with the parts of the body to which they are connected by sensory and motor pathways. The eminent Canadian neurosurgeon, Wilder Penfield, found that a small electrical shock given to different parts of the cerebral cortex of a conscious patient gave rise either to a sensation (e.g. buzzing noise, red light, or tingling in the hand) which the patient later reported, or else to an immediate motor response which the patient claimed was involuntary: jerking the hand, bending the knee, etc. By this technique a detailed map of the specialization of the cortex has been elaborated, in which the occipital lobe is shown to be associated with visual sensation—there is independent corroboration of this in the familiar fact that if one is hit on the back of the head one "sees" stars. The temporal lobe is thought largely to be associated with emotional states. All the parts of the cortex seem to be associated with memory, to a greater or lesser degree.

These neurophysiological findings answer only the question as to what experiences or movements are associated with what parts of the brain. They do not attempt to say *how* it comes about that a certain kind of electrical activity in, say, the occipital lobe gives rise to visual sensations. Questions of that sort are philosophical rather than neurological, and no remotely satisfactory answer has ever been given to them.

BRAILLE. Accidentally blinded at the age of three, he conceived his raised-dot system at 15, while at the National Institute for the Blind in Paris. In 1829 he published a book explaining how his system could be used, not only for reading but also for writing and musical notation.

BRAIN, complex organ which, together with the SPINAL CORD, comprises the central NERVOUS SYSTEM and coordinates all nerve-cell activity. In INVERTEBRATES the brain is no more than a GANGLION; in VERTEBRATES it is more developed—tubular in lower vertebrates and larger, more differentiated and more rounded in higher ones. In higher MAMMALS, including man, the brain is dominated by the highly developed cerebral cortex. The brain is composed of many billions of interconnecting nerve cells (see NEURONS) and supporting cells (neuroglia). The BLOOD CIRCULATION, in particular the regulation of blood pressure is designed to ensure an adequate supply of oxygen to these cells: if this supply is cut off, neurons die in only a few minutes. The brain is well protected inside the SKULL and is surrounded, like the spinal cord, by three membranes, the meninges. Between the two inner meninges lies the CEREBROSPINAL FLUID (CSF), an aqueous solution of salts and GLUCOSE. CSF also fills the four ventricles (cavities) of the brain and the central canal of the spinal cord. If the circulation of CSF between ventricles and meninges becomes blocked, HYDROCEPHALUS results. Relief of this may involve draining CSF to the atrium of the heart.

The human brain may be divided structurally into three parts: (1) the **hindbrain** consisting of the *medulla oblongata*, which contains vital centers to control heartbeat and breathing; the *pons* which, like the *medulla oblongata*, contains certain cranial nerve nuclei and numerous fibers passing between the higher brain centers and the spinal cord; and the *cerebellum*, which regulates balance, posture and coordination. (2) The **midbrain**, a small but important center for REFLEXES in the brain stem, also containing nuclei of the cranial nerves and the *reticular formation*, a diffuse network of neurons involved in regulating arousal: SLEEP and alertness. (3) The **forebrain**, consisting of *thalamus*, which relays sensory impulses to the cortex; the *hypothalamus*, which controls the autonomic nervous system, food and water intake and temperature regulation, and to which the PITUITARY GLAND is closely related (see also PINEAL BODY); and the *cerebrum*. The cerebrum makes up two-thirds of the entire brain and has a deeply convoluted surface; it is divided into two interconnected halves or hemispheres. The main functional zones of the cerebrum are the surface layers of gray matter, the cortex, below which is a broad white layer of nerve fiber connections, and the *basal ganglia*, concerned with muscle control. (Disease of the basal ganglia causes PARKINSON'S DISEASE.) Each hemisphere has a motor cortex, controlling voluntary movement, and a sensory cortex, receiving cutaneous sensation, both relating to the opposite side of the body. Other areas of cortex are con cerned with language (see APHASIA, SPEECH AND SPEECH DISORDERS), memory, and perception of the special senses (sight, smell, sound); higher functions such as abstract thought may also be a cortical function (see also INTELLIGENCE, LEARNING). Diseases of the brain include infections—specifically MENINGITIS, ENCEPHALITIS, syphilis (see VENEREAL DISEASES) and ABSCESSES; also trauma, TUMORS, STROKES, MULTIPLE SCLEROSIS, and degenerative diseases with early ATROPHY, either generalized or localized. Investigation of brain diseases includes X RAYS using various contrast methods, SPINAL TAP (lumbar puncture)—to study CSF abnormalities—and the use of the ELECTROENCEPHALOGRAM. Treatments range from a variety of drugs, including ANTIBIOTICS and STEROIDS, to SURGERY.

BRAINERD, city in central Minn., on the Mississippi R. The seat of Crow Wing Co., it manufactures dairy products. Pop 11 667.

BRAINERD, David (1718–47), colonial American Presbyterian missionary who worked with the Seneca and Delaware Indians in Conn., N.Y., Pa. and N.J. (1744–47).

BRAINTREE, industrial and residential town in Mass., 10mi S of Boston, founded in 1634. Presidents John Adams and John Quincy Adams were born in Braintree. Pop 35 050.

BRAIN TRUST, popular name for the intellectuals advising Franklin D. Roosevelt in his 1932 campaign and first years in office. Professor Raymond MOLEY headed the group, which included Adolph A. BERLE, Jr., Rexford G. Tugwell, Samuel I. Rosenman and Basil O'Connor.

BRAINWASHING, the manipulation of an individual's will, generally without his knowledge and against his wishes. Most commonly, it consists of a combination of isolation, personal humiliation, disorientation, systematic indoctrination and alternating punishment and reward.

BRAKE. See BRACKEN.

BRAKES, devices for slowing or halting motion, usually by conversion of kinetic ENERGY into HEAT energy via the medium of FRICTION. Perhaps most common are **drum brakes**, where a stationary member is brought into contact with the wheel or a drum that rotates with it. They may be either *band brakes*, where a band of suitable material encircling the drum is pulled tightly against its circumference; or *shoe brakes*, where one or more shoes (shaped blocks of suitable material) are applied to the inner or outer circumference of the drum. Similar in principle are **disk brakes**, where the frictional force is applied to the sides of the wheel or a disk that rotates with it. The simplest form is the *caliper brake*, as used on bicycles, in which rubber blocks are pressed against the rim of the wheel. Almost all AIRCRAFT, AUTOMOBILE and RAILROAD brakes are of drum or disk type.

Mechanically operated brakes cannot always be used; as when a single control must operate on a number of wheels, thus involving problems in simultaneity and equality of braking action. In such cases, pressure is applied to a HYDRAULIC system (usually oil-filled), and hence equally to the brakes. Similar in principle are vacuum brakes, where creation of a partial VACUUM operates a PISTON which applies the braking action; and AIR BRAKES. **Fluid brakes**, used mainly in trucks to restrict speed in downhill travel, must be used in combination with mechanical brakes if it is desired to halt the vehicle. They consist of a rotating and a stationary element, between which a liquid (usually water) is introduced. Here it is FLUID, rather than mechanical, friction that converts the kinetic energy. (Cooling is usually performed by circulation through the radiator.) **Electric brakes**, similarly, may only restrict motion. The most common, used on electric trains on downhill runs, consists merely of a GENERATOR driven by the axle (the electricity generated may be used by the train).

In SPACE EXPLORATION there are clearly unique braking problems. In space or when landing on planets with little atmosphere (as on the MOON),

ROCKETS are used. During descent to earth (and eventually other planets) friction between ATMOSPHERE and craft is used, supplemented by PARACHUTES (see ABLATION; HEAT SHIELD).

BRAMAH, Joseph (1749–1814), English engineer who invented the hydraulic press, a machine which made possible many of the 19th century's greatest construction feats.

BRAMANTE, Donato (1444–1514), leading Italian architect who developed the classical principles of High Renaissance architecture. In 1499, he moved from Milan to Rome, where his major designs included the Tempietto of S. Pietro in Montorio (1502) and the Belvedere Court at the Vatican (c1505). His greatest project, the reconstruction of St. Peter's, was not realized.

BRAMBLES, common name given to rambling species of the genus *Rubus*, such as the BLACKBERRY and RASPBERRY. The tangled mass of stems that results in the natural habitat provides shelter for animals. The fruits are valued for food.

BRAMPTON, industrial town in SE Ontario, Canada. It produces lenses and electronic equipment. Pop 41 238.

BRAN, husk removed from grains of wheat, rye, etc., during FLOUR milling. Wheat bran largely comprises carbohydrate, protein and fiber. Bran is used as cattle feeds and is added to some breads as roughage.

BRANCH HERRING. See ALEWIFE.

BRANCUSI, Constantin (1876–1957), Romanian sculptor famous for his simple, elemental, polished forms. Living in Paris from 1904, he rejected Rodin's influence, turning to abstract shape and the example of primitive art. Among his best-known works are *The Kiss* (1910) and *Bird in Space* (1924–49).

BRANDEIS, Louis Dembitz (1856–1941), US jurist, influential in securing social, political and economic reforms, especially while an associate justice of the Supreme Court (1916–39). As a lawyer he crusaded for organized labor against big business interests.

BRANDENBURG, or Brandenburg an der Havel, industrial city and port on the Havel R in East Germany, 38mi SW of Berlin. Manufactures include steel and textiles. Its historic buildings include the 15th-century cathedral. Pop 93 916.

BRANDES, Georg Morris Cohen (1842–1927), Danish literary critic who deeply influenced the course of Scandinavian literature in the late 19th and early 20th centuries. Particularly important was his series of lectures published as *Main Currents in 19th-Century Literature* (1871–87).

BRANDING, burning an identifying mark onto an object with a red-hot iron. A common practice for at least 4 000 years, branding was also once used to mark criminals and slaves.

BRANDO, Marlon (1924–   ), US actor. His first major film role was in *A Streetcar Named Desire* (1952), and international acclaim came with *On the Waterfront* (1954), for which he won an Academy Award. Later successes include *The Godfather* (1971) and *Last Tango in Paris* (1972).

BRANDON, city in Canada, on the Assiniboine R in SW Manitoba. Founded 1879, it is a road and rail center, with food processing, oil refining and chemical industries. Pop 31 500.

BRANDT, Willy (1913–   ), Social Democratic chancellor of West Germany 1969–74, whose *Ostpolitik* (Eastern policy) marked a major step towards East-West detente in Europe. Born Karl Herbert Frahm, he was mayor of West Berlin 1957–66. As chancellor, he secured friendship treaties with Poland and the USSR (1970), with East Germany (1972) and with Czechoslovakia (1974). Brandt's initiative won him the 1971 Nobel Peace Prize. Forced to resign in 1974 over a spy scandal in his own administration, he returned to political life in 1975.

BRANDY, alcoholic drink of distilled grape or other wine, usually matured in wood. Brandies include cognac, from French wines of the Cognac area, kirsch (made from cherries) and slivovitz (made from plums). (See also ALCOHOLIC BEVERAGES.)

BRANDYWINE, Battle of, a British victory in the REVOLUTIONARY WAR. On Sept. 11, 1777, at Brandywine Creek in SE Pa., Gen. William Howe's 15 000 British troops surprised the right flank of Washington's 11 000 men protecting Philadelphia. Washington retreated to Germantown and Howe went on to take Philadelphia.

BRANFORD, town in SE Conn., on Long Island Sound. It is a resort and fishing center. Pop 20 444.

BRANT, Joseph (1742–1807), Mohawk Indian chief, Episcopal missionary and British army colonel. His tribal name was Thayendanegea. He served with the British forces in the FRENCH AND INDIAN WARS and in the REVOLUTIONARY WAR.

BRANT, Sebastian (c1458–1521), German humanist and poet, renowned for his satirical allegory, *The Ship of Fools* (1494), telling of 111 fools led by other fools to a fools' paradise.

BRANTFORD, industrial city and seat of Brant Co., in SE Ontario, Canada. Manufactures include farm equipment and truck bodies. It was named for Joseph BRANT, who was granted land there for an Indian settlement in 1784. Pop 64 421.

BRANT GOOSE, *Branta bernicla*, small N American goose with black head, neck and breast, brown-gray back and white stern. There are pale and dark-bellied forms wintering respectively on the E and W coasts. Both breed in the Arctic.

BRANTING, Karl Hjalmar (1860–1925), Sweden's first Social Democratic premier (1920, 1921–23, 1924–25). He was awarded the 1921 Nobel Peace Prize (with Christian LANGE) for his work for international peace.

BRAQUE, Georges (1882–1963), French painter and sculptor, a seminal figure in modern art. From FAUVISM he went on, together with PICASSO, to evolve CUBISM and to be among the first to use COLLAGE. Among his many major works are *Woman with a Mandolin* (1937) and the *Birds* series (1955–63).

BRAS D'OR LAKE, system of salty lakes in Nova Scotia, Canada, 50mi long and covering 360sq mi in the center of Cape Breton Island. Two channels and a canal link it with the Atlantic Ocean.

BRASÍLIA, federal capital of Brazil since 1960, located on the Paraná R, 600mi NW of the old coastal capital, Rio de Janeiro. It was built to help open up the immense Brazilian interior. Its cross-shaped plan was designed by Lúcio Costa, while such major buildings as the presidential palace and the cathedral are the work of Oscar NIEMEYER. Pop 272 002.

BRAŞOV (formerly Kronstadt), city in the Carpathian foothills of central Romania. A major trade center since the Middle Ages, it is now an industrial center producing chemicals, textiles, vehicles and electrical equipment. Pop 185 000.

BRASS, an ALLOY of COPPER and ZINC, known since Roman times, and widely used in industry and for ornament and decoration. Up to 36% zinc forms α-brass, which can be worked cold; with more zinc a mixture of α- and β-brass is formed, which is less ductile but stronger. Brasses containing more than 45% zinc (white brasses) are unworkable and have few uses. Some brasses also contain other metals: lead to improve machinability, aluminum or tin for greater corrosion-resistance, and nickel, manganese or iron for higher strength.

BRASS, Monumental, memorial marking a tomb, usually engraved with a figure representing the dead. The best examples, often surrounded by ornate inscriptions, motifs and heraldry, date from the late Middle Ages. The brass used, made from zinc carbonate and copper, is known as *latten*.

BRASS, Ornamental, finely worked brassware such as the famous centuries-old Benares ware of India. Islamic countries produced engraved and inlaid brassware in the 7th–15th centuries, an example being the Resulid brazier now at New York's Metropolitan Museum of Art. In 11th-century Belgium, the town of Dinant gave its name to *dinanderie* brassware. During the 16th and 17th centuries BENIN and IFE, in what is now Nigeria, produced some of the best examples of the craft.

BRASSICAS, genus of Old World plants from which many vegetables have been bred, e.g., CABBAGE, CAULIFLOWER, BRUSSELS SPROUTS, BROCCOLI, TURNIP, MUSTARD and RADISH.

BRASS INSTRUMENTS. See WIND INSTRUMENTS.

BRATISLAVA (formerly Pressburg), important industrial center on the Danube R in Czechoslovakia, capital of Slovakia. Manufactures include textiles, timber, processed foods and oil products. The city's historic interest (it was capital of Hungary 1526–1784) and scenic beauty attract many tourists. Pop 283 539.

BRATTAIN, Walter Houser (1902–   ), US physicist who shared the 1956 Nobel physics prize with SHOCKLEY and BARDEEN for their development of the TRANSISTOR.

BRATTLEBORO, town in SE Vt., on the Connecticut R. In a resort area, it also manufactures wood products. Pop 12 239.

BRAUN, Eva (1912–1945), mistress of Adolf HITLER, who married her the day before their joint suicide in 1945. She had little, if any, influence on Hitler's political life and ideas.

BRAUN, Karl Ferdinand (1850–1918), German physicist who shared the 1909 Nobel physics prize with MARCONI for his discovery that certain crystals could act as RECTIFIERS, and for his proposal that these could be used in (crystal-set) RADIOS.

BRAUN, Wernher Magnus Maximillian von (1912–   ), German ROCKET engineer who designed the first self-contained missile, the V-2, which was used against the UK in 1944. In 1945 he went to America, where he led the team that put the first US artificial SATELLITE in ORBIT (1958).

BRAUNSCHWEIG. See BRUNSWICK.

BRAVAIS LATTICES, in crystallography, the 14 different unit cells (arrangements of structurally-significant points) using which regular three-dimensional structures can be built. (See CRYSTALS.)

BRAVO, Nicolás (c1786–1854), Mexican general and statesman, who helped establish Mexican independence. He was among the first of the upper classes to join the peasant struggle for liberation. He was vice-president of the republic 1824–27 and acting president 1839, 1842–43 and 1846.

BRAWLEY, city in SE Cal., S of the Salton Sea, lying 115ft below sea level. It handles the farm produce of the Imperial Valley. Pop 13 746.

BRAZIL, fifth-largest country in the world, covering nearly half of South America. It derives its name from its vast dyewood (*pau-brasil*) forests. Brazil shares borders with all the S American countries except Ecuador and Chile. There are two major geographical regions: the lowlands of the Amazon R basin, mostly tropical rain forests (selvas); and the Brazilian highlands, an extensive mountainous tableland in the S and E making up two-thirds of the country's land area.

The country grew out of the unification of all South America's former Portuguese colonies, differing from its Spanish-speaking neighbors in having a racially integrated population. This consists of a three-fold mixture: the Portuguese intermarried both with the

Amerind woman and children, living in the Mato Grosso, Brazil. The Amerinds' lot has seldom been improved by "assistance" from the outside world.

Rows of luxury hotels and apartment blocks line the sea-front, overlooking the white sands of the world-famous Copacabana Beach near Rio de Janeiro.

Left: Rio de Janeiro is dominated by the enormous concrete statue of Christ the Redeemer on Corcovado Mountain, and by the famous Sugar Loaf Mountain, rising 1,230 ft from the bay.

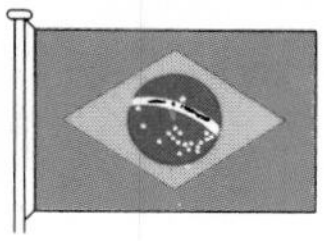

Official Name: Brazil
Capital: Brasilia
Area: 3 286 000sq mi
Population: 93 139 037
Languages: Portuguese
Religions: Roman Catholic
Monetary Unit(s): 1 Cruzeiro = 100 centavos

native Indians and with the Negro slaves imported from W Africa. The majority of Brazilians belong to the Roman Catholic Church, which also runs most state schools.

Although Brazil is rich in natural resources, few of these have been exploited. It is a country of violent social contrasts, and has remained underdeveloped despite international aid. Under its policy of rapid industrialization, however, it has increased the mining of manganese and iron ore deposits, which are among the world's largest. But Brazil is best known as South America's biggest producer of cattle, coffee and cocoa. Cotton and rubber industries have suffered since the development of synthetic substitutes.

Brazil was discovered by the Spanish navigator Vicente Yáñez Pinzón early in 1500, and later in the same year, independently, by Portugal's Pedro Álvares Cabral, but colonization did not begin until after 1532. Slaves were used extensively by the plantation owners, until Jesuit missionaries intervened in the 17th century. The country gained independence in 1822 under its governor, Dom Pedro, who then ruled Brazil as emperor for the next nine years. Largely under military rule after 1889, Brazil made rapid technological progress under President Juscelino KUBITSCHEK, who replaced the previous capital, Rio de Janeiro, by BRASÍLIA in 1960. The civilian government was overthrown in 1964; a new constitution was promulgated in 1967 and amended in 1969.

BRAZIL CURRENT, warm OCEAN CURRENT, fed by the S EQUATORIAL CURRENT, flowing S from the coast of Brazil before turning E around latitude 35°S.

BRAZILNUT, *Bertholletia excelsa*, a tree native to the forests of N Brazil. Numerous seeds are borne in a hard-skinned fruit. The nuts are eaten throughout the world, particularly in the US; they are also the source of a fine lubricating oil. The trees produce a hardwood called Para chestnut.

BRAZILWOOD, popular name for several Brazilian trees that are the source of a water-soluble red dye known as brasil. The wood has a limited use for violin bows.

BRAZING, technique in METALLURGY whereby two pieces of metal are joined using a nonferrous ALLOY (usually of COPPER) of lower MELTING POINT. The process is akin to SOLDERING but is performed at higher temperatures (about 1000 K).

BRAZOS RIVER, 840mi-long river flowing across Tex. to Freeport on the Gulf of Mexico, with dams at Whitney and Kingdom to control the changing water level and provide irrigation and power.

BRAZZA, Pierre Paul François Camille Savorgnan de (1852–1905), Italo-French explorer who founded the French Congo (1891). He explored the Congo and Gabon from 1875, and founded Brazzaville in 1883. He governed the colony 1886–97.

BRAZZAVILLE, river port and capital of the People's Republic of the Congo, formerly capital of French Equatorial Africa. It is mainly an administrative and educational center, with light industries. Pop 175 000.

BREA, city in SW Cal., 20mi SE of Los Angeles. Since the 1890s it has been a center for petroleum-based industries. Pop 18 447.

BREAD, one of humanity's earliest and most important foods, basically comprising baked "dough"—a mixture of FLOUR and water. In developed western societies, WHEAT flour is most commonly used and the dough is "leavened" (i.e., increased in volume by introducing small bubbles of CARBON dioxide throughout) using YEAST. In making bread, the chosen blend of flours is mixed with water, yeast, shortening and salt (and sometimes sugar and milk) to form the dough. This is then kneaded to distribute the GLUTEN throughout the mix, left to rise, kneaded again, molded into shape and left to rise a second time before baking. Bread is generally high in CARBOHYDRATES though low in PROTEIN. The vitamin and mineral content depends on the ingredients and additives used.

BREADFRUIT, the staple food of the East Indian and Pacific islands, it is the fruit of the bread-fruit tree (*Artocarpus altilis*). The melon-like fruit is eaten cooked or dried and ground to a flour that is used in puddings and bread. Some seedless varieties have been bred. Cloth can be made from the inner bark and the wood is used for canoes and furniture.

BREADROOT, *Psoralea esculenta*, also called the prairie turnip, a member of the bean family, native to the prairies and plains of North America. It produces a turnip-shaped root that is rich in starch and eaten as a vegetable.

BREAKSPEAR, Nicholas. See ADRIAN IV.

BREAKWATER, a barrier, made of wood or stone, erected to give protection from heavy seas. It may or may not be connected with the land. Breakwaters built at right angles to the shore are called jetties; those parallel to the shore are moles. They break the waves and help prevent the seabed from shifting.

BREAM, *Abramis brama*, European freshwater fish of the carp family, weighing up to 7.5kg (16.5lb). In the US freshwater sunfish are known as bream, and the marine porgies and wrasses as sea bream.

BREASTED, James Henry (1865–1935), US archaeologist and historian, who advanced archaeological research in Egypt and W Asia. He specialized in Egyptology, and in 1919 organized the Oriental Institute at the U. of Chicago, subsequently sponsoring expeditions at Megiddo and Persepolis.

BREASTS, or mammary glands, the milk-secreting glands in MAMMALS. The breasts develop alike in both sexes, about 20 ducts being formed leading to the nipples, till puberty when the female breasts develop in response to sex HORMONES. In PREGNANCY the breasts enlarge and milk-forming tissue grows around multiplied ducts; later milk secretion and release in response to suckling occur under the control of specific pituitary hormones. Disorders of the breast include mastitis, breast CANCER (see also MASTECTOMY) and adenosis. In humans, the breasts are erogenous zones in both males and females.

BREATHING. See RESPIRATION.

BRÉBEUF, Saint Jean de (1593–1649), patron saint of Canada. A French Jesuit missionary among the Huron Indians for some 20 years, he was martyred by the Iroquois. He was canonized in 1930.

BRECCIA. See CONGLOMERATE; TALUS.

BRECHT, Bertolt (originally, Eugen Berthold Friedrich Brecht; 1898–1956), German Marxist playwright and poet, who revolutionized modern theater with his production techniques and concept of EPIC THEATER. He left Nazi Germany in 1933, returning to East Berlin in 1948 to found the Berliner Ensemble. His plays include *The Threepenny Opera* (1928), *The Life of Galileo* (1938), *Mother Courage* (1939) and *The Caucasian Chalk Circle* (1949).

BRECKINRIDGE, John (1760–1806), US politician, who played a leading role in the KENTUCKY AND VIRGINIA RESOLUTIONS. After beginning his career in Va. and Ky., he entered the Senate in 1801 and became attorney general under Jefferson in 1805.

BRECKINRIDGE, John Cabell (1821–1875), US politician, vice-president of the US 1857–61. He became a congressman from Ky. in 1851, and was elected to the Senate while still vice-president. He was Democratic presidential candidate in 1860, but lost to Lincoln. He joined the Confederate government in the Civil War, becoming a major general and, in 1865, secretary of war.

BREDA, ancient city in North Brabant, the Netherlands, dating from the 13th century. It is a river port and industrial and marketing center. Pop 121 209.

BREDA, Declaration of (April 4, 1660), statement marking the restoration of the English monarchy. A

The Whitney Museum in New York is an example of Marcel Breuer's pioneering work in functionalist architecture. This and many of his other designs have exerted a tremendous influence over modern American architecture and city planning.

conciliatory statement by CHARLES II, it called for liberty of conscience, for an amnesty, settlement of land disputes and full payment of arrears to the army.
BREECHES BUOY, lifesaving device for taking people off ships at sea. It is named for the canvas breeches in which the person to be rescued is secured. The breeches, attached to a pulley, are drawn along a hawser strung between two ships, or from ship to shore.
BREEDER REACTOR, a NUCLEAR REACTOR that produces more nuclear fuel than it consumes, used to convert material that does not readily undergo FISSION into material that does. Commonly, nonfissile URANIUM-238 is converted into PLUTONIUM-239. (See also NUCLEAR ENERGY.)
BREEDING, the development of new strains of plants and animals with more desirable characteristics, such as higher yields or greater resistance to disease and suitability to the climate. Breeding has been practiced since prehistoric times— producing our modern domestic animals—but without firm scientific basis until MENDEL's theory of GENETICS. The breeder first decides which traits he wishes to develop, and observes the range of PHENOTYPES in the breeding population. Discounting variants due to environmental differences, he selects those individuals of superior GENOTYPE. This genetic variation may occur naturally, or may be produced by HYBRIDIZATION OR MUTATIONS induced by radiation or certain chemicals. The selected individuals are used as parent stock for INBREEDING to purify the strain. (See also ANIMAL HUSBANDRY.)
BREEDING BEHAVIOR, any behavior by which animals attract members of the opposite sex for the purposes of reproduction. Such behavior includes visual displays, calls and song and the production of scent for attraction and stimulation. Breeding behavior is found throughout the animal kingdom, but is particularly well developed in birds and mammals. (See also MATING RITUALS.)
BREED'S HILL, site in Mass. of the Battle of BUNKER HILL on June 17, 1775, in the Charlestown district of Boston.
BREMEN, second-largest port in West Germany, situated on both banks of the Weser R. Established as an episcopal see by Charlemagne in 787, it is now capital of Bremen State, and known for shipbuilding and for import and export shipping. Pop 606 500.
BREMERHAVEN, North Sea port in the state of Bremen, West Germany, located at the estuary of the Weser R. Home of West Germany's largest trawler fleet and seafood center. Pop 149 250.
BREMERTON, city in W Wash., 15mi W of Seattle. It produces lumber and dairy products and is the site of Puget Sound Navy Yard. Pop 35 307.
BRENDAN, Saint (c484–578 AD), Irish monk who, according to the 8th-century *Voyages of St. Brendan*, may have reached America 900 years before Columbus.
BRENNAN, William Joseph, Jr. (1906–), US Supreme Court associate justice appointed by Eisenhower in 1956. He championed civil rights and labor relations.
BRENNER PASS, important pass across the Alps, in the Tyrol, linking Innsbruck in Austria with Bolzano in Italy. The first good road along this ancient route was completed in 1772, and the railroad was built 1864–67.
BRENTANO, Clemens (1778–1842), German Romantic poet, novelist and dramatist. Together with Ludwig Joachim von ARNIM he edited the famous *Des Knaben Wunderhorn* (1805–08), a collection of folksongs which greatly influenced later German lyric poetry.
BRENTANO, Franz Clemens (1838–1917), German philosopher and psychologist, a Roman Catholic priest from 1864 to 1873, who founded the school of intentionalism and taught both FREUD and HUSSERL.
BRENT GOOSE. See BRANT GOOSE.
BRENTWOOD, city in E Mo., a residential suburb of St. Louis. Pop 11 248.
BRENTWOOD, unincorporated urban community in SE N.Y., in Islip town, Long Island. Pop 27 868.
BRENTWOOD, residential borough in SW Pa., lying 5mi S of Pittsburgh. Pop 13 732.
BRESCIA, ancient city in N Italy, 56mi E of Milan, producing armaments, textiles and machinery. Pop 214 876.
BRESLAU. See WROCLAW.
BRESSON, Robert (1901–), French film director, noted for the austere, penetrating quality of his work. His films include *The Diary of a Country Priest* (1950) and *The Trial of Joan of Arc* (1962).
BREST, commercial seaport in France's Finistère department, Brittany. A principal naval base, it was used by German submarines and bombed by the Allies in WWII. Pop 154 023.
BREST (formerly Brest-Litovsk), river port in the Belorussian SSR, on the Bug R. It is a rail center with light industry. Pop 122 000.
BREST-LITOVSK, Treaty of, the separate peace imposed on Soviet Russia by Germany and her allies during WWI, signed March 3, 1918, at Brest-Litovsk (now Brest) in Belorussia. By it Russia lost the Ukraine, Finland, and its Polish and Baltic possessions. The treaty was nullified on Nov. 11, 1918.
BRETHREN. See DUNKERS; PIETISTS.
BRETON. See BRITTANY; CELTIC LANGUAGES.
BRETON, André (1896–1966), French poet and critic, a founder of SURREALISM. Associated at first with DADA, he broke with it and in 1924 issued the first of three Surrealist manifestos, becoming the new movement's chief spokesman. Among his works is the poetic novel, *Nadja* (1928).
BRETTON WOODS CONFERENCE, international gathering at Bretton Woods, N.H., in July 1944, at which 44 members of the United Nations planned to stabilize the international economy and national currencies after WWII. They also established the INTERNATIONAL MONETARY FUND and the WORLD BANK.
BREUER, Josef (1842–1925), Austrian physician who pioneered the methods of PSYCHOANALYSIS and collaborated with FREUD in writing *Studies in Hysteria* (1895). He also discovered the role of the semicircular canals of the inner EAR in maintaining balance (1873).
BREUER, Marcel (Lajos) (1902–), Hungarian-born US architect. A student and teacher at the BAUHAUS 1920–28, he moved in 1937 to Harvard, and continued working with GROPIUS. A pioneer of the International Style, he collaborated in the design of the UNESCO headquarters, Paris (1953–58).
BREUGHEL. See BRUEGEL.
BREUIL, Henri Édouard Prosper (1877–1961), French archaeologist, noted for his studies of Paleolithic art. His revision of Paleolithic cultural subdivisions (1912) was particularly important.
BREVIARY, the book of the Divine Office or "Liturgy of the Hours" of the Roman Catholic

The traditional brewing-coppers in a modern brewery. In these coppers malt mashed with water is converted into wort, a sweet halfproduct. After the conversion of starch into sugars the wort is boiled with hops to give the beer the bitter taste.

Church. The last revision (1971) contains the daily service for the canonical hours, each hour consisting of prayers, a hymn, three psalms and a lesson.

BREWING, the process of making ALCOHOLIC BEVERAGES—generally BEER, but also SAKE and PULQUE—from starchy cereal grains. Brewing has been practiced for more than five millennia. The cereal (generally barley) is malted (steeped in moisture and germinated). The malt is then dried, cured at 100°C, and mashed—ground and infused with hot water; in mashing, the ENZYMES produced during malting break down the starch to fermentable SUGARS. The wort (aqueous solution) is filtered and boiled with hops, and then fermented in large vessels with YEAST (see FERMENTATION). When this has almost ceased, the beer is run off and stored to mature; finally, it is filtered, carbon dioxide is added, and the beer is packaged.

BREWSTER, Sir David (1781–1868), Scottish man of science who discovered Brewster's law in optics and did much to popularize science in 19th-century Britain. **Brewster's law** states that the maximum polarization of a ray of light reflected from a transparent surface occurs when the reflected and refracted rays are at right angles. (See POLARIZED LIGHT.)

BREWSTER, William (1567–1644), a leader of the Plymouth Colony, New England. He led the Puritan congregation formed in England in 1606, and sailed with the Pilgrims on the MAYFLOWER in 1620. He played a major part in regulating the civil and religious affairs of the Plymouth Colony.

BREZHNEV, Leonid Ilyich (1906–), USSR statesman, first secretary of the Communist party since 1964, effectively head of the Soviet government. He first became a member of the party central committee in 1952, and was chairman of the presidium of the Supreme Soviet 1960–64. Brezhnev, KOSYGIN and PODGORNY took control when KHRUSHCHEV was ousted in 1964.

BRIAN BORU (941–1014), king of Ireland from 1002. His reign marked the end of Norse domination but unified rule died with him. He was murdered after his victory against the Danes at Clontarf.

BRIAND, Aristide (1862–1932), French statesman, lawyer and socialist leader who was 11 times premier of France. As foreign minister (1925–32), he was the author of the KELLOG-BRIAND PACT. He was awarded the Nobel Peace Prize in 1926.

BRIARD, French sheepdog breed dating back to the 12th century, now often used as a guard or police dog as well as with sheep. Strongly built, it stands 23–27in high. The coat may be any solid color except white (darker shades preferred), and is long and harsh. This lively and intelligent breed is easily offended.

BRICK, a building unit made of kneaded or molded clay, baked by fire or sun, usually rectangular and about 8.5in long, 4in wide and $2\frac{1}{2}$in deep. Bricks were made at least 6000 years ago in Mesopotamia, and their development was a vital step in civilization. The ancient Greeks and Romans used them extensively. There are five major types: **common bricks** for ordinary building, **face bricks** resistant to erosion, **firebricks** (or refractory bricks) to withstand high temperatures, **paving bricks** (larger, harder and more water resistant than the common bricks) and the porous **insulating bricks.**

BRICKER, John William (1893–), governor of Ohio 1939–45 and Republican senator 1947–59, famed for his attempts to amend the constitution. The Bricker amendment, endorsed by the Republican party but opposed by Eisenhower, sought to restrict presidential and executive power.

BRIDALVEIL FALLS, 620ft waterfall in Yosemite National Park in E Cal., named for the "veil" of spray which it creates.

BRIDGE, a card game developed from WHIST. Contract bridge, the form now universally adopted, was perfected by Harold S. Vanderbilt in 1925–26. It is played by two pairs of partners, who before starting play must make bids according to how many tricks they calculate they can win. Demanding great skill, bridge has become immensely popular as a social and competitive game, with international championships controlled by the World Bridge Federation.

The briard is a faithful and intelligent sheepdog. Although still far from common, the briard in fact dates back to the early Middle Ages in France. Its coarse hair stands well out from the body.

BRIDGE, any device that spans an obstacle and permits traffic of some kind (usually vehicular, bridges that carry canals being more generally termed aqueducts) across it.

The most primitive form is the **beam** (or girder) **bridge**, consisting of a rigid beam resting at either end on piers. The span may be increased by use of intermediate piers, possibly bearing more than one beam. A development of this is the **truss bridge,** a truss being a metal framework specifically designed for greatest strength at those points where the load has greatest MOMENT about the piers. Where piers are impracticable, **cantilever bridges** may be built: from each side extends a beam (cantilever), firmly anchored at its inshore end. The gap between the two outer ends may be closed by a third beam. Another form of bridge is the **arch bridge**, essentially an ARCH built across the gap: a succession of arches supported by intermediate piers may be used for wider gaps. A **suspension bridge** comprises two towers that carry one or more flexible cables that are firmly anchored at each end. From these is suspended the roadway by means of vertical cables. **Movable bridges** take many forms, the most common being the **swing bridge**, pivoted on a central pier; the **bascule** (a descendant of the medieval drawbridge), whose cantilevers are pivoted inshore so that they may be swung upward; the **vertical-lift bridge**, comprising a pair of towers between which runs a beam that may be winched vertically upward; and the less common **retractable bridge**, whose cantilevers may be run inshore on wheels. The most common temporary bridges are the **pontoon**, or floating bridge, comprising a number of floating members that support a continuous roadway; and the BAILEY BRIDGE.

BRIDGE, Frank (1879–1941), British composer and conductor, best known for his chamber music. His style gradually evolved towards ATONALITY. His major works include the *Phantasie Quartet* (1910), four string quartets and many songs.

BRIDGE OF SIGHS, famous bridge in Venice, Italy, built c1600 by Antonio Contino. It runs from the Doge's palace to the state prison, and prisoners were taken across it to and from their trials.

BRIDGEPORT, city in SW Conn. on the Pequonnock R. It produces machinery and textiles, and is the site of a university. The showman P. T. Barnum was once mayor of the city. Pop 156 542.

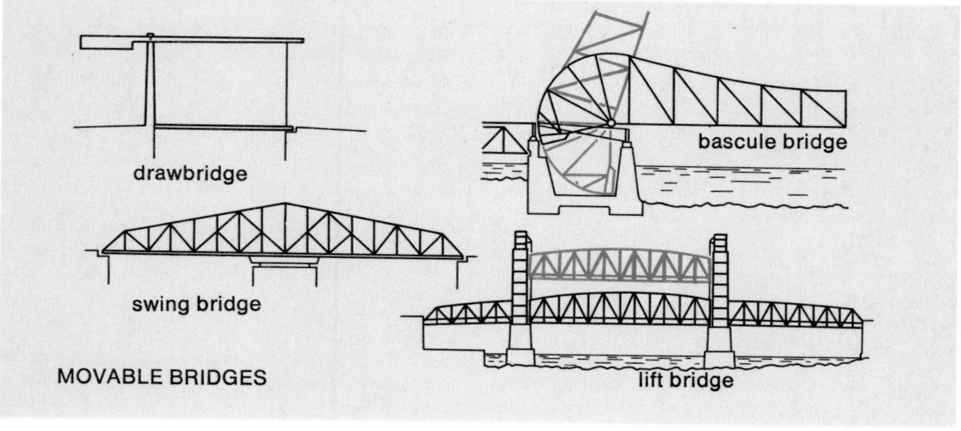

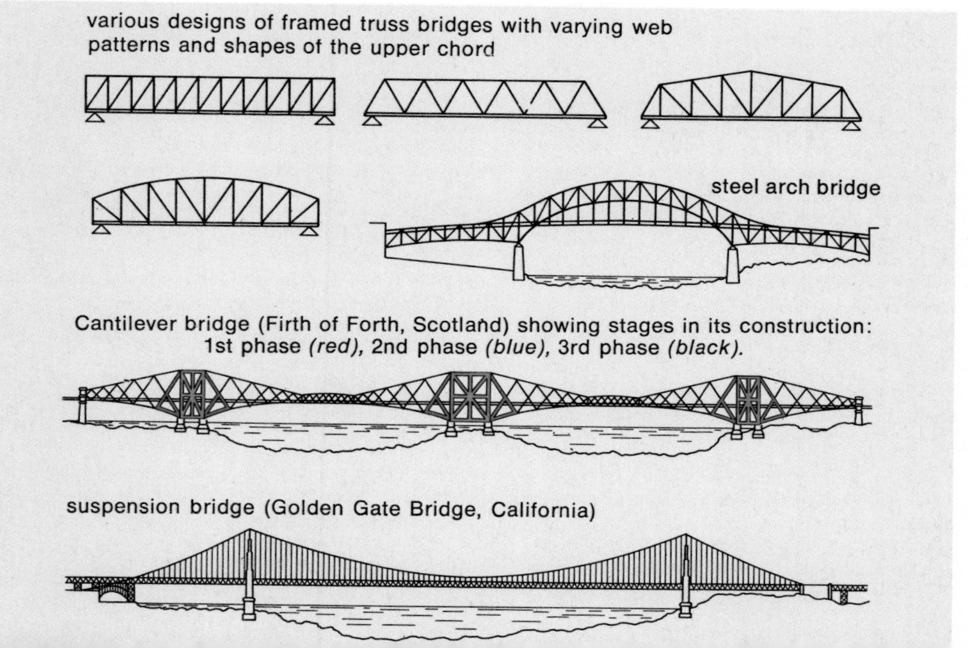

various designs of framed truss bridges with varying web patterns and shapes of the upper chord
steel arch bridge
Cantilever bridge (Firth of Forth, Scotland) showing stages in its construction: 1st phase (red), 2nd phase (blue), 3rd phase (black).
suspension bridge (Golden Gate Bridge, California)

The famous "Bridge of Sighs" in Venice (*above*) has been an example for many similar structures all over Europe, such as this one built in 1831 over the river at St. John's College, Cambridge, England.

BRIDGER, James (1804–1881), US trader, explorer and army scout. He traded in the unexplored American West and Southwest. He discovered Great Salt Lake (1824), and founded Fort Bridger, Wyo.

BRIDGES, Harry (Alfred Bryant Renton Bridges; 1901–), US labor leader, born in Australia. He helped form the International Longshoremen's and Warehousemen's Union (ILWU) in 1937, and as its president fought to improve dock-working conditions. Until 1955 there were many government attempts to deport him as a communist.

BRIDGES, Robert Seymour (1844–1930), English poet laureate, noted for the technical mastery of his verse and his editing of the poetry of Gerard Manley HOPKINS (1916). His works include the philosophical poem, *The Testament of Beauty* (1929).

BRIDGET, Saint (d. c524–28), also known as St. Bride, a patron saint of Ireland, who founded the island's first nunnery. She is the subject of many legends. Her feast day is Feb. 1.

BRIDGET OF SWEDEN, Saint (c1303–1373), also called Birgitta, patron saint of Sweden and founder of the Brigittine Order (1346). A mystic who also engaged in work among the community, she worked to bring the papacy back from Avignon to Rome.

BRIDGETON, town in E Mo., a residential suburb of St. Louis. Pop 19992.

BRIDGETON, city in SW N.J., seat of Cumberland Co. It processes farm products. Pop 20435.

BRIDGETOWN, capital and only port of Barbados, West Indies, founded 1628. It handles sugar, molasses and rum, and is a major tourist center. Pop 8790.

BRIDGE VIEW, village in NE Ill., a residential suburb of Chicago. Pop 12522.

BRIDGEWATER, industrial town in SE Mass., the home of Massachusetts State College. Pop 11829.

BRIDGMAN, Laura (1829–1889), American-born blind-deaf pupil of Samuel Gridley HOWE, the first such person to receive an education. She went on to teach sewing at the Perkin's School for the Blind in Boston, Mass.

BRIDGMAN, Percy Williams (1882–1961), US physicist who won the 1946 Nobel Prize for Physics for his investigation of substances at very high pressures. His work led to the production of synthetic DIAMONDS (1955). In the philosophy of science he championed the view that scientific terms are only meaningful if they can be given "operational definitions."

BRIGGS, Henry (1561–1631), English mathematician who proposed that common (base 10) LOGARITHMS would prove of greater practical use than NAPIER's original natural (base *e*) ones and subsequently calculated and published the appropriate tables (1617).

BRIGHAM CITY, city in NW Ut., seat of Box Elder Co. with textile and canning industries. Pop 14007.

BRIGHT, John (1811–1889), British politician and orator, of Quaker descent. He entered parliament in 1843, and held office under Gladstone. A champion of free trade and of electoral reform, he was a cofounder of the Anti-Corn-Law League and opposed British participation in the Crimean War.

BRIGHTON, popular English resort in East Sussex, on the S coast. Between 1783 and 1827 it was favored by the Prince of Wales (later George IV), who commissioned the Royal Pavilion, rebuilt by John Nash 1815–23 in imitation Indian and Chinese style. Pop 164000.

BRIGHT'S DISEASE, a form of acute NEPHRITIS that may follow infections with certain STREPTOCOCCUS types. Blood and protein are lost in the urine; there may be EDEMA and raised blood pressure. Recovery is usually complete but a few patients progress to chronic KIDNEY disease.

BRILL, Abraham Arden (1874–1948), Austrian-born US psychiatrist, the "father of American PSYCHOANALYSIS," who introduced the Freudian method to the US and translated many of FREUD's works into English.

BRINDISI, major Italian seaport on the "heel" of Italy. The terminus of the Appian Way, it is a busy commercial port with a regular service to Athens and Dubrovnik. Pop 82712.

BRINDLEY, James (1716–1772), self-taught English canal builder who inaugurated the canal age by constructing the Bridgewater Canal. Brindley laid out more than 360mi (580km) of canals before his death, thus providing the transportation system which made possible the INDUSTRIAL REVOLUTION.

BRINE, a concentrated solution of SALT and other compounds. Natural brine occurs as seawater and as underground deposits. It is a major source of salt, BROMINE, IODINE and potassium compounds, and is also used as a food preservative and in refrigeration. (See also EVAPORITES.)

BRINE SHRIMP, *Artemia salina*, a crustacean less than 12mm (0.5in) long, living in very salty water. It swims upside down, propelling itself with 11 pairs of limbs, and sometimes propagates by PARTHENOGENESIS. It is used as fish food, and its eggs are eaten as a paste in N Africa.

BRISBANE, industrial seaport in E Australia, capital of Queensland. Situated on the Brisbane R, about 15mi from the Pacific Ocean, it was founded as a penal settlement in 1824. Pop 699371.

BRISBANE, Albert (1809–1890), US Utopian philosopher and socialist. A disciple of FOURIER, he wrote the influential *Social Destiny of Man* (1840).

BRISEIS, in Greek mythology, female slave over whom ACHILLES and AGAMEMNON quarrelled in the Trojan War.

BRISSOT DE WARVILLE, Jacques Pierre (1754–1793), French revolutionary politician, lawyer and writer, a leader of the GIRONDINS. A dedicated anti-monarchist, he was executed by the JACOBINS.

BRISTLECONE PINE, *Pinus aristata*, slow-growing pine, native to the US Southwest. Some bristlecone pines are more than 4000 years old, which makes them the oldest living trees.

BRISTLETAILS, primitive wingless insects with bristlelike antennae and three "tails." They feed on dead plant material; the silverfish (a common bristletail) is a household pest.

BRISTOL, port and university city in SW England. It was a trade center for textiles from the 14th century, and a hub of the slave trade in the 18th century. The city has many modern industries, including aircraft construction. Pop 422000.

BRISTOL, industrial city in central Conn. on the Pequabuck R. Famous as a clockmaking center, it also manufactures machinery and tools. Pop 55487.

BRISTOL, industrial borough in SE Pa. on the Delaware R. Its products include woolen goods and machinery. Pop 12085.

BRISTOL, port in E R.I. on Narragansett Bay, seat of Bristol Co. Its industries include electrical and rubber goods. Pop 17860.

BRISTOL, city in NE Tenn., contiguous with Bristol, Va. Its manufactures include paper and leather goods. Pop 20064.

BRISTOL, city in SW Va., contiguous with Bristol, Tenn. Its products include textiles and pharmaceuticals. Pop 14857.

BRISTOW, Benjamin Helm (1832–1896), US lawyer and public official. As secretary of the treasury (1874–76) under Grant, he exposed and prosecuted the corrupt WHISKEY RING.

BRITAIN, modern form of the ancient name for the island now comprising England, Scotland and Wales. The Romans referred to the 1st-century BC Celtic inhabitants as *Pritani*, hence their own name for the island, *Britannia*. (See GREAT BRITAIN.)

BRITAIN, Battle of. See BATTLE OF BRITAIN.

BRITANNIA METAL, an ALLOY consisting of 5–10% ANTIMONY, about 1% COPPER and the remainder TIN. It resembles PEWTER, is hard and workable, and is used as a base for electroplated silverware.

BRITISH ANTARCTIC TERRITORY, British colony in Antarctica, covering 652000sq mi and including the South Shetlands and the South Orkney Islands. It is administered from the Falkland Islands.

BRITISH BROADCASTING CORPORATION (BBC), the company running most radio and two of the three television networks in Britain. A publicly financed body responsible to parliament, the BBC first went on the air in 1922 as the British Broadcasting Company.

BRITISH COLUMBIA, province on the W coast of Canada, bounded on the W by the Pacific Ocean and S Alaska and on the E by the province of Alberta. About 500mi from E to W and about 770mi from N to S, it is the most rugged of Canada's provinces. There are two main mountain chains, the Coast Mts in the W and the Canadian Rocky Mts in the E. In the remarkable Rocky Mountain Trench the upper courses of many rivers can be found, notably the Columbia, the Fraser and the Kootenay. The 700mi coastline is broken by fjords, and among the offshore chains of islands Vancouver Island and the Queen Charlotte Islands are the most important. Temperatures and rainfall differ greatly in various parts of the province, with a mild climate near the coast, but temperatures vary between 100°F and −35°F in the interior.

Seventy percent of the population, predominantly of British origin, live in the milder southwest of the province. Forestry, the export of finished-wood

Some of the fine old timepieces that can be viewed in the American Clock and Watch Museum in Bristol, Connecticut, which was once a center for their manufacture.

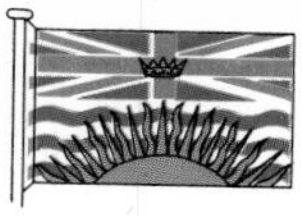

Name of Province: British Columbia
Joined Confederation: July 20, 1871
Capital: Victoria
Area: 366 255sq mi
Population: 2 184 621

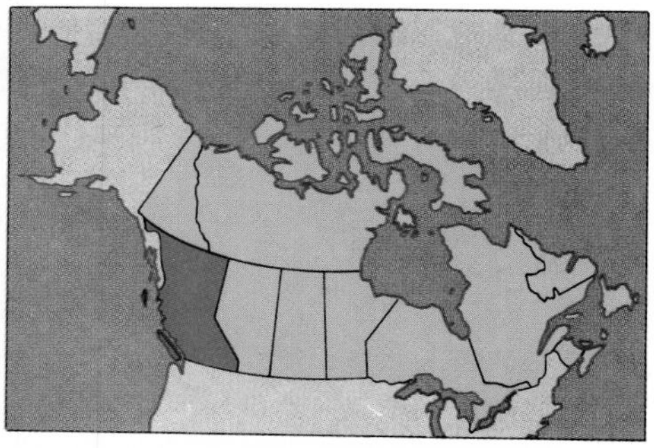

Snow-capped peaks, dense forests and vast lakes of British Columbia, Canada's most westerly state.

products and mining are the biggest industries. British Columbia also supplies about 40% of Canada's fish; and agriculture (often with irrigation) and tourism also contribute to its economy.

The area was first visited by the Spanish explorer Juan Pérez in 1774, and in 1778 Captain Cook anchored in Nootka Sound. Britain commissioned George VANCOUVER to survey the coast in 1792. Other early explorers were Alexander MACKENZIE, David THOMPSON and Simon FRASER. For a time, the region was called New Caledonia, and its trade was controlled by the Hudson's Bay Company after 1821. Settlement increased following the discovery of gold in 1858, when the colony of British Columbia was established. It became a province of Canada in 1871. A new era began in 1885, when the railroad reached Vancouver, which grew to become the capital.

BRITISH COMMONWEALTH OF NATIONS. See COMMONWEALTH OF NATIONS.

BRITISH GUIANA. See GUYANA.

BRITISH HONDURAS. See BELIZE.

BRITISH INDIAN OCEAN TERRITORY, British colony, 30sq mi in land area, established in 1965 to provide defense facilities for Britain and the US. It consists of the Chagos archipelago and Aldabra, Farquhar and Desroches islands. Pop 350.

BRITISH LIBRARY, national library of Britain, established in London in 1753 as part of the BRITISH MUSEUM. It houses some 8.5 million printed books and 150 000 MSS. By law, the library must be sent a copy of every book published in the UK. It became a separate entity in 1973, with several divisions.

BRITISH MUSEUM, national museum of antiquities and ethnography in London. Founded in 1753, when the British government acquired the art collection and library of Sir Hans Sloane, it opened to the public in 1759. Its present Neoclassical premises were built 1823–47 and its natural history section was separated 1881–83. The museum has one of the world's foremost collections.

BRITISH NORTH AMERICA ACT, an act passed by the British parliament in 1867 to create the Dominion of Canada, uniting Canada (Quebec and Ontario), New Brunswick and Nova Scotia under a federal government.

BRITISH THERMAL UNIT (Btu), the quantity of ENERGY required to raise one pound of water through one Fahrenheit degree. The International steam tables define the Btu_{IT} as $251.9958 cal_{IT}$; this is equivalent to 1055.056 joules.

BRITTANY (French: Bretagne), historic peninsular region of NW France. The Romans conquered the area in 56 BC and named it Armorica. It was settled c500 AD by Celtic Britons fleeing the Anglo-Saxon invasion. After struggles for independence from the Franks and from Normandy, Anjou, England and France in turn, it became a French province in 1532. The Bretons retain their own cultural traditions and language.

BRITTANY SPANIEL, French breed of gundog with orange and white or liver and white coat which points game instead of flushing it like the typical spaniel. It stands 20in tall and weighs about 40lb.

BRITTEN, (Edward) Benjamin, 1st Baron Britten of Aldeburgh (1913–), outstanding British composer. His works include several important operas, among them *Peter Grimes* (1945), *Billy Budd* (1951), *The Turn of the Screw* (1954) and *Death in Venice* (1973). Among his many notable instrumental and choral works are the *Variations on a Theme by Frank Bridge* (1937) and *War Requiem* (1962).

BRITTLESTARS, five-armed creatures related to STARFISH, and contained in the order Ophiuroidea, with long arms which can break off and regrow. They trap small particles in the mucus on the arms and pass them to the mouth or use the arms to catch larger animals. Eggs may be fertilized in the sea or in the female's body.

BRNO, second-largest city in Czechoslovakia, capital of the region of Southern Moravia; incorporated in 1243. Its industries include sugar refining, distilling, textiles, chemicals and metal products. Pop 335 918.

BROADCASTING NETWORKS, US, American companies which produce programs for broadcasting to the public over a network or affiliated group of radio or television stations, interlinked by wire or radio relay. The three prime US networks (all commercial) are NBC (National Broadcasting Company), which organized the first radio network (1926), introduced regular TV service in 1939 and began coast-to-coast TV broadcasting in 1951; CBS (Columbia Broadcasting System, Inc.), organized in 1927, which broadcasts radio and TV programs, manufactures electronic equipment and operates hundreds of stations through the US; ABC (American Broadcasting Companies, Inc.), founded 1943; and the Mutual Broadcasting System (MBS), with close to 500 affiliated independently-owned radio outlets which became a coast-to-coast network in 1936. The Public Broadcasting System (PBS) was established in 1969 for educational, noncommercial public TV; it is funded by the federal government and private foundations.

BROADVIEW HEIGHTS, village in NE Ohio, a suburb of Cleveland. Pop 11 463.

BROADWAY, street stretching 150mi from Manhattan Island, New York City, to Albany, N.Y., the longest in the world. In Manhattan it is the center of US commercial theater; it reached its height in the 1920s, with as many as 80 theaters. Its prosperity has greatly lessened since the advent of films and television.

BROCADE, fabric with a raised woven pattern. Originating in the East, it was used for European court clothing in the Middle Ages and Renaissance. It is now mostly seen in upholstery and drapery.

BROCCOLI, fast-growing vegetable of the genus *Brassica*. The most common variety, originating in Italy, is bright green and is now extensively grown in Europe and North America. Dense green, edible flower buds are formed in clusters at the apex of the central stem and branches. (See also BRASSICAS.)

BROCK, Sir Isaac (1769–1812), British general in charge of Upper Canada during the War of 1812. His capture of Detroit from US General William Hull averted the conquest of Upper Canada. He defeated a US force at Niagara, but was killed in the battle.

Festive atmosphere on Thanksgiving Day in Broadway, New York, the longest street in the world. The Times Square area seen here is famous for its profusion of clubs, cinemas and theaters.

BROCKEN, highest peak (3 747ft) in the Harz Mts, East Germany. It is the legendary site of the WALPURGIS NIGHT witches' Sabbath.

BROCKEN SPECTER, phenomenon observed when SHADOWS of aircraft, or of people on a high mountain, are cast on cloud below. An observer's own shadow appears vastly magnified: this is an optical ILLUSION. Those of others appear to him surrounded by rings of color, due to DIFFRACTION by water droplets in the cloud.

BROCKTON, city in SE Mass., 19mi S of Boston. Its manufactures include electronic equipment, clothing, footwear and paper products. Pop 89 040.

BROD, Max (1884–1968), Czech author, best known as editor of the works of his friend Franz KAFKA, which he saved from destruction. His own works include the novel, *The Redemption of Tycho Brahe* (1916) and a biography of Kafka (1937). He emigrated to Palestine in 1939.

BRODERICK, David Colbreth (1820–1859), US politician. A N.Y. TAMMANY HALL politician, he went to Cal. with the FORTY-NINERS and was elected to the US Senate in 1857. He opposed slavery, and was killed in a duel over that issue.

BROGLIE, Louis Victor Pierre Raymond de. See DE BROGLIE, LOUIS VICTOR PIERRE RAYMOND.

BROKEN ARROW, city in NE Okla., 14mi SE of Tulsa. It manufactures tools and trailers, and mines coal and oil. Pop 11 787.

BROKER. See STOCKS AND STOCK MARKET.

BROME GRASS, common name for grasses of the genus *Bromus*. Popular species include smooth brome, a pasture or hay grass which has a high PROTEIN content and is resistant to trampling, and cheatgrass which is valuable as an early spring plant but less palatable than smooth brome.

BROMELIADS, popular name for plants of the pineapple family (Bromeliaceae), many species of which grow in the tropics as EPIPHYTES on trees. Many bromeliads are cultivated as house plants, e.g., *Tillandsia*, AECHMEA and *Billbeigia*, where they prefer a sunny position, although they also do well under strong artificial light. They should be kept at a temperature of 16°C–18°C (61°F–64°F), a humidity of 60% to 70% and should be regularly watered. An unusual feature of bromeliads is that their leaf bases form a reservoir which collects rain in their native habitats; when cultivated, water should be added to this reservoir, but it must be changed each week. Bromeliads form small offsets and these are the best means of propagation.

BROMFIELD, Louis (1896–1956), US novelist, winner of a 1926 Pulitzer Prize for his novel, *Early Autumn*. His other works include *The Rains Came* (1937) and *Pleasant Valley* (1945).

BROMINE (Br), dark-red fuming liquid, toxic and caustic, with a pungent odor; one of the HALOGENS, intermediate in properties between CHLORINE and IODINE. It occurs as bromides, mainly in seawater, from which it is extracted by oxidation with chlorine. Soluble metal bromides (see HALIDES) are used as SEDATIVES; silver bromide, being light-sensitive, is used in PHOTOGRAPHY. Ethylene dibromide, the chief bromine product, is used as a lead scavenger in ANTIKNOCK ADDITIVES. Alkyl bromides (see ALKYL HALIDES) are used as fumigants and solvents. AW 79.9, mp −7°C, bp 59°C, sg 3.12 (20°C).

BRONCHI, tubes through which air passes from the TRACHEA to the LUNGS. The trachea divides into the two primary bronchi, one to each lung, which divide into smaller branches and finally into the narrow bronchioles connecting with the alveolar sacs. The bronchi are lined with a mucus membrane which has motile CILIA to remove dust, etc.

BRONCHITIS, inflammation of BRONCHI. **Acute bronchitis**, often due to VIRUS infection, is accompanied by COUGH and FEVER and is short-lived; ANTIBIOTICS are only needed if there is bacterial infection. **Chronic bronchitis** is a more serious, often disabling and finally fatal disease. The main cause is SMOKING which irritates the LUNGS and causes overproduction of MUCUS. The CILIA fail, and sputum has to be coughed up. Bronchi thus become liable to recurrent bacterial infection, sometimes progressing to PNEUMONIA. Areas of lung become non-functional, and ultimately CYANOSIS and HEART failure may result. Treatment includes PHYSIOTHERAPY, antibiotics and bronchial dilator drugs. Stopping smoking limits damage and may improve early cases.

BRONCHOSCOPE, a tube with a light and lens system, used to examine the TRACHEA and BRONCHI, and also to perform a BIOPSY.

BRONCO. See MUSTANG; RODEO.

BRØNSTED, Johannes Nicolaus (1879–1947), Danish physical chemist principally remembered for formulating (independently of T. M. Lowry) the Brønsted-Lowry theory o ACIDS and bases.

BRONSTEIN, Lev Davidovich. See TROTSKY, LEON.

BRONTË, name of three English novelists, daughters of an Irish-born Anglican clergyman. They lived chiefly in the isolated moorland town of Haworth, Yorkshire. Their lives, marred by the early death of their mother and the dissipations of their brother, Branwell, were closely bound together, and this domestic intensity informed much of their work. **Charlotte Brontë** (1816–1855) published the partly autobiographical *Jane Eyre* (1847) under the name Currer Bell, and met with immediate success. Together with *Shirley* (1849) and *Villette* (1853), it represents an important advance in the treatment of women in English fiction. **Emily Brontë** (1818–1848), using the name Ellis Bell, published a single novel, *Wuthering Heights* (1847), a masterpiece of visionary power. **Anne Brontë** (1820–1849) published two novels, *Agnes Grey* (1847) and *The Tenant of Wildfell Hall* (1848), under the name Acton Bell.

When the 1 595ft Brooklyn bridge was opened in 1883 at a cost of $15 million it was the world's largest suspension bridge. In 1964 the National Park Service designated it a national landmark.

BRONTOSAURUS, a vegetarian DINOSAUR whose fossilized skeleton has been found in the western US. About 20m (66ft) long and calculated to be 35 tonnes in weight, it had a long neck and tail, small head and brain, ponderous body and thick legs.

BRONX, The, one of New York City's five boroughs, named for Jonas Bronck, who acquired the land in 1639. The only mainland borough, it is separated from Manhattan by the Harlem R. It is mainly residential, and contains part of New York U., Hunter College, Fordham U. and the Botanical and Zoological gardens.

BRONZE, an ALLOY of COPPER and TIN, known since the 4th millennium BC (see BRONZE AGE), and used then for tools and weapons, now for machine parts and marine hardware. Statues are often cast in bronze. It is a hard, strong alloy with good corrosion-resistance (the patina formed in air is protective). Various other components are added to bronze to improve hardness or machinability, such as aluminum, iron, lead, zinc and phosphorus. Aluminum bronzes, and some others, contain no tin. (See also BELL METAL; GUN METAL.)

BRONZE AGE, the phase of man's material cultural development following the STONE AGE, and the first phase in which metal was used. The start of the bronze age varies from region to region, but certainly the use of copper was known as early as 6 500 BC in Asia Minor, and its use was widespread shortly thereafter. By about 3 000 BC BRONZE was widely used, to be replaced around 1000 BC by iron.

BROOK, Peter (Stephen Paul) (1925–), English theater and opera director, famed for his reinterpretations of Shakespeare. His productions have included *King Lear* (1962), the *Marat/Sade* (1964) and *A Midsummer Night's Dream* (1970), all for the Royal Shakespeare Company. He has also made several films, among them *Lord of the Flies* (1962).

BROOKE, Alan Francis. See ALANBROOKE, 1ST VISCOUNT.

BROOKE, Edward William (1919–), US senator from Mass., who in 1966 became the first Negro senator since Reconstruction. As attorney general of Mass. (1962–66), he fought corruption.

BROOKE, Sir James (1803–1868), English adventurer who became the ruler of Sarawak, Borneo. Appointed raja in 1841, he founded a dynasty which ruled Sarawak until 1946, when the region was ceded to Britain.

BROOKE, Rupert (Chawner) (1887–1915), English poet, best known for the romantic, patriotic sonnets he wrote before his death in WWI. His verse became highly popular with the publication of *1914 and Other Poems* (1915).

BROOK FARM, US Utopian community, founded at West Roxbury, Mass., by George RIPLEY in 1841. The aim was to create an egalitarian community of workers and thinkers. The community contained a noted progressive school and attracted many leading intellectuals, but lasted only until 1847.

BROOKFIELD, village in NE Ill., 10mi W of Chicago, of which it is a residential suburb. It is the home of the Chicago Zoological Park. Pop 20 284.

BROOKFIELD, city in SE Wis., a suburb of Milwaukee. Mainly residential, but with some important commercial activity and light industry. Pop 32 140.

BROOKHAVEN, city in SW Miss., seat of Lincoln Co. Its industries include timber and dairy products. Pop 10 700.

BROOKHAVEN NATIONAL LABORATORY, center for nuclear research at Camp Upton, Long Island, N.Y. Under the aegis of the US Atomic Energy Commission, it has facilities for medical and agricultural research.

BROOKINGS, city in E S.D., on the Big Sioux R, seat of Brookings Co. It is a center for trade in livestock and grain, and for seed processing and agricultural research. Pop 13 717.

BROOKINGS INSTITUTION, nonprofit-making, public service corporation founded in 1927 in Washington, D.C., for research and information on government and economic problems. It was named for the St. Louis merchant, Robert S. Brookings.

BROOKLINE, town in E Mass., bordering on Boston, Cambridge and Newton. The birthplace of President John F. Kennedy, it is primarily a residential suburb. Pop 58 886.

BROOKLYN, borough of New York City in SE N.Y., seat of Kings Co., SW Long Island. The borough is a residential and heavily industrialized area with major dockyards, including the New York Naval Shipyard. The East R, between the borough and Manhattan, is spanned by the Brooklyn, Manhattan and Williamsburg bridges; the Brooklyn-Battery Tunnel carries traffic under the river. The famous Coney Island sea resort is in Brooklyn. Pop 2 601 852.

BROOKLYN, city in NE Ohio, SW of Cleveland, of which it is a suburb. Pop 13 142.

BROOKLYN BRIDGE, famous suspension bridge in New York City between the borough of Brooklyn and Manhattan Island. It was built in 1869–83 by A. J. Roebling and his son, pioneers in the use of steel-wire support cables, which give the bridge its characteristic spider-web appearance. Its two huge masonry towers are supported by pneumatic caissons, another pioneering feat of the Roeblings.

BROOKLYN CENTER, city in SE central Minn., 8mi NNW of Minneapolis, of which it is a suburb. Pop 35 173.

BROOKLYN PARK, village in SE Minn. It is a northern suburb of Minneapolis. Pop 26 230.

BROOKS, Gwendolyn Elizabeth (1917–), black US poet. Born in Chicago, Ill., she was the first Negro poet to win the Pulitzer Prize, with her semi-autobiographical *Annie Allen* (1948).

BROOKS, Phillips (1835–1893), US Episcopal clergyman, the most famous preacher of his day, with a wide intellectual influence. Many of his sermons were published 1881–1902. He was minister at Trinity Church, Boston, 1869–91, and bishop of Mass. He is known for his hymn, *O Little Town of Bethlehem* (1868).

BROOKS, Preston Smith (1819–1857), US politician, congressman from S.C. from 1857. Enraged by Charles SUMNER's denunciation of Brooks' uncle in an antislavery speech, he beat Sumner senseless with a cane in the Senate, rather than duel with a social inferior. Forced to resign, he was at once reelected. The incident revealed pre-Civil War tensions.

BROOKS, van Wyck (1886–1963), US critic who examined American writers in the context of their contemporary society. In *America's Coming of Age* (1915), he saw the 19th-century US as torn between the idealistic and the materialistic. In biographies of Mark TWAIN, Henry JAMES, EMERSON and others he traced their development in this society.

BROOKS RANGE, N extremity of the Rocky Mts, in N Alaska, extending over 600mi W to E within the Antarctic Circle. Its peaks range from 3 000ft to 9 000ft in height.

BROOM, general name given to a number of LEGUMINOUS PLANTS of the genera *Cytisus* and *Genista*. They are mainly deciduous or almost leafless shrubs that produce a profusion of pea-like flowers. There are many cultivated varieties. Quite unrelated is the Butcher's broom (*Ruscus aculeatus*), a hardy evergreen shrub whose apparent leaves are in fact modified stems (cladodes).

BROOMCORN. See SORGHUM.

BROTHERHOOD WEEK, in the US, celebrated during the week of George Washington's birthday, in Feb. Sponsored by the National Conference of Christians and Jews, it seeks to promote interracial understanding.

John Brown's notorious but abortive attack on this government fort at Harpers Ferry, West Virginia, in 1859, was one sign of the fanatical fervor accompanying abolitionism before the American Civil War.

BROUGHAM AND VAUX, Henry Peter Brougham, 1st Baron (1778–1868), influential Scottish lawyer, social reformer and politician. Cofounder of the *Edinburgh Review* (1802), he was a member of parliament 1810–12 and 1816–30. As lord chancellor 1830–34, he forced both legal reforms and the 1832 REFORM BILL through the House of Lords.

BROUN, Heywood Campbell (1888–1939), US journalist. In his *It Seems To Me* column in the *New York Tribune* and later in *World*, he expounded and defended liberal ideas and causes, such as the SACCO-VANZETTI CASE. He established and headed the American Newspaper Guild.

BROUWER, Adriaen (1605–1638), Flemish painter of humorous peasant scenes such as *The Smokers* (1626), *Drinkers at a Table, Peasant Interior* and *Tavern Brawl*. He was influenced by Pieter BRUEGEL and Frans HALS.

BROWALLIA, a genus of half-hardy annual plants with tubular, violet-shaped blue or white flowers. They are generally grown as house plants where they require a sunny position and will flower in winter as long as the temperature is 13°C to 16°C (55°F to 61°F), but they can be grown as garden plants in mild areas. They should be watered often enough to keep the soil moist, but less in the autumn and winter. Browallias are normally grown from seed, but cuttings can be taken in the summer. The closely-related orange browallia (*Streptosolen jamesonii*) is a tender evergreen shrub, best grown in cool greenhouses against a wall. Family: Solanaceae.

BROWDER, Earl Russell (1891–1973), US Communist party secretary-general 1930–44, and president of the communist political association, 1944–45. Claiming "Communism is 20th-century Americanism" he won great support for the party. Although communist presidential candidate in 1936 and 1940, he was expelled as a deviationist in 1946.

BROWN, Sir Arthur Whitten. See ALCOCK AND BROWN.

BROWN, Benjamin Gratz (1826–1885), US politician. He helped form the Mo. Republican party. As US senator 1863–67, he tried to replace LINCOLN by John FRÉMONT. In 1872 he was the vice-presidential candidate of the LIBERAL REPUBLICAN PARTY.

BROWN, "Capability" (Lancelot Brown; 1715–1783), English garden and landscape designer. His work for English estate-owners was characterized by his use of such natural features or "capabilities" of landscape as tree-clumps, lakes and sloping ground. His best known design is that of Kew.

BROWN, Charles Brockden (1771–1810), one of the first US professional writers. Influenced by William GODWIN, his *Alcuin: a dialogue* (1798) and novel *Edgar Huntly* (1799) plead for social reform. *Wieland*, 1799, is an outstanding Gothic novel.

BROWN, Ford Madox (1821–1893), English literary, religious and historical painter, a precursor of the PRE-RAPHAELITE BROTHERHOOD. He is famous for *Work* (1852–63), and *Pretty Baa-Lambs* (1851).

BROWN, George (1818–1880), Canadian politician and journalist, born in Scotland. In 1844 he founded the Toronto *Globe*, which had great political influence. He supported Canadian confederation.

BROWN, Jacob Jennings (1775–1828), outstanding US general in the War of 1812. He defeated the British at SACKETS HARBOR in 1813. In 1814 he crossed the Niagara and successfully defended Fort Erie. In 1821 he was army commanding general.

BROWN, John (1800–1859), US abolitionist whose exploits helped bring on the Civil War. He was involved in the slave UNDERGROUND RAILROAD in Pa. and then with his five sons moved to Kan. to help the antislavery settlers in 1855. After proslavery men burned down the town of Lawrence, Brown retaliated by murdering five proslavery men at Pottawatamie Creek. During 1857–58 Brown planned to establish a new state in the Va. mountains as a refuge for fugitive slaves and a base for antislavery activity. In October 1859 he seized the government arsenal at Harper's Ferry, Va., and awaited a massive slave insurrection. Instead, the arsenal was stormed; Brown was tried for treason and hanged.

BROWN, Robert (1773–1858), Scottish botanist who first observed BROWNIAN MOTION (1827) and who identified and named the plant CELL nucleus (1831).

BROWN BEAR, *Ursus arctos*, formerly the most widespread species of bear, found in N Europe and Asia and North America. It is now present in small numbers in montane regions of Europe and in the USSR. It is also found with the subspecies, GRIZZLY BEAR and ALASKAN BROWN BEAR, in North America. It has a short neck and a large dog-like head.

BROWN DEER, village in SE Wis., 11mi N of Milwaukee, of which it is a suburb. Pop 12582.

BROWNE, Charles Farrar. See WARD, ARTEMUS.

BROWNE, Robert (c1550–1633), English Puritan clergyman, leader of a separatist group, the Brownists. He taught independence of the Church from secular government and duty to conscience rather than to outward regulation. His writings are considered the first expression of CONGREGATIONALISM.

BROWNE, Sir Thomas (1605–1682), English physician and author. He is most famous for his book, *Religio Medici* (1643), a fine example of ornate English prose which displays religious toleration in an age of intolerance. His other major work is *Urne-Buriall* (1658), a meditation on death and immortality.

BROWNIAN MOTION, frequent, random fluctuation, illustrated by the motion of particles of the dispersed phase of a fluid COLLOID; first described by Robert BROWN (1827) after observation of a SUSPENSION of pollen grains in water. It is a result of the bombardment of the colloidal particles by the MOLECULES of the continuous phase (see KINETIC THEORY): a chance greater number of impacts in one direction changes the direction of motion of the particle. It is believed that all molecules of FLUIDS undergo Brownian motion. Observation of Brownian motion in colloids is of value in studies of DIFFUSION.

BROWNING, Elizabeth Barrett (1806–1861), English poet. In her own day she was second in reputation only to Tennyson. She is now best known for *Sonnets from the Portuguese* (1850), inspired by her romance with Robert BROWNING, who "rescued" her from illness and family tyranny in 1846.

BROWNING, John Moses (1855–1926), US inventor of the Browning automatic guns used by the Allies in WWI and WWII. His 1917 .30 caliber machine gun was recoil-operated and water-cooled. The later .50 caliber version was used in WWII aircraft.

BROWNING, Robert (1812–1889), English poet. He perfected the dramatic monologue in such poems as "Andrea del Sarto" and "Bishop Blougram's Apology" (*Men and Women*; 1855). He also used it in what is considered his masterpiece, *The Ring and the Book* (1868–69), a 17th-century Roman murder story told from several different viewpoints. His psychological insight and use of colloquial language profoundly influenced 20th-century poets.

BROWNSON, Orestes Augustus (1830–1876), US transcendentalist writer on social and religious subjects. He was successively Presbyterian, Unitarian and Roman Catholic; and was interested in labor movements, social reform and emancipation.

BROWNSTONE, reddish-brown variety of SANDSTONE, used for building. Also a house of brownstone: best known are those of New York.

BROWNSVILLE, city and port in S Tex., seat of Cameron Co., 22mi from the mouth of the Rio Grande. It produces chemicals, clothing and petroleum products, and is the W terminus of the Gulf Intracoastal Waterway. Pop 52522.

BROWNSVILLE AFFAIR, an incident in 1906, in which Negro soldiers from Fort Brown, Tex., allegedly entered nearby Brownsville and fired on houses and townspeople. President Theodore Roosevelt ordered the dishonorable discharge of 167 soldiers, a decision reversed by the army in 1972.

BROWN-TAIL MOTH, *Nygmia phaeorrhoea*, a type of moth native to Europe, introduced to North America in about 1868, where it is a pest to foliage. Wings and body are white, but it has a brown abdominal tuft. Larvae hatch in August, hibernate in a white web and scatter as black caterpillars in summer.

BROWNWOOD, industrial city in central Tex., seat of Brown Co. It processes pecans, peanuts, cotton and oil. Pop 17368.

BROZ, Josip. See TITO.

BRUBECK, David Warren (1920–), US jazz pianist and composer. After classical training, in 1951 he formed his own jazz quartet, which became one of the most popular "progressive" groups.

BRUCE, Blanche Kelso (1841–1898), US Negro politician. He was a senator from Mass. in 1874, and was the first Negro to serve a full Senate term.

BRUCE, Sir David (1855–1931), Australian-born British microbiologist who discovered the organisms responsible for undulant fever, nagana and African SLEEPING SICKNESS. The BACILLUS causing the first of these (now known as BRUCELLOSIS) is named *Brucella* in his honor.

BRUCE, James (1730–1794), Scottish explorer who rediscovered the headwaters of the Blue Nile at Lake Tana in 1770. His *Travels to Discover the Source of the Nile* (1790) records his explorations in Egypt and Ethiopia.

BRUCE, Rober the (1274–1329), King Robert I of Scotland. His family's claim to the throne was disputed by John de Baliol, the English nominee. Bruce was crowned in 1306 in defiance of EDWARD I of England, who favored de Baliol. Pursued as a rebel, he defeated Edward II at BANNOCKBURN (1314). English recognition of Scottish independence was eventually granted in 1328.

BRUCELLOSIS, or **Bang's disease**, a BACTERIAL DISEASE of cattle, goats and swine, caused by *Brucella*. It causes ABORTION and affected animals have to be slaughtered to prevent spread. The disease in man (once known as **undulant fever**) is contracted from milk or by contact with infected animals; it is a variable illness, often causing FEVER, malaise and DEPRESSION, and may be treated with ANTIBIOTICS.

BRUCE OF MELBOURNE, Stanley Melbourne Bruce, 1st Viscount (1883–1967), Australian statesman, prime minister 1923–29. He was Australian high commissioner in London 1933–45.

BRUCH, Max (1838–1920), German composer, best known for the *Violin Concerto in G Minor* (1866), *Kol Nidrei* (1880) and two Scottish fantasies (1880).

BRUCKNER, (Josef) Anton (1824–1896), Austrian composer, noted for his nine massive symphonies and his choral music. His deep Catholic piety permeated all his works. A major influence was Richard WAGNER, whom he greatly admired. Bruckner was a professor at the Vienna Conservatory from 1868. A simple and good-natured man, he ranks with MAHLER among the great late Romantic symphonists.

BRUEGEL, family of Flemish artists flourishing from the 16th to the 18th centuries. **Pieter Bruegel the Elder** (c1525–1569) was a great painter of landscapes and peasant scenes. Influenced at first by BOSCH, he was much impressed by the scenery of Italy, which he visited in 1552. His works, some on religious subjects, are often allegorical or satirical, profoundly affected by his view of the human condition. **Pieter Bruegel the Younger** (1564–1638), also called Hell Bruegel, worked in his father's manner, often with an emphasis on the grotesque. **Jan Bruegel** (1568–1625), also called Velvet Bruegel, the second son, painted landscapes and still lifes with great subtlety and delicacy. He often collaborated with RUBENS.

BRUGGE, or Bruges, well-preserved medieval city in

A characteristically grotesque work by Bruegel, in striking contrast to his well known rustic scenes.

NW Belgium. Once a center for wool trade, and in the 15th century home of a school of painting led by the VAN EYCKS and Hans MEMLING, its commercial interest revived in the 19th century when the Zeebrugge Canal to the North Sea was opened. It manufactures lace and textiles. Pop 51 303.

BRUISE, or contusion, a lesion of the SKIN, usually caused by a blow, in which CAPILLARY damage allows blood to leak into the dermis where it is slowly broken down and absorbed. A **hematoma**, a larger blood-filled cavity, may require draining. Bruising without injury may indicate BLOOD disease.

BRÛLÉ, Étienne (c1592–1633), French explorer of North America, the first white man to explore four of the Great Lakes. He accompanied CHAMPLAIN to Canada in 1608 and lived with the Huron Indians 1610–11. In 1629 he piloted the English fleet which took Quebec.

BRUMAIRE, second month of the French Revolutionary calendar. On 18–19 Brumaire (Nov. 9–10, 1799), the DIRECTORY was overthrown and the Consulate under NAPOLEON established in its place.

BRUMMELL, George Bryan "Beau" (1778–1840), English man of fashion. He was a friend of the Prince of Wales (later George IV) and an arbiter of fashion in REGENCY society. He fled to France in 1816 to escape his creditors.

BRUNEI, tropical sultanate on the N coast of Borneo, which controlled all Borneo in the 16th century. It became an English protectorate in 1888, and a 1959 constitution gave it domestic autonomy. The population is 65% Malay and 23% Chinese, the latter running many small businesses. Malay is the chief language, Islam the official religion. Rubber and timber were superseded as main products after petroleum was found in 1929.

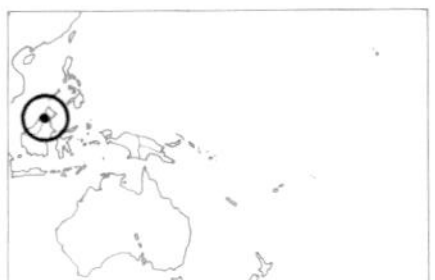

Official Name: The Sultanate of Brunei
Capital: Bandar Seri Begewan
Area: 2 226sq mi
Population: 136 256
Languages: Malay, Chinese, English
Religions: Muslim; Buddhist
Monetary Unit(s): 1 Brunei dollar = 100 cents

BRUNEL, Sir Marc Isambard (1769–1849), French-born British engineer and inventor who built the world's first underwater tunnel (under the River Thames) and devised machines for the mass production of pulley blocks and army boots. His son, **Isambard Kingdom Brunel** (1806–1859), pioneered many important construction techniques, designing the Clifton suspension bridge at Bristol, England laying the Great Western Railway with a controversial 7ft (2.13m) gauge and building iron-hulled steamships, including the giant *Great Eastern*.

BRUNELLESCHI, Filippo (1377–1446), first great Italian Renaissance architect. He devised the rules of linear perspective. Influenced by classical Roman and 11th-century Tuscan Romanesque architecture, his masterpiece is the dome of Florence cathedral (1420–36).

BRÜNHILD, in Germanic mythology, a warrior maiden, heroine of the Old Norse EDDAS and VOLSUNGA SAGA (in which she is portrayed as a VALKYRIE) and prominent in the German NIBELUNGENLIED. The legends, on which WAGNER based his operas, *The Ring of the Nibelungs*, tell of the love between her and Sigurd (or SIEGFRIED) and their tragic deaths.

BRÜNING, Heinrich (1885–1970), German statesman. Chancellor of the Weimar Republic 1930–32, his measures to restore the German economy aroused opposition, and his dismissal from office by President von HINDENBURG led eventually to HITLER's chancellorship.

BRUNNER, Heinrich Emil (1889–1966), Swiss Reformed theologian, an exponent of NEO-ORTHODOXY and an ecumenist. He differed from BARTH in accepting the ideas of BUBER and the limited validity of natural THEOLOGY. Brunner was theology professor at Zurich 1922–53.

BRUNO, Giordano (1548–1600), Italian pantheist philosopher, poet and cosmologist, an apostate Dominican, who taught the plurality of inhabited worlds, the infinity of the universe and the truth of the Copernican hypothesis. Burned at the stake for heresy, he became renowned as a martyr to science—except among scientists.

BRUNSWICK (Braunschweig), historic city in NE West Germany on the Oker R. Chartered in the 12th century, it became an important member of the HANSEATIC LEAGUE. The city now manufactures iron and steel goods. Pop 225 200.

BRUNSWICK, seaport city in SE Ga., seat of Glynn Co. It has fishing and seafood industries and naval stores. It is also a popular resort. Pop 19 585.

BRUNSWICK, town in SW Me., 23mi NE of Portland. It is a resort area, and the site of Bowdoin College and a naval station. It manufactures textiles. Pop 16 195.

BRUNSWICK, city in N Ohio, a suburb of Cleveland. Pop 15 852.

BRUSILOV, Alexei Alexeyevich (1853–1926), Russian general. In WWI he inflicted a massive defeat on Austro-Hungarian forces in E Galicia (1916). After the Russian revolution he aided the Red Army in its war against Poland.

BRUSSELS, Belgian capital city, headquarters of the European Common Market, NATO and the Atomic Energy Commission. First commercially important in the 12th century, it was granted a ducal charter in 1312. From the 16th to the 19th centuries it was subject successively to Spain, Austria and France. It manufactures textiles, lace and furniture and is a transport center. Pop 161 089.

BRUSSELS GRIFFON, wiry-coated Belgian toy breed of dog with a monkey-like face and a beard, developed from a ratting dog. Red, black or black and tan in color, it may weigh up to 9lb and makes a small but lively pet.

BRUSSELS SPROUTS, *Brassica oleracea*, green vegetable of the genus BRASSICA, thought to have been first cultivated in Belgium and descended from the wild cabbage. It is a BIENNIAL grown for the small, close-packed leaf buds that appear in the leaf axils.

BRUTUS, name of an ancient Roman family. **Lucius Junius Brutus** (6th century BC) founded the Roman Republic by expelling King Lucius Tarquinius Superbus in 509 BC. **Decimus Junius Brutus** (d. 43 BC) served with Julius Caesar in Gaul and was one of his assassins. **Marcus Junius Brutus** (85–42 BC) was a highly respected statesman who helped lead the assassination plot against Caesar. He committed suicide after his defeat by Antony and Octavian at Philippi.

BRYAN, city in E central Tex., seat of Brazos Co., the center of an agricultural area. Pop 33 719.

BRYAN, William Jennings (1860–1925), US politician, orator and lawyer. He was an unsuccessful Democratic presidential candidate in 1896, 1900 and 1908 and secretary of state 1913–15. Elected to Congress in 1890, he was influential in the adoption of income tax, popular election of senators and female suffrage. A fundamentalist, he prosecuted at the SCOPES TRIAL in 1925, winning the case against teaching evolution in schools over defense attorney Clarence DARROW.

BRYAN-CHAMORRO TREATY, agreement between the US and Nicaragua in 1914. In return for $3 million, the US gained rights to a canal route and a naval base, and a renewable lease to Great Corn and Little Corn islands and the Gulf of Fonseca.

BRYANSK, USSR city, capital of the Bryansk oblast, on the Desna R. A railroad junction, it has ironworks and locomotive, machine and concrete factories. Pop 338 000.

BRYANT, William Cullen (1794–1878), US poet and journalist. Editor of the New York *Evening Post* from 1829, he campaigned against slavery and for free speech. He wrote pastoral odes, the most famous being *Thanatopsis* (1817), and translated the *Iliad* and *Odyssey* (1870–72).

BRYCE, James Bryce, 1st Viscount (1838–1922), British statesman and historian. He wrote *The Holy Roman Empire* (1864) and *The American Commonwealth* (1888). He was British ambassador to the US 1907–13.

BRYCE CANYON NATIONAL PARK, an area of 36 010 acres in S Ut., created as a park in 1928. It contains extraordinary formations in colorful limestone and sandstone, the result of erosion.

BRYONY, or white bryony, *Bryonia dioca*, climbing plant that is native to Europe and Asia. Also, black bryony (*Tamus communis*), a climbing plant with tuberous roots that have medicinal properties.

This monument commemorating the poet William Cullen Bryant stands in Bryant Park, New York City behind the city library.

BRYOPHYTA, division of the PLANT KINGDOM that contains the most primitive of the green land plants. The Bryophyta are normally divided into three classes: Hepaticae (LIVERWORTS), Anthoceratae (HORNWORTS) and Musci (MOSSES). Bryophytes have a characteristic life cycle in which the GAMETOPHYTE is dominant and the SPOROPHYTE is attached to and dependent on the gametophyte for nutrition. (See also ALTERNATION OF GENERATIONS.)

BRYOZOA, phylum of small plantlike aquatic animals. They live in colonies which encrust seaweeds, stones or submerged wooden objects and sometimes resemble lacy fans. The colonies consist of polyps in a horny tube

BUBBLE CHAMBER, device invented by GLASER (1952) to observe the paths of SUBATOMIC PARTICLES with energies too high for a CLOUD CHAMBER to be used. A liquid (e.g. liquid HYDROGEN or OXYGEN) is held under PRESSURE just below its BOILING POINT. Sudden reduction in pressure lowers this boiling point: boiling starts along the paths of energetic subatomic particles, whose passage creates local heating. At the instant of reduction, their paths may thus be photographed as a chain of bubbles.

BUBER, Martin (1878–1965), Jewish philosopher, born in Austria. Editor of a major German–Jewish journal, *Der Jude*, 1916–24, he was a leading educator and scholar of HASIDISM. An ardent Zionist, he moved to Palestine in 1938. His central philosophical concept is that of the direct "I-Thou" relationship between man and God and man and man.

BUBONIC PLAGUE. See BLACK DEATH; PLAGUE.

BUCARAMANGA, city in N Colombia, in an agricultural region. Founded by Spaniards in 1622, it produces tobacco and coffee. Pop 347 000.

BUCCANEERS, piratical adventurers who preyed on Spanish ships and possessions during the 1600s. Among the most famous were MORGAN, DAMPIER and BLACKBEARD. Operating in American waters, they set up whole communities in the Caribbean area, but died out by 1700.

BUCENTAUR, ornamental barge used for ceremonials by Italian Renaissance princes of Church and state. The most famous was that of the Venetian doge, used annually on Ascension Day.

BUCEPHALUS, Alexander the Great's horse, which accompanied him on campaigns for 18 years. When he died in 326 BC, after the battle of Hydaspes R, Alexander founded the city of Bucephala.

BUCER, Martin (1491–1551), German Protestant reformer who tried to reconcile differences among Protestant sects after the Reformation. He refused to accept a Protestant–Catholic compromise and went to England in 1549.

BUCHAN, John, 1st Baron Tweedsmuir (1875–1940), Scottish author and politician. He wrote historical works, biographies and such classic adventure stories as *The Thirty-Nine Steps* (1915). From 1935 he was governor-general of Canada.

BUCHANAN, Franklin (1800–1874), US Confederate naval officer. He commanded the ironclad *Virginia*, which destroyed two Union ships at the Hampton Roads blockade. Promoted to admiral, he was captured in a heroic fight against Union Admiral David G. FARRAGUT in 1864.

BUCHANAN, James (1791–1868), 15th president of the US. A Pennsylvania lawyer, he was first a Federalist, later a Democrat. He was a US congressman 1821–31, minister to Russia 1831–33, and a US senator 1834–45. While he was secretary of state under President Polk (1845–49), the dispute with Britain over Oregon was settled and the Mexican War broke out, following the annexation of Tex. Under President Pierce he was minister to Britain 1853–56, and with J. Y. Mason and Pierre Soule worked out the controversial OSTEND MANIFESTO, stating that the US must protect its security by acquiring Cuba through purchase or force.

Though morally opposed to slavery, he believed the constitution gave individual states the right to decide the issue, and on this compromise platform won the presidency, serving 1857–61. He attempted to settle Kansas' admission to statehood by "popular sovereignty," allowing popular vote to decide the slavery issue in the territory. His proposal passed the Senate but failed in the House. His upholding of the DRED SCOTT DECISION aroused opposition in both houses. With the Democratic party divided, Abraham Lincoln won the 1860 election. When secession began, Buchanan tried desperately to maintain peace. He disapproved of secession but knew no constitutional authority to prevent it. Believing that federal troops should be used only to protect federal property, he eventually sent troops to Fort Sumter. After Lincoln took office, Buchanan supported the Union.

BUCHAREST, capital of Romania, on the Dâmbovita R. A medieval fortress, it became the residence of the princess of Walachia in 1459 and the capital when the new Romania was formed in 1861. It produces pharmaceutical and electrical goods, machinery and automobiles. Pop 1 525 291.

BUCHENWALD, Nazi concentration camp set up near Weimar in 1937 to hold political and "non-Aryan" prisoners. More than 100 000 (chiefly Jews) died there through starvation, extermination and medical experiment.

BUCHMAN, Frank (1878–1961), US evangelist who founded MORAL RE-ARMAMENT in 1938.

BUCHNER, Eduard (1860–1917), German organic chemist, awarded the 1907 Nobel Prize for Chemistry for his discovery that FERMENTATION did not require the presence of complete YEAST cells but only an extract containing the enzyme ZYMASE. This discovery inaugurated ENZYME chemistry.

BÜCHNER, Georg (1813–1837), German dramatist, forerunner of EXPRESSIONISM. His *Danton's Death* (1835) and *Woyzeck* (1837), use colloquial language and sometimes sordid settings With psychological insight, they trace the powerlessness of isolated individuals, whether against historical forces or society—Woyzeck is a soldier pressured into murdering his unfaithful mistress. *Lenz*, unfinished, is about a dramatist on the verge of madness.

James BUCHANAN

15th US President

Born: April 23, 1791
Died: June 1, 1868
Term of Office: March 4, 1857–March 3, 1861
Political Party: Democratic

BUCK, Pearl Sydenstricker (1892–1973), US author. Most of her novels are set in China, where she lived up to 1934. She won the Pulitzer Prize in 1932 for *The Good Earth* (1931), and the 1938 Nobel Prize for Literature.

BUCKEYE, common name for a number of North American trees of the genus *Aesculus*, the HORSE CHESTNUTS.

BUCKINGHAM, George Villiers, 1st Duke of (1592–1628), English nobleman whose influence over JAMES I and CHARLES I inflamed anti-monarchical feeling. He promoted costly and unsuccessful military ventures, notably the expedition to relieve the Huguenots of LA ROCHELLE. Charles, however, shielded him from impeachment. He was eventually assassinated.

BUCKINGHAM PALACE, London residence of the British royal family, built in 1703 and bought by George III from the Duke of Buckingham in 1761. Queen Victoria, in 1837, was the first monarch to use it as an official residence.

BUCK ISLAND REEF NATIONAL MONUMENT, on St. Croix in the Virgin Islands. It has 850 acres and is famous for its marine gardens.

The London residence of the British Royal Family was built in 1703 and has been restyled a number of times since then. In the foreground stands the Queen Victoria Memorial, designed by Webb and Brock, 1903–1911.

The Daibutsu, or great Buddha at Kamakura near Tokyo is the second largest statue of Buddha, being 42 feet 6 inches in height. Cast in 1252, it was originally housed in a building which was carried away by a tidal wave in 1495. The Daibutsu is a major sanctuary and tourist attraction of Japan.

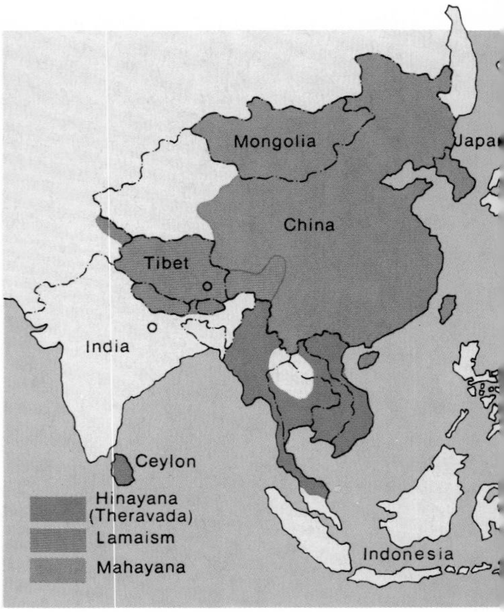

Buddhism is the most important of the religions of Asia.

BUCKLE, Henry Thomas (1821–1862), English historian. With the influential *History of Civilization in England* (1857–61), he broke from the tradition of treating only individuals, wars and politics and considered peoples, cultures and environments.

BUCKLEY, William Frank, Jr. (1925–), US author, editor and lecturer. He founded the weekly *National Review* (1955) to voice often controversially conservative views.

BUCKNER, Simon Bolivar (1823–1914), US Confederate commander and governor of Ky. (1887–91). He surrendered Fort Donelson to General Grant (Feb. 16, 1862) and was later commander of the District of La. His son, **Simon Bolivar Buckner, Jr.** (1886–1945), a general, was killed in action in WWII.

BUCKTHORN, name for trees and shrubs of the genus *Rhamnus*, which are native to Europe, N Africa and N Asia and naturalized in North America. They have small flowers and often red or black edible berries. *Rhamnus purshiana* yields the purgative CASCARA SAGRADA.

BUCKWHEAT, *Fagopyrum sagittatum* (or *esculentum*) and allied species are herbs native to Asia but which are now commonly cultivated in Europe and the US The seed (fruit) is used in the US as a livestock feed or may be ground into a flour that is used for pancakes and cakes.

BUCOLICS, poems idealizing shepherd life, in the PASTORAL tradition of THEOCRITUS (3rd century BC). The term was first used as an alternative title for VERGIL's *Eclogues* (37 BC).

BUCYRUS, city in N central Ohio, on the Sandusky R, settled in 1818. It manufactures farm and highway construction machinery. Pop 13 111.

BUD, a condensed shoot in which the stem is very short, the inner leaves are closely packed and the outer scale leaves form a protective covering. In the spring, the stem elongates rapidly and the leaves unfold. The term bud is also used in zoology for a point from which new growth develops.

BUDAPEST, capital of Hungary, on the Danube R. Two settlements, Buda on the right bank and Pest on the left, date from Roman times but were destroyed by Mongol invaders in 1241. Buda became Hungary's capital in 1361. They declined under the Turks but revived under the Hapsburgs and were united in 1873. Textiles are the main industry. The city was virtually destroyed in WWII. It was the center of the Hungarian uprising in 1956. Pop 2 023 000.

BUDDHA, Gautama (c563–483 BC), founder of BUDDHISM. Son of the raja of Kapilavastu near Nepal, his name was Siddhartha Gautama. At the age of 29, confronting human misery for the first time, he at once set out to find the path to peace and serenity. For six years he studied under BRAHMAN teachers, living as a hermit. Enlightenment came to him while seated under a *bodhi* or pipal tree; he remained there in contemplation of truth some six or seven weeks. Thereafter he preached and gathered disciples as Buddha ("the Enlightened One").

BUDDHISM, religion and philosophy developed from HINDUISM in the 6th century BC by Siddhartha Gautama, the BUDDHA. His monastic disciples shaved their heads, dressed in rags and devoted themselves to the philosophy of Enlightenment.

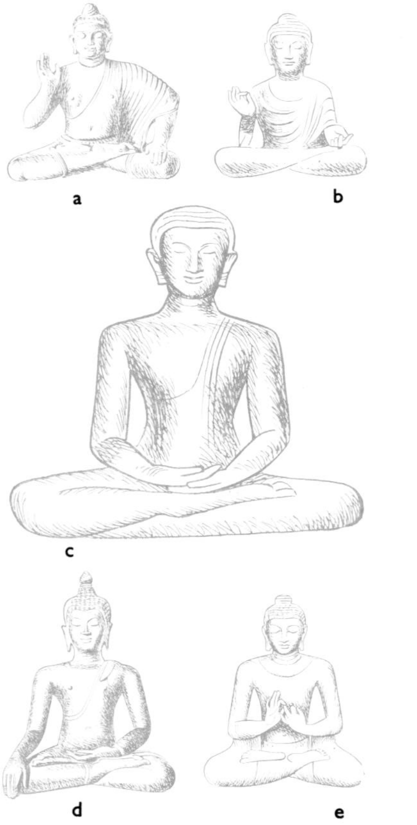

The formal hand gestures, known as *mudras*, shown in these statues symbolise various states of being: *Dhyana mudra* (c), with the hands folded in the lap, is the attitude for meditation. *Abhaya mudra* (a) symbolizes absence of fear, while *Bitarka mudra* (b) is the gesture for argument. The *Bhumi-sparsha mudra* (d) invokes the spirit of the Earth. The *Dharmacakra mudra* (e), symbolizing the setting into motion of the "wheel of the law," is the attitude for preaching.

The Pali canon is the scriptural basis of Buddhism, transcribing from oral tradition Buddha's teaching and monastic rules. It was set down by the first Buddhist council at Rajagaha in the 5th century BC. The next council, at Vesali in the 4th century BC, saw Buddhism divided into two schools because of debate over the stringency of monastic regulations. The third, called by Emperor ASOKA in the 3rd century BC, sent missionaries through India and into Syria, N Africa and Ceylon. Spreading to Tibet in the 7th century AD, Buddhism combined with existing beliefs to form LAMAISM, and in China an Indian Buddhist, Bodhidarma, introduced spontaneous enlightenment, Ch'an (ZEN in Japanese). In the 6th century AD Buddhism reached Japan, where for the first time it was involved with politics.

Buddhist teaching advocates a middle course between self-mortification and pursuit of ambition. Buddha's Four Noble Truths are: life involves suffering; the cause of suffering is desire; elimination of desire leads to cessation of suffering; the elimination of desire is the result of a method or path that must be followed. The Noble Eightfold Path (right mode of seeing things, right thought, right speech, right action, right way of living, right effort, right mindedness, right meditation) leads to the cessation of pain. Through these steps Nirvana is achieved, a state beyond thought which frees one from the perpetual cycle of birth, suffering, death and rebirth. Buddhism has no service, ritual or church. The stricter *Theravada* school is followed in Ceylon, Burma, Thailand and Cambodia, the more lenient *Mahayana* school in Nepal, Korea, Japan and China. The religion numbers 300–500 million followers; many others in the East and West practice Buddhist teaching to achieve self-awareness.

BUDDING, a form of GRAFTING particularly used for roses and fruit trees. The grafted portion, or scion, in this case is a bud which is inserted under the bark of a stock that is usually not more than one year old.

BUDDLEIA, a genus of deciduous or evergreen shrubs and small trees native to China and naturalized in Europe and North America. Buddleias are noted for the profusion of lavender, white or yellow flowers that are produced in globular or plume-shaped clusters.

BUDENNY, Semyon (1883–1973), Russian general. He commanded the Red Cavalry in important revolutionary victories. Made a marshall in 1936, he commanded the SW front in WWII but was badly defeated by the Germans at Kiev.

BUDGE, Donald (1915–), US tennis player. His team won the Davis Cup in 1937, and in 1938 he was the first player to win four top world championships

(US, British, Australian and French). He turned professional in 1938.

BUDGERIGAR, a small Australian PARROT, or parakeet, of the family Psittacidae. They are generally green or blue with black and yellow markings, but white and yellow varieties are bred. Popular cage birds, they can be trained to "talk."

BUDGET, an estimate of income and expenditure over a period of time, usually a year. Governments, corporations and many individuals plan their financial activities around budgets. The American federal budget, drawn up annually by the executive branch, is submitted by the president to congress in Jan. It gives proposals for federal spending and taxation in the next fiscal year, beginning July 1.

BUDGET, Bureau of the. See OFFICE OF MANAGEMENT AND BUDGET, US.

BUELL, Don Carlos (1818–1898), US Union general in the Civil War. Troops under his command contributed to victory in the Battle of Shiloh. At Perryville in 1862 he forced the Confederates to retreat from Ky., but was dismissed because he did not follow up the victory.

BUENA PARK, city in S Cal. Industries include aircraft manufacture and the processing of milk and citrus fruits. Pop 63 646.

BUENA VISTA, a Mexican village 8mi from Saltillo. During the Mexican War, in Feb. 1847, US General Zachary Taylor with 5 000 troops here defeated a Mexican army of 20 000 under General Santa Anna.

BUENOS AIRES, capital of Argentina. On the Rio de la Plata, it is a port for Argentinian agricultural products, meat, hides, wool and cereals. It has a university, an opera house (Teatro Colón) and is the world's leading Spanish language publishing center. Industries include food processing and textiles, automobiles and chemical manufactures. European settlement began in the 16th century, international trade in the 18th century. Pop 2 972 453.

BUFFALO, second-largest city in N.Y., on Lake Erie near Niagara Falls. In the 19th century it gained importance as a junction for road, rail and lake transport from its location between the eastern cities and Chicago. Major industries are flour milling and steel production. Pop 462 768.

BUFFALO, name of several species of wild ox, incorrectly applied to the American BISON. They are members of the mammalian family Bovidae. The domesticated Indian water buffalo or CARABAO is a draft animal and gives milk. It weighs about a ton, is 1.5m (5ft) high and has large curved horns. Other types of Asiatic buffalo are the Philippine TAMARAU and the small ANOA of the Celebes. These are shy, but Cape buffaloes are dangerous big-game animals living in herds. Their populations have been wiped out or reduced by RINDERPEST, a cattle disease.

BUFFALO BERRY, two species of shrubs native to North America, which are noted for their silvery foliage and red or yellow berries.

BUFFALO BILL, nickname of William Frederick Cody (1846–1917), US scout and showman. He claimed to have killed 4 280 buffalo to feed the builders of the Kansas Pacific Railway. He rode with the PONY EXPRESS in 1860 and during the Civil War was a scout in Tenn. and Mo. for the Union army. From 1872 he toured the US and Europe with his Wild West Show.

BUFFALO FISH, *Ictiobus*, fresh-water fish, a variety of sucker. They have large sucking mouths for feeding on the water bottom. Different types range from 0.3–1.2m (1–4ft) long and weigh 9–30kg (20–66lb). They are used for food in the central US.

BUFFALO GRASS, *Buchloe dactyloides*, a low-growing grass abundant in the plains and prairies of North America, where it was the main food for wild herds of BUFFALO and later cattle. It withstands heavy grazing and thrives without irrigation.

BUFFALO GROVE, a village in NE Ill., 25mi NW of Chicago. Pop 11 799.

BUFFER, a solution in which PH is maintained at a nearly constant value. It consists of a relatively concentrated solution of a weak ACID and its conjugate BASE, and works best if their concentrations are roughly equal, in which case the hydrogen ion concentration equals the DISSOCIATION constant of the acid. When a small amount of a different acid or base is added, the buffer equilibrium shifts so that the PH value hardly changes (see LE CHATELIER). One common buffer is acetic acid/sodium acetate. Buffers are used in many chemical and biochemical experiments. Biochemical processes in the body are controlled by natural buffer systems.

BUFFET, Bernard (1928–), French artist, book illustrator and stage designer. His austere, angular naturalistic style won him international fame in his youth, and his work has since been much sought after.

BUFFINGTON, Leroy Sutherland (1848–1931), US architect. He claimed to have invented the skyscraper in 1881 and patented his design for a multi-story steel-framed building in 1888.

BUFFON, Georges Louis Leclerc, Comte de (1707–1788), French naturalist who was the first modern taxonomist of the ANIMAL KINGDOM and who led the team which produced the 44-volume *Histoire naturelle* (1749–1804).

BUG, the name of two rivers rising in the Ukrainian SSR. The Western Bug, 481mi long, rises near Lvov and meets the Vistula by Warsaw. The Southern Bug, 532mi long, rises near Khmelnitsky and flows into the Black Sea.

BUGANDA, region in SE Uganda, formerly one of the historic Bantu kingdoms of Africa, ruled by its kabaka. It covers 25 096sq mi NW of Lake Victoria and contains Kampala, the Ugandan capital. Cotton is the chief crop.

BUGBANE, genus (*Cimicifuga*) of perennial herbs of the BUTTERCUP family, native to eastern North America. They have tall white blooms and an unpleasant odor. The roots of the black snakeroot or black cohosh (*Cimicifuga racemosa*) were once valued as a remedy for snakebites.

BUGGING. See WIRETAPPING.

BUGLE, brass WIND INSTRUMENT. It has a cup-shaped mouthpiece, a conical tube and a five-to-eight note range. It is used mostly for military calls.

BUGLEWEED, plants of the genus *Ajuga*, part of the mint family, which are native to Europe and Asia. They produce dense whorls of white, red, blue or purplish flowers and several species are used as cultivated plants in rock gardens.

BUGS, common name for the insect order Hemiptera. They have beaks for piercing and sucking. Some, like the stinkbug, emit unpleasant odors, others secretions: aphids secrete honeydew; larvae of froghoppers (spittle bugs) secrete protective foam; scale insects secrete a waxy substance used in shellac. Most are plant-feeders and many are pests, attacking crops and transmitting diseases (e.g., squash bugs, lace bugs and whitefly). Some are blood-suckers (e.g., bedbugs and assassin bugs) which transmit disease. Others live on ponds (e.g., water skaters) or under water (e.g., water scorpions). In America the word "bug" often colloquially refers to any insect. (See also APHIDS; BEDBUG; CICADA; WATER BOATMEN; WATER SCORPIONS; WATER SKATERS; WHITEFLY.)

BUILDING. See CONSTRUCTION INDUSTRY.

BUISSON, Ferdinand Édouard (1841–1932), French educationalist. Professor of pedagogy at the Sorbonne, he wrote *Dictionnaire de pédagogie* (1882–93). Active in pacificism and civil rights, he won the Nobel Peace Prize in 1927.

BUJUMBURA, capital and port of Burundi, Africa, at the N end of Lake Tanganyika. It exports coffee, cotton and hides. Pop 107 000.

BUKHARA, ancient Central Asian city in the Uzbek SSR, formerly a great center of Islamic culture, now a center for textiles and the gas industry. Conquered by GENGHIS KHAN (1220) and by TAMERLANE, it became capital of an independent khanate before accepting Russian protection in 1868. Pop 114 000.

BUKHARIN, Nikolai Ivanovich (1888–1938), an early Bolshevik theoretician and friend of Lenin, editor of *Pravda*. A party leader in the 1920s, he was ousted by Stalin in 1929, but was reinstated to edit *Izvestia* in 1934. He wrote several works on political science and economics. He was liquidated in the Great Purge in 1938.

BUKOVINA, Romanian province. Part of the Hapsburg Empire after 1775, it joined Romania in 1919. Some of its territory passed to Russia in 1947 and is now part of the Ukrainian SSR.

BULAWAYO, industrial city in SW Rhodesia, center for Rhodesian Railways. It has iron, steel, textile and cement works and sugar refineries. Pop 70 000.

BULB, a short, underground storage stem composed of many fleshy scale leaves that are swollen with stored food and an outer layer of protective scale leaves. Bulbs are a means of overwintering; in the spring, flowers and foliage leaves are rapidly produced when growing conditions are suitable. Examples of plants producing bulbs are DAFFODIL, TULIP, SNOWDROP and ONION.

BULBULS, tropical songbirds of the family Pycnonotidae, native to Africa and Asia, and popular cage birds. They are pests of fruit crops.

BULFINCH, Charles (1763–1844), US architect, designer of the Mass. statehouse, Boston (1800), University Hall, Harvard U. (1815) and the E portico

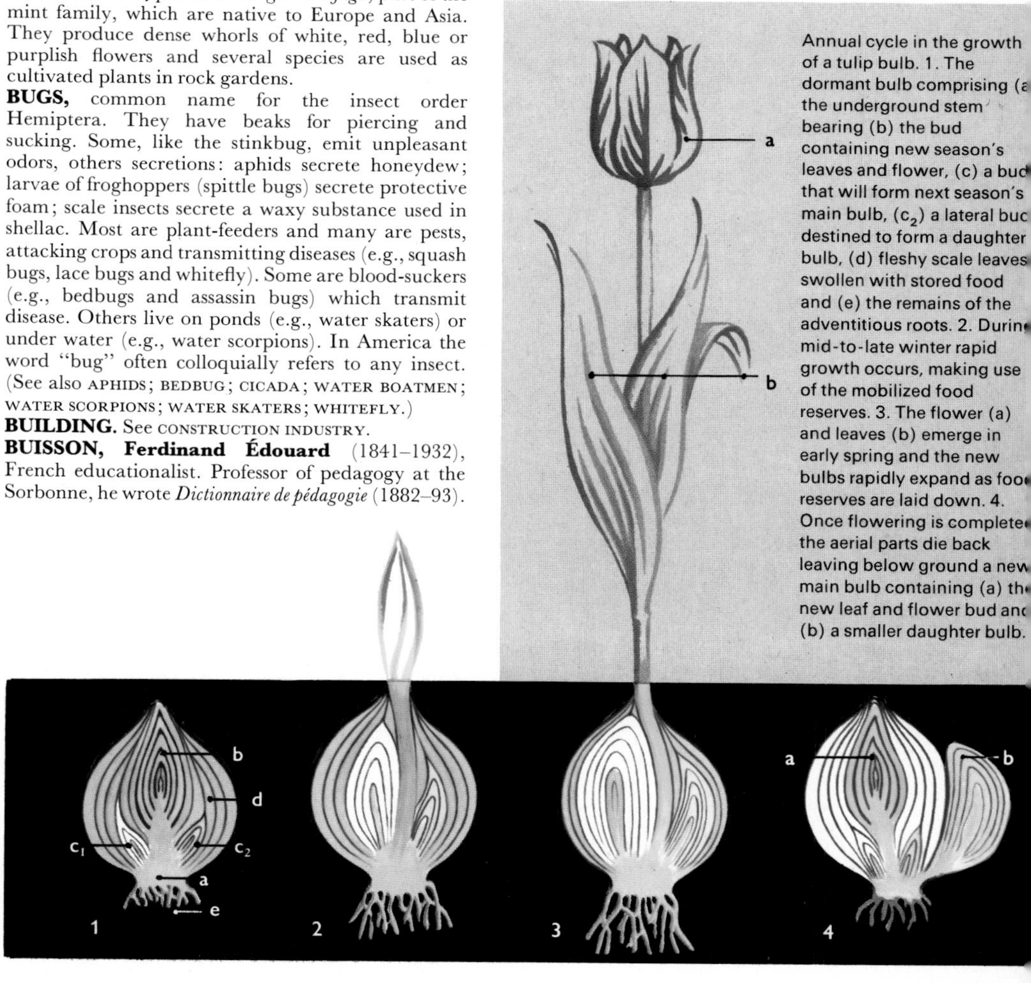

Annual cycle in the growth of a tulip bulb. 1. The dormant bulb comprising (a) the underground stem bearing (b) the bud containing new season's leaves and flower, (c) a bud that will form next season's main bulb, (c_2) a lateral bud destined to form a daughter bulb, (d) fleshy scale leaves swollen with stored food and (e) the remains of the adventitious roots. 2. During mid-to-late winter rapid growth occurs, making use of the mobilized food reserves. 3. The flower (a) and leaves (b) emerge in early spring and the new bulbs rapidly expand as food reserves are laid down. 4. Once flowering is completed the aerial parts die back leaving below ground a new main bulb containing (a) the new leaf and flower bud and (b) a smaller daughter bulb.

of the Capitol, Washington, D.C. (1818). He emphasized the dignified neoclassical style in American civic architecture.

BULFINCH, Thomas (1796–1867), US mythologist. His classic, *The Age of Fable* (1855; "Bullfinch's Mythology"), popularized Greek, Roman, Nordic and oriental mythologies.

BULGAKOV, Mikhail Afanasievich (1891–1940), Russian author and playwright. His work, mostly suppressed until the 1960s, blends realism and fantasy with great humor, as in his most brilliant novel, *The Master and Margarita*, which describes the antics of the devil in modern Moscow.

BULGANIN, Nikolai Alexandrovich (1895–1975), Soviet leader. With the support of Nikita KHRUSHCHEV, he succeeded MALENKOV as premier in 1955. He was expelled from the central committee when Khrushchev became premier in 1958.

BULGARIA, People's Republic in the Balkan Peninsula, bordered by the Black Sea, the Danube and Yugoslavia. The country is traversed by the Balkan and Rhodope Mts; its climate is continental in the N and Mediterranean in the S. Until the 1940s most Bulgarians lived in peasant farming villages, but industrialization has greatly progressed since WWII. Industry produces machinery, textiles and chemicals; and lead, zinc, iron ore, copper and coal are mined. Exports include tobacco, foodstuffs, minerals and machinery. The Black Sea resorts and the country's mineral springs are important tourist attractions.

The Bulgars, a Turkic people, conquered the Slavic population in the 7th century, adopting their language and customs. The Bulgar Empire was a major Balkan force until the 14th century, but from 1396 to 1878 Bulgaria was under rigid Ottoman rule. At the Congress of Berlin (1878), Turkish hegemony was restricted, and in 1908 Bulgaria proclaimed its independence under Ferdinand I. Bulgaria supported Germany in WWI and II, though not against the USSR. In 1944 the USSR occupied the country and the communist Fatherland Front seized power. In 1947 Bulgaria became a People's Republic. A new constitution was adopted in 1971, with Communist party chief Todor Zhivkov as president. Bulgaria has remained a faithful Soviet satellite.

Official Name: The People's Republic of Bulgaria
Capital: Sofia
Area: 42 823sq mi
Population: 8 594 493
Languages: Bulgarian, Turkish
Religions: Bulgarian Orthodox
Monetary Unit(s): 1 Lev = 100 stotinki

BULGE, Battle of the. See BATTLE OF THE BULGE.

BULL. See PAPAL BULL.

BULLDOG, breed of dog native to Britain, used in bullbaiting until the 19th century. A heavybodied breed, it has a large head with a flat drooping face, and is renowned for the great strength of its jaws.

BULLET. See AMMUNITION.

BULLFIGHTING, Spanish national sport and spectacle, also popular in Latin America. Probably developed by the Moors, it was taken over by aristocratic professionals in the 18th century. The modern bullfight stresses the grace, skill and daring of the *matador*. (The most famous matadors have been Juan Belmonte, Joselito, Manolete and El Cordobes.) After a procession, the bull is released. Two mounted *picadors* jab the bull's neck with lances to lower its head for the matador's capework. Then three *banderilleros* thrust decorated wooden goads into the bull's back. The matador, after using his cape to make daring and graceful passes at the bull, kills it with a swordthrust between the shoulders.

Developed in England for the cruel sport of bull-baiting, the bulldog almost disappeared when such sports were outlawed in 1835. Fanciers rescued the breed and bred out its ferocity.

BULLFROG, *Rana catesbeiana*, large aquatic North American frog, noted for the bellowing call of the male. Bullfrogs are a drab greenish color and reach 200mm (8in) in length, with 250mm- (10in-)long hindlegs. Adults will eat almost any suitable food. Two other, quite distinct, species are called bullfrogs: the Indian bullfrog, *Rana tigrina*, and the African bullfrog, *Pyxicephalus adspersus*.

BULLHEADS, four species of North American freshwater catfish, distinguished by their broad, heavy heads and the long BARBELS around their mouths. They reach 0.3m (1ft) in length. The unrelated European miller's thumb is also called bullhead.

BULLINGER, Heinrich (1504–1575), Swiss Protestant reformer. He played an important part in composing the First Helvetic Confession (1536), formulated the *Consensus Tigurinus* with CALVIN (1549) and composed the Second Helvetic Confession (1566), a popular CREED of the Reformation.

BULLITT, William Christian (1891–1967), US diplomat. He was a member of the US peace delegation at the end of WWI, and in 1933 was the first US ambassador to the USSR.

BULLMASTIFF, guard dog created by crossing the Bulldog and the Mastiff, and used by English gamekeepers. With short, broad body and strong legs, it stands 27in high and weighs 130lb. Its short, hard coat can be every shade of brindle fawn and red but the muzzle and ears should be black. Good as a watchdog and with children, it can be unwilling to share its master's affection.

BULL MOOSE PARTY. See PROGRESSIVE PARTY.

BULL RUN, Battles of, two clashes in the American Civil War around Manassas Junction near Bull Run Creek, 25mi SW of Washington, D.C. In the First Battle of Bull Run, July 1861, Union General McDowell was sent against Confederates led by Pierre BEAUREGARD, but was repulsed by them. Gen. "Stonewall" JACKSON was so nicknamed for his tenacity in this battle. In the Second Battle of Bull Run, Aug. 1862, Jackson attacked Union general John Pope. Pope believed his counterattack successful, but heavy artillery fire by Gen. Robert E. LEE forced his retreat. (See also CIVIL WAR, AMERICAN.)

BULL SNAKE, large nonpoisonous North American snake of the genus *Pituophis*, found in S and W states. It reaches a length of 2.5m (8ft) and has a loud whirring hiss. It feeds on rodents but is harmless to humans.

BULL TERRIER, small dog bred from a cross between the English terrier and the bulldog. It weighs 20–60lb, has short hair and may be either white or colored (generally brindle).

BÜLOW, Hans Guido von (1830–1894), German pianist and noted virtuoso conductor. A pupil of LISZT and WAGNER, he championed their music and that of BRAHMS and Richard STRAUSS. He married Liszt's daughter, Cosima, who later left him for Wagner.

BULRUSHES, name given to sedges (*Scirpus*), common plants that grow in wet habitats. Most species produce narrow leaves 1–2m (3.2–6.5ft) long and spiky flowers. The stem is represented by a creeping RHIZOME. (See also SEDGE.)

BULTMANN, Rudolf (1884–   ), German theologian who advocated "demythologizing" the New Testament and reinterpreting it in existentialist terms. He developed a critical approach to the Gospels, studying the oral tradition behind them.

BULWER-LYTTON, Edward George Earle Lytton, 1st Baron Lytton (1803–1873), English author and politician. His best-known works include the historical novels, *The Last Days of Pompeii* (1834) and *Rienzi* (1835), and the Utopian *The Coming Race* (1871).

BUNAU-VARILLA, Philippe Jean (1859–1940), French engineer who organized the Panama Canal Project. He was instrumental in arranging for the canal to go through Panama and then in planning the revolution which led to Panamanian independence. As Panama's minister to the US, he negotiated the HAY-BUNAU-VARILLA TREATY (1903), giving the US control of the canal zone.

BUNCHE, Ralph Johnson (1904–1971), US diplomat. He entered the UN in 1946, and was undersecretary for political affairs in 1958. Having supervised the 1949 Arab-Israeli armistice, he became the first Negro to win the Nobel Peace Prize (1950).

BUNDY, McGeorge (1919–   ), US political aide. He influenced foreign policy as adviser on national security affairs under presidents Eisenhower, Kennedy and Johnson. He resigned in 1966 to become president of the Ford Foundation.

BUNIN, Ivan Alekseyevich (1870–1953), Russian novelist, short-story writer and poet. He is best known for his short stories such as *The Gentleman from San Francisco* (1916). He emigrated to France in 1919, and won the Nobel Prize for Literature in 1933.

BUNION, deformity of the joint of the big toe, generally caused by ill-fitting shoes. Pressure on the tissues at this point creates a BURSA which becomes painfully inflamed. Treatment entails wearing wide shoes, PODIATRY and in some cases surgery.

BUNKER HILL, Battle of, important early encounter of the American Revolutionary War, on June 17, 1775. As part of the encirclement of Boston, American militia under Col. William Prescott occupied Breed's Hill—although the original objective had been Bunker's Hill nearby. The two first British attempts to dislodge them, led by Maj. Gen. William Howe, resulted in heavy losses from close American fire. On the third assault the Americans ran out of ammunition and had to retreat. Though a British victory, the battle damaged British confidence and was a vital boost to American morale.

BUNSEN, Robert Wilhelm Eberhard (1811–1899), German chemist who, after important work on organo-arsenic compounds went on (with G. R. KIRCHHOFF) to pioneer chemical SPECTROSCOPY, discovering the elements CESIUM (1860) and RUBIDIUM (1861). He also helped to popularize the gas burner known by his name.

BUNSEN BURNER, burner, promoted by BUNSEN, used widely in laboratories and sometimes in metal heat-treatment (see METALLURGY). Through a nozzle at the base is introduced slightly pressurized fuel GAS (usually COAL GAS) which is mixed with air (primary air) which the flow induces through adjustable inlets: the usual gas:air ratio is 1:2. The mixture proceeds

The memorial tablet to the Battle of Bull Run and to the 2111 soldiers who were buried on the battlefield where they had fallen.

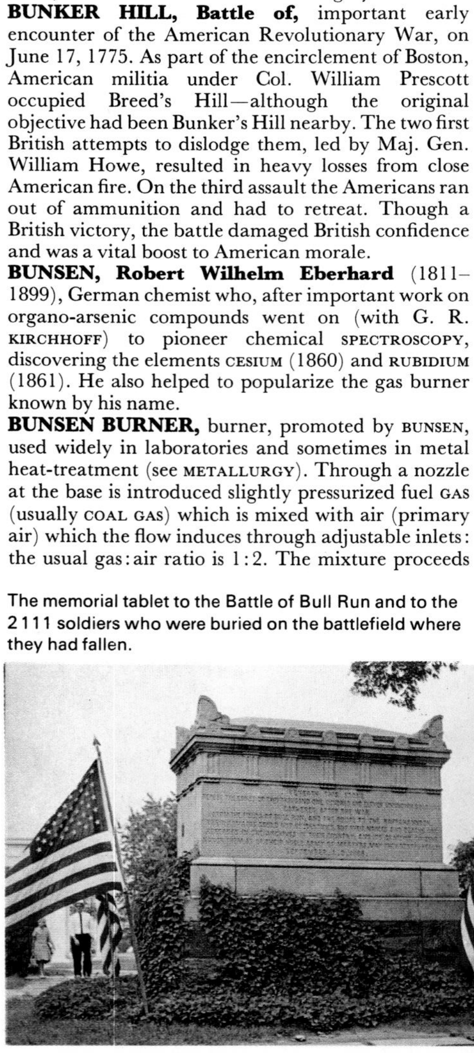

up a short metal tube and is ignited at the top, giving a flame temperature of the order of 2000K. Outer portions of the flame mix with further air (secondary air) to give a cooler, more luminous flame, where the gas:air ratio is about 1:4. The burner is now used mostly in highschools.

BUNTINGS, several varieties of small birds of the finch family (Fringillidae), found in Europe and North America. In North America the name is applied to relatives of the cardinal, the indigo bunting and the painted bunting; while counterparts of the European buntings are called sparrows and finches. They eat seeds and live in woods and grasslands.

BUNTLINE, Ned, pseudonym of American author and adventurer, Edward Zane Carroll Judson (1823–1886). He wrote sensational dime novels, some based on his own escapades. He founded a newspaper, *Ned Buntline's Own*, and was an organizer of the so-called KNOW-NOTHING party.

BUÑUEL, Luis (1900–), Spanish-Mexican director of many outstanding films, often marked by their fierce realism, social criticism and wry humor. Surrealist fantasy has been another recurrent element in his work, ever since his first film, *Un Chien Andalou* (made with Salvador DALI in 1929).

BUNYAN, John (1628–1688), English author. A tinker by trade, he became a Baptist preacher in 1657. While imprisoned for unlicenced preaching (1660–72; 1675) he wrote his most famous work, *The Pilgrim's Progress* (1678), an allegory in simple prose describing Christian's journey to the Celestial City.

BUNYAN, Paul, in US frontier myth a lumberjack, a genial giant who worked with his huge blue ox Babe. By the time the first tall stories about this frontier hero were published in 1910, oral tradition had spread them across the country.

BUONAPARTE. See BONAPARTE.

BUONARROTI, Michelangelo. See MICHELANGELO.

BUONINSEGNA, Duccio di. See DUCCIO DI BUONINSEGNA.

BUOY, an anchored float to guide marine navigators. Buoys indicate locations and mark dangerous areas. They may have a bell, whistle, horn or light to arrest attention at night or in fog. Buoys are sometimes used to support ship moorings.

BURBAGE, Richard (c1567–1619), first great English actor. He played many of Shakespeare's leading roles, including Richard III, Hamlet, Othello and Lear. From his father, **James Burbage** (c1530–1597), builder of the first English theater (The Theatre, 1576), he and his brother Cuthbert inherited the Blackfriars Theatre in London. In 1599 they built the famous Globe Theatre.

BURBANK, city in S Cal., in the San Fernando Valley. It has motion picture and television studios, and manufactures aircraft. Pop 88871.

BURBANK, Luther (1849–1926), US horticulturalist who developed more than 800 varieties of plants, including the Burbank potato.

BURBOT, *Lota lota*, the only freshwater cod. It lives in deep cold waters of North America, Europe and Asia. Its long, narrow body grows to 800m (31in).

BURCHFIELD, Charles Ephraim (1893–1967), US watercolorist known for midwestern landscapes and small town scenes. He was a leader of the realistic movement in American painting.

BURCKHARDT, Jakob Christoph (1818–1897), Swiss cultural historian. He was professor of history and art history at the U. of Basel and is famous for his book, *The Civilization of the Renaissance in Italy* (1860).

BURCKHARDT, Johann Ludwig (1784–1817), Swiss explorer employed by the English African Association. He traveled in Egypt, visited PETRA and, disguised as a Muslim (with the name Sheikh Ibrahim ibn Abdallah), went to Mecca and Medina. Several collections of his writings were published posthumously.

BURDOCK, thistle-like herbs, *Arctium ninus* and *A. lappa*. The burdock grows as a weed, and its prickly seed pods catch on animal hides and people's clothing. (See also BURR.)

BUREAUCRACY, rule by proliferating officialdom. The term is commonly used in a pejorative sense suggesting interminable, meaningless paperwork ("red tape") and unresponsiveness to the individual. It can apply particularly to government.

In the Côte d'Or, a famous wine-growing region, one of the most prized red burgundies comes from the vineyards of Clos Vougeot (pictured here), a château dating from the 16th century.

BURETTE, graduated glass tube with a stopcock, used in VOLUMETRIC ANALYSIS to measure the volume of a liquid, especially of one of the reagents in a TITRATION. A gas burette measures gas volume by the volume of liquid displaced.

BURGER, Warren Earl (1907–), chief justice of the US Supreme Court, nominated in 1969 by President Nixon. He was previously assistant attorney general of the US and chief judge of the US Court of Appeals.

BURGESS, (Frank) Gelett (1866–1951), US humorist and illustrator. He is best known for his nonsense verses and for such works as *Goops and How to Be Them* (1900) and *Are You a Bromide?* (1907).

BURGESSES, House of, the first representative legislative body in the American colonies, and the first in any British colony. It met in Jamestown, Va. (1619–1744), and in 1621 gained legislative powers, with the governor and his council having the power of veto.

BURGHLEY. See CECIL, WILLIAM.

BURGLARY, the crime of breaking and entering with intent to commit a felony. Once confined to acts committed at night, the term now applies to such acts committed at any time of day. In the US, the definition of burglary varies from state to state.

BURGOS, capital of the N Spanish province of Burgos, on the Arlanzón R. In the Spanish Civil War it was the Nationalist capital (1936–39). It has a large textile industry. Pop 119915.

BURGOYNE, John (1722–1792), British general in the American Revolutionary War. He fought in the Seven Years' War (1756–63), and became a fashionable playwright, socialite and politician. Posted to America, he attempted to put into effect his plan to split off the New England colonies but was eventually forced to surrender by Gen. Horatio GATES at Saratoga (1777).

BURGUNDIANS, one of the two opposed political factions of the early 15th century. Under their leader John the Fearless, Duke of Burgundy, they fought the French Orléanist faction of the Armagnacs, led by Bernard VII, Count of Armagnac. The Burgundians allied with the English on Henry V's invasion in 1415. The feud with the Armagnacs continued until 1477.

BURGUNDY (French: Bourgogne), historic region of E France, occupying what are now the departments of Côte-d'Or, Saône-et-Loire and Yonne. It was named for the Burgundians, a Germanic tribe. In 843 the area was divided into the E county of Franche-Comté and the W Duchy of Burgundy, which became virtually an independent state. From 1477 until the Revolution the duchy was a French province. A rich agricultural region, Burgundy is famous for its wines.

BURIAL. See FUNERAL CUSTOMS.

BURIDAN, Jean (c1300–c1385), French philosopher and critic of ARISTOTLE who proposed the impetus theory, often considered to foreshadow NEWTON's first law of motion.

BURKE, Edmund (1729–1797), Irish-born British statesman, political philosopher and outstanding orator. He entered parliament in 1765, and advocated more just policies towards the American colonies, opposing the STAMP ACT and (in 1775) arguing for conciliation. Concerned for justice in India, he promoted the impeachment of Warren HASTINGS (1786–87). His famous *Reflections on the Revolution in France* (1790) presented his rational case against violent change.

BURLESON, Albert Sidney (1863–1937), US postmaster general (1913–21). He favored government control of communications and implemented strict policies for the postal services. He instituted air mail in 1918.

BURLESQUE, form of literary or stage humor characterized by exaggeration or distortion of its subject matter. Aristophanes' comedies are early examples. In mid-19th-century America the term was applied to a low-comedy, sometimes bawdy, entertainment, which developed into a form of variety show. After 1920 striptease acts became the main burlesque attraction.

BURLINGAME, residential city in W Cal. on San Francisco Bay, founded 1868. Pop 27320.

BURLINGAME, Anson (1820–1870), US diplomat. In 1861 he became minister to China. He resigned in 1867 and, because of his sympathy for China's rights, was made head of a Chinese delegation appointed to secure treaties with the West.

BURLINGAME TREATY, treaty between China and the US, signed by Anson BURLINGAME and Secretary of State William H. Seward in 1868. It allowed unlimited Chinese immigration to the US.

BURLINGTON, town in S Ontario, Canada, on Lake Ontario. Its industries include fruit-canning and chemicals. Pop 86125.

BURLINGTON, city in SE Ia. on the Mississippi. A shipping center, it manufactures explosives, electronic equipment and tractors. Pop 32366.

BURLINGTON, town in NE Mass., settled in 1641. It manufactures wood products and machinery. Pop 21980.

BURLINGTON, city in W N.J. on the Delaware R, 11mi SW of Trenton, settled by Quakers in 1677. It is the center of a farming region. Pop 11991.

BURLINGTON, industrial city in N N.C. on the Haw R. Its manufactures include textiles, furniture and chemicals. Pop 35930.

BURLINGTON, city in Vt., seat of Chittenden Co., on Lake Champlain, chartered 1763. A resort, port and industrial center, it manufactures electrical, textile, wood and steel products. Pop 38633.

BURMA, country in SE Asia on the Bay of Bengal, bounded by Bangladesh, India, China, Laos and Thailand. Its official name is the Union of Burma and it comprises five federated states. The country is fringed by high mountain ranges to the E, W and N, which enclose a fertile central plain watered chiefly by the Irrawaddy R and its great delta. Central and N Burma are thickly forested, and much of Burma has a tropical monsoon climate.

The Burmans, a Mongoloid people, form 75% of the population, the Karens and Shans being the other major group. Some 80% of the population live in rural areas, agriculture being the country's mainstay. Rice (grown particularly in the Irrawaddy Basin and

Delta) is the main crop, followed by sugarcane and groundnuts. Forestry provides hardwoods for export. Industry is confined mainly to rice-milling, oil-refining and textiles. Minerals—including oil, lead, tin and tungsten—are poorly exploited.

Burma was settled by the Burmans in the 9th century, establishing a kingdom which reached its height under Buddhist King Anawratha in the 11th century. In 1287 the kingdom fell to KUBLAI KHAN and was later divided among Shan and other rulers, though it was again unified in the 16th century. By 1885 Britain made Burma part of its Indian empire, and in 1937 granted the country separate dominion status. The independent Union of Burma was established in 1948. Its democratic constitution was suspended in 1962 by General Ne Win and a new socialist constitution was announced in Dec. 1973.

Official Name: The Union of Burma
Capital: Rangoon
Area: 261 789sq mi
Population: 28 890 000
Languages: Burmese
Religions: Buddhist
Monetary Unit(s): 1 Kyat = 100 pyas

BURMA ROAD, supply route 681mi long constructed by China in 1937–39 during the Chinese–Japanese war. It was closed when the Japanese conquered Burma in 1942.

BURMESE CAT, an elegant breed of "foreign" type similar to the Siamese but more solid in conformation and with round eyes which should be an intense yellow. The short, satin-like coat may shade almost imperceptibly lighter on the underparts and be slightly darker on face and ears but should otherwise be an even color. Brown, blue, chocolate (champagne) and lilac are recognized in the US but a wider range is known in the UK.

BURNE-JONES, Sir Edward Coley (1833–1898), English artist, a member of the PRE-RAPHAELITE BROTHERHOOD. His paintings (e.g., *King Cophetua and the Beggar Maid*) evince a romantic, dreamy medievalism. In 1858 he worked with ROSSETTI on the Oxford Union frescoes. He also designed many stained-glass windows for William MORRIS.

This magnificently decorated mythical beast guards the inner temple of the Buddhist Shwe Dagon pagoda in Rangoon, capital of Burma.

BURNET, Sir Frank Macfarlane (1899–), Australian physician and virologist who shared the 1970 Nobel Prize for Physiology or Medicine with P. B. MEDAWAR for his suggestion that the ability of organisms to form ANTIBODIES in response to foreign tissues was acquired and not inborn. Medawar followed up the suggestion and performed successful skin transplants in mice.

BURNETT, Frances (Eliza) Hodgson (1849–1924), English-born US author. She is particularly famous for her children's stories, *Little Lord Fauntleroy* (1885–86) and *The Secret Garden* (1910).

BURNEY, Fanny (Frances) (1752–1840), English novelist and diarist. Her first novel, *Evelina* (1778), won her the respect of Samuel JOHNSON. She spent five years from 1786 as a member of Queen Charlotte's household. Her *Early Diary: 1768–78* (1889) and *Diary and Letters: 1778–1840* (1842–46) provide interesting background to the period.

BURNHAM, Daniel Hudson (1846–1912), US architect, a pioneer of city planning. He built some of America's early skyscrapers, including the Masonic Temple Building, Chicago (1892), and the Flatiron Building, New York City (1902). He also designed the plan for the Columbian Exposition in Chicago (1893). Much of his improvement plan for Chicago (1907–09) was subsequently put into effect.

BURNHAM, Sherbourne Wesley (1838–1921), US astronomer noted for his studies of DOUBLE STARS, reported in his *General Catalogue of Double Stars* (1906).

BURNING BUSH, name given to a hardy perennial herb, the gas plant (*Dictamnus albus*), and to the strawberry plant (*Euonymus americanus*), a relative of the spindle tree.

BURNING GLASS. See MAGNIFYING GLASS.

BURNS, Anthony (1834–1862), US fugitive slave. He was arrested in Boston in 1854 under the 1850 FUGITIVE SLAVE LAWS to await return to his Southern owner. The incident provoked a violent local reaction which strengthened the pre-Civil War antislavery movement. Burns later gained his freedom.

BURNS, Arthur Frank (1904–), Austrian-born US economist. An expert on the BUSINESS CYCLE, he served as presidential adviser on economics 1953–56 and on labor management 1961–66. Among his many books, the most influential was *Measuring Business Cycles* (1946), written with Wesley Clair MITCHELL.

BURNS, Robert (1759–1796), famous Scottish poet. The son of a poor farmer, he himself farmed for a living and later worked as a customs official. In 1786 he published *Poems, Chiefly in the Scottish Dialect* (enlarged 1787). His poetry, in Scots-English idiom, deals with rural human experience and feeling. He also wrote satires and radical poems, such as *The Twa Dogs* and *The Jolly Beggars*. Influenced by Scottish folk tradition, he was a master at writing songs to traditional airs—for example, *Auld Lang Syne*. At first taken up by fashionable society, he died neglected and in debt. Among his best-known poems are *Tam O'Shanter*, *To a Mouse* and *The Cotter's Saturday Night*.

BURNS AND ALLEN, US husband and wife comedy team of **Nathan Birnbaum ("George Burns"**; 1896–), and **Grace Ethel ("Gracie") Allen** (1906–1964). They started out in vaudeville in the 1920s and went on to be immensely successful on radio and television. They also made a number of movies.

BURNS AND SCALDS, injuries caused by heat, electricity, radiation or caustic substances, in which protein denaturation causes death of tissues. (Scalds are burns due to boiling water or steam.) Burns cause PLASMA to leak from blood vessels into the tissues and in severe burns substantial leakage leads to SHOCK. In **first-degree burns**, such as mild SUNBURN, damage is superficial. **Second-degree burns** destroy only the epidermis so that regeneration is possible. **Third-degree burns** destroy all layers of SKIN, which cannot then regenerate, so skin-grafting is required. Infection, ulceration, hemolysis, KIDNEY failure and severe scarring may complicate burns. Treatment includes ANALGESICS, dressings and ANTISEPTICS and fluids for shock. Immediate FIRST AID measures include cold water cooling to minimize continuing damage.

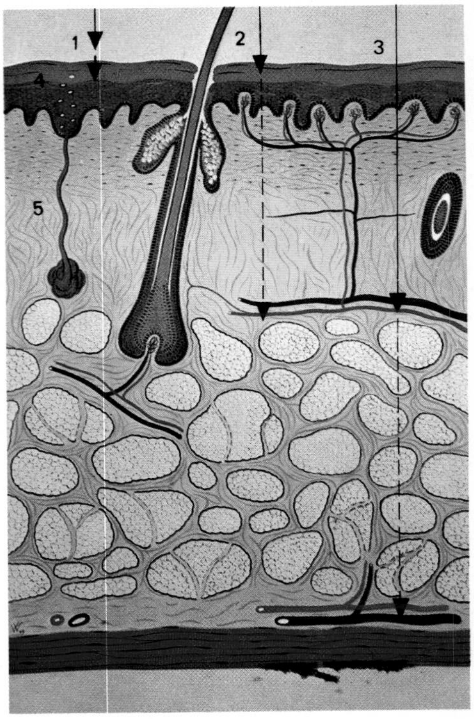

Section through the skin showing the depth to which first (1), second (2) and third (3) degree burns penetrate the epidermis (4) and the dermis (5).

BURNSIDE, Ambrose Everett (1824–1881), Union general in the American Civil War. Succeeding McClellan as general of the Army of the Potomac, he resigned after the Union defeat at FREDERICKSBURG in 1862. He was later governor of R.I. (1866–69) and US senator (1875–81). His whiskers gave rise to the term "sideburns."

BURR, or bur, a seed with barbed spines which catch onto animal fur. Some common burr-producing plants are the burdock, bur marigold, burcock and cocklebur.

BURR, Aaron (1756–1836), brilliant and controversial US vice-president, who killed Alexander HAMILTON in a duel (1804). Hamilton had blocked Burr's election as president in a tie vote with Jefferson in 1800, and (as Burr believed) his election as governor of N.Y. in 1804. Burr was admitted to the New York bar in 1782, was attorney general (1789–91) and US senator (1791–97) while helping to organize the new Republican party. After his term as vice-president (1800–05) he was involved in conspiracies to form an empire in the West, and was tried but acquitted of treason. After 1812 he returned to the law in N.Y.

BURRILLVILLE, town in N R.I., 22mi NW of Providence. It manufactures textiles. Pop 10 087.

BURRITT, Elihu (1810–1879), self-taught US reformer and pacifist, known as "the learned blacksmith." He was an advocate of abolition, temperance and peace, and edited the weekly *Christian Citizen* (1844–51); he formed a plan for compensated slave emancipation.

BURRO. See DONKEY.

BURROUGHS, Edgar Rice (1875–1950), US writer of adventure novels. He is most famous for *Tarzan of the Apes* (1914), whose characters have passed into comic strips, films and television.

BURROUGHS, John (1837–1921), US naturalist and author who made his reputation with philosophical nature essays. His *Notes on Walt Whitman* (1867) was the first biographical study of the poet, who was his friend.

BURROUGHS, William (1855–1898), US inventor of the first practical adding machine (1885). (See also CALCULATING MACHINE.)

BURROUGHS, William Seward (1914–), US novelist associated with the beat and hippie movements; his principal subject matter is drug addiction. He is best known for *The Naked Lunch* (1959), *Soft Machine* (1961) and *Nova Express* (1964).

BURSA, historic Turkish city at the foot of Ulu Dağ, the capital of Bursa province. It is the center for an agricultural and textile-producing area and has a flourishing tourist industry. Pop 276 000.

BURSA, fibrous sac containing SYNOVIAL FLUID which reduces friction where TENDONS move over bones. Extra bursae may develop where there is abnormal pressure or friction.

BURSITIS, inflammation of a BURSA, commonly caused by excessive wear and tear (as in housemaid's knee) or by rheumatoid ARTHRITIS, GOUT or various bacteria. It causes pain and stiffness of the affected part, and may require CORTISONE injections and, if infected, surgical drainage.

BURTON, Richard (1925–), British actor. Starting as a promising Shakespearean at the Old Vic, London, in the 1950s, he appeared on Broadway in *Camelot* (1960) and *Hamlet* (1964) and has made numerous films, including *Look Back in Anger* (1959), *Becket* (1964) and, with Elizabeth TAYLOR, *Who's Afraid of Virginia Woolf?* (1966).

BURTON, Sir Richard Francis (1821–1890), English explorer, linguist and author, famous for his translation of the ARABIAN NIGHTS. Burton was fluent in several Middle Eastern languages. In 1853, disguised as a Muslim, he visited Mecca, an event recorded in his book, *Pilgrimage to Al-Medina and Meccah* (1855). Together with John SPEKE, he discovered Lake Tanganyika (1858).

BURTON, Robert (1577–1640), English clergyman, author of the *Anatomy of Melancholy* (1621), a compendious study of the causes and symptoms of melancholy, which, from the frankness and perception of its section "On Love Melancholy," has led to his being regarded as a precursor of FREUD.

BURUNDI, a small African state on the NE shore of Lake Tanganyika, originally part of Ruanda-Urundi. It consists mostly of high plateau, and is bordered to the N by Rwanda, to the E and S by Tanzania and on the W by Zaire. Burundi has a tropical climate with equable temperatures and irregular rainfall. The economy is based on agriculture, with arabica coffee and cotton the chief exports. There are few towns, no rail system and of about 3 700mi of road, only one stretch is hard-surfaced.

The earliest inhabitants, the Twa hunters, were conquered by the Hutu, who in turn were reduced to

Official Name: The Republic of Burundi
Capital: Bujumbura
Area: 10 747sq mi
Population: over 3 500 000
Languages: Kirundi, French, Swahili
Religions: Roman Catholic, Animist, Muslim
Monetary Unit(s): 1 Burundi franc = 100 centimes

serfdom by the Tutsi. In 1899, Germany claimed the Ruanda–Urundi territory; after WWI it was administered by Belgium as a trust territory under the League of Nations and, after WWII, under the UN. The two states separated in 1962, Burundi being admitted to the UN. In 1966 a republican government replaced the monarchy; in 1973 a short war with Ruanda ended amicably.

BUSH, Vannevar (1890–1974), US electrical engineer, director of the Office of Scientific Research and Development in WWII. In the 1930s he developed a "differential analyzer"—in effect the first analog COMPUTER.

Baby bushbaby clinging to its mother's fur on a nocturnal tree-top. They make interesting, unusual pets providing one is willing to tolerate them sleeping all day and scampering about all night.

BUSHBABIES, four species of small African nocturnal primates of the genus *Galago*, popular as pets. They live in groups in woodlands S of the Sahara and feed mainly on insects. They have round eyes, large ears which fold up, a bushy tail and flattened digits for gripping when they leap from branch to branch.

BUSHEL, a unit of dry measure equal to 64 pints. (See WEIGHTS AND MEASURES.)

BUSHIDO, code of honor among the SAMURAI (warrior) class of Japan, influenced by ZEN and CONFUCIANISM, which stressed military virtues, feudal loyalty and filial piety. It was formulated in the 12th–14th centuries, but the term itself was first used in the 16th century. After the abolition of the samurai class in 1868, it formed a basis for emperor-worship and nationalism.

BUSHMASTER, *Lachesis muta*, a tropical American pit-viper which lays eggs. It is light brown with dark patterns and grows to 3.5m (11.5ft). It feeds on small mammals and its venom is dangerous to man.

BUSHMEN, a people of South Africa related to the pygmies, living around the Kalahari Desert. They average about 5ft in height and have yellowish-brown skin, broad noses and closely curled hair. They are nomadic hunters, living in bands of 25–60. Their language, related to Hottentot and belonging to the Khoisan group, employs a series of "clicks." Bushmen are a musical people, and are also noted for their vivid painting.

BUSHNELL, David (1742–1824), American inventor whose one-man SUBMARINE, *Turtle*, was used against British warships during the American Revolutionary War, but to little effect.

BUSHNELL, Horace (1802–1876), US Congregationalist theologian. His theology is a synthesis of orthodox Puritanism and the Romantic impulses of COLERIDGE, EMERSON and SCHLEIERMACHER. He emphasized a liberal interpretation of Christianity.

BUSINESS CYCLE, periodic fluctuation in the economy of an industrialized nation, between prosperity and recession or depression, with marked variations in growth rate and employment levels. Recession may be caused by overproduction, declining demand, changes in money supply and generally by a loss of confidence. Government interventions to strengthen the economy have become common in recent years.

BUSONI, Ferruccio Benvenuto (1866–1924), Italian pianist and composer. His works include a lengthy piano concerto with chorus (1904) and the opera, *Doctor Faust* (1916–24). He also made many piano transcriptions of works by J. S. Bach and others.

BUSTARDS, large game birds of the family Otidae, native to Europe, Asia and Africa. Plumage on the back and tail is gray and brown. During courtship the male displays the white feathers of his throat and chest. They are turkey-sized and feed on grains, leaves and small animals.

BUTADIENE, or 1,3-Butadiene ($CH_2{=}CHCH{=}CH_2$), gaseous HYDROCARBON made by dehydrogenation of BUTANE and butene. It is mostly polymerized with STYRENE to make synthetic rubber. mp −109°C, bp −4°C. (See also ALKENES; DIELS-ALDER REACTION.)

BUTANE (C_4H_{10}), gaseous ALKANE found in NATURAL GAS and also made by the cracking of PETROLEUM. It is used in BOTTLED GAS and in the manufacture of 1,3-BUTADIENE and high-octane GASOLINE. It has two isomers.

BUTE, John Stuart, 3rd Earl of (1713–1792), favorite of King GEORGE III. Though unpopular, he dominated the King until 1765. As prime minister 1762–63, he ended the SEVEN YEARS' WAR.

BUTENANDT, Adolf Friedrich Johann (1903–), German chemist who shared the 1939 Nobel Prize for Chemistry (with L. RUZICKA) for his work in isolating and determining the chemical structures of the human sex HORMONES estrone, androsterone and progesterone.

BUTLER, industrial city in W Pa., seat of Butler Co. It makes plate glass, railroad cars and steel products, and there are deposits of oil and coal nearby. Pop 18 691.

BUTLER, Benjamin Franklin (1818–1893), US politician and Union general in the Civil War. Because of his harsh autocratic rule as military governor of New Orleans (1862), he was known as "Beast," and he was recalled by President Lincoln. As congressman (1867–75, 1877–79), he supported RECONSTRUCTION and the impeachment of President JOHNSON. A Populist party candidate, he was governor of Mass. (1882) and ran for president (1884).

BUTLER, John (1728–1796), American loyalist leader in the American Revolution. He organized Butler's Rangers, who joined with Britain's Indian allies in frontier raids. After defeating Zebulon BUTLER at Wyoming Valley in Pa., they were blamed for the WYOMING VALLEY MASSACRE.

BUTLER, Nicholas Murray (1862–1947), US educator. He was president of Columbia College (1902–45), and developed it into Columbia U. He was president of the Carnegie Endowment for International Peace (1925–45) and, in 1931, shared the Nobel Peace Prize. He was also active in Republican politics and was president of the AMERICAN ACADEMY OF ARTS AND LETTERS (1928–41).

BUTLER, Samuel (1612–1680), English poet, author of *Hudibras* (1663–78), a mock-heroic, anti-Puritan satire. He attacked the hypocrisy and pedantry of the Puritans of the Commonwealth.

BUTLER, Samuel (1835–1902), English novelist. He considered Darwinism too mechanistic and satirized it in *Erewhon* (1872), his version of Utopia. His major work is *The Way of All Flesh* (1903), an autobiographical novel satirizing Victorian morality.

BUTLER, Walter (1752–1781), loyalist office in the American Revolution, son of John BUTLER. With Indian allies, he led his father's Rangers on a raid culminating in the CHERRY VALLEY MASSACRE (1778).

BUTLER, William Orlando (1791–1880), US general and politician. He served in the War of 1812 and in the Mexican War, and was a US congressman (1839–1843) and an unsuccessful Democratic vice-presidential candidate (1848).

BUTLER, Zebulon (1731–1795), American military leader. He served in the FRENCH AND INDIAN WARS and helped colonize the Wyoming Valley in NE Pa.

BUTTE, mining city in SW Mont., seat of Silver Bow Co., founded in 1864. A mining camp, then a silver-mining center, it gained importance in 1880 with the discovery of copper. Pop 23 368.

BUTTE, small, flat-topped hill formed when EROSION dissects a MESA.

BUTTER, a dairy product (see DAIRY FARMING) made by churning MILK or CREAM, containing fat, protein and water. Made in some countries from the milk of goats, sheep or yaks, it is made in the US from cows' milk only. Continuous mechanized production has been general since the 1940s. After skimming, the cream is ripened with a bacterial culture, pasteurized (see PASTEURIZATION), cooled to 4°C and then churned (see CHURNING), causing the butterfat to separate from the liquid residue, buttermilk. The butter is then washed, worked, colored and salted. World butter production in 1971 was 5.28 million tonnes, of which the US accounted for 10%.

BUTTER-AND-EGGS, common name for *Linaria vulgaris*, a plant with yellow and orange flowers that resemble those of the SNAPDRAGON. It is native to Europe and Asia and is naturalized in North America.

BUTTERCUP, name for a number of species of the genus *Ranunculus*, which are common temperate herbs normally producing yellow or white flowers. The common buttercup (*Ranunculus acris*) has an acrid taste and can be poisonous to cattle. Some species are used as garden flowers.

BUTTERFIELD, John (1801–1869), founder of the American Express Co. (1850). Owner of a stagecoach network, he built up his company by organizing the overland mail route to Los Angeles from 1857. He later invested in the telegraph and railroads.

BUTTERFISH, *Pholis gunnellus*, an elongated BLENNY-like fish found in tidal pools in the N Atlantic from Me. to S.C.

BUTTERFLIES, a large group of INSECTS characterized by wide, brightly colored wings. With MOTHS, they comprise the order LEPIDOPTERA. The life history of the butterfly is composed of several stages, each divided by a METAMORPHOSIS. The EGG grows into a LARVA called a CATERPILLAR, which feeds on vegetation. The next stage, the PUPA, does not feed and eventually produces the adult butterfly.

BUTTERFLY FISH, several small fish with wing-like pectoral fins, used to propel the fish across the surface of the water. They include angelfish and W African freshwater butterfly fish.

BUTTERWORT, common name for *Pinguicula vulgaris*, an INSECTIVOROUS PLANT that grows in wet, boggy habitats in temperate North America and Europe. Each plant has a rosette of fleshy leaves lying flat on the ground. When touched, the leaves secrete a sticky fluid that traps and digests insects; the leaves absorb the nitrogenous compounds so obtained.

BUTTRESS, in architecture, a masonry or brickwork element built against a wall to support it or to take the thrust of a vault or dome. The principle was much developed in the Gothic style. As vaults became higher and walls were pierced by increasingly large windows, the **flying buttress** was evolved. This is a half arch which transfers the thrust to a freestanding masonry member.

BUXTEHUDE, Dietrich (c1637–1707), Danish-born German composer and organist. His cantatas and organ toccatas and chorale preludes influenced J. S. Bach. The evening music concerts he held at Lübeck were famous.

BUXTON, Sir Thomas Fowell, 1st Baronet (1786–1845), English social reformer, successor to WILBERFORCE as leader of the antislavery movement. In parliament he promoted the 1833 act abolishing slavery in the British Empire; he also worked for penal reform.

The buzzard (Buteo) probably had its ancestry in South America, although it is now almost worldwide in distribution, being absent only from Australia and the Indian region.

BUYS-BALLOT'S LAW, in meteorology, states that when an observer stands with his back to the WIND in the N Hemisphere, there is high pressure to his right and low pressure to his left. In the S Hemisphere the reverse holds true. It was named for the Dutch metorologist, **Christoph Hendrik Didericus Buys Ballot** (1817–1890), who published it in 1875. (See also FERREL'S LAW.)

BUZZARDS, a group of medium-sized hawks of the family Accipitridae, easily identifiable by their soaring flight, widespread wings and broad tail. They prey on small mammals by swooping from the air or from a perch. In North America they are called hawks, "buzzard" being applied to VULTURES.

BUZZARDS BAY, inlet of the Atlantic on the SE coast of Mass., 30mi long, 5–10mi wide, connected with Cape Cod Bay by the Cape Cod Canal.

BYBLOS, ancient Phoenician port, trading with Egypt as early as 2800 BC. Now the Lebanese port of Jubayl, it has yielded many early Phoenician inscriptions and other archaeological finds.

BYDGOSZCZ, major industrial Polish city and rail center, on the Brda R. It is Poland's largest inland port. The Bydgoszcz Canal links the Vistula and Noteć rivers. Pop 283 000.

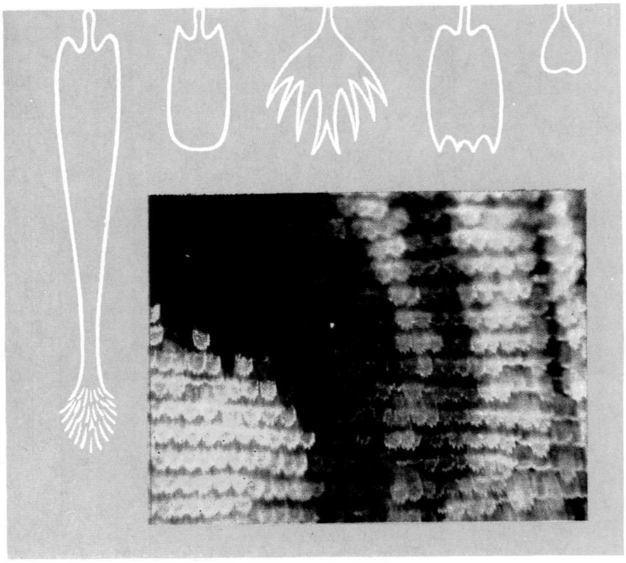

Portion of a butterfly's wing showing scales, overlapping like tiles on a roof, and five variations, shown in outline, in the many shapes scales can assume, according to species.

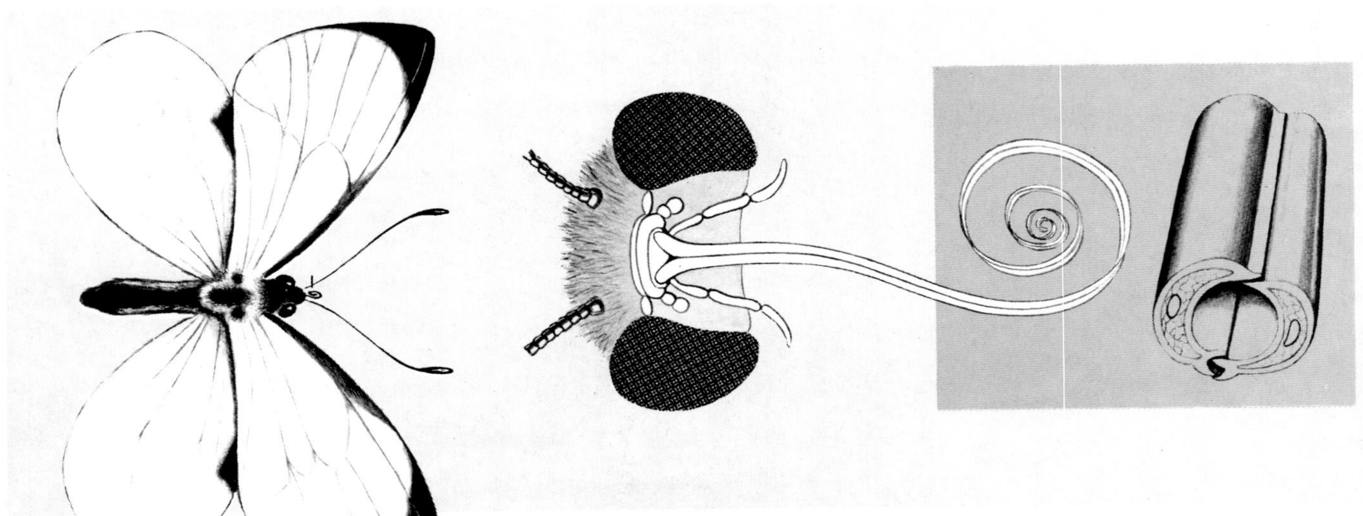

Butterfly (left) with tongue coiled but visible in front of head. Head enlarged (center), with tongue uncoiling. Portion of tongue (right), showing tubular structure achieved by folding it.

BYELORUSSIA. See BELORUSSIAN SOVIET SOCIALIST REPUBLIC.

BYNG, Julian Hedworth George Byng, 1st Viscount (1862–1935), British field marshal and distinguished WWI commander. In 1917 he took Vimy Ridge with the Canadian Corps in France, and later commanded the first-ever large-scale tank offensive. He was governor-general of Canada 1921–26.

BYRD, Harry Flood (1887–1966), US legislator and Democratic governor of Va. 1925–30. During his 32 years in the Senate (1933–65), he advocated stricter government economy and opposed most NEW DEAL programs, foreign aid and integration policies.

BYRD, Richard Evelyn (1888–1957), US aviator, explorer and pioneer of US exploration and research in Antarctica. He led the air unit with D. B. MacMillan's 1925 Arctic expedition and, with Floyd BENNETT, overflew the North Pole (1926); in 1929 he flew over the South Pole. He made five important expeditions to Antarctica (1928–56), established the base camp LITTLE AMERICA there, and worked the whole winter of 1933–34 alone at an advance camp. He headed the US Antarctic program from 1955.

BYRD, William (1543–1623), English composer, one of Europe's greatest masters of POLYPHONY. His choral music includes the "Great Service" for the Anglican Church, three fine Roman Catholic mass settings, some superb motets, *Cantiones Sacrae* (1589; 1591) and many anthems. He also wrote important keyboard music and madrigals. He was closely associated with TALLIS, and in 1575 they were granted a joint monopoly for the printing and sale of music.

BYRD, William (1674–1744), colonial American planter at Westover, Va., active in political and cultural life. He laid out the city of Richmond on part of his family's vast estates. His delightful books and diaries are important records of his times.

BYRNES, James Francis (1879–1972), US statesman. He was director of WWII mobilization 1943–45, and as secretary of state 1945–47 he worked to lessen tensions with the USSR. He was Democratic governor of S.C. 1951–55.

BYRON, George Gordon Byron, 6th Baron (1788–1824), English poet, a leading figure of European ROMANTICISM. Lameness and an unhappy childhood bred morbidity, a scorn for authority and hatred of oppression. His reputation as a libertine drove him to exile in Italy (1816). He later joined the Greek revolt against the Turks, dying of fever at Missolonghi, Greece. *English Bards and Scotch Reviewers* (1809), a savage riposte to his critics, brought overnight fame, and the first two cantos of *Childe Harold's Pilgrimage* (1812), a European reputation. The moody, defiant "Byronic" hero of the poetic drama, *Manfred* (1817), became a great Romantic theme. Major works include the incomplete satiric epic, *Don Juan* (1822), and *The Vision of Judgement* (1819–24), satirizing the poet laureate SOUTHEY and King George III.

BYTOM, city in SW Poland, center of the Katowice mining region. Pop 187 000.

BYZANTINE ART AND ARCHITECTURE, work created in the cultural area of the BYZANTINE EMPIRE in the 4th to early 15th centuries. In architecture, the great church of HAGIA SOPHIA (532–37) in Constantinople (now Istanbul), dominated by its great dome, was a model for later Christian work and for Turkish architects. Other superb Byzantine churches can be seen at S. Vitale in Ravenna, Italy, and Daphne near Athens, while St. Mark's, Venice, is Byzantine-inspired. The interiors of such churches were covered with glowing glass MOSAICS, the supreme Byzantine medium. From dome to floor a strictly ordered scheme of images depicted themes of faith and theology.

Enamels, ivory carving and the art of the goldsmith and silversmith were used to beautify reliquiaries that were the envy of Christendom; many came to Western churches after the Latin sack of Constantinople in 1204. Manuscript illumination, which reached remarkable heights, was a means of diffusing Byzantine styles, and the mystical serenity of the Byzantine masters clearly influenced Italian artists of the medieval Sienese school. The conservative imagery of Byzantine religious art survived for centuries after the fall of Constantinople (1453) in the work of Russian, Greek and Balkan icon painters. Little secular art survives, though Byzantine luxury goods, notably silk, were much sought after in the West. The massive walls of Theodosius at Istanbul are among the monuments to Byzantine military architecture.

During the reign of Justinian (527–565) the Byzantine culture flourished and developed a unique style of art and architecture. These mosaics in the church of San Vitale in Ravenna (6th century) show the emperors surrounded by courtiers, clerics and soldiers.

The Hagia Sophia is another masterpiece of the Byzantine era. It was commissioned by Justinian and designed by Anthemius of Tralles in the 6th century when the empire was at the peak of its glory. This enormous and magnificent church provided the pattern for Byzantine church architecture. The main construction feature of Byzantine churches is the use of pendentives—spherical triangles easing the transition between the circular base of the dome and its polygonal supports. The domes consisted of light stone or even of ceramic bowls covered with cement. Much of the surrounding building, including the two minarets, are additions made since Hagia Sophia became a mosque.

BYZANTINE EMPIRE, historical term for the successor state to the Roman Empire in the East. Its capital was Constantinople (see ISTANBUL), founded by CONSTANTINE I in 330 AD at the ancient Greek BYZANTIUM. Its heartlands were Asia Minor and the Balkans; at its height it ruled S Spain, Italy, Sicily, N Africa, Egypt, Syria, Palestine, the Crimean coast, Cyprus and the Aegean islands. Its religion was Eastern Orthodox Christianity; Byzantine missionaries took Christianity to Russia and Byzantine theologians are among the chief Church Fathers. Its literature was based on the ancient Greek classics. BYZANTINE ART AND ARCHITECTURE influenced W Europe and Turkey, and Byzantine scholars contributed to Western Humanism.

The Roman Empire was divided after the death of Theodosius I in 395. By c500 the Western Empire had fallen, and Germanic invaders occupied Italy, Spain and N Africa. In the East, Roman institutions continued; JUSTINIAN I (527–565) reconquered Italy, S Spain and N Africa and made a great codification of Roman law. However, after c600 fundamental changes displaced Roman with typically Byzantine (Greek) institutions. By 700, S Spain, N Africa, Egypt and Syria were lost to the VISIGOTHS and ARABS, and the LOMBARDS were conquering Italy. Later, Bulgars occupied much of the Balkans and, after the disastrous Byzantine defeat at the Battle of MANZIKERT in 1071, the SELJUKS pushed deep into Asia Minor. A 12th-century recovery ended when, in 1204, Venice and the Fourth Crusade sacked Constantinople. In 1261 MICHAEL VIII regained the city, but the Turkish threat grew. Western Europe, considering the Eastern Church in Schism since a break (1054) between the patriarch of Constantinople and the pope, refused to help. In 1453, the one great Eastern Christian empire fell when the Turks captured Constantinople.

On the rich trade routes from Asia and N Africa to Europe and Russia, Constantinople was the greatest city of the Christian world; its empire rested on a money economy, while feudalism and the Church dominated Western society and government. Byzantine emperors ruled through paid professional administrators, commanded paid professional armies and were supreme in religion as in politics, though affairs were often marked by court intrigues. They controlled early Church Councils and, during the 8th-century ICONOCLASTIC CONTROVERSY, ordered images to be destroyed as idolatrous. Theological debate was a passion with all classes. Military success was expected of emperors and military coups were frequent. Foreign diplomacy was subtle and usually successful. The Byzantines considered themselves to be the heirs to Rome; their high and ancient civilization justified their claim.

BYZANTIUM, ancient capital of the BYZANTINE EMPIRE, renamed Constantinople in 330 AD by Emperor Constantine I. It is now called ISTANBUL.

C

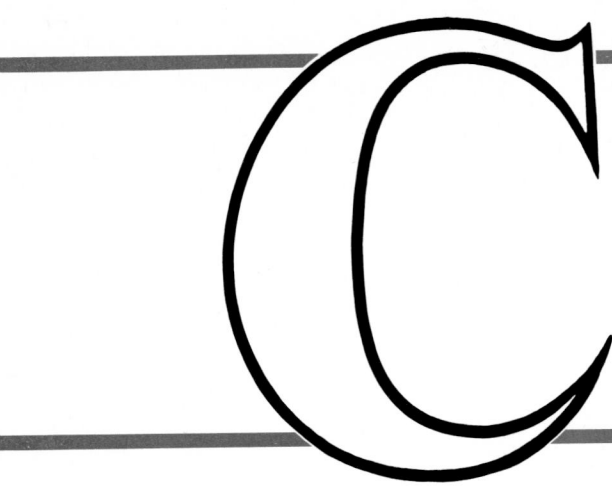

C, third letter of the English alphabet, a rounded form of the Greek *gamma*, used by the Romans instead of *k*. In some languages *c* came to have the sound *s* or *ch*. The English *c* retains both the *k* and *s* sounds (cat, certain, cycle, etc.). C is the chemical symbol for carbon and in Roman numerals equals 100.

CABAL, clandestine group or organization engaged in intrigues; also applied to the intrigues themselves. The term was already used in the 17th century for any secret council of the king. The conduct of English King Charles II's ministers Clifford, Arlington, Buckingham, Ashley and Lauderdale, whose initials spelled "cabal," gave it a sinister sense.

CABALA, or Kabbalah (Hebrew: tradition), a body of esoteric Jewish mystical doctrines dealing with the manifestations of God and his revelation. The Cabala attaches mystical significance to every detail in the TORAH. Its chief books are the *Sefer Yezirah* (Book of Creation; 3rd–6th centuries) and the *Sefer HaZohar* (Book of Splendor; 13th century). The Cabala arose in S France and Spain in the Middle Ages and was later a major influence on HASIDISM.

CABALETTA, short operatic song with a regular rhythm, also the final section of an operatic aria. A fine example is Violetta's "Sempre libera degg'io" in Verdi's *La Traviata*.

CABBAGE, *Brassica olearacea*, a biennial vegetable from which other BRASSICAS, such as KALE, CAULIFLOWER and BROCCOLI have been developed. The cabbage originated many centuries ago from the European wild cabbage. It has a characteristic tight "head" of leaves. Cabbages can be boiled or pickled, or fermented in salt to give Sauerkraut. They are also used as an animal feed.

CABBAGE PALM, *Sabal palmetto*, a common fan-leaved palm tree ranging from N.C. through Middle America. It thrives in swampy regions, such as the Florida everglades, and can grow up to 24m (80ft). The fruit is edible and in some areas the trunks are used for fencing.

CABELL, James Branch (1879–1958), US novelist, who combined an ironic, often anti-romantic style with a strong element of fantasy in plots and settings. His best-known novel is *Jurgen* (1919).

CABER TOSSING, Scottish athletic event which involves throwing a "caber," a stripped stem of a tree up to 20ft long. Held upright against the chest, the caber is "tossed" so that it turns over in the air before striking the ground.

CABET, Étienne (1788–1856), French Utopian socialist, whose novel of an ideal communistic society, *Voyage en Icarie* (1840), gained wide readership. An unsuccessful attempt in 1848 to found an "Icarian" community in Texas was followed by other short-lived colonies, notably one led by Cabet himself (1849–56) at Nauvoo, Ill.

CABEZA DE VACA, Álvar Núnez (c1490–1557), Spanish explorer. Shipwrecked in 1528 after an expedition to Florida, he reached Mexico City after several years among the Indians. He was made governor of the Río de la Plata region in 1540, but after a rebellion against him was recalled to Spain. He was tried and exiled to Africa, but in 1552 he was pardoned by the king.

CABEZÓN, Antonio de (c1510–1566), Spanish composer of keyboard music. Blind from infancy, he served at the Spanish court, writing for the organ, harpsichord and vihuela.

CABINDA, or Kabinda, coastal territory belonging to Angola where there is a separatist movement. It covers 2800sq mi; its economy is traditionally agricultural, based on timber, palm oil, cocoa and coffee but now increasingly on oil. Pop 80857.

CABINET, in the US, top-level advisory council to the president, composed of the heads of the major executive departments. Though not mentioned in the US constitution, the cabinet has been accepted as a consultative body to the executive since George Washington. Normally the cabinet meets weekly with the president, though procedure varies.

Members of the cabinet are appointed by the president and are responsible as individuals to him: they are not members of either house of Congress and may not address them, though they are often called to testify before committees. In Great Britain and most of the Commonwealth the cabinet is a policy-making body of ministers chosen by the prime minister from the political party in power, and collectively responsible to parliament. (See also US Departments of AGRICULTURE; COMMERCE; DEFENSE; HEALTH, EDUCATION AND WELFARE; HOUSING AND URBAN DEVELOPMENT; INTERIOR; JUSTICE; LABOR; STATE; TRANSPORTATION; TREASURY.)

CABINETMAKING, the art of precise and delicate woodworking, exemplified by Thomas CHIPPENDALE in England and Duncan PHYFE in America. Cabinetmaking involves dovetailing, using mortises and tenons, and glue rather than screws or nails, but 20th-century MASS PRODUCTION has led to its steady decline. (See also FURNITURE.)

CABLE, Electric, insulated electric CONDUCTOR used to carry power or signals. In simplest form, a cable has a core of conducting metal (e.g., COPPER), usually several wires stranded together, surrounded by an insulating sheath of PLASTIC or RUBBER. Cable for VHF signals, as used in RADIO, is **coaxial cable**. Here a central core of wire is surrounded by insulation, then by a sheath of wire braid or an ALUMINUM or copper tube, then by a final layer of insulation. For electric power (see ELECTRICITY) simple cables are used in the home. Overhead cables, used to transmit power from power stations, are insulated from the pylons that support them, but between pylons there is generally no insulation around the core. Cables with a number of cores (multicore cables) are used for telephone cables and especially for the great submarine cables that connect countries as far apart as Australia and Canada. The first submarine cable, laid between Dover and Calais in 1850, had a single core insulated with GUTTA PERCHA.

CABLE, George Washington (1844–1925), US novelist, noted for his depiction of the Creole and Negro ways of life in works such as *Old Creole Days* (1879) and *The Grandissimes* (1880).

CABLE CAR, passenger vehicle drawn by a moving cable driven by an exterior power source. The most famous, those of San Francisco, are driven by a continuous cable running beneath the street surface: from each car a grip descends through a slot in the roadway; it can be attached to or detached from the cable by the driver's controls. **Aerial tramways** are used in mountainous regions to span valleys and ascend mountains. On one cable the car is supported by means of PULLEY wheels, which run along the cable; a separate cable provides the motive power. **Ski lifts** are similar, though the car is usually supported by the moving cable alone. The cable-car principle is used by rail transportation on steep gradients in the form of a **funicular**; here an ascending car is usually counterbalanced by a descending car attached to the same cable.

CABLE TELEVISION, or **CATV** (*c*ommunity *a*ntenna *t*ele*v*ision), system used primarily in areas where mountains or tall buildings make TELEVISION reception poor or impossible. Subscribers' sets are connected by coaxial CABLE to a single ANTENNA erected in a suitably exposed position.

CABOT, George (1752–1823), prosperous Mass. merchant who served in the US Senate (1791–96) and led the HARTFORD CONVENTION. Many of his descendants became prominent in public service.

CABOT, John (Giovanni Caboto; c1450–1499), Italian navigator and explorer, probably the first European to reach the North American mainland. In 1497, after receiving letters patent from Henry VII of England authorizing his voyage, Cabot sailed in search of a western route to Asia and reached the coasts of Nova Scotia and Newfoundland. He made a landing and set up the English and Venetian flags. On a second voyage (1498) Cabot may have reached America again, but it is not clear what happened to the expedition. Cabot himself was not mentioned again, though he drew his English annuity for 1499.

CABOT, Sebastian (c1476–1557), explorer and navigator, son of John CABOT. Appointed pilot-major of Spain in 1518, he led an expedition to the Río de la Plata region of South America in 1526. Its failure led to his banishment from Spain. Though eventually reinstated, he went to England in 1548, and later became governor of the Merchant Adventurers Company.

CABRAL, Pedro Álvares (c1467–1520), Portuguese navigator credited with the discovery of Brazil, where he landed in 1500 on a voyage from Lisbon to India. The expedition succeeded in establishing trading posts in India, but after his return in 1501 Cabral was given no other position of authority.

CABRILLO, Juan Rodríguez (d. c1543), Portuguese explorer in the service of Spain, best known for his discovery of California. In 1542 he explored the coastline from Lower California northwards to San Diego Bay, and may have succeeded in landing on some of the islands.

CABRILLO NATIONAL MONUMENT, arm of land forming the W side of San Diego Bay, Cal., first sighted by Juan Rodríguez CABRILLO in 1542. Established in 1913, the monument covers about 123 acres.

CABRINI, Saint Frances Xavier (1850–1917), Italian–American nun, first US citizen to be canonized (1946). She founded the Missionary Sisters of the Sacred Heart in 1880, and established 67 houses of the order throughout the world. In 1889 she immigrated to New York from Italy.

CACAO, *Theobroma cacao*, the tree that produces cacao or cocoa beans. The raw material for CHOCOLATE is prepared by roasting, grinding and pressing the dried seeds (or beans) from the woody cacao fruits. Pressing squeezes out cocoa butter and leaves a solid mass that is reground to make **cocoa** powder. Eating chocolate is made from a blend of ground beans, sugar and cocoa butter, with milk added for milk chocolate. The cacao tree grows in Africa and Middle America and has been cultivated since the time of the Aztecs, who used it for beverages and currency. Christopher Columbus introduced cocoa beans into Europe in 1502 and by the 1700s the hot chocolate drink was popular.

CACOMISTLE, a member of the mammalian family Procyonidae, relative of the RACCOON, found in the US and Mexico. It is 750mm (2.5ft) long, with gray-buff fur and a bushy, black and white ringed tail. The nocturnal cacomistle feeds on small animals and fruit, and is hunted for its fur. It is also known as the "California mink."

CACTI, family of prickly plants (Cactaceae) comprising over 1 500 species, almost all of which are native to America. The succulent cactus is a XEROPHYTE and well adapted to life in the driest desert conditions. It has no leaves, the main source of water loss in other plants, and PHOTOSYNTHESIS takes place in the stem or trunk, which also stores a great deal of water. A network of roots radiating from the stem makes maximum use of brief desert showers. The characteristic spines have two functions: they prevent the stem from being eaten by animals; and where the spines form a dense covering, they help to retain water without obstructing light. Cacti bear beautiful flowers which are shortlived and often open only at night. Cacti are prized as ornamental plants. They are also the source of the drug MESCALINE and some species are edible. As house plants they should be kept in sunny south-facing windows. They tolerate normal house temperatures, although some species require a cold period in winter to set buds. They should be well watered whenever the surface of the soil dries out. They can be propagated by means of seeds, cuttings or by dividing the plants. (See also CEREUS; OLD-MAN CACTUS; PEYOTE; PRICKLY PEAR.)

CADDIS FLIES, worldwide INSECTS of the order Trichoptera, best known in the form of aquatic larvae, or caddis worms. The larvae build tubes or cases of pebbles, snail shells etc. and crawl about to feed; some spin silk cases and trap tiny water organisms in silken nets.

CADDOAN, language-group of North American Indians including the Caddo, Wichita, Arikara and Pawnee tribes. Originating in the fertile areas to the W of the Mississippi R, Caddoan-speaking peoples were mainly sedentary, building conical huts and living by agriculture and hunting. The Caddoan tribes now comprise less than 2 000 people.

CADE, Jack (d. 1450), leader of the Kentish rebellion against Henry VI of England in 1450. His army occupied London for three days, but disbanded after the promise of concessions and pardons. Cade was captured and mortally wounded, and the concessions were revoked.

CADENCE, used in music to describe the notes or chords which close a phrase or movement. It is a melodic or harmonic formula which brings a phrase or passage to a rest.

CADENZA, musical passage at the close of a movement in which a soloist displays his instrumental or vocal skill. In the 18th and 19th centuries, composers would often leave an opening for improvisation by the performer. Eventually cadenzas were written out, whether by the composer or by a famous performer, and became an integral part of the CONCERTO.

CADILLAC, city in NW Mich., on lakes Cadillac and Mitchell, seat of Wexford Co. Its economy combines manufacturing, agriculture and tourism. Pop 9 990.

CADILLAC, Antoine Laumet de la Mothe (c1658–1730), French colonial governor and founder of Detroit (1701). Governor of Mackinac in 1694, he

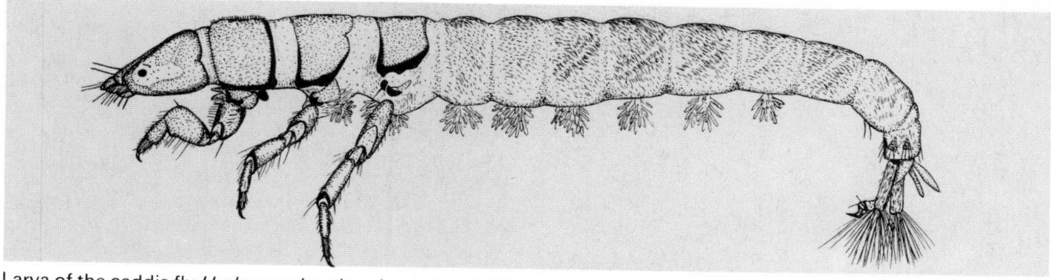

Larva of the caddis fly *Hydropsyche*, showing tufts of gills on thorax and abdomen.

felt the site of Detroit would be a better strategic position. In 1710 he was appointed governor of Louisiana, but was recalled in 1717.

CÁDIZ, ancient city and port in SW Spain, on the Atlantic coast NW of Gibraltar. Founded by the Phoenicians in c1100 BC as Gadir, the city became prosperous under Roman rule. After the discovery of America it became important as the headquarters of the Spanish fleets. It is now a commercial port noted for sherry exports. Pop 135 743.

CADMAN, Charles Wakefield (1881–1946), US composer, inspired by North American Indian music. His works include several operas, the song *From the Land of the Sky-Blue Water* and orchestral suites.

CADMIUM (Cd), soft, silver-white metal in Group IIB of the PERIODIC TABLE; an anomalous TRANSITION ELEMENT. It is found as greenockite (CdS) and in ZINC ores, from which it is extracted as a by-product. Cadmium is intermediate in chemical properties between ZINC and MERCURY, forming mainly Cd^{2+} compounds. Cadmium is used for electroplating to give corrosion-resistance; in storage BATTERIES; in low-melting ALLOYS; and as a moderator in nuclear reactors. Some compounds are used in pigments. AW 112.4, mp 321°C, bp 765°C, sg 8.65 (20°C).

CADMUS, in Greek mythology, the founder of Thebes. Instructed by the oracle at Delphi to found the city, Cadmus first had to slay a dragon which guarded the site. He then sowed the dragon's teeth and warriors sprang up, five of whom helped him build the citadel of Thebes.

CADUCEUS, staff with two serpents entwined around it and topped with wings, symbol of the Greek god Hermes. Resembling the staff of AESCULAPIUS, in classical times it was carried by heralds and envoys.

CADWALLADER (d. 689), semilegendary last king of the Britons. He led his people to Brittany to escape plague in Britain, which was then taken over by the Saxons. After his death he was regarded as a saint.

CAECILIANS, or **apoda,** worm-like amphibians that live in underground burrows. Various species are found in South America, Africa and Asia, the largest growing up to 1.4m (4.6ft).

CAEDMON (7th century), first English Christian poet. After a dream commanding him to "sing the beginning of created things," he spent the rest of his life rendering biblical stories into verse. Only nine lines of his hymn to God survive.

CAELIAN HILL. See SEVEN HILLS OF ROME.

CAEN, capital of the department of Calvados in NW France, on the Orne R, in Normandy. Joined to the coast by a canal about 9mi long, Caen is a major port and trading center for the surrounding area. Pop 110 262.

CAERNARVON, borough in the county of Gwynedd in North Wales, on the Menai Straits. Its castle, built in 1284 by Edward I, is one of the finest examples of medieval fortification in Britain. The town is a popular tourist resort. Pop 9 253.

CAESAR, family name of the Julian clan of Rome. The success of Julius CAESAR made it charismatic, and it was retained as a family name by the first five Roman emperors. The title was kept by later emperors for their heirs designate, and the German *kaiser* and Russian *tsar* were derived from it.

CAESAR, Gaius Julius (100–44 BC), Roman general, politician and writer, one of the most famous of the ancient Romans. Although a member of the ancient patrician Julian clan, he supported the antisenatorial party. His early career through various public offices won him popularity, and in 60 BC he formed the First Triumvirate with POMPEY, who supplied the army, and CRASSUS, who provided the money. With Caesar as consul in 59 BC they succeeded in controlling Roman politics, and in 58 BC he chose Gaul as his proconsular command.

Caesar's successful GALLIC WARS (58–51 BC) gained him great esteem and a loyal and well-trained army. Pompey was given extraordinary powers in Rome and tried to force Caesar to lay down his command, but in 49 BC Caesar crossed the Rubicon R and civil war began. Pompey was finally defeated at Pharsalus in 48 BC, and by 45 BC Caesar had secured the defeat of all the Pompeian forces. In 44 BC he was made dictator for life, but on the IDES OF MARCH he was murdered by a group of senators.

CAESAREA, name of several towns in the Roman Empire, the most important being a Mediterranean port, about 55mi NW of Jerusalem. It was here that the great revolt of the Jews against the Romans began in 66 AD.

CAESARIAN SECTION. See CESARIAN SECTION.

CAETANO, Marcello (1906–), Portuguese statesman, who succeeded Antonio SALAZAR as premier in 1968. In April 1974 Dr. Caetano was deposed and exiled after a military coup.

CAFFEINE, or trimethylxanthine ($C_8H_{10}N_4O_2$), an ALKALOID extracted from coffee, and also found in tea, cocoa and cola. Caffeine stimulates the central NERVOUS SYSTEM and HEART, and is a DIURETIC. It

Bronze statue of Julius Caesar near the ancient Forum in Rome. The initials at the base stand for *senatus populusque Romanus*, the senate and people of Rome. Such statues contributed to Caesar's carefully cultivated public image, as essential to his rule as his military successes.

Cairo's old quarter is still dominated by the domes of its many mosques. Not far away a western style city is developing on either side of the Nile river.

increases alertness, in excess causing insomnia (see SLEEP), and is mildly addictive. mp 238°C.

CAGE, John (1912–), US experimental composer and musical theoretician. He experimented with prolonged silence, improvisation and the chance (aleatoric) element in music. Among his compositions: *Atlas eclipticalis* (1961); *HPSCHD* (1967–69); *Cheap Imitation for Full Orchestra* (1972).

CAGLIARI, ancient Italian seaport, the modern capital of Sardinia. Cagliari is the island's commercial center, exporting salt and minerals—mainly zinc and lead. Pop 231 670.

CAGLIOSTRO, Alessandro di, Count (real name: Giuseppe Balsamo; 1743–1795), Sicilian adventurer who toured the cities of Europe posing as a physician and alchemist. His séances and elixirs duped European society. But he had to flee from Paris after the DIAMOND NECKLACE AFFAIR, and was finally imprisoned in Rome (1789) for freemasonry.

CAGUAS, town in E central Puerto Rico, lying in a fertile agricultural region. Pop 63 215.

CAHAN, Abraham (1860–1951), Russian-born US journalist and novelist, cofounder in 1897 of the Social Democratic party and the influential newspaper, the *Jewish Daily Forward*.

CAHOKIA, residential village in SW Ill., suburb of East St. Louis on the Mississippi R. Founded in 1699 by the French, it became British in 1765. Pop 20 649.

CAHOKIA MOUNDS, a group of prehistoric MOUNDS, mostly in the form of truncated pyramids, near East St. Louis, Ill. The largest of these, Monks Mound, is about 350m by 200m at base and some 30m high, and is the largest mound in the US. More than 300 of the mounds have in recent years been bulldozed to make way for agricultural and municipal expansion, but the 18 largest remain.

CAICOS ISLANDS. See TURKS AND CAICOS ISLANDS.

CAILLÉ, or **Caillié, René Auguste** (1799–1838), French traveler. In 1828, posing as an Arab, he was the first European to survive a journey to Timbuktu.

CAIMANS, reptiles similar to and related to ALLIGATORS. Caimans grow to 5m (16ft) long and live in tropical rivers such as the Amazon. The group is threatened with extinction because their skins are used for the manufacture of handbags.

CAIN, eldest son of ADAM and EVE, who, through jealousy, slew his brother ABEL. He was banished by God from his home and condemned to wander. God, however, gave him an identifying mark for protection, and the promise that, if killed, his death would be avenged sevenfold.

CAINOZOIC. See CENOZOIC.

CAIRN (from Gaelic *carn*, heap), a mound of stones, usually conical in form, used as a marker (as on a mountaintop), a memorial or to cover an ancient burial place. Found all over the world, cairns are sometimes regarded as a form of BARROWS.

CAIRN TERRIER, breed of small, short-legged dog. Usually sandy to black in color, it was developed in W Scotland to drive foxes out of the spaces between rocks in cairns.

CAIRO, or Al-Qāhirah, capital of Egypt. It lies at the head of the Nile delta and is the largest African city. Founded in 969 by the Fatimids, it became and has remained the intellectual center of the Islamic world with the foundation of al-Azhar University (970–78). An allied base during WWII and site of the CAIRO CONFERENCE, it became capital of republican Egypt (1952), and remains a major Arab political, economic and nationalist center. The nearby pyramids, sphinx and Memphis ruins make it a tourist center. Pop 4 961 000.

CAIRO, city in SW Ill., seat of Alexander Co., at the confluence of the Mississippi and Ohio rivers. An important Civil War Union base. Now a trading and shipping center for the surrounding area. Pop 6 277.

CAIRO CONFERENCE, meeting of CHURCHILL, F. D. ROOSEVELT and CHIANG KAI-SHEK in Cairo, Egypt, Nov. 22–26, 1943. The Cairo Declaration (Dec. 1, 1943) asserted that on Japan's defeat her boundaries would revert to what they were before the late-19th-century conquests of Chinese territory.

CAISSON, boxlike structure used primarily in BRIDGE building. **Box caissons** are used where the existing bed is firm. They are open at the top, usually being built on land, floated into position, filled with CONCRETE and sunk. **Open caissons** have neither top nor bottom, their bottom edge being sharp. They are placed on the bed and excavation inside them proceeds. The caisson sinks, and as it does so its walls are built up, the increased weight assisting the sinking. When a firm bed is reached, the caisson is filled with concrete. **Pneumatic caissons** have no bottom, and are filled with air under PRESSURE to prevent the entry of water. Workmen may enter via an AIR LOCK and excavate from within the caisson, which on completion of their task is filled with concrete.

CAISSON DISEASE, or **bends.** See AEROEMBOLISM.

CAJUNS, descendants of expatriate French-Canadians, living in S La. They were deported from Acadia (Nova Scotia) by the British in 1755. They have a distinctive patois: a combination of archaic French forms with English, Spanish, German, Indian and Negro idioms.

CAKEWALK, dance originated by Negro slaves in the southern US before the Civil War. It became a popular dance craze around 1900. Couples walked in a square formation, men on the inside, taking exaggerated high steps. Its music influenced the growth of RAGTIME.

CALABASH, *Crescentia cujete*, tropical American tree that produces fruit similar to the African gourd. It has yellow fluted flowers with red or purple veining. The woody shell of the fruit is used for ornaments and food containers. (See also GOURD.)

CALABRIA, mountainous Italian region; the "toe" of Italy's "boot." Its capital is Catanzaro and other chief cities are Cosenza and Reggio Calabria. It suffered disastrous earthquakes 1783–87, 1905 and 1908. Area: 5 822sq mi.

CALADIUM, a genus of tuberous, herbaceous perennial plants native to the tropics. They are widely cultivated for their ornamental foliage, in containers outdoors during the summer, or more popularly all the year around as house plants. Caladiums have arrowhead-shaped leaves colored in mosaic patterns of white, red and green. Indoors they grow best in moderately sunny positions. During the growing season the temperature must be maintained above 17°C (62°F) and the soil should be kept evenly moist; during the dormant season the temperature can drop to 10°C (50°F) and the soil kept barely damp. Propagation is achieved by tuber divisions. Family: Araceae.

CALAIS, seaport and manufacturing city in Pas-de Calais department, N France. It lies on the Straits of Dover, 170mi from Paris and 21mi from Dover, and is a major Anglo-European transit point. Pop 74 908.

CALAMINE, former name of two ZINC minerals, SMITHSONITE and HEMIMORPHITE. In medicine, calamine lotion (zinc carbonate) is a mild ASTRINGENT used to treat ECZEMA and other itchy skin diseases.

CALAMITY JANE, nickname of Martha Jane Burke (c1852–1903), frontier-town prostitute and camp-follower who roamed the West in male garb. Famous in Deadwood, S.D., during the 1870s gold boom, she claimed she had been an army scout, pony express rider, Custer's aide and Wild Bill Hickok's mistress.

CALAMONDIN, popular name for *Citrus mitis*, a dwarf evergreen shrub native to the Philippines, but widely grown as a pot plant for its fragrant white flowers and small orange-like fruit. It grows well indoors in full sunlight if the temperature is maintained between 16°C and 21°C (60°F and 70°F) and the soil is kept evenly moist. Propagation is achieved by taking root cuttings in spring and summer. Family: Rubaceae.

CALAS, Jean (1698–1762), French Protestant (Huguenot) merchant whose case resulted in the 1788 reform of the Protestants' legal position. In 1762 he was tortured, broken on the wheel and burned for murdering his son, allegedly a Roman Catholic. His cause was championed by VOLTAIRE and became a stimulus for criminal law reform and religious tolerance.

CALATHEA, a genus of evergreen perennials native to South America, but widely grown as house plants for their attractive, dark green, often blotchy or variegated foliage that in some species is maroon on

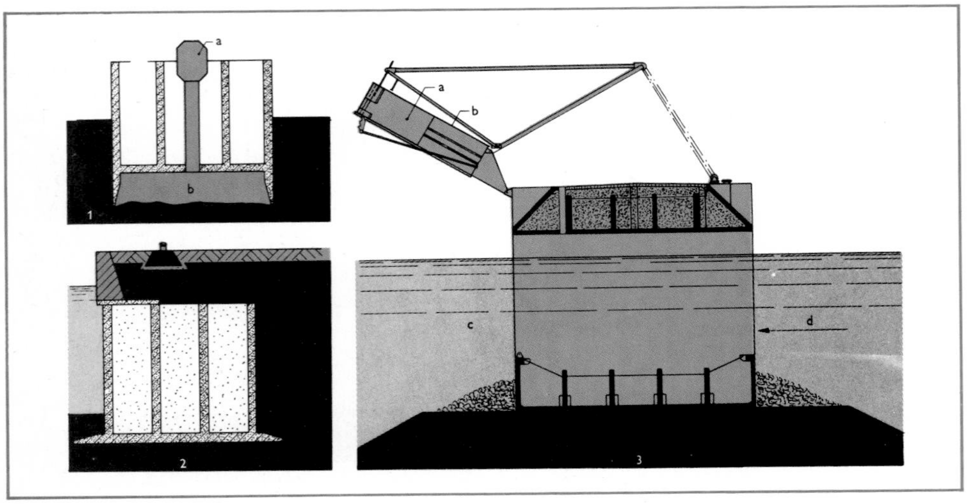

Caissons for various kinds of underwater work. 1. Pneumatic caisson; air pressure maintained by the airlock (a) keeps water out of the work space (b). 2. Box caisson supporting sea wall, jetty or similar structure. 3. Open-sided caisson with a movable gate, containing a float chamber (a) and a valve (b); (c) is the seaward side and (d) the direction of flow at ebb tide. A line of such caissons can control tidal movements to prevent interference with construction without necessarily cutting them off altogether, which might cause environmental damage.

the underside. Indoors they grow best if placed away from direct sunlight, the temperature maintained above 16°C (60°F) and the soil kept evenly moist. The plants are propagated by dividing the crowns in spring and summer. Family: Marantaceae.

CALCEOLARIA, a genus of hardy, half-hardy and tender annuals, biennials and perennials native to Middle and South America, but widely grown as garden and house plants for their freely-produced pouch-shaped yellow, orange or red flowers. Indoors, they should be grown in sunny east- or west-facing windows and maintained at a temperature of 16°C to 21°C (60°F to 70°F) during the winter, but avoiding hot, dry air. The soil should be kept evenly moist. They are propagated from seeds. Calceolarias are commonly known as pocket book plants. Family: Scrophulariaceae.

CALCIMINE. See WHITEWASH.

CALCINATION, the process of heating materials in air to drive off moisture, carbon dioxide or other volatile compounds, and sometimes to oxidize them. Ores are often calcined after grinding, and plaster, cement and some pigments are made by calcination.

CALCITE, mineral form of calcium carbonate (see CALCIUM) of widespread occurrence; hexagonal symmetry. LIMESTONE, MARBLE and CHALK are types of calcite. Iceland spar, a very pure calcite, is transparent and exhibits DOUBLE REFRACTION of light, so being useful in optical instruments. Lime, CEMENT and fertilizers are manufactured from calcite.

CALCIUM (Ca), a fairly soft, silvery-white ALKALINE-EARTH METAL, the fifth most abundant element. It occurs naturally as CALCITE, GYPSUM and FLUORITE. The metal is prepared by ELECTROLYSIS of fused calcium chloride. Calcium is very reactive, reacting with water to give a surface layer of calcium hydroxide, and burning in air to give the nitride and oxide. Calcium metal is used as a reducing agent to prepare other metals, as a getter in vacuum tubes, and in alloys. AW 40.1, mp 839°C, bp 1484°C, sg 1.55 (20°C).

Calcium compounds are important constituents of animal skeletons: calcium phosphate forms the bones and teeth of vertebrates, and many seashells are made of the carbonate. **Calcium Carbonate** ($CaCO_3$), colorless crystalline solid, occurring naturally as CALCITE and aragonite, which loses carbon dioxide on heating above 900°C. It is an insoluble BASE. **Calcium Chloride** ($CaCl_2$), colorless crystalline solid, a by-product of the Solvay process. Being very deliquescent, it is used as an industrial drying agent. mp 782°C. **Calcium Fluoride** (CaF_2), or FLUORITE, colorless phosphorescent crystalline solid, used as windows in ultraviolet and infrared SPECTROSCOPY. mp 1423°C, bp c2500°C. **Calcium Hydroxide** ($Ca(OH)_2$), or **Slaked Lime**, colorless crystalline solid, slightly soluble in water, prepared by hydrating calcium oxide and used in industry and agriculture as an ALKALI, in mortar and in glass manufacture. **Calcium Oxide** (CaO), or **Quicklime**, white crystalline powder, made by calcination of calcium carbonate minerals, which reacts violently with water to give calcium hydroxide and is used in arc lights and as an industrial dehydrating agent. mp 2580°C, bp 2850°C **Calcium Sulfate** ($CaSO_4$), colorless crystalline solid, occurring naturally as GYPSUM and ANHYDRITE. When the dihydrate is heated to 128°C, it loses water, forming the hemihydrate, **plaster of paris**. This re-forms the dihydrate as a hard mass when mixed with water, and is used for casts.

CALCULATING MACHINE, device that performs simple ARITHMETIC operations (see also ALGEBRA). There are two main classes: **adding machines**, for ADDITION and SUBTRACTION only; and **calculators**, able also to perform MULTIPLICATION and DIVISION. They may be mechanical, electromechanical, or electronic.

The forerunner of the calculating machine was perhaps the ABACUS. The first adding machine, invented by PASCAL (1642), was able to add and carry. A few decades later (1671), LEIBNIZ designed a device that multiplied by repeated addition (the device was built in 1694). BABBAGE built a small adding machine (1822): in 1833 he conceived his Difference Engine, a predecessor of the digital COMPUTER, but his device

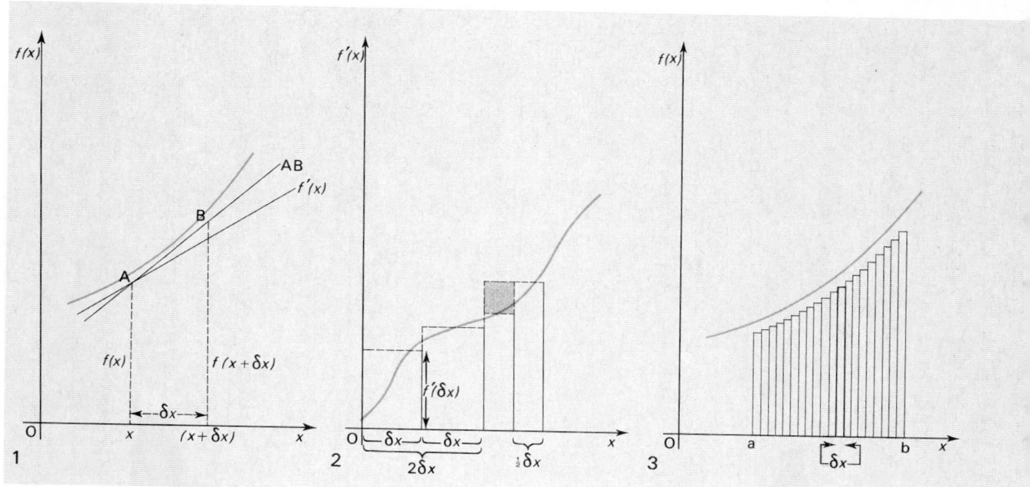

Figure 1: Graph of function $f(x)$, showing geometrical interpretation of a derivative. As δx tends to zero, AB and $f(x)$ coincide. Figure 2: The construction of thin strips under the curve $y=f'(x)$. Each of the strips has an area of approximately $\delta x.f'(n\delta x)$, where n gives the position of the strip. As can be seen, the approximation is more accurate the smaller the value of δx. Figure 3: Integration of a function between bounds $x=a$ and $x=b$.

was never completed. (See also SLIDE RULE.)

CALCULI, or stones, solid concretions of calcium salts or organic compounds, formed in the KIDNEY, BLADDER or GALL BLADDER. They are often associated with infection. There may be no symptoms but they may pass down or block tubes, causing COLIC, or obstruction in an organ. They may pass on unaided with antispasm drugs and ANALGESICS, but may require surgical removal to prevent damage to kidney or liver.

CALCULUS, the branch of MATHEMATICS dealing with continually varying quantities. It can be seen as an extension of ANALYTIC GEOMETRY, much of whose terminology it shares.

Differential Calculus. Consider the FUNCTION $y=f(x)$. This may be plotted as a CURVE on a set of CARTESIAN COORDINATES. Assuming that the curve is not a straight LINE, tangents (see TANGENT OF A CURVE) to it at different points will have different GRADIENTS. Two points close together on the curve, (x, y) and $(x+\delta x, y+\delta y)$, where δx and δy mean very small distances in the x- and y-directions, will usually have tangents of similar, though not identical, gradients. The gradient of the line passing through these two points is given by

$$\frac{(y+\delta y)-y}{(x+\delta x)-x},$$

and is the same as that of a tangent to the curve somewhere between the two points. The smaller δx is, the closer the two gradients will be; and if δx is infinitely small, they will be identical. This LIMIT as $x\to 0$ is the derivative

$$\frac{dy}{dx} \text{ or } f'(x)$$

of the function and is given by (putting $f(x)$ in place of y):

$$f'(x)=\lim_{\delta x\to 0}\frac{f(x+\delta x)-f(x)}{\delta x}.$$

This formula will give the gradient of the curve for $f(x)$ at any value of x. For example, in the parabola (see CONIC SECTIONS) $y=x^2$ the derivative at $x=a$ is given by

$$f'(a)=\lim_{x\to a}\frac{(x^2-a^2)}{(x-a)}=\lim_{x\to a}\frac{(x+a)(x-a)}{(x-a)}$$
$$=\lim_{x\to a}(x+a)=2a.$$

Hence we can say that $f'(x)=2x$ for $f(x)=x^2$. This process is termed differentiation. In general if $f(x)=x^z$ then $f'(x)=z \,.\, x^{z-1}$, and the second derivative,

$$f''(x) \text{ or } \frac{d^2y}{dx^2},$$

the result of differentiating again, is $(z-1) \,.\, z \,.\, x^{z-2}$ — and so on.

Integral Calculus. The derivative of $f(x)$ gives the instantaneous rate of change of $f(x)$ for a particular value of x. Now, consider the plot of $y=f'(x)$, and assume that $f'(x)=0$, $f(x)=0$ when $x=0$. A very thin strip with one vertical side the $f'(x)$-axis and the other the line joining the points $(\delta x, 0)$ and $(\delta x, f'(\delta x))$, will have an area of approximately $\delta x.f'(\delta x)$. A second thin strip drawn next to it will have an area of roughly $\delta x.f'(2\delta x)$, and so on. The area between the curve and the x-axis from $x=0$ to $x=a$ will therefore be roughly $\delta x.f'(\delta x)+\delta x.f'(2\delta x)+\ .\ .\ .\ +\delta x.f'(a-\delta x)+\delta x.f'(a)$. If one plots on a different graph x against (area of strip 1), (area of strips 1+2), (area of strips 1+2+3), etc., one finds that one is plotting a close approximation to $y=f(x)$. This reverse of differentiation is called integration, and $f(x)$ is the integral of $f'(x)$. We find, too, that the integral of x^z is

$$\frac{x^{z+1}}{z+1},$$

which is what we would expect. This is the indefinite integral of x^z since we have not specified how much of the curve we wish to consider, and we must add a constant, c, since the derivative of any constant is 0. As integration is the sum of the areas of the strips described, we symbolize it by an extended S: $\int$. The definite integral of $y=x^z$ between $x=a$ and $x=b$ is therefore expressed as

$$\int_a^b x^z.dx=\int_0^b x^z.dx-\int_0^a x^z.dx.$$

Calculus is one of the most powerful mathematical tools, and is of fundamental importance in many branches of science. (See also EXTREMUM.)

CALCULUS OF VARIATIONS, an extension of CALCULUS concerned with the examination of definite integrals and the calculation of their maximum or minimum values. One of its most famous problems, proposed by BERNOULLI, was the brachistochrone problem, in which it was required to find out the least time taken for a particle to fall, under the influence of gravity alone, between two points at different heights though not vertically above each other. The path is in fact a CYCLOID, the solution involving minimization of the integral that expresses this path.

CALCUTTA, capital of W Bengal and largest Indian city. It lies in the Ganges delta on the Hooghly R. It was founded by the British East India Company (1690) and Fort William was built on the site (1696). It was captured by Siruj-ud-Daula, Nawab of Bengal, in 1756; he imprisoned the British in what is known as the BLACK HOLE OF CALCUTTA. Calcutta was retaken by CLIVE (1757) and was capital of British India 1774–1912. In the 1947 Indian partition, it lost its valuable jute-producing hinterland and received thousands of religious refugees, causing severe

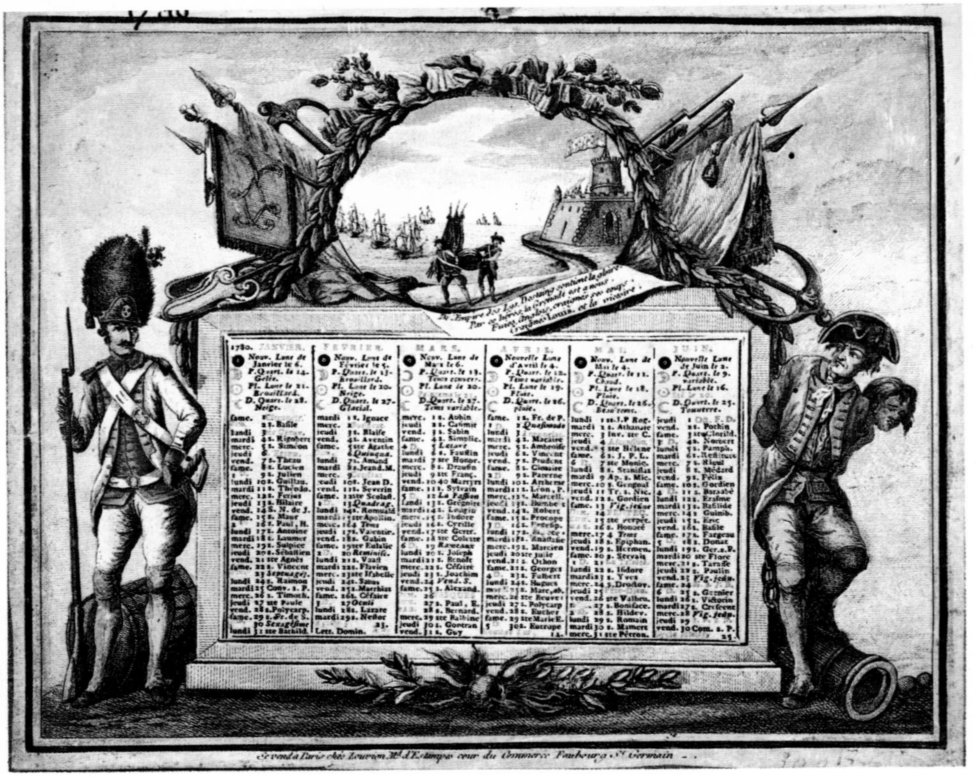

A French 18th-century calendar showing the phases of the moon and indicating the various saints' days.

overcrowding. It remains a major commercial port. Pop 3 141 180.

CALDECOTT, Randolph (1846–1886), British painter and illustrator, particularly of children's books. Among his best-known illustrations are those for Irving's *Old Christmas* (1876) and Cowper's *John Gilpin* (1878). In 1938 the Caldecott Medal was established as an annual award for the best US children's picture book.

CALDER, Alexander (1898–), US abstract sculptor and creator of the "mobile." His mobiles consist of flat metal shapes connected by rods, wire or string, which are hung or balanced and moved by motors or by air currents.

CALDERA, extremely large crater of volcanic (see VOLCANISM) origin, caused by repeated or massive explosion, collapse, or the amalgamation of a number of smaller craters.

CALDERÓN DE LA BARCA, Pedro (1600–1681), Spanish playwright and poet. He and Lope de VEGA were the leading dramatists of Spain's Golden Age. He wrote over 200 plays, distinguished by their heightened style and poetic symbolism, many on religious themes. Among his most famous works are *The Constant Prince* (1629), *Life is a Dream* (1635) and *The Surgeon of His Honor* (1635).

CALDWELL, city on the Boise R in SW Ida., seat of Canyon Co. A trading and shipping center for a rich farming area. Pop 14 219.

CALDWELL, Erskine Preston (1903–), US author noted for his portrayal of poor whites in the South. Famous for *Tobacco Road* (1932), *God's Little Acre* (1933) and *Trouble in July* (1940).

CALEDONIA, Roman name for Britain N of the Antonine Wall, between the firths of Clyde and Forth, roughly corresponding to modern Scotland. The name is now used as a poetic synonym for all Scotland.

CALEDONIAN CANAL, little-used N Scotland ship canal stretching SW–NE from Loch Linnhe to Moray Firth. It links lochs Eli, Lochy, Ness and Oich. Built 1803–47, it is 60mi long, including the lochs.

CALENDAR, a system for reckoning the passing of time. The principal problem in drawing up calendars arises from the fact that the solar DAY, the lunar MONTH and the tropical YEAR—the most immediate natural time units—are not simple multiples of each other. In practice a solution is found in basing the system either on the phases of the moon (lunar calendar) or on the changing of the SEASONS (solar calendar). The difficulty that the days eventually get out of step with the moon or the seasons is got over by adding in (intercalating) one or more extra days or months at regular intervals in an extended cycle of months or years. The earliest Egyptian calendar had a year of 12 months with 30 days each, though later 5 extra days were added at the end of each year so that it approximated the tropical year of 365¼ days. In classical times, the Greeks came to use a lunar calendar in which three extra months were intercalated every eight years (the octennial cycle), though, about 432 BC, the astronomer Meton discovered that 235 lunar months fitted exactly into 19 years (the Metonic cycle), this becoming the basis of the modern Jewish and ecclesiastical calendars. The Roman calendar was reformed under Julius CAESAR in 46 BC, fixing the year at 365 days but intercalating an additional day every fourth year (thus giving an average 365¼-day year). The 366-day year is known as a leap year. This Julian calendar continued in use until the 16th century when it had become about 10 days out of step with the seasons, the tropical year in fact being a little less than 365¼ days. In 1582, therefore, Pope GREGORY XIII ordered that 10 days be omitted from that year. Furthermore, century years would no longer be leap years unless divisible by 400, so that there would be no recurrence of any discrepancy. This Gregorian calendar was only slowly adopted, particularly in non-Catholic countries—the reform waiting until 1752 in England and its American colonies, by which time 11 days had to be dropped. But today it is in civil use throughout the world. Various proposals for further reform have come to nothing.

Years are commonly numbered in Western societies from the birth of Christ—as computed by a 6th-century monk. Years since that epoch are labeled AD, years before, BC. There is no year 0, 1 AD following directly from 1 BC. Astronomers, on the other hand, figure years BC as negative numbers one less than the date BC and include a year 0 (=1 BC). The astronomers' year −10 is thus the same as 11 BC. (See also CHRONOLOGY.)

CALENDERING, process use in the manufacture of TEXTILES, RUBBER, some PLASTICS and especially high-quality PAPER. The substance concerned is passed between a series of pairs of heated rollers, which squeeze it to form a smooth or textured sheet.

CALEXICO, border city in S Cal. It is an entry point from Mexico and a trading center for the Imperial Valley. Pop 10 625.

CALGARY, city on the Bow and Elbow rivers in S Alberta, Canada. Famous for the annual 10-day "Calgary Stampede" rodeo, it is a grain and livestock trading center for a rich farming and ranching region. Nearby coal, gas and oil deposits have led to rapid expansion. Pop 403 319.

CALHOUN, John Caldwell (1782–1850), prominent US statesman and lifelong defender of Southern interests. He was a member of the House of Representatives 1811–17; secretary of war to Monroe 1817–25 and a member of the 1812 War Hawks. He was twice vice-president, under Adams (1825–29) and under Jackson (1829–32). Following Congress' 1828 "Tariff of Abominations," seen as an attack on the South, he wrote his *South Carolina Exposition* (1828), expounding the "doctrine of nullification": when a federal law violates the Constitution, a state can consider the law void. In 1832 he resigned the vice-presidency and became a senator for S.C. (1833–43; 1845–50) and secretary of state under Tyler (1844–45). He was fiercely proslavery, calling slavery the "perfect good." He argued against the 1846 WILMOT PROVISO, saying that slaves were property and property could be moved at will. The last 20 years of his life were spent in fighting ABOLITIONISM.

CALI, city in W Colombia, capital of Valle del Cauca department. A trading center for its rich agricultural and mining region. Pop 1 022 000.

CALIBER. See AMMUNITION.

CALIBRATION, a most important step in preparing a scientific instrument or experimental apparatus for use, in which it is provided with a numerical scale in accordance with an internationally agreed procedure or by comparison with a standard instrument or measure. Thus an ordinary thermometer may be calibrated simply by noting its reading first in freezing and then in boiling water (other conditions being specified), but for greater accuracy, complex calibration procedures must be used to within carefully-controlled tolerances.

CALICO, lightweight plain-weave cotton fabric. It was originally a brightly colored, hand-painted fabric from Calicut, India. It was manufactured in Europe in the late 18th century and much used in the American West.

CALICUT, or Kozhikode, seaport city of central Kerala, S India, on the Malabar coast. Until 1956 it was part of Madras state. Pop 333 980.

CALIFORNIA, fast-growing SW US state, on the Pacific Ocean and Mexican border. It has the largest state population, and is third largest in area. Its capital is Sacramento, but the most important cities are LOS ANGELES and SAN FRANCISCO. Over 50% of California's population lives in the Los Angeles-Long Beach and San Francisco-Oakland metropolitan areas. This high percentage of urban population, its sheer size and the highest per capita income in the US make California an increasingly influential power in national politics.

California's land features are varied, including Mt Lassen, at the head of the Great Valley, which is the only active US volcano outside Alaska and Hawaii. There are occasional earth tremors in California, caused by the San Andreas fault, running two-thirds of the state's length. A major earthquake can be expected every 60–100 years.

People. California has a diverse ethnic population. Before 1849 it was comprised of Indians, Mexicans and Spaniards. The Gold Rush brought an influx of US citizens of European descent, and by 1850 they were the vast majority. Extensive railway and road construction in the 1870s and 1880s brought a large number of Chinese immigrants. By 1900 the Japanese also began to emigrate to California as a labor force. From WWII onwards large numbers of Southern and Eastern Negroes moved to the state. Other significant groups are the Italians, Russians, Filipinos, and Scandinavians.

Compulsory school attendance applies to all children between 8 and 16. The state's system of higher education is constantly expanding. The University of California, founded 1868, moved from Oakland to Berkeley in 1873. Its campuses are located at Berkeley, Los Angeles, Davis, Santa Cruz, Irvine, Riverside, San Diego, Santa Barbara and San Francisco. California has 18 state colleges, plus comprehensive junior colleges.

Although under 5% of California's population lives on farms, and under 9% of the area is cultivated, intensive irrigation gives California the highest state farm income. It produces every major US crop except tobacco, has the largest fishing industry, and produces 85% of US wine and 15% of US petroleum. It also has light and heavy industry.

History. The Spanish explorer CABRILLO is usually credited with California's discovery. In 1542 he named the present state's area Alta (Upper) California. In 1579 DRAKE ineffectively claimed the area for England, calling it New Albion. The first European settlement was the Spanish San Diego Franciscan mission and fort (1769). In 1822 the Californians changed their allegiance from Spain to the new Mexican Congress; and later US presidents Jackson (1835) and Polk (1845) unsuccessfully attempted to buy the area. On June 14, 1846, a group of Californian settlers declared the independent Republic of California in the "Bear Flag" revolt against Mexico. A few weeks later, the Mexican-US War broke out, and from July 7 California was occupied by US forces. On Feb. 2, 1848, the postwar Treaty of GUADALUPE HIDALGO ceded the area to the US. It was admitted to the Union as a free state under the COMPROMISE OF 1850 on Sept. 9, 1850. Before that, on Jan. 24, 1848, gold had been discovered on the American R at Colombo. This caused the 1849 GOLD RUSH and within seven years the state's population leaped from 15000 to 300000. The present constitution was adopted in 1879. There have been over 350 amendments: since 1911 these can be proposed by petition and approved by popular vote. Voters can also propose measures through the power of initiative and challenge a new law by calling a referendum.

There have been various racial problems throughout California's history, at first with Chinese and Japanese immigrants, and in 1965 there were the black Watts ghetto riots in Los Angeles. The 1960s also saw sit-ins and rebellions on the Berkeley and San Francisco State College campuses. The Mexican-American minority has, through a series of strikes, called attention to its exploitation by farm owners.

CALIFORNIA, Gulf of. See GULF OF CALIFORNIA.

CALIFORNIA, Lower. See BAJA CALIFORNIA.

CALIFORNIA CURRENT, cool OCEAN CURRENT, fed by the NORTH PACIFIC CURRENT, flowing from latitude 48°N SE along the W North American coast before joining the N EQUATORIAL CURRENT.

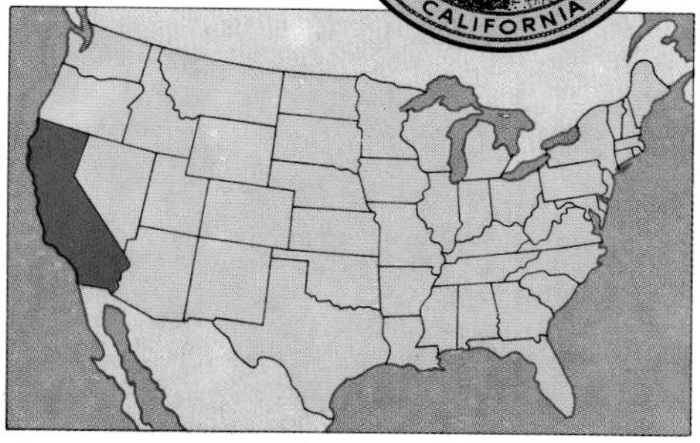

Name of State: California
Capital: Sacramento
Statehood: Sept. 9, 1850 (31st State)
Familiar Name: Golden State
Area: 158 693sq mi
Population: 19 696 840
Elevation: Highest–14 495 ft., Mount Whitney. Lowest–282 ft. below sea level near Badwater in Death Valley
Motto: Eureka ("I have found it")
State Flower: Golden poppy
State Bird: California valley quail
State Tree: California redwood
State Song: "I Love You, California"

CALIFORNIA FAN PALM, or petticoat palm, *Washingtonia filifera*, the only palm native to Cal. The dead leaves remain permanently attached to the tree, so that in older trees they hang down around the trunk in a great mass. (See also PALM.)

CALIFORNIA POPPY, state flower of Cal., once called Cups of Gold. (See POPPY.)

CALIFORNIA SEA LION, *Zalophus californianus*, small N Pacific SEA LION best known as the performing seal in circuses and zoos. It is chocolate brown and native to rocky Pacific coasts from S Mexico to N Cal.

CALIFORNIA TRAIL, trade and travel routes to the early 1850s Cal. goldfield. In particular, the 800mi route from the Oregon Trail near Fort Bridger to Sutter's Fort near Sacramento. Now part of highways 26, 30, 40 and 50.

Ranch in the California mountains. The fertile upland soil provides good grazing land on the slopes as well as supporting dense forest, as seen in the background.

CALIFORNIUM (Cf), a TRANSURANIUM ELEMENT in the ACTINIDE series. Numerous isotopes have been synthesized by various bombardment methods; most undergo spontaneous nuclear FISSION.

CALIGULA (12–41 AD), nickname (meaning "little boots") of Roman Emperor Gaius Caesar, 37–41 AD. He was insanely cruel and despotic and believed he was a god. He reputedly planned to make his horse a consul. His demands that his statue be erected in Jerusalem's temple almost precipitated a revolt in Palestine. He was assassinated by a tribune of his guard.

CALIPERS, devices used in measuring. Simple calipers comprise a pair of metal legs, pivoted about a shared screw at one end, the other ends being turned inward (for outer dimensions) or outward (for inner dimensions). They are usually used in conjunction with a rule. **Vernier calipers** resemble a sliding wrench and incorporate a VERNIER SCALE.

CALIPHATE (Arabic: *khalifa*, successor), highest office in ISLAM. Early caliphs were the successors of MOHAMMED. They were the rulers of the Muslim community throughout the world and guardians of Islamic law. In 632 AD the Muslims of Medina elected Abu Bakr as first caliph. He was succeeded by Omar (634–44), the first caliph to adopt the title "commander of the faithful." Omar was murdered, as were Othman (644–56) and Ali (656–61). The OMAYYAD dynasty of caliphs then ruled from Damascus until 750, when the Shiite Muslims, descendants of Ali who had always claimed their right to the caliphate, massacred the Omayyad family. However, Abd-al-Rahman escaped, fled to Spain, and established an independent emirate at Cordoba which lasted from 750 to 1031. Meanwhile, the Shiite Muslims established the ABBASID family in the caliphate. They ruled from Baghdad until it was sacked by the Mongols in 1258. A puppet Abbasid caliphate also continued in Egypt from 909 until 1520. Until the fall of the Ottoman Empire the Turkish sultans used the title. The caliphate was abolished in 1924 by ATATURK.

CALISTHENICS. See EXERCISE.

CALIXTUS, name of three popes. SAINT **Calixtus I** (d. 222), pope 217–222, was born a Roman slave. His reign was troubled by the Monarchian heresy. He built the shrine of martyrs on the Appian Way. **Calixtus II** (1060–1124), pope 1119–24, was born Guy of Burgundy. He was a reforming pope who negotiated the Concordat of Worms (1122) and called the First Lateran Council (1123). **Calixtus III** (1378–1458), pope 1455–58, was born Alonso Borgia in Spain. He attempted to organize a Crusade against the Ottoman Turks, who had taken Constantinople, and ordered a reappraisal of the case of JOAN OF ARC, resulting in her vindication.

CALLAGHAN, (Leonard) James (1912–), Prime Minister of the UK from 1976. A longtime Labour politician, he was elected party leader on the resignation of Harold WILSON.

CALLAGHAN, Morley Edward (1903–), Canadian novelist and short story writer, with a powerful, precise style influenced by HEMINGWAY. His books include the novel *They shall Inherit the Earth* (1935) and a memoir, *That Summer in Paris* (1963).

CALLA LILY, cultivated perennial plants of the genus *Zantedeschia*, which are native to South Africa. Callas are members of the ARUM family, Araceae. The name calla is also given to *Calla palustris*, the water arum, which also belongs to the family Araceae.

CALLAO, city and seaport capital of Callao province, W Peru, near Lima. Founded in 1537 by Francisco PIZARRO, it is the country's main port, handling over 50% of its foreign trade. Pop 335 400.

CALLAS, Maria (1923–), leading Greek-American operatic soprano, born Maria Kalogeropoulos. Noted for her expressive phrasing and acting ability in a wide variety of roles in over 40 operas.

CALLES, Plutarco Elías (1877–1945), Mexican general and politician, ablest organizer of the Mexican Revolution which ousted President DÍAZ in 1911. President 1924–28, he fought for land reform, educational improvements and greater social welfare. After his presidency he was a power behind the scenes

John Calvin as a young man; portrait from the Historical Museum of the Reformation, Geneva, Switzerland.

until forced into exile in America for a time (1936–41).

CALLICRATES, Greek architect of the 5th century BC who collaborated with Ictinus and Phidias on the PARTHENON. He is credited with the temple of Athena Nike, which is also on the Athenian acropolis.

CALLIGRAPHY, the art of penmanship. Combining beauty with legibility, it evolved in the Far East, where it was a recognized art form as early as 250 BC. In early medieval Europe calligraphy was practiced in monastic communities, which developed the Carolingian and Insular scripts. A high point was reached with the BOOK OF KELLS and the LINDISFARNE gospels. The superb Italian Renaissance manuscripts provided models for the first printed books and roman and italic types. The Englishman Edward Johnston (1872–1944) and his pupil Graily Hewitt (1864–1952) began the remarkable modern revival of calligraphy in the early 1900s.

CALLIMACHUS (c310–240 BC), Greek poet, grammarian and critic, leading member of the Alexandrian school. Only 6 hymns and 64 epigrams of his poetry survive. He also produced the *Pinakes*, the earliest work of systematic bibliography, now lost.

CALLIOPE, fairground organ used to draw crowds with its loud music. Invented about 1850 in the US, the calliope has a keyboard and its pipes are blown by steam generated by a boiler.

CALLIOPE, muse of epic poetry. See MUSES.

CALLISIA, a perennial, trailing, ornamental foliage house plant popularly called WANDERING JEW. Family: Commelinaceae.

CALLISTHENES (c360–328 BC), Greek historian, nephew of Aristotle. The official chronicler of ALEXANDER THE GREAT's Asian expedition, he criticized Alexander's adoption of Oriental customs and was thrown into prison, where he died. None of his works have survived.

CALLISTO, in Greek mythology, the mother of Arcas by Zeus. She was changed into a she-bear by the jealous Artemis, and Arcas would have killed her while hunting if Zeus had not turned them into the constellations of Ursa Major and Minor.

CALLISTUS. See CALIXTUS.

CALLOT, Jacques (c1592–1635), French graphic artist, whose 1500 etchings and engravings are among the greatest of their kind. His masterpiece, the series *Miseries of War* (1633), shows the horrors of the Thirty Years' War. His technical innovations greatly refined engraving techniques.

CALLOWAY, Cabell ("Cab") (1907–), US Negro singer and bandleader. Known as the "King of Hi De Ho," he was famous for *Minnie the Moocher*, and for his versions of *St. James Infirmary Blues* and *Ain't Misbehavin'*.

CALLUS, connective tissue initially formed around a FRACTURE, and slowly ossified as repair proceeds (see BONE).

CALLUS, or Callosity. See CORNS AND CALLUSES.

CALMETTE, Albert Léon Charles (1863–1933), French bacteriologist who with C. GUÉRIN discovered the BCG (bacillus Calmette-Guérin) vaccine, which has greatly reduced the incidence of TUBERCULOSIS.

CALMS, Regions of, areas where the sea is of mirror-like calmness and where the wind-speed is less than 1 knot. Such wind-speed is denoted 0 on the BEAUFORT SCALE. These conditions are characteristic of the HORSE LATITUDES.

CALOMEL, or **mercury (I) chloride.** See MERCURY.

CALONNE, Charles Alexandre de (1734–1802), French statesman and controller general of France 1783–87. At the pre-revolutionary Assembly of Notables in 1787 he proposed a radical financial reorganization, including reduced privileges for the nobility and clergy and a land tax, but his plan was rejected and he was forced into exile.

CALORIC THEORY OF HEAT, the view, formalized by LAVOISIER toward the end of the 18th century, that heat consists of particles of a weightless, invisible fluid, caloric, which resides between the atoms of material substances. The theory fell from favor as physicists began to appreciate the equivalence of WORK and HEAT.

CALORIE, the name of various units of HEAT. The calorie or gram calorie (c or cal), originally defined as the quantity of heat required to raise 1g of water through 1C° at 1 atm pressure, is still widely used in chemical THERMODYNAMICS. The large calorie, kilogram calorie or kilocalorie (Cal or kcal), 1000 times as large, is the "calorie" of dietitians. The 15° calorie (defined in terms of the 1C° difference between 14.5°C and 15.5°C) is 4.184 joules; the International Steam Table calorie (cal_{IT}) of 1929, originally defined as 1/860 watt-hour, is now set equal to 1.1868J in SI UNITS.

CALORIMETRY, the measurement of the HEAT changes associated with chemical reactions and physical processes. This is done using various types of calorimeter. The water calorimeter is a thermally insulated metal cup of known thermal properties containing a known mass of water. When a reaction is carried out in the vessel, any heat liberated or absorbed is taken or given up by the water, the heat changes occurring being monitored by means of a thermometer dipped in the water. Heats of combustion are measured using a bomb calorimeter in which the reaction is carried out in an enclosed, pressurized chamber immersed in the water. Other types of apparatus used to measure SPECIFIC and LATENT HEATS include ice and steam calorimeters. (See also THERMOCHEMISTRY.)

CALOTYPE. See TALBOT, WILLIAM HENRY FOX.

CALPURNIA, third wife of Julius CAESAR, whom she married in 59 BC. According to Plutarch, she tried to dissuade Caesar from going to the Senate on the day of his assassination in 44 BC.

CALUMET. See PEACE PIPE.

CALUMET CITY, industrial city in NE Ill. It lies on the Ind. border and has major chemical and meat-packing plants. Pop 33 107.

CALUMET PARK, village in NE Ill., a residential suburb of Chicago. It lies on the Calumet Sag Channel near Lake Calumet. Pop 10 069.

CALVARY, or Golgotha, Jerusalem hill site of the crucifixion of Jesus. Although archaeologists are not agreed, it is traditionally accepted to be the hill on which Constantine founded the Church of the Holy Sepulcher in the 4th century.

CALVERT, English Roman Catholic family which founded and owned colonial Maryland. **George, 1st Baron Baltimore** (c1580–1632), occupied various public offices until 1625. He founded Ferryland, Newfoundland, in 1621, and lived there 1627–29. Seeking a warmer climate, he established a colony in N Virginia (present-day Md.), for which King Charles I granted a charter to his son Cecil in 1632. **Cecil** (or **Cecilius**), **2nd Baron Baltimore** (c1605–1675), never visited Md., and left its administration to his younger brother **Leonard Calvert** (1606–1647). In 1649, the colony's Act of Toleration was the first practical expression of the principle of freedom of conscience in the New World. **Charles, 3rd Baron Baltimore** (1637–1715), son of Cecil, was governor of Md. from 1661, governed the colony in person 1679–84 and then returned to England. In 1689 his Md. administration was overthrown by a Protestant rebellion, and in 1691 the Crown withdrew his authority to govern.

CALVIN, John (1509–1564), French theologian and reformer. He studied in Paris, and was converted to Reformation doctrines c1533, becoming prominent in the reforming party. He was forced to flee to Basel, where he published his *Institutes of the Christian Religion* (1536). Guillaume FAREL persuaded him to help establish the Reformation in Geneva. They enforced subscription to a confession of faith, but were expelled from the city in 1538. Calvin joined Martin BUCER at Strassburg. Geneva recalled him in 1541, and, despite controversy, he set up a church polity which became the paradigm for PRESBYTERIANISM and the REFORMED CHURCHES. Despite fragile health, Calvin worked unceasingly in preaching, lecturing and advising in the city councils, and aided foreign Protestant refugees. On his death, his work was continued by Theodore BEZA. (See also CALVINISM; REFORMATION; SERVETUS, MICHAEL.)

CALVIN, Melvin (1911–), US biochemist who gained the 1961 Nobel Prize for Chemistry after having led the team that unraveled the details of the chemistry of PHOTOSYNTHESIS.

CALVINISM, the theological system of John CALVIN. Its key principle is that God, not man, is central and supreme. Hence scripture is the source of doctrine. Calvin's *Institutes of the Christian Religion* is a systematic account of biblical teaching, with much in common with early LUTHERANISM, including JUSTIFICATION BY FAITH, PREDESTINATION, assurance of SALVATION, and denial of FREE WILL since the Fall. One distinguishing feature is the view that in Holy COMMUNION the believer participates in Christ in heaven by faith. Calvinism became the doctrine of the REFORMED CHURCHES, which developed Calvin's theology in a scholastic fashion, elevating PRESBYTERIANISM to a

Calvary is often depicted in Christian art, especially in carved shrines such as this one from Brittany, France, where they are common. Such shrines are generally called *calvaires*.

major principle, and emphasizing the divine decrees and COVENANTS. Calvinism has been influential in the CHURCH OF ENGLAND (see THIRTY-NINE ARTICLES), among the PURITANS and nonconformists, and in the EVANGELICAL REVIVAL. Recently Karl BARTH has popularized a modified Calvinism. (See also ARMINIANS; DORT, SYNOD OF; HUGUENOTS; REFORMATION.)

CALX, an old term for the product of calcining a metal or its ore (see CALCINATION). The term thus usually refers to the metal's oxide.

CALYDONIAN BOAR, in Greek mythology, a giant wild boar sent by ARTEMIS to ravage Calydon because its king, Oeneus, had not made the annual sacrifice to her. Oeneus' son MELEAGER summoned a number of heroes (including Theseus, Jason and Nestor) to hunt the boar, which was killed by ATLANTA. The hunt is a favorite subject in Greek art.

CALYPSO, in Greek myth, a water nymph. ODYSSEUS was wrecked on her island, Ogygia, and she offered him immortality if he would stay. But after seven years, with Zeus' help, he left the island.

CALYX. See FLOWER.

CAM, mechanical device which, on rotation, imparts to another member (the follower) a regular, repetitive motion. There are two main types of cams. **Plate cams** (or **disk cams**) are curved, often ovoid, plates mounted on a shaft (the **camshaft**). On rotation, the cam pushes the follower in a direction PERPENDICULAR to the shaft. (The follower is returned to its position by gravity or a SPRING.) **Cylindrical cams** consist of parallel raised lips on the surface of the camshaft and angled such that, when a projection of the follower lies in the groove so formed, rotation of the camshaft imparts to it a motion (usually to and fro) parallel to the shaft. Many engines make use of one or more camshafts: notably, in some forms of INTERNAL-COMBUSTION ENGINE camshafts are used to regulate and actuate the cylinder valves.

CAM (CÃO), Diogo (active 1480–86), Portuguese explorer, who discovered the mouth of the Congo R in 1482. In 1485–86 he made a second voyage along the coast of Africa, reaching Cape Cross in present-day South West Africa (Namibia).

CAMACHO, Manuel Avila. See AVILA CAMACHO, MANUEL.

CAMAGÜEY, city and capital of Camagüey province, E central Cuba. Distribution center of an important cattle-raising and sugar-producing region. Pop 196 854.

CAMARGUE, 300sq mi area of the Rhone delta, S France, with extensive marshes; famous for its rich bird life, bulls and wild horses.

CAMARILLO, city in SW Cal. The main commercial center for the Las Posas, Pleasant and Santa Rosa valleys. Pop 19 219.

CAMBIUM, a meristematic tissue that lies between the XYLEM and PHLOEM in the vascular tissue of plants. In woody plants, a complete ring of cambium develops which produces new xylem cells on the inside and phloem on the outside by a process known as secondary thickening. In some trees, under the epidermis a layer of cork cambium develops which then produces a corky bark. (See BARK; PLANT.)

CAMBODIA, "kingdom" in SE Asia, known as the KHMER REPUBLIC, 1970–75. Laos lies to the N, South Vietnam to the E and Thailand to the W and N.

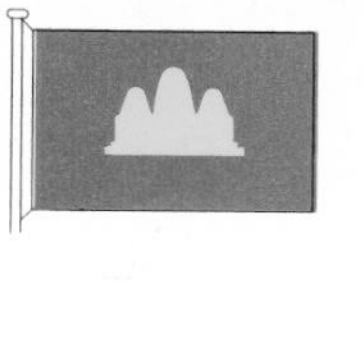

Official Name: Democratic Kampuchea
Capital: Phnom Penh
Area: 69 897sq mi
Population: 6 994 000
Languages: Khmer, English
Religions: Hinayana Buddhist
Monetary Unit(s): 1 Riel = 100 sen

Land. About half Cambodia is tropical forest; at the center of the country the Mekong R flows from N to S, providing 900mi of navigable waterways. During the rainy season, May–Oct., the river backs up to the Tonle Sap Lake, vastly increasing its size and leaving rich fertile silt, excellent for rice production. There are two mountain ranges: the Dong Rek to the N and the Cardamom to the SW.

People. About 85% of the population are Khmers, with sizeable minorities of Chinese and Vietnamese, and smaller groups of Cham-Malays, Mayao-Polynesian and Austro-Asian hill tribes, and Europeans. The official language is Khmer but many people speak French. Cambodia is one of the few countries in SE Asia which is sparsely populated and the majority of the people work in agriculture, the Chinese traditionally controlling the financial sectors. The capital and largest city is Phnom Penh.

Economy. The principal product is rice. Other crops are corn, tobacco, sugar and pepper, and there is extensive fishing. Rubber cultivation is very important to the Cambodian economy and, like rice, is one of the largest exports. The rubber plantations were badly damaged in the fighting in the early 1970s which also seriously affected all exports.

History. The FUNAN kingdom was established in Cambodia for the first six centuries AD, but late in the 6th century the Funans were overcome by the Khmers from the neighboring Chenla state who founded the powerful KHMER EMPIRE. This empire, with its capital at ANGKOR, extended to modern Laos, Thailand and South Vietnam and lasted until the 15th century. From the 14th to the 19th centuries Cambodia's area was reduced by Thai conquests in the N and by the Annamese in the S. In 1863 Cambodia asked for and was placed under French protection. This lasted until 1954 when Cambodia became independent, largely owing to Prince Norodom SIHANOUK's negotiations. Sihanouk, as head of state from 1960, tried to keep Cambodia neutral in the VIETNAM WAR but this proved increasingly difficult. He broke off relations with the US, 1965–69, and allowed the Vietnamese communists to use Cambodia as a supply base. The Cambodian communists (Khmers Rouges) emerged by 1970 as a powerful political group with a standing army of 3 000 men. In 1970 General Lon Nol staged a military coup and established the Khmer Republic, supported by the US. In alliance with the Khmers Rouges Sihanouk formed an exile government—the National United Front of Cambodia—in Peking. Civil war raged between Lon Nol's government forces and the Khmers Rouges, who by 1973 numbered 30 000 and were gaining control of the country despite intensive US bombing until 1973. Fighting was especially heavy at the beginning of 1975; in April Phnom Penh was besieged and surrendered to the Khmers Rouges. "The Royal Government of the National Union of Cambodia (Kampuchea)" returned from exile under Sihanouk (resigned 1976), but reports of intimidation and mass murder of non-communists have continued.

CAMBRAI (Flemish: Kamerijk), industrial city in N France, on the Scheldt R. Once famous for linen goods, especially cambric, it is the center of a rich farming region. Pop 37 532.

CAMBRAI, Battle of, first major British WWI tank offensive (Nov. 20, 1917) and successful German counterattack (Nov. 30) at Cambrai, N France. The battle emphasized the tank's striking power, but also the necessity to consolidate territorial gains.

CAMBRAI, League of, alliance formed in 1508 by Pope Julius II, Louis XII of France, Holy Roman Emperor Maximilian I and Ferdinand II of Aragon. They intended to break the power of the Republic of Venice, but the alliance disintegrated in 1510.

CAMBRIAN, the earliest period of the PALEOZOIC (see GEOLOGY), dated roughly 570–500 million years ago, and immediately preceding the ORDOVICIAN. Cambrian rocks contain the oldest FOSSILS that can be used for dating (see PRECAMBRIAN).

CAMBRIDGE, county town of Cambridgeshire, England, home of a famous university (see CAMBRIDGE, UNIVERSITY OF). On the Cam R 48mi NNE of London, it is a center for British scientific research as well as being a commercial center. The city has many fine medieval buildings. Pop 98 519.

CAMBRIDGE, city and second-largest port of Md., seat of Dorchester Co. It lies on Choptank R, near the E shore of Chesapeake Bay. Pop 11 595.

CAMBRIDGE, city in Mass., on the Charles R opposite Boston, seat of HARVARD UNIVERSITY (founded 1636), Radcliffe College and the Massachusetts Institute of Technology. It became the site of America's first printing plant in 1639 and was the place where Washington took command of the Continental Army in 1775. Pop 100 361.

CAMBRIDGE, city on Wills Creek in Ohio, seat of Guernsey Co. It was settled in 1806 and incorporated in 1837. Pop 13 656.

CAMBRIDGE, University of, one of the world's leading universities, at Cambridge, England. Its history dates from c1209, and its first college, Peterhouse, was established in 1284. Today, the university is coeducational, and has about 9 000 students. It has a total of 29 colleges and approved societies, and is a self-governing body, with authority vested in its senior members.

CAMBRIDGE PLATONISTS, an influential group of philosophers centered on the U. of Cambridge in the mid-17th century, founded by Benjamin Whichcote and including Henry More and Ralph Cudworth. Their philosophy was Platonist, their outlook was tolerant and one of their chief aims was the reconciliation of faith with scientific knowledge and rational philosophy. Their influence long survived their eclipse, and largely inspired the religious and political toleration which was characteristic of Restoration England.

CAMBYSES II (d. 522 BC), king of Persia from 529 BC, of the ACHAEMENID dynasty, son of CYRUS THE GREAT. He brought Phoenicia and Cyprus into the empire and conquered Egypt, but was repulsed in Ethiopia.

CAMDEN, city on the Ouachita R in Ark., seat of Ouachita Co. A manufacturing and processing center in an oil, natural gas and farming area. Pop 15 147.

CAMDEN, port city and industrial center in N.J., seat of Camden Co., located across the Delaware R from Philadelphia, Pa. A major commercial and transportation center, with many important industries. Pop 102 551.

CAMDEN, Battle of, August 16, 1780, during the American Revolution, near Camden, S.C. The Americans, under Gen. Horatio GATES, were badly defeated by the British under Lord CORNWALLIS.

CAMDEN, William (1551–1623), English historian, whose *Britannia* (1586) was a landmark in the topographical study of Britain and in establishing an empirical approach to the study of history.

CAMELIDS, family of cloven-hoofed mammals (Camelidae) in which only the tip of the hoof touches the ground, so that the animal's weight rests on its sole pads. The family includes the Bactrian and Arabian CAMELS and the LLAMA, ALPACA, GUANACO, and VICUNA.

CAMELLIAS, evergreen trees and shrubs native to Asia, but which are easily grown in warm climates. They are valued for their evergreen foliage and fragrant white, pink and red flowers.

CAMELOT, court of King ARTHUR and the Knights of the Round Table in ARTHURIAN LEGENDS. It has been identified variously with Caerleon (Wales), Camelford (Cornwall) and South Cadbury (Somerset), where excavations have taken place.

CAMELS, two species of haired, cud-chewing animals with humped backs, long necks and callosities on knee joints. The one-humped or Arabian camel, or dromedary, *Camelus dromedarius*, of N Africa and the Near East is a widely-kept domestic animal which has even been introduced into desert regions of Australia. The two-humped or Bactrian camel, *C. bactrianus* is found from Asia Minor to Manchuria, and there are still a few living wild in the Gobi Desert. Recorded as being domesticated in Babylonia from about 1100 BC, the animals are invaluable in the desert since they can carry enormous loads and are able to withstand the loss of about one-third of their body fluid without danger (not, however, exclusively from their humps, which are fatty tissue, not water storage vessels).

The Bactrian camel (*left*) has two humps, a thick heavy body and a long coat which is often used to make fine cloth. The Arabian camel (*right*), which lives in warmer areas, has a short coat, a slimmer body and only one hump. It is often called a dromedary, a name strictly applied to one breed only.

CAMEO, a gem or other hard stone carved in low relief, the opposite of INTAGLIO. The stones used include CARNELIAN, AGATE, JASPER, CHALCEDONY and sardonyx. The subjects vary from portrait heads and profiles to elaborate scenes. Cameo-cutting is an ancient art, stretching back to the early Sumerian period (c3100 BC).

CAMERA, device for forming an optical image of a subject and recording it on a photographic film or plate or (in television cameras) on a photoelectric mosaic. The design of modern cameras derives from the ancient camera obscura, represented in recent times by the pinhole camera. This consists of a light-tight box with a small hole in one side and a ground-glass screen for the opposite wall. A faint image of the objects facing the hole is formed on the screen and this can be exposed on a photographic plate substituted for the screen.

Although the image produced in the pinhole camera is distortion-free and perfectly focused for objects at any distance, the sensitive materials used when photography was born in the 1830s required so long exposure times that the earliest experimentalists turned to the already available technology of the LENS as a means of allowing more light to strike the plate. From the start cameras were built with compound lenses to overcome the effects of chromatic aberration (see ABERRATION, OPTICAL) and the subsequent history of camera design has seen constant improvement in lens performance.

Today's simple camera consists of a light-tight box, a fixed achromatic lens, a simple shutter, a view finder and a film support and wind-on mechanism. The lens will focus all subjects more than a few feet distant and the shutter (usually giving an exposure of $\frac{1}{30}$s or $\frac{1}{50}$s) admits sufficient light to expose negative materials on a sunny day. If exposures are to be made for reversal processing (see PHOTOGRAPHY) or of close-by or rapidly moving subjects or in poor light, a more complex camera is required. This may include a movable lens perhaps coupled to a RANGE FINDER (allowing the precise focusing of objects at different distances), a variable diaphragm (aperture) and shutter-speed mechanism (allowing adjustment to meet a wide range of light conditions) perhaps coupled to an exposure meter (LIGHT METER), a flash synchronization unit (allowing use of a flash gun (see FLASH BULB) or a facility for interchangeable lenses (allowing the photographer to alter the width of the camera's field of view). These refinements are realized in a wide range of different types of camera including the miniature camera and the single-lens reflex.

Special types of camera include the POLAROID LAND CAMERA (which produces prints almost instantaneously), stereo cameras (which take pairs of pictures of the same subject from slightly different angles—see PHOTOGRAMMETRY), motion-picture cameras (which make 16 or 24 successive exposures each second on long reels of film) and TELEVISION cameras (See also PHOTOGRAPHY.)

CAMERA LUCIDA AND CAMERA OBSCURA, simple optical devices which assist artists in drawing faithful reproductions of distant scenes, plans and diagrams or microscopic specimens. The principle of the **camera obscura** was known to ARISTOTLE; light admitted through a small hole into a darkened chamber projects a real image of the scene outside on the opposite wall. Later versions have used LENSES and MIRRORS to give an evenly-illuminated horizontal image. The **camera lucida**, invented in 1807 by WOLLASTON, employs a four-sided prism to allow the artist to see a virtual image of an object in the plane of the paper on which he copies the image. It is of particular use in enlarging or reducing artwork and in drawing from the MICROSCOPE.

CAMERON, Simon (1799–1889), US politician. He built a powerful political machine in Pa., was a US senator (1845–49; 1857–61; 1867–77) and served as secretary of war under Lincoln (1860–62). His career was marked by considerable scandal and corruption.

CAMEROON, republic adjoining Nigeria on the W coast of Africa, stretching from the Gulf of Guinea to Lake Chad.

The coastal plain is about 10–50mi wide, dominated by Cameroon Mountain. The S region is a densely forested 1 000ft plateau. In the central region the land rises to the N and the vegetation changes from forest to savanna. The arid far north slopes down to Lake Chad. The entire country is tropical, with average temperatures of 70°–82°F; the S has two rainy seasons, the N only one.

The population is ethnically diverse. In the S are aboriginal pygmies and Bantu farmers, settled in villages; in the N are various Bantu, Sudanese, Hamite and Arab nomads. Some 11% of the population is urban, the main towns being Douala and Yaoundé. Illiteracy is high (85%), though 65% of primary-school-age children attend school; the Federal University at Yaoundé has 2 400 students. Government is by the president and a cabinet which he appoints; there is also a 50-member one-party National Assembly.

The economy is based mainly on agriculture and forestry. Cassava and yams are grown for home consumption, and cattle and sheep are raised; cocoa, coffee, bananas, cotton, timber and rubber are exported. Industry has been developed since independence, and now includes textiles, food processing and aluminum smelting. Export trade is mainly with France. Cameroon's road network is growing but not yet well-developed. There are 520mi of railroads and six airports; Douala is the major seaport.

In 1884 Germany claimed the Cameroon area as a colony. After WWI the League of Nations mandated the larger part to France (Cameroun) and the remainder to Britain (Southern and Northern Cameroons). In 1960 Cameroun became an independent republic. After plebiscites in 1961 Northern Cameroons joined Nigeria, and Southern Cameroons joined Cameroun to form the Federal

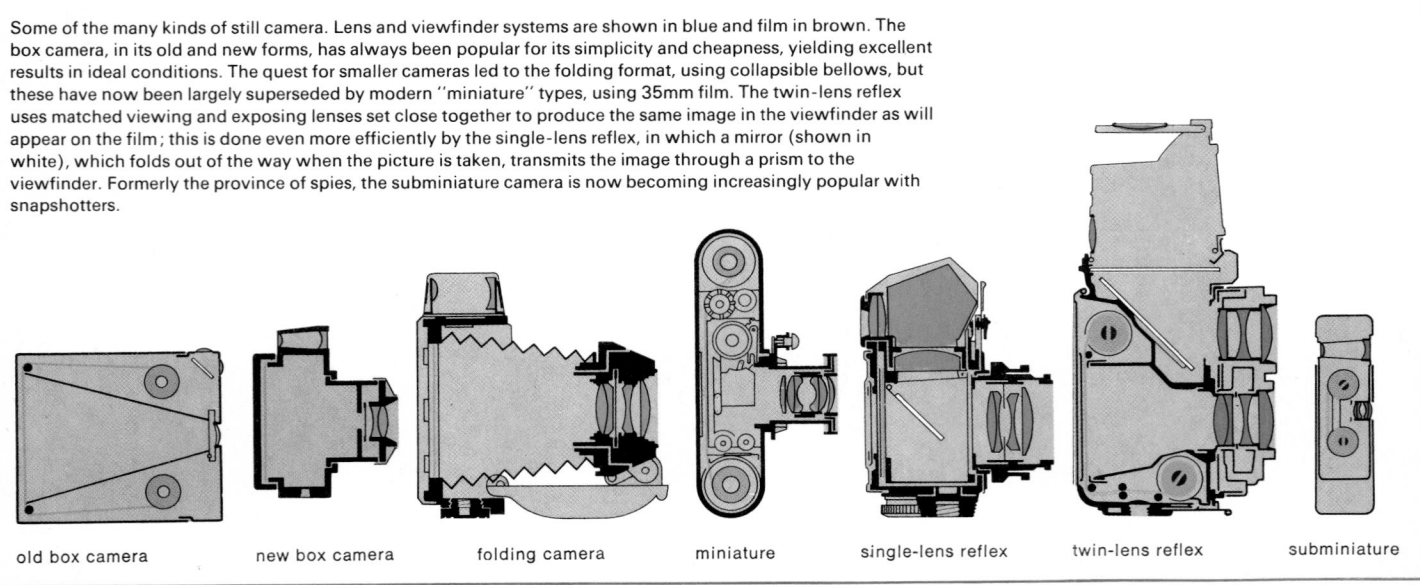

Some of the many kinds of still camera. Lens and viewfinder systems are shown in blue and film in brown. The box camera, in its old and new forms, has always been popular for its simplicity and cheapness, yielding excellent results in ideal conditions. The quest for smaller cameras led to the folding format, using collapsible bellows, but these have now been largely superseded by modern "miniature" types, using 35mm film. The twin-lens reflex uses matched viewing and exposing lenses set close together to produce the same image in the viewfinder as will appear on the film; this is done even more efficiently by the single-lens reflex, in which a mirror (shown in white), which folds out of the way when the picture is taken, transmits the image through a prism to the viewfinder. Formerly the province of spies, the subminiature camera is now becoming increasingly popular with snapshotters.

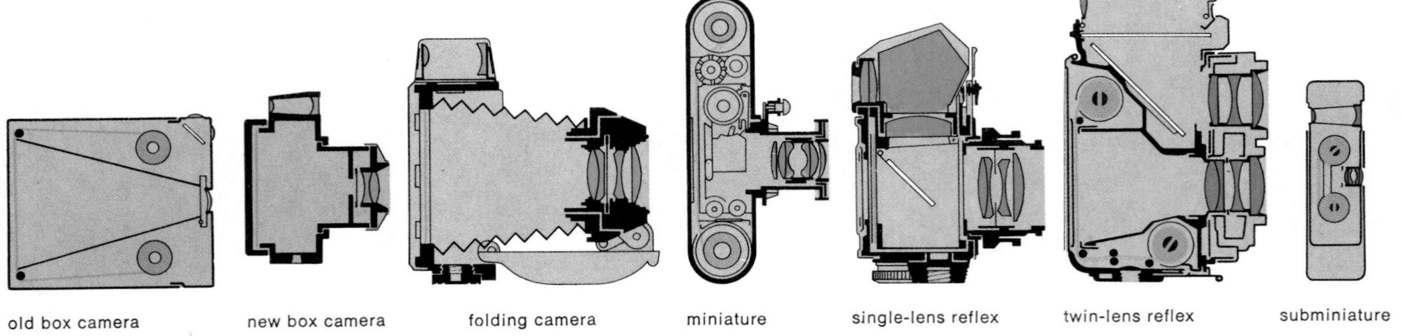

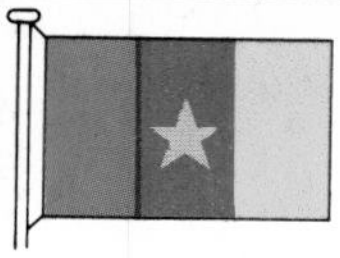

Official Name: The Federal Republic of Cameroon
Capital: Yaoundé
Area: 183 569sq mi
Population: 6 000 000
Languages: French, English
Religions: Animist; Christian, Muslim
Monetary Unit(s): 1 CFA franc = 100 centimes

Republic of Cameroon. After a plebiscite in 1972 the federal system was abandoned in favor of a unitary republic.

CAMEROON MOUNTAIN, volcanic peak in SW Cameroon; the highest point (13 350ft) in W Africa.

CAMÕES (CAMOËNS), Luís Vaz de (1524–1580), Portugal's greatest poet. His epic poem, *The Lusiads* (1572), is a celebration of Portuguese historical glory. Inspired by the AENEID, it centers around the voyages of Vasco da GAMA. Much of the rest of his poetry was published posthumously, in 1595.

CAMOMILE, or chamomile, strong-scented herbs, with daisy-like flowers, of the genera *Anthemis* and *Matricaria*, native to the US and Europe. The leaves of the common camomile (*Anthemis nobilis*) are dried and used medicinally.

CAMORRA, Italian secret society started in the Kingdom of Naples c1830. Although it specialized in extortion, smuggling, robbery and assassination, it was often used by the authorities, and it became very powerful. After unification with Italy in 1861 attempts were made to suppress it, but it survived until 1911.

CAMOUFLAGE, the art of concealment, particularly as used by the military to disguise troops and installations. Formerly, camouflage was confined to such devices as providing protective coloration for soldiers by dyeing their uniforms in irregular earth-and-leaf colored patterns to blend into the terrain, or disguising buildings and emplacements with various materials. Since the development of such camouflage-detecting equipment as infrared photography and electronic sensors, however, more sophisticated chemical and electronic devices have been employed.

CAMP, Walter Chauncey (1859–1925), the father of American FOOTBALL. As a player and coach at Yale U. (1876–92) and Stanford U. (1894–95), Camp helped initiate, implement and develop many of the changes that turned European RUGBY into American football.

CAMPANELLA, Roy (1921–), US baseball player. He caught for the Brooklyn Dodgers 1948–57 and was the National League's Most Valuable Player in 1951–53 and 1955. An automobile accident in 1958 left him paralyzed.

CAMPANELLA, Tommaso (1568–1639), Italian philosopher and poet. A Dominican monk whose humanist theories brought him into conflict with the Church, he died in exile in Paris. His famous *City of the Sun* posits a Utopian society ruled by a philosopher priest.

CAMPANOLOGY, the art of bell-ringing. The two English traditions are ringing single note sequences as chimes ("clocking") or systematic ringing of rounds ("change ringing") involving between 4–12 bells, tuned to the major scale and including the tenor bell. In Europe the Flemish carillon bells are constructed for playing in harmony.

CAMPBELL, city in W Cal., founded in 1885 by Benjamin Campbell; an industrial and trade center in a fruit-growing region. Pop 24 770.

CAMPBELL, city on the Mahoning R in NE Ohio, immediately SE of Youngstown. It is a steel center, known as East Youngstown until 1926. Pop 12 577.

CAMPBELL, Alexander (1788–1866), US clergyman, founder of the DISCIPLES OF CHRIST (Campbellites). The Disciples were formed after a split between Campbell's congregation and the Baptist Church in 1830. He also founded Bethany College in Bethany, W. Va., in 1840.

CAMPBELL, Sir Malcolm (1885–1949), British racing driver, the first racer to average more than 300mph (Bonneville Salt Flats, Ut. 1935). He set three successive water-speed records, finally attaining 141.74mph in 1939. His son, **Donald Malcolm Campbell** (1921–1967), set a water-speed record of 276.33mph in 1964, but was killed trying to establish a new record. All the vehicles of both father and son were called *Bluebird*.

CAMPBELL, Mrs. Patrick (1865–1940), English actress. Popular on stage for over 40 years, she created many classic roles, including Eliza Doolittle in Shaw's *Pygmalion* (1914), a part written for her. She is also remembered for her famous correspondence with Shaw.

CAMPBELL, (Ignatius) Roy (Dunnachie) (1901–1957), South African poet. A romantic by nature, he fought for Franco in the Spanish Civil War. His extrovert verse includes the long poem *Flowering Rifle* (1939).

CAMPBELL, Thomas (1777–1844), Scottish poet. He is known for his patriotic martial verse, particularly his epic *The Pleasures of Hope* (1799).

CAMPBELL, William Wilfred (1861–1918), Canadian poet. He is best known for his nature poems inspired by the countryside around Lake Huron. He was an Anglican clergyman from 1886 to 1891.

CAMPBELL-BANNERMAN, Sir Henry (1836–1908), British prime minister 1905–08 and leader of the LIBERAL party from 1899. He pursued a progressive policy: established old-age pensions, granted self-government to the Transvaal and the Orange Free State and attempted to end the veto power of the House of Lords.

CAMPECHE, state on the Gulf of Mexico in SE Mexico, on the Yucatán peninsula, 21 666sq mi in area. Its main industries are agriculture and fishing. Its capital and largest city is Campeche, built by the Spanish in 1540 on a Mayan site. Pop 250 391.

CAMP FIRE GIRLS, recreational and educational organization for girls from 7 to 18. Founded in 1912 and active in more than 20 countries, it aims to perpetuate the spiritual ideals of the home through homemaking, community projects, sports, study programs and outdoor activities.

CAMPHOR, a white crystalline compound distilled from the wood and young shoots of the camphor tree (*Cinnamomum camphora*). Camphor has a strong characteristic odor which repels insects. It is also used medicinally—internally as an anodyne and antispasmodic and externally in linaments. In large doses it is a narcotic poison.

CAMPIN, Robert (c1378–1444), Flemish painter best known for his religious paintings. His art reflects the influence of manuscript illumination, though with a keener sense of plasticity in rendering the forms. One of his major works is the triptych of the Annunciation (c1428) known as the Mérode Altarpiece.

CAMPINA GRANDE, city in NE Brazil in the state of Paraíba. Its industries include leather and textiles. Pop 195 794.

CAMPINAS, city in Brazil, about 57mi NE of São Paulo. It is an industrial center in a major coffee-growing region. Pop 376 497.

CAMPION, Saint Edmund (c1540–1581), martyred English JESUIT. After a conversion to Roman Catholicism he entered the Society of Jesus in 1573. In 1580 he joined the first mission of Jesuits to England. He was arrested as a spy in 1581, tortured and executed. He was canonized in 1970.

CAMPION, Thomas (1567–1620), English poet, composer and physician. He is best known for his four books of *Ayres*, his lyric poetry and the controversial "attack" on rhyme, *Observations in the art of English Poesie* (1602).

CAMP MEETING, outdoor religious revival meetings in the US which often continued over several days. Originating on the early American frontier, they are still held occasionally, especially in the South.

CAMPOBELLO, island off New Brunswick, Canada, at the entrance to Passamaquoddy Bay, 8mi long and 5mi wide, well known as the former summer home of Franklin D. Roosevelt.

CAMPO FORMIO, Treaty of, agreement made between France and Austria on Oct. 17, 1797, giving France domination over N Italy and Austria's Belgian provinces; and Austria, Venice and its territories. A secret clause also pledged Austria to cede the left bank of the Rhine to France.

CAMPOS, industrial city in SE Brazil, founded 1634, in the state of Rio de Janeiro. It is in a rich agricultural area. Pop 389 045.

CAMSHAFT, a shaft on which a CAM (or cams) is mounted.

CAMUS, Albert (1913–1960), French novelist, essayist, dramatist and philosopher. Through fiction and reflective essays he communicated his vision of man in an absurd universe. He felt that the only true possibility for freedom and dignity lay in the awareness of this absurdity. His major works include the essay *The Myth of Sisyphus* (1942), which elucidated the philosophical basis of his novel *The Stranger* (1942). Other important works are the novels *The Plague* (1947) and *The Fall* (1956), the essay *The Rebel* (1951) and the play *Caligula* (1944). He won the Nobel Prize for Literature in 1957.

CANA, ancient village in Galilee where, at a wedding feast, Jesus performed his first miracle: changing water into wine (John 2:1–11).

CANAAN, early name for PALESTINE, probably meaning Land of the Purple—from the purple dye made in the area. The region was inhabited from the second millennium by Semitic peoples, mainly AMORITES, whose script provides the earliest known alphabet. Their culture was a mixture of Egyptian, Mesopotamian and many other influences. During the 13th century BC Canaan was occupied by the Israelites (see JEWS), though in the next century its coasts were taken by the PHILISTINES. The latter were subdued by King David (1000–961 BC), who extended Israelite rule over all Canaan.

Official Name: Canada
Capital: Ottawa
Area: 3 560 238sq mi
Population: 21 568 311
Languages: English, French
Religions: Roman Catholic, United Church of Canada, Anglican
Monetary Unit(s): 1 Canadian dollar = 100 cents

CANADA, country in North America, largest in the W hemisphere and second-largest in the world after Russia. Ironically it derives its name from *Kanata*, a Huron-Iroquois word meaning a small village. It is bounded on the E by the Atlantic Ocean, on the N by the Arctic Ocean, on the W by the Pacific Ocean and Alaska, and on the S by its 3987mi border with the US.

Canada comprises 10 provinces (Newfoundland, Prince Edward Island, Nova Scotia, New Brunswick, Quebec, Ontario, Manitoba, Saskatchewan, Alberta and British Columbia) and the Yukon and Northwest Territories. It is a Commonwealth country in which the British Crown is represented by a governor-general. The federal capital is Ottawa.

Land. Canada is basically a vast, stepped plain bordered on the W by the Rocky Mts and on the E by

Canada

A nation of many cultures

Sir Wilfrid Laurier, the first French-Canadian prime minister of Canada 1896–1911, once declared that the 20th century would be Canada's century. In the mid-1970s his words seem to be coming true—though possibly not quite as he intended—as Canada, under the leadership of another French-Canadian, Pierre Elliott Trudeau, moves towards a new sense of nationhood and a "just society."

Since he first took office as prime minister in 1968, Trudeau has been a powerful unifying force and has given new direction to Canadian policies at home and abroad. A lawyer educated at Montreal, Harvard, London and Paris, Trudeau has become a charismatic figure; his character and life-style appeal especially to the younger generation. His father's family first came to Canada from France in the 1600s. His mother's British ancestors were Loyalists who moved to Canada at the time of the American Revolution. Trudeau can thus be said to truly represent both founding races of the Dominion, and not least among his measures have been those aimed at reducing the long-standing friction between the two.

The French pioneered the settlement of Canada, founding Quebec in 1608 and Montreal in 1642. After the French came under British rule (1763), their rights to their own language, civil law and religion were recognized by Britain in the Quebec Act (1774), a wise concession which helped to ensure French-Canadian loyalty to Britain during the Revolutionary War. Confederation (1867) was never whole-heartedly accepted by the French-Canadians; they tended to remain shut in upon themselves, nourishing an often extreme nationalism, notably in Quebec province where the majority of them lived (and still live). Feelings ran high in Quebec following the execution of Louis Riel (1885), leader of two *méti* uprisings. (*Métis* are Canadians of French-Indian descent). During both world wars there was friction between the French-speaking and English-speaking communities in Canada over the conscription issue. Separatist sentiment gained ground in Quebec during the 1960s, fanned by French President Charles de Gaulle's provocative reference to "free Quebec" when he visited Montreal in 1967.

Since that time the Canadian government has tried hard to convince French-Canadians that their cultural heritage will not be eroded, nor their distinctive identity submerged. The Official Languages Act (1969) recognized both English and French as official languages. Aimed at enabling the 16 million English-speaking and 6 million French-speaking citizens to participate equally in Canada's future, it led to the establishment of special agencies and programs to help develop bilingualism. But fear that Quebec might secede persisted in the early 1970s, and in 1974 the provincial government put through the controversial Bill 22 making French the official language of Quebec.

Canada is a land of contrast, between its brashly modern cities and its quiet, timeless forests.

The Canadian government has also recognized the desire of the minority ethnic groups to preserve their own cultures. These ethnic groups include more than 561 000 Germans, 538 000 Italians, 310 000 Ukrainians, 145 000 Dutch and 135 000 Poles. Along with lesser groups they are represented in the Consultative Council on Multiculturalism set up in 1973, and their interests are the responsibility of a specially-appointed minister of state. Many multicultural projects, including the Canadian Identities Program, have been established.

The Native Peoples is the commonly-used official description of Canada's original inhabitants, the Indians and the Eskimos (or Inuit). Originally there were six cultural groups of Indians: the nomadic Algonquin hunters and food-gatherers of the eastern woodlands; the more advanced Iroquoian farmers of the eastern woodlands; the buffalo-hunting Algonquin, Athabaskan and Sioux linguistic groups of the plains; the nomadic tribes of the NW; the Athabaskan, Salishan, Kootenayan and Tlingit groups of the NW mountains and plateaus; and the numerous tribes of the West Coast, skilled in totemic art, weaving and basketry, and with a unique and highly stratified social structure. These cultures were shattered by the arrival of the white man. By the end of the 19th century his weapons, diseases and alcohol has reduced the Indian population to only 100 000.

In Canada, the attitude to the Indians was far more paternalistic than in the US, and there were no major Indian wars. From 1871 a series of treaties was concluded with the various tribes which at least ensured their physical survival on small reserves of land. In British Columbia, however, no such treaties were signed, all land, except a few reserves, being taken over by the British Crown. This explains the often-justifiable claims for compensation still periodically made by Coast Indians, on the basis that the land was taken without their consent.

During the present century the Indian population has made a marked recovery and now stands at about 265 000. Organized into 566 bands, they mostly live on about 2 200 reserves covering 6 000 000 acres. Their welfare is the responsibility of the Department of Indian Affairs, but the Indians themselves are increasingly sharing in the decision-making process through band councils and other bodies. They have also formed their own organizations, notably the Native Council for Canada, representing tribes in the treaty reserves, and the National Indian Brotherhood, representing detribalized Indians living in the cities. Significantly the Indians have been pressing land claims, basing their case—with some success—on a proclamation by George III (1763) which has never been repealed and which makes nonsense of the later land treaties. In 1974 Indians and Eskimos in Quebec, with federal government backing, successfully challenged the provincial government over the giant James Bay hydroelectric project, temporarily halting all construction work and finally winning hundreds of millions of dollars in compensation along with 200 000sq mi of reserved lands and valuable hunting and fishing rights.

The Inuit, as the Eskimos prefer to be called, number about 17 000 and have long lived in the Canadian north, mainly along the coasts where they depended on seals, walruses, whales and fish, or inland where they lived on the caribou herds and fished the many lakes. Their first major contact with the white man came in the early 1800s with the arrival of whaling ships and the factors of the Hudson's Bay Company, which still has many posts in the Northwest Territories. In the present century Arctic Canada has been opened up by the development of air transportation, the establishment of radio and meteorological stations and defense installations during and after World War II, and by the exploitation of the considerable mineral resources. The Inuit have benefited from federal government programs covering such services as education, health and housing. They have also been encouraged to exploit local resources and now have more than 30 consumer and producer cooperatives with an annual turnover of more than $C2 000 000. Their inherent artistic talents have been promoted; Inuit sculptures and other works of art now command high prices in world markets.

The Inuit are encouraged to share in the administration of the north. They have elected representatives in the Territorial Council of the Northwest Territories and their settlement councils participate in local community projects. Inuit Tapirisat, the national Inuit organization created to bring the Inuit into full participation in modern society, is backed by federal funds. To turn an Inuit from a tribal hunter into a 20th-century Canadian is an expensive operation. Some Inuit remain suspicious of governmental policy and motives, despite lavish federal expenditure to their interests, even including a special contribution to the Inuit Tapirisat to help research into Inuit land claims and rights.

In spite of the predominance of the two founding races, Canada is a mosaic of peoples without the assimilation that occurred in the US. Canadians seem to rejoice in their differences, rarely aspiring to uniformity. Each province has its distinctive character and attitudes. The Atlantic provinces (New Brunswick, Nova Scotia, Prince Edward Island and Newfoundland) still retain some of their old fierce independence and often feel closer to Britain and the US than to the rest of Canada. Quebec is essentially French Canada and has a long-standing rivalry with Ontario, whose financial power and economic pacesetting are often jealously viewed by the other provinces. Manitoba and Saskatchewan, prospering on wheat, cattle, mining, petroleum and natural gas, are wary of any attempt by the

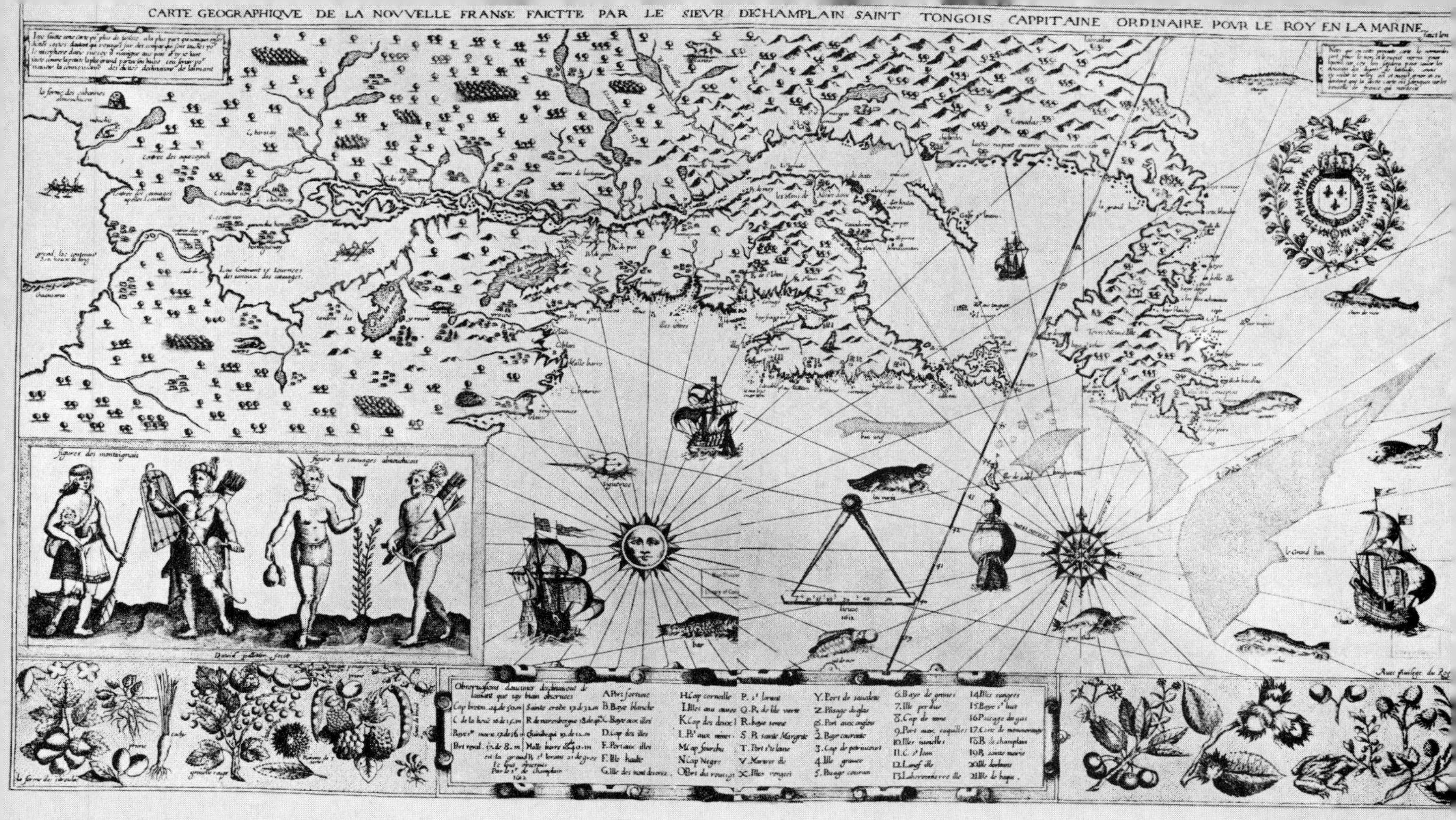

Map of Canada (*top*) by Samuel de Champlain (1612), showing native fauna and flora, and the Great Lakes he was to explore the following year.

federal government to control their natural resources. It has been said that Saskatchewan, a major producer of oil and natural gas, sometimes "behaves like Arabs towards fellow-Canadians" in its fight for higher prices. Alberta, the third prairie province, and one of the most beautiful in Canada is also enjoying an oil boom. British Columbia is to Canada what California is to the US. Although it attracts many immigrants, especially the retired, it tends to be isolationist and slightly resentful of newcomers wishing to share its undoubted beauty and prosperity, though any Canadian over 60 arriving in the province is immediately entitled to a monthly pension of $C213 under a new government program.

The closer the look at Canada, the more apparent the differences between its various peoples and provinces. Nevertheless there is a definite national unity, which has so far proved strong enough to withstand all strains and stresses. It enables presentday Canadians, whose forefathers carved out their country from a vast wilderness, to continue developing the untapped resources which could make Canada one of the world's richest and most prosperous nations.

The history of Canada is far less turbulent than that of most other countries. There are no great convulsions to equal the US Civil War, no drum-and-trumpet heroes. The epics concern explorers, fur traders and pioneers, and achievements like the construction of the Canadian Pacific Railway (completed 1885). But in more recent times Canadians have found it impossible to ignore Europe and have become increasingly involved in world affairs. Canadians fought on the Allied side in both world wars, and for the UN in Korea. Canada has regularly provided troops for UN peace-keeping activities and since 1946 has contributed more than $C500 million to various UN organizations. Canada pioneered NATO, of which she is still a key member although the Trudeau government has scaled down her commitment.

US–Canadian relations are of prime importance to both countries, if only because each is the other's best customer and because of strong financial interdependence. Cooperation on defense, fisheries, agricultural marketing, and on environmental problems along the border area, is handled through a number of permanent bilateral organizations. More migrants move into Canada from the US than from any other country except Britain. Every year more than 30 million Americans visit Canada, and about the same number of Canadians the US.

Canada's attitude to the US, however, has never been entirely cordial. The War of 1812 between Britain and the US began with a US invasion of Canada, and from that time until the early 1900s Canadians were convinced that what they had to fear most was absorption by their powerful southern neighbor. This fear now takes another form—resentment of US economic domination. US investment in Canada, currently about $40 billion, has undoubtedly enabled Canada to maintain a high level of industrialization, but at a cost of increasing depletion of the Dominion's natural resources, large quantities of which are shipped across the border. Many Canadians fear that their industrial plants may soon become mere subsidiaries of powerful US corporations with all key operations and technological developments kept firmly in American hands. The Trudeau administration believes that Canada has ample resources and can afford to let the US have a share, in return for finance for further development, without any threat to her sovereignty or the bright future seemingly in store.

Canada's prosperity rests on natural resources, particularly the vast prairies and the oceans.

Towards the founding of Canada

c986	First sighting of coast of Labrador by Norsemen.
c1000	Leif Ericsson makes abortive attempt to settle in Labrador or Newfoundland.
1497–98	John Cabot's discovery of fishing banks off Newfoundland and exploration of some Canadian coastal areas.
1534	Jacques Cartier claims New France for Francis I. Exploration of St Lawrence River. Attempt to found a colony with Roberval fails but the fur trade with Indians is firmly established.
1604	Samuel de Champlain helps found first French colony in North America at Port Royal (now Annapolis Royal, Novia Scotia), Bay of Fundy.
1608	Champlain founds a settlement at Quebec, which becomes the base for his explorations of the St Lawrence and Ottawa River systems. Fur trade develops and exploration continues but development of a colony stagnates.
1611–15	Jesuit and then Franciscan missions sent to Canada.
1640	Outbreak of Iroquois Wars.
1648–50	Destruction of Huron Confederacy by the Iroquois. Martyrdom of several Jesuit missionaries.
1650s	Explorations of Radisson and Groselliers.
1659	Battle of the Long Sault Rapids.
	New France made a Royal Province with Bishop Laval as first bishop.
	First Intendant: Jean Baptiste Talon (1665–68 and 1670–72).
1660s	Joliet's explorations of the Mississippi.
1670	Incorporation of the Hudson's Bay Company by the English to find a Northwest Passage. The activities of the company in exploration and fur trade led to increasing rivalry between the French and English and their Indian associates.
1672	Frontenac appointed governor.
1682	De la Salle's discovery of the mouth of the Mississippi.
1756	Outbreak of Seven Years' War.
1759	James Wolfe captures Quebec for the English.
1760	Montreal and all of New France surrender to the English.
1763	All of New France east of the Mississippi becomes British save St Pierre, Miquelon and New Orleans.
1776	American Revolutionary War. Attempts to invade Canada fail.
1812–1814	American attempts to invade Canada fail.
1837	Political unrest in Upper Canada (Ontario) over hegemony of the Seven Families leads to brief outbreak of rebellion led by William Lyon Mackenzie.
	Political unrest of French in Lower Canada (Quebec) leads to rebellion.
1840	As a result of the Durham Report, Upper and Lower Canada are united.
1846	Lord Elgin sent to govern Canada.
1867	After years of peaceful agitation and negotiation, Canada achieves confederation on July 1.

Left: The Parliament Building in Ottawa, center of Canada's political life, with the 216ft Peace Tower visible in the background. The present buildings date from 1916, when they were rebuilt after a fire. *Right:* Log boom at Terrace Bay, Ontario. Canadian rivers are an important part of the country's timber industry, transporting millions of logs to mills and market annually.

the Appalachians. The plain narrows northward and in the S continues into the US. Its major feature is the U-shaped CANADIAN SHIELD formation of old and worn rocks, covering about half Canada. In the SE are the Niagara escarpment, the fertile St. Lawrence lowlands and the rolling valleys and uplands of Appalachian Canada. Around the center of the Shield are the lakes and muskegs of the Hudson Bay lowlands.

The Canadian Rockies have at least 30 peaks above 10000ft, but Canada's highest mountain, Mt Logan (19850ft) is in the St. Elias Mts in the Yukon. There are three major drainage systems, the Great Lakes-St. Lawrence, the Saskatchewan-Red-Nelson rivers system and the Mackenzie, Canada's longest river (2635mi). Climate is mainly influenced by distance from the sea and distance north; it runs to extremes. Winters are usually long and cold, though milder on the W and SW coasts. Southern summers are usually warm. Rainfall is heaviest in the W and snowfall heaviest in the E. Vegetation ranges from the tundra of the N to mainly coniferous forest, mixed woodlands and prairie grasslands.

People. Canada's population is predominantly of British or French stock, though it includes many of German, Italian, Ukrainian, Dutch and other origins. Indians number about 265000 and Inuit (Eskimos) about 17000. Most Canadians live within 200mi of the US border and more than 76% are urban-dwelling, the largest cities being Montreal, Toronto, Vancouver, Ottawa, Winnipeg, Hamilton, Edmonton, Quebec and Calgary.

Government. Canada has a parliamentary system of government, with executive power vested in a prime minister and cabinet. The federal legislature comprises a Senate of 102 appointed members and a House of Commons whose 264 members are elected for a 5-year term. Each of the 10 provinces has its own premier and elected legislature. The Yukon and Northwest Territories are governed by federally appointed commissioners and elected councils, and each sends one representative to the federal parliament.

Economy. During the present century Canada has emerged as a major manufacturing country and in the mid-1970s was far more urban and industrial than rural and agricultural. Agriculture, however, remains important, ranking first in terms of employment and providing about 11% of Canada's total exports. Canada is one of the world's chief wheat producers, but also grows other grains, oilseeds, fruit (especially apples), vegetables and tobacco. Beef and dairy cattle, hogs, sheep and poultry are reared. Forestry and fisheries are major industries, and Canada remains a leading source of furs, both farmed and trapped. Mineral resources are rich and include petroleum and natural gas, copper, nickel, iron ore, zinc, lead, silver, gold, asbestos, elemental sulfur and coal. Abundant energy is provided by hydroelectric and thermal power plants, and several nuclear power plants are operating.

In 1972 manufacturing accounted for about 24% of the gross domestic product. In terms of manufacturers' shipments the leading products were automobiles, pulp and paper, meat products, refined petroleum, and iron and steel. Other important products include metals, machinery, chemicals, plastics, electrical equipment and textiles. Among Canada's chief trading partners are the US, Britain, Japan, West Germany, Russia, China, Venezuela and the Netherlands.

History. Visited by 11th-century Vikings, Canada was later penetrated by explorers such as John CABOT, Jacques CARTIER and Samuel de CHAMPLAIN. The French founded Quebec in 1608 and made Canada the royal colony of New France (1663). Anglo-French rivalry culminated in the cession of New France to Britain (Treaty of PARIS, 1763). French rights were guaranteed by the QUEBEC ACT (1774). Only one serious revolt against British rule took place (1837–38), consisting of separate uprisings led by W. L. MACKENZIE in Upper (English-speaking) Canada and Louis PAPINEAU in Lower (French-speaking) Canada. The British North America Act (1867) established Canada as a dominion, the four founding provinces being Quebec, Ontario, Nova Scotia and

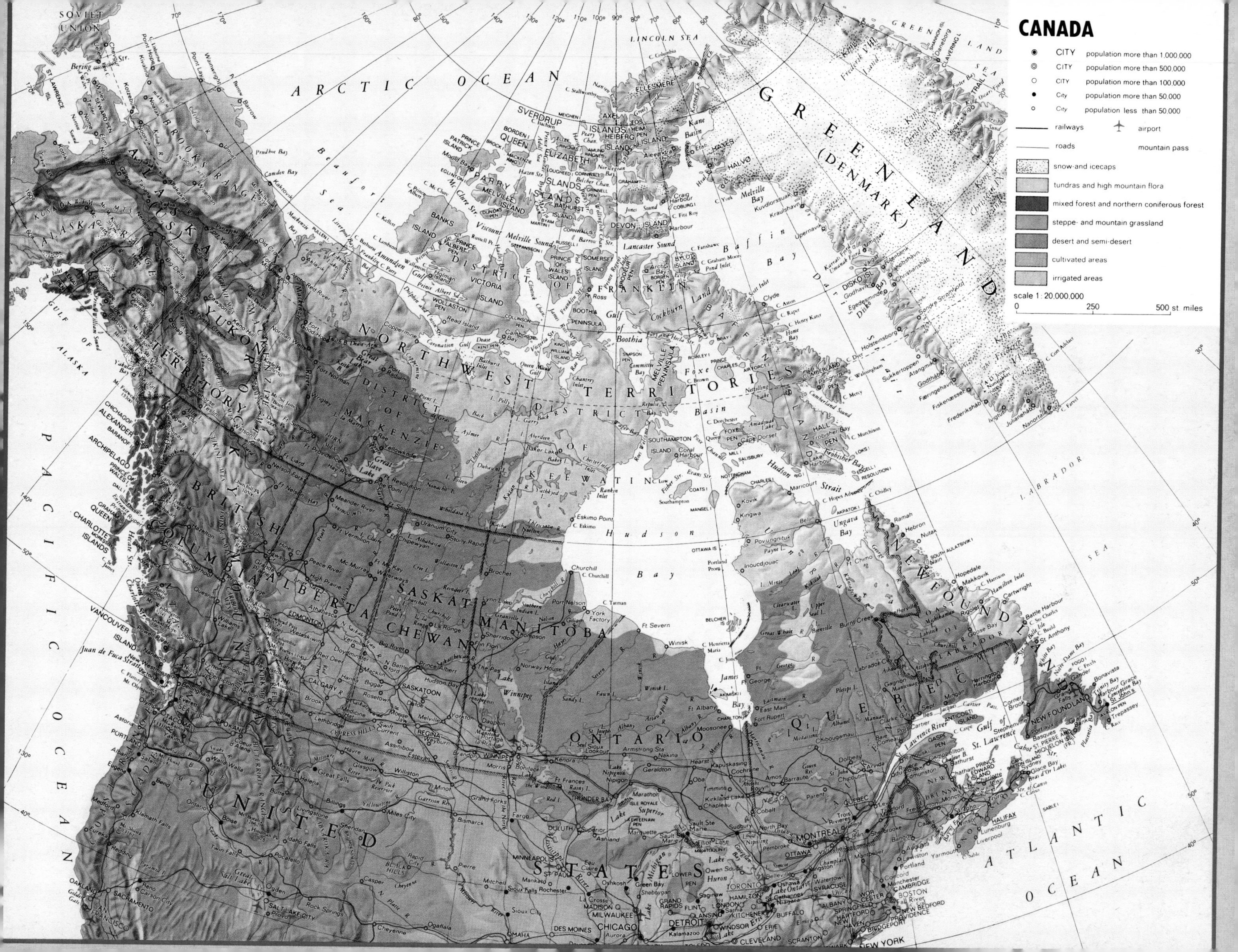
CANADA
CITY population more than 1,000,000
CITY population more than 500,000
CITY population more than 100,000
City population more than 50,000
City population less than 50,000
railways
airport
roads
mountain pass
snow-and icecaps
tundras and high mountain flora
mixed forest and northern coniferous forest
steppe- and mountain grassland
desert and semi-desert
cultivated areas
irrigated areas
scale 1: 20,000,000
0 250 500 st. miles
ARCTIC OCEAN
PACIFIC OCEAN
ATLANTIC OCEAN
GREENLAND (DENMARK)
NORTHWEST TERRITORIES
YUKON TERRITORY
BRITISH COLUMBIA
ALBERTA
SASKATCHEWAN
MANITOBA
ONTARIO
QUEBEC
NEWFOUNDLAND
ALASKA (U.S.)
UNITED STATES
Hudson Bay
Baffin Bay
LABRADOR SEA
Beaufort Sea
GULF OF ALASKA
LINCOLN SEA
SOVIET UNION

A cornfield in Alberta, Canada, seems to stretch as far as the eye can see. Alberta and Saskatchewan have been called "Canada's breadbasket."

New Brunswick. The others entered later: Manitoba (1870), British Columbia (1871), Prince Edward Island (1873), Saskatchewan (1905), Alberta (1905) and Newfoundland (1949). The Northwest Territories, formerly administered by the Hudson's Bay Company, became a federal territory in 1870, and the Yukon was made a separate territory in 1898.

CANADA, United Church of. See UNITED CHURCH OF CANADA.

CANADA ACT, British parliamentary act of 1791, also known as the Constitutional Act, which divided the country into Upper and Lower Canada—thus providing a rough territorial separation of French- and English-speaking settlers, each with their own elected legislature.

CANADA BALSAM, or Canada turpentine, a sticky exudate from the BALSAM FIR (*Abies balsamea*). It is a pale yellow oleoresin that has a refractive index similar to glass and is primarily used as a cement for glass in optics.

CANADA COMPANY, colonizing company founded in 1824 to settle 2.5 million acres of land sold by Upper Canada (Ontario) to pay war debts. Headed by the land agent and author John GALT, it brought settlers into the SW Ontario area, building many roads and townships.

Harzer canary, named for the Harz mountains of Germany, where the best singing canaries have been bred for hundreds of years. All canaries belong to the species *Serinus canaria*.

CANADA COUNCIL FOR THE ARTS, HUMANITIES AND SOCIAL SCIENCES, established by the Canadian government in 1957 with an initial grant of $100 million. It provides aid to colleges and universities, arts groups, publications, exhibitions and gifted individuals.

CANADA GOOSE, *Branta canadensis*, a large migratory bird common to North America, Greenland and parts of Asia. It is recognizable by its long black head and neck and distinctive white cheek bars and is known for its habit of flying in group formations.

CANADA JAY, *Perisoreus canadensis*, also known as the "gray jay" or "whiskey jack," is about 300mm (1ft) long with fluffy gray feathers and black and white head markings.

CANADIAN ARMED FORCES, united body created by the Canadian Forces Reorganization Act, 1967, which merged the Royal Canadian Navy, the Canadian Army and the Royal Canadian Air Force. The strength of the regular forces in early 1974 was 81 727, backed up by a large reserve.

CANADIAN BROADCASTING CORPORATION (CBC), public corporation created in 1936 by the Canadian Broadcasting Act, distributing national network programs through publicly and privately owned radio and television stations throughout Canada.

CANADIAN NATIONAL EXHIBITION, North America's largest fair, held annually on a 350-acre lakeside site near Toronto between mid-Aug. and Labor Day. An international trade fair, it also features an agricultural section and entertainment.

CANADIAN NATIONAL RAILWAYS (CNR), the largest North American transcontinental railroad system, created by an act of parliament in 1922 as a government-owned corporate organization amalgamating five separate systems. It operates over half the country's rail miles and also controls the Canadian National Telegraphs, the Canadian National Steamships and Trans-Canada Air Lines.

CANADIAN PACIFIC RAILWAY, privately owned Canadian railroad company formed by D. J. J. McIntyre in 1880 to build a transcontinental line to the Pacific coast. The line was completed in 1885, but not before a scandal over alleged bribery in the awarding of its contract had forced the resignation of Sir John A. MACDONALD's government. Now concentrating on goods rather than passenger services, it is a large company operating over a third of Canada's rail miles.

CANADIAN RIVER, runs over 900mi through the SW US, from the Sangre de Cristo Mts in N N.M. to the Arkansas R in Okla.

CANADIAN SHIELD, or **Laurentian Shield**, that area of North America (including the E half of Canada and small portions of the US) which has remained more or less stable since PRECAMBRIAN times. Its surface rocks, which are igneous and metamorphic (see IGNEOUS ROCK; METAMORPHIC ROCK), are amongst the oldest in the world, younger structures having disappeared through EROSION, in some areas by GLACIERS of the PLEISTOCENE.

CANALETTO (1697–1768), born Giovanni Antonio Canal, 18th-century Venetian painter. His best-known works are views of Venice, notable for their sense of spaciousness and light, combined with very fine detail. He lived in London 1746–56, and painted many London views of similar quality.

CANALS, man-made waterways used for transportation, drainage and IRRIGATION. They represent one of mankind's earliest attempts to change the environment to suit his convenience. As early as 521 BC a precursor of the Suez Canal joined the Nile to the Red Sea. In China, the Ling Ch'u canal was completed during the 3rd century BC and the Grand Canal, joining the Paiho, Yellow and Yangtze rivers, had sections in use by the 7th century AD. The Romans built many canals to supply their cities with water and canalized a number of European rivers to create an empire-wide transportation system. AQUEDUCTS were widely used long before Roman times to carry water across roads and valleys, but it was the development of the lock which allowed canals to cross other terrain. By the 15th century this simple device for raising boats from one land level to another was already in use, and one of its inventors, LEONARDO DA VINCI, built several canals with locks near the city of Milan.

Although one of the great engineering projects of the 19th century, the SUEZ CANAL to the Red Sea was built entirely without locks, the other great international waterway, the PANAMA CANAL, would not have been possible without them. Locks allowed a canal transport system to be built across England and Europe from the 16th century onwards. In North America, the canal system included the ERIE CANAL, completed in 1825 to link the Hudson R to Lake Erie and, more significantly, to provide an opening to the Middle West. The Welland Canal, opened in 1828 between Lake Erie and Lake Ontario, was the next step in an inland waterway transportation network completed by the opening of the ST. LAWRENCE SEAWAY, of which it is now a part, in 1959.

CANAL ZONE. See PANAMA CANAL ZONE.

CANANDAIGUA, city in W N.Y., seat of Ontario Co., a shipping and industrial center. Lying at the N end of Canandaigua Lake, it is also a popular resort. Pop 10 488.

CANANDAIGUA LAKE, one of the FINGER LAKES. About 15mi long and 2mi across at its widest point, it lies in W N.Y.

CANARIES CURRENT, or **Canary Current**, OCEAN CURRENT fed by the NORTH ATLANTIC DRIFT, flowing SW past the NW African coast, then W to join the N EQUATORIAL CURRENT.

CANARIS, Wilhelm (1887–1945), German admiral, head of military intelligence under the Nazi regime. One of the leaders of the plot to assassinate Hitler, he was executed when it failed.

CANARY, name of several small song birds, particularly a finch native to the Canary Islands. The wild canary is usually gray or green in color, but tame birds have been bred to produce the characteristic "canary yellow." The birds have been kept and bred in Europe since the 16th century and are valued for their lovely song.

CANARY ISLANDS, group of volcanic islands in the Atlantic, about 65mi off the NW coast of Africa. Comprising two Spanish provinces, the main islands are Tenerife, Palma, Gomera, Hierro, Grand Canary, Fuerteventura and Lanzarote; their land area is nearly 3 000sq mi. Main industries are fishing, farming and tourism; Las Palmas and Santa Cruz are the principal ports. They were called "insulae canariae," or "islands of the dogs," by the Romans. The name passed on to the native wild finch, or CANARY. Pop 170 224.

CANASTA, a variation of RUMMY for two to six players. It originated in Argentina, and became very popular in the US in the 1950s.

CANAVERAL, Cape, on the E coast of Fla., site of the John F. Kennedy Space Center, named Cape Kennedy 1963–73. It became famous with the launching of the first US satellite, Explorer I, in 1958; all subsequent US manned space flights have taken off from there.

CANBERRA, federal capital city of the Commonwealth of Australia, built from 1913 onwards in the Australian Capital Territory. Australia's largest inland city, it is located on a plain about 1 900ft above sea level. There are various light industries, but the economy rests mainly on the public service and governmental departments. Pop 156 334.

CANBY, Edward Richard Sprigg (1817–1873), Union general in the US Civil War. He headed a volunteer force in N.M. which, by harassing tactics, blocked a planned Confederate drive into Cal. He maintained order in New York City during the 1863 draft riots and led the capture of Mobile, Ala., in 1865. He was murdered by Indians in Cal. (See also CAPTAIN JACK.)

CANBY, Henry Seidel (1878–1961), US editor, author and literary critic. Canby founded the *Saturday Review of Literature* in 1924 and was its editor until 1936. He also wrote biographies of *Thoreau* (1939) and *Walt Whitman* (1945) and an autobiography, *American Memoir* (1947).

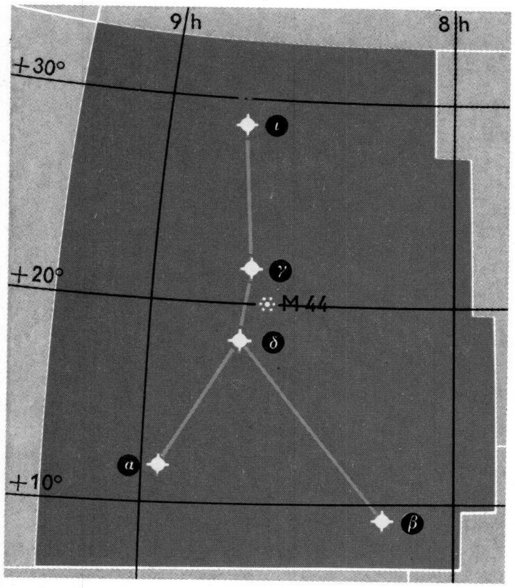

The constellation Cancer, in the Northern Hemisphere of the sky. The sun passes through Cancer from late July to early August.

CANCER (the Crab), a spring constellation in the N Hemisphere, the fourth sign of the ZODIAC. At the time the zodiacal system was adopted, Cancer marked the northernmost limit of the ECLIPTIC. A hazy object near the center of Cancer is a cluster of stars named Praesepe, the Beehive.

CANCER, a group of diseases in which some body cells change their nature, start to divide uncontrollably and may revert to an undifferentiated type. They form a malignant TUMOR which enlarges and may spread to adjacent tissues; in many cases cancer cells enter the BLOOD or LYMPH systems and are carried to distant parts of the body. There they form secondary "colonies" called **metastases**. Such advanced cancer is often rapidly fatal, causing gross emaciation. Cancer may present in very many ways—as a lump, some change in body function, bleeding, ANEMIA or weight loss—occasionally the first symptoms being from a metastasis. Less often tumors produce substances mimicking the action of HORMONES or producing remote effects such as NEURITIS.

Cancers are classified according to the type of tissue in which they originate. The commonest type, **carcinoma**, occurs in glandular tissue, SKIN, or visceral linings. **Sarcoma** occurs in connective tissue, MUSCLE, BONE and CARTILAGE. **Glioma** is a sarcoma of BRAIN neuroglia, unusual in that it does not spread elsewhere. **Lymphoma**, including HODGKIN'S DISEASE, is a tumor of the lymphatic system (see LYMPH); LEUKEMIA can be regarded as a cancer of white blood cells or their precursors. The cause of cancer remains unknown, but substantial evidence points to damage to or alteration in the DNA of CHROMOSOMES. Certain agents are known to predispose to cancer including RADIOACTIVITY, high doses of X RAYS and ULTRAVIOLET RADIATION and certain chemicals, known as **carcinogens**. These include tars, oils, dyes, ASBESTOS and tobacco smoke (see SMOKING). A number of cancers are suspected of being caused by a VIRUS and there appear to be hereditary factors in some cases.

Prevention of cancer is mainly by avoiding known causes, including smoking, excess radiation and industrial carcinogens. People suffering from conditions known to predispose to cancer need regular surveillance. Treatments include surgical excision, RADIATION THERAPY, CHEMOTHERAPY, or some combination of these. The latter two methods destroy cancer cells or slow their growth; the difficulty is to do so without also damaging normal tissue. They have greatly improved the outlook in lymphoma and certain types of leukemia. Treatment can be curative if carried out in the early stages, but if the cancer has metastasized, therapy is less likely to succeed; all that may be possible is the relief of symptoms. Thus, if cure is sought, early recognition is essential.

CANDELA (cd), the photometric base unit in SI UNITS. It is defined as the luminous intensity, in the perpendicular direction, of a surface of 1/600 000 sq m of a black body at the temperature of freezing platinum under a pressure of 101 325 newtons per sq m. (See BLACKBODY RADIATION; PHOTOMETRY.)

CANDLE, one of the oldest forms of lighting, used by the Romans and probably by the Egyptians. It consists of a cylinder of inflammable material (such as paraffin wax or beeswax) with a central wick, usually of plaited cotton fibers. Most candles are now made by molding or by forcing the solid wax through a die under pressure.

CANDLEBERRY. See BAYBERRY.

CANDLEFISH or eulachon, *Thaleichthys pacificus*, an edible freshwater fish of the smelt family, about 300mm (1ft) long, found in the NW of the US. The Indians used its dried flesh to make candles.

CANDLEMAS, the feast of the Purification of the Virgin Mary and the presentation of Jesus in the Temple, on Feb. 2. It takes its name from the consecration of church candles before the mass of the day.

CANDLENUT, seed of the candlenut tree, *Aleurites moluccana*, cultivated in many tropical regions. It yields candlenut oil, used in manufacturing PAINTS, lacquers, VARNISHES and LINOLEUM. The poisonous oil cake is used as a FERTILIZER.

CANDLEPOWER, the ability of a light source to radiate as expressed in CANDELAS.

CANDYTUFT, common name for small annual and perennial herbs of the genus *Iberis*, native to S Europe and W Asia. The flowers are white, red or purple. Candytufts are extensively cultivated as garden plants in North America and Europe.

CANIS MAJOR (the Dog), a constellation of the S Hemisphere visible during winter in N skies. It contains SIRIUS, the brightest star in the night sky. Mythologically, Canis Major and CANIS MINOR were ORION'S hunting dogs.

CANIS MINOR (the Little Dog), a constellation on the celestial equator (see CELESTIAL SPHERE) visible in N skies during winter. It contains the binary star PROCYON (see DOUBLE STAR).

CANISIUS, Saint Peter (1521–1597), Dutch Jesuit theologian active during the COUNTERREFORMATION and writer of the influential *Triple Catechism* (1555–58). He was canonized and made a Doctor of the Church in 1925. His feast falls on April 27.

CANKERWORM, a moth caterpillar whose food is the foliage of fruit, shade and forest trees. Two kinds are found in North America, the spring and fall cankerworms (*Paleacrita vernata* and *Alsophila pometaria*).

CANNABIS. See HEMP; MARIJUANA.

CANNAE, ancient town in S Italy, site of HANNIBAL'S decisive defeat of the Romans in 216 BC. The encircling technique he perfected won him the battle and 10 000 prisoners, and is regarded as a masterpiece of tactics.

CANNAS, large attractive plants of the genus *Canna*, native to the tropics and subtropics of the W Hemisphere. Their unbranched stalks end in a cluster of colorful flowers, each about 150mm (6in) across.

CANNES, French resort and seaport on the Mediterranean coast, in the Alpes Maritime department. Its superb climate makes it a center for tourism and festivals, notably the annual International Film Festival. Pop 68 021.

CANNIBALISM, or **anthropophagy,** consumption by humans of human flesh, common throughout the world at various times in the past and still occasionally practiced, though now generally TABOO. Among PRIMITIVE MAN the motive appears to be belief that eating an enemy or a respected elder transfers to the eater the strength, courage or wisdom of the dead.

CANNING, the process of preserving foods in sealed metal containers, developed by the French chef Nicolas Appert in 1809 and first patented in the US by Ezra Daggett in 1815. The fragile glass jars originally used were replaced by tin-coated iron cans after 1810. Today, a production line process is used. The food may reach the cannery a few hours after picking; it is first cleaned, and then prepared by removing inedible matter. After it has been peeled, sliced or diced as necessary, the food is blanched: hot water and steam are used to deactivate enzymes that might later spoil the flavor and color, and to shrink the product to the desired size and weight. The cans are then filled, and heated to drive out dissolved gases in the food and to expand the contents, thus creating a partial vacuum when they are cooled after sealing. Finally, the cans are sterilized, usually by steam under pressure. (See also FOOD PRESERVATION.)

CANNING, George (1770–1827), British statesman. As foreign secretary 1822–27 (following an earlier tenure, 1807–09), he opposed the HOLY ALLIANCE, pledged support for the independence of the Spanish American colonies (thus provoking the MONROE DOCTRINE) and secured Greek independence. He became prime minister in 1827, but died shortly afterwards.

CANNIZZARO, Stanislao (1826–1910), Italian chemist who discovered the Cannizzaro reaction in which BENZALDEHYDE is converted to BENZYL ALCOHOL and BENZOIC ACID (1853), but he is chiefly remembered for the republication of AVOGADRO'S hypothesis at the Karlsruhe conference of 1860. This at last allowed chemists to distinguish EQUIVALENT WEIGHTS from true ATOMIC WEIGHTS.

CANNON, term used loosely of early ARTILLERY, though some modern devices are still described as cannon. Cannon were present at the Battle of Crécy (1346) but not until the 15th century did artillery power become of note. Early cannon were muzzle-loaded, GUNPOWDER being pushed down the barrel, followed by a pad of material (often cloth), then the stone or metal ball. Flame applied to a touchhole at the rear of the barrel set off the gunpowder. Important developments were increasing maneuverability; the invention of breech-loading; rifling (see RIFLE) of the barrel; and use of explosive AMMUNITION. (See EXPLOSIVES; GUN.)

CANNON, Joseph Gurney (1836–1926), US legislator and speaker of the US House of Representatives 1903–11. Elected to the House by Ill. in 1872, he served for 46 years. As speaker, his arbitrary partisan rules became known as "Cannonism," and he had a dictatorial control of the House which was only finally curtailed when he was excluded from the rules committee in 1910.

CANO, Alonso (1601–1667), Spanish Baroque painter, sculptor and architect. He led a stormy life in Seville and Madrid, and in Granada—where his powerful works include the seven *Mysteries of the Virgin* paintings (1652–54) and the cathedral façade.

CANO, Juan Sebastián del (1476–1526), Basque seaman who commanded the first ship to circumnavigate the globe (1521), after MAGELLAN'S death.

CANOE, long, narrow lightweight boat used on lakes and rivers, today mainly for recreation. The first

Canoes, though invented by primitive cultures, are now popular sports craft. The Eskimo canoe (1), a one-seater, is made from skins and wood. The Canadian canoe, on an Indian design originally made in bark, is now made of wood or fiberglass and seats two or more. The modern touring kayak (3), made of wood, fiberglass or aluminum, seats two.

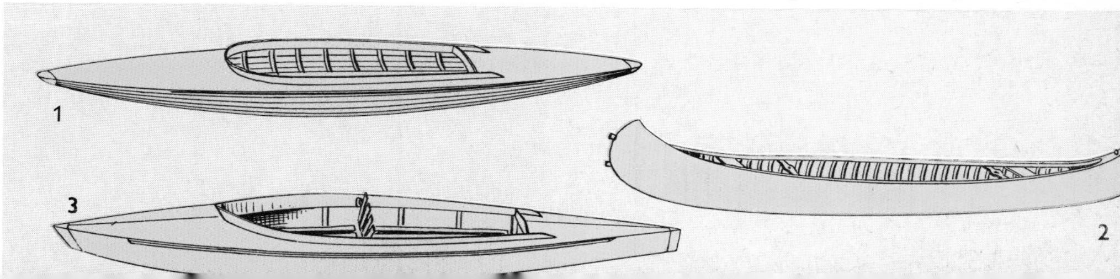

canoes were made from hollowed-out logs; now they are made from canvas, thin wood, glass fiber and aluminum, often weighing no more than 50 pounds. They are 11ft to 20ft long with a beam of about 3ft, drawing about 1ft of water.

CANON, form of musical composition based on the repeated imitation of the initial theme at specified time intervals. Rounds (such as *Three Blind Mice*) are the commonest form. The oldest known canon, composed during the 13th century, is *Sumer is icumen in* (Summer is coming).

CANON, Biblical, books accepted as part of the Bible and usually considered to have divine authority. The Jewish Old Testament canon was completed by the 1st century AD, and St. ATHANASIUS compiled the oldest canonical list of the New Testament in the 4th century.

CANONIZATION, the process by which a Christian church declares a deceased person to be a saint. In the Roman Catholic Church the process involves a long and careful investigation of the individual's life and reputation for sanctity, heroic virtue and orthodoxy. There is also a scrutiny of miracles reputedly effected by the candidate when alive or after death.

CANON LAW, the body of ecclesiastical laws (canons) governing the organization, administration and discipline of a church, most fully developed in the Roman Catholic Church. In the 12th century GRATIAN, a Benedictine monk, compiled the first systematic collection of canon law, based on papal decrees and the proclamations of SYNODS. It was reinforced by further compilations under Pope PIUS X in 1904 and completed under Pope BENEDICT XV in 1917. It contains 2 414 canons.

CANONSBURG, industrial borough in Pa., 20mi SW of Pittsburgh, producing electrical transformers, metal products and pottery. Pop 11 439.

CANOPIC JARS, covered vessels in which, in ancient Egypt, the embalmed viscera removed during mummification (see MUMMY) were placed for burial. After c1000 BC the embalmed viscera were more generally replaced in the mummy and these jars rarely used.

CANOPUS, Alpha Carinae, the brightest star in the S Hemisphere with an apparent magnitude of −0.72. It is 210 times larger than the sun and 30pc from earth.

CANOSSA, castle in N Italy about 17mi SE of Parma, founded in the 10th century to command the Lombardy Plain. The Emperor HENRY IV presented himself as a penitent to Pope GREGORY VII here in 1077. It was razed in 1255.

CANOVA, Antonio (1757–1822), Italian sculptor, a leading exponent of Neoclassicism. His works include *Cupid and Psyche* (1787–92), several statues of his patron Napoleon, and a famous statue of Pauline Bonaparte Borghese as the reclining *Venus Victrix* (1808).

CAN PHUMO. See LOURENCO MARQUES.

CANSO, Strait of, strait between Cape Breton Island and the Canadian mainland, 1mi wide at its narrowest point.

CANTABRIAN MOUNTAINS, Spanish mountain chain running 300mi from the Pyrenees along the N coast. The highest peak is Torre de Cerredo (8 787ft). There are rich iron and coal deposits.

CANTATA (from Italian *cantare*, to sing), originally a piece of music sung, as opposed to one played instrumentally. Now, any work for voices and instruments. Beginning in Italy (1620) the form also developed in France and Germany. One of the earliest composers in this form was Giacomo CARISSIMI, but its most famous exponent is J. S. BACH, who wrote over 300 cantatas.

CANTERBURY, city and county borough of Kent, on the Stour R 55mi SE of London. It was England's ecclesiastical capital from 597AD and the archbishop of Canterbury is Primate of All England. Canterbury has many notable buildings, including the cathedral (where Thomas à BECKET was murdered in 1170), a Norman castle and Kent U. Pop 33 157.

CANTERBURY BELL, *Campanula medium*, a cultivated biennial plant, which produces white, blue, pink or violet, bell-shaped flowers from May to July. (See also BELLFLOWER.)

CANTERBURY TALES, the best-known work of the English poet Geoffrey CHAUCER, written between 1387 and his death in 1400. In 17 000 lines (mostly heroic couplets) it describes a party of 30 pilgrims going to the shrine of St. Thomas à Becket, and their plan to tell four tales each on the journey. Only 24 tales were written, 4 of them unfinished, but the work presents a vivid cross-section of medieval society and the tales cover most medieval literary genres.

CANTICLE, a liturgical song similar to a psalm but based on a passage from elsewhere in the Bible. More recently the name has been given to any short choral work with a religious content.

CANTICLE OF CANTICLES. See SONG OF SOLOMON.

CANTILEVER, beam or structural member supported at one end only. The simplest example is a diving board. (See also BRIDGE.)

CANTON (Kuang-chou), largest city in S China, capital of Kuang-tung province, on the Pearl R about 95mi from Hong Kong. It is the chief seaport and the commercial and industrial center of the area, producing newsprint, textiles, machinery, chemicals, rubber and matches, and also processing many agricultural products. It has been a trading center since the 2nd century AD and was the first to trade with Europeans, in the 16th century. Pop 2 500 000.

CANTON, manufacturing city in Ill., 25mi SW of Peoria; an agricultural trading center also producing agricultural implements. Pop 14 217.

CANTON, town in Mass., 14mi S of Boston; manufacturing electrical and radio products, plastics, rubber goods and woolens. Pop 17 100.

CANTON, city in Miss., 22mi NE of Jackson, seat of Madison Co., agricultural center producing lumber, furniture and pesticides. Pop 10 503.

CANTON, city in Ohio, about 60mi SE of Cleveland, seat of Stark Co. An important industrial center producing rubber, steel, bearings, electrical goods, bricks, paints and motors, it was the home of President James McKinley. Pop 110 053.

CANTON AND ENDERBURY, islands in the S Pacific Ocean, about 2 000mi SW of Hawaii. The largest of the Phoenix Islands, they are under joint Anglo-American control. Canton (3.5sq mi) is the administrative center of the Phoenix Islands.

CANTOR, a singer or chanter in a church or synagogue. The Jewish cantor or *hazan* chants the prayers, but early Christian cantors not only led the singing but soon took charge of all music used in the services, a duty now performed in Anglican cathedrals by the *precentor*.

CANTOR, Eddie (1892–1964), US comedian and song-and-dance man, born Edward Israel Iskowitz. He began his stage career in 1907, and created a character familiar in radio, television and films for several decades.

CANTOR, Georg Ferdinand Ludwig Philip (1845–1918), German mathematician who pioneered the theory of infinite sets (see SET THEORY).

CANTUS FIRMUS, a preexistent musical theme acting as the foundation of a polyphonic structure, deriving from plainsong melodies and usually given to the tenor in 13th and 14th century motets.

CANUTE II THE GREAT (Cnut or Knut; c995–1035), king of England, Denmark and Norway, son of King Sweyn of Denmark. His victory at Ashingdon (1016) won him all England N of the Thames R. Edmund II Ironside's death gave him the south. He succeeded his brother Harold in Denmark (1019), seized the throne of Norway (1028) and was recognized as Scotland's overlord. His attempt to hold back the sea is apocryphal.

CANVAS, heavy woven cloth (see TEXTILES) usually made of cotton or linen fibers, used for centuries as sailcloth, and now also for tents, bags, shoes, hammocks, outdoor chairs, coverings, etc. It can be waterproofed (see WATERPROOFING). Artists' canvas is made of finer material specially treated to take paint.

CANVASBACK, *Aythya vallisneria*, a diving duck found in coastal and inland waters of North America, about 600mm (2ft) long and 1.4kg (3.1lb) in weight. It feeds on aquatic plants, shrimps and small fish.

CANYON, steep-sided VALLEY formed through EROSION by a river of hard rock lying in horizontal strata (see STRATIGRAPHY). The best-known example is the Grand Canyon, Ariz.

Canyon de Chelly in northeastern Arizona. The giant columns of wind-eroded rock in the foreground are known as Spider Rock and are regarded as sacred by the local Indians, who once held religious festivals in this area.

CANYON DE CHELLY NATIONAL MONUMENT, in the Navaho Reservation, NE Ariz., established in 1931 to preserve the ruins of ancient Indian cliff-dwellings. It was an Indian stronghold against first the Spanish, and then the US army.

CANYONLANDS NATIONAL PARK, in E Ut., established in 1964. It covers an area of 215 511 acres and contains much remarkable scenery, including red rock canyons, stone needles, arches and rapids, and also rock carvings.

CAÔ, Diogo. See CAM, DIOGO.

CAOUTCHOUC or "pure rubber," a vegetable gum which is the main constituent of natural RUBBER.

CAPA, Robert (born Andrei Friedmann, 1913–1954). Hungarian-born US photographer, a pioneer of journalistic photography, notably in the Spanish Civil War and the WWII Normandy landings.

CAPABLANCA, José Raoul (1888–1942), Cuban chess grand master and world champion 1921–27. He learned to play chess at the age of four, and spent his adult life in the Cuban diplomatic service.

CAPACITANCE, the ratio of the electric charge (see ELECTRICITY) on a conductor to its POTENTIAL, or, for a CAPACITOR, the ratio of its charge to the potential difference between its plates. Capacitance is measured in farads (F).

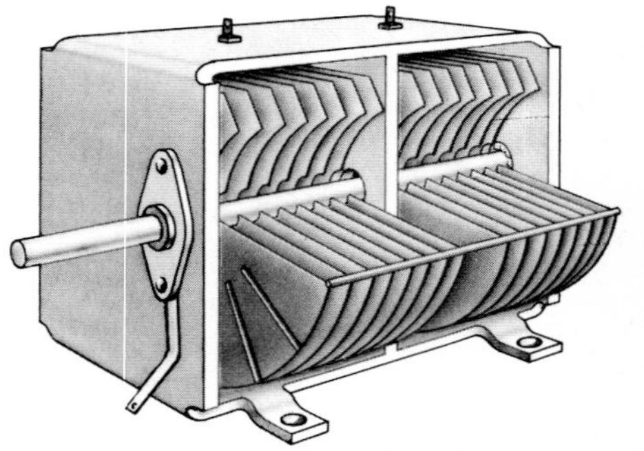

Variable capacitor as used in a radio tuner. The capacitance depends on the effective area of overlap between the moveable metal vanes.

CAPACITOR, or **condenser,** an electrical component used to store electric charge (see ELECTRICITY) and to provide REACTANCE in alternating-current circuits. In essence, a capacitor consists of two conducting plates separated by a thin layer of insulator. When the plates are connected to the terminals of a BATTERY, a current flows until the capacitor is "charged," having one plate positive and the other negative. The ability of a capacitor to hold charge, its capacitance C, is the ratio of quantity of electricity on its plates, Q, to the potential difference between the plates, V. The electric energy stored in a capacitor is given by $\frac{1}{2}CV^2$. The capacitance of a

The Cape of Good Hope, so named because it marked the halfway point on voyages from Europe to India.

capacitor depends on the area of its plates, their separation and the DIELECTRIC constant of the insulator. Small fixed capacitors are commonly made with metal-foil plates and paraffin-paper insulation; to save space the plates and paper are rolled up into a tight cylinder. Variable capacitors used in RADIO tuners consist of movable intermeshing metal vanes separated by an air gap. Electrolytic capacitors, which must be connected with the correct polarity, also find use in flash guns.

CAP-DE-LA-MADELEINE, industrial city on the St. Lawrence R, producing newsprint. It is the site of the shrine of "Our Lady of the Rosary." Pop 31 463.

CAPE BRETON HIGHLANDS NATIONAL PARK, on Cape Breton Island, established 1936. A 400sq mi area, 1700ft above sea level, between the Atlantic and the Gulf of St. Lawrence.

CAPE BRETON ISLAND, in NE Nova Scotia, 110mi long, up to 75mi wide, separated from the Canadian mainland by the Strait of Canso (since 1955 joined by a causeway). Site of CAPE BRETON HIGHLANDS NATIONAL PARK. Local industries include tourism, lumbering, fishing and the mining of coal and gypsum.

CAPE BUFFALO, or African buffalo, *Syncerus caffer*, a massive black mammal with large horns. Formerly found all over Africa, its numbers are now greatly reduced due to disease and hunting.

CAPE COD, peninsula in Barnstable Co., SE Mass., 65mi long, up to 20mi in width, site of the first Pilgrim landing in 1620. Shipping, whaling, fishing and salt production were early industries; today the cape is famous for its cranberries, and its summer resorts such as Provincetown and Hyannis.

CAPE COD CANAL, a 17½mi long channel across CAPE COD (Mass.), privately built (1909–14) and bought by the US Government in 1927. One of the most heavily used toll-free waterways, it shortens the New York City–Boston route by 75mi.

CAPE GIRARDEAU, industrial city in SE Mo., on the Mississippi R, site of Southeast Missouri State College (1873). Pop 31 282.

CAPE HATTERAS, a promontory lying 30mi off the N.C. coast and long known as "the graveyard of the Atlantic" because of its rocky shoals.

CAPE HORN, lower tip of South America, known for its cold, stormy climate. Part of Chile, the cape's bare headland lies well S of the Strait of Magellan on Horn Island.

CAPE HUNTING DOG, *Lycaon pictus*, a large-eared wild dog resembling, but not related to, the hyena, and native to most of Africa. It hunts in packs, pursuing even the larger antelopes.

CAPE KENNEDY. See CANAVERAL, CAPE.

ČAPEK, Karel (1890–1938), Czech writer whose works, known for their humor and anti-authoritarian stand, include the plays *R.U.R.* (*Rossum's Universal Robots*, 1920) and *The Insect Play* (1921) and the novel *War with the Newts* (1936).

CAPELLA, Alpha Aurigae, the fifth brightest star in the night sky. It is a DOUBLE STAR, 13.8pc distant, each component having apparent magnitude +0.85, with possibly two further dim components.

CAPE LOOKOUT NATIONAL SEASHORE, area of 24 500 acres in SE N.C., the oustanding headland S of Cape Hatteras. Noted for its lighthouse, beaches and bird life.

CAPE MAY, city in S N.J., one of the oldest beach resorts in the US. Situated on Cape May Peninsula, 40mi SW of Atlantic City on the Atlantic Ocean, originally it was called Cape Island. Pop 4 392.

CAPE OF GOOD HOPE, rocky promontory near the S tip of Africa, 30mi S of CAPE TOWN, chief navigational hazard in rounding Africa. It was discovered by Bartholomew DIAZ in 1488, who named it Cape of Storms. Vasco da GAMA first sailed around it in 1497 into the Indian Ocean.

CAPER, *Capparis spinosa*, a trailing shrub native to the Mediterranean region, cultivated for its tender aromatic buds, which are pickled for use as pickles or in sauces such as tartare sauce.

CAPERCAILLIE, or capercailzie, *Tetrao urogallus*, a European gamebird of the grouse family, living in coniferous forests and feeding on plants. The cock is mainly gray, with green on the breast; the hen brown with a red patch on the breast.

CAPERNAUM or CAPHARNAUM, a small garrison and customs post of ancient Palestine on the NW shore of the Sea of Galilee, a center of Jesus' ministry. A 2nd- or 3rd-century synagogue has been excavated there.

CAPETIANS, ruling house of France (987–1328) which, by consolidating and extending its power, laid the basis for the French state. HUGH CAPET, founder of the dynasty, was elected king in 987. Though his rule and territory were limited, his successors gradually increased their land and control. Under the Capetian dynasty many basic administration characteristics of the French monarchy were established, including Parliament and the States General.

CAPE TOWN, legislative capital of South Africa and capital of Cape of Good Hope province. Founded by the Dutch East India Company, its first settlers arrived from Holland in 1652. It has a pleasant climate, excellent beaches and attractive scenery, and the country's largest harbor. Among its major exports are gold, diamonds, fruits, wines, skins, wool, mohair and corn. Pop 691 296.

CAPE VERDE ISLANDS, in the Atlantic, 320mi W of the African coast, a Portuguese overseas province until independence was proclaimed in July 1975. Of the 10 principal islands, São Tiago is the largest and contains Praia, the capital. Originally uninhabited, the islands became a slave trade station. Exports include coffee, fish, salt and oranges. Pop 246 000.

CAPE VERDE PENINSULA, in W central Senegal. The peninsula is formed by volcanic offshore islands and a landbridge. It is the westernmost point of Africa.

CAPE YORK PENINSULA, the northernmost point of Australia in NE Queensland, 280mi long, and ending in Cape York on Torres Strait.

CAP-HAÏTIEN, a seaport of N Haiti exporting coffee and sugar. It was the capital of colonial Haiti. Pop 44 123.

CAPILLARIES, minute BLOOD vessels concerned with supplying OXYGEN and nutrients to and removing waste products from the tissues. In the LUNGS capillaries pick up oxygen from the alveoli and release carbon dioxide. These processes occur by DIFFUSION. The capillaries are supplied with blood by ARTERIES and drained by VEINS.

CAPILLARITY, the name given to various SURFACE-TENSION phenomena in which the surface of a liquid confined in a narrow-bore tube rises above or is depressed below the level it would have if it were unconfined. When the attraction between the molecules of the liquid and those of the tube exceeds the combined effects of gravity and the attractive forces within the liquid, the liquid rises in the tube until EQUILIBRIUM is restored. Capillarity is of immense importance in nature, particularly in the transport of fluids in plants and through the soil.

CAPISTRANO, Saint Giovanni di (1386–1456), prominent Italian Franciscan preacher and severe papal inquisitor against the Hussites and other heretics and the Jews.

CAPITAL, the topmost part of a column, providing a structural support for the horizontal member or arch above. The characteristic Greek styles are: Doric, Ionic and Corinthian (See COLUMN.)

CAPITAL, in economics, those goods which are used in production—such as plant and equipment (*fixed capital*) and raw materials, components and semi-finished goods (*circulating capital*)—as opposed to goods intended for immediate consumption. To classical economists, capital was one of three main factors of production, the others being labor and land. Modern economists include "management skill" and "human capital," i.e. education and training. The problem being to find the most profitable combination of resources in the manufacture of goods, the decision to invest in capital is determined by the cost and availability of labor and natural resources, and the cost of capital (e.g. interest on the money used to buy equipment). Other factors, such as the state of the market, are also important. Modern industrial countries are highly capitalized, but, among the less developed countries, the lack of capital is often acute.

CAPITAL GAINS TAX, a tax on the difference between the amount an asset is sold for and its original purchase price, less any allowable depreciation. In the US short-term and long-term capital losses are deductible from capital gains within five years of the loss.

Various forms of capitals: (*left to right*) Doric, Ionic, Corinthian, Roman (cup-shaped), Romanesque, Gothic (root-shaped), Gothic (leaf-shaped).

Central dome of the Capitol in Washington, D.C. Crowned with a statue by Thomas Crawford, representing Freedom, it is made of iron and is over 145ft in diameter; from ground level to the top of the statue it stands 288ft high.

CAPITALISM, the economic system in which goods and services are provided by the efforts of private individuals and groups who own and control the means of production, compete with one another and aim to make a profit. Historically, first merchants, then factory owners and finally bankers have been dominant in the system, though, as defined by Lenin, the predominance of the state within the system is possible. Capitalism is defended by the argument that private ownership and FREE ENTERPRISE, with a minimum of state interference, is the most efficient method of operating the economy; its critics argue that the system produces luxuries for the rich rather than necessities for all.

CAPITAL PUNISHMENT (from Latin *caput*, or head), referring originally to death by decapitation and now to execution in general. Historically, there has been a wide variety of death penalties, but in the US electrocution is the most common, followed by lethal gas and hanging. Capital punishment has long been a center of debate as to whether it deters serious crime or is only a form of revenge. Its use has been declining recently as belief in rehabilitation has grown. In most civilized countries, capital punishment has been discontinued. But those who believe that capital punishment is necessary as a deterrent see their argument supported by recent statistics showing that violent crime has been increasing.

CAPITOL, The, federal government building in Washington, D.C. which houses the US Congress. The Capitol, in classical style, was built on 3½ acres of high ground known as Capitol Hill in Washington's center. Designed by William Thornton in 1792, its construction began the next year when President Washington laid the cornerstone. The Senate occupies the N wing (completed 1800), and the House of Representatives the S wing (completed 1807). The building was severely damaged by the British in 1814. After its reconstruction (completed 1863) no significant alterations were made until 1958–62, when the E facade was extended 32½ feet.

The constellation Capricornus, which in ancient times marked the winter solstice and so gave its name to the Tropic of Capricorn.

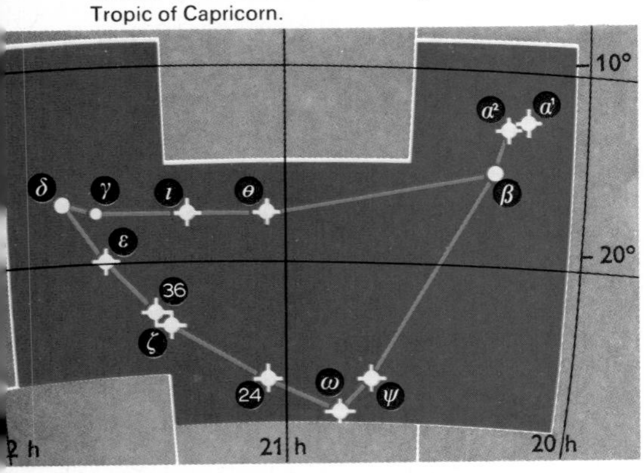

CAPITOL REEF NATIONAL PARK, covering 378sq mi of S Ut. It contains many strangely shaped rocks, cliffs and prehistoric Indian petroglyphs and petrified trees.

CAPITOLINE HILL. See SEVEN HILLS OF ROME.

CAPONE, Al (1899–1947), US gangster, born in Naples, became head of a lucrative Chicago crime syndicate, and was involved in many gang murders, including the St. Valentine's Day Massacre. Because of the difficulty in securing evidence against him he was eventually convicted only of income tax evasion.

CAPORETTO, Battle of (Oct.–Dec. 1917), major defeat of Italian military forces during WWI in NW Yugoslavia. The 600 000 Italian troops, weary after a 2½ year stalemate, either deserted or surrendered to the Austrian-German forces. The defeat caused Italy's allies to send reinforcements and eventually establish a unified Allied command.

CAPOTE, Truman (1924–   ), US writer known especially for *Breakfast at Tiffany's* (1958) and the "non-fiction" crime novel *In Cold Blood* (1965). Among his other works: *Other Voices, Other Rooms* (1948), *The Grass Harp* (1951).

CAPPADOCIA, a mountainous region of central Anatolia, Turkey, watered by the Halys R. A satrapy of the Persian Empire, it became a semi-independent kingdom under Ariarathes III. Caesarea Mazaca was its chief city.

CAPPADOCIAN FATHERS, term applied to three theologians from Cappadocia (BASIL THE GREAT, GREGORY OF NYSSA and GREGORY OF NAZIANZUS) who had great influence in shaping theological doctrine in the second half of the 4th century.

CAPRA, Frank (1897–   ), US film director and three-time Academy Award winner. With a gift for gentle satire and comic improvisation, he directed, among other films, *Mr. Deeds Goes To Town* (1936), *You Can't Take It With You* (1938) and *Lost Horizon* (1937).

CAPRERA, island in the Tyrrhenian Sea, off the NE coast of Sardinia. GARIBALDI lived here from 1856 to 1882.

CAPRI, Italian island resort in the Bay of Naples, site of the Villa Iovis of Roman Emperor TIBERIUS. Capri produces olive oil and wine, but its main industry is tourism. Anacapri, at the island's W end, is approachable from the sea by hundreds of steps, called the "Phoenician Stairs." Pop 8 025.

CAPRICORNUS (the Sea Goat), a fairly inconspicuous constellation of the S Hemisphere, lacking any bright stars, and the tenth sign of the ZODIAC. Lying between AQUARIUS and SAGITTARIUS, Capricornus in ancient times lay at the southernmost limit of the ECLIPTIC.

CAPRIVI STRIP, strip of land 40mi wide in South West Africa (now under mandate to the Union of South Africa), running E some 300mi between Angola and Zambia on the N and Botswana on the S. Formerly part of German South West Africa (1890–1919).

CAPSULE, dry, dehiscent FRUIT, developed from two or more carpels and containing numerous seeds. Seeds are shed by a number of methods including pores at the top of capsule (POPPY) or detachment of the apex (PIMPERNEL).

CAPTAIN JACK (d. 1873), or *Kintpuash*, a chief of the MODOC INDIANS who with a few followers rebelled against their removal by the US government to a reservation in Ore. and returned to their homeland in N Cal., taking refuge in the lava beds. Government attacks led to the Modoc War (1872–73) and the assassination of General Edward CANBY, for which Captain Jack was hanged.

CAPUCHINS, monkeys of the genus *Cebus*, the commonest in South America. Popular as pets, capuchins live in troops and eat fruit and small animals.

CAPUCHINS, Roman Catholic order of friars and an independent branch of the Franciscans. Founded (1525) by Matteo di Basico, a Franciscan who sought a return to the simplicity of St. Francis's life, the order is distinguished by the pointed hood, or *capuccino*.

CAPULIN MOUNTAIN NATIONAL MONUMENT, in NE N.M., established in 1916 in an area of 1.2sq mi. It is the cinder cone of an ancient volcano (8 215ft).

CAPYBARAS, two species of the world's largest RODENT, living in South America. Like a large guinea pig, it can weigh up to 54kg (119lb) and be as high as 540mm (21.3in) at the shoulder. Capybaras live a largely aquatic life.

CARABAO, *Bubalus bubalis*, also known as the Asiatic water buffalo. Probably native to India, the domesticated water BUFFALO is found today from SE Asia to Egypt.

CARACAL, *Caracal caracal*, or Desert Lynx, a medium-sized cat of Africa and S Asia. Fawn colored, the caracal lives in grassland, bush or rocky country.

CARACALLA (188–217 AD), or Marcus Aurelius Antoninus, son of Septimius SEVERUS, tyrannical Roman emperor notable for his edict (212) granting Roman citizenship to all freemen of the Empire. He left the magnificent baths in Rome that bear his name.

CARACARAS, long-legged American hawks, related to FALCONS. They have a bare patch of skin at the base of the bill which is an adaptation for carrion eating, though caracaras also hunt for live prey and will eat fruit.

CARACAS, Venezuelan capital, near the Caribbean Sea at an altitude of 3 020ft, founded in 1567 by Diego de Losada, and the birthplace of Simón BOLÍVAR in 1783. Independence from Spain was achieved in 1821, as part of the Republic of Gran Colombia. In 1829 Caracas became the capital of independent Venezuela.

After WWII and the discovery of oil in Maracaibo, Caracas greatly expanded. Industries include textiles, cement, steel products, paper, leatherwork and furniture. Pop 2 184 000.

The strikingly modern buildings of Caracas, the capital of Venezuela, are evidence of the extensive rebuilding made necessary by the city's dramatic growth over the last four decades.

CARAMEL ($[C_{12}H_{18}O_9]_x$), brown syrupy substance made by heating SUGAR to 180°C with a little water and sometimes sodium carbonate. It is used as a coloring and flavoring in foodstuffs, including a soft candy of the same name.

CARAPACE, the hard outer covering on many INVERTEBRATE and a few VERTEBRATE animals. It is made of bone or the substance **chitin**, which is similar to CELLULOSE. The carapace of insects and other invertebrates forms part of the external skeleton. In vertebrates, such as the turtle, it serves a protective function.

CARAT, a unit of MASS used for weighing precious stones. Since 1913 the internationally accepted carat has been the metric carat (CM) of 200mg. The purity of GOLD is also expressed in carats (usually spelled "karat" in the US). Here one karat is a 24th part; thus, pure gold is 24-karat; "18-karat gold" contains 75% gold and 25% other NOBLE METALS, and so on.

CARAVAGGIO, Michelangelo Merisi da

(1573–1610), Italian Baroque painter who achieved startling and dramatic effects with an interesting technique of shadow and light (see CHIAROSCURO). Among his finest works are the *Death of the Virgin* and *Supper at Emmaus*.

CARAVEL, light wooden ship of about 55 tons, with two or three masts, much used by Spanish and Portuguese explorers of the 15th century. Two of Columbus' ships were caravels.

CARAWAY, *Carum carvi*, a member of the carrot family (Umbelliferae) cultivated in Europe and N Africa for its so-called seed (really a FRUIT), which is used for garnishing and flavoring bread, cakes and cheese. The distilled aromatic oil is used in medicine as a stimulant and carminative and for flavoring liqueurs such as Kümmel.

CARBIDES. See CARBON.

CARBOHYDRATES, a large and important class of ALIPHATIC COMPOUNDS, widespread and abundant in nature, where they serve as an immediate energy source; cellulose is the chief structural material for plants. Most carbohydrates have chemical formulas $(CH_2O)_n$, and so were named as hydrates of carbon—which, however, they are not. Systematic names of carbohydrates end in -ose. They are generally divided into four groups, the simplest being the **monosaccharides** or simple SUGARS and the **disaccharides** or double sugars. The **oligosaccharides** (uncommon in nature) consist of three to six monosaccharide molecules linked together. The **polysaccharides** are POLYMERS, usually homogeneous, of monosaccharide units, into which they are broken down again when used for energy. The main plant polysaccharides are CELLULOSE and STARCH; in animals a compound resembling starch, GLYCOGEN, is formed in the muscles and liver. Other polysaccharides include AGAR, ALGIN, CHITIN, DEXTRIN, GUM acacia, INSULIN and PECTIN. Carbohydrates play an important role in food chains (see ECOLOGY): they are formed in plants by PHOTOSYNTHESIS, and are converted by ruminant animals into PROTEIN. They also form one of the major classes of human FOOD (see also NUTRITION). In Europe and the US they provide a third to a half of the calories in the diet, of which starch and the various sugars supply about half each. In less developed countries carbohydrates, especially starch, are even more important.

CARBOLIC ACID. See PHENOL.

CARBOLOY, a common name for the ultrahard BEARING and cutting-tool material, TUNGSTEN carbide (WC).

CARBON (C), nonmetal in Group IVA of the PERIODIC TABLE. It is unique among elements in that a whole branch of chemistry (ORGANIC CHEMISTRY) is devoted to it, because of the vast number of compounds it forms. The simple carbon compounds described below are usually regarded as inorganic.

Carbon occurs in nature both uncombined (COAL) and as CARBONATES, carbon dioxide in the atmosphere, and PETROLEUM. It exhibits ALLOTROPY, occurring in three contrasting forms: DIAMOND, GRAPHITE and "white" carbon, a transparent allotrope discovered in 1969 by subliming graphite. So-called amorphous carbon is actually microcrystalline graphite; it occurs naturally, and is found as COKE, CHARCOAL and **carbon black** (obtained from the incomplete burning of petroleum, and used in pigments and printer's ink, and to reinforce rubber). Amorphous carbon is widely used for ADSORPTION, because of its large surface area. A new synthetic form is carbon fiber, which is very strong and is used to reinforce plastics and to make electrically-conducting fabrics.

Carbon has several ISOTOPES: C^{12} (used as a standard for ATOMIC WEIGHTS) is much the most common, but C^{13} makes up 1.11% of natural carbon. C^{10}, C^{11}, C^{14}, C^{15} and C^{16} are all radioactive. C^{14} has the relatively long half-life of 5730yr, and is continuously formed in the atmosphere by COSMIC RAY bombardment; it is used in RADIOCARBON DATING.

The element (especially as diamond) is rather inert, but all forms will burn in air at a high temperature to give carbon monoxide in a poor supply of oxygen, and carbon dioxide in excess oxygen. Fluorine will attack

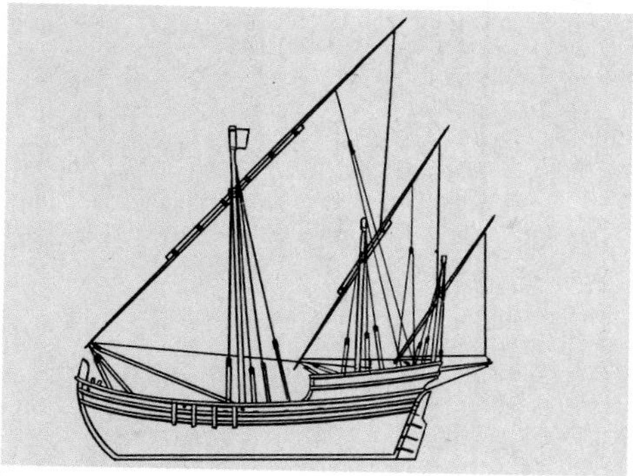

The caravel, a remarkably small vessel, was used by many of the Spanish and Portuguese explorers, including Columbus, on their long and dangerous voyages.

carbon at room temperature to give carbon tetrafluoride, and strong oxidizing agents will attack graphite. Carbon will combine with many metals at high temperatures, forming carbides. Carbon shows a covalency of four, the bonds pointing toward the vertices of a tetrahedron, unless multiple bonding occurs. AW 12.011.

Carbides, binary compounds of carbon with a metal, prepared by heating the metal or its oxide with carbon. Ionic carbides are mainly acetylides (C_2^{2-}) which react with water to give ACETYLENE, or methanides (C^{4-}) which give METHANE. There are also metallic interstitial carbides, and the covalent boron carbide (B_4C) and silicon carbide (see CARBORUNDUM). **Carbon Dioxide** (CO_2), colorless, odorless gas. It is nontoxic, but can cause suffocation. The air contains 0.03% carbon dioxide, which is exhaled by animals and absorbed by plants (see RESPIRATION; PHOTOSYNTHESIS; CARBON CYCLE). Carbon dioxide is prepared in the laboratory by reacting a CARBONATE with acid; industrially it is obtained by calcining LIMESTONE, burning coke in excess air, or from FERMENTATION. At atmospheric pressure, it solidifies at −78.5°C to form "dry ice" (used for refrigeration and CLOUD seeding) which sublimes above that temperature; liquid carbon dioxide, formed under pressure, is used in fire extinguishers. Carbon dioxide is also used to make carbonated drinks. When dissolved in water an equilibrium is set up, with CARBONATE, BICARBONATE and HYDROGEN ions formed, and a low concentration of **Carbonic Acid** (H_2CO_3). **Carbon Disulfide** (CS_2), colorless liquid, of nauseous odor due to impurities; highly toxic and flammable. Used as a solvent and in the manufacture of rayon and CELLOPHANE. mp −111°C, bp 46°C, sg 1.261 (22°C). **Carbon Monoxide** (CO), colorless, odorless gas. It is produced by burning carbon or organic compounds in a restricted supply of oxygen, for example, in poorly-ventilated stoves, or the incomplete combustion of gasoline in AUTOMOBILE engines. It is manufactured as a component of WATER GAS. It reacts with the halogens and sulfur, and with many metals, to give carbonyls. Carbon monoxide is an excellent reducing agent at high temperatures, and is used for smelting metal ores (see BLAST FURNACE; IRON). It is also used for the manufacture of METHANOL and other organic compounds. It is a component of manufactured gas, but not of natural gas. Carbon monoxide is toxic because it combines with hemoglobin, the red BLOOD pigment, to form pink carboxyhemoglobin, which is stable, and will not perform the function of transporting oxygen to the tissues. mp −199°C, bp −191°C. **Carbon Tetrachloride** (CCl_4), colorless liquid, nonflammable but toxic, made by chlorinating carbon disulfide. Used as a fire extinguisher, a solvent (especially for dry-cleaning) and in the manufacture of FREON. mp −23°C, bp 77°C. (See also CYANIDES; CYANOGEN.)

CARBONARI (Italian: charcoal burners), members of a revolutionary secret society in 19th-century Italy. Although originally formed to restore the Bourbons to Naples, the Carbonari later instigated many revolts against conservative regimes in Italy. The name was also used by French, Spanish and Portuguese revolutionaries.

CARBONATES, salts of carbonic acid (see CARBON), containing the CO_3^{2-} ion. A solution of carbon dioxide in water reacts with a base to form a carbonate. Carbonates are decomposed by heating to give the metal oxide and carbon dioxide. They also react with acids to give carbon dioxide. Many minerals are carbonates, the most important being CALCITE, DOLOMITE and MAGNESITE. (For sodium carbonate see SODIUM).

CARBON BLACK. See CARBON.

CARBON CYCLE, in biology, a very important cycle by which carbon, obtained from the atmosphere as carbon dioxide, is absorbed by green plants, synthesized into organic compounds and then returned to the atmosphere as carbon dioxide. The organic compounds, particularly CARBOHYDRATES, are synthesized in plants from carbon dioxide and water in the presence of CHLOROPHYLL and light by a process known as PHOTOSYNTHESIS. The carbohydrates are then broken down to carbon dioxide and water either by the plant during RESPIRATION or after death by putrefying BACTERIA and FUNGI. (See also PLANT.)

CARBON CYCLE, or carbon-nitrogen cycle, in physics, the chain of nuclear FUSION reactions, catalyzed by CARBON nuclei (see CATALYSIS), which is the main source of ENERGY in the hotter STARS, though of minor importance in the SUN and cooler stars where proton–proton fusion is the chief reaction. Overall, four PROTONS are converted to one ALPHA PARTICLE, with destruction of some matter and consequent evolution of energy (see RELATIVITY). Most of the gamma-radiation produced is absorbed within the star, and energy is released as heat and light. The carbon cycle was first described by Hans BETHE.

$$
\begin{aligned}
{}_{6}C^{12} + {}_{1}H^{1} &\rightarrow {}_{7}N^{13} + \gamma \\
{}_{7}N^{13} &\rightarrow {}_{6}C^{13} + e^{+} + \nu \\
{}_{6}C^{13} + {}_{1}H^{1} &\rightarrow {}_{7}N^{14} + \gamma \\
{}_{7}N^{14} + {}_{1}H^{1} &\rightarrow {}_{8}O^{15} + \gamma \\
O^{15} &\rightarrow {}_{7}N^{15} + e^{+} + \nu \\
N^{15} + H^{1} &\rightarrow {}_{2}He^{4} + {}_{6}C^{12}
\end{aligned}
$$

The sequence of reactions in the carbon cycle.

CARBONDALE, city in SW Ill. It is a mining and agricultural center founded in 1852. Pop 22816.

CARBONDALE, city on the Lackawanna R in NE Pa. The world's first underground anthracite mine was inaugurated here in 1831. Pop 13808.

CARBONIFEROUS, collective term used mainly in Europe for the MISSISSIPPIAN and PENNSYLVANIAN.

CARBORANES, compounds derived from polyhedral BORANES by substitution of CARBON for BORON atoms. They are relatively unreactive and thermally stable, and form many derivatives, including highly stable organo-inorganic polymers.

CARBORUNDUM, or silicon carbide (SiC), black, cubic crystalline solid, made by heating COKE with SILICA in an electric furnace. It is almost as hard as DIAMOND (whose structure it resembles), and hence it is used as an abrasive. It is inert, refractory and a good heat conductor, so is used in making high-temperature bricks; at high temperatures it is a SEMICONDUCTOR. subl 2700°C (with decomposition).

CARBOXYLIC ACIDS, a major class of organic compounds, of general formula RCOOH where R is an organic group; those acids where R is a straight-chain alkyl group (see ALKANES) are sometimes known as **fatty acids**, and are named systematically as alkanoic acids from the corresponding alkane. Some carboxylic acids occur free in nature, including FORMIC and ACETIC acids—the two simplest—and CITRIC, LACTIC, MALIC and TARTARIC acids. These, and others including BENZOIC, OXALIC and SALICYLIC acids, are found also as their salts and ESTERS. Many of the fatty acids, including OLEIC, PALMITIC and STEARIC acids, occur in oils and FATS as esters of GLYCEROL (see also SOAPS AND DETERGENTS). Carboxylic acids are made by HYDROLYSIS of esters, ACID ANHYDRIDES or ACID CHLORIDES, or by oxidation of ALDEHYDES or primary ALCOHOLS. They are weak ACIDS, the exact strength depending on the ELECTRONEGATIVITY of the group R. and so are often used with their salts as

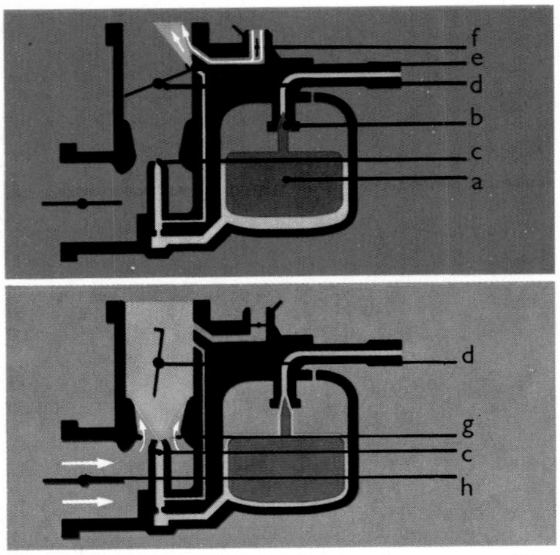

Above: The most basic type of carburetor, shown with the engine in idling position. The float (a), working off the needle valve (b), maintains a constant level of gasoline in the float chamber, which is directly connected to the jet nozzle (c).

The fuel intake valve (d) is closed, but a small amount of gasoline is sucked in from the idling jet (e). The quantity supplied can be regulated at (f) where the air intake can be controlled.

Below: The carburetor as it functions in a moving automobile. The fuel intake valve (d) is open. As the air flows into the carburetor (shown by white arrows), its speed is increased by the venturi (g) and the higher air pressure in the float chamber forces gasoline out through the nozzle (c). Both in idling and in fast running, the choke valve (h) is open; it is closed only for a cold-weather start, when more gasoline and less air flow into the engine.

BUFFERS. Many derivatives of carboxylic acids are important in nature or chemical synthesis: they include acid anhydrides, acid chlorides, AMIDES, esters, NITRILES and peroxyacids (see PEROXIDES). (See also AMINO ACIDS.)

CARBUNCLE. See BOIL.

CARBURETOR, an important element in most automobile engines, the carburetor mixes air and GASOLINE in the correct ratio for most efficient combustion (usually about 15:1, air:gasoline, by weight). Most simply, a carburetor has a tube constricted at one point into a narrow throat, or VENTURI. The speed of air flowing through the venturi increases and hence its pressure decreases: fuel from a reservoir (the float chamber) is therefore sucked in through a hole, or jet, at this point. The fuel mixture then passes through a throttle valve, which controls the rate at which the mixture enters the engine and hence the engine speed. A CHOKE in the air-intake regulates the air supply and thus the richness of the mixture. In practice, carburetors incorporate various means of ensuring constancy of mixture strength during running. High-performance engines may use more than one carburetor or a FUEL INJECTION system. (See also INTERNAL-COMBUSTION ENGINE.)

CARCASSONNE, ancient city in SW France. Originally Roman, it was extended by the Visigoths and in medieval times it became an ALBIGENSIAN stronghold. The extensively restored ramparts around the old town are the most complete medieval fortification extant. Pop 40 580.

CARCHEMISH, ancient city on the W bank of the Euphrates in Syria, commanding an important caravan crossing. First occupied in Neolithic times, it declined after the 6th century BC. It has been the site of many archaeological excavations.

CARCINOGENS. See CANCER.

CARCINOMA. See CANCER.

CARDAMOM, *Elettaria cardamomum*, a spice plant that is native to India and cultivated in Sri Lanka and South America, often as an additional crop on rubber and tea plantations. The seeds are used for flavoring and for medicinal purposes.

CARDANO, Girolamo (1501–1576), Italian physician and astrologer, chiefly remembered for his contributions to mathematics. In particular, he developed and published a general solution for cubic equations.

CÁRDENAS, Lázaro (1895–1970), Mexican soldier and politician. He joined the Mexican revolutionary forces in 1913, rising to the rank of general. President 1934–40, he initiated many radical reforms, including the expropriation of land and nationalization of foreign-owned oil companies.

CARDIAC, relating to the HEART, as in cardiac surgery; also to the cardia or upper part of STOMACH.

CARDIFF, city in S Wales. Established around a Norman castle in the 11th century, it is the administrative center for Wales, and a port exporting Welsh coal, iron and steel. It houses several educational and cultural institutions, and also the National Museum of Wales. Pop 278 221.

CARDIGAN, James Thomas Brudenell, 7th Earl of (1797–1868), British general in the CRIMEAN WAR, who ordered the charge against the Russians at Balaklava in which the Light Brigade was destroyed. A vain and quarrelsome man, he is remembered as an incompetent commanding officer.

CARDINAL, hierarchically high-ranking official of the Roman Catholic Church, whose principal duties include the election of the pope, counseling the papacy and administrating Church government. Cardinals are chosen by the pope, and have the title of Eminence. Their insignia consists of scarlet cassock, sash, biretta (skullcap) and hat, and a ring.

There are three orders: *cardinal bishops* of the sees near Rome; *cardinal priests* (cardinal archbishops) with responsibilities outside the district of Rome; and *cardinal deacons*, who have been titular bishops since 1962. Cardinal bishops and cardinal deacons are members of the CURIA, the central administrative body of the Church. They head the *tribunals*, the courts of the Church. Together, the cardinals form the Sacred College, which elects the pope. The cardinalate originated in early 6th-century Rome. The term cardinal is derived from Latin *cardo*, meaning hinge, reflecting the essential working relationship between this institution and the papacy.

CARDINAL, *Pyrrhuloxia cardinalis*, a North American songbird, about 230mm (9in) long with a pointed crest. Both female and male sing most of the year. They can be a pest, as they feed on fruit and seeds. There may be two or three broods raised each year in southern regions. They nest throughout the year.

CARDINAL NUMBER, one that describes the number of elements in a SET. For example, in the phrase "my 3 oranges," 3 is a cardinal number. (See also ORDINAL NUMBER; TRANSFINITE CARDINAL NUMBER.)

CARDING, process used in TEXTILE manufacture whereby the fibers are laid out parallel to each other, then gathered into strands (card slivers) about 1in (25mm) thick. This process may be followed by **combing**, where the fibers in the sliver below a certain length are removed, those remaining being set more accurately parallel.

CARDOZO, Benjamin Nathan (1870–1938), US jurist and Supreme Court justice (1932–38) after an impressive career at the bar and in the N.Y. courts. He believed that the courts should not merely interpret the law but help create it, particularly in adapting it to changing social conditions. His many significant decisions reflect this view.

CARDS. See PLAYING CARDS.

CARDUCCI, Giosuè (1835–1907), Italian scholar and patriotic poet. His *Hymn to Satan* (1863) is an anticlerical, political satire; the *Barbarian Odes* (1877–89) are perhaps his best work. He won the 1906 Nobel Prize for Literature.

CARE (Cooperative for American Relief to Everywhere, Inc.), a charity founded in 1945, initially for aid to Europe but now operating worldwide. MEDICO (Medical International Cooperation Organization), a medical relief agency, became part of CARE in 1962.

CAREW, Thomas (c1594–1640), English poet and lyricist, in later life a courtier of CHARLES I. His verse, influenced by DONNE, combines a light "cavalier" style with metaphysical elements. He remains best known for his long amatory poem *The Rapture*.

CAREY, James Barron (1911–), US labor leader, past president of the United Electrical, Radio and Machine Workers (UEW) (1936–41) and founder and president of the International Union of Electrical, Radio and Machine Workers (IUE) from 1950 to 1965.

CAREY, Mathew (1760–1839), Irish publisher and editor who fled to America in 1784 to escape prosecution for his criticism of the British government. He founded the *Pennsylvania Herald* (1785) and was prominent in Philadelphia publishing from 1790.

CARGO CULTS, religious movements common among the natives of New Guinea and Melanesia, who believe that, by aping in ritual the European society they do not understand, they can persuade supernatural powers to give them European material wealth—"cargo." Often worshiping John Frum, a messianic figure, the cults have even involved building airstrips to receive the "cargo."

CARIA, ancient area in SW Asia Minor, now the districts of S Aydin and W Mugla in Turkey. Most of it belonged to Greek states; the major cities of Cnidus and Halicarnassus were situated on the coast.

CARIBBEAN CURRENT, warm OCEAN CURRENT, fed by the N EQUATORIAL CURRENT, flowing W through the Caribbean, then E through the Florida Straits as the Florida Current to join the GULF STREAM.

CARIBBEAN SEA, a warm oceanic basin bordered by Central America to the E, South America to the S, and the West Indies to the N and E. The GULF STREAM originates here. Columbus' first landfall was on one of the islands of the West Indies; the region was first explored by Spain and much of it was first colonized by Spaniards. The area was in dispute between various countries, primarily Spain, France, Britain and the Netherlands, until the end of the NAPOLEONIC WARS. The construction of the Panama Canal from 1881 increased trade and traffic in the area.

CARIB INDIANS, inhabitants of the Caribbean before the Spanish conquest, living in the Lesser Antilles and parts of South America. They were farmers and formed villages presided over by headmen. Persistent raiders of other tribes, they ate their captives. The Caribs were practically exterminated after the Spanish settlement, apart from a few on the island of Aruba. Some descendants survive among the area's population today.

CARIBOO MOUNTAINS, in E British Columbia, are the northernmost part of the Columbia mountains. The site of the Wells Gray and Bowron Provincial Parks, they contain extensive mineral deposits.

CARIBOU, city in NE Me., on the Aroostock R near the New Brunswick border. It is a shipping center for a potato-growing area and a winter-sports center, and is known for its wood products. Pop 10 419.

CARIBOU, *Rangifer tarandess*, the only member of the DEER family (Cervidae) in which both sexes bear antlers. They were at one time essential food animals for the Canadian Indians. They live wild in Canada and Siberia, while the semidomesticated reindeer of the same family live in Greenland and Scandinavia. They can travel over boggy or snow-covered ground and they live on lichen, dry grass and twigs.

CARICATURE AND CARTOON. A caricature is a sketch exaggerating or distorting characteristics of its subject for satirical purposes; generally used of pictures, the term may also describe literary works. Caricature became an established form by the 18th century, in the hands of GOYA in Spain and HOGARTH in England, followed by ROWLANDSON, CRUIKSHANK and TENNIEL, and the savagely witty DAUMIER in France. With the freer style of the 20th century it developed into a powerful means of communication. NAST's political caricatures helped topple the Tweed Ring and TAMMANY HALL. Today artists such as MAULDIN, David Levine and Albert Hirschfeld are household names in America. Most prominent in the UK is Ralph Steadman.

Cartoons are related to, and often contain, caricature. Originally meaning a preparatory sketch, the term derives from a series of architectural "cartoons" parodied by *Punch* magazine in 1843. Today it also includes the comic strip, the political cartoon and cartoon ANIMATION. The cartoon has been increasingly adopted as an art form by POP ART. Prominent US cartoonists include Charles ADDAMS, Al Capp, Gahan Wilson, Charles Schultz, John Hart and Walt Kelly; in Britain today the cartoons of Carl Giles and Bill Tidy are among the most popular.

CARIES, decay or softening of hard tissues, usually TEETH, but also used for BONE, especially spinal TUBERCULOSIS. Dental caries is bacterial decay of dentine and enamel (see TEETH), hastened by sugary diet and poor oral hygiene. Fluoride in small quantities protects against caries.

CARILLON, musical instrument, usually permanently set in a bell-tower, consisting of an accurately-tuned series of bells on which tunes can be played from a keyboard and pedal console. It originated in the Netherlands and is very popular in the US today. Electronic carillons create bell tones artificially.

CARISSIMI, Giacomo (1605–1674), Italian composer of cantatas and oratorios, of which he was a pioneer. His masterpiece, *Jephte*, developed the dramatic form of the oratorio and strongly influenced Handel and Bach.

CARLETON, Sir Guy (1724–1808), British soldier and governor-general of Quebec. He was responsible for the QUEBEC ACT of 1774 which guaranteed the French the right to speak French and to practice their religion. During the American Revolution, he led the defense of Quebec against Benedict ARNOLD and later captured Crown Point, N.Y. In 1782 he was appointed commander-in-chief of the British army in North America; he was several times governor-general of Canada.

CARLISLE, borough, seat of Cumberland Co., Pa., 18mi SW of Harrisburg. A major industry is electronics crystal production. Pop 18079.

CARLISTS, Spanish supporters of the claim of Don Carlos (1788–1855) and his successors to the Spanish throne. They were part of the Falange during the Spanish Civil War. The present pretender is Prince Carlos Hugo de Bourbon-Parma.

CARLOS, name of Spanish kings. See CHARLES.

CARLOTA (1840–1927), empress of Mexico, wife of Archduke MAXIMILIAN of Austria. When NAPOLEON III stopped supporting Maximilian as emperor, she returned to Europe to seek other assistance, but failed. After Maximilian's execution she went mad and spent the rest of her life in seclusion in Belgium.

CARLSBAD, resort city in Cal. with mineral springs, beaches and a state park. It produces electronic instruments, winter vegetables and fruit. Pop 14944.

CARLSBAD, resort city in N.M., seat of Eddy Co., near the CARLSBAD CAVERNS. A trading center, it has important potash mines. Pop 21297.

CARLSBAD CAVERNS, a series of underground caves in SE N.M. The caverns consist of a three-level chain of limestone chambers studded with magnificent stalactites and stalagmites. They were discovered in 1901 and are millions of years old. The main chamber is 4000ft long and in places 300ft high; there are over 40mi of explored passages.

CARLYLE, Thomas (1795–1881), Scottish historian and philosopher. His famous *French Revolution* (1837) is a vivid but idiosyncratic presentation of the event rather than a factual account. Believing that man's progress was due to individual "heroes," he scorned egalitarianism, always extolling the right of the stronger. Many of his books, such as *Sartor Resartus* (1833–39), *On Heroes* (1841) and *Past and Present* (1843), are still read, but as literature rather than history.

CARMAN, (William) Bliss (1861–1929), Canadian poet and essayist. He is now best remembered for *Low Tide on Grand Pré* (1893) and *Songs from Vagabondia* (1894, 1896, 1901), volumes of love and nature poems.

CARMEL, Mount, mountain ridge extending into the sea in N Israel. The city of Haifa is at its foot. Carmel is often mentioned in the Old Testament, especially in connection with Elijah. Early Christian hermits lived in caves in the area.

CARMEL-BY-THE-SEA, or Carmel, town in Cal., situated on Carmel Bay, S of Monterey. Famous as an artists' colony, it has been the home of Henry Miller and Joan Baez, among others. Pop 4525.

CARMELITES, Friars of Our Lady of Mount Carmel, a religious order of the Roman Catholic Church. It is named for Mount Carmel, in Israel, where it originated about 1150. The Carmelites' strict rule was based on silence and solitude but it was slightly relaxed by the English prior, Saint Simon Stock (d. 1265). Saint THERESA OF ÁVILA and Saint JOHN OF THE CROSS were members, and in 1593 founded a separate branch, the Discalced (Barefoot) Carmelites. The orders' typical clothing consists of a brown habit and scapular, with a white mantle and black hood.

CARMICHAEL, unincorporated settlement in Sacramento Co., Cal. It is 10mi E of Sacramento. Pop 37625.

CARMICHAEL, Hoagland "Hoagy" (1889–1970), US songwriter, best known for his *Stardust* (1930). He received an Academy Award for *In the Cool, Cool of the Evening* (1951). Many of his tunes have become jazz standards.

CARMICHAEL, Stokeley (1941–   ), US BLACK POWER leader. Prominent in the Civil Rights movement in the 1960s, he then advocated violent revolution and spent some time in exile in Algeria. He later argued for the use of political and economic power to attain black demands.

CARMINA BURANA, a collection of about 300 songs by the Goliards, medieval wandering scholars who begged and sang their way from university to university in the 13th century. (See also ORFF, Carl.)

CARMINE, a red coloring matter found in the COCHINEAL insect. A Franciscan friar discovered the substance in 1756. After boiling the insects the coloring substance is obtained by adding acid.

Young barren-ground caribou in Alaska, distinguished from the woodland caribou by its more delicately branched antlers. Its broad hooves fringed with hair enable it to travel over snow and boggy ground.

CARMONA, António Óscar de Fragoso (1869–1951), Portuguese general and politician who took power in 1926. He outlawed the party system and remained president until his death. He was virtually a dictator but established internal stability.

CARNAC, French town near which are extensive alignments of megaliths (see MEGALITHIC MONUMENTS), a DOLMEN and two BARROWS. The monuments are believed to be of late STONE AGE origin.

CARNAP, Rudolf (1891–1970), German-US logician and philosopher of science, a leading figure in the Vienna Circle (see LOGICAL POSITIVISM), who later turned to study problems of linguistic philosophy and the role of probability in inductive reasoning.

CARNARVON, George Edward Stanhope Molyneux Herbert, 5th Earl of (1866–1923), English Egyptologist. His excavations with Howard Carter in the Valley of Kings area revealed tombs of the 12th and 18th dynasties and, in Nov. 1922, the tomb of TUTANKHAMEN.

CARNATIC (or Karnatik), historic kingdom, a province and linguistic area in S India, between the Eastern Ghats and the Coromandel Coast. Annexed to British India in 1801, it is roughly coextensive with the modern state of Karnataka (formerly Mysore).

CARNATIONS, plants of the genus *Dianthus*, which also includes PINKS and SWEET WILLIAMS. Carnations are very popular garden and greenhouse plants, much prized for their colorful many-petaled, fragrant flowers.

CARNAUBA, *Copernicia cerifera*, the wax palm of Brazil. The name carnauba is also given to an important vegetable wax produced from the young leaves. The wax is used mainly for floor and shoe polish.

CARNÉ, Marcel (1903–   ), French motion-picture maker noted especially for *Quai des Brumes* (1938) and *Les Portes de la Nuit* (1946).

CARNEGIE, borough in SW Pa., a suburb of Pittsburgh. Named for Andrew CARNEGIE, its main manufactures are steel and other metal products and chemicals. Pop 10864.

CARNEGIE, Andrew (1835–1919), US steel magnate and philanthropist. Born in Dunfermline, Scotland, he emigrated with his family and acquired his fortune entirely through his own efforts, rising from bobbin-boy in a cotton factory to railroad manager and then steel producer at a time of great demand. In an essay, *The Gospel of Wealth* (1889), he formulated his belief that the duty of the rich is to distribute their surplus wealth, and in 1900 he began to set up the vast number of charitable and educational institutions for which he is remembered, including libraries, pension funds, educational trusts, grants to universities in Scotland and the US, patriotic funds, a Temple of Peace at The Hague and the CARNEGIE FOUNDATIONS.

CARNEGIE FOUNDATIONS, philanthropic organizations established by Andrew CARNEGIE to advance education, research and world peace. The Carnegie Institution of Washington, D.C., supports research in physical and biological sciences. The Carnegie Foundation for the Advancement of Teaching works to improve higher education, and the Carnegie Corporation of New York endows projects in preschool education and education for the disadvantaged. The Carnegie Endowment for International Peace promotes peace through studies of international law and diplomacy. These and other organizations set a pattern for other major institutions such as the Ford and Rockefeller foundations.

CARNEGIE HALL, concert hall in New York City, named for Andrew CARNEGIE. It was opened in 1891 with a concert conducted by Tchaikovsky, and was the home of the New York Philharmonic Orchestra until 1959. A citizens' group saved the building from demolition in 1960.

CARNELIAN, or **cornelian,** translucent variety of CHALCEDONY, colored red by colloidal HEMATITE; a semiprecious GEM stone widely used in classical times for intaglio signets. (See also SARD.)

CARNIVAL, a festive season, specifically that preceding Lent in many Roman Catholic countries. Today Rome and Venice in Italy, Rio de Janeiro in Brazil and New Orleans in the US have colorful carnivals with their own folklore and tradition. The term is also applied to traveling amusement parks in the US.

CARNIVORA, order of flesh-eating MAMMALS. Daggerlike canine teeth, cutting cheek teeth (*carnassials*) and sharp claws are distinctive features. The cats stalk their prey; dogs run it down. BEARS are now mainly vegetarian, except for the polar bear.

CARNIVORE, any animal that feeds exclusively on other animals. Carnivores are essentially of two types: trappers, that lie in wait for prey, and hunters that actively hunt their prey.

CARNIVOROUS PLANT. See INSECTIVOROUS PLANTS.

CARNOT, Lazare Nicolas Marguerite (1753–1823), French soldier and politician; "Organizer of Victory" for the Revolutionary armies. Disapproving of Napoleon he resigned as minister for war in 1800 and was exiled as a regicide by Louis XVIII in 1816.

CARNOT, Nicholas Léonard Sadi (1796–1832), French physicist who, seeking to improve the EFFICIENCY of the STEAM ENGINE, devised the **Carnot cycle** (1824) on the basis of which Lord KELVIN and R. J. E. CLAUSIUS formulated the second law of THERMODYNAMICS. The Carnot cycle, which postulates a heat engine working at maximum thermal efficiency, demonstrates that the efficiency of such an engine does not depend on its mode of operation but only the TEMPERATURES at which it accepts and discards heat ENERGY.

CARNOTITE, soft, yellow radioactive mineral, potassium uranyl vanadate ($K_2[UO_2]_2[VO_4]_2 \cdot nH_2O$), a major ore of URANIUM and VANADIUM. It is found in Col., Wyo., S.D., Pa., Siberia, Zaire and Australia.

CARO, Joseph ben Ephraim (1488–1575), Jewish talmudist and philosopher whose codification of Jewish law, the *Shulhan 'Arukh* (1565), became the standard authority. Caro's family were Spanish Jews who settled in Constantinople; in later life he became a leader of the Jewish community in Palestine.

CAROB, *Ceratonia siliqua*, a leguminous tree native to the E Mediterranean and used elsewhere as an ornamental. The pods, which have a 50% sugar content, are used as a stock food. They also yield a gum important in making textiles, food, leather, rubber and cosmetics.

CAROL, a rejoicing song, usually religious in content and associated with a religious festival such as Christmas or Easter. The term has denoted a popular religious song since about the 14th century, deriving from the medieval carol, a song with alternating burden (refrain) and chorus.

CAROL, two kings of Romania. **Carol I** (1839–1914), elected prince 1866, became Romania's first king in 1881 when it became independent of the Ottoman Empire. His reign brought economic development but no solution to pressing rural and political problems. **Carol II** (1893–1953) became king in 1930. He established a royal dictatorship to counter the growing Fascist movement, but after losing territory to the Axis powers in WWII, he abdicated in 1940 and went into exile.

CAROL CITY, residential community in SE Fla., a suburb of Miami. There is small-scale dairy and poultry farming in the area. Pop 27 361.

CAROLINE AFFAIR, incident in 1837 in which the US ship *Caroline* was sunk by loyal Canadians, killing a US sailor. The *Caroline* was running supplies to the Canadian rebel leader MACKENZIE. The affair strained relations between Britain and the US, but was settled in 1842 after the Webster-Ashburton treaty.

CAROLINE ISLANDS, archipelago in the W Pacific, administered by the US. There are over 900 islands, the largest being Ponape, Babelthuap, Yap and Truk. In WWII they were the scene of bitter fighting between US and Japanese forces. Pop 70 812.

CAROLINE OF BRUNSWICK (1768–1821), German-born wife of King GEORGE IV of England. Married in 1795 and separated a year later, she was the center of various scandals that resulted in her being denied the position of queen and barred from Westminster Abbey during George's coronation in 1821. The marriage was a bigamous one in that George had secretly married Maria FITZHERBERT in 1785.

CAROLINGIANS, Frankish dynasty named for the Emperor CHARLEMAGNE. Its first members ruled under puppet MEROVINGIAN kings as mayors of the palace, but in 751 Pepin III the Short deposed Childeric III and ruled as king with the blessing of Pope Stephen III. Pepin III's son, Charlemagne, was crowned emperor of the West in 800. His reign was the golden age when the empire had its frontiers on the Elbe, the Danube and the Ebro, and included north and central Italy. However in 843 it was partitioned among his three grandsons, the first of many divisions. The reigns of Charlemagne and his successors are sometimes called "the Carolingian Renaissance" because of their artistic achievements. The superb palatine chapel at Aachen reflects the Carolingian merging of ancient Roman and Byzantine influences; Carolingian manuscripts are among the masterpieces of manuscript illumination, and from the Carolingian minuscule the present small letters are derived. The Carolingians encouraged close church-state relations and fostered feudal ideas which reached their full development in the Middle Ages.

CAROTENOIDS, group of yellow, orange, red and brown pigments found in almost all animals and plants, and responsible for the color of carrots, lobsters, and many flowers and fruits. In leaf CHLOROPLASTS the carotenoid colors are masked by CHLOROPHYLL until this is lost in the fall. The color is due to a long conjugated double-bond system (see ALKENES; RESONANCE) formed by condensation of ISOPRENE units. There are two main types of carotenoids, the oxygen-containing xanthophylls and the hydrocarbon carotenes. VITAMIN A is formed from certain carotenes.

CARP, fish of the carp family (Cyprinidae), particularly one species native to Asia and introduced to Europe and America which grows to 1m (40in), weighs up to 27kg (60lb) and has four BARBELS around the mouth. The wild form is yellowish green and lives in shallow, muddy freshwater. Reared for the table, there are also ornamental varieties such as the golden carp.

CARPACCIO, Vittore (c1460–1526), Venetian Renaissance narrative painter. A major work is the cycle of paintings of the *Legend of St. Ursula* (1490–95), typical of his work in atmospheric use of color and meticulous detail to create fantasy settings. He was an accurate observer and delighted in presenting pageantry.

CARPATHIANS, European mountain range, about 900mi long, running from Czechoslovakia through Poland, the USSR and Romania. Though an extension of the Alps, they are much lower. The N Carpathians are densely forested, with isolated valleys

The evolution of the order Carnivora during the last 65 million years.

inhabited by Slav and Magyar peoples. The S Carpathians (or Transylvanian Alps) are more accessible and have important oilfields.

CARPEL. See FLOWER.

CARPENTARIA, Gulf of, inlet of the Arafura Sea, NE Australia, 480mi long and 420mi wide. It is only 30 to 40 fathoms deep and usually lacks oceanic circulation.

CARPENTER, John Alden (1876–1951), American composer. A businessman until 1936, he composed in his spare time. His ballets *Krazy Kat* (1922) and *Skyscrapers* (1926) and orchestral suite *Adventures in a Perambulator* (1915) were particularly popular.

CARPENTERS' HALL, historic meeting place in Philadelphia, Pa., now within Independence National Historical Park. Seat of the Continental Congress in 1774, it served as a hospital in the Revolutionary War and in the 1790s was occupied by the First Bank of the United States. It has been restored and run by the Carpenters' Company since 1857.

CARPENTERSVILLE, village on the Fox R in NE Ill. It is in a farming area, and has a small steel industry. Pop 24 059.

CARPENTIER, Georges (1894–1975), French light-heavyweight boxer. He beat Battling Levinsky for the world lightweight title in 1920, but in 1921 he lost a challenge to Dempsey for the world heavyweight title.

CARPET. See RUGS AND CARPETS.

CARPETBAGGERS, name give to Northern opportunists who moved into the South after the Civil War to make their fortunes out of postwar chaos and political spoils grabbed from disenfranchised Southerners. They secured many local and state political posts, mobilizing a politically unsophisticated Negro vote, and earned a reputation for graft, wasteful spending and influence-peddling.

CARPET BEETLES, beetles whose larvae feed on clothing, rugs and upholstery. Moth crystals are generally a successful repellent. Most familiar is the common carpet beetle *Anthrenus scrophulariae*.

CARRACCI, family of Bolognese painters. **Lodovico Carracci** (1555–1619), a painter of the Mannerist school, founded an academy of art in Bologna. **Agostino Carracci** (1557–1602) is famous primarily for his prints and *Communion of St. Jerome* (c1590). **Annibale Carracci** (1560–1609) is considered the greatest painter of the family. Much influenced by CORREGGIO, his work, particularly the vast decorations for the Farnese palace (1597–1604), introduced a strong Classical element into a basically Mannerist style.

CARRANZA, Venustiano (1859–1920), Mexican statesman. He became governor of Coahuila state in 1910, and Mexican president in 1917. He was unwilling to introduce reforms, and his restrictions on foreign acquisitions of Mexican property made for uneasy foreign relations. He fled an uprising led by General OBREGÓN, but was assassinated.

CARRARA, city in Tuscany, central Italy, famed from Roman times for the area's white marble, the finest in the world. Carrara's academy of fine arts trains craftsmen in marble work, and the city's beach resort has seaport facilities to handle the stone. Pop 67 540.

CARREL, Alexis (1873–1944), French surgeon who won the 1912 Nobel Prize for Medicine or Physiology for developing a technique for suturing (sewing together) blood vessels, thus paving the way for organ TRANSPLANTS and blood TRANSFUSION.

CARRHAE, Battle of, defeat of the Romans by the Parthians at Carrhae (modern Harran, S Turkey) in 53 BC. The Romans, led by Marcus Licinius Crassus, lost three-quarters of their men, including Crassus himself.

CARRIER, person who carries the agents responsible for infectious DISEASES, and is able to infect others, while often remaining quite well.

CARRIER, Willis Haviland (1876–1950), US industrialist and mechanical engineer, pioneer designer of AIR-CONDITIONING equipment. He invented an automatic humidity-control device first used in a New York printing plant in 1902—arguably the first commercial air-conditioning installation.

CARRIER PIGEON, breed of show pigeon derived from the rock pigeon, not used for message-bearing despite its name. (See also PIGEON.)

CARRION FLOWERS, cactus-like plants of the genus *Stapelier*, native to South Africa. Their pollination is achieved by insects that are attracted to the flowers by the putrid odor they emit.

CARROLL, Charles (1737–1832), US statesman from Md. A delegate to the Continental Congress (1776–79), he signed the Declaration of Independence and later served in the first US Senate (1789–92). At his death he was considered the richest man in the country.

Carpenter's Hall in Philadelphia. Built in 1770 by the Carpenters' Guild, it is now a national monument containing memorabilia from the Revolutionary War.

CARROLL, Daniel (1730–1796), US politician from Md. A delegate to the Continental Congress (1781–83) and the 1787 Constitutional Convention, he signed the Articles of Confederation and the Constitution. He also served in the first US Congress (1789–91).

CARROLL, John (1735–1815), first US Roman Catholic bishop. A strong patriot, he helped establish the Catholic hierarchy in the US. In 1790 he was consecrated bishop of Baltimore, and was made archbishop in 1808. He founded a seminary which became Georgetown U.

CARROLL, Lewis (pseudonym of Charles Lutwidge Dodgson; 1832–1898), English mathematician best known for his childrens' books *Alice in Wonderland* (1865) and *Alice Through the Looking Glass*

James Earl ("Jimmy") CARTER, Jr.
39th US President

Born: October 1, 1924
Term of office: January 20, 1977–
Political party: Democratic

(1872). Lecturer in mathematics at Christ Church, Oxford, from 1854, he was ordained a deacon in 1861 but did not take further orders. The *Alice* books and poems such as *The Hunting of the Snark* (1876) are built on mathematical illogic and paradox. He was also a noted portrait photographer.

CARROLLTON, city in W Ga., seat of Carrol Co., named for Charles CARROLL. Center of a farming area, it manufactures textiles, hosiery, metal products and processed food. Pop 13 520.

CARROLLTON, city in N Tex., NW of Dallas, situated in a wheat farming area. Pop 13 855.

CARROT, *Daucus carota*, a hardy biennial vegetable cultivated for its orange-red taproots, which are rich in carotene, a precursor of VITAMIN A. The carrot is native to Afghanistan, but is now widely grown in the US and Europe.

CARSON, unincorporated urban community in Los Angeles Co., Cal., SE of Los Angeles. Pop 71 150.

CARSON, Christopher "Kit" (1809–1868), US frontiersman, Indian agent, army officer and folk hero. He worked as a hunter and guide in the 1840s and explored Ore. and Cal. with FRÉMONT. He served in the Mexican War, and fought for the Union in the Southwest during the Civil War, finally becoming a brevet brigadier general.

CARSON, Rachel Louise (1907–1964), US marine biologist and science writer whose *Silent Spring* (1962) first alerted the US public to the dangers of environmental POLLUTION.

CARSON CITY, state capital of Nev. and seat of Ormsby Co., named for Kit CARSON. Originally a trading post, it became an important mining center with the discovery of the Comstock Lode in 1859. Pop 15 468.

CARTAGENA, Caribbean seaport on the Bay of Cartagena in N Colombia. An important gold port of the Spanish Empire, it suffered a decline until it became a major oil port in the 20th century. Manufactures include sugar, tobacco and textiles. Pop 348 000.

CARTAGENA, ancient city, seaport and naval base on the Spanish Mediterranean coast, established as a Carthaginian colony in the 3rd century BC. It now exports minerals and vegetable products. In a mining area, it has large smelting works, and manufactures glass and esparto products. Pop 146 904.

CARTE, Richard d'Oyly. See D'OYLY CARTE, RICHARD.

CARTEL, an association, often illegal, of individuals or firms who agree not to compete with each other in the open, domestic or international markets. The price and volume of goods can therefore be fixed and cartel members' profits increased.

CARTER, Elliott Cook (1908–), a major 20th-century American composer. Marked by unusual instrumentation and structure, his work is often complex and experimental. Among his best-known works are the ballet *The Minotaur* (1947), and the *Double Concerto* (1961) and *Concerto for Piano and Orchestra* (1965).

CARTER, Howard (1873–1938), English Egyptologist, famous for the Valley of the Kings' excavations with Lord CARNARVON that led to the discovery of the tomb of TUTANKHAMEN in 1922. Carter spent ten years in careful excavation and exploration of the tomb.

CARTER, James Earl "Jimmy," Jr (1924–), 39th US president, Governor of Georgia 1971–75. A Baptist, Carter grew up on a Georgia farm and graduated from the US Naval Academy in 1946. While in the navy he did graduate work in nuclear physics and worked under Admiral Rickover on the atomic submarine program. He then ran his family's farm and entered community politics. Elected to the State Senate (1962) he built up a reputation both as a liberal on the issue of race relations and as a shrewd and indefatigable committeeman. As governor he simplified the complex system of government of the state in a way that is being emulated in other states and instigated electoral and social reforms. After a successful job as Democratic National Campaign Chairman for the 1974 election, he won the Democratic presidential nomination in 1976 after a success in the primaries which reunited the party. In Nov. 1976, Carter defeated Republican candidate Gerald FORD. He is married with four children.

CARTERET, borough in NE N.J., 11mi S of Newark. It is a center for heavy industry, with metal and oil refining, and steel mills. Pop 23 137.

CARTERET, Sir George (c1610–1680), English politician, admiral and lieutenant-governor of Jersey from 1643. A staunch Royalist, he was rewarded after the RESTORATION with proprietorships in New Jersey and Carolina.

CARTESIAN COORDINATES, the most common system of rectangular coordinates employed in ANALYTIC GEOMETRY. The term is used after DESCARTES.

CARTESIAN PHILOSOPHY. See DESCARTES, RENÉ.

CARTHAGE, ancient N African city which once stood on the Mediterranean coast near the site of modern Tunis. Established around 800 BC by Phoenician traders as an anchorage, by the 5th century BC it had become the capital of a sizeable empire, comprising African colonies, Corsica, Sardinia and much of Sicily and Spain. Greek opposition checked Carthaginian expansion from 480 BC until the 3rd century BC, when the famous rivalry with Rome began. (See PUNIC WARS.)

Although the fortunes of Carthage reached their zenith at this time under HAMILCAR BARCA and his son, HANNIBAL, in 201 BC the city forfeited all but its African possessions, and in 146 BC a Roman army razed it to the ground. Archaeologists have found very few traces of Phoenician Carthage. Julius CAESAR removed the 1st century BC colony to a different site. Roman Carthage had a checkered history passing, after the decline of Rome, through Vandal and Byzantine hands before its final destruction in 698 AD by the forces of Islam.

CARTHAGE, seat of Jasper Co., SW Mo., on the Spring R. A trade center for a farming area, it also has the world's largest Burlington limestone quarries. Pop 11 035.

CARTHUSIANS, contemplative and austere Roman Catholic monastic order founded in France in 1084 by St. Bruno. Each monk spends most of his life in solitude in his private cell and garden. Lay brothers prepare the Chartreuse liqueur which has made the order famous.

CARTIER, Sir George Étienne (1814–1873), Canadian statesman and leading French-Canadian advocate of confederation. Elected to the Canadian parliament in 1848, he was from 1857 to 1862 joint prime minister with Sir John MACDONALD, under whom he later served as minister of defense in the first dominion government.

CARTIER, Jacques (1491–1557), French explorer who, in search of a NORTHWEST PASSAGE, made two important voyages to Canada. In 1534 he explored the Gulf of St. Lawrence and claimed the Gaspé Peninsula for France. In 1535 he explored the St. Lawrence R as far as Mont Royal, which he named.

CARTIER-BRESSON, Henri (1908–), internationally famous French documentary photographer who rose to fame with his coverage of the Spanish Civil War. He has published many books and has also made films, some with Jean RENOIR.

CARTILAGE, tough, flexible connective tissue found in all vertebrates, consisting of cartilage cells (chondrocytes) in a matrix of COLLAGEN fibers and a firm protein gel. The skeleton of the vertebrate embryo is formed wholly of cartilage, but in most species much of this is replaced by BONE during growth. There are three main types of cartilage: hyaline, translucent and glossy, found in the joints, nose, trachea and bronchi; elastic, found in the external ear, Eustachian tube and larynx; and fibrocartilage, which attaches tendons to bone and forms the disks between the vertebrae.

CARTILAGINOUS FISH, fish of the class Chondrichthyes, distinguished by the absence of any true bone in their skeletons, which are composed entirely of cartilage. The class includes SHARKS, dogfishes, skates, RAYS and chimaeras.

CARTOGRAPHY. See MAP.

CARTOON. See ANIMATION; CARICATURE AND CARTOON.

CARTRIDGE, a case of metal or paper (sometimes of cloth) containing the charge for a FIREARM (see also AMMUNITION). For small arms, the term generally embraces also the bullet or shot, a blank cartridge being one without bullet or shot. In larger GUNS, cartridge and projectile are usually loaded separately.

CARTWRIGHT, Edmund (1743–1823), British inventor of a mechanical loom (c1787) that was the ancestor of the modern power loom. He also invented a wool-combing machine (c1790). (See also WEAVING.)

CARTWRIGHT, Peter (1785–1872), US Methodist preacher, frontier circuit rider—the "Kentucky Boy"—and Ill. politician. The life of circuit riders is vividly described in his *Autobiography* (1856).

CARTWRIGHT, Sir Richard John (1835–1912), Canadian statesman and influential advocate of free trade with the US. He was Liberal minister of finance 1873–78, minister of trade and commerce 1896–1911, and acting prime minister in 1907.

CARUSO, Enrico (1873–1921), Italian operatic tenor famous both for his voice and his artistry. He was the first leading singer to recognize the possibilities of the phonograph, and his recordings brought him worldwide fame.

CARVER, George Washington (c1860–1943), black US chemurgist, botanist and educator, born of slave parents in Mo. As director of agricultural research at TUSKEGEE INSTITUTE, Ala., from 1896, he fostered soil improvement by crop rotation, urging an end to the dependence of Southern agriculture on cotton alone. With this in mind he developed hundreds of industrial uses for peanuts and sweet potatoes.

CARVER, John (c1576–1621), leader of the Pilgrim Fathers and first governor of Plymouth Colony (1620–21). In 1620 he and other Separatists commissioned the *Mayflower*, and on the voyage he signed the MAYFLOWER COMPACT, establishing PLYMOUTH COLONY.

CARVER, Jonathan (1710–1780), American explorer and writer. He accompanied an early expedition into the Great Lakes area, commissioned by Major Robert Rogers, which he afterwards described in his popular *Travels Through the Interior Parts of North America in the Years 1766, 1767 and 1768* (1778).

CARY, (Arthur) Joyce (Lunel) (1888–1957), British novelist whose primary theme is the individual's struggle with society. His best-known work is *The Horse's Mouth* (1944).

CARYATID, female statue forming a column, usually supporting a roof. An early example is the Maiden Porch of the Erechtheum in Athens.

CASA GRANDE, city in S Ariz., 43mi SSE of Phoenix. A copper-mining center, it is famous mainly for the Casa Grande Ruins, a pre-Columbian Indian village site established as a National Monument in 1918. Pop 10 536.

CASABLANCA, largest city in Morocco and a major port. Occupied by the French 1907–56, it is a transportation and tourist center with a mixed population of Europeans, Asians and Africans. Its main industries are food, timber and metal processing. Pop 1 506 373.

CASABLANCA CONFERENCE, WWII meeting of Winston Churchill and F. D. Roosevelt (Jan. 1943). It determined Allied strategy in Europe, and established that only unconditional surrender by Germany and Japan would be acceptable.

CASADESUS, Robert (1899–1972), distinguished French pianist and composer, noted for his interpretations of Mozart and Debussy, and also for the two- and three-piano concertos he composed and performed with his wife and eldest son.

CASALS, Pablo (1876–1973), virtuoso Spanish cellist and conductor. In 1919 he founded an orchestra in Barcelona to bring music to the working classes, but left Spain after the Civil War and never returned. He settled in Prades, SW France, and then (1956) in Puerto Rico, organizing annual music festivals in both places. A great interpreter of Bach, he was a model to a whole generation of cellists.

CASANOVA (DE SEINGALT), Giovanni Giacomo (1725–1798), Venetian author and adventurer whose name became a synonym for seducer. His memoirs, both sensual and sensitive, show him as a freethinking libertine; they also give an excellent picture of his times.

CASAS, Bartolomé de Las. See LAS CASAS, BARTOLOMÉ DE.

CASCADE RANGE, mountain range extending from N Cal. to British Columbia in Canada. Its highest peak is Mt Rainier (14 410ft). The range is named for the ferocious rapids in the Columbia R where it crosses the mountains.

CASCADE TUNNEL, longest railroad tunnel in the US, running 7.79mi through the Cascade Mountains in Wash., 55mi NE of Seattle.

CASCARA SAGRADA, a drug obtained from the bark of *Rhamnus purchiana*, a small tree grown in western North America. The drug is used as a laxative.

CASEHARDENING, in METALLURGY, any process applied to the surface of mild STEEL to increase its wear resistance and surface HARDNESS. Most commonly, the steel is packed around with powdered CHARCOAL and heated for a certain period, so that the surface regions absorb CARBON. The steel is then quenched (see QUENCHING) with water. Other techniques include INDUCTION HARDENING and FLAME HARDENING; and **nitriding**, used for certain suitable steels, where the steel is heated in AMMONIA gas or molten CYANIDE salts so that NITROGEN is diffused into its surface regions.

CASEIN, the chief milk PROTEIN, found there as its calcium salt. It is precipitated from skim MILK with acid or RENNET, washed and dried. Highly nutritious, it is used in the food industry. In alkaline solution casein forms a COLLOID used as a glue, a binder for paint pigments and paper coatings, and to dress leather. Casein is also used to make PLASTICS.

CASEMENT, Sir Roger David (1864–1918), Irish politician, knighted for his humanitarian work in the Congo and South America. In WWI he was hanged for an attempt to arrange German support for the 1916 Irish Rising.

CASHEW, edible nut of *Anacardium occidentale*, a tree native to Middle and South America and cultivated in Africa and India. As well as yielding an edible kernel, which has to be roasted before being eaten, the nut produces a caustic oil, which has uses as a lubricant, in insecticides and in plastics manufacture.

CASHMERE, very fine natural fiber, the soft underhair of the Kashmir goat, bred in India, Iran, China and Mongolia. Cashmere is finer than the best wools, although the name may be applied to some soft wool fabrics.

CASIQUIARE RIVER, in S Venezuela, branches off from the Orinoco R below Esmeralda; flows 140mi SW to join the Guainía R and form the Río Negro.

CASKET LETTERS, eight letters and some sonnets supposedly written by MARY QUEEN OF SCOTS to her lover BOTHWELL. They implicate her in the murder of her husband, Lord DARNLEY, but their authenticity is doubtful.

CASLON, William (1692–1766), English typefounder, inventor of Caslon type, for many years the basic typeface. Although superseded by the "new-style" faces of John BASKERVILLE and others, versions of it are much in use today.

CASPER, city in SE Wyo., seat of Natrona Co. An oil center, it is also a shipping center for the area. Pop 39 361.

CASPIAN SEA, the world's largest inland sea (143 000sq mi), in the SW USSR and Iran. Tideless, it is 92ft below sea level. Although fed by several rivers, including the Volga, the level fluctuates because evaporation losses often exceed inflow. Astrakhan and Baku are the main ports. The northern part of the sea is a major sturgeon-fishing area.

CASS, Lewis (1782–1866), US soldier and politician. Born in Exeter, N.H., he rose to the rank of brigadier general in the War of 1812, and then became secretary of war under Andrew Jackson. Minister to France 1836–42, he was elected a senator for Mich. in 1844 and ran as Democratic presidential candidate in 1848. He lost to Zachary TAYLOR, due largely to the defection of the BARNBURNERS to the FREE SOIL PARTY.

CASSANDER (c358–297 BC), king of Macedonia 305–297 BC; son of Antipater, one of the regents who succeeded Alexander the Great. He rebelled against Antipater's successor, seized Macedonia and established his supremacy by military success and the murder of Alexander's family.

CASSANDRA, in Greek mythology, a Trojan prophetess who was cursed by Apollo, who decreed that she was never to be believed. Daughter of King Priam, she was enslaved by AGAMEMNON at the fall of Troy and was later murdered with him.

CASSATT, Mary (1845–1926), American Impressionist painter, strongly influenced by her friend DEGAS. She studied, exhibited and lived mainly in Paris. Most of her paintings are of domestic scenes, especially mother-and-child studies.

CASSAVA, common name for two species of the spurge family, the sweet cassava *Manihot dulcis* and the bitte cassava or **manioc**, *M. esculenta*, native to Middle and South America, and cultivated in W Africa and SE Asia. Many food preparations are obtained from the tuberous roots of the bitter cassava, including Brazilian arrowroot and **tapioca**, but the roots have first to be heat-treated to dissipate the highly poisonous hydrocyanic acid (see CYANIDES) contained in the sap.

CASSETTE. See TAPE RECORDER.

CASSIN, René (1887–1976), French jurist, statesman and writer, winner of the 1968 Nobel Peace Prize and the 1973 Goethe Prize. Principal author of the UN Declaration of the Rights of Man, he was a UN delegate and active on other international bodies.

CASSINI, Giovanni Domenico, or Cassini, Jean Dominique (1625–1712), Italian–French astronomer who discovered four satellites of SATURN, the Cassini division in the ring of Saturn and estimated the scale of the solar system from the PARALLAX of MARS (1672).

CASSINI OVALS, a plane CURVE produced as follows: Consider two points A and B in the same plane, the distance AB equalling $2x$, $x>0$. Consider then a point P moving such that PA . PB$=y^2$, where y is constant and $y^2>x^2$. The figure traced out by the motion of P is a Cassini Oval. If $y^2<x^2$, the figure is in two parts. In the case where $y=x$, the figure traced out, which looks like a figure eight, is called the **Lemniscate of Bernoulli**.

CASSINO, town in central Italy SE of Rome, below Monte Cassino, the famous monastery founded by St. Benedict in 529 AD. Fortified by the Germans in 1944, town and monastery were razed by Allied barrages, but have both been rebuilt. Pop 26 287.

CASSIOPEIA, in Greek mythology, the mother of ANDROMEDA. In astronomy, a northern circumpolar constellation (see CIRCUMPOLAR STARS) whose five principal stars form a prominent "W."

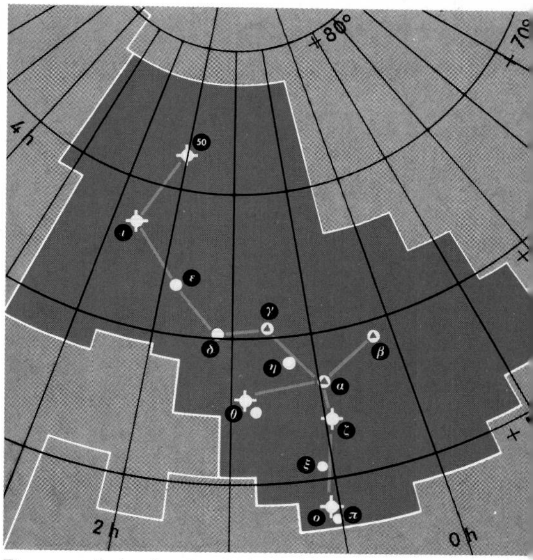

The constellation Cassiopeia, in the Northern Hemisphere. In Greek myth Cassiopeia was a queen who died of grief after offending Poseidon.

CASSIRER, Ernst (1874–1945), German–Jewish philosopher. Based on the ideas of KANT, his work examines the ways in which man's symbols and concepts structure his world. He fled Nazi Germany in 1933, and taught at Oxford, in Sweden and in the US.

CASSITERITE, mineral consisting of stannic oxide (SnO_2) with iron impurity; the chief ore of TIN. It is usually brown to black, with submetallic luster; it forms prismatic crystals (tetragonal), but is usually massive granular. sg 6.8–7.1.

CASSIUS LONGINUS, Gaius (d. 42 BC), Roman general and politician, one of the conspirators against Julius Caesar in 44 BC. After the assassination, he fled to Syria and with his army joined Brutus to fight Octavian and Mark Antony at Philippi in 42 BC. Despairing of victory, he killed himself during the battle.

CASSOWARIES, large, flightless birds of the family Casuariidae, of N Australia and New Guinea, with naked, brightly colored head and neck, wattles and bony helmet. The 1.5m (5ft) tall birds can run at 48km/hr (30mph) and though shy, their claws are

The doubled-wattled cassowary, indigenous to northern Australia and New Guinea. Its large bony crest seems to be used for butting through undergrowth.

formidable weapons. The male, after incubating the eggs, cares for the chicks.

CASTAGNO, Andrea del (c1423–1457), outstanding Florentine painter of church frescoes, portraits and murals. He is best known for his *Last Supper* (1445–50) and *Crucifixion* (1449–50).

CASTANETS, folk instrument made of two shell-shaped pieces of wood or ivory, used in Spanish dancing. They are held in the hands, usually by thumb loops, and tapped by the fingers in a characteristic rippling rhythm.

CASTEL GANDOLFO, town in Italy, on Lake Albano near Rome, politically part of the Vatican City. Its palace, built by Urban VIII in the 17th century, is now the pope's summer residence. Pop 4 814.

CASTELNUOVO-TEDESCO, Mario (1895–1968), Jewish–Italian composer. Forced to leave Italy in 1939, he emigrated to the US. Besides his operas *All's Well That Ends Well* (1957) and *The Merchant of Venice* (1956), he wrote many Shakespeare settings, and also concertos and film music.

CASTEL SANT'ANGELO, fortress in Rome. Originally the tomb of the Emperor Hadrian, it was first fortified in the 5th century AD. It was named for a vision of the Archangel Michael seen there in 590.

CASTE SYSTEM, the division of society into closed groups, primarily by birth, but usually also involving religion and occupation. The most caste-bound society today is probably that of Hindu India; caste divisions are mentioned in the RIGVEDA, dating from 3000 BC, and have not been discouraged until recently. The hierarchy consists of four Varnas (graded classes) with various subdivisions: Brahman (priestly), Kshatriyas (warrior), Vaisyas (merchants and farmers) and Sudras (menials and laborers). There was also a classless element, the outvarnas or untouchables, who performed the lowest tasks. The system solidified social structures by fixing from birth social contacts, thought, diet, ritual, occupation and marriage. Western influences weakened the Indian system in the 19th century; reform was hastened by GANDHI in the 1930s. In India today caste has been drastically modified but not destroyed, despite corrective legislation in the 1950s.

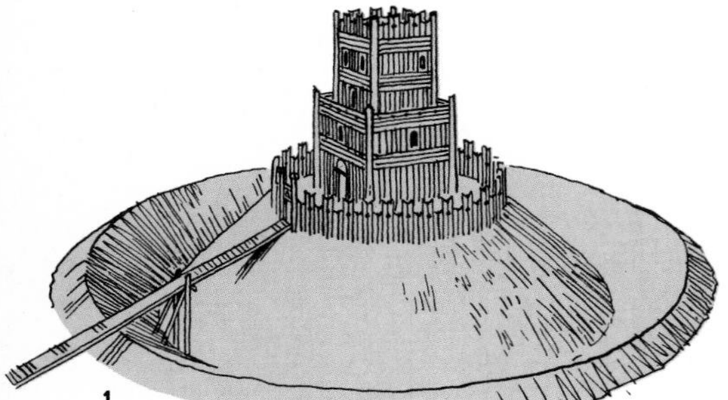

1

2

3

(1) Early castles were merely wooden structures built on a mound (motte) and surrounded by a ditch. (2) A stone shell keep replaced the wooden tower in later "motte and bailey" castles. Here a courtyard (bailey) containing the castle's domestic buildings was constructed at the foot of the mound. (3) In yet later "concentric" castles, there was no central strongpoint, and the domestic buildings were grouped around the inside of a strong "curtain" wall.

CASTIGLIONE, Baldassare (1478–1529), Italian courtier, diplomat and author famed for his *Libro del cortegiano* (1528), a portrait of the ideal courtier and his relationship with the prince he serves. The book greatly influenced Renaissance mores and inspired such writers as Spenser, Sidney and Cervantes.

CASTILE, traditional name for the central region of Spain, formerly the kingdom of Castile. First united in the 10th century, by the 12th century the kingdom was the dominant power in Spain. A royal union between Castile and Aragon (1479) created the core of modern Spain. Madrid, the capital, is in Castile, and the official language is Castilian. A wide plain bounded by mountains, its 54 463sq mi area is largely arid, but some areas support sheep. Wheat is also grown in some parts.

CASTILLA, Ramón (1797–1867), Peruvian statesman and general. A leader in the independence struggle with Spain, he seized power in 1844 and served as president 1845–51 and 1855–62. A benevolent despot, he was essentially conservative but introduced many vital reforms that gave Peru two decades of stability and growth.

CASTILLO DE SAN MARCOS, National Monument and Park in NE Fla., site of the oldest masonry fort in the US. This was built by the Spaniards (1672–96) to protect the city of St. Augustine.

CASTINE, historic fishing and resort town on Penobscot Bay, S Me. It is the site of the Maine Maritime Academy, founded in 1941 to train officers for the US Merchant Marine. Pop 1 080.

CASTING, the production of objects of a desired form by pouring the raw material (e.g., ALLOYS; FIBERGLASS; PLASTICS; STEEL) in liquid form into a suitably shaped mold. Both the mold and the pattern from which it is made may be either permanent or expendable. Permanent-mold techniques include **die casting**, where the molten material is forced under pressure into a DIE; **centrifugal casting**, used primarily for pipes, the molten material being poured into a rapidly rotating mold (see CENTRIFUGE); and **continuous casting**, for bars and slabs, where the material is poured into water-cooled, open-ended molds. Most important of the expendable-mold processes is **sand casting (founding)**: here fine SAND is packed tightly around each half of a permanent pattern, which is removed and the two halves of the mold placed together. The material is poured in through a channel (**sprue**); after setting, the sand is dispersed. In some processes, the mold is baked before use to remove excess water. (See also CAST IRON; METALLURGY.)

CAST IRON, iron ALLOYS containing 1.8–4.5% carbon, used for CASTING; made from PIG IRON in a cupola furnace by melting and purifying it and adding other components. Its properties depend largely on the composition and the ANNEALING process used.

CASTLE, fortified dwelling, built by the ruling classes to dominate and guard a region. The term derives from the Roman *castellum*, meaning fort or frontier stronghold. In Western Europe, most of the extant castles were built between 1000–1500, often on an artificial mound, with a palisaded courtyard. Later, the stockade was replaced by masonry keeps, defensive outer walls, and frequently a moat and drawbridge. With the decline of feudalism the castle evolved into the Renaissance CHÂTEAU, with its emphasis on splendor rather than on fortification.

CASTLE CLINTON, national monument in New York City, originally built in 1808–11 for defense purposes. In 1855–90 it was used as an immigrant landing depot. It became a national monument in 1950.

CASTLEREAGH, Robert Stewart, Viscount (1769–1822), British statesman, creator of the Grand Alliance which defeated Napoleon. As secretary for Ireland, he suppressed the 1798 rebellion and forced through the Act of Union (1800). He was war minister 1805 and 1807–09 and then, as foreign secretary 1812–22, played a major role in the organization of Europe at the Congress of Vienna (1814). Much maligned in his time, he committed suicide.

CASTLE SHANNON, borough in SW Pa., 6mi S of Pittsburgh, of which it is a residential suburb. Pop 11 899.

CASTOR AND POLLUX, twin heroes of classical mythology, also called the *Dioscuri*. Sons of LEDA, brothers of Helen and Clytemnestra, they were inseparable even after Castor's death, when Pollux asked his father Zeus to let him rejoin his brother by releasing him from immortality. (See also GEMINI.)

CASTOREUM, a glandular secretion of the Castor beaver. It is soluble in ETHANOL and is used in the blending of perfumes.

CASTOR OIL, a vegetable oil extracted from the purple-streaked seeds of the castor oil plant (*Ricinus communis*). Once widely used as a laxative, castor oil is now mainly used as a lubricant and in the manufacture of oil and varnish.

CASTRATION, removal of the TESTES of a male animal, usually by surgery but also by constricting their blood supply. It is employed for STERILIZATION, particularly for selective BREEDING; to produce docility; to cause the animal to gain more flesh of better quality; and to prevent secondary sexual characteristics from developing. **Spaying**, removal of the OVARIES of a female animal, has similar uses.

CASTRATION COMPLEX, the nexus of fears (see COMPLEX) concerned with possible or threatened loss of the generative organs, especially the penis (see REPRODUCTION). The term is used analogously to describe fears of loss of sexuality or the capacity for erotic pleasure in either males or females. (See OEDIPUS COMPLEX.)

CASTRATO, a male singer who was castrated to retain his high-pitched prepubescent vocal range. Such male sopranos flourished in Europe in the 17th and 18th centuries. Many major operatic roles were written for them. (See also CASTRATION.)

CASTRO, Cipriano (1858–1924), Venezuelan dictator, who seized Caracas with a private army of cowboys in 1899. He declared himself president in 1902, but was overthrown in 1908 by Juan Vincente Gómez.

CASTRO (RUZ), Fidel (1926–), Cuban premier and revolutionary leader. Born in Oriente, Cuba, after his law studies he led an abortive revolution in 1953 against the Cuban dictator Fulgencio BATISTA, and was imprisoned and exiled. On Dec. 2, 1956, he landed again in Cuba, with 81 men, and, after a guerrilla struggle against overwhelming odds, overthrew the regime and established himself as premier in 1959. He brought about many far-reaching social and economic reforms, becoming increasingly dependent on the USSR for financial support.

CASTRO VALLEY, unincorporated suburban community in W Cal. Pop 44 760.

CASUISTRY, a method of solving ethical questions by reference to a set of closely defined laws. Right conduct is seen in terms of obedience to these laws. Casuistry, in Christianity, fell into disrepute when used to decide the penalties attached to confessed sins. Used by certain Jesuit casuists, it came to appear specious and devoid of all allowances for human feeling. (See also ETHICS.)

CATACOMBS, the name given to underground cemeteries, particularly those of the early Christians. The best known and most extensive are at Rome. The oldest of the catacombs, those of Saint Sebastian and Saint Priscilla, date from the 1st century AD. They also served as a refuge from the religious persecutions of the Roman emperors. Construction was freely permitted provided they were situated outside the city walls. The catacombs extend through rocky soil at depths between 20ft and 65ft, sometimes at several levels, the oldest catacombs usually being uppermost. They form a labyrinthine network of narrow passages, the sides of which are lined with tiers of recesses (*loculi*) and frequently decorated with pictorial and written symbols. After a body had been placed in its recess, the opening was sealed with an inscribed slab of marble or terracotta.

CATALAN, one of the nine Romance languages, and native language of Catalonia in Spain. Also spoken in the French Pyrenees.

CATALAUNIAN PLAINS, Battle of the, defeat of the Huns under ATTILA by the Romans and Visigoths under AETIUS and THEODORIC I in 451 AD, probably near Châlons-sur-Marne in E France. It halted the advance of the Huns in Europe.

CATALEPSY, rare nervous disorder characterized by episodes of rigid immobility.

CATALINA ISLAND. See SANTA CATALINA.

CATALONIA, former province in NE Spain, comprising the modern provinces of Lérida, Gerona, Barcelona and Tarragona. Densely populated, it was occupied by the Romans and Goths, who called it *Gothalonia*. It maintained its own customs and language even after its union with Aragon in 1137. It is now the chief industrial area of Spain, and its dependence on the interior for grain and protected markets mitigates against its tendency to a strong regionalism.

CATALPAS, ornamental trees of the genus *Catalpa* part of the bignonia family (Bignoniaceae). They are native to E Asia, the West Indies and the southern US and are frequently grown as ornamentals. Catalpas have snowy white, yellow or purplish flowers and produce beanlike fruits containing hairy seeds.

CATALYSIS, the changing of the rate of a chemical reaction by the addition of a small amount of a substance which is unchanged at the end of the reaction. Such a substance is called a catalyst, though this term is usually reserved for those which speed up reactions; additives which slow down reactions are called inhibitors. Catalysts are specific for particular reactions. In a reversible reaction, the forward and back reactions are catalyzed equally, and the EQUILIBRIUM position is not altered. Catalysis is either homogeneous (the catalyst and reactants being in the same phase, usually gas or liquid), in which case the catalyst usually forms a reactive intermediate which then breaks down; or heterogeneous, in which ADSORPTION of the reactants occurs on the catalytic surface. Heterogeneous catalysis is often blocked by impurities called poisons. Catalysts are widely used in industry, as in the CONTACT PROCESS, the HYDROGENATION of oils, and the cracking of PETROLEUM. All living organisms are dependent on the complex catalysts called ENZYMES which regulate biochemical reactions.

CATAMARAN, a fast and stable outrigger boat with two hulls, driven by sail or motor. Its forerunner was a primitive fishing craft made of logs, and it is now most used as a racing sailboat.

CATANIA, chief seaport and second-largest city of Sicily. After an earthquake in 1693, the city was rebuilt on a regular plan, with five squares and the largest Baroque church in Sicily. It is mainly commercial and has oil-pressing, fish-canning, engineering, chemical and cement industries. Pop 401 670.

CATAPLEXY, episodic muscular weakness, often precipitated by emotion, its severity relating to depth of emotion. Associated with NARCOLEPSY.

CATAPULT, ancient military weapon used for hurling missiles. Some catapults were large crossbows, with a lethal range of over 400yd, while others (*ballistas*) used giant levers to hurl boulders. In the Middle Ages, catapults were an important part of siege artillery, but were made obsolete by the cannon. A modern steam-powered version of the catapult launches jets from aircraft carriers.

CATARACT, disease of the EYE lens, regardless of cause: the normally clear lens becomes opaque and light transmission and perception are reduced. Congenital cataracts occur especially in children born to mothers who have had GERMAN MEASLES in early PREGNANCY, and in a number of inherited disorders. Certain disturbances of METABOLISM or HORMONE production can cause cataracts, especially DIABETES. Eye trauma and INFLAMMATION are other causes in adults. Some degree of cataract formation is common in old age. Once a cataract is formed, vision cannot be improved until the lens is removed surgically. After this, GLASSES are required to correct loss of focusing power. It is among the commonest causes of BLINDNESS in developed countries.

CATARRH, vague term usually referring to excess MUCUS or discharge of PUS from mucous membranes of NOSE or SINUSES but sometimes referring to sputum.

CATARRHINA, an infraorder containing Old World MONKEYS, apes and MAN. Members are characterized by nostrils that are close together and point downward.

CATASTROPHISM, in geology, the early 19th-century theory that major changes in the geological structure of the earth occurred only during short periods of violent upheaval (catastrophes) which were separated by long periods of comparative stability. The theory fell from prominence after LYELL's enunciation of the rival doctrine of UNIFORMITARIANISM.

CATATONIA, a form of SCHIZOPHRENIA in which the individual oscillates between excitement and stupor. The term is also used for CATALEPSY.

CATAWBA INDIANS, US Indian tribe formerly living around the Catawba R in the Carolinas. Around 1600 they were the most important of the E Siouan groups, and American allies in the Revolutionary War. By 1900 they were almost extinct.

CATBIRDS, garden songbirds related to the MOCKING BIRD, name for the mewing notes in their song. They live in the US and in S Canada, migrating in winter to Middle America or to the West Indies.

CATEAU-CAMBRÉSIS, Treaty of, signed on April 3, 1559, to end the war between France and Hapsburg Spain. By its terms, France had to give up Savoy and Piedmont and renounce its claims on Italy.

CATECHISM, manual of instruction, usually religious, arranged in question and answer form and intended primarily for children and the uneducated. The first catechisms were compiled in the 8th and 9th centuries, and religious reformers like LUTHER and CALVIN wrote catechisms to explain their doctrines.

Fragments taken from early Christian graves in the Roman catacombs. Systematic investigation of the tombs in the 19th century revealed much about the lives of early Christians under persecution.

CATECHU, an astringent brown substance containing TANNIN, made from the bark, wood or fruit of plants like ACACIAS, mainly used as dye for leather and calico.

CATEGORICAL IMPERATIVE, in the ethics of KANT, an absolute moral law, one which is not dependent on ulterior considerations. It was formulated thus: "So act that you could will the maxim of your action to be a universal law."

CATEGORY, a philosophical term given many different meanings by different thinkers. In Aristotelian philosophy, it signifies one of the ultimate classes (e.g., substance, quality, quantity, relation) to which things can be referred. Thus an object might be of the substance, table; the quality, brown, and so on. In the philosophy of KANT, however, the categories are the A PRIORI concepts in terms of which the human mind organizes and interprets its experience of the world. The notions of cause and substance are Kantian categories.

CATERPILLAR, the larva of a moth or a butterfly, with 13 segments, 3 pairs of true legs and up to 5 pairs of soft false legs. (See also INSECTS, LEPIDOPTERA.)

CATFISH, members of 31 families found throughout the world, chiefly in freshwater. Catfish have BARBELS

Some caterpillars spin a silk pad from mouth glands when they are about to metamorphose (1) and attach themselves to it by the rear end. A silk loop is then spun across the upper body (2); thus supported, the caterpillar can change into a chrysalis (3).

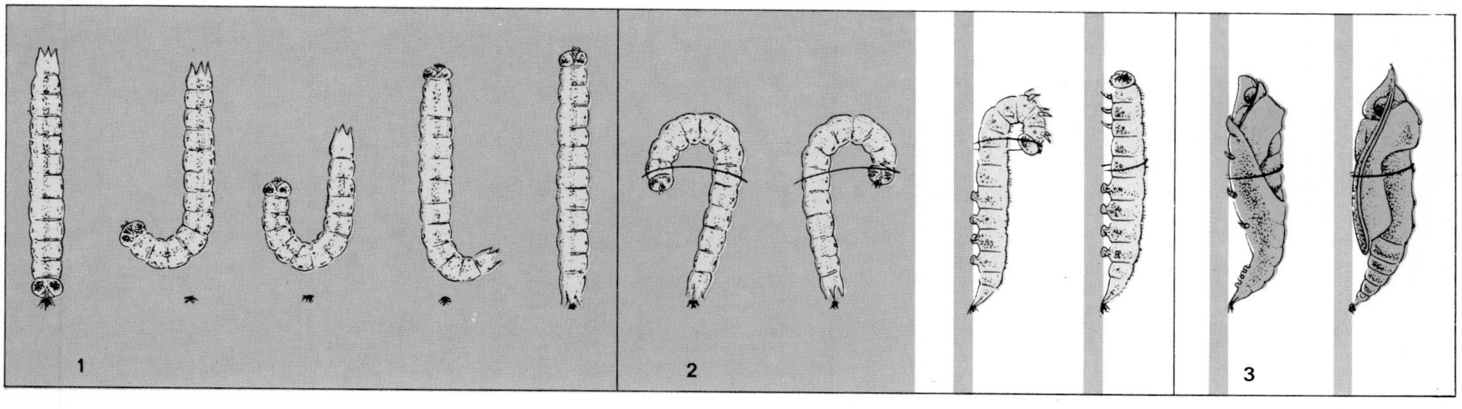

The cathedral of St. Albans, England, originally an eighth century abby. The tower is Norman, made of bricks salvaged from the Roman town of Verulamium.

sometimes resembling cat's whiskers around the mouth, and the bones of the upper jaw are reduced or absent. There are many bizarre forms such as the Upside-down catfish and the transparent Glass catfish.

CATGUT, a strong, thin cord used to string musical instruments and rackets, and to sew up wounds in surgery, made from the intestines of herbivorous animals. In surgery, it has the advantage of being eventually absorbed by the body.

CATHARI, a heretical Christian sect widespread in Europe in the 12th and 13th centuries; called ALBIGENSES in S France. Their philosophy, akin to that of the BOGOMILS, was derived from GNOSTICISM and MANICHAEISM. They saw two principles in the world: good (the spirit) and evil (matter and the body). There were two classes of Cathari, the Believers and the Perfect, the latter practicing extreme asceticism.

CATHARSIS (from Greek *katharsis*, purging), in PSYCHOANALYSIS (where it is also generally termed **abreaction**), the bringing into the open of a previously repressed (see REPRESSION) MEMORY or EMOTION, thus, hopefully, relieving unconscious emotional stress. In medicine, the term is used for the artificial induction of vomiting (see EMETIC). Play, which can be viewed as working off atavistic impulses, is sometimes described as cathartic.

CATHAY, name by which N China was known in medieval Europe. It was derived from *Kitai*, the kingdom of the Khitan Tartars.

CATHEDRAL, the principal church of a diocese, in which the bishop has his *cathedra*, his official seat or throne. A cathedral need not be particularly large or imposing, though its importance as a major center led to the magnificent structures of the Gothic and Renaissance periods. By its prominent position and size, a cathedral often dominated a city and served as the focus of its life. In Europe, most of the older cathedral cities were already important centers in Roman and early Christian times.

CATHEDRAL WINDOWS, popular name for the foliage house plant *Maranta leuconeura massangeana*. Family: Marantaceae. (See MARANTA.)

CATHER, Willa Sibert (1873–1947), US novelist noted for her sagas of pioneer life, such as *My Antonia* (1918) and *Death Comes for the Archbishop* (1927).

CATHERINE, name of two Russian empresses. **Catherine I** (1684–1727), of Lithuanian peasant origin, became the mistress and later the wife of Peter I. On his death in 1725 she succeeded him to the throne. **Catherine II, the Great** (1729–1796), daughter of a minor German prince, became the wife of the heir to the Russian throne, the future Peter III, in 1745. After his deposition and murder in 1762, she became empress and proposed sweeping reforms, but her apparent liberalism was quenched by the PUGACHEV rebellion and the French Revolution. She greatly extended Russian territory, annexing the Crimea (1783) and partitioning Poland (1772–95). She was also a great patron of the arts.

CATHERINE DE MÉDICIS. See MEDICI.

CATHERINE OF ALEXANDRIA, Saint (early 4th century), Christian martyr, probably legendary, who may have died in Alexandria in Egypt. Because of her learned defense against the Emperor Maxentius' priests, she was tortured and then beheaded. She is the patron saint of scholars and philosophers.

CATHERINE OF ARAGON (1485–1536), first wife of HENRY VIII of England. The daughter of Ferdinand and Isabella of Spain, she first married Prince Arthur (1501) and then, after his death, his brother, Henry VIII (1509). Henry's annulment of the marriage in 1533 without papal consent led to the English Reformation. She was the mother of Mary I of England.

CATHERINE OF BRAGANZA (1638–1705), Portuguese wife of King CHARLES II of England. The marriage was intended to promote the Anglo-Portuguese alliance; but she produced no heir and returned to Portugal in 1692.

CATHERINE OF SIENA, Saint (1347–1380), patron saint of Italy and one of the greatest of 14th-century mystics. Her feast day is April 30.

CATHETER, hollow tube passed into body organs for investigation or treatment. **Urinary catheters** are used for relief of BLADDER outflow obstruction and sometimes for loss of nervous control of bladder; they also allow measurement of bladder function and special X-RAY techniques. **Cardiac catheters** are passed through ARTERIES or VEINS into chambers of the HEART to study its functioning and ANATOMY.

CATHODE, a negatively charged ELECTRODE, found particularly in ELECTRON TUBES, CATHODE RAY TUBES, and electrochemical CELLS, and used in combination with its positive counterpart, an ANODE, as a source of ELECTRONS or to produce an electric field.

CATHODE RAYS, ELECTRONS emitted by a CATHODE when heated. First studied by Julius Plücker (1801–1868) in 1858, they can be drawn off in vacuo by the attraction of an ANODE to form a beam which causes fluorescence (see LUMINESCENCE) in appropriately coated screens or X-RAY emission from metal targets.

CATHODE RAY TUBE, the principal component of OSCILLOSCOPES and TELEVISION sets. It consists of an evacuated glass tube containing at one end a heated CATHODE and an ANODE, and widened at the other end to form a flat screen, the inside of which is coated with a fluorescent material. ELECTRONS emitted from the cathode are accelerated toward the anode, and pass through a hole in its center to form a fine beam which causes a bright spot where it strikes the screen. Because of the electric charge carried by the electrons, the beam can be deflected by transverse electric or magnetic fields produced by electrodes or coils between the anode and screen: one such set allows horizontal deflection, and another vertical. The number of electrons reaching the screen can be controlled by the voltage applied to a third electrode, commonly in the form of a wire grid, placed between the cathode and anode so as to divert to itself a proportion of the electrons emitted by the former. It is thus possible to move the spot about the screen and vary its brightness by the application of appropriately timed electrical signals, and sustained images may be produced by causing the spot to traverse the same pattern many times a second. In the oscilloscope, the form of a given electrical signal, or any physical effect capable of conversion into one, is investigated by allowing it to control the vertical deflection while the horizontal deflection is scanned steadily from left to right, while in television sets half-tone pictures can be built up by varying the spot brightness while the spot scans out the entire screen in a series of close horizontal lines.

CATHOLIC, (from Greek *katholikos*, universal), term descriptive of the united communion of the whole Christian Church. Catholic doctrine is that believed "everywhere, always, and by all." The practices of a church are catholic if lineally descended from authentic ancient tradition. The ROMAN CATHOLIC CHURCH regards only itself as truly catholic; the CHURCH OF ENGLAND and the OLD CATHOLICS apply the term also to themselves, the EASTERN ORTHODOX CHURCHES, and the REFORMED CHURCHES—that is, to all who are not heretical or schismatic.

CATHOLIC APOSTOLIC CHURCH, religious body founded in England in the 1830s by a group which included Edward IRVING. Believing the second coming of Christ to be imminent, they appointed 12 "apostles" and proselytized in the US and Germany.

CATHOLIC EMANCIPATION ACT, British law enacted on April 13, 1829, removing most of the civil disabilities imposed on British Roman Catholics. A controversial measure, it was introduced by Sir Robert PEEL, after considerable pressure from Irish campaigners headed by Daniel O'CONNELL.

CATHOLIC LEAGUE, association of German Roman Catholic princes and prelates in the 17th century. It was established by Maximilian of Bavaria in 1609 to offset the Protestant Union. (See also THIRTY YEARS' WAR.)

CATHOLICOS, title of certain dignitaries of the Eastern Christian churches. Having once denoted an archimandrite or bishop, the title later became synonymous with patriarch as applied to the heads of the Armenian and Nestorian churches.

CATHOLIC REFORMATION. See COUNTER REFORMATION.

CATHOLIC YOUTH ORGANIZATION, agency of the Roman Catholic Church providing young people with educational and recreational facilities. It was founded in Chicago in 1930 by Bishop Bernard J. Sheil.

CATILINE (c108–62 BC), Roman aristocrat, who tried to seize power in 63 BC. He was trapped and killed in battle at Pistoia. CICERO attacked him in a series of four celebrated orations.

CATION, a positively-charged ION, normally of a metal, which moves to the CATHODE in ELECTROLYSIS.

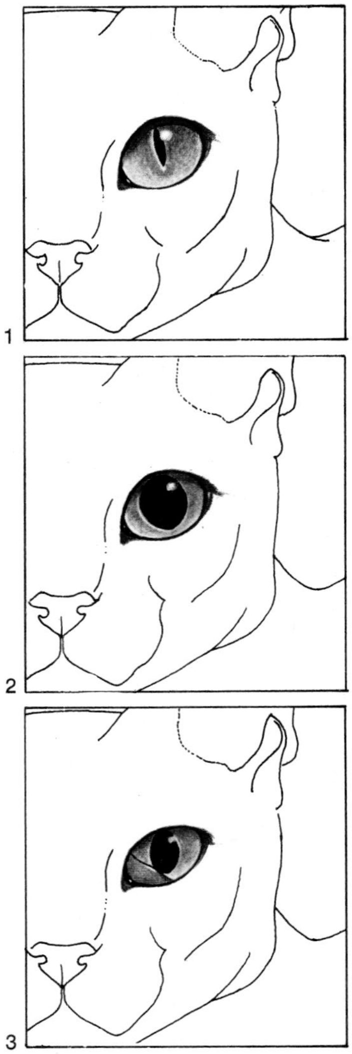

The versatile eye of the cat is able to close up to leave only a narrow slit in bright light (1). However for hunting at night, the pupil enlarges to a full circle (2) allowing it to see in conditions which we would consider pitch darkness. Cats also have an extra eyelid (3) which helps to protect and clean the eye.

CATKIN, type of INFLORESCENCE found on some trees, usually consisting of a spike of unisexual flowers that have no PETALS or SEPALS. POLLINATION is by the wind. Typical examples are found on the HAZEL, BIRCH and WILLOW.

CATLIN, George (1796–1872), US artist, noted for his paintings of American Indian life. His books include *Notes on the Manners, Customs, and Conditions of the North American Indians* (1841).

CATNIP, or catmint, *Nepeta cataria*, a Eurasian mint naturalized in North America, so-named because of its strange attraction for cats. Family: Labiatae.

CATO, name of two Roman statesmen. **Marcus Porcius Cato** (234–149 BC), called the Elder, was an orator and prose writer. He became consul in 195 BC and censor in 184 BC. His only surviving work is a treatise on agriculture. **Marcus Porcius Cato** (95–46 BC), called the Younger (great-grandson of Cato the Elder), was a model Stoic and defender of Roman republicanism. He supported POMPEY against Gaius Julius CAESAR in the Civil War, but after the final defeat of the republican army at Thapsus (46 BC), he killed himself at Utica.

CATONSVILLE, unincorporated residential suburb of Baltimore, Md. Pop 54 812.

CATS, Domestic, popular household pets, thought to be descended from the African cafer (or Bush) cat, mixed with strains from the European wildcat. They were fully domesticated by the time of the ancient Egyptians, who venerated them. Mummies of cats have been found in Egyptian tombs.

The most common type of cat is the tabby (both striped and blotched). Though seemingly derogatory, the term alley or gutter cat (meaning mixed breed) applies to about 90% of cats in the world. Pedigree cats are divided into two groups: shorthaired (including Siamese, Burmese, Russian blue, Manx and Abyssinian) and long-haired (including Persian, Chinchilla and Angora).

Cats are fastidious and independent, and prefer a diet of milk and meat. Their "miaow" is a request for attention; purring indicates contentment.

CATS, members of the family Felidae, all of which are hunting carnivores. They vary in size from the small domestic cat and WILDCATS, through the medium-sized LYNX, PUMA and CHEETAH, to the large LION and TIGER. Cats have large canine teeth, contractible pupils and retractable claws.

CAT'S EYE, any of several GEM stones which, when cut to form a convex surface, show a thin line of light like a cat's eye (chatoyancy). The commonest type is CHALCEDONY; the rarest is cymophane, a green variety of CHRYSOBERYL, found in Sri Lanka. The effect is due to minute parallel inclusions or cavities.

CATSKILL MOUNTAINS, group of low mountains W of the Hudson R in SE N.Y., part of the Appalachian system. Geologically unique, with flat-topped plateaus divided by narrow valleys, they are a popular recreation area. The highest point is Slide Mountain (4 204ft).

CATT, Carrie Lane Chapman (1859–1947), US feminist, suffragette and founder of the LEAGUE OF WOMEN VOTERS. She was also an active advocate of international disarmament. (See also WOMEN'S LIBERATION MOVEMENT.)

CATTAILS, or reed-mace, *Typha latifolia* and allied species, attractive reedlike plants growing in streams, ponds and swamps. They have sword-shaped leaves, a brown, velvety cylinder of minute flowers without any petals and thistle-like down which assists wind distribution of the seeds.

CATTELL, James McKeen (1860–1944), pioneering US psychologist. Having worked in Germany for some years as a disciple of Wilhelm WUNDT, he returned to the US and taught psychology at the U. of Pennsylvania (1888–91) and at Columbia U. (1891–1917).

CATTLE, large ruminant mammals of the family Bovidae, most of which have been domesticated, including BISON, BUFFALO, YAK, ZEBU or Brahman cattle and European cattle. The last two are fully domesticated. Western cattle are derived from the now extinct AUROCHS. By 2500 BC the Egyptians had several breeds of cattle, which may have been used as draft animals, still an important function in many

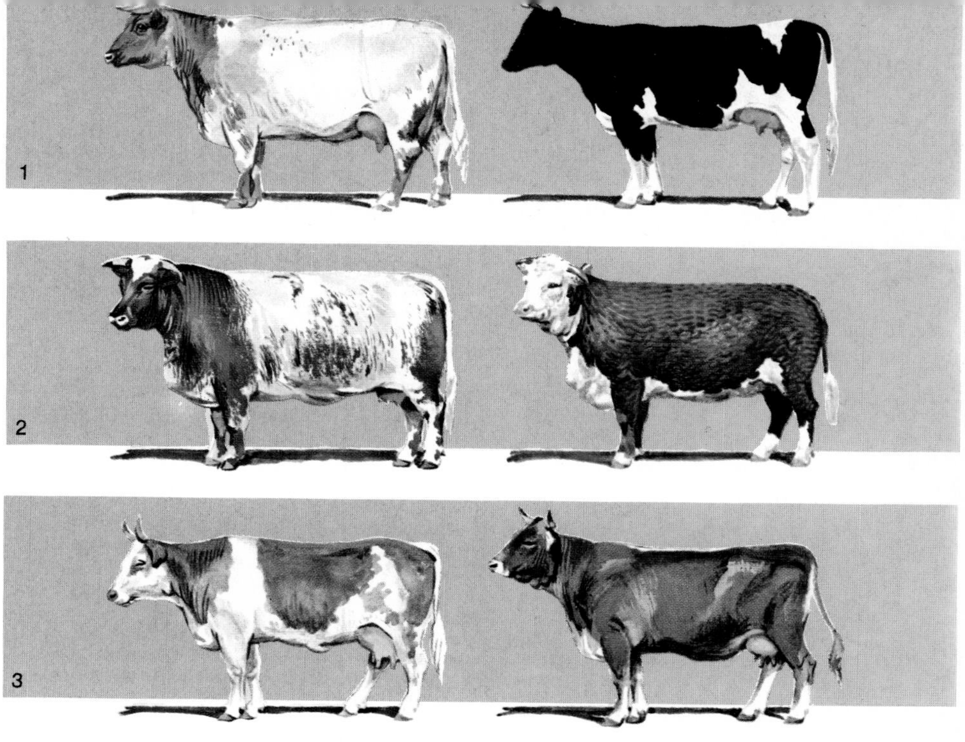

Domestic cattle can be divided into three main types: (1) The dairy breeds including the English Dairy Shorthorn (*left*) and the Holstein-Friesian (*right*). (2) Beef cattle like the Shorthorn (*left*) and the Hereford (*right*) are generally larger than dairy cattle. (3) In areas where separate herds are precluded for reasons of space, both functions are combined as with the Simmenthaler (*left*) and the Brown Swiss (*right*).

places, and for leather. Their dung served as fuel and manure.

Today, beef cattle (like Aberdeen Angus or Hereford) are square, heavily built animals commonly kept on poor grazing land, whereas dairy breeds (like Holstein or Guernsey) are kept on good grazing. Recent breeds are mixed beef and dairy animals. A dairy cow can give as much as 13tonnes of milk in one year.

CATTON, Bruce (1899–), US journalist and Civil War historian. He is best known for his trilogy on the Civil War Army of the Potomac: *Mr. Lincoln's Army* (1951), *Glory Road* (1952) and *A Stillness at Appomattox* (1953). He won the Pulitzer Prize in 1954.

CATULLUS, Gaius Valerius (c84–54 BC), Roman lyric poet, born in Verona, Italy. Influenced by Hellenistic Greek poetry, he wrote passionate lyrics, epigrams, elegies, idylls and vicious satires, of which only 116 survive. He influenced the later Roman poets HORACE and MARTIAL.

CAUCA RIVER, river in W Colombia, rising in the Andes and flowing 600mi N into the Magdalena R.

CAUCASOID, a racial division of man. Caucasoids have straight or curly fine hair, generally mesocephalic (see CEPHALIC INDEX) heads, thin lips, straight faces and well-developed chins. The RACE may have originated in W Asia.

CAUCASUS, mountain range in the USSR between the Caspian and Black seas, 700mi long and up to 120mi wide, including the highest mountain in Europe, Mt Elbrus (18 481ft). Its northern parts belong to Europe, but its southern regions (Transcaucasia), bordering on Turkey and Iran, are part of Asia. The Caucasus is considered to be the cradle of European nations.

CAUCUS, closed party meeting to decide on policy or to select candidates for public office. The etymology of the term is obscure. It was used in the name of an early 18th-century Boston political club. Associations with backroom maneuvring have given it a derogatory flavor.

CAUDILLO (Spanish; chief), name popularly applied to Spanish American political leaders during the wars of liberation. They were generally opportunists who through sheer force of personality commanded loyal military following. The term has become a nickname for dictators. Spain's General FRANCO adopted the term as a title.

CAULIFLOWER, a variety of CABBAGE (*Brassica oleracea*) similar to BROCCOLI. The edible portion consists of large clusters of thick-stalked unopened flowers which develop in the middle of large leaves. (See BRASSICAS.)

CAUSALITY, the philosophical notion that successive events can be related such that the later is dependent on the earlier, the earlier being the cause and the later its effect. According to ARISTOTLE everything has four causes: the material cause, the material substance involved; the formal cause, its shape or structure; the efficient cause, the agency which imposes the shape upon the matter, and the final cause, the end to which it is done (see TELEOLOGY). Modern notions of causation approximate most closely to Aristotle's efficient cause, though many "skeptical" philosophers, notably HUME, have doubted whether there is in fact any "necessary connexion" between the events designated cause and effect. Such thinkers instead argue that the conviction that events can be related as cause and effect has merely been learned from experience. KANT, on the other hand, held that causality was one of the *a priori* CATEGORIES necessary for the ordering of experience.

CAUSTIC SODA, or sodium hydroxide. See SODIUM; ALKALI.

CAUTERIZATION, application of heat or caustic substances. Used for minor SKIN or mucous-membrane lesions (especially of the NOSE and cervix uteri) to remove abnormal tissue and encourage normal healing. Before antiseptics, it was used to sterilize wounds.

CAVAFY, Constantine. See KAVAFIS, KONSTANTINOS.

CAVAIGNAC, Louis Eugène (1802–1857), French republican general who crushed working class unrest in Paris during the JUNE DAYS (1848). Cavaignac was defeated in the presidential election of Dec. 1848 by Louis Napoleon (see NAPOLEON III).

CAVALCANTI, Guido (c1255–1300), Florentine poet, a friend of DANTE. He was a leading exponent of the "sweet new style" and is remembered as the author of some 50 ballads and sonnets, generally dramatic poems about love.

CAVALIER POETS, group of English poets of the 17th century at the court of Charles I. They include Thomas CAREW, Robert HERRICK, Richard LOVELACE and Sir John SUCKLING.

CAVALIERS, armed horsemen. The term was

The best-known species of cavy, the guinea pig, can be smooth-haired, long-haired or shaggy like the one in the picture. Guinea pigs are useful for research into heredity because of their differences in color and hair types and their ability to breed three or four generations in a single year.

applied to the supporters of King Charles I in the English CIVIL WAR. (See also ROUNDHEADS.)

CAVALLI, Pietro Francesco (1602–1676), Italian composer, trained under MONTEVERDI. His 42 operas include *La Didone* (1641) and *Egisto* (1646).

CAVALRY, military force that fights on horseback. It played a key role in warfare from about the 6th century BC to the end of the 19th century when the development of rapid fire rifles began to reduce its effectiveness. The advent of the tank during WWI and subsequent improvements in military hardware have rendered traditional cavalry redundant. The term is retained in the names of some modern armored units.

CAVE, any chamber formed naturally in rock and, usually, open to the surface via a passage. Caves are found most often in LIMESTONE, where rainwater, rendered slightly ACID by dissolved CARBON dioxide from the ATMOSPHERE, drains through joints in the stone, slowly dissolving it. Enlargement is caused by further passage of water and by bits of rock that fall from the roof and are dragged along by the water. Such caves form often in connected series; they may display STALACTITES AND STALAGMITES and their collapse may form a GORGE. Caves are also formed by selective EROSION by the sea of cliff bases. Very occasionally they occur in LAVA, either where lava has solidified over a mass of ice that has later melted, or where the surface of a mass of lava has solidified, molten lava beneath bursting through and flowing on. (See also SPELEOLOGY.)

CAVE ART. See PREHISTORIC AND PRIMITIVE ART.

CAVEAT EMPTOR (Latin: Let the buyer beware), legal maxim expressing the buyer's responsibility for assuring the quality of goods he buys or agreements he enters into. Consumer protection legislation often drastically modifies the principle.

CAVELIER, Robert. See LA SALLE, RENÉ ROBERT, SIEUR DE.

CAVELL, Edith Louisa (1865–1915), British nurse who became a WWI heroine. As matron of the Berkendael hospital in Brussels, she was executed by the Germans for helping Allied soldiers to escape.

CAVEMEN, a term commonly applied to all STONE AGE men, although many of them did not live in caves. (See PREHISTORIC MAN.)

CAVENDISH, Henry (1731–1810), English chemist and physicist who showed HYDROGEN (inflammable air) to be a distinct GAS, water to be a compound and not an elementary substance and the composition of the ATMOSPHERE to be constant. He also used a torsion BALANCE to measure the DENSITY of the earth (1798).

CAVIAR, the salted roe of certain STURGEON, a delicacy because of its scarcity. The best caviar comes from the Beluga sturgeon of the Caspian Sea.

CAVIES, South American RODENTS of the family Caviidae, tailless, with short legs, small round ears and large heads. Cavies include the GUINEA PIG.

CAVITATION, the formation of bubbles of vapor in a liquid, strictly applicable only to formation of bubbles through reduction in PRESSURE without corresponding TEMPERATURE change. Cavitation reduces efficiency in, e.g., TURBINES and PROPELLERS, rapidly erodes (see EROSION) the moving surfaces, and produces unwanted VIBRATIONS.

CAVOUR, Count Camillo Benso di (1810–1861), Italian statesman largely responsible for the creation of a united Italy. Cavour, a native of Turin, founded the liberal newspaper *Il Risorgimento* in 1847 and, under VICTOR EMMANUEL II, became premier of Piedmont in 1852. Cavour sought to unite the country by making piecemeal additions to Piedmont. A subtle diplomat, he exploited NAPOLEON III's ambitions to engineer the defeat of Austria in 1859, through which he secured the central Italian states. He then invaded the Papal States and entered Neapolitan territory. GARIBALDI, who had taken Sicily and Naples, was left with little option but to cede these gains to Cavour. The unification was completed, except for Venice and the Province of Rome, in 1861, only a few months before Cavour's death.

CAWNPORE. See KANPUR.

CAXIAS, city on the Rio Itapicuru in Maranhão state, NE Brazil. It is a commercial center and processes rice and cotton. Pop 31 089.

CAXTON, William (c1422–1491), English printer, trained in Cologne. He produced *The Recuyell of the Histories of Troye* (Bruges, c1475), the first book printed in English, and *The Dictes and Sayenges of the Phylosophers* (1477), the first book printed in England.

CAYENNE, capital of French Guiana, on Cayenne island; a penal colony until 1944. Its port handles gold, rum, cocoa and cayenne pepper. Pop 19 668.

CAYLEY, Sir George (1773–1857), British inventor who pioneered the science of AERODYNAMICS. He built the first man-carrying GLIDER (1853) and formulated the design principles later used in AIRPLANE construction, although he recognized that in his day there was no propulsion unit which was sufficiently powerful and yet light enough to power an airplane.

CAYMAN ISLANDS, British colony in the Caribbean, formerly a Jamaican dependency, now with its own administration in Georgetown on Grand Cayman, the largest of the islands. Tourism and sea-produce are principal industries.

CAYUGA INDIANS, tribe of IROQUOIAN-speaking Indians, members of the Iroquois League. They inhabited the area of Cayuga Lake, N.Y., until the American Revolution. Favoring the British, many then moved to Canada and the others dispersed

CAYUGA LAKE, in W central N.Y., forms the boundary between Cayuga and Seneca counties and is the longest of the FINGER LAKES (about 66.5mi). Its average width is 2mi and greatest depth is 435ft.

CAYUSE INDIANS, tribe of the Sahaptian linguistic family formerly occupying NE Oregon, and closely allied to the Wallawalla and Nez Percé tribes.

CEARÁ, state in NE Brazil on the Atlantic coast; 57 149sq mi in area, its capital is Fortaleza. It has mineral deposits but is largely agricultural, though suffering from periodic droughts.

CEAUŞESCU, Nicolae (1918–   ), president of Romania from 1967. First elected a full member of the Romanian Communist Party central committee in 1948, he became head of the committee in 1965. As president, he instigated a policy of independence within the Soviet bloc.

CEBU, island in the Philippines. Cebu city on the E coast is the provincial capital, and a major port and commercial center; the rest of the island, though hilly, is largely agricultural.

CECIL, Lord (Edgar Algernon) Robert, 1st Viscount Cecil of Chelwood (1864–1958), British statesman, awarded the Nobel Peace Prize in 1937 for his part in the formation of the League of Nations.

CECIL, Robert. See SALISBURY, 1ST EARL OF.

CECIL, William, 1st Baron Burghley (1520–1598), English statesman who rose to power late in Henry VIII's reign. He was appointed chief secretary of state on the accession of Elizabeth I and remained her chief adviser for 40 years, becoming Lord High Treasurer in 1572. He was responsible for the execution of Mary Queen of Scots and for the defensive measures against the Spanish Armada.

CECILIA, Saint, Christian martyr of the 2nd or 3rd century who died in Rome, the patron saint of musicians. Although of dubious authenticity, she has been left in the calendar because of her great popularity.

CECROPIA MOTH, *Hyalophora cecropia*, one of the largest North American MOTHS, with a 150mm (6in) wingspan; the adult has no mouthparts, surviving only long enough to breed. The young feed on broad-leaved vegetation such as apple, elm and maple.

CEDAR, evergreen, cone-bearing trees of the pine family (Pinaceae) with fragrant wood. Unrelated trees are sometimes called "cedars" (see CYPRESS). There are only four true cedars: the cedar of Lebanon (*Cedrus libani*), the Atlantic cedar (*C. atlantica*), the Cyprus cedar (*C. brevifolia*), all native to the Mediterranean area, and the deodar (*C. deodara*), native to the Himalayas.

CEDAR BREAKS NATIONAL MONUMENT, Ut. was founded in 1933 and has an area of 9.6sq mi. It is a vast natural amphitheater created by erosion of the pink limestone cliffs in the area.

CEDAR FALLS, city in E Ia., on the Cedar R 6mi W of Waterloo. Situated in an agricultural area, it produces machinery and metal products. Pop 29 597.

CEDAR GROVE, residential township in NE N.J., 9mi NW of Newark, producing electronic instruments, machine tools and textiles. Pop 15 582.

Branch and cones of the Atlantic cedar, showing the characteristic tufts of needles.

CEDAR RAPIDS, city in E central Ia., the seat of Linn Co., in an area producing corn and livestock. Many of its inhabitants are of foreign descent; Czechoslovak culture flourishes in the area. It has food-processing and electronics industries. Pop 110642.

CELANDINE, *Chelidonium majus*, the greater celandine, which is a member of the poppy family (Papaveraceae), native to Britain and naturalized in North America. Also, the lesser celandine (*Ranunculus ficaria*) which is a member of the BUTTERCUP family (Ranunculaceae), native to Europe.

CELEBES. See SULAWESI.

CELEBES SEA, lying between the Indonesian islands of Kalimantan (Borneo), Sulawesi (Celebes) and Sangihe, and the Philippine island of Mindanao. It is about 165000sq mi in area.

CELERY, *Apium graveolens*, a biennial herb, cultivated as an annual for its crisp, crescent-shaped stalks. Many varieties have been developed, the most popular having white, red or pink stems.

CELESTA, musical instrument resembling a piano, produced during the 19th century as an improvement on the GLOCKENSPIEL. The keys activate hammers which strike metal bars in acoustic chambers, producing a light, bell-like sound.

CELESTIAL SPHERE, in ancient times, the sphere to which it was believed all the stars were attached. In modern times, an imaginary sphere of indefinite but very large radius upon which, for purposes of angular computation, celestial bodies are considered to be situated. The **celestial poles** are defined as those points on the sphere vertically above the terrestrial poles, and the **celestial equator** by the projection of the terrestrial EQUATOR onto the sphere. (See also ECLIPTIC.) Astronomical coordinate systems are based on these great circles (circles whose centers are also the center of the sphere) and, in some cases, on the observer's celestial HORIZON. In the most frequently used, the equatorial system, terrestrial latitude corresponds to declination—a star directly overhead in New York City will have a declination of +41° (S Hemisphere declinations are preceded by a minus sign), New York City having a latitude of 41°N—and terrestrial longitude to right ascension, which is measured eastward from the First Point of ARIES. Right ascension is measured in hours, one hour corresponding to 15° of longitude. (See also SPHERICAL TRIGONOMETRY.)

CELESTINE, name of five popes. **Saint Celestine I** (d. 432), pope 422–432, attacked the Nestorian and Pelagian heresies. His feast day is April 6. **Celestine II** (d. 1144) was pope 1143–1144. **Celestine III** (c1106–1198), pope 1191–1198, crowned Henry VI emperor but severed relations with him after his invasion of Sicily, which threatened papal independence. **Celestine IV** (d. 1241) reigned only 14 days before his death. **Saint Celestine V** (c1209–1296), pope July–Dec. 1294, was the most ascetic of the popes. A political novice, he was persuaded to abdicate by Cardinal Caetani, who succeeded him as Boniface VIII and kept him in confinement until his death.

CELIAC DISEASE, a disease of the small intestine (see GASTROINTESTINAL TRACT), among the commonest causes of food malabsorption. In celiac disease, ALLERGY to part of gluten, a component of wheat, causes severe loss of absorptive surface. In children, failure to thrive and DIARRHEA are common signs, while in adults weight loss, ANEMIA, diarrhea, TETANY and VITAMIN deficiency may bring it to attention. Complete exclusion of dietary gluten leads to full recovery.

CELIBACY, voluntary abstinence from marriage and sexual intercourse. Celibacy of the clergy in the Roman Catholic Church was instituted by Pope Siricius (386), but abandoned by Protestants during the Reformation. In the Eastern Church, married men can be ordained as priests, though bishops must be celibates or widowers. Recently there has been opposition to celibacy among some Catholics.

CÉLINE, Louis-Ferdinand (1894–1961), pseudonym of Louis-Ferdinand Destouches, French novelist. His first novels, *Journey to the End of Night* (1932) and *Death on the Installment Plan* (1936), made his vivid, hallucinatory style famous.

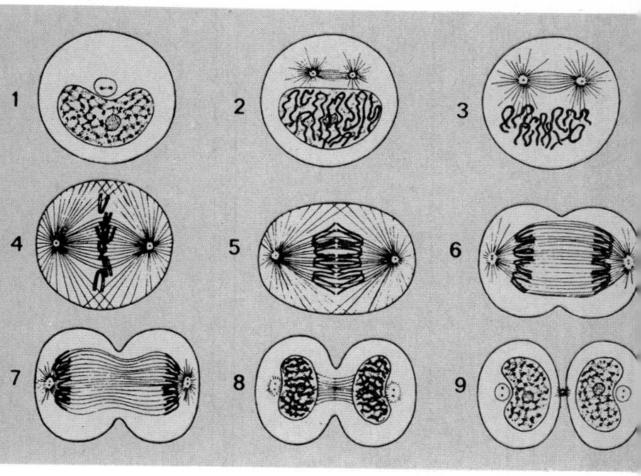

The normal process of cell division (mitosis) is preceded by the duplication of the, as yet invisible, chromosomes. Then, in *prophase* (1–2), the chromosomes become visible, first as fibers and then as coiled rods, in the nucleus. In *metaphase* (2–3), the nuclear membrane dissolves and the centrioles, which in the resting cell (1) lie in the cytoplasm outside the nucleus, draw apart and become the foci for the fibrous spindle. The chromosomes draw themselves up across the equator of the spindle (4). At *anaphase* (5–7), the foci move apart, each drawing an identical set of chromosomes with it. Finally, at *telophase* (8–9), the chromosomes uncoil and disappear within the new nuclear membranes of the identical daughter cells formed as the spindle disappears and the original cytoplasm divides.

CELL, the basic unit of living matter from which all plants and animals are built. A living cell can carry out all the functions necessary for life. BACTERIA, AMOEBA and PARAMECIUM are examples of single-celled organisms. In multicellular organisms cells become differentiated to perform specific functions. All cells have certain basic similarities.

Nearly all cells can be divided into three parts: an outer membrane or wall, a **nucleus** and a clear fluid called CYTOPLASM.

Animal cells are surrounded by a plasma membrane. This is living, thin and flexible. It allows substances to diffuse in and out and is also able to select some substances and exclude others. The membrane plays a vital role in deciding what enters a cell. Plant cells are surrounded by a thick, rigid, non-living CELLULOSE cell wall.

Other types of membrane are found in a cell. Around the nucleus is the nuclear membrane, which has in it tiny pores to allow molecules to pass between the cytoplasm and the nucleus. Another type of membrane is the much-folded endoplasmic reticulum which seems to be a continuation of the cell or nuclear membrane. The endoplasmic reticulum is always associated with the RIBOSOMES where PROTEIN SYNTHESIS takes place, controlled by the CHROMOSOMES which are sited in the nucleus and are mainly made of DNA (see NUCLEIC ACIDS).

The cytoplasm contains many organelles. Among the most important are the rod-shaped **mitochondria**, containing the enzymes necessary for the release of energy from food by the process of RESPIRATION (see also CITRIC ACID CYCLE). Other organelles whose function is still uncertain are the Golgi bodies, which may be involved in the synthesis of cell wall material; and the lysosomes, which may contain enzymes involved in autolysis and controlled destruction of tissues. The cytoplasm of green plants also contains CHLOROPLASTS, where PHOTOSYNTHESIS occurs.

New cells are formed by a process of division called MITOSIS. Each chromosome duplicates and mitosis involves the transfer of this new set of chromosomes to the new daughter cell. Gamete (reproductive) cells are formed by MEIOSIS which is a division that halves the number of chromosomes; thus a human cell that contains 46 chromosomes will produce gamete cells with 23.

Cells differentiate in a multi-cellular organism to produce cells as different as a nerve cell and a muscle cell. Cells of similar types are grouped together into TISSUES.

There are two broad types of cells. Firstly, **prokaryotic cells**, which have the genetic material in the form of loose filaments of DNA not separated from the cytoplasm by a membrane. Secondly, **eukaryotic cells**, which have the genetic material borne on chromosomes made up of DNA and protein that are separated from the cytoplasm by a nuclear membrane. Eukaryotic cells are the unit of basic structure in all organisms except bacteria and blue green algae, which comprise single prokaryotic cells.

CELL, Electrochemical, device for interconverting chemical and electrical ENERGY. For power cells, which transform chemical into electrical energy, see BATTERY. In electrolytic cells the reverse process occurs: by applying an ELECTROMOTIVE FORCE across two electrodes in an electrolyte, a chemical reaction is effected (see ELECTROLYSIS).

CELLINI, Benvenuto (1500–1571), Italian goldsmith and sculptor. Of his work in precious metals little survives except the gold saltcellar made for Francis I of France in 1543. His most famous work of sculpture is *Perseus with the Head of Medusa* (1545–54). His celebrated *Autobiography* (1558–62) is colorful and vigorous, though somewhat exaggerated.

CELLO, or *violoncello*, the second-largest instrument of the violin family, with four strings and a range of three octaves starting two octaves below middle C. It is the deepest-toned instrument in the string quartet (see CHAMBER MUSIC). It dates from the 16th century, but did not become a popular solo instrument until the 17th and 18th centuries. Among the finest music for solo cello are J. S. Bach's six cello suites. Many composers, especially Elgar, Dvořak and Shostakovich, have written cello concertos.

CELLOPHANE, transparent, impermeable film of CELLULOSE used in packaging, first developed by J. E. Brandenburger (1911). Wood pulp is soaked in sodium hydroxide, shredded, aged and reacted with CARBON disulfide to form a solution of viscose (sodium cellulose XANTHATE). This is extruded through a slit into an acid bath, where the cellulose is regenerated as a film. It is dried and given a waterproof coating. If the viscose is extruded through a minute hole, rayon is produced (see SYNTHETIC FIBERS).

Cellini's most famous monumental work is this elegantly mannered bronze sculpture of *Perseus with the Head of Medusa* completed in 1554 in the Loggia dei Lanzi, Florence. Cellini admired Michaelangelo, and worked in the Mannerist style.

CELLULOID, the first commercial synthetic PLASTIC, developed by J. W. Hyatt (1869). It is a colloidal dispersion of NITROCELLULOSE and CAMPHOR. It is tough, strong, resistant to water, oils and dilute acids, and thermoplastic. Used in dental plates, combs, billiard balls, lacquers, spectacle frames and (formerly) photographic films and toys, celluloid is highly inflammable, and has been largely replaced by other plastics.

CELLULOSE, the main constituent of the CELL walls of higher plants, many algae and some fungi; cotton is 90% cellulose. Cellulose is a CARBOHYDRATE with a similar structure to starch. In its pure form it is a white solid which absorbs water until completely saturated, but dissolves only in a few solvents, notably strong alkalis and some acids. It can be broken down by heat and by the digestive tracts of some animals, but it passes through the human digestive tract unchanged and is helpful only in stimulating movement of the intestines. Industrially, it is used in manufacturing textile fibers, CELLOPHANE, CELLULOID, and the cellulose PLASTICS, notably NITROCELLULOSE (used also in explosives), cellulose acetate for toys and boxes and cellulose acetate butyrate for typewriter keys.

CELSIUS, Anders (1701–1744), Swedish astronomer, chiefly remembered for his proposal (1742) of a centigrade TEMPERATURE scale which had 100° for the freezing point and 0° for the boiling point of water. The modern centigrade temperature scale (with 0° for the freezing point and 100° for the boiling point of water) is known as the **Celsius scale** in his honor, temperatures being quoted in "degrees Celsius" (°C).

CELSUS, Aulus Cornelius, 1st-century Roman medical writer, renowned in the Renaissance as the "Cicero of medicine" for the fine Latin style of his *De medicina*. His reputation prompted the 16th-century founder of IATROCHEMISTRY to adopt the name PARACELSUS—beyond Celsus—thus boasting his supposed superiority over his Roman predecessor.

CELTIC ART, art of the Celtic peoples of Europe, chiefly that of the La Tène culture of the 5th to 1st centuries BC. Little Celtic sculpture and architecture has survived, leaving mainly the applied art of the metalworker. This is typified by the use of abstract patterns of interwoven curves and spirals, often absorbing representative forms in an extremely stylized way. Celtic forms persisted in Ireland, where they reemerged in the early Christian art of the 7th and 8th centuries AD.

CELTIC CHURCH, churches organized along monastic lines in Celtic areas (Britain and Brittany) from the 2nd or 3rd century. Cut off from Europe by the Saxon invasion, and differing from Rome in tradition, they were called into line by St. Augustine and submitted to Roman tradition at the Synod of Whitby.

CELTIC LANGUAGES, a major division of the INDO-EUROPEAN LANGUAGES, spoken widely over Europe from pre-Roman times though now confined chiefly to the UK and Brittany. There are two main branches: the now extinct Gaulish, about which little is known, and Insular, to which belong all the modern Celtic tongues. The latter branch is itself split into two: Gaelic, or Goidelic (Irish Gaelic (Erse), Scottish Gaelic and Manx); and Brythonic (Breton, Welsh and Cornish). Recent years have seen a revival in certain of these.

CELTIC RENAISSANCE, literary revival of the Gaelic tongues, particularly in Ireland and Wales, in the 19th and 20th centuries. Linked to the rise of nationalism, it resulted in a large and still growing body of literature and scholarship.

CELTS, a prehistoric people whose numerous tribes occupied much of Europe between c2000 and c100 BC, the peak of their power being around 500–100 BC. No European Celtic literature survives, but the later Irish and Welsh sources tell much about Celtic society and way of life. Primarily an agricultural people, though in local areas crafts and iron smelting developed, they grouped together in small settlements. Their social unit, based on kinship, was divided into a warrior nobility and a farming class, from the former being recruited the priests or DRUIDS, who ranked highest of all. Celtic art mixes stylized heads with abstract designs of scrolls and spirals (but see LA TÈNE). Remnants of CELTIC LANGUAGES are to be found in the forms of Gaelic, Erse, Manx and Welsh. The Celtic sphere of influence declined during the 1st century BC owing to the simultaneous expansion of the Roman Empire and the incursions of the Germanic races.

CEMBALO. See DULCIMER.

CEMENT, common name for Portland cement, the most important modern construction material, notably as a constituent of CONCRETE. In the manufacturing process, limestone is ground into small pieces (about 2cm). To provide the silica (25%) and alumina (10%) content required, various clays and crushed rocks are added, including iron ore (about 1%). This material is ground and finally burned in a rotary kiln at up to 1500°C, thus converting the mixture into clinker pellets. About 5% GYPSUM is then added to slow the hardening process, and the ground mixture is added to sand (for MORTAR) or to sand, gravel and crushed rock (for concrete). When water is added it solidifies gradually, undergoing many complex chemical reactions. The name "Portland" cement arises from a resemblance to stone quarried at Portland, England.

CEMETERY, term derived from the Greek for a burial place which is not a churchyard. It was first used by early Christians for a consecrated burial ground set outside the city walls due to land shortage. Modern cemeteries range from simple fields to elaborate parks such as Forest Lawn in Cal. Some may be reserved for specific denominations or for members of the armed forces, as in the case of Arlington National Cemetery, Va.

CENOBITES, monks who founded the first monastic communities in the 4th century. They differed from their hermit predecessors in that they formed communities rather than living in solitude. Western cenobitic monasticism was introduced by St. Benedict, and was the basis of the Benedictine Order.

CENOZOIC, or **Cainozoic**, the period of geological time containing the TERTIARY and QUATERNARY.

CENSER, vessel for burning incense, usually in religious ceremonies. Various forms have been used all over the world for centuries. In Christian ceremonies censers are most often used by the Eastern Orthodox, Roman Catholic and High Anglican churches.

CENSOR. See CENSORSHIP.

CENSORSHIP, supervision or control exercised by anybody in authority over public communication, conduct or morals. The official responsible is known as the censor. Early censorship in the Greek city-states curbed conduct insulting to the gods or dangerous to public order. In Rome the censor dictated public morality.

Censorship of books was not widespread (although some books were publicly burned) until the invention of printing in the 15th century. The first *Index of Prohibited Books* was drawn up by the Catholic Church in 1559 in an effort to stop the spread of subversive literature. Similar tactics were employed by Protestants and secular authorities. Milton's *Areopagitica* (1644) presented a strong case for freedom of the press, which was won in W Europe during the 18th and 19th centuries, with a few notable exceptions (Spain, Portugal and Ireland). In the US, freedom of the press is provided by the First Amendment to the Constitution, though it is not absolute, and publications deemed obscene are not protected. In recent years film censorship has also become an emotive issue; for a long time it was extremely restrictive, but the trend now is towards more relaxed standards. (See also PORNOGRAPHY.)

CENSORSHIP, in psychoanalysis, the term used by FREUD to describe the process in the UNCONSCIOUS whereby repressed (see REPRESSION) EMOTION, ideas, impulses and MEMORIES are prevented from reaching the CONSCIOUS. (See also SUPEREGO.)

CENSUS, enumeration of persons, property or other items at a given time. Today most countries conduct a regular count of population but these vary greatly in reliability, especially in underdeveloped countries. India, for example, conducts only sample censuses; this is cheaper and allows more detailed examination of the chosen sample. Early censuses, such as those mentioned in the Old Testament, were primarily military inventories. Babylonia, China, Egypt and Rome all made varieties of census for fiscal purposes. The modern concept dates from the 17th and 18th centuries when, in particular, regular censuses were taken in some of the New World colonies. Among the first national censuses was that in the newly-founded US in 1790, to determine each state's representation in Congress; since then, as required by the Constitution, a census has been conducted every 10 years. The UK census began in 1801. Beyond merely determining the size and content of a country's population, the modern census may seek information on economic development and social issues, and is therefore an essential tool in government planning.

CENTAUR, in Greek mythology, a race of beings half human and half horse. They were usually portrayed as wild and barbaric, but one at least, CHIRON, was the wise tutor of gods and heroes.

CENTAURUS, the Centaur, a constellation in the S Hemisphere. (See ALPHA CENTAURI; PROXIMA CENTAURI.)

CENTENNIAL EXPOSITION, International, world's fair held in Philadelphia, Pa., from May to Nov. 1876, celebrating the 100th anniversary of the Declaration of Independence. Exhibits from the arts and sciences were displayed by 49 nations. Mass-production techniques, then being pioneered in the US, were also put on show. The fair attracted almost 10 million visitors.

CENTER LINE, city in SE Mich., 11mi N of Detroit. The site of a US Army arsenal, its economy rests on metalworking and tool plants. Pop 10 379.

CENTER OF GRAVITY, the point about which gravitational FORCES on an object exert no net turning effect, and at which the mass of the object can for many purposes be regarded as concentrated. A freely suspended object hangs with its center of gravity vertically below the point of suspension, and an object will balance, though it may be unstable, if supported at a point vertically below the center of gravity. In free flight, an object spins about its center of gravity, which moves steadily in a straight line; the application of forces causes the center of gravity to accelerate in the direction of the net force, and the rate of spin to change according to the resultant turning effect.

CENTER OF SYMMETRY, a point about which a geometrical figure is symmetrical (see SYMMETRY).

CENTERVILLE, city in Montgomery Co., SW Ohio, 10mi S of Dayton. Pop 10 333.

CENTIGRADE DEGREE (C°), a unit of TEMPERATURE difference equal to 1 kelvin (K), originally defined by dividing the interval between the boiling and freezing points of water into 100 equal divisions. It is used as the basis of the Celsius temperature scale (see CELSIUS, ANDERS).

CENTIMETRE (cm), a unit of length equal to 0.01 metre. (See METRE.)

CENTIPEDES, long-bodied members of the phylum ARTHROPODA with two legs to each of their 15–100 segments. They are usually 25–50mm (1–2in) long, though in the tropics some reach 0.3m (1ft). Normally insectivorous they paralyze their food by injecting poison through a pair of pincers located near the head. Centipedes live in moist places under stones or in soil.

CENTRAL AFRICAN REPUBLIC, landlocked independent republic in Africa. It lies just N of the equator, bounded by Chad to the N and Sudan to the S, on a well-watered plateau 2 500ft above sea level. The country is mostly savanna, with dense tropical rain forest to the S. The chief river, the Ubangi, is the main link with the outside world. There are no railroads and only 50mi of paved road.

The population is composed of various ethnic groups, with mainly Bantu and Nilotic cultures. The main *lingua franca* is Sangho. There are various religious groups, but about 70% of the population are tribal animists. There are few towns, and education and living standards are poor. Exports include diamonds, cotton and coffee but most of the population live by subsistence farming.

Various tribes migrated into the area, most fleeing the slave trade in the 19th century. The French established outposts 1886–87, and the area was

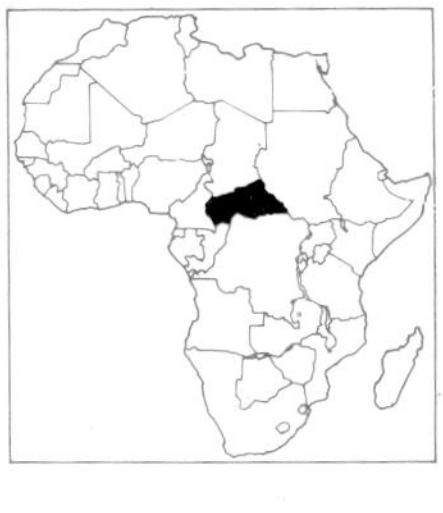

Official Name: Central African Republic
Capital: Bangui
Area: 240 535sq mi
Population: 2 255 536
Languages: French, Sangho
Religions: Animist, Christian, Muslim
Monetary Unit(s): 1 CFA franc = 100 centimes

incorporated into French Equatorial Africa in 1910. It achieved independence on Aug. 13, 1960, under President David Dacko; he was overthrown in 1966 by Colonel Jean-Bedel Bokassa, who in 1972 was appointed president for life.

CENTRAL AMERICA, narrow land bridge linking North and South America, extending from the isthmus of Tehuantepec to the isthmus of Panama. With Mexico and the Caribbean islands (West Indies), it forms the vast region known as MIDDLE AMERICA.

CENTRAL CITY, city in N central Col., seat of Gilpin Co. Formerly a gold-rush boom town, it is now virtually a ghost town kept alive by tourism, especially during the annual music festival. Pop 228.

CENTRAL FALLS, city in NE R.I., in the lower Blackstone valley. It has various industries, including glass and textiles. Pop 18 716.

CENTRALIA, industrial city in S Ill., 93mi SE of Springfield. It lies at the center of an agricultural and oil-bearing region. Pop 15 217.

CENTRALIA, city in SW Wash., 23mi S of Olympia. Its economy rests on lumbering and on dairy, fruit and poultry farming in the area. Pop 10 054.

CENTRAL INTELLIGENCE AGENCY (CIA), established in 1947 by the National Security Act to coordinate, evaluate and disseminate intelligence from other US agencies and to advise the president and the National Security Council on security matters. Though its field of operations widened considerably under Allen Dulles (Director 1953–61), its estimated 15 000 employees spend most of their time in research and analysis at CIA headquarters in Langley, Va. The CIA has done much to further the interests of the US and its allies, but such fiascos as the BAY OF PIGS invasion of Cuba and the capture of the U-2 spy-plane over Russia, in which it was involved, have not helped international relations. Concern over possible misuse of its considerable independence in the wake of "Watergate" led to a major investigation and internal reorganization in 1975.

CENTRAL POWERS, coalition of Germany, Austria–Hungary, Ottoman Turkey and Bulgaria in WWI. (See also ALLIES; TRIPLE ALLIANCE.)

CENTRAL TREATY ORGANIZATION (CENTO), mutual security alliance between Pakistan, Iran, Turkey and the UK, with the US an associate member. It was established by the Baghdad Pact (1955) and, under the name of Middle East Treaty Organization, was based in Baghdad until Iraq withdrew its membership in 1959. Its headquarters are now in Ankara, Turkey.

CENTREVILLE, a residential community in Ill. Scott Air Force Base is 12mi to the E. Pop 11 378.

CENTRIFUGAL FORCE. See CENTRIPETAL FORCE.

CENTRIFUGE, a machine for separating mixtures of solid particles and immiscible liquids of different DENSITIES and for extracting liquids from wet solids by rotating them in a container at high speed. The separation occurs because the centrifugal force experienced in a rotating frame increases with particle density. Centrifuges are used in drying clothes and slurries, in chemical ANALYSIS, in separating cream and in atomic ISOTOPE separation. Giant ones are used to accustom pilots and astronauts to large ACCELERATIONS. The **ultracentrifuge**, invented by T. SVEDBERG, uses very high speeds to measure (optically) sedimentation rates of macromolecular solutes and so determine molecular weights.

CENTRIPETAL FORCE, the FORCE applied to a body to maintain it moving in a circular path. To maintain a body of MASS *m*, traveling with instantaneous VELOCITY *v*, in a circular path of radius *r*, a

centripetal force F, acting *toward the center* of the circle, given by $F=mv^2/r$ must be applied to it. If a body is resting in a rotating frame, it experiences a **centrifugal force**, apparently acting *away from the center* of rotation, numerically equal to the external centripetal force. Because, from the point of view of an observer external to the rotating frame, the centrifugal force has no real existence, it is often termed a fictitious force.

CENTROID, the point of concurrence of the medians of a TRIANGLE (i.e., those lines drawn from each angle to the midpoint of the facing side). The centroid is the CENTER OF GRAVITY of the triangle.

CENTURION, in the armies of the Roman Empire, the commander of a *centuria*, a subdivision of a LEGION consisting of 100 men.

CENTURY OF PROGRESS EXPOSITION, international exhibition celebrating Chicago's centenary, held on the shores of Lake Michigan 1933–34. Primarily concerned with science and technology, it also stimulated design and architecture.

CENTURY PLANT. See AGAVE.

CEPHALIC INDEX, in ANTHROPOMETRY, an index used originally in attempts to classify RACE, now used mainly to indicate possible relationships between small groups. The index is given by

$$\frac{\text{maximum head breadth} \times 100}{\text{maximum head length}}$$

Peoples with broad heads (cephalic index over 80) are classed as brachycephalic; those with long heads (less than 76) as dolichocephalic; and those in between as mesocephalic (mesaticephalic).

CEPHALIZATION, the tendency in the evolution of animals for sense organs and associated nervous tissue to be concentrated at one end of the body—the end that "faces" the environment. Cephalization has led to the development of a distinct head in most animals.

CEPHALOPODA, class of predatory MOLLUSKS including the CUTTLEFISH, OCTOPUS and SQUID. They swim by forcing a jet of water through a narrow funnel near the mouth. Cephalopods have sucker-bearing arms or tentacles and a horny beak. The shell, typical of most mollusks, is absent or reduced.

CEPHEID VARIABLES, stars whose brightness varies regularly with a period of 1–50 days, possibly, but improbably, due to a fluctuation in size. The length of their cycle is directly proportional to their absolute magnitude, making them useful "mileposts" for computing large astronomical distances. (See VARIABLE STAR.)

CERAM, second largest of the Moluccas Islands, E Indonesia. It is a mountainous island, 6 221sq mi in area, and is densely forested. The population is of Malay–Papuan stock; there are Muslim and Christian settlements on the coast. The economy is largely primitive and rests on agriculture and forest produce.

CERAMICS, materials produced by treating non-metallic inorganic materials (originally CLAY) at high temperatures. Modern ceramics include such diverse products as porcelain and china, furnace bricks, electric insulators, ferrite magnets (see SPINEL), rocket nosecones and abrasives. In general, ceramics are hard, chemically inert under most conditions, and can withstand high temperatures in industrial applications. Many are refractory metal OXIDES. Primitive ceramics in the form of pottery date from the 5th millennium BC, and improved steadily in quality and design. By the 10th century AD porcelain had been developed in China. (See also BRICK; CERMETS; CONCRETE; GLASS; POTTERY AND PORCELAIN.)

CERBERUS, in Greek mythology, the triple-headed watchdog of HADES, keeping the living out and the dead in. He was temporarily captured by HERCULES as his 12th labor.

CEREAL CROPS, annual plants of the grass family, including WHEAT, RICE, CORN, BARLEY, SORGHUM, MILLET, OATS and RYE. Their grain forms the staple diet for most of the world. Though lacking in calcium and vitamin A, they have more CARBOHYDRATE than any other food, as well as PROTEIN and other VITAMINS. Cereal crops are relatively easy to cultivate and can cope with a wide range of climates. About 1 757 million acres of the world's arable land are sown with cereal crops each year. The US leads in production of corn, oats and sorghum.

CEREALS, Breakfast, popular foods made from cereal grains. They were first developed in the 19th century as part of the health food movement; W. H. KELLOGG and C. W. Post were the first to make them into massive industries. Some cereals, such as oatmeal, must be cooked before eating; more popular are the ready-to-eat cereals such as cornflakes and puffed wheat, on which milk is usually poured.

CEREBELLUM. See BRAIN.

CEREBRAL PALSY, a diverse group of conditions caused by BRAIN damage around the time of BIRTH and resulting in a variable degree of nonprogressive physical and mental handicap. While abnormalities of MUSCLE control are the most obvious, loss of sensation and some degree of DEAFNESS are common accompaniments. Speech and intellectual development can also be impaired but may be entirely normal. SPASTIC PARALYSIS of both legs with mild arm weakness (diplegia), or of one half of the body (hemiplegia), are common forms. A number of cases have abnormal movements (athetosis) or ATAXIA. Common causes include birth trauma, ANOXIA, prematurity, Rhesus incompatibility and cerebral HEMORRHAGE. PHYSIOTHERAPY and training allow the child to overcome many deficits; deformity must be avoided by ensuring full range of movements at all joints, but surgical correction may be necessary. Sometimes transposition of TENDONS improves the balance of strength around important joints. It is crucial that the child is not deprived of normal sensory and emotional experiences. Improved antenatal care, OBSTETRIC skill and care of premature infants have reduced the incidence.

CEREBROSPINAL FLUID, watery fluid circulating in the chambers (ventricles) of the BRAIN and between layers of the meninges covering the brain and SPINAL CORD. It is a filtrate of BLOOD and is normally clear, containing salts, GLUCOSE and some PROTEIN. It may be sampled and analysed by SPINAL TAP.

CEREBRUM. See BRAIN.

CERENKOV RADIATION, ELECTROMAGNETIC RADIATION emitted when a high-energy particle passes through a dense medium at a velocity greater than the velocity of light in that medium. It was first detected in 1934 by P. A. CHERENKOV.

CERES, in Roman mythology, goddess of food plants and harvest; according to legend her cult was introduced to stem a famine in 496 BC. Cereals are probably named for her. Her Greek counterpart is DEMETER.

CERES, largest of the ASTEROIDS (470mi in diameter) and the one first discovered (by PIAZZI, 1801). Its orbit was first computed by K. F. GAUSS and found to satisfy BODE's Law. Its "year" is 1 681 days and its maximum apparent magnitude is +7.

CEREUS, a genus of columnar CACTI with cylindrical stems, producing fragrant white, funnel-shaped flowers. The plants grow quickly and are easy to cultivate, and hence are commonly grown as house plants.

CERIUM (Ce), most abundant of the RARE EARTHS; one of the LANTHANUM SERIES. AW 140.1, mp 804°C, bp 3257°C, sg 6.657 (25°C).

CERMETS, or **ceramels**, composite materials made from mixed METALS and CERAMICS. The TRANSITION ELEMENTS are most often used. Powdered and compacted with an oxide, carbide or boride, etc., they are heated to just below their melting point, when bonding occurs. Cermets combine the hardness and strength of metals with a high resistance to corrosion, wear and heat. This makes them invaluable in jet engines, cutting tools, brake linings and nuclear reactors.

CERNUNNOS, Celtic horned god, lord of wild things. He bore stag antlers and was often represented in the company of a stag and a ram-horned serpent deity. The Christian Church used him as a symbol of ANTICHRIST.

CERRITOS, city in SW Cal., 28mi SE of Los Angeles. Pop 15 856.

CERRO DE PASCO, Andean mining center, capital of Pasco department, Peru, 112mi NE of Lima. At 14 232ft it is one of the world's highest towns. Pop 21 363.

CERRO GORDO, Battle of, major battle on April 17–18, 1847, in the MEXICAN WAR (1846–48). Winfield SCOTT's 8 500 US troops defeated 12 000 Mexicans led by General SANTA ANNA, 60mi NW of Veracruz. This opened the way to Puebla and ultimately to Mexico City.

CERTIORIARI, Writ of, in COMMON LAW, an order from a higher court to a lower for a reexamination on an action by the lower court, or from an apellate court to obtain information on a case before it.

CERUSSITE, white mineral form of lead (II) carbonate ($PbCO_3$), a major ore of LEAD, found in Spain, SW Africa, Australia and Col. It is formed by weathering of GALENA. **White lead**, used as a paint pigment, is a basic lead (II) carbonate ($PbCO_3+Pb(OH)_2$).

CERVANTES (SAAVEDRA), Miguel de (1547–1616), Spanish novelist and playwright, a major figure of Spanish literature. He left his studies in 1570 to join the army; his left hand was crippled at the sea battle of Lepanto (1571). Captured by pirates in 1575, he was enslaved in Algiers until ransomed in 1580. In 1585 he wrote *La Galatea*, a pastoral novel in verse and prose; after this he entered government service. In 1605 he published the first part of *Don Quixote de la Mancha*, his masterpiece. Not only a masterly debunking of pseudo-chivalric romance but a rich tragi-comic novel, it was an immediate success. He also wrote about 30 plays, of which 16 survive, a volume of short stories and the second part of *Don Quixote* (1615). His last work was *Persilas and Sigismunda* (1617).

CERVERA Y TOPETE, Pascual (1839–1909), Spanish admiral. Minister of marine in 1892, he commanded the Atlantic fleet during the SPANISH-AMERICAN WAR (1898). It was blockaded and sunk at Santiago de Cuba; Cervera was honorably acquitted at his court-martial.

CERYNEAN HIND, in Greek mythology, an incredibly swift deer. HERCULES' 4th labor was to capture it; ARTEMIS, to whom it was sacred, ordered him to free it.

CESARIAN SECTION, BIRTH of a child from the WOMB by abdominal operation. The mother is given an anesthetic and an incision is made in the ABDOMEN and lower part of the uterus; the child is delivered and attended to; the PLACENTA is removed and incisions are sewn up. Cesarian section may be necessary if the baby is too large to pass through the PELVIS, if it shows delay or signs of ANOXIA during labor, or in cases where maternal disease does not allow normal labor. It may be performed effectively before labor has started. With modern ANESTHESIA and BLOOD TRANSFUSION, the risks of Cesarian section are not substantially greater than those of normal delivery. It is believed that Julius Caesar was born in this way.

CESIUM (Cs), a very soft, silvery-white ALKALI METAL, found mainly in the mineral pollucite, and made by reduction of cesium chloride. It is highly reactive, similar to potassium, and burns spontaneously in moist air. When exposed to light it emits electrons, and has applications in television cameras. It is used in vacuum tubes to remove oxygen and water; and a recent application is in ion-propulsion rocket engines. AW 132.9, mp 28°C, bp 678°C, sg 1.873 (20°C).

CETACEA, an order of aquatic MAMMALS which includes the WHALES and DOLPHINS. Cetaceans are fish-like and completely dependent on water, but being mammals, they breathe air and the females bear live young.

CETEWAYO, or Cetshwayo (c1826–1884), fourth and last Zulu king (1873–79). In 1879 he declared war on British and Boer settlers in the Transvaal, but was finally captured and deposed.

CETINJE, city in Yugoslavia. Former capital of Montenegro, it lies about 25mi SW of Titograd. It is a cultural and tourist center. Pop 11 892.

CEUTA, free port and fortified city, a Spanish enclave on the Moroccan coast. Its industries are shipping, fishing and food processing. Pop 67 187.

CÉVENNES, limestone mountain range in S France, on the SE edge of the Massif Central. It stretches for

150mi, rising to Mont Lozère (5 584ft) and the once-volcanic Mont Mézenc (5 755ft).

CEYLON. See SRI LANKA.

CÉZANNE, Paul (1839–1906), French painter, among the most influential of modern times. During his studies in Paris he met and was influenced by Pissarro and other Impressionists. His early work is Impressionist in style, but he later abandoned this to develop a style of his own, lyrical and vibrantly colorful, as in the *Grande Baigneuses* (1905). He sought "to treat nature in terms of the cylinder, sphere and cone . . . ," and to make his paintings autonomous objects. In this he was the prime innovator of modern art, anticipating Cubism and other movements.

CGS UNITS, a metric system of units based on the CENTIMETRE (length), GRAM (mass) and SECOND (time), generally used among scientists until superseded by SI UNITS. Several variants are used for electrical and magnetic problems, including electrostatic units (esu or stat-units—see STATAMPERE), electromagnetic units (emu or ab-units—see ABAMPERE) and the Gaussian system. In this last, ab-units are used for quantities arising primarily in an electromagnetic context, stat-units for electrostatic quantities and both the PERMEABILITY and the PERMITTIVITY of free space are set equal to unity. As a result, the electromagnetic constant (*c*) tends to occur in equations in which electrostatic and magnetic quantities are mixed.

CHABANEL, Saint Noël (1613–1649), French Jesuit martyred by Iroquois Indians while engaged in missionary work in Ontario, Canada, among the Huron tribes. He was canonized in 1930; his feast day is Sept. 26.

CHABRIER, Alexis Emmanuel (1841–1894), French composer best remembered for orchestral works such as *España* (1883) and various piano pieces. He also wrote several operas, partly influenced by Wagner.

CHACO. See GRAN CHACO.

CHACO CANYON NATIONAL MONUMENT, in NW N.M., was established in 1907 to preserve prehistoric remains of the Pueblo civilization. It covers 34sq mi.

CHACONNE, spirited Spanish dance, possibly of Mexican origin, dating from the 17th century, which gave its name to a musical form similar to PASSACAGLIA. Both are usually in triple time and consist of variations on a ground bass.

CHACO WAR, war fought between Paraguay and Bolivia during 1932–35 over possession of part of the Chaco region. It caused significant damage to both countries, with over 200 000 casualties. It was settled by arbitration, largely in favor of Paraguay.

CHAD, landlocked state in N central Africa. Its N part extends into the Sahara desert, where the Tibesti highlands rise to 11 000ft. The S part consists largely of semiarid steppe with wooded grasslands (savannas) near Lake CHAD, watered by the Shari and Logone rivers. In the S rainfall reaches 47in during the rainy season, and most of the population lives there.

The N part of the country is inhabited by nomadic Muslim tribes such as the Fulani, the Wadai and the Toubou. In the S Negroid tribes predominate, the largest being the Sara. Most are animists, speaking tribal languages. There are less than 5 000 Europeans, mainly French; French is the official language. Only about 35% of the children attend school, and over 92% of the population lives in rural areas.

The economy of Chad is based mainly upon agriculture, with the greater part of the population engaged in subsistence farming (though undeveloped uranium deposits are believed to exist). The main crops are millet, sorghum and cassava for local consumption. Cotton, rice, peanuts, meat, hides and fish from Lake Chad are exported. Communications are poor and present a major obstacle to any further development. Most trade was with France, which gave much financial aid, but relations have recently deteriorated.

The French had conquered Chad by 1900, and it became the northernmost of the four territories of Ubanga-Shari-Chad when French Equatorial Africa was formed in 1910. It became an independent republic in Aug. 1960, with François (Ngarta) Tombalbaye as president. He was killed during a military takeover in April 1975.

CGS Units

Quantity	Unit	Symbol	Equivalent in SI units
length	centimetre	cm	0.01 metre
mass	gram	g	0.001 kilogram
time	second	s	1 second
length	angstrom unit	Å	0.1 nanometre
work/energy	erg	erg	10^{-7} joule
force	dyne	dyn	10^{-5} newton
energy	calorie (IT)	$cal_{(IT)}$	4.1868 joule
force	gram-force	gf	9.807×10^{-5} newton

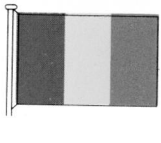

Official Name: The Republic of Chad
Capital: Fort-Lamy
Area: 495 752sq mi
Population: 3 800 000
Languages: French, Arabic
Religions: Muslim, Animist, Christian
Monetary Unit(s): 1 CFA franc = 100 centimes

CHAD, Lake, in W central Africa, is bounded by Cameroon, Chad, Niger and Nigeria and fed by the Shari and Logone rivers. The area of the shallow lake varies from 4 000 to 10 000sq mi at low and high water respectively.

CHADWICK, Sir James (1891–1974), English physicist who was awarded the 1935 Nobel physics prize for his discovery of the NEUTRON (1932).

CHAERONEA, ancient Greek city, once the westernmost city of the district of Boeotia. Nearby is the site of Philip II of Macedon's victory over the Athenians and Thebans in 338 BC and also the site of the Roman general Sulla's victory over Mithridates VI of Pontus in 86 BC.

CHAETOGNATHA. See ARROW-WORMS.

CHAFERS, large, square-bodied BEETLES about 25mm (1in) long, with conical tails protruding beyond the wingcases, fine bristles around the thorax, and antennae ending in a fan of plates. Adults feed on foliage, and their larvae live in the soil and eat roots. Varieties include May bugs, June bugs and the European cockchafer.

CHAGALL, Marc (1887–), Russian-Jewish painter. Influenced at first by his teacher BAKST, his work developed further in Paris 1910–14. His style is characterized by its dreamlike, lyrical fantasy and its bright but never harsh colors. His subjects are often derived from pre-WWI Jewish life in Russia. Chagall left Russia in 1922, and later settled in France.

CHAGAS' DISEASE, PARASITIC DISEASE found only on the American continent, caused by a trypanosome and carried by insects. In the acute form, there is swelling around the eye, FEVER, malaise, enlargement of LYMPH nodes, LIVER and SPLEEN, and EDEMA. Most cases recover fully. The chronic form causes disease of the HEART and GASTROINTESTINAL TRACT.

CHAGRES RIVER, river in Panama, a major water source for the Panama Canal. Flowing SW to join the canal at Gamboa (Gatun Lake), it drains NW into the Caribbean at San Lorenzo.

CHAIN, a series of interlocking links forming a flexible cable. Simple chains are used in, for example, haulage and hoisting. Roller chains are used in power TRANSMISSION (as on a bicycle): here the links of an endless chain mesh with the teeth of toothed wheels called sprockets. EFFICIENCY may be as high as 99%.

CHAIN, Sir Ernst Boris (1906–), German-born UK biochemist who helped develop PENICILLIN for clinical use. For this he shared with FLOREY and FLEMING the 1945 Nobel Prize for Physiology or Medicine.

CHAIN REACTION. See NUCLEAR ENERGY.

CHALCEDON, ancient Greek city in Bithynia, opposite Byzantium (modern Istanbul) on the shores of the Bosporus. The site has changed hands many times and is now Kadiköy, a suburb of Istanbul.

CHALCEDON, Council of, the fourth ECUMENICAL COUNCIL, held Oct. 8–31, 451. It defined Christ as one Person in two natures (divine and human) united "unconfusedly, unchangeably, indivisibly, inseparably;" so opposing Eutyches, the father of MONOPHYSITISM, and the NESTORIANS.

CHALCEDONY, mineral consisting of fibrous microcrystalline QUARTZ. Common in gravels, it

Two Lovers on Horseback, by Marc Chagall. The flowing, dreamlike images and rich colors are typical of his work, particularly after his marriage. Pairs of lovers, modeled on himself and his wife, became a motif.

occurs in several forms, including some semiprecious GEM stones. Notable are BLOODSTONE, CAT'S EYE, ONYX, CHRYSOPRASE, JASPER, CARNELIAN, SARD and AGATE.

CHALCOCITE, dark gray or black mineral, copper (I) sulfide (Cu_2S). A major COPPER ore, it is found (often with BORNITE) in the Ural Mts, Africa, South America, Alaska, Conn. and the southern US.

CHALCOPYRITE ($CuFeS_2$), the most important COPPER ore, very similar to PYRITE, with which it is often associated. It is found in the US, Canada, Australia, W Europe and South America.

CHALDEA, name for S Babylonia, after its occupation by the Chaldeans in the 10th century BC. The Chaldeans were accomplished astronomers and astrologers, and ancient writers often used their name as a synonym for "magician." In 626 BC NABOPALASSAR founded the Chaldean Neo-Babylonian Empire, which held sway over the area until the death of NEBUCHADNEZZAR in 561 BC. (See also BABYLONIA AND ASSYRIA.)

CHALDEAN RITE. See NESTORIANS.

CHALET, type of timber house characteristic of Bavaria and of the Austrian, French and Swiss Alpine regions. It usually has two or three stories, small windows, balconies and a wide overhanging roof.

CHALEUR BAY, an inlet of the Gulf of St. Lawrence in E Canada, about 90mi long and 20mi wide at its widest point; it is an important fishing ground. Major towns on the bay include Bathurst in New Brunswick and New Carlisle in Quebec.

CHALIAPIN, Fyodor Ivanovich (1873–1938), Russian operatic bass. Famous for his acting as well as for his voice, he settled in France after the Russian Revolution. His main successes were as MUSSORGSKY's *Boris Godunov* and Boito's *Mefistofele*.

CHALICE (from Latin *calix*, a cup), vessel used to hold consecrated wine at the celebration of the Christian Eucharist, symbolic of the cup used at the Last Supper. Early Christians used ordinary cups; later chalices are often lavishly ornamented.

CHALK, soft, white rock mainly formed of fine-grained, porous LIMESTONE and containing calcareous remains of minute marine animals. There are large deposits in Tex., Kan. and Ark. Chalk is widely used in lime and cement manufacture and as a fertilizer. It is also used in cosmetics, plastics, crayons and oil paints; school chalk is today usually made from chemically-produced calcium carbonate.

CHALLENGER EXPEDITION, a round-the-world oceanographic-survey cruise made by the steam corvette HMS *Challenger* between 1872 and 1876 under the scientific direction of **Sir Charles Wyville Thomson** (1830–1882), the first and most comprehensive voyage of its type. Its results were published as the 50-volume *Challenger Report* (1881–95).

CHALMERS, Thomas (1780–1847), Scottish theologian, founding member and first Moderator of the Free Church of Scotland (1843). Also a noted economist, he was a pioneer of social work among the poor.

Harvesting grapes that will be made into champagne; a scene near Reims, France, in the heart of the Champagne country.

CHALMETTE NATIONAL HISTORICAL PARK, on the Mississippi R just below New Orleans, La., is the site of Andrew Jackson's defeat of British forces at the Battle of New Orleans, Jan. 8, 1815.

CHÂLONS-SUR-MARNE, Battle of. See CATALAUNIAN PLAINS, BATTLE OF THE.

CHAMBERLAIN, family name of three prominent British statesmen. **Joseph Chamberlain** (1836–1914), entered parliament in 1876 as a Liberal. He held office under Gladstone, but split with him, opposing home rule for Ireland (1886). As colonial secretary 1895–1903, he failed to prevent the Boer Wars. Until his paralysis by a stroke in 1906, he fought for integration of the Empire through preferential tariffs for Empire trade. His son, **Sir Joseph Austen Chamberlain** (1863–1937), entered parliament as a Conservative in 1892, and held various government offices from 1902. As foreign secretary 1924–29 under Baldwin, he helped secure the LOCARNO TREATIES, and shared the 1925 Nobel Peace Prize. Austen's half-brother, **Arthur Neville Chamberlain** (1869–1940), was a Conservative member of parliament from 1918. He held office under Baldwin, and succeeded him as prime minister in 1937. In his efforts to avert war with Germany, he followed a policy of appeasement and signed the MUNICH AGREEMENT, finally abandoning the policy when Hitler seized the rest of Czechoslovakia in March 1939. He resigned on May 10, 1940, during WWII, after the failure of an expedition to help Norway.

CHAMBERLAIN, Houston Stewart (1855–1927), Anglo-German writer. His *Foundations of the Nineteenth Century* (1899) was a racialist glorification of Germanic history from which Hitler and the Nazis drew many ideas. He was a son-in-law of Richard Wagner.

CHAMBERLAIN, Owen (1920–), US physicist who shared the 1959 Nobel physics prize with E. Segrè in recognition of their discovery of the antiproton (see ANTIMATTER).

CHAMBERLAIN, Wilton Norman (1936–), US basketball player, nicknamed "Wilt the Stilt" for his height of 7ft 1in. Among his many records, he was the first to score 25 000 and 30 000 career points in regular-season National Basketball Association games (1968 and 1972).

CHAMBER MUSIC, term applied to a musical composition intended for a small ensemble. Originally it meant domestic music, that is music written by a house composer for his patron. It became established as a special genre during the 17th and 18th centuries. The instrumental combinations are varied, though they do not often exceed a total of 15 instruments. Chamber music is characterized by an intimacy of communication between the performers. The principal form of composition is the string quartet (2 violins, viola and cello), which was developed by HAYDN and MOZART, and expanded to new dimensions by BEETHOVEN.

CHAMBER OF COMMERCE, an association of businessmen set up to improve business conditions and practices, and to protect business interests. The first in the US was the New York Chamber of Commerce (1768) and now most sizeable US cities have one. Activities are coordinated through the US Chamber of Commerce, founded 1912. The International Chamber of Commerce, based in Paris, is mainly concerned with trade problems.

CHAMBERS, (Jay David) Whittaker (1901–1961), US journalist, who exposed Alger HISS as a spy in 1948. Chambers had been a fellow member of the Communist Party 1924–38.

CHAMBERSBURG, borough in S Pa., seat of Franklin Co. Center of an agricultural region, it manufactures clothing and metal and paper products. It is the home of Wilson College. Pop 17 315.

CHAMELEONS, LIZARDS of the family Chamaeleonidae living in Africa and Madagascar with extraordinary adaptations to arboreal life. Their five toes are webbed into two groups of two and three between which they are able to grip branches. Their tails are prehensile, and their eyes can turn independently in all directions. They feed on insects which they catch with their long, sticky tongues, and the color of their skin undergoes swift alteration in response to changes of emotion or temperature. There are over 80 species, some viviparous, ranging in length from 50mm (2in) to 0.6m (2ft).

CHAMIZAL, disputed area (437 acres) on the US–Mexico border, adjoining El Paso, Tex. Technically US territory after a change in the Rio Grande's course, it was finally ceded to Mexico in 1963.

CHAMOIS, *Rupicapra rupicapra*, a goat-like mammal of the family Bovidae found in the mountain forests of Europe and Asia Minor. Chamois are famous for their agility, being capable of leaps of over 6m (20ft). They have thick brown coats and stand about 0.75m (2.5ft) at the shoulder. Their hides were once used for making "shammy" leather.

CHAMOMILE. See CAMOMILE.

CHAMPA, Kingdom of, ancient Indochinese kingdom on the E coast of Vietnam. Originally a Chinese province, it first became prominent under King Bhadravarman c400 AD. In 446 it was subjugated by China. It won independence in the 6th century, and became increasingly powerful until in the 9th century it was threatening Chinese territory and the neighboring Khmer Empire. The Khmers overran it in the 12th century; it then came under Cambodian and later Annamese rule, and by the 17th century it had been absorbed into Annam completely.

CHAMPAGNE, historic province in NE France, famous for the effervescent champagne wines from vineyards between Reims and Épernay. The ruling counts of Champagne were especially powerful during the 12th and 13th centuries, and the region had a central role in French history.

CHAMPAIGN, city in E central Ill., adjoining Urbana. In an agricultural area, it is becoming increasingly industrial. Pop 56 532.

CHAMPLAIN, Lake, narrow lake forming the border between Vt. and N.Y. and jutting partly into Canada. Its area is 435sq mi, excluding 55sq mi of islands. Lake Champlain flows into the St. Lawrence R; though icebound for four months of the year, it is deep enough for commercial navigation. It is both a leisure center and a site for many refining industries. As a major route from N.Y. state to Canada, the lake has often been strategically important.

CHAMPLAIN, Samuel (1567–1635), French explorer, first governor of French Canada. After voyages to the Canary Isles and Central America, he explored the St. Lawrence area in 1603 as far as the Lachine Rapids. In 1604 he settled on the site which is now Annapolis Royal, Nova Scotia. He founded Quebec in 1608 and discovered Lake Champlain in 1609. He was appointed commandant of New France in 1612. When Quebec surrendered to English privateers in 1629, Champlain was imprisoned; on his release in 1633 he returned to Canada as governor.

CHAMPOLLION, Jean François (1790–1832), French linguist and historian, the "father of Egyptology." Professor of history at Grenoble U. 1809–16, he was the first to effectively decipher Egyptian HIEROGLYPHICS, a result of his research on the ROSETTA STONE. A chair of Egyptian antiquities was created especially for him at the Collège de France in 1831.

CHAMPS-ÉLYSÉES, avenue in Paris, France, famous for its spacious elegance. Lined with shops and cafés, it runs for over a mile W from the Place de la Concorde to the Arc de Triomphe.

CHANCE. See PROBABILITY.

CHANCELLORSVILLE, Battle of, fought during the US Civil War, May 1–5, 1863. Gen. Joseph Hooker's Union forces crossed the Rappahonnock R to Chancellorsville, W of Fredericksburg, Va., in a bid to encircle Gen. Robert E. Lee's Confederate forces protecting Fredericksburg. The ploy failed; Lee's counteroffensive led to an indecisive battle claiming 30 000 lives, including that of Gen. "Stonewall" Jackson.

CHANCE MUSIC. See ALEATORY MUSIC.

CHANCERY, Court of, a court corresponding, in those parts of the US where the concept still exists, to the equity court. Because their original function was to provide justice outside the forms of common law, such courts still deal with trust and mortgage law, injunctions and rectification of written instruments.

CHAN CHAN, ruined capital of the pre-Inca Chimú kingdom (1200–1400), on the N Peruvian coast, destroyed by the Incas in the mid-15th century. The ruins are 14sq mi in area, the largest known in South America.

CHAN-CHIANG (Tsamkong), port city in SW Kwangtung province, China. Occupied by the French 1898–1943, it has since become a rail hub and industrial center. Pop 170 000.

CHANDIGARH, joint capital of Punjab and Haryana states, NW India, replacing the former capital, Lahore, now in Pakistan. An ultramodern city largely designed by LE CORBUSIER, it is a communications and industrial center and the seat of Punjab U. Pop 218 743.

CHANDLER, city in S Ariz., 17mi SE of Phoenix. A winter resort, it is otherwise largely an agricultural center. Pop 13 763.

CHANDLER, Raymond Thornton (1888–1959), US detective novelist whose seven novels have received critical acclaim. They combine wit and pace with strong characterization, particularly of their hero Philip Marlowe, a tough but honest private detective.

CHANDLER, Zachariah (1813–1879), US politician, a founder of the Republican Party. He made his fortune as a dry-goods merchant in Detroit and was elected to the Senate in 1857, becoming a firm opponent of slavery and of the Confederate cause in the Civil War.

CHANDRAGUPTA (4th century BC), Indian emperor c321–297 BC, founder of the MAURYA dynasty. He rose to power after Alexander the Great's withdrawal from India, and won territory from the Seleucids, extending his realm into Afghanistan. His grandson was the famous Emperor ASOKA.

CHANDRAGUPTA, name of two emperors of N India. **Chandragupta I** (reigned c320–330 AD) rose from a local chieftainship to rule a prosperous realm covering what is now Bihar, Bengal and Uttar Pradesh. **Chandragupta II** (reigned c380–415), his grandson, took the foreign-controlled Gujarat area, opening the way for extensive trade with Rome. His reign was benevolent and saw a great cultural flowering in India.

CHANEL, Gabrielle ("Coco") (1883–1971), French fashion designer who rose to fame in Paris in the 1920s. She created the "Chanel Look" and the celebrated perfume *Chanel No. 5.*

CHANEY, Lon (1883–1930), US actor whose skill in characterization and makeup won him the title of "Man with a Thousand Faces." His best-known films were *The Hunchback of Notre Dame* (1923) and *The Phantom of the Opera* (1925). His son, **Lon Chaney, Jr.** (1907–1973), also became famous as an actor.

CH'ANG-CHOU, city on Hsi Ch'i R in S Kiangsu province, China, formerly Wutsin. It is now a major commercial center with small local industries. Pop 300 000.

CH'ANG-CH'UN, capital city of Kirin province, N China. Occupied by the Japanese 1931–45, it is now a cultural and industrial center, the nucleus of China's car industry. Pop 1 500 000.

CHANGE OF LIFE. See MENSTRUATION.

CH'ANG-SHA, capital city of Hunan province, S China, on the Siang R. In the center of China's richest rice-growing area, it is a commercial center and river port. It has been a cultural center for over 1 000 years. Pop 900 000.

CHANNEL ISLANDS, archipelago totalling 75sq mi in area, in the English Channel off NW France. Dependencies of the British crown since 1066, they are administered according to their own local constitutions. The two main bailiwicks are Jersey, including Les Minquiers and Ecrehou Rocks, and Guernsey, including Sark, Alderney, Herm, Jethou, Lihou and Brechou. The two main towns are St. Helier on Jersey and St. Peter Port on Guernsey. Pop 125 243.

CHANNEL ISLANDS NATIONAL MONUMENT, consisting of the islands of Santa Barbara and Anacapa, off S Cal. A sea-lion colony and wildlife sanctuary, it has rich fossil beds. Only 2sq mi of the monument's 28sq mi area is land.

CHANNING, William Ellery (1780–1842), US theologian, writer and philanthropist, leader of the Unitarian movement in New England. He led the Unitarian withdrawal from Congregationalism in 1820–25. Active in antislavery, temperance and pacifist causes, he believed that moral improvement was man's prime concern.

CHANSON DE ROLAND (Song of Roland), most famous and probably the earliest of the CHANSONS DE GESTE. Written in the 11th century, probably by the Norman poet Turold, it tells of the death of Roland at the battle of Roncevaux (Roncesvalles) in 778. It was a formative influence on Spanish, Italian and even Icelandic epic poetry.

CHANSONS DE GESTE, medieval French epic poems. Around 80 have survived, and the form and style have given rise to hundreds of other poems in various languages. Most of them deal with "The Matter of France," the legendary exploits of the Emperor CHARLEMAGNE and his knights, the Paladins.

CHANT. See PLAINSONG.

CHANUKAH. See HANUKKAH.

CHANUTE, city in SE Kansas on the Neosho R, named for Octave Chanute. A trade and shipping center, it supplies an agricultural and oil region. It also has some heavy industry. Pop 10 341.

CHANUTE, Octave (1832–1910), US engineer and pioneer aviator. He designed the Union Stockyards in Chicago and the first bridge over the Missouri R. From 1889 on he made many types of glider; these influenced the WRIGHT brothers.

CHAOS, the primordial emptiness that existed before anything came into being in early Greek COSMOGONY. Later this notion was superseded and chaos came to refer to an aboriginal state of confusion. In this sense PARACELSUS applied the term to describe air, hence the modern term, GAS.

CHAPARRAL, a dense thicket of dwarf EVERGREEN trees, usually less than 3m (10ft) high; a locality characterized by such thickets, especially common in the Cal. region.

CHAPEL, place of Christian worship, sometimes a separate building but usually located within a church and separately dedicated. Originally referring to the shrine containing the cloak of St. Martin (*capella*), the word came to denote all places of worship except churches and cathedrals.

CHAPEL HILL, residential town in central N.C. It is the site of North Carolina U., founded in 1789. Pop 25 537.

CHAPLIN, Sir Charles Spencer (1889–), British film actor and director, great comedian of the silent cinema. A vaudeville player, he rose to fame in Hollywood 1913–19 in a series of short comedies, in which he established his "little tramp" character. After 1918 he produced his own feature-length films such as *The Gold Rush* (1925) and, with sound, *Modern Times* (1936) and *The Great Dictator* (1940). Accused of communist sympathies, he left America in 1952 to settle in Switzerland. He was awarded a special Academy Award in 1973 and knighted in 1975.

CHAPMAN, George (c1559–1634), English poet and dramatist. His translations of Homer (1598–1616), although imprecise and full of his own interjections, long remained standard, and they are still recognized as masterpieces. His plays include *Bussy d'Ambois* (1607).

CHAPMAN, John. See APPLESEED, JOHNNY.

CHAPMAN, John Jay (1862–1933), US essayist, poet and dramatist. A perceptive observer of his time, his works include *Emerson and Other Essays* (1898) and *Memories and Milestones* (1915).

CHAPULTEPEC, historic hill near Mexico City. Site of an Aztec royal residence and religious center in the 14th century, it is 200ft high. In 1847 the fort on the hill, built by the Spanish in 1783, was stormed by American forces in the MEXICAN WAR, two days before the occupation of Mexico City. It is now a museum and state residence.

CHAR, or Brook trout, a North American member of the TROUT family, prized for its flesh.

CHARCOAL, form of amorphous CARBON produced when wood, peat, bones, cellulose or other carbonaceous substances are heated with little or no air present. A highly porous residue of microcrystalline GRAPHITE remains. Charcoal is a fuel and was used in BLAST FURNACES until the advent of COKE. A highly porous form, activated charcoal, is made by heating charcoal in steam; it is used for ADSORPTION in refining processes and in gas masks. Charcoal is also used as a thermal insulator and by artists for drawing.

Charles ("Charlie") Chaplin with child star Jackie Coogan while making the silent movie *The Kid* (1920).

CHARCOT, Jean-Baptiste-Étienne-Auguste (1867–1936), French explorer and oceanographer, who in 1904 explored the area W of Graham Land in Antarctica. On a second voyage (1908–10) he discovered Charcot Island and the Fallières Coast. He made other voyages to study marine life and oceanography, and was drowned when his ship sank off Iceland.

CHARCOT, Jean Martin (1825–1893), French physician and founder of modern NEUROLOGY, whose many researches advanced knowledge of HYSTERIA, MULTIPLE SCLEROSIS, locomotor ATAXIA, ASTHMA and aging. FREUD was one of his many pupils.

CHARDIN, Jean-Baptiste-Siméon (1699–1779), French painter best known for his still lifes and for his middle-period genre paintings, affectionate depictions of the everyday life of the bourgeosie. All his work is characterized by a straightforward realism, with atmospheric use of light and color.

CHARGE, Electric. See ELECTRICITY.

CHARGÉ D'AFFAIRES, diplomatic agent of lower rank than an ambassador, minister or resident minister. Accredited to a department of foreign affairs, he deals only with such departments in countries to which he is sent, unless he is deputizing for an ambassador away from his post.

CHARGOGGAGOGGMANCHAUGAGOGGCHAUBUNAGUNGAMAUG, Lake, or Lake Chaubunagungamaug, Indian name for Lake Webster, S Worcester Co., S central Mass.

CHARIOT, light, open, horse-drawn vehicle, usually two-wheeled, used as a weapon of war by many primitive peoples because of its speed. Mesopotamia used chariots c3000 BC, and by c1500 BC Egypt and China made extensive use of them. Chariot racing was a popular sport in ancient Rome.

CHARISMA, New Testament term from the Greek for the gifts of the Holy Spirit, imparted to apostles, prophets and healers to promote God's kingdom. The term has come to mean those personal qualities in certain individuals, such as Napoleon, Lenin or John F. Kennedy, that enable them to win mass support or enthusiastic response from their followers.

CHARITY, Sisters of, Roman Catholic religious

Charles V, emperor of the Holy Roman Empire from 1519 to 1556, was perhaps ruler of more territories than anyone before or since; this portrait, painted by Bernard van Orley, shows him as a young man.

congregation based in Paris. It was founded by St. Vincent de Paul and St. Louise de Marillac in 1633 to care for the sick.

CHARLEMAGNE (Charles the Great; c742–814), king of the FRANKS, founder of the HOLY ROMAN EMPIRE and, in legend, hero of the CHANSONS DE GESTE. In 771, on the death of his co-ruler, his brother Carloman, Charlemagne became sole ruler of the Franks and began to extend the kingdom. In response to an appeal by Pope Adrian I, he waged a successful campaign against Lombardy in 773–74. Bavaria was annexed in 788, and the Saxons and Avars (on the Danube) were subjugated and Christianized after some 30 years of war. In 800 Charlemagne was crowned emperor by Pope Leo III. From his court at AACHEN he not only controlled an efficient administrative system, but also fostered the Carolingian cultural renaissance, which spread through much of present-day France, Germany, Austria, Switzerland, Holland and Belgium.

CHARLEROI, town in S central Belgium. Strategically important in many wars, it was the scene of the first great battle of WWI in 1914. Pop 23 324.

CHARLES, name of seven Holy Roman Emperors. **Charles I** (see CHARLEMAGNE). **Charles II the Bald** (see CHARLES, kings of France). **Charles III the Fat** (839–888), was emperor 881–87. After his overthrow Charlemagne's empire disintegrated. **Charles IV** (1316–1378), was emperor from 1355. Also king of Bohemia, in whose welfare he was most interested. Making Prague his capital, he founded the Charles University there and promulgated the GOLDEN BULL of 1356, which determined the form of elections for the Holy Roman Emperor. **Charles V** (1500–1558), was emperor 1519–56. Ruler of more territory than any of his predecessors (Spain, with its American colonies, the Netherlands, Naples, Sicily and Austria). His reign was marked by struggles with Pope Clement VII and Francis I of France, by attempts to check the Turks and by the REFORMATION. Exhausted and disillusioned, he abdicated in 1556, and retired to Spain. **Charles VI** (1685–1740), was emperor from 1711. With no male heir, he arranged for the succession of his daughter MARIA THERESA by the PRAGMATIC SANCTION. (See AUSTRIAN SUCCESSION, WAR OF THE.) **Charles VII,** or Charles Albert (1697–1745), also known as Charles of Bavaria, was emperor from 1742. He disputed Maria Theresa's succession.

CHARLES, name of 10 kings of France. **Charles I** (see CHARLEMAGNE). **Charles II the Bald** (823–877), reigned as king of the Franks from 843 and as Holy Roman Emperor from 875. Numerous revolts and invasions troubled his reign. It was the last great reign of his dynasty and culturally the last flowering of the Carolingian renaissance. **Charles III the Simple** (879–929), grandson of Charles II, reigned 893–923. **Charles IV the Fair** (1294–1328), reigned from 1322. **Charles V the Wise** (1337–1380), reigned as regent 1356–64 and as king from 1364. Frail and poor in health, he nevertheless put down the JACQUERIE uprising and various plots by his nobles. He regularized taxation and used the increased revenues to build up his armies. He declared war upon England in 1369, and before his death his armies, under the great commander du Guesclin, had regained most French territory occupied by the English. **Charles VI the Mad** (1368–1422), reigned from 1380. He began a disastrous reign at the age of 12. Subject to frequent and severe fits of madness, he allowed corrupt advisors to reign in his stead. England overran most of N France once more, and Charles was forced to name Henry V of England his heir (1420). **Charles VII** (1403–1461), reigned from 1422. The early part of his reign was marked by his unwillingness to challenge the English occupation of France, even to the extent of allowing Joan of Arc to be burned as a heretic. With the influence of new advisers and the end of the Burgundian alliance with England, Charles introduced tax reforms, rebuilt his army and regained all occupied territory except Calais. **Charles VIII** (1470–1498), reigned from 1483. **Charles IX** (1550–1574), who reigned 1560–74, was dominated by his mother, Catherine de Médicis, who instigated the ST. BARTHOLOMEW'S DAY massacre. **Charles X** (1757–1836), reigned 1824–30. He returned to France from exile after the restoration of the monarchy, becoming king on the death of his brother Louis XVIII. He was exiled again after the 1830 revolution, largely provoked by his autocratic rule.

CHARLES I (1227–1285), king of Naples and Sicily from 1266, first of the ANGEVIN dynasty. His last years were marked by a struggle to retain Sicily. As Count of Anjou and brother of the French king, his reign laid the basis for future French claims in Italy.

CHARLES, name of two Stuart kings of Scotland, England and Ireland. **Charles I** (1600–1649), came to the throne in 1625. His absolutist beliefs and Roman Catholic sympathies alienated the Puritan-dominated parliaments. Forced to dissolve parliaments in 1625, 1626 and 1629, he ruled without one until 1640, when increasing fiscal problems made him call the LONG PARLIAMENT, which sought to curtail his powers. This precipitated the Civil War in 1642. Charles was defeated, and captured in 1647. His continual duplicity in dealing with his captors led to his trial and execution. (See CIVIL WAR, ENGLISH.) **Charles II** (1630–1685), returned from exile to succeed his father in 1660 after the death of Cromwell. His pro-Roman Catholic foreign policy, reflecting his own sympathies, made him distrusted, but he was much more tolerant in religious matters than his parliaments. A shrewder man than Charles I, his political expertise and cynicism kept him much of his power. In the end he retained the country's affection, if only for his flamboyant private life.

CHARLES, name of four kings of Spain. **Charles I** (see CHARLES V, Holy Roman Emperor). **Charles II** (1661–1700), last of the Spanish Hapsburgs, reigned from 1665. Feeble and degenerate, he could not produce an heir, and named Philip of Anjou, grandson of Louis XIV, his successor, causing the War of the SPANISH SUCCESSION. **Charles III** (1716–1788), reigned from 1759. A strongly absolutist monarch, his attempts to expand Spanish interests in South America met with defeat at British hands. His enlightened domestic policy, reducing the power of the Church and Inquisition and introducing administrative reforms, was considerably more successful. **Charles IV** (1748–1819), reigned 1788–1808. Spain was largely ruled by his wife, Maria Luisa of Parma, and her lover, Chief Minister Manuel de Godoy. Defeated by France in 1795, Charles allowed Spain to become a satellite of Napoleonic France, and was forced to abdicate in 1808.

CHARLES, name of 15 kings of Sweden. **Charles IX** (1550–1611), reigned from 1607. **Charles X Gustavus** (1622–1660), reigned from 1654. He campaigned in Poland and Denmark, winning Sweden's southern provinces from the Danes. **Charles XI** (1655–1697), king from 1660, established an absolute monarchy and rebuilt Sweden's military and economic power. **Charles XII** (1682–1718), king from 1697, routed Russian invaders at Narva in 1700 and embarked on a series of expansionist campaigns. His death during a siege ended the autocratic monarchy and Sweden's hopes of empire. **Charles XIII** (1748–1818), reigned from 1809. **Charles XIV** (see BERNADOTTE, JEAN). **Charles XV** (1826–1872), reigned from 1859.

CHARLES, Jacques Alexandre César (1746–1823), French physicist who with Nicholas Robert, made the first ascent in a hydrogen BALLOON (1783). About 1787 he discovered **Charles' Law** which, stated in modern terms, records that for an ideal GAS at constant PRESSURE, its VOLUME is directly proportional to its absolute TEMPERATURE.

CHARLES PHILIP ARTHUR GEORGE (1948–   ), PRINCE OF WALES and Duke of Cornwall, heir apparent to the British throne. The first child of Queen Elizabeth II and Prince Philip, he was educated at Gordonstoun and Cambridge.

CHARLES EDWARD STUART (1720–1788), pretender to the throne of England. The grandson of JAMES II, known also as the Young Pretender and, in Scotland, as Bonnie Prince Charlie. After the French refused to support his cause, he rallied the Highland clans to invade England, but was defeated at Culloden in 1746.

CHARLES MARTEL (c688–741), Frankish ruler, who as mayor of the palace (chief minister) from 714, ruled in place of the weak MEROVINGIAN kings. The son of PEPIN II, he received his surname Martel (the hammer) after his famous victory at Tours against the Muslim invaders in 732. His policies assured the Frankish preeminence in N Europe which culminated in his grandson CHARLEMAGNE's coronation as emperor (800).

CHARLES RIVER, river in E Mass. It flows 60mi into Boston Bay from Norfolk Co., separating Boston from Cambridge.

CHARLES THE BOLD (1433–1477), last duke of Burgundy (from 1467). Having failed to defeat him in open war, LOUIS XI of France trapped him in conflicts with other powers, leading ultimately to his death in battle at Nancy.

CHARLESTON, city in E central Ill., seat of Coles Co. Location of Eastern Ill. U. (1895). Industries: shoes, flour and dairy products. Pop 16 421.

The tomb of Charles the Bold, Duke of Burgundy, in Onze Lieve Vrouwe Church, Bruges, Belgium.

The azaleas in this public garden in Charleston typify the flowers which thrive in its subtropical climate.

CHARLESTON, city in S.C., seat of Charleston Co., on a peninsula between the Cooper and Ashley rivers, 3mi from the Atlantic Ocean. A major seaport, it produces fertilizer, cigars, asbestos, pulp, chemicals, paper, textiles and steel. Pop 66 945.

CHARLESTON, capital of W. Va., seat of Kanawha Co., in W central W. Va. at the confluence of the Kanawha and Elk rivers. A distributing point for coal, gas and oil. Pop 71 505.

CHARLESTOWN, since 1874 part of Boston, Mass. Located between the mouths of the Charles and Mystic rivers. Site of US Navy yard. Founded 1628.

CHARLOTTE, largest city in N.C., seat of Mecklenburg Co., 15mi N of the S.C. border. Settled in 1750, chartered in 1768, it is a flourishing commercial, industrial and railroad center. Pop 241 178.

CHARLOTTE (1896–), grand duchess of Luxembourg, elected as ruler by popular vote in 1919, abdicated in 1964 in favor of her son, Jean.

CHARLOTTE AMALIE, capital of the US Virgin Islands, on St. Thomas Island. Founded by Danish colonists 1673, it was bought by the US 1917. Pop 12 372.

CHARLOTTESVILLE, city in Va. in the foothills of the Blue Ridge Mts, seat of Albermarle Co. Founded 1762 and named for the wife of King George III of Britain, it is noted for its agricultural products. Pop 38 880.

CHARLOTTETOWN, capital of Prince Edward Island, Canada, a fishing and shipbuilding center founded 1720 by French colonists. Pop 18 631.

CHARLOTTETOWN CONFERENCE, convened Sept. 1, 1864, at Charlottetown, Prince Edward Island, Canada, first of a series of meetings which led to the formation of the Dominion of Canada.

CHARON, in Greek mythology, the ferryman of dead souls across the rivers ACHERON and STYX to HADES, the underworld. As Charos or Charontas, he is the angel of death in later Greek folklore.

CHARPENTIER, Gustave (1860–1956), French composer, noted for his opera *Louise* (1900), a lyrical work evoking the spirit of Paris.

CHARPENTIER, Marc Antoine (1634–1704), French composer, the most important of his generation. Noted for oratorios, motets and masses.

CHART, a special map used for sea and air NAVIGATION. Aeronautical charts provide data on landmarks and land areas visible to an aircraft in flight. Nautical charts primarily show water areas, hazards and significant coastal features. (See HYDROGRAPHY; MAP).

CHARTER OAK, celebrated oak tree, formerly in Hartford, Conn., in which the Conn. colonial charter was hidden in 1687, to prevent its surrender to the royal governor of New York. In 1865 the Charter Oak was uprooted in a storm. Its age was estimated at 1000 years, and its trunk size was nearly 7ft in diameter.

CHARTISM, a radical and unsuccessful attempt by voteless British laborers, to gain economic and social equality. It was one of the first working-class political movements in Britain. The Chartists took their name from the "People's Charter," drafted in 1838 by William Lovett of the London Workingmen's Association. The demands made were universal male suffrage, equal district representation, vote by ballot, abolition of property qualifications for officeholders, parliamentary salaries and an annual parliament.

CHARTRES, historic city in NW France, capital of the Eure-et-Loire department and commercial center of the Beauce region. It is famous for its Gothic cathedral of Notre Dame. Pop 34 128.

CHARYBDIS. See SCYLLA AND CHARYBDIS.

CHASE, Salmon Portland (1808–1873), US senator 1849–54, 1860–61, governor of Ohio 1855–60, secretary of the treasury 1861–64 and chief justice of the US Supreme Court 1864–73. Born in Cornish, N.H., he became active in the antislavery movement and helped to form the FREE SOIL PARTY. As Lincoln's secretary of the treasury, he instituted a national banking system and issued paper money. Though occasionally a political antagonist of Lincoln, as chief justice he supported the moderate republican view towards RECONSTRUCTION.

CHASE, Samuel (1741–1811), US Supreme Court justice who signed the Declaration of Independence. He was a member of the Maryland legislature and the Continental Congress. In 1804 an unsuccessful attempt to impeach him was made by President Jefferson, who believed Chase conducted his circuit court in a partisan pro-Federalist manner.

CHASE, Stuart (1888–), US author, semanticist and economist, concerned with the problems of living in a technological society. Best-known works: *Men and Machines* (1929), *Tyranny of Words* (1938) and *Power of Words* (1954).

CHAT, name of several birds of the family Parulidae with "chacking" calls. The Yellow-breasted chat is the largest WOOD WARBLER, common in thickets throughout America.

CHÂTEAU, the French term for castle, often applied to any stately mansion. Originally a well-fortified medieval castle with moat (a *château fort*) used for defense rather than residence. By the 17th century the château became a refined and elegant home for royalty and nobility, often distinguished by intricate gardens.

CHÂTEAUBRIAND, François René, Vicomte de (1768–1848), French writer and diplomat, sometimes considered a founder of the Romantic movement in 19th-century French literature. His works include *Atala* (1801), a North American romance, *René* (1802) and *Mémoires d'outre-tombe* (*Memoirs from beyond the Tomb*; 1849–50).

CHÂTEAUGAY RIVER, US and Canada, approximately 60mi long, rises in N N.Y. in the Châteaugay Lakes and flows N to Châteaugay Co., S Quebec, to the St. Lawrence above Montreal. In Canada, site of the Battle of Châteaugay (1813).

CHÂTEAU-THIERRY, town in NE France on the Marne R, scene of the second Battle of the Marne in WWI. Its products include musical instruments. Pop 10 858.

CHATHAM, city in S Ontario, Canada, seat of Kent Co. on the Thames R. Center of a fruit growing and natural-gas producing district. Pop 35 317.

CHATHAM, 1st Earl of. See PITT.

CHATTAHOOCHEE RIVER, 436mi stream flowing from NE Ga. into Fla., where it forms, with the Flint R, the Apalachicola R. It marks almost half the boundary between Ala. and Ga.

CHATTANOOGA, city in S Tenn., on the Tennessee R adjoining Ga. One of the South's major transportation and industrial centers. Aided by cheap hydroelectric power, it produces textiles, chemicals, and steel and iron products. It was an important military objective in the Civil War. Pop 119 082.

CHATTERTON, Thomas (1752–1770), English poet who wrote poems in pseudo-medieval English which he presented as the work of a fictitious 15th-century priest, Thomas Rowley. He was soon found out and, after other poems like *Song of Aella* and the *Ode to Liberty* brought little success, he poisoned himself.

CHAUBUNAGUNGAMAUG, Lake. See CHARGOGGAGOGGMANCHAUGAGOGGCHAUBUNAGUNGAMAUG, LAKE.

CHAUCER, Geoffrey (c1340–1400), one of the first great English poets, who established English as a literary language. His early writing, including an incomplete translation of *Le Roman de la Rose*, shows strong French influence. However, c1370 a new force, due to growing familiarity with BOCCACCIO and DANTE, began to exert itself. This is shown in *The Parliament of Fowls*. His two major works are *Troilus and Criseyde* and the CANTERBURY TALES.

Although the Cathedral of Chartres in North west France is one of the finest examples of Gothic Architecture in Europe, it is in the superb quality of its glass and statuary that it stands in a class of its own. This group of figures from the north portal represents characters from the Old Testament. From left to right: the priest Melchizedek, Abraham with Isaac, Moses holding the tables of the Law, Samuel with the lamb and King David.

CHAUDIÈRE RIVER, S Quebec, Canada, approximately 120mi long; it rises in Lake Megantic, flowing N to the St. Lawrence R immediately above Quebec. The largest of the rapids along its course are the Chaudière Falls.

CHAUMONOT, Pierre Joseph Marie (1611–1693), French Jesuit missionary, who worked

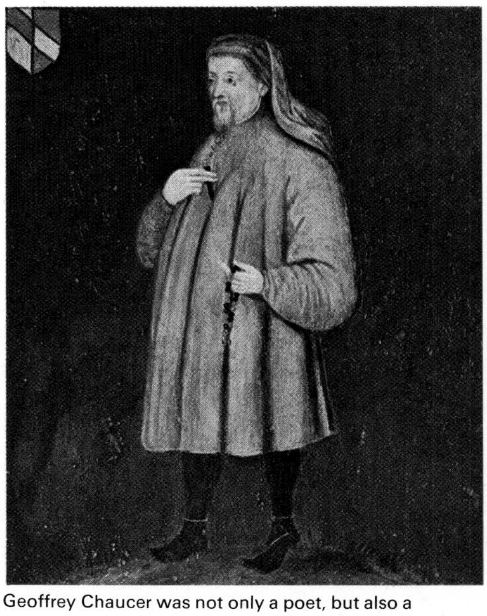

Geoffrey Chaucer was not only a poet, but also a prosperous public servant, clerk of the king's works 1389–91. This picture, from the National Portrait Gallery, London, shows him reciting at court.

among the Huron Indians in Canada and the Onondaga in N.Y. He wrote an autobiography and a Huron grammar.

CHAUNCEY, Isaac (1772–1840), US naval captain, who served in the Tripolitan War (1801–05) and the War of 1812. After a distinguished fighting career he served on the naval commission board in Washington, D.C.

CHAUNCY, Charles (the Elder) (1592–1672), English-born Puritan minister who emigrated to North America. Second president of Harvard College.

CHAUNCY, Charles (1705–1787), influential American Congregationalist minister, a critic of the Great Awakening religious revival.

CHAUSSON, Ernest Amédée (1855–1899), French composer, a major figure in the post-Romantic movement, strongly influenced by FRANCK. Among his best-known works is the *Symphony in B Flat Major* (c1890).

CHAUTAUQUA MOVEMENT, US adult education movement which began at Lake Chautauqua, N.Y., in 1874, as a course for Sunday school teachers. The founders, John H. Vincent, a Methodist minister, and Lewis Miller, a businessman, organized lectures, concerts and recreation activities. (See ADULT EDUCATION; LYCEUM MOVEMENT.)

CHAUVINISM, excessive and blind patriotism, a term derived from Nicholas Chauvin, a soldier blindly devoted to Napoleon who came to represent the militaristic cult of his time. Gradually the term was applied to extreme nationalism of any kind.

CHAVANNES, Puvis de. See PUVIS DE CHAVANNES.

CHÁVEZ, Carlos (1899–), Mexican composer who founded the Orquesta Sinfónica de México (1928). His compositions are strongly influenced by the rhythms and patterns of Mexican-Indian folk music.

CHAVEZ, Cesar Estrada (1927–), revolutionary Mexican–American labor leader who, as head of the United Union of Farmworkers, was instrumental in organizing Cal.'s CHICANO migrant workers. The early history of his union was filled with strikes, picketing and violent clashes with both farmers and the International Brotherhood of TEAMSTERS.

CHAYEFSKY, Paddy (1923–), US TV, film and stage scriptwriter known for his naturalistic depiction of ordinary people. Major plays and films include *Marty* (1953) and *Bachelor Party* (1954).

CHEBOKSARY, capital of the Chuvash republic, USSR, on the Volga R 80mi W of Kazan. Pop 216 000.

The cheetah is credited with being the fastest land animal but it is very difficult to determine its maximum speed accurately since, like other cats, it is a sprinter and will either catch its prey after a short burst of speed or give up. There are records of a cheetah attaining 69mph and over; and on one occasion covering 700 yards in 20 seconds.

CHECK, a bill of exchange directing a bank to pay money as instructed. Checks are the major form of currency exchange in the commerce of developed nations. *Certified* checks and *cashiers'* checks have unquestioned acceptability as they are guaranteed by the depositor's bank. Traveler's checks, however, need two endorsements by the payee.

CHECKERS, called draughts in Britain, a popular game of skill played on a board of 64 alternating light and dark squares. Each of the two players begins with 12 black or white pieces (always identified as such despite the colors used) placed on the 12 dark squares nearest him. It is an ancient game, with roots in Egypt and Greece.

CHECKS AND BALANCES, term used to describe the separation and balance of three branches of government: the legislature which makes the law, the executive which enforces it and the judiciary which interprets it. The idea is based on the theory of SEPARATION OF POWERS advocated by MONTESQUIEU in 1748, which greatly influenced the men who drew up the US Constitution. The SENATE and the HOUSE OF REPRESENTATIVES, as separate organs of the legislature, were to act as checks upon each other in the national Congress.

In practice, however, the powers are not absolutely separated in the working of today's government. Tensions between the branches of government, usually between the president and Congress, often hold up the passage of essential legislation. Some modern critics have pointed out that delay and inefficiency are all too frequently the price that must be paid for a system of checks and balances. In recent years, however, much more criticism has been raised against abuses of power committed by individual branches of government against the spirit of the checks and balances system. (See also WATERGATE.)

CHEESE, nutritious food made from the milk of various animals, with a high protein, calcium and vitamin content. Cheesemaking was already common by 2000 BC. It involves first the curdling of milk by adding an acid or RENNET, so that the fat and protein (mostly CASEIN) coagulate to form the solid curds. After excess liquid whey has been drained off, the curds are compressed and enough moisture is removed to give the cheese the desired degree of hardness. Most cheeses (but not cottage cheese) are then subjected to a period of FERMENTATION, from two weeks to two years, called ripening or curing, during which they are salted and perhaps flavored. The consistency and flavor of the cheese depend on the time, temperature and humidity of storage and on the microorganisms present. Camembert, for instance, is ripened with two molds, *Penicillium candidum* and *P. camemberti*, which make it soft. Process cheese is a blend of several types of cheese melted together.

CHEETAH, *Acinonyx jubatus*, a member of the cat family FELIDAE. It is the fastest land animal, with a speed of up to 110km/hr (68mph). The tawny coat covered with closely set spots makes the cheetah easily recognizable. Once common in Africa and SW Asia the cheetah is fast disappearing through hunting and the reduction in numbers of small deer and antelope, its main prey.

CHEEVER, John (1912–), US writer. His witty novels about the conflicts of suburban life have won major prizes: the National Book Award in 1958 for *The Wapshot Chronicle* and the Howells Medal in 1965 for *The Wapshot Scandal*.

CHEKA, Russian abbreviation of "Extraordinary Commission," the secret police set up by the Bolsheviks in 1917 to eliminate their opponents. Reorganized by STALIN in 1922 and renamed the GPU, it was the ancestor of the modern KGB.

CHEKHOV, Anton Pavlovich (1860–1904), Russian dramatist and short story writer. Between 1898 and 1904 his four major plays were produced by the MOSCOW ART THEATER: *The Seagull, Uncle Vanya, The Three Sisters* and *The Cherry Orchard*. These plays realistically explore the frustrations and unhappiness of life, particularly among the Russian rural upper and middle classes of the time. His work (both plays and short stories) has exerted an immense influence on modern literature.

CHELATE, chemical complex formed from a polydentate LIGAND and a metal ION, thus making a ring. They are more stable than the corresponding unidentate complexes, and are used to sequester metal ions (see HARD WATER), as well as in chemical ANALYSIS and for separating metals. Some biochemical substances, including CHLOROPHYLL and HEMOGLOBIN, are chelates.

CHELMSFORD, town in NE Mass. 4mi SSW of Lowell. Main industries: textiles and furniture. Pop 31 432.

CHELSEA, industrial city in E Mass. It manufactures chemicals, wood products and rubber and plastic goods. Pop 30 625.

CHELYABINSK, city in the USSR, on the Miass R. The second-largest city in the central Urals, it has a large rail complex, and metal and machine industries. Pop 874 000.

CHELYUSKIN, Cape, the northernmost point of the continent of Asia, on the Taimyr Peninsula in the NW USSR.

CHEMICAL AND BIOLOGICAL WARFARE, the use of poisons and diseases against an enemy, either to kill or disable personnel or to diminish food supply, natural ground cover, etc. According to legend, SOLON defeated a Megaran army c600 BC by poisoning their drinking water. THUCYDIDES records that the Spartans in the 5th century BC used in attack the fumes produced by burning wood, sulfur and pitch. Julius CAESAR mentions with disapproval the use of poisons in warfare. GREEK FIRE was in use from about the middle of the 7th century AD. In the US during the FRENCH AND INDIAN WAR, infected blankets were given to the Indians to spread SMALLPOX among them. During the CIVIL WAR, John Doughty proposed the use of an artillery shell containing the choking, corrosive gas CHLORINE. Chemical warfare on a large scale was first waged by the Germans in WWI at YPRES (1915), using chlorine against the Allies. Gas warfare on both sides escalated throughout the remainder of WWI; despite the use of the GAS MASK, around 100 000 may have died as a result of chlorine, PHOSGENE and MUSTARD GAS attacks. During WWII the Germans developed nerve gases, which attack the NERVOUS SYSTEM, but these (Sarin, Soman and Tabun) were not used. More deadly nerve gases have since been developed in the US: some may linger for months and kill in seconds. In the VIETNAM WAR, TEAR GASES were used in combat as distinct from their more normal role in riot control. Also in Vietnam, defoliants were sprayed from aircraft on enemy crops and on vegetation to deprive guerrillas of cover (see also NAPALM).

Waging of biological warfare has been rare, mainly because its effects are hard to control. Nevertheless, most developed countries have encouraged military research in this field. Available preparations could, if used, unleash pneumonic PLAGUE, pulmonary ANTHRAX, and BOTULISM, among other fatal diseases; it has been estimated that 1oz (about 30g) of these would, if well distributed, be sufficient to kill the entire population of North America. Less fatal diseases, such as TULAREMIA, and certain HALLUCINOGENIC DRUGS are also available for such use.

Of the international agreements outlawing the use of chemical and biological warfare, the oldest is the 1925 Geneva Protocol; the UK accepted its strictures only in part, reserving the right to retaliate; and the US, although they signed the agreement in 1925, did not ratify until 1975. The Protocol was contravened by Italy against Ethiopia (1936) and by Japan against China (1943). Most countries have signed the Biological Weapons Convention (1972), agreeing to cease production of biological weapons and destroy existing stockpiles.

CHEMILUMINESCENCE, LUMINESCENCE caused by a chemical reaction, usually oxidation, as of phosphorus in air. The molecules are excited to a high ENERGY LEVEL, and emit light as they return to the ground state. This process in living organisms is called BIOLUMINESCENCE.

CHEMISTRY, the science of the nature, composition and properties of material substances, and their transformations and interconversions. In modern terms, chemistry deals with ELEMENTS and compounds, with the ATOMS and MOLECULES of which

Cheeses of the world

Variety	Origin	Type
Aura	Finland	Veined blue
Brick	USA	Semisoft, mild
Brie	France	Soft, white, surface-ripened, almost liquid inside
Caerphilly	Wales	Semihard, mild, white
Camembert	France	Soft, yellow, surface-ripened, almost liquid inside
Cheddar	England	Hard, white to yellow
Cheshire	England	Hard, crumbly, white or orange
Danish blue	Denmark	Veined blue, pungent
Edam	Holland	Semihard, mild, yellow
Emmental	Switzerland	Hard, large eyes, mild
Gjetost	Norway	Goat's milk cheese, brown, sweet
Gorgonzola	Italy	Semisoft, veined blue, sharp
Gouda	Holland	Semihard, mild, yellow
Gruyère	Switzerland	Hard, small eyes, mild
Limburger	Belgium	Semisoft, white, pungent
Münster	Alsace	Semisoft, sharp
Parmesan	Italy	Very hard, sharp
Roquefort	France	Ewe's milk cheese, semihard, veined blue
Stilton	England	Semihard, veined blue

they are composed, and with the reactions between them. It is thus basic to natural phenomena and modern technology alike. Chemistry may be divided into five major parts: ORGANIC CHEMISTRY, the study of carbon compounds (which form an idiosyncratic group); INORGANIC CHEMISTRY, dealing with all the elements except carbon, and their compounds; chemical ANALYSIS, the determination of what a sample contains and how much of each constituent is present; BIOCHEMISTRY, the study of the complex organic compounds in biological systems; and PHYSICAL CHEMISTRY, which underlies all the other branches, encompassing the study of the physical properties of substances and the theoretical tools for investigating them. Related sciences include GEOCHEMISTRY and METALLURGY.

Practical chemistry originated with the art of the metallurgists and artisans of the ancient Middle East. Their products included not only refined and alloyed metals but also dyes and glasses, and their methods were and remain shrouded in professional secrecy. Their chemical theory, expressed in terms of the prevailing theology, involved notions such as the opposition of contraries and the mediation of a mediating third. Classical Greek science generally expressed itself in the theoretical rather than the practical, as the conflicting physical theories of THALES and ANAXAGORAS, ANAXIMENES and ARISTOTLE bear witness. An important concept, that matter exists as atoms—tiny individual material particles—emerged about this time (see ATOMISM) though it did not become dominant for another 2 000 years. During the HELLENISTIC AGE a new practical chemistry arose in the study of ALCHEMY. These early alchemists sought to apply Aristotelian physical theory to their practical experiments. Alchemy was the dominant guise of chemical science throughout the medieval period. Like the other sciences, it passed through Arab hands after the collapse of the Roman world, though, unlike the case with some other sciences, great practical advances were made during this time with the discovery of alcohol DISTILLATION and methods for preparing NITRIC and SULFURIC ACIDS. Chemical theory, however, remained primitive and practitioners sought to guard their secret recipes by employing obscure and even mystical phraseology. The 16th century saw new clarity brought to the description of metallurgical processes in the writings of Georgius AGRICOLA and the foundation by PARACELSUS of the new practical science of IATROCHEMISTRY with its emphasis on chemical medicines. Jan Baptist van HELMONT, the greatest of his successors, began to use quantitative experiments. In the 17th century mechanist atomism enjoyed a revival with Robert BOYLE leading a campaign to banish obscurantism from chemical description. The 18th century saw the rise and fall of the PHLOGISTON theory of combustion, promoted by STAHL and adopted by all the great chemists of the age: BLACK, SCHEELE and PRIESTLEY (all of whom found their greatest successes in the study of GASES). The phlogiston theory fell before the oxygen theory of LAVOISIER and his associated binomial nomenclature, and the new century (the 19th) saw the proposal of DALTON's atomic theory, AVOGADRO's hypothesis (neglected for 50 years until revived by CANNIZZARO) and the foundation of ELECTROCHEMISTRY which, in the hands of DAVY, rapidly yielded two new elements, SODIUM and POTASSIUM. During the 19th century chemistry gradually assumed its present form, the most notable innovations being the periodic table of MENDELEYEV, the BENZENE ring-structure of KEKULÉ, the systematic chemical THERMODYNAMICS of GIBBS and BUNSEN's chemical SPECTROSCOPY. In the opening years of the present century the new atomic theory revolutionized chemical theory and the interrelation of the elements was deciphered. Since then successive improvements in experimental techniques (e.g., CHROMATOGRAPHY; isotopic labeling; MICROCHEMISTRY) and the introduction of new instruments (infrared, nuclear-magnetic-resonance and mass spectroscopes) have led to continuing advances in chemical theory. These developments have also had a considerable impact on industrial chemistry and biochemistry. Perhaps the most significant recent change in the chemist's outlook has been that his interest has moved away from the nature of chemical substance itself towards questions of molecular structure, the energetics of chemical processes and REACTION MECHANISMS.

CHEMNITZ. See KARL-MARX-STADT.

CHEMOTHERAPY, the use of chemical substances to treat disease. More specifically, the term refers to the use of nonantibiotic antimicrobials and agents for treating CANCER. The drug must interfere with the growth of bacterial, parasitic or TUMOR cells, without significantly affecting host cells. In antimicrobial chemotherapy, the work of P. ERLICH on aniline dyes and arsenicals (SALVARSAN) and of G. DOMAGK on Prontosil led to the development of sulfonamides (see SULFA DRUGS). Many useful synthetic compounds are now available for BACTERIAL and PARASITIC DISEASE, although ANTIBIOTICS are often preferred for bacteria. Cancer chemotherapy is especially successful in LEUKEMIA and lymphoma; in carcinoma it is usually reserved for disseminated tumor. Nitrogen mustard, ALKALOIDS derived from the periwinkle, certain antibiotics and agents interfering with DNA METABOLISM are used, often in combinations and usually with STEROIDS.

CHEMURGY, the application of science to both the development of new agricultural products (and the realization of the potential of previously uncultivated plants) and the derivation of new uses to which existing products may be put (see also AGRICULTURE; AGRONOMY). As such, the chemurgist deals not only with techniques of plant and animal BREEDING but also with ways of processing foods and feeds, industrial and agricultural uses of what were previously regarded as agricultural waste by-products, etc.

CHEN-CHIANG, city in E China. Situated 43mi below Nanking on the Yangtze R, the city is about 2 000 years old. Pop 250 000.

CHENG-CHOU, city in China. It is the capital of Hunan province and an important railway junction. Pop 1 500 000.

CH'ENG-TU, city in S central China. A former imperial capital, it is capital of Szechwan province and a major port, trade and industrial center for the surrounding Ch'eng-tu plains. Pop 2 000 000.

CHÉNIER, André Marie de (1762–1794), French poet who renewed the classical tradition in French poetry. His work forms a bridge between CLASSICISM and ROMANTICISM, with many of the best characteristics of both. He was guillotined during the French Revolution.

CHENNAULT, Claire Lee (1890–1958), US pilot, founder of the WWII *Flying Tigers*. In 1937 he went to China to organize CHIANG KAI-SHEK's air force in the war against Japan. He reentered US service in 1942 as commander of the US air forces in China.

CH'EN TU-HSIU (1879–1942), founder of the Chinese Communist Party. He was a professor at Peking University, but resigned and founded the party in 1920. In his last years he denounced Soviet communism and outlined China's need for true socialist democracy.

CHEOPS. See KHUFU.

CHERBOURG, French seaport and naval station 190mi NW of Paris. It is a base for French fishing fleets and a port of call for oceangoing vessels. Pop 38 243.

CHERENKOV (or CERENKOV), Pavel Alekseyevich (1904–), Russian physicist who first observed CERENKOV RADIATION (1934). He shared the 1958 Nobel Prize for Physics with FRANK and TAMM who correctly interpreted this phenomenon in 1937.

CHEREPOVETS, city in SW Vologda Oblast, USSR. It is an important manufacturing and communications center. Pop 189 000.

CHERNOVTSY (German: Czernowitz), city in the W Ukraine, USSR, with textile, food and engineering industries. Pop 187 000.

CHERNOZEM (Russian: black earth), a group of neutral SOILS with a dark surface layer rich in HUMUS. It occurs in the Russian steppes, Argentina, and in a wide belt from E Kan. to N Alberta. It is the best soil for cereal growing.

CHERNYSHEVSKY, Nikolai Gavrilovich (1828–1889), Russian critic and radical journalist of the 1850s and 1860s. His work laid the foundation of revolutionary populism, and ultimately of Bolshevik ideology.

CHEROKEE INDIANS, North American tribe of the IROQUOIS linguistic group. Once numerous in Ga., N.C., S.C. and Tenn., they were decimated by smallpox and conflicts with settlers in the 18th century. Deprived of their land, thousands died on a march west in 1838. Today about 40 000 Cherokee live in the West and another 3 000 in the East.

A section of Chesapeake Bay Bridge-Tunnel, completed in 1964. Carrying truck and auto traffic between the Delmarva Peninsula and Norfolk, Va., it was opened in 1964. A series of causeways connect to underwater tunnels via artificial islands in the Bay.

CHEROKEE NATION v GEORGIA, legal battle fought in 1831, when the Cherokee appealed to the Supreme Court to prevent Georgia settlers encroaching on their lands. The court denied their case on the grounds that as a dependent nation they were not protected by Article I of the Constitution and therefore Georgia could deal with them without federal interference.

CHEROKEE STRIP, strip of land along the S border of Kan. which was guaranteed by treaty to the CHEROKEE INDIANS. In 1891 the US bought the land and added it to Okla.

CHERRY, general name for a number of deciduous trees of the genus *Prunus*, native to North America, Europe and Asia. The trees are widely cultivated for their succulent fruits containing a single hard seed. Most cultivated cherries originated from two wild cherries, *Prunus avium* and *P. cerasus*. The trees are also grown for their attractive blossom and fine-grained wood. Family: Rosaceae.

CHERRY HILL, an urban township in Camden Co., W central N.J. Pop 14395.

CHERRY VALLEY MASSACRE, incident during the American Revolution, in which the loyalist BUTLER'S RANGERS and their MOHAWK allies, led by Walter BUTLER, on Nov. 11, 1778, massacred 30 men during a siege in Cherry Valley, N.Y.

CHERT. See FLINT.

CHERUBIM, powerful spirits (sometimes with animal attributes) appearing in many religions, particularly JUDAISM, where they are guardian angels of holy places. Renaissance art mistakenly represents them as winged angelic children.

CHERUBINI, Maria Luigi (1760–1842), Italian composer who spent most of his life in France. Now remembered mainly for his opera *Medea* (1797), and the *Requiem in D major* (1836).

CHERUSCI, major N German tribe who lived between the Elbe R and Weser R in the 1st centuries BC and AD; one of their chiefs was ARMINIUS. Roman vengeance under GERMANICUS (AD 16) caused their decline.

CHERVIL, common name given to two species of the family Umbelliferae: the salad chervil (*Anthriscus cerefolium*), which is used as a culinary herb; and the tuberous-rooted chervil (*Chaerophyllum bulbosum*), which is cultivated for its edible carrot-shaped roots.

CHESAPEAKE, independent city in SW Va., formed by the merger of S Norfolk city and Norfolk Co. Its industries are meat packing, cement and fertilizer. Pop 89580.

CHESAPEAKE, US frigate involved in two major incidents between Britain and the US. The first was the boarding of the frigate by H.M.S. *Leopard* (1807) and the impressment of four crewmen as British deserters. This aroused much ill-feeling in the US. In the WAR OF 1812 the *Chesapeake* was captured by H.M.S. *Shannon* after a very brief battle.

CHESAPEAKE AND DELAWARE CANAL, small canal running about 14mi from Chesapeake City, Md., to Delaware City, Del., connecting the two bays.

CHESAPEAKE AND OHIO CANAL, waterway running along the Potomac R between Washington, D.C., and Cumberland, Md. It was planned as a route to the Midwest, but went bankrupt because of competition with the railroads. The canal was taken over by the government in 1938 and established as a national monument in 1961.

CHESAPEAKE BAY, large inlet on the E coast of the US in both S Md. and N Va., an important trade route for oceangoing vessels. Baltimore, Norfolk and Newport, important shipping and industrial towns, are on its shores. The bay, formed by the submergence of the lower Susquehana R, separates the Md.–Del. peninsula from mainland Md. and Va. The area is famous for its waterfowl and seafood.

CHESAPEAKE BAY BRIDGE-TUNNEL, complex of highways, bridges and tunnels stretching 17.5mi across Chesapeake Bay. It links the Md. peninsula with mainland Va. without obstructing shipping. The project cost 200 million dollars.

CHESAPEAKE BAY RETRIEVER, medium-sized sporting dog, one of the few breeds developed in the US. Its short and thick coat ranges from brown to dull yellow in color.

CHESHIRE, residential town in central New Haven Co., Conn. Formerly a mining center, it is now agricultural rather than industrial. Pop 19051.

CHESS, game for two players, each with 16 pieces, played on a board of 64 squares, colored light and dark alternately. Each chessman moves in a certain way. Chess is thought to have originated in India c500 AD, and to have spread to Europe by 1300, perhaps through Byzantium and the Moors; many piece names are of Eastern origin. Chroniclers in N Europe often used the name chess for any board game. Chess as we know it dates from 15th-century Italy and Spain. In the 18th century France was the game's chief center. Chess today has been given a popularity by publicized international contests, such as those between FISCHER and Spassky.

CHEST, upper part of the trunk, between the neck and ABDOMEN. The chest wall consists of ribs articulating with the spinal column and sternum, and the related muscles. The DIAPHRAGM separates the chest from the abdomen. The LUNGS fill much of each side of the chest while the HEART, the AORTA and other large vessels lie centrally, the heart slightly to the left; the TRACHEA and ESOPHAGUS pass into the chest from the neck.

CHESTER, oldest city in Pa., 12mi WSW of Philadelphia. In 1681 William Markham, deputy governor to William PENN, made it Pennsylvania Colony's seat of government. Modern Chester manufactures ships, steel, locomotives and munitions. Pop 56331.

CHESTERFIELD, Philip Dormer Stanhope, 4th Earl of (1694–1773), English statesman and wit. He is chiefly remembered for his *Letters to His Son*, which give a vivid and often amusing insight into the morality of the age.

CHESTERTON, Gilbert Keith (1874–1936), English author and critic, noted for his lyrical style and delight in paradox. He wrote many poems, short stories, novels, and essays condemning the moral and political evils of his day. He is best known for his Father Brown detective stories.

CHESTNUTS, general name for four species of deciduous trees of the genus *Castanea*. The American chestnut (*Castanea dentata*) was common in the E US, but since 1904 has been virtually wiped out by a blight introduced from Asia. The Spanish or sweet chestnut (*C. sativa*) native to Europe is prized for its nuts, and the Japanese (*C. crenata*) and Chinese (*C. mollissima*) chestnuts are now cultivated in the US. Chestnuts are valued for their wood, nuts and bark, which was used in the tanning of leather.

CHETNIKS, name given to members of WWII Yugoslav resistance group. Led by Draža MIHAJLOVIĆ, they opposed both the Nazis and communist partisans. After loss of Allied support, they were crushed by the partisans.

CHEVALIER, Maurice (1888–1972), popular French singer and film star. He gained international fame in the 1930s as a singer of light French songs. His films include *Gigi* (1958) and *Can-Can* (1959).

CHEVES, Langdon (1776–1857), US politician and banker. He rose from humble origins to become speaker of the House of Representatives and president of the Second Bank of the US, which he saved from financial ruin in 1819.

CHEVIOT, city in Hamilton Co. SW Ohio, about 8mi NW of Cincinnati. Pop 11135.

CHEVIOT HILLS, range of hills extending 35mi NE to SW along the English–Scottish border. The Cheviot breed of sheep is famous.

CHEVROTAINS, or Mouse deer, small deer-like animals of the family Tragulidae. The four species are found in forests and scrub in W Africa and S Asia. They are timid, swim well and climb trees. They eat leaves, and, surprisingly for ruminant animals, insects and meat.

CHEVY CHASE, fashionable residential suburb of Washington, D.C., in Md. It is under the jurisdiction of Montgomery Co. Pop 10600.

CHEWING GUM, confection made from sweetened and flavored sap. For centuries Indian tribes chewed CHICLE (gum from the juice of the sapodilla tree) or spruce resin. Early settlers adopted the habit, and chewing gum has been made commercially in the US since the 1860s. Modern gum contains chicle, other resins and waxes, sugar and corn syrup. US annual consumption is now about 200 sticks per person.

CHEYENNE, capital of Wyo., seat of Laramie Co., in the SE corner of the state. It processes agricultural produce and has large oil refineries. The district is a key site for US intercontinental ballistic missiles. Pop 40419.

CHEYENNE INDIANS, North American tribe of the ALGONQUIAN linguistic group. By the mid-19th century they had become nomadic hunters on the Great Plains and fierce fighters against neighboring tribes and, after 1860, the encroaching whites. A history of Cheyenne raids and punitive actions by the government (see SAND CREEK MASSACRE), of broken promises and starvation culminated in the defeat of General CUSTER in 1876 by the Sioux and Northern Cheyenne. Eventually all the Cheyenne were resettled in Okla. and Mont.

CHEYENNE RIVER, river flowing some 500mi from Wyo. into the Missouri R. It forms part of the Missouri R basin project.

Chess sets are often extremely beautiful, like this 16th-century Bavarian set made from gemstones.

CHIAI, city of S Taiwan. It processes timber from nearby forests and distributes the agricultural products of the region. Pop 200 000.

CHIANG CH'ING (1913–), Chinese communist leader, wife of MAO TSE-TUNG. Originally an actress, she fought in the Revolution and thereafter held various offices. An active supporter of Mao's policies, particularly during the Cultural Revolution, she became a leadership contender after his death.

CHIANG KAI-SHEK (1887–1975), Chinese soldier and politician. As aide to SUN YAT-SEN, he supported the KUOMINTANG or Nationalist party during the Nationalist Revolution of 1911. He rose to the leadership of the Kuomintang and became leader of China in 1928, despite guerrilla attacks by communist terrorists. However, when Japan invaded China in 1937, Chiang made peace with communist forces to fight the common enemy. After the war the communists forced him to leave the mainland and with US help he set up a nationalist state in TAIWAN in 1949, which represented China at the UN until 1971.

CHIANG SOONG MAYLING (1898–), wife of CHIANG KAI-SHEK. She was her husband's closest adviser and is believed to have had great influence on his policies. Educated in the US, she was a key figure in securing American support for his cause.

CHIANTI, a mountainous district in central Italy, part of the Appenines. Its slopes produce the famous red and white Chianti wines.

CHIAPAS, state in S Mexico on the Pacific Ocean. Chiapas produces coffee, rubber and cattle but its remoteness prevents major exploitation of its forests of hardwood and dyewood. There are many remains of the MAYAS, especially near the town of Palenque.

CHIAROSCURO, the relationship between light and shade in a work of art. It can determine the degree to which objects seem three-dimensional. CARAVAGGIO and REMBRANDT were major exponents of the chiaroscuro style.

CHIBA, city in Japan, 25mi from Tokyo on Tokyo Bay. It has a steel mill, and produces cotton goods and paper products. Pop 482 133.

CHIBCHA or MUYSCA INDIANS, the inhabitants of the plateau of Bogota in central Colombia. Their society was based on farming and the worship of the Sun God. The Spaniards destroyed their culture in the 16th century. Over a million of their descendants survive in the area today.

CHICAGO, city situated on Lake Michigan in Ill. Two branches of the Chicago R divide it into three parts, known as the North, South and West sides. Chicago is the hub of the US road, rail and air systems; the city's wholesale outlets handle more goods than any city except New York. Industry is diverse and immense, including the famous meat-packing plants, grain elevators and chemical, metal and printing industries. Chicago has large public libraries and many museums and art galleries. It is the home of the U. of Chicago, the Chicago Symphony Orchestra and was the major center of "Urban Blues" music.

Chicago grew as a French trading post in the 1700s, but it was not until after the BLACK HAWK WAR (1832) that the Indian threat was ended and a city developed. The arrival of the railroads in the mid-19th century placed Chicago in the path of the nation's economic expansion as the commercial hub of the vast northern plains. Even the Great Fire of 1871, which destroyed 2 000 acres of property, could not end the vitality of Chicago's growth. With sudden economic growth a tradition of violence grew up, coming to a climax in the 1920s and 1930s in open gang warfare. A large influx of blacks during WWI and WWII has created serious problems, culminating in severe rioting. Unemployment is high and Chicago's West and South sides have some of the worst slums in the US. Pop 6 979 000.

CHICAGO, University of, a private, non-denominational, coeducational institution of Chicago, Ill., incorporated in 1890. The university has about 7 500 students and employs well over 1000 teaching staff. It is famous for research in most subjects.

CHICAGO HEIGHTS, industrial city in NE Ill., 23mi SE of Chicago. It has iron, steel, chemical and textile industries. Pop 40 900.

CHICAGO RIVER, small river in Chicago, Ill. It has two branches, North and South; the South branch is connected to the Des Plaines R by the Chicago Drainage canal. This canal has been known as the Sanitary and Ship Canal since 1930.

CHICANO, originally a pejorative nickname for an American of Mexican descent, derived from the common name "Chico." Like the word "black," it has now been accepted as a proud acknowledgement of racial identity.

CHICHA, alcoholic drink used by South American Andean Indians. It is made by fermenting a mixture of water, sugar and masticated grain. In pre-Columbian times it was used in religious rites.

CHICHÉN-ITZÁ, important archaeological remains of a Maya city, in Yucatan state, Mexico. The ruins indicate two periods of prosperity. The first was around 1000 AD when Chichén-Itzá was a modest Maya city and a member of the League of Mayapan. A second period (with strong Toltec-Mexican influences) saw the construction of an astronomical observatory and the huge pyramid temples for the worship of the god QUETZALCOATL, or Kukulcan.

CHICHERIN, Georgi Vasilievich (1872–1936), Russian diplomat, foreign minister 1918–30. He served under the Tsars but left Russia in 1904 to help revolutionary activity in Europe. He returned in 1918 and joined the Bolsheviks.

CHICHESTER, Sir Francis Charles (1901–1972), British yachtsman and aviator. In 1931 he became the first to fly solo across the Tasman Sea. His most famous achievement was his solo circumnavigation of the world in 1966–67.

CHICHIHAERH, or Tsitsihar, a Chinese city and port, situated on the left bank of the Nen R, 170mi NW of Harbin. Pop 1 200 000.

CHICKADEES, common garden birds, of the family Paridae, with dark caps and bibs and white faces, noted for their tameness and agility. Their simple song can be heard throughout most of the year. They nest in tree cavities or nest boxes.

CHICKAHOMINY RIVER, flows for 90mi through SE Va. to join the James R. It was the scene of heavy fighting in the Civil War PENINSULAR CAMPAIGN.

CHICKAMAUGA, Battle of, Confederate victory in the American Civil War, fought in N Ga. in Sept. 1863. After the victories of GETTYSBURG and Vicksburg in July, Union troops under General ROSECRANS drove on Chattanooga, Tenn., a key railway hub. The Confederates under General Braxton BRAGG retreated south of the city, regrouped, and in the ensuing battle along Chickamauga Creek routed the Federals, despite the firm stand of Union General G. H. THOMAS. Both sides lost heavily.

CHICKASAW INDIANS, one of the FIVE CIVILIZED TRIBES of North American Indians of the Muskogean linguistic group. They were moved from N Miss. to Okla. with the Choctaws. Both tribes fought for the Confederacy in the Civil War and lost one third of their territory as a punishment.

CHICKASHA, city in central Okla. on the Washita R. The main industry is cotton ginning and the production of cottonseed oil. Pop 14 190.

CHICKENPOX, or **varicella**, a VIRUS disease due to *Varicella zoster*, affecting mainly children, usually in EPIDEMICS. It is contracted from other cases or from cases of SHINGLES and is contagious. It causes malaise, FEVER and a characteristic vesicular rash—mainly on trunk and face—and cropping occurs. Infrequently it becomes hemorrhagic or LUNG involvement occurs. Chickenpox is rarely serious in the absence of underlying disease but it is important to distinguish it from SMALLPOX.

CHICKENS, domestic birds derived from the Red jungle fowl, *Gallus gallus*, raised for their flesh and eggs. They were first domesticated in India by 2 000 BC. Champion layers like the White Leghorn produce over 300 eggs a year. Chickens raised for meat are sold as broilers and fryers at under three months old and as roasters at 4–8 months.

CHICK-PEA, *Cicer arietinum*, a plant of the family Leguminosae, cultivated for its round seeds which are used as food in India, South America and N Africa. The seeds are boiled or roasted.

View of midtown Chicago, showing one of its most striking modern buildings, the Marina City apartment complex, designed by Bertrand Goldberg. The 60-story twin circular towers overlooking the Chicago River house shops and restaurants as well as providing accommodation and parking spaces.

CHICKWEED, *Stellaria media*, a low-growing member of the family Caryophyllaceae, with white star-shaped flowers, often found on roadsides and lawns. Native to Europe, it has become naturalized in North America. Other members of the family are also called Chickweed.

CHICLE, gum obtained from the SAPODILLA tree, *Achras zapota*, the raw material for CHEWING GUM. The latex is obtained by cutting grooves in the bark. The tree is native to Middle America and mainly cultivated in the Yucatan peninsula.

CHICO, city in N Cal. It processes nuts grown in the area and also produces lumber, conveyor systems and toothpaste tubes. Pop 19 580.

CHICOPEE, city in SW Mass., founded 1641. In the 19th century it became a manufacturing center and now has diversified industries, including rubber. Pop 66 676.

CHICORY, *cichorium intybus*, a hardy perennial plant with sky-blue flowers, native to Europe and naturalized in the US. It is cultivated for its leaves, which grow in a firm conical shape and are used in winter and spring salads, and for its roots, which are dried, roasted and added to coffee to increase its color, bitterness and body.

CHICOUTIMI, city in SE Quebec on the Saguenay R. A growing tourist and commercial city, it is the center of the Saguenay hydroelectric development, and has various manufacturing industries. Pop 32 990.

CH'IEN LUNG (1711–1799), Chinese emperor, fourth of the Ch'ing (Manchu) dynasty (ruled 1736–96). He fostered Western trade but allowed no penetration. Under him China prospered and reached its greatest extent.

CHIGGER, the name of two American parasites. The chigger mite, chigoe or Red mite is found in central and southern US. It penetrates the skin of birds and mammals to suck lymph, causing irritation and spreading disease. The female Sand flea (also called the chigger) which has spread to many tropical countries, burrows into the flesh to lay her eggs. This causes pain and sores and may cause severe infection.

CHIGNECTO BAY, an inlet in the Bay of Fundy, Canada. It is noted for its 50ft tides, which are among the highest in the world.

CHIHUAHUA, largest state of Mexico, bordering Tex. and N.M. Its 95 400sq mi contain forests, deep canyons and rich grasslands which make it Mexico's leading cattle-raising state. There are also rich gold and silver mines.

CHIHUAHUA, capital of Chihuahua state, founded as a mining community in 1701 and now an agricultural center. Pop 364 000.

CHIHUAHUA, world's smallest breed of dog,

The tiny chihuahua, a popular lap dog, typically saucy-looking and alert, is much sturdier than it at first seems. It was probably derived from the Techichi, a small Toltec dog without a bark.

standing about 5in tall and weighing up to 6lb. Descended from a Toltec breed, it is named for the Mexican state.

CHILBLAIN, itchy or painful red swelling of extremities, particularly toes and fingers, in predisposed subjects. A tendency to cold feet and exposure to extremes of temperature appear to be factors in causation. Treatment is symptomatic.

CHILDBIRTH. See BIRTH.

CHILD LABOR, the employment of children in industrial or agricultural work to an extent detrimental to their health, education and general well-being. The practice was rampant in the US in the 19th century and, despite public outrage, commercial interests opposed legislation until the Fair Labor Standards Act was passed in 1938. This act, with the 1961 amendment, forbids the employment of children under 16 in heavy industry, transport or commerce, and under 18 in occupations detrimental to health.

CHILDREN'S CRUSADE (1212), a sad attempt by 30 000 children to conquer the Holy Land after their elders had failed. Defying king, priests and parents, they set out from France and Germany, led by the youths Stephen of Vendôme and Nicholas of Cologne. Those who survived disease, starvation and the grueling journey over the Alps were mostly sold into slavery by unscrupulous sea captains when they reached the Mediterranean ports.

CHILE, South American republic. The main topographic feature of the country is the Andes Mts, which run the length of E Chile. The North, Central and South parts of Chile form three distinct natural regions: the North is dominated by desert and has rich mineral deposits in its dry saline basins. Central Chile is made up of well-watered valleys and has a Mediterranean climate. The South is wetter and cooler, containing dense rain forests and rolling grasslands in the Southeast.

Nine out of ten Chileans live in the Central area, many in Santiago, the capital, and Valparaiso, the chief port. 70% of the population is of mixed Spanish-Indian blood, the other 30% being mainly of Spanish or other European origin. Spanish is spoken by the great majority. Because of the rapid growth of the population and the fact that Chile is not agriculturally self-supporting, there is much poverty, though the average standard of living compares favorably with the rest of South America. Chile's chief source of wealth is mining, of iron ore, nitrates, lead, zinc, gold, silver, manganese and copper; Chile is the world's largest producer of copper. Agriculture employs one third of the labor force, but outdated methods hinder productivity. Other industries include iron and steel, paper, petroleum products, cement and chemicals. The economy is lamed by communication problems, raging inflation and heavy debt repayments to creditor nations (chiefly the US). Chile's main trading partners are the US, Japan, Argentina and W Europe.

The original inhabitants of Chile were the Araucanian Indians. Settled by the Spanish, Chile was dominated by Spain until 1818 when Bernardo O'HIGGINS and José de SAN MARTÍN led a successful war of independence. In 1821 the powerful landholders rejected O'Higgins' rule and set up their own autocracy. The addition of the valuable northern area to Chile after the WAR OF THE PACIFIC (1879–83) heralded a period of industrial expansion. During the depression of the 1920s many Chileans were attracted by left-wing policies. After a series of left-wing presidents, Salvador Allende, a Marxist, was elected in 1970. The subsequent collapse of the economy and a widespread famine caused an army-led rebellion, in which Allende committed suicide (1973). The military remains in control.

Official Name: The Republic of Chile
Capital: Santiago
Area: 286 397sq mi
Population: 10 044 940
Languages: Spanish
Religions: Roman Catholic
Monetary Unit(s): 1 Chilean escudo = 100 condores

CHILE SALTPETER, an impure form of sodium nitrate (see SODIUM) occurring in large quantities in Chile.

CHILI, or chilli, the fruit of several species of the genus *Capsicum*, notably the red pepper (*Capsicum annuum*), which are native to tropical America. Many varieties are in cultivation, differing in the shape and color of fruit produced. Family: Solanaceae.

CHILL HARDENING, technique used in CASTING whereby the mold is chilled. This accelerates the cooling of the molten metal poured into it, thereby increasing its surface HARDNESS.

CHILLICOTHE, city in S Ohio, seat of Ross Co. It is a marketing center for the area's agricultural produce and an industrial city. Pop 24 842.

CHILLON, a castle on Lake Geneva in Switzerland, built in the 13th century for the dukes of Savoy. It was the prison of Frąnois de Bonnivard, inspiring BYRON's poem *The Prisoner of Chillon*.

CHILTERN HILLS, range of chalk hills in the S Midlands of England. They extend for about 50mi and are noted for their fine beech woods. The highest point is Coombe Hill (850ft).

CHILTERN HUNDREDS, ancient stewardship of the British Crown, now a purely nominal office usually granted to members of parliament on request. It provides a way for them to resign (which technically they cannot do) since they are not allowed to hold any paid Crown office.

CHILUNG (Keelung), in N Taiwan, the principal port of the island and of the capital Taipei. Its industries are shipbuilding, fishing and minerals. Pop 324 040.

CHIMAERAS, or ratfishes or rabbitfishes, cartilaginous fish related to SHARKS. Males have claspers on their heads which may aid copulation. Their teeth are composed of three pairs of large, flat plates.

CHIMBORAZO, highest peak in Ecuador (20 561ft). An inactive, snowcapped volcano, it was first climbed by Edward WHYMPER in 1880.

CHIMERA, a fire-breathing monster of Greek mythology, with the forequarters of a lion, the middle of a goat and the hindquarters of a dragon. She was killed by BELLEROPHON in Lycia. Today the term is used for any imaginary monster.

CHIMKENT, USSR, capital of Chimkent region in Kazakh SSR, one of Central Asia's major industrial cities with metal, chemical, machine and textile industries. Pop 247 000.

CHIMPANZEE, *Pan troglodytes*, an intelligent ape, the smaller of the two African apes related to Man. Chimpanzees inhabit woodland or grassy savanna, and feed mainly on vegetable matter. They live in large societies of as many as 60 or 80 individuals.

CHIMU, name of two pre-Inca cultures of coastal Peru. The first (Mochica) lasted c500–1000 AD. The second developed after 1200, and ended with the INCA conquest in the 15th century. They were periods of technological advance and population expansion.

CH'IN, Chinese dynasty (221–207 BC) whose first emperor, SHIH-HUANG-TI, unified China, and also completed the GREAT WALL OF CHINA and built new canals and roads. The Ch'in standardized Chinese script, abolished feudalism and initiated local government.

CHINA, republic in E Asia, the world's most populous country.

Land. China is surrounded by natural barriers; sea to the E, and mountains and deserts to the SW and N. Within this framework are three natural regions: the W, an area of high plateaus and desert, the N, fertile plains, and the S, mostly hills and valleys. The two main rivers, the Yangtze R and the Yellow R, flow from the Tibetan plateau, and are of great economic importance. The climate and vegetation are varied, with monsoons and subtropical rain forest in the SE, and areas of grassland and desert in the NW.

People. The Chinese belong to the Mongoloid race, and 95% are Chinese-speaking, though there are sizeable minorities of Mongols and Tibetans, who speak their own languages. The principal dialect is now MANDARIN, taught in all schools. (See also CHINESE.)

The traditional religions are TAOISM, based on the teachings of LAO-TSE (6th century BC), BUDDHISM, introduced in the 3rd century AD, and CONFUCIANISM, based on the teachings of CONFUCIUS (551–479 BC); of these, Confucianism was most responsible for building the very strong family ties, based on patriarchal dominance, that characterized Chinese society. These ties have been replaced under communism by loyalty to the commune and state; and the status of women in society has greatly improved.

Although China is still an agriculturally-based nation, with only 1 in 5 living in cities, there are many large cities: in the N, Peking, the capital (pop 8 000 000), Tientsin (pop 4 500 000), Lü-ta (pop 4 000 000), and in the S, Shanghai (pop 11 000 000) and Canton (pop 2 300 000); many of them are badly overcrowded.

Economy. The communist government is trying to raise the economy from subsistence to prosperity by a combination of industrialization and improved agriculture, despite the problems of the vast population, which is increasing by 12 million a year.

Although China is the third-largest food producer in the world, raising sheep and growing rice, corn, wheat, vegetables, tea and cotton, it has barely enough to feed the population; but increasing production is difficult as all available land is under cultivation, and there is not enough profit to finance large-scale irrigation.

Fishing, sea and fresh water, is an important food source. Timber resources have fallen, though reforestation is under way.

Surveys have shown that mineral resources are very rich, and production of coal and iron ore has dramatically increased. More heavy machinery is being built, giving China a sound basis for industrial expansion. Power sources are largely coal and hydroelectricity, as extensive oil resources are largely undeveloped, and much heavy work is still done by hand.

Transport is largely by canal and river and rail, as the road network is poor. Nearly all trade is by sea, main exports being raw materials and textiles, and imports being oil and wheat.

History. PEKING MAN and Lan-t'ien man lived in China well over 500 000 years ago, but the earliest farming settlements date from c4 000 BC.

The SHANG dynasty (c1523–1028 BC), ruling near the Yellow R, marks the beginning of the historical period and the Bronze Age; it was succeeded by the CHOU dynasty (1027–256 BC), who were powerful war lords. A period of local wars followed, which only ended when the powerful CH'IN dynasty (221–207 BC) united China. Under the subsequent HAN dynasty

(202 BC–220 AD), China expanded S to Vietnam and W to central Asia.

The arts and sciences flourished for two centuries, but army revolts and barbarian invasions brought chaos, and not until the T'ANG dynasty (618–906 AD) reinstated strong government did trade and civilization thrive again. Prosperity continued through the SUNG dynasty (960–1279), but an invasion by mounted Mongol archers made China part of the great MONGOL EMPIRE. Soon, however, the Mongol Empire broke up and a Chinese ruling house, the MING dynasty (1368–1644), drove the Mongols deep into Asia, and China resumed power in her own right.

The rich empire was again invaded by northern barbarians, this time the MANCHUS, who set up the CH'ING dynasty (1644–1911), the last in Chinese history. Prosperity continued until the mid-19th century, when European expansion led to unfavorable competition. China lost wars against Britain, Russia and Japan, and nationalist revolts against the Manchus caused the fall of the empire.

A new republic was declared in 1912, led first by SUN YAT-SEN and then by YUAN SHIH-KAI. However it was not until 1928 that the nationalists under CHIANG KAI-SHEK, with the help of the communists led by MAO TSE-TUNG, gained control from the Chinese war lords. Though Chiang turned on the communists in 1928, they rejoined forces to fight the Japanese invasion in 1937, and fought together during WWII.

After WWII the communists gained control and drove the nationalists off the mainland to TAIWAN (then Formosa) in 1949. They then consolidated their position, and under the strong leadership of Chairman MAO TSE-TUNG, Vice-Chairman LIU SHAOCH'I and Premier CHOU EN-LAI have kept control since. In that time they have reorganized land and factory ownership on a communal basis and made great improvements in conditions at home. Abroad they have encouraged communist movements in Asia, Africa and South America, and notably in Vietnam. However an easing of relations between China and the West led to her entry into the UN (1971), and an exchange of visits between Chinese and Western politicians. President Nixon visited China in 1972, President Ford in 1974.

Official Name: The People's Republic of China
Capital: Peking
Area: 3 704 400sq mi
Population: 824 960 000
Languages: Mandarin, local dialects
Religions: No official religion
Monetary Unit(s): 1 Yuan = 100 cents

CHINA, Great Wall of. See GREAT WALL OF CHINA.

CHINABERRY TREE, *Melia azedarach*, a tree with blue flowers and large leaves, which is native to Asia and is grown as an ornamental in the southern US.

CHINA CLAY. See KAOLIN.

CHINA SEA, W part of the Pacific Ocean, along the E coast of Asia. Taiwan divides it into the E China Sea, 485 300sq mi in area, whose maximum depth is 9 126ft; and the S China Sea, whose area is 895 400sq mi, and maximum depth is 15 000ft. Major seaports are Canton and Hong Kong.

CHINAWARE. See CERAMICS; POTTERY AND PORCELAIN.

CHINCH BUG, highly destructive insects of North America whose young, hatched in the spring, feed on wheat. When that becomes too tough for them, they migrate to young corn, where a second generation will feed.

CHINCHILLA, *Chinchilla laniger*, a South American RODENT once common in the Andes, but now decimated for its soft fur. Chinchillas are reared now on fur farms, 100 skins being needed for one coat. Females bear 5 or 6 fully-furred young at a time.

Above: one of several royal palaces in Peking built during the Ming Dynasty (1368–1644). These palaces formed part of the so-called "Forbidden Town." *Above right:* schoolroom in modern China. Since 1952 educational facilities have been much enlarged and the country is moving towards quite a high rate of literacy. The main subjects studied, however, are still revolutionary history and Marxist economics. *Right:* workers in a Chinese cotton mill applaud a speaker. Although conditions are still relatively poor, the morale of workers is high, and China is gradually outgrowing its traditional agricultural economy and becoming a major industrial nation.

CHINCHONA. See CINCHONA.

CHINCHOU (formerly Chinhsien), city in SW Liaoning province of NE China, at the head of the Gulf of Chihli. Pop 400 000.

CHINCOTEAGUE ISLAND, E Va., between Assateague Island and the mainland. Its shellfishing industry is important; the annual pony roundup is a major tourist attraction. Pop 1 867.

CHINESE, a group of languages of the Sino-Tibetan family. MANDARIN, China's official language, is the most commonly used in the world, being spoken by nearly 700 million people. Other dialects include Cantonese, Hakka and Wu. Except for borrowing European technical terms, Chinese is self-sufficient; Japanese and Korean use a version of its writing system. There is evidence of its existence from c2000 BC. The earliest examples date from c1400 BC. The written Chinese of CONFUCIUS' time is still used in literature and scholarship, but the spoken word has developed differently, and is the basis for the new literary form, introduced in 1911. The writing system developed from pictorial representation into conventionalized designs, one character being composed of between one and 32 strokes. In the 20th century attempts have been made to simplify the script. Chinese literature spans 3 000 years, and is written in two styles: the classical and, since 1911, the vernacular.

CHINESE ART, one of the major cultural heritages of the world, spanning 3 000 years. In the SHANG dynasty (c1523–1028 BC) artists decorated pottery, cast bronze, and carved wood and ivory. Most painting was done on silk in ink and watercolor, until the invention of paper in the 2nd century AD. Three characteristic forms in painting were the wall scroll, the horizontal hand scroll and the album. No examples of painting survive from the HAN dynasty (202 BC to 220 AD), but tomb and pottery decorations indicate that the human form and portrayals of gods were major subjects. In the T'ANG dynasty (618–906 AD) BUDDHISM flourished and temples were lavishly decorated. In the SUNG dynasty (960–1279) landscape painting emerged. The art of the MING dynasty (1368–1644) was scholarly, with court artists returning to earlier traditions, and writing books on technique. Sculpture, which had developed with painting, declined by the end of the Ming dynasty. Art in China today is regulated by the state for the purpose of political, social and economic indoctrination. The scope of the artist has thus been greatly narrowed.

CHINESE CABBAGE, a quick-growing cabbage, native to the Far East where it is an important crop. Used principally in salads, it is now popular in North America. (See also BRASSICAS; CABBAGE.)

CHINESE EVERGREEN, popular name for several species of the genus *Aglaonema*, which are evergreen, perennial greenhouse and house plants cultivated for their arum-like flowers and variegated ornamental foliage. These are very easy plants to grow since they thrive in dim light (even surviving with only artificial light) and at temperatures as low as 13°C (55°F). The soil should be kept wet to evenly moist. Propagation is by seeds or cuttings. Family: Araceae.

CHINESE EXCLUSION ACTS, name of two acts to limit immigration of Orientals to the US. The first, passed in 1879, stemmed from anti-Chinese agitation on the W coast of the US. President HAYES vetoed the act on the grounds that it abrogated the BURLINGAME

Chinese art: a vase from the K'ang-si period (c1700 AD), elaborately decorated in cloisonné enamel.

China

The new China

China's transformation since 1949, when Mao Tse-tung and the communists came to power, is truly awesome. The old feudal society with its rigid class structure and *kao-shang* (corruption) has been swept away. In its place an entirely new social system based on Maoism, the distinctively Chinese form of communism, has been established. It is possibly the most remarkable social revolution ever witnessed. The watchword of this revolution has been "struggle"—against the opponents of change, against the environment—with, at the heart of the matter, the struggle of the individual to measure up to the ideals of Maoist thought. "If there were no contradictions and no struggle," said Mao, "there would be no world, no progress, no life. There would be nothing at all."

The upheaval in China has seen periods of orderly development alternating with periods of violence and confusion. Collectivization was introduced hastily in 1956, "socialist education" in 1962. A notable failure was the "Great Leap Forward" (2nd Five-year Plan, 1958). Other stimuli have been the "Cultural Revolution" (1966) directed against "rightists" and "anti-party intellectuals," and the campaign against the dead defense minister Lin Piao, once named as Mao's heir apparent, and against Confucianism (1974).

In emphasizing "struggle," Mao may have been seeking an answer to what William James, the American psychologist, called "the human need for a moral equivalent to war." By 1975, however, the Chinese people, alive to their impressive achievements in agriculture and industry, in education, public health and other fields, seemed to have lost some of their revolutionary zeal. Some Sinologists predicted a new age of greater stability and more peaceful progress. However, the death of Mao (1976) following the deaths of Chou En-lai and Chu Teh makes a struggle for leadership between the "moderates" and "radicals" seem inevitable, with the more numerous moderates likely to win.

In Jan. 1975, the National People's Congress, China's parliament, met in Peking for the first time in 10 years and its 2885 delegates unanimously approved a new constitution, along with a new corporate leadership which would take over when Mao died. The new constitution, much shorter than that of 1954, institutionalized many features of Mao's revolution. The communist party, which previously had been overshadowed by the army, was proclaimed "the core of the leadership" and supreme command of the armed forces was vested in the chairman of its central committee. The office of head of state was abolished. China, formerly designated a "democratic state," was redefined as a "socialist state of the dictatorship of the proletariat," with its attitudes determined by "Marxism-Leninism-Mao-Tse-tung Thought."

The constitution gave legal recognition to such Maoist institutions as the communes and (administrative) revolutionary committees. The communes, groups of villages containing 5000–10000 families, are responsible for local government and the organization of farm and other production, and now number about 74000. The revolutionary committees were a feature of the Cultural Revolution. Although the peasants are permitted small private plots, many of the clauses in the 1954 constitution which allowed the ownership of private property do not appear in the new constitution.

Freedom of speech, of the press and of religious belief, and the right to strike, were all guaranteed. The "masses" may discuss, criticize and "write big-character posters" as they did during the Cultural Revolution. But to what extent religious freedom and the right to strike will prevail has yet to be seen. The constitution warns that loyalty to the Communist party and the socialist system is the first duty of every citizen.

Written into the constitution is Mao's hostility to Russia, in an opening clause which castigates "socialist imperialism." The constitution states that China does not intend to become a superpower.

The meeting of the National People's Congress was also an occasion for appointments and elections to the high offices of state. Not surprisingly the communist party emerged with a much stronger presence in the corridors of power. Although radicals were represented, the list of the new hierarchy suggested an overall victory for moderate policies.

In his "state of the nation" speech to the Congress, Premier Chou En-lai reported record increases in agricultural and industrial output and forecast the completion of an independent and relatively comprehensive economic system, "without servility to things foreign," by 1980.

The success of the commune system was reflected in increased agricultural production, up 51% by value over 1964. China is essentially an agricultural country; of the total population of over 800000000, about 500000000 are peasants. It was Mao's profound understanding of the peasant mind that enabled him to win power and to replace the old way of life, based on the *hsiang* (village), with cooperative "socialist agriculture" centered on the commune. Today, in the tens of thousands of communes scattered across the vast country, the peasants are organized in production "brigades" and teams which not only till the land, sow the seed and tend the crops, but also—after harvest-time—toil at construction projects, perhaps for river-control and irrigation, or terrace neglected hillsides to marginally increase the arable land of their commune. Only rarely is machinery available for such projects, but the lack is made good by the large numbers working on them.

A vital role in China's green revolution is played by the network of national agricultural institutes and experimental farms and plots. More than 33% of the technical work force of the institutes is constantly out on the land with the peasants, introducing new seed varieties and more scientific farming techniques. Young people are also sent from the cities to work alongside the farmers and "peasant agrotechnicians." Multiple cropping and the transplantation of wheat have been introduced, increasing yields in some northern areas by more than 20%. Hogs are bred in increasing numbers, both cooperatively and on the peasants' private plots, the target being one hog per person. Hogs are valued as a source of both food and organic fertilizer. Chemical fertilizers are also used, but supplies as yet are limited.

The zest for experiment has also spread to other rural activities, notably fish-breeding and "intercropping" (breeding several species in the same pond or canal). Many areas where fish was formerly unknown now have it as a regular item of diet. In her freshwater and sea fisheries China ranks second only to Japan.

For more than a decade the Chinese, while knowing periods of hunger, have been spared the famines that were once a regular feature of their lives. Despite drought and other problems, food production has consistently increased to the point where it can more than cope with the growth of population (now feeling the effects of the family-planning program). Other countries with large peasant communities, such as India, might well have much to learn from the Chinese example.

Gross industrial output has increased by 190% over 1964, and petroleum production by 650%. China has rejected financial cooperation with the West in favor of "self-reliance," even though this has made progress more gradual and often involved improvization and painful trial and error. The policy of self-

TREATY. But in 1882 the second act suspended immigration for 10 years, and in 1902 the suspension was made indefinite.

CHINESE-JAPANESE WARS. See SINO-JAPANESE WARS.

CHINESE LANTERN, *Physalis alkekengii*, an Asian plant cultivated for the lantern-like, membraneous calyx that contains a single berry. It is a popular decorative flower since the lanterns retain their orange-red color for several months.

CH'ING, MANCHU dynasty that ruled CHINA after seizing Peking in 1644. It was overthrown by Chinese nationalists in 1911.

CH'INHUANGTAO, major coal and fishing port on the Gulf of Chihli in the NE Hopeh province of NE China. Pop 210000.

CHINO, city in SE Cal., 37mi E of Los Angeles. It is a major trade center for fruit growing. Pop 20411.

CHINOISERIE, European art style using Chinese designs in architecture, ceramics, furniture and decorating, usually in conjunction with BAROQUE and ROCOCO styles. It reached its peak in the mid-18th century, and thereafter waned except for a brief revival in the 1930s.

CHINOOK, settlement of North American Indians living in the NW along the N bank of the Columbia R. The Chinook were first encountered in 1805 by the LEWIS AND CLARK EXPEDITION. A version of their language was used by Pacific coast traders and other Indian tribes. The Chinook became almost extinct after a smallpox epidemic in 1829 which killed 80% of their people.

CHINOOK, FOEHN wind blowing eastward from the Rocky Mountains, mainly in winter. The term is also applied to the warm, wet WIND coming off the Pacific before it passes over the Rockies.

CHIOS, Greek island, 321sq mi in area, lying off the W coast of Turkey. It is both mountainous and fertile, growing fruit, especially figs. With adjacent islands it forms a department of Greece. Pop 60061.

CHIPEWYAN INDIANS, once the largest Athabascan-speaking tribe living in the Churchill R area, N Canada. Loosely organized in small bands with little material culture, they hunted CARIBOU for their staple food. Stricken by disease, only about 5000 remain today.

CHIPMUNKS, small striped ground-living SQUIRRELS. There are 16 species in North America, and one in Asia. They feed on fruits and nuts which they carry to a store in their cheek pouches; they may also eat small animals. Without hibernating, they sleep for long periods in winter.

CHIPPENDALE, Thomas (c1718–1779), famous English cabinetmaker whose elegant, individual style blended aspects of GOTHIC, ROCOCO and CHINOISERIE. He also worked from designs by Robert ADAM.

CHIPPEWA, common name for the OJIBWA Indians.

CHIPPEWA FALLS, industrial city in W Wis., on the Chippewa R, seat of Chippewa Co. Potato growing and brewing are the main industries. Pop 12351.

CHIRICAHUA NATIONAL MONUMENT, SE Ariz. Founded in 1924, it occupies 17sq mi. There are

The great annual October 1 parade in Peking, commemorating the foundation of the People's Republic.

reliance was born of sheer necessity when Russia withdrew her technicians. It has also involved national pride. A typical example of its successes is the large Taching oil field in the northeast region which was developed by a huge work force numbered in thousands and manhandling obsolete machines after the Russians had pulled out in 1960. Self-sufficient in oil, China expects to be exporting up to 50 million tons of crude yearly to Japan by 1978.

Self-reliance, however, has recently become the subject of debate. With the prospect of lucrative oil exports, it is argued that China will have ample funds to import all the foreign plant and technology she needs, and to quicken the pace of industrial development. China, in fact, has already imported complete petrochemical, steel and other plants with varying success. Steel output, of high importance at the present time when there is urgent need of better transportation and more farm machinery, has been disappointing. The average of 20–30 million tons per year is far short of the target figure of 100 million tons annually.

Nevertheless industrial progress is impressive and is reflected in the increasing number of trucks and electrical machines, like generators, coming off the assembly lines, and also in limited production of sophisticated electronically-controlled machines. But the technology gap remains wide. As might be expected in a society where wages are low, consumer goods (along with food and clothing) are cheap, but there is little choice.

An interesting pointer to China's long isolation from the outside world is that prices have been stable for the past 20 years. By 1974, however, there was evidence that China was beginning to feel the impact of the world recession. The expected large deficit in trade with noncommunist countries suggested a cutback in Chinese imports in 1975, and probably also in 1976.

Life in China is probably more egalitarian than anywhere else in the world, but the apparent classlessness is not so real as it might seem. Society is stratified by pay differentials and by the jealously-guarded powers and privileges of the elite. A Western visitor would find the standard of living low and housing poor. But remembering the past, he would understand the general satisfaction of the people at the rate of progress. The family, while reluctantly recognized as a stabilizing social institution, is officially disliked as a link with rejected traditions and a source of resistance to change. It is common for husband and wife to work far from each other, meeting only occasionally, and for children to be educated in schools well away from parental influence. Reared by the state, a new generation is emerging which is dedicated to its service.

During the period of international isolation, China pursued an aggressive foreign policy, occupying Tibet (1950), intervening in the Korean War, briefly invading India (1962), and encouraging communist movements in Asia, Africa and South America, notably in Vietnam. Her long dispute with Russia has not been limited to which country is the rightful heir to Marx and Lenin, and so leader of the communist world, but has also involved repeated border clashes in areas of disputed territory. China has also sought to extend her influence by trade and aid, notably in Africa and the Mediterranean (Malta). In Europe, tiny Albania has long been a faithful ally.

After Mao came to power, the US withheld recognition from the communist regime, and a thaw in Chinese-American relations did not begin until 1971. Although presidential and other visits improved understanding between the two nations, full normalization of relations was still snagged down in early 1975 by the question of Taiwan and the US policy of detente with Russia.

Taiwan has always been regarded by the Chinese as an integral part of the People's Republic. That the US should guarantee Taiwan's security by a defense treaty (1954) and continue recognition of the Nationalist "Republic of China" has always seemed to Peking an interference in China's internal affairs.

China's unrelenting hostility to Russia, now enshrined in the constitution, has led her to denounce Russo-US attempts at detente as a fraud, though Chinese fears of a Russian attack have diminished since China became a nuclear power. Using the abundant uranium of the mineral-rich Sinkiang-Uighur autonomous region and expertise initially gleaned from the Russians, China was able to develop an atomic bomb (1964), a hydrogen bomb (1967) and a space satellite (1970). By early 1975 China had the capacity to devastate Moscow and other cities west of the Urals with intercontinental ballistic missiles and had deployed other nuclear weapons to cover traditional invasion routes from Siberia.

As for the rest of the world, China has strived to maintain her position as champion of the Third World, a role which some African countries have questioned, and has pledged support to what Chou En-lai called "the second world," meaning developed nations opposed to "superpower control." Thus China has favored further development of the EEC.

many curious natural rock formations due to volcanic action.

CHIRICO, Giorgio de (1888–), Italian painter who, as a founder of the *scuola metafisica,* was a forerunner of SURREALISM. He abandoned this style after 1930 in favor of Renaissance-type art.

CHIRIKOV, Alexei Ilich (1703–1748), Russian explorer, commander of BERING's second expedition to discover whether Asia was joined to North America by land. He made the first sighting of ALASKA on July 15, 1741.

CHIROMANCY. See PALMISTRY.

CHIRON, a centaur in Greek mythology, famous for his knowledge of healing. Accidentally wounded by HERCULES, he gave up his immortality to PROMETHEUS and was placed in heaven as the constellation SAGITTARIUS.

CHIROPODY. See PODIATRY.

CHIROPRACTIC, a health discipline based on a theory that disease results from misalignment of VERTEBRAE. Manipulation, massage, dietary and general advice are the principal methods used. It was founded by Daniel D. Palmer in Davenport, Ia., in 1895 and has a substantial following in the US.

CHIROPTERA. See BATS.

CHISHOLM TRAIL, 19th-century route for cattle drives and wagon trains between Tex. and Kan., named after the scout and trader Jesse Chisholm. It was superseded by the spread of the railroads.

CHI-SQUARED TEST, in STATISTICS, a test of the closeness of an observed result to an expected result, and hence how closely a model corresponds to a particular sample of n members of a population. χ^2 is given by

$$\chi^2=\frac{(n-1)s^2}{\sigma^2},$$

where s^2 is the observed sample VARIANCE and σ is the STANDARD DEVIATION of the model. Values of χ^2 have been tabulated for a range of values of n, and their distributions (chi-square distributions with $(n-1)$ DEGREES OF FREEDOM) derived in each case.

CHITA, city in USSR, capital of Chita oblast, situated on the Chita R in E Siberia. It has a machine factory and produces textiles. Pop 242 000.

CHITIN. See CARAPACE.

CHITONS, primitive limpet-like MOLLUSKS with shells of eight overlapping plates. Found all over the world, they range from 12mm (0.5in) to 330mm (13in) in length. They live by the shore, where they feed on algae scraped from rocks.

CHITTAGONG, city and chief port in Bangladesh on the Karnaphuli R 12mi from the Bay of Bengal. Much of the city was destroyed in 1971 by West Pakistan troops. Pop 488 300.

CHIVALRY, knightly code of conduct in medieval Europe combining Christian and military ideals of bravery, piety, honor, loyalty and sacrifice. These virtues were particularly valued by the crusaders, who founded the earliest chivalric orders. Chivalry was also associated with ideals of courtly love, and it was this, together with changing methods of warfare, that led to its degeneration and decline during the late Middle Ages.

Miniature by Jacob van Maerlant showing the Knights of the Cross attacking Jerusalem in 1099. The Crusades turned the knights into something like an international brotherhood.

CHIVES, *Allium schoenoprasam*, edible perennial herb related to the GARLIC, LEEK and ONION. The leaves are used for flavoring salads, soups and other dishes.

CHLOE. See DAPHNIS AND CHLOE.

CHLORAL, or trichloroacetaldehyde (CCl_3CHO), colorless, oily liquid made by reacting CHLORINE and ETHANOL or ACETALDEHYDE, used chiefly in the manufacture of DDT. MW 147.4, mp −57.5°C, bp 98°C. **Chloral hydrate** ($CCl_3CH(OH)_2$), colorless crystalline solid made by reacting chloral and water and used as a SEDATIVE, since it is a DEPRESSANT of the central nervous system. It is toxic in excess, and especially when mixed with alcohol to make "Mickey Finns" or "knockout drops." Habitual use produces DRUG ADDICTION and GASTRITIS. mp 57°C.

CHLORINE (Cl), greenish-yellow gas with a pungent odor, a typical member of the HALOGENS, occurring naturally as chlorides (see HALIDES) in seawater and minerals. It is made by electrolysis of SALT solution, and is used in large quantities as a bleach, as a disinfectant for drinking water and swimming pools, and in the manufacture of plastics, solvents and other compounds. Being toxic and corrosive, chlorine and its compound PHOSGENE have been used as poison gases (see CHEMICAL AND BIOLOGICAL WARFARE). Chlorine reacts with most organic compounds, replacing hydrogen atoms (see ALKYL HALIDES) and adding to double and triple bonds. AW 35.5, mp −101°C, bp −35°C. **Chlorides,** the commonest chlorine compounds, are typical HALIDES except for carbon tetrachloride (see CARBON), which is inert (see STEREOCHEMISTRY). Other chlorine compounds include a series of oxides, unstable and highly oxidizing, and a series of oxyanions—HYPOCHLORITE, chlorite, chlorate and perchlorate—with the corresponding OXY-ACIDS, all powerful oxidizing agents. Calcium hypochlorite (see BLEACHING POWDER) and sodium chlorite are used as bleaches; chlorates are used as weedkillers and to make matches and fireworks; perchlorates are used as explosives and rocket fuels. (See also HYDROGEN CHLORIDE.)

CHLORITE, group of green CLAY minerals, related to the MICAS, and consisting of alternate single layers of BIOTITE, containing ferrous iron (Fe^{2+}), and brucite $[(Mg,Al)_6(OH)_{12}]$. They are widespread alteration products.

CHLOROFORM, or trichloromethane ($CHCl_3$), dense, colorless, volatile liquid made by chlorination of ETHANOL or ACETONE. One of the first anesthetics (see ANESTHESIA) in modern use (by Sir James SIMPSON, 1847), it is now seldom used except in tropical countries, despite its potency, since it has a narrow safety margin and is highly toxic in excess. It is also used in cough medicines and as an organic solvent; it is nonflammable. MW 119.4, mp −64°C, bp 61°C.

CHLOROMYCETIN, or chloramphenicol, the first broadspectrum ANTIBIOTIC. Owing to risk of aplastic ANEMIA it is restricted to use in TYPHOID FEVER or serious *Hemophilus* infections and for tropical use.

CHLOROPHYLL, various green pigments found in plant CHLOROPLASTS. They absorb light and convert it into chemical energy, thus playing a basic role in PHOTOSYNTHESIS. Chlorophylls are CHELATE compounds in which a magnesium ion is surrounded by a PORPHYRIN system.

CHLOROPLAST, a PLASTID body containing CHLOROPHYLL, found in plant cells. Higher plant cells contain up to 50 chloroplasts, while most algal cells have only one. Variously shaped, they are of the order of 5μm in diameter, and are surrounded by a semipermeable membrane. They contain ordered stacks of membranes within which all PHOTOSYNTHESIS reactions take place.

CHLOROQUINE, antimalarial drug derived from QUININE, acting on the red-cell phase of the parasite. Probably the most commonly used drug for both the prevention and treatment of MALARIA. It is effective against all varieties of malarial parasite.

CHMIELNICKI, Bohdan (c1595–1657), Ukrainian hetman who led a successful Zaporozhian COSSACK revolt against Polish rule (1648). He established a Cossack principality in the Ukraine but in 1651 was defeated by the Poles. He sought Russian aid in return for which he swore allegiance to the tsar (1654), so forfeiting Cossack hopes for independence.

CHOATE, Joseph Hodges (1832–1917), US lawyer who fought some of the most famous US court cases, also a diplomat. In 1871 he served on the Committee of Seventy which exposed the New York fraud ring led by William TWEED. He successfully contested the constitutionality of the 1894 income tax law. Choate was US ambassador to Britain 1899–1905.

CHOATE, Rufus (1799–1859), US lawyer and congressman from Mass. A master of oratory, his forte was criminal law. He was a Whig in the House of Representatives 1830–34 and in the Senate 1841–45.

CHOCOLATE, popular confectionary made from CACAO beans. Fermented beans are roasted and the outer husks removed by a process that breaks the kernels into fragments called nibs. Chocolate is made from ground nibs, cocoa butter (the fat released when the nibs are subjected to hydraulic pressure), sugar and sometimes milk. It is a high energy food that contains a small amount of the stimulant CAFFEINE. Chocolate may be molded into bars or used as a beverage and in some liqueurs.

CHOCTAW, North American Indian tribe which originated in what is now SE Miss. They remained at peace with the US government but, following the Removal Act of 1830, were forced, as members of the FIVE CIVILIZED TRIBES, to sell their lands and move to what is now Okla.

CHOKE, or **inductor**, device used in electric CIRCUITS to oppose changes in the magnitude or direction of current flow (see ELECTRICITY); i.e., it is a coil of high self-inductance (see INDUCTANCE). The term is also used for the VALVE regulating the air supply to the CARBURETOR of an INTERNAL-COMBUSTION ENGINE.

CHOKEBERRY, name of several eastern North American ornamental shrubs of the genus *Aronia*. They bear small apple-shaped fruits and the leaves turn red in the autumn. Family: Rosaceae.

CHOLA, ancient Tamil dynasty in S India which, after some centuries in obscurity, reemerged in the 9th century AD and by the 11th century had conquered most of peninsular India. The Chola Empire reached its greatest power under Rajaraja I (reigned 985–1016) and Rajendracola Deva I (reigned 1016–42) when it included Ceylon, virtually all S India, the Deccan and parts of the Malay peninsula and archipelago. The dynasty survived until 1279.

CHOLERA, a BACTERIAL DISEASE causing profuse watery DIARRHEA, due to *Vibrio cholerae*. It is endemic in many parts of the East and EPIDEMICS occur elsewhere. A water-borne infection, it was the subject of a classic epidemiological study by John Snow in 1854. Abdominal pain and diarrhea, which rapidly becomes severe and watery, are main features, with rapidly developing dehydration and SHOCK. Without rapid and adequate fluid replacement, death ensues rapidly; ANTIBIOTICS may shorten the diarrheal phase. It is a disease due to a specific TOXIN; a similar but milder disease occurs due to the El Tor Vibrio. VACCINATION gives limited protection for six months.

CHOLESTEROL ($C_{27}H_{46}O$), STEROL found in nearly all animal tissue, especially in the NERVOUS SYSTEM, where it is a component of MYELIN. Cholesterol is a precursor of BILE salts and of adrenal and sex HORMONES. Large amounts are synthesized in the liver, intestines and skin. Cholesterol in the diet supplements this. Since abnormal deposition of cholesterol in the arteries is associated with ARTERIOSCLEROSIS, some doctors advise avoiding high-cholesterol foods and substituting unsaturated for saturated FATS (the latter increase production and deposition of cholesterol). It is a major constituent of gallstones (see CALCULI).

CHOMSKY, Avram Noam (1928–), US linguist whose theory of "transformational grammar" has revolutionized the study of language structure. (See LINGUISTICS.)

CHONDRULE, small, roughly spherical granules of OLIVINE, PYROXENE, GLASS or other MINERALS found in members of that class of stony meteorites (see METEOR) known as **chondrites**.

CH'ONGJIN, town in NE North Korea, capital of North Hamgyong province. Situated on the Sea of Japan, it is one of the republic's largest industrial centers. Pop 250 000.

CH'ONJU, town in central South Korea, capital of North Cholla province. Located in a rich rice-growing region, the city is also developing light industries. Pop 263 000.

CHOPIN, Frédéric François (1810–1849), Polish composer and pianist who wrote chiefly for the solo piano. His music is Romantic, inspired by introspection and concern for the fate of his native Poland. Chopin gave his first public performance at the age of eight, in Warsaw. In 1831 he moved to Paris (his father was French) where he began serious composition. His solo pieces, written in a wide variety of forms, and including 21 nocturns, nearly 60 mazurkas and 26 preludes, display an often startling technical virtuosity. In 1837 he began his famous friendship with the novelist George SAND. Their relationship ended unhappily in 1847 and Chopin, already ill with tuberculosis, died in Paris two years later.

CHORALE, metrical hymn set to a simple tune, associated with the Reformation in Germany. Designed for congregational singing, chorales were often derived from earlier PLAINSONG melodies. LUTHER is credited with having written chorales. Later composers, notably J. S. BACH, reharmonized existing ones.

CHORAL MUSIC, music sung by a choir or chorus. The unaccompanied choral music sung in monasteries and abbeys during the early Christian era is known as PLAINSONG. Choral music continued to be performed without accompaniment through the 16th century. Some of the finest works of this period were written by the Italian PALESTRINA. The development of instrumental accompaniment in the 17th and 18th centuries culminated in J. S. BACH's orchestrated CANTATAS and PASSIONS and the ORATORIOS of HANDEL. Choral music lost some popularity with the development of secular and orchestral music but choral works continued to be written. BEETHOVEN's innovatory inclusion of a choir in the finale of his *Ninth Symphony* (1817–23) marks a turning point in the history of music. Notable among 20th-century choral works are ELGAR's *Dream of Gerontius* (1900) and STRAVINSKY's *Symphony of Psalms* (1930).

CHORD. See CIRCLE.

CHORD. See HARMONY.

CHORDATES, group of animals comprising the phylum Chordata. They include all VERTEBRATES and little-known animals such as AMPHIOXUS, the HEMICHORDATES and the TUNICATES. At some stage in their development, all possess a stiff rod called the NOTOCHORD.

CHOREA, abnormal, nonrepetitive involuntary movements of the limbs, body and face. It may start with clumsiness, but later uncontrollable and bizarre movements occur. It is a disease of basal ganglia (see BRAIN). **Sydenham's chorea**, or **Saint Vitus' dance**, is a childhood illness associated with STREPTOCOCCUS infection and RHEUMATIC FEVER; recovery is usually full. **Huntingdon's chorea** is a rare hereditary disease, usually coming on in middle age and associated with progressive dementia.

CHOREOGRAPHY, composition of steps and movements for dancing, especially BALLET. The most influential choreographers of the early decades of the 20th century created ballets for DIAGHILEV and included Michel FOKINE, NIJINSKY and George BALANCHINE. Pioneers in modern dance, such as Martha GRAHAM and Jerome ROBBINS, helped to free the dance theater from the restrictions of classical steps. Teaching is traditionally by demonstration and written records of early dance steps are scant. A notation system was published 1699 by Raoul Feuillet (c1670–c1730) and in the 20th century Rudolf von Laban developed his *Labanotation*.

CHORZÓW, city in SW Poland. It lies in Katowice province and is a manufacturing and mining center of the Upper Silesian industrial region. Pop 152 000.

CHOU, Chinese dynasty that ruled from Hao, near present-day Sian, (c1122–770 BC) and then from Loyang (770–256 BC). The two periods, known respectively as the Western and Eastern Chou, were, despite political turmoil, a time of fundamental cultural growth. Irrigation projects were established, great advances were made in iron-casting techniques, and a money economy was evolved. Literature and philosophy flourished, particularly during the Eastern Chou which became the classical age of Chinese philosophy. (See CONFUCIUS; CHUANG-TZU; LAO-TSE; MENCIUS.)

CHOU EN-LAI (1898–1976), first prime minister of the People's Republic of China. Born into the gentry, he became a Marxist after studying in China, Japan and Paris. In 1924 he became political director of the Whampoa Military Academy while CHIANG KAI-SHEK was commandant. In 1926 he organized the Shanghai Strike for Chiang and escaped when Chiang betrayed the communists. He became a Comintern liaison man organizing the proletariat and eventually director of military affairs for MAO TSE-TUNG's guerrilla forces. After commanding the first stages of the LONG MARCH (1934–35), he became Mao's champion and thereafter always deferred to his authority. As foreign minister (as well as prime minister) until 1958, he won support for China in the Third World. He was a moderating influence during Mao's Cultural Revolution in the 1960s and a major force in taking China into the UN (1971). Seeking to balance worsening Sino-Soviet relations, he was responsible for the rapprochement with the US, symbolized by President Nixon's visit to China in 1972.

CHOUTEAU, family of fur traders who helped to open up the Middle West. **(René) Auguste Chouteau** (1749–1829), co-founded with Pierre Laclède the trading post which was to become St. Louis (1764). Auguste's brother, **(Jean) Pierre Chouteau** (1758–1849), an Indian agent for all tribes W of the Mississippi R, co-founded the St. Louis Missouri Fur Company (1809). His son, **Auguste Pierre Chouteau** (1786–1838), was an Indian treaty commissioner and made many expeditions into the West. Auguste Pierre's brother, **Pierre Chouteau** (1789–1865), headed the AMERICAN FUR COMPANY from 1834. By pioneering the use of steamboats he monopolized trade on the Missouri R.

CHOW (or Chow-Chow), a medium-sized red or black dog with a rough coat, lion-like mane and paws, and a plumed tail curling over its back.

CHRÉTIEN DE TROYES (c1135–1183), French poet who wrote romances rooted in ARTHURIAN LEGEND. His five romances, *Erec, Cligès, Lancelot, Yvain* and the unfinished *Percevel*, were seminal, greatly influencing French and English literature through the next two centuries.

CHRIST (Greek *Christos*, anointed one), translation from the Hebrew *Mashiah* or Messiah. (See JESUS CHRIST; MESSIAH.)

CHRISTCHURCH, city in New Zealand on the E coast of South Island. It is the island's largest city and the second largest in New Zealand. Founded in 1850, it developed as a grain, meat and wool center but is now also a major manufacturing city. Pop 281 000.

CHRISTIAN, name of 10 Danish kings who at various periods also ruled Iceland, Norway and Sweden. **Christian I** (1426–1481), king of Denmark 1448–81, Norway 1450–81 and Sweden 1457–64. He founded the Oldenburg dynasty which ruled Denmark until 1863. He failed in his attempt to control Sweden (1471). **Christian II** (1481–1559), king of Denmark and Norway 1513–23 and Sweden 1520–23. His reign marked the end of the KALMAR UNION (1397–1523). He regained Sweden only to be defeated by the Swedes after massacring some 80 nobles. In 1523 he was deposed by the Danes and later imprisoned until his death. **Christian III** (1503–1559), king of Denmark and Norway 1534–59. He brought LUTHERANISM to Denmark. **Christian IV** (1577–1648), king of Denmark and Norway 1588–1648. He fought costly wars against Sweden (1611–13 and 1643–45) and in the THIRTY YEARS' WAR unsuccessfully invaded Germany (1625). **Christian V** (1646–1699), king of Denmark and Norway 1670–99. He fought Sweden unsuccessfully (1675–79). **Christian VI** (1699–1746), king of Denmark and Norway 1730–46. He formed alliances with Sweden, England and France. **Christian VII** (1749–1808), king of Denmark and Norway 1766–1808. Soon after his accession he became insane and in 1771 his physician Struensee gained control. After the latter's fall from power in 1772, Christian ruled only nominally and in 1784 his son, Frederick, acted as regent. **Christian VIII** (1786–1848), king of Denmark 1839–48, governor and king-elect of Norway (1814) which was then returned to Sweden. In 1846 he revised the status of Schleswig (see SCHLESWIG-HOLSTEIN). **Christian IX** (1818–1906), king of Denmark 1863–1906. He annexed Schleswig, thus precipitating war with Prussia and Austria (1864) by which he lost both Schleswig and Holstein. **Christian X** (1870–1947), king of Denmark 1912–47 and of Iceland 1918–44. In WWII he became a symbol of Danish resistance to Nazi rule. In 1944 Iceland became a republic.

CHRISTIAN BROTHERS, Roman Catholic teaching order founded in 1802 by Edmund Ignatius Rice at Waterford, Ireland, to care for poor Catholic boys. The order now has schools and colleges in many countries.

CHRISTIAN CHURCH (denomination). See DISCIPLES OF CHRIST.

CHRISTIAN ENDEAVOR, an international and interdenominational organization established in 1881 by the Rev. Francis Edward Clark at Portland, Me., to promote the observance of Christian virtues among young people.

CHRISTIANITY, a major world religion; arising out of JUDAISM, and founded on the life, death and resurrection of JESUS CHRIST. Christians total some 28% of the world's population. Half of all Christians are in Europe, most of the rest in North and South America. The central Christian proclamation (see KERYGMA) is that by the grace of God men are saved (see SALVATION) through faith in Christ, their sins are forgiven, and they receive new and eternal life in the fellowship of the CHURCH. Arising out of this are the various aspects of Christian life and teaching, broadly divided into worship (see LITURGY), THEOLOGY, MISSION and personal and social obedience to God's will—that is, the practice of righteousness, love and mercy. The whole Church regards the BIBLE as authoritative, but the place given to TRADITION and reason varies.

After Jesus' resurrection and ascension (c30 AD), his APOSTLES and other followers traveled widely, spreading and developing Christian beliefs and worship. Christian communities emerged throughout the Roman Empire, meeting weekly for prayer and Holy COMMUNION. Soon an ecclesiastical structure began to evolve. Meetings were led by bishops, assisted by elders (see PRESBYTERS). Later the elders presided over local congregations and bishops had wider authority (see MINISTRY). Regions were organized into dioceses and provinces.

The chow-chow is one of the oldest breeds of dog, dating back over 2 000 years to the Han dynasty in China; compactly built with a thick coat, it differs from every other breed in having a blue-black tongue.

Christians suffered persecution until the Emperor CONSTANTINE proclaimed freedom of worship throughout the Roman Empire (313 AD). He made Christianity Rome's official religion in 324 AD, and in 325 called the first ECUMENICAL COUNCIL at Nicaea to settle major doctrinal disputes. In the 4th century MONASTICISM spread from Egypt to the West.

Almost from the beginning the Church had been divided into the Greek-speaking East and the Latin-speaking West, with divergent traditions. The WESTERN CHURCH came to recognize the preeminence of the pope, the bishop of Rome, as the direct successor of St. Peter. But the EASTERN CHURCH looked to the patriarch of Constantinople as its head. This division finally led to the GREAT SCHISM of 1054. The MONOPHYSITE CHURCHES had previously separated from the Eastern ORTHODOX CHURCHES in the 6th century. The advance of ISLAM was an increasing threat to all the Eastern Churches.

In medieval Western Europe the increasing secular power and corruption of the Roman Church helped to spark off the 16th-century REFORMATION, from which PROTESTANTISM emerged as various national churches separated from the ROMAN CATHOLIC CHURCH, which responded by its own COUNTER-REFORMATION. The LUTHERAN and REFORMED CHURCHES came to dominate northern Europe. The Roman Catholic Church and (two centuries later) Protestant churches embarked on a vigorous missionary program to the Americas, Africa and Asia, often closely connected with colonial expansion.

Today, Christian churches, though still divided by differences of doctrine and practice, work together

Christianity's humble beginnings in a stable are traditionally sited where this elaborate altar in the Church of the Nativity in Bethlehem now stands.

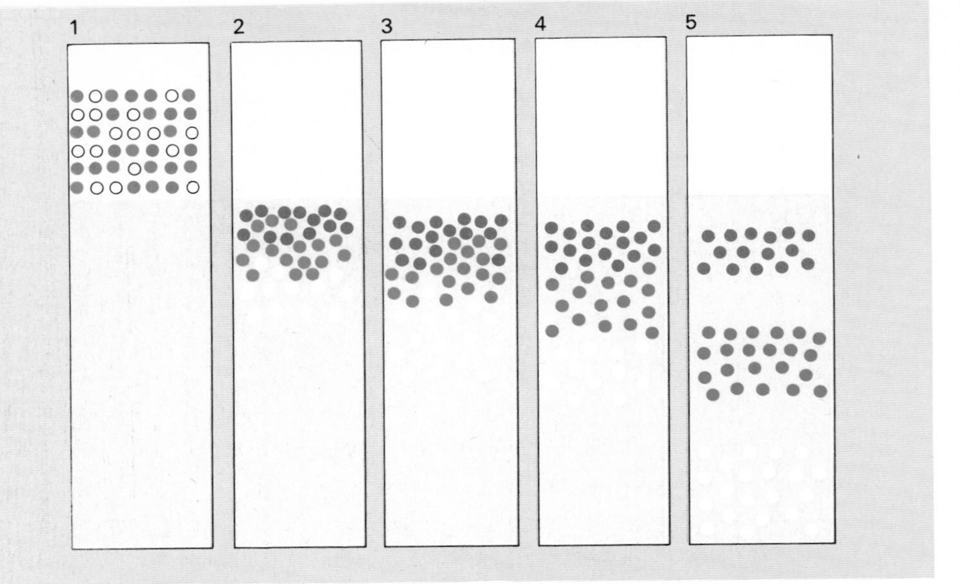

Schematic representation of liquid-solid chromatography. (1) A sample containing three components (colored dots) is introduced at the top of the chromatographic column (a tube packed with an adsorbant solid as the stationary phase). (2–5) A liquid eluant is allowed to flow through the tube. As the three components are adsorbed by the stationary phase to varying degrees, the eluant carries them down the column at different rates. This results in a gradual separation of the components.

and share a concern for worldwide social justice, and the ECUMENICAL MOVEMENT offers hope of eventual reunion.

CHRISTIAN REFORMED CHURCH, Protestant denomination founded in 1857 by Dutch immigrants in the US who separated from the Protestant Dutch Church (now the Reformed Church in America). Originally known as the True Holland Reformed Church, the present name was adopted in 1890.

CHRISTIAN SCIENCE, a religious movement which believes in the power of Christian faith to heal sickness. It was founded by Mary Baker EDDY, who organized the first "Church of Christ, Scientist" at Boston, Mass., in 1879. There are now many affiliated churches throughout the world. The *Christian Science Monitor* is a widely respected international daily newspaper.

CHRISTIANSTED, town in the Virgin Islands of the US on the NE coast of St. Croix Island. It was briefly the capital of the former Danish West Indies. Tourism has largely replaced the production of rum and sugar as the main industry. Pop 2 966.

CHRISTIE, Agatha (1891–1976), British writer of popular detective novels and plays. Her two central characters are the egotistical Hercule Poirot and the elderly Miss Jane Marple. Her play *The Mousetrap* opened in London in 1952 and was still being performed in 1976, the world's longest continuous run.

CHRISTINA (1626–1689), queen of Sweden 1632–54, successor to Gustavus Adolphus. She was a lavish patron of the arts and attracted many scholars to her court, among them Descartes. Christina refused to marry and in 1654 she abdicated, leaving the country in male disguise. She was received into the Roman Catholic Church at Innsbruck in the following year and settled in Rome. She failed in two attempts to regain her throne (1660 and 1667).

CHRISTINA, Fort, Swedish settlement, now WILMINGTON, Del., founded in 1638 in the Delaware Valley, captured by the Dutch in 1655, then seized by Britain in 1664. The fort was later a Civil War military prison.

CHRISTMAS (Christ's Mass), annual Christian festival observed on Dec. 25 in the Western Churches to commemorate the birth of Jesus Christ. It is a public holiday in Christian countries, usually marked by the exchange of gifts—tokens of the gifts of the three wise men to the infant Jesus. Christmastide lasts from Dec. 25 to Jan. 6 (EPIPHANY).

CHRISTMAS ISLAND, Australian territory in the Indian Ocean occupying 52sq mi. There are phosphate deposits. Britain annexed the island in 1888. It passed to Australia in 1958. Pop 3 361.

CHRISTMAS ISLAND, largest coral atoll in the Pacific Ocean (234sq mi) and one of the Line Islands. Captain Cook discovered it in 1777. Both the UK and US claim sovereignty and both have held nuclear tests there. Pop 367.

CHRISTOPHE, Henri (1767–1820), Negro king of N Haiti. He became president of Haiti in 1806, after the murder of DESSALINES. Opposed by Alexandre Pétion, after 1811 he ruled only N Haiti, as King Henri I, building the mountain fortress of La Ferrière. Faced with a revolt, he shot himself.

CHRISTOPHER, Saint (c3rd century AD), by tradition a Christian martyr and patron of travelers because, according to a popular legend, he once carried the Christ child across a river. The Roman Catholic Church has removed Christopher from its calendar of saints for lack of historical evidence as to his existence.

CHRISTUS, Petrus (d. 1473?), leading Flemish painter, early Netherlandish school. His work, strongly influenced by Jan VAN EYCK, was important in the 15th-century development of realistic perspective.

CHRISTY, Edwin P. (1815–1862), US actor who organized the highly successful Christy Minstrels troupe at Buffalo, N.Y. in 1842. He established the basic format of the MINSTREL SHOW, popular in the 19th century.

CHROMATIC ABERRATION. See ABERRATION, OPTICAL.

CHROMATIC SCALE, musical scale consisting of all 12 semitones within an octave. It contains every tone commonly used in Western music. (See also SCHOENBERG, ARNOLD; TWELVE TONE MUSIC.)

CHROMATOGRAPHY, a versatile technique of chemical separation and ANALYSIS, capable of dealing with many-component mixtures, and large or small amounts. The sample is injected into the moving phase, a gas or liquid stream which flows over the stationary phase, a porous solid or a solid support coated with a liquid. The various components of the sample are adsorbed (see ADSORPTION) by the stationary phase at different rates, and separation occurs. Each component has a characteristic velocity relative to that of the solvent, and so can be identified. In **liquid-solid chromatography** the solid is packed into a tube, the sample is added at the top, and a liquid eluant is allowed to flow through; the different fractions of effluent are collected. A variation of this method is ion-exchange chromatography, in which the solid is an ION-EXCHANGE resin from which the ions in the sample are displaced at various rates by the acid eluant. Other related techniques are paper chromatography (with an adsorbent paper stationary phase) and thin-layer chromatography (using a layer of solid adsorbent on a glass plate). The other main type of chromatography—the most sensitive and reliable—is **gas-liquid chromatography (glc)**, in which a small vaporized sample is injected into a stream of inert eluant gas (usually nitrogen) flowing through a column containing nonvolatile liquid adsorbed on a powdered solid. The components are detected by such means as measuring the change in thermal conductivity of the effluent gas.

CHROMITE, a hard, black SPINEL mineral, an iron (II) chromium (III) mixed OXIDE ($FeCr_2O_4$); the chief ore of CHROMIUM. It is found in southern Africa, USSR, Turkey and the Philippines.

CHROMIUM (Cr), silvery-white, hard metal in Group VIB of the PERIODIC TABLE; a TRANSITION ELEMENT. It is widespread, the most important ore being CHROMITE. This is reduced to a ferrochromium alloy by carbon or silicon; pure chromium is produced by reducing chromium (III) oxide with aluminum. It is used to make hard and corrosion-resistant ALLOYS and for chromium ELECTROPLATING. Chromium is unreactive. It forms compounds in oxidation states +2 and +3 (basic) and +6 (acidic). Chromium (III) oxide is used as a green pigment, and lead chromate (VI) as a yellow pigment. Other compounds are used for tanning leather and as mordants in dyeing. (See also ALUM.) AW 52.0, mp 1890°C, bp 2482°C, sg 7.20 (20°C).

CHROMOSOMES, threadlike bodies in cell nuclei, composed of GENES, linearly arranged, which carry genetic information responsible for the inherited characteristics of the organism (see HEREDITY). Chromosomes consist of the NUCLEIC ACID DNA (and sometimes RNA) attached to a protein core. All normal cells contain a certain number of chromosomes characteristic of the species (46 in man), in homologous pairs (DIPLOID). GAMETES, however, are HAPLOID, having only half this number, one of each pair, so that they unite to form a ZYGOTE with the correct number of chromosomes. In man there is one pair of sex chromosomes, females having two X chromosomes, males an X and a Y; thus each EGG cell must have an X chromosome, but each spermatozoon (see SPERM) has either an X or a Y, and determines the sex of the offspring. In cell division, the chromosomes replicate and separate (see MEIOSIS; MITOSIS). Defective or supernumerary chromosomes cause various abnormalities, including MONGOLISM. (See also MUTATION; PROTEIN SYNTHESIS.)

CHROMOSPHERE. See SUN.

CHRONICLES, two Old Testament books summarizing Jewish history from Adam through the Babylonian captivity. The first consists mainly of genealogies up to Saul, and the second is largely a history of the Kingdom of Judah.

CHRONOLOGY, the science of dating involving the accurate placing of events in time and the definition of suitable timescales. In Christian societies, events are dated in years before (BC) or after (AD—*Anno Domini*) the traditional birth date of Christ. In scientific use, dates are often given BP (Before Present). In ARCHAEOLOGY, dating techniques include DENDROCHRONOLOGY and RADIOCARBON DATING. In GEOLOGY, rock strata are related to the geological time scale by examination of the FOSSILS they contain (see also POTASSIUM).

CHRONOMETER, an extremely accurate clock, especially one used in connection with celestial NAVIGATION at sea (see also CELESTIAL SPHERE). It differs from the normal clock in that it has a **fusee**, by means of which the power transmission of the mainspring is regulated such that it remains approximately uniform at all times; and a balance made of metals of different coefficients of EXPANSION to minimize the effects of temperature changes. The device is maintained in gimbals to reduce the effects of rolling and pitching. A chronometer's accuracy is checked daily and its error noted; the daily change in error is termed the **daily rate**. Chronometers are always set to GREENWICH MEAN TIME. The first chronometer was invented by John HARRISON (1735). (See also ATOMIC CLOCK; CLOCKS AND WATCHES.)

CHRYSALIS, the PUPA stage in the life-history of many insects, during which the LARVA undergoes METAMORPHOSIS to produce the features characteristic of the adult.

CHRYSANTHEMUM, genus of popular flowering herbaceous plants of the daisy family (Compositae). The large showy flowers are usually white, yellow, pink or red. Each flower consists of a number of florets. Chrysanthemums are native to temperate and subtropical areas. Many cultivated varieties have been developed.

CHRYSOBERYL, mixed OXIDE mineral of BERYLLIUM and ALUMINUM ($BeAl_2O_4$), forming hard crystals in the orthorhombic system, and found mainly in Brazil. ALEXANDRITE and CAT'S EYE are GEM varieties.

CHRYSOPRASE, a GEM variety of CHALCEDONY, colored apple-green by colloidal nickel silicate. It is found in Silesia and Cal.

CHRYSOSTOM, Saint John (c3y7–407 AD), one of the CHURCH DOCTORS, called Chrysostom ("golden mouthed") for his powers of oratory. He was patriarch of Constantinople (398–404) and became its patron saint.

CHRYSOTILE, mineral forming the chief variety of ASBESTOS, a fibrous SERPENTINE.

CHUANG-TZU (c369–286? BC), Chinese Taoist philosopher, noted for the *Chuang-tzu*, an original interpretation of TAOIST beliefs. Many chapters, though, were probably written by his disciples. (See also LAO-TSE.)

CHUB, any of several kinds of freshwater fish of the family Cyprinidae, related to the MINNOW. Species include the common or creek chub of E North America which may weigh 1kg (2.2lb) and the European chub which reaches 5.5kg (12lb).

CHUBB CRATER. See NEW QUEBEC CRATER.

CHUCKWALLA, *Sauromalus obesus*, a lizard of the SW deserts of North America. The chuckwalla is herbivorous and grows to 0.3m (1ft). When alarmed it wedges itself in a crevice by inflating its body.

CHUGACH MOUNTAINS, mountain range in S Alaska forming part of the COAST RANGES. The mountains hug the coast from Cook Inlet to the W end of the St. Elias Mts. The highest peak is Mt Marcus Baker (13 200ft).

CHUKAR, *Alectoris cukar*, a partridge with a black eye stripe and barred flanks, native to S Europe and W Asia. It now breeds in desert mountain ranges of western US.

CHUKOTSKI PENINSULA, the extreme NE of Siberia, facing Alaska across the Bering Sea. The peninsula forms part of the Chukot National Okrug in the USSR. Its peoples are mainly Chukchi and Eskimo hunters and fishermen.

CHULA VISTA, city in extreme SW Cal. It produces missile and aircraft parts and chemicals. Pop 67 901.

CHUMASHAN INDIANS, Indians of the Hokan linguistic group who lived in what is now SW Cal. They occupied the N islands in the Santa Barbara group and the coast from Malibu Canyon to Estero Bay. Their numbers fell from 10 000 in 1770 to 14 by 1930.

CHUNGKING, (Ch'ung-ch'ing), city in S China, in SE Szechwan province at the confluence of the Yangtze and Chia-ling rivers. A major trading center with well-developed heavy industry, it was the political capital of China 1938–45. Pop 4 400 000.

CHURCH, the community of Christian believers, a society founded as such by Jesus Christ (though springing from the Jewish community). The term is used both for the universal Church and for its national and local expressions. Governed and served by its MINISTRY, the Church is established by the Holy Spirit through the Scriptures and the SACRAMENTS. Its life, ideally characterized by holiness, is expressed in WORSHIP, teaching, MISSION and doing good. The Church consists not only of its present members (the "Church Militant") but also of those departed, the "Church Triumphant" in heaven and (disputedly) the "Church Expectant" in purgatory. The traditional marks of the Church, as in the Nicene Creed, are that it is one, holy, CATHOLIC and apostolic; the first is challenged by schism and the last by heresy. Protestant churches, while generally accepting the visible organization of the Church, have stressed more its spiritual nature, attempting to distinguish true Christians from nominal. (See also CHRISTIANITY; EASTERN CHURCH; WESTERN CHURCH.)

CHURCH, Frederick Edwin (1826–1900), US romantic landscape painter. He was a student of Thomas COLE and the most famous member of the HUDSON RIVER SCHOOL.

CHURCH DOCTORS, saints whose writings on Christian doctrine have special authority. The four great doctors of the E Church are saints ATHANASIUS of Alexandria, BASIL THE GREAT of Caesarea, GREGORY OF NAZIANZUS, and John CHRYSOSTOM. The four great doctors of the W Church are saints AMBROSE, AUGUSTINE, Gregory the Great (Pope GREGORY) and JEROME. The W has 20 other doctors, including saints Thomas AQUINAS, BONAVENTURA, CATHERINE OF SIENA and TERESA OF AVILA. The last two were declared doctors in 1970 by papal decree.

CHURCHES OF CHRIST, US religious denomination based on the primitive Church. It holds that the Church of Christ was founded at PENTECOST and refounded by Thomas CAMPBELL (1763–1854). There are over 17 000 independent churches and 2 290 000 members.

CHURCH FATHERS, eminent early Christian bishops and teachers whose writings deeply influenced Church doctrine. They include the eight great CHURCH DOCTORS and the APOSTOLIC FATHERS.

CHURCHILL, Lord Randolph Henry Spencer (1849–1895), British politician, father of Sir Winston Churchill, famous in the 1880s for advocating a more democratic and reformist Conservative Party. He founded a Fourth Party, which lasted from 1880 to 1885. A brilliant orator, he became chancellor of the exchequer in 1886, but resigned the same year and never again held office.

CHURCHILL, Sir Winston Spencer Leonard (1871–1965), greatest modern British statesman, as a war leader the architect of victory in WWII. He was the son of Lord Randolph Churchill. After an early career as an army officer and war correspondent he became a Conservative member of Parliament, changing to the Liberals in 1905. He was home secretary 1910–11, a dynamic first lord of the admiralty 1911–15 and held various government posts 1917–22. He was Conservative chancellor of the exchequer 1924–29 but in the 1930s his unpopular demands for war preparedness kept him from power. In WWII he was first lord of the admiralty 1939–40 and premier 1940–45. As such he became one of the greatest-ever war leaders; his oratory maintained Britain's morale, and he was one of the main shapers of Allied strategy. A postwar reaction cost him the 1945 election, but he was again premier 1951–55, remaining a nationally loved and revered figure for the rest of his life.

CHURCHILL RIVER (formerly Hamilton R), river flowing some 250mi from Churchill Falls (Canada's highest) in Labrador through Lake MELVILLE to the Atlantic. Above the falls (over 200mi more) it is called Ashuanipi R.

CHURCHILL RIVER, river in W Canada. It flows 1000mi E and then NE, from Lake la Loche in NW Saskatchewan to Hudson Bay in Manitoba. It has numerous rapids and flows through Churchill Lake and other lakes.

CHURCH OF CHRIST, SCIENTIST. See CHRISTIAN SCIENCE.

CHURCH OF ENGLAND, the English national church. Its doctrine is basically Protestant and its hierarchy and ceremony are rooted in Catholic tradition. The Church broke with Rome in 1534 (see REFORMATION) when HENRY VIII assumed the title of head of the Church. In the 16th and 17th centuries the Church was troubled by PURITAN agitation and later by nonconformity. But it remains the established state church with a nominal membership of 25–30 million (active members perhaps total only 10% of this figure). The 26 senior bishops (lords spiritual) sit in the House of Lords, and are led by the archbishop of Canterbury. (See also ANGLICANISM; MINISTRY.)

Although the Church of England was not directly founded by King Henry VIII, who was a staunch Catholic, it was Rome's refusal to grant him a divorce from Catherine of Aragon that led to the creation of an autonomous English national church. Since his time all English monarchs have borne the title, Defender of the Faith. This statue of King Henry is in Trinity College, Cambridge.

CHURCH OF SCOTLAND, the Scottish national church, based on PRESBYTERIANISM. It is governed by the General Assembly, which is elected from the presbyteries. Parishes are presided over by kirk sessions elected by the congregation. Membership totals some 1 300 000. (See also KNOX, JOHN; COVENANTERS; CHALMERS, THOMAS.)

CHURCH OF THE NAZARENE, Protestant evangelical denomination created in its present form in Tex. in 1908 when three groups merged. Its headquarters is in Kansas City, Mo.

CHURCH YEAR, or ecclesiastical CALENDAR, the division of the year into seasons related to the Christian festivals, used in many churches as a basis for liturgy and ritual.

CHURNING, process, known since prehistoric times, for converting cream to BUTTER. Cream is an EMULSION of water in oils: agitation in a butter churn makes it an oil-in-water emulsion, and the fatty

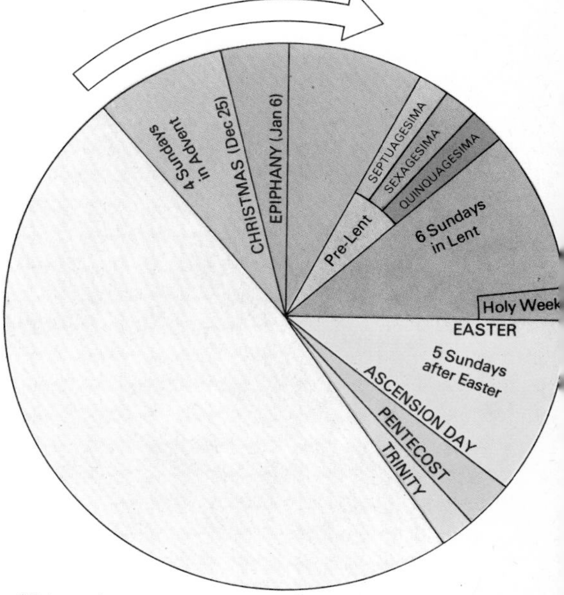

All the major feasts and seasons of the church year occupy approximately half the year. The church year begins with the season of Advent, and celebrates the major events in the life of Christ. The exact position of Easter, and of the other "movable feasts" dependent on it, changes from year to year.

This mausoleum is the traditional burial place of Cicero by the Appian Way, near Formia, north of Naples. He was murdered nearby in 43 BC.

globules coagulate. The remaining buttermilk may then be skimmed.

CHURRIGUERA, José Benito (1665–1725), Spanish architect who gave his name to the Spanish Baroque style, better known as Churrigueresque (1650–1740). Churriguera designed grandiosely theatrical altars and the entire town of Nuevo Baztán, Madrid.

CHURUBUSCO, Battle of, a conflict in the MEXICAN WAR. On Aug. 20, 1847 Winfield Scott's US forces crushed Santa Anna's Mexican troops at Churubusco, a suburb of Mexico City.

CIANO, Count Galeazzo (1903–44), Italian Fascist statesman. He married Mussolini's daughter (1930) and became propaganda minister (1933). As foreign minister (1936–43), he was overshadowed by Mussolini. Dismissed, he voted against Mussolini at the 1943 Fascist Grand Council. He was caught by the Nazis, handed over to the Fascists in N Italy and shot.

CIARDI, John (1916–), US poet, translator and teacher. He made notable translations of Dante's *Inferno* (1954), *Purgatorio* (1961) and *Paradiso* (1970).

CIBBER, Colley (1671–1757), English actor-manager and dramatist who introduced sentimental comedy to the theater in *Love's Last Shift* (1696). His moral comedies were a reaction against Restoration drama. Cibber was made poet laureate in 1730.

Statue of El Cid, the great hero of Spanish history and literature, outside the Museum of Natural History in New York. El Cid was regarded as the prototype of the chivalrous Christian warrior.

CIBOLA, Seven Cities of, golden cities reported in the Southwest of North America in the 16th century. The legend attracted Spanish exploration, notably by Coronado with 300 Spanish cavalry and 1000 Indian allies (1540). In fact the cities were five or six Zuñi pueblos.

CICADA, family (Cicadidae) of large bugs well-known for the monotonous, whining song of the males. This song is produced by rapidly vibrating drum-like membranes on the abdomen. The periodical cicada or 17-year locust spends 17 years underground as a larva.

CICERO, industrial town in NE Ill. It is a suburb of Chicago, with metallurgical and electrical industries. Pop 69 130.

CICERO, Marcus Tullius (106–43 BC), Roman orator, statesman and philosopher. As consul (63 BC) he championed POMPEY and saved Rome from civil war by crushing the CATILINE conspiracy. His refusal to submit to the First Triumvirate ruined his political career in 58 BC. Cicero's tacit approval of Caesar's murder and his defense of the Republic in his *First and Second Philippics* led Mark ANTONY to have him killed.

CICHLIDS, family of 650 flattened, perchlike fish (Cichlidae) native to Africa and South and Central America. They are often brightly colored, and are popular aquarium fish.

CID, El ("the Lord"), title given to Rodrigo Días de Vivar (c1043–1099), a Castilian Spanish national hero. He led the forces of Sancho II of Castile and Alfonso VI of León. Banished by Alfonso in 1081, he fought for the Moorish king of Saragossa and captured Valencia (1094), which he ruled until his death. His romanticized exploits appear in much literature, notably in *The Song of the Cid* (c1140) and CORNEILLE's *Le Cid* (1637).

CIDER, an ALCOHOLIC BEVERAGE made from fermented sour apples (see FERMENTATION). In the US this is known as "hard" cider, whereas "sweet" cider is a commercially-prepared nonalcoholic apple juice.

CIERVA, Juan de la (1895–1936), Spanish aviator, the inventor of the AUTOGIRO. He was killed in an airplane crash at Croydon, England.

CILIA, hair-like outgrowths from the surfaces of cells, which provide the means of locomotion for many small animals such as PROTOZOA and WORMS. In higher animals, cilia provide means for moving fluids over the surfaces of cells, such as in the respiratory tract. Flagella is the name used for longer forms of cilia.

CILICIA, ancient region of SE Asia Minor, now in Turkey. It lay between the Taurus Mts and the Mediterranean, straddling a major route to Syria and the E. The chief cities were Tarsus and Seleucia. Assyrians, Persians, Greeks and Romans ruled the area in turn.

CIMABUE, Giovanni (c1240–1302?), Italian fresco painter of the 13th-century Florentine school. His work links Italian Byzantine and early Renaissance art. He possibly taught GIOTTO.

CIMAROSA, Domenico (1749–1801), prolific Italian composer famous for his comic operas, notably *Il Matrimonio Segreto* ("The Secret Marriage") of 1792. He was court composer to Catherine the Great of Russia, 1787–91.

CIMARRON RIVER, river that rises in NE N.M. It flows 500 mi across SW Kan. and central Okla. to the Arkansas R in N Okla.

CIMBALON. See DULCIMER.

CIMBRI, Germanic tribe from Jutland, a danger to Rome in the late 2nd century BC. With the Teutoni, they defeated four Roman armies (113–105 BC) and, in 103 BC, prepared to invade Italy from S Gaul. Gaius MARIUS destroyed the Teutoni in Gaul (102 BC) and the Cimbri in N Italy (101 BC).

CIMMERIANS, an ancient semilegendary people of S Russia. In the 8th century BC, the Scythians drove them into Asia Minor, where they destroyed the Phrygian kingdom and were themselves defeated by the Lydian King Alyattes in the 7th century BC.

CINCHONA, or **chinchona**, genus of tropical evergreen trees and shrubs that are native to the Amazonian slopes of the Andes from Colombia to Bolivia. The main importance of these trees lies in the bark, which yields medicinal ALKALOIDS, notably QUININE, used as a cure for malaria. Cinchona seeds from Bolivia formed the basis of major plantations established in Jawa by the Dutch. Jawa is the chief source of cinchona bark today.

CINCINNATI, second-largest city in Ohio, and seat of Hamilton Co. It stands in SW Ohio on the Ohio R. Founded 1788, the city was named for the Society of the Cincinnati (see CINCINNATI, SOCIETY OF THE). By the mid-19th century it was the nation's largest pork packing center, nicknamed "Porkopolis." Cincinnati is now a commercial, manufacturing and railroad center, site of the University of Cincinnati and home of the Cincinnati Symphony Orchestra. Pop 452 524.

CINCINNATI, Society of the, hereditary patriotic association of officers formed by members of the Continental Army in 1783, at the end of the Revolutionary War. Many Americans saw it as an attempt to establish a military aristocracy. There are societies in each of the original 13 states and one in France. George Washington was the first president-general.

CINCINNATUS, Lucius Quinctius (c519–439? BC), early Roman hero renowned for selfless patriotism. He was twice appointed dictator (458 and 439 BC) to save Rome from disaster. Both times he reputedly defeated Rome's enemies and then resigned, rejected all rewards and returned to his farm.

CINDERELLA, fairy tale heroine. Her fairy godmother helps her escape domestic drudgery to attend a prince's ball. He falls in love, loses her, then finds her by means of a glass slipper which only she can wear. This version of an old Chinese tale comes from Perrault's *Mother Goose* (1697). His slipper became "glass" by a mistranslation from the French.

CINEMA. See MOTION PICTURES.

CINNA, Lucius Cornelius (c130–84 BC), Roman consul at the time of MARIUS and SULLA who became virtual dictator of Rome after the death of Marius (86 BC). He was killed by mutinous troops he had assembled to oppose his rival, Sulla.

CINNABAR, red SULFIDE mineral consisting of mercury (II) sulfide (HgS), the chief ore of MERCURY, found in Spain, Italy, Peru and Cal. as massive deposits or hexagonal crystals. It is used as the pigment vermilion. A black, cubic form of mercury (II) sulfide, **metacinnabar**, also occurs.

CINNAMON, dried, aromatic bark of the cinnamon tree (*Cinnamomum zeylanicum*), which is native to Sri Lanka and India. Cinnamon has been long prized as a spice and is still used for flavoring bakery goods. Cinnamon oil is mainly used to flavor medicines and may have medicinal properties.

CINQUEFOIL, general name for herbs and shrubs of the genus *Potentilla*, family Rosaceae. They are so-named from their "five-fingered" leaves. They are native to N temperate zones of the world and many varieties are used as garden plants.

CINQUE PORTS, originally five, but ultimately thirty-two towns along the S coast of England which from the 11th–17th centuries enjoyed certain privileges in return for providing the crown with ships and men. England had no royal navy at this time.

CIPHERS. See CODES AND CIPHERS.

CIRCADIAN RHYTHM. See BIOLOGICAL CLOCKS.

CIRCASSIANS, a pastoral and fruit-growing mountain people living in the NW Caucasus E of the Black Sea. Today they number over 350 000: 80% live in the Soviet Union, the rest live in Turkey and are descended from Muslims who fled there when Russia annexed Circassia in 1829.

CIRCE, in Greek mythology, the enchantress daughter of Helios and the nymph Perse. She lived on the island of Aeaea, and changed the companions of ODYSSEUS into swine before he outwitted her.

CIRCLE, a CURVE so drawn that all points on its perimeter are at an equal distance, the **radius**, from a single point, the **center**. A straight line cutting the circle is known as a **secant**, the area within the circle cut off by the secant being termed a **segment**. A secant passing through the center is called a **diameter**. The part of a secant lying with a circle is a **chord**, the part of the perimeter between the two points of intersection of the secant and the circle being termed an **arc**. A line in the same plane touching the circle at a single point is a **tangent** (see TANGENT OF A CURVE). A **central angle** is the angle between two radii, and the area between them is termed a **sector**. The length of the perimeter is the circle's **circumference**. The AREA of a circle is πr^2 (see PI), where r is the radius; and its circumference is $2\pi r$. (See also CYLINDER; MENSURATION; SPHERE; SPHERICAL GEOMETRY.)

CIRCLEVILLE, city in S central Ohio and seat of Pickaway Co. It makes paper, fluorescent lamps, animal feeds and plastics. Pop 11 687.

CIRCUIT, Electric, assemblage of electrical CONDUCTORS (usually wires) and components through which current from a power source such as a BATTERY or GENERATOR flows (see ELECTRICITY). Components may be connected one after another (in series) or side by side (in parallel). If current may flow between two points their connection is a closed circuit; if not, an open circuit; and if RESISTANCE between them is virtually zero, a short circuit: a switch when off is a closed circuit, when on a short circuit. Short circuits between the terminals of the power source are dangerous (see CIRCUIT BREAKER; FUSE). (See also ELECTRONICS; KIRCHHOFF'S LAWS.)

CIRCUIT BREAKER, device now often used in place of a FUSE to protect electrical equipment from damage when the current exceeds a desired value, as in short-circuiting. The circuit breaker opens the CIRCUIT automatically, usually by means of a coil that separates contacts when the current reaches a certain value (see ELECTROMAGNETISM). One advantage of the circuit breaker is that the contacts may be reset (by hand or automatically) whereas a fuse has to be replaced. Small circuit breakers are used in the home (as in many TELEVISION sets), larger ones in industry .

CIRCUIT RIDER, an itinerant preaching clergyman, usually of the Methodist Church, who rode out to visit scattered frontier communities unable to form a church congregation of their own. The practice was originated in England by John WESLEY.

CIRCULATION OF THE BLOOD. See BLOOD CIRCULATION.

CIRCUMCENTER, the point of concurrence of the lines drawn perpendicular to and through the midpoints of the sides of a TRIANGLE. This point is equidistant from the triangle's vertices and hence the center of the circle that may be circumscribed about it (see CIRCUMSCRIPTION).

CIRCUMCISION, removal of the foreskin of the penis, either as a religious requirement (notably among Jews and Muslims) or as a surgical measure for sanitary or other reasons (for example, to relieve tightness of the foreskin). In ancient Egypt circumcision was regarded as an initiation into puberty. For the Jews it symbolizes an infant's induction into the covenant between God and Abraham.

CIRCUMPOLAR STARS, those stars which can be seen every night of the year from any particular latitude, and which appear to circle the celestial pole (see CELESTIAL SPHERE).

CIRCUMSCRIPTION, in plane GEOMETRY, the construction of a CIRCLE such that all vertices of a particular POLYGON lie on its circumference, the polygon then being said to be inscribed (see INSCRIPTION) within the circle. All regular polygons and all TRIANGLES may be circumscribed. In three dimensions circumscription implies the construction of a SPHERE such that on its surface lie all the vertices of a POLYHEDRON.

CIRCUS, an entertainment involving equestrian, acrobatic, animal, trapeze and clown acts. The modern circus first appeared in London in 1768, when Philip Astley launched an equestrian show to which other acts were added. The first US circus was opened by an Englishman, J. W. Ricketts, in Philadelphia in 1793. Its imitators often formed traveling shows, performing under an enormous tent, the "Big Top." The most famous American circuses, later combined, were those of BARNUM and Bailey and the RINGLING BROTHERS. (See also CIRCUS, ROMAN.)

CIRCUS, Roman, an oblong racetrack with tiered seating on three sides, used for chariot races and other spectacles. In Rome, the oldest and most important was the Circus Maximus, but there were circuses in many cities of the Roman Empire.

CIRE PERDUE ("lost wax"), a casting technique used in sculpture, probably invented about 5 000 years ago in Mesopotamia. The work is modeled in wax, coated in clay, and fired until the clay has baked hard and the wax has melted, leaving a hollow mold into which molten bronze is poured.

CIRQUE, corrie or **cwm,** steep-sided hollow formed by glacial erosion, usually occupied by a lake where the GLACIER has retreated, or by névé where the glacier is still present. (See also EROSION.)

CIRRHOSIS, chronic disease of the LIVER, with disorganization of normal structure and replacement by fibrous scars and regenerating nodules. It is the end result of many liver diseases, all of which cause liver-cell death; most common are those associated with ALCOHOLISM and following some cases of hepatitis, while certain poisons and hereditary diseases are rare causes. All liver functions are impaired, but symptoms often do not occur until early liver failure develops with EDEMA, ascites, JAUNDICE, COMA, emaciation, or gastrointestinal-tract HEMORRHAGE; BLOOD clotting is often abnormal and PLASMA proteins are low. The liver damage is not reversible, but if recognized early in the alcoholic, abstention can minimize progression. Treatment consists of measures to protect the liver from excess protein, DIURETICS and the prevention and treatment of hemorrhage.

CISTERCIANS, or White Monks, Roman Catholic religious order founded at Cîteaux, France, in 1098 by St. Robert of Molesme and at its height in the 12th and 13th centuries. Cistercians eat and work in silence and abstain from meat, fish and eggs.

CITIZENSHIP, a legal relationship between an individual and the country of his nationality, usually acquired by birth or naturalization. The terms for acquiring citizenship vary in different countries, but usually depend on a person's place of birth and the nationalities of the parents. In the US, anyone born on American soil is an American citizen, unless born of foreign parents having diplomatic status. If born outside the US, the child can acquire US citizenship through either parent, by birth if at least one parent maintains residence in the US, or by residing in the US for at least five years between ages 13 and 21 if only one parent is an American citizen. A person may become a naturalized citizen of the US by residing there for five years under permanent status. The citizen is given a passport, government protection and constitutional rights, and must pay taxes and be ready to serve in the armed forces.

CITRANGE, hardy ornamental tree that yields a juicy, highly acid fruit mainly used to flavor drinks and in cooking. The tree is a hybrid of the sweet orange (*Citrus sinensis*) and the trifoliate orange (*Poncirus trifoliata*). The rootstock is used to bud other citrus varieties. (See also CITRUS.)

CITRIC ACID ($C_6H_8O_7$), colorless crystalline solid, a CARBOXYLIC ACID widespread in plant and animal tissue, especially citrus fruits. It is made commercially by FERMENTATION of crude sugar with the fungus *Aspergillus niger*, and is used in the food, pharmaceutical and textile industries, and for cleaning metals. It is vital in cell METABOLISM (see CITRIC ACID CYCLE). MW 192.1, mp 153°C.

CITRIC ACID CYCLE, or **Krebs cycle,** or tricarboxylic acid cycle, a vital cycle of chemical reactions forming the final stage in the oxidation of food in cells (see METABOLISM; RESPIRATION) and thus producing energy for BIOSYNTHESIS. The previous stages of oxidation produce the acetyl derivative of coenzyme A (see ENZYMES). The acetyl group then adds to oxaloacetic acid to produce citric acid, which in a sequence of enzyme-catalyzed oxidation reactions is converted back to oxaloacetic acid. The net result of the cycle is total oxidation of one ACETIC ACID molecule to carbon dioxide and water. The oxidizing agents are pyridine NUCLEOTIDES, which accept hydrogen atoms and are then reoxidized by CYTOCHROMES, the energy produced being stored as ATP (see NUCLEOTIDES). Except in microorganisms, the enzymes needed in the cycle are located in the mitochondria (see CELL).

CITRON, *Citrus medica*, small tree or shrub cultivated in Corsica, Sicily, Greece and the West Indies for its lemon-like fruits, the rind of which is used in making candies. The citron is closely related to other CITRUS fruit trees.

This Fourth of July circus parade with its antique wagons is part of the annual "Day in Old Milwaukee" put on by the Circus World Museum at Baraboo, southern Wisconsin, where the Ringling brothers began their Big Top shows in 1884 and later set up their winter quarters.

CITRUS, genus of trees that provide some of our most important fruits. These include the CITRANGE, citron, GRAPEFRUIT, LEMON, LIME, ORANGE, SHADDOCK and TANGERINE.

CITTERN, an instrument similar to the guitar, popular in the Middle Ages and Renaissance. It usually had eight or nine wire strings, plucked with fingers or plectrum. The body was pear-shaped with a flat back and the neck had fixed metal frets.

CITY, any large center of population distinguished from a town or village by differentiation of economic, administrative or religious functions within it; or a center officially designated as a city for purposes of local government. Cities first developed in the Middle East, notably in what is now Mesopotamia. One of the earliest true cities was UR in Sumer, dating back to at least 3 500 BC. Thereafter cities proliferated throughout the Middle East and in any parts of the world where civilization developed, either as religious or governmental centers, or centering trade, transportation, markets and manufacturing. Few

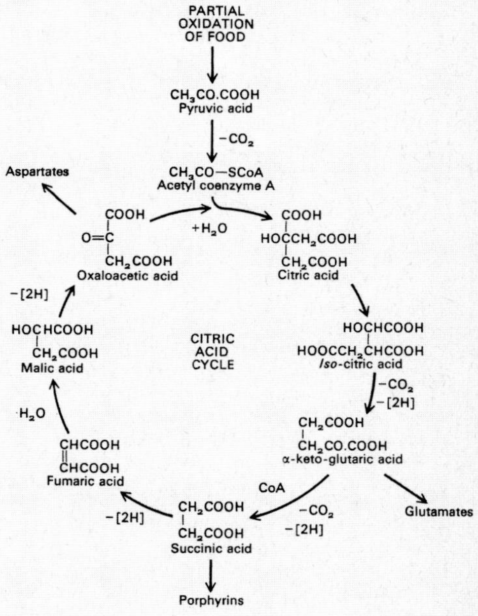

City

"This great hive, the city" *Abraham Cowley*

Cities are as old as human civilization. Ur in Mesopotamia, founded about 3500 BC, contained all the functions that cities have had through to the present, providing a trading, administrative, defensive, religious and cultural center for the region surrounding it. It was in the city that man first began to practice that division of labor that so sets man apart from most other species. Specialized crafts and large-scale political and religious domination were possible only after men adopted permanent settlements, supported on the surplus products that farmers brought to exchange in the market place. Trade could only grow after the founding of cities, offering fixed and specialized markets for merchants to travel between in days when their journeys might last for several years.

After the decline of the Roman Empire, urban life in Europe was virtually nonexistent until the 11th century, although in the Orient and the Islamic world cities remained an important element in social organization. With the gradual breakup of the feudal system in the west, a drift of population from the countryside into the towns began, which, although hesitant at first, has gained momentum ever since. A wealthy and increasingly powerful merchant class began to develop and slowly wrested political power from the rural landholders. Urban architecture re-blossomed as a living art-form as the emergent cities vied with each other to display their commercial wealth in ever grander magnificence.

It was not until the 19th century that the industrial revolution in western Europe accelerated the process of urbanization. The city became as much the location of industry as it had ever been the center for trading. Vast populations in the cities were crowded into dismally inadequate houses as the factories' appetite for labor grew insatiably and the countryside progressively became the mere larder of the towns.

The influx into the cities brought with it new problems of housing, sanitation, education, air pollution, traffic congestion, urban poverty and urban crime. Cities today retain many of these problems—and have discovered new ones—as the process of urbanization has spread like a contagion throughout the developed and developing world.

Recent urbanization has brought its gains as well as its losses. Were it not for the city, the world could probably not carry its present population because labor-intensive agriculture tends to be inefficient. Cities are necessary to provide both the pool of labor that industry requires to man its processes and the major consumer-markets of the world—conveniently close to the urban centers of manufacture.

Probably the most significant feature of the city in the 20th century is its ability to provide an increasing range and intensity of service functions. It is not just the public utilities—gas, electricity, water, postal and telecommunications services—that are most efficiently provided within the urban context, but educational, medical, legal, financial and welfare services are also best provided where a population is not too widely scattered. Wholesale and retail distribution is a further sector where the comprehensiveness of the service can increase in direct proportion to the total population within economic range.

A major problem confronting many cities in recent years has been the difficulty experienced in persuading key workers—doctors, teachers, transportation and local government employees—to live in the inner city. Attention is consequently being directed to making the urban environment an attractive place in which to live and work, chiefly by improving city transportation systems and increasing recreational facilities.

Most established cities in the western world center around a central business district which provides administrative, commercial and retail functions on sites of high value and consequently tall buildings. The retail core is traditionally surrounded by an area of wholesale facilities and inner-city industries with perhaps considerable space given over to railroad freight yards. Residential areas range from inner-city slums through middle-income residential suburbs to exclusive outer suburbs. Usually housing densities fall with land values as the distance from the city center increases. Other large uses of urban land include suburban factory estates, recreation space (parks and sportsfields) and horticulture.

early cities had more than 20 000 inhabitants and even Rome, the largest in the Empire, had no more than 800 000. Urban life decayed in Western Europe during the Dark Ages, but proliferated elsewhere. Around the 6th to 8th centuries AD Ch'ang-an, the T'ang capital in China, was the largest and most cosmopolitan city in the world; Teotihuacan in Mexico had possibly 200 000 inhabitants, and somewhat later Chan-Chan in Peru had possibly 250 000. In Europe the RENAISSANCE was ushered in by the revival of the cities as centers of trade and culture, but the giant cities of today were strictly a product of the INDUSTRIAL REVOLUTION.

In the US, city government originated in the colonial settlements, granted borough or city charters by the state legislatures after the Revolution, and governed usually by a mayor, a city council or similar body and a city judiciary (on the pattern of national government). In the 19th century the Industrial Revolution caused a tremendous population movement into the cities which is still continuing on a worldwide basis. In the US in 1800 only 5% of the population lived in cities, then defined as settlements with more than 8 000 inhabitants; by 1960 70% of the population was urban; and by 1970 the New York metropolitan area alone exceeded 11.5 million inhabitants. This influx has caused considerable problems, including pollution, overcrowding, insufficient recreation areas, deteriorating school standards and a lack of funds for essential services, which offset the many advantages of urban living.

CITY PLANNING, planning for the growth of a city or town to take into consideration the physical, social and economic aspects of its environment. Most Roman cities, and many earlier ones in the ancient world, were built on a gridiron pattern, with the public buildings centrally and strategically placed. The cities of the Middle Ages, however, were rarely planned unless powerful monied interests made this possible. The Renaissance, especially in Italy, saw a revival of grandiose city planning, usually intended to glorify a ruler or to strengthen his military position. The Industrial Revolution and the enormous population movements it generated caused rapid piecemeal development, and the situation had become critical before any attempt was made to deal with it.

In the US various civic reform movements were already active before the Civil War, leading to legislation to enforce slum clearance and provide better educational and recreational facilities, while designers such as Frederick L. OLMSTED and Daniel BURNHAM (planner of the Chicago World's Exposition of 1893) stimulated their fellows to more imaginative efforts. Unfortunately the teams responsible for such work tended to impose their own class and moral values on other social classes. More recently efforts have been made to avoid such mistakes; large federal subsidies have been made available, notably for low-cost housing and city center renewal projects, and planning has begun to take human as well as physical factors into account. Local government has become increasingly professional in planning ahead, and over 30 American universities now offer courses in city planning.

CITY-STATES, politically independent communities controlling the lives of their own citizens and dominating the surrounding countryside. They flourished in three major areas of Western culture: among the ancient civilizations of the Middle East, notably in Sumeria (ancient Babylonia), and Phoenicia; in the classical period of Greece (emerging about 700 BC); and in Europe from the 11th to the 16th centuries, notably in Italy and Germany.

CIUDAD BOLÍVAR, city in NE Venezuela, on the Orinoco R 250mi from the sea. It is the capital of Bolívar state and exports rubber, coffee, cocoa, sugar, tobacco, cattle, hides, pharmaceuticals and gold. Pop 109 600.

CIUDAD JUÁREZ. See JUÁREZ.

CIUDAD OBREGÓN, town in NW Mexico. It is in Sonora state, 65mi SE of Guaymas. Pop 138 506.

CIVETS, weasel-like carnivorous mammals of the family Viverridae, found in Africa and S Asia. The African civet, *Civettictis civetta*, is reared for the musky-smelling oily substance used as a base for perfumes that is produced by glands under the tail.

CIVICS, the study of the rights and duties of CITIZENSHIP, usually taught as a branch of political science. Civics deals with the national and economic workings of political and economic systems.

CIVIL AERONAUTICS BOARD (CAB), an independent US federal agency which regulates civil aviation, established as the Civil Aeronautics Authority in 1938. The five board members, appointed by the president and confirmed by the Senate, serve for six years. They supervise air safety, airline rates and practices and domestic air routes and negotiate international air agreements.

CIVIL AIR PATROL (CAP), an 80 000 strong volunteer civilian auxiliary of the US Air Force, established by Congress in 1946. It has a massive radio network and cooperates with Red Cross and Civil Defense personnel in search and rescue operations and disaster relief programs.

CIVIL DEFENSE, measures taken to protect the civilian population and its resources from enemy attack. Civil defense programs were launched in several countries just before WWII, when the potential danger of air strikes was first realized. In the US civil defense is directed by the Office of Civil Defense, under the Department of Defense. Measures include nuclear shelter construction, a national attack warning system of 400 stations, an Emergency Broadcast System (EBS) to transmit information and instructions, a radiation monitoring network to determine when it is safe to leave the shelters, and inexpensive gas masks to help deal with CHEMICAL AND BIOLOGICAL WARFARE.

CIVIL DISOBEDIENCE, a form of political action involving intentional violation of the law in order to draw attention to alleged injustices. The aim is to enlist public sympathy, and the idea probably dates

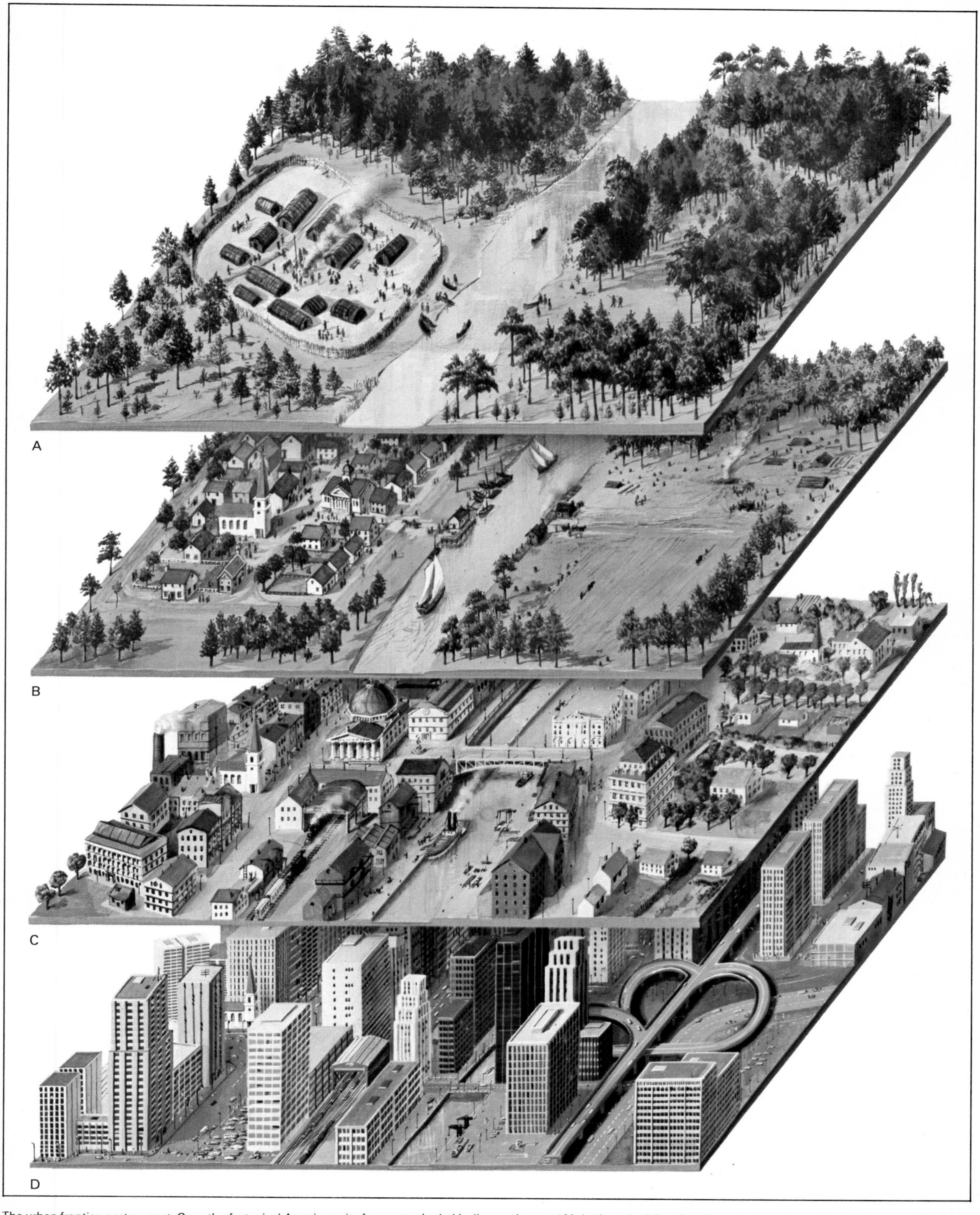

The urban frontier, east or west. Growth of a typical American city from a stockaded Indian settlement (A), in the colonial period, through the early and late 19th century (B–C), to the glass and steel metropolis of today (D).

back to the essay *On Civil Disobedience* by the 19th-century American writer Henry David THOREAU. It was successfully used by the Indian leader GANDHI to help gain independence for India, and has been employed by movements as diverse as the Suffragettes and the Vietnam-War protesters, not always accompanied by Gandhi's technique of "passive resistance." In the US the civil rights movement has made the most widespread and striking use of civil disobedience.

CIVIL ENGINEERING, that branch of engineering concerned with the design, construction and maintenance of stationary structures such as buildings, bridges, highways, dams, etc. The term "civil engineer" was first used c1750 by John Smeaton, who built the Eddystone Lighthouse. Nowadays, civil engineering incorporates modern technological advances in the structures required by industrial society. The branches of the field include: SURVEYING, concerned with the selection of sites; hydraulic and sanitary engineering, dealing with public WATER SUPPLY and SEWAGE disposal, etc.; TRANSPORTATION engineering, which deals with highways, airports and so on; structural engineering, which is concerned with the actual planning and construction of permanent installations; and environmental, town or city planning, which improves existing urban environments and plans the development of new areas.

CIVILIAN CONSERVATION CORPS (CCC), federal agency initiated in 1933 by President F. D. Roosevelt to combat unemployment during the Great Depression by providing jobs in forestry and conservation schemes. Projects included pest control, flood prevention and reforestation. The CCC was abolished in 1942.

CIVIL LAW, law dealing with private rights of individual citizens in contrast to branches of law, such as CRIMINAL LAW, which regulate relationships between individuals and the state. Thus civil law includes mortgages, marriage, inheritance, citizenship and property (COMMERCIAL LAW is often separate). The term civil law is also used for codified legal systems derived from Roman Law, not from the COMMON LAW.

The Romans distinguished civil law (*jus civile*) from international or public law (*jus gentium*). Codified by JUSTINIAN but replaced by customary laws in the Dark Ages, Roman law was rediscovered in the 12th century. It influenced France's CODE NAPOLÉON (1804), soon copied by other West European nations. Today, Western countries comprise civil law nations (most of Europe and Latin America) and common law countries (notably Great Britain, Canada and the US). In civil law countries, courts base judgements on codified principles rather than on precedents, and they do not feature trial by jury or the law of evidence.

CIVIL LIBERTIES UNION. See AMERICAN CIVIL LIBERTIES UNION.

CIVIL RIGHTS AND LIBERTIES, rights and privileges held by citizens of a nation, whether deemed natural and inviolable or part of what is legally owed to them.

Origins of Civil Rights. England's MAGNA CARTA, 1215, and BILL OF RIGHTS, 1689, established a basis in common law for the inviolable liberties of citizens. NATURAL LAW theorists of the 17th and 18th centuries (notably John LOCKE and Jean-Jacques ROUSSEAU) reinforced such concepts, which became enshrined in the US DECLARATION OF INDEPENDENCE.

Civil Rights in the United States. The basis for civil rights in the US is the Constitution and its first 10 amendments, the BILL OF RIGHTS. This deals, for example, with freedom of speech, press, religion and assembly; freedom from unreasonable seizure and searches; right to a speedy, public trial; and prohibition of double jeopardy and self-incrimination.

Progress on minority rights included the 13th amendment abolishing slavery (1865) and the 19th amendment giving women the vote in Federal elections (1920). But continuing racial discrimination led to civil rights bills in and after the 1950s and to key Supreme Court decisions, notably those rejecting the doctrine of "separate but equal facilities" for whites and blacks in state schooling (1954) and ordering immediate integration in schools (1969). Meanwhile such bodies as the AMERICAN CIVIL LIBERTIES UNION worked to ensure and extend individuals' civil liberties. In 1964 a Supreme Court decision reapportioned Congressional districts to maintain the "one man, one vote" principle, and a sweeping civil rights act against discrimination was passed. In 1966 the Miranda case ruling made illegally-obtained confessions inadmissible as evidence in a court of law and established that an arrested person must be made aware of his constitutional rights and able to exercise them. A bill of 1970 lowered the voting age from 21 to 18. (See also WOMEN'S LIBERATION MOVEMENT; WOMEN'S RIGHTS.)

Civil Rights in Canada are based on acts, common law tradition and court decisions. A Bill of Rights (1960) largely parallels that of the US.

International Civil Rights Movement. The UN's Universal Declaration of Human Rights (1948) lists civil rights that should be available to all people everywhere. Bodies working for such goals have included UNESCO, the INTERNATIONAL LABOR ORGANIZATION, European and Inter-American commissions on human rights, the International Commission of Jurists and the International League for the Rights of Man.

CIVIL SERVICE, the permanent body of civilian employees of a government, usually excluding elected officials, judges and military personnel. Appointment and promotion are generally based on merit, to secure efficiency and freedom from political influence. Civil services date from ancient China and Rome, and a civil service bureaucracy has become increasingly important as the functions of national governments have increased in scope and complexity.

In the US the civil service's integrity and continuity suffered from the SPOILS SYSTEM (gifts of government jobs as political rewards), firmly established from 1828 under President Andrew Jackson. Attempts to establish a merit system failed until the PENDLETON ACT (1883) set up the Civil Service Commission to administer a merit system of federal employment. The HATCH ACTS of 1939 and 1940 forbade federal employees to play any active part in politics beyond voting. Since the 1880s many states, cities and countries have set up civil service systems for public employees.

CIVIL WAR, American (1861–1865), conflict between 11 Southern states known as the CONFEDERATE STATES OF AMERICA, and the US Federal government. Because the 11 states had attempted to secede from the Union, the conflict was officially called the "War of Rebellion" in the North. Since it was a sectional struggle, it is also known, particularly in the South, as the "War between the States."

Significance. The Civil War was one of the most crucial events in American history. It was fought for total aims: restoration of the Union or independence for the South. The conflict destroyed slavery and the agrarian society of the South which depended on it, stimulated northern industry and ensured the supremacy of the Federal government over the states. Military historians often see the struggle as the first modern, or "total" war. More than 4 million men took part, over 600 000 died and new weapons and military tactics made their appearance. The American Civil War was probably the greatest sustained combat in history before WWI.

Origins. The immediate cause of the war was the North's refusal to recognize STATES' RIGHTS regarding secession from the Union. The war's underlying cause lay in the socio-economic division between North and South. The economy of the South, based on the plantation system of agriculture, depended on slave labor, which became increasingly distasteful to the more industrialized, non-slave-owning North. Political differences between the two sides came to a head over the question of westward expansion—whether slavery should be permitted in the new states and territories or remain confined to the South. Attempts to settle this question produced the MISSOURI COMPROMISE (1820) and the COMPROMISE OF 1850 which was nullified by the KANSAS-NEBRASKA ACT (1854). The DRED SCOTT DECISION (1857) and Lincoln's election as president (1860) inflamed the situation. Fearing that a Republican president would enforce abolition, S.C. seceded from the Union on Dec. 20, 1860 and was soon followed by six other states. The CONFEDERATE STATES elected Jefferson Davis provisional president, and after Lincoln ordered supplies to Federal-held Fort Sumter, in Charleston (S.C.) Harbor, Confederate guns opened fire on the fort on April 12. The fort surrendered, and four more states (N.C., Va., Ark. and Tenn.) joined the Confederacy. So began what Senator James M. Mason of Va. aptly called "a war of sentiment and opinion by one form of society against another form of society."

The war. The determination of both sides led to over 2 400 named battles. The war involved 1 600 000 Federal troops and nearly 1 000 000 Confederates. There were over 600 000 dead, Union armies suffering more than 600 000 casualties, the Confederates nearly half as many. The North outnumbered the South by 22 000 000 to 9 000 000 and was constantly reinforced by immigration from Europe. The North also had superior manufacturing, transportation and other facilities. The South had a poor railroad system, few good harbors and little industry. The North set out to crush the South by naval blockade and offensive war—waged both in the East and the West.

Congress gave Lincoln authority to recruit 500 000

Above left: monument in Nashville, Tennessee, to the memory of all the Confederate soldiers who died during the American Civil War (1861–65). The text on the monument reads: "Duty Done, Honor Won."

Left: the field at Gettysburg, with monuments and reminders of the famous battle (July 1–4, 1863), which changed the course of the Civil War and spelled the end of the Confederacy.

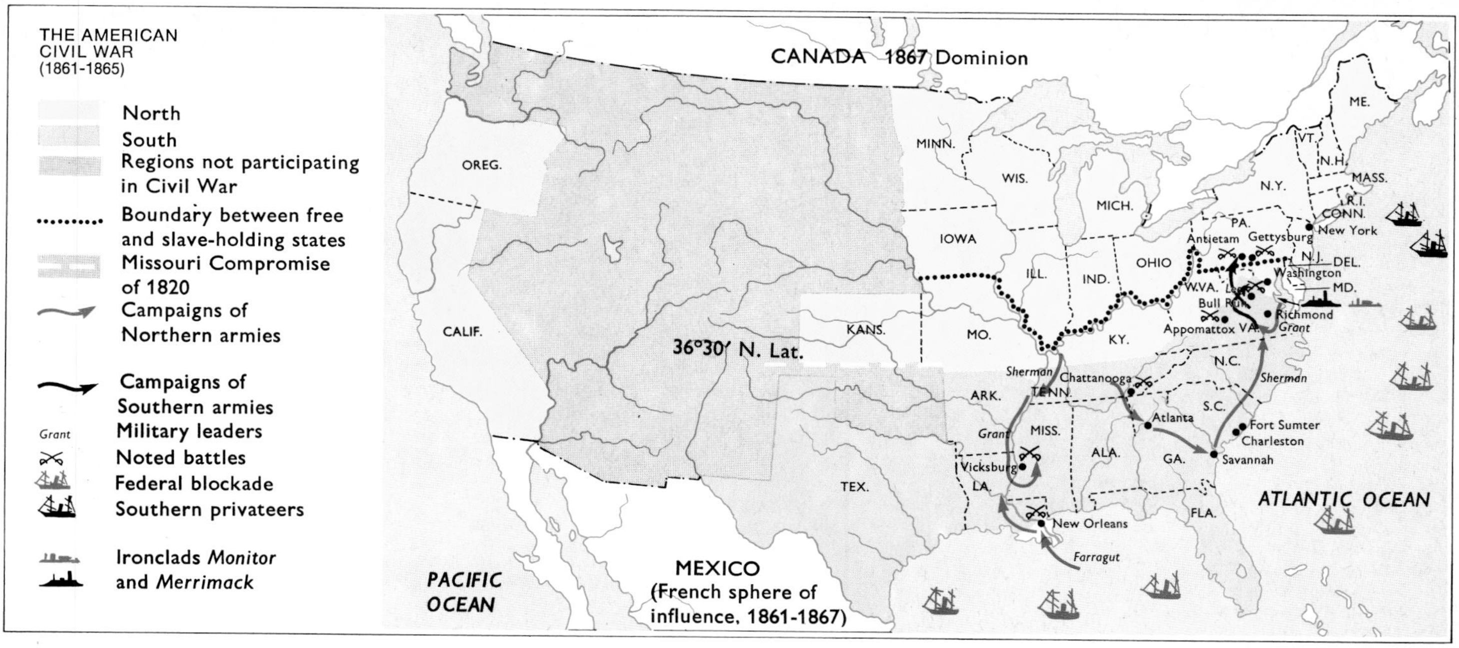

men. As volunteers failed to come forward, the first national conscription act in American history was passed in March 1863. The South, too, brought in conscription. As the world's major cotton exporter, the South expected financial and diplomatic support from abroad, and what it lacked in numbers and equipment it largely made up for in the quality of its soldiers and their leaders.

The campaigns. The war, which opened in the East with the Federal disaster at BULL RUN, was won by the superior numbers and hard fighting of the Federals against the brilliant tactics of the South, and by the crippling naval blockade (see MONITOR AND MERRIMACK). Britain and France stayed neutral (though British aid to the South provoked the TRENT AFFAIR and ALABAMA CLAIMS). The war really began with the PENINSULA CAMPAIGN (1862) of G. B. MCCLELLAN which bogged down close to Richmond. The great southern commander, Robert E. LEE, now harassed McClellan in the SEVEN DAYS' BATTLES, then blunted a Federal thrust, again at BULL RUN; but his own northward drive was stopped at ANTIETAM. (The victory gave LINCOLN the occasion to issue the preliminary EMANCIPATION PROCLAMATION.) Undaunted, Lee defeated the Federals at FREDERICKSBURG and CHANCELLORSVILLE (where he lost his brilliant commander, "Stonewall" JACKSON) and moved north again. In the war's climactic battle, Lee was turned back at GETTYSBURG, Pa. (July 1863). Meanwhile in the West Ulysses S. GRANT moved down into W Tenn. to win the battle of SHILOH (1862), and W. S. ROSECRANS pushed Braxton BRAGG through Tenn. E into Ga. at MURFREESBORO and CHICAMAUGA. New Orleans fell to David FARRAGUT. Grant's objective was VICKSBURG on the Mississippi R. When it fell, a day after Gettysburg, Grant became Supreme Commander and began relentlessly pounding at Lee in the East. From the West W. T. SHERMAN moved on Atlanta, marched to the sea, laying waste the countryside, then north to join Grant. Caught in a pincers, Lee surrendered at APPOMATTOX COURT HOUSE, April 9, 1865.

The South was devastated, its economy in ruins, but the North emerged stronger than before. Slavery was abolished, but the balance of power between the states and the Federal government remained a problem. (See also CIVIL RIGHTS AND LIBERTIES; RECONSTRUCTION.)

CIVIL WAR, English (1642–51), the conflict between Royalists and Parliamentarians that led to the defeat and execution of CHARLES I, and the establishment of the Commonwealth under Oliver CROMWELL. It is also called the Puritan Revolution, because the king's opponents were mainly Puritan, and his supporters chiefly Episcopalian and Catholic. But the constitutional issue at stake was whether England should be effectively ruled by parliament or by a monarch claiming supreme authority by virtue of the DIVINE RIGHT OF KINGS. War between parliament's ROUNDHEADS and Charles' CAVALIERS began after Charles opposed the LONG PARLIAMENT's efforts to curb his powers. No clear-cut social or geographical boundaries divided the forces.

In the first major battle, Charles' army held back Parliamentarian troops under Robert Devereux, Earl of Essex, at EDGEHILL near Warwick (1642). This enabled Charles to establish headquarters at Oxford. But Prince RUPERT lost to Cromwell's "Ironsides" at Marston Moor (1644). On June 14, 1645, FAIRFAX and Cromwell destroyed the Royalist army at Naseby, and by autumn 1646 parliament held most of England. Fighting flared up again after Charles' capture (1646), but Cromwell routed Scottish invaders at Preston. After Charles' execution (1649) fighting recurred. Cromwell brutally subdued Ireland (1649–50), crushed Scottish troops at Dunbar (1650) and defeated CHARLES II's Scottish forces at Worcester (1651). This was the last battle of the war.

CIVIL WAR, Spanish. See SPANISH CIVIL WAR.

CLAIBORNE, William (c1587–1677?), English-born fur trader from Virginia, who seized and briefly held Maryland (1644–46). His insurrection ousted the Catholic governor, Leonard Calvert, and in the 1650s he was one of four commissioners of England's Puritan government governing the colony.

CLAIBORNE, William Charles Coles (1775–1817), first and only governor of the Territory of Orleans (1804–12) and first governor of La. (1812–16). Elected to the US Senate, he died before taking his seat. (See also LOUISIANA PURCHASE.)

CLAIMS, Court of. See COURT OF CLAIMS.

CLAIR, René (René Chomette; 1898–   ), French film director, producer and writer, especially of screen comedies. Born in Paris, he worked on both silent and "talkie" films, including *Sous les toits de Paris* (1930).

CLAIRTON, city in SW Pa., SE of Pittsburgh, founded 1770. Products: coal by-products, chemicals and steel. Pop 15051.

CLAIRVOYANCE, ("second sight"), alleged ability to perceive things outside the range of ordinary senses. (See also ESP.)

CLAM, the general name given to many two-shelled BIVALVE mollusks, particularly to the jack-knife clam, the quahog and the pismo-clam. Giant clams on coral reefs may reach a diameter of 1.2m (4ft) and weigh 0.25 tonnes.

CLAN, a social group whose membership is restricted to those claiming descent from a common ancestor, usually through the male line though sometimes through the female line. Clans are often exogamous (see ENDOGAMY AND EXOGAMY) and usually have a TOTEM or other emblem. The most sophisticated clans currently in existence are those in Scotland.

CLAPHAM SECT, evangelical Christian group, active 1790–1830, responsible for abolishing slavery and pioneering other social reforms. Founded in Clapham, London, by the banker H. Thornton, and led by William WILBERFORCE, the group included many members of parliament.

CLARE, Saint (or Clara; 1194–1253), Italian founder of the POOR CLARES and patron saint of television. She was born at Assisi, and was influenced by St. FRANCIS OF ASSISI. Canonized 1255.

CLARE, John (1793–1864), English Romantic poet of the English rural scene, notably in *The Shepherd's Calendar: with Village Stories, and Other Poems* (1827). Clare was a poor, largely self-taught farm laborer. He was more or less insane from 1837.

CLAREMONT, city in SW Cal., 28mi E of Los Angeles, specializing in fruit packing. Home of the six Claremont Colleges. Pop 23464.

CLAREMONT, city in W N.H., summer vacation center. Products: mining machinery, shoes. Pop 14221.

CLARENDON, Edward Hyde, 1st Earl of (1609–1674), English statesman and historian, author of the *History of the Rebellion*, a personal account of the English Civil War. As lord chancellor 1660–67, he was a chief adviser and minister of Charles II, but lost favor and fled to France.

CLARENDON CODE, penal laws against nonconformists, enacted in England 1661–65 during the RESTORATION to strengthen the Anglican Church. The code was named for Charles II's lord chancellor, the 1st Earl of CLARENDON (who opposed much of it).

CLARINET, woodwind instrument comprising a tube (usually wooden) with a flared bell and tapered mouthpiece with a single reed. Different tones are produced by the fingers opening and closing holes (some covered by keys) in the tube. Clarinets feature in dance bands, military bands, woodwind groups, symphony orchestras and as solo instruments. The clarinet was invented in Germany by Johann Christoph Denner early in the 18th century.

CLARK, Alvan Graham (1832–1897), US lens-maker and astronomer who first saw the white dwarf companion (see STAR) of Sirius (1862). In 1897 he directed the construction of the world's largest refracting TELESCOPE, the 40in instrument at the Yerkes observatory.

CLARK, George Rogers (1752–1818), US frontiersman and Revolutionary War general who led the campaign against the British in the Northwest Territory. In 1778, with about 175 volunteers, he set out to capture the British forts north of the Ohio R. Clark

Civil War

Lincoln and the civil war

The American Civil War was the first of the modern wars. So far-flung were its operations, so shattering its effects, so pervasive its implications that only in recent years have Americans been able to gain a measure of perspective on it. The pivotal military fact of the war, for instance, is that the North, despite its blundering, always-too-late leadership, despite defeat after defeat in the first years of the war, was consistently on the offensive around the whole perimeter of the South. The Confederacy, on the other hand, sought only to ensure its existence as an independent nation, and its military planning, despite bold forays into the North, was therefore primarily defensive. Yet so brilliant were the tactics of a Lee or a Jackson—probing and feinting with their smaller, mobile forces, aiming always at the enemy's morale rather than at his numbers—that at the time it was hard to believe the North stood any chance of victory at all.

In fact the task of the North, despite its superiority in numbers and immensely greater resources, was by far the more difficult one. It had to crush a rebellion. To win, it had to invade the Confederacy, destroy its armies and force the surrender of its government—but the South, with the advantage of interior lines of communication, had only to keep the enemy off while hoping for a miracle in the form of foreign intervention or the internal collapse of the North. And this it did brilliantly—far more persistently and effectively than anyone at that time could have imagined. Often it was touch and go for the North.

For the North to mount an offensive operation against the South required strategic planning on a scale seldom envisaged in Lincoln's day. No wonder the North fumbled, hesitated and was often defeated. But in time a winning strategy did emerge, carried through by generals who knew what they were doing; and behind this winning strategy lay the pertinacity and vision of one man, Lincoln. The ungainly backwoodsman, with no military experience worth mentioning, is now recognized as one of the first strategists of modern, total war. Year after year, in the distant west as well as in the east, Lincoln struggled with generals who, as he said, got the "slows," who bickered among themselves instead of fighting the enemy, who made unreasonable demands for reinforcements and supplies and then lost their nerve in battle. If his military aides could not straighten them out, he would step in. "During the entire war," wrote one of his telegraph operators, "the files of the War Department telegraph office were punctuated with short, pithy despatches from Lincoln."

In 1862, when the war began, the United States had practically no army, an outmoded system of command and very few officers who knew anything about fighting a war. Most of the best generals seem to have gone with the Confederacy; and its president—and also commander-in-chief in the American tradition—was Jefferson Davis, a West Pointer and veteran of the Mexican War. Lincoln was of course commander-in-chief and president in the North. Unlike Davis, he was totally inexperienced in military affairs. Yet Davis was an indifferent war leader while Lincoln turned out to be a brilliant war president.

Much, but not all, can be explained by the inborn genius which this tall, gangling, self-educated product of the midwestern frontier had in generous measure. Very early in the war he seemed to have grasped its larger meaning. If the North was to restore the Union by force, it would have to fight an offensive war, and here the superior numbers and resources of the North would play a vital

A contemporary photograph showing Union troops exercising in their winter camp. The troops were well disciplined and well trained on both sides during the Civil War. Sophisticated training, supply lines and armaments, as well as the mass deployment of men and trench warfare, helped to make this the first of modern wars.

was never paid for his services, and remained in debt for the rest of his life.

CLARK, James Beauchamp (1850–1921), US Congressman, Democratic Party leader and speaker of the House of Representatives. Born in Ky. but representing Mo. (1893–1921), "Champ" Clark helped to oust dictatorial House Speaker J. G. CANNON, whom he succeeded (1911–19).

CLARK, Kenneth Bancroft (1914–), US educationist whose 1950 report on school segregation was cited in the Supreme Court's 1954 ruling against segregation. More recently he has become a civil rights leader and youth worker in New York City's Harlem. (See CIVIL RIGHTS AND LIBERTIES.)

CLARK, Kenneth MacKenzie, Baron Clark of Saltwood (1903–), British art critic, director of the National Gallery 1934–45 and chairman of the Arts Council 1953–60. He has held many other important posts, but became most widely known through his television series *Civilisation* (1969).

CLARK, Mark Wayne (1896–), US general, commander of Allied ground forces in Italy in WWII and commander of UN operations in the Korean War (1952–53). He led the invasion of Italy in 1943.

CLARK, Tom Campbell (1899–), US lawyer from Dallas, Tex., who was attorney general 1945–49 and an associate justice of the US Supreme Court (1949–67).

CLARK, William (1770–1838), US explorer, a leader of the LEWIS AND CLARK EXPEDITION 1804–06, and brother of George Rogers CLARK. Previously a frontier soldier (1791–96), he was subsequently superintendant of Indian affairs and governor of Missouri Territory (1813–21).

CLARKE, Arthur Charles (1917–), British science fiction and science writer, best knowm as the author of the film *2001: A Space Odyssey* (1968) and for his detailed design for communications satellites in 1945. His best-known novel is *Childhood's End* (1953).

CLARKE, John (1609–1676), English Baptist clergyman, one of the founders of Rhode Island (1638) and a co-founder of Newport. With Roger WILLIAMS he helped to keep Rhode Island's government basically democratic and liberal, securing its royal charter in 1663.

CLARKE, Marcus Andrew Hislop (1846–1881), Australian journalist, author of *For the Term of His Natural Life* (1870–72), a powerful novel about convict life in Tasmania.

CLARKSBURG, city in NW Va., seat of Harrison Co., an industrial center producing coal, natural gas, part, provided they were used relentlessly to destroy the enemy's forces, not just to gain his territory. Thus when the amateurish disaster of First Bull Run in July, 1861 showed up the incompetence of the Union forces and their generals, Lincoln acted. He called up 500 000 men and proclaimed a naval blockade of the Southern ports, hoping thus to bring the superior naval and military forces of the Union upon the South to end the war. And he appointed General George B. McClellan, who had a reputation as a professional soldier, to command the armies around Washington. Lincoln's protracted search for a general who would fight had begun. Meantime he himself as commander-in-chief would direct the war until he found a general who could carry out his ideas.

Two years later when he had found his man in Ulysses S. Grant, Lincoln told Grant in their first talk together: "... he had never professed to be a military man or to know how campaigns should be conducted, and never wanted to interfere in them; but that procrastination on the part of commanders, and the pressure from the people at the North and Congress ... forced him into his series of 'Military Orders' ... All he wanted or had ever wanted was someone who would take the responsibility and act."

As always, Lincoln was far too modest. Faced at the beginning of the war with the task of directing its strategy, he had begun to read military treatises drawn from the Library of Congress and had talked to any officer he could find who seemed to know something about the theory of war. "This poor President!" wrote W. H. Russell. "He is to be pitied ... trying with all his might to understand strategy, naval warfare, big guns, the movements of troops, military maps ... and all the technical details of the art of slaying." In January 1862, Lincoln told a Senator that "he was thinking of taking the field himself, and suggested several plans of operation." He was, as he had always done, educating himself, and his quick mind had soon grasped the essentials.

But it is surprising to find that these military ideas which he was to put into practice throughout the war were hardly the accepted theories of warfare current in his day; they were the now familiar concepts of "total war"—to destroy the enemy's forces, his morale and his resources with unrelenting violence, using all means at hand—as enunciated by Karl von Clausewitz in his book *On War*, published in 1833, and later adopted by the Prussian General Staff. Lincoln could scarcely have read Clausewitz, since his book was not translated into English until 1873, and his doctrines were not generally known in America until the early 1900s. Had Lincoln run across some echo of Clausewitz in his reading or in his talks with military men? Or was it a case of inborn genius, two fertile minds separately drawing the same conclusions from the lessons of the past?

When McClellan came to Washington he seemed to be the very general Lincoln was looking for. Quickly dubbed by the press the "Young Napoleon," he was handsome, a born leader, an experienced officer and superlative at organization. But war for him was a gentlemanly game of maneuver, fought by professionals—hardly Lincoln's concept of "total" war—and he was cautious, always over-estimating his needs and the size of the forces opposing him. Lincoln's interference annoyed him, and he began openly to insult the president whom he called "nothing more than a well-meaning baboon." But the president said, "I will hold McClellan's horse if he will only bring us success."

The army, now over 160 000 strong, three times the size of the Confederate army near Washington, was at last well-organized and trained; but McClellan would not move. Lincoln suggested a frontal attack, but McClellan preferred a move towards the enemy capital, Richmond, from a base on the Virginia rivers. It took 113 steamers, 188 schooners and 88 barges to move McClellan's huge army by water in April of 1862 and set it down before enemy-held Yorktown. There he spent weeks entrenching and setting up his batteries, while Lincoln urged him to attack. When he did storm the city the enemy forces, about half the size of McClellan's, had slipped away, leaving him an empty shell. It was an inauspicious beginning to the Peninsula Campaign. McClellan did manage to get within five miles of Richmond, but when he was sharply attacked by the Confederates and then attacked again, this time by the great Southern general Robert E. Lee, he executed a masterly withdrawal to the banks of the James and there he sat, effectively ending the campaign.

Disgusted, Lincoln withdrew most of McClellan's troops and put them under the dashing John Pope in a new army near Washington. He also brought General H. W. Halleck in to act as a strategic director for the whole farflung war. But Pope was ignominiously crushed by Lee at the second battle at Bull Run in August, 1862, and disappeared from history, while Halleck rapidly degenerated into little better than a "first-rate clerk," as Lincoln put it later. The war was right back on Lincoln's hands again. As Pope's defeated forces streamed back into a panicky Washington, Lincoln decided to reinstate McClellan. At least he was "an organizer and a good hand at defending a position," he said. Instead, McClellan was soon forced to confront Lee, who had moved up into Maryland. He did turn Lee back at Antietam, but allowed him to escape, and then again dawdled for months. In November, his patience exhausted, Lincoln dismissed McClellan.

"The fact is the people have not yet made up their minds that we are at war with the South," said Lincoln after Antietam. "General McClellan thinks he is going to whip the rebels by strategy; the army has got the same notion. They have no idea that the War is to be carried on and put through by hard, tough fighting, that it will hurt somebody ..."

Lincoln resumed his search for a fighting general. Ambrose Burnside reluctantly accepted the post, ran into a Confederate trap at Fredericksburg and lost 12 000 men. He had to go. Lincoln's next choice was "Fighting Joe" Hooker, an intriguer who with others had been talking against Lincoln and calling for a national dictator. But Lincoln would take Hooker, braggadocio and all, if he was the man he needed. Hooker, however, suffered a crushing defeat at Chancellorsville, and when Lee, still holding the initiative, again pushed north into the heart of the Union, Hooker was allowed to resign. It was George Meade, a solid and dependable soldier, who fought the pivotal battle of the war at Gettysburg, Pa., in July of 1863. The Union army, at last a seasoned fighting machine, performed magnificently. Lee fell back, and when a few days after Gettysburg the news flashed east that Grant had taken the great fortress of Vicksburg on the Mississippi, the North went wild.

Lincoln alone was in despair; he alone seemed to have grasped the significance of Gettysburg. He wrote Meade a letter (but he never sent it): "I do not believe you appreciate the magnitude of the disaster involved in Lee's escape. He was within your easy grasp, and to have closed upon him would, in connection with our other successes, have ended the war." Now the war would go on indefinitely.

In the west it had been the same story. Lincoln tried one general after another, but all in one way or another failed. Then in February 1862 came a victory. Grant captured forts Henry and Donelson on the Tennessee and Cumberland rivers, opening a way south. Though he was surprised at Shiloh and barely held his own, he continued to move inexorably on Vicksburg, the fortress that dominated the last stretch of the Mississippi held by the South. It took Grant almost a year to capture Vicksburg, but with its fall the whole river was in Union hands and Lincoln's aim of encircling and isolating the South was virtually accomplished. Moreover the Union armies around Chattanooga were now poised to attack the heart of the Confederacy in Georgia. It had all been Grant's doing. When urged to remove him after Shiloh, Lincoln had said, "I can't spare this man; he fights."

In February 1864 he made him general-in-chief of all the Union armies and brought him east to face Lee. Not without opposition, however; for Grant in appearance was hardly a McClellan. "He's the quietest fellow you ever saw ..." Lincoln said after he first met him, "The only evidence you have that he's in any place is that he makes things *git*! Wherever he is, things move!" He had "rather a scrubby look," another observer reported. "He had a cigar in his mouth, and rather the look of a man who did, or once did, take a little too much to drink." In fact Grant did have a drinking problem. When a delegation came to Lincoln to demand Grant's removal as a drunkard, Lincoln quipped, "If I knew what kind of liquor Grant drinks, I would send a barrel or so to some other generals."

There was a year more of fighting until the surrender at Appomattox in April, 1865. Sherman marched through Georgia, laying waste the countryside in a chilling preview of total war, then swung north to join Grant in a fatal pincers movement. Grant himself hammered at Lee, pushing him mile by mile beyond Richmond to Petersburg. The casualties were enormous, the combat unrelenting. This was the "dark summer" of '64 and the North was nearing exhaustion. Lincoln in the White House was gaunt and haggard, upset by the slaughter, sleepless. For Lincoln was a compassionate man. War for him, as also for Clausewitz, was not an end in itself but a necessary extension of policy. And his single policy was to preserve the Union. Once accomplished, he would make an end to killing, to hating, he would forgive and forget. "With malice toward none;" he had said at his Second Inaugural, "with charity for all; with firmness in the right, as God gives us to see the right, let us strive on to finish the work we are in; to bind up the nation's wounds ..."

He had been the nation's greatest war president; but the greater task of binding up the nation's wounds was denied him. On Good Friday, April 14, shortly after the surrender, he was struck down by an assassin's bullet.

oil, glass, cement. Pop 24 684.

CLARKSDALE, city in NW Miss., seat of Coahoma Co., an important cotton-processing center. Pop 21 673.

CLARKSON, Thomas (1760–1846), English abolitionist who helped to end the international African slave trade by researching and publicizing its evils. Author of books on the slave trade, partly based on his travels.

CLARKSVILLE, town in S Ind., on the Ohio R opposite Louisville, Ky. Pop 13 806.

CLARKSVILLE, city in N Tenn., on Lake Barkley. Seat of Montgomery Co.; it produces tobacco and limestone. Pop 31 719.

CLASSICAL ORDERS, in architecture, the names given to various styles of COLUMN and adjoining parts, notably the ENTABLATURE. They are: **Doric** (the oldest, without base, used in the PARTHENON), **Ionic** (developed in Asia Minor around the 6th century BC, then taken to Greece), **Corinthian** (the most ornate, appearing in Greece in the 4th century BC, but fully developed by the Romans and revived in the RENAISSANCE), **Tuscan** (the simplest, supposedly derived from the Etruscans) and **Composite** (a late-Roman blend of Ionic and Corinthian). As outlined by VITRUVIUS (1st century BC) and described by SERLIO (16th century AD), the classical orders deeply influenced architectural design in and after the Renaissance.

CLASSICISM, art forms and cultural periods characterized by the conscious emulation of classical antiquity, particularly the art and literature of ancient Greece and Rome. Emphasizing order, clarity, restraint and harmony of form, the most notable epoch of classicism was the Renaissance, the "rebirth" of classical civilization. After the Mannerist and Baroque periods, classicism reappeared in the 18th–19th-century movement known as NEOCLASSICISM. Influenced by Johann WINCKELMANN, principal exponents of the movement included Antonio CANOVA, J. L. DAVID and Robert ADAM. (See illustration page 250.)

CLASSIFICATION OF LIVING THINGS. See TAXONOMY.

CLAUDE, Albert (1899–), Belgian-US biologist who shared the 1974 Nobel Prize for Physiology or Medicine with G. E. PALADE and C. de DUVE for demonstrating the usefulness of the ELECTRON MICROSCOPE and the CENTRIFUGE in biological studies. He pioneered the study of the internal structure of CELLS.

Classicism: The wing of the Capitol in Washington, D.C., seen here, is a fine example of the Neoclassical style, emphasizing harmony, order and clarity and recalling the grandeur of the ancient Greek and Roman civilizations.

CLAUDEL, Paul (1868–1955), French Roman Catholic dramatist, poet and diplomat. Influenced by RIMBAUD and intensely religious, he drew inspiration for his sensuous, lyrical verse from nature and Oriental thought.

CLAUDE LORRAIN (real name, Claude Gellée; 1600–1682), was a founder of French romantic landscape painting, who lived and worked mostly in Rome. His works usually show a biblical or classical scene dominated by an idyllically-lit landscape. His later works are almost visionary in their intensity.

CLAUDIUS, name of two Roman emperors. **Claudius I** (Tiberius Claudius Nero Germanicus; 10 BC–54 AD), reigned 41–54 AD. A sickly nephew of TIBERIUS, he was a scholar and writer. He invaded Britain (43 AD), annexed Mauretania, Lycia and Thrace (41–46 AD), improved Rome's legal system and encouraged colonization. He was poisoned by his second wife, Agrippina. **Claudius II, Gothicus** (Marcus Aurelius Claudius; 214–270 AD), reigned 268–70. An army officer, he succeeded Gallienus.

CLAUSEWITZ, Karl von (1780–1831), Prussian general, strategist and military historian, known mainly as the author of *On War* (1833), which revolutionized military thinking after his death. He defined war as an extension of diplomacy and urged the destruction of enemy forces, morale and resources. He has thus been called the prophet of total war (although he favored defensive fighting).

CLAUSIUS, Rudolf Julius Emanuel (1822–1888), German theoretical physicist who first stated the second law of THERMODYNAMICS (1850) and proposed the term ENTROPY (1865). He also contributed to KINETIC THEORY and the theory of ELECTROLYSIS.

CLAUSTROPHOBIA, an intense feeling of fear or panic experienced by certain people in enclosed places. (See PHOBIA.)

CLAVICHORD, a stringed keyboard instrument used primarily between the 15th and 18th centuries. Its sound is produced by brass blades (tangents) hitting against pairs of strings. Although small-toned, it is especially sensitive and responsive. It was the usual household musical instrument in 16th–18th-century Germany.

CLAVICLE. See COLLAR BONE.

CLAWSON, city in SE Mich., a suburb of Detroit. Products: tools, including machine tools. Pop 17 617.

CLAY, any SOIL material with a particle size of less than 2–4μm in diameter, i.e. finer-grained than SILT or SAND; an earthy material which becomes plastic when wet, including mud (which is used in oil drilling). Clays are used as catalysts (see CATALYSIS) in PETROLEUM refining, for making molds for CASTING and, when molded and fired, for CERAMICS, POTTERY AND PORCELAIN, bricks and TILES. They are also used in making CEMENT and RUBBER, and as ION-EXCHANGE agents for softening HARD WATER. (See also FULLER'S EARTH.) Clay rocks, including mudstones and SHALES, are microcrystalline rocks composed mainly of clay-size particles. Their mineralogical composition is highly variable, but they usually contain a high proportion of **clay minerals**, hydrated aluminum and magnesium SILICATES including BENTONITE, CHLORITE, diaspore (hydrated ALUMINUM oxide), illite (hydrated MICA—see also GLAUCONITE), KAOLINITE and MEERSCHAUM.

CLAY, Cassius. See MUHAMMAD ALI.

CLAY, Cassius Marcellus (1810–1903), US abolitionist, politician and statesman, founder of the antislavery journal *True American*, in Lexington, Ky., 1845. He was a founder of the Republican Party, 1854, and US ambassador to Russia (1861–62 and 1863–69).

CLAY, Henry (1777–1852), US statesman, famous for his attempts to reconcile North and South in the pre-Civil War period. Born near Richmond, Va., Clay served as both US representative and senator from Ky. 1806–1852, and secretary of state 1825–29. He helped produce the MISSOURI COMPROMISE on slavery (1820). In 1844 he was Whig presidential candidate but lost the election by alienating New York abolitionists on the issue of the annexation of Tex. as a slave state. His career culminated in the COMPROMISE OF 1850, a complex package of "slave" and "free" provisions. Known as "the great compromiser," Clay lost support as the nation became more bitterly divided. He is also remembered as one of the WAR HAWKS of 1812 and for his controversial AMERICAN SYSTEM, a series of radical economic proposals.

CLAY, Lucius Dubignon (1897–), US general assigned to govern the American zone of West Germany 1947–49. He also supervised the BERLIN AIRLIFT.

CLAYTON, city in Mo., seat of St. Louis Co. It is a residential suburb 8mi W of St. Louis. Pop 16 222.

CLAYTON, John Middleton (1796–1856), US secretary of state who negotiated the CLAYTON-BULWER TREATY. He served (1849–1850) under President Zachary Taylor.

CLAYTON ANTITRUST ACT, a law passed by Congress in 1914 to supplement the SHERMAN ANTITRUST ACT of 1890. The Clayton act specified illegal monopolistic practices, among them certain forms of interlocking directorates and holding companies. It also legalized peaceful strikes, picketing and boycotting. In 1921, however, the Supreme Court interpreted the act as doing no more than legalize labor unions and not their practices. (See MONOPOLY AND UNFAIR COMPETITION.)

CLAYTON-BULWER TREATY, an Anglo-American agreement of 1850 concerning a proposed canal across the Isthmus of Panama. Both sides agreed to control, finance and maintain the canal jointly, and "not to occupy, or fortify, or colonize . . . any part of Central America." But differing interpretations of the treaty produced friction and, after the second HAY-PAUNCEFOTE TREATY (1901), the US built the PANAMA CANAL alone.

CLEAR AIR TURBULENCE (CAT). See AIR TURBULENCE.

CLEARFIELD, city in N Ut. It lies in an agricultural area and is the site of Hill Air Force Base. Pop 13 316.

CLEARINGHOUSE, name of the type of institution through which banks and other corporations that do extensive business with each other settle their accounts. Clearinghouses operate by offsetting transactions, thus minimizing payment settlements. America's first bank clearinghouse was set up in New York in 1853. The Federal Reserve bank of New York is the major bank clearinghouse in the US.

CLEARWATER, city in W Fla., seat of Pinellas Co. on the Gulf of Mexico. It handles citrus fruit and flowers, has an electronics industry and is a center for tourism. Pop 52 074.

CLEAVAGE, of a MINERAL, the tendency to split along a definite PLANE parallel to an actual or possible CRYSTAL face: e.g., GALENA, whose crystals are cubic, cleaves along three mutually PERPENDICULAR planes (parallel to 100, 010, 001). Such cleavage is useful in identifying minerals. ROCK cleavage generally takes place between roughly parallel beds whose resistance under deformation to internal SHEARING differs.

CLEAVELAND, Moses (1754–1806), US soldier and frontiersman who founded the city of Cleveland, Ohio. Cleaveland led the initial exploring party to "New Connecticut" in 1796, and planned the site at the mouth of the Cuyahoga R. The settlement's name was spelled as Cleaveland until the 1830s.

CLEAVER, (Leroy) Eldridge (1935–), US black militant, a leader of the BLACK PANTHER PARTY. His autobiographical *Soul on Ice* (1968) deals with his own experience of racial hatred and of the US penal system. It was to avoid further experience of the latter that Cleaver jumped bail in 1968 and fled first to Cuba and then to Algeria where, until 1972, he organized an international wing of the Black Panthers. In 1975 he returned voluntarily to the US to stand trial.

CLEBURNE, city in N Tex., the seat of Johnson Co. It is an agricultural trading center. Pop 16 015.

CLEFT PALATE, a common developmental deformity of the PALATE in which the two halves do not meet in the midline; it is often associated with HARELIP. It can be familial or follow disease in early PREGNANCY, but may appear spontaneously. It causes a characteristic nasal quality in the cry and voice. Plastic SURGERY can close the defect and allow more normal development of the voice and TEETH.

CLEISTHENES, two ancient Greek statesmen. **Cleisthenes of Sicyon**, tyrant of the house of Orthagoras, ruled c600–570 BC. He vigorously opposed and ridiculed the Argive Dorian ascendancy. During his rule DELPHI became a center of the Delphic AMPHICTYONY. His grandson **Cleisthenes of Athens** (late 6th century BC) is generally held to be the founder of Athenian democracy. He built upon SOLON'S reforms and broadened the base of government, which nevertheless may be seen as somewhat aristocratic when compared with that of his grandson PERICLES.

CLEMATIS, genus of deciduous and evergreen woody flowering climbers of the family Ranunculaceae. The flowers bear four large colorful sepals but no petals. Many hybrid garden varieties have been bred.

CLEMENCEAU, Georges (1841–1929), French statesman and journalist, a founder of the Third Republic and twice French premier, 1906–09 and 1917–20. Clemenceau was a committed republican. He worked with GAMBETTA (1870) for the overthrow of the Second Empire and supported ZOLA in the DREYFUS AFFAIR. During his second premiership he made a major contribution to the Allied victory in WWI and to the drafting of the Treaty of VERSAILLES.

CLEMENS, Samuel Langhorne. See TWAIN, MARK.

CLEMENT, name of 14 popes and 3 antipopes. **Saint Clement I**, pope 88–97 or 92–101. He was one of the Apostolic Fathers and probably knew St. Peter. His *Epistle to the Corinthians* (c96) is one of the most important works of the early Church. A martyr, he was the subject of many later legends. **Clement II** (d. 1047), was pope 1046–47. **Clement III** (c1025–1100), antipope 1080–1100. He was appointed by a synod formed by Henry IV of Germany. **Clement III** (d. 1191), pope 1187–91. He preached the Third Crusade and made the Scottish Church dependent on Rome. **Clement IV** (d. 1268), pope 1265–68. His involvement in Italian and German politics was harmful to the papacy. **Clement**

V (c1260–1314), pope 1305–14. His papal court at Avignon, France, initiated the BABYLONIAN CAPTIVITY. **Clement VI** (c1291–1352), pope 1342–52. He reigned from Avignon where, during the BLACK DEATH, he granted shelter to Jews. By supporting Charles IV of Germany's election as Holy Roman Emperor he strengthened links between the empire and the papacy. **Clement VII** (1342–1394), antipope 1378–94. He was the first antipope of the GREAT SCHISM. **Clement VII** (1478–1534), pope 1523–34. The papacy suffered from his indecision and involvement in European power politics—in 1527 the Emperor Charles V sacked Rome. The REFORMATION increased in strength during his reign. His delay in annulling the marriage of England's Henry VIII to Catherine of Aragon led Henry to sever the English Church from Rome. **Clement VIII** (d. 1446), antipope 1423–29. Spanish by birth, he succeeded Antipope Benedict XIII, his election being urged by King Alfonso V of Aragon. **Clement VIII** (1536–1605), pope 1592–1605. He promoted the COUNTER-REFORMATION and, by absolving Henry IV of France, reduced Spanish influence on the papacy. **Clement IX** (1600–1669), was pope 1667–69. **Clement X** (1590–1676), was pope 1670–76. **Clement XI** (1649–1721), pope 1700–21. He took measures against JANSENISM and condemned the Chinese and Malabar rites. **Clement XII** (1652–1740), pope 1730–40. He condemned MASONRY and Jansenism, and did much to develop missionary training colleges. **Clement XIII** (1693–1769), pope 1758–69. He unsuccessfully tried to prevent the suppression of JESUITS in France, Spain, Portugal, Parma and Naples. **Clement XIV** (1705–1774), pope 1769–74). Under political pressure from the BOURBONS he formally suppressed the Jesuit order, although he had himself received a Jesuit education. The ban lasted until 1814.

CLEMENTI, Muzio (1752–1832), Italian composer and pianist, known as "the father of the piano". He enjoyed a successful concert career throughout Europe. John FIELD was among his pupils. In 1799, in London, he became a partner in one of the first firms ever to manufacture pianos.

CLEMENT OF ALEXANDRIA (c150–c215 AD), theologian of the early Christian Church. His most important work is the trilogy *Exhortation to the Greeks*, the *Tutor* and *Miscellanies*. Born in Athens, Clement spent most of his life as a teacher in Alexandria.

CLEON (d. 422 BC), Athenian leader who represented the commercial classes of Athens and opposed PERICLES. He assumed power on the latter's death and took the offensive in the PELOPONNESIAN WAR, leading a successful expedition against Sparta in 425 BC. He was killed in the battle of Amphipolis.

CLEOPATRA, name of several queens of the Ptolemaic dynasty, the most famous being the Egyptian Queen Cleopatra VII (69–30 BC) who, as mistress of Julius CAESAR and later wife to Mark ANTONY, had a profound influence on Roman politics. Her marriage to Mark Antony contributed to Egypt's defeat by Rome, which in turn led to the couple's tragic suicide. A celebrated *femme fatale*, she is the subject of dramatic works by Shakespeare and G. B. Shaw.

CLEOPATRA'S NEEDLES, two large stone obelisks erected by Thutmose III at Heliopolis in Egypt, c1500 BC. One now stands on the Thames Embankment in London; the other is in Central Park, New York City.

CLEPSYDRA, or **water clock,** an instrument in which the discharge of water from a storage tank is monitored in order to measure the passing of time. They were used from ancient times until the Renaissance.

CLERESTORY, architectural term for any windowed wall set above the level of a building's main walls or, in the case of a large building, its main roofline, in order to light the interior. The device has been used since the 2nd century BC. It was an important feature in ROMANESQUE and GOTHIC architecture. The clerestory at Amiens cathedral is a fine example.

CLERGY, Benefit of. See BENEFIT OF CLERGY.

CLERIHEW, humorous biographical verse composed in two rhyming couplets. Clerihews were named for their inventor Edmund Clerihew Bentley (1875–1956). They play upon awkward, whimsical rhymes and unequally accented lines.

CLERMONT, name of Robert FULTON's steamboat, the first commercially successful vessel of its kind. The *Clermont*, completed in 1807, operated on the Hudson R between Albany and New York City.

CLERMONT, Council of, Church reform assembly at Clermont-Ferrand in France in 1095. It was at this assembly that Pope Urban II urged the undertaking of the First Crusade.

CLERMONT-FERRAND, city in S central France. An important industrial center, its products include rubber goods, chemicals, linen and machinery. It has a 13th-century Gothic cathedral. Pop 160 800.

CLETUS, Saint. See ANACLETUS, SAINT.

CLEVELAND, city in NW Miss., seat of Bolivar Co. It is a cotton trading center. Pop 13 327.

CLEVELAND, city in NE Ohio, seat of Cuyahoga Co., on Lake Erie at the mouth of the Cuyahoga R. It was founded by Moses CLEAVELAND in 1796 but developed only with the completion of the Ohio and Erie Canal (1832), and the coming of the railroad in the 1840s. During the Civil War the city's iron and petroleum industries mushroomed. Later Cleveland became the home of the Standard Oil Company. Today the city produces steel, automobile parts, chemicals, precision machinery, petroleum products and electrical goods. In recent years much effort has been expended on urban renewal. In 1967 Cleveland became the first major American city to elect a Negro mayor, Democrat Carl B. STOKES. Pop 750 879.

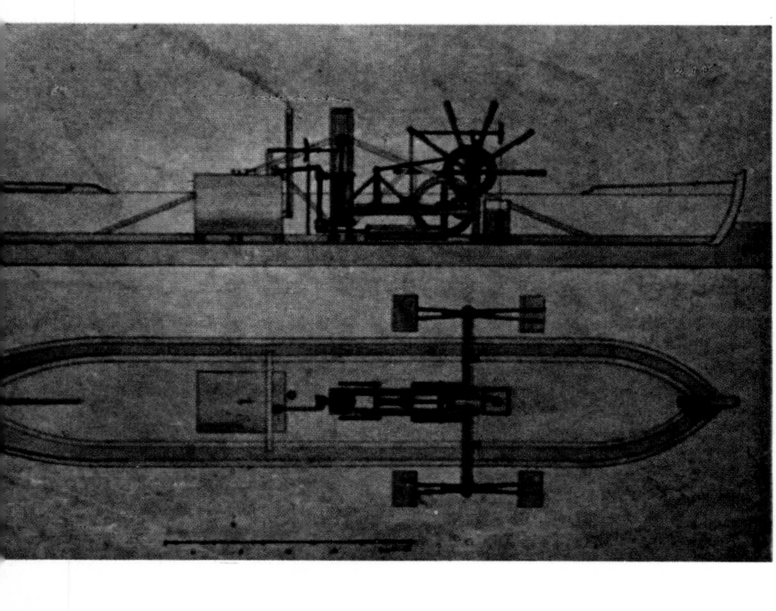

The S.S. *Clermont*, designed by Robert Fulton in 1803, was the first commercially successful steamboat. Because of its extraordinary appearance it was mockingly referred to in New York as "Fulton's Folly."

Stephen Grover CLEVELAND

24th US President

Born: March 18, 1837
Died: June 24, 1908
Terms of Office: March 4, 1885–March 3, 1889
March 4, 1893–March 3, 1897
Political party: Democratic

CLEVELAND, city in SE Tenn., seat of Bradley Co. It has manganese and silica mines. Pop 20 651.

CLEVELAND, (Stephen) Grover (1837–1908), twice Democratic president of the US, remembered for his unswerving honesty in government. Grover Cleveland was born in Caldwell, N.J. In 1855 he moved to Buffalo and entered the legal profession. In 1881 he was elected mayor of Buffalo, and little more than a year later was catapulted into the job of governor of N.Y. state. There his opposition to graft and opportunism earned him a countrywide following and, in 1884, despite the efforts of TAMMANY HALL, the Democratic presidential nomination.

First Term (1885–89). Cleveland became president after more than 20 years of all-too-often lazy and corrupt Republican government. His adherence to principle often lost him political support. He implemented the Pendleton Civil Service Act (1883), cutting by almost 12 000 the number of posts previously controlled by political patronage, and this cost him much of his own party's backing. Cleveland also angered Western timber companies, cattle ranchers and railroaders by exposing illicit land deals. And by trying to reduce tariffs, he antagonized Eastern bankers and industrialists. Losing the presidential election of 1888, Cleveland was readopted by the Democratic Party, once more in spite of Tammany Hall, in 1892.

Second Term (1893–97). Cleveland took office just as the US was beginning to experience severe economic depression. He saw the SHERMAN SILVER PURCHASE ACT (1890) as a major factor in causing the depression and forced its repeal in 1893, but this measure had little impact. Cleveland then attempted to replenish the treasury by buying gold from private financiers. Again, this proved to be no remedy. The situation deteriorated for Cleveland with the outbreak of labor troubles. He lost support by turning away Jacob COXEY and his "army" of unemployed citizens, and by using troops to break the PULLMAN STRIKE (1894). In 1896, with the president's popularity at its lowest ebb, FREE SILVER supporters gained control of the Democratic Party, nominating William Jennings Bryan for the presidency. Cleveland retired to Princeton, where he died.

CLEVELAND HEIGHTS, city in N Ohio, a residential suburb 7mi to the W of Cleveland. Pop 60 767.

CLIBURN, Van (Harvey Lavan, Jr.; 1934–), US concert pianist. He became world famous after winning the International Tchaikovsky Piano Competition in Moscow in 1958.

CLICK BEETLES, any of 7 000 species contained in

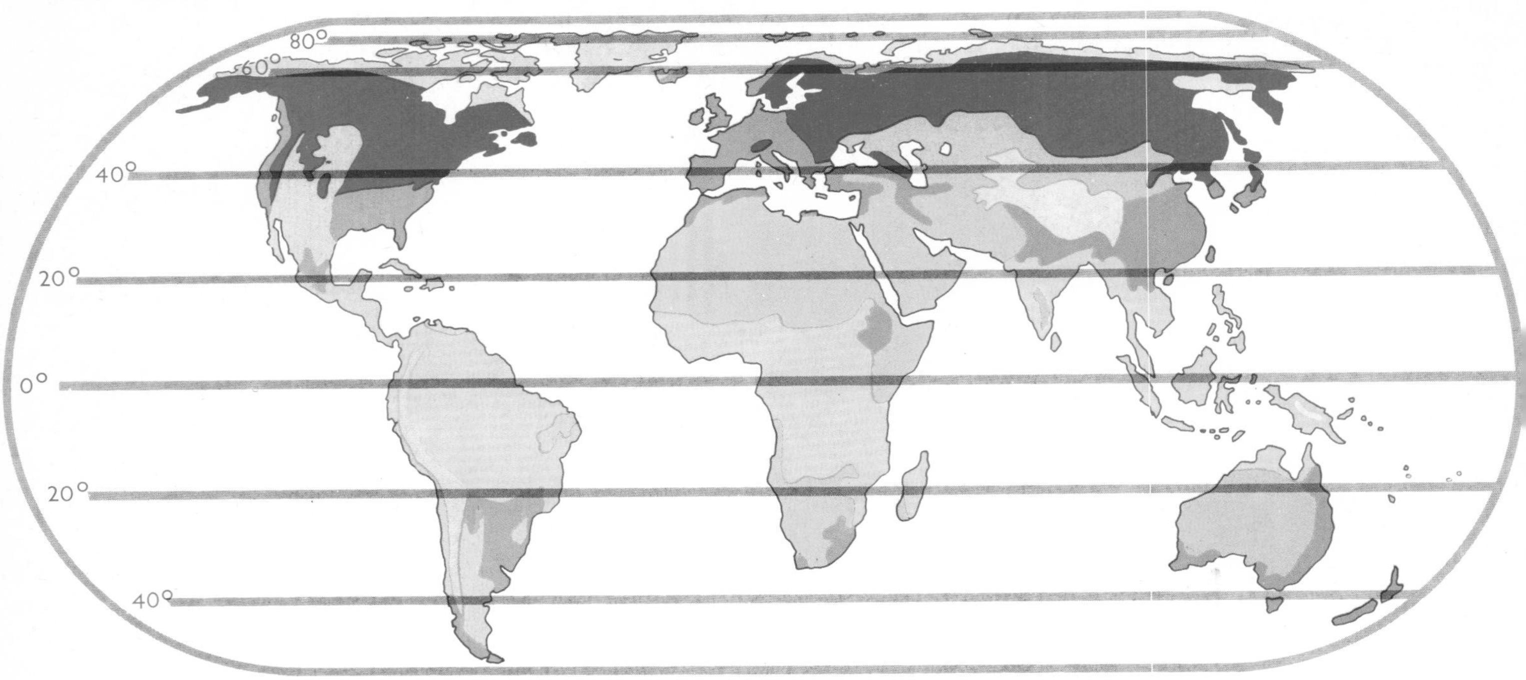

the genus *Agriotes*. Click beetles have short legs and long bodies, and produce a click sound (the result of sudden movement between the first and second segments of the THORAX) when they leap. The larvae of click beetles are WIRE-WORMS, serious agricultural pests.

CLIFF DWELLERS, prehistoric Indians who built multi-roomed houses, sheltered beneath overhanging cliffs, in the American Southwest. Most of the dwellings date from about 1000 AD. The Cliff Dwellers were a peaceful agricultural community whose settlements, built high above the canyon floors, were inaccessible to roving tribes. When the Spanish arrived in the Southwest in the 16th century, they found the settlements abandoned. The Cliff Dwellers are considered to be members of the PUEBLO culture. Cliff Dweller ruins are found in Mesa Verde National Park, Col., and in national monuments in Ariz., N.M. and Ut.

CLIFFSIDE PARK, residential borough in NE N.J., on the Hudson R opposite New York City. It is 8mi NE of Jersey City. Pop 18891.

CLIFTON, industrial town in N N.J., until 1917 part of the city of Passaic. It manufactures steel, textiles and chemicals. Pop 82437.

CLIMATE, the sum of the weather conditions prevalent in an area over a period of time. Weather conditions include temperature, rainfall, sunshine, wind, humidity and cloudiness. Climates may be classified into groups. The system most used today is that of Vladimir Köppen, with five categories (A, B, C, D, E), broadly defined as follows:

A Equatorial and tropical rainy climates;
B Arid climates;
C Warmer forested (temperate) climates;
D Colder forested (temperate) climates; and
E Treeless polar climates.

These categories correspond to a great extent to zoning by LATITUDE; this is because the closer to the EQUATOR an area is, the more direct the sunlight it receives and the less the amount of ATMOSPHERE through which that sunlight must pass. Other factors are the rotation of the earth on its axis (diurnal differences) and the revolution of the earth about the sun (seasonal differences).

PALEOCLIMATOLOGY, the study of climates of the past, has shown that there have been considerable long-term climatic changes in many areas: this is seen as strong evidence for CONTINENTAL DRIFT (see also PLATE TECTONICS). Other theories include variation in the solar radiation (see SUN) and change in the EARTH's axial tilt. Man's influence has caused localized, short-term climatic changes. (See CLOUDS; METEOROLOGY; RAIN; TROPIC; WEATHER FORECASTING; WIND.)

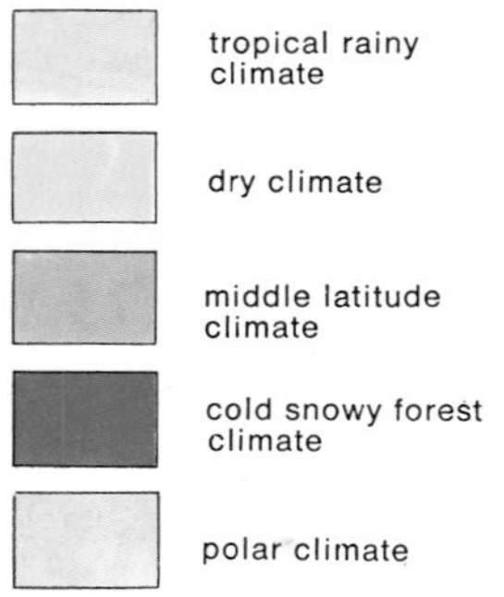

The climates of the world according to the classification of Vladimir Köppen. This takes temperature patterns, rainfall and vegetation into account.

CLIMBING FERNS, common name for a small number of vine-like ferns of the genus *Lygodium*. The Hartford fern (*Lygodium palmatum*) is native to the eastern US.

CLIMBING PERCH, *Anabas testudinosus*, a fish resembling a true PERCH which inhabits oriental freshwaters. It can wriggle over land from pool to pool, breathing air through its enlarged gill cavities.

CLINGMAN'S DOME, mountain peak in the Great Smoky Mts. At 6643ft, it is the highest in Tenn.

CLINTON, town in S Conn., on Long Island Sound, settled in 1663. It produces cosmetics. Pop 10267.

CLINTON, city in E Ia., the seat of Clinton Co. It is an industrial and rail center, processing corn and making steel and cellophane. Pop 34719.

CLINTON, town in central Mass., settled in 1654. Industries are printing, publishing, metal and plastic goods and textile manufacture. Pop 13383.

CLINTON, De Witt (1769–1828), US politician who promoted the building of the ERIE CANAL and the Champlain–Hudson Canal. As mayor of New York for most of 1803–15 and N.Y. governor, 1817–23 and 1825–28, he set up important civic and political reforms and social relief for the Roman Catholics, slaves and the poor. He had Federalist and Republican support for his presidential candidacy in 1812, but lost to James Madison.

CLINTON, George (1739–1812), US vice-president, statesman and revolutionary soldier, often called the "father of New York state." He built up N.Y.'s economy during seven terms as governor. He was a leading opponent of the Federal Constitution. He was vice-president for 1804–12 and presidential candidate in 1804.

CLINTON, Sir Henry (c1738–1795), English general appointed (in 1778) commander-in-chief of British forces during the American Revolution after distinguishing himself at BUNKER HILL. He captured Charleston in 1780 but resigned in 1781. He was blamed for the British surrender at YORKTOWN in that year.

CLIO, the muse of history. See MUSES.

CLIPPER SHIPS, 19th-century sailing ships, the fastest ever built. They evolved from the Baltimore clippers and were built in the US and later in Britain.

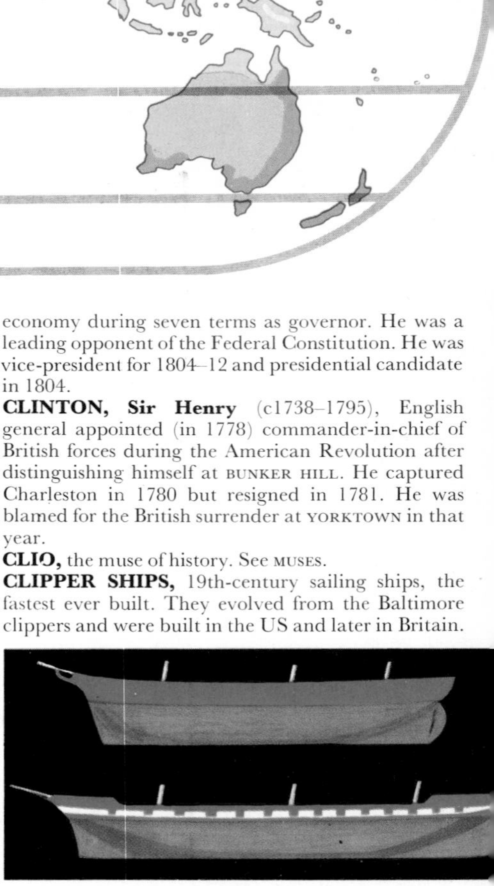

Evolution of clipper ship hulls in the 19th century.

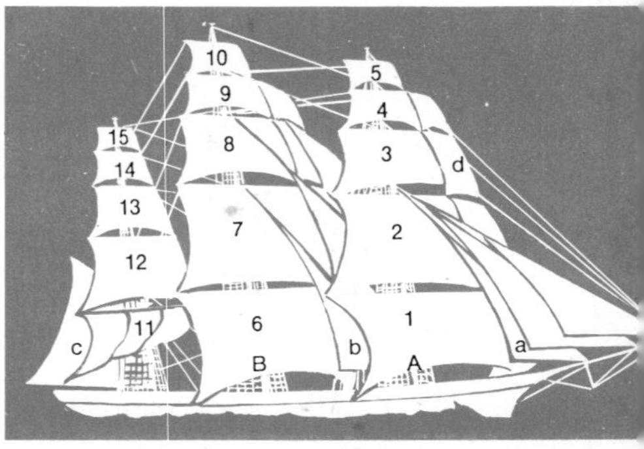

A Clipper ship in full sail. A. Fore mast B. Main mast C. Mizzen mast (a) jib (b) staysails (c) spanker (d) lee sails
Yard sails: 1. Fore sail, 2. Fore top sail, 3. Fore topgallant sail, 4. Foreroyal, 5. Fore-skysail, 6. Mainsail, 7. Main topsail, 8. Main topgallant sail, 9. Main royal, 10. Main skysail, 11. Mizzen sail, 12. Mizzen topsail, 13. Mizzen topgallant sail, 14. Mizzen royal, 15. Mizzen skysail.

They had a very large area of sail, relied on a good crew, and traded with China and Australia where speed paid off. Two famous ships were Donald MCKAY'S "Lightning" and the British "Cutty Sark" (now at Greenwich, England).

CLIVE OF PLASSEY, Robert Clive, 1st Baron (1725–1774), British soldier and administrator, twice governor of Bengal, who established British power in India. He defeated both the French at Arcot (under DUPLEIX) and the Bengal nawab, Siraj-ud-Daula, at Plassey, thus securing all Bengal for the EAST INDIA COMPANY. He reformed administrative corruption in Bengal. Although acquitted by parliament of the charge of dishonesty when in office, he afterwards committed suicide.

CLOCKS AND WATCHES, devices to indicate or record the passage of time; essential features of modern life. In prehistory, time could be gauged solely from the positions of celestial bodies; a natural development was the SUNDIAL, initially no more than a vertical post whose SHADOW was cast by the sun directly onto the ground. Other devices depended on the flow of water from a pierced container (see CLEPSYDRA); the rates at which marked candles, knotted ropes and oil in calibrated vessels burned down; and the flow of sand through a constriction from one bulb of an HOURGLASS to the other. Mechanical clocks were probably known in Ancient China, but first appeared in Europe in the 13th century AD. Power was supplied by a weight suspended from a rope, later by a coiled spring; in both cases an escapement being employed to control the energy release. Around 1657–58 HUYGENS applied the PENDULUM principle to clocks; later, around 1675, his hairspring and balance-wheel mechanism made possible the first portable clocks—resulting eventually in watches. Jeweled bearings, which reduced wear at critical points in the mechanism, were introduced during the 18th century, and the first CHRONOMETER was also devised in this century. Electric clocks with synchronous motors are now commonly found in the home and office, while the ATOMIC CLOCK, which can be accurate to within one second in 3 million years, is of great importance in science.

CLOISONNÉ, decorative combination of metal and enamel. Metal strips are soldered edgewise to a metal surface forming compartments, or *cloisons*, that are filled with colored enamel paste. The enamel is fused to the surface by heating, and then highly polished to a smooth pattern. The technique, first known in MYCENAE, was developed by the Byzantines and then by the Chinese.

CLOISTER, a courtyard surrounded by vaulted and arcaded walkways. Cloisters feature prominently in Romanesque and Gothic churches and monasteries, where they were used for study, recreation and as covered ways between buildings.

CLOSED SHOP, an establishment where the employer accepts only members of a specified union as his employees, and continues to employ them only if they remain union members. The TAFT-HARTLEY ACT of 1947 forbids closed shops in industries involved in or affecting interstate commerce.

CLOTHES MOTHS, small MOTHS whose caterpillars feed on woolen or fur clothes, especially if these are soiled. The adults can reach clothes in closed chests and closets. Thus the best method of control is by dry-cleaning, mothballs or INSECTICIDES.

CLOTHING. See COSTUME; GARMENT INDUSTRY.

CLOTTING, the formation of semisolid deposits in a liquid by coagulation, often by the denaturing of previously soluble ALBUMEN. Thus clotted cream is made by slowly heating milk so that the thick cream rises; the curdling of skim milk to make CHEESE is also an example of clotting. Clotting of BLOOD is a complex process set in motion when it comes into contact with tissues outside its ruptured vessel. These contain a factor, **thromboplastin**, which activates a sequence of changes in the PLASMA clotting factors (12 enzymes). Alternatively, many surfaces, such as glass and fabrics, activate a similar sequence of changes. In either case, factor II (prothrombin, formed in the liver), with calcium ions and a platelet factor, is converted to **thrombin**. This converts factor I (fibrinogen) to **fibrin**, a tough, insoluble polymerized protein which forms a network of fibers around the platelets (see BLOOD) that have stuck to the edge of the wound and to each other. The network entangles the blood cells, and contracts, squeezing out the serum and leaving a solid clot. (See also ANTICOAGULANTS; EMBOLISM; HEMOPHILIA; HEMORRHAGE; THROMBOSIS.)

CLOTURE (or closure), procedure for ending discussion and securing an immediate vote on an issue in a deliberative assembly. In the US Senate a motion to invoke cloture must be supported by a petition signed by 16 senators and passed by two-thirds of those present and voting. It is used against a delaying FILIBUSTER.

CLOUDBERRY, *Rubus chamaemorus*, a creeping herbaceous plant similar to the BLACKBERRY, native to mountains of N temperate regions. It grows 75–250mm (3–10in) high and its shallow white flowers, borne singly, give rise to red or yellow berries. Family: Rosaceae.

CLOUD CHAMBER, device, invented by C. T. R. WILSON (1911), used to observe the paths of subatomic particles. In simplest form, it comprises a chamber containing saturated VAPOR (see SATURATION) and some liquid, one wall of the chamber (the window) being transparent, another retractable. Sudden retraction of this wall lowers the temperature, and the gas becomes supersaturated (see SUPERSATURATION). Passage of SUBATOMIC PARTICLES through the gas leaves charged IONS that serve as seeds for CONDENSATION of the gas into droplets. These fog trails (condensation trails) may be photographed through the window. (See also BUBBLE CHAMBER; SPARK CHAMBER.)

CLOUDS, visible collections of water droplets or ice particles that, because they fall so slowly, may be regarded as suspended in the ATMOSPHERE. Clouds whose lower surfaces touch the ground are usually called FOG. The water droplets are very small, indeed of colloidal size (see COLLOID; AEROSOL); they must coagulate or grow before falling as rain or snow. This process may be assisted by **cloud seeding**;

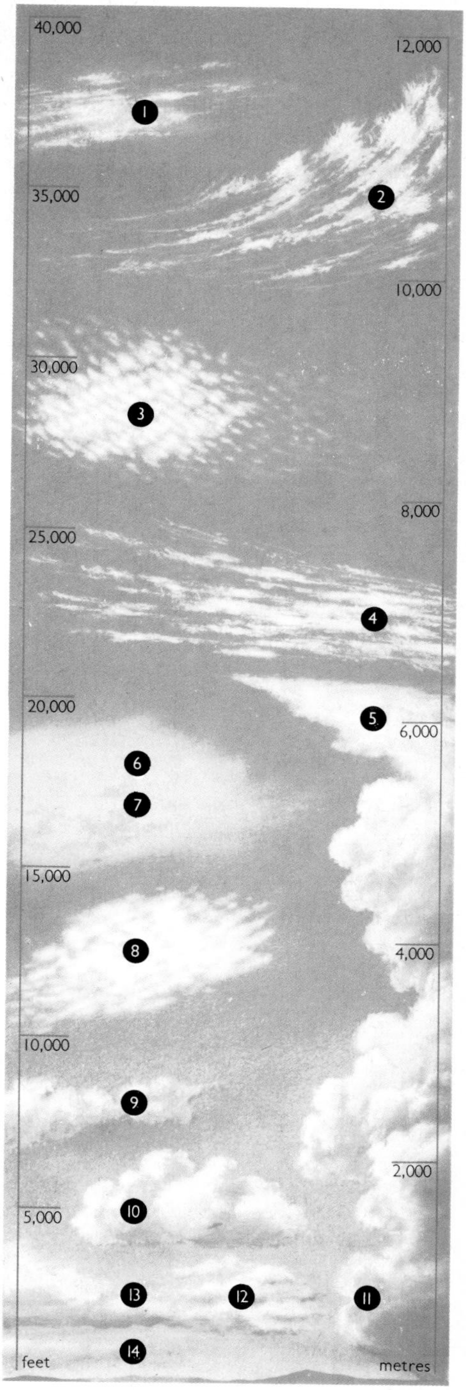

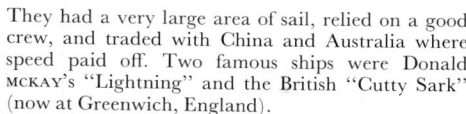

Clouds are classified according to their altitude and the factors which have stimulated them to form. The cumulonimbus cloud (*top left*) shows a well developed anvil head. Such clouds, towering up to 6000m, are often associated with thunderstorms. Altocumulus clouds (*top center*) usually occur between 3000 and 5000m. *Above right:* The altitudes at which different types of clouds occur: (1) iridescent; (2) cirrus; (3) cirrocumulus; (4) cirrostratus; (5) anvil head of cumulonimbus; (6) altostratus; (7) fractostratus patches; (8) altocumulus; (9) nimbus; (10) cumulus; (11) cumulonimbus; (12) stratocumulus; (13) nimbostratus; (14) stratus.

supercooled clouds are seeded with particles of (usually) dry ice (i.e., solid CARBON dioxide) to encourage CONDENSATION of the droplets, ideally causing RAIN OR SNOW.

Cloud Formation. Clouds are formed when air containing water vapor cools in the presence of suitable condensation nuclei (e.g., dust particles).

This may occur through CONVECTION, when warm, moist air from near the earth's surface penetrates upward into regions of lower PRESSURE; here they expand, thus cooling past the dew point (see CONDENSATION), the temperature at which SATURATION of water in air is reached. The vapor condenses out to form cloud droplets. They may also form when warm air flows over a mountain; the air travels in a vertical wave (see WAVE MOTION), parts of which may be higher than its condensation level, resulting in a stationary cloud at the crest of the wave. Other modes of formation occur. (See METEOROLOGY.)

Types of Clouds. There are three main cloud types: Cumulus (heap) clouds, formed by convection, often mountain- or cauliflower-shaped, are found from about 600m (2000ft) up as far as the tropopause, even temporarily into the stratosphere (see ATMOSPHERE). Cirrus (hair) clouds are composed almost entirely of ice crystals. They appear feathery, and are found at altitudes above about 6000m (20000ft). Stratus (layer) clouds are low-lying, found between ground level and about 1500m (5000ft). Other types of cloud include cirrostratus, cirrocumulus, altocumulus, altostratus, cumulonimbus, stratocumulus and nimbostratus.

CLOUET, Jean (c1485–1540?), Flemish artist who was chief portrait painter at the court of Francis I of France. However, only one unsigned painting and about 130 drawings can be assigned to him.

CLOVE, *Eugenia caryophyllata*, evergreen tree grown in the East Indies and Mauritius. Also the name of its dried unopened flowers used as flavoring and in medicine. Oil of cloves is used to flavor toothpastes and as a pain-killer and antiseptic.

CLOVER, small plants of the genus *Trifolium*, family Leguminosae, commonly found in lawns and pastures and along paths and roads. Many species are native to North America. Others, notably the red clover (*Trifolium pratense*), have been introduced from Europe. Clovers normally have leaves divided into three parts and are grown for forage and for hay. Clover roots contain nitrogen-fixing bacteria which enrich the soil. (See also NITROGEN FIXATION.)

CLOVIS, city in S central Cal., 10mi NE of Fresno. It handles fruit and forest products and makes concrete pipes. Pop 13856.

CLOVIS, city in E N.M., the seat of Curry Co. It is a trading center for cattle and wheat and their products, and also a railroad division point. Pop 28945.

CLOVIS I (c466–511 AD), Frankish king, founder of the Frankish monarchy. He amassed a huge kingdom from the Rhine R to the Mediterranean, defeating the Romans at Soissons (486) and the Visigoths under Alaric II of Spain at Vouillé (507). He became a Christian in c498. Clovis compiled the SALIC LAW, followed by his successors the MEROVINGIANS.

CLOWN, a comedy figure of the pantomime and circus. Modern clowns possibly derived from the vice figures of medieval miracle plays, but clowns were also known in ancient Greece and Rome, and as jesters or fools in medieval courts. They later featured as harlequins in the COMMEDIA DELL' ARTE; but their grotesque makeup, baggy clothes and slapstick and tumbling (see Joseph GRIMALDI) only developed fully in the 1800s.

CLUBFOOT, deformity of the FOOT, with an abnormal relationship of the foot to the ankle; most commonly the foot is turned in and down. Abnormalities of fetal posture and ligamentous or muscle development, including CEREBRAL PALSY and SPINA BIFIDA, may be causative. Correction includes gentle manipulation, PHYSIOTHERAPY, plaster splints and sometimes SURGERY.

CLUB MOSSES, primitive vascular plants of the order Lycopodiales, related to the ferns. They have creeping stems that branch dichotomously and small leaves arranged spirally. These are found mainly in the tropics, but some occur in temperate climates.

CLUBROOT, a plant disease affecting cabbages and other members of the mustard family (Cruciferae). It is caused by the SLIME MOLD *Plasmodiophora brassicae*. Club-like bodies form on the roots. Clubroot is avoided by growing resistant plant strains and adding lime to the soil. (See also PLANT DISEASES.)

CLUJ, city in NW Romania on the Someşul Mic R. Founded about the 12th century, it was the historic capital of TRANSYLVANIA. It makes chemicals, textiles, ceramics and machinery. Pop 202715.

CLUMBER SPANIEL, old breed of sporting dog named for Clumber Park in northern England, where it was developed. Its long coat is white, with light lemon patches, preferably on the head and fore-muzzle. It stands 18in high and weighs 55–70lb.

CLUNY, small town in E central France, 12mi NW of Mâcon. Its Benedictine abbey (910–1790) was the parent house of the Cluniac order. Only a part of its great basilica, once the largest church in W Europe, remains. Pop 4300.

CLUSTER. See STAR CLUSTER.

CLUTCH. See TRANSMISSION.

CLYDE, Scotland's most important river. It rises in N Dumfries and flows 106mi N then NW to the Firth of Clyde. From Hamilton on, the Clyde valley is occupied by heavy industry, notably shipbuilding and iron and coal mining. GLASGOW stands at the head of its navigable channel.

CLYMER, George (1739–1813), American revolutionary patriot and statesman. He was a Pennsylvania signer of the Declaration of Independence and of the US Constitution, and served in the first House of Representatives.

CLYTEMNESTRA, in Greek mythology, wife of AGAMEMNON and mother of ORESTES, ELECTRA and IPHIGENIA. Seduced by Aegisthus, her husband's cousin, she helped him to murder Agamemnon when he returned from Troy. In revenge Orestes killed both her and Aegisthus.

CNIDARIA, a phylum of mainly marine animals once included with the CTENOPHORES in the phylum COELENTERATA. They include the freshwater HYDRA and the marine JELLYFISH, SEA ANEMONES, CORALS, Seafirs and Sea fans. Cnidarians have bodies composed of two layers of cells and most species exist in a variety of forms, a phenomenon known as ALTERNATION OF GENERATIONS. The main forms are the polyp, which is cylindrical and sessile, and the hydranth or medusa, which is bell-or saucer-shaped and free swimming.

CNOSSUS. See KNOSSOS.

COACHELLA VALLEY, valley in SE Cal., between the brackish Salton Sea and the San Bernardino Mts. Irrigation has developed date and citrus fruit gardens. In the N is the resort city of Palm Springs.

COAHUILA, dry upland state in NE Mexico (capital: SALTILLO). Irrigation permits the cultivation of cotton, corn, wheat, beans and grapes. Iron and steel production and coal mining are important, and there are rich mineral ores of copper, iron, zinc, silver and lead.

COAL, hard, black mineral burned as a FUEL. With its by-products COKE and COAL TAR it is vital to many modern industries.

Coal is the compressed remains of tropical and subtropical plants, especially those of the CARBONIFEROUS and PERMIAN periods. Changes in the world climatic pattern explain why coal occurs in all continents, even Antarctica. Coal formation began when plant debris accumulated in swamps, partially decomposing and forming PEAT layers. A rise in sea level or land subsidence buried these layers below marine sediments, whose weight compressed the peat, transforming it under high-temperature conditions to coal; the greater the pressure, the harder the coal.

Coals are analyzed in two main ways: the "ultimate analysis" determines the total percentages of the elements present (carbon, hydrogen, oxygen, sulfur and nitrogen); and the "proximate analysis" gives an empirical estimate of the amounts of moisture, ash, volatile materials and fixed carbon. Coals are classified, or ranked, according to their fixed-carbon content, which increases progressively as they are formed. In ascending rank, the main types are: **lignite**, or brown coal, which weathers quickly, may ignite spontaneously, and has a low calorific value (see FUEL), but is used in Germany and Australia; **subbituminous coal**, mainly used in generating stations; **bituminous coal**, the commonest type, used in generating stations and the home, and often converted into COKE; and **anthracite**, a lustrous coal which burns slowly and well, and is the preferred domestic fuel.

Coal was burned in Glamorgan, Wales, in the 2nd millennium BC, and was known in China and the Roman Empire around the time of Christ. Coal mining was practiced throughout Europe and known to the American Indians by the 13th century AD. The first commercial coal mine in the US was at Richmond, Va., (opened 1745) and anthracite was mined in Pa. by 1790. The INDUSTRIAL REVOLUTION created a huge and increasing demand for coal. This slackened in the 20th century as coal faced competition from abundant oil and gas, but production is now again increasing. Annual world output is about 3 billion tonnes, 500 million tonnes from the US. World coal reserves are estimated conservatively at about 7 trillion tonnes, enough to meet demand for centuries at present consumption rates. (See also MINING.)

COAL GAS, a mixture of gases produced by the destructive distillation of COAL, consisting chiefly of hydrogen, methane and carbon monoxide. Other products are COKE and COAL TAR. Coal gas is used as a domestic fuel, but has been largely superseded by NATURAL GAS.

COAL TAR, a dense black viscous liquid produced by the destructive distillation of COAL; COKE and COAL GAS are other products. Fractional distillation of coal tar produces a wide variety of industrially important substances. These include ASPHALT (pitch) and CREOSOTE, a wood preservative; also various oils used as fuels, solvents, preservatives, lubricants and disinfectants. Specific chemicals that can be isolated include benzene, toluene, xylene, phenol, pyridine, naphthalene and anthracene—the main source for the pharmaceutical and other chemical industries.

COAST AND GEODETIC SURVEY, US. See NATIONAL OCEANIC AND ATMOSPHERIC ADMINISTRATION.

COAST GUARD, US, branch of the armed services supervised in peacetime by the Department of Transportation, in war by the navy. It helps to maintain law and safety wherever the US has jurisdiction on the high seas and navigable inland waters. Formed in 1915 by a union of the Life Saving Service and the Revenue Cutter Service, its duties are the following: search and rescue operations, maintaining weather ships and navigational aids, including the LORAN radio network, collecting meteorological and oceanographic data, ice-breaking in inland waters and patrolling the N Atlantic for icebergs, enforcing navigation and shipping laws and marine safety regulations for seamen and the construction and equipment of ships, and operating against smugglers. In wartime the coast guard assumes the regular duties of the navy.

COAST GUARD ACADEMY, US, an institution of higher education training career officers for the US COAST GUARD, located in New London, Conn. Students take a four-year course leading to a Bachelor of Science degree and an ensign's commission in the US coast guard.

COAST RANGES, a series of mountain ranges along the Pacific coast of North America from Kodiak Island, S Alaska, to S Cal. The mountains are of widely varied geological composition. The highest peak in the entire series is Canada's Mt Logan (19850ft).

COATESVILLE, city in SE Pa., 30mi W of Philadelphia. It produces steel and textiles and has a Veterans Administration hospital. Pop 12331.

COATI, three species of a small carnivorous, arboreal mammal, with long, erectly-held tails. They are related to the raccoon, and live in forest areas from Arizona to South America. Females and young live in groups, males are solitary.

COBALT (Co), silvery-white, hard, ferromagnetic (see MAGNETISM) metal in Group VIII of the PERIODIC TABLE; a TRANSITION ELEMENT. It occurs in nature largely as sulfides and arsenides, and in nickel and copper ores; major producers are Canada, Zaire and Zambia. An ALLOY of cobalt, aluminum, nickel and iron ("Alnico") is used for magnets; other cobalt alloys, being very hard, are used for cutting tools. Cobalt is used as the matrix for tungsten carbide in drill bits. Chemically it resembles IRON and NICKEL: its characteristic oxidation states are +2 and +3. Cobalt compounds are useful colorants (notably the artists' pigment cobalt blue). Cobalt CATALYSTS facilitate HYDROGENATION and other industrial processes. The RADIOISOTOPE cobalt-60 is used in RADIATION THERAPY. Cobalt is a constituent of the vital VITAMIN B12. AW 58.9, mp 1495°C, bp 2870°C, sg 8.9 (20°C).

COBALT BOMB, device used in CANCER treatment as a source of gamma rays (see RADIOACTIVITY; RADIATION THERAPY). It uses Co^{60}, a RADIOISOTOPE of cobalt. Because of its long half-life, Co^{60} is used widely as a radioactive tracer; and gives its name to a theoretical nuclear weapon (see ATOMIC BOMB; NUCLEAR WARFARE), also called the cobalt bomb, whose fallout might remain deadly for years.

COBB, Tyrus Raymond (1886–1961), the "Georgia Peach," one of baseball's greatest players. In 24 years with the Detroit Tigers and the old Philadelphia Athletics he appeared in more games, batted more times and made more hits than any other major leaguer; his lifetime average was a record .367.

COBBETT, William (1763–1835), British radical writer and reformer, best known for his *Rural Rides* (1830), which portrayed the misery of rural workers. His radical views forced him to live in the US 1793–1800 and 1817–19. His *Weekly Political Register* (founded 1802) was the major radical newspaper of its day. He was elected to parliament after the 1832 Reform Act.

COBDEN, Richard (1804–1865), British politician and reformer. A textile merchant, he was known as "the Apostle of Free Trade". He was a founder member of the Anti-Corn Law League 1838–39, and its chief spokesman in parliament 1841–46. In two pamphlets, *England, Ireland and America* (1835) and *Russia* (1836), he surveyed international relations and argued against British interventionist policies.

COBLENZ. See KOBLENZ.

COBOL (Common Business-Orientated Language), COMPUTER language designed primarily for business use. It has the advantage that it can be easily learned and understood by people without technical backgrounds; and that a program designed for one computer may be run on another with minimal alteration.

COBRAS, poisonous snakes of the family Elapidae that spread the ribs of the neck to form a hood when alarmed. The king cobra, the longest poisonous snake, is about 5.5m (18ft) long. The Egyptian and Indian cobras are the traditional snake-charmer's snakes. They respond to movement, not to music, as they are deaf.

COCA, a shrub, *Erythroxylon coca*, whose leaves contain various ALKALOIDS, especially COCAINE. Native to the Andes, it is widely cultivated elsewhere. The leaves have been chewed by South American Indians for centuries to quell hunger and to refresh. Cocaine-free coca extracts are used in making cola drinks (see KOLA).

COCAINE, an ALKALOID from the coca leaf, the first local anesthetic agent and model for those currently used; it is occasionally used for surface ANESTHESIA. It is a drug of abuse, taken for its euphoriant effect by chewing the leaf, as snuff or by intravenous INJECTION. Although physical dependence does not occur, its abuse may lead to acute psychosis. It also mimics the actions of the sympathetic NERVOUS SYSTEM.

COCCYX, bone at the base of the spine, vestigial in man. If large in rare cases it causes difficulties in childbirth. It may even cause pain, requiring its excision.

COCHABAMBA, capital city of Cochabamba department, Bolivia. Founded in 1574, it is the area's cultural, educational and political center. Apart from oil refining there is little industry. Pop 180 000.

COCHIN CHINA, colony of French Indochina 1862–1948, now part of South Vietnam. It covered the outer Mekong delta area and surrounding country; its chief city was Saigon, the country's capital.

COCHINEAL, a red coloring agent obtained from dried bodies of female scale insects. Synthetic ANILINE dyes have largely replaced cochineal commercially.

COCHISE (c1815–1874), Chiricahua Apache chief. Wrongly antagonized by soldiers, he began a savage campaign against whites in Ariz. in 1861 and effectively drove them from the area. In 1862 he was driven back by troops to the Dragon Mts, which he held until his capture by Gen. CROOK in 1871. He escaped, but gave himself up when the Chiricahua Reservation was formed in 1872.

Among the most popular of spaniels, the cocker was so named because it was used by hunters to flush birds, notably the woodcock, from cover; it is a compact and sturdily built dog with a merry disposition.

COCHLEA, part of the inner EAR, concerned with the mechanism of hearing. It is a spiral structure containing fluid and specialized membranes on which receptor nerve cells lie. Sound is conducted to the fluid by the tiny bones of the middle ear.

COCHRAN, Jacqueline (1912?–), US pilot. She obtained her pilot's license in 1932, after only three weeks' flying. First woman to fly in a Bendix transcontinental race (1934), she won it in 1938. She organized and headed the Women's Airforce Service Pilots (WASP) in WWII, and was the first woman to fly faster than sound.

COCHRANE, Gordon Stanley "Mickey" (1903–1962), one of baseball's greatest catchers. He played for the old Philadelphia Athletics and was catcher-manager for the Detroit Tigers. His lifetime batting average was .320.

COCKAIGNE, Land of, imaginary medieval Utopia with rivers of wine, streets of pastry and so on. The name has been jokingly applied to London, as in Elgar's *Cockaigne* overture.

COCKATOOS, PARROTS with erectile crests. Their plumage is usually white, sometimes black, pink or yellow. They live in and around Australia, and are good talkers.

COCKATRICE. See BASILISKS.

COCKCROFT, Sir John Douglas (1897–1967), English physicist who first "split the atom." With E. T. S. WALTON, he built a particle ACCELERATOR and in 1932 initiated the first man-made nuclear reaction by bombarding LITHIUM atoms with PROTONS, producing ALPHA PARTICLES. For this work Cockcroft and Walton received the 1951 Nobel Prize for Physics. In 1946 Cockcroft became the first director of the UK's atomic research laboratory at Harwell, and in 1959, the first Master of Churchill College, Cambridge.

COCKERELL, Sir Christopher Sydney (1910–), British engineer who rediscovered the hovercraft principle and stimulated worldwide interest in the possibilities of the AIR-CUSHION VEHICLE.

COCKER SPANIEL, smallest breed of hunting spaniel, named for the woodcocks it was bred to hunt. Standing 14–16in at the shoulder, it can weigh from 22 to 28lb. It has a soft coat, usually thick and curly.

COCKER SPANIEL, English, one of the oldest English breeds of sporting dog but now largely kept as house dogs. Lively animals with appealing faces framed by pendulous ears, their long smooth coat may be a variety of colors or multicolored. Shortish in the leg, they stand 15–16in high and weigh about 28lb.

COCKFIGHTING, sport in which two gamecocks are set to fight each other, usually to the death. The specially-bred birds wear metal spurs, making the contest especially vicious. Cockfighting seems to have originated in the East, and to have spread through Greece to Europe. In the US it was popular, but was soon outlawed by most states; in Britain it was prohibited in 1849. Devotees have included Henry VIII, Washington and Jefferson. It is generally unlawful in most Western countries today.

COCKLEBUR, clotbur or burweed, any of several annual weeds of the genus *Xanthium*, family Compositae. They produce bristly balls of seeds called BURRS. The seedlings are poisonous to livestock, but they can be controlled by herbicides. (See also BURDOCK.)

COCKLES, bivalve marine MOLLUSKS with cupped shells ornamented with grooves radiating from the hinges. They live buried in mud or sand, digging in with a muscular foot that they can protrude between the shells. There are many species along the coasts of North America, ranging in size from 100mm (4in) to 6mm (0.24in).

COCKNEY, nickname for a Londoner, especially one born within the sound of the bells of St. Mary-le-Bow church. It derives from a derogatory term used c1500 of anyone city-bred.

COCKROACHES, running, flat-bodied insects of the family Blattidae with long antennae and hardened forewings that protect the hindwings, as in BEETLES. They feed on fungi and on plant and animal remains, but also come indoors to eat exposed food, book bindings or even wood. Cockroaches are often a pest in the older neighborhoods of large American cities. There are about 70 species in America.

COCKS-OF-THE-ROCK, strikingly handsome birds of the family Cotingidae, native to mountain forests in N and NW South America. They have bright orange and black plumage and a helmet-like crest. (See also COTINGAS.)

COCOA, city in E Fla., on the Indian R. Its economy rests on the aerospace industry and on fruit, tourism, fishing and livestock. Pop 16 110.

COCOA. See CACAO.

COCO-DE-MER, *Lodoicea maldivica*, palm tree native to the Seychelles. It produces large double fruits which are the largest known fruit and take ten years to ripen. The husks of the fruit were found floating in the Indian Ocean long before the actual tree was known.

COCONUT PALM, *Cocus nucifera*, an economically valuable tree found on many tropical coasts. It has a long trunk crowned by a cluster of large fronds. The fruits, coconuts, take one year to develop and a single palm normally produces up to 100 nuts in one year. Each nut is surrounded by a thick fibrous husk and contains a white kernel surrounding the "coconut milk." The kernel is dried to produce **copra**, which is the source of coconut oil, a vegetable oil much used in the US and Europe in detergents, edible oils, margarine, brake fluid etc. The fibers of the husk are used for mats and ropes.

COCOON, the protective capsule enclosing the eggs of many animals; also, the stage in the life history of many insects called the PUPA or CHRYSALIS. In butterflies and moths the cocoon enclosing the chrysalis is formed by secretions of SILK.

COCOS ISLANDS (or Keeling Islands), two coral atolls in the E Indian Ocean. Declared a British possession in 1857, they were granted in perpetuity to

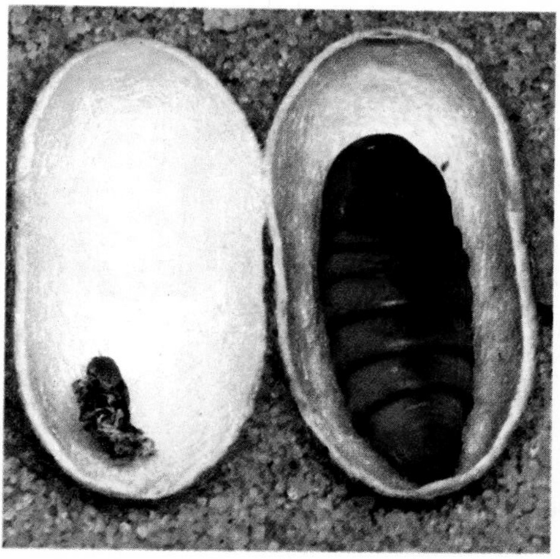

The cocoon of the silk moth cut open to show the pupa inside. These cocoons are the sole source of the material silk.

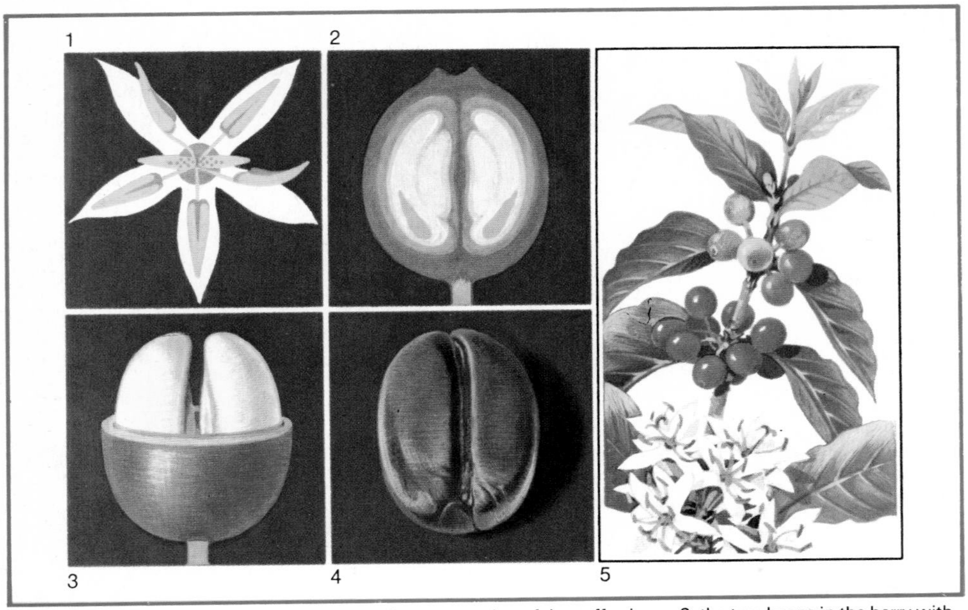

Five aspects of the coffee plant: 1. The flower, 2. cross-section of the coffee berry, 3. the two beans in the berry with their flat sides facing each other, 4. roasted bean, 5. branch with blossoms and berries.

the Clunies-Ross family, who had settled there in 1827. They passed to Australia in 1955 and in 1972 John Clunies-Ross surrendered authority to the Australian government. Most of the population are Malays employed on the coconut plantations.

COCTEAU, Jean (1889–1963), French author, artist and film director. He first rose to fame with poetry, ballets such as *Parade* (1917), and the novel *Thomas l'Imposteur* (1923). After overcoming opium addiction, he produced some of his most brilliant work, such as the play *Orphée* (1926) and the novels *Les Enfants Terribles* (1929) and *La Machine Infernale* (1934). A prolific writer in many fields, he also made several films, of which *Le Sang d'un Poète* (1932) is the most adventurous.

COD, members of the family Gadidae, important food fish of the N Atlantic and the Pacific, weighing up to 90kg (200lb). Cod form dense shoals, feeding on other fish and bottom-living animals. Females lay up to 6 million eggs at a time. The "cod banks" off New England and Newfoundland stimulated colonization of North America. The cod were salted, their livers yielded vitamin-rich COD LIVER OIL and the swim-bladder produced isinglass, a pure form of GELATIN.

CODDINGTON, William (1601–1678), English colonist in North America. He left Massachusetts in 1637 and founded Portsmouth (1638) and Newport (1639) on what is now Rhode Island, becoming their governor in 1639. He opposed union with Providence and Warwick in 1644, but was chief magistrate of the Rhode Island colonies 1674–75 and 1678.

CODE, systematic and usually comprehensive set of legal rules. Many early bodies of law, such as that of HAMMURABI (c1800 BC), took this form. Roman law was codified in the TWELVE TABLES and again by the Emperor JUSTINIAN in the 6th century AD. The law reform movement in modern CIVIL LAW countries chose the code as the most accessible form of law; first of these was the CODE NAPOLÉON of 1804–10. Britain, the US and other COMMON LAW countries have made only limited use of codes.

CODEINE, a mild NARCOTIC, ANALGESIC and COUGH suppressant related to MORPHINE. It reduces bowel activity causing CONSTIPATION and is used to cure DIARRHEA.

CODE NAPOLÉON, French legal CODE, officially the *Code Civil*. Napoleon I, as first consul, appointed a commission to devise a replacement for the confused and corrupt local systems formerly in force. The code, made up of 2281 articles arranged in three books, was enacted in 1804 and, although much altered, is still in force today. Revision commissions were appointed in 1904 and 1945. The code has been the model for nearly all codes in CIVIL LAW countries. The La. civil code (1825) is closely based on it.

CODES AND CIPHERS, devices for conveying information secretly, mostly used in wartime and for espionage. In ciphers, individual letters or numerals that make up a message are transposed or replaced by other letters or numerals. But ciphers can often be "broken" because each letter of the alphabet tends to occur with a particular frequency.

Codes are based on units that may vary in length from letters to sentences. These units are given arbitrary code equivalents known to sender and receiver, who use identical code books listing code words and symbols. Machines have often been used to create complex codes and ciphers; today computers are entering the field. It is not clear how often cryptoanalysts break cryptographers' ciphers and codes, since successes are seldom made public, but Allied cryptoanalysts undoubtedly contributed to victory in WWII.

CODEX, earliest example of the book form, a number of manuscript sheets stitched together. It replaced the more cumbersome scrolls and tablets. The term is also used for a legal CODE.

CODICIL, addition to a will which modifies any part of that will not in accordance with it.

CODLING MOTH, *Laspegresia pomonella*, a nocturnal moth whose caterpillars feed on APPLES. Infested orchards need repeated spraying with INSECTICIDES.

COD LIVER OIL, an oil rich in VITAMINS A and D, a convenient way of enriching diets which contain inadequate amounts, particularly used for children. Both vitamins are dangerous in excess.

CODON, the basic "vocabulary" unit in the genetic code which controls PROTEIN SYNTHESIS. Each molecule of messenger-RNA (see NUCLEIC ACIDS) consists of an ordered sequence of NUCLEOTIDES. There are only four different nucleotides in RNA, not enough to code individually for the 20 AMINO ACIDS which make up proteins. So the nucleotides are grouped in threes, giving 64 different combinations called codons. Of these, 61 code for amino acids—several codons usually coding for the same amino acid—and 3 signal for termination of the protein chain. The code appears to be the same for all organisms.

CODY, William Frederick. See BUFFALO BILL.

COEDUCATION, education of both sexes in the same school. It became quite usual in Protestant countries for very young children, but for older children it is a modern development. The US took the lead over Europe; the first coeducational college was established at Oberlin in 1833 and by 1900 70% of colleges were coeducational, as are most public schools now. Other countries vary widely, but generally more public schools than private are coeducational. Universities in most countries are now coeducational.

COEFFICIENT, any FACTOR in an algebraic expression. Usually, coefficients are considered to be CONSTANTS by which terms involving one or more VARIABLES must be multiplied for all values of the variable. Thus, in ax^3+bx^2+cx+d the numbers a,b,c are coefficients. The values of coefficients are as important as the values of variables in most POLYNOMIALS and FUNCTIONS (see also EQUATION).

COELACANTHS, fish, common as 70-million-year-old fossils, thought to be extinct until rediscovered by scientists in 1938 off the E African coast, where fishermen knew one species, *Latimeria chalumnae*, well. Coelacanths are not ancestors of land vertebrates as was once suggested.

COELENTERATA, a phylum of primitive animals, now divided into two groups, the CNIDARIA and the CTENOPHORES.

COELOM, a body cavity found in most animals—the so-called coelomate animals. The main organs of the body are contained within the coelom.

COERCIVE ACTS. See INTOLERABLE ACTS.

COEUR, Jacques (c1395–1456), French merchant and banker who enjoyed great power at the court of Charles VII. In 1439 he became royal financial comptroller and in 1442 a member of the king's council. He was arrested on false charges in 1451 and imprisoned. He escaped to Rome, where he had great influence with Pope Calixtus III, and died in the latter's service.

COEUR D'ALENE, city in NW Ida., seat of Kootenai Co. It was originally a lead and silver mining center, but its economy now rests on lumbering and tourism. Pop 16228.

COEUR D'ALENE INDIANS, Indian tribe who lived around Coeur d'Alene Lake in Ida. A peaceful people, they belonged to the Plateau cultures and spoke a Salish language. Their descendants live on a reservation in the area.

COEUR D'ALENE LAKE, 24mi-long lake in Kootenai Co., N Ida. In a mountainous area, it is a popular beauty spot.

COFFEE, drink produced from the roasted fruit (beans) of the coffee plant. The coffee tree (or bush) belongs to the genus *Coffea*, the most extensively cultivated species being *Coffea arabica*. The coffee tree probably originated in Abyssinia. Its use as a drink rapidly spread through Arabia in the 13th century and it became popular in Europe during the 16th and 17th centuries. The US is now the largest market for coffee. Coffee is grown in many tropical countries. Brazil produces more coffee than any other country, but its share is becoming less. For many Latin American, African and Asian countries it is a very important export commodity. After picking, the ripe red berries are either naturally dried and the hulls, pulp and parchment removed (dry process), or are squeezed out of their skin and soaked when slight fermentation takes place, washed and then dried (wash process). The processed berries are roasted, which induces the coffee color and aroma, partly through the formation of CAFFEINE.

The coffee bush can also be grown as a house plant, requiring several hours sunlight in the winter, although young plants thrive under fluorescent light. Indoors, the temperature should not drop below 13°C (53°F) and the soil should be kept evenly moist. Propagation is by seeds and shoot tip cuttings.

COFFERDAM, temporary DAM used to divert the stream in early stages of dam-building. The term is used also for a structure similar to an open CAISSON.

COFFEYVILLE, city in SE Kan. An important commercial center, it has various industries and lies in an oil and gas-producing area. Pop 15116.

COFFIN, Levi (1789–1877), US abolitionist, "president" of the UNDERGROUND RAILROAD in Newport (now Fountain City), Ind.

COGNAC, historic town in Charente department, W France. It gives its name to the famous brandy distilled in the area. Pop 21137.

COHAN, George Michael (1878–1942), US popular songwriter, actor, playwright and producer. He is best known for the songs he composed during WWI, notably *Give My Regards to Broadway, I'm a*

Yankee-Doodle-Dandy and *Over There*, for which Congress awarded him a special medal in 1940.
COHEN, Leonard Norman (1934–), Canadian popular songwriter, poet and novelist. Among his best-known poetry collections are *Parasites of Heaven* (1966) and *The Energy of Slaves* (1973). He has recorded many poems set to his own music.
COHEN, Morris Raphael (1880–1947), Russian-born US philosopher. He taught at the College of the City of New York 1912–38 and at the University of Chicago until 1942. His best-known works include *Reason and Nature* (1931 and 1953) and *Law and the Social Order* (1933).
COHESION, the tendency of different parts of a substance to hold together. This is due to forces acting between its MOLECULES: a molecule will repel one close to it but attract one that is farther away; somewhere between these there is a position where WORK must be done to either separate the molecules or push them together. This situation results both in cohesion and in ADHESION. Cohesion is strongest in a SOLID, less strong in a LIQUID, and least strong in a GAS.
COHN, Ferdinand Julius (1828–1898), German botanist renowned as one of the founders of BACTERIOLOGY. He showed that BACTERIA could be classified in fixed species and discovered that some of these formed endospores which could survive adverse physical conditions. He was also the first to recognize the value of KOCH's work on the ANTHRAX bacillus.
COHOES, city in E N.Y., at the Mohawk R Falls. Cohoes Dam, at the falls, provides power for the city's diesel industries. It is a major textile center. Pop 18653.
COHOSH. See BANEBERRY.
COIMBATORE, city in Tamil Nadu state, S India. A trade and manufacturing center, it supplies the surrounding cotton-producing and agricultural area. Pop 353469.
COIMBRA, historic city in N central Portugal, capital of the country 1139–1260. It has many light industries, and one of Europe's oldest universities. Pop 24350.

This statue on Broadway, New York City, was erected to the memory of George Cohan, the versatile man of the theater whose most famous song was "Give my regards to Broadway."

COIN, piece of stamped metal, of fixed value and weight, issued to serve as money. Coins were probably invented in Lydia, Asia Minor, in the 8th century BC. Their use spread through the civilized world, and coins remained the main medium of exchange until the introduction of bank notes. Coins are made in licensed government mints. They carry a design on both sides, traditionally including inscriptions giving their value and the name of the issuing ruler or state. Gold, silver and copper are the traditional metals, often alloyed with harder metals to reduce wear. Unscrupulous debt-laden rulers also practiced debasement—reducing a coin's precious metal content without changing its face value. The Massachusetts Bay Colony produced the first US coins in 1652. The first US mint was established in Philadelphia in 1792. (See also MONEY.)
COKE, form of amorphous CARBON (also containing ash, volatile residues and sulfur) remaining when bituminous COAL is heated in special furnaces to distill off the volatile constituents. Before the exploitation of NATURAL GAS, much COAL GAS was thus produced. In the US 95% of coke is used in METALLURGY, mostly in BLAST FURNACES. Such coke must be strong (to support the weight of the charge), porous and relatively pure. Some coke is used as a smokeless fuel, and to make WATER GAS.
COKE, Sir Edward (1552–1634), English lawyer and parliamentarian who defended the supremacy of the common law and the rights of parliament and the judiciary against the attempts of JAMES I and CHARLES I to govern by royal prerogative. He drafted the PETITION OF RIGHT in 1628 setting out the rights of a citizen.
COLA. See KOLA.
COLBERT, Jean Baptiste (1619–1683), French statesman, finance minister and comptroller general under LOUIS XIV. He transformed the finances of the state by reforming taxation, correcting abuses in the administration and encouraging industry and trade. He introduced protective tariffs, developed roads and canals and was a patron of culture.
COLCHICINE ($C_{22}H_{25}NO_6$), poisonous ALKALOID found in the autumn crocus or MEADOW SAFFRON (*Colchicum autumnale*). It is used to stimulate genetic changes in plants and animals. mp 156°C.
COLCHIS, region at the E end of the Black Sea, now part of Georgia, USSR. In mythology it was the home of MEDEA. The GOLDEN FLEECE, sought by JASON and the Argonauts, was guarded in Colchis by an unsleeping dragon.
COLD, Common, or coryza, a mild illness of the NOSE and throat caused by various types of VIRUS. General malaise and RHINITIS, initially watery but later thick and tenacious, are characteristic; sneezing, COUGH, sore throat and headache are also common, but significant FEVER is unusual. Secondary bacterial infection of EARS, SINUSES, PHARYNX or LUNGS may occur, especially in predisposed people. Spread is from person to person. Mild symptomatic relief only is required.
COLD-BLOODED ANIMALS, or poikilotherms, animals, in particular fish, amphibians and reptiles, that cannot maintain a constant body TEMPERATURE and which are therefore greatly affected by climatic changes.
COLDEN, Cadwallader (1688–1776), colonial American physician, administrator and naturalist. As lieutenant governor of N.Y. colony, he became unpopular for defending the British position during the STAMP ACT riots of 1765. He produced a botanical classification of American plants which was published by LINNEAUS in Sweden, and wrote a study of the IROQUOIS Indians, *History of the Five Indian Nations of Canada* (1727).
COLD FRAME, artificial enclosure for delicate plants and seedlings to protect them from wind, rain, hail, snow and extremes of temperature.
COLD HARBOR, locality in E central Va., 10mi ENE of Richmond. It was the scene of two Civil War battles: GAINES' MILL (1862) and Cold Harbor (1864), in which Robert E. LEE forced General GRANT's troops to withdraw with massive losses.

A dramatic symbol of the Cold War. US soldiers look on as East Germany works on the erection of the Berlin Wall in August 1961.

COLD SORE, vesicular SKIN lesion of lips or NOSE caused by *Herpes simplex* VIRUS. Often associated with periods of general ill-health or infections such as the COMMON COLD or PNEUMONIA. The virus, which is often picked up in early life, persists in the skin between attacks. Recurrences may be reduced by special antivirus drugs, applied during an attack.
COLD WAR, state of tension between countries, featuring mutually antagonistic policies but stopping short of actual fighting. The term is usually used to describe postwar relations between the Western powers led by the US and the communist bloc led by the USSR. Both sides built powerful alliances. The US established the NORTH ATLANTIC TREATY ORGANIZATION and the USSR organized the WARSAW PACT. Meanwhile a nuclear arms race gained momentum. Famous incidents in the Cold War included the BERLIN AIRLIFT (1948–49), the Cuban missile crisis (1962), in which the US forced Russia to dismantle its missile bases in Cuba, and the Russian invasion of Hungary (1956). Since the emergence of communist China as a world power, the US and the USSR have tried to improve relations with each other, partly from fear of China, partly for economic advantage.
COLE, Nat "King" (1919–1965), black US singer and jazz pianist. Born Nathaniel Adams Coles, he first became known as a pianist in the "Chicago Blues" manner, but his throaty individual singing brought him his greatest fame.
COLE, Thomas (1801–1848), British-born painter who founded the HUDSON RIVER SCHOOL. His best-known works are views of the Catskills and the White Mountains. Cole's grandiose, Italianate paintings of the wilderness introduced landscape as a serious subject for US painting.
COLEMAN, Ornette (1930–), black US musician, one of the most creative of the saxophonists. He plays in small groups, including his own trio, and has developed an advanced, original style. (See also JAZZ.)
COLEOPTERA. See BEETLES.
COLERIDGE, Samuel Taylor (1772–1834), leading English poet, essayist and critic. With WORDSWORTH he published *Lyrical Ballads* (1798), a landmark in early ROMANTICISM, in which Coleridge's major contribution was "The Rime of the Ancient Mariner," a tale in verse of the sea and fate. He is also remembered for an unfinished dream poem, "Kubla Khan," published in 1816. He gave notable lectures on Shakespeare and his *Biographia Literaria* (1817) criticizes the philosophy of KANT, FICHTE and SCHELLING and the poetry of Wordsworth. Opium addiction blighted his early life.
COLET, John (c1466–1519), English theologian, dean of St. Paul's and founder of St. Paul's School, London. He was a friend of Thomas MORE and ERASMUS and a proponent of the new Renaissance HUMANISM.

The collie is a working dog bred in England, probably by the 18th century. The rough-coated variety was used to guard and herd sheep and the smooth-coated was used to drive livestock to market. It is a purebred dog but not recognized by the American Kennel Club.

COLETTE, Sidonie-Gabrielle (1873–1954), French writer and music-hall actress known for her sensuous and subtle characterizations of people, especially of slightly disreputable women in the demimonde which she knew so well. Her brilliant style was admired by PROUST. Her best-known heroine is Claudine, a thinly veiled self-portrayal.

COLEUS, a genus of evergreen perennial plants native to the Old World tropics. Two species, *Coleus blumeri* and *C. thrysoidens* are widely cultivated in the greenhouse and home for their ornamental variegated foliage in shades of red, bronze, brown, purple, yellow, white and green and for their spikes of blue or white flowers. Flower buds should be pinched out if the plant is to remain bushy and if the foliage is to be retained in a healthy condition. Coleus should be placed in sunny east-, south- or west-facing windows, though they grow quite well under fluorescent lights. They grow best at temperatures above 13°C (55°F), and the soil should be evenly moist. Propagation is by seeds or shoot cuttings. Family: Labiatae.

COLFAX, Schuyler (1823–1885), US congressman (1855–69), speaker of the House of Representatives (1863–69) and vice-president of the US (1869–73) during Ulysses S. GRANT's presidency, when his alleged involvement in the CRÉDIT MOBILIER OF AMERICA railroad scandal ended his political career.

COLIC, intermittent pain; generally experienced as bouts of severe pain with pain-free intervals. It is due to irritation or obstruction of hollow viscera, in particular the GASTROINTESTINAL TRACT, ureter (see KIDNEY) and GALL BLADDER or bile ducts (see LIVER). Treatment of the cause is supplemented by ANALGESICS and drugs to reduce smooth muscle spasm.

COLIGNY, Gaspard de (1519–1572), admiral of France and French Protestant leader. As Huguenot commander in the second of the French Wars of RELIGION, he concluded the Treaty of St. Germain (1570) which favored the Protestants. But CHARLES IX turned against him and he was a victim in the massacre of St. Bartholomew's Day. (See SAINT BARTHOLOMEW'S DAY, MASSACRE OF.)

COLIMA, name of Pacific coast state in SW Mexico, and of its capital. Its climate is hot and humid. Products include cotton, rice and leather goods. City pop 64 851.

COLISEUM. See COLOSSEUM.

COLITIS, INFLAMMATION of the colon (see GASTROINTESTINAL TRACT). Infection with VIRUSES, BACTERIA or PARASITES may cause it, often with ENTERITIS. Inflammatory colitis can occur without bacterial infection in the chronic diseases, ulcerative colitis and Crohn's disease. Impaired blood supply may also cause colitis. Symptoms include COLIC and DIARRHEA (with slime or blood). Severe colitis can cause serious dehydration or SHOCK. Treatments include ANTIBIOTICS, and, for inflammatory colitis, STEROIDS, ASPIRIN derivatives or occasionally SURGERY.

COLLAGE, modern art form in which various objects and materials are glued onto a canvas or board and sometimes painted. Pablo PICASSO and Georges BRAQUE extended it to CUBISM in 1912–13, and DADAISM developed it further. Collage gave rise to "assemblage," a modern art form using scrap-metal objects and wood.

COLLAGEN, tough, fibrous PROTEIN occurring as a major component of the connective TISSUE of many animals. Animal hide is chiefly collagen, converted by tanning into LEATHER. When collagen is boiled it yields GELATIN and GLUE.

COLLARBONE, or **clavicle**, a bone which forms part of the shoulder girdle in many vertebrates. Man has two S-shaped collarbones running between the breastbone and the shoulder blade. In birds the two collarbones are joined to form the furcula or **wishbone**.

COLLARDS, *Brassica oleracea*, a variety of CABBAGE that differs from KALE only in its leaf characters. The plant is more adaptable than kale and is extensively grown in the southern US. It is a rich source of VITAMINS A and C. (See also BRASSICAS.)

COLLECTIVE BARGAINING, process by which labor unions and management arrange wages and conditions of work directly between themselves or their representatives without the involvement of an arbitrator or other third party. In the US the NATIONAL LABOR RELATIONS ACT (1935) actively encouraged collective bargaining.

COLLECTIVE FARM, state-organized farm, usually in communist countries, notably the USSR where there are about 32 000 collectives. Such farms were created to replace private farms and raise agricultural ouput on a communal basis. Though the land is worked collectively, members may retain small plots for their own use.

COLLECTIVE SECURITY, system whereby nations band together to guarantee each others' security against aggression. It was a basic principle of both the LEAGUE OF NATIONS and the UNITED NATIONS. However it has not been successful in preventing aggression.

COLLECTIVE UNCONSCIOUS, term used, especially by JUNG, for those parts of the UNCONSCIOUS derived from racial, rather than individual, experience.

COLLECTIVISM, political doctrine which places control of economic activity in the hands of the community or the government, as opposed to CAPITALISM, which emphasizes private ownership. Collectivists, beginning with ROUSSEAU, hold that it is only through submission to the community that the individual can fulfill himself and that economic power is too important to be left to the self-interest of individuals.

COLLEGE PARK, city in NW Ga., 8mi SSW of Atlanta. Pop 18 203.

COLLEGE PARK, city in Md., 8mi NE of Washington, D.C. It is the site of the U. of Md. Pop 26 156.

COLLEGE STATION, city in E central Tex., site of the Texas Agricultural and Mechanical U. Pop 17 676.

COLLEONI, Bartolomeo (1400–1475), general-in-chief of the Venetian Republic and CONDOTTIERE, among the greatest of 15th-century soldiers. He devised new battle tactics and forms of field artillery.

COLLIE, type of sheepdog originating in the UK. It is of medium size, with a long tapering head and bushy tail. Color is often black or brown and white. Both rough- and smooth-coated varieties are found.

COLLINGDALE, borough in SE Pa., 7mi WSW of Philadelphia. Pop 10 605.

COLLINGSWOOD, residential borough in SW N.J., SE of Camden. It was settled by Quakers in 1682 and incorporated in 1888. Pop 17 422.

COLLINS, Michael (1890–1922), Irish revolutionary leader. Imprisoned for opposing the British in the EASTER RISING of 1916, he later became a SINN FEIN leader and intelligence chief of the guerrilla IRISH REPUBLICAN ARMY. Collins helped to negotiate the treaty with Britain which set up the Irish Free State in 1921, and briefly headed the Irish army and government, but was ambushed and shot by Irish opponents.

COLLINS, Michael (1930–), US astronaut who piloted the historic Apollo 11 moon mission. He remained in the command module while Neil ARMSTRONG and Edwin ALDRIN took the first steps on the moon (July 20, 1969).

COLLINS, (William) Wilkie (1824–1889), English novelist. A friend of DICKENS, he established his reputation in 1860 with the publication of *The Woman in White*, one of the first English detective stories.

COLLINSVILLE, city in SW Ill. Once a center of coal mining, it now has zinc-smelting, canning and clothing industries. Pop 18 015.

COLLODION, solution of pyroxyline in ETHANOL and diethyl ETHER which evaporates to form a fine film impervious to water; used for protection of wounds and BURNS. Inhalation should be avoided.

COLLOID, or **colloidal solution**, a system in which two (or more) substances are uniformly mixed so that one is extremely finely dispersed throughout the other. A colloid may be viewed intuitively as a halfway stage between a SUSPENSION and a SOLUTION, the size of the dispersed particles being larger than simple MOLECULES, smaller than can be viewed through an optical MICROSCOPE (more precisely, they have at least one diameter in the range 1μm–1nm). Typical examples of colloids include FOG and BUTTER. Colloids may be classified in two ways: one by the natures of the particles (dispersed phase) and medium (continuous phase); the other by, as it were, the degree of permanency of the colloid. In the latter case, one may define a **lyophilic colloid** as one that forms spontaneously when the two phases are placed in contact; and a **lyophobic colloid** as one that can be formed only with some difficulty and maintained for a moderate elapse of time only under special conditions. Colloids have interesting properties, perhaps the most notable of which is light DISPERSION: it is due to colloidal particles in the atmosphere that the sky is blue in the daytime and the sunset red. Moreover, the property of ADSORPTION of molecules and IONS at the interface between particles and continuous phase plays a major part in water purification (see WATER SUPPLY). (See also AEROSOL; BROWNIAN MOTION; DIALYSIS; ELECTROPHORESIS; OSMOSIS; TYNDALL; ULTRAMICROSCOPE.)

COLLOTYPE, PRINTING process, akin to LITHOGRAPHY, whereby photographs may be reproduced without a HALFTONE screen. A GLASS or ALUMINUM plate is coated in a light-sensitive GELATIN and POTASSIUM bichromate (dichromate, $K_2Cr_2O_7$) solution. On exposure, the gelatin hardens most in areas of brightest light. The plate is soaked in GLYCEROL which is absorbed most in the softest areas; during printing, the plate is kept moist by a glycerol-water mixture, the glycerol-soaked areas absorbing the moisture and repelling the INK. Collotype printing is slow and the plate lacks durability (print run at most about 5 000).

COLOGNE (Köln), river port and leading industrial city in West Germany, on the Rhine R in the W of the country. Its products range from heavy machinery to toilet water (Eau de Cologne). Cologne's prosperity dates from its membership of the HANSEATIC LEAGUE. The cathedral of St. Peter (1248–1880) is its most renowned landmark. Pop 862 000.

COLOMBIA, republic in NW South America. It is the only South American country with both Pacific and Caribbean coastlines.

Land. Colombia has four major regions: the Andes; the Caribbean coastal lowlands; the Pacific coastal lowlands; and the E plains. Some 80% of the people live in the Andean region. Three *cordilleras* (mountain ranges) branch out northwards from the Pasto knot in the S, some peaks exceeding 16 000ft. BOGOTÁ, the capital and largest city, stands on a plateau at an altitude of 8 563ft. The Caribbean lowlands are drained by sluggish rivers that frequently flood, but in the dry season big herds of cattle find good grazing here. The Pacific lowlands are wet and scantily populated. The N section of the E region forms part of the South American *llanos* or tropical grasslands; the S section is equatorial rain forest containing Leticia, Colombia's only port on the Amazon R. The country's climate varies from extreme cold to humid heat according to altitude and proximity to the coast.

People. Most Colombians are Europeans or mestizos

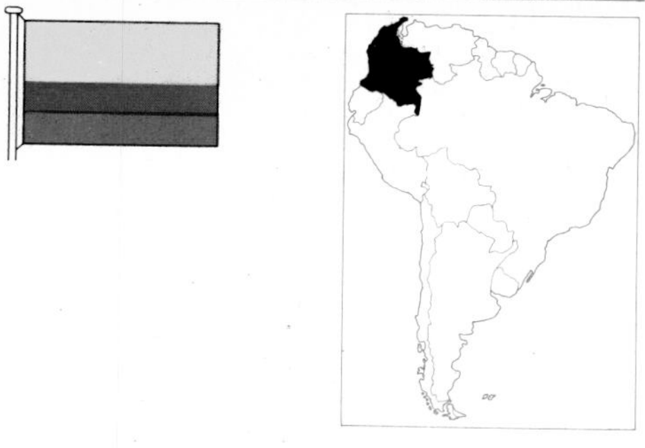

Official Name: The Republic of Colombia
Capital: Bogotá
Area: 456 535sq mi
Population: 23 210 000
Languages: Spanish
Religions: Roman Catholic
Monetary Unit(s): 1Colombian peso = 100 centavos

(of mixed European and Amerindian ancestry); there are minorities of mulattoes and Negroes. Education is free but not compulsory, and existing schools can hold only half of all eligible children. Housing conditions are locally poor.

Economy. Colombia is a major world coffee producer as well as growing other tropical crops. It is also South America's second largest producer of oil, and Colombian mines yield precious metals, coal, iron ore and rock salt. Leading industrial centers are Medellín and Bogotá. Transportation is hindered by mountain ranges, but cities are joined by road, rail or river and an advanced air network.

History. CHIBCHA INDIANS of the E Cordilleras had a highly developed culture before the Spanish arrived in the early 16th century. Spain ruled the area until independence, which followed Simón BOLÍVAR's Boyacá victory over Spanish colonial forces (1819). At the end of the 19th century thousands died in fighting between Liberals and Conservatives—Colombia's two main political parties. A system of alternating Liberal and Conservative presidents brought an uneasy peace by the 1960s.

COLOMBO, capital and largest city of Sri Lanka (Ceylon). A port on the W coast of the island, it exports tea, rubber and coconut products and imports rice, sugar, textiles and machinery. Pop 562 000.

COLOMBO PLAN, cooperative program for economic development in S and SE Asia, inaugurated in 1951 at Colombo. The first participants were members of the British Commonwealth, who were joined by the US, Japan and some SE Asian countries. A consultative committee meets annually to discuss national accomplishments and plans.

COLÓN, second-largest city of Panama, at the Atlantic end of the Panama Canal. It is a large tourist center and exports fruit through its port of Cristobal. Pop 95 308.

COLON. See GASTROINTESTINAL TRACT.

COLONIAL HEIGHTS, city in SE Va. facing Petersburg across the Appomattox R. It was incorporated in 1948. Pop 15 097.

COLONIAL NATIONAL HISTORICAL PARK, area in SE Va. containing major historic sites, notably YORKTOWN, JAMESTOWN and WILLIAMSBURG. It was founded in 1936 and covers over 9 000 acres.

COLONNA, medieval noble Roman family, enemies of the Caetani and Orsini and generally antipapalist. **Sciarra Colonna** (d. 1329), assisted the arrest of the Caetano pope, BONIFACE VIII. **Oddone Colonna** (1368–1431), became Pope MARTIN V, and richly endowed his family with land. **Vittoria Colonna** (1492–1547), was a poetess and a confidante of Michelangelo.

COLOPHON, an inscription at the end of a MS, or on the title or final page of a printed book; also a printer's or publisher's identifying device.

COLOR, the way the brain interprets the wavelength distribution of the LIGHT entering the eye. The phenomenon of color has two aspects: the physical or optical—concerned with the nature of the light—and the physiological or visual—dealing with how the eye sees color.

The light entering the eye is either emitted by or reflected from the objects we see. Hot objects emit light with wavelengths occupying a broad continuous band of the electromagnetic SPECTRUM, the position of the band depending on the temperature of the object—the hotter the object, the shorter the wavelengths emitted (see BLACKBODY RADIATION). (We tend to think of the spectrum of visible light in terms of the band of colors revealed by NEWTON when he split up a beam of sunlight using a PRISM; in these terms, the shorter the wavelength, the bluer the light.) Other objects emitting light do so either at particular wavelengths or in narrow bands of the spectrum (see SPECTROSCOPY). Where these emission bands fall within the visible spectrum, such objects appear colored, otherwise black. Objects reflecting diffuse light appear colored in virtue of combined SCATTERING and ABSORPTION effects, though the nature of the light source is also important.

The EYE can only see colors when the light is relatively bright; the rods used in poor light see only in black and white. The cones used in color VISION are of three kinds, responding to light from the red, green or blue portions of the visible spectrum. The brain adds together the responses of the different sets of cones and produces the sensation of color. The three colors to which the cones of the eye respond are known as the three primary colors of light. By mixing different proportions of these three colors, any other color can be simulated, equal intensities of all three producing white light. This is known as the production of color by addition, the effect being used in color TELEVISION tubes where PHOSPHORS glowing red, green and blue are employed. Color pigments, working by transmission or reflection, produce colors by subtraction, abstracting light from white and displaying only the remainder. Again a suitable combination of a set of three pigments—cyan (blue-green), magenta (blue-red) and yellow (the "complementary" colors of the three primaries)—can simulate most other colors, a dense mixture of all three producing black. This effect is used in color photography but in color printing an additional black pigment is commonly used.

Most colors are not found in the spectrum. These nonspectral colors can be regarded as intermediates between the spectral colors and black and white. Many schemes have been proposed for the classification and standardization of colors. The most widely used is that of Albert Henry Munsell which describes colors in terms of their hue (basic color); saturation (intensity or density), and lightness or brightness (the degree of whiteness or blackness).

COLORADO, a W central state of the US bounded on the N by Wyo. and Neb., on the E by Kan., on the S by Okla. and N.M. and on the W by Ut. It is the highest state in the US.

Colorado has three main areas. To the E, plateaus rise to meet the Rocky Mts. Denver, Colorado Springs and Pueblo, the three largest cities, are situated in the narrow Piedmont (foothills) zone between the plateaus and the mountains. Ranges of the Rocky Mts crisscross central Colorado from N to S, and include the state's highest point, Mt Elbert (14 431ft). To the W, along the Ut. border, lies a region of lower mountains and plateaus crossed by rivers flowing in deep canyons. The Colorado, South Platte, Arkansas and upper Rio Grande are the state's main rivers. The climate is largely dry and sunny; average annual rainfall is only 17in and water is scarce, restricting agriculture. Three million acres are irrigated for the cultivation of sugar beet, vegetables and fruit; another 40 000 acres provide grazing for cattle and sheep and land for dry crops such as wheat and hay.

Mining has always been important to Colorado's economy; discoveries of gold and silver were followed by zinc, oil, natural gas, molybdenum, vanadium and uranium. Manufacturing includes food processing, sugar manufacture and the production of metals, machinery and aerospace equipment. Agriculture ranks after manufacturing in value of output.

Scientific understanding of color dates from the late 1660s when Isaac Newton discovered that a beam of white light could be split up into a spectrum of pure colors using a prism.

Tourism is also important, with spectacular mountain scenery and skiing the major attractions.

Traces of an ancient Indian culture in Colorado are evident in the MESA VERDE and other cliff dwellings. In the 1500s Spanish explorers entered the territory to be followed by the French. US trappers hunting beaver and buffalo came in the early 1800s and after the LOUISIANA PURCHASE (1803), explorers like Zebulon PIKE and traders like William BENT began to open up the territory. In the MEXICAN WAR (1848) the US conquered further Colorado territory and the discovery of gold near Denver in 1858–59 brought a rush of prospectors. In 1876 Colorado became the Union's 38th state.

Now one of the nation's most prosperous regions, Colorado is still governed according to its original constitution. Governor and lieutenant governor are elected for a four-year term, and members of the Senate and House of Representatives serve four- and two-year terms respectively.

COLORADO BEETLE or potato bug, *Leptinotarsa decemlineata*, a serious insect pest of potato crops. The adult is a small yellow beetle with black stripes. The larva is orange-red. Both feed on potato leaves. In the US the beetle originally fed on buffalo burrs in the Rocky Mountains but spread eastward after potato

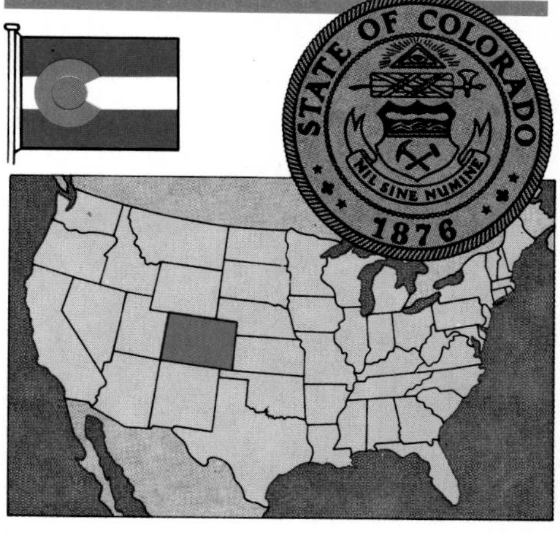

Name of state: Colorado
Capital: Denver
Statehood: Aug. 1, 1876 (38th state)
Familiar name: Centennial State
Area: 104 247sq mi
Population: 2 195 887
Elevation: Highest—14 431ft, Mount Elbert. Lowest—3 350ft, Arkansas River
Motto:: Nil Sine Numine ("Nothing without Providence")
State flower: Rocky Mountain columbine
State bird: Lark bunting
State tree: Colorado blue spruce
State song: "Where the Columbines Grow"

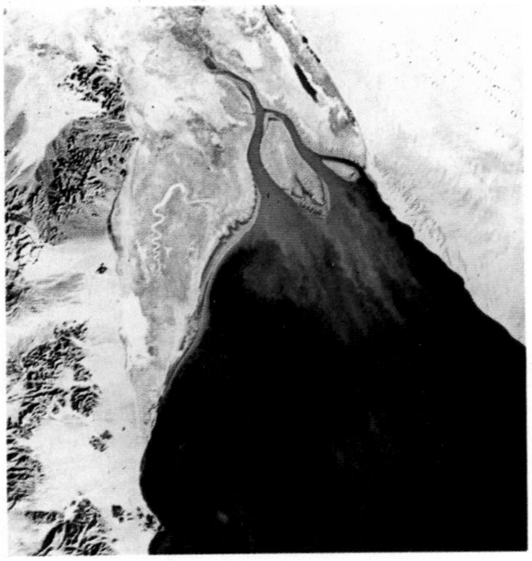

The estuary of the Colorado River in the Gulf of California, photographed by the crew of the Apollo IX spacecraft at a height of 110 miles.

cultivation arrived. The beetles can be controlled by INSECTICIDES.

COLORADO DESERT, arid area of 2000sq mi in SE Cal. Temperatures reach 125°F and rainfall averages only 4in. The area includes the SALTON SEA and the Imperial and Coachella valleys, irrigated from the Colorado R.

COLORADO NATIONAL MONUMENT, desert area in W Col. of some 17000 acres. The monument includes monoliths, canyons, prehistoric remains and a wildlife preserve. It was established in 1911.

COLORADO PLATEAU, 45000sq mi of upland covering parts of Ut., Col., N.M. and Ariz. Lightly-watered grazing land is intersected by canyons such as the GRAND CANYON of the Colorado R.

COLORADO RIVER, a major US river, rising in the Rocky Mts of N Col. and flowing 1450mi SW to enter the Gulf of Cal. Features include the GRAND CANYON and the HOOVER DAM, one of a series of dams that provide irrigation for seven states.

COLORADO SPRINGS, city in E central Col. and seat of El Paso Co. A dramatic setting under PIKES PEAK makes it a popular resort. It produces chemicals, tools and airplane parts. Colorado College and the USAF Academy are sited here. Pop 135060.

COLORATURA, elaborate ornamentation in vocal music, especially opera. The term also describes music

Part of the ruins of the gigantic Colosseum in Rome, showing the seats for spectators and the network of tunnels and chambers beneath the former floor level.

characterized by this style and singers, especially sopranos, who specialize in it.

COLOR BAR. See APARTHEID; INTEGRATION.

COLOR BLINDNESS, inability to discriminate between certain COLORS, an inherited trait. It is a disorder of the RETINA cones in the EYE. The commonest form is red-green color blindness (Daltonism), usually found in men (about 8%), the other types being rare.

COLORIMETRY, the techniques for measuring and describing the phenomena of COLOR. Since the experience of color is largely subjective and similar experiences can occur with quite different sets of physical phenomena, many different instruments (colorimeters) and criteria are employed. Of two basic approaches, one involves the visual comparison of colors (using color comparators), while the other employs the instruments and techniques of PHOTOMETRY and SPECTROSCOPY.

COLORPOINT SHORTHAIR CATS, name given by some authorities to cats which others recognize as Lynx (Tabby) Point, Red Point and Tortoiseshell Point Siamese.

COLOSSEUM, huge oval amphitheater in Rome which held 45000 spectators on several tiers of seats supported by arches. Built by the Flavian Emperor Vespasian and completed by his son, the Emperor Titus, 80 AD, it was used for gladiatorial, wild beast and other displays up to the 5th century. It has been damaged by earthquakes and its marble was quarried as building stone in the Middle Ages.

COLOSSIANS, Epistle to the, book of the New Testament written by St. Paul to the Christians of Colossae in SW Asia Minor. It resembles EPHESIANS.

COLOSSUS OF RHODES, huge bronze statue of Helios, the sun god, and one of the SEVEN WONDERS OF THE WORLD. It was made c280 BC by the Greek sculptor Chares and stood over 100ft high at Rhodes harbor (not straddling the harbor entrance as a late account claimed). An earthquake toppled the statue c224 BC; the ruin was broken up only in 653 AD.

COLOSTRUM, the first thin watery fluid secreted by the BREAST after the BIRTH of a child. Although low in FAT, it is rich in PROTEIN, including ANTIBODIES which are important in giving temporary passive IMMUNITY, notably in cattle and other ungulates.

COLT, Samuel (1814–1862), US inventor and industrialist who devised the REVOLVER, a single barreled pistol with a revolving multiple breech (bullet chamber), in the early 1830s. His factories pioneered mass-production techniques and the use of interchangeable parts.

COLTER, John (c1775–1813), US trapper and guide, the first white man to cross the Wind River Mts and Teton Range (1807), now in Yellowstone National Park. He guided the 1803 LEWIS AND CLARK EXPEDITION and other expeditions up the Missouri R.

COLTON, city in S Cal., near San Bernardino. It handles and processes fruit and makes concrete pipes. Pop 20016.

COLTRANE, John (1926–1967), leading US jazz tenor and also soprano saxophonist. He worked with Dizzy GILLESPIE, Miles DAVIS and Thelonious MONK. In his last years he experimented in free forms.

COLTSFOOT, *Tussilago forfara*, a perennial herb of the family Compositae, named for its hoof-shaped leaves (once used as a folk remedy for asthma). Coltsfoot bears pale yellow flowers on leafless stems. It is native in Eurasia and is naturalized in eastern North America.

COLUGO. See FLYING LEMUR.

COLUMBA, St. (c521–597 AD), Irish missionary to Scotland. After founding Irish monasteries at Derry and Kells, he made the island of IONA a base for the conversion of N Scotland.

COLUMBIA, city in central Mo., seat of Boone Co. It is a major Midwest educational center and the home of the U. of Mo. Pop 58804.

COLUMBIA, an industrial borough in SE Pa. Its factories produce textiles, metal and glass products. Pop 12075.

COLUMBIA, city in W central S.C.; capital and largest city of S.C. and seat of Richland Co. It produces or handles textiles, lumber and corn. It houses the U. of S.C. and five other institutions of higher education. Pop 113542.

COLUMBIA, District of. See WASHINGTON, D.C.

COLUMBIA BROADCASTING SYSTEM, INC. (CBS). See BROADCASTING NETWORKS, US.

COLUMBIA HEIGHTS, residential city in Minn., 5mi N of Minneapolis. It manufactures air compressors and hydraulic systems. Pop 23837.

COLUMBIAN EXPOSITION (World's Fair, Chicago Fair), held in Chicago in 1893 to commemorate the 400th anniversary of Columbus' landfall in America. Some 150 buildings, designed by such important architects as C. F. MCKIM and L. H. SULLIVAN, housed exhibits from 72 countries. The fair had 27 million visitors.

COLUMBIA PLATEAU, one of the world's largest lava plateaus, in the states of Wash., Ore. and Ida., between the N Rocky Mts and the Cascade Mts. The uneven surface includes plains, valleys, hills and mountain ranges and is broken by deep canyons carved by the Columbia, Snake and other rivers.

COLUMBIA RIVER, rises in the Rocky Mts of SE British Columbia, Canada. It flows 460mi to the US border and thence 745mi to the Pacific Ocean, forming the Wash.-Ore. border. The numerous dams of the Columbia basin project form one of the world's largest irrigation, hydroelectric and flood control schemes.

COLUMBIA UNIVERSITY, New York City, one of the nation's major private universities. Founded as King's College in 1754, it was renamed Columbia College in 1784 and became a university in 1896. Its schools and faculties include important research institutes for international relations and schools of journalism, business and social work. Its libraries hold valuable rare books and MS collections. It has some 20000 students.

COLUMBINE, plants of the genus *Aquilegia*, family Ronunculaceae, producing yellow, white, red or blue flowers on a slender stem. They are cultivated and found wild in the US, mainly in the Rocky Mts.

COLUMBITE, lustrous black OXIDE mineral of iron, manganese and niobium [$(Fe,Mn)Nb_2O_6$], the chief ore of NIOBIUM, found mainly in W Australia, Zaire, Madagascar and S. D. TANTALUM replaces niobium in all proportions up to 100% (tantalite). Columbite crystallizes in the orthorhombic system.

COLUMBIUM, former name of NIOBIUM, especially in the US.

COLUMBUS, city in W Ga., seat of Muscogee Co. and Ga.'s second largest city. It is a textile center and also serves a farming area. Educational institutions include Columbus College. Pop 155028.

COLUMBUS, city in central Ind., seat of Bartholomew Co. It makes diesel engines, furniture and leather. Pop 27141.

COLUMBUS, city in E Miss., seat of Lowndes Co. It is an agricultural center; industries include lumber and automobile parts. Pop 25795.

COLUMBUS, city in E Neb., seat of Platte Co., and headquarters of the Loup River Public Power Project. Pop 15741.

COLUMBUS, city in central Ohio, the state's capital and second-largest city, and the seat of Franklin Co. Major industries include the manufacture of plastics, aircraft components and automobile parts. Columbus has Ohio State U., other higher education centers, a fine museum, an art gallery and a symphony orchestra. Pop 540025.

COLUMBUS, Christopher (1451–1506), Genoese explorer generally credited with the discovery of America. An experienced navigator, he hoped to sail W across the Atlantic to pioneer a new short route to the spice-rich East Indies (formerly reached by sailing E). Columbus failed to win Portuguese backing but Queen Isabella and King Ferdinand of Spain eventually agreed to finance the voyage.

On Aug. 3, 1492, Columbus, commanding the *Santa María* and accompanied by the *Niña* and *Pinta*, sailed from SW Spain for the Canary Islands. On Sept. 6 he set out due W and on Oct. 12 landed on Watling Island, in the Bahamas. After discovering Cuba and Hispaniola, he returned to Spain where he was created an admiral and governor of the new lands discovered and to be discovered.

Columbus made three further voyages to the New

World. On Oct. 1493 he left Spain with 17 ships, planning to set up trading posts and colonies and carrying hundreds of colonists. He colonized Hispaniola, discovered Puerto Rico, Jamaica, the Virgin Islands and some of the Lesser Antilles and explored the S coast of Cuba. On his third voyage, 1498, he sighted South America and discovered Trinidad. But the Hispaniola colonists' discontent with living conditions threatened to break into revolt. Complaints against Columbus reached Spain, disorders continued, and Francisco de Bobadilla was sent out to replace him as governor. Columbus was sent back to Spain in disgrace. His fourth and last voyage (1502–04) was again intended to find the elusive route to the East Indies. Instead he came upon the Central American coast at Honduras and followed it E and S to Panama. Columbus died two years after his last journey, poverty-stricken and almost forgotten.

COLUMBUS DAY, Oct. 12, the anniversary of COLUMBUS' arrival in the New World in 1492. It is observed as a holiday in the US and in parts of Latin America and Canada.

COLUMN, in architecture, slim vertical structural support, usually cylindrical, consisting of a base, shaft and a capital. Columns support the ENTABLATURE on which the roof rests. A row of columns forms a colonnade. Widely used in early architecture, columns were characteristic of Egyptian temples and of classical Greek architecture. The three main Greek forms were the Doric, Ionic and Corinthian orders (see CLASSICAL ORDERS).

COLUMNEA, a genus of tender, evergreen, epiphytic sub-shrubs and climbers, several species of which are popularly grown as house plants for their showy hooded, red, orange or yellow flowers and green, reddish or brownish foliage. To flower, they require a few hours of direct sunlight each day and do not tolerate temperatures below 13°C (55°F). The soil should be kept evenly moist. Plants are usually propagated by shoot tip cuttings. Family: Gesnariaceae.

COLVILLE RIVER, river in N Alaska, some 375mi long. It rises on the N flank of the Brooks Range, flows E, then turns N to the Beaufort Sea.

COMA, state of unconsciousness in which a person cannot be roused by sensory stimulation and is unaware of his surroundings. Body functions continue but may be impaired, depending on the cause. These include POISONING, head injury, DIABETES, and BRAIN diseases, including STROKES and CONVULSIONS. Severe malfunction of LUNGS, LIVER or KIDNEYS may lead to coma.

COMA, in optics. See LENS.

COMANCHE, North American Indians, closely related to the SHOSHONE INDIANS. Brilliant horsemen and fierce warriors, they were dominant among the S Great Plains peoples, warring as far afield as Mexico. They stubbornly defended the buffalo hunting grounds against white incursions until the 1870s. Some 3000 Comanche still live in W Okla.

COMBINATIONS. See PERMUTATIONS AND COMBINATIONS.

COMBINATORIAL ANALYSIS, the branch of mathematics dealing with subdivisions of sets (see SET THEORY): its primary concerns are PERMUTATIONS AND COMBINATIONS and partitions. A **partition** of a number n is its expression in the form of a SUM of positive INTEGERS: i.e., setting

$$n=a_1+a_2+\ldots+a_m.$$

For example, the number 5 has 7 partitions: (1+1+1+1+1), (2+1+1+1), (2+2+1), (3+1+1), (3+2), (4+1) and (5). By extension, **combinatorial topology** is the study of complex forms in terms of their being built up from combinations of basic geometric figures. (See TOPOLOGY.)

COMBINE HARVESTER, machine which cuts, threshes and winnows a crop as it moves over a field. Modern models cut a swathe up to 20ft wide. Most kinds of grain can be harvested in this manner, also soybeans and legumes. Heads of grain pass by conveyor from cutter bar to threshing unit, then sieves and an air blast separate the grain from the chaff. Combines were developed in Mich. in the 1830s, but became widespread only in the 1930s. Self-powered models were introduced in the 1940s.

COMBING. See CARDING.

COMB JELLIES. See CTENOPHORES.

COMBUSTION, or **burning**, the rapid OXIDATION of FUEL in which heat and usually light are produced. In slow combustion (e.g., a glowing charcoal fire) the reaction may be heterogeneous, the solid fuel reacting directly with gaseous oxygen; more commonly, the fuel is first volatilized, and combustion occurs in the gas phase (a flame is such a combustion zone, its luminance being due to excited particles, molecules and ions). In the 17th and 18th centuries combustion was explained by the PHLOGISTON theory, until LAVOISIER showed it to be due to combination with oxygen in the air. In fact the oxidizing agent need not be oxygen: it may be another oxidizing gas such as nitric oxide or fluorine, or oxygen-containing solids or liquids such as nitric acid (used in rocket fuels). If the fuel and oxidant are premixed, as in a BUNSEN BURNER, the combustion is more efficient, and little or no SOOT is produced. Very rapid combustion occurs in an explosion (see EXPLOSIVES), when more heat is liberated than can be dissipated, or when a branched chain reaction occurs (see FREE RADICALS). Each combustion reaction has its own ignition temperature below which it cannot take place, e.g. c400°C for coal. Spontaneous combustion occurs if slow oxidation in large piles of such materials as coal or oily rags raises the temperature to the ignition point. (See also INTERNAL-COMBUSTION ENGINE.)

COMECON, Council for Mutual Economic Assistance (CMEA), set up in 1949 by the USSR and E European communist countries. Mongolia and Cuba joined later. The nine member countries cooperate in the areas of trade, finance, currency and industry.

COMEDY, literary work which aims primarily to amuse, often using ridicule, exaggeration or criticism of human nature and institutions, and usually ending happily. One of the two main traditional categories of drama (see also TRAGEDY), comedy also describes nondramatic art forms.

Comedy evolved in ancient Greece from the festivals of DIONYSUS and from the SATYR PLAYS, and developed in the satiric plays of ARISTOPHANES. It then became more consciously literary, employing stock characters and situations, as in the works of MENANDER, who was later imitated by the Roman poets PLAUTUS and TERENCE. Classical comedy elements survived the Middle Ages in folk plays and festivals. Roman comedies were revived in the Renaissance and influenced Italian COMMEDIA DELL'ARTE and the comedies of Spain's Lope de VEGA and the Elizabethans Ben JONSON and SHAKESPEARE. In 17th-century France MOLIÈRE wrote comic and satiric drama; the COMEDY OF MANNERS stemmed from his work and influenced CONGREVE and other writers of RESTORATION COMEDY. In the 18th century SHERIDAN and GOLDSMITH and Italy's Carlo GOLDONI wrote satiric, witty and more realistic comedies. From the 19th century onwards, outstanding writers of comedy included Oscar WILDE, who wrote English drawing-room comedies; G. B. SHAW, who wrote unique comedies of ideas; James BARRIE, who wrote romantic comedies; J. M. SYNGE and Sean O'CASEY, who wrote native Irish comedy; Noel COWARD, who wrote witty farces; and George S. KAUFMAN and

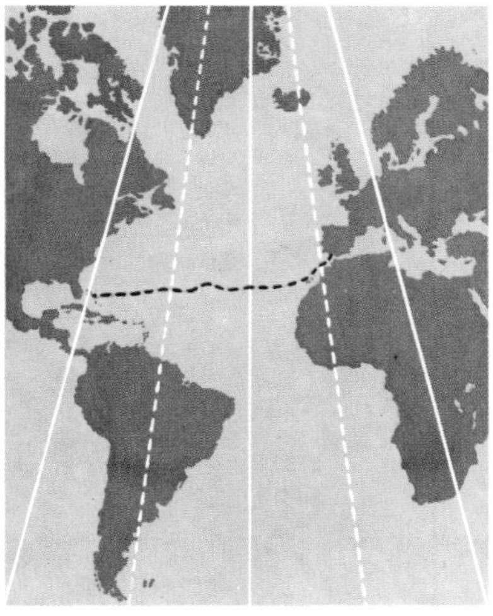

A

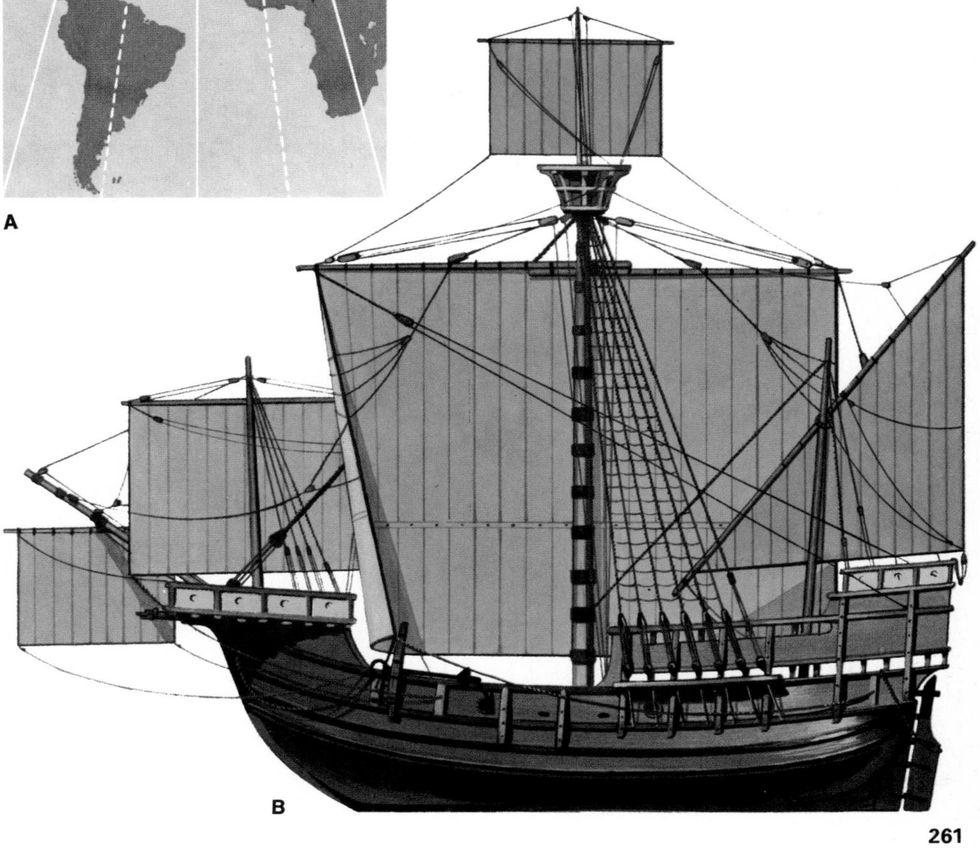

B

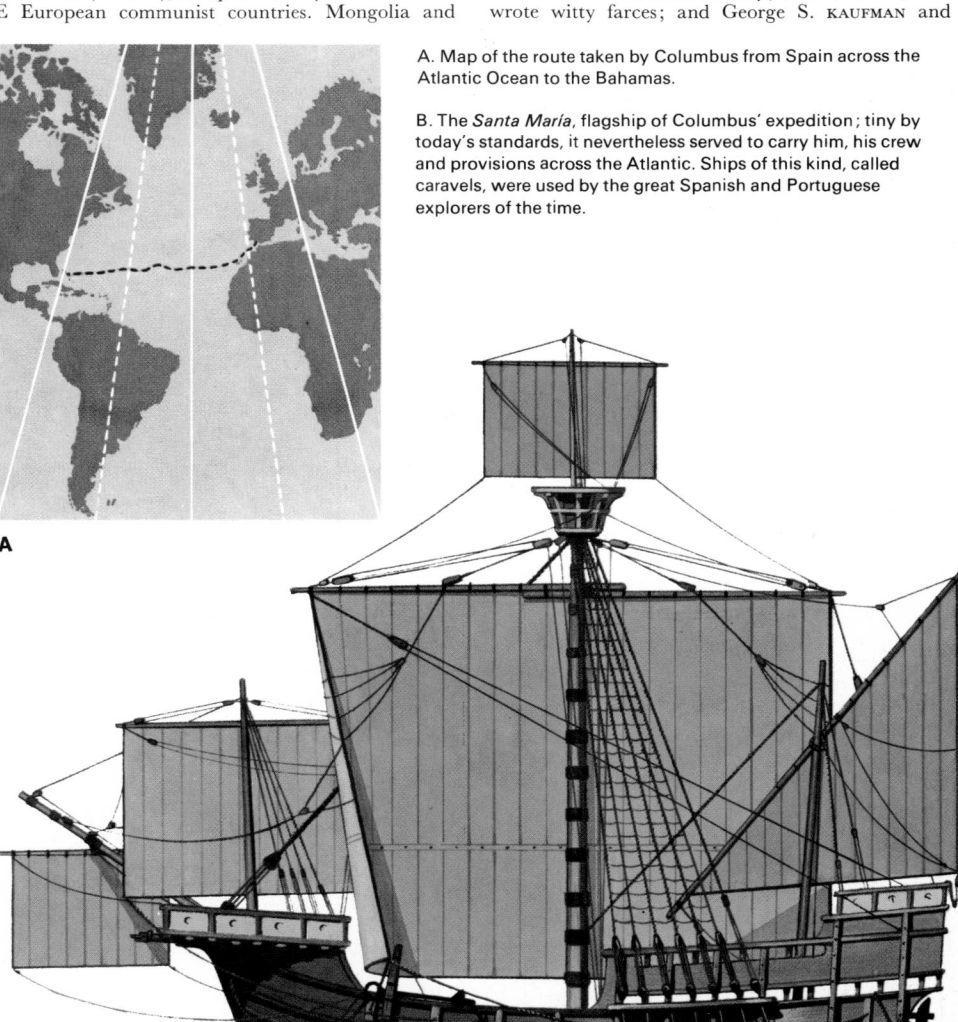

A. Map of the route taken by Columbus from Spain across the Atlantic Ocean to the Bahamas.

B. The *Santa María*, flagship of Columbus' expedition; tiny by today's standards, it nevertheless served to carry him, his crew and provisions across the Atlantic. Ships of this kind, called caravels, were used by the great Spanish and Portuguese explorers of the time.

Thornton WILDER, who both combined modern humor with serious social commentary. (See also BURLESQUE; FARCE; SATIRE.)

COMEDY OF HUMORS, type of satiric comic drama such as *Every Man In His Humour* (1598) by Ben JONSON. The characters display exaggerated qualities of one of the four HUMORS.

COMEDY OF MANNERS, comedy which ridicules the manners and fashions of a particular social class or set. Witty, artificial and often licentious, it originated in the work of MOLIÈRE, but the term usually applies to English RESTORATION COMEDY such as CONGREVE's *The Way of the World* (1700).

COMENIUS (Jan Amos Komenský); 1592–1670), Czech educational reformer and theologian; last bishop of the old MORAVIAN CHURCH. He advocated universal education, teaching in the vernacular and Latin as a common language. His most famous books are *The Great Didactic* (1628–32) and *The Visible World* (1658–59).

COMET, a nebulous body which orbits the sun. In general, comets can be seen only when they are comparatively close to the sun, though the time between their first appearance and their final disappearance may be as much as years. As they approach the sun, a few comets develop tails (some comets develop more than one tail) of lengths of the order 1–100Gm, though at least one tail 300Gm in length—more than twice the distance from the earth to the sun—has been recorded. The tails of comets are always pointed away from the sun, so that, as the comet recedes into space, its tail precedes it. For this reason it is generally accepted that comets' tails are caused by the SOLAR WIND.

The head of the comet is known as the nucleus. Nuclei may be as little as 100m or as much as 100km in radius, and are thought to be composed primarily of frozen gases and ice mixed with smaller quantities of meteoritic material. Most of the mass of a comet is contained within the nucleus, though this may be less than 0.000001 that of the earth. Surrounding the nucleus is the bright coma, possibly as much as 100Mm in radius, which is composed of gas and possibly small particles erupting from the nucleus.

Cometary orbits are usually very eccentric ellipses, with some perihelions (see ORBIT) closer to the sun than that of MERCURY, aphelions as much as 100 000 AU from the sun. The orbits of some comets take the form of hyperbolas, and it is thought that these have their origins altogether outside the SOLAR SYSTEM, that they are interstellar travelers.

In Greco-Roman times it was generally believed that comets were phenomena restricted to the upper atmosphere of the earth. In the late 15th and 16th centuries it was shown by M. Mästlin and BRAHE that comets were far more distant than the moon. NEWTON interpreted the orbits of the comets as parabolas, deducing that each comet was appearing for the first time. It was not until the late 17th century that HALLEY showed that at least some comets returned periodically.

COMICS, cartoon drawings in a single panel or series of panels (strips), with consistent characters—involved in brief incidents or continuous stories. Captions or dialogue are often set in "balloons." The concept originated with satirical cartoons (18th–19th centuries), but developed in 20th-century America as a device to increase newspaper circulation. Early successes were *The Yellow Kid* (1895) and *The Katzenjammer Kids* (1897), while the 1970s' most popular comic was Charles M. Schulz's *Peanuts*. Comics range from humor or farce to adventure, crime and horror stories, science fiction, classics and satire and social criticism.

COMINES, or **Commynes, Philippe de** (c1447–1511), French historian and diplomat; adviser to Louis XI. His *Mémoires* (1524) acutely analyzed the characters of contemporary monarchs.

COMINFORM, Communist Information Bureau, an organization set up in 1947 to create unity among and assert Soviet influence over communist countries. Membership was limited to representatives of the communist parties of the USSR, its E European satellites, and France and Italy. Khrushchev disbanded the Cominform in 1956.

COMINTERN. See INTERNATIONAL, THE.

COMITIA, elective and legislative assemblies of the ancient Romans. The *comitia centuriata* elected CONSULS and PRAETORS; the *comitia curiata* ratified wills and adoptions; the *comitia tributa* elected minor magistrates and enacted laws.

COMMACK, urban community in SE N.Y., on central Long Island. Pop 22 507.

COMMAGER, Henry Steele (1902–), US historian who widely influenced the study of American history. His works include the standard textbook, *The Growth of the American Republic* (1930, with MORISON), and *The American Mind* (1950).

COMMANDO, military unit specializing in raids into enemy territory, and in hand-to-hand and night fighting. The British army took the name from Boer units in South Africa, and formed commando battalions which played an important role in liberating Europe in WWII. Commandos are now part of the British Royal Marines. US army RANGERS were modeled on British units.

COMMEDIA DELL'ARTE, form of Italian COMEDY which originated in the Middle Ages and flourished in the 16th–18th centuries. Traveling professional actors (often wearing masks) improvised action and dialogue around outline plots with stock characters. The *commedia* spread through Europe and had a lasting influence on the theater.

COMMENSALISM, form of SYMBIOSIS in which one organism—the commensal—benefits from the partnership while the other neither gains nor loses. The commensal often gets shelter, transport and food from its host. (See also EPIPHYTE.)

Picture of the comet Humason, discovered in 1961 when it was visible as a bright star in the Southern Hemisphere. The diagonal bars are due to the apparent motion of stars during the exposure.

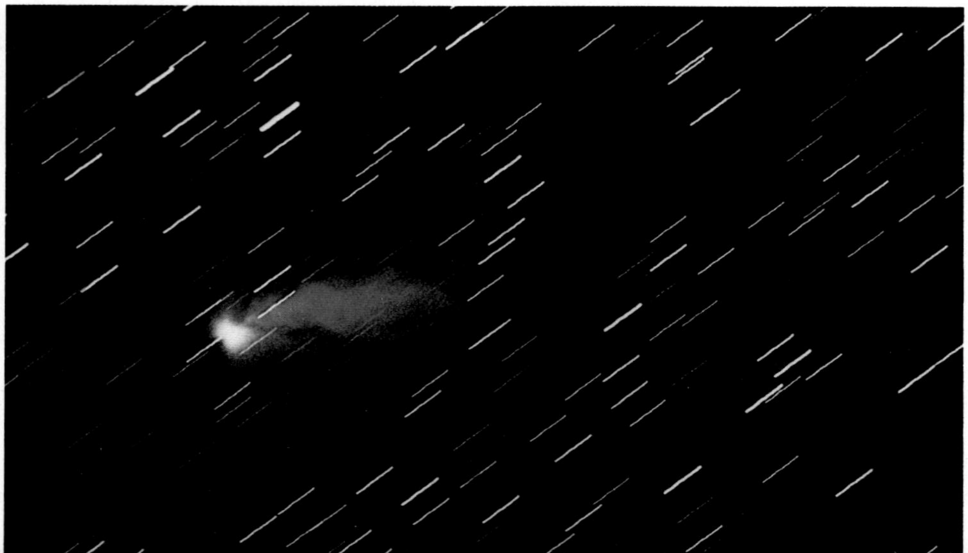

COMMERCE, city in SW Cal., 4mi SE of downtown Los Angeles. A suburban and industrial area. Pop 10 536.

COMMERCE, Chambers of. See CHAMBERS OF COMMERCE.

COMMERCE, US Department of, the executive department of the government responsible for fostering and regulating domestic and foreign commerce. Its present name dates from 1913. The secretary of commerce, a member of the cabinet appointed by the president as chief adviser on federal policies affecting trade and industry, is aided by an under secretary and five assistant secretaries. The department operates the MARITIME ADMINISTRATION, Office of Business Economics, Economic Development Administration, BUREAU OF INTERNATIONAL COMMERCE, National Oceanic and Atmospheric Administration, Office of Telecommunications, BUREAU OF THE CENSUS, NATIONAL BUREAU OF STANDARDS, PATENT OFFICE, and Office of Equal Opportunity, among others.

COMMERCE TOWN, city in NE central Col., NE of Denver. Pop 17 407.

COMMERCIAL ART, art which helps sell a product, service or point of view; also "advertising art." It involves design, drawing and type matter in advertisements and illustrations for books, magazines and newspapers, posters and packages, display and exhibition material, television and films. Commercial artists need a wide knowledge of art techniques and reproduction methods. (See also ADVERTISING; GRAPHIC ARTS.)

COMMERCIAL LAW, body of law governing commercial transactions and commercial organizations. Transactions are governed largely by the law of CONTRACTS dealing with the negotiation, breach and performance of legally enforceable business agreements. The laws governing commercial organizations lay down the legal forms in which business bodies may be constituted, such as the incorporation of companies. The law of AGENCY, making it possible for a person or corporation to transact business through employees, is important in this area.

Commercial law is as old as large-scale trade, but it expanded and consolidated after the Middle Ages. English mercantile law was gradually incorporated into the COMMON LAW and so inherited by the US, where it grew with the expansion of interstate trade in the 19th century, necessitating uniform legislation. Many states have adopted the Uniform Commercial Code of 1952 in an attempt to systematize national practice.

COMMISSAR, USSR Communist Party people's representative on a local or regional level; also a minister of state. In 1946 STALIN replaced the commissars by the Soviet council of ministers. From 1917 to 1920 commissars were Bolshevik (see BOLSHEVISM) political agents attached to military units.

COMMITTEE OF PUBLIC SAFETY, committee elected by the Convention in April 1793 during the FRENCH REVOLUTION to enforce revolutionary law and govern the country. Under ROBESPIERRE's leadership, the committee used its despotic power to crush "counter revolution" (see also REIGN OF TERROR).

COMMITTEES, Legislative, bodies composed of members of legislative assemblies, intended to expedite lawmaking by providing expert and considered advice and by giving continuous attention to complex issues in a restricted field. A typical legislature has committees which consider problems of finance, labor, agriculture and so on with the help of professional experts. There are three principal kinds of committee: the **standing committee**, a permanent group with changing membership, which gives preliminary and day-to-day consideration to problems within a broad field, e.g., foreign relations; the **temporary** or **select committee**, created to investigate a single issue; and the **committee of the whole**, the name given to an entire legislative assembly when it considers a matter using the committee approach rather than purely formal debate.

The committee system of the US Congress typifies the way committee systems operate. The Senate has

15 standing committees, the House of Representatives 19. Each member of Congress serves on at least one committee. Each committee is headed by an influential chairman, who is usually a senior member of the majority political party. The committees hear expert witnesses, debate issues and frame final bills for consideration by the whole house.

COMMITTEES OF CORRESPONDENCE, groups set up by colonies and towns before and during the American Revolution to spread anti-British propaganda. As the rift with Britain grew, the committees served as agents of state legislatures and acted as revolutionary governments; their role was taken over by the COMMITTEES OF SAFETY.

COMMITTEES OF SAFETY, bodies appointed by the American colonies' assemblies to carry on certain government business during the Revolution. They performed the role of the executive branch of government between 1775 and about 1777.

COMMODITY MARKET, a formal market for dealings in raw materials and foods. Such exchanges trade simultaneously in present and future supplies, thus minimizing price variations caused by supply fluctuation and reducing the risks to traders. Coffee, tobacco, cotton, grain, livestock and metals are some of the commodities sold in this way. The largest commodity markets are in Chicago, New York City, and London. Their prices largely determine world prices. (See also FUTURES MARKET.)

COMMODUS, Lucius Aelius Aurelius (161–192 AD), Roman emperor 180–92. The son of MARCUS AURELIUS, Commodus' reign was marked by barbarian threats, economic decline, public discontent and his own insanity. He was assassinated on his mistress' instigation.

COMMON LAW, body of law based upon custom and the established precedent of court decisions. Developed in England since early medieval times, it is the basis of the law of many other countries today, including the US. In late Anglo-Saxon and early Norman England, the growth of centralized government created a law common to all areas, administered by royal justices. Henry II and Edward I (12th–13th centuries) strengthened the law, laying the foundations of many modern practices and principles. Common law gradually absorbed much of English mercantile, sea and CANON LAW. By the 15th century, however, adherence to outdated, narrow and unsuitable legal formalities created many injustices. The lord chancellor, therefore, on behalf of the king, set up a court to "restore the equity" between parties involved in such situations. This created the modern body of EQUITY law, in which such concepts as TRUST and MORTGAGE are based.

At the same time, the custom of relying on precedents—preceding decisions—was becoming a firm principle, to be modified only by statute or a higher court. This contrasted with the CIVIL LAW system, derived from Roman law, which was popular in Europe. In this, the main legal rules are embodied in a central code such as the CODE NAPOLÉON, which courts theoretically apply without references to previous decisions. However, civil law often relies on precedent, just as many common law rules are codified by statute for convenience. Common law spread throughout the British colonies. It was generally adopted in the US, although La. state law is based upon the Code Napoléon and other states have partially codified systems.

COMMON MARKET, European, officially the European Economic Community (EEC), an economic union of W European nations. The Common Market grew out of the chaos created in Europe by WWII. W European nations sought new forms of cooperation in order to revive their war-damaged economies. The first step was the foundation of the EUROPEAN COAL AND STEEL COMMUNITY, set up in 1952 by the six future members of the EEC. The TREATY OF ROME creating the EEC was signed in 1957 by West Germany, France, Italy, Belgium, the Netherlands and Luxembourg. In 1973 "The Six" were joined by Great Britain, Ireland and Denmark.

The market's aims are to eliminate tariffs between member countries, to develop common policies for agriculture, free movement of labor, social welfare, transport and foreign trade, and to abolish trusts and cartels. The union is thus partly political, and many politicians see the Common Market developing into a United States of Europe, with economic and political power to rival that of the USSR or the US. The structure of the EEC includes an executive commission, the European Parliament and the Court of Justice. (See also EUROPEAN FREE TRADE ASSOCIATION.)

COMMON PRAYER. See BOOK OF COMMON PRAYER.

COMMONS, House of. See HOUSE OF COMMONS.

COMMONS, John Rogers (1862–1945), US labor economist and historian. He founded the U. of Wisconsin School of History and helped draft the exemplary reform legislation of the state of Wis.

COMMON SENSE SCHOOL, in philosophy, a group of Scottish thinkers, including Thomas REID and Dugald STEWART, who, reacting against the idealism of BERKELEY and the skepticism of HUME, affirmed that the truths apparent to the common man—the existence of material objects, the reality of CAUSALITY, and so on—were genuine, reliable and not to be questioned.

COMMONWEALTH, form of government based on the consent of the people ("common weal" means common well-being). In the US, the states of Mass., Pa., Va. and Ky. are known as commonwealths. Various nations are associated with Britain in the COMMONWEALTH OF NATIONS; and the federated states of Australia form the Commonwealth of Australia. In English history, the Commonwealth was a period of republican rule (1649–60).

COMMONWEALTH FUND, philanthropic fund for the welfare of mankind, set up in 1918 by Mrs. Stephen V. HARKNESS, with headquarters in New York City. It assists medical education, community health and international understanding. US fellowships are given to students from the British Commonwealth and W Europe.

COMMONWEALTH OF NATIONS, free association of Britain and over 30 former colonies, now independent states, and their dependencies. It is not governed by a constitution or specific treaty; member countries are linked by a common heritage and economic and cultural interests and recognize the British sovereign as symbolic head of the Commonwealth. Commonwealth prime ministers and other officials meet at periodic conferences and exchange views on international economic and political affairs of mutual interest. Member nations range in size from Canada, Australia and India to tiny Tonga and Fiji. Membership tends to increase as more British colonies gain independence and opt to join. Burma chose to remain outside the Commonwealth; Ireland, South Africa and Pakistan have withdrawn.

COMMUNE, cooperative community formed for ideological, political or religious reasons. The self-governing towns of medieval Europe were known as communes; the term is also used of the period's religious communities, and of those in 17th-century America. In the 19th century, with the growth of Utopian socialism, a number of experimental communes were established, notably NEW HARMONY and BROOK FARM in the US. The farm collective of China is a form of commune, as is the Israeli KIBBUTZ.

Map of the Common Market showing the member countries. The union, which is intended to be political as well as economic, grew out of attempts to end postwar chaos.

COMMUNE OF PARIS. See PARIS COMMUNE.

COMMUNICABLE DISEASES. See DISEASE.

COMMUNION, Holy (Lord's Supper, Eucharist), the SACRAMENT of the body and blood of Jesus Christ received by eating and drinking consecrated bread and wine, as at the LAST SUPPER. Whether this receiving is physical or only virtual has been much disputed (see TRANSUBSTANTIATION). Nonconformists, following ZWINGLI, see Holy Communion as merely a symbolic memorial. The manner in which it is a SACRIFICE, if at all, is equally controversial. In Holy Communion, the central act of all Christian worship, the Church celebrates the ATONEMENT made by Christ as the basis of its common life and faith. (See also CONFIRMATION; MASS.)

COMMUNISM, political doctrine based on the writings of Karl MARX and Friedrich ENGELS, developed along a number of different lines during the course of the 20th century by various communist states and parties throughout the world. The term

Title page and first page of the Communist Manifesto, written by Karl Marx and Friedrich Engels and published in London in 1848. It sought to show that the inevitable outcome of history would be the perpetual dominance of the working classes.

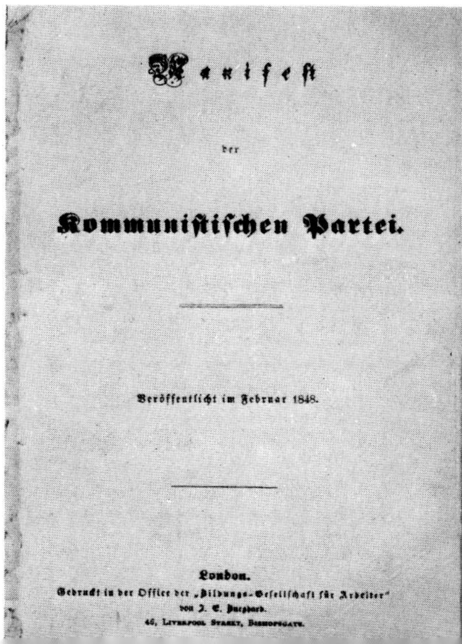

Manifest

der

Kommunistischen Partei.

Veröffentlicht im Februar 1848.

London.

Gedruckt in der Office der „Bildungs-Gesellschaft für Arbeiter"

von J. E. Burghard.

46, Liverpool Street, Bishopsgate.

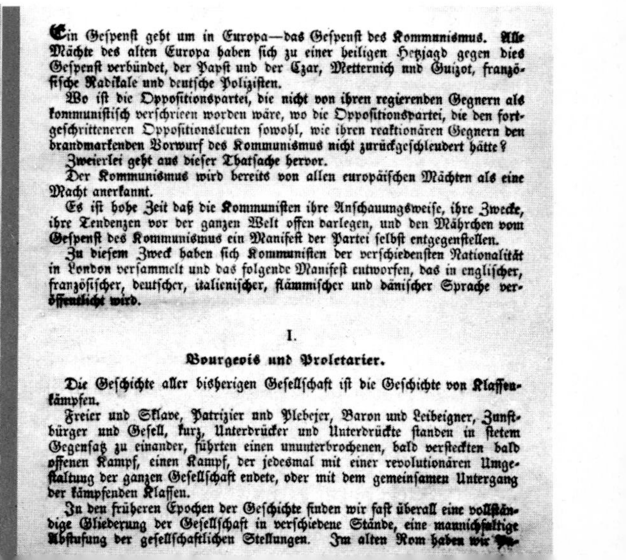

Ein Gespenst geht um in Europa—das Gespenst des Kommunismus. Alle Mächte des alten Europa haben sich zu einer heiligen Hetzjagd gegen dies Gespenst verbündet, der Papst und der Czar, Metternich und Guizot, französische Radikale und deutsche Polizisten.

Wo ist die Oppositionspartei, die nicht von ihren regierenden Gegnern als kommunistisch verschrieen worden wäre, wo die Oppositionspartei, die den fortgeschritteneren Oppositionsleuten sowohl, wie ihren reaktionären Gegnern den brandmarkenden Vorwurf des Kommunismus nicht zurückgeschleudert hätte?

Zweierlei geht aus dieser Thatsache hervor.

Der Kommunismus wird bereits von allen europäischen Mächten als eine Macht anerkannt.

Es ist hohe Zeit daß die Kommunisten ihre Anschauungsweise, ihre Zwecke, ihre Tendenzen vor der ganzen Welt offen darlegen, und den Mährchen vom Gespenst des Kommunismus ein Manifest der Partei selbst entgegenstellen.

Zu diesem Zweck haben sich Kommunisten der verschiedensten Nationalität in London versammelt und das folgende Manifest entworfen, das in englischer, französischer, deutscher, italienischer, flämmischer und dänischer Sprache veröffentlicht wird.

I.

Bourgeois und Proletarier.

Die Geschichte aller bisherigen Gesellschaft ist die Geschichte von Klassenkämpfen.

Freier und Sklave, Patrizier und Plebejer, Baron und Leibeigner, Zunftbürger und Gesell, kurz, Unterdrücker und Unterdrückte standen in stetem Gegensatz zu einander, führten einen ununterbrochenen, bald versteckten bald offenen Kampf, einen Kampf, der jedesmal mit einer revolutionären Umgestaltung der ganzen Gesellschaft endete, oder mit dem gemeinsamen Untergang der kämpfenden Klassen.

In den früheren Epochen der Geschichte finden wir fast überall eine vollständige Gliederung der Gesellschaft in verschiedene Stände, eine mannichfaltige Abstufung der gesellschaftlichen Stellungen. Im alten Rom haben wir Pa-

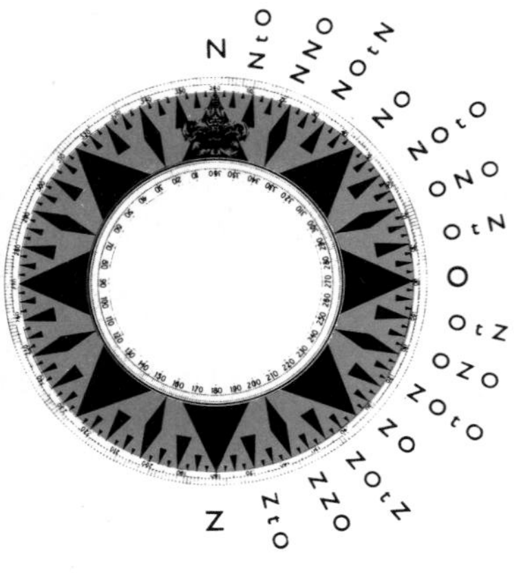

(*Left*) A compass card with 17 of the 32 traditional "points of the compass" labeled. Today the graduations dividing the card into 360° are of much greater importance than the compass points. In this card the inner graduations are labeled with reversed numerals for use with an optical system allowing the direct sighting of an object onto the card. (*Right*) Schematic representation of the earth's magnetic field, the continuous red lines indicating the magnetic meridians with which magnetic compasses align. The broken red lines represent the return field lines through the center of the earth from the north to the south magnetic poles. (The terrestrial north magnetic pole is, of course, a south-seeking magnetic pole, since it attracts compass north-seeking poles toward it.) The black vertical line indicates the earth's axis of rotation.

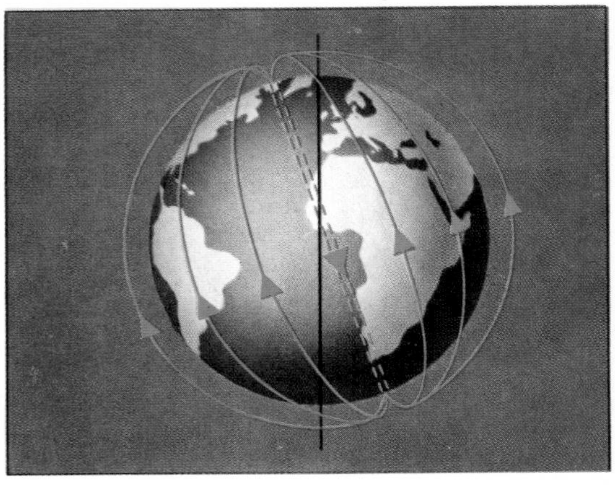

communism was originally used of communities, generally small and short-lived, whose members enjoyed common ownership of all property and material provision for all according to need. All communist parties share the general belief that a state-run economy is superior to private enterprise and that land should be organized for communal cultivation.

Marx and Engels saw communism as an advanced stage of SOCIALISM and the term first acquired its modern associations with the appearance of their COMMUNIST MANIFESTO in 1848 (see MARXISM). The RUSSIAN REVOLUTION (1917) was the world's first successful communist revolution. It was led by LENIN, who had built upon 19th-century revolutionary POPULISM to create a disciplined Marxist movement (see BOLSHEVISM). Russia became the center of world communism.

The Comintern or Third INTERNATIONAL was founded in Moscow in 1919. It was to have been the spearhead of the world revolution which many saw as imminent. However, by March 1921 discontent at home and opposition to communism by European socialist parties forced Lenin to draw in his horns. He introduced the New Economic Policy, a compromise policy which meant a "temporary" abandoning of the world revolution and in time proved the seed of schism between right and left. On Lenin's death (1924), this schism broke out in the form of a power struggle between STALIN, whose priority was to strengthen socialism within Russia, and the internationalist TROTSKY. It was the first great rift in the world communist movement.

Stalin's repressive policies produced further rifts, such as that between Yugoslavia and the USSR, throughout the European communist bloc as well as among communist parties in non-communist countries. The 1968 Soviet invasion of Czechoslovakia had much the same result. The second great schism in world communism came after the success in 1949 of the Chinese Revolution, under the leadership of MAO TSE-TUNG.

Communism differs from what is in the West generally called socialism in its adherence to the doctrine of revolution. Movements such as that in Chile led by Salvador ALLENDE and the advances made in the last 10 years by the Italian Communist Party indicate the difficulties involved in making democratic progress towards communism. (See also COLD WAR.)

COMMUNIST MANIFESTO, credo of the early communist movement, by Karl MARX and Friedrich ENGELS. It explains how violent revolution, led by the exploited PROLETARIAT, will inevitably overthrow CAPITALISM. The manifesto was originally published in German, in 1848. (See also COMMUNISM.)

COMMUNIST PARTY, US, American political organization devoted to the ideals of COMMUNISM. Two parties, the Communist Labor Party and the Communist Party of America, emerged in 1919. They were united in 1921 and by 1925 were known as the Workers Party. In 1929 the party was renamed the Communist Party of the US, under the leadership of William Z. FOSTER. It became the leading revolutionary organization in the US, though post-depression economic recovery and the Nazi–Soviet pact of 1939 greatly reduced its appeal (see also BROWDER, EARL RUSSELL). With the end of WWII and the onset of the COLD WAR, anti-communist legislation, for example the TAFT-HARTLEY ACT (1947), increased (see also McCARTHYISM). The party was virtually outlawed in 1954 but in 1966 it resumed open activity.

COMMUNITY CHEST, organization coordinating fund raising by different groups to help voluntary and welfare agencies. This method of financing charities originated in Liverpool, England, in 1873.

COMMUNITY PROPERTY, under the laws of some US states, property owned jointly by husband and wife. This is broadly defined as property received through the efforts of either or both, and generally does not apply to gifts, legacies or property owned before the marriage. In case of death or divorce it must be equally divided; only one's own half may be disposed of by will.

COMMUTATIVE LAW. See ALGEBRA.

COMMYNES, Philippe de. See COMINES, PHILIPPE DE.

COMNENA, Anna. See ANNA COMNENA.

COMO, Lake, mountain lake in N Italy, N of Milan. It covers 56sq mi and has a maximum depth of 1 345ft. Many resorts border the lake, among them Bellagio and Varenna.

COMORIN, Cape, headland in Tamil Nadu state, and the southernmost point in India. The temple of Kanya Kumari is a famous place of pilgrimage.

COMORO ISLANDS, group of volcanic islands off E Africa, in the Mozambique Channel. The islands, declared a French overseas territory in 1947, were granted internal autonomy in 1960, independence in December 1975. Their products include copra, sisal, sugar and vanilla. The capital is Moroni. Pop 290 000.

COMPACT THEORY. See SOCIAL CONTRACT.

COMPASS, device for determining direction parallel to the earth's surface. Most compasses make use of the EARTH's magnetic field (see GEOMAGNETISM); if a bar magnet (see MAGNETISM) is pivoted at its center so that it is free to rotate horizontally, it will seek to align itself with the horizontal component in its locality of the earth's magnetic field. A simple compass consists of a magnet so arranged and a compass card marked with the four cardinal points and graduated in degrees (see ANGLE). In ship compasses, to compensate for rolling, the card is attached to the magnet and floated or suspended in a liquid, usually alcohol. Aircraft compasses often incorporate a GYROSCOPE to keep the compass horizontal. The two main errors in all magnetic compasses are **variation** (the angle between lines of geographic longitude and the local horizontal component of the earth's magnetic field) and **deviation** (local, artificial magnetic effects, such as nearby electrical equipment). Both vary with the siting of the compass, and may be with more or less difficulty compensated for. (See also GYROCOMPASS; NAVIGATION.) A **radio compass**, used widely in aircraft, is an automatic radio DIRECTION FINDER, calibrated with respect to the station to which it is tuned.

COMPASSES, instrument used in EUCLIDEAN GEOMETRY and technical draftsmanship to measure off distances and to draw CIRCLES or parts thereof. A compass whose two legs are tipped by sharp points is called a **divider**, the term compass (or pair of compasses) being usually reserved for instruments with one leg tipped by a pen or pencil.

COMPETITION, in economics, an ideal market situation, in which prices are fixed by SUPPLY AND DEMAND, not by individual buyers or sellers. Theoretically it ensures that resources are used efficiently. In practice, however, free competition can lead to poor conditions of employment hence the growth of labor movements, and the tendency towards more state control in some Western industrial countries. (See also MONOPOLY AND UNFAIR COMPETITION.)

COMPETITIVE INHIBITION. See ENZYMES.

COMPIÈGNE, tourist center and manufacturing town in N France, 47mi NNE of Paris. It is famous for its château and forest where the WWI armistice was signed in Marshall FOCH's rail roach. Hitler accepted France's surrender in the same coach on June 22, 1940. Pop 28 381.

COMPILER. See COMPUTER.

COMPLEMENTARITY PRINCIPLE, a philosophical thesis proposed in 1927 by Niels BOHR, seeking to make intelligible the then newly-developed WAVE MECHANICS. Bohr recognized that the hardware used in any subatomic-physics experiment materially affected the results obtained and inferred from this that atomic systems could only be described and understood in terms of a series of complementary partial views.

COMPLEX, a nexus of ideas and feelings from both the CONSCIOUS and UNCONSCIOUS which has an effect, favorable or adverse, on the actions or emotional state of the individual. ADLER used the term in connection with the superiority and INFERIORITY COMPLEXES, FREUD in connection with the CASTRATION COMPLEX and OEDIPUS COMPLEX.

COMPLEX NUMBERS. See IMAGINARY NUMBERS.

COMPOSITAE, the largest family of flowering

plants, which includes the ASTER, DAISY, DANDELION and SUNFLOWER. The apparently single flower consists of a large number of florets. The florets are of two types, ray florets with a strap-shaped corolla and disk florets with a small tubular corolla. In some species there are only ray florets, e.g., dandelion, in some, disk florets, e.g., BURDOCK, and in the majority both ray and disk florets, e.g., daisy. (See also FLOWER.)

COMPOSITION, Chemical, the proportion by weight of each ELEMENT present in a chemical compound. The **law of definite proportions**, discovered by J. L. PROUST, states that pure compounds have a fixed and invariable composition. A few compounds, termed non-stoichiometric, disobey this law: they have lattice vacancies or extra atoms, and the composition varies within a certain range depending on the formation conditions. The **law of multiple proportions**, discovered by DALTON, states that, if two elements A and B form more than one compound, the various weights of B which combine with a given weight of A are in small whole-number ratios. (See also BOND, CHEMICAL; EQUIVALENT WEIGHT.)

COMPOST. See MANURE.

COMPOUND EYE, a type of eye found in the phylum ARTHROPODA, so-called because it consists of a number of organs called *ommatidia*. Each ommatidium perceives part of the visual field so that the animal's view of the world is composed of a mosaic of images that is more complete the greater the number of ommatidia that are present. Predatory insects such as dragonflies have compound eyes composed of several thousand ommatidia.

COMPRESSION RATIO, in INTERNAL-COMBUSTION ENGINES, the RATIO between the volumes in a cylinder when the piston is at the bottom of its stroke and when it is at the top of its stroke. In AUTOMOBILE engines this ratio is about 8:1, while in truck DIESEL ENGINES it is around 16:1.

COMPRESSOR, device for increasing the pressure of a gas or vapor, important in, for example, GAS TURBINES and pneumatic tools. Gases under very high pressure may liquefy; liquefied gases are of great importance in many fields of everyday life. **Reciprocating compressors** have a cylinder in which runs a piston driven by a crankshaft; their principle of operation is similar to that of a PUMP. Simple **rotary compressors** have a rotating cylinder mounted eccentrically in a cylindrical casing. Vanes are mounted on the cylinder such that they slide in and out of slots as compelled by the walls of the chamber. Gas is introduced at one side of the chamber and drawn round by the vanes; the volume between cylinder and chamber decreases as the cylinder turns, and thus pressurized gas is released at the outlet on the other side of the chamber. A device known as a compressor is used in TELEPHONE systems to reduce the effects of INTERFERENCE.

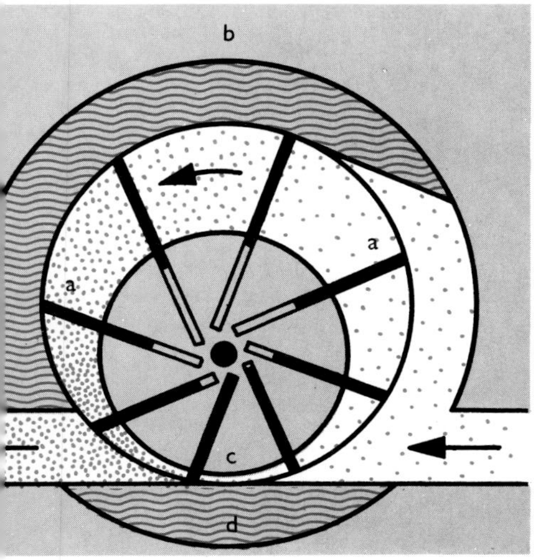

This ingenious type of rotary compressor augments the pressure of a gas by trapping it between vanes which reduce it in volume as the impeller rotates around an axis eccentric to the casing:
(a) diffuser; (b) casing; (c) impeller; (d) water coolant.

COMPROMISE OF 1850, attempt by the US Congress to reconcile North and South in the pre-CIVIL WAR period on the question of extending slavery to new territories. Approved by Congress in Sept. 1850, Senator Henry CLAY's compromise Omnibus Bill admitted Cal. as a free state; prohibited slave trade in the District of Columbia; proposed a stricter FUGITIVE SLAVE LAW; deferred a decision on slavery in Ut. and N.M. until they applied for statehood; and paid the slave state of Tex. $10 million to relinquish much of its western territory to the federal government. The Compromise temporarily saved the Union; the factions were too entrenched for it to do any more.

COMPTON, industrial city in SW Cal., 13mi S of Los Angeles. It produces steel castings, chemicals and aircraft components. Pop 78611.

COMPTON, Arthur Holly (1892–1962), US physicist who discovered the Compton effect (1923), thus providing evidence that X RAYS could act as particles as predicted in QUANTUM THEORY. Compton found that when monochromatic X rays were scattered by light elements, some of the scattered radiation was of longer wavelength, i.e., of lower ENERGY than the incident. Compton showed that this could be explained in terms of the collision between an X-ray PHOTON and an ELECTRON in the target. For this work he shared the 1927 Nobel physics prize with C. T. R. WILSON.

COMPTON-BURNETT, Dame Ivy (1892–1969), English novelist who portrayed late-Victorian upper middle class life. Her novels dealt with familial corruption, property and greed and proceed almost entirely through mannered yet dramatically flexible dialogue. Among her best-known works are *Men and Wives* (1931) and *Mother and Son* (1955).

COMPTROLLER GENERAL OF THE UNITED STATES, head of the general accounting office, directly responsible to Congress for auditing all government spending. The comptroller is appointed by the president, with the advice and consent of the Senate, for one term of 15 years.

COMPTROLLER OF THE CURRENCY, US government office in the Treasury department. The comptroller supervises all existing national banks and vets new ones. The office dates from 1863.

COMPULSION, an irresistible UNCONSCIOUS force which makes an individual perform conscious (see CONSCIOUSNESS) thoughts or actions which he would not normally perform, perhaps even against his will. The force may also come from outside, i.e., from someone whose character dominates the individual (see also BRAINWASHING; OBSESSIONAL NEUROSIS).

COMPURGATION, medieval legal defense in which the accused summoned a number of people, usually 12, to swear to his veracity. Compurgation was abolished in English COMMON LAW in 1164; it is a distant ancestor of the JURY system.

COMPUTER, any device which performs calculations. In this light, the ABACUS, CALCULATING MACHINE and SLIDE RULE may all be described as computers; however, the term is usually limited to those electronic devices that are given a program to follow, data to store or to calculate with, and means with which to present results or other (stored) information.

Programming. A computer program consists essentially of a set of instructions which tells the computer which operations to perform, in what order to perform them, and the order in which subsequent data will be presented to it; for ease of use, the computer may already have subprograms built into its memory, so that, on receiving an instruction such as LOG X, it will automatically go through the program necessary to find the LOGARITHM of that piece of data supplied to it as X. Every model of computer has a different machine language or code; that is, the way in which it should ideally be programmed; however, this language is usually difficult and cumbersome for an operator to use. Thus a special program known as a **compiler** is retained by the computer, enabling it to translate computer languages such as ALGOL, COBOL and FORTRAN, which are easily learned and used by operators and programmers, into its own machine code. Programmers also make extensive use of ALGORITHMS to save programming and operating time.

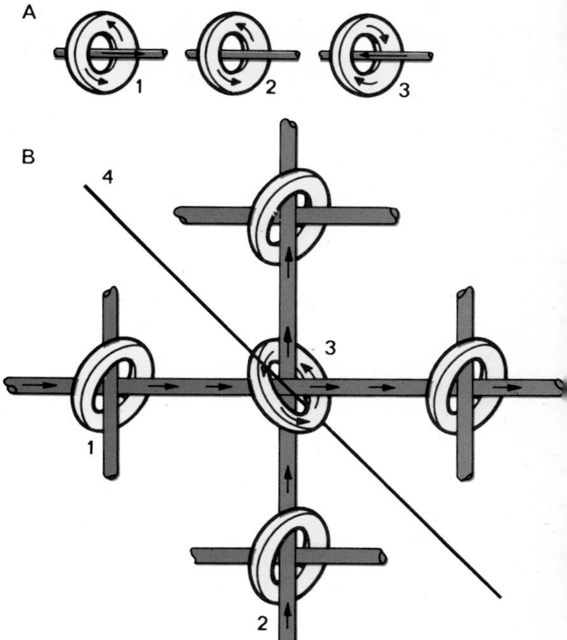

The magnetic core store memory of a digital computer comprises thousands of tiny ferrite rings threaded on a matrix of wires. (A) When a current pulse is passed through a ring (1), it adopts a certain polarity, which it retains (2) after the pulse has passed. The polarity is reversed (3) only when a pulse is passed in the opposite direction. (B) In a core store each ring stores one bit of information, its polarity representing the value of the bit. By pulsing the two wires (1) and (2) defining a particular core's position in the matrix, its polarity is switched. Its value can then be read using a sense wire (4).

Input. Programs and data are fed into computers using either the medium of punched tape or, more commonly in recent years, that of punched cards. In both cases it is the positions of holes punched in the medium which carry the information. These are read by a card or tape reader which usually consists of a light shining through the holes and activating PHOTOELECTRIC CELLS on the far side. (Mechanical readers exist but are generally regarded as less reliable.) The computer "reads" the resulting electrical pulses.

Storage. Machine languages generally take the form of a binary code (see BINARY NUMBERS), so that the two characters 0 and 1 may be easily represented by + and −. Thus the ideal medium for data storage is magnetic, and may take the form of tapes, disks or drums. Magnetic tapes are used much as they are in a TAPE RECORDER; a magnetic head "writes" on the tape by creating a suitable magnetic flux, and can "read" the spots so created at a later date, retransmitting them in the form of electric pulses. Magnetic disks and drums work on a similar principle; the former are flat disks mounted in groups of up to twenty on a shared shaft, looking rather like a stack of phonograph records; drums are, as the name suggests, cylindrical, and are coated with a magnetic medium. Both drums and stacks of disks rotate constantly while the computer is in use, so that the maximum time taken for the read/write head to locate any specific area is that for one revolution. In all cases, each datum must be identified and given a specific "address" in the storage system, so that instructions for its retrieval may be given to the computer and so that the operator may take precautions against erasing it. (See INFORMATION RETRIEVAL.)

The computer's "memory," for longer-term storage, usually takes the form of arrays of cores: tiny (about 0.5mm in diameter) doughnut-shaped magnetic objects. Once again, each core in the array is uniquely identifiable by the computer.

Data processing. All the operations performed by the computer on the information it receives are collectively described as data processing. The main element of data processing is, of course, computation. This is almost exclusively done by addition, and performed using binary arithmetic (see BINARY NUMBERS). More complicated procedures, such as integration (see CALCULUS) or finding ROOTS, are performed algorithmically, suitable subprograms being built into the computer. Again the characters 0 and 1 are represented by + and −, where this may refer to a closed or open switch, a direction of magnetic flux (see MAGNETISM), etc. Moreover, the computer contains logic circuits so that it may evaluate information while performing a calculation. If, for example, it were performing an algorithm to find $\sqrt{2}$ to a specified number of decimal places (see APPROXIMATION), it has to have a system whereby it can check at the end of each cycle of the algorithm whether or not its result is correct to the accuracy required. These circuits are designed using an application of Boolean algebra (see LOGIC; BOOLE, GEORGE): the three elements are AND, NOT and OR. Information wil be passed by the AND and OR elements (switches) if, respectively,

$$a \wedge b \leftrightarrow I,$$
$$a \vee b \leftrightarrow I$$

(for pulses a and b). The NOT switch is also called the **inverter**, and its function is to convert a into a', or vice versa (i.e., + into − or − into +). Combinations of these three switches are capable of handling any logical operation required.

Output. Before being fed out, the information must be converted from machine code back into the programmer's computer language, numerical data being translated from the binary into the DECIMAL SYSTEM. The information is then fed out in the form of paper tape, punched cards or, using an adapted TELEPRINTER, as a printout.

Types of computer. We have been talking almost exclusively about the **digital computer**, since this is the most widely-encountered and certainly the most versatile type. As we have seen, it requires information to be fed into it in "bits." Contrarily, the other main type of computer, the **analog computer**, is designed to deal with continuously varying quantities, such as lengths or voltages; the most everyday example of an analog computer is the slide rule. Electronic analog computers are usually designed for a specific task; as their accuracy is not high, their greatest use is in providing models of situations as bases for experiment. (See also CYBERNETICS; DICTIONARY.)

COMSTOCK, Anthony (1844–1915), US moral crusader and a founder of the New York Society for the Suppression of Vice (1873). He successfully campaigned for stricter legislation against gambling and prostitution in N.Y. and the mailing of obscene matter.

COMSTOCK LODE, rich vein of silver discovered in the 1850s in W Nev. and named for Henry T. P. Comstock, one of the lode's first claimants. For some 30 years after its discovery it produced about half the US's silver output.

COMTE, Auguste (1798–1857), French philosopher, the founder of POSITIVISM and a pioneer of scientific sociology. His thinking was essentially evolutionary; he recognized a progression in the development of the sciences: starting from mathematics and progressing through astronomy, physics, chemistry and biology towards the ultimate goal of sociology. He saw this progression reflected in man's mental development. This had proceeded from a theological stage to a metaphysical one. Comte now sought to help inaugurate the final scientific or positivistic era. His social thinking reflected that of Henri de Saint-Simon and in turn his own works, particularly the *Philosophie positive* (1830–42), became widely influential in both France and England.

COMUS, in Greek and Roman mythology, a minor deity of mirth and revelry. In John MILTON's *Comus* he is represented as the son of BACCHUS and CIRCE.

CONAKRY, capital and main port and trading city of the Republic of Guinea, on Tombo Island. It is linked to the mainland by a causeway; it handles alumina, bananas, palm kernels and coffee. Pop 197 267.

CONANICUT ISLAND, island in SE R.I., in Narragansett Bay. It is coextensive with Jamestown.

CONANT, James Bryant (1893–), US chemist and educator, president of Harvard U. 1933–53. He conducted important research into the structure of CHLOROPHYLL, and during WWII was involved in the development of the ATOMIC BOMB. Conant was US ambassador to West Germany 1955–57.

CONANT, Roger (c1592–1679), English-born American colonist. He left PLYMOUTH COLONY in 1625 and became manager of the New England Plantation at Cape Ann. When that site proved unsuitable, he went on to lead the group which in 1626 founded Salem, Mass.

CONCENTRATION CAMP, term now most commonly associated with the forced-labor and extermination camps of Nazi Germany and the USSR. It was first applied to British internment camps in the Boer War 1899–1902. Some 6 million Jews perished in Hitler's concentration camps. Among the most notorious Nazi camps were those at Auschwitz, Buchenwald and Treblinka.

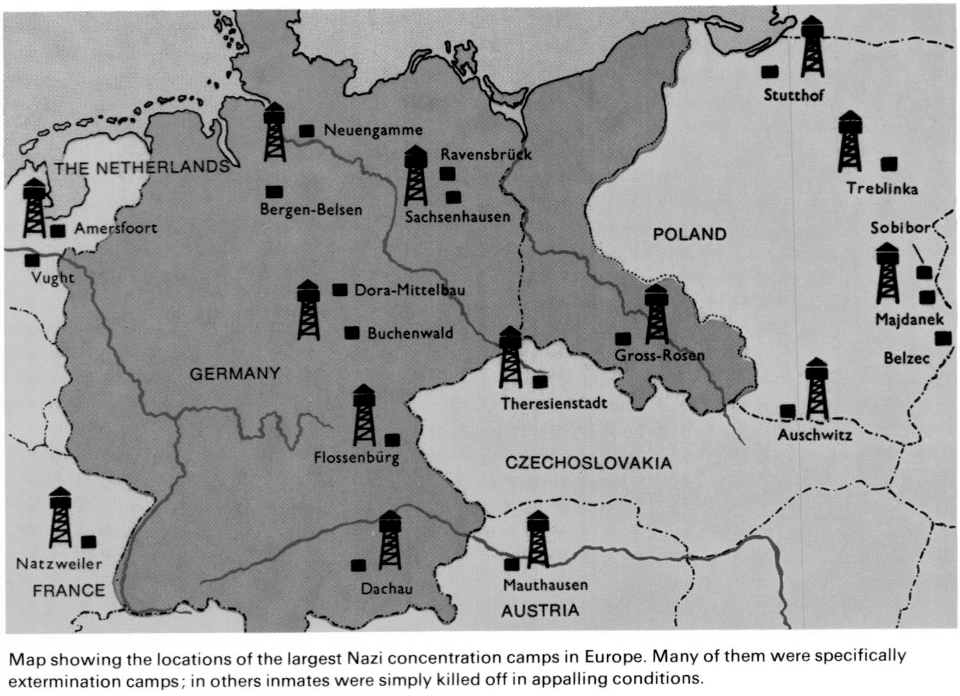

Map showing the locations of the largest Nazi concentration camps in Europe. Many of them were specifically extermination camps; in others inmates were simply killed off in appalling conditions.

CONCENTRICITY, in GEOMETRY, the situation in which two or more figures share a common center.

CONCEPCIÓN, city in S central Chile, capital of Concepción province. The country's third largest city, it is a major industrial, distribution and educational center. It is served by the ports of Tomé and Talcahuano. Pop 192 000.

CONCEPTUALISM, a modern term describing a position in scholastic philosophy with respect to the status of universals that was intermediate between the extremes of both NOMINALISM and REALISM. To a conceptualist, UNIVERSALS (general concepts such as chair-ness) indeed exist, but only as concepts common to all men's minds and not as things in the world of particular objects (such as chairs).

CONCERTINA, musical instrument patented in 1829 by Sir Charles WHEATSTONE. It consists of a hexagonal bellows stopped at each end by boards in which are set a number of reeds. The concertina is played between the hands, by expanding and contracting the bellows and so forcing air through the reeds. A series of buttons on the end boards is used to select the required notes. (See also ACCORDION.)

CONCERTMASTER (from the German *Konzertmeister*), leader of the first violins in an orchestra, and assistant conductor.

CONCERTO, composition opposing unequal musical forces, usually on solo instrument against a large orchestra. The three-movement orchestral form was elaborated by J. S. Bach out of the *concerto da camera*, a type of CHAMBER MUSIC. Handel added the CADENZA as a regula feature. Mozart set the style for the modern concerto: the orchestra announces an opening subject with a *tutti,* a passage for full orchestra, then takes a subordinate position when the solo instrument enters, thus establishing the pattern of interchanges. Beethoven added many novel touches to Mozart's basic form; others, including Mendelssohn, Schumann, Chopin, Brahms and Elgar have developed the concerto, using a wide range of solo instruments. The form remains popular with more recent composers such as Bartók, Prokofiev, Stravinsky and Shostakovitch.

CONCERT OF EUROPE, philosophy of cooperation shared by the major 19th-century European powers, aimed at maintaining the balance of power and settling disputes through negotiation. It originated in the Treaty of Chaumont 1814 (see also QUADRUPLE ALLIANCE) and remained intact until the CRIMEAN WAR 1854–56. The spirit of the Concert of Europe, however, may be said to have lasted through to the outbreak of WWI.

CONCH, marine MOLLUSCS with conical shells that are widely collected. Large conch shells were used as trumpets in South America and Japan and figure in Greek mythology, being used by Neptune's trumpeter.

CONCHOID, or **Conchoid of Nicomedes**, a shell-shaped CURVE constructed as follows: consider a point O a PERPENDICULAR distance a from a fixed straight line PQ on which there is a moving point A. In each direction along the line AO measure out a distance b, so that $AB' = AB = b$, which distance is fixed. If the line B′ABO is pivoted about O the points B′ and B trace out a conchoid, whose shape depends on the relationship of b to a.

CONCHOID FRACTURE, a form of ROCK and MINERAL fracture producing a curved, ribbed surface resembling the shell of certain MOLLUSKS.

CONCLAVE, assembly of Roman Catholic cardinals, who meet in Rome within 21 days of the death of a pope to choose his successor. The assembly meets in total seclusion and may not disperse until a two-thirds majority has been reached.

CONCORD, city in W Cal., 20mi E of Oakland. It is a residential and industrial suburb of San Francisco, developed since 1853. Pop 85 164.

CONCORD, residential town in NE Mass., on the CONCORD RIVER 19mi NW of Boston. Founded 1635, home of the MINUTEMEN and scene of a famous revolutionary skirmish (see CONCORD, BATTLE OF), it

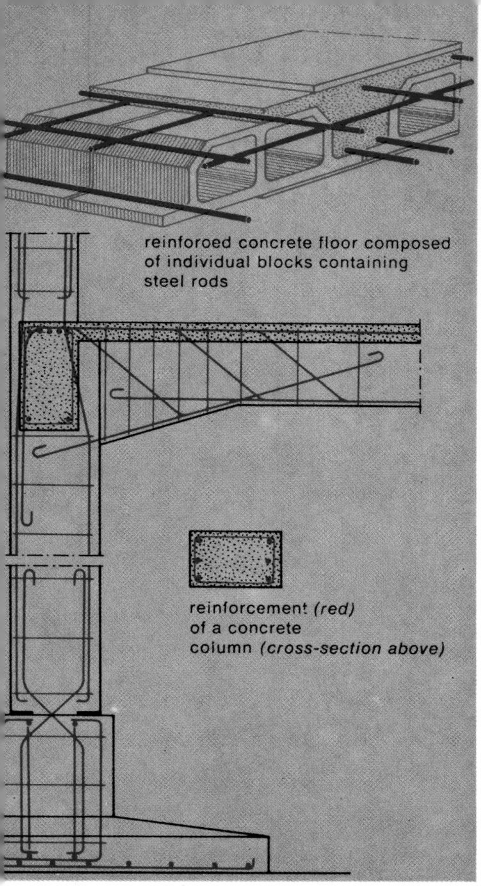

became the home of EMERSON, THOREAU and HAWTHORNE. WALDEN POND is nearby. Pop 16 148.

reinforced concrete floor composed of individual blocks containing steel rods
reinforcement (red) of a concrete column (cross-section above)

CONCORD, city in S central N.H., capital of N.H. and of Merrimack Co. Industries: printing, leather goods, electronic products, granite. Founded in 1727 as Pennycook, it was later called Rumford (1733–65). Pop 30 022.

CONCORD, city in S central N.C., seat of Cabarrus Co. It is a center for agricultural products and home of Barber-Scotia College. Pop 18 464.

CONCORD, Battle of, second engagement in the American Revolutionary War, after Lexington (see LEXINGTON, BATTLE OF). Both were fought on April 19, 1775. The British, 700 strong, marched on CONCORD, Mass. to destroy military stores. The Americans retreated, but returned on seeing smoke from burning supplies. Under Major John Buttrick, they met the British at North Bridge and routed them, raising American morale. Casualties for both battles totaled 273 British, 95 Americans.

CONCORDANCE, alphabetical index of key words from a book (particularly the Bible) or from the collected works of a famous writer, citing the passages where they occur.

CONCORDAT, agreement between the pope and the secular government of a state regulating religious affairs within the state, for instance appointment of bishops and status of church property. The first concordat was the Concordat of WORMS, in 1122. The best-known recent concordat is the LATERAN TREATY (1929), establishing the sovereign state of the Vatican within Italy.

CONCORDAT OF WORMS. See WORMS, CONCORDAT OF.

CONCORD RIVER, river in NE Mass. formed by the confluence of the Sudbury and Assabet rivers. It flows N to the Merrimack R.

CONCRETE, versatile structural building material, made by mixing CEMENT, AGGREGATE and water. Initially moldable, the cement hardens by hydration, forming a matrix which binds the aggregate. Various other ingredients—admixtures—may be added to improve the properties of the concrete; air-entraining agents increase durability. Since concrete is much more able to resist compressive than tensile STRESS, it is often reinforced with a steel bar embedded in it which is able to bear the tension. **Prestressed concrete** is reinforced concrete in which the steel is under tension and the concrete is compressed; it can withstand very much greater stresses. Concrete is used for all building elements and for bridges, dams, canals, highways etc., often as precast units.

CONCRETE MUSIC. See ELECTRONIC MUSIC.

CONCRETION, irregularly-shaped nodule of rock embedded in sedimentary rock of a different composition, in which it grew by deposition on a nucleus. Examples include FLINT in chalk.

CONCUSSION, a state of disturbed consciousness following head injury, characterized by AMNESIA for events preceding and following the trauma. Permanent BRAIN damage is only found in cases of repeated concussion, as in boxers who develop the punch-drunk syndrome.

CONDÉ, Louis II de Bourbon, Prince de (1621–1686), "the Great Condé," outstanding French general of the THIRTY YEARS' WAR, related to the royal family. He turned against MAZARIN, led troops in the FRONDE rebellion, and served with Spain; but was pardoned and fought for Louis XIV in the DUTCH WARS.

CONDENSATION, passage of substance from gaseous to liquid or solid state: CLOUDS are a result of condensation of water vapor in the ATMOSPHERE (see also RAIN). Warm air can hold more water vapor than cool air; if a body of air is cooled it will reach a temperature (the DEW POINT) where the water vapor it holds is at SATURATION level. Further decrease in temperature without change in pressure will initiate water condensation. Such condensation is greatly facilitated by the presence of condensation nuclei ("seeds"), small particles (e.g., of smoke) about which condensation may begin. **Condensation trails** behind high-flying jet aircraft result primarily from water vapor produced by the engines increasing the local concentration (see also CLOUD CHAMBER; GAS; VAPOR). Condensation is important in all processes using steam; and in DISTILLATION, where the liquid is collected, and condensed by removal of its LATENT HEAT of vaporization, in an apparatus called a **condenser**. In chemistry a **condensation reaction** is one in which two or more MOLECULES link together with elimination of a relatively small molecule, such as water.

CONDENSER, term sometimes used for CAPACITOR. (See also CONDENSATION.)

CONDILLAC, Étienne Bonnot de (1715–1780), French philosopher, who broke with the teaching of LOCKE to found the doctrine of SENSATIONALISM, holding that all knowledge is derived from the senses.

CONDITIONED REFLEX. See REFLEX.

CONDITIONING, term used to describe two quite different LEARNING processes. In the first, a human or animal response is generated by a stimulus which does not normally generate such a response (see conditioned REFLEX; PAVLOV). In the second, animals (and by extension humans) are trained to perform certain actions to gain rewards or escape punishment (see LEARNING).

CONDOMINIUM, in real estate, individual ownership in property, such as an apartment, which is part of a larger complex owned in common. In international law, joint control over another nation or territory (as the US and Britain control CANTON AND ENDERBURY ISLANDS).

CONDORCET, Marie Jean Antoine Nicholas de Caritat, Marquis de (1743–1794), French philosopher, mathematician and revolutionary politician chiefly remembered for his theory that the human race, having risen from barbarism, would continue to progress toward moral, intellectual and physical perfection. His principal mathematical work was in the theory of probability. He played a prominent role in the Revolution, though his moderate opinions led to his outlawry and suicide.

CONDORS, two species of New World vultures, the California condor *Gymnogypes californianus* and the Andean condor *Vultur gryphus*. The California condor is extremely rare, there being only 40 extant individuals.

CONDOTTIERE, mercenary soldier of 14th- and 15th-century Italy. Powerful condottieri raised armies and sold their services to the highest bidder among warring states. Famous leaders were Francesco Sforza, Bartolomeo COLLEONI and an Englishman, Sir John Hawkwood.

CONDUCTANCE, a measure of the ability of a body to conduct ELECTRICITY. Measured in SIEMENS, it is the RECIPROCAL of RESISTANCE. (See also CONDUCTIVITY.)

CONDUCTING, the art of directing a group of musicians. Conducting evolved with the increasing complexity of music. Choirs had leaders by the 15th century, while by HANDEL's day CONTINUO players guided orchestral works; but the idea of a conductor whose sole task was training and directing an orchestra emerged in the time of BEETHOVEN (who conducted his own works). Conducting became a virtuoso skill in the 19th century.

CONDUCTION, Heat, passage of heat through a body without large-scale movements of matter within the body (see CONVECTION). Mechanisms involved include the transfer of vibrational ENERGY from one MOLECULE to the next through the substance (dominant in poor conductors), and energy transfer by ELECTRONS (in good electrical conductors) and PHONONS (in crystalline solids). In general, solids, especially metals, are good conductors, liquids and gases poor. (See also RADIATION.)

CONDUCTIVITY, or specific conductance, the CONDUCTANCE of a 1-metre cube of a substance, measured between opposite faces. Measured in siemens per metre, conductivity is the RECIPROCAL of resistivity (see RESISTANCE), and expresses the

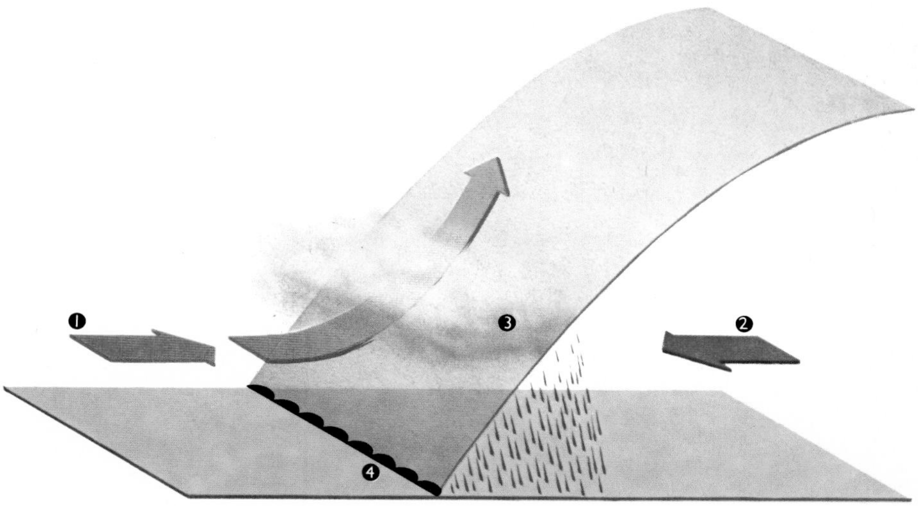

Condensation: A warm front occurs when a body of moist warm air (1) advances against a mass of dry cold air (2). The warm air is pushed upwards and, as it becomes cooler, condensation takes place, resulting in a band of rainfall preceding the front (3). Although the front is in fact an inclined plane, it is represented on weather charts by the symbol shown at (4).

substance's ability to conduct electricity. The **equivalent conductivity** Λ of an electrolytic solution is the conductivity of a solution divided by its concentration in gram-equivalents (see EQUIVALENT WEIGHT) per cubic metre, and is usually measured with an electrolytic CELL in a WHEATSTONE BRIDGE. The degree of ionic DISSOCIATION (α) was found by ARRHENIUS to be given by

$$\alpha = \frac{\Lambda}{\Lambda_0},$$

where Λ_0 is the value of Λ extrapolated to zero concentration; this equation has since been shown to apply only to weak electrolytes (see ELECTROLYSIS).

CONDUCTORS, Electric, substances (usually metals) whose high CONDUCTIVITY makes them useful for carrying electric current (see ELECTRICITY). They are most often used in the form of WIRES or CABLES. The best conductor is SILVER, but, for reasons of economy, COPPER is most often used. (See also SEMICONDUCTORS; SUPERCONDUCTIVITY.)

CONE, a solid geometrical figure traced by the rotation of a straight line A (the generator) about a fixed straight line B which it intersects, such that each point on A traces out a closed CURVE. A cone has therefore two parts (nappes) which touch each other at the point of intersection, termed the vertex of the cone, of lines A and B; the two parts being skew-symmetrical (see SYMMETRY) about the vertex and of infinite extent. Usually one considers only one of these parts, limited by a PLANE which cuts it. The tracing of the closed curve of rotation on this plane is the directrix and the part of the plane bounded by the directrix is the base of the cone. The lines joining the vertex to each point of the directrix are the cone's elements. The PERPENDICULAR line from the vertex to this plane is the altitude or height of the cone; the line joining the vertex to the center of the base (if it has a center) is the axis, and in most cases coincides with line B. Should axis and altitude coincide, the cone is a right cone; otherwise it is oblique. A cone whose directrix is a circle is a circular cone, its volume being given by $\pi r^2 h/3$ where r is the radius of the directrix and h is the altitude. (See also CONIC SECTIONS.)

CONE-BEARING TREES. See CONIFERS.

CONE SHELLS, MOLLUSCS of the genus *Conus* found mainly in warm marine waters of the Indo-Pacific, often on CORAL reefs.

CONESTOGA INDIANS (Susquehanna or Minqua tribe), extinct IROQUOIAN Indians of the lower Susquehanna R area in what are now Pa. and Md. They were exterminated in Indian wars and a final white-led massacre in Lancaster Co., Pa., in 1763.

CONESTOGA WAGON, large covered wagon used by American pioneers. Originating about 1725 in the Conestoga region of Pennsylvania, it became the chief means of transporting settlers and freight across the Alleghenies until about 1850. It had big, broad-rimmed wheels and a canvas roof supported by wooden hoops, and was pulled by four to six horses.

CONEY, name applied to the HYRAX, PIKA, RABBIT and a species of GROUPER.

CONEY ISLAND, seaside resort in the borough of Brooklyn, New York City. Millions annually visit its famous beaches, boardwalk and amusement park.

CONFEDERATE STATES OF AMERICA, government formed by the Southern states which seceded from the United States of America, Dec. 1860–May 1861. S.C. was the first state to leave the Union after the election of President LINCOLN and was followed by Miss., Fla., Ala., Ga., La., Tex., Va., Ark., Tenn and N.C. Rebels from Mo. and Ky. (both of which remained in the Union) set up their own governments-in-exile under the Southern banner and brought the number of Confederate states hypothetically to 13.

A constitutional convention was called for Feb. 4, 1861, in Montgomery, Ala., which became the Confederate capital. Jefferson DAVIS (Miss.) and Alexander STEPHENS (Ga.) were elected president and vice-president. A constitution much like that of the US—but with strong "states' rights" provisions—was produced on March 11.

War with the North began on April 13 with the bombardment of Union-held Fort Sumter. Davis was reelected in Nov. and inaugurated on Feb. 22, 1862, in the new capital, Richmond, Va. He led some 9 000 000 people—of whom about 3 500 000 were slaves—at war with the nearly 23 000 000 citizens of the Union. By April he had been forced to initiate the draft and his need for wide wartime powers brought clashes with his "states' rights" Congress.

As the war continued, the government's problems deepened. Reluctant to impose taxes, it issued vast amounts of currency and war bonds which caused ruinous inflation. The essentially agricultural South suffered an increasingly desperate shortage of munitions, heavy industrial goods, domestic supplies and even of food, worsened by a successful Union naval blockade which hampered export of cotton, the country's one major crop. The South's chief cotton consumer, Britain, sent ships and munitions but refused to enter the war.

Superb military leadership provided the South's early victories and kept the conflict alive into 1865. After several desperate peace initiatives, the Confederacy had to acknowledge total military surrender. By then much of its land was devastated and the economy was in ruins. (See also CIVIL WAR, AMERICAN.)

CONFEDERATION, Articles of. See ARTICLES OF CONFEDERATION.

CONFEDERATION OF THE RHINE, association of 16 German principalities, formerly in the HOLY ROMAN EMPIRE, set up in 1806 under the protection of NAPOLEON I. The confederation was dissolved in 1813 after the French defeat in the NAPOLEONIC WARS.

CONFESSING CHURCH (*Bekennende Kirche*), German Lutheran movement founded in 1933 to uphold the "true confession" against the Nazi-controlled established church. Leaders such as Martin NIEMÖLLER and Dietrich BONHOEFFER opposed euthanasia and antisemitism, but by WWII the church had been split and forced underground.

CONFESSION, admission of sin, an aspect of repentance and thus required for ABSOLUTION. General confession may be made in a congregation; private confession may be made to God, or also to a priest. The latter is a SACRAMENT of the Roman Catholic and Eastern churches, also observed in some Lutheran and Episcopalian churches.

CONFIRMATION, a rite of certain Christian churches, usually administered in adolescence. The candidates confirm the promises made in their BAPTISM and the bishop lays his hands on them, invoking the HOLY SPIRIT upon them. First COMMUNION generally follows. In the Roman Catholic and Eastern churches confirmation is a SACRAMENT.

CONFLICT OF INTEREST, usually refers to a situation in which a public official also has private interests which may conflict with the best interests of the state. The term may also apply to many private legal and business situations.

CONFLICT OF LAWS, conflict between the laws of different nations or subdivisions of a nation, each with a claim to jurisdiction, and the resolution or mediation of the conflict. Examples are divorce and child custody cases between nationals or residents of different nations, or of different US states.

CONFORMATIONAL ANALYSIS, the study of molecular conformations, i.e. the spatial arrangements of the atoms that can be interconverted merely by rotation about single bonds (see BOND, CHEMICAL). In general, different conformations are transient and nonisolable, unlike different configurations (see STEREOCHEMISTRY). But if large substituents, such as bromine or phenyl groups, are attached to adjacent atoms, steric hindrance or interference may cause the eclipsed conformation to be less stable than the staggered. This may affect reaction rates. Conformational effects are most important in ALICYCLIC COMPOUNDS.

CONFUCIANISM, philosophical system based on the teachings of CONFUCIUS and practiced throughout China for nearly 2 000 years. Confucianism teaches a moral and social philosophy and code of behavior based on peace, order, humanity, wisdom, courage and fidelity. Confucius refused to consider the question of God but Confucianists hold there is a state of heavenly harmony which man can attain by cultivating virtues, especially knowledge, patience, sincerity, obedience and the fulfillment of obligations between children and parents, subjects and ruler. Confucianism's encouragement of the acceptance of the *status quo* is at odds with the ideology of continuing revolution of the Communist Chinese government.

CONFUCIUS (c551–479 BC), *K'ung Fu-tzu,* founder of the Chinese ethical and moral system CONFUCIANISM. Born in the feudal state of Lu, he was poor and self-educated but began teaching and gathering disciples when aged about 20. Distressed by political disunity and oppressive rule, over the next 30 years he evolved a system of "right living," a guide for wise government preserved by his disciples in a collection of his sayings, the Confucian *Analects.* Confucius became a magistrate of the city of Chang-tu but resigned from what proved to be a position of impotence. Little else is reliably known of his life.

CONGER, large marine eel, *Conger conger,* found in the N and S Atlantic, the Mediterranean and the Indo-Pacific region. Females grow to a length of 2.7m (9ft) and weigh as much as 38kg (84lb).

CONGLOMERATE, type of company participating in widely varied and generally unrelated industries, usually formed by merger and acquisition. Conglomerates may achieve efficiency by centralizing management, and they avoid breaking antitrust laws because they are not monopolies. (See also CARTEL; HOLDING COMPANY.)

CONGLOMERATE, or pudding stone, in geology, a consolidated GRAVEL consisting of rock fragments (rounded by transportation) cemented in a sedimentary matrix. If the fragments are angular it is

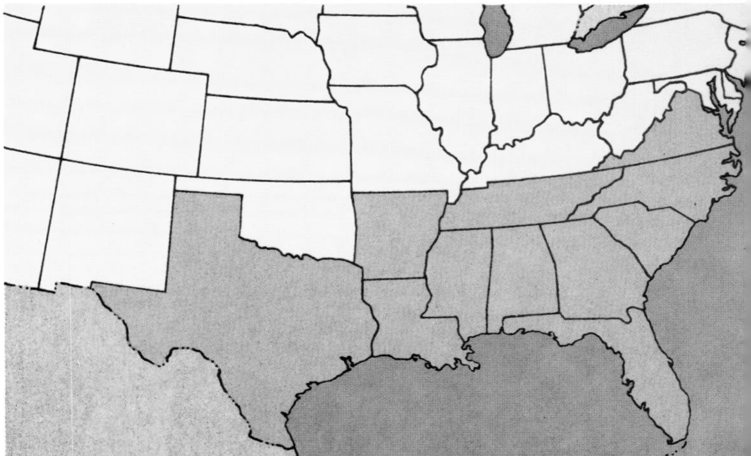

Map showing (in grey) the Confederate States of America. Apart from the 11 states shown as part of the Confederacy, dissident elements in Kentucky and Missouri set up governments-in-exile under the Confederate flag, bringing the total number of states to 13—the same number as the original states of America.

known as **breccia.** The fragments vary in size from boulders to small pebbles, grading into SANDSTONE. Poorly-sorted conglomerates, having fragments of many different rocks, include **tillite** (of glacial origin) and **graywacke.** (See also AGGLOMERATE.)

CONGO, republic in W central Africa, formerly part of French Equatorial Africa. It is about the size of Mont. and lies on the equator E of Gabon and the Atlantic and W of Zaire.

Land. A low, treeless plain along the coast gives way inland to the Mayombé Escarpment, a mountainous rain forest. There is a savanna plateau in the N, and the Ubangi and Congo (Zaire) rivers and their hot, humid forests border the E and S.

People. Some 60% of the population is rural, but there has been a major drift to the towns, of which the largest are the capital Brazzaville and Pointe-Noire, the Atlantic port. Most people are Bantu speakers, notably the Bakongo whose roughly 15 tribes make up nearly half the population. Other main Bantu-speaking tribal groups are the Batcke and M'Bochi. French is the official language. The illiteracy rate is still high, but there is a university in Brazzaville.

Economy. There is little manufacturing industry and the country chiefly exports raw materials, notably hardwoods, diamonds, crude oil, palm oil and sugar. Peanuts, coffee, cacao, bananas, rice, corn, cassava and sweet potatoes are also grown and minerals (not all exploited) include tin, iron, potash, bauxite, lead, zinc, copper and gold. The Congo R is still the major means of transportation, although there are roads, airfields and a railroad.

History. The region was once subject to the African kingdom of the Kongo discovered by the Portuguese in the 15th century, later broken up into small states and exploited by European slave traders. The region became a French colony in 1891, an overseas territory of France in 1946 and an independent republic in 1960. Periodic civil strife from 1963 onward led to an army takeover in 1968. A National Council of the Revolution (CNR) was formed and the Congolese Workers' Party became the supreme source of political authority, the president of the party's central committee acting as president of the republic.

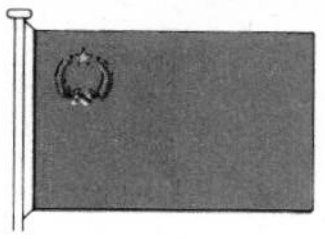

Official Name: The Republic of Congo
Capital: Brazzaville
Area: 128 127sq mi
Population: 1 250 000
Languages: French, Lingala, Kongo
Religions: Animist, Roman Catholic
Monetary Unit(s): 1 CFA franc = 100 centimes

CONGO (Kinshasha). See ZAIRE.

CONGO RIVER, second-longest river in Africa. It exceeds 2 700mi from its source in the Chambezi R, Zambia, to the Atlantic Ocean in W Zaire. It drains 1 425 000sq mi, and in volume of water is second only to the Amazon. The Congo proper and its longest navigable portion (1000mi) begins below Boyoma (Stanley) Falls near Kisangani (Stanleyville) and runs to Pool Malebo (Stanley Pool), linked by channels to BRAZZAVILLE and KINSHASA. Below Livingstone Falls the Congo is navigable for 95mi from Matadi to the Atlantic. The river mouth was discovered by Diogo CAM in 1482, and David LIVINGSTONE explored its upper reaches in 1866–71. Henry Morton STANLEY first traced its course in 1874–77. It was renamed the Zaire by President Mobutu in 1971.

CONGREGATIONAL CHURCHES, Protestant churches which hold that each local church (congregation) should have complete autonomy, though they may form loose associations. In the 16th century Robert BROWNE first stated Congregational doctrine. In the 17th century Congregationalists established churches in the New England colonies and founded Harvard and Yale universities. Most US Congregationalists merged (1931) with the Christian Church (see DISCIPLES OF CHRIST) and then with the EVANGELICAL AND REFORMED CHURCH (1957) to form the UNITED CHURCH OF CHRIST. (See also MATHER; SEPARATISTS.)

CONGRESS, Library of. See LIBRARY OF CONGRESS.

CONGRESSIONAL COMMITTEES. See COMMITTEES, LEGISLATIVE.

CONGRESSIONAL RECORD, daily publication put out by the US GOVERNMENT PRINTING OFFICE since 1873. It contains the debates and proceedings of the US Congress and other material, such as presidential messages and speeches.

CONGRESS OF RACIAL EQUALITY (CORE), US interracial organization founded in 1942 by James FARMER to promote black CIVIL RIGHTS AND LIBERTIES through nonviolent direct action projects. Its voter registration drives and "freedom rides" in the South led to civil rights legislation in the 1960s. In the 1970s CORE became more militant (see also BLACK POWER).

CONGRESS OF THE CONFEDERATION, governing body of the American states (1781–89) under the ARTICLES OF CONFEDERATION. It was replaced by the Congress established by the UNITED STATES CONSTITUTION.

CONGRESS OF THE UNITED STATES, legislative branch of the US federal government. It consists of two houses, the Senate and the House of Representatives. Under the UNITED STATES CONSTITUTION, the powers vested in Congress are to introduce legislation, to assess and collect taxes, to regulate interstate and foreign commerce, to coin money, to establish post offices, to maintain armed forces and to declare war. Congress convenes on Jan. 3 and is in session until adjournment, usually in the fall. A single Congress is two sessions; the first Congress met in 1789–90.

House of Representatives. Membership was 65 in 1789 and is now fixed at 435. Each state has at least one representative; the total number per state is proportional to state population as determined by official census; state legislatures set the boundaries for congressional districts. A representative must be over 25, a US citizen for at least seven years and resident in the state (and usually the district) which elects him.

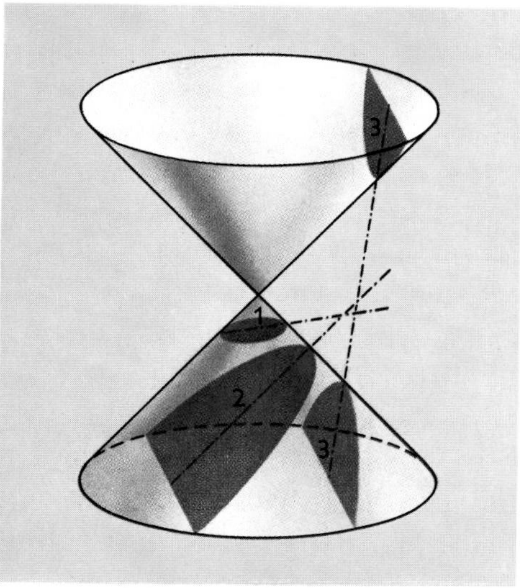

Conic sections are created by the intersection of a plane and a right circular cone. (1) An ellipse is formed when the angle between plane and axis is greater than the angle between axis and generator (side) of the cone. (2) A parabola results when the two angles are the same. (3) A hyperbola is created when the angle between plane and axis is less than the angle between axis and generator.

Elections for representatives are held every two years on the Tuesday after the first Monday in Nov. The House has special powers to impeach federal officials (who are then tried by the Senate), originate revenue bills and elect the president if no candidate gains a majority in the ELECTORAL COLLEGE.

The Senate. There are 100 senators, two from each state. Direct popular elections were introduced in 1913. Until then senators had been elected by state legislatures. Senators serve overlapping six-year terms, one-third being elected every two years. They must be over 30, citizens for at least nine years and resident in the state which elects them. The Senate's special powers are to advise and consent on the appointments of important government officials, including ambassadors and federal judges, and to approve treaties. Through its foreign relations committee, the Senate wields large influence on the conduct of foreign affairs. Officially the vice-president presides over the Senate, but often delegates the task.

The Work of Congress. For a bill to become law it must be approved by both the House and Senate and signed by the president. If he vetoes the bill, Congress may pass it by a two-thirds majority in each house. When the House and Senate disagree on a bill, a joint committee may resolve the differences in a compromise bill, or the bill may die. Each house has committees for drafting and studying bills (see COMMITTEES, LEGISLATIVE). They are then debated by the house which originated them, and votes are taken to pass, reject or defer them. Debate is freer in the Senate than in the House because of the Senate's smaller numbers; a bill may be killed by FILIBUSTER unless a two-thirds majority can be reached to close the debate (see CLOTURE).

CONGRESS OF VIENNA. See VIENNA, CONGRESS OF.

CONGRESS PARTY (Indian National Congress), Indian political party which came to power in 1947 with India's independence from Britain. The Indian National Congress was founded in 1885. It developed a wide national following under the leadership of Mahatma GANDHI and NEHRU. The latter headed the Congress Party as India's prime minister 1947–64. He was succeeded by Indira GANDHI.

CONGREVE, Sir William (1772–1828), English inventor of the Congreve ROCKET (1805), an incendiary rocket used with great effect against Boulogne (1806) and Copenhagen (1807).

CONGREVE, William (1670–1729), English Restoration dramatist, master of the COMEDY OF MANNERS. Among his comedies are *The Old Bachelor* (1693), *Love for Love* (1695) and his masterpiece *The Way of the World* (1700), which is often performed today.

CONGRUENCE, in GEOMETRY, the situation in which two geometrical figures are identical except for their positions in space. (See also MODULUS.)

CONIC SECTIONS, plane CURVES formed by the intersection of a PLANE with a right circular or right elliptical CONE: the three curves are the ellipse, the parabola and the hyperbola. An **ellipse** occurs when the ANGLE between the axis of the cone and the plane is greater than the angle between the axis and the generator (in special cases a CIRCLE may be produced). It may be defined as the locus of a point P about two fixed foci (singular, focus) F and F′, such that PF+PF′=c, where c is a constant greater than the distance FF′. The major axis of an ellipse is its axis of SYMMETRY concurrent with FF′; its minor axis is the axis of symmetry perpendicular to this, their point of intersection being defined as the center of the ellipse. If the length of the minor axis is 2b, b being a constant, then $c^2=(FF')^2+b^2$. The eccentricity of an ellipse is given by the distance FF′ divided by the length of the major axis. A **parabola** occurs when the angle between the axis and the plane equals the angle between the axis and generator (in special cases a straight line may be produced). It may be defined as the locus of a point P such that its distance from a fixed focus F is constantly equal to its PERPENDICULAR distance from a fixed straight line XY. The curve, which has only one axis of symmetry, perpendicular to XY and passing through F, is of infinite extent. The **hyperbola** occurs when the angle between axis and plane is less than that between axis and generator (in special cases a pair of intersecting straight lines may be produced). It may be defined as the loci of two points, P and P′, about two foci, F and F′, such that $PF' - PF = c = P'F - P'F'$, where c is a constant less than the distance FF′. The curve, which is of infinite extent, has a real axis of symmetry passing through F and F′, and an imaginary axis of symmetry passing perpendicularly through the midpoint of FF′. The hyperbola, though of infinite extent in the direction of its real axis, is bounded in the direction perpendicular to this (see ASYMPTOTE).

CONIFERS, trees and some shrubs of the order Coniferales. Important genera include *Pinus* (PINE), *Picea* (SPRUCE), *Cedrus* (CEDAR), *Sequoia* (REDWOOD), *Cupressus* (CYPRESS), *Larix* (LARCH), *Taxus* (YEW), *Abies* (FIR) and *Tsuga* (HEMLOCK). Conifers are characterized by the production of cone-like reproductive bodies, which gives them their name **cone-bearing trees**. (See also GYMNOSPERMS.)

CONJUGATE, of one ROOT OF AN EQUATION, another number that is a root of the same EQUATION. Thus, if $x^2+2x-3=0$, the numbers 1 and -3 are conjugates. If one root of an equation is a complex number (see IMAGINARY NUMBERS) of the form $a+ib$, then it is a fundamental theorem of algebra that it has a conjugate of the form $a-ib$, also a root of the equation. **Conjugate binomials** (see POLYNOMIAL) are those such as $(a+b)$ and $(a-b)$ which differ only by one sign. Another conjugate of $(a+b)$, though not of $(a-b)$, is $(-a+b)$.

CONJUGATION, primitive mode of REPRODUCTION occurring in single-celled organisms—bacteria, protozoa, and some algae and fungi—in which two similar cells link and then exchange nuclear material containing CHROMOSOMES, or fuse, or one cell may absorb the contents of the other. This first step towards SEX often occurs only after many generations of reproduction by FISSION.

CONJUNCTION occurs when the earth, the sun and a planet are in a straight line (as projected onto the plane of the solar system). A planet on the far side of the sun is in superior conjunction, a planet between earth and sun in inferior conjuction (see also OPPOSITION). Planets may be in conjunction with each other (see ASTROLOGY).

CONJUNCTION, in mathematical LOGIC, the assertion that two statements are both true. For statements *a* and *b*, this is written $a \wedge b$, read "*a* is true and *b* is true." In terms of Boolean algebra (see BOOLE, GEORGE), $a \leftrightarrow I$ and $b \leftrightarrow I$ implies $a \wedge b \leftrightarrow I$.

CONJUNCTIVITIS, INFLAMMATION of the conjunctiva, or fine skin covering the EYE and inner eyelids. It is a common but usually harmless condition caused by ALLERGY (as part of HAY FEVER), foreign bodies, or infection with VIRUSES or BACTERIA. It causes irritation, watering and sticky discharge, but does not affect VISION. Eye drops may help, as can ANTIBIOTICS if bacteria are present.

CONJURING. See MAGIC.

CONKLING, Roscoe (1829–1888), US lawyer and Republican politician. He served as congressman (1858–62; 1864–66) and then senator (1867–81) from N.Y. state. A radical advocate of RECONSTRUCTION, he became boss of New York's political machine when given control of the state's federal patronage by President Grant.

CONNALLY, John Bowden, Jr. (1917–), US politician. He was secretary of the navy (1961–62) and Democratic governor of Tex. (1963–69). In 1971–72 he served as secretary of the US Treasury, under President Nixon, and in 1973 joined the Republican party. Connally was badly wounded during the incident in which President Kennedy was killed at Dallas, Nov. 1963.

CONNALLY, Tom (Thomas Terry Connally; 1877–1963), US politician. He served five terms in the House from 1916 and was a senator from 1928 to 1953. Chairman of the Senate's foreign relations committee (1941–47; 1949–53), he helped secure ratification of the UN Charter, and was a US delegate to the UN General Assembly (1945–47).

CONNEAUT, city in NE Ohio, on Lake Erie. Settled in 1799, it is a coal, steel and ore port. Pop 14 552.

CONNECTICUT, the southernmost New England state; one of the original 13 states. Connecticut covers about 5 000sq mi from the Taconic Mts in the NW to a coastal plain along Long Island Sound and the neighboring states of Mass., R.I. and N.Y. The climate is temperate and changeable. Although about two-thirds of the state is forested, it is generally a highly urbanized area with many New York City commuter-residents. Until 1818 the Congregational Church was the established church; Roman Catholics are now the largest religious group. Most of the state's prosperity comes from industry: Connecticut produces guns, thread, needles and pins, textiles, metal products, helicopters, jet engines and submarines. Hartford, the state capital, is the insurance center of the US. Yale, founded in 1701, was the nation's third university.

Under the 1965 state constitution a governor and other officials are elected every four years. The General Assembly, consisting of 36 senators and 177 representatives, is elected biennially. Local government is conducted by townships and cities.

The Connecticut R was first explored in 1614 by the Dutchman Adriaen BLOCK and in 1633 a Dutch fur trading post was established at Hartford. In the 1630s, Puritans from Massachusetts Bay Colony settled Wethersfield, Hartford, Windsor and Saybrook, while Congregationalists from the Bay Colony founded New Haven Colony, restricting voting rights there to members of the Congregational Church. The river towns joined to form the Connecticut Colony in 1639 to which New Haven also belonged after 1665. Colonial agriculture prospered in the Connecticut Valley and in the 18th century manufacturing developed with production of iron and tin products (the state supplied men and munitions for the revolution), and also textiles and clothing.

In 1788 Connecticut became the fifth state of the new Union. It opposed Jefferson's EMBARGO ACT of 1807 and the WAR OF 1812. The HARTFORD CONVENTION, set up to protect New England interests during the War of 1812, was dissolved when the war ended and the new state constitution (1818) was introduced. In the Civil War, Connecticut supported the Union. The war increased industry, immigration and urbanization. WWI aided industrial expansion and WWII revived the economy after the depression of the 1930s. Population and prosperity have since steadily increased throughout the state.

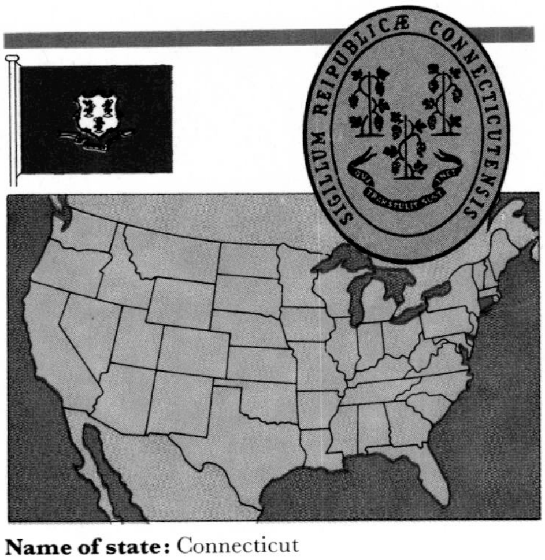

Name of state: Connecticut
Capital: Hartford
Statehood: Jan. 9, 1788 (5th state)
Familiar name: Constitution State; Nutmeg State
Area: 5 009sq mi **Population:** 2 987 950
Elevation: Highest—2 380ft. Mount Frissell. Lowest—sea level, Long Island Sound.
Motto: Qui Transtulit Sustinet ("He who transplanted still sustains")
State flower: Mountain laurel
State bird: American robin
State tree: White oak
State song: The Hills of My Connecticut

CONNECTICUT RIVER, longest river in New England. It rises in N.H., flows 407mi through Mass. and Conn. and empties into Long Island Sound. It was discovered in 1614 by Adriaen BLOCK.

CONNECTICUT WITS. See HARTFORD WITS.

CONNECTIVE TISSUE. See TISSUE.

CONNELLSVILLE, city in SW Pa., on the Youghiogheny R, settled 1770. It produces coal, metal castings and plastics. Pop 11 643.

CONNELLY, Marc (Marcus Cook Connelly; 1890–), US playwright, best known for his Pulitzer prize-winning play, *The Green Pastures* (1930). He collaborated with George S. KAUFMAN on several plays, including *Beggar on Horseback* (1924).

CONNERSVILLE, city in E central Ind., seat of Fayette Co., on the Whitewater R. A market center, it manufactures machinery and refrigerators. Pop 17 604.

CONNOLLY, James (1870–1916), Irish nationalist, Marxist and labor leader, shot by the British for his part in the EASTER RISING. Connolly worked with James Larkin to create the Irish Transport Workers Union. While living in New York City (1903–10), he helped organize the INDUSTRIAL WORKERS OF THE WORLD.

CONQUISTADORS, 16th-century military adventurers who founded Spain's empire in the Americas. Most famous among them were BALBOA, Hernán CORTÉS and Francisco PIZARRO.

CONRAD, Charles, Jr. (1930–), US astronaut. He piloted the Gemini 5 expedition (1965) to gain information on long-term space flights and commanded the successful Apollo 12 moonshot (1969).

CONRAD, Joseph (Józef Teodor Konrad Korzeniowski; 1857–1924), Polish-born English novelist. He went to sea from 1874 to about 1894 and became a British citizen (1886). Conrad is best known for his studies of individuals and also of small groups or communities (such as those on board ship or in isolated jungle settlements) at moments of extreme moral crisis. His works include *The Nigger of the "Narcissus"* (1897), *Lord Jim* (1900), *Heart of Darkness* (1902), *Typhoon* (1903), *Nostromo* (1904) and *The Secret Agent* (1907).

CONROE, city in SE Tex., seat of Montgomery Co., 38mi N of Houston. It is a trading center for a lumber- and oil-producing area. Pop 11 969.

CONSCIENCE WHIGS, members of the US WHIG party who joined the FREE SOIL PARTY (1847–54) which opposed the extension of slavery into new territories.

CONSCIENTIOUS OBJECTOR, person who refuses to bear arms and opposes military training or service. The position of objectors is based on conscience, according to their religious, political or philosophical beliefs. Groups refusing to bear arms have been persecuted at various periods in history. Most countries now have legal provisions for objectors, who are generally drafted into alternative noncombatant military duty or socially useful civilian work. (See also DRAFT, MILITARY; PACIFISM.)

CONSCIOUS, in psychoanalysis, the structure of the mind in which logical, conscious thought takes place. Because of confusion over the roles of conscious, CONSCIOUSNESS, UNCONSCIOUS and UNCONSCIOUSNESS (e.g., in dreams), the conscious is now often referred to as the EGO.

CONSCIOUSNESS, in psychology and psychoanalysis, man's capacity for self-awareness as contrasted with its lack in other animals. According to FREUD, it differs from UNCONSCIOUSNESS in that it applies and abides by rules, and in that it recognizes distinctions of space and time.

CONSCRIPTION. See DRAFT, MILITARY.

CONSERVATION, the preservation of the ENVIRONMENT, whether to ensure the long-term availability of natural resources such as FUEL or to retain such intangibles as scenic beauty for future generations.
History. The conservation movement was born in the 19th century as a result of two developments: acceptance of the theory of EVOLUTION and the concept (later proved erroneous) of the BALANCE OF NATURE. It was estimated in that century that over 100 million acres of land in the US had been totally destroyed through EROSION of SOIL caused by the reckless destruction of forests; Congress passed the Forest Reserve Act (1891) and the Carey Land Act

(1894) but both were rendered ineffectual by commercial interests. The first genuinely conservationist president was Theodore ROOSEVELT, whose Newlands Reclamation Act of 1902 began the struggle for American conservation in earnest. More recently, where officialdom has been dilatory, conservation has been brought to the people by groups such as Friends of the Earth, earning through their efforts a powerful international membership.

The Part of Science. ECOLOGY, the study of the interrelationships of elements of an environment, has enabled many scientific disciplines to play a part in conservation. In AGRICULTURE, where protection of the soil from erosion is clearly of paramount importance, crop rotation, strip-cropping and other improvements in land use have been made. Important in all fields of human existence and endeavor is the conservation of WATER for IRRIGATION, industrial, drinking and other purposes. Careful use, plus the prevention or amelioration of POLLUTION, especially by industry, are essential. Conservation of raw materials is more complicated, since they cannot be replaced; however, much has been done in the way of good management, and science has developed new processes, artificial substitutes and techniques of RECYCLING. Conservation of wildlife, however, is probably the most dramatically successful of all conservation in this century. Many species, such as the koala and American bison, that were in danger of extinction are now reviving; and most governments are vigilant in areas such as hunting and industrial pollution. Important to all these efforts is the retention of the human population within reasonable limits. In this, CONTRACEPTION has a large part to play, and many governments are now active in their encouragement of it.

CONSERVATISM, term for social and political philosophies or attitudes, stressing traditional values and continuity of social institutions and rejecting sudden radical change, while at the same time maintaining ideals of progress. It was first used in the early 19th century of the policies of the British TORY party. Modern conservative political parties include the British Conservative and Unionist Party, the Canadian PROGRESSIVE-CONSERVATIVE PARTY and the American REPUBLICAN PARTY.

CONSERVATIVE PARTY, Canadian. See PROGRESSIVE-CONSERVATIVE PARTY.

CONSHOHOCKEN, borough in SE Pa., on the Schuylkill R, 13mi NW of Philadelphia. It manufactures iron and steel products, textiles and tires. Pop 10 195.

CONSIDÉRANT, Victor Prosper (1808–1893), French socialist. He promoted the doctrines of Charles FOURIER, edited *La Phalange*, the journal of Fourierism, and published *Destinée sociale* (1834–38) and *Principes du socialisme* (1847). He tried to establish a communistic community near Dallas, Tex. (1855–57).

CONSISTENCY. See LOGIC.

CONSONANT, SPEECH sound characterized by partial or total obstruction of the breath channel. In English, all the letters of the ALPHABET save the five VOWELS are considered consonants, though *h* is truly an aspirate and *y* may be used as a vowel.

CONSPIRACY, agreement between two or more persons to commit an unlawful act; this act need not necessarily be carried out. Each conspirator is criminally responsible for the results of the act, intended or not. Conspiracy in Britain and the US tends to be a vague and ill-defined offense. Labor unions were once held to be conspiracies, and today the dispute over what exactly constitutes a conspiracy has assumed new importance with the growth of politically-motivated terrorism.

CONSTABLE, John (1776–1837), English painter. He and J. M. W. TURNER were England's two greatest landscapists. Believing that painting should be pursued scientifically, he explored techniques of rendering landscape from direct observation of nature under different effects of light and weather. His naturalist approach had some influence on the French BARBIZON SCHOOL.

CONSTANCE, Council of, western ECUMENICAL COUNCIL held (1414–18) at Constance in West Germany which ended the GREAT SCHISM caused by rival claimants to the papacy (John XXIII, Gregory XII and Benedict XIII). John and Benedict were deposed, while Gregory abdicated; Martin V was then elected. The teachings of WYCLIFFE and HUS were condemned as heresy and Hus was burned at the stake.

CONSTANCE, Lake, or Bodensee, bordered by Austria, West Germany and Switzerland. It is about 46mi long, up to 8mi wide, and is a popular tourist site. Remains of Bronze Age pile dwellings have been found on the shores.

CONSTANT, a mathematical quantity that is not VARIABLE. Constants occur in almost all POLYNOMIALS, in the form of either COEFFICIENTS or ADDENDS. Thus in ax^3+bx^2+cx+d each of a,b,c,d is a constant; should the expression be set to ZERO (see EQUATION) then the values of the constants determine the values of x for which the equation holds (see ROOTS OF AN EQUATION); should the expression be a FUNCTION then the constants determine the values of x for which $f(x)$ is defined. Constant addends are usually symbolized by c,C,k or K, though this is by no means universal.

Some constants are naturally occurring. One such is π (see PI), which is of considerable importance in MENSURATION; another is e (see EXPONENTIAL). Physical quantities whose SCALAR magnitude is constant, such as c, the velocity of LIGHT (the electromagnetic constant), or G, the universal

The Hay Wain, by John Constable, a richly atmospheric evocation of the English landscape first exhibited in Paris in 1824; his work was then far better received in France than in England.

gravitational constant, are termed **physical constants**.

CONSTANT, Benjamin (1767–1830), Swiss-born French writer and liberal political leader. Henri Benjamin Constant de Rebecque is remembered for *Adolphe* (1816), an analytical novel about his relations with Mme de STAËL, and for *Cécile*.

CONSTANTA, seat of Constanta district, SE Romania, on the Black Sea. Founded by Greeks in the 7th century BC, it is Romania's chief port. Pop 172 464.

CONSTANTINE, capital of Constantine province, NE Algeria. It was the ancient Numidian capital of Cirta in the 2nd century BC, rebuilt by Constantine 313 AD. Pop 245 621.

CONSTANTINE (d. 715), pope 708–15. He upheld Roman authority over Ravenna's archbishop and refused to accept canons established by a church council under Justinian II.

CONSTANTINE, name of two Greek kings. **Constantine I** (1868–1923), king of the Hellenes from 1913. He was expelled in 1917 by the Allies for his neutralist attitude in WWI, but recalled by a plebiscite in 1920. An army rebellion in 1922 forced his abdication. **Constantine II** (1940–), succeeded to the throne in 1964. A military coup led by George PAPADOPOULOS in 1967 deprived him of power and he went into exile in Rome. In 1973 the monarchy was abolished.

CONSTANTINE I (c280–337 AD), Roman emperor, known as the Great. He promoted and accepted Christianity, and transferred the empire's capital from Rome to Constantinople. He became Caesar in the W after the death of his father Constantius (306), who had been Augustus in the W. He defeated Maximian, emperor of the W, in 310, and then his son Maxentius at the battle of the Milvian Bridge (312), where he is said to have had a vision of a cross against the sun, which he adopted as his standard. In the *Edict of Milan*, Constantine, now Augustus in the W, and Licinius, Augustus in the E, agreed to tolerate Christianity in the empire. In 324 Constantine defeated Licinius and became sole emperor. His council at Arles (314) condemned DONATISM and the first general council of the Church at NICAEA (325) dealt with ARIANISM. He rebuilt Byzantium, inaugurating it as his eastern capital in 330 and renaming it Constantinople. He instituted a centralized bureaucracy, separated military from civil government and introduced many legal reforms.

This head from a colossal statue of Constantine the Great stands in the courtyard of the Museo dei Conservatori in Rome. Constantine was the first Roman emperor to espouse Christianity.

CONSTANTINE, Donation of. See DONATION OF CONSTANTINE.

CONSTANTINOPLE. See ISTANBUL.

CONSTANTINOPLE, Latin Empire of (1204–61), feudal empire set up by leaders of the Fourth Crusade, the Venetians and Latins. Throughout this disastrous period of Byzantine history, the city suffered massacres and pillages until its recapture by Greek Emperor Michael VIII. (See CRUSADES.)

CONSTELLATION, a group of stars forming a pattern in the sky, though otherwise unconnected. In ancient times the patterns were interpreted as pictures, usually of mythic characters. The ECLIPTIC passes through twelve constellations, known as the zodiacal constellations (see ZODIAC).

CONSTELLATION, 36-gun US warship used in an undeclared naval war with France (1798–1801). It is now a public memorial at Baltimore, Md.

CONSTIPATION, a decrease in the frequency of bowel actions from the norm for an individual; also increased hardness of stool. Often precipitated by inactivity, changed diet or environment, it is sometimes due to GASTROINTESTINAL TRACT disease. Increased dietary fiber, and taking of fecal softeners or intestinal irritants are usual remedies; enema may be required in severe cases.

CONSTITUTION, fundamental rules, written or unwritten, for the government of an organized body such as a nation. The US constitution defines the rights of citizens and of states, and the structure and powers of the federal government. It exists in documentary form, but those of many other nations do not. The British constitution is embodied in tradition and the law of the land. Some constitutions, such as that of the US, may only be altered by special procedures, while others, such as that of Britain, may be altered by a simple act of the legislature.

CONSTITUTION, US. See UNITED STATES CONSTITUTION.

CONSTITUTION, U.S.S., American frigate carrying 44 guns, known as "Old Ironsides." Launched in Boston in 1797, she served in the war with Tripoli and the War of 1812. In 1828 a plan to dismantle the warship provoked Oliver Wendell Holmes' poem "Old Ironsides." She was rebuilt, berthed in Boston, and opened to the public in 1934.

CONSTITUTIONAL LAW, US, body of law which interprets the US Constitution. The original constitution did not precisely define the roles or the limits of power of government institutions. Constitutional law studies their historical development and relates it to contemporary issues. **Judicial review** deals with the power of the courts, ultimately the SUPREME COURT, to determine the constitutionality of laws or acts of government. Although the Constitution did not provide for this activity, the Supreme Court has claimed it since Chief Justice John MARSHALL's decision in MARBURY V MADISON (1803). He claimed that since the Constitution is the supreme law, and it is the courts' duty to uphold the law, the courts must invalidate any law or action they consider in conflict with the Constitution. This power is exercised with restraint. **Separation of powers** (formulated by MONTESQUIEU) combats arbitrary exercise of governmental power by dividing it up (see SEPARATION OF POWERS). Thus legislative power is granted to Congress, judicial power to the courts and executive power to the president. Each is supreme in its own sphere, but the 20th century has seen growth in executive power, which now initiates legislation. **The federal system** divides governmental powers between the federal and state governments. The Constitution designated the federal government's powers and reserved all others to the states. Recently the use by Congress of its right to make all laws necessary and proper to carry out its constitutional function and to regulate interstate commerce has enormously increased federal power. The conflict between centralized and state power is reflected in US political parties: Democrats tend to favor centralized power and financial control, while Republicans favor STATES' RIGHTS and decentralized financial administration.

CONSTITUTIONAL UNION PARTY, US political party (the Do-Nothing Party), formed from remnants of the Whig and American (Know-Nothing) parties, active 1859–60. Its platform upheld the Constitution and the Union, while ignoring the slavery issue. As a result, the vote in 1860 was split and LINCOLN was elected by the ELECTORAL COLLEGE, the first president without a popular majority.

CONSTRUCTIVISM, artistic movement which was developed in Russia 1913–20 by TATLIN, LISSITZKY, PEVSNER and GABO. Partly influenced by CUBISM and FUTURISM, it was related to technology and industrial materials. The geometric abstract work of Russian constructivists was influential in Germany (in the BAUHAUS), France, England and the US.

CONSUBSTANTIATION, doctrine that in the Eucharist the blood and body of Christ coexist substantially with the bread and wine of the sacrament. This was introduced by LUTHER in opposition to belief in TRANSUBSTANTIATION, the changing of the water and wine into the body and blood of Christ.

CONSUL, public official who protects his nation's interests, especially economic, in a foreign country, and performs functions such as issuing visas (see FOREIGN SERVICE). The modern office of consul derives from officials who settled trade disputes in medieval Italy and France.

CONSUL, Roman, the two chief magistrates of the Roman Republic, elected annually by the COMITIA centuriata. Consuls were the heads of state from the fall of the kings, c509 BC, until 27 BC; under the empire consulship became an honorary office.

CONSULATE, the French Republic's government from 1799–1804; in reality a military dictatorship under NAPOLEON, who became first consul and was then elected consul for life in 1802. The consulate ended when he became emperor.

CONSUMER AFFAIRS, Office of, agency established in 1970 under the executive branch of the US government. It coordinates consumer activity in government agencies and departments, advises on consumer policy and handles complaints.

CONSUMER PROTECTION, the body of laws and voluntary codes setting standards for goods and services sold and the agencies enforcing them, as well as the efforts of consumer groups. In the 1960s and 1970s widespread recognition was given to the fact that the common law maxim "let the buyer beware" (*caveat emptor*) was no longer valid in superindustrial societies; today's buyer cannot necessarily protect his own best interests by judicious purchasing. The need for consumer protection arose because of the dangers of price-fixing by monopolies, of fraud and of the increasing difficulty in judging the quality or suitability of goods as technological production, packaging and sales techniques grow more sophisticated.

There are over 1000 consumer protection programs in the US under federal, state and local agencies. The federal government sets standards for weights and measures, product safety, packaging, food and drug composition and advertising descriptions. The FOOD AND DRUG ADMINISTRATION is the best known of the federal agencies. The departments of Justice, Transportation, Commerce, Housing and Urban Development, and the Federal Power Commission, Trade Commission, Communications Commission and Interstate Commerce Commission are among those involved in consumer protection.

Consumer movements. The National Consumers' League was formed in 1899 to encourage purchase of articles made under good working conditions and of good standard. Its work inspired such books as *The Great American Fraud* by Samuel Hopkins ADAMS, which contributed to the passage of the Food and Drug Act in 1906 and the founding of the American Home Economics Association (1908). Upton SINCLAIR's *The Jungle* (1906) exposed meat-packing industry conditions. *Your Money's Worth* (1924) discussed the relative merits of various brands of products. E. J. Schlinck, one of its authors, founded a Consumer's Club which became Consumers Research Inc. in 1929; it tested goods and published findings in

CONSTELLATIONS of the northern sky	CONSTELLATIONS of the southern sky
1. Pisces	1. Cetus
2. Pegasus	2. Aquarius
3. Cetus	3. Eridanus
4. Aries	4. Piscis Austrinus
5. Triangulum	5. Capricornus
6. Aquila	6. Phoenix
7. Delphinus	7. Grus
8. Cygnus	8. Orion
9. Andromeda	9. Lepus
10. Cassiopeia	10. Columba
11. Perseus	11. Hydrus
12. Taurus	12. Pavo
13. Lyra	13. Sagittarius
14. Draco	14. Aquila
15. Cepheus	15. Monoceros
16. Ursa Minor	16. Canis Major
17. Auriga	17. Puppis
18. Orion	18. Carina
19. Ophiuchus	19. Vela
20. Hercules	20. Crux
21. Draco	21. Centaurus
22. Gemini	22. Lupus
23. Serpens	23. Ara
24. Corona Borealis	24. Scorpius
25. Boötes	25. Ophiuchus
26. Ursa Major	26. Serpens
27. Cancer	27. Hydra
28. Canis Minor	28. Crater
29. Virgo	29. Corvus
30. Leo	30. Virgo
31. Hydra	31. Libra

variable stars
double stars
globular clusters
nebulae

NORTHERN SKY

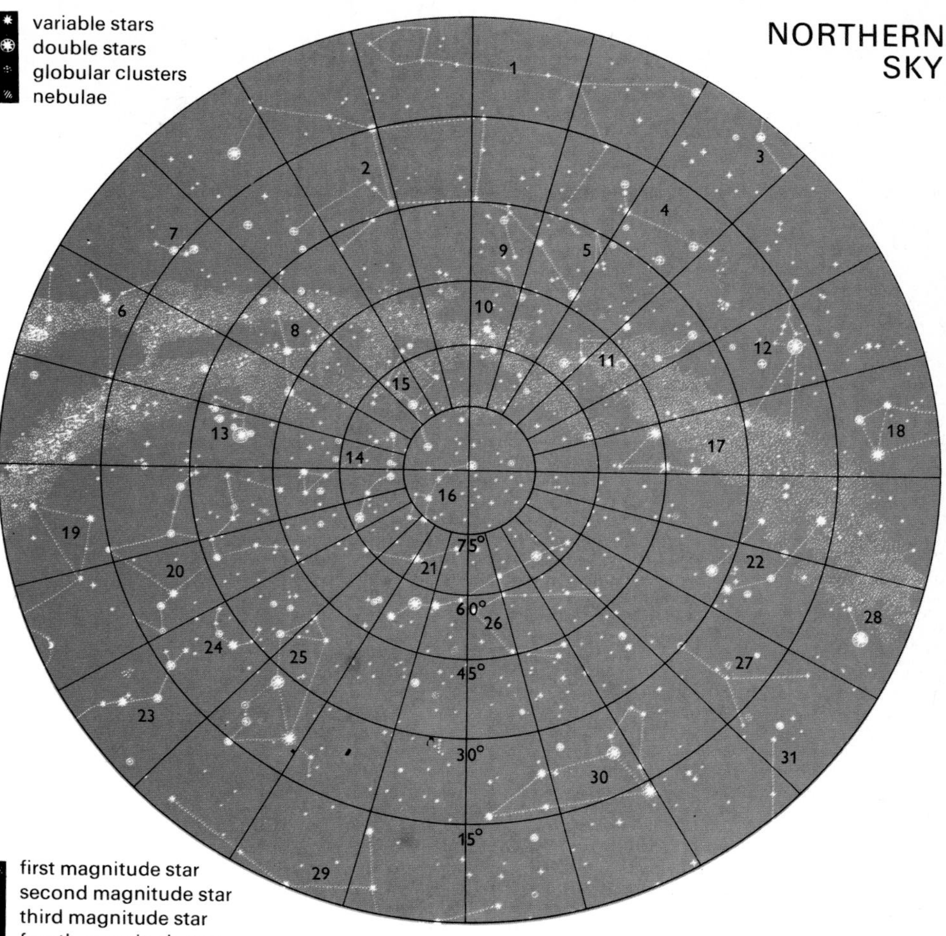

first magnitude star
second magnitude star
third magnitude star
fourth magnitude star
fifth magnitude star

SOUTHERN SKY

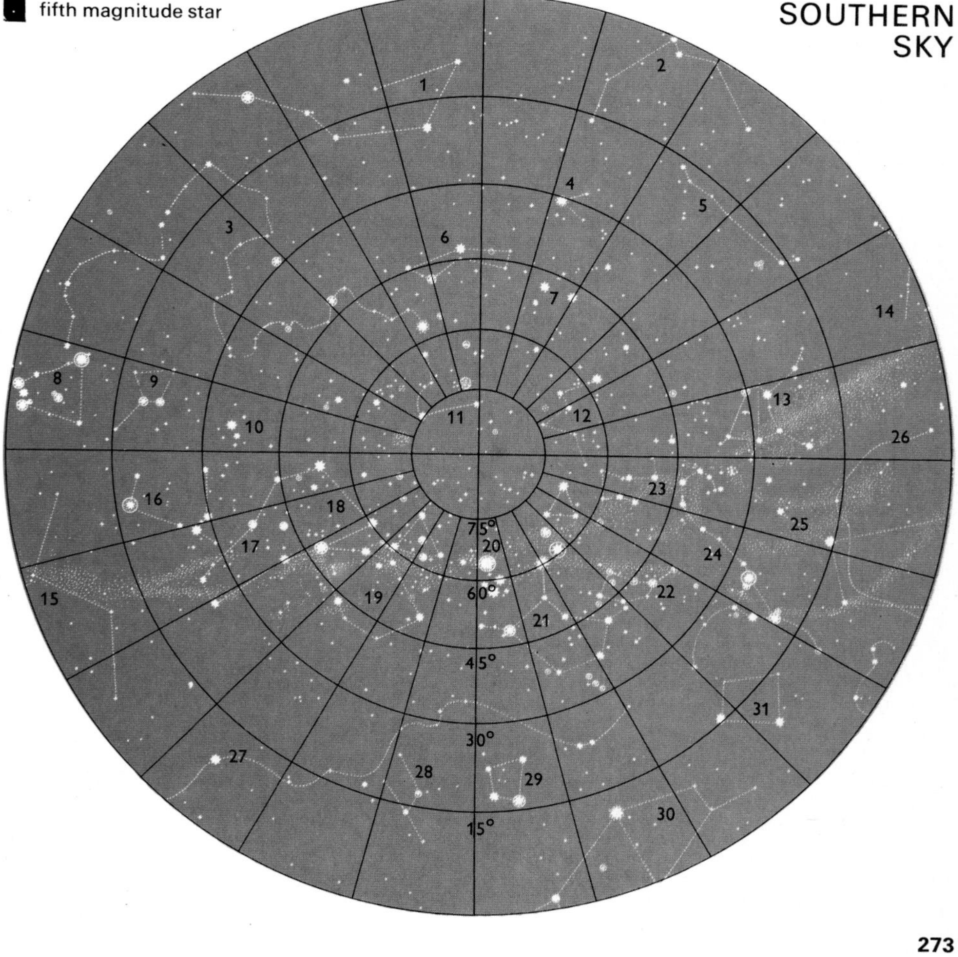

Consumer Reports. The Food, Drug and Cosmetic Act was passed in 1938.

Consumerism. Ralph NADER exposed the automobile industry in *Unsafe at Any Speed* (1965), and financed investigation of other products. With "Nader's Raiders," his volunteer assistants, he aroused consumer awareness, which was consolidated in boycotts and group lawsuits. Such action was at first bitterly opposed, but later won positive response from government, industry and the public. New York City established an Office of Consumer Protection and other cities reinforced similar institutions. The Food and Drug Administration studied food additives and regulated them more strictly. Congress introduced an Auto Safety Act (1965) and Consumer Credit Protection Act (1969) and investigated packaging and advertising. Courts have heard "class action" suits by groups of consumers. Some companies have begun to manufacture products less harmful to consumers and to the environment, such as biodegradable detergents, lead-free gasoline, returnable bottles and foods free from chemical additives.

CONSUMPTION, an obsolete term for TUBERCULOSIS.

CONTACT LENS, a small LENS worn directly on the cornea of the EYE under the eyelid to correct defects of VISION. Generally made of transparent plastic, they sometimes give better results than GLASSES and are certainly less noticeable. (See *illustr.*, p 274.)

CONTACT PROCESS, major process for manufacturing SULFURIC ACID. SULFUR is burned in air to give sulfur dioxide, which is then oxidized to sulfur trioxide with a vanadium pentoxide or platinum catalyst. Arsenic, which poisons the catalyst, must first be removed. The sulfur trioxide is absorbed in concentrated sulfuric acid to yield oleum, which is diluted with water to the concentration required. Direct reaction of sulfur trioxide with water is too violent.

CONTAINERIZATION, transport of cargo in unbroken unit loads, a growing trend from the 1960s. The cargo is packaged in containers which can be transferred from one mode of transport to another without unpacking. This has led to greater integration of shipping, railroad and road transport facilities.

Consumer Protection

Action to protect the buyer

"The business of making and selling," said the Molony Report on Consumer Protection, published in Great Britain in 1962, "is highly organized, often in large units, and calls to its aid at every step complex and highly expert skills. The business of buying is conducted by the smallest unit, the individual consumer, relying on the guidance afforded by experience, if he possesses it, and if not, on instinctive but not always rational thought processes."

The 20th century has seen a rapid increase in the manufacture of consumer goods and the provision of consumer services as well as in new methods in the distribution of consumer products. At the same time, the development of modern sales methods, advertising, mail order, supermarkets, self-service and prepackaging has made it difficult for the consumer to base a valid choice upon his own, unaided experience and judgment. Because the economic and political organization of most countries has been biased in favor of producers (manufacturers, agriculturalists and the providers of services) with a strong profit motive, it has become clear that the uninformed consumer needs "protection" from these powerful groups, either by law or by organizations established for the purpose.

During the early years of this century legal protection for the consumer was the aim, but later emphasis began to be placed on the information and education of the consumer. Now, the term "consumerism" rather than "consumer protection" more accurately describes the wide-ranging efforts to aid the individual consumer.

In most societies laws have existed to protect the purchaser: they include penalties against usury and the manipulation of markets, as well as the more obvious practices of the short weighting or adulteration of goods. But until recently the maxim for relations between seller and buyer has been "let the buyer beware." The onus was on the consumer to protect his own interests. This principle of laissez-faire capitalism assumes that the buyer is best served by competition between sellers.

The last hundred years has seen, it is true, important legislative measures for the protection of the consumer concerned primarily with food and drugs rather than with the more sophisticated consumer durables and services for which it has been difficult to devise and enforce effective regulation.

For non-food products, government bodies and national standards institutions have been of only indirect assistance to the consumer. In the United States, the General Services Administration (1949) laid down specification and quality standards that had to be satisfied before the federal government purchased equipment; thus the GSA assisted the consumer only in so far as the government was itself a consumer. In Britain, the British Standards Institute (1901) was established for the convenience of manufacturers, laying down *minimum* applicable standards. For example, a piece of electrical apparatus would have to meet certain BSI safety requirements, but its efficient operation would not receive consideration. Moreover, these standards were in general voluntary and not legally enforceable. The standards bureaus of over 70 countries belong to the International Organization for Standardization (ISO) set up in Geneva, Switzerland, in 1946, which draws up product standards for use by all countries, but which are not universally adopted. The attitudes of governments have been generally that the manufacturer should test goods to his own satisfaction, while the retailer should be responsible for them at the point of sale. It is only in the 1970s that the responsibility for goods vis-à-vis manufacturer and retailer is being legally revised in numerous countries.

Other areas of consumer anxiety have been consumer credit (loans and installment purchase) and advertising. In the past, there was little redress against exorbitant interest rates, deception and fraud. In the field of advertising, the consumer can become a prey to beguiling modern techniques, which today dominate radio and television, particularly. Advertising can and does enable the consumer to make some sort of choice between brands and retailing outlets by the information it provides, but it can also create artificial desires and disguise superficial wants as real needs. There has been little legal control by governments over the claims and methods of advertising, although the Federal Trade Commission in the US has the power to stop misleading advertising. In Britain, more effective control is exercised by the Independent Television Authority (ITA) which can ban advertising and which actively regulates content. But advertising world-wide is largely under voluntary control which is far from satisfactory.

Similarly, the control of sales methods has been lax. Door-to-door sales may involve the consumer in extensive financial commitments. The labeling of products has often been deceptive; and a lack of uniform unit pricing makes comparison between brands difficult.

It was in the United States, before World War II, the awareness of consumers' specific needs first took a practical form. During the war consumerism could not be effectively pursued, but afterwards American influence spread to Europe and, later, Japan, resulting in the formation of private consumer movements and more determined attention from governments. From the 1960s on, Great Britain forged ahead in attention to consumer problems, especially in the area of product research to determine quality and suitability for consumer use.

Historically, some of the important acts affecting consumers in the US have been:

1848: An act to prevent the importation of adulterated and spurious drugs and medicines. It stated that "all drugs and medicines, etc., shall, before passing the

Inserting a contact lens: the cleaned lens is laid on its convex side on the tip of the second or third finger (A); a droplet of special wetting agent is applied to its concave side (B); and the head is bent towards a mirror; the third or fourth finger of the hand holding the lens is placed on the rim of the lower lid and pulls it downward; one finger of the other hand is placed on the rim of the upper lid and pulls it upward (C); while looking at the lens, the second or third finger on which the lens rests moves towards the cornea and presses the lens against it; the head is raised and the eyes rolled downward for a few seconds to overcome the initial discomfort.

CONTAINMENT, US strategic policy toward the USSR outlined by George F. KENNAN in 1947. It argued that attempts by the USSR to expand beyond certain geographical limits should be countered with force. (See TRUMAN DOCTRINE.)

CONTEMPT OF COURT, an action insulting to or obstructing the proceedings of a court of law. Such actions are punishable by fine or imprisonment. Contempt can be direct (inside a court) or indirect (occurring outside, especially in refusal to obey a court order); criminal (interfering with judicial authority) or civil (depriving someone of a court's relief) or both.

CONTINENT, one of the seven major divisions of land on earth: Africa, Antarctica, Asia, Australia, Europe, North America, South America. These continents have evolved during the earth's history from a single landmass, PANGAEA (see also CONTINENTAL DRIFT; PLATE TECTONICS; GONDWANALAND; LAURASIA). (See also CONTINENTAL SHELF.)

CONTINENTAL ARMY, American force in the REVOLUTIONARY WAR, organized (1775) and commanded by George WASHINGTON. It consisted of about 5000 volunteers, joined at irregular intervals by state militia, sometimes raising the number to around 20000. It was financed by individual states and foreign loans, and was always short of money, food,

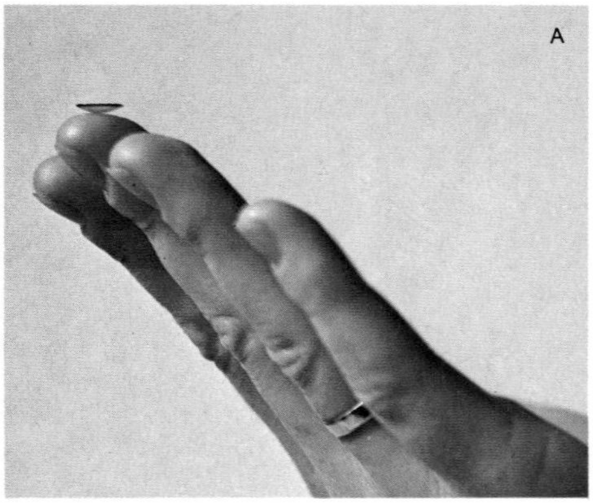
A

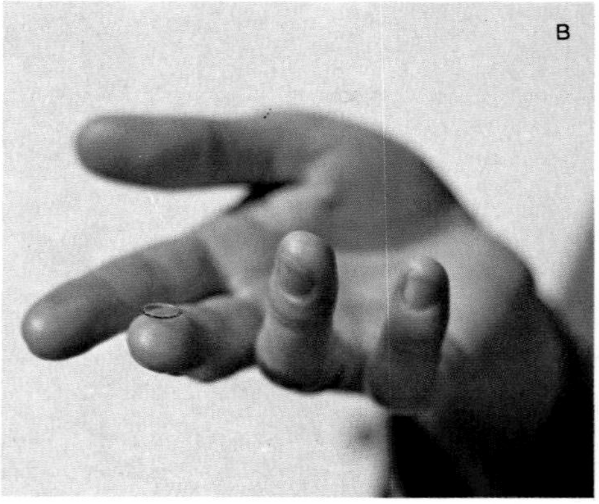
B

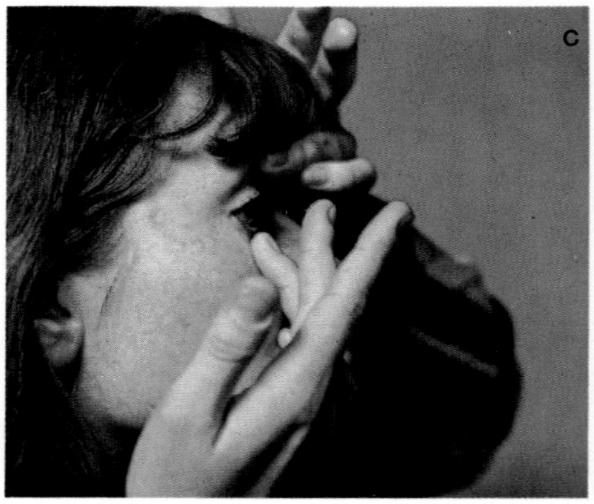
C

Custom-house, be examined and appraised."

1890: An act providing for an inspection of meats for exportation and "prohibiting the importation of adulterated articles of food or drink, and authorizing the President to make proclamation in certain cases. . . ."

1906: The *Federal Meat Inspection Act* and the *Pure Food and Drug Act*.

1938: The *Federal Food, Drug and Cosmetic Act*. There have also been acts in the individual states, aimed at preventing misleading descriptions of goods in labeling and in advertising and in stores.

The first independent organization was Consumers' Research in the US from which a splinter group formed the Consumers' Union of the United States, (1936). An important inspiration was publication of the best seller *Your Money's Worth* (1928) by Stuart Chase and F. J. Schlink, which investigated the work of the National Bureau of Standards. The Consumers' Union is independent of both industry and government. It is nonprofit-making and financed solely by its members. It set out to investigate the cost, quality and efficiency of goods and services and to protect the consumer from unwarranted or unscrupulous advertising. It aimed to provide information so that the consumer was in a position to help himself. This aim has been followed and developed by consumer movements throughout the world. The Consumers' Union has increasingly concerned itself with obtaining justice for the consumer. It has attacked, for example, dishonest practices such as the packaging of goods designed to make the quality appear greater than it really is.

A movement in the US, pioneered by lawyer Ralph Nader, has become increasingly significant. Nader has sought by direct action to benefit the consumer by lobbying and law suits, and has attacked through the mass media the power held by advertisers, industrialists and politicians. He obtained support, at first, mainly from young idealists who gathered information on suspected abuses in American governmental and corporate institutions. These helpers became known as "Nader's raiders." With his book *Unsafe at Any Speed* (1965), which exposed defects in car design and the fact the manufacturers gave speed priority over safety, he attracted immense publicity and support for the consumer cause. Nader became the center of a network of organizations which concerned themselves with a much wider scope of operations than the original consumer protection organizations and which have penetrated social, ecological and environmental fields. Nader's successes include startling danger from color TV and food and drug hazards.

Consumer movements outside the US have had different characteristics. In the Scandinavian countries consumerism has always had active and detailed governmental participation. In Japan there is an extensive, organized system of independent consumer groups engaged in active boycotting of products and manufacturers. In Great Britain the independent Consumers' Association (CA) has been highly effective, particularly in bringing about governmental action and in spreading consumerism in European countries and to the third world. CA was originated by Americans Ray and Dorothy Goodman, living in Britain, who found it difficult to obtain information on goods and services. The Consumers' Union supported the CA's early work with a small grant and acted as a successful model for the CA.

At many levels, locally, nationally and internationally, there is no doubt that consumer associations influence policy and practice. An important task is to develop ways in which consumer advice can be successfully communicated to lower income groups. One method of doing this is through locally organized and financed consumer advice centers. Also local consumer groups can make a contribution to local government policy and advise consumers about specialist regional differences.

The International Organization of Consumers Unions (IOCU), established in 1960 with headquarters at the Hague, Netherlands, coordinates the work and research of consumer organizations throughout the world. Originally set up to exchange test methods, plans and publications, and to carry out joint projects, it broadened its scope, became affiliated to the United Nations, and now holds world conferences. The consumer needs of emergent countries, many becoming productive on their own account, present special problems to IOCU.

The effectiveness of voluntary effort in pressurizing governments to take up the cause of the consumer has resulted in much recent consumer legislation. In the US, the *Consumer Products Safety Act* (1972) has been described as "a sweeping new challenge from the federal government." A Consumer Product Safety Commission has been assigned the task of assuring that the numerous products and components covered by the law are safe or even safer than the law requires. It is armed with comprehensive authority to set safety standards, ban products that cannot be made safe, rid the market of potentially hazardous products, require record keeping by manufacturers and retailers and examine such records, call for reports, inspect business premises, impose warning and instructional direction on product labels and demand safety certification—and more. The commission is backed up by enforcement devices— civil and criminal penalties and, of course, consumer law suits. The act also encourages active participation by industry, consumers and their organizations in insuring safe products.

The British government, as well as passing several consumer protection acts between 1968 and 1975, set up a Department of Prices and Consumer Protection (1974) charged with securing ways in which the consumers' voices can be heard at a national level.

Although the involvement of governments is a great step forward, education of the public is required for its support. Various magazines and reports in the US help in this respect: *Consumer Reports, Consumer Research,* the *Kiplinger News Letter* and publications of the Council on Consumer Education. Other countries publish consumer magazines and reports too. However, more formal consumer education is logically needed, and a beginning is being made. Programs are being established by consumer groups, businesses, government agencies and educational institutions to instruct individuals in the basic areas of efficient consumerism: (1) effective use of income; (2) choosing between alternative products; (3) learning how to make the best use of products; (4) the relationship between individual and social consumption; (5) effective "buymanship."

It is essential that the public should discern deception as well as be able to appreciate intrinsic worth. The consumer will need throughout his life to make informed choices and decisions, not only in his personal life but also in a world in which consumer goods are increasingly complex and which calls for skill in the equitable distribution and consumption of goods and services, some of which will become sparse in the future.

clothing and ammunition.

CONTINENTAL CONGRESS (1774–89), body of delegates representing the colonies which was summoned before and during the American REVOLUTIONARY WAR. The First Continental Congress met in Philadelphia, Sept. 5, 1774, to seek relief from England's commercial and political oppression. There were 56 delegates, from all colonies except Georgia. The congress drafted a declaration of rights setting forth the colonists' demands as British subjects, and formulated a "plan of association," denounced "taxation without representation" and agreed to boycott trade with England until their demands were met. When the Second Continental Congress met on May 10, 1775, battles had already been fought at Lexington and Concord, Mass. It appointed George Washington commander-in-chief of the army. It approved the Declaration of Independence on July 4, 1776, and drafted the ARTICLES OF CONFEDERATION, which served as a US constitution from 1781 until the present constitution was drawn up (1787). In the meantime, the Continental Congress acted as a federal government in maintaining an army, issuing currency and dealing with foreign policy.

CONTINENTAL DIVIDE, imaginary line which divides a continent at the point where its rivers start flowing in opposite directions and empty into different oceans. In North America it follows the Rocky Mts, in South America the Andes.

CONTINENTAL DRIFT, theory first rigorously formulated by WEGENER, later amplified by DUTOIT, to explain a number of geological and paleontological phenomena. It suggests that originally the land on earth composed a single, vast CONTINENT, PANGAEA, which broke up. Continental drift is now recognized to be a consequence of the theory of PLATE TECTONICS.

CONTINENTAL SHELF, the portion of a landmass that is submerged in the OCEAN to a depth of less than 200m (650ft), resulting in a rim of shallow water surrounding the landmass. The outer edge of the shelf slopes towards the ocean bottom (see ABYSSAL PLAINS), and is called the continental slope.

CONTINENTAL SYSTEM, attempted economic blockade of England initiated in 1806 by Napoleon. It was defeated by a counter-blockade by England's superior naval power. The British blockade interfered with American continental trade and was a major cause of the WAR OF 1812. (See also NAPOLEONIC WARS.)

CONTINGENCY, in LOGIC, the property whereby a statement may be either true or false, its truth or falsity depending upon the actual state of the world. The statement "the paper in this book is white" is contingent in that although it is in fact true, it is conceivable that it might have been, say, pale green. (See also NECESSITY.)

CONTINUO, or thoroughbass, in 17th- and 18th-century European music, continuous accompaniment of a musical work, underlining its harmony and rhythm. Played on the harpsichord, double bass, cello, bassoon or other instruments, continuo involved a degree of improvisation, particularly in the harmonization.

CONTINUOUS CREATION. See COSMOLOGY.

CONTRABASS. See DOUBLE BASS.

CONTRACEPTION, the avoidance of conception, and thus of PREGNANCY. Many different methods exist, none of which is absolutely certain. In the **rhythm method**, sexual intercourse is restricted to the days immediately before and after MENSTRUATION, when fertilization is unlikely. **Withdrawal** (*coitus interruptus*) is removal of the PENIS prior to ejaculation, which reduces the sperm released into the vagina. The **condom** is a rubber sheath, fitting over the penis, into which ejaculation occurs; the diaphragm is a complementary device which is inserted into the vagina before intercourse. Both are more effective with **spermicide creams**. **Intrauterine devices** (IUDs) are plastic or copper devices which are inserted into the WOMB and interfere with IMPLANTATION. They are convenient but may lead to infection, or increased blood loss or pain at menstruation. **Oral contraceptives** ("the Pill") are sex HORMONES of the ESTROGEN and PROGESTERONE type which, if taken regularly through the menstrual cycle, inhibit the release of eggs from the ovary. While they are the most reliable form of contraception, they carry a small risk of venous THROMBOSIS, raised blood pressure and possibly other diseases. When the Pill is stopped, periods and ovulation may not return for some time, and this can cause difficulty in assessing fetal maturity if pregnancy follows without an intervening period. While the more effective forms of contraception carry a slightly greater risk, this must be set against the risks of pregnancy and induced ABORTION in the general context of FAMILY PLANNING. Indeed, many risky and costly abortions could be avoided, if more thought were given to contraception.

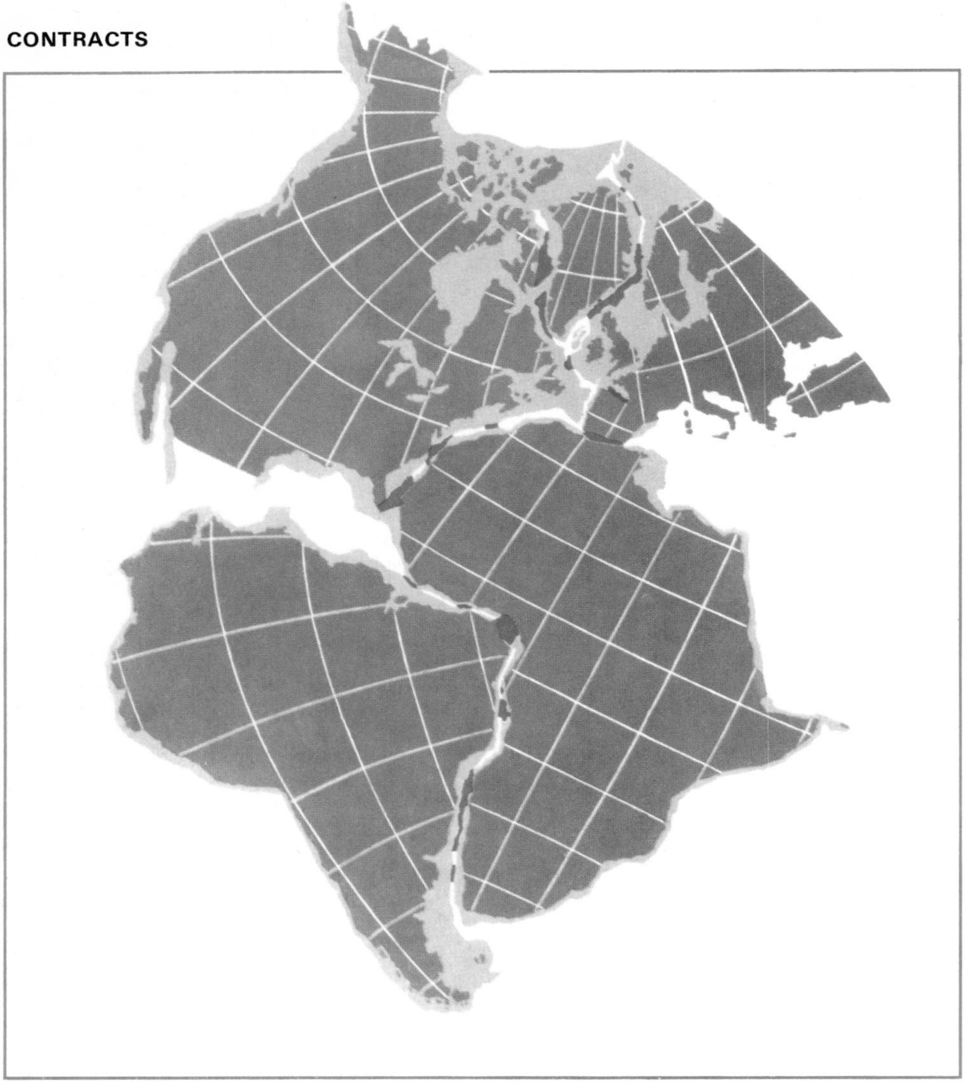

resembles the eye in mammals.

CONVERTIBILITY, an arrangement under which currencies of different countries can be exchanged for each other. The rate of exchange may be either fixed or floating (changing from day to day). After WWII some European countries were forced to restrict convertibility. However, most major currencies are freely convertible.

CONVERTIPLANE, a VERTICAL TAKEOFF AND LANDING AIRCRAFT capable of high forward speeds.

CONVICT LABOR, use of convicted prisoners as a work force. Until the 19th century it was primarily a form of punishment, and a means of reimbursing the state for the prisoners' keep. In the West, it is now used to keep prisoners usefully occupied. In some prison systems convict labor serves as vocational training and rehabilitation.

CONVOLVULUS, genus of twining plants, family Convolvulaceae, with large trumpet-shaped flowers. They are widely distributed in temperate and tropical regions. (See also BINDWEEDS; DODDER; MORNING GLORY.)

CONVOY, fleet of merchant or other unarmed vessels escorted by warships. In WWI (but only from 1917) convoys protected Allied merchant shipping against German surface and submarine attack. Development of the convoy system helped to achieve Allied victory in WWII.

CONVULSIONS, or seizures, abnormal involuntary movements, usually rhythmic and associated with disturbance of consciousness; also, a popular term for EPILEPSY.

Left: Continental drift. The jigsaw puzzle formed by the continents now bordering the Atlantic ocean when the mechanisms underlying continental drift were beginning to force them apart, some 190 million years ago. The red areas indicate continental-shelf overlap. The continental-drift hypothesis proposed by Alfred Wegener in 1912 accounted for various transoceanic parallels in the distribution of geological and paleontological evidence but did not explain convincingly why the continents should move at all. It was not until the 1960s that the first plausible driving mechanisms were postulated.

CONTRACTS, legally enforceable promises or agreements. Most are written, but verbal contracts may be equally binding in law. A contract is a bargain in which one party agrees to the terms offered by another party. To be binding there must be consideration: one party promises to do something in return for something of value promised by the other. Contracts are usually enforced under civil rather than criminal law. A party failing to fulfill his contracted promises is in breach of contract, and the court may award financial damages to the other party.

CONTRERAS, Battle of, engagement in the MEXICAN WAR, near Contreras, 8mi SW of Mexico City. Finding his advance on Mexico City blocked by generals Santa Anna and Valencia, US Maj. Gen. Winfield Scott outflanked and attacked Valencia, scattering his troops. Scott thus gained control of roads to Mexico City.

CONVECTION, passage of heat through a fluid by means of large-scale movements of material within the body of the fluid (see CONDUCTION). If, for example, a liquid is heated from below, parts close to the heat source expand and, because their DENSITY is thus reduced, rise through the liquid; near the top, they cool and begin to sink. This process continues until HEAT is uniformly distributed throughout the liquid. Convection in the ATMOSPHERE is responsible for many climatic effects (see METEOROLOGY). (See also RADIATION.)

CONVENT, monastic community of monks, friars or nuns. The term is now loosely used for nuns' residences. The first convents were established in the 4th century. (See also MONASTICISM.)

CONVENTION, business, political or other assembly of people met for a common purpose. In US politics the term usually applies to meetings of delegates to nominate candidates for political office. No provision for political parties exists in the US constitution. Originally a caucus of party members in Congress chose candidates for office. In the 1830s this system was replaced by the more democratic national convention system. In the early 1900s conventions were replaced by direct primary elections for Congressional and state offices, but the national convention to select presidential candidates survives. At its national convention, each party chooses a presidential and a vice-presidential candidate. Each US state, district or possession sends delegates to the convention to propose and vote on candidates. In early ballots delegates must vote for the candidates chosen by local party officials or elected in state primary elections. In later ballots they may support the candidate most likely to secure the final majority.

CONVERGENCE, of a SEQUENCE, the tending of its terms toward a LIMIT; of a SERIES, the tending of its consecutive partial sums toward a limit. The sequence $\frac{1}{2}, \frac{1}{4}, \frac{1}{8}, \ldots, (\frac{1}{2})^n$ is convergent, since $\lim_{n\to\infty} (\frac{1}{2})^n = 0$. Similarly, the series $\sum_{n=1}^{\infty} (\frac{1}{2})^n$ is convergent, its limit being 1. A sequence or series which does not converge is said to diverge: one such sequence is $1, -1, 1, -1, \ldots, (-1)^n$ though the sequence $1, -\frac{1}{2}, \frac{1}{4}, -\frac{1}{8}, \ldots, (-\frac{1}{2})^n$ is convergent, with limit 0. An example of a divergent series is

$$\sum_{n=1}^{\infty} (-1)^n.$$

CONVERGENT EVOLUTION, the process by which unrelated animals or plants come to resemble one another. Convergence is due to the similar effects of NATURAL SELECTION on the organisms living under the same conditions. An example of convergence is seen in the evolution of the octopus eye; this closely

Portrait of James Cook (*below*) and a map (*right*) showing the routes Cook followed during his three great voyages. The *Endeavour* was the ship that carried him on his first voyage. On his second and third voyages he sailed on the *Resolution*.

CONWAY, city in central Ark., seat of Faulkner Co., settled 1865. It makes shoes, metal products and furniture and handles farm produce. Pop 15 510.

CONWAY CABAL, plot to oust George Washington as commander-in-chief of the Continental Army in 1777, during the American Revolution. Washington had lost at Brandywine and Germantown, but General Horatio Gates had won at Saratoga. Washington intercepted a letter from Gen. Thomas Conway to Gates criticizing Washington and revealing plans by an army and Congressional cabal to replace Washington by Gates. Washington published the letter and rallied Congressional support. Conway was forced to resign his command.

CONY. See HYRAX.

COOK, Frederick Albert (1865–1940), US explorer who claimed to have climbed Mt McKinley in 1906, and to have discovered the North Pole in 1908, before Peary. Neither claim was widely believed.

COOK, James (1728–1779), English navigator and explorer who led three celebrated expeditions to the Pacific Ocean (1768–71; 1772–75; 1776–80), during which he charted the coast of New Zealand (1770), showed that if there were a great southern continent it could not be so large as was commonly supposed, and discovered the Sandwich Islands (1778). He died in an attack by Hawaiian natives.

COOK, Mount, mountain in NW Canada, in SE Yukon Territory. It is 13 760ft high.

COOK, Thomas (1808–1892), English travel agent, founder of Thomas Cook & Son and pioneer of packaged travel. He started tours in England (1841) and on the Continent (1855). In 1884 his firm transported a military expedition up the Nile.

COOKE, Jay (1821–1905), US financier who helped the federal government finance the Civil War. He formed the banking firm Jay Cooke & Co. in 1861, and sold over $1 billion in war bonds. His firm later underwrote the construction of the Northern Pacific Railway but failed in the financial crisis of 1873. Cooke made a second fortune in silver mining, 1878–79.

COOKEVILLE, town in N central Tenn., 80mi N of Chattanooga, seat of Putnam Co. and home of the Tennessee Technological U. Products include lumber, sports equipment and pottery. Pop 14 270.

COOK INLET, arm of the Pacific Ocean in the Gulf of Alaska, about 150mi long by up to 80mi wide. First explored by Capt. James Cook in 1778.

COOK ISLANDS, two groups of coral islands in the S Pacific, discovered 1773 by Capt. James Cook; a British protectorate (1888), then part of New Zealand (1901), and a self-governing dependency since 1965. The population is Polynesian. Exports include citrus fruit, copra and jewelry.

COOK STRAIT, channel 16–90mi wide separating New Zealand's North Island and South Island. Discovered 1770 by Capt. James Cook.

COOLIDGE, (John) Calvin (1872–1933), 30th president of the US (1923–29), a moderately conservative Republican who continued Warren G. Harding's policies but replaced corruption with honesty. Born at Plymouth, Vt., he became a lawyer in Mass. and rose in local political office. He was mayor of Northampton 1910–11, state senator 1912–15, lieutenant governor of Mass. 1916–18 and governor 1919–20. His firm handling of the BOSTON POLICE STRIKE gave him national prominence, and in 1920 he was chosen US vice-president, succeeding to the presidency on the death of Harding. He was elected president in 1924 over Democrat John W. Davis and Progressive Robert M. La Follette. His administration was characterized by caution, governmental efficiency and delegation of responsibility to such able men as Secretary of Commerce Herbert Hoover, Secretary of the Treasury Andrew Mellon, and Secretary of State Frank B. Kellogg.

Disapproving of government interference in economic affairs and believing in government frugality, Coolidge vetoed the McNary Haugen Bill for relief to agriculture. He lowered taxes, reduced the national budget and the national debt and protected industry with high tariffs, creating a short-lived prosperity. He handled with restraint and integrity the oil-lease scandals of the Harding administration. In foreign affairs the country's policy was isolationist. The US kept out of the League of Nations but took part in League-sponsored conferences. Coolidge's wish for US participation in the World Court was blocked by Senate opposition. He sponsored the KELLOGG-BRIAND PACT (1927) outlawing war. His administration passed the DAWES PLAN to lend Germany money to rebuild its economy. Coolidge let stock market speculation proceed but probably foresaw the Great Depression.

Calvin COOLIDGE

30th US President

Born: July 4, 1872
Died: January 5, 1933
Term of Office: August 3, 1923–March 3, 1929
Political Party: Republican

COONHOUND, US dog breed, black and tan in color, developed from bloodhound-type dogs to hunt raccoon and opossum. Of medium body length on long legs, it stands 24–27in high with long, folded, pendulous ears.

COON RAPIDS, city in SE Minn., N of Minneapolis; incorporated 1952. Home of Anoka-Ramsey State Junior College. Pop 30 505.

COOPER, Anthony Ashley. See SHAFTESBURY.

COOPER, James Fenimore (1789–1851), first major US novelist, best known for adventures of the American frontier. The series of *Leatherstocking Tales* (1823–41), with their hero the scout Natty Bumppo, includes *The Pioneers, The Last of the Mohicans, The Prairie, The Pathfinder* and *The Deerslayer*. His attitude to frontier life is romantic, characterization shallow, dialogue stilted. He also invented the sea romance and wrote works of social criticism.

COOPER, Leon P. (1930–), US physicist who shared the 1972 Nobel Prize for Physics with J. BARDEEN and J. R. SCHRIEFFER for their development of a theory accounting for SUPERCONDUCTIVITY.

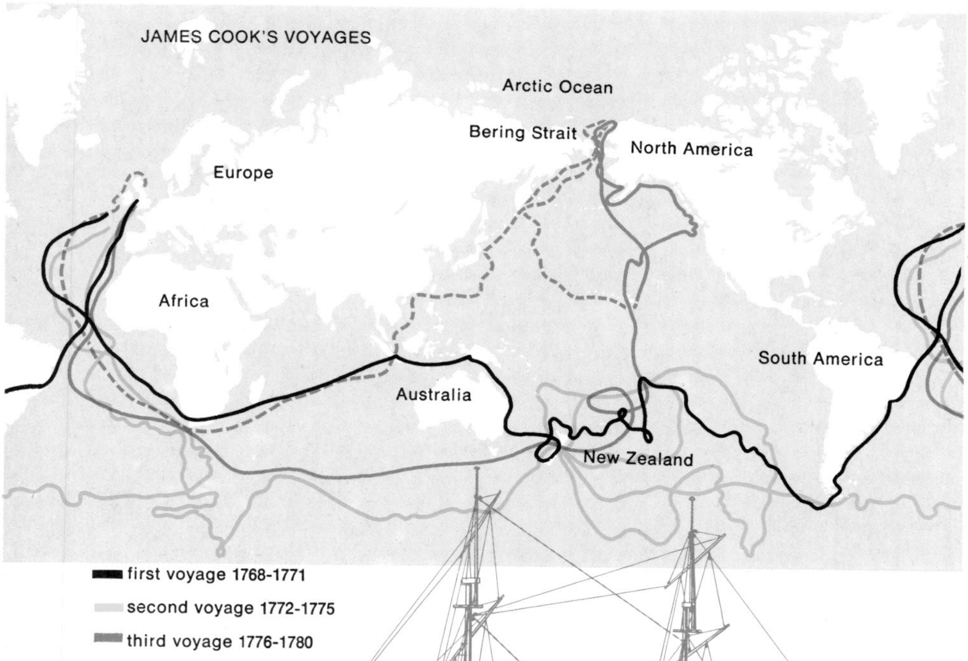

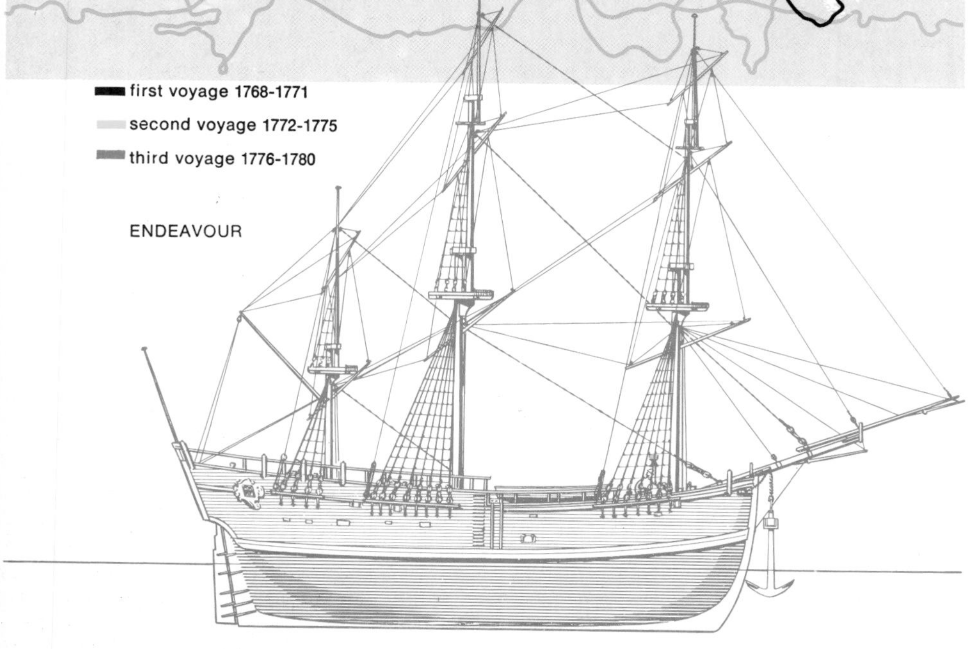

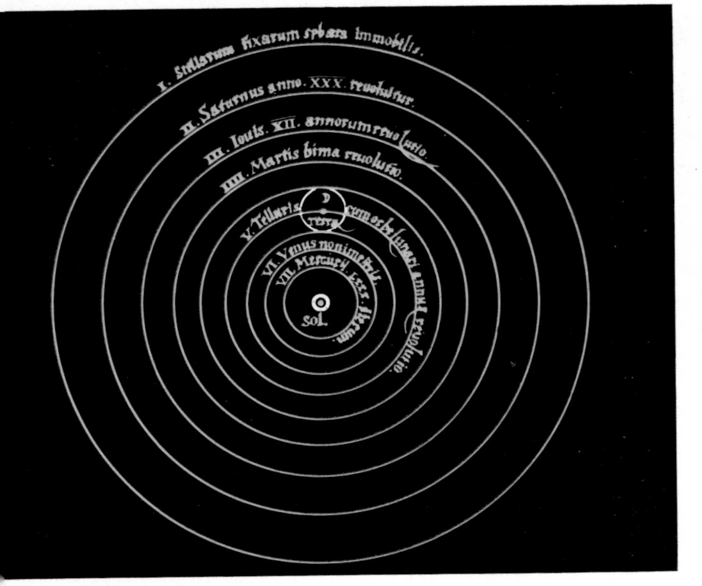

The heliocentric system of astronomy proposed by Nicolaus Copernicus, illustrated here from his great work *De Revolutionibus Orbium Coelestium*, published in 1543. The sun, at the center, is surrounded by the six planets known in Copernicus' time: Mercury, Venus, Earth (with the Moon), Mars, Jupiter and Saturn. The periods of revolution indicated are 80 days, 9 months, and 1, 2, 12 and 30 years. On the outside is what was thought to be the sphere of the fixed stars.

COOPER, Leroy Gordon, Jr. (1927–), US astronaut, the first man to make more than one space orbit. In 1963 he orbited the earth 22 times in the capsule *Faith 7.* In 1965 he completed 120 orbits with Charles CONRAD in *Gemini 5.* He resigned in 1970 to enter business.

COOPER, Peter (1791–1883), US industrial innovator and philanthropist. His Baltimore iron works built the first US steam locomotive, *Tom Thumb* (1830). He introduced structural iron beams and popularized the BESSEMER PROCESS. In 1854 he founded Cooper Union in New York City for free instruction in arts and sciences. In 1876 he was GREENBACK PARTY presidential candidate.

COOPER, Thomas (1759–1839), British-born American lawyer, educator, scientist and political philosopher. He was fined and imprisoned for attacking the ALIEN AND SEDITION ACTS (1798). He advocated freedom of speech and supported states' rights.

COOPERATIVE COMMONWEALTH FEDERATION (CCF). See NEW DEMOCRATIC PARTY.

COOPERATIVE, an association of producers or manufacturers and consumers to share profits which would otherwise go to middlemen. The pioneer Rochdale Society of Equitable Pioneers, founded in England 1844, set precedents of unrestricted membership, democratic organization, educational facilities and service at cost. The National Grange, founded in the US 1867, promoted Rochdale principles (see GRANGE, THE). Current US cooperative activity consists of farmers' purchasing and marketing, credit and banking, mutual insurance, wholesaling, group medical programs and consumer cooperatives. There are over 800 000 cooperative societies in the world.

COOPERSTOWN, village in central N.Y., seat of Otsego Co. It is the site of the National Baseball Museum and Hall of Fame and the supposed hometown of baseball. Pop 2 403.

COORDINATES. See ANALYTIC GEOMETRY; CELESTIAL SPHERE; SPHERICAL COORDINATES.

COOSA RIVER, navigable river 286mi long, formed in NW Ga. from the Etowah and Oostanaula rivers. It flows S into Ala. through man-made lakes to become the Alabama R.

COOS BAY, city in SW Ore., on Coos Bay inlet. A fishing port and shipping center, handling lumber. Pop 13 466.

COOTS, water birds of the rail family (Rallidae). They have black plumage with a white head patch. With lobed feet they swim and dive for food. The Common coot is found in S Canada to northern South America. Giant and Horned coots occur in South America.

COPACABANA, beach resort in Brazil, in SE Rio de Janeiro. It lies on the Atlantic Ocean W of Guanabara Bay.

COPENHAGEN (Kφbenhavn), seaport capital of Denmark, on Sjaelland and Amager islands. It handles most of Denmark's trade, exporting ham, bacon, porcelain, silverware and furniture. Its main industries are shipping, shipbuilding, brewing and light manufacturing. The Royal Copenhagen porcelain factory and Georg Jensen handmade silverworks are famous. Landmarks include Amalienborg Palace, Tivoli amusement park, national museums and academies of art. The university, founded 1478, is a major center for research in theoretical physics. A small fishing port until the 11th century, Copenhagen grew as a center on the Baltic trade route. In 1443 it became the royal residence and expanded under Christian IV (1577–1648). It was occupied by the Germans 1940–45. Pop 625 678.

COPENHAGEN, Battle of, naval action of April 2, 1801, when a British fleet under Sir Hyde Parker and Lord NELSON attacked the Danish forts and fleet at Copenhagen. The battle forced Denmark to leave the Northern Convention, in which Denmark, Russia, Prussia and Sweden had declared neutrality in the French Revolutionary Wars and resisted Britain's claim to right of search at sea.

COPERNICUS, Nicolaus, or Niklas Koppernigk (1473–1543), Polish astronomer who displaced the earth from the center of man's conceptual universe and made it orbit a stationary sun. Belonging to a wealthy German family, he spent several years in Italy mastering all that was known of mathematics, medicine, theology and astronomy before returning to Poland where he eventually settled into the life of lay canon at Frauenburg. His dissatisfaction with the earth-centered (geocentric) cosmology of PTOLEMY was made known to a few friends in the manuscript *Commentariolus* (1514), but it was only on the insistence of Pope Clement VII that he expanded this into the *De revolutionibus orbium coelestium (On the revolutions of the heavenly spheres)* which, when published in 1543, announced the sun-centered (heliocentric) theory to the world. Always the theoretician rather than a practical observer, Copernicus' main dissatisfaction with Ptolemy was philosophical. He sought to replace the equant, EPICYCLE and deferent of Ptolemaic theory with pure circular motions, but in adopting a moving-earth theory he was forced to reject the whole of the scholastic physics (without providing an alternative—this had to await the work of GALILEO) and postulate a much greater scale for the universe. Although the heliocentric hypothesis was not immediately accepted by the majority of scientists, its proposal did begin the period of scientific reawakening known as the Copernican Revolution.

COPIAGUE, unincorporated urban community in SE N.Y., on Long Island, near Lindenhurst. Pop 19 578.

COPLANAR, in GEOMETRY, lying in the same PLANE. It is possible to construct a plane through any set of three POINTS, but this is true of sets of four points only in special cases. Any two intersecting or parallel straight LINES are coplanar (see INTERSECTION; PARALLEL LINES).

COPLAND, Aaron (1900–), US composer using a distinctively American idiom. His lyrical and exuberant music incorporates jazz and folk tunes. His works include the ballet scores *Billy the Kid* (1938) and *Appalachian Spring* (1944), the song cycle *Twelve Poems of Emily Dickinson* (1950), the opera *The Tender Land* (1954), symphonies, piano and chamber works, and film scores.

COPLEY, John Singleton (1738–1815), American portrait painter who brilliantly depicted colonial personalities. In 1774 he left America and settled in London. He became a member of the Royal Academy and painted large canvases with historical themes, including *The Death of Chatham* (1779–80).

COPPER (Cu), soft, red metal in Group IB of the PERIODIC TABLE; a TRANSITION ELEMENT. Copper has been used since c6500 BC (see BRONZE AGE). It occurs naturally as the metal in the US, especially Mich., and as the ores CUPRITE, CHALCOPYRITE, ANTLERITE, CHALCOCITE, BORNITE, AZURITE and MALACHITE in the US, Zambia, Zaire and Chile. The metal is produced by roasting the concentrated ores and smelting, and is then refined by electrolysis. Copper is strong, tough, and highly malleable and ductile. It is an excellent conductor of heat and electricity, and most copper produced is used in the electrical industry. It is also a major component of many ALLOYS, including BRASS, BRONZE, GERMAN SILVER, cupronickel (see NICKEL) and beryllium copper (very strong and fatigue-resistant). Many copper alloys are called bronzes, though they need not contain tin: copper + tin + phosphorus is phosphor bronze, and copper + aluminum is aluminum bronze. Copper is a vital trace element: in man it catalyzes the formation of HEMOGLOBIN; in mollusks and crustaceans it is the basic constituent of HEMOCYANIN. Chemically, copper is unreactive, dissolving only in oxidizing acids. It forms cuprous compounds (oxidation state +1), and the more common cupric salts (oxidation state +2), used as fungicides and insecticides, in pigments, as mordants for dyeing, as catalysts, for copper plating, and in electric cells. **Copper (II) Sulfate** ($CuSO_4 \cdot 5H_2O$), or **Blue Vitriol**, blue crystalline solid occurring naturally as chalcanthite; used as above. AW 63.5, mp 1083°C, bp 2567°C, sg 8.96 (20°C).

COPPERAS, or Iron (II) Sulfate. See IRON.

COPPERAS COVE, town in central Tex., about 50mi SW of Waco. A farm and ranch center. Pop 10 818.

COPPERHEAD, *Agkistrodon contortrix*, a pit viper living in hill country of the eastern US. It is 0.6–1.2m (2–4ft) long and shows copper-colored hourglass markings on a dark brown background. It is a poisonous snake whose bite is dangerous but seldom fatal. It usually eats warm-blooded animals but occasionally frogs and insects.

COPPERHEADS, Northern Democrats who opposed the Lincoln administration's Civil War policy and advocated peace with the Confederates. The term originated in a newspaper article depicting them as poisonous copperhead snakes. Most urged peace through negotiation, but some secret societies (KNIGHTS OF THE GOLDEN CIRCLE, Order of American Knights, SONS OF LIBERTY) harassed Northern sympathizers, helped deserters and sabotaged Union supplies.

COPPER LEAF, *Acalypha wilkesiana macafeana*, a popular house plant that produces attractive red-brown leaves with pinkish-copper to rosy-orange variegations and insignificant flowers. Copper leaf requires a sunny position but direct sunlight should be avoided in the summer. It grows best between temperatures of 13°C and 24°C (55°F and 75°F), and should be watered regularly to keep the soil evenly moist. Propagation is by shoot tip cuttings taken in the spring and summer. Family: Euphorbiaceae.

COPPERMINE RIVER, river in Canada's Northwest Territories, in Mackenzie District. It rises N of Great Slave Lake and flows 525mi NW then N to Coronation Gulf on the Arctic Ocean.

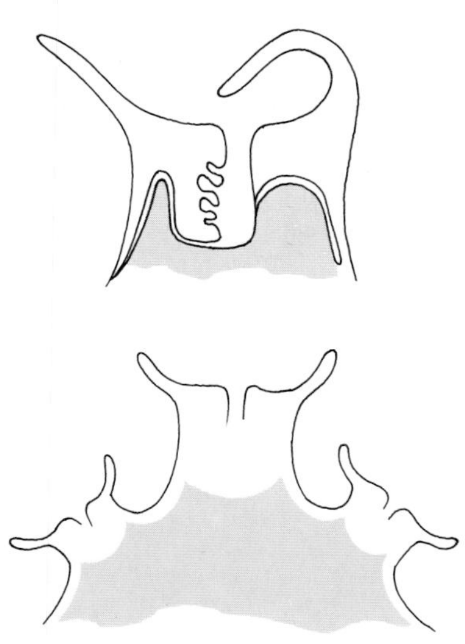

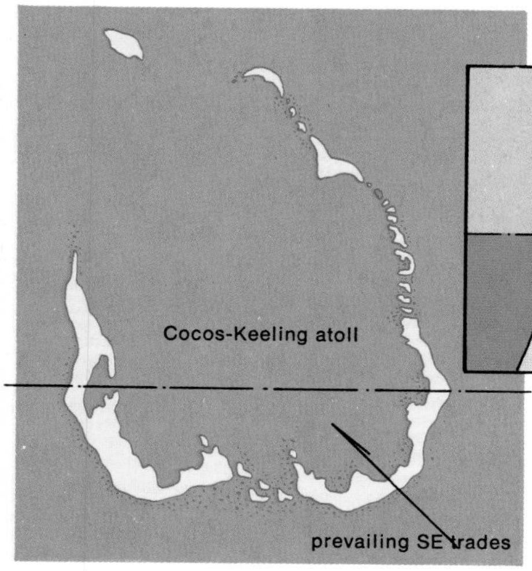

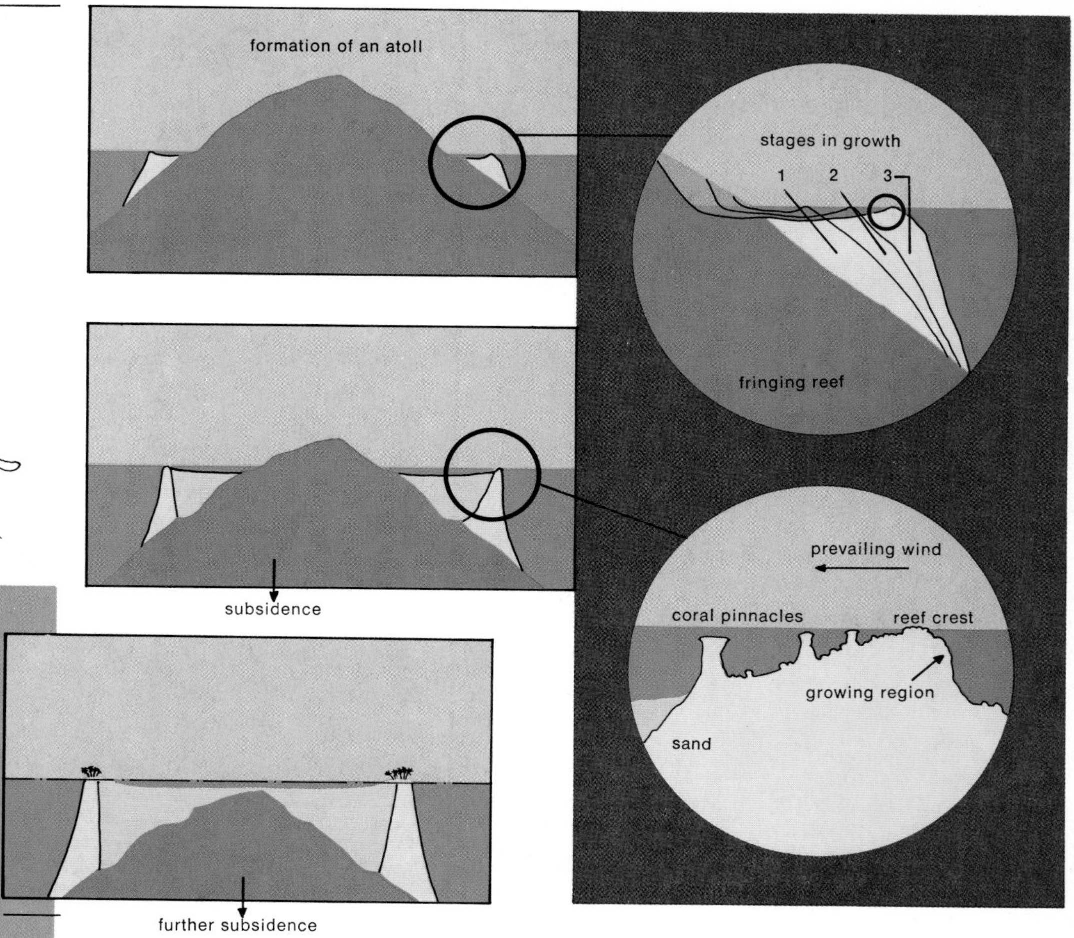

From the secreted mineral skeletons of individual corals (*top left*) the vast coral reefs of the world have been slowly built over thousands of years. Some reefs fringe a land mass, but where, as Charles Darwin suggested, the land has subsided, the reef often forms an atoll. Darwin landed on the Cocos-Keeling atoll during his famous voyage on HMS *Beagle*.

COPPER PYRITES. See CHALCOPYRITE.

COPRA. See COCONUT PALM.

COPTIC CHURCH, chief Christian church in Egypt, led by a patriarch in Cairo and 12 diocesan bishops. Services are held in Greek, Arabic and the otherwise dead language Coptic, based on ancient Egyptian. The Copts broke from the Roman Church when the Council of Chalcedon in 451 rejected their doctrine of MONOPHYSITISM. After the 7th-century Arab conquest many Copts became Muslims. The Ethiopian Church derives from the Coptic.

COPYRIGHT, exclusive right of an author, artist or publisher to publish or sell a work. Anyone reproducing a copyrighted work without permission of the copyright holder is liable to be sued for damages and ordered to stop publication or distribution. Books, plays, musical compositions, periodicals, motion pictures, photographs, designs and other works of art, maps and charts, speeches and lectures may be copyrighted in the US. This involves publishing the work with the statutory copyright notice (usually © followed by the year and copyright owner's name). Copies and a registration fee must be lodged with the US Copyright Office.

The first US Copyright Act of 1790 protected only books, maps and charts, but later legislation included other works. Current US copyright law grants exclusive rights for 28 years, renewable for another 28 years, after which the work becomes public domain. International agreements protect rights of authors in the markets of other countries. The Buenos Aires Convention protects copyright among 17 Western countries including the US. The Universal Copyright Convention covers over 50 nations including the US. (See also BERNE CONVENTION.)

CORACLE, ancient type of one-man fishing boat, resembling an Amerindian bullboat. Hides covered its bowl-shaped wooden frame. Coracles (now often covered by canvas sealed with tar) are still found in Wales, Ireland and Iraq.

CORALBERRY, popular name for an evergreen shrub of the genus *Ardisia*, which is frequently grown as a house plant for its waxy, crinkled leaves, fragrant pink or white flowers, and particularly for its persistent red berries. The plants should be kept in a sunny position although direct sunlight must be avoided in the summer. It tolerates temperatures up to 21°C (70°F) and should be watered regularly to keep the soil evenly moist. Coralberries can be grown from seeds or by taking shoot cuttings. Family: Myrsinaceae.

CORAL GABLES, city in SE Fla., 5mi SW of Miami. A residential and manufacturing center, it also houses the U. of Miami. Pop 42 494.

CORALS, small marine invertebrates of the class Anthozoa (phylum COELENTERATA) whose limestone skeletons form coral **reefs** and islands in warm seas. Most corals join together in colonies and secrete external LIMESTONE skeletons. Branches and successive layers are formed by budding and by the addition of new members produced sexually which swim freely before attaching themselves and secreting their skeletons. Older members of the colony gradually die, leaving their skeletons behind. Vegetation, such as coraline algae, cements the discarded skeletons, forming coral reefs, of which there are three types: *fringing reefs* along the shore, *barrier reefs* offshore and *atolls*, circular reefs enclosing a lagoon.

CORAL SEA, SW part of the Pacific Ocean, enclosed by NE Australia, Papua New Guinea, the Solomon Islands, New Hebrides and New Caledonia. Coral reefs abound.

CORAL SEA, Battle of the, battle between US and Japanese naval forces in the Coral Sea May 4–8, 1942. Fought by aircraft launched from carriers, it was the first naval engagement in which opposing vessels never saw each other. US losses were the heavier, but the battle checked the Japanese advance towards New Guinea.

CORAL SNAKES, poisonous SNAKES with black, yellow or white and red rings. They feed on small reptiles and insects. Two species inhabit the southern US (*Micrurus julvius* and *M. euryxanthus*).

COR ANGLAIS (English horn), large, low-pitched type of OBOE.

CORBETT, James John (1866–1933), US world heavyweight boxing champion, known as "Gentleman Jim." In 1892 he knocked out John L. Sullivan, to become the first man to win the world heavyweight championship under Marquess of Queensberry Rules. He lost his title to Bob Fitzsimmons in 1897. Later he took up a stage and film career.

CORBUSIER, Le. See LE CORBUSIER.

CORCYRA. See CORFU.

CORD, unit of cut firewood, often of 128cu ft (4ft wide, 4ft high, 8ft long).

CORDAY, Charlotte (1768–1793), French assassin of the French revolutionary Jean Paul MARAT. Objecting to Marat's persecution of the GIRONDINS, she stabbed him to death in his bath on July 13, 1793. She was guillotined by order of the revolutionary tribunal.

CORDELE, city in S central Ga., 35mi NE of Albany, seat of Crisp Co. It processes and handles farm produce. Pop 10 733.

The Corinth Ship Canal, opened in 1893, links the Gulf of Corinth with the Aegean Sea and separates the mainland of Greece from the Peloponnesus.

CORDELIERS, political club of the French Revolution, active 1790–94, led by DANTON and MARAT, and later by HÉBERT. It espoused extremist policies, helping to overthrow the GIRONDINS in 1793 and disintegrating in 1794 after its leaders were executed for trying to seize power by force.

CORDILLERA, an extended mountain system, often composed of a number of parallel ranges, associated with a GEOSYNCLINE. In some parts of the world they appear only as chains of islands.

CORDITE, smokeless propellant EXPLOSIVE containing NITROCELLULOSE and NITROGLYCERINE, with petroleum jelly as a stabilizer. Other nitrates were partially substituted for nitroglycerine in WWII to reduce gun-barrel erosion.

CÓRDOBA, city in N central Argentina on the Primero R. It is Argentina's second-largest city; a road and rail center, agricultural market, resort and manufacturing center (textiles, cement and glass), with two universities. Founded 1573. Pop 802 000.

CÓRDOBA, city in SW Spain, capital of Córdoba province, noted for its Moorish cathedral. It makes machinery, pottery, woolens, gold and silver filigree and leather work. Probably founded by Carthaginians, it was Rome's first Spanish colony. Under Muslim rule (711–1236) it became capital of Moorish Spain and W Europe's chief intellectual center. Pop 236 000.

CORELLI, Arcangelo (1653–1713), Italian composer and violinist, pioneer of the concerto grosso form which led to the CONCERTO. He wrote largely for violin, viola and cello—instruments then replacing the older VIOL family.

CORFU (Kerkira), fertile Greek island (229sq mi) in the Ionian Sea off NW Greece and SW Albania. Settled by Corinthians c700 BC, it was occupied (as Corcyra) by Rome 229 BC, and later by Byzantines, Sicilians, Venetians and the British, being ceded to Greece in 1864. It produces olives, fruit and grain.

CORGI, Welsh dog used for cattle droving, now known in two distinct breeds: Cardiganshire and Pembrokeshire, named for the counties in which they were developed. Both are long bodied and short legged with rather foxy heads. The Cardiganshire is somewhat heavier (26lb), has a long tail like a fox's brush, stands 12in high and may be any color except white. Pembrokeshires may be red, sable, fawn or black and tan, sometimes with white markings on legs, neck and breast, and have a short, docked tail, slightly longer coat and weigh 24lb. The British Royal Family has greatly popularized this breed, which is intelligent and good with children.

CORI, Carl Ferdinand (1896–), Czech-born US biochemist who shared the 1947 Nobel Prize for Medicine or Physiology with his wife, **Gerty Theresa Radnitz Cori** (1896–1957), for their joint elucidation of the processes by which GLYCOGEN is broken down and reformed in the body. (B. A. HOUSSAY also shared in the 1947 physiology prize.)

CORIANDER, *Coriandrum satiuum*, a relative of the carrot, native to S Europe and Asia Minor. The aromatic oil from its fruit is used as a flavoring in medicine, curries, sauces and liqueurs.

CORINTH, ancient Greek city on the Isthmus of Corinth. Established under Dorian rule (9th century BC), it founded Syracuse and other colonies in the 7th century BC and was the chief Greek merchant city until outstripped by Athens. Destroyed by Rome in 146 BC, it was rebuilt by Julius Caesar in 44 BC. Modern Corinth (Kórinthos) was founded in 1858 after an earthquake destroyed the old city. Pop 20 773.

CORINTH, city in NE Miss., seat of Alcorn Co. and site of a Civil War battle. It manufactures dairy products and textiles. Pop 11 581.

CORINTH, Battle of, Civil War battle at the rail junction of Corinth, Miss., on Oct. 3–4, 1862. Union forces under Rosecrans repulsed Confederates under generals Van Dorn and Price.

CORINTH, Gulf of, inlet of the Ionian Sea about 80mi long, 3–20mi wide, between the Peloponnese and central Greece.

CORINTHIANS, Epistles to the, two letters, the 7th and 8th books of the New Testament, written by St. Paul c52–55 AD to the Christian church of Corinth, Greece. The first discusses the discipline and organization of the divided church and ways of restoring unity. The second largely defends Paul's work and authority as an apostle.

CORINTH SHIP CANAL, canal in Greece, cut (1881–93) 4mi through the Isthmus of Corinth. It connects the Gulf of Corinth with the Saronic Gulf.

CORIOLANUS, Gaius Marcius (5th century BC), legendary Roman patrician, hero of Shakespeare's *Coriolanus*. He was named for Corioli, a town he allegedly won for Rome from the Volscians in 493 BC. Exiled for his anti-plebeian attitude, he led a Volscian attack on Rome until his mother and wife persuaded him to relent.

CORIOLIS EFFECT, a FORCE which, like a centrifugal force (see CENTRIPETAL FORCE), apparently acts on moving objects when observed in a frame of reference which is itself rotating. Because of the rotation of the observer, a freely moving object does not appear to move steadily in a straight line as usual, but rather as if, besides an outward centrifugal force, a "Coriolis force" acts on it, perpendicular to its motion, with a strength proportional to its MASS, its VELOCITY and the rate of rotation of the frame of reference. The effect, first described in 1835 by **Gaspard de Coriolis** (1792–1843), accounts for the familiar circulation of air flow around CYCLONES, and numerous other phenomena in METEOROLOGY, oceanography and BALLISTICS.

CORK, seaport city in SW Ireland at the mouth of the Lee R. Seat of County Cork, it produces and handles beer, whiskey, petrochemicals and dairy products. Cobh is its port for ocean steamers. Pop 128 235.

CORK, protective, waterproof layer of dead cells that have thick walls impregnated with suberin, a waxy material. Cork is found as the outer layer of stems and roots of older woody plants. The cork oak (*Quercus suber*) of S Europe and North Africa produces a profuse amount of cork, which is harvested commercially every 3 to 4 years. (See also CAMBIUM; OAK.)

CORLISS, George Henry (1817–1888), US inventor. He invented a sewing machine predating Elias HOWE's, and designed improvements for steam engines, including a reliable GOVERNOR.

CORM, short, stout, underground stem. It is an organ of vegetative reproduction consisting of a stem base swollen with food material and bearing buds in the remains of the leaves of the previous year's growth. Examples are found in the CROCUS and GLADIOLUS. (See also BULB; RHIZOMES; TUBER.)

CORMORANTS, or shags, birds of the family Phalacrocoracidae related to PELICANS. Cormorants have long necks and bills, are usually black, and dive for fish food in coastal regions and in the larger lakes and rivers of the world. There are 30 species.

CORN, or **maize,** *Zea mays*, a grain crop native to the New World, but now cultivated throughout the world and second among the world's crop plants to WHEAT in terms of acreage planted. The major area of cultivation is in the Midwest cornbelt of the US. Five main types of corn have been developed. Most of the US yield is dent corn (so-called from the indentation in the crown of each kernel) used for animal feed. Flint corn grows in colder climates, such as Canada. It has a hard kernel and is used for animal feed. Sweet corn, containing sugar, is a familiar vegetable. Popcorn kernels have hard outer coatings to prevent moisture escape. When heated the internal steam pressure causes them to burst. Flour corn, grown in Peru, Bolivia and Ecuador, has soft kernels and is used for flour and corn meal. The plants grow 0.9–4.5m (3–15ft) high and require a frost-free growing season of at least 100 days. Each plant develops 1–3 ears. The male flowers are in tassels on top of the stem. The female inflorescences consist of a number of rows of ovaries; each ovary is crowned by a silk that projects from the top of the "cob." Pollination is by the wind, the pollen falling on the silks. Corn is subject to numerous diseases. Fungi attack young plants and improperly stored ears and bacterial leaf blights cause wilting. RUST, SMUT and VIRAL DISEASES also attack the crop. The CORN BORER is the worst insect pest. Corn is mainly used in the US as an animal feed, but elsewhere it is a major human food. Corn is ground for feeding to animals and for human consumption. It is rolled and flattened for breakfast cereals. Cornbread, hominy, mash, griddle cakes and confections are made from corn. Industrially corn is processed to make alcohol, syrup and oil and is used in manufacturing plastics. The stalk is sometimes used in paper and wall board manufacture. The term "corn" is also used locally to indicate the CEREAL CROPS most important in the district, e.g., in England corn refers to wheat and in some parts of Scotland to OATS. (See also AGRICULTURE; PLANT DISEASES.)

CORN BORERS, any one of several moths whose caterpillars feed on plants, including beet, beans and corn. Native to Europe, they attacked Indian corn introduced there and were transported to North America in 1907, where they are serious pests.

CORNEA, the transparent part of the outer EYE, through which VISION occurs and the iris may be seen; it is responsible for much of the focusing power of the eye. Made of specialized cells and connective tissue, it may be replaced after trauma or infection by a graft from a cadaver.

CORN EARWORM. See BOLLWORM.

CORNEILLE, Pierre (1606–1684), French dramatist, creator of French classical verse tragedy. His masterpiece, *Le Cid* (1637), though controversial in its time, was a great popular success. His many other plays included *Horace* (1640), *Cinna* (1641) and *Polyeucte* (1643). His popularity faded with the rise of his younger rival, RACINE.

CORNELIAN. See CARNELIAN.

CORNELIUS, Saint (d. 253 AD), pope 251–253. Opposed (251) by Antipope Novatian, he was exiled under the Emperor Gallus. His feast day (shared with that of his friend St. CYPRIAN) is Sept. 16.

CORNELL, Alonzo Barton (1832–1904), US businessman and politician, son of Ezra CORNELL. He was director and vice-president of the Western Union Telegraph Company 1868–99, chairman of the N.Y. Republican Party 1870–78 and governor of N.Y. 1880–83.

CORNELL, Ezra (1807–1874), US businessman, a pioneer in telegraphy. He created America's first (Baltimore–Washington) telegraph line (1844) with Samuel MORSE, and was founder and director of the Western Union Telegraph Company (1855). His gifts helped create Cornell U., Ithaca, N.Y. (1868).

CORNELL, Katharine (1898–1974), US actress, noted for her major roles in serious dramas, often directed by her husband Guthrie McClintic. Her most famous part was Elizabeth Barrett Browning in *The Barretts of Wimpole Street* (1931).

CORNER BROOK, city in W Newfoundland, Canada, on the Humber estuary. Its products include cement, paper, gypsum and fish. Pop 26 309.

CORNET, valved brass WIND INSTRUMENT somewhat like a trumpet. It has a mellow tone controlled by lip vibration at the cupped mouthpiece, a two-and-a-half octave range and is usually tuned to B flat. Cornets are used in brass bands but rarely in orchestras.

CORNFLOWER, or **bachelor's button**, *Centaurea cyanus*, annual flower of the COMPOSITAE, reaching 0.3–0.6m (1–2ft) in height and generally producing blue flowers. It is native to Europe and naturalized in North America.

CORNFORTH, John Warcup (1917–), Australian-born British biochemist who shared the 1975 Nobel Prize for Chemistry with V. PRELOG for his work on the STEREOCHEMISTRY of enzyme-catalyzed reactions.

CORNING, industrial city in SW N.Y., on the Chemung R. Home of Corning Glass Works and Corning Community College. It produces glass, lenses, electronic equipment and precision instruments. Pop 15 792.

CORNISH. See CELTIC LANGUAGES.

CORN ISLANDS, two small islands (4sq mi) in the Caribbean Sea, part of Nicaragua. The BRYAN-CHAMORRO TREATY leased them to the US (1916–71) as a naval base.

CORN LAWS, various laws regulating English import and export of grain from the 14th century to 1849. After the Napoleonic Wars the corn price was raised to offset agricultural depression. But protests from the poor and from manufacturers objecting to agricultural subsidy helped COBDEN and BRIGHT, leaders of the Anti-Corn Law League (1839–46), to persuade Prime Minister Sir Robert PEEL to repeal the Corn Laws (1846 and 1849).

CORNPLANTER (c1732–1836), Seneca Indian chief, son of a Dutch trader and a Seneca mother. He led Indian parties for the British in the Revolutionary War but in 1784 ceded Indian lands to the US. Pa. gave him a pension and a land grant on the upper Allegheny R.

CORNS AND CALLUSES, localized thickenings of the horny layer of the SKIN, produced by continual pressure or friction. **Calluses** project above the skin and are rarely troublesome; **corns** are smaller, and are forced into the deep, sensitive layers of skin, causing pain or discomfort.

CORNSTALK (c1720–1777), Shawnee Indian chief. He fought sporadically against Virginian settlers until 1763, and in 1774 led a major rising, but made peace after a defeat at Point Pleasant. Later held hostage there, he was killed in reprisal for an Indian ambush.

CORNUCOPIA, horn of plenty. In classical art figures hold the horn from which pours fruit or grain, symbolizing plenty, fertility or liberality.

CORNWALL, southwesternmost county in England, and a duchy of the heir to the throne. It is a peninsula between the Atlantic Ocean and English Channel, with fishing, farming and tourism.

CORNWALL, manufacturing city and port in SE Ontario, Canada, on the St. Lawrence R. It produces chemicals, textiles, paper and flour. Pop 47 116.

CORNWALLIS, Charles Cornwallis, 1st Marquis of (1738–1805), British general, whose surrender to Washington at Yorktown (Oct. 19, 1781) ended the Revolutionary War. Earlier, he had defeated Nathanael Greene in the Carolinas. He later gave important service as governor-general of India 1786–93 and 1805, and as viceroy of Ireland 1798–1801.

COROLLA. See FLOWER.

COROMANDEL COAST, SE coast of India, low-lying, surf-beaten and lacking natural harbors. Ports include Madras, Nellore and Pondicherry.

Ears and seeds of three of the most widely cultivated types of corn: (1) "flat" corn, also known in the US as "dent"; (2) sweet corn; and (3) popcorn. Corn is the most important crop in the US, which annually harvests some four billion bushels—almost half the world's total production. The main corn-growing region in the US—the "corn belt"—includes the whole of Iowa and parts of Illinois, Indiana, Ohio, Missouri, Kansas, Nebraska, South Dakota and Minnesota.

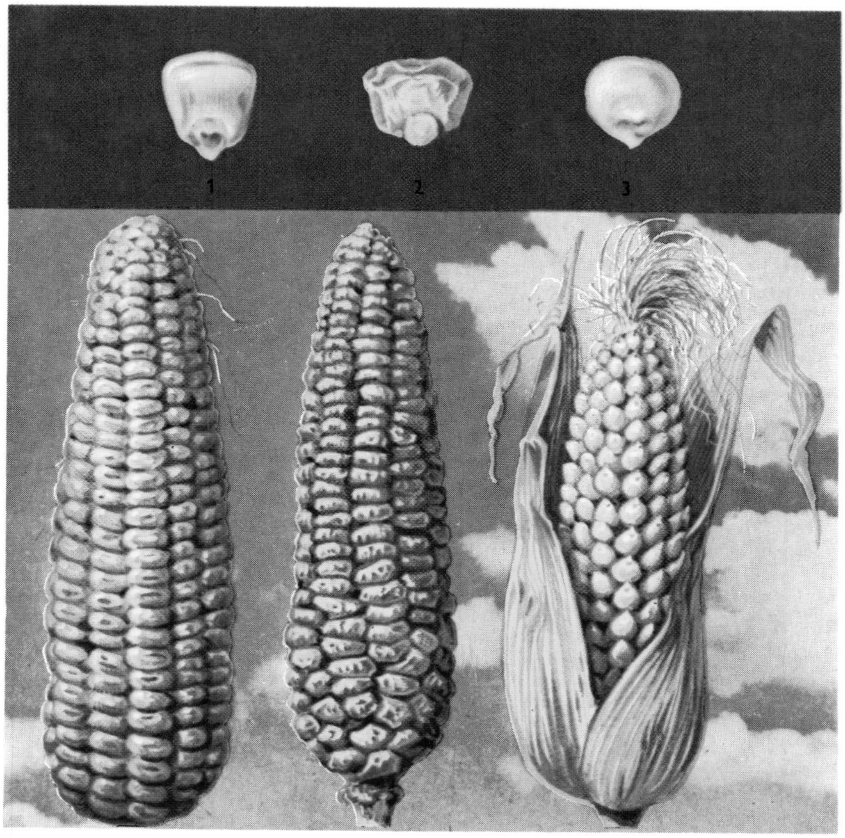

CORONA, city in SW Cal., founded 1898. It produces die castings and handles citrus fruit. Pop 27 519.

CORONA, outer atmosphere of the SUN or other STAR. The term is used also for the halo seen around a celestial body due to DIFFRACTION of its light by water droplets in thin CLOUDS of the earth's ATMOSPHERE; and for a part appended to and within the corolla of some FLOWERS. Around high-voltage terminals there appear a faint glow due to the ionization (see ION) of the local air. The result of this ionization is an electrical discharge known as **corona discharge**, the glow being called a corona.

CORONADO, city in S Cal., W of San Diego Bay. A beach resort and residential city. Pop 20 910.

CORONADO, Francisco Vázquez de (1510–1554), Spanish explorer of SW North America. While governor of Nuevo Galicia (in Mexico) in 1540 he subdued the so-called Seven Cities of CIBOLA. Fruitlessly seeking gold, his expedition probed what is now N.M., Ariz., Tex. and Kan., and discovered the Grand Canyon.

CORONARY THROMBOSIS, myocardial infarction, or heart attack, one of the commonest causes of serious illness and death in Western countries. The coronary ARTERIES, which supply the HEART with OXYGEN and nutrients, may become diseased with ARTERIOSCLEROSIS which reduces BLOOD flow. Significant narrowing may lead to superimposed THROMBOSIS which causes sudden complete obstruction, and results in death or damage to a substantial area of heart tissue. This may cause sudden death, usually due to abnormal heart rhythm which prevents effective pumping. Severe persistent pain in the center of the CHEST is common, and it may lead to SHOCK or LUNG congestion. Characteristic changes may be seen in the ELECTROCARDIOGRAPH following myocardial damage, and ENZYMES appear in blood from the damaged heart muscle. Treatment consists of rest, ANALGESICS and drugs to correct disordered rhythm or inadequate pumping; certain cases must be carefully observed for development of rhythm disturbance. Recovery may be complete and normal activities resumed. Predisposing factors, including OBESITY, SMOKING, high blood pressure, excess blood FATS (including CHOLESTEROL) and DIABETES must be recognized and treated.

CORONATION, ceremony of crowning a sovereign. The ritual usually has religious as well as temporal significance and includes anointment, investiture with symbols of royalty, swearing a coronation oath and enthronement.

COROT, Jean Baptiste Camille (1796–1875), French landscape painter, who broke with classical tradition to achieve subtle lighting effects by painting directly from nature. He won fame with his misty gray-green landscapes, and influenced the BARBIZON SCHOOL and IMPRESSIONISM.

CORPORAL PUNISHMENT, punishment inflicted on the offender's body. Whipping, branding, mutilation and imprisonment in the stocks were common until c1800, when the concept of more humane punishment gained currency.

CORPORATE STATE (corporatism), theory which holds that a community consists of functional or economic groups rather than of individuals. It has been part of authoritarian governmental ideology in Fascist Italy, Nazi Germany, Spain and Portugal. In theory each group (labor unions, business firms, etc.) names representatives to a governing body which takes its views into account. In fact corporate ideology was usually a slogan giving dictatorship a veneer of respectability. Thus in Italy corporations were created under state direction.

CORPORATION, group of persons forming a legal entity independent of the individuals owning or managing it. As a legal "person" it may hold property, sue and be sued. Corporations may be public or private. Municipal corporations such as school districts and cities perform some governmental functions. National public corporations carry out large-scale enterprises. Private corporations carry on a vast range of business and other activities. Advantages of a corporation are that it can deal in its

Detail of Correggio's *The Mystic Marriage of St. Catherine*, painted 1518–19, and now in the Capodimonte Museum, Naples. Correggio's work was much influenced by Leonardo da Vinci and is seen as a forerunner of the Baroque and later schools with its graceful emphasis on expression and pose.

own name without risking the personal finances of its officers or stockholders; it has a permanence lacking in a partnership or individually owned business; and it may raise large amounts of capital by sale of stocks.

Corporations are chartered by state governments and usually managed by officers named by a board of directors elected by the votes of a stockholders' majority. Thus anyone owning 51% of the stock controls a corporation. Business corporations grew out of the great trading companies of 16th- and 17th-century England. In the US, N.Y. passed the first general corporation law in 1811.

CORPUS CHRISTI, city in SE Tex., on Corpus Christi Bay. Seat of Nueces Co., it is a major port and industrial center (oil and gas fields, and metal refineries), a fishing resort and home of the U. of Corpus Christi. Pop 204 525.

CORPUS CHRISTI, Feast of, festival of the Roman Catholic Church honoring Christ's presence in the Eucharist. It was instituted in 1264 and is celebrated on the Thursday after Trinity Sunday. It was marked by a procession, once followed by the performance of miracle and MYSTERY PLAYS.

CORPUSCLE. See BLOOD.

CORPUS JURIS CIVILIS, the code of Roman law. Compiled in the 6th century under the Emperor Justinian, it enshrined 1000 years of legal development in its *Institutes, Digest, Codex* and *Novels*. Rediscovered in the 11th century, it is the basis of CIVIL LAW in much of Europe.

CORREGGIO (real name: Antonio Allegri; c1494–1534), Italian Renaissance painter who influenced the BAROQUE style. His works (including most of his Parma frescoes) are primarily devotional, and are noted for softness and use of CHIAROSCURO.

CORREGIDOR, fortified rocky island (2sq mi) in the Philippines, at the entrance to Manila Bay. Under US control from 1898, it fell to the Japanese in May 1942 after four months of fierce fighting. Recaptured in 1945, it is now a WWII memorial.

CORRELATION, Statistical, the inter-dependent variation of two or more VARIABLES. Positive correlation between two variables occurs when increase in the value of one implies increase in the value of the other, decrease similarly implying decrease. Negative correlation occurs when increase in the value of one implies decrease in the value of the other. (See also STATISTICS.)

A measure of the correlation between two variables is given by their **correlation coefficient**, r, given by

$$r=\frac{\sum_{i=1}^{n}(a_i-\bar{a})(b_i-\bar{b})}{\sqrt{\sum_{i=1}^{n}(a_i-\bar{a})^2\sum_{i=1}(b_i-\bar{b})^2}}$$

where a and b are the variables, and $\bar{a}$ and $\bar{b}$ are their mean values (see MEAN, MEDIAN AND MODE). r varies between -1 and $+1$; $r=-1$ indicating perfect negative correlation, $r=0$ the mutual independence of the variables, and $r=+1$ perfect positive correlation.

CORROSION, the insidious destruction of metals and alloys by chemical reaction (mainly OXIDATION) with the environment. The annual cost of corrosion is more than $5 billion in the US alone. In moist air most metals form a surface layer of oxide, which, if it is coherent, may slow down or prevent further corrosion. **Tarnishing** is the formation of such a discolored layer, mainly on copper or silver. (**Rust**—hydrated iron (III) oxide, $FeO(OH)$—offers little protection, so that iron corrodes rapidly.) Industrial AIR POLLUTION greatly speeds up corrosion, oxidizing and acidic gases (especially sulfur dioxide) being the worst culprits. Corrosion is usually an electrochemical process (see ELECTROCHEMISTRY): small cells are set up in the corroding metal, the potential difference being due to the different metals present or to different concentrations of oxygen or electrolyte; corrosion takes place at the anode. It also occurs preferentially at grain boundaries and where the metal is stressed. Prevention methods include BONDERIZING; a protective layer of paint, varnish or electroplate; or the use of a "sacrificial anode" of zinc or aluminum in electrical contact with the metal, that is preferentially corroded. **Galvanizing**—coating iron objects with zinc—works on the same principle.

CORROSIVE SUBLIMATE, or **mercury (II) chloride.** See MERCURY.

CORRUPT PRACTICES ACTS, US federal and state legislation designed to stop unethical electioneering. The major Act of 1925 regulated US Congressional elections. It limited campaign expenditure for would-be senators and representatives, forbade contributions from national banks and corporations and obliged treasurers of political committees and candidates for office to report contributions and expenditures. (See also HATCH ACTS.)

CORSAIRS, Muslim pirates from the BARBARY STATES who preyed on Mediterranean and Atlantic shipping, especially Christian vessels. Corsairs flourished in the 16th–19th centuries, after BARBAROSSA had used Turkish aid to make Algiers and Tunis strong pirate bases.

CORSET, stiff, close-fitting undergarment controlling the figure, sometimes for surgical reasons. It developed from the medieval laced bodice. In the 16th century corsets were of bone-stiffened leather. In the 19th century both men and women wore corsets.

CORSICA, Mediterranean island and French department N of Sardinia, off W Italy, occupying 3352sq mi. It is largely mountainous, with much Mediterranean scrub and forest. Its products include olive oil, wine and citrus fruits. The capital is Ajaccio. Its rulers have included Carthaginians, Romans, Vandals, Goths, Saracens and (1347–1768) the Genoese, who sold it to France. There is strong nationalist feeling on the island. Napoleon Bonaparte was born here.

CORSICANA, city in central Tex., seat of Navarro Co. It has flour-milling and oil-refining industries and local oil and gas wells. Pop 19 972.

CORTES (Spanish: courts), representative assembly of Spain. It originated in the medieval kingdoms' assemblies of nobles, clergy and burghers. The Cortes instituted in 1942 by General FRANCO had little power. Portugal under the monarchy had legislative bodies called cortes.

CORTÉS, Hernán (1485–1547), Spanish explorer, conqueror of Mexico. In 1504 he settled in Hispaniola (Santa Domingo) and in 1511 joined the conquest of Cuba, becoming mayor of Santiago. Sent to explore Yucatán, in 1519 he marched on the AZTECS' capital Tenochtitlán, where MONTEZUMA greeted him as the white god QUETZALCOATL. Cortés took Montezuma prisoner, but the latter was killed in an uprising against the Spaniards. Cortés retreated, but returned in 1521 and conquered the capital, ending the Aztec Empire. He later explored Honduras and Lower California.

CORTEX, in plant STEMS and ROOTS, the layer of mostly unspecialized packing cells between the EPIDERMIS and the PHLOEM. It is used to store food and other substances including resins, oils and tannins; in stems it may contain CHLOROPLASTS; in roots it transports water and ions inwards. The term is used for the outer layer of the BRAIN, KIDNEYS or ADRENAL GLANDS.

CORTISOL, principal natural STEROID HORMONE.

CORTISONE, minor STEROID, converted to CORTISOL.

CORTLAND, city in central N.Y., on the Tioughnioga R, seat of Cortland Co. It is the home of the State University College, and produces canned food, vehicles and clothing. Pop 19 621.

CORTONA, historic town of central Italy, in Arezzo province. It has Etruscan ruins, Roman baths, Gothic churches, a cathedral and paintings by Luca Signorelli and Fra Angelico. Pop 23 564.

CORTOT, Alfred Denis (1877–1962), French pianist, conductor and teacher, a leading interpreter of Romantic piano works. With CASALS and Jacques Thibaud, he formed a famous trio in 1905. In 1918 he founded the École Normale de Musique in Paris.

CORUÑA, La (Corunna). See LA CORUÑA.

CORUNDUM, or α-alumina, rhombohedral form of aluminum oxide (see ALUMINUM), occurring worldwide (see also EMERY); transparent varieties include RUBY and SAPPHIRE. Artificial corundum, or β-alumina, is made by calcining BAUXITE. Corundum is the hardest natural substance after diamond (Mohs hardness 9), and is used as an abrasive and for BEARINGS.

CORVALLIS, city in NW Ore., on the Willamette R. Seat of Benton Co. and home of Oregon State U., it makes dairy and forest products. Pop 35 056.

CORVETTE, escort warship smaller than a frigate. In sailing days corvettes were flush-deck vessels with one row of guns.

COSECANT. See TRIGONOMETRY.

COSGRAVE, Liam (1920–), Irish politician, prime minister of Eire from 1973. A member of the Dáil from 1943, he was minister for commerce and industry 1948–54, minister for external affairs 1954–57 and leader of the Fine Gael Party from 1965.

COSGRAVE, William Thomas (1880–1965), Irish statesman, president of the Irish Free State 1922–32. He was in the 1916 EASTER RISING, served in the first republican ministry 1919–21 and, as president, brought stability to the Irish nation.

COSHINE (COSH). See HYPERBOLIC FUNCTIONS.

COSHOCTON, city in central Ohio, seat of Coshocton Co. It makes enamelware, rubber, paper, iron and textile products. Pop 13 747.

COSINE. See TRIGONOMETRY.

COSINE RULE, in any plane TRIANGLE, with angles P, Q, R, and sides p, q, r,

$$p^2=q^2+r^2-2qr\cos P;$$

i.e., the SQUARE of any one side is equal to the sum of the squares of the other two sides less twice the product of those two sides and the cosine (see TRIGONOMETRY) of the ANGLE they include. In SPHERICAL TRIGONOMETRY the cosine rule as applied to the sides of a spherical triangle is

$$\cos p=\cos q\cos r+\sin q\sin r\cos P$$

and, as applied to angles,

$$\cos P=-\cos Q\cos R+\sin Q\sin R\cos p.$$

(See also SINE RULE.)

COSMAS AND DAMIAN, Saints (4th century), patron saints of physicians. By tradition, the brothers were physicians of Asia Minor who refused payment for services, and were martyred under Diocletian. Roman Catholic feast day: Sept. 27.

COSMIC EGG. See COSMOLOGY; LEMAÎTRE.

COSMIC RAYS, ELECTRONS and the nuclei of HYDROGEN and other ATOMS which isotropically bombard the earth's upper ATMOSPHERE at VELOCITIES close to that of light. These primary cosmic rays interact with molecules of the upper atmosphere to produce what are termed secondary cosmic rays, which are considerably less energetic and extremely shortlived: they are SUBATOMIC PARTICLES that change rapidly into other types of particles. Initially, secondary cosmic rays, which pass frequently and harmlessly through our bodies, were detected by use of the GEIGER COUNTER, though now it is more common to employ a SPARK CHAMBER. It is thought that cosmic rays are produced by SUPERNOVAS, though some may be of extragalactic origin.

COSMOGONY, the science or pseudoscience of the origins of the UNIVERSE.

COSMOLOGY, the study of the structure and evolution of the universe. Ancient and medieval cosmologies were many, varied and imaginative, usually oriented around a stationary, flat earth at the center of the universe, surrounded by crystal spheres carrying the moon, sun, planets and stars, although ARISTARCHUS understood that the earth was spherical and circled the sun. With increasing sophistication of observational techniques and equipment, more realistic views of the universe emerged (see COPERNICUS; BRAHE; KEPLER; GALILEO; NEWTON). Modern cosmological theories, which take into account EINSTEIN's Theory of RELATIVITY and the recession of galaxies shown by the RED SHIFT in their spectra (see SPECTRUM), divide into two main types.

Evolutionary Theories. The most important of these is the **Big Bang Theory** resulting from HUBBLE's observations of the galaxies. This theory proposes that initially the universe existed as a single compact ball of matter, the **cosmic egg**, that exploded to form a mass of gaseous debris which eventually began to condense to form stars. An alternative theory is of an **oscillating universe** that periodically reaches a maximum size, then begins to shrink until it is once more in the form of a cosmic egg, which in turn explodes to create a new universe.

Continuous Creation. The **Steady State Theory** of BONDI, GOLD and HOYLE, first put forward in 1948, proposes that the universe has existed and will exist forever in its current form, the expansion being caused by the continuous creation of new matter so that the average density and appearance of the universe remain the same at all times. This would necessitate a reexamination of the Law of Conservation of ENERGY.

In 1965 A. Penzias and R. Wilson discovered that the universe possesses an inherent radio "background noise," and it was suggested by R. Dicke that this was the relic of the RADIATION produced by the Big Bang. Further researches have indicated the probability that space is filled with uniform BLACKBODY thermal radiation corresponding to a temperature of around 3K. This would support an evolutionary theory and, though it still has adherents, the Steady State Theory has now largely been abandoned. (See also ASTRONOMY; BLACK HOLE; PULSAR; QUASAR.)

COSMOTRON, large proton SYNCHROTRON used to accelerate (see ACCELERATOR) PROTONS to energies in the 1 GeV range (see ELECTRON VOLT).

COSSACKS, Russian warrior peasants living on the Ukranian steppe and famed for horsemanship. Self-governing under leaders like CHMIELNICKI, they resisted outside authority, but served the tsars as irregular cavalry, pioneered in Siberia and fought the Bolsheviks 1918–21. Collectivization broke up their communities in the 1930s, but Cossack cavalry served in WWII.

COST. See PRICE.

COSTA BRAVA, the rugged coast of Catalonia in NE Spain, a popular tourist area. Inland lies a rich farming and cork-growing region.

COSTAIN, Thomas Bertram (1885–1965), Canadian-born US author of historical novels. His works include *The Black Rose* (1945), *The Silver Chalice* (1952), and *The Last Plantagenets* (1962).

COSTA MESA, city in SW Cal., on the coast near Santa Ana. It makes electronic equipment, machine tools and plastics. Pop 72 660.

COSTA RICA, small republic in S Central America. Its topography varies from wet tropical plains on the coast to the temperate central plateau at about 3 000ft, surrounded by two chains of volcanic mountains rising to over 12 000ft. The population is largely of Spanish descent, with a smaller number of mixed Spanish-Indian descent than in other South American countries and a few thousand Negroes on the Caribbean coast. About two-thirds live in rural areas, largely on small farms. Coffee is Costa Rica's most important cash crop, monopolizing 95% of the arable land in the central plateau; bananas are grown in coastal areas. Agricultural exports bring in most of the country's foreign exchange. A lack of mineral resources has created an emphasis on light industry, producing for the home market, but large sulfur deposits are now being exploited and some gold and silver is mined.

Columbus discovered Costa Rica in 1502, but due to its lack of resources it escaped the ravages of the Conquistadors. Since few Indians survived, the white farmers worked their own land, establishing a significant middle class and avoiding the semifeudal peonage system so destructive in other South American countries. In 1821 Costa Rica declared independence from Spain, joining first the Mexican Empire and then a Central American republic which dissolved into anarchy in 1838. A power struggle followed, complicated by the invasion of the American adventurer William WALKER, defeated in 1857. Despite internal strife in 1919 and 1948, the country's history has been peaceful and its politics democratic. This has encouraged foreign investment, especially from the US, leading to national prosperity.

Official Name: The Republic of Costa Rica
Capital: San José
Area: 19 653sq mi
Population: 1 336 274
Languages: Spanish
Religions: Roman Catholic
Monetary Unit(s): 1 Costa Rica colon = 100 centimos

COST-BENEFIT ANALYSIS, a systematic comparison of the cost of a project with the benefits resulting or likely to result from it. Its prime use is to assess the viability of projects and their priority over the other projects with lower cost-benefit ratios.

COST-OF-LIVING INDEX, index relating the present cost of typical goods and services with their cost at a previous time, called the base period. It is now more accurately called the "consumer price index" in the US. The cost of the goods in the base period is usually represented as 100 units, and the subsequent cost calculated proportionally. Many governments compute the index monthly or quarterly, to detect and measure inflation; some wage contracts alter wages in proportion to it.

COSTUME, style or fashion in clothing, prevailing at different times and places; also official, ceremonial and theatrical attire. Clothes, it seems, are not worn simply for protection against the elements, since natives of Tierra del Fuego, for example, wear no clothes in a cold climate. Nor only out of modesty, for there is little agreement among societies upon which parts of the body may or may not be exposed. The idea appears to be to accentuate bodily characteristics considered attractive. Nudity in primitive societies is not considered attractive in itself. The emphasis is always on decoration with paints, tattoos, beads and so on, even to the point of actual physical distortion, such as the insertion of plugs to stretch ears and lips.

Similarly, in sophisticated societies changes in fashion draw attention to different features; tight-laced waists give "hour glass" figures, deep décolletage emphasizes the bosom, miniskirts accentuate the legs and so forth. Male costume has usually tended to emphasize codpieces, padded shoulders and, in general, as much ornament as women. Not all changes in costume are due to these influences. For example, some particularly extravagant fashions were designed to show that the wearer did not have to work for a living, and had servants to help him or her dress; the severity of 17th- and 18th-century Puritan dress in England and America was a reaction against such extravagances.

Information about costumes in the past can be gained from contemporary writings and the visual arts. The study of costume may yield clues about the society in which it was worn, as, for example, whether the court or the merchants set the fashion. Research into the sources of materials used may help to indicate trade routes and details of economic history. See illustration page 284.

COTANGENT. See TRIGONOMETRY.

CÔTE D'AZUR, originally the French Mediterranean coast between Cannes and Menton, now loosely used for the French Riviera, especially the E end. An important tourist area, it is also a fruit-growing region and has a perfume industry.

COTENTIN, peninsula on the NW coast of France, a region of NORMANDY. Its chief town is Cherbourg. It was the scene of fierce fighting after the Normandy landings in June 1944 in WWII.

COTINGAS, a large family of ornate birds (Cotingidae), found mainly in the Amazon region, though the Rose-throated becard reaches the southern US. The family includes the Three-wattled bellbird, and the Umbrella-bird. They live in forests, some species living on fruit, others on insects. (See also COCKS-OF-THE-ROCK.)

COTMAN, John Sell (1782–1842), English watercolorist and etcher, member of the "Norwich School." A melancholy character, he was not widely known in his time, but works such as *Greta Bridge* are now recognized as among the finest English landscape paintings.

COTOPAXI, the highest active volcano in the world, 19 347ft high. It is situated in the Andes in Ecuador, and last erupted in 1942.

COTSWOLDS, ridge of limestone hills in Gloucestershire, England, about 50mi long and rising to 1000ft. An important medieval wool-producing area, the hills are now a tourist attraction for their scenery and picturesque villages.

COTTAGE GROVE, village in E Minn., 11mi SE of St. Paul, of which it is a residential suburb. Pop 13 419.

COTTAGE INDUSTRY, a term used for the spinning and weaving industry in Britain before the INDUSTRIAL REVOLUTION. A trader distributed wool and cotton among peasant homes to be woven and spun by the women and children. Arkwright's spinning frame (1769) encouraged the transfer of spinning to factories, although weaving remained a cottage industry until the 1820s.

COTTON, a subtropical plant of the genus *Gossypium*, grown for the soft white fibers attached to its seed, which can be woven into cloth. The seeds are planted in the early spring and the plants bloom after four months. The white flowers redden and fall in a few days, leaving the seed pods, which are fully grown in another month or so. These pods then burst, showing the white lint, which is picked either by hand or mechanically. Each fiber is a single cell, with numerous twists along its length, which give it excellent spinning characteristics.

A number of species and their varieties are grown. Cultivated varieties of *Gossypium barbodense* produce fibers 36–64mm (1.4–2.5in) long, *G. hirsutum* (the American upland cotton) fibers 21–32mm (0.8–1.3in) and the Asiatic species *G. herbaceum* and *G. arboreum*

1340
1370
1385
1415
1460
A
B
C
D
E
F
1485
1490
1500
1525
1539
1570
1580
G
H
J
K
L
M
1628
1635
1643
1665
1665
1694
N
O
P
Q
R
S
T
1696
1718
1735
1735
1776
1777
1785
1795
V
W
X
Y
Z
Aa
Bb

Costume, 1300–1800: In the 13th century the French Gothic style developed and became widespread in Europe. The tunic was still the most important costume (kirtle for women and gipon for men), often covered by a sleeveless outer garment, the surcoat (A). This was the age of chivalry and the bright colors and designs of heraldry started to appear in clothing for both sexes. Many incorporated the use of *miparti* (differing colors for left and right half of the costume), a fashion that remained popular into the Renaissance (F, G, J). Shortly after 1300 the gipon grew progressively closer fitting and shorter (B). By mid-century two new garments had evolved, the doublet (with padded bodice) for men, and the opensided surcoat for women (C). By the end of the 14th century, longer and wider sleeves and long pointed shoes had become fashionable (D). From 1400–1490, when the Burgundian court dictated fashion, clothing became far more extravagant. The houppelande (E) was an essential garment for both sexes, and heavy padding widened men's shoulders (E, F). After 1440 the men's doublet began to get shorter. In contrast to the pointed and exaggerated late Gothic styles, the Italian Renaissance dress displayed a tendency to adopt more natural forms following the lines of the body. Materials were often luxurious and magnificently patterned, offset by small flashes of contrasting color which showed through sleeve slits from colored undergarments (G). As Renaissance ideas swept through Europe, so did the new clothing styles (H). In the period 1510–50, however, German and Swiss mercenaries took over the earlier Italian idea of slashing overgarments, carrying it to such extremes that entire garments seemed to have been constructed of ribbons (J). During the same period costumes became wider and broader, favoring voluminous decorative sleeves on jerkin or gown (K). Another striking feature of male costumes of the time is the large codpiece, which sometimes doubled as a pocket (J, K). In the period 1550–1600, more stiffly stylized Spanish costumes began to influence European fashions. The Spanish hooped skirt (verdugado) (L) was perfectly conical, ignoring completely the natural body lines. In France the codpiece was assimilated into the doublet in the panseron (M). Englishwomen began to favor the skirt with a wheel farthingale (N), while Dutchwomen wore a roll farthingale on the hips (O). As Renaissance styles gave way to Baroque, Spanish influence on costumes lessened and new expansively theatrical fashions developed. Cavalier's riding boots became real show-pieces (Q) and were worn indoors as well as outdoors, spurs and all. After 1630 the flat-lying Van Dyck collar (P) gained popularity. The waist was placed high and there was a definite movement towards harmony of line and color (O, P). At about 1650 the waist was returned to its normal position, but the doublet became even shorter, like a balero, showing the shirt underneath. Breeches were flared into petticoat shapes (R), women's necklines were almost horizontal, and a neckerchief or wide horizontal collar was worn (S). Towards the end of the century, fitting knee-breeches (*culotte*) (T) came into fashion and remained popular until the end of the 18th century. Female clothing became stiff and more formal and the high-piled hair of the men was paralleled by a *fontange* (U) for women. In the 1700s, fashions tended towards more elegance and frivolity. The graceful "Watteau gown" (V) became the central model of the period; men's fashions (W) changed less after this time. Powdered wigs with curls for men were extremely popular, while women wore their own hair close to the head with small kerchiefs or lace bonnets, in the first half of the century (V, X), though after 1760 their hairstyles became more elaborate and wigs came back into fashion (Y, Z). Women's court dress became wider with the enormous domed skirt supported by a whalebone scaffolding worn on the hips (X, Y). After 1780 English fashions became more influential (Aa). In men's fashion this is still true today. At the end of the century there was again a period of flamboyance in women's costumes (Bb), in which one can discern elements of the Empire style popular at the beginning of the 19th century.

The cotton plant. (1) Branch of the cotton bush with a flower and one open and one closed cotton boll; (2) flower seen from above; (3) fruit with seed pappi; (4) seed with fibers (enlarged); and (5) transverse section through a fiber. Cotton is ready for harvesting when the bolls open. To encourage the bolls to open at the same time and to facilitate mechanical picking, the leaves are usually first removed by chemical means.

fibers 9–19mm (0.4–0.8in). Cotton is produced in more than 60 countries; total world production exceeds 55 million bales annually, each bale weighing 222.6kg (490lb).

Cotton is prone to many pests and diseases, which cause enormous damage to the crop (averaging nearly 300 million dollars in the US every year). The main insect pests are the BOLLWEEVIL in the US and the PINK BOLL WORM in India and Egypt. Destructive fungus diseases that attack the plant include fusarium and verticillium wilt and Texas root rot. Boll rots can cause severe damage to the crop. Mechanization of the cotton processing industry was one of the first stages of the Industrial Revolution. It is still an important industry, although consumption of cotton has not risen since the development of man-made textiles. However, 80% of the yarn from spinning mills is still made into cloth, the remainder being used in industry. The seed is now used for oils and cattle food, while small fibers are made into cellulose. (See also COTTON GIN; PLANT DISEASES; TEXTILES.)

COTTON, John (1584–1652), powerful Puritan minister of Boston, Mass., noted for his didactic writings. Born in England, Cotton fled to the colonies in 1632 to avoid religious persecution. He was later to become involved in the banishment of Ann HUTCHINSON and Roger WILLIAMS for their heretical views.

COTTON GIN, device for separating cotton fibers from the seeds, invented by Eli WHITNEY (1793), which revolutionized the cotton industry in the US South. Whitney's original gin comprised a rotating drum on which were mounted wire spikes that projected through narrow slits in a wire grid. The spikes drew the fibers through these slits, leaving behind the seeds, which are broader. A revolving brush removed the fibers from the drum. In 1794, Hodgen Holmes replaced the wire spikes by a circular SAW; and modern cotton gins still work on this principle.

COTTON GRASS, or cotton sedge, sedges of the genus *Eriophorum* which grow in swamps and bogs. The flower clusters bear fine white hairs that look like cotton bolls. (See SEDGE.)

COTTONMOUTH. See MOCCASIN.

COTTONWOODS, name for several large trees of the genus *Populus*, family Salicaceae. They are so-named from the cottonlike fibers produced around the seed. *P. deltoides,* native to the E US, produces attractive heartshaped foliage and grows very rapidly. (See also ASPEN; POPLAR; WILLOW.)

COTTRELL, Frederick Gardner (1877–1948), US chemist who invented the ELECTROSTATIC PRECIPITATOR used to reduce AIR POLLUTION from factory flues (1910), and founded the nonprofit Research Corporation to plow back the profits of invention into further scientific research (1912).

COTYLEDON, leaf forming part of the embryo in seeds. In MONOCOTYLEDONS there is only one cotyledon and in DICOTYLEDONS there are two. They often contain food reserves used in the early stages of GERMINATION and normally they are brought above the ground, turn green and carry out PHOTOSYNTHESIS, but soon fall off. They bear no resemblance to normal foliage leaves. (See also PLANT; SEED.)

COUBERTIN, Pierre de (1863–1937), French scholar and educator largely responsible for reviving the Olympic Games in 1896, in the belief that they would foster international goodwill.

COUÉ, Émile, French pharmacist who developed a method of psychotherapy involving autosuggestion and hypnotism, which became briefly popular in England and the US in the 1920s.

COUGAR. See PUMA.

COUGH, sudden explosive release of air from the

Eli Whitney's cotton gin, an original machine, in the Smithsonian Institute's National Museum of History and Technology. Historians have argued that it was the very simplicity and efficiency of Whitney's invention which led to the almost exclusive cultivation of cotton in the US South and so to the institutionalization of slavery.

LUNGS, which clears respiratory passages of obstruction and excess MUCUS or PUS; it occurs both as a REFLEX and on volition. Air flow may reach high velocity and potentially infectious particles spread a great distance if the mouth is uncovered. Persistent cough always implies disease.

COUGHLIN, Charles Edward (1891–), Roman Catholic priest who became a national figure in the US in the 1930s with his radio broadcasts, attacking first the financial leaders he believed to be responsible for the Depression, and later F. D. ROOSEVELT. He formed the Union Party in 1936 in opposition to Roosevelt; its presidential candidate received 2% of the popular vote. In 1942 his activities were curbed by the Church, worried by his apparent Nazi sympathies.

COULOMB (C), the SI UNIT of electric charge, defined as the quantity of ELECTRICITY transported in one second by a one-ampere current.

COULOMB, Charles Augustin de (1736–1806), French physicist noted for his researches into FRICTION, TORSION, ELECTRICITY and MAGNETISM. Using a torsion BALANCE, he established **Coulomb's Law** of electrostatic forces (1785). This states that the force between two charges is proportional to their magnitudes and inversely proportional to the square of their separation. He also showed that the charge on a charged conductor lies solely on its surface.

COUNCIL, Ecumenical. See ECUMENICAL COUNCIL.

COUNCIL BLUFFS, city in SW Ia., seat of Pottawattamie Co., situated on the E side of the Missouri R. Once a staging area for travel to the W coast, it became the eastern terminus for the Union Pacific Railroad in 1863, and is now an important railroad center and grain market. Pop 60 348.

COUNCIL FOR NEW ENGLAND, English body formed by Sir Ferdinando GORGES in 1620 to organize settlement in New England. King James I granted it all the country from sea to sea between latitudes 40°–48°N. The council made its first grants in 1622, but surrendered its charter in 1635.

COUNCIL GROVE, city in E central Kan., seat of Morris Co., situated 25mi NW of Emporia. Named for the site of a treaty with the Osage Indians in 1825, it is now a grain and poultry center. Pop 2403.

COUNCIL OF ECONOMIC ADVISERS, three-member commission established in the US in 1946 to help prevent postwar depressions. It advises the president on economic and monetary problems.

COUNCIL OF NICAEA. See NICAEA, COUNCIL OF.

COUNCIL OF TRENT. See TRENT, COUNCIL OF.

COUNTERFACTUAL CONDITIONALS, or contrary-to-fact conditionals, in LOGIC, statements known to be false of which the consequences are nevertheless explored. The epistemic status of these conclusions is hotly debated by philosophers.

COUNTERFEITING, the forging of money in an attempt to pass it off as genuine. Since this threatens the monetary basis of any economy it is a serious offense, punishable by death in the USSR and China. As it requires a high degree of technical skill it is seldom successful as organized crime; successful counterfeiters are more often eccentric individuals rather than habitual criminals.

COUNTERGLOW or **Gegenschein**. See ZODIACAL LIGHT.

COUNTERPOINT, in music, a term for the art of combining two or more different melodic lines simultaneously in a composition. The term derives from Latin *punctus contra punctum*, meaning "note against note." Originating in the *organum* style of the 10th century, it reached its zenith in BAROQUE music, especially that of J. S. BACH. It remains a widely used form; a mastery of counterpoint is considered essential for a composer.

COUNTER-REFORMATION, reform movement in the Roman Catholic Church during the 16th and 17th centuries, springing as much from internal demands for reform as from reaction to the Protestant REFORMATION. Many organizations, such as the Oratory of Divine Love, the CAPUCHINS and the URSULINES, were founded in an attempt to infuse more spiritual life into the Church. Most notable among these were the JESUITS, founded in 1534, whose emphasis on action and education did much to slow the spread of Protestantism. The reform movement within the Church culminated in the Council of TRENT, convened by Pope Paul III in 1545. Its reaffirmation of doctrine and its disciplinary reforms did much to improve the standing of the Church. The establishment of the congregation of the INQUISITION in Rome by Paul III helped check Protestant influence; there was also a revival of missionary work. A revival in the arts, which fostered BERNINI and PALESTRINA among others, accompanied the movement.

COUNTERTENOR, adult male alto voice. Strictly, it should be produced without falsetto, but this is seldom the case. It was popular in the 15th to 17th centuries, and has been written for by modern composers, including Benjamin BRITTEN.

COUNTERVAILING POWER, an economic concept, introduced by J. K. GALBRAITH, which regards the controlling influence in modern capitalism not as direct competition between sellers, but as the checking of one large firm by the growth of another. The same principle has been extended to unions and businesses.

COUPERIN, François (1668–1733), French composer, most celebrated member of an illustrious musical family. He wrote supremely for the harpsichord, which he taught to the French royal family. His authoritative treatise, *The Art of Harpsichord Playing* (1716), influenced J. S. BACH.

COUPLET, two lines of verse, usually related by rhyme. The Heroic couplet (rhymed, in iambic pentameter) has been widely used in English literature from CHAUCER to POPE and DRYDEN; other forms are less common. The Alexandrine couplet (iambic hexameter with a caesura in mid-line) has featured equally widely in French literature.

COURBET, Gustave (1819–1877), French painter noted for his development of the "Realist" style in paintings such as *The Burial at Ornans* (1849) and *The Studio* (1855). Influenced by the Dutch genre painters of the 17th century, he emphasized everyday life and landscape in his work, as a reaction to the Classical and Romantic schools.

COUREURS DE BOIS, illicit traders in 17th- and 18th-century French Canada, largely responsible for the corruption of the Indian population. In defiance of government regulations they ruthlessly exploited the fur trade, selling the Indians cheap alcohol at exorbitant rates.

COURNAND, André Frédéric (1895–), French-born US physiologist who shared the 1956 Nobel Prize for Physiology or Medicine with D. W. RICHARDS and W. FORSSMANN for the development of heart catheterization (see CATHETER) and other work which has led to a much fuller understanding of heart and lung diseases.

COURT-MARTIAL, tribunal for the trial of members of the armed forces for offenses under military (and in some cases civil) law. Under the US Uniform Code of Military Justice there are three types—*summary*, for minor offenses; *special*, for more serious offenses; and *general*, which may try any offense under the Uniform Code and may impose the maximum penalties prescribed, including death.

COURT OF CLAIMS, special federal court established in 1855 to hear all claims founded on any act of Congress, any regulation of any executive department, any contract with the US Government, and any torts or wrongs committed by an officer of the US.

COURTRAI, city in West Flanders, Belgium, 26mi SW of Ghent on the banks of the Lys river. It was the site of the French defeat by the Flemish at the Battle of the Golden Spurs in 1302. The town has been famous for its lace and fine linen since medieval times and is still a major textile center. Pop 44 998.

COURTS, official assemblies for the administration of justice. A typical US court will consist of a judge, jury (when required), attorneys representing both parties to the dispute, a bailiff or marshal to carry out court orders and keep order, and a clerk to record the proceedings.

Though many nations have developed various types of judicial assembly, the court in Western countries is descended from the king's court, in which he dispensed justice. Since his justices were theoretically deputizing for him, their assemblies were still *curiae regis*—the king's courts. Unlike their European counterparts, the English courts did not base themselves upon Roman law but developed the system of legal interpretation known as the COMMON LAW, and this, with its accompanying judicial system, became one of Britain's most important and lasting exports to her colonies, including the US and Canada.

The US has two related court systems: federal and state. The federal court system covers cases involving the Constitution, the nation, foreign nationals, federal laws, interstate disputes and ships at sea. Federal courts comprise a SUPREME COURT, intermediate courts of appeals, and many district courts, as well as special courts such as the Tax Court, Court of Claims and the Court of Customs and Patent Appeals. In an individual state, the state court system deals with that state's affairs in both civil and criminal matters. Inferior (lower) state courts include magistrates' courts in urban areas, courts run by justices of the peace in rural areas, and juvenile and family courts, traffic courts, probate courts, rent courts and small-claims courts. Above these stand the county and municipal courts and other superior courts, and above these there are often appellate courts reviewing lower court decisions. The highest court in the state is the state supreme court.

The US court system is a carefully designed judicial apparatus, but by the 1970s it was so overstrained that some defendants were waiting years for a trial. Expansion and procedural streamlining may improve the position.

Like the US, Canada has two related court systems: federal and provincial. The federal system features the Supreme Court (the highest court of appeal) and Exchequer Court (dealing largely with cases involving the national government). The provincial courts handle cases of federal and provincial law.

The INTERNATIONAL COURT OF JUSTICE meets at the Hague, in the Netherlands, to deal with cases under INTERNATIONAL LAW. Its 15 judges, each from a

The pride of the English city of Coventry is its great modern cathedral, consecrated in 1962. A number of major British designers and artists cooperated on the building, including the architect Sir Basil Spence, the sculptor Jacob Epstein and the painter Graham Sutherland.

different country, are elected for nine-year terms by the UN Security Council.

COURTSHIP. See MATING RITUALS.

COURT TENNIS, indoor tennis game also called royal or real tennis; it originated in 12th–15th-century France. It is played in a roofed indoor court. Two or four players, using pear-shaped rackets, serve a solid ball across a sagging net and bounce it off a penthouse roof on three sides of the court. They score by hitting the ball into one of several demarcated winning areas. A more complex ancestor of modern tennis, it is now a minority sport.

COUSTEAU, Jacques-Yves (1910–), French naval officer and oceanologist who pioneered underwater exploration, coinventor of the aqualung and an underwater television system. His popular cinema and television films have made him world-famous.

COUVADE, a custom in many primitive societies throughout the world in which a prospective father imitates the prospective mother's confinement and labor, perhaps as a ritual stressing of the male reproductive role.

COVENANT, in law, a formal agreement entered into by deed, much used in land law to restrict the uses to which land may be put or to assure a buyer of his title. In theology, it refers to the sacred covenant between God and Israel and the new covenant established with mankind by Christ.

COVENANT, Ark of the. See ARK OF THE COVENANT.

COVENANTERS, 16th- and 17th-century Scottish Presbyterians pledged by covenants to defend their religion against Anglican influences. They were suppressed, both by Cromwell and the Stuart kings. Their savage persecution after the Restoration was known as the "killing time".

COVENTRY, cathedral city in the west Midlands, England, ESE of Birmingham. An industrial center, much of it was shattered by WWII air raids but has since been rebuilt, most notably the cathedral. Pop 335 238.

COVENTRY, town in central R.I., 15mi SW of Providence. Now mainly residential, it has textile and chemical industries. Pop 22 947.

COVERDALE, Miles (1488–1569), English Protestant reformer, royal chaplain to Edward VI and later bishop of Exeter. While studying in Europe, he produced in 1535 the first complete printed English translation of the Bible, revising large portions of it for inclusion in the Great Bible he prepared for Thomas Cromwell in 1539–40.

COVINA, residential city in SW Cal., 23mi E of Los Angeles, formerly a major citrus-growing and shipping center. Pop 30 380.

COVINGTON, city in N central Ga., seat of Newton Co. It lies 30mi SE of Atlanta in a lumber-producing area. Pop 10 267.

COVINGTON, city in N central Ky., seat of Kenton Co., on the Ohio R opposite Cincinnati. An agricultural market, it has also become an industrial center. Pop 52 535.

COVINGTON, city in W Va., seat of Alleghany Co. It produces paper and textiles. Pop 10 060.

COWARD, Sir Noel (Peirce) (1899–1973), English actor, playwright and composer. He is famous for his witty comedies of manners, such as *Private Lives* (1930) and *Blithe Spirit* (1941), revues, musicals and serious plays such as *The Vortex* (1924). Their prevailing cynicism is offset by patriotic works such as the film *In Which We Serve* (1942).

COWBIRDS, birds of the family Icteridae, relatives of the grackles, so named because they follow cattle and feed on the insects they stir up. Two species live in the US but most are South American. Most lay eggs in the nests of other birds that hatch and raise their young.

COWELL, Henry Dixon (1897–1965), US experimental composer. Like John CAGE, he sought to explore new sonorities in his music, as with "tone clusters," produced on the piano by striking groups of keys with the forearm.

COWLEY, Abraham (1618–1667), English poet and essayist, whose work bridged the gap between the extravagance of the METAPHYSICAL POETS and the cooler rationalism of the Neoclassical school. He was associated with the Royal Society, though never a member, and his love of philosophy and science was reflected in his work. Among his collections of poetry are *The Mistress* (1647), *Miscellanies* (1656) and *Pindaric Odes* (1656).

COWPEA, or black-eyed pea, *Vigna sinensis* and *V. catjang*, a trailing tender BEAN grown as a forage crop and for its edible beans. Native to India and Iran, varieties of the cowpea are cultivated in the S US. (See also LEGUMINOUS PLANTS.)

COWPENS, Battle of, tactical victory in the Revolutionary War, fought on Jan. 17, 1781 in S.C. American troops under Gen. Daniel Morgan attacked Col. Banastre Tarleton's British troops in the Cowpens area. The Americans then withdrew, but met the British counterattack with bayonets and a flank attack, surrounding them. The British surrendered with 200 casualties to the Americans' 72.

COWPER, William (1731–1800), English poet. His work anticipates Romanticism in its lyrical delight in nature, expressed directly and simply. His best-known serious poem is *The Task* (1785). He also wrote many hymns, but is remembered for his comic ballad *John Gilpin* (1783).

COWPOX, a disease of cattle, caused by a VIRUS related to the smallpox virus. It was by noting the IMMUNITY to SMALLPOX conferred on humans who contracted cowpox by milking infected cattle that JENNER popularized VACCINATION against smallpox.

COWRIES, MOLLUSKS with a glossy shell whose spire is hidden by the final dome-shaped twist. Most live in warm seas. Their shells are used as money in parts of Africa.

COWSLIP, popular name for several unrelated herbs, including the **marsh marigold** (*Caltha palustris*), a marsh plant with big yellow flowers; the Virginia cowslip (*Mertensia virginica*), a marsh plant with blue flowers; and the European cowslip (*Primula veris*) a yellow-flowered meadow plant.

COX, Archibald (1912–), US lawyer, special prosecutor (1972–73) appointed by President Nixon to probe the WATERGATE scandal, but sacked by him for demanding "presidentially privileged" tape recordings. He was professor of law at Harvard, and US solicitor-general 1961–65.

COX, James Middleton (1870–1957), US politician and journalist who championed liberal reform. He became nationally known as a newspaper publisher, Democratic congressman (1909–13) and governor of Ohio (1913–15; 1917–21). In 1920 he stood as Democratic presidential candidate but lost heavily to Warren G. Harding.

COXEY, Jacob Sechler (1854–1951), US self-made businessman who, with revivalist Carl Browne, led a "living petition" of 500 unemployed to Washington from Massillon, Ohio, in 1894, in support of his plan for national reconstruction. The march of "Coxey's Army," or the "Commonweal of Christ," ended when Coxey was jailed for demonstrating on the Capitol lawn.

COYOTE, *Canis latrans*, a wild dog that looks like a small wolf and has a characteristic howl. It has spread from the plains of NW America to the Atlantic coast. Coyotes hunt small mammals or live as urban scavengers, some interbreeding with dogs.

COYPU, *Myocastor coypus*, a large South American RODENT, farmed in North America and Europe for its fine underfur ("nutria"). It has webbed hindfeet, and swims in marshes and streams.

COZZENS, James Gould (1903–), US novelist. His books, such as *By Love Possessed* (1957) and *Ask Me Tomorrow* (1940), deal with moral problems of the professional classes, seen by Cozzens as the custodians of social stability. *Guard of Honor* (1948) won him a Pulitzer Prize.

CRAB APPLE, fruits and plants of the genus *Malus*, the APPLE genus, family Rosaceae. They are chiefly grown as ornamentals for their white or pink blossom and for their small acid fruits used for making jelly. There are about 25 species native to temperate regions of North America and Eurasia.

CRABBE, George (1754–1832), English poet. His long narrative poems, such as *The Village* (1783) and *The Borough* (1810), seek to convey the harsh realities of village life as opposed to the conventional "poetic" view then popular.

CRAB GRASS, any of several European GRASSES of the genus *Digitaria*, which are native to Europe and established as weeds in North America. They have reclining stems that root at the joints, which makes eradication difficult. Family: Graminae.

CRAB NEBULA (M1), a bright NEBULA in the constellation TAURUS, the remnants of the SUPERNOVA of 1054. It is 1 223pc from the earth and is associated with a PULSAR.

CRABS, crustaceans with 10 pairs of legs, the first pair usually modified as pincers. They are closely related to LOBSTERS and SHRIMPS and start life as small, swimming, lobster-like larvae that repeatedly molt before settling on the bottom and becoming adult crabs. The adults have rounded protective shells covering head and thorax, the abdomen curling under the body to form a series of plates. Most of the 4 500 species live in the sea or brackish water, eating small animals and carrion. They range in size from the tiny Pea crabs that live in oyster shells to the Giant crab of the Pacific, a Spider crab with a leg span of up

Five different species of crab showing variations of size and shape that reflect the way each creature has adapted to its particular environment. (1) The Chinese woolly-handed crab (*Eriocheir sinensis*), which has a carapace measuring about 90mm across. (2) The tiny breakwater crab (*Heteropanope tridentata*), about 35mm long. (3) *Hyas araneus*, around 150mm long. (4) The edible sea-crab (*Cancer pagurus*), 300mm across. (5) A beach crab (*Carcinus maenas*), 80mm across. Some crabs spend a considerable amount of time out of water: fiddler crabs live in holes in mud flats, and another species—the robber crab—even climbs trees.

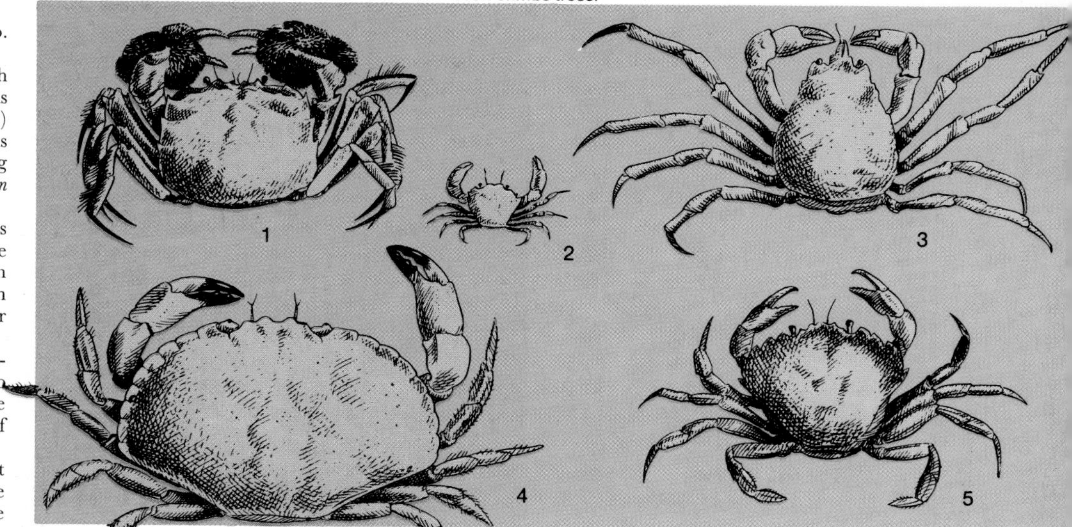

Cranes belong to an order of birds which are quite diverse in appearance but share a number of anatomical similarities, such as a functional appendix and nasal openings that are not separated by septum. Illustrated here is the crowned crane, *Balearica pavonina*, a native of Africa. Cranes are easily recognized in flight, their wings flapping slowly yet powerfully, their long necks stretched forward and their legs held parallel to the ground, flying either in V-formation or a straight line. The sectional diagram through a crane's body shows how the windpipe lies coiled in a partially or completely hollow breastbone, a configuration which produces the birds' unmistakable trumpeting calls which, in flight, are believed to be warnings to birds straying too far from the main group.

to 3.8m (12.5ft). (See also FIDDLER CRAB; HERMIT CRAB; KING CRAB.)

CRACKING, process by which heavy HYDROCARBON molecules in PETROLEUM are broken down into lighter molecules and isomerized, by means of high temperatures or CATALYSIS. It yields branched-chain ALKANES and ALKENES of high OCTANE rating for GASOLINE, and also simple gaseous alkenes for chemical synthesis.

CRACOW. See KRAKÓW.

CRAIG, Edward Gordon (1872–1966), English stage director and designer who helped to revolutionize theater production. He stressed the director's unifying role and abandoned realism in favor of a stark abstract style relying for its effects on lighting and mass.

CRAIOVA, regional center in S Romania, 115mi W of Bucharest. An industrial center, it also has a university and cathedral. Pop 179 000.

CRAMP, the painful contraction of muscle—often in the legs. The cause is usually unknown. It may be brought on by exercise or lack of SALT; it also occurs in muscles with inadequate BLOOD supply. Relief is by forcibly stretching the muscle or by massage.

CRANACH, Lucas (1472–1553), major German Renaissance painter and engraver. His early paintings are mainly on biblical themes and set in romantic landscapes; later mythological treatments introduced his characteristic sinuous female nudes. A great portraitist, especially for the Saxon court, he produced many propagandist woodcuts for his friend Martin Luther.

CRANBERRY, several low, berrybearing shrubs related to the BLUEBERRY, native to N Eurasia and North America. The American cranberry (*Vaccinium macrocarpon*) is cultivated in Mass., N.J. and Wis., the berries being used in sauces and as a relish for meats, particularly turkey.

CRANE, an important device used for hoisting heavy loads, a familiar sight in warehouses, at docks, on building sites and elsewhere. It has a WINCH or winding mechanism operating a rope (usually steel) attached to a PULLEY block on which there is a hook. In many cranes the rope passes over a pulley at the far end of a boom or **jib** from the winch; in others it hangs from a horizontal beam or girder. A **derrick** is a crane where the distance of the end of the jib from the crane's vertical support (e.g., pillar) may be varied: simplest is the ship's derrick, where the jib is pivoted near the base of a braced or guyed mast. The tower derrick is similar, though here the pivoted end of the jib may be moved up and down the pillar as needed. Mobile cranes move on rails or caterpillar tracks: in particular, the **gantry crane** is shaped like a bridge, the two verticals having wheels and the pulley block being suspended from the horizontal. In **traveling bridge cranes** the horizontal runs on wheels on tracks mounted high on facing walls of, say, a workshop. Cranes may also be mounted on trucks, railroad freight cars or ships.

CRANE, (Harold) Hart (1899–1932), a major US poet. His masterpiece was *The Bridge* (1930), an attempted epic of the American experience that influenced Ezra Pound and Wallace Stevens. Beset by personal problems, he drowned himself on a return voyage from Mexico.

CRANE, Stephen (1871–1900), US novelist, short story writer and poet, best known for *The Red Badge of Courage* (1895), a sensitive study of a young man's development towards manhood during the Civil War. *Maggie: A Girl of the Streets* (1893) frighteningly describes a girl's poverty, seduction and suicide in New York's slums. Crane died of tuberculosis at 28.

CRANE, Walter (1845–1915), English artist, most famous as an illustrator. His imaginative designs for children's books were influenced by Renaissance and Pre-Raphaelite painting and Japanese color prints. He was also an influential teacher.

CRANES, large birds of the family Gruidae, with long necks and legs, both of which project in flight. Most are mainly white or gray and some have partly naked heads. Their coiled windpipe helps to produce a trumpeting call. Cranes eat small animals and grasses in marshes and on plains, and perform graceful leaping courtship dances. Most of the 14 species spread around the world are now rare. The sandhill crane and the nearly extinct whooping crane are found in North America.

CRANFORD, township in NE N.J., 5mi W of Elizabeth. It has cosmetics and plastics industries, but is largely residential. Pop 27 391.

CRANIAL NERVES. See NERVOUS SYSTEM.

CRANMER, Thomas (1489–1556), first Protestant archbishop of Canterbury and leader of the English Reformation. He favored the ascendancy of state over church and obtained royal favor by helping Henry VIII to divorce his second, third, fourth and fifth wives. As counselor to Edward VI, Cranmer compiled the first Book of Common Prayer (1549), his most enduring monument. Under the Roman Catholic regime of Mary Tudor he was stripped of office and burned at the stake as a heretic.

CRANNOG. See LAKE DWELLING.

CRANSTON, city in R.I., on the W shore of Narragansett Bay. A residential suburb of Providence, it produces textiles, rubber, machinery and beer. There are various prisons in the city, and a major hospital. Pop 73 037.

CRAPE MYRTLE, or "Lilac of the south," *Lagerstroemia indica*, an Asian shrub of the loosestrife family (Lythraceae) grown in the southern US. It produces large pink, purple or white clustered flowers.

CRAPPIES, freshwater SUNFISH which anglers have introduced throughout the US from the east. The Black crappie prefers clear water, the White crappie turbid water.

CRASHAW, Richard (c1613–1649), English poet, whose poetry combined religious fervor with sensuous imagery. At first a High Church Anglican, he later became a Roman Catholic convert, and died as canon of Santa Casa Cathedral at Loreto.

CRASSUS "DIVES", Marcus Licinius (c115–53 BC), Roman consul, a shrewd businessman and political manipulator, who with Caesar and Pompey formed the First Triumvirate (60 BC). Crassus had enjoyed some military success by defeating SPARTACUS (71 BC), but ultimately overreached himself and died in a vainglorious attempt to conquer Parthia.

CRATER LAKE NATIONAL PARK, a 250sq mi area centered on Crater Lake in the Cascade Mts in SW Ore., established as a park in 1902. The crater, which is volcanic, measures 6mi across and the lake within it, noted for its vivid blue color, reaches a depth of 1 932ft.

CRATERS OF THE MOON NATIONAL MONUMENT, an area of 83sq mi in south central Ida., named for its resemblance to a lunar landscape. Among its lava structures are cones more than 6 000ft high and craters almost half a mile across and some hundreds of feet deep.

CRAWFORD, Thomas (1813–1857), US Neoclassical sculptor who worked mainly in Rome. His monumental figure *Freedom*, cast posthumously, surmounts the dome of the capitol in Washington, D.C.

CRAWFORD, William Harris (1772–1834), US lawyer and senator, one of four candidates in the indecisive 1824 presidential election after which the House of Representatives chose John Quincy Adams for the presidency. Crawford was secretary of war 1815–16 and secretary of the treasury 1816–25.

CRAWFORDSVILLE, city in Ind., seat of Montgomery Co. It is a center for local agricultural trade and also has printing and bookbinding industries. Pop 13 842.

CRAYFISH, or crawfish, several species of lobsterlike, decapod, freshwater CRUSTACEA. They are nocturnal, omnivorous scavengers found in the temperate Americas, Eurasia and Australasia.

CRAZY HORSE (c1840–1877), chief of the Oglala Sioux Indians and the inspiration behind Indian resistance to the white man's invasion of the N Great Plains. He led the SIOUX and CHEYENNE victory over Gen. George CROOK at Rosebud R (June 17, 1876) and eight days later led the Sioux massacre of Gen. CUSTER's forces at Little Bighorn. Arrested on his surrender in 1877, he was killed some months later while attempting to escape.

CREAM OF TARTAR. See TARTARIC ACID.

CREATION, Biblical. See GENESIS.

CREATION MYTHS, accounts of the creation of the earth, or of man's known world, and of man himself. They often form a basis for religious doctrine and as such have determined the structure of particular societies. Supreme deity myths are typified by the biblical account in GENESIS. Emergence myths, such as that of the Navajo Indians, are analogous to gestation and birth, seeing creation as a gradual unfolding of forces within the earth. Hindu and other Asian cultures represent the moment of creation in terms of the breaking of an egg. World-parent myths generally deal in personifications of the earth (mother) and the sky (father) and include the Babylonian *Enuma Elish* myth. Diving myths posit a watery chaos with mud as the stuff of creation. In accounts by the Crow Indians a duck dives for the mud; a Romanian version has the devil in the role of diver. Antagonism between newly-emergent life forms is a common mythological feature and serves to account for life's subsequent imperfections.

CRÉCY, Battle of (Aug. 26, 1346), battle in the HUNDRED YEARS' WAR near Crécy-en-Ponthieu in N France. Edward III of England's smaller army, with its high percentage of longbowmen, devastated Philip VI's French forces (mainly mounted knights) after some of them launched a premature attack.

CREDIT, in business and economics, the ability of a borrower to raise funds, or the funds themselves. The lender (creditor) generally makes a charge (interest) for his service to the borrower (debtor). Creditors often expect the debtor to pledge goods, stocks or other property (collateral) as a sign of good faith. Today, commercial banks and insurance and finance companies are the chief credit source. Credit created in this way is part of the money supply; it is therefore linked with general economic activity and must be controlled if an attempt is made to prevent inflation or recession. (See also BANKING; MONEY.)

CRÉDIT MOBILIER OF AMERICA, company involved in the construction of the Union Pacific railroad (1865–69). The subject of a financial scandal involving Congressman Oakes AMES, Crédit Mobilier came to symbolize corruption in US business during and after the RECONSTRUCTION period.

CREDIT UNION, a cooperative bank formed under government charter generally by groups of employees or members of a particular association or community. Members buy shares in the bank in return for which they can borrow at interest rates lower than those of commercial banks.

CREED, formal, authorized statement of religious belief, found in all major world religions, used in worship and to define and maintain doctrine. The Christian creeds grew out of early formulas of belief used in BAPTISM, and became standards of orthodoxy. The three "ecumenical creeds," accepted by virtually all WESTERN CHURCHES, the APOSTLES', NICENE and ATHANASIAN CREEDS, all express belief in God the Father, Son and Holy Spirit, the first two creeds having thus three sections. The Protestant Confessions of the 16th and 17th centuries, including the AUGSBURG CONFESSION, the THIRTY-NINE ARTICLES and the WESTMINSTER CONFESSION, are longer creeds defining controverted points, as is the Roman Catholic *Decrees and Canons* of the Council of TRENT.

CREE INDIANS, North American Indian tribe of the ALGONQUIAN group. Originally they were all woodland Indians, hunting and trapping in the forests of S Manitoba, Canada, but in time part of the tribe moved onto the plains of Alberta, Canada, and into the N US, where they hunted buffalo.

CREEK INDIANS, confederacy of North American Indian tribes of the MUSKOGEAN linguistic family. An agricultural people, they lived in the SE US, occupying a large area including most of present-day Ala. and Ga. Under chief TECUMSEH they resisted white domination in the Creek War (1813–14), but were routed at the Battle of HORSESHOE BEND and as a result lost most of their lands. By 1840 they had been moved to the INDIAN TERRITORY as one of the FIVE CIVILIZED TRIBES.

CREEL, George Edward (1876–1953), US journalist, appointed head of American propaganda in WWI by President Wilson. Creel, who made his reputation as a MUCKRAKER, also represented Wilson at a number of major conferences.

CREEPERS, birds of the family Certhiidae, which can climb up treetrunks or even stone walls. They have long, thin, downcurved bills and dull plumage. Creepers are found throughout the N Hemisphere. They eat insects and insect eggs.

CREMATION. See FUNERAL CUSTOMS.

CREMER, Sir William Randal (1838–1908), English labor union leader and pacifist, winner of the 1903 Nobel Peace Prize. Cremer was secretary of the First International in Britain and of the Workmen's Peace Association, which he formed in 1870. He was a member of parliament 1885–95.

CREMONA, Italian city, capital of Cremona province, Lombardy, on the Po R, an agricultural market center. It was the home of the violin-making families of AMATI, STRADIVARI and GUARNIERI. Pop 84475.

CREOLE, term first used in the 16th century to describe people of Spanish parentage born in the West Indies. It is now far less specific, serving to describe the descendants of Spanish, Portuguese and French settlers in the West Indies, Latin America and parts of the US—where in La., for example, the term applies to French-speaking people of either French or Spanish descent. French- and Spanish-based patois are known as Creole languages. (See PIDGIN.)

CREON, in Greek mythology, brother of Jocasta and successor to OEDIPUS as king of Thebes. Another legend represents him as king of Corinth and father of Glauce (or Creusa), wife of Jason.

CREOSOTE, distillation product of COAL TAR or wood tar. Coal-tar creosote is a mixture of HYDROCARBONS, PHENOLS (see also CRESOL) and other compounds, used to preserve wood used outdoors, and often applied under pressure. Wood creosote is an oily mixture of phenols formerly used as an ANTISEPTIC and food preservative.

CREOSOTE BUSH, *Larrea tridentata*, an evergreen desert shrub common in dry regions of Mexico and the southwestern US. Its creosote odor deters animals from eating it. (See also GREASEWOOD.)

CRESAP, Michael (1742–1775), American frontiersman accused of massacring the family of the Ohio River Indian chief James John LOGAN and so starting Lord Dunmore's War (1774).

CRESOL, or methylphenol ($CH_3C_6H_4OH$), a member of the PHENOLS; there are three isomers, synthesized from TOLUENE. Distillation of CREOSOTE or PETROLEUM yields a mixture of cresols and xylenols ("cresylic acid") used as a disinfectant and in the manufacture of resins and tricresyl phosphate (used to make gasoline additives and plasticizers).

CRESS, several plants of the mustard family (Cruciferae) with strong-flavored leaves that are used in salads, seasonings and garnishes. **Watercress** (*Nasturtium officinale*) is native to Europe but is naturalized elsewhere.

CRESTWOOD, city in E Mo., a residential suburb of St. Louis, in a truck-farming area. Pop 15398.

CRETACEOUS, final period of the MESOZOIC, about 135 to 65 million years ago, lying after the JURASSIC and before the CENOZOIC. (See GEOLOGY.)

CRETE, mountainous but fertile Greek island in the E Mediterranean at the southern end of the Aegean. The largest of the Greek islands, it covers some 3189sq mi. Agriculture is the mainstay, with grapes, oranges and olives the only significant cash crops. The island is of great historical interest, being the home of the ancient MINOAN CIVILIZATION, which had KNOSSOS, with its famous palace, as its leading city. The present-day capital is Canea.

CRETINISM, congenital disease caused by lack of THYROID HORMONE in late fetal life and early infancy, which interferes with normal development, including that of the BRAIN. It may be due to congenital inability to secrete the hormone or, in certain areas of the world, to lack of dietary IODINE (which is needed for hormone formation). The typical appearance, with coarse SKIN, puffy face, large tongue and slow responses, usually enables early diagnosis. It is crucial that replacement therapy with thyroid hormone should be started as early as possible to minimize or prevent the mental retardation that occurs if diagnosis is delayed.

CRÈVECOEUR, Michel-Guillaume Jean de (1735–1813), French-born writer and settler in America—where he was known as J. Hector St. John. His popular *Letters from an American Farmer* (1782) is an important documentary source on the period. He was French consul in New York 1783–90.

CRIBBAGE, card game essentially for two people, played with the standard deck and a special board with pegs for marking the score. Picture cards are valued at 10 points and all others at their face value. Each player discards two of his six cards, to create a spare hand, or crib, which goes to the dealer. The object is to make the pool of cards in play add up to no more than 31.

CRICK, Francis Harry Compton (1916–), English biochemist who, with J. D. WATSON, proposed the double-helix model of DNA. For this, one of the most spectacular advances in 20th-century science, they shared the 1962 Nobel Prize for Physiology or Medicine with M. H. F. WILKINS, who had provided them with the X-ray data on which they had based their proposal. Crick's subsequent work has been concerned with deciphering the functions of the individual CODONS in the genetic code.

CRICKET, field game that originated in England before 1700 and is now most popular in Commonwealth countries. It is too complex to explain here in detail, but basically it is played

Two scenes at Knossos, Crete. *Below left:* the throne of Minos virtually as it was on the day that the palace was destroyed (c1400 BC); carefully excavated and restored by the archaeologist Sir Arthur Evans. *Below:* pithoi in the west magazine of the palace, used for storing oil, wine and grain.

Criminal Law

The nature of crime

Concern about soaring crime rates is not a new phenomenon in the US. A hundred years ago it was written of San Francisco: "No decent man is in safety to walk the street after dark; while at all hours, both day and night, his property is jeopardised by incendiarism and burglary." Policemen in the Broadway area of New York walked "only in pairs and never unarmed." Almost every decade has seen a new "crime wave" scare: the looting of New York in the 1863 draft riots, the murders at the time of the 1877 rail strike, the lynchings of the 1880s, through the Jesse James era, prohibition, race riots and so on to the muggings of the present day.

The US has kept national statistics on crime only since 1930, and only since 1958 have they been reasonably reliable. It is therefore difficult to tell whether such crime waves were real or created by exaggeration in the press and elsewhere. But despite such problems it is certain that the sixties and early seventies have seen a rapid increase in crimes against the person, particularly aggravated assault and forcible rape. In 1966 a Presidential Commission estimated that in any year the average American's chances of suffering a serious personal attack were about 1 in 550— although the risk for slum-dwellers was well above, and that for rural and suburban population well below this figure. The situation has further deteriorated since then, and there are few signs of a reversal.

This may prove to be as temporary a crisis as those of the past, but the search for its causes gives rise to grave concern. New theories draw attention to two major factors—the rapid postwar growth of cities and the race problem.

Violent crime is overwhelmingly a big city problem. Generally speaking the larger a city the higher the rate of offences per 100 of the population. The difference between the rates for burglary and robbery in cities of over one million as compared to the rates in small towns is dramatic: the recorded rate for burglary is 30% higher in the city, but that for robbery is more than 450% higher. Statistics vary widely between the cities themselves, of course; highest rates of robbery are recorded in Chicago, Washington and Detroit, while Houston, Philadelphia and Milwaukee suffer far less than their size would suggest. The reason for this is uncertain; various authorities have suggested differing levels of poverty, ethnic composition, quality of city management, corruption and police behavior, and even less obvious variables, such as the population's age structure, local tradition and the physical layout of the city.

What is agreed, though, is that it is the poorest areas of every city which breed the most violent crime. Offences, victims and offenders are to be found in areas characterized by bad housing, overcrowding, low level of education, and high unemployment, most frequently the inner city. Every year the population of US metropolitan areas swells by about 3 million. Of these new city dwellers, the poorest are forced to live in the cheaper city centers, the remainder further out towards the suburbs. The centers thus deteriorate and the suburbs improve. The developing pattern has implications which cannot be overlooked in any study of the growth of crime.

Many slum-dwellers are black migrants from the rural south and their offspring. Between 1940 and 1967 around 4 million Negroes moved from the South to the cities; Negroes are responsible for about two-thirds of convictions for assault. Other ethnic groups coming to the cities in the past, such as Irish and Italians, also underwent the experience of slum living and achieved notoriety for crime and violence, but within one or two generations most had managed to acquire a sufficient stake in society to escape to a more settled existence. Why is the same not happening to the black people?

One reason is that there have been major changes in the employment market, with automation greatly reducing the demand for unskilled labor. Education is more necessary than ever for a good job, and in this competitive field Negroes have suffered both as late-comers and from discrimination. Frustrated ambition and lack of hope contribute to a "nothing-to-lose" attitude, often manifesting itself in drug addiction, alcoholism and gratuitous violence. The reaction this has provoked both from the other ethnic groups and within the black community itself has only worsened the situation. This vicious spiral is an example of the process

between two teams of eleven. A pair of batsmen from one side defend two wickets, one at each end of a 22yd pitch. The other team act as fielders. A hard ball is "bowled" (thrown overhand with a straight arm) at the defended wicket from the other; the batsman tries to hit out into the field to give himself time to score by running between wickets. If the ball strikes his wicket either directly or while he is running, or if it is caught off his bat, he is out. When all the batsmen are out the teams exchange functions and the "innings" ends; a game consists of not more than two innings per team. The side with most runs wins and the game is drawn if the innings cannot be completed.

CRICKETS, a large group of orthopterous INSECTS. Male ground-dwelling crickets make a chirping sound (stridulation) by rapidly rubbing together the front edge of their wing covers. Crickets have long antennae. Most species have wings, and most have hind legs developed for jumping. An exception is the mole cricket, whose hind legs are undeveloped, but whose fore legs are adapted for burrowing. Field crickets can attack crops. Tree crickets damage trees by laying eggs in the twigs. (See also KATYDID.)

CRIMEA, peninsula 10 425sq mi in area on the N side of the Black Sea, an *oblast* (province) of the Ukrainian Republic, USSR; it is connected to the Ukrainian mainland by the Perekop Isthmus. Its population today is about 70% Russian and 20% Ukrainian, the indigenous Tatars having been absorbed or exiled.

Around 60% of the population lives in the major urban areas, which include the capital, Simferopol, Kerch, Sevastopol, Balaklava and Yalta. The Crimea is largely agricultural, but has important fisheries and mines, and the S is a popular resort area. The area belonged to the Ottoman Empire until 1783, when Catherine the Great annexed it to Russia. It was the scene of major battles in the CRIMEAN WAR, Russian Revolution and WWII.

CRIMEAN WAR (1853–56), war between Russia and an alliance of Britain, France, Turkey and later Sardinia. A chief cause was Russia's desire to expand to Constantinople and gain access to Mediterranean ports, justified by a claim to be protector of Christians in the Ottoman Empire. In July 1853, the Russians occupied the Turkish provinces of Moldavia and Walachia. In Oct., Turkey declared war on Russia. In March 1854, Britain and France allied with Turkey, out of concern at the general Russian threat to their interests elsewhere. On Oct. 17, the Allies began the siege and bombardment of Sevastopol. Major battles, chaotic and with heavy losses on both sides, followed at Balaklava (Oct. 25) and Inkerman (Nov. 5). The siege of Sevastopol ended in Sept. 1855 with Allied victory. After continued fighting, an armistice was concluded in Feb. 1856 and the Treaty of PARIS signed in March. It was the first conflict reported by war correspondents and photographers.

CRIMINAL LAW, defines those acts considered to be offenses against the state as distinct from civil wrongs committed against an individual. It also regulates legal procedures for the apprehension and trial of suspected offenders and limits the penalties of those convicted.

Modern US criminal law derives from the English common law system, with which it concurs on the broad definition of crime. An act cannot be a crime unless it contravenes a rule of law, customary or statutory, in two elements. The *actus reus* is the act (or failure to act) itself; it must be voluntary, but it is worth noting that self-induced incapacity (as through drugs or alcohol) is held to be reckless of consequences and therefore voluntary. The *mens rea* requires intention to commit the act, rather than mere mistake. Recklessness or carelessness is usually held to be sufficient *mens rea*, however.

The US system relies less on judicial precedent than its British ancestor. In several states, for example, no person may be tried for an offense not specified by statute in that state, although in other states offenses founded only on precedent, such as breach of the peace and conspiracy, still exist. In general, the flexible common law is not well adapted to the federal system of the US because it leads to inconsistencies between states. Since the 1800s La., Wis., Ill., Minn., N.M., N.Y. and Mich. have adopted penal codes on the lines of the CODE NAPOLÉON and other European codes, and many other states are studying them, especially the drafts produced by the American Law Institute in 1962 and the National Commission on Reform of Federal Criminal Laws in 1970.

CRINOIDS, about 700 living and 4 000 fossil species of stalked ECHINODERMS. The extinct crinoids are usually called stone lilies and the existing ones **sea lilies**. Some sea lilies are attached to the sea bottom by a stalk. Others (**feather stars**) break away as adults and become free-moving.

CRISPIN AND CRISPINIAN, Saints, 3rd- or 4th-century Christian martyrs. According to legend they were two Roman brothers, shoemakers at Soissons in Gaul, who were beheaded for preaching Christianity. They are patrons of shoemakers and tanners, and their feast is Oct. 25.

CRITICAL MASS, the MASS of a radioactive material needed to achieve a self-sustaining FISSION process. This requires that the NEUTRONS emitted by a given nuclear fission are more likely to encounter further fissionable nuclei than to escape. It is of the order of several kilograms for URANIUM-235.

CRITTENDEN, John Jordan (1787–1863), US politician, sponsor of the 1860 CRITTENDEN COMPROMISE. A supporter of the Union, he nevertheless opposed antislavery measures. He first entered the Senate in 1817, and was US attorney general in 1841 and 1850–53, and governor of Ky, 1848–50.

CRITTENDEN COMPROMISE, measure sponsored by Senator John J. CRITTENDEN in Dec. 1860 in an attempt to avert the Civil War. It proposed the abolition of slavery N of 36°30′, and the protection of slavery S of that line. The domestic slave trade was to be free of all restriction; there was also to be a constitutional amendment preventing Congress from interfering with slave states. The compromise failed in committee and Crittenden won no support for a national referendum.

CRIVELLI, Carlo (c1430–1495), Italian painter. A

sometimes called "deviancy amplification." While halting the process might not solve the entire problem it is certain that the problem cannot be solved unless it is halted.

Another aspect of the escalation of crime has been the rise in crimes, usually of violence, with a real or assumed political motive, as in the assassination of the Kennedy brothers, Martin Luther King, the attempt on George Wallace and the "Manson Family" murders and many others. Yet criminologists have been reluctant to include criminals of this kind in their studies, chiefly because they are not easily explained in terms of existing theory. When the dividing line between "political" and "criminal" acts becomes blurred, the law itself is called into question in a way seldom occurring in "ordinary" criminal cases. Criminals have not been slow to exploit this, with the resulting public interest, and have further confused the issue.

Defining a crime, and hence criminality, is difficult without recourse to moral norms; since these differ widely from society to society an overall definition is impossible. A view popular among modern sociologists is that who and what is "criminal" is determined by society in its evaluation of and reaction to deviant acts.

Some theorists believe that crimes reported to the police are only the tip of an enormous iceberg, and that of these only a tiny fraction are fully processed through all the stages of report to the police, identification as crime, investigation, arrest, decision to prosecute, trial, verdict and sentence. It is often claimed that men with criminal records are subject to excessive surveillance, sometimes harassment, and that some ethnic groups are more privileged than others in their relationships with law enforcement agencies. If this is so, those people convicted and imprisoned do not constitute a reasonable sample of all criminals. Statistical analyses of personal facts about prisoners in order to find the secret of their "criminality" may therefore be of less value than many criminologists formerly believed.

They are now trying to analyse the "process" through which a man may become a hardened criminal. For example, how far does the experience of conviction and confinement in an institution—particularly as a juvenile—encourage a man to see himself as a criminal, and thus tend to increase rather than reduce criminal behavior? Frank Tannenbaum referred to this process in 1938, calling it the "dramatization of evil," but it was not generally regarded as a central issue until after Edwin Lemert's work in the 1950s and Howard S. Becker's challenging book, *Outsiders*, published in 1963. Tannenbaum wrote: "The first dramatization of evil which separates the child out of his group for special treatment plays a greater role in making the criminal than any other. . . . He now lives in a different world. He has been tagged."

This notion of "tagging" has been taken up by some criminologists and developed into the "labelling theory." Society tends to reject a man with a criminal background even if he is attempting to "go straight;" this attitude reinforces the criminal "label" or self-image, leading to behavior which reinforces it further, both to society and to himself.

Another theory regards criminal behavior as *learned behavior*. Thus it has much in common with non-criminal behavior, and must be explained within the same general framework used to explain other human behavior. Edwin Sutherland did much to develop this notion with his theory of "differential association." A child growing up among thieves or pickpockets or prostitutes is likely to learn a set of values, expressed perhaps in apparently insignificant ways such as turns of phrase, gestures or jokes, but which in time combine to influence his whole personality and pattern of behavior. Just as a child brought up on a ranch sees the world differently from one who grows up in a palace, so constant contact with criminal patterns and isolation from anti-criminal patterns give a child a radically different perspective.

This theory has had great influence in directing criminological research towards attempts to understand the interaction between confirmed criminals, their organization and value systems, the way new "apprentices" are recruited and trained, and so on. It has also indirectly helped along the trend in public policy towards probation and community service as serious alternatives to prison, even for apparently unrepentant criminals. A year working in a non-criminal environment, it is thought, might produce new patterns of thinking and behavior, where prison might simply bolster and reinforce existing ones.

Penal reform, however is always slow. Many criminologists see public attitudes as the major barrier to new methods, but the protection of society must be weighed against the possibility of rehabilitating an offender. While the notion of innate criminality is at present out of favor, it may be that social causes alone do not account for criminal behavior. At the moment nothing certain can be said, but the search for a more just, humane and effective system of treating criminals continues.

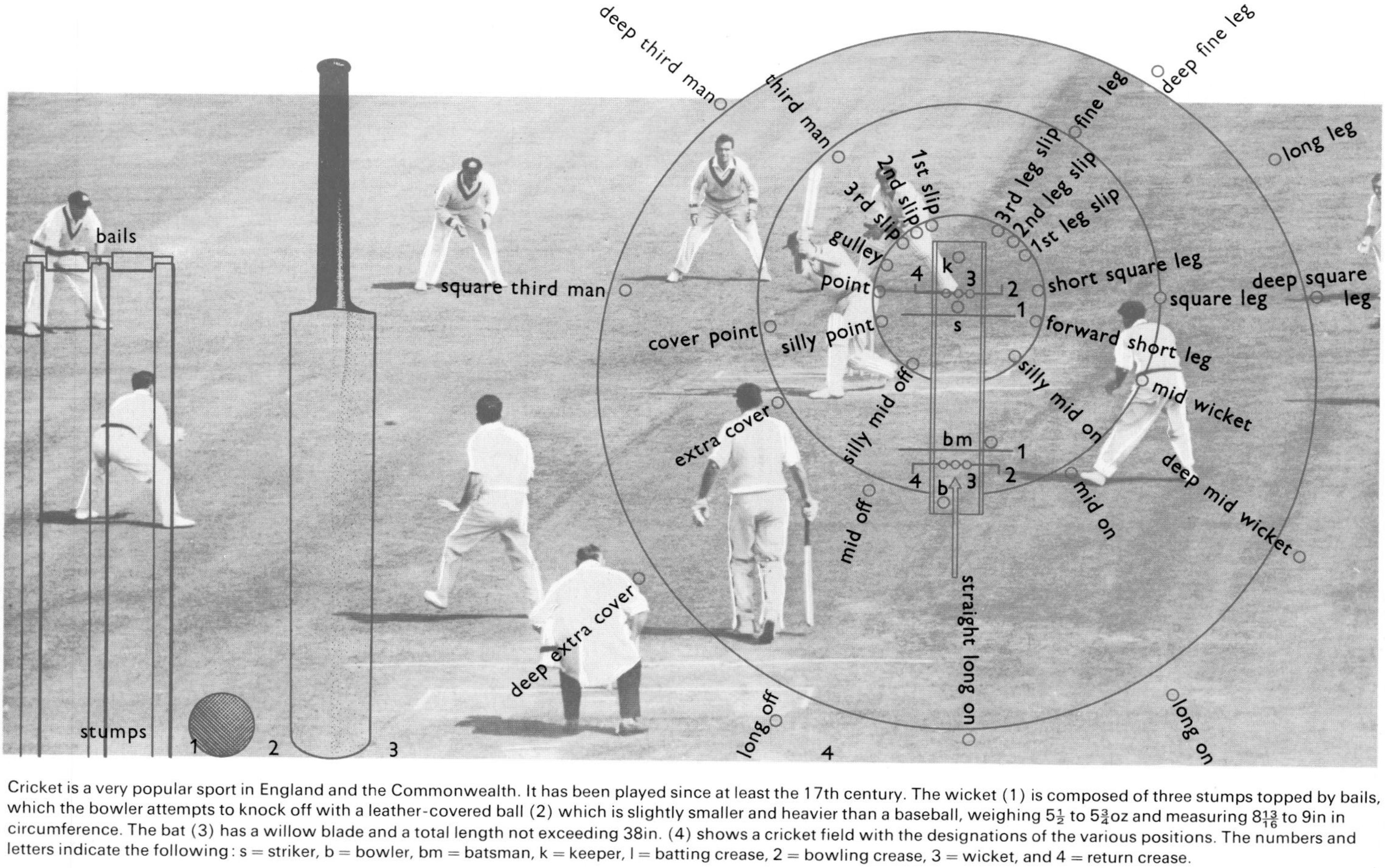

Cricket is a very popular sport in England and the Commonwealth. It has been played since at least the 17th century. The wicket (1) is composed of three stumps topped by bails, which the bowler attempts to knock off with a leather-covered ball (2) which is slightly smaller and heavier than a baseball, weighing $5\frac{1}{2}$ to $5\frac{3}{4}$oz and measuring $8\frac{13}{16}$ to 9in in circumference. The bat (3) has a willow blade and a total length not exceeding 38in. (4) shows a cricket field with the designations of the various positions. The numbers and letters indicate the following: s = striker, b = bowler, bm = batsman, k = keeper, l = batting crease, 2 = bowling crease, 3 = wicket, and 4 = return crease.

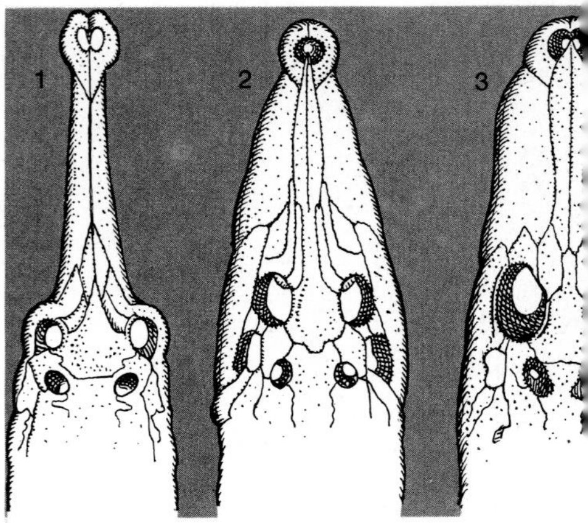

True crocodiles, members of the family Crocodylidae, should be distinguished from other members of the order Crocodilia—alligators, caymans and gavials. *Above left:* a true crocodile, the Nile crocodile, *Crocodylus niloticus*, with its affable grin (top); and the plump, lounging form of the spectacled cayman, *Caiman sclerops*. The Nile crocodile, found practically everywhere in Africa, can attain lengths of 16ft or more. The spectacled cayman, which receives its name from the appearance of the bony structures in the area of its eye-sockets, may grow to about 9ft in length. *Left:* the main difference between the crocodile and the alligator lies in the construction of the snout and jaws. The crocodile (a) has a narrow snout and the large fourth lower tooth fits into a groove in the side of the upper jaw, remaining visible when the jaw is closed. The alligator (b) has a broad snout, its large lower teeth fit into pockets in the upper jaw, and the large fourth lower tooth is not visible when the mouth is closed. *Above:* the gavial's snout (1) is specifically designed for eating fish, whereas the crocodile's (2) and alligator's (3) are adapted for eating larger animals as well.

Venetian, he worked in exile in the March of Ancona. In his intensely religious paintings, outlines are sharp and ornamentation rich and varied, though his figures are somewhat flat and stylized.

CROAKERS, several species of saltwater fish of the family Sciaemidae, found in shallow temperate and tropical seas. Their characteristic croaking, hissing or whistling noise is produced by the swim bladder, which is vibrated by special muscles. One of the best-known species is the Atlantic croaker or Hard head.

CROATAN, member of a group of people of mixed ethnic origins, living largely in Robeson Co., E N.C. Of predominantly Indian and Negro descent, they also have some white ancestry; this may have come from members of the LOST COLONY on Roanoke Island, N.C.

CROATIA, a constituent republic of Yugoslavia, 21 829sq mi in area. Political and religious friction between the Croats and Serbs led to Croatia's temporary autonomy during WWII. In 1946 Croatia, Serbia and Slovenia formed the new state of Yugoslavia. Present-day Croatian agitation for greater autonomy led to political crises and terrorist activity in 1971–74.

CROCE, Benedetto (1866–1952), major Italian philosopher, historian and literary critic. Influenced by HEGEL and VICO, he was a leading exponent of Neo-Idealist philosophy and founder of the review *La Critica* in 1903. He was an active critic of fascism before and during WWII, and in 1943 refounded the Italian Liberal Party, becoming its president; he held various government posts after 1944.

CROCHET, method of making fabrics, garments, lace-like dress trimmings and rugs from yarn or, more rarely, straw, by a series of looped chain stitches made with a special hook. Silk, cotton, wool, or artificial-fiber yarn may be used. Many primitive cultures, including the American Indians, used some form of crochet work; it became popular in the modern US when reintroduced by Irish immigrants.

CROCKETT, Davy (David) (1786–1836), US frontiersman, politician and folk hero. A farmer and Tenn. politician, he was elected to Congress as a Democrat 1827–31, but in 1833 was returned as a Whig. The Whigs built him up as a "backwoods" alternative to Andrew Jackson, and he became famous for his shrewd and humorous speeches, and his memoirs of frontier life. He lost his seat in 1835, and led a Tenn. volunteer force to the ALAMO, where he was killed.

CROCODILE, a family (Crocodylidae) of aquatic reptiles closely related to the ALLIGATOR and GAVIAL. There are over a dozen species, which are distinguished from alligators by their narrower snout. True crocodiles are members of the genera *Crocodylus*, *Osteoblepharon* and *Osteolaemus*. They are found in the warmer areas of the world. Young crocodiles feed on small creatures such as frogs or insects, then graduate to fish and, finally, to mammals and birds. Large prey is knocked down and drowned; man-eating has been known to occur.

CROCODILE BIRDS, plover-like birds which are seen frequently with the Nile crocodile (*Crocodylus niliticus*.) The bird removes parasites from the mouth and skin of the crocodile and emits warning cries when there is danger nearby.

CROCUS, genus of over 70 species of perennial flowers of the iris family (Iridaceae) which are native to Eurasia. All produce a thickened underground stem called a CORM. They are popular ornamental flowers that either flower in the spring or in the autumn. The autumn-flowering saffron crocus (*Crocus sativus*) yields the dye SAFFRON.

CROESUS, last king of Lydia, c560–546 BC, and last of the Mermnad dynasty, proverbial for his wealth and generosity. At his height he ruled a large part of Asia Minor, but he was overthrown by Cyrus the Great c546 BC. He apparently became an honored courtier of Cyrus.

CROFTER, in the Highlands and Islands of Scotland, a tenant farmer of a small-holding. In 1886 special rights in land were granted to crofters to alleviate hardship, but this damaged the crofting system by making it uneconomical.

CROKER, Richard (1841–1922), US politician and TAMMANY HALL boss 1885–1901. In the late 1860s he was leader of New York's "Young Democracy" faction of Tammany Hall Democrats who opposed "Boss" Tweed. After Tweed's downfall he built a strong political machine, but the election of reformist mayor Seth Low (1901) ended Croker's career.

CROLY, Herbert David (1869–1930), US editor and political theorist. His attacks on political complacency and stagnation influenced presidents Theodore Roosevelt and Wilson. In 1914 he founded *The New Republic* magazine.

CRO-MAGNON MAN, a race of primitive man named for Cro-Magnon, France, dating from the Upper Paleolithic (see STONE AGE) and usually regarded as AURIGNACIAN, though possibly more recent. Coming later than Neanderthal Man (see PREHISTORIC MAN), Cro-Magnon Man was dolichocephalic (see CEPHALIC INDEX) with a high forehead and a large brain capacity, his face rather short and wide. He was probably around 1.7m tall, powerfully muscled and robust.

CROME, John (1768–1821), English landscape painter, also called Old Crome, founder of the Norwich School. He was almost entirely self-taught. His best works, such as *Mousehold Heath* (1815) and *Poringland Oak* (1817–21), were done in later life. His main influences were HOBBEMA and other Dutch painters.

CROMER, Evelyn Baring, 1st Earl of (1841–1917), British colonial administrator, who ruled Egypt as consul general 1883–1907. His progressive policies brought the economic and social advances he believed were essential for political progress, but he was distrusted by nationalists. He retired in 1907, becoming leader of the free-trade group in the Unionist party.

CROMPTON, Samuel (1753–1827), English inventor of the SPINNING mule (1779), so-called because it was a cross between ARKWRIGHT's water-frame machine and HARGREAVES' spinning jenny. Although the mule was a great advance on its progenitors, it made little money for its inventor.

CROMWELL, Oliver (1599–1658), Lord Protector of the Commonwealth of England, Scotland and Ireland 1653–58. A minor landowner, he became prominent in the early days of the English Civil War as a member of parliament and as commander of the "Ironsides" cavalry regiment he had created. Largely responsible for victory at Marston Moor (1644), he became lieutenant general of the New Model Army, leading his men to victory at Naseby and Langport in 1645. At first inclined to negotiate with Charles I, the king's untrustworthiness so infuriated him that he lent all his weight to the latter's trial and execution. As lord lieutenant of Ireland he led a campaign there (1649) marked by appalling massacres, and as captain general and commander-in-chief of the army defeated the Scots at Dunbar in 1650. He summarily dissolved the oligarchic and bigoted RUMP PARLIAMENT in 1653. Its beleaguered successor handed power over to him as Lord Protector; he refused the crown in 1657.

Essentially a dictator, his wish to rule through parliament was continually thwarted by the intransigence of the Puritan politicians. His regime, though benevolent, suppressed rather than solved the nation's problems and they broke out anew at his death.

CROMWELL, Richard (1626–1712), son of Oliver Cromwell, on whose death he became Lord Protector of England (1658). He was deposed by military coup in 1659, and went into exile for 20 years.

CROMWELL, Thomas, Earl of Essex (c1485–1540), English statesman under Henry VIII. A ruthless administrator and the main agent for destroying papal power in England, he supervised the king's break with Rome under the Act of Supremacy (1534) and the dissolution of the monasteries (1536–39). He arranged the king's marriage with Anne of Cleves, and on its failure he was executed without trial on charges of heresy and treason trumped up by his many enemies.

CRONIN, A(rchibald) J(oseph) (1896–), Scottish doctor who devoted himself to writing after the success of his first novel, *Hatter's Castle* (1931). His other novels include *The Citadel* (1937) and *The Keys of the Kingdom* (1942).

CRONSTEDT, Axel Fredrik, Baron (1722–1765), Swedish chemist who discovered the element NICKEL, introduced the use of the blowpipe into chemical ANALYSIS and published one of the first chemical classifications of minerals.

CRONUS, in Greek mythology, youngest of the TITANS and son of URANUS, whom he overthrew to rule heaven. When told that he too would be overthrown by one of his children, he swallowed them, except for Zeus, hidden by his mother. Zeus overthrew Cronus and condemned him to Tartarus.

CROOK, George (1829–1890), US cavalry officer. After service in the Civil War, he led campaigns against the Apache Indians in Ariz. (1871–74) and the Sioux and Cheyenne forces led by Sitting Bull and Crazy Horse (1875–77). From 1883 Crook led a temporarily successful campaign to subdue Geronimo.

CROOKES, Sir William (1832–1919), English physicist who discovered the element THALLIUM (1861), invented the RADIOMETER (1875) and pioneered the study of CATHODE RAYS. By 1876 he had devised the **Crookes tube**, a glass tube containing two ELECTRODES and pumped out to a very low gas PRESSURE. By applying a high voltage across the electrodes and varying the pressure, he was able to produce and study cathode rays and various glow discharges.

CROP, or craw, in some birds, a pouch-like enlargement of the gullet or of the alimentary canal. In it, food can be stored, or receive partial preparation, before digestion.

CROP DUSTING, the spraying of farm and garden crops with INSECTICIDES and herbicides (see WEEDKILLER). It aims to protect them from pest attack and competition of uneconomic plants. In recent years, concern has been expressed over the use of poisonous chlorinated and phosphate insecticides, which may cause human and animal injury. (See also PESTICIDES; PLANT DISEASES.)

CROP INSURANCE. See FEDERAL CROP INSURANCE CORPORATION.

CROQUET, lawn game of French origin that became popular in 19th-century England. Competitors have to drive colored balls with a long-handled mallet in strict sequence against each other and through a series of iron hoops stuck into the ground.

CROSBY, Bing (Harry Lillis Crosby; 1904–), US popular singer and actor. He became known as a big-band singer with Paul Whiteman's "Rhythm Boys" and as a "crooner" on radio (1931–49). His many films include the famous *Road* series with Bob Hope and Dorothy Lamour, and he won an Oscar for his performance in *Going My Way* (1943).

CROSS, symmetrical figure consisting of two intersecting lines, although this basic form is often elaborated upon. Crosses have often been used as mystical and religious symbols. In Christianity from the 4th century they symbolize the Cross used to execute Jesus Christ (see CRUCIFIXION).

CROSSBILLS, finches of the genus *Loxia* found chiefly in the colder regions of the N Hemisphere. They have overlapping, scissor-like bills which they use to tear open pine-cones and extract the seeds.

CROSSBOW, medieval weapon consisting of a small but very powerful box fixed transversely on a stock, grooved to take the missile. Its bowstring latched onto a trigger mechanism, often by a lever or winch. It fired a shaft called a bolt or quarrel, about 10in long; some varieties also fired stones. It had less range and accuracy than the LONGBOW and was slower to load.

CROSS-EYE. See STRABISMUS.

CROSSING OVER, exchange of genes between the members of a homologous pair of CHROMOSOMES, resulting from breakage and rejoining of the chromosomes, usually during MEIOSIS. It can alter the LINKAGE groups.

CROSSOPTERYGIAN FISH, a fish group of the DEVONIAN and CARBONIFEROUS. They were the ancestors of land VERTEBRATES. One species, the COELACANTH, has survived until the present day.

CROSS-SECTION, Nuclear, a measure of the strength of the interaction between two atomic or SUBATOMIC PARTICLES. A beam of one kind of particle is directed at a particle of the other kind, and the number of particles scattered or absorbed is measured as an equivalent area (often in BARNS) presented to the beam by the target particle within which all incident particles are affected.

CROTON, genus of tropical herbs, shrubs and trees of the spurge family (Euphorbiaceae). The seeds of *Croton tiglium* yield croton oil, once used as a purgative but now considered dangerous. The bark of *C. eluteria* provides cascarilla, which has medicinal uses. The closely related house plant crotons belong to the genus *Codiaeum* and are popular for their ornamental foliage, particularly *Codiaeum variegatum*, which has green leaves variously colored with white, pink, orange and near-black blotches and spots. Ideally, they should be grown in a sunny position, at temperatures not below 16°C (60°F), and should be well watered whenever the surface of the soil dries out. They are propagated by means of shoot-tip cuttings.

CROTON AQUEDUCT, in SE N.Y., the first artificial water source for New York City. Built 1839–42, it carried water 38mi. It was supplemented by the underground New Croton Aqueduct, built 1885–90.

CROUP, a condition common in infancy due to VIRUS infection of LARYNX and TRACHEA and causing characteristic stridor, or spasm of larynx when the child breathes in. Often a mild and short illness, it occasionally causes so much difficulty in breathing that OXYGEN is needed.

CROWFOOT. See BUTTERCUP.

CROW INDIANS, North American Indian tribe of the Siouan linguistic group, first encountered in Mont. and Wyo. A nomadic plains tribe living mainly by hunting bison and buffalo, they originally broke away from the Hidatsa tribe, and had two main divisions: the Mountain and River Crow. They now occupy a reservation in S Mont.

CROWLEY, city in S La., seat of Acadia Parish. In a rice-growing area, it is an important milling and distribution center. Pop 16 104.

As befits the headdress of great spiritual or temporal ruler, crowns have been made in a wide variety of lavish and beautiful forms. Shown here are (1) the Byzantine imperial crown, (2) the Byzantine imperial diadem as worn by Empress Theodora, (3) the crown of England (St. Edward's crown), now used at coronations, (4) the royal crown of the Netherlands, (5) the German imperial crown, (6) the Austrian imperial crown, (7) the Hungarian crown of St. Stephen and (8) the crown of Charlemagne.

CROWN, ornamental headdress, usually the symbol of sovereignty. In Classical times, distinguished athletes, soldiers and citizens were often crowned with flowers or leaves, sometimes gilded or of real gold. Egyptian pharaohs wore elaborate gold headdresses; Roman emperors wore jewelled diadems. Popes and patriarchs also wear crowns or diadems. The term is also used to denote the office of a crowned ruler.

CROWN OF THORNS, a large STARFISH. It has 15 to 17 arms which may span 0.6m (2ft). Each arm has rows of poisonous, 50mm (2in) spines. Crown of thorns feed on CORAL, killing about 0.2m² (2sq ft) per day. In the late 1960s, an alarming increase in their numbers in the Pacific area gave rise to the fear that the Great Barrier Reef may be destroyed.

CROWN POINT, city in NW Ind., seat of Lake Co. It lies in an agricultural area growing mainly cereal crops. Pop 10 931.

CROWN POINT, resort town in NE N.Y. It was the site first of a trading post, then of a French fort (1731–59), and finally of a British fort occupied and recaptured during the Revolutionary War.

CROWS, a large group of black songbirds which are found worldwide. The true crows are members of the family Corvidae, related to ravens and jays. They are omnivorous and are regarded as pests in agricultural

The distinctive footprints of members of the crow family are virtually identical in all respects except that of size. Shown here are the tracks of the black crow (Corvus corone).

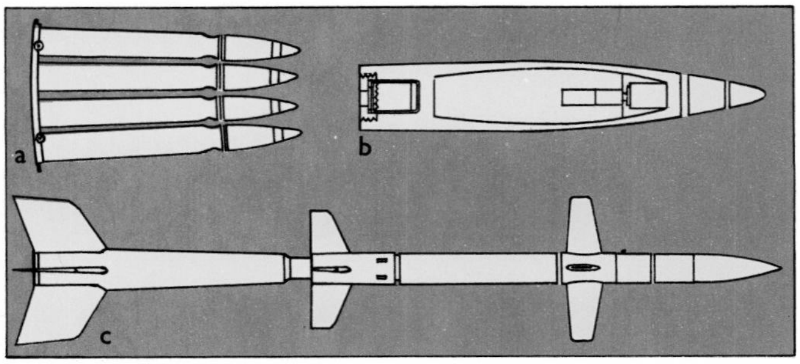

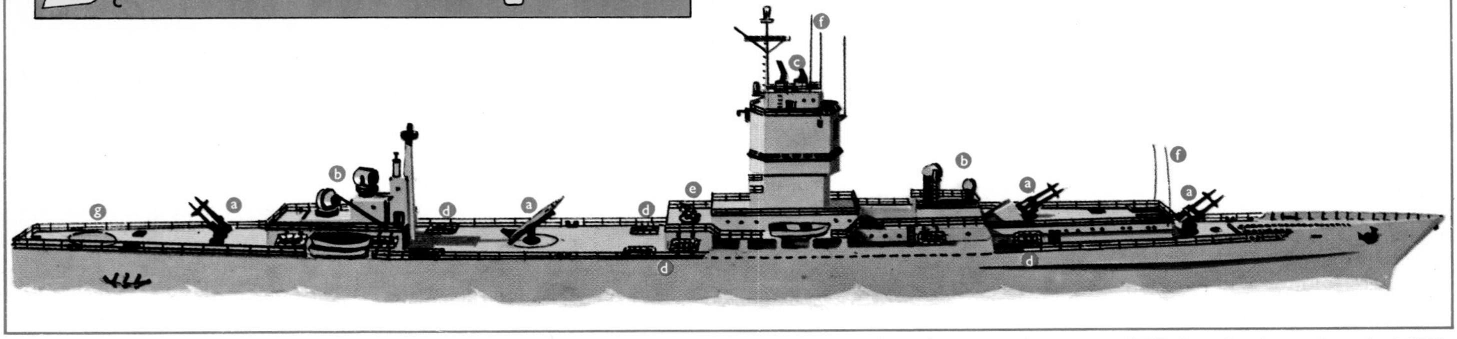

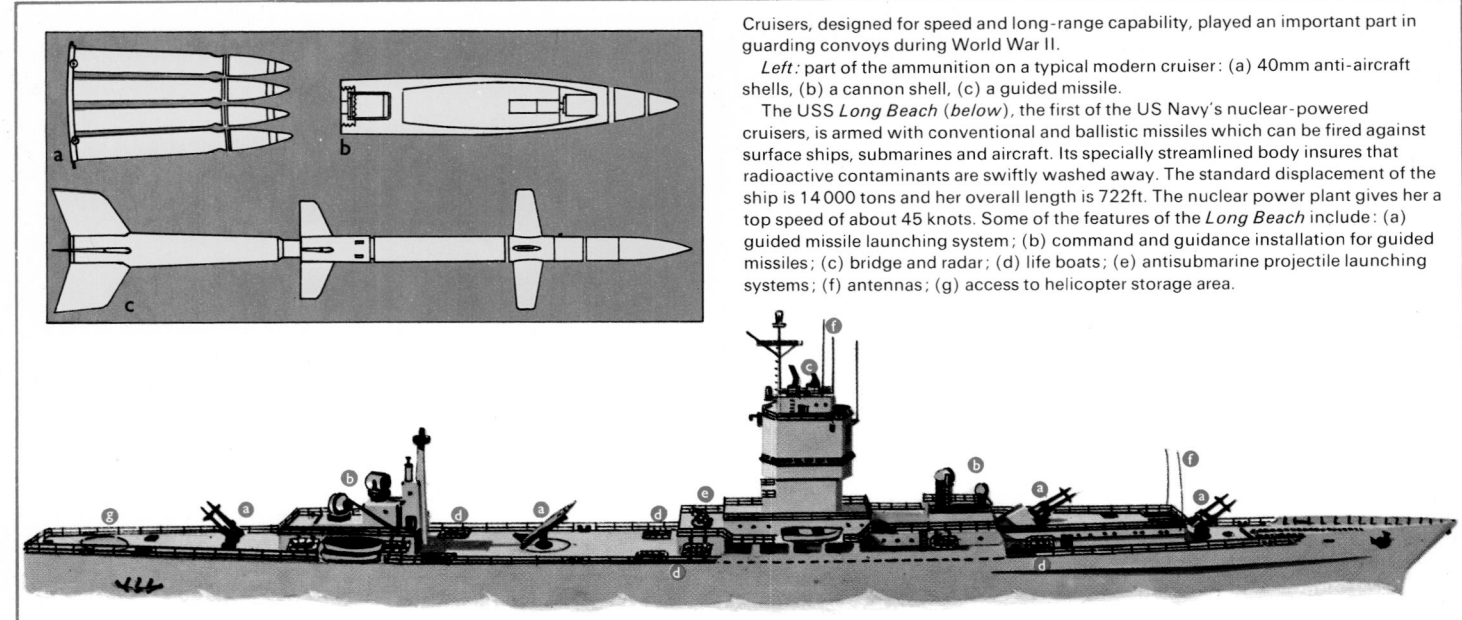

Cruisers, designed for speed and long-range capability, played an important part in guarding convoys during World War II.

Left: part of the ammunition on a typical modern cruiser: (a) 40mm anti-aircraft shells, (b) a cannon shell, (c) a guided missile.

The USS *Long Beach* (*below*), the first of the US Navy's nuclear-powered cruisers, is armed with conventional and ballistic missiles which can be fired against surface ships, submarines and aircraft. Its specially streamlined body insures that radioactive contaminants are swiftly washed away. The standard displacement of the ship is 14 000 tons and her overall length is 722ft. The nuclear power plant gives her a top speed of about 45 knots. Some of the features of the *Long Beach* include: (a) guided missile launching system; (b) command and guidance installation for guided missiles; (c) bridge and radar; (d) life boats; (e) antisubmarine projectile launching systems; (f) antennas; (g) access to helicopter storage area.

areas. Crows are highly intelligent. They can imitate sounds and, with training, the human voice. The clough, jackdaw and rook are common forms of Eurasian crow.

CRUCIBLE, a container used for chemical reactions at high temperatures, for CALCINATION, or for melting metals. Crucibles are made of earthenware, porcelain, quartz or graphite; or of metals such as iron, platinum, nickel or silver. Metal crucibles may be damaged by alloy formation if metals are melted in them. Industrial crucibles are generally large and lined with refractory materials.

CRUCIFIX, model of the Cross bearing the image of Christ crucified. Some early crucifixes showed Christ in a king's robes and wearing a crown, but by the 11th century the figure had become more realistic.

CRUCIFIXION, execution by being nailed or tied to a cross by the limbs or, more specifically, the execution in this manner of Jesus Christ. Many countries of the ancient world used it as their most painful method of execution. The victim often suffered for days; death resulted from shock, exhaustion or exposure. The Romans inflicted crucifixion only on lower-class non-Roman criminals and on political agitators.

CRUIKSHANK, George (1792–1878), English artist and satirical caricaturist. He first won fame with his numerous political cartoons (1811–25), then turned to book illustration. His superb illustrations included those for Dickens' *Sketches by Boz* (1836–37) and *Oliver Twist* (1838).

CRUISER, warship designed for speed and long-range attack, in size between the destroyer and aircraft carrier. Used as a small battleship in WWII, its function has been to maintain lines of sea communication and to defend carriers against air attack. The three traditional types of cruiser, heavy, light and antiaircraft, with 8in, 6in and 5in guns respectively, are being converted to or replaced by guided-missile cruisers, and the first such cruiser with nuclear power, USS *Long Beach*, was launched 1959.

CRUMHORN, double-reed WIND INSTRUMENT popular in the 16th and 17th centuries. A wooden pipe, curved upward at the lower end and fingered like a recorder, it was an ancestor of the oboe.

CRUSADES, a series of religious wars from the end of the 11th to the 13th century, organized by European powers to recover Christian holy places in Palestine from the Muslims. Crusades arose from religious reform and revival, and because the SELJUKS of Asia Minor, who had taken Jerusalem (1071), were now threatening the Byzantine Empire, ruled by ALEXIUS I. There was an enthusiastic response to Pope URBAN II's appeal at the Council of CLERMONT to recover Jerusalem, but political and commercial interests on the part of European rulers confused the issues of religious zeal and wars of conquest.

The **First Crusade** (1095–99) was fought initially by French and German peasants, but they were massacred in Asia Minor. A second force of four large European armies routed the Turks at Dorylaeum (1097) and, led by GODFREY OF BOUILLON, captured Jerusalem in 1099, slaughtering thousands of Muslims and Jews. The Crusaders set up the Latin kingdom of Jerusalem, with fiefs at Tripoli, Antioch and EDESSA. The Turkish recapture of Edessa in 1144 caused the **Second Crusade** (1147–48), led by Louis VII of France and Conrad III of Germany. Their attack on Damascus failed because of mutual jealousy. The Muslims under SALADIN captured Jerusalem in 1187, thus provoking the **Third Crusade** (1189–92), led by the Holy Roman Emperor Frederick I, Philip II of France and RICHARD I of England. Disunited by rivalry, they were unable to take Jerusalem. However, Richard won Acre, gained a few coastal towns and made a truce with Saladin giving pilgrims access to Jerusalem.

The **Fourth Crusade** (1201–04) was diverted by Venetians and claimants to the Byzantine throne from Egypt to Constantinople. The Crusaders pillaged the city, and set up the Latin Empire of Constantinople (1204). The **Children's Crusade** (1212) was a fiasco: some children died on the way, others were sold into slavery. The **Fifth Crusade** (1218–21), against Egypt, the center of Muslim power, was the last launched by a papal legate. The invasion failed when the Crusaders had to be evacuated from floodwaters near Cairo. On the peaceful **Sixth Crusade** (1228–29), the Holy Roman Emperor Frederick II claimed his title to Jerusalem and secured the city for the Christians; but it again fell to the Muslims in 1244. LOUIS IX, leading the **Seventh Crusade** (1248–54) to Egypt, was captured at Mansura; he undertook the **Eighth Crusade** in 1270 but died at Tunis. The last Christian city, Acre, fell to

Map showing the various routes followed by the Crusaders in the eight Crusades mounted during the period 1095–99 AD. Although the Crusaders failed in their attempts to wrest the Christian holy places permanently from the Muslims, European culture was greatly enriched by the contact with the East.

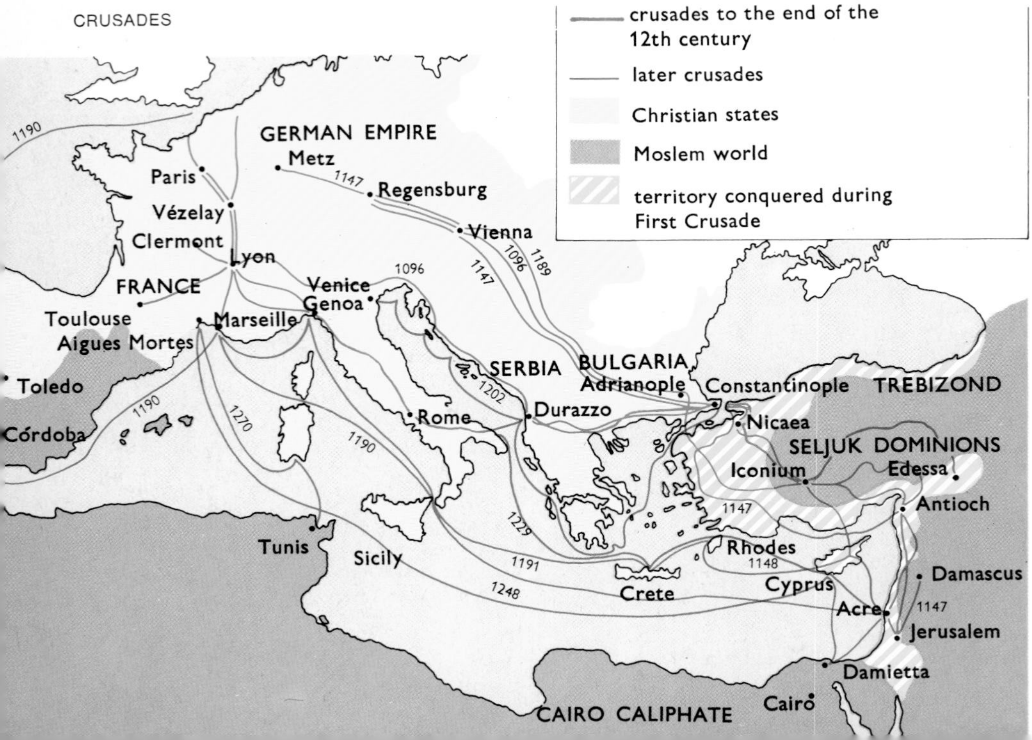

the Muslims in 1291 and there were no further large-scale Crusades. Although the Crusades were a military failure, Western Europe was profoundly affected by the prolonged contact with the East, which stimulated culture and trade. (See also KNIGHTS OF SAINT JOHN; KNIGHTS TEMPLAR; TEUTONIC KNIGHTS.)

CRUSTACEA, class of animals in the phylum ARTHROPODA, with jointed legs, including CRABS, SHRIMPS, WATERFLEAS, BARNACLES and WOODLICE. A few live on land or are parasitic, but most are aquatic, breathing by gills or through the skin and bearing paired series of antennae and limbs down the body. They are vital to the economy of the sea, forming the food of many marine animals.

CRYOGENICS (from Greek *kruos*, frost), the branch of physics dealing with the behavior of matter at very low temperatures, and with the production of those temperatures. Early cryogenics relied heavily on the Joule–Thomson effect (named for James JOULE and William Thomson, later Lord KELVIN) by which temperature falls when a gas is permitted to expand without an external energy source. Using this, James DEWAR liquefied HYDROGEN in 1895 (though not in quantity until 1898), and H. K. Onnes liquefied HELIUM in 1908 at 4.2K (see also ABSOLUTE ZERO). Several cooling processes are used today. Down to about 4K the substance is placed in contact with liquefied gases which are permitted to evaporate, so removing HEAT energy (see LATENT HEAT). The lowest temperature that can be reached thus is around 0.3K. Further temperature decrease may be obtained by paramagnetic cooling (adiabatic demagnetization). Here a paramagnetic material (see PARAMAGNETISM) is placed in contact with the substance and with liquid helium, and subjected to a strong magnetic field (see MAGNETISM), the heat so generated being removed by the helium. Then, away from the helium, the magnetic field is reduced to zero. By this means temperatures of the order of 10^{-2}–10^{-3}K have been achieved (though, because of heat leak, such temperatures are always unstable). A more complex process, nuclear adiabatic demagnetization, has been used to attain temperatures as low as 2×10^{-7}K.

Near absolute zero, substances can display strange properties. Liquid helium II has no VISCOSITY (see SUPERFLUIDITY) and can flow up the sides of its container. Some elements display SUPERCONDUCTIVITY: an electric current started in them will continue indefinitely. (See also CRYOTRON.)

Low temperatures can be used to preserve foods for periods of years. Recently, much publicity has surrounded the idea of freezing people with terminal illnesses, so that at some date in the future, when medical science has advanced sufficiently, they may be revived and cured. Another idea mooted is that of freezing travelers on interstellar spacecraft.

CRYOLITE, a mineral found in Greenland: chemical formula Na_3AlF_6, white monoclinic crystals. Molten cryolite is used to dissolve bauxite ore in the electrolytic production of aluminum (see HALL-HÉROULT PROCESS).

CRYOTRON, miniature switching device used in computers. It makes use of the property of SUPERCONDUCTIVITY exhibited by metals at very low temperatures (see CRYOGENICS). About a single wire of one metal (e.g., TANTALUM) is a coil of another (e.g., NIOBIUM): both are bathed in liquid HELIUM at about 4K. Current passed through the coil creates a magnetic field (see MAGNETISM) which renders the tantalum non-superconductive (niobium can tolerate a greater magnetic field without loss of superconductivity). Such switching can be performed extremely rapidly.

CRYPT, vault or chamber, usually beneath a church, sanctuary or choir, and used as a chapel or for burial. In Latin, *crypta* meant a vaulted building below ground level, but the present use comes from the custom of building a church over the grave and chapel of a saint or martyr. Medieval crypts were often extensive, as at Canterbury Cathedral, England.

CRYPTIC COLORATION, coloration that aids the concealment of animals. In many, the coloration matches the animal's natural background, but in others it serves to break up or distort the otherwise easily recognizable outline of the animal.

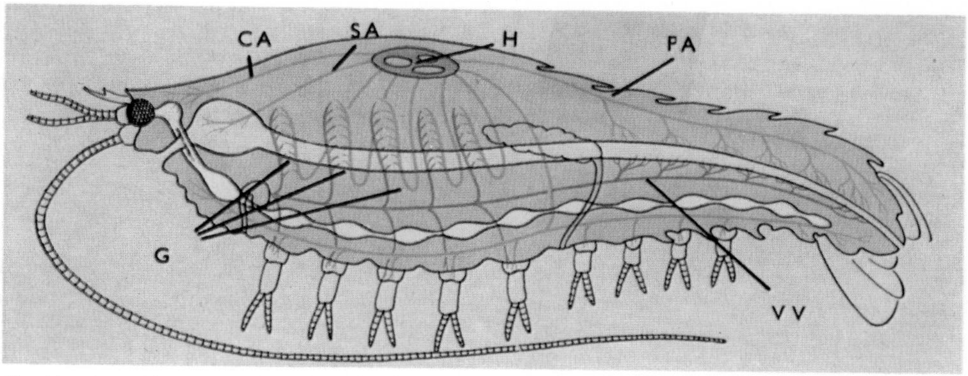

The blood vascular system in a generalized crustacean. The heart (H) lies dorsally in the thorax. A main artery (CA) carries oxygenated blood to the head region, another, the sternal artery (SA) carries blood to the thorax and a third (PA) runs to the abdomen. These connect with a ventral vein (VV) from which capillaries take the impure blood to the gills (G) where carbon dioxide is lost to the surrounding water and oxygen is taken in, the oxigenated blood being to the heart for circulation through the body.

The seven crystal Systems

Name	*Symmetry axes*	*Crystallographic axes*
triclinic	none	$a \neq b \neq c$ $\alpha \neq \beta \neq \gamma$
monoclinic	one diad axis	$a \neq b \neq c$ $\gamma \neq \alpha = \beta = 90°$
orthorhombic	three diad axes	$a \neq b \neq c$ $\alpha = \beta = \gamma = 90°$
tetragonal	one tetrad axis	$a = b \neq c$ $\alpha = \beta = \gamma = 90°$
cubic	four triad axes	$a = b = c$ $\alpha = \beta = \gamma = 90°$
trigonal	one triad axis	$a_1 = a_2 = a_3 \neq c$ $90° = \alpha \neq \gamma = 120°$
hexagonal	one hexad axis	$a_1 = a_2 = a_3 \neq c$ $90° = \alpha \neq \gamma = 120°$

CRYPTOGAM, name given by early botanists to plants such as ALGAE, FUNGI, MOSSES, LIVERWORTS and FERNS, which do not have prominent organs of reproduction when compared to the GYMNOSPERMS and the ANGIOSPERMS.

CRYPTOGRAPHY. See CODES AND CIPHERS.

CRYPTOZOIC, in GEOLOGY, the aeon in which life first appeared (see EVOLUTION) and PRECAMBRIAN rocks were formed. The rocks do not contain FOSSILS that can be used for dating (see CAMBRIAN; CHRONOLOGY); hence the name Cryptozoic (hidden life). By contrast the aeon of visible life, from the end of the Cryptozoic to the present, is called the PHANEROZOIC.

CRYSTAL, village in SE central Minn., 15mi W of Minneapolis. Pop 30 295.

CRYSTAL LAKE, city in N Ill., 28mi WSW of Waukegan. It is chiefly a tourist and summer resort. Pop 14 541.

CRYSTAL PALACE, vast glass exhibition hall designed by Sir Joseph PAXTON for the Great London Exhibition of 1851. An innovative work, it was both the first cast-iron frame building and the first for which structural units were prefabricated and then assembled on site. It was destroyed by fire in 1936.

CRYSTALS, homogeneous solid objects having naturally-formed plane faces. The order in their external appearance reflects the regularity of their internal structure, this internal regularity being the keynote of the **crystalline state**. Although external regularity is most obvious in natural crystals and those grown in the laboratory, most other inorganic solid substances (with the notable exceptions of PLASTICS and GLASS) also exist in the crystalline state although the crystals of which they are composed are often microscopic in size. True crystals must be distinguished from cut gemstones which, although often internally crystalline, exhibit faces rather chosen according to the whim of the lapidary than developed in the course of any natural growth process. The study of crystals and the crystalline state is the province of **crystallography**. Crystals are classified according to the symmetry elements that they display. (See SYMMETRY; an alternative method of reaching the same classification uses the crystallographic axes used in describing the crystal's faces). This gives the 32 crystal classes, which can be grouped into the seven traditional crystal systems (six if trigonal and hexagonal are counted together). Crystals are allotted to their proper class by considering their external appearance, the symmetry of any etch marks made on their surfaces, and their optical and electrical properties (see DOUBLE REFRACTIONS; PIEZOELECTRICITY). Although such observations do enable the crystallographer to determine the type of "unit cell" which, when repeated in space, gives the overall LATTICE structure of a given crystal, they do not allow him to determine the actual dispositions of the constituent ATOMS or IONS. Such patterns can only be determined using X-RAY DIFFRACTION techniques. When a crystal is composed solely of particles of a single species and the attractive forces between molecules are not directionally localized, as in the crystals of many pure metals, the atoms tend to take up one of two structures which both allow a maximum degree of close-packing. These are known as hexagonal close packed (hcp) and face-centered cubic (fcc) and can both be looked upon as different ways of stacking planes of particles in which each is surrounded by six neighbors. Where there is a degree of directionality in the bonding between particles (as in DIAMOND) or more than one particle species is involved (as in common SALT), the crystals exhibit more complex structures, single substances often adopting more than one structure under different conditions (POLYMORPHISM). Although much crystallography assumes that crystals perfectly exhibit their supposed structure, real crystals, of course, contain minor defects such as grain boundaries and DISLOCATIONS. Many of the most important properties and uses of crystals depend on these defects (see SEMICONDUCTOR).

CSARDAS. See CZARDAS.

CTENOPHORES, small group of INVERTEBRATES forming the phylum Ctenophora, found in all seas at a depth of up to 3 000m (10 000ft); often known as **comb jellies** or sea walnuts and confused with true jellyfish. They are transparent, composed of eight "combs" or plates used for swimming, and most give off a greenish light at night (see BIOLUMINESCENCE). They eat the larvae of shellfish and crustacea.

CTESIPHON, ancient city on the Tigris R, Iraq, near Baghdad; a capital of PARTHIA and the SASSANIANS. It has the ruins of a great vaulted palace hall probably built by KHOSRAU I. After the Arab occupation (637–763 AD), the city was deserted.

CUBA, republic and largest island in the Caribbean Sea, at the entry to the Gulf of Mexico and 90mi S of Florida Keys. It has three mountain ranges, the Sierra de los Organos in the W, the Sierra de Trinidad in the center and the Sierra Maestra in the SE—where Turquino, Cuba's highest peak, rises to 6 560ft. Cuba has many rivers, but only a few are major navigable waters. There are deep bays and natural harbors. The warm climate (temperatures being between 72°F and 82°F), the usually plentiful rainfall, severe hurricanes and the rich soil give Cuba a very wide variety of plant life (over 8 000 species) and great mountain forests.

People. The population is about 55% white, of Spanish origin, and 45% mulatto and Negro, descendants of the imported slaves. More than half the population live in cities or towns. Havana has more than 1.75 million inhabitants and other large cities are Santiago de Cuba, Santa Clara, Camagüey, Holguín and Cienfuegos. Most of the rural population lives near sugar factories.

Economy. Cuba is dependent upon one crop, sugar, although in the 1970s there were disastrously poor harvests. Tobacco is the second most important crop and the agriculture has been further diversified by the production of coffee, citrus fruit and rice crops. The fisheries are a growing industry. The largest mineral resource is iron ore, and there are also deposits of nickel, cobalt, copper and manganese. Before 1959 industrialization was limited; after a period of rapid development (1959–63) it has progressed slowly. All trade, commerce and industrial production is nationalized, and most of the cultivated land has been reorganized as state cooperatives. Cuba benefits from an extensive transport network.

History. COLUMBUS discovered Cuba in 1492 and it became important as the base for Spanish exploration of America and as a harbor for Spanish treasure ships. The native Indians, decimated by ill-treatment and disease, were replaced as a work force by West African Negro slaves, particularly in the 18th century when the sugar plantations developed rapidly. In the 19th century Spain's colonial policy led to a series of nationalist uprisings, and after the SPANISH-AMERICAN WAR (1898) Cuba became an independent republic, though it was under US military occupation 1899–1902 and 1906–09. In return for rights of intervention (see PLATT AMENDMENT), the US organized public services and invested heavily in Cuba's economy. This flourished until set back by the Depression, but there were continuous political troubles, corruption, poverty and unemployment.

Between 1924 and 1959 Cuba was under virtually continuous dictatorship. Fulgencio BATISTA, who had come to power in 1933, was overthrown by Fidel CASTRO in 1959, aided by "Che" GUEVARA. Castro, as premier, established a socialist state and instituted sweeping land, industrial and educational reforms. After US firms had been nationalized, the US supported the abortive BAY OF PIGS invasion and enforced an economic blockade. Thereafter, the USSR and the communist bloc replaced US trade and provided great economic support. In 1962 Cuba accepted Russian nuclear missiles, which led to a major confrontation between US and USSR until the missiles were withdrawn. The ORGANIZATION OF AMERICAN STATES (OAS) expelled Cuba in 1962. In 1965 the Cuban Communist Party became the government party. Despite many setbacks Castro's policies have in general benefited the island. Recently there has been a rapprochement between Cuba and the US and the OAS.

Official Name: The Republic of Cuba
Capital: Havana
Area: 44 206sq mi
Population: 7 800 000
Languages: Spanish
Religions: Roman Catholic
Monetary Unit(s): 1 Cuban peso = 100 centavos

The American yellow-billed cuckoo (*Coccyzus americanus*), unlike its somewhat ill-mannered European relatives, builds its own nest and raises its own brood. Although it is sometimes found in Europe, it breeds only in the US and Canada.

CUBE, a regular hexahedron (see POLYHEDRON). In ALGEBRA, the cube (x^3) of a number, x, means $x \times x \times x$: e.g., $10^3 = 10 \times 10 \times 10 = 1000$.

CUBEB, the small berries of *Piper cubeba*, a scrambling shrub native to the tropics. Oil of Cubeb extracted from the berries is used as an antiseptic and expectorant and for flavoring foods and cigarette tobaccos. Family: Piperaceae.

CUBE ROOT. See ROOT.

CUBISM, influential modern art style created by PICASSO and BRAQUE in Paris between 1907 and 1914. Until 1912, in the "analytic" period, Cubist paintings represented subject matter in the pictorial form of an elaborately faceted surface. After 1912, in the "synthetic" period, Cubists also stuck objects to their canvases, instead of representing them, and stressed color, texture and construction in COLLAGE. Cubism had a wide effect on all the arts. (See also ABSTRACT ART.)

CUBIT, the name of various ancient units of length, originally the length of the human forearm and typically about 525mm. (See WEIGHTS AND MEASURES.)

CUBOID, a rectangular PARALLELEPIPED.

CUCHULAIN, mythological hero in the Irish Ulster cycle, renowned for his great beauty and prodigious strength. He defended Ulster single-handed against the armies of the rest of Ireland.

CUCKOO, family of birds (Cuculidae), including the anis, coucals, guiras and roadrunners. The Common cuckoo of Europe, Asia and Africa lays its eggs in other species' nests where they are reared by their foster-parents. The North American species raise their own broods.

CUCUMBER, *Cucumis sativus*, low-growing vine, probably originating in N India, with edible long, green, succulent fruits. Many cultivated varieties have been developed. The West Indian gherkin (*C. anguria*) produces small fruit with worts and spines; these fruit are pickled.

CUCUTA, city in NE Colombia near the Venezuelan border. It was destroyed by earthquake in 1875 and rebuilt. It is a shipping, trading and agricultural center. Pop 249 000.

CUDAHY, city in SW Cal., 20mi SE of Los Angeles. Pop 16 998.

CUDAHY, city in Wis., on Lake Michigan 7mi S of Milwaukee. Industries include meat-packing, tanning and foundry products. Pop 22 078.

CUERNAVACA, capital of Morelos state, Mexico. A historic city and tourist center, it is also the marketing and processing center for rice, sugarcane and fruit. Pop 160 000.

CUESTA, or (British) escarpment, a ridge or hill with one side gently sloping, the other a steep cliff (SCARP), formed by selective EROSION in areas where the ROCK strata are tilted. (See also HOGBACK.)

CUI, César Antonovich (1835–1918), Russian composer, music critic and military engineer. He was a champion of Russian nationalist music and wrote ten operas, though he is now best known for his short piano pieces and songs.

CUISENAIRE METHOD, system used in teaching basic mathematics. The students may, by manipulation and comparison of rods of ten different lengths and ten corresponding colors, derive for themselves fundamental laws and relations.

CULEBRA CUT. See GAILLARD CUT.

CULIACÁN, or Culiacán-Rosales, capital of Sinaloa state, W Mexico. A commercial and agricultural center, it was founded in 1531 on the Culiacán R. Pop 358 812.

CULLEN, Countee (1903–1946), US Negro poet and member of the HARLEM RENAISSANCE. He wrote about the "New Negro" who has proud roots in an African past. Among his works are *Color* (1925) and a novel, *One way to Heaven* (1932).

CULLMAN, city in N Ala., 45mi N of Birmingham, sea of Cullman Co. It is an agricultural and manufacturing center. Pop 12 601.

CULLODEN MOOR, site of the battle near Inverness, N Scotland, where CHARLES EDWARD STUART, the Young Pretender, and the JACOBITES were finally defeated in 1746 by the Duke of Cumberland. About 1000 of the 5 000 Scots were slaughtered.

CULPEPER, Thomas Culpeper, 2nd Baron (1635–1689), English colonial governor of Virginia (1675–83), who ruled through deputies until compelled to go there after BACON'S REBELLION (1680). Uprisings because of the low tobacco prices led to a

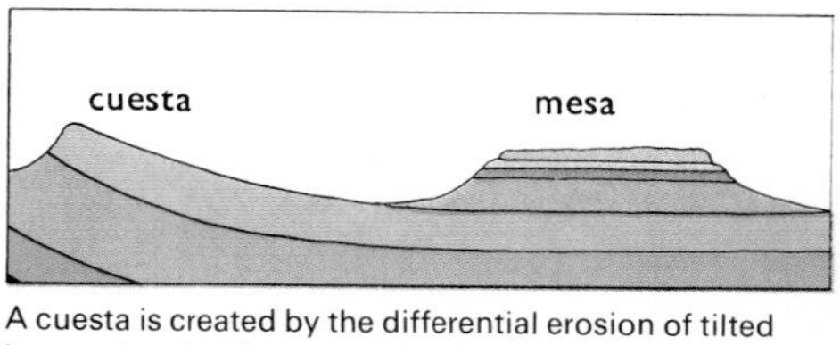

A cuesta is created by the differential erosion of tilted layers of rock, where a very hard capping layer is underlaid by softer rock. When the layers are horizontal, a mesa is formed.

quarrel with the colonists, which resulted in his removal from office.

CULPEPER'S REBELLION (1677–79), early colonial uprising in N Carolina. The people of Albemarle Colony, denied a free market for their tobacco, were led by John Culpeper to imprison their governor, and maintained their own government for two years.

CULTURE, a controlled growth of living cells in an artificial medium, often in a PETRI DISH. The cells may be microorganisms isolated and studied in a pure culture, or made to compete with each other under various environmental and nutritional conditions (see MICROBIOLOGY); or they may be cells from animal or plant tissue cultivated for studies of heredity and function. The culture medium usually contains water, GELATIN or AGAR, salts and various nutrients.

CULTURE. See ANTHROPOLOGY.

CULVER CITY, city in SW Cal. It is the home of MGM film studios and has aircraft and light engineering industries. Pop 34 526.

CUMAE, ancient city near Naples; the oldest Greek colony in Italy, founded 750 BC. Its power and prosperity brought on defeat at the hands of the Samnites (428 BC) and then the Romans (338 BC). The SIBYL's cave, one of the most important sanctuaries in antiquity, may still be seen there.

CUMANS, medieval Turkic race originating from NW Asiatic Russia, which conquered S Russia and Walachia in the 11th century, and settled along the steppes of the Black Sea. They were defeated by the Mongols in c1245 and sought refuge in Hungary and Bulgaria.

CUMBERLAND, city in W Md., on the Potomac R, seat of Allegany Co. An industrial center for coal, iron and steel, and synthetic fibers. Pop 29 724.

CUMBERLAND, town in N R.I. Industries include metal and fiberglass products and textiles. Pop 26 605.

CUMBERLAND GAP, a natural pass, 1 640ft high, through the Cumberland Mts near where Ky., Tenn. and Va. meet. Daniel Boone's WILDERNESS ROAD ran through the Gap, and it was one of the three early major routes to the West through the Appalachian Mts. In the Civil War it was a strategic point.

CUMBERLAND MOUNTAINS, or Plateau, the W division of the Appalachians extending 450mi, from SW Va. to NE Ala., and cut by the Tennessee R. Principal products are coal and timber.

CUMBERLAND RIVER, river 687mi long, rising in SE Ky. and joining the Ohio R in W Ky. The TENNESEE VALLEY AUTHORITY exploits the river for hydroelectric power.

CUMBERLAND ROAD. See NATIONAL ROAD.

CUMIN, *Cuminum cyminum*, a small, slender herb, of the family Umbelliferae, with white or rose flowers, grown in India, China, Mexico and the Mediterranean. Cumin seeds are used as a condiment, and an oil produced on distillation is used for flavoring in perfumery and medicinally.

CUMMINGS, Edward Estlin (1894–1962), US poet known as **e. e. cummings,** famous for his innovations in language, punctuation and typography. The content of his poems is often traditional and romantic, though colored by wit and satire. His major work is *Poems 1923–1954*.

CUMULUS. See CLOUDS.

CUNARD, Sir Samuel (1787–1865), Canadian ship-owner, founder of the Cunard line. He pioneered regular transatlantic steamship lines from 1840 after he had won a contract to carry British and North American mail.

CUNAXA, Babylonian town where King ARTAXERXES II of Persia slew his rebellious brother, CYRUS THE YOUNGER, in 401 BC. Cyrus' army fled, but his Greek mercenaries were led by XENOPHON in the heroic "retreat of the ten thousand" described in the *Anabasis*.

CUNEIFORM (from Latin *cuneus*, wedge, and *forma*, shape), one of the earliest known fully developed writing systems. Each character is formed by a combination of wedge- or nail-shaped strokes. Invented probably by the Sumerians (see SUMER) before 3000 BC, it was soon adopted by the Akkadians and then by other peoples, such as the Hittites and the Persians. The characters are stylizations of earlier pictographs, and were impressed in clay. Cuneiform was first deciphered in detail by RAWLINSON in 1846.

CUNNINGHAM, Merce (1919–), US dancer and choreographer whose avant-garde style emphasizes experimental music and abstract movement. Much of his work is set to the music of John CAGE.

CUPERTINO, city in Santa Clara Valley, Cal., 8mi W of San Jose. It is in a fruit-growing area and manufactures electronic goods. Pop 18 216.

CUP FUNGI, FUNGI of the class Ascomycetes, which produce a cup-shaped fruiting body called an apothecia. These fungi are mainly SAPROPHYTES growing in soils and on dead trees. They are frequently brightly colored, particularly red or orange.

CUPID, or Amor, in Roman mythology, the god of love, identified with the Greek Eros and the son and companion of Venus. He is usually depicted as a small boy, winged, naked and armed with bow and arrow. Those wounded by him fall in love.

CUPPING, a former medical technique for drawing BLOOD to the surface of the body by producing a partial VACUUM inside a "cupping glass" applied to the skin by burning a few drops of denatured alcohol in it.

CUPRITE, red mineral consisting of copper(I) oxide (Cu_2O); a major ore of COPPER, found in Europe, Australia, Ariz., SW Africa and South America. It is formed by oxidation of copper sulfide ores.

CURAÇAO, largest island (182sq mi) of the Netherlands Antilles, West Indies, 60mi N of NW Venezuela. It is flat and barren. The chief industries are oil-refining and phosphate mining. The liqueur *Curaçao* originated here. The capital is Willemstad.

CURARE, arrow-poison used by South American Indian hunters, extracted from various plants, chiefly of the genera *Strychnos* and *Chondodendron*, killing by respiratory paralysis. Curare is a mixture of ALKALOIDS, the chief being *d*-tubocurarine. By competing with ACETYLCHOLINE it blocks nerve impulse transmission to muscles, producing relaxation and paralysis. It has revolutionized modern surgery by producing complete relaxation without a dangerous degree of ANESTHESIA being required. (See also TETANUS.)

CURASSOWS, large gallinaceous game birds of the family Cracidae, found almost exclusively in South America. Curassows are heavily built, with strong bills, powerful legs and broad tails. They live in flocks in trees and feed on insects, fruits, leaves and small animals.

CURB MARKET, a stock market which carries on its business in the streets. The American Stock Exchange originated in this way—hence its former name, Curb Exchange.

CURCULIO, insect of the beetle family, found only in North America, which causes great damage to stone fruits, particularly plums. The eggs are laid in a cut made in the skin of the fruit and further growth of the fruit is stopped at the site.

CURFEW (from the French *couvre-feu*, "cover fire"), regulation clearing the streets for a prescribed period and usually imposed during civil unrest. The original curfew was a bell warning medieval townsmen to extinguish fires at night to prevent conflagrations.

CURIA, properly Curia Romana, administrative and judicial organization that helps the pope govern the Roman Catholic Church. Directed by cardinals, it includes a secretariat of state, three tribunals, five sacred offices, various secretariats and 10 departments (sacred congregations). In ancient Rome a curia comprised several families within a tribe, and formed a political unit in the COMITIA Curiata. Curia eventually became synonymous with Senate. (See also CURIA REGIS.)

CURIA REGIS, royal household, or king's great council, especially of the Norman kings of England, representing the center of national government. Out of it grew all the modern departments of state, including PARLIAMENT.

CURIE (Ci), a unit of RADIOACTIVITY now defined as the quantity of a radioactive material in which 3.7×10^{10} disintegrations per second are occurring.

CURIE, Marie (1867–1934), born Marja

The bridge over the Cumberland River at Fort Nashborough. The river flows past the Tennessee shipyards and is an important transportation route.

Sklodowska, Polish-born French physicist who, with her French-born husband **Pierre Curie** (1859–1906), was an early investigator of RADIOACTIVITY, discovering the radioactive elements POLONIUM and RADIUM in the mineral PITCHBLENDE (1898). For this the Curies shared the 1903 Nobel physics prize with A. H. BECQUEREL. After the death of Pierre, Marie went on to investigate the chemistry and medical applications of radium and was awarded the 1911 Nobel Prize for Chemistry in recognition of her isolation of the pure metal. She died of LEUKEMIA, no doubt contracted in the course of her work with radioactive materials. Pierre Curie is also noted for the discovery, with his brother Jacques, of PIEZOELECTRICITY (1880) and for his investigation of the effect of TEMPERATURE on magnetic properties. In particular he discovered the **Curie point**, the temperature above which ferromagnetic materials display only PARAMAGNETISM (1895). The Curies' elder daughter, Irène JOLIOT-CURIE, was also a noted physicist.

CURITIBA, city in S Brazil, capital of Paraná state. It is 70mi inland and 3 000ft above sea level. It makes paper and furniture and has two universities. Pop 498 000.

CURIUM (Cm), a TRANSURANIUM ELEMENT in the ACTINIDE series. It is prepared by bombarding plutonium-239 with ALPHA PARTICLES or americium-241 with neutrons. Cm^{244} is used as a compact power source for space uses, the heat of nuclear decay being converted to electricity. mp c1340°C, sg 13.51.

CURL of a vector (see VECTOR ANALYSIS), the vector product of DEL with the vector. Thus

$$\text{curl}\,\mathbf{V} = \nabla \times \mathbf{V} = \mathbf{i}\left(\frac{\partial v_z}{\partial y} - \frac{\partial v_y}{\partial z}\right) + \mathbf{j}\left(\frac{\partial v_x}{\partial z} - \frac{\partial v_z}{\partial x}\right) + \mathbf{k}\left(\frac{\partial v_y}{\partial x} - \frac{\partial v_x}{\partial y}\right)$$

(in CARTESIAN COORDINATES).

CURLEW, name of several moorland birds of the family Scolopacidae related to the woodcock and plover and found in America, Europe, Africa and Australia. They are generally dull brown, about 0.6m (2ft) long and have long curved bills. The eggs are laid in a nest on the ground.

CURLEY, James Michael (1874–1958), Democratic "boss" and mayor of Boston, Mass. for many years; also US congressman and governor of Mass. In 1947 he was convicted for fraudulent use of the mails, but his sentence was later commuted by President Truman. He was fully pardoned in 1950.

CURLING, game introduced from Scotland to North America over 100 years ago. Two teams of four players grasp handles attached to rounded 40lb stone *granites* and slide them down 138ft-long ice *rinks* at a *tee*—the marked center of a circle called the *house*. World championships date from 1959.

CURLY-COATED RETRIEVER, breed of

moderately long-legged sporting dog, good for water work. It stands 25–27in high and its black or liver coat is dense and tightly-curled, except on the forehead and muzzle.

CURRANTS, deciduous shrubs of the genus *Ribes* native to the temperate and cool regions of many parts of the world. They are grown for their berries, which are rich in VITAMIN C. Cultivated black currants originate from *Ribes nigrum*, red currants from *R. sativum* and white currants from *R. petraeum*. Family: Grossulariaceae.

CURRENT, Electric. See ELECTRICITY.

CURRENT, Ocean. See OCEAN CURRENTS.

CURRIE, Sir Arthur William (1875–1933), commander of Canadian forces in Europe in and after WWI (1917–19). Later, he was inspector general of the Canadian Militia and (1920–33) principal and vice-chancellor of McGill U., Montreal.

CURRIER AND IVES, firm of American lithographers which produced over 7000 different prints showing lively scenes from 19th-century American life. Nathaniel Currier (1813–1888), became known in 1835 by producing a lithograph of a major New York City fire only four days after the event. James Merritt Ives (1824–1895), became Currier's bookkeeper in 1852, his partner in 1857.

CURTIS, Benjamin Robbins (1809–1874), US lawyer, associate justice in the US Supreme Court 1851–57, and President Andrew Johnson's leading counsel during his impeachment trial, 1868.

CURTIS, Charles (1860–1936), 31st vice president of the US (1929–33) under Hoover. He became a lawyer in 1881 and was a Republican representative in Congress 1893–1907 and senator 1907–13, 1915–29.

CURTIS, Cyrus Hermann Kotzschmar (1850–1933), US founder of a publishing empire. From the age of 12, he started or bought magazines and newspapers including *The Saturday Evening Post, The Ladies' Home Journal* and the *New York Evening Post*.

CURTIS, George William (1824–1892), US journalist, lecturer and reformer. He wrote humorous essays and spoke on national issues. He became political editor of *Harper's Weekly* (1863–92), chairman of the commission on civil service reform (1871), and chancellor of New York U. (1890).

CURTISS, Glenn Hammond (1878–1930), US aircraft manufacturer and inventor of the AILERON (1911). In 1908 he won a trophy for the first public flight of more than 1km in the US.

CURVATURE, at any point P on a plane CURVE, the difference between the angle θ made by the tangent (see TANGENT OF A CURVE) at that point with a fixed straight line, and the angle $\theta+\delta\theta$ made by the tangent at the adjacent point P' with the same straight line. The curvature at P may therefore be defined as the rate of change, k, of θ at that point. In terms of DIFFERENTIAL CALCULUS, for the curve $y=f(x)$,

$$k=\frac{\pm d^2y/dx^2}{[1+(dy/dx)^2]^{3/2}}.$$

The curvature of a curved surface in a specified direction is defined similarly.

CURVE, in mathematics, the map of an infinite set of points $(x_1, x_2, \ldots x_\infty)$ into a space S such that each point satisfies a FUNCTION, $f(x)$. In plane GEOMETRY, should $f(x)$ be a polynomial (see ALGEBRA), the curve is described as an algebraic curve; others are termed transcendental curves. Although most curves are of infinite extent in at least one direction, it is generally useful to consider only that section of it lying between two points, $f(p)$ and $f(q)$: a curve on which for every $f(p)$ an $f(q)$ can be chosen which coincides with $f(p)$, $p\neq q$, is a closed curve and may be finitely bounded in all directions (though possibly of infinite extent); curves which do not satisfy these conditions are described as open.

The most commonly encountered algebraic curves are the hyperbola, parabola, ellipse (see CONIC SECTIONS), the CIRCLE, which is a special case of the ellipse, and the straight LINE. The most common transcendental curves are those of the trigonometric functions (see TRIGONOMETRY) sine, cosine and tangent and those of the logarithmic and exponential functions (see LOGARITHM; EXPONENT). In CARTESIAN COORDINATES these are:

(hyperbola)	$y=\pm b\sqrt{x^2-a^2}/a$,
(parabola)	$y=ax^2+bx+c$,
(ellipse)	$y=\pm b\sqrt{a^2-x^2}/a$,
(circle)	$y=\pm\sqrt{a^2-x^2}$,
(straight line)	$y=ax+b$,
(sine curve)	$y=a.\sin x+b$,
(cosine curve)	$y=a.\cos x+b$,
(tangent curve)	$y=a.\tan x+b$,
(log curve)	$y=a.\log_b x+c$,
(exponential curve)	$y=a.b^x+c$,

where in each case a, b, c are CONSTANTS.

CURZON, George Nathaniel Curzon, 1st Marquess of Kedleston (1859–1925), British statesman, viceroy of India 1898–1905 and foreign secretary 1919–24. His reforms while viceroy included reorganizing government finance. (See also CURZON LINE.)

CURZON LINE, an E boundary proposed for Poland at the VERSAILLES Peace Conference, 1919, and championed by Lord CURZON of Kedleston, July 1920, as a Polish—Soviet armistice line. By defeating Russia, Poland gained over 50000sq mi E of this line in the treaty of Riga, 1921.

CUSA, Nicholas of. See NICHOLAS OF CUSA.

CUSCUS, six species of arboreal Australasian MARSUPIALS about the size of a domestic cat. They have large eyes, a pouch and a prehensile tail, and are covered in soft fur.

CUSH, Kingdom of, Egyptian-influenced Sudanese state flourishing c1000 BC—350 AD. Cushite kings, reigning from the capital, Napata, conquered Egypt, ruling as its 25th dynasty (8th–7th centuries BC). The later capital, MEROË, was Negro Africa's first major iron-making center until its destruction in the 4th century AD.

CUSHING, Caleb (1800–1879), US politician, lawyer and diplomat, who negotiated a treaty opening five Chinese ports to US trade. Member of the US House of Representatives 1835–43, first US commissioner to China 1843–45; US attorney general 1853–57; US counsel at the ALABAMA CLAIMS conference 1871–72.

CUSHING, Harvey Williams (1869–1939), US surgeon who pioneered many modern neurosurgical techniques and investigated the functions of the PITUITARY GLAND. In 1932 he described **Cushing's Syndrome**, a rare disease caused by STEROID imbalance and showing itself in obesity, high blood pressure and other symptoms.

CUSHING, Richard James (1895–1970), US cardinal (from 1958), archbishop of his native Boston, Mass., (from 1944) and a friend of the Kennedy family. He was noted for his missionary and social work.

CUSHING, William Barker (1842–1874), Union naval officer, a hero in the American Civil War. He torpedoed the Confederate ironclad *Albemarle* (1864), barely escaping alive when his launch sank. He became a commander at the age of 30.

CUSP, a point on a CURVE at which the CURVATURE is infinite.

CUSTARD APPLE, the fruit of several trees and shrubs of the genus *Annona*, native to tropical America. The pulp of the common custard apple (*Annona reticulata*) has edible, sweet pulp with a very soft custard-like consistency.

CUSTER, George Armstrong (1839–1876), controversial American cavalry officer, killed in a famous battle with Indians. He proved himself an outstanding Union cavalry leader during the Civil War. Made a lieutenant colonel in 1866, he joined General Hancock's successful expedition against the Cheyenne Indians in Kan. and subsequently saw western patrol duty. In 1876 Custer and the 7th US Cavalry Regiment moved to herd Sioux Indians in Mont. into government reservations. Underestimating the size of an Indian village, Custer refused to await expected reinforcements and attacked, recklessly dividing his force into three columns. His own column was entirely wiped out. (See also CRAZY HORSE; LITTLE BIGHORN, BATTLE OF.)

CUSTER BATTLEFIELD NATIONAL MONUMENT, 765 acres in SE Mont. on the Little Bighorn R, scene of General CUSTER's defeat and death. A national cemetery 1876–1946, it is now a national monument.

CUSTIS, George Washington Parke (1781–1857), playwright, the stepgrandson and adopted son of George Washington. His daughter married Robert E. LEE. His former estate opposite Washington, D.C., is now ARLINGTON NATIONAL CEMETERY.

CUSTOMS, taxes levied on goods entering or leaving a country. The term may cover any TARIFF but is often used for duties on goods brought into a country as personal baggage or sent through the mails to an individual.

CUSTOMS UNION, a grouping of independent nations which abolish tariffs between themselves to improve trade. Examples have included the ZOLLVEREIN, BENELUX, EUROPEAN FREE TRADE ASSOCIATION (EFTA), EEC (see COMMON MARKET, EUROPEAN) and the Latin American Free Trade Association.

CUTHBERT, Saint (d. 687), English bishop renowned for his piety. A Northumbrian shepherd, he became prior of Melrose Abbey, then of LINDISFARNE (661–676); a hermit of Farne Island (676–684); then bishop of Hexham and finally of Lindisfarne (685–687). He retired to Farne.

CUTLER, Manasseh (1748–1823), US Congregationalist clergyman with wide-ranging accomplishments as botanist, lawyer, pioneer, merchant, teacher, physician. He classified New England flora and helped organize the second OHIO COMPANY (1786) to settle land in the NORTHWEST TERRITORY.

CUTLER RIDGE, unincorporated town in SE Fla., SSW of Miami. Pop 17441.

CUTLERY, general term used for edged cutting instruments such as knives, axes and scissors. PREHISTORIC MAN used cutlery of sharpened stones, SHELLS and FLINTS, as does PRIMITIVE MAN today. Gradually implements of bronze, iron (see BRONZE AGE; IRON AGE) and, later, STEEL became current. Modern table cutlery may be made of SILVER, STAINLESS STEEL, SHEFFIELD PLATE, any of a number of PLASTICS, or other suitable material. (See also FORGING; GRINDING AND POLISHING; METALLURGY.)

CUTTACK, city in E India, largest in Orissa state. It is Orissa's main trade center and former capital, noted for filigree work and historic buildings. Pop 194000.

CUTTLEFISH, *Sepia officinalis*, small marine CEPHALOPODS found in coastal waters. The feet are modified into short arms and a pair of tentacles surround the head. The cuttlebone is an internal calcified structure. When disturbed cuttlefish expel a jet of dark fluid and dart sharply backward.

CUTWORM, caterpillar of owlet moths that feeds on young plants, cutting them off near the ground. It sometimes climbs into trees and eats new buds. It is mainly nocturnal. (See ARMY WORM.)

CUVIER, Georges Léopold Chrétien Frédéric Dagobert, Baron (1769–1832), French comparative anatomist and the founder of PALEONTOLOGY. By applying his theory of the "correlation of parts" he was able to reconstruct the forms of many fossil creatures, explaining their creation and subsequent extinction according to the doctrine of CATASTROPHISM. A tireless laborer in the service of French Protestant education, Cuvier was perhaps the most renowned and respected French scientist in the early 19th century.

CUYAHOGA FALLS, city in NE Ohio, 5mi N of Akron. A residential town, it also produces machinery, tools, rubber and plastics. Pop 49678.

CUYP, Aelbert Jacobsz (1620–1691), outstanding member of a family of Dutch painters. His glowing river scenes with cattle are particularly fine, but he also painted portraits, still lifes and seascapes. He influenced later English landscape artists, and many of his best works are in Britain.

CUZCO, city of S Peru, capital of Cuzco department and former capital of the INCA Empire. Located 11024ft above sea level, it is an agricultural center with textiles, metalwork; and tourism based on Inca ruins and Spanish colonial architecture. Pop 109 000.

CYANAMIDE PROCESS, process for NITROGEN FIXATION. Calcium carbide (CaC_2) is made by heating CALCIUM carbonate with COKE. Nitrogen is passed through the finely-divided calcium carbide at 1000°C, giving calcium cyanamide ($CaCN_2$), which is then decomposed by steam to give calcium carbonate (for recycling) and AMMONIA.

CYANIDES, compounds containing the CN group. Organic cyanides are called NITRILES. Inorganic cyanides are salts of **hydrocyanic acid** (HCN), a volatile weak ACID; both are highly toxic. Sodium cyanide is made by the Castner process: ammonia is passed through a mixture of carbon and fused sodium. The cyanide ion (CN^-) is a PSEUDOHALOGEN, and forms many complexes. Cyanides are used in the extraction of GOLD and SILVER, ELECTROPLATING and CASEHARDENING.

CYANOGEN (C_2N_2), colorless, toxic gas, a PSEUDOHALOGEN, prepared by oxidizing a CYANIDE. It is reactive, and polymerizes to paracyanogen. mp −27.9°C, bp −21.2°C.

CYANOSIS, the bluish tinge of SKIN and mucous membranes seen when there is too little OXYGEN bound to HEMOGLOBIN in the BLOOD. If generalized it may be due to inadequate oxygen reaching the blood or failure of the BLOOD CIRCULATION; this may be chronic or acute, the latter often needing early treatment or resuscitation. If it is only at the extremities, it indicates slow blood flow due to vasoconstriction.

CYAXARES (d. c585 BC), king of Media (from c625 BC) and founder of the Median Empire. Uniting Iranian tribes, he overcame the Scythians and defeated Assyria with Babylonian help. Media and Babylonia shared the Assyrian Empire.

CYBELE, Great Mother of the Gods, supreme goddess of the Phrygians in Asia Minor. About 430 BC her orgiastic cult spread to the Greeks (who sometimes identified her with CRONUS's sister Rhea or with DEMETER). In 205 BC the cult reached Rome. (See also ATTIS.)

CYBERNETICS, a branch of INFORMATION THEORY which compares the communication and control systems built into mechanical and other man-made devices with those present in biological organisms. For example, fruitful comparisons may be made between DATA PROCESSING in COMPUTERS and various of the BRAIN functions; the fundamental theories of cybernetics may be applied with equal validity to both.

CYCADS, trees and tree ferns of the order Cycadales. They resemble palm trees and are the most primitive living seed plants. The stem is normally unbranched and crowned by large fern-like leaves. The seeds, cones and trunks of some species are ground into flour or meal that is rich in starch. A type of SAGO is produced from the trunk of the sago palm (*Cycas revoluta*). Their fern-like appearance makes Cycads popular ornamental plants. (See also GYMNOSPERMS.)

The Dutch painter Aelbert Cuyp's *River Valley*, painted c1660; now in the Boymans-Van Beuningen Museum, Rotterdam. It is not known whether Cuyp ever ventured far from his hometown, Dordrecht, but some critics consider his style to have been influenced by Jan van Goyen and Claude Lorraine.

CYCLADES, circular group of more than 200 mountainous islands in the S Aegean Sea. From the 5th century AD they were successively under Byzantines, Venetians and Turks, and have been part of Greece since 1829. The main islands include ANDROS, DELOS, NAXOS, PAROS, Syres, Tenos and THERA. Pop 99 959.

CYCLADIC CIVILIZATION. See AEGEAN CIVILIZATION.

CYCLAMATES, the sodium or calcium salts of N-cyclohexylsulfamic acid ($C_6H_{11}NHSO_3H$), white crystalline solids widely used as potent SWEETENING AGENTS until they were found to cause CANCER in rats. They were banned in the US in 1969.

CYCLAMEN, genus of tuberous plants of the family Primulaceae, native to the Mediterranean region and mountainous parts of central Europe. They are popular ornamental plants producing heart-shaped leaves and red, pink or white flowers.

CYCLOID, the CURVE traced by a point on the circumference of a rolling CIRCLE. The curve resembles a succession of arches, with CUSPS separated by distances equal to the circumference of the circle. The cycloid is of architectural interest since it forms the strongest known ARCH. (See also EPICYCLOID; HYPOCYCLOID.)

CYCLONE, an atmospheric disturbance in regions of low pressure (see ATMOSPHERE; METEOROLOGY) characterized by a roughly circular ground plan, a center towards which ground WINDS move, and at which there is an upward air movement, usually spiraling. Above the center, in the upper TROPOSPHERE, there is a general outward movement.

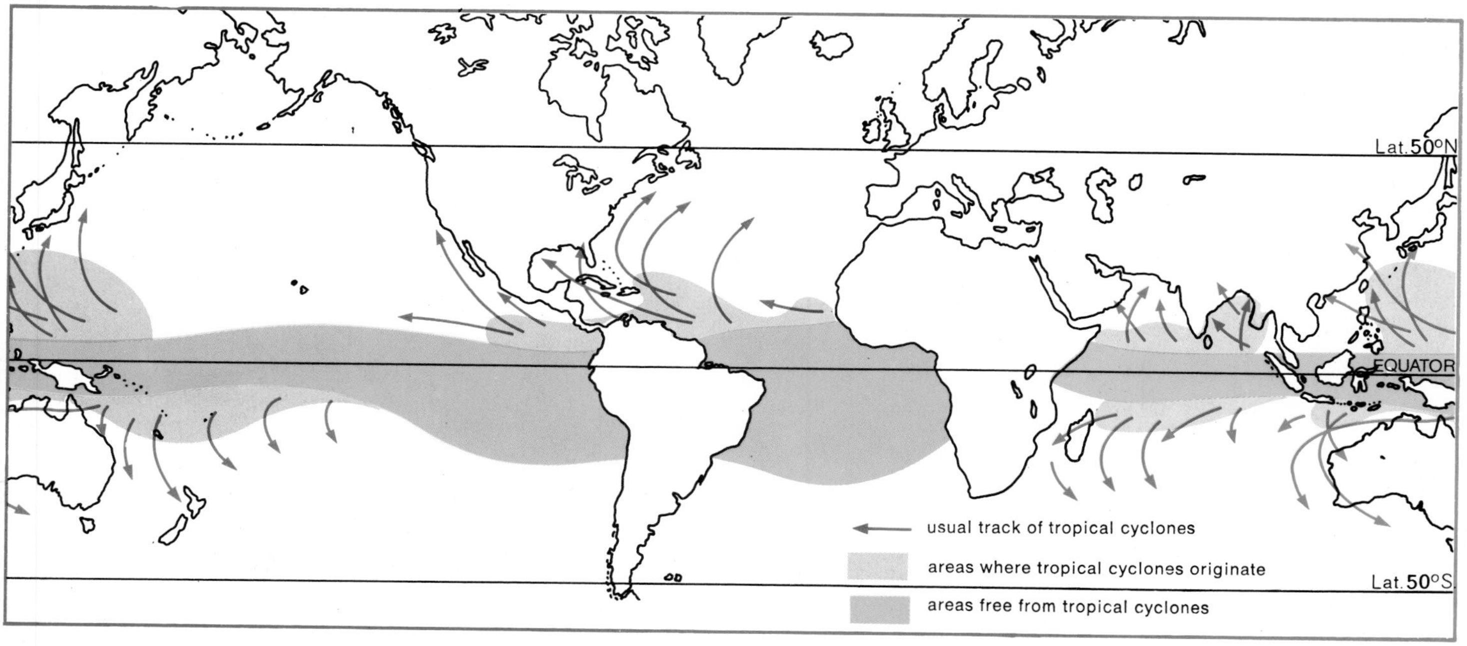

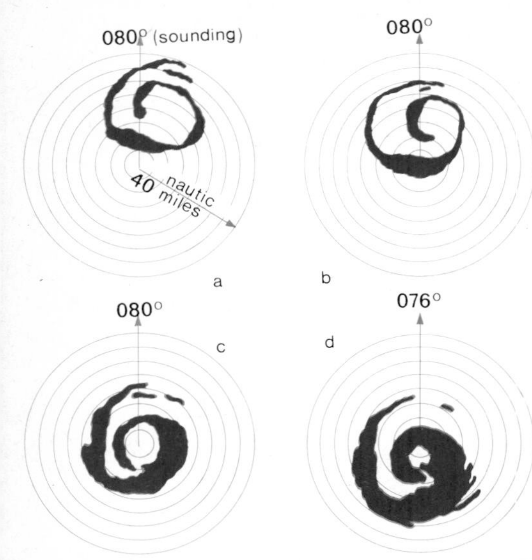

Radar images of a developing tropical cyclone, or hurricane, showing its distinctive spiral configuration.

The direction of spiraling is counterclockwise in the N Hemisphere, clockwise in the S Hemisphere, owing to the CORIOLIS EFFECT. **Anticyclones**, which occur in regions of high pressure, are characterized by an opposite direction of spiral. (See also HURRICANE; TORNADO.)

CYCLONITE. See RDX.

CYCLOPEAN ARCHITECTURE, masonry work of massive, irregular, usually uncemented stone blocks. It is named for the CYCLOPS and is typical of the Mycenaean civilization and of INCA Peru.

CYCLOPS, in Greek mythology, a one-eyed giant. Homer's Cyclopes were (probably Sicilian) shepherds and included POLYPHEMUS, whom Odysseus met. Other legends speak of them as blacksmith sons of Uranus who made Zeus' thunderbolts, and as builders of the mighty walls of Tiryns and Mycenae.

CYCLOSTOMATA, a class of aquatic VERTEBRATES with fixed open mouths, consisting of LAMPREYS and HAGFISH. Cyclostomes are related to the most primitive living vertebrates. They inhabit waters of the temperate zones.

The Cypress, an elegant tree with fragrant wood, is found around the world. Pictured here are the cones and leaves of the Mediterranean cypress (*Cupressus sempervirens*), which are comparatively small, 1 to 1.5in in diameter.

CYCLOTRON, a type of charged particle ACCELERATOR in which the particles travel a spiral path in a strong magnetic field, thus repeatedly traversing the same electric field regions (dees) and achieving energies much greater than those attainable with a linear accelerator.

CYGNUS (the Swan), a large, approximately cruciform constellation of the N Hemisphere containing Deneb (absolute magnitude −7) and Albireo.

CYLINDER, the geometrical solid formed of two congruent (see CONGRUENCE) two-dimensional geometric figures lying in parallel PLANES and the lines (elements) joining each point on the boundary of one to the equivalent point on the boundary of the other. The volume of a cylinder is given by the area of its base multiplied by the vertical distance between the two planes. The most common form of cylinder is the right circular cylinder, whose bases are circles to which the elements are perpendicular (see ANGLE). A cylinder whose elements are not perpendicular to the bases is termed oblique. In ANALYTIC GEOMETRY a cylinder is formed of the lines cutting a plane CURVE, each being parallel to a fixed line not in the plane of the curve, the curve being open or closed.

CYLINDRICAL COORDINATES, coordinate system in which a point is located by its height z above a reference PLANE and the polar coordinates (see ANALYTIC GEOMETRY) of its PROJECTION onto that plane, (r, θ). (r, θ, z) can be related to rectangular CARTESIAN COORDINATES by $x=r\cos\theta$, $y=r\sin\theta$, and $z=z$ (where the original reference plane corresponds to the xy-plane).

CYMBALS, percussion instruments of ancient origin. They consist of two shallow concave metal disks, swept or clashed together, or struck individually. Modern cymbals are made in different sizes—with a diameter of between 10 and 20in—to produce sounds of varying pitch and intensity.

CYMBELINE (Cunobelinus; d. c43 AD), pre-Roman British king, father of Caractacus and an ally of Augustus. Shakespeare fictionalized him in his *Cymbeline*, based on Holinshed's *Chronicles*.

CYNICS, members of an ascetic Greek philosophical sect following DIOGENES (4th century BC), and influenced by SOCRATES. They ignored conventional standards, preached self-control, condemned immorality and renounced worldly comfort, living as simply as animals (hence, probably, their name: *kynikos* means "doglike"). Their movement vanished in imperial Roman times but gave rise to STOICISM.

CYPRESS, city in SW Cal., 9mi NE of Long Beach; mainly a residential center. Pop 31 894.

CYPRESS, common name for ornamental, evergreen conifers of the family Cupressaceae, native to warm temperate and subtropical parts of the world. The young shoots characteristically have no buds and bear small scale-like leaves. The Mediterranean cypress (*Cupressus sempervirens*) is tall and tapering, often reaching 25m (82ft). Through the ages this species has been regarded as a symbol of mourning. (See also ARBORVITAE; JUNIPER.)

CYPRIAN, Saint (Thascius Caecilianus Cyprianus; c200–258 AD), bishop of Carthage (248–258) and martyr, one of the CHURCH FATHERS. Converted to Christianity c246, Cyprian wrote and spoke influentially on order and conduct in the Church, stressing Church unity and episcopal authority. Feast day: Sept. 16.

CYPRUS, island republic in the NE Mediterranean, about 40mi from the S Turkish coast. It is the third-largest island in the Mediterranean after Sicily and Sardinia. The island consists of fertile central lowlands with rugged mountains to the N and S. The N range comprises the Kyrenia and Karpas mountains (Akromandra, 3 357ft). In the SW, the Troodos massif has Mt Olympus (6 403ft), the island's highest peak. On the Mesaoria lowland between the mountain systems is Nicosia, the capital. The mountains are partly forested (pine, cypress and juniper) and have much poor pasture. The climate is typically E Mediterranean.

People. The population is about 80% Greek and 20% Turkish. Both Greek and Turkish are official languages and English is widely spoken. In 1973 nearly 37% of the people lived in the six district capitals: Nicosia, Limassol, Famagusta, Larnaca, Paphos and Kyrenia, but recent events have changed the pattern.

Official Name: The Republic of Cyprus
Capital: Nicosia
Area: 3 572sq mi
Population: 645 000
Languages: Greek, Turkish
Religions: Greek Orthodox, Turkish Muslim
Monetary Unit(s): 1 Cyprus pound = 1 000 mils

The economy normally depends heavily upon irrigated agriculture (citrus fruits, vines, tobacco, cereals and vegetables). Mineral resources include cupreous and iron pyrites, asbestos, chromite and gypsum. Tourism was formerly important.

History. Ruled successively by the Ottoman Turks (1570–1878) and Great Britain, Cyprus became an independent republic, with Archbishop Makarios III as president, in 1960. But strife between Greek and Turkish Cypriots continued, and in 1974 a military coup organized by Greek army officers favoring *enosis* (union with Greece) briefly ousted Makarios, whereupon Turkey invaded the island and occupied the NE third, seeking the permanent partition of Cyprus between the two communities. Stalemate still prevailed in mid-1976.

CYRANO DE BERGERAC, Savinien de (1619–1655), French author. He gave up a military career to write plays and prose. A freethinker, influenced by GASSENDI, he satirized contemporary society in ingenious fantasies about voyages to the sun and moon. Edmond ROSTAND, in his play *Cyrano de Bergerac*, made him into a flamboyant Romantic hero.

CYRENAICA, historic region of E Libya. The chief town is Benghazi. Originally a Greek kingdom ruled from CYRENE, Cyrenaica came successively under Rome, Arab, Turkish and Italian rule. Many battles were fought here in WWII.

CYRENAICS, members of a Greek school of philosophy centered in Cyrene in the 3rd and 4th centuries BC. Its founder, Aristippus (c435–356 BC), advocated seeking pleasure and avoiding pain. Pleasure was the only absolute good, but wisdom was a vital path to its attainment. Theodorus, Hegesias and Anniceris were major Cyrenaic philosophers who succeeded Aristippus, and each founded sects. Cyrenaic philosophy gave rise to EPICUREANISM.

CYRENE, ancient Greek city of N Africa, near the coast of E Libya. Founded c630 BC, it was the original capital of CYRENAICA, becoming a great trade and cultural center.

CYRIL AND METHODIUS, Saints (c827–869 and c825–884), Greek missionaries, apostles to the Slavs, who deeply influenced Slavic culture. Invited to Moravia, from 863 the brothers rivaled Latin-speaking German missionaries in the Danube region, preaching in the local Slavic tongue, pioneering the Glagolitic script (precursor of Cyrillic) and translating biblical texts into Old Church Slavonic. Their feast day is July 7.

CYRILLIC ALPHABET. See ALPHABET.

CYRIL OF ALEXANDRIA, Saint (c375–444), patriarch of Alexandria 412–44, one of the CHURCH DOCTORS. He stressed the unity of God and man in Christ, and led the Council of Ephesus (431) which condemned Nestorius. Roman feast day: Feb. 9.

The desolately beautiful tomb of Cyrus the Great at Pasargadae in Iran; it was restored by Alexander the Great. At the time of his death, Cyrus's empire stretched from the Black Sea and Caspian in the north to the Arabian desert and Persian Gulf in the south.

CYRIL OF JERUSALEM, Saint (c315–386), patriarch of Jerusalem from c350, one of the CHURCH DOCTORS. Thrice deposed for supporting orthodoxy against ARIANISM, he expounded Christian doctrine in his 24 *Catecheses*. Feast day: March 18.

CYRUS, name of three rulers of ancient Persia. **Cyrus I** was king of Anshan in the late 7th century BC. **Cyrus II the Great** (c590/580–529 BC) was the son of Cambyses I and founder of the empire of the ACHAEMENIANS. Ruler of Anshan from c559 BC, he conquered Media, Lydia (c547 BC) and Babylonia (539 BC), building an empire from the Black Sea and the Caspian to the Arabian Desert and Persian Gulf (see also PERSIA, ANCIENT). **Cyrus the Younger** (d. 401 BC) was the second son of DARIUS II. Pardoned after unsuccessfully trying to oust his elder brother, ARTAXERXES II, he rebelled and was killed by Artaxerxes at the Battle of Cunaxa.

CYST, a fluid-filled sac, lined by fibrous connective tissue or surface EPITHELIUM. It may form in an enlarged normal cavity (e.g., sebaceous cyst), it may arise in an embryonic remnant (e.g., branchial cyst), or it may occur as part of a disease process. They may present as swellings or may cause pain (e.g., some ovarian cysts). Multiple cysts in KIDNEY and LIVER occur in inherited polycystic diseases; here kidney failure may develop.

CYSTIC FIBROSIS, an inherited disease presenting in infancy or childhood causing abnormal GLAND secretions; chronic LUNG disease with thick sputum and liability to infection is typical, as is malabsorption with pale bulky feces and MALNUTRITION. Sweat contains excessive salt (the basis for a diagnostic test) and heat exhaustion may result. Significant disease of LIVER, SINUSES and salivary glands occurs. Prompt treatment of chest infection with PHYSIOTHERAPY and appropriate ANTIBIOTICS is crucial to minimize lung damage; concentrated PANCREAS extract and special diets encourage normal digestion and growth, and extra salt should be given in hot weather. Although long-term outlook in this disease has recently improved, there is still a substantial mortality before adult life.

CYSTITIS, INFLAMMATION of the BLADDER, usually due to infection. A common condition in women, sometimes precipitated by intercourse. It occasionally leads to pyelonephritis, or upper urinary tract infection. Burning pain and increased frequency of urination are usual symptoms. ANTIBIOTICS are often needed. Recurrent cystitis may suggest an underlying disorder of bladder or its nervous control.

CYTOCHROMES, colored proteins which transfer energy within cells. They contain a CHELATE complex of an iron ion and a PORPHYRIN system, and so include HEMOGLOBIN. Cytochromes undergo a series of OXIDATION AND REDUCTION reactions, transferring electrons from a substrate to each other and finally to an electron-acceptor. In cellular RESPIRATION the substrates are the hydrogen-acceptors in the CITRIC ACID CYCLE, the electron-acceptor is oxygen, and the energy produced is stored as ATP. (See also PHOTOSYNTHESIS.)

CYTOLOGY, the branch of BIOLOGY dealing with the study of CELLS, their structure, function, biochemistry, etc. Techniques used include tissue CULTURE and ELECTRON MICROSCOPY. (See also HISTOLOGY.)

CYTOPLASM, the PROTOPLASM of which a CELL is made, excluding the nucleus and the boundary membrane.

CZAR. See TSAR.

CZÁRDÁS, a Hungarian dance, or its music. It is in $\frac{2}{4}$ time, but features violent changes of tempo. A slow movement (*lassu*) is usually followed by a quick one (*friss*).

CZECH, one of the two official languages of Czechoslovakia, spoken in Bohemia, Moravia and Silesia. It is a member of the Western branch of the SLAVONIC LANGUAGES.

CZECHOSLOVAKIA, central European communist republic between Poland on the N and Hungary and Austria on the S. The USSR lies to the E, West Germany to the W and East Germany to the NW.

Land. It comprises four distinct geographical regions: Bohemia, Moravia, the Carpathians and Slovakia. Bohemia is the W plateau fringed by mountains—the Böhmer Wald (Bohemian Forest), Erzgebirge (Ore Mountains), the Sudetic Mountains (Sněžka, 5 256ft) and the Bohemian–Moravian Heights. Cutting through the uplands in the S is the Vltava R, which flows through Prague, the Czech capital, on its way to the Elbe. Moravia, E of Bohemia, has rolling hills and fertile soils and is drained by the Morava R and its tributaries and, in the N, by the Oder R. The forested arc of the Carpathians dominates N Slovakia, its ridges separated by the Váh, Nitra and Hron rivers, all flowing to the Danube. In the High Tatra is Gerlachovka (8 711ft), the republic's highest peak. Slovakia's plains in the SW and SE are extensions of the Danube–Tisa (Pannonian) plain. The climate is central European, with hot, thundery summers and long, cold winters.

People. More than 60% of the population are Czech and nearly 30% Slovak, with Hungarians, Germans, Poles and Ukrainians accounting for the remainder. Prague is the only city with more than 1 million inhabitants. Other large cities are Brno, Bratislava, Ostrava, Plzeň and Košice.

Economy. Industry provides about 40% of the Gross National Product, agriculture about 12%. Heavy industry, especially engineering and chemicals, has been greatly expanded since WWII. Steel, armaments, machinery, precision instruments, electrical goods, glass, textiles and footwear are among Czechoslovakia's many products. Limited mineral resources (coal, oil, natural gas, iron ore, uranium and lead-zinc ores) are supplemented by imports of bituminous coal, iron ore, oil and natural gas, mainly from the USSR. There are valuable forests (mainly spruce and beech). Agriculture has been collectivized and provides cereals, sugar beets, potatoes, hops, grapes, fruit and beef and dairy cattle.

History. With the disintegration of Austria–Hungary at the end of WWI, the Czechs and Slovaks proclaimed the independent republic of Czechoslovakia (1918), which developed as a Western-style democracy. Seized by Nazi Germany (1938–39), Czechoslovakia came under Russian domination after WWII, and a communist regime took power. In 1968–69 an attempt by the Communist Party leader Alexander Dubček to liberalize the country was crushed by invading Russian and other Warsaw Pact troops. Dubček and other progressives were purged and the staunchly pro-Soviet Gustáv Husák put in control.

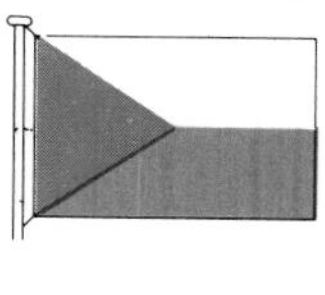

Official Name:
The Socialist Republic of Czechoslovakia
Capital: Prague
Area: 49 365sq mi
Population: 14 500 000
Languages: Czech, Slovak
Religions: Roman Catholic, Czechoslovak Church, Protestant
Monetary Unit(s): 1 Koruna = 100 halérii

CZERNY, Karl (1791–1857), Austrian pianist, teacher and composer. He studied under Beethoven and taught Liszt. Czerny wrote over 1 000 works, but is best remembered for his piano exercises.

CZĘSTOCHOWA, city in S Poland, 125mi SW of Warsaw. It is an iron and steel and railroad center with textile, paper and chemical industries. Pop 189 000.

CZOLGOSZ, Leon (1873–1901), US anarchist, assassin of President William McKinley, whom he shot at Buffalo, N.Y., on Sept. 6, 1901. He was convicted of the crime and executed.

D

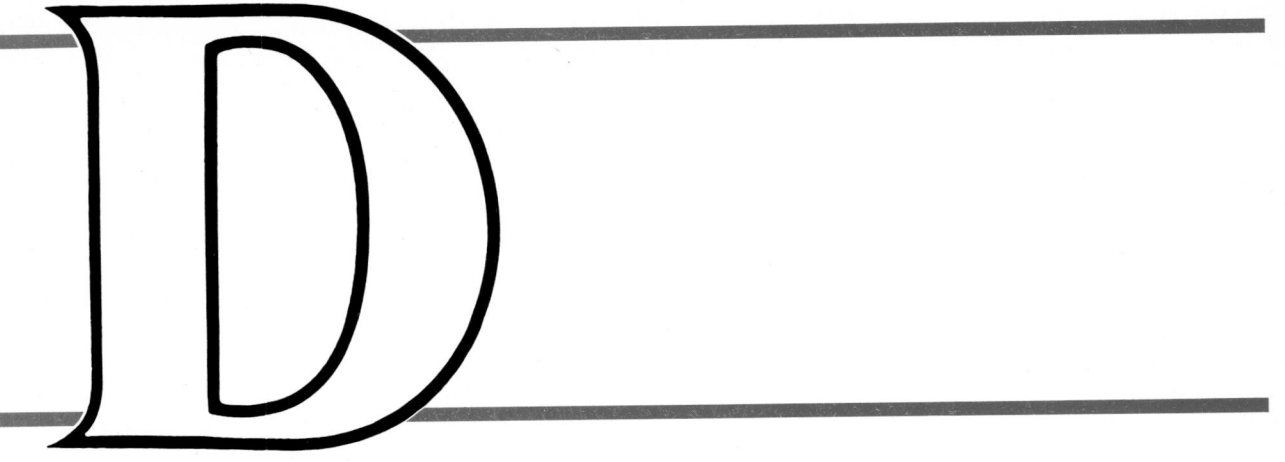

D, fourth letter of the English alphabet, originally derived from the triangular Semitic symbol *daleth* (meaning door). The present form comes from the Latin alphabet. In chemistry D stands for DEUTERIUM; it is the second note of the musical scale of C, and the Roman numeral for 500.

DABLON, Claude (1618–1697), French priest who set up a mission among the IROQUOIS of N.Y. in 1655. As superior of the Jesuit missions, he sent MARQUETTE with JOLIET to explore the Mississippi.

DACCA, capital of Bangladesh, a port located on the Burhi Ganga R. The country's commercial and industrial center, it produces textiles, rubber goods and jewelry. It has been important since about 1600. Pop 1 500 000.

DACHAU, town in Bavaria, West Germany, 10mi NW of Munich. Many thousands were murdered at the Nazi concentration camp set up nearby in 1933, some in brutal medical experiments. Pop 32 713.

DACHSHUND, a dog originally bred in Germany to pursue small, burrowing animals. It has a long body, short legs, pointed nose, long ears and usually a reddish-brown or black-and-tan coat. It may be miniature (9lb) or standard size (12–28lb).

DACIA, ancient kingdom between the Danube R and the Carpathian Mts, in present-day Romania. Subjugated by Rome c107 AD, Dacia remained a Roman province until c270.

DACRON, or **Terylene,** a polyester SYNTHETIC FIBER.

DADA, artistic movement which arose in Zurich and New York in 1915–16, spreading to Berlin and Paris. The name was first used in Zurich by the poet Tristan TZARA, the artists Jean ARP and Marcel Janco, and the writers Hugo Ball and Richard Huelsenbeck. Dada was deliberately provocative, aiming at the destruction of aesthetic preconceptions. The Dadaists experimented with "ready-mades," phonetic or nonsense poetry, collage, anarchic typography and outrageous theater events. Dada was a prelude to SURREALISM and, though it effectively ended in 1923, it influenced many later artistic developments.

DADDI, Bernardo (c1290–1355), Florentine painter of the early Renaissance. The lyrical grace of his works shows the influence of GIOTTO and of Sienese artists such as LORENZETTI.

DADDY LONG LEGS, name referring to two types of unrelated insects: the craneflies and the harvestmen. Craneflies are FLIES but harvestmen close relatives of SPIDERS.

DAEDALUS, mythical Greek artist and inventor who built a labyrinth for King MINOS. After offending the king, Daedalus and his son ICARUS were imprisoned in the maze, but escaped by using wings fastened with wax.

DAFFODIL, bulbous, perennial plants of the genus *Narcissus*, family Amaryllidaceae, producing yellow trumpet-shaped flowers. They are native to Europe and North Africa, but are now an important ornamental crop grown throughout the world. (See also NARCISSUS.)

DAFYDD AP GWILYM (c1325–1385), medieval Welsh poet, born to noble parents in S Wales and trained in Welsh bardic art. His themes were love and nature. About 150 of his poems survive.

DA GAMA, Vasco. See GAMA, VASCO DA.

DAGESTAN, constituent republic of the USSR, located in the Caucasus Mts on the W shore of the Caspian Sea. It has a warm, dry climate and produces wine, fruit and vegetables. It was established in 1921. Pop 1 429 000.

DAGOBERT I (c604–639), last of the MEROVINGIANS to rule the Frankish empire in more than name only. He enlarged and stabilized the empire, while contributing to the cultural life of his subjects.

DAGON, god worshiped by the PHILISTINES and other ancient Near Eastern peoples. Dagon was a god of crop fertility, and was depicted with a human head and a fish's tail.

DAGUERRE, Louis Jacques Mandé (1789–1851), French theatrical designer and former partner of NIÉPCE who in the late 1830s developed the DAGUERREOTYPE process, the first practical means of producing a permanent photographic image.

DAGUERREOTYPE, the first practical photographic process, invented by DAGUERRE in 1837 and widely used in portraiture until the mid-1850s. A brass plate coated with silver was sensitized by exposure to iodine vapor and exposed to light in a CAMERA for several minutes. A weak positive image produced by mercury vapor was fixed with a solution of salt. Hypo soon replaced salt as the fixing agent and after 1840 gold (III) chloride was used to intensify the image. (See PHOTOGRAPHY.)

A daguerreotype of Louis Daguerre, the inventor who rapidly became famous after the French government made public the details of his process in 1839, having acquired them in exchange for a pension agreement.

DAHLGREN, John Adolphus Bernard (1809–1870), American Civil War admiral and inventor of the Dahlgren gun. He served as chief of the US Navy Bureau of Ordnance and adviser to Lincoln. He also developed the use of rockets for naval warfare.

DAHLIA, genus of half-hardy tuberous perennials of the family COMPOSITAE, much prized as ornamentals. There are many cultivated varieties, all of which are descended from a single Mexican species, *Dahlia variabilis*.

DAIBUTSU ("Great Buddha"), Japanese Buddha images fashioned after the Chinese statues. The oldest (c747 AD), in Nara near Kyoto, is over 53ft high and weighs 452 tons. The most famous is the Kamakura Buddha (1252), 42ft high, weighing 103 tons. The interior of the statue is hollow.

DÁIL ÉIREANN, (Assembly of Ireland), Eire legislative assembly, established 1918. It consists of about 145 members elected every five years through universal suffrage by proportional representation. The assembly has more power than the Senate.

DAIMLER, Gottlieb Wilhelm (1834–1900), German engineer who devised a high-speed INTERNAL-COMBUSTION ENGINE (1883) and used it in building one of the first AUTOMOBILES about 1886.

DAIMYO, Japanese feudal barons who first acquired land in the 8th century. Their power grew and reached its zenith by about the middle of the 15th century. In the 17th century they were united and controlled by the SHOGUN Ieyasu. They survived the Shogunate's fall in 1867, but surrendered their domains to the new Meiji regime shortly afterwards.

DAIREN. See PORT ARTHUR-DAIREN.

DAIRY FARMING, the business of producing milk and milk products. It includes the selection, breeding, feeding and milking of cows and other RUMINANTS, and the packaging and distribution of merchandise. Dairy farming has always been economically important to man, but has only recently become highly mechanized. Most countries stringently regulate the hygienic standards and the quality of milk. Cows are bred to ensure maximum yield, and in the US a cow produces an annual average of more than 1 000 gallons of milk. The best-known breeds are Ayrshires, Guernseys, Jerseys and Friesians. They are fed on grass, hay, silage, roots and grain. Domestic cattle were introduced to the US by the Jamestown colonists in 1607. Dairy farming has since become important in N.Y., Pa., Cal., Tex. and in the north central region. Main dairy farming areas of the world are North America, Europe, India, Australasia and parts of South America, but efforts have been made recently to improve milk production in some of the underdeveloped countries.

DAISY, common name given to several plants of the family COMPOSITAE. The common daisy (*Bellis perennis*) is native to Europe, and ornamental varieties are popular in North America and Europe. Similarly, the ox-eye daisy (*Chrysanthemum leucanthemum*) is native to Europe, naturalized in North America and many varieties are in cultivation.

DAKAR, capital of Senegal, W Africa, seaport located on Cape Verde Peninsula. Built as a fort by

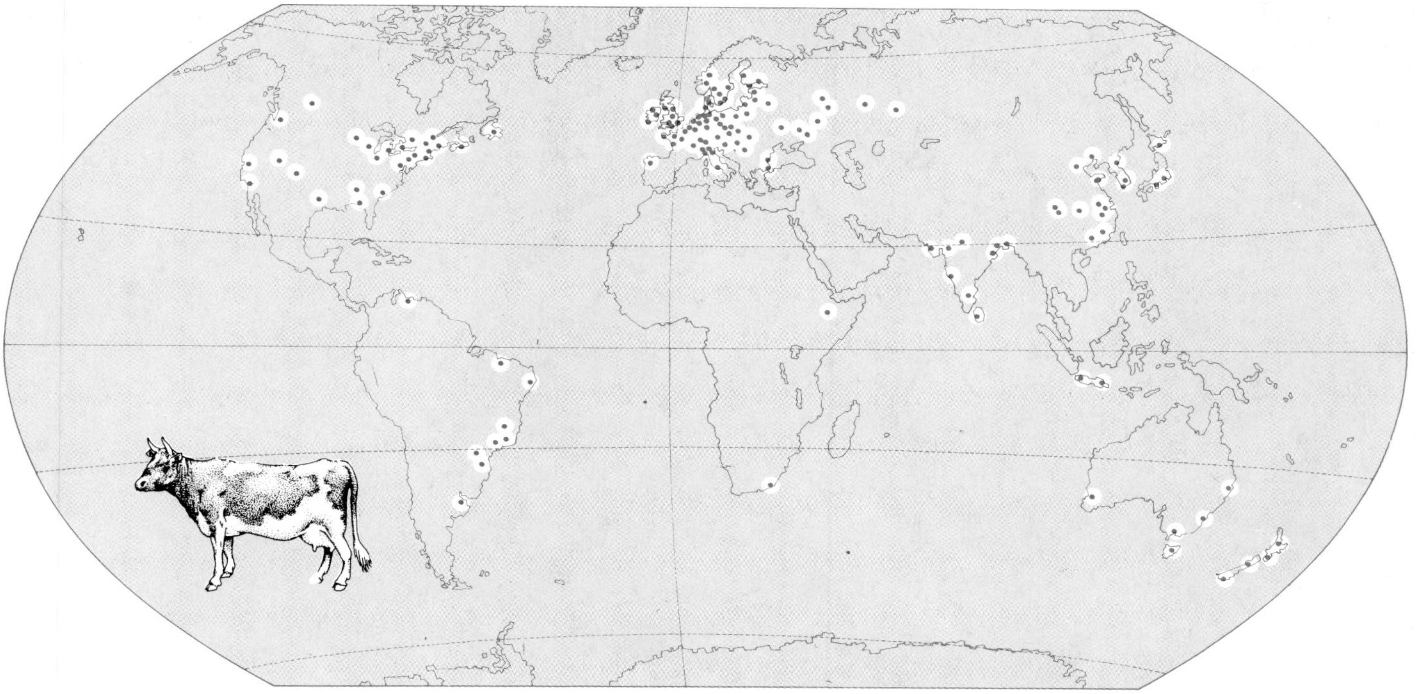

Map of the world showing the major dairying areas. The greatest concentration of dairy farms is in northwest Europe.

the French in 1857, Dakar is Africa's westernmost city and a major maritime and air center. It is also an important trading port for W African goods, and a leading medical and cultural center. Pop 581 000.

DAKOTA INDIANS. See SIOUX INDIANS.

DALADIER, Édouard (1884–1970), French statesman and premier of France who, with Neville CHAMBERLAIN, signed the MUNICH AGREEMENT abandoning Czechoslovakia to Hitler. Premier in 1933, 1934 and 1938–40, he resigned in 1940 after failing to aid Finland against Russia. He was imprisoned by the Germans 1943–45, and later became leader of the Radical Party.

DALAI LAMA, traditional religious and political leader of Tibet. The title (meaning "ocean") was first conferred on a lama by Altan Khan in 1578. The Dalai Lama acquired temporal power in 1642. Tibetans believe that the Dalai Lama is reincarnated in a male child born between 49 days and two years after the Dalai Lama's death. Once the new leader is chosen, he is rigorously trained and takes office on his 18th birthday. Tibet was invaded by China in 1950 and after an abortive Tibetan revolt in 1959 the Dalai Lama fled to India.

DALE, David (1739–1806), Scottish industrialist and philanthropist, who founded his own religious community in 1770. His cotton mills at New Lanark were acquired by his son-in-law Robert OWEN, who went on to form his model community there.

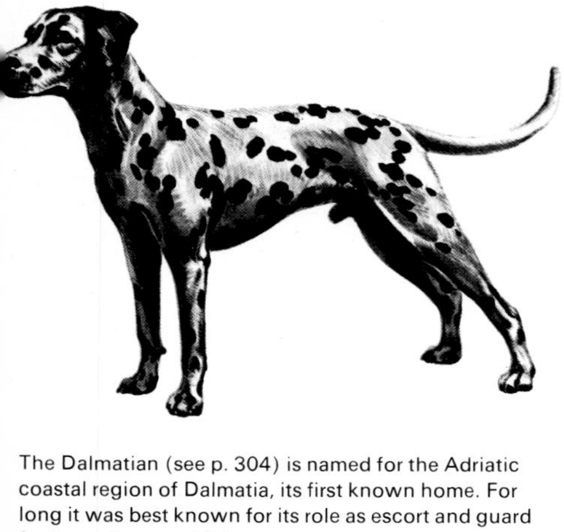

The Dalmatian (see p. 304) is named for the Adriatic coastal region of Dalmatia, its first known home. For long it was best known for its role as escort and guard for horsedrawn vehicles.

DALE, Sir Henry Hallet (1875–1968), British biologist who discovered ACETYLCHOLINE and described its properties together with those of HISTAMINE. In 1936 he shared the Nobel physiology or medicine prize with Otto LOEWI, having identified the chemical that Loewi had found to be secreted by certain nerve endings as acetylcholine and demonstrated its role in transmitting nerve impulses.

DALE, Sir Thomas (d. 1619), British soldier, acting governor (1611; 1614–16) and marshal of the Virginia colony (1611–16). He enforced a rigorous legal code and restored order. He also encouraged tobacco cultivation.

D'ALEMBERT, Jean Le Rond. See ALEMBERT, JEAN LE ROND D'.

D'ALEMBERT'S PRINCIPLE, the observation that NEWTON's third law of motion (that to every action there is an equal and opposite reaction) applies not only to systems in static EQUILIBRIUM but also to those in which at least one component is free to move. Thus when a FORCE **F** is applied to an unconstrained body of MASS m endowing it with ACCELERATION **a**, there is an equal inertial reaction $-m\mathbf{a}$.

DALÉN, Nils Gustaf (1869–1937), Swedish engineer who was awarded the 1912 Nobel physics prize in recognition of his invention of the automatic "sun valve." This device, which rapidly went into worldwide use, allowed the gas lights in unmanned buoys and lightships to be controlled by the amount of natural light.

DALEY, Richard Joseph (1902–), American Democratic politician, mayor of Chicago since 1955. Born in Chicago, he was a state senator 1939–43, director of revenue 1948–50 and clerk of Cook Co. 1950–55 before becoming mayor. He improved Chicago in many ways, but was criticized for his failure to curb racial segregation and for his handling of demonstrators at the 1968 Democratic Convention. He was an adviser to presidents Kennedy and Johnson.

DALI, Salvador (1904–), Spanish surrealist painter whose works mix images as in dreams and hallucinations. Strongly influenced by Sigmund FREUD, Dali sought to portray the elements of the UNCONSCIOUS by using unusual methods and rich fantasy, combined with a polished technique.

DALLAPICCOLA, Luigi (1904–1975), Italian composer who adapted the 12-tone technique to his own emotionally expressive and melodic approach. His works include vocal compositions and operas.

DALLAS, second-largest city in Tex., founded by John Neely Bryan in 1841 on the Trinity R and named for George Mifflin DALLAS. In the 1870s the railroads brought Dallas growth and lasting importance as a cotton processing and shipping center. When oil was discovered in E Tex. in the 1930s, Dallas became a major oil center. The banking and insurance capital for the Southwest, it also has many thriving industries (textiles, paper, machinery), and cultural and educational institutions. Pop 869 600.

Distinctive skyline of Dallas, a thriving center for industry, commerce and finance. Its Cotton Exchange is one of the world's largest buildings. The city also holds a great number of important convention centers and has outstanding cultural facilities.

DALLAS, George Mifflin (1792–1864), US politician, born in Philadelphia. He served as a state senator 1831–33, as vice-president to James Polk 1845–49, and as minister to Russia 1837–39 and to the UK 1856–61. The city of Dallas, Tex., is named for him.

DALMATIA, region in W Yugoslavia consisting of a mountainous strip bordering the Adriatic, and including about 300 islands. The area has been dominated by the Romans (1st century BC–5th century AD), Venetians (1420–1797), Austrians (1815–1918) and many other foreign powers. The present, largely Croatian population lives on tourism, fishing and farming. They produce wine, olive oil, cotton, ships, bauxite and limestone. Dalmatia became part of Yugoslavia in 1920.

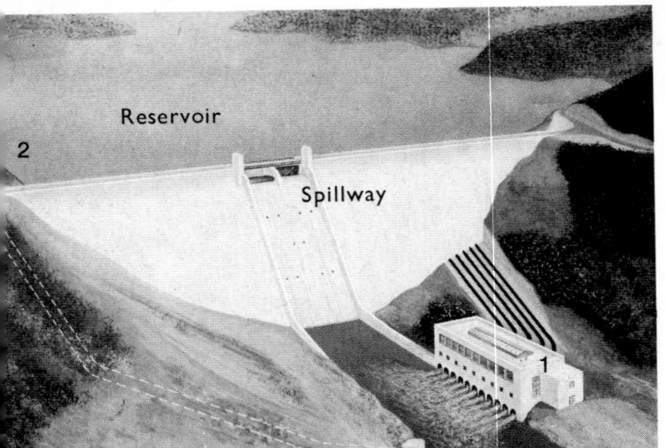

The colossal Hoover Dam (*above*) on the border of Arizona and Nevada; its vast hydroelectric power plant supplies much of the west coast with electricity.

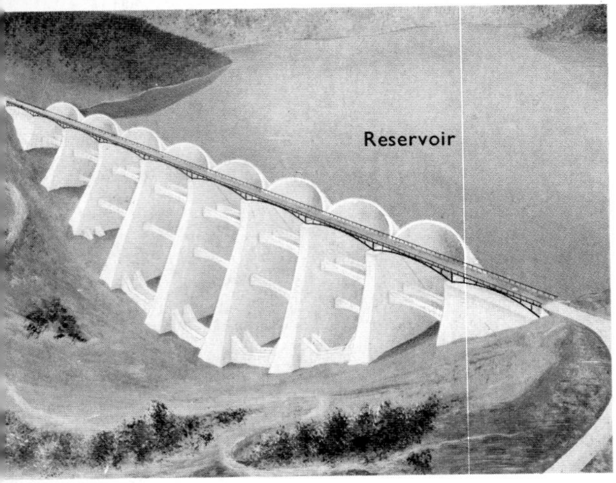

Modern dams (*above left*) are frequently allied with hydroelectric plants (1) in the production of cheap electricity. In most cases there is a diversion tunnel—shown by broken lines (2)—in addition to a central spillway. Enormous reservoirs, often with an area of several hundred square miles, are created by the dammed-up waters. This type of dam-hydro installation is common in the United States. A simpler type of dam (*left*) uses a series of hollow, semicircular arches backed by buttresses and cross-members. The advantage of such a structure is that it utilizes less building material, puts less strain on the foundations and allows simplified inspection and maintenance.

DALMATIAN, strong, muscular dog with a smooth white, black-spotted coat. Dalmatians weigh 50–55lb, and stand 20–23in in height. They are often used as fire-station mascots. Their supposed origin is Dalmatia, in modern Yugoslavia.

DALTON, city in NW Ga., 75mi NW of Atlanta; seat of Whitfield Co. Manufactures candlewick bedspreads, carpets and textiles; has cotton and lumber mills. Pop 18872.

DALTON, John (1766–1844), English Quaker scientist renowned as the originator of the modern chemical atomic theory. First attracted to the problems of GAS chemistry through an interest in meteorology, Dalton discovered his **Law of Partial Pressures** in 1801. This states that the PRESSURE exerted by a mixture of gases equals the sum of the partial pressures of the components and holds only for ideal gases. (The partial pressure of a gas is the pressure it would exert if it alone filled the volume.) Dalton believed that the particles or ATOMS of different ELEMENTS were distinguished from one another by their weights, and, taking his cue from the laws of definite and multiple proportions (see COMPOSITION, CHEMICAL), he compiled and published in 1803 the first table of comparative ATOMIC WEIGHTS. This inaugurated the new quantitative atomic theory. Dalton also gave the first scientific description of COLOR BLINDNESS. The red-green type from which he suffered is still known as **Daltonism**.

DALY CITY, city in Cal., S of San Francisco, developed after the San Francisco earthquake 1906. It has metal and machine works. Pop 66922.

DAM, a structure confining and checking the flow of a river, stream or estuary to divert its flow, improve navigation, store water for irrigation or city supplies or raise its level for use in power generation. Often a recreation area is made as a by-product. Dams are one of the earliest known man-made structures, records existing from c2900 BC of a 15m-high dam on the Nile. Construction methods were largely empirical until 1866, when the first scientifically designed dam was built in France. Dams are classified by profile and building material, these being determined by availability and site. They must be strong enough to hold back water; withstand ice, silt and uplift pressures, and stresses from temperature changes and EARTHQUAKES. The site must have stable earth or rock that will not unduly compress, squeeze out or let water seep under the dam. Borings, seismic tests, structural models and computer simulations are all design aids. **Masonry** or **concrete dams** are typically used for blocking streams in narrow gorges. The highest are around 300m high. A **gravity dam** holds back water by its own weight and may be solid, sloping downstream with a thick base, or buttressed, sloping upstream and strengthened by buttresses which transfer the dead weight sideways; these require less concrete. **Arch dams**, with one or more ARCHES pointing upstream, are often built across a canyon and transfer some water pressure to its walls. Hoover Dam, built in 1936, is a combination of arch and gravity types. **Embankment** or **earthfill dams** are large barriers of rock, sand, silt or clay for controlling broad streams. As in a gravity dam, their weight deflects the horizontal water thrust downward toward the broad base. The materials may be uniformly mixed or there may be zones of waterproof material such as CONCRETE either on the upstream face or inside the dam. During construction, temporary **cofferdams** are built to keep water away from the site. Automatic **spillways** for disposing of excess water from the dam, intakes, gates and bypasses for fish or ships are all important parts of a dam complex.

DAM, Carl Peter Henrik (1895–), Danish biochemist who discovered and investigated the physiological properties of VITAMIN K. For this he shared the 1943 Nobel Prize for Physiology or Medicine with E. A. DOISY who isolated the vitamin and determined its structure.

DAMASCENING, inlaid ornamentation of gold, silver or copper on the surface of metal objects; the process originated in Damascus, Syria before the 12th century. The surface is undercut with a chisel, and wires or chips of metal are hammered in. The term also applies to watered patterns on sword blades, etc., made from Damascus steel.

DAMASCUS, capital city of Syria, founded c2000 BC and reputed to be the oldest continuously inhabited city in the world. An oasis by the Anti-Lebanon Mts, it has been a halt for desert caravans since c1000 BC; it is still a market center, dealing in both produce and industrial products. The city's northern section is modern, the southern ancient, with the famous Great Mosque and a medieval citadel. The city has been controlled by Greeks, Macedonians, Romans, Arabs, Mongols, Turks, British and French until it became the capital of independent Syria in 1946. Pop 836668.

DAMASUS, name of two popes. **St. Damasus** (c304–384), pope 366–384, commissioned a revised Latin translation of the Bible from St. Jerome, which became the VULGATE. In his reign Roman doctrine was established as orthodox and the primacy of the Roman see was established. **Damasus II** was pope from July–Aug. 1048.

DAMAVAND, Mount, extinct volcano in N Iran, some 40mi NE of Teheran. The highest peak in the Elburz Mts, it rises to 18934ft.

D'AMBOISE, Jacques (1934–), American dancer and choreographer of the New York City Ballet. A pupil of George Balanchine, he has become known to a wider public through stage and screen musicals.

DAMIAN, Saint. See COSMAS AND DAMIAN, SAINTS.

DAMIAN, St. Peter (1007–1072), 11th century Italian leader of church reform. A teacher and prior of Fonte Avellana (1045), he became cardinal in 1057 and was papal legate under three popes. In 1828 he was named a Doctor of the Church, but has never been formally canonized.

DAMIEN, Father (Joseph de Veuster; 1840–1889), Belgian Roman Catholic missionary who spent his life in the leper colony of Molokai Island, Hawaii, which he turned from a mere refuge into a thriving community. He died of leprosy himself, having refused to be cured because he would have had to leave Molokai.

DAMIETTA, Egyptian city on the Nile Delta, formerly an important port. In the 13th century it was moved 4mi inland from the Mediterranean to prevent raids by the crusaders. There is a flourishing textile industry and also a shoe factory. Pop 101600.

DAMOCLES, in Greek legend, a courtier of Dionysius the Elder of Syracuse. To illustrate the precariousness of power and position he made Damocles sit at a banquet on a throne over which a sword hung by a single thread. Hence the phrase "sword of Damocles."

DAMON AND PYTHIAS, in Greek legend the prototypes of true friendship. Damon surrendered himself to stand trial for Pythias, sentenced to death by Dionysius of Syracuse, while Pythias settled his affairs. Dionysius was so impressed when Pythias returned that he freed them both and sought their friendship.

DAMP, various noxious gases found in mines. **Firedamp** is METHANE, a colorless gas forming a highly explosive mixture with air. Sir Humphry DAVY's safety lamp reduced the danger of such explosions. **Afterdamp** is a mixture of carbon dioxide and nitrogen which results from firedamp explosions. **Chokedamp** (or **blackdamp**) is also mainly carbon dioxide.

DAMPIER, William (1652–1715), English adventurer, explorer and author. For 11 years he sailed the Atlantic and Pacific as a buccaneer, then was commissioned by the British Admiralty to explore the SW Pacific. He was the first Englishman to reach Australia. He described his voyages in *A New Voyage Round the World* (1697) and other books.

DAMROSCH, Walter (1862–1950), German-born US conductor. As conductor at the Metropolitan Opera, he directed the first US performances of *Parsifal* and other Wagner operas; until 1927 he conducted the New York Symphony Orchestra. He also composed several operas.

DAMSELFISHES, small tropical fish that inhabit CORAL reefs. Damselfish are often brilliantly colored. American species include the Sergeant major, the garibaldi and the Anemone fishes. The Anemone fish are covered with mucus that protects them from the stings of SEA ANEMONES among which they live.

DAMSELFLIES, insects related to the DRAGONFLIES but distinguishable from them by their weak fluttering flight and by their habit of holding the wings erect when resting. Damselflies are small, laying their eggs on water plants and feeding on small insects.

DAN, in the Old Testament, Jacob's first son by Bilhah. He became leader of the Danites, one of the 12 tribes of Israel, who conquered Laish in N Palestine, renaming it Dan; it is now Tell-el-Qadi, Israel.

DANA, Charles Anderson (1819–1897), American journalist who developed the "human interest" story. From 1841–46 he lived in the Utopian BROOK FARM; he then joined the *New York Tribune*, and in 1849 became its managing editor. From 1864–65 he was assistant to the secretary of war. As editor of the *New York Sun* in 1868, he became a national figure.

DANA, Francis (1743–1811), US diplomat and jurist. He was a member of the Massachusetts provincial council and a delegate to the Continental Congress 1776–78. After missions to Europe and Russia, he became a justice of the Massachusetts Supreme Court in 1785 and Chief Justice in 1791.

DANA, Richard Henry, Junior (1815–1882), American lawyer, social reformer and author of *Two Years Before the Mast* (1840), grandson of Francis DANA. Written after he had sailed to Cal. round Cape Horn, it exposed in realistic and readable detail the harsh treatment of sailors and started a reform campaign. He was a founder of the FREE SOIL PARTY.

DANAE, see PERSEUS.

DANAIDS, in Greek mythology, the 50 daughters of Danaus. His twin brother Aegyptus forced them to marry his 50 sons. They obeyed, but murdered their husbands on their bridal night, except for Hypermnestra, who allowed hers to escape.

DA NANG, one of the chief seaports and third largest city in Vietnam. It was an important US naval base in the Vietnam war. Pop 437 668.

DANBURY, city in SW Conn. A military storage depot during the revolution, it was burned by the British in 1777. Once a center of hat-making and called the Hat City, it now produces electrical and metal goods, furniture, paper and textiles. Pop 50 781.

DANBURY HATTERS' CASE, a Supreme Court decision of 1908, important in US commercial law, upholding a suit by a non-union Danbury hat manufacturer against the hatters' union for boycotting his product. He contended that their boycott was in violation of the Sherman Anti-Trust Act (1890) outlawing restrictive practices in interstate and foreign trade.

DANCE, the art of moving the body rhythmically, usually to music. The movements may be enjoyed for their own sake, they may express an idea or emotion or tell a story, or they may be employed to induce a frenzied or trancelike state in the dancer. These possibilities of dance have made it a central feature of the religious, social and artistic life of most cultures. From earliest times dance has played an important part in courtship rituals—the root of most popular dances in the West today—and in the celebration of notable public and private occasions. Among primitive peoples a belief in the magical potency of dance found expression in fertility and rain dances, in dances of exorcism and resurrection, and in dances preparatory to hunting or fighting. Religious dance, associated with paganism, has been played down by the Christian Church since the 12th century. In contrast, in the East traditional dancing is wholly religious in origin and there is little tradition of social dancing. Communal dance as a powerful symbol of group cooperation and mutual regard underlies enduring traditions in FOLK DANCING. Classical BALLET had its origins in the court dances in 15th and 16th-century Italy and France, which were increasingly elaborated into complete entertainments. The 19th century saw the development of the waltz, in which social dancing reached the height of popularity. 20th-century dance styles, promoted by the syncopated rhythms of popular music, have become increasingly free and uninhibited, often resembling primitive dances. One conspicuous innovation has been the conscious invention and commercial promotion of dance styles.

DANDELION, *Taraxacum officinale* and related species of the family COMPOSITAE, with worldwide distribution. They are common weeds producing a sessile rosette of spreading leaves and an inflorescence of yellow flowers and fluffy heads of seeds. The name is derived from the French *dent-de-lion* (lion's teeth), referring to the points on each leaf. The roots and leaves are sometimes eaten and wine is made from the flowers.

DANDIE DINMONT TERRIER, working dog from the English–Scottish border, named for a character in a novel of Walter Scott who kept a pack of these tough vermin killers. The breed stands 8–11in tall and weighs 18lb. Its 2in-long coat mixes hard and soft hair with a soft and silky tuft on its domed head. Shortlegged, with a longish body and pendulous ears, it has a pepper or mustard color coat.

DANDOLO, Enrico (1108–1205), doge of Venice 1192–1205. He founded Venice's colonial empire and was active in the Fourth Crusade which led to the sack of Constantinople by the crusaders.

DANDRUFF, scaling of the SKIN of the scalp, part of the chronic skin condition of seborrheic DERMATITIS; scalp involvement is usually diffuse and itching may occur. The condition is lifelong but usually little more than an inconvenience. Numerous remedies are advertised but few are effective.

DANEGELD, tax levied in Anglo–Saxon England to buy off Danish invaders, created in 868 and made a regular institution by ETHELRED THE UNREADY. It later came to mean military taxes levied by the Anglo–Norman kings until 1162.

DANELAW, Anglo–Saxon name for areas of England colonized by Danish Viking forces in the 9th century, during the reign of Alfred the Great. The W Saxon king Edgar (959–975) granted autonomy to the Danelaw in return for fealty, and a Danish customary law developed in the area.

DANIEL, Book of, Old Testament book, placed among the Prophets in the Christian BIBLE, but in the Hebrew Bible placed in the Writings. Parts of it are in Aramaic. It is the story of Daniel, thought to have been a Judaean noble brought to Nebuchadnezzar's court during the BABYLONIAN CAPTIVITY, and of his exploits and his apocalyptic visions.

DANIEL, Saint Antoine (1600–1648), French Jesuit missionary to the HURON INDIANS in North America; he went with Champlain to Quebec in 1633. He was killed as he walked to meet the Iroquois attacking a Huron village. He was beatified in 1925 and canonized 1930.

DANIEL, Yuri (1926–), Soviet writer sentenced in 1966 with Andrei Sinyavsky to five years in a labor camp for publishing abroad (under the pen-names Arshak and Tertz) works allegedly slandering the Soviet Union.

DANIELL CELL. See BATTERY.

DANIELS, Josephus (1862–1948), US public official and newspaperman. Editor of the Raleigh, N.C., *News and Observer*, he was active in the campaigns of William Jennings Bryan and Woodrow Wilson, who made him secretary of the navy, 1913–21. He was ambassador to Mexico, 1933–42.

DANILOVA, Alexandra (c1906–), Russian-born American ballerina, who studied at the Leningrad ballet schools. She rose to fame in Paris in Diaghilev's Ballet Russe, making her US debut in 1933. Her most famous role is Odette in *Swan Lake*.

DANISH. See SCANDINAVIAN LANGUAGES.

DANISH WEST INDIES. See VIRGIN ISLANDS.

D'ANNUNZIO, Gabriele (1863–1938), Italian writer and adventurer. His poetry first made him famous, its sensuous imagery reflecting his life-style. His novel *The Flame of Life* (1900) is an account of his long liaison with Eleonora DUSE. As a politician he helped bring Italy into WWI on the Allies' side, himself serving in the air force, and in 1919 he occupied the Dalmatian port of Fiume, ruling it as dictator until 1920.

DANTE (Dante Alighieri; 1265–1321), Italy's greatest poet, author of the *Divine Comedy*. Scion of an old Florentine family, he mastered the art of lyric poetry at an early age. He probably attended Bologna University during 1287. His first major work is *The New Life* (c1292) which describes his early life and great love for Beatrice—probably Beatrice Portinari, whom he had known since he was nine; she died in 1290, but remained his lifelong inspiration. He married Gemma Donati c1285. Politically, he was active in Florentine affairs, and was exiled from Florence in 1302. He finally settled in Ravenna in 1318 and died there. *The Divine Comedy* (probably written between 1308 and 1320) is an account of the poet's travels through Hell and Purgatory, and his final glimpse of Heaven. A poetic masterpiece in itself, it is also a diatribe against the corruption Dante saw in the world around him.

DANTON, Georges Jacques (1759–1794), one of the leaders of the FRENCH REVOLUTION. A lawyer, a powerful orator and, in the end, a moderate, Danton strove to reconcile the GIRONDINS and JACOBINS. He dominated the first Committee of Public Safety, but by 1793 began to lose power to the militant Robespierre. Believing the revolution won, he was unable to stop the Reign of Terror, was accused of treason and executed by the Jacobins.

DANUBE RIVER, European river, second only to the Volga in length. From its official source near Donaueschingen in West Germany, it flows 1 750mi through Austria, Czechoslovakia, Hungary, Yugoslavia, Romania, Bulgaria and Russia before emptying into the Black Sea. With over 300 tributaries, it drains almost one-tenth of Europe and provides a major transport system. It was a major natural boundary for the Roman Empire and a useful highway for invaders from the east. The river becomes navigable at Ulm in Bavaria and flows through three capitals—Vienna, Budapest and Belgrade. Since 1856, international agreements have regulated its use, but seasonal obstructions and Europe's East–West political split have limited its traffic.

DANVERS, town in NE Mass., originally Salem Village, scene of the witch trials in 1692. It is today a residential area, but has some light manufacturing. Pop 26 151.

DANVILLE, city in E Ill., seat of Vermilion Co. Originally a mining center, it is now largely agricultural. Pop 42 570.

The water flea *Daphnia* seen here under a microscope, showing the body enclosed in a bivalved carapace.

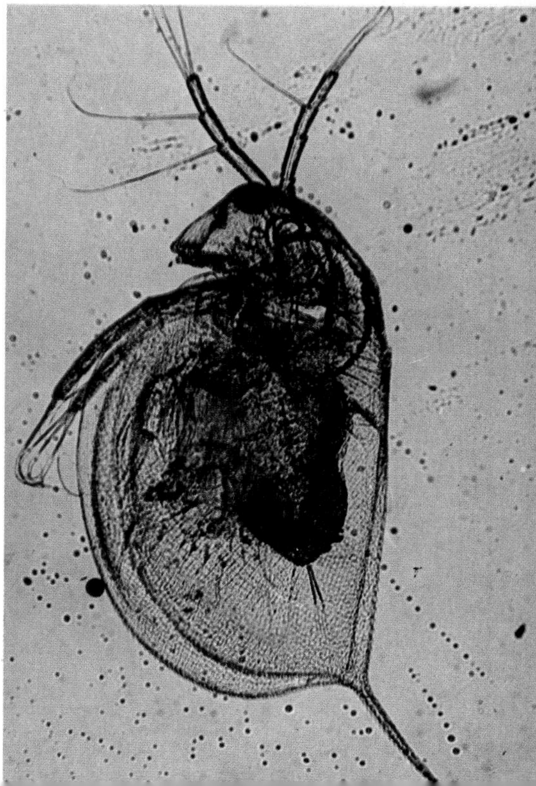

Charles Darwin as an old man; portrait by the English painter John Collier.

DANVILLE, historic city, seat of Boyle Co., central Ky. It is a trade center for tobacco, livestock and horses. Pop 11 542.

DANVILLE, city in S central Va., an industrial center in a tobacco-growing area; its other industries include textiles, tires, gypsum products and glassware. Pop 46 391.

DANZIG. See GDANSK.

DAPHNE, in Greek mythology, a nymph who was changed into a laurel tree rather than submit to the god Apollo. The laurel thereafter was sacred to Apollo, who wore the leaves as a crown; this made the awarding of a laurel crown a special mark of distinction.

DAPHNIA, small freshwater CRUSTACEA, often called **Water fleas**. Their bodies are enclosed in a transparent shell and they move by propelling themselves with their two antennae. Dried daphnia are sold as aquarium food.

DA PONTE, Lorenzo (1749–1838), Italian poet, author of the librettos for Mozart's *Marriage of Figaro* (1786), *Don Giovanni* (1787) and *Cosi Fan Tutte* (1790). In 1805 he went to the US, where he taught Italian language and literature, after 1830, at the newly-founded Columbia U.

DARBY, a residential borough, suburb of Philadelphia in SE Pa. It was settled in 1682 by the Quakers. Pop 13 729.

DARBY, family of English ironmasters. **Abraham Darby** (1677–1717) pioneered IRON smelting using COKE rather than charcoal. His grandson, **Abraham Darby** (1750–1791) built the world's first cast-iron bridge over the Severn R at Ironbridge, Salop.

DARDANELLES, narrow strait 44mi in length in NW Turkey, separating Asia Minor from Europe, formerly called the Hellespont; it is bordered on the W by the GALLIPOLI PENINSULA. It links the Sea of Marmora with the Aegean and is part of the waterway from the Black Sea to the Mediterranean.

DARDANELLES CAMPAIGN. See GALLIPOLI PENINSULA.

DARDANUS, in Greek mythology, a son of Zeus who married the King of Phrygia's daughter and founded Dardania, which became TROY.

DARE, Virginia (b. 1587), the first white child of English parentage to be born in America. Her parents were members of the settlement established by Sir Walter Raleigh on Roanoke Island, N.C., all of whom met an unknown fate.

DAR ES SALAAM, largest city and former capital of Tanzania (formerly Tanganyika). A modern city, it is a commercial center with a fine harbor providing an outlet for exports of cotton, sisal, coffee, diamonds and gold. Pop 396 700.

DARIEN, residential and commuting town in SW Conn., on Long Island Sound. Pop 20 411.

DARIEN, Spanish settlement, also traditionally the E end of the Isthmus of Panama. From 1510–19 the colony was a base for exploration of the American mainland, notably by BALBOA. Santa Maria la Antigua del Darién, the original colony, soon declined, and some colonists moved to a site now called Porto Bello.

DARIEN SCHEME, a program promoted by the Scottish Darien Company in 1698–99 under the economist William Paterson to establish a settlement and a trade route for Scotland across the Isthmus of Darien (now Panama). The settlement failed because of disease, attacks by Darien Spaniards, and the hostility of English merchants who feared competition.

DARÍO, Rubén, pen name of Felix Rubén García Sarmiento (1867–1916), Nicaraguan poet. He introduced the *modernista* movement which revolutionized Spanish and Spanish–American literature; it is characterized by direct language, exotic themes and imaginative use of imagery and of form. His best-known works are *Profane Hymns* (1896) and *Songs of Life and Hope* (1905).

DARIUS, three Persian kings of the Achaemenid dynasty. **Darius I, the Great**, reigned from 522–486 BC. An able ruler, he reorganized his empire into 20 satrapies under officials responsible to him who were supervised by ministers and secret police; he introduced efficient transport, taxation, coinage and legal systems. He attacked the SCYTHIANS, overran Thrace and Macedonia, then attempted to subdue Greece but was finally defeated at MARATHON in 490. **Darius II** reigned from 423 BC until his death in 404 BC; his reign was corrupt, but he achieved much influence in Greece in an alliance with Sparta against Athens. **Darius III** (reigned 336–330 BC) was the last ruler of an independent Persia. Defeated by ALEXANDER THE GREAT, he was murdered by one of his own satraps.

DARJEELING, capital of Darjeeling district in W Bengal, India, and processing center for the famous Darjeeling tea. A mild climate, and its position at 7 000ft in the Himalayan Mts, with views of Everest, make it a popular resort. Pop 42 662.

DARK AGES, general term for the centuries of decline in Europe, c500–1000 AD, after the fall of the Roman Empire. Documentation for the period is sparse because, in the general instability, classical culture was stifled, though remnants of Greek and Roman tradition were preserved by Christian monks in Ireland, Italy, France and Britain. Charlemagne's rule (800–814) briefly reunited Europe but the true flowering of the MIDDLE AGES came till after 1000.

DARLAN, Jean François (1881–1942), French admiral who held various posts in the Vichy government, becoming vice premier, foreign minister and heir-designate to Pétain in Feb. 1941. In Nov. 1942 he surrendered French North Africa to the Allies, but was soon afterward assassinated.

DARLING RIVER, the longest (1 702mi) tributary of the Murray R in Australia, flows mainly through New South Wales and in its early stages forms the boundary with Queensland.

DARMSTADT, industrial city in the state of Hesse, West Germany, largely rebuilt after bombing in WWII. It is the center for a number of chemical and engineering industries as well as wine-making and agriculture. Pop 141 847.

DARNLEY, Henry Stuart, Lord (1545–1567), became second husband of MARY QUEEN OF SCOTS in 1565; their son became James VI of Scotland and JAMES I of England. His intrigues for the Scottish crown led to an early death by violence.

DARROW, Clarence Seward (1857–1938), US lawyer, a renowned defense attorney. After 20 years defending the interests of organized labor, he changed his practice to criminal cases. None of his clients on murder charges received the death penalty. His eloquence saved Leopold and Loeb in 1924 from the electric chair; and he won acclaim in 1925 for upholding the right of academic enquiry in his defense of John Scopes for teaching Darwin's theory of evolution.

DARTERS, long necked, cormorant-like birds which catch fish with their bills. See ANHINGAS.

DARTERS, small, often colorful, bottom-living perch-like fishes of North America. The largest is 220mm (9in) long.

DARTMOUTH, city in S Nova Scotia standing on the E shore of Halifax Harbor in Canada. Its industries include oil refining, shipbuilding and aircraft parts. Pop 64 002.

DARTMOUTH, town in SE Mass., an agricultural community and a summer resort on Buzzards Bay. Pop 18 800.

DARTMOUTH COLLEGE, in Hanover, N.H., is one of America's oldest universities, chartered by George III in 1769. The College is known for its liberal arts curriculum, but also has schools of medicine, business and civil engineering.

DARTMOUTH COLLEGE CASE, US Supreme Court decision of 1819 which denied a state legislature's right to alter the charter of a private college without its consent. The case was brought by the College's trustees against the N.H. legislature. The decision safeguarded private education in the US and gave business corporations a measure of freedom from state interference.

DARWIN, administrative capital of the Northern Territory, Australia and port for the vast hinterland. It serves farming and mining areas, notably the uranium center of Rum Jungle. Founded as Palmerston in 1869.

DARWIN, Charles Robert (1809–1882), English naturalist, who first formulated the theory of EVOLUTION by NATURAL SELECTION. Between 1831 and 1836 the young Darwin sailed round the world as the naturalist on board H.M.S. BEAGLE. In the course of this he made many geological observations favorable to LYELL's uniformitarian geology, devised a theory to account for the structure of coral islands and was impressed by the facts of the geographical distribution of plants and animals. He became convinced that species were not fixed categories as was commonly supposed but were capable of variation, though it was not until he read MALTHUS' *Essay on the Principle of Population* that he discovered a mechanism whereby ecologically favored varieties might form the basis for new distinct species. Darwin published nothing for 20 years until, on learning of A. R. WALLACE's independent discovery of the same theory, he collaborated with the younger man in a short Linnean–Society paper. The next year (1859) the theory was set before a wider public in his *Origin of Species*. The rest of his life was spent in further research in defense of his theory, though he always avoided entering the popular controversies surrounding his work and left it to others to debate the supposed consequences of "Darwinism."

DARWIN, Erasmus (1731–1802), English physician, philosopher, scientist and poet who proposed a theory of EVOLUTION by the inheritance of ACQUIRED CHARACTERISTICS in his *Zoonomia* of 1794–96. Perhaps the foremost physician of his day, he was a leading member of the LUNAR SOCIETY of Birmingham. Charles DARWIN was his grandson.

DASSIN, Jules (1911–), French film director and actor, born in the US. Noted for *Rififi* (1954) and *Never on Sunday* (1960).

DASYURES, small arboreal carnivorous marsupials of the family Dasyuridae, found in Australia and New Guinea. They are becoming rare.

DATA PROCESSING. See COMPUTER.

DATE LINE, International, an imaginary line on the earth's surface, with local deviations, along longitude 180° from Greenwich. As the earth rotates, each day first begins and ends on the line. A traveler going east over the line sets his calendar back one day, and one going west adds one day.

DATE PALM, *Phoenix dactylifera*, a tall palm tree native to drier regions of North Africa and Asia, and introduced to Middle and North America. The date palm produces a large number of edible fruits, which have been locally staple in many desert regions for many centuries and are an important commercial crop. All parts of the plant are economically valuable.

DATING. See CHRONOLOGY; DENDROCHRONOLOGY; RADIO CARBON DATING.

DAUDET, Alphonse (1840–1897), French writer noted for his stories of his native Provence. He wrote

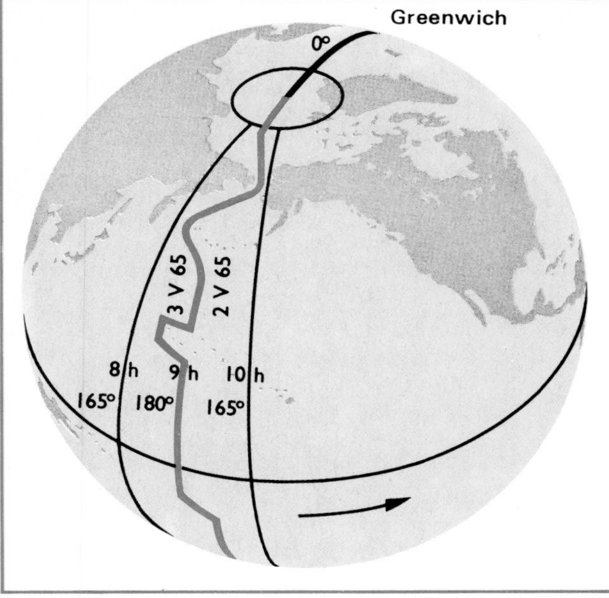

The International Date Line (shown here in red) follows an irregular course approximating to the 180th meridian. This is in order to avoid the confusion it would cause if it crossed land areas. To the west of the line it is one day later than it is to the east.

with humor and compassion about the poor, and is best remembered for *Lettres de Mon Moulin* (1866) and *Tartarin de Tarascon* (1872).

DAUGHERTY, Harry Micajah (1860–1941), US politician, manager of Warren Harding's campaign in 1920 and attorney general 1921–24. Impeachment attempts for his part in the TEAPOT DOME scandal failed. He was tried for conspiracy to defraud the government, but his case was dismissed twice, after juries disagreed.

DAUGHTERS OF THE AMERICAN REVOLUTION (DAR), US conservative women's organization aiming to foster education and patriotism, made up of direct descendants of patriots who "rendered aid" during the Revolutionary War. Founded 1890, its headquarters is in Washington D.C.

DAUMIER, Honoré (1808–1879), French caricaturist, painter and sculptor. In some 4000 lithographs he satirized the bourgeoisie and contemporary politicians. He was one of the first to paint scenes from modern life. In 1832 his cartoon of King Louis-Philippe earned him six months in jail.

Details of the foliage, fruit and flowers of the date palm: the feather-like leaf (a); the fruit, seen here in section (b); the male flower (c); the female flower (d); and a cluster of fruit (e). Each tree has flowers of one sex only. The world's leading producer and exporter of dates is Iraq. Algeria and Tunisia are also major producers.

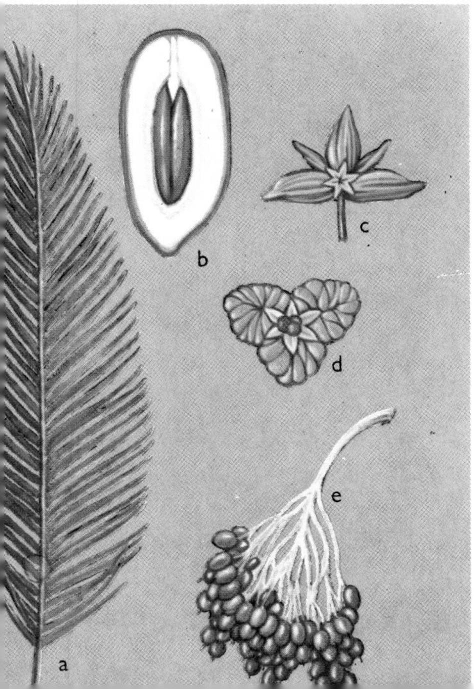

DAUPHIN, title given to the heir to the French throne after Philip VI purchased Dauphiné from the Count of Viennois in 1349. The title was renounced in 1830 following the abdication of Charles X.

DAUPHINÉ, historical region of SE France, now covering the departments of Drôme, Isère and Hautes Alpes. The Rhone valley is the main wine center; Grenoble the capital, manufacturing and cultural center.

DAVAO, largest city on Mindanao Island in the Philippines. Its port is the outlet for the area's coffee, Manila hemp, copra and rubber. Founded 1849. Pop 392473.

DAVENANT, Sir William (1606–1668), English poet, playwright and theater manager, who presented the first English opera, *The Siege of Rhodes*, in 1656. He also introduced painted stage sets and pioneered heroic tragedy.

DAVENPORT, city in E Ia. on the Mississippi R. The largest of four cities comprising an extensive urban area, it processes food products and makes farm equipment. Pop 98467.

DAVENPORT, John (1597–1670), American Puritan minister who was prominent in the theological debates of the day and founded a new colony, New Haven, leading it till it joined Conn.

DAVID, Saint (d. c600), patron saint of Wales, who founded many monasteries of strict rule in the 6th century.

DAVID, (d. c961 BC), King of Israel. A Judaean from Bethlehem, he became arms bearer to King Saul of Israel, and an intimate friend to Saul's son Jonathan. David killed the Philistine giant Goliath, and his subsequent popularity aroused Saul's envy and wrath. After years as an outlaw, he was chosen king of Judah on Saul's death, soon extending his authority over the northern tribes. David then seized Jerusalem, making it the religious and political capital of Israel and of a large empire. His highly prosperous reign lasted forty years. David was the prototype of the MESSIAH through whom God mediated his blessing to Israel, and an ancestor of Jesus Christ. He is the reputed author of many of the psalms.

DAVID, name of two Scottish kings. **David I** (c1084–1153), king from 1124, was the son of Malcolm III and St. Margaret of Scotland. He strengthened the feudal system and reorganized the Church. He invaded England twice. **David II** (1324–1371), king from 1329, was the son of ROBERT THE BRUCE. Supplanted in 1334 by Edward de Balliol and exiled to France, he returned in 1341. After an abortive invasion of England in 1346, he was held captive for 11 years.

DAVID, Gerard (c1460–1523), last great master of the 15th-century Bruges school of painting. He is noted for his emotional power and depth, and accomplished technique, as in the altarpieces, *Rest on Flight into Egypt* and *Madonna with Angels and Saints*.

DAVID, Jacques Louis (1748–1825), French painter and leader of the French neoclassical movement. His style, which combines formal perfection with romantic feeling and didactic purpose, is exemplified in his *Oath of the Horatii* and *Death of Marat*. He appealed to the French Revolutionary spirit and was appointed painter to Napoleon. Exiled by Louis XVIII, he died in Brussels.

DAVID, star of or **Mogen David** (Hebrew: the shield of David), a Jewish symbol of a six-pointed star formed by two crossed triangles. Though without any original religious significance, it has come to symbolize God's protection of Israel.

DAVIDSON, Jo (1883–1952), US sculptor, born N.Y. city, but lived in Paris. Among famous sitters for his portrait busts were Gertrude Stein, Will Rogers, Walt Whitman and Franklin Roosevelt.

DAVIE, William Richardson (1756–1820), American soldier and statesman. Commissary-general in the Revolutionary War. He helped secure N.C.'s cession of Tennessee to the Union in 1789 and was governor of N.C. 1798–99. Concluded treaty with Tuscarsora Indians 1802.

DAVIES, Arthur Bowen (1863–1928), US painter in the romantic-idealist tradition. A leader in the modern movement and a member of the ASHCAN SCHOOL. Chief organizer of the 1913 ARMORY SHOW. Noted for the lyrical and abstract *Unicorns* and *Dreams* (1908).

DAVIES, Sir Louis Henry (1845–1924), Canadian jurist. A member of Parliament in 1882, he was minister of fisheries 1896–1901, a judge of the Supreme Court, and chief justice from 1918.

DAVIES, William Henry (1871–1940), British poet, lyrical author of *The Autobiography of a Super-Tramp* (1908), who wrote about nature and the plight of the poor.

DÁVILA, Pedrarias (c1440–1531), Spanish conquistador, noted for his cruelty. He conquered large areas of Costa Rica and Nicaragua, founded Panama City (1519), and from 1526 ruled despotically in Nicaragua.

DA VINCI, Leonardo. See LEONARDO DA VINCI.

DAVIS, city in central Cal., Yolo Co. Industries include food processing and steel products. The U. of Cal. at Davis is there. Pop 23488.

DAVIS, Alexander Jackson (1803–1892), US architect and exponent of the Gothic Revival style. With his partner, Ithiel Town, he built the New York Customs House, and the capitols of Ill., Ind. and Ohio.

DAVIS, Benjamin Oliver, Jr., (1912–), the first Negro general in the US army (1940). He was appointed brigadier-general and supervised the desegregation of Negro troops.

DAVIS, Bette (1908–), US movie actress. She won Academy awards for *Dangerous* (1935) and *Jezebel* (1938), and in the 1960s won new fame in psychological thrillers. Her other films include *Dark Victory* (1939), *All About Eve* (1950).

DAVIS, David (1815–1886), US politician and Supreme Court justice 1862–77. Born in Cecil Co. Md., he was a circuit court judge in Ill. 1848–62 and managed Lincoln's campaign for the presidential nomination at the 1860 Republican convention.

DAVIS, Dwight Filley (1879–1945), US public official and donor of the Davis Cup for international tennis. He was secretary of war under Coolidge and governor general of the Philippines 1929–32.

DAVIS, Henry Winter (1817–1889), US Congressman and leader of the pre-Civil War Know Nothing party. A staunch Unionist who served in the House of Representatives from 1855–61 and 1863–65, he criticized Lincoln's lenient Reconstruction program for the South. With Benjamin Wade, he succeeded in getting his own Reconstruction bill through Congress, but Lincoln refused to sign it.

DAVIS, Jefferson (1808–1889), president of the Confederate States of America during the Civil War,

The home of Jefferson Davis in Montgomery, Alabama, was known as the White House of the Confederacy when he was president of the South during the Civil War. It is now a museum.

born in Fairview, Ky. He represented Miss. in the US Senate (1847–51 and 1857–61) and was a leading defender of slavery and states' rights. He was a nationalist secretary of war, 1853–57, but when the Southern states began their secession Davis resigned from the Senate in Jan. 1861, withdrawing Miss. from the Union. His peace delegation to Lincoln was rebuffed and he ordered the attack on Fort Sumter, N.C., which opened the war. On Feb. 18, 1861 he became president of the Confederacy for a six-year term. Although his leadership was criticized, he made the best of inferior numbers and poor industrial resources. In 1865 Davis was captured, and after two years in prison was released on bail.

DAVIS, John (d. 1605), English navigator and one of the greatest early Arctic explorers. He discovered the Davis Strait between Greenland and Baffin Island as well as the Falkland Islands. He was also the author of valuable aids to navigation.

DAVIS, John William (1873–1955), US public official and lawyer, unsuccessful Democratic presidential candidate (1924); US solicitor-general 1913–18 and adviser to President Woodrow Wilson. He opposed the New Deal and argued a record number of cases before the US Supreme Court.

DAVIS, Miles Dewey (1926–), US trumpeter and composer, associated with bebop jazz in the 1940s and cool jazz in the 1950s. He pioneered improvisations that were guided by scales rather than chords.

DAVIS, Stuart (1894–1964), US abstract painter, illustrator and lithographer, studied in New York. A forerunner of the pop art movement, his style is characterized by brilliant colors the use of printed words and interlocking shapes.

DAVIS, William Morris (1850–1934), US geographer and leading geomorphologist of the late 19th century. Davis is best remembered for his erosion-cycle concept, characterizing the successive stages in the history of a newly uplifted landmass as its youth, its maturity and its old age (see EROSION).

DAVIS CUP, silver bowl trophy for international tennis given by Dwight Filley Davis who organized the tournament in 1900. Eliminating rounds are played in zones, and the final round is settled in four singles and one doubles match.

DAVISSON, Clinton Joseph (1881–1958), US physicist who shared the 1937 Nobel physics prize with G. P. THOMSON for his demonstration of the DIFFRACTION of ELECTRONS. This confirmed DE BROGLIE's view that matter might act in a wavelike manner in appropriate circumstances.

DAVIS STRAIT, separates Greenland from North America and joins Baffin Bay and the Labrador Sea. It is named for John Davis, who discovered it in 1585.

DAVITT, Michael (1846–1906), Irish nationalist, who in 1879 organized the Irish Land League, which sought to better the lot of the Irish tenant farmers. He was elected to Parliament in 1892 and 1895 but resigned in 1899 over the South African War.

DAVY, Sir Humphry (1778–1829), English chemist who pioneered the study of ELECTROCHEMISTRY. Electrolytic methods yielded him the elements SODIUM, POTASSIUM, MAGNESIUM, CALCIUM, STRONTIUM and BARIUM (1807–08). He also recognized the elemental nature of and named CHLORINE (1810). His early work on nitrous oxide (see NITROGEN) was done at Bristol under T. BEDDOES but most of the rest of his career centered on the ROYAL INSTITUTION where he was assisted by his protégé, M. FARADAY, from 1813. A major practical achievement was the invention of a miner's SAFETY LAMP, known as the **Davy Lamp**, in 1815–16. From his Bristol days, Davy was a friend of S. T. Coleridge.

DAVY JONES, sailors' name for a malevolent sea-demon responsible for the sea's treacherous nature. "Davy Jones' locker" is the ocean floor, the grave of those drowned or buried at sea.

DAVYS, John. See DAVIS, JOHN.

DAWES, Charles Gates (1865–1951), US statesman who shared the 1925 Nobel Peace Prize for his DAWES PLAN. Vice-president under Calvin Coolidge 1925–29, he was ambassador to Great Britain from 1929 until 1932, when he became chairman of the Reconstruction Finance Corporation. He resigned the same year and entered banking.

DAWES, William (1745–1799), American patriot. On the night of April 18, 1775, he rode with Paul REVERE and Samuel Prescott to warn of the British advance at the start of the REVOLUTIONARY WAR.

DAWES ACT, also called the General Allotment Act, passed by the US Congress in Feb. 1887 to encourage American Indians to settle as farmers. It gave 160 acres of land to each head of family in certain tribes. The land had to be cultivated for 25 years before the Indians could own it.

DAWES PLAN, plan developed by Charles Gates DAWES in 1924, to enable Germany to pay off WWI reparations by means of an international loan and mortgages on German industry and railways.

DAWSON, city in W Yukon Territory, Canada. A boom town created by the 1898 gold rush, it has since dwindled to a local supply center. Pop 745.

DAWSON, Sir John William (1820–1899), Canadian geologist and educator who specialized in the geology of Nova Scotia; a determined opponent of Darwinian theory. His son **George Mercer Dawson** (1849–1901), also a geologist, directed the Canadian Geological Survey from 1895.

DAWSON CREEK, city in NE British Columbia, Canada, the starting point of the Alaskan Highway. Pop 11 488.

DAY, term referring either to a full period of 24 hours (the civil day) or to the (usually shorter and varying) period between sunrise and sunset when a given point on the earth's surface is bathed in light rather than darkness (the natural day). Astronomers distinguish the sidereal day from the solar day and the lunar day depending on whether the reference location on the earth's surface is taken to return to the same position relative to the stars, to the sun or to the moon respectively. The civil day is the mean solar day, some 168 seconds longer than the sidereal day. In most modern states the day is deemed to run from midnight to midnight, though in Jewish tradition the day is taken to begin at sunset.

DAY, Clarence (Shepard) (1874–1935), US writer and humorist, best known for *This Simian World* (1920), *Life with Father* (1935) and *Life with Mother* (1936).

DAY (or DAYE), Stephen (c1594–1668), American printer who set up in Cambridge, Mass., the first printing press in the American colonies. Forerunner of Harvard University Press, it printed the *Freeman's Oath* (1639) and the BAY PSALM BOOK (1640).

DAY, William Rufus (1849–1923), US politician and lawyer, a member of the Supreme Court 1903–23. He was briefly secretary of state in 1898, and then headed the commission which made peace with Spain the same year.

DAYAK, or Dyak, the native people of Borneo. They include the N coastal Iban (Sea Dayak) and the Land Dayak of the SW interior. Most live in communal longhouses and eat rice supplemented by fish and game. They were formerly headhunters.

DAYAN, Moshe (1915–), Israeli military leader and politician. Active in Israel's War of

These diagrams show how the length of the natural day varies with latitude at the equinoxes (1) and the solstices (2 and 3).

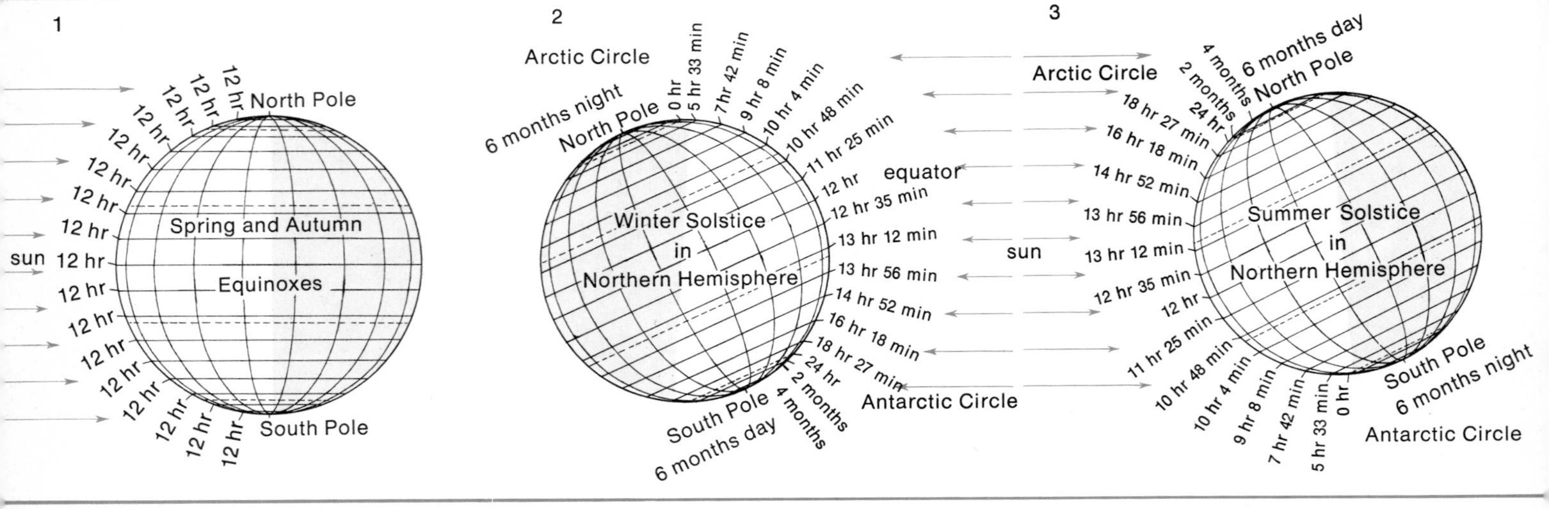

Independence (1948), he commanded the Israeli army in the 1956 Sinai Campaign. He was minister of defense during the Six-Day War of 1967 and from 1969 to 1974, when he resigned over the Yom Kippur War.

DAY LEWIS, C. See LEWIS, CECIL DAY.

DAYLIGHT SAVING TIME, system that adjusts the clock to make maximum use of seasonal daylight; it was first adopted as a WWI fuel conservation measure.

DAYTON, city in SW Ohio, seat of Montgomery Co., on the Miami R. It has over 800 manufacturing plants and is a production center for precision products such as refrigerators, calculating machines and cash registers; the electric self-starter was invented there. The Wright brothers started their bicycle business in the city. Pop 243 601.

DAYTON, Jonathan (1760–1824), US politician, who at 26 became the youngest signatory of the US Constitution. He was a member of the House of Representatives 1791–99, and a senator from N.J. 1799–1805. Dayton, Ohio, is named for him.

DAYTONA BEACH, resort city in NE Fla., with a 23mi hard beach used for speed trials since 1903. Bethune–Cookman College, a famous Negro college, is located here. Pop 45 327.

D-DAY, in WWII, June 6, 1944, the day fixed for the Allied landing in Normandy beginning the invasion of Europe, under the command of General EISENHOWER. Over 5 000 ships were used, from which 90 000 British, American and Canadian troops landed; around 20 000 more were delivered by parachute and glider. After some initial difficulties, the forces had linked up in a solid front by June 11. The invasion, code-named *Overlord*, was one of the most complex feats of organization and supply in history.

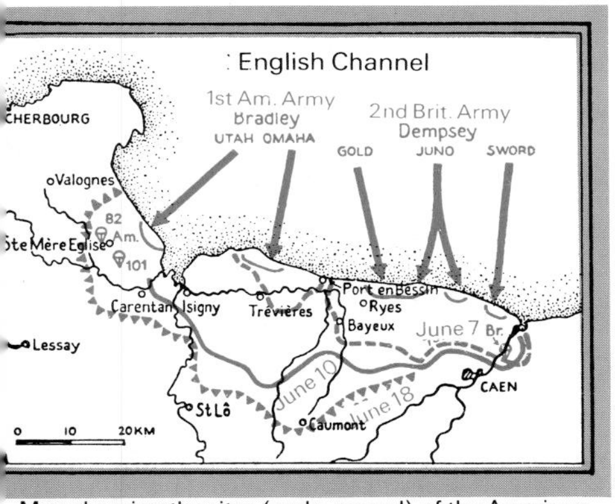

Map showing the sites (code-named) of the American, British and Canadian landings on D Day, on the Normandy coast. With surprise on their side, the allies swiftly formed an unbroken front against the Germans, isolated the Cotentin peninsula with Cherbourg at its head, and moved on into the heart of France.

DDT, dichlorodiphenyltrichloroethane, a synthetic contact INSECTICIDE which kills a wide variety of insects, including mosquitoes, lice and flies, by interfering with their nervous systems. Its use, in quantities as great as 100 000 tonnes yearly, has almost eliminated many insect-borne diseases, including MALARIA, TYPHUS, YELLOW FEVER and PLAGUE. Being chemically stable and physically inert, it persists in the environment for many years. Its concentration in the course of natural food chains (see ECOLOGY) has led to the buildup of dangerous accumulations in some fish and birds. This prompted the US to restrict the use of DDT in 1972. In any case the development of insect strains resistant to DDT was already reducing its effectiveness as an insecticide. Although DDT was first made in 1874, its insecticidal properties were only discovered in 1939 (by P. H. MÜLLER).

DEACON, lowest rank in the threefold MINISTRY in episcopally-organized Christian churches, an elected lay official in some Protestant churches. Traditionally deacons have administered alms. Since the Second Vatican Council, a permanent office of deacon in the Roman Catholic Church has become open both to celibate and married men, where formerly it was a transitional rank as a step towards priesthood. In some Lutheran churches an assistant minister is called a deacon although fully ordained.

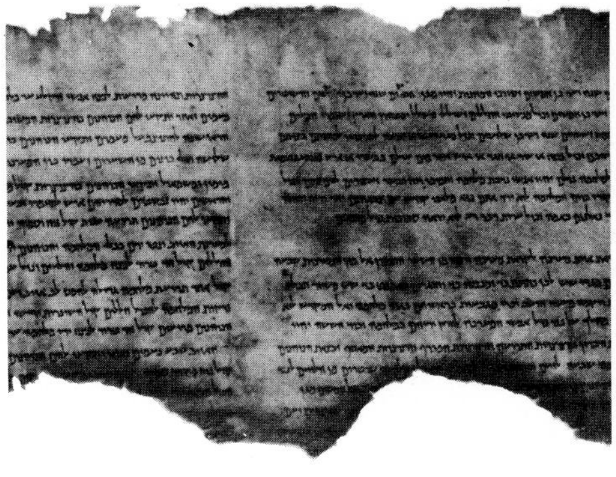

The ultra-modern interior (*above*) of the Hechal Hasefer museum in Jerusalem specially built to house the Dead Sea Scrolls. The scrolls (*right*), discovered in 1947, include two copies of the Old Testament Book of Isaiah, and are nearly 1 000 years older than previously discovered biblical texts.

DEAD, Book of the. See BOOK OF THE DEAD.

DEADLY NIGHTSHADE. See BELLADONNA.

DEAD SEA, salt lake on the Israeli–Jordan border. It extends around 50mi S from the mouth of the Jordan R (its main affluent) and is up to 11mi wide. Much of it is more than 1000ft deep, and with a surface 1 302ft below sea level it is the lowest point on earth. Its biblical name of Salt Sea derives from its extremely high salt content (over 20%), resulting from the rapid evaporation in the area's hot climate. Some minerals are extracted from it commercially.

DEAD SEA SCROLLS, manuscripts on papyrus and leather (and even one on copper) discovered in five sites in what is now Israel and Israeli-occupied territory. The first discovery was made by shepherds at Khirbat Qumran on the NW shore of the Dead Sea. These scrolls were possibly part of the library of a Jewish sect, the Essenes, that flourished from c200 BC to 68 AD. The area's 11 caves contained hundreds of manuscripts, including large portions of the Hebrew Old Testament. This has proved that the modern Hebrew Bible has hardly changed in 2 000 years. Another site at Wadi al-Murabba'ah, a few miles away, contained both religious and secular documents dating from the anti-Roman rebellion led by Bar Cochba in 132–135 AD. They were probably left by fugitives from his army, as were those at a third site near Ein Gedi.

A cave near Jericho and an excavation at Masada produced further documents that, together with the other finds, clarify much of the complex history of the area and throw new light on the beginnings of Christianity. The manuscripts are not well preserved, and their transcription and interpretation is made more difficult by the necessity of carefully unrolling the ancient scrolls, and of salvaging and putting together pieces often smaller than postage stamps.

DEADWOOD, mining city and tourist center in S.D., seat of Lawrence Co. Originally a frontier boom town, it was the home of many legendary Western characters. Pop 2 409.

DEADWOOD DICK, "pulp" fiction hero of the 1880s. He was created by the popular novelist E. L. Wheeler, probably based on Dick Clark, an adventurer from Deadwood, S.D.

DEAF MUTE. See DUMBNESS.

DEAFNESS, or failure of hearing, may have many causes. Conductive deafness is due to disease of outer or middle EAR, while perceptive deafness is due to disease of inner ear or nerves of hearing. Common physical causes of **conductive deafness** are obstruction with wax or foreign bodies and injury to the tympanic membrane. Middle ear disease is an important cause: in *acute otitis*, common in children, the ears are painful, with deafness, FEVER and discharge; in *secretory otitis* or glue ear, also in children, deafness and discomfort result from poor Eustachian tube drainage; *chronic otitis*, in any age group, leads to a deaf discharging ear, with drum perforation. ANTIBIOTICS in adequate courses are crucial in acute otitis, while glue ear is relieved by tubes or "grommets" passed through the drum to drain the middle ear. In both, the ADENOIDS may need removal to relieve Eustachian obstruction. In chronic otitis, keeping the ears clean and dry is important and antibiotics are used for secondary infection, while SURGERY, including reconstitution of the drum, may be needed to restore hearing. *Otosclerosis* is a common familial disease of middle age in which fusion or ANKYLOSIS of the small bones of the ear cause deafness. Early operation can prevent irreversible changes and improve hearing. **Perceptive deafness** may follow infections in PREGNANCY (e.g., GERMAN MEASLES) or be hereditary. Acute VIRUS infection and trauma to the inner ear (e.g., blast injuries or chronic occupational noise exposure) are important causes. Damage to the ear blood supply or the auditory nerves by drugs,

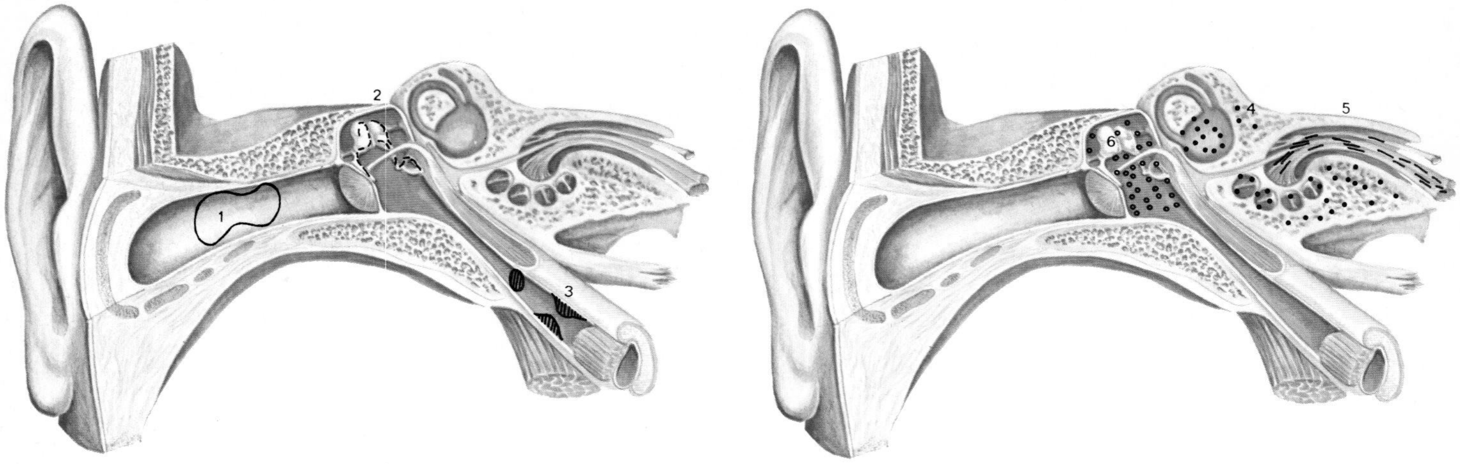

Locations of some potential causes of deafness: (1) obstruction in the external auditory canal; (2) degeneration of the auditory ossicles; (3) plugging of the eustachian tube; (4) inflammation of the inner ear extending to the petrous bone; (5) infection of the auditory nerve; (6) middle-ear inflammation. External ear (blue); middle ear (red); inner ear (green).

TUMORS or MULTIPLE SCLEROSIS may lead to perceptive deafness, as may the later stages of MÉNIÈRE'S DISEASE. Deafness of old age, or *presbycusis*, is of gradual onset, mainly due to loss of nerve cells. Early recognition of deafness in children is particularly important as it may otherwise impair learning and speech development. HEARING AIDS are valuable in most cases of conductive and some of perceptive deafness. Lip-reading, in which the deaf person understands speech by the interpretation of lip movements, and sign language are useful in severe cases.

DEÁK, Ferenc (1803–1876), Hungarian statesman who negotiated the 1867 Compromise with the Austrian emperor, giving Hungary internal autonomy within the dual monarchy of AUSTRIA–HUNGARY. A lawyer, he entered the Diet in 1833. In the 1848 revolution he became minister of justice, but resigned in disagreement with the revolutionary KOSSUTH the same year. He returned to the Diet in 1861, becoming the country's acknowledged leader.

DEAKIN, Alfred (1856–1919), Australian statesman. He was a teacher, lawyer and journalist before he entered the Victoria legislature in 1880; he was prime minister 1903–04, 1905–08 and 1909–10.

DEAN, Dizzy (Jay Hanna Dean; 1911–), American baseball pitcher who played for the St. Louis Cardinals and Chicago Cubs 1932–41, winning 30 games in 1934, when the Cardinals won the World Series. He retired in 1941, and became a popular sports commentator.

Monument commemorating Fort Dearborn, on the Chicago River bridge adjacent to the original site of the fort. During the Indian raid in 1812, when the fort was destroyed, all but one of its defenders lost their lives.

DEAN, James (1931–1955), American actor, who became a cult hero after his death in a car crash. The films *East of Eden* (1955), *Rebel Without a Cause* (1955) and *Giant* (1956), characterized him as the symbol of rebellious youth.

DEAN, William Frische (1899–), US major-general who was captured while fighting a vital delaying action during the Korean War in July 1950. Imprisoned in North Korea for three years, he resisted privation and torture.

DEANE, Silas (1737–1789), American diplomat, first envoy to Europe. He was sent to France in 1776 to recruit officers and obtain arms. He was recalled on profiteering charges; these were never proved, but he went into exile in England.

DEARBORN, industrial city in Mich. on the Rouge R near SW Detroit. Birthplace of Henry Ford, it began a rapid expansion with the establishment of the Ford Motor Company there in 1917; it now has many other manufacturing industries. Pop 104 199.

DEARBORN, Fort, military post built on the future site of Chicago in 1803, named for Secretary of War Dearborn, who ordered its construction. In 1812 it was destroyed in an Indian raid, but was rebuilt 1816–17.

DEARBORN, Henry (1751–1829), American politician and army officer. Secretary of war 1801–09, he was appointed senior major general commanding the NE front (1812), but was recalled for incompetence in 1813, and in 1815 resigned his commission. He was minister to Portugal 1822–24.

DEARBORN HEIGHTS, city in Mich., 8mi SE of Detroit. Pop 80 069.

DEATH, the complete and irreversible cessation of LIFE in an organism or part of an organism. Death is conventionally accepted as the time when the HEART ceases to beat, there is no breathing and when the BRAIN shows no evidence of function. Ophthalmoscopic examination of the EYE shows that columns of BLOOD in small vessels are interrupted and static. Since it is now possible to resuscitate and maintain heart function and to take over breathing mechanically, it is not uncommon for the brain to have suffered irreversible death but for "life" to be maintained artificially. The concept of "brain death" has been introduced, in which reversible causes have been eliminated, when no spontaneous breathing, no movement and no specific REFLEXES are seen on two occasions. When this state is reached, artificial life support systems can be reasonably discontinued as brain death has already occurred. The ELECTROENCEPHALOGRAPH has been used to diagnose brain death but is now considered unreliable.

After death, ENZYMES are released which begin the process of autolysis or decomposition, which later involves BACTERIA. In the hours following death, changes occur in muscle which cause rigidity or RIGOR MORTIS. Following death, anatomical examination of the body (AUTOPSY) may be performed. Burial, embalming or cremation are usual practices for disposal of the body in Western society.

Death of part of an organism, or necrosis, such as occurs following loss of blood supply, consists of loss of cell organization, autolysis and GANGRENE. The part may separate or be absorbed but if it becomes infected, this is liable to spread to living tissue. Cells may also die as part of the normal turnover of a structure (e.g., SKIN or blood cells), after POISONING or infection (e.g., in the LIVER), from compression (e.g., by TUMOR), or as part of a degenerative disease. They then undergo characteristic involutionary changes.

DEATH PENALTY. See CAPITAL PUNISHMENT.

DEATH'S HEAD MOTH, *Acherontia atropos*, a large moth native to Europe. the markings on the thorax of which resemble a skull. It is also one of the only moths to produce sound, a squeaking call, which has added to its reputation as being an evil omen.

DEATH VALLEY, arid valley in Inyo Co., Cal. The highest recorded US temperature—134°F—was recorded here in 1913. Located near the Nevada border, it is 140mi long, and up to 15mi wide. The lowest point in the W Hemisphere, Badwater (282ft below sea level) is at the heart of the valley. Since rainfall is only 2in per year, it supports little vegetation. Large deposits of borax were discovered there in the late 19th century. In 1933 it was made part of the Death Valley National Monument.

The arid landscape of Death Valley, the lowest, hottest and driest place in North America. It was given its name by a group of emigrants who tried to cross it in 1849 and nearly died in the attempt.

DEATHWATCH BEETLES, a family of BEETLES that bore into wood, especially that of old buildings and furniture.

DEBENTURE, in US finance, a bond issued for an unsecured loan; this is issued by the borrower and depends upon his credit for its worth. Most government bonds, not being secured by public property, are of this type, although not usually referred to as such. In Britain a debenture is a secured bond, and in international trade a duty refund on reimported goods.

DEBORAH, Old Testament prophetess who inspired the Israelites to victory over the Canaanites at the battle of Mount Tabor (Judges 4 and 5). The *Song of Deborah* (Judges 5) may not have been composed by her but is a great poem of its time.

DE BOW, James Dunwoody Brownson (1820–1867), US publisher and pioneering statistician, who founded the *Commercial Review of the South and Southwest* (also known as *De Bow's Review*) in New Orleans in 1846. He prepared the *Statistical View of the United States* (1854).

DEBRAY, Régis (1941–), French Marxist journalist jailed in Bolivia in 1967 for spying, but released in 1970. After a stay in Chile he returned to Paris in 1973 to pursue nonviolent revolutionary politics.

DEBRÉ, Michel Jean Pierre (1912–), French statesman and political writer. Active in the Resistance in WWII he became an unswerving Gaullist and was De Gaulle's minister of justice in 1958. Principal author of the constitution of the 5th Republic, he became its first prime minister 1959–62, and later minister of economics and finance 1966–68, foreign minister May 1968 and defense minister 1969–73.

DEBRECEN, city in E Hungary, 140mi E of Budapest. Here in 1849 KOSSUTH declared Hungary's shortlived independence from the Hapsburgs. Originally an important market center, its economy is now based on manufacturing and crafts. Pop 170 000.

DE BROGLIE, Louis Victor Pierre Raymond, Prince (1892–), French physicist who was awarded the 1929 Nobel Prize in Physics for his suggestion that acknowledged particles should display wave properties under appropriate conditions in the same way that ELECTROMAGNETIC RADIATION sometimes behaved as if composed of particles.

DEBS, Eugene Victor (1855–1926), American labor organizer and socialist political leader. He was a national leader of the Brotherhood of Locomotive Firemen and in 1893 founded the American Railway Union. Debs was jailed in 1895 for defying a federal court injunction against strike action which interfered with the mails. Five times a socialist candidate for the presidency, he fought his last and most successful campaign in 1920 while still imprisoned under the WWI Espionage Act (1917) for his opposition to the war.

DEBUSSY, Claude (1862–1918), born Achille-Claude. French composer whose impact on the history of music was revolutionary. He involved music in the Impressionist movement (see IMPRESSIONISM) which was affecting painting and poetry at this time. His ideas on harmony and his innovations in orchestration and the use of the piano were highly influential in the development of 20th-century music. His works include songs, some outstanding piano music, an opera, *Pelléas et Mélisande* (1902), and the orchestral pieces *Prélude a l'après-midi d'un faune* (1892–94) and *La Mer* (1905).

DEBYE, Peter Joseph Wilhelm (1884–1966), Dutch-born German–US physical chemist chiefly remembered for the Debye-Hückel theory of ionic solutions (1923). He was awarded the 1936 Nobel Prize for Chemistry.

DECALOGUE. See TEN COMMANDMENTS.

DECAMERON, The, collection of 100 stories by the 14th-century Italian writer, Giovanni BOCCACCIO, one of the outstanding works in Italian literature. Amusing and often bawdy, the tales provide a shrewd commentary on 14th-century Italian life.

DECATHLON, ten-event contest in modern Olympic games. It consists of the 100-metre dash; the 400-metre and 1 500-metre flat races; the 110-metre hurdle race; pole vaulting; discus throwing; shot putting; javelin throwing; and the long and high jumps.

DECATUR, city in N Ala., seat of Morgan Co. It lies on the Tennessee R, 75mi N of Birmingham, and is a transportation and trading center. Pop 38 044.

DECATUR, city in NW Ga., seat of De Kalb Co. It is a residential suburb 5mi E of Atlanta. Pop 21 943.

DECATUR, city in central Ill., seat of Macon Co. It lies on the Sangamon R, 35mi E of Springfield. THE GRAND ARMY OF THE REPUBLIC was organized here in 1866. It is a major communication center relying on industrial and agricultural trading. Pop 90 397.

DECATUR, Stephen (1779–1820), American naval hero. He was responsible for many victories in the BARBARY WARS, and later in the WAR OF 1812 until forced to surrender to the British in 1815. After the war he was sent to subdue Algiers, and then served as a US navy commissioner until his death in a duel. He is famous for his reply to a toast: "Our country, right or wrong."

DECAY, Radioactive. See RADIOACTIVITY.

DECCAN, peninsula of India, strictly the plateau between the Narmada and Krishna rivers. Crops include cotton in the north and tea and coffee in the south.

DECEMBER, 12th month of the year in the Gregorian calendar, taking its name from the 10th month in the Roman calendar. The winter solstice occurs about Dec. 21, and traditionally it is the month for celebrations, including CHRISTMAS.

DECEMBRIST REVOLT, unsuccessful uprising against the tsar of Russia (Dec. 1825). In the unrest following the French Revolution and the Napoleonic Wars, groups of officers and aristocrats formed secret revolutionary societies. On this occasion they attempted to take advantage of the confusion accompanying the accession of Nicholas I. They lacked effective organization and were quickly suppressed, but the uprising served as an inspiration to later Russian revolutionaries.

DECEMVIRS, in ancient Rome, a body of 10 men acting as an official commission on political, judicial or religious matters. Especially well-known are the decemvirs of 451–449 BC who drew up the Laws of the Twelve Tables, Rome's first written law code.

DECIBEL (dB), a unit used to express power ratio, equal to one-tenth of a BEL, widely used by acoustics and telecommunications engineers. It is commonly employed in describing NOISE levels relative to the threshold of hearing. Doubling the noise level adds 3 to the decibel rating.

DECIDUOUS TREES, shrubs and trees that shed their leaves at a certain season, generally in the autumn when the environmental conditions are becoming unsuitable to active growth and just before the tree enters a period of dormancy. (See also EVERGREENS.)

DECIMAL SYSTEM, a number system using the POWERS of ten; our everyday system of numeration. The digits used are 0, 1, 2, 3, 4, 5, 6, 7, 8, 9; the powers of 10 being written $10^0=1$, $10^1=10$, $10^2=100$, $10^3=1000$, etc. To each of these powers is assigned a place value in a particular number; thus $(4\times10^3)+(0\times10^2)+(9\times10^1)+(2\times10^0)$ is written 4092. Similarly, FRACTIONS may be expressed by setting their DENOMINATORS equal to powers of 10—

$$\frac{3}{4}=\frac{75}{100}=\frac{7}{10}+\frac{5}{100}=(7\times10^{-1})+(5\times10^{-2}),$$

which is written as 0.75. Not all numbers can be expressed in terms of the decimal system: one example is the fraction $\frac{1}{3}$ which is written 0.333 3 . . . , the row of dots indicating that the 3 is to be repeated an infinite number of times. Fractions like 0.333 3 . . . are termed **repeating decimals**. APPROXIMATION is often useful when dealing with decimal fractions.

The decimal system probably came about through the number of digits on a pair of hands. In recent years it has been suggested that a more efficient number system would be one using the powers of twelve (see DUODECIMAL SYSTEM).

DECIUS, Gaius Messius Quintus Trajanus (c201–251 AD), Roman emperor 249–251. Proclaimed emperor by his troops, apparently against his will, he killed the reigning Emperor Philip in battle. He was the first Roman emperor to organize persecutions of Christians throughout the empire, which however only strengthened the movement. He died in battle against the Goths.

DECKER, Thomas. See DEKKER, THOMAS.

DECLARATION OF HUMAN RIGHTS, Universal, adopted by the UN General Assembly on Dec. 10, 1948. UN members pledged to guarantee not only civil rights such as life, liberty and freedom from arbitrary arrest, but also so-called social rights such as the rights to work and to education, on the principle that "all human beings are born free and equal in dignity and rights."

DECLARATION OF INDEPENDENCE, manifesto in which the representatives of the 13 American colonies asserted their independence and explained the reasons for their break with Britain. It was adopted on July 4, 1776. The date has since been celebrated annually as Independence Day.

American discontent with British attempts at taxation began in the 1760s, but in these disputes colonists demanded only their "rights" as Englishmen. Even after the military confrontations at Lexington and Concord (1775), the Second Continental Congress convened at Philadelphia in May disavowed any desire for independence. However, after continued British provocations in 1775, opinion began to shift. Thomas Paine's pamphlet *Common Sense* (1776), which attacked the monarchy and called for independence, was extremely influential. During 1776 definite moves towards independence were taken.

On June 7 Richard Henry Lee of Virginia resolved before the Congress that "These United Colonies are, and of right ought to be, free and independent States." A committee consisting of Thomas Jefferson, Benjamin Franklin, John Adams, Robert Livingston and Roger Sherman was selected to draft a formal declaration of independence. The draft, almost wholly Jefferson's work, passed on July 2, with 12 colonies voting in favor and New York temporarily abstaining. The ensuing debate made the most significant changes in omitting the clauses condemning the British people as well as their government, and, in deference to the Southern delegates, an article denouncing the slave trade.

In Europe, including Britain, the Declaration was greeted as inaugurating a new age of freedom and self-government. As a manifesto for revolution it gave place to the French DECLARATION OF THE RIGHTS OF MAN AND THE CITIZEN, although its importance increased in the US. After the federal union was organized in 1789 it came to be considered as a statement of basic political principles, not just of independence.

DECLARATION OF THE RIGHTS OF MAN AND THE CITIZEN, key philosophical document of the French Revolution, adopted by the National Assembly on Aug. 26, 1789. It reflects the French Enlightenment's rejection of the rule of absolute monarchy in favor of natural rights. These included fair taxation, self-determination in government and personal liberty under the rule of law. It was made the preamble to the 1791 Constitution.

DECLARATORY ACT, assertion by the British parliament (1766) of its authority to make laws binding on the American colonies. It was passed by the Marquess of Rockingham's government simultaneously with repeal of the Stamp Act to satisfy sections of British opinion which favored taxing the colonies.

DECLINATION, the angular distance of a celestial

The Assembly Room of Independence Hall in Philadelphia where the Declaration of Independence was signed in 1776.

Declaration of Independence

Thomas Jefferson and the Appeal to Reason

These few and simple words were inscribed, at his own request, on the tombstone of Thomas Jefferson, third president of the United States: *"Here was buried Thomas Jefferson, Author of the Declaration of American Independence, of the Statute of Virginia for Religious Freedom, and Father of the University of Virginia."* Jefferson's choice of these few examples from his many accomplishments was most fitting, for all three reflected his lifelong philosophy, the philosophy of the European Enlightenment which he, more than any other of the Founding Fathers, brought to practical fruition in America. It was a philosophy of human equality, of confidence in the good sense of man, of freedom and progress, and it was nowhere more elegantly and succinctly expressed than in the Preamble to the Declaration of Independence:

"We hold these truths to be self-evident, that all men are created equal, that they are endowed by their Creator with certain unalienable Rights, that among these are Life, Liberty and the pursuit of Happiness.—That to secure these rights, Governments are instituted among Men, deriving their just powers from the consent of the governed.—That whenever any Form of Government becomes destructive of these ends, it is the Right of the People to alter or to abolish it, and to institute new Government, laying its foundation on such principles and organizing its powers in such form, as to them shall seem most likely to effect their Safety and Happiness."

In Jefferson's day the heart of the Declaration was the long, tedious catalogue of the crimes of George III, a prince who was intent upon establishing "an absolute Tyranny over these States." This was considered its most important part, for it provided the immediate justification for the break with Britain. But it has long since been forgotten, whereas the brief Preamble has not, and some 200 years later still wields influence as an ideal, albeit rather attenuated, over these overgrown and rather different states. For the voice of the Preamble, in its confident, ringing statement of democratic principles was the voice of young America, an America growing by leaps and bounds—rapidly increasing in wealth and sophistication, its population doubling every 20 or 25 years, with territory enough for everybody and plenty to spare, no real poverty, no crowded, festering cities (though Philadelphia had already become the second city in size to London in the British Empire), no manufactures to speak of, no kings or princes, courts and palaces, and every man his own master (except the Negro slaves). Immigration was only part of the reason for this burgeoning population and wealth. In the words of Dr. Franklin it was rather "the salubrity of the air, the healthiness of the Climate, the Plenty of good provisions, the Encouragement of early Marriages by the certainty of Subsistence in cultivating the Earth."

Indeed this is what the War of Independence, just getting under way, was really all about. The American colonies were becoming too big, too rich, too independent to submit to direct rule by the Mother Country except on the basis of a large measure of autonomy—and this the British would not grant. The "Colonies" were on the way to becoming a new country, newly styled the United States of America, and in the eyes of Jefferson and his friends this new country was a testing ground for the future where men at last could put into actual practice the rational principles that the enlightened minds of the Old World had been preaching but could not carry out. The Old World, they thought, was the prisoner of history, but in the New World man was making his own history. "We can no longer say there is nothing new under the sun," Jefferson wrote. "This whole chapter in the history of man is new. The great extent of our Republic is new. Its sparse habitation is new." Here the good life might at last be achieved. Here men were to be treated as equals, with certain unalienable rights. Here, to secure these rights—among them life, liberty and the pursuit of happiness—a new government had been deliberately constituted, and with the consent of the governed.

Independence Hall, Philadelphia, Pa. The provincial state house where the Second Continental Congress declared the colonies independent.

In the Declaration Jefferson had elevated the rather minor quarrel with Britain into a movement dedicated to a new day for mankind; no wonder he invoked not only "the opinion of mankind" but "the powers of the earth" and "the Laws of Nature and of Nature's God," and grandly places his little revolution "in the Course of human events."

Of course Jefferson was also a practical politician, and he appreciated, as did the other members of the committee, that the high tone he had taken in the Declaration was just what was needed to explain and justify the rather risky break with Britain—not only to the British and to the world at large, particularly to possible future allies like the French—but also to the American public; for there were still many waverers who continued to treasure the British bond. How better to bring them around than to preach a vision of a new world which could only be obtained through independence? But then all great manifestos operate on a number of different levels, and the Declaration is no exception. If the idealistic philosophy of the Enlightenment was precisely what was needed to ennoble the sordid fact of rebellion and to sell it in the right quarters, it is also true that Jefferson and his colleagues believed profoundly in just this philosophy—and no one more so than Jefferson himself.

It is fashionable these days to dismiss the *philosophes* of the Enlightenment—d'Alembert, Diderot, even Voltaire and Locke—for their rather simple-minded and over-optimistic view of man and society. Yet some of the basic ideas of their philosophy are still working strongly today in the West, and in the American consciousness in particular: the essential equality of all men (at birth at least); the basic common sense of the people taken as a whole, whose will must be allowed to prevail over that of minorities if the body politic is to remain healthy; the superiority of a form of government elected by and responsive to the governed; the concept of progress, of progressive improvement as an ideal in every area (still strong, though under attack today); above all the danger of tyrannies of any kind, tyranny of the state, of religion, of class, or tyranny of any kind over the mind of man.

Jefferson himself devoted a lifetime to the abolition of tyranny in one form or another, and it was for this reason that he listed on his tombstone the three accomplishments in which he took the greatest pride. First came the Declaration of Independence, which as a whole denounced in effect the attempted tyranny of the Old World over the New. Speaking for the colonies, he wrote: "But when a long train of abuses and usurpations, pursuing invariably the same Object evinces a design to reduce them under absolute Despotism, it is their right, it is their duty, to throw off such Government, and to provide new Guards for their future security." These "new Guards" included, as we have seen, the idea of human equality and the sovereignty of the people, the natural rights of man and the right of revolution. These were the fundamental ideas upon which the new nation was built, and 200 years later they have not yet lost their force.

Next on his list came the Statute of Virginia for Religious Freedom, which was enacted into law in his home state of Virginia in 1786 after he had battled for ten years to get it passed. The Declaration was a great public document, but on a personal basis nothing gave Jefferson more satisfaction than the enacting of this Statute, which was directed not so much against religion per se as against the pernicious idea that "the operations of the mind as well as the acts of the body, are subject to the coercion of the laws." He was against any form of tyranny over the human mind. "Reason and free inquiry are the only effectual agents against error." True, the immediate objective of the Statute was to disestablish the Anglican church in Virginia; but compared with the established churches of Europe, the Anglican state church in Virginia had been but a weak thing. None of the established churches in the colonies exercised much actual power. But Jefferson, far ahead of his time, was after bigger game, to build "a wall of separation between Church and State." To Jefferson religion was a private matter, and coercion could have no part in it.

Americans today, who take the principle of the separation of church and state for granted, probably do not realize how radical a proposal this was in Jefferson's day. Even the enlightened *philosophes* of Europe—Rousseau for instance—believed in the need for a powerful state church; their only quarrel was with the *abuse* of power by any church. Yet Jefferson's lead, to his satisfaction, was well-received among the liberals of Europe. "It is comfortable" he wrote, "to see the standard of Reason at length erected, after so many ages, during which the human mind has been held in vassalage by kings, priests and nobles, and it is honorable for

IN CONGRESS, JULY 4, 1776. 5

The unanimous Declaration of the thirteen united States of America,

When in the Course of human events, it becomes necessary for one people to dissolve the political bands which have connected them with another, and to assume among the powers of the earth, the separate and equal station to which the Laws of Nature and of Nature's God entitle them, a decent respect to the opinions of mankind requires that they should declare the causes which impel them to the separation. —— We hold these truths to be self-evident, that all men are created equal, that they are endowed by their Creator with certain unalienable Rights, that among these are Life, Liberty and the pursuit of Happiness. — That to secure these rights, Governments are instituted among Men, deriving their just powers from the consent of the governed, — That whenever any Form of Government becomes destructive of these ends, it is the Right of the People to alter or to abolish it, and to institute new Government, laying its foundation on such principles and organizing its powers in such form, as to them shall seem most likely to effect their Safety and Happiness. Prudence, indeed, will dictate that Governments long established should not be changed for light and transient causes; and accordingly all experience hath shewn, that mankind are more disposed to suffer, while evils are sufferable, than to right themselves by abolishing the forms to which they are accustomed. But when a long train of abuses and usurpations, pursuing invariably the same Object evinces a design to reduce them under absolute Despotism, it is their right, it is their duty, to throw off such Government, and to provide new Guards for their future security. — Such has

Top: detail of the American artist John Trumbull's painting *Declaration of Independence*, completed in 1794. The five standing figures grouped together formed the committee appointed by the Second Continental Congress on June 11, 1776, to draw up a formal Declaration of Independence. They are, from left to right: John Adams of Massachusetts (US President 1797–1801); Roger Sherman of Connecticut; Robert R. Livingston of New York; Thomas Jefferson of Virginia (US President 1801–1809); and Benjamin Franklin of Pennsylvania, the colonies' most widely renowned citizen. It was Adams who insisted that Jefferson, a noted literary stylist, should draft the Declaration. *Bottom:* the opening lines of the Declaration document.

us to have produced the first legislature who had the courage to declare that the Reason of man may be trusted with the formation of its own opinions."

But if man is to exercise his reason in a free society, he must be educated. Again in contrast to the European Enlightenment, popular education took a prominent position in the philosophy of American leaders like Jefferson, because it was essential for the success of popular government in the United States that the tyranny of ignorance be fought on every level. "Enlighten the people generally, and tyranny and oppression of body and mind will vanish like spirits at the dawn of day" he wrote when he was old. He had tried, and failed, to put through a comprehensive system of public education in Virginia in the 1780s, but in his old age he did succeed in establishing the University of Virginia at Charlottesville, organized on quite an original plan. It opened in 1825, and he was not only its founder and responsible for its plan, but also its architect and first Rector. No wonder he placed this achievement third on his tombstone, and with justifiable pride. He had done what he could to combat the tyranny of ignorance.

In fact all three accomplishments he listed were *practical* acts. Jefferson and the other Founding Fathers were exceptionally learned men; they all possessed large and well-chosen libraries, and from their extensive reading they had absorbed the basic tenets of the Enlightenment as set forth in the classic writings of Europe—Locke, Sidney, Milton, Montesquieu, Voltaire and many others. But they were also at the center of power in America and had the great advantage of being able to put these tenets into practice in the laboratory of the new United States. As John Adams wrote, "they *realized* the theories of the wisest writers."

Some of these theories, however, fell by the wayside or proved to be impractical. Jefferson above all was a firm believer in the common myth that true civic virtue was to be found only in agrarian societies: "Those who labor in the earth are the chosen people of God . . ." he wrote. Evil lay in industry, commerce and the swarming cities of the Old World. "Generally speaking, the proportion which the aggregate of the other classes of citizens bears in any state to that of its husbandmen, is the proportion of its unsound to its healthy parts." In the United States, then predominantly agrarian, he foresaw the ideal agrarian state of the future. But he was wrong. In this respect Hamilton, not Jefferson, was the prophet of the American future, because he believed in the kind of social structure which has actually evolved in America. Similarly, the current preoccupation with the unalienable right of "happiness," which was closely related to the idea of progress based upon material abundance, seems to us in hindsight naive. Happiness to Jefferson seems to have been the end-product of all the virtues proclaimed by the Enlightenment.

Yet the young Jefferson (he was only 33), who stood at a portable desk in his rented rooms in Philadelphia and produced the Declaration of Independence in only two weeks, turning "neither to book nor pamphlet" as he said later, did manage to capture in words some profound realities. It did not matter that the ideas came from others. The important thing is that they had never been better expressed.

body from the celestial equator (see CELESTIAL SPHERE) along the MERIDIAN through the body. Bodies north of the equator have positive declinations, those south, negative. Together with right ascension, declination defines the position of a body in the sky.

DECLINATION, Magnetic. See EARTH.

DECOMPOSITION, Biological. See PUTREFACTION.

DECOMPOSITION, Chemical, a reaction in which a chemical compound is split up into its elements or simpler compounds. Heat, or light of a suitable wavelength, will decompose many compounds, and some decompose spontaneously. Ionic compounds may be decomposed by ELECTROLYSIS. **Double decomposition** is a reaction of the type

$$AC + BD \rightarrow AD + BC$$

in which radicals are exchanged.

DECOMPRESSION SICKNESS, or **Bends.** See AEROEMBOLISM.

DECONGESTANT DRUGS are used to relieve the stuffy nose and RHINITIS of the COMMON COLD or HAY FEVER. They reduce swelling and secretion of affected mucous membrane and lessen symptoms, but prolonged use leads to chronic changes in mucous membranes.

DECORATED STYLE, in English medieval Gothic architecture, the second, more ornamental style (c1250–1375) of the three main periods. The previous problems of vaulting were solved by increased use of ribs and buttresses, making possible lighter walls pierced by larger windows. One of the distinctive features was the window tracery, at first geometric but later more curving and flamboyant.

Windows illustrating the two main phases in the development of the Decorated Style: the Geometric and the Curvilinear.

DECORATION DAY. See MEMORIAL DAY.

DECORATIONS AND MEDALS, awards for exceptional bravery in civil or military service. The highest US civil decoration is the Presidential Medal of Freedom; the Medal for Merit is also for outstanding services. The highest US military award, "for conspicuous gallantry at the risk of life" is the Congressional Medal of Honor. Soldiers wounded in action receive the Purple Heart. Important foreign decorations include the Victoria Cross and the George Cross (Britain and the Commonwealth), the Croix de Guerre and Legion of Honor (France), the Order of Merit for civilians (the German Federal Republic), the Order of Lenin (USSR), the Order of the Chrysanthemum (Japan) and the Order of the People's Liberation Army (China).

DÉCOUPAGE (from French *découper*, to cut out), a form of surface decoration. The craft originated as a form of furniture decoration in France during the 17th century. Engravings were cut out, colored, glued to the surface of pieces of furniture and then "sunk" under numerous coats of varnish or lacquer so that the final effect closely resembles that of fine inlay work.

DECRETALS, written replies by the pope to bishops or private persons, in disputed cases involving doctrine or Church discipline. They served as precedents for similar, later cases and were thus an important source of canon law.

DEDEKIND, Julius Wilhelm Richard (1831–1916), German mathematician who contributed to the theory of numbers. He proposed the method of "Dedekind cuts" for defining all the REAL NUMBERS in terms of RATIONAL NUMBERS.

Two species of deer: the Fallow deer (*Dama dama*) (*above left*), now established in most parts of Europe; and the American elk, or wapiti, (*Cervus canadensis*), once found over most of North America south of the tundra region. Deer are found in most parts of the world, generally living in small groups in wooded or park-like areas, and are well known for their beauty and grace.

DEDHAM, town in E Mass., seat of Norfolk Co. A residential suburb 9mi SW of Boston, it was one of the earliest settlements (1635) of the Massachusetts Bay colony. Pop 26 938.

DE DUVE, Christian René (1917–), English-born Belgian-US biochemist who shared the 1974 Nobel Prize for Physiology or Medicine with A. CLAUDE and G. PALADE for their pioneer studies of CELL anatomy. De Duve's particular contribution was the discovery of LYSOSOMES.

DEE, John (1527–1608), English mathematician and astrologer to Elizabeth I of England who encouraged the practical application of mathematics and supported the theory of COPERNICUS.

DEED, formal document which transfers ownership of real property. The careful formality required for a valid deed is designed to avoid the need for any further proof of the transaction.

DEEP-SEA ANIMALS. See ABYSSAL FAUNA.

DEER, cloven-hoofed mammals of the family Cervidae, found in Europe, Asia and the Americas. The most remarkable characteristic of the deer family, which contains about 40 species, is the ANTLERS of the males. Only the Musk deer and the Chinese water deer lack antlers, while both sexes of the CARIBOU and the REINDEER are antlered. The smallest deer is the Chilean PUDU (320mm (13in) at the shoulder) and the largest the North American MOOSE (up to 2.1m (7ft), and over 450kg (1000lb) in weight). Though many species are abundant, some, such as the Axis deer of India and Ceylon, are fast becoming rare and the Chinese Pere David's deer survives only in ZOOS. (See also CHEVROTAIN; ELK; FALLOW DEER; MULE DEER; RED DEER; ROE DEER; WAPITI; WHITE-TAILED DEER.)

DEERE, John (1804–1886), US inventor who developed and marketed the first steel plows.

DEERFIELD, village in NE Ill., 25mi NW of Chicago, a residential community. Pop 18 949.

DEERFIELD, town in NW Mass., in the Connecticut R valley. It was the scene of several Indian attacks, including the Bloody Brook Massacre (1675) and a raid in 1704 in which the Indians and French invaded the town and took many of the inhabitants to Canada. Pop 3 850.

DEERFIELD BEACH, town in SE Fla. on the Atlantic coast, 40mi N of Miami. It is a residential and tourist resort. Pop 17 130.

DEERFLIES. See HORSEFLIES.

DEERHOUND, rugged breed of hound, related to the IRISH WOLFHOUND. It can weigh over 100lb and stand up to 32in at the shoulder. Its coat, gray to wheaten in color, is usually about 3in in length.

DEER MICE, or white-footed mice, any of over 50 species of mouse found in North America and classified in the genus *Peromyscus*. Between 125mm and 380mm (5–15in) long, Deer mice vary in color from white to near black. They are nocturnal and omnivorous.

DEER PARK, unincorporated residential town in N.Y., on Long Island. Pop 31 120.

DEER PARK, city in Tex., 15mi E of Houston. It manufactures plastics and refrigerators and also caters for local truck farmers. Pop 12 773.

DEFAMATION. See LIBEL.

DEFENESTRATION OF PRAGUE, incident on May 23, 1618, considered to mark the start of the THIRTY YEARS' WAR, when a group of Protestant Bohemian nobles threw two of the imperial councillors out of a window of Prague Castle, in protest at interference in their religious liberty. It was the beginning of a Bohemian revolt against Hapsburg authority.

DEFENSE, US Department of, executive department responsible for national security. It is the

The deerhound, a large rough-haired dog, was once widely used in Europe for hunting red deer; hence its name. Although now rarely used for hunting, it is still a valued breed.

largest of the federal departments and receives the major part of the federal budget. It was created by the National Security Act of 1947 as a National Military Establishment, bringing together the three previously separate departments of the Army, Navy and Air Force. It was established in its present form in 1949 with the aim of achieving a more unified defense structure. It is headed by a civilian secretary of defense, appointed by the president, who is a member of his cabinet.

DEFENSE MECHANISM, any measure or measures taken by the individual's UNCONSCIOUS to protect his EGO from unpleasant or humilating situations: for example, SUBLIMATION, REPRESSION or PROJECTION. The more embracing term, **defense reaction**, describes the behavior resulting from such measures and also from analogous conscious measures.

DEFERENT. See EPICYCLE.

DEFIANCE, city in NW Ohio, seat of Defiance Co. It is a market and manufacturing center. Pop 16281.

DEFICIENCY DISEASES. See DISEASE; VITAMINS.

DEFICIT FINANCING, deliberate government policy of allowing expenditure to exceed income. First advocated by J. M. KEYNES to reduce unemployment in a depressed economy, it is now common even at times of full employment.

DEFLATION, decline in prices owing to oversupply of goods. It usually leads to unemployment and a lessening in production. Government measures, like increased expenditure and tax reductions, are usually introduced to encourage business investment and consumer purchases.

DEFOE, Daniel (1660–1731), English author, one of the founders of the English novel. Originally a merchant, he took to writing essays and pamphlets, including a satire against the Anglican High Church for which he was fined and pilloried. He was nearly 60 when he began writing the realistic novels for which he is best known, including *Robinson Crusoe* (1719), *Moll Flanders* (1722) and *A Journal of the Plague Year* (1722).

DE FOREST, John William (1826–1906), American writer, outstanding for his ability to achieve realism in fiction. A captain in the Civil War, his war reports for *Harper's Monthly* were brilliant. His best-known novel is *Miss Ravenel's Conversion from Secession to Loyalty* (1867).

DE FOREST, Lee (1873–1961), US inventor of the TRIODE (1906), an electron tube with three ELECTRODES (CATHODE, ANODE and grid) which could operate as a signal AMPLIFIER as well as a RECTIFIER. The triode was crucial to the development of RADIO.

DEGAS (Hilaire-Germain Edgar de Gas; 1834–1917), French painter and sculptor associated with IMPRESSIONISM. The paintings of INGRES were the source of Degas' linear style, but his asymmetrical compositions were influenced by Japanese prints. His favorite subjects were ballet dancers and women at their toilet. From the 1880s, Degas worked regularly in pastel, and produced small bronze sculptures of dancers and horses. Among his best-known paintings are *The Rehearsal* (1872) and *The Millinery Shop* (c1885).

DE GASPERI, Alcide (1881–1954), Italian statesman, premier 1945–53. Active in political life from 1911, he was twice imprisoned for his opposition to the fascist regime. He clandestinely organized the Christian Democratic Party during WWII and as its leader became the first premier of the new Italian Republic in 1945.

DE GAULLE, Charles André Joseph Marie (1890–1970), French soldier and statesman, president 1945–46 and 1958–69, noted for his sense of personal destiny and unswerving devotion to France. De Gaulle was trained at Saint-Cyr military academy, and served under PÉTAIN as a captain in WWI. He then taught military history at Saint-Cyr, developing his advanced tactical theories. When France fell in 1940, he started the Free French movement in England. In 1944, his provisional government took over liberated France and did much to restore national morale. After resigning in 1946 he returned the following year with a new party, but met with little success and retired in 1953. On June 1, 1958, he was named premier at the height of the Algerian crisis; he assumed new and wide powers and passed many reforms which strengthened the economy. The Algerian crisis worsened, but De Gaulle was largely responsible for its resolution in 1962. He failed in his aim to make France the leader of a European political community, and during the 1960s pursued a policy of national independence. He resigned in 1969 on the defeat of a referendum designed to give him further powers for constitutional reforms.

DEGAUSSING, removing the magnetization (see MAGNETISM) of a permanent magnet or other object by withdrawing it slowly from a strong oscillating magnetic field, so that it is repeatedly magnetized in opposite directions but to progressively smaller degrees.

DEGENERATION, a term sometimes, but erroneously, applied to the evolution of parasitic organisms. Parasitic animals often lack features found in their free-living relatives, but they always possess others that suit them for their specialized way of life. (See PARASITE.)

DEGENERATIVE DISEASES. See DISEASE.

DEGREE, in ALGEBRA, of a POLYNOMIAL such as

$$ax^4+bx^2+cx+d$$

the highest POWER to which the VARIABLE x is raised—in this case, 4. (See also EQUATION.)

DEGREE, in GEOMETRY. See ANGLE.

DEGREE, Academic, title conferred by a university or college as a formal recognition of academic competence. In the US the first degree usually confers the status of Bachelor. Master's and Doctor's degrees are usually awarded for research work undertaken after a first degree. Honorary degrees are awarded as a recognition of distinction without reference to academic achievement. In the US special excellence in the Bachelor's degree is recognized by the Latin terms *cum laude*, *magna cum laude* and *summa cum laude*.

DEGREES OF FREEDOM, the minimum number of independent VARIABLES in a system whose values must be specified in order to define the system. The number of degrees of freedom equals the number of variables less the number of independent relations between them (constraints). Thus OHM'S LAW provides one relation between three variables, and there are two degrees of freedom: if the resistance of a wire and the current through it are specified, both degrees of freedom have been used, and the voltage across the wire is fixed. In STATISTICS, for a sample of n members, the distribution has $(n-m)$ degrees of freedom where there are m constraints on the distribution. (See also CHI-SQUARED TEST; PHASE EQUILIBRIA; STUDENT'S t-DISTRIBUTION.)

DE HAVILLAND, Sir Geoffrey (1882–1965), British aeronautical engineer, designer and manufacturer of De Havilland airplanes. His firm produced the famous *Moth* biplane and in WWII the *Mosquito* bomber. In the early 1950s De Havilland also produced the pioneering *Comet* jet airliner.

DE HOOCH, Pieter. See HOOCH, PIETER DE.

DEHUMIDIFIER, a device for removing water vapor from air, by passing the air over cooling fins to promote CONDENSATION, or by ADSORPTION by such materials as SILICA GEL or alumina. It is a standard part of AIR-CONDITIONING systems in hot climates, where low humidity is desirable.

DEHYDRATION, or drying, the removal of WATER from a substance. To remove the elements of water, as in the dehydration of ALCOHOLS to ETHERS, requires a powerful dehydrating agent such as concentrated SULFURIC ACID. Generally, however, water is present as such, as a HYDRATE or merely absorbed, in which case milder methods suffice, such as equilibration in a desiccator with SILICA GEL or deliquescent compounds (see DELIQUESCENCE). Dry air may be passed over solids in heated drums, causing EVAPORATION. Gases are dried (for AIR CONDITIONING, or before liquefying them) by compression and refrigeration. Foods are preserved by drying; this is done for convenience and compactness. Milk and eggs are dried by spraying into hot air. Modern freeze drying—sublimation of ice from frozen foods under vacuum—retains texture and flavor. In medicine, dehydration of the body occurs through DIARRHEA, VOMITING, CHOLERA or merely lack of water to replace PERSPIRATION.

DEIANIRA, in Greek myth the wife of HERCULES. Tricked by the centaur NESSUS into causing the hero's death, she committed suicide.

DEIMOS, the outer moon of MARS, circling the planet in 30.3h at a distance of 23500km. Its diameter is about 8km.

DEIRDRE, in Irish legend the betrothed of King Conchobar of Ulster. She fell in love with Naisi, his nephew, and they eloped to Scotland. They were tricked into returning and Conchobar had Naisi murdered. Deirdre then killed herself.

DEISM, religious system developed in the 17th and 18th centuries, expounded by VOLTAIRE and Jean Jacques ROUSSEAU. Deists believed in a Creator God, but rejected PROVIDENCE, REVELATION and the supernatural, holding that religious truth is known by reason and the light of nature. (See also THEISM).

DE KALB, city on the Kishwaukee R, N Ill. The economy rests on agriculture and on various manufactures, including wire; barbed wire was first made here. Pop 32949.

DE KALB, Johann. See KALB, JOHANN.

DEKKER, Thomas (c1570–c1632), English dramatist and pamphleteer. On many plays he collaborated with Philip MASSINGER, Thomas MIDDLETON, John FORD and John WEBSTER. His best-known work is the comedy *The Shoemaker's Holiday* (1600). He was a vigorous pamphleteer and witty observer of London life.

DE KOONING, Willem (1904–), Dutch-born US painter, a founder of ABSTRACT EXPRESSIONISM. Influenced by GORKY, MIRO and PICASSO, he painted abstract and figurative pictures with thickly applied pigment. One famous work is *Woman I* (1952).

DE KRUIF, Paul (1890–1971), US bacteriologist and science writer whose *Microbe Hunters* (1926) and later books telling the story of recent advances in medical science achieved large circulations.

DEL (also known as **alted** and **nabla**), the vector operator ∇, expressed in CARTESIAN COORDINATES as

$$\nabla=\mathbf{i}\frac{\partial}{\partial x}+\mathbf{j}\frac{\partial}{\partial y}+\mathbf{k}\frac{\partial}{\partial z}.$$

The product of ∇ and a SCALAR S yields a VECTOR FIELD called grad S (the gradient of S):

$$\text{grad } S=\mathbf{i}\frac{\partial S}{\partial x}+\mathbf{j}\frac{\partial S}{\partial y}+\mathbf{k}\frac{\partial S}{\partial z}.$$

The scalar product (see VECTOR ANALYSIS) of ∇ with a vector $\mathbf{V}$ is the divergence of $\mathbf{V}$ (see DIV); the vector product of ∇ with $\mathbf{V}$ is the CURL of $\mathbf{V}$.

DELACROIX, Ferdinand-Victor-Eugène (1798–1863), French painter whose literary and

Self-portrait by Delacroix, an aristocratic figure in Parisian circles. It was painted in 1842, and now hangs in the Uffizi Gallery, Florence. Delacroix's romanticism, his brilliant use of color and his love of dramatic lighting effects are all clearly in evidence.

George Washington crossing the Delaware River on Christmas night, 1776. Landing on the New Jersey shore in a storm, the Americans marched on Trenton and surprised the Hessian troops, routing them completely. (Painting by E. Leutze now in museum at Washington's Crossing State Park, near Philadelphia.)

historical themes are typical of ROMANTICISM. Such early works as *The Massacre of Chios* (1824) were influenced by GÉRICAULT, but his mastery of rich color schemes and handling of paint was largely learned from RUBENS, as shown by *Death of Sardanapalus* (1827), *The Justice of Trajan* (1840) and the many official decorative schemes he undertook. His frescoes for Saint-Sulpice, Paris, influenced IMPRESSIONISM.

DELAGOA BAY, inlet of the Indian Ocean on the SE coast of Mozambique, upon which the country's capital, Maputo, is situated.

DE LA MARE, Walter John (1873–1956), English poet and novelist. His work, much of which was intended for children, is characterized by its power to evoke the atmosphere of dreams and the supernatural. His best-known works are the novel *Memoirs of a Midget* (1921) and the childrens' poetry collection *Peacock Pie* (1913).

DE LANCEY, James (1703–1760), US jurist and politician. Chief justice of the N.Y. Supreme Court from 1733, he was accused of bias against the defendant during the trial of John P. ZENGER. He was lieutenant-governor of N.Y. 1753–55 and from 1757.

DE LAND, city in E Fla., seat of Volusia Co. The economy rests mainly on packing and shipping of locally-grown citrus fruits and on lumbering. It is also a winter resort. Pop 11 641.

DELANO, city in SE Cal., center of a grape-growing and wine-making area. The economy is mainly agricultural, but there is some industry. Pop 14 559.

DELANY, Martin Robinson (1812–1885), US Negro leader. A newspaper publisher until 1849, he received a medical degree from Harvard in 1852, one of the first Negroes to do so. He wrote and worked for abolitionist causes such as the UNDERGROUND RAILROAD and Negro emigration. In the Civil War he became an army surgeon, the first Negro to reach the rank of major. He later joined the FREEDMEN'S BUREAU and became a trial judge in Charleston, S.C.

DELAUNAY, Robert (1885–1941), French abstract painter who with his wife Sonia founded the Orphist movement in 1910. His pictures comprised forms of brilliantly contrasting color. His *Windows* (1912) developed the Cubist style.

DELAWARE, first state to ratify the US Constitution. One of the original 13 colonies, it is the second smallest state in area but is also one of the fastest growing and richest in the nation. Most of the state is part of the Atlantic coastal plain, long and narrow in shape The greater part consists of lowland, but the Piedmont area in the NW has rolling hills. The main river is the Delaware, running down the E boundary of the state. It has many other rivers and lakes. The climate is temperate but humid with quite mild winters and hot summers. The state has become mainly urban, and its population, swelled by interstate migration, is chiefly concentrated in the Wilmington metropolitan area.

Until 1920 the economy was mostly rural, but now agriculture (corn, fruit, vegetables and broiler chickens) accounts for only a fraction of the state's production, while the chemical industry is the state's largest producer of goods. Shipbuilding, leather tanning, paper making and oil refining are also important. Corporation taxes are unusually low, attracting many companies whose main business is often not in Del. Public education made slow progress in the 19th century, and only in 1907 did school attendance become compulsory. The state legislature, the General Assembly, consists of a Senate of 19 members, elected for four-year terms, and a House of Representatives with 39 members who serve for two years.

The first Englishman to sail into the Delaware R was Samuel ARGALL, who named it for Baron DE LA WARR, then governor of Virginia (1610). The area was occupied by the Dutch and the Swedes until seized by the English in 1604; it was ruled as part of Pennsylvania until acquiring its own assembly in 1704. After the Revolution Delaware prospered; flour-milling was then the leading industry. Gunpowder mills were built by DU PONT in 1802, becoming the basis of the state's chemical industry.

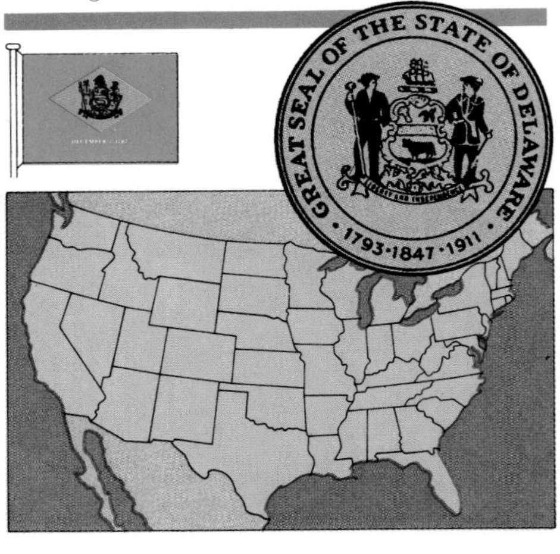

Name of state: Delaware
Capital: Dover
Statehood: Dec. 7, 1787 (1st state)
Familiar name: First State; Diamond State; Blue Hen State
Area: 2 057sq mi
Population: 542 979
Elevation: Highest—442ft, New Castle County. Lowest—sea level, Atlantic coast
Motto: Liberty and Independence
State flower: Peach Blossom
State bird: Blue hen chicken
State tree: American holly
State song: "Our Delaware"

Quaker influence around Wilmington meant that many slaves were freed by 1860. WWI stimulated production of explosives and the population became concentrated in the industrialized N part of the state.

DELAWARE, city in central Ohio, seat of Delaware Co. A 19th-century health resort with sulfur springs, it now has some industry. Ohio Wesleyan U. was founded here in 1842. Pop 15 008.

DELAWARE AQUEDUCT, water tunnel running 105mi SE from Rondout Reservoir in the Catskill Mts to Hillview Reservoir in Yonkers, supplying New York City. Sunk deep in bedrock, it was built 1937–53 and extended to its present length by 1965.

DELAWARE BAY, inlet of the N Atlantic on the E coast of the US. It extends out from the mouth of the Delaware R with N.J. to the N and Del. to the S and W. It is about 50mi long and 30mi at its widest.

DELAWARE INDIANS, tribe of the ALGONQUIAN linguistic group who lived in the Delaware R basin area until driven out into Ohio in the 18th century by the incursions of colonists and the FRENCH AND INDIAN WARS. An agricultural tribe, they had a sophisticated culture and were respected by other tribes. Today their descendants are scattered through reservations in Okla. and Ontario, Canada.

DELAWARE RIVER, rises in the Catskill Mts of SE N.Y. and flows 300mi S into Delaware Bay. Forming the boundaries between Pa. and N.Y. and N.J., and between N.J. and Del., it is an important shipping channel for Philadelphia and the great industrial area of N.J. It has a serious pollution problem.

DELAWARE WATER GAP, deep gorge, 3mi in length, cut by the Delaware R through the Kittatinny ridge of the Appalachian Mts. The area's scenic beauty makes it a popular tourist resort.

DE LA WARR, Thomas West, 12th Baron, (1577–1618), first governor of the Va. colony. Appointed for life in 1610, he revitalized the failing settlement despite a serious illness which forced his return to England in 1611. He continued to work for Va. and died while making a return voyage. The state of Delaware is named for him.

DELBRÜCK, Max (1906–), German-born US biologist whose discovery of a method for detecting and measuring the rate of mutations in BACTERIA opened up the study of bacterial GENETICS.

DEL CITY, eastern residential suburb of Oklahoma City, Okla., founded in 1946. Pop 27 133.

DE LEON, Daniel (1852–1914), US Marxist leader. An emigrant from Curaçao, he edited the Socialist Labor Party organ, *The People*, for some years. A cofounder of the INDUSTRIAL WORKERS OF THE WORLD in 1905, he was expelled from it in 1908, after which his influence declined.

DELESCLUZE, Louis Charles (1809–1871), French revolutionary activist and journalist. He was involved in uprisings against the monarchy in 1830 and 1848, and against Napoleon III in 1849; his journalistic attacks led to his deportation in 1853. He joined the Paris Commune revolt in 1871 and was killed at a barricade.

DELFT, industrial town in the Netherlands, sited on land reclaimed from the sea along the banks of the Schie R. A historic town and tourist center, it has been famous for its DELFTWARE pottery from the early 16th century. The industry declined there after 1700 but has been revived in the 20th century. Pop 86 189.

DELFTWARE, earthenware covered with an opaque white glaze made from tin oxide, first produced in the Netherlands and particularly at Delft in the 16th century. Designed to imitate Chinese porcelain, the style spread to England and remained popular until the 18th century, when porcelain was manufactured in the West.

DELHI, city in N India, its capital 1912–31. Adjacent to NEW DELHI, Delhi dates from the 17th century and has many historic buildings, such as the Red Fort, dating from that time. There are several light industries, and the city's craftwork in ivory, jewelry and pottery is famous. Most new building is now confined to New Delhi, and much of the old city, which has a much larger population, has become a slum. Pop 3 279 955.

DELIAN LEAGUE, confederacy of Greek states formed by Athens 478–477 BC to follow up the Hellenic league's victories against Persia. It was nominally governed by a council in which each member state had one vote, but was in fact entirely Athenian dominated. After considerable success

A fine example of blue Delft pottery, modeled on the exquisite Chinese porcelain designs and made in the historic Dutch city which gives it its name. Although the production of Delftware has been revived in the 20th century, it has proved hard to match the individuality of the originals.

against Persia, Athens began to turn the League into an empire, using its fleet to subjugate reluctant states such as Naxos. The so-called League endured until Athens was defeated by Sparta in the PELOPONNESIAN WAR. An attempt to revive it in 377 BC was crushed by Philip II of Macedon in 338 BC.

DELIBES, Clément Philibert Léo (1836–1891), French composer. Best known at first for his lighter works and operettas, some written in collaboration with OFFENBACH, he set a new high standard of ballet music with *Coppélia* (1870) and *Sylvia* (1876). His masterpiece is the grand opera *Lakmé* (1883).

DELILAH, in the Old Testament a Philistine woman who became the mistress of SAMSON. She duped him into revealing that the secret of his strength lay in his long hair, and so betrayed him to the Philistines.

DELINQUENCY. See JUVENILE DELINQUENCY.

DELIQUESCENCE, the absorption of atmospheric moisture by a solid until it dissolves to form a saturated solution. If it merely forms a crystalline HYDRATE it is termed **hygroscopic**. The phenomenon depends on the relative HUMIDITY: sugar, for example, deliquesces above 85% humidity. (See also EFFLORESCENCE.)

DELIRIUM, altered state of consciousness in which a person is restless, excitable, hallucinating and is only partly aware of his surroundings. It is seen in high FEVER, POISONING, drug withdrawal, disorders of METABOLISM and organ failure. SEDATIVES and reassurance are basic measures.

DELIRIUM TREMENS, specific delirium due to acute alcohol withdrawal in ALCOHOLISM. It occurs within days of abstinence and is often precipitated by injury, surgery or imprisonment. The sufferer becomes restless, disorientated, extremely anxious and tremulous; FEVER and profuse sweating are usual. Characteristically, hallucinations of insects or animals cause abject terror. Constant reassurance, SEDATIVES, well-lit and quiet surroundings are appropriate measures until the episode is over. Treatment of dehydration and reduction of high fever may be necessary, though fatalities do occur.

DELIUS, Frederick (1862–1934), English composer An orange-grower in Fla. 1884–86, he studied in Leipzig, where he met and was influenced by Edward GRIEG. He is best known for orchestral pieces such as *Florida* (1886–87) and *Brigg Fair* (1907), and for tone poems such as *Summer Night on the River* (1911) and *Sea Drift* (1903). His best-known opera is *A Village Romeo and Juliet* (1900–01). In old age he became blind and paralysed, but continued to compose by dictation.

DELLA FRANCESCA, Piero. See PIERO DELLA FRANCESCA.

DELLA QUERCIA, Jacopo. See QUERCIA, JACOPO DELLA.

DELLA ROBBIA. See ROBBIA, DELLA.

DELLO JOIO, Norman (1913–), US composer whose style blends neoclassicism and late romanticism. His orchestral work *Meditations on Ecclesiastes* (1956) won a 1957 Pulitzer Prize. He has composed operas such as *Blood Moon* (1961), choral works, ballet scores and much chamber music, as well as television scores.

DELMARVA PENINSULA, peninsula between Chesapeake Bay and Delaware Bay. It includes most of Del. and parts of Md. and Va., and its name is a compound of their names.

DE LONG, George Washington (1844–1881), US naval officer and Arctic explorer. De Long died of starvation after his ship had been crushed by ice N of Siberia. His journal, discovered after his death, was published by his widow in 1883, under the title *Voyage of the "Jeannette."*

DELOS, small Greek island of the Cyclades group in the S Aegean Sea. In Greek mythology Delos was said to be the birthplace of ARTEMIS and APOLLO. After the wars against Persia, it was the headquarters of the DELIAN LEAGUE from 478 to 404 BC. In Roman times Delos became an important port and center of the slave trade.

DELPHI, Classical Greek site located on the lower slopes of Mt PARNASSUS. Delphi was considered by the Greeks to be the center of the world, and was the seat of the most important ORACLE in ancient Greece. The oracular messages often had a strong influence on state policy. Excavations begun in 1892 revealed the magnificent temple of Apollo, now partially reconstructed, treasuries, a theater and a stadium.

DELPHINIUM, genus of plants of the BUTTERCUP family (Ranunculaceae), cultivated examples being the annual LARKSPURS and perennial hybrids of *Delphinium elatum*.

DELPHINUS (the Dolphin), a small summer constellation in N skies, four of whose stars form a diamond sometimes known as Job's Coffin.

DELRAY BEACH, city and tourist resort in SE Fla., on the Atlantic coast. It is a center for deepsea fishing and truck farming. Pop 19 366.

DEL RIO, city and seat of Val Verde Co. in SW Tex. It is a port and agricultural trading center on the Rio Grande. Pop 21 330.

DEL SARTO, Andrea. See ANDREA DEL SARTO.

DELTA, a flat alluvial plain at a rivermouth or at the confluence of two rivers, formed of fertile mud deposited by the slow-moving water. Typically, the stream divides and subdivides until a fan-shaped plain covered by a complex of channels results. The form of a delta depends on the rates of SEDIMENTATION and of EROSION by the sea. (See also ESTUARY.)

DELTA RAYS, short ELECTRON tracks surrounding the track left by a fast charged particle in CLOUD CHAMBERS, BUBBLE CHAMBERS, or photographic emulsions. The primary particle dislodges electrons from the ATOMS of the medium concerned, and the faster of these leave short tracks of their own before being brought to rest.

DEMAND. See SUPPLY AND DEMAND.

DE MAUPASSANT, Guy. See MAUPASSANT, (HENRY RENÉ ALBERT) GUY DE.

DEMENTIA, loss of the ability to reason, as distinct from AMNESIA. (See KORSAKOV'S PSYCHOSIS.) *Dementia Praecox* is an obsolete term roughly corresponding to SCHIZOPHRENIA.

DEMETER, in Greek mythology, the goddess of agriculture, identified with the Roman CERES. Demeter was sister of ZEUS and mother of PERSEPHONE and the presiding deity of the ELEUSINIAN MYSTERIES.

DEMETRIUS, name of two kings of Macedonia. **Demetrius I Poliorcetes** (336–283 BC), son of ANTIGONUS I, reigned 294–288 BC. He destroyed the naval power of Egypt by defeating PTOLEMY at Salamis (Cyprus) in 306 BC. **Demetrius II** (c276–229 BC), son of Antigonus II, reigned from 239 BC. His failure against the Aetolian and Achaean confederacy weakened the kingdom of Macedon.

DEMETRIUS, name of three kings of Syria. **Demetrius I Soter** (187–150 BC) reigned from 162 BC. In 161 he defeated the rebel general Timarchus and was recognized as king by Rome. His son **Demetrius II Nicator** (c161–125 BC) reigned 145–139 and 129–125 BC. He was captured in war and after 129 BC controlled only part of Syria. **Demetrius III** (d. 88? BC), called Eukairos and Philometer, reigned 95–88 BC.

DE MILLE, Agnes George (1909–), US dancer and choreographer. She pioneered the combination of ballet and American folk music, often within the framework of modern musical comedy. Her productions include *Rodeo* (1942), *Oklahoma!* (1943) and *Fall River Legend* (1948).

DE MILLE, Cecil Blount (1881–1959), US motion picture producer and director, noted for his use of spectacle. He directed such epics as *The Ten Commandments* (1923), *Samson and Delilah* (1949) and *The Greatest Show on Earth* (1952).

DEMOCRACY, system of government which recognizes the right of all members of society to influence political decisions, either directly or indirectly. Direct democracy, in which political decisions are made by the whole citizen body meeting together, is only possible where the population is small. (See GREECE, ANCIENT.) The direct democracy of some ancient Greek city-states has had little influence on the development of modern representative democracies, in which political decisions are made by elected representatives responsible to their electors.

Representative democracy began to evolve during the 18th and 19th centuries, in Britain, Europe and the US. Its central institution is the representative parliament, in which decisions are effected by majority vote. Institutions intrinsic to representative democracy are: regular elections with a free choice of candidates, universal adult suffrage, freedom to organize rival political parties and independence of the judiciary. Freedom of speech and the press, and the preservation of civil liberties and minority rights are also implicit in the idea of liberal representative democracy. The American and French revolutions, and the growth of the middle classes following the INDUSTRIAL REVOLUTION, were important influences in the formation of modern democracies. The concepts of natural rights and political equality expressed by such philosophers as John LOCKE in the 17th century, VOLTAIRE and Jean Jacques ROUSSEAU in the 18th century, and BENTHAM and J. S. MILL in the 19th century, are vital to the theory of representative democracy. (See also CONSTITUTION; PARLIAMENT; REPUBLIC; TOTALITARIANISM; UNITED STATES CONSTITUTION.)

DEMOCRATIC PARTY, one of the two major political parties in the US. Democrats trace their history back to the Democratic Republican Party (1792) of Thomas JEFFERSON, who favored popular control of the goverment. Following the inauguration of Andrew JACKSON in 1828, the party's base was broadened, with representation from the new West as

The treasury of Athens on the slopes of mount Parnassus at Delphi, re-erected by archaeologists between 1903 and 1906. Delphi was an important religious center in the ancient Greek world, containing, among many shrines and temples, the famous oracle of Apollo. In this building the votive offerings of the Athenians were deposited.

well as the East. Jackson was a man of the people, and his administration marked the beginning of a period of dominance for the Democrats that only ended with the election in 1860 of Abraham Lincoln, the first successful candidate of the new REPUBLICAN PARTY. The slavery controversy and the Civil War split the party into northern and southern sections and, apart from the success of Woodrow WILSON in WWI, it was not until the election of Franklin D. ROOSEVELT in 1932 that the party reemerged with its old vigor. Roosevelt's NEW DEAL transformed the party's traditional policies, introducing broad governmental intervention in the economy and social welfare. This approach was continued on Roosevelt's death in 1945 by Harry S. TRUMAN, whose FAIR DEAL measures were, however, largely thwarted by a coalition of Republicans and Southern Democrats. In the 1950s, under Eisenhower's Republican administration, the party was led by Adlai E. STEVENSON. It controlled both houses of Congress from 1954, but the "solid South" alliance began to fracture under the drive towards improved civil rights. The election of John F. KENNEDY in 1960 led to important legislation in this sphere, but also contributed further to the breakup of the traditional alliance. On Kennedy's assassination in 1963, Vice-president Lyndon B. JOHNSON came to power. By 1968 the party was riven by dissent, particularly over policy in Vietnam. In 1968 Hubert H. HUMPHREY lost the presidential election to Richard M. NIXON, and in 1972 he was replaced as leader of the party by George S. McGOVERN, The Democrats retained control of Congress. In 1976 Jimmy CARTER became leader.

DEMOCRATIC REPUBLICAN PARTY. See DEMOCRATIC PARTY; JEFFERSON, THOMAS.

DEMOCRITUS OF ABDERA (c460–370 BC), Greek materialist philosopher, one of the earliest exponents of ATOMISM, who maintained that all phenomena were explicable in terms of the nomic motion of atoms in the void.

DEMOGRAPHY, a branch of sociology, the study of the distribution, composition and internal structure of human populations. It draws on many disciplines (e.g., genetics, psychology, economics, geography), its tools being essentially those of STATISTICS: the sample and the census whose results are statistically analyzed. Its prime concerns are birth rate, emigration and immigration. (See also POPULATION.)

DE MOIVRE, Abraham (1667–1754), French-born English mathematician chiefly remembered for **De Moivre's Theorem** which states that for a rational number *n*,

$$(\cos\theta + i\sin\theta)^n = \cos n\theta + i\sin n\theta.$$

DEMOLAY, Order of, international organization sponsored by Masonic orders to promote high ideals and character among boys from 14 to 21 years of age. It was founded in 1919 at Kansas City, Mo.

DEMONS AND DEMONOLOGY, supernatural and generally malignant beings, and their study. Demons (from Greek *daimōn*) vary in their attributed power and significance from culture to culture. The demons of ancient Greece, for example, were represented as vengeful spirits of the dead, or implacable agents sent to exact the justice of the gods (see FURIES; HARPIES), while by the Romans they tended to be considered as more amenable spirits. The early Judaic tradition believed in such demons as AZAZEL and LILITH. In Christianity, demons are fallen angels, the servants of SATAN. Northern European myths of Slavic, Teutonic and Celtic origin are haunted by many shadowy and powerful demon figures (see for example WEREWOLF). Demon cults flourished in 16th- and 17th-century Europe (see WITCHCRAFT). Many primitive societies still practice cults in which demons play a central role (see ANIMISM).

DEMOSTHENES (384–322 BC), famous Athenian orator and statesman. Demosthenes was the author of the *Philippics* (351–341 BC) and the *Olynthiacs* (349–348 BC)—speeches designed to awaken the Athenians to the danger of conquest by Philip II of Macedon. Demosthenes' most famous speech was *On the Crown* (330 BC) in which he vindicated himself against charges brought by AESCHINES of financial corruption, cowardice in battle and indecisiveness in policy.

DEMPSEY, Jack (1895–), US boxer, one of the great heavyweights. He won the world championship from Jess WILLARD in 1919 at Toledo, Ohio, and held the title until defeated by Gene TUNNEY in 1926. Again defeated by Tunney in 1927, he retired from the ring in 1928.

DEMUTH, Charles (1883–1935), US painter and illustrator. Demuth, who was influenced by both CUBISM and EXPRESSIONISM and worked in a number of styles, is best known for his precise and delicate watercolor studies of flowers. He is also noted for his illustrations for the works of Poe, Zola and Henry James.

DENATURED ALCOHOL. See ETHANOL.

DENBY, Edwin (1870–1929), US lawyer and politician. He was appointed secretary of the navy in 1921, but was forced to resign in 1924 on charges of incompetence, as a result of the TEAPOT DOME scandal.

DENDRITE, a branched, treelike CRYSTAL form, common in ice (especially frost) and certain minerals, and chiefly important in metals, which often consist of dendrites embedded in a matrix of the same or (for alloys) different composition. In anatomy, a dendrite is a tapering receptor branch of a NEURON.

DENDROCHRONOLOGY, the dating of past events by the study of tree-rings. A hollow tube is inserted into the tree trunk and a core from bark to center removed. The ANNUAL RINGS are counted, examined and compared with rings from dead trees so that the chronology may be extended further back in time. Through such studies important corrections have been made to the system of RADIOCARBON DATING.

DENGUE FEVER, or breakbone fever, a VIRUS infection carried by mosquitoes, with FEVER, headache, malaise, prostration and characteristically severe muscle and joint pains. There is also a variable skin rash through the roughly week-long illness. It is a disease of warm climates, and may occur in EPIDEMICS. Symptomatic treatment only is required.

DENIER, a unit used to describe the mass per unit length of silk or nylon yarn. The denier number of a yarn is its weight in grams per 9km length.

DENIKIN, Anton Ivanovich (1872–1947), Russian leader of the anti-Bolshevik "White" forces in the civil war following the RUSSIAN REVOLUTION of 1917. In 1918 he succeeded KORNILOV as commander of the Whites in S Russia, but was convincingly defeated at Orel, 250mi from Moscow, in 1919. Denikin resigned his command the following year and fled to France. He emigrated to the US in 1945.

DENIS, Saint, patron saint of France and martyr. He is thought to have lived in the 3rd century and to have been the first bishop of Paris. His feast day is Oct. 9.

DENISON, city in Tex. It is a center for agriculture in the Red R valley, and is famous as the birthplace of Dwight D. Eisenhower. Pop 24 923.

DENMARK, kingdom on the Jutland peninsula, between the North and Baltic seas in NW Europe. It includes 482 islands off the peninsula, the two largest of which are Zealand (where Copenhagen is situated) and Fyn, and also the FAEROE ISLANDS and GREENLAND. Denmark's 42mi S land boundary is with West Germany. Her E and N neighbors are respectively Sweden and Norway. Denmark is the smallest of the Scandinavian countries.

The W half of the country, which is fairly flat, consists of coastal dunes and lagoons and relatively infertile plains with sandy soil and peat bogs. The E has hilly moraines, cut by deep inlets and valleys, a pattern continued in the islands. The soils in this region are loamy and fertile. Climate is moist, with cool summers and, for the latitude, relatively warm winters.

People. Denmark's population is almost entirely Scandinavian. A German minority of about 30 000 lives in SW Jutland, while some 40 000 Danes live in German Schleswig. The majority of people live in the towns, with Greater Copenhagen the most densely populated district. Hinterlands are restricted and the Danes have become increasingly aware of the extent to which fertile farmland is being swallowed up. Denmark has a highly developed state education

Official Name: The Kingdom of Denmark
Capital: Copenhagen
Area: 16 629sq mi
Population: 5 007 538
Languages: Danish
Religions: Lutheran
Monetary Unit(s):
1 Krone = 100 øre

system and advanced social security schemes.

Economy. Agriculture was the chief support of the economy until recently, and although some 60% of the country is given over to intensive farming, manufacturing now supplies more than 60% of Denmark's total exports. About 20% of the Gross National Product is provided by industry, 9% by agriculture and 16% by commerce. Industry employs about 30% of the work force, agriculture about 11%.

Among the major products are foodstuffs (particularly dairy products), furniture, glass, silverware, leather goods and clothing. There are important shipbuilding and agricultural engineering industries, while fishing and tourism also make an important contribution to the economy. Denmark depends heavily on imported raw materials, particularly iron, coal and oil. From 1958–72 she was a member of the EUROPEAN FREE TRADE ASSOCIATION; in 1973 she joined the COMMON MARKET.

History. Denmark has a rich early history as the center of VIKING expansion. She maintained her influence through to the 16th century, as a dominant partner in the KALMAR UNION. From about 1600 Danish power waned, under Swedish pressure. Prussia and Austria wrested Schleswig-Holstein from the Danes (1864), who eventually recovered N Schleswig after a plebiscite (1920). During WWII Denmark was occupied by Germany (1940–45).

DENOMINATOR, the DIVISOR of a common FRACTION.

DENSITY, the ratio of MASS to volume for a given material or object. Substances that are light for their size have a low density, and vice versa. Objects whose density is less than that of water will float in water, while a hot air BALLOON will rise when its average density becomes less than that of air. The term is also applied to properties other than mass: e.g., **charge density** refers to the ratio of electric charge (see ELECTRICITY) to volume.

DENTISTRY, the branch of MEDICINE concerned with the care of TEETH and related structures. Dental CARIES is responsible for most dental discomfort. Here the bacterial dissolution of dentine and enamel leads to cavities, especially in molars and premolars, and these allow accumulation of debris which encourages further bacterial growth; destruction of the tooth will gradually ensue unless treatment restores a protective surface. Each tooth contains sensitive nerve fibers extending into the dentine; exposure of these causes toothache, but the fibers then retract so that the pain often recedes despite continuing caries. The dentist removes all unhealthy tissue under ANESTHESIA and fills the cavity with metal AMALGAM which hardens and protects the tooth, although a severely damaged tooth may require extraction. Traumatic injury to teeth is repaired by a similar process. In some instances a tooth may be reconstructed on a "peg" of the original by using an artificial "crown." Maldeveloped or displaced teeth may need extraction or, during childhood, braces or plates to encourage realignment with growth. Wisdom teeth (rearmost molars), in particular, may need extraction if they erupt out of alignment or if they interfere with the normal bite. Infection of tooth pulp with ABSCESS formation destroys the tooth; PUS can only be drained by extraction. False teeth or dentures, either fitted individually or as a group on a denture plate that sits on the gums, are made to replace lost teeth, to allow effective bite and for cosmetic purposes. Dentistry is also concerned with the prevention of carious decay and periodontal disease by encouragement of oral hygiene, including regular adequate brushing of teeth. Fluoride and protective films are important recent developments in preventive dentistry.

DENTITION. See TEETH.

DENTON, city in N Tex., seat of Denton Co. It is a manufacturing and agricultural center and the site of two universities. Pop 39 874.

D'ENTRECASTEAUX ISLANDS, volcanic island group in the SW Pacific Ocean off the SE coast of New Guinea, with an area of about 1 200sq mi. It produces copra and is part of Papua New Guinea.

DENVER, state capital and largest city in Col., seat of Denver Co. It is located to the east of the foothills of the Rocky Mts, a mile above sea level. Settled in 1858, Denver is known today as the commercial center of the Rocky Mountain region, with large sheep and cattle markets and modern industries, including aerospace, mining machinery and printing. It is also the site of numerous federal agencies and educational establishments, including the U. of Denver. The fine dry climate and opportunities for skiing make it a popular tourist resort. Pop 514 678.

DENVER, James William (1817–1892), US governor of the Territory of Kansas 1858. He brought law and order to Colorado and Kansas, and Denver, Col., was named for him.

DEODAR, *Cedrus deodora*, cedar tree native to the Himalayas where it grows in extensive forests and is a valuable lumber tree. The deodar is also grown as an ornamental. Family: Pinaceae. (See also CEDAR.)

DEODORANT, a substance used to counteract unpleasant body smells. Deodorants may simply mask a smell, as air fresheners in rooms, or may destroy the bacteria that live in PERSPIRATION and are the cause of the smell (see ANTISEPTICS). However, body odors are most easily prevented by regular washing. Antiperspirants, usually aluminum chlorohydroxide, are ASTRINGENTS.

DEOXYRIBONUCLEIC ACID (DNA). See NUCLEIC ACIDS.

DE PERE, city in E Wis. It is an agricultural and industrial center. Pop 13 309.

DEPEW, village in N.Y. It is an industrial suburb 9mi E of Buffalo. Pop 22 158.

DEPORTATION, expulsion of an alien from a country for criminal or other undesirable activities, or because he has entered the country illegally. He may be returned to the country of his origin, or the place where he lived previously. In the US, an alien who has been deported may not reenter the country without the attorney general's consent.

DEPRECIATION, of an asset, reduction in its value brought about by factors such as age, use, action of the elements and obsolescence. It is allowed for in calculating tax liability, whether the assets are machinery, real estate and the like, or intangibles like leaseholds and copyrights. Depreciation of MONEY is a reduction in its exchange value caused by a rise in commodity prices (see also DEVALUATION).

DEPRESSANT, an agent that depresses any organ, but specifically the functioning of the central NERVOUS SYSTEM. Reduction of the level of consciousness and impaired control of breathing are serious effects, usually seen in overdosage. Many drugs including alcohol, BARBITURATES and SEDATIVES are depressants. The loss of inhibition associated with their use may be due to a differential depressant effect.

DEPRESSION, a common psychiatric disease with pathologically depressed mood and characteristic somatic and sleep disturbance. It is divided into those due to external factors, and those where depression arises without obvious cause, including manic-depressive illness. SHOCK THERAPY, ANTIDEPRESSANTS and psychotherapy are usually successful.

DEPRESSION, Economic, major decline in business activity. It involves sharp reductions in industrial production, bankruptcies, massive unemployment and a general loss of business confidence. Although minor recessions occur regularly among the industrial nations, the most widespread was the GREAT DEPRESSION commencing in 1929.

DEPTH CHARGE, explosive device for use against submarines and other underwater targets, developed by Britain to counter the U-boat menace in WWI. The charge explodes not on contact but at a preset depth, relying on concussive effect.

DEPTH OF FIELD, in PHOTOGRAPHY, the distance between the nearest and farthest planes from the CAMERA for which the image formed in the film plane is reasonably in focus. The available depth of field depends both on the quality of the LENS employed and on the aperture stop. The greater the aperture (the lower the *f*/number), the shorter the depth of field, and vice versa.

DE QUINCEY, Thomas (1785–1859), English essayist and critic, author of *Confessions of an English Opium Eater* (1821), in which he recounted his experiences under opium. His output, affected by lifelong opium addiction, was erratic, but included some penetrating essays and powerful descriptions of drug-inspired dreams.

DERAIN, André (1880–1954), French painter, one of the original Fauves (see FAUVISM). He was also attracted for a time to CUBISM. Later, rejecting non-representational extremes, he returned to a more traditional style.

DERBY, borough in N central England, seat of Derbyshire, on the Derwent R. It is a railroad center, famous for the manufacture of porcelain. Pop 219 348.

DERBY, town in central Col., Adams Co., a suburb of Denver. Pop 10 206.

DERBY, city in S Conn. It manufactures rubber, hardware and metal goods. Pop 12 599.

DERBY, classic annual horse race at Epsom, England, instituted in 1780 by the 12th Earl of Derby. (See also KENTUCKY DERBY.)

DERBY, Edward (George Geoffrey Smith) Stanley, 14th Earl of (1799–1869), British statesman and Conservative prime minister 1852, 1858 and 1866–68. His third and last administration saw the passing of the REFORM BILL of 1867, which increased the franchise.

DERIVATIVE. See CALCULUS.

DERMATITIS, SKIN conditions in which INFLAMMATION occurs. These include ECZEMA, contact dermatitis (see ALLERGY) and seborrheic dermatitis (see DANDRUFF). Acute dermatitis leads to redness, swelling, blistering and crusting, while chronic forms usually show scaling or thickening of skin. Cool lotions and dressings, and ointments are used in acute cases, whereas tars are often useful in more chronic conditions. Avoidance of allergens in contact or allergic dermatitis is essential.

DERMATOLOGY, subspeciality of MEDICINE concerned with the diagnosis and treatment of SKIN DISEASES: a largely visual speciality, but aided by skin BIOPSY in certain instances. Judicious use of lotions, ointments, creams (including STEROID creams) and tars is the essence of treatment, while the recognition of ALLERGY, infection and skin manifestations of systemic disease are tasks for the dermatologist.

DERRICK. See CRANE.

DERRINGER, short-barreled pocket pistol of large caliber. It was designed by Henry Derringer, Jr. (1786–1868), a Philadelphia gunsmith.

DERRY, town in SE N.H. It manufactures shoes and wood products. Robert Frost wrote some of his best known poems there. Pop 11 712.

DERVISH, a Muslim mystic, member of one of the Sufi brotherhoods that emerged in about the 12th century. Members served a period of initiation under a teacher and each order had its own ritual for inducing a mystic state which stressed their dependence on the unseen world. The best known are the "whirling" and "howling" dervishes, who used forms of dancing and singing. (See also SUFISM.)

DERZHAVIN, Gavrila Romanovich (1743–1816), one of the greatest poets of 18th-century Russia. He held high office under Catherine the Great, whom he praised in the ode, *Felitsa* (1782). His lyrics and odes also include the *Ode to the Deity* (1784).

DESALINATION, or **desalting**, the conversion of salt or brackish water into usable fresh water. DISTILLATION is the most common commercial method; heat from the sun or conventional fuels vaporizes BRINE, the vapor condensing into fresh water on cooling. Reverse OSMOSIS and electrodialysis (see DIALYSIS) both remove salt from water by the use of semipermeable membranes; these processes are more suitable for brackish water. Pure water crystals may also be separated from brine by freezing. The biggest problem holding back the wider adoption of desalination techniques is that of how to meet the high ENERGY costs of all such processes. Only where energy is relatively cheap and water particularly scarce is desalination economic, and even then complex energy conservation procedures must be built into the plant.

DESCARTES, René, or **Renatus Cartesius** (1596–1650), mathematician, physicist and the foremost of French philosophers, who founded a rationalist, à priorist school of philosophy known as **Cartesianism**. After being educated in his native France and spending time in military service (1618–19) and traveling, Descartes spent most of his creative life in Holland (1625–49) before entering the service of Queen Christiana of Sweden shortly before his death. In mathematics Descartes founded the study of ANALYTIC GEOMETRY, introducing the use of CARTESIAN COORDINATES. He found in the deductive logic of mathematical reasoning a paradigm for a new methodology of science, first publishing his conclusions in his *Discourse on Method* (1637). The occult qualities of late scholastic science were to be done away with; only ideas which were clear and distinct were to be employed. To discover what ideas could be used to form a certain basis for a unified A PRIORI science, he introduced the method of universal doubt; he questioned everything. The first certitude he discovered was his famous *cogito ergo sum* (I think therefore I am) and on the basis of this, the existence of other bodies, and of God, he worked out his philosophy. In science, Descartes, denying the possibility of a VACUUM, explained everything in terms of motion in a plenum of particles whose sole property was extension. This yielded his celebrated but ultimately unsuccessful VORTEX theory of the solar system and statements of the principle of INERTIA and the laws of ordinary REFRACTION. In psychology Descartes upheld a strict DUALISM: there were no causal relationships between physical and mental substances. In biology, his views were mechanistic; he regarded animals as but complex machines.

DESCHUTES RIVER, river in central and N Ore., 250mi long. It rises in SW Deschutes Co., and flows N into the Columbia R. It is used for hydroelectric power and irrigation.

DESCRIPTIVE GEOMETRY, the branch of GEOMETRY concerned with the representation of three-dimensional objects on a PLANE, the basis of architectural drawing (see ARCHITECTURE). There are two main systems of projection: the PERSPECTIVE view, in which the object is projected from a POINT onto a plane (see PROJECTIVE GEOMETRY); and orthographic projection, where the object is projected from one plane into another. In **orthographic projection**, two planes are considered, at right ANGLES to each other, the vertical plane and the horizontal plane, intersecting in a line termed the ground line. From each point of the object, PERPENDICULARS are dropped to each of the two planes, giving the horizontal and vertical coordinates of that point. The representation of this on a plane surface is achieved by considering the two planes to be hinged along the ground line so that the horizontal plane may be rotated through 90° to coincide with the vertical, thus providing a graphical representation of the object.

DESEGREGATION. See INTEGRATION.

DESERET, State of, name chosen by the MORMONS in 1849 for the state they had settled. The US Congress, however, rejected their application for admission to the Union.

DESERTS, areas where life has extreme difficulty in surviving. Deserts cover about one third of the earth's land area. There are two types.

Cold Deserts. In cold deserts, water is unavailable during most of the year as it is trapped in the form of ice. Cold deserts include the Antarctic polar icecap,

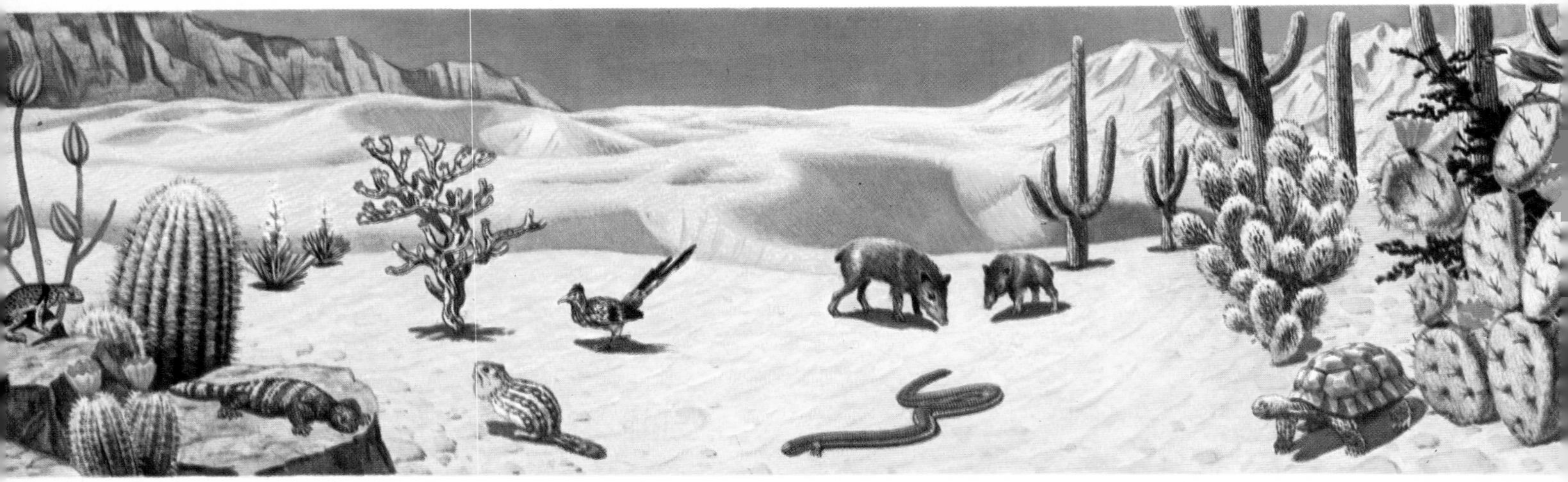

The desert has two different faces: during the day (*top*) cacti are a commonly visible feature of most deserts. To adapt to desert conditions, herbivorous animals absorb water from desert plants, carnivorous creatures find moisture in the blood of their prey, while cacti cope with the extreme dryness by developing long roots which absorb as much of the available water as possible, and spines to prevent its evaporation. At night (*bottom*) the picture changes—animals that hide from the sun during the day appear, and there is even a cactus, the Wilcoxia (*extreme left*), which only flowers at night.

the barren wastes of Greenland, and much of the TUNDRA. (See also GLACIER.) Eskimos, Lapps and Samoyeds are among the ethnic groups inhabiting such areas in the N Hemisphere. Their animal neighbors include seals and the polar bear.

Hot Deserts. These typically lie between latitudes 20° and 30° N and S, though they exist also farther from the equator in the centers of continental landmasses. They can be described as areas where water precipitation from the ATMOSPHERE is greatly exceeded by surface EVAPORATION and plant TRANSPIRATION. The best known, and largest, is the Sahara. GROUNDWATER exists but is normally far below the surface; here and there it is accessible as SPRINGS OR WELLS (see ARTESIAN WELL; OASIS). In recent years, IRRIGATION has enabled reclamation of much desert land. Landscapes generally result from the surface's extreme vulnerability to EROSION (see also SOIL EROSION). Features include arroyos, BUTTES, DUNES, MESAS and WADIS. The influence of man may assist peripheral areas to become susceptible to erosion, and thus temporarily advance the desert's boundaries. (See also DUST BOWL; SANDSTORM.)

Plants may survive by being able to store water, like the cactus; by having tiny leaves to reduce evaporation loss, like the paloverde; or by having extensive ROOT systems to capture maximum moisture, like the mesquite. (See also DRY FARMING.) Animals may be nomadic, or spend the daylight hours underground. Best adapted of all is the camel.

DESERTION, unjustified abandonment of an obligation. In civil law, desertion is abandonment of a spouse or children of the marriage without the consent of the other party or parties. If continued for a specified period, marital desertion is grounds for DIVORCE in most states of the US.

DE SEVERSKY, Alexander Procofieff (1894–), Russian-born US aviator and aeronautical engineer. He founded the Seversky Aero Corporation in 1922, and has served as an adviser to the US government.

DE SICA, Vittorio (1901–1974), Italian film director. His earlier films, such as *The Bicycle Thief* (1948), are outstanding for their compassionate treatment of social problems in the Neorealist style. The later films are not thought to be of the same standard, though many, like the *Garden of the Finzi Continis* (1971), have won international acclaim.

DESIDERIO DA SETTIGNANO (c1430–1464), one of the foremost Italian sculptors of the Early Renaissance. His delicate style with its wealth of detail is exemplified in fine works in the churches of Santa Croce and San Lorenzo, both in Florence.

DESIDERIUS (ruled 757–774), last king of the Lombards, in N Italy. He invaded papal lands in 771, but Charlemagne (his former son-in-law) supported the pope and Desiderius was defeated. Italy became part of Charlemagne's empire.

DE SITTER, Willem. See SITTER, WILLEM DE.

DESMANS, two species of aquatic mammals related to the moles and included in the family Talpidae, *Desmana moschata* and *Galemys pyrenaicus*. Found in Europe, they live in holes in river banks. They are hunted in Russia for their fur.

DE SMET, Pierre Jean (1801–1870), Belgian-born Jesuit missionary to the North American Indians. His work among several tribes won their friendship, and he often acted as a peacemaker for the government, as when he started negotiations with SITTING BULL and the SIOUX INDIANS.

DES MOINES, capital and largest city of Ia., seat of Polk Co. Founded in 1843, it is now an important commercial, educational, governmental and communications center. Industries include plastics, chemicals, printing and agricultural implements. Pop 200 587.

DESMOULINS, Camille (1760–1794), journalist and leader in the FRENCH REVOLUTION. His oratory helped incite the mob to storm the BASTILLE in 1789, and his writing helped to radicalize public opinion. He and DANTON led the moderate faction in 1793–94, and were eventually arrested and guillotined.

DE SOTO, Hernando (1500–1542), Spanish explorer, discoverer of the Mississippi R. He served as second in command in PIZARRO's conquests in Peru (1531–35), and supported the Inca emperor ATAHUALPA. He returned to Spain with a fortune and set out again to explore the Florida region. He landed in 1539 at Charlotte Harbor and spent two years exploring what is now the SE US. He reached the Mississippi R in May 1541, and the expedition went on to Arkansas and Louisiana, where De Soto died.

DES PLAINES, city in NE Illinois, a suburb of Chicago. It is a manufacturing center. Pop 57 239.

DESPOTISM, system of government where one person rules without any constitutional controls. The term is now used in a pejorative sense, but in the 18th century the concept of "enlightened" or "benevolent" despotism was fashionable. (See also ABSOLUTISM; DICTATORSHIP.)

DES PRÉS, Josquin. See JOSQUIN DES PRÉS.

DESSALINES, Jean-Jacques (1758–1806), first Negro emperor of Haiti. Brought to Haiti as a slave, he took part in the rebellion against the French in the 1790s. After the final expulsion of the French in 1803 he became governor-general. In 1804 he proclaimed an independent country and took the title of Emperor

Jacques I. His rule, characterized by extreme hostility to whites, ended when he was killed in a mulatto revolt.

DESSAU, city in S central East Germany, 70mi SW of Berlin. It is a manufacturing center, and was the seat of the BAUHAUS school 1925–32. Pop 98 100.

DE STIJL, modern art movement in the Netherlands taking its name from the magazine *De Stijl* (*The Style*). Founded in 1917 by a group of artists including MONDRIAN and Van DOESBURG, it stressed purity of line and the use of primary colors. Its theories were also applied to interior decoration, furniture and architecture, of which the Schröder House in Utrecht (1924) is a good example.

DESTROYER, small, fast naval vessel which evolved in the 1890s out of earlier torpedo boats. In the two world wars destroyers were used principally as escorts for convoys and for attacking submarines. Some of the modern destroyers are nuclear-powered and many carry guided missiles.

DETERGENTS. See SOAPS AND DETERGENTS.

DETERMINANT, a square array of numbers, each a member of a FIELD F, used to represent another number in F. Consider the four numbers a_1, a_2, b_1, b_2. The determinant

$$\begin{vmatrix} a_1 & b_1 \\ a_2 & b_2 \end{vmatrix} = |\mathbf{A}|$$

(see MATRICES) is described as a determinant of order 2 over F and defined to have value

$$+a_1b_2 - a_2b_1.$$

Notice that transposition (i.e., exchange of rows for columns) does not affect the value of $|\mathbf{A}|$:

$$\begin{vmatrix} a_1 & a_2 \\ b_1 & b_2 \end{vmatrix} = +a_1b_2 - b_1a_2 = |\mathbf{A}|$$

(since multiplication in F is commutative: see ALGEBRA). This is true also of higher order determinants, so that every theorem applied to the columns of a determinant may equally be applied to its rows, and vice versa. Notice also that each of the terms in $+a_1b_2 - a_2b_1$ contains exactly one number from each row and one from each column; thus the value of a determinant of order 2 has 2 terms, one of order 3 has 6 terms, and one of order n has $n!$ terms (see FACTORIAL). Other properties of determinants include:

(1) If the elements of any row are multiplied by a factor c, then the new determinant has a value c times that of the original.

(2) Interchanging two rows of a determinant creates a new determinant with a value equal to that of the original multiplied by (-1).

(3) If two rows of a determinant are proportional the determinant has a value 0 (a special case of this is when two rows are identical).

(4) Addition of the elements of one row to the elements of another does not alter the value of the determinant.

The theory of determinants closely parallels that of linear simultaneous EQUATIONS. Consider

$$a_1x + b_1y + c_1 = 0,$$
$$a_2x + b_2y + c_2 = 0.$$

These imply that

$$a_2(a_1x + b_1y + c_1) - a_1(a_2x + b_2y + c_2) = 0,$$
$$b_2(a_1x + b_1y + c_1) - b_1(a_2x + b_2y + c_2) = 0.$$

These may be restated, respectively, as

$$(a_1b_2 - a_2b_1)y - (c_1a_2 - c_2a_1) = 0,$$
$$(a_1b_2 - a_2b_1)x - (c_2b_1 - c_1b_2) = 0.$$

The solutions, assuming that

$$\begin{vmatrix} a_1 & b_1 \\ a_2 & b_2 \end{vmatrix} \neq 0,$$

may therefore be expressed in the form

$$x = \frac{\begin{vmatrix} b_1 & c_1 \\ b_2 & c_2 \end{vmatrix}}{\begin{vmatrix} a_1 & b_1 \\ a_2 & b_2 \end{vmatrix}}, \quad y = \frac{\begin{vmatrix} c_1 & a_1 \\ c_2 & a_2 \end{vmatrix}}{\begin{vmatrix} a_1 & b_1 \\ a_2 & b_2 \end{vmatrix}}.$$

DETERMINISM, the philosophical theory that all events are determined (inescapably caused) by preexisting events which, when considered in the context of inviolable physical laws, completely account for the subsequent events. The case for determinism has been variously argued from the inviolability of the laws of nature and from the omniscience and omnipotence of God. Determinism is often taken to be opposed to the principles of FREE WILL and indeterminacy.

DETONATOR, a small explosive device used to initiate the explosion of a main explosive charge in quarrying, mining or tunneling operations and in AMMUNITION. Safer, i.e., less sensitive, EXPLOSIVES need stronger detonators. The typical detonator comprises a thin-walled metal or plastic tube containing a charge of MERCURY fulminate ($Hg(ONC)_2$) or, now more common, LEAD azide (PbN_6), often mixed with other chemicals. The detonator is set off by a flame from a safety fuze or electrically, by passing a current through an attached resistance wire.

DETROIT, city in SE Mich., situated on the W bank of the Detroit R, directly opposite the city of Windsor, Canada. The fifth-largest city in the US and the world's largest automobile manufacturing center: over a quarter of all America's cars are built there. It is also the country's third-ranking overseas trade port and a major Great Lakes shipping center. A major steel center, Detroit produces a wide variety of metal goods and machine tools; pharmaceuticals, paints and chemicals are other important industries. One of the largest salt mines in the US lies beneath the city. Detroit is also a prominent educational and cultural center: Wayne State U. and the U. of Detroit, the city's symphony orchestra and the Detroit Institute of Arts are nationally known.

The city's history began in 1701 with the founding by Antoine CADILLAC, at "la place détroit," of a French trading post. It rapidly gained in importance and was a British possession 1706–96. Rebuilt after a fire in 1805, it was capital of Mich. until 1847; it achieved city status in 1815. Auto building had already begun by 1896, and within 10 years such famous firms as Cadillac, Ford, Oldsmobile and Packard were well established. Pop 1 511 482.

DETROIT RIVER, important commercial waterway in SE Mich., about 31mi long, flowing from Lake St. Clair S to Lake Erie. It separates SE Mich from S Ontario and so forms part of the international boundary between the US and Canada.

DEUCALION, in Greek mythology, the son of PROMETHEUS. Acting on his father's advice, he and his wife, Pyrrha, built an ark—in time to escape a flood ordained by Zeus which drowned the rest of mankind. After their landing on Mt Parnassus, they obeyed an oracle and threw some stones behind them. Deucalion's became men, Pyrrha's women.

The destroyer USS *William R. Rush.* Destroyers evolved in the late 19th century from torpedo boats and torpedo-boat destroyers; many are now equipped with nuclear weapons and are capable of speeds of up to 37 knots.

DEUSDEDIT. See ADEODATUS.

DEUTERIUM (D or $_1H^2$), or "heavy hydrogen," an ISOTOPE of HYDROGEN discovered in 1931, whose nucleus (the deuteron) has one PROTON and one NEUTRON (see also TRITIUM). It forms 0.014% of the hydrogen in naturally occurring hydrogen compounds, such as water, and is chemically very like ordinary hydrogen, except that it reacts more slowly. It is obtained as HEAVY WATER by the fractional electrolysis of WATER. Deuterium is the major fuel for nuclear FUSION (see HYDROGEN BOMB) and is used in tracer studies. (See also NUCLEAR REACTORS.) AW 2.0, mp −254.6°C, bp −249.7°C.

DEUTEROMYCETES, or fungi imperfecti. See FUNGI.

DEUTERONOMY, fifth book of the Old Testament and last book of the PENTATEUCH. Supposedly a testament left by Moses to the Israelites about to enter Canaan, it is primarily a recapitulation of moral laws and laws relating to the settlement of Canaan. Much of it was written long after Moses, parts being added during the reforms under King JOSIAH (621 BC). It may have been the "Book of the Law" discovered by Hilkiah in the Temple at that time.

DEUTSCHER, Isaac (1907–1967), Polish-born English historian and influential journalist who in 1939 escaped from Poland to England. An expert on Soviet affairs, his main works are his biography of Stalin (1949) and his trilogy on the life of Trotsky (1954, 1959 and 1963).

DEUTZIA, genus of deciduous flowering shrubs native to Mexico, Japan, China and the Himalayas, now widely cultivated for their white, pink and purple flowers. Many hybrids have been bred.

DEUXIÈME BUREAU, French security and intelligence department controlled by the ministry of defense. The armed services each have a *deuxième bureau* which gathers and transmits intelligence to the ministry. The *securité militaire* is responsible for security within the services themselves.

DE VACA, Álvar Nuñez Cabeza. See CABEZA DE VACA, ÁLVAR NUÑEZ.

DE VALÉRA, Eamon (1882–1975), Irish statesman, prime minister 1937–48, 1951–54, 1957–59; and president of Ireland 1959–73. Born in New York City, he was raised in Ireland, and became an ardent republican. Only his US citizenship saved him from execution after the 1916 EASTER RISING. He was imprisoned by the IRISH FREE STATE for refusing to recognize the Anglo-Irish treaty of 1922; in 1927 he organized the FIANNA FÁIL party which won power in 1932. In 1937 he declared Ireland independent of Britain, and during WWII preserved Irish neutrality.

DE VALOIS, Dame Ninette (Edris Stannus; 1898–), British dancer and choreographer, founder of the company at Sadler's Wells which, in 1956, became the Royal Ballet. She directed the company 1931–63.

DEVALUATION, official reduction by a country of the value of its currency in relation to gold or other currencies. It is a swift way of enhancing the competitiveness of a country's exports when a BALANCE OF PAYMENTS crisis threatens.

DE VEGA, LOPE. See VEGA, LOPE DE.

DEVENTER, city in the Netherlands, on the IJssel R, about 65mi E of Amsterdam. An important commercial and industrial center, producing textiles, carpets and chemicals. Thomas à Kempis and Erasmus studied there. Pop 66 318.

DEVEREUX, ROBERT. See ESSEX, 2ND EARL OF.

DEVIL (from Greek *diabolos*, slanderer or accuser), in Western religions and sects, the chief spirit of evil and commander of lesser evil spirits or DEMONS. Dualistic systems (see DUALISM)—notably ZOROASTRIANISM, GNOSTICISM and MANICHAEISM—have regarded the devil as the uncreated equal of God, engaged in an eternal war for evil against good. Such beliefs, often leading to devil worship, have appeared sporadically in connection with the OCCULT. In Judaism, Christianity and Islam, the devil, SATAN, is a fallen angel, powerful but subordinate to God, who opposes God and tempts mankind, but is to be utterly defeated and bound at the LAST JUDGMENT. (See also EXORCISM; MAGIC.)

George Dewey's flagship, the USS *Olympia*, is now preserved as a naval museum in Philadelphia. An American naval hero, Dewey succeeded in destroying the entire Spanish eastern fleet as it lay at anchor in Manila harbor.

DEVIL RAYS, large ray-like cartilaginous fishes which have wing-like pectoral fins. They are surface-feeding fishes eating small crustaceans and plankton. Despite their large size and a devilish appearance, they are generally harmless to man. Family: Mobulidae.

DEVIL'S ADVOCATE. See ADVOCATUS DIABOLI.

DEVIL'S ISLAND, small island off the coast of French Guiana. Formerly the site of a notorious French penal colony for political prisoners, among whom was Alfred DREYFUS. The penal colony was abolished in 1938.

DEVILS POSTPILE NATIONAL MONUMENT, on the San Joaquin R in central Cal., is a cliff about 60ft high and a fifth of a mile long, formed of hexagonal-sectioned basaltic columns.

DEVILS TOWER NATIONAL MONUMENT, in NE Wyo., is an exposed volcanic plug, rising 865ft above the ridge on which it stands. Flat-topped and fluted, it resembles a huge tree stump. Established in 1906, it was the first US national monument.

DEVOLUTION, War of (1667–68), conflict between Spain and France over the right of succession to the Spanish Netherlands. LOUIS XIV claimed that by an old law of devolution the territory should have reverted to his wife MARIE THÉRÈSE upon the death of her father, Philip IV. Although his military campaign was successful, Louis was forced to withdraw in the face of the Triple Alliance of England, the United Provinces and Sweden; and the matter was settled in 1668 (see AIX-LA-CHAPELLE, TREATIES OF), Spain ceding to France 12 small fortified towns along the French border.

DEVONIAN, the fourth period of the PALEOZOIC, which lasted from about 400 to 345 million years ago. (See GEOLOGY.)

DE VOTO, Bernard Augustine (1897–1955), US journalist and author. He won national fame as a contributor to *Harpers Magazine*. His books include *Mark Twain's America* (1932), *Across the Wide Missouri* (1948 Pulitzer Prize) and the novel *The Crooked Mile* (1924).

DEVOY, John (1842–1928), Irish-American journalist and dedicated Irish patriot and propagandist. He founded, in the US, the *Irish Nation* (1881) and the *Gaelic-American* (1903). A supporter of the SINN FEIN party during WWI, he organized backing for the Easter Rising of 1916.

DE VRIES, Hugo. See VRIES, HUGO DE.

DEW, water droplets produced on clear calm nights by CONDENSATION of water vapor in the air. It is deposited on surfaces freely exposed to the sky which have cooled by RADIATION of heat. Dew forms when the air TEMPERATURE falls to the **dew point**. This, the temperature at which the air becomes saturated with water vapor, rises rapidly with the HUMIDITY. Dew is an important source of moisture for desert plants.

DEWAR, Sir James (1842–1923), British chemist and physicist who proposed various structures (including the "Dewar structures") for BENZENE, invented the VACUUM FLASK (Dewar bottle—1892) and pioneered the techniques of low-temperature physics. He developed methods for liquifying gases and discovered the magnetic properties of liquid OXYGEN and OZONE.

DEWBERRY, species of the genus *Rubus*, family Rosaceae, with stems that trail along the ground. They are closely related to the BLACKBERRY and are frequently called trailing blackberries.

DEWEY, George (1837–1917), US naval hero promoted admiral of the navy—the highest possible rank—for his victory at the Battle of Manila Bay and the capture of the Philippines from Spain. On May 1, 1898, during the SPANISH-AMERICAN WAR, Dewey led the Asiatic squadron into Manila Bay and, without losing a man, destroyed the Spanish eastern fleet. In August, aided by Filipino rebels and US army forces, he received the surrender of Manila; the Philippines then fell to the US. Dewey later served as president of the general board of the Navy Department.

DEWEY, John (1859–1952), US philosopher and educator, the founder of the philosophical school known as INSTRUMENTALISM (or experimentalism) and the leading promotor of educational reform in the early years of the 20th century. Profoundly influenced by the PRAGMATISM of William JAMES, Dewey developed a philosophy in which ideas and concepts were validated by their practicality. He taught that "learning by doing" should form the basis of educational practice, though in later life he came to criticize the "progressive" movement in education, which, in abandoning formal tuition altogether, he felt had misused his educational theory.

DEWEY, Melvil (1851–1931), US librarian who, at Amherst College, devised the DEWEY DECIMAL SYSTEM (published 1876). He founded the *Library Journal* (1883) and, at Columbia College, the first school of librarianship.

DEWEY, Thomas Edmund (1902–1971), US lawyer and Republican politician, defeated for the presidency in 1948 by Harry S. Truman, although his election had been thought a foregone conclusion. In the 1930s, as US attorney for the southern district of N.Y. state and then as special prosecutor in New York City, Dewey gained a national reputation for successful campaigning against organized crime. He was governor of N.Y. 1943–55. He declined the post of chief justice under Richard M. Nixon (1968).

DEWEY DECIMAL SYSTEM, a system devised by Melvil DEWEY (1851–1931) for use in the classification of books in libaries, and based on the DECIMAL SYSTEM of numbers. Dewey divided knowledge into ten main areas, each of these into ten subdivisions, and so on. Thus a book could fall into one of a thousand categories, from 000 to 999. Extensions of this system added further classificatory numbers after the decimal point.

DE WITT, Jan (1625–1672), Dutch statesman, grand pensionary (ruler) of Holland 1653–72, and republican opponent of the House of Orange. In 1667 he made peace with England (see BREDA, DECLARATION OF) and, in 1668, negotiated the Triple Alliance with England and Sweden against Louis XIV, to end the War of DEVOLUTION. After the victory of the Orange party, he and his brother **Cornelius De Witt** (1623–1672) were brutally murdered by a mob.

DEW LINE (*D*istant *E*arly *W*arning Line), joint Canadian-United States defense chain of about 60 radar posts, mainly along or near the 70th parallel, some on land, some on ships or planes. Completed in 1958, it was designed to give up to two hours' advance warning of the approach of hostile aircraft and 15–30 minutes' warning of an intercontinental ballistic-missile attack.

DEXTRIN, a polysaccharide (see CARBOHYDRATES) obtained from STARCH by heating or partial HYDROLYSIS with acids, DIASTASE or the bacterium *Bacillus macerans*. Soluble in water, it is used as an adhesive and a size for paper and textiles.

DEZHNEV, Cape. See EAST CAPE.

DHARMA, important concept in HINDUISM, BUDDHISM and JAINISM. To Hindus, it denotes the universal law ordaining religious and social institutions, the rights and duties of individuals or, simply, virtuous conduct. Buddhists consider it the universal truth proclaimed to all men by Buddha. In Jainism, it also represents an eternal substance.

DHAULAGIRI, Himalayan mountain peak in N Nepal. The seventh highest (26 810ft) in the world, it was first climbed in 1960 by a Swiss expedition.

DHOLE, Sinhalese name for the wild dog of southern Asia. Dholes live in packs and run down their prey; females rear their young in communal dens. They are almost untamable.

DIABASE, or **dolerite,** dark IGNEOUS ROCK intermediate in grain size between BASALT and GABBRO. Consisting of plagioclase FELDSPAR and PYROXENE, it is a widespread intrusive rock, quarried for crushed and monumental stone (known as "black granite").

DIABETES, a common systemic disease, affecting between 0.5 and 1% of the population, and characterized by the absent or inadequate secretion of INSULIN, the principal hormone controlling BLOOD sugar. There are many causes, including heredity, VIRUS infection, primary disease of the PANCREAS and OBESITY. Though it may start at any time, two main groups are recognized: juvenile (beginning in childhood, adolescence or early adult life)—due to inability to secrete insulin; and late onset (late middle life or old age)—associated with obesity and with a relative lack of insulin. High blood sugar may lead to coma, often with keto-ACIDOSIS, excessive thirst and high urine output, weight loss, ill-health and liability to infections. The disease may be detected by urine or blood tests and confirmed by a glucose tolerance test. It causes disease of small blood vessels, as well as premature ARTERIOSCLEROSIS, RETINA disease, CATARACTS, KIDNEY disease and NEURITIS. Poor blood supply, neuritis and infection may lead to chronic leg ULCERS. Once recognized, diabetes needs treatment to stabilize the blood sugar level and keep it within strict limits. Regular medical surveillance and education is essential to minimize complications. Dietary carbohydrate must be controlled and for late onset cases this may be all that is needed; in this group, drugs that increase the body's insulin production are valuable. In juvenile and some late onset cases, insulin itself is needed, given by subcutaneous injection by the patient. Regular dosage, adjusted to usual diet and activity, is used but surgery, PREGNANCY and infection increase insulin requirement. Control can be assessed by a simple urine test. Insulin overdose can occur, with sweating, confusion and COMA, and prompt treatment with sugar is crucial. EYE complications should be recognized early, especially in juvenile onset cases, as early intervention may prevent or delay BLINDNESS.

DIADOCHI, the generals of ALEXANDER THE GREAT who, after his death in 323 BC, divided his empire among themselves. They included ANTIGONUS, ANTIPATER, PTOLEMY and Seleucus (see SELEUCIDS).

DIAGHILEV, Sergei Pavlovich (1872–1929), Russian impresario and founder (Paris, 1909) of the Ballets Russes which inaugurated modern BALLET. His magazine *World of Art* (1899–1904) led a movement for Russian involvement in Western European arts. He moved to Paris in 1906. The Ballets Russes broke with the formalism of classical choreography and aimed to unify music, dance and stage design. Its productions included the dancers and choreographers FOKINE, PAVLOVA, NIJINSKY and MASSINE, the composers STRAVINSKY and PROKOFIEV and the designers BENOIS and BAKST. MATISSE, PICASSO, DEBUSSY and RAVEL also worked for Diaghilev.

DIAGONAL, in plane GEOMETRY, a straight line joining two non-consecutive vertices of a POLYGON.

DIAGNOSIS. See DISEASE.

DIALECTIC, in philosophy, variously: a method of forcing a respondent to alter his opinion by leading him into self-contradiction (SOCRATES); the process of getting to know the world of ideal forms (PLATO); sound reasoning from generally accepted opinions rather than from self-evident truths (ARISTOTLE); argument exposing the folly of reasoning that employs the categories of the understanding outside the world of experience (KANT), or a dynamic logic, common to true philosophy and historical process, in which

apparent contradictories—theses and antitheses—are reconciled in syntheses (HEGEL).

DIALECTICAL MATERIALISM, a general theory based on the works of MARX and ENGELS which is the official philosophy of the USSR and other communist states (see also MARXISM). It holds that the material world has reality independently of the mind, and that mental and spiritual states are reflections of material conditions (contrary to HEGEL); that all things in the material world contain opposing aspects and are in a state of tension, which leads to transformation and development. The theory is used to explain change in human society (historical materialism): every phase of society develops as a dialectical process, so that the capitalist state produces the proletarian class which is necessarily opposed to it and which eventually overthrows it.

DIALYSIS, process of selective DIFFUSION of ions and molecules through a semipermeable membrane which retains COLLOID particles and macromolecules. It is accelerated by applying an electric field (see ELECTROPHORESIS). Dialysis is used for DESALINATION and in artificial kidneys (see ARTIFICIAL ORGANS). (See also OSMOSIS.)

DIAMAGNETISM, very weak magnetization (see MAGNETISM) of a material in a direction opposing the magnetizing field, due to ELECTRON orbital distortion. It is a property of all materials, though sometimes masked by stronger PARAMAGNETISM or ferromagnetism.

DIAMETER, the LINE joining any two points on the surface of a geometrical figure and passing through its center. The term is most often used in connection with the CIRCLE and SPHERE, all of whose infinitely many diameters have equal length.

DIAMOND, allotrope of CARBON (see ALLOTROPY), forming colorless cubic crystals. Diamond is the hardest known substance, with a Mohs hardness of 10, which varies slightly with the orientation of the crystal. Thus diamonds can be cut only by other diamonds. They do not conduct electricity, but conduct heat extremely well. Diamond burns when heated in air to 900°C; in an inert atmosphere it reverts to GRAPHITE slowly at 1000°C, rapidly at 1700°C. Diamonds occur naturally in dikes and pipes of KIMBERLITE, notably in South Africa (Orange Free State and Transvaal), Tanzania, and in the US at Murfreesboro, Ark. They are also mined from secondary (alluvial) deposits, especially in Brazil, Zaire, Sierra Leone and India. The diamonds are separated by mechanical panning, and those of GEM quality are cleaved (or sawn), cut and polished. Inferior, or industrial, diamonds are used for cutting, drilling and grinding. Synthetic industrial diamonds are made by subjecting graphite to very high temperatures and pressures, sometimes with fused metals as solvent. sg 3.51.

DIAMOND HEAD, extinct volcano forming a 761ft high promontory on the SE shore of Oahu, Hawaii. An ancient burial ground, it is now the site of US Fort Ruger.

In 1919, the mathematician Tolkówsky computed how a gem diamond could best be cut to give the maximum reflection and brilliance (*below left*).

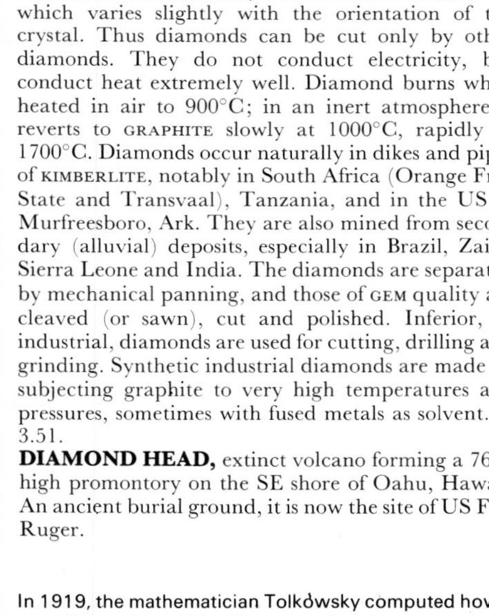

Below right: a diamond crystal embedded in kimberlite rock, found in the great Kimberley diamond mine in South Africa. This crystal is about 10mm across.

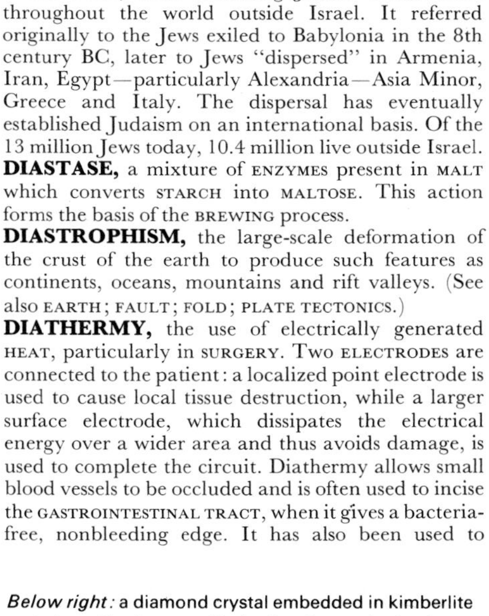

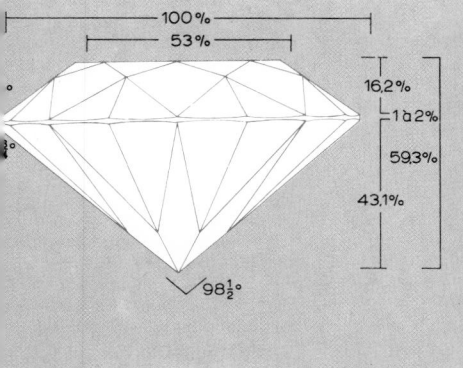

DIAMOND NECKLACE AFFAIR, celebrated scandal at the French court in 1785 which seriously discredited Queen MARIE ANTOINETTE. The comtesse de La Motte duped Cardinal de Rohan into acquiring a necklace for the queen, but in fact kept it for herself. There was uncertainty about the queen's involvement but the cardinal's trial and Louis XVI's handling of the case suggested government weakness and corruption.

DIANA, Roman goddess of the moon, forests, animals and women in childbirth, identified with the Greek goddess ARTEMIS. She is usually represented as a huntress, accompanied by a deer or a hound. Her most famous shrine was near modern Ariccia, Italy.

DIAPHRAGM, thin muscular and fibrous structure dividing the contents of the CHEST from those of the ABDOMEN. It is involved to a varying degree in quiet breathing and also contracts during deep breathing and straining. Through it pass the ESOPHAGUS, AORTA and inferior VENA CAVA, the first by a small opening or hiatus, through which part of the STOMACH may slide into the chest causing a hiatus HERNIA.

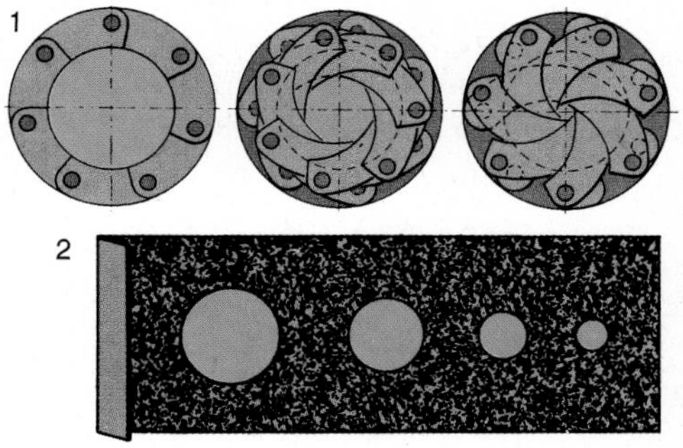

In photography, the term diaphragm refers to devices used in cameras and enlargers to control the amount of light falling on the sensitive film or paper. Commonest is the iris type (1), but inexpensive cameras often use a sliding (2) or revolving (3) diaphragm.

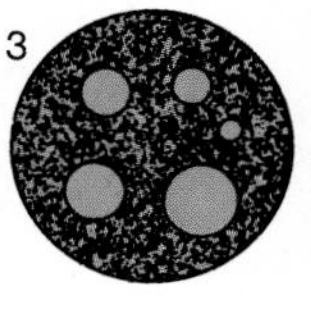

DIARRHEA, loose and/or frequent bowel motions. A common effect of FOOD POISONING, GASTROINTESTINAL TRACT infection (e.g., DYSENTERY, CHOLERA) or INFLAMMATION (e.g., COLITIS, ENTERITIS, ABSCESS), drugs and systemic diseases. Benign or malignant TUMORS of the colon and rectum may also cause diarrhea. Slime or blood indicate severe inflammation or tumor.

DIAS (or Diaz), Bartholomeu (d. 1500), Portuguese navigator and explorer who, in 1488, discovered the sea route around Africa past the Cape of Good Hope to India. He explored much of the W coast of Africa. In 1500 he took part in Pedro CABRAL's expedition, which discovered Brazil.

DIASPORA, term describing Jewish communities throughout the world outside Israel. It referred originally to the Jews exiled to Babylonia in the 8th century BC, later to Jews "dispersed" in Armenia, Iran, Egypt—particularly Alexandria—Asia Minor, Greece and Italy. The dispersal has eventually established Judaism on an international basis. Of the 13 million Jews today, 10.4 million live outside Israel.

DIASTASE, a mixture of ENZYMES present in MALT which converts STARCH into MALTOSE. This action forms the basis of the BREWING process.

DIASTROPHISM, the large-scale deformation of the crust of the earth to produce such features as continents, oceans, mountains and rift valleys. (See also EARTH; FAULT; FOLD; PLATE TECTONICS.)

DIATHERMY, the use of electrically generated HEAT, particularly in SURGERY. Two ELECTRODES are connected to the patient: a localized point electrode is used to cause local tissue destruction, while a larger surface electrode, which dissipates the electrical energy over a wider area and thus avoids damage, is used to complete the circuit. Diathermy allows small blood vessels to be occluded and is often used to incise the GASTROINTESTINAL TRACT, when it gives a bacteria-free, nonbleeding edge. It has also been used to remove hairs, but the FOLLICLES may be scarred.

DIATOMS, single-celled fresh and salt water ALGAE, important as food to many small animals. Over millions of years, their skeletons have formed deposits on the sea bed, one in California being over 300m (1000ft) thick. These deposits are excavated as fuller's or diatomaceous earth and the fine silica grains used in metal polishes and toothpaste. Diatom deposits are sometimes associated with the occurrence of petroleum deposits.

DÍAZ, Porfirio (1830–1915), Mexican general and president. Renowned for his part in the war against the French (1861–67), he came to oppose Benito JUÁREZ and gained power in 1877. President until 1880 and again from 1884, he was politically ruthless. However, his policies and foreign investment brought stability and prosperity, although peasant conditions were wretched. He was overthrown in 1911 and died in exile in Paris.

DÍAZ DEL CASTILLO, Bernal (c1492–c1581), Spanish soldier and historian, who settled in Guatemala. He served Hernán CORTÉS in the conquest of Mexico (1519–21), and in his old age wrote *The True History of the Conquest of New Spain* (first published 1632), a lively and detailed account of events and scenes of the conquest.

DIAZONIUM COMPOUNDS, salts containing the cation $R{-}\overset{+}{N}{\equiv}N$ where R is an aryl group (see AROMATIC COMPOUNDS), made by reacting a primary aromatic AMINE with nitrous acid (see NITROGEN). Their sensitivity to light is exploited in the **diazo process** or OZALID PROCESS. They couple with phenols and amines to give AZO COMPOUNDS. The aliphatic diazo compounds have the related structure $R_2C{=}\overset{+}{N}{=}\overset{-}{N}$.

DÍAZ ORDAZ, Gustavo (1911–), politician and president of Mexico (1964–70), a member of the dominant Partido Revolucionario Institucional (PRI). Formerly interior minister, he instituted economic, industrial and welfare development plans.

DICK, George Frederick (1881–1967) and **Gladys Henry Dick** (1881–1963), US physicians (husband and wife) who discovered the organism responsible for causing SCARLET FEVER (1923) and developed a means (the **Dick test**) for estimating an individual's susceptibility to the disease.

DICKCISSEL, small bird of the American prairies. A member of the bunting family (Fringillidae), it resembles a colorful sparrow, feeds on insects and migrates to South America in winter. The dickcissel is so named for its song.

DICKENS, Charles John Huffam (1812–1870), one of the great English novelists. His brief childhood experience of a debtor's prison and work in a blacking factory shaped his future imagery and sympathies. Trained as a stenographer and lawyer's clerk, he began his literary career in London as a magazine contributor, under the pseudonym "Boz," publishing

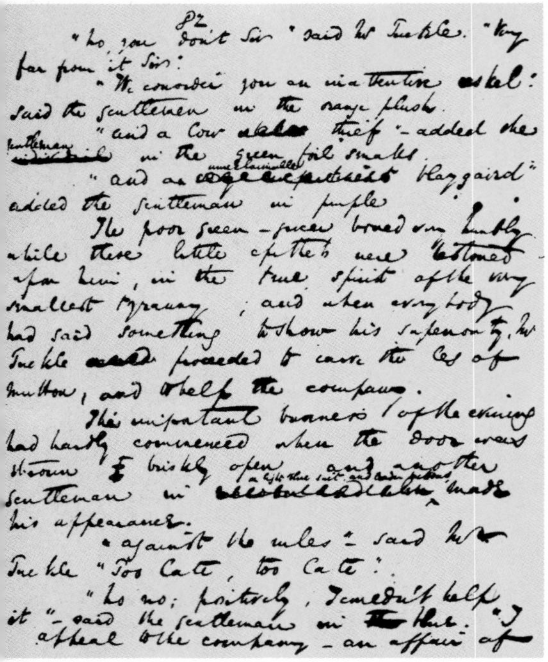
82

"No, you don't Sir" said Mr Tuckle. "Very far from it Sir:"
"We consider you an inattentive [illegible]" said the gentleman in the orange plush.
"And a Cow [illegible] thief" - added the [illegible] in the green foil smalls.
"And an [illegible] blaggaird" added the gentleman in purple.
The poor green-grocer bowed very humbly while these little epithets were bestowed upon him, in the true spirit of the very smallest tyranny; and when everybody had said something to show his superiority, Mr Tuckle proceeded to carve the leg of mutton, and to help the company.
This important business of the evening had hardly commenced when the door was thrown briskly open, and another gentleman in [illegible] made his appearance.
"Against the rules" said Mr Tuckle "Too late, too late."
"No no; positively, I couldn't help it" - said the gentleman in [illegible]. "I appeal to the company - an affair of

A leaf from the manuscript of *The Posthumous Papers of the Pickwick Club,* in Dickens' handwriting. This was the work which first established Dickens as a novelist. It originally appeared in monthly installments. This fragment is in the British Library.

Sketches by "Boz" in 1836. His comic work *The Pickwick Papers* (1837) made him famous. Most of his novels were published first in monthly installments, for popular consumption, and this affected their structure and style. His chief concern was the effect of moral evil, crime and corruption on society. He created some memorable comic characters, as in *David Copperfield* (1850), which was based on his own experiences. His works include *Oliver Twist* (1838), *Bleak House* (1853), *Little Dorrit* (1857), *Great Expectations* (1861) and *Our Mutual Friend* (1865). Dicken's novels were dramatized, and he made successful reading tours of England and the US. His works influenced the Russian writer DOSTOYEVSKY.

DICKINSON, city and seat of Stark Co. in SW N.D. It ships livestock and wheat and has coal, brick and pottery industries. Pop 12405.

DICKINSON, Emily Elizabeth (1830–1886), important American poet. She spent most of her life secluded in her father's home in Amherst, Mass. Her concise lyrics, witty and aphoristic in style, simple even sentimental in expression, and remarkable for metrical variations, are chiefly concerned with immortality and nature. Of 1775 poems, only seven were published during her lifetime.

DICKINSON, Goldsworthy Lowes (1862–1932), English author, pacifist and early advocate of the LEAGUE OF NATIONS. His works include *The Greek View of Life* (1896) and *The International Anarchy, 1904–1914* (1926).

DICKINSON, John (1732–1808), American colonial statesman and political writer, who opposed British colonial policy but was against separation from Britain. He wrote *Letters from a Farmer in Pennsylvania* (1767 and 1768) and, while a member of the CONTINENTAL CONGRESS 1774–76, probably drew up the *Declaration of the Causes of taking up Arms.* He also wrote the first draft of the ARTICLES OF CONFEDERATION, in 1776. Dickinson refused to sign the DECLARATION OF INDEPENDENCE but supported the Constitution.

DICOTYLEDONS, flowering PLANTS or ANGIOSPERMS that produce SEEDS with two seed leaves (COTYLEDONS) and thus differ from MONOCOTYLEDONS in which only one is produced. They also have net-veined leaves, a ring of bundles in the stem vascular system and flowering parts in fours or fives or multiples of these.

DICTATING MACHINE, device for recording and subsequently reproducing spoken messages; normally used in offices. Letters or messages are dictated into a MICROPHONE and recorded on magnetic tape, plastic disk or belt. This is played back on a reproducing unit (usually separate from the recording unit) for transcription by a typist.

DICTATORSHIP, form of government in which one person holds absolute power and is not subject to the consent of the governed. The term derives from the Roman *dictator* who was a magistrate appointed to govern for a six month period, following a state emergency. Both SULLA and Julius CAESAR, however, abolished the constitutional limits to their dictatorial power. In the 20th century, HITLER and STALIN assumed dictatorial powers and committed hideous atrocities; there have also been dictatorships in Portugal, Spain and Greece and in many South American and African countries. (See also DESPOTISM; TOTALITARIANISM.)

DICTIONARY, alphabetically-arranged book giving the orthography, syllabication, pronunciation, meanings and uses, and etymology of words. Until the 18th century, dictionaries amounted to little more than lists, furnishing simple glossaries. The first large-scale compilation was *A New English Dictionary* (1702), containing 38000 entries. Nathan Bailey's *Universal Etymological English Dictionary* (1721), besides containing etymologies, marked word stress and syllabication and established a methodology of word collection. In 1755 Samuel JOHNSON published the famous *Dictionary of the English Language,* in two volumes, the first English language dictionary to give literary examples of usage. Johnson's work was expanded by Noah WEBSTER in the US, who produced *An American Dictionary of the English Language* (1828). In 1857 Richard Chenevix Trench proposed *A New English Dictionary on Historical Principles* known, since 1894, as the *Oxford English Dictionary.* Its 12 volumes were published between 1884 and 1928, with supplements appearing in 1933 and 1973. Bilingual and special subject dictionaries are also made.

DICTIONARY, in text processing or analysis by COMPUTER, a section of the computer's memory devoted to common phrases, punctuation, different uses of words spelled similarly, synonyms, etc. Comprehensive dictionaries are not yet practicable, but restricted ones are of great value in some fields of information storage and retrieval (see INFORMATION RETRIEVAL).

DIDEROT, Denis (1713–1784), French encyclopedist, philosopher and man of letters. His versatility as a novelist, playwright and art critic made him prominent in the ENLIGHTENMENT. His fame rests on the *Encyclopédie,* which he edited with d'ALEMBERT and published between 1751 and 1771. The *Encyclopédie,* comprising 17 volumes of text and 11 of engravings, contained essays on the sciences, arts and crafts by such eminent contributors as BUFFON, CONDORCET, Jean Jacques ROUSSEAU and VOLTAIRE, as well as by d'Alembert and Diderot themselves. It presented the scientific discoveries and more advanced thought of the time. As a result the French government tried to suppress it, in 1759. Diderot's works included the play *Le Père de Famille* (1761) and the novel *Jacques le Fataliste* (1796).

DIDO, legendary queen and founder of Carthage in N Africa, where she fled after her brother PYGMALION murdered her husband. She killed herself to escape marriage to Iarbas the Numidian king, or, according to VERGIL in the Aeneid, because AENEAS abandoned her.

DIE, a mold or tool used in the shaping of metals, plastics and other materials. Dies are used in countless areas of METALLURGY, including CASTING, FORGING and EXTRUSION. Rather different are the gripper dies used in the making of NAILS and elsewhere. **Blanking and punching dies** are used together for trimming or punching holes in metal sheet. Both the blanking die and the punch have sharp edges: the workpiece is placed on the blanking die and the punch brought down with sufficient force to shear the metal (see SHEARING). **Deep-drawing** is similar, but the punch, though of the same cross-sectional shape as the die, is smaller, and both have rounded edges. The flat workpiece is placed on the die, into which it is forced by the punch. Cup-shaped and other parts can be produced in this way. WIRE can be produced by **drawing**, being pulled through one or a series of tapered dies to reduce cross-section and improve surface. (See also MATERIALS, STRENGTH OF.)

DIEFENBAKER, John George (1895–), Canadian politician and premier 1957–63. After repeated attempts he succeeded in being elected to parliament from Saskatchewan, in 1940. Becoming leader of the PROGRESSIVE CONSERVATIVE PARTY in 1956, he headed a minority government in 1957, after 22 years of Liberal rule. The 1958 election produced a record government majority. He instituted agricultural reforms but the economic recession, the Cuba missile crisis, and the nuclear arms debate, which aggravated relations with the US under Kennedy, brought on his defeat in 1963 by Lester PEARSON and the Liberals.

DIELECTRIC, an electrical insulator in which the application of an electric field (see ELECTRICITY) causes polarization which in turn produces a field opposed to the original field, thus reducing the resultant field strength by a factor known as the **dielectric constant** for the material concerned. Their properties are exploited in CAPACITORS, and to reduce dangerously strong fields. They also have optical applications, since refractive index (see REFRACTION) is the square ROOT of dielectric constant.

Some approximate dielectric constants

Air*	1.0005
Paraffin wax	2.3
Natural rubber	2.4
Diamond	5.7
Soda glass	7.0
Water	80

* at room temperature and atmospheric pressure.

DIELS, Otto Paul Hermann (1876–1954), German organic chemist who discovered carbon suboxide (C_3O_2) in 1906 and who with Kurt ALDER discovered the DIELS-ALDER REACTION (1928). For this latter work he and Alder shared the 1950 Nobel chemistry prize.

DIELS-ALDER REACTION, or diene synthesis, reaction discovered by Otto DIELS and Kurt ALDER, important in making plastics, insecticides and fungicides. A conjugated diene (see ALKENES; RESONANCE), such as 1, 3-BUTADIENE or ISOPRENE, adds readily to a "dienophile" containing a double or triple bond activated by an adjacent NUCLEOPHILE group.

DIEM, Ngo Dinh (1901–1963), American-backed president of the South Vietnam republic 1954–63. His Roman Catholic regime's harsh oppression of the Buddhist majority (leading to cases of self-immolation), his corrupt politics and failure to effect land reform, led to a withdrawal of US support. He was assassinated in a coup led by his own generals.

DIEN BIEN PHU, military outpost, in northern Vietnam, where in 1954 France was finally defeated in the Indochina war. During a 55-day siege, the French army lost 15000 men in their bid to resist the onslaught of Gen. Vo Nguyen Giap's Vietminh forces. France formally withdrew from Indochina at the GENEVA CONFERENCE (1954).

DIEPPE, historic French port in Seine-Maritime department, on the English Channel, important for commerce and fishing. In 1942 during WWII, Allied troops made a tragic and unsuccessful attempt to capture the city from the Germans. Pop 29829.

DIESEL ENGINE, oil-burning INTERNAL-COMBUSTION ENGINE patented by **Rudolf Diesel** (1858–1913), a German engineer, in 1892 after several years of development work. Air enters a cylinder and is compressed by a piston to a high enough TEMPERATURE and PRESSURE for spontaneous combustion to occur when fuel is sprayed in. This method of operation differs from that of a gasoline engine in which air and fuel are mixed before entering the cylinder, there is less compression and a spark is needed to initiate combustion. In the first (intake) stroke of the cycle of a 4-stroke diesel engine, the piston moves down, drawing in air through a valve. In the second (compression) stroke, the piston returns up, compressing the air and heating it to over 300°C. (The exact value depends on the compression ratio, which may be between 12:1 and 22:1.) Near the end of the stroke, fuel is sprayed into the cylinder at high pressure through a nozzle and ignites in the hot air. In the third (power) stroke, the burning fuel–air mixture increases the pressure in the cylinder, pushing the piston down and driving the crankshaft. Then, in the fourth (exhaust) stroke, the piston moves up again and drives the burnt gases out of the cylinder. There are also 2-stroke diesel engines. These have only compression and power strokes, the exhaust gases being scavenged and new air introduced by a blower while the piston is at the bottom of its stroke. Diesel engines are less smooth-running, heavier and initially more expensive than gasoline engines but make more efficient use of cheaper fuel. They are widely used in ships, heavy vehicles and power installations.

DIET, legislative or deliberative council. The Diet of the Holy Roman Empire, founded in 1356, was attended by princes, electors and delegates from the imperial cities. Famous diets were at worms (1521), speyer (1529) and Augsburg (1530) (see augsburg confession). The Diet lost its legislative power after the Peace of westphalia (1648), and after 1806 was replaced by various German legislatures. Danish, Hungarian, Japanese and Swedish parliamentary bodies are also called diets.

DIET. See dieting; dietetic foods; nutrition.

DIETETIC FOODS, special foods for conditions in which normal diet leads to disease or ill-health, or where dietary manipulation modifies disease. Gluten-free diet for celiac disease; polyunsaturated fat diet for excess blood fats and arteriosclerosis; milk avoidance in lactose intolerance; carbohydrate restriction in diabetes; low phenylalanine foods for phenylketonuria, and low protein diet for kidney or liver failure are important examples. Vitamin- or protein-enriched diets may be required for certain conditions, and a high-fat (ketogenic) diet can be used to treat epilepsy. Numerous diets exist which have no proven value.

DIETING, a term usually applied to the restriction of food intake in treatment of obesity, although the use of dietetic foods is strictly included. Many special diets have been recommended, but simple calorie restriction is the essence of weight reduction. Abstinence from potatoes, most root vegetables, rice, pasta, bread, cakes, biscuits, sugar, candies, cream and alcohol is usually effective; lean meat and green vegetables should be the staple diet. Occasionally more extreme dieting under supervision is needed.

DIETRICH, Marlene (1904–   ), German-born US film actress and cabaret artist. Her classic role was that of the "femme fatale" nightclub singer in the German film *The Blue Angel* (1930). She became famous for her sultry glamor and sophistication.

DIEZ, Friedrich Christian (1794–1876), German philologist and pioneer in study of the Romance languages. He wrote a *Grammar* (1836–44) and an *Etymological Dictionary* (1853).

DIFFERENCE EQUATIONS, in the calculus of finite differences, equations which play a role analagous to that played by differential equations in calculus. The calculus of finite differences deals with discrete quantities; unlike calculus, which deals with continuous quantities. For a function $f(x)$ at a particular value x_n, we define $\Delta f(x_n)$ as $f(x_{n+1}) - f(x_n)$, where Δ is called the difference operator. From this, we find that $\Delta^2 f(x_n)$—i.e., $\Delta(f(x_{n+1}) - f(x_n))$—can be expressed as $f(x_{n+2}) - 2f(x_{n+1}) + f(x_n)$; and so forth for $\Delta^3 f(x_n), \ldots, \Delta^m f(x_n)$. A difference table may be constructed showing values of $\Delta f(x_n)$, $\Delta^2 f(x_n), \ldots, \Delta^m f(x_n), \ldots$, and from this a relationship between the differences may be deduced. Generally, then, a difference equation is any equation which expresses such a relationship; and use may be made of it to find discrete values for $f(x)$ which lie outside the known range. Approximation of a differential equation to a suitable difference equation is often a powerful tool in the solution of the former.

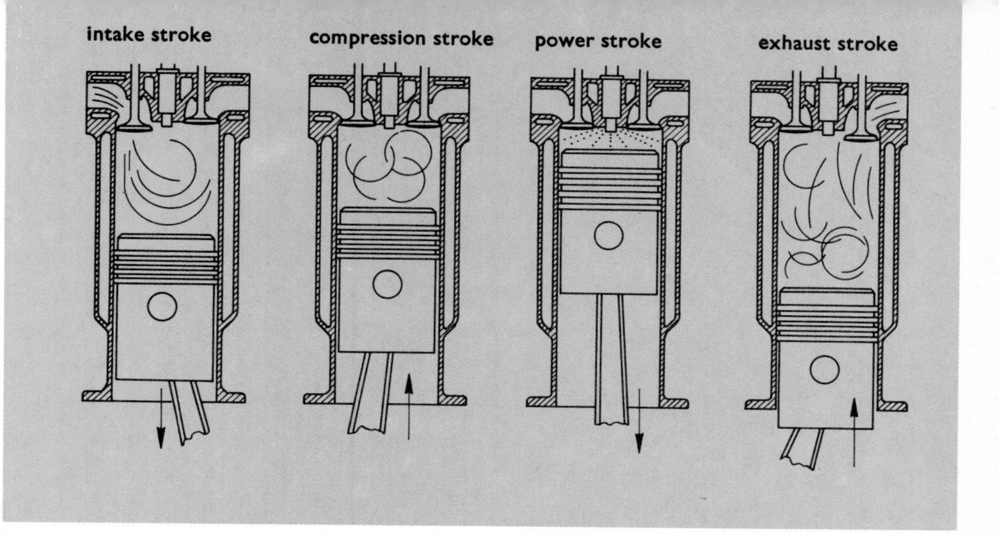

The operating cycle of a four-stroke diesel engine. In the intake stroke, the piston travels downward while the intake valve is open; this draws air into the cylinder. Then, during the compression stroke, the piston returns upward, compressing, and thus heating, the air in the cylinder. Now the fuel is injected; it mixes with the air and ignites, driving the piston violently down in the power stroke. Lastly, the piston again rises, this time with the exhaust valve open, forcing out the waste gases in the exhaust stroke.

DIFFERENTIAL, in automobiles and trucks, an assembly of gears which permits the two wheels on a driven axle to rotate at slightly different rates during cornering.

DIFFERENTIAL, in differential calculus, either of dy and dx where $dy/dx = f'(x)$.

DIFFERENTIAL EQUATIONS, equations involving derivatives (see calculus). Consider a body accelerating (see acceleration) uniformly at 40 m/s². After a time t it has a velocity of $40t$, assuming a stationary start. This velocity may also be expressed as ds/dt, the instantaneous rate of change of distance, s, from the starting point. Thus

$$40t = \frac{ds}{dt}.$$

To find out the distance traveled by the body after a time t we can integrate to find

$$20t^2 + \mathrm{k} = s + \mathrm{c}$$

or

$$s = 20t^2 + (\mathrm{k} - \mathrm{c})$$

where k and c are constants. However, we have assumed a stationary start; i.e., that when $t=0$, $s=0$ and hence, by substitution, $(\mathrm{k}-\mathrm{c})=0$. Therefore, to find out how far the body has traveled after a given period of time, we need merely to substitute the value of t into

$$s = 20t^2.$$

This is the solution of a very simple first-order differential equation. In some problems there occur second derivatives of the form d^2y/dx^2, and these involve solution of **second-order differential equations**. Equations involving nth derivatives, d^ny/dx^n, are called nth-order equations, most important of which are the equations of the form

$$f(x) = \mathrm{A}y + \mathrm{B}\frac{dy}{dx} + \mathrm{C}\frac{d^2y}{dx^2} + \cdots + \mathrm{N}\frac{d^ny}{dx^n}$$

where A, B, C, . . . , N are constants. This is termed a **linear *n*th-order differential equation**. Differential equations occur in many, if not most, physical problems. (See difference equations.)

DIFFERENTIAL GEOMETRY, the branch of geometry dealing with the basic properties of curves and surfaces, using the techniques of calculus and analytic geometry.

DIFFERENTIATION. See calculus.

DIFFRACTION, the property by which a wave motion (such as electromagnetic radiation, sound or water waves) deviates from the straight line expected geometrically and thus gives rise to interference effects at the edges of the shadows cast by opaque objects, where the wave-trains that have reached each point by different routes interfere with each other. Opaque objects thus never cast completely sharp shadows, though such effects only become apparent when the dimensions of the obstruction are of the same order as the wavelength of the wave motion concerned. It is diffraction effects which place the ultimate limit on the resolving power of optical instruments, radio telescopes and the like. Diffraction is set to work in the diffraction grating. Here, light passed through a series of very accurately ruled slits or reflected from a series of narrow parallel mirrors produces a series of spectrums by the interference of the light from the different slits or mirrors. Gratings are ruled with from 70 lines/mm (for infrared work) to 1800 lines/mm (for ultraviolet work).

DIFFUSION, the gradual mixing of different substances placed in mutual contact due to the random thermal motion of their constituent particles. Most rapid with gases and liquids, it does also occur with solids. Diffusion rates increase with increasing temperature; the rates at which gases diffuse through a porous membrane vary as the inverse of the square root of their molecular weight. Gaseous diffusion is used to separate fissile uranium-235 from nonfissile uranium-238, the gas used being uranium hexafluoride (UF_6).

DIGESTIVE SYSTEM, the mechanism for breaking down or modifying dietary intake into a form that is absorbable and usable by an organism. In unicellular organisms this is by phagocytosis and enzyme breakdown of large molecules; in larger animals it occurs outside cells after liberation of enzymes. In higher animals, the digestive system consists structurally of the gastrointestinal tract, the principal absorbing surface which also secretes enzymes, and the related organs: the liver and pancreas, which secrete into the tract via ducts. Different enzymes act best at different pH, and **gastric juice** and bile respectively regulate the acidity of the stomach and alkalinity of the small intestine. Proteins are broken down by pepsin in the stomach and by trypsin, chymotrypsin and peptidases in the small intestine. Carbohydrates are broken down by specialized enzymes, mainly in the small intestine. Fats are physically broken down by stomach movement, enzymatically by lipases and emulsified by bile salts. Food is mixed and propelled by peristalsis, while nerves and locally regulated hormones, including gastrin and secretin, control both secretion and motility. Absorption of most substances occurs in the small intestine through a specialized, high-surface-area mucous membrane; some molecules pass through unchanged but most in altered form. Absorption may be either by an active transport system involving chemical or physical interaction in the gut wall, or simply by a passive diffusion process. Some vitamins and trace metals have specialized transport systems. Most absorbed food passes via the portal system to the liver, where much of it is metabolized and toxic substances

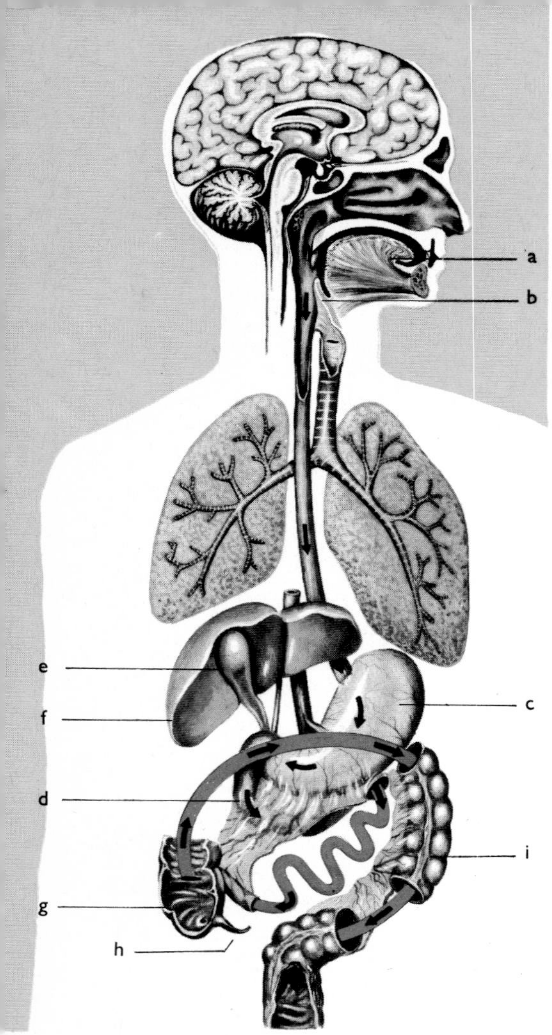

Most of the processes of the digestive system take place in the gastrointestinal tract. Food passes from the mouth (a) through the esophagus (b) to the stomach (c) where it mixes with the gastric juice. Absorption continues in the duodenum (d) where bile from the gall bladder (e) and liver salts from the liver (f) are introduced. The food then passes to the cecum (g), to which the appendix (h) is attached, and then enters the colon (i) where most of the water is absorbed. The residue is then eliminated through the rectum.

removed. Some absorbed fat is passed into the LYMPH. BACTERIA colonize most of the small intestine and are important in certain digestive processes. **Malabsorption** occurs when any part of the digestive system becomes defective. Pancreas and liver disease, obstruction to bile ducts, alteration of bacteria and inflammatory disease of the small intestine are common causes.

DIGGERS, or True Levellers, 17th-century English radical cooperative movement, followers of Gerrard WINSTANLEY. In April 1649, following the execution of King Charles I after the Civil War, they occupied the common land on St. George's Hill, Surrey, and began to cultivate it. They claimed land should be given to the poor and held in common. They were dispersed in 1650.

DIGITALIS, drug derived from the FOXGLOVE and acting on the muscle and conducting systems of the HEART. WITHERING in 1785 described its efficacy in heart failure or dropsy; it increases the force of cardiac contraction. It is also valuable in treatment of some abnormal rhythms; however, overdosage may itself cause abnormal rhythm, nausea or vomiting.

DIHEDRAL ANGLE, the figure formed by the intersection of two PLANES, described by a point on one of the planes, the line of intersection (edge), and a point on the other plane. Should a point P on one of the planes be so positioned that the line through it PERPENDICULAR to the edge, E, intersects E at the same point as a line drawn perpendicular to E through a point P′ on the other plane, then the angle PEP′ is the **plane angle** of the dihedral angle. All plane angles of a dihedral angle are equal.

DIJON, city in E France. Its industries include local, Burgundy, wine. It was capital of the ducal province of Burgundy, and the palace of the dukes of the House of VALOIS (1364–1477) is now the Hôtel de Ville and museum. Ducal patronage made the Charterhouse of Champmol at Dijon center of a school of sculpture led by Claus SLUTER. Pop 145 357.

DIK-DIKS, small African ANTELOPES, standing only 350mm (14in) at the shoulder. Males have short horns. They live in groups in dense undergrowth.

DIKE, embankment to control water flow, often equipped with gates for farmland irrigation. Dikes are common features of the Dutch landscape, as most of the country is below sea level. Originally referring to a trench, "dike" later also came to mean the embankment thrown up while excavating it.

DIKE, or **dyke**, a tabular body of IGNEOUS ROCK which, unlike a SILL, cuts across the beds of surrounding rock. Dikes commonly occur in swarms, which may be parallel or radial.

DILL, *Peucedanum graveolens*, annual herb of the parsley family (Umbelliferae), native to the Mediterranean region and cultivated in Europe and North America. The leaves are used for flavoring and the seeds as a condiment and drug.

DILLINGER, John (1903–1934), notorious US gangster, who terrorized the Midwest in 1933 after escaping from jail. He was responsible for 16 killings and was shot in Chicago in 1934.

DILLON, John (1851–1927), Irish statesman, a member of the British Parliament 1880–83 and 1885–1918, who, with PARNELL, worked for Irish independence by constitutional means. In 1918 he became leader of the Irish Nationalist Party, but it was defeated at the elections by the SINN FEIN.

DILTHEY, Wilhelm (1833–1911), German philosopher who sought to achieve for "historical reason" (the human sciences: law; religion; history; psychology and the arts), what KANT had achieved for the natural sciences in the *Critique of Pure Reason*.

DIMAGGIO, Joseph Paul (1914–), US baseball outfielder. He played for the New York Yankees from 1936 until his retirement in 1951, set a new record with consistent safe-hitting in 56 consecutive games (1941), hit 361 home runs and had a career batting average of .325. He entered the Baseball Hall of Fame in 1955.

DIMENSIONAL ANALYSIS, the branch of applied MATHEMATICS concerned with the analysis of physical problems in terms of DIMENSIONS such as mass, length and time. Its fundamental theorem is that the dimensions of the quantities appearing on opposite sides of an equation are the same.

DIMENSIONS, in GEOMETRY, the three properties of geometrical figures: length, breadth and depth. A POINT is defined as having no dimensions, a straight LINE as having only one, length, a PLANE figure as having two, length and breadth, and a solid figure as having all three. In terms of ANALYTIC GEOMETRY, an object has as many dimensions as it requires AXES to define its spatial position. In RELATIVITY there is considered to be a fourth dimension, TIME. (See also DIMENSIONAL ANALYSIS.)

DIMENSIONS, as applied to a physical quantity, an indication of the role it plays in equations. The dimensions of a mechanical quantity, in terms of mass [M], length [L] and time [T], can be deduced from the units in which it is expressed. Thus VELOCITY, measured in m/s, has dimensions [L]/[T]. Dimensions are purely conventional, having no real physical significance. This is clear in the case of electromagnetic quantities where dimensions vary according to the units system employed. Dimensions nevertheless find use in DIMENSIONAL ANALYSIS.

DIME NOVEL, fast-moving melodramatic tale of adventure, usually about the American Revolution, the frontier period or the Civil War. Sold for 10 cents, dime novels were popular in the US from 1860 to the 1890s.

DIMINISHING RETURNS, Law of, economic law which states that, in the production of a commodity, if any one input (e.g. capital or labor) is increased while the others remain fixed, the return on this varying factor will eventually diminish. This assumes that technology remains unchanged.

DIMITROV, Georgi Mikhailovich (1882–1949), Bulgarian communist leader. A member of the Moscow Comintern in 1921, he was active in Germany and was accused of arson in the REICHSTAG fire (1933). He won acquittal at his trial, ably defending himself against the Nazi prosecution. He ensured the success of the 1946 Bulgarian communist coup and was premier 1946–49.

DINARIC ALPS, mountain range in S Europe, part of the E Alpine system. Its rocky and largely barren limestone ridges run 400mi down the E coast of the Adriatic Sea, from NW Yugoslavia into Albania. The highest peak is Mt Durmitor (8 274ft).

D'INDY, (Paul Marie Théodore) Vincent (1851–1931), French composer and teacher, a pupil of César FRANCK and cofounder of the Schola Cantorum academy, Paris (1894). He thought French 19th-century music superficial, admiring the German classics and Renaissance polyphony. He urged a renovated French style derived from folk idioms. His works include *Symphony on a French Mountain Air* (1886).

DINESEN, Isak, pseudonym of Karen Christence Dinesen, Baroness Blixen-Finecke (1885–1962), Danish author of romantic tales of mystery, such as *Seven Gothic Tales* (1934). The autobiographical *Out of Africa* (1937) was based on her 20 years in E Africa as a planter.

DINGHY, small boat, built for stability rather than

The Age of Reptiles, when dinosaurs were the dominant large animals, lasted 120 million years and ended 80 million years ago. With the aid of abundant plant and animal fossils

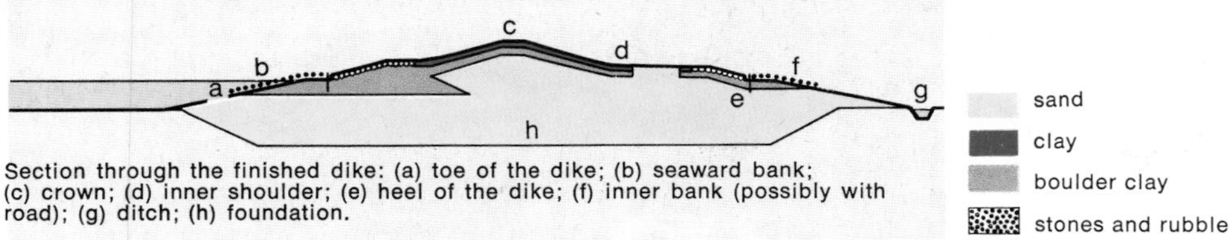

Section through the finished dike: (a) toe of the dike; (b) seaward bank; (c) crown; (d) inner shoulder; (e) heel of the dike; (f) inner bank (possibly with road); (g) ditch; (h) foundation.

speed. Though usually rowed, dinghies can be fitted with sails or an outboard motor. They are made from various materials and can be inflatable.

DINGO, Australian wild dog, probably introduced by the aborigines. The size of a small wolf, dingos commonly attack livestock but unlike wolves, they rarely hunt in packs.

DINOFLAGELLATES, microscopic single-celled organisms, occurring in vast numbers in fresh and salt water. Some dinoflagellates contain CHLOROPHYLL, others do not, so they may be classed as plants or animals. They are propelled by two whip-like hairs (flagella) and each one is covered by a layer of cellulose; they are important as food for many animals, though some are poisonous.

DINOSAUR NATIONAL MONUMENT, an area of national parkland in NE Ut. and NW Col., covering some 200 000 acres. The monument was established in 1915 and is of vast scientific interest, being rich in quarries of well-preserved fossils.

DINOSAURS, extinct REPTILES that flourished for 120 million years from the TRIASSIC to the CRETACEOUS periods. They ranged in size from small forms no larger than a domestic chicken to giants such as *Diplodocus* which was 27m (90ft) long and weighed about 30 tonnes. Early in their history two distinct dinosaur groups evolved: the Saurischia and the Ornithischia.

The **Saurischians** (or lizard-hipped dinosaurs) had pelvic girdles typical of lizards, with three prongs to each side. They included the two-legged carnivorous theropods, such as *Tyrannosaurus* and *Allosaurus*, with enormous skulls and large teeth; and the four-legged herbivorous sauropods, such as *Brontosaurus* and *Diplodocus*, with very small heads and long necks and tails.

The **Ornithischians** (or bird-hipped dinosaurs) had bird-like pelvic girdles, with four prongs to each side. All were herbivorous. Four-legged types include the stegosaurs, with triangular bony plates along the back, and the armadillo-like ankylosaurs. The two-legged duck-billed dinosaurs were well equipped for swimming.

At the end of the Cretaceous period, about 80 million years ago, dinosaurs disappeared. The reasons for this sudden extinction are not known and are the subject of much debate and controversy among paleontologists.

DINWIDDIE, Robert (1693–1770 AD), British colonial administrator in Bermuda, the Bahamas and America, governor of Virginia 1751–58. He sent George Washington to resist French encroachments, but his position was considerably weakened after Washington's defeat at Fort Necessity in 1754.

DIO CASSIUS (c150–235 AD), ancient Roman administrator and historian. His history of Rome (of which 19 volumes survive), written in Greek, covers late republican and early imperial times.

DIOCLETIAN (Gaius Aurelius Valerius Diocletianus; c245–316), Roman emperor from 284 to 305, when he abdicated. He reformed the army and administration, dividing the empire into four regions (293), ruled by two emperors and two caesars. Much of his great palace at Split, Yugoslavia, survives. In 303 he initiated the last universal persecution of the Christians.

DIODE, originally an ELECTRON TUBE having two ELECTRODES (CATHODE and ANODE) used as a RECTIFIER, but now extended to include SEMICONDUCTOR devices performing a similar function (See ELECTRONICS.)

DIODORUS SICULUS (d. after 21 BC), Sicilian-born ancient Greek author of a 40-volume world history. Only 15 volumes survive.

DIOECIOUS PLANTS, those in which the male and female organs are borne in separate flowers which are on separate plants. Examples are WILLOW, HEMP and ASPARAGUS. (See also MONOECIOUS PLANTS.)

DIOGENES (c412–323 BC), Greek philosopher, living in Athens. He rejected tradition and social conventions. Contemptuous of his contemporaries and their values, he was nicknamed "the Dog" and his followers the CYNICS (*kynikos*, "doglike"). He abandoned all his possessions, begged his living and reputedly lived in a barrel. Supposedly, when Alexander the Great asked what he could do for him, Diogenes answered, "Just step out of my light."

DIOGENES LAERTIUS (3rd century AD), ancient Greek author. His 10-book *Lives and Opinions of Famous Philosophers* contains invaluable biographical and bibliographical details.

DIOMEDE ISLANDS, two small islands in the Bering Strait, separated by the international dateline and the boundary between Alaska and the Soviet Union. They were discovered in 1728 by Vitus Bering and are icebound for half the year.

DIOMEDES, name of two figures in Greek legend. **Diomedes**, son of Tydeus, was one of the principal heroes of the TROJAN WAR. **Diomedes**, son of Ares, was king of Thrace. His fearful man-eating mares were captured by HERCULES in his eighth labor. Diomedes died trying to protect them.

DIONYSIA, ancient Greek festivals honoring DIONYSUS, god of wine. The Anthesteria was held in early spring, the City Dionysia in late spring, the Rural Dionysia in December and the Lenaea in winter. The City Dionysia and the Lenaea were marked by dramatic performances.

DIONYSIUS, Saint (d. 268), pope 259–68. His major task was the reorganization of the Church after the persecution of VALERIAN.

DIONYSIUS, name of two Greek tyrants of Syracuse, Sicily. **Dionysius the Elder** (c430–367 BC), reigned from 405 BC and campaigned against Carthaginian garrisons in Sicily and against S Italian cities. He patronized learning and wrote some minor plays. His son, **Dionysius the Younger**, ruled 367–356 BC and 354–344 BC, but was finally expelled to Corinth after a turbulent reign. Plato had tried to train him as the ideal philosopher–king.

DIONYSIUS OF HALICARNASSUS (flourished 20 BC), Greek rhetorician and historian. He wrote a detailed Roman history up to the First Punic War (the *Roman Antiquities*). Books I–IX are intact.

DIONYSIUS THE AREOPAGITE, Saint (1st century AD), converted by St. Paul and traditionally the first bishop of Athens. In the 6th century certain Greek philosophical treatises were wrongly attributed to him. These books by the **Pseudo-Dionysius** introduced important themes of neo-Platonism into Western Scholastic philosophy.

DIONYSIUS THE GREAT, of Alexandria, Saint (c200–265), bishop of Alexandria from 247. Exiled under the purge of Emperor VALERIAN, he returned in 260 to enter into bitter doctrinal controversies.

DIONYSUS, Greek god of wine and fertility, also called BACCHUS, a son of Zeus. He founded the art of vine culture. In early times his devotees, notably the MAENADS, practiced an orgiastic cult of divine possession. (See also DIONYSIA.)

Portion of a mosaic showing the Greek god of wine, Dionysus, dressed in eastern costume and riding a leopard; it was discovered in the Dionysus house in Delos. Dionysus is supposed to have traveled to India in a chariot drawn by panthers.

DIOPHANTUS OF ALEXANDRIA, mathematician, probably of the 3rd century AD, whose fame rests on his use of an algebraic notation and his

it is possible to reconstruct the landscape of those times together with its major inhabitants.

interest in **Diophantine equations**. These are formulations of problems such as that of finding all the right-angled TRIANGLES whose sides are INTEGERS (e.g., 3, 4, 5). Diophantes indeed solved this problem.

DIOPTRE, or reciprocal metre, a unit used to express the focal power of optical lenses. The power of a converging LENS in dioptres is a positive number equal to the reciprocal of its focal length in metres. Diverging lenses have negative powers.

DIOR, Christian (1905–1957), French fashion designer, whose "New Look" of 1947 helped to reestablish Paris as the leader of fashion after WWII. His salon opened in 1946 and Dior rapidly became the undisputed leader of world fashion.

DIPHTHERIA, BACTERIAL DISEASE, now uncommon, causing FEVER, malaise and sore throat, with a characteristic "pseudomembrane" on throat or PHARYNX; also, the LYMPH nodes may enlarge. The LARYNX, if involved, leads to a hoarse voice, breathlessness and stridor; this may progress to respiratory obstruction requiring tracheostomy. The bacteria produce TOXINS which can damage nerves and HEART muscle; cardiac failure and abnormal rhythm, or PARALYSIS of palate, eye movement and peripheral NEURITIS may follow. Early treatment with ANTITOXIN and use of ANTIBIOTICS are important. Protection is given by VACCINATION.

DIPLOCOCCUS, spherical or ovoid nonmotile BACTERIA, so named because they occur in pairs. PNEUMONIA, MENINGITIS and gonorrhea (see VENEREAL DISEASES) are caused by types of diplococcus bacteria.

DIPLODOCUS, quadruped vegetarian DINOSAUR found in the Jurassic strata in the US. It had a long tail and a small head and was up to 27m (90ft) long.

DIPLOID. See MEIOSIS.

DIPLOMACY, conduct of negotiations and maintenance of relations in time of peace between sovereign states. A diplomatic mission is generally headed by an ambassador, supported by attachés, chargés d'affaires and other officials specializing in economic, political, cultural, administrative and military matters. An embassy building is considered to have "extraterritoriality," that is, to be outside the jurisdiction of the receiving state. Accredited diplomats are immune from prosecution and customs regulations. Abuse of this privileged diplomatic immunity can lead to a diplomat being asked to quit the host country as *persona non grata*. The most common abuse is espionage. The whole body of diplomats in a capital is known as the diplomatic corps and its spokesman is the longest serving ambassador.

International contacts have been handled by diplomats since ancient times. In medieval Europe they were generally appointed for the duration of specific missions. The first permanent residential missions were established by the Italian city states c1400. Diplomatic protocol and the forms of accreditation owed much to the practice of papal missions from the Vatican. Latin was the official language of diplomacy until the 17th century, when it was superseded by French, later joined by English. The Congress of Vienna (1815) further clarified diplomatic procedure. The traditional formulas of diplomatic exchange allow sharp expressions of protest without ruptures in international dealing. Improved communications have strengthened direct links between governments and diplomacy is now often conducted at "summit conferences" between heads of state. (See also INTERNATIONAL RELATIONS.)

DIP NEEDLE, or inclinometer, an instrument for measuring magnetic dip (see EARTH), consisting of a magnetic needle mounted free to pivot in the vertical plane within a graduated circle. For use, the instrument is carefully leveled and oriented into the magnetic meridian.

DIPOLE, in radio; see ANTENNA.

DIPOLE MOMENT. An electric dipole is a pair of equal and opposite electric charges a short distance apart (see ELECTRICITY). All ordinary manifestations of MAGNETISM are the result of magnetic dipoles, whether these arise in the context of permanent magnets or ELECTROMAGNETS. In either case the dipole moment is a VECTOR quantity descriptive of the dipole. Atomic nuclei and asymmetric molecules often exhibit dipole or other multipole properties.

DIPPERS, birds of the family Cinclidae which appear to walk under water. In fact they swim underwater, with the help of their legs. The American dipper is found by mountain streams in the western US. Oil glands keep the thick plumage waterproof.

DIPSOMANIA. See ALCOHOLISM.

DIRAC, Paul Adrien Maurice (1902–), English theoretical physicist who shared the 1933 Nobel physics prize with E. SCHRÖDINGER for their contributions to WAVE MECHANICS. Dirac's theory (1928) took account of RELATIVITY and led him to postulate the existence of the positive ELECTRON or positron, later discovered by C. D. ANDERSON. Dirac was also the codiscoverer of FERMI-DIRAC STATISTICS.

DIRECTION FINDER, device used to locate the direction of an incoming RADIO signal. Usually a loop ANTENNA is rotated until maximum reception strength is achieved, giving the line of the transmission. If this is repeated from a different position, the transmitting station may be located. The **radiocompass** used in air and sea NAVIGATION is a direction finder: position is determined by finding the directions of two or more transmitters.

DIRECTOIRE, French decorative style of the DIRECTORY period (1795–99). It was a transitional phase between the heavy and ornate style of Louis XVI and the Neoclassical style of the Empire, and stressed simple designs with accents on straight lines and minimal ornament.

DIRECTORY, name given to the government of Revolutionary France 1795–99. It consisted of five directors appointed by the bicameral legislature. Military failures, international disorders and growing internal corruption made it unpopular, enabling Napoleon to seize power with the assistance of the director Sieyès.

DIRIGIBLE. See AIRSHIP.

DIRKSEN, Everett McKinley (1896–1969), US legislator and a leading Republican. He entered Congress in 1933, becoming a senator in 1950, and was noted for the quality of his rhetoric. Senate minority leader from 1959, he was spokesman for conservative Republican support of bipartisan legislation, notably over the Civil Rights Act of 1964.

DIS, Roman god of the dead, counterpart of PLUTO.

DISARMAMENT, the abolition, reduction or limitation of military forces and weapons. The aim of disarmament provisions may be to reduce the likelihood of war by reducing the military capabilities of contracting parties, to prevent a defeated aggressor from again disturbing the peace, or to ban the use of some weapon considered especially inhumane. Probably the first instance of this was a papal promulgation of 1139 against the use of the crossbow in war between Christians. More recently, the 1925 Geneva Protocol, ratified by over 40 nations, prohibited the use of chemical and biological weapons; and the 1972 Convention on Prohibition and Destruction of Bacteriological Weapons came into force in 1975.

Attempts to restrain aggressors have rarely been successful. After WWI the victors imposed crippling arms limitations on Germany, but inadequate inspection procedures, a recurrent problem in disarmament agreements, and considerable ingenuity in design enabled the German arms industry to circumvent them. After WWII, a ban was imposed on the arms industries of defeated Japan. General disarmament agreements have had little effect. The HAGUE PEACE CONFERENCES (1899 and 1907) failed to restrain the arms race in Europe. At the WASHINGTON CONFERENCE (1921–22), the US, Britain, Japan, France and Italy agreed to naval limitations for a 15-year period. After WWII, East–West confrontation led to a renewed arms buildup, reaching a climax of tension in the 1962 Cuban Missile Crisis. In 1963 the US, Britain and the USSR signed a Nuclear Test Ban Treaty, banning atomic tests in the atmosphere, underwater and in space. The UN Disarmament Committee drafted the Nuclear Non-Proliferation Treaty in 1968; by 1975 it had been ratified by 94 countries, including the US and the USSR. Development of new weapons systems has threatened to upset the balance of power between the US and the USSR, and the Strategic Arms Limitation Talks (SALT) in Helsinki and Vienna began in 1969. In May 1972 President Nixon signed two agreements in Moscow, limiting each nation to two antiballistic missile sites and prohibiting any increase in the development of long-range offensive missiles. An agreement in 1975 placed limitations on future additions to the already massive arsenals of the superpowers.

DISCIPLES OF CHRIST, now the International Convention of Christian Churches, US religious body founded (1832) by followers of Alexander CAMPBELL. It has no formal ministry or creed, teaching simple, personal faith in the Bible and the primitive gospel of Christ. This, it holds, should be the basis for union of Christian churches. It has missions all over the world. Its membership in North America is about 1 600 000.

DISCOUNT, in finance, the percentage discounted from promissory notes or bills of exchange when they are cashed in advance. The **discount rate** is the interest charged by central banks on funds lent to commercial banks; it regulates borrowing and lending costs, and thus serves as a measure of credit conditions.

DISCOVERY. See EXPLORATION.

DISCRIMINANT, in a POLYNOMIAL equation, a number calculated from the COEFFICIENTS which can tell much about the roots (see ROOTS OF AN EQUATION). For a quadratic EQUATION of the standard form $ax^2+bx+c=0$ the discriminant, D, is b^2-4ac; for a cubic equation ax^3+bx^2+cx+d, $D=18abcd-4b^3d+b^2c^2-4ac^3-27a^2d^2$. For a cubic or quadratic, $D<0$ implies that there are two imaginary roots (see IMAGINARY NUMBERS); $D\geqslant 0$ that the roots are all real (see REAL NUMBERS); $D=0$ that at least two of these are equal.

DISCUS, wooden disk used in the sport of discus throwing. It has a smooth metal rim and brass plates set in its sides; the men's discus weighs not less than 4lb 6.5oz and the women's 2lb 3.25oz. The sport dates from Classical times, and is now an Olympic Games track-and-field event.

DISEASE, disturbance of normal bodily function in an organism. MEDICINE and SURGERY are concerned with the recognition or diagnosis of disease and the institution of treatment aimed at its cure. Disease is usually brought to attention by symptoms, in which a person becomes aware of some abnormality of, or change in, bodily function. Pain, HEADACHE, FEVER, COUGH, shortness of breath, DYSPEPSIA, CONSTIPATION, DIARRHEA, loss of BLOOD, lumps, PARALYSIS, numbness and loss of consciousness are common examples. **Diagnosis** is made on the basis of symptoms, signs on physical examination and laboratory and X-RAY investigations; the functional disorder is analyzed and possible causes are examined. Causes of physical disease in man are legion, but certain categories are recognized: trauma, congenital, infectious, inflammatory, vascular, tumor, degenerative, deficiency, poison, metabolic, occupational and iatrogenic diseases.

Trauma to body may cause SKIN lacerations and BONE FRACTURES as well as disorders specific to the organ involved (e.g., CONCUSSION). **Congenital diseases** include hereditary conditions (i.e., those passed on genetically) and diseases beginning in the FETUS, such as those due to drugs or maternal infection in PREGNANCY. **Infectious diseases** include VIRAL DISEASE, BACTERIAL DISEASE and PARASITIC DISEASE, which may be acute or chronic and are usually communicable. Insects, animals and human carriers may be important in their spread and EPIDEMICS may occur. INFLAMMATION is often the result of infection, but **inflammatory disease** can also result from disordered IMMUNITY and other causes. In **vascular diseases**, organs become diseased secondary to disease in their blood supply, such as ARTERIOSCLEROSIS, ANEURYSM, THROMBOSIS and EMBOLISM. **Tumors,** including benign growths, CANCER and LYMPHOMA are diseases in which abnormal growth of a structure occurs and leads to a lump, pressure on or spread to other organs and distant effects such as emaciation, HORMONE production and NEURITIS. In **degenerative disease**, DEATH or premature ageing in parts of an organ or system lead to a gradual impairment of function. **Deficiency diseases** result from inadequate intake of nutrients, VITAMINS, minerals, calcium, iron and trace substances; disorders of their fine control and that of hormones leads to **metabolic disease**. **Poisoning** is the toxic action of chemicals on body systems, some of which may be particularly sensitive to a given poison. An increasingly recognized side-effect of industrialization is the occurrence of **occupational diseases**, in which chemicals, dusts or molds encountered at work cause disease—especially PNEUMOCONIOSIS and other LUNG disease, and certain cancers. **Iatrogenic disease** is disease produced by the intervention of doctors, in an attempt to treat or prevent some other disease. The altered ANATOMY of diseased structures is described as **pathological**. **Psychiatric disease**, including psychoses (schizophrenia and depression) and neuroses, are functional disturbances of the BRAIN, in which structural abnormalities are not recognizable; they may represent subtle disturbances of brain metabolism. **Treatment** of disease by SURGERY or DRUGS is usual, but success is variable; a number of conditions are so benign that symptoms may be suppressed until they have run their natural course.

DISINFECTANTS. See ANTISEPTICS.

DISLOCATION, a CRYSTAL defect in which the normal crystal lattice is distorted (e.g., by the interposition of an extra half plane of atoms—an edge dislocation). The type and number of dislocations in a crystal help to determine its electrical and mechanical properties.

DISMAL SWAMP, coastal region of some 750sq mi in SE Va. and NE N.C. It has a rich and varied tree cover, though most of the swamp is now drained and used for lumbering and agriculture. In the center of the swamp is Lake Drummond.

DISNEYLAND, amusement center at Anaheim, Cal., built by Walt DISNEY. The park was opened in 1955 and now includes 160 acres of amusements and recreations based on Disney films and cartoon characters. There is a larger counterpart in Fla.

DISNEY, Walt (Walter Elias Disney; 1901–1966), US pioneer of animated film cartoons. Starting in the 1920s, the Disney studios in Hollywood created the famous cartoon characters Mickey Mouse, Pluto, Donald Duck and Goofy. Disney's first full-length cartoon feature, *Snow White and the Seven Dwarfs* (1938), was followed by *Pinocchio* (1940), *Fantasia* (1940) and *Bambi* (1942) among others. He also produced many popular nature and live-action films.

DISPENSATIONALISM, the doctrine, commonly held in FUNDAMENTALISM, that human history is divided into seven ages ("dispensations") in each of which man is tested by God in terms of a different standard of obedience, the current requirement being faith in Jesus Christ.

DISPERSION, in optics, the separation of a mixture of LIGHT radiations according to COLOR (i.e., wavelength). This can occur in REFRACTION (when it is responsible for the RAINBOW and the production of a SPECTRUM with a PRISM), in DIFFRACTION (as is applied in the grating spectroscope), or in SCATTERING (giving rise, e.g., to the blue color of the sky). The dispersive power of an optical medium is a measure of the extent to which its refractive index varies with wavelength.

Characters from Disney films walk the streets of Disneyland, the world-famous amusement park in California. Visitors enter along Main Street, a recreation of a 19th-century small town, to reach the park's four main areas, Adventureland, Frontierland, Fantasyland and Tomorrowland.

DISPLACEMENT ACTIVITY, term used by ethologists for actions performed by an animal in stressful situations that appear to be irrelevant to prevailing conditions. An example is grooming in a situation where fighting would normally be expected. A possible explanation of such activity is that it results from the effects of conflicting stimulae. This diversion of impulses is due either to conflict between opposing drives or the presence of a strong drive in the absence of an appropriate external object for its relief.

DISRAELI, Benjamin, 1st Earl of Beaconsfield (1804–1881), British Conservative statesman of Jewish descent, prime minister 1868 and 1874–80. A member of Parliament from 1837, he was chancellor of the exchequer 1852, 1858 and 1865. His influence was crucial in the passing of the 1867 Reform Bill, which enfranchised some 2 million working-class voters. His brief first ministry ended when the Liberals under GLADSTONE won the 1868 elections. His second period of office included domestic reforms: slum clearance, public-health reform and improvement of working conditions. Abroad, Disraeli fought imperial wars, bought control of the Suez Canal (1875), had Queen Victoria proclaimed Empress of India(1876) and annexed the Transvaal (1877). In the confrontation between Russia and Turkey (1877–78), he forced concessions on Russia (see BERLIN, CONGRESS OF). A prolific writer, he published many books, notably the novels *Coningsby* (1844) and *Sybil* (1845)—both on social and political themes.

DISSENTERS. See NONCONFORMISTS.

DISSOCIATION, in chemistry, the reversible decomposition of a compound, often effected by heat. **Ionic dissociation** is the dissociation of a covalent compound—a weak electrolyte (see ELECTROLYSIS)—into IONS when dissolved in water or other ionizing SOLVENTS. It accounts in part for the phenomena of electrolytic CONDUCTIVITY.

DISSONANCE, in acoustics, the simultaneous sounding of two or more tones which, because of BEATING, seem unpleasant to the human ear. Which musical intervals are considered dissonant is largely a matter of cultural and historical relativism.

DISTANCE MEASURING EQUIPMENT (DME), instrument used in aerial NAVIGATION to determine distance from a RADIO beacon by measuring the time taken for a pulse to reach the beacon and return.

DISTANT EARLY WARNING SYSTEM. See DEW LINE.

DISTEMPER, term applied to several animal diseases, but particularly referring to a specific VIRAL DISEASE of dogs. It commonly occurs in puppies, with FEVER, poor appetite and discharge from mucous membranes; bronchopneumonia and ENCEPHALITIS may be complications. VACCINATION is protective.

DISTILLATION, process in which substances are vaporized and then condensed by cooling, probably first invented by the ALEXANDRIAN SCHOOL and used in ALCHEMY, the still and the ALEMBIC being employed. It may be used to separate a volatile liquid from nonvolatile solids, as in the production of pure WATER from seawater, or from less volatile liquids, as in the distillation of liquid air to give oxygen, nitrogen and the noble gases. If the boiling points of the components differ greatly, **simple distillation** can be used: on gentle heating, the components distill over in order (the most volatile first) and the pure fractions are collected in different flasks. Mixtures of liquids of similar boiling points require **fractionation** for efficient separation. This technique employs multiple still heads and fractionating columns in which some of the vapor is condensed and returned to the still, equilibrating as it does so with the rising vapor. In effect, the mixture is redistilled several times; the number of theoretical simple distillations, or theoretical plates, represents the separating efficiency of the column. The theory of distillation is an aspect of PHASE EQUILIBRIA studies. For ideal solutions, obeying RAOULT's law, the vapor always contains a higher proportion than the liquid of the more volatile component; if this is not the case, an AZEOTROPIC MIXTURE may be formed. When two immiscible liquids are distilled, they come over in the proportion of their VAPOR PRESSURES at a temperature below the boiling point of either. This is utilized in **steam distillation**, in which superheated steam is passed into the still and comes over together with the volatile liquid. It is useful when normal distillation would require a temperature high enough to cause decomposition, as is **vacuum distillation**, in which the pressure reduction lowers the boiling points. A further refinement is **molecular distillation**, in which unstable molecules travel directly in high vacuum to the condenser.

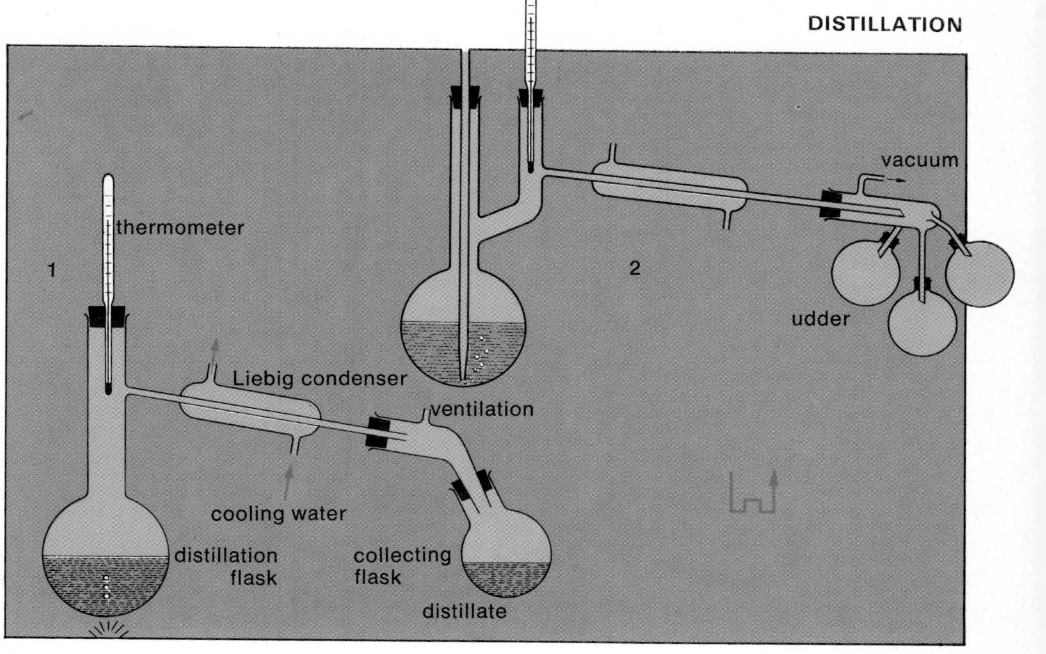

(1) Simple laboratory distillation apparatus comprising a distillation flask with thermometer, a Liebig condenser and a collecting flask (receiver). (2) Vacuum distillation apparatus. A capillary tube allows some air to "bleed" into the flask and a rotating "udder" allows several distillate fractions to be collected without breaking the vacuum. Vacuum distillation is invaluable when thermally unstable liquids have to be distilled.

Large-scale production of distilled liquor: a row of whisky stills in a Scottish distillery. Scotch whisky, probably the world's most widely consumed distilled beverage, is a distillate of malted barley.

DISTILLED LIQUOR, an ALCOHOLIC BEVERAGE of high ETHANOL content produced by DISTILLATION of a fermented mixture (see BREWING; FERMENTATION). Crude distilling of rice beer was practiced in the Far East several centuries BC; in the West distilled mead and wine were made by 500 AD. Whiskey and brandy production flourished in the later Middle Ages, and in the 16th century fractional distillation was introduced. Modern production is in large, continuous stills. As well as ethanol and water, the distillate contains FUSEL OILS and other compounds which give flavor and aroma, further improved by several years' maturation in oak casks. The alcohol content is expressed in the "proof" system: in the US one degree proof equals 0.5% ethanol by volume.

DISTRIBUTIVE LAW. See ALGEBRA.

DISTRIBUTOR, in AUTOMOBILES, a device operated off the CAMSHAFT which ensures that the cylinders of the INTERNAL-COMBUSTION ENGINE are fired in the correct sequence and at the optimum time.

DISTRICT ATTORNEY, US lawyer and public official who acts as public prosecutor for a particular district, usually a county. A federal D.A. is usually responsible for a substantial part of a state. His main duties are to decide whether and on what charges the accused is to be prosecuted, and to act as prosecutor. He may also appear for the government in civil cases. A D.A. may be elected or appointed. Federal attorneys are appointed by the president and responsible to the attorney general.

DISTRICT OF COLUMBIA. See WASHINGTON, D.C.

DISULFIRAM. See ANTABUSE.

DITHYRAMB, ancient Greek choral song, originating in the 7th century BC, improvised in honor of DIONYSUS. The term was later used for writing or speech in an unrestrained, passionate style.

DITTERSDORF, Karl Ditters von (1739–1799), Austrian composer and violinist. He composed light operas, establishing the *singspiel* form, and various other works. Among his works are the operas *Doctor und Apotheker* (1786), *Hieronymus Knicker* (1789) and *Das Rote Kappchen* (1790).

DIURETICS, drugs that increase urine production by the KIDNEY. Alcohol and CAFFEINE are mild diuretics. Thiazides and other diuretics are commonly used in treatment of HEART failure, EDEMA, high blood pressure, LIVER and KIDNEY disease.

DIV, in VECTOR ANALYSIS, divergence. Div **V** is defined as the scalar product of DEL with the vector **V**: ∇.**V**. Hence, in CARTESIAN COORDINATES,

$$\operatorname{div}\mathbf{V}=\nabla.\mathbf{V}=\frac{\partial v_x}{\partial x}+\frac{\partial v_y}{\partial y}+\frac{\partial v_z}{\partial z}.$$

DIVERGENCE, of a SEQUENCE or SERIES. See CONVERGENCE. See also DIV.

DIVERTIMENTO, a primarily 18th-century musical form for string and wind instruments, characterized by its light and enjoyable nature. Among others, Mozart, Haydn, Beethoven and Schubert wrote in this form.

DIVIDE, water parting, or **watershed**, a region of high ground that lies between and determines the flow of two unconnected drainage systems. The **Continental Divide** of North America is formed by the Rocky Mountains.

DIVIDEND, a number that is divided (see DIVISION) by another number, the DIVISOR. In a FRACTION such as $\frac{a}{b}$ the dividend, a, is called the numerator.

DIVINATION, the term applied to various methods of foretelling the future, by means of oracles, omens or signs. These methods include dream interpretation, astrology, investigation of parts of the body, (e.g., palmistry, phrenology), the study of animal entrails, and the interpretation of the cries of birds and animals (augury). Divination is one of the most ancient of practices, and has been found in almost all societies. (See ASTROLOGY; FORTUNE-TELLING; ZODIAC.)

DIVINE, Father. See FATHER DIVINE.

DIVINE COMEDY. See DANTE.

DIVINE RIGHT OF KINGS, the theory that a sovereign's right to rule comes directly from God, and that he is responsible only to God. A rebellion against such a sovereign is seen as rebellion against God. This justification for ABSOLUTISM survived until the 1800s. Included among its principal theorists were BOSSUET and FILMER.

DIVING. See SWIMMING AND DIVING.

DIVING, Deep Sea, the descent by divers to the sea bed, usually for protracted periods, for purposes of exploration, salvage, etc. Skin diving is almost as old as man and the Romans had primitive diving suits connected by an air pipe to the surface. This principle was also known in the early 16th century. A breakthrough came when John Lethbridge devised the forerunner of the armored suits used today in deepest waters (1715): it looked much like a barrel with sleeves and a viewport, and was useless for depths of more than a few metres. In 1802 William Forder devised a suit where air was pumped to the diver by bellows. And in 1837 (improving his earlier design of 1819) Augustus Siebe (1788–1872) invented the modern diving suit, a continuous airtight suit to which air is supplied by a pump. The diving suit today has a metal or fiberglass helmet with viewports and inhalation and exhalation valves, joined by an airtight seal to a metal chestpiece, itself joined to a flexible watertight covering of rubber and canvas; and weights, especially weighted boots, for stability and to prevent the diver shooting toward the surface. Air or, more often, an oxygen/helium mixture is conveyed to him via a thick rubber tube. In addition, he has either a telephone wire, or simply a cord which he can tug, for communication with the surface. Nowadays SCUBA diving, where the diver has no suit but carries gas cylinders and an AQUALUNG, is preferred in most cases since it permits greater mobility. In all diving great care must be taken to avoid the bends (see AEROEMBOLISM) through too-rapid ascent to the surface. (See also BATHYSCAPHE; BATHYSPHERE.)

DIVINING ROD, a forked rod (usually of wood) used in DOWSING. The dowser holds the forked end, one prong in each hand, and is allegedly able to detect underground water, metal, etc., by the directions and magnitudes of convulsions of the rod.

DIVISION, the INVERSE operation of MULTIPLICATION, the determination of the number of times one number must be multiplied to equal another number. If DIVIDEND and DIVISOR have like positive or negative sign, then the QUOTIENT is positive; if their signs are different, the quotient is negative:

$$\text{e.g.,}\quad \frac{6}{3}=\frac{-6}{-3}=2,\quad\text{and}\quad \frac{-6}{3}=\frac{6}{-3}=-2.$$

Division involving two POWERS of a number or VARIABLE is performed by subtracting the EXPONENT of the divisor from that of the dividend:

$$x^4/x^2=x^{4-2}=x^2;$$

the division of the COEFFICIENTS being carried out in the normal way:

$$ax^7/bx^9=\frac{a}{b}x^{-2}.$$

In the division of INTEGERS, where an integral quotient is required, it may well be that the divisor does not divide exactly into the dividend: thus $\frac{7}{3}=2$ REMAINDER 1 (or, in REAL NUMBERS, $2\frac{1}{3}$).

Division of a polynomial by a binomial can be performed by factoring if the binomial is a FACTOR of the POLYNOMIAL. If not, a more complex procedure is used. To divide a polynomial by a monomial, divide each term separately by the monomial. Thus $ax^4y^2+bxy^3-cx$ divided by $-dxy$ is

$$-\frac{a}{d}x^3y-\frac{b}{d}y^2+\frac{c}{d}(y^{-1}).$$

DIVISOR, a number by which another number, the DIVIDEND, is divided (see DIVISION). In a FRACTION such as $\frac{a}{b}$, the divisor, b, is called the denominator.

DIVORCE, legal dissolution of a valid marriage, as distinct from SEPARATION, in which the partners remain married but live apart, and ANNULMENT, in which the marriage is deemed to be invalid. In most cases, divorce leaves the partners free to remarry, sometimes after a set period. Divorce has existed in most cultures, but its availability and the grounds for it have varied widely. Christianity regards marriage as a sacrament which may not lightly be set aside, and this view has affected the Western concept of divorce. The Roman Catholic Church still does not allow it,

Cutaway of a bathyscaphe capable of diving up to 10 000m. (a) Snorkels; (b) and (k) electromagnets; (c) propeller; (d) and (l) air release valves; (e) gasoline buoyancy tank; (f) observation light; (g) and (n) iron shot silos; (h) viewing lights; (i) viewing port; (j) conning tower; (m) rudder; (o) crew ladder; (p) air lock; (q) observation cabin.

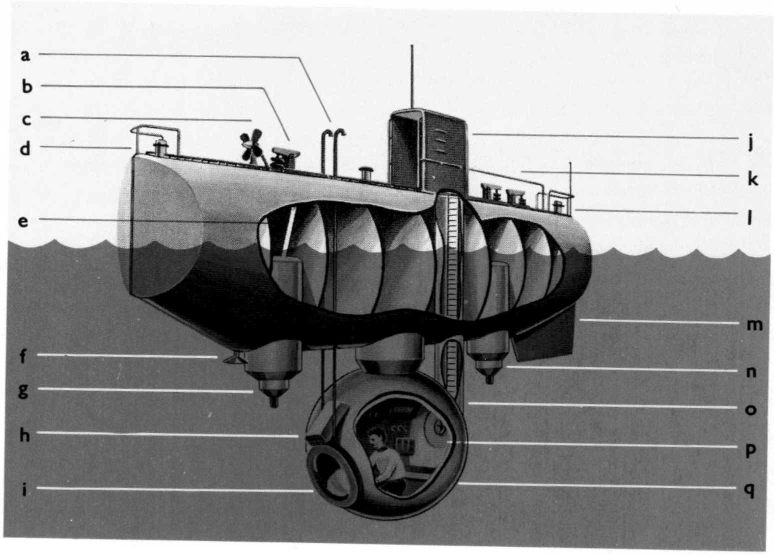

but most other churches now allow divorce. In the US each state makes its own divorce laws and there is great divergence. The trend has been towards a liberal view, but it has created the migratory or "quickie" divorce, for which Nevada is renowned. Adultery is the most widely accepted ground for divorce; others include cruelty, alcoholism, insanity, desertion and conviction of a serious crime. A modern trend is to make irreparable breakdown of the marriage another ground, without involving the misconduct of either party; the first states to introduce this were California and Iowa. Divorce is a major social problem in the US; it has been estimated that it ends one in every four marriages. The possible effect of such marital instability upon the children involved and upon society is giving rise to serious concern.

DIX, Dorothea Lynde (1802–1887), US social reformer and crusader for the humane and scientific treatment of mental illness. In 1841 she was shocked to see mentally sick people in jail and launched a successful campaign to establish mental hospitals.

DIX, Otto (1891–1969), German painter and leader of the "New Objectivity" school of social realism. His most famous work is the cycle of 50 etchings entitled *Der Krieg* (The War; 1924) depicting WWI horrors. He was jailed (1939–45) by the Nazi government. In later years he turned to a form of religious mysticism in his work.

DIXIE, popular term for the Southern states of the US, particularly those that formed the Confederacy. Many theories exist about the term's origin. The most popular, among Southerners, is that it is a corruption of "Mason-Dixon Line," the boundary between the free and the slave states. It is also the title of a popular melody which became the favorite marching song of the Confederate army.

DIXIECRATS, Southern faction of the US Democratic Party which opposed the 1948 party platform on civil rights. They ran their own candidates, Governor Strom Thurmond of S.C. for president and Governor Fielding Wright of Miss. for vice-president, against the incumbent President Truman, and received 1 169 000 national and 39 electoral votes.

DIXIELAND, the name given to one of the earliest jazz styles. It originated in New Orleans as an attempt by white musicians to copy early Negro jazzmen. Dixieland music is bright and extrovert, but with time it has become a slick and commercialized reflection of the New Orleans style.

Elevation plans of two floating dry docks: a large U-shaped dock capable of raising an ocean liner out of the water; and a smaller L-shaped dock on which lighter vessels can quickly and conveniently undergo hull repairs below the waterline. In both cases the vessel is floated on to the partially submerged dock which then discharges its water ballast.

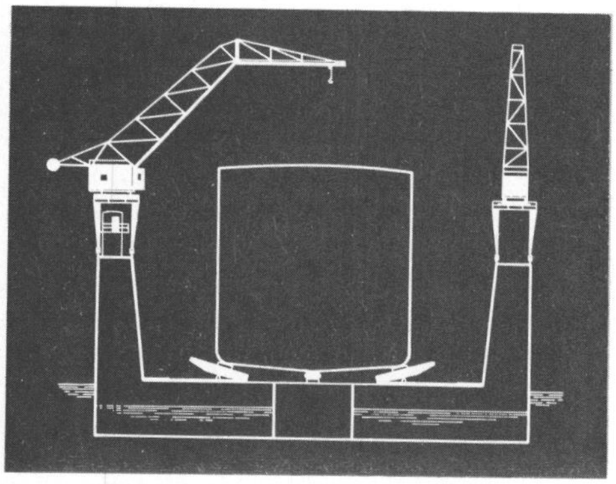

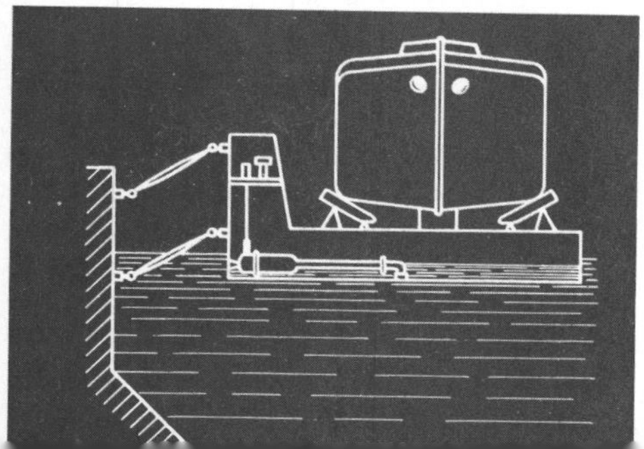

DIXON, city in N Ill., seat of Lee Co. Its industries include cement and electronic equipment. Pop 18 147.

DIXON, Jeremiah. See MASON-DIXON LINE.

DIXON, Joseph (1799–1869), US manufacturer, the inventor of the high-temperature GRAPHITE crucible and other graphite products.

DJAKARTA. See JAKARTA.

DJIBOUTI, capital and largest city of the French Territory of Afars and Issas (formerly French Somaliland). It stands on the westernmost part of the Gulf of Aden and, as a free port, is the main export center for Ethiopia. Pop 62 000.

DJILAS, Milovan (1911–), Yugoslav communist leader and writer. He was a leading WWII partisan alongside TITO, and became a vice-president after the war. But because of his outspoken criticisms of the regime he was imprisoned 1956–66. Among his works are *The New Class* (1957) and *Conversations with Stalin* (1962).

DJINN. See GENIE.

DMITRI, name of several pretenders to the Russian throne, claiming to be the son of Ivan IV the Terrible, Dmitri (1582–1591), who had died in mysterious circumstances. The first became tsar with Polish aid in 1605, after the death of Boris GODUNOV, but was killed by a mob in 1606. The second, also called the Thief of Tushino, challenged Tsar Shuisky from 1607 with Polish support, until murdered by a follower in 1610.

DNA, deoxyribonucleic acid, a NUCLEIC ACID comprising two strands of NUCLEOTIDE wound around each other in a double helix, found in all living things and VIRUSES.

DNEPRODZERZHINSK, formerly Kamenskoye, city in the Ukraine, USSR, on the Dnieper R. It makes steel, cement and chemical products. Pop 227 000.

DNEPROPETROVSK, formerly Ekaterinoslav, city in the Ukraine, USSR, on the Dnieper R. It is a major industrial center (with iron and steel) and houses several institutes of higher education. It was founded in 1787 by Potemkin. Pop 863 000.

DNIEPER RIVER, second-longest river in the European USSR, about 1 400mi long. Rising in the Valdai Hills, it flows SW to empty into the Black Sea E of Odessa. Leading tributaries are the Desna, Pripyat, Berezina and Sozh. It is a major water transport route, and also has many hydroelectric plants.

DNIESTER RIVER, river in the USSR, about 877mi long. It rises in the Carpathian Mts in the Ukraine and empties into the Black Sea W of Odessa. It carries timber and grain and has hydroelectric potential.

DOBBS FERRY, village in SE N.Y., on the Hudson R, a residential suburb of New York City. It houses Children's Village, a home for emotionally disturbed children. Pop 10 353.

DOBERMAN PINSCHER, a German breed of dog much used by police forces. Its hard, smooth coat is black and brown in coloring. It has clipped ears and tail, and a strong square build. Its height is about 25in and its weight is about 60–65lb.

DOBSON, William (1610–1646), English portrait painter, one of the first significant English painters. He was much influenced by Venetian works, and worked for King Charles I at Oxford 1642–46.

DOBSON FLY, *Corydalis cornutus*, a relative of the ALDERFLIES which is remarkable for its large size—its wingspan is 100mm (4in)—and for its marked sexual dimorphism. The larvae are aquatic.

DOBZHANSKY, Theodosius (1900–), Russian-born US biologist, famed for his study of the fruit fly, *Drosophila*, which demonstrated that a wide genetic range could exist in even a comparatively well-defined species. Indeed the greater the "genetic load" of unusual genes in a species, the better equipped it is to survive in changed circumstances. (See EVOLUTION; HEREDITY.)

DOCK, an enclosure of water in a port or harbor in which a ship may be berthed for maintenance or loading. Where access to the hull is required, a **dry dock** may be used. Usually this is a basin of water dug into the shore of a water channel, from which it can be closed off by a gate: the ship is floated in, the gate closed and the water pumped out. **Floating dry docks** are trough-like structures which can, by use of ballast, be partly submerged: with the ship inside, the dock is drained and the ballast discarded. In all cases, the ship must be supported before pumping dry.

DOCK, large-leafed, herbaceous plants of the genus *Rumex*, distinguished from the sorrels by having nonacid tasting leaves and bisexual flowers. Docks have worldwide distribution and most are classed as weeds. Family: Polygonaceae. (See also WOOD SORREL.)

DOCTOR, Medical. See MEDICINE.

DOCTORFISH, fishes of the family Teuthididae, that are found in warm waters, especially in S Asian seas. They are related to Moorish Idols and on each side of their body they have one or two sharp spines.

DODDER, parasitic, twining plants of the genus *Cuscuta*, family Convolvulaceae, with no chlorophyll. They are widely distributed in temperate and warmer climates. They obtain nourishment through suckers that penetrate the host plant. Some species can be pests in crops such as FLAX, CLOVER and BEANS. (See also CONVOLVULUS; PARASITE.)

DODECAHEDRON. See POLYHEDRON.

DODECANESE, group of Greek islands in the SE Aegean Sea off Turkey. There are 12 main islands, and, except for Rhodes and Cos, they are largely rocky and infertile. Italy seized the group in 1912 from the Turks, but after WWII they were ceded to Greece.

DODECAPHONIC MUSIC. See TWELVE-TONE MUSIC.

DODGE, Grenville Mellen (1831–1916), US military and civil engineer, who built many of the first railroads in the West and Southwest. After serving as a Union general in the Civil War, he was chief construction engineer for the Union Pacific Railroad (1866–70). He later worked with Jay GOULD on railroad construction in the Southwest.

DODGE, Mary Elizabeth Mapes (1831–1905), US children's author, who founded and edited the magazine *St. Nicholas* (1873). She is best known for her book *Hans Brinker, or The Silver Skates* (1865), a classic of children's literature.

DODGE CITY, city in SW Kan. on the Arkansas R, seat of Ford Co. In the late 1800s it was a cattle center on the Sante Fe Trail, at the head of the Santa Fe Railroad, and it became notorious for its wild frontier life. It now has railroad shops and makes agricultural implements. Pop 14 127.

DODGSON, Charles Lutwidge. See CARROLL, LEWIS.

DODO, *Raphus cucullatus*, an extinct bird that was native to Mauritius. The dodo was about the size of a turkey, had a bulky body, short legs and feet and reduced wings. The head was most unusual, being large and carrying a heavy, strongly hooked, dark colored bill. The dodo was first discovered in 1507 but, mainly due to the effects of man and the animals he introduced, it was extinct by 1681.

DODONA, ancient Greek town in Epirus, the site of the oldest of Greek oracles, dedicated to Zeus. The rustling of oaktree leaves or the echoing of a bronze gong were interpreted by priests as omens.

DOENITZ, Karl (1891–), German admiral, head of the WWII U-boat service and later commander in chief of the German navy (1943–45). On Hitler's death in 1945 he became head-of-state, and subsequently surrendered to the Allies. He was tried for war crimes at Nuremberg and sentenced to 10 years in prison.

DOESBURG, Theo van (real name: Christian Emil Marie Küpper; 1883–1931), Dutch painter and author, a leader of the DE STIJL group. He turned to abstraction in 1916, influenced at first by MONDRIAN. He taught at the BAUHAUS 1921–23.

DOG, carnivorous mammal of the family Canidae, with long legs, long muzzle and bushy tail, that lives by chasing its prey. Many live in packs. Wild dogs include the Raccoon dog of Asia and several South American forms like the Bush dog and the Maned wolf.

DOGBANE, herbaceous perennial plants of the genus *Apocynum*, native to North America. They produce bell-like white, pink or greenish flowers and oval leaves. Family: Apocynaceae.

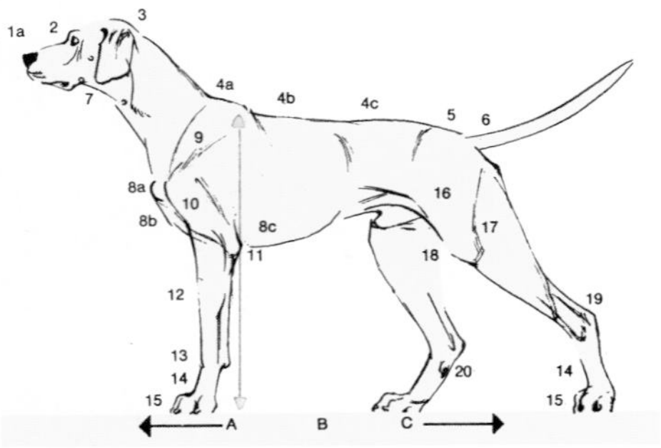

Parts of the dog: (A) forequarters; (B) middle part; (C) hindquarters; (1) muzzle; (1a) nose; (2) stop; (3) occiput; (4) back; (4a) withers; (4b) back; (4c) loin (seen from above) and coupling (seen from the side); (5) croup; (4a, 4b, 4c and 5 together) topline; (6) tail root; (7) cheek and throat wart; (8) chest; (8a) breastbone; (8b) forechest; (8c) brisket or lower chest; (9) shoulder; (10) upper arm; (11) elbow; (12) forearm; (13) wrist or pastern joint; (14) front pastern; (15) forefoot or paw; (16) upper thigh; (17) second thigh or gaskin; (18) knee or stifle; (19) hock joint or point of hock; (20) dewclaws; (4a–A) the dog's height, measured at the withers.

DOGE, title of the heads of the republics of Venice (from the early 8th century) and Genoa (from 1339). The Venetian doge ruled for life; his dictatorial powers were increasingly restricted from the establishment of the Council of Ten in 1310. In Genoa, Andrea DORIA in 1528 reduced the doge's term of office to two years. Both offices were abolished by Napoleon when he overthrew the republics (1797).

DOGFISH, small sharks up to 1.5m (5ft) long which feed near the sea bottom on worms, shrimps, fish and mollusks. They have the typical head shape and rough skin of the shark, and lay their eggs in horny cases. They are sold as grayfish or rock salmon for food.

DOGGER BANK, large shoal in the North Sea about 60mi off the NE coast of England. It is some 60mi long and 65mi wide, and is 50ft below sea level at its highest point. Cod, haddock and herring have been fished here since the Middle Ages.

DOGMA, in Roman Catholic theology, those teachings considered as divine revelation and laid down by the Church as essential tenets of faith. In a more general sense, dogma describes the principal tenets of any authoritarian Christian church.

DOG RACING, sport in which specially bred dogs (usually greyhounds) chase a mechanical hare around a fixed circuit. One of the major gambling sports, it derives from the English custom of live hare coursing. The modern dog track was first developed by the American, Oliver P. Smith, in 1919. In the US the sport is most popular in Fla.; it is widely followed in Britain and various other European countries and in Australia. The standard US track is 440yd long; in Britain it may be up to 1 200yd.

DOGRIB INDIANS, members of the ATHABASCAN language group who lived by hunting game in the Mackenzie R area of the Northwest Territories of Canada.

DOGSLED, type of dog-drawn vehicle, used in Arctic regions since ancient times. Huskies, samoyeds, Eskimo dogs or Alaskan malamutes are used, harnessed either in line or in a "fan," with a separate lead for each dog. Dogsled racing is popular in Norway, Canada, Alaska and the northern US.

DOG STAR. See SIRIUS.

DOGTOOTH VIOLET, common name for plants of the genus *Erythronium,* native to North America. Unbranched stems are produced in the spring from a deep-sited CORM. *Erythronium americanum* produces lily-like flowers. Family: Liliaceae.

DOGWOODS, creeping shrubs, shrubs and trees of the genus *Cornus*, family Cornaceae, various species of which are native to North America, Asia and Europe, cultivated as ornamentals for their colorful foliage.

DOHNÁNYI, Ernst von (1877–1960), Hungarian-born composer and pianist, conductor of the Budapest Philharmonic Orchestra (1919–44). His music, influenced by Brahms, includes the light-hearted *Variations on a Nursery Song* (1913) and *Ruralia Hungarica* (1924), both for piano and orchestra.

DOISY, Edward Adelbert (1893–), US biochemist who first crystallized the female sex HORMONE estrone (1929). He shared the 1943 Nobel Prize for Physiology or Medicine with H. DAM after isolating, determining the structure of, and synthesizing VITAMIN K (1936).

DOLCI, Danilo (1924–), Italian writer and social reformer. Since 1952 he has worked to improve the lot of the Sicilians, despite opposition from both the authorities and the Mafia. He won the 1957 Lenin Peace Prize. His books include *To Feed the Hungry* (1959) and *"Where There's Smoke..."* (1971).

DOLDRUMS, regions of low wind, calms and strong upward air movement around the EQUATOR, produced by the convergence of the SE and NE TRADE WINDS. Sailing ships were often becalmed there.

DOLE, Robert J. (1923–), US politician, unsuccessful Republican vice-presidential candidate in 1976 as running mate of Gerald FORD. Twice decorated in WWII, he was Republican national chairman 1971–73 and senator from Kan. from 1974.

DOLE, Sanford Ballard (1844–1926), US judge and leader of the Republic of Hawaii. In 1893, he led the movement which overthrew Queen Liliuokalani and resulted in the establishment of the Hawaiian republic, of which Dole was proclaimed president (1894–1900). After US annexation in 1898, he served as territorial governor 1900–03.

DOLERITE. British term for DIABASE.

DOLIN, Anton (born Patrick Healey-Kay; 1904–), British dancer and choreographer. He made his debut in DIAGHILEV's *The Sleeping Princess* (1921). In 1931 he began his renowned partnership with Alicia MARKOVA. Dolin worked with the Ballet Theater, New York, 1940–46, and in 1949, with Markova, founded the London Festival Ballet.

DOLL, a miniature representation of the human form, used as a toy or, in some societies, a sacred object. The practice of making dolls is an ancient one. Some of the earliest examples, made from a wide range of substances including wood, bone, ivory and clay, have been found in Pakistan at MOHENJO-DARO (c3000 BC) and on Babylonian, Egyptian and Aztec sites. In ancient societies dolls were often entombed with the dead. In America, they are still used in Hopi and Zuni Indian rites.

The modern doll has its origin in medieval doll nativity scenes and in the 14th-century fashion dolls of France and England. During the 16th century, Nuremberg in Germany became a major center of doll making, noted particularly for its figures carved from wood. Papier-mâché and wax were used in the 19th century as ideal materials for fashioning dolls' heads. Present-day dolls are made from a variety of synthetic materials, their designs incorporating such sales gimmicks as "voices," working limbs and moving eyelids.

DOLLAR, name for the monetary units of the US, Canada, Australia and many other countries. The word is said to derive from the German *taler*, meaning silver coin. Since WWII the US dollar has been the world's principal RESERVE CURRENCY and medium of international trade. (See also GOLD STANDARD.)

DOLLFUSS, Englebert (1892–1934), Austrian chancellor and fascist dictator (1933–34). He allied with Mussolini to keep Austria independent of Hitler and banned the Austrian Nazi party. In Feb. 1934, his Fatherland Party decimated the Social Democrats in street fighting. Dollfuss was assassinated in an unsuccessful Nazi *putsch* the following July.

DÖLLINGER, Johann Joseph Ignaz von (1799–1890), German Roman Catholic historian and theologian, excommunicated (1871) for rejecting the doctrine of papal infallibility. He was professor of ecclesiastical history and law at Munich U. (1826–71). His books include *The Pope and the Council* (1869), a collection of letters and articles criticizing papal authoritarianism. (See OLD CATHOLICS.)

DOLMEN, Neolithic (see STONE AGE) tomb in a roughly table-like form, with one horizontal slab of stone supported by three or more vertical slabs, beneath which is the burial chamber. It is possible that dolmens are manifestations of a megalithic religion that spread from the Aegean.

DOLMETSCH, Arnold (1858–1940), French-born British musicologist and instrument builder. A pioneer of the revival of early music and musical instruments, he wrote *The Interpretation of the Music of the 17th and 18th Centuries* (1915).

DOLOMITE, a common mineral, calcium magnesium carbonate ($CaMg(CO_3)_2$), with white or colorless rhombohedral crystals, often found associated with limestone and MARBLE and in magnesium-rich metamorphic rocks. It is used as an ornamental and building stone, and is a source of magnesium.

DOLOMITES, Alpine mountain range in NE Italy mainly composed of vividly-colored dolomitic limestone. The highest peak is Marmolada (10 965ft). A popular tourist and climbing resort, its main center is Cortina d'Ampezzo.

DOLPHINS, a group of aquatic mammals. Dolphins are small toothed WHALES living in schools and feeding mainly on fish. The largest, the KILLER WHALE, also feeds on seals and the largest whales. The Pilot whale is another large dolphin, but the most well-known member of the family (Delphinidae) is the Bottle-nosed dolphin, a highly intelligent mammal with an amazingly developed system of echolocation (see

The bottle-nosed dolphin, considered by some scientists to be the most intelligent animal in the world next to man, has come to be a familiar sight in marine parks in many countries, delighting audiences with extraordinary displays of acrobatic skill.

ECHO) for finding food and avoiding obstacles. A second family of dolphins (Platanistidae) lives in fresh water, and includes the Chinese Lake dolphin and the Blind susu or Ganges dolphin. (See also PORPOISE.) The Pacific spout fish of the family Corphaenidae is also known as the dolphin. It has a blunt head and forked tail, and can swim at great speed. It is a popular Hawaiian food fish.

DOLTON, village in NE Ill., 18mi S of Chicago on the Calumet R. It manufactures glass and metal products. Pop 25 937.

DOMAGK, Gerhard (1895–1964), German pharmacologist who discovered the antibacterial action of the dye Prontosil Red. This led to the discovery of other SULFA DRUGS. In recognition of this Domagk was offered the 1939 Nobel Prize for Physiology or Medicine, though he was not allowed to accept it at the time.

DOMAIN. See SET THEORY.

DOMAINS, Magnetic. See MAGNETISM.

DOME, in architecture, an oval or hemispherical vault, used to roof a large space without interior supports. The first domes were built around 1000 BC by the Persians and Assyrians but these were small and the dome did not become architecturally significant until Roman times. The PANTHEON, in which the dome rests on a drum-shaped building, is an outstanding example of the large-scale dome. The Byzantine architects of HAGIA SOPHIA in Constantinople evolved the pendentive, a device enabling the construction of a great dome over a square central area. Brunelleschi's dome on the cathedral in Florence has an inner and an outer shell; Sir Christopher Wren's dome for St. Paul's London, has three shells. Modern techniques and lightweight materials permit the spanning of vast areas, as at the Houston Astradome.

The dome has been a persistent feature in the architecture of most civilizations since the Assyrians and Persians innovated the form over 3 000 years ago. The magnificent white-painted iron dome of the Capitol in Washington D.C., seen here, was designed by Thomas Walter and is based on the dome of St. Peter's Basilica in Rome.

DOMENICHINO (born Domenico Zampieri; 1581–1641), Italian Baroque painter from Bologna, noted for the landscape settings of his pictures. Trained by the CARRACCI brothers, he painted large fresco schemes, notably *The Life of St. Cecilia* (1613–14), in palaces and churches in Rome.

DOMESDAY BOOK, a survey of most of England compiled for William I the Conqueror in 1085–86. It describes "ploughland and habitations ... men ... both bond and free," housing conditions, services and rents owned by gentry and peasants, land values and every detail of rural economy in the years 1066 and 1085. It was compiled largely by itinerant commissioners with the aid of juries of inquiry. A statistical record unique in medieval Europe, it is an invaluable source for English national and local history.

DOMESTICATION, the process by which some animals have been adapted to the uses of man. Domestication implies the rearing of animals in captivity or semicaptivity but also usually involves changes in the animals concerned. (See also ARTIFICIAL SELECTION.)

DOMINANCE HIERARCHY, the organization of animals, notably PRIMATES, within groups according to social status. This order is usually established by mutual threatening or warning signals that make fighting for dominance unnecessary. The dominant animal has priority over members of the group in feeding, sex relations, and other activities.

DOMINIC, Saint (c1170–1221), Spanish churchman, founder of the DOMINICAN ORDER. From 1207 he was leader of a mission to the ALBIGENSIAN heretics of S France. In 1216 the pope approved Dominic's plans for a new preaching order based on ideals of poverty and scholarship. The order grew rapidly and Dominic spent the rest of his life supervising it. He was canonized in 1234. His feast day is Aug. 4.

DOMINICA, largest island in the Windward Islands of the Lesser Antilles group, between Guadeloupe and Martinique. It is crossed from N to S by a mountain range which contains Morne Diablotin (4 747ft), the highest point in the Lesser Antilles. Dominica enjoys high temperatures and heavy rainfall and has a rich volcanic soil. Bananas, cacao and spices are the chief exports. Discovered by Columbus in 1493 and colonized by France in the early 17th century, it was acquired by Britain in 1805 and became internally self-governing in 1967. Pop 70 302.

DOMINICAN ORDER, officially the Order of Preachers (O.P.), Roman Catholic order of FRIARS. It was founded (1216) by St. DOMINIC, with approval from Pope Honorius III, as a band of highly trained priests, pledged to poverty, study and itinerant preaching. The first friaries were intended as hostels, not permanent residences. The "Black Friars," as they were popularly named for the black cloak they wore over their white habit while preaching, played a major role in the medieval INQUISITION and produced many great missionaries and theologians, notably AQUINAS. There were associated orders of nuns (see CATHERINE OF SIENA) and of lay men and women. The religious reformer SAVONAROLA was a Dominican.

DOMINICAN REPUBLIC, independent republic of the West Indies occupying the eastern two-thirds of the island of Hispaniola, which it shares with Haiti. Parallel mountain chains run from NW to SE. The biggest of these, the Cordillera Central, contains Pico Duarte, which at 10 490ft is the highest point in the West Indies. The main rivers (the Yaque del Norte, Yaque del Sur and the Yuna) also rise here. To the N of the range lie the Cibao and Vega Real lowlands, the main agricultural area. The climate is subtropical, with an annual rainfall averaging 50in which is heaviest in the N. Hurricanes tend to occur between Aug. and Nov.

About 65% of Dominicans are mulattoes, 20% are Negroes and 15% are Caucasians. About two-thirds of the people live in rural areas, especially the Cibao and Vega Real lowlands. Over 60% of the population are illiterate. Agriculture employs 80% of the population, with sugar, coffee and cacao forming a similar percentage of the republic's total exports. Industry is concentrated around the capital, and apart from agricultural processing includes cement, textile and plastic manufacture. There is also some mining of bauxite, iron ore and nickel.

Hispaniola was discovered by Columbus in 1492. The E part remained Spanish, while the W part was ceded to France in 1697. After centuries of turmoil the independent Dominican republic emerged in 1844, but continued to be torn by internal troubles under a succession of dictators and revolutions. It was occupied by the US Marines (1916–1924). In 1930 an army revolt put General TRUJILLO in power. His dictatorship ended with his assassination in 1961. Free elections followed, but the new left wing government of Juan BOSCH was overthrown by a military coup in 1963. An attempt to reinstate Bosch prompted US intervention in the form of armed occupation of Santo Domingo (1965). In 1966 Dr. Joaquín Balaguer became president. He was reelected in 1970.

Official Name: Dominican Republic
Capital: Santo Domingo
Area: 18 700sq mi
Population: 4 188 000
Languages: Spanish
Religions: Roman Catholic
Monetary Unit(s): 1 D.R. peso = 100 centavos

DOMINION DAY, July 1, Canadian national holiday commemorating the creation of the independent Dominion of Canada under the BRITISH NORTH AMERICA ACT (1867).

DOMINOES, a game for two or more people played with flat rectangular blocks whose faces are divided into two sections and marked with pips in every possible combination from 0–0 to 6–6. In the best-known version of the game, players try to match a block or "domino" in their hand with one of the two exposed ends on the table. The first to dispose of his hand wins the game.

DOMITIAN (51–96 AD), Roman emperor, 81–96, son of VESPASIAN and brother of TITUS, whom he succeeded. He governed efficiently but harshly, his last years amounting to a reign of terror. He was assassinated at the instigation of his wife.

DONATELLO (c1386–1466), Florentine sculptor, a major figure of the Italian Renaissance. He trained as a metal worker with GHIBERTI, and as a marble sculptor. His many commissions for the Duomo of Florence include the famous *putti* for the singing gallery. Other major works are *St. George Slaying the Dragon* (1415–17), the graceful bronze *David* (c1432) in the Bargello, Florence, and the equestrian statue known as the Gattamelata Monument (1447–53), in Padua.

DONATI, Giovanni Battista (1826–1873), Italian astronomer who first studied the spectra of COMETS (1864). He discovered several comets including "Donati's comet" of 1858.

DONATION OF CONSTANTINE, document purporting to be addressed to Pope Sylvester I by

Emperor Constantine I (d. 337), but forged, probably in the 8th century. According to it, Constantine, the first Christian emperor, renounced imperial political authority in Italy and spiritual authority in the Church in favor of the pope. The forgery was exposed by Lorenzo VALLA in c1440, though the document's authenticity was contested on into the 18th century.

DONATISM, schismatic Christian sect in North Africa founded in 316 by the followers of a Bishop Donatus. During DIOCLETIAN's persecution (303–05) some churchmen collaborated with the authorities. Bishop Donatus protested when in 311 one such collaborator consecrated Caecilian bishop of Carthage. He argued that a "traitor" to the faith could not legitimately administer the sacraments. Donatism survived until the spread of Islam through North Africa, in the early 7th century.

DONAU, German name for the DANUBE RIVER.

DONELSON, Fort, Confederate camp on the Cumberland R at Dover, Tenn., commanded by Gen. BUCKNER. Its capture by Gen. GRANT on Feb. 16, 1862, and the fall of Fort HENRY ten days earlier, opened the river passage into Tenn. and forced the evacuation of Nashville.

DONETS BASIN, or Donbass, region along the Donets and lower Dnieper rivers in the USSR. It has the USSR's richest coalfield, covering nearly 9 000sq mi and supplying about 35% of the country's coal. It also produces more iron and steel than any other region in the USSR.

DONETSK, capital city of the Donetsk *oblast* in the Ukraine, USSR. One of the largest industrial centers of the Donets Basin, it has enormous metallurgical plants, foundries and chemical works. There are also important cultural and educational amenities. Pop 905 000.

DONETS RIVER (also Northern Donets R), in the USSR. Rising in E Kurst *oblast*, it flows 631mi through the Donets Basin to join the Don R. It is navigable for much of its length, and is a means of transportation for heavy industry.

DONGAN, Thomas, 2nd Earl of Limerick (1634–1715), colonial governor of New York 1682–88. He called a representative assembly and issued a "Charter of Liberties" granting religious toleration and city government. He negotiated with the Iroquois Confederacy and secured New York against the French.

DONIPHAN, Alexander William (1808–1887), US soldier and lawyer. In 1838, commanding the Mo. state militia, he refused orders to execute Joseph SMITH and other Mormon leaders. In 1846–47, during the Mexican War, he led his men on a celebrated long march of 3 600mi, from Santa Fe, N.M., to Chihuahua, Mexico (which he captured) and then back to Mo.

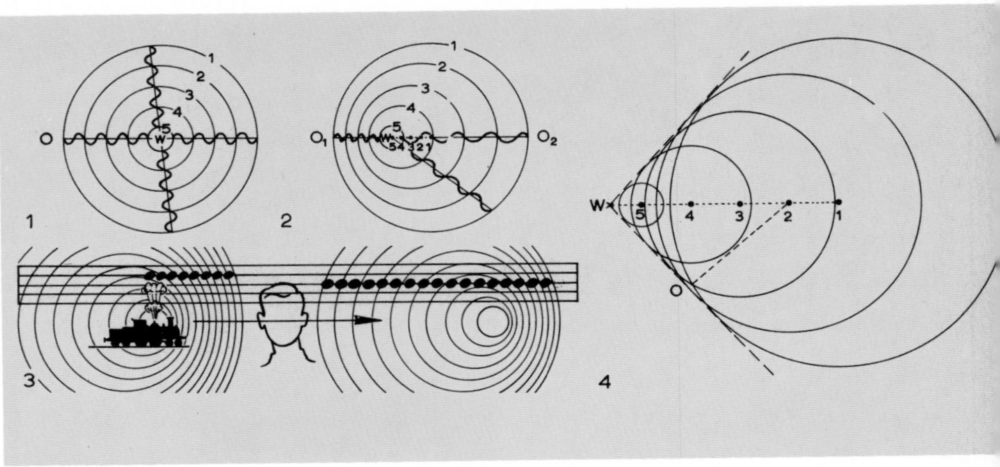

Doppler effect is the name given to phenomena related to the movement of a wave source (such as light or sound) relative to its observer. When the wave source is at rest, as in (1), the waves radiate equally in all directions, represented here by a series of concentric circles (1–5). The same number of waves will pass the observer (O) in any given time, whatever his position relative to the source. However, when the source is moving (2), the circles representing each wave have different centers. Consequently, the waves bunch together in front of the source and spread out behind it. When the source moves toward the observer (O_1), more waves pass in any given time, and the frequency observed will be higher. When the source moves away from the observer (O_2), fewer waves pass and the frequency observed is lower. A common example of the Doppler effect is the falling pitch of a passing train whistle (3). A special case of the Doppler effect occurs when the source is moving faster than the wave motion itself (4), as with a plane traveling faster than the speed of sound. The waves form a common front and the observer is assaulted by so many waves simultaneously that he cannot distinguish them and hears only a "sonic boom."

The donkey, a slow and gentle animal, has been used as a beast of burden since time immemorial and is still an important form of transportation in many parts of the world.

DONIZETTI, Gaetano (1797–1848), Italian opera composer. Influenced by ROSSINI, he developed the traditions of serious and comic opera. His operas include *L'Elisir d'Amore* (1832), *Lucia di Lammermoor* (1835) and *Don Pasquale* (1843). He influenced VERDI.

DON JUAN, legendary libertine, often the subject of dramatic works in which, after a dissolute life, he was led off to hell. The earliest-known dramatization is TIRSO DE MOLINA's *The Rake of Seville* (1630). Other versions are by MOLIÈRE, MOZART (*Don Giovanni*), BYRON and G. B. SHAW (*Man and Superman*).

DONKEY, the domesticated form of the wild ass, descended from the African wild ass of Ethiopia. The donkey is related to the horse, but has long ears, a large head and a short mane, a tuft of hair on the end of the tail and no callosities on the hind legs. A dark band usually runs along the back and another over the shoulders. Crossbreeding with the horse produces the MULE or the HINNY, which is sterile. It is surefooted and intelligent and much used as a pack animal.

DONKEY'S-TAIL, *Sedum morganiacum*, a popular house plant grown for its small succulent leaves and stems. It grows best in sunny east-, south- or west-facing windows and should only be watered when the soil surface becomes dry. It tolerates a temperature range between 13°C and 24°C (55°F and 75°F) and is propagated by means of leaf and shoot tip cuttings taken in the spring or summer. Family: Crassulaceae.

DONNE, John (1572–1631), English METAPHYSICAL POET and divine. His love poems and religious verse and prose are characterized by sophisticated argument, complex metaphors and a passionate and direct tone. His imagery relies upon both Scholastic philosophy and 17th-century scientific thought. After a long period of exclusion from court life he took orders in 1615 and became dean of St. Paul's, London, where he gave many fine sermons. His most famous writings are the love-lyrics *Songs and Sonnets*, and the religious works *Holy Sonnets*, *Sermons* and *Devotions*.

DONNELLY, Ignatius (1831–1901), US politician and writer. A Republican Congressman for Minn. 1863–69, he later led the GREENBACK PARTY and in the 1890s the Populist Party. He wrote the party platform and was the Populist nomination for vice-president in 1900. He wrote several speculative works, including the Utopian novel *Caesar's Column* (1891).

DONNER PARTY, group of 87 settlers from Ill., led by George Donner, who were trapped by snow in the Sierra Nevada, N Cal., in the winter of 1846–47. When food ran out, the surviving members resorted to cannibalism. Only about half the group were rescued.

DON QUIXOTE. See CERVANTES SAAVEDRA, MIGUEL DE.

DON RIVER, river in the USSR, about 1 224mi long. Rising SE of Tula (about 100mi S of Moscow) it flows SE to within 48mi of the VOLGA, to which it is linked by the VOLGA-DON CANAL, and then SW to the Sea of Azov. It is mostly navigable and carries coal, timber and grain. The Don is rich in fish and has many fishing villages on its banks. It has a fertile drainage basin of 170 849sq mi.

DONUS (d. 678), pope from 676, successor to ADEODATUS II, who ended the schism of Ravenna caused by attempts to make it an independent see.

DOODLEBUGS. See ANT LIONS.

DOOLEY, Mr. See DUNNE, FINLEY PETER.

DOOLEY, Thomas Anthony (1927–1961), US physician, author and a founder of MEDICO, an international medical aid organization for underdeveloped countries. In *Deliver us from Evil* (1956) he tells how he supervised care for 600 000 Vietnamese refugees in Haiphong in 1954–55.

DOOLITTLE, Hilda (1886–1961), US poet, known as **H.D.** She lived in Europe after 1911. H.D. was one of the first IMAGISTS in America, and she continued to develop the Imagist style in her later poetry. Her works include *Sea Garden* (1916), *The Walls Do Not Fall* (1944) and the novel *Bid Me To Live* (1960).

DOOLITTLE, James Harold (1896–), US pilot and WWII air hero. Famous as a racing pilot in the 1920s and early 1930s, he led the first air raid on Tokyo on April 18, 1942, thereby slowing the Japanese offensive.

DOPPLER EFFECT, the change observed in the wavelength of a sonic, electromagnetic or other wave (see WAVE MOTION) because of relative motion between the wave source and an observer. As a wave source approaches an observer, each pulse of the wave is closer behind the previous one than it would be were the source at rest relative to the observer. This is perceived as an increase in frequency, the pitch of a sound source seeming higher, the color of a light source bluer. When a sound source achieves the speed of sound, a SONIC BOOM results. As a wave source recedes from an observer, each pulse is emitted farther away from him than it would otherwise be. There is hence a drop in pitch or a reddening in COLOR (see LIGHT; SPECTRUM). The Doppler Effect, named for

Christian Johann Doppler (1803–1853) who first described it in 1842, is of paramount importance in astronomy. Observations of stellar spectra can determine the rates at which stars are moving towards or away from us, while observed red shifts in the spectra of distant galaxies are generally interpreted as an indication that the universe as a whole is expanding (but see RED SHIFT).

DORADO (the Swordfish or Goldfish), a southern hemisphere constellation containing the Greater Magellanic Cloud (see MAGELLANIC CLOUDS).

DORATI, Antal (1906–), Hungarian-born US conductor, musical director of the Washington National Symphony Orchestra since 1969 and of the Royal Philharmonic Orchestra, London, from 1975. He has recorded all Haydn's symphonies.

DORCHESTER HEIGHTS, hill near Boston, Mass. Its occupation by George Washington's forces in March 1776 ended the BOSTON SIEGE of British troops.

DORDOGNE, department in SW France, in PÉRIGORD. Much of the region is agricultural, and it also produces truffles and walnut oil. It has many prehistoric remains, such as the LASCAUX CAVES.

DORDOGNE RIVER, river in SW France, 293mi long, which flows SW and W to join the Garonne R near Bordeaux. It is navigable for about 190mi.

DORDRECHT, also Dordt or Dort, city in the SW Netherlands, about 12mi ESE of Rotterdam. It has shipbuilding, engineering and chemical industries and is a commercial center. Founded in 1008, it is one of Holland's most historic cities. Pop 102 000.

DORÉ, Paul Gustave (1832–1883), French engraver, illustrator and painter. He created dreamlike, grandiose scenes in a fantastic, bizarre style. He illustrated editions of Balzac's *Contes Drolatiques* (1855), Dante's *Inferno* (1861), Cervantes' *Don Quixote* (1863) and the Bible (1866).

DORIA, Andrea (1466–1560), Genoese admiral, CONDOTTIERE and statesman. After fighting for the French 1519–27, he joined Emperor CHARLES V to prevent French domination of Italy. He secured independence for Genoa, where he ruled with absolute power and instituted a new constitution. (See DOGE.)

DORIANS, people of ancient Greece. Originating from the lower Balkans, they probably defeated the ACHAEANS and conquered the Peloponnese between 1100 and 950 BC, subsequently extending their influence to the Aegean Islands, Crete, Sicily and parts of Asia Minor, Africa and Italy.

DORMANCY, a resting state that occurs in animals and plants, when growth stops and the internal processes, principally RESPIRATION, are slowed down. In animals, dormancy during the winter is termed HIBERNATION, while dormancy in the summer or dry season, such as in the lung fish and earthworm, is termed **aestivation** (or **estivation**). In plants, dormancy during adverse conditions is manifest in the lack of growth of perennial plants such as grasses, the loss of foliage by deciduous trees and the production of underground perennating organs such as BULBS, CORMS and TUBERS.

DORMONT, residential borough in SW Pa., 4mi S of Pittsburg. Pop 12 856.

DORMICE, RODENTS of the family Gliridae that are intermediate in appearance between squirrels and mice. They are nocturnal, and live in trees and shrubs in Asia, Africa and Europe.

DORR, Thomas Wilson (1805–1854), US constitutional reformer and leader of Dorr's Rebellion. Elected to the R.I. state legislature in 1834, he became head of a popular party agitating for the extension of voting rights. In 1842 the R.I. state legislature and Dorr's party formed separate administrations, but Dorr's administration collapsed after an armed confrontation. He was jailed for treason 1844–45.

DORT, Synod of (1618–19), assembly of the DUTCH REFORMED CHURCH, held at Dordrecht (Dort), which rejected the ARMINIANS' doctrines. It affirmed unconditional election, limited atonement, man's total depravity, God's irresistible grace, and the impossibility of falling from grace.

DORTMUND, industrial and mining city in West Germany, in the Ruhr valley, producing steel, heavy machinery, coal and beer. Built on the Ems R, it is connected to the North Sea by canal. It was rebuilt after extensive damage in WWII. Pop 639 634.

DORVAL, a residential town of S Quebec, Canada, 10mi WSW of Montreal. Pop 20 471.

DOSIMETER, a device worn by persons working in situations where they are exposed to ionizing radiations (see RADIOACTIVITY), which measures the dose of radiation to which they have been exposed.

DOS PASSOS, John (Roderigo) (1896–1970), US novelist and writer of American social history. His trilogy, *U.S.A.* (1937), paints 20th-century American life until 1929, and makes use of reportage techniques. Other works are *Manhattan Transfer* (1925), *District of Columbia* (a trilogy; 1952) and *Midcentury* (1961).

DOSSI, Dosso (real name: Giovanni di Lutero; c1490–1542), Italian Renaissance painter of allegorical scenes set in landscapes. His style and handling were influenced by GIORGIONE and TITIAN.

DOSTOYEVSKY, Fyodor Mikhailovich (1821–1881), major Russian novelist. He spent several years in the army but resigned his commission in 1844 to devote himself to writing. Arrested in 1849 as a member of a socialist circle, Dostoyevsky was condemned to be shot; however, the sentence was commuted in the execution yard to four years' hard labor in Siberia. During the 1860s he founded two journals and traveled in Europe after his consumptive wife and his brother had died, and after he had incurred large gambling debts. He did not finally return to Russia until 1871. In 1876 he edited his own monthly *The Writer's Diary*. Suffering from epilepsy for most of his life, he died after an epileptic attack. Dostoyevsky's major novels, *Crime and Punishment* (1866), *The Idiot* (1868), *The Devils* (1871–72) and *The Brothers Karamazov* (1879–80), reveal his deep understanding of the complex psychology of human character and the problems of sin and suffering.

DOTHAN, city in SE Ala., seat of Houston Co. An agricultural trading center, it also manufactures fertilizers, cigars and peanut oil. Pop 36 733.

DOU, Gerard (1613–1675), Dutch painter. Trained as a glassmaker, and a pupil of REMBRANDT, he developed the tradition of small minutely-finished pictures, with enamel-like surfaces, painting GENRE scenes, portraits, still lifes and landscapes. He influenced METSU.

DOUAI, city in N France, 19mi S of Lille, on the Scarpe R. Its industries include steel, engineering, chemical products, railroad equipment and printing. The DOUAY BIBLE was prepared here. Pop 47 347.

DOUALA, the main port of Cameroon, on the Bight of Biafra. Its industries are beer, textiles and metalworking. It was capital of German Kamerun 1884–1916, and then under French control until 1960. Pop 250 000.

DOUAY BIBLE, first official Roman Catholic English version of the Bible. It was translated from St. JEROME's Latin VULGATE Bible by English Catholics exiled in Douai. The New Testament was published in 1582, the Old Testament in 1609–10. The translation was revised by Bishop Challoner 1749–72.

DOUBLE-BASS, stringed musical instrument, contrabass of the violin family. About 6ft high, it has four strings tuned in fourths; a fifth string or an extension at the neck is sometimes added. The double-bass is usually bowed, but jazz basses are plucked.

DOUBLEDAY, Abner (1819–1893), US Union general, credited with the invention of baseball in 1839 at Cooperstown, N.Y. He fired the first Union gun in defense of Fort Sumter and was a hero of the Battle of Gettysburg.

DOUBLE INTEGRAL, the integral (see CALCULUS) used to treat two FUNCTIONS that are of different VARIABLES. More than two such functions are treated together by use of a multiple integral.

DOUBLE JEOPARDY, principle embodied in the 5th Amendment of the US Constitution, protecting a person against being tried twice on the same charge, or on another charge arising from the same circumstances, unless there is more than one offense, as with robbery and murder.

DOUBLE REFRACTION, or **birefringence**, the property of certain CRYSTALS to split a ray of unpolarized light into two rays plane-polarized at right-angles to each other (see POLARIZED LIGHT). One of these, the ordinary ray, is refracted according to the ordinary laws of REFRACTION, but the other, the extraordinary ray, is refracted with a refractive index that depends on the direction from which the original ray was incident. Double refraction in Iceland spar is used in the NICOL PRISM to produce plane-polarized light.

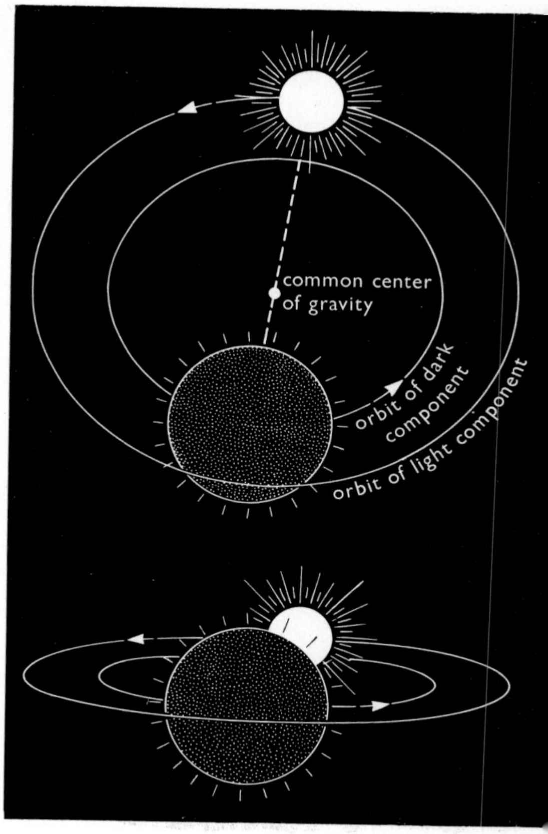

Two stars revolving around a common center of gravity are referred to as binary, or double, stars. Here a binary system is seen both from above, with the orbital paths around the center marked, and edge on, showing how one star periodically eclipses the other when it moves in front of it. These stars are known as eclipsing binaries.

DOUBLE STAR or **binary star**, a pair of stars revolving around a common center of gravity. Less frequently the term "double star" is applied to two stars that merely appear close together in the sky though in reality at quite different distances from the earth (optical pairs) or to two stars whose motions are linked but which do not orbit each other (physical pair). About 50% of all stars are members of either binary or multiple star systems, in which there are more than two components. It is thought that the components of binary and multiple star systems are formed simultaneously. **Visual binaries** are those which can be seen telescopically to be double. There are comparatively few visual binaries, since the distances between components are small relative to interstellar distances, but examples are CAPELLA, PROCYON, SIRIUS and ALPHA CENTAURI. **Spectroscopic binaries**, while unable to be seen telescopically as doubles, can be detected by RED SHIFTS in their spectra, their orbit making each component alternately approach and recede from us. **Eclipsing binaries** are those whose components, due to the orientation of their orbit, periodically mutually eclipse each other as seen from the earth.

DOUBLE-STOPPING, the simultaneous playing of two or more tones on adjacent strings of a violin or a related instrument. The term is also used to describe the double sound when one or both strings are not stopped.

DOUGH, thick, elastic mixture of flour, water or milk and other ingredients, often including YEAST, shortening, sugar, salt and eggs, used to make bread, pastry and cakes. Leavened dough (see LEAVEN) undergoes FERMENTATION to make it rise. **Batter** is a thinner, pourable mixture used to make pancakes, scones, biscuits etc. and as a coating for fried foods and fritters.

DOUGHTY, Charles Montagu (1843–1926), English writer, traveler and poet. *Travels in Arabia Deserta* (1888), written in Elizabethan style, describes his experiences living and traveling in Arabia in the mid-1870s.

DOUGHTY, Thomas (1793–1856), US landscape painter, a founder of the HUDSON RIVER SCHOOL. His pictures of woodlands, river valleys and lakes have a silvery light. Among his works are *On the Hudson* and *A River Glimpse*.

DOUGLAS, city in SE Ariz., on the Mexican border. Its industries include copper and lead smelting and stockraising. Pop 12 462.

DOUGLAS, city of S Ga., seat of Coffee Co., 35mi WNW of Waycross. One of Georgia's most important tobacco markets and an agricultural center. Pop 10 195.

DOUGLAS, (George) Norman (1868–1952), British essayist and novelist. In the late 1890s he settled in Capri. *Old Calabria* (1915) combines themes of travel, history and philosophy. His famous and witty novel *South Wind* (1917) is about life in Capri.

DOUGLAS, Sir James (1803–1877), Canadian trader and colonial governor, known as "the father of British Columbia." After being in charge of the Hudson's Bay Company operations W of the Rockies he was governor of Vancouver Island 1851–64 and of the new colony of British Columbia 1858–64.

DOUGLAS, Stephen Arnold (1813–1861), US politician, affectionately known as the "Little Giant." He is remembered for his debates with Abraham Lincoln (see FREEPORT DOCTRINE) in the Ill. Senate elections (1858) which brought Lincoln to public attention. He was a Democratic congressman from Ill. 1843–46, and senator 1847–61. Involved in the issue of slavery in the new states, he helped draft the COMPROMISE OF 1850, based on SQUATTER SOVEREIGNTY, and the KANSAS-NEBRASKA LAW (1854). In 1860 he was unsuccessful Democratic presidential candidate, but later supported Lincoln and the Union.

DOUGLAS, Tommy (Thomas Clement Douglas; 1904–), Canadian politician. Horrified by Depression conditions, he was a founder of the Cooperative Commonwealth Federation (CCF) in 1932, and was first CCF premier of Saskatchewan 1944–61. He instituted important social welfare reforms. In 1961 he became the first leader of the NEW DEMOCRATIC PARTY.

DOUGLAS, William Orville (1898–), justice of the US Supreme Court since 1940. He was chairman of the SECURITIES AND EXCHANGE COMMISSION in 1938. He gained a reputation as a leading liberal, especially on civil rights affairs.

The distinguished 19th-century abolitionist orator and writer Frederick Douglass. He was the first black citizen of the US to hold high office in government.

DOUGLAS FIR, *Pseudotsuga menziesii*, an evergreen CONIFER, native to the western US, growing up to 90m (300ft). The tree is highly valued for its wood which yields a major portion of US lumber. The related large-coned Douglas fir (*P. macrocarpa*) has larger cones up to 180mm (7in) long. The much smaller Japanese Douglas fir (*P. japonica*) is native to Japan. (See also FIRS.)

DOUGLAS-HOME, Alec (Alexander Frederick), Baron Home of the Hirsel of Coldstream in Berwick (1903–), British Conservative prime minister 1963–64. After being foreign secretary 1960–63, he renounced six peerages in order to become premier. He followed a moderate anti-communist policy and achieved some compromise on Commonwealth racial issues.

DOUGLASS, Frederick (1817–1895), US escaped slave (born Frederick Augustus Washington Bailey) who became a leading abolitionist and orator. He lectured for an antislavery society in Mass. and published *The Narrative of the Life of Frederick Douglass* (1845). He campaigned in England, purchased his freedom and returned to establish his own newspaper, *North Star*. In the Civil War he recruited Negroes for the North, and during Reconstruction pressed for Negro civil rights. He held various federal posts and was US minister to Haiti 1889–91.

DOUKHOBORS, Russian pacifist religious sect, now settled in Canada. Founded in the 18th century, the sect rejected all forms of religious, ecclesiastical and secular authority in favor of individual direct revelation. The Doukhobors were often exiled and persecuted by the tsars. In 1898, assisted by their leader Peter Verigin and by Leo TOLSTOY, over 7 000 emigrated to Saskatchewan, some moving later to British Columbia. Their communities have developed economically, but there has been continuous trouble with the Canadian government, particularly from the extremist splinter group, Sons of Freedom, over issues of technology and compulsory education.

DOUM PALM, or doom palm, palm trees of the genus *Hyphaene*, native to tropical Africa. They produce edible reddish fruit about the size of an apple, tasting like gingerbread.

DOURO RIVER, Iberian river rising in N Spain (where it is called the Duero), and flowing generally W to the Atlantic, for 556mi. It forms about 70mi of the Spanish–Portuguese border. The Portuguese section has been developed for hydroelectric power.

DOVE, the name sometimes given to small members of the PIGEON family, e.g., the Rock dove.

DOVER, borough and seaport in Kent, England, on the English Channel. Settled by the Romans, as Dubris, it was used by the Saxons and later the Normans. Dover is the major UK port for cross-channel ferries. Pop 34 322.

DOVER, city in Del., state capital and seat of Kent Co., on the St. Jones R, 40mi S of Wilmington. It is a major industrial and commercial center and is the site of the Dover Air Force Base. Manufactures include chemicals and spacesuit equipment. Pop 17 488.

DOVER, city in N.H., seat of Stafford Co., 11mi NNW of Portsmouth. Among its products are shoes, plastics and textiles. Pop 20 850.

DOVER, city in N.J., 8mi NNW of Morristown. It is the center of an iron-ore area and produces explosives. Pop 15 309.

DOVER, city in Ohio. Situated in a coal-mining area, it manufactures chemicals and steel and refines oil. Pop 11 516.

DOVER, Strait of, narrow passage separating SE England from N France, connecting the English Channel with the North Sea. It is around 19mi across at its narrowest point. The chief ports are Dover, Folkestone, Calais and Boulogne. Of great strategic importance, the strait was the scene of the first repulse of the Spanish ARMADA (1588), the Dover (antisubmarine) Patrol of WWI and the evacuation from DUNKERQUE (1940).

DOVZHENKO, Alexander (1894–1956), Ukrainian motion-picture director. With such films as *Ivan* (1932), *Frontier* (1935) and *Shors* (1939), he earned international recognition for the Soviet cinema. He won two Stalin prizes.

DOW, Herbert Henry (1866–1930), Canadian-born US chemist and industrialist who developed an electrolytic method for extracting BROMINE from certain natural BRINES. He founded the Dow Chemical Company to exploit this process in 1897.

Details of the foliage, cones and seeds of the Douglas fir, one of the most common evergreens in western North America: pendulous branch (a), to which needle-like leaves are attached directly, terminating in a cone; male bud (b); female bud (c); seeds (d); and needles (e).

DOWDING, Hugh Caswall Tremenheere, 1st Baron (1882–1970), British air chief marshal responsible for the buildup of Fighter Command in the RAF. His leadership helped win the Battle of Britain. He retired in 1942 and was created Baron in 1943.

DOWLAND, John (c1563–1626), English composer and lutenist, best known for his songs and the collection of lute pieces *Lachrimae* (1604). He traveled to France, Italy, Germany and Denmark in the

Downing Street, London, on which at No. 10 (guarded by two policemen) the British prime minister has his official residence, was named for Sir George Downing, who served Charles II as envoy to Holland and as secretary to the treasury. When in 1671 Downing was sent to Holland with instructions to provoke a conflict, he succeeded so well that he was obliged to flee for his life—and incur a brief imprisonment in England for deserting his post.

service of various kings and princes. From 1612, he served in the court of James I.

DOWNERS GROVE, village in Ill., 20mi W of Chicago. It produces tools and furniture and is the home of George Williams College. Pop 32 751.

DOWNEY, city in Cal., SE of Los Angeles. Its manufactures include electronic equipment, aircraft and missiles. Pop 88 445.

DOWNING, Andrew Jackson (1815–1852), US architect, landscape designer and horticulturalist. He planned the grounds of the White House and the Smithsonian Institution in 1851.

DOWNING, Sir George (1623–1684), English diplomat for whom London's Downing Street is named. He was educated in America at Harvard College. Charles II appointed him envoy to Holland where his aggressive behavior contributed to the outbreak of the First and Second DUTCH WARS. As secretary to the treasury (1667), he introduced important reforms.

DOWRY, property brought by a wife to her husband or his family upon marriage, consolidating relations between the two families. In primitive societies, it corresponded to the bridewealth paid by the husband's family to the bride's. Legislation safeguarding the bride's interests was first introduced in the US in 1839, in Miss. (See also COMMUNITY PROPERTY.)

DOWSING, the detection, usually with a DIVINING ROD, of hidden (usually underground) resources of water, metals, etc. Another frequently-used technique employs a PENDULUM held in the dowser's hand; the direction and magnitude of swing provides information as to the material beneath the ground, the bob itself being made of suitable material. Laboratory tests (see PARAPSYCHOLOGY) have shed little light on dowsing, though some dowsers have remarkable records of success.

DOWSON, Ernest Christopher (1867–1900), English poet, one of the so-called decadents of the 1890s. From a life of misery and squalor he produced a delicate, mellifluous poetry on themes of love and lost childhood. He influenced the early work of W. B. YEATS.

DOYLE, Sir Arthur Conan (1859–1930), British writer, creator of the detective Sherlock Holmes, in many short stories and four novels. A doctor, soldier and campaigner for law reform, he also wrote historical novels such as *Micah Clarke* (1889) and science fiction, as in *The Lost World* (1912). In later life he became an adherent of spiritualism.

D'OYLY CARTE, Richard (1844–1901), English impresario who produced GILBERT AND SULLIVAN'S first operetta *Trial by Jury*, in 1875. In 1878 he founded the D'Oyly Carte Opera Company, and in 1881 built the Savoy Theatre, London, as a stage for works by Gilbert and Sullivan.

DRACAENA, a genus of evergreen shrubby plants, frequently grown as house plants for their ornamental foliage. *Dracaena deremensis* has sword-like glossy green leaves with two longitudinal silver stripes, while *D. fragrans massangeana* has golden-green stripes. *D. godseffiana* has green obovate leaves spotted with cream, the spots coalescing in the variety "Florida Beauty." In *D. marginata* and *D. sanderiana*, the sword-like leaves are edged with burgundy and silver respectively. Dracaenas grow well in sunny E- or W-facing windows, although *D. fragrans* adapts to the low light intensity in the interior of rooms. They grow well between temperatures of 13°C and 27°C (55°F and 80°F) and should be watered regularly to keep the soil evenly moist. Propagation is by cuttings or air layering. Family: Agavaceae.

DRACO (the Dragon), a large N Hemisphere constellation. Alpha Draconis was the POLESTAR c3000 BC (see PRECESSION). Gamma Draconis is the bright star Eltanin. Draco also contains the planetary NEBULA NGC 6543.

DRACO (7th century BC), lawgiver in Athens. His code (c621 BC) made both serious and trivial crimes punishable by death—hence the term "Draconian" to describe any harsh legal measure. SOLON later repealed all the laws except those dealing with homicide.

DRACULA, in the book of that name by Bram STOKER, a Transylvanian VAMPIRE count, subject of many horror films. The name, meaning "demon," was applied to Vlad IV the Impaler, a 15th-century Walachian prince upon whom Stoker based the character.

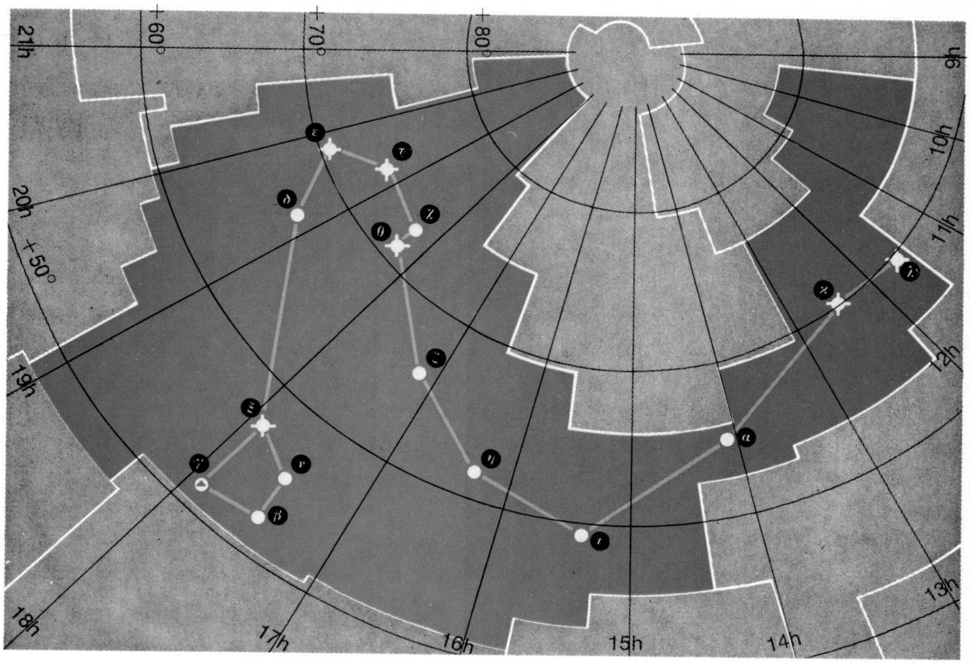

The long, faint constellation of Draco lies near the north pole of the sky. The star α Draconis, also called Thuban, was once the pole star (about 3000 BC), and the Great Pyramid at Giza in Egypt was aligned with respect to it.

DRACUT, town in Mass., on the Merrimack R, 2mi N of Lowell. It manufactures textiles and chemicals. Pop 18 214.

DRAFT, Military, or conscription, system of raising armed forces by compulsory recruitment. The modern practice is more aptly described as selective service. Obligatory military service dates back to ancient times but conscription as we know it began to evolve only in the late 18th century when, in France, Napoleon I imposed universal conscription of able-bodied males. Conscription in Prussia 1807–13 was used to build up large reserves of trained men. Peacetime conscription became standard practice in the 19th century, except in Britain where it was not imposed until prior to WWII (wartime conscription was practiced in both Britain and the US during WWI). During the American Civil War both North and South used conscription, but mainly to encourage volunteering. In the US peacetime conscription was first introduced in 1940 and, though dropped briefly in 1947, continued through to 1973 to meet the demands of the Korean and then the Vietnamese commitment. Conscription has frequently given rise to civil protest (see NEW YORK DRAFT RIOTS). During Johnson's presidency (1963–69), anti-draft demonstrations, with mass burning of draft cards, became a popular form of protest against involvement in Vietnam. (See also CONSCIENTIOUS OBJECTOR; IMPRESSMENT.)

DRAFTING. See MECHANICAL DRAWING.

DRAFT RIOTS. See NEW YORK DRAFT RIOTS.

DRAGO, Luis Maria (1859–1921), Argentinian jurist and minister of foreign affairs (1902–03). He formulated the Drago doctrine which stated that European nations should not use the public debt of American states as a justification for armed intervention in, or occupation of those states, a principle now accepted in international law.

DRAGON (from Greek *drakōn*, serpent), legendary monster, usually represented as a fire-breathing, winged serpent or lizard, with crested head and large claws. Apart from the wingless Chinese and Japanese dragons, which were beneficent, dragons were usually regarded as symbols of evil, and dragon-slayers, for example Saint GEORGE, as saints and heroes.

DRAGONFLIES, predatory flying insects with a long, slender abdomen, two pairs of transparent wings, and large compound eyes which may contain 30 000 separate facets. The LARVA is aquatic and may live under water for a year or more before hatching into the adult. Dragonflies are included with the DAMSELFLIES in the order Odonata.

DRAGON'S BLOOD, a reddish resin obtained from a number of plants. Once used in medicine for its astringent properties, it is now mostly used in China to give a red facing to writing paper. Its main commercial source is an Indonesian rattan palm, *Daemonorops draco*.

DRAINAGE, the runoff of water from an area, either naturally or, in agriculture, under artificial control. In nature, drainage generally takes the form of a pattern of streams, which feed rivers and lakes and flow, usually, to the sea (see HYDROLOGIC CYCLE). An area all of whose rainwater drains into a particular body of water is called a watershed or catchment basin. (See also GROUNDWATER.) Systems of artificial drainage depend on the nature of the SOIL as well as local topography. Two main systems are used: surface and subsurface. Surface systems usually comprise a pattern of ditches; subsurface systems a pattern of conduits and tunnels. These usually lead to a natural stream or river. (See also IRRIGATION; LAND RECLAMATION.)

DRAKE, Edwin Laurentine (1819–1880), US oil-industry pioneer who drilled the world's first oil well at Oil Creek, Titusville, Pa. in 1859. (See PETROLEUM.)

DRAKE, Sir Francis (c1543–1596), English admiral and explorer, the first Englishman to sail around the world (1577–80). During his circumnavigation aboard the *Golden Hind*, Drake seized a fortune in booty from Spanish settlements along the South American Pacific coast. He was knighted on his return by Queen Elizabeth I. In 1587 he destroyed a large part of the Spanish fleet at anchor in Cadiz harbor. The following year he was joint commander of the English fleet which, with the help of a storm, dispersed and destroyed the Spanish ARMADA.

DRAKENSBURG MOUNTAINS, range in the Republic of South Africa. It extends 700mi SSW from the Transvaal to the Cape of Good Hope, and forms the border with Lesotho. Thabana Ntlenyana, at 11 425ft, is the highest peak.

DRAMA. See THEATER.

DRAPER, John William (1811–1882), English-born US chemist who investigated the chemical action of light, first photographed the moon (1840) and obtained a photograph of the solar spectrum

(1844). His son, **Henry Draper** (1837–1882), US physician and amateur astronomer, obtained the first photograph of a nonsolar stellar spectrum (1872) and the first photograph of a NEBULA (the Orion) in 1880.

DRAUGHTS. See CHECKERS.

DRAVIDIANS, subgroup of the Hindu race, some 100 000 000 people of (mainly) S India. They are fairly dark-skinned, stocky, have rather more NEGROID features than other Indics, and are commonly dolichocephalic (see CEPHALIC INDEX). (See also RACE.) The **Dravidian languages** are a family of some 22 languages, perhaps the most important from a philological point of view being Tamil, texts in which date back to at least the 1st century BC (see also PHILOLOGY).

DRAWING, the art of delineating a representation or pattern on a surface, usually paper. Two general types of medium are used: dry mediums such as graphite, metalpoint, charcoal, chalks and crayons, and wet mediums, inks and washes, applied by pen or brush. Drawings have traditionally served as preparatory studies for paintings, sculptures or works of architecture. Artists like the 13th-century architect Villiard d'Honnecourt or the Renaissance painter PISANELLO, drew and collected together many detailed studies for use in other works. LEONARDO DA VINCI drew to create and elaborate his artistic ideas, and like RAPHAEL, DÜRER, MICHELANGELO and REMBRANDT made drawing an art form in its own right. During the 17th century, drawing evolved into an important artistic discipline. In the 19th century, INGRES was a major exponent of this discipline. Modern masters of drawing include PICASSO, KLEE and MATISSE.

DRAYTON, Michael (1563–1631), English poet who wrote skillfully in a wide variety of manners upon conventional Elizabethan themes. He was best known in his day for the sequence of love poems *England's Heroical Epistles* (1597) and for the lengthy historical and topographical poem *Poly-Olbion* (1612; 1622).

DREADNOUGHT, British battleship (1906) of revolutionary design. Weighing 18 000 tons and capable of traveling at 21 knots, the *Dreadnought* carried ten 12in guns. At the time of her completion there was nothing afloat to match her for speed and firepower. By the outbreak of WWI nine *Dreadnought*-class ships and 12 other big-gun battleships were in service in the British navy.

DREAMS, fantasies, usually visual, experienced during sleep and in certain other situations. About 25% of an adult's sleeping time is characterized by rapid eye movements (REM) and brain waves that, registered on the ELECTROENCEPHALOGRAPH, resemble those of a person awake (EEG). This REM-EEG state occurs in a number of short periods during sleep, each lasting a number of minutes, the first coming some 90min after sleep starts and the remainder occurring at intervals of roughly 90min. It would appear that it is during these periods that dreams take place, since people woken during a REM-EEG period will report and recall visual dreams in some 80% of cases; people woken at other times report dreams only about 40% of the time, and of far less visual vividness. Observation of similar states in animals suggests that at least all mammals experience dreams. Dreams can also occur, though in a limited way, while falling asleep; the origin and nature of these is not known. **Dream interpretation** seems as old as recorded history. Until the mid-19th century dreams were regarded as supernatural, often prophetic; their possible prophetic nature has been examined in this century by, among others, J. W. Dunne. According to FREUD, dreams have a *latent content* (the fulfilment of an individual's particular UNCONSCIOUS wish) which is converted by *dreamwork* into *manifest content* (the dream as experienced). In these terms, interpretation reverses the dreamwork process. (See also HALLUCINATION; SLEEP.)

DREDGING, the excavation of material from the bottom of harbors and navigation channels, generally with the aim of keeping them open for shipping. In the **bucket dredge** an endless chain of buckets extends down into the bottom mud: the buckets dig into the mud and carry it up to be discharged on board. The **grab dredge** operates just as a CRANE with a grab bucket; the **dipper dredge** much as an EXCAVATOR. In the **hydraulic dredge** the material is drawn up through a pipe by suction.

DRED SCOTT CASE, suit brought by Scott, a slave from Mo., on the grounds that temporary residence in a territory in which slavery was banned under the MISSOURI COMPROMISE had made him free. The US Supreme Court, under Chief Justice TANEY, decided (1857) that Scott's voluntary return to Mo. left him still a slave. This alone could have resolved the case, but seven Democrat judges laid down that Congress had no constitutional power to enact the Compromise, and Taney and two others held that a slave was not a citizen under the Constitution. The two Republican judges held that these two points were *obiter dicta*, mere opinions without legal effect. The decision inflamed and divided national feeling and helped precipitate the Civil War.

DREISER, Theodore (1871–1945), US novelist whose naturalistic fiction, concerned with the dispossessed and criminal, dealt with the grimmer realities of American life. Dreiser's work, often artistically raw, has at its best a massive energy and power. His novels include *Sister Carrie* (1900) and *An American Tragedy* (1925).

DRESDEN, city in East Germany, capital of Dresden district, on the Elbe R. It is a communications and cultural center containing world-famous art museums, and many historic buildings, extensively restored since WWII. It produces optical and electrical equipment and has food processing industries. The famous DRESDEN CHINA is manufactured nearby. Pop 500 100.

DRESDEN CHINA, also known as Meissen ware, after the town near Dresden where china has been

Dresden china, or Meissen ware, has been manufactured since the early 18th century, when the production of true porcelain was introduced into Europe. Initially based on Chinese shapes and motifs, Dresden china later developed its famous floral patterns and rococo decorations. Pieces like this Meissen shepherdess are now valuable collectors' items.

made since 1710. Europe's first true porcelain, the process of its manufacture was discovered by Johann Friedrich Böttger c1707. (See POTTERY AND PORCELAIN.)

DRESS. See COSTUME; GARMENT INDUSTRY.

DREW, Charles Richard (1904–1950), US Negro physician, surgeon and medical researcher who founded the American Red Cross blood bank.

DREW, Daniel (1797–1879), US financier, notorious for his speculative dealing in connection with the Erie railroad, of which he became a director (1857). With Jay GOULD and James FISK, Drew conspired to thwart the ambitions of Cornelius VANDERBILT.

DREYFUS AFFAIR, notorious French political scandal of the Third Republic. In 1894, Alfred Dreyfus (1859–1935), a Jewish army captain, was convicted of betraying French secrets to the Germans. Further evidence pointed to a Major ESTERHAZY as the traitor; but when tried (Jan. 1898), he was acquitted on further secret, and forged, evidence. Dreyfus' conviction had aroused ANTI-SEMITISM; and although evidence against him had been forged, the army was reluctant to admit error. As public interest in the case was aroused, it became known that the Roman Catholic Church supported the conviction. After Esterhazy's acquittal, Émile ZOLA published an attack on the army's integrity, *J'accuse*, which roused intellectual and liberal opinion to a furor. With the suicide of an army officer who acknowledged the forgeries and Esterhazy's flight from France, a new trial began, but Dreyfus was found "guilty with extenuating circumstances" (Aug. 1899). Public opinion was outraged, and in Sept. the government gave him a pardon. He served in WWI and retired a lieutenant-colonel. The scandal had thrown the government, army and Church into disrepute. Legislation followed which led to separation of Church and State (1905). The original verdict against Dreyfus was quashed in 1906.

DRIFT, the material left behind on the retreat of a GLACIER. The unstratified material deposited directly on land is called TILL; fluvio-glacial drift, well stratified, is that transported by melted waters of the glacier. Drift may be composed of particles from fine sand up to huge boulders, and may be up to 100m deep.

DRILL, a BABOON (*Mandrillus leucophaeas*) closely related to the MANDRILL, which inhabits the inland forests of E Africa. They live mainly on the forest floor, but also climb trees and eat fruit, berries, bark and roots.

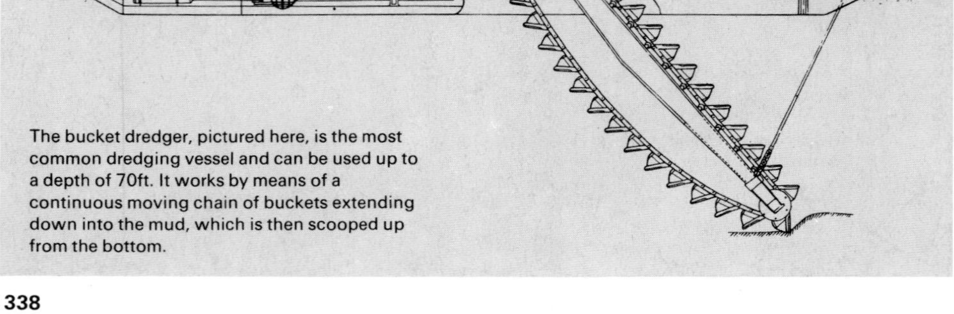

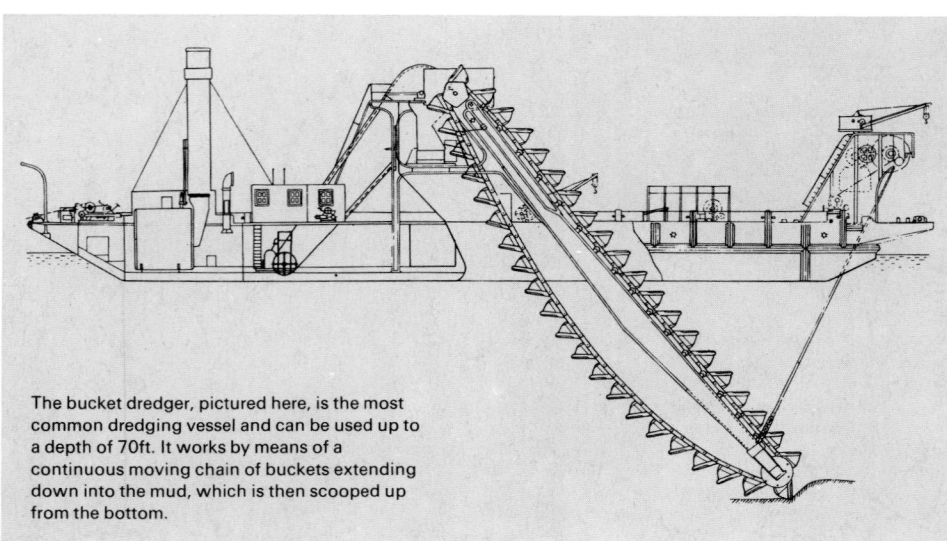

The bucket dredger, pictured here, is the most common dredging vessel and can be used up to a depth of 70ft. It works by means of a continuous moving chain of buckets extending down into the mud, which is then scooped up from the bottom.

DRILLS, tools for cutting or enlarging holes in hard materials. There are two classes: those that have a rotary action, with a cutting edge or edges at the point and, usually, helical fluting along the shank; and those that work by percussive action, where repeated blows drive the drill into the material. **Rotary drills** are commonly used in the home for wood, plastic, masonry and sometimes metal. They are usually hand-turned, though electric motors are increasingly used to power drills in home workshops. In metallurgy the mechanical drilling machine or *drill press* is one of the most important MACHINE TOOLS, operating one or several drills at a time. As great heat is generated, LUBRICATION is very important. Most metallurgical drills are of high-speed STEEL. Dentists' drills rotate at extremely high speeds, their tips (of TUNGSTEN carbide or DIAMOND) being water-cooled: they are powered by an electric motor or by compressed air. Rotary drills are used for deeper oil-well drilling: a cutting bit is rotated at the end of a long, hollow drill pipe, new sections of pipe being added as drilling proceeds. **Percussive drills** are used for rock-boring, for concrete and masonry, and for shallower oil-well drilling. Rock drills are generally powered by compressed air, the tool rotating after each blow to increase cutting speed. The pneumatic drill familiar in city streets is also operated by compressed air. *Ultrasonic drills* are used for brittle materials; a rod, attached to a TRANSDUCER, is placed against the surface, and to it are fed ABRASIVE particles suspended in a cooling fluid. It is these particles that actually perform the cutting. (See also ULTRASONICS.)

DRIVE, in psychology and psychoanalysis, term used for a human or animal INSTINCT.

DROGHEDA, seaport in S County Louth, NE Eire, on the Boyne R 4mi from the Irish Sea. Its main industries are cement works, textile mills, tanneries and breweries. Pop 19 762.

DROMEDARY. See CAMEL.

DROPSY. See EDEMA.

DROSOPHILA. See FRUIT FLIES.

DROUGHT, temporary, often disastrous climatic condition of extreme dryness when an area's natural water supplies are insufficient for plant, specifically crop, needs. It occurs when loss of water from the SOIL by EVAPORATION or otherwise greatly exceeds the water precipitation from the atmosphere; this may result from high winds, low HUMIDITY and heat. Areas with a well-defined dry season suffer **seasonal drought** (see DRY FARMING). (See also DESERT; DUST BOWL.)

DROWNING, immersion in water causing DEATH by ASPHYXIA, metabolic or blood disturbance, following inhalation of water. On immersion, REFLEX breath-holding occurs but is eventually overcome; if immersion continues, water is taken into the LUNGS. Spasm of LARYNX leads to further asphyxia and abnormal HEART rhythm. If death does not follow, water absorbed from the lungs alters the mineral concentration of BLOOD and red blood cells may be damaged. ACIDOSIS, lung EDEMA and distension of STOMACH may occur. Prompt resuscitation at an early stage by clearing the airway, ARTIFICIAL RESPIRATION and, if necessary, cardiac massage and correction of blood abnormalities, may be successful.

DRUG ADDICTION, an uncontrollable craving for a particular DRUG, usually a NARCOTIC, which develops into a physiological or sometimes merely psychological dependence on it. Generally the individual acquires greater tolerance for the drug, and therefore requires larger and larger doses, to the point where he may take doses that would be fatal to the nonaddict. Should his supply be cut off he will suffer **withdrawal symptoms** ("cold turkey") which are psychologically gruelling and often physically debilitating to the point where death may result. Many drugs, such as ALCOHOL and TOBACCO, are not addictive in the strictest sense but more correctly HABIT forming (but see ALCOHOLISM; DIPSOMANIA). Others, such as the OPIUM derivatives, particularly HEROIN and MORPHINE, are extremely addictive. With others, such as LSD (and most other HALLUCINOGENIC DRUGS), COCAINE, HEMP and the AMPHETAMINES, the situation is unclear: dependence may be purely psychological, but it may be that these drugs interfere with the chemistry of the BRAIN; for example, the hallucinogen MESCALINE is closely related to ADRENALINE. The situation is even less clear with such drugs as MARIJUANA which appear to be neither addictive nor habit forming. An inability to abstain from regular self-dosage with a drug is described as a **drug habit**.

DRUGS, chemical agents that affect biological systems. In general they are taken to treat or prevent disease, but certain drugs, such as the OPIUM NARCOTICS, AMPHETAMINES, BARBITURATES and cannabis, are taken for their psychological effects and are drugs of addiction or abuse (see DRUG ADDICTION). Many drugs are the same as or similar to chemicals occurring naturally in the body and are used either to replace the natural substance (e.g., THYROID HORMONE) when deficient, or to induce effects that occur with abnormal concentrations as with STEROIDS or oral CONTRACEPTIVES. Other agents are known to interfere with a specific mechanism or antagonize a normal process (e.g., ATROPINE, CURARE). Many other drugs are obtained from other biological systems; FUNGI or BACTERIA (ANTIBIOTICS) or plants (DIGITALIS), and several others are chemical modifications of natural products. In addition, there are a number of entirely synthetic drugs (e.g., barbiturates), some of which are based on active parts of naturally occurring drugs (as with some antimalarials based on QUININE).

In devising drugs for treating common conditions, an especially desirable factor is that the drug should be capable of being taken by mouth; that is, that it should be able to pass into the body unchanged in spite of being exposed to STOMACH acidity and the ENZYMES of the DIGESTIVE SYSTEM. In many cases this is possible but there are some important exceptions, as with INSULIN which has to be given by INJECTION. This method may also be necessary if VOMITING or GASTROINTESTINAL-TRACT disease prevent normal absorption. In most cases, the level of the drug in the BLOOD or tissues determines its effectiveness. Factors affecting this include: the route of administration; the rate of distribution in the body; the degree of binding to PLASMA PROTEINS or FAT; the rates of breakdown (e.g., by the LIVER) and excretion (e.g., by the KIDNEYS); the effect of disease on the organs concerned with excretion, and interactions with other drugs taken at the same time. There is also an individual variation in drug responsiveness which is also apparent with undesired **side-effects**. These arise because drugs acting on one system commonly act on others. Side effects may be nonspecific (nausea, DIARRHEA, malaise or SKIN rashes); allergic (HIVES, ANAPHYLAXIS), or specific to a drug (abnormal HEART rhythm with digitalis). Mild side-effects may be suppressed but others must be watched for and the drug stopped at the first sign of any adverse effect. Drugs may cross the PLACENTA to reach the FETUS during PREGNANCY, interfering with its development and perhaps causing deformity as happens with THALIDOMIDE.

The hemp or cannabis plant, from which two of the most common "soft" drugs are obtained: marijuana is made from its leaves, hashish from the resin. The plant grows wild in many parts of the world and is easily cultivated.

A drumlin near Soudus, in New York State. The occurence of drumlins in swarms, which may consist of as many as ten thousand individuals, all with the same orientation, gives rise to what is known as "basket-of-eggs topography." Drumlins may be several miles long, but rarely exceed 200ft in height.

Drugs may be used for symptomatic relief (ANALGESICS, antiemetics) or to control a disease. This can be accomplished by killing the infecting agents; by preventing specific infections; by restoring normal control over MUSCLE (anti-Parkinsonian agents) or mind (ANTIDEPRESSANTS); by replacing a lost function or supplying a deficiency (e.g., VITAMIN B_{12} in pernicious ANEMIA); by suppressing inflammatory responses (steroids, ASPIRIN); by improving the functioning of an organ (digitalis); by protecting a diseased organ by altering the function of a normal one (e.g., DIURETICS for heart failure), or by toxic actions on CANCER cells (cancer CHEMOTHERAPY). The scientific study of drugs is the province of PHARMACOLOGY.

DRUIDS, ancient Celtic priestly order in Gaul (France), Britain and Ireland, respected for their learning in astronomy, law and medicine, for their gift of prophecy and as lawgivers and leaders. Little is known of their religious rites, though human sacrifice may have been involved. Because of their power, they were banned by the Romans.

DRUM, musical instrument of the percussion family, common to most cultures. It consists of a shell, usually cylindrical, with a membrane, or skin, stretched over one or both ends. The skin is struck with the hand or with sticks. The principal drum in the symphony orchestra is the kettledrum, or tympanum, which can be tuned to a definite pitch. Other types include the tenor, snare and bass drums. The last two also feature in jazz, where they are important in the rhythm section.

DRUMLINS, elongate hillocks, formed of TILL, found usually in swarms in lowland areas formerly covered by GLACIERS. They usually taper away from a steep slope that faced the oncoming ice.

DRUMMONDVILLE, city in S Quebec, Canada, on the St. Francis R, 60mi E of Montreal. Manufactures textiles and other goods. Pop 31 813.

DRUNKENNESS. See INTOXICATION.

DRUPE, fleshy FRUIT comprising an outer skin (exocarp), a fleshy pulp (mesocarp) and an inner hard and woody stone (endocarp) enclosing a single seed. Examples are found in the CHERRY, PEACH and PLUM. (See also BERRY.)

DRURY LANE THEATER, famous theater in Covent Garden, London, first opened in 1663 as the Theatre Royal and rebuilt three times. The second theater was rebuilt by WREN in 1674; the present building dates from 1812. GARRICK and SHERIDAN were among its many famous actors and managers.

DRUSUS, Julius Caesar (c13 BC–23 AD), only son of the Emperor TIBERIUS. He was consul in 15 AD and commander in Illyricum (a Roman province on the Balkan peninsula) 17–20 AD, but was poisoned after being indicated as Tiberius' successor.

DRUSUS, Nero Claudius (38–9 BC), younger

brother of the Emperor TIBERIUS. As governor of Gaul he completed a census in 13 BC. He commanded Roman forces in Germany 12–9 BC, and after his death near the Elbe R was given the surname Germanicus.

DRUZES, Islamic sect of about 300 000 living in the Lebanon, Syria, Israel and the US. They form a closed community, and most of their doctrines are jealously guarded secrets. They have their own scriptures, and profess MONOTHEISM and the divinity of al-Hakim, 6th caliph (996–1021) of the Egyptian FATIMID dynasty.

DRYADS, in Greek mythology, young mortal female nature spirits, the NYMPHS of woods. Hamadryads were tree nymphs who were supposed to die when the trees they inhabited died.

DRY CELL. See BATTERY.

DRY CLEANING, process of cleaning fabrics with nonaqueous SOLVENTS and detergents, removing grease-based stains and retaining the shape and texture of the garments. Modern dry cleaning dates from the mid-19th century. GASOLINE was first used, but has been replaced by less inflammable solvents such as Stoddard solvent (a petroleum distillate), or the nonflammable chloroethylenes. Carbon tetrachloride, being highly toxic, is seldom used. The process is analogous to the use of a washing machine which spins and tumble-dries.

DRYDEN, John (1631–1700), English poet and dramatist, also considered the father of English literary criticism. Dryden's career began around the time of the RESTORATION (1660). He became Poet Laureate in 1668 and Historiographer Royal in 1670. One of his best-known plays is *All for Love* (1677); his famous critical *Essay of Dramatick Poesie* appeared in 1668. *Absalom and Achitophel* (1681) and *Mac Flecknoe* (1682) are brilliant satirical poems. After the accession of William of Orange, Dryden worked largely on translations, notably of Vergil (1697).

DRY DOCK. See DOCK.

DRY FARMING, the raising of crops in semiarid areas without making use of IRRIGATION. The essential principle of dry farming is the encouragement of efficient retention of moisture by the SOIL, coupled with selection of crops that can make best use of that moisture. Among the techniques employed are tilling the land and eradicating weeds; wide spacing of crops; leaving the stubble after harvest to act as a snow-trap over winter; letting clods of earth or dry vegetable matter lie on the land so as to reduce water runoff and SOIL EROSION; contouring of fields; and, occasionally, allowing fields to lie fallow in alternate years. Crops may be of two types: those whose GROWING SEASONS permit them to evade the summer DROUGHT; and those which are able to survive the drought by reduction of their own moisture loss.

DRY ICE, solid CARBON dioxide, used as a refrigerant for transporting perishables. It is made by compressing carbon dioxide gas to about 7MN/m² at −57°C, when it liquefies; it is then expanded adiabatically to atmospheric pressure and cools, solid carbon dioxide "snow" separating. This is compressed into blocks. subl −78.5°C.

DRYOPITHECUS, European representative and type of a fossil ape group which inhabited Europe, India and Africa from the MIOCENE to the late PLIOCENE epoch. It is thought to be ancestral to modern ANTHROPOID APES.

DRY POINT. See ENGRAVING.

DRY ROT, form of wood decay found in houses, resulting in loss of strength of timbers. The causal agents are the basidiomycete fungi *Merulius lacrymans* (in Britain) and *Poria incrassata* (in North America). Preventative measures include ensuring that conditions ideal for growth of the fungus are avoided, i.e., relative HUMIDITY is kept low, no free moisture is allowed and wood surfaces are covered. Treatment for the disease includes painting the wood surface with CREOSOTE and using FUNGICIDES to kill the fungus.

DRY TORTUGAS, coral island group, part of Monroe Co., Fla., 50mi SW of the mainland at the entrance to the Gulf of Mexico. Named by the Spanish for their abundant tortoise population and lack of fresh water. (See also FORT JEFFERSON NATIONAL MONUMENT.)

DUALISM, any religious or philosophical system characterized by a fundamental opposition of two independent or complementary principles. Among religious dualisms are the unending conflict of good and evil spirits envisaged in ZOROASTRIANISM and the opposition of light and darkness in Jewish apocalyptic, GNOSTICISM and MANICHAEISM. The Chinese complementary principles of *yin* and *yang* exemplify a cosmological dualism while the mind–body dualism of DESCARTES is the best-known philosophical type. Dualism is often opposed to MONISM and pluralism.

DUANE, James (1733–1797), American political leader. A staunch patriot, he nevertheless favored maintaining relations with Britain in the Revolutionary War period. He was mayor of New York City 1784–89, and a N.Y. federal judge, 1789–94.

DUANE, William (1760–1835), US journalist; powerful editor of the Philadelphia *Aurora*, a Jeffersonian journal. He was accused of sedition for newspaper attacks on the FEDERALISTS; the charges were dropped when Jefferson became US president.

DUARTE, city in SW Cal., 16mi ENE of Los Angeles. It is the center of a citrus fruit, avocado and poultry farming area. Pop 14 981.

DUBAI, one of the sheikhdoms of the UNITED ARAB EMIRATES which extends about 45mi along the Persian Gulf, bordered on the S and W by Abu Dhabi. Over 90% of the population live in the capital, Dubai, a port with an international airport and a commercial center. Oil and trade in gold are the mainstay of the economy. Pop 80 000.

DU BARRY, Marie Jeanne Bécu, Countess (1743–1793), the last mistress of LOUIS XV of France. Her years as mistress (1769–74) were marked by her generosity and good nature but little political influence. She was executed in Paris for coming out of retirement to aid royalist émigrés during the French Revolution.

DUBČEK, Alexander (1921–), Czechoslovak statesman. As first secretary of the Communist Party in 1968, he led popular measures to liberalize and "de-Stalinize" communism in Czechoslovakia. But USSR and Warsaw Pact forces invaded and put an end to hopes for "socialism with a human face." In 1975 Dubček was expelled from the Communist Party.

DU BELLAY, Joachim (1522–1560), French poet, whose *Defense et illustration de la langue française* (1549) acted as a manifesto for the PLÉIADE group. With *L'Olive* (1549) he created the first French sonnet-sequence. His most famous sonnet-collections, *Antiquités* and *Regrets* (1558) are the elegaic reflection of an unhappy stay in Rome.

DUBINSKY, David (1892–), Polish-born US labor leader. As president (1932–66) of the International Ladies' Garment Workers' Union, he stabilized the industry, crushed communist influence and pioneered union welfare activities. He became a founding vice-president of the American Federation of Labor (AFL) when it joined the Congress of Industrial Organizations (CIO) in 1955.

DUBLIN (Baile Átha Cliath), capital of the Irish Republic (Eire) and of County Dublin. Located at the mouth of the Liffey R and Dublin Bay on the Irish Sea, Dublin is the political and cultural center of Ireland. Its fine buildings include the Four Courts, the Custom House, Trinity College, the National Library, Museum and Gallery and the Royal Irish Academy, in addition to many Georgian streets and squares. There is also a famous medical center and zoological gardens dating from 1830, as well as the Abbey Theatre and University College. English rule, which severely restricted Dublin's commercial development, was finally removed after the EASTER RISING (1916) and the establishment of the Irish Free State (1921). Dublin is an industrial seaport and the city manufactures stout, whiskey and textiles. There is a direct rail and steamer link to London. Pop 566 000.

DUBLIN, city in central Ga., seat of Laurens Co. It is a railroad center and processes lumber, wool and cottonseed. Pop 15 143.

DU BOIS, industrial city in W central Pa., 46mi NNW of Altoona. It is a coal mining and manufacturing center. Pop 10 667.

DUBOIS, Marie Eugène François Thomas (1858–1940), Dutch paleontologist who discovered Java Man (*Pithecanthropus erectus*) in 1894. (See PREHISTORIC MAN.)

DU BOIS, William Edward Burghardt (1868–1963), US Negro educator and author, who helped transform the Negro view of the black man's role in America. Professor of economics and history at Atlanta U., 1897–1910, and head of its sociology department, 1934–44, he wrote *The Philadelphia Negro* (1899), *The Souls of Black Folk* (1903) and *Black Reconstruction* (1935). A hero of black intellectuals, he became increasingly alienated from the US and died in Ghana in self-imposed exile.

DUBOS, René Jules (1901–), French-born US microbiologist who discovered tyrothricin (1939), the first ANTIBIOTIC to be used clinically.

DUBROVNIK, Dalmatian seaport in SW Yugoslavia, in the republic of Croatia. The old city wall and streets and a promontory setting make it a picturesque tourist resort. It was a flourishing medieval trading port and Slav cultural center, and an independent republic until 1808, becoming part of Yugoslavia after WWI. Pop 31 106.

DUBUFFET, Jean (1901–), French artist influenced by spontaneous, primitive amateur art, *art brut* ("raw art"). He uses gravel, tar etc. to produce fantastic impasto paintings.

DUBUQUE, city in NE Iowa, on the Mississippi R, seat of Dubuque Co. It is a railroad and manufacturing center (farm machinery, processed food and lumber) and home of the U. of Dubuque. It is one of Iowa's oldest cities, settled 1833. Pop 62 853.

DUBUQUE, Julien (1762–1810), French-Canadian pioneer, first white settler in Iowa. The Fox Indians let him mine lead near present-day Dubuque. In 1796 he received 189sq mi from Spain, which then owned the area.

DUCCIO DI BUONINSEGNA (c1255–c1319), Italian painter, first great master of the Sienese school. Combining Byzantine austerity with French Gothic grace, Duccio's work strongly influenced the development of Renaissance painting. The altarpiece *Maestà* is regarded as his masterpiece.

DUCE, Il. See MUSSOLINI, BENITO.

DU CHAILLU, Paul Belloni (c1831–1903), French-born US explorer and author. His botanical–zoological expedition to central Africa (1856–59) covered 8 000mi and collected the first gorillas to be shown in North America. He made a second journey, 1863–65.

DUCHAMP, Marcel (1887–1968), French artist, a pioneer of DADA, CUBISM and FUTURISM, initially influenced by CÉZANNE. His *Nude Descending a Staircase*, No. 2, shocked the American public in 1913. He settled in New York in 1915 and in 1923 abandoned art for chess. He became an American citizen in 1955.

DUCK-BILLED PLATYPUS. See PLATYPUS.

DUCKING STOOL, a stool on the end of a pole pivoted so that a woman strapped to the stool could be ducked under water. Used in the 17th–19th centuries to punish any crime from scolding to witchcraft.

DUCKS, aquatic birds comprising most of the smaller members of the family Anatidae which also contains the GEESE and SWANS. The word "duck" also is used to describe the females of many members of the Anatidae, the males being called drakes. Ducks are, broadly, of two types: surface-feeding or dabbling, and diving ducks. The most familiar ducks are dabblers and include the MALLARD which is found throughout the N Hemisphere and is the ancestor of the domestic duck. Many ducks are killed for sport and food. Their down, particularly that of the EIDER, is of commercial importance in the furniture industry.

DUCKWEED, species of the genera *Lemna*, *Spirodela*, *Wolffia* and *Wolffiella*, of the family Lemnaceae. The simple plants, which consist of an oval, floating frond and hanging root, are found floating in great masses on the surface of ponds and ditches.

DUCOMMUN, Élie (1833–1906), Swiss writer and editor, famous for his work for peace and European unity. He founded the International Bureau of Peace at Bern, 1891, and shared the Nobel Peace Prize, 1902.

DUCTILITY, the property of metals, alloys and some other substances to be drawn out or extruded (see EXTRUSION) without rupture or loss of strength. GOLD is the most ductile metal at normal temperatures. (See MALLEABILITY; MATERIALS, STRENGTH OF.)

DUCTLESS GLANDS. See ENDOCRINE GLANDS.

DUDLEY, Joseph (1647–1720), American colonial administrator. As royal governor of Massachusetts 1702–15 he clashed with the Massachusetts general court. He was chief of the council of New York then chief justice of New York, 1691–92.

DUEL, prearranged combat between two armed people. It is usually fought according to rules and before witnesses, to decide a quarrel or avenge an insult. Dueling originated in Europe in the early Middle Ages as trial by combat. The defendant challenged his accuser and victory theoretically went to the innocent party. Private duels, though generally illegal, persisted into the 19th century, particularly in France. In a famous American duel of 1804, Aaron BURR killed Alexander HAMILTON.

DUE PROCESS, constitutional guarantee of fairness in the administration of justice. This concept can be traced back to MAGNA CARTA, and is embodied in the 5th Amendment to the US Constitution: "No person shall be ... deprived of life, liberty or property without due process of law." The 14th Amendment extended this limitation on the federal government to include the states. Due process has two aspects. *Procedural* due process guarantees fair trial in the courts, and *substantive* due process places limitations on the content of law. It is under this latter heading that the Supreme Court has struck down many state laws restricting civil liberties as infringements of the Bill of Rights. (See also CIVIL RIGHTS AND LIBERTIES; UNITED STATES CONSTITUTION.)

DUFAY, Guillaume (c1400–1474), Flemish composer, the greatest of his period. Attached to Cambrai Cathedral from 1445, he wrote church music and songs, developing the mass in a graceful, expressive style, much influenced by John DUNSTABLE.

DUFF, Sir Lyman Poore (1865–1955), Canadian chief justice, 1933–44, a Supreme Court of Canada judge from 1906. He was chairman of the "Duff Commission" of 1931–32 on railroad problems.

DUFY, Raoul (Ernest Joseph) (1877–1953), French painter influenced by FAUVISM, CUBISM and CÉZANNE. He is best known for gay sporting scenes in brilliant colors.

DU GARD, Roger Martin. See MARTIN DU GARD, ROGER.

DUGONG, *Dugong dugong*, an ugly, seal-like aquatic mammal, which lives in family groups around the coasts of the Indian Ocean. They eat sea plants, and have been reduced in numbers by being hunted for their oil.

DUHAMEL, Georges (1884–1966), French writer who stressed human values and distrusted material progress. Works include war stories and two cycles of novels: *Salavin* (1920–32) and *The Pasquier Chronicle* (1933–45).

DUIKERBOK, genus of small African ANTELOPES with crested heads, large muzzles, and short conical horns. They frequent thick forests.

DUISBURG, city in West Germany, in North Rhine-Westphalia, at the confluence of the Rhine and Ruhr rivers. It is Europe's biggest inland port, and a major coal, iron and steel center. It was heavily bombed in WWII. Pop 487 000.

DUKAS, Paul Abraham (1865–1935), French composer of the colorful orchestral piece, *The Sorcerer's Apprentice*. He also wrote a symphony, a ballet, an opera and piano works.

DUKE, James Buchanan (1856–1925), US industrialist and philanthropist, member of a family with expanding tobacco interests. In 1890 he became president of the powerful merger-built American Tobacco Company. He helped found Duke U. in N.C. and endowed colleges, churches and hospitals.

DUKHOBORS. See DOUKHOBORS.

DULBECCO, Renato (1914–), Italian-born Anglo-American physiologist who shared the 1975 Nobel Prize for Physiology or Medicine with D. BALTIMORE and H. TEMIN for their work on cancer-causing VIRUSES.

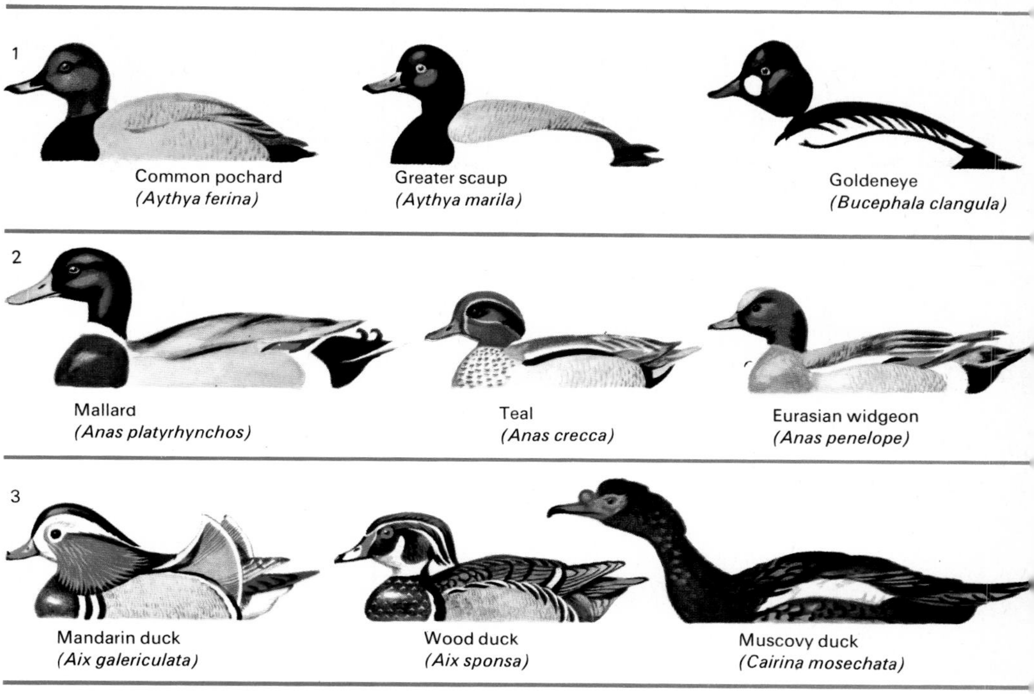

Nine duck species, here represented in each case by the drake of the species. In the family Anatidae there are 147 species of birds, most of which, comprising the subfamily Anatinae, are true ducks. Three groups of such ducks are exemplified: (1) diving ducks; (2) surface-feeding or dabbling ducks; and (3) perching ducks. By far the most widespread and numerous group are the surface-feeding or dabbling ducks, which do not dive, except in unusual circumstances, but obtain all their food at or near the water surface or on damp ground or vegetation. The commonest duck of all is the mallard.

DULCIMER, musical instrument with a set of strings stretched across a thin, flat soundbox and struck with mallets. Of ancient origin, it is still used in the folk music of Central Europe. The Kentucky dulcimer, a US folk instrument, is plucked.

DULLES, name of two prominent US brothers. **John Foster Dulles** (1888–1959), lawyer, US secretary of state under Eisenhower (1953–59), employed a strong foreign policy to block communist "cold war" expansion. He was legal counsel at the WWI peace conference, worked on the UN charter during WWII and negotiated the Japanese peace treaty, 1951. **Allen Welsh Dulles** (1893–1969), US lawyer and intelligence official, negotiated the Nazi surrender in Italy in WWII. He directed the CENTRAL INTELLIGENCE AGENCY 1953–61, considerably influencing foreign policy, as in the American-backed BAY OF PIGS invasion of Cuba.

DULONG, Pierre Louis (1785–1838), French chemist who with A. T. Petit discovered **Dulong and Petit's Law**. This states that the SPECIFIC HEATS of elements are inversely proportional to their ATOMIC WEIGHTS, and is equivalent to the observation that the atomic heats of most elements are about 26.4J/K.mol.

DULUTH, city in NE Minn. at the W end of Lake Superior, seat of St. Louis Co. The biggest Great Lakes port in tonnage handled, it exports iron ore, grain and oil, and imports coal. Products: iron, steel, machinery and processed foods. Pop 100 578.

DULUTH, Daniel Greysolon, Sieur (1636–1710), French explorer around Lake Superior from 1679. He befriended and influenced the OJIBWA and SIOUX Indians, and claimed the Great Lakes area for France. Duluth, Minn., was named for him.

DUMA, elected assembly in tsarist Russia, instituted by Nicholas II in 1906. The first two dumas were radical, and were swiftly dissolved. The third and fourth (1907–12 and 1912–17), though restricted, introduced some reforms. Revolution in 1917 did away with the institution.

DUMAS, name of two 19th-century French authors, a father and his illegitimate son. **Alexandre Dumas** (1802–1870), "Dumas père," wrote the famous historical novels *The Three Musketeers* (1844) and *The Count of Monte Cristo* (1845). Historically inaccurate and lacking in depth, their adventures nevertheless remain popular. **Alexandre Dumas** (1824–1895), "Dumas fils," won fame with his tragic play *La Dame aux Camélias* (known in English as *Camille*, 1852) which formed the basis of Verdi's opera *La Traviata*. He also wrote moralizing plays aimed at the reform of such social evils as prostitution and illegitimacy.

DUMAS, Jean Baptiste André (1800–1884), French organic chemist who discovered that CHLORINE could substitute for HYDROGEN in HYDROCARBONS and was thus led to propose his "law of substitution" (1834) which revolutionized the theory of organic chemistry. From 1868 he was secretary of the Academy of Sciences.

DU MAURIER, name of two English novelists. **George Louis Palmella Busson du Maurier** (1834–1896), caricaturist, illustrator and novelist, best known for *Peter Ibbetson* (1891), and *Trilby* (1894). **Daphne du Maurier** (1907–), George's granddaughter, has written romantic novels. Her most famous work is *Rebecca* (1938).

DUMBARTON OAKS CONFERENCE, meeting of diplomats of the "Big Four" (China, the US, USSR and UK), held Aug. 24–Oct. 7, 1944, at the Dumbarton Oaks estate in Washington, D.C. Its discussions were the first major step towards establishing a postwar international security system (see UNITED NATIONS).

DUMBCANE, *Dieffenbachia amoena*, a perennial shrubby plant frequently grown as a house plant for its green leaves variegated with white or a pale chartreuse color. For healthy growth the plant requires a sunny position in an east- or west-facing window, although direct sun should be avoided in the summer. Dumbcanes fail to thrive at temperatures below 16°C (60°F), and should be watered often enough to keep the soil evenly moist. Propagation is by shoot tip cuttings or air-layering. Family: Araceae.

DUMBNESS, inability to speak. Failure of speech development, usually associated with congenital DEAFNESS (deaf-mute) is the most common cause in childhood. APHASIA and hysterical mutism are the usual adult causes. If comprehension is intact, writing and sign language are alternative forms of communication, but in aphasia language is usually globally impaired. (See SPEECH AND SPEECH DISORDERS.)

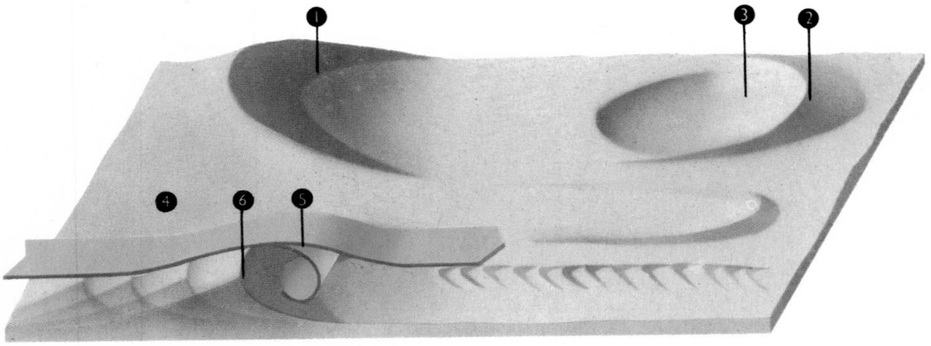

Wind is important in shaping the landscape by sand-dune formation behind depositional coastlines and in deserts. Sand dunes can be crescentic or barchan (1), parabolic (2), or hairpin (3). A crescentic dune (4) over which the wind usually blows in one particular direction (5) advances as its ridge (6) migrates forwards.

DUMDUM BULLET, a bullet so devised as to expand on impact, creating greater damage. Most simply, a cross is scored on the bullet's nose. Their military use was outlawed by the Hague Conference, 1899.

DUMONT, a borough in NE N.J., 9mi E of Paterson. Pop 20 155.

DUMOURIEZ, Charles François du Périer (1739–1823), French revolutionary general. A Seven Years' War veteran, in the French Revolution he became foreign minister (1792), defeated Prussia and Austria at VALMY and JEMAPPES, but lost at Neerwinden. Rightly suspected of seeking to restore royal power, he deserted in 1793 and eventually settled in England.

DUNANT, Jean Henri (1828–1910), Swiss philanthropist, founder of the RED CROSS. Horrified by unrelieved suffering at the Battle of SOLFERINO (1859) he publicized the need for effective aid for injured in war and peace. His efforts led to the Geneva Convention of 1864 (see GENEVA CONVENTIONS) and to the formation of the Red Cross. He shared in the first Nobel Peace Prize in 1901.

DUNBAR, Battle of, battle fought in SE Scotland on Sept. 3, 1650, between the English army under Oliver CROMWELL, and the Scots under David Leslie. Leaving a commanding position, the Scots were routed. (See CIVIL WAR, ENGLISH.)

DUNBAR, Paul Laurence (1872–1906), US Negro poet and novelist who expressed the Negroes' feelings sensitively in Negro dialect poems and short stories.

DUNBAR, William (c1460–1520), greatest of the old Scottish poets. He became a priest, employed by James IV on court business. His mainly short poems show great satiric power, originality, versatility and wit.

DUNCAN, city in S Okla., seat of Stephens Co. It serves local farms and oil fields, producing cottonseed oil, asphalt, gasoline and oil field equipment. Pop 19 718.

DUNCAN, two Scottish kings. **Duncan I** (d. 1040) succeeded his grandfather, Malcolm II, in 1034. Challenged by MACBETH, Mormaer of Moray, he was defeated and killed. **Duncan II** (d. 1094), grandson of Duncan I, was crowned in 1094 with Anglo-Norman support, but was murdered soon after by agents of Donaldbane, his uncle and rival.

DUNCAN, Isadora (1878–1927), US dancer, a pioneer of modern dance, encouraging a spontaneous personal style. She danced in a loose tunic, barefoot, to symphonic music. After European concert successes, she founded schools of dancing in Germany, the USSR and the US. She was strangled by a scarf caught in a car wheel.

DUNCANVILLE, town in NE Texas, 12mi SW of Dallas. It is a dairy farming and cotton center. Pop 14 105.

DUNDALK, a Baltimore suburb in N Md., in Baltimore Co. Pop 85 577.

DUNDAS, town in SE Ontario, Canada, 5mi NW of Hamilton. It is a manufacturing center in a farming area. Pop 17 211.

DUNDEE, seaport in E Scotland, in Tayside Region, on the Firth of Tay. Great Britain's major jute processor (canvas, carpets, etc), it also produces ships, machinery, linen and preserves. Pop 182 084.

DUNE, hillock of sand built up by a prevailing WIND, found mostly in DESERT areas. They have several forms, commonest being **barchans**, crescent shaped with the horns pointing downwind; and **transverse**, elongate dunes at right angles to the wind direction. (See also SAND.)

DUNEDIN, city in New Zealand, in SE South Island, on Otago harbor. It is a residential, university and industrial center, exporting farm produce. Pop 82 216.

DUNEDIN, city in W Fla., on the Gulf of Mexico, 20mi NW of St. Petersburg. A winter resort and citrus fruit center. Pop 17 199.

DUNG BEETLES, a group of beetles which roll balls of dung into underground chambers, where they are eaten or have eggs laid within them. They include the "divine scarab" of ancient Egypt.

DUNKERQUE (Dunkirk), seaport in N France, on the English Channel, 10mi from Belgium. A shipbuilding, oil-refining and food processing center, and railway terminus. In WWII (May 29–June 2, 1940) some 1000 vessels evacuated 337 000 trapped British and Allied troops from here. Pop 27 504.

DUNKERS (Dunkards), any of several bodies of Brethren, or German Baptists. They are theologically rooted in 17th-century Lutheran PIETISM and named for their practice of triple baptismal immersion. The movement began in 18th-century Germany but most members went to America where they now number over 230 000, most in the Church of the Brethren.

DUNKIRK. See DUNKERQUE.

DUNKIRK, city in SW N.Y., on Lake Erie, 35mi SW of Buffalo. It is a port and producer of textiles, machinery and farm products. Pop 16 855.

DUNLAP, William (1766–1839), US artist and the first professional American playwright. He studied art in London under Benjamin West. Later he wrote or adapted about 60 plays and a *History of the American Theater* (1832).

DUNLOP, John Boyd (1840–1921), British inventor who devised the first commercially successful pneumatic TIRE. This was patented in the UK in 1888.

DUNMORE, borough in NE Pa., 3mi E of Scranton. It manufactures textiles and footwear. Pop 17 300.

DUNMORE, John Murray, 4th Earl of (1732–1809), English governor of New York (1770–71), Virginia (1771–75) and the Bahamas (1787–96). He launched "Lord Dunmore's War" (1774) against the Indians. Opposing the rebels, he three times dissolved the Virginia assembly (1772–74) but in 1776 an uprising forced him out of Virginia.

DUNNE, Finley Peter (1867–1936), US journalist and humorist. He created "Mr. Dooley," an Irish–American saloonkeeper, whose amusing and satirical comments on current events Dunne first published in the press, then in books such as *Mr. Dooley in Peace and War* (1898).

DUNNING, John Ray (1907–1975), US physicist who first measured the ENERGY released in nuclear FISSION (1939) and the next year demonstrated the fission of URANIUM-235. He later helped to develop the gas-diffusion method of ISOTOPE separation used in making the first two ATOMIC BOMBS.

DUNS SCOTUS, John (c1265–1308), Scottish philosopher and theologian. He joined the Franciscans (1280), was ordained in 1291 and taught at Cambridge, Oxford, Paris and Cologne. His system of thought, embodied chiefly in his commentary on LOMBARD's *Sentences*, was adopted by the Franciscans and was highly influential. Typical of SCHOLASTICISM, it differs from AQUINAS in asserting the primacy of love and the will over reason. He was the first in the West to defend the IMMACULATE CONCEPTION.

DUNSTABLE, John (c1385–1453), English composer whose flowing, harmonious works influenced European music. He wrote some 60 works, including motets and secular part-songs.

DUNSTAN, Saint (c909–988), archbishop of Canterbury from 960. A powerful national administrator under kings Edred and Edgar, he worked to strengthen royal power, reformed monastic life on strict Benedictine lines and founded and rebuilt churches. His feast day is May 19.

DUNSTER, Henry (1609–1659), English-born American clergyman, first president of Harvard College, 1640–54. Educated at Cambridge, he emigrated in 1640 and soundly established Harvard before his unorthodox Baptist beliefs caused his dismissal.

DUODECIMAL SYSTEM, a number system using the POWERS of twelve, which are allotted place values as in the DECIMAL SYSTEM. The number written in decimals 4092 can be expressed as $(2\times12^3)+(4\times12^2)+(5\times12^1)+(0\times12^0)$ or, in duodecimals, 2450. Fractions are expressed similarly. Two extra symbols are needed for this system to represent the numbers 10 and 11; these are generally accepted as X (dek) and Σ (el) respectively. The advantage of this system can be realized by consideration of the integral (see INTEGERS) FACTORS of 10 and 12: 10 has two (2,5) while 12 has four (2,3,4,6). The most common examples of everyday use of this system are the setting of 12 inches to the foot, 12 months to the year.

DUODENUM, the first part of the small intestine, leading from the STOMACH to the jejunum (see GASTROINTESTINAL TRACT). The BILE and pancreatic ducts end in it and its injury may result in a FISTULA. Peptic ULCERS are common in the duodenum.

DUPLEIX, Joseph François (1696–1763), governor-general of French possessions in India, 1742–54. He tried to extend French influence in central and S India by supporting Indian rulers against their British-backed rivals. Defeated by CLIVE, Dupleix was discredited and returned to France to die in poverty.

DUPLESSIS, Maurice Le Noblet (1890–1959), Canadian politician, premier of Quebec from 1936. He founded the Union Nationale Party, which urged French-Canadian self-government, and became premier of Quebec when it won the 1936 election. Anti-war policies lost him the 1939 election but he was again premier 1944–59.

DUPLICATING MACHINE, machine to produce copies from an original master. A stencil comprising a porous backing sheet coated on one side with an ink-resisting waxy plastic is clamped round an inked drum: ink seeps through where the plastic has been displaced using a stylus or typewriter. In the **spirit process**, the master sheet bears the impression in a strong dye: the copy paper is moistened with spirit which dissolves some of the dye, so taking the copy. (See also XEROGRAPHY.)

DUPLICATION OF THE CUBE, one of the classical problems of ancient GEOMETRY. Given a CUBE A with edges of length a, the problem is to find the length, b, of the edges of a cube, B, whose VOLUME is twice that of A: i.e., $b^3=2a^3$. This may be expressed as $b^3/a^3=2$, or $b/a=\sqrt[3]{2}$. It is impossible with the tools of classical geometry, the straight edge and compass, to evaluate a cube ROOT (see also IRRATIONAL NUMBERS).

DU PONT, US industrial family of French origin. **Pierre Samuel du Pont de Nemours** (1739–1817), French economist and statesman, publicized the PHYSIOCRATS' doctrines. He was a reformist member of the Estates General (1789) and secretary general of the provisional government (1814). He fled to the US in 1799 and, having returned in 1802, fled again in 1815. His son

Éleuthère Irénée du Pont (1771–1834) established a gunpowder factory near Wilmington, Del., in 1802. The company expanded enormously during the Mexican, Crimean and Civil wars under Éleuthère's son **Henry du Pont** (1812–1889), who in 1872 organized the "Gunpowder Trust" which soon controlled 90% of explosives output. **Alfred Irénée du Pont** (1864–1935), **Thomas Coleman du Pont** (1863–1930) and **Pierre Samuel du Pont** (1870–1954) reorganized the firm in 1902, and after WWI it exploited the valuable dye-trust patents confiscated from Germany. Under Pierre's brothers **Irénée du Pont** (1876–1963) and **Lammont du Pont** (1880–1952) the firm built up an immensely powerful synthetic chemicals industry, developing rayon, cellophane, neoprene, nylon and other materials.

DUPRÉ, Marcel (1886–1971), French organist and composer, director of the Paris Conservatoire 1954–56. His compositions include symphonies and many organ works.

DUQUE DE CAXIAS, city in SE Brazil, in Rio de Janeiro State. It is a N suburb of Rio de Janeiro. Pop 259 000.

DUQUESNE, city in SW Pa., on the Monongahela R, 10mi ESE of Pittsburg. It is a major steel-production center. Pop 11 410.

DURALUMIN, aluminum-based ALLOY typically containing 4% copper, 1% magnesium, 0.7% manganese and 0.5% silicon. After heat treatment and aging it is hard and strong as steel, and, being light, is used in aircraft construction.

DURAND, Asher Brown (1796–1886), US painter and engraver, a founder of the HUDSON RIVER SCHOOL. He made his name by engraving John Trumbull's painting *The Signing of the Declaration of Independence* (1820). He painted realistic landscapes and portraits, and also designed banknotes.

DURANGO, state in N central Mexico. It is largely dry plateau, and produces silver, gold, iron, copper and other minerals. Crops include cotton, corn and wheat.

DURANGO (Victoria de Durango), city in N central Mexico, capital of Durango state. It is a university city and a leading mining and commercial center, producing iron, textiles, flour and sugar. It was founded in 1563. Pop 193 000.

DURANGO, city in SW Col., seat of La Plata Co. An oil-mining, lumber-processing and trade center. Pop 10 333.

DURANT, city in S Okla., 125mi SE of Oklahoma City, seat of Bryan Co. Its industries include cotton processing, packaging and furniture. Pop 11 118.

DURANT, Thomas Clark (1820–1885), US railroad pioneer, chief founder of the Union Pacific Railroad (1862). Founder president of the CRÉDIT MOBILIER OF AMERICA (1863–67), he was ousted by rivals, but remained a Union Pacific director till 1869.

DURANT, William Crapo (1861–1947), US automobile executive who founded the General Motors Corporation in 1916 with the aid of Louis Chevrolet (1879–1941). He lost control in 1920.

DURANT, Will(iam James) (1885–), US educator and popular historian. He wrote the stylishly lively bestseller *The Story of Philosophy* (1926) and, with his wife, the 10-volume *The Story of Civilization* (1935–67).

DURANTE, Jimmy (1893–), US entertainer, born James Francis Durante, famous for his outsized nose. He began in show business in 1910 and has appeared in many films and musicals.

DURAS, Marguerite (1914–), French novelist, playwright and scriptwriter, associated with the New Wave French writers of the 1950s and 1960s. Her works include the novels *The Sea Wall* (1950) and *Moderato Cantabile* (1958) and the film script *Hiroshima, Mon Amour* (1960).

DURBAN, city in South Africa, in E Natal, on the Indian Ocean. It is South Africa's major seaport, exporting coal, ores and farm products, and producing fertilizers, textiles, metalware, sugar and petroleum. A university city and leading tourist resort, it was founded 1824. Pop 495 000.

DÜRER, Albrecht (1471–1528), German artist who introduced Italian Renaissance outlook and style to Germany, though tempered by Gothic tradition. Bellini, Mantegna and Leonardo da Vinci all influenced Dürer after his visits to Venice (1494–95 and 1505–07). He became court painter to the emperors Maximilian (1512) and Charles V (1520), and produced a huge output of masterly, vividly detailed drawings, engravings, woodcuts and paintings. His themes included religious subjects, plant and animal studies and evocative landscapes in watercolor.

DURHAM, city in NE England, seat of Durham county. It is dominated by its fine cathedral (begun 1093) and its castle (founded 1072), now occupied by the U. of Durham. Pop 24 744.

DURHAM, city in N central N.C., 20mi NW of Raleigh, seat of Durham Co. The world's chief cigarette manufacturer, it also produces cotton textiles, machinery and pharmaceuticals. It has Duke U. and North Carolina U. Pop 95 438.

DURHAM, John George Lambton, 1st Earl of (1792–1840), English statesman, author of DURHAM'S REPORT. A radical Whig, he was lord privy seal 1830–33 and helped draft the Reform Bill of 1832. Governor general of Canada 1838, he was criticized for his leniency towards rebels, and resigned.

DURHAM'S REPORT, report by Lord Durham which laid down the basic principles of British colonial administration. *The Report on the Affairs of British North America* (1839) urged the union of Canada and the granting of internal self government.

DURKHEIM, Émile (1858–1917), pioneer French sociologist who advocated the synthesis of empirical research and abstract theory in the social sciences and developed the concepts of "collective consciousness" and the "division of labor."

DUROCHER, Leo Ernest "Lippy" (1906–), US baseball player and manager. Beginning in 1925, he played shortstop for major league teams, then managed the Brooklyn Dodgers (world champions 1941), New York Giants (world champions 1951 and 1954) and Chicago Cubs.

DURRA. See SORGHUM.

DURRELL, Lawrence (George) (1912–), English novelist and poet, known for the sensuous lyricism and rhythmic vitality of his style. His works include *The Alexandria Quartet*, four novels—*Justine* (1957), *Balthazar* (1958), *Mountolive* (1958) and *Clea* (1960)—exploring one story from different viewpoints; *Tunc* (1968) and several volumes of poetry.

DÜRRENMATT, Friedrich (1921–), Swiss playwright and novelist. His often bizarre tragicomedies employ biting satire, and include *The Visit* (1956) and *The Physicists* (1962). He has also written crime novels.

DURRËS, chief seaport of Albania, and capital of Durrës province, on the Adriatic Sea, 19mi W of Tiranë. Pop 53 800.

DURYEA, Charles Edgar (1861–1938), pioneer US AUTOMOBILE manufacturer who with his brother, **J. Frank Duryea** (1870–1967), produced the first successful car in the US.

DU SABLE, Jean Baptiste Point (c1745–1818), Haitian–American pioneer and explorer regarded as the first settler of Chicago. He built a trading post on the N bank of the Chicago R in 1779.

DUSE, Eleonora (1859–1924), Italian dramatic actress, rivaling Sarah Bernhardt as the greatest actress of her period, notably in plays by Ibsen and by Duse's lover Gabriele D'Annunzio.

DUSHANBE (formerly Stalinabad), capital of the Soviet republic of Tadzhikistan, a leading cotton-textile center and a university city. Pop 400 000.

DÜSSELDORF, city in West Germany, capital of the state of North Rhine-Westphalia. It is a leading port on the Rhine, a major center for communications, finance and industry (iron, steel, chemicals, textiles and machinery) and has a famous academy of arts. Pop 663 586.

DUST, fine particles, usually inorganic, which may be easily picked up by the wind and remain suspended in the air for long periods. It may be produced by volcanic action (dust from the Krakatoa explosion of 1883 circled the earth several times, some taking years to settle), by wind EROSION (see DUST BOWL; SANDSTORM), by the breaking up of meteoroids (see METEOR) in the atmosphere, by salt spray from the oceans, and by industrial processes and auto exhausts (see AUTOMOBILE EMISSION CONTROL). POLLEN is an example of an organic dust. Many dusts are serious health risks, especially the radioactive dust present in nuclear FALLOUT. (See also AIR POLLUTION; INTERSTELLAR MATTER.)

DUST BOWL, area of some 400 000km² in the S Great Plains region of the US which, during the 1930s, the Depression years, suffered violent dust storms owing to accelerated SOIL EROSION. Grassland was plowed up in the 1910s and 1920s to plant wheat: a severe drought bared the fields, and high winds blew the topsoil (see SOIL) into huge dunes. (See SANDSTORM.) Despite rehabilitation programs, farmers plowed up grassland again in the 1940s and 1950s, and a repetition of the tragedy was averted only by the action of Congress.

DUTCH, West Germanic language spoken in the Netherlands and (as FLEMISH) in N Belgium, also in Surinam and the Dutch Antilles. AFRIKAANS, spoken in South Africa, is derived from Dutch. Dutch evolved largely from the speech of the Franks, who settled in the Low Countries in the 4th–5th centuries. About 20 million people speak Dutch.

DUTCH EAST INDIES, former Dutch overseas territory, now INDONESIA. Colonized by the Dutch East India Company in the 17th century, the area came under Dutch government in 1798, was occupied by Japan in WWII and gained independence in 1949 after a nationalist struggle.

DUTCH ELM DISEASE. See ELM.

DUTCH GUIANA. See SURINAM.

DUTCH REFORMED CHURCH, largest and oldest Protestant church of the Netherlands and dominant church in South Africa. It was the first reformed church from mainland Europe to be established in North America. (See also REFORMED CHURCHES.)

DUTCH WARS, three 17th-century wars fought by the Dutch and English for maritime supremacy. The

Dürer was largely responsible for bringing the art of the Italian Renaissance to Germany and became the most influential German artist of his time. His *Adoration of the Kings*, pictured here, hangs in the Uffizi Gallery, Florence.

First Dutch War (1652–54) began after England's First Navigation Act (1651) excluded the Dutch from trade with English possessions. The English temporarily lost control of the English channel and failed to sustain a blockade. War ended with the Treaty of Westminster (1654). British attacks on Dutch colonies provoked the *Second Dutch War* (1665–67), in which the French aided the Dutch. Impoverished by plague and the Great Fire of London, England signed the Treaty of Breda (1667). This gave the Dutch Surinam and relaxed the navigation laws, but gave England New Netherland (New York). In the *Third Dutch War* (1672–74), the English and French attacked the Dutch but failed to subdue the Dutch fleet. France invaded the Dutch Republic until halted by deliberate flooding and a powerful alliance including Austria, Spain and Brandenburg. Disheartened by lack of success, England made peace with the Dutch in 1674. But Franco-Dutch fighting continued until 1678.

DUTCH WEST INDIA COMPANY, association of Dutch merchants incorporated in 1621 to monopolize Dutch trade with Africa and the Americas and to found colonies there. It colonized Caribbean islands (1634–48) and Surinam (1667). Harassed by Spain, Portugal and England, it lost other New World possessions and was dissolved in 1674. Reorganized in 1675, it was absorbed by the Dutch state in 1791 and finally dissolved in 1794.

DUTCH WEST INDIES. See NETHERLANDS ANTILLES.

DUVALIER, François ("Papa Doc"; 1907–1971), autocratic president of Haiti 1957–71. A physician turned politician, he was elected to power as a reformer but ruled as dictator, helped by a political police force, the Tonton Macoutes. He made himself president for life in 1964.

DUVEEN OF MILLBANK, Joseph Duveen, 1st Baron (1869–1939), English art dealer who advised wealthy American collectors such as MELLON and John D. ROCKEFELLER. He largely created and satisfied the American taste for fine old masters, now represented in many American art museums.

DE VIGNEAUD, Vincent (1901–), US biochemist who was awarded the 1955 Nobel Prize for Chemistry in recognition of his synthesis of the hormone OXYTOCIN (1954). He had earlier worked out the structure of the VITAMIN biotin (1942).

DUXBURY, resort town in SE Mass., 30mi SE of Boston. It was founded c1624 by some of the Plymouth colonists. Pop 7636.

DVINA, name of two rivers in the USSR. The Northern Dvina flows about 460mi through N European Russia into the White Sea at Arkhangelsk. The Western Dvina rises near Moscow and flows 630mi into the Gulf of Riga on the Baltic sea. Both are navigable.

DVOŘÁK, Antonín (1841–1904), major Czech composer, who developed the national style founded by SMETANA. A viola player, his richly lyrical music began to win him acclaim in the 1870s. He spent 1892–95 in the US, as director of the National Conservatory of Music, New York City. His works include 9 symphonies, 10 operas, concertos, the Slavonic dances and other orchestral compositions, choral works and chamber music.

DWARFISM, or small stature. This may be a family characteristic or associated with congenital disease of CARTILAGE or BONE development (e.g., achondroplasia). Failure of growth-HORMONE (see PITUITARY GLAND) or THYROID-hormone production during growth, and excess STEROID, ANDROGEN or ESTROGEN can cause small stature by altering control of bone development. The condition can also arise from spine or limb deformity (e.g., SCOLIOSIS), MALNUTRITION, RICKETS, chronic infection or visceral disease.

DWARF STAR. See STAR.

DWARF TREE. See BONSAI.

DWIGGINS, William Addison (1880–1956), US designer and calligrapher whose new typefaces and layouts revolutionized book and magazine design. He created Alfred A. Knopf's house style and wrote the influential *Layout in Advertising* (1928) and *MSS by WAD* (1949).

DWIGHT, Theodore (1764–1846), American author, one of the HARTFORD WITS. He served in Congress 1806–07 and was secretary of the HARTFORD CONVENTION (1814–15). His journal on the convention was published in 1833.

DWIGHT, Timothy (1752–1817), American clergyman, teacher and author; like his brother Theodore, one of the HARTFORD WITS. He was president of Yale from 1795 and became one of the leading figures of the period's religious revival movement.

DYAK. See DAYAK.

DYER, Mary (d. 1660), Quaker martyr in Massachusetts. A supporter of Anne HUTCHINSON, she visited imprisoned Quakers and preached in Boston, despite orders banishing her from the settlement. She was reprieved in 1659, but was rearrested the following year and sentenced to be hanged.

DYER, Reginald Edward Harry (1864–1927), British general whose harsh measures reinforced anti-British feeling in India. On April 15, 1919, following violent rioting and the imposition of martial law, he ordered troops in Amritsar to fire on an unarmed Indian crowd. Some 380 people died and many more were wounded. Dyer was stripped of his command.

DYERSBURG, city and seat of Dyer Co. in NW Tenn. It is an agricultural center, producing flour, cottonseed oil and textiles. Pop 14523.

DYES AND DYEING. Dyes are colored substances which impart their color to textiles to which they are applied and for which they have a chemical affinity. They differ from PIGMENTS in being used in solution in an aqueous medium. Dyeing was practiced in the FERTILE CRESCENT and China by 3000 BC, using natural dyes obtained from plants and shellfish. These were virtually superseded by synthetic dyes—more varied in color and applicability—after the accidental synthesis of mauve by PERKIN (1856). The raw materials are AROMATIC hydrocarbons obtained from COAL TAR and PETROLEUM. These are modified by introducing chemical groups called chromophores which cause absorption of visible LIGHT (see also COLOR). Other groups, auxochromes, such as amino or hydroxyl, are necessary for substantivity—i.e., affinity for the material to be dyed. This fixing to the fabric fibers is by HYDROGEN BONDING, ADSORPTION, ionic bonding or covalent bonding in the case of "reactive dyes" (see BOND, CHEMICAL). If there is no natural affinity, the dye may be fixed by using a MORDANT before or with dyeing. Vat dyes are made soluble by reduction in the presence of alkali, and after dyeing the original color is re-formed by acidification and oxidation; INDIGO and ANTHRAQUINONE dyes are examples. Dyes are also used as biological stains (see MICROSCOPE), INDICATORS and in PHOTOGRAPHY. (See also AZO DYES; FLUORESCEIN; INK.)

Bob Dylan, pictured here playing (with Leon Russell) at the Bangladesh benefit concert (New York, 1971), is generally considered to be one of the major figures in 20th century popular music. His powerful and poetical lyrics have helped to raise the whole standard of "pop" music.

DYKE. See DIKE.

DYLAN, Bob (born Robert Zimmerman; 1941–) US folk singer and composer. His distinctive blues style had a strong influence on popular music in the 1960s. He later turned to country and ballad music.

DYNAMICS, the branch of mechanics concerned with the actions of forces on bodies, with particular respect to the motions produced. (See MECHANICS.)

DYNAMITE, high EXPLOSIVE invented by Alfred NOBEL, consisting of NITROGLYCERIN absorbed in an inert material such as KIESELGUHR or wood pulp. Unlike nitroglycerin itself, it can be handled safely, not exploding without a DETONATOR. In modern dynamite SODIUM nitrate replaces about half the nitroglycerin. Gelatin dynamite, or **gelignite**, contains also some NITROCELLULOSE.

DYNAMO. See GENERATOR, ELECTRIC.

DYNAMOMETER, any of various devices used to measure the POWER output of a MACHINE.

DYNE (dyn), the unit of FORCE in the CGS SYSTEM, equal to 0.00001 newtons in SI UNITS.

DYSENTERY, a BACTERIAL or PARASITIC DISEASE causing abdominal pain, DIARRHEA and FEVER. In children, **bacillary dysentery** due to *Shigella* species is a common endemic or EPIDEMIC disease, and is associated with poor hygiene. It is a short-lived illness but may cause dehydration in severe cases. The organism may be carried in feces in the absence of symptoms. ANTIBIOTICS may be used to shorten the attack and reduce carrier rates. **Amebic dysentery** is a chronic disease, usually seen in warm climates, with episodes of diarrhea and CONSTIPATION, accompanied by MUCUS and occasionally BLOOD; constitutional symptoms occur and the disease may resemble noninfective COLITIS. Treatment with emetine, while effective, is accompanied by a high risk of toxicity; metronidazole is a less toxic antiamebic agent introduced recently.

DYSLEXIA, difficulty with reading, often a developmental problem possibly associated with suppressed left-HANDEDNESS, and spatial difficulty; it requires special training. It may be acquired by BIRTH injury, failure of learning, visual disorders or as part of APHASIA (see SPEECH AND SPEECH DISORDERS).

DYSPEPSIA, or indigestion, a vague term usually describing abnormal visceral sensation in upper ABDOMEN or lower CHEST, often of a burning quality. Relationship to meals and posture is important in defining its origin; relief by ANTACIDS or milk is usual. HEARTBURN from esophagitis and pain of peptic (gastric or duodenal) ULCERS are usual causes.

DYSPHASIA. See APHASIA; SPEECH AND SPEECH DISORDERS.

DYSPROSIUM (Dy), one of the LANTHANUM SERIES. AW 162.5, mp 1409°C, bp 2335°C, sg 8.550 (25°C).

DZERZHINSK, city in the USSR, in Gorki Oblast, 20mi W of Gorki on the Oka R. It is a major chemicals center. Pop 228000.

DZERZHINSKI, Felix Edmundovich (1877–1926), Polish-born revolutionary, one of the founders of the USSR. From 1917 until his death he organized and headed the CHEKA, the Soviet secret police, known after 1922 as the OGPU. He also became commissar of transport 1921 and was head of the supreme economic council 1924.

DZHAMBUL (formerly Aulie Ata), city and capital of Dzhambul Oblast in the USSR, 130mi NE of Tashkent. Food processing and the manufacture of fertilizers are the chief industries. Pop 205000.

DZHUGASHVILI, Josef Vissarionovich. See STALIN, JOSEPH.

DZUNGARIA, semidesert region in W China, in the Sinkiang Uighur Autonomous Region, N of the Tien Shan mountain range. Conquered by the Mongol Dzungars in the 17th century, it was absorbed by China in 1758–59. Agriculture, the chief occupation, is concentrated in the rich I-li R valley.

E

E, fifth letter of the English alphabet, derived from an ancient Semitic letter and the Greek *epsilon*. It is a vowel and can be long as in *feet*, or short as in *met*, or it can lengthen the preceding vowel as in *bite*. In music, *E* is the note *mi* in the scale of *C*.

e. See EXPONENTIAL.

EADS, James Buchanan (1820–1887), US engineer whose jetty system opened the Mississippi R to big oceangoing vessels (1879). He also built ironclad Union gunboats in the Civil War and spanned the Mississippi at St. Louis with the first major US steel arch bridge (1874).

EAGLE PASS, city in SW Tex. It is a port on the Rio Grande, and the seat of Maverick Co. It stood on a major Cal. goldrush route. Pop 15 364.

EAGLES, powerful BIRDS OF PREY found in many highland regions such as North America, Scotland and Asia. Their nests (eyries) are found between 275 and 600m (900–2 000ft). The eagles comprise four groups: Sea and Fish eagles; Snake eagles; Crested eagles; and "true" or Aquiline eagles. All have characteristic soaring flights made possible by broad wings with spans of up to 2m (6.5ft). Being carnivores, eagles have hooked beaks and clawed feet. They are diurnal. Eagles have frequently figured in mythology, especially of North American Indians.

EAGLETON, Thomas Francis (1929–   ), US lawyer and Democratic senator who became MCGOVERN's vice-presidential running-mate after the 1972 primaries. Disclosures of past psychiatric treatment forced his withdrawal.

EAKER, Ira Clarence (1896–   ), US general and pioneer aviator. He set a world flight record for endurance (1929) and made the first "blind" transcontinental flight (1936). In WWII he led the first US air attack on the Germans (1942) and commanded Mediterranean Allied Air Forces (1944–45).

EAKINS, Thomas (1844–1916), major US realist painter. Among his most famous paintings is *The Gross Clinic* (1875). Eakins was also an early action photographer.

EAMES, Charles (1907–   ), US designer, who influenced contemporary furniture design. He created plywood and fiberglass form-fitting chairs, and the upholstered "Eames chair."

EAR, a special sense organ in higher animals, concerned with hearing and balance. It may be divided into the outer ear, extending from the tympanic membrane or ear drum to the pinna, the inner ear embedded in the SKULL bones, consisting of cochlea and labyrinth, and between them the middle ear, containing small bones or ossicles. The cartilaginous pinna varies greatly in shape and mobility in different animals; a canal lined by skin leads from it and ends with the thin tympanic membrane stretched across it. The middle ear is an air-filled space which communicates with the PHARYNX via the **Eustachian tube**. This allows the middle ear to be at the same pressure as the outer and also secretions to drain away. The middle ear is also connected with the MASTOID antrum. Three ossicles (malleus, incus, stapes) form a bony chain articulating between the ear drum and part of the cochlea; tiny muscles are attached to the drum and ossicles and can affect the intensity of SOUND transmission. The inner ear contains both the cochlea, a spiral structure containing fluid and specialized membranes on which hearing receptors are situated, and the labyrinth which consists of three semicircular canals, the utricle and the saccule, all of which contain fluid and receptor cells. Nerve fibers pass from the cochlea and labyrinth to form the eighth cranial nerve.

The golden eagle (*Aquila chrysaetos*), found in the US along the Pacific coast and in the Rockies.

In **hearing**, sound waves travel into the outer ear, funneled by the pinna, and cause vibration of the ear drum. The drum and ossicular chain, which transmits vibration to the cochlea, effect some amplification. The vibration set up in the cochlear fluid is differentially distributed along the central membrane according to pitch. By a complex mechanism, this membrane movement causes certain groups of receptor cells to be preferentially stimulated, giving rise to auditory nerve impulses, which are conducted via several coding sites to higher centers for perception. These centers can in turn affect the sensitivity of receptors by means of centrifugal fibers. In **balance**, rotation of the head in any of three perpendicular planes causes stimulation of specialized cells in the semicircular canals as fluid moves past them. The utricle and saccule contain small stones which respond to gravitational changes and affect receptor cells in their walls. All these balance receptor cells cause impulses in the vestibular nerve, and this connects to higher centers.

Disease of the ear usually causes DEAFNESS or ringing in the ears. Peripheral disorders of balance include VERTIGO and ATAXIA, which may be accompanied by NAUSEA OR VOMITING. MÉNIÈRE'S DISEASE is an episodic disease affecting both systems.

EARHART, Amelia (1898–1937), US pioneer aviator. She was the first transatlantic woman passenger (1928), first solo transatlantic woman pilot (1932) and made the first ever solo flight from Hawaii to the US mainland (1935). She disappeared over the Pacific Ocean on an attempted around-the-world flight in 1937.

EARL, Ralph (1751–1801), American portrait painter. His distinctively rugged portraits were influenced by John Singleton COPLEY. He is noted for his Revolutionary War battle scenes.

EARLY, Jubal Anderson (1816–1894), Confederate general, famous for his advance on Washington (1864), in which he cleared the Shenandoah Valley of Union forces. His army was subsequently forced to retreat and defeated by Union troops under Philip SHERIDAN.

EARLY CHRISTIAN ART AND ARCHITECTURE. Little is known of the first two centuries of Christian art. It derived from the Classical tradition of the late Roman Empire. The earliest extant

Cutaway of the human ear showing (a) the semicircular canals which provide the sense of balance; (b) the cochlea, containing the cochlear fluid which activates the hearing receptor cells; and (c) the tympanic membrane or ear drum, which vibrates with incoming sound.

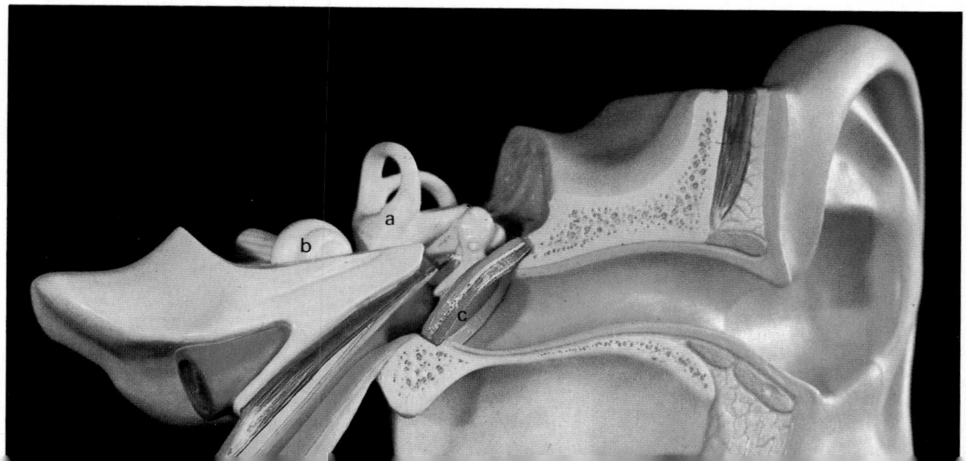

examples are the 3rd-century wall paintings and sarcophagi of the Roman CATACOMBS which mostly featured biblical figures. Great emphasis was placed on the production and illumination of books. In the 4th and 5th centuries, after the official recognition of Christianity, monumental BASILICA-type churches appeared. Externally they were plain, but inside they were resplendent with wall mosaics of glass and colored marble. After the 5th century these features reached a peak in BYZANTINE ART AND ARCHITECTURE in the East and ROMANESQUE ART AND ARCHITECTURE in the West.

EARLY ENGLISH STYLE, late 12th- and 13th-century architectural style marking a transition from Romanesque to mature Gothic. It featured high, slim openings and steeply pointed arches. Salisbury cathedral (begun 1220) is one of the finest examples. (See also GOTHIC ART AND ARCHITECTURE.)

EARP, Wyatt Berry Stapp (1848–1929), US frontier lawman and folk hero. He was deputy sheriff and US marshal in several Kan. and Ariz. "cow towns." He is most famous for the gunfight at O.K. Corral in Tombstone, Ariz. (1881).

EARTH, the largest of the inner planets of the solar system, the third planet from the sun and, so far as is known, the sole home of life in the solar system. To an astronomer on Mars, several things would be striking about our planet. Most of all, he would notice the relative size of our MOON: there are larger moons in the SOLAR SYSTEM, but none so large compared with its planet—indeed, some astronomers regard the earth as one component of a "double planet," the other being the moon. Our Martian astronomer would also notice that the earth shows phases, just as the moon and Venus do when viewed from earth. And, if he were a radio astronomer, he would detect a barrage of radio "noise" from our planet—clear evidence of the presence of intelligent life.

The earth is rather larger than VENUS. It is slightly oblate (flattened at the poles), the equatorial diameter being about 12 756.4km, the polar diameter about 12 713.6km. It rotates on its axis in 23h 56min 4.09s (one **sidereal day**), though this is increasing by roughly 0.000 01s annually due to tidal effects (see TIDES); and revolves about the sun in 365d 6h 9min 9.5s (one **sidereal year**: see SIDEREAL TIME). Two other types of year are defined: the **tropical year**, the interval between alternate EQUINOXES (365d 5h 48min 46s); and the **anomalistic year**, the interval between moments of perihelion (see ORBIT), 365d 6h 13min 53s. The earth's equator is angled about 23.5° to the ECLIPTIC, the plane of its orbit. The direction of the earth's axis is slowly changing owing to PRECESSION. The planet has a mass of about 5.98×10^{21} tonnes, a volume of about 1.08×10^{21} m^3, and a mean DENSITY of about 5.52 tonnes/m^3.

Like other planetary bodies, the earth has a magnetic field (see MAGNETISM). The magnetic poles do not coincide with the axial poles (see NORTH POLE; SOUTH POLE), and moreover they "wander." At or near the earth's surface, **magnetic declination** (or **variation**) is the angle between true N and compass N (lines joining points of equal variation are **isogonic lines**); and **magnetic dip** (or **inclination**) the vertical angle between the MAGNETIC FIELD and the horizontal at a particular point. **Isomagnetic lines** can be drawn between points of equal intensity of the field. There is also evidence to suggest that the direction of the field reverses from time to time. These changes are of primary interest to the paleomagnetist (see PALEOMAGNETISM). The earth is surrounded by radiation belts, probably the result of charged particles from the sun being trapped by the earth's magnetic field (see VAN ALLEN RADIATION BELTS; AURORA).

There are three main zones of the earth: the ATMOSPHERE; the HYDROSPHERE (the world's waters); and the LITHOSPHERE, the solid body of the world. The atmosphere shields us from much of the harmful radiation of the SUN, and protects us from excesses of heat and cold. Water covers much of the earth's surface (over 70%) in both liquid and solid (ice) forms (see GLACIER; OCEANS). There are permanent polar icecaps. The earth's solid body can be divided into

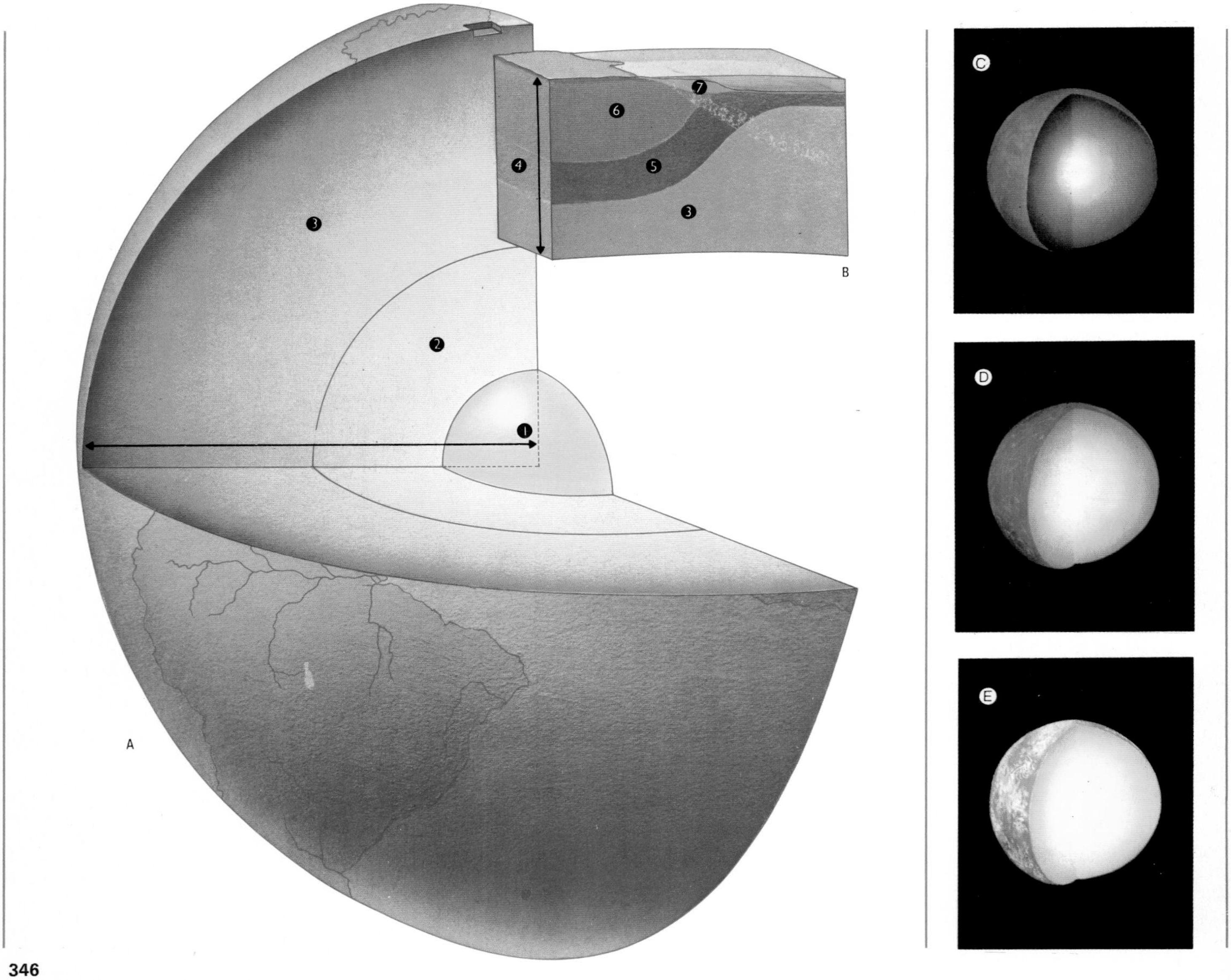

(A) The earth probably comprises a solid core (1), an outer liquid core (2), and a solid mantle (3) composed of iron and magnesium silicates. (B) An enlarged section of the outermost layers of the earth (4). The upper part of the mantle (3) is fairly plastic. Above this occurs the earth's crust: basaltic material up to 5mi thick forms the oceanic crust (5) while granitic material underlies the continental land masses (6). Recent sediments (7) result from erosion. Early in the earth's formation (C) the materials compressed near its center melted to produce a molten core. As the earth cooled (D), the crust was formed. With more cooling (E), the three layers separated out: core, mantle and crust.

three regions: The **core** (diameter about 7000km), at a temperature of about 3000K, is at least partly liquid, though the central region (the inner core) is probably solid. Probably mainly of NICKEL and IRON, the core's density ranges between about 9.5 and perhaps over 15 tonnes/m³. The **mantle** (outer diameter about 12686km), probably mainly of OLIVINE, has a density around 5.7 tonnes/m³ toward the core, 3.3 tonnes/m³ toward the **crust**, the outermost layer of the earth and the one to which all human activity is confined. It is some 35km thick (much less beneath the oceans) and composed of three types of ROCKS: IGNEOUS ROCKS, SEDIMENTARY ROCKS and METAMORPHIC ROCKS. FOSSILS in the strata of sedimentary rocks give us a geological time scale (see GEOLOGY). The earth formed about 4550 million years ago; life appeared probably little more than 570 million years ago, and man around 4 million years ago. Life has thus been present for about 12.5% of the earth's history, man for about 0.09%, and civilization for less than 0.0001%.

It is now known that the earth's configuration of continents and oceans has changed radically through geological time—as it were, the map has changed. Originally, this was attributed to continents drifting, and the process was called CONTINENTAL DRIFT (see also Alfred WEGENER). However, although this term is still used descriptively, the changes are now realized to be a manifestation of the theory of PLATE TECTONICS, and so a result of the processes responsible also for EARTHQUAKES, MOUNTAIN building and many other phenomena.

EARTHENWARE. See POTTERY AND PORCELAIN.

EARTHQUAKE, a fracture or implosion beneath the surface of the earth, and the shock waves that travel away from the point where the fracture has occurred. The immediate area where the fracture takes place is the **focus** or **hypocenter**, the point immediately above it on the earth's surface is the **epicenter**, and the shock waves emanating from the fracture are called seismic waves.

Earthquakes occur to relieve a stress that has built up within the crust or mantle of the EARTH; fracture results when the stress exceeds the strength of the rock. The reasons for the stress build-up are to be found in the theory of PLATE TECTONICS. If a map is drawn of the world's earthquake activity, it can be immediately seen that earthquakes are confined to discrete belts. These belts signify the borders of contiguous plates; shallow earthquakes being generally associated with MID-OCEAN RIDGES where creation of new material occurs, deep ones with regions where one plate is being forced under another.

Seismic waves are of two main types. Body waves travel from the hypocenter, and again are of two types: P (compressional) waves, where the motion of particles of the earth is in the direction of propagation of the wave; and S (shear) waves, where the particle motion is at right angles to this direction. Surface waves travel from the epicenter, and are largely confined to the earth's surface; Love waves are at right angles to the direction of propagation; Rayleigh waves having a more complicated, backward elliptical movement in the direction of propagation.

The experienced intensity of an earthquake depends mainly on the distance from the source. Local intensities are gauged in terms of the Mercalli Intensity Scale, which runs from I (detectable only by SEISMOGRAPH) through to XII ("Catastrophic"). Comparison of intensities in different areas enables the source of an earthquake to be located. The actual magnitude of the event is gauged according to the RICHTER SCALE.

The study of seismic phenomena is known as **seismology**. (See also FAULT; TSUNAMI.)

EARTHWORMS, members of the phylum ANNELIDA, the best-known being *Lumbricus terrestris*. Earthworms come to the surface to copulate at night and the eggs develop in cocoons. Earthworms feed on vegetable matter from the soil surface and are beneficial in that, by burrowing, they enhance the mixing of the soil, and masticate plant material to a fine state.

EARWIGS, over 500 species of insects included in the order Dermaptera. They are omnivorous and show parental care of both eggs and young. The eggs are laid in the early spring and adults emerge in the summer. The adults are characterized by pincer-like organs situated at the hind end of the body.

Damage to freeway, San Francisco. California has been subjected to several earthquakes and this picture of San Francisco shows the considerable damage caused by one to a freeway in 1971.

EASEMENT, in law, a limited right over another's land. A positive easement, for example, may allow access across it to one's own land; a negative easement may prevent building or other activity on it that will damage one's own land. Easements may be granted or be held by a court to arise out of long usage or necessity.

EASLEY, city in NW S.C. It lies in a cotton and general agricultural area. Pop 11175.

EAST BERLIN. See BERLIN.

EAST CAPE, name of three locations: the easternmost point of North Island, New Zealand; the easternmost point of New Guinea; the easternmost point of Asia and the USSR, on the Chukotski Peninsula (also called Cape Dezhneva).

EAST CHICAGO, industrial city and port in NW Ind. E of Chicago. It lies on Lake Michigan and is part of the Calumet steel-producing area. Pop 46982.

EAST CLEVELAND, city in NE Ohio, ENE of Cleveland. It is a residential suburb with some light industry. Pop 34600.

EAST DETROIT, residential city in SE Mich., N of Detroit. It manufactures steel and tools. Pop 45920.

EASTER, chief festival of the Christian CHURCH YEAR, celebrating the RESURRECTION of Jesus Christ, and subsuming the Jewish PASSOVER. Despite early variation, Easter has been observed, since the Council of NICAEA, on the Sunday next after the first full moon following the vernal EQUINOX. It traditionally included a night vigil and the BAPTISM of catechumens.

EASTER ISLAND, easternmost island of Polynesia. This small, grassy, volcanic island features hundreds of colossal stone statues up to 40ft high, carved and raised on burial platforms by a pre-Columbian culture, which have been the subject of much speculation. Easter Island was discovered on Easter Sunday, 1722, by the Dutch admiral Jakob Roggeveen and annexed by Chile in 1888. Pop 1400.

EASTER LILY, *Lilium longiflorum*, a tall LILY with fragrant white trumpet-shaped flowers. Hothouse plants bloom before Easter. Family: Liliaceae.

EASTERN CHURCH, one of the two great branches of the Christian Church. From the apostolic age itself a natural distinction arose between the Greek-speaking church of the eastern Roman empire and the Latin-speaking church of the west (see WESTERN CHURCH). The Eastern Church developed its own liturgical traditions, patriarchal government, outlook and ethos, and resisted the increasing claims of the papacy. It became a family of ORTHODOX CHURCHES, finally breaking with Rome in the GREAT SCHISM of 1054. The non-orthodox MONOPHYSITE CHURCHES separated in the 5th and 6th centuries but share the common eastern tradition. (See also CHRISTIANITY.)

EASTERN QUESTION, the international political problems raised in the 19th century by the decline of the OTTOMAN EMPIRE. The rival ambitions of Russia, Austria-Hungary, Britain and France in the E Mediterranean led to the CRIMEAN WAR (1854–56) and BALKAN WARS (1912–13) and were partly responsible for the outbreak of WWI.

EASTER RISING, Irish rebellion against British rule, begun on Easter Monday, 1916. Although itself abortive, it proved a turning point in the Irish struggle for Home Rule. Sir Roger CASEMENT tried in vain to obtain arms from Germany, but the rising went ahead at the insistence of CONNOLLY and PEARSE and some 1500 volunteers seized public buildings, notably the Post Office, in Dublin. The British suppressed the rebellion after fierce street fighting and executed its leaders, an act which further fueled the nationalist cause.

The traditions of the Eastern Church have culminated in the splendid ritual of modern Orthodoxy. Here a Greek Orthodox priest dons his bejewelled miter in preparation for the Sunday service—always an occasion of great splendor and ritual in the Orthodox churches.

Earthquakes

Prediction and control

As many as 60000 people died in Lisbon on All Saints' Day, 1755, in what was probably the most violent earthquake on record. At least two major tremors struck the city, causing enormous structural damage and sending the waters of the River Tagus rushing through the streets. The death toll was especially high because the churches were packed, and because of the fire that ravaged the city after the tremors had passed.

Earthquakes are probably the most dramatic of man's natural enemies; and for that very reason they are worth our study. By developing an understanding of both the causes and effects of earthquakes we can hope to reduce the horrifying toll of lives in the future, not only by selecting suitable building materials and sites but also by playing an active part in modifying the earthquake itself. Before taking any steps in this direction, we have to be able to predict where earthquakes are likely to occur.

If the locations of major quakes are plotted on a map of the world, differentiating between shallow, intermediate and deep events, two things become immediately apparent. The first is that the distribution is strictly limited to a number of belts; the second that the deep earthquakes are virtually all associated with ocean trenches and island arc structures bordering the Pacific Ocean. Why should this be so?

The answer lies in the theory of plate tectonics. This theory had its genesis in the theory of continental drift and in studies of earthquake and volcanic activity, and the effects of its general acceptance have in recent years radically altered our ideas about the planet we live on. Briefly, the theory implies that the earth's crust consists of a number of semi-rigid plates that are in motion relative to each other. At margins where plates are meeting, one edge is forced under the other; and this is compensated for by the emergence of new material in mid-ocean in the process known as sea-floor spreading.

The belts of deep earthquakes are an indication of where oceanic plates and the lighter continental blocks are meeting. As the oceanic plate is forced under, arcs of volcanic islands, mountains and deep ocean trenches are formed. Coupled with this, there is as one might expect deep seismic activity. In a similar way, the belts of shallow earthquakes indicate areas of active seafloor spreading. The rather more scattered earthquakes throughout Europe, the Middle East and the Himalayas are a result of the collision of two continental blocks.

There is a similar correlation between plate movements and earthquake magnitude. In general, the larger events—those with Richter magnitudes greater than 5 or 6—do not occur in regions of plate creation but are associated only with the more violent process of plate underthrusting. A clear example of this is the zone of activity along the west coast of North America, which defines a region of lateral slip between the Pacific plate and the American plate. The San Andreas fault system of California is a clear expression of this; and the San Francisco earthquake of 1906, in which 500 died and half a billion dollars' worth of damage was done, was a direct result.

Detailed information about the present distribution of earthquakes has been a major factor in the study of plate tectonic processes. In addition, a technique known as the determination of fault-plane solutions has played a large part in confirming the theory.

When a volume of rock fractures along a fault plane, the amount of seismic energy recorded by an observer will depend on the direction, relative to the fault plane, of his observation. Moreover, the sense of the first motion (that is, whether it is a push or a pull, a compression or a dilation) will be compressional in the directions of motion and consequently dilational in the opposite directions.

So here we have a way of inferring the orientation of the faulting surface. Observations from stations in different parts of the world can be correlated, and from these it is fairly simple to work backwards to find the direction of the fault plane. There is only one problem: exactly the same results would be obtained for a fault at right angles to this where the sense of the faulting was reversed. This is less of a problem than it might seem, since what we are in general really interested in is the direction of maximum compression, and, at right angles to this, the direction of maximum tension.

The fault-plane technique was applied very early to the phenomenon, then only beginning to be accepted, of sea-floor spreading. Spreading occurs along the mid-ocean ridges. At intervals along these there are discontinuities, where sections appear to have been displaced "sideways." It had been suggested that a feature called a transform fault lay between the end of one portion of ridge and the beginning of the next.

If these offsets were due to simple displacement along a fault the sense of motion would be parallel to the fault in both directions; but if new oceanic crust were being formed at the crests of the ridges and then spreading away, the sense of motion in the region of the fault would be outward in both directions from each of the sections of ridge. Fault-plane solutions were determined for earthquakes located along certain of these faults, and the results conformed perfectly with the hypothesis that new material was being created. Sea-floor spreading is one of the foundations of plate tectonic theory, and so these studies were a substantial contribution towards our understanding of the nature of the earth.

Knowledge of where earthquakes are likely to occur is only part of the battle; we also want to know when; and, if possible, whether or not there is anything that can be done to modify the effects of the fracture.

In 1966 an increase in the number of small local earthquakes was observed in the vicinity of Denver, Colorado, and it appeared that this increase was related to the disposal of fluid waste down a deep borehole. At roughly the same time it was shown that underground nuclear explosions at the Nevada test site were responsible for a similar increase there: the explosions were thought to act as a trigger, disturbing an existing distribution of stress that was already close to some critical value.

It wasn't long before somebody suggested that it would be a good idea to bore holes along the San Andreas Fault and pump water down them, on the principle that a number of small earthquakes now is preferable to the catastrophically large one that is bound to happen at some point in the future. The firing of a number of small explosions along the fault seemed an equally good idea, for exactly the same reasons. However, the uncertainties were—and still are—much too great, and the consequences of error too serious, for an exercise of this type to be carried out.

For earthquake prediction to be possible, we need some measurable and unambiguous phenomenon that precedes the fracture. Fortunately there is one. Large earthquakes are often heralded by smaller events, known as foreshocks. These seem to be the first signs of a major stress redistribution, which they in fact trigger. (It is equally logical to expect the period before a major quake to be seismically quiet while energy is steadily accumulated, and this "ominous silence" has also been observed in some cases. In particular instances this may be just as useful for prediction purposes.)

Foreshocks seem to be due to a phenomenon known as dilatancy hardening. Anyone who has walked across wet sand at the seaside will recall how a dry patch appears round each footprint. The sand grains, which had been closely packed together by the sea, have been disturbed by the pressure of the foot. Space between the grains has increased, and for this reason the intergranular water pressure has dropped, resulting in the apparent dryness.

The same sort of process occurs in rocks, and it is called dilatancy. Other studies have shown that decreasing the pore pressure increases the resistance of rock to fracturing, and this increase in strength is, logically enough, termed dilatancy hardening.

It is believed that as stress buildup approaches a critical value cracks begin to open and so the pore pressure drops. This results in dilatancy hardening and so the earthquake proper is delayed until water has had time to percolate into the region of low pressure from the surrounding rock. This theory has been tested both by observation of changes in the seismic waves received and by electrical testing of the wetness of local rocks, and the results of these experiments bear out the theory admirably.

Despite successes of this kind, earthquake prediction is still a long way from becoming a practical reality. Recent researches have shown that precursory phenomena are often very dependent on the orientation of the cracks and the shape of the dilatant region, and for these and other reasons they might go unnoticed. The converse is also true: a region can show all the symptoms of preparation for a quake—and then no quake occurs! As if to add to the present infeasibility of accurate prediction, some workers suggest, and for very good reasons, that the dilatancy-hardening model may be invalid. Nevertheless, we can say with confidence that comparatively soon geologists will be able to accurately predict and ameliorate the effects of earthquakes.

Earth is not alone in experiencing quakes. Seismometers placed on the surface of the moon during the Apollo missions have detected hundreds of seismic signals believed to be due to "moonquakes." They are all of fairly low magnitude—indeed, quakes of the same size would probably go unnoticed on earth, even by people close to the focus.

There is no evidence of any currently active tectonic processes on the moon similar to those operating on earth. However, a strong correlation exists between the times of closest earth/moon approach and moonquake activity, and it would therefore seem likely that tidal forces act as a trigger to the release of strain within the moon. The origin of this strain itself is not known.

This correlation suggests an interesting question: does the presence of the moon influence the pattern of quakes on the earth? So far there is no evidence of such an effect, but it will probably be some time before a definitive answer can be given.

EAST GRAND RAPIDS, city in W Mich. It is a residential suburb of Grand Rapids. Pop 12 565.

EASTHAMPTON, town in W Mass., 12mi NNW of Springfield, close to the Mt Tom State Reservation. Pop 13 012.

EAST HARTFORD, town in N Conn. on the E bank of the Connecticut R. It is a suburb of Hartford and makes aircraft engines and furniture. Pop 57 583.

EAST HAVEN, suburban residential town in Conn. It lies on Long Island Sound, just E of New Haven. Pop 25 120.

EAST INDIA COMPANY, name of several private trading companies chartered by 17th-century European governments to develop trade in the E Hemisphere, after the discovery of a sea route to India. They competed for commercial supremacy and eventually aided European colonial expansion. **The Dutch East India Company** (1602–1798) dominated trade with the East Indies but failed to survive the French invasion of Holland in 1795. **The British East India Company** (1600–1858) monopolized trade with India and, in the 18th century, gained administrative control of most of India. Its power was curbed by William PITT in 1784 and successive British governments took complete control of the Company and made India an imperial possession.

EAST INDIES, the former Dutch East Indies, now Indonesia. The name can also be used to describe India and Indochina, but modern usage confines the term to the Malay Archipelago. It is the largest island group in the world.

EAST KILDONAN, city in Manitoba, Canada; a residential suburb of Winnipeg. Pop 29 722.

EASTLAKE, city in NE Ohio. It lies on Lake Erie and is a residential suburb of Cleveland. Pop 19 690.

EASTLAND, James Oliver (1904–), US senator from Miss. and lawyer. In 1948, he and Miss. governor F. L. Wright led the DIXIECRAT revolt when the state voted for the States Rights Party. Though a Democrat, he consistently opposed civil rights legislation.

EAST LANSING, residential suburb and city in S Mich. It lies on the Red Cedar R and is the seat of Michigan State U. Pop 47 540.

EAST LIVERPOOL, city in E Ohio, on the Ohio R. Formerly called Fawcettstown, it produces pottery and porcelain. Pop 20 020.

EAST LONGMEADOW, residential town in SW Mass., 5mi SE of Springfield. Pop 13 029.

EAST LOS ANGELES, unincorporated urban community in Los Angeles Co., SW Cal. Pop 105 033.

EAST LYME, residential town in SE Conn. It lies on Long Island Sound. Pop 11 399.

EASTMAN, George (1854–1932), US inventor and manufacturer who invented the Kodak CAMERA, first marketed 1888. Earlier he perfected processes for manufacturing dry photographic plates (1880) and flexible, transparent film (1884). He took his own life in 1932. (See also PHOTOGRAPHY.)

EASTMAN, Max (1883–1969), US author and editor. He edited two influential socialist magazines and was a Communist Party member until 1923. He became a critic of Stalinism in the 1930s and 1940s.

EAST MASSAPEQUA, unincorporated urban community in N.Y., part of the Oyster Bay township on Long Island. Pop 15 926.

EAST MEADOW, unincorporated urban community in N.Y., part of the Hempstead township on W Long Island. Pop 46 352.

EAST MOLINE, city in NW Ill. It lies on the Mississippi R in an agricultural and coal mining area. Pop 20 832.

EAST NORTHPORT, unincorporated urban community in N.Y. It lies on Long Island, and is the site of a US veterans' hospital. Pop 12 392.

EASTON, manufacturing town in SE Mass. Nearby is Stonehill College. Pop 12 157.

EASTON, industrial city and seat of Northampton Co., E Pa. It lies at the junction of the Lehigh and Delaware rivers. Pop 30 256.

EAST ORANGE, residential city in NE N.J., a suburb of Newark and New York City. It is a leading insurance center, and also has light industries. Pop 75 471.

EAST PAKISTAN. See BANGLADESH.

EAST PATERSON, industrial borough in NW N.J., a suburb of Paterson. It manufactures communications equipment. Pop 20 511.

EAST PEORIA, industrial city in N central Ill., on the Illinois R. Nearby is Fort Creve Coeur State Park. Pop 18 455.

EAST POINT, industrial city in NW Ga. It played a major part in the defense of Atlanta by the Confederates (1864). Pop 39 315.

EAST PROVIDENCE, industrial city in N R.I., on the Providence and Seekonk rivers. Pop 48 207.

EAST PRUSSIA, historic region of Europe, bounded, (between WWI and WWII,) by the Baltic Sea, Poland, Lithuania and Danzig. It was a stronghold of the Teutonic Knights in the Middle Ages, and later belonged variously to Poland, Prussia and Germany. East Prussia was separated from the rest of Germany from 1918 to 1939 by the "Polish Corridor," and after WWII it was partitioned between the USSR and Poland.

EAST RIDGE, town in SE Tenn., a residential suburb of Chattanooga. It lies near the Ga. border. Pop 21 799.

EAST RIVER, 16mi-long navigable strait connecting Long Island Sound with New York Bay, and joined to the Hudson R by the Harlem R. It separates the New York City boroughs of Manhattan and the Bronx from Brooklyn and Queens. The river is also an important arm of New York harbor.

EAST ROCKAWAY, residential village and resort in SE N.Y. It lies on the Rockaway Peninsula of Long Island, fronting Hewlett Bay. Pop 10 323.

EAST SAINT LOUIS, manufacturing city and railroad center in SW Ill. It lies on the Mississippi R, facing St. Louis, Mo. Pop 69 996.

EATON, Cyrus Stephen (1883–), Canadian industrialist. After amassing a fortune as founder and head of many corporations, he became a philanthropist and advocate of nuclear disarmament.

EATON, Dorman Bridgman (1823–1899), US lawyer, civil servant, and civic reformer. As chairman of the first US Civil Service Commission (1873–75), he tried to end the corruption then prevalent in public service, and helped to establish the civil service merit system by the PENDELETON ACT (1883).

EATON, John Henry (1790–1856), US politician and diplomat. Secretary of war in Andrew Jackson's first cabinet (1829), he was forced to resign in 1831 when his wife, Margaret O'NEILL, was found socially unacceptable by cabinet colleagues, including Vice-President Calhoun. Eaton was governor of Fla. 1834–36 and minister to Spain 1836–40.

EATON, Theophilus (c1590–1658), North American colonial governor. With John DAVENPORT, he founded NEW HAVEN (1638) and was its governor 1639–58. He drew up the colony's strictly Puritan legal code—the Connecticut BLUE LAWS (1655).

EATONTOWN, residential borough in E central N.J. It lies in a fruit and vegetable area. Pop 14 619.

EAU CLAIRE, commercial and industrial city, seat of Eau Claire Co., W central Wis. It lies on the Eau Claire and Chippewa rivers. Pop 44 619.

EBAN, Abba Solomon (1915–), Israeli politician. Born in South Africa and educated in England, he became Israel's first UN delegate (1949–59) and ambassador to the US (1950–59). He was then minister of education 1960, deputy prime minister 1963–65 and foreign minister 1966–74.

EBBINGHAUS, Hermann (1850–1909), German psychologist who developed experimental techniques for the study of rote LEARNING and memory. In later life he devised means of intelligence testing and researched into color VISION.

EBERT, Friedrich (1871–1925), first president (1919–25) of the German WEIMAR REPUBLIC. A lifelong Social Democrat and moderate Marxist, he initiated many social reforms and helped to reconstruct Germany after WWI.

EBONY, extremely hard, deep black heartwood from trees of the genus *Diospyros*, which are native to tropical parts of the world. Ebony is used mainly for cabinetmaking, carvings and inlays. Family: Ebenaceae.

EBRO RIVER, second-largest river of Spain, 565mi long. It rises in the Cantabrian Mts and flows ESE through Santander, Navarre, Saragossa and Tarragona provinces to the Mediterranean Sea. It is partly navigable, but is mainly important as a source of irrigation.

George Eastman's house in Rochester, New York, now a museum of photography. Eastman invented the dry-plate photographic process, manufacturing the world famous Kodak camera in 1888.

EÇA DE QUEIROZ, José Maria (1845–1900), Portuguese author. His novels pioneered a new realist literature in Portugal, in reaction against the established conventions.

ECBATANA, capital of ancient Media, now called Hamadan (Iran). From the 6th century BC it was the summer residence of Persian and Parthian kings, notably CYRUS THE GREAT and CAMBYSES.

ECCENTRICITY, in Geometry. See CONIC SECTIONS.

ECCLES, Sir John Carew (1903–), Australian physiologist who shared the 1963 Nobel Prize for Physiology or Medicine with Alan HODGKIN and Andrew HUXLEY. Using their findings, he had been able to establish the chemical bases of the electrical changes during transmission of nervous impulses across the SYNAPSES (see also NERVOUS SYSTEM).

ECCLESIASTES, Old Testament "wisdom" book, pessimistic and skeptical in tone. It was traditionally attributed to King Solomon, but modern experts favor a much later author, possibly of the 3rd century BC.

ECCLESIASTICUS, Old Testament book included in the APOCRYPHA by Jews and Protestants. It was written c180 BC by Jesus son of Sirach, and is a collection of instructive observations, influenced by the Book of PROVERBS.

ECDYSIS. See MOLTING.

ECHEGARAY Y EIZAGUIRRE, José (1832–1916), Spanish dramatist and politician. Having served in government, he began writing plays in 1874. He shared the 1904 Nobel Prize for Literature.

ECHEVERRÍA, Luís (1922–), Mexican lawyer and politician. After holding several political and academic posts, he became president of Mexico in 1970 for a 6-year term.

ECHIDNA or Spiny anteater, one of two members of the order Monotremata. Echidnas are almost unique among MAMMALS because they lay eggs. They are hedgehog-like in appearance, up to 450mm (17.7in) long, with spines, a long snout and tongue evolved for feeding on ants, and clawed feet with which they break up ant nests. Like other monotremes, the echidna retains a number of features typical of REPTILES, and is found only in Australasia.

ECHINODERMS, members of a phylum of marine invertebrates, Echinodermata. They include STARFISH, CRINOIDS, SEA CUCUMBERS and SEA URCHINS. Their body form is generally radially

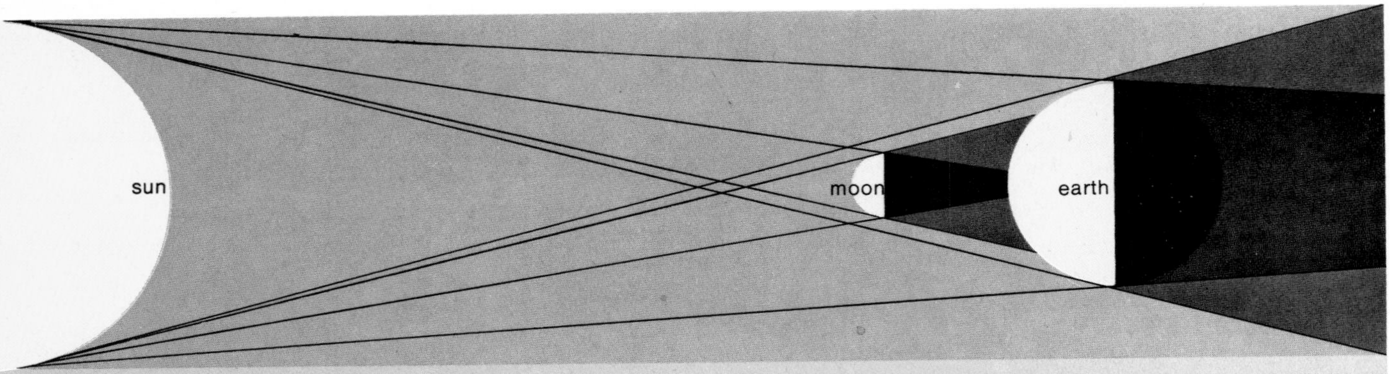

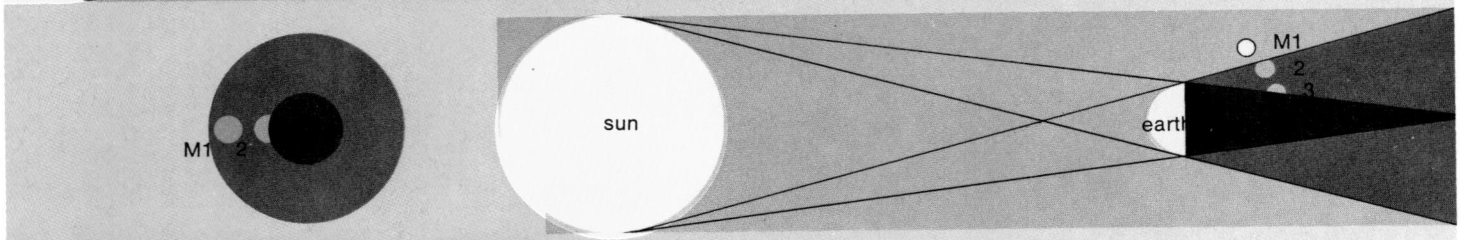

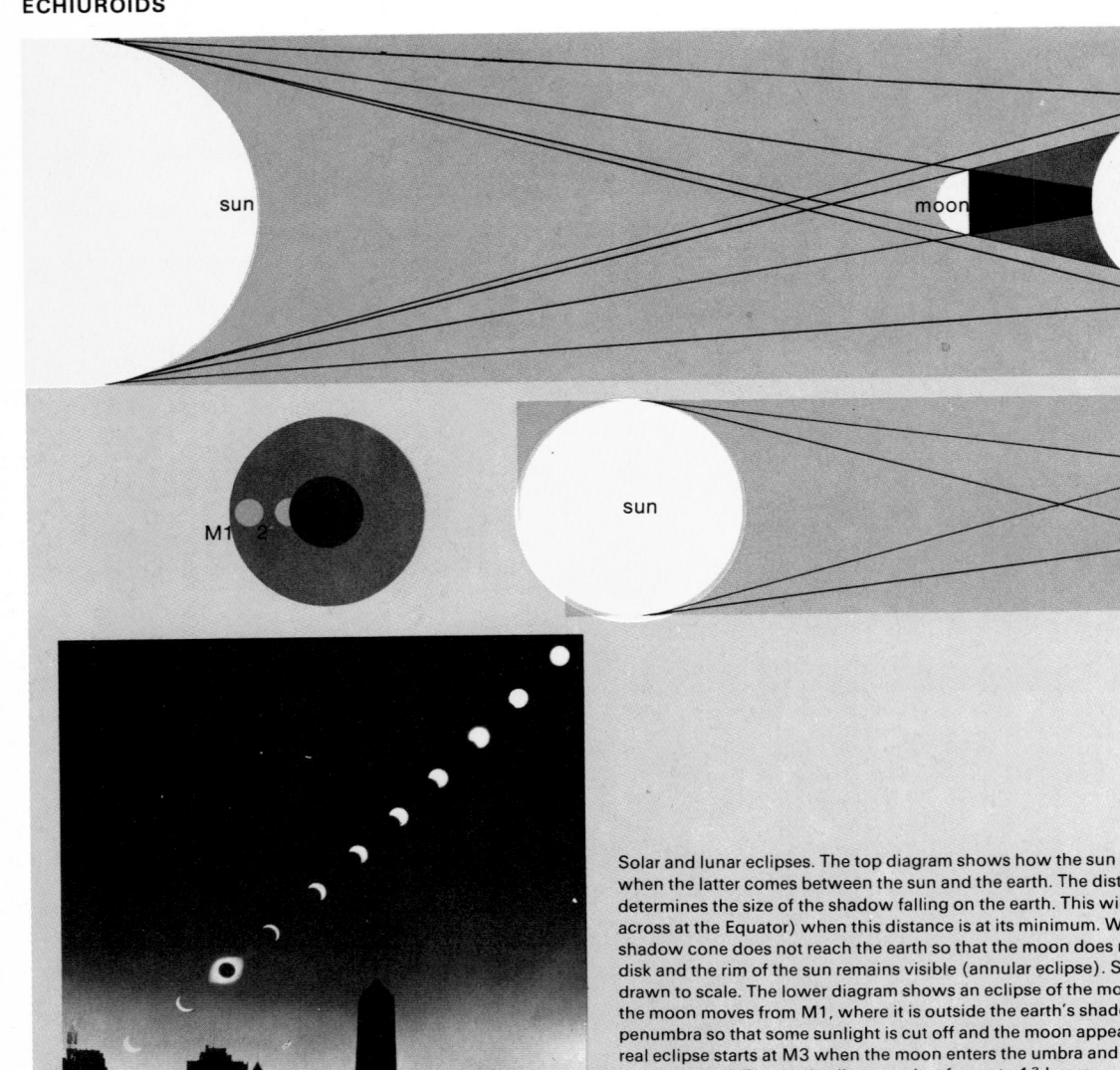

Solar and lunar eclipses. The top diagram shows how the sun can be eclipsed by the moon when the latter comes between the sun and the earth. The distance of the moon from us determines the size of the shadow falling on the earth. This will be largest (about 167 miles across at the Equator) when this distance is at its minimum. When it is at its maximum the shadow cone does not reach the earth so that the moon does not cover the whole of the sun's disk and the rim of the sun remains visible (annular eclipse). Sizes and distances are not drawn to scale. The lower diagram shows an eclipse of the moon by the earth. During its orbit the moon moves from M1, where it is outside the earth's shadow, to M2, entering the earth's penumbra so that some sunlight is cut off and the moon appears less bright than usual. The real eclipse starts at M3 when the moon enters the umbra and is partially eclipsed. At M4 the eclipse is total. The total eclipse can last for up to 1¾ hours.
Left: a series of short exposures at intervals of 15 minutes recording a total eclipse of the sun at Chicago on June 30, 1954. At the third exposure the sun is completely masked and only the corona is visible.

symmetrical; they move slowly by means of tube feet and the majority possess a calcite skeleton. The sexes are generally separate; most are suspension feeders, but some prey on mollusks.

ECHIUROIDS, unsegmented marine worms sometimes included in the phylum ANNELIDA, but generally thought to have uncertain affinities. A well-known genus, *Borellia,* exhibits sexual dimorphism, the female having an ovoid body with a long proboscis leading to the mouth through which it feeds. The male is minute and enters the female's body to effect fertilization.

ECHO, in Greek mythology, a mountain nymph who fell in love with NARCISSUS. When her love was not returned, she faded away to a mere voice.

ECHO, a wave signal reflected back to its point of origin from a distant object, or, in the case of RADIO signals, a signal coming to a receiver from the transmitter by an indirect route. Echoes of the first type can be used to detect and find the position of reflecting objects (echolocation). High-frequency SOUND echolocation is used both by bats for navigation and to detect prey and by man in marine SONAR. RADAR, too, is similar in principle, though this uses UHF radio and MICROWAVE radiation rather than sound energy. The range of a reflecting object can easily be estimated for ordinary sound echoes: since sound travels about 340m/s through the air at sea level, an object will be distant about 170m for each second that passes before an echo returns from it.

ECHO SOUNDER, device for determining the depth of water under a ship's keel from the time taken for SOUND pulses beamed vertically downward from the ship to be reflected from the sea-bed; an application of SONAR.

ECK, Johann (1486–1543), German scholar and theologian. Though advocating church reform, he was a bitter opponent of LUTHER and the REFORMATION. He influenced the 1520 papal bull against Luther, and presented the Roman Catholic case at the Diet of Augsburg (1530).

ECKERMANN, Johann Peter (1792–1854), German writer and literary assistant of GOETHE. Notable for his *Conversations With Goethe* (3 volumes, 1836–48.)

ECKHART, Johann (c1260–1327), also called Meister Eckhart, German Dominican theologian, regarded as the founder of German mysticism. He was influenced by neoplatonism and by the works of Saint AUGUSTINE and Thomas AQUINAS.

ECLECTICISM, principle of combining different ideas from diverse sources. The term has been particularly applied in art and philosophy: e.g., the 18th and 19th-century Classical and oriental revivals in art; and the thought of some Greek and Roman philosophers, especially Cicero and the neoplatonists.

ECLIPSE, the partial or total obscurement of one celestial body by another; also the passage of the moon through the earth's shadow. The components of a binary star (see DOUBLE STAR) may eclipse each other as seen from the earth, in which case the star is termed an eclipsing binary. The moon frequently eclipses stars or planets, and this is known as OCCULTATION.

A **lunar eclipse** occurs when the moon passes through the umbra of the earth's SHADOW. This happens usually not more than twice a year, since the moon's orbit around the earth is tilted with respect to the ECLIPTIC. The eclipsed moon is blood-red in color due to some of the sun's light being refracted by the earth's atmosphere into the umbra. A partial lunar eclipse occurs when only part of the umbra falls on the moon.

In a **solar eclipse**, the moon passes between the sun and the earth. A total eclipse occurs when the observer is within the umbra of the moon's shadow: the disk of the sun is covered by that of the moon, and the solar corona (see SUN) becomes clearly visible. Total eclipses are particularly important since only during them can astronomers study the solar corona and prominences. The maximum possible duration of a total eclipse is about 7½min. Should the observer be outside the umbra but within the penumbra, or should the earth pass through only the penumbra, a partial eclipse will occur.

An **annular eclipse** is seen when the moon is at its farthest from the earth, its disk being not large enough to totally obscure that of the sun. The moon's disk is seen surrounded by a brilliant ring of light.

ECLIPTIC, the great circle traced out on the CELESTIAL SPHERE by the apparent motion of the sun during the year, corresponding to the motion of the earth around the sun. The ecliptic passes through 12 constellations, known as the constellations of the ZODIAC.

ÉCOLE DES BEAUX ARTS, world-famous school of fine arts in Paris, France. It was formed in 1795 by combining the École Académique (founded 1648) and the École de l'Académie d'Architecture (founded 1671). It greatly influenced American art.

ECOLOGY, the study of plants and animals in relation to their ENVIRONMENT. The whole earth can be considered as a large ecological unit: the term BIOSPHERE is used to describe the atmosphere, earth, surface, oceans and ocean floors within which living organisms exist. However, it is usual to divide the biosphere into a large number of ecological sub-units or **ecosystems**, within each of which the organisms making up the living community are in balance with the environment. Typical examples of ecosystems are a pond, a deciduous forest or a desert. The overall climate and topography within an area are major factors determining the type of ecosystem that develops, but within any ecosystem minor variations give rise to smaller communities within which animals and plants occupy their own particular niches. Within any ecosystem each organism, however large or small, plays a vital role in maintaining the stability of the community.

The most important factor for any organism is its source of energy or food. Thus, within any ecosystem, complex patterns of feeding relationships or **food chains** are built up. Plants are the primary source of food and energy; they derive it through PHOTOSYNTHESIS, utilizing environmental factors such as light, water, carbon dioxide and minerals. Herbivores then obtain their food by eating plants. In their turn, herbivores are preyed upon by carnivores, who may also be the source of food for other carnivores. Animal and plant waste is decomposed by microorganisms (BACTERIA, FUNGI) within the habitat and this returns the raw materials to the environment. The number of links within a food chain are normally three or four, with five, six and seven less frequently. The main reason for the limited length of food chains is that the major part of the energy stored within a plant or animal is wasted at each stage in the chain. Thus if it were possible for a carnivore to occupy, say, position 20 within a food chain, the area of vegetation required to supply the energy needed for the complete chain would be the size of a continent.

The plants within an ecosystem, as well as the major environmental features, help create habitats suitable for other organisms. Thus, in a forest ecosystem, the humid, dimly illuminated environment covered by a thick canopy is suitable for mosses, lichens and ferns and their associated fauna. Within any ecosystem the raw materials nitrogen, carbon, oxygen and hydrogen (in water) are continually being recycled via a number of processes including the NITROGEN CYCLE, CARBON CYCLE and photosynthesis.

Most natural ecosystems are in a state of equilibrium or balance so that few changes occur in the natural flora and fauna. However, when changes occur in the environment, either major climatic changes or minor alterations in the inhabitants, an imbalance results and the ecosystem changes to adapt to the new situation. The sequence of change that leads to a new period of equilibrium is called a succession and may take any length of time from a few years, for the establishment of a new species, to several centuries, for the change from grassland to forest.

Over millions of years, nature has moved toward the overall creation of stable ecosystems. Natural changes, such as adaptations to the slow change of climate, tend to be gradual. However, man often causes much more sudden changes—the introduction of a disease to a hitherto uninfected area, the cutting down of a forest or the polluting of a river. The effects of this type of change upon an ecosystem can be rapid and irreversible. Up to now these changes have not been too serious on a worldwide scale but there is an increasing awareness of what could happen if a worldwide disturbance in the biosphere occurred.

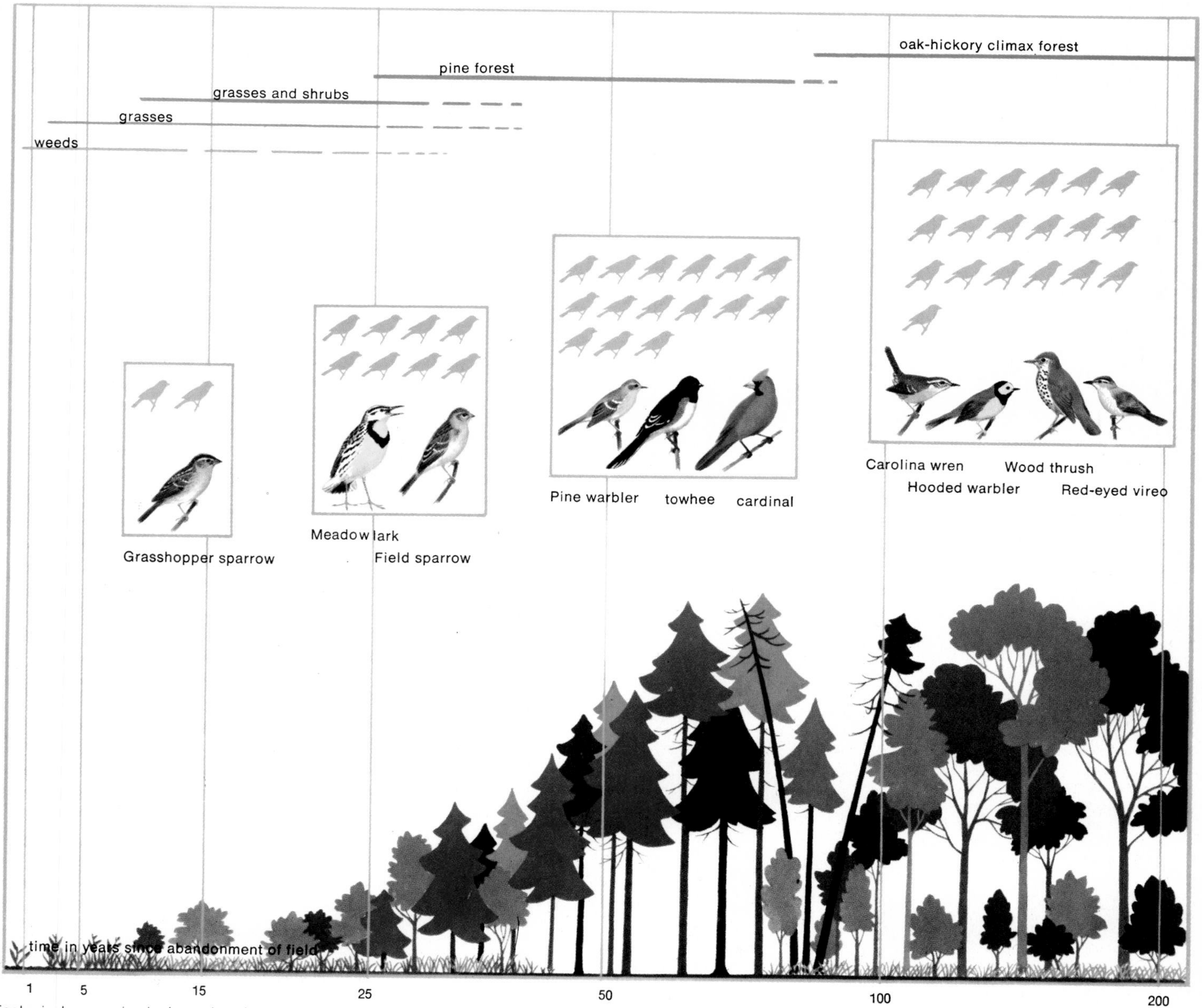

Ecological succession is shown here by a schematic representation of the change from a meadow to woodland over a period of 200 years. Changes in the kinds of birds inhabiting the area are indicated, as are the numbers of individuals. The combined changes in total amount of vegetation and animals represent changes in the biomass.

The forms of life as they are known today depend entirely upon the sensitive balance within the environment and any change with worldwide effects could have devastating consequences for man and life in general.

ECONOMETRICS, branch of economics specializing in the use of mathematics and statistics to describe economic phenomena and test economic theories. The international Econometric Society was founded in 1930 to provide governments with reliable information on which to base attempts to alleviate the economic Depression.

ECONOMIC ADVISERS, Council of. See COUNCIL OF ECONOMIC ADVISERS.

ECONOMICS, is basically concerned with the most efficient use of scarce resources (factors of production such as land, labor, capital) in producing various types of goods and services to satisfy numerous different and competing demands. The American economist Paul SAMUELSON has called economics the study of how, what and for whom to produce. The difficulty of defining economics precisely stems from the various concerns that have characterized the evolution of economic thought. Analytical economics began with XENOPHON who coined the word *oikonomikos*, a combination of two Greek words meaning home or household, and the verb to manage or rule. While theologians in the Middle Ages have written about economic matters, serious and organized economic studies date only from the 17th century. Since then there have been seven principal schools of economic thought: Mercantilists (17th and 18th centuries); PHYSIOCRATS (mid-18th century); Classicists (18th and 19th centuries); Marxists (19th and 20th centuries); Neoclassicists (19th and 20th centuries); Keynesians, and Post-Keynesians (both of them 20th century).

Mercantilists were concerned with trade, especially foreign trade and argued for a surplus of exports over imports. They also advocated development of local industries protected by tariffs from foreign competition as a means of reducing unemployment and minimizing the reliance on imports in times of national emergency. In contrast, the Physiocratic school is best known for the *Tableau économique*, a work by its founder François QUESNAY. In this school the economy is visualized in terms of circular flows of outputs and income among its members, thus displaying the general interdependence of industries in the economy. The Physiocrats were eventually eclipsed by the work of the three most eminent Classicists: Adam SMITH who favored free trade and competition (LAISSEZ-FAIRE); Thomas MALTHUS and David RICARDO, whose treatises on rent and the labor theory of value have influenced all subsequent discussions on problems of distribution and value.

A separate school of thought, MARXISM, developed during this period. However, the work of its two founders, Karl MARX and Friedrich ENGELS, was preoccupied with describing and analyzing how the capitalist economy behaves. They used philosophical and sociological principles to postulate "inexorable laws of development," and concluded that capitalism was doomed and that socialism was inevitable.

The Neoclassicists, of which the most famous were William Stanley JEVONS in England, Karl Menger in Austria and Léon Walras in Switzerland, were concerned with diverse theoretical aspects of the problems of value and distribution, and for the first time applied mathematics to the study of economics in systematic fashion. In the 20th century, two new schools of thought came into being. The Keynesians applied basic principles of supply and demand to analyze problems of national income, unemployment and inflation. The Post-Keynesians concern themselves with issues of post-WWII economic development. Among these are growth economics (at what rate should the economy grow and what is the rate of investment needed); economic planning (guidance and control of the economy to achieve certain objectives); monetary and fiscal economics (role of money supply and government spending to influence economic performance); and development economics (how can developing countries industrialize).

ECONOMIC SANCTIONS, the partial or complete cessation of international trade and/or aid to a country, either by international agreement or by BLOCKADE. Notable were the UN's partial sanctions against South Africa (from 1963) and Rhodesia (from 1966).

ECORSE, city in SE Mich., on the Detroit R. Its main products are steel, chemicals and automobile parts. Pop 17515.

ECOSYSTEM. See ECOLOGY.

ECTOPLASM, the outer layer of cellular CYTOPLASM (see also CELL). In PARAPSYCHOLOGY, a substance thought to be emitted by mediums when in trance.

ECUADOR, republic in NW South America, lying S of Colombia and N and W of Peru, on the Pacific coast. Its territory includes the GALAPAGOS ISLANDS in the Pacific. Ecuador is divided by two Andes ranges running N to S, between which lie about 10 plateaus around 8000ft high. This is the most densely populated region of the country, and the capital, Quito, is situated in its N part. Between the Andes and the Pacific lie the coastal lowlands, also well populated, while to the E of the Andes there are thinly populated equatorial forests. The central Andean area has a mild climate all the year around, but the lowlands are hotter and wetter.

People. Of the population, roughly 10% are white, 10% Negro, 40% Indian and 40% mestizo—people of mixed Indian and white ancestry. The official language is Spanish but Quechua is more widely spoken. Most people are Roman Catholics. Personal incomes average about $200 a year, and most Ecuadorians live near subsistence level either by working their own small landholdings or more commonly as laborers on large estates and plantations. The educational system is poor—the illiteracy rate being about 30%.

Economy. Ecuador can be divided into two economic regions. In the tropical coastal lowlands, sugarcane, rice, cacao and bananas and other fruits are grown for export. The temperate highlands produce potatoes and grain for domestic consumption and fishing is also important. But only 5% of the land in Ecuador is currently productive. Enough petroleum is produced to satisfy the country's own needs, but in general mineral resources are underdeveloped. Industrialization has proceeded slowly in the face of political instability, insufficient capital and transportation difficulties. Most transportation equipment, iron and steel products, chemicals and consumer goods must be imported.

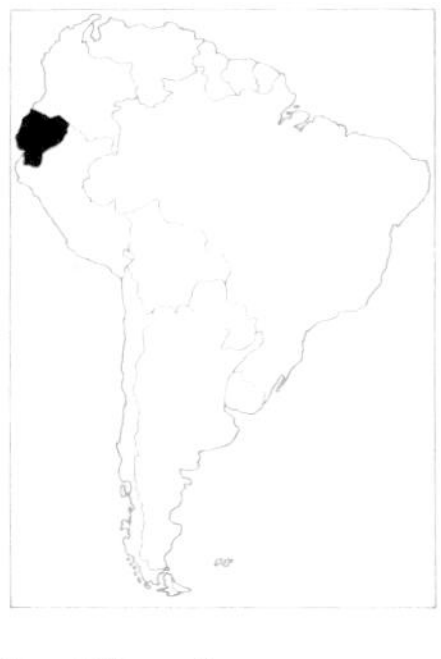

Official name: The Republic of Ecuador.
Capital: Quito
Area: c104505sq mi (excluding Galápagos Islands)
Population: 6508000
Languages: Spanish
Religions: Roman Catholic
Monetary unit(s): 1 Sucre = 100 centavos

History. Following the conquest of the Incas by PIZARRO in 1533, Ecuador became part of the Spanish Empire. It has been an independent republic since 1830, but has always suffered from political instability, marked by conflict between the landed bourgeoisie of the Andean region, the mercantile interests centered in the leading port of Guayaquil and, more recently, the urban working classes. Military coups have been common—the most recent successful one in January 1976. This instability is a major cause of Ecuador's underdevelopement.

ECUMENICAL COUNCIL, a general council of the leaders of the entire Christian Church. The first was at Nicaea (325) and there have been 20 since. The Orthodox Churches recognize only those that were truly ecumenical—the first seven, with the Trullan Synod (692), and give them supreme authority; the Roman Catholic Church recognizes also the 14 later Western councils, the last being the Second Vatican Council (1962–65), but denies their authority unless confirmed by the pope. Protestants generally honor the first four.

ECUMENICAL MOVEMENT, modern movement among the Christian churches to encourage greater cooperation and eventual unity. Various organizations such as the International Missionary Council, and the Life and Work and the Faith and Order conferences (after WWI) studied the churches' doctrinal differences. But substantial progress was not made until 1948, when representatives of 147 world churches agreed to form the WORLD COUNCIL OF CHURCHES. Most Protestant and Orthodox churches have since joined the council, and the Roman Catholic Church, though not a member, participates in some joint studies.

ECZEMA, form of DERMATITIS, usually with redness and scaling. It is often familial, being worst in childhood, and is associated with HAY FEVER and ASTHMA.

EDDA, name of two works of Old Icelandic literature known as the *Prose (Younger) Edda* and the *Poetic (Elder) Edda*. The *Prose Edda* was written c1200 by SNORRI STURLUSON for aspiring court poets as a guide to the subject matter and techniques of SKALDIC POETRY. The *Poetic Edda*, compiled later in the 13th century, contains 34 mainly alliterative poems written between c800 and 1200. It represents the finest extant body of ICELANDIC literature.

EDDINGTON, Sir Arthur Stanley (1882–1944), English astronomer and astrophysicist who pioneered the theoretical study of the interior of STARS and who, through his *Mathematical Theory of Relativity* (1923), did much to introduce the English-speaking world to the theories of EINSTEIN.

EDDY, Mary Baker (1821–1910), US founder of CHRISTIAN SCIENCE. After a period of study under Phineas QUIMBY she began to formulate her own ideas on spiritual healing and published these in *Science and Health* (1875). She founded the *Christian Science Monitor* newspaper in 1908.

EDDY CURRENTS, electric currents induced in solid conductors in rapidly varying MAGNETIC FIELDS or when moving through nonuniform magnetic fields. They cause heating and power loss in motors and transformers but are exploited in induction furnaces.

EDELMAN, Gerald Maurice (1929–), US biochemist who shared with Rodney PORTER the 1972 Nobel Prize for Physiology or Medicine for his researches into the chemical structures of antibodies (see ANTIBODIES AND ANTIGENS).

EDELWEISS, *Leontopodium alpinum*, a small perennial herb native to the European Alps, but cultivated in lowland areas. It has small white flowers surrounded by white woolly bracts and woolly stems and leaves. Family: COMPOSITAE.

EDEMA, the accumulation of excessive watery fluid outside the cells of the body, causing swelling of a part. Some edema is seen locally in INFLAMMATION. The commonest type is gravitational edema (**dropsy**), where fluid swelling is in the most dependent parts, typically the feet. HEART or LIVER failure, MALNUTRITION and nephrotic syndrome of the KIDNEY are common causes, while disease of VEINS or LYMPH vessels in the legs also leads to edema. Serious edema may form in the LUNGS in heart failure and in the BRAIN in some disorders of METABOLISM, trauma, TUMORS and infections. DIURETICS may be needed in treatment.

EDEN, agricultural town in N.C. It processes and ships corn, wheat and tobacco. Pop 15871.

EDEN, Garden of, in biblical tradition, the garden paradise created by God for ADAM and EVE. In the Old Testament book of Genesis it is described as being watered by four streams, including the Tigris and the

Ecumenical Councils

Date	Council
325	Nicaea I
381	Constantinople I
431	Ephesus
451	Chalcedon
553	Constantinople II
680–681	Constantinople III
787	Nicaea II
869–870	Constantinople IV
1123	Lateran I
1139	Lateran II
1179	Lateran III
1215	Lareran IV
1245	Lyons I
1274	Lyons II
1311–1312	Vienne
1414–1417	Constance
1438–1445	Ferrara-Florence
1512–1517	Lateran V
Trent	1545–1563
1869–1870	Vatican I
1962–1965	Vatican II

After 787 the councils, previously recognized by both the Eastern Orthodox and the Roman Catholic churches, were recognized by the Roman Catholic church only.

Euphrates, which suggests that it was set somewhere in ancient Mesopotamia.

EDEN, Robert Anthony, Earl of Avon (1897–), British statesman and prime minister (1955–57), renowned for his part in the SUEZ CANAL crisis of 1956. Eden became foreign secretary in 1935 but resigned in 1938 in protest against Chamberlain's negotiations with Hitler and Mussolini. He served again at the foreign office 1940–45. As prime minister he promoted an invasion of Egypt (1956) to restore Anglo-French control of the Suez Canal after the Egyptians had nationalized it. He resigned the following year because of ill health.

EDENTATES, a South American order of MAMMALS including the SLOTHS, ARMADILLOS, and ANTEATERS. They generally have long snouts and tongues with reduced teeth, and extra articulation between the vertebrae. Bizarre external coverings aid in temperature regulation.

EDERLE, Getrude Caroline (1906–), US swimmer, the first woman to swim the English Channel. She broke all previous records, crossing the 35mi from France to England on Aug. 6, 1926, in 14hr 31min.

EDESSA, or Vodena, city in NE Greece. The earliest seat of the ancient Macedonian kings, today it is a crop trading center with textile factories. Pop 15 534.

EDESSA, city in SE Turkey, now called Urfa. Situated in N ancient Mesopotamia, the city has been successively controlled by Syrians, Persians, Romans, Muslims, crusaders and the Turks (from 1637). It is a frontier trading center. Pop 100 231.

EDGAR or Eadgar (c943–975), king of Mercia and Northumbria (from 957); king of the West Saxons (from 959); known as king of the English. With St. DUNSTAN he initiated the monastic revival in England. His orderly and prosperous reign earned him the title of Edgar the Peaceful.

EDGAR ATHELING (c1060–1125?), English prince and claimant to the English throne. After the death of King HAROLD in 1066, he was chosen king but acknowledged WILLIAM THE CONQUEROR in 1067. After periods of exile he made his peace with William and later William II. He joined Robert, duke of Normandy, in the 1099 crusade and in a war against Henry I of England, during which he was captured (1106) but later released.

EDGEHILL, Battle of, the first great conflict of the English CIVIL WAR. On Oct. 23, 1642, near the Oxford-Warwickshire border, the Royalists fought the Parliamentarians in an inconclusive battle.

EDGERTON, Harold Eugene (1903–), US electrical engineer known for his development of rapid-flash STROBOSCOPES and application of them to high-speed PHOTOGRAPHY.

EDGEWORTH, Maria (1767–1849), Anglo-Irish novelist. Her gifts for social observation and colorful, realistic portrayal of Irish domestic life and young people influenced many later novelists including Sir Walter SCOTT. Among her works are *Tales of Fashionable Life* (1809–12).

EDINA, suburban village in E central Minn., 8mi SW of Minneapolis. It manufactures electronics equipment. Pop 44 046.

EDINBURG, city in S Tex., seat of Hidalgo Co., in the fertile lower Rio Grande valley. Surrounding areas are rich in gas and oil deposits. Pop 17 163.

EDINBURGH, capital of Scotland, the seat of Midlothian Co., and the second largest Scottish city, located on the S shore of the Firth of Forth. The Old Town, dominated by Edinburgh Castle, dates from the 11th century, but has remains of fortifications from c617. The city became Scotland's capital in 1437. It has always been Scotland's cultural center. HOLYROOD HOUSE is situated here; Edinburgh U. was founded in 1583. The city has many public and private buildings which are beautiful examples of Neoclassical architecture. Since 1947 Edinburgh has been world-famous for its annual summer arts festival. Today the city is a thriving commercial center for banking, insurance and finance; its industries include brewing, distilling, engineering, printing and publishing. Pop 453 422.

EDIRNE, formerly Adrianople, capital of Edirne province, W Turkey. Now a commercial and manufacturing center in an agricultural region, the city has occupied its strategic position between Asia Minor and the Balkans since at least the 6th century BC. Pop 54 885.

EDISON, urban township in central N.J., which includes Menlo Park where Thomas Alva EDISON perfected the incandescent light bulb (1879). Pop 67 120.

EDISON NATIONAL HISTORIC SITE, 14 acres in NE N.J. designated of special importance in 1962 in connection with pioneer inventor Thomas Alva EDISON. It contains his late-Victorian family home, Glenmont, his West Orange laboratory and a museum of the hundreds of inventions developed in Edison's laboratories.

EDISON, Thomas Alva (1847–1931), US inventor, probably the greatest of all time with over 1 000 patents issued to his name. His first successful invention, an improved stock-ticker (1869), earned him the capital to set up as a manufacturer of telegraphic apparatus. He then devised the diplex method of TELEGRAPHY which allowed one wire to carry four messages at once. Moving to a new "invention factory" (the first large-scale industrial-research laboratory) at Menlo Park, N.J., in 1876, he devised the carbon transmitter and a new receiver which made A. G. BELL's TELEPHONE commercially practical. His tin-foil PHONOGRAPH followed in 1877 and in the next year he started to work toward devising a practical incandescent lightbulb. By 1879 he had produced the carbon-filament bulb and electric LIGHTING became a reality, though it was not until 1882 that his first public generating station was supplying power to 85 customers in New York.

Moving his laboratories to West Orange, N.J., in 1887 he set about devising a motion-picture system (ready by 1889) though he failed to exploit its entertainment potential. In all his career he made only one important scientific discovery, the **Edison effect**—the ability of ELECTRICITY to flow from a hot filament in a vacuum lamp to another enclosed wire

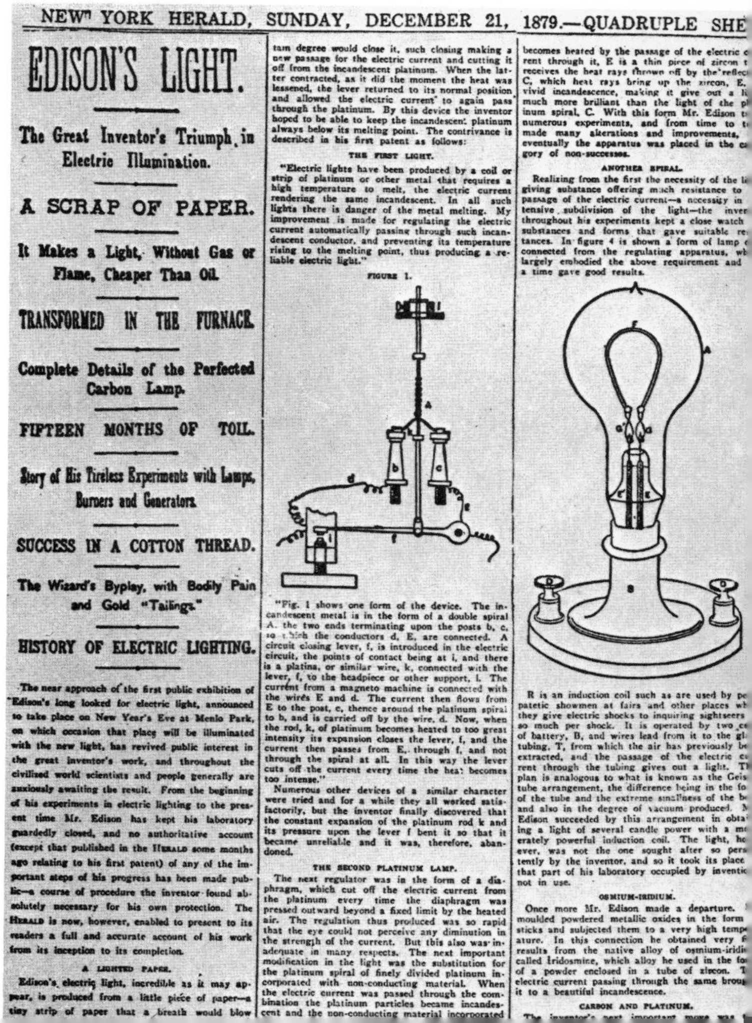

NEW YORK HERALD, SUNDAY, DECEMBER 21, 1879.—QUADRUPLE SHE

EDISON'S LIGHT.

The Great Inventor's Triumph in Electric Illumination.

A SCRAP OF PAPER.

It Makes a Light, Without Gas or Flame, Cheaper Than Oil.

TRANSFORMED IN THE FURNACE.

Complete Details of the Perfected Carbon Lamp.

FIFTEEN MONTHS OF TOIL.

Story of His Tireless Experiments with Lamps, Burners and Generators.

SUCCESS IN A COTTON THREAD.

The Wizard's Byplay, with Bodily Pain and Gold "Tailings."

HISTORY OF ELECTRIC LIGHTING.

The near approach of the first public exhibition of Edison's long looked for electric light, announced to take place on New Year's Eve at Menlo Park, on which occasion that place will be illuminated with the new light, has revived public interest in the great inventor's work, and throughout the civilized world scientists and people generally are anxiously awaiting the result. From the beginning of his experiments in electric lighting to the present time Mr. Edison has kept his laboratory guardedly closed, and no authoritative account (except that published in the HERALD some months ago relating to his first patent) of any of the important steps of his progress has been made public—a course of procedure the inventor found absolutely necessary for his own protection. The HERALD is now, however, enabled to present to its readers a full and accurate account of his work from its inception to its completion.

A LIGHTED PAPER.

Edison's electric light, incredible as it may appear, is produced from a little piece of paper—a tiny strip of paper that a breath would blow

tain degree would close it, such closing making a new passage for the electric current and cutting it off from the incandescent platinum. When the latter contracted, as it did the moment the heat was lessened, the lever returned to its normal position and allowed the electric current to again pass through the platinum. By this device the inventor hoped to be able to keep the incandescent platinum always below its melting point. The contrivance is described in his first patent as follows:

THE FIRST LIGHT.

"Electric lights have been produced by a coil or strip of platinum or other metal that requires a high temperature to melt, the electric current rendering the same incandescent. In all such lights there is danger of the metal melting. My improvement is made for regulating the electric current automatically passing through such incandescent conductor, and preventing its temperature rising to the melting point, thus producing a reliable electric light."

FIGURE 1.

"Fig. 1 shows one form of the device. The incandescent metal is in the form of a double spiral A. the two ends terminating upon the posts b, c, to which the conductors d, E, are connected. A circuit closing lever, f, is introduced in the electric circuit, the points of contact being at i, and there is a platina, or similar wire, k, connected with the lever, f, to the headpiece or other support, l. The current from a magneto machine is connected with the wires E and d. The current then flows from E to the post, c, thence around the platinum spiral to b, and is carried off by the wire, d. Now, when the rod, k, of platinum becomes heated to too great intensity its expansion closes the lever, f, and the current then passes from E, through f, and not through the spiral at all. In this way the lever cuts off the current every time the heat becomes too intense."

Numerous other devices of a similar character were tried and for a while they all worked satisfactorily, but the inventor finally discovered that the constant expansion of the platinum rod k and its pressure upon the lever f bent it so that it became unreliable and it was, therefore, abandoned.

THE SECOND PLATINUM LAMP.

The next regulator was in the form of a diaphragm, which cut off the electric current from the platinum every time the diaphragm was pressed outward beyond a fixed limit by the heated air. The regulation thus produced was so rapid that the eye could not perceive any diminution in the strength of the current. But this also was inadequate in many respects. The next important modification in the light was the substitution for the platinum spiral of finely divided platinum incorporated with non-conducting material. When the electric current was passed through the combination the platinum particles became incandescent and the non-conducting material incorporated

becomes heated by the passage of the electric c rent through it, E is a thin piece of zircon t receives the heat rays thrown off by the reflec C, which heat rays bring up the zircon, E, vivid incandescence, making it give out a li much more brilliant than the light of the pl inum spiral, C. With this form Mr. Edison t numerous experiments, and from time to t made many alterations and improvements, eventually the apparatus was placed in the ca gory of non-successes.

ANOTHER SPIRAL.

Realizing from the first the necessity of the li giving substance offering much resistance to passage of the electric current—a necessity in tensive subdivision of the light—the inver throughout his experiments kept a close watch substances and forms that gave suitable re tances. In figure 4 is shown a form of lamp connected from the regulating apparatus, wh largely embodied the above requirement and a time gave good results.

R is an induction coil such as are used by pe patetic showmen at fairs and other places wh they give electric shocks to inquiring sightseers so much per shock. It is operated by two ce of battery, B, and wires lead from it to the gl tubing, T, from which the air has previously be extracted, and the passage of the electric cu rent through the tubing gives out a light. Th plan is analogous to what is known as the Geis tube arrangement, the difference being in the fo of the tube and the extreme smallness of the b and also in the degree of vacuum produced. M Edison succeeded by this arrangement in obta ing a light of several candle power with a mo erately powerful induction coil. The light, ho ever, was not the one sought after so pers tently by the inventor, and so it took its place that part of his laboratory occupied by inventio not in use.

OSMIUM-IRIDIUM.

Once more Mr. Edison made a departure. moulded powdered metallic oxides in the form sticks and subjected them to a very high tempe ature. In this connection he obtained very f results from the native alloy of osmium-iridi called Iridosmine, which alloy he used in the fo of a powder enclosed in a tube of zircon. T electric current passing through the same broug it to a beautiful incandescence.

CARBON AND PLATINUM.

Extract from an article in the *New York Herald* of December 21, 1879, announcing that Edison's system of electric lighting will be switched on for the first time at Menlo Park on New Year's Eve. The article also contains a scientific explanation of the principles of electric lighting and the problems Edison had to overcome.

but not the reverse (1883)—and, because he saw no use for it, he failed to pursue the matter. His success was probably more due to perseverance than any special insight; as he himself said: "Genius is one percent inspiration and ninety-nine percent perspiration."

EDMOND, city in central Okla., 13mi N of Oklahoma City. It has gas fields and one of the world's largest oil fields is W of the city. Pop 16653.

EDMONDS, suburb of Seattle, Wash., located on Puget Sound. It produces logging equipment. Pop 23998.

EDMONTON, capital of Alberta, Canada, on the N Saskatchewan R. The city developed from a trading post founded in 1795 by the HUDSON'S BAY COMPANY and prospered after the railroad arrived in 1891. Today it is a transportation and agricultural marketing center; its main industries include oil refining and the production of petrochemicals and plastics. The U. of Alberta is located at Edmonton. Pop 438152.

EDMUND, Saint (c1175–1240), archbishop of Canterbury from 1233. His opposition to King Henry III's French allies nearly led to civil war in England. His feast day is Nov. 16.

EDMUND I (921–946), king of the English, 939–46. He spent much of his reign recovering territory in the N from the VIKINGS. He also established a secure border and peaceful relations with Scotland by entrusting Strathclyde, which he captured in 945, to the Scots king, Malcolm I.

EDMUND IRONSIDE (c993–1016), king of the English, April–Nov., 1016. Edmund staunchly opposed the Danish invasion led by CANUTE, hence his name "Ironside." After Canute defeated his troops at Ashingdon, Essex, peace was established and Edmund retained WESSEX while the Danes held the lands N of the Thames R.

EDMUND THE MARTYR, Saint (c841–870), king of East Anglia from 855. He was captured by the Danes, tortured and beheaded for refusing to share his Christian kingdom with pagans. His feast day is Nov. 20.

EDOM, ancient country along the borders of SE Israel and SW Jordan extending from the Dead Sea to the Gulf of Aqaba. The Old Testament says that this barren, mountainous land was given to ESAU (or Edom). Edom's chief town was Sela; its ruins were discovered in 1812.

EDRED or Eadred (d. 955), king of the English, 946–955. During his reign, Northumbria, the last remaining Scandinavian kingdom in England, submitted to English rule. Edred assisted the monastic revival of St. DUNSTAN.

EDUCATION, the process of leading people from the darkness of ignorance to the light of knowledge. The word education comes from the Latin *educare*, meaning "to lead out." In its broadest sense, education, whether formal or informal, includes anything that enlarges people's understanding of themselves and of the world they live in.

The mainstream of Western education was fed from four springs: Israel, Greece, Rome and the Christian Church. During the BABYLONIAN CAPTIVITY after the destruction of Jerusalem, the exiled Jews preserved their faith by writing down their laws and by founding teaching centers or synagogues in which to study. In ancient Greece education for free men in the Athenian democracy included gymnastics and sports, music, mathematics, poetry, philosophy and the art of political dispute. These subjects were the foundation of Classical education which has influenced western civilization for centuries. The city of Athens produced the first great educators, among them the philosophers SOCRATES, ARISTOTLE and PLATO. Greek culture was absorbed by the Romans, who in turn spread Graeco-Roman education and culture throughout the known world. After the fall of Rome, the Christian Church kept education alive in the Dark Ages and deeply influenced Europe's first medieval universities. The RENAISSANCE and the REFORMATION contributed to a wider demand for education and knowledge and public and private schools as well as PAROCHIAL SCHOOLS were established to educate a larger number of people. With the development of

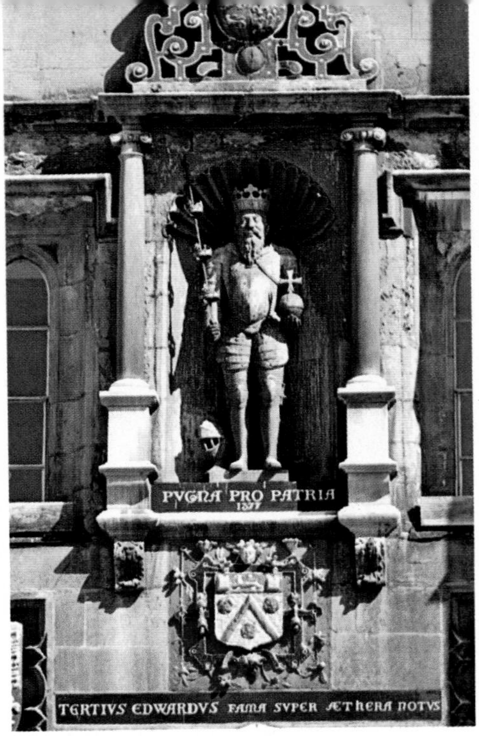

Statue of King Edward III of England which stands in an ornamented niche on the clock tower over one of the gates of the Great Court of Trinity College, Cambridge.

scientific interest and inquiry, the traditional Classical curriculum was expanded to include scientific studies. Later came the pioneers of modern educational theory, including ROUSSEAU, PESTALOZZI, who founded modern elementary education, HERBART, FROEBEL, who founded the KINDERGARTEN, Maria MONTESSORI and Jean PIAGET. The American John DEWEY (1859–1952) rejected authoritarian teaching and advocated PROGRESSIVE EDUCATION. In the 19th century, public education expanded widely in the W. The education systems of modern industrially advanced nations now cater for pupils of all ages and abilities in institutions offering a bewildering variety of studies.

The foundations of American education were laid by the Puritans of New England. The famous Boston Latin School (founded 1635) was modeled on the English grammar school, and Harvard U. (founded 1636) began as a college in the English tradition. In the colonial period and the decades following the Revolutionary War, ELEMENTARY SCHOOLS were run with the cooperation of civil and religious authorities. In 1812 New York became the first state to take responsibility for providing public education. By the 1860s most states had accepted the principle of providing free public education, maintained by taxation and administered by school boards of locally elected officials. The structure of American education has not changed fundamentally since then; it is essentially decentralized, although the federal government plays an important role in school finance at all levels. The 20th century has seen additions to the many universities and colleges founded in the previous century, the establishment of numerous new educational institutions, as well as the establishment of schools for the handicapped and widespread ADULT EDUCATION and training programs. The drive for universal education and higher standards in the US received an unprecedented boost from the G.I. BILL OF RIGHTS (1944) to provide education for war veterans and also from the NATIONAL DEFENSE EDUCATION ACT (NDEA, 1958), which encouraged instruction in mathematics, science and foreign languages.

Today some 60000000 people are enrolled in educational institutions in the US (excluding those outside the age group 3–34). One of the biggest problems of American education in the mid-1960s involved enforcement of the 1954 Supreme Court ruling outlawing racial segregation. Much has now been accomplished in school integration, thus providing better education for racial minorities. Also, by the 1970s there were massive federally-funded programs designed to provide for the special educational needs of minority groups such as Blacks, Mexican-Americans and Puerto Ricans, in urban and in rural areas. The educational projects HEADSTART and FOLLOW THROUGH, for example, were designed to improve minority group educational standards. Then, too, efforts have been made especially in big cities to break down large school districts and to increase parental (see PARENT-TEACHER ASSOCIATION) and community participation in education. (See AUDIOVISUAL EDUCATION; COEDUCATION; NURSERY EDUCATION; PROGRAMMED LEARNING; VOCATIONAL EDUCATION; see also LAND-GRANT COLLEGES.)

EDWARD, eight kings of England. (See also EDWARD THE CONFESSOR.) **Edward I** (1239–1307), reigned 1272–1307. He subjugated Wales and, inconclusively, Scotland, centralized the national administration and reduced baronial and clerical power. **Edward II** (Edward of Caernarvon; 1284–1327), reigned 1307–27. He spent his reign trying to resist the barons and an increasingly powerful parliament. In 1326 he was unseated in a revolt led by his wife, Queen Isabella, and her paramour Roger de Mortimer. Edward was imprisoned, and forced to abdicate in favor of his son, and was probably murdered. **Edward III** (1312–1377), reigned 1327–77. Edward's claim to part of Guienne in France was one of the causes of the HUNDRED YEARS' WAR. He financed the war through parliament, which used the situation to increase its power. In 1348–49, the BLACK DEATH decimated the population, resulting in major economic and social upheavals. **Edward IV** (1442–1483), reigned 1461–70 and 1471–83, during the Wars of the ROSES. A Yorkist, Edward deposed the Lancastrian Henry VI in 1461 and again in 1471 after the latter had been restored in 1470 by the Earl of WARWICK. Edward reestablished the power of the monarchy, improved administration and law enforcement and increased England's trade and prosperity. **Edward V** (1470–1483?), reigned April–June, 1483, one of the "princes in the tower." He is believed to have been murdered at the order of his uncle and protector, Richard Duke of Gloucester, who became Richard III. Edward acceded to the throne as a minor and was immediately a victim of a ruthless power struggle between his uncles Gloucester and Earl Rivers. **Edward VI** (1537–1553), Henry VIII's only son, reigned 1547–53. A sickly child who was to die of consumption, he succeeded to the throne as a minor. Struggles over the succession, and between Protestants and Roman Catholics soon engulfed him. His reign saw the introduction, under Archbishop CRANMER, of the first *Book of Common Prayer* (1549). **Edward VII** (1841–1910), king of Great Britain and Ireland, 1901–10. A popular king, with a reputation as a *bon vivant*, he was particularly concerned with Britain's role in Europe and he helped to promote ENTENTES with France and Russia. **Edward VIII** (1894–1972), king of Great Britain and Ireland, Jan. 20–Dec. 11, 1936. Edward enjoyed great popularity as Prince of Wales and heir, but his association with the American divorcée Mrs. Wallis Warfield Simpson, was treated as a scandal by the press and met stern opposition from government and Church. Edward acceded to the throne but to avoid a constitutional crisis abdicated, becoming Duke of Windsor. He married Mrs. Simpson in 1937 and thereafter lived mainly in France.

EDWARDIAN ERA, in British history the period from the accession of Edward VII in 1901 until 1914. It was characterized by a relaxation of Victorian standards and more general peace and prosperity, with a new consciousness of social issues.

EDWARD, Lake, lake on the Uganda–Zaire border. About 47mi long and up to 32mi wide, it was discovered by H. M. STANLEY in 1889 and named for Edward, Prince of Wales. In Uganda it is known as Lake Idi Amin Dada.

EDWARDS, Jonathan (1703–58), American theologian, and philosopher of wide-ranging interests (see also ENLIGHTENMENT). A Calvinist in the Puritan tradition, he furthered the GREAT AWAKENING by his preaching, but was dismissed by his church in 1749 for his opposition to the HALF-WAY COVENANT. In 1757 he became president of the College of New Jersey (Princeton U.). Influenced by LOCKE, he wrote many works of philosophical theology, most notably on *The Freedom of the Will* (1754) and the *Religious Affections* (1746).

EDWARDSVILLE, city in SW Ill., seat of Madison Co. In an agricultural area, its economy rests on coal mining and light industry. Pop 11 070.

EDWARD, the Black Prince (1330–1376), Prince of Wales, son and heir of Edward III. His nickname may derive from the color of his armor; he is remembered mainly as a brilliant soldier. Given his first independent command in France in 1355, he won the battle of POITIERS in 1356, capturing the French king. Made Prince of Aquitaine in 1362, he alienated his subjects by inept rule and had to return to England in 1371. He died there a year before his father.

EDWARD THE CONFESSOR, Saint (c1003–1066), king of England from 1042. Brought up in Normandy, he was respected for his piety but was dominated throughout his reign by the powerful Earl GODWIN. Edward alienated the country by attempting to exile Godwin and introduce Normans into the government. He had named William of Normandy as his heir, but on his deathbed chose HAROLD, Godwin's son, precipitating the NORMAN CONQUEST.

EDWARD THE ELDER (d. 924), king of the West Saxons from 899, son of ALFRED THE GREAT. He continued his father's expulsion of the Danes; in 917–18 he drove them out of East Anglia and the Midlands. He inherited Mercia in 918, and subdued Northumbria in 920. At his death he controlled most of England.

EDWARD THE MARTYR, Saint (c963–978), elected king of England in 975 against the claims of his younger brother Ethelred. He was assassinated while visiting Ethelred, who succeeded him.

EDWY (d. 959), king of England 955–57 and of Kent and Wessex from 957. Apparently an unpopular king, he drove St. DUNSTAN into exile. In 957 Mercia and Northumbria installed his brother Edgar as king, leaving him only the S kingdoms.

EELGRASS, grass-like marine perennials of the genus *Zostera* with creeping or tuberous RHIZOMES. They are found in shallow coastal salt water in temperate regions and are an important food for water fowl. Family: Zosteraceae.

EELS, long slender fish of the order Anguilliformes, without pelvic fins and with dorsal and ventral fins joining the tail fin. They include the CONGER, moray, snake, snipe and freshwater eel families. Some eels are covered in slime, and some have tiny scales in the skin. Moray eels live in warm water and are a danger to divers. American and European freshwater eels spawn in the Sargasso Sea. The leaf-like larvae cross the ocean, and enter rivers as young eels or elvers. When adult they swim back to the Sargasso Sea to spawn and die.

EELWORMS, threadlike roundworms of the class Nematoda, less than 0.5mm (0.02in) long. They live in vast numbers in soil, fresh water and on the seashore. Some are serious crop pests, notably the stem and bulb eelworm.

EFFICIENCY, in THERMODYNAMICS and the theory of MACHINES, the ratio of the useful WORK derived from a machine to the ENERGY put into it. The mechanical efficiency of a machine is always less than 100%, some energy being lost as HEAT in FRICTION. When the machine is a heat engine, its theoretical thermal efficiency can be found from the second law of thermodynamics but actual values are often rather lower. A typical gasoline engine may have a thermal efficiency of only 25%, a STEAM ENGINE 10%.

EFFIGY MOUNDS NATIONAL MONUMENT, area in NE Ia. containing many preColumbian Indian burial mounds, some in animal or bird shapes. Many have yielded tools and other relics. Farming destroyed hundreds of mounds before the monument was established in 1949.

EFFLORESCENCE, in chemistry, spontaneous loss of water from a crystalline HYDRATE, which crumbles on its surface to an anhydrous powder. SODIUM carbonate and sulfate are common examples. Like its converse, DELIQUESCENCE, it depends on the relative HUMIDITY, occurring if the partial VAPOR PRESSURE of water at the solid exceeds that of the air.

EGBERT (d. 839), king of the West Saxons from 802. He inherited the kingdoms of Kent, Sussex, Essex and Surrey. His defeats of Mercia in 825 and 829 laid the foundations of Wessex's political ascendancy in England.

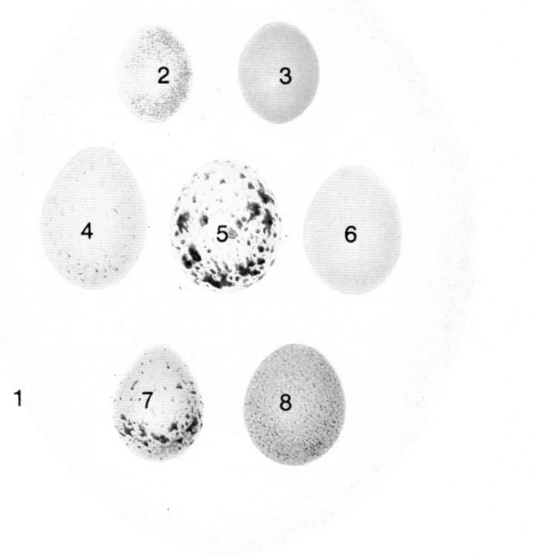

Eggs of various bird species compared: (1) extinct elephant bird (*Aepyornis maximus*); (2) glossy ibis (*Plegadis falcinellus*); (3) common bittern (*Botaurus stellaris*); (4) European spoonbill (*Platalea leucorodia*); (5) osprey (*Pandion haliaetus*); (6) Steller's eider (*Polysticta stelleri*); (7) long-tailed skua (*Stercorarius longicaudus*); (8) gyrfalcon (*Falco rusticolus*).

EGG, the female GAMETE, germ cell or OVUM found in all animals and in most plants. Popularly, the term is used to describe those animal eggs that are deposited by the female either before or after fertilization and develop outside the body, such as the eggs of reptiles and birds. The egg is a single cell which develops into the EMBRYO after FERTILIZATION by a single sperm cell or male gamete. In animals, it is formed in a primary sex organ or GONAD called the ovary. In fishes, reptiles

Diagrammatic section across the North Atlantic (*below left*), showing the migration and breeding cycle of the common eel. At 5–10 years of age the eels undergo changes in outward appearance and are then known as silver eels (A). They migrate to the sea where they become sexually mature (B) and swim across the Atlantic, converging on the Sargasso Sea (*below right*). There they spawn at a depth of 1 600ft and die. Larvae hatching from the eggs are known as leptocephali, those of the American eel taking one year to reach the American coast from the spawning ground. There they change into elvers. The larvae of the European eel take three years to make the corresponding journey to Europe. Their growth in length during this period is indicated.

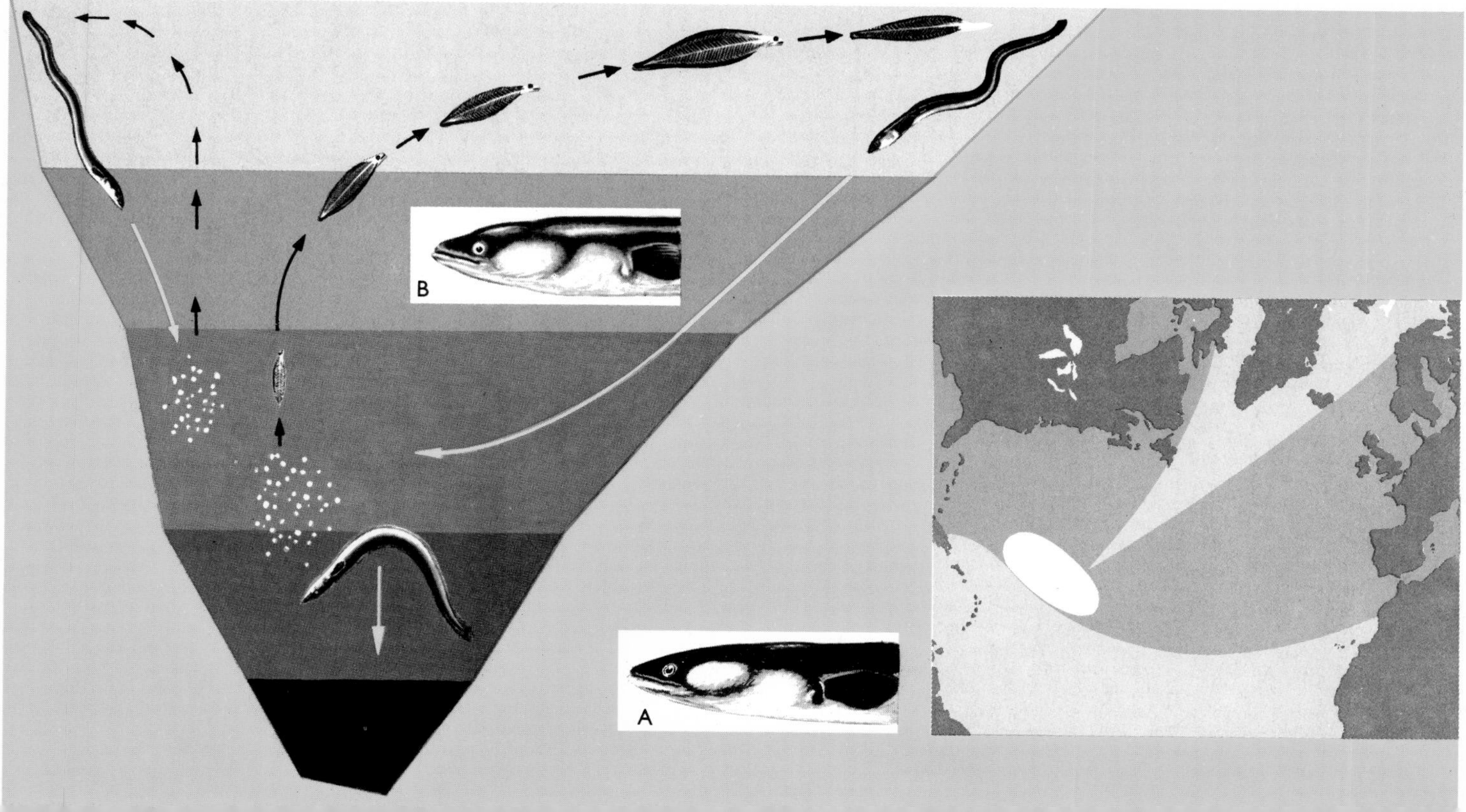

and birds there is a food store of yolk enclosed within its outer membrane. In ANGIOSPERMS, the female reproductive organs form part of the FLOWER. The egg cell is found within the ovules, which upon fertilization develop into the embryo and SEED. (See also POLLINATION, REPRODUCTION.)

EGGLESTON, Edward (1837–1902), US novelist, historian and clergyman. In novels such as *The Hoosier Schoolmaster* (1871) he sought to portray frontier life accurately. His *Beginners of a Nation* (1896) and *Transit of Civilization from Europe to America* (1900) are seminal works of social history.

EGGPLANT, *Solanum melongena*, bushy perennial plant native to S and E Asia, but now widely cultivated in warm climates for its large, egg-shaped fruit that are purple in cultivated varieties. The fleshy fruit, which are eaten as vegetables, are also known as eggfruit or aubergines. Family: Solanaceae.

EGLANTINE. See SWEET BRIAR.

EGLEVSKY, André (1917–), Russian-born US virtuoso ballet dancer and teacher. A member of the Ballet Russe de Monte Carlo 1939–42 and the New York City Ballet 1951–58, he has appeared with many of the world's greatest companies.

EGMONT, Lamoral, Count of (1522–68), popular Flemish nobleman, a Catholic, who attempted to take a moderate stand in the Dutch independence movement. He favored loyalty to Philip II of Spain but made a personal protest to him about the persecution of Protestants. When this was ignored he withdrew from the Council of State in 1565, but put down uprisings against the Spanish in Flanders. In 1568 the Duke of ALVA, attempting to suppress the independence movement, had him beheaded.

EGO, the structured part of the individual's psychic makeup, developing, according to FREUD, from the ID through experience. Closely related in concept to the CONSCIOUS, it can be viewed as the objective equivalent of IDENTITY. (See also SUPEREGO.)

EGRETS, certain HERONS, usually with all-white plumage. The size and body shape of egrets vary considerably and they do not constitute a natural group. They are widely distributed in the tropics and warm temperate regions. Most egrets nest colonially and feed on fish, frogs and sometimes insects.

EGYPT, Arab republic in NE Africa, bordered on the N by the Mediterranean, on the NE by Israel and the Red Sea, on the S by the Sudan and on the W by Libya. The Suez Canal and Gulf of Suez separate the Sinai Peninsula from the rest of Egypt.

Land is mostly desert, only some 13 800sq mi being habitable. The chief physical feature, the fertile Nile R valley, runs narrowly for about 800mi from the Sudanese frontier to the Mediterranean, developing, N of Cairo, into a large alluvial delta where most of the population lives. The Nile separates the Western Desert (260 000sq mi) from the Eastern Desert where the Red Sea Mts (Gebel Sha'ib, 7 175ft) parallel the coast. Egypt's highest peak, Gebel Katherina (8 652ft) is in the thinly-populated Sinai Peninsula. The climate everywhere is arid and hot. Rainfall is low, being 3in annually or even less in most of the S.

People are mainly of Hamitic origin. There are small Greek and Armenian communities. The largest cities are Cairo, the capital and Alexandria. Other important towns are Giza, Port Said, Suez and Ismailia. Arabic is the official language, but most educated Egyptians also speak French or English. At least 70% of the population is illiterate. Most Egyptians are Sunni Muslims, but Coptic Christians are numerous.

Economy. Agriculture (especially cotton, wheat, corn, millet and rice) depends mostly on irrigation from the Nile and provides over 29% of the GNP. Mineral resources include petroleum, iron ore, manganese, phosphates and titanium. Leading industries are food processing, textiles, petroleum products, chemicals and iron and steel. Tourism is highly developed. The ARAB–ISRAELI WARS have severely strained the economy, piling up an estimated debt of $10 350 million, owed mainly to Russia. Following the reopening of the Suez Canal (1975), Egypt sought foreign investment to redevelop the canal area.

History (see also EGYPT, ANCIENT). After the Arab invasion (641 AD), Egypt had a variety of rulers including the Mamluks and Ottomans. Financially insolvent after the opening of the Suez Canal (1869), Egypt was made a British protectorate 1914–36. From 1948 it played a major role in the Arab–Israeli conflict. In 1952 an army coup deposed King Farouk and the republic was proclaimed in 1953, Col. Gamal Abdel NASSER becoming president in 1956. He used aid from the USSR to modernize the army and to a lesser extent industry, building the Aswan High Dam. Much Egyptian territory was lost in the Six-Day War. On Nasser's death (1970) Anwar al-SADAT became president; he regained much lost territory in the Yom Kippur War of 1973 and through a 1975 pact with Israel. He expelled the Russians from Egypt and sought closer links with the US.

EGYPT, Ancient, one of the cradles of world civilization. Egyptian civilization began more than 5 000 years ago in the fertile Nile Valley. Actual dates are much disputed, but Upper and Lower Egypt seem to have been united c3110 BC under MENES, a southern ruler; he made his capital at Memphis, on the boundary between the two. In this period HIEROGLYPHICS developed.

The Old Kingdom (3rd-6th dynasties). The 4th dynasty of pharaohs developed the PYRAMID as a royal tomb. Under them Egypt became a massive and powerful state. Official worship centered on the sun

The Dynasties of Ancient Egypt

Period	Date	Dynasty and names of important rulers	
Predynastic Period	c5000–3100 BC		
Archaic Period	c3100–2890 BC	1	Menes (Narmer)
	c2890–2686 BC	2	
Old Kingdom	c2686–2613 BC	3	Djoser; Huni
	c2613–2494 BC	4	Sneferu; Cheops; Chephren; Mycerinus
	c2494–2345 BC	5	Sahure; Neuserre; Unas
	c2345–2181 BC	6	Pepi I; Pepi II
First Intermediate Period	c2181–2173 BC	7	(Memphite)
	c2173–2160 BC	8	(Memphite)
	c2160–2130 BC	9	(Heracleopolitan) Achthoes
	c2130–2040 BC	10	(Heracleopolitan) Achthoes
	c2133–1991 BC	11	(Theban) Mentuhotep Nebhepetre I
Middle Kingdom	1991–1786 BC	12	Amenemmes I, II, III; Sesostris I, II, III
Second Intermediate Period	1786–1633 BC	13	
	1786–1603 BC	14	(Xois)
	1674–1567 BC	15	(Hyksos) Khyan; Apophis; Jacob-el
	c1684–1567 BC	16	(Hyksos) Khyan; Apophis; Jacob-el
	c1650–1567 BC	17	(Theban) Sequenenre; Kamose
New Kingdom	1567–1320 BC	18	Amosis I; Amenophis I, II, III; Thutmose I, II, III, IV; Hatshepsut; Akhenaton (Amenophis IV); Tutankhamen; Horemheb
	1320–1200 BC	19	Sethod I; Ramses II; Merenptah
	1200–1085 BC	20	Ramses III
Late Period	1085–945 BC	21	Psusennes I; Herihor (high-priest)
	945–730 BC	23	(Bubastis) Shoshenk I; Osorkon I
	817?–730 BC	23	(Tanis) Pedubast
	720–715 BC	24	(Sais) Bochchoris
	751–668 BC	25	(Ethiopian) Pi'ankhy; Shabaka; Taharqa
	664–525 BC	26	(Sais) Psammetichus I, II; Necho II; Apries (Hophra); Amasis
First Persian Period	525–404 BC	27	(Persian) Cambyses; Darius I; Xerxes; Artaxerxes
Late Period	404–399 BC	28	(Sais) Amyrteos
	399–380 BC	29	(Mendes)
	380–343 BC	30	(Sebennytos) Nectanebo I and II
Second Persian Period	343–332 BC	31	(Persian) Artaxerxes III; Arses; Darius III
Conquest by Alexander The Great	332 BC		
Ptolemaic Period	332–30 BC		(Ptolemies); Ptolemy I; Soter I; Ptolemy VII; Euergetes II; Cleopatra
Conquest by Romans Octavius rules Egypt	30 BC		

god RA. The 94-year reign of Pepi II seems to have led to civil war, foreign infiltration and the breakup of the kingdom. After a century of anarchy a stable kingdom was set up in Middle Egypt.

The Middle Kingdom (11th–13th dynasties). The restoration of stability was completed by the 11th dynasty. Under the 12th dynasty the country flourished. Irrigation became more systematic, resulting in increased food production and raised standards of living. Trade extended to Crete and cultural activity reached a new peak. But the 13th dynasty evidently lost power to foreign nomadic rulers, the HYKSOS, who were overthrown by the 17th and 18th dynasties.

The New Kingdom (18th–21st dynasties). The 18th dynasty completed the reconquest, and under THUTMOSE III Egypt ruled from the Sudan to the Euphrates. AKHENATON, rejecting traditional polytheism, introduced the sun worship of ATON and founded a new capital at Akhetaton (now TELL EL AMARNA). Traditional religion revived under his son-in-law TUTANKHAMEN. Incursions by Hittites, Libyans and other foreign tribes were now weakening Egypt, despite revivals under RAMSES II and III.

The Late Period (21st dynasty–641 AD). Egypt now came increasingly under foreign control, divided between Libyan rulers and CUSH. Invaded by Assyria (668 BC), Egypt was later annexed by Persia (525 BC), then taken by Alexander the Great (332 BC). Alexander founded Alexandria and made his general PTOLEMY governor of Egypt. He fathered the Ptolemaic dynasty of Macedonian rulers which persisted until the death of Cleopatra in 30 BC. Egypt then became a Roman province. In the 4th century AD the country became Christian and c395 it passed under the control of the Byzantine Empire. Byzantine misrule made Arab conquest easy in 641. Egypt became a province of the Arab empire, from which it takes its present character. (For recent history see EGYPT.)

For over 3 000 years the civilization of ancient Egypt flourished, producing some of the most impressive examples of art and architecture in the world. *Right:* the earliest step pyramid (3rd dynasty), precursor of the true pyramid. It was designed by the architect Imhotep as a new kind of stone tomb for his master, King Djoser. *Below:* over 1 000 years later is the mortuary temple of Ramses III at Medinet Habu. The vast relief sculptures show the pharaoh striking his enemies.

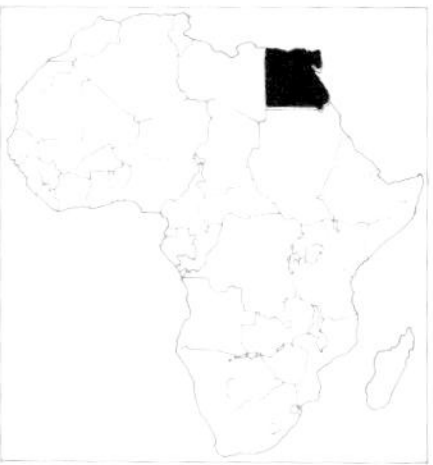

Official name: Arab Republic of Egypt
Capital: Cairo
Area: 386 198sq mi
Population: 34 383 000
Languages: Arabic
Religions: Muslim; Coptic Orthodox
Monetary unit(s): 1 Egyptian pound = 100 piastres

Most of Egypt is barren desert except for a narrow strip of agricultural land which is irrigated by the flood waters of the Nile. This aerial view of the Nile shows the fertile Black Land beside the river and the desert Red Land beyond.

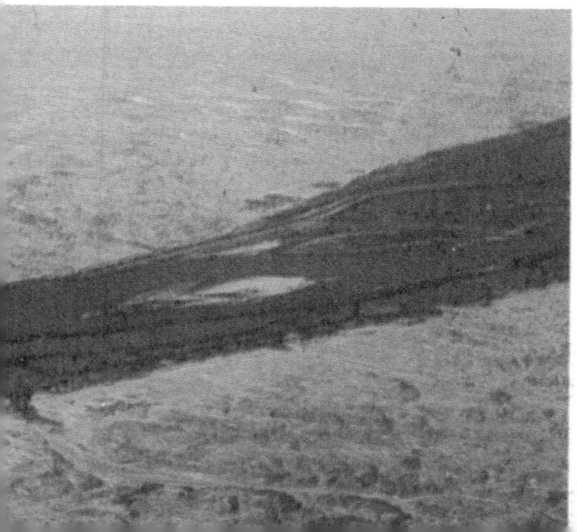

EGYPTIAN ART AND ARCHITECTURE, flourished c3500 BC to c30 BC. In that time much of it changed remarkably little, because both art and architecture were valued primarily as religious expression; much of the finest work is in temples and tombs.

Architecture. Early buildings were of clay and reeds, and later buildings often copied these. The pillar shaped like papyrus reeds became a common motif. Most domestic buildings were of brick, as were at first larger buildings, such as the MASTABA tombs. In the later Old Kingdom, however, stone was introduced. The step-pyramid built by IMHOTEP at Sakkara is the oldest known building entirely in stone. Middle Kingdom pyramids were also of stone, but New Kingdom tombs were usually carved from the side of a cliff, as in the Valley of the Kings. The New Kingdom built great temples such as those at ABU SIMBEL and KARNAK.

Art. Art was a religious matter in Egypt because painting and sculpture were the means of supplying the dead with what was needed in the afterlife and affirming their status. Thus tombs are decorated with familiar scenes and testimonials to the achievements of the dead. Such was the wealth buried with the pharaohs that tomb-robbing became a trade. Jewelry so buried is among the finest examples of Egyptian art surviving. The characteristic conventions in painting and sculpture, idealized and generally non-representational, developed in the Old Kingdom; by the New Kingdom they had become less rigorous, until the reign of the apostate AKHENATON ushered in a whole new and experimental school of representational art. With the resurgence of the old religion this faded, taking with it much of the vitality in Egyptian art.

EGYPTIAN MAU, cat breed created to reproduce the type which appears in ancient Egyptian paintings and sculpture. Conformation is of "foreign" type but not so extreme as in the Siamese, nor are the oval eyes fully oriental. The coat is spotted with either sloe-black markings on a silver ground or dark brown on light bronze.

EHRENBURG, Ilya Grigoryevich (1891–1967), Russian author. He emigrated to Paris in 1911 and did not return to Russia until 1924; he then lived in Europe as a journalist until 1941. He received the Stalin Prize for the anti-Western novel *The Fall of Paris* (1942). The novel *The Thaw* (1954) was a major work of the post-Stalin liberalization.

EHRLICH, Paul (1854–1915), German bacteriologist and immunologist, the founder of CHEMOTHERAPY and an early pioneer of HEMATOLOGY. His discoveries include: a method of staining (1882), and hence identifying, the TUBERCULOSIS bacillus (see also Robert KOCH); the reasons for immunity in terms of the chemistry of ANTIBODIES AND ANTIGENS, for which he was awarded (with METCHNIKOFF) the 1908 Nobel Prize for Physiology or Medicine; and the use of the drug SALVARSAN to cure syphilis (see VENEREAL DISEASES), the first DRUG to be used in treating the root cause of a disease (1911).

EHRLICH, Paul Ralph (1932–), US biologist and ecologist, author of *The Population Bomb* (1968).

EICHMANN, Adolf (1906–1962), lieutenant-colonel in the GESTAPO, head of the Jewish Division from 1939. He was responsible for the deportation, maltreatment and murder of European Jews in WWII. He escaped to Argentina, but was abducted, tried and executed in Israel.

EICHOLTZ, Jacob (1776–1842), US painter. A pupil of Gilbert STUART, he is remembered for his portraits of eminent contemporaries such as John MARSHALL.

EIDERS, several species of DUCK which are native to northern coastal regions. The female lines her nest with soft breast down. Eiderdown is collected commercially for high-quality quilting, particularly in Iceland.

EIDETIC IMAGE, an exceptionally vivid mental image which the individual "sees" either projected onto a suitable background (e.g., a wall) or with eyes closed in a darkened room. The image may be a MEMORY (eidetic memory) or a fantasy, and may be either voluntary or spontaneous. Eidetic imagery is most common among children.

The best known feature of the Paris skyline, the Eiffel Tower, which since its completion in 1889 has become an emblem of the city and tourist attraction. State-owned since 1909, it is now used as a meteorological observation post and a radio and television tower.

EIFFEL, Alexandre Gustave (1832–1923), French engineer best known for his design and construction of the Eiffel Tower, Paris (1887–89), from which he carried out experiments in AERODYNAMICS. In 1912 he founded the first aerodynamics laboratory.

EIFFEL TOWER, tower in Paris designed and built by Gustave EIFFEL for the Centennial Exposition of 1889. Constructed from four latticework columns of iron on a masonry base, it dominates the city's skyline, rising to a height of 984ft topped by a 55ft television antenna.

EIGEN, Manfred (1927–), German physicist awarded, with Ronald NORRISH and George PORTER, the 1967 Nobel Prize for Chemistry for studies of extremely fast chemical reactions.

EIGHT, The. See ASHCAN SCHOOL.

EIJKMANN, Christiaan (1858–1930), Dutch pathologist. Following a trip to Indonesia (1886) to investigate BERIBERI he was able to show that the disease resulted from a dietary deficiency. This led to the discovery of VITAMINS. For his work he was awarded (with Sir F. G. HOPKINS) the 1929 Nobel Prize for Physiology or Medicine.

EILAT, port city and beach resort at Israel's southern extremity, on the Gulf of Aqaba. Israel's only direct access to E Africa and the Far East, it has often been blockaded by Egypt. Pop 14 600.

EINDHOVEN, city in Noord-Brabant province, S Netherlands. On the Dommel R about 55mi SE of Rotterdam, it is a major industrial center built up largely by the electrical industry established there in 1891. Pop 189 613.

EINEM, Gottfried von (1918–), Austrian composer best known for his operas *Danton's Death* (1947) after BUCHNER, *The Trial* (1953) after KAFKA, and *The Old Lady's Visit* (1971) from the play by DÜRRENMATT.

EINHARD (c770–840), Frankish historian, architect and court scholar under CHARLEMAGNE and LOUIS I; both kings made him abbot of several monasteries. He is best known for his *Vita Caroli*, a life of Charlemagne modeled on SUETONIUS.

EINHORN, David (1809–1879), Bavarian-born rabbi and theologian who in 1855 emigrated to the US, where he became a leading figure in the establishment of Reform Judaism and a noted Abolitionist.

EINSTEIN, Albert (1879–1955), German-born Swiss-American theoretical physicist, the author of the theory of RELATIVITY. In 1905 Einstein published several papers of major significance. In one he applied PLANCK'S QUANTUM THEORY to the explanation of photoelectric emission. For this he was awarded the 1921 Nobel Prize for Physics. In a second he demonstrated that it was indeed molecular action which was responsible for BROWNIAN MOTION. In a third he published the special theory of relativity with its postulate of a constant VELOCITY for LIGHT (c) and its consequence, the equivalence of MASS (m) and ENERGY (E), summed up in the famous equation $E=mc^2$. In 1915 he went on to publish the general theory of relativity. This came with various testable predictions, all of which were spectacularly confirmed within a few years. Einstein was on a visit to the US when Hitler came to power in Germany and, being a Jew, decided not to return to his native land. The rest of his life was spent in a fruitless search for a "unified field theory" which could combine QUANTUM MECHANICS with GRAVITATION theory. After 1945 he also worked hard against the proliferation of nuclear weapons, although he had himself, in 1939, alerted President F. D. Roosevelt to the danger that Germany might develop an ATOMIC BOMB, and had thus contributed to the setting up of the Manhattan Project.

EINSTEINIUM (Es), a TRANSURANIUM ELEMENT in the ACTINIDE series, first found in the debris from the first HYDROGEN BOMB, and now prepared by bombardment of lighter actinides.

EINTHOVEN, Willem (1860–1927), Dutch physiologist awarded the 1924 Nobel Prize for Physiology or Medicine for his invention of, and investigation of heart action with, the ELECTROCARDIOGRAPH. In 1903 he devised the **string galvanometer**, a single fine wire placed under tension in a MAGNETIC FIELD. Current passed through the wire causes a deflection which can be measured, for greater accuracy, by microscope. This GALVANOMETER was sensitive enough for him to use it to record the electrical activity of the HEART.

EIRE. See IRELAND, REPUBLIC OF.

EISENACH, city in East Germany, former capital of the Thuringian Landgraves, whose castle, the WARTBURG, still dominates the town. It is now a tourist center with important automobile and electronics industries. Pop 51 000.

EISENHOWER, Dwight David (1890–1969), "Ike," 34th president of the United States (1953–1961) and supreme commander of Allied troops in Europe during WWII.

Born in Denison, Tex., the third of seven sons, he spent most of his childhood in Abilene, Kan. He left Abilene in 1909 to attend West Point. The year after his graduation he married Mary (Mamie) Geneva Doud, by whom he had two sons, Doud David (1917–1921) and John Sheldon Doud (1922–). In 1926 he graduated first out of 275 from the Fort Leavenworth Staff School. By 1941 he had become a brigadier-general, and in the summer of 1943 he was sent to London as commanding general of US forces in the European theater of operations. As supreme commander of the Allied Expeditionary Force he directed the D-Day assault in 1944, and received the German surrender at Rheims in 1945. He headed the occupation force until 1948, when he became president of Columbia University, taking leave of absence to serve as supreme commander of NATO in 1950.

He became the Republican presidential candidate in 1952 and was elected by a large margin. Domestically he sought "moderation," appealing, often fruitlessly, for bipartisan support from a Democratic Congress which consistently rejected such Republican programs as the repeal of the TAFT–HARTLEY ACT and a reduction in tariffs.

The CIVIL RIGHTS legislation of 1957 and 1960 was among the most significant measures of his presidency. Although he had sent troops to Little Rock, Ark., to enforce an antisegregation court order, he personally doubted the ability of such legislation to effect social change. One of his first foreign-policy moves was to arrange a truce in the KOREAN WAR. He also, however, supported the COLD WAR strategy of his secretary of state, John Foster DULLES, which resulted in some of the highest peacetime military budgets ever proposed. Einsenhower himself warned of the massive potential for "misplaced power" such military expenditures entailed, in his famous "military-industrial complex" speech, given when he retired at the age of 70—the oldest president to complete his term in office.

Dwight David EISENHOWER

34th US President

Born: October 14, 1890
Died: March 28, 1969
Term of office: January 20, 1953–January 19, 1961
Political party: Republican

EISENHOWER, Milton Stover (1899–), American educator, brother of Dwight D. EISENHOWER. He became president of Kansas State College in 1943, of Pennsylvania State College in 1950 and of Johns Hopkins University in 1956. He was chairman of the president's Committee on Causes and Prevention of Violence, created in 1968.

EISENHOWER DOCTRINE, policy approved by Congress in 1956 which gave the president powers to send aid and troops to any country requesting help against a threatened communist takeover. It was first exercised in the Lebanon in 1958.

EISENSTAEDT, Alfred (1898–), pioneering American photojournalist who worked for *Life* magazine for over 30 years. From the early 1930s he helped to develop news and candid photography from mere reportage into an art form.

EISENSTEIN, Sergei Mikhailovich (1898–1948), Soviet film director who was a major influence on the development of the cinema. He extended editing techniques, especially the use of montage. His films—especially *Battleship Potemkin* (1925), *Alexander Nevsky* (1938) and *Ivan the Terrible* (1944–46)—are undisputed classics.

EISNER, Kurt (1867–1919), German-Jewish journalist and poet who led a socialist uprising which overthrew the Bavarian monarchy in 1918. He then became the head of the new Bavarian republic, but was assassinated by a Prussian nationalist in the following year.

EISTEDDFOD, ancient Welsh poetry festival which died out after the 16th century, though enough of the "bardic" tradition survived to revive it in the 19th century; it is now a festival of all the arts. A National Eisteddfod is held each summer in N or S Wales alternately.

ELAGABALUS. See HELIOGABALUS.

EL-ALAMEIN, Battle of, decisive British victory in the N African campaign in WWII. The 8th Army under General MONTGOMERY forced the Axis troops under Field-Marshal ROMMEL to withdraw from Egypt and Libya into E Tunisia, thus paving the way for their total defeat soon after.

ELAM, biblical name for an ancient kingdom of Babylonia which covered the plain of SW Persia, an area roughly corresponding to the modern Iranian province of Khuzestan. Probably established in the 4th millennium, it became a large and important nation which overthrew Babylonia in the 18th century BC and reached the height of its power in the 14th century BC. Its capital was at SUSA. The Elamites were defeated by the armies of ASHURBANIPAL 645 BC and Elam was absorbed into the Persian Empire.

ELAND, members of the genus *Taurotragus*, the largest ANTELOPES. Native to central and southern Africa, they may reach a height of 1.8m (6ft) and have spirally twisted horns.

ELASTICITY, the ability of a body to resist tension, torsion, shearing or compression and to recover its original shape and size when the stress is removed. All substances are elastic to some extent, but if the stress exceeds a certain value (the elastic limit), which is soon reached for brittle and plastic materials, permanent deformation occurs. Below the elastic limit, bodies obey Hooke's Law (see MATERIALS, STRENGTH OF).

ELASTOMER, any POLYMER suitable for use as a synthetic RUBBER.

ELATH. See EILAT.

ELBA, Italian island in the Mediterranean, 6mi SW of Tuscany, famous as the place to which NAPOLEON I was exiled. The island is about 20mi long and less than 10mi wide, and is very mountainous. Industries include iron mining, marble quarrying, fishing and agriculture.

ELBE RIVER, major river in central Europe. It rises in the Riesengebirge in NW Czechoslovakia and flows 725mi N through East and West Germany into the North Sea beyond Hamburg. The river is navigable for some 525mi and is connected by a canal system to the Oder. Important cities on the Elbe include Hamburg, Dresden and Magdeburg.

ELBERT, Mount, in central Colorado, the highest peak in the Rocky Mountains (14 433ft).

ELBRUS, Mount, the highest mountain in the Caucasus, and in Europe. Its two extinct volcanic peaks are 18 481ft and 18 356ft high.

ELBURZ MOUNTAINS, range in N Iran between the S shore of the Caspian and the central plateau. Mt Demavand (18 655ft) is the highest peak

EL CAJON, city in S Cal., about 15mi E of San Diego. It produces electronic equipment and aircraft components. Pop 52 273.

EL CANEY, Battle of, decisive American victory in the Spanish-American War. Fought in E Cuba on July 1, 1898, El Caney and the victory at SAN JUAN HILL on the same day assured American control of Santiago de Cuba.

EL CAPITAN, name of three different mountain peaks in the US, one in Yosemite Valley, Cal. in the Sierra Nevada (7 569ft); one in W Mont. (9 983ft); one in the Guadalupe Mts, W Tex. (8 078ft).

EL CENTRO, city in S California's famous Imperial Valley farming region, about 10mi N of the Mexican border. Pop 19 272.

EL CERRITO, city in W Cal. on San Francisco Bay about 6mi N of Oakland, of which it is a residential suburb. Pop 25 190.

EL CID. See CID, EL.

ELDER, popular name for hardy deciduous trees with compound leaves of the genus *Sambucus*, family Caprifoliaceae, which are native to Europe, Asia and North America. Their berries are used in preserves, wines and medicines.

ELDER, an office in the early church (see PRESBYTER) and in the REFORMED CHURCHES. In PRESBYTERIANISM there are two kinds of elders: preaching elders or ministers; and ruling elders, laymen who assist the minister in the government of the congregation. Certain other Protestant churches also have elders.

EL DORADO (Spanish: the gilded one), South American Indian chief who was reputed to cover himself with gold dust at festivals and then, as a sacrifice, wash it off in a lake into which his subjects also threw gold. Much of the Spanish exploration and conquest of South America was fired by the quest for the legendary city of El Dorado.

EL DORADO, city in Ark., about 15mi N of the La. border. An oil center, it also produces lumber, chemicals and cotton. Pop 25 283.

EL DORADO, city in SE Kan. An oil-refining center about 25mi NE of Wichita, the area also produces grain and livestock. Pop 12 308.

ELEANOR OF AQUITAINE (c1122–1204), daughter and heiress of William, Duke of Aquitaine; queen consort first to Louis VII of France (marriage annulled 1152) and then to Henry II of England. Her marriage to Henry in 1152 brought almost all of W France under English domination. In 1173 she supported her sons (later kings Richard I and John) in rebellion against their father and was afterwards kept in captivity until Henry's death.

ELEANOR OF CASTILE (1246–1290), daughter of Ferdinand II of Castile and queen consort to Edward I of England, whom she accompanied on his Crusade. After her death he erected "Eleanor crosses" at each place in England where her funeral cortege had rested on its way to London.

ELEATICS, pre-Socratic school of Greek philosophy mentioned by PLATO and ARISTOTLE. Founded by PARMENIDES, it also included ZENO OF ELEA and Melissus, taking its name from Elea, their native city. The central Eleatic doctrine, in contrast to the theory of HERACLITUS, is that the world is one uniform whole, an abstract "being" remaining unchangeable and absolute, and change a mere illusion of the senses. Because the Eleatics were the first to develop purely formal arguments they are often regarded as the founders of LOGIC.

ELECAMPANE, *Inula helenium*, a coarse herb with yellow flowers, of the family COMPOSITAE, native to Europe, Asia and North America. Its thick fleshy roots have been used medicinally.

ELECTION, method of choice by poll, often used by democratic bodies, including states, to select office-holders. Some public officials in ancient Greece and Rome were elected, but the modern system of government by elected representatives derives largely from the British parliamentary system and the American system based on it.

When the American states adapted the British system, however, they wished to avoid having a hereditary head of state and upper house, but did not wish to "degrade" these offices by putting them up for straightforward competitive election. President and Senate were therefore to be chosen by indirect election. The Senate is no longer elected by the state legislatures, but the president is technically still elected by the ELECTORAL COLLEGE.

PRIMARY ELECTIONS, a reform adopted by a number of states in the late 19th century, might also be considered a form of indirect election, since voters actually elect a delegate of a particular party, who is usually then pledged to vote in convention for those voters' candidate for the party's nomination. The general tendency in American government has been to extend the franchise, by giving all citizens, regardless of color, sex, etc., the right to vote, and individual representation has been channeled to the various people for whom each citizen votes—local officials, county officials, some judges, state governors and legislators, US Representatives and Senators etc.

A system of proportional representation, as opposed to the plurality system, operates by awarding parties seats in a national legislature, for example, on the basis of the proportion of the total popular vote each party has received. Although operated widely in Europe, proportional representation has only been used experimentally in the US, except in the special case of some primary elections.

ELECTOR (German: *Kurfurst*), title given to members of a group or "college" of German princes who elected the Holy Roman Emperor from the 12th to the beginning of the 19th century. (See also HOLY ROMAN EMPIRE.)

ELECTORAL COLLEGE, body created to elect the president and vice president of the US. The college was conceived as a compromise between direct popular elections for the nation's highest office and rule by appointment or inheritance. It was originally intended in the Constitution that the electors would be chosen by the state legislatures. But this has been modified so that the electors are chosen by the voters of each state—often without their names appearing on the ballot—by the indirect method of allowing voters to indicate their choice for president and vice president and then allowing the winning party's electors to cast the states' votes for the candidates chosen. Each state has as many votes in the college as the total number of its senators and representatives. If no candidate receives a majority of electoral votes, the

The major preliminaries to the 1976 presidential election, the Democratic (*top*) and Republican conventions. The atmosphere of these conventions, a strange mixture of Madison Avenue, Mardi Gras and hard politics, often gives rise to fears that they are only obscuring the real party forums, the so-called "smoke-filled rooms."

House of Representatives elects the president from among the top three candidates. This happened twice in the 19th century—in 1800, when Thomas Jefferson was chosen by the House, and in 1824, when John Quincy Adams was chosen. Since the winning candidate in each state receives all that state's electoral votes, it is mathematically possible for the losing presidential candidate to receive more popular votes than the man elected by the college. This happened in 1824 with Jackson and Adams, in 1876 (see ELECTORAL COMMISSION 1877) with Tilden and Hayes and in 1888 when Benjamin Harrison defeated Grover Cleveland. There has been constant dissatisfaction with the electoral college, but the institution still survives. (See also UNITED STATES CONSTITUTION.)

ELECTORAL COMMISSION (1877), body created to settle the disputed presidential election of 1876 between Samuel J. Tilden (Democrat) and Rutherford B. Hayes (Republican), because the 22 electoral votes of Fla., La., S.C. and Ore. were in doubt. The commission (composed of eight Republicans and seven Democrats) eventually decided to award all the disputed ballots to Hayes, which provoked allegations of prejudice.

ELECTRA, in Greek legend, the daughter of AGAMEMNON and CLYTEMNESTRA. With her brother ORESTES, she slew her mother and her mother's lover, who had connived to kill her father. The legend is the subject of three tragedies—by EURIPIDES, AESCHYLUS and SOPHOCLES.

ELECTRICAL ENGINEERING, branch of technology dealing with the practical applications of ELECTRICITY and ELECTRONICS, and thus concerned with generation of electric POWER, design and construction of electrical and electronic components, and the use of these components in integrated, functional systems. **Power engineers** are important in modern industry as electric MOTORS are an integral part of most factory work, and electric LIGHTING and AIR CONDITIONING play a vital role in maintaining good working conditions. **Communications engineers** deal with construction of TELEVISIONS, TELEPHONES and other electronic equipment: perhaps their greatest success is the COMPUTER.

proposition for urban transportation.

ELECTRIC CURRENT. See ELECTRICITY.

ELECTRIC EEL. See ELECTRIC FISH.

ELECTRIC EYE, popular name for a PHOTOELECTRIC CELL.

ELECTRIC FIELD, what is said to exist where stationary electric charges (see ELECTRICITY) experience a force: the field is defined with the strength and direction of the force on a unit charge. Electric fields are produced by (other) electric charges, and by changing magnetic fields (see ELECTROMAGNETISM).

ELECTRIC FISH, several unrelated groups of fish which are able to generate electric currents in organs that appear to be composed of modified muscle tissue. Fish such as the Marine stargazer, the Electric catfish and the Electric ray use this power to stun prey and immobilize their enemies. The **Electric eel** of the Amazon (not a true eel), in addition to being able to deliver some 500 volts against an enemy, discharges a very weak current to form an ELECTROMAGNETIC FIELD around itself which allows it to detect the approach of other fish. The African Elephant-snout fish and knifefish also have this facility.

Black electric ray (*Torpedo nobiliana*) gliding just above the Mediterranean seabed. The largest of the electric rays, this species may reach 5ft in length and attain a weight of 100lb. The electric organs are in the wing-like pectoral fins and can produce a current of 200 volts, quite enough to stun the small crustaceans and fishes on which they feed.

ELECTRIC ARC, a high-current electric discharge between two ELECTRODES. The current is carried by the gas PLASMA maintained by the discharge. Sodium and neon lights exemplify large relatively cool arcs, while arc-welding uses a small very hot arc between a slowly consumed electrode and the workpiece. LIGHTNING is a naturally occurring arc. (See also ARC LAMP.)

ELECTRIC-ARC PROCESS, process for NITROGEN FIXATION, now largely uneconomical. Air (see ATMOSPHERE) is blown through an ELECTRIC ARC at 1000°C, and nitric oxide (see NITROGEN) is formed. It is converted into NITRIC ACID as in the OSTWALD PROCESS.

ELECTRIC BELL. See BELL, ELECTRIC.

ELECTRIC CAR, an automobile driven by electric MOTORS and (usually) using storage BATTERIES as the ENERGY source. Although an electrically-powered carriage was built as long ago as 1837, it was only in the 1890s that electric cars became common. After WWI they lost ground to AUTOMOBILES with INTERNAL-COMBUSTION ENGINES although, particularly in Europe, electric traction has remained popular for urban delivery vehicles. With increasing concern being felt at the energy- and pollution-costs of the gasoline automobile, renewed interest is being shown in the electric car in spite of its relatively short range between charges. It is pollution-free, robust and simple to drive and maintain. The only difficulty is its low power-to-weight ratio, largely due to the weight of the lead-acid storage batteries commonly used. Much research is being put into finding alternative, lighter battery systems or powerful-enough FUEL CELLS to make electric cars once again an attractive

ELECTRIC FURNACE, any of various industrial furnaces heated electrically. In an **arc furnace**, batches of steel are melted by the heat of ELECTRIC ARCS struck between GRAPHITE ELECTRODES and the charge. In **induction furnaces**, used mainly for remelting batches of steel, a refractory crucible is surrounded by a large water-cooled copper coil. When this is connected to a high-frequency AC supply, eddy currents are induced in the batch which heat it. Often a lower-frequency field is also applied to help stir the charge. **Chamber furnaces** are simply large electric ovens, heated from the walls.

ELECTRIC GENERATOR. See GENERATOR, ELECTRIC.

ELECTRICITY, the phenomena of charged particles at rest and in motion. Electricity provides man with a highly versatile form of ENERGY, electrical devices being used in heating, LIGHTING, machinery, telephony and ELECTRONICS. **Electric charge** is an inherent property of matter, ELECTRONS carrying a negative charge of 1.602×10^{-19} coulomb and atomic nuclei normally carrying a similar positive charge for each electron in the ATOM. When the balance is disturbed (in the case of glass, by rubbing it, for example), a net charge is left on an object, and the study of such isolated charges is called **electrostatics**. Like charges repel and unlike charges attract each other with a FORCE proportional to the two charges and inversely proportional to the square of their separation (the inverse square law): electrostatic repulsion, for example, will be familiar in newly combed hair. The force is normally interpreted in terms of an ELECTRIC FIELD produced by one charge with which the other interacts. The fields produced by any number of charges may be superposed independently, and the result conveniently represented graphically by field lines, beginning at positive and ending at negative charges, showing by their direction that of the field, and by their density its strength. Pairs of equal but opposite charges separated by a small distance are called dipoles, the product of charge and separation being called the DIPOLE MOMENT. These experience a TORQUE in an electric field tending to align them with the field, but no net force unless the field is nonuniform. The amount of work done in moving a unit charge from one point to another against the electric field is called the electric potential difference or **voltage** between the points, and is measured in VOLTS (volts (V) = joules/coulomb). The ratio of a charge added to a body to the voltage produced is called the CAPACITANCE of the body; for most practical purposes, the earth provides a reference potential with an infinite capacitance.

In some materials, known as electric CONDUCTORS, there are charges free to move about—for example, valence electrons in metals, or IONS in salt solutions—and in these, the presence of an electric field produces a steady flow of charge in the direction of the field (negative charges moving the opposite way); such a flow constitutes an **electric current**, measured in AMPERES (amperes (A) = coulombs/second). The field implies a voltage between the ends of the conductor, which is normally proportional to the current (OHM'S LAW), the ratio being called the RESISTANCE of the conductor, and measured in OHMS (ohms (Ω) = volts/amps); it normally rises with TEMPERATURE. Materials with high resistance to currents are classed as **insulators**. (See also SEMICONDUCTOR, DIELECTRIC.) The energy acquired by the charges in falling through the field is dissipated as HEAT—and LIGHT, if a sufficient temperature is reached—the total POWER output being the product of current and voltage. Thus, for example, a 1 kW fire supplied at 110 V draws a current of about 9 A, and the hot element has a resistance of about 12 Ω.

Electric sources such as BATTERIES or GENERATORS convert chemical, mechanical, or other energy into electrical energy (see ELECTROMOTIVE FORCE), and will pump charge through conductors much as a water pump circulates water in a radiator heating system (see CIRCUIT, ELECTRIC). Batteries create a constant voltage, and so produce a steady or **direct current** (DC); many generators on the other hand provide a voltage which changes in sign many times a second, and so produce an **alternating current** (AC) in which the charges move to and fro instead of continuously in one direction. This system has advantages in generation, transmission and application, and is now used almost universally for domestic and industrial purposes.

An electric current is found to produce a MAGNETIC FIELD circulating around it, to experience a force in an externally generated magnetic field, and to be itself generated by a changing magnetic field; for more details of these properties on which most electrical machinery depends, see ELECTROMAGNETISM.

Static electricity was known to the Greeks; the inverse square law was hinted at by J. PRIESTLEY in 1767 and later confirmed by H. CAVENDISH and C. A. COULOMB. G. S. OHM formulated his law of conduction in 1826, though its essentials were known before then. The common nature of all the "types of electricity" then known was demonstrated in 1826 by M. FARADAY, who also originated the concept of electric field lines.

ELECTRIC LIGHT. See LIGHTING.

ELECTRIC METER, a single-phase AC watt-hour meter used to measure the amount of ELECTRICITY used by domestic consumers. It is a sort of simple electric MOTOR with a disk free to rotate in the magnetic field set up by two sets of coils, one in series with (the current coil), and the other in parallel to (the potential coil), the applied load. The rate of rotation is proportional to the POWER being used and

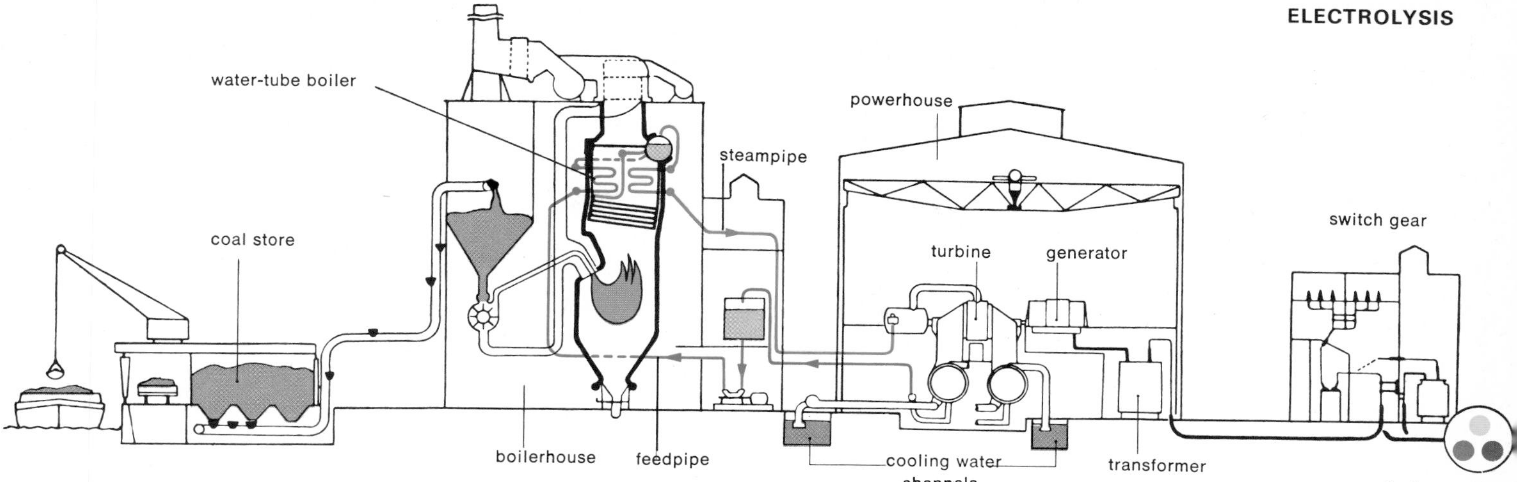

Cutaway of a typical fossil-fuel-fired electricity generating plant. Over 40% of US electric power is generated in coal-fired plants such as this. An automatically stoked water-tube boiler supplies superheated steam to a steam turbine which drives an electric generator. The output transformer then steps up the output voltage to the 100–765kV customary for primary three-phase transmission.

so, by counting the rotations mechanically, the total ENERGY consumption can be measured.

ELECTRIC MOTOR. See MOTOR, ELECTRIC.

ELECTRIC POWER. See ELECTRICITY; POWER.

ELECTRIC SHOCK, passage of a small electric current through the body, usually causing unpleasant sensations, powerful MUSCLE spasm and sometimes stunning. Low energy shocks are rarely fatal but may cause superficial burns; high energy shocks cause ELECTROCUTION. Small electric shocks are used in SHOCK THERAPY and in defibrillation of the HEART.

ELECTROCARDIOGRAPH, instrument for recording the electrical activity of the HEART, producing its results in the form of multiple tracing called an electrocardiogram (ECG). These are conventionally recorded with twelve combinations of ELECTRODES on the limbs and CHEST wall. The electrical impulses in the conducting tissue and muscle of the heart pass through the body fluids, while the position of the electrodes determines the way in which the heart is "looked at" in electrical terms. ECGs allow CORONARY THROMBOSIS, abnormal heart rhythm, disorders of the heart muscle and PERICARDIUM to be detected, as well as diseases of the METABOLISM that affect the heart.

ELECTROCHEMICAL SERIES, or electromotive series, a sequence of elements (chiefly metals) listed in order of their standard redox potentials—i.e., the potential developed by an electrode of the element immersed in a molar solution (see MOLECULAR WEIGHT) of one of its salts (see ELECTROCHEMISTRY; OXIDATION AND REDUCTION). Metals high in the series are generally more reactive than those lower down, and displace them from aqueous solutions of their salts. (See also ELECTRONEGATIVITY; IONIZATION POTENTIAL.)

ELECTROCHEMISTRY, branch of PHYSICAL CHEMISTRY dealing with the interconversion of electrical and chemical energy (see CELL, ELECTROCHEMICAL). Many chemical species are electrically-charged IONS (see BOND, CHEMICAL), and a large class of reactions—OXIDATION AND REDUCTION—consists of electron-transfer reactions between ions and other species. If the two half-reactions (oxidation, reduction) are made to occur at different ELECTRODES, the electron-transfer occurs by the passing of a current through an external circuit between them (see BATTERY; FUEL CELL). The ELECTROMOTIVE FORCE driving the current is the sum of the electrode potentials (in volts) of the half-reactions, which represent the free energy (see THERMODYNAMICS) produced by them. Conversely, if an emf is applied across the electrodes of a cell, it causes a chemical reaction if it is greater than the sum of the potentials of the half-reactions (see ELECTROLYSIS). Such potentials depend both on the nature of the reaction and on the concentrations of the reactants. Cells arising through concentration differences are one cause of CORROSION. (See also CONDUCTIVITY; ELECTROMETALLURGY; ELECTROPHORESIS.)

ELECTROCUTION, the usually fatal effect of passing a high-energy electric current through the body. ELECTRICITY passing through the body fluid, which acts as a resistor, causes BURNS at sites of connection and along the electrical pathway. CONVULSIONS and rhythm disturbance in the heart are usual; the latter are the cause of immediate death. ARTIFICIAL RESPIRATION with cardiac massage must be started immediately if resuscitation is to be successful.

ELECTRODE, a component in an electric CIRCUIT at which current is transferred between ordinary metal conductors and a gas or electrolyte. A positive electrode is an ANODE and a negative one a CATHODE.

ELECTRODYNAMICS, the study of the interaction of charged particles with ELECTROMAGNETIC FIELDS, as summarized in the definitions of ELECTRIC and MAGNETIC FIELDS through the FORCES experienced by charged particles and described by the MAXWELL Equations.

ELECTROENCEPHALOGRAPH, instrument for recording the BRAIN's electrical activity using several small electrodes on the scalp. Its results are produced in the form of a multiple tracing called an electroencephalogram (EEG). The "brain waves" recorded have certain normal patterns in the alert and sleeping individual. Localized brain diseases and metabolic disturbances cause abnormal wave forms either in particular areas or as a generalized disturbance. The abnormal brain activity in EPILEPSY, both during CONVULSIONS and when the patient appears normal, usually allows diagnosis. The interpretation of EEGs requires skill and experience.

ELECTROFORMING, process for making an exact replica of an object. A wax mold is made and electroplated with copper (see ELECTROPLATING). Masters for pressing records and duplicate plates (**"electrotype"**) for letterpress PRINTING are made thus, the copper shells being backed with lead.

ELECTROLUMINESCENCE, the emission of LIGHT from some PHOSPHORS (particularly ZnS) and SEMICONDUCTORS under the influence of an applied ELECTRIC FIELD. Electrophotoluminescent screens (in which the effect is PHOTON activated) are used medically to intensify X-ray pictures. (See also LUMINESCENCE.)

ELECTROLYSIS, Cosmetic, treatment designed to remove cosmetically unwanted HAIR—usually from the face—by a form of DIATHERMY, in which electric current is passed into the hair causing destruction of the hair follicle, and thus preventing regrowth. Permanent scarring may be an undesired end result.

ELECTROLYSIS, production of a chemical reaction by passing a direct current through an electrolyte—i.e., a compound which contains IONS when molten or in solution. (See ELECTROCHEMISTRY.) The CATIONS move toward the CATHODE and the ANIONS toward the ANODE, thus carrying the current. At each electrode the ions are discharged according to FARADAY's laws: (1) the quantity of a substance produced is proportional to the amount of electricity passed; (2) the relative quantities of different substances produced are proportional to their EQUIVALENT WEIGHTS. Hence one gram-equivalent of any substance is produced by the same amount of electricity, known as a **faraday** (96 500 coulombs). Electrolysis is used to extract electropositive metals from their ores (see ELECTROCHEMICAL SERIES), and to

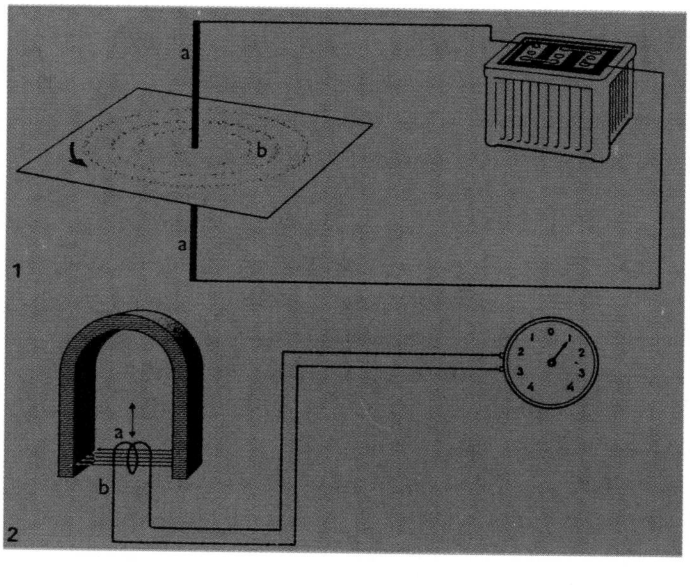

The close relationship between electricity and magnetism can be demonstrated in a number of ways. 1, When an electric current is passed through a wire conductor (a) it gives rise to a radial magnetic field. If iron filings are spread on a sheet of paper with the wire passing perpendicularly through a hole at its center and the paper is gently tapped, the filings will display the magnetic field pattern (b). 2, While a probe coil is moving through a magnetic field, an electromotive force is induced in it. If the circuit is completed via a galvanometer, it will reveal that a current flows while the coil is moving.

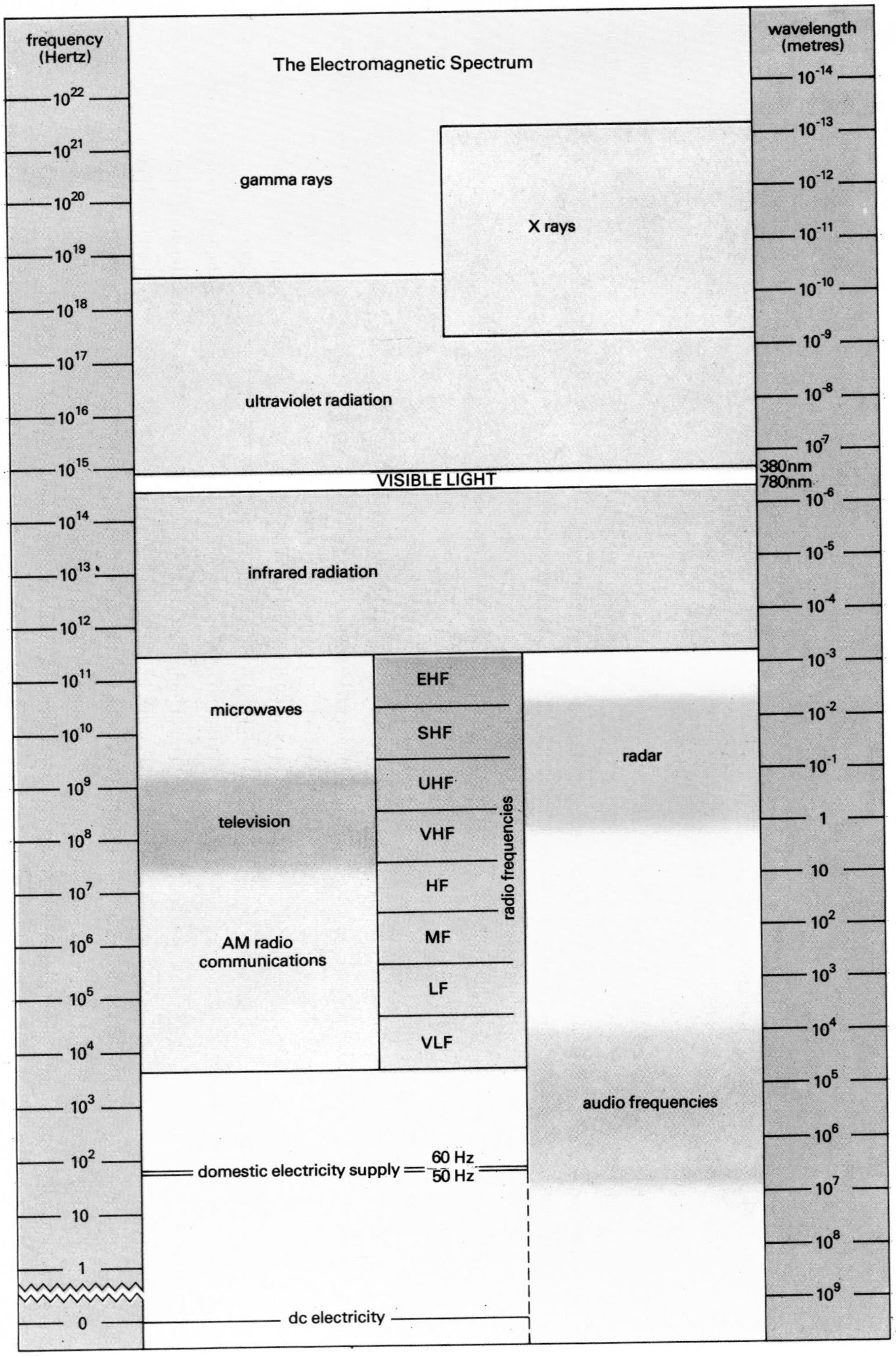

refine less electropositive metals; to produce SODIUM hydroxide, CHLORINE, HYDROGEN, OXYGEN and many other substances; and in ELECTROMETALLURGY.

ELECTROMAGNET, a magnet produced (and thus easily controlled) by the electric current in a coil of wire which is usually wound on a frame of highly permeable (see PERMEABILITY) material so as to reinforce and direct the MAGNETIC FIELD appropriately.

ELECTROMAGNETIC FIELD, any combination of ELECTRIC and MAGNETIC FIELDS, the two being closely related physically.

ELECTROMAGNETIC RADIATION, or radiant energy, the form in which ENERGY is transmitted through space or matter using a varying ELECTROMAGNETIC FIELD. Classically, radiant energy is regarded as a WAVE MOTION. In the mid-19th century MAXWELL showed that an oscillating (vibrating) electric charge would be surrounded by varying electric and magnetic fields. Energy would be lost from the oscillating charge in the form of transverse waves in these fields, the waves in the electric field being at right-angles both to those in the magnetic field and to the direction in which the waves are traveling (propagated). Moreover, the VELOCITY of the waves would depend only on the properties of the medium through which they passed; for propagation in a vacuum its value is a fundamental constant of physics—the **electromagnetic constant,** $c =$ 299 792.5km/s. At the beginning of the 20th century PLANCK proposed that certain properties of radiant energy were best explained by regarding it as transporting energy in discrete amounts called quanta. EINSTEIN later proposed the name PHOTON for the electromagnetic quantum. The energy of each photon is proportional to the frequency of the associated radiation (see QUANTUM THEORY).

The different kinds of electromagnetic radiation are classified according to the energy of the photons involved, the range of energies being known as the electromagnetic SPECTRUM. (Looked at in other ways, this spectrum arranges the radiations according to wavelength or frequency.) In order of decreasing energy the principal kinds are GAMMA RAYS, X-RAYS, ULTRAVIOLET RADIATION, LIGHT, INFRARED RADIATION, MICROWAVES and RADIO waves. In general, the higher the energies involved, the better the properties of the radiation are described in terms of particles (photons) rather than waves. Radiant energy is emitted from objects when they are heated (see BLACKBODY RADIATION) or otherwise energetically excited (see LUMINESCENCE; SPECTROSCOPY); man uses it to channel and distribute both energy and information (see INFORMATION THEORY). (See also ABSORPTION.)

ELECTROMAGNETISM, the study of ELECTRIC and MAGNETIC FIELDS, and their interaction with electric charges and currents. The two fields are in fact different manifestations of the same physical field, and are interconverted according to the speed of the observer. Apart from the effects noted under ELECTRICITY and MAGNETISM, the following are found:

1. Moving charges (and hence currents) in magnetic fields experience a FORCE, perpendicular to the field and the current, and proportional to their product. This is the basis of all electric MOTORS, and was first applied for the purpose by M. FARADAY in 1821.

2. A change in the number of magnetic field lines passing through a circuit "induces" an electric field in the circuit, proportional to the rate of the change. This is the basis of most GENERATORS, and was also established by M. Faraday, in 1831.

3. An effect analogous to the above, but with magnetic and electric fields interchanged, and usually much smaller. This was hypothesized by J. C. MAXWELL, who in 1862 deduced from it the possibility of self-sustaining electromagnetic waves traveling at a speed which coincided with that of LIGHT, thereby identifying the nature of visible light, and predicting other waves such as the RADIO waves found experimentally by H. HERTZ shortly afterwards.

ELECTROMETALLURGY, branch of METALLURGY which uses electricity. It includes the use of ELECTRIC FURNACES, and also the use of ELECTROLYSIS for extracting and refining metals, ELECTROPLATING, ANODIZING and ELECTROFORMING.

ELECTROMOTIVE FORCE (emf), loosely, the voltage produced by a BATTERY, GENERATOR or other source of ELECTRICITY, but more precisely, the product of the current it produces in a circuit and the total circuit RESISTANCE, including that of the source itself. The actual voltage across the source is usually somewhat lower.

ELECTRON, a stable SUBATOMIC PARTICLE, with rest MASS 9.1091×10^{-31}kg (roughly 1/1836 the mass of a HYDROGEN atom) and a negative charge of 1.6021×10^{-19}C, the charges of other particles being positive or negative integral multiples of this. Electrons are one of the basic constituents of ordinary MATTER, commonly occupying the ORBITALS surrounding positively charged atomic nuclei. The chemical properties of ATOMS and MOLECULES are largely determined by the behavior of the electrons in their highest-energy orbitals. Both CATHODE RAYS and BETA RAYS are streams of free electrons passing through a gas or vacuum. The unidirectional motion of electrons in a solid conductor constitutes an electric current. Solid conductors differ from nonconductors in that in the former some electrons are free to move about while in the latter all are permanently associated with particular nuclei. Free electrons in a gas or vacuum can usually be treated as classical particles, though their wave properties become important when they interact with or are associated with atomic nuclei. The anti-electron, with identical mass but an equivalent positive charge, is known as a positron (see ANTIMATTER).

ELECTRONEGATIVITY, the relative power of an

atom in a molecule to attract electrons. A concept variously defined and estimated since its proposal by L. PAULING, it depends on the atom's VALENCE state (see BOND, CHEMICAL) and is useful only as a qualitative guide to polarity of bonds and molecules. Electropositive metals are generally high in the ELECTROCHEMICAL SERIES. (See also NUCLEOPHILES.)

ELECTRON GUN, that part of an ELECTRON TUBE which produces, accelerates, focuses and deflects a beam of ELECTRONS. A CATHODE emits electrons which pass through a grid to the steering ANODES.

ELECTRONIC FLASH, a glass tube containing inert gas, used as a light source in photography and having a useful life of over 10 000 flashes. A high-voltage pulse applied to electrodes at either end creates a discharge through the gas, giving a daylight-type flash lasting from 1ms to 1μs.

ELECTRONIC MUSIC, compositions in which musicians use sounds created solely on electronic equipment. **Concrete Music** uses recordings of natural sounds as the basis for composition; and works mixing both approaches are called "tape music." Experiments with electronic composition began as early as the 1890s but widespread production began only after WWII, as universities and broadcasting authorities in many countries began setting up studios to encourage this use of modern technology. John CAGE, Karlheinz STOCKHAUSEN and Edgar VARÈSE have produced important works in this field.

ELECTRONICS, an applied science dealing with the development and behavior of ELECTRON TUBES, SEMICONDUCTORS and other devices in which the motion of electrons is controlled; it covers the behavior of electrons in gases, vacuums, conductors and semiconductors. Its theoretical basis lies in the principles of ELECTROMAGNETISM and solid-state physics discovered in the late 19th and early 20th centuries. Electronics began to grow in the 1920s with the development of RADIO. During WWII, the US and UK concentrated resources on the invention of RADAR and pulse transmission methods and by 1945 they had enormous industrial capacity for producing electronic equipment. The invention of the TRANSISTOR in 1948 as a small, cheap replacement for vacuum tubes led to the rapid development of COMPUTERS, transistor radios, etc. Now, with the widespread use of integrated circuits, electronics plays a vital role in communications (TELEPHONE networks, information storage, etc.) and industry. All electronic circuits contain both active and passive components and transducers (e.g., MICROPHONES) which change ENERGY from one form to another. Sensors of light, temperature, etc., may also be present. **Passive components** are normally conductors and are characterized by their properties of RESISTANCE (R), CAPACITANCE (C) and INDUCTANCE (L). One of these usually predominates, depending on the function required. **Active components** are electron tubes or semiconductors; they contain a source of power and control electron flow. The former may be general-purpose tubes (DIODES, TRIODES, etc., the name depending on the number of ELECTRODES) which rectify, amplify or switch electric signals. Image tubes (in TELEVISION receivers) convert an electric input into a light signal; photoelectric tubes (in television cameras) do the reverse. Semiconductor diodes and transistors, which are basically sandwiches made of two different types of semiconductor, now usually perform the general functions once done by tubes, being smaller, more robust and generating less heat. These few basic components can build up an enormous range of circuits with different functions. Common types include: power supply (converting AC to pulsing DC and then smoothing out the pulsations); switching and timing (the logic circuits in computers are in this category); AMPLIFIERS, which increase the amplitude or power of a signal, and oscillators, used in radio and television transmitters and which generate AC signals. Demands for increased cheapness and reliability of circuits have led to the development of microelectronics. In **printed circuits**, printed connections replace individual wiring on a flat board to which about two components per cm^3 are soldered. INTEGRATED CIRCUITS assemble about 10^5 components and interconnections per cm^3 in a single structure, formed directly by evaporation or other techniques as films about 0.03mm thick on a substrate. In monolithic circuits, components are produced in a tiny chip of semiconductor by selective diffusion.

ELECTRON MICROSCOPE, a microscope using a beam of ELECTRONS rather than LIGHT to study objects too small for conventional MICROSCOPES. First constructed by Max Knoll and Ernst Ruska around 1930, the instrument now consists typically of an evacuated column of magnetic lenses with a 20–1 000 kV electron gun at the top and a fluorescent screen or photographic plate at the bottom; it can thus be thought of as a kind of CATHODE RAY TUBE. The various lenses allow the operator to see details almost at the atomic level (0.3 nm) at up to a million times magnification (though many specimens deteriorate under the electron bombardment at these limits), and to obtain DIFFRACTION patterns from very small areas. In the scanning electron microscope, the beam is focused to a point and scanned over the specimen area while a synchronized television screen displays the transmitted or scattered electron intensity. Electron microscopes are used for structural, defect and composition studies in a wide range of biological and inorganic materials.

ELECTRON TUBE, or **valve,** an evacuated glass or metal tube which may contain gas at low pressure, through which ELECTRONS flow between two or more ELECTRODES. A heated filament, the cathode, emits electrons which are attracted to the positively-charged anode. By varying the voltage on intermediate (grid) electrodes, the electron flow can be regulated and the tube made to work as an AMPLIFIER. (See also DIODE; CATHODE-RAY TUBE; RECTIFIER; TRIODE.)

ELECTRONVOLT (**eV**), a unit of ENERGY used in atomic and high-energy physics, defined as the kinetic energy acquired by an ELECTRON in passing through a POTENTIAL difference of 1 volt in a vacuum. The electronvolt is about $1.602\,19 \times 10^{-19}$ joules.

ELECTROPHILES. See NUCLEOPHILES.

ELECTROPHORESIS, the DIFFUSION of charged particles through FLUIDS or GELS under the influence of an ELECTRIC FIELD. Particles with different sizes and charges diffuse at different rates, so that the effect can be used to separate and identify large MOLECULES such as PROTEINS.

ELECTROPLATING, process of depositing a thin metal coating on base-metal objects, to improve their appearance or CORROSION resistance (see also ELECTROFORMING). The object is made the CATHODE of a cell containing a salt of the metal to be deposited, which is made the ANODE; on ELECTROLYSIS the metal dissolves from the anode and deposits on the object. Chromium, nickel, copper, silver and gold are commonly used. In **electropolishing**, the reverse process, the object is made the anode; preferential solution of irregularities yields a high polish. (See also ANODIZING.)

ELECTROSCOPE, gold leaf, an instrument used (mainly historically) for the measurement of electric charge or potential (see ELECTRICITY), based on one or two fine gold foils suspended vertically and free to deflect under electrostatic repulsion when an electric charge was applied. Although never very accurate, the instruments could sometimes detect as little as 10^{-14} coulombs and were also used to measure radiation intensity through the rate of charge leakage caused by ionization of the air.

ELECTROSTATIC GENERATOR, an instrument producing a very high direct voltage, particularly that developed by Robert J. van de Graaff (1901–1967). An insulating belt is driven around a pair of rollers some distance apart, a small electric discharge at one end producing positively charged IONS which are carried by the belt to the other end and lifted off by a small metal comb, the charge accumulating on a polished metal sphere surrounding this end. Such generators can develop up to 20MV with a 15m sphere and are used in various ways as particle ACCELERATORS.

ELECTROSTATIC PHOTOGRAPHY. See XEROGRAPHY.

ELECTROSTATIC PRECIPITATOR, a device for removing solid or liquid particles from gases, capable of cleaning dirty ventilating air or removing tar or dust from the smoke of coal-burning plants. An electrical discharge is produced in the gas and the ELECTRONS released collide with the suspended particles carrying them toward the ANODE, where they accumulate for periodic removal.

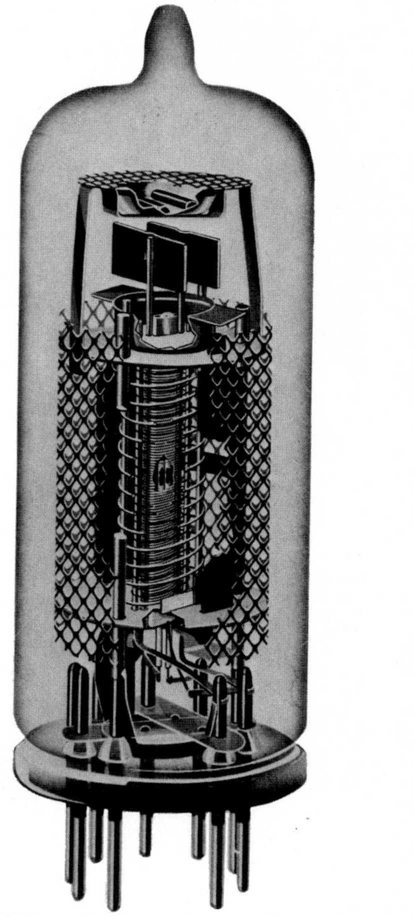

Cutaway diagram of a compact electron tube. This one is a pentode, having five electrodes. Outward from the center are the heater, the cathode, the three grids, the solid anode and, enclosing all, a mesh screen. At the top are cooling fins, the getter and a further screen.

ELECTROSTATICS, the study of static ELECTRICITY.

ELECTROTYPING. See ELECTROFORMING.

ELECTRUM, pale yellow ALLOY of GOLD with up to 40% SILVER, occurring naturally as gold ore, and used for ornament. The term has been used for AMBER.

ELEGY, in classical poetry, refers to a lyric poem of alternate two-line stanzas written in a distinctive meter on a variety of themes. However, the term has been used since the Renaissance to describe any poem expressing sorrow, particularly about death, such as Milton's *Lycidas* (1637) or Thomas Gray's *Elegy Written in a Country Churchyard* (1750).

ELEMENT, Chemical, simple substance composed of ATOMS of the same atomic number, and so incapable of chemical degradation or resolution. They are generally mixtures of different ISOTOPES. Of the 106 known elements, 88 occur in nature, and the rest have been synthesized (see TRANSURANIUM ELEMENTS). The elements are classified by physical properties as METALS, METALLOIDS and NONMETALS, and by chemical properties and atomic structure according to the PERIODIC TABLE. Most elements exhibit ALLOTROPY, and many are molecular (e.g., oxygen, O_2). The elements have all been built up in STARS from HYDROGEN by complex sequences of nuclear reactions, e.g., the CARBON CYCLE.

ELEMENTARY PARTICLES. See SUBATOMIC PARTICLES.

ELEMENTARY SCHOOL, grades 1–8 in the US

Electronics

Integrated circuits

A few years ago a calculator was something that sat on your desk; now you can carry one in your shirt pocket, wear a digital wristwatch or take your holiday snapshots with a computerized camera. Next year your automobile may be computer-controlled to regulate pollution and increase performance while reducing fuel consumption.

The key to much of this development is the integrated circuit, which has three advantages over conventional components: very small size, low cost and great reliability. For these reasons integrated circuits are being used in domestic products ranging from televisions to washing machines and in industrial equipment from cash registers to satellites.

Before World War II all electronic circuits were made with vacuum tubes which were large and mechanically fragile and which used a lot of power. In 1948 Shockley, Bardeen and Brattain of Bell Telephone Laboratories published the details of what is now known as the "transistor." They were subsequently awarded the Nobel Prize for this discovery. The transistor was made entirely within a single crystal of germanium, although today silicon is preferred. Being entirely solid (hence the term "solid state") the transistor is more robust than the tube. It is also much smaller and consumes about one-hundredth of its power. At first, like most new products, it was rather temperamental, but after many years of refining the manufacturing technique it has become the principal component in use today. The integrated circuit is a direct development from the transistor.

A transistor has three layers: the base, the collector and the emitter (see Fig. 1). A small current, made to flow into the base and out of the emitter, will control a much larger current in the collector-emitter circuit. The small current is therefore amplified. It is by this means that the small signals received by a transistor radio set can be amplified and converted to audio-frequency to emerge as sound from the speaker. The "sandwich" construction of a transistor is made entirely within a single, ultra-pure crystal of silicon. The layers of the sandwich are former by impurities placed in the crystal by a process which will be described later. The type of impurity described in each layer is different; there are two sorts: the n-type, such as phosphorus, which supplies extra electrons to the lattice; and the p-type, such as boron, which absorbs electrons from the lattice. These modifications control the conducting properties of the lattice. A transistor sandwich is either n-p-n or p-n-p. The transistor we have described is an n-p-n sandwich. A p-n-p sandwich works in just the same way but the current flows in the opposite direction (see Fig. 2).

The whole device is a "chip" of silicon about 20-thousandths of an inch square and a few thousandths thick. However, if you buy a transistor in your local radio store, you will find that it is apparently much larger. Cut it open and you will see why—it's all packaging! No one could handle bare transistors, because they are too small. The packaging makes them big enough and strong enough to withstand even the most clumsy fingers. If we could build some more components into the chip of silicon the package would still be no larger, and would probably cost no more, because the packaging is much more expensive than the transistor itself.

Necessity, economic or otherwise, is the mother of invention—people soon began to put more components on the chip and the integrated circuit was born. It began in a fairly small way but has grown quite remarkably during the 1970s. At first there were 10 components on the chip, then 50, then 1 000, and recently several tens of thousands.

As one may guess from the name, an integrated circuit (i.c.) is a complete circuit in one package. This would otherwise have been built with diodes, resistors, capacitors and inductors as well as transistors. It can be seen from Fig. 3 that diodes and resistors can be made in a similar way to transistors. Capacitors are more difficult to fabricate, and a satisfactory method for including inductors in an integrated circuit has yet to be found. Much attention is therefore devoted to avoiding their use.

Not only is the packaging the major cost in making a transistor, but it is also the cause of most of the failures. The failure rate of a whole integrated circuit is almost exactly the same as that of an individual transistor. Suppose that an integrated circuit contains the equivalent of 1 000 components. If you built a version with individual components and discovered that one component failed every six months, you could expect the integrated circuit version to fail once about every 500 years!

Integrated circuits, like transistors, are made from silicon, a metallic-looking solid. The silicon used must be very pure, and special techniques have been developed for refining it. The principal method is zone-refining, which relies on the impurities being soluble in molten silicon and remaining in the melt rather than solidifying with the silicon. A coil is placed around a crystal rod of nearly pure silicon (Fig. 4). A very-high-frequency alternating current is then passed through the coil, which causes the rod to heat up, and a thin section inside the coil melts. The coil is moved slowly down the rod, melting the part inside it as it goes. The silicon solidifies again as the coil moves on, but the impurities remain in the molten silicon and so are carried to the end of the rod. This is repeated many times until the silicon is sufficiently pure, and then the end of the rod, which now contains all the impurities, is cut off. The purity of the silicon used today is better than one part of impurity in ten billion (10 000 000 000) parts of silicon—about the same as one grain of sand in a ton of sugar. The pure silicon thus made is then melted, and a tiny "seed" crystal is dipped into the melt. The seed is slowly rotated and pulled out of the melt, growing over a period of hours into a single crystal of silicon about nine inches long. In the late 1960s such crystals were about one inch thick; now they can be made three inches thick, producing larger wafers and better yield. The crystal is once more zone-refined and the ultra-pure crystal is sliced. The disks produced, which are about six-thousandths of an inch long, are polished ready to be made into integrated circuits.

To make a disk—or "wafer" as it is called—into an integrated circuit, layers of impurities must be placed inside to form the components. These layers are inserted one at a time starting with the deepest. Within each layer the location of the impurity is defined by the opaque material in a "mask" like a stencil.

The masks are first drawn many times actual size so that the circuit is about two feet across. Even at this stage a draftsman could not draw them accurately enough without the aid of a machine called a coordinatograph. This large pattern is photographed and reduced in size. Since many circuits will be made from each wafer, hundreds of copies of this pattern are assembled, photographed and reduced in size again. The actual mask is made on a glass carrier, and the pattern, originally two feet across, is now about a tenth of an inch.

The mask is transferred to the crystal by another photographic process (see Fig. 5). A layer of silicon dioxide is grown on the surface of the wafer by heating it in oxygen. This in turn is covered by a layer of photoresist, and the wafer, with the mask on top, is exposed to ultraviolet radiation. Where the photoresist is irradiated through the transparent parts of the mask, it hardens, whereas under the opaque sections it is still soft and is quickly washed off. The unprotected silicon dioxide is now etched away to expose bare silicon. Finally the hardened resist is removed so that it does not interfere with the rest of the process, leaving a mask of silicon dioxide attached to the surface of the wafer.

The principal method of implanting the impurities or "doping" the silicon is by diffusion. The wafer is heated in a furnace in an atmosphere of the impurity required. The high temperature opens up the crystal lattice slightly and atoms of impurity slowly diffuse in. By controlling the temperature of the furnace and the concentration of impurity in the atmosphere, both the depth and concentration of impurities in the silicon can be controlled. No impurities diffuse through the silicon dioxide layer. The last stage of diffusion is to grow another layer of silicon dioxide over the surface ready for the next mask.

A more recent method of inserting the impurities, which is gaining in popularity, is ion implantation. In this process the diffusion furnace is replaced by a "gun" which fires the impurity atoms at the crystal. Some of the atoms penetrate the lattice through the gaps in the silicon dioxide layer and lodge inside. The gun is easier to control than the furnace, so it is more suited to very precise "light" doping of circuits. Light doping is used to give low power consumption in circuits such as those used for wristwatches.

After the last layer has been added the circuit is complete except for a few remaining connections between parts of the circuit and some metalized areas to which the leadout wires are bonded. Aluminum is evaporated onto the wafer for these and is insulated from the circuit, except where contact is required, by a layer of silicon dioxide which fortunately is an electrical insulator. The wafer is finally scribed with a diamond and broken up into individual circuits to be packaged and tested ready for sale.

In this description of the manufacture of an integrated circuit two problems have been left aside, the solutions of which are interrelated. These problems are registration and yield.

If you look at a cheap comic book you will see many examples of bad registration. The red of the heroine's lips is not in place below her nose but slightly to the left of it. Not only that but the same red used for the villain's blood is coming from a hole to the left of the bullet-hole made by the hero. In a similar way the masks used in the manufacture of an integrated circuit will never match up exactly. Since things must be arranged so that the maximum number of circuits work, the smallest size of component is limited to that at which the effects of bad registration are just becoming noticeable. If registration can be improved the circuit can be smaller. This means either that there are more circuits per wafer and each circuit is cheaper, or that there are the same number of circuits each costing the same as before, and that each circuit is more complicated (for example, the calculator circuit may now have a memory as well).

Assuming that the registration and the diffusion are right, why don't all the circuits work? The answer is that the original crystal had imperfections in it. The imperfections will ruin some circuits, but the more circuits per chip the greater the yield—the percentage of those that work (see Fig. 6). So the smaller the circuit, the greater the yield and the more circuits there are per wafer—a two-way winner. Manufacturers are therefore always looking for ways to improve registration—or to reduce the number of masks, which has the same effect. The rapid introduction of the "field-effect transistor" into integrated circuits has been because it uses fewer masks than a conventional transistor.

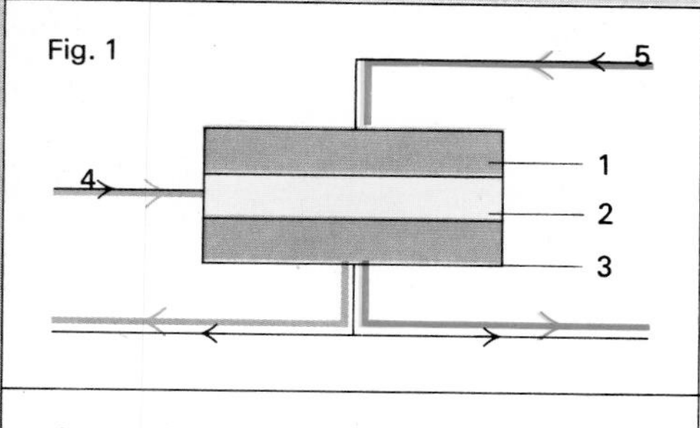

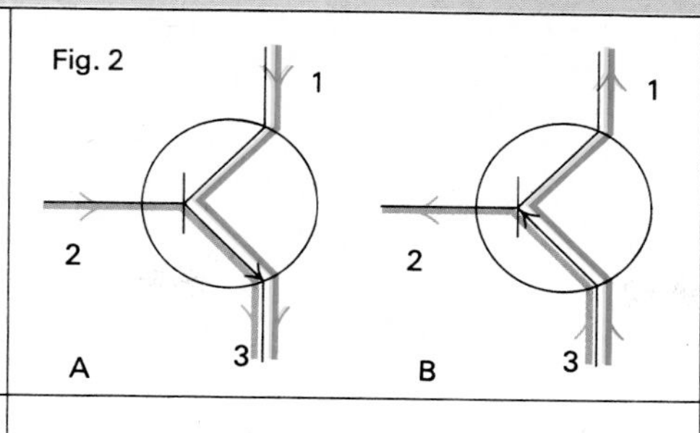

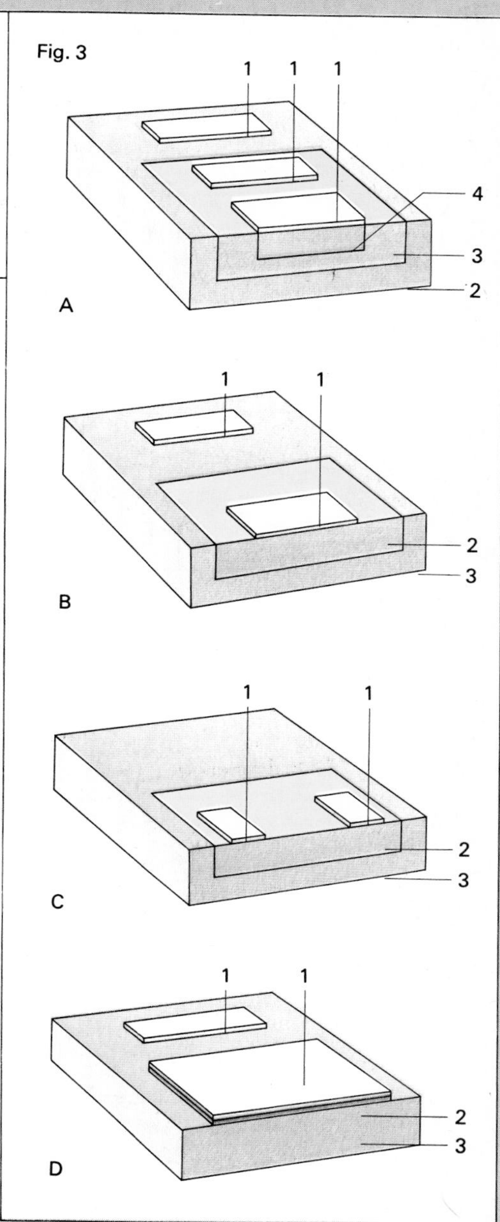

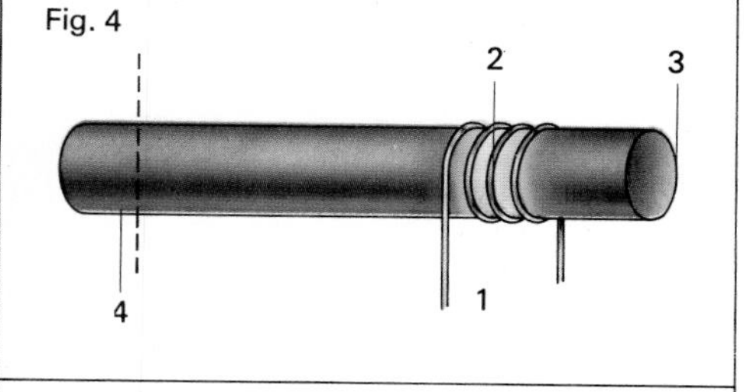

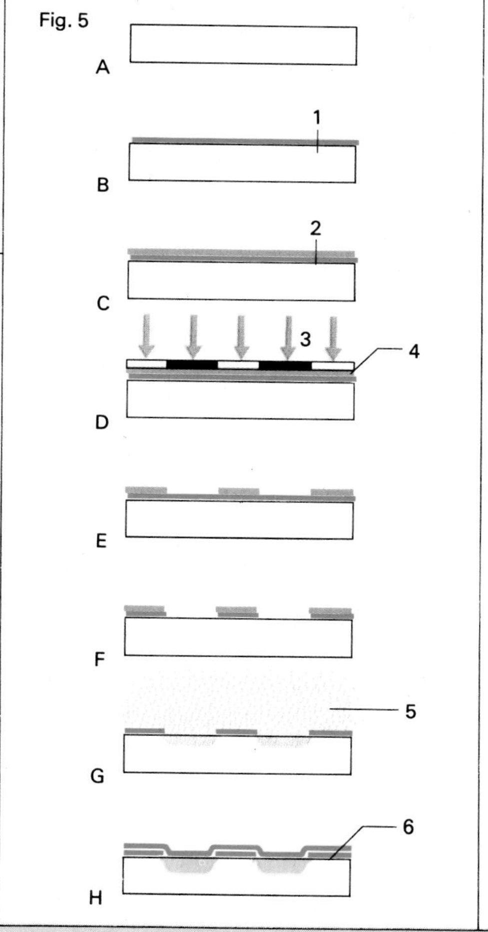

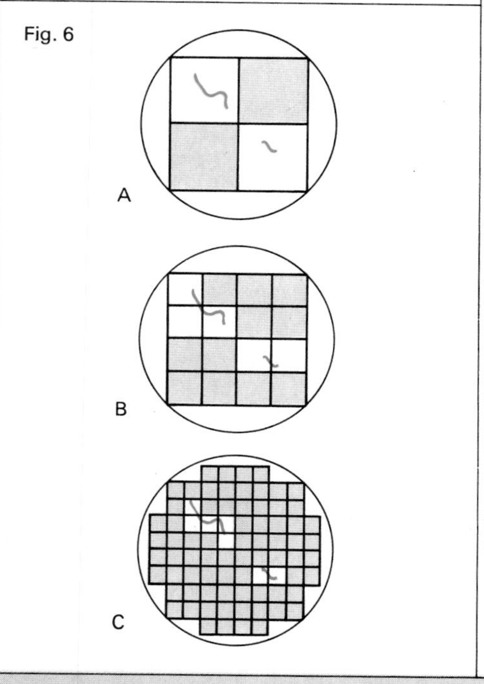

1. A schematic diagram of a transistor, with collector (1), base (2) and emitter (3). The small current (4) controls a much larger current (5). **2.** The symbols for a transistor in a circuit diagram, with collector (1), base (2) and emitter (3). (A) shows an n-p-n transistor; (B) a p-n-p transistor. The arrow on the emitter is said to remind the engineer which way the current is flowing! **3.** Components in integrated form (about 350 × actual size). The leadout wires are attached to the metallized areas (1) in each case. (A) A "diffused" transistor, with collector (2), base (3) and emitter (4). (B) A diode, with p-type anode (2) and n-type cathode (3). (C) A resistor of p-type material (2) in an n-type substrate (3). (D) A capacitor, with a thin layer of silicon dioxide (2) acting as the dielectric; the substrate (3) may be p- or n-type. **4.** Zone-refining. The heating coil (1), with a thin molten section inside it (2), is moved slowly from the pure end of the rod (3) to the other (4), which is cut off. **5.** The stages in implanting impurities in a silicon wafer by diffusion. The wafer (A) is heated in oxygen, acquiring (B) a layer of silicon dioxide (1). (C) A layer of photoresist (2) is added; and (D) is exposed to ultraviolet radiation (3) through a mask (4). The parts of the photoresist that remain soft are washed off (E). Etching (F) removes also the corresponding parts of the silicon dioxide layer. (G) The selected impurities (5) are allowed to diffuse in. (H) Further heating in oxygen yields a further layer of silicon dioxide (6), ready for the process to be repeated. **6.** Imperfections in a wafer cause circuits containing them to be spoiled, but the percentage wasted decreases as the number of circuits increases. (A) 4 circuits, 50% spoiled. (B) 16 circuits, 31% spoiled. (C) 80 circuits, 9% spoiled.

Integrated circuits are ideal for use in equipment where a single circuit is repeated many times. The first widespread use was in computers and other numerical machines which use many identical circuits, perhaps tens of thousands. As manufacturers became more confident, larger circuits were put onto one chip and the number of packages was reduced. Engineers naturally responded by building more complex machines; so these days, computers no longer get smaller: they get faster, more powerful and more sophisticated. The pocket calculator was a valuable by-product of this progression, which is affecting the whole of Western society. The market for these devices appears to be so large that it has become a field of its own, and progress has been both great and fast. Last year's model and perhaps even last month's model are already out-of-date! One can imagine future generations finding it very difficult to add without the help of a calculator.

By no means all integrated circuits are used in computers. There are a vast number known as "linear" circuits which are used in non-numerical equipment. Development in this field has been slower than the explosive expansion of the digital types. Linear circuits are now used in TV sets, radios and Hi-Fi sets, and shortly will be used in washing machines and other domestic equipment.

What of the future? It is hard to predict what will happen next. Undoubtedly the integrated circuit can be made to do far more than has yet been achieved, but we may have to wait for some other fields to catch up. It will soon be possible to talk to a computer using your voice instead of a typewriter. You will then be able to dial-a-computer and tell it your problems if the calculator in your wristwatch can't give you the answer. Perhaps the next development will be in data-handling which, using your TV set and telephone, could call a library larger than the National Library of Congress into your living room, select your book, and "open" it to the right page. Perhaps your car will be capable of driving itself and finding its own parking space. Whatever the next development, you can be sure that somewhere inside will be an integrated circuit or two running the show.

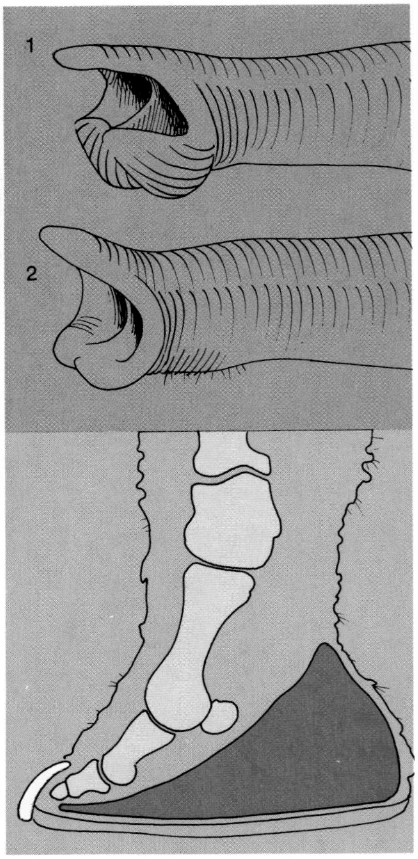

The African elephant, seen here, has much larger ears than its Indian cousin; the first one seen in America was brought over by the famous showman P. T. Barnum, in the 1870s, and rapidly became the most popular animal in his circus. Its nickname, Jumbo, has since stuck as a pet name for any elephant. The most peculiar feature of the elephant is its arm-like trunk with a snout which can be used to pick up even quite small objects. The trunk tip of an African elephant (1) has a double "lip," while the Indian elephant (2) has a single lip. Below is a section through the lower part of an elephant's powerful leg showing bones of the foot.

educational system, designed to teach children the "elements" of learning. Elementary public education began in Mass. in the 1640s with a law ordering that all children should be taught to read. However, "common schools" were few and poor until the 1830s when the workingmen's societies took up the cause for public education. Universal literacy became a principle of Jacksonian democracy and the emphasis shifted from religious instruction to preparation for enlightened citizenship. This attitude of government responsibility led to the establishment of the US Office of Education in 1867 and finally to national standards of compulsory elementary schooling. (See also EDUCATION.)

ELEPHANT BIRDS, *Aepyornis*, flightless birds of Madagascar, recently extinct. Resembling massive ostriches, they stood up to 3m (10ft) high and may have inspired the legend of the giant roc.

ELEPHANT FISH, three genera of the Elephant or Rabbit fish, so called because of their extraordinary pectoral fins which are large and lie high on the sides of the body. They are oviparous as in the SHARK family. Distribution is widespread from Scandinavian waters to the Tropics.

ELEPHANTIASIS, disease in which there is massive swelling and hypertrophy of the SKIN and subcutaneous tissue of the legs or scrotum, due to the obstructed flow of LYMPH. This may be a congenital DISEASE, due to trauma, CANCER, or infection with FILARIASIS, TUBERCULOSIS and some VENEREAL DISEASES. Recurrent secondary bacterial infections are common and chronic skin ULCERS may form. Elevation, elastic stockings, DIURETICS and treatment of infection are basic to relief, while some cases are helped by SURGERY.

ELEPHANTINE, now Jazirat Aswān, an island in the Nile opposite Aswan. Papyruses from the 5th century BC describing a colony of Jewish mercenaries were found here (1903). Important as a frontier post in ancient times, it was also the site of a temple and a nilometer built to gauge the level of the Nile.

ELEPHANTS, the largest living land mammals, comprising two species, the African *Loxodonta africana* and the Indian *Elephas maximus*. The African elephant is up to 3.3m (11ft) tall and may weigh 6 tonnes; the Indian species is slightly smaller. Both species are characterized by their trunks, elongated extensions of the nose and upper lip, and by huge incisor teeth in the males prized as the source of ivory. The African elephant has large ears that distinguish it from the Indian species. Both live in herds feeding on grass and foliage. In spite of, and because of, its size the Indian elephant has long been tamed as a beast of burden.

ELEPHANT SEALS, large SEALS, up to 6.7m (22ft) long, named for their large snouts that resemble an elephant's trunk. The northern species is found along the Pacific coast near Cal. and the Southern elephant seal lives in subantarctic waters, especially near the Falkland Islands.

ELEPHANT SHREW, name given to several insect-eating RODENTS of Africa, so-called because of their elongated, pointed snouts. There are more than 15 species which have brown or gray fur and long tails.

ELEUSINIAN MYSTERIES, secret religious rites of the seasons in ancient Greece. They were originally performed in honor of DEMETER at Eleusis near Athens and dramatized the descent of PERSEPHONE into the underworld. Later the rites were performed in Athens.

ELEUSIS, ancient and present-day Greek city about 14mi NW of Athens. It was the scene of extensive excavations from 1882 onwards which uncovered the sacred precinct where the ELEUSINIAN MYSTERIES were performed.

ELEUTHERA, one of the BAHAMAS islands (164sq mi in area) settled in the mid-17th century by religious dissenters from Bermuda. It is primarily agricultural, and the principal city is Governor's Harbour.

ELEUTHERIUS, Saint, pope from c175–189, who was the source of many legends. He was born in Epirus, Greece and his feast day is May 26.

ELEVATOR, in aeronautics, one of the three basic control surfaces of an AIRPLANE, used to control pitch. Elevators are usually pivoted on the stabilizer.

ELEVATOR, or **lift,** a device installed in a building for carrying passengers and freight vertically between levels. Most modern lifts are electrically powered and many are now electronically controlled. The MOTOR is now usually mounted at the top of the elevator well with the elevator car slung below. The weight of the empty car plus about 40% of its designed load is offset by a traveling counterweight at the other end of the suspension cable. Modern elevator installations feature a galaxy of safety devices including automatic door locks, emergency brakes and buffers at the foot of the well.

ELGAR, Sir Edward William (1857–1934), English composer. In general Elgar followed the German orchestral and choral traditions of the 19th century, but his *Enigma Variations* and *Pomp and Circumstance* marches reflected a style which was clearly English in character. His other works include the oratorio *The Dream of Gerontius*, two symphonies, violin and cello concertos, and the concert overture *Cockaigne*.

ELGIN, city in NE Ill., on the Fox R. It is an industrial center, particularly known for watchmaking, and is the home of Elgin Academy and Elgin Community College. Pop 55691.

ELGIN, James Bruce, 8th Earl of (1811–1863), British Governor-General of Canada (1847–54) who implemented limited self-government. He also served as envoy to China and Japan and was viceroy of India (1861–63).

ELGIN MARBLES, ancient sculptures (mostly from the Athenian ACROPOLIS) brought to Britain by Thomas Bruce, 7th Earl of Elgin and British envoy at Constantinople (1799–1802). Now in the British Museum, they include a frieze from the Parthenon and parts of the Erechtheum temple.

EL GRECO. See GRECO, EL.

ELI, high priest of the temple of Shiloh, according to the Old Testament. The prophet SAMUEL was entrusted in boyhood to his care.

ELIJAH, Hebrew prophet of the late 9th century BC, mentioned in the Koran and the Old Testament Book of Kings. He fought against the worship of BAAL introduced from Phoenicia during the reign of King Ahab of Israel by his Queen, JEZEBEL. In the New Testament Elijah appears with Christ at the TRANSFIGURATION.

ELIJAH MUHAMMAD. See MUHAMMAD, ELIJAH.

ELIMINATION, the technique used in the solution of simultaneous equations by which n equations in n VARIABLES are reduced to one solvable equation in one variable, the process being repeated until all the equations are solved for all the variables. The process may be performed by establishing the value of one variable in terms of another and substitution; or by the addition to or subtraction from one equation of another. Thus

if $\quad x-6=y \quad$ (1)

and $\quad 2x+3=y \quad$ (2)

we can substitute the value of y in equation (1) into equation (2) to give

$$2x+3=x-6$$

and hence $\quad x=-9.$

Substituting this value into equation (1) gives $y=-15$. (See also EQUATION.)

ELIOT, Charles William (1834–1926), US educator, President of Harvard University from 1869–1909 and editor of the original *Harvard Classics* series. Eliot had a profound influence on American education.

ELIOT, George (1819–1880), pseudonym of the famous English novelist, Mary Ann Evans. Her work, notably *Adam Bede* (1859), *The Mill on the Floss* (1860), *Silas Marner* (1861), *Middlemarch* (1871–72) and *Daniel Deronda* (1876) brought a new breadth of intellect, technical sophistication and moral scope to the English novel and greatly influenced later novelists. Her creative work was encouraged by writer and editor George Henry Lewes, with whom she lived for 24 years, defying convention. She was a friend of Herbert SPENCER, was subeditor of the *Westminster Review* (1851–53) and a notable translator of German works.

ELIOT, John (1604–1690), Puritan clergyman known as the "apostle to the Indians." Born in England, he emigrated to Mass. in 1631 and devoted himself to the conversion of local Indians. He established over a dozen missions in New England, most of which were destroyed in KING PHILIP'S WAR.

ELIOT, Sir John (1592–1632), English radical politician. He was an eloquent Parliamentary critic of royal policies, but his advocacy of such reforms as the PETITION OF RIGHT (1628) angered CHARLES I who ordered Eliot's imprisonment in the Tower of London, where he died.

ELIOT, Thomas Stearns (1888–1965), major 20th-century poet and critic. Born in St. Louis, Mo., he settled permanently in England. He was a leading modernist who found his own poetic voice as early as *Prufrock and Other Poems* (1917). His most famous poem, *The Waste Land*, appeared in 1922, and was noted for its portrayal of chaos and squalor in modern life. His criticism (*The Sacred Wood*, 1920) stated beliefs in tradition and the life of the spirit, however. Increasingly meditative and philosophical poetry followed (e.g. *Ash Wednesday*, 1930 and his masterpiece the *Four Quartets*, 1944). He wrote successful poetic dramas such as *Murder in the Cathedral* (1935) and *The Cocktail Party* (1950). He was awarded the Nobel Prize for Literature in 1948.

ELISHA, Hebrew prophet, a disciple of and successor to ELIJAH. Greatly gifted as a soothsayer and healer, he was successful in driving out BAAL worship from the northern state of Israel.

ELIZABETH, city in NE New Jersey on Newark Bay, 12mi SW of New York City. New Jersey's oldest settlement (from 1664) and the original site of Princeton University, it is now a large industrial center. Pop 112654.

ELIZABETH, Saint, mother of JOHN the Baptist and wife of the priest Zechariah. She bore her son in old age after an angel foretold the event.

ELIZABETH (1837–1898), Empress of Austria from 1854 and consort to the Emperor FRANCIS JOSEPH. She disliked Viennese court life, preferring Hungary, and fostered the Austro-Hungarian Union of 1867. Her only son, Rudolf, committed suicide and the Empress herself was assassinated by an anarchist.

ELIZABETH (1709–1762), Empress of Russia from 1741, daughter of PETER the Great. In 1741 she staged a coup against her cousin, the regent and reasserted her father's principle of government. She rid the court of German influence, founded Moscow University, and pursued the SEVEN YEARS WAR against Prussia.

ELIZABETH I (1533–1603), Queen of England and Ireland 1558–1603, and the last TUDOR monarch. A daughter of HENRY VIII, who had broken with the Catholic Church to marry ANNE BOLEYN, her mother, her initial task as queen was to reestablish her supremacy over the English Church after the reign of her Catholic sister, MARY I. The defeat by her navy of the Spanish ARMADA (1588) established England as a major European power. At home industry, agriculture and the arts (especially literature) throve under conditions of relative peace and financial stability, while colonization of the New World was encouraged. The settlement of the Protestant succession became the *bête noire* of the reign as Elizabeth was unmarried and childless. After the execution of her Catholic cousin, MARY QUEEN OF SCOTS, a possible heir, Elizabeth finally acknowledged the succession of JAMES VI of Scotland, Mary's son, thus securing the peaceful Union of England and Scotland.

Anonymous portrait of Queen Elizabeth I from the National Portrait Gallery, London. During her long reign, England flowered into the most culturally and politically powerful country in the world.

ELIZABETH II (1926–   ), Queen of the United Kingdom of Great Britain and Northern Ireland (from 1952) and head of the COMMONWEALTH OF NATIONS. One of the world's few remaining monarchs, she is extremely popular at home and abroad and has traveled extensively as her country's representative. She is married to Philip Mountbatten, Duke of Edinburgh, and has four children.

ELIZABETH CITY, city in NE North Carolina, the seat of Pasquotank Co. It manufactures textiles and furniture and has a good harbor and fisheries. Pop 14381.

ELIZABETH ISLANDS, group of 16 small islands in SE Mass., forming the town of Gosnold. They lie SW of Cape Cod, between Vineyard Sound and Buzzards Bay, and are a popular vacation resort.

ELIZABETH OF HUNGARY, Saint (1207–1231), daughter of Andrew II, king of Hungary. In 1227, after the death of her husband Louis IV of Thuringia, she joined the Third Order of St. Francis, at Marburg, and devoted herself to piety and charity. Her feast day is Nov. 19.

ELIZABETHTON, industrial city in NE Tenn. and seat of Carter Co., 9mi E of Johnson City, on the Watauga R. Rayon is the chief product. Pop 12269.

ELIZABETHTOWN, city in central Ken. and seat of Hardin Co. It manufactures plastics and metal goods. Pop 11748.

ELK, large member of the DEER family Cervidae. It inhabits some of the forest areas of N Europe and Asia and is closely related to the larger American MOOSE.

ELK GROVE VILLAGE, suburb of NW Chicago, Ill. It manufactures electrical goods and paper products. Pop 21907.

ELKHART, industrial city in Ind. It produces musical instruments, proprietary medicines and electrical equipment. Pop 43152.

ELK HILLS, US oil reserve of 46000 acres in Cal., now leased to the navy. Dubious lease arrangements for the reserve, and that at TEAPOT DOME, became the subject of Senate investigations in 1923.

ELKINS, Stephen Benton (1841–1911), US Republican politician. He served in Congress as a territorial delegate from 1873–77, and was secretary of war 1891–93 and Senator from W.Va. 1895–1911. He drafted the Elkins Act (1903), designed to prevent secret railroad REBATES.

ELK ISLAND NATIONAL PARK, covers 75sq mi in central Alberta, Canada. Situated about 30mi E of Edmonton, it was established in 1913 as a conservation area for prairie animals.

ELKS, American fraternal and charitable organization, formally titled Benevolent and Protective Order of Elks, founded in New York (1868) and now Chicago-based. The Elks National Foundation was set up to direct benevolent works, including college scholarships and aid to war veterans.

ELLENSBURG, industrial city in Wash. and seat of Kittitas Co. It is a meat-packing and coal-mining center. Pop 13568.

ELLESMERE ISLAND, northernmost Canadian Arctic island off the W coast of N Greenland. Covering 82119sq mi, it is the largest of the Elizabethan Island group. The terrain is mountainous with deep fjords and icecapped plateaus. Settlements include those of Alert and Eureka.

ELLICE ISLANDS. See GILBERT AND ELLICE ISLANDS.

ELLINGTON, Edward Kennedy "Duke" (1899–1974), US jazz musician. After a formal musical education, Ellington formed his first band in 1918 and by the 1930s enjoyed an international following. His insistence on classical standards of discipline and technique together with his own exceptional talents as a player, arranger and composer, made him a master of mainstream big-band jazz.

Sadly, the elm tree in America and Europe is in great danger of extinction from Dutch elm disease, caused by a fungus. In its healthy state the tree grows to a height of about 120ft and has long graceful branches which curve down slightly. (a) Flowers and leaf buds; (b) twig with leaves; (c) fruit.

ELLIPSE. See CONIC SECTIONS.

ELLIPSOID, a three-dimensional geometrical figure whose intersection with any plane is an ellipse (see CONIC SECTIONS). It has three mutually PERPENDICULAR axes of SYMMETRY; taking these as the AXES defining a set of CARTESIAN COORDINATES, the equation of an ellipsoid is $x^2/a^2+y^2/b^2+z^2/c^2=1$, where a, b, c are CONSTANTS. If any one of a, b, c equals any other, the figure is an ellipsoid of revolution or spheroid, sections parallel to the plane defined by two of its axes of symmetry being circular. If $a=b=c$ the figure is a SPHERE.

ELLIS, Henry Havelock (1859–1939), British writer chiefly remembered for his studies of human sexual behavior and psychology. His major work was *Studies in the Psychology of Sex* (1897–1928).

ELLIS ISLAND, island of about 27 acres in upper New York Bay, within the boundaries of New York City. Bought by the government in 1808, it was the site of a fort and later an arsenal, until 1892, when it was established as an immigration station. Some 20 million immigrants passed through Ellis Island in the next 50 years. In 1943–54, the island was used as a detention center for aliens and deportees.

ELLISON, Ralph Waldo (1914–   ), US Negro writer. He is best known for his novel *Invisible Man* (1952), a story of black alienation in a hostile white society.

ELLSWORTH, Lincoln (1880–1951), US polar explorer and the first man to cross both the Arctic and Antarctic by air. He flew from Spitsbergen to Alaska with AMUNDSEN and NOBILE, in the dirigible *Norge* (1926), and in 1935 he made a 2300mi flight over the Antarctic in a single-engine airplane.

ELLSWORTH, Oliver (1745–1807), American statesman and jurist reputedly responsible for the use of the term "United States" in the American Constitution. He represented Conn. at the Constitutional Convention (1787), where he helped promote the "Connecticut compromise," providing equal state representation in the Senate. He was Senator from Conn. 1789–96, and chief justice of the US 1796–1800.

ELM, large deciduous trees of the genus *Ulmus*, family

Ulmaceae, which are native to Eurasia and North America. Both American and European elms are particularly susceptible to **Dutch elm disease** which can kill a mature tree in a single year. The disease is caused by fungus *Ceratocystis ulmi* and is spread by beetles of the genus *Scolytus*. There is no cure for the disease and it has ravaged elm populations in Europe and North America.

ELMAN, Mischa (1891–1967), Russian-born US violinist. He made his international debut in Berlin (1904), and first performed in the US in 1908. He became an American citizen in 1923.

ELMHURST, residential suburb in Ill., 17mi W of Chicago. It is a truck farming center. Pop 50 547.

ELMIRA, manufacturing city in N.Y. and seat of Chemung Co., on the Chemung R. It is a coal shipping point and manufactures a wide range of products including automobile parts and electrical equipment. Pop 39 945.

EL MISTI, a dormant volcano (19 031ft) in S Peru, NE of Arequipa. It was held sacred by the Incas.

ELMONT, residential city on Long Island in N.Y. It manufactures clothing. Pop 29 363.

EL MONTE, manufacturing city in Cal., 12mi E of Los Angeles. It produces electronic equipment, aircraft accessories and metal goods. Pop 69 852.

EL MORRO NATIONAL MONUMENT, area of 1 278 acres in Valencia Co., N.M. It contains castle-like sandstone remains inscribed by early Spanish explorers, and houses of Pueblo Indian CLIFF DWELLERS. It was established in 1906.

ELMWOOD PARK, residential village in Ill., a suburb of Chicago. It manufactures metal goods. Pop 26 160.

EL PASO, industrial city in Tex., seat of El Paso Co. It is a port of entry on the Rio Grande on the Mexican border. Industries include oil and copper refining, smelting and food processing. Fort Bliss is nearby. Pop 322 261.

EL RENO, industrial city in Okla. and seat of Canadian Co., 27mi W of Oklahoma City. It is a wheat and cotton market center. Pop 14 150.

EL SALVADOR, smallest Central American republic, bordered by Guatemala and Honduras, and having a Pacific coastline. It is densely populated with people of Spanish and Indian descent.

Two parallel volcanic mountain ranges cross the country from SE to NW enclosing high fertile plateaus and valleys irrigated in the W by the Lempa R. To the E of the narrow coastal plain the Gulf of Fonseca forms a natural harbor for the chief port, La Unión.

Economy. El Salvador depends on agriculture, which supports most of its population at subsistence level. Corn, rice, sugar, cotton and beans are grown, and coffee, from the rich volcanic areas of the highlands, is the chief export. The developing industries include food processing and the production of textiles, cement and asbestos. The country trades mainly with the US, importing machinery, foodstuffs and chemical products, and since 1961 has been a member of the Central American Common Market.

The government consists of a unicameral legislative

Official name: The Republic of El Salvador
Capital: San Salvador
Area: 8 236sq mi **Population:** 3 541 000
Languages: Spanish
Religions: Roman Catholic
Monetary unit(s): 1 Salvadoran colón = 100 centavos

assembly of 52 members elected by popular vote for two years. This has the power to overrule the president, who is elected for a five-year term and appoints governors to head the 14 departments of the country.

History. El Salvador was discovered in 1524 by a Spanish expedition led by ALVARADO. Unrest during the early 19th century led to independence from Spain in 1821. After brief involvement in the Mexican Empire, El Salvador joined the first Central American Federation 1823–39. It became an established independent republic in 1856. From the beginning the nation was beset by ideological disputes, political rivalries and military coups. The urgent need for reform led to some social improvement in the 1960s.

EL SEGUNDO, industrial city in Cal., 15mi SW of Los Angeles. Founded by the Standard Oil Company (1911), it now produces chemicals. Pop 15 620.

ELSINORE. See HELSINGØR.

ÉLUARD, Paul (1895–1952), pen name of the French poet Eugène Grindel. He rejected SURREALISM, of which he had been a leading exponent in the 1920s and early 1930s, and turned to more socially committed writing. In 1942 he joined the French Communist Party.

ELWOOD, industrial city in central Ind., 40mi NW of Indianapolis, and center of a truck farming region. Pop 11 196.

ELY, city in Cambridgeshire, England, 18mi NE of Cambridge on the Ouse R. It is an agricultural market center and processes beet sugar. Its famous cathedral dates from c1083. Pop 9 969.

ELY, Richard Theodore (1854–1943), US political economist. He advanced the study of economics and helped found the American Economic Association (1885). As a leader of the Society of Christian Socialists, he supported the growth of the labor unions.

ELYOT, Sir Thomas (c1490–1546), English scholar. He wrote *The Boke Named the Governour* (1531), a treatise on the type of education fit for a gentleman of the governing class, and produced the influential Latin–English *Dictionary of Sir Thomas Elyot* (1538).

ELYRIA, industrial city in Ohio, seat of Lorain Co., 23mi SW of Cleveland. It manufactures plastics, machinery and auto parts. Pop 53 427.

ELYSÉE PALACE, official residence in Paris of the presidents of France. It was built in 1718 for Henri La Tour d'Auvergne and was once the home of Madame de Pompadour.

ELYSIAN FIELDS (Elysium), Greek mythological paradise where those blessed by the gods were sent after death. It was depicted by Homer as a meadow at the western edge of the earth, a land of sunlight and perfect happiness. Later it was regarded as part of the underworld.

ELZEVIER (Elsevier), family of Dutch publishers in Leiden (1587–1713) famous for finely-printed pocket editions of classical writers. The name is today continued by a major Dutch publishing house specializing in encyclopedias and scientific texts.

EMANATION, metaphysical concept of divine influence in the world as continuous and out-flowing. Like ripples on a pond, emanations become weaker the further they get from the center. The concept, which is in conflict with Judeo-Christian belief, is used in connection with NEOPLATONISM and GNOSTICISM.

EMANCIPATION PROCLAMATION, decree issued by Abraham Lincoln on Jan. 1, 1863, during the Civil War. It abolished slavery in the rebel states, although Lincoln was not an Abolitionist and pledged in 1860 not to interfere with slavery. It was a shrewd military and political maneuver designed to deprive the Confederacy of its economic base, namely slavery. Nevertheless, the proclamation boosted the Abolitionist cause and three years later the 13th Amendment brought all slavery in America to an end. (See also CIVIL WAR, AMERICAN.)

EMBALMING, a process by which a corpse is prevented, at least temporarily, from decomposing. Under some circumstances bodies may be naturally embalmed, but artificial embalming first appeared in ancient Egypt (see MUMMY). Modern embalming began after HARVEY's discovery of the blood circulation (1628). Embalming fluid is injected into an artery (arterial fluid) while blood is drained from a vein, then a stronger fluid (cavity fluid) is injected into bodily orifices and hollow organs.

EMBARGO, strictly, a country's order forbidding merchant vessels leaving its ports, but more generally, the prohibition of trade with a particular country by sea, air or land. Since WWII, embargoes have been used by the US against hostile or offending states such as Cuba, North Vietnam and Rhodesia. They are sometimes enforced by BLOCKADE.

EMBARGO ACT, statute of Dec. 1807, forbidding foreign commerce and confining US merchant ships to port. Sparked off by the CHESAPEAKE affair, it was Jefferson's attempt to force England into recognizing American rights. The Act, which lasted 15 months, caused hardship and was not only unpopular but also unsuccessful. It was replaced by the NONINTERCOURSE ACT (1809).

EMBASSY, the office or mission of an AMBASSADOR, representing his own country in another. (See DIPLOMACY; EXTRATERRITORIALITY.)

EMBER DAYS, days traditionally set apart by the Anglican and Roman Catholic churches for fasting and prayer, originally to sanctify each season of the year, now to prepare for ensuing ORDINATIONS.

EMBEZZLEMENT, misuse by a person for his own profit of property entrusted to him by another. Originally this was only a crime if the property was in its owner's possession at the time. Otherwise the offender could only be sued for damages. In the 18th century the growth of modern business led to the offense of embezzlement being created by statute.

EMBOLISM, the presence of substances other than liquid BLOOD in the BLOOD CIRCULATION, causing obstruction to ARTERIES or interfering with the pumping of the HEART. The commonest embolism is from atheromatous plaques (see ARTERIOSCLEROSIS) or THROMBOSIS on a blood vessel or the HEART walls. FAT globules may form emboli from bone MARROW after major bone FRACTURES, and amniotic fluid may cause embolism during childbirth. STROKE or transient cerebral episodes, pulmonary embolism, CORONARY THROMBOSIS and obstruction of limb or organ blood supply with consequent cell DEATH are common results, some of them fatal. Some may be removed surgically, but prevention is preferable.

EMBOSSING, mechanical production of a raised pattern on a surface: suitable materials are plastic, thin metal, paper, leather, fabric, etc. A male DIE is machined such that the required pattern is raised, and a female die such that a mirror image of the pattern is engraved into it. When the two dies are forced together the pattern is embossed on the material between.

EMBROIDERY. See NEEDLEWORK.

EMBRYO, the earliest stage of the life of a FETUS, the development from a fertilized EGG through the differentiation of the major organs. In man, the fertilized egg divides repeatedly, forming a small ball of cells which fixes by IMPLANTATION to the wall of the WOMB; differentiation into PLACENTA and three primitive layers (endoderm, mesoderm and ectoderm) follows. These layers then undergo further division into distinct organ precursors and each of these develops by a process of migration, differentiation and differential growth. The processes roughly correspond to the phylogeny or evolutionary sequence leading to the species. Much of development depends on formation of cavities, either by splitting of layers or by enfolding. The HEART develops early at the front, probably splitting into a simple tube, before being divided into separate chambers; the gut is folded into the body, although for a long time the bulk of it remains outside. The NERVOUS SYSTEM develops as an infolding of ectoderm, which then becomes separated from the surface. Facial development consists of mesodermal migration and modification of the bronchial arches, remnants of the GILLS in phylogeny; primitive limb buds grow out of the developing trunk. The overall control of these processes is not yet understood; however, infection (especially GERMAN MEASLES) in the mother, or the taking of certain DRUGS (e.g., THALIDOMIDE) during PREGNANCY may lead to abnormal development and

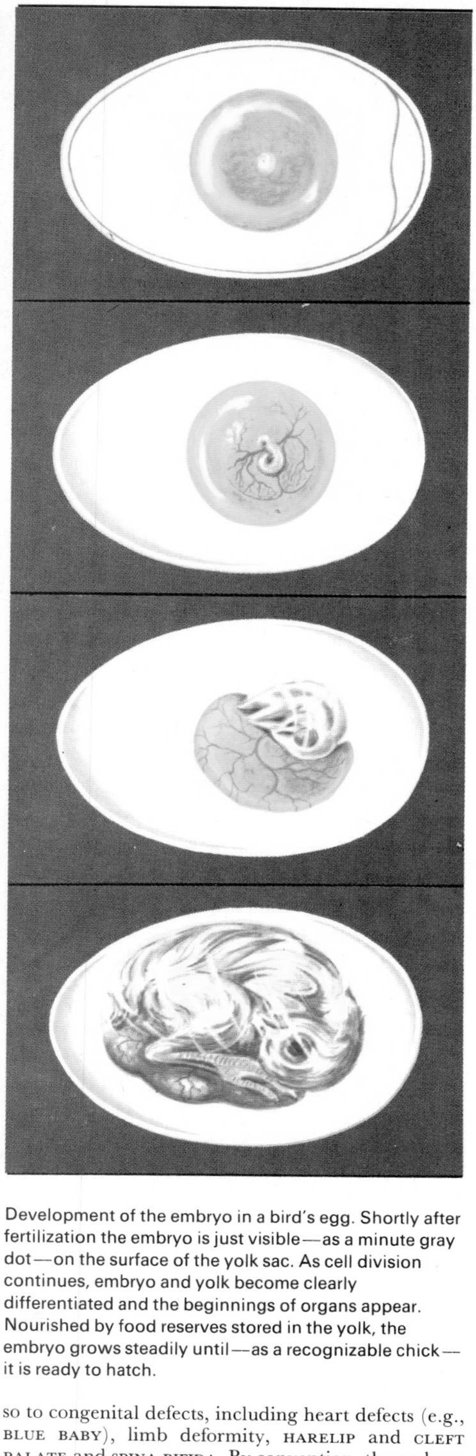

Development of the embryo in a bird's egg. Shortly after fertilization the embryo is just visible—as a minute gray dot—on the surface of the yolk sac. As cell division continues, embryo and yolk become clearly differentiated and the beginnings of organs appear. Nourished by food reserves stored in the yolk, the embryo grows steadily until—as a recognizable chick—it is ready to hatch.

so to congenital defects, including heart defects (e.g., BLUE BABY), limb deformity, HARELIP and CLEFT PALATE and SPINA BIFIDA. By convention, the embryo becomes a fetus at three months gestation.

EMBRYOLOGY, the study of the development of EMBRYOS of animals and humans, based on anatomical specimens of embryos at different periods of gestation, obtained from animals or from human ABORTION. The development of organ systems may be deduced and the origins of congenital defects recognized, so that events liable to interfere with development may be avoided. It may reveal the basis for the separate development of identical cells and for control of growth. The ANATOMY of an organism may be better understood and learnt by study of embryology. The principal embryologists of past ages have included ARISTOTLE; William HARVEY and Marcello MALPIGHI in the 17th century, and Karl Ernst von BAER in the 19th century.

EMBRYOPHYTE, any plant of the subkingdom Embryophyta, which is a group characterized by having an embryo and multicellular sex organs. Included in the Embryophyta are MOSSES, LIVERWORTS, FERNS, GYMNOSPERMS and ANGIOSPERMS. (See also PLANT KINGDOM.)

EMERALD, valuable green GEMstone, a variety of BERYL. The best emeralds are mined in Colombia, Brazil and the USSR. Since 1935 it has been possible to make synthetic emeralds.

EMERGENCY BANKING RELIEF ACT, measure taken to ease the US banking crisis of March 1933. All banks were closed and federal support was given to the stronger banks. Within three days confidence was restored and most banks had reopened.

EMERSON, Ralph Waldo (1803–1882), US philosopher and poet, a seminal essayist and lecturer. He resigned a Unitarian pastorate (1831) and, after traveling in Europe, settled in Concord, Mass. His *Nature* (1836) was the strongest motivating statement of American TRANSCENDENTALISM. After 1837 he became renowned as a public speaker and as editor of the Transcendentalist journal, *The Dial*. He later adjusted his idealistic view of the individual to accommodate the American experience of man's historical and political limitations, especially over the issue of slavery.

EMERY, an impure CORUNDUM containing MAGNETITE and other minerals, occurring on Naxos island and in Asia Minor. It is used as an abrasive (Mohs hardness 8), and as a non-skid material in floors and stairs.

EMETIC, any agent that causes vomiting. Salt solution or stimulation of the PHARYNX are emetics used from antiquity, while drugs such as ipecacuanha and apomorphine are also effective. They are used when a POISON such as an overdose of tablets has been recently ingested; they should not be used when the poison taken causes damage to the ESOPHAGUS or LUNGS.

EMIGRANT AID COMPANY, organization to encourage free-state settlement of Kansas Territory, founded in 1854. Supported by politics and businessmen from the Northeast, it antagonized the South by its crusade against slavery and succeeded in settling only a few thousand people. The Emigrant Aid movement petered out by the Civil War.

EMILIA-ROMAGNA, fertile, low-lying historic region of about 8 500sq mi in N Italy, bounded by the Po R, the Adriatic and the Apennines. Though mainly farmland, the area also has large deposits of oil and natural gas.

EMINENT DOMAIN, in US law, the right to expropriate private property for public use without the owner's consent. Under the 5th and 14th Amendments to the Constitution this must be done by due process of law and compensation must be paid. The right may be used to acquire either the whole title to the property or merely an interest in it such as an EASEMENT.

EMIN PASHA, Mehmed (1840–1892), German physician and explorer. Born Eduard Schnitzer, he changed his name while a surgeon in the Turkish army (1865–74). In the Sudan from 1876, he was made chief medical officer by Gen. Gordon, and then governor of the Upper Nile regions (1878–89). He was killed by Arab slave-traders in central Africa.

EMMAUS, borough in E Pennsylvania. Founded by Moravians c1740, it produces textiles and electrical products. Pop 11 511.

EMMET, Robert (1778–1803), Irish patriot. After a poorly planned uprising against the British in 1803, Emmet was tried and hanged for treason, which assured his fame as a martyr and romantic hero.

EMMETT, Daniel Decatur (1815–1904), US songwriter, who wrote *Dixie*, which became the unofficial Confederate anthem in the Civil War. He cofounded an early minstrel troupe, the Virginia Minstrels.

EMOTION, in psychology, a term that is only loosely defined. Generally, an emotion is a sensation which causes physiological changes (as in pulse rate, breathing) as well as psychological changes (as disturbance) which result in, usually, compulsive (see COMPULSION) adaptations in the individual's behavior. Some psychologists differentiate types of emotion: one such classification is into primary (e.g., fear), complex

Dwarfing even the colossi of New York's skyline stands the Empire State Building. It is visited by over a million tourists each year and, on a clear day, there is a fifty-mile view. The building, desiged by the architectural firm Shreve, Lamb and Harmon, was completed in 1931.

(e.g., envy) and sentiment (e.g., love, hate); but such schemata are controversial. The causes of emotion are not fully understood, but the emotional effects of certain drugs suggest that emotions are the result of biochemical change in various parts of the body. (See also IDEA; INSTINCT.) Modern psychoanalysts generally prefer the term **affect** for emotion.

EMPEDOCLES (c490–430 BC), Sicilian Pythagorean philosopher who developed the notion that there were four fundamental elements in matter—earth, air, fire and water. In medicine he taught that blood ebbed and flowed from the heart and that health consisted in a balance of the four HUMORS in the body.

EMPEROR PENGUIN *Aptenodytes torsteri*, largest species of the PENGUIN family, standing at about 1.2m (4ft) and weighing some 41kg (90lb). The Emperor penguin is found only in the Antarctic, where it breeds on floating ice, the male incubating the single egg on its feet.

EMPHYSEMA, condition in which the air spaces of the LUNGS become enlarged, due to destruction of their walls. Often associated with chronic BRONCHITIS, it is usually a result of SMOKING but may be a congenital or occupational disease. Subcutaneous emphysema refers to air in the subcutaneous tissues.

EMPIRE STATE BUILDING, famous skyscraper on 5th Avenue, New York City. Completed in 1931, it is 1 250ft high, with 102 stories. It remained the world's tallest building until overtaken by the World Trade Center (New York) and the Sears Tower (Chicago).

EMPIRE STYLE, Neoclassical style in architecture, interior decoration and furniture design which reached its peak during the Napoleonic empire (1804–14). In architecture, Roman grandeur was imitated; mahogany and gilt were favored materials for furniture; and costume design was inspired by Classical drapery. The style evolved into the German BIEDERMEIER and the English REGENCY styles. (See also NEOCLASSICISM.)

EMPIRICISM, in philosophy, the view that knowledge can be derived only from sense experience.

Enameling is the decoration of glass, earthenware and metal objects in brilliant and highly durable colors. The process was known to the ancient Egyptians, although its finest exponents were the Chinese, who produced much fine enamel ware (like the piece pictured) on metal.

Modern empiricism, fundamentally opposed to the RATIONALISM that derives knowledge by deduction from principles known À PRIORI, was developed in the philosophies of LOCKE, BERKELEY and HUME. Other thinkers in the "British empiricist tradition" include J. S. MILL and the Americans J. DEWEY and W. JAMES.

EMPLOYMENT BUREAU, privately or publicly owned organization to help unemployed persons to find employment and employers to find workers. Private services charge a fee, often paid by the employer. The first US public employment service was that of New York City, opened in 1834. State agencies, now totaling some 2000 offices, were established nearly 60 years later; federal efforts did not become important until the Depression years of the 1930s, and federal and state services are now coordinated by the Department of Labor.

EMPORIA, city in E Kansas, seat of Lyon Co. and site of Kansas State Teachers' College. It is an important livestock trading center. Pop 23327.

EMS DISPATCH, telegram which helped precipitate the Franco-Prussian War (1870–71). It was BISMARCK's edited version of the account he had received of the French ambassador's demands to King William I of Prussia. It indicated that the French required Prussia's unconditional pledge not to support any future HOHENZOLLERN candidate for the Spanish throne. The dispatch inflamed feelings on both sides.

EMU, *Dromains novae-hollandiae*, flightless, brown ostrich-like bird of Australia. Emus live in small groups, feeding on plants and insects. The male assumes the task of incubating the blue-green eggs, after driving his mate from the nest.

EMULSION, a COLLOID in which both phases are initially liquid.

ENABLING ACTS, legislation empowering individuals or groups to act when they would otherwise have no authority. The US, for example, used such legislation to set up governments in the territories prior to their joining in the Union.

ENAMEL, vitreous glaze (see CERAMICS; GLASS) fused on metal for decoration and protection. Silica, potassium carbonate, borax and trilead tetroxide (see LEAD) are fused to form a glass (called flux) which is colored by metal oxides; tin (IV) oxide makes it opaque. The enamel is powdered and spread over the cleaned metal object, which is then fired in a furnace until the enamel melts.

ENAMELING, the decoration of metal or pottery by fusing enamel on to it, comprising several techniques. CLOISONNÉ, of ancient Egyptian origin, involves enclosing the enamel in metal strips to prevent color-mixing. In the **champlevé** method enamel is placed in cavities cut into the metal. This process was revived in the 12th century at Limoges, which later became famous for its **painted enamels.** The Greek technique of **encrusted enamel** was also revived during the Renaissance, and paintings on enamel became popular in the 17th century.

ENCEPHALITIS, infection affecting the substance of the BRAIN, usually caused by a VIRUS. It is a rare complication of certain common diseases (e.g., mumps, herpes simplex) and a specific manifestation of less common viruses, often carried by insects. Typically an acute illness with HEADACHE and FEVER, it may lead to evidence of patchy INFLAMMATION of brain tissue, such as personality change, EPILEPSY, localized weakness or rigidity. It may progress to impairment of consciousness and COMA. A particular type, *Encephalitis lethargica*, occurred as an EPIDEMIC early this century leading to a chronic disease resembling PARKINSON'S DISEASE but often with permanent mental changes.

ENCKE, Johann Franz (1791–1865), German astronomer who discovered one of the divisions in the rings of SATURN and, using observations of a transit of Venus, established a good value for the distance of the sun. He also discovered **Encke's Comet**, whose period is only 3.3yr (see COMET).

ENCLOSURE, in Britain especially, the practice of fencing off land formerly open to common grazing or cultivation. It began in the 12th century and increased from the 15th century onwards as land values rose, often causing social dislocation and hardship in the countryside.

ENCOMIENDA, system of tributary labor imposed by the Spanish in South America in the 16th century. Spanish settlers, *encomenderos*, were assigned groups of Indians, from whom they exacted tribute and labor. The Spaniards were ostensibly supposed to pay the Indians, protect them and Christianize them. The system died out in the 18th century.

ENCYCLICAL, letter from the pope, originally for general circulation within the Roman Catholic Church, now more often addressed to the bishops. It is usually a guide to the application of church doctrines, and Roman Catholics are officially bound to follow its direction. The best known encyclicals of recent years have been *Pacem in Terris* (1963), on Church and State relations, issued by John XXIII; and *Humanae Vitae* (1968) by Paul VI, on birth control.

ENCYCLOPEDIA, reference work comprising alphabetically or thematically arranged articles on the whole or part of human knowledge. The earliest extant encyclopedia is the *Natural History* of PLINY the Elder (1st century AD) in 37 volumes. The most famous medieval encyclopedia was the *Speculum Majus* of Vincent de Beauvais (13th century), and in 1481 William CAXTON issued one of the earliest encyclopedias in English, the *Mirror of the World*. Ephraim Chambers' *Cyclopaedia* (1728) used specialist writers and formed the basis of the most ambitious and influential work of its kind, the French *Encyclopédie* (1751–72; see DIDEROT, DENIS). The *Encyclopaedia Britannica*, which first appeared 1768–71, is now probably the most comprehensive world encyclopedia.

ENDECOTT, John (c1588–1665), governor of Massachusetts Bay Colony. An English settler, he established the colony at Naumkeag (later Salem), Massachusetts, in 1628. He was governor 1629–30 and at various periods after 1644. A zealous Puritan, he persecuted other sects in the colony.

ENDERBURY ISLAND. See CANTON AND ENDERBURY ISLANDS.

ENDERBY LAND, part of the Antarctic coast, from Prince Olav Coast to Edward VIII Bay. First sighted by John Biscoe in 1831.

ENDERS, John Franklin (1897–), US microbiologist who shared the 1954 Nobel Prize for Physiology or Medicine with F. C. ROBBINS and T. H. WELLER for their cultivation of POLIOMYELITIS virus in non-nerve tissues, so opening the gate for the development of polio vaccines.

ENDICOTT, village in S central N.Y., on the Susquehanna R. One of the Triple Cities (with Binghampton and Johnson City). Pop 16556.

ENDIVE, *Cichorium endivia*, low-growing salad plant, closely related to CHICORY and resembling LETTUCE. Family: COMPOSITAE.

ENDOCRINE GLANDS, ductless glands in the body which secrete HORMONES directly into the BLOOD stream. They include the PITUITARY GLAND, THYROID and PARATHYROID GLANDS, ADRENAL GLANDS and part of the PANCREAS, TESTES and OVARIES. Each secretes a number of hormones which affect body function, development, mineral balance and METABOLISM. They are under complex control mechanisms including FEEDBACK from their metabolic function and from other hormones. The pituitary gland, which is itself regulated by the HYPOTHALAMUS, has a regulator effect on the thyroid, adrenals and gonads.

ENDOGAMY AND EXOGAMY, social rules requiring a person to marry within (endogamous) or without (exogamous) his or her social, religious or ethnic group. A well-known example of endogamy is to be found among Hindus, where inter-caste MARRIAGES are forbidden (see CASTE SYSTEM). In biology, endogamy means INBREEDING, and exogamy

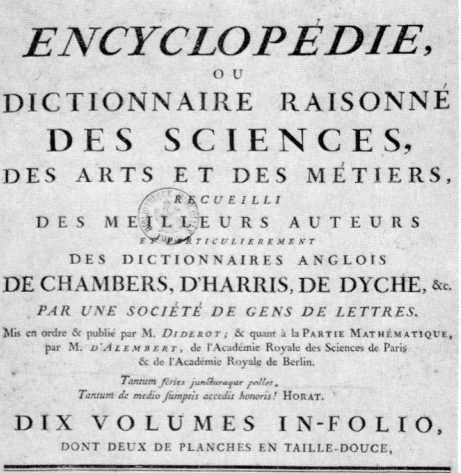

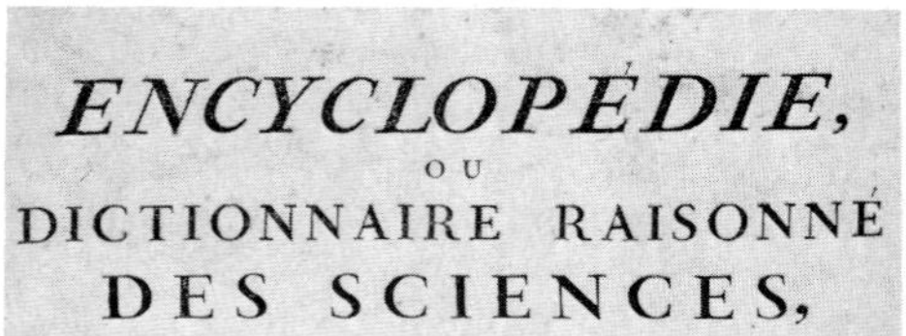

ENCYCLOPÉDIE,
OU
DICTIONNAIRE RAISONNÉ
DES SCIENCES,
DES ARTS ET DES MÉTIERS,
RECUEILLI
DES MEILLEURS AUTEURS
ET PARTICULIEREMENT
DES DICTIONNAIRES ANGLOIS
DE CHAMBERS, D'HARRIS, DE DYCHE, &c.
PAR UNE SOCIÉTÉ DE GENS DE LETTRES.
Mis en ordre & publié par M. *DIDEROT*; & quant à la PARTIE MATHÉMATIQUE, par M. *D'ALEMBERT*, de l'Académie Royale des Sciences de Paris & de l'Académie Royale de Berlin.
Tantum séries juncturaque pollet,
Tantum de medio sumptis accedit honoris! HORAT.
DIX VOLUMES IN-FOLIO,
DONT DEUX DE PLANCHES EN TAILLE-DOUCE,
PROPOSÉS PAR SOUSCRIPTION.
A PARIS, Chez BRIASSON, *rue Saint Jacques, à la Science.*
DAVID l'aîné, *rue Saint Jacques, à la Plume d'or.*
LE BRETON, Imprimeur ordinaire du Roy, *rue de la Harpe.*
DURAND, *rue Saint Jacques, à Saint Landry, & au Griffon.*
M. DCC. LI.
AVEC APPROBATION ET PRIVILEGE DU ROY.

Title page of the prospectus for the famous and immensely influential *Encyclopédie* of Diderot and d'Alembert. The first of its 28 volumes appeared in 1751 and from then until its completion in 1772 it was constantly under attack for irreligion. Parts of it were censored by the printer himself.

Endangered Species

Positive measures to protect our wildlife

During the past 600 million years, the evolutionary process has been responsible for the production of many thousands of plant and animal species. Many have become extinct, but those that survive today do so because they are particularly suited to the environments that have existed since the last Ice Ages. Although many of these species are able to survive in a variety of environments, even more have become adapted to living in particular habitats to which their structure, behavior and ways of life are ideally fitted.

Man, one of the most recent animals to have evolved, has been enormously successful because of his ability to change the environment to suit his needs. Because of this, however, many other species are now in danger of premature extinction, and only recently has man become concerned about his responsibility for these species and for their conservation.

There are four reasons why man threatens the existence of a large number of plant and animal species: he kills individuals of some species because they provide him with raw materials; he removes species from the habitats to which they have become adapted to alien surroundings; he destroys natural habitats to suit his own ends; and, finally, he introduces animal and plant species to new areas where they then threaten the naturally-occurring populations.

Examples of species threatened because of overkilling by fishermen, hunters and trappers are well-known and have received much recent publicity. The African elephant, prized for the ivory of its tusks, and the Blue whale, hunted for its blubber and whalebone, are but two. Killing on an even greater scale is the result of the indiscriminate use of insecticides and herbicides in an attempt to force increasingly high crop yields from regions that must support an ever-growing human population.

A misguided interest in "pets" has led to the trapping of large numbers of animals, especially birds, which are then removed from their natural environments to spend the rest of their lives in cages, whether in private homes or zoos. In a similar way, many plants, for example cacti, have been collected to be sold as house plants.

Even greater than the threat to individual species is man's threat to habitats. When a habitat disappears, whole communities of animals and plants are endangered. Activities that are particularly harmful include the harvesting of timber from forests, the flooding of river valleys for hydroelectric schemes, the irrigation of dry regions, the overgrazing of grasslands, and the drainage of wet lands. In addition, the use of destructive fires and the prevention of natural fires, strip mining, general industrial pollution and the taking over of land for agricultural, urban and industrial development all contribute to the same effect.

Finally, man, by his introduction of species into different regions, has threatened indigenous populations. For example, the successful introduction of the Water hyacinth from tropical South America to almost all regions of the world, including the southern states of the US, has endangered many freshwater plants of ponds, canals and slow-flowing rivers.

During the last decade, there has been an upsurge of interest throughout the world in animal and plant conservation. In the US, the Endangered Species Act of 1973 authorized and directed the Smithsonian Institution to review both the species of plants that were endangered or threatened, and the means of conserving them. The Smithsonian Institution reported to Congress in Jan. 1975 after a year-long study. In this report they listed 761 species in the continental US as endangered, that is, in danger of imminent extinction. In addition, they listed as many as 1 238 plant species as being threatened, that is, likely to become endangered. A further 77 species were identified as being commercially exploited, particularly cacti and orchids. In all, these lists constitute 10% of the entire flora of the continental US. In Hawaii the situation is even worse, with some 50% of the flora in danger of extinction. A similar analysis has produced a list of about 120 animal species from the US that are now deemed to be threatened with extinction.

The identification of endangered species does much to awaken the public's awareness of an acute problem. Action to preserve these species is often more difficult to stimulate because, inevitably, large sums of money must be spent, and business enterprises are sometimes hostile to interference with what they consider to be their legitimate interests.

Sound conservation requires that land-use programs be preceded by comprehensive surveys and research, to determine the best use for all categories of land within a given region. Modification of existing development plans or practices is often enough to eliminate any environmental damage which might otherwise result. For example, the replacement of clear felling by selective felling systems in forested water-catchment zones permits exploitation without the risk of water pollution or soil erosion. Similarly, construction of fish ladders at hydroelectric dams allows the passage of spawning fish to streams above the dam. Investigation may show that certain areas make their most profitable contribution to human welfare by being left undisturbed. For example, the return likely to be obtained from the drainage of small areas of wetland for agriculture is often small, compared with the value of the areas to migratory waterfowl, which provide food, sport and enjoyment for us all.

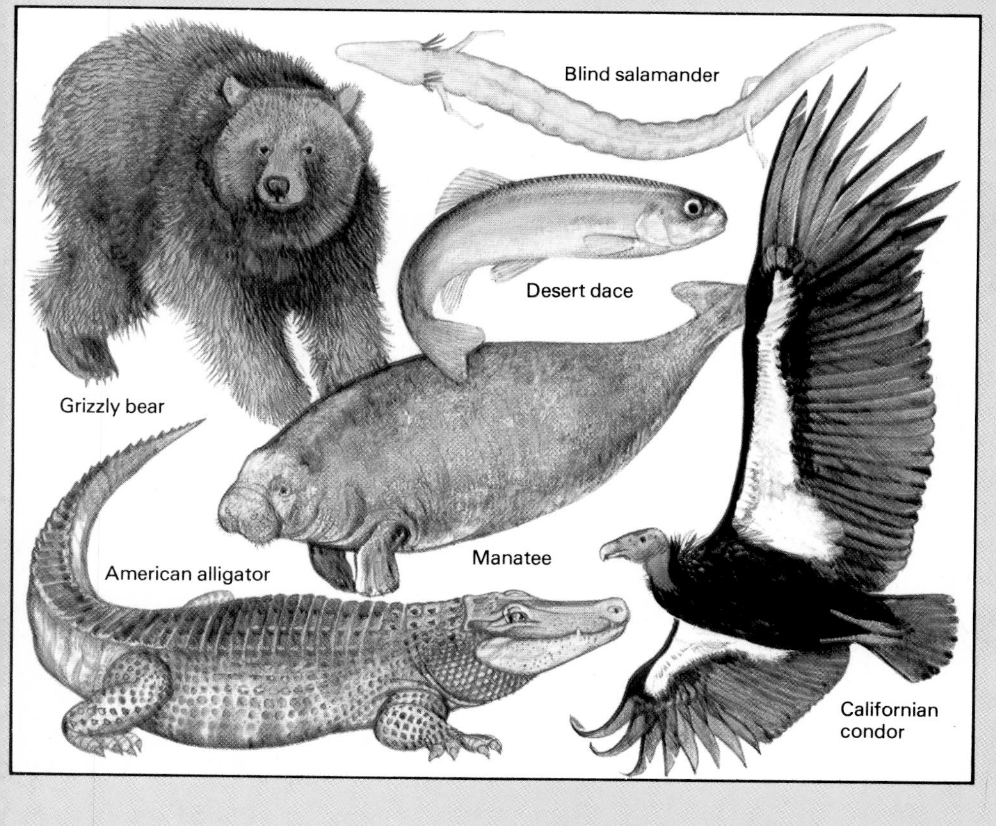

Left: Some of the endangered species in the United States today. In each case it is human interference that is to blame, whether because the animal is a potential threat, like the grizzly, or of commercial value, like the alligator. *Below:* US Department of the Interior publications on conservation, a sign of the increasing governmental concern in this area.

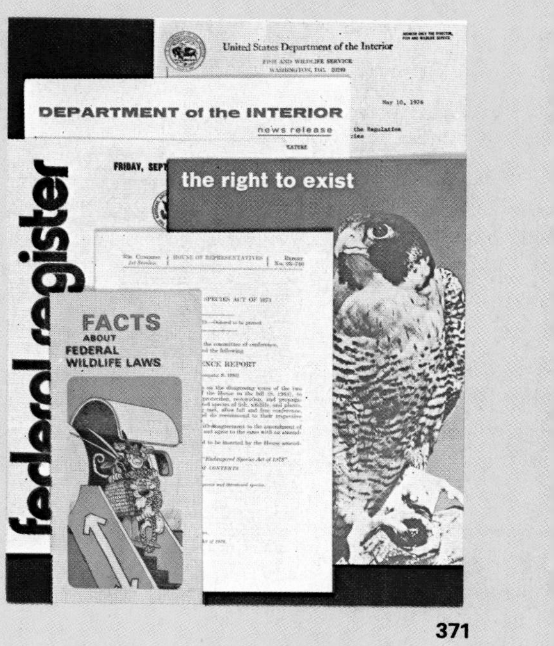

Energy exploitation: both the water mill powering the 18th-century knife-grinding workshop (*above*) and the turbines at the foot of the Oroville Dam on California's Feather River (*below*) represent man's efforts to extract work from the hydrologic cycle. But whereas the water mill turns in virtue of the kinetic energy of the water rushing down the sluice, the turbines exploit the potential energy of the water stored behind the dam.

outbreeding, or breeding between individuals not closely related.

ENDOR, Witch of. See WITCH OF ENDOR.

ENDOSKELETON, any SKELETON that is enclosed within an animal's body. (See also EXOSKELETON).

ENDOWMENT, fund set aside by a person or an organization for a specific purpose. Usually it provides an income for an individual or institution, and the money is invested to provide a continuing income. (See FOUNDATIONS; TRUST.)

ENDYMION, in Greek mythology, a beautiful youth who was put to sleep forever by Zeus, from whom he had asked eternal youth, on Mt Latmus. He was visited nightly by the moon goddess, Selene. It is also the title of a major poem of John KEATS.

ENERGY, to the economist, a synonym for fuel; to the scientist, one of the fundamental modes of existence, equivalent to and interconvertible with MATTER. The MASS-energy equivalence is expressed in the Einstein equation, $E=mc^2$, where E is the energy equivalent to the mass m, c being the electromagnetic constant (speed of LIGHT). Since c is so large, a tiny mass is equivalent to a vast amount of energy. However, this energy can only be realized in nuclear reactions and so, although the conversion of mass may provide energy for the STARS, this process does not figure much in physical processes on earth (except in nuclear power installations). The law of the conservation of mass-energy states that the total amount of mass-energy in the UNIVERSE or in an isolated system forming part of the universe cannot change. In an isolated system in which there are no nuclear reactions, this means that the total quantities both of mass and of energy are constant. Energy then is generally conserved.

Energy exists in a number of equivalent forms. The commonest of these is HEAT—the motion of the MOLECULES of matter. Ultimately all other forms of energy tend to convert into thermal motion. Another form of energy is the motion of ELECTRONS, ELECTRICITY. Moving electrons give rise to electromagnetic fields and these too contain energy. A pure form of electromagnetic energy is ELECTROMAGNETIC RADIATION (**radiant energy**) such as light. According to the QUANTUM THEORY, the energy of electromagnetic radiation is "quantized," referable to discrete units called PHOTONS, the energy E carried by a photon of radiation of FREQUENCY ν being given by $E=h\nu$, where h is the PLANCK CONSTANT. When macroscopic bodies move, they too have energy in virtue of their motion; this is their **kinetic energy** and is given by $\frac{1}{2}mv^2$ where m is the mass and v the velocity of motion. To change the velocity of a moving body, or to set it in motion, a FORCE must be applied to it and work must be done. This work is equivalent to the change in the kinetic energy of the body and gave physicists one of their earliest definitions of energy: the ability to do work. When work is done against a restraining force, **potential energy** is stored in the system, ready to be released again. The restraining force may be electromagnetic, torsional, electrostatic, tensional or of any other type. On earth when an object of mass m is raised up to height h, its gravitational potential energy is given by mgh, where g is the acceleration due to gravity. If the object is let go, it falls and it will strike the ground with velocity v, its potential energy having been converted into kinetic energy $\frac{1}{2}mv^2$. SOUND energy is kinetic energy of the vibration of air. Chemical energy is the energy released from a chemical system in the course of a reaction. Although all forms of energy are equivalent, not all interconversion processes go with 100% EFFICIENCY (the energy deficit always appears as heat—see THERMODYNAMICS). The SI UNIT of energy is the joule.

ENERGY LEVEL, a stationary state of a physical system characterized by its having or being able to have a fixed quantity of ENERGY. QUANTUM MECHANICS assumes that physical systems can only exist in a well-defined set of energy levels. The emission of ELECTROMAGNETIC RADIATION is associated with transitions of electronic and molecular systems between energy levels (see SPECTROSCOPY).

ENERGY RESEARCH AND DEVELOPMENT ADMINISTRATION, US government agency set up in 1974 to supervise research into energy conservation, nuclear energy, fossil fuels and advanced energy systems, and to relate this to safety and the environment.

ENESCO (Enescu), Georges (1881–1955), Romanian composer and violinist. Strongly influenced by folk music, he is best known for his two Romanian Rhapsodies.

ENFIELD, town in N Conn., on the Connecticut R. It is a manufacturing center, producing textiles, plastics and tobacco. Pop 46 189.

ENGELS, Friedrich (1820–1895), German socialist, philosopher and close associate of Karl MARX. Born into a wealthy German family, he went to England in 1842 as the manager of a family factory and there became interested in SOCIALISM. In 1844 he met Marx, whom he supported both financially and politically. Four years later he and Marx published the influential COMMUNIST MANIFESTO. Engels edited the 2nd and 3rd volumes of Marx's *Capital*, and among other works wrote *Anti-Duehring: Socialism, Utopian and Scientific* (1878) and *The Origin of the Family, Private Property and the State* (1884).

ENGHIEN, Louis de Bourbon-Condé, Duc d' (1772–1804), French prince, unjustly executed by Napoleon. The incident, which involved the abduction of the prince from Bremen to face charges of conspiracy, was widely condemned. It ended all possibility of reconciliation between Napoleon and the BOURBONS.

ENGINE, a device for converting stored ENERGY into useful WORK. Most engines in use today are heat engines which convert HEAT into work, though the EFFICIENCY of this process, being governed according to the second law of THERMODYNAMICS, is often very low. Heat engines are commonly classified according to the fuel they use (as in gasoline engine); by whether they burn their fuel internally or externally (see INTERNAL-COMBUSTION ENGINE), or by their mode of action (whether they are reciprocating, rotary or reactive). (See DIESEL ENGINE; GAS TURBINE; JET PROPULSION; STEAM ENGINE; TURBINE.)

ENGINEERING, essentially, the managing of ENGINES. The term also describes the application of the sciences (including mathematics), and the development and uses of technology, to the service of man. Branches include: aeronautical engineering (see AERONAUTICS); chemical engineering, using chemical knowledge and processes in the conversion of raw materials into desired products (see CHEMISTRY); CIVIL ENGINEERING; ELECTRICAL ENGINEERING; HUMAN ENGINEERING; marine engineering, the design and construction of structures and processes for naval purposes; mechanical engineering, the design and use of MACHINES, with its tool, MECHANICAL DRAWING; and nuclear engineering (see NUCLEAR ENERGY).

ENGINEERS, Army Corps of, technical and combatant corps of the US army. It performs civil as well as military construction and maintenance operations on projects such as harbors, waterways, airfields and missile bases. In war it provides combat and supply support.

ENGLAND, largest and most populous part of the UK, covers 50 333sq mi and has a multiracial population of over 46 million. It is bounded on the S by the English Channel, on the N by Scotland, on the W by the Atlantic Ocean, Wales and the Irish Sea, and on the E by the North Sea. It includes the Isle of Wight and the Scilly Isles, and its coast is much indented. Physical features include the Pennine Chain (Cross Fell 2 930ft) running N from Derbyshire; the Cumbrian Mts containing the country's highest point (Scafell Pike 3 210ft); and numerous lowlands and low hills such as the London basin between the Chiltern Hills and North Downs, the Fens bordering on the Wash and, in the SW, the Cotswold Hills, Exmoor, Dartmoor and Bodmin Moor. Among the largest cities are London, capital of both England and the UK, Birmingham, Manchester, Liverpool, Newcastle, Sheffield, Leeds and Bradford, all centers of industry. Leading industries, some now state-controlled or nationalized, include mining (especially coal), iron and steel, chemicals, and manufacturing of all kinds (including automobiles, ships and aircraft). Agriculture is important, but much food—and industrial raw materials, too—has to be imported. (See also GREAT BRITAIN.)

ENGLAND, Church of. See CHURCH OF ENGLAND.

ENGLEWOOD, residential city in central Col., 5mi S of Denver. Situated in a farming area, it manufactures machinery and chemicals. Pop 33 695.

ENGLEWOOD, city in NE N.J., near the Hudson R. It was incorporated in 1895. Pop 24 985.

ENGLISH, language native to the British Isles, spoken there and in North America and Australasia, also in parts of Africa, in India and throughout many other former British colonies. English is taught as the first foreign language in numerous countries over six continents. It is the foremost international language. Several centuries of British colonial expansion facilitated its dispersal while, given the stability this expansion ultimately afforded, the language's qualities of relative simplicity and flexibility enhanced its chances of taking root and surviving in foreign lands.

English is of the INDO-EUROPEAN LANGUAGE family, its parent tongue being referred to as Proto-Indo-European, and it evolved from West Germanic (as did Dutch, Flemish and Frisian). The first steps in its development may be traced back to the Jute, Saxon and Angle settlement in Britain during the 5th and 6th centuries, a settlement gradually given cohesion by the spread of Christianity, and hence of Latinate influences, which followed St. Augustine's landing in Kent in 597. The language that evolved from this settlement is known as Anglo-Saxon or Old English, of which there were four dialects: Northumbrian, Mercian, West Saxon and Kentish. Of these, West Saxon, the dialect of Wessex in which the period's literature has survived, is referred to as standard Old English. It is the language of such works as BEOWULF and the ANGLO-SAXON CHRONICLE. Incursions by VIKING invaders in the 9th century left their mark on the language in the form of numerous Scandinavian loan words.

The Middle English period begins with the Norman Conquest of 1066 and extends to the 15th century, the death of CHAUCER in 1400 being chosen as a convenient closing point. The language absorbed many French (and thereby also many Latin) influences during the period. Two factors are of key importance: the requirement through the Statute of Pleading (1362) that all court proceedings should be in English, and the fact that Chaucer chose to write his major works not in Latin or French, nor even Italian, but in the East Midlands English dialect then spoken in London.

After 1400, there followed a century of transition in which London speech became established, the language undergoing a process of standardization which was to be aided by the introduction of printing by CAXTON in 1476.

With the RENAISSANCE, a host of Greek and Latinate words were introduced and, amid considerable controversy, the English vocabulary expanded. By Shakespeare's time the language was only a little more inflected than it is today. The King James Bible appeared in 1611 and just under a century and a half later Dr. Johnson's *Dictionary* (1755) was published. (See also DICTIONARY.)

American English dates from the 17th century. It diverges to a degree in spelling, being often more accurate phonetically, and is also idiomatically different. Its influence on the language has been considerable, especially in the sphere of new coinages, among which scientific words predominate.

ENGLISH CHANNEL, an arm of the Atlantic Ocean separating England and France, called *La Manche* by the French. About 300mi long, it varies in width from about 112mi to about 21mi. Its principal islands are the Isle of Wight and the Channel Islands.

ENGLISH CIVIL WAR. See CIVIL WAR, ENGLISH.

ENGLISH HORN. See OBOE.

ENGLISH LITERATURE. Early English literature divides into two periods. ANGLO-SAXON literature ends roughly with the Norman Conquest (1066). Poems which survive, such as the epic BEOWULF (8th century), the religious and quasi-mystical *Dream of the Rood*, and the historical narrative *The Battle of Maldon*, remind us both of the rich culture that produced them and of the pre-literary oral traditions that influenced them. The prose ANGLO-SAXON CHRONICLE is a major chronicle of the age of King Alfred. After the Conquest, as the language developed, the literature widened in range and subject matter. *Sir Gawain and the Green Knight* is perhaps the finest Arthurian poem in the 14th century and such poets as GOWER and LANGLAND were notable, but Geoffrey CHAUCER (c1340–1400) is the indisputable genius of the era. He is accessible to modern readers because he wrote in the Midlands dialect upon which modern English is based (see ENGLISH) and because his style and temperament have the timeless quality of all great writers. Modern literature can be said to begin with his work which was the first in English to synthesize successfully a number of widespread European influences. The Middle English period ends by 1476 when CAXTON's press became a decisive factor in completing the standardization of the language. Poetry in the 15th century is dominated by the name of John SKELTON (c1460–1529) although there was a steady production of anonymous lyrics and ballads. Memorable prose of this period includes MALLORY's *Morte d'Arthur* (c1470) and the Paston letters; while the MYSTERY and MORALITY PLAYS presaged the drama.

The continuing political stability after the WARS OF THE ROSES permitted a belated appearance of RENAISSANCE humanism under the TUDORS. In this period PROTESTANTISM was established; the language, like the country, grew prosperous, confident and eclectic; in every genre a rich flair for linguistic experimentation and development of new forms reflected the spirit of adventure of a country that was exploring the globe. Sir Thomas WYATT (1503–1542) and Henry Howard, Earl of Surrey (c1517–1547) introduced Italian literary influences into England, particularly adapting the SONNET, and Surrey's early experiments with blank verse were of major importance to dramatists. As important to the linguistic temperament of the era were Sir Philip SIDNEY's *Arcadia* (1590) and *Defence of Poesie* (1595), both widely known in manuscript before publication. The quintessential Renaissance allegory, uniting moral vision with aesthetic virtues, is Edmund SPENSER's *The Faerie Queene* (1590–96). The specific voice of Puritanism appeared, among other places, in ASCHAM's *The Schoolmaster* (1570). Prose works like LYLY's *Euphues* (1578–80) and Robert Greene's fiction seemed to presage development of the novel, but it was in the field of drama that the glory of the age was expressed. In the theater, human insight and poetic development united to entertain and stir an insatiable audience. In one generation the theater progressed from tentative efforts such as Sackville and Norton's blank verse tragedy *Gorboduc* (1562) and the anonymous farce *Gammer Gurton's Needle* (1575) to the plays of KYD, MARLOWE, DEKKER, Ben JONSON, MARSTON, and, of course, the consummate artistry of SHAKESPEARE. The impetus given to drama after the building of theaters in the 1570s carried through to the Civil War and the closing of the theaters in 1642, adding such names as BEAUMONT AND FLETCHER, WEBSTER, MIDDLETON, MASSINGER and FORD to the list of major dramatists. It was also the period of such offshoots of theater as the MASQUE. A flowering of Elizabethan and Jacobean prose was reached with the Authorized Version of the BIBLE (1611), but the English genius for discursive prose continued to develop in Robert BURTON's *Anatomy of Melancholy* (1621), the work of Sir Thomas BROWNE (1605–1682), and Thomas HOBBES's *Leviathan* (1651).

The dual trauma of the English Civil War and the Puritan Commonwealth produced a profound shift in sensibility. The diaries of Samuel PEPYS (1644–1703) reflect the social flavor of the Restoration period. In the theater a brief flourish of sophisticated, artificial RESTORATION COMEDY gave way by c1800 to a taste for sentiment and prudery that constrained the English drama until the 20th century, except for the brief resurgence of wit in the plays of SHERIDAN and GOLDSMITH in the late 18th century. The great poet of the Puritan movement was John MILTON (1608–1674), who, in retirement after the Restoration, wrote the incomparable Christian epic *Paradise Lost* (1667), a study of the origin of evil which is Homeric in scope. John DRYDEN (1631–1700) was another pivotal writer of the times. Inheritor and supreme exponent of the ideals of the Renaissance, he produced prose, poetry and drama which looked forward to the tone and ambitions of the succeeding era of Neoclassicism. BUNYAN's *The Pilgrim's Progress* (1678) is, perhaps, the major achievement of Puritan prose literature.

The first years of the prosperous 18th century were the years of ADDISON and STEELE's suave prose and fashionable periodicals. Alexander POPE (1688–1744) was the most famous and admired poet of his era, subtle in his experimentation, wide-ranging in his wit, irony and compassion, while his friend Jonathan SWIFT (1667–1745), also a considerable poet, was a master prose-satirist. His *Gulliver's Travels* (1726) can be seen along with fictitious narratives by Daniel DEFOE (1660–1731)—such as *Robinson Crusoe* (1719) and *Moll Flanders* (1722)—as prime stimulators of the growth of the novel. Coincidental with the increase in economic and political dominance of the middle classes, the new genre was established with the epistolary novels of RICHARDSON (*Pamela*, 1740) and the satirical novels of FIELDING (*Joseph Andrews*, 1742). Tobias SMOLLETT (1721–1771) and Laurence STERNE (1713–1768) were also among the first professional novelists. Increasingly in the 18th century, prose literature in all forms dominated the taste and outlook of the age, the labors and personality of Samuel JOHNSON (1709–1784) being of major importance along with BOSWELL's *Life of Dr. Johnson* (1791–99), and GIBBON's monumental *History of the Decline and Fall of the Roman Empire* (1776–88). Following upon the Gothic mysteries of Horace WALPOLE (1717–1797) and Mrs. RADCLIFFE (1764–1823), precursors of ROMANTICISM, the novels of Jane AUSTEN (1775–1817) are rooted in the 18th-century standards of moderation and elegance, while they established new complexities of irony, psychology and social observation. Later novelists were to develop the territory which she mapped out and to take as models her achievement in formal and technical skills.

The 19th century began with the impact of the Romantic era in poetry: WORDSWORTH, COLERIDGE, BYRON, SHELLEY and KEATS reflected both German literary and French Revolutionary movements. The novels of Sir Walter SCOTT (1771–1826) are as much in keeping with Romantic restlessness, gusto and individuality of utterance as are the criticism of HAZLITT, LAMB and COLERIDGE and the confessional writings of Thomas DE QUINCEY (1785–1859). The Victorian Age which followed, seemingly more staid, was troubled by the early results of the industrial revolution and the political consequences of expanding imperialism in the post-Napoleonic era. Despite adherence to certain conventions, the mid-century poetry of TENNYSON, BROWNING and ARNOLD is innovative in content as well as style. Thomas MACAULAY and Thomas CARLYLE (1795–1881) satisfied the Victorian taste for heavy and moralizing non-fiction. The controversies instigated by Cardinal John Henry NEWMAN (1801–1890) and Charles DARWIN (1809–1882) raged with much publicity and rebuttal and reached wide audiences. It was also an age of popular and literary magazines, in which many of the most famous novels first appeared as serials. The great novels of DICKENS, THACKERAY, Emily and Charlotte BRONTË and George ELIOT dominated the period 1830–75 and reflected the major social, political, psychological and historical debates of the country.

Transitional novels by TROLLOPE (1815–1882), MEREDITH (1828–1909) and GISSING (1857–1903) lead to the novels of Thomas HARDY (1840–1928) and American-born Henry JAMES (1843–1916) who in their different ways usher in the modern era. Joseph CONRAD (1857–1924), a Pole who chose to write in English, and E. M. FORSTER (1879–1970) were among those who even before WWI introduced foreign influences into English literature. It was about this time, however, that a split began to occur between "serious" and "popular" literature: the more journalistic fiction of Arnold BENNETT (1867–1931), John GALSWORTHY (1867–1933) and H. G. WELLS (1866–1946), along with imperialistic and conservative prose and poetry by Rudyard KIPLING (1865–1936), Hilaire BELLOC (1870–1953) and G. K. CHESTERTON (1874–1936), were also more widely read. This division has been exacerbated since WWI by the increasing complexity of various schools of "modernism." Symbolism, Expressionism and Vorticism were but three experiments in literature (and the visual arts) of the first decades of the 20th century. James JOYCE (1882–1941), Virginia WOOLF (1882–1941) and D. H. LAWRENCE (1885–1930) came to dominate fiction in the interwar period (1918–1939) while YEATS (1865–1939) and T. S. ELIOT (1888–1965) established the new voice of modern poetry. For the first time in 200 years there was a major revival in drama (coinciding with the European revival led by IBSEN, STRINDBERG and CHEKOV), headed by the Irishmen Oscar WILDE (1854–1900) and George Bernard SHAW (1856–1950) in London and J. M. SYNGE (1871–1909), Sean O'CASEY (1884–1964), and Yeats in association with the ABBEY THEATRE in Dublin.

By WWII a new generation of writers had begun to appear. Concern about the tortured politics of Europe was reflected by poets such as W. H. AUDEN (1907–1973) and C. Day LEWIS (1904–1972) and the journalist-novelists Arthur KOESTLER (b. 1905) and George ORWELL (1903–1950). Graham GREENE (b. 1904), Christopher ISHERWOOD (b. 1904) and Evelyn

Energy

The power to do work

Industrial man is nothing without energy. The story of his progressive mastery of his environment is the history of his discovery and development of new sources of useful energy—for cooking his food, to warm his shelter, draw his water and transport his person. The first breakthrough in energy technology came with the harnessing of steam power for pumping out mines in the 18th century. Within a century coal-raised steam was displacing all former energy sources—muscle, wood, wind and water—from their traditional employment. Steam both powered the factories and made mass transportation a reality, releasing men from the age-old constraint of locality.

The 20th century may have seen the passing of the age of steam but western man has become more than ever dependent on plentiful supplies of available energy. "Available" is the key to the understanding of energy, for although the total quantity of energy (or, more strictly, mass-energy) in the universe is constant—energy can neither be created nor destroyed—only a certain proportion of any given quantity can be converted into useful work.

A heat-engine is a machine which converts energy from one form to another. Typically it extracts chemical energy from a fuel (which is merely a convenient source or store of energy), puts some of it to work—in accelerating an automobile, turning a lathe or spinning a phonograph turntable—and expels the unusable energy in the form of waste (low-temperature) heat. But although a fuel may be used up its energy is never annihilated, for even the energy usefully converted into mechanical work is ultimately "degraded" to unemployable heat. One solution to any energy shortage is to find ways of improving the efficiency of energy conversion—to discover how to get the maximum work out of the fuel.

Most of the world's energy resources ultimately originate in the solar radiation arriving at the top of the atmosphere. The sun is a massive nuclear furnace emitting energy in the form of heat and light radiation. Some of the energy reaching the earth warms the seas and land-surface, powering the winds and ocean-currents, while a minute proportion fuels the growth of plants.

Although the potential for the direct conversion of solar energy is great, man has hitherto employed little ingenuity in harnessing this energy. Instead, while he still fuels his own body with vegetable foods and in many countries keeps himself warm by burning contemporary wood, 96% of his current energy consumption is supplied by burning "fossil fuels"—the remains of plants which converted solar energy into carbohydrates many ages ago.

The principal fossil fuels are coal, petroleum oil and natural gas. Their importance to modern man is reflected both in the technological lengths to which he will go to get them out of the ground and in the political price he is willing to pay to secure access to adequate supplies. Although the stocks of any fossil fuel must ultimately become exhausted if the capital is being eroded faster than it is replenished, recent experience has shown that known reserves tend to increase the more effort is put into looking for them. Further, the soaring price of any fossil fuel that appeared to be running out would force a switch to other sources of energy long before supplies were actually exhausted.

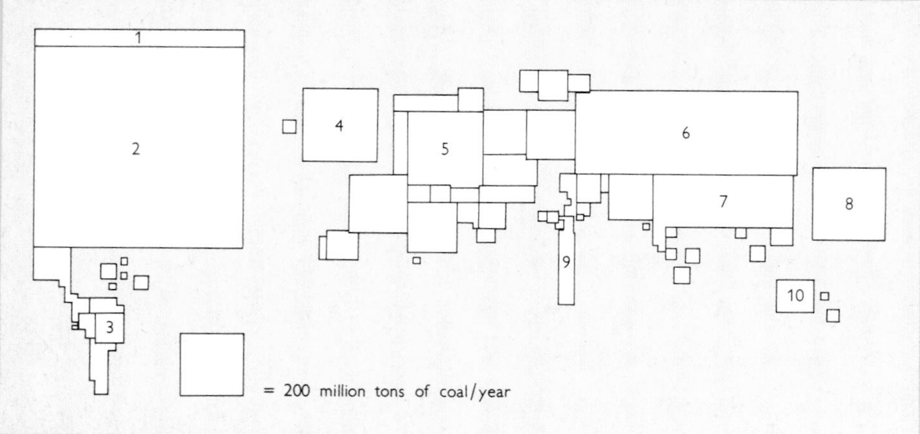

Above: the geothermal power plant at Waisakei, New Zealand. Here, as in certain locations in Iceland and Italy, energy from the hot interior of the earth can be converted for the benefit of mankind.
Left: cartogram of world energy consumption. The disproportionate share of the world's energy consumed by the industrialized nations is highlighted on this diagram on which the size of each country is drawn in proportion to its energy consumption. (1) Canada, (2) the US, (3) South America, (4) the UK, (5) Europe, (6) the USSR, (7) China, (8) Japan, (9) Africa, (10) Australia.
Right: The distribution of the world's major power plants. Most are concentrated in Western Europe and the northeast US. Coal-fired plants (black) are distinguished from hydroelectric (blue) and nuclear (red).

A four-column rotative beam steam engine, preserved at Combe, near Oxford, England. Engines such as this, built in 1852 and installed to power a saw-mill, provided man with vastly increased potential for the manipulation of his environment.

Although it is virtually impossible to store in useful quantities, the most versatile form of energy is electricity. The "great blackout" which struck the northeastern US in November 1965 dramatically illustrates western man's dependence on electrical power. For 12 hours 30 million people were plunged into darkness and chaos resulted. While at present most electricity is generated by the conversion of fossil fuels, as these become more expensive there will probably be a switch to greater dependence on nuclear and water power. Most hydroelectric power is at present won by interrupting the hydrological cycle in which water evaporated from the oceans is precipitated on hills before flowing back down rivers into the oceans, but in future more electricity will be generated by trapping tidal energy behind barrages built across the mouths of large estuaries. In the long run nuclear fuels and the more efficient interception of solar energy offer fuller solutions to current energy shortages and the present fossil fuels will be released to serve as valuable raw materials for plastics and fibers manufacture.

Although potential energy supplies are not infinite (and there are serious problems regarding for instance nuclear waste disposal), if the necessary technology is developed, man need not fear that his energy requirements can be met throughout the foreseeable future.

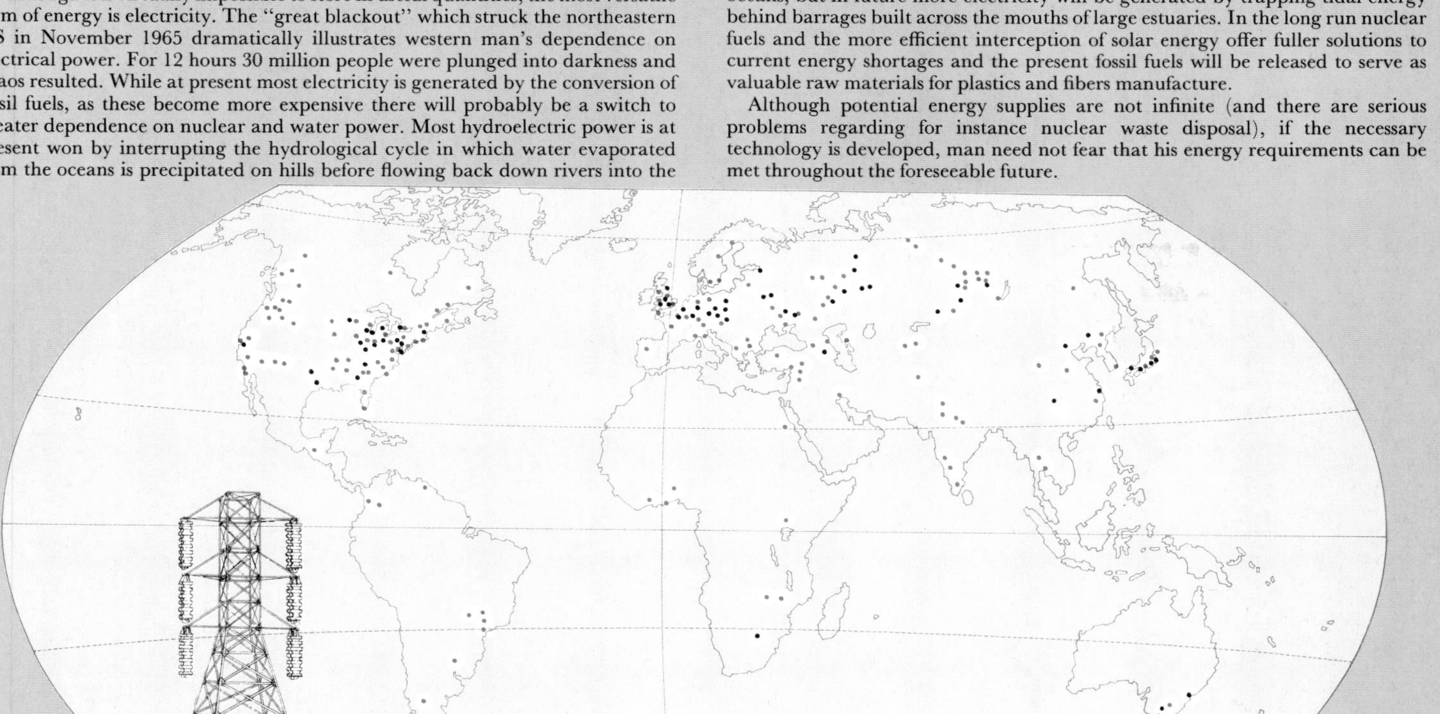

WAUGH (1903–1966) were among the most interesting novelists of the same generation.

Since the war, the most consistently lively activity in England has been in the theater: John OSBORNE (b. 1929), Harold PINTER (b. 1930), Athol FUGARD (b. 1932) and Tom STOPPARD (b. 1937) have produced striking work. Individual works in other genres have attracted attention. William GOLDING (b. 1911) and Doris Lessing (b. 1919) among novelists, and Philip Larkin (b. 1922) and Seamus Heaney (b. 1937) among poets have been of particular interest. It has also become evident that the critical writings of T. S. ELIOT, William Empson (b. 1906) and F. R. LEAVIS (b. 1895) among others, have established a new age of the prose essay in English literature.

ENGLISH SETTER, long-legged sporting dog standing up to 27in high, weighing 56–66lb. Its long, silky coat may be white with black, lemon or liver, or black, white and tan. One of the oldest bird dog breeds, it crouches on the ground when it scents game and creeps up on the birds. Affectionate, it makes a good pet but needs plenty of exercise.

ENGRAVER BEETLES, or **Bark beetles,** BEETLES that burrow through the bark of trees, excavating large chambers in which eggs are laid. Many species cause serious damage to timber, one transmitting the fungus disease Dutch ELM disease.

ENGRAVING, various craft and technological techniques for producing blocks or plates from which to print illustrations, banknotes etc.; also, an individual print made by one of these processes. Line engraving refers to preparing a plate by scratching its smooth surface with a highly-tempered steel tool called a burin or graver. If the desired design is left standing high as is common with woodcuts and linocuts, this is known as a relief process. If the ink is transferred to the paper from lines incised into the plate, the surface of the inked plate having been wiped clean, this is known as intaglio. Drypoint and mezzotint are mechanical engraving processes developed from line engraving; other techniques, including AQUATINT, involve chemical ETCHING processes. (See also LITHOGRAPHY.)

ENGROSSING, in English law, the criminal offence of buying or acquiring a monopoly of goods for the purpose of selling at an excessive profit.

ENID, city in N Okla., seat of Garfield Co. Its industries include meat packing, oil refining and grain storage. Pop 44986.

ENISEI RIVER. See YENISEY RIVER.

ENIWETOK, Pacific atoll at the NW end of the Ralik Chain of the NW Marshall Islands. Since 1947 it has served as a US test site for atomic weapons.

ENLIGHTENMENT, The, also known as The Age of Reason or *Aufklärung*, a term applied to the period of European intellectual history centering on the mid-18th century. The empiricist philosophy of LOCKE and scientific optimism following the success of NEWTON's *Principia* provided men with the confidence to deem reason supreme in all the departments of intellectual enquiry.

ENNIS, industrial city in NE central Tex. It produces cottonseed oil. Pop 11046.

ENNIUS, Quintus (239–169 BC), classical Roman poet. His most important work was the *Annales*, a history of Rome beginning with the fall of Troy and ending with his own times, of which only about 600 lines have survived. It was the national poem of Rome until the *Aeneid* of VERGIL.

ENOCH, Books of, three books describing experiences and visions of the Old Testament patriarch Enoch. The first, complete only in an Ethiopic version, is one of the Jewish PSEUDEPIGRAPHA. It is an important aid to New Testament study. The second is written in Slavonic and the third, which is sometimes anti-Christian in tone, is in Hebrew.

ENOSIS, the Greek word for "unification." It is applied to the campaign by Greek Cypriots, chiefly under the leadership of Archbishop MAKARIOS, to unite Cyprus with Greece.

ENSILAGE. See SILAGE.

ENSOR, James Sydney, Baron (1860–1949), Belgian painter and forerunner of modern EXPRESSIONISM. He is noted for the bizarre, often morbid treatment of his subjects, and for a bold use of color. Among his best-known work is *Entry of Christ into Brussels* (1888).

ENTABLATURE, in architecture, the horizontal moldings set above the columns of classical buildings, or similar features in other styles. They consist, in ascending order, of the architrave, frieze and cornice.

ENTAIL, legal term for the restriction of inheritance to a limited class of heirs, through several generations. Feudal in origin, it was generally used to ensure that estates remained intact, rather than being dispersed among several heirs. Most states in the US have abolished the practice. Where it is retained, it is limited to one generation.

ENTENTE (French: understanding), political term for a friendly relation between countries, based on diplomatic agreement rather than formal treaty. The term originated in the 17th century, and has been applied particularly to the relationship between Britain and France, the Entente Cordiale (1904) which in 1907, when it included Russia, became the TRIPLE ENTENTE.

ENTERITIS, INFLAMMATION of the small intestine (see GASTROINTESTINAL TRACT) causing abdominal COLIC and DIARRHEA. It may result from VIRUS infection, certain BACTERIAL DISEASES or FOOD POISONING, which are in general self-limited and mild. The noninfective inflammatory condition known as **Crohn's disease** causes a chronic relapsing regional enteritis, which may present with weight loss, ANEMIA, abdominal mass or VITAMIN deficiency, as well as colic and diarrhea. In bacterial enteritis, ANTIBIOTICS may help, while Crohn's disease is sometimes helped by anti-inflammatory drugs or STEROIDS; SURGERY may also be required, but is often hazardous and may lead to FISTULA formation.

ENTERPRISE, city in SE Ala. It is situated in a livestock and food crop producing area. Pop 15591.

ENTERPRISE, the first nuclear-powered aircraft carrier, commissioned by the US Navy in 1961.

ENTOMOLOGY, the study of INSECTS. In a broader sense the term is sometimes erroneously used to describe studies on other arthropod groups. Entomology is important, not only as an academic discipline, but because insects are among the most important pests and transmitters of disease.

ENTREPRENEUR, term for a person who assumes the risks and heads the management of a firm or industry, often used of one who undertakes an entirely new venture. It originated in the 18th century, in connection with the Industrial Revolution. Individual entrepreneurial flair enjoys less freedom today owing to the increasingly large scale on which business tends to operate.

ENTROPY, the name of a quantity in THERMODYNAMICS, statistical mechanics and INFORMATION THEORY variously representing the degree of disorder in a physical system, the extent to which the ENERGY in a system is available for doing WORK, the distribution of the energy of a system between different modes, or the uncertainty in a given item of knowledge. In thermodynamics ABSOLUTE entropies cannot be determined, only changes in entropy. The infinitesimal entropy change δS when a quantity of HEAT δQ is transferred at absolute TEMPERATURE T is defined as $\delta S = \delta Q/T$. One way of stating the second law of thermodynamics is to say that in any change in an isolated system, the entropy (S) increases: $\Delta S \geqslant 0$. This increase in entropy represents the energy that is no longer available for doing work in that system.

The famous amphitheater at Epidaurus, marvellously preserved. Dating from the 4th or early 3rd century BC, this finely proportioned structure, nearly 400ft in diameter, is thought to have been designed by the architect Polyclitus the Younger.

ENUGU, capital of Central-Eastern state in Nigeria. It is an important coal-shipping center en route to Port Harcourt. It served for a brief period during 1967 as capital of the breakaway region of BIAFRA. Pop 167339.

ENVER PASHA (1881–1922), also known as Enver Bey, Ottoman leader who organized the Young Turk revolution of 1908 and one of the triumvirate that ruled Turkey from 1913–18. As minister of war he took Turkey into WWI on Germany's side (1914). Edged from power by Mustafa Kemal (see ATATURK), he died leading Turkish Uzbek factions against Russia.

ENVELOPE, a CURVE or curves TANGENT to every member of a family of curves. For example, the CIRCLE $x^2+y^2=r^2$ (see ANALYTIC GEOMETRY) is envelope to the family of LINES $x \cos\theta + y \sin\theta = r$.

ENVIRONMENT, the surroundings in which animals and plants live. The study of organisms in relation to their environment is called ECOLOGY. Organisms are affected by many different physical factors in their environment, such as temperature, water, gases, light, pressure and also biotic factors such as food resources, competition with other species, predators and disease.

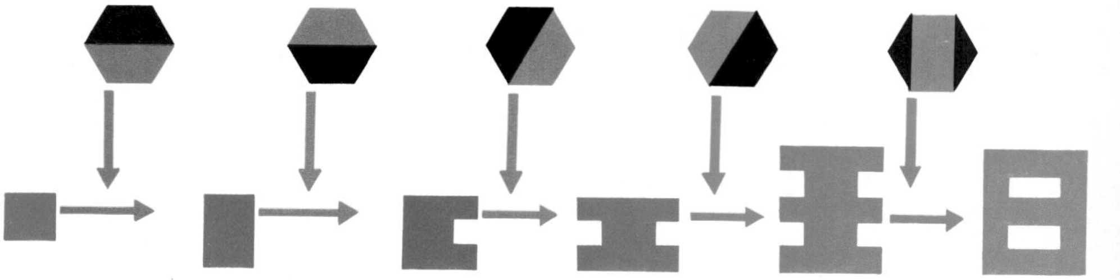

Without the catalyzing effect of enzymes in metabolic processes life would not be possible. This diagram demonstrates the principle of enzyme function in building up large molecules. Red and black hexagons represent a series of closely related enzymes. The blue shapes signify the stages in building up the product. Starting from a simple molecule a complex substance is built up in a number of chemical reactions. Each step is catalyzed by an enzyme. Although the enzymes in the series are closely related, each one can catalyze only a single reaction.

ENVIRONMENTAL PROTECTION AGENCY, US agency established in 1970 to coordinate government action on environmental issues. It absorbed several existing agencies and as well as serving as the public's advocate in pollution cases also coordinates research by state, local government and other groups.

ENZYMES, PROTEINS that act as catalysts (see CATALYSIS) for the chemical reactions upon which LIFE depends. They are generally specific for either one or a group of related reactions. Enzymes are responsible for the production of all the organic materials present in living CELLS, for providing the mechanisms for energy production and utilization in MUSCLES and in the NERVOUS SYSTEM, and for maintaining the intracellular environment within fine limits. They are frequently organized into subcellular particles which catalyze a whole sequence of chemical events in a manner analogous to a production line. Enzymes are themselves synthesized by other enzymes on templates derived from NUCLEIC ACIDS. An average cell contains about 3000 different enzymes. In order to function correctly, many enzymes require the assistance of metal IONS or accessory substances known as **coenzymes** which are produced from VITAMINS in the diet. The action of vitamins as coenzymes explains some of the harmful effects of a lack of vitamins in the diet. A majority of enzymes function in a neutral aqueous environment although some require different conditions. For instance, those which digest food in the stomach require an ACID environment. Cells also contain special activators and inhibitors which switch particular enzymes on and off as required. In some cases a substance closely related to the substrate (the substance on which the enzyme acts) will compete for the enzyme and prevent the normal action on the substrate; this is termed **competitive inhibition**. Again, the product of a reaction may inhibit the action of the enzyme so that no more product is produced until its level has dropped to a particular threshold, this being known as FEEDBACK control. Enzymes either synthesize or break down chemical compounds or transform them from one type to another. These differing actions form the basis of the classification of enzymes into oxidoreductases, transferases, hydrolases, lyases, isomerases and synthetases. Enzymes normally work inside living cells but some (e.g., digestive enzymes) are capable of working outside the cell. Enzymes are becoming important items of commerce and are used in "biological" washing powders, food processing and brewing.

EOCENE, the second epoch of the TERTIARY, lasting from about 55 million to about 40 million years ago. (See also GEOLOGY.)

EOHIPPUS, a small fossil mammal of the EOCENE period, the size of a dog and thought to be ancestral to the modern horse. *Eohippus* is found in the US and is identical to the European *Hyracotherium*.

EOKA (Ethniki Organosis Kipriakou Agonos; National Organization of Cypriot Struggle), Greek Cypriot terrorist movement. Established in 1955 by Colonel George GRIVAS, it was dedicated to ending British rule in Cyprus, and to ENOSIS (union with Greece). The organization, officially disbanded in 1959, made a brief reappearance in the summer of 1973.

EOS, Greek goddess of dawn. She was under a curse by APHRODITE that made her insatiable in her lust for young men.

EPAMINONDAS (c410–362 BC), Theban statesman and general. He defeated the Spartans at the Battle of Leuctra (371 BC), thus depriving them of their supremacy over Greece. He died of wounds received in the otherwise successful battle against the Spartans at Mantinea in 362 BC.

EPÉE, Charles Michel, Abbé de l' (1712–1789), French pioneer in the teaching of deaf-mutes and inventor of a sign language enabling them to communicate and receive instruction.

EPHEDRINE, a drug related to ADRENALINE. It may act as a central nervous system STIMULANT and is used to dilate the BRONCHI in ASTHMA, to dilate the pupils, and occasionally for its effects on BLADDER function. Recently it has been largely replaced by other drugs.

EPHESIANS, Epistle to the, New Testament book attributed to the apostle Paul, closely resembling COLOSSIANS. Probably written during Paul's first imprisonment in Rome c60 AD, its main theme is the universality and unity of the church, Jewish and Gentile Christians alike being saved in Christ.

EPHESUS, ancient Greek city, at its prime the major seaport of Asia Minor, whose ruins lie near what is now Izmir in Turkey. It changed hands many times before its final destruction by the Goths in 262 AD. Its temple of ARTEMIS was one of the Seven Wonders of the Ancient World. It became a center of Christianity; St. Paul stayed there 53–56 AD.

EPHORS, elected magistrates of ancient Sparta. Popular representatives, the five ephors had wide judicial, executive and legislative powers and could even impeach the two kings of Sparta. The office diminished but survived until late Roman times.

EPHRAIM, one of the TWELVE TRIBES OF ISRAEL, descended from and named for the second son of JOSEPH. They occupied a fertile central area of Palestine. Ephraim led the ten tribes that founded the northern kingdom of Israel.

EPHRATA, borough in SE Pa., about 55mi W of Philadelphia. Founded as a German Seventh-Day Baptist colony in 1732, it is now an agricultural and trading center with some light industry. Pop 9662.

EPIC, long narrative poem concerned with heroism, either of individuals or of a people. GILGAMESH, the earliest known epic, dates from c2000 BC, but epics were considered the highest literary form until at least the 14th century. Many, such as the ODYSSEY and ILIAD, and BEOWULF, must have existed as oral tradition before being written down; the KALEVALA was only collated in the 19th centry. Others, such as VERGIL's *Aeneid*, SPENSER's *Faerie Queene* and MILTON's *Paradise Lost*, draw on traditional material but are very much individual works. Many epics, such as the NIBELUNGENLIED, are nationalistic in flavor, blending actual history with myth and fable. (See also, for example, ARTHURIAN LEGENDS; CHANSON DE GESTE; CHANSON DE ROLAND; SAGA.)

EPICENTER, the point on the earth's surface directly above the focus of an EARTHQUAKE.

EPICTETUS (c55–135 AD), Greek Stoic philosopher. An educated Roman slave, after he was freed he taught philosophy, but was expelled with other philosophers by Emperor Domitian in 90 AD, moving to Nicopolis in Greece. His teachings, recorded by his pupil ARRIAN, indicate that the key to conduct is self-control and acceptance of the natural order—itself the will of God. (See also STOICISM.)

EPIC THEATER, form of theater developed by PISCATOR and BRECHT, emphasizing the narrative and political aspect of staged events. Brecht's theories stressed the arousal of a critical response by alienating the spectator from the staged action.

EPICUREANISM, philosophy propounded by EPICURUS in the 4th century BC. It regarded the purpose of human life as the attainment of pleasure, by which was meant contentment and peace of mind in a frugal life. The school was viciously attacked, particularly by Christians; and this has debased the name into merely signifying sensual hedonism.

EPICURUS (c341–270 BC), Athenian philosopher, the author of Epicureanism. Reviving the ATOMISM of DEMOCRITUS, he preached a materialist, sensationalist philosophy which emphasized the positive things in life and remained popular for more than 600 years.

EPICYCLE, a circle whose center lies on the circumference of a larger circle. In geocentric cosmologies, such as that of PTOLEMY, the planets were thought to move around the earth in epicycles, the centers of which lay on larger circles known as **deferents**.

EPICYCLOID, the CURVE traced by a point on the circumference of a CIRCLE that is rolling along the outside of another, fixed, circle. (See also CYCLOID; HYPOCYCLOID.)

EPIDAURUS, ancient Greek seaport on the Saronic Gulf, 25mi E of Argos. Site of a sanctuary dedicated to ASCLEPIUS, the town's ruins include a very well-preserved theater where Classical plays are still produced.

EPIDEMIC, the occurrence of a disease in a geographically localized population over a limited period of time; it usually refers to INFECTIOUS DISEASE which spreads from case to case or by carriers. Epidemics arise from importation of infection, after environmental changes favoring infectious organisms or due to altered host susceptibility. A **pandemic** is an epidemic of very large or world-wide proportions. Infectious disease is said to be **endemic** in an area if cases are continually occurring there. Travel through endemic areas may lead to epidemics in nonendemic areas.

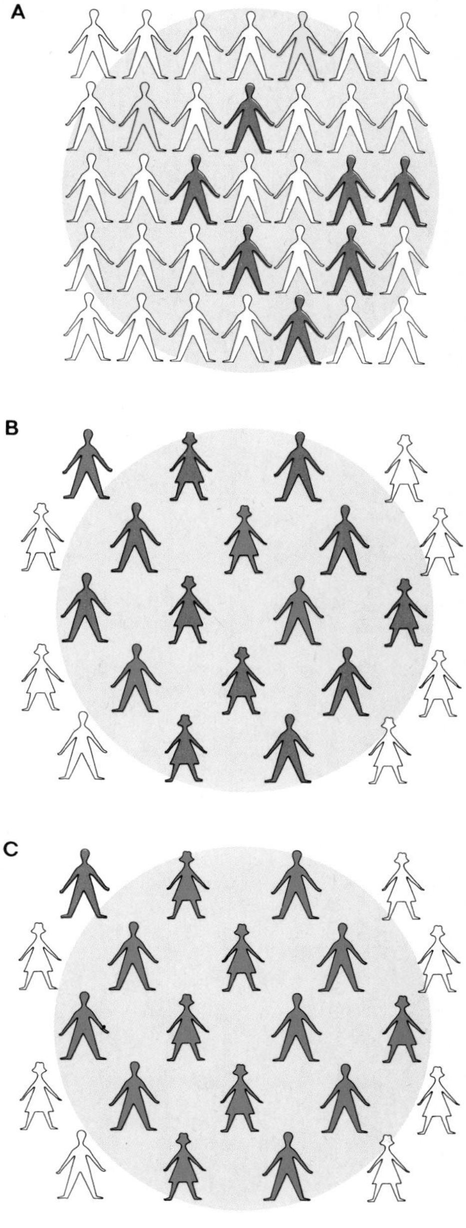

The occurrence of an epidemic and the form it takes depend on the nature of the disease, the disease-carriers involved, the density of the population and the degree of immunity in the population. (A) represents a closely-knit group in which the disease is spread by a few carriers (*yellow*), who do not show symptoms of the disease, to other members of the group (*red*). (B) shows how a disease introduced to a population (*blue circle*) from outside affects all (*red*) who are not immune (*green*). If the whole population is immune (C), there is no epidemic, though there may be a few isolated cases.

EPIDERMIS, the outermost layer of the SKIN.

EPIGENESIS, the succession of changes by which an embryonic organism passes through stages, more or less distinct from each other, in which new parts and organs appear that were not preformed. The slow acquisition of the characteristic form and function of the individual is called morphogenesis.

EPIGLOTTIS, a structure made of CARTILAGE and covered with mucous membrane, situated in the PHARYNX in front of the glottis or upper windpipe, from which it tends to divert food. It becomes swollen and inflamed in the childhood condition of acute epiglottitis and may cause respiratory obstruction.

EPIGRAM, terse and pointed saying in either prose or verse, often in couplet form. It is named for Greek monumental inscriptions, but the modern form was established by the Romans, particularly CATULLUS and MARTIAL. COLERIDGE defined it thus:

What is an epigram? A dwarfish whole.
Its body brevity, and wit its soul.

EPIGRAPHY, the study of ancient writings inscribed on hard or durable material. (See PALEOGRAPHY.)

EPILEPSY, the "sacred disease" of HIPPOCRATES, a chronic disease of the BRAIN, characterized by susceptibility to CONVULSIONS or other transient disorders of NERVOUS-SYSTEM function and due to abnormal electrical activity within the cerebral cortex. There are many types, of which four are common. **Grand mal** convulsions involve rhythmic jerking and rigidity of the limbs, associated with loss of consciousness, urinary incontinence, transient cessation of breathing and sometimes CYANOSIS, foaming at the mouth and tongue biting. **Petit mal** is largely a disorder of children in which very brief episodes of absence or vacancy occur, when the child is unaware of the surroundings, and is associated with a characteristic ELECTROENCEPHALOGRAPH disturbance. In **focal or Jacksonian epilepsy**, rhythmic movements start in one limb, progress to involve others and may lead to a grand mal convulsion. **Temporal lobe or psychomotor epilepsy** is often characterized by abnormal visceral sensations, unusual smells, visual distortion or memory disorder, and may or may not be followed by unconsciousness. **Status epilepticus** is when attacks of any sort occur repetitively without consciousness being regained in between; it requires emergency treatment.

Epilepsy may be either primary due to an inborn tendency, often appearing in early life, or it may be symptomatic of brain disorders such as those following trauma or brain SURGERY, ENCEPHALITIS, cerebral ABSCESS, TUMOR, or vascular disease. The ELECTROENCEPHALOGRAPH is the cornerstone of diagnosis in epilepsy, helping to confirm its presence and localize its origin, and suggesting whether there is a structural cause. If epilepsy is secondary, the cause may respond to treatment such as surgery, but all cases require anticonvulsant medication in the long term. Phenytoin (Dilantin), Phenobarbitone (see BARBITURATES), ethosuccimide, carbamazepine, diazepam and related compounds are important anticonvulsants, suitable for different types. DIETARY FOOD (ketogenic diet) may be effective in some cases.

EPINEPHRINE. See ADRENALINE.

EPIPHANIUS, Saint (c315–403), Greek Father of the Church, a native of Palestine. Made bishop of Salamis in 367, he was a friend of St. Jerome and a vigorous opponent of ARIANISM.

EPIPHANY (from Greek *epiphania*, manifestation), feast of the CHURCH YEAR held on 6 Jan. Originating in the 3rd century in the Eastern Church, where it commemorates Christ's baptism, it came into the Western Church in the 4th century and there celebrates the manifestation of Christ to the gentiles, represented by the MAGI.

EPIPHYSES, the ends of the long bones of the body (e.g., the FEMUR or HUMERUS) which are growth centers during growth and form the articulating surfaces at JOINTS. Each epiphysis remains partly cartilaginous during growth. The CARTILAGE is eventually converted into mature BONE which is then incorporated into the main shaft. Bone-growth disorders such as RICKETS and some HORMONE disorders affect the epiphyses.

EPIPHYTE, or **airplant**, a plant that grows on another but which obtains no nourishment from it. Various LICHENS, MOSSES, FERNS and ORCHIDS are epiphytes, particularly on trees. Epiphytes thrive in warm, wet climates. (See also COMMENSALISM; PARASITE.)

EPIRUS, ancient region in NW Greece, now partly in S Albania, along the coast of the Ionian Sea. A wet and mountainous region with many deep and narrow valleys, it is primarily pastureland and produces livestock and timber, though cereals and tobacco are grown. The area has had a turbulent history and has never kept independence for long.

EPISCIA, a relative of the AFRICAN VIOLET, frequently grown as a house plant for its variegated green, bronze, silver or pink foliage and white, yellow, pink, orange, red or blue flowers. It requires a few hours direct sun in the winter, but indirect light is sufficient in the summer. It suffers at temperatures below 17°C (60°F) and should only be watered often enough to keep the soil moist. Episcia produces numerous runners which are the main means of propagation. Family: Gesnariaceae.

EPISCOPAL CHURCH, Protestant, US denomination that formed itself from the remnants of the Church of England in the colonies after the Revolutionary War, and was finally given a constitution at a convention in Philadelphia in 1789. It now has 100 dioceses and a membership of around 3 500 000. Its administrative body is the Executive Council in New York, and it is governed by the triennial General Convention, composed of a House of Bishops and a House of Clerical and Lay Deputies. It is part of the Anglican Communion, and in recent years has been prominent in the ecumenical movement and in social action among minority groups.

EPISTEMOLOGY, the branch of philosophy dealing with the theory of knowledge. Its fundamental questions enquire as to the sources and status of our knowledge. It thus differs from **ontology** which is concerned with the being of things, the nature of things-in-themselves.

EPISTLE, a formal letter, often a literary form, addressed to a particular person or group but usually meant for publication. The 21 epistles of the New Testament are concerned with problems of the early Christian Church. The verse epistle was an important literary genre in France and Britain in the 17th and 18th centuries.

EPITAPH, literary form deriving from funerary inscriptions, although many epitaphs are witty or satirical and never seriously intended for tombstones. Many of those that are can be unintentionally comic, and form an entire genre of black humor.

This bust of the great violinist Yehudi Menuhin made in 1943 by Jacob Epstein is typical of the once-controversial sculptor's later work in rough-textured portraiture. It is now in the collection of the Peter Stuyvesant Foundation in Amsterdam.

EPITHELIOMA, CANCER of the skin EPITHELIUM.

EPITHELIUM, surface tissue covering an organ or structure. Examples include skin and the mucous membranes of the LUNGS, gut and urinary tract. A protective layer specialized for water resistance or absorption, depending on site, it usually shows a high cell-turnover rate.

E PLURIBUS UNUM (Latin: out of many, one), motto referring to the unification of the original 13 American colonies. Chosen for the Continental Congress by John Adams, Franklin and Jefferson, it is now inscribed on the great seal of the US and on many US coins.

EPOXY RESIN, class of thermoplastic POLYMERS of the polyether type, formed from epichlorhydrin and a dihydric ALCOHOL or PHENOL (e.g. bisphenol-A), and cross-linked by a curing agent. Inert, strong, adhesive, and good insulators, they are mixed with fillers and plasticizers and used for construction, coating and bonding.

EPSOM SALTS, or epsomite, the mineral MAGNESIUM sulfate heptahydrate, found at Epsom, England, and elsewhere. It has been used as a LAXATIVE.

EPSTEIN, Sir Jacob (1880–1959), US-born sculptor, living in London, whose work often caused controversy. His early sculptures were influenced by African sculpture, Constantin BRANCUSI and VORTICISM, but after 1915 he turned, in more conventional style, to religious subjects and portraiture. His works include *Rock Drill* (1913) and *Ecce Homo* (1935).

EQUAL EMPLOYMENT OPPORTUNITY COMMISSION. See FAIR EMPLOYMENT PRACTICES.

EQUALITY, in mathematics, two or more expressions which represent the same thing. Thus $3+4=7$ is an equality. For CONSTANT nonzero a, b, c, the equality $a=b$ implies:

$$b=a,$$
$$a+c=b+c,$$
$$ac=bc,$$

and if $b=c$ then $a=c$. (See also EQUIVALENCE.)

EQUATION, a statement of equality. Should this statement involve a VARIABLE it will, unless it is an invalid equation, be true for one or more values of that variable, though those values need not be expressible in terms of REAL NUMBERS: $x^2+2=0$ has two imaginary (see IMAGINARY NUMBERS) roots, $+\sqrt{-2}$ and $-\sqrt{-2}$.

Linear equations are those in which no variable term is raised to a POWER higher than 1. Solution of linear equations in one variable is simple. Consider the equation $x+3=7$. The equation will still be true if we add or subtract equal numbers from each side (see EQUALITY):

$$x+3=7,$$
$$x+3-3=7-3$$

and $$x=4.$$

Linear equations are so called because, if considered as the equation of a CURVE (see ANALYTIC GEOMETRY), they can be plotted as a straight LINE (see also FUNCTION).

Quadratic equations are those in a single variable which appears to the power 2, but not higher. A quadratic equation always has two roots (see ROOTS OF AN EQUATION) though these roots may be equal.

Cubic equations are those in a single variable which appears to the power 3, but not higher. Cubic equations always have three roots, though two or all three of these may be equal.

Degree of an equation. Linear, quadratic and cubic equations are said to be of the 1st, 2nd and 3rd degrees respectively. More generally, the degree of an equation is defined as the SUM of the EXPONENTS of the variables in the highest-power term of the equation. In $ax^5+bx^3y^3+cx^2y^5=0$, the sums of the exponents of each term are, respectively, 5, 6 and 7; hence cx^2y^5 is the highest-power term, and the equation is of the 7th degree.

Radical equations are those in which ROOTS of the variables appear: e.g., $a\sqrt[p]{x}+b\sqrt[q]{x}+c=0$.

Radical equations can always be simply converted into equations of the nth order, where $n = 1, 2, 3 \ldots$, by raising both sides of the equation to a power, repeating the process where necessary.

Simultaneous equations. A single equation in two or more variables is generally insoluble. However, if there are as many equations as there are variables, it is possible to solve for each variable. Consider

$$2x + xy + 3 = 0 \qquad (1)$$

and

$$x + 2xy = 0. \qquad (2)$$

Multiplying equation (1) by 2 we have

$$4x + 2xy + 6 = 0 \qquad (3)$$

and, subtracting equation (2) from this,

$$3x + 6 = 0.$$

Hence

$$x = -2.$$

Substituting this value into equation (1) we find the value $y = -\frac{1}{2}$. More complicated simultaneous equations can be solved in the same way (see also ELIMINATION). (See also DIFFERENCE EQUATIONS; DIFFERENTIAL EQUATIONS.)

EQUATION OF A CURVE. See ANALYTIC GEOMETRY.

EQUATOR, an imaginary line drawn about the earth such that all points on it are equidistant from the N and S poles (see NORTH POLE; SOUTH POLE). All points on it have a latitude of 0°. (See also CELESTIAL SPHERE; LATITUDE AND LONGITUDE.)

EQUATORIAL CURRENT, collective name for a complex system of ocean currents flowing in the environs of the equator in the Atlantic, Pacific and Indian Oceans. In all three there are W-flowing currents roughly N and S of the EQUATOR, with an E-flowing countercurrent between. There are also E-flowing undercurrents beneath the main W-flowing currents. In the Pacific, the N Equatorial Current is part of the clockwise OCEAN CURRENT system with the JAPAN CURRENT, NORTH PACIFIC CURRENT and CALIFORNIA CURRENT. Similarly in the Atlantic, the N Equatorial Current is part of the clockwise system with the GULF STREAM, Azores Current and CANARIES CURRENT.

EQUATORIAL GUINEA, small republic between Gabon and Cameroon on the W coast of Africa, consisting of the coastal province of Mbini (10 040sq mi), the island of Macías Nguema (785sq mi) and other small islands in the Gulf of Guinea. Most of the indigenous population belongs to the Fang ethnic group, but there are many immigrant workers. The country's main resources are volcanic soils and timber; its main products are cocoa, coffee, bananas, palm oil and timber. Formerly Spanish colonies, the territories became provinces in 1960 and became fully independent in 1968.

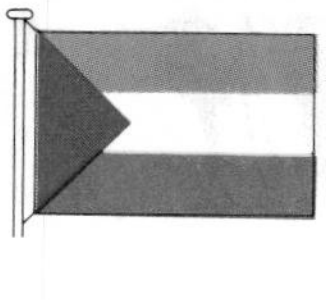

Official name: The Republic of Equatorial Guinea
Capital: Malabo
Area: 9 828sq mi
Population: 300 000
Languages: Spanish; Fang, Bubi, Ibo
Religions: Roman Catholic; Protestant, Muslim, Animist
Monetary unit(s): 1 Guinea peseta = 100 centimos

EQUILATERAL POLYGON, a POLYGON all of whose sides are of equal length. The term is most frequently applied when describing a TRIANGLE.

EQUILIBRIUM, a state in which a mechanical, electrical, thermodynamic or other system will remain if undisturbed. In "stable equilibrium" (as with a well sprung automobile body) the system returns to its original position if disturbed; the position of stable equilibrium thus determines the rest position of the system. In "unstable equilibrium" (as with a tall pole balanced on one end) it moves farther away. Stable and unstable equilibria correspond to configurations with minimal and maximal ENERGY respectively. Systems in thermodynamic equilibrium, e.g., the contents and air in an unheated room, have the same TEMPERATURE throughout.

EQUILIBRIUM, Chemical, the EQUILIBRIUM condition of a reversible reaction, in which the concentrations of the reactants and products have no tendency to change. In this case, the free energy of the system (see THERMODYNAMICS) is a MINIMUM, and it may be shown that for the general reaction $aA + bB \rightleftharpoons cC + dD$ there is an equilibrium constant K given approximately by

$$K = [C]^c [D]^d / [A]^a [B]^b$$

where [A] is the concentration of A, and so on. Chemical KINETICS yields the same equation, since at equilibrium the rates of the forward and back reactions are equal, and so K is also given by the ratio of the rate constants of these two reactions $(K = k_1/k_{-1})$.

EQUINOXES, (1) the two times each year when day and night are of equal length. The spring or **vernal equinox** occurs in March, the **autumnal equinox** in September. (2) The two intersections of the ECLIPTIC and equator (see CELESTIAL SPHERE). The vernal equinox is in PISCES (see also First Point of ARIES), the autumnal between VIRGO and LEO.

EQUITES, Roman term for "cavalrymen," which came to mean members of the *ordo equester*, a privileged social and political class. They were at first recruited as an elite cavalry corps, but by the 1st century BC they had become a distinct officer class. The class came to denote the middle nobility, especially those engaged in commerce rather than government. Under the empire it was gradually transformed into an elite civil service, but was later debased and gradually died out.

EQUITY, legal term for the application of certain principles by the judiciary to prevent injustice that would result from strict application of the law. In fact, however, in English and US COMMON LAW these principles have hardened into rules of law and have been incorporated into the system. They originated in the judicial remedies of the English Court of CHANCERY, which introduced and shaped such essential legal forms as the TRUST, EASEMENT and MORTGAGE.

EQUIVALENCE, a relationship * such that if a*b then b*a, and if a*b and a*c then b*c. Moreover, a*a and b*b. One example of equivalence is the relation EQUALITY; another CONGRUENCE. The sign for equivalence is ≡, as in $\frac{1}{4} \equiv 25\%$.

EQUIVALENT WEIGHT, the weight of an element or compound which combines with or displaces the equivalent weight of any other element or compound; for an element, it equals the atomic weight (see ATOM) divided by the VALENCE. This presupposes the **law of equivalent proportions**, which states that the ratio of the weights of two elements A and B which combine with the same weight of an element C, is the same as the ratio of the weights of A and B which combine with each other, or a small integral multiple of it. Since an element may have more than one valence, and a compound may react in more than one way, they may have more than one equivalent weight. The **normality** of a solution is its concentration in gram-equivalent weights per litre; a solution whose normality is 1 is called normal. (See also ELECTROLYSIS; MOLECULAR WEIGHT.)

ERA OF GOOD FEELINGS, a newspaper's term for the two administrations of President James Monroe, 1817–25. Coined after Monroe's friendly reception by Boston Federalists, it was belied by the ill-feeling and discord in the Republican administration among Monroe's potential successors.

ERASISTRATUS (3rd century BC), Greek physician of the ALEXANDRIAN SCHOOL who is credited with the foundation of PHYSIOLOGY as a separate discipline.

ERASMUS, Desiderius (c1466–1536), Dutch Roman Catholic humanist and advocate of church and social reform. The illegitimate son of a priest, he was forced by his guardians to enter a monastery and was ordained in 1492. Studies in Paris imbued him with a deep dislike of Scholastic theology, and on a visit to England in 1499 he met and was influenced by the humanists John COLET and Thomas MORE. He published *The Christian Soldier's Handbook* (1503), with an emphasis on spiritual simplicity. *In Praise of Folly* (1509) is a light, witty satire on Church corruptions, paving the way for the REFORMATION. The foremost scholar of his time, Erasmus produced the first critical edition of the Greek New Testament (1516) and edited the works of the Fathers. Although a moderate reformer, he called for religious peace, and opposed LUTHER in his *Diatribe on Free Will* (1524), which drew a crushing reply from Luther. Erasmus died embittered by the Reformation controversies, accepted by neither side.

One of the intellectual leaders of the Renaissance in northern Europe, Erasmus was among the first "men of letters" to achieve widespread recognition through the printed word. This portrait of him by Holbein now hangs in the Galeria Nazionale in Parma, Italy.

ERASTIANISM, doctrine that the state should have complete control over the affairs of the Church. It is named for ERASTUS who, in fact, believed only that a Christian state could administer church discipline.

ERASTUS, Thomas (1524–1583), Swiss physician for whom ERASTIANISM was named, although he never subscribed to it. An adherent of ZWINGLI, he clashed with the Calvinists, particularly over the practice of excommunication, which he opposed in his *Explicatio gravissimae quaestionis* (1589).

ERATO, Muse of Love. See MUSES; POETRY.

ERATOSTHENES OF CYRENE (273–192 BC), the Librarian of the ALEXANDRIAN LIBRARY, remembered for his remarkably accurate determination of the circumference of the earth and for his map of the then-known world.

ERBIUM (Er), one of the LANTHANUM SERIES. AW 167.3, mp 1522°C, bp 2510°C, sg 9.066 (25°C).

EREBUS, in Greek mythology, the son of CHAOS and personification of darkness. The name was also given to the hinterlands of Hades.

EREBUS, Mount, active volcano on Ross Island in Antarctica, around 13 200ft high. It has three cones, only one of which is active.

ERECH, biblical name of Uruk, an ancient city in Mesopotamia, now S Iraq. Founded c4500 BC near the Euphrates R, it was the city of the epic hero GILGAMESH. It is believed to have survived and prospered until at least 70 BC.

ERECHTHEUM, temple dedicated to Athena and the mythical king ERECHTHEUS, on the Acropolis in Athens. It was built 421–05 BC as a multiple shrine. Much of it still stands, including the famous Porch of the Caryatids.

ERECHTHEUS, in Greek mythology, a king of Athens who sacrificed his youngest daughter in order to win a war. His other daughters committed suicide and he was destroyed by the gods.

ERFURT, historic city in SW East Germany, capital of Erfurt district. Dating from the Frankish Empire, the town has long been a cultural and artistic center, noted for its architecture. Its main industries are machinery, electrical equipment and clothing. Pop 196200.

ERG, the unit of WORK in the CGS system (see CGS UNITS), equal to 10^{-7} joules in SI UNITS.

ERGONOMICS. See HUMAN ENGINEERING.

ERGOT, disease of GRASSES and SEDGES caused by fungal species of the genus *Claviceps*. Also, the masses of dormant mycelia (sclerotia) formed in the flower heads of the host plant. Ergots contain toxic ALKALOIDS which if eaten by animals or man, can cause serious poisoning (ergotism or St. Anthony's fire).

ERHARD, Ludwig (1897–   ), West German economist and statesman. Forced out of academic life by the Nazis in 1942, he was appointed to various posts by the occupying powers in 1945–49. In 1949 he became economics minister under Konrad ADENAUER, and in this post he was the prime architect of West Germany's post-WWII revival. He succeeded Adenauer as chancellor in 1963, but was removed from chancellorship and party leadership in 1966.

ERICSON, Leif (flourished 999–1002 AD), Norse explorer, son of ERIC THE RED. Tradition holds that after his conversion to Christianity, Ericson tried to spread the religion in Greenland. On his return voyage in 1000 AD, he discovered some part of the North American coast (called VINLAND in old Norse sagas). Modern scholars do not agree on the location of Vinland, but excavation at a Norse site in Newfoundland in the 1960s lends credence to the story.

ERICSSON, John (1803–1889), Swedish-born US engineer and inventor who developed the screw PROPELLER (patented 1836). He designed and built the *Monitor* (1862), the first warship to bear an armored revolving gun turret. Later he pioneered researches into tapping solar energy for power.

One of the leading, and most original, members of the Surrealist school, Ernst innovated many techniques in his painting, including *decalcomania* (an offshoot of *frottage*), an example of which is seen here in his *Landscape* (1941).

ERIC THE RED (10th century AD), Norse chieftain and discoverer of Greenland. He settled in Iceland with his exiled father, but was banished for manslaughter about 980. Eric sailed W and discovered Greenland, then returned to Iceland where he organized a voyage about 985 to colonize Greenland. He founded settlements near present-day Julianehaab and Osterbygd, which may have survived for as long as 500 years.

ERIDANUS (the River), large, long CONSTELLATION of the S celestial hemisphere. Of particular interest is Epsilon Eridani: this, at 3.31pc, is the closest star to us to resemble our SUN.

ERIE, city in NW Pa., seat of Erie Co., on Lake Erie. Founded in 1795 on the site of a French fort, Erie is now a major port and industrial center, producing processed foods, locomotives, paper and rubber products. Pop 129231.

ERIE, Battle of Lake, major naval engagement in the WAR OF 1812. The US forces, led by Commodore Oliver Hazard PERRY, defeated the British at Put-in-Bay, Ohio, Sept. 10, 1813. The victory gave the US control of Lake Erie and the NE.

ERIE, Lake, one of the five GREAT LAKES of North America, bordered by N.Y., Pa., Ohio, Mich. and Ontario, Canada. Named for the ERIE INDIANS, it is the shallowest and fourth-largest (9940sq mi) of the Great Lakes. Erie is icebound much of the year and is heavily polluted by waste from industry and large cities. Some of its chief ports are Buffalo, N.Y., Erie, Pa., Cleveland and Toledo, Ohio. The US–Canadian boundary passes through the center of the lake. (See also SAINT LAWRENCE SEAWAY.)

ERIE CANAL, former major artificial waterway in the US, connecting Buffalo, N.Y., on Lake Erie with Albany, N.Y., on the Hudson R. The NEW YORK STATE BARGE CANAL now follows part of the old Erie Canal route, which was completed in 1825 as a result of the political support of N.Y. Governor DeWitt CLINTON. The canal, originally 365mi long, facilitated settlement and shipping between the East and the Midwest, and stimulated the growth and financial development of New York and many Midwestern cities.

ERIE INDIANS, North American tribe, related to the IROQUOIS, which occupied areas SE of Lake Erie (named after them) in N.Y., Pa. and Ohio. In the early 17th century they numbered about 14000, but the Iroquois practically exterminated them by 1656, and adopted or enslaved the survivors.

ERIGENA, John Scotus (c810–877), Irish theologian and philosopher who taught at Paris, probably the most advanced thinker of his time. He attempted to combine Christian theology and NEOPLATONISM.

ERIKSON, Eric Homburger (1902–   ), German-born US psychoanalyst who defined eight stages, each characterized by a specific psychological conflict, in the development of the EGO from infancy to old age. He studied also the IDENTITY, introducing the concept of the identity crisis.

ERINYES. See FURIES.

ERITREA, province of N Ethiopia, on the W coast of the Red Sea. Eritrea is populated by many ethnic groups, with diverse socio-cultural systems. Less than 5% of this hot, dry, mountainous region is cultivated. The capital, Asmara, produces some food products, textiles and hide. Roads, a railroad and air service link the province with the Sudan and the rest of Ethiopia. Eritrea became an Italian colony in 1890 and an Ethiopian province in 1962. Since then sporadic warfare has been carried on by rebels to gain independence from Ethiopia.

ERIVAN. See YEREVAN.

ERLANDER, Tage Fritiof (1901–   ), Swedish statesman and prime minister, 1946–68. During his administration, Erlander expanded social welfare legislation, maintained Sweden's neutrality in the COLD WAR and friendly relations with the West.

ERLANGER, city in N central Ky. Mainly a residential suburb, it is 4mi SE of Cincinnati's main airport. Pop 12676.

ERLANGER, Joseph (1874–1965), US physiologist who shared with Herbert GASSER the 1964 Nobel Prize for Physiology or Medicine for their discovery that different nerve fibers have different functions, carrying different types of impulses and at different speeds. (See NERVOUS SYSTEM.)

ERMINE, term for any WEASEL which turns white in winter. In the Middle Ages ermine fur was used only by royalty; it was later associated with high-court judges. Ermine fur is obtained from the Russian STOAT and several species of North American weasel.

ERNST, Max (1891–1976), German artist, leader of the DADA movement in Cologne (1919) and one of the founders of SURREALISM in Paris (1931). Best known for his COLLAGE work, Ernst also developed the technique of "frottage," whereby he created unusual patterns by rubbing paper placed over surfaces like wood and stone with pencil or charcoal.

EROS. See CUPID.

EROS, an ASTEROID measuring roughly $35 \times 16 \times 8$km discovered in 1898 by G. Witt. Eros' eccentric orbit brings it close to earth every seven

Erosion is one of the most potent influences in shaping the landscape. At Dead Horse Point, Utah (*left*), the Colorado River has cut a deep canyon in the slowly uplifted Colorado plateau. Glacier National Park, Montana (*right*), contains spectacular valleys displaying the U-shaped cross-section characteristic of glacial erosion. These have been excavated by former glaciers, usually following the course of preexisting V-shaped river valleys. Except on the high shoulders of the valleys, no remnants of the original valley slopes remain, the new valley floor lying much below the level of its predecessor.

years, sometimes within 22 million km. Its orbital period is 643 days.

EROSION, the wearing away of the earth's surface by natural agents. Running water constitutes the most effective eroding agent, the process being accelerated by the transportation of particles eroded or weathered farther upstream: it is these that are primarily responsible for further erosion. GROUNDWATER may cause erosion by dissolving certain minerals in the rock (see also KARST). OCEAN WAVES and especially the debris that they carry may substantially erode coastlines. GLACIERS are extremely important eroding agents, eroded material becoming embedded in the ice and acting as further abrasives (see ABRASION). Many common landscape features are the results of glacial erosion (e.g., DRUMLINS, FJORDS). Rocks exposed to the atmosphere undergo **weathering**: mechanical weathering usually results from temperature changes (e.g., in **exfoliation**, the cracking off of thin sheets of rock due to extreme daily temperature variation); chemical weathering results from chemical changes brought about by, for example, substances dissolved in RAIN water. Wind erosion may be important in dry, sandy areas. (See also SOIL EROSION.)

ERYMANTHIAN BOAR, in Greek mythology, a savage beast who was captured by the hero HERCULES as one of his 12 labors.

ERYSIPELAS, or St. Anthony's fire, a SKIN infection, usually affecting the face, caused by certain types of STREPTOCOCCUS. It is common in infancy and middle age. ERYTHEMA and swelling spread with a clear margin and cause blistering. It is a short illness with FEVER; if it affects the trunk it may however cause prostration and can prove fatal. PENICILLIN is the ANTIBIOTIC of choice.

ERYTHEMA, redness of the SKIN due to increased CAPILLARY BLOOD flow; it occurs in INFLAMMATION including DERMATITIS, and numerous rashes.

ERYTHROCYTE, or red BLOOD cell, a discoid cell without a nucleus, that contains HEMOGLOBIN and is responsible for OXYGEN transport in the body.

ERZERUM, or Erzurum, capital of Erzurum province, E Turkey. A military fortress since the 5th century, today it is an important agricultural and railroad center. Pop 134 655.

ESAKI, Leo (1925–), Japanese-born US physicist awarded, with I. GIAEVER and B. JOSEPHSON, the 1973 Nobel Prize for Physics for his work on tunneling (see WAVE MECHANICS).

ESARHADDON (d. 669 BC), king of Assyria from 681 BC, son of SENNACHERIB. A powerful ruler, he enlarged the Assyrian empire by subduing CHALDEA and ELAM and by conquering Egypt (673–670).

ESAU, son of ISAAC and REBECCA, elder twin brother of JACOB to whom he sold his birthright for a meal of "red pottage." According to the Old Testament, Esau was a coarse man and a hunter, and the ancestor of the Edomites.

ESCALANTE, Silvestre Vélez de (flourished 1768–79), Spanish Franciscan missionary and explorer. Based in what is now N.M., he sought an overland route to Monterey, Cal., and rediscovered the Grand Canyon. He was the first Spanish explorer in Ut.

ESCALATOR, a moving stairway to transport passengers or goods from one level to another. Most simply, it comprises steps mounted on an endless belt such that they fold flat at top and bottom to allow passengers more easily to step on and off. (See also ELEVATOR.)

ESCANABA, city in the Upper Peninsula of N Mich., seat of Delta Co. It ships large amounts of iron ore on the Great Lakes. Pop 15 391.

ESCAPE VELOCITY, the velocity that a less massive body must achieve in order to escape from the gravitational attraction of a more massive body; sometimes known as the parabolic velocity. The earth's escape velocity is 11.2km/s. Less massive planets have smaller escape velocities (Mars: 5.1km/s), more massive planets greater escape velocities (Jupiter: 61.0km/s).

ESCARPMENT. See SCARP.

ESCHATOLOGY, the study of the "last things." A universal theme in religion, especially Christianity and Judaism, eschatology deals with the meaning of history and the final destiny of the world, mankind and the individual. Old Testament eschatology centers in the expected MESSIAH. Christian eschatology includes the doctrines of death, RESURRECTION, HEAVEN, HELL, the SECOND COMING of Christ and the LAST JUDGMENT (see also MILLENNIUM). The benefits of the "age to come" are in part realized now in the Church (see KINGDOM OF GOD).

ESCHEAT, term in English feudal land law which meant return of a tenant's property to the lord of the land. In the US, property escheats to the state, country or city if no legitimate heirs claim it when the owner dies without a will.

ESCHENBACH, Wolfram von. See WOLFRAM VON ESCHENBACH.

ESCOFFIER, Georges-Auguste (1846–1935), world-famous French chef, director of the Carlton and Savoy Hotel kitchens (London), and author of many cookbooks, including *Ma Cuisine* (1924), he was awarded the *Légion d'Honneur* (1920) for his culinary achievements.

ESCONDIDO, city in S Cal., 28mi N of San Diego. It produces wine, dairy products and fruit, and has chemical and electronic industries. Pop 36 792.

ESCORIAL, monastery and palace in central Spain, 26mi NW of Madrid. One of the most magnificent buildings in Europe, it was built (1563–84) by PHILIP II and houses a church, palace, college, library and a mausoleum in which many Spanish kings are buried. Its famous art collection contains works by VELÁSQUEZ, EL GRECO and TINTORETTO, among others.

ESDRAELON, Plain of, fertile lowland in N Israel, separating Galilee and Samaria. Esdraelon, also known as Jezreel, was a battleground for centuries (1500 BC–1918 AD). It is the site of the first large KIBBUTZ and is a rich agricultural area.

ESDRAS, the Greek form of EZRA, a Jewish priest often called the "second Moses." Esdras is the name given to four Old Testament books, two in the Jewish canon (Ezra and Nehemiah) and two in the Protestant APOCRYPHA (1 and 2 Esdras, called 3 and 4 Esdras in the Vulgate). (See also PSEUDEPIGRAPHA.)

ESHKOL, Levi (1895–1969), Israeli political leader and prime minister, 1963–69. He emigrated from Russia to Palestine (1914), helped found one of the first *kibbutzim* (1920) and *Histadrut* (the labor federation). He succeeded BEN-GURION as prime minister, unified the labor parties in Israel to gain a majority in the KNESSET and led the country in the SIX DAY WAR (1967).

ESKER, serpentine ridge of glacial DRIFT, up to several kilometres long, formed from deposits at the mouth of a subglacial stream as the GLACIER retreated.

ESKIMO, a Mongoloid race native to the Arctic coasts of Greenland, North America and NE Asia, believed to have crossed the Bering Strait from Asia in about 2000 BC. Considering their widespread distribution, the Eskimos, who speak dialects of the Eskimo-ALEUT language family and today number some 70 000, have preserved their cultural identity to a remarkable degree. Although the white man's influence has been important in education and medical welfare and in the establishment of cooperatives, the Eskimos have only intermarried with white settlers, to any significant extent, on Greenland. Many still live by hunting and fishing, using traditional skills to exploit the unyielding Arctic environment. Seals, fish, walrus and whales are hunted for food, fuel and clothing. Travel on land is by DOG-SLED and on the water by KAYAK or *umiak*, a skin boat. During hunting expeditions, temporary IGLOO shelters are sometimes built, but the basic home, in which the Eskimos live in small communal groups, is made of sod, driftwood and stone. Tents of hide or sealskin are used in the summer. The traditional Eskimo religion draws heavily on a rich folklore. On Greenland, many Eskimos are Christian. SHAMANISM is also practiced.

ESKIŞEHIR, city in Turkey, 128mi W of Ankara. It produces farm machinery, refined sugar and meerschaum pipes. Pop 173 882.

ESOPHAGUS, the thin tube leading from the PHARYNX to the STOMACH. Food passes down it as a bolus by gravity and PERISTALSIS. Its diseases include reflux esophagitis (HEARTBURN), ULCER, stricture and CANCER.

An eskimo obtaining drinking water from the snow at Sachs Harbor in the Arctic Circle. Eskimos have many different words for such important elements in their lives as snow, ice and water.

ESP, or **Extrasensory Perception,** the perception other than by the recognized SENSES of an event or object; and, by extension, those powers of the mind (such as **telekinesis**, the moving of distant objects by the exercise of willpower) that cannot be scientifically evaluated. The best known and most researched area of ESP is **telepathy**, the ability of two or more individuals to communicate without sensory contact: though laboratory tests (see PARAPSYCHOLOGY) have been inconclusive, it seems probable that telepathic communication between individuals can exist. Analogous is **empathy**, the communication across distance of EMOTIONS. Another important area of ESP is **precognition**, the prior knowledge of an event: again, despite a mass of circumstantial evidence, laboratory tests have been inconclusive. The term **clairvoyance** is sometimes used for ESP.

ESPALIER, name given to any plant that is trained to grow against a support, either for ornamental purposes or in orchards for maximum use of space and light. Also, term used for the device on which the plants are trained.

ESPARTO, *Stipa tenacissima*, coarse feathery grass native to sandy areas of N Africa and Spain. The fiber produced from the grass is used in making rope, mats, sandals and high-quality paper. Esparto fiber is also produced from a similar grass *Lygeum spartium*.

ESPERANTO, artificial language created by Dr. L. L. ZAMENHOF of Poland to enable people of different linguistic backgrounds to communicate more easily and with less misunderstanding. Consisting of "root words" derived from Latin, Greek and the Romance and Germanic languages, Esperanto is easy to learn and has enjoyed more popularity since its introduction in 1887 than other artificial "universal" languages such as Volpük and Interlingua. Probably around 8 million people speak Esperanto. (See also BASIC ENGLISH.)

ESPIONAGE, clandestine attempt to gather confidential information, usually of a political, military or industrial nature. Espionage is an ancient practice; it is mentioned in the Bible and in the *Iliad*. Espionage activities are primarily carried on by individual nations to gain data on other nations, although industrial espionage is becoming widespread. Undercover espionage may be severely penalized; although espionage is not illegal under international law, every country has laws against it. (See also CENTRAL INTELLIGENCE AGENCY; INTELLIGENCE SERVICE; NATIONAL SECURITY COUNCIL; OFFICE OF STRATEGIC SERVICES.)

ESPÍRITO SANTO, state in E Brazil, on the Atlantic coast, with an area of 17 605sq mi. It produces coffee, sugarcane, cotton, tobacco and lumber.

ESQUILINE HILL. See SEVEN HILLS OF ROME.

The ruins of Qumran in western Jordan on the shores of the Dead Sea, thought to have once been an Essene community owing to its proximity to the site where the Dead Sea Scrolls were discovered. The scrolls sparked off much speculative debate about the exact nature of the Essenes and their relationship with historical Judaism and Christianity.

ESSEN, city in West Germany, North Rhine-Westphalia state. Originally the site of a convent, Essen was the home of German industrialist Friedrich KRUPP and is now the largest industrial center in the RUHR coal field, producing iron, steel, chemicals and glass. Pop 704 800.

ESSENCE, in philosophy, a term referring to the permanent actuality of a thing, the that-by-which it can be recognized, whatever its outward appearance. Different philosophers have used the term with various detailed significations; LOCKE, for instance, distinguished a thing's real essence, the what-it-is-in-itself, from its nominal essence, the what-it-appears-to-be, the name men give it.

ESSENES, ascetic sect which flourished in Palestine from about 200 BC to about 100 AD. Gathered in small monastic communities, the Essenes held property in common and observed the law of Moses strictly. The DEAD SEA SCROLLS may have been written by a community of Essenes.

ESSENTIAL OILS, volatile oils produced by many plants, flowers and fruits which give them their characteristic odor or flavor. A great number of chemical compounds have been identified from various essential oils. They are used commercially for flavoring food and in perfumes; some have medicinal properties.

ESSEQUIBO RIVER, longest river in GUYANA, flowing from the Brazilian border N for about 630mi to the Atlantic Ocean. The river drains over 50% of Guyana and forms a vital part of its transportation system.

ESSEX, suburb of Baltimore, Md., E of the city, on the Back R. Pop 38 193.

ESSEX, town in NW Vt., 5mi E of Burlington, incorporating Essex Junction which is an industrial village. Fort Ethan Allen is located close by. Pop 10 951.

ESSEX, Robert Devereux, 2nd Earl of (1567–1601), a favorite of Queen ELIZABETH I. He acquired some fame in European military campaigns and was knighted in 1589 and made lord lieutenant of Ireland in 1599, a post he lost by failing to crush the Earl of Tyrone's rebellion. Unfailingly ambitious for power, he later attempted a coup to establish his own party at court, was defeated and then executed.

ESSEX JUNTO, name of a group of US New England Federalist property owners who supported Alexander HAMILTON and earlier had opposed Mass. radicals in the American Revolution. They were regarded as traitors by many Americans.

ESTAING, Jean Baptiste Charles Henri Hector, Comte d' (1729–1794), French admiral, commander of a French fleet which assisted the Americans in the REVOLUTIONARY WAR. In 1779 he took part with General Benjamin LINCOLN in the abortive attack on Savannah.

ESTATE, general legal term for property. A man's estate is the total value of his property less his total financial liabilities.

ESTATES GENERAL. See STATES GENERAL.

ESTERHAZY, noble Magyar family important in Hungarian history. **Count Pál** (1635–1713), defended Vienna against the Turks in 1683 and was made a prince of the Holy Roman Empire. **Count Miklós Jozsef** (1714–1790), received the title of prince for himself and his heirs, modeled the family castle on the palace of Versailles, and employed HAYDN as his musical director. **Prince Miklós** (1765–1833), declined to accept Napoleon I's offer of the crown of Hungary (1809).

ESTERS, organic compounds formed by CONDENSATION of an ACID (organic or inorganic) with an ALCOHOL, water being eliminated. This reaction, esterification, is acid-catalyzed; its reverse, HYDROLYSIS, is acid- or base-catalyzed; an EQUILIBRIUM is set up in aqueous solution. Many esters occur naturally: those of low molecular weight have fruity odors and are used in flavorings, perfumes and as solvents; those of higher molecular weight are FATS and WAXES.

ESTHER, Old Testament book. It tells of Esther, formerly named Hadassah, a Jewess, queen of the Persian King Ahasuerus (probably XERXES I) who prevented the king's favorite, Haman, from massacring all Persian Jews. Instead the Jews' enemies were slain. The story is the origin of the feast of PURIM.

ESTHETICS. See AESTHETICS.

ESTIVATION. See HIBERNATION.

ESTONIA, or Estonian Soviet Socialist Republic, constituent republic of the USSR, S of the Gulf of Finland and E of the Baltic Sea. The largest cities are Tallin, the capital, Tartu and Pärnu. A third of the land, which consists of plains and low plateaus, is forested. The climate is temperate. Estonians are ethnically and linguistically related to the Finns. More than half the population is urban, although agriculture, especially dairying, is the chief industry. Other important industries are shipbuilding, electrical engineering, cement and textiles. Ruled at various times by the Danes, the TEUTONIC KNIGHTS, the Swedes and the Russians, Estonia became independent in 1918. Its annexation by the USSR in 1940 is not recognized by the US.

ESTORIL, resort town in Portugal, on the Atlantic, 15mi W of Lisbon. It enjoys a mild climate and is popular throughout the year. Pop 15 740.

ESTOURNELLES DE CONSTANT, Paul Henri Benjamin Balluat, Baron d' (1852–1924), French diplomat and pacifist, co-winner of the 1909 Nobel Peace Prize. He strove for international cooperation and disarmament and attended the HAGUE PEACE CONFERENCES of 1899 and 1907.

ESTROGENS, female sex HORMONES concerned with the development of secondary sexual characteristics and maturation of reproductive organs. They are under the control of pituitary-gland GONADOTROPHINS and their amount varies before and after MENSTRUATION and in PREGNANCY. After the menopause, their production decreases. Many pills used for CONTRACEPTION contain estrogen, as do some preparations given to menopausal women. Their administration may lead to venous THROMBOSIS, and some other diseases.

ESTUARY, the typically funnel-shaped part of a river near its mouth where fresh- and seawater mix and which is affected by TIDES. At ebb tide both tide and river current assist in the EROSION of the estuary Estuaries may also form by local subsidence of the coast. (See also FIRTH.) Many estuaries provide important harbors.

ETCHING, an ENGRAVING technique in which acid is used to "bite" lines into a metal plate which is then printed, usually intaglio. The plate, usually copper or zinc, is first coated with a resin "ground" through which the design is drawn with a needle. Only the exposed metal is etched away. Different line thicknesses can be obtained by selective stopping out and repeated exposure to the acid. (See also AQUATINT.)

ETHANE (C_2H_6), an ALKANE occurring in natural gas and formed in petroleum CRACKING. It is catalytically dehydrogenated to produce ETHYLENE. MW 30.1, mp −183°C, bp −89°C.

ETHANOL (C_2H_5OH), or ethyl alcohol, also known as grain alcohol, the best-known ALCOHOL; a colorless, inflammable, volatile, toxic liquid, the active constituent of ALCOHOLIC BEVERAGES. Of immense industrial importance, ethanol is used as a solvent, in ANTIFREEZE, as an ANTISEPTIC and in much chemical

Simeon with the baby Jesus in the Temple by Rembrandt, an incomparable example of the etcher's art, showing the great artist's mastery of chiaroscuro and (*inset*) the boldness of the intricate lines which make up the picture.

synthesis. Its production is controlled by law, and it is heavily taxed unless made unfit for drinking by adulteration (denatured alcohol); see METHANOL. Most industrial ethanol is the AZEOTROPIC MIXTURE containing 5% water. It is made by FERMENTATION of sugars or by catalytic hydration of ETHYLENE. MW 46.1 mp −112°C, bp 78°C. (See also DISTILLED LIQUOR.)

ETHELBALD (d. 757), king of MERCIA, 716–57. He had conquered the region S of the Humber R by 731. He attacked NORTHUMBRIA in 740 and Wales in 743, but was defeated by WESSEX in 752.

ETHELBALD (d. 860), king of WESSEX, 856–60. He seized the throne from his father ETHELWULF.

ETHELBERT (d. 616), king of Kent, 560–616. Converted to Christianity by Saint AUGUSTINE of Canterbury, he was the first Christian king to rule in Anglo-Saxon England. He promulgated the first extant code of Anglo-Saxon laws which established the legal rights of clergy.

ETHELBERT (d. c865), king of Kent and WESSEX succeeding to the thrones of his father ETHELWULF (858) and of his brother ETHELBALD (860). His kingdom was regularly raided by the Danes.

ETHELRED, Saint (c1109–1166), English monk known as the "English St. Bernard." He was abbot of the CISTERCIAN monastery at Rievaulx 1146–66. He wrote Edward the Confessor's biography.

ETHELRED THE UNREADY (968?–1016), king of England, 978–1016. His name refers to his lack of sound counsel. He succeeded his brother EDWARD THE MARTYR, whom he possibly murdered. Danish power spread in England during his reign and he paid DANEGELD to the Danes. Ethelred fled when the Danes ruled England, 1013–14, and then negotiated his restoration in a pact with his subjects.

ETHELWULF (d. 858), king of WESSEX (839–56) and overlord of Kent (825–39; 856–58). He defended his kingdom against the Danes, defeating them at Aclea, Surrey, in 851. His son Ethelbald deposed him as king of Wessex. Another son was ALFRED THE GREAT.

ETHER, a hypothetical medium postulated by late-19th-century physicists in order to explain how LIGHT could be propagated as a wave motion through otherwise empty space. Light was thus thought of as a mechanical WAVE MOTION in the ether. The whole theory was discredited following the failure of the MICHELSON–MORLEY EXPERIMENT to detect any motion of the earth relative to the supposed stationary ether.

ETHEREGE, Sir George (1634?–1691), English dramatist, an important writer of RESTORATION COMEDY, who influenced both CONGREVE and WYCHERLEY. His three plays are *The Comical Revenge* (1664), *She Wou'd if She Cou'd* (1668) and *The Man of Mode* (1676).

ETHERS, organic compounds of general formula R-O-R′, where R and R′ are HYDROCARBON radicals. They are prepared by catalytic dehydration of ALCOHOLS, catalytic hydration of ALKENES, or by reacting an ALKYL HALIDE with a sodium alkoxide (see ALCOHOLS). Ethers are chemically fairly inert, though they are split by hydrogen HALIDES, and form explosive PEROXIDES on standing in air. **Diethyl ether** $(C_2H_5)_2O$, the most important, is used as an anesthetic (see ANESTHESIA) and an industrial solvent. It is a volatile, inflammable liquid, partially miscible with water. MW 74.1, mp −116°C, bp 35°C.

ETHICAL CULTURE, movement based on the belief that ethical tenets are not necessarily dependent on philosophical or religious dogma. Ethical Culture has undertaken programs of social welfare, education and race relations. The movement was founded by Felix ADLER in 1876 in New York City and has now spread throughout the world.

ETHICS, principles or moral values of a person or a group of people which guide their actions and behavior. The term comes from the Greek word *ethos* which in the plural means character.

Ethical actions may be approved of in that they are "good," "desirable," "right" or "obligatory," or disapproved of because they are "bad," "wrong," "undesirable" or "evil." In philosophy ethics is the study of moral principles. A traditional philosophical discussion has centered on the problem of whether a person has innate moral sense of the principles of right and wrong or whether he acquires these principles from experience.

Like other Idealist philosophers, including HEGEL, PLATO held that the "good" was a metaphysical idea and that the study of it was the purpose of all philosophy (see IDEALISM). ARISTOTLE, on the other hand, regarded ethics as a separate branch of philosophy concerned with concepts like "virtues" and "habits." SPINOZA thought that the principles of ethics could be discovered by a process of deduction. KANT's "categorical imperative" was an attempt to formulate moral principles as imperative statements that were applicable to all human beings. John Stuart MILL and the Utilitarians (see UTILITARIANISM) held that the correct action was determinable in that it was one whose consequences produced the greatest amount of happiness for the greatest number of people.

In the 20th century G. E. MOORE began the modern study of ethics by denying that "good" was an aspect of the natural world as it was investigated by science, and said that "good" was a simple, indefinable concept, thereby altering the philosophical discussion of ethics to the investigation of the meaning of the concept "good."

ETHIOPIA, East African state lying between Sudan and the Red Sea, with Kenya and Somalia to the S and E, formerly known as Abyssinia. It consists basically of mountainous W and E highlands divided by the GREAT RIFT VALLEY. In the center of the W highlands, or Abyssinian Plateau, is the capital Addis Ababa, 8000ft above sea level. Spectacular river gorges, including that of the Abbai R (or Blue Nile) which runs from Lake Tana, cut through the Plateau. Ras Dashan in the N is Ethiopia's highest peak (15 158ft). In the SE is the great plain of the Ogaden and the Haud. Average highland rainfall is 40in, but overall rainfall varies from 80in in the S and W to 4in on the Red Sea Coast. The lowlands are tropical.

People. The Ethiopians comprise many linguistic, cultural and racial groups. The Galla are the largest single group (33% of the population) but the Amhara and the Tigre (together 37%) have been historically and politically the most important peoples. Other significant groups are the Walamo, the Somali and the Gurage. Although education is now expanding, less than 10% of the population is literate. The majority of the population is concentrated in the fertile high-rainfall area of the highlands. About a tenth of the population is town-dwelling and the chief towns are Addis Ababa, Asmara, Dire Dawa and Harer.

Economy. About 80% of the working population are employed in agriculture and pastoralism, which form the basis of the economy. Coffee provides over half the export trade and skins and hides about 10%. Principal industries include the sugar and cotton plantations along the lower valley of the Awash R, but industrial development has been hindered by the lack of local raw materials. The discovery of gas and oil fields on the Egyptian Red Sea coast has stimulated oil prospecting. Ethiopia's tremendous hydroelectric potential is being gradually exploited. Imports exceed exports, the deficit being met by development loans. Severe drought drastically affected the economy in the early 1970s.

According to local legend the Ethiopian dynasty descended from Menelik I, son of King Solomon and the Queen of Sheba, and the national emblem was thus the Lion of Judah. This statue of the Lion, by the sculptor Morris Calka, stands in the center of Addis Ababa.

History. Ethiopia is one of the most ancient kingdoms of the world. Former kings claimed descent from the son of King Solomon and the Queen of Sheba. The kingdom of Aksum, prominent from the 1st to the 8th century, was converted to Coptic Christianity in the 4th century. In medieval times Ethiopia was isolated and was thought to be the realm of PRESTER JOHN. Frequent Muslim invasions and internal feuds for long undermined Ethiopian power but MENELIK II reconsolidated the empire and defeated the Italians in 1896 at ADOWA. The Italians remained in ERITREA and in 1935–36 invaded Ethiopia, which was liberated in 1941, when Emperor HAILE SELASSIE was restored to the throne. Ethiopia made considerable economic and technical advances, but after unrest the army mutinied in 1974 and Haile Selassie was deposed. In 1975 a socialist one-party state replaced the military government. Unrest has continued in Eritrea where there is a strong movement for secession.

Official name: Ethiopia
Capital: Addis Ababa
Area: 471 778sq mi
Population: 25 248 000
Languages: Amharic, English
Religions: Ethiopian Orthodox; Muslim, Animist
Monetary unit(s): 1 Ethiopian dollar = 100 cents

ETHNOGRAPHY, in ANTHROPOLOGY, the descriptive study of different human cultures, as distinct from the more theoretical ETHNOLOGY. The terms ethnology and ethnography are often now used interchangeably, and the latter is gradually falling out of use.

ETHNOLOGY, the science dealing with the differing races of man, where they originated, their distribution about the world, their characteristics and the relationships between them. More generally, the term is used to mean cultural ANTHROPOLOGY.

ETHOLOGY, meaning literally the "study of behavior," is applied particularly to the European school of behavioral scientists. Their concern is the behavior of the animal in the wild, paying special attention to patterns of behavior, or "instinctive" behavior. This contrasts with the interests of most American behaviorists whose work stems largely from comparative psychology and is concentrated on the study of the learning process, studies which are mainly if not entirely laboratory based. The founders of ethology were Konrad LORENZ and Nikolaas TINBERGEN, whose ideas on instinctive behavior supplied the stimulus for renewed study of animals in the wild.

ETHYL COMPOUNDS, organic compounds containing the ethyl group, C_2H_5 (see ALKANES). The most important are: ETHANOL, diethyl ETHER, ethyl ACETATE, LEAD tetraethyl, and the ethyl halides (see ALKYL HALIDES). Ethyl chloride is a refrigerant and local anesthetic.

ETHYLENE (C_2H_4), or ethene, the simplest ALKENE, made by CRACKING of ETHANE and PROPANE. It is a colorless gas, used to ripen fruit and to make ETHANOL, diethyl ETHER, ethyl chloride, POLYETHYLENE and STYRENE. MW 28.05, mp −169°C, bp −104°C. It is oxidized by air over a silver catalyst to **ethylene oxide**, a reactive gas used as a fumigant and to make

Ethology

The scientific study of animal behavior

The study of animal behavior is fascinating not only because it may shed light on human behavior—indeed, such analogies are as often as not incorrect—but because it reveals the degree of sophistication present even in the actions of lower animals, and the ease with which they may respond to both familiar and unfamiliar situations. Fish are the lowest class of vertebrates, and yet may easily cope with quite complex problems. The male jewel fish (*Hemichromis bimaculatus*) gathers up its young by inhaling them into its mouth, then swims with them to the nest hole over which the female hovers and spits them in. The air bladders of young that have been spat into the nest deflate, so making them heavier than water and able to remain together in a group. As a male fish under observation swam about the laboratory tank looking for stray young, he saw some food, part of an earthworm, which he seized and started to chew. Before he had finished, one of his young swam in front of him, and he went after it and inhaled it. So the fish found himself in a dilemma, with one thing in his mouth destined for the nest, the other for the stomach. One might imagine that in this situation the fish would either swallow the whole contents of his mouth, or spit it all into the nest. The fish found a better solution. He spat out the whole of the contents of his mouth; the worm fell to the bottom, and the offspring, deflating its air bladder as though it had been spat into the nest, did the same. The male parent unhurriedly ate up the worm, but kept an eye on the young lying on the bottom. After that he inhaled the young again and returned it to the nest. In a conflict between his desire to eat and his desire to ensure that the young was out of danger the fish produced a solution as apparently intelligent and even ingenious as any a human might.

This distinctive piece of behavior, exhibited by a "lower" vertebrate, is only one illustration of the great complexity of animal behavior—a complexity not studied scientifically until the 1920s and 1930s. In the 50 years since then the study of ethology has increased so rapidly that by the 1970s it had become one of the largest branches of zoology.

In the late 19th century, scientists had widely differing approaches. The physiologists relied heavily on the concept of the *reflex arc* to explain behavior—a sense cell receives a stimulus, transmits it through nerve cells along a given path to a muscle cell or effector, resulting in an invariable response. A typical example of a reflex action is the salivation of a hungry dog in response to the sight of food. Russian physiologists therefore evolved the theory of fixed or inherited animal behavior patterns.

Psychologists in the 19th century, on the other hand, were largely concerned with human things, the mind, emotions and feelings—concepts which could not readily be quantified. They later concentrated on the idea of association and learning; cats and dogs were confined in puzzle boxes where they had to learn to depress catches to get out or obtain food. In the 1920s J. B. Watson, in the US, developed this into *Behaviorism*, characterized by a rigid mechanistic outlook in which there was no room for such vague concepts as "mind." The work of Pavlov provided an important advance. He showed how simple reflexes could be conditioned, so that the hungry dog salivated now not at the sight of food but at the sound of a bell, which had been associated with the production of food. For the first time it seemed that adaptive behavior could be explained, chains of conditioned and simple reflexes being responsible for the complex reaction of an animal to its environment.

This, however, left the phenomenon of instinct unexplained. This type of behavior is not produced solely in response to the environment but seems to come about because the animal is urged on by some internal drive. Such activities as the migration of certain birds, and the almost universal search for food or for a mate come into this category. Neither conditioned reflex nor mechanistic behaviorism supplied any answer.

Seeking to avoid viewing behavior over-analytically, Wertheimer and his colleagues enunciated the theories that formed the basis of Gestalt psychology: animals must be studied as a whole, since "the whole is greater than the sum of the parts." In the late 1930s, Konrad Lorenz, joined by Niko Tinbergen, evolved from this the basis of the modern ethological approach. Since there was no adequate physiological explanation for instinct, ethologists had to tackle the problem more or less from scratch. They concentrated on studying the behavioral repertoire of species thoroughly, and exposed as they did so a host of puzzling activities which were not directly related to the environment, and could not be explained away as "conditioned." Some of these are the subject of intense study today. In *vacuum activities*, for example, behavior is produced in the absence of external stimulation. A nesting rat in breeding condition, but denied access to nesting material, will repeatedly carry its own tail to the nest site and away again. In *displacement activities* irrelevant actions are produced in the middle of an otherwise continuous piece of behavior, as when cocks while fighting each other, will stop, briefly peck the ground, and then continue fighting. In *appetitive behavior* (seeking behavior) the external stimulus is actively sought, as with predatory animals who seek out and then hunt their prey.

Lorenz suggested that instinct had two components: a *fixed action pattern* which often formed the end-point or "consummation" of an instinctive action, such as copulation with a mate, and a more flexible appetitive behavior, such as the seeking out of the mate with which to copulate. He also suggested the existence of the *innate releasing mechanism* (IRM) to account for the fact that instinct is adjusted to the external environment, postulating the existence of a mechanism in the central nervous system which blocks an instinctive drive unless the appropriate environmental stimulus exists to release it.

The idea of the IRM gave rise to the study of "releasers"—the constituents of the external environment which allow the correct piece of instinct to be exhibited. By the use of models these can be analyzed into simpler sign stimuli. A newly hatched herring-gull, for example, pecks for food at the adult parent's bill, which is yellow with a round red patch on the mandible. Cardboard models are produced with differing head color, head shape, bill color, color of the patch on the mandible or degree of contrast of that patch against the bill. By counting the number of pecks each model receives in a given time from the chicks, it is possible to analyse which sign stimuli matter most. Here, the chick responded most strongly to the red color, and to the color contrast between patch and mandible. The color of the bill and the shape and color of the parent's head seem to be unimportant.

With increasing research it has become clear that we can no longer make Lorenz's clear distinction between "rigid" and "flexible" instinct. His concept of the IRM, though useful, has been found to be too simple; on this hypothesis one would expect chains of instinctive action to be halted when the eliciting stimulus is removed, but this does not always happen. The "drive" concept has been overworked; what once might have appeared to be internally activated, as for example the return of a digger wasp to its nest hole, now appears to result from external influences. Tinbergen found the wasp oriented to a ring of fir-cones placed round the nest; if these were moved to one side, the wasp missed its hole.

Last but not least, the internal drive may not be affected by external influences directly, but instead indirectly, by hormones themselves activated by the environment. Drives may also be under the direct control of the central nervous

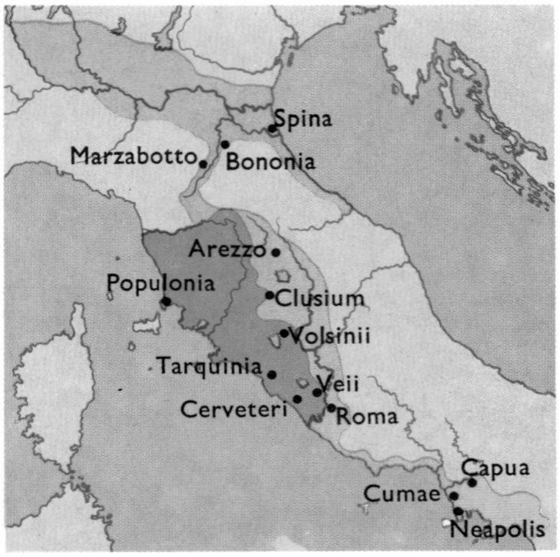

plastics and emulsifiers, and hydrated to ETHYLENE GLYCOL.

ETHYLENE GLYCOL ($HOCH_2CH_2OH$), colorless syrupy liquid, an ALCOHOL, made from ETHYLENE. It is used to make polyester POLYMERS, and, mixed with water, as an ANTIFREEZE and deicer. MW 62.1, mp −12°C, bp 198°C.

ETNA, active volcano in NE Sicily, highest Italian peak S of the Alps. Its height (about 10 900ft) varies with eruptions. The peak is snow-covered through much of the year. The fertile lower slopes are intensely cultivated.

ETON, town in Berkshire, England, on the Thames R, near Windsor, most famous for Eton College. Founded in 1440–41 by Henry VI, the college is possibly the most prestigious private school for boys in Britain. Pop 3 954.

ETRUSCANS, ancient race of Etruria which was located in what is now modern Tuscany, Italy. Their civilization lasted from the 8th to the 1st century BC but had begun to decline from the beginning of the 5th century BC. It is generally accepted that the Etruscans migrated from the Aegeo-Asian region to Italy in the 8th century BC, although some may have settled there as early as the 13th century BC. The Etruscans called themselves the "Rasenna" but the Romans named them the "Tusci" or "Etrusci."

No Etruscan literary works are extant and, even though some documents and funerary inscriptions remain, so far it has only been possible to understand a few words. Etruria comprised 12 "populi" or city-states, including Arretium, Caere, Perusia, Tarquinii, Veii, Volci, Volsinii and Volterrae. The cities were associated in a league but each controlled its own political power. The early governments were monarchical and changed subsequently to republican states which were controlled by oligarchies. The Etruscans were extremely powerful. They enjoyed extensive maritime trade with the Greeks and Phoenicians, and had colonies in Sicily, Corsica, Sardinia, the Balearic Islands and Spain. Another source of wealth were the rich mine deposits,

system. A good example of this is the behavior in set circumstances of the male Three-spined stickleback, which may be related to his environment and the external stimuli it produces, his endocrine glands and the hormones produced, and his central nervous system.

Sticklebacks are often chosen in ethology experiments because they are easy to keep in captivity and can be readily induced to come into breeding condition. The male's characteristic behavior patterns relate to the stage reached in his reproductive cycle. He builds a nest of weeds, looks for a female, courts her with a zig-zag dance, leads her to the nest entrance, and induces her into the nest. She lays her eggs, which the male fertilizes; he then drives her away, and she has nothing further to do with the next generation. The male alone looks after the eggs and hatched young.

In this experiment, males were brought into breeding condition and observed from their refractory (non-reproductive) state up to the time of building the nest. Before the experiment started, the fish were divided into two groups: crowded (six fish per tank) and isolated (one fish per tank). The isolates (I) all built nests within the experimental period, while the crowded divided into two groups: *crowded dominant* (C+), which acquired a territory and built nests, and *crowded suppressed* (C−), which failed to nest-build and spent their time hiding in weeds from their aggressive companions. Behaviorally, then, the (C+) and the (I) fish, the nest builders, were markedly different from the (C−) ones. The experiment proceeded until all fish which were going to build under these conditions had done so. Microscopic slide preparations were then made of each fish's pituitary gland (the endocrine organ "controlling" the other endocrines). Attention was focused on certain acidophilic cells in the intermediate or middle lobe of the pituitary, because their size varied markedly between pre-experimental fish and the post-experimental groups. They were larger in the former and smaller in the latter, the inference being that as the fish became reproductively active, so the hormones produced by these cells were used up, and the cells became smaller. But whereas there was no significant difference in acidophilic cell size between (C+) and (C−) groups, there was a highly significant difference between the (C+) and (C−), considered as a single group, and the (I). The important point is, therefore, that behaviorally the (C+) and the (I) fish were similar and the (C−) different, but endocrinologically the (C+) and (C−) were similar and the (I) different. Here, then, the environment apparently has a different effect on behavior and on hormone release. What hormone was actually involved could not be positively determined, for attempts to compare or homologize the stickleback pituitary with that of mammals, where the function of cells is better known, could not yield sufficiently precise results. Where does the central nervous system come in? In the case of (C+) and (C−), it is found that if (C−) fish are taken away from (C+) fish and put in tanks on their own, then they will almost immediately build nests. It seems likely, then, that in this instance the act of nest building is under nervous and not hormonal control, since nervous control allows quick behavior changes, hormonal relatively slower.

This practical example shows the kind of link ethology is forming with allied disciplines, the gaps in our knowledge, and the care that is necessary over the interpretation of results in this rapidly expanding field.

The female Three-spined stickleback plays a minor role in breeding. The male, distinguished by his red belly, builds a nest (*top left*) of water weeds glued together with secretions from his kidneys. When a female approaches, he comes out to court her (*middle*). After the eggs have been laid, the male guards the nest (*bottom*).

especially those of copper, lead and iron. The Etruscans are famous for their gold and bronze craftsmanship and for their black *bucchero* ceramic ware. They decorated their tombs with large mural paintings. After the 5th century BC the Etruscan cities were absorbed by the expanding Roman state.

ETYMOLOGY (from Greek *etymos*, true meaning, and *logos*, word), the history of a word or other linguistic element; and the science, born in the 19th century, concerned with tracing that history, by examining the word's development since its earliest appearance in the language; by locating its transmission into the language from elsewhere; by identifying its cognates in other languages; and by tracing it and its cognates back to a (often hypothetical) common ancestor. **Cognates** (from Latin *co*, together, and *nasci*, to be born) of English words appear in many languages: our "father" is cognate with the German "*Vater*" and French "*père*," all three deriving from the Latin "*pater*." An **etymon** is the earliest known form of a word, though the term is sometimes applied to any early form. (See also LINGUISTICS; PHILOLOGY.)

EUBOEA, second largest island in the Greek archipelago, 1411sq mi in area. In the Aegean Sea close to the E coast of Greece, it is dominated by three mountain ranges with fertile and well-wooded valleys and plains.

EUCALYPTUS, several hundred species of trees commonly known as **gum trees**. The majority of

Originally, the area inhabited by the Etruscans (*opposite*) lay between the Arno and the Tiber (*brown*). Later this area extended further to the north and south (*orange*). Etruscan art reached its highest levels in the 6th and 1st centuries BC, being clearly influenced, especially architecturally, by the cultures of Asia Minor, Egypt and Greece, as can be seen from their domed tombs (*right*), built at a time when other Italians cremated their dead. The tombs were lavishly decorated inside.

species are native to Australasia, but many are cultivated throughout the world. Fast-growing and with attractive blue-green leaves, they can reach a height of over 90m (300ft). Eucalyptus oil obtained from the leaves is used for clearing head colds and the bark is used in papermaking and for tanning. Family: Myrtaceae.

EUCHARIST. See COMMUNION, HOLY.

EUCKEN, Rudolf Christoph (1846–1926), German Idealist philosopher, winner of the Nobel Prize for Literature in 1908. A great interpreter of ARISTOTLE, he believed that man must continually aim towards spiritual ends.

EUCLID (c300 BC), Alexandrian mathematician whose major work, the *Elements*, is still the basis of much of geometry (see EUCLIDEAN GEOMETRY): its fifth postulate (the Euclidean axiom) cannot be proved, and this lack of proof gave rise to the NON-EUCLIDEAN GEOMETRIES. Other ascribed works include *Phaenomena*, on SPHERICAL GEOMETRY, and *Optics*, treating vision and PERSPECTIVE.

EUCLID, city in Ohio, by Lake Erie. Since WWII it has become a manufacturing center. Pop 71 552.

EUCLIDEAN GEOMETRY, the branch of GEOMETRY dealing with the properties of three-dimensional space. It is commonly split up into plane geometry, which is concerned with figures and constructions in two or less dimensions (such as the POLYGON; CIRCLE; ellipse (see CONIC SECTIONS); CURVE; LINE and POINT), and solid or three-dimensional geometry, which deals with three-dimensional figures (such as the POLYHEDRON; SPHERE and ELLIPSOID) and the relative spatial positions of figures of three dimensions or less. It takes its name from EUCLID, whose *Elements,* written c300 BC, summarized all the mathematical knowledge of contemporary ancient Greece into 13 books; those on geometry were taken as the final, authoritative word on the subject for well over a millennium and still form the basis for many school geometry textbooks. (See also ANGLE; AREA; CONGRUENCE; CYLINDER; DUPLICATION OF THE CUBE; GOLDEN SECTION; PLANE; PYRAMID; PYTHAGORAS' THEOREM; TRIANGLE; VOLUME.)

EUDEMUS OF RHODES (4th century BC), Greek mathematician and anatomist, a pupil of ARISTOTLE and a friend of THEOPHRASTUS. He probably edited *Eudemian Ethics*, one of the three works in which Aristotle's ethical statements are preserved.

EUDOXUS OF CNIDUS (c400–c350 BC), Greek mathematician and astronomer who proposed a system of homocentric crystal spheres to explain planetary motions; this system was adopted in ARISTOTLE's cosmology (see ASTRONOMY). He was probably responsible for much of the content of Book V of EUCLID's *Elements*.

EUGENE, city in W Ore., seat of Lane Co. Home of Oregon U., the city is a tourist center with lumber and manufacturing industries. Pop 78 389.

EUGENE, name of four popes. **Saint Eugene I** (d. 657), pope 654–57. **Eugene II** (d. 827), pope 824–27. **Eugene III** (d. 1153), pope 1145–53, a Cistercian abbot. He proclaimed the disastrous Second CRUSADE. **Eugene IV** (1383–1447), pope from 1431, spent most of his reign in conflict with the reformist Council of BASEL. In 1439 he achieved a short-lived union of the Eastern and Western churches.

EUGENE OF SAVOY, Prince (1663–1736), Austrian general, one of Europe's greatest commanders. He served the emperors Leopold I, Joseph I and Charles VI, and won many victories, most notably over the Turks at Zenta (1697), Peterwardein (1716) and Belgrade (1717). He was also a great statesman and patron of learning and the arts.

EUGENICS, the study and application of scientifically directed selection in order to improve the genetic endowment of human populations. Eugenic control was first suggested by Sir Francis GALTON in the 1880s. People supporting eugenics suggest that those with "good" traits should be encouraged to have children while those with "bad" traits should be discouraged or forbidden from having families. But who is to decide which traits are "good?"

EUGÉNIE (1826–1920), Empress of France 1853–70 as wife of NAPOLEON III. The daughter of a Spanish noble, she was a major influence on her husband and was three times regent in his absence. After his downfall she escaped to England.

EUGLENA, microscopic, single-celled organism found mainly in stagnant water, with plant and animal characteristics: like plants, they make their own food and are capable of PHOTOSYNTHESIS; like animals, they can move freely, propelled by whiplike organelles called flagella.

EUKARYOTE; eukaryotic cell. See CELL.

EULENSPIEGEL, Till, trickster hero of a group of German tales originally published c1515. The historic Till may have been a 13th-century Brunswick peasant. His pranks demonstrated peasant cunning triumphing over establishment figures of his day.

EULER, Leonhard (1707–1783), Swiss-born mathematician and physicist, the father of modern ANALYTIC GEOMETRY and important in almost every area of mathematics. He introduced the use of analysis (especially CALCULUS, a field which he also profoundly affected) into the study of MECHANICS; and made major contributions to modern ALGEBRA. **Euler's Relation** links the logarithmic and trigonometric functions: $e^{ix} = \cos\ x + i\ \sin\ x$, or, more generally, $e^{ikx} = \cos\ kx + i\ \sin\ kx$ (see IMAGINARY NUMBERS; TRIGONOMETRY). *e*, the EXPONENTIAL, is often named **Euler's Number** for him; and the VENN DIAGRAM is sometimes called the **Euler Diagram**. He worked also on a theory to explain the motions of the MOON and pioneered the science of HYDRODYNAMICS.

EULER, Ulf Svante von (1905–), Swedish physiologist, President of the Nobel Foundation from 1965, who shared with AXELROD and KATZ the 1970 Nobel Prize for Physiology or Medicine for their independent work on the chemistry of the transmission of nerve impulses (see NERVOUS SYSTEM).

EULER-CHELPIN, Hans Karl August Simon von (1873–1964), German-born Swedish biochemist who shared with Arthur HARDEN the 1929 Nobel Prize for Chemistry for their work on ENZYME action in the FERMENTATION of sugar.

EULESS, village in N Tex. Its economy rests on agriculture and light industry. Pop 19 316.

EUMENIDES. See FURIES.

EUNICE, town in S central La. Its economy rests upon supplying the surrounding oil area and on agriculture. Pop 11 390.

EUNUCH, castrated male human. In the Far and Middle East they were employed as harem officials, and often rose to positions of great power and influence, as in China. In classical times the priests of CYBELE were eunuchs. Some early Christians, such as ORIGEN, castrated themselves to avoid sin. (See also CASTRATO.)

EUPHORBIA, a genus of some 2 000 species of annual, biennial and perennial sub-shrubs and deciduous and evergreen shrubs. Euphorbias are popular house plants and although they have insignificant flowers some have colorful bracts, e.g. POINSETTIA. Some have pencil-like shoots, e.g. *Euphorbia tirucalli*, some are cactuslike, e.g. *E. milli* (the crown-of-thorns) while others have candelabralike forms, e.g. *E. lactea* (the **hatrack plant**). Most species prefer a sunny position in a south-facing window and grow well at temperatures above 13°C (55°F). They should be watered well and then no more added until the surface becomes dry, although cactus types tolerate dryer and hotter conditions. They are normally propagated by means of shoot tip cuttings. Family: Euphorbiaceae.

EUPHRATES RIVER, 2 235mi long, is the largest in SW Asia. It rises in NE Turkey and crosses the plains of Iraq where it finally joins the TIGRIS R to form the SHATT-AL-ARAB. It fostered the great civilizations of MESOPOTAMIA.

EUPHROSYNE. See GRACES.

EUPHUISM, affected and convoluted prose style. Named for the style developed by John LYLY, it was popular in England in the 1580s but soon became synonymous with bad writing.

EURASIA, landmass composed of Asia and Europe, politically and culturally separate continents. In fact there is hardly any physical division, although the Ural and Caucasus Mts may be taken as a border.

EURATOM (European Atomic Energy Community), organization formed by France, Belgium, Luxembourg, The Netherlands, Italy and West Germany in 1958 to develop the peaceful uses of nuclear energy and establish a nuclear industry on a European scale, supervising and coordinating trade, research and development. Military applications are outside its scope.

EUREKA, port city in NW Cal., seat of Humboldt Co. Its economy rests on lumber, fishing, dairying and on tourism. Pop 24 337.

EURIPIDES (c480 BC–406 BC), one of the greatest Greek playwrights. He appears to have been unpopular in Athens in his lifetime, possibly because of his agnostic and cynical views. He is thought to have written 92 plays, of which 19 have survived. The best-known are *Medea, The Trojan Women, Electra, Orestes* and *The Bacchae*.

EURODOLLARS, dollar deposits in a European bank obliged to pay out withdrawals in dollars. The bank in effect receives a balance with a US bank and can therefore make dollar loans.

EUROPA, in Greek myth the daughter of King Agenor of Phoenicia. Zeus, in the form of a white bull, carried her off to Crete. She bore him three sons, MINOS, RHADAMANTHUS and Sarpedon.

EUROPE, the world's second smallest continent after Australia, is bounded on the N by the Arctic Ocean, on the W by the Atlantic and on the S by the Caucasus Mts and Black and Mediterranean seas. Because its E boundary, conventionally the Ural Mts and Ural R, is not generally agreed, and because Europe has thousands of offshore islands (including the British Isles and Iceland), estimates of its area range from 3 800 000sq mi to over 4 000 000sq mi. With Asia it forms a vast, single landmass (Eurasia).

The Land is dominated by great mountain systems including the Kjolen Mts and other peaks in Scandinavia, and the Hercynian system—the mosaic of plateaus, uplands and mountains extending E from Brittany and the Iberian peninsula and embracing the Central Massif of France, the Bohemian plateau and the Urals. Alpine Europe, including the Pyrenees, Alps, Carpathians and Caucasus, has many high peaks such as Mont Blanc (15 777ft) in the Alps and Elbrus (18 481ft) in the Caucasus, Europe's highest peak. Peninsular Italy has the Apennines, and the Dinaric fold mountains swing through Yugoslavia and into Greece. Volcanoes occur in Iceland and in Mediterranean Europe (especially Italy), and earthquakes and tremors are common in the Balkans. The most prominent lowland is the North European Plain, which broadens eastward from Belgium and The Netherlands reaching across N Poland and into Russia. Other lowlands are associated with major rivers like the Rhine and Danube. Europe's longest river is the Volga. Other important rivers include the Rhône, Elbe, Oder, Vistula and Don.

Climate and Vegetation. Most of Europe has a relatively mild climate, though winters in the N and E are long and severe. Rainfall is mostly plentiful. Mediterranean lands are known for their hot, dry summers and mild, wet winters. Vegetation ranges from the tundra plants and coniferous forests of the N to the alpine plants and varied forests of the high mountains, and the olives, cypress and scrub of the Mediterranean lands. The W has much natural grassland.

People. Some 659 000 000 people, about 17% of the world's population, live in Europe. It is the most densely-populated continent. Its peoples are of many different ethnic and linguistic groups. It has 34 countries and more than 60 languages. Some areas, owing to their harsh environments, are thinly populated. Rural densities of population are highest in the lowlands, while the highest concentrations are centered on coal fields and industrial centers. In most areas people are tending to move from the countryside and into the towns. The pattern has also been changed by the influx of millions of migrant workers from the Mediterranean lands into highly-industrialized W countries like France and West Germany. Though it has more than 4 000 000 Jews and about 13 000 000 Muslims, Europe is mainly a Christian continent, Roman Catholics being by far the most numerous.

EUROPE
political
CITY population more than 1,000,000
CITY population more than 500,000
CITY population more than 100,000
City population more than 50,000
City population less than 50,000
railways
roads
scale 1 : 20,000,000
0 250 500 st. miles
ARCTIC OCEAN
ATLANTIC OCEAN
BARENTS SEA
WHITE SEA
NORTH SEA
BALTIC SEA
GULF OF BOTHNIA
Gulf of Finland
Gulf of Riga
ENGLISH CHANNEL
BAY OF BISCAY
MEDITERRANEAN SEA
TYRRHENIAN SEA
ADRIATIC SEA
IONIAN SEA
AEGEAN SEA
BLACK SEA
GREENLAND
Arctic Circle
Jan Mayen (Norway)
Bear Island (Norway)
Novaya Zemlya
North Cape
Hammerfest
Pechenga
MURMANSK
ARKHANGELSK
N.Dvina
Pechora
Kotlas
Lake Onega
Lake Ladoga
ICELAND
Reykjavik
FAEROE ISLANDS
SHETLAND ISLANDS
ORKNEY ISLANDS
HEBRIDES
NORWAY
SWEDEN
FINLAND
Narvik
Kiruna
Kemi
TRONDHEIM
Sundsvall
BERGEN
OSLO
Stavanger
UPPSALA
STOCKHOLM
VÄSTERÅS
NORRKÖPING
Gotland
Öland
GÖTEBORG
Lake Väner
Lake Vätter
TAMPERE
TURKU
HELSINKI
Vyborg
LENINGRAD
TALLINN
RIGA
PSKOV
VOLOGDA
RYBINSK
YAROSLAVL
IVANOVO
GORKIY
KALININ
MOSCOW
RYAZAN
Oka
Volga
TULA
SMOLENSK
VITEBSK
W.Dvina
BRYANSK
OREL
Don
VORONEZH
KAUNAS
VILNIUS
KALININGRAD
MINSK
UNION OF SOVIET SOCIALIST REPUBLICS
KHARKOV
KIEV
Dnepr
DNEPROPETROVSK
ZAPOROZHYE
DONETSK
KRIVOY-ROG
VINNITSA
Dnestr
KISHINEV
ODESSA
Perekop
SEVASTOPOL
LVOV
BREST
BIALYSTOK
ABERDEEN
DUNDEE
GLASGOW
EDINBURGH
N. IRELAND
BELFAST
DUBLIN
IRELAND
Cork
UNITED KINGDOM
LIVERPOOL
LEEDS
MANCHESTER
SHEFFIELD
BIRMINGHAM
LONDON
Thames
CARDIFF
BRISTOL
PLYMOUTH
SOUTHAMPTON
AARHUS
COPENHAGEN
DENMARK
MALMÖ
Bornholm (Dk.)
HAMBURG
BREMEN
Elbe
HANNOVER
A'DAM
R'DAM
NETHERLANDS
BELGIUM
BRUSSELS
LILLE
ESSEN
COLOGNE
BONN
Rhine
G.F.R.
G.D.R.
BERLIN
LEIPZIG
DRESDEN
FRANKFURT
Luxembourg
NURNBERG
STUTTGART
MUNICH
Danube
GDANSK
SZCZECIN
Oder
Weichsel
POLAND
POZNAN
WARSAW
LODZ
Vistula
WROCLAW
KRAKOW
Neisse
PRAGUE
CZECHOSLOVAKIA
OSTRAVA
BRNO
KOSICE
BRATISLAVA
VIENNA
AUSTRIA
LINZ
GRAZ
BUDAPEST
MISKOLC
DEBRECEN
HUNGARY
CLUJ
ARAD
BRASOV
ROMANIA
PLOESTI
BUCHAREST
CONSTANTA
IASI
Prut
LE HAVRE
ROUEN
Seine
PARIS
BREST
STRASBOURG
NANTES
Loire
ORLEANS
DIJON
FRANCE
BASEL
SWITZERLAND
BERN
LIECHTENSTEIN
GENEVA
LYON
BORDEAUX
ST.-ETIENNE
Rhône
GRENOBLE
TOULOUSE
MONACO
Monte Carlo
NICE
MARSEILLE
TOULON
ANDORRA
TURIN
MILAN
VENICE
Po
GENOA
BOLOGNA
SAN MARINO
FLORENCE
ITALY
ROME
NAPLES
BARI
TARANTO
Ajaccio
CORSICA
SARDINIA
CAGLIARI
PALERMO
SICILY
MESSINA
CATANIA
Valletta
MALTA
TRIESTE
ZAGREB
YUGOSLAVIA
SARAJEVO
BELGRADE
NIS
SKOPJE
ALBANIA
TIRANE
SOFIA
BULGARIA
VARNA
PLOVDIV
Danube
ISTANBUL
GREECE
THESSALONIKI
ATHENS
IZMIR
Samos
Rhodes
CRETE
CYPRUS
LA CORUÑA
Cape Finisterre
VIGO
SANTANDER
BILBAO
PORTO
PORTUGAL
Douro
VALLADOLID
Ebro
ZARAGOZA
Tagus
MADRID
LISBON
SPAIN
BARCELONA
VALENCIA
Mallorca
PALMA
BALEARIC ISLANDS
CORDOBA
SEVILLA
GRANADA
MURCIA
CARTAGENA
CADIZ
MALAGA
TANGIER
Gibraltar (Br.)
CASABLANCA
ALGERS
TUNIS

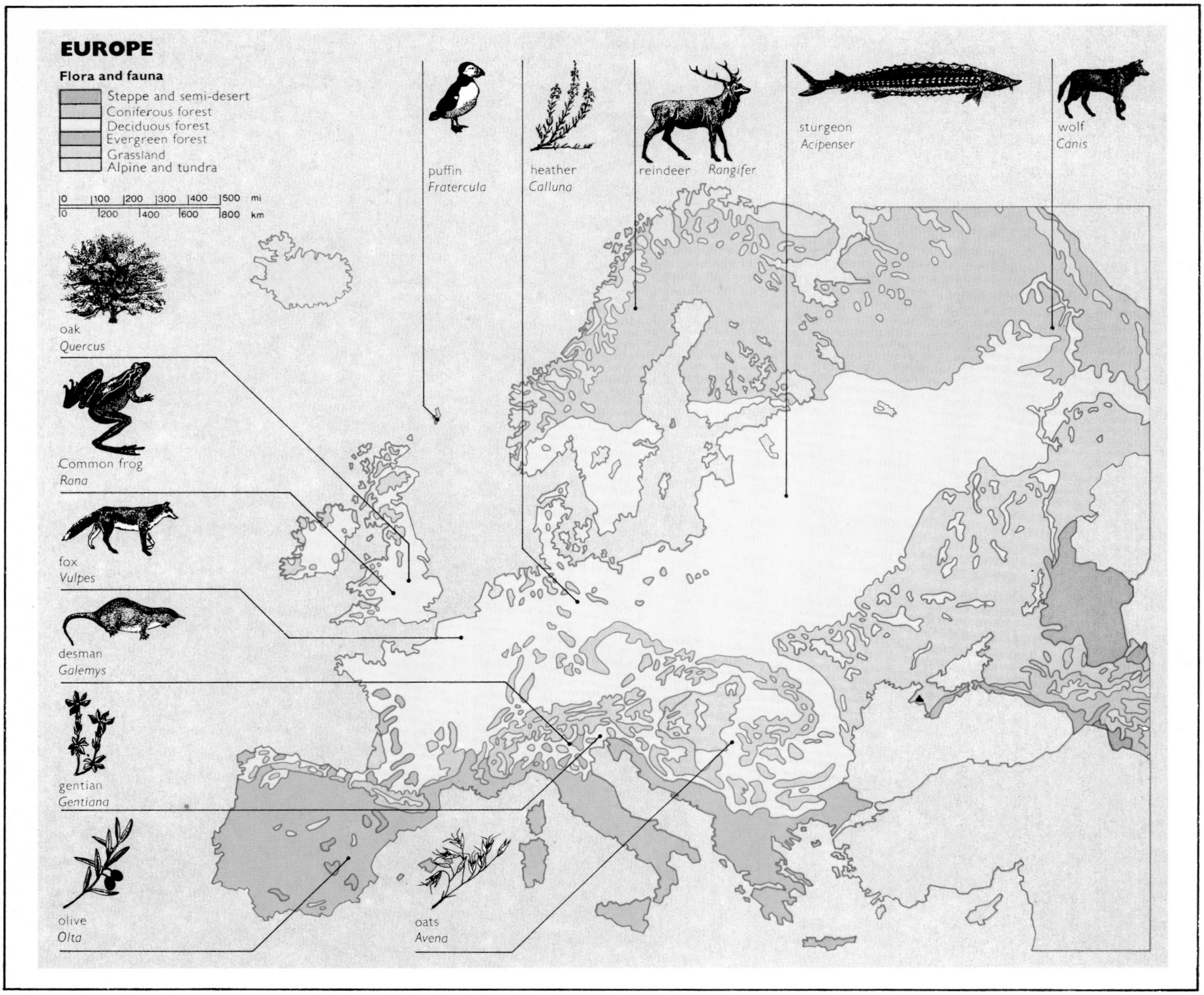

Economic Development. Agriculture has long been important, especially in Great Britain, N France, Belgium, The Netherlands, Denmark and parts of the two Germanys, also in Poland and the Ukraine (USSR). The main fisheries are the North Sea, also a source of oil and natural gas, and the Atlantic coastal waters. Europe has rich coal fields (especially in Great Britain, N France, West Germany, Poland and the Ukraine) and iron ore (especially in France, Luxembourg, Sweden and the Ukraine) and other minerals. There are many large steel plants and manufacturing centers. Pipelines for oil and natural gas have stimulated the growth of new industrial centers away from the coal fields with petrochemical and other plants.

History. Europe has influenced the world more than any other continent. It was the birthplace of Western civilization, the launching pad for great voyages of discovery, and, in Great Britain, the scene of the world's first industrial revolution. Since WWII it has become politically divided by the creation of Soviet satellite states in the E.

EUROPE, Council of, organization of 17 Western European nations, founded in 1949 to discuss items of mutual interest and promote European unity, protection of human rights, and social and economic progress. Greece was expelled in 1969.

EUROPEAN COAL AND STEEL COMMUNITY (ECSC), international agency established in 1952 to integrate the coal and steel industries of France, West Germany, Italy, The Netherlands, Belgium and Luxembourg. In 1967 its executive body was merged with those of the European COMMON MARKET and EURATOM.

EUROPEAN ECONOMIC COMMUNITY (EEC). See COMMON MARKET, EUROPEAN.

EUROPEAN FREE TRADE ASSOCIATON (EFTA), customs union and trading group formed in 1960 by Austria, Britain, Denmark, Norway, Portugal, Sweden and Switzerland to promote free trade between members. Finland became an associate member in 1961, and Iceland joined in 1970. Denmark and Britain seceded by joining the COMMON MARKET in 1973, but the Market as a unit maintains agreement with individual EFTA countries.

EUROPEAN RECOVERY PROGRAM. See MARSHALL PLAN.

EUROPIUM (Eu), one of the LANTHANUM SERIES. AW 152.0, mp 822°C, sg 5.243 (25°C).

EUROPOORT, large-scale port complex begun opposite the Hoek van Holland, on the SW coast of the Netherlands, in 1958.

EURYDICE. See ORPHEUS.

EURYNOME. See GRACES.

EURYTHMICS, art of expressing musical rhythms through body movement. It was developed by the Swiss professor of music Émile Jaques-Dalcroze in an attempt to increase his students' awareness of rhythm, and has been a major influence on modern dance and in education.

EUSEBIUS OF CAESAREA, bishop, 4th-century scholar, remembered for his *Ecclesiastical History*, a primary source for the early history of the Church. Originally an Arian sympathizer, he was exonerated of heresy by the Council of NICAEA (325).

EUSTACHIAN TUBE. See EAR.

EUSTACHIO, Bartolomeo (1524–1574), Italian anatomist. Aiming at first to vindicate GALEN against VESALIUS and others, he brought a new skill and accuracy to dissection. The eustachian tube of the EAR is named for him. (See also ANATOMY.)

EUTAW SPRINGS, Battle of, Revolutionary War engagement (Sept. 8, 1781) near Charleston, S.C. It prevented a British force from leaving the area to link up with the main body under CORNWALLIS.

EUTERPE, Muse of Lyric Poetry. See MUSES.

EUTHANASIA, the practice of hastening or causing the DEATH of a person suffering from incurable DISEASE. While frequently advocated by various groups, its practical and legal implications are so contentious that it is illegal in most countries.

EUTROPHICATION, the increasing concentration of plant nutrients and FERTILIZERS in lakes and estuaries, partly by natural drainage and partly by POLLUTION. It leads to excessive growth of algae and aquatic plants, with oxygen depletion of the deep water, causing various undesirable effects.

EVANGELICAL AND REFORMED CHURCH, Protestant church formed by the union of the Reformed Church of America and the Evangelical Synod of North America (1934); since 1957 part of the UNITED CHURCH OF CHRIST.

EVANGELICALISM, meaning "pertaining to the Gospel," the name of a theological movement, found in most Protestant denominations, that emphasizes the primary authority of the Bible. It stresses Christ's atoning death, human sinfulness, JUSTIFICATION BY FAITH, the necessity of personal conversion and expository preaching, and opposes Roman and Anglo-Catholicism.

EVANGELICAL REVIVAL, religious reawakening that occurred in the 18th century in Europe (see PIETISM), America (see GREAT AWAKENING), and in Britain, both in the Church of England and in the movement that became METHODISM.

EVANGELICAL UNITED BRETHREN (EUB), Protestant church, essentially Methodist, formed by the merger (1946) of the Evangelical Church and the Church of the United Brethren in Christ. In 1968 they became part of the UNITED METHODIST CHURCH.

EVANGELIST, New Testament term for a person sent out to preach the gospel, used likewise today for an itinerant preacher. From the 3rd century it has been applied to the Gospel writers, Matthew, Mark, Luke and John.

EVANS, Sir Arthur John (1851–1941), English archaeologist famous for his discovery of the MINOAN CIVILIZATION from excavations at KNOSSOS in Crete. He was curator of the Ashmolean Museum, Oxford 1884–1908 and professor of prehistoric archaeology at Oxford from 1909.

EVANS, Dame Edith (1888–), British actress famous for her work in classical and contemporary theater and in films, of which the best-known are *The Importance of Being Earnest* (1953) and *The Whisperers* (1967). Her first stage appearance was in 1912.

EVANS, George Henry (1805–1856), English-born US reformer and publisher of popular labor papers such as the *Daily Sentinel*.

EVANS, Mary Ann. See ELIOT, GEORGE.

EVANS, Maurice (1901–), Welsh-American actor famous for his performances of Shakespeare and Shaw, and in many films and television plays.

EVANS, Oliver (1755–1819), US engineer who constructed the first high-pressure STEAM ENGINE in America (c1802), and possibly the first continuous production-line system.

EVANS, Walker (1903–), US photographer who documented the Depression in the southern US. He published his work in *Now Let Us Praise Famous Men* (1941) and in *Fortune Magazine* of which he was an editor.

EVANSTON, city in NE Ill., 15mi N of Chicago, a residential and educational center. It is the headquarters of Rotary International and the National Women's Christian Temperance Union. Pop 79 808.

EVANSVILLE, city in SW Ind., seat of Vanderburgh Co. on the Ohio R. Principal industries are aluminum, chemicals and plastics. Pop 138 764.

EVAPORATION, the escape of molecules from the surface of a liquid into the vapor state. Only those molecules with above-average ENERGY are able to overcome the cohesive forces holding the liquid together and escape from the surface. Eventually all the molecules left in the liquid have below-average energy; its temperature is now lower. In an enclosed space, the pressure of the vapor above the surface eventually reaches a maximum, the saturated vapor

1

2

3

4

5

6

Europe is a continent of rich variety and contrast, embracing every aspect of Western civilization, from ancient monuments, like the Roman Forum (1), to the fiery furnaces symbolic of our technological age, which have turned areas like the Ruhr in Germany (2) into industrial centers of world importance. For centuries, Europe's highest mountains, the Alps, formed a natural barrier, holding apart the northern and southern countries; today they are easily crossed by modern highways through the passes (3), like the one pictured which crosses over one of the oldest passes, the St. Gotthard. Areas like the grain-producing plains of Silesia in southwest Poland (4) and the rich vineyards of France (5), help to make Europe a major exporter of agricultural products. Copenhagen (6), like many other European cities, teems with rambling old buildings full of history, narrow, shady streets and twisting waterways.

pressure (SVP). This varies according to the substance concerned and, together with the rate of evaporation, increases with temperature, equalling atmospheric pressure at the liquid's BOILING POINT.

EVAPORITES, sedimentary deposits of salts that have been precipitated from solution owing to the evaporation of a body of water (see EVAPORATION; SOLUTION). Evaporite deposits have the least soluble salts at the bottom (CALCIUM salts), followed by the very soluble halite (common SALT) and MAGNESIUM and POTASSIUM salts. Most important commercially are GYPSUM ($CaSO_4.2H_2O$), ANHYDRITE ($CaSO_4$) and halite (NaCl). (See also SALT DOME; SEDIMENTATION.)

EVARISTUS, Saint (d. c107 AD), pope from c97 to 107. According to tradition he was martyred but this is unproven.

EVARTS, William Maxwell (1818–1901), US lawyer and politician famous for his role in important US trials. He attempted to prosecute Jefferson DAVIS after the CIVIL WAR, defended President Andrew JOHNSON in his impeachment proceedings (1868) and represented the US in the ALABAMA CLAIMS, 1872. He was counsel for Rutherford HAYES at the electoral commission in 1877. US secretary of state 1877–81, he was subsequently N.Y. state senator 1885–91.

EVE, the first woman, according to the Bible, wife of ADAM from whose rib God created her. She is the subject of Jewish, Christian and Muslim legend.

EVELYN, John (1620–1706), English writer and humanist whose *Diary*, published in 1818, is one of the most important sources for English life in the 17th century.

EVENING PRIMROSE, collective name for plants of the genus *Oenothera*, native to temperate regions of the W Hemisphere. They have white, yellow or rose flowers that open in the afternoon and close at dawn. They are not related to the PRIMROSE.

EVENT HORIZON, the boundary of a BLACK HOLE beyond which an outside observer can detect nothing.

EVEREST, Mount, highest mountain in the world (29 028ft), situated in the Himalayas on the Nepalese-Tibetan border. It is named for Sir George Everest, British surveyor general of India 1830–43. After several unsuccessful attempts, it was first climbed on May 29, 1953 by Edmund HILLARY and Tenzing Norkay.

EVERETT, city in NE Mass., 3mi N of Boston. It stores petroleum and coal and manufactures paint and chemicals. Pop 42 485.

EVERETT, industrial city in NW Wash. on the Puget Sound, seat of Snohomish Co. It has shipyards, lumberyards and fisheries. Pop 53 622.

EVERETT, Edward (1794–1865), US statesman and orator. He became professor of Greek at Harvard in 1815, was a congressman, 1825–35, governor of Mass., 1836–39, minister to England, 1841–45, president of Harvard, 1846–49, secretary of state, 1852–53 and in 1860 the Constitutional Union Party's vice-presidential candidate.

EVERGLADES, swampy region in S Fla. Covering an area of about 5 000sq mi, the Everglades extend from Lake Okeechobee in the N to the S end of the Florida peninsula. The flooded sawgrass swamps support abundant wild animals and plants, many peculiar to the area. Indians inhabited the Everglades before the 1500s. In the 1830s the US tried to drive the SEMINOLE Indians out. Part of the Everglades was drained in the late 19th century, producing rich agricultural land, but drainage now conflicts with conservation plans. In 1947 the Everglades National Park was established in the S.

EVERGREEN, a plant that retains its leaves all the year around, although they are continually being shed and replaced. Examples are the HOLLY, LAUREL and PINE. (See also DECIDUOUS TREES.)

EVERGREEN PARK, village in NE Ill., 10mi SW of Chicago and named for the many pine trees growing in the area. Pop 25 487.

EVERS, name of two US Negro civil rights leaders. **(James) Charles Evers** (1922–), was first black mayor of Fayette, Miss. in 1969, and in 1971 ran for governor of Miss. **Medgar Wiley Evers** (1925–1963), his brother, was first black field secretary of the National Association for the Advancement of Colored People and organized the registration of black voters. He was assassinated by a sniper.

EVERYMAN, late 15th-century English morality play about a man (Everyman) who, when summoned by Death, finds that of all his friends only Good Deeds aided by Knowledge accompanies him. The allegory has been often used by dramatists.

EVIDENCE, in law, that which is advanced by parties to a legal dispute as proving, or contributing to the proof, of their case. To be admissible in court evidence must conform to various rules in order to ensure a clear and fair presentation of it to the trier of fact, a jury or a judge. Such evidence may consist of the oral testimony of witnesses summoned by either side, of documentary evidence or of physical objects, as for example an alleged murder weapon. The evidence may be direct, supporting the facts of the case, or it may be circumstantial, evidence from which those facts may reasonably be deduced. An eyewitness account of an auto accident is direct evidence; unaccountable damage to the defendant's auto may be circumstantial evidence. Evidence may be excluded for three main reasons—if it is not sufficiently relevant, if it arises out of privileged circumstances, and if it is hearsay—"second-hand" evidence arising out of a statement made outside court by a person not called as a witness, who cannot therefore be cross-examined. Business and public records likely to be accurate are exempted from this, as in some circumstances is a statement made by a dying person. Privileges protect certain interests, such as the right not to incriminate oneself, and certain relationships considered essential to society, such as that between a husband and wife.

EVOLUTION, the process by which living organisms have changed since the origin of life. The formulation of the theory of evolution by NATURAL SELECTION is credited to Charles DARWIN, whose observations while sailing around the world on H.M.S. BEAGLE, when taken together with elements from MALTHUS' population theory and viewed in the context of LYELL's doctrine of UNIFORMITARIANISM, led him to the concept of natural selection, but the theory also later occurred independently to A. R. WALLACE. Other theories of evolution by the inheritance of ACQUIRED CHARACTERISTICS had earlier been proposed by E. DARWIN and LAMARCK. Darwin defended the mechanism of natural selection on the basis of three observations: that animals and plants produced far more offspring than were required to maintain the size of their population; that the size of any natural population remained more or less stable over long periods, and that the members of any one generation exhibited variation. From the first two he argued that in any generation there was a high mortality rate, and from the third that, under certain circumstances, some of the variants had a greater chance of survival than did others. The surviving variants were, by definition, those most suited to the prevailing environmental conditions. Any change in the environment led to adjustment in the population such that certain new variants were favored and gradually became predominant.

The missing link in Darwin's theory was the mechanism by which heritable variation occurs. Unknown to him, a contemporary, G. MENDEL, had demonstrated the principle of GENETICS and had deduced that the heritable characters were controlled by discrete particles. We now know these particles to be GENES which are carried on the CHROMOSOMES. Mendel's variants were caused by RECOMBINATION and MUTATION of the genes. Natural selection acts to eradicate unfit variants either by mortality of the individual or by ensuring that such individuals do not breed. How then can natural selection lead to the evolution of a new character? The key is that a character that is advantageous to an individual in the normal environment may become disadvantageous if the environment changes. This means that individuals that happen through variation to be well adapted to the new set of circumstances will tend to survive and thus become the norm.

An example of natural selection at work is provided by studies carried out recently on North American sparrows. Large numbers of sparrows were trapped and their various characteristics recorded. In this way the "normal" sparrow was identified. A further collection was made of dead sparrows which had succumbed to the adverse conditions of a particularly severe winter. It was found that the individuals in the second sample were all different in some important respect from the "normal" sparrow. Natural selection could thus be seen to be maintaining a population that was ideally suited to the North American environment.

Today, the evidence for evolution is overwhelming and comes from many branches of biology. For instance, the comparative anatomy of the arm of a man, the foreleg of a horse, the wing of a bat and the flipper of a seal reveals that these superficially different organs have a very similar internal structure, this being taken to indicate a common ancestor. Then, the study of the embryos of mammals and birds reveals that at some stages they are virtually indistinguishable and thus have common ancestors. Again, vestigial organs such as the appendix of man and the wing of the ostrich are of no use to these mammals, but in related species such as herbivores and flying birds they clearly are of vital importance. Evidently these individuals have progressively evolved in different ways from a common ancestor. The hierarchical classification of plants and animals into species, genus, family etc. (see TAXONOMY) is a direct reflection of the natural pattern that would be expected if evolution from common ancestors occurred. Again, the geographical distribution of animals and plants presents many facts of evolutionary significance. For example, the tapir is today centered in two widely separated areas, the E Indies and South America. However, it probably evolved in a single center, migrated across the world and then became extinct in many areas as habitats changed. Indeed FOSSILS of tapirs have been found in Asia, Europe and North America. Fossils in general provide convincing evidence of evolution. Thus, the

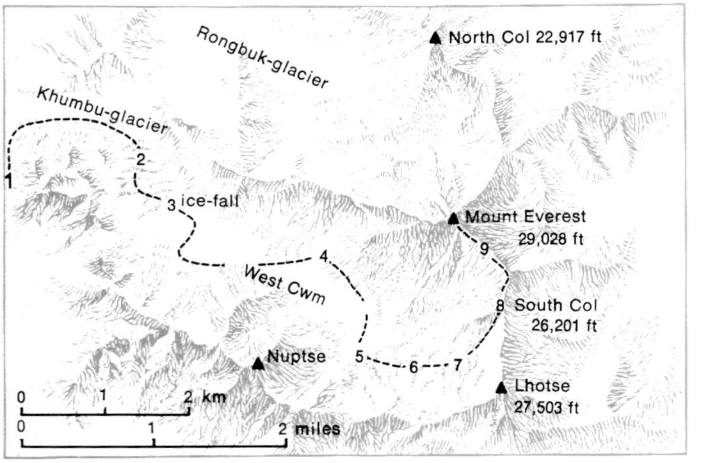

The route to the summit of Mount Everest followed by the Hunt expedition in 1953, the numbers 1–9 on the map indicating camps set up on the way. Two members of the expedition, Edmund Hillary and the Nepalese Sherpa Tenzing Norkay, became the first men ever to reach the summit. Seven previous expeditions had failed to conquer the mountain. Since 1953, however, there have been a number of successful assaults on Everest.

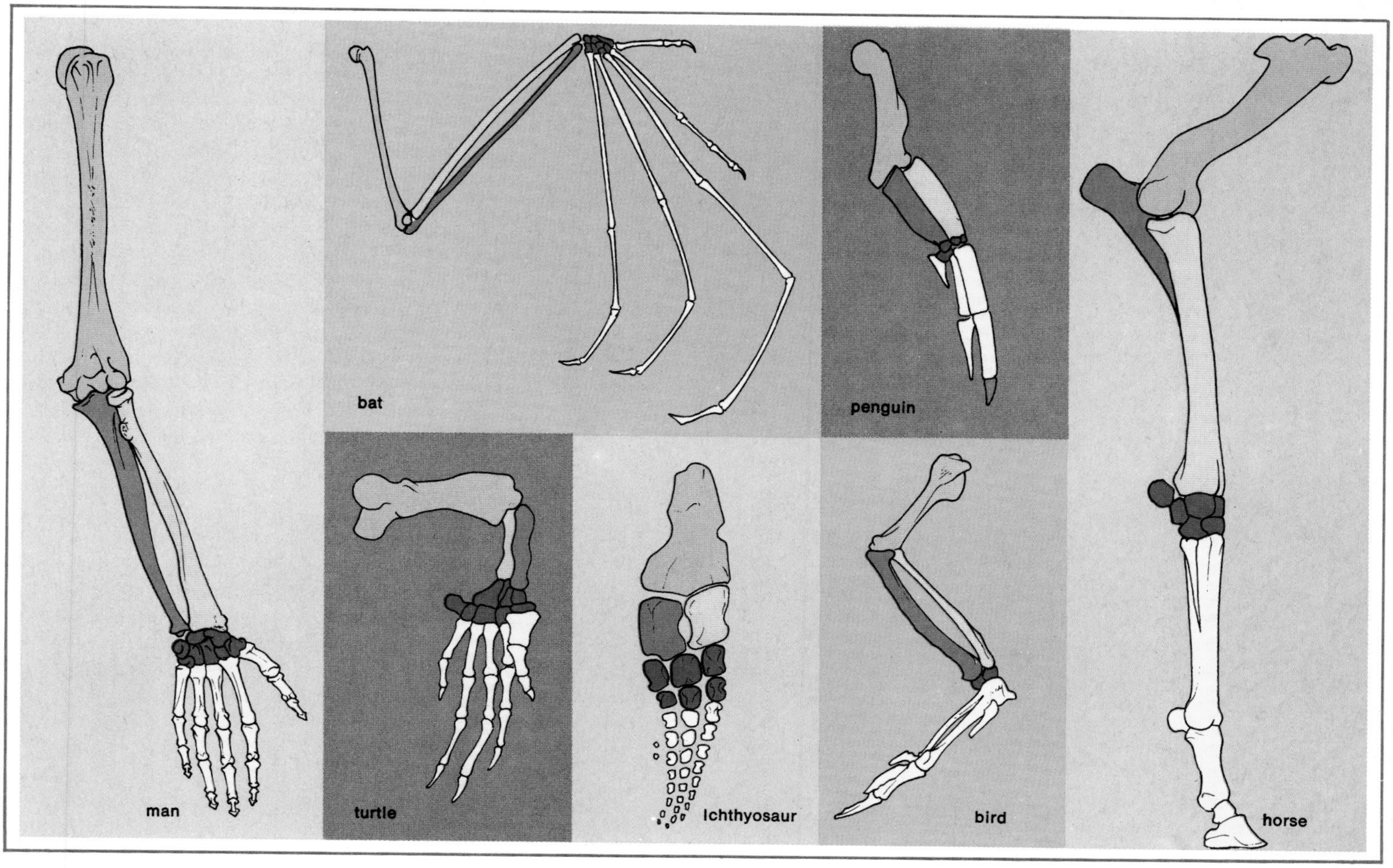

The theory of evolution receives powerful supporting evidence from the essential similarity of the basic plans of various reptiles, birds and mammals, despite wide differences in appearance. Shown here are outline drawings of their forelimbs.

theory of the evolution of birds indicates descent from now extinct reptiles. The fossil ARCHAEOPTERYX, a flying reptile with some bird-like features, was believed to represent the missing link in this development.

LIFE probably first evolved from the primeval soup some 3000–4000 million years ago when the first organic chemicals were synthesized due to the effects of lightning. Primitive ALGAE capable of synthesizing their own food material have been found in geological formations some 2000 million years old. Simple forms of animals and fungi then evolved. From that time there has been a slow evolution of multicellular organisms.

EVORA (or Ebora), historic commune, capital of the district of Evora in SE central Portugal, producing textiles and steel. Pop 47 806.

EVTUSHENKO, Evgeny. See YEVTUSHENKO, Yevgeny.

EWELL, Richard Stoddert (1817–1872), US Confederate general who served with distinction throughout the Civil War. He fought in "Stonewall" JACKSON's Shenandoah Valley Campaign. After losing a leg he led the second corps in the battle of GETTYSBURG and in the battle of the WILDERNESS.

EWING, township in W central N.J., NNW of Trenton. Pop 32 831.

EXARCH, Byzantine title for ecclesiastical and state officials and for governors of North Africa and Italy. It was adopted by the Orthodox Church for patriarchs with authority overseas.

EXCALIBUR, legendary magic sword of King ARTHUR, who drew it out of a stone in which it was embedded. After Arthur's death Excalibur was thrown into a lake and was caught by a hand which rose mysteriously from the water.

EXCAVATORS, machines used for digging ditches, trenches or holes in the ground, as well as for removing heaps of rubble or banks of earth. At the end of a jointed boom (or jib) is a bucket whose angle to the boom may be altered: power is usually supplied by a hydraulic system (see HYDRAULICS). Smaller excavators usually resemble a tractor with the addition of the boom; larger ones comprise a **slewing platform** mounted on caterpillar tracks. The **backhoe** is used usually for digging below the working surface: the bucket is forced into the ground, then drawn back toward the base. In the **face shovel**, used usually to excavate above the working surface, the bucket is forced forward, then lifted toward the base.

EXCESS PROFITS TAX, a tax on profits which are in excess of "normal" income, established during WWI to prevent excess war profits being acquired unfairly by businessmen; also applied by the US in WWII and the Korean War.

EXCHEQUER, British government revenue department, established after the Norman Conquest as part of the king's court. It was named for the checkered table on which calculations were made.

EXCISE, a tax levied on the sale of certain commodities when transacted within a country. Excise taxes were known in ancient Egypt and were levied in the Middle Ages. They were favored by the Dutch who introduced them into their American colonies.

EXCLUSION ACT, passed by Congress in 1882, banned further importation of Chinese laborers. Chinese imported to work on railway projects had aggravated unemployment in Cal., resulting in rioting and persecution. (See also IMMIGRATION; KEARNEY, DENIS.)

EXCLUSION PRINCIPLE, the law accounting for the different chemical properties of the ELEMENTS and numerous other phenomena. Applying to those particles called fermions (see FERMI-DIRAC STATISTICS), particularly ELECTRONS, it is a consequence of the fact that particles of the same kind are indistinguishable, and states that only one such particle can occupy a given quantum state (see QUANTUM MECHANICS) at a time. In a system of such particles, the lack of empty neighboring states often prevents most particles from contributing to the system properties, which thus depend only on the states bordering the filled ones—i.e., those at the **Fermi surface**. (See also PAULI, W.)

EXCOMMUNICATION, expulsion from a religious group, enforced by ancient pagans, Jews and Christians, and a common form of ecclesiastical punishment in the Middle Ages. The Roman Catholic Church retained the rule until the Vatican Council II (1962–65) when it was virtually abandoned.

EXCRETION, the removal of the waste products of METABOLISM either by storing them in insoluble forms or by removing them from the body. Exretory organs are also responsible for maintaining the correct balance of body fluids. In VERTEBRATES the excretory organs are the KIDNEYS: blood flows through these and water and waste products are removed as URINE. Other forms of excretory organs include the Malpighian tubes of insects, arachnids and myriapods, the contractile vacuoles of Protozoa and the nephridia of annelids. In plants, excretion usually takes the form of producing insoluble salts of waste products within the cells.

EXECUTIVE, that part of government which carries out the business of governing. In the US it shares power with the LEGISLATURE and the JUDICIARY. Under the Constitution it is charged with taking care "that the laws be faithfully executed." It is headed by the president, who appoints all executive officers, usually subject to Senate approval. His cabinet, federal departments such as the defense department, foreign ambassadors and hundreds of boards and commissions come under the jurisdiction of the executive. The term is also used of that part of a private organization or company that manages and controls its business. (See also SEPARATION OF POWERS.)

EXECUTIVE ORDER, authoritative order issued by the president of the US. The system dates from c1850. Executive orders are now consecutively numbered, and published in the *Federal Register*.

EXECUTORS, persons appointed to administer the

estate of a deceased person. Usually the person making a will chooses his own executors, who are required to dispose of the property in accordance with the provisions of the will. If neither a will is made nor executors named, the court may appoint administrators to dispose of the estate.

EXERCISE, or physical exertion, the active use of skeletal muscle in recreation or under environmental stress. In exercise, MUSCLES contract actively, consuming OXYGEN at a high rate, and so require increased BLOOD CIRCULATION; this is effected by increasing the HEART output by raising the PULSE and increasing the blood expelled with each beat. Meanwhile, the CAPILLARIES in active muscles dilate. The raised demand for oxygen and, more especially, the increased production of carbon dioxide in the muscles increase the rate of RESPIRATION. Some energy requirements can be supplied rapidly without oxygen but, if so, the "oxygen debt" must be made good afterward. GASTROINTESTINAL TRACT activity is reduced during exercise. Changes in the autonomic and central NERVOUS SYSTEMS, HORMONES and local regulators are responsible for adaptive changes in exercise. In athletes, exercise increases muscle efficiency and cardiac compensation.

EXETER, chief city of Devonshire, England, on the Exe R. Built on a pre-Roman site and Roman settlement, it has a fine cathedral dating from the 12th century. Its economy relies on tourism, printing and leatherwork. Pop 95 598.

EXILE, The. See BABYLONIAN CAPTIVITY.

EXISTENTIALISM, twentieth-century branch of philosophy which stresses that since "existence precedes essence," man is what he makes himself and is also responsible for what he makes of himself. It is a rejection of traditional metaphysical thought such as that of Immanuel KANT or Georg HEGEL which considers man's relation to God and to the external world. The important precursor of Existentialism was Søren KIERKEGAARD, who held that man's sense of dread and despair arose from his responsibility for his own decisions and for his relationship with God. Theologians influenced by Kierkegaard are Karl BARTH, Martin BUBER, Karl JASPERS, Gabriel MARCEL, Reinhold NIEBUHR and Paul TILLICH. Edmund HUSSERL's philosophy of PHENOMENOLOGY influenced his two students Martin HEIDEGGER and Jean-Paul SARTRE to consider the nature of human experience and of responsibility and freedom. Sartre, who eventually became a Marxist, influenced Albert CAMUS and Simone de BEAUVOIR.

EXOBIOLOGY, or **xenobiology**, the study of life beyond the earth's atmosphere. Drawing on many other sciences (e.g., biochemistry, physics), it is for obvious reasons a discipline dealing primarily in hypotheses (though FOSSIL organic matter has been found in certain meteorites—see METEOR). An important branch deals with the effects on man of nonterrestrial environments.

EXOCRINE GLANDS. See GLANDS.

EXODUS, second book of the Old Testament, and of the TORAH. The book describes the escape of the Israelites from slavery in Egypt, the covenant made at Mt Sinai between Moses and Yahweh and includes the Ten Commandments.

EXOGAMY. See ENDOGAMY AND EXOGAMY.

EXORCISM, the expulsion of DEMONS from places or persons, common in pagan religions, and found also in Judaism and Christianity. In the New Testament, Jesus cast out demons from the possessed by a word, and the apostles did likewise in his name. In the early Church anyone so gifted could exorcise; in the 3rd century exorcism was restricted to ordained clergy, in particular a minor order called **exorcists**, finally suppressed in 1972. Now somewhat controversial, exorcism is practiced as a last resort and with medical advice. Regulated by canon law and requiring episcopal permission, it is a ceremonial rite with set prayers. An exorcism to ward off evil (not presupposing possession) forms part of the Roman Catholic service of baptism.

EXOSKELETON, any skeletal material that lies on the surface of the animal's body. In this position it not only performs the mechanical functions common to any other SKELETON but, in addition, affords protection. Exoskeletons are particularly well developed in arthropods such as crabs, lobsters and insects.

Extinct birds. (1) *Ichthyornis;* (2) *Hesperornis;* (3) *Archaeopteryx;* (4) *Diatryma;* (5) *Teratornis;* (6) Great auk *Alca impennis;* (7) Reunion starling *Fregilupus varius;* (8) Passenger-pigeon *Ectopistes migratorius;* (9) Huia *Heterolocha acutirostris;* (10) Moa *Dinornis maximus;* (11) Elephant-bird *Aepyornis titan* or *A. maximus;* (12) Dodo *Raphus cucullatus;* and (13) Madagascar coua *Coua delandei.*

EXOSPHERE, the outermost zone of the earth's ATMOSPHERE (ALTITUDE greater than 500km) where terrestrial GRAVITATION is too weak an effect to prevent the escape of uncharged particles.

EXOTIC SHORTHAIR, deliberately created US cat breed with Persian body type but with short hair. All Persian colors and patterns (except Peke-faced red) are recognized in the US.

EXPANDING UNIVERSE. See COSMOLOGY; UNIVERSE.

EXPANSION, the increase in volume of a body as a result of changing conditions, normally increasing TEMPERATURE or decreasing PRESSURE, the latter being more important for GASES. Contraction is the reverse process. In most solids and liquids, increasing temperature increases the random thermal motion of their atoms, which tend to move apart, i.e., expansion occurs. The amount of expansion is usually expressed as a coefficient of expansion—the fractional change in length or volume per unit temperature change—and is specific for a given material. Water is unusual in that it expands on cooling from 4°C to 0°C. This means that ice floats on water at 0°C and rivers freeze from the surface downward.

EX PARTE MILLIGAN. See MILLIGAN, EX PARTE.

EXPATRIATION, the renunciation or deprivation of all rights of, and duties to, one's native country. It may be the voluntary decision of an emigrant, who then becomes a citizen of another country, or a government decree to punish certain crimes.

EXPERIMENT. See SCIENTIFIC METHOD.

EXPLOITS RIVER, largest river in Newfoundland, Canada, flowing for c150mi NE through the Red Indian Lake into Exploits Bay.

EXPLOSIVES, substances capable of very rapid COMBUSTION (or other exothermic reaction—see THERMOCHEMISTRY) to produce hot gases whose rapid expansion is accompanied by a high-velocity shock wave, shattering nearby objects. The detonation travels 1000 times faster than a flame. The earliest known explosive was GUNPOWDER, invented in China in the 10th century AD, and in the West by Roger BACON (1242). Explosives are classified as **primary explosives**, which explode at once on ignition, and are used as DETONATORS; and **high explosives**, which if ignited at first merely burn, but explode if detonated by a primary explosion. The division is not rigid. Military high explosives are usually mixtures of organic nitrates, TNT, RDX, PICRIC ACID and PETN, which are self-oxidizing. Commercial blasting explosives are less-powerful mixtures of combustible and explosive substances; they include DYNAMITE (containing NITROGLYCERIN, ammonium nitrate and sometimes NITROCELLULOSE), ammonals (ammonium nitrate+aluminum) and Sprengel explosives (an oxidizing agent mixed with a liquid fuel such as nitrobenzene just before use). Obsolete explosives include the dangerous chlorates and perchlorates, and the uneconomical liquid oxygen explosives (LOX). Explosives which do not ignite firedamp (see DAMP) are termed "permissible," and may be used in coal mines. Propellants for guns and rockets are like explosives, but burn fast rather than detonating.

EXPO. See FAIRS AND EXPOSITIONS.

EXPONENT, a number such as x in the expression a^x, a being a number to be used as a FACTOR x times: e.g., $a^3 = a.a.a$. In the expression, a is termed the base. (See also POWER.)

Exponential equation, in ALGEBRA, an equation of the form $a^x = b$ where a and b are numbers. For example, if $3^x = 81$ we can solve for x by restating 81 as $9.9 = 3.3.3.3$, and so $x = 4$. More difficult problems are solved using LOGARITHMS: e.g., if $4^x = 15$, then $x \log_e 4 = \log_e 15$. Therefore $1.3863x = 2.7081$ and $x = 1.9535$ (to 4 decimal places).

Exponential function, in ANALYTIC GEOMETRY, a FUNCTION of the form $f(x) = a^x$ where x is positive and does not equal 1. In terms of differential CALCULUS, $f'(x) = a^x \log_e a$ if $f(x) = a^x$.

Exponential growth. Since the value of a^x increases considerably with increase in x, the term exponential growth is used loosely in STATISTICS to refer to the very rapid growth in number of a quantity over a period of time. More accurately, it refers to an increase which, if plotted against units of time, would approximate closely to an exponential CURVE (the plotting of an exponential function).

Exponential notation, the expression of a number by means of a base and an exponent; e.g., 16 expressed as 4^2. (See also EXPONENTIAL.)

EXPONENTIAL, the base of the natural LOGARITHMS, known also as EULER's number and always symbolized by the letter e. It is defined as the REAL NUMBER such that $\int_1^e x^{-1}dx = 1$, and is an IRRATIONAL NUMBER whose value to six decimal places is 2.718284. (See also EXPONENT.)

EXPONENTIAL SERIES, the SERIES $1/0! + 1/1! + 1/2! + 1/3! + \ldots + 1/n! + \ldots$ (see FACTORIAL). The LIMIT of the series as $n \to \infty$ is e (see EXPONENTIAL).

EXPORT-IMPORT BANK OF THE UNITED STATES (Eximbank), US government agency set up in 1934 to assist foreign exports. It makes loans to foreign borrowers who wish to buy US goods and services. After developing world trade and particularly that of Latin America and the Allied countries after WWII, Eximbank now supports US exports especially to developing countries.

EXPORTS. See INTERNATIONAL TRADE.

EXPOSITIONS. See FAIRS AND EXPOSITIONS.

EX POST FACTO LAW, law acting retrospectively, most commonly to make actions illegal which were legal when committed. The US Constitution prohibits *ex post facto* criminal laws; in English law they are permitted but are rare. The NUREMBURG TRIALS were based on *ex post facto* legislation.

EXPOSURE METER. See LIGHT METER.

EXPRESSIONISM, early 20th-century movement in art and literature which held that art should be the expression of subjective feelings and emotions. Expressionist painters preferred intense coloring and primitive simplified forms, in that these seemed to convey emotions directly. VAN GOGH, ENSOR and MUNCH influenced the movement which developed in both France and Germany after 1905. In France the style was represented by the Fauvists (see FAUVISM), MATISSE and ROUAULT, and in Germany by Die Brücke and the BLAUE REITER artists like KANDINSKY, KIRCHNER, KOKOSCHKA, NOLDE, GROSZ, and MARC. Expressionist writers include STRINDBERG, WEDEKIND and KAFKA.

EXTERIOR ANGLE, the angle between one side of a POLYGON and the extension of the side adjacent to it. The exterior angle at any VERTEX is the supplement of the INTERIOR ANGLE there (see ANGLE). The sum of the exterior angles of a convex polygon is always equal to 360° in plane geometry.

EXTINCT ANIMALS. See PREHISTORIC ANIMALS.

EXTINCTION, the disappearance of any species or group of organisms. Extinction may be the result of a number of factors including physical changes in the environment, and competition from other species—during recent times notably from man.

EXTORTION, seeking to obtain money from a person by non-physical intimidation, often by the threat of a criminal charge or the exposure of some secret. Physical intimidation is usually considered ROBBERY. Some specific kinds of extortion are usually known as blackmail.

EXTRACTION, method of separating a desired substance from a SOLUTION containing one or more other substances. The solution is shaken with a solvent immiscible with it, into which the solute required (but not the others) is largely transferred, according to the distribution law that its concentrations in the two phases are in a constant ratio. The process is repeated if necessary. Continuous extraction is used if the distribution ratio is small. Metal ions are extracted as a CHELATE by adding a ligand to the solvent.

EXTRADITION, formal surrender of an alleged criminal by one country to another. This is generally not allowed when the alleged offense is of a political nature. The US Constitution provides for interstate extradition, but in practice this is left to the discretion of the state governor.

EXTRAPOLATION. See INTERPOLATION AND EXTRAPOLATION.

EXTRASENSORY PERCEPTION. See ESP.

EXTRATERRITORIALITY, privilege granted by a country to resident foreign nationals, allowing them to remain under the jurisdiction of the laws of their own country only. Generally extended only to diplomatic agents, this may be withdrawn if abused.

EXTRAVERSION. See INTROVERSION AND EXTRAVERSION.

EXTREME UNCTION, or **Anointing of the Sick,** a SACRAMENT of the Roman Catholic and Eastern Orthodox churches; a rite including anointing with oil, laying on of hands and prayer for healing. From the Middle Ages until recently in the Roman Catholic Church it was administered chiefly to the dying as preparation for death, but its healing use is now emphasized. It is practiced in some other churches.

EXTREMUM, a point on a CURVE $f(x)$ at which there is an instantaneous change of sign of the derivative $f'(x)$ (see CALCULUS; FUNCTION). If $f'(x)$ is defined at this point it has value 0. There are two types of extrema: maxima and minima. At a **maximum** $f'(x)$ changes from positive to negative with increasing x; at a **minimum** $f'(x)$ changes from negative to positive. Points of INFLECTION are not extrema.

EXTRUSION, a way of producing metal and plastic components of constant cross-section (e.g., tubes, sheets) by forcing the material through a DIE. In **cold extrusion** a billet of metal is surrounded by liquid LUBRICANT in a suitable chamber; hydrostatic PRESSURE is increased, forcing the metal through orifices at one end of the chamber. In **hot extrusion**, used for plastics, the material is melted throughout before being forced through a die and rapidly cooled.

EYCK, Jan van. See VAN EYCK, JAN.

EYE, the specialized sense organ concerned with VISION. In all species it consists of a lens system linked to a LIGHT receptor system connected to the central NERVOUS SYSTEM. In man and mammals, the eye is roughly spherical in shape, has a tough fibrous capsule with the transparent CORNEA in front, and is moved by specialized eye muscles. The exposed surface is kept moist with tears from lacrymal glands. Most of the eye contains VITREOUS HUMOR—a substance with the consistency of jelly—which fills the space between the lens and the retina, while in front of the lens there is watery or AQUEOUS HUMOR. The colored iris or aperture surrounds a hole known as the pupil. The focal length of the lens can be varied by specialized ciliary muscles. The RETINA is a layer containing the nerve cells (rods and cones) which receive light, together with the next two sets of cells in the relay pathway for vision. The optic nerve leads back from the retina to the BRAIN. Rods and cones receive light reflected from a pigment layer and contain pigments (e.g., RHODOPSIN) which are bleached by light and thus set off the nerve-cell reaction.

EYE BANK, a department in a hospital or some other organization where eyes or corneas are stored (for up to three weeks) for use in corneal grafts by ophthalmic surgeons. Sometimes removed in a necessary operation on someone living, the eyes usually come from the dead (within 10 hours of decease) by permission either of a will or of surviving relatives.

EYEGLASSES. See GLASSES.

EYRE, Edward John (1815–1901), British explorer, later a colonial governor. He discovered an overland route from the S to the W of Australia; many places there, such as Lake Eyre, are named for him. As governor of Jamaica (1864–66) he was censured for taking excessive reprisals against a Negro revolt.

EYRE, Lake, large salt pan in NW South Australia. About 3600sq mi in area, its occasionally flooded basin lies about 40ft below sea level. Its specialized ecology is of great scientific interest.

EZEKIEL, early 6th-century BC Hebrew priest and prophet. He lived in Jerusalem but in 597 BC was taken by Babylon. The Old Testament book which bears his name foretells the destruction of Jerusalem, pronounces judgment on foreign nations and predicts the restoration of Israel.

EZRA, 5th-century BC Babylonian Jewish priest and religious leader, whose teachings are recorded in the Old Testament Book of Ezra. He advocated an exclusive and legalistic doctrine, prohibiting marriages between Jews and gentiles.

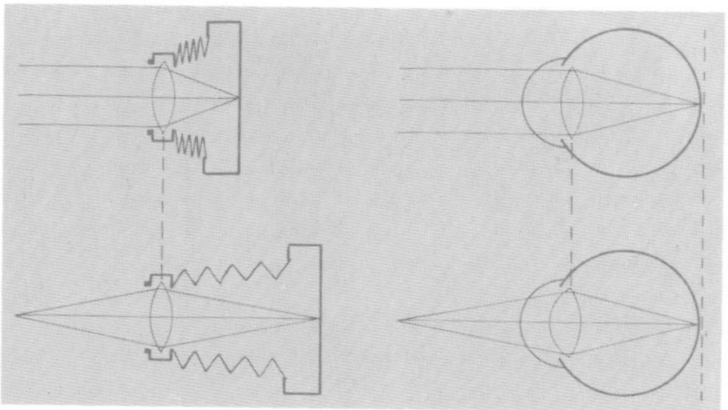

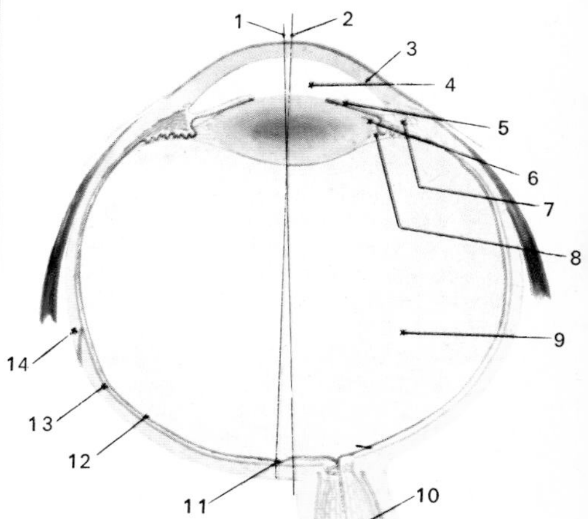

Above: in some respects the optical system of the eye (right) resembles that of a bellows camera (left). But whereas the camera lens is of fixed focal length and accommodation is by adjusting the lens-film distance, the eye employs a lens of variable focal length and a fixed lens-retina separation. *Right* : a horizontal section through a human eye shows (1) optical axis; (2) visual axis; (3) cornea; (4) anterior chamber (aqueous humor); (5) iris; (6) posterior chamber; (7) ciliary body; (8) lens capsule; (9) vitreous humor; (10) optic nerve; (11) fovea; (12) retina; (13) choroid; (14) sclera.

F

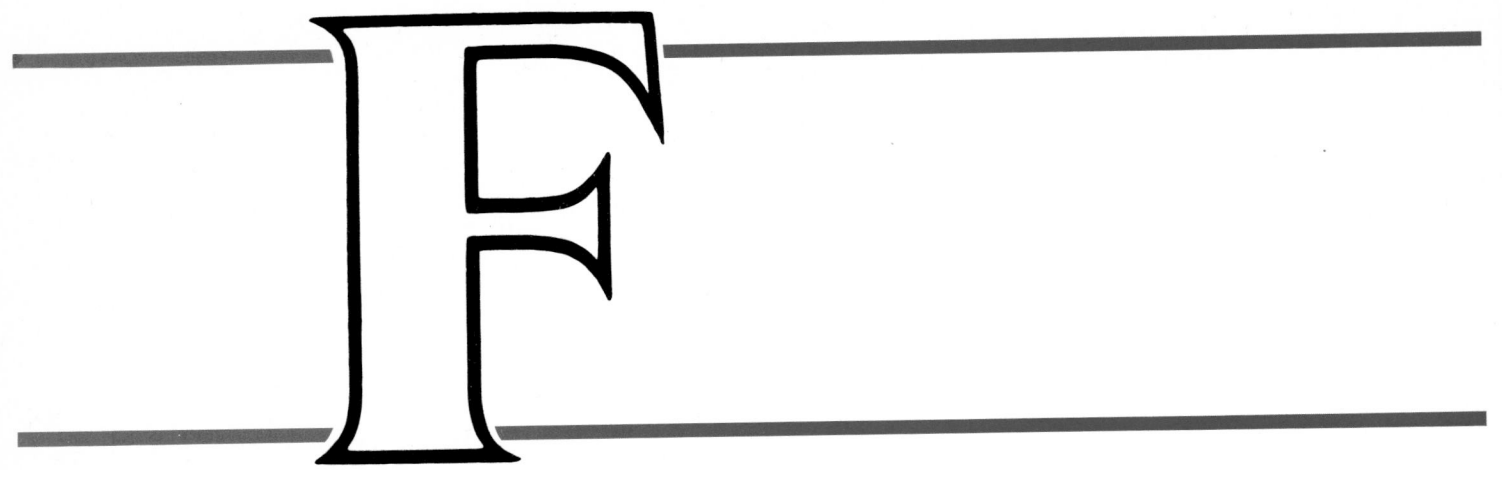

F, sixth letter of the English alphabet, and also of the Roman and early Greek alphabets. In science, F is the symbol for farad, the SI unit of capacitance, and °F for degrees Fahrenheit.

FABERGÉ, Peter Carl (1846–1920), Russian goldsmith famous for the jewelry he made for the Russian Tsars and other royalty, especially the bejeweled "Easter Eggs." He went into exile in 1917.

FABIAN, Saint (d. 250 AD), pope from 236. The first to develop an ecclesiastical organization in Rome and to record the deeds of the martyrs, he was himself martyred. His feast day is Jan. 20.

FABIAN SOCIETY, English society for the propagation of socialism, established 1883–84, taking its name from the delaying tactics of FABIUS CUNCTATOR. Fabians rejected violent revolution, seeking to change society gradually. They helped form the Labour Representation Committee which became the Labour Party in 1906. Leading Fabians were Sidney and Beatrice WEBB and G. B. SHAW.

FABIOLA, Saint (d. c399 AD), Roman noblewoman. A Christian scholar, she studied under St. Jerome and is said to have founded the first public hospital in W Europe, at Rome. Her feast day is Dec. 27.

FABIUS CUNCTATOR (Quintus Fabius Maximus Verrucosus; d. 203 BC), Roman general, famous for his delaying tactics in the war against HANNIBAL. He harassed the Carthaginian army but avoided pitched battle, giving Rome time to recover its strength.

FABLE, a fictional story, generally one illustrating a moral. The characters are often animals whose behavior caricatures human folly. Famous collections of fables are those by AESOP and Jean de LA FONTAINE.

An example of Italian faience, from the collection of the Museo del Bargello, Florence. It is the work of the school of Luca della Robbia (1400–82) and portrays the Madonna with infant Jesus and John the Baptist. The white figure and the clear blue background are typical of these beautiful faience reliefs.

FABRE, Jean Henri (1823–1915), French entomologist who used direct observations of insects in their natural environments in his pioneering researches into insect instinct and behavior.

FABRICIUS, David (1564–1617), German Protestant minister and astronomer who discovered the first VARIABLE STAR (1596). His son, **Johannes Fabricius** (1587–1615), was one of the first to observe SUNSPOTS and hence report the SUN's rotation.

FABRICIUS AB AQUAPENDENTE, Hieronymus, or Girolamo Fabrizi (1537–1619), Italian physician, the pupil and successor of FALLOPIUS at Padua and teacher of William HARVEY. Fabricius made a detailed study of the valves in VEINS and pioneered the modern study of EMBRYOLOGY.

FACE, front part of the head, bordered by hairline and chin, and consisting of the EYES, NOSE, mouth, EARS, forehead, cheeks and jaw. It is particularly concerned with sensibility and communication: it bears the special sense organs of VISION, hearing, SMELL, TASTE and balance, as well as especially sensitive SKIN. VOICE and facial expression (fine facial movements) are mediated via the face. Neck mobility allows these organs to be directed quickly and easily toward an object without turning the body.

FACSIMILE, in telecommunications, the transmission of graphic images (photographs, diagrams, maps, manuscript or printed matter, etc.) by wire or RADIO, as used by governmental, weather or news agencies and business firms. The copy for transmission is scanned to give an electrical analogue signal in terms of a large number of dot areas and this signal is modulated onto a carrier for transmission. At the receiving station the original image is reconstituted using CATHODE-RAY TUBES, pressure-sensitive paper, XEROGRAPHY, etc.

FACTOR, an INTEGER which may be divided into another integer without REMAINDER. Thus the factors of 12 are 1, 2, 3, 4 and 6, since each of these may be divided exactly into 12. In general it is of use to consider only the factors of a number which are NATURAL NUMBERS. The prime factors of a number are those PRIME NUMBERS which are its factors. The prime factors of 12 are 1, 2 (twice), 3, since $4=2.2$ and $6=3.2$.

In ALGEBRA the factors of a POLYNOMIAL are found by a mixture of guesswork and rules of thumb. This is helped by certain standard rules:

$$x^2-y^2=(x+y)(x-y)$$
$$x^3-y^3=(x-y)(x^2+xy+y^2)$$
$$x^3+y^3=(x+y)(x^2-xy+y^2)$$
$$x^2+2xy+y^2=(x+y)^2.$$

Moreover, to find the factors of a polynomial of the form x^2+bx+c we know that, if the factors are $(x+p)$ and $(x+q)$, $p+q=b$ and $p.q=c$. Hence x^2-3x+2 has factors $(x-2)$ and $(x-1)$, since $(-2)+(-1)=(-3)$ and $(-2)(-1)=2$. (See also FACTORIAL.)

FACTORIAL, a system of notation in which, for a NATURAL NUMBER n, $n!$ (or $\lfloor n$), read "n factorial," represents the PRODUCT of all the natural numbers up to n. Thus
$12! = 1.2.3.4.5.6.7.8.9.10.11.12 = 479\,001\,600$. Additionally, $0!$ is defined as 1.

FACTORY, establishment for the manufacture of goods in quantity. In the US most goods are factory-made and almost 25% of the population is employed in factories. Factories as we know them originated in the INDUSTRIAL REVOLUTION and were soon focal points for over-crowding and slums caused by the massive influx of workers into urban areas. Working conditions were often bad and had to be improved by legislation. The factory today is attacked because of the POLLUTION it can cause, and because a town may become economically dependent on a few factories and so suffer disproportionately in a recession.

FADEYEV, Aleksander Alexandrovich (1901–1956), Russian novelist, an influential Stalinist literary politician. In 1918 he fought for the Bolsheviks in Siberia, the setting of his best-known novel, *The Nineteen* (1927). He committed suicide when destalinization began.

FAENZA, historic city in N Italy near Bologna, famous for the manufacture of FAIENCE. Pop 54 733.

FAEROE ISLANDS, group of islands in the N Atlantic, self-governing since 1948 but linked with Denmark. They lie 190mi NW of the Shetlands and 250mi SE of Iceland. The islanders speak Faeroese, related to Old Norse. The economy rests on the fishing industry and on agriculture, especially sheep-raising. Pop 38 681.

FAFNIR, in Norse mythology a great dragon who guards an accursed hoard of gold. He is slain by the hero Sigurd (or SIEGFRIED).

FAHRENHEIT, Gabriel Daniel (1686–1736), German-born Dutch instrument maker who introduced the mercury-in-glass THERMOMETER and discovered the variation of BOILING POINTS with atmospheric PRESSURE, but who is best remembered for his **Fahrenheit temperature scale**. This has 180 divisions (degrees) between the freezing point of water (32°F) and its boiling point (212°F). Although still commonly used in the US, elsewhere the Fahrenheit scale has been superseded by the Celsius scale (see CELSIUS, ANDERS).

FAIENCE, earthenware with a tin oxide glaze, made from a coarse clay and fired several times. The name, originally French, derives from the Italian town of FAENZA, famous for such earthenware since the 14th century. Egyptian blue-glazed ware is often also called faience.

FAINTING, or **syncope,** transient loss or diminution of consciousness associated with an abrupt fall in blood pressure. In the upright position, head and BRAIN are dependent on a certain blood pressure to maintain BLOOD CIRCULATION through them; if the pressure falls for any reason, inadequate flow causes consciousness to recede, often with the sense of things becoming more distant. The body goes limp and falls, so that, unless artificially supported, the effect of gravity on brain flow is lost and consciousness is rapidly regained. Fainting may result from sudden emotional shock in susceptible individuals, HEMORRHAGE, ANEMIA or occur with transient rhythm disorders of the HEART.

FAIRBANKS, city in E central Alaska, a supply center for the interior. Major industries are mining and lumbering. Pop 14 771.

FAIRBANKS, Charles Warren (1852–1918), US lawyer and politician, vice-president of the US under Roosevelt 1905–09. A conservative, he was the dominant figure in the Ind. Republican Party from 1896 and senator 1897–1905.

FAIRBANKS, Douglas, Sr. (1883–1939), US film actor famous for his romantic and swashbuckling roles in films such as *Robin Hood* (1922) and *The Black Pirate* (1926). In 1919 he founded United Artists Studio with his wife Mary PICKFORD, Charlie CHAPLIN, and D. W. GRIFFITH.

FAIRBORN, city in SW Ohio, a suburb of Dayton. In an agricultural area, it has various light industries. Pop 32 267.

FAIR DEAL, reform program put before Congress by President Truman 1945–48, covering civil rights, education, health services, agriculture and employment. Congress rejected many of the proposals as being too expensive, but the 1946 Employment Act and other social measures resulted.

FAIR EMPLOYMENT PRACTICES COMMITTEE (FEPC), US government agency established 1941–46 by President Roosevelt to prevent employment discrimination in order to mobilize maximum manpower in war industries. In 1964 the Equal Employment Opportunity Commission was established with a similar function.

FAIRFAX, city in NE Va., seat of Fairfax Co. Pop 21 970.

FAIRFAX, Thomas, 6th Baron (1693–1781), English peer, proprietor of the Northern Neck of Va. which he inherited from his grandfather, Baron CULPEPER, Colonial Governor of Va. He and his cousin William Fairfax were patrons to the young George Washington.

FAIRFIELD, industrial city in Ala., laid out as a suburb of Birmingham by the US Steel Corp. Pop 14 369.

FAIRFIELD, city in Cal., seat of Solano Co. It developed as an agricultural center, but now has some industry also. Pop 44 146.

FAIRFIELD, town in SW Conn., beside Bridgeport on Long Island Sound. A summer resort, it has some manufacturing industry. Pop 56 487.

FAIRFIELD, city in SW Ohio, a local industrial center. Pop 14 680.

FAIRHAVEN, resort town in SE Mass. on Buzzards Bay. Until 1812 part of New Bedford, it was a whaling center in the 19th century. Pop 16 332.

FAIR ISLE, island, 3sq mi in area, lying between the Orkneys and Shetlands NE of Scotland. The island's 60-odd CROFTER inhabitants still knit the famous patterned wool garments named for the island.

FAIR LABOR STANDARDS ACT, passed in 1938 by the Roosevelt administration to ensure for most workers a minimum wage and a 44hr maximum working week. The act was subsequently extended and improved.

FAIR LAWN, residential borough in NE N.J., a pioneer of community planning. Industrial development is strictly zoned. Pop 37 975.

FAIRMONT, city in S central Minn., seat of Martin Co. It has diverse industries and is a lake resort. Pop 10 751.

FAIRMONT, city in NW Va., seat of Marion Co., on the Monongahela R. A coal mining center, it also has other industry. Pop 26 093.

FAIR OAKS, Battles of, two battles in the American Civil War fought May 31–June 1, 1862, near Richmond, Va. Confederate troops under Gen. J. E. JOHNSTON unsuccessfully tried to drive Union troops led by Gen. G. B. MCLELLAN out of the area before they could be reinforced.

FAIRS AND EXPOSITIONS, gatherings at which goods from many areas are brought together for sale, or to foster trade and the prestige of the producing country. Fairs date from early times when they were accompanied by holidays and festivities, and some old fairs, such as the Frankfurt Book Fair, have survived until the present. Massive international fairs, or expositions, began with the Great Exhibition, held at the Crystal Palace, London, in 1851. The first large exposition in the US was the CENTENNIAL EXPOSITION at Philadelphia in 1856. Many other world fairs followed, such as Expo 67 at Montreal and Expo 70 in Tokyo.

FAIR TRADE LAWS (or resale price maintenance laws), laws permitting manufacturers of certain branded goods to fix a minimum resale price. In the US the practice became widespread in the 1930s, when 45 states passed such laws, but they have become less common since WWII.

FAIRVIEW, borough in NE N.J., a center for the clothing industry. Pop 10 698.

FAIRVIEW PARK, city in N Ohio, a residential suburb SW of Cleveland. Pop 21 681.

FAIRY, in folklore of many nations, particularly northern, a supernatural being skilled in magic and generally either indifferent or hostile to humans. Originally regarded as powerful and terrible beings it was unwise to name, they have degenerated into characters in children's stories.

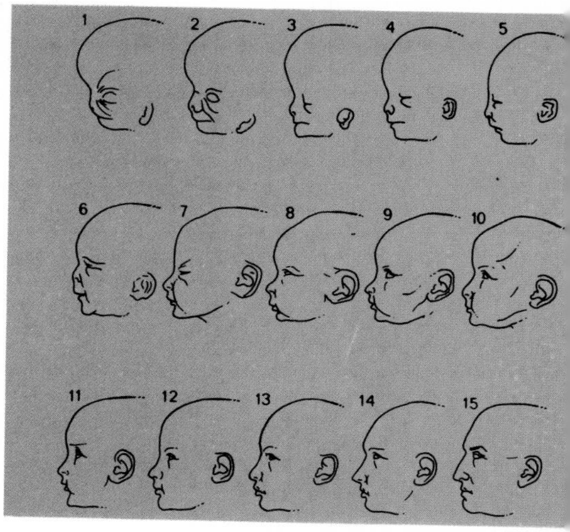

The development of the shape of the face before and after birth, seen in profile. 1. Embryo at $1\frac{1}{2}$ months; 2. at 2 months; 3. at $2\frac{1}{2}$ months; 4. at 3 months; 5. at $4\frac{1}{2}$ months; 6. embryo at $5\frac{1}{2}$ months; 7. new-born baby; 8. baby aged 4 months; 9. child aged 1 year; 10. aged 2 years; 11. aged 4 years; 12. aged 7 years; 13. aged 10 years; 14. aged 14 years; 15. adult.

FAIRY RING, a complete circle or an arc of fruiting bodies of FUNGI, particularly AGARICS, which commonly appear in fields and lawns. Each colony of fungi is derived from a single spore from which the hyphae grow out in all directions forming an invisible circular colony that only becomes visible when fruiting bodies are formed at its periphery. The name is derived from the old superstition that mushrooms growing in a circle represent the path of dancing fairies.

FAIRY SHRIMPS, CRUSTACEA which lack a CARAPACE and bear stalked eyes. Found in pools from desert regions to the Arctic, they swim by rhythmic beating of flattened, jointed legs. Food particles are filtered by fine hairs or setae on the edges of the legs.

FAIRY TALE, general term for a tale involving fantastic events and characters, not necessarily fairies. Many of these originate in myth and folklore, but an equal number have been written or collected to provide sophisticated adult entertainment, among them those by Charles PERRAULT, the brothers GRIMM, GOETHE, E. T. A. HOFFMAN and some by Hans ANDERSEN. Many modern writers, such as J. R. R. TOLKIEN and C. S. LEWIS, invented and incorporated fairy-tale elements in their works.

FAISAL, or Feisal, two kings of Iraq. **Faisal I** (1885–1933), took part in the Arab revolt against the Ottoman Turks in 1915 and was king 1921–33. **Faisal II** (1935–58), reigned from 1939. His uncle, Abdul Ilah, ruled Iraq as regent till 1953. In 1958 they were both murdered in a revolution.

FAISAL, or Feisal (1905–1975), king of Saudi Arabia from 1964, when his brother King Saud was forced to abdicate. A pious, moderate and able ruler, Faisal instituted a far-ranging program of social reform. Friendly to the West, he nevertheless joined the campaign against Israel and supported the Arab oil cartel. He was assassinated by a nephew in March 1975.

FAITH, confidence or trust, or that which is reliable and trustworthy. In Christianity, "faith" is applied objectively to the content of Christian doctrine, the faith which is to be believed; and also, especially in St. Paul's theology, subjectively to the human response of acceptance of Divine truth by mind and will, and trust in Jesus Christ as savior. In the latter sense, faith is an act possible only by GRACE, leading to JUSTIFICATION and to obedience to God. Faith differs from belief in that while the former is absolute and unconditional, the latter, involving rational assent upon probable evidence, admits of degrees, and lies on a continuum with the shades of doubt.

FAITH HEALING, the treatment of DISEASE by the evocation of faith, usually induced during a public ceremony or meeting; chanting and laying on of hands are common accompaniments. Greatest success is often with disease that tends to remit spontaneously and in HYSTERIA; in some instances, patients are helped to come to terms with disease. Substantiation of cures is rare.

FAJARDO, town in NE Puerto Rico, a tobacco and sugar center. Pop 18 249.

FAKIR, in Islamic countries, a mendicant holy man or dervish. Fakirs often display great feats of self-control and endurance, such as lying on nails or walking through fire.

FALAISE, historic market town in Normandy, NW France. It was the site of a major battle soon after the Allied landings in 1944; severely bombed, it has been restored. Pop 7 599.

FALANGE (Phalanx), Spanish political party set up in 1933 as the *Falange Española*. It espoused Fascist principles and pledged itself to aggressive tactics. In the Civil War of 1936–39 it supported FRANCO, and after the war it became his official party. It was renamed the National Movement in 1967.

FALASHAS, Jewish Ethiopians who claim descent from Solomon's son Menelik I and the Queen of Sheba. About 20 000 of them now live in the area N of Lake Tana. They know and follow the Old Testament but not the Talmud.

FALCONET, Étienne Maurice (1716–1791), French sculptor. Under the patronage of Madame de POMPADOUR he became director of the SÈVRES porcelain factory. He is noted for his *Milo of Crotona* (1744) and his statue of Peter the Great.

FALCONRY, the hunting of game using trained falcons and other birds of prey. An ancient sport, it was popular with the medieval nobility. Training a falcon is a long and difficult process; the bird must become familiar with its trainer, return to him after flights and learn not to eat its prey. Interest in falconry has recently revived after a period of decline.

FALCONS, name generally applied to about 60 species of hawk, though the true falcons of the family Falconidae number about 35 species. They are BIRDS OF PREY, feeding mainly on other birds which they kill in the air. They inhabit most parts of the world, making their nests on rocky ledges or tree forks. Falcons in the US include the Prairie falcon and the Sparrowhawk.

FALKLAND ISLANDS, self-governing British colony, a group of islands totalling 4 700sq mi in the S Atlantic about 480mi NE of Cape Horn. Possesion is disputed with Argentina.They number about 200, the largest of which are E Falkland and W Falkland. The inhabitants are mostly of British descent; the economy rests largely on sheep and cattle raising. The islands are noted for their abundant wild life. Capital: Stanley. Pop 2 045.

FALL, Albert Bacon (1861–1944), US politician, senator 1912–21 and secretary of the interior 1921–23. He resigned over the TEAPOT DOME scandal and in 1931 was convicted of accepting a bribe and jailed.

FALL, The. See ORIGINAL SIN.

FALLA, Manuel de (1876–1946), major Spanish composer. He studied in Madrid and Paris. His work was heavily influenced by RAVEL and native Andalusian folk music, evident in the famous ballets *El Amor Brujo* (1915) and *The Three-Cornered Hat* (1919). Other famous works are the opera *La Vida Breve* (1905) and *Nights in the Gardens of Spain* (1919), for piano and orchestra.

FALLADA, Hans (pseudonym of Rudolf Ditzen; 1893–1947), German novelist. His most popular books were *Little Man, What Now?* (1932) and *The World Outside* (1934).

FALLEN ARCHES. See FLATFOOT.

FALLEN TIMBERS, Battle of, fought in 1794 in NW Ohio between settlers led by Gen. Anthony WAYNE and the Northwestern Indian Confederation. The Indians, who had opposed settlement beyond the Ohio R, were defeated and the NW frontier was secured. (See also GREENVILLE, TREATY OF.)

FALLING STAR. See METEOR.

FALL LINE, a line along which a number of nearby rivers have WATERFALLS, marking the progress of the rivers from hard to softer rock. Since this marks the farthest inland point navigable from the sea, and because the falls can supply HYDROELECTRIC POWER, many important industrial centers have sprung up along fall lines.

FALLOPIAN TUBE, narrow tube leading from the surface of each ovary within the female PELVIS to the WOMB. Its abdominal end has fimbria which waft peritoneal fluid and eggs into the tube after ovulation. Fertilization may occur in the tube, and if followed by IMPLANTATION there, the PREGNANCY is ectopic and ABORTION, which may be life-threatening, is inevitable. In STERILIZATION, the tubes are divided.

FALLOPIUS, Gabriel, or **Fallopia** (1523–1562), Italian anatomist, a supporter of VESALIUS. He carried out important work on many anatomical structures; and is best known for his descriptions of the FALLOPIAN TUBES, whose function he discovered.

FALLOUT, Radioactive, deposition of radioactive particles from the ATMOSPHERE on the earth's surface. Three types of fallout follow the atmospheric explosion of a nuclear weapon. Large particles are deposited as intense but short-lived local fallout within about 250km of the explosion; this dust causes radiation burns. Within a week, smaller particles from the TROPOSPHERE are found around the latitude of the explosion. Long-lived RADIOISOTOPES such as strontium-90, carried to the STRATOSPHERE by the explosion, are eventually deposited worldwide.

(1) The largest of the falcons, the gyrfalcon (*Falco rusticolus*), which may grow to a length of 24in. It is found in the Arctic region, in the northern US and Europe and in central Asia. (2) The merlin, or pigeon hawk, (*Falco columbarius*), which grows to about 12in and is found in North America and in northern Europe and Asia.

FALLOW DEER, two species of DEER with flat, notched antlers and spotted coats. One species is distributed worldwide, the other is rare and found in S Iran.

FALLOW LAND, cropland that is not cultivated, usually only as a temporary measure for the purposes of improving the soil. Periodic leaving of some land fallow is common to most farming systems, though where SOIL EROSION is a threat the land may be planted (e.g., with hay). FERTILIZERS now permit more intensive cultivation.

FALL RIVER, city in SE Mass., one of three seats of Bristol Co. In the 19th century it became and has remained a major textile center. Pop 96 569.

FALLS CHURCH, independent city in NE Va., residential center of a truck gardening and poultry-farming area. Pop 10 772.

FALMOUTH, town in SE Mass., on the SW tip of Cape Cod. Formerly a whaling center, it is now a residential town and a resort. Pop 15 942.

FALSE-COLOR PHOTOGRAPHY, the processing of special photographic emulsions to display information using unnatural colors, used in terrestrial infrared PHOTOGRAPHY (e.g., vegetation studies) and astronomy. False-color ultraviolet photographs of the sun can be obtained using the SPECTROHELIOGRAPH.

FALSE IMPRISONMENT, the unlawful detention of a person against his will. His release can be obtained through a writ of HABEAS CORPUS, and he may obtain redress through a civil action.

FALSETTO, "artificial" vocal tone produced by male singers to enable them to sing higher than their natural range. It was much written for in Renaissance music. A falsetto singer in the alto range is called a COUNTERTENOR.

FALSTAFF, Sir John, comic and half-tragic figure in Shakespeare's *Henry IV* and *The Merry Wives of Windsor*, companion of Prince Hal. A roguish and cowardly knight, he remains likeable because of his wit, good nature and humanity.

FAMAGUSTA, historic port on the E coast of Cyprus. Under British administration 1878–1960, it was extensively developed. Pop 43 600.

FAMILY, a social unit comprising a number of persons in most cases linked by birth or MARRIAGE. There are four main types of families: the conjugal or nuclear family, a single set of parents and their children; the extended or consanguine family, which includes also siblings and other relations and generations (e.g., brothers, grandparents, grandchildren, uncles and aunts); the corporate family, a group organized around an important activity such as hunting, sharing of shelter, religion or customs; and the experimental family, a group whose members are generally unrelated to each other genetically, but who choose to live together and perform the traditional roles of the nuclear or consanguine family. The *kibbutzim* of Israel and the commune are examples of experimental families.

The descent within a family is usually either patrilineal, through its male members, or matrilineal, through its female members. Occasionally descent is bilineal, through either male or female lines, or bilateral, through both males and females.

By far the most common forms of families are the **nuclear** and **consanguine**. There are sound reasons for this: psychological security through membership of a close, intimate group; ready sexual and emotional satisfaction between husband and wife; and physical security based on a family's sense of duty and willingness to protect its members. Moreover, it would seem that these types of families are the most efficient insofar as childrearing is concerned, with older generations or siblings acting as mentors during the child's formative years. In the West, the nuclear family has in recent years become generally more democratic, the male's absolute authority being tempered to permit wives and children greater freedom and responsibility.

FAMILY, in the classification of living things. See TAXONOMY.

FAMILY COMPACT, alliances between the Bourbon rulers of France, Spain, Naples and Parma in

1733, 1743 and 1761. All three engaged Spanish help against Britain. (See also SEVEN YEARS' WAR.)

FAMILY PLANNING, the practice of regulation of family size by judicious use of CONTRACEPTION, STERILIZATION and, occasionally, induced ABORTION; increased survival of children and increasing world population have created the need for such an approach. Planning of numbers and timing to accord with economic and social factors are greatly aided by modern methods of contraception, so unwanted PREGNANCY should be a rarity. However, ignorance and neglect have prevented the realization of this ideal. ADOPTION, ARTIFICIAL INSEMINATION and treatment of infertility are used for parents unable to conceive.

FAMINE, acute food shortage resulting in widespread starvation. It is usually caused by natural disasters such as drought, floods or plant diseases, causing crop failure. Famines have often dramatically influenced the course of history. One such was the Irish famine (1846–47) caused by potato blight. Millions died and around a million and a half emigrated, mostly to the US. Recently there have been crippling famines in Bangladesh and Ethiopia.

FAN, device to produce a current of air. Originally, fans were hand-held, a small screen mounted on a stick. Later came the folding fan, a number of sticks held together by a pin at one end, and connected by paper or fabric. Modern **electric fans** are of two types: axial-flow, whose principle is roughly that of a PROPELLER; and centrifugal, where air is introduced along the rotation axis and forced outward by the rotation.

FANDANGO, rapid Andalusian folk dance, probably of Moorish origin, in 3/4 or 6/8 time. Often accompanied by castanets, the dance is an expression of passion. A sung form of fandango exists, its melodies improvised within set rules.

FANEUIL HALL, given by Boston merchant Peter Faneuil (1700–1743) to Boston, Mass. Site of many events leading to the American Revolution, it is known as the "cradle of liberty." Famous speeches were made here by Daniel WEBSTER, and J. F. KENNEDY, among others.

FANFANI, Amintore (1908–), Italian Christian Democratic statesman, premier in 1954, 1958–59 and 1960–63. A confirmed supporter of the COMMON MARKET, he was foreign minister in 1965 and 1966–68. He was secretary of the Christian Democratic Party 1954–59 and 1973–75.

FANJET or **Turbofan.** See JET PROPULSION.

FANNIN, James Walker (c1804–1836), US soldier. A colonel in the Texan army, he was active in the revolutionary movement against Mexico. He was captured on March 19, 1836 and by order of SANTA ANNA he and most of his men were shot.

FANNING, Edmund (1769–1841), US sea-captain who during a profitable trading expedition in 1797–98 discovered Fanning Island and others in the Pacific. He promoted and participated in the growth of South Sea trade.

FANON, Frantz Omar (1925–1961), French Negro psychoanalyst and social philosopher. He condemned racism in his book *Black Skin, White Masks* (1952). In *The Wretched of the Earth* (1961) he advocated extreme violence against whites as a cathartic expression for black peoples.

FANTIN-LATOUR, Ignace Henri (1836–1904), French painter known for his flower-paintings, his illustrations of the work of WAGNER and BERLIOZ, and his portraits of other artistic celebrities such as *A Studio at Batignolles* (1870), featuring MANET, MONET, RENOIR and ZOLA.

FARAD (F), the SI UNIT of CAPACITANCE, defined as the capacitance of a CAPACITOR for which a one coulomb charge raises its potential by one volt. The capacitance of most practical capacitors is measured in micro- or picofarads.

FARADAY, Michael (1791–1867), English chemist and physicist, the pupil and successor of H. DAVY at the ROYAL INSTITUTION, who discovered BENZENE (1824), first demonstrated electromagnetic INDUCTION (see also HENRY, JOSEPH) and invented the dynamo (1831—see GENERATOR, ELECTRIC), and who, with his concept of magnetic lines of force, laid the foundations of classical field theory later built upon by J. Clerk MAXWELL. In the course of many years of researches, he also discovered the laws of ELECTROLYSIS which bear his name and, in showing that the plane of polarization of plane POLARIZED LIGHT was rotated in a strong magnetic field, demonstrated a connection to exist between LIGHT and MAGNETISM.

FARCE, comedy based on exaggeration and broad visual humor. Its traditional ingredients are improbable situations and characters developed to their limits. Farcical elements are present in the plays of ARISTOPHANES, PLAUTUS, SHAKESPEARE, MOLIÈRE and many others, but only through such 19th-century writers as Georges Feydeau and W. S. GILBERT, did farce become a respectable theatrical form.

FAREL, Guillaume (1489–1565), French reformer, converted to REFORMATION doctrines c1520. A powerful preacher, he was a leader in the REFORMED CHURCHES of French-speaking Switzerland, and brought John CALVIN to Geneva. From 1538 he worked at Neuchâtel.

FARGO, city in N.D., seat of Cass Co. Founded by a railway company in 1871, it is now a transport hub and food processing center. Pop 53 365.

FARGO, William George (1818–1881), cofounder of Wells and Company (later Wells-Fargo), the pioneer express service, in 1844. In 1850 it merged with other companies to become the American Express Company, of which he was president until his death.

FARIBAULT, city in SE Minn., seat of Rice Co. It is an industrial and trading center for the surrounding agricultural area. Pop 16 595.

FARLEY, James Aloysius (1888–1976), politician and businessman who managed the presidential campaigns of F. D. ROOSEVELT in the 1930s. He opposed Roosevelt's third-term candidacy and resigned from the chair of the Democratic National Committee in 1940.

FARMAN, Henri (1874–1958), French aviator who perfected the aileron. With his brother Maurice (1877–1964) he designed and built many aircraft, including the first long-distance passenger airliner.

FARM BUREAU FEDERATION, US organization for promoting and protecting the interests of farmers. Founded in 1920, it was made up of voluntary organizations from most states. It has an effective Washington lobby and provides insurance and marketing, export and investment advice facilities, as well as various publications.

FARM CREDIT ADMINISTRATION, US federal agency formed in 1933 by President Franklin D. ROOSEVELT out of other agencies to provide adequate finance facilities to revive farming. Part of the Department of Agriculture 1939–53, it then became independent again.

FARMER, Fannie Meritt (1857–1915), US cookery instructor, author of the *Boston Cooking School Cook Book* (1896) which introduced standard level measurements. She served as the director of the Boston Cooking School 1891–1902, when she opened a school of her own.

FARMER, James Leonard (1920–), US civil rights leader who led the CONGRESS OF RACIAL EQUALITY 1942–66, when he joined the War on Poverty. In 1969 President Nixon appointed him assistant secretary of the Department of Health, Education and Welfare.

FARMER-LABOR PARTY, minor US political party, which represented the interests of small farmers and city workers 1918–44. Particularly active in Minn., where its candidate F. B. Olsen was elected governor in 1930, 1932 and 1934, it merged with the Democratic Party in 1944.

FARMERS' ALLIANCE, US agrarian movement comprising many groups 1890–91 which protested against both big business and traditional political parties. In 1891 it became a wing of the new Populist party.

FARMERS BRANCH, city in Tex., a NW suburb of Dallas. Pop 27 492.

FARMERS ORGANIZATION, National (NFO), US farmers' union which acts as a bargaining agent in negotiating farm produce prices. It was formed in Ia. in 1955.

FARMERS UNION, National, the Farmers Educational and Cooperative Union of America, an organization founded in Tex. in 1902 to lobby for farming interests and develop cooperative business methods in farming.

FARMINGTON, town in central Conn. In the 19th century it was an important textile and manufacturing center, but is now mainly residential. Pop 14 390.

FARMINGTON, city in Mich., a residential and shipping center with light industries. Pop 10 329.

FARMINGTON, city in NW N.M., an oil and natural gas center. There are Indian reservations in the area. Pop 21 979.

FARNABY, Giles (c1565–1640), English composer best known for his madrigals and virginal music. His work, marked by a free style and brilliant virtuosity, places him among the great composers of his day.

FARNESE, Alessandro, Duke of Parma (1545–1592), regent of the Netherlands under Philip II of Spain. By force and diplomacy he managed to maintain Spanish rule in the rebellious N, capturing Antwerp in 1585.

FARNSWORTH, Philo Taylor (1906–1971), US radio engineer known especially for his early work in the development of TELEVISION.

FARO, port city on the S Atlantic coast of Portugal. A historic city, its economy rests on agriculture, fishing, viniculture and tourism. Pop 21 581.

FAROE ISLANDS. See FAEROE ISLANDS.

FAROUK I (1920–1965), king of Egypt 1936–52. He was weak and incompetent, and his administration was marked by corruption, the alienation of the military and many internal rivalries. This led to a military coup headed by Gamar Abdel NASSER, which forced Farouk's abdication.

FARQUHAR, George (1678–1707), English comic dramatist. His most successful plays, *The Recruiting Officer* (1706) and *The Beaux' Stratagem* (1707), are characterized by vigorous language and pungent satire, and more realism than was then fashionable.

FARRAGUT, David Glasgow (1801–1870), US admiral, a Civil War hero. In 1862 he captured New Orleans, a Confederate supply center, by a bold maneuver. In 1863 he gained control of the Mississippi R. In a daring attack on Mobile Bay, Ala., in 1864 he gave the now proverbial command "Damn the torpedoes! Full speed ahead!"

FARRELL, industrial city in W Pa., a steel center. Pop 11 022.

FARRELL, James Thomas (1904–), US writer. He is known for his social novels, particularly the *Studs Lonigan* trilogy (1932–35), which depicts the often harsh life of the Irish on the Chicago South Side.

FARS, formerly Farsistan, a province in SW Iran. It consists mainly of limestone mountain ridges divided by fertile valleys. Settled since Neolithic times, it has deteriorated in the last 300 years. Its economy is almost totally agricultural.

FARSIGHTEDNESS. See HYPEROPIA.

FASCES, bundles of rods tied around the handle of an ax, carried before magistrates in ancient Rome as a sign of punitive authority. They were later adopted by generals and emperors. The term FASCISM derives from the adoption of the fasces as the symbol of the Italian revolutionaries under MUSSOLINI.

FASCISM, strictly, the political social system of Italy under MUSSOLINI 1922–45 (the name is derived from the FASCES); more generally, an authoritarian and anti-democratic political philosophy placing the corporate society, as embodied in the party and the state, above the individual, and stressing absolute obedience to a glorified leader. It is a reaction against the achievements of the ENLIGHTENMENT, the FRENCH REVOLUTION and LIBERALISM. It rejects both the 19th-century neutral state based on economic laissez-faire and also socialism, because fascism denies to separate social groups any independent political and economic activity. Instead it promotes an organic social order whereby the individual will find his own place in family, profession and society according to his character and ability. Nationalism and militarism are its logical products and thus it has close ties with NAZISM. "Fascist" has become a term of abuse for

Family Planning

Responsibility for ourselve

The policy of regulating the birth of children has now been adopted in many countries of the world.

The spread of family planning has been closely connected with concern about the capacity of the world's resources to supply an ever-increasing population. In states where overpopulation (either present or potential) is a problem it is usually national policy to encourage family planning by disseminating information on contraceptive measures, and sometimes by providing free facilities and even economic incentives. Birth control is part of government policy in the US, Britain, Sweden, Japan, the USSR, China, India, Pakistan and many others. Family planning is also promoted by international organizations, notably the International Planned Parenthood Federation.

On a personal level, sexual partners may wish to control the spacing as well as the number of their children. Many married couples in America, for example, wait some years before they have their first child, and they plan the arrival of subsequent offspring in the light of such varied factors as the family's economic situation, the wife's desire to complete her education or to go to work, and the needs of the children themselves.

Family planning is achieved by natural restraint or by contraception. Any couple choosing to practice birth control now has a number of well-established meods to consider. Factors which may play a part in their choice are: simplicity, reliability, safety to health, moral or religious beliefs, and sexual satisfaction.

Methods of birth control

"Natural" methods. There are some contraceptive methods which make no use of mechanical or chemical barriers to fertilization. These are, on the whole, the least reliable.

Withdrawal of the penis before ejaculation (*coitus interruptus*) is widely practiced, but very often fails to prevent the sperm, which are produced in millions, reaching the ovum. Withdrawal is also likely to be sexually unsatisfying to both partners.

The simple douche, or flushing out of the vagina after intercourse, is usually ineffective and often positively harmful to the delicate membranes.

The "rhythm" method requires restriction of sexual intercourse to the woman's so-called safe period: that is, the time in her monthly cycle of egg production when no egg is available for fertilization. It is difficult (and for some women impossible) to determine this time with adequate precision because there are many variables: the exact day of ovulation, the length of life of the ovum, the number of days the sperm survive in the uterus, and the regularity of the menstrual cycle itself. The complications of this method are such that it is usually only used by those whose religion forbids other methods.

The obvious way of preventing pregnancy by abstaining from intercourse requires caution: if semen comes into contact with the moist vaginal lips of the woman, some sperm may journey up into the uterus. Man has tried for centuries to produce an effective barrier between the sperm and the uterine cavity of the female while otherwise allowing full intercourse. From primitive beginnings, various forms of appliances have been devised.

Foaming pessary. This comes in tablet, cream, or aerosol form and is inserted into the vagina just before intercourse. The natural moisture of the vaginal secretions causes it to produce gas bubbles of carbon dioxide which form a partial barrier to the spermatozoa. The pessary also contains a chemical spermicide which kills the sperm coming into contact with it. However, used on its own, it is relatively unreliable in preventing fertilization.

The condom. This is a sheath of rubber or plastic which is pulled onto the erect penis just before insertion into the vagina. A loose teat is left at the end of the condom to hold the seminal fluid after ejaculation. The condom or "french letter" is an effective method of contraception only if it is used carefully. It must be unrolled over the penis while the penis is fully erect but before it enters the vulva or vagina. Because sperm can leak out with the male's secretions, produced long before ejaculation, the condom is not entirely reliable if used just for the final orgasm. Care must also be taken when removing the condom from the flaccid penis to prevent any leakage of semen near the vagina, since the moistness of the whole vagina area means the sperm deposited outside the woman's body might still be able to swim to the uterus for fertilization. The efficiency of the condom is increased when it is used in conjunction with a spermicidal cream.

The diaphragm. The diaphragm, or Dutch cap, is a fine membrane of rubber or plastic attached to a thin spring at its margin. It is inserted into the vagina by the woman before intercourse. The pliable cap is squeezed into a narrow oval and pushed into the vaginal opening; when it reaches the top it opens and presses gently against the walls, preventing the entry of spermatozoa into the uterus. The diaphragm is normally smeared with a spermicidal cream before use, which (as with the condom) greatly increases its efficiency.

The size of the vagina varies in different women, and in the same woman after childbirth, and with age. Deciding on the right size of cap is thus crucial and requires the help of a doctor. Proper care as well as proper use of the appliance is essential, and both should be learned from the doctor.

A disadvantage of this method, as with the condom, is that it is not always possible to predict when intercourse will happen, and to have the cap ready in place; so it may be necessary to break off sexual pleasures to insert it. The cap must be left in the vagina for at least six hours after intercourse to allow time for the sperm either to die naturally or to be killed by the spermicide.

Intrauterine device. For centuries it has been realized that a foreign body in the uterus prevents conception. However, this method of contraception has only been developed and refined since the 1920s. Today the interuterine device (or I.U.D.) comes in various forms, most commonly either a loop or a coil, about one inch across, made of pliable plastic material, stainless steel or silver. Until recently these devices were large, and only suitable for women who had had children, since the cervix needs to be slightly open when it is inserted. However the new I.U.D. is now available to women who have not had children.

The insertion of an I.U.D. must be done by a doctor. The device is threaded into a long narrow bore tube which is passed through the cervix. A plunger then pushes the device out of the tube to its resting place in the uterus just above the cervix, the natural springiness giving the device its original shape. Hanging from each device are some long threads which remain in the vagina so that the woman can check with a finger that her I.U.D. is still in place. It is advised that this should

The importance of contraception for the future of mankind is shown by a study made by a major US computer center for the Club of Rome, an international group of scientists which first met in Rome in 1970. The left-hand graph shows how the world may develop if no measures are taken to stop population growth. World population will increase slightly, but will then drop sharply as food shortages increase. Affected by famine and pollution, the average life expectancy will fall below what it had attained by 1900; on average man will live for only 25 years. The right-hand graph portrays a situation that should result if strict birth control is practiced before 1980. In this case an equilibrium will eventually be reached in which all the lines on the graph run parallel. This should then allow the average lifespan to increase considerably.

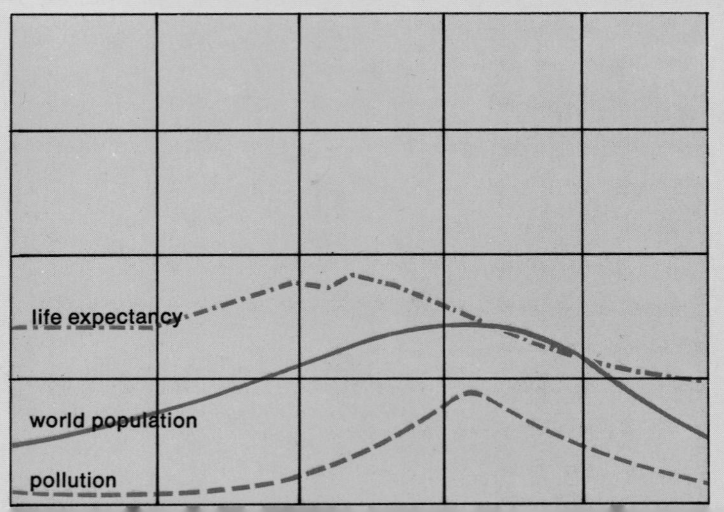

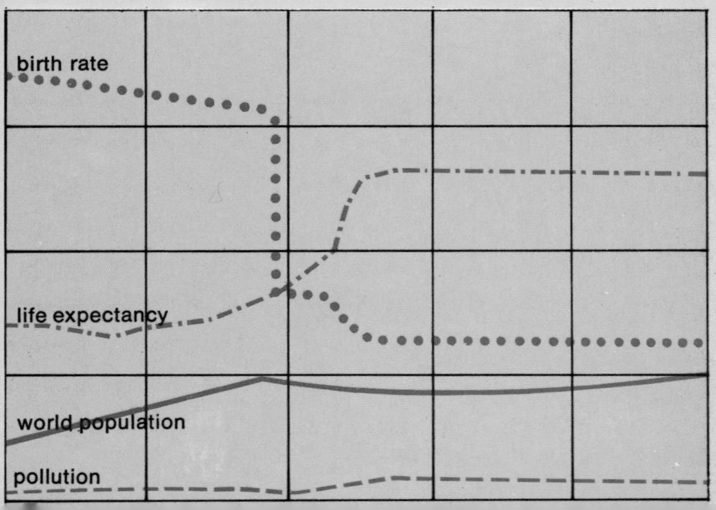

be done once a week. To remove the device (which must also be done by a doctor), the threads are simply pulled.

The mode of action of these devices is still not well understood. The most likely explanation is that the presence of the coil prevents the implantation of a fertilized egg. Other authorities believe that the I.U.D. alters the speed at which the ovum is carried down the Fallopian tubes so that a fertilized egg reaches the uterus at too young a stage to implant itself. These theories give rise to the ethical question of whether prevention of implantation constitutes abortion.

Twenty per cent of women cannot use the I.U.D. because they expel it or it causes undue bleeding. However, for those women who can use the intrauterine device it is second only to the pill in its efficiency as a contraceptive method.

All the more reliable methods of birth control mentioned so far (the condom, cap and I.U.D.) require the use of artificial devices. Many people do not find them acceptable, and lose sexual pleasure when they are used. In the last 20 years enormous advances have been made to control the production of the female gamete—the ovum—by the use of the contraceptive "pill."

The pill. In a normal woman one ovum is produced every 28 days in a regular cycle. The whole ovarian cycle is controlled by hormones produced by the pituitary, a tiny gland at the base of the brain. The pituitary produces three hormones in a carefully regulated sequence to bring about ripening and liberation of an ovum from either ovary each month. The stimulation of the ovary by pituitary hormones also makes it produce the ovarian hormones, estrogen and progesterone, which prepare the uterus for the event of implantation of the fertilized egg. When estrogen and progesterone levels in the blood stream rise they actually prevent the pituitary producing its egg-ripening hormones. Professor Pinkus exploited this natural phenomenon by producing a pill which contained estrogen and progesterone. Any woman then taking the pill had a continual artificially-high level of ovarian hormones thus preventing the pituitary hormone production which in turn prevented egg production.

To be effective the contraception pill must be taken from well before the time of ovulation. It is usually taken from the fifth to the twenty-fifth day of the cycle. When the hormone levels fall as the pill is stopped the woman sheds the lining of her uterus as a menstrual period in the usual way.

Apart from sterilization the pill is by far the most effective method of birth control. Much long-term research is being carried out at the moment to investigate the possible side effects of the pill. The most recent results seem to indicate that given adequate physical examination and twice-yearly medical checks, the dangers of taking the pill are negligible and many women even feel better on it. For women with high blood-pressure, the risk of thrombosis with the pill is very much less than the risk encountered during pregnancy and childbirth. However, some conditions may be aggravated by the pill.

The production of the "mini" pill has helped a great deal. It contains the minimum necessary quantities of estrogen needed to suppress ovulation and also cuts down any possible side effects of the hormone.

Sterilization. The methods so far described are all reversible, so that a couple need only stop using these methods if they wish to regain their chances of having a child. However, for those who either do not want children or who have all the family they desire or can afford, sterilization may be the answer.

In women sterilization has for a long time involved an abdominal incision (under a general anesthetic) to remove a portion of each of the Fallopian tubes. However, there is now a method of cauterizing the tubes (known as the *laparoscopy technique*), which requires much less surgery. Both methods result in an absolute barrier between the gametes, making conception impossible; but there is no interference with ovulation or menstruation. The ovary sheds ova into the body cavity where they disintegrate harmlessly.

In men sterilization involves cutting the tube (vas deferens) which leads from the sperm-producing tissue in the testes to the penis. This operation, called a vasectomy, prevents the sperm from reaching the outside of the body. The cut is made in the skin at the root of the penis, and, the tubes being much more accessible than the woman's Fallopian tubes, the operation is a simple one requiring only a local anesthetic. There is no interference with the glands which make the seminal fluid, thus ejaculation continues to function normally.

The future. Modern research into methods of birth control is mostly based on chemical contraception in one form or another.

For women, there is some likelihood of a "morning-after" pill which would interfere with the implantation of the already fertilized egg. By changing to such a pill, women who take the standard daily pill could lessen the quantity of hormone or chemical material taken into the body. A "morning-after" pill would be ethically unacceptable to some because it acts after fertilization has taken place.

There is also the possibility of a monthly pill consisting of a slow-release compound or capsule which would inhibit pituitary hormones.

It has been observed during the use of the standard pill that the mucus of the cervix becomes sticky and viscid, thus actually forming a barrier to the sperm. This observation has led to attempts to produce a substance which might alter the cervical secretions to prevent the ascent of sperm, but at the same time not interfere with pituitary, ovary or uterus. There has been some limited success with a chemical called chlormadinone.

The idea of a pill for men is not a new one, but great difficulties have been experienced in its production. Although the male system and its control is seemingly easier to modify than the female, no one has yet developed a satisfactory chemical which would prevent the production of sperm but have no unpleasant side effects. So far chemical contraception has been less intensively researched for men than for women.

There is, however, a great overall increase in contraceptive research, and it is expected that new methods will be produced and some of the existing ones perfected.

many because of the ugly aspects of fascism, and is often used of anyone whose views are right-wing.

The roots of fascism in Italy lay in the stagnant political situation with its chronic poverty, social unrest and manifold dissensions, worsened by the fact that the country had "won the war (WWI) but lost the peace." In 1919 Mussolini founded the *Fasci Italiani di Combattimento*, mainly ex-soldiers in black shirts who strove to overthrow the government by means of street fighting units. Regular fights ensued during 1921 between them and the communists. On 28 Oct. 1922, Mussolini, with four companions and followed by thousands of supporters, marched on Rome from Naples, where the king refused the prime minister's request for extraordinary powers, thus making way for Mussolini's first cabinet three days later.

Fascist movements spread to most western countries between WWI and WWII following in the wake of the economic crisis. Dollfuss and Schuschnigg headed a fascist government in Austria from 1933 until its incorporation into Germany in 1938, Horthy led one in Hungary, Pilsudski in Poland, Metaxas in Greece and Perón in Argentina. The longest surviving fascist regimes were in Portugal under Salazar and in Spain under Franco and the Falange.

FASHODA INCIDENT, confrontation between the French and British (Sept. 18, 1898), at the small town of Fashoda in the Sudan, over the desire of both nations to consolidate their African territories. The British under KITCHENER forced the French to relinquish claims to the region.

FAST, Howard Melvin (1914–), US novelist best known for his strong stand on social issues. His works include *Citizen Tom Paine* (1943) and *Spartacus* (1952). A communist, he was imprisoned by the House Un-American Activities Committee in 1950. In *Naked God* (1957) he recounted his disillusion with communism.

FASTING, abstention, wholly or in part, from food or drink, a practice common to many religions, usually linked with PRAYER and PENANCE. YOM KIPPUR is a major Jewish fast and RAMADAN the main Muslim fast. Christians fast at various times, such as during LENT and before Holy Communion, to aid spirituality and self-discipline. Fasting is also used as a form of peaceful political protest.

FATALISM, a philosophical attitude which sees everything in human affairs as preordained by some inscrutable and unknowable agency, termed Fate. The individual is thus unable to influence the course of events. This attitude is implicit in STOICISM, absolute IDEALISM and many Oriental philosophies such as VEDANTA and TAOISM.

FATA MORGANA, a MIRAGE sometimes seen above cold water surfaces; images of a far shoreline may be seen in the air in magnified and elongated forms. The effect was named for the Italian form of Morgan le Fay, the enchantress of the ARTHURIAN LEGENDS.

FATES (Greek: *Moirai*), in Greek mythology the three goddesses of destiny, Clotho who spins the thread of life, Lachesis who decides its length and Atropos, who cuts the thread. The Romans called them the *Parcae* (for *Parca*, goddess of birth) and they were invoked at a child's birth.

FATHER DIVINE, pseudonym of George Baker (c1877–1965), black US religious leader whose Peace Mission sect, popular on the East Coast in the 1930s, demanded worship of him as God incarnate and communal celibate living.

FATHER'S DAY, originated in the US (1910), where it is observed on the third Sunday in June.

FATHERS OF THE CHURCH. See CHURCH FATHERS.

FATHOM, a unit of length used to describe depth at sea. One fathom equals six feet (1.8288m).

FATHOMETER, trade name for a recording ECHO SOUNDER.

FATIGUE, or tiredness, a vague term indicating an inability to perform EXERCISE or even normal tasks due to previous exertion or DISEASE. This may consist of general weakness, specific muscular weakness or shortness of breath. Physiological fatigue after exertion may be due to accumulation of waste products of METABOLISM. Virtually any disease may cause fatigue, in particular FEVER, visceral disease, DIABETES, ADDISON'S DISEASE and MUSCULAR DYSTROPHY. MYASTHENIA GRAVIS is characterized by excessive muscle fatigability.

FATIGUE, Metal. See METAL FATIGUE.

FATIMA, village and sanctuary in central Portugal, famous for its shrine of the Virgin Mary. The shrine was created after several apparitions of the Virgin were reported here in 1917. Pop 6 433.

FATIMAH (c606–632), youngest daughter of MOHAMMED, the Prophet of Islam. She is an object of great veneration by Shi'ite Muslims.

FATIMIDS, Muslim dynasty which ruled a N African empire from its conquest of Egypt in 969 AD until 1171. The first rulers claimed descent from FATIMAH. In 969 al-Mu'izz established his capital at Cairo, bringing a religious and cultural renaissance to the city. At one time all of N Africa, Sicily and Syria was under Fatimid rule, but the dynasty was overthrown in 1171 by SALADIN.

FATS, ESTERS of CARBOXYLIC ACIDS with GLYCEROL which are produced by animals and plants and form natural storage material. Fats are insoluble in water and occur naturally as either liquids or solids; those liquid at 20°C are normally termed **oils** and are generally found in plants and fishes. Oils generally contain esters of OLEIC ACID which can be converted to esters of the solid STEARIC ACID by HYDROGENATION in the presence of finely divided nickel. This process is basic to the manufacture of MARGARINE. Fats are the most concentrated sources of energy in the human diet, giving over twice the energy of STARCHES. Diets

Famine

The growing threat of mass starvation

Famine is defined as a protracted shortage of food in a community or country, usually marked by a significant increase in deaths from starvation or from diseases previously held in check by adequate individual nutrition. Throughout the developing world, some 460 million people are believed to be suffering from malnutrition. As highlighted by the United Nations World Food Conference held in Rome in 1974, populations in many developing countries now face severe shortages of food, but these shortages are not normally considered famines. Such populations must be considered at risk, however, since it requires only a minor reduction in food supplies to push them into a state of famine.

Major famines are usually characterized by a high death toll; migration of large numbers of people out of the stricken areas; and, very often, an inability to bury the dead either through weakness of the survivors or because of the large numbers of victims. There may be evidence of cannibalism, particularly in remote and isolated communities.

The history of famine is long and dreadful: between 10 AD and 1846, the British Isles had over 200 famines; and between 108 BC and 1911 AD, China suffered 1828. If anything, recent times have been notable for the rarity of famine. Although political upheavals such as those in West Africa and South-east Asia can still lead to widespread starvation, several major famines have been averted by international action. Emergency food and medical supplies prevented serious famine during an Indian crop failure in 1966, and helped to reduce the death toll in Bangladesh during the early 1970s following catastrophic flooding and crop failures.

Although the worst effects of famine can be reduced by international action, it has not yet succeeded in completely preventing deaths on a massive scale through starvation. During famines in 1973 and 1974 at least 500000 people are believed to have died: some 150000 in Africa, mainly in the Sahel countries, but spreading to Ethiopia, Somalia, Kenya and Tanzania; and about 350000 in South Asia. Without outside help, the death toll could easily have been much higher. The fact that so many people still did die, however, reflects the difficulty of mobilizing emergency food aid and getting it to people in the remote parts of developing countries.

The most common cause of famine has been drought, especially when one drought has followed another in successive years. Between 1876 and 1879, up to 13 million Chinese died in a famine caused by prolonged drought. Drought was also the cause of the recent Sahel famine. Too much rain and floods can cause extensive damage to food crops, but, like other natural disasters such as earthquakes, hurricanes and volcanic activity, their greatest impact is through the disruption of communications. Famine conditions may well prevail among the stricken populations until new supply routes are opened up to deliver food and other vital materials.

Crop pests and diseases can also greatly reduce supplies of food. Future production of sorghum, rice and the millets in some semi-arid areas of Africa could well depend upon what happens to the millions of red-billed weaver birds *Quelea quelea* that flock to fields in the savanna region and feed on the maturing grain. Infestations of stored foods such as peanuts, brazil nuts and corn by the mold *Aspergillus flavus* can make them unfit for human consumption by contaminating them with poisonous aflatoxins produced by the fungus. Generally, however, such unwanted organisms contribute to famine rather than being the sole cause.

The locust is one of the few animal pests known to have caused major famine. A combination of drought, war and locusts in Western India during 1803 to 1804 produced a famine in which thousands of people died. In 1889, when the British were at war in the Sudan, a plague of locusts struck the fields beside the Nile with disastrous results. The inhabitants of Omdurman had nothing left to eat. Some turned cannibal, but many more died in the streets or on the banks of the river which became polluted with putrefying bodies.

The late blight which struck the potato crop of Ireland between 1846 and 1847 is probably the only plant disease to have caused a major famine. The late blight, an infestation by the fungus *Phytophthora infestans*, occurs in cool, moist regions wherever potatoes are grown. Normally, it is kept in check by cultural techniques, including spraying with fungicides and sowing blight-free seed potatoes. The disease tends to be localized, but an epiphytotic outbreak in Ireland brought about severe famine. Over one million people died and nearly a fifth of the population fled the country seeking refuge mainly in the United States.

In the past, famines have been isolated incidents that could usually be explained in simple terms—the result of drought, warfare, natural disasters and poor husbandry. There is a fear now that the world is entering a period when famine will threaten continuously as the demand for food outstrips production. The present crisis emerged in 1972 when food output declined for the first time in more than 20 years. The output of cereals, for example, fell by 33 million tons (eight million tons more than the average annual increase needed to meet rising world demand). The wheat reserves of the main exporting countries fell from 49 million tons in 1971–72 to 29 million tons within a year. Rice reserves were practically exhausted. The solution, according to the World Food Conference, was to increase investment in agricultural development, to establish a network of food reserves, and to stabilize the world trade in agricultural products.

Efforts to resolve the disparities between food production, distribution and needs are far from new. In 1946, Lord Boyd-Orr, then Director General of the Food and Agriculture Organization of the United Nations, proposed the creation of a World Food Board. In 1954 the UN General Assembly called for the establishment of a World Food Reserve. In 1955 the United States suggested that the UN should set up a World Food Bank. World Food Congresses in 1963 and 1970 also tackled the problem, but, apart from setting up the World Food Programme, failed to mobilize adequate resources. Following the World Food Conference, a World Food Council has been established to provide a high political body dealing exclusively with food.

According to Russian estimates, the world could feed as much as ten times its present population. The fact that instead millions of people still go hungry inevitably raises doubts as to the will and ability of nations to eradicate famine from the world. Increases in food production arising from the introduction of high-yielding crop varieties have begun to level out. Initial increases were startling as progressive farmers in many developing countries started to grow the new varieties of rice, wheat and maize, but since 1970 the so-called Green Revolution has been losing momentum. Increases in agricultural production in many developing countries have failed to match the growth in demand. Instead of diminishing, the threat of famine seems to be growing again in the modern world.

containing high levels of animal fats have been implicated as causative factors in heart disease, and replacement of animal fat by plant oils (e.g., peanut oil, sunflower oil) has been suggested. Fats particularly of fish and plant origin represent important items of commerce, and world production in 1976 should reach 49 million tonnes. Of major importance are soybean oil (9–10 million tonnes), sunflower, palm, peanut, cottonseed, rapeseed and coconut oil (2.5–4 million tonnes each) and olive and fish oil (over 1 million tonnes each). Major producers include the US (soybean oil), the USSR (sunflower oil and cottonseed oil) and India (peanut oil).

FATSHEDERA, a perennial shrub produced by crossing the English IVY (*Hedera helix*) with ARALIA (*Fatsia japonica*). It is a popular house plant requiring a few hours direct sun in the winter, but avoiding direct sunlight in the summer. It grows best in cool parts of the house, avoiding temperatures above 21°C (70°F) and should be watered often enough to keep the soil evenly moist. Propagation is by shoot tip cuttings. Family: Araliaceae.

FATTY ACIDS. See CARBOXYLIC ACIDS.

FAULKNER, William Cuthbert (1897–1962),

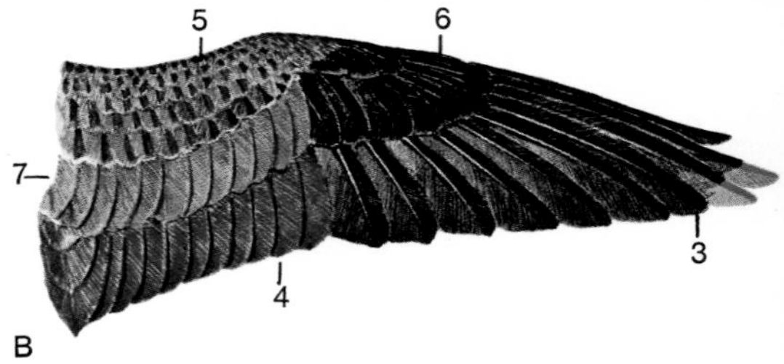

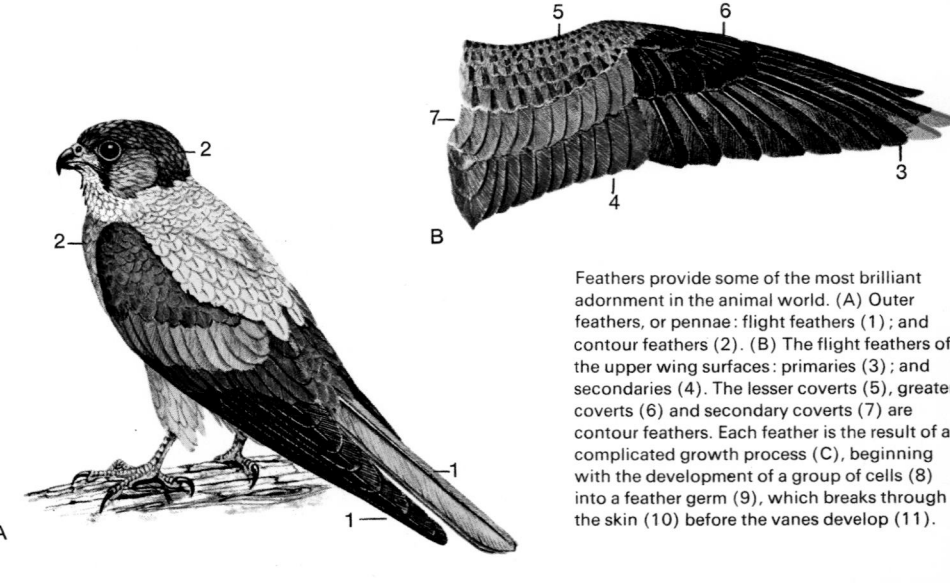

Feathers provide some of the most brilliant adornment in the animal world. (A) Outer feathers, or pennae: flight feathers (1); and contour feathers (2). (B) The flight feathers of the upper wing surfaces: primaries (3); and secondaries (4). The lesser coverts (5), greater coverts (6) and secondary coverts (7) are contour feathers. Each feather is the result of a complicated growth process (C), beginning with the development of a group of cells (8) into a feather germ (9), which breaks through the skin (10) before the vanes develop (11).

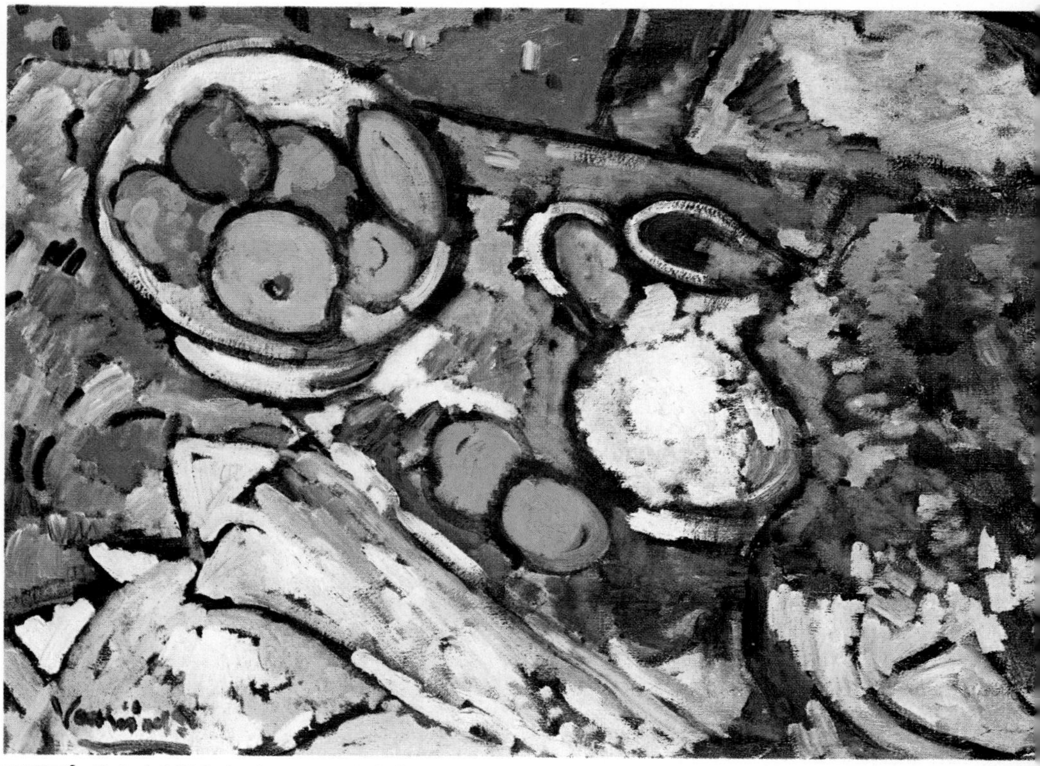

Two paintings in the style of Fauvism, both painted in 1905: *The Open Window* (*above*)—a view of the harbor at Collioure—by Matisse, the leading figure among the Fauves; and *Still Life* (*right*) by Vlaminck, executed with characteristic vigor.

major US writer, known for his vivid and complex characterization and his adventurous style. His most famous work is the cycle of stories set in the fictional Yoknapatawpha Co., Miss., and most of all the novel *The Sound and the Fury* (1929), an experimental work influenced by James JOYCE. He painted a vivid picture of the decadent and dying South, seeing in it a microcosm of human destiny. In 1949 he was awarded the Nobel Prize for Literature, and in 1955 the Pulitzer Prize.

FAULT, a fracture in the earth's crust on either side of which there has been relative movement (see EARTH). Faults seldom occur along a single PLANE: usually a vast number of roughly parallel faults take place in a belt (fault-zone) a few hundred metres across. The side of a fault on which the strata have moved relatively downward is the *downthrow* side; the other the *upthrow* side. The difference in vertical height between the sides is the *throw*, the lateral displacement the *heave*. The angle between the horizontal and the fault plane is the *dip*: where this is roughly 90°, the fault is a *normal fault*. (See also DIASTROPHISM; HORST; RIFT VALLEY.)

FAUN, in Roman mythology a woodland spirit resembling the Greek SATYR, humanoid but with a goat's legs and horns. Fauns were followers of the god Faunus, a Roman analogue of PAN.

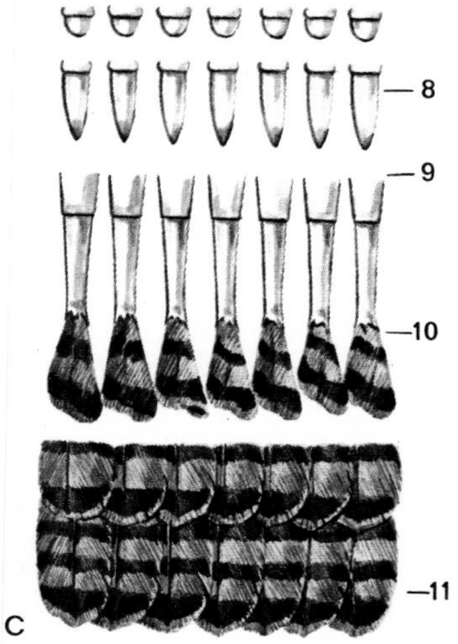

FAURÉ, Gabriel Urbain (1845–1924), influential French composer, director of the Paris Conservatory 1905–20. He is famous for his songs, chamber music and large-scale works such as the *Requiem Mass* (1887).

FAUST, legendary German enchanter, based on a 16th-century charlatan, who sold his soul to the devil Mephistopheles for knowledge and pleasure. Faust has been a favorite literary subject; its greatest exponents have been MARLOWE, who in *Dr. Faustus* (c1590) made the tale a tragedy of human presumption, and GOETHE. In *Faust* (1808 and 1832) he made Faust a Romantic idealist whose sins are forgiven because of his continual striving after good.

FAUVISM, art movement that developed in early 20th-century France, characterized by its bold use of brilliant color and rhythmic line. Hostile critics dubbed the group of artists painting in the style "*fauves*," wild beasts. Its main members were MATISSE, DERAIN, BRAQUE, ROUALT, VLAMINCK and DUFY. The movement, lasting c1898–c1908, was largely transitional; some Fauvists moved on to CUBISM.

FAVRE, Jules Gabriel Claude (1809–1880), liberal French statesman. A republican deputy 1848–51 and 1858–71, he was a strong opponent of Napoleon III. After the latter's downfall in 1870, Favre became vice-president and negotiated an unpopular treaty with Prussia.

FAWKES, Guy (1570–1606), Roman Catholic Englishman, hired by the GUNPOWDER PLOT conspirators as an explosives expert while he was serving in the Spanish army. Arrested while setting explosives beneath the House of Lords, he was tortured and hanged. In England he is burnt in effigy on Guy Fawkes Day, Nov. 5.

FAYETTEVILLE, city in NW Ark., seat of Washington Co. A summer mountain resort, its manufactures include wood products and agricultural machinery. Pop 30 729.

FAYETTEVILLE, city in SW N.C., seat of Cumberland Co. On the Cape Fear R, it is a wood and textile center. Pop 53 510.

FAYUM, or Al-Faiyum, city in N Egypt, capital of Fayum province. A trade and administrative center, its economy depends largely on locally-grown cotton. Pop 151 000.

FEAR, Cape, point on Smith Island, N.C., at the mouth of Cape Fear R.

FEATHER, the structure which forms the outer covering of BIRDS. No other animal possesses feathers. Feathers function to insulate and waterproof the body, provide flight surfaces and colors that are important as camouflage and in displays. There are two types of feather: pennae which are composed of contour and flight feathers; and plumulae or down feathers.

FEATHER STARS, ECHINODERMS that are related to SEA LILIES, but which are not attached to the sea-bed by a stalk. There are about 600 species.

FEBRUARY, the second month of the year. Before Julius Caesar decreed that the year should begin in January, February was the last month of the year. The name is from the Latin *febrarius*, purification; the month was then a time of religious purification for the new year.

FEBRUARY REVOLUTION, French. See REVOLUTIONS OF 1848.

FEBRUARY REVOLUTION, Russian. See RUSSIAN REVOLUTION.

FECHNER, Gustav Theodor (1801–1887), German physicist and founder of experimental psychology, usually remembered for his reformulation of Ernst Heinrich Weber's (1795–1878) conclusions concerning the increase in a stimulus needed to make someone aware that there was a difference. **Fechner's law** (or the Weber-Fechner law) states that the perceived intensity of a sensation increases with the logarithm of its stimulus.

FEDERAL ARTS PROJECTS, four projects begun by the US Work Projects Administration in 1935 to relieve the arts. The Art Project (1935–43) had around 5 000 employees, and produced artwork for public buildings and exhibitions. The Music Project (1935–43) operated many orchestras, bands and other organizations. The Theater Project (1935–39) put on performances of many old and new works, but was disbanded for its political bias. The Writers' Project (1935–39) produced hundreds of books on all aspects of US life.

FEDERAL AVIATION ADMINISTRATION (FAA), an agency of the US Department of Transportation created in 1958 to regulate air traffic. It shares responsibility with the CIVIL AERONAUTICS BOARD. The agency's main responsibility is the operation and maintenance of the national air traffic control system in the interests of efficiency and safety.

FEDERAL BUREAU OF INVESTIGATION (FBI), investigative branch of the US Department of Justice. Established in 1908, it is headed by a director appointed by the president, subject to Senate confirmation. Its headquarters are in Washington,

The impressive facade of New York City's Federal Hall, a national memorial. On this site in 1789 George Washington, whose statue now stands there, was inaugurated as President.

DC. In general, the FBI is responsible for the investigation of possible violations of all federal laws except those for which enforcement is specifically assigned to another agency, and is also concerned with internal security and counterespionage. It seeks to use the most up-to-date investigative techniques. FBI history is dominated by J. Edgar HOOVER, director 1924–72, a conservative figure who held the post until his death.

FEDERAL COMMUNICATIONS COMMISSION (FCC), an independent agency of the federal government, directly responsible to the US Congress, which regulates communication by radio, television, wire and cable. Created in 1934, it has seven members appointed by the president. Its most important functions are the licensing of commercial radio and television stations, the assignment of broadcasting frequencies, the supervision of other radio services and regulation of interstate communications services.

FEDERAL CROP INSURANCE CORPORATION, agency of the US Department of Agriculture, created by the 1938 Crop Insurance Act. It insures farmers against crop loss caused by natural hazards; loss through bad farming is not so covered and profit is not guaranteed.

FEDERAL DEPOSIT INSURANCE CORPORATION (FDIC), federal corporation which insures almost all bank deposits in the US, created by the 1933 Banking Act. All FEDERAL RESERVE SYSTEM banks must insure with FDIC. In the case of failure of an insured bank, the FDIC reimburses each depositor up to a maximum sum. It also acts as a watchdog over banking practices.

FEDERAL HALL NATIONAL MEMORIAL, stands on Wall and Nassau streets, Manhattan Island, New York City. The site was first occupied by the colonial city hall, which became the first US capitol 1781–89; it was rebuilt as Federal Hall. The present building was completed in 1842 and designated a national memorial in 1955.

FEDERAL HOUSING ADMINISTRATION (FHA), a division of the Department of Housing and Urban Development (HUD), an agency created by President Roosevelt in 1934. Seeking to raise housing standards, it insures loans for private residential building operations. The FHA is also in charge of land development, mortgage insurance and the rent supplement program.

FEDERALIST PAPERS, collection of American political essays written in support of the proposed US Constitution, published serially 1787–88. Written anonymously by Alexander HAMILTON, James MADISON and John JAY, the papers were later collected in book form and published under the title, *The Federalist*. They provide a classic exposition of the US federal system.

FEDERALIST PARTY, first true US political party. Founded by Alexander HAMILTON c1789, it was in general supported by prosperous citizens who wanted a strong central government. It dominated the government 1794–1800 but lost support among the lower middle class to Thomas JEFFERSON's Democratic Republican Party. After Jefferson won the election of 1800, the Federalist Party endured until 1816 only, remaining as a New England party until the 1820s.

FEDERAL MARITIME COMMISSION, federal agency established in 1961 to regulate rates, services and charters of US ships, enforce shipping laws and keep the US shipping industry on an internationally competitive basis.

FEDERAL MEDIATION AND CONCILIATION SERVICE, independent federal agency established as a result of the 1947 TAFT-HARTLEY ACT to promote the amicable settlement of labor disputes. The agency has no coercive powers and cannot dictate a settlement, but strives to bring the parties together and break deadlocks.

FEDERAL MUSIC PROJECT. See FEDERAL ARTS PROJECTS.

FEDERAL POWER COMMISSION (FPC), independent regulatory agency which oversees the electricity and natural gas industries. The FPC regulates rates and business practices of all public utilities and wholesale supplies of gas and electricity in interstate commerce. It is also responsible for regulating hydroelectric projects.

FEDERAL RESERVE SYSTEM, central US banking authority, created by the Federal Reserve Act of 1913. It consists of a board of governors, 12 Federal Reserve banks, the Federal Open Market Committee and Advisory Council, and the member banks, which account for about 85% of the country's banking. All national banks must belong to the System; state banks may also join. The System is the basic arm of the monetary side of national economic management. By buying securities it expands bank reserves, enabling banks to expand loans and stimulate economic activity. When it sells, it contracts bank reserves, reducing lending and slowing the economy (these are called open-market operations). The System may also affect the volume of banks' lending by changing the statutory amount of reserves they must hold and by changing the rate at which member banks may borrow from the System.

FEDERAL STYLE, US architectural style, seen in such buildings as the Capitol at Richmond, Va. and the University of Virginia. Neoclassical, and based on an idealization of the Roman state, it was popular from c1785 until the mid-19th century.

FEDERAL THEATER PROJECT. See FEDERAL ARTS PROJECTS.

FEDERAL TRADE COMMISSION (FTC), a federal agency established in 1914 to prevent unfair business practices, particularly monopolies, and to maintain a competitive economy. Its five commissioners are appointed by the president subject to Senate confirmation. The FTC studies the effects of business mergers and price agreements, issuing cease and desist orders if their effects prove undesirable. It also attempts to prevent misleading advertising and protect public health.

FEDERAL WRITERS' PROJECT. See FEDERAL ARTS PROJECTS.

FEDIN, Konstantin Alexandrovich (1892–), Soviet novelist. His best-known works, such as *First Joys* (1950), depict the plight of the Russian intellectual after the revolution. In the 1920s a member of the unconventional literary group, the Serapion Brotherhood, he has since tended to follow official policy.

FEEDBACK, the use of the output of a system to control its performance. Many examples of feedback systems can be found in the life sciences, particularly in ecology, biochemistry and physiology. Thus the population of a species will grow until it overexploits its food supply. Malnutrition then leads to a reduction in population. In the design of machines, SERVOMECHANISMS and GOVERNORS also exemplify feedback systems. The most important application of the feedback concept in modern technology comes in ELECTRONICS where it is common practice to feed some of the output of an AMPLIFIER back to the input to help reduce NOISE, distortion or instability. Most often used is "negative feedback" in which the effect of the feedback is to reduce the amplifier's output while stabilizing its performance. The howling that can occur when too much sound from a LOUDSPEAKER enters the MICROPHONE of a public address system is an example of positive feedback.

FEHLING'S SOLUTION, reagent composed of COPPER (II) sulfate, Rochelle salt (see TARTARIC ACID) and sodium hydroxide, used in chemical ANALYSIS to detect ALDEHYDES, including some SUGARS. It is reduced to a copper (I) oxide precipitate, from whose amount the quantity of sugar can be determined.

FEININGER, Lyonel (1871–1956), US artist. Influenced by CUBISM, his style is based on interpenetrating prismatic planes of color. He lived in Germany 1887–1936, teaching at the BAUHAUS 1919–32.

FEISAL. See FAISAL.

FEKE, Robert (c1706–1750), itinerant American colonial portraitist. Little is known of his life. His portraits, though stiff, surpass those of his contemporaries in composition, vitality and color.

FELDSPAR, widely distributed mineral group. Potash feldspars, principally ORTHOCLASE and MICROCLINE, are potassium aluminum silicates where sodium or barium may partly replace potassium. Plagioclase feldspars form a series derived from sodium aluminum silicate (ALBITE) with calcium replacing sodium in all proportions up to 100% (ANORTHITE). Feldspar is used in making glass and glazes.

FELIDAE. See CATS.

FELIX, three popes and two antipopes. **Saint Felix I** (d. 274), reigned from 269. **Felix II** (d. 365), was antipope during the banishment of Liberius 355–58 and was forced to retire on his return. **Saint Felix III** (d. 492), reigned from 483. **Saint Felix IV** (d. 530), reigned from 526. **Felix V** (Amadeus VIII of Savoy) (1383–1451), antipope 1440–49, elected by the Council of BASEL when it deposed Eugenius IV.

FELLER, Robert William Andrew (1919–), US baseball star, a pitcher with the Cleveland Indians 1936–42 and 1944–56. In 1946 he set a season record of 348 strike-outs. He was elected to the Baseball Hall of Fame in 1962.

FELLINI, Federico (1920–), Italian film director. His early films, such as *La Strada* (1954) and *La Dolce Vita* (1960), portray human disillusionment in a corrupt society. Later films such as *8½* (1963),

Gelmeroda VIII, painted in 1921 by Lionel Feininger. His work is built not around the human figure but around strong architectural forms, showing the influence of the Bauhaus school.

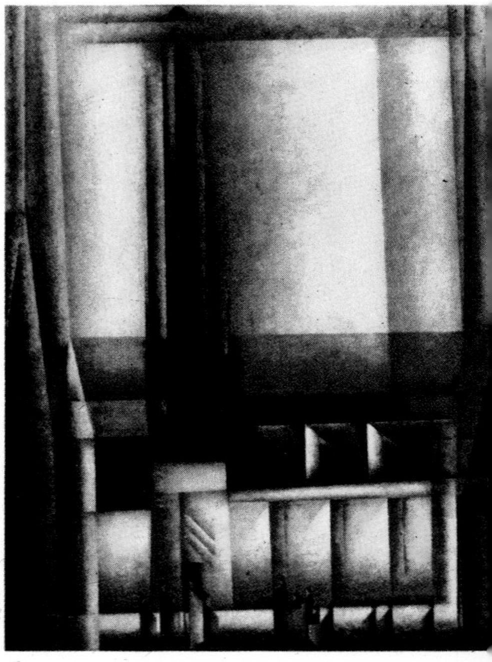

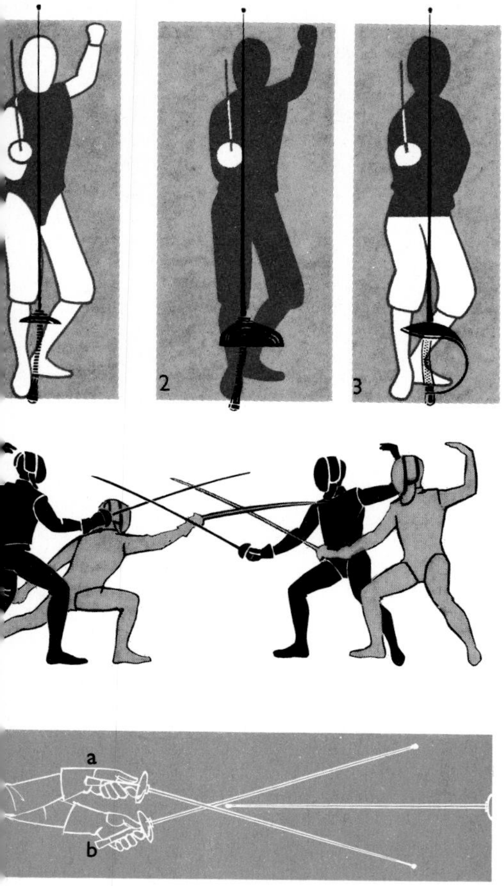

Three different weapons are employed in fencing: the foil (1); the épée (2); and the saber (3). Each of the three forms of fencing has its own rules, including restrictions on the areas of the body which may be "touched." The permitted areas for the three weapons are shown in blue in the diagrams (1)–(3). The normal distance between fencers requires a lunge (4) to touch the target area. A fencer may counter a lunge with a defensive action known as a parry, of which two varieties are shown in (5).

Juliet of the Spirits (1964), *Satyricon* (1970) and *Amaracord* (1974), have a more personal style, often dream-like and fantastic.

FELONY, a criminal offense more serious than a MISDEMEANOR. In US law the distinction between the two categories is generally the severity of the prescribed penalty for the offense. HOMICIDE, ROBBERY, BURGLARY, theft and rape are the main felonies.

FELT, fabric made from wool, hairs and fur. The fibers are matted together by rolling and pressing under heat. Hat felts are of wool or fur. Other types include padding felts and carpet underfelts. Jute roofing felt is not true felt.

FEMINISM. See WOMEN'S RIGHTS.

FEMUR, in vertebrates the proximal BONE of the hind leg, or thigh bone. In the human skeleton it is the largest and longest bone.

FENCING, sport of combat with swords. It is descended from the DUEL, but in fencing the object is only to touch, not to wound, one's opponent. Fencers wear protective clothing and masks. Three weapons are used; the light, rectangular foil, the stiffer, triangular épée and the triangular two-edged saber. Only the tip of the foil and épée may be used to score hits; saber scores may be made with the point or by a cut. In foil and saber fencing hits may only be made on certain parts of the body. Matches take place on a measured strip or *piste*. In men's bouts the first to be hit five times loses, in women's four times.

FÉNELON, François de Salignac de la Mothe- (1651–1715), French theologian, archbishop of Cambrai from 1695. His reform writings were far in advance of their day. He opposed JANSENISM. He tutored the duke of Burgundy, heir of Louis XIV, and wrote for him *Fables: Dialogues of the Dead* (1690) and *Telemachus* (1699).

FENIAN BROTHERHOOD, Irish-American revolutionary society, founded in 1858 by Irish exile John O'Mahony. The movement achieved little in Ireland but made sporadic terrorist attacks in Canada 1866–71. It collapsed with O'Mahony's death in 1877.

FENELLOSA, Ernest Francisco (1853–1908), US orientalist, who lived in Japan 1878–90. He did much to reawaken declining Japanese interest in their own culture, but was little appreciated there. In the US he wrote and lectured on Japanese art.

FENNEC, *Fennecus zerda*, the smallest fox, of N Africa and Arabian deserts; it has long ears and lives for long periods without water.

FENNEL, *Foeniculum vulgare*, an aromatic European perennial herb, the leaves of which are used for flavoring. Also, *F. vulgare dulce*, grown as an annual, the swollen stems of which are used as a vegetable.

FENS, 15 500sq mi low-lying marshy region in E England, S and W of the Wash. Much of it was drained in the 17th and 19th centuries to provide rich farmland. The drainage has proved hard to maintain owing to land subsidence.

FENUGREEK, *Trigonella foenum-graecum*, a yellow-flowered annual plant of Mediterranean origin, which is cultivated as food and as flavoring. Its seeds are the main ingredient of "condition powder" for livestock. Family: Papilionaceae.

FERBER, Edna (1887–1968), US author popular for her epic novels set in the 19th- and 20th-century US such as *So Big* (1924), for which she won a 1925 Pulitzer Prize, *Showboat* (1926), *Cimarron* (1930), *Saratoga Trunk* (1941) and *Giant* (1952).

FER-DE-LANCE, *Bothrops atrox*, a dangerous relative of the rattlesnake, found in Middle and South America and in the West Indies. It has a powerful venom and measures from 1.2m to 2.4m (4–8ft).

FERDINAND, name of three Holy Roman Emperors. **Ferdinand I** (1503–1564), emperor 1558–64, was king of Bohemia and Hungary from 1526. His agreement to the Peace of AUGSBURG ended the crippling religious conflict in Germany. Elected emperor after his brother Charles V abdicated, he stabilized the unwieldy empire by capable administration. **Ferdinand II** (1578–1637), was elected emperor in 1619. An advocate of the COUNTER-REFORMATION, his attempts to enforce Catholicism in Protestant Bohemia led to a revolt in 1619, which began the THIRTY YEARS WAR. In the Peace of Prague (1635) he was forced to make concessions to the Protestants. **Ferdinand III** (1608–1657), succeeded his father Ferdinand II as emperor in 1637. A capable ruler, he compromised with the Protestant powers in the Peace of WESTPHALIA (1648).

FERDINAND, name of three kings of Spain. **Ferdinand II of Aragon** (1452–1516), married Isabella of Castile in 1469, becoming her consort in Castile in 1474. In 1492 he conquered the Moorish kingdom of Granada, becoming effective king of Spain. A supporter of the Spanish Inquisition, he expelled the Jews from Spain. Isabella, rather than he, was COLUMBUS' sponsor. **Ferdinand VI** (1713–1759), came to the throne in 1746. A capable ruler and patron of the arts, he carried out many administrative reforms and managed to keep Spain neutral during the SEVEN YEARS WAR. **Ferdinand VII** (1784–1833), acceded in 1808 when his father Charles IV was deposed by a revolt; he was himself deposed by Napoleon two months later and imprisoned until his restoration in 1814. A cruel and repressive absolutist, he was deposed 1820–23 and only restored by a French army. Of limited ability, he was unable to prevent the complete loss of Spain's American possessions.

FERENCZI, Sándor (1873–1933), Hungarian psychoanalyst, and an early colleague of FREUD, best known for his experiments in PSYCHOTHERAPY, in course of which he broke away from Freud's classic psychoanalytic theory. (See PSYCHOANALYSIS.)

FERGUS FALLS, city in W central Minn., seat of Otter Tail Co. A summer resort, it has a primrily agricultural economy. Pop 12443.

FERGUSON, Adam (1723–1816), Scottish philosopher and historian, friend of David HUME. Formerly a clergyman, he became professor of natural philosophy (1759) and of mental and moral philosophy (1764) at Edinburgh University. His emphasis on social relationships made him an ancestor of sociology.

FERGUSON, James Edward (1871–1944), US politician. Elected Democratic governor of Texas on an antiprohibition platform in 1914, he was re-elected in 1916, but impeached and removed by the state legislature for corruption (1917). He then managed to have his wife "Ma" elected governor in 1924 and 1932.

FERLINGHETTI, Lawrence (c1919–   ), US poet of the "Beat Generation," founder of the *City Lights* bookstore and publishing house. His poetry was generally a means of political expression. The best known collection is *A Coney Island of the Mind* (1958).

FERMAT, Pierre de (1601–1665), French mathematician best remembered for **Fermat's Principle**, that the path of light traveling between two points by REFLECTION is that taking least time; and **Fermat's Last Theorem**, that $x^n + y^n - z^n = 0$, where $x, y, z \neq 0$ and $n > 2$, is impossible for integral x, y, z and n.

FERMENTATION, the decomposition of CARBOHYDRATES by microorganisms in the absence of air. Louis PASTEUR first demonstrated that fermentation is a biochemical process, each type being caused by one species (see also BUCHNER, EDUARD). It is an aspect of bacterial and fungal METABOLISM, in which GLUCOSE and other sugars are oxidized by ENZYME catalysis to pyruvic acid (see CITRIC ACID CYCLE). Pyruvic acid is then reduced to LACTIC ACID or degraded to carbon dioxide and ETHANOL. Considerable energy is released in this process: some is stored as the high-energy compound ATP (see NUCLEOTIDES), and the rest is given off as heat. Fermentation by YEAST has been used for centuries in BREWING and making bread and wine; fermentation by lactic acid bacteria is used to make cheese. Special fermentations are used industrially for the manufacture of ACETONE, butanol (see ALCOHOLS), GLYCEROL, CITRIC ACID, glutamic acid (see MONOSODIUM GLUTAMATE) and many other compounds. (See also RESPIRATION.)

FERMI, Enrico (1901–1954), Italian atomic physicist who was awarded the 1938 Nobel Prize for Physics. His first important contribution was his examination of the properties of a hypothetical gas whose particles obeyed Pauli's EXCLUSION PRINCIPLE; the laws he derived can be applied to the ELECTRONS in a metal, and explain many of the properties of metals (see FERMI-DIRAC STATISTICS). Later he showed that NEUTRON bombardment of most elements produced their RADIOISOTOPES.

FERMI-DIRAC STATISTICS, in QUANTUM MECHANICS, the statistical behavior of a system of indistinguishable particles with a number of discrete states, each of which may be occupied at any one time by a

Huge fermentation tanks in the cellar of a large brewery. The albumen foam seen on top of the fluid is formed by escaping carbon dioxide gas.

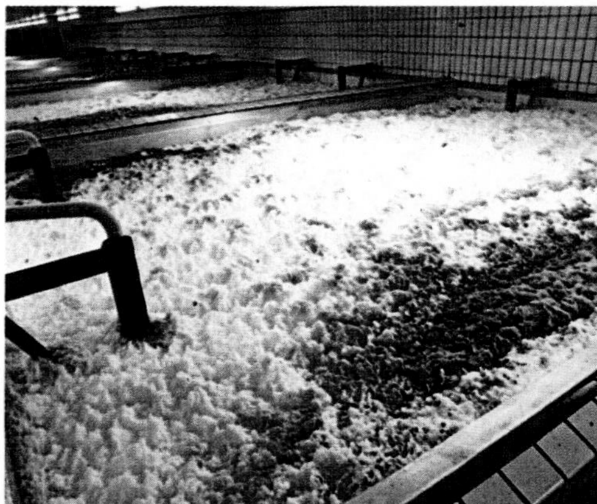

single particle only. SUBATOMIC PARTICLES that show this behavior are termed **fermions**. (See also BOSE–EINSTEIN STATISTICS.)

FERMIUM (Fm), a TRANSURANIUM ELEMENT in the ACTINIDE series, found in the debris from the first HYDROGEN BOMB, and now prepared by bombardment of lighter actinides.

FERNS, nonflowering plants of the class Filicineae having creeping or erect RHIZOMES or an erect aerial stem and large conspicuous leaves. Spores are produced on the underside of the leaf within sporangia and germinate to form the GAMETOPHYTE or sexual stage of the life cycle. Ferns are widely distributed throughout the world, but the majority grow in the tropics. Many ferns are popular house plants, e.g. *Nephrolepis* (Boston ferns), *Pteris* (maidenhair ferns), *Platycerium* (staghorn ferns) and *Asplenium* (bird's nest ferns). Indoors they require a reasonably bright position but avoiding direct sunlight; they flourish under fluorescent lighting. They grow best at temperatures between 16°C and 21°C (60°F and 70°F) and will tolerate temperatures as high as 24°C (75°F) so long as the air is fresh and humid. They should be watered often enough to keep the soil evenly moist and most benefit from daily misting. They can be propagated from spores, but normally by division of the plant or by rhizome cuttings.

FERNANDO PO, island in the Gulf of Guinea, a province of Equatorial Guinea.

FERNDALE, city in Mich., a manufacturing center and suburb of Detroit. Pop 30 850.

FERRAR, Nicholas (1592–1637), English founder and leader of a famous religious community at Little Gidding, Huntingdonshire. Among his followers was George HERBERT, whose poems he published. His community, much admired by Charles I, was dedicated to useful work and religious observance.

FERRARA, historic capital city of Ferrara province, N Italy. Always an agricultural center, it has become industrialized since WWII. Pop 154 923.

FERRARA-FLORENCE, Council of (1438–1445), the last medieval attempt to reunite the Roman Catholic and Greek Orthodox churches. In a feud between the Council of BASEL and Pope Eugenius IV, the papal party gained the upper hand and resolved their disagreements with the Greeks. They signed a decree of union in 1439, but the Greeks repudiated this soon after.

Four different species of ferns: (1) *Osmunda regalis*; (2) *Adiantum capillusveneris*; (3) *Athyrium filix-femina*; and (4) *Phyllitis scolopendrium*.

FERREL'S LAW, the proposition that moving air masses tend to be deflected to the right in the northern hemisphere and to the left in the southern, first proposed by US meteorologist, **William Ferrel** (1817–1891). (See also BUYS-BALLOT'S LAW.)

FERRET *Mustelo furo*, a domesticated POLECAT, normally about 350mm (13.8in) long, which is bred in Europe to kill vermin and, in hunting, to drive rabbits from burrows. The wild, Black-footed ferret of the western US is a close relative.

FERRIER, Kathleen (1912–1953), brilliant British contralto singer. She appeared in oratorio, opera and under the direction of Bruno WALTER specialized in the works of MAHLER. After a brief career she died of throat cancer.

FERRIS WHEEL, amusement park ride consisting of a huge, upright wheel with seats on its outer rim revolving around a fixed center. It is named for its designer, George W. Ferris (1859–96).

FERROMAGNETIC MATERIALS. See MAGNETISM.

FERROMAGNETISM. See MAGNETISM.

FERROUS SULFATE, or Iron (II) Sulfate. See IRON.

FERRY, Jules François Camille (1832–1893), French statesman. A republican opponent of the Second Empire, he held many offices in the Third Republic, becoming premier 1880–81 and 1883–85. He sought to exclude the clergy from education, and directed the acquisition of many colonies.

FERTILE CRESCENT, area in the Middle East, extending in an arc or crescent from the N coast of the Persian Gulf to the E coast of the Mediterranean. Natural irrigation made this semi-arid land fertile; it gave birth to the Sumerian, Phoenician and Hebrew civilizations. (See also MESOPOTAMIA.)

FERTILIZATION, the union of two GAMETES, or male and female sex cells, to produce a CELL from which a new individual, animal or plant, develops. The sex cells contain half the normal number of CHROMOSOMES, and fertilization therefore produces a cell with the normal number of chromosomes for any particular species. Fertilization may take place outside the organism's body (external fertilization), or inside the female (internal fertilization) as a result of copulation.

FERTILIZERS, materials added to the SOIL to provide elements needed for plant NUTRITION, and so to enable healthy growth of crops with high yield. The elements needed in large quantities are NITROGEN, PHOSPHORUS, POTASSIUM, SULFUR, CALCIUM and MAGNESIUM; the last three are usually adequately supplied in the soil or incidentally in other fertilizers. Small amounts of TRACE ELEMENTS are also needed, and usually supplied in fertilizers. The choice of compounds or materials containing nitrogen, phosphorus and potassium depends mainly on cost. The traditional natural fertilizers—BONE MEAL, GUANO and MANURE—are now too expensive to be much used outside HORTICULTURE. Potassium is supplied as potassium chloride, widely available as SYLVITE. Phosphorus fertilizers are obtained from mineral PHOSPHATES, especially APATITE; some is used as such, but most is converted to ammonium phosphate or superphosphate (see PHOSPHATES). Nitrogen is supplied as AMMONIA (injected under pressure), ammonium salts, NITRATES (ammonium nitrate being most useful) and UREA (see also NITROGEN CYCLE; NITROGEN FIXATION). Fertilizers in excess may harm crops and cause EUTROPHICATION.

FESCUE, common name for GRASSES of the genus *Festuca*. Commonly found in temperate and cold climates, they are important pasture and hay crops.

FESSENDEN, William Pitt (1806–1869), US politician, a founder of the Republican Party. He served in the House of Representatives 1841–43 and as senator from Me. 1854–64 and 1865–69. In the interval he was secretary of the Treasury. An opponent of slavery, he advocated RECONSTRUCTION. He opposed the impeachment of President JOHNSON.

FETISH, in abnormal psychology, any object or focus of obsession onto which has been projected an exaggerated power to erotically stimulate. The term also applies to the abnormal attraction itself.

FETISH, in anthropology, an object in which a spirit is thought to reside, distinct from an AMULET whose supernatural power is believed to be externally derived. Unlike idols, fetishes are not intended to be a likeness of the spiritual being.

FETTERMAN MASSACRE, ambush and massacre by Sioux Indians in 1866 of an 80-man escort party from Fort Phil Kearney, Wyo., led by Captain William Judd Fetterman, an officer of proven ability but no frontier experience who disobeyed strict orders against leaving the trail.

FETUS, the developing intrauterine form of an animal, loosely used to describe it from the development of the fertilized egg (EMBRYO), but strictly referring in man to the period from three months gestation to BIRTH. During fetal life, organ development is consolidated and specialization extended so that function may be sufficiently mature at birth; some organs start to function before birth in preparation for independent existence. During the fetal period most increase in size occurs, both in the fetus and in the PLACENTA and WOMB. The fetus lies in a sac of AMNIOTIC FLUID which protects it and allows it to move about. BLOOD CIRCULATION in the fetus is adapted to the placenta as the source of OXYGEN and nutrients and site for waste excretion, but alternative channels are developed so that within moments of birth they may take over. Should the fetus be delivered prematurely, immaturity of the LUNGS may cause respiratory distress, that of the LIVER, JAUNDICE.

FEUDALISM, system of social, economic and political relationships that shaped society in medieval Europe. It originated in the 8th century and flourished from the 10th to the 13th centuries. Thereafter it declined, although in Europe and Russia many feudal institutions persisted into the 19th century. The system rested on the obedience and service of a vassal to his lord in return for protection, maintenance and, most particularly, a tenancy of land (a *fief*). The duty owed by a vassal included military service, counsel and attendance at court, and contribution towards the lord's extraordinary expenditures such as ransoms or dowries. At the apex of the social pyramid was the king, vassal only to God. His vassals were his great nobles, holding land or some other source of income in fief from him. They in turn invested, or *enfeoffed* (so, "feodal" or "feudal") their own vassals, the lords of the manor. At the base of the pyramid were the serfs, or villeins, permanently tied to the land. They worked both for the lord and for themselves, unpaid; serfdom offered a degree of security in that if a serf could not leave the land, neither could it be taken from him.

In effect feudalism tended to allow vassal lords unrestricted freedom, at least in their own holdings. With the tendency towards centralized government this liberty was curbed. The system assumed a subsistence economy; the growth of trade and of economically powerful towns attacked it, and by the 15th century it was dying out.

FEUERBACH, Ludwig Andreas (1804–1872), German materialist philosopher, a major influence on MARX. He rejected HEGEL's Idealism, and in such works as *The Essence of Christianity* (1841) he analyzed the Christian concept of God as an illusory fulfilment of human psychological needs.

FEUILLANTS, reformed branch of the Cistercian monastic order, founded at Les Feuillants, France, in 1577 by Jean de la Barrière (1544–1600). The name was also given to two conservative political clubs in the French Revolution because they met at a former Feuillant convent 1789–92.

FEVER, raising of body TEMPERATURE above normal (37°C or 98.6°F in man), usually caused by DISEASE. Infection, INFLAMMATION, heat stroke and some TUMORS are important causes. Fever is produced by pyrogens, which are derived from cell products, and alter the set level of temperature-regulating centers in the HYPOTHALAMUS. Fever may be continuous, intermittent or remittent, the distinction helping to determine the cause. Anti-inflammatory drugs (e.g., ASPIRIN) reduce fever; STEROIDS mask it.

FEVERFEW, *Chrysanthemum parthenium*, a European species of perennial flowering plants belonging to the family COMPOSITAE. It has white flowers and several varieties are in cultivation. It was once used as a folk remedy for feverish conditions.

FEYNMAN, Richard Phillips (1918–), US physicist awarded with SCHWINGER and TOMONAGA the 1965 Nobel Prize for Physics for their independent work on quantum electrodynamics (see QUANTUM MECHANICS). With GELL-MANN he has proposed the quark as a basic component of all SUBATOMIC PARTICLES.

FEZ, or Fes, historic city in N Morocco, long important as a trading center and as a center for Islamic studies. It has over 100 mosques, of which the Qarawiyin, dominating the university, is reputedly the largest in Africa. Pop 325 327.

FIANNA FÁIL (Gaelic: Warriors of Ireland), Irish political party, formed in 1926 in opposition to the terms of the 1921 Anglo-Irish treaty. Led by Eamonn DE VALERA, it came to power in 1932 and, except for the periods 1948–51 and 1954–57, remained in government until 1973.

FIAT MONEY, money made legal tender by government *fiat* (decree), having less purchasing power than money redeemable in gold or silver. Fiat money tends to foster inflation, as with continental currency during the Revolution, and German marks in the 1920s.

FIBER, a thin thread of natural or artificial material. **Animal fibers** include wool, from the fluffy coat of the sheep, and silk, the fiber secreted by the silkworm LARVA to form its cocoon. **Vegetable fibers** include COTTON, FLAX, HEMP, JUTE and SISAL: they are mostly composed of LIGNIN, though CELLULOSE is also important. **Mineral fibers** are generally loosely termed ASBESTOS. These fibrous mineral SILICATES are mined in South Africa, Canada and elsewhere. **Man-made fibers** are of two types: regenerated fibers, extracted from natural substances (e.g., rayon is cellulose extracted from wood pulp); and SYNTHETIC FIBERS. Most PAPER is made from wood fiber. (See also COTTON GIN; SPINNING; WEAVING.)

FIBERBOARD, two types of board made by reducing woodchips to fibers which are then compacted with adhesives. **Hardboard**, strong and fairly dense, is used for, e.g., wall paneling. Less dense **insulating board** is used for soundproofing, etc.

FIBERGLASS, GLASS drawn or blown into extremely fine fibers that retain the tensile strength of glass while yet being flexible. The most used form is fused QUARTZ, which when molten can be easily drawn and which is resistant to chemical attack. Most often, the molten glass is forced through tiny orifices in a platinum plate, on the far side of which the fine fibers are united (though not twisted) and wound onto a suitable spindle. Fiberglass mats (**glass wool**) are formed from shorter fibers at random directions bonded together with a thermosetting RESIN: they may be pressed into predetermined shapes. Known in ancient Egypt, fiberglass is now used in INSULATION, automobile bodies, etc.

FIBIGER, Johannes Andreas Grib (1867–1928), Danish pathologist awarded the 1926 Nobel Prize for Physiology or Medicine for his discovery of a technique of inducing CANCER in rats.

FIBONACCI, Leonardo, or **Leonardo of Pisa** (c1180–c1240), Italian mathematician whose *Liber Abaci* (1202) was probably the first European account of the mathematics of India and Arabia, including some material on ALGEBRA. He also devised the FIBONACCI SEQUENCE.

FIBONACCI SEQUENCE, often misleadingly termed **Fibonacci Series**, an infinite SEQUENCE in which each term $u_n = u_{n-2} + u_{n-1}$. The first few terms are thus 1, 1, 2, 3, 5, 8, 13, ... The term is sometimes applied to other recursive sequences, such as 1, 1+a, 2+a, 3+2a, . . ., as in 1, 4, 5, 9, 14, . . ., where a = 3.

FIBRIN. See CLOTTING.

FIBULA, the smaller of the two BONES in the lower LEG, apposed to the TIBIA, and part of the ankle JOINT.

FICHTE, Johann Gottlieb (1762–1814), German philosopher, an early exponent of ethical idealism. His work influenced HEGEL and SCHOPENHAUER, among others. Some of his theories prefigured socialism; his concept of the nation as a manifestation of divine order, combined with his fanatical patriotism, stimulated German nationalism.

FICINO, Marsilio (1433–1499), Italian philosopher who headed the Renaissance revival of Platonism. He translated all of PLATO into Latin, and under the aegis of Cosimo de MEDICI taught a form of Platonism reconciled with Christianity.

FICTION. See NOVEL; SHORT STORY.

FIDDLER CRABS, or calling crabs, small tropical CRABS of the family Decapoda, which make a high-pitched sound by rubbing their claws together. Males threaten rivals and attract females by waving their one outsize claw.

FIEDLER, Arthur (1894–), US conductor, famous for his concerts and records of high quality light music with the "Boston Pops" Orchestra. A player in the Boston Symphony Orchestra 1915–30, he became the "Pops" conductor in 1930.

FIELD, US family prominent in law and industry in the 19th century. **Cyrus West Field** (1819–1892), an industrialist, financed the laying of the first permanently operational transatlantic telegraph cable in 1866. His elder brother **David Dudley Field** (1805–1894), a jurist, was appointed by N.Y. in 1857 to draw up civil, political and penal codes, the last of which was subsequently adopted. Other states adopted all three. In 1873, he became the first president of the International Law Association. A third brother, **Stephen Johnson Field** (1816–1899), was also a distinguished jurist. He rose to become chief justice of Cal. and in 1863 was appointed to the US Supreme Court.

FIELD, influential US mercantile and publishing family. **Marshall Field I** (1834–1906) established one of the world's first and largest department stores. His donations established the U. of Chicago and the city's Art Institute and Field Museum of Natural History. **Marshall Field III** (1893–1956), publisher and philanthropist, began the *Chicago Sun* (later *Sun-Times*) in 1941, and published the *World Book Encyclopedia*, and various magazines. **Marshall Field IV** (1916–1965), expanded and increased the Field publishing concerns.

FIELD, a set (see SET THEORY) F with two operations, $+$ and $\times$, in which: (1) both $+$ and $\times$ are associative and commutative, and the operation $\times$ is distributive over $+$ (see ALGEBRA); (2) there are two identity elements in F, 0 relative to $+$ and 1 relative to $\times$, such that $a+0=a$ and $a\times 1=a$ for any element a of the field; (3) every element a has an inverse $-a$, also a member of the set, such that $a+(-a)=0$; (4) every nonzero element a has an inverse a^{-1}, also a member of the set, such that $a\times a^{-1}=1$. Examples of fields include the RATIONAL NUMBERS and the REAL NUMBERS with, in each case, the operations ADDITION and MULTIPLICATION. A set (with two operations) which satisfies the conditions (1), (2) and (3) but not (4) is an **integral domain**: an example is the set of all INTEGERS under addition and multiplication. (See also GROUP.)

FIELD, Eugene (1850–1895), US humorous journalist and poet, famous for his column *Sharps and Flats* in the *Chicago Morning News*. His popular collections *A Little Book of Western Verse* (1889) and *With Trumpet and Drum* (1892) were partly taken from this column.

FIELD, John (1782–1837), Irish virtuoso pianist and composer. Famous in his time, he created the piano nocturne, a form much used by CHOPIN, whose style Field anticipated.

FIELD-EMISSION MICROSCOPE, a lower-resolution relative of the FIELD-ION MICROSCOPE, in which the image is produced by ELECTRONS emitted by the tip itself when negatively charged.

FIELD GLASS. See BINOCULARS.

FIELD HOCKEY, a stick and ball game played on a field by two teams of eleven. Each team defends its own goal and the object of the game is to hit the 5½oz white ball into the opponents' goal as many times as possible. The game, of uncertain origin, was nationally organized in England in 1886. It was introduced into the US in 1902, and is today a popular sport in over 70 countries.

FIELDING, Henry (1707–1754), English novelist, dramatist and essayist. His satirical comedies angered the Whig premier Sir Robert WALPOLE, and Fielding had to abandon the stage and turn to the law. He then wrote two novels, *Joseph Andrews* (1742) and *Tom Jones* (1749). Robustious, picaresque works, they burlesque the stilted sentimentality then fashionable. He became a magistrate in 1748; he helped organize the Bow Street Runners, an early police force.

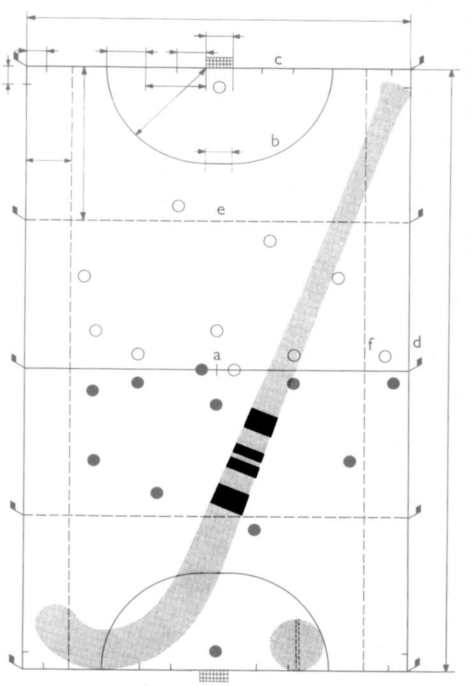

The field-hockey field is 90 to 100yd long and 50 to 60yd wide. There are 6 lines marked on the field: (a) the center line; (b) the striking circle—an attacking player must have touched the ball within this circle to be able to score a goal; (c) the goal line; (d) the side line; (e) the 25yd line; (f) the 7yd line. The normal length of a hockey stick is from 36 to 38in; it is curved at the end with one flat surface, which is the only side used to strike the ball. The ball is hard and made of leather with a circumference of about 8 to 9in.

FIELD-ION MICROSCOPE, an instrument producing very beautiful pictures of the arrangement of individual ATOMS in materials drawn out into, or evaporated on to, a fine tip, typically 40nm in radius. Invented by Erwin Wilhelm Müller (1911–) in 1936, the microscope is lensless, the image being produced on a fluorescent screen by IONS created in a low-pressure gas by the intense ELECTRIC FIELD at the tip when it is positively charged to a few kilovolts.

FIELD OF CLOTH OF GOLD, extravagantly-staged meeting between Henry VIII of England and Francis I of France in 1520. Elaborate temporary palaces were set up in fields near Calais. The meeting, though an impressive demonstration of wealth, produced little political result.

FIELD SPANIEL, British breed of sporting dog which resembles a stoutly-built COCKER SPANIEL and stands about 18in high, weighing 35–50lb. Its silky, flat and close-fitting coat is usually black, but may be liver, black and tan, liver and tan or liver roan.

FIELDS, W. C., pseudonym of Claude William Dukenfield (1880–1946), US deadpan comedian, characterized both on and off stage as a cantankerous but witty misogynist and child-hater. He began in VAUDEVILLE but rose to fame in movies, many of which he wrote himself. He was acclaimed for his portrayal of Mr. Micawber in *David Copperfield* (1935).

FIESOLE, historic hill town in N central Italy, 4mi NE of Florence. It has many Roman and Renaissance buildings, and few industries beyond tourism. Pop 14 138.

FIESOLE, Mino da. See MINO DA FIESOLE.

FIFTH COLUMN, agents and sympathizers of one side in a war engaged in subversion and sabotage in the home territory of the other side. The term originated in the Spanish Civil War, describing the sympathizers within Madrid of the four Nationalist columns advancing on the city.

FIFTH MONARCHY MEN, fanatical 17th-century English sect which aimed to bring in the "Fifth Monarchy" prophesied by Daniel, the reign of Christ on earth (see MILLENNIUM). The group first supported Cromwell, then opposed him, and dissolved after its leaders were executed following abortive coups (1657 and 1661).

FIFTY-FOUR FORTY OR FIGHT!, US expansionist slogan in the 1844 dispute with Britain over the Oregon territory (to latitude 54° 40′ N) especially in the election campaign of James A. POLK.

FIGS, shrubs and trees belonging to the genus *Ficus*, family Moraceae, particularly *Ficus carica*, the common fig, which is widely cultivated in SW Asia and the Mediterranean. The edible fruits are in fact a mass of male and female flowers enclosed in a fleshy receptacle. Dried figs are used medicinally as laxatives and poultices and are a staple food in Mediterranean regions. *F. elastica* (rubber tree) and *F. benjamina* (weeping fig) are popular house plants, the former producing large dark green leaves, and the latter small leaves on a much more compact bush. They grow best at average house temperatures in sunny east or west windows or a short distance from south-facing windows. They should be well watered whenever the soil surface dries out and are propagated by air layering or taking shoot tip cuttings.

FIGHTING FISH, fish of the genus *Betta*. The males, which are 50mm to 75mm (2–3in) long, build and guard nests made of bubbles, and display remarkable aggression in the presence of other males. In Thailand males of *Betta splendens* are often matched like gamecocks.

FIGURED BASS, or *basso continuo*, or thoroughbass, a system of musical notation in which figures placed under the bass notes indicate how the CONTINUO should improvise his part. Devised in Italy in the 17th century, the system is mainly associated with the scoring of BAROQUE music.

FIGWORTS, popular name for plants of the family Scrophulariaceae, many of which are common wild flowers. The family includes FOXGLOVES and SNAPDRAGONS. Species of the genus *Scrophularia* are tall plants with an unpleasantly pungent scent.

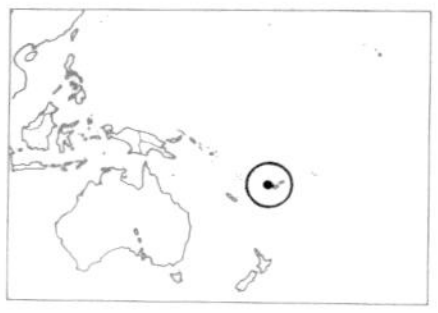

Official name: Fiji
Capital: Suva
Area: 7 055sq mi
Population: 476 727
Languages: Fijian; Hindustani; English
Religions: Christian; Hindu
Monetary unit(s): 1 Fiji dollar = 100 cents

FIJI, since 1970 an independent state within the British Commonwealth, an island group in the SW Pacific. It contains around 100 inhabited islands, of which the largest are Viti Levu, with the capital city Suva, and Vanua Levu. The larger islands are volcanic in origin, the rest are coral atolls or reefs. The climate is tropical, rainfall averaging over 100in a year and temperatures 65°–95°F. The original Melanesian and Polynesian inhabitants are now only 40% of the population, outnumbered by Indian immigrants.

Sugarcane and coconuts are the main crops; dairying is increasingly important. Industries are less important, but include mining, sugar milling and copra processing. First visited by Abel TASMAN in 1643 and James COOK in 1774, the islands were offered to Britain by a chieftain in 1858 but not accepted until 1874. Pop 531 000.

FILAMENT, in flowers, the stalk of the stamen that bears the anther at its apex. (See FLOWER.) Also, the thread-like row of cells found in certain ALGAE.

FILAMENT, a length of tungsten resistance wire which glows white-hot on carrying a suitable electric current, used in incandescent filament lamps (see LIGHTING for early history). Lamp filaments, from 0.015 to 0.045mm in thickness, are coiled once or twice (coiled coil) before being fused into the neck of the lamp. Heater filaments in ELECTRON-TUBE cathodes operate at only red heat.

FILARIASIS, a group of PARASITIC DISEASES of warm climates, transmitted by MOSQUITOS, causing FEVER, LYMPH node enlargement, ABSCESSES, epididymal inflammation and signs of ALLERGY; ELEPHANTIASIS may result. A specific type, onchocerciasis, or river blindness, leads to SKIN rash, EYE disease, sometimes causing BLINDNESS, and muscle pains or nodules. Some cause LUNG disease and increased BLOOD eosinophils. Diagnosis is by special staining of blood films and skin tests. Treatment and prevention are with diethylcarbamine; mosquito control is needed.

FILBERT. See HAZELS.

FILEFISH, certain genera of marine fishes of the family Balistidae. They have a single dorsal spine and a tough skin studded with tiny, hard scales, like sandpaper. With their small, sharp teeth they can break off corals and pierce mollusk shells.

FILENE, Edward Albert (1860–1937), US merchant who, as president of William Filene's Sons, Boston, pioneered such new methods of retailing as the "bargain basement." He was also a founder of the US Chamber of Commerce.

FILIBUSTER, legislative device for prolonging debate to prevent the adoption of a measure. The tactic is an especial feature of the US Senate, which seeks not to limit debate.

FILIBUSTERING, term (probably derived from the Dutch *vrijbuiter*, freebooter) originally applied to buccaneers and later to 19th-century adventurers who led expeditions from the US against Cuba, Mexico and Central and South America, usually for personal gain.

FILICINEAE. See FERNS.

FILIGREE, decorative metalwork formed of delicate gold and silver wire wrought into fine floral designs or network. The style was popular in ancient Mesopotamia, Greece and Rome; much of the best filigree work has come from the Far East.

FILLMORE, Millard (1800–1874), 13th US president. Fillmore stepped into office on the death of President Zachary Taylor in 1850. He served only 2½ years and assumed the role of moderator in the fierce national and congressional debates of the pre-Civil War period.

Born in Summerhill, N.Y., and trained as a lawyer, Fillmore was first elected to the US House of Representatives in 1832, serving from 1833–35 and again from 1837–43. In 1848 he was elected to the vice-presidency on the Whig ticket under Taylor. His principal achievement as president 1850–53 was a trade agreement with Japan. He supported the COMPROMISE OF 1850 as avoiding a North–South clash, although himself against slavery. This damaged his reelection chances, and on March 4, 1853, Fillmore left office after failing to win renomination with the Whig party. He finally retired from public life in 1856 after an unsuccessful candidature for the KNOW-NOTHING Party.

FILM. See MOTION PICTURES.

FILM, Photographic. See PHOTOGRAPHY.

FILMER, Sir Robert (c1588–1653), English Royalist political writer. His *Patriarcha; or The Natural Power of Kings* (1680), although much criticized by LOCKE and others, is a valid picture of the development of society up to his time.

FILSON, John (c1753–1788), American pioneer. His *Discovery, Settlement and Present State of Kentucky* (1784) included a pseudo-autobiographical account of the adventures of Daniel BOONE and established the frontiersman in American legend.

FILTER, Color. See PHOTOGRAPHY.

FILTER, Electric, an arrangement of electronic components used in a circuit to transmit signals within a given frequency range, rejecting others, used in RADIOS, TELEVISION receivers, TELEPHONE systems, etc. A **low-pass filter** transmits frequencies below a specified cut-off and blocks out higher frequencies; typically it consists of an inductor (see INDUCTANCE) in series with and a CAPACITOR shunted across the load to short out high-frequency current. In a **high-pass filter** the inductor and capacitor are interchanged and only high frequencies are transmitted. A **band-pass filter** blocks all frequencies outside two limits.

FILTRATION, separation of solid particles from a liquid or gas by passing it through a porous mesh on which the solid collects. Commonly used are filter cloths, filter paper, wire mesh, sintered glass, or—where a large volume of water is to be filtered—sand beds. Filters have many varied uses, including use in cigarettes, vacuum cleaners, gasoline and diesel engines, coffee-making, air-conditioning units, water-purification systems, and chemical preparation and analysis. A magnetic filter is used to remove iron or steel particles from oils etc. in machine tools and some engines. (See also ELECTROSTATIC PRECIPITATORS.)

FINBACK WHALE, a rorqual or whalebone (baleen) WHALE, *Balaenoptera physalus*, so called because of its prominent dorsal fin. Finbacks reach a maximum of 20–24m (66–79ft) in length and constitute about 50% of the world whale catch, most being taken in Antarctica.

FINCHES, small seed-eating birds of the family Fringillidae—canaries, grosbeaks, sparrows, cardinals, crossbills and buntings. Finches are characterized by their conical bills, used for opening seeds. Many members of the family number among the familiar songbirds of town and country.

FINDLAY, industrial city in NW Ohio, seat of Hancock Co. In the 1880s, it expanded rapidly as an oil and gas center. Pop 35 800.

FINE ARTS, term used to distinguish painting, sculpture, architecture and sometimes literature and music from the applied arts, on the grounds of their non-utilitarian nature.

FINE ARTS, Commission of, independent US Federal agency set up in 1910 to advise on the aesthetic aspects of the public buildings, parks and general appearance of Washington D.C. There are seven commissioners, appointed for four-year terms by the president.

FINE GAEL, Irish political party. It supplied the *taoiseach* (prime minister) for the coalition governments of 1948–51 and 1954–57. In 1973 a Fine Gael–Labor Party coalition government was formed.

FINGAL'S CAVE, sea cave, about 230ft long and 42ft wide, on the island of Staffa, Inner Hebrides, off the W coast of Scotland. Its walls are of hexagonal basalt columns. It inspired a famous overture by MENDELSSOHN.

FINGER LAKES, eleven narrow, glacially-formed lakes in N.Y. The largest are Seneca, Cayuga and Canandaigua. The lakes are situated in rolling, wooded countryside, with many resorts.

FINGERPRINTS, impressions of the loops and whorls of the papillary ridges of the fingertips, a valuable police tool. The earliest police system was developed by Jean Vucetich (1888, Argentina) and is still in use in the Spanish-speaking world. The system most in use today was developed by Sir Edward Richard Henry from the work of Sir Francis GALTON. Replacing the anthropometric techniques of BERTILLON, it was adopted in the UK in 1901, the US in 1903. In **dactyloscopy** (fingerprinting) the tips are well cleaned, rolled on printer's ink spread on a glass sheet and then onto coated cards.

FINISTERRE, Cape, promontory on the Atlantic coast of NW Spain, the scene of British naval victories over the French in 1747 and 1805.

FINK, Mike (1770?–1823), US frontiersman and folk hero. A Mississippi keelboatman and famous sharp-shooter, he was renowned for his drinking, brawling and bragging. He was murdered by a friend of a man he had killed in a drunken game.

FINLAND, independent republic in N Europe, bordered by arms of the Baltic Sea in the SW and W, by the USSR in the E and by Norway and Sweden in the N and NW. An independent country only since 1917, it has made great contributions to European culture, among them the music of Jan SIBELIUS and the work of architects Alvar AALTO and Eliel and Eero SAARINEN.

Land. The central plateau, glacial relatively

recently, is low-lying. Lakes, which cover about 9% of the whole country, extend over about 20%–50% of the central lakeland, creating a labyrinth of waterways. The N uplands, about 40% of the country, pass from forest into swamplands, and then into barren Arctic tundra; 30% of the country lies above the Arctic circle. The coastal lowlands are fertile, with a mild climate fostered by the Gulf Stream. The major cities, Turku and Helsinki, are situated here, as is most of the country's farmland. The coastal archipelago is largely barren.

People. The Lapps, nomadic reindeer herders, live in the N, numbering only about 1 500. There is a Swedish-speaking minority along the coasts, but the remaining 92% of the people are Finns. Around 60% of the population is now urban, compared with 9% in 1880. Educational standards have long been high and illiteracy is minimal; there are five universities. Most of the population belongs to the Lutheran National Church. Government is by elected president and single-chamber parliament.

Economy. Before WWII Finland remained predominantly agricultural, but manufacturing has now expanded until agriculture and forestry account for around only 15% of the national output. It is largely private enterprise, but the government has often intervened because of capital shortage. Forests remain the most important national resource, covering 70% of the total land area.

History. Finland was colonized from the S, and by the 9th century formed three tribal states, Karelia, Tavastenland and Suomi. Sweden progressively colonized the area and after the 14th century Finland became a Swedish grand duchy. In 1809 Sweden was forced to cede it to Russia. Tsar Alexander I maintained the country as a grand duchy but allowed it considerable autonomy under a governor-general. This period saw the rise in nationalism: the Swedish language was replaced by Finnish, particularly after the publication of the national folk-epic, the KALEVALA. In 1863 the legislative Diet was revived and political parties developed. Under Alexander III a policy of "Russification" was adopted and generally bitterly resisted until WWI. In 1917 the parliament declared independence from the new regime in Russia, and Bolshevik forces were defeated in a brief civil war. In 1919 a republic was declared. In 1939, in breach of a non-aggression pact, the USSR invaded Finland and set up a puppet junta government; but was stalled by fierce resistance. For the German aid Finland then received it was made to pay massive postwar reparations to the USSR and lost S Karelia. Postwar politics, dominated by the Social Democratic Party and the Agrarian Party under KEKKONEN, have sought a peaceful rapprochement with the USSR, despite much interference in Finnish affairs.

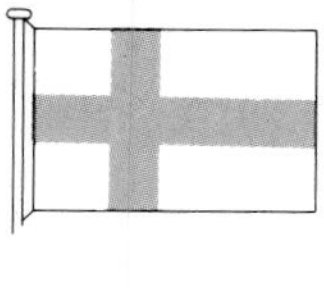

Official name: Finland
Capital: Helsinki
Area: 130 094sq mi
Population: 4 684 000
Languages: Finnish, Swedish: Lappish
Religions: Evangelical Lutheran Church
Monetary unit(s): 1 Markka = 100 penni

FINLAND, Gulf of, branch of Baltic Sea, running around 260mi W to E between Finland and the USSR. Cities on it include HELSINKI and LENINGRAD.

FINLAY, Carlos Juan (1833–1915), Cuban physician who first proposed (1881) that YELLOW FEVER is transmitted by the MOSQUITO. Despite his considerable research, this was unproved until 1900.

FINNEY, Charles Grandison (1792–1875), US evangelist, president of Oberlin College, Ohio, 1851–66. A former lawyer, he brought his courtroom technique to revivalist preaching, first under Presbyterian and later Congregational polity.

FINNISH, the most important of the UGRO-FINNIC LANGUAGES, spoken by around 5 million people in Finland. It has a written tradition dating from the 16th century but only achieved official status in the 19th century.

FINNISH-RUSSIAN WARS. See RUSSO-FINNISH WARS.

FINNO-UGRIC LANGUAGES. See UGRO-FINNIC LANGUAGES.

FINSEN, Niels Ryberg (1860–1904), Danish physician awarded the 1903 Nobel Prize for Physiology or Medicine for his discovery and use of the curative properties of certain wavelengths of LIGHT.

FIRBANK, (Arthur Annesley) Ronald (1886–1926), English novelist known for his eccentric and often innovatory style and his fluent verbal wit. Among his best-known works are *Vainglory* (1915), *Inclinations* (1916) and *Valmouth* (1919).

FIRDAUSI, penname of the great Persian poet Abu Qasim Mansur (c940–1020), author of the *Shah-Nameh* (Book of Kings), Persia's national epic. The poem, 60 000 verses long, took him 30 years and appears to have ruined him financially.

FIRE. See COMBUSTION.

FIRE ANTS, mainly tropical ants with extremely painful stings. Two species, one introduced from Argentina, are found in the southern US, and are a pest in fruit plantations.

FIREARMS, weapons in which missiles are projected by firing explosive charges. They are classified as either ARTILLERY or small arms. The latter seem to have originated in 14th-century Europe in the form of metal tubes, closed at one end, into which GUNPOWDER and the missile were packed, the charge being ignited via a touch hole. The heavy **harquebus** was one of these. The 15th century saw the introduction of the **matchlock** in which a spring-loaded lever mechanism was used to introduce a smoldering match (a hemp cord soaked in SALTPETER) to the powder. This was superseded by the **wheel lock** in the next century. In this a serrated wheel rotated against a flint and ignited the powder with a spark. In the 17th century the **flintlock** was introduced. Here a flint held in a spring-loaded arm, or cock, struck a metal hammer, or frizzen, to produce the spark. The perfecting of the gas-tight breechblock and the modern percussion lock in the early 19th century led to the development of the breech-loading RIFLE and the repeating pistol (see REVOLVER). By the end of the century, MACHINE GUNS were in an advanced state of development. SHOTGUNS, used mainly for sport, fire a cartridge containing numerous small pellets. (See also AIR GUN; AMMUNITION; PISTOL.)

FIREBALL, a particularly bright METEOR, especially a bolide. The term is also applied to LIGHTNING of globular form.

FIREBRICK, bricks made in a variety of shapes from refractory materials and used in constructions, particularly FURNACES, designed for the treatment of molten GLASS and metals. (See METALLURGY; REFRACTORY.)

FIRE CLAY, type of CLAY which, being refractory (mp above 1500°C), is used to make FIREBRICK. It has a high content of ALUMINUM oxide and SILICA.

FIRE CONTROL, the techniques and operations ensuring that a missile, shell or depth charge lands on target. When the target is visible and stationary the problem is relatively simple (see BALLISTICS), and accurate sights, firing tables, etc., are used. In other cases such devices as RADAR, SONAR, RADIO and TELEPHONE communications and COMPUTER control are employed.

FIREDAMP. See DAMP.

FIRE-EATERS, in US history, term applied to a number of vociferous extremists and secessionists in the Southern slave states in the years before the Civil War.

FIRE EXTINGUISHER, a portable appliance for putting out small fires. Extinguishers work either by cooling or by depriving the fire of OXYGEN (as typified by the simplest, a bucket of water or bucket of sand), and most do both. The **soda-acid extinguisher** contains a SODIUM bicarbonate solution and a small, stoppered bottle of SULFURIC ACID: depression of a plunger shatters the bottle, mixing the chemicals so that CARBON dioxide (CO_2) gas is generated, forcing the water out of a nozzle. **Foam extinguishers** employ a foaming agent (usually animal PROTEIN or certain detergents) and an aerating agent: they are effective against oil fires, as they float on the surface. **Carbon dioxide extinguishers** provide a smothering blanket of CO_2; and **dry chemical extinguishers** provide a powder of mainly sodium bicarbonate, from which the fire's heat generates CO_2.

Millard FILLMORE

13th US President

Born: January 7, 1800
Died: March 8, 1874
Term of office: July 10, 1850–March 3, 1853
Political party: Whig

FIREFLIES, mainly tropical soft-bodied BEETLES which produce an intermittent greenish light in their abdominal organs. The light is created by the oxidation of luciferin under the influence of an ENZYME, luciferase. In some species females are without wings and are known as **glowworms**. The lights serve to attract mates.

FIRE ISLAND, a sandspit off the S central coast of Long Island, N.Y., about 30mi long, ½mi wide, separating Great South Bay from the Atlantic. It is the site of Fire Island National Seashore and a summer resort.

FIRENZE. See FLORENCE.

FIREPROOFING, the techniques and materials used in rendering an object, building, etc., resistant to COMBUSTION. One of the commonest for fabrics, etc., is WATER GLASS. Substances such as ASBESTOS may be used to protect structural elements of buildings from excesses of heat.

FIRE PROTECTION, the prevention and control of fires, one of the most essential community services. Volunteer firefighting organizations are known to have existed in ancient Egypt, Rome and many other countries, but the first attempts to cope with fires in the modern fashion began after the Great Fire of London in 1666. After this the first regulations controlling building materials and techniques to avoid fire risks were passed. Also at this time the flourishing fire insurance companies set up brigades with pumps mounted on handcarts, to attend to their customers only. In the early 19th century fast horsecarts were used to carry the pumps, and soon after steam-driven pumps were introduced. The extensible ladder was developed c1800, and the

Fine Art

A new movement

In the history of the fine arts painting and sculpture have been for many centuries the most prominent aesthetic forms of representative or abstract visual expression. Painters have painted subjects on frescoed walls, with tempera on wooden panels and with oil paints or acrylic on canvas. Sculptors have carved objects out of wood or stone, modeled with plaster, cast or welded with metals. New materials have become available to artists through technical or industrial developments and artists have often seen new materials as a means of reinterpreting and enlivening the subject matter of their works. The traditional view is that, however strange and unconventional an artist's themes, styles and materials may seem to his public, nevertheless a work of art is necessarily an object made by an artist, who designed it expressly to embody his ideas.

Recently there have been heated arguments between artists, critics and the public about certain works of modern art. During the past 10 years many artists throughout the world have adopted means of visual expression that differ considerably from the traditional forms of painting and sculpture. This movement is known usually as "conceptual" art, but it may also be known as "dematerialized" art because it rejects the traditional view that art must be embodied in an object. Like many labels in art, "conceptual art" is inexact and does not define the kind of works that are accepted as "conceptual" nor the intentions of the artists in making them. Once the label was coined, however, it was adopted by artists internationally.

As opposed to the view that an artist's creative ideas and physical activity must result in a work of art that is an object, the "conceptual" art movement holds that a work of art simply can be the artist's creative idea or physical act itself. Consequently there are works of "conceptual" art that are artists' plans, instructions, discussions; or performances of artists dancing, singing, drinking, walking. Usually the creative ideas and performances are "documented" or recorded in such materials as videotapes, color slides, photographs, maps, diagrams, texts and sound cassettes. It might be more accurate to say that the ideas and performances are "worked out" in such materials since the artists take the materials into account in their presentation of ideas and physical activities. Also, whatever the medium of presentation, the artists nevertheless adopt the traditional aesthetic qualities of composition, color, texture, usually associated with the arts of painting and sculpture.

A form of art that places so much importance on artists' ideas, apparently to the exclusion of their artifacts, may seem radical. However, such an emphasis can be traced back to some artists' muddled interpretations of Neoplatonic thought in the 16th century. They felt that the artist could never hope to realize in mere paintings or sculpture the divine, creative ideas that inspired them. There are more immediate sources for "conceptual" art in 20th-century art movements such as Dada and Surrealism. Both these movements were noted for bizarre performances organized by artists, and for the value artists placed on automatic or unconscious acts to reveal innate aesthetic behavior. Marcel Duchamp's exhibitions of "ready-mades" indicated that the public would accept any kind of object, including a urinal, which the artist chose to exhibit as a work of art. This is not a situation like that of "the emperor's new clothes;" rather it shows that the artist often recognizes aesthetic qualities, even traditional ones, in objects which might seem to the public to be completely devoid of artistic values.

Keith Arnatt's *Self Burial* (1969); Tate Gallery, London.

The Minimal Art movement, which took place in the US in the early 1960s, developed an artistic belief important in "conceptual" art that an artist might be able to express more clearly, and his public recognize more easily, his artistic ideas if he worked in simple forms and materials; this would prevent the artist from indulging in "romantic" gestures in painting and sculpture. The American artists Robert Morris and Sol Lewitt thought that the works they exhibited in the room of an art museum should not be any more aesthetically conspicuous than the floor of the room or a chair in it. This belief led "conceptual" artists to adopt what might be regarded as "neutral" documenting materials like videotapes, sound cassettes or color slides. Such materials as these are not conventionally used by practitioners of the fine arts, and so are not burdened with a history of use and handling, which may interfere with the expression and interpretation of the artist's themes.

"Conceptual" artists have used subjects not formerly considered the province of art. These include anthropology, history, philosophy, sociology, aesthetics, linguistics, semantics and scientific theories. In 1971 an exhibition of the works of the American artist Hans Haacke, planned to be held at the Guggenheim Museum, New York, was canceled by the director on the grounds that some of the documentary works included concerned "specific social situations" not considered art. There were two particular works which upset the director. One comprised photographs and documentation of a large Manhattan real estate office whose holdings were mainly slum-located properties. The other was a poll of the Guggenheim's visitors consisting of 10 demographic questions (age, sex, education, etc.) and 10 questions on current socio-political issues. The cancellation caused mass demonstrations by artists and outrage in art circles throughout the world. It was widely felt that although an artist might take a political stand in his work (and artists have been doing this for centuries) a museum had no such right in respect to its artists, and their choice of subject matter.

Philosophy has provided themes for many "conceptual" artists. The English artist Keith Arnatt and the American Mel Bochner have made use of photographs or diagrams to illustrate philosophical paradoxes. The Art Language Group parodied the work of philosophers by attempting to arrange and order philosophical problems in a vast filing system. The "philosophical" relationships and analogies which the Art Language Group established are in fact based on over-simplified connexions, but the Group's extraordinary undertaking has disguised the issue of whether they have discovered any new philosophical truths.

There are "conceptual" artists whose interests are primarily in the fine-arts tradition because of their concerns with landscape and the human body. The English artists Richard Long and Hamish Fulton have visited ancient sites in England and Scotland and also in Peru where they studied the curious desert markings of the Nazca culture. Long's documentation of such a journey takes the form of a map of his travels, one or more photographs of special places and a list of his feelings, thoughts and experiences during the walk. Jan Dibbets, a Dutch artist, photographed the changing effects of natural light in particular places, altering the angle of the camera for each shot.

In performances and photograph series the German Klaus Rinke, using his own facial expressions and bodily movements, developed an elaborate sequence of abstract, sometimes fantastic, visual patterns. His work *Mutations* (1970) is presented either in performance, or on videotape, or in the form of 112 photographs, each 23in by 16in. Many "conceptual" artists have presented one activity in several different forms and media, although on each occasion adjusting it to the techniques and demands of the media. The American Bruce Nauman has drawn attention by the use of videotapes and sound cassettes to the possible expressive force and humor of pinching his thigh, as in *Thighing*. He has constructed corridors for performances by museum visitors; the narrowness of the corridor restricts the performer's movements which are recorded on videotape.

Two English sculptors, Gilbert and George, have made their life the theme of their work. Their artistic activities of dancing, singing, drinking in bars, and walking in the countryside have been exhibited in videotapes, photographs, drawings and books. Since all their life is devoted to art, a casual meeting with them raises the problem of whether one is experiencing a work of art or encountering two performers!

Since "conceptual" artists have adopted subject matter and materials that are not traditionally those of the visual or fine arts, their works frequently involve commercial difficulties; for what does it mean to buy an artist's idea without the accompanying physical embodiment? "Conceptual" art is still developing as a branch of the fine arts and it will probably take about 50 years to establish what constitutes its publicly acceptable subject matter, materials and forms. In the meantime "conceptual" art will doubtless continue to be controversial.

wheeled escape ladder in 1837. In 1865 the communal fire department of the insurance companies was taken over and expanded into the London Metropolitan Fire Brigade, ancestor of modern brigades. In the US the trend was similar. The first volunteer fire organization in America was founded by Benjamin Franklin in Philadelphia in 1736. In the US also it was the insurance companies which established fire brigades, and these were eventually taken over by the municipalities. Small towns, however, often still have a wholly or partly volunteer service.

FIRESTONE, Harvey Samuel (1868–1938), US industrialist, founder of one of the largest rubber companies in the world, the Firestone Tire & Rubber Company. His million-acre rubber plantation in Liberia played a large role in the country's economic development from 1926.

FIRESTORM, condition where flames from multiple fires combine as a single column. Owing to CONVECTION, violent winds blow in from around, fanning the flames to very high temperatures. In populated areas, firestorms, used as a weapon by the Allies in WWII, caused phenomenal loss of life: in the raid on Dresden (1945) up to 135 000 died.

FIREWEED, a number of weedy plants that grow rapidly after a forest fire. The most common species in North America and N Europe is the great, or rose bay, willow herb (*Epilobium angustifolium*).

FIREWORKS, combustible or explosive preparations used for entertainment, probably first devised in ancient China to frighten off devils. Their initial European use was as weaponry (see GREEK FIRE) and not until after about 1500 were they employed for entertainment. Compounds of CARBON, POTASSIUM and SULFUR are the prime constituents in fireworks, colors being produced by metallic salts (e.g., blue, COPPER; yellow, SODIUM; red, LITHIUM or STRONTIUM; green, BARIUM), sparks and crackles by powdered IRON, CARBON or ALUMINUM, or by certain LEAD salts. (See also EXPLOSIVES; GUNPOWDER.)

FIRE WORSHIP, a pagan religious practice popular through the ages in many continents; it appears universally in mythologies. Fire was often associated with the sun and worship was a recognition of its purifying and protective powers. Ancient Rome venerated the sacred fire of Vesta, goddess of the hearth. The Aztecs worshiped a fire god and a goddess of volcanoes. Hindus venerated the fire-god Agni.

FIRN. See NÉVÉ.

FIRS, EVERGREEN trees of the genus *Abies*, family Pinaceae. They are mostly conical in shape and have erect cones. There are 40 to 50 species native to North America and Eurasia. *Abies* wood is sold as (white) deal. (See also BALSAM FIR; CONIFERS; DOUGLAS FIR; PINE.)

FIRST AID, treatment that can be given by unqualified people in the event of accident, injury and sudden illness, until more skilled persons arrive or the patient is transferred to hospital. Recognition of the injury or the nature of the illness and its gravity are crucial first measures, along with prevention of further injury to the patient or helpers. Clues such as medical bracelets or cards, tablets, lumps of sugar, alcohol and evidence of external injury should be sought and appropriate action taken. Arrest of breathing should be treated as a priority by clearing the airway of dentures, gum, vomit and other foreign material and the use of ARTIFICIAL RESPIRATION; likewise CARDIAC massage may be needed to restore BLOOD CIRCULATION if major PULSES cannot be felt. In traumatic injury, FRACTURES must be recognized and splinted to reduce pain; the possibility of injury to the spine must be considered before moving the patient to avoid unnecessary damage to the SPINAL CORD. External HEMORRHAGE should be arrested, usually by direct pressure on the bleeding point; tourniquets are rarely needed and may be dangerous. Internal hemorrhage may be suspected if SHOCK develops soon after collapse or trauma without obvious bleeding. BURNS AND SCALDS should be treated by immediately cooling the burnt surface to reduce the continuing injury to SKIN due to retained heat. The use and, if necessary, improvization of simple dressings, bandages, splints and stretchers should be known; simple methods of moving the injured, should this be

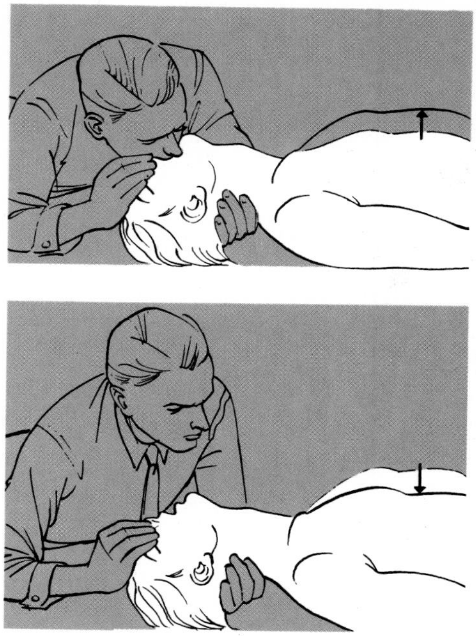

The "kiss of life," a first-aid measure when, as a result of electric shock, near-drowning or some other cause, the victim has stopped breathing. The person administering aid blows through the victim's mouth as shown, ensuring that the chest first rises and then falls. The cycle is repeated until natural breathing is induced.

necessary, must also be understood. Accessory functions such as contacting ambulances or medical help, direction of traffic and different aspects of resuscitation should be delegated by the most experienced person present. The inquisitive should be kept away and a calm atmosphere maintained.

Prevention as a part of first aid includes due care in the home: avoiding highly polished floors and unfixed carpets, obstacles on or near stairs, loose flex, overhanging saucepan handles, unlabeled bottles of poison and DRUG cupboards accessible to children. Attention to fireguards, adequate lighting and suitable education of children are also important. Effective first aid depends on prevention, recognition, organization and, in any positive action, adherence to the principle of "do no harm."

FIRTH, term used primarily in Scotland to describe usually a long narrow ESTUARY, often a FJORD, and sometimes a STRAIT. The best known are those of the rivers Forth, Clyde and Tay; the Solway Firth, into which several rivers drain; the Moray Firth, between the NE tip of Loch Ness and the North Sea; and the Pentland Firth, the strait between NE Scotland and the Orkney Islands.

FISCHER, Bobby (Robert James Fischer; 1943–), US chess player. In 1958, he became the youngest player (age 15) to attain the rank of international grand master. In 1972 in Iceland, he was the first American to win the world championship, defeating the Russian Boris Spassky in a widely-publicized tournament.

FISCHER, Emil (1852–1919), German organic chemist and pioneer of BIOCHEMISTRY, awarded the 1902 Nobel Prize for Chemistry for his work on the structures of SUGARS and PURINES, simple members of both of which families he synthesized. He also synthesized PEPTIDES and studied ENZYME action in the breaking down of PROTEINS.

FISCHER, Ernst Otto (1918–), German chemist awarded with G. WILKINSON the 1973 Nobel Prize for Chemistry for their work on ORGANOMETALLIC COMPOUNDS.

FISCHER, Hans (1881–1945), German organic chemist awarded the 1930 Nobel Prize for Chemistry for his elucidation of the structure of, and synthesis of, hemin—a substance closely related to heme (see HEMOGLOBIN). He later worked on the analysis of the CHLOROPHYLLS.

FISCHER-DIESKAU, Dietrich (1925–), German baritone. He achieved international fame in the 1950s as an opera singer and an interpreter of German lieder (see SONG), notably those of SCHUBERT and WOLF.

FISCHER VON ERLACH, Johann Bernhard (1656–1723), Austrian architect, who served the Hapsburgs and was a leading exponent of the Austrian BAROQUE style. Among his works are the original Schönbrunn Palace (Vienna) and the Kollegienkirche (Salzburg). He wrote *A Plan of Civil and Historical Architecture* (1721).

FISH, Hamilton (1808–1893), US statesman. A governor and US senator for New York, Fish was a Whig who joined the Republicans (1856) as an anti-slavery moderate. He served as an extremely capable secretary of state under President U. S. Grant and helped bring about the 1871 Treaty of Washington which settled the ALABAMA CLAIMS with Britain.

FISH AND WILDLIFE SERVICE, US federal agency within the Department of the Interior, created in 1956, concerned with conservation and development of fish and wildlife resources, wilderness areas and river basins. It maintains waterfowl refuges and fish hatcheries, prepares federal hunting regulations, performs research for the fishing industry, protects threatened wildlife, manages the fur seal herds of Alaska and administers international agreements.

FISHER, or pekan, *Martes pennanti*, North American MARTEN valued for its fur. Fishers feed on small mammals such as squirrels and grow to a length of 1m (3.3ft)—larger than any other marten.

FISHER, Dorothy Canfield (1879–1958), US author of novels, short stories and notable children's fiction about rural New England and the Midwest. Among her best known works are *The Bent Twig* (1915) and *Understood Betsy* (1916).

FISHER, Fort, a complex earthwork and wood fort that guarded Wilmington harbor, SE N.C., during the Civil War. In 1865 a Union military and naval expedition stormed it, thereby closing the last Confederate seaport for receiving European war supplies.

FISHER, Irving (1867–1947), US economist. He applied mathematics to economic theory, and propounded the idea of a "compensated dollar" which would have stable, constant purchasing power.

FISHER, John (c1469–1535), English cardinal, saint and martyr. As bishop of Rochester (1504–34), he refused to recognize Henry VIII's claim to royal ecclesiastical supremacy, was imprisoned in the Tower and later beheaded.

FISHER, John Arbuthnot Fisher, 1st Baron (1841–1920), British admiral, who as second and then first sea lord (1902–10), introduced wide-ranging naval reforms, including the encouragement of submarine development. His measures helped ensure British naval superiority in WWI.

FISHERIES, the commercial harvesting of marine and freshwater animals (and some plants) to provide food for men and animals. The main catch is of FISHES, but shellfish and marine mammals including seals and whales are also important. The world harvest now totals about 70 million tonnes per year, and has risen annually by about 6% since WWII. About 75% is caught in the cold and temperate zones of the Northern Hemisphere. The chief fishing nations are Peru, China, the USSR, Norway, Japan and the US; in the next rank are Canada, India, Spain, Great Britain and Iceland. Inland fisheries—in lakes, rivers and ricefields—account for less than 10% of recorded catches. The most important groups of fish caught are herring and its relatives, and cod and its relatives. Modern fishing vessels are equipped with radar, depth sounders and echo sounders to locate fish shoals; increasingly used are factory ships which process the fish and freeze or can them. Modern nets are very strong, being made from synthetic fibers. Trawlers draw a bag-shaped net behind them; drift nets are fastened to a buoy; lining involves trailing many-hooked lines in deep water; and in seining a large net encircles the fish and is gradually closed as it is drawn in. The supply of fish can no longer be regarded as practically inexhaustible: it is depleted by the vast catches of efficient modern fishing and also by POLLUTION. Conservation is therefore important, and there are international agreements against overfishing and to regulate the meshes of nets so that young fish can escape. Fish farming is also being developed. International disputes have often arisen over fishing rights in coastal waters.

FISHERS ISLAND, resort at the NE end of Long Island Sound, N.Y., 7mi from the mainland. It is about 8mi long and 1mi wide and has a permanent population of around 500.

FISHES, a large group of cold-blooded aquatic vertebrates that breathe by means of GILLS, and whose bodies bear a vertical tail fin. Most fishes fall within this definition, but a few breathe atmospheric air by means of a lung or lung-like organ, some species have a body temperature slightly above that of the surrounding water and in certain fishes the tail may be missing or reduced to a filament. There are four classes of fish-like vertebrates: the jawless fishes (Agnatha); the placoderms (Placodermi); the cartilaginous fishes (Chondrichthyes), and the bony fishes (Pisces).

The AGNATHA are now represented solely by the lampreys and hagfishes. When they first appeared, during the Ordovician period 530 million years ago, they were fish-like in shape, but had poorly formed fins and lacked jaws.

The Placoderms are now entirely extinct. They are known only as fossils, mainly from rocks of Devonian age (about 400 million years old). They had jaws and paired fins, and ossified skeletons.

The Chondrichthyes include the SHARKS, RAYS and CHIMAERAS as well as certain fossil forms. They are characterized by skeletons that are composed of cartilage, gills that are located in pouches and tooth-like scales.

The most widespread class comprises the Pisces or bony fish, which include the COELACANTH, LUNGFISHES and ray-finned fishes. Ray-finned fishes contain the chondrosteans (bichirs, sturgeons and one entirely fossil order); the holosteans (bowfins and five fossil orders), and finally the teleosteans. The overwhelming majority of present-day fishes are teleosts. There are at least 20 000 different species of teleosts and countless millions of individuals inhabiting the seas, lakes and rivers of the world. They show an amazing diversity of form, from eels to the Sea horse, but have a number of characteristics in common. They range in size from a total length of over 6m (20ft) in the oarfish and a weight of over 2 tonnes in the Ocean sunfish, to an adult length of only 13mm ($\frac{1}{2}$in) in a Philippine goby (*Paudaka pygmaea*), the latter qualifying as the smallest of all vertebrates. Typically, the body is streamlined, rising smoothly from the head and tapering gently to the tail, but in particular cases the body shape reflects the mode of life of the fish. In most fishes swimming is achieved by throwing the body into a series of lateral undulations which travel along the length of the body growing in amplitude toward the tail. The tail provides the final thrust and evens out the oscillations of the body. One characteristic (but not invariable) feature of fishes is the presence of scales on the body.

Sports fishing boat off Small Point, Maine. Such boats are generally used for trolling for larger fish in deep waters. The high "pulpit" above the cockpit aids visibility.

FISH HAWK. See OSPREY.

FISHING, the catching of fish for consumption or for sport. It is one of the world's most popular participant sports. There are millions of fishermen (almost 30 million in the US alone), or anglers, who fish for recreation or in competition. World records by weight, length and girth exist for every type of fish. The first fishing club in America was the Schuylkill Fishing Company of Philadelphia (established 1732). There are three main types of sports fishing: game, coarse and sea angling. Game anglers fish trout, salmon and other fish in fast-moving streams which require accurate casting of the right lure. Coarse anglers fish in slow, deep rivers. Sea anglers generally fish for shark, tuna, tarpon or barracuda.

FISK, James (1834–1872), US financial speculator, notorious for stock manipulation. With Jay GOULD he engaged in a brutal stock market struggle for control of the Erie Railroad and together their attempt to corner the gold market in 1869 led to the BLACK FRIDAY scandal. He was shot by a business associate and rival for the affections of an actress.

FISKE, John (1842–1901), born Edmund Fisk Green, US historian and philosopher who wrote popular accounts of Colonial America and attempted to show that evolutionary theory was compatible with religious ideas.

FISSION, the division of CELLS, or sometimes multi-cellular organisms, to produce identical offspring. Binary fission results in the production of two equal parts and multiple fission in the production of more than two equal parts. The term is normally applied to the reproduction of multicellular organisms such as members of the phylum PROTOZOA.

FISSION, Nuclear, the splitting of the nucleus of a heavy ATOM into two or more lighter nuclei with the release of a large amount of ENERGY. Fission power is used in NUCLEAR REACTORS and the ATOMIC BOMB.

FISTULA, an abnormal communication between two internal organs, or from an organ to the outside of the body. Infection, inflammatory disease (e.g. Crohn's disease—see ENTERITIS), TUMORS, trauma and SURGERY may lead to fistula. The GASTROINTESTINAL TRACT (particularly DUODENUM), PANCREAS, BLADDER and female genital tract are particularly susceptible.

FITCH, John (1743–1798), US inventor and engineer who built the first viable steamboat (1787), larger vessels being launched in 1788 and 1790. All were paddle-powered; his later attempt to introduce the screw PROPELLER was a commercial failure.

FITCHBURG, city in N Mass., on the N branch of the Nashua R, named for John FITCH. Its paper-making industry was established in 1805. Pop 43 343.

FITTONIA, a genus of creeping perennial plants native to South America and widely cultivated as house plants for their ornamental green leaves with the veins picked out in ivory or brilliant carmine. They should have 2–3 hours of sunlight in the winter, but will adapt to fluorescent light. They grow well at average room temperatures. They should be watered often enough to keep the soil evenly moist, and are propagated by means of shoot tip cuttings. Family: Acanthaceae.

FITZGERALD, Edward (1809–1883), English poet and scholar. FitzGerald is famous for his "translation" of OMAR KHAYYAM's *Rubaiyat* (1859) in which he managed to capture the spirit of the original while at the same time creating a new masterpiece using his own images and structure.

FITZGERALD, Ella (1918–   ), US jazz singer. Internationally known as a great original interpreter of jazz and blues, she possessed a clear, sweet yet paradoxically powerful voice and unique rhythmic control.

FITZGERALD, F. Scott (Francis Scott Key Fitzgerald; 1896–1940), US novelist and short story writer. The "spokesman" of the Jazz Age in the 1920s, his works deal with the frenetic life style of the post-WWI generation and the spiritual bankruptcy of the so-called American Dream. His celebrated novel *The Great Gatsby* (1925) explores the ruthless society of the 1920s. *Tender is the Night* (1934) draws upon his experience of American expatriates in Paris and upon the schizophrenic gaiety and breakdown of his wife, Zelda. He spent his last years as a Hollywood script-writer.

FITZHERBERT, Maria Anne (1756–1837), first wife of the British king, George IV. Twice widowed, she married the Prince of Wales secretly in 1785, but her Roman Catholicism invalidated the marriage. They were estranged for a time, when he married Princess CAROLINE OF BRUNSWICK (1795), but Mrs. Fitzherbert later lived with the king as his mistress.

FITZHUGH, George (1806–1881), US editor and author. In such works as *Sociology for the South* (1854), a collection of proslavery essays and *Cannibals All! or, Slaves Without Masters* (1857) he criticized Northern laissez-faire capitalism and praised the Southern social order and slave system.

FITZPATRICK, Thomas (c1799–1854), US fur trader and guide. One of the famous MOUNTAIN MEN who helped open up the West, he worked with Western fur companies in the 1820s and 30s. From 1834, he was a guide for wagon trains, FRÉMONT's second expedition into Ore. and Cal. and Stephen KEARNY's Army of the West in the Mexican War.

FITZROY, Robert. See BEAGLE, H.M.S.

FITZSIMMONS, Robert Prometheus (called "Bob" or "Ruby Robert"; 1863–1918), English world boxing champion. Middleweight (1891–97), heavyweight (1897–99) and light-heavyweight (1903–05) champion of the world, he fought in New Zealand and Australia and in the US from 1890.

FIUME. See RIJEKA.

FIVE, The, name for a group of Russian composers who created a national school of music in the late 19th century. They were: Mili BALAKIREV, César CUI, Alexander BORODIN. Nikolai RIMSKY-KORSAKOV and Modest MUSSORGSKY.

FIVE CIVILIZED TRIBES, term for the CHEROKEE, CHICKASAW, CHOCKTAW, CREEK and SEMINOLE Indian tribes of North America. Between about 1830–50 they were forced to settle in INDIAN TERRITORY but were recognized as domestic dependent nations with constitutions and laws based on those of the US. After the Civil War they were restricted to areas in E Okla. and the US followed a detribalization policy which left the five with little autonomy.

FIVE FORKS, Battle of, last major American Civil War battle, fought April 1, 1865, SW of Petersburg, Va. Two Union corps under SHERIDAN defeated LEE's right wing under PICKETT, leading to the capture of Richmond and Lee's surrender.

FIVE-YEAR PLANS, programs for a nation's economic development, specifically those enacted in the USSR since 1928. They usually aim to raise production by a certain percentage over a given period. Similar plans have been initiated in other, mainly communist, countries.

FIXATION, an ambivalent (see AMBIVALENCE) attachment to an object or habit typical of an earlier stage of psychological development. Specific examples are REGRESSION to infantile behavior during stress, and COMPULSION toward objects reminiscent in some way of the individual's childhood.

FJORD, narrow, deep sea inlet, steep-sided and bounded by mountains, formed by past glacial EROSION of a stream or river valley. Usually there is a shallow rock threshold, probably of terminal MORAINE, at the seaward entrance.

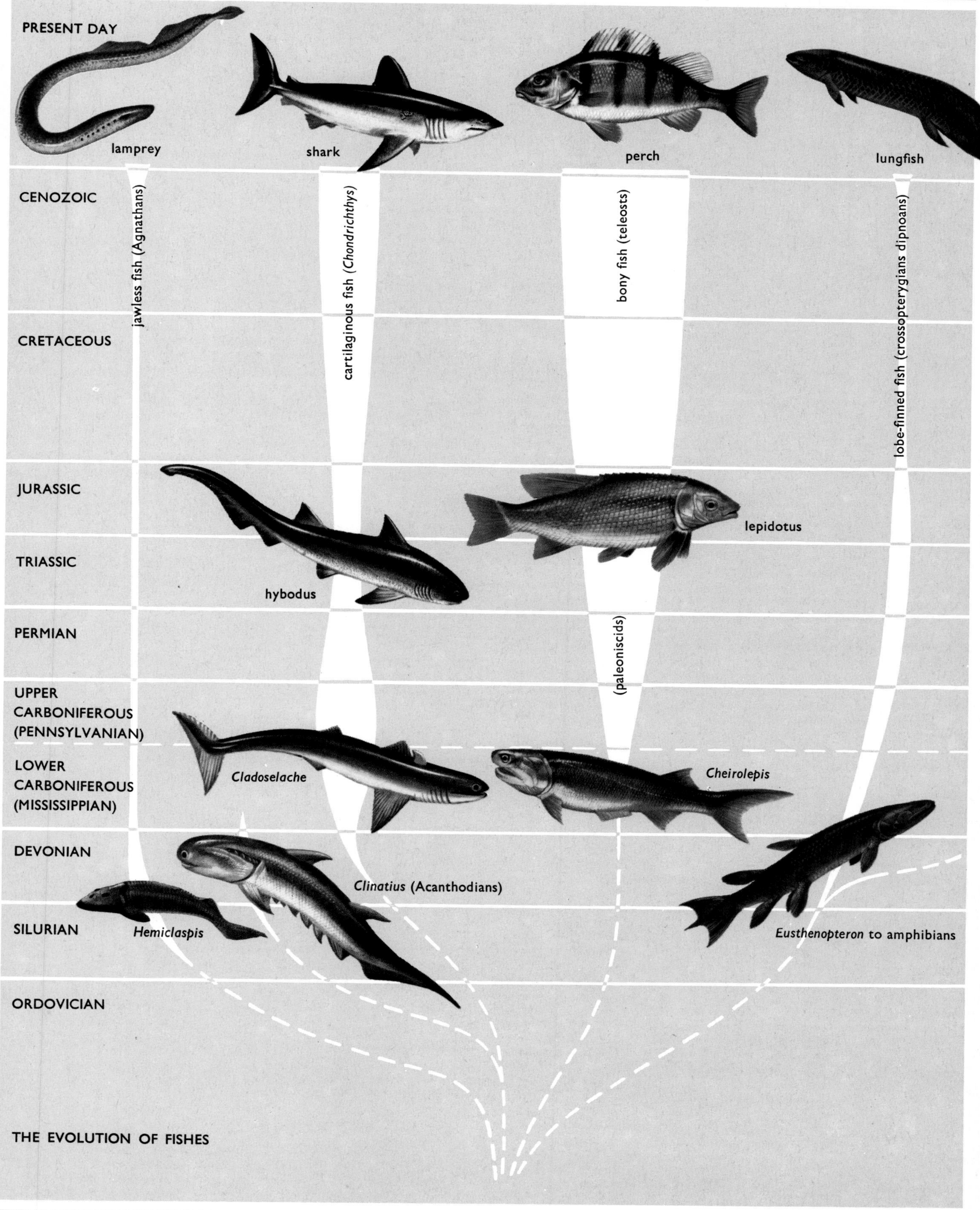

PRESENT DAY
lamprey
shark
perch
lungfish
CENOZOIC
jawless fish (Agnathans)
cartilaginous fish (*Chondrichthys*)
bony fish (teleosts)
lobe-finned fish (crossopterygians dipnoans)
CRETACEOUS
JURASSIC
lepidotus
TRIASSIC
hybodus
PERMIAN
(paleoniscids)
UPPER CARBONIFEROUS (PENNSYLVANIAN)
LOWER CARBONIFEROUS (MISSISSIPPIAN)
Cladoselache
Cheirolepis
DEVONIAN
Clinatius (Acanthodians)
SILURIAN
Hemiclaspis
Eusthenopteron to amphibians
ORDOVICIAN

THE EVOLUTION OF FISHES

According to a probably spurious tradition, Betsy Ross sewed the first US flag at the request of George Washington. Weigerber's painting *The Birth of Our Nation's Flag*, hanging in the Betsy Ross house in Philadelphia (*right*), shows her displaying her flag to Washington, Robert Morris and her husband George.

FLAG, a piece of cloth or other material, usually rectangular, bearing a distinctive design and displayed as a symbol or signal. Regimental flags date back to ancient battle standards—symbolic objects borne on poles. Personal standards of heads of state derive from the heraldic banners of medieval knights. Early national flags often used royal insignia like the FLEUR-DE-LIS of France, or religious devices. The United Kingdom's *Union Jack* combines the crosses of St. George (England), St. Andrew (Scotland) and St. Patrick (Ireland). The *Stars and Stripes* of the US, officially adopted by Congress on June 14, 1777, now consists of 13 alternate red and white stripes for the original colonies, and 50 stars for the present states. Betsy ROSS supposedly made the first *Stars and Stripes*. International organizations, including the Red Cross and UN, have their own flags. Other internationally used flags include the white flag of surrender and the yellow flag for infectious disease (representing Q in the international code of signals used at sea).

FLAG, popular name for several plants of the genus *Iris*, family Iridaceae. (See IRISES.)

FLAG DAY, June 14, anniversary of the adoption in 1777 of the *Stars and Stripes* as the US flag.

FLAGELLANTS, medieval religious zealots who scourged themselves to expiate their sins and the sins of the world. A big flagellant movement started in Italy in 1260, and later spread through Europe during the BLACK DEATH. Heretical aspects of this movement led to its suppression by the Church.

FLAGELLATES, single-celled organisms that have whip-like extensions called flagella which they wave about to swim or catch food. Some have one flagellum, but others have many. (See PROTOZOA.)

FLAGEOLET. See WIND INSTRUMENTS.

FLAGG, James Montgomery (1877–1960), US artist famous for a WWI recruiting poster. It showed Uncle Sam beckoning and saying "I want YOU." Flagg also drew homely scenes of American life, in a vigorous pen-and-ink technique.

FLAGLER, Henry Morrison (1830–1913), US financier who helped develop Fla. In partnership with John D. Rockefeller, he helped form the Standard Oil Company in 1870, then built hotels and railways that made Fla. a vacation center.

FLAG OF CONVENIENCE, foreign flag under which a merchant vessel is registered to avoid strict safety regulations, heavy taxes or labor restrictions in its country of ownership. The largest such registrations (by tonnage) are with Liberia and Panama.

FLAGSTAD, Kirsten (1895–1962), Norwegian singer, one of the greatest Wagnerian sopranos. She made her New York debut as Sieglinde in *The Valkyrie* in 1935 and retired from public singing in 1953, though she continued making records.

FLAGSTAFF, city in N Ariz., seat of Coconino Co. A health resort, it has lumber mills and is the home of Lowell Observatory and Northern Arizona U. Pop 26 117.

FLAHERTY, Robert Joseph (1884–1951), US pioneer documentary filmmaker. He is chiefly famous for *Nanook of the North* (1922), a study of Eskimo life, and *Man of Aran* (1934), about life on the Aran Islands of Ireland.

FLAMBOYANT STYLE, last stage of French Gothic architecture, named for the wavy flame-like lines of its window tracery. Influenced by the English DECORATED STYLE, it stressed reversed curves, lavishly detailed flowing tracery and interpenetrating moldings. It flourished late 14th–early 16th centuries.

FLAME. See COMBUSTION.

FLAME HARDENING, surface hardening technique in which a steel workpiece is heated using an oxyacetylene flame and then quickly cooled with water.

FLAMENCO, type of sensuous folk music and dancing from Andalusia in S Spain, performed especially by gypsies. Dancers, stamping and clapping, interpret songs, accompanied by forceful guitar playing. It is probably of Moorish origin.

FLAME TEST, preliminary test in qualitative chemical ANALYSIS. A small amount of the sample is introduced into a nonluminous flame; certain metal ions, on excitation, impart a characteristic color to the flame, e.g. yellow for sodium, red for strontium, green for copper. For **flame photometry** see SPECTROPHOTOMETRY.

FLAMETHROWER, a device—basically a SYRINGE—that propels a petroleum fuel, commonly NAPALM, through a nozzle, igniting it as it emerges, so that a burning stream lands on the enemy. Compressed air provides the driving force. A portable flamethrower has a range of 50m, and a mechanized flamethrower 150m. (See also CHEMICAL AND BIOLOGICAL WARFARE.)

FLAMINGO, several species of colorful water birds, of the family Phoenicopteridae, related to HERONS. They have long spindly legs and necks, and large bills with bristles which they use to sift their food from the water. Their plumage is white, pink and black. They live in large flocks on alkaline lakes in America, Africa and S Eurasia.

FLAMINIAN WAY, the great northern road of ancient Italy, begun in 220 BC by the censor Gaius Flaminius. It ran some 240mi from the Flaminian Gate of Rome (now *Porta del Popolo*) to Ariminum (Rimini) on the Adriatic coast.

FLAMSTEED, John (1646–1719), the first Astronomer Royal, appointed 1675 with the foundation of the GREENWICH OBSERVATORY. In course of compiling his major star catalog, *Historia Coelestis Britannica*, he was pestered for his data by NEWTON: Newton prevailed, and a muddled version, edited by HALLEY, was published in 1712. Flamsteed's own edition appeared posthumously (1725).

FLANAGAN, Edward Joseph (1886–1948), Irish-born US Roman Catholic priest who founded BOYS TOWN, a self-governing community of homeless boys, near Omaha, Neb., in 1917. After WWII he helped organize youth facilities abroad for the US government.

FLANDERS, medieval county on the coast of NW Europe, largely corresponding to N Belgium, with smaller portions in the Netherlands and France. In the 14th and 15th centuries, wealth from trade and textile manufacture enriched the chief towns (Antwerp, Ypres, Bruges and Ghent) and made Flanders a major cultural center. Its famous artists included Bruegel, Rubens and Van Dyck.

FLANDERS, Ralph Edward (1880–1970), Vt. senator who opposed the anti-communist campaign methods of fellow Republican senator Joseph Raymond MCCARTHY. Flanders' resolution led to the US Senate's censure of McCarthy (Dec. 1954), contributing to McCarthy's loss of political power.

FLANNEL, in TEXTILES, a soft all-wool fabric with a slightly raised (fluffy) surface used for blankets and clothing. **Flannelette** is a cotton fabric having a similar finish.

FLAPPER, in the 1920s, the popular term for any lively young woman scorning conventional dress and conduct, and identified by short skirts, swinging beads and bobbed or shingled hair.

FLAPS, AIRPLANE control surfaces fixed at the trailing edges of the wings, lowered to improve control in landing. When lowered, flaps improve the AIRFOIL's lift but at the cost of increased drag. They are consequently raised for normal flying.

FLARE, Solar, a temporary brilliance in the SUN's chromosphere associated with a sunspot or group of sunspots. Large flares may last for as long as an hour or more, small ones only a few minutes. During the flare X RAYS and RADIO waves are emitted from the solar corona, as are slower-moving ALPHA PARTICLES and PROTONS.

FLASHBULB, a light source used in PHOTOGRAPHY to give a brief intense flash of light. A switch in the CAMERA shutter mechanism discharges a CAPACITOR in the flash gun through a tungsten filament in the oxygen-filled bulb, igniting the mass of aluminum, magnesium or zirconium wire present. Bulbs are lacquered to prevent shattering, blue lacquering being used to balance the light for color work. **Flash cubes**, comprising four flash bulbs mounted in one expendable unit, are percussion-ignited by a pin in the camera body. More versatile is the **electronic flash gun** which employs a discharge lamp (see LIGHTING) which can be used repeatedly.

FLASH PHOTOLYSIS, technique for investigating very fast chemical reactions (see KINETICS, CHEMICAL). A very intense flash of light of very short duration (from a LASER or flash lamp) is passed through a reaction mixture, usually gaseous. Instant dissociation occurs, producing FREE RADICALS, whose subsequent fast reactions are followed by automatic spectroscopy. (See also PHOTOCHEMISTRY.)

FLASH POINT, the lowest temperature at which the VAPOR above a volatile LIQUID forms a combustible mixture with the OXYGEN in the air. At the flash point the TEMPERATURE is too low for sustained COMBUSTION to occur, but when a pilot flame is introduced to the mixture a brief flash occurs.

FLAT-COATED RETRIEVER, breed of sporting dog standing 25–27in high and weighing 60–70lb, similar to other retrievers except for its flat coat, which may be black or liver.

FLATFISHES, plate-shaped fish with both eyes on the upper side of the head. They begin life as normal fish, with one eye on either side, but after a few days one eye migrates to its new position. Flatfish live on the sea bottom and often have camouflaged uppersides. (See also FLOUNDERS; HALIBUT; SOLE; TURBOT.)

FLATFOOT, deformity of FOOT in which the longitudinal or transverse arches of the feet are flattened or lost; this results in loss of spring and the inefficient use of the feet in walking or running. It may result from muscle weakness or be congenital. Corrective exercises and shoe wedges may relieve the condition.

FLATHEAD INDIANS, North American tribe of the Salish linguistic family inhabiting W Mont. The name derives from the head-flattening practiced by tribes from whom the Flatheads took slaves. The Flatheads were early converts to Christianity, and most now live at Flathead Lake, Mont.

FLATTERY, Cape, promontory in NW Wash., S of the entrance to Juan de Fuca Strait. James Cook discovered it in 1778.

FLATWORMS, members of the phylum Platyhelminthyes, invertebrates which include free-living turbellarian worms and parasitic FLUKES and TAPEWORMS. Turbellarians and flukes have flat, leaf-like bodies, but tapeworms are elongated with numerous segments or proglottids behind a well-developed head.

FLAUBERT, Gustave (1821–1880), French novelist; a scrupulous observer and stylist, whose work influenced much subsequent French writing. His first work, *Madame Bovary* (1856–57), brought him immediate fame. The vividly naturalistic tragedy of a provincial wife who attempts to live out her fantasies, it was unsuccessfully prosecuted as an offense against public morality in 1857. The exotic Carthaginian setting of *Salammbô* (1862) showed an equal mastery of Romantic style. His *Three Tales* (1877), set in modern, medieval and ancient times, combined both Romanticism and realism.

FLAX, *Linum usitatissimum*, an important temperate and subtropical plant, grown for fiber and LINSEED OIL. The native flax of Eurasia is a straw-like annual, 600–900mm (2–3ft) high, whose white, blue or pink flowers ripen into seed bolls. The crop is usually harvested after about 14 weeks, when the fiber is separated from the seed. The fibers are then soaked and scraped away from the woody stem and the longer ones are combed out and spun into yarn, which is turned into LINEN. The seeds are squeezed to give oil. The USSR is the chief producer of fiber flax and a leading producer of seed flax. Family: Linaceae.

FLAXMAN, John (1755–1826), English sculptor and illustrator, chief exponent of the Neoclassical style in England. He illustrated works by Homer, Dante and Aeschylus, designed pottery for Wedgwood and produced monumental sculpture.

FLEABANE, popular name for herbs of the genus *Erigeron*, family COMPOSITAE, native to temperate parts of the world. Some species are cultivated as garden ornamentals.

FLEAHOPPER, common name for any of several small jumping bugs which feed on plants. The garden fleahopper *Halticus bracteatus* is widely distributed and feeds on foliage, causing white spots. The cotton fleahopper *Psallus seriatus* is a mirid bug which feeds on young cotton plants.

FLEAS, wingless INSECTS with legs developed for jumping, and a laterally compressed body. They suck the blood of host animals, and can carry such diseases as the bubonic PLAGUE. The flea survives its early stages in insanitary conditions; when newly emerged, adults leap onto passing hosts.

FLEMING, Sir Alexander (1881–1955), British bacteriologist, discoverer of lysozome (1922) and penicillin (1928). Lysozome is an ENZYME present in many body tissues and lethal to certain bacteria; its discovery prepared the way for that of ANTIBIOTICS. His discovery of PENICILLIN was largely accidental; and it was developed as a therapeutic later, by Harold FLOREY and Ernst CHAIN. All three received the 1945 Nobel Prize for Physiology or Medicine for their work.

FLEMING, Ian (Lancaster) (1908–1964), English novelist and journalist. He created the fictional British secret-service agent James Bond—who became a popular cult figure.

FLEMING, Sir Sandford (1827–1915), Scottish-born Canadian railway engineer. He was responsible for the Northern and Intercolonial railways, and made surveys for the Canadian Pacific Railway. He also pioneered the system of STANDARD TIME.

FLEMISH, the form of DUTCH traditionally spoken in N Belgium. Given official equality with French in 1898, it became the official language of N Belgium in 1934. (See also FLANDERS.)

FLETCHER, John. See BEAUMONT, FRANCIS AND FLETCHER, JOHN.

FLETCHER v. PECK, the first case (1810) in which the Supreme Court invalidated a state law as unconstitutional. The Ga. legislature had sought to rescind a corruptly-made grant of state land. (See also YAZOO FRAUD.)

FLEUR-DE-LIS (or Fleur-de-Lys), "lily flower," stylized emblem on the French royal coat of arms c1147–1789. It may represent the white iris, an arrowhead or a spearhead, and was first used in ancient Egypt.

FLEXNER, Abraham (1866–1959), US educator who profoundly changed medical teaching in the US. His survey of medical schools (1910) led to drastic reorganization. He was founder and first director (1930–39) of the Institute for Advanced Study, Princeton, N.J.

FLEXNER, Simon (1863–1946), US medical scientist who did important work in bacteriology and pathology, especially on the nature of POLIOMYELITIS, and contributed toward the development of a serum treatment for spinal MENINGITIS.

FLICKERS, small American woodpeckers of the genus *Colaptes*, well known for their colorful plumage and loud calls. Their main food is ants.

FLIES, members of the INSECT order Diptera which number about 85 000 species, and whose second pair of wings has been reduced to a pair of halteres or balancing organs which act as GYROSCOPES. These give flies great agility. They have two compound eyes; the antennae act as tactile, and possibly also smelling and hearing, organs. Their mouths are adapted either for sucking (as in the House fly), or piercing (as in mosquitoes). Their larvae are called MAGGOTS, and live on plants or decaying flesh. Adults feed on NECTAR, other insects, decaying matter or animal blood. The MOSQUITO and TSETSE FLY carry MALARIA and SLEEPING SICKNESS respectively.

FLIGHT, the ability to travel through the air during long periods. The only animals that are capable of sustained flight are the extinct PTERODACTYLS; some insects; a few fish and mammals, and most birds. Very few insects are completely wingless, and most have two pairs of wings that flap together. In flies and beetles one pair is modified. Usually muscles distort the thorax, forcing the wings up and down at rates of up to 1000 beats per second in midges.

The only true flying fish are certain freshwater hatchetfishes and Butterfly fishes. The tropical flying fish in fact glides. In birds, power for flying comes

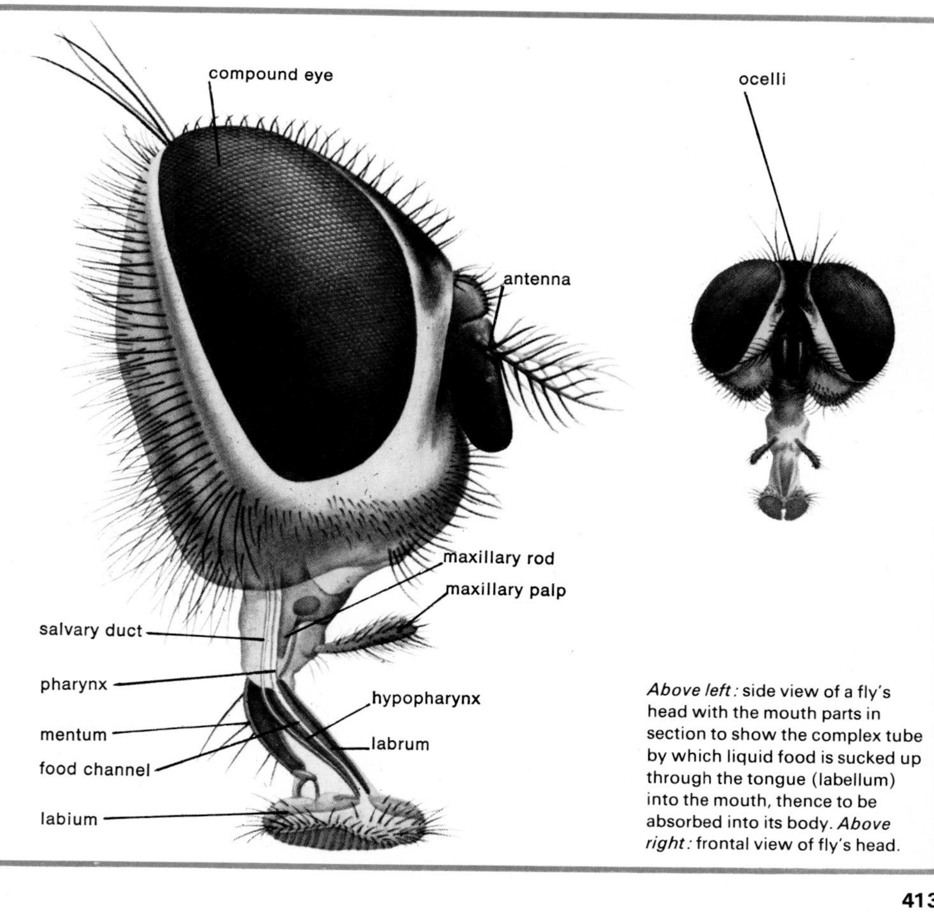

Above left: side view of a fly's head with the mouth parts in section to show the complex tube by which liquid food is sucked up through the tongue (labellum) into the mouth, thence to be absorbed into its body. *Above right:* frontal view of fly's head.

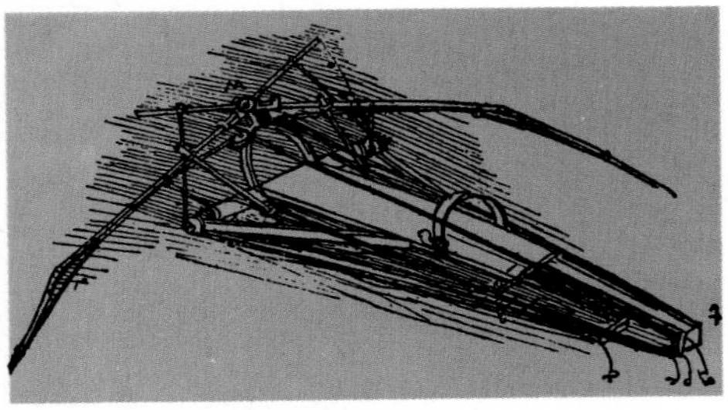

(1) Design for a flying machine by Leonardo Da Vinci. His designs, usually modeled after birds, were feasible but impractical in his time because there was no suitable power source. (2) Very unlike Leonardo's concept, the Wright Brothers' *Flyer*, first successful powered airplane. (3) Larger and faster than either Leonardo or the Wrights could have foreseen, the Anglo-French Concorde, first supersonic passenger airliner, prepares for takeoff.

from the breast muscles, which control both the up and down strokes of the wing. Wing shape depends on the kind of flight; narrow for gliding and broad for soaring.

The only flying mammals are the BATS, whose wings are composed of skin stretched between the finger and back legs.

FLIGHT, History of. LEONARDO DA VINCI was the first man to attempt the scientific design of flying machines. But in his time no motor was available which was powerful enough to lift a man into the air. Man's first ascents from the ground had to await the late 18th century and the invention of the MONTGOLFIER brothers' hot-air BALLOON and J. CHARLES' hydrogen balloon (1783). The addition of steam engines to the balloon gave the first maneuverable AIRSHIP (1852). Meanwhile G. CAYLEY designed and built flying GLIDERS (1810–1853) and William Henson designed a steam-powered model airplane with twin PROPELLERS (1842). It was not until the advent of the gasoline INTERNAL-COMBUSTION ENGINE, though, that the powered heavier-than-air machine became a practical possibility. The first successful controlled airplane flight was made by the WRIGHT BROTHERS near Kitty Hawk, N.C., on December 17, 1903 and within a few years there were many competing manufacturers and fliers of airplanes. Airplane technology was greatly stimulated by WWI and after 1919 commercial aviation developed rapidly. Meanwhile, the AUTOGIRO was invented by J. de la CIERVA (1923), to be followed by SIKORSKY'S HELICOPTER in 1939. JET PROPULSION was developed in several countries during WWII and by the mid-1950s had come to be used in the majority of military and commercial airplanes. RADAR navigation systems came into general use in this period. The early 1970s saw the introduction of wide-bodied jet airliners (jumbo jets) with vastly increased carrying capacity and the development of the first supersonic jet airliners. (See also AIR TRANSPORTATION.)

FLIGHTLESS BIRDS, birds whose wings can no longer be used to fly. They include the OSTRICH, CASSOWARIES, EMU and KIWI of Australia, and the RHEA of South America. The PENGUIN'S wings are used as paddles in water. The many species of extinct flightless birds include the MOA of New Zealand, the ELEPHANT BIRDS of Madagascar, the GREAT AUK, and the DODO.

FLINDERS, Matthew (1774–1814), English navigator who charted the S and E coasts of Australia (1795–1803), discovering BASS STRAIT and circumnavigating Tasmania in 1798–99. He wrote *A Voyage to Terra Australis* (1814).

FLINDERS RIVER, longest river in Queensland, Australia. It flows 520mi from the Great Dividing Range NW to the Gulf of Carpentaria.

FLIN FLON, town in Canada, on the Manitoba–Saskatchewan border. It is situated in a copper, zinc, gold, silver and cadmium mining area and has a smelting industry. Pop 9 307.

FLINT, city and seat of Genesee Co. in Mich. Once a fur-trading post, it is now a major automobile manufacturing center and also produces airplane engines, steel and paints. Pop 193 317.

FLINT, or **chert**, sedimentary rock composed of microcrystalline QUARTZ and CHALCEDONY. It is found as nodules in LIMESTONE and CHALK, and as layered beds, and was mainly formed by alteration of marine sediments of silicaceous organisms, and by replacement, preserving many FOSSIL outlines. A hard rock, flint may be chipped to form a sharp cutting edge, and was used by STONE AGE man for their characteristic tools.

FLINTLOCK, firearm developed in the 17th century and named for its use of flint ignition. It had a cock or hammer containing a piece of flint. When the trigger was pulled the flint struck a steel *frizzen* and the resulting spark ignited the charge. It was superseded by the percussion system which was introduced in the 19th century.

FLOATING EXCHANGE RATE, in international finance, the exchange rate for a national currency as determined by SUPPLY AND DEMAND and not by fixed PARITY. It is sometimes used to allow a currency to find a stable level. (See also GOLD STANDARD.)

FLODDEN FIELD, Battle of, English victory in which James IV of Scotland and at least 10 000 of his troops were killed near Branxton in NE England, on Sept. 9, 1513. They had invaded England to support their ancient ally, France.

FLOODS AND FLOOD CONTROL. River floods are one of mankind's worst enemies. In 1887, when the Hwang Ho overflowed, around 900 000 lost their lives; and, as recently as 1970, 200 000 died in E Pakistan when a cyclone struck the Ganges delta. Clearly the development of ways to control and contain floods must be a preoccupation of man.

Often floods are caused by unusually rapid thawing of the winter snows: the river, unable to hold the increased volume of water, bursts its banks. Heavy rainfall may have a similar effect. Coastal flooding may result from an exceptionally high TIDE combined with onshore winds, or, of course, from a TSUNAMI.

River floods can be forestalled by artificially deepening and broadening river channels or by the construction of suitably positioned DAMS. Artificial levees may also be built (in nature, levees occur as a result of sediment deposited while the river is in flood; they take the form of built-up banks). Vegetation planted on uplands helps to reduce surface runoff (see DRAINAGE).

Flood control can create new problems to replace the old. In Egypt the Aswan Dam has halted the once regular flooding of the Nile, thus robbing farmlands of a rich annual deposit of silt. But flood control made possible the civilization of ancient Mesopotamia and plays a vital rôle in modern water conservation. (See also RIVERS AND LAKES.)

FLORAL PARK, residential village in SE N.Y., on Long Island. It is best known for horticulture. Pop 18 422.

FLORENCE (Firenze), historic city in central Italy, capital of Firenze province, on the Arno R at the foot of the Apennines. A town on the Cassian Way during Roman times, it grew to become a powerful medieval republic, dominating Tuscany. Florence was a major commercial and artistic center during the Renaissance. It retains many architectural and other art treasures which, together with the proximity of the Apennines, serve to make the city an important tourist center. Famous figures associated with Florence include BRUNELLESCHI, DANTE, GIOTTO, MACHIAVELLI, MASACCIO, MICHELANGELO and SAVONAROLA. Glass and leatherware, pottery, furniture and precision instruments are among its products. In 1966 floods seriously damaged many of Florence's art treasures. Pop 482 000.

FLORENCE, city in NW Ala., seat of Lauderdale Co. It produces textiles and fertilizers and has food packing and lumber processing industries. Pop 34 031.

FLORENCE, city in N Ky., SW of Cincinnati, Ohio. It is situated in a farming area. Pop 11 661.

FLORENCE, city and seat of Florence Co. in S.C. It is a railroad center, produces fertilizer and markets local farm products. Pop 25 977.

FLORENCE, Council of. See FERRARA-FLORENCE, COUNCIL OF.

The historic skyline of Florence, dominated by Brunelleschi's magnificent cathedral dome with the bell-tower and ancient baptistery to its left, and in the distance the Apennine foothills.

FLORES, mountainous island in Indonesia's Lesser Sunda Islands group. It is 224mi long and up to 37mi wide. The people are chiefly of Malay and Papuan origin. Agriculture is the main occupation with corn and rice the chief crops.

FLOREY, Howard Walter, Baron (1898–1968), Australian-born British pathologist who worked with E. B. CHAIN and others to extract PENICILLIN from *Penicillium notatum* mold for use as a therapeutic drug (1938–44). He shared with Chain and Alexander FLEMING the 1945 Nobel Prize for Physiology or Medicine.

FLORIDA, southeastern coastal state of the US, one of the nation's fastest-growing states. It is a major resort area, attracting over 20 million tourists a year, and has important manufacturing industries, many of them related to agriculture which ranks as Florida's third most important source of income.

The greater part of the state consists of a low 400mi-long peninsula between the Gulf of Mexico and the Atlantic, with the Straits of Florida skirting its S coast. The state's land boundaries are with Ala. to the W and N, and with Ga. to the N. Sandbars and islands flank the smooth E coast. The string of islands known as the Florida Keys and the Dry Tortugas Islands extend SW from Biscayne Bay on the S coast. The W coast is indented and swampy. The central plains run from the NW to central Florida. Big Cypress Swamp and the EVERGLADES are situated in the marshlands of the S. There are some 30 000 lakes, including the 700sq mi OKEECHOBEE, and numerous rivers. Florida enjoys a subtropical climate. Hurricanes are frequent between July and Oct.

People and Economy. Three-fourths of the people live in rapidly expanding urban areas, such as Miami, Palm Beach, St. Petersburg and Fort Lauderdale. The state is administered by a governor elected for 4 years, a 40-member Senate and a 120-member House of Representatives. Education is compulsory for ages 7–16. The 66 institutions of higher learning include the U. of Florida and Miami U.

Tourism, manufacturing (processed foods, paper, chemicals, electrical products) and agriculture, which produces 80% of the nation's citrus fruit, are the three leading industries. Phosphate and titanium mining and fisheries are also important. Cape Canaveral is located midway along the E coast. Florida's transportation system includes 17 airports with scheduled flights, 5 railroads and numerous deepwater harbors. Lake Okeechobee links the ATLANTIC INTRACOASTAL WATERWAY to the Gulf of Mexico, via the Caloosahatchee and St. Lucie canals and rivers.

History. Juan PONCE DE LEÓN discovered and named Florida in 1513, landing to claim it for Spain on April 3. Early European settlements met with failure, but in 1565 Spain founded Saint Augustine, which survives as the oldest permanent white settlement in the US. Spain soon controlled all Florida. Britain held it from 1763 until 1783 when it was returned to Spain. American colonists began moving in and in 1819 Spain ceded Florida to the US. Resistance to white settlement by Seminole Indians culminated in the brutal Second Seminole War (1835–42). Admitted to the Union in 1845, Florida seceded in 1861. It was readmitted in 1868. Major economic growth began only late in the 19th century when an expanding railroad system encouraged the development of tourism and of the citrus fruit industry. Economic expansion has been phenomenal since WWII, putting increasing strains upon social services, public utilities, transportation and the dwindling tracts of subtropical wilderness.

FLORIDA, Straits of, channel between Fla. and Cuba. About 90mi wide, it links the Atlantic Ocean with the Gulf of Mexico.

FLORIDA CURRENT. See CARIBBEAN CURRENT.

FLORIDA KEYS, chain of about 20 small coral islands off S Fla. Their arc curves SW from Biscayne Bay S of Miami to KEY WEST. Causeways bearing some 160mi of highway link most of the islands, which support fishing and farming and attract vacationers.

FLORIO, John (c1553–1625), English translator and lexicographer, of Italian parentage. He is noted for his Italian–English dictionary *A Worlde of Wordes*

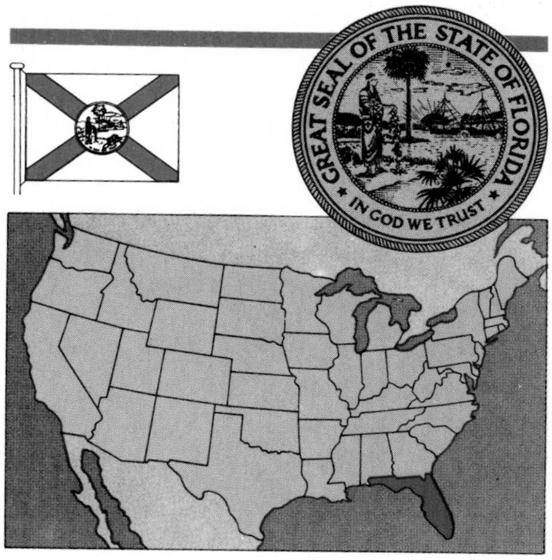

Name of state: Florida
Capital: Tallahassee
Statehood: March 3, 1845 (27th state)
Familiar name: Sunshine State
Area: 58 560sq mi (ranks 22nd)
Population: 6 671 162 (1970— 9th)
Elevation: Highest—345ft., Walton County. Lowest—sea level, Atlantic and Gulf coasts
Motto: In God We Trust
State flower: Orange blossom
State bird: Mockingbird
State tree: Sabal Palmetto
State song: Swanee River

(1598), and for his translation of MONTAIGNE's essays (1603) which directly influenced Shakespeare.

FLORISSANT FOSSIL BEDS NATIONAL MONUMENT, area of 5 992 acres in central Col., noted for its Oligocene fossils and petrified trees. It was authorized in 1969.

FLOTATION, Froth, a process used to recover valuable minerals from low-grade areas. The pulverized ore is mixed with water and flotation reagents. When air is pumped into the mixture, the mineral particles that preferentially adhere to the air bubbles rise to the surface in a froth which can then be skimmed off.

FLOTSAM, JETSAM AND LAGAN, goods lost at sea. In maritime law the term flotsam refers to such goods that remain floating while those that sink are known as jetsam. Lagan refers to items of jetsam that have been marked with a buoy to show that the owner has claimed them. Pieces of flotsam and jetsam need not be returned to their owner unless he lays specific claim to them. (See SALVAGE.)

FLOUNDERS, edible FLATFISHES of the Pacific and Atlantic. They include members of the family which have eyes on the left side of the body, and the Pleuronectidae which have eyes on the right side.

FLOUR, fine powder ground from the grains or starchy portions of WHEAT, RYE, CORN, RICE, POTATOES, BANANAS or BEANS. Plain white flour is produced from wheat; soft wheat produces flour used for cakes and hard wheat, with a higher GLUTEN content, makes flour used for bread. Flour is made from the endosperm, which constitutes about 84% of the grain; the remainder comprises the BRAN, which is the outer layers of the grain, and the germ, which is the embryo. Grain used to be milled by hand between two stones, until the development of wind, water or animal driven mills. In modern mills, the grain is thoroughly cleaned and then tempered by bringing the water content to 15%, which makes the separation of the bran and germ from the endosperm easier. The endosperm is broken up by rollers and the flour graded and bleached. It may then be enriched with VITAMINS. Byproducts are used mainly for cattle food, although wheat germ is an important source of vitamin E.

FLOUR BEETLE, common name of various beetles which feed on flour and grain. Many of them are serious pests in flour mills because their small size

These marshy stretches lying between Talahassee and the Gulf of Mexico are typical of the large areas of swampland in Florida. These areas abound in plant, animal and bird life.

3mm ($\frac{1}{8}$in) prevents their being readily noticed, and because they reproduce rapidly. They can be controlled by frequent fumigation.

FLOWER, the part of an ANGIOSPERM that is concerned with REPRODUCTION. There is a great variety of floral structure, but the basic organs and structure are similar. Each flower is borne on a stalk or pedicel, the tip of which is expanded to form a receptacle that bears the floral organs. The **sepals** are the first of these organs and are normally green and leaflike. Above the sepals there is a ring of **petals**, which are normally colored and vary greatly in shape. The ring of sepals is termed the **calyx** and the ring of petals the **corolla**. Collectively the calyx and corolla are called the **perianth**. Above the perianth are the reproductive organs comprising the male organs, the **stamens** (collectively known as the **androecium**) and female organs, the **carpels** (the **gynoecium**.) Each stamen consists of a slender stalk, or FILAMENT, which is capped by the pollen-producing **anther**. Each carpel has a swollen base, the **ovary**, which contains the **ovules** that later form the **seed**. Each carpel is connected by a **style** to an expanded structure called the **stigma**. Together, the style and stigma are sometimes termed the **pistil**.

There are three main variations of flower structure. In hypogynous flowers (e.g. BUTTERCUP) the perianth segments and stamens are attached below a superior ovary, while in perigynous flowers (e.g. ROSE) the receptacle is cup-like enclosing a superior ovary, with the perianth segments and stamens attached to a rim around the receptacle. In epigynous flowers (e.g. DANDELION) the inferior ovary is enclosed by the receptacle and the other floral parts are attached to the ovary. In many plants, the flowers are grouped together to form an INFLORESCENCE.

Pollen produced by the stamens is transferred either by insects or the wind to the stigma where POLLINATION takes place. Many of the immense number of variations of flower form are adaptions that aid either insect or wind pollination. (See also PLANT KINGDOM.)

FLOWERING ALMOND, a number of ornamental trees and shrubs of the genus *Prunus*, family Rosaceae, such as *Prunus amygdalo-persica*, a hybrid of the PEACH and ALMOND and *P. glandulosa*, native to China. They have white or pink flowers produced in the spring.

FLOWERING MAPLES, herbs and shrubs of the genus *Abutilon*, family Malvaceae. They are not related to the MAPLE. Native to South Asia and South America, some naturalized in North America. Fiber is produced from some species.

FLOWERING PLANTS. See ANGIOSPERMS.

FLOWERING TOBACCO, annual and perennial plants of the genus *Nicotiana*, native to South America, but cultivated in warm climates. The yellow, purple, red or white flowers have a very sweet scent. Family: Solanaceae.

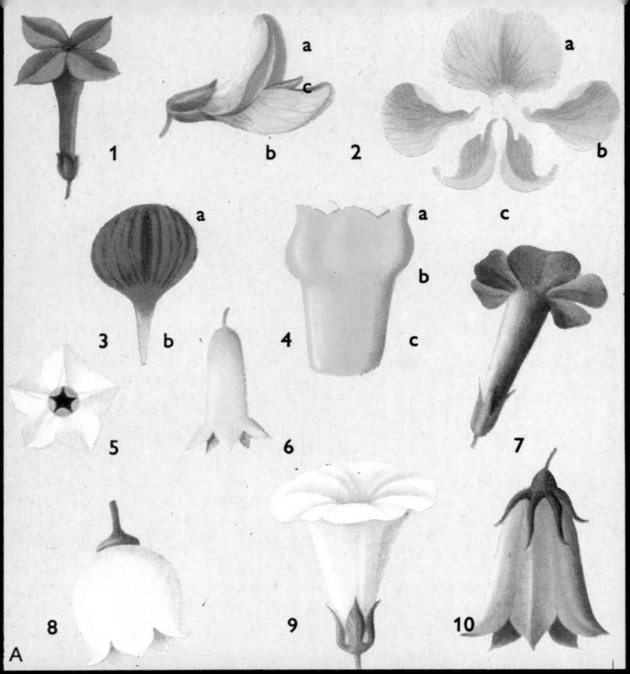

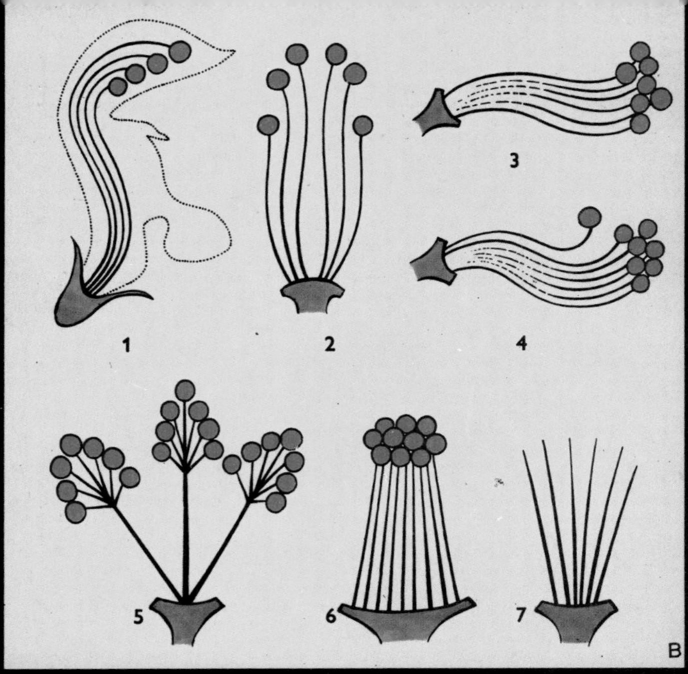

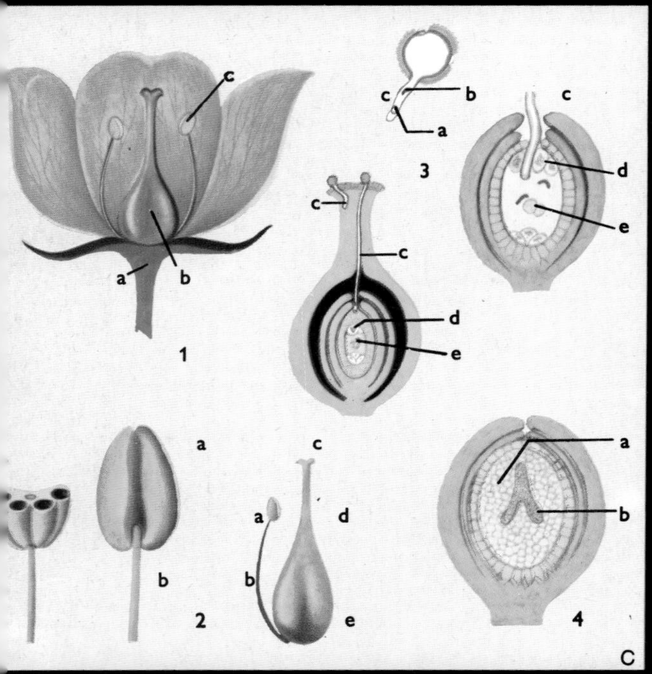

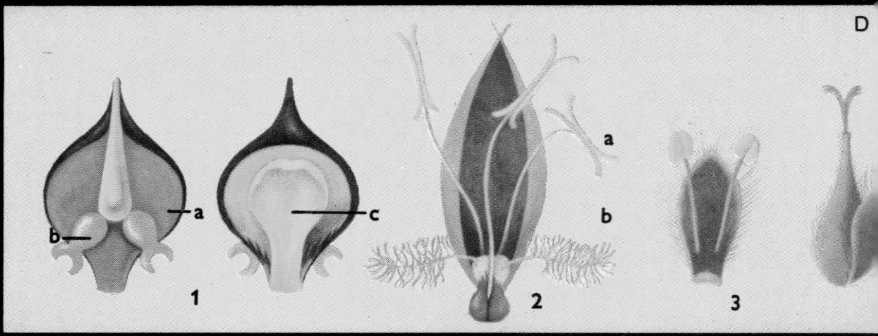

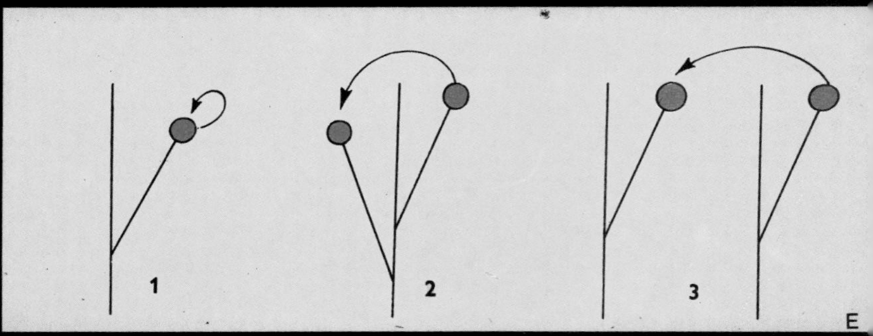

(A) The envelopes (perianths) may take many forms: (1) multilateral symmetry; (2) bilateral symmetry, with (a) banner, (b) wing, (c) keel; (3) petal consisting of a broad lamina (a) and a narrow claw (b); (4) connate (grown together) corolla, with (a) limb, (b) throat, and (c) tube; (5) rotate; (6) tubular; (7) salverform; (8) cup-shaped; (9) funnelform; (10) campanulate. (B) Types of stamens include (1) didynamous, (2) tetradynamous, (3) monadelphous, (4) diadelphous, (5) polydelphous, (6) syngenesious, (7) antherless (sterile). (C) Fertilization. (1) location of pistil and stamens in a flower, with (a) receptacle, (b) pistil, (c) stamen; (2) pistil and stamen separately, with (a) anther, (b) filament, (c) stigma, (d) style, (e) ovary; (3) germinating pollen grains, with (a) tube nucleus, (b) sperm, (c) pollen tube, (d) egg cell, (e) embryo sacs; (4) seed, with (a) endosperm, (b) placenta. (D) Special flower forms include (1) a primitive flower of a conifer; (2) the flower of a grass, with (a) stamen, (b) feathered stigma; (3) flower of male willow tree; (4) flower of female willow. (E) Pollination methods include (1) self-pollination, (2) pollination from another flower on same plant, and (3) cross-pollination.

FLU. See INFLUENZA.
FLUENT. See FLUXIONS.
FLÜGELHORN. See HORN.

FLUID, a substance which flows (undergoes a continuous change of shape) when subjected to a tangential or shearing FORCE. LIQUIDS and GASES are fluids, both taking the shape of their container. But while liquids are virtually incompressible and have a fixed volume, gases expand to fill whatever space is available to them.

FLUID COUPLING, or fluid flywheel, a device for transmitting TORQUE between rotating shafts comprising an oil-filled case connected to the driving shaft and with impeller vanes on the inside, and an opposing turbine mounted on the driven. The only coupling between these elements is by means of oil thrown by the impeller against the turbine. Modified forms of this device known as the fluid converter and the converter coupling (torque converter) and including a third stator or reactor element are used in the TRANSMISSIONS of construction machinery and AUTOMOBILES respectively.

FLUID MECHANICS, the study of moving and static FLUIDS, dealing with the FORCES exerted on a fluid to hold it at rest and the relationships with its boundaries that cause it to move. The scope of the subject is wide, ranging from HYDRAULICS, concerning the applications of fluid flow in pipes and channels, to aeronautics, the study of airflow relating to the design of AIRPLANES and ROCKETS. Any fluid process, such as flow around an obstacle or in a pipe, can be described mathematically by a specific equation that relates the forces acting, the dimensions of the system and its properties such as TEMPERATURE, PRESSURE and DENSITY. Newton's laws of motion and VISCOSITY, the first and second laws of THERMODYNAMICS and the laws of conservation of MASS, ENERGY and MOMENTUM are applied as appropriate. Much use is also made of experimental evidence from models, wind tunnels, etc., to determine the process equation. Many types of flow occur: in laminar flow in a closed pipe, distinct layers of fluid slide over each other, their velocity decreasing to zero at the pipe wall; in turbulent flow the fluid is mixed by eddies and vortices and a statistical treatment is needed. (See also ARCHIMEDES; BERNOULLI; PASCAL'S LAW; REYNOLDS NUMBER.)

FLUKES, parasitic FLATWORMS, some of which are important disease carriers. The Sheep liver fluke lives in the bile duct of mammals. Its eggs pass out of the intestine into water, where the larvae infect water snails, then wait on vegetation to be eaten by mammals. The blood fluke bilharzia is responsible for the disease SCHISTOSOMIASIS, which is thought to affect 250 million people throughout the world.

FLUORESCEIN, synthetic DYE made by fusing RESORCINOL with phthalic anhydride (see ACID ANHYDRIDES) and zinc chloride catalyst. A red crystalline solid, it dissolves in alkalis to give a deep red solution showing very intense yellow-green FLUORESCENCE, visible at very low concentrations. It is used as a water tracer, and was used in WWII to mark spots on the sea.

FLUORESCENCE. See LUMINESCENCE.

FLUORESCENT LIGHTING. See LIGHTING.

FLUORIDATION, addition of small quantities of fluorides (see FLUORINE) to public water supplies, bringing the concentration to 1 ppm, as in some natural water. It greatly reduces the incidence of tooth decay by strengthening the teeth. Despite some opposition, many authorities now fluoridate water. Toothpaste containing fluoride is also valuable.

FLUORINE (F), the lightest of the HALOGENS, occurring naturally as FLUORITE, CRYOLITE and fluorapatite (see APATITE). A pale-yellow toxic gas, fluorine is made by electrolysis of potassium fluoride in liquid HYDROGEN FLUORIDE. It is the most reactive, electronegative and oxidizing of all elements, reacting with almost all other elements to give fluorides (see HALIDES) of the highest possible oxidation state. It displaces other nonmetals from their compounds. Most nonmetal fluorides are highly reactive, but sulfur hexafluoride (used as an electrical insulator) and carbon tetrafluoride are inert (see STEREOCHEMISTRY). Fluorine is used in rocket propulsion, in URANIUM production, and to make FLUOROCARBONS. (See also FLUORIDATION.) AW 19.0, mp −220°C, bp −188°C.

FLUORITE, a common mineral composed of calcium fluoride (see CALCIUM), also called fluorspar. It forms cubic crystals with a wide color range. Fluorite is used as a flux in the iron and steel industries, and as a FLUORINE ore.

FLUOROCARBONS, HYDROCARBONS in which hydrogen atoms are replaced (wholly or in part) by fluorine. Because of the stability of the carbon-fluorine bond, they are inert and heat-resistant. Thus they can be used in artificial joints in the body, and where hydrocarbons would be decomposed by heat, such as in spacecraft heatshields, the coating of nonstick pans or as lubricants. Liquid fluorocarbons are used as refrigerants. (See also TEFLON; FREON.)

FLUOROSCOPE, device used in medical diagnosis and engineering quality control which allows the direct observation of an X-RAY beam which is being passed through an object under examination. It contains a fluorescent screen which converts the X-ray image into visible light (see LUMINESCENCE) and, often, an image intensifier.

FLUTE, reedless woodwind instrument of ancient origin. The modern concert flute is a transverse or side-blown instrument, the earlier form being, like the RECORDER, end-blown. It was in widespread use by the end of the 18th century. The C flute with a three octave range is the standard instrument. Other types include the piccolo and the bass flute.

FLUTTER AND WOW. See HIGH-FIDELITY.

FLUX, in WELDING and SOLDERING, a material used to clean the surface of the workpieces, particularly to remove OXIDE films; also, in metallurgical processes, a material (such as the LIMESTONE used in IRON smelting) added to a melt to abstract impurities in the form of a SLAG.

FLUXIONS, term used by NEWTON for CALCULUS. In his terminology, later abandoned in favor of that of LEIBNIZ, what we now call a FUNCTION was called a fluent, its derivative a fluxion.

FLY. See FLIES.

FLY AGARIC, or fly amanita, *Amanita muscaria*, deadly poisonous mushroom found in pastures and fields. It has a bright red or orange cap with white scales and a white stalk with a bulbous base. (See FUNGI.)

FLYCATCHERS, members of the families Tyrannidae and Muscicapidae, birds that feed on insects, though larger species feed on lizards, mice and small birds.

FLYING, History of. See FLIGHT, HISTORY OF.

FLYING BUTTRESS. See BUTTRESS.

FLYING DRAGON, a genus, *Draco*, of tree-dwelling lizards found in S Asia, also known as flying lizards. The Flying dragon uses a thin fold of skin along the sides of its body to glide up to 9m (30ft) between trees. They average 130mm (5.1in) in length.

FLYING DUTCHMAN, a ghost ship said to appear to ill-fated sailors in storms off the Cape of Good Hope. One version has it that the ship's captain is doomed to sail forever for having committed blasphemy. COLERIDGE and WAGNER both made use of the legend.

FLYING FISHES, members of the family Exocoetidae, tropical fish which propel themselves out of the sea by an elongated lobe of the tail. They can glide on their fins for over 0.4km (0.25mi) but the flights are usually 55m (180ft) or less. The reason for flying is to escape predatory fish.

FLYING FOXES, members of the family Pteropidae, large fruit BATS ranging from Madagascar to the Philippines. The largest has a 1.5m (5ft) wingspan. They roost in trees and fly out in the evenings to feed on flowers and fruit.

FLYING LEMUR, or **colugo,** *Cynocephalus volans*, an unusual mammal in the family Dermoptera unrelated to the lemurs. It has flaps of skin between fore and hindlimbs which enable it to glide 140m (460ft) from one tree to another. It feeds on leaves and flowers.

FLYING PHALANGERS, members of the marsupial family Phalangeridae. These pouched mammals skim on a parachute of skin between their fore and hind legs from tree to tree. They are found mainly in Australia, where they are known as squirrel gliders.

FLYING SAUCER, popular term for Unidentified Flying Object (UFO). UFOs have been reported for many years, but only caught the public imagination in the 1950s "Saucer Scare." Most sightings are obviously erroneous but a number by reliable observers remain unexplained.

FLYING SQUIRRELS, members of the family Sciuridae, a family of SQUIRRELS which glide on a web of skin between their legs. They use their tails to balance and as a rudder. Flying squirrels are found throughout the world but are most common in SE Asia. Their habits are similar to those of other squirrels.

FLYING TIGERS, group of US volunteer pilots (officially the American Volunteer Group) who fought for China before the US entered WWII. It was commanded by Claire Lee CHENNAULT. Most of its members later joined the US Army Air Force.

FLY RIVER, chief river of New Guinea, navigable for over 500mi. It flows 650mi S and SE through Papua New Guinea to the Gulf of Papua.

FLYWHEEL, a device used for storing mechanical ENERGY and for smoothing the POWER output of an engine, comprising a heavy shaft-mounted wheel. Since energy is stored as kinetic energy of rotation, it is advantageous for the wheel to have as large as possible a MOMENT OF INERTIA, and thus for its MASS to be concentrated near the rim.

FM (Frequency Modulation). See RADIO.

FOAM RUBBER, a material used widely for cushioning and sometimes for thermal INSULATION. It is about 10% rubber, 90% air. Usually LATEX is whipped into a froth, then gelled and vulcanized in a mold. For insulation, hydrogen PEROXIDE is introduced into latex: this liberates oxygen during vulcanization to form unlinked cells.

FOCAL LENGTH. See LENS, OPTICAL.

FOCH, Ferdinand (1851–1929), outstanding French army marshal. His courageous stand against the Germans at the Marne in 1914 led to his appointment as Gen. JOFFRE's assistant. He commanded the Allied armies in France, April–Nov., 1918, launching the Aisne-Marne offensive which ended WWI.

FOCUS (Geometry). See CURVE.

FOCUS (Optics). See LENS, OPTICAL.

FOCUS OF EARTHQUAKE. See EARTHQUAKE.

FOEHN, or **föhn,** dry, warm wind coming down the leeward slopes of mountains due to air having lost its moisture while ascending the windward slope, then warming on its descent. (See also CHINOOK.)

FOETUS. See FETUS.

FOG, in essence, a cloud touching or near to the earth's surface. A fog is a SUSPENSION of tiny water (sometimes ice) particles in the air. Fogs are a result of the air's HUMIDITY being high enough that CONDENSATION occurs around suitable nuclei; and are found most often near coasts and large inland bodies of water. In industrial areas, fog and SMOKE may mix to give **smog**. Persistent **advection fogs** occur when warm, moist air moves over cold land or water. (See also CLOUDS; MIST.)

FOIL, Metal, metal rolled or beaten into a very thin sheet. Commonest is ALUMINUM foil (having largely replaced TIN foil), used extensively in packaging and in the home in the storage or cooking of food. GOLD foil is used decoratively and in electronics (see also GOLD LEAF); LEAD foil as a radiation shield.

FOKINE, Michel (1880–1942), Russian-born US dancer and choreographer, a founder of modern ballet. Influenced by the work of Isadora DUNCAN, he stressed the total effect of expressive dancing, costume, music and scenery. He worked in Paris as chief choreographer of DIAGHILEV's Ballets Russes 1909–14, and from 1925 directed his own company in the US.

FOKKER, Anthony Herman Gerard (1890–1939), Dutch-American pioneer in aircraft design. In WWI he designed pursuit planes for Germany,

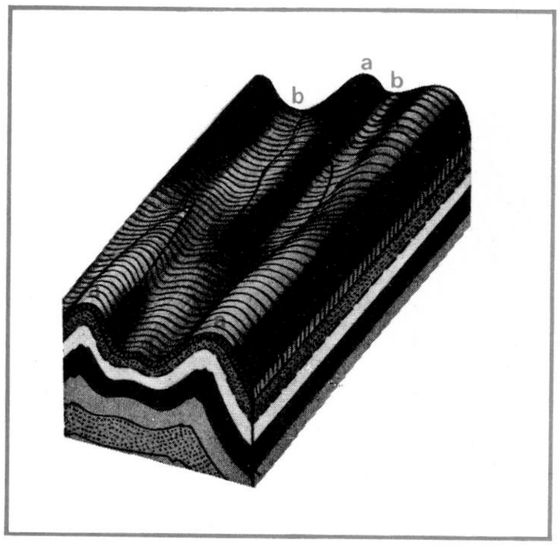

Sometimes folds in rock layers are clearly visible, as on this rock face near Lulworth Cove in Dorset, England, where the chalk layers have become distorted into wave-like forms. Pressures within the earth's crust can fold layers of rock which were originally flat, creating (a) upfolds (anticlines) and (b) downfolds (synclines).

developing a synchronizer mechanism by which guns could be fired from directly behind a plane's propeller blades. In 1922 Fokker emigrated to the US where he designed for the Army Air Corps and built transport planes, such as the Fokker T-2, which in 1923 made the first nonstop flight across the US.

FOLD, a buckling in rock strata. Folds convex upward are called **anticlines**; those convex downward, **synclines**. They may be tiny or up to hundreds of kilometres across. Folds result from horizontal pressures in the EARTH's crust. The upper portions of anticlines have often been eroded away. (See also GEOSYNCLINE; MOUNTAIN.)

FOLGER, Henry Clay (1857–1930), US lawyer and industrialist, founder of Washington D.C.'s Folger Shakespeare Library (1932). He was president of the Standard Oil Company of New York 1911–23 and chairman 1923–28.

FOLIC ACID. See VITAMINS.

FOLK DANCING, traditional popular dancing, often stylistically peculiar to a nation or region. Folk dances derive variously from ancient magic and religious rituals and also from the sequences of movement involved in certain forms of communal labor. Famous national dances include the Irish JIG, Italian TARANTELLA and Hungarian CZARDAS. The American Folk Dancing Society popularizes American folk dances, notably the SQUARE DANCE where an expert "caller" gives rhyming instructions. Many US dances have European origins, but their barn dance setting is authentically American. (See also DANCE.)

FOLKLORE, a culture's traditional beliefs, customs and superstitions handed down informally in fables, myths, legends, proverbs, riddles, songs and ballads. Folklore studies were developed in the 1800s, largely through collection and collation of material by the GRIMM brothers, and folklore societies were set up in Europe and the US. The American Folklore Society was founded in 1888. The extent to which folktale themes are echoed and paralleled between distinct and isolated cultures is truly remarkable. One of the major studies of this phenomenon is Sir James FRAZER's *Golden Bough* (1890). (See also FABLE; MYTHOLOGY.)

FOLK MUSIC, traditional popular music stylistically belonging to a regional or ethnic group. Compositions are usually anonymous and, being in the main orally transmitted, often occur in several different versions. Folk music of the US includes the English ballads of Kentucky, Mexican music of the Southwest, and Black music of the South. Among classical composers influenced by folk music are BARTÓK, KODALY and Vaughan WILLIAMS.

FOLLICLE, dry single-seeded FRUIT that splits along one margin only to liberate the seeds, e.g., LARKSPURS, COLUMBINE. (See also LEGUME.) Also, in animals, deep pit surrounding the root of a HAIR.

FOLLICLE-STIMULATING HORMONE, or FSH, a pituitary-gland GONADOTROPHIN, concerned with ovarian follicle and SPERM development in females and males.

FOLSOM CULTURE, prehistoric (c8000 BC) American Indian culture named for Folsom, N. M., where stone arrow- or spearheads were discovered in the 1920s in close association with the bones of an extinct breed of bison. Other tools, such as stone scrapers, bone needles, etc., have been found; and it is thought that the culture was a nomadic, hunting one.

FONDA, family of US actors. **Henry Fonda** (1905–), made many Hollywood films including *Grapes of Wrath* (1940) and *Twelve Angry Men* (1957). His daughter **Jane Fonda** (1937–), who campaigned vigorously against the Vietnam War, starred in *Cat Ballou* (1964) and *Barbarella* (1968). Her brother **Peter Fonda** (1939–), co-produced, coauthored and starred in *Easy Rider* (1969).

FOND DU LAC, city in E Wis., seat of Fond du Lac Co. It has a variety of manufacturing industries and handles dairy products. Pop 35 515.

FONESCA, Gulf of, inlet of the Pacific, in Central America, bounded by El Salvador, Honduras and Nicaragua. It is about 50mi long and offers sheltered anchorages. Amapala and La Unión are among its chief ports.

FONT, basin, usually of stone, used to hold the water for Christian BAPTISM. Fonts vary in type from small raised chalices to troughs large enough for an adult's total immersion.

FONTAINEBLEAU, French town 37mi SSE of Paris, in the department Seine-et-Marne. A tourist center in the Forest of Fontainebleau, it is best known for its magnificent, mainly 16th-century chateau which was once a royal residence and is now a presidential summer home. Pop 20 580.

FONTANA, city in S Cal., W of San Bernardino. It produces steel, electronic equipment and clothing. Pop 20 673.

FONTANA, Domenico (1543–1607), Italian architect and civil engineer. As chief architect to Pope Sixtus V he completed the dome of St. Peter's (1585–90) and designed the Lateran Palace and the Vatican Library (1588). He discovered remains of POMPEII.

FONTENELLE, Bernard le Bovier de (1657–1757), French writer best known as a popularizer of new scientific ideas. As secretary of the Royal Academy of Sciences (1699–1741) and through such works as *Conversations on the Plurality of Inhabited Worlds* (1686) he paved the way for the skeptical philosophers of the French ENLIGHTENMENT.

FONTEYN, Dame Margot (Dame Margot Fonteyn de Arias; 1919–), English prima ballerina of the Royal Ballet. She made her debut in 1934 and first won widespread international acclaim in 1949 with *The Sleeping Beauty* during her US debut. Her partnership with NUREYEV is particularly famous.

FOOCHOW, major seaport on the coast of SE China; it is the capital of FUKIEN province. An important commercial and industrial center, it is famous for exporting black bohea tea. Pop 900 000.

FOOD, any substance that is used by an organism to produce ENERGY or that makes possible GROWTH or REPRODUCTION. Foods are usually complex chemical compounds that have to be broken down in the DIGESTIVE SYSTEM before they can be assimilated. Animals that are specialized to feed on other animals are called carnivores, those that feed on plants are herbivores, and those that feed on both, omnivores. Plants are able to synthesize food from inorganic material using energy derived from sunlight, a process called PHOTOSYNTHESIS. (See also NUTRITION.)

FOOD AND AGRICULTURE ORGANIZATION (FAO), agency of the UN, established in 1945. It provides member nations with information on food and agricultural problems and with technical and financial aid.

FOOD AND DRUG ADMINISTRATION, US, Federal agency in the Department of Health, Education and Welfare, set up in 1940 to enforce the laws maintaining standards in the sale of food and drugs. Originally concerned largely with preventing adulteration and poor food hygiene, the FDA is now also involved in testing the safety, reliability and usefulness of drugs and chemicals, and assessing the effects on health of "accidental additives" such as PESTICIDES.

FOOD CHAIN. See ECOLOGY.

FOOD POISONING, disease resulting from ingestion of unwholesome food, usually resulting in COLIC, VOMITING, DIARRHEA and general malaise. While a number of VIRUS, contaminant, irritant and allergic factors may play a part in some cases, three specific types are common: those due to STAPHYLOCOCCUS, Clostridium and SALMONELLA bacteria. Inadequate cooking, allowing cooked food to stand for long periods in warm conditions and contamination of cooked food with bacteria from humans or uncooked food are usual causes. **Staphylococci** may be introduced from a BOIL or from the NOSE of a food handler; they produce a TOXIN if allowed to grow in cooked food. Sudden vomiting and abdominal pain occur 2–6 hours after eating. *Clostridium* poisoning causes colic and diarrhea, 10–12 hours after ingestion of contaminated meat. *Salmonella* enteritis causes colic, diarrhea, vomiting and often fever, starting 12–24 hours after eating; poultry and human carriers are the usual sources. BOTULISM is an often fatal form of food poisoning. In general, food poisoning is mild and self-limited and symptomatic measures only are needed; ANTIBIOTICS rarely help.

FOOD PRESERVATION, a number of techniques used to delay the spoilage of food. There are two main causes of spoilage: one is the PUTREFACTION that follows the death of any plant or animal; the other over-ripening, the result of the action of certain plant ENZYMES. Heating destroys these enzymes and the BACTERIA responsible for putrefaction but, before it cools, the food must be isolated in cans or bottles from air-borne bacteria. Freezing slows the enzyme action and the REPRODUCTION of the bacteria and preserves flavor better. DEHYDRATION, IRRADIATION and preservatives are also used. Traditional means of preservation include smoking, salting and pickling (see VINEGAR). (See also FOOD POISONING; REFRIGERATION.)

FOOLS, Feast of, festival celebrated in Europe, particularly in France, on or around new year's day, from the 5th to the 15th centuries. It derived from the Roman SATURNALIA and consisted of mocking church and clergy through burlesque religious ceremonies.

FOOL'S GOLD. See PYRITE.

FOOT, weight-bearing structure of animal LEGS, and, in man, of the lower limbs only. It consists of numerous BONES which are connected at the ankle with the bones of the lower leg. Muscles and tendons in the feet are concerned with walking and running and in sustaining the transverse and longitudinal arches. Muscles in the calf act across the ankle JOINT to move the foot. The SKIN of the sole is thickened.

FOOT (ft), an old Imperial and US Customary unit of length equal to one-third of a yard or 0.304 8m.

FOOT, Samuel Augustus (1780–1846), US politician. In 1829 his Senate resolution inquiring into limiting the sale of public lands led to a fierce debate between Daniel WEBSTER and Robert HAYNE. Later, Foot was governor of Conn. 1834–35.

FOOT AND MOUTH DISEASE. See HOOF AND MOUTH DISEASE.

FOOTBALL, popular US sport, played with a leather-covered oval-shaped ball, by two teams of 11 men, on a field 120yd long by 53yd 1ft wide. Playing time is 60min, divided into two halfs of two quarters each. To score, a team must run, pass or kick the ball to a goal. A touchdown (running or passing the ball over the goal line) scores six points; a field goal (kicking the ball over the opponents' goal from a scrimmage) three points. After touchdown, the scoring team can try for more points (a conversion). Possession of the ball is the key to scoring; the offensive team has four plays, or downs, to advance 10yd and keep possession; a new first down begins when 10yd are gained. The defense obtains the ball by blocking the advance, intercepting a pass or recovering a fumble.

Early US football was similar to SOCCER, but today's game evolved from RUGBY, which allowed handling of the ball. In the 1880s US football began to take on its own form; many rules and tactics were devised by Walter Camp of Yale U., the "father of American football." The sport became popular, but public criticism of physical violence brought about a meeting of President Theodore Roosevelt with college team representatives, which resulted in banning mass formations and other dangerous tactics (Sept. 1906). Forward passing of the ball was legalized, opening up the game.

By the 1920s professional football was flourishing; the National Football League was organized in 1921. The Depression and WWII retarded the NFL's development, but television made the pros' faster, more skillful, harder style of play popular with the masses. Game attendance soared from the 1950s on. In 1972, over 15 059 364 spectators attended pro games.

FOOT-CANDLE, in PHOTOMETRY a former unit of illumination. It represents the illumination of a surface receiving an incident luminous flux of 1 lumen per square foot.

FOOT-POUND (weight) or **foot-pound-force** (ft lbf), a unit of WORK, that done when a MASS of one pound is lifted through one foot against gravity, equal to 1.35582 joules.

FOOTE, Andrew Hull (1806–1863), US naval officer. During the Civil War, he organized the

Mississippi squadron and commanded Union operations on the river, capturing Fort Henry (see HENRY, FORT).

FORAKER, Joseph Benson (1846–1917), US politician, governor of Ohio 1885–89, and US Senator 1902–08. Foraker planned Puerto Rico's civil government and fought President Roosevelt's reform program. His public career ended with evidence that he had been paid by Standard Oil Company while in the Senate.

FORAKER, Mount, mountain (17400ft) in the Alaska Range, Mt McKinley National Park, Alaska.

FORAMINIFERA, single-celled sea animals. Each species has a limy shell which sinks when the foraminifer dies. These shells form deposits of Foraminiferan ooze which cover one third of the ocean floor.

FORBES, John (1710–1759), British general in the FRENCH AND INDIAN WARS. In 1758 he commanded an expedition, which included a detachment led by George Washington, from Halifax, Nova Scotia, against Fort Duquesne, on the Ohio R. Despite great hardship Forbes' troops took the fort, renaming it Fort Pitt (now Pittsburgh, Pa.). Emaciated and exhausted, Forbes was taken to Philadelphia where he died.

FORBIDDEN CITY, walled enclosure in Peking, China, containing the imperial palace, its grounds, reception halls and state offices. In imperial times, the Forbidden City was closed to the public.

FORCE, in mechanics, the physical quantity which, when it acts on a body, either causes it to change its state of motion (i.e., imparts to it an ACCELERATION), or tends to deform it (i.e., induces in it an elastic strain—see MATERIALS, STRENGTH OF). Dynamical forces are governed by NEWTON's laws of motion, from the second of which it follows that a given force acting on a body produces in it an acceleration proportional to the force, inversely proportional to the body's MASS and occurring in the direction of the force. Forces are thus VECTOR quantities with direction as well as magnitude. They may be manipulated graphically like other vectors, the sum of two forces being known as their resultant. The SI UNIT of force is the newton, a force of one newton being that which will produce an acceleration of $1 m/sec^2$ in a mass of 1 kilogram.

FORCE ACTS, or force bills, name for several 19th century US laws. The first bill was enacted in 1833 to enforce protective tariffs in S.C. (see NULLIFICATION). In the 1870s, three acts attempted to enforce Negro civil and voting rights, guaranteed under the 14th and 15th amendments to the US Constitution. The acts failed because of Southern intransigence and Northern apathy.

FORCING, the technique of bringing plants into a flowering or fruiting condition out of season. By artificially changing such environmental conditions as heat, light and moisture, plants can be forced into growth and the production of fruits and flowers at times when they would not do so under natural conditions.

FORD, Ford Madox (1873–1939), influential English man of letters, born Ford Madox Hueffer. His novels *The Good Soldier* (1915) and *Parade's End* (1924–28), a tetralogy, described the decline of the English upper classes before WWI. As first editor of *The English Review* (1908–11), he encouraged such writers as Conrad, T. S. Eliot, Pound, Frost, Hemingway and D. H. Lawrence.

FORD, Gerald Rudolph, Jr. (1913–), 38th president of the US. Born Leslie King, Jr. in Omaha, Neb., Ford was adopted and renamed before he was two by his mother's second husband. Ford grew up in Grand Rapids, Mich., graduated from the U. of Michigan, where he had been a star player on the varsity football squad, worked his way through Yale U. Law School as a coach, and returned home to practice law in 1941. In the same year he joined the navy, serving four years during WWII, and becoming a lieutenant-commander. After service he resumed his law practice.

At the urging of Senator Arthur VANDENBERG, Ford ran for Congress in 1948, scoring a victory over the incumbent Republican. Ford arrived on Capitol Hill in 1949 with a new bride, Elizabeth Bloomer. He became a hard-working Congressman and remained in the House of Representatives for 25 years. He obtained a seat on the powerful House Appropriations Committee, and was known as a conservative and an internationalist. Slowly he became a prominent Republican spokesman. In 1963 he was appointed to the WARREN COMMISSION investigating President Kennedy's assassination. In 1964 Ford became Republican Minority Leader of the House.

Several times Ford was considered as a possible vice-presidential nomineee, but he remained in the House; the highest offices in the US came to him unexpectedly and unsought. On Oct. 12, 1973, President Nixon nominated Ford to succeed Spiro Agnew as vice-president. On Aug. 9, 1974, Nixon resigned the presidency over the WATERGATE crisis and Ford took the oath of office, declaring, "Our long national nightmare is over . . . Our Constitution works." Ford proved himself to be a competent president, but lost popularity for his pardon of Nixon and occasional lack of tact; his general policies alienated liberals. He lost the 1976 election to the charismatic James CARTER.

Far removed from its sedate English namesake, American football is one of the toughest, fastest and most exciting games in the world. The picture shows one of the most skilled teams, the New York Giants, in action.

Gerald Rudolph FORD

38th US President

Born: Omaha, Nebraska; July 14, 1913

Term of office: August 9, 1974–January 20, 1977

Political party: Republican

FORD, Henry (1863–1947), American automobile production pioneer. He produced his first automobile in 1896 and established the Ford Motor Company, Dearborn, Mich., in 1903. By adopting mass-assembly methods, and introducing the moving assembly line in 1913, Ford revolutionized automobile production. Ford saw that mass-produced cars could sell at a price within reach of the average American family. His Model T sold 15 million (1908–26). Ford was a paradoxical and often controversial character. Although a proud anti-intellectual, he set up several museums and the famous FORD FOUNDATION. A violent anti-unionist, he reduced the average working week, introduced profit-sharing and the highest minimum daily wage of his time. In 1938 he accepted a Nazi decoration and became a leading isolationist. At the oubreak of war, however, he built the world's largest assembly plant, to produce B-24 bombers.

FORD, John (1586–1640?), English dramatist. Three tragedies, *'Tis Pity She's a Whore, The Broken Heart* and *Love's Sacrifice*, are his best-known works. Considered decadent by earlier critics because of his lack of moral comment, Ford's insight into human passion has been admired in the 20th century.

FORD, John (1895–1973), US motion picture director. In 1917 he began directing the first of his more than 100 films, most of them Westerns. He won Academy awards for *The Grapes of Wrath* (1941), *How Green Was My Valley* (1942), *The Informer* (1936) and *The Quiet Man* (1953).

FORD FOUNDATION, philanthropic corporation founded by Henry Ford in 1936. With assets of over $3 billion, it is the world's largest philanthropic trust. The foundation uses its funds for educational, cultural, scientific and charitable purposes in the US and abroad.

FORDNEY-McCUMBER TARIFF ACT (1922), US protectionist law which restored high tariff rates and gave the president unique power to adjust individual duties up to 50%, on the advice of the Tariff Commission (see TARIFFS).

FOREBRAIN, in EMBRYOLOGY, the division of the BRAIN that develops into the cerebral cortex (particularly large in man), the basal ganglia, THALAMUS, HYPOTHALAMUS, olfactory bulbs, RETINA and optic nerves.

FOREIGN AID PROGRAMS, financial and other aid given by one country to another. The first major foreign aid programs were loans from the US to Europe during and after WWII. The LEND-LEASE program provided over $40 billion to US allies. After the war the MARSHALL PLAN strengthened the weakened economies of Western Europe. In 1949 the POINT FOUR PROGRAM initiated US aid to underdeveloped countries, particularly in Asia. Credit facilities were set for these nations in 1957 with the creation of the DEVELOPMENT LOAN FUND. The 1960s saw a diversification of US aid programs (in Asia, Africa and Latin America), and establishment of the PEACE CORPS and the ALLIANCE FOR PROGRESS.

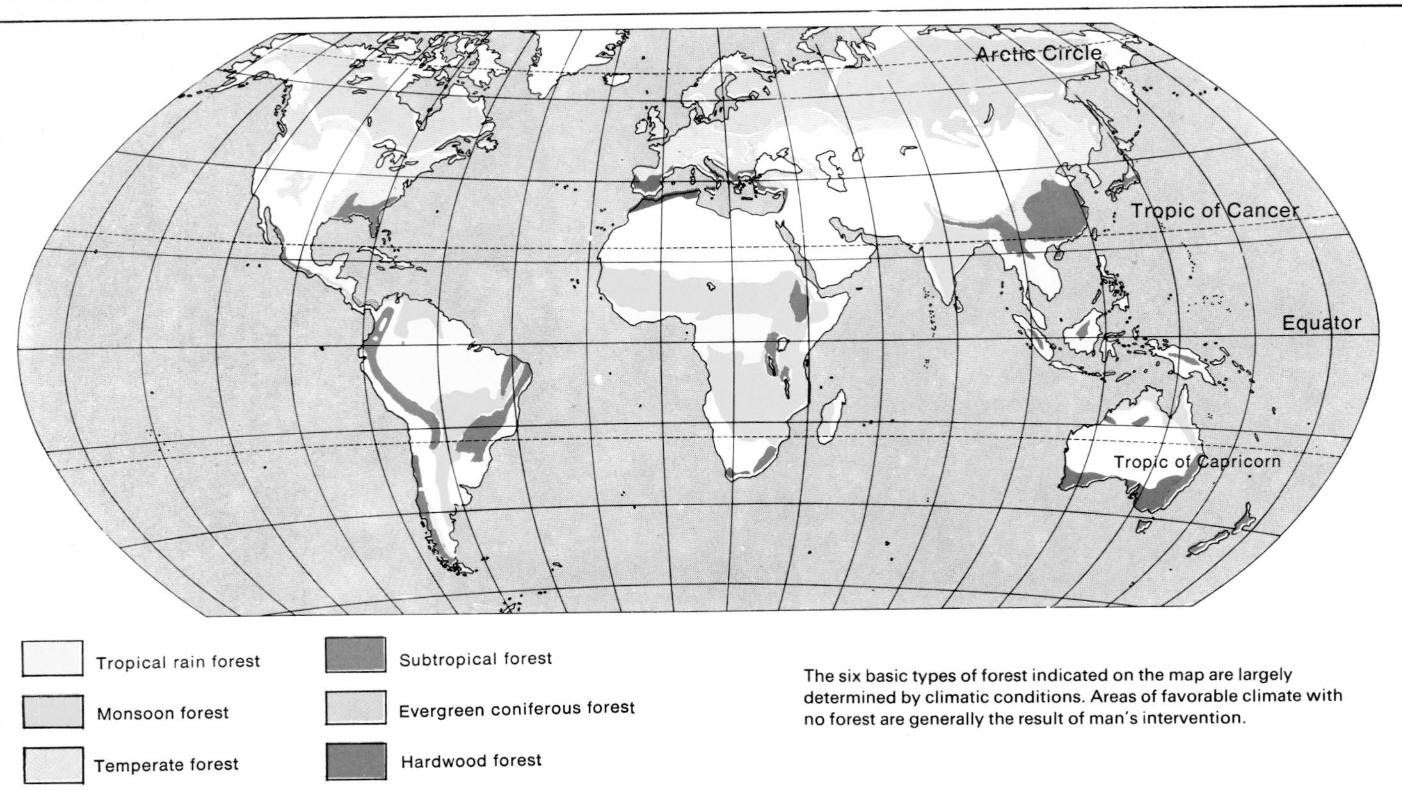

The six basic types of forest indicated on the map are largely determined by climatic conditions. Areas of favorable climate with no forest are generally the result of man's intervention.

Since 1945 US foreign aid has totaled over $119 billion; recent balance-of-payment difficulties have caused cutbacks in expenditure. Apart from bilateral aid, the US is involved in multilateral aid programs, acting with other countries through the UN and other agencies. The US contributes about half the budget of the ORGANIZATION FOR ECONOMIC COOPERATION AND DEVELOPMENT. OECD member-countries provide $6–7 billion per year in aid. Increasingly, the nations of Western Europe and Canada, Japan, Australia and the US have been coordinating their foreign aid programs, through such agencies as the WORLD BANK, to help narrow the gap between rich and poor nations.

FOREIGN LEGION, elite mercenary army created in 1831 by the French to save manpower in Algeria. The legion fought mainly outside France until Algerian independence (1962): in Morocco, Madagascar, Spain, Mexico, the Crimea and Indo-China.

FOREIGN SERVICE, diplomatic and consular employees of the US Department of State. They staff embassies and consulates, promote friendly relations between the US and countries where they serve, advise on political and economic matters, protect and aid US citizens abroad and deal with aliens seeking entry to the US. (See also STATE, US DEPARTMENT OF.)

FOREIGN TRADE. See INTERNATIONAL TRADE.

FORENSIC MEDICINE, the branch of MEDICINE concerned with legal aspects of DEATH, DISEASE or injury. Forensic medical experts are commonly required to examine corpses found in possibly criminal circumstances. They may be asked to elucidate probable cause and approximate time of death, to investigate the possibility of POISONING, trauma or suicide, to analyse links with possible murder weapons and to help to identify decayed or mutilated bodies.

FORESTER, Cecil Scott (1899–1966), English novelist, best known for his popular Captain Hornblower novels set in the Napoleonic period. An earlier novel, *The African Queen* (1935), was made into an Academy award-winning film in 1951.

FORESTERS, INDEPENDENT ORDER OF, US fraternal, benevolent society created in 1874. Following the Civil War, numerous societies such as the Foresters, the Elks and the Moose began to offer members social activities and other benefits.

FORESTERS, THE SOCIETY OF AMERICAN, founded in 1900 to promote good forestry practice. It is the accrediting agency for professional forestry training, and publishes the *Journal of Forestry*.

FOREST FIRES, despite a reduction of 60% in the last 20 years, fire still destroys some six million acres a year in the US. Chief cause is man's carelessness; lightning, the main natural cause, accounts for only 5% of all fires. Wind direction and strength are the most important factors in fire control, for sudden changes make control difficult. If a blaze cannot be put out, fire fighters try to restrict its area—often by creating treeless channels called firebreaks. (See also FIRE FIGHTING.)

FOREST PARK, town in NW Ga., 10mi S of Atlanta. The Atlanta Army Depot and State Farmer's Market are located there. Pop 19994.

FOREST PARK, residential suburb of Chicago, in NE Ill. Pop 15472.

FOREST PARK, residential town in SW Ohio, 12mi N of Cincinnati. Pop 15139.

FORESTRY, management of forests for productive purposes. In the US, a forestry program emerged in the 1890s because of fears of a "timber famine" and following exploitation of the Great Lakes pine forests. Congress authorized the first forest reserves in 1891; creation of the FOREST SERVICE in 1905 put forestry on a scientific basis.

The most important aspect of forestry is the production of lumber. Because of worldwide depletion of timber stocks, it has become necessary to view forests as renewable productive resources, and because of the time scale and area involved in the growth of a forest, trees need more careful planning than any other crop. Forestry work plans for a continuity of timber production by balancing planting and felling. Other important functions are disease, pest, fire and flood control. The forester must control the density and proportions of the various trees in a forest and ensure that man does not radically disturb a forest's ecological balance.

The science of forestry is well advanced in the US, which is the world's largest timber producer and has more than 25 forestry schools across the country. However, only 20% of the world's forests are being renewed, and timber resources are declining. (See also CONSERVATION; FORESTS.)

FOREST SERVICE, US, Department of Agriculture agency, created in 1905 to manage and protect the national forests. Nearly 190 million acres of national forests and grasslands, as well as 480 million acres of forests and watersheds belonging to state and local governments and private owners, benefit from the service's conservation, research, development and advisory programs.

FORESTS, extensive tracts of land whose vegetation is composed most notably of trees. They are of considerable importance to man: they have provided fuel and building material since prehistory; their fruits have served as food; and, particularly today, they play a valuable role in countering SOIL EROSION (see also CONSERVATION).

Coniferous Forests have as characteristic trees the pine, spruce and fir (see CONIFERS), and are found in temperate regions as far N as the edges of the TUNDRA. They are similarly distributed in the S Hemisphere.

Deciduous Forests, found in temperate zones, are characterized by DECIDUOUS TREES with some conifers. They contribute most of the world's commercially important hardwood; e.g., oak, elm, beech and birch.

Fossil or Petrified Forests, best known of which is that of E Ariz., occur where collections of trees have been petrified, usually by mineralization (see FOSSILS).

Monsoon Forests are found in MONSOON regions, and resemble rain forests except that they are more open. Their trees have adapted to the marked dry season. They are a source of teak, a commercially important hardwood.

Rain or Equatorial Forests (*Selvas*) are found in equatorial regions, where there is no dry season. These dense jungles support the wild RUBBER tree, and are important as sources of mahogany and ebony.

Thorn Forests occur in tropical and subtropical areas where rainfall is insufficient to maintain larger trees. They are characterized by shrubs and small trees; e.g., mesquite, acacia. The thorn forest of Brazil is known as the *caatinga*.

(See also DENDROCHRONOLOGY; TREES; WOOD.)

FORGERY, in law, the making or altering of a written instrument with intent to defraud. As a general term it is used of anything, such as a work of art or literature, made or altered with intent to deceive whether fraudulently or not. This is usually not criminal unless done for some kind of gain. Art forgeries are common, but are easier to detect than is commonly supposed; literary forgeries, such as CHATTERTON's "Rowley" poems, have seldom survived for long. Forgeries are usually detected through errors in either content or substance. It is almost impossible, for example, to age paper or canvas artificially. The most successful modern art forger, however, the Dutchman Hans van Meegeren, was detected only when he confessed to forgery to escape a charge of selling art treasures to the Nazis. The term for forgery of money is COUNTERFEITING.

FORGET-ME-NOTS, popular name for annual and perennial plants of the genus *Myosotis*, native to North America and Eurasia and widely cultivated as garden plants. They normally produce many blue flowers, but some white and pink-flowered forms occur. Family: Boraginaceae.

FORGING, the shaping of metal by hammering or pressing, usually when the workpiece is red hot (about 700–1000K) but sometimes when it is cold. Unlike CASTING, forging does not alter the granular structure of the metal, and hence greater strength is possible in forged than in cast metals. The most basic method of forging is that of the blacksmith, who heats the metal in an open fire (forge) and hammers it into shape against an anvil. Today, metals are forged between two DIES, usually impressed with the desired shape. Techniques include: **drop forging**, where the workpiece is held on the lower, stationary die, the other being held by a massive ram which is allowed to fall; **press forging**, where the dies are pressed together; and **impact forging**, where the dies are rammed horizontally together, the workpiece between. (See also METALLURGY.)

FORMALDEHYDE (HCHO), colorless, acrid, toxic gas; the simplest ALDEHYDE, more reactive than the others. It is made by catalytic air oxidation of METHANOL vapor or of NATURAL GAS. Formaldehyde gas is unstable, and is usually stored as its aqueous solution, **formalin**, used as a disinfectant and preservative for biological specimens; on keeping, formalin deposits a polymer, **paraformaldehyde**, which regenerates formaldehyde on heating. Formaldehyde is condensed with UREA and PHENOLS to make PLASTICS, with AMMONIA to give hexamethylenetetramine (a urinary ANTISEPTIC also used to make RDX), and with ACETALDEHYDE to give pentaerithrytol and hence PETN. It is also used in TANNING and textile manufacture. MW 30.0, mp −92°C, bp −21°C.

FORMIC ACID (HCOOH), colorless, acrid liquid; the simplest CARBOXYLIC ACID, a stronger ACID than the others. It occurs in the stings of ants and nettles. It is made (via sodium formate) by heating sodium hydroxide with carbon monoxide under pressure, and used in TANNING, as a latex coagulant and to reduce dyes. MW 46.0, mp 8°C, bp 101°C.

FORMOSA. See TAIWAN.

FORMOSUS (c816–896), pope 891–96. Under STEPHEN VII, political enemies declared Formosus' pontificate invalid. Later popes reversed the decision.

FORMULA, Chemical, a symbolic representation of the composition of a MOLECULE. The **empirical formula** shows merely the proportions of the atoms in the molecule, as found by chemical ANALYSIS, e.g., water H_2O, acetic acid CH_2O. (The subscripts indicate the number of each atom if more than one.) The **molecular formula** shows the actual number of atoms in the molecule, e.g., water H_2O, acetic acid $C_2H_4O_2$. The atomic symbols are sometimes grouped to give some idea of the molecular structure, e.g., acetic acid CH_3COOH. This is done unambiguously by the **structural formula**, which shows the chemical BONDS and so distinguishes between ISOMERS. The **space formula** shows the arrangement of the atoms and bonds in three-dimensional space, and so distinguishes between STEREOISOMERS; it may be drawn in PERSPECTIVE or represented conventionally. Loosely-associated compounds, such as LIGAND complexes, are often shown with a dot, e.g., copper (II) sulfate pentahydrate, $CuSO_4.5H_2O$. Special symbols are sometimes used for common groups and ligands, e.g., ethyl Et, phenyl Ph, ethylenediamine en.

FORREST, Edwin (1806–1872), prominent American tragedian; the first US actor actively to encourage native playwrights. His feud with English actor William Macready led to a notorious riot at New York's Astor Place Opera House on May 8, 1849.

FORREST, Nathan Bedford (1821–1877), Confederate cavalry general, esteemed for bravery and brilliant leadership. His troops committed a massacre of Negroes at Fort Pillow, near Memphis, Tenn., on April 12, 1864.

FORRESTAL, James Vincent (1892–1949), US financier and statesman. He became an assistant to President Roosevelt (1940) and secretary of the navy (1944). Appointed the first US secretary of defense (1947), he reorganized and tried to unify the armed services.

FORREST CITY, city in E Ark., seat of St. Francis Co., producing timber, corn and sweet potatoes. Pop 12521.

FORSSMAN, Werner (1904–), German surgeon awarded, with A. COURNAND and D. W. RICHARDS, the 1956 Nobel Prize for Physiology or Medicine for his discovery of the technique of introducing medicine directly into the heart via a CATHETER.

FORSTER, E. M. (1879–1970), Edward Morgan Forster, a major English novelist of the early 20th century. His novels are *Where Angels Fear to Tread* (1905), *The Longest Journey* (1907), *A Room With a View* (1908), *Howard's End* (1910), *A Passage to India* (1924) and *Maurice* (1971). Forster's major themes concern conflict in human relations—between truth and falsehood, "culture" and instinct or emotion, and the inner and outer life. His *Aspects of the Novel* (1927) was an influential critical work.

FORSYTHIA, genus containing seven species of deciduous shrubs that are widely cultivated for the yellow flowers produced in the spring before the leaves open. Family: Olearaceae.

FORTALEZA, city in NE Brazil, port of Ceará state, founded 1609 by the Portuguese. It exports sugar, coffee, cotton, rum, fruit, rubber and hides. Pop 842231.

FORT . . . Forts usually appear alphabetically under their identifying names, except when part of a city's or national monument's name.

FORTAS, Abe (1910–), US public official. Under-secretary of the interior 1942–46, he was appointed to the US Supreme Court in 1965. He resigned in 1969, after allegations of conflict of interest in private financial dealings.

FORT BRIDGER, historic trading post and fort in SW Wyo. Built in 1843 by James BRIDGER, it was an important post on the OREGON TRAIL. A US army post 1858–90, it is now the site of a state park.

FORT CAROLINE NATIONAL MEMORIAL, fortified settlement near St. Johns R, Fla. Founded in 1564, its Huguenot settlers were massacred by Spanish forces in 1565. In 1568 the Spanish garrison was wiped out by avenging French forces.

FORT COLLINS, city in N Col., seat of Larimer Co., 65mi N of Denver. Produces canned goods, sugar, plastics and light industrial products. Pop 43337.

FORT-DE-FRANCE, capital and chief port of Martinique, an island in the West Indies. The city's favorable climate and French atmosphere attract many tourists. Pop 100000.

FORT DODGE, city in N central Iowa, seat of Webster Co., about 90mi N of Des Moines. Produces agricultural equipment and products. Pop 31263.

FORT DUQUESNE, fort in Pa., at the junction of the Allegheny and Monongahela rivers. Begun in 1754 by Virginians, it was seized and completed by the French who routed George Washington's militia-men nearby, starting the last of the FRENCH AND INDIAN WARS. Pittsburgh, Pa., now stands on the site.

FORTESCUE, Sir John (c1385–1479), English chief justice 1442–61, who wrote *In Praise of the Laws of England* (c1470) to instruct the son of the deposed HENRY VI in exile. He made the famous remark: "It is better that the guilty escape than that the innocent be punished."

FORT FREDERIKA NATIONAL MONUMENT, site of a British fort on the W coast of St. Simons Island, Ga., built (1736–48) by James OGLETHORPE to protect Ga. from the Spanish in Fla.

FORT GEORGE RIVER (Big River), runs through Quebec province, Canada. Rising in Lake Nichicun, it flows N 60mi then W 420mi into James Bay. The Hudson's Bay Company traded at the river's mouth before 1800.

FORTH, Firth of. See FIRTH.

FORTIFICATION, military construction for defense or protection. Two main types are permanent fortification (forts, castles, defense zones), usually built in peacetime, and field works, temporary defense systems in combat zones. Permanent structures such as walls, forts or castles have been important in most countries throughout world history. Artillery revolutionized fortification: walls and towers became lower and thicker; bastions and gun platforms were set at calculated angles in walls; and concrete came into use (see MAGINOT LINE). Field works can be hasty (fox or shell hole, shallow trench) or deliberate (rampart, trench, bunker, obstacles such as mines or wire), and have been used in war since ancient times. Modern developments include chemical defoliation, bugging devices and underground installations.

FORTIN, Jean, French physicist. See BAROMETER.

FORT JEFFERSON NATIONAL MONUMENT, site on Garden Key, Dry Tortugas islands, 68mi W of Key West, Fla. Established in 1935, it has a marine exhibit and remains of a fort, begun in 1846, which served as a federal prison.

FORT KNOX, is a US military reservation in N Hardin Co. N central Ky., 33000 acres in size and established in 1917 as a training camp. It has been a permanent military post since 1932, and the site of the US Gold Bullion Depository since 1936. Godman Air Force Base is also there.

FORT-LAMY. See NDJAMENA.

FORT LAUDERDALE, city in SE Fla., seat of Broward Co., 20mi N of Miami. A yachting and fishing resort, with almost 300mi of waterways and 5mi of public ocean beach. Pop 139590.

FORT LEE, borough in Bergen Co., N.J. on the Hudson R opposite New York City. Site of a Revolutionary War fort. Pop 30,631.

FORT MADISON, city in SE Iowa, on the Mississippi R, one of two seats of Lee Co., and an important industrial and trade center. Pop 13996.

FORT MATANZAS NATIONAL MONUMENT, on Matanzas Inlet, NE Fla., S of St. Augustine. Built (c1836) by the Spaniards on a small island, the fort houses relics of the Spanish occupation of Fla.

FORT McHENRY NATIONAL MONUMENT AND HISTORIC SHRINE, fort in Baltimore harbor, Md. During the War of 1812, it withstood overnight bombardment by a British fleet. This inspired Francis Scott Key, a spectator, to write the words to *The Star-Spangled Banner*, which became the US national anthem.

FORT MYERS, city in SW Fla., seat of Lee Co., manufactures electronics equipment, cigars and lumber. Pop 27351.

Mural depicting a reconstructed Spanish fort in the Apalache Historical Memorial, south of Talahassee, Florida. Simple forts in this style have been in use for thousands of years in many different cultures all over the world.

The bombardment of Fort Sumter by Southern forces on April 12, 1861, opened the Civil War. After a 36-hour bombardment the garrison of 68 under Major Robert Anderson surrendered honorably. The fort, which was subsequently regained by Union forces, is now a national monument.

FORT PECK DAM, the largest earth structure in the world, in NE Mont., on the Missouri R 15mi from Frazer. It is 250ft high with a crest length of 21 026ft, and was built to improve river navigation and control floods.

FORT PIERCE, city in E Fla., seat of St. Lucie Co.; produces fertilizer, lumber and canned fruit. Pop 29721.

FORT PULASKI NATIONAL MONUMENT, on Cockspur Island, at the mouth of the Savannah R, E Ga. Built in 1829–47, it was captured by Union troops who used it to blockade Savannah harbor in the Civil War.

FORTRAN (*for*mula *tran*slation), one of the most widely used COMPUTER languages. Originally developed for purely scientific work, it is now, as Fortran IV, used also in commerce and elsewhere.

FORT RANDALL DAM, on the Missouri R, 80mi upstream from Yankton, S.D. Part of the Missouri R basin development program, the dam is 165ft high with a crest length of 10 700ft.

FORT SMITH, city in W Ark., on the Arkansas R just E of the Oklahoma border. A diversified manufacturing center sited in a rich coal, gas and timber area. Pop 62802.

FORT SUMTER NATIONAL MONUMENT, site of a US fort in Charleston harbor, S.C., where the first shots in the Civil War were fired on April 12, 1861. When S.C. seceded from the Union (1860), US Maj. Robert Anderson received a rebel summons to surrender his garrison. He refused, Sumter was fired upon, and the war had begun. The fort was retaken when Confederates evacuated Charleston in Feb. 1865.

FORT THOMAS, residential city in N Ky., 5mi SE of Cincinnati, Ohio. Pop 16 338.

FORTUNA, popular ancient Roman goddess of fortune and good luck, later associated with the Greek goddess Tyche. Originally a fertility deity, she was often represented holding a CORNUCOPIA.

FORTUNATE ISLES, ancient name for the CANARY ISLANDS.

FORTUNE TELLING, prediction of future events by nonscientific or mystical means. ASTROLOGY, PALMISTRY, crystal gazing, the reading of TAROT and other cards and of tea leaves and coffee grounds, and various methods of DIVINATION such as clairvoyance are popular methods of attempting to foretell the future. In recent times there has been a popular resurgence in fortune telling, despite scientific skepticism, and some methods (such as clairvoyance) have been considered subjects for serious research.

FORT UNION NATIONAL MONUMENT, in NE N.M., 60mi from Santa Fe. Built 1851 on the SANTA FE TRAIL, to protect settlers from Indian attack, it supplied army posts throughout the Southwest.

FORT WALTON BEACH, city in NW Fla. on the Gulf of Mexico. Eglin Air Force Base is nearby. Pop 19994.

FORT WAYNE, city in NE Ind., seat of Allen Co., located on the Maumee R with access to major waterways, E and W. In a rich farm and dairy area, it is a major industrial and railroad center. Named for Gen. Anthony WAYNE. Pop 177671.

FORT WILLIAM. See THUNDER BAY.

FORT WORTH, city in N Tex., seat of Tarrant Co., on the Trinity R 33mi W of Dallas. A major SW grain-storage and flour-milling center, it lies in an important producing area. Site of a large aircraft factory and the biggest stockyards and meat packing plants in the South. Pop 393476.

FORTY-NINERS, name given to those who went to California following the gold strike Jan. 24, 1848. By 1849 people from all over the world joined the gold rush, and the population of California soared from 20000 to over 107000.

FORUM, the principal public square or market place in ancient Roman cities, where citizens gathered to discuss important issues and transact judicial and other public business. The forum usually contained colonnades, shops, and temples and other important buildings.

Northwest corner of the Forum Romanum, the forum of ancient Rome. The triumphal arch is that of the emperor Septimius Severus. It was erected in 203 AD to celebrate the tenth anniversary of his reign and also to glorify his victories and those of his two sons Caracalla and Geta.

FOSDICK, Harry Emerson (1878–1969), American clergyman, leading exponent of Protestant liberalism. A professor at Union Theological Seminary 1908–46, he became the first pastor of Riverside Church, New York City (1926–46).

FOSSA, *Cryptoprocta ferox*, a cat-like member of the civet family Viverridae, found only in Madagascar. Its reddish brown coat gives it the appearance of a small brown puma. It is a nocturnal forest dweller, spending much time in trees. It eats small lemurs and birds.

FOSSILS, the remains, traces or impressions of living organisms that inhabited the earth during past ages. Traces may be, for example, footprints, burrows or preserved droppings.

Fossil remains take a number of forms. **Petrification** describes two ways in which the shape of hard parts of the organism may be preserved. In **permineralization**, the pore spaces of the hard parts are infilled by certain minerals (e.g., SILICA, PYRITE, CALCITE) that infiltrate from the local GROUNDWATER. The resulting fossil is thus a mixture of mineral and organic matter. In many other cases, **mineralization** (or **replacement**) occurs, where the hard parts are dissolved away but the form is retained by deposited minerals. Where this has happened very gradually, even microscopic detail may be preserved; but generally only the outward form remains.

Exceptional fossils are those where the organism has been preserved in its entirety: e.g., MAMMOTHS in the Siberian PERMAFROST, or insects in AMBER (though dehydrated). Sometimes teeth and shells may be preserved unaltered.

Often the organism is dissolved entirely, so that only a cast or impression remains in the rock. In the process of **carbonization**, the tissues decompose leaving only a thin CARBON film that shows the outline of the organism's form. (See also PALEONTOLOGY; PREHISTORIC ANIMALS; PREHISTORIC MAN; RADIOCARBON DATING.)

FOSTER, Sir George Eulas (1847–1931), Canadian statesman; minister of trade and commerce 1911–21, and representative at the Paris Peace Conference (1918–19). He was vice-president of the first Assembly of the League of Nations (1920–21).

FOSTER, Stephen Collins (1826–1864), US composer of over 200 songs and instrumental pieces. His *Oh! Susannah*, *My Old Kentucky Home* and *Old Black Joe* and other Southern dialect songs are essentially so simple that they are often considered folk music.

FOSTER, William Zebulon (1881–1961), US communist leader, organizer of the 1919 steel strike. He joined the Communist Party (c1921) and was its candidate for president (1924; 1928; 1932) and for governor of N.Y. (1930).

FOSTORIA, city in NW Ohio, 34mi S of Toledo. A manufacturing city, where Fostoria glass was first made. Pop 16307.

FOUCAULT, Jean Bernard Léon (1819–1868), French physicist best known for showing the rotation of the earth with the FOUCAULT PENDULUM, inventing the GYROSCOPE and for the first reasonably accurate determination of the velocity of LIGHT.

FOUCAULT PENDULUM, a PENDULUM comprising an iron ball at the end of a long steel wire which, on being set swinging, maintains its direction of swing while the earth rotates beneath it. When one was demonstrated by J. B. L. FOUCAULT in 1851, it provided the first direct evidence for the rotation of the earth. Foucault pendulums are demonstrated in several major science museums.

FOUCHÉ, Joseph (1759–1820), French revolutionary and police minister. As a member of the National Convention, he voted for Louis XVI's execution (1793). He helped overthrow ROBESPIERRE (1794) and supported the JACOBINS 1795–99, deserting them to back Napoleon. He served the BOURBONS briefly after 1815 but was exiled as a regicide in 1816.

FOU-HSIN (Fusin), city in NW Liaoning province, Manchuria, NE China. It is situated in a major coal mining and agricultural area. Pop 290000.

FOULARD, a lightweight twill or plain-woven silk fabric, used for scarves and dresses; also, a garment

The Foucault Pendulum in the hall of the United Nations building in New York, a gift from the Dutch government. The path the pendulum follows as it oscillates serves as a constant reminder of the rotation of the earth.

made of foulard. Imitation foulards are made of mercerized cotton or synthetic fibers.

FOUNDATIONS, nonprofit corporations or charitable trusts which distribute private wealth for public purposes. Though primarily modern institutions, foundations have a long history, from the ENDOWMENT set up for the library at Alexandria in Hellenistic Egypt, through medieval church charitable funds, to funds set up by Benjamin Franklin in the 18th century. A pioneer in the field was Andrew CARNEGIE, who gave about $300 million to funds and set an example for John D. ROCKEFELLER and Henry Ford. There are approximately 22 000 charitable foundations in the US. The larger ones, such as the FORD FOUNDATION, have a wide social impact. Foundations are usually financed from invested capital. Those which use only income from investments are called perpetuities. Liquidating foundations must use their capital and income within a specified time limit.

FOUNDING. See CASTING.

FOUNTAIN, a device which allows water to flow into a basin, or a more complex system from which water is forced into the air through a jet or jets. Fountains were used in ancient Greece as shrines and as public water supply points and by the Romans both to supply water and as civic decoration. The Italian Renaissance opened a new era of grandeur in fountain design. These featured tiered basins and elaborate sculptures and tableaus. BERNINI's Baroque Fountain of the Rivers (1648–51) and the Trevi Fountain (1762) are among Rome's many famous fountains. Other fine examples are those by LE NÔTRE at VERSAILLES in France, and by the modern designer Carl MILLES in New York and Chicago.

FOUNTAIN OF YOUTH, a rejuvenating spring located according to legend on the BIMINI ISLANDS off the coast of Fla. The Spaniard PONCE DE LEON discovered Florida in 1513, probably on an expedition to find the fountain.

FOUNTAIN VALLEY, city in SW Cal., 28mi SE of Los Angeles, named for its artesian wells. It has light industries. Pop 31 826.

FOUQUET, Jean (c1415–1481?), French painter who helped bring the Italian Renaissance style to France. His miniatures, panels, portraits and manuscript illuminations are realistic and precisely-detailed. One of his finest works is the *Melun Diptych* (c1450).

FOUR-COLOR PROBLEM, an unsolved topological (see TOPOLOGY) problem concerning the minimum number of colors required to color any map on a PLANE surface such that no two adjoining regions are in the same color. It can be proved that five colors will always be sufficient; and one can easily draw maps requiring more than three colors; but a general proof that four colors will always be sufficient has not yet been given. On non-plane surfaces, more colors may be required: a map on a TORUS, for example, may require up to seven.

FOUR-EYED FISHES, freshwater fishes of the family Anablepidae, found in Middle America, which appear to have two pairs of eyes. In fact, each eye is divided horizontally into two parts, one for vision in air and one for vision under water. They include the *Anablebs*.

FOUR FREEDOMS, freedom of speech, freedom of worship, freedom from want, freedom from fear. These principles were first presented by President Roosevelt in 1941 as a basis for world peace. After WWII the freedoms became enshrined in the UN Charter. (See DECLARATION OF HUMAN RIGHTS.)

FOUR-H CLUBS, educational organizations for young people from 9–19 years, who live primarily in rural areas. Started in 1914 by the US Department of Agriculture, the clubs undertake projects in farming, home economy, science and community services. The four "H's" are contained in the oath: "I pledge my *head* to clearer thinking, my *heart* to greater loyalty, my *hands* to larger service and my *health* to better living, for my club, my community and my country."

FOUR HORSEMEN OF THE APOCALYPSE, allegorical biblical figures in the book of Revelation (often called the Apocalypse) 6:1–8. The red horse's rider represents war, the black is famine, the pale horse death, while the rider on the white horse is usually taken to represent Christ.

FOUR HUNDRED, The, term used to describe elite society in New York City, or generally. The phrase is derived from Ward MCALLISTER's controversial comment (1892) that there were only about 400 important members of N.Y. society.

FOURIER, François Marie Charles (1772–1837), French Utopian socialist. Rejecting CAPITALISM, he devised a social system based on cooperative, primarily farming COMMUNES of about 400 families. Fourierism gained considerable following in France and the US, but attempts to put his theories into practice, as at BROOK FARM, were short-lived. (See also UTOPIA.)

FOURIER, Jean Baptiste Joseph, Baron (1768–1830), French mathematician best known for his equations of HEAT propagation and for showing that all periodic OSCILLATIONS can be reduced to a SERIES of simple, regular WAVE MOTIONS, as represented by Fourier Series, which have the general form

$$\tfrac{1}{2}a_0+\sum_{n=1}^{\infty}(a_n \cos nx + b_n \sin nx).$$

FOURNIER, Pierre Simon (1712–1768), French engraver and type founder. He devised the first point system for measuring type, designed several type faces and wrote *Manuel Typographique* (1764–66). (See also PRINTING; TYPOGRAPHY.)

FOUR-O'CLOCK PLANT, or marvel of Peru, *Mirabilis jalapa*, a tender perennial plant native to tropical America. It is widely cultivated as an annual for its trumpet-shaped flowers which open in the late afternoon. Family: Nyctaginaceae.

FOURTEEN POINTS, war objectives for the US, proposed by President Wilson in Jan. 1918, incorporated in the armistice of Nov. 1918. The points were that there should be: open covenants of peace; freedom of the seas; abolition of trade barriers; general disarmament; settlement of colonial claims; evacuation of conquered Russian territories; evacuation and restoration of Belgium; return of Alsace-Lorraine to France; readjustment of Italian frontiers; autonomy for the subject peoples of Austria-Hungary; guarantees for the integrity of Serbia, Montenegro and Rumania; autonomy for the subject peoples of the Ottoman Empire; an independent Poland; and a general association of nations. These points formed the basis of the Treaty of VERSAILLES and the LEAGUE OF NATIONS.

FOURTH DIMENSION. See SPACE-TIME.

FOURTH ESTATE, name for the public press, ranking it with the three traditional orders of society: the nobility, the clergy and the commonalty. The term, often wrongly attributed to Edmund Burke, was probably first used by MACAULAY, who wrote in 1828: "The gallery in which the reporters sit has become a fourth estate of the realm."

FOURTH OF JULY. See INDEPENDENCE DAY.

FOVEA, the tiny area in the macula (the area of the RETINA used for central VISION) where the retina is thinned of nonreceptor cells and there are no rods. The concentration of cones and lack of additional tissue makes this the most sensitive part of the retina for both acuity and color vision.

FOWLER, Henry Watson (1858–1933), distinguished English lexicographer, best-known for his masterly *A Dictionary of Modern English Usage* (1926). Fowler collaborated with his brother on several books, including *The Concise Oxford Dictionary of Current English* (1911).

FOX, Charles James (1749–1806), English statesman and orator, champion of political and religious freedom and fierce opponent of George III and the power of the crown. He served from 1768 as a Tory and as a Whig, both in and out of government and in coalitions. He championed the colonists in the REVOLUTIONARY WAR (1775–83) and in the 1790s supported the French Revolution.

FOX, George (1624–1691), English religious leader, founder of the Society of Friends or QUAKERS (1652). Although frequently harassed and imprisoned by the authorities, Fox traveled widely in Europe and North America preaching his doctrine—derived from his conversion experience (1646)—that truth comes through the inner light of Christ in the soul. (See also MYSTICISM.)

FOX, Luke (1586–1635), English navigator, who in 1631 attempted to find the NORTHWEST PASSAGE to the E. He returned to England unsuccessful, after exploring the Hudson Bay and Baffin Island area.

FOXBORO, town in SE Mass., 23mi SW of Boston. Settled in 1704, the town now manufactures time recording equipment. Pop 14 218.

FOXE, John (1516–1587), English Puritan, author of *The Book of Martyrs*, a history of English Protestant martyrs published in 1563 as the *Acts and Monuments of These Latter and Perilous Days* and officially installed in churches. Its general reliability has been vindicated. Forced to flee to Europe in Mary Tudor's reign, he was ordained in 1560.

FOXES, small members of the dog family Canidae, noted for their cunning and solitary habits; foxes feed mainly on small mammals. The common Red fox of the N Hemisphere is the quarry of British fox-hunts; American foxes include the Gray fox, the desert Kit fox and the now rare Swift fox. The Arctic fox lives in northern tundras and has a white winter coat. Africa offers the insect-eating Bat-eared fox and South America the Crab-eating fox.

FOXGLOVES, common name for plants of the genus *Digitalis*, which are native to Europe. *Digitalis purpurea*, the purple foxglove, is cultivated commercially as the source of the drug DIGITALIS. Family: Scrophulariaceae.

FOXHOUND, versatile, strong, fast hunting dog standing up to 25in at the shoulder, weighing up to 70lb, with a short coat that may be a mixture of black, tan and white. Usually kept in packs for FOX HUNTING, the American and English breeds are very similar.

FOX HUNTING, popular sport among horsemen in Britain, North America and elsewhere. Members of a hunt, led by a pack of foxhounds, pursue a wild fox to the death. The excitement of a chase comes from pitting the wits of the hounds against the fox. Hunts are often opposed by animal welfare and anti-blood-sports groups.

FOX INDIANS, small North American tribe of Algonquian stock related to the SAUK INDIANS. They were first contacted by white men in c1660 near Green Bay, Wis. The Fox took part in the BLACK HAWK WAR (1832), after which they moved to reservations in Kan. and then in Ia.

FOX ISLANDS, easternmost group of the ALEUTIAN ISLANDS, extending for about 300mi SW from the tip of the Alaska Peninsula.

FOX RIVER, river in SE central Wis. It rises in N Columbia Co. and flows about 175mi SW to a canal link with the Wisconsin R, then NE via Lake

Winnebago into Green Bay and Lake Michigan. The Mississippi-Wisconsin-Fox formed an important early water route to the Great Lakes.

FOXTAIL, common name for annual and perennial grasses of the genera *Alopecurus* and *Setaria*, the latter formerly being known as bristlegrasses. *Alopecurus pratensis*, the meadow foxtail, is widely cultivated as a forage crop in Europe and North America. Family: Poaceae.

FOX TALBOT, William Henry. See TALBOT, WILLIAM HENRY FOX.

FOX TERRIER, dog bred in smooth and wire-haired varieties, originally used in the 19th century by English fox hunters to pursue its quarry into its lair. It stands around 15in at the shoulder and is predominantly white, marked with black or tan.

FOXX, James Emory (1907–1967), US baseball player. Jimmy "the Beast" Foxx played (1926–45) for the Philadelphia Athletics, Boston Red Sox, Chicago Cubs and Philadelphia Phillies, hitting 534 home runs. He was elected to the Baseball Hall of Fame in 1951.

FRA ANGELICO. See ANGELICO, FRA.

FRACTION, a RATIONAL NUMBER that cannot be expressed as an INTEGER. Fractions are normally expressed either as RATIOS between two integers (e.g., $\frac{3}{4}$) or in the DECIMAL SYSTEM (e.g., 0.75). Fractions greater than 1 are usually expressed as an integer plus a fraction less than 1: e.g., $\frac{10}{9} = 1\frac{1}{9}$; $\frac{22}{3} = 7\frac{1}{3}$. Fractions less than -1 are treated analagously.

FRACTIONATION. See DISTILLATION.

FRACTURES, mechanical defects in BONE caused by trauma or underlying DISEASE. Most follow sudden bending, twisting or shearing forces, but prolonged stress (e.g., long marches) may lead to small fractures. Fractures may be *open*, in which bone damage is associated with SKIN damage, with consequent liability to infection; or *closed*, in which the overlying skin is intact. Comminuted fractures are those in which bone is broken into many fragments. *Greenstick* fractures are partial fractures where bone is bent, not broken, and occur in children. Severe pain, deformity, loss of function, abnormal mobility of a bone and HEMORRHAGE, causing swelling and possibly SHOCK, are important features; damage to nerves, ARTERIES and underlying viscera (e.g., LUNG, SPLEEN, LIVER and BRAIN) are serious complications. Principles of treatment are: reduction, or restoring the bone to satisfactory alignment, by manipulation or operation; immobilization, with plaster, splints or internal fixation with metal or bone prostheses, until bony healing has occurred, and rehabilitation, which enables full recovery of function in most cases. Early recognition and appropriate treatment of associated soft tissue injury is crucial. **Pathological fractures** occur when congenital defect, lack of mineral content, TUMORS etc. weaken the structure of bone, allowing fracture with trivial or no apparent injury.

FRAGONARD, Jean-Honoré (1732–1806), French ROCOCO painter, and noted portraitist. His work is characterized by a lightness of touch and a use of radiant color. Among his masterpieces are *The Swing* (1766) and *Fête at St. Cloud* (1775).

FRAMINGHAM, town in NE Mass., 18mi WSW of Boston. It manufactures chemicals, automobiles, paper products and carpets. Pop 64 048.

FRANCE, officially the French Republic, the largest country in W Europe, covering some 211 000sq mi. It is bordered on the N by the English Channel; on the NE by Belgium and Luxembourg; on the E by West Germany, Switzerland and Italy; on the S (where Monaco forms a small enclave) by the Mediterranean, Spain and Andorra; and on the W by the Atlantic Ocean; and it includes the island of Corsica. The whole area is known as metropolitan France, and is divided administratively into 95 departments grouped into 22 regions. In addition, the former colonies of Guadeloupe, French Guiana, Martinique and Réunion rank as overseas departments.

Land. More than 50% of metropolitan France is lowlying and less than 25% is highland. The main mountain ranges form natural frontiers: the Pyrenees in the SW, the French Alps (with Mont Blanc, 15 781ft, the highest peak in W Europe) in the SE, and the Jura and Vosges (separated by the Belfort Gap, an important routeway) in the E. A major physical feature is the Massif Central (central plateau) W of the Saône and Rhône rivers and terminated in the S by the Cévennes Mts. Its features include lava plateaus and *puys* (ash and lava cones). In the NW is the small and much lower Armorican Massif. The lowlands are mainly in the N and W and include the Paris Basin (about 29 000sq mi) between the English Channel and the Massif Central, the Ile-de-France, a fertile plateau and the triangular Aquitaine lowland in the SW.

Draining the country are five major river systems: the Seine (historically and commercially France's most important river), Loire, Garonne-Gironde, Rhône-Saône, and Rhine. Most have important canal links and some provide hydroelectric power, notably the Rhône. Coastal features include the *rias* (long inlets) of the Armorican Massif, the sand dunes and lagoons of the Landes in the SW, and the marshy lagoons of the Rhône delta.

The climate is mainly mild but has many regional variations. More than half of France has less than 80 days with frost annually and most areas average 20–50in of rain yearly. The Riviera and Corsica have a typically Mediterranean climate. Vegetation ranges from the beech and oak of N and central France to the drought-resistant scrub and wild olives of Mediterranean areas.

People. Due to invasions by Romans, Celts, Franks and Mediterranean peoples, the French are of mingled racial types. Distinctive groups include the Celtic Bretons of Brittany and the Basques living along the Spanish frontier. The population of over 52 600 000 also includes more than 750 000 Algerians and some 3 500 000 migrant workers, including many Spaniards and Italians. More than 70% of the population lives in the cities and towns; the largest is Paris, the capital. The Paris megapolis has more than 15% of the total population. Other large conurbations are Lyons, Marseilles and Lille-

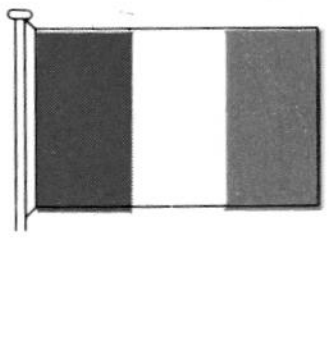

Official name: The French Republic
Capital: Paris
Area: 211 208sq mi
Population: 51 590 000
Languages: French
Religions: Catholic, Protestant, Jewish
Monetary unit(s): 1 French franc = 100 centimes

Roubaix-Tourcoing. People are increasingly moving from the rural areas into the towns.

Most French people are baptized Roman Catholic, but many of them are not practicing Catholics. Minority groups include Protestants, Jews and Muslims. The French are justly proud of their education system; illiteracy is negligible. French culture has had worldwide influence on social intercourse, diplomacy, learning, the arts and crafts and architecture since the Middle Ages.

Economy. France is a major agricultural and industrial country, leading W Europe in food production, especially grain, beef, sugar beets and wine. Leading crops include wheat (especially in the Paris Basin and Flanders), oats, rye and corn, sugar beets (Brittany and Flanders), rice (the Camargue) and all kinds of fruits. Millions of beef and dairy cattle, sheep and hogs are reared. The NW is known for its dairy products. France is the world's third-largest silk-producer and leads in the production of high-quality wines from such areas as Champagne, Bordeaux and lower Burgundy. About 20% of the land is forested, and fisheries, centered on such ports as Boulogne and Lorient, are important. France has coal (Nord, Pas de Calais, Lorraine), oil (Parentis), natural gas (Lacq), abundant iron ore (mainly Lorraine but also in Normandy), bauxite and other minerals. Industry includes iron and steel production, mainly in the N and E (especially Dunkerque) but also in the S (Fos-sur-Mer), oil refining (mainly of imported oil) and petrochemicals, aircraft and automobiles, textiles (Lyons, Roubaix, Lille, Tourcoing, Castres), clothing and most other consumer products. Paris is the chief manufacturing center. Tourism is important, and so is the production of high fashion clothing, gloves, perfume, jewelry and watches.

History. Among early inhabitants were the Stone Age hunter-painters of such caves as Lascaux (Dordogne) and the megalith builders in Brittany. Greeks founded Marseilles about 600 BC. The country was progressively settled and unified under the Gauls, Romans, Franks, and Charlemagne. On Charlemagne's death (814 AD) his empire disintegrated and feudal rulers became powerful. Their territories were increasingly welded together under the CAPETIANS (987–1328), and the HUNDRED YEARS' WAR (1338–1453) saw the eviction of the English. Under Louis XI (1461–83) and later monarchs, royal power was strengthened, reaching its zenith with Louis XIV (1643–1715). Continuing royal extravagance culminated in the French Revolution (1789), the execution of Louis XVI and the establishment of the First Republic. The Bourbon restoration following on the downfall of Napoleon (1815) was short-lived and Louis Philippe was put on the throne (July Revolution, 1830). After his deposition, Louis Napoleon headed the Second Republic (1848), then made himself Emperor Napoleon III (1852). Defeat in the Franco-Prussian War (1870) led to his downfall and to the Third Republic. WWI left France victorious but devastated and in WWII the country was occupied by Germany (1940). The Fourth Republic (1946) proved unstable and Gen. Charles DE GAULLE was recalled to head the Fifth Republic (1958). The once-great French empire was now breaking up, though some remnants still remain under French rule—Afars and Issas, French Polynesia, New Caledonia, Comores, Saint-Pierre and Miquelon, Wallis and Futuna Islands, the Southern and Antarctic Territories (see also NEW HEBRIDES). When De Gaulle resigned over a constitutional issue (1969), his successor as president was another Gaullist, Georges POMPIDOU, who was concerned with modernizing the French nation. When Pompidou died (1974), Valéry GISCARD D'ESTAING was elected to the presidency and dedicated himself to preserving what was best in French society while removing many of the injustices and abuses.

FRANCE, Anatole (Jacques Anatole François Thibault; 1844–1924), French novelist and critic, a renowned stylist. Though he believed in and worked for social justice, his work is deeply pessimistic. Among his best-known books are *Penguin Island* (1908) and *The Revolt of the Angels* (1914). He won the 1921 Nobel literature prize.

FRANCESCA, Piero della. See PIERO DELLA FRANCESCA.

FRANCESCA DA RIMINI (d. 1285?), Italian beauty, immortalized in DANTE's *Divine Comedy (Inferno)*. She married the Lord of Rimini but then fell in love with his brother Paolo. When Rimini found this out he killed them both.

FRANCHISE, in business, a contractual privilege such as a public utility contract awarded by a municipality, or the right to open a store under the trade-name of a chain.

FRANCHISE. See ELECTION; VOTING.

FRANCIS, name of two Holy Roman Emperors. **Francis I** (1708–1765), Holy Roman Emperor from 1745, was consort of Maria Theresa of Austria from 1736. **Francis II** (1768–1835), last Holy Roman Emperor (1792–1806) and first emperor of Austria (from 1804). Defeated by Napoleon in 1796, 1805 (AUSTERLITZ) and 1809, he then sided with him until 1813, when he joined the anti-Napoleonic side. At the CONGRESS OF VIENNA, through the diplomacy of

METTERNICH, he regained most of the Austrian territories.

FRANCIS, two kings of France. **Francis I** (1494–1547), king from 1515, strengthened royal power at the expense of the nobility. He conducted costly wars against the Hapsburgs, including abortive Italian campaigns. He suppressed Protestantism but fostered Renaissance ideals; he was a great patron of art and letters, and a great builder of palaces. **Francis II** (1544–1560), king from 1559, first husband of MARY QUEEN OF SCOTS. A weak-willed man, he was dominated by the House of Guise and his mother, Catherine de MEDICI.

FRANCIS BORGIA, Saint (1510–1572), fourth duke of Gandia in Spain. He joined the JESUITS in 1546, disposing of his estates. He became Commissar General for Spain, Portugal and the Indies, and in 1565 third General of the order. His feast day is Oct. 10.

FRANCISCANS, largest order in the Roman Catholic Church. Three orders were founded by St. FRANCIS OF ASSISI in 1209. They were called Grey Friars for the color of their habits; modern habits are dark brown. Dissension within the First Order divided it into three main branches, the Observants, Conventuals and CAPUCHINS. The Second Order are nuns, known as Poor Clares for their foundress St. Clare. The Third Order is mainly a lay fraternity, but some members live in community under vows.

FRANCIS FERDINAND. See FRANZ FERDINAND.

FRANCIS JOSEPH. See FRANZ JOSEF.

FRANCIS OF ASSISI, Saint (c1181–1226), Italian Roman Catholic mystic, founder of the FRANCISCANS. In 1205 he turned away from his extravagant life and wealthy merchant family to a wandering religious life of utter poverty. With his many followers he preached and ministered to the poor in Italy and abroad, stressing piety, simplicity and joy in creation, and the love of all living things. Given oral sanction by Pope Innocent III, his order expanded beyond the control of its founder; he relinquished the leadership in 1221. His feast day is Oct. 4.

FRANCIS OF SALES, Saint (1567–1622), Roman Catholic bishop of Geneva-Annecy from 1603. Author of popular works such as *Introduction to the Devout Life* (1608), he was respected even by the Calvinists for his good nature and humility. He helped found the Order of the Visitation (1610). His feast day is Jan. 24.

FRANCIS XAVIER, Saint (1506–1552), Spanish missionary. A friend of St. Ignatius LOYOLA, he was a founder member of the JESUITS. In 1541 he set out as a missionary, reaching the East Indies, Goa, India, Malacca and Ceylon. In 1549 he established a Jesuit mission in Japan and in 1552 sought to extend his work to China, but died before he reached there. His feast day is Dec. 3.

Photograph of Anne Frank and a fragment of one of the pages of her famous diary. This entry, in Dutch, was written on October 18, 1942.

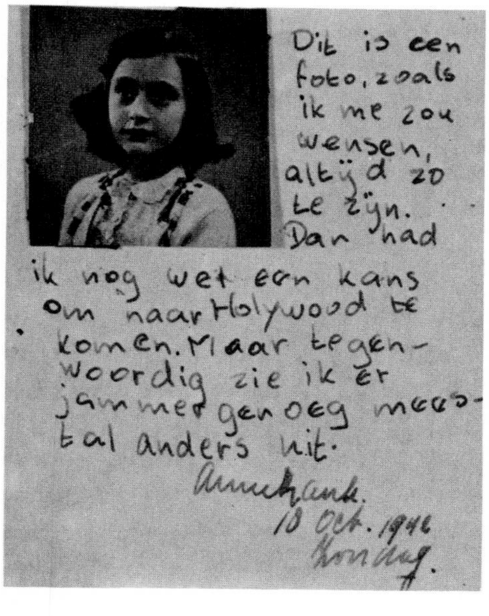

FRANCIUM (Fr), a radioactive ALKALI METAL, resembling CESIUM, which has been obtained only in tracer quantities. Its most stable isotope, Fr^{223}, has a half-life of 21 minutes.

FRANCK, César Auguste (1822–1890), Belgian-French composer. Organist of St. Clotilde, Paris, from 1858, he became a professor at the Paris Conservatory in 1872. Though at first little appreciated, his compositions greatly influenced French Romantic music. Among his famous works are the tone poem *The Accursed Hunter* (1882) and the *Symphony in D minor* (1888).

FRANCK, James (1882–1964), German physicist who shared with G. HERTZ the 1925 Nobel Prize for Physics for their experiments showing the internal structure of the atom to be quantized (see QUANTUM THEORY). With E. V. Condon, he was responsible for the **Franck-Condon principle**, which assumes that the nuclei in vibrating molecules do not have time to move during electronic transitions.

FRANCO, Francisco (1892–1975), Spanish general, *caudillo* (Spanish: leader, head of state) of Spain from 1939. Kept in foreign commands by left-wing governments, he joined the 1936 military revolt in Spain from Morocco and in 1937 became leader of the FALANGE party. After the fall of leftist-held Madrid he became head of state. Although he had been aided against the Soviet-backed Loyalists by Germany and Italy he remained neutral in WWII. In the postwar period his rule became less totalitarian but he retained all his power. In the late 1960s increasing unrest caused him to harden the regime once more; he remained in control until shortly before his death, when he was succeeded by Prince JUAN CARLOS as king.

FRANCOLINS, birds closely related to partridges, up to 300mm (12in) long. They have large bills and most are dull brown in color. Five species are found in Asia and 36 in Africa.

FRANCONIA MOUNTAINS, western range of the White Mts, W N.H. The highest peak is Mount Lafayette (5 249ft) on the E side of the FRANCONIA NOTCH.

FRANCONIA NOTCH, gorge 6mi long between the Franconia and Kinsman Mts., N.H. The Pemigewasset R flows through it. Granite formations and mountain scenery make the area a beauty spot.

FRANCO-PRUSSIAN WAR (July 1870–May 1871), arose from BISMARCK's desire to unify the German states against a common enemy and NAPOLEON III's fear of an alliance against him if a Prussian prince succeeded to the Spanish throne. Provoked by the EMS DISPATCH, France declared war; the more efficient Prussians trapped a large French army at Metz, and in Sept. 1870 captured the main French army and Napoleon himself at Sedan. The Second Empire fell and Paris was besieged; despite vigorous resistance led by Leon GAMBETTA it capitulated in Jan. 1871. William II of Prussia was declared German emperor at Versailles. The PARIS COMMUNE revolt followed. In the treaty, France lost Alsace-Lorraine and incurred crushing indemnities.

FRANGIPANI, shrubs and small trees of the genus *Plumeria*, family Apocynaceae. They are native to Middle America, but are widely cultivated for their ornamental flowers that may be produced all the year round.

FRANK, Anne (1929–1945), German Jewish girl who with her family lived in hiding from the Nazis in Amsterdam 1942–44; betrayed and sent to a concentration camp, she died there of typhus. Her diary, published in 1947, provided the material for a popular play and film.

FRANK, Ilya Mikhailovich (1908–), Russian physicist who, with TAMM, provided an explanation for CERENKOV RADIATION (1937), first observed by CHERENKOV (1934). For their work all three shared the 1958 Nobel Prize in Physics.

FRANKENSTEIN, novel by Mary SHELLEY. In an attempt to recreate life, its title character makes a hideous, suffering creature who wavers between good and evil and finally kills his creator. The name has become attached to the creature, particularly as portrayed on film by Boris KARLOFF.

A flowering frangipani tree with its small fragrant blossoms—used in India to decorate temples. Although the American variety originated in Central America, it now grows in other warm regions.

FRANKFORT, city in central Ind., seat of Clinton Co. Its economy rests on oil refining and heavy manufacturing. Pop 14 596.

FRANKFORT, city in central Ky., capital of the commonwealth and seat of Franklin Co. It has various industries, especially whiskey distilling, and is the trading center of the surrounding agricultural area. Pop 21 902.

FRANKFURT AM MAIN, historic city on the Main R in West Germany, since medieval times a world center of commerce, industry and finance. Its prosperity was founded on the textile trade, and on the great medieval trade fairs; the city remained independent until taken by Prussia in 1866. It was largely devastated in WWII but some old buildings, including its Gothic cathedral, still survive. A major river port, it is a rail and road junction with Germany's busiest airport. It has a wide range of industries. Pop 669 600.

FRANKFURT AN DER ODER, industrial city in East Germany, on the Oder R, S of Berlin. It has been seriously depopulated since WWII. Pop 62 011.

FRANKFURTER, Felix (1882–1965), US Supreme Court Justice 1939–62, legal adviser to presidents Wilson and F. D. Roosevelt. Known for his liberal views, he advocated the doctrine of judicial restraint, minimizing the judiciary's role in the process of government; he was equally opposed to attempts to obstruct "progressive" legislation and to attempts to further it by undue interpretation.

FRANKINCENSE, an aromatic gum produced from the trunks of trees of the genus *Boswellia*. It is used as INCENSE, for fumigation and in perfumes, and was once thought to have medicinal properties. It was one of the MAGI's gifts to the infant Jesus.

FRANKLIN, city in central Ind., seat of Johnson Co. It has various industries and processes agricultural produce from the surrounding area. Pop 11 477.

FRANKLIN, township in E Mass., an industrial and trade center for an agricultural area. Pop 17 830.

FRANKLIN, industrial city in SW Ohio. Pop 10 075.

FRANKLIN, city in SE Wis., a residential suburb of Milwaukee. Pop 12 247.

FRANKLIN, Benjamin (1706–1790), American writer, printer, philosopher, scientist and politician of the American revolution. Tolerant, urbane and intellectual, he combined the spirit of the ENLIGHTENMENT with his puritan upbringing. Born of a poor family in Boston, Mass., he moved to Philadelphia (1723) and married Deborah Read, by whom he had two children. By his own efforts he made enough money as a publisher and printer to retire at the age of 42 and devote himself entirely to writing, science and public life. His writings include letters, journals, satires, economic and social essays, a revealing *Autobiography* and the aphoristic *Poor Richard's Almanack* (1732). A founder of the American

Philosophical Society (1743), he was an enthusiastic researcher and inventor. Experiments in electrostatics (1750–51) led to his famous kite experiment, which proved that lightning was a form of electricity; from this he invented the lightning conductor. He also invented bifocal spectacles, the glass harmonica and the efficient Franklin stove, and developed theories of electricity, heat absorption, meteorology and ocean currents.

In Philadelphia's civic affairs he helped found an insurance company, a hospital, a night watch and in 1747 the first militia. He became deputy postmaster general of the colonies (1753) and in 1754 organized defenses in the FRENCH AND INDIAN WARS. His respect for Britain declined when he lived there as a colonial agent 1757–75.

When he returned home, he helped draft the Declaration of Independence. He was the rebel colonies' commissioner in the French court from 1776 and his diplomatic skill gained them vital French support in the war. He led the independence negotiations and returned home in 1785 to serve as president of the Pennsylvania Executive Council. Franklin supported the abolition of slavery and at 81 attended the Constitutional Convention, where despite ill-health he helped formulate the compromise that made the US Constitution possible.

FRANKLIN, District of, in the NORTHWEST TERRITORIES, Canada, is 549 253sq mi in area. It includes the Boothia and Melville peninsulas and the sparsely populated islands N of the Canadian mainland.

FRANKLIN, John Hope (1915–), US Negro historian, educator and author of books on Negro history, including *From Slavery to Freedom* (1947) and *The Emancipation Proclamation* (1963).

FRANKLIN, Sir John (1786–1847), British rear admiral and explorer who in expeditions during 1819–22 and 1825–27 charted much territory from Hudson Bay N to the Arctic. He set out in 1845 with two ships to find the NORTHWEST PASSAGE; trapped in the ice, the entire expedition perished and was not traced until 1859.

FRANKLIN, State of, self-proclaimed US state 1784–88, named for Benjamin Franklin. Statehood was sought by the inhabitants of territory ceded by N.C., to the federal government. John SEVIER was elected governor, but Congress refused to recognize Franklin. It broke up in disorder, but was incorporated into Tenn. with Sevier as governor, in 1796.

FRANKLIN PARK, village in Ill., an industrial suburb NW of Chicago. Pop 20 497.

FRANKLIN'S GULL, *Larus pipixcan*, a gull found in large colonies on inland marshes of the western prairies of the US and Canada. Known as the prairie dove, Franklin's gull feeds on insects, and is small with a dark head.

FRANKLIN SQUARE, incorporated community in

Left: a lithograph of the famous portrait of Benjamin Franklin, by his contemporary the French painter Joseph S. Duplessis. It is now in the Boston Museum of Fine Arts. Benjamin Franklin is buried in the Christ Church cemetery, Philadelphia (*above*). His grave lies alongside those of other signatories of the Declaration of Independence: Francis Hopkinson, Benjamin Rush, Joseph Hewes and George Ross.

SE N.Y., in the town of Hempstead on Long Island. Pop 32 156.

FRANKS, Germanic tribes, living originally E of the Rhine. In the 3rd–5th centuries AD they repeatedly invaded Gaul and finally overran it. CLOVIS I united the disparate tribes under his rule, founding the Christian MEROVINGIAN dynasty; this was weakened by internal conflict, and finally deposed by the CAROLINGIANS in the 8th century. Under the rule of CHARLEMAGNE the Franks reached the height of their power. France and Franconia in Germany are named for them.

FRANZ FERDINAND (1863–1914), Archduke of Austria and heir to the Austro-Hungarian Empire. His children's right of succession was forfeited by his morganatic marriage to Sophie Chotek of the lesser nobility. Their assassination at Sarajevo triggered off WWI.

FRANZ JOSEF (1830–1916), Emperor of Austria from 1848 and King of Hungary from 1867. He came to the throne in a year of revolutions and was at first highly absolutist. He suppressed a Hungarian revolt in 1849, but in 1867 further unrest forced him to create the Dual Monarchy, giving Hungary internal autonomy. Alliance with Germany (1879) and Italy (1882) created the TRIPLE ALLIANCE. His harsh policies against Serbia were among the causes of WWI. A conservative autocrat but a patron of arts and learning, he was generally liked and respected by his subjects.

FRANZ JOSEF LAND, archipelago in the Arctic, owned by the USSR but discovered by Austria in 1873. It consists of about 187 islands; they have scanty vegetation, but abundant bird life, and are the site of Soviet weather stations.

FRASCH PROCESS, process for extracting SULFUR from sulfur-bearing CALCITE deposits, invented by Herman Frasch in 1891. Three concentric pipes are lowered down a bore-hole to the ore. Superheated water at 165°C is pumped down the outer pipe and compressed hot air is blown down the inner pipe. This forces a frothy mixture of molten sulfur and water up the middle pipe. Very pure sulfur is produced.

FRASER, city in SE Mich., an industrial suburb of Detroit. Pop 11 868.

FRASER, James Earle (1876–1953), US sculptor. He studied in Chicago, and is now known mainly for his monumental bronze *The End of the Trail* (1915), and for his design for the Indian-head nickel.

FRASER, Simon (1776–1862), Canadian fur-trader who in establishing a chain of trading posts explored the interior of British Columbia. In 1808 he sailed down most of the British Columbia R (now the FRASER RIVER). In 1816 he was acquitted of the massacre of the RED RIVER SETTLEMENT.

FRASER RIVER, in British Columbia, rises in the Rocky Mts and flows in a winding course around the Cariboo Mts to the Strait of Georgia S of Vancouver. About 850mi in length, it is named for Simon FRASER.

FRAUD, in law a willful deception with intent to deprive the deceived of something of value. It is actionable both under criminal and civil law; in COMMON LAW a milder form, deceit, is only actionable under civil law. The deception may be an explicit lie, a concealment or a statement made in reckless disregard of its likely accuracy.

FRAUNCES TAVERN, historic building in New York City. A tavern in Revolutionary times, it was named for its owner, the West Indian "Black Sam" Fraunces. A rendezvous for patriot groups, it was Washington's headquarters in Dec. 1783. Since 1904 it has been a museum run by the Sons of the Revolution.

FRAUNHOFER, Joseph von (1787–1826), German optician who mapped the dark lines (FRAUNHOFER LINES) in the solar spectrum and reinvented the DIFFRACTION grating.

FRAUNHOFER LINES, dark lines that appear in the SPECTRUM of the SUN. They are due to the ABSORPTION of the radiation of particular FREQUENCIES (and thus ENERGIES) by ATOMS in the outer layers of the solar ATMOSPHERE. Analysis of the solar spectrum thus leads to the identification of these atoms. The lines were first accurately mapped by J. von FRAUNHOFER. The more prominent are denoted by letters: A and B being due to terrestrial OXYGEN; C to HYDROGEN; D to SODIUM; E to IRON, and so on.

FRAZER, Sir James George (1854–1941), British social anthropologist. In *The Golden Bough: A Study in Magic and Religion* (1890; enlarged 1907–15) he proposed a parallel evolution of thought in all peoples: from magic through religion to science, each with its distinct notion of cause and effect. Despite the apparent error of his conclusions, his work in surveying primitive customs and beliefs was of great value to cultural anthropology.

FRAZIER, Edward Franklin (1894–1962), US sociologist, known for his studies of US Negroes, particularly *The Negro Family in the United States* (1939), which examines the effects of slavery and persecution on Negro family life.

FRAZIER, Joe (1944–), US boxer declared world champion in 1970 after Muhammad ALI's deposition. His title was disputed, but he defeated Ali in the ring in 1971. In 1973 he lost the title to George Foreman.

FRECKLE, small brown pigmented spot in the SKIN of exposed areas, numerous in some individuals; they are brought out by sunlight and are benign.

FREDERICK, city in N Md., seat of Frederick Co. An agricultural market center, it has an important lime-cement industry. Pop 23 641.

FREDERICK, name of three Holy Roman Emperors. **Frederick I Barbarossa** (c1123–1190) was elected king of Germany in 1152. Having pacified Germany, he occupied Lombardy and was crowned king of Italy in 1154 and Holy Roman Emperor in 1155. He was drowned while leading the Third Crusade, and passed into legend as Germany's savior. **Frederick II** (1194–1250) became king of Sicily in 1198 and of Germany in 1211. He was crowned Holy Roman Emperor in 1220. Made titular king of Jerusalem in 1227, he acquired territory in the Holy Land and was crowned in 1229. He was continually at odds with the papacy and was excommunicated three times. A capable administrator, scholar and patron of the arts, he went into a decline after a serious defeat at Parma in 1248. **Frederick III** (1415–1493) was chosen king of Germany in 1440 and obtained election as Holy Roman Emperor in 1452 by making concessions to the papacy, weakening the Empire.

FREDERICK, name of nine kings of Denmark; six also ruled Norway, ceded to Sweden in 1814. **Frederick I** (1471–1533), reigned from 1523. **Frederick II** (1534–1588), reigned from 1559. **Frederick III** (1609–1670), king from 1648, established the monarchy as hereditary and absolute rather than elective. **Frederick IV** (1671–1730), reigned from 1699. **Frederick V** (1723–1766), reigned from 1746. **Frederick VI** (1768–1839), was regent 1783–1808. Slavery and serfdom were abolished in his reign. His policy of neutrality and then support for Napoleon I led to crushing English attacks on Copenhagen and the cession of Norway to

Sweden. **Frederick VII** (1808–1863), king from 1848, agreed to a constitution creating a constitutional monarchy in 1849. **Frederick VIII** (1843–1912), reigned from 1906. **Frederick IX** (1889–1972), remained in Denmark during the German occupation and actively supported the resistance. He acceded in 1947.

FREDERICK, name of three kings of Prussia. **Frederick I** (1657–1713), Elector of Brandenburg from 1688, sought the title of king from the Emperor Leopold I. In 1700 he obtained it in exchange for military aid and crowned himself king of Prussia, the major part of his domain, in 1701. **Frederick II the Great** (1712–1786), was one of the greatest 18th century monarchs. As a boy his inclinations were artistic rather than military. His father, Frederick William II, resented this and so maltreated the prince that he attempted to escape. He was captured, imprisoned and forced to watch the execution of a friend. Eventually he was readmitted to court and succeeded his father in 1740. He almost immediately used his father's strong army to win Silesia from Austria, thus precipitating the War of the AUSTRIAN SUCCESSION. There followed a period of peace, which he used to strengthen Prussia, encouraging both arts and commerce. Fearing attack by an alliance of Austria, Russia and France, he made a preemptive attack on Saxony in 1756, beginning the SEVEN YEARS' WAR, from which Prussia emerged unscathed but exhausted. Frederick rebuilt the economy at considerable personal expense. Through the partition of Poland and the War of the Bavarian Succession he made further territorial gains for Prussia. By the end of his reign he had doubled the country's area and left it rich, powerful, more humanely governed and dominant in Germany. **Frederick III** (1831–1888), son of Emperor William I, was a cultivated and liberal man. A distinguished army commander, he was a determined opponent of BISMARCK's imperial policies. Much was expected of his reign, but he died of cancer only three months after his coronation.

FREDERICK, Harold (1856–1898), US journalist and author, best known for his realistic novels of life in upstate N.Y., such as *The Copperhead* (1893), and *The Damnation of Theron Ware* (1896) about a young clergyman's loss of faith.

FREDERICKA, Fort. See FORT FREDERICKA NATIONAL MONUMENT.

FREDERICK BARBAROSSA. See FREDERICK I (Holy Roman Emperor).

FREDERICK HENRY (1584–1647), Prince of Orange and Stadholder of the Dutch Republic from 1625, the son of William the Silent. His military success against the Spanish led to a treaty in 1647 in which they effectively capitulated to the Dutch nationalists.

FREDERICKSBURG, a residential town on the Rappahannock R in NE Va., 41mi SW of Alexandria. Pop 14450.

FREDERICKSBURG, Battle of, Confederate victory in the Civil War, at Fredericksburg, Va., on Dec. 13, 1862. Outnumbered Confederate forces under Gen. Robert E. LEE inflicted heavy casualties on the Union Army of the Potomac, led by Gen. BURNSIDE.

FREDERICK THE GREAT. See FREDERICK II (King of Prussia).

FREDERICK WILLIAM (1620–1688), Elector of Brandenburg from 1640, known as the Great Elector. By skillful shifting of alliances in an attempt to establish a balance of power he was able to shield his country from the worst of the THIRTY YEARS' WAR and add Prussia to Brandenburg. This and the modern army he created laid the foundations for the country's future predominance in Germany.

FREDERICK WILLIAM, name of four kings of Prussia. **Frederick William I** (1688–1740), king from 1713, centralized and radically reformed his administration. He spent freely on building up a powerful army but was otherwise frugal to the point of miserliness. **Frederick William II** (1744–1797), reigned from 1786. Nephew of Frederick the Great, he lacked his uncle's military and administrative skill, being most noted as a patron of the arts. Prussia made large territorial gains in his reign, however, by inheritance and through the partition of Poland. **Frederick William III** (1770–1840), reigned from 1797. He resisted demands for internal reforms until the collapse of Prussia in the Napoleonic Wars. **Frederick William IV** (1795–1861), reigned from 1840, a time of unrest and the growth of the movement for German unity. He resisted most demands for reform until forced by the 1848 revolution to make drastic changes.

FREDERICTON, capital city of New Brunswick, Canada, and seat of York Co. An administrative and trade center, it also has some light industry. The U. of New Brunswick was founded here in 1785. Pop 24254.

FREDONIA, village in the township of Pomfret, W N.Y. Its economy rests mainly on the area's vineyards. Pop 10326.

FREDONIAN REBELLION, first attempt to make the Tex. area independent of Mexico. After a dispute over land titles with the Mexican government, Benjamin Edwards, a settler from La., took over the town of Nacogdoches on the Mexican border but was forced to flee when Mexican troops approached.

FREE ASSOCIATION, the ideas which occur spontaneously in the CONSCIOUSNESS without concentration on the part of the individual. The encouragement in a patient of free ASSOCIATION is one of the primary techniques of PSYCHOANALYSIS.

FREE CITY, (German: *freie Stadt*), town in the medieval HOLY ROMAN EMPIRE free of all except imperial rule and not liable to pay taxes. Among the greatest of these were Nuremberg, Augsburg, Hamburg and Frankfurt. Their independence lasted from the 13th to the 17th century, and many became great trade and cultural centers.

FREEDMEN'S BUREAU, the US Bureau of Refugees, Freedmen and Abandoned Lands (1865–72), established during RECONSTRUCTION to act as a welfare agency for freed slaves in the South. It was headed by Major O. O. HOWARD. Handicapped by inadequate funding and personnel, the bureau nevertheless built Negro hospitals, schools and colleges. It had little success in improving civil rights, due to judicial and congressional hostility; its influence had declined by the time it was dissolved.

FREEDOM OF THE PRESS, right of private individuals to print and distribute information and opinions without interference, subject only to laws against indecency, libel and in extreme cases sedition. (See also BILL OF RIGHTS.)

FREEDOM OF RELIGION, right to believe and worship freely, without legal restraint. Religious practices considered contrary to public interest, such as Mormon POLYGAMY, are usually forbidden in the US. (See also BILL OF RIGHTS; FOUR FREEDOMS).

FREEDOM OF SPEECH, right to express facts and opinions without legal restraint. In practice this is usually limited by the laws of libel, and in extreme cases sedition. (See also BILL OF RIGHTS; FOUR FREEDOMS).

FREEDOM OF THE SEAS, concept in international law to describe the legal status of the high seas as free from the sovereignty of any nation. The high seas are held to be those areas outside the territorial waters of all nations. The concept has never been generally accepted and is increasingly called into question in the matter of sea and seabed resources, such as fish and minerals.

FREE ENTERPRISE SYSTEM, economic doctrine advocating unrestricted freedom for individuals and companies to determine what they produce and how. It relies upon competition and the discrimination of the consumer market to check abuses of this freedom. (See also CAPITALISM.)

FREEHOLD, borough in E N.J., seat of Monmouth Co. Its economy rests on truck farming and home light industry. Pop 10545.

FREEHOLD, in law, an interest in property involving ownership, as opposed to leasehold, in which the property is leased (see LEASE). Freehold in fee simple is as absolute an ownership of land as the law allows; freehold with a life estate is ownership for life only.

FREEMASONRY. See MASONRY.

FREE-PISTON ENGINE, a type of DIESEL ENGINE in which the power output is extracted from a TURBINE driven by the exhaust gases and not via any direct rod and crank drive. The combustion chamber is formed between two opposed pistons in a closed metal tube, the pistons oscillating in and out in phase with each other, regularly exposing the exhaust and air-inlet ports. Fuel is injected at the midpoint. The engine, which has a good power-to-weight ratio and is used in some ships, has the advantage that the gasifier and turbine units need not be sited adjacently.

FREE PORT, area, usually part of a port or airport, in which goods may be imported, handled or fabricated without coming under customs regulations and incurring duty. The concession is extended to attract a greater volume of trade and promote use of the port's facilities.

FREEPORT, city in NW Ill., seat of Stephenson Co. During the railroad boom it became an important trade and shipping center, and now has many light industries. Pop 27736.

FREEPORT, village in SE N.Y. on the S shore of Long Island. A residential community, it has some light manufacturing. Pop 40374.

FREEPORT, city at the mouth of the Brazos R, SE Tex. A deepwater port, it serves the Brazosport industrial complex. Pop 11997.

FREEPORT DOCTRINE, doctrine advanced by Stephen A. DOUGLAS during a series of debates with Abraham Lincoln at Freeport, Ill. in 1858, holding that in spite of the DRED SCOTT CASE slavery could be barred by local legislatures. This lost him much support in the South.

FREER, Charles Lang (1856–1919), US industrialist and art collector. He built the Freer Gallery in Washington, D.C. to house the magnificent art collection, including the world's largest collection of WHISTLER's work, that he gave to the SMITHSONIAN INSTITUTION in 1906.

FREE RADICALS, molecules or atoms which have one unpaired electron (see ORBITAL), and hence an unused VALENCE. Most are very reactive and shortlived, but if the odd electron can be delocalized by RESONANCE (e.g., in triphenylmethyl) they may be stable. Free radicals can be studied by SPECTROSCOPY, chiefly electron-spin resonance. They are produced by heat, irradiation, FLASH PHOTOLYSIS and ELECTROLYSIS, and are important in forming POLYMERS and in explosive chain reactions.

FREESIA, genus of bulbous sweet-scented flowering plants, native to S Africa, hybrids of which are widely cultivated. Family: Iridaceae.

FREE SILVER, 19th century US political issue

Fredericksburg, Virginia, a beautiful city with many historic buildings, including the homes of George Washington's mother and sister and of John Paul Jones, as well as the Rising Sun tavern, a famous meeting place of the patriots.

started by Western silver interests in an attempt to boost the price of silver, which had been hit by world prices and demonetization in 1873. The idea of "free silver" as an economic panacea was nonsensical but had great appeal among the economically ignorant and those whose debts would be lessened by a cheaper dollar. After the 1893 depression (which it in fact helped precipitate) it became the major issue of the 1896 presidential campaign, with William Jennings BRYAN as its most fervent advocate. (See also BIMETALLISM.)

FREE SOIL PARTY, a short-lived US coalition party (including the BARN BURNERS), formed in N.Y. in 1848 to oppose the extension of slavery into the territories. It attracted many famous men, including President Martin VAN BUREN but polled few votes in the 1848 and 1852 elections, and most members merged with the Republican Party in 1854.

FREETOWN, capital of Sierra Leone; a port on the Atlantic. It is an administrative, commercial and transport center and has some heavy industry. The site was first settled 1787–92 by former slaves. Pop 178600.

FREE TRADE international trade, free from tariffs, quotas or other legal restriction, except non-restrictive tariffs levied for revenue only. The opposite of free trade is PROTECTIONISM. Among early advocates of free trade were the PHYSIOCRATS, Adam SMITH, David RICARDO and J. S. MILL. Modern economists generally accept free trade but advocate varying degrees of protection to safeguard employment and developing industries, as in the theories of J. M. KEYNES. The US has traditionally been protectionist but since WWII has become committed to freer trade.

FREE VERSE (from French *vers libre*), verse without conventional rhythm or meter, relying instead upon the cadences of the spoken language. It was first developed in 19th century France as a reaction to the extreme formality of accepted styles. Among its many exponents in English are Walt WHITMAN, D. H. LAWRENCE, Ezra POUND and T. S. ELIOT.

FREE WILL, in philosophy, a faculty that man is alleged to require if he is to be able to make moral choices. Philosophical theories in which man is assumed to have free will formally conflict with those in which his actions are considered to be determined by causes beyond his control. However, the choice between theories of free will and DETERMINISM may admit of other, intermediate alternatives.

FREEZE DRYING, FOOD processing technique in which the produce is deep frozen before being pumped down to a high vacuum so that constituent ice sublimes out as water vapor leaving a high-quality dehydrated product.

FREEZING POINT, the TEMPERATURE at which a liquid begins to solidify—not always well-defined or equal to the melting point (see FUSION). It usually rises with PRESSURE, solids being slightly denser than liquids, though water is a notable exception; it is lowered by solutes in the liquid, the amount providing an accurate means of determining MOLECULAR WEIGHTS. The solid separating from a solution usually has a different composition from the liquid, and repeated freezing can be used to separate substances. Pure substance can often be "supercooled" below their freezing point for limited periods, as the formation of the solid CRYSTAL requires enucleation by rough surfaces in contact with or particles suspended in the liquid.

FREGE, Gottlob (1848–1925), German logician, father of mathematical LOGIC. Inspired by the similar, earlier work of LEIBNIZ, he tried to show that all mathematical truths could be derived logically from a few simple axioms. After RUSSELL's criticism that his system allowed at least one paradox, he wrote little more; but his work influenced later thinkers such as PEANO, Russell and WHITEHEAD. (See also LOGICAL POSITIVISM.)

FREIBURG (Freiburg im Breisgau), city in W Germany, on the Rhine R. A historic city founded in 1120, it is now a commercial and tourist center with a famous university. Pop 163509.

FRELINGHUYSEN, Frederick Theodore (1817–1885), US statesman, one of the founders of the Republican Party in N.J. A senator 1866–69 and 1871–77, he was secretary of state 1881–85. He was a leading member of the conservative "Stalwart" group and a supporter of Ulysses S. GRANT.

In the French and Indian War many American colonists gained military experience with British forces that was to prove invaluable in the Revolutionary War. Outstanding among them was a young captain of militia, George Washington, shown in this painting, mounted, on the right.

FREMONT, city in Cal, on the SE shore of San Francisco Bay. Its industries include automobile manufacture and brewing. Pop 100869.

FREMONT, a city in E Neb., seat of Dodge Co. On the Platte R, it is a market and processing center for prairie produce. Pop 22962.

FREMONT, city in N Ohio, seat of Sandusky Co. on the Sandusky R. A market center, it has diverse light industries. Pop 18490.

FRÉMONT, John Charles (1813–1890), US explorer, general, politician and popular hero. He mapped much of the territory between the Mississippi valley and the Pacific during the early 1840s. He was caught up in the struggle with Mexico over California, being at one moment appointed military governor and the next convicted of mutiny (1847–48), a sentence later commuted by President Polk. Frémont stood as the Republican Party's first presidential candidate (1856) but was defeated by James BUCHANAN. He had to resign as commander of the Department of the West in Mo. during the Civil War for exceeding his office by declaring martial law. He was governor of Arizona territory 1878–83.

FRENCH, Romance language spoken in France and parts of Belgium, Switzerland, Canada and former French colonies; it is the official language of 21 countries. It developed from Latin during and after the Roman occupation and also from Celtic and Germanic elements. By the 11th century two dialects had developed: in the south the *langue d'oc*, in the north the *langue d'oil*. From the latter came *francien*, the Paris dialect which became modern French as spoken and written since the 17th century.

FRENCH, Daniel Chester (1850–1931), US sculptor best known for his monumental statuary, such as his first work, *The Minute Man* (1875) in Concord, Mass., and the seated *Lincoln* (1922) in the Lincoln Memorial, Washington, D.C.

FRENCH, John Denton Pinkstone, 1st Earl of Ypres (1852–1925), British field marshal, commander of the British Expeditionary Force at the beginning of WWI. He was relieved of his command after the costly retreat from Mons and the battles of Ypres and Loos 1914–15.

FRENCH ACADEMY. See ACADEMIE FRANÇAISE.

FRENCH AND INDIAN WARS, struggle for supremacy in North America between the British and French and their respective Indian allies. Both countries sought to expand from their initial settlements; their clashes reflected European wars but in general arose from local problems. The first three wars were named for the British monarch of the day. **King William's War** (1689–97) was the American phase of the War of the League of AUGSBURG. It consisted of bloody but disorganized raids on both sides, and was inconclusively ended by the Treaty of RYSWICK. **Queen Anne's War** (1702–13) reflected the War of the SPANISH SUCCESSION. French raids on British territory in the N were beaten off and Acadia Nova Scotia) taken. In the S French and Spanish forces unsuccessfully attacked Charleston, S.C. In the Peace of UTRECHT much territory was theoretically ceded to Britain. **King George's War** (1744–1748) was the American phase of the War of the AUSTRIAN SUCCESSION. After much disorganized raiding, New England Troops captured Louisbourg in 1745; it was returned in the treaty of AIX-LA-CHAPELLE, which restored the status quo. **The French and Indian War** (1754–63) was the American arena of the SEVEN YEARS WAR, and the final British-French clash. It centered on the upper Ohio valley, territory claimed by both sides. The French sought to encircle the British colonies by linking their territory along the St. Lawrence R and the Great Lakes with their Mississippi territory, confining the British E of the Appalachian Mts. In 1753 the French began constructing a line of forts to do this, some on territory claimed by Va. An expedition to build a competing fort there, led by George Washington, was forced back in 1754. In 1755 Gen. Edward BRADDOCK's expedition to attack Fort Duquesne was ambushed and he was killed; the few successes before 1757 were by colonial troops. In 1758 William PITT came to power in Britain and developed a new strategy; in 1758 Forts Frontenac, Duquesne and Louisbourg were taken, cutting the French lines of communication. In 1759 Gen. James WOLFE captured Quebec. Montreal fell in 1760, and in 1763 the Treaty of PARIS ceded all Canada and a large part of La. to Britain. By thus freeing the colonists from the French threat and giving their troops war experience, the French and Indian War paved the way for the REVOLUTIONARY WAR.

FRENCH BULLDOG, variety of BULLDOG, first bred in France in the 19th century. Standing around 12in high, it may weigh up to 28lb. Its coat may be brindle or white and brindle.

FRENCH COMMUNITY, created in 1958 to replace the French Union. It now links the independent African states of Chad, Congo (Brazzaville), Central African Republic, Malagasy Republic, Gabon and Senegal with the 5th French Republic, its overseas territories and departments, on matters of defense and foreign, fiscal, economic and communications policies.

FRENCH EQUATORIAL AFRICA, federation of four French overseas territories 1910–59. It included Gabon, Middle Congo (now the Congo Republic), Chad and Ubangi-Sharif (now the Central African Union).

FRENCH GUIANA, French overseas department on the NE coast of South America. Until 1938 the chief town, Cayenne, had penal settlements, of which DEVIL'S ISLAND was part. It is bounded by Surinam on the W and Brazil on the E and S, and consists of a strip of lowland along the 200mi Atlantic coastline and a hilly interior stretching c225mi inland. Its economy rests on the timber trade from its massive forests, and on shrimp fishing. Pop 50 400.

FRENCH HORN. See HORN.

FRENCH POLYNESIA, French territory in the E Pacific, consisting of the Society, Gambier, Austral and Marquesas islands and the Tuamotu Archipelago. They export phosphates, copra, coffee and mother-of-pearl. The capital is Papeete, on Tahiti in the Society Islands. Pop 119 168.

FRENCH REVOLUTION (1789), the first major revolution of modern times. It overthrew the most famous monarchy in Europe, executed the Royal Family, ended the privileged position of the nobility and replaced the traditional institutions of France with new ones based upon popular sovereignty and democratic rights. Subsequently through its wars, the Revolution spread the explosive ideas of the sovereignty of the people, liberty of the individual and equality before the Law throughout Europe. Although the immediate sequel to the Revolution was the establishment of the Napoleonic empire, its impact survived the Napoleonic interlude, and inaugurated the liberal and democratic movements of the 19th century.

By 1788, in a time of rapid economic growth and the consequent rise of the middle classes the country was still ruled by the privileged nobility and clergy, the two upper Estates of the STATES-GENERAL. The tax burden fell on the Third Estate, made up of the middle classes and the landowning peasantry; this was further increased by the corruption of the fiscal system. Into this situation the philosophy of the ENLIGHTENMENT introduced the ideal of progress, scientific materialism and the concepts of constitutional monarchy and republicanism on the British and American models. When the nobility thwarted attempts by the royal ministers to reform government finance the king was forced to summon the Estates-General for the first time since 1614. The Third Estate, which outnumbered the other two chambers, demanded that votes be counted individually and not by chamber, giving them a majority; when this was not immediately granted the Third Estate, with sympathetic members of the other two, declared itself the National Assembly on June 20, 1789. Louis XVI agreed to this, but brought troops to Versailles; mobs stormed the BASTILLE prison on July 14, and pillaged the nobility's country estates. On Aug. 4 the Assembly abolished the feudal system and approved the DECLARATION OF THE RIGHTS OF MAN; the royal family was threatened by mobs, the Church disestablished and largely suppressed. The royal family fled in June, hoping to join their sympathizers who had fled abroad, but were arresed at Varennes and returned to Paris. In Oct. 1791 the Legislative Assembly convened under a new constitution, and became increasingly radical in form. Threat of attack from abroad precipitated the FRENCH REVOLUTIONARY WARS. In the face of this crisis the mob again threatened the king, forcing him to replace the Assembly with a radical Convention elected in Sept. 1792, during mob massacres of jailed royalists. The king was tried for treason and executed in Jan. 1793. In the face of royalist insurrection and foreign hostility the JACOBINS now seized power from the more moderate GIRONDINS, transferring power from the Convention to arbitrary bodies such as the Committees for Public Safety and General Security. Dominated by DANTON and ROBESPIERRE, these brought about the REIGN OF TERROR. This ended with Robespierre himself being executed by the Convention in July 1794. The Convention then introduced a new constitution, setting up the DIRECTORY, which proved ineffectual and corrupt. In 1799 it was overthrown by the army, led by the popular general NAPOLEON. He established the CONSULATE, effectively ending the revolutionary period.

FRENCH REVOLUTIONARY WARS, waged by Revolutionary France before the accession of NAPOLEON I. In 1789 France preemptively declared war on and defeated Austria. The First Coalition (Austria, Britain, Prussia, Russia, Spain, and the Netherlands) was defeated 1793–95, France showing surprising if costly military strength. The Second Coalition of Britain, Austria and Russia was defeated 1799–1800, although Napoleon's strike at British-held Egypt failed.

FRENCH SOUTHERN AND ANTARCTIC TERRITORIES, French territory (established 1955) in Antarctica and the South Indian Ocean, comprising the Kerguelen and Crozet archipelagos, the islands of St. Paul and Nouvelle-Amsterdam, and the Adélie Coast.

FRENCH TERRITORY OF AFARS AND ISSAS, French overseas territory on the Gulf of Aden between Ethiopia and the Somali Republic. In area 8 500sq mi, it is largely desert; the economy rests on agriculture and on the major port facilities at Djibouti, the capital. It is also the terminus of a railroad from Addis Ababa.

FRENCH WEST AFRICA, federation of eight French overseas territories, 1895–1958. Its members were Dahomey, Guinea, Ivory Coast, Mauritania, Niger, Senegal, Sudan (now Mali) and Upper Volta.

FRENCH WEST INDIES, comprises two islands: MARTINIQUE and GUADELUPE. They were French colonies until 1946.

FRENEAU, Philip Morin (1752–1832), US journalist and "poet of the American Revolution." Best known in his time for his savage satires, he attempted to develop a distinctively American poetical idiom.

FREON, trade name for a group of volatile CARBON compounds (derivatives of METHANE and ETHANE) containing fluorine and chlorine or bromine. They are nonflammable and nontoxic, and are used as refrigerants and aerosol propellants.

FREQUENCY, the rate at which a periodic WAVE MOTION executes complete cycles of its variation. Frequencies are measured in hertz (Hz), i.e., in cycles per second. Musical sounds typically have frequencies in the range 30–20 000Hz; alternating-current ELECTRICITY supply is at 60Hz in the US, but usually 50Hz in the rest of the world. According to QUANTUM THEORY, the frequency (ν) of ELECTROMAGNETIC RADIATION provides a measure of the ENERGY (E) of its quanta (PHOTONS): $E = h\nu$, where h is the PLANCK CONSTANT. Again, the wavelength (λ), frequency (f) and velocity (v) of a harmonic wave are related by the equation $v = f\lambda$.

FREQUENCY CURVE. See HISTOGRAM.

FREQUENCY MODULATION (FM). See RADIO.

FREQUENCY POLYGON. See HISTOGRAM.

FRESCO, type and technique of wall painting common in ancient Crete and China, and in Europe from the 13th to the 17th centuries. In true fresco, dry earth pigments mixed with water were painted on fresh wet lime-plaster, setting with it. Preparatory drawings (*sinopia*) were often done in red paint on an underlying layer. In *fresco secco* (dry fresco) varnishes are painted on a smooth, non-absorbent surface. Among famous fresco painters are GIOTTO and MICHELANGELO.

FRESCOBALDI, Girolamo (1583–1643), Italian organist, an early master of organ and instrumental composition. His style is bold but logical. He was organist of St. Peter's, Rome, 1608–28 and from 1634.

FRESNEL, Augustin Jean (1788–1827), French physicist who evolved the transverse-wave theory of LIGHT through his work on optical INTERFERENCE. He worked also on REFLECTION, REFRACTION, DIFFRACTION and POLARIZATION, and developed a compound LENS system still used for many lighthouses.

FRESNO, city in central Cal., seat of Fresno Co. A commercial center, it processes the produce of the San Joaquin Valley, especially its grapes. Pop 165 972.

FREUD, Anna (1895–), Austrian-born British

The storming of the Bastille by the Parisian mob and the National Guard on July 14, 1789, depicted (*above*) on a contemporary etching. *Left:* painting of the luckless Louis XVI at the foot of the scaffold, January 21, 1793, about to be guillotined.

pioneer of child psychoanalysis. Her book *The Ego and Mechanisms of Defense* (1936) is a major contribution to the field. After escaping with her father Sigmund FREUD from Nazi-occupied Austria (1938), she established an influential child-therapy clinic in London.

FREUD, Sigmund (1856–1939), Austrian neurologist and psychiatrist, founder and author of almost all the basic concepts of PSYCHOANALYSIS. He graduated as a medical student from the University of Vienna in 1881; and for some months in 1885 he studied under J. M. CHARCOT. Charcot's interest in HYSTERIA converted Freud to the cause of psychiatry. Dissatisfied with HYPNOSIS and electrotherapy as analytic techniques, he evolved the psychoanalytic method, founded on DREAM analysis and FREE ASSOCIATION. Because of his belief that sexual impulses lay at the heart of NEUROSES, he was for a decade reviled professionally, but by 1905 disciples such as Alfred ADLER and Carl Gustav JUNG were gathering around him; both were later to break away. For some thirty years he worked to establish the truth of his theories, and these years were especially fruitful. Fleeing Nazi anti-Semitism, he left Vienna for London in 1938, and there spent the last year of his life.

FREY, in Norse myth the god of rain and sunshine, and hence of peace and fertility. The brother of FREYA, he was worshiped at the winter solstice, especially in Sweden.

FREYA, in Norse myth the goddess of love, beauty and fertility, sister of FREY. Portrayed unfavorably in some tales, in others she is a patroness of heroes equal to ODIN.

FRIAR, member of any of the medieval Roman Catholic mendicant orders, forbidden to hold property in common, not bound to one convent, and having various controversial ecclesiastical privileges. Some were distinguished by the color of their habits as Black Friars (DOMINICANS), Grey Friars (FRANCISCANS) and White Friars (CARMELITES); the other main order was the AUGUSTINIANS or Austin Friars.

FRIAR'S BALSAM, or tincture of benzoin, a resin, taken by inhalation, used to ease COUGH and loosen MUCUS secretion in respiratory diseases.

FRICK, Henry Clay (1849–1919), US industrialist and art collector. He started a coke business in 1868, and in 1882 he became an associate of Andrew CARNEGIE and managed his steel company 1889–99. He bequeathed his extensive art collection, housed in his New York mansion, for public exhibition.

FRICTION, resistance to motion arising at the boundary between two touching surfaces when it is attempted to slide one over the other. As the FORCE applied to start motion increases from zero, the equal force of "static friction" opposes it, reaching a maximum "limiting friction," just before sliding begins. Once motion has started, the "sliding friction" is less than the limiting. Friction increases with the load pressing the surfaces together, but is nearly independent of the area in contact. For a given pair of surfaces, limiting friction divided by load is a dimensionless constant known as the coefficient of friction. LUBRICATION is used to overcome friction in the BEARINGS of machines.

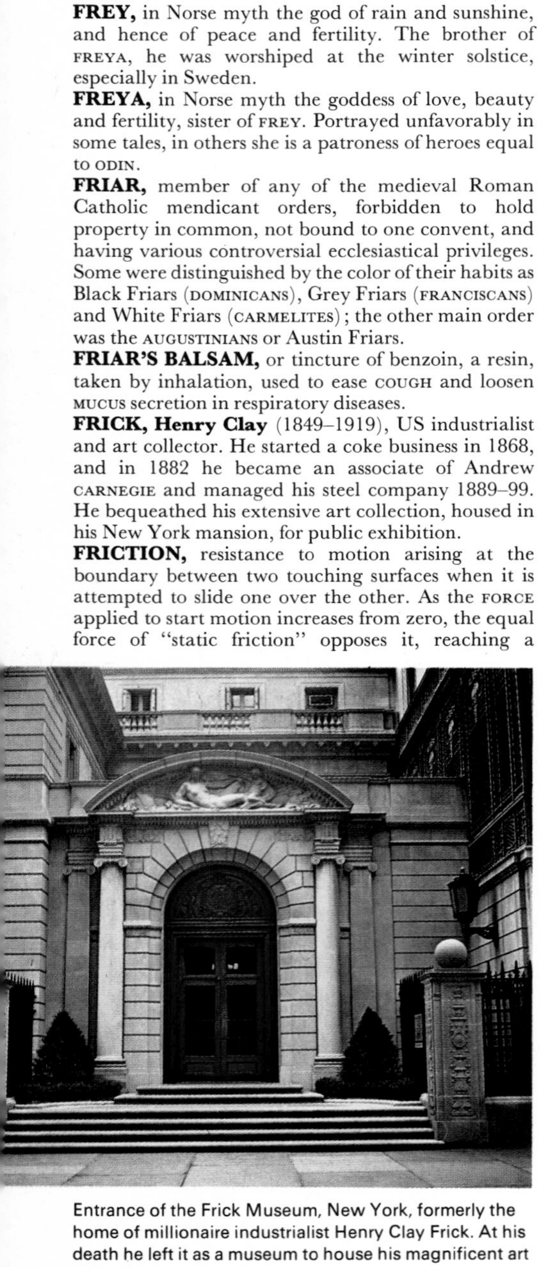

Entrance of the Frick Museum, New York, formerly the home of millionaire industrialist Henry Clay Frick. At his death he left it as a museum to house his magnificent art collection.

Drawing of a typical 19th century frigate, showing the sleek lines that made this class ideal for fast strike actions, where speed was more important than firepower.

FRIDAY, sixth day of the week. The name derives from the Latin *Veneris dies* (day of VENUS); in translation the name of FRIGG, Norse sky goddess, was substituted for Venus, resulting in "Frigg's Day."

FRIDLEY, residential city in E Minn., a suburb of Minneapolis. Pop 29 233.

FRIED, Alfred Hermann (1864–1921), Austrian pacifist, founder of the journals *Die Waffen Nieder!* (1891) and *Die Friedenswarte* (1899). He was awarded the 1911 Nobel Peace Prize.

FRIEDEL-CRAFTS REACTION, class of substitution reactions, catalyzed by acidic metal halides (e.g., aluminum chloride); an ALKYL HALIDE or an ACID CHLORIDE reacts with an AROMATIC COMPOUND, the alkyl or acyl group replacing a hydrogen atom on the aromatic ring: the carbonium ion formed attacks the ring as an electrophile (see NUCLEOPHILES). (See also ALKYLATION.)

FRIEDLAND, Battle of, defeat of Russian forces by the French Grand Army under Napoleon I. Fought on June 4, 1807, at Friedland (now Pravdinsk, USSR), it resulted in the Treaty of Tilsit between Napoleon and Tsar Alexander I.

FRIEDMAN, Milton (1912–), US economist, a proponent of the monetarist theory; this regards the money supply as the central controlling factor in economic development. A columnist in *Newsweek* magazine, he has taught at Chicago U. since 1946 and is a staff member of the National Bureau of Economic Research.

FRIEDRICH, Caspar David (1774–1840), German Romantic painter, known for the land and seascape compositions he imbued with rich light effects and deep religious symbolism, such as *Cross in the Mountains* (1807) and *Man and Woman Gazing at the Moon* (1809).

FRIENDS, Society of. See QUAKERS.

FRIENDLY ISLANDS. See TONGA.

FRIEND OF THE COURT. See AMICUS CURIAE.

FRIES, John (c1750–1818), American ex-militia captain of Millford township, Pa. Sentenced to death for leading armed but relatively peaceful demonstrations in 1799 against a federal property tax, he was pardoned in 1800 by President Adams.

FRIEZE, in classical architecture the middle division of an ENTABLATURE, or, more generally, any long, narrow decorative band set horizontally upon a wall, or around pottery, etc.

FRIGATE, originally a fast, three-masted vessel used in the 18th and 19th centuries for cruising and scouting, with its main gun battery on the upper deck only. Since WWII the name has been given in Britain to small, well-armed escort destroyers, and in the US to larger missile carriers.

FRIGATE BIRDS, large sea birds of the family Fregatidae with long pointed wings, forked tails and weak legs. They spend most of their lives in the air and breed in tropical seas. In the mating season, the male has a red throat pouch which can be inflated.

FRIGG (or Frigga), in Norse mythology the goddess of the sky and, as wife of ODIN, protectress of marriage. She was the mother of BALDER.

FRIJOLES, the popular name for a small, black bean, *Phaseolus vulgaris*, grown in Mexico and Latin American countries. It is probably a native of South America and is an important food plant.

FRILLED LIZARD, a large AGAMID lizard of N Australia and New Guinea. If threatened it extends a wide frill of skin around the neck. It can also run on its hind legs.

FRIML, (Charles) Rudolf (1879–1972), Czech-born US composer of widely popular operettas and film scores. His best-known works include *The Firefly* (1912), *Rose Marie* (1924) and *The Vagabond King* (1925).

FRISCH, Karl von (1886–), Austrian zoologist best known for his studies of bee behavior, perception and communication, discovering the "Dance of the Bees." With TINBERGEN and LORENZ he was awarded the 1973 Nobel Prize for Physiology or Medicine for his work.

FRISCH, Max (Rudolf) (1911–), Swiss architect, journalist and playwright best known for his play *Biedermann and the Fireraisers* (1958) and his novels *Stiller* (1954) and *Homo Faber* (1957). His dominant theme is the destructive effect of modern society upon individuals.

FRISCH, Ragnar (1895–1973), Norwegian economist, one of the founders of the Econometric Society. He won the first Nobel Memorial Prize for Economic Science, in 1969.

FRISIAN, West Germanic language closely related to English. Formerly spoken along the North Sea Coast and on the islands of the Netherlands and Germany, it is now in decline except in the Dutch province of Friesland, where it is a flourishing official language.

FRISIAN ISLANDS, chain of about 30 islands in the North Sea, from 3mi to 20mi off the coasts of the Netherlands, Germany and Denmark. Their economy is largely agricultural, often on land reclaimed from the sea.

FRITIGERN, or Fridigern (d. c382 AD), Visigoth chieftain, possibly a Christian, who rebelled against Roman domination. He was one of the Visigoth generals who defeated and killed the Emperor Valens at Adrianople in 378.

FRITILLARY, popular name for hardy bulbous plants of the genus *Fritillaria*, family Liliaceae. They have bell-shaped hanging flowers. Also, name for several species of butterfly.

FRIULI-VENEZIA GIULIA, region in NE Italy, covering an area of 3 028sq mi. It was granted limited autonomy in 1963. Its capital is the great port city of TRIEST; this and its other towns are mainly industrial. The land is poor, but livestock production flourishes.

FROBISHER, Sir Martin (c1539–1594), English

navigator and explorer. In search of a NORTHWEST PASSAGE to the Pacific, he led three expeditions to N Canada 1576–78, landing at Labrador and Frobisher Bay and at Greenland.

FROEBEL, Friedrich Wilhelm August (1782–1852), German educator noted as the founder of the kindergarten system. He believed in play as a basic form of self-expression, and in the innate nature of mystical understanding. Though much criticized, he has profoundly influenced later educators.

FROGFISH, or Fishing frog, name used for the Common ANGLERFISH, *Lophius piscatorius*.

FROGHOPPER. See SPITTLE BUG.

FROGS, jumping, tailless AMPHIBIA. Strictly, the name applies only to true frogs, members of the family Ranidae, but other members of the order Anura (which also includes the TOADS) are sometimes called frogs. True frogs are characterized by shoulder-girdles that are fused down the midline. They are found throughout the world except in the southern parts of South America and Australia.

FROHMAN, Charles (1860–1915), US theater manager whose Theatrical Syndicate was the major power in American theater 1900–1910. He fostered the careers of many famous actors and playwrights, such as Ethel BARRYMORE and David BELASCO. He was killed in the sinking of the *Lusitania*.

FROISSART, Jean (c1338–1410?), French poet and chronicler who traveled widely in search of material for his *Chronicles of France, England, Scotland and Spain*, which present a colorful picture of events between 1325 and 1400. His poetry ranges from light verse to the romance *Meliador*.

FROMM, Erich (1900–), German-born US psychoanalyst who combines many of the ideas of Freud and Marx in his analysis of human relationships and development in the context of social structures and in his suggested solutions to problems such as alienation.

FRONDE, a series of uprisings against the French crown 1648–53. At first largely popular uprisings against heavy taxation, they were later fomented by the *parlements* and discontented members of the aristocracy, such as Prince Louis II de Condé, against the autocratic chief minister, Cardinal MAZARIN whose decisive intervention in 1653 finally crushed the Fronde.

FRONT, a boundary between two air masses, one cold and dense, the other warm and less dense. Fronts are regions of uncertain weather: cloud and rain, variable HUMIDITY and WIND direction, and low air pressure (see ATMOSPHERE). A **warm front** is where warm air advances, displacing cold; the reverse happens in a **cold front**. An **occluded front** occurs often toward the end of a system of STORMS: a mass of warm air is surrounded and forced upward by cold air.

In the N Hemisphere the **polar front** separates the W-moving cold air of polar regions from the E-moving warm air flowing up from the TROPICS. Warm air flows into "bays" in the front, then cold air in from the rear, resulting in the rotating air system known as a **depression**. (See also METEOROLOGY.)

FRONTAL LOBE, the foremost of the four main lobes of cerebral cortex in the BRAIN of man. It is concerned with personality and behavior, and with the emotional aspects of perception. Its removal by LOBOTOMY leads to a disinhibited type of behavior.

FRONTENAC, Fort, log fort in New France, originally called Cataraqui, built in 1673 by the Comte de FRONTENAC and renamed for him in 1675. Kingston, Ontario, now stands on its site.

FRONTENAC, Louis de Buade, Comte de Palluau et de (1622–1698), French soldier who became governor of New France in 1672. He badly mismanaged Indian relations, and damaged the fur trade. Recalled to France in 1682, he returned in 1689 and in the FRENCH AND INDIAN WARS successfully held Quebec. He maintained the French position in New France up to the Treaty of RYSWICK (1697).

FRONTIER, in American history, the boundary between the settled and unsettled areas of the country. It was constantly expanding as the descendants of the original settlers of the 13 Colonies spread out N, S and especially W. In the early days expansion was slow, consisting largely of migrations into the Appalachians area and into what is now Pa. By the time of Independence, Ky. had been settled and the frontier was in Tenn. The new government provided for surveying, settlement and administration of new areas. The frontier moved steadily W, and new states were formed in quick succession until by 1846 Mexico had been forced to cede the SW, and the W coast was effectively settled. The Indians suffered badly under the government's policy of moving them to make way for settlers, and struggled to resist it. After the Civil War, Indian wars broke out again, but by the 1870s and 1880s the growth of cities and the enclosure of much of the land meant that the settlers were firmly established. In 1890 the Bureau of the Census officially declared the frontier closed; its way of life and the peculiar mythology it created have had a great influence on American society.

FROST, frozen atmospheric moisture formed on objects when the temperature is below 0°C, the freezing point of water (see FREEZING POINT). **Hoarfrost** forms in roughly the same way as DEW but, owing to the low temperature, the water VAPOR sublimes (see SUBLIMATION) from gaseous to solid state to form ice crystals on the surface. The delicate patterns often seen on windows are hoarfrost. **Glazed frost** usually forms when RAIN falls on an object below freezing: it can be seen, for example, on telegraph wires. **Rime** occurs when supercooled (see SUPERCOOLING AND SUPERHEATING) water droplets contact a surface that is also below 0°C; it may result from FOG or drizzle. The first frost of the year signifies the end of the GROWING SEASON. (See also ICE; SNOW.)

FROST, Robert (1874–1963), eminent US poet. For most of his life he supported himself by farming and part-time academic work. His first two volumes of poetry *A Boy's Will* (1913) and *North of Boston* (1914) were published during a stay in England. His reputation grew in America, and he won many honors, including four Pulitzer prizes. His style is individual, clearly influenced by rural life, religion and much personal tragedy. Frost's complete poems were published in 1967.

FROSTBITE, damage occurring in SKIN and adjacent tissues caused by freezing. (The numbness caused by cold allows considerable damage without pain.) DEATH of tissues follows and they separate off. Judicious rewarming, pain relief and measures to maximize skin blood flow may reduce tissue loss.

FROZEN FOODS. See FOOD PRESERVATION; BIRDSEYE, CLARENCE.

FRUCTOSE ($C_6H_{12}O_6$), or "fruit sugar," a naturally occurring simple SUGAR (monosaccharide) found in a wide variety of fruits and in honey. It is the sweetest of the simple sugars.

FRUIT, botanically, the structure that develops from the ovary and accessory parts of a FLOWER after FERTILIZATION. True fruits are formed from the

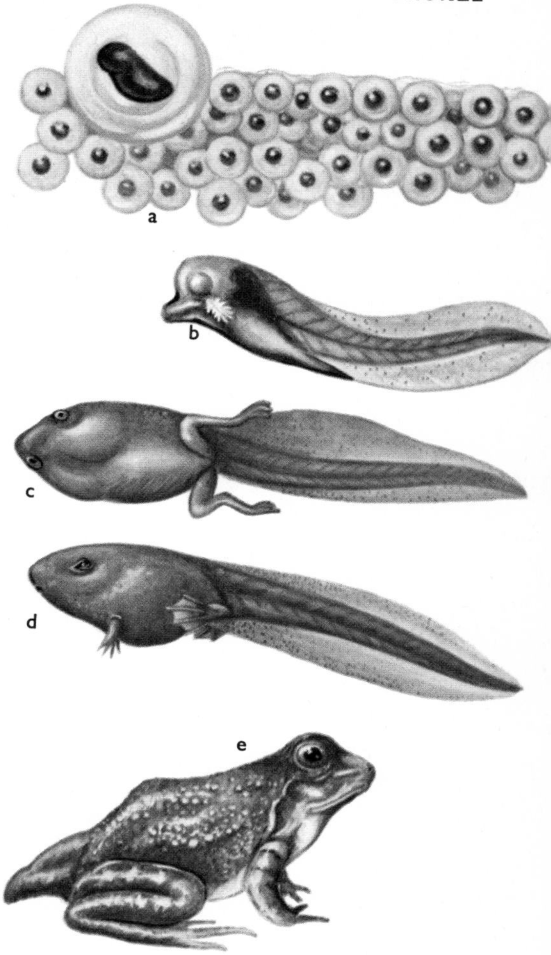

A frog passes through several different forms before reaching maturity. The eggs or spawn (a) are laid in water and surrounded by a protective layer of jelly upon which the developing embryo also feeds, until it emerges as a tadpole (b) which has external gills and a sucker enabling it to hold on to plants and scrape algae from them with an organ in its mouth. Hind legs develop at the base of the tail (c), and then the forelegs (d). The tail gradually disappears (e), leaving the tiny body which will grow into a mature frog. Over this early period the feeding habits also change radically as the frog changes from a vegetarian into a carnivore.

As the frontiersmen forged steadily westward, they faced increasing resistance from the Indian tribes and often had to build stockaded forts, like this one in Nashville, Tennessee.

carpels, while in false fruits other parts of the flower are involved, for example in apple the fleshy pulp is derived from the receptacle (see POME). Fruits may be simple (derived from the ovary of one pistil), aggregate (formed by a single flower with several separate pistils, e.g. RASPBERRY) or multiple (formed from the flowers of an INFLORESCENCE, e.g. FIG). Simple fruits may be fleshy or dry. Fleshy fruits include the BERRY and the DRUPE. Dry fruit may split open to disperse the seeds (dehiscent), the main types being the LEGUME (or pod), FOLLICLE, CAPSULE and SILIQUE. Some dry fruits do not break open (indehiscent) the main types here being the ACHENE, GRAIN, SAMARA and NUT.

The main function of the fruit is to protect the seeds and disperse them when ripe.

FRUIT FLIES, small FLIES of the genus *Drosophila*, which feed on decaying vegetation and ripe fruit, sometimes causing great damage to crops. Some species are used for genetics experiments because they breed rapidly. As a result, the fruit fly is one of the most studied animals in the world today.

FRUMENTIUS, Saint, 4th century bishop of Aksum, a native of Tyre, He and his brother St. Aedesius established the COPTIC CHURCH in Ethiopia.

FRUNZE, city in the USSR, capital of Kirgiz SSR, 300mi NE of Tashkent. An industrial and administrative center, it was formerly called Pishpek. M. V. FRUNZE was born here. Pop 431 000.

FRUNZE, Mikhail Vasilyevich (1885–1925), Soviet military leader and theorist, an outstanding commander in the civil war 1919–20. An opponent of TROTSKY, he replaced him as people's commissar for war in 1925.

FRUSTUM, the base of a cone; more rigorously, a part of one nappe of a CONE lying between two PLANES, usually parallel, that intersect the cone.

FRY, Christopher (1907–), British verse dramatist, whose plays, although often in ancient or medieval settings, deal with contemporary themes. His best-known play, *The Lady's Not For Burning* (1948), is a dry comedy centering on witchcraft hysteria. *A Sleep of Prisoners* (1951) and *The Dark is Light Enough* (1955) are essentially religious plays.

FRY, Elizabeth Gurney (1780–1845), British Quaker philanthropist who made great advances in the treatment of the imprisoned and the insane, inspecting prisons all over Britain and Europe. Her proposed reforms of London's notorious Newgate prison, calling for segregation of the sexes and the provision of employment and religious instruction, were largely accepted.

FRY, Roger Eliot (1866–1934), British painter. A member of the London Group, he is most remembered as a critic. He was a champion of CÉZANNE and POSTIMPRESSIONISM. In 1933 he was appointed Slade Professor of Fine Art at Cambridge.

FUAD I (1868–1936), modern Egypt's first monarch, son of the khedive Ismail Pasha. He became sultan on his brother's death in 1917 and assumed the title of king when the British protectorate ended in 1922.

FUCHOU. See FOOCHOW.

FUCHS, Klaus Emil (1911–), German-born British physicist, jailed 1950–59 as a communist spy. He began passing secrets to the Russians after 1943 while working on the atomic bomb in the US and continued after 1945 as head of theoretical physics at Harwell in Britain. Fuchs admitted the charges against him and on his release went to East Germany.

FUCHS, Sir Vivian Ernest (1908–), British geologist and explorer, who led the British Commonwealth Trans-Antarctic expedition that made the first overland crossing of Antarctica 1957–58.

FUCHSIA, genus of trees and shrubs native to Middle and South America and New Zealand. Many hybrids are cultivated for their attractive pendulous flowers. Family: Onagraceae.

FUCHSIN. See MAGENTA.

The snowcapped crest of Mount Fuji, the great sacred mountain of Japan, situated about 50m SW of Tokyo. While it remains a formidable volcano, its last eruption occurred some 270 years ago. Still a place of pilgrimage, it now chiefly attracts climbers and tourists. The city of Fuji lies at its foot.

FUEL, a substance that may be burned (see COMBUSTION) to produce heat, light or power. Traditional fuels include dried dung, animal and vegetable oil, wood, PEAT and COAL, supplemented by the manufactured fuels CHARCOAL, COAL GAS, COKE and WATER GAS. In this century PETROLEUM and NATURAL GAS have come into widespread use. The term "fuel" has also been extended to include chemical nuclear fuels (see FUEL CELL; NUCLEAR ENERGY), although these are not burned. Specialized high-energy fuels such as HYDRAZINE are used in ROCKET engines. The chief property of a fuel is its **calorific value**—the amount of heat produced by complete combustion of a unit mass or volume of fuel. Also of major importance is the proportion of incombustibles—ASH and moisture—and of sulfur and other compounds liable to cause AIR POLLUTION.

FUEL CELL, a direct-current power source similar to a BATTERY but differing in that a chemical fuel must be supplied while the CELL is in use. Various chemical reactions are utilized in different types of cell. The most common is the hydro-oxygen cell in which HYDROGEN reacts with hydroxyl (HYDROXIDE) ions in the electrolyte to form water at the ANODE, and OXYGEN reacts with water to form hydroxyl ions at the CATHODE, the overall reaction resulting in the formation of water and a flow of ELECTRONS through an external circuit. The cell is divided into three compartments by the ELECTRODES, the two outer ones containing the hydrogen fuel and the oxygen, and the central one the aqueous electrolyte. The electrodes are porous so that the gases can penetrate to meet the electrolyte. Platinum and nickel are typical catalysts. Fuel cells are much more efficient converters of chemical energy than heat ENGINES.

FUEL INJECTION, various systems for delivering a metered quantity of fuel into the cylinder of an INTERNAL-COMBUSTION ENGINE, usually driven by pumps run off the CAMSHAFT and controlled from the throttle. Fuel injection has always been essential in DIESEL ENGINES but it is only in recent years that it has begun to replace the CARBURETOR in gasoline-engined passenger cars. Some recent systems have been electronically controlled.

FUGGER, Germany family of merchant bankers. The business was founded in Augsburg in the 14th century by Johann Fugger, a Swabian weaver. The fortunes of his descendants flourished during the 15th and 16th centuries. Jakob Fugger (1459–1525) materially assisted Charles V's election as Holy Roman Emperor. The family included many distinguished soldiers, statesmen and clerics.

FUGITIVE SLAVE ACTS, laws passed by Congress in 1793 and 1850 to deter slaves from fleeing to Abolitionist states. The 1793 act denied runaway slaves the benefit of jury trial. The 1850 measure was a reaction to the growing opposition this provoked. It imposed severe fines and imprisonment on US marshals and citizens who helped or failed to apprehend runaway slaves. The acts only hardened opposition and were another divisive factor between North and South.

FUGITIVES, the group of American poets who contributed to a literary magazine *The Fugitive,* published in Nashville, Tenn., 1922–25. The principal members of the group were John Crowe RANSOM, Allen TATE and Robert Penn WARREN.

FUGUE, a musical form in which two or more parts (voices) combine in introducing and developing a theme. The principal idea behind fugal composition is that of developing contrasts which produce a specific texture and density. The fugue's history dates from the 16th century CANON and round. The greatest achievements in this form are by J. S. BACH whose unfinished *The Art of Fugue* (1748–50) is a major study of fugal form.

FUGUE STATE. See AMNESIA.

FUJAIRAH, emirate on the Oman promontory, one of the United Arab Emirates. Its independence was not recognized by the British until 1952, despite *de facto* independence since 1886. It has few mineral resources and is largely agricultural. Pop 14 000.

FUJI, industrial and agricultural city in S central Honshu, Japan. Pop 180 639.

FUJI, Mount (or Fujiyama), highest mountain in Japan (12 388ft), long considered sacred by the Japanese and a source of inspiration to artists and poets. A dormant volcano crowned by a wide crater, it last erupted in 1707.

FUJISAWA, residential and industrial city in Honshu, Japan. It now produces automobiles and electrical appliances. Pop 228 978.

FUKIEN, a maritime province of SE China, covers 47 529sq mi of hilly terrain. Its capital FOOCHOW lies near the mouth of the Min River. Fishing is the basic source of livelihood; however Fukien is famous for providing tea and wood. Pop 17 000 000.

FUKUI, city in central Honshu, Japan. It is the country's major textile center. Its silk-weaving industry dates back to the 10th century. Pop 200 509.

FUKUOKA, port city on the N coast of Kyushu island, Japan. It is also a commercial and administrative center for the region. Pop 853 270.

FUKUSHIMA, town in N Honshu, Japan, about 150mi N of Tokyo. It is a trade center for raw silk, textiles and agricultural goods. Pop 227 451.

FUKUYAMA, city in SW Honshu, Japan. A commercial port on the Ashidia delta, it is also an industrial center. Pop 225 086.

FULANI, an ancient people of W Africa found over a wide area from Senegambia to W Sudan. They include nomadic pastoralists as well as settled communities. The Fulani have a deep-rooted culture based on Islam and have strong ties with the HAUSA. They number some 7 million.

FULBERT, Saint (c960–1028), medieval scholar and cleric associated with the Cluniac reform movement. Fulbert studied under Gerbert (later Pope Silvester II) at Reims and from 990 directed the cathedral school at Chartres, where in 1006 he became bishop.

FULBRIGHT, James William (1905–), US politician and lawyer, initiator of the FULBRIGHT SCHOLARSHIPS. After teaching law at Arkansas U. Fulbright was elected to the House of Representatives in 1942, and served in the Senate 1944–75. He was chairman of the Senate Foreign Relations Committee 1959–74.

FULBRIGHT SCHOLARSHIPS, grants made possible by the Fulbright Act of 1946 to encourage the exchange of students and teachers between the US and other countries. The grant program was conceived by Senator J. W. FULBRIGHT and together with subsequent legislation has been strengthened and extended by the Mutual Educational and Cultural Exchange Act (Fulbright-Hays Act) of 1961.

FULLER, Richard Buckminster (1895–), US inventor, philosopher, author, mathematician and perhaps the 20th century's most original and prolific thinker. He is best known for his concept "Spaceship Earth" and for inventing the GEODESIC DOME.

FULLER, John Frederick Charles (1878–1966), British soldier and military historian. In WWI he directed the first successful use of tanks in battle, at Cambrai in 1917. He pioneered the concept known as BLITZKRIEG. His chief work is *Military History of the Western World* (1954–56).

FULLER, Margaret (1810–1850), influential American critic and advocate of female emancipation. A friend of EMERSON, she edited the Transcendentalist magazine *The Dial* 1840–42. She was literary critic for the New York *Tribune* (1844) and in the same year published *Women in the Nineteenth Century*. She was drowned with her husband and child in a shipwreck off FIRE ISLAND.

FULLER, Melville Weston (1833–1910), Chief Justice of the US Supreme Court, 1888–1910. A strong advocate of states' rights, in two of his most significant judgments he declared the 1894 federal income tax law unconstitutional and weakened the 1890 Sherman Antitrust Act. He was a member of the Hague Court of International Arbitration 1900–10.

FULLER'S EARTH, natural CLAY material of variable composition, once used to clean wool and cloth (fulling); now used for decolorizing OIL of all sorts by selective chemical ADSORPTION, and also as a pesticide carrier, and in drilling muds.

FULLERTON, city in S Cal. It grew up as a citrus center and is now an industrial city. California State U. was founded here in 1959. Pop 85 987.

FULMARS, gull-like seabirds of the family Procellariidae found in the N Atlantic and Pacific. The fulmar *Fulmarus glacialis* is now the commonest bird of the Atlantic region, and lives largely on offal thrown from fishing boats. It reaches about 460mm (18in) in length.

FULMINATE, or **mercury (II) cyanate.** See MERCURY.

FULTON, city in central Mo., seat of Callaway Co. A trade center in an agricultural area, it has various light industries. Pop 12 148.

FULTON, city in N central N.Y., on the Oswego R. Its industries are food-canning, paper-mill machinery and chocolate and light container manufacture.

FULTON, Robert (1765–1815), US inventor who improved both the submarine and the steamboat. His submarine *Nautilus* was launched at Rouen, France (1800), with the aim of using it against British warships: in fact, these repeatedly escaped and the French lost interest. His first steamship was launched on the Seine (1803), and after this success he returned to the US, launching the first commercially successful steamboat (see FITCH, John), the *Clermont*, from New York (1807). He built several other steamboats and the *Demologus*, the first steam warship (launched 1815).

FUMAROLE, found in volcanic regions, a hole in the ground that emits steam, carbon dioxide and other vapors typical of volcanic eruption. (See GEYSER; VOLCANISM; VOLCANO.)

FUMITORY, popular name for species of the genus *Fumaria*, especially *Fumaria officinalis*, a weed native to Eurasia, but naturalized in North America. The leaves have a bitter saline taste and are used as a tonic and diaphoretic, notably in provincial France. Family: Fumariaceae.

FUNABASHI, city in Honshu, Japan, on Tokyo Bay, a suburb of Tokyo. An agricultural center, it has developed metal industries since WWII. Pop 325 426.

FUNAN, ancient kingdom by the Mekong Delta which grew into a powerful empire from the 3rd to the 6th centuries AD. It was a center of Hindu civilization and Buddhist religion.

FUNCHAL, city, capital of the Madeira Islands. On the S coast of the principal island, it is an important port and tourist resort noted for its wines, fruit and fish. Pop 105 791.

FUNCTION, a rule in which each element of one set (see SET THEORY) is assigned one or more elements, not necessarily unique, of another set. (On occasion, the two sets may share some or all elements.) In CARTESIAN COORDINATES a function may be plotted by setting x along one axis and $f(x)$ (read "function of x") along the other. (See also ANALYTIC GEOMETRY; CALCULUS; VARIABLE.)

A function may be thought of as a rule. If the rule is SQUARE the number, add twice the number and subtract three, this is expressed as $y = x^2 + 2x - 3$, or more usually $f(x) = x^2 + 2x - 3$.

A TRANSCENDENTAL FUNCTION is one that cannot be expressed algebraically (see ALGEBRA; CURVE). For example, sin x (see TRIGONOMETRY) cannot be expressed in algebraic terms and hence, if $f(x) = \sin x$, $f(x)$ is a transcendental function.

FUNCTIONAL GROUP, a group of connected atoms whose presence in a molecule gives rise to characteristic chemical properties and infrared absorptions; e.g., hydroxyl —OH, carboxyl =C=O. The properties of a molecule are roughly the sum of those of its constituent functional groups, though their interactions are also significant.

FUNCTIONALISM, the principle that all design should be dictated by the function of what is being designed, all unnecessary elements being discarded. This was derived from a dictum of the architect Louis SULLIVAN, "form follows function," and was a moving principle of the BAUHAUS school. Functionalism influenced many modern architects, notably Frank Lloyd WRIGHT, and LE CORBUSIER.

FUNDAMENTALISM, US conservative Protestant movement, upholding EVANGELICALISM against MODERNISM, which has flourished, particularly in the South, since the early 20th century. Its chief doctrines, set out in a series of pamphlets, *The Fundamentals* (1910–1912), are Christ's virgin birth, physical resurrection and second coming, the substitutionary theory of the atonement, and the absolute infallibility of the Bible. The last led to a denial of biblical criticism and the theory of evolution. Leading advocates of the movement included W. J. BRYAN and the theologian John Gresham Machen. Modern fundamentalism is mostly anti-intellectual, dispensationalist, pietist and revivalist.

Some of the best aspects of Functionalism are expressed in the purity and simplicity of the interior of the architect Le Corbusier's Chapelle de Notre Dame in Ronchamp, France, although the irregular and gracefully curved exterior may appear to depart from the principles of the movement.

FUNDAMENTAL ORDERS, charter adopted in 1639 by the towns of Hartford, Windsor and Wethersfield. in the Connecticut R Valley. They were superseded by the royal charter of 1662.

FUNDED DEBT, a short-term floating debt which has been converted to a long-term negotiable debt, as for example bonds, mortgages and notes. A long-term debt is usually taken to be one maturing after more than a year. The term is often used of the national debt.

FUNDY, Bay of, an arm of the Atlantic Ocean between New Brunswick and Nova Scotia about 94mi long and about 50mi at its widest. It is remarkable for a massive fluctuation in tidal level, which has reached 70ft. Its chief harbor is St. John, in New Brunswick.

FUNDY NATIONAL PARK (established 1948) lies on the Bay of Fundy, Canada, between St. John and Monckton. It covers about 80sq mi of shoreline and forest country which reaches an altitude of about 1 000ft.

FUNERAL CUSTOMS, appear to be as old as man himself, and as diverse. They have generally been determined by religious beliefs and ideas of the afterlife. The practice of burying with the dead implements useful to them in the afterlife originated during the Old Stone Age and reached its most elaborate form among the ancient Egyptians. Disposal of the body has taken many forms, including ritual cannibalism. Parsees (see ZOROASTRIANISM) leave their dead to be eaten by vultures. Preservation, usually with a view to bodily resurrection, was practiced in its most extreme form by the ancient Egyptians. The commonest forms of disposal are burial (where posture and orientation often have ritual significance) and cremation.

FUNGAL DISEASES, DISEASES caused by FUNGI which, apart from common SKIN and nail ailments such as ATHLETE'S FOOT, tinea cruris and RINGWORM, develop especially in people with disorders of IMMUNITY or DIABETES and those on certain DRUGS (STEROIDS, immunosuppressives, ANTIBIOTICS). THRUSH is common in the MOUTH and vagina but rarely causes systemic disease. Specific fungal diseases occur in some areas (e.g., HISTOPLASMOSIS, blastomycosis) while aspergillosis often complicates chronic LUNG disease. In addition, numerous fungi in the environment lead to forms of ALLERGY and lung disease.

FUNGI, a subdivision (Eumycotina) of the PLANT KINGDOM which comprises simple plants that reproduce mostly by means of SPORES and which lack CHLOROPHYLL, hence are either SAPROPHYTES or PARASITES.

The closely related SLIME MOLDS produce naked (no cell walls) amoeboid states, and the YEASTS are single-celled, but the majority of true fungi produce microscopic filaments (hyphae) that group together in an interwoven weft, the mycelium or spawn. REPRODUCTION is sometimes by budding (yeasts) but more normally by the production of asexual and sexual spores. Some fungi produce large fruit bodies, which are the structures commonly associated with fungi. The classification of fungi is complicated and several systems have evolved, mostly based on the types of spore produced. Fungi belong to the division MYCOTA, which also includes the Myxomycetes or slime molds. The true fungi are divided into a number of classes, the main ones being: the Chytridomycetes, which produce motile gametes or zoospores that have a single flagellum; the Oomycetes, which have biflagellate zoospores and produce dissimilar male and female reproductive organs and gametes; Zygomycetes, which do not produce motile zoospores

The fulmar, a common seabird of the northeast Atlantic which, like the shearwater, flies low over the wave crests. If disturbed when nesting the fulmar spits out a stream of oil, which may also serve as a means of eliminating excess vitamin A.

Fusion Power

Energy from the sea

Everyone knows that the world community faces an energy crisis, but few would claim to know how it can be solved. Unless civilization is redesigned in terms of lower energy requirements—at best an unpopular prospect—new power sources must be developed or old ones revitalized. The proposals for geothermal, tidal or solar power share the common disadvantages of being ultimately limited: if an expanding technology is to be maintained into the next millenium, the less restricted possibilities of fusion power must be explored.

The arguments in favor of fusion include its theoretical cheapness, safety, and the practical inexhaustibility of its supply of fuel—heavy hydrogen—from the sea. The major mark against it is the fact that, up to now, nobody has produced a working fusion-power generator. However, various lines of approach are actively being researched in laboratories all over the world. These research programs and some of the problems they face are described below.

Nuclear Forces and Binding Energy

The source of all nuclear power lies not so much in the basic nuclear particles (the *nucleons*: protons and neutrons) as in the forces that hold them together. An examination of these forces is necessary to the understanding of fusion power.

Imagine two magnets in contact: to separate them we must exert a force and "do work" on the system. This means that energy must be added: the magnets have a greater energy when pulled apart. The energy we must add to pull them apart is a measure of the strength of the magnetic bond between them, and can be called their "binding energy" (BE).

To zoom in from a couple of magnets to the deuterium nucleus (or deuteron) involves an enormous change of scale, but the principle remains the same. Deuterium—heavy hydrogen ${}_1H^2$—has a nucleus containing a proton and a neutron held together, not by magnetism, but by the "strong nuclear force." (The exact nature of this force is not understood, but it is effective only over very short distances.) As with the magnets, work must be done to separate the nucleons—the binding energy must be supplied.

As Einstein taught, $E=mc^2$: mass is equivalent to energy. The deuteron has lower energy than the neutron and proton separately, and this difference appears as a mass difference: ${}_1H^2$ weighs less than its component parts!

It is more convenient to talk about binding energy per nucleon than about total BE. The binding energy per nucleon is the energy needed to detach a single proton or neutron from a nucleus. A plot of binding energy against atomic mass number (showing how BE varies through the various chemical elements—the famous "BE curve"), peaks in the middle left: here are the most stable elements. To the far left, BE falls off for lack of things to bind to. Ordinary hydrogen ${}_1H^1$, with only a single nucleon, has zero binding energy. To the far right, a different factor comes into play. Protons have a positive charge. Now, like charges repel. As the number of protons in a nucleus increases, so does the electrostatic force which resists the binding of the nucleus and tries to burst it apart. This happens spontaneously with uranium-235, for example.

(A) The DD reaction. (B) The DT reaction.
(C) The BE curve.

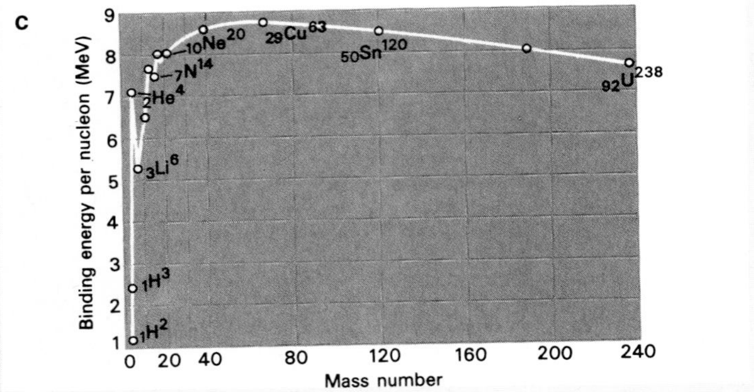

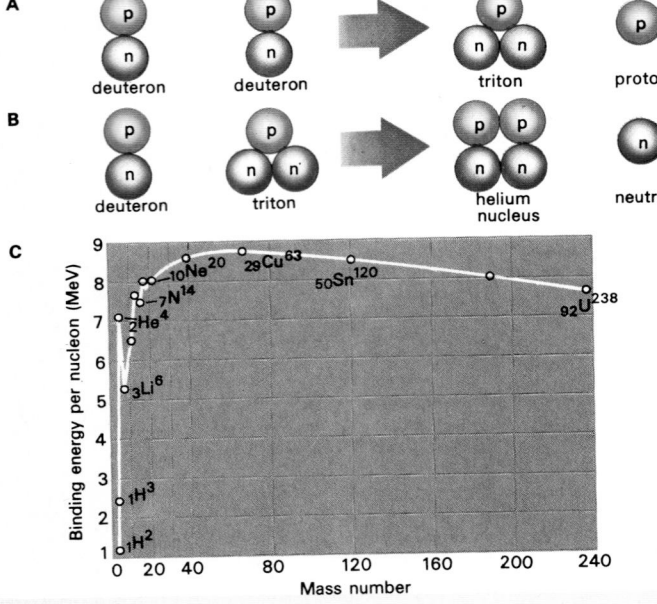

Fission and Fusion

When the uranium-235 nucleus splits up—"nuclear fission"—we get two lighter nuclei which lie closer to the center of the BE curve. Their combined BE is greater than that of the uranium and the difference is released as energy in the form of electromagnetic radiation and the kinetic energy of the "daughter nuclei."

Now, working instead from the left of the curve, by fusing very light nuclei together to form heavier ones, the overall BE can again be increased and external energy become available. This is the basic principle of fusion power. Note that, because the BE curve dips much more steeply to the left than it does to the right, the BE changes in fusion are much greater than those encountered in fission. Fusion thus is potentially a much more prolific source of power than fission.

Conditions for Fusion

Fusion does not take place easily. This is fortunate, for the sea is full of suitable material! Again, electrostatic force is the villain: the nuclear force is very short-range and the repulsion of like charges prevents nuclei closing to within this range. To initiate fusion we must accelerate them and then slam them violently together to overcome this repulsion.

The easiest way to speed up nuclei is to heat them. And if large numbers are to be handled, this is the only way. But although at very high temperature and pressure fusion will take place, the temperatures involved are really enormous: for the DT reaction (see below), temperatures of about 100 000 000 kelvins are needed.

The Fusion Bomb

The sun is a fusion reactor. Gravity provided the original high temperature and pressure, and now the reaction is self-sustaining. Man's nearest approach to solar conditions is the fireball of a fission (atomic) bomb. Such a weapon can be used to touch off the vastly greater power of fusion (as in the hydrogen bomb), just as ordinary explosives are used to initiate fission. But this provides raw, uncontrollable power, useless from a commercial standpoint: a viable fusion reactor must be incapable of explosion. But there is no need for alarm at the prospect of a commercial fusion reactor going wrong. American researchers recently calculated that the worst imaginable accident that could occur with a hypothetical fusion reactor would have practically no effect even at a distance of only 200 metres. In small-scale fusion, the difficulty is in producing any power at all.

Fusion Reactions

In the original fusion bomb, the reaction used, the "DD reaction" (so called because both reacting particles are deuterium nuclei), was

${}_1H^2 + {}_1H^2 \rightarrow {}_1H^1 + {}_1H^3$ energy release 3.174 mega-electron-volts (MeV)

The deuterium, in the form of solid lithium deuteride, was fused to produce ordinary hydrogen and tritium, ${}_1H^3$.

But a reaction which is more productive, and easier to initiate, is

${}_1H^2 + {}_1H^3 \rightarrow n + {}_2He^4$ energy release 17.577MeV

This, the "DT reaction" (named for its reagents: deuterium and tritium) is frequently used as a source of neutrons (n). The other product is the helium nucleus, ${}_2He^4$.

There are many other nuclear reactions. The sun, for instance, is believed to be powered by the "nuclear carbon cycle," a series of six nuclear reactions involving isotopes of carbon and nitrogen, the overall result of which is the conversion of ordinary hydrogen into helium, together with the liberation of positrons, neutrinos and gamma rays.

Controlled Fusion

At the present time three main avenues to the production of useful power from nuclear fusion are being explored. The traditional approach, *plasma confinement*, involves confining a superheated, ionized gas (a plasma) using very strong magnetic fields. (The temperatures required are such as would melt any material container.) Either a linear "magnetic bottle" or a toroidal (doughnut-shaped) "tokamak" are used. The gas is heated either by radio-frequency induction or by passing a heavy electric current through it. The main difficulty is instability: using a magnetic field to contain a gas at 100 000 000 kelvins is rather like trying to hold water in the air using air-jets alone. It is theoretically possible, but extremely difficult in practice.

Under the same general heading should come the relatively new theory of "migma fusion." Here a particle accelerator is used rather than simple heating, and deuterium nuclei are magnetically constrained into colliding orbits. So far, however, successful migma fusion is yet to be reported.

A second approach to controlled fusion involves the *compression* of a pellet of fusible material (frozen deuterium, deuterium-tritium mixture, or a deuterium-substituted plastic) using multiple lasers or electron beams. In theory—and according to computer predictions—the expanding gases boiled off the pellet surface will reinforce the compression, driving the nuclei together to the point of fusion. The lasers so far available are not powerful enough to succeed in this and although electron beams of great power can be produced, the beam intensity can be built up only slowly, so that the pellet simply boils away rather than suffering the required violent compression. As larger and more powerful lasers are

The Culham Conceptual Tokamak Reactor Design Mk II. Research aimed at designing an economic nuclear fusion power plant is being undertaken at laboratories in the USA, USSR, Japan and Western Europe. Seven EEC countries, including France, the UK and West Germany, are banded together in the Euratom fusion power program. Britain's contribution to this is centered on Culham Laboratory near Oxford. Before a working reactor can be built, a whole new nuclear fusion technology must be developed; research problems in both physics and engineering must first be identified and then solved. The Fusion Reactor Studies program at Culham extrapolates the results of the latest available research and uses such data to produce "conceptual" reactor designs, study of which reveals the areas requiring further research effort. The design illustrated here is for a reactor producing about 2 000MW of electricity from the DT reaction. The tritium fuel is bred from lithium contained in a neutron-absorbing blanket surrounding the torus. Heat extraction is by helium gas at high pressure (this gives up its heat to steam which then powers a turbogenerator). The "tokamak" method of plasma confinement is used. Here the plasma is confined within a torus by a magnetic field having two components: a toroidal component induced by external field coils, and a poloidal component induced by the heating current flowing toroidally through the plasma. (1) toroidal field coils; (2) poloidal field coils; (3) core; (4) blanket module; (5) cooling ducts; (6) duct joints; (7) shield structure and vacuum wall; (8) shield door; (9) shield cooling; (10) shield support; (11) servicing floor; (12) injector, refuel and control access.

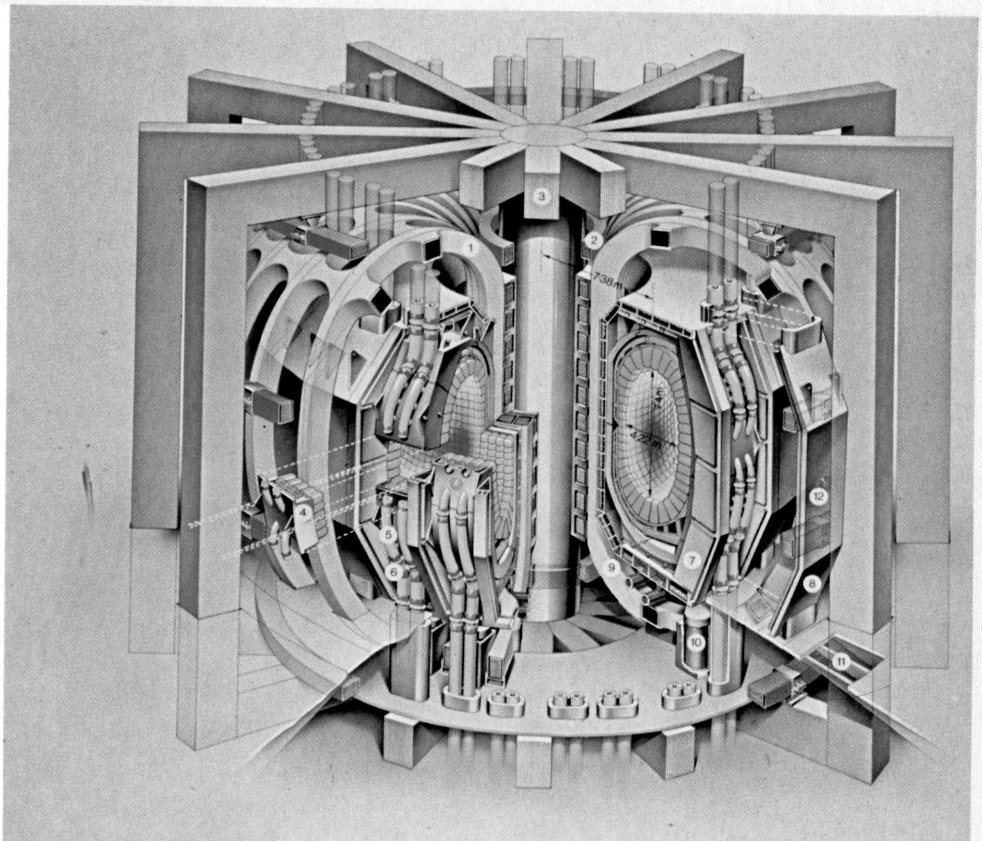

Culham Conceptual Tokamak Reactor Mk II

developed, however, it seems inevitable that laser fusion will one day be a fact. But even then the work will only be half done, for the vast engineering problems associated with fuel injection and power conversion will remain to be solved.

The third and most elegant approach to the production of a high-temperature plasma involves the *z-pinch.* Here an electron beam is fired into, or a high voltage is discharged through, the fusion fuel in the form of a high-pressure gas. The current simultaneously ionizes, heats and—through the magnetic-field "pinch" it produces—confines the plasma. Fusion on a very small scale has been achieved using the z-pinch effect, but again much development work remains to be done.

The Future

Today we can, without too great difficulty, cause fusion, but only too little or too much. The problem is power gain: the need to extract more energy than we put in. The only power gain achieved so far is in the catastrophic case of the hydrogen bomb; small-scale fusion uses up far more power than it produces. We have, then a club—the fission trigger—and an assortment of tweezers in the form of lasers, electron beams and magnetic fields. What is needed is a strong pair of pliers, and these will perhaps become available very soon.

There are still hazards—the inevitable release of neutrons and the need for radioactive tritium—but these are believed to be minor. For one thing, all reactors produce neutrons, and screening is not difficult. Again, tritium is not a strongly radioactive material, and has a half-life of only 12.3 years—very short indeed when compared with those of toxic fission wastes. There is no question of bequeathing danger to our descendants.

As reserves of fossil fuels dwindle and unease concerning fission grows, we may yet find ourselves working against time to solve the fusion problem: the greatest challenge yet faced by science. And it has been said that even if a workable fusion device were available tomorrow, it would take twenty years before a significant portion of our power came from this source.

The Bird of Time has but a little way
To fly; and lo! the Bird is on the wing.

The Culham DITE (Divertor and Injection Tokamak Experiment) tokamak. This machine is an experimental tokamak designed to test the feasibility of certain design features proposed for use on the projected large-scale JET (Joint European Torus) tokamak. DITE will test the "neutral-particle injection" method of plasma heating and the "bundle divertor" method of removing impurities and possibly spent gases from the plasma. It is expected that the neutral-beam heating method will raise the JET reactor plasma temperature to that required for the fusion reaction (>100 000 000K). Research into building practical fusion reactors is slow and costly: full power (1.5MW neutral beam injection) on the DITE experiment is scheduled for 1978—and this is only one of many individual studies contributing to the JET reactor program.

Futurology

Discovering the shoals ahead

In the last quarter of the twentieth century, the future is like a kaleidoscope. Twist it one way, and you view a brave new world of material affluence and technological miracles in which humanity leaves the earth to begin voyages to the stars. Twist again, and you slip over into the bleak landscape of a polluted planet, overburdened with people, and close to exhausting its fragile stores of energy, food and raw materials. Another turn and our future is virtually non-existent—but for the few ragged survivors of a world which has gone over the nuclear edge.

However it is viewed, we are more conscious of the future than at any time in history. Future issues encroach more upon present decisions whether collectively, in locating a nuclear power plant or, individually, in planning a career or choosing a retirement place. Even the past is not immune to the future, as its long-term changes may be re-interpreted in the light of their future consequences. There is a widespread feeling that we have now reached a major turning point in our affairs, in which the future of society may be radically different from anything we have known so far. Some feel exhilarated by the challenge, others voice anxiety and concern, all share in a global restlessness which is expressed in different ways.

This awareness of the future is, in itself, comparatively new. Until the 18th century the future was for most people essentially a continuation of the past. Life was short, change slow and difficult and the capacity to intervene in future events was very limited. Probing the future was largely the job of the religious prophet, the fortune teller or the divine oracle. Utopian visions, of more recent origin, were located in the distant future to serve as imaginary models of conditions to which we might ideally aspire, but had little hope of realizing in practice.

All this has changed within living memory. The distant future appears to become the present more swiftly and with greater impact. A speeding up of the change process has become visible in a single lifetime; those who grew up with the horse and buggy now travel in automobiles and jets, and have watched men landing on the moon in living color.

In less than a generation, we have had a series of scientific technical, social and economic revolutions cresting one upon another. Our previous world of distant, loosely linked, independent nations has suddenly shrunk into a small, interdependent neighborhood in which any major event has swift global repercussions. In transforming the planet to human use, we have moved into the air to travel above its surface and beyond its atmosphere. We have gone below the land, and downwards into the oceans, to extract and consume more energy and materials in the past century than in all history. A crucial aspect of this transition is that it marks the stage at which human activities have grown to such a level as to potentially threaten the overall ecological balance of life on earth. The capability to influence and shape the future is literally within our hands. The range, scale and complexity of our actions now force us to view them in terms of their longer range consequences and implications.

Against this background, probing the future is no longer confined to crystal balls, dependence on divine oracles, or tea leaf patterns, but has become a field of serious intellectual enquiry, of corporate investment and of governmental concern.

The last ten years, particularly, has been marked by a remarkable upsurge of studies of the future, not only in the shorter term of the next decade, but extending to the year 2000 and beyond.

The terms used to describe the field vary considerably. *Futures research*, *futurology*, *forecasting*, and *futuristics* are all used widely and interchangeably. The Russians and East Europeans also use *prognostics* to describe their work and the French have a preference for *futuribles*. One essential difference between future studies and the fiction of visionaries like Jules Verne or H. G. Wells is that today's futurists are not so much concerned with prophesying what some particular future will be, but rather more with exploring the kinds of futures that might emerge as a consequence of our decisions and actions, or be brought about by choice.

Though all studies of the future tend to be lumped together there may be considerable differences of approach and method. They fall into three main categories. Descriptive studies embrace all conjectural and speculative studies, ranging from essays on the future in general to imaginative projections of future developments in some particular sphere of human activity. Exploratory studies are restricted to the more methodical extrapolation of past and present trends into the future, including economic and technological forecasts. Prescriptive studies are those in which some specific future is presented with a strong argument in favor of this or that direction. In practice, of course, all three approaches may be involved in the same study.

There has been a distinct shift in the past five years from an emphasis on predicting and forecasting some specific set of future events towards considering the range of alternative futures available to us, and their positive or negative implications, costs and benefits. Studies have also increasingly recommended which directions should be taken to avoid future catastrophe or to ensure some alternative future.

This change in emphasis has been accompanied by a swift expansion of the field in terms of the numbers and kinds of people and organizations engaged in studying the future and in the range and volume of their activities.

The first world congress held by the World Futures Research Federation in Oslo

and reproduce sexually by fusion of identical gametes; the Ascomycetes, including yeasts, which reproduce asexually by budding or by the production of spores (conidia) and sexually by the formation of ascospores within sac-like structures (asci) that are often enclosed in a fruiting body or ascocarp; the Basidiomycetes, including BRACKET FUNGI and AGARICS in which the sexual spores are produced or enlarged cells called basidia, that often occur on large fruiting bodies; and the Deuteromycetes, or Fungi Imperfecti, which are only known to reproduce asexually, although sexual forms are often classified in the Ascomycetes and Basidiomycetes. (See also FUNGAL DISEASES; MOLD; PLANT DISEASES; RUST; SMUT.)

FUNGICIDE, substance used to kill FUNGI and so to control FUNGAL DISEASES in man and plants. In medicine some ANTIBIOTICS, SULFUR, CARBOXYLIC ACIDS and potassium iodide are used. In agriculture a wide variety of fungicides is used, both inorganic—BORDEAUX MIXTURE and sulfur—and organic—many different compounds, generally containing sulfur or nitrogen. They are applied to the soil before planting or around seedlings, or are sprayed or dusted onto foliage. (See also PESTICIDE.)

FUNGI IMPERFECTI or Deuleromycetes. See FUNGI.

FUNK, Casimir (1884–1967), Polish-born biochemist. Following the work of C. EIJKMAN and F. G. HOPKINS, he proposed that BERIBERI, RICKETS, SCURVY and PELLAGRA arose from lack of certain trace dietary constituents, which he christened vitamines, or "life-amines." (See also AMINES; VITAMINS.)

FUNNY BONE, part of the ulna at the elbow over which passes the ulnar nerve. If this point is struck sharply, it causes transient unpleasant, electric shock-like tingling and numbness in the ARM and SKIN area served by the ulnar nerve.

FUNSTON, Frederick (1865–1917), American soldier, awarded the Congressional Medal of Honor

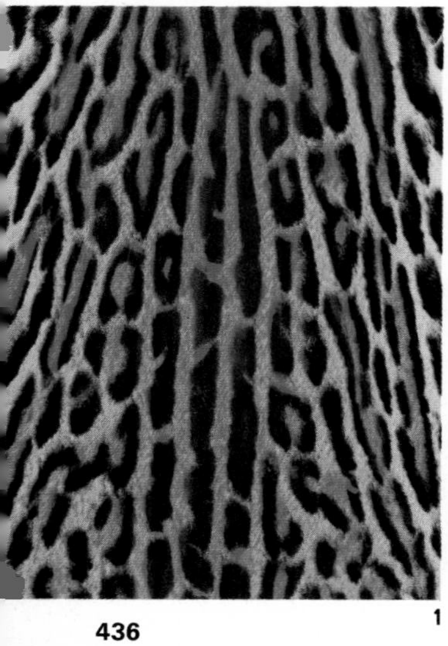

1

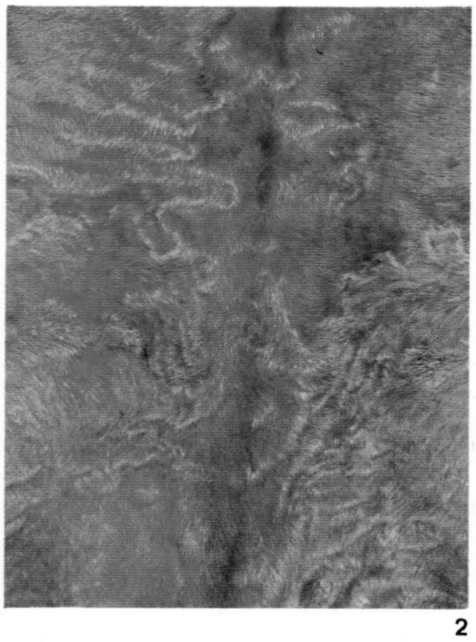

2

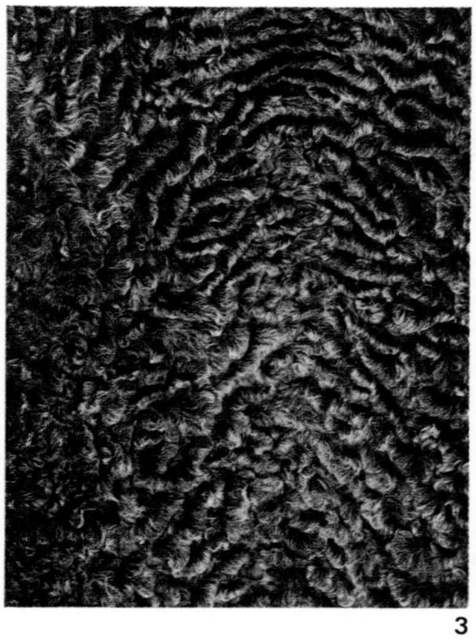

3

4

(1967) had about 30 participants, the second, in Kyoto (1970) had 250 and the third, in Bucharest (1973) attracted over 300. In parallel with these meetings of the World Futures Research Federation, the US-based World Futures Society has grown from a few hundred members in 1967 to 18000 in 1975; its last annual assembly drew over 2000 participants. In addition to specialized gatherings, a growing number of voluntary, professional and commercial organizations now have futures sections in their yearly meetings.

Where the earlier balance of academic disciplines in futures work was mainly drawn from the physical sciences, engineering and mathematics, more recent additions to the field have come from the social sciences and humanities. As academic interest has widened there has been a corresponding rise in the number of journals and newsletters devoted to the future, such as *Futures* in the UK, *The Futurist* and *Technological Forecasting and Social Change* in the US, *Futuribles* in France, *Polska 2000* in Poland and many others. In the US alone, upwards of 300 courses on the future are now being offered in universities, colleges and other parts of the educational system.

The futures field itself has broadened, particularly in the past five years, to merge at one end with corporate and governmental long range planning, and at the other with the wider and less specialized involvement of large numbers of people concerned with the future in general, or with some specific problem such as environmental protection, population control or simply the quality of life.

There are now a growing number of futures secretariats and commissions at national governmental levels in W and E Europe and Japan, and several regional study groups such as *Europe Plus 30*. Many of these activities have been linked in part to the international concerns expressed in the various United Nations world conferences on environment, population and food which have focused attention on longer term global problems and issues.

The Club of Rome has also been an important influence on these developments with internationally sponsored and widely publicized studies on *The Limits to Growth* and *Mankind at the Turning Point*.

In the US, where interest and support for futures work has been strongest, Congress has been active in setting up its Office of Technology Assessment to monitor the long range impacts of technical developments, and in the adoption of a "foresight" provision in its committees to consider the long-term consequences of legislative actions. Many industrial corporations now have their own futures "think tanks" not only to explore future products and markets but to study wider socio-economic issues. Several US institutes have played a pioneer role in the overall development of the futures field. Some are more or less independent entities like the Rand Corporation, the Hudson Institute and The Futures Group; others are linked to academies, such as the 1967 "Commission on the Year 2000" of the American Academy of Arts and Sciences, or are university-based like the Institute for the Future, the Center for Integrative Studies and the Center for Futures Research. Another aspect of growing US interest in the future has been the revival of the utopian commune movement, by those not only interested in studying the future but by attempting to anticipate it.

Methods used in more formal probing of the future range from individual "brainstorming" and straightforward trend projection to techniques such as the "Delphi" which correlate the probability of occurrence of future events given by expert panels and calculate their cross-impacts. Some use gaming methods in which alternative futures are played out to examine their consequences; others construct elaborate scenarios combining various approaches. The emphasis is less on the success or failure of prediction than on the ways in which different possibilities can be explored and their costs and benefits estimated. Given our present human prospects, the problem is not one of prophesying but rather of inventing the future.

Public involvement and concern with the future has undoubtedly been generated by bestselling books such as *Future Shock*, *The Limits to Growth*, *The Population Bomb*, *Our Plundered Planet*, *The Chasm Ahead* and *The Doomsday Book*, whose very names sound like a drum roll for the coming apocalypse. In general, the message is that we have come too far and too fast on a world facing exhaustion. However negative their approach they helped create a wide awareness of long-term problems. Signs that the tide of pessimism has now abated are evident; Herman Kahn's *The Next 200 Years* suggests not only that we may survive the future but that it may be more prosperous and more secure for more people, and Earl Hubbard's *Our Need for New Worlds*, which sees our long range prospects as lying beyond the earth, in the exploration of other planets and systems.

In conjunction with the steady growth of futuristic themes in literature and films, works such as these provide a wide range of arresting metaphors and images of possible futures within which a large public audience can identify their personal and collective concerns. This generalized concern for the future has now begun to evolve into a social movement. Again, in the US particularly, we have had the emergence of large scale citizen involvement in futures speculation at state and regional levels. The first event of this kind was Hawaii 2000, followed by Iowa 2000, the Puget Sound Regional Conference and others. All seek to explore and plan the future in a manner which is at once a creative challenge and a threat to established political procedures.

Apart from totalitarian societies with their traditional five- and twenty-year plans, the political process has been somewhat immune to the future. Where political office previously depended on short-range policies and decisions, politicians are now increasingly faced with issues and problems which go far beyond their given period of office. How to cope with the long-range consequences of today's decisions in a world of rapid and turbulent change is now a central political dilemma.

Many of our present technical and socio-economic problems require the commitment of relatively enormous investments over longer and longer time spans. Nuclear energy planning, for example, may involve the secure storage of radioactive wastes as a dubious legacy to future generations; the supersonic aircraft debate goes far beyond local noise levels to involve possible long-term deterioration of the ozone layer. In managing the present, we now realize that our choices may also affect the future in ways which may limit the choices of the next generation.

The study of the future today is a far cry from the utopianism of yesterday. Its central challenge is to provide the longer range navigational aids and early warning systems with which we may avoid the shoals ahead and ensure not only that we have a future but that we retain the possibility of many diverse and alternative futures for mankind.

in the Philippines Campaign in 1899. In 1901 he captured Emilio Aguinaldo, the insurgents' leader, in a daring raid.

FUR, the soft, dense, hairy undercoat of certain mammals. Fur is an excellent heat insulator and protects against the cold of the northern regions where most furbearing animals are found. It is generally interspersed with guard HAIRS, longer and stiffer, that form a protective outer coat and prevent matting. Skins or pelts are cleaned, softened and converted to a leatherlike state by "dressing," a process resembling TANNING. In some cases the guard hairs are sheared or plucked. The pelt is then dyed or bleached and then glazed, chemically or by heat, to give it a lustrous sheen. To make the furs into a garment, they are matched for color and texture, cut to shape, sewn together, and finally dampened and nailed to the pattern to dry smooth and the exact shape wanted. Fur clothing has long been valued for its beauty and warmth, and was an aristocratic luxury until the discovery of America, in whose exploration and economic development trapping and fur trading played a major role. Demand is still high, threatening some furbearing species with extinction; this has led to fur-farming of suitable animals such as mink and to the development of artificial furs made of synthetic fibers.

FURFURAL ($C_4H_3O.CHO$), colorless liquid, an ALDEHYDE similar to BENZALDEHYDE and a HETEROCYCLIC COMPOUND derived from furan. It is made by digesting corncobs, oat and rice hulls, etc. with acid, and is used as a solvent, a pesticide, and an intermediate in making PLASTICS and other compounds.

FURIES (or Erinyes), in classical mythology Tisiphone, Alecto and Megaera, avenging goddesses who carried out the curses pronounced on criminals and tortured the guilty. They are portrayed in the *Orestes* of EURIPIDES and the *Eumenides* of AESCHYLUS. They were called *Eumenides* (the Kindly Ones) although there was nothing kindly about them.

FURNACE, a construction in which heat can be generated, controlled and used. The heat may be produced by burning a fuel such as coal, oil or gas; by electricity; by concentrating the heat of the sun; or by atomic energy (see FISSION, NUCLEAR). Simple furnaces are often used in the home to heat water; but much larger ones are used in industry, particularly in the heat treatment of metals (see METALLURGY). These are usually lined with FIREBRICKS (see also REFRACTORY), which may also be water-cooled. (See also BESSEMER PROCESS; BLAST FURNACE; ELECTRIC FURNACE; OPEN-HEARTH PROCESS.)

FUR SEALS, two distinct genera of SEALS. *Arctocephalus* is found in the S Hemisphere, *Callorhinus* only in the N Pacific, notably on the Pribilof Islands in the

Opposite: four different kinds of fur: (1) short-haired (ocelot); (2) moiré (foalskin); (3) curly (Persian lamb); and (4) long-haired (silver fox).

Right: female Kerguelen fur seal on the island of South Georgia. A rush of sealers to the southern seas brought the Kerguelen fur seal to the point of extinction by the end of the 19th century; but the animal's numbers have increased dramatically since 1933, when a small colony was discovered on Bird Island, off South Georgia.

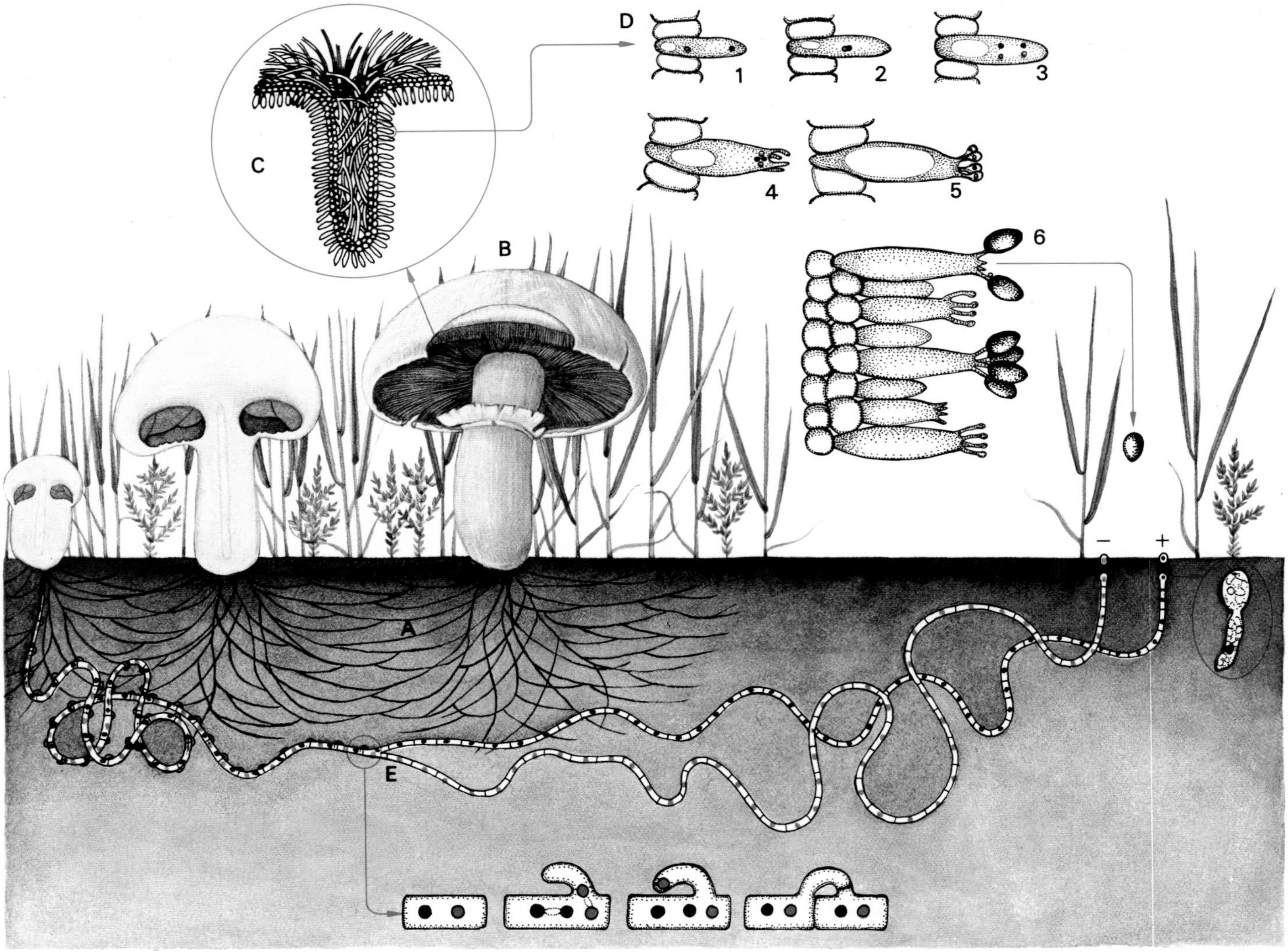

A common form of sexual reproduction in the mushrooms: an example of reproduction in fungi. The actual "body" (A) is the spawn (mycelium). This gives rise to (B) a fruitbody (basidiocarp) on either side of whose gills is a layer of basidia (C). Each young basidium contains two separate nuclei (D1). They fuse together (2) and subsequently divide again (3), then migrating to the developing spores (4 & 5). These spores drop off (6) and germinate to produce what is known as a hypha. If a (+) spore hypha meets up with a (–) spore hypha, they fuse (E) and reproduce.

Bering Sea. Both have been threatened with extinction by sealers. *Callorhinus* is now protected.

FUR SEAL CONTROVERSY. See BERING SEA CONTROVERSY.

FURTWÄNGLER, Wilhelm (1886–1954), German conductor whose free, passionate style made him one of the great interpreters, particularly of Beethoven and Wagner.

FURZE, common name for shrubs of the genus *Ulex*, several species of which are in cultivation as ornamentals. Common furze, or gorse (*Ulex europaeus*) is abundant on heaths and commons in W Europe and produces a mass of yellow flowers in the spring. Family: Leguminosae.

FUSE, safety device placed in an electric circuit to prevent overloading. It usually comprises a wire of low-melting-point metal mounted in or on an insulated frame. Current passing through the wire heats it (see RESISTANCE); and excessive current heats it to the point where it melts, so breaking the CIRCUIT. In most domestic plugs, the fuse consists of a cylinder of glass, capped at each end by metal, with a wire running between the metal caps. Similar, but larger, cartridge fuses are used in industry.

FUSEL OIL, a mixture mainly of amyl and butyl ALCOHOLS, produced as a by-product of FERMENTATION. It helps to flavor alcoholic beverages, but is separated by DISTILLATION from industrial ETHANOL, and used for solvents.

FUSELI, Henry (1741–1825), Anglo-Swiss painter and writer, appointed professor of painting at the Royal Academy in 1799. His paintings, of which the most famous is probably *The Nightmare* (1781), are highly stylized and have an often sinister sensuality.

FU-SHUN, city in China in central Liaoning province, S Manchuria. Sited 28mi E of Mukden in an agricultural area, it has the richest coalfields in China. Pop 1 091 000.

FUSION, the process of melting, or passing from the solid state to liquid state. This is accompanied by an absorption of LATENT HEAT and usually occurs at a well-defined TEMPERATURE, the **melting point** which rises slightly with PRESSURE and chemical purity. Many amorphous solids like GLASS have no melting point, and simply reduce their VISCOSITY over a wide temperature range.

FUSION, Nuclear, a nuclear reaction in which the nuclei of light ATOMS combine to produce heavier, more stable nuclei, releasing a large quantity of ENERGY. Fusion reactions are the energy source of the SUN and the HYDROGEN BOMB. If they could be controlled and made self-sustaining man would have a safe and inexhaustible energy source using DEUTERIUM OR TRITIUM extracted from seawater. Only small amounts of fuel would be needed and the products are not radioactive. But if they are to fuse, the light, positively charged nuclei must collide with sufficient energy to overcome their electrostatic repulsion. This can be done by using a particle ACCELERATOR, but to get a net energy release the material must be heated to very high temperatures (around 10^9K) when it becomes a PLASMA. However, plasmas are difficult to contain and, as yet, no apparatus has been designed which allows more energy to be extracted than is used in heating and containing the plasma. (See also NUCLEAR ENERGY.)

FUST, Johann (or Faust) (c1400–1466?), German pioneer printer. He financed GUTENBERG's development of the printing press, then sued him, seized the press and printed his own 350-page Psalter in 1457.

FUSTEL DE COULANGES, Numa Denis (1830–1889), French historian whose books *The Ancient City* (1864) and *Political Institutions of Ancient France* (1888–92), though now superseded, encouraged and helped develop a modern approach to historical studies in France.

FUSTIAN, term formerly applied to a fabric with a linen warp and cotton weft but now referring to heavy-piled cotton fabrics including velveteen and corduroy.

FUSTIC, a yellow heartwood obtained from *Chlorophora tinctoria*, a tree native to the West Indies and Tropical America. Also, the dye extracted from the wood which is used to produce yellow, brown and olive colors for wool dyeing.

FUTURES MARKET, commodity market through which futures contracts are bought and sold. Futures contracts are for the delivery of standardized goods at a time, place and price determined when the contract is drawn up. The first such market in the US was the Chicago Board of Trade, though the idea originated in Venice and Alexandria in the 16th century.

FUTURISM, 20th-century Italian art movement based on two manifestos of Futurist poetry and painting, issued in 1909 and 1910 by the poet Filippo MARINETTI and an allied group of artists. It sought to express the speed, violence and dynamism of a mechanical age.

FUZE, primary explosive charge set off by electrical, chemical or mechanical means which detonates the main charge of an explosive device. Commonly fuzes operate on the principle of the firecracker fuze. **Proximity fuzes** may be set in a moving projectile, to function when it is a certain distance from target. (See also AMMUNITION.)

G

G, seventh letter of the English alphabet, developed from the Semitic *ghimel* and a differentiated form of the Greek *gamma*. English has a hard "g" sound as in "go" and a soft "g" sound, mostly before e, i, and y, as in "gentle." In music G is the fifth note in the scale of C.

G, the Universal Gravitational Constant. See GRAVITATION.

g, acceleration due to gravity. See ACCELERATION.

GABBRO, a dense IGNEOUS ROCK, resembling BASALT, composed of coarse-grained plagioclase FELDSPAR with PYROXENE and OLIVINE. Often rhythmically banded, it arises from fractional crystallization of MAGMA.

GABELLE, French term for a tax levied from the 14th century to the Revolution; from the 15th century specifically the salt tax. Hated because it was too heavy and unequally applied, it was a major popular grievance against the French crown.

GABLE, Clark (1901–1960), US film star, winner of a 1934 Academy Award for a comedy role in *It Happened One Night*. His most famous role was Rhett Butler in *Gone with the Wind* (1939).

GABO, Naum (born Naum Pevsner; 1890–), Russian sculptor, a pioneer of CONSTRUCTIVISM. With his brother Anton PEVSNER, he issued the *Realist Manifesto* (1920). He left Russia and taught at the BAUHAUS (1922–32). In 1946 he emigrated to the US. He is noted for his kinetic sculptures and geometrical constructions in metal, plastic and nylon.

GABON, small republic on the Atlantic coast of W Africa. Most of the country, lying across the Equator, is rain forest; a mountain range separates the narrow coastal area from the heartland plateaus. The climate is hot and humid, with heavy rainfall. The country has a wide range of ethnic groups; the largest, the Fang, constitutes about 30% of the population and dominates politics and industry. Most of the people are village dwellers, but over 15% live in the main towns of Libreville, Port-Gentil and Lambarene, site of Albert SCHWEITZER's famous hospital. Until the 1960s Gabon's main natural resource was timber, but mineral reserves, especially manganese, petroleum and uranium, have been increasingly exploited. Uranium deposits appear to be nearly depleted, but iron ore may become equally important. The main industry is timber and mineral processing. Due to the weakness of Gabonese agriculture, much food is imported.

The Omyene peoples dominated Gabon until gradually displaced by the Fang in the 19th century. France maintained a naval base on the coast from 1843, but only occupied the country when its economic possibilities became apparent. A French colony from 1886, Gabon was exploited both by commercial interests and by native leaders, who made much use of forced labor. Only in and after WWII did conditions improve. In 1946 it became an overseas territory of France. It achieved self-government in 1958, independence in 1960, and became a one-party state in 1968.

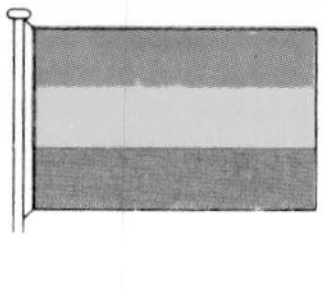

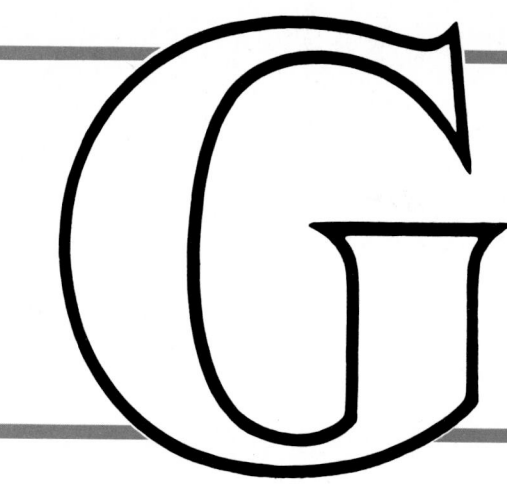

Official Name: Gabon Republic
Capital: Libreville
Area: 103 088sq mi
Population: 500 000
Languages: French, Fang, Bantu
Religions: Roman Catholic, Animist, Muslim
Monetary Unit(s): 1 CFA franc = 100 centimes

GABOON VIPER, *Bitis gabonica*, a venomous snake found in tropical Africa, about 750mm (30in) long with a thick body. It moves by throwing its body forward in loops. When approached it makes a blowing sound through its nostrils. Its markings are in shades of brown, yellow and purple.

GABOR, Dennis (1900–), Hungarian-born UK physicist who invented HOLOGRAPHY, for which he was awarded the 1971 Nobel Prize for Physics. He had developed the basic technique in the late 1940s, but practical applications had to wait for the invention of the LASER (1960) by C. H. TOWNES.

GABORONE, capital of the republic of Botswana in S Africa since 1965. It is now an administrative and cultural center. Pop 18 436.

GABRIEL (Hebrew: divine hero or man of God), name of one of the ARCHANGELS in the Bible and the Koran. In the Bible he appears to Daniel and to Zacharias, and to Mary in the ANNUNCIATION. In the Koran he is the medium of revelation to Mohammed.

GABRIELI, family of Italian composers. **Andrea** (c1520–1586), organist at St. Mark's, Venice, composed sacred motets and psalms, madrigals and organ works. **Giovanni** (c1556–1612), Andrea's nephew and successor at St. Mark's, composed vocal and instrumental music noted for its dramatic style and use of counterpoint.

GAD, son of Jacob and his wife's maid Zilpah (Gen. 30). He gave his name to one of the TWELVE TRIBES OF ISRAEL.

GADDAFI, Muammar el-. See QADAFFI, MUAMMAR AL-.

GADDI, Taddeo (c1300–1366), Florentine painter, a pupil of GIOTTO, whom he succeeded as decorator of S. Croce in Florence. His frescoes of the lives of Christ, St. Francis and St. Bonaventure, are perhaps his greatest works.

GADFLIES, blood-sucking FLIES such as HORSEFLIES and WARBLE FLIES. They attack livestock.

GADOLINIUM (Gd), element of the LANTHANUM SERIES. AW 157.3, mp 1313°C, bp 3266°C, sg 7.9004 (25°C).

GADSDEN, city in NE Ala., seat of Etowah Co. Local mineral resources are exploited and metal, textiles and rubber products manufactured. Pop 53 928.

GADSDEN, James (1788–1858), US soldier and diplomat who, as minister to Mexico, negotiated the GADSDEN PURCHASE. In the WAR OF 1812 he served against the Seminole Indians and was in charge of their removal to S Fla. in 1825 and to the W in 1832.

GADSDEN PURCHASE, Mexican territory bought by the US in 1853, to add to their territorial gains in the war of 1848. The extra land, some 30 000 sq mi, cost $10 million. It provided a rail route through the conquered land to the Pacific. The purchase was negotiated by James GADSDEN.

GADWALL, common name for a type of duck popular for eating. It breeds in N and E Europe, N Asia and North America in ponds, lakes and marshes. Its coloring is drab, its head small and body long.

GAEA (Ge), goddess in Greek mythology, personification of the earth. Mother and wife to URANUS, she gave birth to the CYCLOPS, TITANS and ERINYES. She was worshiped as the universal Mother.

GAELIC, or Goidelic, group of CELTIC LANGUAGES, native to Ireland (Irish Gaelic), the Isle of Man (Manx) and the Scottish Highlands (Scottish Gaelic).

GAELIC LITERATURE, writings in the Gaelic language. There are two main traditions. Irish Gaelic is divided into three periods, Old Irish (up to c10th century); Middle Irish (up to mid-15th century) and Modern Irish. The early literature consists chiefly of lyric verse and sagas, of which the *Ulster Cycle* is a famous example. Scottish Gaelic diverged from the Irish tradition in c1300 and developed an impressive body of poetry, with some prose work. (See also OSSIAN; MACPHERSON, JAMES.)

GAELS, or Goidels, the Gaelic-speaking Celtic peoples of Ireland, and Scotland and the Isle of Man, as opposed to the Celtic people of Wales, Cornwall or Brittany, who speak Brythonic.

GAFFNEY, city, seat of Cherokee Co., N S.C. It is a market center for peaches and grain, and manufactures textiles, bricks and metal goods. Pop 13 253.

GAGARIN, Yuri Alekseyevich (1934–1968), Soviet astronaut, first man in space. His capsule was launched on April 12, 1961, and orbited the earth once. A deputy to the Supreme Soviet from 1962, he died in a plane crash.

GAGE, Thomas (1721–1787), British general, from 1763 commander-in-chief of British forces in North America and military governor of Mass. from 1774. In April 1775 his attempt to take an arms depot at Concord resulted in the first battles (at Lexington and Concord) of the REVOLUTIONARY WAR. He resigned after the debacle at BUNKER HILL.

GAG RULES, resolutions passed in the US House of Representatives 1836–40 to prevent discussion in the House of petitions regarding slavery. The rules infringed the right of petition; they were repealed in 1844 as the result of a campaign led by John Quincy ADAMS and Joshua GIDDINGS.

GAHANNA, village in central Ohio, in an agricultural area 5mi NE of Columbus. Pop 12 400.

GAILLARD, David Du Bose (1859–1913), US engineer. An authority on hydraulics and channel

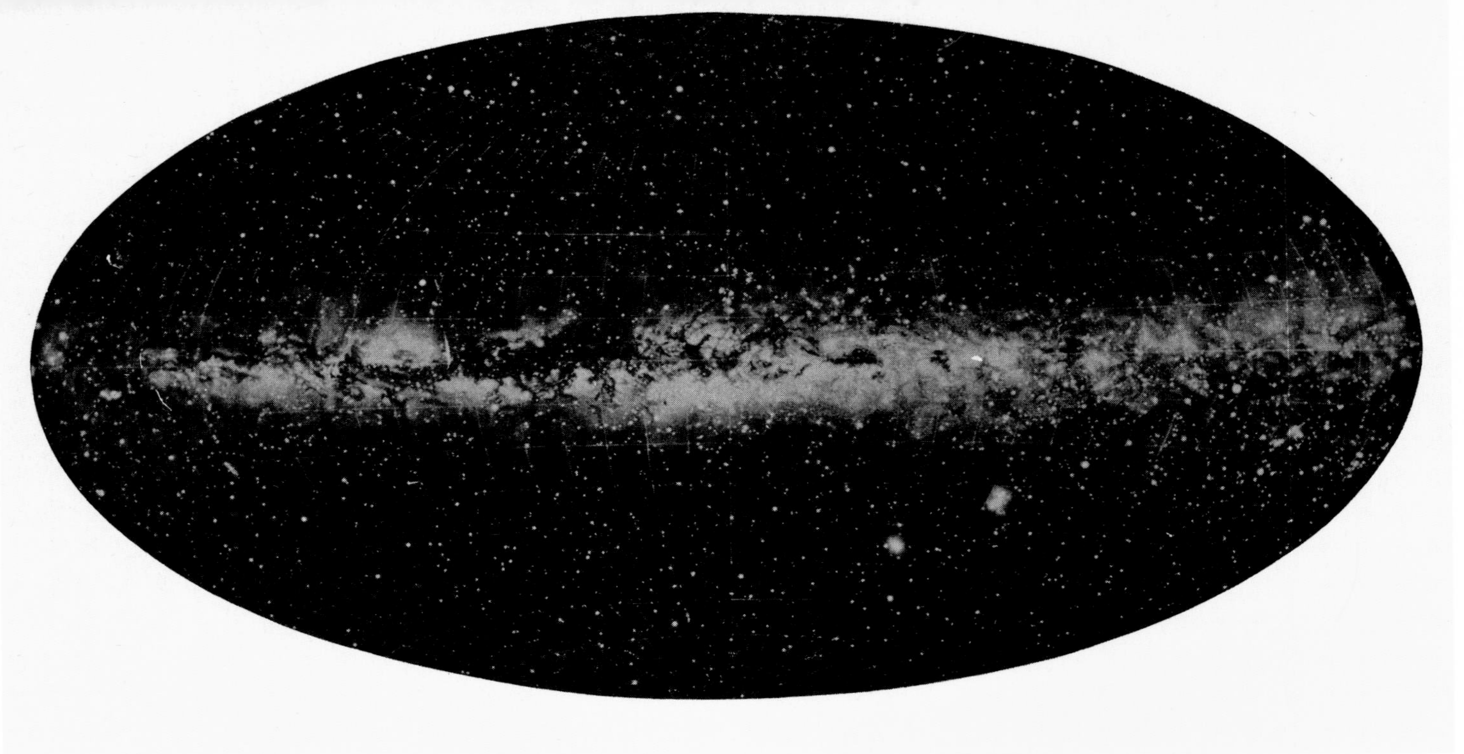

The Milky Way, a reconstruction of which seen edge-on is shown here, is a large spiral galaxy. At the speed of light it would take about 100 000 years to cross it from edge to edge. Our sun is only one of the 100 billion or so stars it contains. Fewer than 7 000 stars appear in the photograph.

dredging, he took charge, under GOETHALS, of the central division of the Panama Canal excavations, including the Culebra cut, since named for him.

GAILLARD CUT, 8mi excavated gorge, 50ft deep by 500ft wide, part of the PANAMA CANAL. Formerly the Culebra Cut, it was named for David Du Bose GAILLARD.

GAILLARDIA, genus of North American annual and perennial herbs producing showy yellow or yellow-red flowers with purple centers. Several species are popular garden flowers. Family: COMPOSITAE.

GAINES'S MILL, Battle of, in the American Civil War, part of the Confederate counter-offensive to end the PENINSULAR CAMPAIGN, near Richmond, Va. On June 27, 1862, forces led by Generals Jackson and Longstreet attacked and routed Union forces under Gen. Fitz-John Porter.

GAINESVILLE, city in N Fla., seat of Alachua Co. home of the U. of Fla. It manufactures electronic equipment and wood products. Pop 64 510.

GAINESVILLE, city in N central Ga., seat of Hall Co. A textile center, it also manufactures furniture. Pop 15 459.

GAINESVILLE, city in N Tex. on the Trinity R, seat of Cooke Co. It is an industrial and oil-refining center, with cotton and grain processing. Pop 13 830.

GAINSBOROUGH, Thomas (1727–1788), English portraitist and landscape painter. He painted numerous society portraits; in 1780 he was commissioned to portray George III and Queen Charlotte. Many of his portraits are actually set in landscapes, which were his primary interest. His work influenced CONSTABLE and English landscape painting in the 19th century.

GAISERIC. See GENSERIC.

GAITSKELL, Hugh (Todd Naylor) (1906–1963), British politician, Labour Party leader 1955–63. He entered Parliament in 1945 and was chancellor of the exchequer in 1950. In opposition he was a leading critic of Conservative policies and managed to reunite the party after a split in 1960.

GAIUS, Saint, pope c283–c296. His feast day is April 22.

GAIUS, Roman jurist of the 2nd century AD, author of the *Institutes*, an authoritative exposition of Roman law in his time. This served as a source for the *Institutes* and *Digest* commissioned by JUSTINIAN.

GALACTIC CLUSTERS, clusters of stars lying in or near the galactic plane, each of which contains a few hundred stars. Due to their irregular shape they are also termed **open clusters**. The best known galactic cluster in N skies is the PLEIADES.

GALAGO, or Bushbaby. See BUSHBABIES.

GALAHAD, Sir, in ARTHURIAN LEGEND the personification of spiritual purity. As the HOLY GRAIL legend took on a more spiritual significance, so its original hero Sir Perceval (PARSIFAL) was replaced by the more spiritual Sir Galahad.

GALÁPAGOS ISLANDS, group of volcanic islands in the Pacific, on the equator W of Ecuador. They were named for the giant tortoises found there in 1535 by the Spaniard Thomas de Berlanga. They have unique vegetation and wildlife, the study of which confirmed Charles DARWIN in his theory of evolution. There are large marine and land iguanas, scarlet crabs, penguins, a flightless cormorant, unique finches and the giant tortoises, now rare. The main islands are Isabella, Santa Cruz, Fernandina, San Salvador and San Cristobal; they are now a national park and wildlife sanctuary.

GALATEA, in Greek mythology a NEREID loved by the Cyclops Polyphemus. He murdered her lover Acis, but she changed Acis' blood into a river. Galatea was also the name of PYGMALION's living statue.

GALAŢI, city on the Danube R in E Romania. An inland port and naval base, it manufactures metal, chemical and textile goods. Pop 179 189.

GALATIA, an ancient territory of central Asia Minor overrun by Gauls in the 3rd century BC. Subjugated by Rome in 189 BC, it became part of the Roman province of Galatia (which extended south) in 25 BC, and by 200 AD had merged with Anatolia.

GALATIANS, Epistle to the, ninth book of the NEW TESTAMENT, a letter written by St. Paul to the Christians in N or S Galatia to counter the influence of Judaizers who taught that Christians must keep all the law of Moses. It sets forth the basis of Christian freedom, man's union with Christ through faith.

GALAX, *Galax aphylla*, an evergreen perennial herb found in wooded areas of the southeastern US. The small white flowers are borne on a spike. The heart-shaped leaves turn bronze in the fall and are often used for decoration. Family: Diapensiaceae.

GALAXY, the largest individual conglomeration of matter, containing stars, gas, dust and planets. Galaxies start life as immense clouds of gas, out of which stars condense. Initially a galaxy is **irregular** in form; that is, it has neither a specific shape nor any apparent internal structure. It contains large amounts of gas and dust in which new stars are constantly forming. It rotates and over millions of years evolves into a **spiral** form, looking rather like a flying saucer, with a roughly spherical nucleus surrounded by a flattish disk and orbited by GLOBULAR CLUSTERS. In the nucleus there is little gas and dust and a high proportion of older stars; in the spiral arms a great deal of gas and dust and a high proportion of younger stars (our SUN lies in a spiral arm of the MILKY WAY). Over further millions of years the spiral arms "fold" toward the nucleus, the end result being an **elliptical** galaxy containing a large number of older stars and little or no gas and dust. The ultimate form of any galaxy is a sphere, after which it possibly evolves into a BLACK HOLE. The nearest external galaxy to our own is the ANDROMEDA Galaxy. Similarly spiral, though rather larger, it has two satellite galaxies which are elliptical in form. Originally it was thought to be a NEBULA within our own galaxy, but in 1924 HUBBLE showed that it was a galaxy in its own right. Study of the Andromeda Galaxy is important as it enables us better to understand our own, most of which is obscured from us by clouds of gas and dust. Galaxies emit radio waves, and the strongest sources are known as **radio galaxies**. One group of these, spiral with active nuclei, are named **Seyfert galaxies** for the US astronomer Carl Seyfert. (See also PULSAR; QUASAR.) Galaxies tend to form in clusters. The Milky Way and the Andromeda Galaxy are members of a cluster of around 20 galaxies.

GALBRAITH, John Kenneth (1908–   ), US economist and author, ambassador to India 1961–63. In *American Capitalism* (1952) he introduced the concept of COUNTERVAILING POWER. In *The Affluent Society* (1958) he argued that resources used in the production of superfluous consumer goods should be diverted into public and social sectors.

GALDOS, Benito Perez. See PEREZ GALDOS, BENITO.

GALEN OF PERGAMUM (c130–c200 AD), Greek physician at the court of the Emperor Marcus Aurelius. His writings drew together the best of classical medicine and provided the form in which the science was transmitted through the medieval period to the Renaissance. He himself contributed many original and careful observations in anatomy and physiology.

GALENA, gray mineral consisting of lead (II) sulfide (PbS), forming cubic crystals; the main ore of LEAD. Deposits occur in Germany, the US, Britain and Australia.

GALENA PARK, city in S Tex., an industrial suburb of Houston. Pop 10 479.

GALESBURG, city in W Ill., seat of Knox Co. It is a trade and railroad center in an agricultural and coal mining area. Pop 36 290.

GALICIA, historic region in E central Europe N of the Carpathian Mts, now part of Poland and of

Russia's Ukrainian SSR. It is both rich in minerals and a productive agricultural area. Annexed by Austria in the 18th century, it was named in the 19th century as a province of the Austrian empire. It was ceded to Poland in 1919 and after WWII the E passed to the USSR.

GALICIA, mountainous region of NW Spain, one of the ancient kingdoms of Castile. A distinctive school of lyric poetry in the Galician-Portuguese language flourished in the 13th century. Santiago de Compostella has been a pilgrimage center since the 9th century. Agriculture and fishing are the chief occupations.

GALILEE, hilly region of N ancient Palestine between the Sea of Galilee and the Jordan R. It was the homeland of Jesus, who was sometimes referred to as the Galilean.

GALILEE, Sea of (Lake Tiberias), lake in N Israel, 104sq mi in area, fed by the Jordan R. The only body of fresh water in Israel, it has been a fishing center since biblical times. Many sites on its shores are associated with Jesus' ministry.

GALILEO GALILEI (1564–1642), Italian mathematical physicist who discovered the laws of falling bodies and the parabolic motion of projectiles. The first to turn the newly invented TELESCOPE to the heavens, he was among the earliest observers of SUNSPOTS and the phases of Venus. A talented publicist, he helped to popularize the pursuit of science. However, his quarrelsome nature led him into an unfortunate controversy with the Church. His most significant contribution to science was his provision of an alternative to the Aristotelian dynamics. The motion of the earth thus became a conceptual possibility and scientists at last had a genuine criterion for choosing between the Copernican and Tychonic hypotheses in ASTRONOMY.

GALION, city in N central Ohio. Sited in a farming area, it has a diverse manufacturing industry. Pop 13 123.

Two sketches of the moon's cratered surface made by Galileo himself. He was the first man to use the recently invented telescope to observe the heavens. His discovery of the Medici planets (four moons of Jupiter) and the phases of Venus leant great support to the antagonists of the geocentric theory.

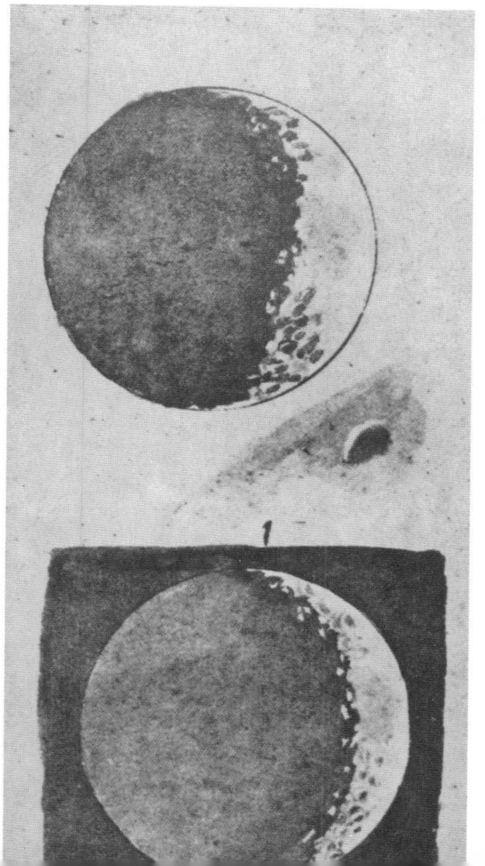

GALIUM, genus of mostly perennial slender herbs native throughout the world. They are commonly called BEDSTRAW because they were once used for filling mattresses. Family: Rubiaceae.

GALL, Saint, 7th century Irish monk, companion of St. Columban on a mission to France. He then lived as a hermit with the Alamanni tribe in N Switzerland. His feast day is Oct. 16.

GALL (c1840–1894), Sioux Indian chief, principal war chief at LITTLE BIGHORN. In 1880 he settled as a farmer on the Standing Rock Reservation, S.D., and became a judge of the Indian Court there in 1889.

GALL, Franz Joseph (1758–1828), German-born Viennese physician who was one of the earliest proponents of the theory of cerebral localization (that different areas of the BRAIN control different functions) and who founded the pseudoscience of PHRENOLOGY.

GALLA PLACIDIA (c388–450), Roman empress of the West. Daughter of THEODOSIUS I, she was captured by the Visigoths in 410. She later married the future Constantius III and after his death was regent for her son Valentinian III.

GALLATIN, town in N Tenn., seat of Sumner Co. It raises tobacco and livestock and breeds horses. Pop 13 271.

GALLATIN, (Abraham Alfonse) Albert (1761–1849), Swiss-born American statesman and diplomat. As congressman 1795–1801 he defended US relations with France during the XYZ AFFAIR. Secretary of the treasury 1801–13, he objected to the drain on national economy caused by the War of 1812 and helped negotiate the Treaty of GHENT, 1814. He was minister to France 1816–23 and Britain 1826–27.

GALLAUDET, Thomas Hopkins (1787–1851), US educator of the deaf. After study at the Royal Institute for Deaf-Mutes in Paris, he founded the first free school for the deaf in the US at Hartford, Conn.

GALL BLADDER, small sac containing BILE, arising from the bile duct which leads from the LIVER to DUODENUM. It lies beneath the liver and serves to concentrate bile. When food, especially fatty food, reaches the STOMACH, local HORMONES cause gall bladder contraction and bile enters the GASTROINTESTINAL TRACT. In some people the concentration of bile favors the formation of **gall stones**, usually containing CHOLESTEROL. These stones may cause no symptoms; they may obstruct the gall bladder causing biliary COLIC or INFLAMMATION (cholecystitis), or they may pass into the bile duct and cause biliary obstruction with JAUNDICE or, less often, pancreatitis. Acute episodes are treated with ANALGESICS, antispasmodics and ANTIBIOTICS, but SURGERY is frequently necessary later. Recent advances suggest that in some instances stones may be dissolved by DRUG therapy.

GALLEGOS, Rómulo (1884–1968), Venezuelan novelist and statesman. Elected president of Venezuela in 1948, he was almost immediately overthrown by a military coup. His short stories and novels, of which the best known is *Dona Barbara* (1929), are primarily didactic and ideological works concerned with social reform.

GALLEON, strictly, a 16th-century warship with reduced fore and sterncastles and a three or four mast rig. Much trimmer and less top-heavy than previous types, the galleon combined size with speed, paving the way for future designs.

GALLEY, a long, narrow craft propelled mainly by large banks of oars, usually with sails as a reserve. Used by most Mediterranean nations from ancient Egypt, Greece and Rome to 18th century Genoa, Venice and France, they were usually rowed by slaves, convicts and prisoners of war.

GALLFLY, any INSECT which causes galls in plants. These include gall midges, fruitflies, gall wasps and certain aphids. The type of insect can generally be identified from the size and shape of the gall.

GALLIARD, a court dance originating in the 15th century and continuing until the 16th century. Usually following a PAVAN, it was a lively dance on five basic steps, performed to music in triple-time.

GALLIC ACID, or 3,4,5-trihydroxybenzoic acid, $[(HO)_3C_6H_2COOH]$, an acid occurring in plants, including oak galls, sumach and tea. Obtained from

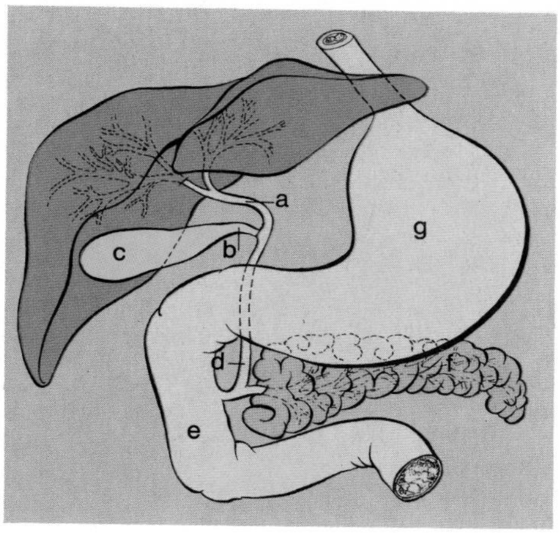

Diagram showing the connection between the gall ducts and the intestine. The ducts from the right and left lobes of the liver join together to form the hepatic duct (a), through which bile passes into the gall bladder duct (b) and the gall bladder (c). From here, concentrated bile passes out again and, together with fresh bile from the hepatic duct, travels through the bile duct (d) to the duodenum (e). Also shown are the pancreas (f) and stomach (g).

TANNINS by HYDROLYSIS, it is used in INK, dyes and as a mild ANTISEPTIC and ASTRINGENT. On heating it gives **pyrogallol**, a photographic developer.

GALLIC WARS, a series of campaigns by Julius CAESAR, 58–51 BC. The name is derived from Caesar's propagandist *Commentaries on the Gallic War* (c50 BC). As governor of Transalpine Gaul, Caesar carried out a combined strategy of driving out invading German tribes and in the process occupying more territory in Gaul, until almost the whole country was in Roman hands (55 BC). In 53–52 BC he put down revolts by the chieftains Ambiorix and VERCINGETORIX. The latter's defeat at Alesia (52 BC) effectively ended the wars.

GALLIENI, Joseph Simon (1849–1916), French general, governor of French Sudan and then Madagascar (1896–1905). Military governor of Paris 1914–15, his strategy precipitated the Battle of the Marne, which saved the city. He was minister of war 1915–16.

GALLIENUS, Publius Licinius Egnatius (c218–268 AD), Roman emperor 253–268. Under pressure from German, Persian and Gothic invasions and provincial revolutions, he reorganized the army and reduced the power of the Senate. He ended official persecution of the Christians. Gallienus was assassinated in Milan while quelling a revolt.

GALLINULE, a type of medium-sized walking or swimming bird inhabiting dense vegetation at the edge of fresh water. Gallinules have short bodies and long legs and are usually purple or dark blue in color. They are members of the RAIL family.

GALLIPOLI PENINSULA, a 50mi long strip of land in European Turkey between the Aegean Sea and the Dardanelles. A strategic point of defense for Istanbul, it was fought over during the Crimean War and WWI. In 1915 an Allied expedition of British, Australian, French and New Zealand forces failed to dislodge Turkish troops in an effort to gain control of the Dardanelles.

GALLIUM (Ga), bluish-white metal in Group IIIA of the PERIODIC TABLE, resembling ALUMINUM; found as a trace element in SPHALERITE, PYRITE, BAUXITE and germanite. Gallium forms trivalent salts and a few monovalent compounds. It contracts on melting, and is liquid over a greater temperature range than any other element. Its few uses include doping SEMICONDUCTORS and producing TRANSISTORS. AW 69.7, mp 29.78°C, bp 2403°C, sg 5.904 (29.6°C), 6.095 (29.8°C).

GALLON (gal), name of various units of volume. The US gallon is 0.003 785m^3. The UK gallon, the volume of 10lbf of pure water under specified conditions, is 0.004 546m^3 or 1.201 US gallons.

GALLOWAY, Joseph (1731–1803), American

loyalist statesman. A member and speaker of the Pennsylvania Assembly 1756–76, he proposed at the First CONTINENTAL CONGRESS a plan for legal settlement of differences between Britain and the colonies, but was forced by the war to join the Loyalists.

GALLS, growth abnormalities that occur in plants caused by insects, mites, nematodes, fungi and bacteria. By definition, galls are self-limiting growths requiring the continued presence of the inciting organism for full development. They thereby differ from TUMORS, where abnormal growth continues in the absence of the inciting organism. However, in crown gall disease of crucifers (e.g., cabbage), the bacterium *Agrobacterium tumefaciens* is required for the initiation of the gall, but subsequent growth becomes tumorous and does not require the presence of the bacterium.

GALLSTONES. See GALL BLADDER.

GALLUP, city on the Puerco R in NW N.M., seat of McKinley Co. Largely a trade center, it lies near several Indian reservations. Pop 13 779.

GALLUP, George Horace (1901–), American journalist. In 1935 he established the American Institute of Public Opinion which undertakes the Gallup polls, periodic samplings of public opinion on current issues.

GALOIS, Évariste (1811–1832), French mathematician best-known for applying GROUP theory in his investigations of the solubility of EQUATIONS. He received no encouragement from his contemporaries and died after a duel at 20, but his work profoundly influenced many later algebraists.

GALSWORTHY, John (1867–1933), English novelist and playwright. His works, especially the famous cycle of novels *The Forsyte Saga*, are concerned with the life and attitudes of the wealthier English middle casses, typified by the "man of property" Soames Forsyte. He was awarded the Nobel Prize for Literature in1932.

GALT, industrial city in SW Ontario, Canada, lying in a rich agricultural region on the Grand R. It was named for John GALT. Pop 38 134.

GALT, Sir Alexander Tilloch (1817–1893), Canadian statesman who supported the confederation of Canada. (See BRITISH-NORTH AMERICA ACT.) He was Conservative Finance Minister 1858–62 and 1864–67, and Canada's first High Commissioner to Britain 1880–83.

GALT, John (1779–1839), Scottish novelist best known for his studies of Scottish rural life in such novels as *The Ayrshire Legatees* (1821). As agent for a land company Galt traveled in Canada, where he founded the town of Guelph, Ontario in 1827.

GALTON, Sir Francis (1822–1911), British scientist, the founder of EUGENICS and biostatistics (the application of statistical methods to animal populations); the coiner of the term "anticyclone" and one of the first to realize their meteorological significance; and the developer of one of the first FINGERPRINT systems for identification.

GALVANI, Luigi (1737–1798), Italian anatomist who discovered "animal electricity" (about 1786). The many varying accounts of this discovery at least agree that it resulted from the chance observation of the twitching of frog legs under electrical influence. A controversy with VOLTA over the nature of animal electricity was cut short by Galvani's death.

GALVANIZING. See CORROSION.

GALVANOMETER, an instrument used for detecting and measuring very small electric currents. Most modern instruments are of the moving-coil type in which a coil of fine wire wrapped around an aluminum former is suspended by conducting ribbons about a soft iron core between the poles of a permanent magnet. When an electric current flows through the coil, a magnetic field is set up which interacts with that of the permanent magnet producing a TORQUE. This turns the coil until it is fully resisted by the suspension, the displacement produced being proportional to the current. The result is read from a scale onto which a light beam is reflected from a mirror carried on the suspension ribbons. If all electromagnetic and mechanical damping can be eliminated from such an instrument, it can also be used as a **ballistic galvanometer** to measure small charges and CAPACITANCES. (See also AMMETER.)

GALVESTON, seaport city in coastal Texas on the Gulf of Mexico. Seat of Galveston Co., it is a fishing and shipping center whose industries include oil refining and shipbuilding. Pop 61 809.

GALVESTON BAY, inlet of the Gulf of Mexico extending about 25mi N of Galveston. First explored in the 18th century by Spaniards, it was the haunt of buccaneer Jean LAFITTE and is today an important commercial waterway.

GÁLVEZ, Bernardo de (c1746–1786), Spanish governor of La. and viceroy of New Spain (now Mexico). At the outbreak of war between Spain and Britain in 1779 he captured much of the Gulf area, forcing Britain to cede E and W Fla.

GALWAY, town in the W of Ireland, capital of Co. Galway on Galway Bay. A seaport and commercial center since c1270, it has many links with mainland Europe, particularly architecturally. Local industries, including iron, wool, chemicals and fishing, are small but prosperous. Pop 26 896.

GAMA, Vasco da (c1469–1524), Portuguese navigator whose discovery of a new sea-route around the Cape of Good Hope and destruction of the Muslim trade monopoly made possible large-scale European trade with the East. In his first voyage (1497–99) his trade negotiations in India were thwarted by Muslim merchants. On his second voyage (1502–03) his fleet established Portuguese supremacy in the area by a ruthless destruction of the Malabar Muslim fleet. Later appointed viceroy to India, he died soon after his arrival there.

GAMALIEL, name of three rabbis, leaders of the Sanhedrin. **Gamaliel I** (1st century AD) taught the Apostle Paul. He interceded for the Apostles when they were arrested by the Sanhedrin. **Gamaliel II** (early 2nd century AD) enforced HILLEL's lenient interpretation of the law, and strengthened and unified Judaism in a time of turmoil. **Gamaliel III** (early 3rd century AD) completed the editing of the Mishna, the compilation of the Jewish Oral law.

GAMBETTA, Léon Michel (1838–1882), French republican statesman who assumed virtually dictatorial power after Napoleon III's defeat at Sedan, but was unable to prevent capitulation to Prussia. Premier in 1881, he was distrusted as an opportunist and lasted only three months in office.

GAMBIA, republic in W Africa, smallest state on the continent. It extends for around 200mi from the W coast narrowly along the Gambia R, almost bisecting Senegal. A low-lying country, it varies between the mangrove areas beside the river to the interior scrublands. The Mandingo peoples constitute around 40% of the population; others are the Fulani, Wolof, Jola and the Serahuli. They are mostly small farmers producing millet, corn and rice for home consumption; goats and sheep are raised, but few cattle. The economy rests on the only cash crop, peanuts. There is little industry, and commerce is dominated by the Syrian and Lebanese communities. Gambia was born out of the struggle between Britain and France for supremacy in W Africa. The French territory became Senegal and the British Gambia. The first legislative assembly was elected in 1960. Independence came in 1965; the country became an independent republic within the British Commonwealth in 1970, with Sir Dauda Jawara as its first president.

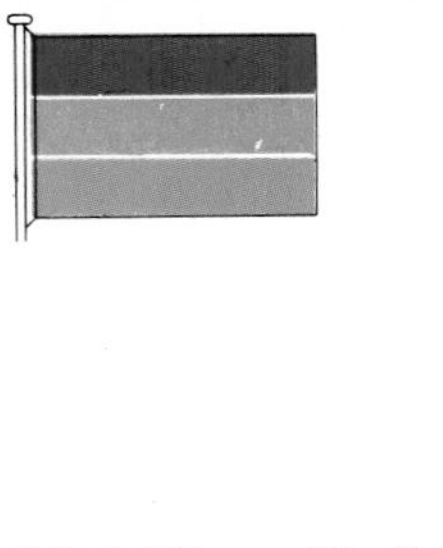

Official Name: The Gambia
Capital: Banjul
Area: 4 361sq mi
Population: 374 770
Languages: English; Malinke; Wolof
Religions: Muslim; Animist; Christian
Monetary Unit(s): 1 Dalasi = 100 butut

Neon lights beneath the desert skies of Las Vegas, Nevada, a paradise for gamblers. Fifteen million people, spending over $400 million, visit Las Vegas each year. They have little choice—the only other US resort for legal gambling is in Puerto Rico.

GAMBIA RIVER, a W African waterway, providing Gambia's main transport artery. Rising in Guinea, it flows 700mi down to the Atlantic, emerging at St. Mary's Island, Gambia, near Banjul.

GAMBIER ISLANDS, a group of coral islands and atolls in the S Pacific nearly enclosed by a single reef. The largest is Mangareva. Discovered by the British in 1797, they were annexed by France in 1881, and are part of French Polynesia.

GAMBLING, wagering of money or valuables on a chance outcome, usually in connection with an organized game or sport; horse racing is the most popular. Gambling is generally regarded by governments as an ineradicable social evil to be strictly controlled, usually by taxation or outright ban. In the US the high turnover in gambling (about $50 billion a year) results in many corrupt practices. Casino gambling is legal only in Nev. and Puerto Rico. Lotteries, raffles and bingo, more socially acceptable forms of gambling, are often used in charity fund-raising. Gambling can become a neurotic compulsion; Gamblers Anonymous was founded in 1948 to help those so afflicted.

GAMELAN, Indonesian orchestra. Apart from the *rabab*, a viol-like instrument, and the *suling*, a bamboo flute, it is composed of a wide variety of percussion instruments. Its distinctive sound has influenced Western composers such as DEBUSSY.

GAME THEORY, an application of mathematical LOGIC to decision-making in games and, by extension, in commerce, politics and warfare. In singular games (e.g., solitaire) the player's strategy is determined solely by the rules. In dual games (e.g., chess, football) one side's strategy must take into account the possible strategies of the other. Dual games are usually zero-sum: one side's gain exactly equals the other's loss. In practical situations, however, they may be non-zero-sum, as where two conflicting nations negotiate a truce that benefits both. Two major strategies are available to players of dual games: the minimax, in which a player evaluates his probable maximum loss and attempts to minimize it; and the maximin, in which a player evaluates his probable minimum gain and attempts to maximize it. VON NEUMANN showed in his minimax theorem (first stated 1928) that, since, statistically, minimax and maximin strategies negate each other, most dual games are not worth playing in that their outcome is determined solely by the rules.

In plural or *n*-person games (e.g., poker), an individual's gain does not necessarily imply another's loss; and more complex considerations must affect each player's choice of action. Moreover, the outcome may be affected by the formation of coalitions, possibly reducing the *n*-person game to a dual one.

GAMETE, or **germ cell**, a sexual reproductive CELL capable of uniting with a gamete of the opposite sex to form a new individual or ZYGOTE; this process is termed FERTILIZATION. Each gamete contains one set of dissimilar chromosomes and is said to be HAPLOID. Thus when gametes unite, the resultant cell contains a DIPLOID or paired set of CHROMOSOMES. The gametes of some primitive organisms are identical cells capable of swimming in water, but in most species only the male gamete (sperm) is mobile while the female gamete (ovary or egg) is a larger static cell. In higher PLANTS the male gametes or pollen are produced by the anthers and the female gametes (ovules) by the ovary. In animals gametes are produced by the GONADS, namely the testes in the male and ovaries in the female.

GAMETOPHYTE, phase of the life cycle of a plant representing the haploid generation. (See ALTERNATION OF GENERATIONS.)

GAMMA GLOBULIN, the fraction of BLOOD PROTEIN containing antibodies (see ANTIBODIES AND ANTIGENS). Several types are recognized. Although they share basic structural features they differ in size, site, behavior and response to different antigens. Absence of all or some gamma globulins causes disorders of IMMUNITY, increasing susceptibility to infection, while the excessive formation of one type is the basis for **myeloma**, a disease characterized by BONE pain, pathological FRACTURES and liability to infection. Gamma globulin is available for replacement therapy, and a type from highly immune subjects is sometimes used to protect against certain diseases (e.g., serum hepatitis, TETANUS). (See also GLOBULINS.)

GAMMA RAYS, high-energy PHOTONS of wavelength shorter than 0.1nm emitted from atomic nuclei during radioactive decay (see RADIOACTIVITY). Usually their emission follows the ejection of an electron (BETA RAY) from the nucleus. The most penetrating of the radioactive emissions, gamma rays find use in engineering quality control—as a source for exposing RADIOGRAPHS—and in RADIATION THERAPY.

GAMOW, George (1904–1968), Russian-born US physicist and popular science writer, best known for his work in nuclear physics, especially related to the evolution of STARS; and for his support of the "big bang" theory of COSMOLOGY. In GENETICS, his work paved the way for the discovery of the role of DNA.

GANDHI, Indira Priyadarshini (1917–), first woman prime minister of India. Daughter of Jawaharlal NEHRU, she became president of the Congress Party in 1959. Regarded as a moderate, she became prime minister in 1966. In 1975, she was found guilty of electoral malpractice. During the ensuing constitutional crisis she declared a state of emergency during which she briefly jailed nearly 700 of her political opponents. The Indian Supreme Court overruled the verdict against her and upheld her electoral and constitutional changes.

GANDHI, Mohandas Karamchand "Mahatma" (1869–1948), Indian nationalist leader. After studying law in London, he went to South Africa, where he lived until 1914 becoming a driving force in the Indian community's fight for civil rights. During this campaign he developed the principle of SATYAGRAHA, nonviolent civil disobedience, and held to it despite persecution and imprisonment. When he returned to India he had achieved substantial improvements in civil rights and labor laws. In India he became leader of the Congress Party, initiating the campaign which led to the independence of India after WWII. He was assassinated by a Hindu fanatic who disapproved of his tolerance of Muslims.

GANGES RIVER, in India the most sacred Hindu river, believed to be the reincarnation of the goddess Ganga. It rises in the Himalayas and flows through N and NE India, following a SE course across the plain of India. It joins the Brahmaputra R in Bangladesh, then continues through the vast Ganges delta to empty into the Bay of Bengal. The river waters irrigate a populous agricultural area. Many cities line the river's banks, including the holy cities of Vārānasi (Benares) and Allahābād.

GANGLION, a small collection of nerve cells, sometimes with SYNAPSE formation, common in autonomic or peripheral NERVOUS SYSTEMS. Also, a benign lump, often at the WRIST, found close to TENDONS and containing jelly-like fluid. Traditionally treated by a blow from the family Bible, they are less likely to recur after surgical removal.

GANGRENE, DEATH of tissue following loss of blood supply, often after obstruction of ARTERIES by trauma, THROMBOSIS OR EMBOLISM. **Dry gangrene** is seen when arterial block is followed by slow drying, blackening and finally separation of dead tissue from healthy. Its treatment includes improvement of the blood flow to the healthy tissue and prevention of infection and further obstruction. **Wet gangrene** occurs when the dead tissue is infected with BACTERIA. **Gas gangrene** involves infection with gas-forming organisms (*Clostridium*) and its spread is particularly rapid. ANTIBIOTICS, HYPERBARIC CHAMBERS and early AMPUTATION are often required.

GANGTOK, capital of the Indian state of SIKKIM, in the Himalayas, 28mi NE of Darjeeling. It was a commercial center on the India-Tibet trade route until the Chinese occupation of Tibet in 1962. Pop 9 000.

GANNETS, large seabirds, weighing nearly 3kg (7lb), which spend much of their time on the wing and feed by plunge-diving for fishes from the air, a habit for which they are well adapted. They belong to the genus *Morus* and are related to the BOOBIES.

GANNETT, Henry (1846–1914), US geographer and a founder of the National Geographic Society (1883). He was chief geographer of the US Geological Survey, 1882–1914, and from 1880 to 1900 geographer of the US censuses. He greatly contributed to the science of mapmaking in America.

GANYMEDE, in Greek mythology, a beautiful youth whom ZEUS, in the form of an eagle, carried off to be immortal cupbearer to the gods on Olympus. He is identified with the constellation Aquarius.

GAPON, Georgi Apollonovich (1870–1906), Russian priest, concerned in the 1905 revolution. He helped set up a workers' association to deal with grievances. On Jan. 22, 1905, (known as "Bloody Sunday") he led workers to the Winter Palace in St. Petersburg to petition the tsar for better conditions, but troops shot over 100 people. He was murdered in Finland by socialist revolutionaries.

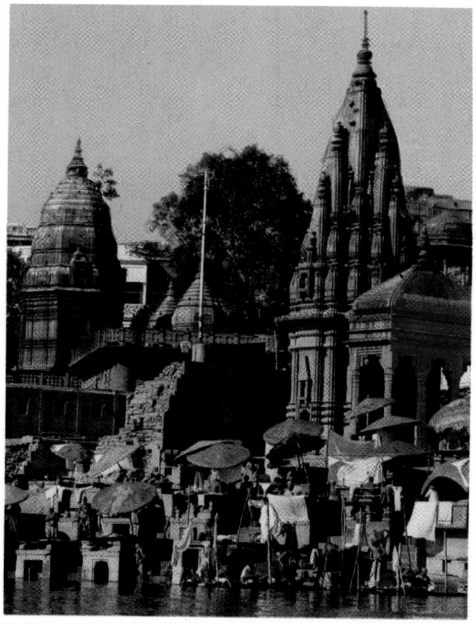

Millions of Hindu pilgrims visit the holy city of Vārānasi each year to bathe in the purifying waters of the river Ganges which are believed to wash away sins and prepare one for a more spiritual life. In Hindu scripture the river is said to flow from the hair of the great god Siva, destroyer of evil.

GAR, or garpikes, primitive fish of the genus *Lepisosteus* with long thin bodies covered with thick, diamond-shaped scales. Gars are found in North America, the largest reaching a length of 3.3m (10ft). In Europe, gar refers to the **needlefish** of the family Belonidae, of the Mediterranean and Black Seas.

GARAMOND, Claude (c1480–1561), French type designer and publisher. He created typefaces which helped establish roman in place of Gothic or black letter as standard type. His royal Greek and italic types were also highly influential. (See also TYPOGRAPHY.)

GARBAGE DISPOSAL. See WASTE DISPOSAL.

GARBO, Greta (1905–), Swedish–American film actress, born Greta Lovisa Gustafsson. She was a talented actress known for her aura of glamour and mystery; her 24 films included *Anna Christie* (1930), *Camille* (1937) and *Ninotchka* (1939). She retired in 1941, and was given an Academy Award in 1954.

GARCIA, Carlos Polestico (1896–1971), fourth president of the Philippines, 1957–61. Elected vice-president as a Nacionalista Party candidate in 1953, he became president on the death of President MAGSAYSAY. He maintained the traditional policy of strong ties with the US.

GARCÍA LORCA, Federico. See LORCA, FEDERICO GARCÍA.

GARCÍA y ÍÑIGUEZ, Calixto (1839–1898), Cuban revolutionary. He commanded Cuban forces in the Ten Years War (1868–78) against Spain. After being imprisoned in Spain, he helped lead the Cuban revolt in 1895–98 which led to the SPANISH-AMERICAN WAR. His name became a famous byword in the US after publication of a magazine article, *A Message to Garcia* (1899), dealing with an incident in the war.

GARDA, Lake, largest N Italian lake, in the Alps, 34mi long and up to 11mi wide. The Sarca R enters it from the N and the Mincio flows out at the S into the Po R. It lies in a temperate fruit-growing and resort area.

GARDENA, city in SW Cal., a suburb of Los Angeles which manufactures aircraft, missile parts and electronic equipment. Pop 41 021.

GARDEN CITY, city in SW Kan. on the Arkansas R. A trading and manufacturing city in an agricultural region. Pop 14 790.

GARDEN CITY, residential city in SE Mich., 15mi W of Detroit, of which it is a suburb. Pop 41 864.

GARDEN CITY, residential village on Long Island, SE N.Y., 18mi E of New York City. Planned as a model town in 1869, today it is a printing and publishing center. Pop 25 373.

GARDEN CITY, a concept in town planning developed in 1898 by British social reformer Sir Ebenezer HOWARD. This new type of urban development was to be surrounded by a rural belt and would accommodate residences, industry and agriculture, preventing urban congestion. Two such cities were founded in England: Letchworth (1903) and Welwyn Garden City (1919–20). Howard's ideas influenced town planning in England and spread to the US where Radburn, N.J., was one of the first planned satellite towns (of New York City).

GARDEN GROVE, city in SW Cal., S of Anaheim, in an area growing citrus fruit and beans. Pop 122 524.

GARDENIA, genus of evergreen flowering shrubs native to subtropical Asia and Africa. *Gardenia jasminoides* and its varieties are cultivated outdoors in greenhouses and as house plants. They produce fragrant white blooms much favored as cut flowers. Indoors they should be grown in full sunlight, except in the summer, and the temperature maintained at about 21°C (70°F) during the day, with a drop to 17°C (62°F) at night. They should be watered often enough to keep the soil evenly moist, avoiding extremes of dryness or wetness; they benefit from frequent misting. They are propagated by taking shoot tip cuttings in spring and summer. Family: Rubiaceae.

GARDENS, land cultivated for flowers, herbs, trees, shrubs and vegetables. Early man made the first gardens when he discovered he could plant and then harvest edible roots, greens and fruits. The Hanging Gardens of Babylon (about 600 BC) were considered one of the seven wonders of the ancient world. Ancient

Greek, Roman and medieval monastic gardens cultivated herbs for medicinal uses. The Greeks had the first potted plant gardens and the Romans planted roof gardens. The elaborate gardens of Renaissance Italy were copied in Tudor England. The formal gardens of Versailles were the most impressive of 17th century French LANDSCAPE ARCHITECTURE. In 18th and 19th century England, idealized natural landscapes were created by landscape gardeners such as Lancelot "Capability" BROWN. The US tended to imitate English and European garden design, but after WWI emphasis was on private suburban gardens. "Garden apartments" with shared parklike facilities became increasingly common after WWII. (See also BOTANICAL GARDENS; HORTICULTURE.)

GARDINER, Stephen (c1490–1555), English bishop of Winchester. By the end of HENRY VIII's reign he was regarded as the chief opponent of the REFORMATION in England. Secretary to Cardinal WOLSEY and then to Henry, he aided negotiations for the king's annulment from Queen Catherine and accepted royal supremacy over the English church; but he opposed many of CRANMER's reforms, was jailed under Edward IV, and became Lord High Chancellor under MARY I.

GARDINERS ISLAND, an island in Gardiners Bay, off E Long Island, N.Y., about 90mi E of New York City. It was the first permanent settlement (1639) of the English in N.Y. State.

GARDNER, city in N central Mass., 60mi NW of Boston. It has a furniture industry dating from 1805. Pop 19 748.

GARDNER, Erle Stanley (1889–1970), US mystery writer, creator of lawyer-detective Perry Mason. Gardner wrote over 140 novels under his own name and the pseudonym A. A. Fair.

GARDNER, Isabella Stewart (1840–1924), US art collector. Her home in Boston, Mass., was built as a 15th-century Venetian palace; it was opened in 1903 as a public museum to display her collection which includes works by Cellini, Raphael, Rembrandt and Titian.

GARFIELD, industrial city in NE N.J. on the Passaic R, 5mi SE of Paterson. It manufactures textiles, chemicals, metal and paper products. Pop 30 797.

GARFIELD, James Abram (1831–1881), 20th president of the US, the second to be assassinated in office. He was born in a log cabin near Orange in Cuyahoga Co., Ohio, the son of pioneer farmers. In his youth he worked as a farmer and on canal boats. He graduated from Williams College in 1856 and then became a teacher and principal of Hiram College (Ohio), and was admitted to the bar. A distinguished officer of Ohio volunteers in the Civil War, he was commissioned major general in the Union army (1863). He resigned to take a seat in the House of Representatives (1863–80). During his years in Congress he was chairman of the House appropriations committee (1871–75), Republican House leader and helped establish an Office of education (1867), served as a Smithsonian Institution regent and helped create the US Geological Survey. He favored a conservative policy on money, fought inflation and supported RECONSTRUCTION measures against the South. In 1880 he was elected to the Senate, but the same year was chosen as compromise Republican presidential candidate and defeated W. S. HANCOCK in the election. Garfield's brief term of office was notable for the start of friendlier US–Latin American relations under Secretary of State James G. BLAINE and for exposure of STAR ROUTE mail frauds in the W. He gained prestige by asserting presidential power in a patronage struggle with New York state Republican Party boss Roscoe CONKLING. When the president was shot, the nation was outraged, and the postal and civil service reforms he had advocated were hastened (supported by his successor Chester A. ARTHUR). (See also SPOILS SYSTEM.)

James Abram GARFIELD
20th US President

Born: November 19, 1831
Died: September 19, 1881
Term of office: March 4, 1881–September 19, 1881
Political party: Republican

GARFIELD HEIGHTS, city in N Ohio, 6mi SSE of Cleveland. It manufactures iron and steel, abrasives and has oil refineries. Pop 41 417.

GARGOYLE, in architecture, a decorative projecting water spout on a building's parapet. Gargoyles appeared on ancient Greek and Roman buildings, but the term now mainly describes grotesque, often humanoid figures on GOTHIC buildings.

GARIBALDI, Giuseppe (1807–1882), Italian patriot and general, one of the creators of modern Italy. As a young man he joined the republican Young Italy society set up by MAZZINI. In 1834 he first fought in a republican uprising in Genoa and then fled to South America. There he became famous as a guerrilla leader in revolutions in Brazil and Uruguay. In 1848, the "year of revolutions," he returned to Italy to fight against Austrian, French and Neapolitan armies in support of Mazzini's short-lived Roman Republic. On its collapse, Garibaldi fled to the US until 1854. Again returning to Italy, from 1859–62 he led brilliant guerrilla campaigns against Austria and captured Sicily and Naples (see KINGDOM OF THE TWO SICILIES) with a volunteer army, his famous "Red Shirts," in the most decisive campaign of the RISORGIMENTO. He surrendered the territories to King VICTOR EMMANUEL, which effectively unified Italy. Twice (in 1862 and 1867) Garibaldi unsuccessfully tried to capture Rome from the pope. Subsequently he fought for the French against Prussia (1870). In 1874 he was elected to the Italian parliament, but retired in 1876.

GARLAND, town in NE Tex., 14mi NE of Dallas. It manufactures electronic equipment for aircraft missiles and equipment for oilfields. Pop 81 437.

GARLAND, Augustus Hill (1832–1899), US lawyer. Barred as an ex-Confederate during RECONSTRUCTION from practicing law before the US Supreme Court, he won the right to resume practice in the court's famous *Ex parte Garland* case (1866). He was US senator from Ark. (1876–85) and US attorney general (1885–89).

GARLAND, (Hannibal) Hamlin (1860–1940), US writer. His fiction portrays pioneering Middle Western farm life with bitterness and realism. Among his best work is the story collection *Main Travelled Roads* (1891) and his autobiographical "Middle Border" stories (4 vols., 1917–1928).

GARLAND, Judy (1922–1969), US singer and movie actress, born Frances Gumm. Famous for her performances of popular songs such as "You Made Me Love You," she starred in *The Wizard of Oz* (1939) and many other films.

GARLIC, *Allium sativum*, a close relative of the ONION. The small BULBS have a very strong aroma and are used to flavor salads, soups, fish and meat dishes. It yields "oil of garlic," used as an antiseptic and expectorant for numerous minor complaints.

GARMENT WORKERS' UNION. See INTERNATIONAL LADIES' GARMENT WORKERS' UNION.

GARMISCH-PARTENKIRCHEN, ancient town in West Germany, an important ski and winter sports resort in the Bavarian Alps where the 1936 Winter Olympics took place. Pop 63 600.

GARNEAU, François-Xavier (1809–1866), French-Canadian historian. His *Histoire du Canada* (1845–48) introduced scientific methods of investigation to Canadian history and revived QUEBEC's ethnic pride and the public's interest in French-Canadian culture.

GARNER, Erroll (1921–), US jazz musician and composer. He created a piano style of spread chords and melodic variations on popular tunes. His most famous work is the ballad "Misty."

GARNER, John Nance (1868–1967), US vice-president, 1933–40 under Franklin ROOSEVELT. A Democratic member of the US House of Representatives (1903–35) and its speaker from 1931, he was a skillful behind-the -scenes political legislator. He ran unsuccessfully for the Democratic presidential nomination in 1940.

GARNET, common SILICATE mineral group of general formula $M_3^{II}M_2^{III}(SiO_4)_3$, having six end-members It is found in metamorphic and some igneous rocks, often as rhombododecahedral crystals. It is hard, and used as an ABRASIVE. The color is variable; GEM varieties are red, green or transparent. The garnet is popularly the birthstone for January.

GARNIER, Saint Charles (1606–1649), French Jesuit missionary to the Canadian HURON Indians from 1636. He was killed during an intensive Iroquois campaign against the Hurons. Canonized in 1930, his feast day is Sept. 26.

GARNIER, Tony (1869–1948), French architect, a pioneer in the use of reinforced concrete (patented in France, 1867). Architect of Lyons, he introduced new concepts in city planning, which were published in *Cité Industrielle* (1917).

GARNISHMENT, a legal process for collecting debts. By court order, a debtor's property may be attached or a portion of his wages deducted by his employer to pay off a debt incurred. The US Consumer Protection Act, 1970, decreed that the amount deducted should not exceed 25% of wages and that an employee may not be fired for a single garnishment.

GARONNE, river in SW France flowing from the Pyrenees into the Bay of Biscay. It is 357mi long and runs N and NE to Toulouse and then NW to Bordeaux. Beyond Bordeaux it joins the Dordogne R and forms the Gironde estuary. A canal from Toulouse connects the river with the Mediterranean.

GARRETT, Patrick Floyd "Pat" (1850–1908), US frontier sheriff. He arrested BILLY THE KID in 1880, and after "the Kid's" escape from jail in N.M. pursued and shot him in 1881.

GARRICK, David (1717–1779), English actor-manager and dramatist. He introduced a more natural acting style to the English stage in roles such as Hamlet and partially restored the original versions of Shakespeare's plays. From 1747–1776 he was manager of the DRURY LANE THEATRE.

GARRISON, William Lloyd (1805–1879), US leader of the abolitionist movement. From 1831–65 he published *The Liberator*, an influential crusading journal which opposed slavery, war and capital punishment and supported temperance and women's rights. (See ABOLITIONISM; see also EMANCIPATION PROCLAMATION.)

GARRISON DAM, an earth embankment about 2mi long and 210ft high built 1956–62 as part of the Missouri R basin project, near Riverdale, N.D. It provides regional flood control and hydroelectric power. The dam, one of the largest of its type, holds back Lake Sakajawea.

GARTER, Order of the, the highest order of British knighthood, established in the mid-14th century by King Edward III. It consists of the sovereign, the Prince of Wales, 25 knights companions and such foreign rulers and others as the monarch may name. Its patron is St. George and its famous motto is *Honi soit qui mal y pense* ("Shame to him who thinks ill of it").

GARTER SNAKES, harmless snakes of the genus *Thamnophis*. They are the most common, and among the most colorful, snakes of North America, growing usually to a length of 500–750mm (20–30in) and feeding on frogs or salamanders. They are semi-aquatic and kept as pets.

GARVEY, Marcus Moziah (1887–1940), US Negro leader, born in the British West Indies. In 1914 he founded the Universal Negro Improvement Association in Jamaica and in 1916 introduced it to the US where it gained a widespread following. It emphasized the kinship of all Negroes and a "back to Africa" movement. He promoted the Black Star Line, a shipping company for trade with Africa but in 1925 was convicted of mail fraud in connection with its funds.

GARY, industrial city in NW Ind. on Lake Michigan, bordering on Chicago. It is the site of the chief plants of the US Steel Corporation which laid out the city in 1906. Pop 175415.

GARY, Elbert Henry (1846–1927), US lawyer and industrialist. He organized the US Steel Corporation and was its chairman, 1901–27. He founded the city of GARY, Ind., named for him, and promoted good working conditions, but opposed unions.

GARY, Romain (1914–), French novelist of Russian origin, born Romain Kacev. He fought in WWII and was a diplomat. His works include *The Roots of Heaven* (1956) and *Promise at Dawn* (1960).

GAS, one of the three states (solid, liquid, gas) into which nearly all matter above the atomic level can be classified. Gases are characterized by a low DENSITY and VISCOSITY; a high compressibility; optical transparency; a complete lack of rigidity, and a readiness to fill whatever volume is available to them and to form molecularly homogeneous mixtures with other gases. Air and STEAM are familiar examples. At sufficiently high temperatures, all materials vaporize, though many undergo chemical changes first. Gases, particularly steam and CARBON dioxide, are common products of COMBUSTION, while several available naturally or from PETROLEUM or COAL (e.g., HYDROGEN, METHANE) are used as fuels themselves. The great bulk of the universe is gaseous, in the form of interstellar hydrogen. Gases will often dissolve in liquids, the solubility rising with PRESSURE and falling with TEMPERATURE; a little dissolved carbon dioxide is responsible for the bubbles in soda.

In contrast to solids and liquids, the MOLECULES of a gas are far apart compared with their own size, and move freely and randomly at a wide range of speeds of the order of 100m/s. For a given temperature and pressure, equal volumes of gas contain the same number of molecules ($2.7 \times 10^{25}\,m^{-3}$ at room temperature and atmospheric pressure). The impacts of the molecules on the walls of the container are responsible for the pressure exerted by gases, which is much larger than is often appreciated: the atmosphere exerts on everything a pressure many times larger than a person's weight and without it we would quite simply boil and burst.

For a given mass of an **ideal gas** (i.e., one in which the molecules are of negligible size and exert no forces on each other), the product of the pressure (P) and the volume (V) is proportional to the absolute temperature (T):

$$PV = RT \text{ (the general gas law).}$$

The constant of proportionality (R) is known as the **universal gas constant** and has the value 8.314 joules/kelvin-mole. The general gas law and most of the other properties of gases can be explained in terms of the KINETIC THEORY without reference to the internal structure of the molecules. Real gases deviate from this ideal behavior at high pressures because of the actual presence of small intermolecular forces.

GAS, Fuel, combustible GAS used as FUEL for domestic or industrial heating, furnaces, engines etc. The main types are NATURAL GAS, COAL GAS, PRODUCER GAS and WATER GAS (blue gas). Town gas, now little used, is a mixture of coal gas and water gas. (See also BOTTLED GAS.)

GAS CHAMBER, method of execution used by some states in the US because it was considered more humane than other methods. The criminal was strapped to a chair in a sealed room and died rapidly from inhaling fumes of deadly prussic acid (hydrogen cyanide). It was introduced in 1924. In WWII the Nazis murdered millions of Jews and other minorities in gas chambers. (See also CAPITAL PUNISHMENT.)

GASCONY, historic region of SW France. Once occupied by the Romans and settled by the Basques, it was semi-independent of France until the 17th-century.

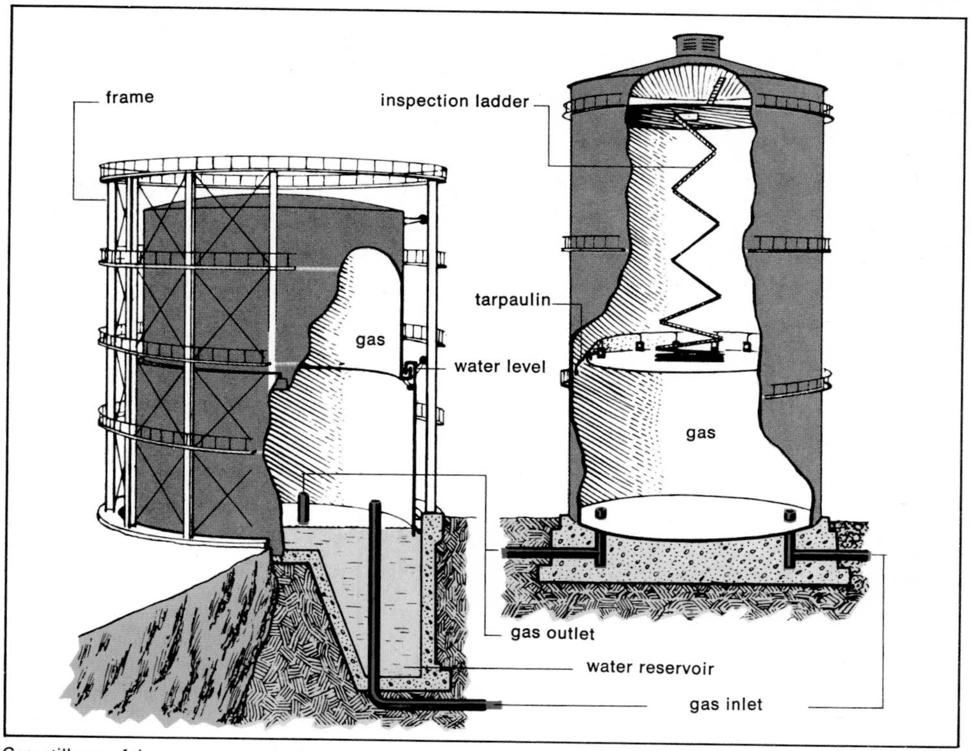

Gas, still one of the most economical sources of energy for domestic purposes, is stored in a number of different ways. *Left:* a variable capacity storage holder in a frame. *Right:* a storage holder with an internal piston (and a folding inspection ladder) that rises and falls as the demand for gas fluctuates.

GAS GUN. See AIR GUN.

GASKELL, Elizabeth Cleghorn (Stevenson) (1810–1865), English novelist. Her most famous works are *Cranford* (1853), about middle-class village life, and *North and South* (1855), a social portrayal of industrial towns.

GAS MASK, or **respirator**, head-piece to protect the wearer from poisonous fumes or gases. It essentially comprises a filter of CHARCOAL, through which air enters; plastic eyepieces; and a VALVE for exhalation. Various chemicals are added to the charcoal to render specific poisons harmless; e.g., hopcalite (mixed copper and manganese oxides) to oxidize CARBON monoxide (CO) to carbon dioxide (CO_2). (See also CHEMICAL AND BIOLOGICAL WARFARE.)

GASOLINE, or petrol, a mixture of volatile HYDROCARBONS having 4 to 12 carbon atoms per molecule, used as a FUEL for INTERNAL-COMBUSTION ENGINES, and as a solvent. Although gasoline can be derived from oil, coal and tar, or synthesized from carbon monoxide and hydrogen, almost all is produced from PETROLEUM by refining, CRACKING and ALKYLATION, the fractions being blended to produce fuels with desired characteristics. Motor gasoline boils between 30°C and 200°C, with more of the low-boiling components in cold weather for easy starting. If, however, the fuel is too volatile, vapor lock can occur—i.e., vapor bubbles form and hinder the flow of fuel. Aviation gasoline contains less of both low- and high-boiling components. The structure of gasoline components is also carefully controlled for maximum power and efficiency, as reflected in the OCTANE rating; this may be further improved by ANTIKNOCK ADDITIVES. Other additives include lead scavengers (ethylene dibromide and dichloride), antioxidants, metal deactivators (which remove metal ions that catalyze oxidation), anti-icing agents, and detergents. Total US gasoline production in 1972 was 272 million tonnes.

GASOLINE ENGINE. See INTERNAL-COMBUSTION ENGINE.

GASPÉE, British revenue cutter burned by Colonists in 1772. Under Lieutenant Dudingston it came to Rhode Island to enforce revenue laws and suppress smuggling in Narragansett Bay. After being run aground on the Namquat peninsula it was burned in a raid led by the merchant John Brown in an act of pre-Revolutionary defiance.

GASPÉ PENINSULA, mountainous peninsula, c170mi long, in SE Quebec, Canada, projecting into the Gulf of St. Lawrence. Its forested interior with lakes and rivers provides excellent hunting and fishing.

GAS POISONING. See CHEMICAL AND BIOLOGICAL WARFARE; POISONING.

GASSENDI, or **Gassend, Pierre** (1592–1655), French philosopher important for his role in tipping the balance away from the old and toward the new science. A friend and ally of KEPLER and GALILEO, he attacked the prevalent Aristotelianism and supported ATOMISM. He also made a number of important astronomical observations, and named the *aurora borealis* (see AURORA).

GASSER, Herbert Spencer (1888–1963), US physiologist who shared with Joseph ERLANGER the 1964 Nobel Prize for Physiology or Medicine for their investigations of the functions of nerve fibers.

GASTONIA, city in SW N.C., sea of Gaston Co. It has foundries and chemical and plastics industries. Pop 47142.

GASTRIC JUICE. See DIGESTIVE SYSTEM.

GASTRIN, group of HORMONES, derived from part of the STOMACH, that stimulate acid secretion by the stomach, PANCREAS secretion, and possibly GALL-BLADDER contraction. Its secretion is stimulated by food in the stomach, and the vagus nerve.

GASTROENTERITIS, group of conditions, usually due to viral or bacterial infection of upper GASTRO-INTESTINAL TRACT, causing DIARRHEA, VOMITING and abdominal COLIC. While these are mostly mild illnesses, in young infants and debilitated or elderly adults, dehydration may develop rapidly and fatalities may result. (See also ENTERITIS; FOOD POISONING.)

GASTROINTESTINAL SERIES, X-RAY examination of the GASTROINTESTINAL TRACT using radio-opaque substances, usually barium salts. In **barium swallow** and **meal**, an emulsion is taken and the ESOPHAGUS, STOMACH and DUODENUM are X-rayed. A follow-through may be performed later to outline the small intestine. For **barium enema**, a suspension is passed into rectum and large intestine. CANCER, ULCERS, diverticulae and forms of ENTERITIS and COLITIS may be revealed.

GASTROINTESTINAL TRACT, or gut, or **alimentary canal**, the anatomical pathway involved in the DIGESTIVE SYSTEM of animals. In man it starts at the PHARYNX, passing into ESOPHAGUS and STOMACH. From this arises the small intestine, consisting of the DUODENUM and the great length of the jejunum and ileum. This leads into the large bowel, consisting of the cecum (from which the vermiform APPENDIX arises), colon and rectum. The parts from the stomach to the latter part of the colon lie suspended on a MESENTERY, through which they receive their blood supply, and lie in loops within the peritoneal cavity of the ABDOMEN. In each part, the shape, muscle layers and epithelium are specialized for their particular functions of secretion and absorption. Movement of food in the tract occurs largely by PERISTALSIS, but is controlled at key points by SPHINCTERS. There are many gastrointestinal tract diseases. In GASTROENTERITIS, ENTERITIS and COLITIS, gut segments become inflamed. Peptic ULCER affects both the duodenum and stomach, while CANCER of the esophagus, stomach, colon and rectum are relatively common. Disease of the small intestine tends to cause malabsorption. Methods of investigating the tract include GASTROINTESTINAL SERIES, and endoscopy, in which viewing tubes are passed in via the mouth or anus to examine the gut epithelium.

GASTROPODA, a class of MOLLUSKS whose shells and internal organs are spiraled. The body consists of a head with tentacles, a dorsal foot and a ventral mantle which secretes the shell. There are terrestrial varieties, such as the snail and slug, and marine varieties, such as water snails and whelks.

GASTROTICHA, a class of minute aquatic animals. Some live in fresh water, others in salt water. They are long and thin, moving along the bottom by means of cilia. They eat bacteria and organic debris. Some forms are hermaphroditic.

GAS TURBINE, a heat ENGINE in which hot gas, generated by burning a fuel or by heat exchange from a nuclear reactor, drives a TURBINE and so supplies power. Straightforward and reliable, they were developed in the late 1930s, and are now used to power aircraft, ships and locomotives, to generate electricity and to drive compressors in pipelines. The fuel used may be fuel GAS, gasoline, kerosine or even powdered coal. Some gas turbines are external-combustion engines, the working gas being heated in a heat exchanger and passed round the system in a closed cycle. Most, however, are INTERNAL-COMBUSTION ENGINES working on an open cycle: in the combustors fuel is injected into compressed air and ignited; the hot exhaust gases drive the turbines and are vented to the atmosphere, heat exchangers transferring some of their heat to the air from the compressors. (See also JET PROPULSION.)

GATES, Horatio (c1727–1806), American Revolutionary War general. As a commander of the Army of the North he gained fame by defeating General Burgoyne at the battle of SARATOGA in 1777, after which the CONWAY CABAL plotted to replace Washington by Gates as commander-in-chief. Gates took command in the South in 1780 and was badly defeated at CAMDEN, by General Cornwallis.

GATES, Sir Thomas (d. c1621), English colonial governor of the Virginia colony 1611–14. In 1606 he was one of the first petitioners granted a charter for the LONDON COMPANY to settle Virginia. After Virginia was almost abandoned in 1610, Gates helped to reestablish the colony in 1611.

GATINEAU, R in SW Quebec, Canada, rising in the Laurentians and flowing for 240mi to the Ottowa R at Hull. Lumber is transported along the river.

GATLING, Richard Jordan (1818–1903), US inventor of the Gatling gun, a multi-barreled MACHINE GUN capable of a high rate of fire (patented 1862). After decades in eclipse, it is now returning to use where extremely rapid fire (up to 7000 shots/min) is required.

GATT. See GENERAL AGREEMENT ON TARIFFS AND TRADE.

GATUN LAKE, artificial lake, part of the Panama Canal system. It was formed and is now controlled by the Gatun dam built across the Chagres R in 1912. It has an area of 166sq mi.

GAUCHO, cowboy of the South American pampas who flourished in the 18th and 19th centuries. Gauchos were skilled riders, and were usually employed to herd cattle. Their function ceased with the fencing of the pampas and reorganization of the cattle industry, but like the US COWBOY they survived as local folk heroes.

GAUDÍ, Antonio (1852–1926), Spanish architect, born Antonio Gaudí y Cornet. The fluidity, intricacy and bizarre aspect of his designs are an expression of ART NOUVEAU. He used glazed tiles to color his architecture. He worked mostly in Barcelona where he created the Milá House, the Güel Park and the Church of the Holy Family.

GAUDIER-BRZESKA, Henri (1891–1915), French sculptor, born Henri Gaudier. Working in England, his abstract animal sculptures attracted the interest of Ezra POUND and Wyndham LEWIS and he became an exponent of VORTICISM. He was killed in WWI.

GAUGAMELA, Battle of, battle in 331 BC near modern Mosul, Iraq, where ALEXANDER THE GREAT defeated the larger army of DARIUS III of Persia. This battle, sometimes called the Battle of Arbela, marked the final overthrow of the Persian Empire.

GAUGUIN, Paul Eugène Henri (1848–1903), French post-impressionist painter noted for his pictures of Polynesian life. After painting in a symbolist style at Pont-Aven, Brittany and working with VAN GOGH, he went to Tahiti and the Marquesas in 1891 where he lived for the rest of his life. He painted scenes in brilliant colors and flattened, simplified forms. His concept of primitivism in art influenced EXPRESSIONISM.

GAUL, ancient designation for a region in W Europe comprising present-day France, Belgium, western Germany and northern Italy. The region was named for the invaders the "Galli" (Celts) who conquered it. Northern Italy, *Cisalpine Gaul* (Gaul this side of the Alps), was conquered in the 5th century BC by Celts who were subjected by Rome in 222 BC. The inhabitants were given Roman citizenship in 49 BC. *Transalpine Gaul* (Gaul the other side of the Alps), now France and parts of Germany, Belgium, Holland and Switzerland, was gradually conquered by the Celts from the 8th to the 5th century BC. However, by 121 BC Rome had occupied the S portion. In his GALLIC WARS, 58–51 BC, Julius Caesar defeated incursions of Germanic tribes and conquered all the Gallic tribes. Under Roman dominion Gaul prospered; roads were built and cities founded. In the 5th century AD it was overrun by Germanic tribes.

Bouquet of Flowers by Paul Gauguin, now in the National Gallery, London. Gauguin's work shows an extraordinary sense of the vigor to be found in nature and in people living close to nature.

GAULLE, Charles de. See DE GAULLE, CHARLES.

GAUNT, John of. See JOHN OF GAUNT.

GAUR, *Bos gaurus*, the largest species of wild ox, usually about 1.9m (6.2ft) high at the shoulder. It is found in forested hills of SE Asia where it feeds on grasses. A domesticated variety is known as the **gayal**.

GAUSS (Gs), unit of magnetic flux density in CGS UNITS, equalling one maxwell per square centimetre.

GAUSS, Johann Karl Friedrich (1777–1855), German mathematician who discovered the method of LEAST-SQUARES (for reducing experimental errors), made many contributions to the theory of NUMBERS (including the proof that all algebraic equations have at least one root of the form $(a+ib)$ where i is the IMAGINARY OPERATOR and a and b are real numbers), and discovered a NON-EUCLIDEAN GEOMETRY. He won fame when he showed how to rediscover the lost ASTEROID Ceres (1801), and later (1831) turned to the study of MAGNETISM, particularly terrestrial magnetism. He is also remembered for his contributions to STATISTICS and CALCULUS.

GAUSSIAN DISTRIBUTION. See NORMAL DISTRIBUTION.

GAUSSIAN SYSTEM. See CGS UNITS.

GAUTIER, Théophile (1811–1872), French poet, novelist and critic. He was a supporter of the aesthetic movement, "art for art's sake," which he explained in the preface to his novel *Mademoiselle de Maupin* (1835–36). He wrote outstanding art, drama and ballet criticism. His volumes of verse include *Enamels and Cameos* (1852).

GAVIAL, or **gharial**, *Gavialis gangeticus*, a relative of alligators and crocodiles. It has a slender nose, grows to 6m (20ft) and lives in Indian rivers where it eats fish. The false (Sunda) gharial is a SE Asian crocodile.

GAVOTTE, lively French folk dance with skipping steps, danced at Louis XIV's court. COUPERIN and J. S. BACH used its rhythms in their music.

GAWAIN, one of the knights of the Round Table, nephew to King ARTHUR in the ARTHURIAN LEGENDS. He is most notably represented in the 14th-century anonymous romance *Sir Gawain and the Green Knight*.

GAY, John (1685–1732), English poet and dramatist, author of *The Beggar's Opera* (1728). Using English ballads for the music, he satirized Italian operatic forms and contemporary politics in a comedy of highwaymen, thieves and prostitutes.

GAYA, city in Bihar state, NE India, 57mi S of Patna.

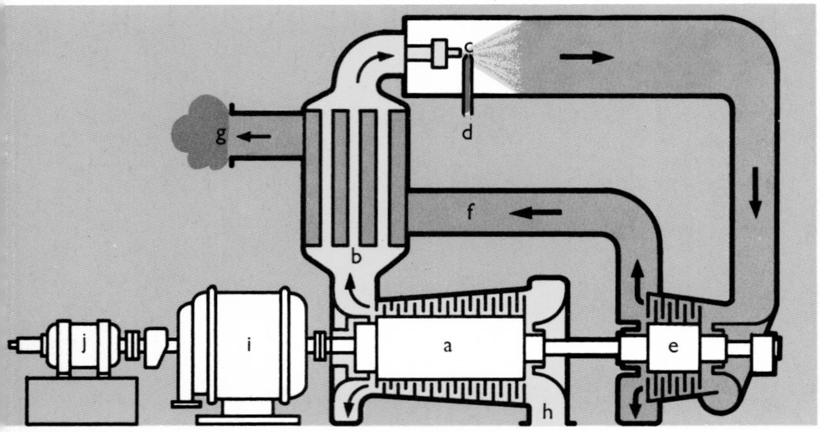

The many different functions of gas turbines include generating electricity and producing compressed air for blast furnaces. The diagram shows a typical open-cycle gas turbine, with (a) air compressor, (b) heat exchanger, (c) combustion chamber, (d) fuel injector, (e) turbine, (f) exhaust gas channel, (g) exhaust, (h) air intake, (i) dynamo and (j) starting motor.

It is in a sacred Hindu and Buddhist region, and 7mi N of Buddh Gaya, the place of Buddha's enlightenment.

GAYAL. See GAUR.

GAY-LUSSAC, Joseph Louis (1778–1850), French chemist and physicist best known for **Gay-Lussac's Law** (1808), which states that, when gases combine to give a gaseous product, the ratio of the volumes of the reacting gases to that of the product is a simple, integral one. AVOGADRO's hypothesis is based on this and on DALTON's law of multiple proportions (see COMPOSITION, CHEMICAL). He also showed, independently of CHARLES, that all gases increase in volume by the same fraction for the same increase in temperature, 1/273.2 for 1C°; and (once with BIOT) made two balloon ascents to investigate atmospheric composition and the intensity of the EARTH's magnetic field at altitude. His many important contributions to inorganic chemistry include the identification of CYANOGEN.

GAZA, city in the Philistia Plain near the Mediterranean, once a Philistine site whose temple Samson destroyed. It has long been of commercial and administrative importance. Pop 118 300.

GAZA STRIP, narrow piece of land in the former SW Palestine, about 26mi long, 4–5mi wide. After the Arab–Israeli war in 1948, it was granted to Egypt and numerous Arab refugees fled there. Israel occupied the area in 1967. Some of the Arab population has been resettled.

GAZELLE, a slender, graceful ANTELOPE of Asia and Africa. Males are horned; females may have short spikes. They are usually 600–900mm (2–3ft) high at the shoulder, swift and light-footed. They inhabit dry open country. Thompson's and Grant's gazelles live in Africa; the Goitered gazelle, so called from a swelling in the throat, in Asian deserts; Speke's gazelle, with an inflatable nose, in Somali deserts. The gerenuk or Giraffe-necked gazelle has a long neck and legs.

GAZIANTEP, capital of Gaziantep province, S Turkey, a textile center. It was an ancient Hittite city. In 1920–21 it was the base of Turkish resistance to the French. Pop 225 881.

GDÁNSK (formerly Danzig), large Polish industrial city and port on the Baltic Sea with some of the world's largest shipyards. Its economy rests on mechanical engineering and chemical industries. Once a major city in the Hanseatic League, since 1772 Gdánsk has alternated several times between being a free city and under German or Polish control. Pop 364 285.

GDYNIA, city in N Poland. Formerly a German village ceded to Poland in 1920, it was made a port in 1924 to avoid Polish dependence on Gdánsk, which had a hostile German population. Pop 190 125.

GE. See GAEA.

GEAR, machine part—a toothed wheel—used to transmit rotation from one shaft to another without slip. They are used in pairs, or in threes if both shafts are to rotate in the same sense. The **gear ratio**, the ratio of the number of teeth on the two gears, is equal to the ratio of the TORQUES (neglecting friction), and the inverse of the ratio of the angular velocities. (In the rare case of noncircular gears the torque and angular velocity vary periodically.) Gear teeth are designed to mesh and turn with minimal friction: thus their sides are shaped as involutes of the circular wheel, so that they roll on each other. The commonest type of gear for parallel shafts is the spur gear, with straight teeth parallel to the axis; the helical gear has teeth cut along sections of a HELIX, the double helical gear—the most efficient type—having a herring-bone-like arrangement to avoid axial thrust. Bevel gears, whose tapering teeth are set on a FRUSTUM of a cone, connect intersecting shafts. Skew shafts are connected by a gear and **worm**: the worm is a SCREW, equivalent to a one-toothed gear, so the gear ratio is high.

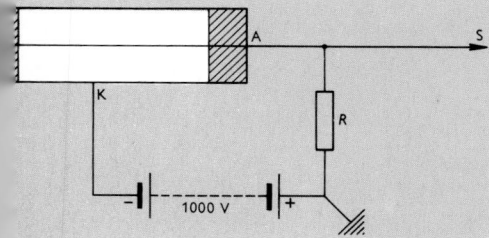

The Geiger counter, used to detect and measure ionizing radiation, consists of a gas-filled metal tube—the cathode (K)—and a wire anode (A). Radiation entering the tube through a window detaches electrons from the gas molecules. The resulting electron "avalanche" creates an electrical impulse which passes through an amplifier (R) and is registered on a pulse counter at (S).

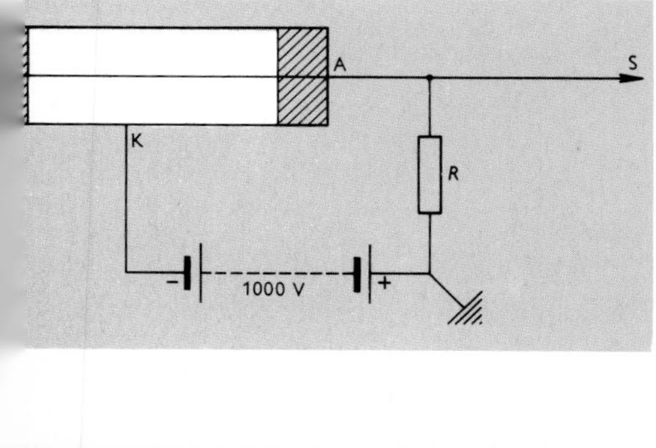

The graceful Thomson's gazelle is still a familiar sight in African parks, but not in the once-common herds of several thousand. Like many other animals, it is gradually losing its territory to man's need to cultivate more and more land for his own food.

GEBER, Ibn-Hayyan. See JABIR.

GECKOES, small lizards living in warm climates all over the world. They appear in the US in Fla. and Cal. They are about 150mm (6in) long, eat insects and are able to climb vertical surfaces by means of suction pads and minute hairs on the feet. They can change color to match their background. Most live in trees, but some are found in the desert.

GEDDES, Norman Bel (1893–1958), US industrial and stage designer famous for his "streamlined" style. He designed over 200 stage and film sets, and after the 1920s theaters, trains and automobiles.

GEDDES, Sir Patrick (1854–1932), Scottish biologist and sociologist who played a formative role in early sociological and urban planning studies.

GEERTGEN TOT SINT JANS (c1465–c1495), Netherlandish painter. His dramatic style, brilliant coloring, the individuality of his figures and lyrical landscapes prefigure later developments in Dutch art.

GEESE, water birds of 14 species closely related to DUCKS and SWANS. There are two natural groups of true geese: Gray geese of the genus *Anser*, and Black geese (genus *Branta*). They are all confined to the N Hemisphere, breeding in arctic or subarctic regions. They are gregarious, feeding and migrating in large flocks. In flight a flock usually adopts a characteristic V-formation. Geese feed by grazing on the banks of rivers and lakes, or may fly quite a distance from water to feed on grain or in stubble. Domestic geese are derived from the Graylag goose, *A. anser*.

GE'EZ, Semitic language of N Ethiopia, now used only as a literary language and as the liturgical language of the Ethiopian Church. It has been extinct as a spoken tongue since around the 13th century.

GEGENSCHEIN, or **Counterglow.** See ZODIACAL LIGHT.

GEHENNA, valley near Jerusalem where Israelites sacrificed children to the god MOLOCH between the 10th and 6th centuries BC. The word has come to be synonymous with HELL in Jewish, Christian and Islamic tradition.

GEHRIG, "Lou" (Henry Louis; 1903–1941), US baseball player. As first baseman for the New York Yankees he set a record by playing 2 130 consecutive games. He had a .361 batting average in seven world series, a lifetime average of .341 and 493 home runs.

GEIGER, Abraham (1810–1874), German rabbi and theological scholar, a leader of the Reform movement in JUDAISM. He wrote many historical studies on the Bible.

GEIGER COUNTER, or **Geiger-Müller tube,** an instrument for detecting the presence of and measuring radiation such as ALPHA PARTICLES, BETA-, GAMMA- and X-RAYS. It can count individual particles at rates up to about 10 000/s and is used widely in medicine and in prospecting for radioactive ores. A fine wire ANODE runs along the axis of a metal cylinder which has sealed insulating ends, contains a mixture of ARGON or NEON and METHANE at low pressure, and acts as the CATHODE, the potential between them being about 1kV. Particles entering through a thin window cause ionization in the gas; ELECTRONS build up around the anode and a momentary drop in the inter-electrode potential occurs which appears as a voltage pulse in an associated counting circuit. The methane quenches the ionization, leaving the counter ready to detect further incoming particles.

GEIKIE, Sir Archibald (1835–1924), Scottish geologist, Director General of the Geological Survey of Great Britain (1882–1901) and President of the Royal Society (1908–12), best known for books such as *A Textbook of Geology* (1882) and *The Ancient Volcanoes of Great Britain* (1897).

GEISEL, Theodor. See SEUSS, DR.

GEISHA, Japanese professional female entertainer, especially for businessmen's parties in restaurants. The name means "art person" and a Geisha's accomplishments include singing, dancing, playing instruments and conversation, ranging in subject from a knowledge of history to contemporary gossip. Geishas are not prostitutes. Training for the profession, which has existed since the 18th century, begins early with a highly-organized apprenticeship.

GEISSLER TUBE, a forerunner of the modern ELECTRON TUBE, invented in 1858 by Heinrich Geissler (1849–1879). It is a glass tube containing a gas at low pressure which glows with a characteristic COLOR when a high voltage is applied to the metal ELECTRODES at the ends of the tube. Modified forms are used as spectroscopic light sources and in neon or argon signs.

GEL, a COLLOID in which one phase is initially solid, the other initially liquid, but in which both phases are continuous. (See also SOL.) A gel has usually a solid or semisolid form.

GELASIUS, name of two popes. **Saint Gelasius I** (d. 496 AD), pope from 492. He defended Rome's ecclesiastical supremacy over Constantinople. His doctrine that the authority of the priesthood and of kings were both divinely inspired but independent in their own sphere was revolutionary. **Gelasius II** (d. 1119), pope 1118–19. Because of controversy between the popes and Holy Roman emperors over the right to grant ecclesiastical titles, Emperor Henry V opposed his election, and chose antipope Gregory VIII in his stead, forcing Gelasius into exile.

GELATIN, yellowish animal PROTEIN, derived from COLLAGEN and obtained by treating animal hides and bones with acid or alkali and boiling them. It dissolves in hot water to form a sol (see COLLOID) which sets to a GEL on cooling. It is used in jellies, soups and other foods, capsules for pharmaceuticals, photographic emulsion, lithography and plastics.

GELIGNITE. See DYNAMITE.

GELL-MANN, Murray (1929–), US physicist awarded the 1969 Nobel Prize for Physics for his work on the classification of SUBATOMIC PARTICLES (notably K-mesons and hyperons) and their interactions. With FEYNMAN he has proposed the quark as a basic component of all subatomic particles.

GELSENKIRCHEN, city, North Rhine-Westphalia, West Germany, on the Rhine-Herne canal. It is a mining center and inland port of the industrial Ruhr area. Pop 348 292.

GEMARA (Aramaic: completion), the second part of the TALMUD, the compilation of Jewish oral law. It is a commentary on sections of the MISHNAH, the first part of the Talmud. There is a Palestinian Gemara, completed c400 AD, and a Babylonian Gemara completed a century later.

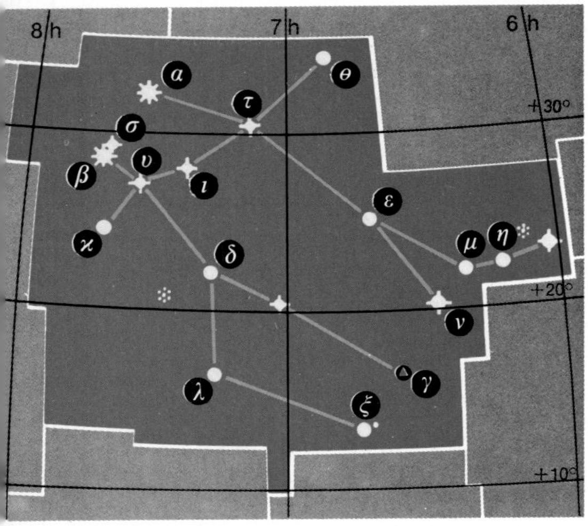

Position of the constellation Gemini in the northern hemisphere of the sky. The stars it is named for, Castor and Pollux, twins in Greek mythology.

GEMINI (the Twins), a constellation on the ECLIPTIC named after its two brightest stars, Castor and Pollux. The third sign of the ZODIAC, Gemini gives its name to the Geminid METEOR shower.

GEMINI MISSIONS, US space program designed to develop docking and rendezvous procedures, a vital preparation for the Apollo Project (see SPACE EXPLORATION). Gemini 1 was launched April 8, 1964; 3 (the first manned), March 23, 1965; 12 (the last), Nov. 11, 1966. From Gemini IV E.H. White II became the 2nd man ever to float free in space.

GEMINIANI, Francesco (c1687–1762), Italian composer and violinist. He moved to London where he gained a considerable reputation for performing and composing, and wrote several theoretical works on music, notably the influential *The Art of Playing on the Violin* (1731).

One of the most complex technical feats ever performed by man was the docking of two separate space capsules in orbit during the Gemini program. The success of this venture paved the way for the historic Apollo series and the moon landing.

GEMS, stones prized for their beauty, and durable enough to be used in jewelry and for ornament. A few—AMBER, CORAL, PEARL and JET—have organic origin, but most are well-crystallized MINERALS. Gems are usually found in IGNEOUS ROCKS (mainly pegmatite dikes) and in contact METAMORPHIC zones. The chief gems have HARDNESS of 8 or more on the Mohs scale, and are relatively resistant to CLEAVAGE and fracture, though some are fragile. They are identified and characterized by their SPECIFIC GRAVITY (which also determines the size of a stone with a given weight in CARATS) and optical properties, especially refractive index (see REFRACTION). Gems of high refractive index show great brilliancy (also dependent on transparency and polish) and prismatic DISPERSION ("fire"). Other attractive optical effects include chatoyancy (see CAT'S EYE), dichroism (see DOUBLE REFRACTION), opalescence and asterism—a star-shaped gleam caused by regular intrusions in the crystal lattice. Since earliest times gems have been engraved in intaglio and cameo. Somewhat later cutting and polishing were developed, the cabochon (rounded) cut being used. Not until the late Middle Ages was faceting developed, now the commonest cutting style, its chief forms being the brilliant cut and the step cut. Some gems are dyed, impregnated, heated or irradiated to improve their color. Synthetic gems are made by flame-fusion or by crystallization from a melt or aqueous solution.

GEMSBOK, *Oryx gazella*, a species of ORYX living in SW Africa.

GENEALOGY, the study of the origins and history of families, by means of pedigree charts showing lines of descent. It is a skilled profession, also a hobby, which developed after 1500. Genealogy is a tool of the historian and is useful for determining legal cases involving inheritance. It is fundamental to such hereditary organizations as the DAUGHTERS OF THE AMERICAN REVOLUTION.

GENE POOL, the total amount of information present at any time in the GENES of the reproductive members of a biological population. The frequency of any particular gene in the gene pool changes owing to NATURAL SELECTION, MUTATION and GENETIC DRIFT. This change forms the basis of evolutionary change.

GENERAL ACCOUNTING OFFICE (GAO), an independent agency of the US Congress, created in 1921 for auditing government spending. Headed by the US Comptroller General, it sets up accounting and management standards, settles claims for or against the government, collects debts and assesses the practicability and legality of public expenditures of most government agencies.

GENERAL AGREEMENT ON TARIFFS AND TRADE (GATT), a set of agreements which aim to abolish quotas and reduce tariffs and other restrictions on world trade, originally agreed to by 23 countries in 1947. By the 1970s there were 78 nations participating in GATT. The "Kennedy round" of GATT negotiations in 1964–67 provided for a reduction in import duties over five years. Tariffs among steel-producing countries were agreed upon, export prices for grain controlled and an international anti-dump code established.

GENERAL GRANT NATIONAL MEMORIAL, the tomb of US president and Civil War general Ulysses S. Grant and his wife Julia, in New York City on the Hudson R. An impressive mausoleum, it was authorized as a memorial in 1958.

GENERAL SAN MARTÍN, city, E central Argentina. It is a major industrial center in NE Buenos Aires province. Pop 278 751.

GENERAL SARMIENTO, city, E central Argentina. It is a NNW suburb of metropolitan Buenos Aires. Pop 167 160.

GENERAL SERVICES ADMINISTRATION (GSA), an independent US federal agency, established 1949, to maintain government property and records. Its five branches deal with quality-controlled supplies for government use, emergency stockpiles of strategic materials, erection and management of public buildings, transportation and telecommunications and the preserving of historical records and archives.

GENERAL WILL, a doctrine that in a democratic society the will of the majority should prevail. It was postulated by Jean Jacques ROUSSEAU in the 18th century that men achieve civil liberty by means of a social contract in which authority is vested in society. Hence the general will of citizens reflects the common interest and must be supreme in decision-making.

GENERATOR, Electric, or **dynamo**, a device converting mechanical ENERGY into electrical energy. Traditional forms are based on inducing ELECTRIC FIELDS by changing the MAGNETIC FIELD lines through a circuit (see ELECTROMAGNETISM). All generators can be, and sometimes are, run in reverse as electric MOTORS.

The simplest generator consists of a permanent magnet (the **rotor**) spun inside a coil of wire (the **stator**); the magnetic field is thus reversed twice each revolution, and an AC voltage is generated at the frequency of rotation (see also MAGNETO). In practical designs, the rotor is usually an ELECTROMAGNET driven

Manned missions of the Gemini programme

Mission Number	Crew	Date(s) (hr:min)	Weight lb[kg]	Orbits	Maximum Distance from Earth mi[km]
3*	Virgil I. Grissom, John W. Young	March 23, 1965 (4:53)	7 111[3 225]	3	140[225]
4	James A. McDivitt, Edward H. White II	June 3–7, 1965 (97:56)	7 879[3 573]	62	184 [296]
5	L. Gordon Cooper, Jr Charles Conrad, Jr	August 21–29, 1965 (190:55)	7 947[3 604]	120	217[349]
7	Frank Borman, James A. Lovell, Jr	December 4–18, 1965 (330:35)	8 076[3 663]	206	204[328]
6-A	Walter M. Schirra, Jr. Thomas P. Stafford	December 15–16, 1965 (25:51)	7 817[3 545]	16	193[310]
8	Neil A. Armstrong David R. Scott	March 16, 1966 (10:41)	8 351[3 787]	6½	186[299]
9-A	Thomas P. Stafford Eugene A. Cernan	June 3–6, 1966 (72:21)	8 268[3 750]	45	194[312]
10	John W. Young Michael Collins	July 18–21, 1966 (70:47)	8 248[3 741]	43	476[766]
11	Charles Conrad, Jr Richard F. Gordon, Jr	September 12–15, 1966 (71:17)	8 509[3 859]	44	853[1 373]
12	James A. Lovell, Jr Edwin E. Aldrin, Jr	November 11–15, 1966 (94:35)	8 297[3 763]	59	187[301]

*The Gemini Program was inaugurated with two unmanned flights on April 8, 1964 and August 8, 1964.

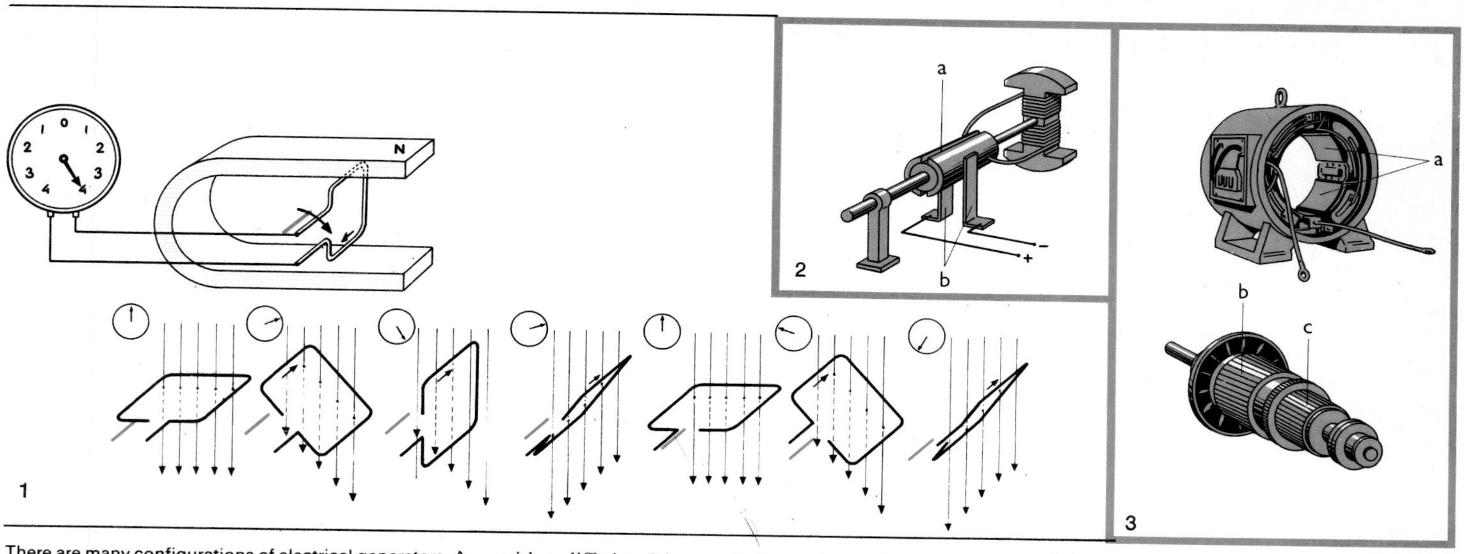

There are many configurations of electrical generators. A simple generator (1) consists of a coil turning in the field of a permanent magnet; the current produced is an alternating current, i.e., it changes direction every time the coil turns through 180°. With a commutator (2) it is possible to obtain a direct current: the collector (a) consists of two half slip rings which distribute the current by means of "brushes" (b). In a large DC generator (3) stationary field coils (a) are used to create the magnetic field; armature coils (b) move through this field, and current is taken off via the collector (c).

by a direct current obtained by rectification of a part of the voltage generated, and passed to the rotor through a pair of CARBON **brush**/slip ring contacts. The use of three sets of stator coils 120° apart allows generation of a three-phase supply. (See also ARMATURE.)

Simple DC generators consist of a coil rotating in the field of a permanent magnet: the voltage induced in the coil alternates at the frequency of rotation, but it is collected through a **commutator** —a slip ring broken into two semicircular parts, to each of which one end of the coil is connected, so that the connection between the coil and the brushes is reversed twice each revolution—resulting in a rapidly pulsating direct voltage. A steadier voltage can be achieved through the use of multiple coil/commutator arrangements, and except in very small generators, the permanent magnet is again replaced by an electromagnet driven by part of the generated voltage.

For large-scale generation, the mechanical power is usually derived from fossil-fuel-fired steam TURBINES, or from dam-fed water turbines, and the process is only moderately efficient. The magnetohydrodynamic generator, currently under development, avoids this step, and has no moving parts either. A hot conducting fluid (treated coal gas, or reactor-heated liquid metal) passes through the field of an electromagnet, so that the charges are forced in opposite directions producing a DC voltage. In another device, the electrogasdynamic generator, the voltage is produced by using a high speed gas stream to pump charge from an electric discharge, against the electric field, to a collector. (See also ELECTROSTATIC GENERATOR.)

Generators originated with the discovery of induction by M. FARADAY in 1831; the considerable advantages of electromagnets over permanent magnets were first exploited by E. W. von SIEMENS in 1866.

GENES, the carriers of the genetic information which is passed on from generation to generation by the combination of GAMETES. Genes consist of chain-like molecules of NUCLEIC ACIDS, DNA in most organisms and RNA in some VIRUSES. The genes are normally located on the CHROMOSOMES found in the nucleus of the CELL. The genetic information is coded by the sequences of the four bases present in nucleic acids, with a differing 3-base code for each AMINO ACID so that each gene contains the information for the synthesis of one PROTEIN chain.

GENESIS (Greek: origin or generation), the first book of the OLD TESTAMENT and of the PENTATEUCH. It tells of the creation, the Fall (see ORIGINAL SIN), the Flood (see NOAH), the origins of the HEBREWS, and the early PATRIARCHS with whom God made his COVENANT. The book accounts for the Israelites' presence in Egypt, and so leads into EXODUS.

GENÊT, Edmond Charles Édouard (1763–1834), French diplomat. He tried to bring the US into the war against Britain during the FRENCH REVOLUTION thus creating the first international crisis for America. "Citizen Genêt" was sent as minister to the US (1792–94). His demands were opposed by President Washington.

GENET, Jean (1910–), French playwright and novelist. He spent much of his life in prisons. His writing concerns the homosexual underworld of France and the borderline between acceptable and unacceptable social behavior. His works include the novel *Our Lady of the Flowers* (1944), *The Thief's Journal* (1948) and the plays *The Balcony* (1956) and *The Blacks* (1958).

GENETIC DRIFT, a process by which genetic information controlling certain features is lost from a population because it is not transmitted to the offspring. It only occurs in small isolated populations. In large populations any specific trait is carried by so many individuals that unless it is unfavorable its loss is highly unlikely. The almost total absence of BLOOD group B in American Indians may be due to genetic drift.

The General Grant National Memorial is in Riverside Park, New York and was built between 1891 and 1897 in the classic style. It is usually known as Grant's Tomb and holds the remains of General Grant and his wife, Julia Dent Grant.

GENETICS, the branch of biology dealing with HEREDITY, which studies the way in which GENES operate and the way in which they are transmitted from parent to offspring. Genetics can be subdivided into a number of more specialized subjects including classical genetics (which deals with the inheritance of parental features in higher animals and plants), cytogenetics (which deals with the cellular basis of genetics), microbial genetics (which deals with inheritance in microorganisms), molecular genetics (which deals with the biochemical basis of inheritance) and human genetics (which deals with inheritance of features of social and medical importance in man). **Genetic counseling** is a branch of human genetics of growing importance. Here couples, particularly those with some form of inherited defect, are advised on the chances that their children will have similar defects.

GENETS, a group of carnivorous mammals related to civets and mongooses and similar in appearance to the domestic cat. There are six species; best known is the Feline or Spotted genet *Genetta genetta* found in Africa, Spain and southern France. It is up to 1m (3.3ft) long, and has soft black to brown fur.

GENEVA, city and capital of Geneva canton, SW Switzerland, on Lake Geneva at the Rhône R outlet. It is the headquarters of the WORLD HEALTH ORGANIZATION, the INTERNATIONAL LABOR ORGANIZATION, the WORLD COUNCIL OF CHURCHES and the International RED CROSS. It is an important cultural, scientific, theological, industrial and banking city and the center of the Swiss watchmaking industry. The Collège de Genève was founded (1559) by John CALVIN. Pop 173 618.

GENEVA, city, W central N.Y., on Seneca Lake, settled around 1785. It has two private colleges and varied light industry. Pop 16 793.

GENEVA, Lake, or Lac Léman, largest Alpine lake in Europe, at an altitude of 1 200ft, between SW Switzerland and SE France and the Jura Mts. The Rhône R enters at the E end of the beautiful crescent-shaped lake, emerging at Geneva.

GENEVA CONFERENCE, name of several international conferences held in Geneva, Switzerland. Among the most significant is that of April–July 1954, between the US, Britain, the USSR, France, Communist China, SE Asian countries and other interested parties to discuss settlement of the French–Indochinese and the Korean wars. Cease-fires were agreed for Cambodia, Laos and Vietnam, which was divided into North and South. (See VIETNAM WAR.)

GENEVA CONVENTIONS, four international agreements for the protection of soldiers and civilians from the effects of war, signed by 58 nations and the Holy See in Aug. 1949, at Geneva, Switzerland. Convention I derived from a conference in 1864 in which the work of Jean DUNANT, founder of the RED

The shape of things to come—Buckminster Fuller's geodesic dome at the Montreal Expo '67. The dome is based on a study of spherical structures and the manner in which such structures as cells and bubbles group together. The resulting unit is actually stronger when under pressure from the elements than it is in calm conditions.

CROSS, led to an agreement to improve conditions for sick and wounded soldiers in the field. Convention II deals with armed forces at sea, Convention III with treatment of prisoners of war and Convention IV with protection of civilians.

GENEVIÈVE, Saint (c442–c512), patron saint of Paris, reputed to have saved Paris from Attila the Hun in 451 through prayer and fasting.

GENGHIS KHAN (1167?–1227), Mongol ruler of one of the greatest empires in world history, born Temujin. After 20 years of tribal warfare, he was acknowledged Genghis Khan (Universal Ruler) in 1206. He campaigned against the CH'IN empire in N China (1213–15) and in 1218–25 he conquered Turkistan, Iran, Afghanistan and S Russia until his empire stretched from the Caucasus Mts to the Indus R and from the Caspian Sea to Peking. He was not only a fearsome warrior, but also a skilled political leader. (See MONGOL EMPIRE.)

GENIE (or djinn), in Arabic folklore, an invisible spirit or demon with superhuman powers, capable of assuming human or animal form. Genies, which could be good or evil spirits, often feature in Near East tales. In the *Arabian Nights* the spirit of Aladdin's lamp is a genie.

GENOA, capital of Genoa province and of Liguria, NW Italy, 71mi SSW of Milan. It is Italy's largest port and is second only to Marseilles on the Mediterranean. In ancient times it was the headquarters of the Roman fleet. In the 12th and 13th centuries it was an independent republic with its own fleet and possessions in the LEVANT. The city's principal industries include shipbuilding, iron and steel making and oil and sugar refining. Pop 812 206.

GENOA, Gulf of, large inlet in NW Italy, forming the N Ligurian sea. The city of Genoa lies at its head.

GENOA CONFERENCE, convention of 34 nations at Genoa, Italy, in 1922, to discuss European economic reconstruction. Instigated by British Prime Minister Lloyd George, it was the first attempt of the USSR to join in European affairs after the Russian Revolution. It failed, however, because of disagreements over war debts and distrust of the USSR, increased by the signing of the German–Russian Treaty of RAPALLO, by which both nations mutually canceled all prewar debts and war claims.

GENOCIDE, (from Greek *genos,* race) the deliberate extermination of a racial, ethnic, political or religious group of people. The term is widely credited to the Polish–American scholar Raphael Lemkin. He believed that Nazi persecution of the Jews and other groups called for an international code on the subject. This was achieved when the UN General Assembly in 1948 approved the Convention on the Prevention and Punishment of the Crime of Genocide. (See also ANTI-SEMITISM.)

GENOTYPE, the total genetic makeup of a particular organism consisting of all the GENES received from both parents. For any individual the genotype determines their strengths and weaknesses during their whole life and is unique and constant for each individual. Duplication of the genotype except in identical twins is statistically impossible except in the simplest organisms. (See also PHENOTYPE.)

GENOVA. See GENOA.

GENRE, form of painting which takes its subjects from everyday life. The term derives from the French *de tout genre* (of every kind). Dutch, Flemish and Italian genre schools flourished in the 16th and 17th centuries. Among the great artists of the genre are Pieter BRUEGEL, VERMEER, WATTEAU, LONGHI and GAINSBOROUGH. The 19th and 20th centuries saw their own genre movements, such as the American ASHCAN SCHOOL.

The first edition of Ptolemy's *Geographia* to include this map of the coast and islands of the New World was published in 1513, twenty-one years after the discovery of the American continent. Of the islands was written, "Once known as the enchanted isles, they have very distinct vegetation and wildlife and were named after the famous large tortoises which are found there."

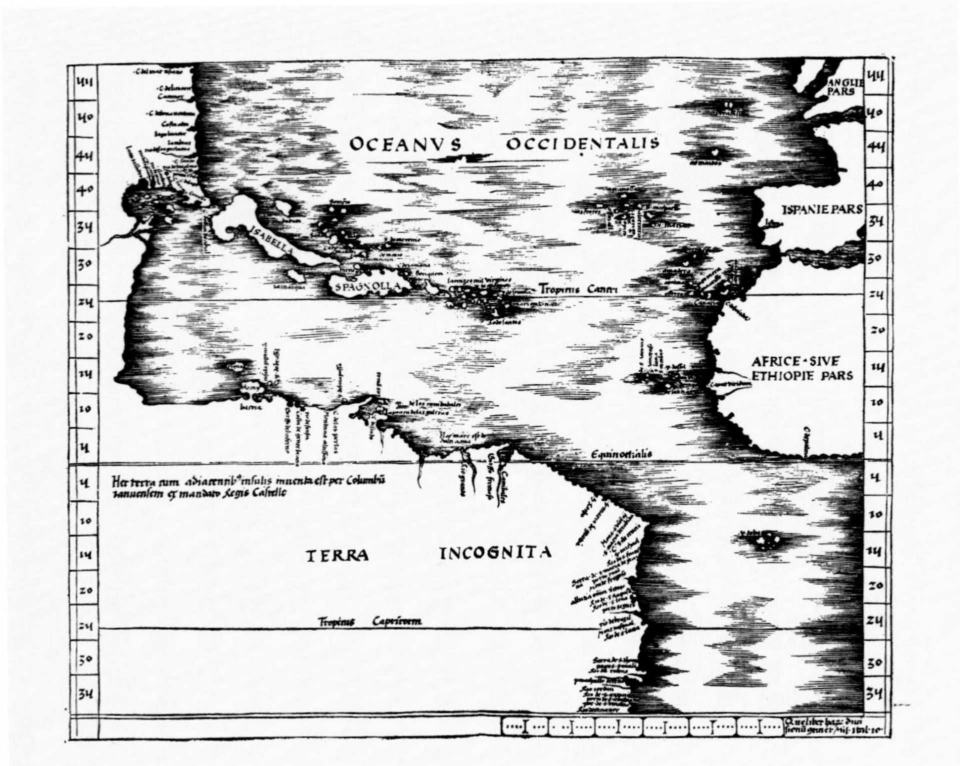

GENSERIC or **Gaiseric** (c390–477 AD), king of the VANDALS and the ALANI from 428. He led his people from S Spain to N Africa, took Carthage in 439, gained control of the Mediterranean and in 455 sacked Rome. By the time of his death he controlled Sardinia, Corsica, Sicily, Roman Africa and the Balearic Islands.

GENTIANS, a number of annual and herbaceous perennial plants of the genus *Gentiana,* which have worldwide distribution, except Africa. Many produce decorative trumpet-shaped flowers and several species are in cultivation, particularly in rock gardens. Family: Gentianaceae.

GENTIAN VIOLET, or methylrosaniline chloride, green powder used in aqueous solution (violet) as an ANTISEPTIC and medicinal FUNGICIDE, and against intestinal WORMS (see PARASITIC DISEASES).

GENTILE, Giovanni (1875–1944), Italian educator and philosopher. He wrote for Benedetto CROCE's *La Critica* and became known as the philosopher of FASCISM. As Fascist education minister (1922–24), he reformed the public educational system; in the period 1925–43 he edited the *Enciclopedia italiana.*

GENTILE DA FABRIANO (c1370–1427), Italian painter, a major exponent of the International Gothic style. His rich, exotic style with its profusion of color and gilt is seen in his masterpiece, the *Adoration of the Magi* (1423), now an altarpiece in the Uffizi, in Florence.

GENTLEMEN'S AGREEMENT, an informal agreement between Japan and the US in 1907. The US promised to discourage any laws restricting Japanese immigration and the Japanese agreed to stop unrestricted emigration to America. It lapsed in 1924 when the US Congress restricted Japanese immigration. The term also applies to any informal agreement not legally binding.

GENUS. See TAXONOMY.

GEOCHEMISTRY, the study of the CHEMISTRY of the EARTH (and other planets). Chemical characterization of the earth as a whole relates to theories of planetary formation. Classical geochemistry analyzes rocks and MINERALS. The study of PHASE EQUILIBRIA has thrown much light on the postulated processes of ROCK formation. (See also GEOLOGY.)

GEODE, a hollow mineral formation found in certain rocks. Typically, it is almost filled by inward-growing crystal "spikes," usually of QUARTZ. Geodes range between 20mm and 1m across.

GEODESIC DOME, architectural dome-like structure composed of polygonal (usually triangular) faces of lightweight material. It was developed by Buckminster FULLER. A geodesic dome housed the US exhibit at Expo '67 (Montreal).

GEODESY, the branch of geophysics concerned with the determination and explanation of the precise shape and size of the EARTH. The first recorded measurement of the earth's circumference that approximates to the correct value was that of ERATOSTHENES in the 3rd century BC. Modern geodesists use not only the techniques of SURVEYING but also information received from the observations of artificial SATELLITES.

GEODUCK, an edible CLAM of the Pacific coasts that may weigh over 2.3kg (5lb).

GEOFFREY OF MONMOUTH (c1100–1155), British bishop and chronicler whose *History of the Kings of Britain* (c1135) is a romantic and fictional account of early Britain. Highly popular in medieval Europe, it introduced the ARTHURIAN LEGENDS to the continent.

GEOFFREY PLANTAGENET (1113–1151), Duke of Normandy from 1135 and Count of Anjou, Maine and Touraine from 1131. In 1128 he married Matilda, daughter of Henry I of England; their son Henry thus became Henry II of England, founding the line of PLANTAGENETS.

GEOFFROY DE SAINT-HILAIRE, Étienne (1772–1844), French naturalist who argued, against G. CUVIER, for "unity of plan," the notion that all animals contain the same anatomical elements, some of these being developed at the expense of others in particular species. He acknowledged that there had been development in previously existing species.

GEOGRAPHY, the group of sciences concerned with the surface of the earth, including the distribution of life upon it, its physical structures, etc. Geography relies on surveying and mapping, and modern cartography (mapmaking) has rapidly adapted to the new needs of geography as it advances and develops. (See MAP; SURVEYING.) **Biogeography** is concerned with the distribution of life, both plant and animal (including man), about our world. It is thus clearly intimately related to BIOLOGY and ECOLOGY. **Economic geography** describes and seeks to explain the patterns of the world's commerce in terms of production, trade and transportation, and consumption. It relates closely to economics. **Mathematical geography** deals with the size, shape and motions of the EARTH, and is thus linked with ASTRONOMY (see also GEODESY). **Physical geography** deals with the physical structures of the earth, also including CLIMATOLOGY and OCEANOGRAPHY, and is akin to physical GEOLOGY. **Political geography** is concerned with the world as nationally divided; **regional geography** with the world in terms of regions separated by physical rather than national boundaries. **Historical geography** deals with the geography of the past: PALEOGEOGRAPHY at one level, exploration or past political change or settlement at another. **Applied geography** embraces the applications of all these branches to the solution of socioeconomic problems. Its subdivisions include urban geography and social geography; and it contributes to the science of SOCIOLOGY. (See also ETHNOLOGY; HYDROLOGY; METEROLOGY.) **Development of Geography.** Geography had its origins in the Greek attempts to understand the world in which they found themselves. Once it was realized that the earth was round, the next step was to estimate its size. This was achieved in the 3rd century BC by ERATOSTHENES. The classical achievement in geography, like that in astronomy, was summed up by Claudius PTOLEMY. His world MAP was used for centuries. Geographical knowledge next leapt forward in the age of exploration that opened with the voyages of Dias and Columbus. The 17th century saw continuing discovery and greatly improved methods of survey. The earliest modern geographical treatises, including that of Varenius, also appeared in this era. The 19th century brought with it the works of F. H. A. von HUMBOLDT and Karl Ritter, the former stressing physical and systematic geography, the latter the human and historical aspects of the science. Encompassing so many different studies, geography since the mid-19th century has become a battleground for the strife between different schools of geographers. While some have encouraged a regional approach, others have preferred to develop a landscape-concept. Others have stressed the study of the physical environment while others still have concentrated on political and economic factors.

aeon	era	period	epoch	time since commencement (million years)
Phanerozoic	Cenozoic	Quaternary	Holocene (Recent)	0.01
			Pleistocene	4
		Tertiary	Pliocene	10
			Miocene	25
			Oligocene	40
			Eocene	55
			Paleocene	65
	Mesozoic	Cretaceous		135
		Jurassic		190
		Triassic		225
	Paleozoic	Permian		280
		Pennsylvanian } Carboniferous		315
		Mississippian } Carboniferous		345
		Devonian		400
		Silurian		440
		Ordovician		500
		Cambrian		570
Cryptozoic	Proterozoic	Precambrian		
	Archeozoic (Archean)			
Azoic				4550

Perhaps the most recent group to come to the fore favors the collection of precise numerical data. With this they try to build mathematical models of geographic phenomena.

GEOID, geodesic model of the earth, the shape the earth would have to have for the pull of GRAVITY to be constant for all points, taken at sea level over the oceans and at corresponding level on land. The result is an oblate spheroid (see ELLIPSOID; OBLATENESS) with irregularities due to differing local densities. (See also EARTH; GEODESY.)

GEOLOGICAL SURVEY, US government bureau, established in 1879, responsible for the location and control of water and mineral resources on federal land, and for the chartering of water resources and the location of potential problem areas. It carries out and supervises research in the earth sciences.

GEOLOGY, the group of sciences concerned with the study of the earth, including its structure, long-term history, composition and origins.

Physical Geology deals with the structure and composition of the EARTH and the forces of change affecting them. The sciences that make up physical geology thus include GEODESY, GEOMORPHOLOGY, GEOPHYSICS and seismology (see EARTHQUAKE). Much of modern physical geology is based on the theory of PLATE TECTONICS.

Historical Geology deals with the earth in past ages, and with the EVOLUTION of life upon it. It embraces such sciences as PALEOCLIMATOLOGY, PALEOMAGNETISM, PALEONTOLOGY and STRATIGRAPHY; and relies heavily on dating (see CHRONOLOGY), events being related to the geological time scale, whose derivation is primarily stratigraphical, to a lesser extent paleontological.

Economic Geology lies between these two, and borrows from both. Concerned with the location and exploitation of the earth's natural resources (see ORE),

In recent years, geologists have learned much from studying the ocean floor. Here is a section of a deep-sea trench and its accompanying arc of volcanic islands. The dense oceanic plate (1) is being subducted beneath the lighter continental plate (2) in accordance with the theory of plate tectonics. Deep earthquake activity and the formation of an island arc results. The basaltic rocks of the oceanic plate are overlain by pelagic sediments, and, close to the trench, these are in turn overlain by turbidites (3). Island arcs such as this are common in the western Pacific Ocean. Examples include the Mariana Islands, the Kuril Islands and the New Hebrides.

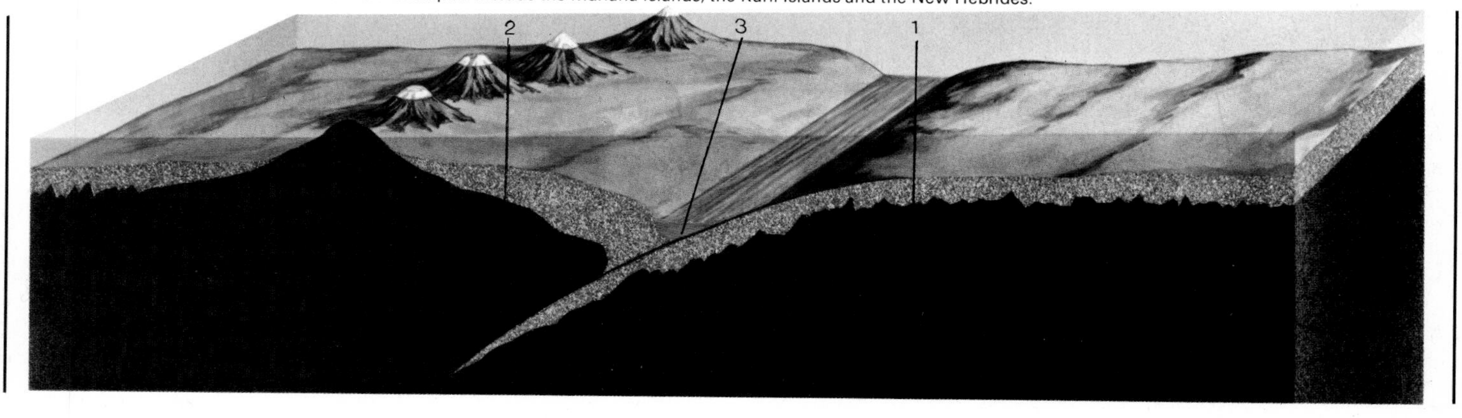

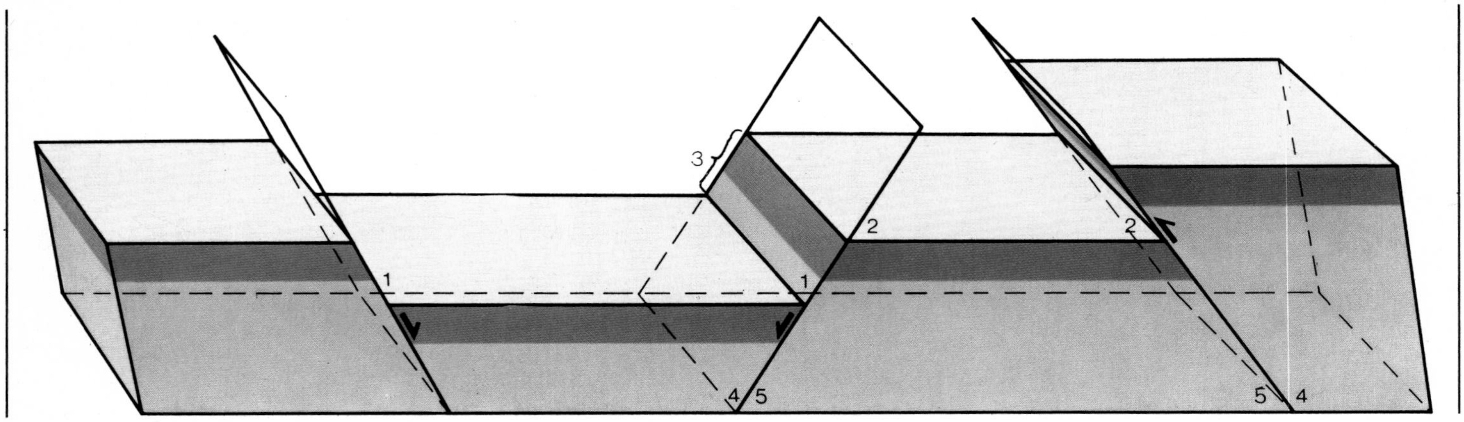

Above: terms used to describe geological faulting: (1) normal fault; (2) reverse fault; (3) displacement; (4) hanging wall; (5) foot wall. *Below:* the development of plateau formations through erosion, where a roughly horizontal mass of resistant rock lies in more easily eroded rocks (A). Initially a tabletop (B) is produced; later, this is fragmented by further erosion, forming buttes and mesas (C).

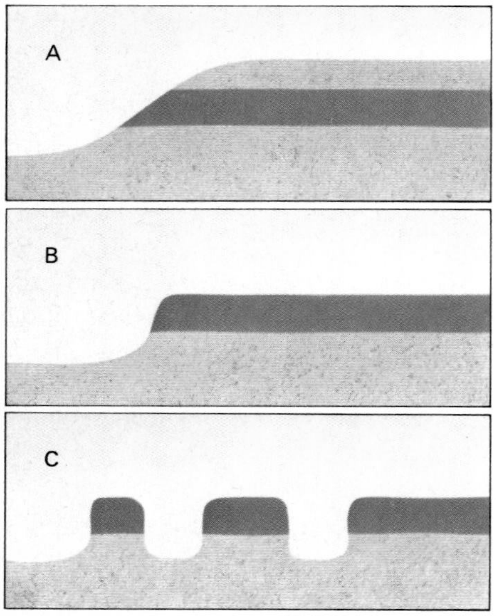

it is generally taken to include also the disciplines of crystallography, mineralogy and petrology (see CRYSTAL; MINERALS; ROCKS). Its practical manifestations are PROSPECTING and MINING.

Geology of other Planets. Except with the MOON, it is not yet possible to examine the rocks of other planets, but telescope and spectroscopic examinations have revealed much, as have those of unmanned probes. VOLCANISM is known on the moon and MARS (one volcano is some 600km across), and "moonquakes" have been detected.

Development of Geology. Most early geological knowledge came from the experience of mining engineers, some of the earliest geological treatises coming from the pen of Georgius AGRICOLA. The interest of the 16th century in FOSSILS was also reflected in the writings of K. von GESNER. In the 17th century the biblical timescale of about 6000 years from the Creation to the present largely constrained the many speculative "Theories of the Earth" that were issued. The century's most notable geological observations were made by N. STENO. The late 18th century saw the celebrated controversy between A. G. WERNER's "Neptunists" and J. HUTTON's "Plutonists" as to the origin of the rocks. The first decades of the 19th century, however, witnessed the decline of speculative geology as field observations became ever more detailed. William Smith (1769–1839), the "father of stratigraphy," showed how the succession of fossils could be used to index the stratigraphic column, and he and others produced impressive geological maps. C. LYELL's classic *Principles of Geology* (1830–33) restated the Huttonian principle of UNIFORMITARIANISM and provided the groundwork for much of the later development of the science. L. AGASSIZ pointed to the importance of glacial action in the recent history of the earth (1840), while mining engineering continued to contribute to the pool of geologic data. The most significant recent development in the earth sciences has been the acceptance of the theory of PLATE TECTONICS, foreshadowed in A. WEGENER's 1912 theory of CONTINENTAL DRIFT.

GEOMAGNETISM, the magnetic field of the EARTH; and the study of it, both as it is in the present and as it was in the past (see PALEOMAGNETISM). (See also GEOPHYSICS; MAGNETISM.)

GEOMETRIC STYLE, use of simple geometric forms to decorate pottery and ceramics, usually in abstract designs. First found in early Greek pottery, the style appears in most Neolithic cultures.

GEOMETRY, the branch of MATHEMATICS which studies the properties both of space and of the mathematical constructs—lines, curves, surfaces and the like—which can occupy space. Today it divides into ALGEBRAIC GEOMETRY; ANALYTIC GEOMETRY; DESCRIPTIVE GEOMETRY; DIFFERENTIAL GEOMETRY; EUCLIDEAN GEOMETRY; EUCLIDEAN GEOMETRY, and PROJECTIVE GEOMETRY, but many of these divisions have grown up only in the last few hundred years. The name geometry reminds us of its earliest use—for the measurement of land and materials. The Babylonian and Egyptian civilizations thus gained great empirical knowledge of elementary geometric figures, including how to construct a right-angled triangle. The Greek philosophers transformed this practical art into an intellectual pastime through which they sought access to the secrets of nature. About 300 BC EUCLID collected together and added to the Greek rationalization of geometry in his *Elements*. Later

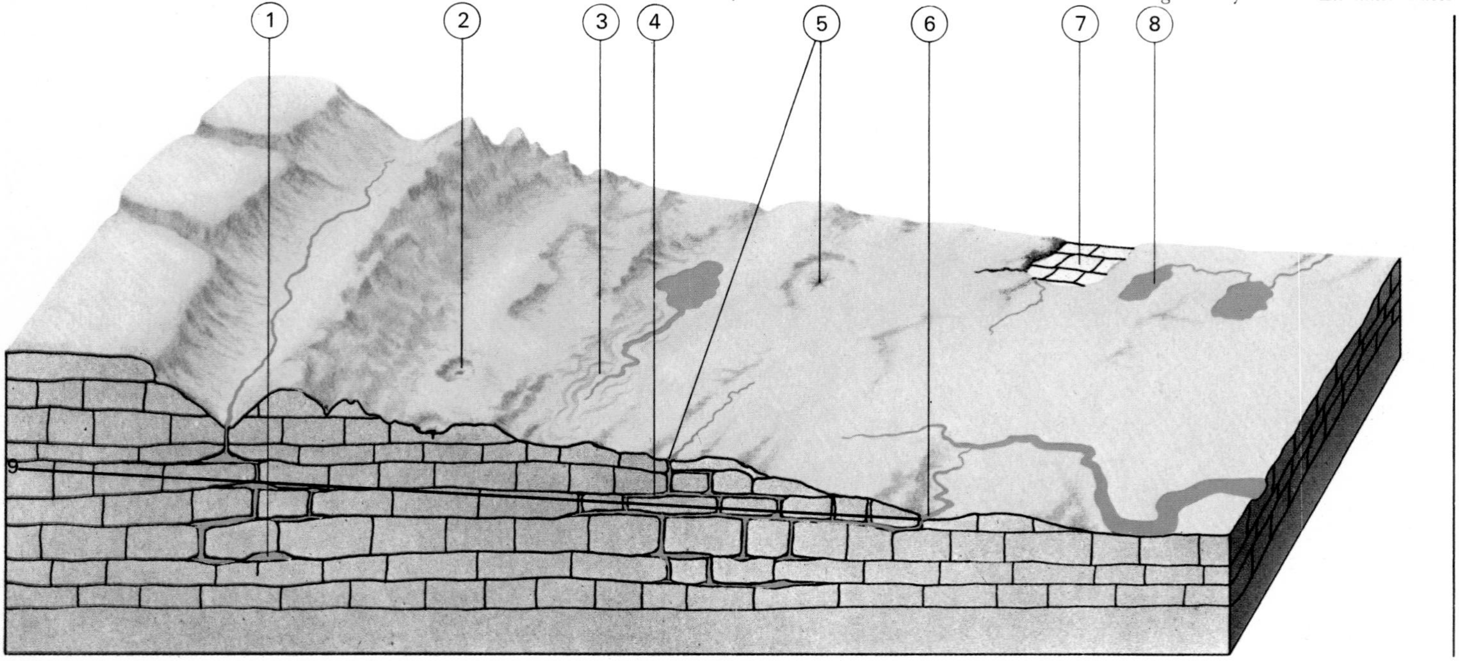

Alexandrian geometers began to develop TRIGONOMETRY. The revival of interest in life-like painting in the Renaissance led to the development of projective geometry, though it is to the philosopher–scientist DESCARTES that we owe the invention of the algebraic (coordinate) geometry which allows algebraic FUNCTIONS to be represented geometrically. The next new branch of geometry to be developed followed fast upon the invention of CALCULUS: differential geometry. The greatest upset in the history of geometry came in the 19th century. Men such as J. K. F. GAUSS, N. I. LOBACHEVSKI and BOLYAI Janós began to question the Euclidean parallel-lines axiom and discovered hyperbolic geometry, the first non-Euclidean geometry. The elliptic non-Euclidean geometry of G. F. B. RIEMANN aided A. EINSTEIN in the development of the theory of general RELATIVITY.

GEOMORPHOLOGY, the surface features of the EARTH; and their study, especially as to their origins and the processes acting on them. (See GEOLOGY.)

GEOPHYSICS, the physics of the EARTH, as such including studies of the ATMOSPHERE, EARTHQUAKES and VOLCANISM, as well as GEODESY, GEOMAGNETISM, HYDROLOGY and OCEANOGRAPHY.

GEOPOLITICS, the study of politics in relation to geography and demography. The term was originally applied to the theories of the biologist and geographer Friedrich RATZEL, who sought to apply evolutionary theory to the rise and fall of nations. In the 1900s the British geographer Sir Halford MACKINDER extended these, seeing the international struggle for survival as hanging on control of the heartlands, or interior lands, of the world's great landmasses, particularly the "World Island" of Eurasia. The German Karl HAUSHOFER combined these theories to preach the eventual regeneration of Germany through her inevitable demand for *Lebensraum* (German: living space, space to expand), which would have to be sacrificed by the seaboard countries to the more dynamic countries of the heartland. This was seized upon by Adolf Hitler and became a cornerstone of Nazi doctrine, thus entirely discrediting the theory.

GEORGE, Saint, the patron saint of England. He is an obscure figure, possibly a Christian convert martyred in 303. Many medieval legends became connected with his name, including his rescue of a maiden from a dragon. His feast day was April 23, but since 1969 the Roman Catholic Church has merely commemorated him on Jan. 1.

GEORGE, name of six kings of Britain. **George I** (1660–1727), Elector of Hanover from 1698, came to the throne in 1714. Shrewd and not very popular, he never learned English; this left much power in the hands of his chief minister Sir Robert WALPOLE. **George II** (1683–1760), born in Hanover, succeeded his father, George I, in 1727. He was considerably more popular. Strongly in favor of peace, he allowed the country to be drawn into the War of Austrian Succession (1740–48), losing influence and prestige. After 1750 he took little interest in politics, becoming a great patron of musicians such as HANDEL; Parliament was dominated by the Whigs WALPOLE and PITT the elder. **George III** (1738–1820), king from 1760. Much of his reign was spent in conflict with the Whig oligarchy in Parliament, which had become entrenched under his father's rule. Ironically, he became the American colonists' principal symbol of English oppression although Whig policy was really responsible. Before the onset of insanity in his later years, George III was a well-meaning ruler in a time of great stress abroad and at home. **George IV** (1762–1830), regent from 1811 and king from 1820. A loose-living dandy, he cared little about government. The scandal surrounding his divorce from Caroline of Brunswick lowered public esteem of the monarchy. **George V** (1865–1936), ascended the throne in 1910. He was immediately thrown into a constitutional crisis over the power of the House of Lords, in which he played a moderating role. He proved a popular monarch in WWI, seeking to unify the country; he later played an important part in the formation of a coalition government in the economic crisis of 1931. **George VI** (1895–1952), ascended the throne after the abdication crisis of 1936. He and his consort did much to restore confidence in the monarchy; during WWII they were a tireless example of devotion to duty. In 1939 George VI became the first reigning monarch to visit the US.

◁ Geomorphology is the branch of geology which studies the surface features of the earth: their shape; the way in which they are formed, and the processes which are continually influencing the evolution of the landscape. One of the classic studies of geomorphology is karst topography: the landforms which develop through the solution of limestone by rainwater. Limestone is composed mainly of calcium carbonate ($CaCO_3$) which does not readily dissolve in water. However, rainwater contains dissolved carbon dioxide (CO_2), part of which reacts with water giving hydrogen and bicarbonate ions (H_3O^+ and HCO_3^-). The presence of these ions permits the calcium carbonate to be dissolved as the bicarbonate, which is soluble in water. This strange chemical behavior allows water to dissolve out complex systems of underground channels in limestone, usually following zones of natural weakness in the rock. Features of particular interest in karst geomorphology include: (1) phreatic zone; (2) sinkhole or doline; (3) polje; (4) vadose region; (5) swallow holes; (6) vauclusian spring; (7) limestone pavement; (8) kamenitza.

GEORGE, name of two kings of Greece. **George I** (1845–1913), king of Greece from 1863. During his reign much of Thessaly and part of Epirus were incorporated into the kingdom. He was assassinated in Salonika. **George II** (1890–1947), king of Greece from 1922–23 and 1935–47. Deposed by a military coup in 1923, he was recalled by a plebiscite in 1935. The rest of his reign was dominated by METAXAS.

GEORGE, Henry (1839–1897), US journalist whose *Progress and Poverty* (1879) saw the prime cause of inequality as the possession of land. His proposed SINGLE TAX on land was never endorsed by economists but won him popular support.

GEORGE, James Zachariah (1826–1897), Democratic senator for Miss. from 1880, known as the "Great Commoner." A Confederate brigadier-general in the Civil War, he wrote the GRANDFATHER CLAUSE in the state constitution which nullified Negro suffrage.

GEORGE, Lake, lies in NE N.Y., in the foothills of the Adirondack Mountains; it is 32mi in length. Surrounded by fine scenery, it is a popular summer resort.

GEORGE, Stefan (1868–1933), German lyric poet. Associated with the PRE-RAPHAELITES and symbolists, he based his poetry on classical Greek humanism, free of naturalistic influences.

GEORGE, Walter Franklin (1878–1957), Democratic senator from Ga. 1922–56. Chairman of the foreign relations committee in the eighty-fourth Congress, he became Eisenhower's ambassador to NATO in 1957.

GEORGETOWN, capital and chief port of Guyana on the NE coast of South America. A cultural and recreational center, the city exports locally-produced sugar, rice and fruit, and minerals. Pop 66 070.

GEORGE TOWN. See PENANG.

GEORGETOWN, city, seat of Georgetown Co., S.C. It is a trading and shipping center for the surrounding farming and lumbering area. Pop 10 449.

GEORGETOWN, former town in the District of Columbia, now incorporated into the city of Washington, D.C. A historic residential area of great character, it is the site of Georgetown U.

GEORGE WASHINGTON BIRTHPLACE NATIONAL MONUMENT, a large estate in Westmoreland Co., Va. Established in 1930, it includes the Washington family burial ground and the site of the house (burnt down in 1780) in which Washington was born.

GEORGE WASHINGTON BRIDGE, suspension bridge across the Hudson R at New York City. Designed by Othmar AMMANN, it was completed in 1931. It has a main span 3 500ft in length.

GEORGE WASHINGTON CARVER NATIONAL MONUMENT, estate in Mo., birthplace and childhood home of the famous chemist, botanist and educator G. W. CARVER. The monument was established in 1951.

GEORGIA, state in SE US, sometimes called the "Peach State." More than half consists of warm humid plains, which extend from the Atlantic coast to the Piedmont region. The rest consists of rolling hill country. On the coastal plains, average temperatures range from a winter low of 54°F to a summer high of 82°F; the Piedmont is a little cooler in winter.

People. The majority of Georgians live in urban areas—over one million live within the urban area of Atlanta, the capital. Until the late 1950s Georgia was primarily rural in character, but today fewer than 10% of Georgians live on farms, and most of the rural population commute to work in the towns.

Economy. The structure of Georgia's economy has changed radically in the last 30 years; the volume of manufacturing has more than sextupled since WWII. Leading industries include textiles, lumber and paper products, production of pine oil resin and turpentine, and food processing. Agriculture still accounts for about a quarter of the state's income. No longer totally dependent on cotton, however, it produces peanuts, peaches, tobacco and broiler chickens; cattle raising is also of importance.

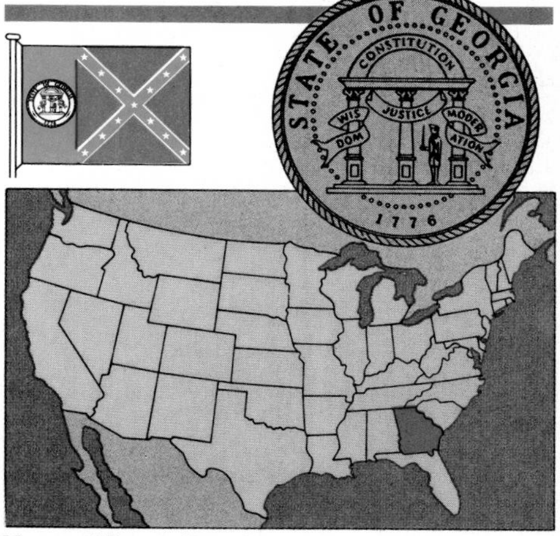

Name of State: Georgia
Capital: Atlanta
Statehood: Jan. 2, 1788 (4th state)
Familiar Name: Peach State, Empire State of the South
Area: 58 876sq mi
Population: 4 589 575
Elevation: Highest—4 784ft, Brasstown Bald Mountain. Lowest—Sea level, Atlantic Ocean
Motto: Wisdom, Justice and Moderation
State Flower: Cherokee rose
State Bird: Brown thrasher
State Tree: Live oak
State Song: "Georgia"

History. The first permanent settlement in Georgia was made by the English in 1733. In 1749 a ban on the importation of slaves was removed and Georgia quickly prospered; she ratified the US Constitution in 1788. Before the Civil War Georgia was one of the world's leading cotton producers. Her economy was based on slave labor; by 1860 almost half of the state's million inhabitants were black slaves. Georgia seceded from the Union on Jan. 19, 1861, and suffered greatly in the Civil War. After the war, resentment aroused by harsh RECONSTRUCTION measures ensured Democratic control over the state's politics for a century. Little changed fundamentally until the combined effects of crop destruction by the boll weevil and low cotton prices in the 1920s and 1930s drove thousands of smaller farmers from the land. Since WWII Georgia has enjoyed rapid industrialization but has tended to ignore federal demands for integration.

GEORGIA, constituent republic of the USSR, located in the SW of the country E of the Black Sea.

The Caucasus Mts run across the N of the republic. Georgia has a subtropical climate and the lowland areas near the Black Sea produce tea, fruit, wine, tobacco and cereals. Georgia provides the Soviet Union with petroleum and many essential minerals. There is much heavy industry, with steel and other metals, textiles and chemicals the main products. Around two-thirds of the population still work on the land. The Georgian people have a long cultural history. The ancient kingdom of Georgia, ravaged by Turkey and Persia, was annexed to Russia in 1801; an attempt to regain independence after the Revolution was crushed in 1921. Georgia was the home of STALIN.

GEORGIA, Strait of, narrow channel from NW US to SW Canada, between Vancouver and British Columbia. It is part of the INSIDE PASSAGE sea-route between Wash. and Alaska.

GEORGIAN ARCHITECTURE, 18th-century architectural style in Britain and the British North American colonies. In Britain it refers to the classically formal and elegant style, influenced by the Italian PALLADIO, popular during the reigns of the first three Georges. In the US it refers to the style prevailing between 1700 and the Revolution, deriving more from WREN and the baroque; Palladian influences entered later. Fine examples are INDEPENDENCE HALL, Philadelphia (1745) and King's Chapel in Boston (1754).

GEORGIAN BAY, NE arm of Lake Huron, Ontario, Canada. It is separated from the lake itself by the Bruce peninsula on the SW and Manitoulin Island to the N. The bay is about 150mi long by 50mi wide.

GEORGIAN BAY ISLANDS NATIONAL PARK, about 30 islands in Georgian Bay, Ontario, Canada. The area's dense woodlands and the good fishing has made the park a popular tourist area.

GEOSYNCLINE, a large basin or syncline (concave FOLD in the rock strata) which has become filled with sediment and whose floor has subsided, so that it contains vast thicknesses of SEDIMENTARY ROCKS. (See also MOUNTAIN; OROGENIES.)

GEOTROPISM. See TROPISMS.

GERANIUM, genus of cosmopolitan hardy perennial herbs, some of which are cultivated in gardens and as house plants. Geranium is also the name given to popular pot and bedding plants of the genus *Pelargonium.* Common or zonal geraniums (hybrid races derived from *Pelargonium zonale*) have white, salmon pink or red, flowers single or semi-double, some with bronze or maroon zones on the leaves. A range of dwarf or miniature varieties are available in this group. Another decorative-leaved variety is the ivy-leaved geranium (*P. peltatum*). Indoors, geraniums grow well in sunny south-facing windows, and the miniature varieties are particularly suited to fluorescent-light gardens. Ideally, geraniums should grow at temperatures between 16°C and 21°C (60°F and 70°F) and they should be well watered whenever the soil surface becomes nearly dry, making sure that the soil never completely dries out. Propagation is by seeds and taking shoot tip cuttings. Family: Geraniaceae.

GERASA. See JARASH.

GERBILS, small RODENTS found in arid areas of Africa and Asia. Known as sand rats, they have fine, dense fur, long tails and can move fast by hopping.

GERIATRICS, the branch of MEDICINE specializing in the care of the elderly. Although concerned with the same DISEASES as the rest of medicine, the different susceptibility of the aged and a tendency for multiple pathology make its scope different. In particular the psychological problems of old age differ markedly from those encountered in the rest of the population and require special management. The social and medical aspects of long-term care involve the coordination of family, voluntary and hospital services; the geriatrician must nevertheless seek to maximize the individuality and freedom available to the geriatric patient.

GÉRICAULT, (Jean Louis André) Théodore (1791–1824), French painter whose style combined a massive, dynamic romanticism with a minutely detailed realism. His best-known works are his studies of lunatics, his horse paintings and the *Raft of the Medusa* (1818–19).

The Independence Hall in Philadelphia, with the typically red brick walls and white framed windows of early American Georgian architecture, dates from 1745.

GERM, microorganism capable of causing disease, including VIRUSES, BACTERIA, PARASITES and PROTOZOA.

GERMAN, official language of Germany and Austria and an official language of Switzerland and Luxembourg, native tongue of more than 100 million people. Modern German is descended from two main forms. Low German, spoken mainly in the N, is the ancestor of both Dutch and Flemish. High German, spoken in central and S Germany is, historically, the classical German. A large part of medieval German literature, such as the 12th and 13th century epics, is in Middle High German. Today the written language is standardized but there are still great differences between spoken N and S German. Modern German is a highly inflected language with three genders and four cases, and requires agreement in number, gender and case, as in Latin. Many words are formed by compounding.

GERMAN-AMERICAN BUND, US pro-Nazi paramilitary organization that flourished 1936–41. Composed chiefly of descendants of German immigrants, it tried to rally American support for the Nazis. Some of its leaders were imprisoned during WWII. (See NAZISM.)

GERMAN DEMOCRATIC REPUBLIC. See GERMANY, EAST.

GERMAN FEDERAL REPUBLIC. See GERMANY, WEST.

GERMANIUM (Ge), silvery-gray metalloid in Group IVA of the PERIODIC TABLE; brittle crystalline solid whose structure resembles that of DIAMOND. It occurs naturally in sulfide ores of SILVER, COPPER and ZINC, and in COAL, and is extracted as a by-product of processing them. Its chemical properties are intermediate between those of SILICON and TIN; it reacts with the halogens, oxidizes in air at 600°C, and is attacked by concentrated oxidizing acids and by fused alkalis. Germanium is a SEMICONDUCTOR, and is used in electronic devices, especially TRANSISTORS; it is also used in alloys and for lenses and windows for INFRARED RADIATION. AW 72.6, mp 937°C, bp 2830°C, sg 5.323 (25°C).

Germanium forms covalent tetra- and divalent compounds. **Germanium (IV) Oxide** (GeO_2) is used in high-refractive-index GLASS. mp 1086°C. **Germanium (IV) Chloride** ($GeCl_4$), colorless liquid intermediate in the extraction of germanium and the preparation of most of its compounds. mp −50°C, bp 84°C. **Germanes**, series of volatile hydrides resembling silanes (see SILICON).

The German shepherd is one of the most popular dogs in the United States today. It's combined qualities of loyalty, obedience, intelligence and strength make it an excellent choice both as a guard dog and as a pet.

GERMAN MEASLES, or **rubella**, mild VIRUS infection, usually contracted in childhood and causing FEVER, SKIN rash, malaise and LYMPH node enlargement. Its importance lies in the fact that infection of a mother during the first three months of PREGNANCY leads to infection of the EMBRYO via the PLACENTA and is associated with a high incidence of congenital DISEASES including CATARACT, DEAFNESS and defects of the HEART and ESOPHAGUS. VACCINATION of intending mothers who have not had rubella is advisable. If rubella occurs in early pregnancy, ABORTION may be induced to avoid the BIRTH of malformed children.

GERMAN POINTER, Short-haired, versatile gundog created from the heavy old German gundog and the Spanish Pointer. Its coat is usually speckled liver and white or black and white and it stands up to 26in high and weighs 55–70lb.

GERMAN POINTER, Wire-haired, a heavier and more rugged dog than the Short-haired, for it carries less pointer blood, this is Germany's leading sporting dog and is increasingly popular in the US. The harsh, water-repellent coat is solid liver in color or liver and white. It stands about 24in high (smaller than the Short-haired).

GERMAN SHEPHERD (or Alsatian), a breed of dog developed in Germany, known for its strength, loyalty and intelligence. It has a long body, with black and tan or grey hair, and a rather wolf-like head. It is much used by police and military and as a guide dog for the blind.

GERMAN SILVER, or **nickel silver**, an ALLOY composed of copper, nickel and zinc. It resembles silver, and is used for cheap jewelry, cutlery etc., and as the base for silver-plated ware.

GERMANTOWN, Battle of, fought on Oct. 4, 1777, during the REVOLUTIONARY WAR. American troops under Washington sought to regain the Philadelphia area from the English under Burgoyne and Cornwallis, but were routed and driven off.

GERMANY, nation in western Europe now divided into two effectively independent states, East and West Germany. It occupies the heartland of Europe and is composed of the North German Plain in the N, and highlands in the center and S. West Germany has a maritime climate with average temperatures in July 64°F and in January 32°F. In East Germany the temperature varies more widely. About 28% of Germany is still forest and about 39% is farmland; the soil, however, is fairly poor in most areas.

People. The German people are of two distinct strains: the tall, fair-skinned, blue-eyed Nordic people of the N, and darker, stockier Alpine types of the S; the two types are well mingled throughout the country. About three-quarters of the population now lives in urban areas. Germans are known for their liking of outdoor sports and also for their folk traditions. German culture has made major contributions to European art, thought, science, and especially music, through such composers as BEETHOVEN and WAGNER.

Economy. Germany's greatest natural asset has been her coal. The soft coal mines of the Ruhr supply much of the fuel needed for the whole W European steel industry. Other important minerals are salt, potash, silver, copper, lead, zinc and nickel. The Ruhr is still one of the centers of heavy industry in W Europe. More traditional industries include the making of fine clocks, toys and cameras.

History. Although Rome conquered the left bank of the Rhine, the Teutonic tribes of central Germany were never brought into the empire. CHARLEMAGNE united most of the territory of modern France and

Germany into the Frankish empire, which was eventually divided among his three grandsons; the area E of the Rhine went to Louis the German. From the 10th to the 13th centuries attempts to retain a united Germany were unsuccessful, and until the 19th century Germany was generally composed of independent states, united in name only as the Holy Roman Empire. The foundation of modern Germany was largely the work of Otto von BISMARCK, prime minister of Prussia from 1862. By defeating Austria in 1866 and France in 1871, he created enough nationalist feeling to promote unity in a Prussian-dominated empire. In the last decades of the 19th century there was massive industrial development in Germany; she began to compete with Britain and France, a competition that culminated in WWI. Germany was defeated and the WEIMAR REPUBLIC was declared on Nov 9, 1918. However, resentment aroused by the harsh Treaty of VERSAILLES (1919), economic chaos in the 1920s and 1930s and lack of democratic traditions all served to undermine support for the Republic.

HITLER became chancellor in 1933 and quickly established a dictatorial, one-party regime. His aggressive expansionist policies led to war in Sept. 1939 and although German armies overran most of Europe in 1939 and 1940, the war ended with Germany's unconditional surrender. The US, France, Britain and the USSR divided the defeated country into four zones of occupation, the first three of which became West Germany, the fourth, Russian zone becoming East Germany. The former capital, Berlin, although situated in East Germany, was divided between the Western powers and East Germany. (See also GERMANY, EAST and GERMANY, WEST.)

A picturesque village in the Haardtgebirge, an important wine producing and agricultural area near Bad Dürkheim in the Rhineland of Germany. Although this region is rapidly becoming industrialized it still contains some of the most beautiful scenery in Europe.

GERMANY, East, customary name for the German Democratic Republic. The population has dropped by around two million since 1948 due to emigration to West Germany before the erection of the Berlin Wall in 1961. The standard of living is much lower than that in West Germany. East Germany's free educational system stresses science, mathematics and public service.

Economy. The East German economy is socialized, though there are private firms in the retail trade and in handicrafts. Over 90% of industrial output comes from state-owned establishments. East Germany's industrial output is now approaching that of other European countries, largely the result of injections of

Official Name: German Democratic Republic
Capital: East Berlin
Area: 41 768sq mi
Population: 17 040 926
Languages: German
Religions: Protestant; Roman Catholic
Monetary Unit(s): 1 Mark (M) = 100 pfennige

Russian capital in the 1950s. Important industries are chemicals, electronics, textiles and metallurgy. Trade is oriented towards the USSR, which accounts for about half the country's imports and exports. Agriculture is now highly mechanized; main products are rye, wheat, barley, potatoes and sugar beet. Livestock is also important.

History. The German Democratic Republic came into being in 1949. It lacked popular support and a revolt in 1953 by students and workers was violently suppressed with the help of Soviet troops. East Germany was unrecognized by the Western world in the 1950s and 1960s and there were continual crises, particularly over the status of West Berlin. However, recent years have seen a certain relaxation in the austerity which has so far characterized the East German way of life. The 1970s have seen considerable steps towards improvements of relations between East Germany and the rest of the world, and in Sept. 1973, East Germany was admitted as an independent member of the UN. (See also GERMANY and GERMANY, WEST.)

GERMANY, West, customary name for the Federal Republic of Germany, a member of NATO and the COMMON MARKET. West Germany has a well-developed state educational system; there are very few private schools.

Economy. The country's economic progress since WWII has been so striking that it has become known as the *Wirtshaftswunder* (economic miracle). West Germany now has one of the highest living standards in the world. This is the result of the German capacity for hard work, injections of American capital in the COLD WAR period, and a good supply of immigrant labor. West Germany's vast and diverse industries include automobiles, electronics, oil refining, textiles, chemicals and shipbuilding. German exports have caused such surpluses in her trade balance that in 1969 and 1971, under international pressure, the West

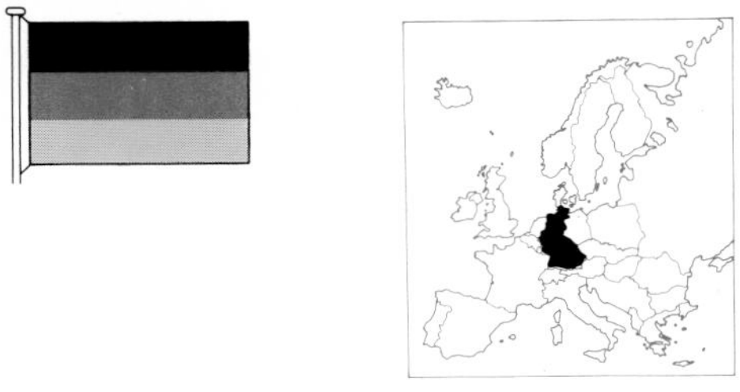

Official Name: Federal Republic of Germany
Capital: Bonn
Area: 95 985sq mi
Population: 61 809 400
Languages: German
Religions: Protestant; Roman Catholic
Monetary Unit(s): 1 Deutsche Mark (DM) = 100 pfennige

German mark was revalued. West Germany has to import many of her foodstuffs.

History. The Federal Republic of Germany came into being in 1949. The Christian Democratic Party leader, Konrad ADENAUER, became chancellor, and held office for 14 years. In the early years West Germans hoped above all for the reunification of their country, and to this end refused to recognize East Germany. In recent years, however, the existence of two German states has come to be seen as inevitable, at least for the time being. The Brandt government in 1969 took the first steps towards improving relations with East Germany. This resulted in a nonaggression pact with the USSR (1970) and a treaty recognizing East Germany (1972). (See also GERMANY and GERMANY, EAST.)

GERM CELL. See GAMETE.

GERM-FREE ANIMALS. See GNOTOBIOTICS.

GERMICIDES. See ANTISEPTICS.

GERMINATION, the resumption of growth of a plant embryo contained in the SEED after a period of reduced metabolic activity or dormancy. Conditions required for germination include an adequate water supply, sufficient oxygen and a favorable temperature. Rapid uptake of water followed by increased rate of respiration are often the first signs of germination. During germination, stored food reserves are rapidly used up to provide the energy and raw materials required for the new growth. The embryonic root and shoot which break through the seed coat are termed the radicle and plumule, respectively. There are two general forms of germination: hypogeal and epigeal. In the former, the seed leaves, or COTYLEDONS, remain below the ground, as in the broad bean, while in the latter they are taken above the ground and become the first photosynthetic organs, as in the castor oil seed.

GERMISTON, city in S Transvaal Province, South Africa. Its economy rests on the Rand gold refinery, largest in the world. Pop 139 471.

GERM PLASM, a special type of PROTOPLASM present in the reproductive cells or gametes of plants and animals, which A. WEISMANN suggested passed on unchanged from generation to generation. Although it gave rise to the body cells, it remained distinct and unaffected by the offspring.

GERM WARFARE. See CHEMICAL AND BIOLOGICAL WARFARE.

GERONIMO (1829–1909), greatest war leader of the APACHE INDIANS of Ariz. When his tribe was forcibly removed to a barren reservation he led an increasingly large band of hit-and-run raiders 1876–86. Twice induced to surrender by Lt.-Col. George CROOK, he was driven to escape again by maltreatment. Persuaded to surrender a third time by Gen. Nelson MILES, he was summarily exiled to Fla. and resettled in Okla., where he became a farmer.

GERRY, Elbridge (1744–1814), US politician for whom the GERRYMANDER was named. He signed the Declaration of Independence and attended the Constitutional Convention (1787), was a member of Congress 1789–93, governor of Mass. 1810–12 and vice-president under Madison from 1812. (See also XYZ AFFAIR.)

GERRYMANDER, an unfair practice usually employed by a party in power, involving a redivision of electoral boundaries in its favor. The term originated during Elbridge GERRY's governorship of Mass. in 1812, when the state senatorial districts were reapportioned to produce a majority in his favor.

GERSHWIN, George (1898–1937), major US popular composer. From a Jewish immigrant family, he first rose to fame as a songwriter and then with musical shows such as *Lady Be Good!* (1924), his first Broadway success, and the satirical *Of Thee I Sing* (1931) among many others. His orchestral pieces, such as *Rhapsody in Blue* (1924) and his *Piano Concerto* (1925), and his masterpiece, the folk opera *Porgy and Bess* (1935), remain in the repertoire of serious music, among the first jazz pieces to do so.

GERSHWIN, Ira (1896–), US lyricist known primarily for his collaborations with his brother George in the 1920s and 1930s on many shows, songs and the opera *Porgy and Bess* (1935). After George's death he collaborated with Kurt WEILL and others.

This Franciscan church marks one of the several possible locations of the Garden of Gethsemane, where Christ passed the night in prayer before his crucifixion. It stands on the western slope of the Mount of Olives, near Jerusalem.

GERYON, in Greek mythology a three-headed giant. HERCULES as his 10th labor killed him and stole his cattle.

GESNER, Konrad von (1516–1565), Swiss naturalist whose major work, *Historia Animalium* (4 vols., 1551–58), an encyclopedic study of many varieties of animals, is considered the foundation stone of modern zoology.

GESSO, a paste used to prepare surfaces for painting or gilding, made by mixing CHALK or whiting with GLUE.

GESTALT PSYCHOLOGY, a school of psychology concerned with the tendency of the human (or even PRIMATE) mind to organize PERCEPTIONS into "wholes"; for example, to hear a symphony rather than a large number of separate notes of different tones. Gestalt psychology, whose main proponents were WERTHEIMER, KOFFKA and KÖHLER, maintained that this was due to the mind's ability to complete patterns from the available stimuli. The school emerged as a reaction against such schools as BEHAVIORISM.

GESTAPO, abbreviated form of *Geheime Staatspolizei* (Secret State Police) the executive arm of the Nazi police force 1936–45, with almost unlimited power. Under the overall control of Heinrich HIMMLER, it shared responsibility for internal security and administered the concentration camps. It was declared a criminal organization at the NUREMBERG TRIALS.

Scene from the bloody battle of Gettysburg on the great cyclorama in the Gettysburg Memorial, Pennsylvania. The three-day-long battle marked a turning point in the Civil War, although both sides suffered heavy losses.

GESTATION, the development of young mammals in the mother's uterus from FERTILIZATION to BIRTH. With some exceptions, the gestation period is proportional to the adult size of the animal, thus, for the human young the gestation period is about 270 days, but for the elephant it is closer to two years. (See EMBRYO; FETUS; PREGNANCY.)

GESUALDO, Don Carlo (1560–1613), Italian composer a master of the MADRIGAL form. Of his five collections (1594–1611) the last two are noted for their revolutionary use of harmony and handling of chromaticism and dissonance.

GETHSEMANE (from Hebrew *gat semanim*, oil press), the garden across the Kidron valley, on the Mount of Olives, E of the old city of Jerusalem, where Jesus prayed on the eve of his crucifixion, and was betrayed. Gethsemane was probably an olive grove; its precise location is disputed.

GETTYSBURG, Battle of, the major conflict of the US Civil War, fought July 1–3, 1863. In a daring maneuver Confederate General Robert E. LEE had struck deep into Union territory, reaching Pa. in June 1863. He and the Union Army of the Potomac, under Gen. George S. MEADE, converged upon Gettysburg, Pa. On July 1 and 2 there were many inconclusive attacks and counterattacks; Union reinforcements arrived on July 2. On July 3 suicidal Confederate attacks broke the Union line on Cemetery Ridge, but were driven back in disorder. On July 4, after a day of stalemate, Lee retreated under cover of night and rain. Union losses were over 23 000, around 25%; Confederate losses were around 20 000, a similar percentage. The costly battle marked a reversal in the fortunes of the Confederacy which paved the way for the eventual Union victory.

GETTYSBURG ADDRESS, speech delivered by President LINCOLN at the dedication of the national cemetery at Gettysburg, Pa., on Nov. 19, 1863. A brief masterpiece of oratory, it combined the themes of grief for the dead with the maintenance of the principles they had died to uphold.

GETZ, Stanley (1927–), US jazz musician, a tenor saxophonist with Woody HERMAN, Benny GOODMAN and Stan Kenton. In the 1950s he became famous with his own group.

GEYSER, a hot spring, found in currently or recently volcanic regions (see VOLCANISM), that intermittently jets steam and superheated water into the air. It consists essentially of a tube leading down to a heat source. GROUNDWATER accumulates in the tube, that near the bottom being kept from boiling by the PRESSURE of the cooler layers above. When the critical temperature is reached, bubbles rise, heating the upper layers which expand and well out of the orifice. This reduces the pressure enough for substantial STEAM formation below, with subsequent eruption. The process then recommences. The famous Old Faithful used to erupt every 66½min, but has recently become less reliable. (See also FUMAROLE; HOT SPRINGS; SPRING.)

GHANA, republic in West Africa, on the Gulf of Guinea, formerly the British Gold Coast dependency. Generally a low-lying country, it has a narrow coastal plain, the Kwahu plateau inland, and rolling savanna in the N. The country is drained by the Volta R, much of it dammed to make a lake. Ghana has a hot climate with, generally, one rainy season in the N and two in the S.

People. The population is made up of various tribal groups. Compared with other African states, Ghana has a high level of education with 10 years of free and compulsory basic schooling and subsidized further education. Most Ghanians still live on the land, but large numbers have moved to the cities in recent years.

Economy. Ghana has one of the highest per capita incomes in Africa and is the world's leading producer of cocoa, upon which the country's economy rests. Corn, millet, rice and cassava are grown for local consumption; while export crops include coffee, rubber, bananas and mahogany from the upland forests. Gold, diamonds, bauxite and manganese have been exported but since the completion of the Volta R hydroelectric project in 1965, aluminum smelting has become a major industry.

FOUR SCORE and seven years ago our fathers brought forth on this continent, a new nation, conceived in Liberty, and dedicated to the proposition that all men are created equal.
Now we are engaged in a great civil war, testing whether that nation or any nation so conceived and so dedicated, can long endure. We are met on a great battle-field of that war. We have come to dedicate a portion of that field, as a final resting place for those who gave their lives that that nation might live. It is altogether fitting and proper that we should do this.
But, in a larger sense, we can not dedicate—we can not consecrate—we can not hallow—this ground. The brave men, living and dead, who struggled here, have consecrated it, far above our poor power to add or detract. The world will little note, nor long remember what we say here, but it can never forget what they did here. It is for us the living, rather, to be dedicated here to the unfinished work which they who fought here have thus far so nobly advanced. It is rather for us to be here dedicated to the great task remaining before us—that from these honored dead we take increased devotion to that cause for which they gave the last full measure of devotion—that we here highly resolve that these dead shall not have died in vain—that this nation, under God, shall have a new birth of freedom—and that government of the people, by the people, for the people, shall not perish from the earth.

The Gettysburg Address delivered by President Abraham Lincoln at the dedication of the national cemetery on the Civil War battlefield, November 19, 1863.

History. In 1482 the Portuguese began trading at Elmina in gold, ivory and then slaves. The Gold Coast was then controlled by the French, Dutch, and finally the British, under whom the economy expanded, bringing prosperity. Ghana was the first West African country to become independent, on March 6, 1957, with Kwame NKRUMAH as premier. In 1960 he declared the country a republic, with himself as life president. While he made reforms in education, transportation and other social services, he maintained an absolute dictatorship which became increasingly inefficient, brutal and corrupt until in 1966 he and his government were overthrown in a coup, which had popular support. In 1969 democratic elections were held, and Kofi Busia elected premier. In 1972 he was deposed by a left-wing military coup.

Official Name: Republic of Ghana
Capital: Accra
Area: 92 100sq mi
Population: 8 545 561
Languages: English; Twi; Fanti; Ga; Hausa and others
Religions: Animist; Christian; Muslim
Monetary Unit(s): 1 New cedi = 100 pesawas

GHANA, Ancient Empire of, former empire in West Africa, located between the Niger and Senegal rivers. Founded in the 4th century AD, it reached its height in the 10th century, but was eclipsed by the rise

of the Mali empire in the 13th century. At one point, the Ghanaian empire stretched from the Atlantic as far as Timbuktu.
GHARIAL. See GAVIAL.
GHATS, Eastern and Western, two mountain ranges forming the E and W boundaries of the Deccan Plateau of peninsular India. The Western Ghats receive between 200in and 400in of rain a year from the monsoons and are the source of several rivers. Both ranges are between 3000 and 5000ft high, and about 1000mi long.
GHEE, a semifluid butter made in India and neighboring countries, usually from buffalo milk. Ghee is used mainly for cooking.
GHELDERODE, Michel de (1898–1962), Belgian avant-garde dramatist. His style is characterized by a fantastic and often macabre medievalism with elements of the morality play, as in *Barabbas* (1929), *Chronicles of Hell* (1929) and *Hop, Signor!* (1935).
GHENT, historic city in Belgium, at the junction of the Lys and Scheldt rivers. Former capital of Flanders, it was the textile center of medieval Europe; the textile industry is still important, along with paper, chemical and metal production. It also has a major port. In the 16th and 17th centuries it was a center of Flemish art. Pop 149265.
GHENT, Treaty of, concluded on Dec. 24, 1814, in Ghent, Belgium, formally ending the WAR OF 1812 between Britain and the US. Because the war had developed into a military stalemate, the treaty was essentially a return to prewar status. No concession was made over the impressment of former British citizens from US ships, a major US grievance, but the resulting British withdrawal from interference in the affairs of the American Northwest opened the frontier to westward expansion.
GHETTO, (from Hebrew *get*, divorce) section of a city to which Jewish residence was restricted. In N Europe many ghettos came into existence before the Middle Ages and some, such as the famous Warsaw Ghetto, lasted until WWII. Today the term is often used to refer to slum areas in which one ethnic group, such as Negroes or Puerto Ricans, is dominant.
GHIBELLINES. See GUELPHS AND GHIBELLINES.
GHIBERTI, Lorenzo (c1378–1455), Italian sculptor, goldsmith, painter, writer and architect. A Florentine, he was one of the leading figures of the early Renaissance. His most famous work is probably his second pair of bronze doors for the Florence baptistery, known as the *Gates of Paradise* (1425–52).
GHIRLANDAIO, Domenico (1449–1494), Florentine Renaissance painter said to have taught MICHELANGELO. Probably his most famous frescoes are those of *Saint Jerome* (1480) and the *Last Supper* (1480), both in the Church of Ognissanti, Florence. He is also noted for his portraits, among them *Grandfather and Grandson*.
GHOST DANCE, millenarian cult originating among the PAIUTE INDIANS in W Nev. in 1870, named for its ceremonial dance. It was led by WOVOKA who prophesied the rebirth of the dead and the restoration of the Indians to their lands. The massacre of Ghost Dance believers at WOUNDED KNEE in 1890 did much to suppress the cult.
GHOST TOWNS, abandoned communities, usually mining towns vacated when the mineral deposits ran out. Found in Canada and Australia, they are most common in the W US, where many are now tourist attractions.
GHOSTS, disembodied spirits of the dead, often said to haunt the places they frequented when alive. The concept of ghosts varies from culture to culture and is usually linked to religious beliefs. (See also POLTERGEIST.)
G.I., common term for enlisted soldier in the US Army. In WWI the initials stood for *galvanized iron*; they later came to mean *general issue* and hence anything utilitarian and unattractive.
G.I. BILL OF RIGHTS, the Serviceman's Readjustment Act of 1944, which provided government aid for demobilized servicemen. It was designed to prevent a repetition of the social problems that had resulted after WWI. It provided financial aid for the purchase of houses, farms and businesses, and for veterans' hospitals; unemployment benefits; and

The Giant's Causeway in Northern Ireland. It is not difficult to see why this extraordinary structure was explained as the work of giants: according to some legends it was intended as a road which would enable the giants to cross to Scotland.

vocational training. Most significant, however, was the educational aid, which in effect paid for four years of college education, including basic living expenses.
GIACOMETTI, Alberto (1901–1966), Swiss-born sculptor and painter who spent most of his life in Paris. He is best known for his elongated and skeletal human figures which convey a sense of extreme spiritual isolation. His early work was influenced by primitive art and SURREALISM.
GIAEVER, Ivar (1929–), Norwegian-born US physicist awarded, with L. ESAKI and B. JOSEPHSON, the 1973 Nobel Prize for Physics for his work on tunneling (see WAVE MECHANICS).
GIANNINI, Amadeo Peter (1870–1949), US banker, founder (1930) of the Bank of America National Trust and Savings Association. One of the largest US banks, it was based on the Transamerica chain which Giannini built up after founding his Bank of Italy in San Francisco (1904).
GIANT PANDA. See PANDA.
GIANTISM. See GIGANTISM.
GIANTS, semi-human creatures of great size and strength; they feature in the myth and folklore of almost every culture, usually as survivors of races that lived before mankind. The Greek TITANS were to some extent personifications of elements and natural forces. Other giants, such as the biblical GOLIATH, are probably exaggerated memories of very large and fierce men.
GIANT SALAMANDER, *Megalobatrachus japonicus*, the largest living amphibian, reaching a length of 1.5m (5ft) and found in Japan. It lives in cool, swift streams and feeds on fish, other salamanders and crayfish.
GIANT'S CAUSEWAY, spectacular rock structure near Portrush, Northern Ireland, formed by cooling LAVA. Initially, generally hexagonal cracks appeared on the surface, formed by localized contractions toward discrete centers: these developed downward, forming columns, as the rest of the BASALT mass cooled.
GIANT STAR. See STAR.
GIAUQUE, William Francis (1895–), US chemist who discovered the isotopes of OXYGEN (1929). He has also contributed to the science of CRYOGENICS by inventing and applying the process of adiabatic demagnetization, for which he was awarded the 1949 Nobel Prize for Chemistry.
GIBBERELLINS, a group of plant HORMONES mainly found in the seeds, young leaves and roots of green plants and in certain fungi. They were originally isolated from a Japanese fungus (*Gibberella fujikuroi*) which lengthens the stems of rice plants. **Gibberellic acid**, found in green plants, is involved in the "bolting" of plants like carrots. Various attempts to use gibberellins commercially to increase crop yield have been unsuccessful.
GIBBON, the smallest of the apes, distinguishable by its very long arms. It is the only ape to walk upright with ease. There are six species living in SE Asia from Borneo to Assam. They can leap over 9m (30ft) and swing along the branches of trees in which they live without pausing between bounds. (See also ANTHROPOID APES.)
GIBBON, Edward (1737–1794), English historian, author of the *History of the Decline and Fall of the Roman Empire* (1776–88), the greatest historical work of the 18th century and a literary masterpiece. The *Decline and Fall* is particularly well known for its skeptical treatment of Christianity. Gibbon served somewhat unsuccessfully as a member of Parliament (1774–82).
GIBBONS, Grinling (1648–1721), English carver and sculptor. While still a young man he was engaged by WREN to work on St. Paul's Cathedral. His wood carvings decorate many of England's country houses, among the most notable being at Petworth, Sussex.
GIBBONS, James (1834–1921), US Roman Catholic cardinal and archbishop, author of *The Faith of Our Fathers* (1876), a popular work of Catholic apologetics. In 1886 Pope Leo XII made him cardinal; he was only the second American to hold this office.
GIBBONS, Orlando (1583–1625), English composer, one of the last of the polyphonic school. A talented keyboard player, he was made organist of the Chapel Royal when only 21. In 1623 he became organist of Westminster Abbey. He composed madrigals, motets and music for viol and for virginals.
GIBBONS v. OGDEN, US Supreme Court decision of March 2, 1824, important in defining the power of Congress. Ogden, a steamship operator, held a license from a company given a monopoly of steamship traffic by the N.Y. legislature. He sought to prevent Gibbons, who held a license from the federal government, from competing with him. Chief Justice Marshall's decision favored Gibbons and the federal case, holding the monopoly to be unconstitutional.
GIBBS, James (1682–1754), Scottish architect, designer of the present church of St. Martin-in-the-Fields, London, and the Radcliffe Camera, Oxford. Trained in Rome, he developed a simple but striking style unlike the then fashionable Palladian architecture. His *Book of Architecture* (1728) was a major influence in the 18th century.
GIBBS, Josiah Willard (1839–1903), US physicist best known for his pioneering work in chemical THERMODYNAMICS. In *On the Equilibrium of Heterogeneous Substances* (2 vols., 1876 and 1878) he states Gibbs' Phase Rule (see PHASE EQUILIBRIA). In the course of his research on the electromagnetic theory of LIGHT, he made fundamental contributions to the art of VECTOR ANALYSIS.
GIBRALTAR, self-governing British colony, 2.5sq mi in area, on the Rock of Gibraltar at the S tip of the Iberian peninsula. The population is mixed; natives are of English, Genoese, Portuguese and Maltese descent. The economy rests on light industry,

The towering Rock of Gibraltar seen from the port. In days gone by it was a site of the greatest strategic importance, overlooking the entrance to the Mediterranean quite near to the point where the strait narrows to less than 9 miles across.

shipping and tourism, and on the important British naval and airbases. Gibraltar was captured from Spain in 1704. A 1967 referendum showed overwhelming opposition to a return to Spanish rule. Pop 27 965.

GIBRALTAR, Strait of, channel connecting the Mediterranean to the Atlantic. It is 36mi long and 9–14mi wide. Its fast eastward current keeps the Mediterranean a sea rather than a salt lake.

GIBRAN, Kahlil (1883–1931), Lebanese–American essayist, philosopher–poet and painter who blended elements of Eastern and Western mysticism. He was influenced by BLAKE and NIETZSCHE. His best-known work is *The Prophet* (1923).

GIBSON, Althea (1927–), US tennis player. She was the first black player to win the US women's championship singles (1957), was British champion the same year, and retained both titles in 1958.

GIBSON, Charles Dana (1867–1944), US artist, a fashion illustrator who created the "Gibson Girl." Based on his wife, she was an elegant and high-spirited figure who came to typify the ideal of American womanhood in the early 20th century.

GIDE, André Paul Guillaume (1869–1951), French writer and moralist, whose relentless examination of his own standard and assumptions, and the resulting inner conflicts, made him one of the foremost figures in French literature in the first half of the 20th century. In 1947 he was awarded the Nobel Prize for Literature. Among his best-known works are *The Immoralist* (1902) and *The Counterfeiters* (1927).

GIDEON, or **Jerubbaal,** leader and judge of Israel; his story is told in the Book of Judges. He became a national hero after the defeat of the Midianites.

GIDEONS INTERNATIONAL, laymens' organization supplying free Bibles for hotel rooms, prisons, schools, and sometimes the US Armed Forces. It was formed in Janesville, Wis. in 1899.

GIELGUD, Sir (Arthur) John (1904–), British actor, producer and director, famous early in his career for his Shakespearean roles, especially Hamlet and Richard III. He made his debut in 1921 at the Old Vic theater in London. Famous for his versatility, he created many modern roles in his maturity in numerous stage, film and television appearances.

GIEREK, Edward (1913–), Polish politician, first secretary of the Polish Communist Party since 1970, and a Politburo member since 1956. He was appointed to improve the standard of living following food riots in late 1970.

GIFFARD, Henri (1825–1882), French engineer who built the first steam-powered AIRSHIP, flown in Paris in 1852; and invented (1859) an injector for steam boilers, used for many decades.

GIFU, city in central Honshu, Japan. In an agricultural area, it has diverse industries and is famous for the cormorant fishing on the Nagara R. Pop 385 727.

GIGANTISM, or abnormally large stature starting in childhood, may be caused by a constitutional trait or by HORMONE disorders during growth. The latter are usually excessive secretion of growth hormone or thyroid hormone before the EPIPHYSES have fused.

GIGUE. See JIG.

GIJÓN, historic seaport in NW Spain. It has many old buildings, including Roman baths and much Moorish architecture. El Musel, the port, is also an industrial center. Pop 187 612.

GILA CLIFF DWELLINGS NATIONAL MONUMENT, Pueblo Indian CLIFF DWELLER settlement in SW N.M., about 30mi N of Silver City. Dating from the 10th century, it was built in natural cavities of a 150ft cliff; it was made a national monument in 1907.

GILA MONSTER, an ugly, stout-bodied lizard, up to 0.6m (2ft) long. It and the related BEADED LIZARD, are the only poisonous lizards. Both live in the deserts of the SW states and in Mexico. The gila monster is so rare that it is protected by law.

GILA RIVER, rises in the Elk Mountains, N.M., and flows over 630mi WSW to join the Colorado R at Yuma. It is stopped near Globe, Ariz., by the Coolidge dam which irrigates the Casa Grande Valley.

GILBERT (Gb), unit of magnetomotive force in CGS UNITS, equalling $10/4\pi$ ampere-turns.

The famous Woolworth building on Broadway, New York, designed by Cass Gilbert and opened in 1913. Combining neoclassical elements with Gothic detail, it was until 1931 the tallest building in the city.

GILBERT, Cass (1859–1934), US architect most famous for the Woolworth Building in New York (1913). His characteristic neoclassical style appears also in his other designs, such as the Supreme Court Building in Washington, D.C.

GILBERT, Sir Humphrey (c1537–1583), English soldier and explorer who founded England's first North American colony, at St. John's, Newfoundland (1583). He was granted a royal charter to colonize unclaimed lands in North America (1578). His first expedition had to turn back after being attacked by the Spanish. He went down with his ship while returning from his second, otherwise successful voyage.

GILBERT, William (1544–1603), English scientist, the father of the science of MAGNETISM. Regarding the earth as a giant magnet, he investigated its field in terms of dip and variation (see EARTH), and explored many other magnetic and electrostatic phenomena. The GILBERT is named for him.

GILBERT, Sir William Schwenck (1836–1911), English author and humorist who collaborated with Sir Arthur SULLIVAN on the cycle of comic operettas named for them. He combined facetiousness with a mordant wit in satires more vigorous in their day than they appear to modern audiences.

GILBERT AND ELLICE ISLANDS, British crown colony of about 40 islands and atolls in a 2 000 000sq mi area of the SW Pacific. The inhabitants are mainly Micronesians, with some Polynesians and Europeans and a few Chinese. The economy is based on phosphate and copra exports. A protectorate since 1892, the islands became a colony in 1916; they were given local self-government in 1970. In 1976 the Ellice Islands achieved administrative separation and took the name Tuvalu. Pop 53 517.

GILBERT AND SULLIVAN. See GILBERT, SIR WILLIAM SCHWENCK; SULLIVAN, SIR ARTHUR SEYMOUR; D'OYLY CARTE, RICHARD.

GILDED AGE, sardonic name for the post-Civil War period up to around 1880 in the US, a time of rampant corruption in politics and commerce. The term derives from the title of a novel by Mark TWAIN and C. D. WARNER.

GILEAD, mountainous area of ancien Palestine, E of the Jordan R. The home of the prophet ELIJAH, it was settled by the Hebrew tribes of Reuben and Gad, and the half-tribe Manasseh.

GILELS, Emil Grigorevich (1916–), Russian pianist, winner of the Stalin Prize in 1946 and the Lenin Prize in 1962. Noted for his crystalline technique, he was one of the first Soviet artists to tour the US (1955) after WWII.

GILES, Saint, 8th century hermit and, according to legend, abbot. No reliable details of his life exist, but he is regarded as the patron of cripples, beggars and smiths. His feast day is Sept. 1.

GILGAMESH, Epic of, the earliest known epic poem, written in the Akkadian language and originating in Mesopotamia in the 3rd millennium BC. The fullest surviving text, carved on tablets, was found in a 7th-century BC library at Nineveh in 1872. Other poems in Sumerian from the 2nd millennium are known. It tells of the semi-divine hero Gilgamesh (a historical 3rd-millennium king of Uruk), and of his friend Enkidu. They clash with the gods, who cause Enkidu's death. Gilgamesh then goes on a quest to find the secret of eternal life, which in the end eludes him. The epic contains a flood story with close parallels to that in Genesis (see NOAH).

GILL, Eric (1882–1940), English sculptor, engraver and typographic designer, famous for the *Perpetua* (1925) and *Gill Sans Serif* (1927) faces. His *Stations of the Cross* (1914–18), bas-reliefs for Westminster Cathedral, are perhaps his most famous sculptures.

GILL (gi), name of various units of volume, usually equalling one-fourth of a pint. The US gill is 0.118 3 litres; the Imperial gill is 0.142 1 litres.

GILLESPIE, (John Birks) Dizzie (1917–), US jazz trumpeter and composer who in the 1940s pioneered, with Charlie PARKER, the BOP style. He is noted for his technically brilliant and original style. He became in 1956 the first jazz musician to have a foreign tour sponsored by the US government.

GILLRAY, James (1757–1815), English caricaturist whose violent and often scurrilous cartoons both expressed and influenced public opinion in his time. He reduced all the major political figures of his day, including George II and the royal family, to ridiculous grotesques.

GILLS, the respiratory organs of many aquatic animals. They take in OXYGEN from the water and give off CARBON dioxide waste. They are thin-walled so that gases pass easily through and usually take the form of thin flat plates or finely divided feathery filaments. The higher invertebrates, crabs and lobsters for instance, have gills protected by an EXOSKELETON and maintain an adequate oxygen supply by pumping water over them. The gills of fish are protected by a bony operculum and movements of the throat provide a water current over them. (See RESPIRATION.)

GILMAN, Daniel Coit (1831–1908), US educator. He taught physical and political geography at Yale and in 1872 became president of the U. of California at Berkeley. He was first president of Johns Hopkins U. 1875–1901 and then first president of the Carnegie Institute until 1904.

GILROY, city in W Cal., 30mi SE of San Jose. A truck-farming and agricultural center, it is the home of Gavilan College. Pop 12 665.

GILSON, Étienne Henri (1884–), French historian and philosopher. A neo-Thomist, most of his writings are either studies of medieval Christian philosophy or applications of Thomist principles to modern data. He became a member of the French Academy in 1947.

GILSONITE, natural asphaltic BITUMEN found in veins near the Col./Ut. border, in the Uinta Basin. It is a lustrous black solid, used in paints and coating and insulating materials, and, more recently, converted to coke, gasoline and gas.

GIN, liquor distilled from grain flavored with juniper berries. Sometimes coriander, orange or lemon peel, cardamon and orris roots are added as flavoring agents. It contains 40–47% alcohol (80–94 US Proof). It originated in the Netherlands, apparently from a juniper-berry medicine. (See ALCOHOLIC BEVERAGES.)

GIN. See COTTON GIN.

GINASTERA, Alberto (1916–), leading Argentinian composer. Despite his advanced techniques he is an essentially nationalistic composer, making much use of local idioms. His best known work is his opera *Don Rodrigo* (1964).

GINGER, *Zingiber officinale*, an East Indian reed-like, perennial plant, now widely cultivated in the Old and New World tropics, particularly Jamaica. The peeled, partly-boiled and dried rhizomes are used as a condiment, for flavoring and medicinally for the relief of stomach upsets. Green ginger is produced by boiling the rhizomes in sugar to preserve them. Family: Zingiberaceae.

GINGIVITIS, or gum INFLAMMATION, due to BACTERIAL INFECTION (e.g., VINCENT'S ANGINA) or disease of the TEETH and poor mouth hygiene.

GINKGO, *Ginkgo biloba*, the **maidenhair tree**, primitive deciduous tree with fan-shaped leaves. Native to China, it is widely cultivated as an ornamental in temperate regions. The roasted seeds are eaten in China.

GINSBERG, Allen (1926–), US poet. An outspoken member of the BEAT GENERATION, his works include *Howl* (1956), *Kaddish and Other Poems* (1961) and *The Yage Letters* (an exchange with William BURROUGHS; 1963).

GINSENG, popular name for two small flowering herbs, *Panax ginseng* (Asian) and *P. quinquefolius* (American) whose roots are ground to make a tea reputed to have strong tranquilizing and calming effects. Family: Araliaceae.

GIORGIONE (c1478–1510), Italian Renaissance painter. A native of Venice, he studied under Giovanni BELLINI. He painted with a soft subordination of line to light and color, and achieved a unity of human figures with landscape which greatly influenced TITIAN and other painters. Among the works attributed to him are *The Tempest* (c1505), *Madonna and Child Enthroned* (1504) and *The Three Philosophers* (1510).

GIORGI SYSTEM. See MKSA UNITS.

GIOTTO (Giotto di Bondone; c1266–1337), Italian painter of the Florentine school. He had a profound influence on his own time and on future generations. Breaking away from the Byzantine style of graceful but static representation, he painted monumental figures dramatically and emotionally, giving his vast FRESCO scenes a sense of movement and spatial depth. Among his famous works are frescoes in Padua, Florence and the Church of St. Francis at Assisi.

GIPSY. See GYPSIES.

GIRAFFE, *Giraffa camelopardalis*, the tallest living mammal, reaching 5.5m (18ft) in the male, some 2m (6.6ft) of which are taken up by the head and extremely long neck. Its coat is a neutral buff color spotted with red-brown patches. A short, rather bristly mane runs along its spine from head to tail. Giraffes live by grazing, often on trees, aided by their long necks and tongues. They are speedy runners. Giraffes are related to deer as is evidenced by their short horns.

GIRARD, city in NE Ohio, on the Mahoning R, about 5mi NW of Youngstown. It has produced steel and iron since 1866. Pop 14 119.

GIRARD, Stephen (1750–1831), US merchant banker and philanthropist. He helped finance the WAR OF 1812, and later helped raise capital for the Second Bank of the US (1816). He gave several million dollars to Philadelphia, Pa., and founded Girard College.

GIRAUD, Henri Honoré (1879–1949), French general. He was commander of French North and West Africa during WWII and co-president (1943–44) of the French Committee of National Liberation with Gen. DE GAULLE, who virtually forced Giraud to retire.

GIRAUDOUX, (Hippolyte) Jean (1882–1944), French playwright. Known for his imaginative, satirical dramas, his major works include *Tiger at the Gates* (1935) and *Electra* (1937), both based on Greek mythology, and *The Mad Woman of Chaillot* (1945).

GIRL SCOUTS AND GIRL GUIDES, organizations in almost 70 countries which form an international movement, The World Association of Girl Guides and Girl Scouts. The Girl Guides were founded in England (1909) by Lord BADEN-POWELL, who also founded the BOY SCOUTS, in Canada in 1910 and in the US (as Girl Scouts) in 1912 by Juliette Gordon LOW. Girls learn to become good citizens, they practice useful skills, develop self-reliance and enjoy a continuing, well-rounded program of companionship, work, service to others and play, from age seven through the late teens.

GIRONDINS, or Girondists, French political group of republicans, representing the middle classes and favoring a federal republic, prominent in the FRENCH REVOLUTION. The group's original members came from the Gironde department in SW France. They came into power under the 1791 Constitution but lost ground to the JACOBINS. In June 1793, a Jacobin-led mob forced the expulsion of 29 Girondins from the National Convention; many Girondins were guillotined in the REIGN OF TERROR.

GIRTY, Simon (1741–1818), American frontiersman called the "Great Renegade." He was captured by the Seneca Indians at age 15. During the REVOLUTIONARY WAR, he deserted the Colonists to serve the British as a scout and interpreter and led numerous, often brutally savage Indian raiding parties.

GISCARD D'ESTAING, Valéry (1926–), French political leader; became president of France in 1974. At 29 he became a member of the national assembly. In 1959, under President DE GAULLE, he became deputy finance minister. From 1962–66 he was minister of finance, a post he resumed (1969) under Georges POMPIDOU, supporting the Common Market and closer ties with the US. He ran for president as an independent Republican with Gaullist support.

GISH, Lillian Diana (1896–), and **Dorothy** (1898–1968), American sisters, famous stage and screen actresses who appeared in silent films and the pioneering epics of D. W. GRIFFITH. In *The Birth of a Nation* (1915), Lillian won world fame; she appeared in many notable plays, including *All the Way Home* (1960) and *Uncle Vanya* (1973).

GISSING, George Robert (1857–1903), English novelist. He is noted for his starkly realistic studies of late Victorian lower and middle class life. His most famous novel *New Grub Street* (1891), depicts much of the drudgery and hardship he himself experienced as an aspiring writer.

GIST, Christopher (c1706–1759), American frontiersman, who explored parts of Ky. 18 years before Daniel BOONE and was the first to explore and map the Ohio R Valley in Western Va. He served in the FRENCH AND INDIAN WARS, during which he is said to have twice saved George Washington's life.

GIULIO ROMANO, (born Giulio Pippi; c1492–1546), Italian painter and architect in the style of MANNERISM. RAPHAEL's pupil, his masterpiece is the Palazzo del Té, Mantua where his architecture is highly fanciful, and the frescoes exciting examples of illusionism.

GIZA, or Al-Gizeh, ancient city in N Egypt, on the W bank of the Nile R opposite Cairo. It is an important manufacturing and market center. The Great PYRAMIDS and the SPHINX are nearby. Pop 345 261.

GIZZARD, part of the alimentary canal developed by a variety of animals for the mechanical breakdown of food. Situated before the main digestive region of the gut it has very muscular walls. Fragmentation of the food may be by chitinous "teeth" in the inner wall or by stones and grit, swallowed expressly for this purpose.

GJELLERUP, Karl Adolph (1857–1919), Danish poet and novelist, who shared the 1917 Nobel

The coat patterns of giraffes vary widely with different sub-species, and can serve to provide camouflage against different types of background. *Top left:* the coat pattern of the Reticulated giraffe *Giraffa camelopardalis reticulata*, of Ethiopia and Kenya. *Bottom left:* Masai giraffe *G. c. tippelskirchi*, of the southern areas of East Africa. *Center:* despite the length of its neck, the giraffe has only the usual seven cervical vertebrae typical of mammals, but each vertebra is nearly 16in long. *Below:* a solitary giraffe on an East African plain. Unlike many animals of the plain, giraffes do not have a recognizable herd structure.

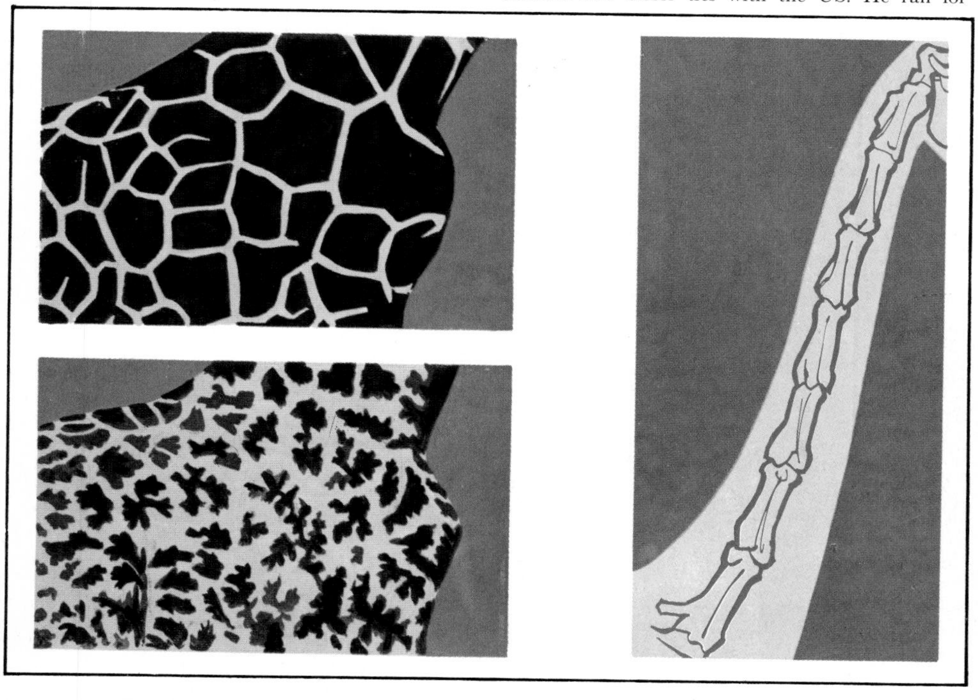

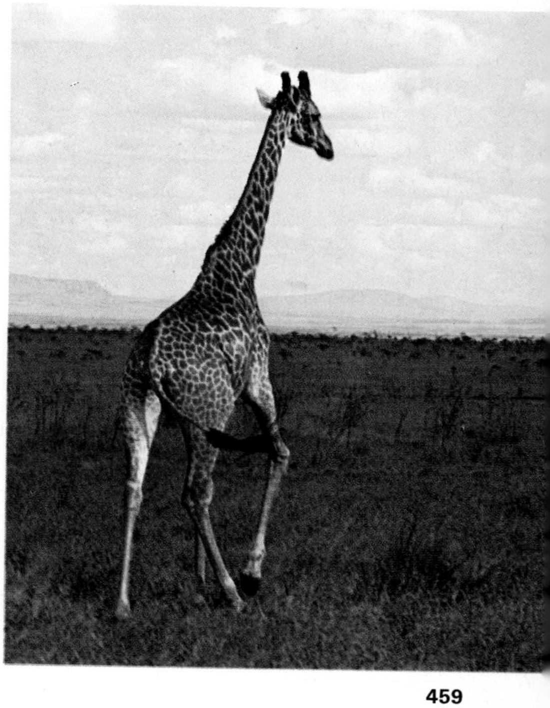

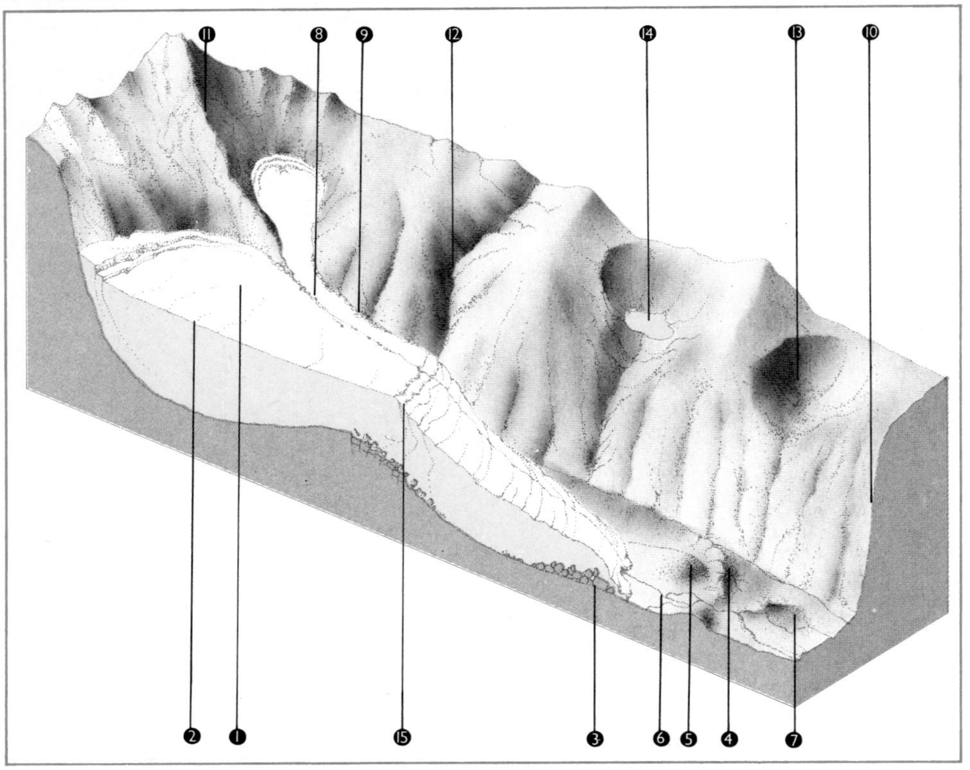

Features associated with glaciers and glaciated landforms: (1) head of glacier; (2) firn or névé; (3) region of ground moraine deposition; (4) terminal moraine; (5) drumlin; (6) braided stream; (7) kettle; (8) medial moraine; (9) lateral moraine; (10) U-shaped valley; (11) arête; (12) hanging valley; (13) cirque; (14) tarn; and (15) ice fall. Based on the Mount Temple glacier, Alberta, Canada.

literature prize. His novels, radical and idealist in tone, include *An Idealist* (1878), *Minna* (1889) and *The Pilgrim Kamanita* (1906).

GLACE BAY, port on Cape Breton Island, Nova Scotia, Canada. It is the center of a coal mining and deep-sea fishing region. Pop 22 440.

GLACIER, a large mass of ice that can survive for several years. In most cases, glaciers are heavy enough to flow downhill under their own weight. There are three recognized types of glacier: ice sheets and caps; mountain or valley glaciers; and piedmont glaciers. Glaciers form wherever conditions are such that annual PRECIPITATION of snow, sleet and hail is greater than the amount that can be lost through evaporation or otherwise (see ABLATION). The occurrence of a glacier thus depends much on latitude (see LATITUDE AND LONGITUDE) and also on local topography: there are several glaciers on the EQUATOR. Glaciers account for about 75% of the world's fresh water, and of this the Antarctic ice sheet accounts for about 85%. **Mountain glaciers** usually result from snow accumulated in CIRQUES coalescing to form glaciers; and **piedmont glaciers** occur when such a glacier spreads out of its valley into a contiguous lowland area. (See also DRIFT; DRUMLIN; EROSION; ESKER; FJORD; ICE; ICE AGES; ICEBERG; MORAINE; NÉVÉ; TILL.)

GLACIER BAY NATIONAL MONUMENT, region of 2 803 840 acres in SE Alaska, established in 1925. It is noted for its numerous coastal glaciers.

GLACIER NATIONAL PARK, glaciated area covering 521sq mi., in the Selkirk Mts, SE British Columbia, Canada, established in 1886. It includes the Illecilliwaet glacier.

GLACIER NATIONAL PARK, wilderness area of over 1 million acres in the Rocky Mts, NW Mont. Part of the Waterton-Glacier International Peace Park, it is noted for its spectacular peaks and glacier-fed lakes. It was established in 1910.

GLACKENS, William James (1870–1938), US illustrator and painter. A member of the ASHCAN SCHOOL in New York City, he painted GENRE subjects and landscapes. Among his works are: *Hammerstein's Roof Garden* (1901) and *Chez Mouqin* (1905).

GLADDEN, Washington (1836–1918), US Congregational minister and social reformer. His many books and public lectures popularized the idea of a Christian solution to modern social problems.

GLADIATORS, warrior-entertainers of ancient Rome. They fought in public arenas against each other and against wild beasts with a variety of weapons including swords (Latin *gladius*, a short sword), three-pronged tridents and nets, for the favor of the crowds. They were recruited from prisoners of war, slaves, criminals and sometimes freemen. The tradition survived into the 5th century AD.

GLADIOLUS, genus of tall, large-flowered, bulbous plants with long, narrow leaves. Many hybrids are used as ornamental and cut flowers, with colors ranging over a wide spectrum. The CORMS are eaten locally. Family: Iridaceae.

GLADSTONE, city in NW Mo. It is a residential suburb of Kansas City with some manufacturing businesses. Pop 23 422.

GLADSTONE, William Ewart (1809–1898), British statesman; four times prime minister (1868–74; 1880–85; 1886; 1892–94). Originally a TORY, he later dominated the LIBERAL PARTY, 1868–94. He was a powerful and popular orator, a dedicated social reformer and a deeply religious man. Among his many accomplishments from the time he

A representative example of "The Eight" or "Ashcan" school of painting is the *Soda Fountain* by William Glackens, an impressionist social-realist painter heavily influenced by Renoir.

entered Parliament (1833) were the introduction of the secret ballot, the extension of the franchise, the abolition of sales of army concessions, the first Education Act, the Irish Land Act and the disestablishment of the Anglican Church in Ireland. (See also REFORM BILLS.)

GLANDERS, BACTERIAL DISEASE of horses, rarely transmitted to man. In horses, ABSCESSES are common and are a source of infection, which causes FEVER, ulceration of the NOSE and PHARYNX, and multiple abscesses. PNEUMONIA, LUNG abscess, ARTHRITIS and MENINGITIS occur; without ANTIBIOTICS, death ensues.

GLANDS, structures in animals and plants specialized to secrete essential substances. In plants they may discharge their secretions to the outside of the plant (via glandular hairs), or into special secretory canals. External secretions include NECTAR and insect attractants; internal secretions, PINE resin and RUBBER latex. In animals they are divided into ENDOCRINE GLANDS, which secrete HORMONES into the BLOOD stream, and **exocrine glands** which are the remainder, usually secreting materials via ducts into internal organs or onto body surfaces. LYMPH nodes are sometimes termed glands. In man, SKIN contains two types of gland: *sweat glands*, which secrete watery fluid (PERSPIRATION) and *sebaceous glands* which secrete sebum. *Lacrimal glands* secrete TEARS. The cells of mucous membranes or the EPITHELIUM of internal organs secrete MUCUS, which serves to lubricate and protect the surface. *Salivary glands* (parotid, submandibular and sublingual) secrete SALIVA to facilitate swallowing. In the GASTROINTESTINAL TRACT, mucus-secreting glands are numerous, particularly in the STOMACH and colon, where solid food or feces need lubrication. Other stomach glands secrete hydrochloric acid and pepsin as part of the DIGESTIVE SYSTEM. Small-intestinal juices containing ENZYMES are similarly secreted by minute glandular specializations of the epithelium. The part of the PANCREAS secreting enzyme-rich juice into the DUODENUM may be regarded as an exocrine gland. Analysis of gland secretion may be helpful in diseases of digestion, of the EYES and salivary glands and in CYSTIC FIBROSIS.

GLANDULAR FEVER. See MONONUCLEOSIS.

GLASER, Donald Arthur (1926–), US physicist awarded the 1960 Nobel Prize for Physics for his invention of the BUBBLE CHAMBER (1952).

GLASGOW, Scotland's largest city and principal port, on the Clyde R. It is a major commercial and industrial center for shipbuilding, metal working and manufacturing of locomotives, machinery, chemicals, paper, leather, whisky and textiles. Glasgow U. was founded in 1451. Pop 896 958.

GLASGOW, seat of Barren Co., S central Ky. It manufactures oil, lumber and tobacco and is in the center of a farming region. Pop 11 301.

GLASGOW, Ellen Anderson Gholson (1873–1945), US novelist, winner of the Pulitzer Prize in 1941 for *In This Our Life*. Her realistic novels about the American South satirized the code of Southern chivalry. They include *The Descendants* (1897) and *Barren Ground* (1925).

GLASS, material formed by the rapid cooling of certain molten liquid so that they fail to crystallize (see CRYSTAL) but retain an amorphous structure. Glasses are in fact supercooled LIQUIDS which, however, have such high viscosity that they behave like solids for all practical purposes. Some glasses may spontaneously crystallize or devitrify. Few materials form glasses, and almost all that are found naturally or used commercially are based on SILICA and the SILICATES. Natural glass is formed by rapid cooling of MAGMA, producing chiefly OBSIDIAN, or rarely by complete thermal metamorphism (see also TEKTITES). The earliest known manufactured glass was made in Mesopotamia in the 3rd millennium BC. Glass was shaped by molding or core-dipping, until the invention of **glassblowing** by Syrian craftsmen in the 1st century BC. Essentially still used, the process involved gathering molten glass on the end of a pipe, blowing to form a bubble, and shaping the vessel by further blowing, swinging, or rolling it on a surface. They also blew glass inside a shaped mold; this is now the chief process used in mechanized automatic

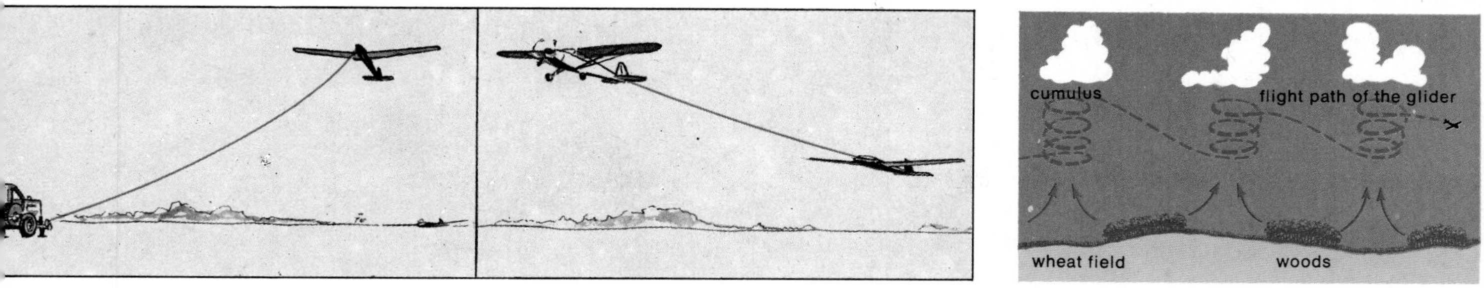

Gliders, being unpowered, have to be towed up into the air. This may be done using a winch (*left*) or an airplane tow (*center*). To stay airborne (*right*) the pilot is dependent on wind and upward-moving air currents, such as thermals, which frequently occur over open plains and cities.

glassblowing. Modern glass products are very diverse, including windows, bottles and other vessels, optical devices, building materials, fiberglass products, etc. Most are made of **soda-lime glass**. Although silica itself can form a glass, it is too viscous and its melting point is too high for most purposes. Adding soda lowers the melting point, but the resultant sodium silicate is water-soluble (see WATER GLASS), so lime is added as a stabilizer, together with other metal oxides as needed for decolorizing etc. The usual proportions are 70% SiO_2, 15% Na_2O, 10% CaO. **Crown glass**, used in optical systems for its low DISPERSION, is of this type, with BARIUM oxide (BaO) often replacing the lime. **Flint glass**, or **crystal**, is a brilliant clear glass with high optical dispersion, used in high-quality glassware and to make lenses and prisms. It was originally made from crushed flints to give pure, colorless silica; later, sand was used, with increasing amounts of lead (II) oxide. For borosilicate glass, used where high thermal stresses must be withstood, see PYREX. The manufacture of the various kinds of glass begins by mixing the raw materials—sand, limestone, sodium nitrate or carbonate, etc.—and melting them in large crucibles in a furnace. The molten glass, having been refined (free from bubbles) by standing, is formed to the shape required and then annealed (see ANNEALING). Some SAFETY GLASS is not annealed, but rapidly cooled to induce superficial compressive stresses which yield greater strength. **Plate glass** is made by passing a continuous sheet of soft glass between rollers, GRINDING AND POLISHING it on both sides, and cutting it up so as to eliminate flaws. A newer method (the float glass process) involves pouring the molten glass onto molten metal, such as tin, and to allow it to cool slowly: the surface touching the metal is perfectly flat and needs no polishing. Special glass products include **foam glass**, made by SINTERING a mixture of glass and an agent that gives off a gas on heating, used for insulation; **photosensitive glass**, which darkens reversibly in bright light; and FIBERGLASS. (See also ENAMEL.)

GLASS, Carter (1858–1946), US congressman from Va., 1902–18, senator 1920–46, and secretary of the treasury 1918–20. He helped set up the FEDERAL RESERVE SYSTEM and the FEDERAL DEPOSIT INSURANCE CORPORATION. He was a major opponent of President Roosevelt's NEW DEAL program.

GLASSBORO, borough in SW N.J. One of the earliest glass factories in the US here began the city's primary industry. President Lyndon Johnson met Soviet Premier Alexei Kosygin at Glassboro State College in 1967. Pop 12 938.

GLASSES, or spectacles, LENSES worn in front of the EYES to correct defects of VISION or for protection. Converging lenses have been worn to correct farsightedness (HYPEROPIA) since the late 13th century and diverging lenses for shortsightedness (MYOPIA) since the 16th. Glasses with cylindrical lenses are used to correct ASTIGMATISM and those having bifocal lenses (i.e., having two different powers in the upper and lower areas of each lens) or even trifocals (three powers) may be worn for PRESBYOPIA. Most spectacle lenses are worn in a metal or plastic frame which rests on the nose and ears, though in some cases CONTACT LENSES fitting directly onto the eyeball may be suitable. Protective glasses include sunglasses and safety glasses.

GLASS HARMONICA, a musical instrument which evolved from drinking glasses, filled with different levels of water, whose rims were rubbed to create tones. The glass harmonica developed by Benjamin FRANKLIN was a treadle-operated instrument with glass bowls on spindles to which a keyboard was added.

GLASSMAKING. See GLASS.

GLASS SNAKES, not true snakes but a group of legless lizards with wide geographical distribution. The tail in these lizards is very long and in most species it is shed when the animal is disturbed. Legend has it that these creatures can travel at great speed by bowling like a loop with the tail in the mouth. In fact they move only slowly. Genus: *Ophisaurus*.

GLASSWORT, leafless plants, with greenish petalless flowers, of the genus *Salicornia*, family Chenopodiaceae. They grow in salt marshes and near the seashore in many parts of the world. Soda ash used in the manufacture of GLASS and SOAP was once obtained from these plants.

GLASTONBURY, historic town in Somerset, SW England, famous for its abbey. It stands on a peninsula which is alleged to be the Isle of Avalon of ARTHURIAN LEGEND. Tradition and legend also suggest that JOSEPH OF ARIMATHEA founded England's first Christian church here. Pop 6 571.

GLASTONBURY, town in central Conn., on the Connecticut R, SE of Hartford. It is a light industrial manufacturing center. Pop 20 651.

GLAUBER, Johann Rudolf (1607–1670), German chemist who prepared a wide variety of organic and inorganic compounds to make use of their (often non-existent) medicinal powers. In preparing hydrochloric acid from sulfuric acid and common salt, he found a residue which he claimed as a cure-all. In fact it was sodium sulfate, a mild laxative, and still often called **Glauber's salt**.

GLAUCOMA, raised fluid pressure in the EYE, leading in chronic cases to a progressive deterioration of VISION. It arises from a variety of causes, often involving block to aqueous humor drainage. Glaucoma is relieved using drugs or surgically.

GLAUCONITE, a CLAY mineral of the illite type, a hydrated MICA containing considerable iron and magnesium. Formed by alteration of BIOTITE in a shallow, reducing marine environment, it commonly occurs as small green pellets in sedimentary deposits. **Greensand** is a mixture of glauconite with quartz SAND. (See also MARL.)

GLAZE. See POTTERY AND PORCELAIN.

GLAZUNOV, Aleksandr Konstantinovich (1865–1936), Russian composer. A pupil of RIMSKY-KORSAKOV, he was director 1906–17 of the St. Petersburg Conservatory. He wrote eight symphonies and numerous other works including the ballet *The Seasons* (1889).

GLEE CLUB, in the US, a choral group or organization, often a male choir associated with a college which sings secular part songs in harmony, usually unaccompanied. Glee societies were first formed in England, mainly between 1750 and 1830.

GLEN CANYON DAM, dam on the Colorado R in N Ariz. Completed in 1964, it is 710ft high and is one of the largest concrete dams in the world; it regulates the river flow and generates electricity.

GLENCOE, the Coe R valley, N Argyll, Scotland. Here in Feb. 1692 the MacDonald clan were treacherously massacred by Campbell soldiers.

GLENCOE, a residential village in NE Ill., 22mi N of Chicago on Lake Michigan. Pop 10 675.

GLEN COVE, city SE N.Y., on the N shore of Long Island. A residential area, it has some light industries. Pop 25 770.

GLENDALE, a city, SW central Ariz., 8mi NNW of Phoenix. Its industries include food processing and shipping. Pop 36 228.

GLENDALE, a suburb of Los Angeles, S Cal. It is an industrial center which produces aerospace equipment and has film studios. Pop 132 752.

GLENDALE, city in SE Wis., on the Milwaukee R. It is a suburb of Milwaukee with some light industry. Pop 13 426.

GLENDALE HEIGHTS, residential village in NE Ill., 22mi W of Chicago. Pop 11 406.

GLENDORA, city, SW Cal., a suburb of Los Angeles. Once important for its citrus production, it is now primarily residential. Pop 31 349.

GLENDOWER, Owen (c1354–c1416), the last independent prince of Wales, a Welsh national hero. He led one of the last Welsh rebellions against English rule (1400–13), exploiting baronial unrest in England against Henry IV. His gains were finally recovered by Henry V.

GLEN ELLYN, village in NE Ill., 22mi W of Chicago, of which it is a residential suburb. Pop 21 909.

GLENN, John Herschel, Jr. (1921–), first US astronaut to orbit the earth. He served as a pilot in WWII and in the Korean War. On Feb. 20, 1962, in the space capsule *Friendship 7*, he orbited the earth three times in 4hr 56min. Active in Ohio politics, he became a Democratic senator in 1974.

GLEN ROCK, borough in NE N.J., 4mi NNE of Paterson. It is a residential suburb of New York City, with some light industry. Pop 13 011.

GLENS FALLS, city in E central N.Y., near 50ft high falls on the Hudson R. It has limestone and marble quarries and also produces paper, textiles, cement and chemicals. Pop 17 222.

GLENSIDE, city in SE Pa. It has stone quarries and manufactures paints, toys, rubber and wood products. Pop 17 353.

GLENVIEW, village, NE Ill., a suburb of Chicago. A US naval air station is located nearby. Pop 24 880.

GLIDER, or **sailplane,** nonpowered airplane which, once launched by air or ground towing, or by using a winch, is kept aloft by its light, aerodynamic design and the skill of the pilot in exploiting "thermals" and other rising air currents. Sir George CAYLEY built his first model glider in 1804 and in 1853 he persuaded his coachman to undertake a short glide—the first manned heavier-than-air flight. Otto LILIENTHAL made many successful flights in his hang-gliders (planes in which the pilot hangs underneath and controls the flight by altering his body position, hence moving the craft's CENTER OF GRAVITY) from 1891 until his death in a gliding accident in 1896. Later, the WRIGHT brothers developed gliders in which control was achieved using moving control surfaces, as a prelude to their experiments with powered flight. Gliding as a sport was born in Germany after WWI and is now popular throughout the world. Recent years have seen a particular resurgence of interest in hang gliding.

GLIÈRE, Reinhold Moritzovich (1875–1956), Russian composer whose pupils included PROKOFIEV.

Among his works are the opera *Shah Senem* (1934), the ballet *The Red Poppy* (1927) and *Symphony No. 3* (1911).

GLINKA, Mikhail Ivanovich (1804–1857), Russian composer. His two operas, *A Life of the Tsar* (1836) and *Russlan and Ludmilla* (1842), marked the start of a nationalistic Russian school of music.

GLIOMA, TUMOR of glial cells, the supporting cells of the BRAIN. They never metastasize (see CANCER), but produce signs of focal damage to the brain, such as weakness, visual disturbance, personality change or EPILEPSY, and often a characteristic type of HEADACHE. SURGERY and RADIATION THERAPY may be helpful, but glial cell destruction cannot be reversed.

GLIWICE, city in SW Poland, 14mi W of Katowice, chartered in 1276. Its major industries are coal mining and steel. Pop 170 900.

GLOBE, a representation of the earth as a small sphere, mounted on an axis so that it may revolve. The oldest extant globe is from Nuremberg, 1492. Celestial and lunar globes are also made.

GLOBEFISH, fish of warm seas, also known as PUFFERS or PORCUPINE FISH. Globefish possess sacs which can be filled with water or air, distending the body and erecting the spines which cover the skin.

GLOBEFLOWER, popular name for hardy herbaceous perennials of the genus *Trollius*, from the BUTTERCUP family Ranunculaceae. They have large globe-shaped yellow or orange flowers and some hybrids are in cultivation.

GLOBE THEATRE, the principal public theater of the Elizabethan acting company, the Lord Chamberlain's Men, where most of SHAKESPEARE's plays were first performed. It was an open-air theater with three galleries and a platform stage and stood on the S bank of the Thames. Built in 1598, it was destroyed by fire in 1613, rebuilt in 1614 and finally destroyed in 1644 by the Puritans.

GLOBIGERINA, a single-celled organism found floating on the surface of the oceans. It is of the order Foraminiferida (see FORAMINIFERA). It has a perforated shell, through which it can extend PSEUDOPODIA. After death, the shells sink to the OCEAN floor to form much of the organic OOZES.

GLOBULAR CLUSTERS, apparently ellipsoidal densely packed clusters of up to a million stars orbiting a GALAXY. The MILKY WAY and the ANDROMEDA Galaxy have each around 200 such clusters. They contain high proportions of cool red stars and RR Lyrae VARIABLE STARS. Study of the latter enables the distances of the clusters to be calculated.

GLOBULINS, PROTEINS insoluble in water but soluble in dilute solutions of mineral salts. They are widely distributed in plants and animals, e.g., lactoglobulin in milk and plant globulins in seeds. In man, serum globulins (in BLOOD) are concerned in resistance to disease and in various ALLERGIES.

GLOCKENSPIEL, German term for a percussive musical instrument, meaning "play of bells." It originally consisted of a set of bells, but the modern version is made of metal bars of different lengths, and is similar to the XYLOPHONE and the CELESTA.

GLORIOUS REVOLUTION, or the Bloodless Revolution, events of 1688–89, which drove King James II from England and brought William III of Orange and his wife Mary to the throne. Distrusting Parliament, the Catholic James had kept a large standing army. The birth of his son threatened to turn England into a permanent Catholic monarchy. This finally caused the Whigs and Tories to unite and invite the Dutch prince to take over. James fled to France after his army deserted him. In 1689, Parliament redefined and restricted royal powers in the BILL OF RIGHTS.

GLOSSOLALIA, speech in an unknown or fabricated language uttered by individuals under HYPNOSIS, suffering from certain MENTAL ILLNESSES or in trance, or by groups undergoing religious ecstasy. In the Christian Church, glossolalia has sometimes accompanied revivals, and characterizes the PENTECOSTAL CHURCHES. A spiritual gift (see CHARISMA) common in the early Church, its use was regulated by St. Paul.

GLOUCESTER, city in NE Mass., on Cape Ann. A fishing port and port of entry, it also has granite quarries. Pop 27 941.

GLOUCESTER, Humphrey, Duke of (1390–1447), youngest son of Henry IV of England. He fought with his brother King Henry V at AGINCOURT in 1415, and in the absence of his brother the duke of Bedford, was protector of the realm 1422–29. He was called "good Duke Humphrey" because of his support of scholars and scholarship.

GLOUCESTER CITY, city in SW N.J. on the Delaware R, opposite Philadelphia, Pa. It manufactures paper products, asbestos and chemicals. Pop 14, 707.

GLOVERSVILLE, city in E N.Y., known for its glove making since the 18th century. Pop 19 677.

GLOW WORM. See FIREFLY.

GLOXINIA, *Sinningia speciosa,* popular garden and house plants native to Brazil. Many hybrids are in cultivation with blue, purple, pink, crimson or white flowers. Indoors, they should be placed in sunny windows avoiding direct sunlight in the summer; they thrive in fluorescent-light gardens. The temperature should be maintained between 18°C and 24°C (65°F and 75°F) and the soil kept evenly moist, except for resting periods of a least two months every year when water is withheld. Gloxinias are propagated from seeds, leaf and shoot cuttings or by tuber division. Family: Gesneriaceae.

GLUBB, Sir John Bagot (1897–), British soldier and Arabist. As commander of the Arab Legion for nearly 20 years, "Glubb Pasha" was a stabilizing influence on Jordanian affairs and a symbol of Britain's influence in the Middle East until the beginning of the 1956 ARAB-ISRAELI WAR.

GLUCAGON, HORMONE produced by specialized cells in the PANCREAS, tending to counteract the effect of INSULIN on blood sugar, but having other actions.

GLUCK, Christoph Willibald von (1714–1787), German operatic composer. His first 10 operas were produced in Italy, and he traveled extensively in Europe before he settled in Vienna. In *Orfeo ed Euridice* (1762) he discarded many of the artificial operatic conventions of the previous hundred years and made the opera a unified dramatic musical performance. In the preface to *Alceste* (1767) he set out his ideas for operatic reform which considerably influenced later operatic composers such as MOZART.

GLUCOSE ($C_6H_{12}O_6$), also dextrose or "grape sugar," a naturally occurring simple SUGAR (monosaccharide) found in honey and sweet fruits. It circulates in the BLOOD of mammals, providing their cells with energy. Other sugars and CARBOHYDRATES are converted to glucose by digestion before they can be utilized.

GLUES, widely used adhesive substances of animal or vegetable origin. Animal glues are made from bones, hides, fish bones, fish oil, or the milk protein CASEIN; vegetable glues from natural GUMS, STARCH (e.g., flour and water) or soybeans. Though in use for millennia, it is not yet fully understood how glues work. Nowadays, synthetic RESINS are replacing glues for many purposes. (See also ADHESIVES.)

GLUTEN, a mixture of two proteins (gliadin and glutenin) found in wheat and other cereal flours. In the rising of BREAD gluten forms an elastic network which traps the carbon dioxide, giving a desirable crumb structure on baking. The proportion of gluten in wheat flour varies from 8% to 15%. The level determines the suitability of the flour for different uses. The high gluten content of hard wheat is right for bread and pasta, while soft wheat (low gluten) is used for biscuits.

GLYCEROL, or **glycerin,** colorless, viscous liquid with a sweet taste; a trihydric ALCOHOL. Its fatty-acid esters constitute natural FATS and OILS, from which glycerol is obtained as a by-product of SOAP manufacture; it is also synthesized from propylene, a petroleum product. It is used to make resins for paints and varnishes, in foods, medicines and cosmetics, as a moistening agent and plasticizer, and to make NITROGLYCERIN.

GLYCOGEN, or animal starch, a soluble CARBOHYDRATE consisting of chains of glucose units. It is produced by all vertebrates and stored in muscle and in the liver where it forms a readily available reserve of GLUCOSE.

GLYCOL, or diol, class of dihydric ALCOHOLS, the lower members being viscous, hygroscopic liquids. ETHYLENE GLYCOL is the most important; propylene glycol has similar uses, but being nontoxic is also used in foods, pharmaceuticals and cosmetics.

GLYCOLYSIS, an enzyme-mediated cellular process by which GLUCOSE is broken down to pyruvate. In all, 10 different steps are involved. The process does not require the presence of OXYGEN. In some anaerobic organisms it is the sole source of energy.

GLYPTODONTS, a group of extinct South American edentates up to 3m (10ft) long. The body was extremely well-armored with small plates of bone formed in the skin, an unusual feature in mammals. Herbivores, glyptodonts were also the only hooved edentates.

GNATS, minute two-winged dancing flies very like MOSQUITOES. But true gnats do not bite.

GNATCATCHERS, a group of warblers common in the woodlands of the US. These birds are mainly insectivorous although they may eat fruits, particularly in winter.

GNEISS, broad class of coarse-grained METAMORPHIC ROCKS with a banded, foliated structure and poor CLEAVAGE (see also SCHIST). Their composition is variable, but often approximates to that of GRANITE.

GNOME, a dwarf-like creature in mythology and folklore. Gnomes dwell within the earth, mine precious minerals and fashion intricate metal ornaments and weapons, hence their reputation as guardians of hidden treasure. They are generally depicted as misshapen.

GNOSTICISM, syncretic religious system of numerous pre-Christian and early heretical Christian sects. A form of DUALISM, Gnosticism held that matter (created by the Demiurge) is evil and spirit good, and that salvation comes from secret knowledge (gnosis) granted to initiates. A large Gnostic library was found in Egypt in 1945. The sources of Gnostic beliefs range from Babylonian, Egyptian and Greek mythology to the CABALA and ZOROASTRIANISM. Gnosticism threatened early Christianity, but declined after the 2nd century AD. (See also MANICHAEISM.)

GNOTOBIOTICS, term used to describe laboratory organisms which are either free of all known contaminating organisms (e.g., BACTERIA, FUNGI, YEASTS)—and which are thus "germ-free"—or germ-free organisms specifically contaminated with a known organism. Animals which are not contaminated with a specific organism (but otherwise normal), the so-called Specific Pathogen Free (SPF) animals, are not gnotobiotic. SPF and gnotobiotic animals are widely used in medical research.

GNU, or **wildebeest,** ungainly-looking African ANTELOPES of the genus *Connochaetes*. The White-tailed gnu, a southern species, is now rare outside captivity while the Brindled gnu (Blue wildebeest) still roams the plains of E Africa in vast herds—a major prey of the LION.

A herd of gnu grazing on an African plain. When frightened, gnus characteristically dash a few yards and then wheel to face the danger.

GOA, former Portuguese colony on the W coast of India. Since Dec. 1961 it has been part of the Union Territory of Goa, Daman and Diu in the Republic of India. The union's capital is Panaji in Goa. The area's main crops are rice, cashews and coconuts. Pop 857 180.

GOATS, members of the Bovidae closely related to SHEEP. Goats are widely kept as domestic stock and, as

This magnificent, richly colored tapestry was made by Gobelin weavers in the 17th century and shows King Louis XIV visiting their Paris workshop. It now hangs in the Palace of Versailles, in France.

browsers (feeding on the twigs and leaves of bushes), they can be kept in areas not suitable for other domestic stock. They will eat anything, and the barrenness of many Mediterranean countries is largely due to overgrazing by goats. Probably the earliest-domesticated ruminant, the domestic goat is derived from the wild goat (*Capra aegagrus*) of Western Asia.

GOAT'S BEARD, popular name for hardy herbaceous perennials of the genus *Aruncus* (formerly *Spirea*), family Rosaceae, which have long plumes of white flowers. Also a popular name for *Tragopogon porifolius* or the OYSTER PLANT.

GOATSUCKERS, alternative name for NIGHTJARS used commonly in North America. The name is based on the erroneous but long-held belief that the birds sucked milk from goats and cows at night.

GOBAT, Charles Albert (1843–1914), Swiss statesman and lawyer who shared the 1902 Nobel Peace Prize. A writer on international law, he helped found an international peace bureau.

GOBELIN, French family of clothmakers and dyers. Their workshops, established in the mid-15th century, were bought by Louis XIV (1662) whose finance minister COLBERT created from them a factory to make fine TAPESTRY and furniture. The Gobelin factory is still state-controlled.

GOBI, vast desert in central Asia, which lies mainly in Mongolia, but extends to N China. It covers about 500 000sq mi in the Mongolian plateau and has an average altitude of between 3 000ft and 5 000ft. Parts of the desert's steppeland fringes are inhabited by Mongol herdsmen.

GOBIES, small fishes found in coastal waters in almost every part of the world. Gobies are stocky little fishes in which the pelvic fins are fused to form a sucking disk. This enables them to stick to the bottom and thus hold their position in strong currents.

GOBINEAU, Joseph Arthur, Comte de (1816–1882), French diplomat and author. His essay on *The Inequality of the Human Races* (1853–55) propounded a pseudo-scientific theory of Nordic superiority which, as *gobinisme*, enjoyed some popularity in Germany. He is today more admired for his novel *The Pleiads* (1874).

GOBLIN, or hobgoblin, a dwarf-like sprite in folklore and legend, grotesque in appearance. A household mischief-maker, the goblin is sometimes evil. (See also FAIRY.)

GOD, a supernatural being worthy of worship; especially, the supreme being who is the creator of the universe and on whom all else depends. Many religions are based on POLYTHEISM, having a pantheon of many gods which are generally local, tribal or which have particular functions. Behind some such pantheons lies a more or less explicit belief in a supreme being, which idea comes to fruition in the MONOTHEISM of Judaism, Christianity and Islam; and, in a different form, in the Good Power of DUALISM, who is not merely one of many gods, yet not wholly supreme. Many scholars have supposed that religions evolve from ANIMISM through polytheism to monotheism. In monotheistic religions and philosophies the knowledge of God (absent from AGNOSTICISM—and impossible in ATHEISM) has been approached via reason, in particular the classical arguments for the existence of God (see NATURAL THEOLOGY), via God's self-disclosure (see REVELATION), or via an existential encounter in which the knowledge is personal rather than intellectual. The attributes of God as held by traditional monotheism— though now often questioned—are derived partly from revealed scripture, partly from the results of controversy with pagans, and partly from Greek philosophy. God is described as one, eternal, all-powerful, all-knowing, omnipresent, self-existent, unchangeable, and perfectly good, just, holy and true. Being infinite, his nature is ineffable, and the human mind is incapable of fully grasping it. The relation of God to the world is differently held in DEISM, PANTHEISM and THEISM; theism, as in orthodox Christianity, balances God's IMMANENCE and transcendence. Christianity also teaches that God is a TRINITY—that the one God exists as three Persons—a doctrine which in early and modern Christianity has been controversial, and which is rejected by Jews, Muslims and Unitarians as being inconsistent with the absolute unity of God. (See also RELIGION; THEOLOGY.)

GODARD, Jean-Luc (1930–), French film director. His film *Breathless* (1959) pioneered the French "new wave" school of the cinema. Godard's personal use of imagery and innovative camera work were highly influential on films in the late 1960s.

GODAVARI RIVER, river sacred to Hindus in Maharashtra state, W central India. About 900mi long, it flows SE across the Deccan plateau into the Bay of Bengal.

GODDARD, Robert Hutchings (1882–1945), US pioneer of rocketry. In 1926 he launched the first liquid-fuel rocket. Some years later, with a Guggenheim Foundation grant, he set up a station in N.M., there developing many of the basic ideas of modern rocketry: among over 200 patents was that for a multistage rocket. He died before his work received US Government recognition.

GÖDEL, Kurt (1906–), Austrian-born US mathematician who in 1931 proposed GÖDEL'S THEOREM, arguably the most significant mathematical achievement of the 20th century.

GÖDEL'S THEOREM, theorem showing the futility of attempting to set up a complete axiomatic formalization of mathematics. GÖDEL proved (1931 onward) that any consistent mathematical system must be incomplete; i.e., that in any system formulae must be constructed that can be neither proved nor disproved within that system. Moreover, no mathematical system can be proved consistent without recourse to axioms beyond that system. Gödel's Theorem has had profound effects on attitudes toward the foundations of MATHEMATICS. (See also LOGIC.)

GODEY, Louis Antoine (1804–1878), US magazine publisher. *Godey's Lady's Book*, founded in Philadelphia in 1830, contained notable fiction and fashion pictures in color, and was the first successful US periodical for women.

GODFREY OF BOUILLON (c1058–1100), a leader of the FIRST CRUSADE. On the capture of Jerusalem from the Muslims in 1099, he was elected Protector of the Holy Sepulcher. He became a legendary figure and the hero of several CHANSONS DE GESTE.

GODIVA, Lady (c1040–80), noted for her legendary ride through Coventry, England. Her husband Leofric, Earl of Mercia, promised to reduce the people of Coventry's heavy taxes if she rode naked through the city streets on a white horse. "Peeping Tom" alone essayed to gaze upon the spectacle.

GODKIN, Edwin Lawrence (1831–1902), US newspaper editor. He founded the influential weekly review the *Nation* (1865). He was chief editor of the *New York Evening Post* by 1883 and became famous as an independent, incorruptible social and political critic.

GODOLPHIN, Sidney, 1st earl of (1645–1712), English statesman. A powerful court politician from 1679 to 1710, he maintained the treasury with great financial expertise during a constitutionally unstable period, and supported the Duke of MARLBOROUGH's campaigns. The unpopular WAR OF THE SPANISH SUCCESSION eventually led to his downfall.

GODPARENTS, in Christian BAPTISM, sponsors who take on the responsibility of being spiritual parents to the baptized child. They also make the baptismal confession and spiritual promises on the child's behalf.

GODTHÅB, or **Godthaab,** capital of Greenland, on the Godthåb fjord off Davis strait. The city has an ice-free harbor and is the center of a fishing area. Pop 7 166.

GODUNOV, Boris Fedorovich (c1551–1605), tsar of Russia (1598–1605). A close adviser to IVAN IV ("the Terrible") and regent for Feodor I, Ivan's son and heir, Boris was virtual ruler of Russia. On Feodor's death (1598), Boris was elected tsar and continued Ivan IV's policies of subjugating the BOYARS and expanding Russian boundaries. His life is the subject of a drama by PUSHKIN upon which MUSSORGSKY based his famous opera.

GODWIN, or **Godwine,** (d. 1053), earl of Wessex. The chief adviser to CANUTE, on the king's death (1035) Godwin became the most powerful earl in England. He challenged the power of EDWARD THE CONFESSOR and was exiled (1051); in 1052, he led an armed invasion of England and regained his former power. He was succeeded by his son HAROLD, who became King of England in 1066.

GODWIN, Mary Wollstonecraft. See WOLLSTONECRAFT, MARY.

GODWIN, William (1756–1836), English political theorist and novelist. In his *Enquiry Concerning Political Justice* (1793) and in his novels such as *The Adventures of Caleb Williams* (1794), Godwin rejected all government as corrupting and expressed his belief that humans are rational beings able to live without laws and institutions. He was the father of Mary SHELLEY.

GODWIN-AUSTEN, Mount. See K2.

GODWITS, four species of large wading birds related to sandpipers, curlew and snipe, occurring in Europe and the Americas. Godwits may undertake long migrations from their breeding grounds to wintering quarters. Genus: *Limosa.*

GOEBBELS, Paul Joseph (1897–1945), German Nazi propaganda chief. He had a brilliant academic career before joining the Nazi party. Appointed minister of propaganda by Hitler in 1933, Goebbels skillfully organized political campaigns and used the mass media to promote NAZISM throughout WWII. He committed suicide with his family in Berlin in 1945.

GOEPPERT-MAYER, Maria. See MAYER, MARIA GOEPPERT.

GOERDELER, Karl Friedrich (1884–1945), German resistance leader against the Nazi regime. A former mayor of Leipzig, he plotted Hitler's assassination with Ludwig BECK, and would have become chancellor if the plot on July 20, 1944, had not failed. He was hanged at Plötzensee.

GOERING, Hermann Wilhelm (1893–1946), German political leader and Hitler's deputy, 1939–45. He organized the STORM TROOPS and the GESTAPO and, as commander of the German Air Force, prepared for the aerial *blitzkrieg* campaigns of WWII. By 1936 Goering was economic dictator of Germany, but his power dwindled when he failed to stop Allied air attacks. Convicted of WAR CRIMES at the NUREMBERG TRIALS in 1946, he poisoned himself in his prison cell.

GOES, Hugo van der. See VAN DER GOES, HUGO.

GOETHALS, George Washington (1858–1928), US army engineer who completed construction of the PANAMA CANAL, 1907–14. Apart from solving the complicated technical problems of the project, Goethals successfully overcame unexpected difficulties caused by the climate, disease and the labor force. He served as governor of the Canal Zone, from 1914–16.

GOETHE, Johann Wolfgang von (1749–1832), German poet, novelist and playwright, one of the giants of world literature, and perhaps the last European to embody the ideal of the Renaissance man. His monumental work ranges from poems, novels, plays, and a famous correspondence with SCHILLER to 14 volumes of scientific studies and is crowned by *Faust* (part I, 1808; part II, 1833), written in stages during 60 years, in which he synthesized his life and art in a poetic and philosophical statement of man's search for complete experience and knowledge.

Goethe's birthplace in Frankfurt-am-Main, completely restored in 1949, is now a museum.

Born in Frankfurt-am-Main, Goethe achieved national recognition with his STURM UND DRANG play *Götz von Berlichingen* (1773) and the romantic novel *The Sorrows of Young Werther* (1774). From 1775 until his death, he lived at the ducal court of Saxe-Weimar, where he published, among many other works, *The Apprenticeship of Wilhelm Meister* (1795–96), a novel of the maturing artist to which he later wrote a sequel. A visit to Italy in 1786–88 gave Goethe inspiration for the plays *Iphegenie auf Tauris* (1787) and *Egmont* (1788). Thomas CARLYLE is among his notable English translators; the Weimar edition of Goethe's complete works was published in 133 volumes, 1887–1919.

GOETHITE, brown OXIDE mineral of composition FeO(OH); a major IRON ore of widespread occurrence, formed in bogs or by weathering of other iron minerals. Goethite is very similar to LIMONITE, but is crystalline (in the orthorhombic system). X-RAY DIFFRACTION analysis has shown that much supposed limonite is in fact goethite.

GOFFE, William (d. c1679), English Puritan soldier and signatory to the death warrant of Charles I. An administrator in the PROTECTORATE, Goffe fled to America on the RESTORATION (1660) and lived in seclusion at Haley, Mass.

GOG AND MAGOG, in the Bible, two nations or two warriors, who wage war on the kingdom of Christ (see Rev. 28:8). In Ezek. 38:2 Gog is an enemy nation (probably the Scythians) of the people of God from the land of Magog. In medieval legend they are two giants captured by "Brutus the Trojan" who acted as porters to the royal palace at London.

GOGH, Vincent van. See VAN GOGH, VINCENT.

GOGOL, Nikolai Vasilievich (1809–1852), Russian short story writer, novelist and dramatist. Considered the father of Russian realism, his comic stories of Ukrainian peasant life and later more bizarre and intense tales set in St. Petersburg, such as *The Overcoat* (1872), put him among the most original of Russian authors. Adverse reaction in Russia to his satirical drama *The Inspector-General* (1836) drove Gogol into a self-imposed exile abroad, where he wrote more macabre stories and also his masterpiece, the picaresque novel, *Dead Souls* (1834–52), of which only the first part survives.

GOIÂNIA, capital of Goiás state, S central Brazil. It is the commercial center of an agricultural, ranching and mining region. Pop 388 926.

GOIÁS (formerly Goyaz), state in S central Brazil. With the transfer in 1956 of the national capital to BRASILIA, the surrounding state of Goiás began to develop rapidly. It has extensive mineral (largely nickel) deposits and livestock, tobacco and lumber processing industries.

GOITER, enlargement of the THYROID gland in the neck, causing swelling below the LARYNX. It may represent the smooth swelling of an overactive gland in **thyrotoxicosis** or more often the enlargement caused by multiple CYSTS and nodules without functional change. **Endemic goiter** is enlargement associated with IODINE deficiency, occurring in certain areas where the element is lacking in the soil and water. Rarely, goiter is due to CANCER of the thyroid. If there is excessive secretion or pressure on vital structures SURGERY may be needed, although DRUG or RADIATION THERAPY for excess secretion are often adequate.

GOLD (Au), yellow NOBLE METAL in Group IB of the PERIODIC TABLE; a TRANSITION ELEMENT. Gold has been known and valued from earliest times and used for jewelry, ornaments and coinage. It occurs as the metal and as tellurides, usually in veins of QUARTZ and PYRITE; the chief producing countries are South Africa, the USSR, Canada and th US. The metal is extracted with CYANIDE or by forming an AMALGAM, and is refined by electrolysis. The main use of gold is as a currency reserve (see GOLD STANDARD). Like SILVER, it is used for its high electrical conductivity in printed circuits and electrical contacts, and also for filling or repairing teeth. It is very malleable and ductile, and may be beaten into GOLD LEAF or welded in a thin layer to another metal (rolled gold). For most uses pure gold is too soft, and is alloyed with other noble metals, the proportion of gold being measured in CARATS. Gold is not oxidized in air, nor dissolved by alkalis or pure acids, though it dissolves in AQUA REGIA or cyanide solution because of LIGAND complex formation, and reacts with the HALOGENS. It forms trivalent and monovalent salts. Gold (III) chloride is used as a toner in photography. AW 197.0, mp 1063°C, bp 2966°C, sg 19.32 (20°C).

GOLD-DUST PLANT, a perennial evergreen shrub of the genus *Aucuba*, native to China but widely grown as an ornamental plant for its dark green foliage spotted with yellow. It can tolerate low winter temperatures and high atmospheric pollution, so is a popular outdoor plant in cities, such as New York. Shrubs of this genus are unisexual, so male and female plants must be planted close together if the ornamental red berries are to be produced. Indoors, gold-dust plants require a few hours sun in the winter and bright indirect light in the summer. They grow well at cool temperatures, not exceeding 21°C (70°F). The soil should be kept evenly moist, and propagation is normally by shoot tip cuttings. Family: Cornaceae.

GOLD, Thomas (1920–), Austrian-born US cosmologist who, with Hermann BONDI, proposed (1948) the steady-state model of the universe (see COSMOLOGY).

GOLDBERG, Arthur Joseph (1908–), US labor lawyer and public servant. He served as secretary of labor (1961), associate justice of the Supreme Court (1962–65) and US representative to the United Nations (1965–68). Goldberg was instrumental in the 1955 merger of the AMERICAN FEDERATION OF LABOR and the Congress of Industrial Organizations (AFL-CIO).

GOLDBERG, "Rube" (Reuben Lucius Goldberg; 1883–1970), US cartoonist and sculptor. Known for his bizarre "inventions" of ridiculously complicated machinery to perform everyday tasks. In 1948 he won the Pulitzer Prize for political cartoons.

GOLDBERGER, Joseph (1874–1929), American physician. He is known for his research on PELLAGRA, a vitamin deficiency disease. He discovered that it could be prevented by eating food rich with niacin.

GOLD COAST. See GHANA.

GOLDEN AGE, in Greek mythology, the timeless

paradise that preceded recorded history, especially as seen by HESIOD and OVID—a bygone era of prosperity, innocence and peace. The term is also applied to the particular period in which a nation reaches its cultural peak. (See also AGES OF MAN.)

GOLDEN BULL, name applied to any medieval document bearing a golden seal (*bulla*). The most famous bull was issued by the Holy Roman Emperor Charles IV in 1356. It formulated the procedures by which the emperor would be selected by the Electors (the heads of the chief German principalities); guaranteed the Electors considerable territorial sovereignty; and excluded papal influence from elections of the German ruler. (See also HOLY ROMAN EMPIRE.)

GOLDEN CALF, an idol (usually a young bull) worshiped by Old Testament Israelites. A calf was fashioned by AARON in the "wilderness," but was destroyed by MOSES because the worship of any "graven image" was forbidden by the TEN COMMANDMENTS.

GOLDEN CLUB, *Orontium aquaticum*, an aquatic plant native to shallow ponds and swamps in North America, and sometimes used in water gardens. It has fleshy leaves and produces a spike of bright yellow flowers. Family: Araceae.

GOLDEN EAGLE, *Aquila chrysaetos*, large BIRD OF PREY, widely distributed in the N Hemisphere. See EAGLES.

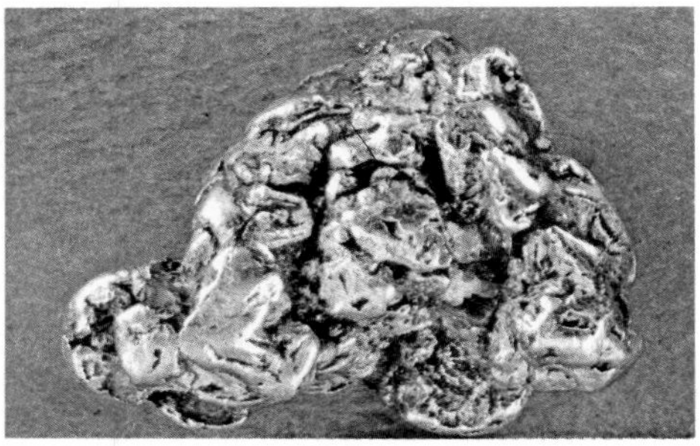

The large estate (*top*) houses miners working on adjacent goldmines, near Johannesburg, South Africa. Gold is normally extracted from ores, but relatively pure gold is sometimes found in nuggets, such as this exceptionally large one (*middle*) weighing 375 grams, from Colombia. *Bottom:* intricately wrought gold weights of the Ashanti, representing a ceremonial sword in its scabbard, a fan, and the frame of a shield.

GOLDENEYE, a diving DUCK found on coastal waters and often, as an ornamental species, on inland lakes. A strikingly-marked bird, (the male is brilliant black and white), it breeds in holes in trees or banks.

GOLDEN FLEECE, in Greek mythology, the golden and magical wool of a sacred winged ram. Guarded by a dragon, the fleece hung in a grove in Colchis near the Black Sea. The hero JASON set sail in search of the fleece with his ARGONAUTS, and after many trials, finally captured the prize.

GOLDEN GATE, a navigable strait connecting San Francisco Bay, Cal., with the Pacific Ocean. It is over 4mi long, 1–2mi wide, and reaches a maximum depth of 414ft.

GOLDEN GATE BRIDGE, bridge spanning the entrance to San Francisco Bay, Cal., built in 1933–37. Its 4 200ft central span, between two 746ft towers, is the second longest in the world and carries six traffic lanes 220ft above the water.

GOLDEN HORDE, name for the Mongol rulers of much of Russia from the 13th to the 15th century, and their *khanate* or empire. Led by BATU KHAN, the horde swept across Russia in 1237–40. The *khanate* slowly came under Turkish influence, but at the end of the 14th century was reconquered by TAMERLANE. (See also MONGOL EMPIRE; TARTARS.)

GOLDEN MOLE, insectivorous, burrowing mammal with powerful spadelike hands found in South and Central Africa where it replaces the Common MOLE of Europe and the various American species. It differs little in structure or habit from the other moles, except that the fur has a coppery sheen.

GOLDEN RETRIEVER, breed of hunting dog, popular as a gundog in the US and UK. First bred in Scotland c1870, it has a thick golden tan coat. Adults may stand up to 24in high at the shoulder and weigh from 60–75lb.

GOLDENRODS, tall plants of the genus *Solidago*, producing masses of yellow or white flowers in the autumn. There are many species, some native to Europe and South America, but most are found in North America, particularly on the Great Plains. Family: COMPOSITAE.

GOLDEN RULE, the precept stated by Jesus in the SERMON ON THE MOUNT: "Always treat others as you would like them to treat you." The name, implying that this is the chief ethical principle, has been used since the 16th century. The golden rule is not peculiarly Christian, and is also found (in a negative form) in Jewish writers, Confucius, Aristotle, Plato, Isocrates and Seneca.

GOLDEN SEAL, *Hydrastis canadensis*, or orangeroot, long-growing perennial herb of the BUTTERCUP family, Ranunculaceae, which is native to the eastern US and Japan. The rootstock yields an ALKALOID that is used as a tonic.

GOLDEN SECTION, a proportion of interest in classical GEOMETRY. If a straight line AB is cut at a point P so that AP:AB = PB:AP, the division is described as a golden section or divine proportion.

$$\frac{AP}{AB} \simeq 0.618,$$

the SEQUENCE 1/1, 1/2, 2/3, 3/5, 5/8, 8/13, 13/21, . . . , the DENOMINATORS of whose terms form a FIBONACCI SERIES, providing successively closer approximations to this ratio.

GOLDEN STOOL, ceremonial ruler's seat, a symbol of the unification of the ASHANTI peoples of Ghana. The solid gold seat is decorated with historical scenes and legend ascribes to it a divine origin. An attempt by the governor of Ghana to seize it in 1900 led to an Ashanti revolt, and the stool was hidden until 1940.

GOLDEN VALLEY, village in SE central Minn., 5mi W of Minneapolis, of which it is a suburb. Pop 24 246.

GOLDFISH, *Carassius auratus* a common pet fish related to the CARP. In the wild state, the goldfish—native to the rivers and streams of China—is dull brown in color. Chance MUTATION produces a form in which all pigments are missing except red (a form of albinism (see ALBINO) well-known in carp-like species). Such mutants breed true, and goldfish have now been kept as pets for over 2 000 years.

GOLDING, William (Gerald) (1911–),

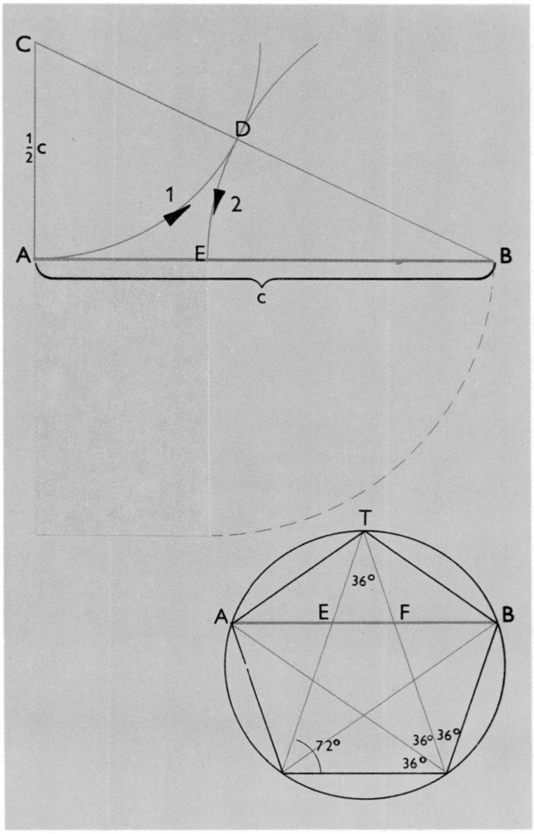

Line AB (*top*) is divided at point E into two portions that illustrate the golden section: AB : BE = BE : AE = $1 : \frac{1}{2}(\sqrt{5}-1)$ = 1.618 to 1 or roughly 8 to 5. To determine point E, bisect AB (= c). Then lay off AC (= $\frac{1}{2}$c) at right angles to AB. Using C as a center and CA as radius, strike off an arc intersecting CB at point D. Using B as a center and BD as radius, strike an arc intersecting AB at point E, which then divides AB into two parts having the proportions of the golden section.

To construct a rectangle the sides of which are in golden section, merely continue in the same figure. AE is the width of the desired rectangle, while EB is the length. Hence simply lay off the length EB at right angles to AE, using E as the center of an arc (dashed line). The pink rectangle then has width and length which are in the golden ratio. The yellow box of this illustration also has dimensions that are in the golden ratio.

The concept of the golden section probably developed from study of the pentagon (lower portion of diagram), the diagonals of which form a pentagram (red) that contains a large number of golden sections. Thus EB : AB = AE : AF = EF : AE, etc.

English novelist. His powerful allegorical works explore the nature of mankind, and include *Lord of the Flies* (1954), *The Inheritors* (1955), *The Spire* (1964) and *The Pyramid* (1967).

GOLD LEAF, thin GOLD foil produced by beating gold ribbon placed between vellum and animal skins until the leaf is only 0.1μm thick. It is used for decorative gilding, lettering on leather-bound books, and for coating artificial satellites etc. to reflect infrared radiation.

GOLDMAN, Emma (1869–1940), Russian-born anarchist who worked in the US c1890–1917. She was imprisoned (1893, 1916, 1917) for inciting riots, advocating birth control and obstructing the draft. She was temporarily deported (1919) and later lived in England and Canada and was active in the Spanish civil war, 1936.

GOLDONI, Carlo (1707–1793), Italian dramatist. His type of character comedy led to the decline in popularity of the rival COMMEDIA DELL' ARTE. Goldoni directed the Comédie Italienne in Paris, 1762–64. Among his 150 comic plays are *The Mistress of the Inn* (1753) and *The Fan* (1763).

GOLD RUSH, general term for an influx of gold prospectors following the discovery of a new gold field. From 1848–1915, in the Americas, Australia and South Africa, there were numerous gold rushes. Three main North American gold strikes attracted thousands of prospectors: in California (1849; see FORTY-NINERS), Colorado (1858–59) and the Klondike (1897).

GOLDSBORO, city in E central N.C., seat of Wayne Co., 46mi SE of Raleigh. It produces tobacco, textiles, furniture, bricks, fertilizers and farm tools. Pop 26810.

GOLDSMITH, Oliver (c1730–1774), Anglo-Irish man of letters. His best known works are the novel *The Vicar of Wakefield* (1766), the comedy *She Stoops to Conquer* (1773) and the pastoral poem *The Deserted Village* (1770). An unsuccessful physician, he achieved both a considerable literary reputation and widespread popularity in his day. His works attacked pedantry and sentimentalism and stressed the simple virtues of humility, courage and humor.

GOLD STANDARD, a monetary system whereby a standard currency unit equals a fixed weight of gold and central banks must be prepared to exchange currency for gold and vice versa. In an *internal* gold standard system, gold coins circulate in a country as LEGAL TENDER. In an *international* system, gold (or gold-based currency) is used for making international payments. Since WWII most countries no longer have an internal gold standard, but do use a limited international standard in which they convert their currencies into gold or US dollars for international payments.

GOLDWATER, Barry Morris (1909–), leading US conservative senator from Ariz. since 1952. As Republican presidential candidate in 1964, Goldwater won only six states in the election campaign against Lyndon B. JOHNSON. Goldwater's writings include *The Conscience of a Conservative* (1960) and *Why Not Victory?* (1962).

GOLDWYN, Samuel (1882–1974), Polish-born US motion picture pioneer. He produced over 70 films and in 1916 founded a unit in the future Metro-Goldwyn-Mayer film company, though he worked as an independent producer after 1924. He won an Academy Award (1947) for *The Best Years of Our Lives.*

GOLEM, in Jewish medieval legend, an effigy (often of clay) magically endowed with life. The golem was a faithful mechanical servant, protecting its owner in times of danger. The most famous golem, supposedly created by Rabbi Löw in 16th-century Prague, was a forerunner of the creature FRANKENSTEIN.

GOLF, the most popular outdoor sport in the US, a game in which individual competitors drive a small hard ball with variously-shaped clubs towards and into a hole. A game consists of playing into either 9 or 18 consecutive holes spread over an extensive ground known as a golf course or links. The winner of individual stroke (or medal) play is the player who holes his ball in the fewest strokes over the course; in match play the winner is the player who wins the most individual holes. Playing a hole involves driving the ball from a raised peg or *tee* across the fairway towards the distant closely-mown *putting green* around the hole (which may be 100 to 600yd from the tee). The player seeks to keep the ball on the intervening mown fairway, avoiding the flanking "rough"—water and sand trap hazards. A player's score is based on *par*, the number of strokes an expert golfer would need to hit the ball from the tee into the hole in a given distance and course difficulty. Par varies from three to six strokes per hole. An expert golfer would average a score of 72 strokes for 18 holes—or an average of four per hole.

Written records of golf date from the 15th century in Scotland, where the traditional international rule-making body, the Royal and Ancient Club of St. Andrews, was founded (1754). Early Scottish colonists probably introduced golf to the US in the 17th century. The game slowly gained popularity, and the Professional Golfers' Association (PGA) championship began in 1916. American golfers have tended to dominate the world game, from Bobby JONES to Ben HOGAN, Arnold PALMER and Jack NICKLAUS. More than 10 million Americans play golf, which is a multi-million dollar leisure business.

GOLGI, Camillo (1844–1926), Italian histologist who developed a staining technique (1873) with which he was able to explore the NERVOUS SYSTEM in great detail. He shared with RAMÓN Y CAJAL the 1906 Nobel Prize for Physiology or Medicine.

GOLIAD, city in S Tex., seat of Goliad Co., 22mi W of Victoria. It is an historic site of the Mexican revolt against Spain (1812–13). In the Texas revolt against Mexico in 1836, James FANNIN's troops were massacred at Goliad on SANTA ANNA's orders. Pop 1709.

GOLIATH, in the Old Testament, a giant Philistine warrior. He challenged the Israelites to send a champion to fight him, and was killed by the youthful DAVID, armed only with faith and a slingshot.

GOMEL, capital of Gomel administrative area, W European USSR, on a tributary of the Dnieper R, 140mi N of Kiev. It is a major port and an industrialized railroad center. Pop 272000.

GÓMEZ, Juan Vicente (1857–1935), Venezuelan caudillo or dictator, 1908–35. Seizing power from Cipriano CASTRO, he encouraged foreign investment and the oil industry and turned Venezuela into a modern nation. However, he corruptly enriched himself, and largely ignored pressing social needs.

GOMORRAH. See SODOM AND GOMORRAH.

GOMPERS, Samuel (1850–1924), pioneer American labor leader. A leader in the cigar makers' union, he helped found and became first president, 1886–94, 1896–1924, of the AMERICAN FEDERATION OF LABOR (AFL). Gompers led the labor fight for higher wages, shorter working time and more freedom. He opposed militant political unionism and as head of the War Committee on Labor (WWI), he greatly helped organized labor gain respectability in the US.

GOMULKA, Wladyslaw (1905–), Polish communist leader. He helped organize communist underground resistance in WWII, became Poland's deputy premier, 1945–49, and cochairman of the COMINFORM (from 1947). A Polish nationalist, he opposed Russian domination and was imprisoned, 1951–54. After the Poznan uprising (1956) he became first secretary of the Polish Communist Party (1956–70), encouraging some social and economic freedoms for Poles while maintaining close ties with the USSR. He resigned following food price riots.

GONADOTROPHINS, HORMONES secreted by the PITUITARY GLAND and PLACENTA, which stimulate the production of sex hormones by gonads: ESTROGEN and PROGESTERONE in females and ANDROGENS in males. They control the maturation and release of EGGS from the ovaries and the development of SPERM. Gonadotrophin secretion is controlled by releasing hormones from HYPOTHALAMUS.

GONADS, the reproductive organs of animals, which produce GAMETES. The female gonad is the OVARY, producing eggs, and the male gonad the testis (see TESTES), producing spermatozoa. (See also REPRODUCTION.)

GONCHAROV, Ivan Aleksandrovich (1812–1891), Russian novelist. His novel, *Oblomov* (1859), satirized realistically the indolence of Russian landed gentry in the 1860s. As a result, the Russian word *oblomovism* was coined to describe the hero's typical aristocratic laziness.

GONCOURT, two French brothers, known as "les deux Goncourt," art historians and pioneer authors of the naturalist school of fiction. **Edmond Louis Antoine Huot de Goncourt** (1822–1896) and **Jules Alfred Huot de Goncourt** (1830–1870) wrote novels exploring aspects of French society, notably *Germinie Lacerteux* (1864), a study of working-class life. They also wrote perceptively on art and social history and published a famous journal depicting Parisian society, 1851–95. Edmond provided money in his will for the Goncourt Academy which annually awards the prestigious literary Goncourt Prize.

GONDOLA, long, slim Venetian boat with high, pointed ends. A gondolier standing in the stern propels it with a long, narrow-bladed oar or sweep. Gondolas have traditionally plied as taxis on the canals of Venice, Italy, but are being partially superseded by motorboat taxis.

GONDWANALAND, hypothetical S Hemisphere supercontinent formed after the split of PANGAEA (see also CONTINENTAL DRIFT; LAURASIA). Stratigraphic and FOSSIL evidence suggest it comprised what are now Antarctica, Australia, India, South America and other, smaller, units.

GONG, or tam-tam, ancient oriental percussion instrument. It comprises a suspended disk, usually bronze, struck by a mallet or a drumstick. Gongs have been used in orchestras since 1791 and also in jazz bands and as burglar alarms and other signals.

GÓNGORA Y ARGOTE, Luis de (1561–1627), Spanish poet. Often called the greatest poet of Spain's cultural Golden Age, he created an ornate, difficult poetic style called Gongorism. His greatest work, *Las Soledades* (1613), led to long controversy over his grandiose and abstruse, yet technically skilled and never dull style.

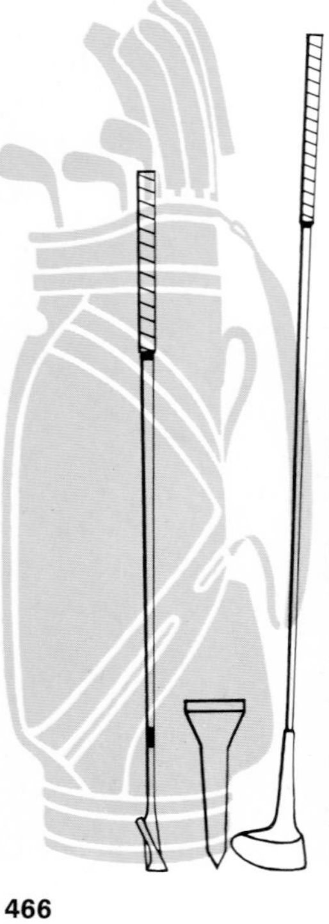

Left: the golfer may use a maximum of 14 clubs, of which four usually have wooden heads (right) and the rest metal heads (left). The first stroke or drive on each hole is generally made from a tee (center; not to scale). *Right:* a golf ball. *Below:* view of a golf course.

GONIOMETER, instrument for measuring ANGLES, especially those between CRYSTAL faces. The simplest form is the **contact goniometer**, a protractor whose base is laid against one face, a movable arm being turned until it contacts the adjacent face. The more accurate **reflecting goniometer** mounts the crystal axially on a graduated circle, or more usually two graduated circles, horizontal and vertical, rotatable independently. The crystal is rotated until each face in turn reflects a collimated light beam into a fixed telescope, and so the direction of the normal to each face is determined. (The term may also be used for the DIRECTION FINDER.)

GONORRHEA. See VENEREAL DISEASES.

GONZAGA, Saint Aloysius (1568–1591), Italian Jesuit, patron saint of Roman Catholic youth. He died of plague in Rome after nursing victims of the disease.

GONZALES, Richard Alonzo "Pancho" (1928–), American tennis champion. One of the great world-class players, he won the US men's singles championship (1948, 1949), then turned professional and was US professional champion and an active player from 1954 through the 1960s.

GONZÁLEZ, Julio (1876–1942), Spanish sculptor. His surrealist work (see SURREALISM) such as *Woman Combing Her Hair* (1932) or the realistic *Montserrat* (1936–37) were constructed from welded metal.

GOOBER. See PEANUT.

GOOD FRIDAY, the Friday in HOLY WEEK before Easter, observed in most Christian churches as a day of fasting and repentance in commemoration of the CRUCIFIXION of Jesus Christ, of which it is the anniversary. Its observance dates from the 2nd century.

GOOD HOPE, Cape of. See CAPE OF GOOD HOPE.

GOODMAN, Benny (Benjamin D. 1909–), American clarinetist and band leader. One of the most famous jazz soloists and danceband leaders of the 1930s and 1940s "swing" era. His virtuoso playing inspired classical compositions for the clarinet, notably *Contrasts* (1938) by Bela BARTÓK and concertos by COPLAND and HINDEMITH.

GOOD NEIGHBOR POLICY, pact signed at the 1933 Pan-American conference by the US and Latin American countries, as outlined by President Franklin D. ROOSEVELT. Ending the "gun-boat diplomacy" long practiced by the US to protect its interests in Latin America, the policy stated that no nation would interfere in another's affairs. Exchange programs were set up for teachers and technical experts and the US agreed to help develop Latin American agriculture, business, education and health facilities. (See also ALLIANCE FOR PROGRESS.)

GOODWILL INDUSTRIES OF AMERICA, nonprofit welfare organization, founded 1902, to provide training and employment for the handicapped in the US, Canada and Mexico. Clothing and appliances donated by the public and reconditioned in Goodwill workshops are resold in more than 150 Goodwill stores in the US.

GOODYEAR, Charles (1800–1860), US inventor of the process of VULCANIZATION (patented 1844). In 1839 he bought the patents of Nathaniel Manley Hayward (1808–1865), who had had some success by treating RUBBER with SULFUR. Working on this, Goodyear accidentally dropped a rubber/sulfur mixture onto a hot stove, so discovering vulcanization.

GOOKIN, Daniel (1612–1687), American magistrate and protector of Indians in Mass. He was superintendent of Indians in the colony, 1656–87, and as a result suffered unpopularity during the Indian wars. He rose to become major general of the Mass. militia.

GOONEY-BIRD, the Black-footed ALBATROSS, *Diomedea nigripes.*

GOOSE. See GEESE.

GOOSEBERRY, hardy shrub bearing green, fleshy fruit that are covered by a fine down. The fruits are either eaten fresh or used to make jams and pies. There are many hybrids in cultivation in the N Hemisphere, but it is banned in certain states in the US because it carries BLISTER RUST of white pine. Family: Grossulariaceae (Saxifragaceae).

GOOSEFLESH, fanciful description of SKIN appearance in cold or acute anxiety; contraction of tiny muscles causes the HAIRS to be erected and the papillae to rise, looking like pimples. Cold prompts reflex contraction as a means of increasing skin insulation, while anxiety leads to stimulation of the muscles by the sympathetic NERVOUS SYSTEM.

GOOSEFOOT, or **pigweed,** popular name for species of the genus *Chenopodium*, family Chenopodiaceae, most of which are common weeds. *Chenopodium bonus-henricus* has large leaves used as a cooked vegetable.

GOPHERS, the name applied in North America to any burrowing rodent, but properly referring to the Pocket gophers, a group confined to arid areas of North America. Gophers are solitary animals feeding on bulbs and roots collected in their underground tunnels. They possess fur-lined cheek pouches for storing food, which open on the outside of each cheek.

GORAKHPUR, city in N central India, SE Uttar Pradesh, on the Rapti R. It is an amalgamation of farming villages and a railroad center. Pop 230 701.

GORALS, the east-Asian representative of the CHAMOIS group of "goat-antelopes." They are coarse-haired and mountainous in habit—occurring up to altitudes of 3 700m (12 000ft).

GORDIAN KNOT, in Greek mythology, an intricate knot by which King Gordius of Phrygia joined the yoke and pole of an oxcart. A prophecy held that anyone undoing the knot would rule all Asia. The knot defied all comers until the conqueror ALEXANDER THE GREAT severed it with his sword. Hence, "cutting the Gordian knot" describes any problem solved by bold, unorthodox action.

GORDON, Charles George (1833–1885), British soldier, popularly known as "Chinese Gordon." He helped suppress the TAIPING REBELLION (1863–64) in China, was governor of the Sudan (1877–80), where he established law, improved communications and attempted to suppress the slave trade. In 1885 he defended Khartoum against the MAHDI's forces for 10 months, but was killed on Jan. 26 before relief arrived on Jan. 28. British indignation over his abandonment led to the collapse of GLADSTONE's government.

GORDON, Lord George (1751–1793), English Protestant agitator. In June 1780 he instigated the violent Gordon riots in London that destroyed Roman Catholic homes, chapels and other buildings and caused over 450 deaths.

GORDON, John Brown (1832–1904), US Confederate soldier and politician. He rose from infantry captain to major general and led the last charge at APPOMATTOX in 1865. Later he dominated state politics in Ga., as US senator, 1873–80, 1891–97 and governor, 1886–90.

GORDON SETTER, hunting dog, bred in Scotland before the 17th century and named for Sir Alexander Gordon. A pointer, it has a long black and tan coat, slightly waved, and may stand up to 27in high at the shoulder and weigh 45–80lb.

GORGAS, William Crawford (1854–1920), US Army sanitarian. After Walter REED's commission had proved (1900) Carlos FINLAY's theory that YELLOW FEVER is transmitted by the MOSQUITO, Gorgas conducted in Havana a massive control program; he repeated this in Panama (1904–1913), facilitating the digging of the Panama Canal.

GORGES, Sir Ferdinando (c1566–1647), English colonizer. He helped found the PLYMOUTH COMPANY (1606) and the Council of New England (1620) for colonizing eastern North America between lat. 40°N–48°N, and supported numerous colonizing and trading ventures in North America. In 1639 he received a royal charter for the province of Me. After his death, his grandson sold all rights in Me. to Mass. (1677).

GORGIAS (c483–376 BC), Greek sophist and teacher of rhetoric. He believed that objective truth or knowledge was impossible, and hence that the ability to argue on either side of a question was of prime value to an educated man. He is a central figure of Plato's *Gorgias* dialogue. (See SOPHISTS; see also CYNICS; SKEPTICISM.)

GORGON, in Greek mythology, three monster sisters. The gorgons Stheno, Euryale and MEDUSA were daughters of the seagod Phorcus and had writhing snakes for hair. Anyone looking at a gorgon's head was turned to stone, but PERSEUS killed Medusa, who was mortal.

GORILLA, (*Gorilla gorilla*) the largest of the PRIMATES, with a scattered distribution throughout central Africa. They live in groups with a single dominant "silverback" male, feeding on vast quantities of vegetable material as they wander over their range of 25–40km² (10–15sq mi). Gorillas are quadrupedal, rising to two legs only when displaying. They spend most of their time on the ground, but may make nests on the ground or in trees to sleep in at night. Though huge apes, (a male weighs 160–200kg (350–440lb) they are peaceable and will not attack unprovoked. The well-known chest-beating display is not a threat, but an intraspecific social signal.

GORKI, city in the USSR, about 250mi E of Moscow, capital of Gorki Oblast. It is a major industrial center at the confluence of the Volga and Oka rivers. It produces planes, automobiles, machinery and plastics. Maxim GORKI was born here. Pop 1 213 000.

GORKI, Maxim (1868–1936), pen name of Aleksey Maksimovich Peshkov, Russian author recognized as the father of SOCIALIST REALISM. His works, noted for their optimism and stark naturalism, include the play *Lower Depths* (1902), the novel *Mother* (1907) and the autobiographical trilogy *Childhood* (1914), *In the World* (1916) and *My Universities* (1923).After the Revolution, Gorki headed state publishing up to 1921.

GORKY, Arshile (1904–1948), Armenian-born US painter, a pioneer of ABSTRACT EXPRESSIONISM. His seemingly spontaneous, organic abstracts influenced the work of Jackson POLLOCK and Willem DE KOONING.

GORLOVKA, city in the USSR, in the Ukrainian SSR, N of Donetsk. It is a coalmining center in the Donets Basin. Pop 337 000.

GORTON, Samuel (1592–1677), English Puritan, leader of the radical religious Gortonites and founder of Showamet (Warwick, R.I.), 1642. Jailed and then banished by the Mass. authorities for his radical opinions, he gained English legal backing for his land claims, and returned to Showamet, which he renamed Warwick, in 1648.

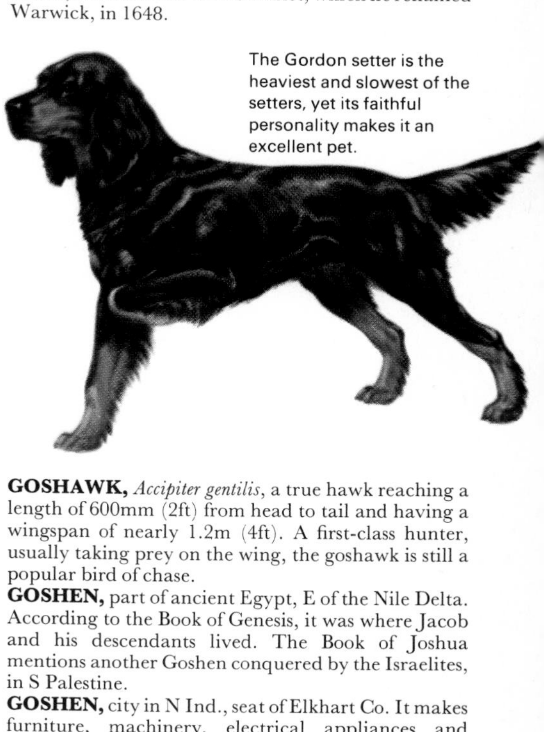

The Gordon setter is the heaviest and slowest of the setters, yet its faithful personality makes it an excellent pet.

GOSHAWK, *Accipiter gentilis*, a true hawk reaching a length of 600mm (2ft) from head to tail and having a wingspan of nearly 1.2m (4ft). A first-class hunter, usually taking prey on the wing, the goshawk is still a popular bird of chase.

GOSHEN, part of ancient Egypt, E of the Nile Delta. According to the Book of Genesis, it was where Jacob and his descendants lived. The Book of Joshua mentions another Goshen conquered by the Israelites, in S Palestine.

GOSHEN, city in N Ind., seat of Elkhart Co. It makes furniture, machinery, electrical appliances and rubber products. Pop 18 004.

GOSNOLD, Bartholomew (d. 1607), English navigator, who in 1602 explored the New England coast S from Maine to Buzzard's Bay and named CAPE COD. He died of malaria at Jamestown in Virginia, a settlement he had opposed for its unhealthy location.

GOSPELS, The, first four books of the NEW TESTAMENT, named for their reputed authors:

Matthew, Mark, Luke and John. Each is a collection of the acts and words of Jesus. Didactic in intention rather than biographical, they were written to help spread the gospel ("good news") of Christian salvation. All broadly cover the key events of Jesus' life, death and resurrection, but narrative styles and details, and intended readership, differ. The Gospel—an excerpt from the Gospels—is one of the readings at Holy COMMUNION. (See also SYNOPTIC GOSPELS.)

GOSSAERT, Jan. See MABUSE, JAN DE.

GÖTEBORG, city in SW Sweden on the Kattegat. Sweden's leading seaport and second largest city, it is linked to Stockholm by canal. Shipbuilding is a major industry and timber, iron, steel products, textiles and porcelain are also made. There is a university and a cathedral. Pop 445 483.

GOTHIC, an ancient E Germanic language spoken in S Europe, in the 4th and 5th centuries AD. Fragments of Bishop Ulfilas' 4th-century Gothic version of the Bible represent the earliest written record of a Germanic language.

Notre Dame cathedral in Paris, built between 1163 and 1313, is one of the finest existing examples of Gothic architecture. It is especially notable for its flying buttresses and its great rose window.

GOTHIC ART AND ARCHITECTURE. The Gothic style of art and architecture flourished in Europe, particularly in France, from the mid-12th century to the end of the 15th century. The style was first referred to as "gothic" in the Renaissance by artists and writers who sought to condemn it as barbaric.

Gothic architecture in fact developed from the Romanesque, combining the latter's barrel vault and the stone rib to produce its most characteristic feature, the rib vault. This was first perfected at the Abbey Church of St. Denis near Paris, in 1140. It made possible a lighter, almost skeletal building. The flying buttress, also characteristic, was first used at Notre Dame in Paris. During the 13th century, High Gothic was perfected and cathedrals with higher vaults and more slender columns and walls were constructed, as at Chartres and Reims in France, Salisbury in England and Cologne in Germany. In the 14th and 15th centuries Gothic became more elaborate and ornate. (See DECORATED STYLE; FLAMBOYANT STYLE; PERPENDICULAR STYLE.)

Sculptural decoration was an essential part of Gothic architecture, as were stained glass windows, among the most notable examples of which are at Chartres. The period is also noted for its manuscript illumination in missals, books of hours, Bibles and psalters.

GOTHIC NOVEL, genre of novel in which romantic stories are given a supernatural setting. The term now embraces a wide range of popular fiction. Early examples of the genre are Horace WALPOLE's *Castle of Otranto* (1765) and Ann RADCLIFF's *The Mysteries of Udolpho* (1794).

GOTHIC REVIVAL, 18th and 19th-century revival of interest in medieval culture, chiefly in England and the US. It involved a somewhat dilettante liking for such phenomena as the GOTHIC NOVEL and pseudo-medieval country houses, but there was also a more serious appeal to the standards of the Middle Ages, as by the architect Pugin and by John RUSKIN.

GOTHS, ancient Germanic peoples, reputed to have originated in S Scandinavia, who invaded and settled in Roman Spain and Italy in the 5th century AD. In the 2nd century AD, they settled on the N and NW Black Sea coast and during the next century occupied the Roman province of DACIA. The Goths in Dacia became known as VISIGOTHS and those around the Black Sea as OSTROGOTHS.

GOTLAND, Swedish island in the Baltic Sea off SE Sweden. The economy rests on agriculture, fishing and tourism. The historic port of Visby belonged to the HANSEATIC LEAGUE.

GOTTFRIED VON STRASSBURG, 13th century German poet famous for his masterpiece *Tristan* (c1210), an epic based on Celtic legend, and stressing the ennobling ideals of courtly love. Richard WAGNER used the work as the basis of his opera *Tristan and Isolde* (1859).

GÖTTINGEN, city in West Germany, in S Lower Saxony, on the Leine R. Its manufactures include precision instruments. Göttingen's famous university was founded in 1737. Pop 108 991.

GOTTSCHALK, Louis Moreau (1829–1869), US composer and pianist, internationally celebrated as a virtuoso. He studied in Europe, toured there and in North and South America, and wrote operas, orchestral works and piano pieces.

GOUACHE, watercolor paint made opaque by adding white pigment. Easier to work than ordinary watercolor, it was probably first used by the ancient Egyptians.

GOUJON, Jean (c1510–1568?), French sculptor and architect. He is famous for his elongated and elegant statues. His finest work, part of which is in the Louvre in Paris, is generally agreed to be the *Fontaine des Innocents* (1547–49).

GOULD, Glenn (1932–), Canadian virtuoso pianist, famous for his performances of BACH, BEETHOVEN and BRAHMS. From the late 1960s he abandoned live performances, making records and documentary films.

GOULD, Jay (1836–1892), US railroad speculator. He denied Cornelius VANDERBILT control of the Erie Railroad by selling stock illegally. With James FISK he tried cornering the gold market (1869) and triggered the BLACK FRIDAY panic. From 1872 he built up the Gould railroad system in the SW, which included the Union Pacific. He also gained a controlling interest in the Western Union Telegraph Company.

GOULD, Morton (1913–). US avant-garde composer and conductor who attempted to combine popular musical styles with modern techniques. His works include three symphonies and stage music.

GOUNOD, Charles François (1818–1893), French composer, best known for the operas *Faust* (1859) and *Romeo and Juliet* (1867). He wrote 10 other operas, also oratorios, masses, songs and piano pieces in a melodic and often sentimental style.

GOUPIL, Saint René (c1607–1642), French Jesuit, a surgeon and missionary in Canada. He and Father JOGUES were tortured and killed by the Iroquois. Canonized in 1930, his feast day is Sept. 26.

GOURAMIS, tropical freshwater fish found from India to Malaya, and very popular with aquarists. They are highly colorful fishes with a long filamentous pelvic ray. The best-known species, the Kissing gourami (*Helostoma temmincki*), places its mouth against those of other individuals, probably as a threat display.

GOURD, vine-like annual plants of family Cucurbitaceae, which produce hard-shelled fruit used as carriers, bowls, and in making some musical instruments. Hybrid varieties of *Cucurbita pepo* produce fruit with a wide range of color and shape, which are used as ornaments.

GOUT, a DISEASE of PURINE metabolism characterized by elevation of uric acid in the BLOOD and episodes of ARTHRITIS due to uric acid crystal deposition in SYNOVIAL FLUID and the resulting INFLAMMATION. Deposition of urate in CARTILAGE and subcutaneous tissue (as *tophi*) and in the KIDNEYS and urinary tract (causing stones and renal failure) are other important effects. The arthritis is typically of sudden onset with severe pain, often affecting the great toe first and large JOINTS in general. Treatment with allopurinol prevents recurrences.

GOVERNMENT PRINTING OFFICE (GPO), US government agency in Washington D.C., one of the world's largest printing establishments. Created in 1860, it prints and publishes official documents and supplies stationery to other government agencies.

GOVERNOR, executive official, notably the elected head of each of the 50 US states, ordinarily serving a four or two-year term. He is the state's chief executive, responsible for administration and appointment of non-elective officials and judges.

GOVERNOR, device that maintains the speed of a machine constant despite load variation, often by controlling the fuel supply. The common flyball governor works by the centrifugal force of two rotating weights, acting against a spring. (See also SERVOMECHANISM.)

GOVERNORS ISLAND, island in New York Bay, S of the East R. Former residence of colonial governors, and site of Castle William (1811), it is now a military base.

GOWER, John (c1330–1408), English poet, a friend of CHAUCER. He is best known for his narrative poem in English *Confessio amantis* (c1390), but he also wrote in French and Latin. His work, characterized by its moral tone, was widely influential.

GOWON, Yakubu (1934–), Nigerian general, head of state (1966–75). He crushed secessionist BIAFRA in a bloody civil war (1967–70), then announced an amnesty and launched a reconciliation program. He was replaced by Brigadier Muritala Mohammed (d. 1976) after a bloodless coup.

GOYA Y LUCIENTES, Francisco José de (1746–1828), Spanish painter and etcher, famous as much for his delightful paintings and portraits for the Spanish court as for his grim depictions of the French invasion of Spain in 1808–14. During the 1790s he painted some of his most delicately and brilliantly-colored portraits, including *La Tirana* (1794) and, after he became first court painter in 1799, the *Family of Charles IV* (1800). The etchings *Caprices* (1793–98) and *Disasters of War* (1810–14) are scenes of absurd and savage human behavior.

Goya's *The Battle Against the Mameluk Knights* (1814), reproduced here, hangs in the Prado, Madrid. Much of Goya's work depicts the inhumanity of man to man.

GOYEN, Jan Josephszoon van (1596–1656), Dutch landscape painter. Exploiting a narrow range of colors, he depicted Dutch rural, city, coast and winter scenes, using low horizons surmounted by delicately atmospheric skyscapes.

GOZZOLI, Benozzo (Benozzo di Lese; 1420–1497), Italian painter and goldsmith. He assisted Fra ANGELICO and is best known for his frescoes in which he treated contemporary Florentine life. His finest work is in the Medici Palace chapel, Florence.

GRABEN. See RIFT VALLEY.

GRACCHUS, family name of two Roman brothers, reformers and statesmen, known as the Gracchi.

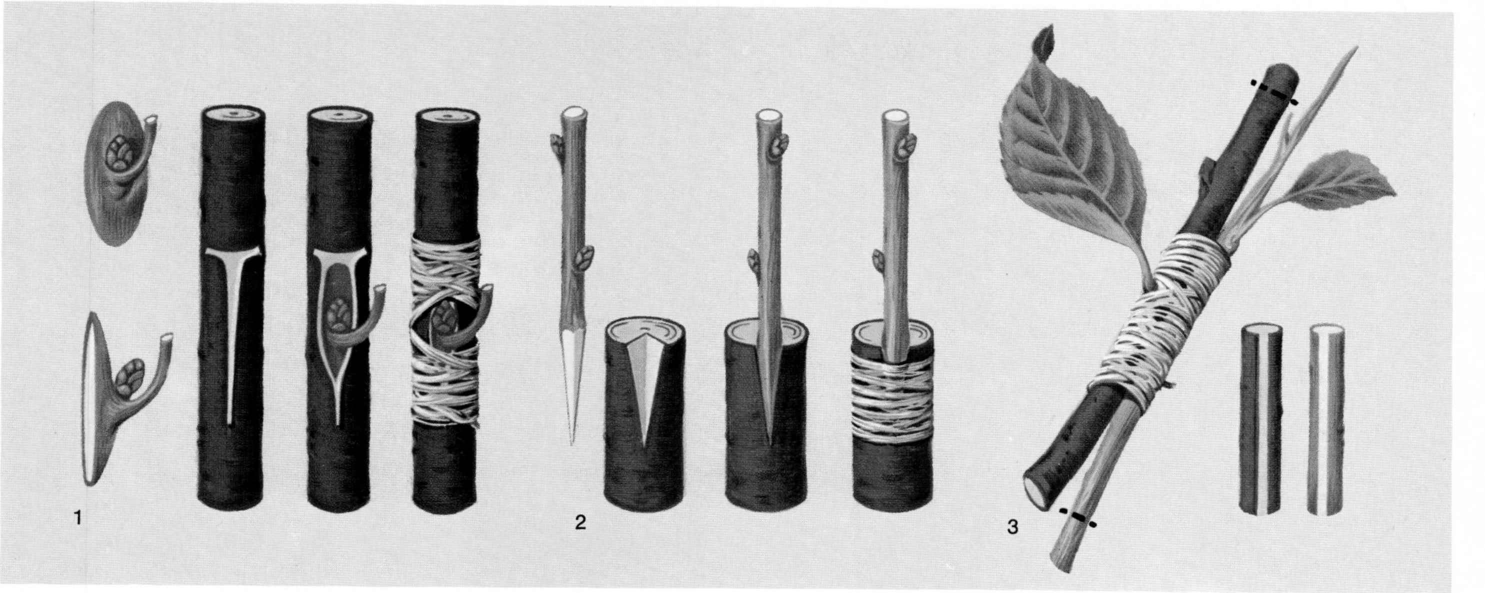

There are a number of different methods used in grafting, related to the characteristics of the plants concerned. A scion bud may be fitted onto the stock (1); or a scion shoot may be side grafted (2), the scion being trimmed to a point to fit into a long notch cut in the side of the stock. Alternatively, a slice may be cut in both the scion and the stock (3) which are then bound together and left to unite before each is cut as indicated by the dotted lines.

Tiberius Sempronius (163–133 BC), was elected a tribune of Rome in 133 and proposed a law redistributing public land (largely farmed by rich senators) to landless citizens. To push his law through he interfered with senatorial powers. A mob of senators killed him, believing his popular reforms a threat to political stability. Gaius Sempronius (154–121 BC) was elected a tribune in 123 and 122. He, too, tried to restrict the powers of the Senate and to help the poor and the underprivileged middle class—for instance by issuing cheap grain, establishing overseas colonies and proposing Roman citizenship for all free Italians and Latins. The Senate moved to revoke his bills, fighting broke out, and Sempronius was killed.

GRACE, in Christian theology, the undeserved favor of God shown towards needy and sinful men in Jesus Christ. In biblical thought, especially in St. Paul, grace is at the heart of SALVATION, and is necessary for faith and good works; the relation between them has been controversial (see ARMINIANS; AUGUSTINE; CALVINISM; PELAGIANISM). The "means of grace" include holy scripture, the sacraments, prayer and Christian fellowship. The term is also used for thanksgiving for food.

GRACE, W. G. (William Gilbert; 1848–1915), English cricketer, a highly colorful and popular figure who became a legend in his lifetime. He scored 54 896 runs, took 2 876 wickets and was one of the founders of modern batting technique.

GRACE, William Russell (1832–1904), Irish-born US shipping magnate. He created a Latin American shipping empire. As mayor of New York from 1880 and 1884 he opposed TAMMANY HALL.

GRACES, Greek goddesses of fertility, personifying charm, beauty and grace, also known as the Charites. They usually number three: Aglaia (radiance), Euphrosyne (joyfulness) and Thalia (bloom)—daughters of Zeus and Hera. The Graces sometimes attended Aphrodite, goddess of love, and sang with the Muses and Apollo, and hence were linked with the arts.

GRACKLES, medium-sized perching birds of the New World. Most have iridescent plumage, long tails and rather heavy bills. They are birds of lightly wooded country favoring parkland and suburban areas. They are omnivorous, feeding on insects, the eggs of other birds and refuse. Grackles nest in colonies; polygamy is widespread and males play little or no part in raising the young.

GRAD. See DEL; GRADIENT.

GRADIENT, in plane ANALYTIC GEOMETRY, an increase in *y* corresponding to a unit increase in *x*. The gradient of a CURVE may be found at any point along it by use of differential CALCULUS. Gradient is a VECTOR quantity. In vector notation, the gradient of a SCALAR field *W* is the vector field

$$\text{grad } W = \mathbf{i}\frac{\partial W}{\partial x} + \mathbf{j}\frac{\partial W}{\partial y} + \mathbf{k}\frac{\partial W}{\partial z},$$

that is, ∇W (see DEL).

GRADY, Henry Woodfin (1850–1889), US journalist and orator who encouraged reconciliation between North and South after the Civil War. He delivered a famous Speech, *The New South*, in New York City in 1886.

GRAF, Urs (c1485–1527), Swiss goldsmith and artist influenced by DÜRER. A pioneer in the use of white-line engraving, he is noted for his vigorous and humorous style.

GRAFFITO or **sgraffito**, from Italian, "scratching," in the visual arts a technique (and its results) in which a second covering of color is partially scraped away to reveal a primary covering of color below. In archaeology, the term graffito is used to mean a casual writing on an interior or exterior wall. Graffiti are found in great numbers on ancient Egyptian monuments, the walls of Pompeii, etc., and are of special interest in PALEOGRAPHY as they show the corruptions and transmutations of alphabetical characters. Ancient graffiti, like their modern counterparts, are mainly of a political or obscene nature.

GRAF SPEE, German "pocket battleship." A fast, heavily-armored cruiser, she sank nine British merchantmen in the S Atlantic in the first three months of WWII. Finally trapped by British warships off the Rio de la Plata, she was allowed four days sanctuary in neutral Uruguay's Montevideo harbor. Her captain then scuttled her, on Dec. 17, 1939.

GRAFT, Surgical. See PLASTIC SURGERY; TRANSPLANTS.

GRAFTING, the technique of propagating plants by attaching the stem or bud of one plant (called the scion) to the stem or roots of another (the stock or rootstock). Only closely related varieties can be grafted. ROSES and fruit trees are often grafted so that good flowering or fruiting varieties have the benefit of strong roots.

GRAFTON, town in central Mass. It is a residential suburb ESE of Worcester, and makes textiles and plastics. Pop 11 659.

GRAHAM, Billy (1918–), William Franklin Graham, US evangelist. Ordained a Southern Baptist minister, 1939, he gained national prominence on the revivalist circuit about 1949 and went on to establish an international reputation as a leader of mass religious rallies.

GRAHAM, Martha (1895–), American dancer and choreographer, a major pioneer of modern dance. Influenced by Isadora DUNCAN, Ruth SAINT DENIS and Ted SHAWN, she made her solo concert debut in 1926. She choreographed over 100 works, most notably *Appalachian Spring* (1944) and *Clytemnestra* (1958).

GRAHAM, Sylvester (1794–1851), US temperance advocate who recommended the use of coarsely-ground unsifted flour, often now called **graham flour**.

GRAHAM, Thomas (1805–1869), British chemist who formulated **Graham's Law**: the DIFFUSION rate of a gas is proportional to the inverse of the square ROOT of its density. While working further on diffusion and OSMOSIS he discovered the colloidal state, coining the term colloid (see COLLOID).

GRAHAME, Kenneth (1859–1932), British writer, author of the famous children's story *The Wind in the Willows* (1908), featuring animals with appealingly human characters.

GRAHAM LAND (or Palmer Peninsula), N part of Antarctica's Antarctic Peninsula, annexed by Great Britain 1831–32; but also claimed by Argentina and Chile.

GRAIL. See HOLY GRAIL.

GRAIN, or caryopsis, a dry one-seeded FRUIT, usually containing a high percentage of starch, produced by, for example, CORN, OATS, BARLEY, RYE and other CEREAL CROPS. Grain crops have a high food value, store well and are a primary food stuff, contributing over half the world's calorie intake. (See also FLOUR.)

GRAIN (gr), the fundamental Anglo-American unit of weight, shared between the avoirdupois, troy and apothecaries' systems. The Imperial grain is defined equal to 0.064 798 91 grams exactly. (See WEIGHTS AND MEASURES.)

GRAIN ELEVATOR, tall structure in which grain is stored, cleaned and mixed; also a machine for lifting grain. Most of the storage bins are more than 100ft high. Storage elevators, usually of steel or concrete, range from 10 000-bushel *farm elevators*, through 25 000–100 000-bushel *country elevators* in grain towns, to 1–20-million-bushel *terminal elevators* at major grain shipping centers and markets.

GRAINGER, Percy Aldridge (1882–1961), Australian-born composer and pianist, a naturalized American from 1919. Influenced by his friend GRIEG, he collected and edited English folk music, basing short orchestral pieces upon it.

GRAIN WEEVILS, small brown or black BEETLES infesting stored products such as grain or flour. There are many species which between them show worldwide distribution. In many areas their numbers reach pest proportions.

PARTS OF SPEECH

Noun: a word used as the name of a person, place, thing or concept (e.g.: Mary, house, cat, song)

Verb: a word that expresses action or a state of being (e.g.: runs, is)

Adjective: a word which qualifies (adds meaning to) a noun or pronoun (e.g.: good, happy)

Pronoun: a word used in place of a noun (e.g.: he, she, it, I, you, we, which, who)

Adverb: a word which modifies a verb or adjective (e.g.: swiftly, very)

Preposition: a word with a noun or pronoun to show its relation with some other word in the sentence (e.g.: on, by, at, from)

Conjunction: a word joining words, phrases or clauses (e.g.: and, but, although)

Interjection: an exclamatory word bearing no formal relation to the rest of the sentence (e.g.: oh! alas! whew!)

Definite article: the

Indefinite article: a or an

SENTENCE ANALYSIS

Each sentence has a **subject** (the thing, person or idea the sentence is about) and a **predicate** (what is said about the subject). A **clause** is a group of words containing a subject and predicate but not forming a complete sentence by itself. A **simple** sentence has only one clause. A **compound** sentence has more than one clause of equal force. A **complex** sentence has one main clause and one or more subordinate clauses. A **phrase** is a small group of words equivalent to a noun, adjective or adverb.

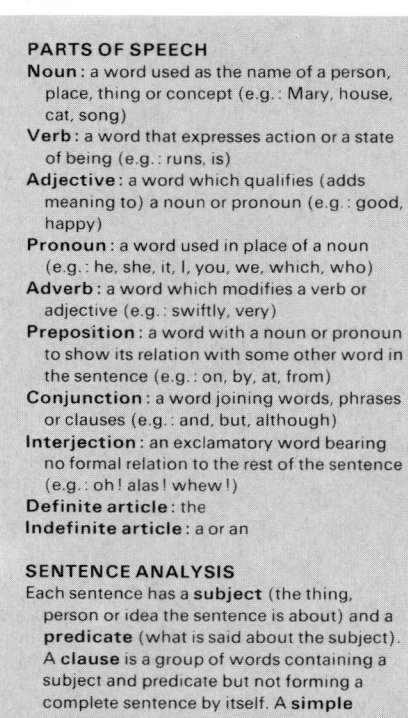

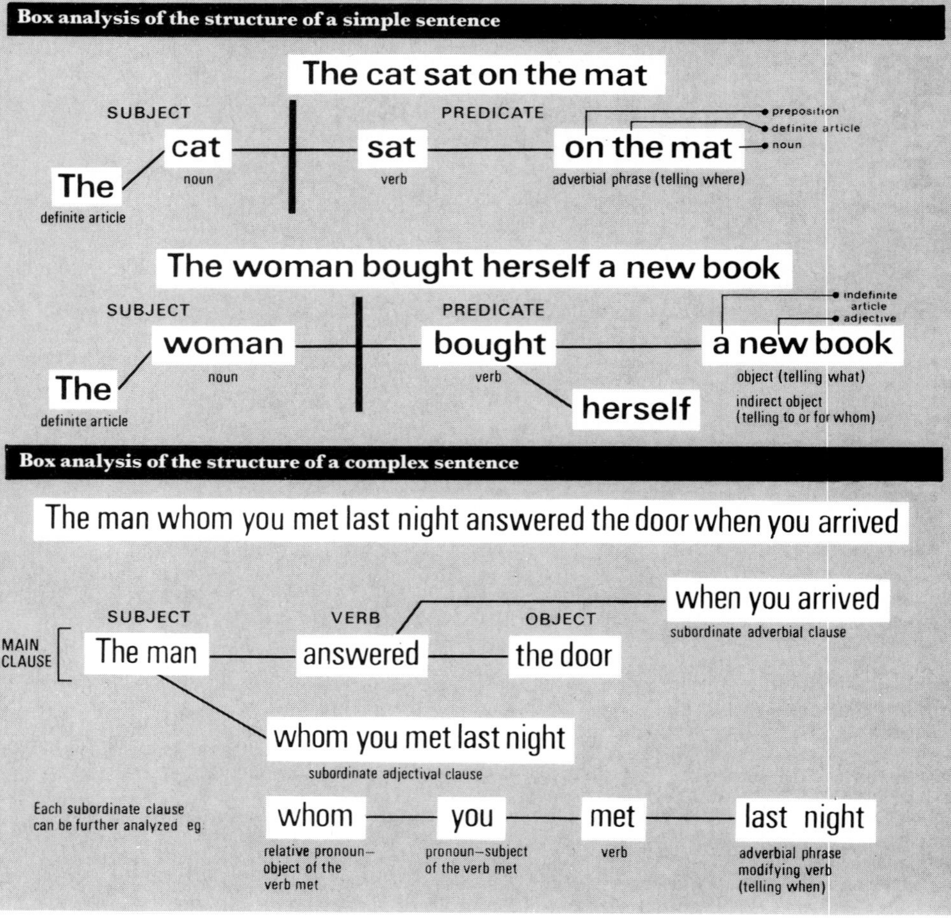

GRAM (g), the fundamental unit of mass in the CGS version of the METRIC SYSTEM. It approximates to the mass of a cubic centimetre of water.

GRAMICIDIN, an ANTIBIOTIC contained in the tyrothricin first prepared by DUBOS in 1939. It is rarely used today since less toxic alternatives exist.

GRAMMAR, the structures of language and of its constituents; and the science concerned with the study of those structures. The grammarian concentrates on three main aspects of language: syntax, the ways that words are put together to form sentences; accidence, or morphology, the ways that words alter to convey different senses, such as past and present or singular and plural (see INFLECTION); and phonology, the ways that sounds are used to convey meaning.

Syntax. In English, the simplest sentence has a noun followed by a verb: "Philip thinks." More complicated is "Philip seldom thinks," where the verb is qualified by an adverb. In both of these, order is important: in "Seldom, Philip thinks" the change in order has brought about a change in meaning. In contrast, sentences of widely different outward form may have the same meaning (for example, using active and passive forms of the verb), and this suggests to many grammarians that superficial structure is not ultimately important, that there is a deep-lying structure of language which can be resolved into a few basic elements whose combinations can be used to produce an infinite number of sentences. Here grammatical studies are probing at the very roots of the human psyche; and ethnographical studies of the syntaxes of different languages, primitive and civilized, have been of primary importance in cultural ANTHROPOLOGY. (See also CHOMSKY; ETHNOGRAPHY.)

Accidence. Most English nouns have different endings for singular and plural: "knight" and "knights." Again, there is a change of ending for the genitive (possessive) case: "knight's" (the obsolete full form is "knightes") and "knights'." Most other cases are dealt with by prepositions: "to the knight" (dative); "from the knight" (ablative). Similarly, verb-endings are changed for two tenses only, past and present, the remainder being dealt with by use of the "auxiliary" verbs "to be" and "to have." Most other languages have a profusion of noun-and verb-endings to deal with different cases and tenses, and so have a lesser flexibility than English.

Phonology. Much of our speech depends for meaning on our tone of voice: "Philip is thinking" may have several meanings, depending on the stress placed on each of the words. These stresses are thus an important part of grammar, less so in English than in many other tongues: in the Sino-Tibetan languages, for example, a word may have two utterly different meanings depending upon the tone of voice in which it is said. (See also ETYMOLOGY; LANGUAGE; LINGUISTICS; MORPHEME; PHILOLOGY; PHONEME; PHONETICS; PRONUNCIATION; PUNCTUATION; SEMANTICS.)

GRAMPIANS, S edge of the central Highlands of Scotland, overlooking the Lowlands. They consist of schists, gneisses and granites, reach 3 757ft high at Ben Alder and form a range 100mi long, pierced only by deep narrow passes.

GRAMPUS, an alternative name for the KILLER WHALE, the largest of the dolphin family.

GRAMSCI, Antonio (1891–1937), Italian left-wing intellectual, cofounder (with TOGLIATTI) of the Italian Communist Party, 1921. He edited the left-wing journal *L'Ordine Nuovo* and led communists in the Chamber of Deputies (1924–26). He was arrested under fascism and imprisoned for 11 years.

GRAM'S STAIN, a stain for BACTERIA which divides them into Gram-positive and Gram-negative groups. Since the cell walls determine not only the staining difference but also behavior and ANTIBIOTIC sensitivity of bacteria, the stain has considerable medical value.

GRANADA, city in S Spain, N of the Sierra Nevada, capital of Granada Province and a former Moorish capital. Landmarks include a cathedral, university and the ALHAMBRA. Its industries are tourism and consumer goods manufacture. Pop 190 429.

GRANADA, Kingdom of, medieval Moorish kingdom in S Spain. Founded 1238 by the Nasrid Dynasty, who made GRANADA its capital, the state pursued an independent Moorish policy, and was a center of Moorish culture. In the 15th century internal dissensions furthered Castile's slow conquest, completed when BOABDIL surrendered to Ferdinand and Isabella in 1492.

GRANADOS, Enrique (1867–1916), Spanish composer and pianist who helped create a distinctively Spanish musical style. He is best known for his songs and the *Goyescas* piano pieces (1912–14), inspired by Goya's paintings, and used in one of Granados' seven operas.

GRANBY, industrial city in Canada, in S Quebec, 45mi E of Montreal. Products: textiles, plastics, furniture. There is a prominent zoo. Pop 33 958.

GRAN CHACO, lowland region in central S America, occupying 300 000sq mi between the Amazon forests and Argentinian pampa. Prone to droughts and flooding, it is mostly scrub with areas of swamp, grassland and desert.

GRAND ALLIANCE, War of the. See AUGSBURG, WAR OF THE LEAGUE OF.

GRAND ARMY OF THE REPUBLIC (GAR), fraternal society of Union Civil War veterans, founded 1866. It helped veterans and their families, and by 1890 had 400 000 members forming a powerful political pressure group that secured the Disability Pension Act. The last member died in 1956.

GRAND BANKS, underwater plateau in the N Atlantic Ocean, extending 350mi off Newfoundland, where the Labrador Current and Gulf Stream meet. Averaging 240ft in depth, the shallow waters abound in plankton that directly and indirectly support millions of food fish, notably cod. This is one of the world's richest fishing grounds.

GRAND CANAL, chief waterway of Venice, Italy. It is a natural, winding channel 2½mi long, lined by over 100 old palaces and crossed by three bridges, including the historic RIALTO Bridge.

GRAND CANAL, ancient artificial waterway in NE China, about 1200mi long, connecting Peking and Hangchow. Parts date from the 5th century BC. Once a major route, it is now largely silted up, but the S and middle parts are still in use.

GRAND CANYON, spectacular gorge cut by the Colorado R in NE Ariz. It is about 217mi long, 4–18mi wide, up to 1mi deep, and flanked by a plateau 5000–9000ft above sea level. The main canyon contains smaller canyons, peaks and mesas, and is walled by colorful, horizontal rock strata dating back to the PRECAMBRIAN era. It is an important geological site, contains a wealth of animal and plant life, and attracts 1500000 visitors a year. The most impressive part forms the 673575-acre Grand Canyon National Park.

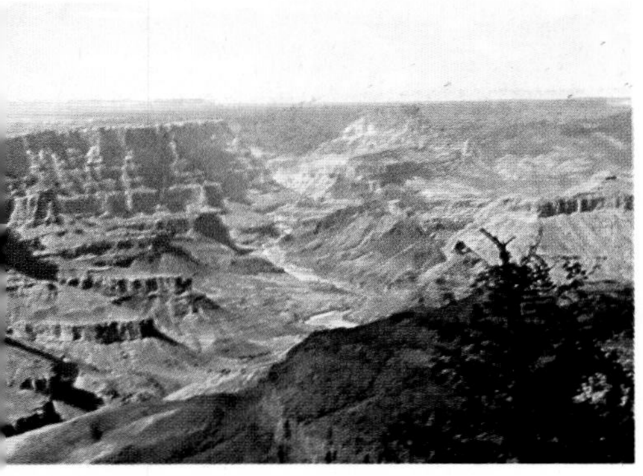

The Grand Canyon, Arizona, one of the most spectacular natural formations on earth. It is the result of erosion over millions of years, as the land around the Colorado River slowly rose.

GRAND COULEE DAM, concrete dam on the Columbia R, Wash., 85mi WNW of Spokane. Built 1934–42, it is one of the world's largest dams, providing irrigation, flood control and hydroelectric power for all the Northwest.

GRANDFATHER CLAUSE, legal device used in Southern states to deny Negroes the vote, by giving it to males with high literacy and property qualifications or to those whose fathers and grandfathers had been qualified to vote on Jan. 1, 1867 (before the 15th Amendment had enfranchised Southern blacks). First used in S.C. in 1895, it was declared unconstitutional in 1915.

GRAND FORKS, city in E N.D., seat of Grand Forks Co. and of the U. of North Dakota. Products: beet sugar, feed, flour. Pop 39008.

GRAND HAVEN, city in W Mich., on Lake Michigan, seat of Ottawa Co. Summer resort and port, with light industry. Pop 11844.

GRAND ISLAND, city in SE central Neb., seat of Hall Co., Railroad shipping center for grain and livestock. Products: processed foods, farm equipment. Pop 31269.

GRAND JUNCTION, city in W Col., seat of Mesa Co. It processes Grand Valley farm products and is a trade center for W Col. and E Ut. Pop 20170.

One of the world's largest dams, the Grand Coulee on the Columbia River, floodlit at night to provide a dramatic sense of the vast power present in the head of water behind the spillway. The hydroelectric plant has a capacity of nearly 2000 megawatts.

GRAND JURY. See JURY.

GRAND MAL. See EPILEPSY.

GRAND'MÈRE, city in Canada, in S Quebec, 20mi NNW of Trois Rivières. It has paper, pulp and textile mills and a hydroelectric plant. Pop 17144.

GRAND NATIONAL, most famous steeplechase in horse-racing, held annually since 1834 at the Aintree race course in England. The difficult and dangerous 4½mi course includes 30 jumps, and many participants fail to finish.

GRAND OLD PARTY (GOP). See REPUBLICAN PARTY.

GRAND PORTAGE NATIONAL MONUMENT, 770 acres at Grand Portage, NE Minn., on Lake Superior. The site commemorates the longest (9mi) canoe portage between Montreal and the Rockies, and a major British NORTH WEST COMPANY fur-trading center founded here in the 1780s. The National monument dates from 1960.

GRAND PRAIRIE, city in NE Texas, 13mi W of Dallas. It makes aircraft, boats and rubber goods. Pop 50904.

GRAND PRÉ, village in Canada, in W Nova Scotia, on the S coast of Minas Basin. Founded c1675, it was a settlement of ACADIA (as such the scene of Longfellow's *Evangeline*). Britain seized it in 1755.

GRAND RAPIDS, city in W Michigan, on the Grand R, seat of Kent Co. "Furniture capital of the US," it also produces machinery, tools electrical equipment, paper and chemicals. There are dozens of printing works. Pop 197649.

GRAND TETON NATIONAL PARK, spectacular area of the Rocky Mts in NW Wyo., jus S of Yellowstone National Park. It comprises major peaks of the TETON RANGE and the valley of JACKSON HOLE from which the peaks rise abruptly. Created in 1929, the park occupies c500sq mi. It is a major tourist area and wildlife preserve.

GRANDVIEW, city in W Mo., 5mi S of Kansas City. It serves a farming area. Pop 17456.

GRANDVILLE, city in W Michigan, 5mi SW of Grand Rapids. It is a farming center, with light industries. Pop 10764.

GRANGE, (Harold Edward) "Red" (1903–   ), American football player, one of the most prolific scorers of touchdowns. He played for the University of Illinois, Chicago Bears and New York Yankees, and was All-American halfback 1923–24, and quarterback 1925.

GRANGE, The, American farmers' organization, officially the National Grange of the Patrons of Husbandry. Founded as a fraternal order in 1867, in the 1870s it led the Granger Movement to protect farmers against the railroad monopolies, who fixed high prices on freight and storage. Soon individual states pioneered laws to curb these charges. Upheld in the GRANGER CASES, such laws led to government regulation of transportation and utilities. The Grange united farmers throughout the country as a political force, encouraged technical and educational exchanges and laid a basis for farm cooperatives. It is now a social and educational organization, still representing farmers' interests when necessary. (See also FARMERS' ALLIANCE.)

GRANGER CASES, six supreme court cases in 1876 which established a state's right to regulate privately-owned services affecting the public interest. The cases arose from the Granger Movement which aimed at curbing high prices imposed on farmers by business monopolies. The first and most important Granger case was *Munn* v. *Illinois*, a landmark in US law. (See also GRANGE, THE.)

GRANGER MOVEMENT. See GRANGE, THE.

GRANICUS, Battle of the, first great victory of ALEXANDER THE GREAT. In 334 BC his highly-trained troops defeated a larger Persian army, near the Granicus R in NW Asia Minor.

GRANIT, Ragnar Arthur (1900–   ), Finnish-born Swedish physiologist who shared the 1967 Nobel Prize for Physiology or Medicine with H. K. HARTLINE and G. WALD. Granit demonstrated that individual nerves in the EYE could distinguish light of different colors.

GRANITE, coarse- to medium-grained plutonic IGNEOUS ROCK, composed of FELDSPAR (orthoclase and microcline predominating over plagioclase) and QUARTZ, often containing BIOTITE and AMPHIBOLE. It is the type of the family of **granitic rocks**, plutonic rocks rich in feldspar and quartz, of which the CONTINENTS are principally made. Most granite was formed by crystallization of MAGMA, though some is METAMORPHIC, and some was formed by replacement ("granitization"). It occurs as DIKES and SILLS, large masses, and enormous BATHOLITHS. A hard, weather-resistant rock, usually pink or gray, granite is used for building, paving and road curbs.

GRANITE CITY, industrial city in SW Ill., 9mi NE of St. Louis. It makes sheet steel, metal products, chemicals and processed foods. Pop 40440.

GRAN QUIVIRA NATIONAL MONUMENT, 611-acre site in Torrance Co., central New Mexico, established in 1909. It has Pueblo ruins, and the ruins of an early Spanish mission.

GRANT, Duncan James Corrowr (1885–   ), Scottish painter and designer, whose pictures feature bright colors and bold brushwork. He was influenced by POSTIMPRESSIONISM, and his friendship with the BLOOMSBURY GROUP.

Ulysses Simpson GRANT

18th US President

Born: April 27, 1822
Died: July 23, 1885
Term of Office: March 4, 1869–March 3, 1877
Political party: Republican

GRANT, Ulysses Simpson (1822–1885), 18th president of the US 1869–77, and military leader who secured Union victory in the Civil War. A man of great personal integrity, he led an administration infiltrated by corruption.

Army career. Son of an Ohio farmer and tanner, he entered West Point in 1839, graduated four years later and first saw action in 1846 as a second lieutenant in the MEXICAN WAR. He then returned to St. Louis, and married his fiancée, Julia Dent. Though made a captain in 1853, he resigned from the army in 1854, disheartened by an uncongenial posting. For the next seven years he wandered from job to job, but on the outbreak of the Civil War became a colonel in the 21st Illinois Regiment. Promoted to brigadier general, he fought at Paducah, Ky. (1861), then won victories at forts Henry and Donelson (1862)—the first major Union successes. His subsequent victories at Shiloh, Vicksburg and Chattanooga eventually cut the Confederacy in two. Lincoln made Grant a lieutenant-general in 1864, with command of the entire Union Army and control of the Virginia campaign that eventually ended the war.

The politician. Created a full general in 1866, Grant

The characteristic flavors of different groups of wines are basically due to the different kinds of grape from which they are pressed, such as Muscadine (1), Riesling (2) and Frankenthaler (3). Every bud (4) produces a floweret (5), which, after pollination, produces a grape that will ripen in the sun, forming first one pip (6) then a second, by which time it is ready for picking (7). Any visitor to wine-growing areas will have noticed the assortment of techniques employed in training the vines (8–10). The growing vine branch (11) shows inflorescence (a), a tendril (b), the main stem (c), a side branch (d) and part of the woody stem (e).

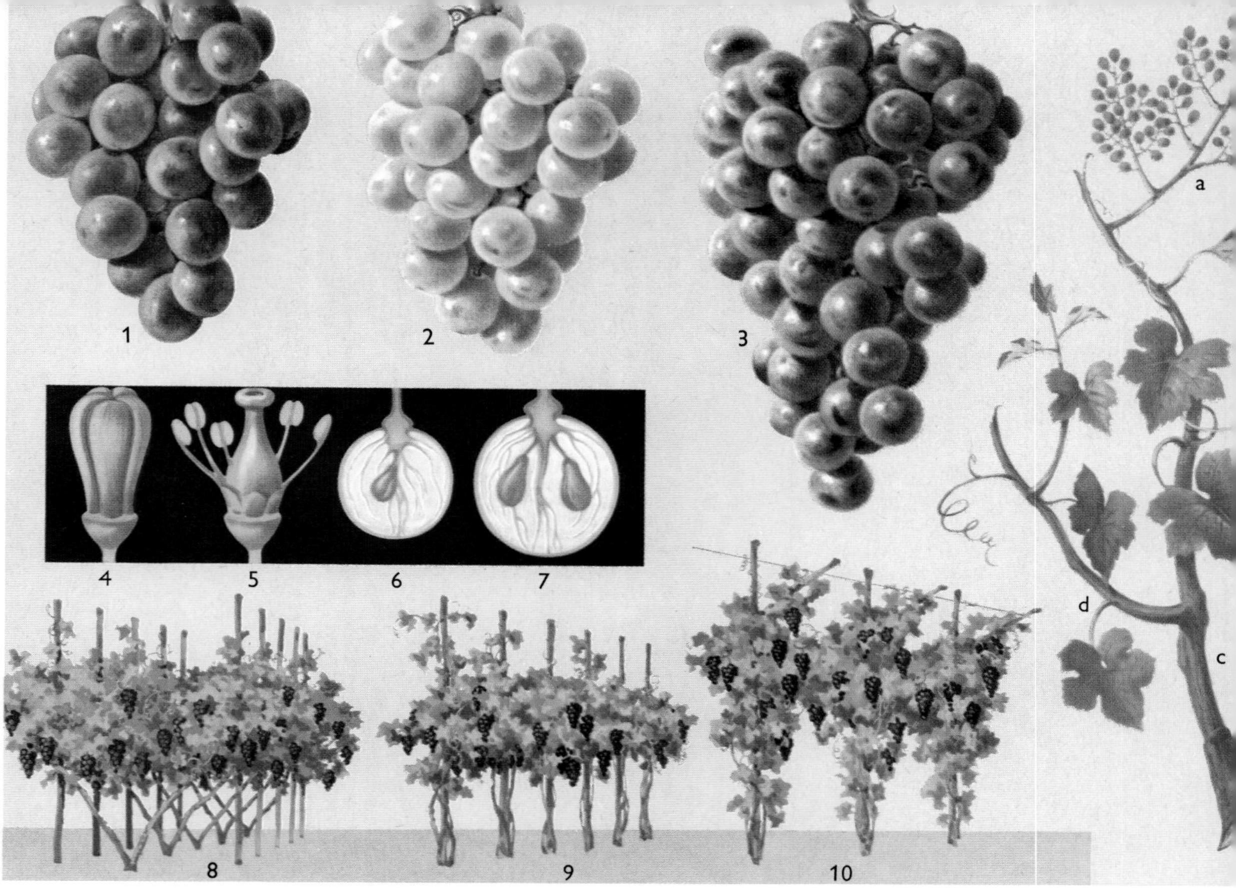

was now a national hero. He impressed Republicans by opposing President Johnson's unpopular attempt to oust Edwin M. Stanton as secretary of war and to put Grant in his place. Becoming the Republican presidential candidate, Grant defeated Democrat Horatio Seymour in the 1868 election by a small popular majority. He was reelected in 1872, defeating Horace Greeley. As president, Grant pursued a lenient RECONSTRUCTION policy, reduced the national debt and worked to prevent a currency crisis. His administration improved relations with Britain (see WASHINGTON, TREATY OF). But Grant's scheme to annex Santo Domingo foundered, and his FORCE ACTS failed to help Southern Negroes. Above all, corruption affected the government—partly because the inexperienced Grant chose personal friends rather than the most able Republicans to fill government offices. Grant's own brother-in-law helped in an attempt to corner the gold market that led to the 1869 business panic (see BLACK FRIDAY). BELKNAP resigned as secretary of war to avoid impeachment for taking bribes. The CRÉDIT MOBILIER OF AMERICA frauds and the WHISKEY RING were among other scandals, though none of these touched Grant personally. After leaving the presidency, Grant undertook a world tour, then lost all his capital in an investment swindle. Virtually penniless and suffering from throat cancer, he wrote two volumes of Civil War memoirs that helped to ensure his family's financial security.

GRANTH ("the book"), the Sikh scriptures. It consists of hymns (mainly in Punjabi or Hindi) set to music, and gathered in the early 1600s by the fifth Sikh guru, Arjan, and in 1705–06 by the tenth guru, Gobind Singh. The hymns proclaim selfless service to others as a means of uniting the soul with its maker. (See also SIKHS.)

GRANTS PASS, city in SW Ore., seat of Josephine Co. The main industry is lumbering; otherwise it is an agricultural center. Pop 12 455.

GRANT'S TOMB. See GENERAL GRANT NATIONAL MEMORIAL.

GRANULATION TISSUE, the bright red, granular tissue that develops during healing. The tissue consists initially of fine blood vessels and therefore bleeds easily. Later, fibrous tissue is laid down and a SCAR replaces the granulation tissue.

GRANVILLE-BARKER, Harley (1877–1946), English actor, director, playwright and seminal Shakespeare critic. He produced several of G. B. SHAW's plays for the first time. His best-known plays include *The Voysey Inheritance* (1905), *Waste* (1907) and *The Madras House* (1910).

GRAPE, *Vitis vinifera* and other species of the genus *Vitis*, family Vitaceae. The grapevine is a hardy deciduous climber cultivated for its edible golden-green or red-purple fruits that are used as table fruit, dried as raisins and used for making WINE. The grapevine is native to temperate regions of W Asia, N Africa and S Europe and many varieties are cultivated throughout the temperate regions of the world, France, Italy and Spain having the greatest areas planted. Grapes grow best in sandy, fertile, well-drained soils in open, sunny areas. They are propagated from cuttings or by GRAFTING. A number of insect pests and diseases can cause serious losses, notably grape PHYLLOXERA, an insect pest.

GRAPE-IVY, *Cissus rhombifolia*, a woody, evergreen climber that is popular as a house plant and tolerates some neglect. It should receive a few hours sun in the winter and adapts well to light from a north window or from fluorescent tubes. The soil should be kept evenly moist, avoiding extreme wetness or dryness; it grows well at normal house temperatures, suffering above 24°C (75°F). Propagation is by shoot tip cuttings. Family: Vitidaceae. (See also KANGAROO VINE.)

GRAPEFRUIT, *Citrus paradisi*, tree that produces the popular yellow CITRUS fruits. Probably native to Jamaica, it is now extensively grown in the US, West Indies, Israel, Jordan, South Africa and Brazil.

GRAPHITE, allotrope of CARBON (see ALLOTROPY), forming soft, black, metallic crystals, in which the atoms are arranged in layers of hexagons that easily slide over each other. It is found naturally in GNEISS and SCHIST, and synthesized from COKE. Graphite is a good conductor of HEAT and ELECTRICITY. It is used for ELECTRODES, nuclear-reactor moderators and lubricants. subl 3660°C, sg 2.25 (20°C).

GRAPHOLOGY, the study of handwriting, particularly the deduction, from its form, of information about the character of the writer.

GRAPHS, plottings of sets of points whose coordinates are of the form $(x, f(x))$, where $f(x)$ is a FUNCTION of x (see ANALYTIC GEOMETRY). These points may define a CURVE or straight LINE. Graphs are a powerful tool of STATISTICS, since it is often profitable to plot one variable (such as age) along one axis, against another (such as height) plotted along the other (see also NORMAL DISTRIBUTION): the points on statistical graphs need not define a continuous curve (see HISTOGRAM). The AXES on a graph are not always marked off regularly: in some cases it is useful to mark off one or both on a nonlinear scale—e.g., using logarithmic (see LOGARITHM) or exponential (see EXPONENT) scales.

GRAPTOLITES, a class of extinct marine colonial organisms superficially resembling the HYDROZOA. The feeding and reproductive polyps were protected by an external skeleton of chitin. Graptolites are thought to be related to early CHORDATES.

GRASS, Günter Wilhelm (1927–), German novelist. His works, deeply affected by the post-WWII sense of national guilt, are usually centered around grotesque motifs with a strong moral content. His best-known works include *The Tin Drum* (1959), *Dog Years* (1963) and *Local Anaesthetic* (1969).

GRASSE, François Joseph Paul, Comte de (1722–1788), French naval commander whose fleet made possible Washington's decisive victory over the British at the siege of YORKTOWN (1781). Grasse landed 3 000 troops to aid the siege, and remained off Chesapeake Bay to keep the British fleet from aiding the British force under Cornwallis.

GRASSES, large group of ANGIOSPERMS that are of great importance to man. Strictly speaking grasses only include those species belonging to the family Graminae, but the name applies to any plant with a similar growth habit. Grasses are wind- or self-pollinated and have hollow or pithy, jointed stems, bearing lanceolate leaves. The fruit is a GRAIN. Grasses include CEREAL CROPS, such as WHEAT, RICE and CORN, SUGARCANE, SORGHUM, MILLET and BAMBOO.

GRASSHOPPERS, active jumping INSECTS related to the CRICKETS. The hindlegs are greatly enlarged for jumping. Adults usually have two pairs of fully-developed wings; these are lacking in immature stages. Many grasshoppers can produce sounds by rubbing the hind legs against the folded wings. Grasshoppers feed entirely on grasses and other plants. A few species form large migratory swarms and are known as LOCUSTS.

GRASSLAND, the areas of the earth whose predominant type of vegetation consists of GRASSES, rainfall being generally insufficient to support higher plant forms. There are three main types: SAVANNA, or tropical grassland, has coarse grasses growing 1m to 4m high, occasional clumps of trees and some shrubs; it is found in parts of Africa and South America. PRAIRIE has tall, deep-rooted grasses and is found in Middle and North America, Argentina, the Ukraine, South Africa and N Australia. STEPPES have short grasses and are found mainly in Central Asia. Grasslands are of great economic importance as they provide food for domestic animals and often excellent cropland for cultivation.

GRATIAN, early 12th-century Italian monk, who founded CANON LAW with his *Concordia discordantium canonum* (c1140), the first attempt to resolve over 3000 conflicting texts on ecclesiastical discipline.

GRATTAN, Henry (1746–1820), Irish nationalist politician. An eloquent champion of economic reform and Roman Catholic emancipation, he served both in the Irish and British parliaments.

GRAVEL, in geology, a collection of rock particles whose diameter ranges from 2mm to 4mm. In general terms, gravel particles may be as large as pebbles. Gravel is used commercially in the making of CONCRETE (see also CONGLOMERATE; SAND).

GRAVES, Morris Cole (1910–), US painter whose interest in Eastern art and American Indian mythology is seen in his delicate images of, for example, blind birds, pine trees and waves. His best-known work is probably the *Little Known Bird of the Inner Eye* (1941).

GRAVES, Robert James (1796–1853), Irish physician remembered for his work on exophthalmic GOITRE (Graves' disease).

GRAVES, Robert Ranke (1895–), English poet and novelist, best known for his novels set in imperial Rome, *I, Claudius* (1934) and *Claudius the God* (1934). Less popular but equally successful was *Goodbye to All That* (1929) which described his experiences in WWI. He was professor of poetry at Oxford from 1961–66.

GRAVIMETER, an instrument for detecting small variations in the earth's gravitational field, frequently used in mineral and oil prospecting. Variations in the gravitational FORCE on a weight suspended from a SPRING cause it to stretch or be deflected in a way which is then measured.

GRAVIMETRIC ANALYSIS, method of quantitative chemical ANALYSIS in which the substance to be estimated is converted to a substance which can be separated pure and entire, and which is then weighed. Commonly a highly insoluble precipitate is formed, filtered off, washed and dried (see DEHYDRATION). The weight of substance sought is calculated from the weight and composition of the precipitate.

GRAVITATION, one of the fundamental forces of nature, the force of attraction existing between all MATTER. It is much weaker than the nuclear or electromagnetic forces and plays no part in the internal structure of matter. Its importance lies in its long range and in its involving all masses. It plays a vital role in the behavior of the UNIVERSE: the gravitational attraction of the SUN keeps the PLANETS in their orbits, and gravitation holds the matter in a STAR together. NEWTON's **law of universal gravitation** states that the attractive FORCE F between two bodies of MASSES M_1 and M_2 separated by distance d is $F = GM_1M_2/d^2$ where G is the **Universal Gravitational Constant** (6.670×10^{-11} N m^2 kg^{-2}). The force of gravity on the earth is a special case of the attraction between masses and causes bodies to fall toward the center of the earth with a uniform ACCELERATION $g = GM/R^2$ where R and M are the radius and mass of the earth. Assuming, with Newton, that the inertial mass of a body (that which is operative in the laws of motion) is identical with its gravitational mass, application of the second law of motion gives the WEIGHT of a body of mass m, the force with which the earth attracts that body, as mg. Bodies on the earth and moon thus have the same mass but different weights. Again, the gravitational force on a body is proportional to its mass but is independent of the type of material it is. Newton's theory explains most of the observed motions of the planets and the TIDES and is still sufficiently accurate for most applications. The Newtonian analysis of gravitation remained unchallenged until, in the early 20th century, EINSTEIN introduced radically new concepts in his theory of general RELATIVITY. According to this, mass deforms the geometrical properties of the space around it. Einstein reaffirmed Newton's assumption regarding the equivalence of gravitational and inertial mass, proposing that it was impossible to distinguish experimentally between an accelerated coordinate system and a local gravitational field. From this he predicted that LIGHT would be found to be deflected toward massive bodies by their gravitational fields and this effect indeed was observed for starlight passing close to the sun. It was also predicted that accelerated matter should emit gravitational waves with the velocity of light but the existence of these has not as yet been demonstrated.

GRAVITY. See GRAVITATION.

GRAVURE. See PRINTING.

GRAY, Asa (1810–1888), the foremost of 19th-century US botanists. Being a prominent Protestant layman, his advocacy of the Darwinian thesis carried special force. However, he never accepted the materialist interpretation of the evolutionary mechanism and taught that NATURAL SELECTION was indeed consistent with a divine TELEOLOGY.

GRAY, Elisha (1835–1901', US inventor whose claim to have invented the device used by BELL in his telephone led to a famous legal battle. The invention appears to have been almost simultaneous; Gray's device was in fact the more practical of the two, but the legal battle was won by Bell.

GRAY, George (1840–1925), US jurist, a senator 1885–99. After a distinguished legal career he entered the Senate as a Democrat and was known for his work on foreign relations, including the American–Mexican Commission of 1916.

GRAY, Robert (1755–1806), sea captain, first American to circumnavigate the world. Between 1787–90 Gray sailed westward around the world, starting from Boston. In 1792 he penetrated the mouth of the Columbia R and established the American claim to the Oregon territory.

GRAY, Thomas (1716–1771), English poet. His *Elegy Written in a Country Churchyard* (1750) is one of the most popular English poems; among his other main works are the odes *The Progress of Poesy* and *The Bard* (both 1757).

GRAYLAG GOOSE, *Anser anser*, the type species of the gray GEESE, from which the barnyard goose was domesticated. The largest of the true geese, it breeds on the tundra of arctic or subarctic regions, migrating long distances to temperate areas in the fall.

GRAYLING, *Thymallus thymallus*, a salmon-like freshwater fish found in arctic and temperate regions. A river fish, the grayling feeds on insects, worms and snails. Normally a gray color, in the breeding season the body has a green-gold sheen and the dorsal fins and tail become deep purple.

GRAY MATTER, the parts of BRAIN that are rich in nerve-cell bodies, as opposed to white matter which is mainly nerve fibers, sheathed by MYELIN. The cerebral cortex, basal ganglia, nuclei of the brain stem and the center of the SPINAL CORD are major gray areas.

GRAY SEAL, or Atlantic seal, *Halichoerus grypus*, a large SEAL up to 3m (10ft) in length. This mammal is now becoming increasingly rare, the bulk of the population being restricted to the northern British Isles. The gray seal pup has a white coat at birth, replaced later by the typical gray coat with dark spots.

GRAYWACKE. See CONGLOMERATE.

GRAZ, second largest city in Austria, on the Mur R, 90mi SW of Vienna. An ancient city, Graz today is a commercial and industrial center producing iron and steel, paper, textiles and chemicals. Pop 248 500.

GREASE. See LUBRICATION.

GREASEWOOD, popular name for shrubs of the genus *Sarcobatus*, family Chenopodiaceae, native to North America. *Sarcobatus vermiculatus*, the black greasewood, grows in the desert plains of the western US. The CREOSOTE BUSH is also called greasewood.

GREAT AMERICAN DESERT, a term applied to the desert areas of SW US and N Mexico. Beginning in S Cal., it stretches N along the E side of the Sierra Nevada into Ida. and Ore. It continues E to the Rockies and S into Mexico where the Lower California peninsula and the E shore of the Gulf of California are desert.

GREAT AUK, *Alca impennis*, an extinct flightless seabird of the North Atlantic. About the size of a domestic goose, it was highly adapted to aquatic life: the legs were set well back for swimming and it was very ungainly on land. It was thus very vulnerable to predation by man, and it is thought that hunting contributed greatly to its extinction. The last Great Auk was recorded in 1844.

GREAT AUSTRALIAN BIGHT, large bay on the S coast of Australia, about 600mi wide. It lies off the

A desert expanse in southwest Arizona, part of the Great American Desert. Typical of the hottest, dryest parts of America, country such as this receives barely 3in of rain a year.

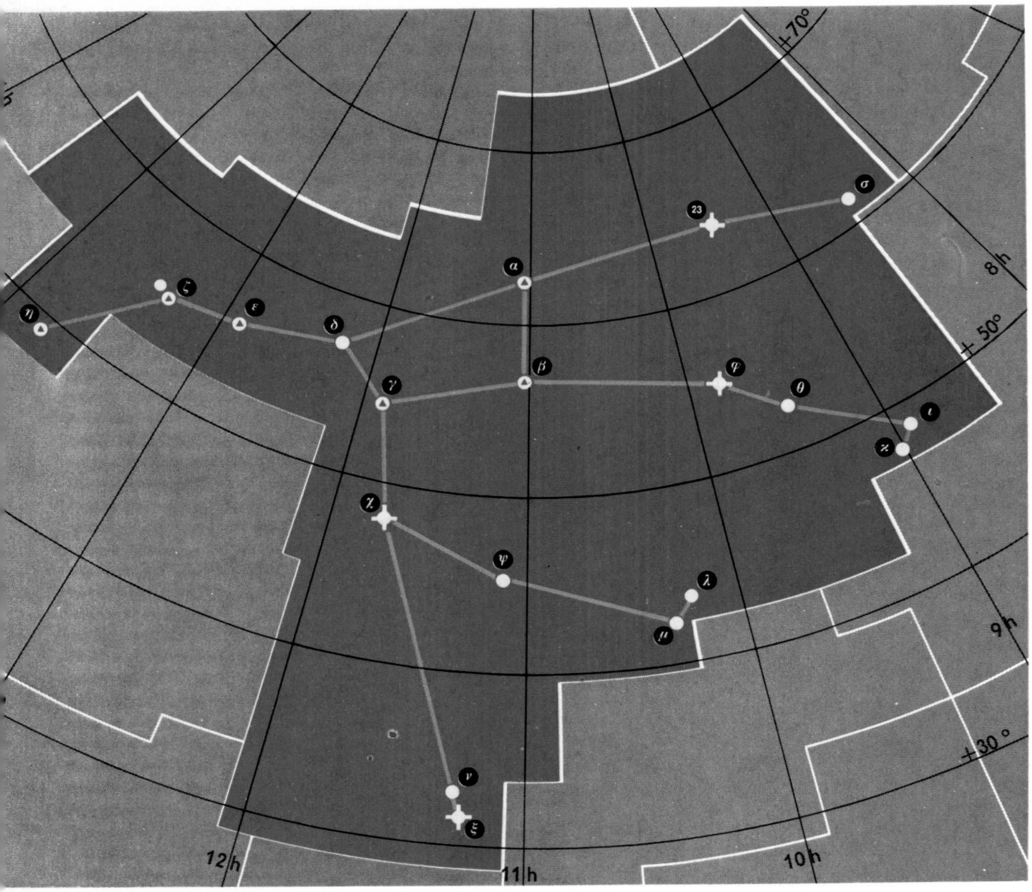

The Great Bear (Ursa Major) is one of the most familiar constellations of the Northern hemisphere. Its seven brightest stars form the plow or "big dipper." The two brightest (α and β) point due north.

Nullarbor Plain and is skirted by 200ft high cliffs. It is renowned for its winter storms.

GREAT AWAKENING, an intense and widespread religious REVIVAL in 18th-century America, forming part of the EVANGELICAL REVIVAL. Starting in N.J. (c1726), the movement quickly spread across New England. In reaction to the prevailing rationalism and formalism, its leaders—notably Jonathan EDWARDS and George WHITEFIELD—preached evangelical CALVINISM and discouraged excessive emotionalism. The 1740s saw the zenith of the Awakening, which led to the rapid growth of the Presbyterian, Baptist and Methodist churches, continuing to the end of the century. A similar revival beginning in the 1790s is known as the Second Great Awakening.

GREAT BARRIER REEF, series of massive coral reefs off the NE coast of Australia, extending for about 1 250mi. The reef, which is the world's largest coral formation, can only be safely crossed at certain passages, the chief of which is Raines Inlet.

GREAT BASIN, desert region in the W US, occupying W Ut., E Cal., S Ore., S Ida. and nearly all of Nev. The basin contains Death Valley, Reno, Las Vegas and Salt Lake City. Mineral mining and agriculture are the main industries.

GREAT BEAR (Ursa Major), a large N Hemisphere constellation containing the seven bright stars known as the **Plow** or **Big Dipper**. Two of these, the **Pointers**, form roughly a straight line with POLARIS and are hence of navigational importance. Five stars of the Plow are, with SIRIUS, members of a widely separated GALACTIC CLUSTER.

GREAT BEAR LAKE, in Northwest Territories, Canada. The lake is about 200mi by 120mi and is frozen for several months of the year. On the E shore is Port Radium, the site of important uranium ore deposits, now running low.

GREAT BEND, city on the Arkansas R in central Kan., seat of Barton Co. It processes locally-produced grain and oil. Pop 16 133.

Official Name: United Kingdom of Great Britain and Northern Ireland
Capital: London
Area: 94 217sq mi
Population: 55 348 364
Languages: English; Welsh, Gaelic
Religions: Church of England, Roman Catholic, Church of Scotland
Monetary Unit(s): 1 Pound = 100 pence

GREAT BRITAIN, or the United Kingdom of Great Britain and Northern Ireland, a constitutional monarchy of NW Europe occupying the whole of the British Isles except the Republic of Ireland. The United Kingdom (UK) thus comprises England, Scotland and Wales and Northern Ireland. The Isle of Man and the Channel Islands are both Crown dependencies and are not strictly part of the UK. Great Britain is also the name of the largest of the British Isles, comprising mainland England, Scotland and Wales.

Land. England, largest country in the UK, has a hilly backbone—the Pennines—running N from Derbyshire to the Scottish border. This extends from the Solway Firth to Berwick-upon-Tweed. W of the N Pennines (Cross Fell, 2 930ft), is the scenic Lake District, set amid the Cumbrian Mts, and containing England's highest point (Scafell Pike, 3 210ft) and largest lake (Windermere 5.69sq mi). Lowlands, sometimes with low hills, stretch across the rest of England. Among them are the fertile Fens bordering on the Wash and, SE of the Chiltern Hills, the London basin with the Thames R.

Scotland has rolling southern uplands, and fertile central lowlands deeply penetrated by the firths (estuaries) of the Clyde R (leading to Glasgow) and the Forth R (leading past Edinburgh, the capital city). The Tay (118mi) is Scotland's longest river. N of the Ochil hills are the rugged Scottish Highlands. Ben Nevis (4 406ft), in the Grampian Mts, is the highest peak in the British Isles. SE of Glen More (the Great Glen) and its chain of lochs, are the Cairngorm Mts (Ben Macdhui, 4 296ft). Scotland's many islands include the Inner and Outer Hebrides to the NW and the Orkney and Shetland groups to the N.

Wales centers on the Cambrian Mts (Snowdon 3 560ft). The many rivers flowing from the Welsh massif include the Severn (220mi), the UK's longest river.

Northern Ireland is often called Ulster because it occupies most of that ancient province. Lough Neagh (153sq mi) is the largest lake in the British Isles. To the SE are the granite Mourne Mts (Slieve Donard, 2 796ft). The Erne R drains the SW.

Climate. Britain enjoys a mainly mild climate with changeable weather. The warm N Atlantic Drift and prevailing westerly winds are major influences. Rainfall, heaviest in the W and mountains, averages 40in yearly. Winter temperatures average 40°F, summer averages ranging from 54°F in the far N, to 61°F in the usually warmer S.

People. With an estimated population of over 57 million, the UK is one of the world's most densely populated countries. More than 46 million live in England. Most British are urban-dwelling, with London, the nation's capital, the largest of some eight major conurbations.

As a result of immigration the UK now has a multiracial society. Mainly colored immigrants from India, Pakistan, the West Indies and other Commonwealth countries number at least 1 500 000.

Government. MAGNA CARTA and the English CIVIL WAR checked the power of the monarch. Cabinet government and parliamentary democracy developed during the 18th and 19th centuries. Today the supreme legislative body is Parliament, comprising the House of Commons, whose 630 members are elected for a five-year term by all citizens over 18, and the House of Lords with about 1 078 members. The government is conducted by a prime minister and cabinet, usually provided by the majority party in the Commons from among its members of Parliament.

Culture and Beliefs. Education is free and compulsory from 5 to 16. English is the universal language, but Welsh is widely spoken in Wales, and Gaelic survives in Scotland. There are two established churches, the CHURCH OF ENGLAND and CHURCH OF SCOTLAND. The many other religious groups include Roman Catholics, Methodists, Baptists, Unitarians, Congregationalists, Quakers, Jews and Muslims.

Economy. Scene of the world's first industrial revolution in the 18th century, the UK based its economic development on its coal and iron deposits. Recently North Sea oil and natural gas have been exploited. Industrial raw materials and food, however, often have to be imported. (British farms, though efficient, provide only some 50% of the nation's food.) To pay for imports the UK exports manufactured goods and provides services like banking, insurance and shipping. Major industries include iron and steel, engineering, textiles, chemicals and shipbuilding. Most industries are privately owned, but some of the most important, like coal-mining, iron and steel, electric power, railroads and the chief airlines, are wholly or partly owned by the state. Since WWII the UK has failed to keep pace in economic growth with other W European countries. Membership of the EEC (1973) did not solve her chronic balance of payments difficulties and in 1976 the problem of inflation was exacerbated by a severe drought.

History. After the Roman occupation (c100–400 AD) England was invaded by Angles, Saxons, Jutes and Danes. The Norman conquest (1066) introduced the feudal system and the first centralization of power. Wales, conquered in 1282, was legally joined to England in 1536. Scotland was united with England under the monarchy of James VI and I (1603) and then by Act of Union (1707). Northern Ireland remained part of the UK after the S became independent (1922).

Maritime expansion began under Elizabeth I (1558–1603) and reached its height in the 1700s and 1800s, building up the 19th-century British Empire. British power was greatly weakened by both world wars, and with successive grants of independence from 1945, the empire was transformed into the Commonwealth of Nations. Remaining colonies include the Falkland Islands (claimed by Argentina), Gibraltar (claimed by Spain) and Hong Kong.

One of the most colorful and popular traditions in England is the "Trooping of the Colour" ceremony on the reigning monarch's official birthday, when regiments of the royal guard parade in traditional uniform.

GREAT CIRCLE ROUTES, routes of prime importance in air travel as they describe the shortest distances between two points on the earth's surface. Great circles are circles on the surface of a sphere whose centers coincide with the center of the sphere (see SPHERICAL GEOMETRY): the EQUATOR is an example (see also LATITUDE AND LONGITUDE). Great circle navigation is aided by use of MAPS drawn to a **gnomonic projection**, where the center of PERSPECTIVE is the center of the earth. On such maps, great circles appear as straight lines.

GREAT DANE, breed of large dog, standing up to 36in at the shoulder and weighing up to 150lb. The Great Dane, first developed in Germany, has a short smooth coat and is bred in blue, black, brindle, fawn and black-and-white.

GREAT DEPRESSION, a period of US and world economic depression during the 1930s which was immediately precipitated by the disastrous stockmarket collapse in Wall Street on BLACK FRIDAY, Oct. 29, 1929. This heralded a period of high unemployment, failing businesses and banks and falling agricultural prices. Millions of workers were unemployed during the period (some 16 million in the US alone in 1933). There were many causes of the depression: easy credit had led to widespread stock speculation; the world had not completely recovered from WWI; US economic policies under President HOOVER had created domestic overproduction and less foreign trade. Franklin ROOSEVELT, elected president in 1932, brought in the NEW DEAL measures, but full recovery of the economy only occurred with the beginnings of defense spending immediately prior to WWII.

GREAT DIVIDE. See CONTINENTAL DIVIDE.

GREAT EASTERN, a revolutionary British steamship constructed of iron and designed by Isambard Kingdom BRUNEL. Launched in 1858, it was four times larger than any other contemporary ship, with room for 4 000 passengers and displacing 22 500 tons.

GREAT ELECTOR. See FREDERICK WILLIAM.

GREAT FALLS, city in N central Mont., seat of Cascade Co., on the Missouri R, E of the Rocky Mts. It is a mining and agricultural center. Pop 60 091.

GREAT LAKES, chain of five freshwater lakes in North America, forming the largest lake group in the world and covering an area of 95 170sq mi. From E to W the lakes are: Ontario, Erie, Huron, Michigan and Superior. They are connected by several channels, forming a waterway including the St. Lawrence R that stretches from Duluth, Minn., on Lake Superior to the Atlantic. The lake system is used for the transportation of iron ore, steel, petroleum, coal, grain and heavy manufactured goods. Trading ports on the waterways include Duluth, Chicago, Detroit, Cleveland, Buffalo, Port Arthur, Toronto and Montreal. In recent years, the lakes, particularly Lake Erie, have suffered from serious pollution.

GREAT MEADOWS, Battle of, a battle fought 10mi SE of Uniontown, SW Pa., early in the FRENCH AND INDIAN WAR, on July 3, 1754. George Washington attempted to take Fort Duquesne, but had to surrender to a superior force of French and Indians.

GREAT MOTHER, in ancient religions, a goddess worshiped as the mother of all life, and hence as the source of earth's fertility. In some cults, a male god, for example ADONIS, was also worshiped. The idea of a Great Mother is familiar in most countries and religions, from the ancient CYBELE to the Greek DEMETER and Roman CERES, to the Virgin Mary.

GREAT NECK, a residential village, SE N.Y., on N shore of Long Island, 15mi NE of New York City. Pop 10 724.

GREAT PLAINS, large plateau in W central North America, extending for over 1 500mi from the Saskatchewan R in NW Canada to the Rio Grande in Mexico and the Gulf coastal plain in the S US. The plateau slopes gently downwards from the Rockies in the W, extending about 400mi E. The natural vegetation is buffalo grass, and the area generally has hot summers and cold winters with an average annual rainfall of 20in. The plains are known as the "granary of the world" owing to their vast wheat production; livestock is also important.

GREAT PYRENEES, breed of large dog, thought to have been developed from the Tibetan mastiff. Originally a shepherd and guard dog, it is a large animal, standing up to 32in at the shoulder and weighing up to 125lb. The coat is thick and in some cases wavy.

GREAT RIFT VALLEY, a large depression or geological fault extending more than 3 000mi from N Syria to SE Africa. In Asia, the Sea of Galilee, the Jordan R, the Gulf of Aqaba, the Red Sea and the Gulf of Aden are in the Great Rift Valley. In Africa the valley ranges across Ethiopia, Kenya, Tanzania and Malawi to the Zambesi R in Mozambique.

GREAT SALT LAKE, a shallow saline inland sea in NW Ut., about 5mi NW of Salt Lake City. Its size and depth vary yearly, but on average the lake is 72mi long and 30mi across at its widest point, with a maximum depth of 27ft. It is the largest brine lake in North America. Industrial plants along the shore extract some 300 000 tons of salt from the lake every year, and plans are under way for tapping other mineral resources.

GREAT SALT LAKE DESERT, a salt desert in NW Ut., about 140mi long by 80mi wide, bordering on the SW corner of Great Salt Lake. The Bonneville Salt Flats, famous as an auto racing site, occupy its W central area.

GREAT SAND DUNES NATIONAL MONUMENT, about 35 000 acres in S Col., in San Luis Park, Sangre de Cristo Mts, containing the largest, highest inland sand dunes in the US. The monument was established in 1932.

GREAT SCHISM, two divisions in the Christian Church. The first was the breach between the EASTERN CHURCH and the WESTERN CHURCH. Long-standing divergences in tradition, combined with political and theological disputes, came to a head in 1054 when Pope Leo IX sent legates to refuse the title of Ecumenical Patriarch to the Patriarch of Constantinople and to demand acceptance of the *filioque* ("and from the Son") clause in the Nicene Creed (see HOLY SPIRIT). The Patriarch refused and rejected the claim of papal supremacy. Reciprocal excommunications and anathemas followed. Later Councils were unsuccessful in healing the breach.

The second Great Schism was the division within the Roman Catholic Church from 1378 to 1417, when there were two or three rival popes and antipopes (see PAPACY), each with his nationalistic following. The Council of Constance ended the schism by electing Martin V sole pope.

GREAT SLAVE LAKE, large lake in the Northwest Territories, Canada. Fed by the Slave and Hay rivers and drained by the Mackenzie, it covers about 11 000sq mi. Lead, gold and zinc mines are located on its shores, and there are important fisheries.

GREAT SMOKY MOUNTAINS, range of the Appalachian Mts, forming the border between N.C. and Tenn. The "Great Smokies" are almost entirely within the 800sq mi Great Smoky Mountains National Park, established 1934. The mountain valleys are often filled with a smoky-blue haze, from which the name of the range derives.

GREAT SPIRIT. See MANITOU.

GREAT STONE FACE, a stone profile formed by erosion on Profile Mt in the Franconia range of the White Mts, N N.H. Also known as the "Old Man of the Mountain," the Great Stone Face is a tourist attraction.

GREAT TREK, a migration between 1835 and 1845 of about 14 000 Afrikaners out of Cape Colony, South Africa, to escape British domination. They set up Natal, but when in 1843 it was taken by Britain, they trekked on across the Drakensberg Mts to form the ORANGE FREE STATE and the TRANSVAAL.

GREAT WALL OF CHINA, the world's longest wall fortification, N China. It extends over 1 500mi, roughly following the S border of the Mongolian

The Great Wall of China, the largest fortification ever built. Dating from the 4th century BC, it was substantially rebuilt in the 15th and 16th centuries.

plain. Construction was begun in the CH'IN dynasty to defend China against invasion from the N and mostly completed during the MING dynasty. Its average height is 25ft; it is wide enough (about 12ft) for horsemen to ride along it.

GREBES, a group of highly specialized aquatic birds all closely related; family: Podicipedidae. They are diving birds of lakes or coastal waters; the feet are not webbed but "lobed" with flaps along the toes. Many of the grebes are highly ornamental birds, brightly colored and bearing tufts or crests. Courtship displays are often complex and extremely spectacular. All grebes eat quantities of their own feathers which collect around fishbones in the gut allowing these indigestible remains to be formed into a pellet and cast.

GRECHKO, Andrei Antonovich (1903–1976), Russian marshal; Soviet minister of defense from 1967. He commanded Soviet troops in East Germany (1953) and organized the invasion of Czechoslovakia (1968). He became a member of the POLITBURO in 1973.

GRECO, El (1541–1614), one of the greatest and most individual Spanish painters of religious subjects, born Domenikos Theotokopoulos. First in Venice, where he was influenced by TINTORETTO, and later in Toledo, Spain, he developed his distinctive style of painting, characterized by dramatically elongated figures and contrasting colors. Among his most famous works are *The Burial of the Count of Orgaz* (1586), the *Portrait of Cardinal Niño de Guevara* (c1600), and *View of Toledo* (1608).

Official Name: Greece
Capital: Athens
Area: 50 943sq mi
Population: 8 957 000
Languages: Greek
Religions: Greek Orthodox; Muslim
Monetary Unit(s): 1 Drachma = 100 leptae

GREECE, a European republic which occupies the S part of the Balkan peninsula and the surrounding islands in the Ionian, Mediterranean and Aegean seas. Of the country's total land area, almost 20% is accounted for by islands, among them Corfu, the Ionian Isles, Crete, the Cyclades, Sporades and Dodecanese. Over 75% of the land is mountainous; the Pindus range runs SE down the length of the country and then continues S into the Peloponnesus. The S and coastal areas of Greece have hot summers and mild winters, but Macedonia and the mountainous northern interior have cold winters. Much of Greece receives only about 15in of rain a year, but W Greece can receive as much as 50in.

People and Economy. The Greek people, who call themselves Hellenes, are a racial mixture of the many peoples who invaded the Balkans before and after classical times. Language and culture, rather than race, define the Greeks. Half of Greece's population lives in rural communities of fewer than 2 000 inhabitants, and about 48% is engaged in agriculture. In the last two decades there has been a trend towards urbanization. The capital, Athens, with its port Piraeus, is the largest city. The official language is modern Greek. Religious life is dominated by the Greek Orthodox Church. Elementary and secondary education are free, but private secondary schools are widespread. The country's two biggest universities are at Athens and Salonika.

The Bouzouki (small lute) is a traditional Greek instrument used in folk music; local resinated wine (*retsina*) completes this Greek café scene.

The leading farm products are fruit and vegetables, wheat, cotton, tobacco, wine and olive oil, but Greece is not self-sufficient in food. Both sheep and goats are raised in large numbers. The country is rich in mineral resources which have not been fully exploited. The bulk of the country's manufacturing is located in or near Athens, but efforts are being made to develop industrialization and thus provide a wider economic base for future growth. Greece has traditionally had a prosperous shipping industry; in 1973 it merchant fleet ranked fifth in the world. In recent years tourism has become increasingly important to Greece's economy. In 1962 Greece signed an association agreement establishing a customs union with the European Economic Community.

History. It was not until after the War of Independence (1821–32) that an independent Greece was established with a constitutional monarchy. Thereafter Greece was characterized by political instability and conflict between monarchists and republicans. In WWI the country fought against Germany and Turkey. During WWII Greece was invaded by Germany in 1941 and occupied until Oct. 1944. A civil war was fought between 1944 and 1949, and US intervention was a major factor in ensuring the victory of the monarchists over communist and other left-wing groups. Political instability continued during the 1950s and 1960s leading to a military coup and eventual dictatorship in April 1967. The monarchy was abolished in July 1973, and another military coup in Nov. of that year overthrew the dictatorship. In 1974 the Greek people voted for a constitutional republic rather than a reinstatement of the monarchy and a new constitution was adopted in June 1975.

GREECE, Ancient, the independent cities and states of classical times occupying the Balkan peninsula and the surrounding islands. The name Greece comes from the Greek *graikoi*—the original inhabitants of the area around Dodona, the most ancient shrine of ZEUS. The Greeks called their land Hellas and themselves Hellenes. Ancient Greek culture is recognized as profoundly significant for Western man, for it provided the foundation of civilization in the West.

Greece was settled by about 3500 BC, and the Greek people probably moved into the area around 2000 BC. These settlers were strongly influenced by the MINOAN CIVILIZATION on the island of Crete. In the next few centuries the Mycenaean Civilization (named after the city of Mycenae on the mainland; see AEGEAN CIVILIZATION) flourished (1600–1200 BC). The writings of HOMER provide a vivid picture of Mycenaean times. In the period between 1200–750 BC (known as the "Dark Ages" of Greek history), Dorian invaders overwhelmed the culture of Mycenae, bringing with them the knowledge of working with iron. In the 8th and 7th centuries the first Greek CITY-STATES emerged, generally consisting of a fortified hilltop such as the Athenian ACROPOLIS and the surrounding market town and countryside. Trade with Egypt, Syria and Phoenicia grew and the city-states formed colonies throughout the Mediterranean area. From the 6th century ATHENS and SPARTA became the two most powerful city-states, embodying, respectively, a liberal and an authoritarian approach to government and society. Athens became a DEMOCRACY; Sparta became a military state. The 5th century BC began with attempted invasions of Greece by the Persians. The Persians were defeated on land at the Battles of Marathon (490 BC) and Plataea (479 BC) and at sea near Salamis. Athens emerged as the undisputed leader of Greece and led a number of Ionian cities in the formation of the DELIAN LEAGUE, whose purpose was to protect commerce and resist any further Persian invasions. From this league the Athenian empire emerged. The latter half of the 5th century, especially during PERICLES' leadership, was the Golden Age of Athens—a period of unparalleled cultural activity ranging from the building of the PARTHENON (see also PHIDIAS) to the ideas of SOCRATES. However, growing resentment against Athenian power led eventually to Athens' defeat by Sparta in

The temple of Athena Nikè, dating from 425 BC, on the Acropolis in Athens, is an excellent example of the Ionic style. The building has been heavily restored, but part of the original frieze remains.

the PELOPONNESIAN WAR (431–404 BC).

In the 4th century BC Athens' artistic and intellectual achievements continued to flourish under PLATO, ARISTOTLE, the sculptor PRAXITELES and others. However, in 338 BC Philip of Macedon became ruler of Greece, depriving the people of political liberty they were not to regain for more than 2000 years. Philip's son Alexander the Great (356–323 BC) carried out a plan of conquest which would have far-reaching effects on the world. In the period that followed his death, the HELLENISTIC AGE, Greek culture and civilization spread over all the known world. Macedonia controlled Greece for more than a hundred years, although some city-states joined two confederations to restore a measure of their lost power: the Aetolian League (see AETOLIA) and the Achaean League (see ACHAEANS).

Rome first became involved in Greek affairs in 220 BC in support of the Aetolian League against Macedonia, and in 197 BC the leagues helped the Romans defeat Macedonia. The Romans were hailed as liberators, but afte the revolt of the Achaean League against Rome (146 BC), Greece was dominated by Rome and in 27 BC became the Roman province of Achaea. Greece still remained the cultural and intellectual center of the Mediterranean world, but economically and politically was unable to regain her former power. From 395 AD when the Roman Empire was divided into W and E, Greece was incorporated into the BYZANTINE EMPIRE (395–1453 AD). In the DARK AGES (from the 4th to the 9th centuries), Greece suffered from barbarian incursions, and after the fall of Constantinople in 1453 she became part of the Turkish OTTOMAN EMPIRE.

GREEK, the language of ancient and modern Greece, one of the oldest INDO-EUROPEAN LANGUAGES. The ancient and modern tongues use the same alphabet (which the Greeks adopted from the Phoenicians in the 8th century BC), but differ greatly in grammar, vocabulary and pronunciation. The earliest known records of ancient Greek date from around 1400 BC and use a form of writing known as MINOAN LINEAR SCRIPT. Classical Greek is based on Athenian dialects spoken from the 6th to the 4th centuries BC. During Hellenistic times a simplified Greek known as Koine became the common language of the civilized world. There are two forms of modern Greek: Koine for everyday use and an official state language which incorporates classical forms and words.

GREEK ART AND ARCHITECTURE. The art of ancient Greece was the tangible expression of its religion and philosophy. Greek culture is essentially humanist, and the expressive possibilities of the human figure played a preeminent part in Greek art. Gods took human forms and abstract qualities were personified.

Sculpture. The Greeks first began to carve large-scale marble sculptures around 650 BC. Their finest achievements date from the Classical Age beginning about 480 BC—idealized majestic figures of great harmony and fluidity. Notable examples are MYRON's *Discus Thrower,* POLYCLITUS' *Spearbearer* and PHIDIAS' PARTHENON sculptures and his *Zeus*, a 40ft statue of gold and ivory at Olympus, one of the seven wonders of the ancient world. From the 4th century, Greek sculpture embodied emotional appeal, as in PRAXITELES' *Aphrodite of Cnidus*, the Hellenistic *Venus de Milo* and *Winged Victory of Samothrace.*

Vase Painting. The history of Greek painting in which portraiture and perspective were skilfully developed is illustrated primarily from painted pottery which has survived from about 900 BC. The earliest Dipylon vases, decorated with human figures in funeral and battle scenes, were grave markers. In the 7th century BC black-figure ware appeared, with carefully incised silhouette forms. In the mid-6th century BC Athenian red-figure ware appeared with carefully painted-on details and scenes which conformed to the shape of the pottery.

Architecture. Classical Greek architecture, which flourished in the 5th century BC, had its origins in the 6th century when stone and then marble replaced wood in civic buildings and temples. Greek architecture is characterized by harmony and symmetry. There are three specific styles of decoration: the earliest Doric style has great columns with wide flutes as in the Parthenon of Athens; the later Ionic and Corinthian styles have slenderer columns with more elaborate capitals (see CLASSICAL ORDERS).

GREEK FIRE, liquid mixture of unknown composition that took fire when wet, invented by a Syrian refugee in Constantinople in the 7th century AD and used by the Byzantine Empire and others for the next 800 years. Thrown in grenades or discharged from syringes, it wrought havoc in naval warfare until superseded by gunpowder. It appears to have been a petroleum-based mixture. (See also INCENDIARY BOMB.)

GREEK REVIVAL, a movement in art and architecture, in Europe and America, during the late 18th and 19th centuries, characterized by renewed interest in classical antiquity. Private and public buildings were modeled on Classical designs. Notable examples include the U. of Va. by Thomas JEFFERSON and the WASHINGTON MONUMENT. (See also NEO-CLASSICISM.)

GREELEY, seat of Weld Co., at the foot of the Rocky Mts Front range, N. Col. It is a processing and shipping center for a farming region. Pop 38 902.

Statue of Horace Greeley, founder of the New York Tribune, on the site of the paper's old offices.

GREELEY, Horace (1811–1872), US journalist and reformer, founder and editor of the popular New York *Tribune* (1841). One of the most influential figures of the pre-Civil War period, he endorsed abolitionism, helped found the Republican Party and was instrumental in the candidature and election of Lincoln. However, his popularity was diminished during and after the Civil War by his confused attitude towards the South, and by his pleas for total amnesty for the Confederacy.

GREELY, Adolphus Washington (1844–1935), US army officer and explorer. In 1881–89 he was one of only six survivors from an expedition to establish observation stations near the N pole. Chief signals officer from 1887, he introduced radio telegraphy to the Signal Corps.

GREEN, Thomas Hill (1836–1882), English idealist philosopher who was the leading critic of the empiricist philosophies of J. S. MILL and H. SPENCER in mid-Victorian Oxford. His influence long survived his death, declining only with the resurgence of the empirical approach in the 20th century.

GREEN, William (1873–1952), US labor leader. A union official from an early age, he served as president of the AMERICAN FEDERATION OF LABOR (1924–52).

GREENBACK, the first paper currency not backed by specie, issued by the US Treasury. Greenbacks were introduced in 1862 to help finance the Civil War. Because they were not backed by gold or silver, their issue was controversial and their value fell during the war. Since 1878 issue has been frozen at $346 681 016.

GREENBACK PARTY, US political group active between 1876 and 1884. Founded largely by farmers, its main aim was to expand the circulation of GREENBACK currency to bring about inflation, and thus end the depressed agricultural prices and make debts easier to pay. In 1878 the party sent 14 congressmen to Washington but it rapidly declined in the 1880s. Many of the party's supporters and leaders turned to POPULISM in the 1890s.

GREEN BAY, port city in NE Wis., on S end of Green Bay at the mouth of Fox R., seat of Brown Co. Its main industries are paper, machinery and food processing. Pop 87 809.

GREEN BAY, arm of NW Lake Michigan, on the S boundary of the Mich. peninsula and the NE boundary of Wis. It extends inland for about 120mi.

GREENBELT, town in central Md., 11mi NW of Washington, D.C. It was built in the 1930s by the US government to provide low-cost housing. Pop 18 199.

GREENBERG, Hank, (1911–), American League baseball batting champion. Born in New York, Greenberg played 15 seasons at first base with the Detroit Tigers (1933–47). He was elected to the Baseball Hall of Fame in 1956.

GREENBRIER, popular name for climbing vines with prickly leaves of the genus *Smilax*, family Liliaceae, distributed throughout the world. *Smilax rotundifolia*, the common greenbrier, is a weed in the woodlands of eastern North America.

GREEN CRAB, or shore crab, *Carcinus maenas*, a common scavenger of beaches and shorelines. A typical crustacean with specialization of limbs and the development of a CARAPACE, the first of five pairs of legs is developed as a pair of powerful pincing claws.

GREENDALE, residential village in SE Wis., government-built in the 1930s as an experiment in city planning and low-cost housing. Pop 15 809.

GREENE, Graham (1904–), British novelist, best-known for the works he defined as his "entertainments," such as *The Third Man* (1950) and *Our Man in Havana* (1958). His more serious work is influenced by Roman Catholicism, expressing the need for faith and the possibility of personal salvation, as in *The Power and the Glory* (1940), *The Heart of the Matter* (1948) and *A Burnt-Out Case* (1961).

GREENE, Nathanael (1742–1786), American military commander in the REVOLUTIONARY WAR. Washington's second-in-command, he became general of the Southern army in 1780. His strategy at the battles of Guildford Court House, Hobkirk's Hill and Eutaw Springs in 1781 did not bring outright victory, but wore out the British forces.

GREENEVILLE, city in NE Tenn., seat of Greene Co. A tobacco growing and processing center, the city has other light industries. It was the home of President Andrew Johnson. Pop 13 722.

GREENFIELD, town in NW Mass. on the Connecticut R, seat of Franklin Co. It is a manufacturing center in a productive agricultural area. Pop 18 116.

GREENFIELD, largely residential city in E Wis., a suburb of Milwaukee. Pop 24 424.

GREENFIELD VILLAGE, in Dearborn, Mich., 15mi W of Detroit, is a collection of about 100 restored homes and workshops of famous Americans. Founded by Henry FORD in 1929 as a tribute to his friend Thomas EDISON, it includes Edison's laboratory complex from Menlo Park, N.J., and the bicycle shop where the WRIGHT BROTHERS planned their first airplane.

GREENHOUSE, building used for growing plants in a controlled environment, protecting them from extreme heat and cold. At first, in the 17th century, they were built of brick or wood, but later glass in a wood or metal frame was used for light, and today transparent plastic is common. Greenhouses are heated artificially and by the sun, whose radiation passes through the glass and is absorbed by the objects inside, which warm the air by convection; some heat is reradiated at longer wavelengths but this is trapped by the glass.

GREENHOUSE EFFECT, a phenomenon whereby the temperature at the earth's surface is some 18C° warmer than would otherwise be the case. Sunlight radiated at visible and near-ultraviolet wavelengths provides most of the earth's energy income. After absorption it is reradiated, but at longer, infrared wavelengths, the earth being much cooler than the sun (see BLACKBODY RADIATION). Although the ATMOSPHERE is transparent to the incoming solar radiation, that reradiated from the earth's surface is strongly absorbed by atmospheric water vapor and carbon dioxide. That absorbed is again reradiated, the majority back toward the surface. A similar effect may account for VENUS' high surface temperature.

GREENLAND, the world's largest true island, part of the kingdom of DENMARK. It is located mainly N of the Arctic Circle, to the NE of Canada. An ice cap which may reach a depth of over 1mi covers four-fifths of the island; the only habitable areas are two small coastal strips. Vegetation is sparse, but there is a variety of Arctic fauna such as musk ox and caribou. About 90% of the population live on the SW coast, near the capital Godthaab. Greenlanders have in general a blend of ESKIMO and Danish blood, but enjoy a distinct racial identity and have their own language. W Greenland has local government; the country sends two representatives to the Danish parliament. Health services and education are free. Known mineral resources are now largely exhausted and the economy rests on fishing and agriculture.

It is uncertain when Eskimo tribes first arrived from N Canada. VIKINGS, led by ERIC THE RED, established a colony in Greenland in around 982, but the settlers appear to have died out in the 14th century. Greenland was rediscovered in the 16th century; it became a Danish colony in 1815 and a Danish settlement was established in 1894. The island was made an integral part of Denmark in 1953. It was defended by the US during WWII. There is still a US airbase and research station at Thule in the NW.

GREENLINGS, strong-swimming marine fishes of the New World. The diet consists of bottom-living invertebrates, particularly bivalve MOLLUSKS, of which the greenling bites off the foot—eating the rest of the animal if the shell then opens. Some species are believed to care for their young.

GREEN MOUNTAIN BOYS, organization formed in the Green Mountains of what is now Vt. in the 1760s. Led by Ethan ALLEN, its original purpose was to assault and rob N.Y. state officials and settlers in areas disputed between N.Y. and N.H. In the REVOLUTIONARY WAR the Green Mountain Boys directed their activities against the British, and helped take Crown Point and Fort Ticonderoga.

GREEN MOUNTAINS, mountain range, part of the Appalachians, running S to N the length of Vt. The mountain valleys are used for agriculture, while the higher regions are heavily forested, producing timber. Much is in the Green Mountain National Forest.

GREENOUGH, Horatio (1805–1852), US neoclassical sculptor and art critic who spent most of his working life in Italy. His best-known work is the grandiose statue of George Washington in the Smithsonian Institution (1841).

GREEN REVOLUTION, an agricultural trend of recent years which has greatly increased crop production in India, Pakistan and Turkey. It is based on the introduction of new varieties of crops and is dependent on the use of large quantities of PESTICIDES and FERTILIZERS. It was once hoped that the Green Revolution could solve the problem of feeding the world's increasing population, but these hopes have faded in the face of high prices and of secondary ecological effects. (See POLLUTION.)

GREEN RIVER, in W US. It flows 730mi S from Wind River Range, W Wyo., through Ut., into Col. and out into Ut. again, joining the Colorado R in SE Ut.

GREENSAND. See GLAUCONITE.

GREENSBORO, second largest city in N.C., seat of Guildford Co. A major industrial and commercial center, it is named for Nathanael GREENE. Pop 144 076.

GREENSBURG, city in SW Pa., seat of Westmoreland Co. It produces machinery, steel and other metal products and has various lighter industries. Pop 15 870.

GREEN SNAKES, two species of small harmless snakes common through the US. They occur in grassland and scrub where their bright coloration provides excellent camouflage. Curious among the snakes in being entirely insectivorous, green snakes feed on crickets, grasshoppers and caterpillars.

GREEN'S THEOREM, in VECTOR ANALYSIS, an extension of the divergence theorem, which latter states

$$\iiint \nabla . \mathbf{V}\, dt = \iint \mathbf{V} . d\mathbf{S}$$

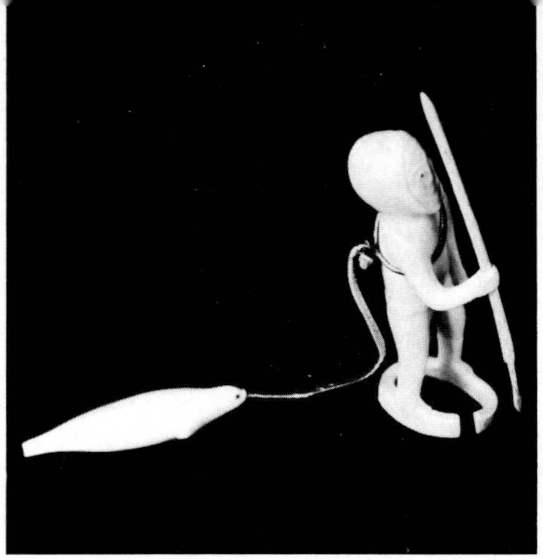

Left: the inhospitable wastes of Greenland. About 80% of the land is covered by an enormous ice sheet, which only the highest mountain peaks (called nunataks) penetrate. The Eskimo inhabitants of the east coast make small, often grotesque, figures known as "tupilaks" out of walrus tusk, such as this seal hunter (*right*).

where **V** is a VECTOR and $d\mathbf{S}$ an element of a surface. If **V** has components (x, y, z), for a volume v and a surface S, Green's theorem states

$$\iiint (x\nabla^2 y - y\nabla^2 x)\, dv \quad = \quad \iint (x\nabla y - y\nabla x) . d\mathbf{S}.$$

(See also CALCULUS; DEL; DIV; SURFACE INTEGRAL.)

GREEN TURTLE, or **Edible turtle,** *Chelonia mydas*, an edible species of marine TURTLE now in danger of extinction, feeding on algae and other marine plants of tropical waters. The young turtles head unerringly for the water as soon as they hatch from eggs buried in the sand of the beach.

GREENVILLE, city in W Miss., seat of Washington Co. It processes lumber, produces auto components and has important fisheries. Pop 39 648.

GREENVILLE, city in E N.C., seat of Pitt Co. Industry is tending to displace agriculture, although the area is still an important tobacco producer. Pop 29 063.

GREENVILLE, city in W Ohio., seat of Drake Co. Its economy is basically agricultural, but there is some light industry in the area. Pop 12 380.

GREENVILLE, city in NW S.C., seat of Greenville Co. The textile industry dominates its economy, but agriculture is still important. Pop 61 438.

GREENVILLE, city in NE Tex., seat of Hunt Co., NE of Dallas. It is a trade center of a rich agricultural area, with some industry. Pop 22 043.

GREENVILLE, Treaty of, agreement signed on Aug. 3, 1795, by Gen. Anthony WAYNE and the chiefs of the Indian tribes of the Ohio area after their defeat at Fallen Timbers. It opened up most of Ohio and parts of Ind. for peaceful settlement.

GREEN VITRIOL, or Iron (II) Sulfate. See IRON.

GREENWICH, a borough of Greater London, on the Thames R. The meridian of zero longitude is located here on the site of the Royal Observatory (1657–1948). The borough, including Woolwich, is an industrial and residential area long associated with the armed forces. Pop 216 441.

GREENWICH, town on Long Island Sound, SW Conn. To an extent a residential suburb of New York, it is also a flourishing commercial center with some industry. Pop 59 775.

GREENWICH MEAN TIME (GMT), local mean time along the Greenwich meridian, used as a TIME standard throughout the world.

GREENWICH OBSERVATORY, Royal, observatory established in 1675 at Greenwich, England, by Charles II to correct the astronomical tables used by sailors and otherwise to advance the art of NAVIGATION. Its many famous directors, the "astronomers royal," have included J. FLAMSTEED (the first), E. HALLEY, and Sir George Airy. The original Greenwich building, now known as Flamsteed House and run as an astronomical museum, was designed by Sir C. WREN. The Observatory is presently sited at Herstmonceux, Sussex, to where it was moved 1948–1957. The Observatory itself is thus no longer sited on the Greenwich meridian, the international zero of longitude.

GREENWICH VILLAGE, area between Spring and West 14th Streets in New York City, famous since the 19th century as an "artist's colony." The area's Bohemian atmosphere has made it a popular tourist attraction.

GREENWOOD, residential town in central Ind., 10mi S of Indianapolis. It has some manufacturing industries. Pop 11 408.

GREENWOOD, city in W Miss., seat of Keflore Co. Its economy has been based on cotton since before the Civil War. Pop 22 400.

GREENWOOD, city in W S.C., seat of Greenwood Co. It is a rail hub and textile center. Pop 21 069.

GREER, city in NW S.C., in the foothills of the Blue Ridge Mountains. An agricultural center, it has textile and other light industries. Pop 10 642.

GREETING CARD, a card, usually with some illustration or design, sent in celebration of an event or as an expression of goodwill. Greeting cards first became fashionable in the early 19th century in Britain. In the US they have become a major industry, supplying cards for every conceivable occasion.

GREGG, John Robert (1867–1948), inventor of the Gregg system of shorthand, using the phonetic principle and the forms of ordinary handwriting. Easy

An intricately carved ivory plaque dating from the 9th or 10th century showing Pope Gregory I, the Great, at his writing table. Gregory was the first monk to be chosen as pope, and the 14 years of his pontificate paved the way for the medieval papacy and for centuries afterward remained an inspiration and guide to the best among the clergy, his claim to be "the servant of the servants of God" being adopted by popes ever since. His idea of a Christian society was heavily influenced by St. Augustine's famous work *The City of God.*

to learn, it is now taught in most US schools, and is adopted for use in 20 languages.

GREGG, Josiah (1806–1850), Santa Fé trader, author of *Commerce of the Prairies* (1844), a classic of the frontier. He led various exploratory expeditions in N Cal., and during one of these was killed falling from his horse.

GREGG, William (1800–1867), industrialist who established cotton-milling in the South to provide a livelihood for the "poor whites." His first mill opened at Graniteville, S.C., in 1846. He provided schools, libraries and housing for his workers.

GREGORIAN CALENDAR. See CALENDAR.

GREGORIAN CHANT. See PLAINSONG.

GREGORY, Lady Isabella Augusta (1852–1932), Irish dramatist and director, largely responsible for the production of YEATS' and SYNGE'S plays at the famous ABBEY THEATRE in Dublin. Their works have tended to overshadow her own plays, such as *The Rising of the Moon* and *The White Cockade* (1904–08).

GREGORY, name of 16 popes. **Gregory I, Saint** (c540–604), pope 590–604. Called Gregory the Great, his papacy laid the foundation for the political and moral authority of the medieval papacy. He reorganized the vast papal estates scattered all over Italy, providing economic foundation for the Church's power. In 596 he sent St. AUGUSTINE to Britain, beginning its conversion to Christianity. His feast day is March 12. **Gregory II, Saint** (c669–731), pope 715–731. Held office at a time of increasing conflict between Rome and Byzantium, and eventually excommunicated Patriarch Anastasius of Byzantium. His feast day is Feb. 11. **Gregory III, Saint** (d. 741), pope 731–41, continued to be involved in conflicts with Byzantium, excommunicating Byzantine Emperor Leo III. His feast day is Nov. 28. **Gregory IV** (d. 844), was pope 827–44. **Gregory V** (d. 999), pope 996–99 was the first German to become pope. **Gregory VI**, (d. 1048), was pope 1045–46. **Gregory VII, Saint** (c1025–1085), called Hildebrand, pope 1073–85. He was one of the great medieval reform popes; he attacked corruption in the Church, insisted on the celibacy of the clergy and on the sole right of the Church to appoint bishops and abbots. These reforms threatened the power of the German monarchy, leading to disputes and war with Henry IV of Germany. In 1084 Henry seized Rome, forcing Gregory to flee. His feast day is May 25. **Gregory VIII** (d. 1187), was pope during 1187. **Gregory IX** (c1170–1241), pope 1227–41. His papacy was marked by conflict with Holy Roman Emperor Frederick II, leading eventually to war in Italy between Imperial and papal factions. **Gregory X** (1210–1276), was pope 1271–76. **Gregory XI** (1329–1378), was pope 1370–78. Elected pope in Avignon, he managed to return the papal court to Rome in 1377. **Gregory XII** (c1325–1417), was pope 1406–1415. **Gregory XIII** (1502–1585), pope from 1572–85, promoted the COUNTER-REFORMATION through his pledge to execute the decrees of the Council of Trent. A patron of the Jesuits, he is remembered for the calendar reform he sponsored and for his lavish building program, which emptied the papal treasury. He celebrated the massacre of Huguenots on St. Bartholomew's Day, 1572, with a *Te Deum.* **Gregory XIV** (1535–1591), was pope 1590–91. **Gregory XV** (1554–1623), was pope 1621–23. **Gregory XVI** (1765–1846), pope 1831–46. He strengthened the papacy, aligning it with Austria under METTERNICH, with whose help he suppressed a revolt in the Papal States. He opposed the introduction of gas lighting and railroads.

GREGORY OF NAZIANZUS, Saint (c330–c390), one of the CAPPADOCIAN FATHERS, delegate to the Council of Constantinople and bishop of that see in 381. A prolific writer, he laid the foundations of Eastern theology in his *Orations.*

GREGORY OF NYSSA, Saint (4th century), philosophical theologian and orthodox leader of the Eastern Church. One of the CAPPADOCIAN FATHERS, he was made bishop of Nyssa in 372, and figured prominently at the Council of Constantinople in 381.

GREGORY THE ILLUMINATOR, Saint (240–332), pioneer evangelist of Armenia and founder of the Armenian Church.

GRENADA, southernmost of the Windward Islands in the West Indies, 90mi N of Trinidad, area 120sq mi. It is an independent state which includes the S group of the GRENADINES. Its capital is St. George's. It was discovered by Columbus in 1498. It exports cocoa, nutmeg, mace, lime oil and bananas. Pop 94 500.

GRENADE, small BOMB (of all sorts) thrown by hand or propelled by a grenade launcher (a specialized gun), used in warfare at short range.

GRENADINES, a group of c600 small islands, part of the WINDWARD ISLANDS in the West Indies, between Grenada and St. Vincent. The N group, and the N part of Carriacou (the largest island) belong to St. Vincent. The S Group belongs to Grenada.

GRENFELL, Sir Wilfred Thomason (1865–1940), English physician, missionary and author who devoted himself to establishing hospitals, nursing stations and schools in Labrador and Newfoundland. He founded the International Grenfell Association. His books include *Forty Years for Labrador* (1932).

GRENOBLE, city in SE France on the Isère R at the foot of the Alps, 60mi SE of Lyons. Famous for its university (founded 1339), it is now the center of hydroelectric power in France. It produces electrical machinery, chemicals and metals, and has a large nuclear research station. Pop 161 616.

GRENVILLE, George (1712–1770), English statesman who tried to impose internal taxation on the American colonies by means of the STAMP ACT, which was a precipitant of the American Revolution. He was prime minister 1763–65.

GRENVILLE, Sir Richard (1542–1591), Elizabethan "sea dog." He commanded RALEIGH'S first expedition (1585) to colonize Roanoke Island, N.C. When his ship the *Revenge* became isolated in a British attempt (1591) to intercept Spanish treasure ships off the coast of the Azores, Grenville held an entire Spanish fleet in combat for 15 hours before he was captured and died.

GRESHAM, city in NW Ore., 14mi E of Portland, an agricultural and manufacturing center. Pop 10 030.

GRESHAM, Sir Thomas (c1519–1579), English financier, merchant and government official. He restored the coinage (devalued under Henry VIII) and proposed stabilization of the pound. He was founder of the Royal Exchange.

GRESHAM, Walter Quintin (1832–1895), US statesman. His appointments included that of postmaster general (1883), secretary of the treasury (1884) and circuit judge (1884). He broke with the Republican Party over the tariff issue, and from 1893 to 1895 served as President Cleveland's secretary of state.

GRESHAM'S LAW, the economic principle (erroneously attributed to Sir Thomas Gresham) that "bad money drives out good." This means that when coins of the same face-value but of different market-value circulate together, the coins of higher market-value will disappear from circulation to be hoarded or used as an open-market commodity.

GRETNA, city in SE La., on the Mississippi R, the seat of Jefferson parish. It is now a suburb of New Orleans. It produces industrial alcohol and cottonseed oil. Pop 24 875.

GREUZE, Jean-Baptiste (1725–1805), French painter who started a vogue with his sentimental and moralistic GENRE painting, e.g. *The Village Bride* (1761). He is also known for his popular erotic studies of young girls, such as *The Broken Pitcher* (c1773).

GREVILLE, Charles Cavendish Fulke (1794–1865), British diarist whose writings are a main source of information on British politics of his time. He was clerk of the privy council under George IV, William IV, and Victoria.

GREVILLE, Sir Fulke, 1st Baron Brooke (1554–1628), English court official under Elizabeth I and James I and literary patron and writer. He was a friend of Sir Philip SIDNEY, whose biography he wrote. He is remembered for a tragedy, *Mustafa* (1609).

GREW, Nehemiah (1641–1712), English plant anatomist and physician who introduced the term "comparative" anatomy (1676) and was a principal founder of his science. His main work, *The Anatomy of Plants*, appeared in 1682.

GREY, Charles, 2nd Earl Grey (1764–1845), English prime minister responsible for the passage of the REFORM BILL (1832), which extended the franchise to the middle classes. A long-time leader of the liberal Whig party in opposition, he was in office from 1830 to 1834.

The greyhound, introduced by the Celts into England, where it was formerly used on long hunts. It has now been bred into the most popular dog for racing.

GREY, Lady Jane (1537–1554), queen of England for nine days in 1553. The Duke of Northumberland, her father-in-law and powerful adviser to the dying Edward VI, persuaded the king to name Jane heir to the throne. She reluctantly accepted the crown, but Mary Tudor, Edward's half-sister, had the country's support, and was proclaimed queen by the Lord Mayor of London. Lady Jane and her husband were beheaded for treason.

GREY, Zane (1875–1939), US author of sagas about the American West. His 54 novels, of which *Riders of the Purple Sage* (1912) is the most popular, have sold over 15 million copies.

GREYHOUND, hunting dog bred originally for speed, and today raced for sport. The family existed in ancient Egypt, and includes many varieties, as for example the SALUKI. Greyhounds have an arch-backed slender body with a narrow waist and long wiry legs. The coat is short and may be various colors. Adults can weigh up to 70lb.

GREY OF FALLODEN, Edward Grey, Viscount (1862–1933), British foreign secretary who engineered a conference of the Great Powers during the BALKAN WARS, and attempted similarly to avert WWI after the assassination of Archduke Ferdinand. He was responsible for the Treaty of London that brought Italy into WWI in 1915.

GRIBBLE, *Limnoria lignorum*, marine woodboring CRUSTACEANS which cause extensive damage to piers and breakwaters. They bore into the wood for shelter, the chips they rasp off forming their staple food. While most wood-eaters have cellulose-digesting BACTERIA in their gut, gribbles are unusual in secreting their own cellulolytic ENZYMES.

GRIBOYEDOV, Aleksandr Sergeyevich (1795–1829), Russian playwright whose verse satire *Wit Works Woe* (written 1822–24) is considered by many to be the finest of Russian comedies.

GRIEG, Edvard Hagerup (1843–1907), Norwegian composer who based his work on traditional national folk music. He wrote many songs and piano pieces. His best known orchestral works are: the *Piano Concerto* (1869), the *Peer Gynt* suites (1876) and the *Holberg Suite* (1885).

GRIERSON, John (1898–1972), British pioneer of the documentary film in England. The influential *Drifters* (1929) was the only film he directed himself, but Grierson organized and supervised information films in WWII and later.

GRIFFES, Charles Tomlinson (1884–1920), US composer. His style, at first impressionist, became both eclectic and individual. His works include: *White Peacock* (1917), and the *Pleasure-Dome of Kubla Khan* (1919).

GRIFFIN, city in W central Ga., 42mi SSE of Atlanta, seat of Spalding Co. It has textile mills and canneries. Pop 22 734.

GRIFFIN, mythological animal having a lion's body with the head and wings of an eagle. In heraldry it is a symbol of vigilance and strength.

GRIFFITH, town in NW Ind., 8mi S of Gary. It manufactures metal products. Pop 18 168.

GRIFFITH, Arthur (1872–1922), Irish nationalist who founded SINN FEIN, a major force in Ireland's struggle for independence from England. He was the first vice-president of the Irish Republic and, in 1922, succeeded De Valera as president.

GRIFFITH, D. W. (David Wark Griffith; 1880–1948), US silent film director and producer, often considered the father of modern cinema. His immensely popular *Birth of a Nation* (1915) introduced major principles of film technique. Griffith also pioneered the film "spectacular." Among his other films are *Intolerance* (1916), *Way Down East* (1920) and *Orphans of the Storm* (1922).

GRIFFON, Wire-Haired Pointing, versatile breed of sporting dog originating in the Netherlands. It stands about 23in high and weighs 56lb. Its distinctive coat, with each hair stiff like wire, is usually blue-gray with brown patches.

GRIGNARD, François Auguste Victor (1871–1935), French chemist who shared with SABATIER the 1912 Nobel Prize for Chemistry for his discovery of GRIGNARD REAGENTS, complex compounds used in the synthesis of many important organic chemicals.

GRIGNARD REAGENTS, ORGANOMETALLIC COMPOUNDS of great importance in laboratory and industrial chemical synthesis. Made by reacting ALKYL (or aryl) HALIDES with MAGNESIUM in an ETHER solution, they are commonly represented as RMgX where R is an alkyl (see ALKANES) or aryl (see AROMATIC COMPOUNDS) group. They are powerful NUCLEOPHILES, and react with many compounds, introducing the group R.

The strange and often frightening fairy tales of the brothers Grimm, Wilhelm (*left*) and Jakob, were illustrated in an appropriately haunting Gothic style by Ludwig Grimm, as can be seen from this depiction of an episode in *Little Red Riding Hood*.

GRILLPARZER, Franz (1791–1872), Austria's foremost dramatist. His poetic tragedies introduced a new realism to the romantic tradition out of which they grew. His major works include *Hero and Leander* (1831), and *A Dream is Life* (1834).

GRIMALDI, Joseph (1779–1837), English clown. Born of a family of pantomimists, he first appeared on stage at age two. His legendary success (1806) in *Mother Goose* established him as one of the comic masters of all time.

GRIMKÉ, Angelina Emily (1805–1879), and **Sarah Moore** (1792–1873), US abolitionists and women's rights crusaders. Angelina's *An Appeal to the Christian Women of the South* and Emily's *An Epistle to the Clergy of the Southern States* (both 1836) urged opposition to slavery.

GRIMM, Jakob (1785–1863) and **Wilhelm** (1786–1859), German philologists, most famous for their collections of folk tales, notably *Grimm's Fairy Tales* (1812–1815). Jakob's *German Grammar* (1819–37) formulated a linguistic law (Grimm's Law) explaining the systematic sound-changes of consonants in the Germanic languages from their Indo-European roots. In 1838 the brothers began work on the great *German Dictionary* which was not completed until 1960.

GRIMMELSHAUSEN, Hans Jakob Christoffel von (1625–1676), German novelist whose picaresque romance *Simplicissimus* (1669), set in the Thirty Years' War, ranks as the great 17th-century German novel.

GRINDING AND POLISHING, the removal of material by friction, using an ABRASIVE, to shape an object and give it a smooth surface. Substances commonly ground include glass (e.g., for lenses), ceramics and stone for building, but the chief industrial process is the grinding and polishing of metals. The grindstone—a rotated sandstone wheel—has been used since ancient times, notably for sharpening CUTLERY. Modern machines use a fast-rotating grinding wheel consisting of abrasive granules of suitable size bonded together with a material such as clay or resin designed to hold the granules until they become blunt. Grinding fluids—oils or alkaline aqueous solutions—are used to cool the workpiece, dissipating frictional heat, and to remove the abrasive dust. The part is first roughly cut and shaped with a coarse wheel, and is then precision-ground. A surface grinder produces a plane surface by passing the workpiece to and fro as it is ground by the edge or flat face of the wheel. Cylindrical grinding, external and internal, requires the workpiece to be rotated on its axis against the wheel. Centerless grinders do not hold the workpiece, but allow it to rest on a support between the grinding wheel and a tilted regulating wheel that rotates it and moves it slowly along; they are suitable for mass production. Polishing uses very finely powdered abrasive such as emery or rouge.

GRIPPE. See INFLUENZA.

GRIS, Juan (1887–1927), Spanish cubist painter, born José Victoriano González. A follower of PICASSO, he developed the style known as Synthetic CUBISM, which he applied to still lifes in increasingly free compositions.

GRISAILLE, technique of monochrome painting done in shades of gray. It was used, especially by Renaissance artists, to give the effect of architectural or sculptural relief. *Grisaille* can also mean a monochrome base in an oil painting.

GRIS-NEZ, Cape, a headland in N France extending into the Strait of Dover, 15mi S of Calais. It is the point nearest to England.

GRISONS, two species of small terrestrial weasel-like mammals with a striking black and white pattern, found in tropical America. They live in small social groups in open grasslands, feeding on small rodents, birds, eggs and insects. Partially webbed paws enable them to wade when searching for insects in mud.

GRISSOM, Virgil Ivan (1926–1967), US astronaut who was the first man to make two flights in space. On July 21, 1961 he made a suborbital flight as part of Project Mercury. In March 1965 he commanded the first manned mission of the Gemini program. He died in a fire during a ground test for the first Apollo mission.

GRISWOLD, Roger (1762–1812), US politician and leader of the New England FEDERALISTS. A strong critic of Jefferson, he was a congressman from 1794 to 1805. He was lieutenant governor of Connecticut (1809–11) and governor (1811–12).

GRITS. See HOMINY.

GRIVAS, Giorgios (1898–1974), Greek-Cypriot leader of the guerrilla army known as EOKA, which fought (1955–59) to end British rule in Cyprus. Favoring union with Greece (ENOSIS), he actively opposed President MAKARIOS.

GRIZZLY BEAR, *Ursus arctos horribilis*, one of the largest of the North American brown bears. The name refers to the grizzled coat rather than to the beast's temper, but despite this the grizzly has more or less been exterminated in the US. Though classed with the CARNIVORA, the grizzly is largely vegetarian and rarely eats flesh. An imposing, even terrifying, animal, the grizzly plays a big role in the legends of the North American pioneers.

A grizzly bear looks on while a puma feeds in the snowy wastes of Alaska, where the bears are still abundant. Though basically vegetarian, the grizzly will occasionally eat meat, especially carrion.

GROFÉ, Ferde (1892–1972), US composer and pianist. His best known work is the *Grand Canyon Suite* (1931) and the orchestration of George GERSHWIN's *Rhapsody in Blue* (1924).

GROMWELL, popular name for hardy plants of the genus *Lithospermum*, family Boraginaceae. The roots of several species yield red or purple dyes. The common gromwell (*Lithospermum officinale*) has dull whitish flowers and is a common roadside weed in the N Hemisphere.

GROMYKO, Andrei Andreyevich (1909–), prominent Soviet diplomat, and foreign minister from 1957. Under KHRUSCHEV he was spokesman for a new conciliatory attitude to the US, reflected in the Test Ban Treaty of 1963.

GRONINGEN, a city in NE Netherlands, capital of Groningen province. It is an important commercial center. Pop 171 334.

GRONLUND, Laurence (1846–1899), Danish-American socialist whose *Cooperative Commonwealth* (1884), was the first full English-language discussion of Marxist socialism.

GROOTE, Gerhard (1340–1384), Dutch monastic reformer and founder of the Brethren of the Common Life. A mystic, he stressed simple piety.

GROPIUS, Walter (1883–1969), German-American architect and teacher who originated the profoundly influential BAUHAUS style, characterized by a marriage of form and function, and the use of modern materials (especially glass). His designs include the Bauhaus in Dessau (1926) and (in collaboration) the Pan Am Building in New York.

GROPPER, William (1897–), US satirical cartoonist and painter, whose theme was social and economic injustice. In the 1930s his expressionist paintings won widespread recognition.

GROSBEAKS, large-billed FINCHES of a variety of species, feeding on large fruits. The heavy beak enables the bird to deal with extremely hard tree fruits. The group includes the Hawfinch of Europe and the migratory Evening grosbeak of the New World.

GROSEILLIERS, Médard Chouart, Sieur des (c1618–c1690), French fur-trader. Working for the English, he led an expedition (with his brother-in-law Pierre Radisson) to the Hudson Bay area of Canada in 1668, which resulted in the formation of the Hudson's Bay Company.

GROSSE POINTE FARMS, a residential city in SE Mich., 10mi E of Detroit on Lake St. Clair. Pop 11 701.

GROSSE POINTE PARK, a residential city in SE Mich. Pop 15 585.

GROSSE POINTE WOODS, a residential suburb of Detroit in SE Mich. Pop 21 878.

GROSS NATIONAL PRODUCT (GNP), the total value of goods and services produced by a national economy before any deduction has been made for depreciation (the *net national product*). The annual growth of the GNP is often taken as an indicator of the state of a country's economy, but its significance is limited because it does not reveal price changes, and thus does not register benefits to the consumer, but only comparative national wealth.

GROS VENTRE INDIANS, two different groups of North American Indians: the ATSINA and the HIDATSA. The French term, meaning "big belly Indians," apparently originated as a misinterpretation of Indian sign language.

GROSZ, George (1893–1959), German–American satirical artist. He was a member of the DADA movement. His caricatures, especially those attacking corruption and militarism in post-WWI Germany, are among the most persuasive expressions of misanthropy in the 20th century.

GROTIUS, Hugo (1583–1645), Dutch jurist, considered the father of international law. In 1619 he was condemned to life imprisonment for his political activity, but he escaped to Paris. There he wrote *On the Law of War and Peace* (1625). This was a study of all the laws of mankind with an emphasis on rules of conduct applying to states, nations and individuals.

GROTON, town in SE Conn., on the Thames R estuary. It is noted for the construction of submarines. The nuclear-powered NAUTILUS was launched from there in 1954. Pop 38 244.

GROUND, Electrical, an electrical connexion between apparatus and the earth or an equivalent conducting body at zero POTENTIAL. Electricity supply systems are grounded to avoid overvoltage and to improve performance. Metal cases, frames etc. of electrical equipment are grounded to minimize risk of ELECTRIC SHOCKS in case a fault should make the exposed part "live."

GROUND-EFFECT MACHINE (GEM). See AIR-CUSHION VEHICLE.

GROUNDHOG, a familiar North American member of the ground squirrels popularly referred to as the WOODCHUCK.

GROUNDHOG DAY, in US tradition Feb. 2. On this day, according to legend, the groundhog emerges from hibernation. If he does not see his shadow when he first pokes his head out of the hole then spring has come. If he does, he is supposed to jump back in fright and sleep for six more weeks, and spring is delayed until he awakens again.

GROUND IVY, *Glechoma hederacea*, herbaceous perennial of the mint family, Labiatae. Native to Eurasia and naturalized in North America it is a prolific weed that is difficult to eradicate. The leaves when made into a tea were once used as a home cure for indigestion.

GROUNDNUT. See PEANUT.

GROUNDSEL, many herbs and shrubs of the genus *Senecio*, family COMPOSITAE, with worldwide distribution. Most species have small yellow flowers and produce fruit (ACHENES) with a hairy pappus.

GROUND SLOTHS, an extinct group of EDENTATES probably ancestral to present-day SLOTHS and ANTEATERS. Ground sloths were found in both Americas; the Giant ground sloth *Megatherium* was some 6m (20ft) long and weighed 5 tonnes.

GROUND SQUIRRELS, the large proportion of the squirrel family (Sciuridae) which live on the ground, including PRAIRIE DOGS, WOODCHUCKS and GOPHERS. Usually social animals, their burrows are often grouped in colonies. They frequently raise themselves on their hindlegs to watch for danger, and give a sharp whistle in warning when danger approaches.

GROUNDWATER, water accumulated beneath the earth's surface in the pores of rocks, spaces, cracks, etc. It may be *meteoric*, rainwater having soaked down from above, or *juvenile*, where water has risen from beneath. Permeable, water-bearing rocks are AQUIFERS; rocks with pores small enough to inhibit the flow of water through them are aquicludes. Build-up of groundwater pressure beneath an aquiclude makes possible construction of an ARTESIAN WELL. The uppermost level of groundwater saturation is the water table. (See also PERMAFROST; SPRING; WELL.)

GROUP, a set of algebraic elements in which there is an operation * such that: (1) for all elements a, b, in the set, * is associative (see ALGEBRA) and $a*b$ is a member of the set; (2) there is an identity element e defined by $a*e=a$ for every element a of the set; (3) every element a has an inverse a^{-1}, also a member of the set, where $a*a^{-1}=e$. If * is commutative, the group is an ABELIAN GROUP. The set of all INTEGERS under the operation ADDITION (+) is such a group; it is not, however, a group under, say, DIVISION, since division is not associative. (See also FIELD; RING; SET THEORY.)

GROUP, in psychology, a collection of individuals that can be regarded as a single unit. The behavior of a group (usually a social unit) or an individual acting in response to his membership of the group is termed **group behavior**; the stimulus that produces such response being **group consciousness**. The study of group behavior and group consciousness is termed **group psychology** or **social psychology**: important factors include the presence of an exterior common enemy, and identification of the individual with not only the group but also another individual within it regarded as leader. An application of this to SOCIOLOGY is **group dynamics**, whose chief proponent was LEWIN. In his field theory he analogized the forces acting on an individual in a group at any given time to a VECTOR FIELD; and extended this to treat the group as a whole. Other key concepts are locomotion (the aims of the group and their achievement of them); cohesiveness (the field of forces binding each member to the group); and communication between members, the nature and extent of which determines the group's structures, hierarchy and cohesiveness. **Group therapy** is a technique of PSYCHOANALYSIS in which several patients are treated by an analyst simultaneously, with the aim that individuals within the group will assist each other in the treatment; recent amateur applications have tended to bring the technique into popular disrepute. The term "group" is also used in GESTALT PSYCHOLOGY to describe a pattern of PERCEPTIONS. Found in primitive societies (see PRIMITIVE MAN) and occasionally more advanced ones is **group marriage**, where a number of individuals of each sex marry in common.

GROUPERS, large perch-like marine fish of temperate and tropical seas. Bulky fish with enormous mouths, they live among coral reefs, many of them being able to change color to match their background. Also called sea-basses or merous, groupers are considered valuable food fishes.

GROUP OF TEN. See INTERNATIONAL MONETARY FUND.

GROUP THEATER, New York City theatrical organization that from 1929–41 produced new plays, largely on contemporary social themes. It laid great emphasis on the STANISLAVSKI method in acting, and was a revitalizing influence on US theater of the time, presenting plays such as Clifford ODET's *Golden Boy* for the first time.

GROUSE, a family (Tetraonidae) of game birds usually brown, gray or black in plumage. They are ground birds living on open moorland or heath, and are well-camouflaged. Three species moult into a white or parti-colored winter plumage for camouflage in snow. Grouse feed largely on plant material—shoots, buds and fruits—but will also eat insects. In many species males perform elaborate courtship displays at established display grounds, or "leks." These lek species, and many others, are polygamous.

A cock Sage grouse inflating his throat sac in an extraordinary courtship display. Although grouse are among the most popular game birds, various species are now protected in many countries.

GROVE, Frederick Philip (1871–1948), Canadian author known for his realistic novels about pioneer life in the W of Canada. A casual laborer and teacher in his youth, he wrote for many years but his first book, *Over Prairie Trails*, was only published in 1922. Perhaps his best-known works are *Our Daily Bread* (1928) and *The Yoke of Life* (1930).

GROVE, Lefty (1900–), US baseball player. Born Robert Moses Grove, he got his nickname from his left-handed pitching. He played with the Philadelphia Athletics 1925–33 and the Boston Red Sox 1934–41, totaling 300 victories. He was elected to the Baseball Hall of Fame in 1947.

GROVE CITY, city in central Ohio, SSW of Columbus. Center of a rich farm area, it is a well-known venue for horse-racing. Pop 13 911.

GROVES, city in E Tex., adjoining Port Arthur to the S as a suburban residential community. Pop 18 067.

GROVES, Leslie Richard (1896–1970), US army officer who headed the MANHATTAN PROJECT to develop the atomic bomb, and was responsible for the vast construction program involved. Before the war he supervised all US military construction, including the building of the PENTAGON.

GROWING SEASON, the period of the year in which most active plant growth occurs. In temperate zones it lasts from the final frost of spring through to the first frost of autumn. The length of the growing season in a particular year or in a particular area is of agricultural importance.

GROWTH, the increase in the size of an organism, reflecting either an increase in the number of its CELLS, or one in its protoplasmic material, or both. Cell number and protoplasmic content do not always increase together; cell division can occur without any increase in PROTOPLASM giving a larger number of smaller cells. Alternatively, protoplasm can be synthesized with no cell division so that the cells become larger. Any increase in protoplasm requires the synthesis of cell components such as nuclei, mitochondria, thousands of enzymes, and cell membrane. These require the synthesis of macromolecules such as PROTEINS, NUCLEIC ACIDS and polysaccharides from AMINO ACIDS, SUGARS and fatty acids. These subunits must be synthesized from still simpler substances or obtained from the environment. **Growth curves**, which plot time against growth (such as the number of cells in a bacterial culture, the number of human beings on earth, the size or weight of a plant seedling, an animal or an organ of an animal) all have a characteristic S-shape. This curve is divided into three parts: the lag phase, during which cells prepare for growth; the exponential phase when actual growth occurs, and the stationary phase when growth ceases. The time any particular cell or group of cells remains in any phase depends on their type and the particular condition prevailing. The *lag phase* represents a period of rapid growth of protoplasm so that the cells become larger without any increase in their number. The duration of the lag phase depends on the resynthesis of the enzyme systems required for growth and the availability of the necessary raw materials. Basically each original cell must obtain sufficient components to form two new cells. During the *exponential phase*, each cell gives rise to two cells, the two to four and so on, so that the number of cells after n generations is 2^n. The generation or doubling time for any particular cell is constant throughout the exponential phase. The time for organisms to double their mass ranges from 20 min for some bacteria to 180 days for a human being at birth. If exponential growth were unlimited, one bacterial cell in 24 hours would give rise to some 4 000 tonnes of bacteria. However, the exponential growth usually ceases (giving the *stationary phase*) either because of lack of an essential nutrient or because waste products produced by the cells pollute the environment. Again, in higher animals population growth is often slowed by parasite-carried epidemics.

The S-type growth pattern can be readily seen in unicellular organisms. Although growth in organisms containing different types of cells obeys the same basic rules, the relationships of the different types of cells complicate the pattern. But although all parts of a multicellular organism do not grow at the same rate or stop growing at the same time, the overall growth curve is still S-shaped.

GROZNY, city in the USSR in the Caucasus 300mi NW of Baku. It is the administrative center of an oil-producing district; its main industries are oil and timber processing. Pop 341 000.

GRUB, the name given to the larval stage of certain insects. Grubs are typically legless, the body is largely undifferentiated, and movement is through muscular contractions of the whole body.

GRUENING, Ernest Henry (1887–1974), US journalist, first Alaskan senator. Territorial governor of Alaska 1939–53, he lobbied for statehood, and was elected as Democratic senator after this was achieved in 1958. He is the author of *The State of Alaska* (1954).

GRUENTHER, Alfred Maximilian (1899–), US general who after distinguished service in WWII became Chief of Staff for NATO forces in 1951 and supreme commander of the Allied powers in Europe 1953–56. On his retirement he became President of the US Red Cross 1957–64.

GRUNDTVIG, Nikolai Frederik Severin (1783–1872), Danish theologian, poet and educationalist who pioneered the study of the Nordic myths. He was the first to translate *Beowulf* and the works of SNORRI STURLUSON and SAXO GRAMMATICUS into Danish. His ideas on religious and educational reform had a far-reaching influence in his time.

GRÜNEWALD, Matthias (c1470–1528), German painter. He and his contemporary DÜRER are considered the great masters of the German Renaissance. His most characteristic theme is the crucifixion, a subject in which he combined beauty and delicacy of style with a savage and harrowing realism. His masterpiece is the altarpiece for St. Anthony's monastery at Isenheim, with subjects such as the *Resurrection* and the *Temptation of St. Anthony* (1513–15).

GRUNION, *Leuresthes tenuis*, small marine fish related to the SILVERSIDES, living in shallow water along the shores of Lower California. They have remarkable breeding habits: the adults allow themselves to be washed high up the beach in spring tides and burrow into the sand where the eggs are laid and fertilized. The eggs remain in the sand till wetted by the next spring tides, when they hatch, and the larvae escape back to the sea.

GRUNTS, perch-like fish of tropical and subtropical seas. They are vocal fish, producing a variety of noises by grinding together their throat or pharyngeal teeth. The sound is amplified by the swimbladder. The color pattern in grunts is distinctive, and varies with age.

GRYSBOKS, *Raphicerus melanotis* and *R. sharpei* (Sharp's grysbok), medium-sized ANTELOPES related to the STEINBOK, and found in parts of southern and eastern Africa. They are usually solitary except during the mating season. Both species will squat when in danger, disappearing in the long grass by lying flat on the ground, or even entering AARDVARK holes.

GUADALAJARA, second-largest city in Mexico, capital of Jalisco state. A major industrial center, it produces foodstuffs, chemicals, textiles, metal products, ceramics and much else. It is also an extremely beautiful city, with historic buildings in many styles dating back as far as the 16th century. Pop 31 917.

GUADALCANAL, largest of the British SOLOMON ISLANDS group in the S Pacific. Volcanic in nature, it supports extensive coconut plantations which are the economic mainstay; copra and timber are the main exports. The island was the scene of a decisive battle of WWII in 1943, when it was recaptured from its Japanese occupiers. Pop 23 996.

GUADALQUIVIR RIVER, rises in the Sierra de Cazorla, S Spain, and flows 375mi across Andalusia to the Atlantic below Sanlúcar de Barrameda. It is navigable as far as Córdoba, and has tidal effects as far as Seville.

GUADALUPE HIDALGO. See GUSTAVO A. MADERO.

GUADALUPE HIDALGO, Treaty of, was signed by the US and Mexico at this Mexican town in 1848 to end the Mexican War. Mexico agreed to cede what are now Tex., Cal., Utah., Nev., and parts of N.M., Ariz., Col., and Wyo. to the US in return for $15 million and other benefits. The treaty guaranteed Mexicans' land rights, but these were not respected.

GUADALUPE MOUNTAINS NATIONAL PARK, covers 128.6sq mi of Tex. E of El Paso. An area of geological interest, particularly for its limestone formations, it contains prehistoric Indian ruins and a wide variety of wildlife; established 1966.

GUADELOUPE, overseas department of France composed of two islands in the Leeward group, Grande-Terre and Basse-Terre. With some smaller islands they cover a total area of 687sq mi. A French settlement captured by the British in the Seven Years' War, it was confirmed as French in 1815; the largely Negro population speaks a French patois. Bananas, coffee, cacao and vanilla are produced. Pop 325 965.

GUAM, largest of the MARIANA ISLANDS group in the Pacific Ocean 6000mi W of San Francisco, and US territory since 1898. Captured by the Japanese in 1941, it was recaptured by the US in 1944; the island is now an important US base. Its people were awarded full US citizenship in 1950. Local products include sugar, bananas, breadfruit and coconuts. The island has an area of about 209sq mi. Capital: Agaña. Pop 84 996.

GUANABARA, state in SE Brazil, effectively an appendage of its capital, Rio de Janeiro, since 1960. Covering an area of 524sq mi, it is an important industrial and administrative region.

GUANACO, *Lama guanicoe*, a wild form of the LLAMA found in South America. It is the only llama which thrives not only at high altitude but also on the plains. Guanacos live in family groups forming herds of up to 20 led by a stallion. Guanacos are often found grazing with RHEAS, which give them warning of danger.

GUANAJUATO, state in central Mexico. It has extensive mineral deposits, especially silver, for which it was known during the colonial period. Wheat, corn and many vegetables are grown in the fertile plains of the S. It covers an area of 11 805sq mi.

GUANCHES, STONE AGE culture first found by the Conquistadores (15th century) in the W group of the Canary Islands. Thought to have been of Cro-Magnon (see CRO-MAGNON MAN) origin, possibly having come from E or Central Europe in ancient times, they no longer exist as a distinct race.

GUANINE, or 2-amino-6-oxypurine, a PURINE first found in GUANO. It is an important component of several NUCLEOTIDES.

GUANO, a naturally occurring fertilizer composed mainly of the excrement of sea birds; bat and seal guanos are also used. Because of the cheapness of other FERTILIZERS, guano is now little used. (See also MANURE.)

GUANTÁNAMO, city in SE Cuba 40mi E of Santiago, the center of an agricultural region producing sugarcane and coffee. Pop 130 061.

GUANTÁNAMO BAY, large natural harbor in Cuba, site of a US naval base strategically placed with access to the Caribbean and Panama. It has been leased to the US since 1903 but since 1960 has been isolated and harassed by the hostile Castro regime.

GUARANI INDIANS, group of primitive South American tribes, linked by language, who once lived in an area now covered by parts of Paraguay, Brazil and Argentina. Conquered by Spain in the 16th century, their numbers have been reduced by disease. Their language, however, is now the second language of Paraguay.

GUARANTY, in law, an agreement by a third party to indemnify a creditor against the debtor's failure to pay. The agreement is made between the third party and creditor, rendering the debtor liable to the third party. Guarantors are usually people or corporate bodies of firm financial standing.

GUARDI, Francesco (1712–1793), Venetian landscape and figure painter, noted for his romantic, visionary views of Venice. His early work came from the studio he shared with his brothers, but his characteristic work, typified by his *Feast of the Ascension at Venice* (c1763), was done in later life.

GUARDIAN, in law, a person entrusted with the care of another who through minority or mental incapacity is unable to handle his own affairs. Parents are held to be "natural guardians." A guardian may be appointed in parents' wills, or by the courts where other guidance is lacking. Guardians are usually individuals, but may also often be corporate bodies such as trust companies.

GUARINI, Guarino (1624–1683), influential Italian architect, one of the masters of the Baroque. Most of his major works were churches and palaces in Turin, such as San Lorenzo, the Capella della Sacra Sindone, and the Palazzo Carignano.

GUARNERI, family of violin makers of Cremona in Italy. **Andrea** (c1626–1698) (with STRADIVARI an apprentice of AMATI), founded the dynasty. His sons **Giuseppe** (1666–1739?) and **Pietro Giovanni** (1655–c1740), and **Pietro** (1695–c1765) a grandson, continued the trade, but the most renowned member of the family was the eccentric and experimental **Giuseppe** "del Gesu" (c1687–1745).

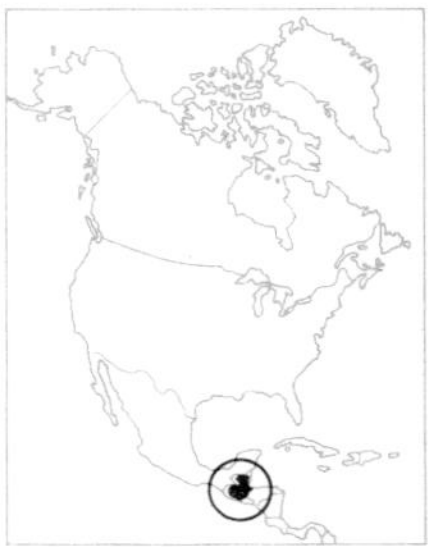

Official Name: Republic of Guatemala
Capital: Guatemala City
Area: 42 042sq mi
Population: 5 600 000
Languages: Spanish; Maya-Quiché dialects
Religions: Roman Catholic
Monetary Unit(s): 1 Quetzal = 100 centavos

Guerrilla Warfare

Increasingly an offensive tactic

The advent of the atomic age after WWII radically changed the nature of war. For the first time in history man was faced with the possibility that "total" war might devastate most or all of a country—or even the world. This has so far brought neither dreaded holocaust nor hoped-for peace, even though conventional warfare has been made a less practical instrument of national policy by the growth of defensive alliances and the fear of escalation into nuclear war. Instead, the rivalries of the major powers are reflected in the struggles of lesser states through politics, revolution and the increasing use of guerrilla warfare.

In the past guerrilla warfare was a mainly defensive weapon, used as a rule by the weaker and worse-equipped side in a conflict. In a nuclear situation, however, it has distinct advantages; by avoiding large-scale confrontations it is less likely to lead to escalation. For the aggressor it is less costly than all-out war; also, it is often easier to avoid responsibility for it. A relatively small amount of war material and a degree of ideological and moral support is usually sufficient for a guerrilla campaign. A prime example is the success of communist campaigns in Cuba and Angola; these have shown that decisive changes in the balance of world power can be engineered by inciting and supporting guerrilla campaigns in areas far distant from established communist countries. Some authorities believe that a successful guerrilla campaign may break an enemy's will to resist to the point where conventional and even nuclear war might be used without fear of reprisal.

The term *guerrilla* is Spanish in origin, meaning "little war." It came into general use during the Peninsular War of 1808–14 to describe the Spanish partisans who harassed the invading French army, the first example of partisan operations on a large scale. Despite humiliating defeats inflicted by the French on the Spanish regular forces, the Spaniards, particularly in rural areas, continued to resist the invader. Central to this patriotic resistance were the *guerrilleros*, of whom there were about 30000, in groups varying from several thousand to a mere handful. These were fiercely independent and reluctant to cooperate with each other or with regular forces.

Despite their lack of coordination the guerrillas made an important contribution to the war. French dispatches were intercepted, convoys were ambushed and senior officers killed. French troops were committed to weary searches across badly-mapped terrain, with no help from the peasants. The partisans attacked outright only when they could do so with overwhelming numbers; when threatened, they disbanded. One partisan leader, "El Empecinado", boasted that he never lost a man in action, and indeed it was very rare that the French managed to bring guerrilla bands to battle on anything like equal terms.

In 1812 a second major guerrilla war against the French broke out in Russia. Throughout the disastrous retreat from Moscow, Napoleon's Grand Army was harassed by partisans and Cossack cavalry. These raids did far more damage to the French than did all the efforts of the Russian regular forces.

The modern strategy of total war has fueled popular resistance on many occasions. An early example of this was in the US Civil War. The Shenandoah Valley was a fertile area through which several Southern armies had advanced to attack Washington. In 1864 Northern troops under General Phil Sheridan were ordered to devastate the whole area so thoroughly that "a crow flying across the Valley would have to carry its own rations." This was duly done, but the result was a savage and bloody guerrilla campaign waged by the local inhabitants against the Northern troops. The same pattern was repeated in other areas and, ill-organized though they were, the partisans could have prolonged the war considerably had it not been for the decision of the Southern leaders not to resort to all-out guerrilla war when their regular forces collapsed in 1865.

Measures used against guerrillas gradually became more thorough. In the South African War (1899–1902) Boer guerrillas continued to fight after the formal annexation of their territories by the British. The country was vast and poorly mapped, the Boers were well mounted, accustomed to living off the country and were crack shots. In an attempt to prevent the partisans from obtaining supplies from their farms, the British swept the Boer noncombatants into internment camps and burned the farms. This policy failed because it strengthened the Boers' will to resist and it relieved the guerrillas of the burden of caring for their families. A second innovation was more successful; a network of about 10000 blockhouses connected by fences was set up in the Boer territories. This restricted the guerrillas' mobility and their numbers gradually dwindled. When terms were finally agreed in May, 1902, 20000 guerrillas were faced by almost half a million Imperial soldiers.

In the 19th century guerrilla warfare was seen purely as a defensive measure against an invader. Partisans took up arms spontaneously against an occupying power, often provoked by the marauding and brutality of invading troops. Once resistance had begun, steps might be taken to organize it, but central organization was not an essential feature. The motives of these resistance fighters were patriotic rather than ideological. In the present century, however, a new type of guerrilla campaign has emerged, the revolutionary guerrilla war. This differs from the traditional patriotic resistance movement in that it is aggressive rather than defensive and is motivated by ideology rather than patriotism.

Revolutionary guerrilla movements are not spontaneous; they must be organized before the fighting can begin. A revolutionary movement can therefore be effectively suppressed if it is caught in its early stages. Spontaneous resistance movements, on the other hand, can rarely be destroyed completely.

The first application of revolutionary guerrilla warfare on a large scale was by Mao Tse-Tung in China 1927–49. Mao saw this type of campaign as developing in three merging phases. The first of these is devoted to organization, consolidation and preservation of regional base areas situated in difficult terrain. Here training and indoctrination of volunteers takes place and from here agitators and propagandists set forth to enlist the support of the local population. The aim is to surround each base with sympathizers who provide information, food and recruits. During this phase military operations are sporadic. In the second phase, fighting becomes more important. Acts of sabotage and terrorism multiply; collaborators and reactionary elements are liquidated. Weakly-defended police and military posts are attacked in order to obtain weapons, ammunition and other equipment. Political agents indoctrinate the inhabitants of further regions which will soon be added to the "liberated area." Local vigilante groups are then formed in this area; lacking the training and equipment of the true guerrillas, their function is to collect taxes and to liquidate government agents and collaborators. The final phase, the destruction of the enemy, requires the transformation of a portion of the guerrilla army into regular formations capable of engaging in conventional warfare. Usually enough equipment has been captured by this stage to permit the formation of artillery and armored units as well as infantry.

In WWII almost all the countries invaded by the Germans produced resistance movements. These were largely patriotic in origin; they arose spontaneously and only later were they organized. Their effect on the war was considerable; in Yugoslavia, for instance, the partisans tied down at least 10 German divisions. Even in comparatively densely-populated areas of Western Europe resistance flourished, although the risks run by the urban fighters were immense. The Allies recognized the value of the resistance and, where possible, supplies and technical assistance were provided for the partisans.

Attempts were made to convert many wartime resistance movements into revolutionary movements; among the most successful examples of this were Yugoslavia and, later, Vietnam. Such attempts failed, however, in Western Europe during WWII despite the presence of large numbers of communist partisans in, for example, France. In August 1944 British, US and Free French troops advanced through N and SE France. In the rest of the country the task of liberation fell to the resistance fighters, which included the communist FTP (French: *Francs-Tireurs Partisans*). Civil authority broke down over much of the country; newly-appointed prefects failed to prevent some 20000 summary executions of so-called "collaborators," many of which were merely the settling of personal scores or simple banditry. In this chaotic situation there was a risk that some southern areas might secede from the central power altogether. The FTP in the Dordogne received orders to proclaim the "Republic of the Soviets of the South of France." Nevertheless, the varying levels of inter-unit cooperation in the FTP and the strong patriotic elements in the organization made many unwilling to oppose de Gaulle's government, reducing the effectiveness of the threat. There were exchanges of fire between communist and government troops, but in the end the conflict fell short of open war.

In Yugoslavia, on the other hand, the monarchist Cetniks and communist partisans at first cooperated in a guerrilla campaign against the Germans. After mutual accusations of treachery, however, fighting broke out between the groups and the Cetniks eventually broke off action against the Germans to concentrate on the communists. Because the communists, led by Tito, were now the only opposition to the Germans, the Allies had little choice but to support them. When the Germans began to withdraw from Yugoslavia, British forces along the coast were also withdrawn at the communists' request, leaving them in effective control. The monarchists, divided and discredited, were unable to influence events.

Since WWII revolutionary guerrilla movements have been organized with varying degrees of success in many parts of the world. Experience suggests that once such a movement has survived the organization and consolidation phase and has gained the support of a significant segment of the population (perhaps 15–20%), there is little prospect of destroying it. In the Malayan Emergency of 1948–60 the government was able to prevent the guerrillas from gaining control of the rural peasants; villages were fortified and food was rationed to stop supplies going to the guerrillas. The communists were then defeated by energetic military action. In Cuba, however, the guerrillas easily gained public support at the expense of the corrupt and reactionary Batista regime, which was duly destroyed.

In the face of nuclear stalemate, guerrilla war seems likely to become still more important in deciding the future of the world. Many Western armies are ill adapted for this form of war; the huge administrative "tail" required to keep comparatively small numbers of combat troops in the field offers an excellent target for guerrillas. Such countries, it seems, must heed the words of the Roman Vegetius, paraphrased by the great military historian, Captain Liddell Hart: "If you wish for peace, *understand* war . . ." The form of war they must learn to understand is undoubtedly guerrilla warfare.

GUATEMALA, northernmost republic in Central America, a mountainous country composed largely of volcanic highland at altitudes of from 2000–6000ft, although mountain peaks such as Mount Tajumulco (13845ft) rise much higher. The E and W highlands are not very fertile, lacking the rich volcanic soils of the coast or the cooler climate and high rainfall of the N central area. To the N is the Petén, a rain forest plateau with areas of savanna covering a third of the country. The climate varies from the tropical Petén and coastal areas to the subtropical and temperate highlands. The native Indians moved into the highland areas as Spanish colonizers occupied the valleys, and many of them still live there. Today they account for over 54% of the population, only 4% being white; the remainder are the largely half-breed *Ladinos*.

The Indians maintain a traditional family-oriented village culture, speaking mainly their own dialects. Many of them provide the work-force on the coffee plantations that account for almost half the nation's revenues. Cotton is also an important product, having superseded banana cultivation since the 1930s. Corn and cattle account for the rest of the country's agriculture. Guatemala has only limited mineral resources; some chromate, silver, lead and zinc are produced. Manufacturing industries are mainly devoted to the processing of local produce, but they are steadily expanding. Although Guatemala joined the Central American Common Market in 1961, the US remains its principal trading partner, taking about 75% of its exports and providing about 66% of its imports.

From 300–900 AD the Indian MAYAS ruled the area, and their ruins still stand. Their civilization declined, however, and they were unable to offer much resistance to the invading Spaniards under ALVARADO in 1524. With the breakup of the Spanish New World, Guatemala became independent in 1823. The tyrannical but efficient Rafael CARRERA held power 1838–65; the Liberal coup in 1871 established a line of less efficient dictators. Post-WWII democracy was increasingly threatened by Cuban-sponsored terrorism, resulting in conclusive election victories for right-wing presidents, who have had to cope with right- and left-wing insurgency.

GUATEMALA CITY, capital of Guatemala and largest city in Central America, the country's political, cultural and commercial hub. In the center of an agricultural region, it has a wide range of light industries. The city was razed by earthquakes 1917–18 and has been largely rebuilt. Pop 790000.

GUAVA, common name for tropical trees and shrubs of the genus *Psidium*. Also the fruit, which is rich in vitamin C, and used in jellies, jams and preserves. Family: Myrtaceae.

GUAYAMA, town in SE Puerto Rico, 5mi from the Caribbean coast. Important local products include sugar, coffee and tobacco. Pop 20318.

GUAYAQUIL, city and chief port of Ecuador, on the Guayas R, about 40mi inland from the Pacific. Exports from the port include bananas, cocoa, coffee and rubber. The city is a center for textile, cement and iron production. Pop 794300.

GUAYULE, *Parthenium argentatum*, desert shrub of the family COMPOSITAE, native to Mexico and Texas. It has been used as a source of RUBBER, but production has never been commercially viable.

GUDERIAN, Heinz (1888–1954), German army officer whose tank warfare and *blitzkrieg* techniques were successful in the German invasion of Poland (1939) and of France (1940).

GUELPH, city in SE Ontario, Canada, at the center of a diversified agricultural area. It has a wide range of industries. Pop 60087.

GUELPHS AND GHIBELLINES, two opposing political factions in 13th- and 14th-century Italy. The Guelphs supported the pope, while the Ghibellines backed imperial Germany. Both originated in 12th century Germany, in opposition over territories of the Holy Roman Empire. After 1268, the rivalries became purely political between cities and families. In Florence the ruling Guelphs split into rival groups of Whites and Blacks.

GUENONS, the most common MONKEYS of the African forest and savanna. They are small monkeys with round faces and long tails; the group includes the vervets, Sykes', Patas and Mona monkeys. Guenons tend to live in troops and have complex social organizations and social display.

GUERICKE, Otto von (1602–1686), German physicist credited with inventing the vacuum pump. His best-known experiment was with the Magdeburg hemispheres (1654): he evacuated a hollow sphere composed of two halves placed together, and showed that two 8-horse teams were insufficient to separate the halves. (See PUMPS.) He is also credited with inventing the first electric GENERATOR.

GUÉRIN, Camille (1872–1961), French bacteriologist who, with CALMETTE, developed the BCG VACCINE, which is used to counter TUBERCULOSIS.

GUERNICA, town in N Spain in the Basque province, destroyed by bombing in 1937 by German planes fighting for FRANCO in the Spanish Civil War. PICASSO's picture commemorating the event is in the Museum of Modern Art, New York. Pop 14678.

GUERNSEY, second largest of the CHANNEL ISLANDS, 60mi from France. It produces fruit, tomatoes, flowers and dairy goods, and attracts many tourists.

GUERRERO, state in S Mexico on the Pacific coast. Its chief towns are Chilpancingo, Acapulco and Taxco. It has two distinct regions: the tropical coastal area and the mountainous zone of the Sierra Madre del Sur. The economy is based on agriculture, mining and tourism.

GUERRILLA WARFARE, is waged by irregular forces in generally small-scale operations, often in enemy-held territory. The term (Spanish: little war) originally applied to the tactics of Spanish–Portuguese irregulars in the Napoleonic Wars. Traditional guerrilla warfare is generally waged against larger and better-equipped conventional forces; it is usually part of a wider strategy, as for example the activities of the resistance movements in Nazi-occupied Europe, which were part of overall Allied strategy. The guerrilla fighter must avoid open battle as much as possible, exploiting the mobility gained from lack of equipment and supply lines. To compensate for these he must have a wide degree of popular support. He must rely on hit-and-run tactics, ambush, sabotage and the psychological effects of unpredictable attack. Recent years have seen the development of the "urban guerrilla," usually motivated by ideology alone, whose desire is not to expel an invader by a general insurrection but to so disorganize the fabric of society that a faction can seize power without relying on popular support. To this end ambush, hijacking and bombing, directed both at specific targets and simply at the populace at large, have become increasingly common.

GUEUX, name given to Dutch nobles and burghers who signed the Compromise of Breda, 1566, protesting that Spain had curtailed Dutch liberties. The name (French: beggars) was also applied to the Dutch privateers—the Sea Beggars—who harassed Spanish ships in the 1570s.

GUEVARA, Che (Ernesto Guevara Serna; 1928–1967), Argentinian-born Cuban communist revolutionary and guerrilla leader, who helped organize CASTRO's coup in 1959. After serving as president of the Cuban national bank and minister of industry, he went to Bolivia in 1966 to direct the guerrilla movement there. He was captured by the Bolivian army and executed.

GUGGENHEIM, name of a family of US industrialists and philanthropists. **Meyer** (1828–1905), emigrated to Philadelphia from Switzerland in 1847 and set up a business importing Swiss lace. Aided by his seven sons he later established large smelting and refining plants. One son, **Daniel** (1856–1930), extended the concern internationally and set up an aeronautics research foundation. Another son, **Simon** (1867–1941), was a senator for Col. and established a memorial foundation awarding fellowships to artists and scholars. The fourth son, **Solomon Robert** (1861–1949), founded the GUGGENHEIM MUSEUM.

GUGGENHEIM MUSEUM, museum of modern art in New York. It was set up in 1939 and in 1959 moved to the building designed by Frank Lloyd WRIGHT which centers around a spiral ramp gallery.

GUIANA, British. See GUYANA.

GUIANA, Dutch. See SURINAM.

GUIANA, French. See FRENCH GUIANA.

GUIANA HIGHLANDS, mountainous plateau in South America, covering most of the Guianas, the S part of Venezuela and part of N Brazil. It is made up of old crystalline rocks topped by lava and sandstone. The area has spectacular waterfalls. Mt Roraima (9219ft) is the highest peak.

GUICCIARDINI, Francesco (1483–1540), Italian Renaissance historian and statesman noted for his *History of Italy* and *History of Florence*. He was governor of Modena and president of the Romagna but retired to write after Italy's defeat by Charles V.

GUIDANCE COUNSELING, advice on educational, vocational and related personal matters. Career advice is available commercially in most US cities, but it is concentrated in secondary schools where it has been established since 1958. Trained counselors test students for career and educational aptitude and suggest possible courses of action.

GUIDE DOG. See SEEING-EYE DOG.

GUIDED MISSILE. See MISSILE.

GUIDO D'AREZZO (c990–1050), Italian musical theorist and monk whose great work *Micrologus* (c1025) reformed musical notation. He introduced a four-line staff so that certainty of pitch in notation was established.

GUILD, association of merchants or craftsmen in the same trade or craft to protect the interests of its members. Guilds have both economic and social purposes and flourished in Europe in the Middle Ages. Merchant guilds were often very powerful, controlling trade in one area, or in the case of the HANSEATIC LEAGUE much of N Europe. The guilds of individual craftsmen such as goldsmiths, weavers or shoemakers, regulated wages, quality of production and working conditions for APPRENTICES. Wealthy guilds built extensive headquarters for themselves, some of which still stand. The guild system declined from the 16th century because of changing trade and work conditions.

GUILFORD, town in S Conn., on Long Island Sound, 13mi E of New Haven. Its industries include fishing and metal products. Pop 12033.

GUILFORD COURTHOUSE, Battle of, battle in the Revolutionary War in North Carolina on March 15, 1781, between the Southern Army under Nathanael GREENE and the British under CORNWALLIS. Greene was defeated, but the British suffered great losses and withdrew, abandoning the drive to capture the center of the state.

GUILLAUME, Charles Édouard (1861–1938), Swiss-born French physicist best known for discovering INVAR, an iron-nickel alloy which expands and contracts only very slightly with temperature change. For his work on ferronickels he was awarded the 1920 Nobel Prize for Physics.

GUILLEMOTS, three closely related species of diving seabirds, well-adapted to aquatic life. Guillemots can "fly" underwater: the wings are used as paddles and the large webbed feet used for steering. They are highly social birds, living and breeding in colonies on steep cliffs. They make little or no nest and the single egg is laid on a bare rock ledge.

GUILLOTINE, method of beheading whereby an oblique blade between two upright posts falls, when a supporting cord is released, onto the victim's neck below. It was widely used in the French Revolution after Joseph Ignace Guillotin (1738–1814) called for a more humane form of execution.

GUIMARD, Hector (1867–1942), French ART NOUVEAU architect and designer. He is famous for the Castel Béranger (1894–98), an apartment building in Paris, and the Paris métro station decorative cast-iron gates (c1900).

GUINEA, West African republic, between Guinea-Bissau and Sierra Leone, and with frontiers with Senegal, Mali, Ivory Coast and Liberia. It is a tropical country. The Atlantic coastline has many estuaries and mangrove swamps, which have been reclaimed for the cultivation of rice and bananas. Behind the narrow coastal plain is the high and extensive Fouta Djallon plateau, the slopes of which

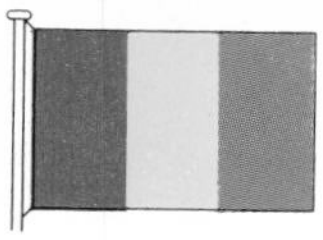

Official Name: Republic of Guinea
Capital: Conakry
Area: 95 000sq mi
Population: 4 010 000
Languages: French; Soussou; Manika
Religions: Muslim; Animist; Christian
Monetary Unit(s): 1 Sily = 100 corilles

are densely forested. Mt Nimba in the SE is the highest peak (5 800ft). The annual rainfall is especially heavy in the coastal region, the average being 169in. The climate and vegetation support a richly varied wildlife.

People and Economy. The population is made up of about 16 ethnic groups, notably the Fulani, Malinke, Soussou and Kissi. The majority of Guineans are Muslims, but many are animist. Most of the people live in villages and about 90% are illiterate. Besides the capital Conakry, the principal towns are Kankan and Kindia.

There are very valuable bauxite and iron ore deposits, and bauxite production and export is being developed. Agriculture is also important. Rice, corn, oil palms, bananas and pineapples are grown, the latter two being chief export crops. Large herds of small Ndama cattle are bred on the plateau.

History. Portuguese exploration began in the 15th century and by the 17th there was extensive trade with Europe. Guinea became independent in 1958, whereupon France stopped supplying aid, which was subsequently accepted from both communist and non-communist countries. Politics are dominated by the president and there is only one political party, the Democratic Party of Guinea. Several unsuccessful attempts have been made to overthrow the regime, and many Guineans are in exile.

GUINEA, Equatorial. See EQUATORIAL GUINEA.

GUINEA, Gulf of, inlet of the Atlantic Ocean on the W coast of Africa, located between Upper Guinea and Lower Guinea. It contains the bights of Benin and Biafra and the mouth of the Niger R.

GUINEA, Portuguese. See GUINEA-BISSAU.

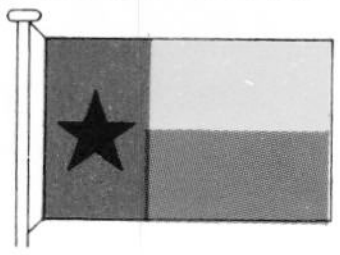

Official Name: Guinea-Bissau
Capital: Madina do Boe
Area: 13 948sq mi
Population: 487 448
Languages: Cape Verde-Guinean Crioulo; Portuguese
Religions: Animist; Muslim
Monetary Unit(s): 1 Escudo = 100 centavos

The modern acoustic guitar is almost entirely derived from the Spanish form, and by the late 18th century had much the shape and construction we know today. As this 19th-century guitar (1) shows, however, it was still handcrafted, usually highly ornamented and often rather delicate. Mass production created the sturdier but less elegant type most common today (2). With the advent of electrical amplification the soundbox was reduced or abandoned in the electric guitar (3), the vibrations of the strings being transmitted through a magnetic pickup (4) to an external amplifier and speakers.

GUINEA-BISSAU, formerly Portuguese Guinea, independent republic in W Africa, bordered by Senegal, Guinea and the Atlantic. Low-lying and crossed by many rivers, it consists of coastal swamps, a heavily forested central plain, and savanna grazing land to the E. The climate is hot and monsoonal, with heavy rains May–Oct. The population is 98% black, and mostly engaged in agriculture. There is no significant industry, except bauxite mining. Agriculture includes rice, groundnut, coconut and palm oil cultivation and cattle-rearing. The chief export is groundnuts. The largest town and main port is Bissau.

First visited by the Portuguese in 1446–47, the country became a Portuguese colony and a center of the slave trade. It became an overseas province of Portugal in 1951, and in 1963 the black nationalists started a war of independence which continued for 10 years. The republic of Guinea-Bissau was proclaimed in 1973 and recognized by Portugal in 1974, under the presidentship of Luis de Almeida Cabral.

GUINEA COAST, the old name for the West African coast between Senegal and Angola. The territory was divided into regions named for their trade: the Grain Coast, the Ivory Coast, the Gold Coast and the Slave Coast.

GUINEA FOWL, a family of game birds (Numididae) about the size of domestic fowl and characterized by featherless or ornamented heads, and spotted iridescent plumage. They are found in Africa, usually occurring in open country. They take a variety of foods including seeds and insects.

GUINEA PIG, *Cavia porcellus*, a domestic pet related to the CAVIES of South America. The plump body, absence of tail and extremely short legs are quite distinctive. Guinea pigs feed on vegetable matter of any sort, although, if they are caged, it is necessary, for reasons not fully understood, to provide them with hay, whatever else they are given to eat.

GUINEVERE, the wife of King ARTHUR. In most versions of the Arthurian legend she falls in love with LANCELOT, thus contributing to the disintegration and downfall of Arthur's kingdom.

GUINNESS, Sir Alec (1914–   ), English stage and screen actor, remarkable for his versatility in both classical and contemporary drama. His films include *Kind Hearts and Coronets* (1950) and *Bridge on the River Kwai* (1957) for which he won an Academy Award.

GUISCARD, Robert. See ROBERT GUISCARD.

GUISE, French ducal family prominent in the 16th century. A branch of the house of Lorraine, they exercised great power in many areas of France. Famous members include **François** (1519–1563), who together with his brother **Charles**, Cardinal of Lorraine, (c1525–1577), controlled the French government during the reign of Francis II; **Henri** (1550–1588), a Catholic leader who planned the SAINT BARTHOLOMEW'S DAY Massacre of the Huguenots, 1572; Henry subsequently organized the CATHOLIC LEAGUE against the future HENRY IV. Declining in power in the 1600s, the family died out in 1675.

GUITAR, stringed musical instrument, related to the lute and cither, played by plucking. Its curved sides form a waisted shape. The Moors introduced the guitar into Spain about the 13th century, and the Spanish guitar with five strings evolved in the 1500s, becoming the Spanish national musical instrument. The modern guitar has six, sometimes metal, strings.

GUITEAU, Charles Julius (1841–1882), US assassin of President James GARFIELD. Because of disappointments in obtaining diplomatic office he shot the president on July 2, 1881.

GUITRY, Sacha (1885–1957), Russian-born French actor, playwright and film producer. His prolific output included 130 comedies. His best-known films are *The Comedian* (1921) and *The Cheat* (1935).

GUIZOT, François Pierre Guillaume (1787–1874), French statesman and historian. Under the restored monarchy after Napoleon Guizot held various offices, notably the education and foreign ministries, 1832–48, and led the conservative faction in power, until forced to resign in 1848.

GUJARATI, INDO-ARYAN LANGUAGE of the Indian states of Gujarat and Maharashtra. Spoken by around 20 000 000 people, it is written in a form of Devanāgāri script.

GUJRĀNWĀLA, city in W Punjab, NE Pakistan, a commercial and manufacturing center of an agricultural district, producing mainly grain. Pop 266 000.

GULF INTRACOASTAL WATERWAY, system of navigable waterways, both natural and man-made, running about 1 100mi along the Gulf of Mexico from Apalachee Bay, Fla., to Brownsville, Tex.

GULF OF CALIFORNIA, 700mi arm of the Pacific Ocean separating Baja (Lower) California, Mexico, from the Mexican states of Sonora and Sinaloa to the E.

GULF OF MEXICO, off the SE coast of North America between the US and Mexico, and bounded to the E by Cuba. It is linked to the Atlantic by the Strait of Florida and to the Caribbean by the Strait of Yucatan.

GULF OF SAINT LAWRENCE, gulf on the Atlantic coast of Canada, extending 250mi from Newfoundland across the mouth of the St. Lawrence R to New Brunswick and Nova Scotia. Containing many islands, it is linked to the Atlantic by the Strait of Belle Isle and by the Cabot and Canso Straits.

GULF OF TONKIN RESOLUTION, put before the US Congress on Aug. 4, 1964 by President Lyndon B. JOHNSON, following unprovoked attacks by North Vietnamese vessels on US destroyers in the Gulf. The resolution declared the maintenance of peace in SE Asia to be essential to US interests and therefore gave the president power to take measures necessary to repel other attacks and prevent aggression. The resolution was later seen as the beginning of full-scale US involvement in the VIETNAM WAR and was attacked for giving excessive power to the president. In July 1970 the Senate voted to revoke its authorizations.

GULFPORT, port city in SE Miss., on the Gulf of Mexico, seat of Harrison Co. It has various manufacturing industries and became a sea resort after the construction of a beach. Pop 40 791.

The herring gull (*Larus argentatus*) is the commonest species of gull along the Atlantic coastline of the Northern Hemisphere. It is primarily a scavenger, feeding on garbage and sewage, but is remarkably versatile in its feeding habits: here a herring gull is seen dropping cockles onto a rock in order to break them open.

GULF STREAM, warm ocean current flowing N, then NE, off the E coast of the US. Its weaker, more diffuse continuation is the E flowing **North Atlantic Drift**, which is responsible for warming the climates of W Europe. The current, often taken to include also the CARIBBEAN CURRENT, is fed by the N EQUATORIAL CURRENT, and can be viewed as the western part of the great clockwise water circulation pattern of the N Atlantic. (See also OCEAN CURRENTS.)

GULFWEED, brown SEAWEEDS of the genus *Sargassum*, principally *Sargassum natans*, which grows as free-floating masses kept afloat by air-filled bladders.

GULLAH, descendants of freed slaves who settled in the coastal districts of S.C. and Ga. The name is also used for their Creole dialect, a blend of various African languages and English; it resembles neither very closely.

GULLS, strong-flying and swimming seabirds forming the subfamily Larinae. The plumage is basically white with darker wings and back. Some species develop a dark hood in the breeding plumage. There are altogether some 40 species of gulls and the group is widespread. Gulls are a very successful and adaptable group and many species have now become common inland as scavengers on refuse, or on plowed land.

GULLSTRAND, Allvar (1862–1930), Swedish opthalmologist awarded the 1911 Nobel Prize for Physiology or Medicine for his work on the REFRACTION of light in the EYE. Von HELMHOLTZ had shown that the lens's surface curvature altered for focusing: Gullstrand showed that also the internal components of the lens adjust, accounting for about a third of the accommodation.

GULPERS, fish belonging to three families of deep-sea eels. Gulper eels live in all oceans, usually at depths of between 1 200–3 000m (4 000–10 000ft). All have large mouths and in at least one genus the stomach is elastic and distends to accommodate large prey items.

GUM, sticky substances containing CARBOHYDRATES, exuded from some trees, shrubs, seeds and SEAWEEDS. Gum arabic is produced by the African tree *Acacia senegal*. AGAR is a dried mucilaginous gum extracted from seaweeds.

GUMBO. See OKRA.

GUM TREES. See EUCALYPTUS.

GUN, weapon able to project a missile by means of an EXPLOSIVE charge (see AMMUNITION; BALLISTICS). Heavy guns, or ARTILLERY, include cannons, howitzers and mortars; lighter guns such as machine guns, pistols, revolvers and rifles count as FIREARMS.

GUNCOTTON, a NITROCELLULOSE with a high nitrate content; an EXPLOSIVE.

GUN METAL, a type of BRONZE, normally 88% copper, 10% tin, 2% zinc. Formerly used for cannons, it is now used for gears, bearings and steam fittings, being wear- and corrosion-resistant.

GUNNISON RIVER, rises in Gunnison Co., Col., flowing 150mi through W central Col. to join the Colorado R. (See also BLACK CANYON OF THE GUNNISON.)

GUNPOWDER, or **black powder**, a low EXPLOSIVE, the only one known from its discovery in the West in the 13th century until the mid-19th century. It consists of about 75% POTASSIUM (or SODIUM) nitrate, 10% SULFUR and 15% CHARCOAL; it is readily ignited and burns very rapidly. Gunpowder was used in fireworks in 10th-century China, as a propellant for firearms from the 14th century in Europe and for blasting since the late 17th century. It is now used mainly as an igniter, in fuses and in fireworks.

GUNPOWDER PLOT, conspiracy of a group of English Roman Catholics led by Robert Catesby to blow up King James I, his family and government in the Houses of Parliament on Nov. 5, 1605. Guy FAWKES was arrested while setting charges under the Houses of Parliament and under torture disclosed the names of the conspirators, who were executed. In England Nov. 5 is celebrated with bonfires, fireworks and the burning of effigies.

GUNTHER, John (1901–1970), US journalist and author. His background as a foreign correspondent enabled him to write the highly successful "Inside" books, the first being *Inside Europe* (1936); in describing various countries these blended personal observation with historical and economic analysis to provide a vivid picture.

GUNTUR, city in SE India. A trade center in an agricultural area around the Krishna R, it is also a local administrative center. Pop 269 941.

GUPPY, *Lebistes reticulatus*, a small, livebearing fish from the fresh waters of the West Indies and parts of South America, now a popular aquarium fish. The females are dull olive, but the males are brightly colored and have large, fanlike tails. In the male, as in all the livebearing toothcarp, the anal fin is modified into a copulatory organ for the transfer of sperm.

GUPTA DYNASTY, N Indian dynasty which ruled c320–50 AD, a period which produced some of the finest Indian art and literature. From a small area in the Ganges valley they spread out to rule most of India, and under CHANDRAGUPTA II (385–414) scholarship, law and art reached new heights. The White Hun invasion c450 reduced the Gupta empire to a portion of Bengal.

GURKHAS, dominant Hindu race in Nepal, and its ruling dynasty. The name has become attached to the Nepalese soldiers serving in the British army. Gurkha regiments are famous for their great courage, endurance, discipline and loyalty. The Gurkhas carry the famous *kukhri*, a long knife with a hooked blade.

GURNARDS, a family (Triglidae) of marine bottom-living fishes with strongly armored, spined heads. They are known as Sea robins in the US. Gurnards are found in all tropical and temperate seas and many of them are able to produce noises by vibrating the muscular walls of the swimbladder.

GURU, in Hinduism a religious and spiritual mentor, in many sects venerated as a leader and near-deity. He instructs pupils and followers in religious knowledge and techniques of meditation. The first ten leaders of the SIKHS also bore the title of *guru*.

GUSTAVO A. MADERO, since 1931 official name of Guadalupe Hidalgo, city in central Mexico. It has various industries, but is best known for its shrine of the Virgin Mary, a major object of pilgrimage. Pop 1 182 895.

GUSTAVUS, name of six kings of Sweden. **Gustavus I Vasa** (1496?–1560), was founder of the modern Swedish nation. A Swedish noble, he led the successful revolt against the Danes 1520–23 and was elected king. Through the establishment of Lutheranism and the growth of the economy he took firm control of the country and established hereditary monarchy. **Gustavus II Adolphus** (1594–1632), reigned from 1611; he made Sweden a great European power. When he acceded Sweden was at war with Denmark, Russia and Poland. In 1613 he ended the Danish war and in 1617 the Russian. With his chancellor OXENSTIERNA he introduced wide internal reforms. He joined the THIRTY YEARS WAR in 1631, scoring the first Protestant victory at Breitenfeld (1631). He was killed at Lützen in 1632. **Gustavus III** (1746–1792), became king in 1771, at a time of factionalism and unrest. He regained much of the monarchy's lost power in 1772, and ruled well, introducing many liberal reforms. He was assassinated by a conspiracy of discontented nobles. **Gustavus IV** (1778–1837), reigned 1792–09. In 1805 he joined a coalition against Napoleon and lost Swedish Pomerania and territory in Germany; despite English help he lost Finland to Russia in 1808. He was then deposed and exiled. **Gustavus V** (1858–1950) reigned from 1907. **Gustavus VI Adolphus** (1882–1973), reigned from 1950. He was an able and popular monarch; in 1971 the monarchy was stripped of its powers, but this was deferred during his reign. He was also a noted archaeologist.

GUSTON, Philip (c1913–   ), Canadian-born US painter, a follower of ABSTRACT EXPRESSIONISM; his *White Painting* series is often reminiscent of MONET.

GUTENBERG, Johann (c1400–1468), German printer, usually considered the inventor of PRINTING from separately cast metal types. By 1450 he had a press in Mainz, financed by **Johann Fust** (c1400–c1466) but in 1455 he handed over the press (and his invention) to Fust in repayment of debts. By now the Gutenberg (or Mazarin) Bible was at least well under way: each page has two columns of 42 lines. Gutenberg possibly founded another press some time later.

GUTHRIE, Sir (William) Tyrone (1900–1971), influential British stage director, famous for his experimental approach to traditional works. His Shakespeare productions and his vigorous and realistic opera productions such as *Peter Grimes* (1946) and *Carmen* (1949 and 1952), set new standards in their time. The Tyrone Guthrie Theater was established in 1963 at Minneapolis, Minn., under his direction.

GUTHRIE, Woody (Woodrow Wilson Guthrie; 1912–1967), US folksinger whose compositions and guitar style have had enormous influence on modern folk music. He developed his characteristic themes as a migrant worker in the 1930s, becoming a left-wing agitator and developing his "protest" songs.

GUTTA PERCHA, brownish, leathery solid used in the manufacture of golf balls, in dentistry and to insulate marine cables and electrical equipment. It is prepared from the latex obtained from trees native to Malaysia.

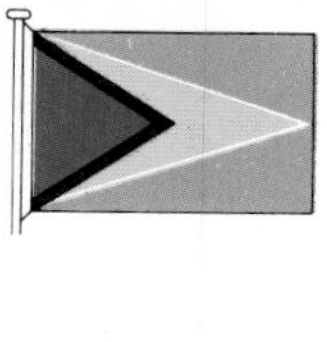

Official Name: Guyana
Capital: Georgetown
Area: 83 000sq mi
Population: 740 000
Languages: English; Indian; Chinese; Portuguese also spoken
Religions: Christian; Hindu; Muslim
Monetary Unit(s): 1 Guyana dollar = 100 cents

GUYANA, independent republic on the NE coast of South America, largest of the three countries in the Guiana region.

Land. The sparsely settled interior is largely massive sandstone plateaus, up to 500ft in height, sloping up to the Guiana Highlands in the S. Much of the more densely populated coastal strip, 10–40mi in width, lies below sea level; some of it is reclaimed land. About 85% of the country is tropical rain forest. Heat is constantly around 80°F with average humidity of about 75%; rainfall at the coast is around 90in a year.

People. More than 90% of the population lives along the coast, more than 20% in the capital. The main ethnic groups are East Indians (descendants of imported labor), Negroes and mulattoes; there are about 30 000 Amerindians. Many of the professional classes are European or Chinese. Education is compulsory between 6 and 14, and literacy is around 80%.

The Economy rests on agriculture, especially sugarcane grown on plantations near the coast. With rice this comprises about 50% of exports. Important mineral reserves include bauxite, diamonds and manganese. Hardwood from the enormous forests is also becoming an important resource.

History. Guyana's original inhabitants were Carib and Arawak Indians. The Dutch were the first to colonize the area, setting up POLDERS to reclaim land and importing Negro slaves to cultivate sugar and tobacco. At the end of the 18th century the British took over the area. British Guiana was created in 1831; slavery was abolished there in 1834 and East Indian labor imported. Moves towards self-government began after WWII; full internal self-rule was achieved in 1961, but independence was delayed by political problems and serious racial unrest between Negroes and East Indians. Under a new and fairer system of proportional representation, the People's National Congress, led by Forbes Burnham (a Negro), was elected; Burnham continued as premier after Guyana gained total independence in 1970. Serious border disputes with Venezuela and Surinam were not entirely resolved.

GUYOT, submarine table-mountain, found especially in the Pacific. It is thought that guyots originate as volcanic islands associated with MID-OCEAN RIDGES. Wave EROSION reduces the island, and SEA-FLOOR SPREADING causes the guyot to be further submerged. (See also VOLCANISM.)

GWALIOR, historic city in N India. Centered around a fortress built c500 AD, the city has many ancient buildings. It is now a national center for transport, commerce and industry. Site of several colleges, Gwalior is a famous cultural center, especially for music. Pop 384 772.

GWIN, William McKendree (1805–1885), US politician. Congressman from Miss. 1841–43, he moved to Cal. in 1849. He championed statehood there and was elected senator 1850–55 and 1857–61. A defender of slavery, he was imprisoned as a Confederate supporter during the Civil War.

GWYN, Nell (1650–1687), English actress, favorite mistress of Charles II from 1669. Daughter of a brothel-keeper, she became an orange-seller in the Theatre Royal, and 1666–69 its most popular actress. She bore Charles two sons.

GYMNASIUM, a building designed to provide suitable space and equipment for individual or group physical exercise and indoor sports such as basketball, volleyball, badminton, boxing and wrestling. The *gymnasium* (literally "school for naked exercise") originated in ancient Greece, where physical training was considered important. The ancient gymnasium was also a place for conversation, and philosophers taught there; the term has thus become applied to a type of high school in modern Europe.

GYMNASTICS, a system of exercise designed not only to maintain and improve the physique, but also as a sport. In ancient Greece gymnastics were important in education, including track and field athletics and training for boxing and wrestling. Competitive gymnastics are a series of exercises on set pieces of apparatus: parallel bars, horizontal bar, side and vaulting horses, beam and asymmetric bars. The US system, derived from the German, is designed to assist physical growth; the Swedish system aims at rectifying posture and weak muscles; and the Danish system seeks general fitness and endurance.

GYMNOSPERMS, the smaller of the two main classes of seed-bearing plants, the other being the ANGIOSPERMS. Gymnosperms are characterized by having naked seeds usually formed on open scales produced in cones. All are perennial plants and most are EVERGREEN. There are several orders, the main ones being the Cycadales, the CYCADS or sago palms; the Coniferales, including PINE, LARCH, FIR and REDWOOD; the Ginkgoales, the GINKGO; and the Gnetales, tropical shrubs and woody vines.

GYNECOLOGY, branch of MEDICINE and SURGERY, specializing in diseases of women, specifically disorders of female reproductive tract; often linked with OBSTETRICS. CONTRACEPTION, ABORTION, STERILIZATION, infertility and abnormalities of MENSTRUATION are the commonest problems. The early recognition and treatment of CANCER of the WOMB cervix after PAPANICOLAOU smears have become important. Other TUMORS of womb or ovaries, benign or malignant, and disorders of genital tract or closely related BLADDER following PREGNANCY, commonly require gynecological surgery. Dilatation of the cervix and curettage of womb endometrium (D and C) is used frequently for diagnosis and sometimes for treatment of menstrual disorders or postmenopausal bleeding. HYSTERECTOMY or removal of the womb is the commonest major operation of gynecologists.

GYNOECIUM. See FLOWER.

GYPSIES, nomadic people of Europe, Asia and North America. They are believed to have originated in India; their language, ROMANY, is related to Sanskrit and Prakrit. The gypsies probably began their westward migration about 1000 AD. By the 15th century they had penetrated the Balkans, Egypt and North Africa. In the 16th century they were to be found throughout Europe. Often known as thieves and tricksters, they have met with little toleration. In WWII many European gypsies were executed by the Nazis. There is a strong gypsy tradition of folklore, legend and song, and this, combined with the independence of their lives, has inspired the romantic imagination of many musicians, artists and writers.

GYPSUM, mineral consisting of CALCIUM sulfate dihydrate. It occurs worldwide as monoclinic crystals of various colors (SELENITE), or as fibrous or massive forms (ALABASTER). Gypsum is used in building and CEMENT.

GYPSY LANGUAGE. See ROMANY.

GYPSY MOTH, *Porthetria dispar*, a pretty moth originating in Europe and later introduced to North America. Here, in the absence of natural enemies, it has become a serious pest: the caterpillars feed on the leaves of deciduous trees, particularly fruit trees, and their occasional mass outbreaks can lead to complete defoliation.

GYRFALCON, *Falco rusticolus*, the largest, strongest and most beautiful of the FALCONS, found in Greenland, Iceland and Scandinavia. The long narrow wings and slender tail are typical of all falcons and allow extremely rapid flight. The beak is short, curved, and "toothed."

GYROCOMPASS, a continuously-driven GYROSCOPE which acts as a COMPASS. It is unaffected by magnetic variations and is used for steering large ships. As the earth rotates the gyroscope experiences a TORQUE if it is out of the meridian. The resulting tilting is sensed by a gravity sensing system which itself applies a torque to the gyroscope which returns it to the N–S meridian. The sensitivity of such instruments decreases with latitude away from the equator.

GYROPILOT, an automatic device for keeping a ship or airplane on a given course using signals from a gyroscopic reference. The marine version operates a ship's rudder by displacement signals from the GYROCOMPASS. In an airplane, the device is usually known as an **automatic pilot** and consists of sensors to detect deviations in direction, pitch and roll, and pass signals via a computer to alter the controls as necessary.

GYROSCOPE, a heavy spinning disk mounted so that its axis is free to adopt any orientation. Its special properties depend on the principle of the conservation of angular MOMENTUM. Although the scientific gyroscope was only devised by FOUCAULT in the mid-19th century, the child's traditional spinning top demonstrates the gyroscope principle. The fact that it will stay upright as long as it is spinning fast enough demonstrates the property of **gyroscopic inertia**: the direction of the spin axis resists change. This means that a gyroscope mounted universally, in double gimbals, will maintain the same orientation in space however its support is turned, a property applied in many navigational devices. If a FORCE tends to alter the direction of the spin axis (e.g., the weight of a top tilting sideways), a gyroscope will turn about an axis at right-angles to the force for as long as it is applied; this movement is known as **precession**. Instrument gyroscopes usually consist of a wheel having most of its mass concentrated at its rim to ensure a large moment of inertia and which is kept spinning in frictionless bearings by an electric motor. Once the wheel is set spinning its response to applied TORQUES can be monitored or used in control servomechanisms.

GYROSTABILIZER, a gyroscopic device for stabilizing a ship, airplane or instrument mounting. Originally giant gyroscopes (up to 4m in diameter) were used to counteract roll in ships, but they were found to be too cumbersome. Now fins protruding from the ship's hull are moved hydraulically to oppose roll under the control of signals from small GYROSCOPES that sense roll angle and velocity.

H

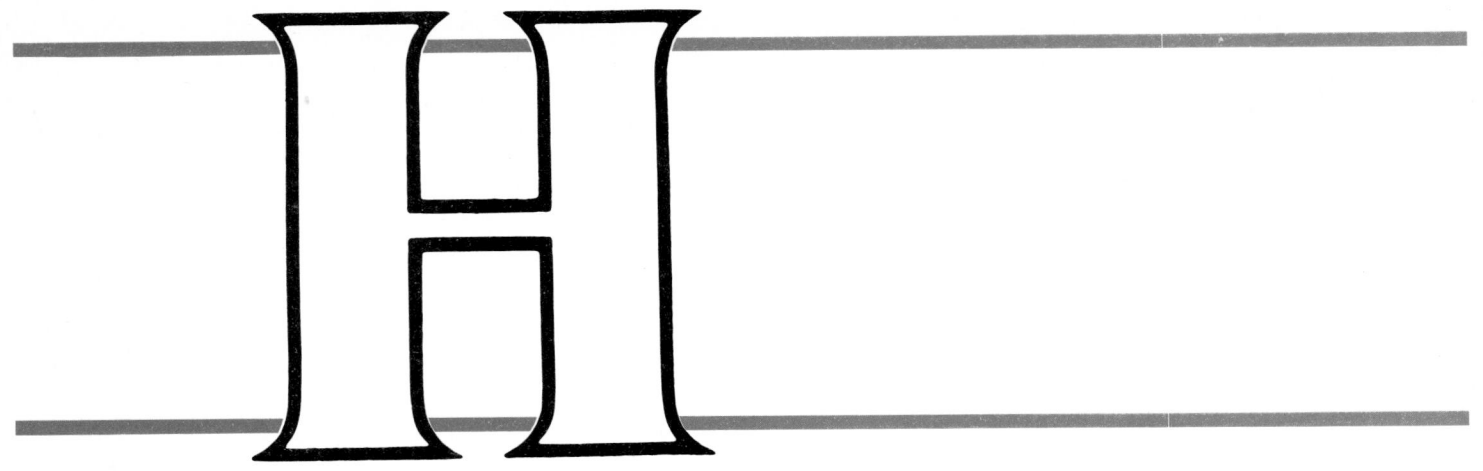

H, eighth letter of the English alphabet, derived from the Semitic letter *cheth.* Usually a glottal spirant, it is silent in many Romance languages. In thermodynamics it is the symbol for enthalpy.

HAAKON VII (1872–1957), king of Norway from 1905. A Danish prince, he was elected constitutional monarch when Norway became independent of Sweden. He resisted the German invasion in 1940; forced to flee to England, he reigned from there until 1945, becoming the much-respected symbol of his country's resistance.

HAARLEM, historic capital city of North Holland Province, W Netherlands. A great cultural center, it has become a prosperous industrial city in a major tulip-growing area. Pop 172 612.

HABAKKUK, Book of, the eighth of the Old Testament MINOR PROPHETS, dated probably late 7th century BC. Nothing is known of Habakkuk himself. The first part explores the problem of God's using the evil Chaldeans to punish Judah, and includes the influential statement, "The righteous shall live by his faith." The final chapter is a psalm.

HABEAS CORPUS (Latin: you have the person), in COMMON LAW a writ issued by the judiciary to compel a person held in custody to be brought before a court, so that it may determine whether or not the detention is lawful. Habeas corpus originated in medieval England, becoming a major civil right through the 1679 Habeas Corpus Act. Embodied in the US Constitution, it may not be suspended except in cases of rebellion or invasion. President Lincoln suspended it in 1861, at the onset of the Civil War. The writ may also be used in some non-judicial cases, as by an inmate in a mental hospital.

HABER, Fritz (1868–1934), German chemist awarded the 1918 Nobel Prize for Chemistry for synthesizing AMMONIA from the elements nitrogen and hydrogen. (See also HABER PROCESS.)

HABER PROCESS, industrial synthesis of AMMONIA invented by HABER and developed by BOSCH. NITROGEN (from the atmosphere) is mixed with HYDROGEN (from natural gas or water gas) and heated to about 500°C under 200–1000atm pressure, with a catalyst of finely divided iron containing aluminum oxide and potassium oxide. The ammonia formed is frozen out, and the unreacted gases recycled. See also NITROGEN FIXATION.

HABIT, in psychology, a REFLEX response to a frequently experienced stimulus; e.g., lighting a cigarette before using the telephone, or singing in the bath. The term is sometimes used loosely for CONSCIOUS reactions to situations. **Habit interference** is the conflict within an individual between two responses to a situation that differs slightly from one to which he has a habitual response. The process of acquiring a habit is **habit formation**. (See also DRUG ADDICTION.)

HABITAT, an area with certain physical characteristics which support a particular community of animals and plants. In general, a habitat can be defined in physical terms, e.g., rocky seashore or sandy desert, but as far as any one animal or plant species is concerned, the habitat cannot be defined without reference to the other animals and plants in the community. (See also ECOLOGY.)

HABSBURG. See HAPSBURG, HOUSE OF.

HACHINOHE, city in N Honshu, Japan, on the Pacific coast. A deep-sea fishing port, it has some other industries. Pop 208 801.

HACKBERRY, popular name for trees of the genus *Celtis,* family Ulmaceae, bearing inedible green or purple fruits. The common hackberry (*Celtis occidentalis*) is native to the E US and is cultivated in Europe. The wood is used for fencing and for making furniture.

HACKENSACK, city in NE N.J., seat of Bergen Co. and an industrial suburb of Jersey City. Pop 35 911.

HADASSAH, US Zionist women's organization. Founded in 1912, it supports educational and charitable work in the US and relief and refugee welfare in Israel.

HADDOCK, *Melanogrammus aeglefinus,* a cod-like fish found throughout the N Atlantic. Economically among the most important food fishes of countries fishing the North Sea, they live in shoals on sandy bottoms, feeding on shellfish, urchins and small fish. The black spot on the side of the haddock is said to be the thumbprint of St. Peter.

The mausoleum of Hadrian in Rome, now called the Castel Sant'Angelo. It was built by Hadrian as part of his building program in Rome 135–139 AD and was intended not only for himself but for succeeding emperors. Its appearance has altered greatly since it was built because it was made into a fortress by successive popes.

HADDON, township in SW N.J., SSE of Camden. Pop 18 192.

HADDONFIELD, historic borough in SW N.J.; a residential suburb of Camden, it was settled in 1682. Pop 13 118.

HADES, in Greek mythology, the pitiless god of the underworld, ruling with PERSEPHONE his queen over the dead. The term *hades* is used in the Greek Old Testament to render the Hebrew *sheol,* and so in late Judaism and Christianity means the realm of departed spirits. (See also HELL.)

HADHRAMAUT, region in E central Yemen, bounded by desert and the Gulf of Aden. An arid area, its economy rests on fishing and some agriculture.

HADJ. See HAJJ.

HADRIAN, name of six popes. See ADRIAN.

HADRIAN (76–138), Publius Aelius Hadrianus, Roman emperor from 117, successor of TRAJAN. He traveled the empire for 12 years, reforming and restoring imperial rule. An able administrator and soldier, he was a talented poet and an admirer of Greek civilization. His plan to build a new city at Jerusalem, however, sparked off a Jewish revolt 132–135, which he savagely repressed. His later years were saddened by the death of his favorite, Antinoüs.

HADRIAN'S WALL, Roman fortification built by Emperor HADRIAN, running 74 miles across the N of England. Intended to exclude the dangerous northern tribes, it had a series of forts along its length. Twice breached, it was abandoned after 383.

HADRONS, a class of SUBATOMIC PARTICLES including the BARYONS and the mesons. They are influenced by strong interactions (the FORCES binding PROTONS and NEUTRONS within the nucleus), GRAVITATION and, if charged, electromagnetic forces. Protons and neutrons are relatively stable but other hadrons (e.g., π-mesons) produced by collision processes are short-lived.

HAECKEL, Ernst Heinrich (1834–1919), German biologist best remembered for his vociferous support of DARWIN's theory of EVOLUTION, and for his own theory that ontogeny (the development of an individual organism) recapitulates phylogeny (its evolutionary stages), a theory now discarded. (See ONTOGENY AND PHYLOGENY.)

HAFNIUM (Hf), hard TRANSITION ELEMENT in Group IVB of the PERIODIC TABLE, found in ores of ZIRCONIUM, which it closely resembles. It is used in nuclear reactor control rods. AW 178.5, mp 2150°C, bp c4000°C, sg 13.31 (20°C).

HAFIZ, Shams ud-Din Mohammed (c1325–c1390), great Persian lyric poet, a courtier at Shiraz. He adopted the hitherto frivolous verse form *ghazal,* using it to express a sensuality and gaiety heightened by the philosophical mysticism of SUFISM.

HAGANAH, (Hebrew: defense) Jewish volunteer

militia in Palestine, formed after WWI to protect the Jewish community there. Although outlawed by the British, it was moderate and well-disciplined. It fought alongside the Allies in WWII and against the Arabs in 1947; in 1948 it was made into the Israeli national army.

HAGEN, city in North Rhine-Westphalia, in the E Ruhr district of West Germany, an industrial center since the 18th century. Pop 203 000.

HAGEN, Walter Charles (1892–1969), US professional golfer. He won the US Open championship twice, the British Open four times and the US P.G.A. championship five times. A colorful personality, he did much to make professional golf more respectable.

HAGENBECK, Karl (1844–1913), German animal collector and trainer. His touring animal show demonstrated animal intelligence rather than savagery. The zoo he founded near Hamburg in 1907 pioneered the use of barless, "natural" housing for animals.

HAGERSTOWN, city in N Maryland, seat of Washington Co., a manufacturing and transport center for an agricultural area. Pop 35 862.

HAGFISH, one of the two surviving groups of jawless fishes, AGNATHA. Eel-shaped fishes of colder seas, hagfish feed on dead and dying fish into which they burrow with the aid of a rasping tongue and horny teeth. Very flexible fishes—the skeleton is entirely cartilaginous—they usually live in burrows in muddy areas. As a means of defense hagfish can produce copious secretions of slime.

HAGGADAH (Hebrew: narration), rabbinical literature excluding the Law, including legendary and proverbial matter. It also refers to the Passover narration of the EXODUS. (See also MIDRASH; TALMUD.)

HAGGAI, Book of, the tenth of the Old Testament MINOR PROPHETS, dated 520–519 BC. It consists of four oracles urging the Jews to rebuild the Temple at Jerusalem and attributing their economic plight to their delay in doing so, and prophesying the glories of the Messianic Age.

HAGGARD, Sir Henry Rider (1856–1925), British novelist, best known for *King Solomon's Mines* (1885), *She* (1887) and other romantic adventure novels with an authentic African background. He was also a pioneering agriculturalist.

HAGGIS, traditional Scots pudding, made of the heart, liver and lungs of a sheep with oatmeal and suet, seasoned and cooked in the sheep's stomach (a plastic skin is sometimes used today). A cheap, tasty and long-lasting winter food, it should be eaten with vegetables and beer—*not* with neat whisky.

HAGIA SOPHIA, or Santa Sophia, massive cathedral raised at Constantinople (now Istanbul) by JUSTINIAN I; completed in 537, it became a mosque after the Turkish conquest (1453). Now a museum, the domed basilica, richly decorated, is the finest remaining example of Byzantine architecture.

HAGUE, The (Dutch: 'S Gravenhage or Den Haag), historic city, seat of government of the Netherlands and capital of South Holland province. It has many ancient buildings and is one of the country's handsomest cities, with many parks and woodland areas. The Binnenhof palace houses the two chambers of the legislature. The economy rests more on the administration than on industry. The city is also an educational and cultural center. Pop 537 643.

HAGUE, Frank (1876–1956), US politician, mayor of Jersey City, N.J. 1917–47 and boss of one of the most powerful party machines. He was elected to the Democratic National Committee in 1922. Accused of corruption and intimidation, he was ousted in 1952.

HAGUE PEACE CONFERENCES, two conferences held in 1899 and 1907 at The Hague, the Netherlands, at Russia's request. They achieved little beyond some clarification of belligerency rules and war conventions, but established the International Permanent Court of Arbitration (the HAGUE TRIBUNAL).

HAGUE TRIBUNAL, an international Permanent Court of Arbitration. Established by the first HAGUE PEACE CONFERENCE (1899), it is now supported by 71 nations, each of which may appoint up to four jurists. The court will supply arbitrators to decide international disputes submitted to them by international agreement. After WWI it was supplemented by the World Court and later the INTERNATIONAL COURT OF JUSTICE.

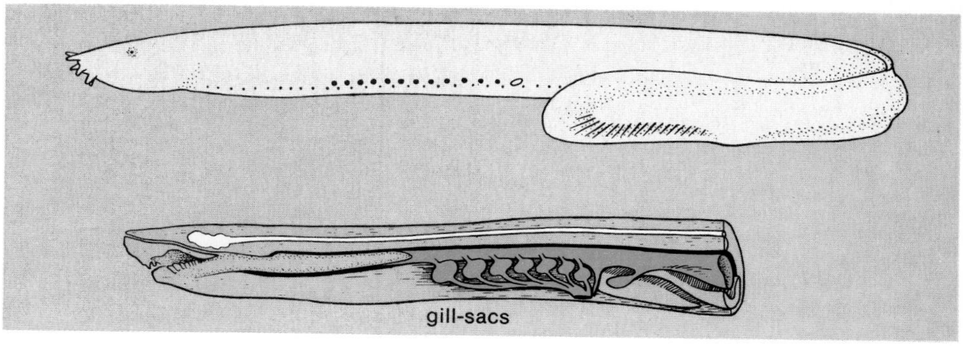

The hagfish *Myxine glutinosa* (*top*) and (*bottom*) dissected section showing the way in which its gill-sacs are linked to a common external opening.

HAHN, Otto (1879–1968), German chemist awarded the 1944 Nobel Prize for Chemistry for his work on nuclear FISSION. With Lise MEITNER he discovered the new element PROTACTINIUM (1918); later they bombarded URANIUM with NEUTRONS, treating the uranium with ordinary barium. Meitner showed that the residue was radioactive BARIUM formed by the splitting (fission) of the uranium nucleus.

HAHNEMANN, Christian Friedrich Samuel (1755–1843), German physician, the father of HOMEOPATHY, which has as its basis the fact that the induction by drugs of the symptoms of a disease appears to immunize an individual against that disease.

HAHNIUM (Ha), a TRANSURANIUM ELEMENT in Group VB of the PERIODIC TABLE, atomic number 105. The priority of its discovery is disputed between the USSR and the US, as in the case of RUTHERFORDIUM. American scientists claimed in 1970 to have synthesized hahnium-260 (half-life 1.6s) by bombarding californium-249 with nitrogen-15 ions.

HAIDA, Indian tribe of the N Pacific coast area of British Columbia and Alaska. The Haida lived mainly by salmon and cod fishing, and by hunting. Their native art, especially carving, is sophisticated and commands high prices today. Their society was based on two subdivided clans. Social status was gained through the POTLATCH system. Today their numbers have been reduced by disease to around 800.

HAIFA, city in NE Israel, the country's principal port on the Mediterranean. It existed in the 1st century BC and probably earlier. It is now a flourishing industrial center, especially in the port area; the city's upper region, on Mt Carmel, is largely residential. The population includes Muslim and Christian minorities, and is the world headquarters of the BAHA'I FAITH. Pop 217 400.

HAIG, Douglas Haig, 1st Earl (1861–1928), field-marshal, British commander in WWI. He has been unfairly blamed for the misconduct of the Somme and Ypres campaigns 1916–17. Hampered by the hostility of British premier LLOYD GEORGE, he was denied effective command until 1918, when he displayed far greater generalship.

HAIKU, traditional Japanese verse form, consisting of three lines of 5, 7 and 5 syllables each. Developed by MATSUO BASHO and others around the 17th century from an older 31-syllable form, it is now considered the major traditional form. Typically a *haiku* uses an image, often drawn from nature, to suggest or evoke a mood or feeling; a good *haiku* is compact and intense.

HAIL, PRECIPITATION of pellets of ice, often associated with thunderstorms. Hailstones have diameters of 2–250mm, 2–5mm being most common. They require a strong updraft, raising them to colder regions, to form. Often this happens several times, the hailstone collecting a new layer of ice each time it rises, until it is too heavy to support and falls to the ground. Larger hailstones may have alternate layers of clear and white ice, due to different rates of freezing. (See also ICE; RAIN; SNOW.)

HAILE SELASSIE (1892–1975), reign-name of Ras Tafari, emperor of Ethiopia 1930–74. A benevolent despot, he won great popularity by his determined resistance to the Italian invasion of Ethiopia 1935–41, when British forces restored him to his throne. Efficient at first, his autocracy degenerated in later years. In the face of a nationwide famine he was deposed by his army in 1974 and died in captivity.

HAINAN, island in the S China Sea, part of Kwangtung province, China. Mountainous and tropical, it is inhabited by the aboriginal Li in the S and by many Chinese immigrants. It is a major rubber producer and a rich mineral center.

HAIPHONG, major seaport city in North Vietnam. It became prosperous during the French occupation; since 1954 it has become dependent on Chinese-financed industry, particularly after heavy bombing from the S until 1974. Pop 390 000.

HAIR, nonliving filamentous structure made of KERATIN and pigment, formed in the skin hair FOLLICLES. Facial and genetic factors determine both

Diagram of the structure of the skin and hair. (I) Epidermis; (II) dermis; (III) subdermal tissue. (a) Stratum corneum; (b) stratum papillare cutis; (c) connective tissue; (d) sebaceous gland; (e) muscle fiber in the skin; (f) tiny blood vessels; (g) shaft of hair; (h) cross section of hair; (i) hair papilla; (j) fatty tissue.

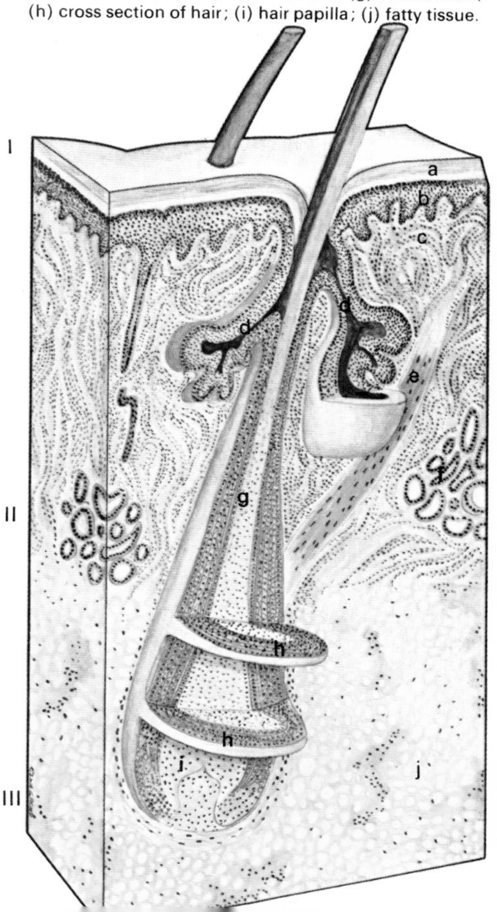

coloring and shape (by heat-labile sulfur bridges). In man all skin surfaces except the palms and soles are covered with very fine hair. This assists in TOUCH reception. In the cold, these hairs are erected (see GOOSEFLESH) to create extra insulation. Scalp hair is prominent in man. Pubic and axillary hair develop at PUBERTY in response to sex HORMONES and their patterns differ in the sexes; facial hair is ANDROGEN-dependent. Hair growth is more rapid in the summer. Hormone abnormalities alter hair distribution, while BALDNESS follows hair loss.

HAIRWORMS, very slender worms about 1mm (0.04in) in diameter and from 300–900mm (1–3ft) long. Free-living as adults, all hairworms are parasitic in their larval stages, the larvae of freshwater forms infesting insects, those of marine forms parasitic in crabs. The alimentary system is degenerate or absent in both juveniles and adults.

Official name: Republic of Haiti
Capital: Port-au-Prince
Area: 10 700sq mi
Population: 4 969 000
Languages: French; Creole spoken by majority
Religions: Roman Catholic.
Voodoo is the folk religion
Monetary unit(s): 1 Gourde = 100 centimes

HAITI, independent republic in the Caribbean Sea, the W portion of the island of Hispaniola, which it shares with the Dominican Republic. Haiti is mainly mountainous; the coastline has beaches, coral reefs, mangrove swamps and cliffs. The climate is tropical, with two rainy seasons. There are extensive forests, mainly rain forest with many coffee and fruit plantations on the coast. The people are mostly of African descent, with a powerful mulatto minority. The official language is French, but the main tongue is CREOLE. The official religion is Roman Catholicism but VOODOO dominates the life of the people. Only about 10% of the population is literate and education, although theoretically compulsory, is scant. The standard of living is low; government, army and professions are in the hands of the mulattoes.

The economy is poor, based on subsistence agriculture. Coffee is the major cash crop and some sisal, sugarcane, cotton and cocoa are processed and exported, as are wood and, on a small scale, minerals. The tourist trade is developing.

Columbus claimed Haiti for Spain in 1492. Spanish exploitation wiped out the aboriginal ARAWAK INDIANS. The island was ceded to France in 1697, and became a plantation center to which African slaves were imported. In 1804 a slave revolt led by TOUSSAINT L'OUVERTURE and Jacques DESSALINES finally won independence. Political chaos then continued until the US occupation 1915–47. In 1957 François DUVALIER became dictator, and with the brutal backing of his *tontons macoutes* (secret police) held power until his death in 1971; he was succeeded by his son, under whom little changed.

HAJJ, pilgrimage to Mecca, obligatory for every able, adult Muslim at least once in his life. The pilgrimage takes place during the last month of the Islamic year. Various rites are performed at Mecca, the central one being a circling of the KAABA.

HAKE, *Merluccius merluccius*, a deep-water fish of the cod family found in the N Atlantic. Predatory on other fishes, hake are migratory, and differ from other codlike fishes in that the second dorsal and the anal fins are single and not split into two.

HAKLUYT, Richard (c1552–1616), pioneering British geographer. He published many early accounts of the Americas and a major account of English voyaging and discoveries. He lectured on geography at Oxford.

HAKODATE, port city on the SW tip of Hokkaido, Japan. A historic city, its economy rests on the port, shipyards and fishing. Pop 241 663.

HALACHAH (Hebrew: law) the body of Jewish law relating to religious observance, life and conduct. It is held to stem directly from the revelation on Mt Sinai. (See also TORAH.)

HALCYON DAYS, a time of peace and prosperity. The term derives from the period of calm weather which in Greek myth was given by the gods to the kingfisher (*halcyon*) as a breeding season.

HALDANE, John Burdon Sanderson (1892–1964), British geneticist whose work, with that of Sir Ronald Aylmer Fisher (1890–1962) and Sewall WRIGHT, provided a basis for the mathematical study of population GENETICS.

HALDANE, John Scott (1860–1936), British physiologist best known for his researches into industrial (especially mining) diseases caused by poor ventilation. He also contributed to a technique for dealing with the "bends" (see AEROEMBOLISM).

HALDANE, Richard Burdon Haldane, 1st Viscount (1856–1928), British statesman and lawyer, a Liberal member of Parliament 1885–1911. As secretary of state for war 1905–12 he introduced sweeping army reforms, founding the Territorial Army and national and imperial general staffs. He was Lord Chancellor 1912–15 and in 1924. A founder of the London School of Economics (1895), he wrote several philosophical works.

HALDIMAND, Sir Frederick (1718–1791), Swiss-born British general, governor of Quebec 1778–86. A former mercenary, he commanded the British North American Army 1773–74. In Quebec he managed to prevent any revolutionary outbreaks at the time of the REVOLUTIONARY WAR.

HALE, Edward Everett (1822–1909), US Unitarian clergyman and writer. Trained as a journalist, he wrote a vast number of books, pamphlets and other works; he is best known for his short story *The Man Without a Country* (1863). He was chaplain to the Senate from 1903.

HALE, George Ellery (1868–1938), US astronomer who discovered the magnetic fields of SUNSPOTS, and who invented at the same time as Henri Alexandre Deslandres (1853–1948) the SPECTROHELIOGRAPH (c1892). His name is commemorated in that of the HALE OBSERVATORIES.

HALE, Nathan (1755–1776), American revolutionary. A former schoolteacher, he was caught in disguise behind the British lines on Long Island, and hanged as a spy on Sept. 22, 1776. His last words are said to have been that he regretted having but one life to lose for his country; the quotation actually comes from Joseph ADDISON's play *Cato*.

HALE, Sarah Josepha (1788–1879), US feminist journalist. Editor of *Ladies' Magazine* (1828–37) and *Godey's Lady's Book* (from 1837), she championed higher education for women.

HALEAKALA NATIONAL PARK, inactive volcano crater on Maui Island, Hawaii, 20mi in circumference. It has spectacular scenery and unusual plant life.

HALE OBSERVATORIES, formerly the Mt Wilson and Palomar Observatories, renamed (1970) for G. E. HALE and since 1948 operated jointly by the Carnegie Institution and the California Institute of Technology. At Mt Wilson (Cal.) are two reflecting TELESCOPES and two solar towers; at Palomar Mountain (Cal.) a 200-in reflector, until 1973 the largest in the world, and two Schmidt telescopes.

HALES, Alexander of. See ALEXANDER OF HALES.

HALES, Stephen (1677–1761), English plant physiologist and chemist who, in accordance with the Newtonian quantitative paradigm, devised experiments to measure blood pressure in animals, and, realizing the importance of careful weighing and measuring in chemical experiments, applied these principles in his investigations of the life of plants. His *Vegetable Staticks* was published in 1727.

HALEVI, Jehuda. See JUDAH HA-LEVI.

HALF-BEAKS, small marine and freshwater fishes of tropical and temperate regions. The lower jaw is elongated and beak-like, projecting far beyond the short upper jaw. Closely related to the flying fishes, half-beaks too may skitter along the water surface and even leap into the air.

HALF-LIFE, the time taken for the activity of a radioactive sample to decrease to half its original value, half the nuclei originally present having changed spontaneously into a different nuclear type by emission of particles and energy. After two half-lives, the radioactivity will be a quarter of its original value and so on. Depending on the type of nucleus and method of decay, half-lives range from less than a second to over 10^{10} years. The half-life concept can also be applied to other systems undergoing random decay, e.g. certain biological populations.

HALFTONE, reproduction of a photograph or other picture containing a range of continuous tones, by using dots of various sizes but uniform tone. The dots are small enough to blend in the observer's vision to give the effect of the original. The picture is photographed through a screen on which a fine rectangular grid has been scribed (2 to 6 lines/mm); the dots arise by DIFFRACTION. From the screened negative is made a halftone plate used for PRINTING by all processes.

HALF-WAY COVENANT, a religious-political compromise adopted by the New England Congregationalists (Puritans) in 1662, which allowed baptized persons not publicly professing conversion to be regarded as church members in a sense, though not admitted to Holy Communion. This gave them political rights, and entitled their children to baptism and membership. In the 18th century the churches reverted to the stricter policy of requiring for membership a statement of personal conversion.

HALIBUT, *Hippoglossus hippoglossus*, largest of the N Atlantic flatfishes, reported to reach 2.7m (9ft) and to weigh up to 270kg (600lb). The related Pacific halibut (*H. stenolepsis*) is somewhat smaller. Halibut are carnivorous, feeding on other fishes, squids and crabs. Important as a food fish, the halibut is the subject of one of the most successful fish-management projects.

HALICARNASSUS, ancient Greek city, capital of Caria, Asia Minor; its site is now Bodrum, Turkey. HERODOTUS was born here. The monumental tomb of

Among the many monuments to Nathan Hale, one of the most tragic figures of the Revolution, is this statue in front of a Chicago newspaper building.

the Carian king Mausolus, the original MAUSOLEUM, was built here c355 BC.

HALIDES, binary compounds of the HALOGENS with oxidation number −1. Metal halides are mostly ionic salts (X^-), usually very soluble. Nonmetal halides, and a few metal halides such as tin (IV) chloride, are volatile covalent compounds, highly reactive, often violently hydrolyzed by water, and used as halogenating agents. Halide ions form stable LIGAND complexes. Their reducing power increases down the group. Halide minerals include SALT, SYLVITE, FLUORITE, APATITE and CRYOLITE. (See also ALKYL HALIDES; HYDROGEN CHLORIDE; HYDROGEN FLUORIDE.)

HALIFAX, port city, capital of Nova Scotia, E Canada. A major British military base from 1749, it was taken over by Canada in 1906 and remained a naval base in WWI and WWII. It now has various industries, many connected with the port, and is a cultural and educational center. Pop 122 035.

HALIFAX, Edward Frederick Lindley Wood, 1st Earl of (1881–1959), British statesman, a Conservative member of Parliament 1910–25. As viceroy of India 1925–31 he was sympathetic to the independence movement. Foreign secretary 1938–40, he advocated APPEASEMENT of Hitler, helping to negotiate the MUNICH PACT. He was ambassador to the US 1941–46.

HALITE, or **Rock Salt.** See SALT.

HALITOSIS, or bad breath, a condition often caused by excessive bacterial growth in the mouth, e.g., in TONSILLITIS, and associated with poor oral hygiene. Disease of the GASTROINTESTINAL TRACT, including ULCER and APPENDICITIS, may also cause halitosis.

HALL, Charles Martin (1863–1914), US chemist who discovered (c1886), independently of HÉROULT, the electrolytic method of isolating pure aluminum now known as the HALL-HÉROULT PROCESS.

HALL, Fort, historic fur-trading port on the Snake R, SE Idaho, an important landmark and garrison post on the OREGON TRAIL. It was built in 1834 and operated until 1855.

HALL, Granville Stanley (1844–1924), US psychologist and educator best known for founding the *American Journal of Psychology* (1887), the first US psychological journal. He was first president of the American Psychological Institute (1894), a body whose foundation he had assisted.

HALL, James (1811–1898), US geologist and paleontologist, the father of American STRATIGRAPHY. His major work was on the paleontology of the SILURIAN and DEVONIAN of New York State, *The Paleontology of New York* (13 vols., 1847–94).

HALL, James Norman. See NORDHOFF AND HALL.

HALLANDALE, city in SE Fla., on the Atlantic coast N of Miami. In a fruit-growing area, its economy rests more on tourism. Pop 23 849.

HALLE, industrial city in E Germany, on the right bank of the Saale R. It is also a historic cultural center, dating back at least to the 10th century. Pop 257 300.

HALLECK, Henry Wager (1815–1872), US Civil War general and military theorist, whose *Elements of Military Art and Science* (1846) was an influential training manual in the Civil War. After service in the Mexican War he left the army in 1853 to practice law. At the onset of the Civil War he was appointed major-general in command of the Western theater and in 1862 general in chief. In 1864 he was relieved, and served as chief of staff until 1865.

HALL EFFECT, the POTENTIAL difference that develops across a METAL OR SEMICONDUCTOR placed in a transverse magnetic field when an electric current flows in it. This voltage is at right-angles to both the current and magnetic field directions, and arises from the deflection of moving charge carriers (ELECTRONS or holes) by the magnetic field.

HALLER, Albrecht von (1708–1777), Swiss biologist, best known for his work on human anatomy and physiology, and also a poet. A pupil of BOERHAAVE and much influenced by him, he is credited with being the founder of experimental ANATOMY. In physiology he investigated RESPIRATION, the BLOOD CIRCULATION, the NERVOUS SYSTEM and the irritability and sensibility of different types of body tissue; in all cases relying on experiment.

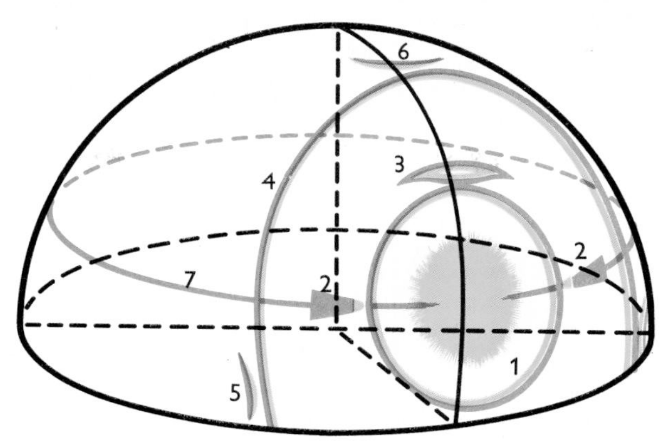

Halo phenomena may take many forms. Besides the common 22° halo (1) we may sometimes see parhelia ("mock suns"), luminous spots about 22° on either side of the sun (2). A tangent arc (3) is often associated with the 22° halo. (4) The large, less luminous halo with an angular radius of 46°; (5) the tangent arc to the 46° halo; and (6) the circumzenithal arc, centered on the zenith and parallel to the horizon. The parhelic circle ("mock sun ring"), which passes through the sun and may extend completely across the sky, is seen at (7).

HALLEY, Edmund (1656–1742), English astronomer. In 1677 he made the first full observation of a transit of Mercury; and in 1676–79 prepared a major catalog of the S-hemisphere stars. He persuaded NEWTON to publish the *Principia*, which he financed. In 1720 he succeeded FLAMSTEED as Astronomer Royal. He is best known for his prediction that the comet of 1680 would return in 1758 (see HALLEY'S COMET), based on his conviction that COMETS follow elliptical paths about the sun.

HALLEY'S COMET, the first periodic comet to be identified (by HALLEY, late 17th century) and the brightest of all recurring comets. It has a period of about 76 years. Records of every appearance of the comet since 240 BC, except that of 163 BC, are extant; and it is featured on the BAYEUX TAPESTRY. It will next reappear in 1986.

HALL-HÉROULT PROCESS, main ALUMINUM production method. Pure aluminum oxide, extracted from BAUXITE, is dissolved in molten CRYOLITE at 970°C, and electrolyzed (see ELECTROLYSIS) with a current of about 100kA through carbon electrodes. Molten aluminum is formed at the cathode and withdrawn from the bottom of the cell. The process was invented independently in 1886 by Charles HALL in the US and by Paul HÉROULT in France.

HALLMARK, symbols stamped on gold and silverware to indicate its conformity to legal standards of purity, usually indicating the maker, date and assaying authority. Hallmarking was officially initiated in Britain in 1300, and in the US has been under federal supervision since 1906.

HALL OF FAME, shrine established in 1901 on the New York University campus, to commemorate prominent Americans; busts and tablets of them are placed in a large semicircular hall. Those so honored, chosen by an Electoral College, must have been dead at least 25 years.

HALLOWEEN, festival on Oct. 31, eve of All Saints' Day or Hallowmas, originally a Celtic festival to mark the new year, welcoming the spirits of the dead and assuaging supernatural powers. It was introduced to the US by Scots and Irish immigrants, and is now a children's festival famous for "trick-or-treat."

HALLSTATT, term referring to the late BRONZE AGE and early IRON AGE in W and Central Europe, from Hallstatt, Austria, where there is a prehistoric cemetery and salt mines which have been in constant operation since 2500 BC. It was characterized by extremely fine, decorated pottery, though the quality deteriorated toward the end of the period.

HALLSTEIN, Walter (1901–), West German statesman and jurist. Professor of Law at Rostock (1930–41) and Frankfurt (1941–44) he was president of the influential European Economic Community Commission (see COMMON MARKET) 1958–67.

HALLUCINATION, an experience similar to a normal PERCEPTION but with the difference that sensory stimulus is either absent or too minor to explain the experience satisfactorily. Certain abnormal mental conditions (see MENTAL ILLNESS) produce hallucinations, as does taking of HALLUCINOGENIC DRUGS. They may also result from exhaustion or FEVER; or may be experienced while falling asleep (hypnogogic) or waking (hypnopompic), and also by individuals under HYPNOSIS. A **negative hallucination** is lack of perception despite adequate stimulus. **Mass hallucination** is hallucination shared by the members of a GROUP; it may particularly result from mass hypnosis. (See also EIDETIC IMAGE; ILLUSION.)

HALLUCINOGENIC DRUGS, DRUGS which cause hallucinations or illusions, usually visual, together with personality and behavior changes. The last may arise as a result of therapy, but more usually follow deliberate exposure to certain drugs for their psychological effects ("trip"). Lysergic acid diethylamide (LSD), HEROIN, MORPHINE and other OPIUM NARCOTICS, MESCALINE and PSILOCYBIN are commonly hallucinogenic and cannabis sometimes so. The type of hallucination is not predictable and many are unpleasant ("bad trip"). Recurrent hallucinations may follow use of these drugs; another danger is that altered behavior may inadvertently cause death or injury. Although psychosis may be a result of their use, it may be that recourse to drugs represents rather an early symptom of SCHIZOPHRENIA.

HALMAHERA, largest island of the Moluccas group, E Indonesia. Partly volcanic in origin, the island is mountainous. The inhabitants live in tribal societies, by hunting and subsistence agriculture.

HALO, a luminous ring or series of arcs sometimes seen around the sun or moon, the result of REFRACTION OF REFLECTION (or both) of their light by crystals of ICE in high, thin clouds. Commonest is the 22° halo, of angular diameter 22° and centered on the sun or moon. (See also CORONA.)

HALOGENS, highly reactive nonmetals in Group VIIA of the PERIODIC TABLE, comprising FLUORINE, CHLORINE, BROMINE, IODINE and ASTATINE; the general symbol X is often used. The elements have molecular formular X_2. They show a regular gradation of physical and chemical properties: with increasing atomic number, they become less volatile, darker in color, less reactive (in particular, less strongly oxidizing), and less electronegative (see ELECTRONEGATIVITY). The typical compounds of the halogens are the HALIDES, with oxidation number −1; compounds with positive oxidation numbers (usually 1, 3, 5 and 7) are also formed, with increasing stability down the group. The halogens react vigorously with almost all other elements and always occur combined in nature. (See also INTERHALOGENS; PSEUDO-HALOGENS; ALKYL HALIDES; ACID CHLORIDES.)

HALOGETON, genus of salt-tolerant herbs of the goosefoot family (Chenopodiaceae). *Halogeton glomeratus* was introduced to Nevada from Europe and Asia and has become a problematical weed that is poisonous to sheep and cattle.

HALOPHYTES, plants that are tolerant to saline conditions, found on the seashore and salt marshes, such as GLASSWORT and eel-grasses (*Zostera*).

HALS, Frans (c1580–1666), Dutch painter, one of the great portraitists. In his time he was not especially famous, known mainly in his native Haarlem. Many of his greatest works, such as the *Lady Governors of the Old Men's Home* (1664), are civic portraits. His later works have a somber serenity, but many portraits and genre scenes, such as *Banquet of the Officers of St. George* (1616) and the so-called *Laughing Cavalier* (1624), are infused with a rich joviality.

HALSEY, William Frederick "Bull", Jr. (1882–1959), US admiral, WWII. After commanding a Pacific carrier division with great distinction 1940–42, he took command of the Pacific theater. As commander of the 3rd Fleet he helped destroy the Japanese fleet at LEYTE GULF in 1944. He resigned as fleet admiral in 1947 and entered business.

HÄLSINGBORG, seaport city in S Sweden, on the Øresund. A medieval fortified town, it is now a prosperous commercial center. Pop 100 305.

HALTOM CITY, village in N Tex., a suburb of Fort Worth. Pop 28 127.

HAMA, commercial city in W central Syria, on the Orontes R. The biblical Hamath, it is now the center of a rich agricultural region. Pop 137 000.

HAMADAN, historic city in W Iran, on the site of Ectabana, a Median capital. It is now a major commercial center and summer resort. Pop 140 000.

HAMADRYADS. See DRYADS.

HAMADRYAS BABOON, or Sacred baboon, *Papio hamadryas hamadryas*, a small BABOON occurring in Somalia, Eritrea and southwestern Arabia. Hamadryas baboons forage in small groups during the day, each group consisting of a single male and several females, but gather into big troops of 100 or more at night.

HAMAMATSU, city in S Honshu, Japan, near Nagoya. A manufactory and marketing center, it produces textiles and musical instruments. Pop 432 221.

HAMBLETONIAN, US standardbred horse, 1849–1876. Bred in Chester, N.Y., he sired the dominant breed of trotting horses. The Hambletonian trotting event takes place in Du Quoin, Ill.

HAMBURG, historic seaport, now the largest city in West Germany, near the mouth of the Elbe R. Probably founded by CHARLEMAGNE, it was a dominant member of the HANSEATIC LEAGUE, and always a flourishing commercial center. Devastated in WWII, it has been rebuilt and now has shipyards and a wide range of industries. A transport hub, it is the center of the country's fishing industry. Pop 1 793 823.

HAMBURG, village in W N.Y., a residential town for nearby Buffalo. Pop 10 215.

HAMDEN, residential town in SW Conn. An early rail center, it now has some light industry. Pop 49 357.

HAMELN (Hamelin), historic city in West Germany, on the Weser R. Once an influential member of the HANSEATIC LEAGUE, it is now a river port and industrial center. Pop 47 100.

HAMILCAR BARCA (d. c228 BC), Carthaginian general, father of HANNIBAL. He became commander of Sicily in 247 BC, in the First PUNIC WAR, and from there harassed the mainland. In 241 he returned to Carthage; he quelled a mercenary revolt and became a political leader. In 238 he led a successful occupation of Spain, but was later killed there.

HAMILTON, port city on Bermuda Island, capital of Bermuda. A governmental center, its economy rests mainly on tourism. Pop 2 127.

HAMILTON, major industrial city in SE Ontario, Canada. It is a transport, commercial and financial center and site of McMaster U. Pop 309 173.

HAMILTON, industrial city in SW Ohio, seat of Butler Co. Pop 67 865.

HAMILTON, Alexander (c1755–1804), a founding father of the US. Successively a revolutionary, first secretary of the treasury, founder of the first American political party, adviser to Washington and a powerful statesman, he was one of the most important figures in the new nation. His hauteur and elitist political outlook antagonized many people, but his integrity was beyond doubt. The young republic would have had less chance of surviving without his determination to make it fiscally sound with a strong central government.

A pamphleteer for the Revolution, he joined the army and became Washington's aide-de-camp in 1777. After the war he campaigned for central government, and served in Congress and the New York legislature, becoming its delegate to the ANNAPOLIS CONVENTION and the Constitutional Convention of 1787. With John JAY and MADISON he wrote the *Federalist Papers* (1787–88), still considered classics of political theory. Not a democrat, he advocated an intellectual aristocracy maintained by the "enlightened self-interest" of the wealthy. This brought him into conflict with JEFFERSON, who supported the French Revolution and sought to abolish privilege. As first secretary to the treasury from 1789, Hamilton created the Bank of the United States (1791) and became leader of the Federalist Party; Jefferson and Madison led the Republicans, the Hamiltonians becoming the Federalists. Hamilton left the cabinet in 1795 but he continued to influence the executive from behind the scenes until John ADAMS became president. When the latter lost his bid for reelection, an electoral tie occurred between Aaron BURR and Jefferson. The Federalists in Congress wanted Burr, but Hamilton intervened in favor of his old opponent and Burr lost. Burr challenged him to a duel, in which Hamilton was killed.

The designated setting of Shakespeare's *Hamlet*, Castle Kronborg in Helsingor (Elsinore), Denmark. Appropriately, the play is performed in this courtyard every year.

HAMILTON, Andrew (1676–1741), Philadelphia lawyer, whose successful defense of the publisher John Peter ZENGER on a libel charge in 1735 established a precedent that contributed towards freedom of the press in America.

HAMILTON, Edith (1867–1963), US educator and classical scholar. Founder and headmistress of Bryn Mawr School for girls in Baltimore, she wrote her first and most influential book, *The Greek Way*, a survey of Greek culture, in 1930.

HAMILTON, Emma, Lady (1765–1815), celebrated beauty who became the mistress of Lord NELSON. A blacksmith's daughter, she was the wife of Sir William Hamilton, British envoy in Naples. She exercised great influence over Nelson. After his death she lived extravagantly, but died in poverty.

HAMILTON, Henry (c1732–1796), British army officer, lieutenant-governor of Detroit (1775). Much hated by the Americans during the Revolution, he was captured by George Rogers CLARK at Vincennes in 1779.

HAMILTON, Patrick (c1504–1528), Scottish Lutheran scholar, the first martyr of the Scottish Reformation. He fled to Germany in 1527, but on his return to Scotland he was burned as a heretic.

HAMILTON RIVER, former name of the CHURCHILL RIVER.

HAMITES, in the Old Testament, the descendents of Ham, Noah's son and father of Canaan, Cush, Mizraim and Put. Today the term is sometimes applied to N and E African peoples speaking the HAMITIC LANGUAGES.

HAMITIC LANGUAGES, a group within the **Hamito-Semitic** language family, including Berber, Cushite and Ancient Egyptian (the former two still being spoken today). Other Hamito-Semitic Languages include SEMITIC and Chadic. (See also LANGUAGE.)

HAMLET, Danish prince in SHAKESPEARE's tragedy of that name. The story is that of Amleth, whose vengeance on his usurping uncle is recounted in SAXO GRAMMATICUS' *History of Denmark* (12th century). The legend of the prince who feigns madness to outwit a tyrant, however, has origins in Roman and Eastern legend. Shakespeare probably found the story in François de Belleforest's *Histoires Tragiques* (1570) or in a play, now lost, drawn from it.

HAMLIN, Hannibal (1809–1891), US vice-president under Lincoln 1861–65. A Democrat at first, he joined the Republicans in 1856 because of his antislavery views. He was a senator from Me. 1848–56 and 1869–81, and an ardent Reconstructionist.

HAMMARSKJÖLD, Dag (Hjalmar Agne Carl) (1905–1961), Swedish statesman and economist, UN secretary general 1953–61. He greatly increased UN power and prestige. He was instrumental in negotiations over the Korean War truce and the Suez crisis of 1956. In 1960 he directed UN attempts to end the fighting in the Congo, and his actions were condemned by the USSR. He refused to resign, but was killed in an air-crash in the Congo. He was posthumously awarded the 1961 Nobel Peace Prize.

HAMMERFEST, town in N Norway, the northernmost in Europe. Commercial center of W Finnmark, its industries are fishing and fish processing, tourism and livestock raising. Pop 7 136.

HAMMERHEAD SHARKS, *(Sphyrna spp)*, curious sharks of warm seas with the eyes set at the tips of two flat platelike outgrowths of the head. The function of this strange-shaped head is unknown. Hammerheads are all livebearers, and in some species the young are even nourished in the uterus before birth.

HAMMERKOP, or **hammerhead,** *Scopus umbretta*, a curious ibis-like bird of lake and stream margins in Africa, feeding on frogs, tadpoles and large insects. A heavy crest "balancing" the bill gives the head the appearance of a blunt pickax. A huge roofed nest is built in the fork of a tree in the breeding season, and courtship includes a curious "false mounting."

HAMMERSTEIN, name of two US theatrical producers. **Oscar Hammerstein I** (1846–1919), was a German-born tobacco magnate who became an opera impresario, opening theaters in New York, London and Philadelphia. **Oscar Hammerstein II** (1895–1960), his grandson, became famous as a writer and producer of musical comedies in partnership with Richard RODGERS and others. Among their greatest successes were *Oklahoma!* (1943), *Carousel* (1945), *South Pacific* (1949), *The King and I* (1951) and *The Sound of Music* (1959).

HAMMER THROWING. See TRACK AND FIELD.

HAMMETT, (Samuel) Dashiel (1894–1961), US detective-story writer and left-wing political activist. His novels are "hard-boiled" and realistic. His main character, Sam Spade, became the prototype of the fictional American detective, especially as portrayed by Humphrey Bogart in the film of Hammett's best-known work, *The Maltese Falcon* (1930). *The Thin Man* (1932) featured more amiable detectives, Nick and Nora Charles.

HAMMOND, city in NW Ind., on the Grand Calumet R near Lake Michigan. It is in a steel producing area, and is a major manufacturing center. Pop 107 790.

HAMMOND, city in SE La., about 45mi E of Baton Rouge. It is in a truck-farming area famous for its strawberries. Pop 12 487.

HAMMOND, James Henry (1807–1864), US politician and journalist. He was a S.C. plantation owner and an advocate of Southern secession. Congressman 1835–36, governor of S.C. 1842–44 and senator 1857–60, he resigned on Lincoln's election, to support the Confederacy.

HAMMONTON, town in S N.J., 28mi NW of Atlantic City. In a fruit and vegetable growing area, it has canning and clothing industries. Pop 11 464.

HAMMURABI, more correctly Hammurapi (d. 1750 BC or 1686 BC), 6th king of the 1st dynasty of Babylon, from 1792 BC or 1728 BC. Over many years of wars and alliances he conquered and united Mesopotamia, though his empire did not long survive him. An able administrator, he was responsible for the Code of Hammurabi, a compilation and expansion of earlier laws which is the fullest extant collection of Babylonian laws. The best source of the code is a black diorite stela found at Susa, Iran, in 1901.

HAMPDEN, John (1594–1643), English Parliamentary leader. He provoked a test case by refusing to pay ship money, a royal tax not approved by Parliament, in 1636. King Charles I's attempted seizure of him and other Parliamentary leaders in 1642 was one of the incidents which provoked the English Civil War, in which Hampden was killed.

HAMPTON, city in SE Va., a seaport at the mouth of the James R. Its economy rests largely on a number of federal and military installations. Pop 120 779.

HAMPTON, Wade (1818–1902), US politician and soldier. Although opposed to secession, he joined the Confederate army, becoming famous as General LEE's cavalry commander. He advocated postwar reconciliation, and in his 1876 gubernatorial campaign led the "Red Shirt" movement which ended RECONSTRUCTION in S.C. He was a senator 1879–91.

HAMPTON COURT CONFERENCE, meeting held at Hampton Court Palace in 1604 to consider Puritan demands for reform in the Church of England, especially of the episcopal system of Church government and the *Book of Common Prayer*. James I rejected most of these, but agreed to sponsor a new translation of the Bible, which became the Authorized Version now also named for him.

HAMPTON COURT PALACE, palace built by Cardinal Wolsey in 1515 as his private residence, outside the then limits of London. In 1529 he was coerced into presenting it to Henry VIII, whose favorite residence it became. Subsequently enlarged, it was a royal residence until the time of George II and is now open to the public.

HAMPTON ROADS, natural harbor in SE Va. formed by the estuary of the James R and subsidiaries flowing into Chesapeake Bay. The cities of Norfolk News and Hampton are on the N shore and Portsmouth and Norfolk on the S, all with extensive port and dockyard installations. Several important military bases are located in the area.

HAMPTON ROADS, Battle of. See MONITOR AND MERRIMACK.

HAMPTON ROADS PEACE CONFERENCE, informal peace talks held on board a ship in the Hampton Roads in Feb. 1865, in an attempt to reconcile the Union and the Confederacy. Abraham Lincoln and William H. SEWARD represented the Union, and Alexander H. STEPHENS led the Confederate delegates. The talks broke down over the question of reunion, upon which Lincoln insisted.

HAMSTERS, short-tailed RODENTS of Europe and Asia. Living in dry areas—STEPPE country or the edge of deserts—hamsters feed chiefly on cereals, but also on fruits, roots and leaves. Large cheek pouches are used for carrying food back to their nests—where it may be stored against the winter. The most familiar species, the Golden hamster, *Mesocricetus auratus*, makes an attractive pet, though both it and the related Common hamster, *Cricetus cricetus*, are nocturnal.

HAMSUN, Knut (1859–1952), Norwegian novelist. In his youth he led a wandering life, which became the theme of many of his novels, such as *Hunger* (1890). His masterpiece, *Growth of the Soil* (1917), brought him the Nobel Prize for Literature in 1920.

HAMTRAMCK, city in SE Mich., surrounded by Detroit. Its economy rests on the automobile industry. Pop 27 245.

HANCOCK, John (1737–1793), American revolutionary leader. President of the Continental Congress (1775–77) and first signer of the Declaration of Independence, he used much of his inherited wealth to support the American cause. Governor of Mass. 1780–93, he presided over the convention that ratified the US Constitution in 1788.

HANCOCK, Winfield Scott (1824–1886), US general and politician. As commander of the 2nd Corps, Army of the Potomac, he distinguished himself in the Civil War and was wounded at Gettysburg. Democratic nominee for the presidency in 1880, he was narrowly defeated by James A. GARFIELD.

HAND, structural specialization of the end of the ARM, enabling grip and the fine motor tasks which characterize higher primates, especially man. Numerous small BONES arise from the WRIST in five radiations, which divide into four fingers and, at right-angles to them, the thumb. Manual dexterity reflects the existence of these two planes of operation and the particular mobility of the thumb JOINT. Small MUSCLES in the hand are used in finer tasks, while grip and joint stabilization are controlled by the forearm muscles. The SKIN of the hand is specially sensitive, essential for fine motor tasks and enabling the hand to explore at a distance from the body.

HAND, (Billings) Learned (1872–1961), prominent US jurist noted for his profoundly reasoned rulings in almost 3 000 cases. He served 52 years as a New York federal district judge and, from 1924, member and later chief of the federal Court of Appeals. Although never a Supreme Court judge, he was greatly influential.

HANDBALL, court game played between two or four people; it requires both stamina and coordination. There are one-wall and four-wall versions of the game. Players attempt to hit a hard rubber ball against one or more walls so as to prevent opponents from returning it before it bounces twice on the floor. The ball is only $\frac{7}{8}$in in diameter and reaches very high speeds. The game is popular in the US; it was probably imported from Ireland in the 1880s. The first world championship, won by the US, was staged in New York City in 1964.

HANDEDNESS refers to the side of the body, and in particular to the hand, that is most used in motor tasks. Most people are right-handed and few are truly ambidextrous (either-handed). In the BRAIN, the paths for sensory and motor information are crossed, so the right side of the body is controlled by the left cerebral hemisphere and vice versa. The left hemisphere is usually dominant and also contains centers for speech and calculation. The nondominant side deals with aspects of visual and spatial relationships, while other functions are represented on both sides. In some left-handed people, the right hemisphere is dominant. Suppression of left-handedness may lead to speech disorder.

HANDEL, George Frederick (1685–1759), German-born composer who settled in England in 1712. He is considered one of the greatest composers of the Baroque period; he enjoyed both public favor and royal patronage in his lifetime. Established as an

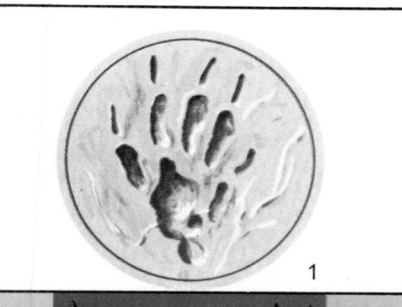

Hamsters, although they make lovable pets, are a serious pest to farmers, who know when they have been around from the typical footprint (1) that they leave. In the wild the hamster lives in elaborate underground burrow systems (2) in which a number of chambers are connected by galleries. Three types of hamster are relatively common in various parts of the world: *Cricetus cricetus* (3) is found in central and eastern Europe; *Cricetulus migratorius* (4) is a Chinese species. *Mesocricetus auratus* (5), the golden hamster, is unknown in the wild but is a popular pet, safe, clean and relatively easy to feed and look after. This and their high breeding rate has made them invaluable laboratory animals also.

opera composer in Germany and Italy, he turned to oratorio to suit British taste. His most famous such works are *Saul* (1739), *Israel in Egypt* (1739), *The Messiah* (1742) and *Belshazzar* (1745). Among the rest of his vast output, the *Water Music* (1717) and the *Music for the Royal Fireworks* (1749) are best known. His career was ended by blindness in 1751–52.

HANDSOME LAKE (c1735–1815), Seneca Indian chief and prophet who advocated giving up the Indian way of life. His doctrine, a mixture of Puritanism, Quakerism and tribal mythology, stressed the importance of the family rather than the tribe. Although sometimes opposed by missionaries, his cult has helped maintain a sense of identity among its Indian adherents.

HANDWRITING. See CALLIGRAPHY; GRAPHOLOGY; WRITING, HISTORY OF.

HANDY, W(illiam) C(hristopher) (1873–1958), US songwriter, band leader and jazz composer; he progressively lost his sight after 1903. He conducted his own band 1903–21. In 1912 he published one of the first popular blues songs, *Memphis Blues*, and in 1914 wrote the famous *St. Louis Blues*. He became a music publisher in the 1920s.

HAN DYNASTY, powerful Chinese dynasty lasting from 206 BC to 220 AD. Usually divided into Western Han and the later Eastern Han, it was founded by Liu Pang after a period of oppressive centralized rule under the Chi'in dynasty. At the height of its expansion, the dynasty extended from Korea and Vietnam to Uzbekistan, and presided over a period of great cultural growth.

HANFORD, city in central Cal., seat of Kings Co. Its economy is basically agricultural, but tires and petroleum products are made there. Pop 15 179.

HANGCHOW, port and provincial capital at the mouth of the Fu-ch'un R in E China. A historic city of great beauty, it has been a cultural center since the Five Dynasties (907–60 AD). Noted for its silk, it also processes tea and has heavy industry. Pop 960 000.

HANGING, method of execution by being hanged by the neck from a noose. In primitive forms death results from slow strangulation. In more sophisticated methods the victim is dropped through a trap, and the resultant jerk dislocates the cervical vertebrae, causing almost immediate unconsciousness. One of the most common methods of execution, it was used in some states of the US and in Britain until recently.

HANGING GARDENS OF BABYLON, terraced roof gardens traditionally built by Nebuchadnezzar II of Babylon for his queen in the 6th century BC. Considered one of the Seven Wonders of the World in Classical times, no certain remains of them have yet been discovered.

HANGING VALLEY. See VALLEY.

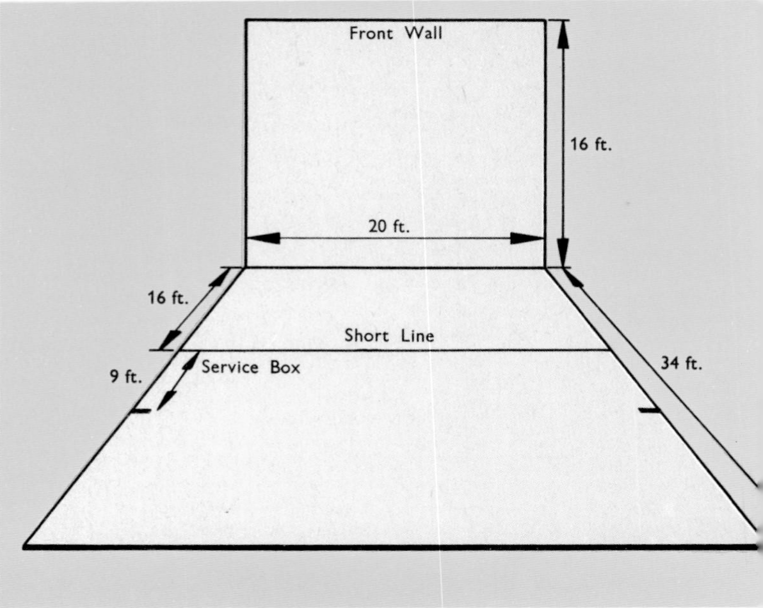

Diagram showing the dimensions of a one-wall handball court. The game derives from Rugby "Fives," under which name it has long been played in England and Ireland. An Irish star, Phil Casey, is usually credited with introducing the game to the United States when he emigrated to Brooklyn in the 1880s. National championships were inaugurated in 1919.

HANKOW. See WUHAN.

HANNA, Marcus Alonzo "Mark" (1837–1904), US Republican politician and industrialist whose financial backing of William MCKINLEY brought about the latter's victory over William Jennings BRYAN in the 1896 presidential elections. Hanna was appointed and subsequently elected US Senator from Ohio 1897–1904 and remained a close presidential adviser.

HANNIBAL (247–183 BC), brilliant Carthaginian general who almost defeated Rome in the Second PUNIC WAR. Son of the great general HAMILCAR BARCA, he commanded Carthaginian forces in Spain when Rome declared war in 218 BC. He set off across the Pyrenees with around 40 000 seasoned troops and a force of elephants. In an extraordinary feat of organization, he took his forces across the Alps in wintry conditions and defeated Roman forces under SCIPIO at the Trebia R, then won great victories at Lake Trasimene (217 BC) and at CANNAE (216 BC). Rome then detained him by harassing tactics while Roman armies reduced Carthaginian possessions in Spain and began to strike at Carthage itself. Hannibal was recalled, only to be defeated at Zama in 202 BC. Driven into exile c195 BC, he was hounded by Roman agents to Syria and Bithynia, where he poisoned himself.

HANNIBAL, city in NE Mo. on the Mississippi R. The boyhood home of Mark TWAIN, it was the location of many of his novels. Pop 18 609.

HANNO (5th century), Carthaginian navigator and trader who sailed through the Straits of Gibraltar and down the W coast of Africa. His accounts of the voyage, however, were deliberately confused to keep information from his competitors.

HANOI, capital of North Vietnam 1954–76 and of Vietnam from 1976. Dating from the 7th century, it is an important shipping, industrial and transport center on the Red R., part European and part Annamese in style. The city suffered from US bombings during the Vietnam War. Pop 920 000.

HANOVER (Hannover), historic city in West Germany, capital of Niedersachsen state. Largely destroyed during WWII, it has been rebuilt and is today an important industrial, commercial and transport center. Pop 517 000.

HANOVER, town in SE Mass. on the North R 10mi E of Brockton. Its economy is based on dairy produce, poultry and a metal works. Pop 10 107.

HANOVER, borough of York Co., SE Pa., settled in 1763. Produces shoes, furniture and cigars. Pop 15 623.

HANOVER, House of, reigning family of Hanover, Germany, and of Great Britain (1714–1901). In 1658 the 1st Elector of Hanover married Sophia, granddaughter of James I, named heir to the British throne by the ACT OF SETTLEMENT, 1701. Her son became GEORGE I of Britain. By Salic law, Victoria could not become queen of Hanover, and from 1837 the thrones separated. On Edward VII's accession the family name became Saxe-Coburg (after Prince Albert) and in 1917 was changed to WINDSOR.

HANOVER PARK, village in NE Ill., 27mi WNW of Chicago. Pop 11 916.

HANSARD, official report of the British Parliament's debates, named for the Hansard family, who began printing Parliamentary papers in 1774. From 1909, *Hansard* became an official verbatim government report, published daily for sale to the public.

HANSBERRY, Lorraine (1930–1965), US playwright, first black woman to have a play produced on Broadway. *Raisin in the Sun* (1959) won the New York Drama Critics' Circle Award, and was later made into a film and a musical, *Raisin* (1973).

HANSEATIC LEAGUE, a medieval confederation (c1157–1669) organized by N German towns and merchants to protect their trading interests in the Baltic Sea and throughout Europe. The town of Lübeck on Germany's N coast was the League's administrative center. Diets were held there to decide on monopolies, trading rights and other policy matters. From the late 13th to 14th centuries, the *hanse* (or guild) had over 100 members and exercised wide commercial powers, backed by monopoly and

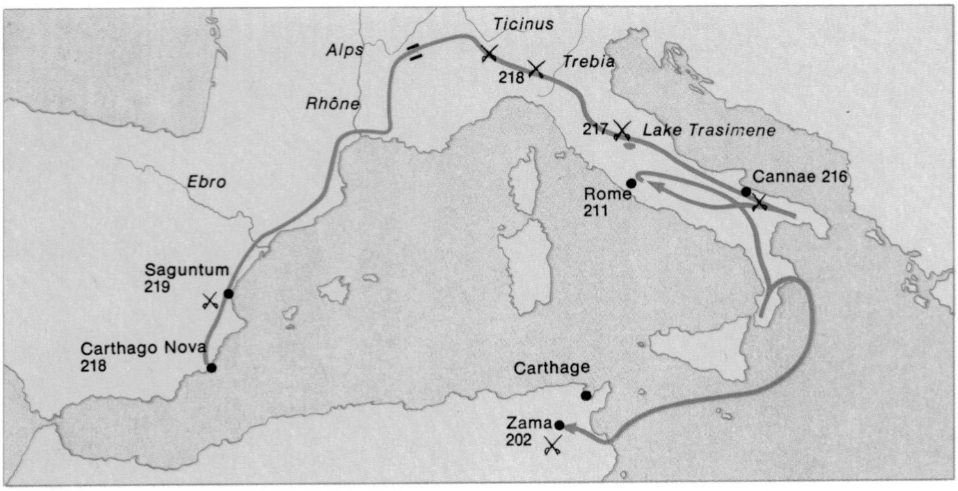

Hannibal's long campaign in the Second Punic War. Starting from his home at Carthago Nova in Spain he attacked Saguntum, an ally of Rome, in 219 BC, precipitating war. He made his way north and with amazing skill took his forces (including the famous elephants) across the river Rhône on rafts and over the Alps in winter, probably by the Great St. Bernard Pass. He beat off Roman forces at Ticinus and the Trebia river, and scored decisive victories at Lake Trasimene and Cannae. Thwarted in his march on Rome by Roman harassment, he was recalled to defend Carthage and defeated by Scipio Africanus.

boycott, and strong political influence. Members of the *hanse* established commercial centers in numerous foreign towns such as Bergen (Norway), London and Novgorod (Russia). The League's strength declined with the rise of nationalism in Europe.

HANSEN, Alvin H(arvey) (1887–1975), US economist; acknowledged leader in the development of John Maynard KEYNES's economic theory between 1938 and 1960. He was a professor at the U. of Minnesota and at Harvard and held various advisory posts under Franklin D. Roosevelt. His writings aimed to join economic theory to practical needs.

HANSEN'S DISEASE. See LEPROSY.

HANSON, Howard (1896–), US conductor, teacher and composer in the Romantic tradition. He won a Prix de Rome (1921) and was director of the Eastman School of Music, Rochester, N.Y., 1924–64. Hanson's Fourth Symphony won a Pulitzer Prize in 1944.

HANSON, John (1721–1783), American Revolutionary political leader from Maryland, first president of Congress under the Articles of Confederation (1781). Before he retired (1782), peace terms with Britain were agreed, treaties signed and US government departments set up.

HANUKKAH, Jewish Feast of Dedication in Nov.–Dec., which marks the rededication (164 BC) of the Temple in Jerusalem after Judas Maccabaeus' victory over Antiochus IV (see MACCABEES, BOOK OF). This "Festival of Lights" is celebrated by lighting candles, one on the first night, two on the second and so forth, for eight days.

HANYANG. See WUHAN.

HAPLOID, term applied to any CELL which contains a single set of unpaired CHROMOSOMES in each nucleus. The number of chromosomes present is termed the haploid number. Haploid cells are produced by MEIOSIS and are typified as GAMETES.

HAPSBURG, House of, European dynasty from which came rulers of Austria (1278–1918), the HOLY ROMAN EMPIRE (1436–1806), Spain (1516–1700), Germany, Hungary, Bohemia and other countries. Count Rudolf, elected king of Germany in 1273, founded the imperial line. Thereafter Hapsburg power and hereditary lands grew until under CHARLES V they included most of Europe (excepting France, Scandinavia, Portugal and England). After Charles, the Hapsburgs were divided into Spanish and imperial lines. When the Spanish line died out, Charles V's granddaughter, MARIA THERESA, gained the Austrian title. Her husband, Francis I (Duke of Lorraine). became Holy Roman Emperor (1745); the Hapsburg-Lorraine line ruled the Holy Roman Empire until its demise. The last Hapsburg ruler, Charles I, emperor of Austria and king of Hungary, abdicated in 1918.

HARAHAN, city on the E bank of the Mississippi R, SE La. An industrial and warehousing center near the port of New Orleans. Pop 13037.

HARA-KIRI, or *seppuku,* ancient Japanese act of ceremonial suicide, in which a short sword was used to slash the abdomen from left to right, then upwards; used by warriors to escape capture by the enemy, and also by the Samurai (warrior) class to avoid dishonorable execution after breaking the law. The Japanese favored hara-kiri to avoid capture even during WWII.

HARAPPA, site of the prehistoric Indus Valley or Harappan culture (c2500–1500 BC), about 100mi SW of Lahore, in the Punjab, Pakistan. Harappa was the first such site to be discovered and was identified in 1921. (See also MOHENJO-DARO.)

HARBIN, industrial port in NW China, capital of Heilungkiang province, on the S bank of the Sungari R. Largely built by Russians engaged in construction of a railroad from Siberia to Vladivostock, Harbin is now the largest city in the NE. It produces machinery, steel, chemicals, textiles, paper, foodstuffs and forest products. Pop 1670000.

HARBOR, sheltered body of water with a navigable entrance and suitable depth to give boats or ships a safe anchorage, allowing transfer of cargo, passengers or supplies, and repair work. Natural harbors are found in bays protected by headlands (San Francisco); in anchorages protected by an island (Isle of Wight); and in river mouths (New York City). Modern ships require greater drafts (water depths), so artificial harbors are now important. Engineering techniques improve existing harbors and make new ones: DREDGING provides greater depth and BREAKWATER construction softens the impact of waves on ships at anchor. Harbor design is complicated and expensive, but vital for modern worldwide shipping.

HARDECANUTE (c1019–1042), king of Denmark (from 1028) and last Danish king in England, the son of Canute II and Emma of Normandy. On his father's death (1035) Hardecanute, in Denmark, laid claim to the English throne, but his half brother, Harold I, succeeded. On Harold's death (1040), Hardecanute reigned with the support of GODWIN of Wessex.

HARDEN, Sir Arthur (1865–1940), British biochemist awarded with EULER-CHELPIN the 1929 Nobel Prize for Chemistry for their work on ENZYME action in the FERMENTATION of sugars. Harden demonstrated the existence of coenzymes, and Euler-Chelpin determined the structure of the first found, cozymase.

HARDENING OF THE ARTERIES. See ARTERIOSCLEROSIS.

HARDIE, James Keir (1856–1915), pioneer British socialist and first leader of the Labour Party. A mine worker from age 10, he was elected the first independent Labour member of Parliament (1892) and helped form the Labour Party in 1906.

HARDIN, John (1753–1792), American army officer in the Revolutionary and Indian wars. He campaigned with George Rogers CLARK against Indians in the Northwest Territory and was murdered by Miami Indians near present-day Hardin, Ohio.

HARDIN, John Wesley (1853–1895), US Western outlaw, born in Bonham, Tex. He killed over 30 men, served a prison term and was pardoned in 1894.

Warren Gamaliel HARDING
29th US President

Born: November 2, 1865
Died: August 2, 1923
Term of office: March 4, 1921—August 2, 1923
Political party: Republican

HARDING, Warren Gamaliel (1865–1923), 29th president of the US. He died after only 30 months in office, during which his administration was marred by high-level corruption, culminating in the TEAPOT DOME oil reserve scandal, which involved Secretary of the Interior Albert B. Fall accepting large bribes.

Born in Ohio and educated at a backwater college, Harding became part owner of the Marion, Ohio, *Star* (1884), which he turned into a successful small-town daily. In 1891 he married Mrs. Florence Kling

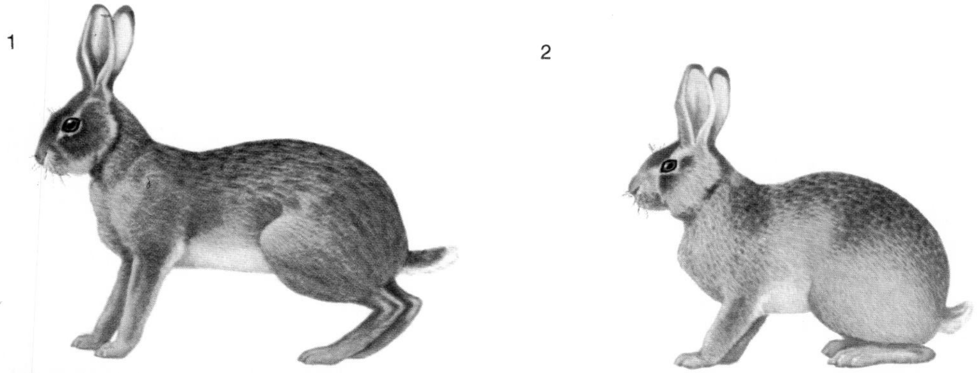

Hares are usually solitary in their habits and do not burrow like rabbits. Their young are born above ground, fully furred and with the eyes open; they are able to run within a short time. Two of the best-known species are: (1) the common hare, *Lepus europaeus,* and (2), the blue or varying hare, *Lepus timidus,* which turns white in winter and has a mat of hair under its feet so that it can walk over snow. *Below:* when threatened the hare attempts to escape by rapid flight in a straight line, reaching speeds of up to 30mph. Before moving, it crouches to escape notice for as long as possible. When detection is imminent it begins its rapid flight, making great leaps with its strong hind legs.

DeWolfe; their domestic life was unhappy and led to Harding's involvement in liaisons which hurt his personal reputation. A genial man with a flair for vague rhetoric, Harding entered politics, becoming a Republican state senator and Ohio's lieutenant-governor. Defeated in the 1910 gubernatorial race, but elected US Senator in 1914, he was a conservative and popular member of Congress though he did little of consequence.

In 1920 he was adopted as a presidential candidate when the Republican convention became deadlocked over the leading contenders. He won a sweeping victory on a "return to normalcy" platform, appealing to a nation weary of wartime restraints. Many of Harding's political appointments were disastrous; he rewarded political cronies with office, and their corruption and dishonesty seriously damaged both his administration and the reputation of the Republican Party. Harding's cabinet did include some distinguished political figures: Charles Evans Hughes (State), Herbert Hoover (Commerce), Andrew Mellon (Treasury) and Henry C. Wallace (Agriculture). He also appointed former President Taft as chief justice and created the Bureau of the Budget, introducing modern budgetary systems into government. Determined that America should join the League of Nations' World Court, despite Congressional disapproval, Harding set out on a cross-country tour to take the issue to the people. Already suffering from a serious heart condition, Harding died in San Francisco on Aug. 2, 1923, during the tour. After his death, the scandals of his administration and personal life that came to light destroyed his reputation. Harding is now recognized as a well-intentioned, ingenuous man who did not have the leadership capabilities to fulfill the office of president.

HARDNESS, the resistance of a substance to scratching, or to indentation under a blow or steady load. Resistance to scratching is measured on the **Mohs' scale**, named for Friedrich Mohs (1773–1839), who chose 10 MINERALS as reference points, from TALC (hardness 1) to DIAMOND (10). The **modified Mohs' scale** is now usually used, with 5 further mineral reference points. Resistance to indentation is measured by, amongst others, the Brinell, Rockwell and Vickers scales. (See also MATERIALS, STRENGTH OF.)

HARD WATER, water containing CALCIUM and MAGNESIUM ions and hence forming scum with soap and depositing scale in boilers, pipes and kettles. **Temporary hardness** is due to calcium and magnesium BICARBONATES; it is removed by boiling, which precipitates the carbonates. **Permanent hardness** (unaffected by boiling) is due to the sulfates. Hard water may be softened by precipitation of the metal ions using CALCIUM hydroxide and SODIUM carbonate, followed by sodium PHOSPHATE; or by a ZEOLITE OR ION-EXCHANGE column, which exchanges the calcium and magnesium ions for sodium ions.

HARDWOOD. See FORESTS; WOOD.

HARDY, Oliver. See LAUREL AND HARDY.

HARDY, Thomas (1840–1928), English novelist and poet. Born in Dorset (Wessex in his novels), he practiced architecture until the popular success of his novel *Far From the Madding Crowd* (1874). Nine novels, including *The Return of the Native* (1878) and *Tess of the d'Urbervilles* (1891), appeared in the next 20 years. *Jude the Obscure* (1894), partially autobiographical, so offended Victorian morality that Hardy abandoned writing novels and continued writing poetry. His heroic verse drama *The Dynasts* (1903–08) and later lyric poetry are as highly regarded as his novels. The "last of the great Victorians," Hardy directly influenced 20th-century English literature. His view of life was essentially tragic; his characters often seem victims of malignant fate, especially if they rebel against "nature." Hardy is almost unsurpassed in his skill at describing rustic life and the English countryside.

HAREBELL. See BLUEBELL.

HARELIP, a congenital DISEASE with a cleft defect in the upper lip due to impaired facial development in the EMBRYO, and often associated with CLEFT PALATE. It may be corrected by plastic SURGERY.

HAREM, from the Arabic *harim* (meaning forbidden), the secluded part of a Muslim dwelling reserved for the women of a household. An ancient Semitic practice, the harem was fostered by Muslims, who practiced polygamy and concubinage. Today, harems are dying out as Muslim women move out of their seclusion and attain more social freedom.

HARES, *Lepus spp*, animals resembling RABBITS and including the JADE RABBITS, adapted for swift running and characterized by long ears, long, powerful hindlegs and feet and short tails. Hares are herbivorous, living entirely above ground in grasslands in Eurasia, Africa and North America and, by introduction, in South America, Australia and New Zealand. Various species molt into a white pelage over winter. Male European hares indulge in wild boxing matches during the rut—the origin of the expression "Mad as a March hare." Young hares, leverets, are born well-developed, alert and capable of independent movement.

HARGREAVES, or **Hargraves, James** (c1720 1778), British inventor of the spinning jenny (c1764), a machine for SPINNING several threads at once. Public uproar forced him to flee his native Blackburn for Nottingham (1768), where he patented the jenny (1770). In 1777 he adopted ARKWRIGHT'S more sophisticated machinery.

HARKNESS, family of US philanthropists noted for their support of museums, colleges and hospitals. **Stephen Vanderburg Harkness** (1818–1888), became a partner of John D. Rockefeller, Sr., and with his wife, **Anna M. Harkness**, founded the Commonwealth Fund to support medical education and the Harkness Fellowships for foreign students. Their son, **Edward Stephen Harkness** (1874–1940), gave away about $100 000 000; Harvard U. received a substantial proportion.

HARLAN, two associate justices of the US Supreme Court, grandfather and grandson. **John Marshall Harlan** (1833–1911), appointed in 1877, served 34 years. A court independent, he is best known for his 1896 dissenting opinion that Jim Crow laws which established the principle of "separate but equal" racial segregation, in fact deprived black citizens of equal protection at law. **John Marshall Harlan** (1899–1971), was appointed to the court by President Eisenhower in 1955. He had been an assistant US attorney, chief counsel to the N.Y. State Crime Commission and member of the US Court of Appeals.

HARLEM, densely populated, primarily Negro community, in the N part of Manhattan borough, New York City. A Dutch settlement from 1658 (Nieuw Haarlem), it was a rural and then a fashionable residential area. From the 1900s it became chiefly black; overcrowding helped turn Harlem into a notorious slum. Government-funded programs since the 1960s have attempted to improve conditions there.

HARLEM GLOBETROTTERS, famous US professional basketball team, organized in 1927 by Abe Saperstein. The squad has toured the US and abroad, playing against college All-Star and professional teams. Their games have been widely televised, and their popularity is due to adroit handling of the ball and extraordinary clowning on the playing court.

HARLEM HEIGHTS, Battle of, Sept. 16, 1776, skirmish in the struggle for Manhattan Island during the American Revolutionary War. The repulse of the British momentarily revived American spirits and William HOWE, the British commander, gave up the idea of frontal attack.

HARLEM RENAISSANCE, period of cultural development among US Negroes, centered in Harlem, New York City, in the 1920s. In this period black American literature changed from works in dialect and imitations of white writers to penetrating analyses of Negro culture and protest, displaying racial pride. Notable writers included Countee CULLEN, Langston HUGHES and Richard WRIGHT.

HARLEQUIN, comic character who usually performed in PANTOMIME, often wearing a standard costume of multicolored diamond-shaped patches. He is derived from Arlecchino, a character of the COMMEDIA DELL'ARTE in the 16th–17th centuries.

HARLEQUIN, a striking sea DUCK—the male of the species sports a bizarre "harlequin" pattern of white spots and streaks on a dark gray head and neck. Harlequins breed socially on islands in swift rivers, wintering along steep coasts where they dive in rough surf.

HARLEQUIN BUG, a North American species of shield bug occurring in large numbers on cultivated cruciferous plants, e.g., cabbages and turnips. Harlequin bugs are brilliant red and black HEMIPTERA, which feed on plant juices, sucking the contents of the cells through specialized piercing mouthparts.

HARLINGEN, city in S Tex., 21mi NNW of Brownsville, near the Mexican border. A barge port and trading center for the lower Rio Grande valley. Pop 33 503.

HARMATTAN, wind blowing W or SW from the S Sahara. In winter it transports vast quantities of dust over the Atlantic Ocean. In summer it interacts with NE-blowing MONSOON winds, often causing TORNADOES.

HARMONICA, or mouth organ, a wind instrument with metal reeds inside a small flat box. The player moves the box horizontally across the lips, inhaling or exhaling air to produce musical tones and chords.

HARMONIC MOTION. See SIMPLE HARMONIC MOTION.

HARMONIC POINTS, four POINTS A, B, C, D, which divide a LINE such that

$$\frac{AC/BC}{AD/BD} = -1.$$

(The negative is possible only if there are positive and negative directions along the line; e.g., BC = −CB.)

HARMONICS, vibrations at FREQUENCIES which are INTEGER multiples of that of a fundamental vibration: the ascending notes C,, C, G, C′, E′, G′ comprise a fundamental with its first five harmonics. Apart from their musical consonance, they are important because any periodically repeated signal—a vowel sound, for example—can be produced by superposing the harmonics of the fundamental frequency, each with the appropriate intensity and time lag.

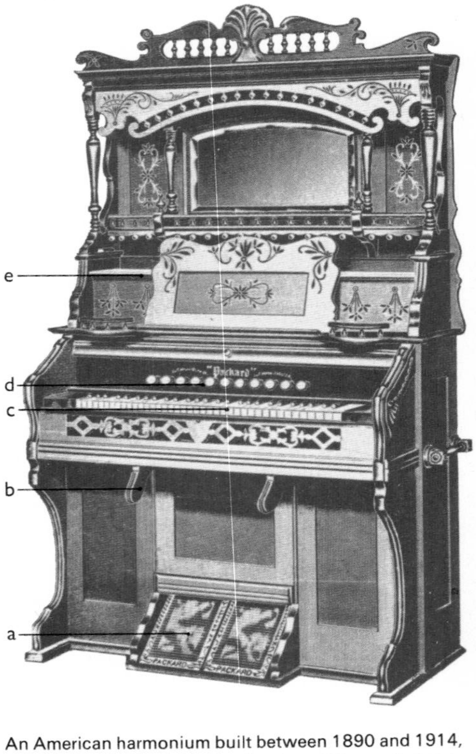

An American harmonium built between 1890 and 1914, with pedals (a) for pumping the air past the reeds, knee swells (b) enabling the person playing to control volume with his knees, the keyboard (c), the stops (d) which control the tone of the sound, and a space for music books behind the stand (e). This type of harmonium would have been mainly used in church services when no proper organ was available.

HARMONIUM, portable wind instrument, related to the organ and resembling a small upright piano, with pedals to pump air past single metal reeds. It was popular in the late 19th century.

HARMONY, in music, the simultaneous sounding of two or more tones or parts; also the structure, relation and progression of chords and the rule governing their relationship. Traditional harmony is based upon a triad, a three-tone musical structure, with notes named for their position on the musical SCALE: the lowest tone is called the root, the middle tone is called the third (located a third scale tone above the root), the next is called the fifth (a fifth scale tone above the root). The triad becomes a chord in four-part writing when one tone is doubled. Chords can be erected on any note of the traditional eight-note scale. In the 20th century, harmonic rules and standards, developed over the preceding 400 years, were largely discarded. (See also ATONALITY; HARMONICS; PROGRESSION.)

HARMONY SOCIETY, or Rappites, religious group of 600 German immigrants to the US, led by George RAPP, which established Utopian communities in Pa. and Ind. (1804–1906). They held property in common and believed in Christ's imminent coming. The celibate society prospered until Rapp's death (1847), but thereafter attracted few converts.

HARNACK, Adolf von (1851–1930), influential German church historian. A professor at Leipzig, Gressen, Marburg and Berlin, his masterpiece was the *History of Dogma* (1885–89). He advocated a return to the simplicity of the Gospels.

HARNESS, working gear of any draft animal, which hitches an animal to machinery or wagons; used mainly with horses. The main parts are the *collar* and *hames*, resting on the horse's shoulders or chest; the *traces* or *shafts* which extend from the collar along the horse's sides to the vehicle; the *saddle pad* or *back band*, held by the girth and crupper, which retains the traces or shafts; and the *headgear*, the bit, bridle, blinkers and reins or lines.

HARNESS RACING. See HORSE RACING.

HAROLD I HAREFOOT (d. 1040), illegitimate son of King CANUTE of England. In 1035 he became regent in the absence of his legitimate half-brother, HARDECANUTE. In 1037 Harold was declared king in his place, but died before Hardecanute could depose him.

HAROLD II (c1020–1066), last Anglo-Saxon king of the English, son of GODWIN and earl of East Anglia, Wessex and Kent. Harold accepted the crown on the death of Edward the Confessor. Nine months later, he was killed at the Battle of HASTINGS when William, duke of Normandy, began his conquest of England.

HARP, stringed instrument, usually triangular in shape, with a resonating chamber nearly perpendicular to the plane of the strings. The harp is of ancient origin, although the Greeks and Romans favored the LYRE. The modern "double-action" harp, developed in 1800, is chromatic throughout its range.

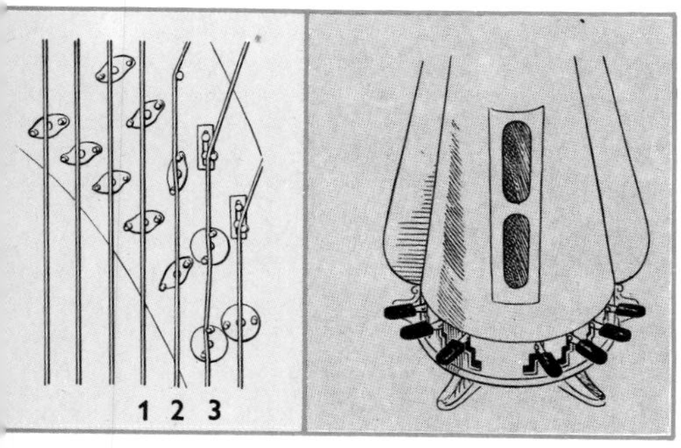

The modern double-action harp, much larger than older types, has seven pedals, three for the left foot and four for the right, each of which controls one string in every octave. Depressing a pedal effectively shortens the open string (1) by turning the first studded lever or disk to grip it (2) and so raising its pitch a semitone. Depressing a pedal further turns the second disk (3), raising the pitch by a full tone.

To alter their pitch, strings are shortened by means of seven pedals.

HARPERS FERRY, town in NE W.Va., scene of John BROWN's raid in Oct. 1859. Its location at the confluence of the Potomac and Shenandoah rivers made it an important Civil War strongpoint. It changed hands many times; its spirited resistance in 1862 seriously delayed Robert E. LEE's march N. The Civil War sites are preserved in the Harpers Ferry National Historical Park. Pop 423.

HARPER WOODS, city in SE Mich., NE of Detroit. Its economy rests on automobiles. Pop 20 186.

HARPIES, in Greek mythology, bird-like monsters with the heads of women. Originally they may have been tomb demons, but in the myths they are agents of divine punishment.

HARPOON, spearlike weapon used in hunting sea creatures such as whales, seals and fish. Most designs have a heavily barbed head and a long line attached to the shaft. Modern whaling harpoons are usually fired from a gun, and often have explosive tips which kill more quickly.

HARPSICHORD, keyboard instrument in which the strings are plucked, rather than hit as in a piano. The range is small, but tonal effects are achieved by stops or "registers." Larger harpsichords have two keyboards. The harpsichord was very popular from c1550 until the advent of the piano in the early 1800s, and much great music was written for it, most notably by Bach, Couperin and Scarlatti. It is now enjoying renewed popularity.

HARPY EAGLE, *Harpya harpyja*, largest and most powerful of the EAGLES, inhabiting the rain forests of tropical South America. It is a fast and agile bird moving short distances from tree to tree in pursuit of prey—primarily monkeys and sloths. Juveniles remain dependent on the adults for up to ten months.

HARQUEBUS, or arquebus, smoothbore matchlock firearm with a shaped stock for bracing against the shoulder. First used in 15th-century Spain, it was more accurate than earlier hand guns fired from the chest. Used in ranks, a high firing rate was possible. (See also FIREARMS.)

HARRIER, breed of dog, closely related to foxhounds and beagles. A scent- rather than a sight-hound, it was bred for hunting hares. Its smooth coat may be black, white, tan or a combination of these; an adult weighs 40–50lb.

HARRIERS, *Circus spp*, medium-sized, diurnal birds of prey, with long narrow wings and a long tail. There are ten species distributed through America and the Old World, occupying a variety of open habitats over which they hunt at low level in search of ground prey. Most Old-World species are migratory, traveling south for the winter. In the breeding season the males perform spectacular display flights. Later on, food brought to the incubating female is also exchanged in flight.

HARRIMAN, father and son prominent in US commerce and government. **Edward Henry Harriman** (1848–1909), formed syndicates to buy the Union Pacific railroad in 1898 and the Southern Pacific in 1901, and created a Wall Street panic in his fight for the Northern Pacific in 1901. His son, **William Averall Harriman** (1891–), board chairman of Union Pacific 1933–46, served under Franklin D. Roosevelt in the NATIONAL RECOVERY ADMINISTRATION, and carried on lend-lease negotiations in Britain 1941–42. Named US ambassador to Moscow in 1943, he took part in all the major wartime conferences. Ambassador to London in 1946, he became secretary of commerce and in 1954 governor of N.Y. Under the Kennedy administration he was instrumental in the Laos peace talks 1961–62 and in achieving the limited test ban treaty in 1963. In 1968–69 he took part in the Vietnam peace talks.

HARRINGTON, James (1611–1677), English philosopher, best known for his *Commonwealth of Oceana* (1656), a treatise on the ideal state and ideal ruler. In 1661 he was arrested on a charge of plotting Charles II's overthrow, but this was never proved.

HARRIS, Frank (1856–1931), British writer, editor of three London newspapers 1892–98. A prolific writer, he is best remembered for his biographies of Shakespeare, Oscar Wilde and G. B. Shaw, and for his humorous, erotic and unreliable autobiography *My Life and Loves* (1925–29).

HARRIS, George Washington (1814–1869), US dialect humorist, a metalsmith in Tenn. A selection of his short newspaper pieces, *Sut Lovingood's Yarns* (1867), was named for his central character.

HARRIS, Joel Chandler (1848–1908), US journalist and author. The popularity of his tales of plantation life, many centering around the old slave and folk philosopher Uncle Remus, has tended to obscure his portrayal of the fading plantation life and its mythology.

HARRIS, Roy Ellsworth (1898–), US composer who studied in Paris with Nadia BOULANGER. Well known as a teacher, he was twice awarded the Guggenheim Fellowship (1927–28). The *Third Symphony* (1937) is perhaps his best known work.

HARRIS, Townsend (1804–1878), US diplomat. A New York merchant, he settled in the Far East in 1847, becoming the first US consul-general in Japan 1855. He negotiated a preferential commercial treaty with the shogunate in 1858.

HARRIS, William Torrey (1835–1909), US educator, a leading neo-Hegelian philosopher. US commissioner of education 1889–1906, he helped to establish the first public kindergarten in the US in 1873, and began the introduction of fine and manual arts into public schools.

HARRISBURG, city in S central Pa., seat of Dauphin Co. and state capital since 1812. A commercial city and steel center, it nevertheless has many attractive residential areas. Pop 68 061.

HARRISON, industrial town in NE N.J. on the Passaic R opposite Newark. It has many heavy and manufacturing industries. Pop 11 811.

HARRISON, town in SW Pa., on the Allegheny R. Lying 20mi NE of Pittsburgh, it is a steel center. Pop 14 448.

Benjamin HARRISON

23rd US President

Born: August 20, 1833
Died: March 13, 1901
Term of office: March 4, 1889—March 3, 1893
Political party: Republican

HARRISON, Benjamin (1833–1901), 23rd president of the US (1889–93). Grandson of William Henry Harrison, 9th president, he studied law in Cincinnati, and in 1854 began practice in Indianapolis. There he became active in the new Republican Party, was elected city attorney in 1857, and became reporter of the Ind. Supreme Court in 1860. During the Civil War, he served heroically in Sherman's Atlanta campaign of 1864. He returned to his law practice and politics, supporting Garfield in

1880 and entering the US Senate in 1881. There he backed high tariffs, helped to create the Interstate Commerce Commission and worked to expand the national park system. In 1888 he won the Republican presidential nomination, to oppose the then president, Grover Cleveland. The ensuing election was fought largely on the tariff issue; Harrison defeated Cleveland in the electoral vote, although trailing in the popular vote. As president, Harrison pursued a vigorous foreign policy. US claims to Samoa were established; the first and highly successful Pan-American conference was held in Washington. A dispute with the UK over Bering Sea fur-seal exploitation went to arbitration. He had less influence over domestic legislation, although he signed the SHERMAN ANTITRUST ACT and the McKinley Tariff Act, convinced that the nation wanted high import duties. In 1890, the Democrats captured Congress, due to low farm prices, the rise of the Populist party and the rising cost of living. This made Harrison's last years in office unfruitful and lost him personal popularity; he was reluctantly renominated in 1892. His wife died two weeks before the election. Growing agrarian unrest and bitter labor disputes helped to give Cleveland an easy victory; Harrison returned to Indianapolis to pursue a distinguished legal career.

HARRISON, John (1693–1776), British inventor of the marine CHRONOMETER (1735). A prize of £20 000 had been offered for a device to allow the accurate determination of longitude at sea: this he won with his No. 4 Marine Chronometer of 1759.

HARRISON, Peter (1716–1775), foremost American architect of his time. He introduced a strong Palladian influence, as may be seen in such buildings as Christ Church, Cambridge, Mass., and King's Chapel in Boston.

HARRISON, Wallace Kirkman (1895–), US architect, who coordinated work on the UN building and the Lincoln Center. His First Presbyterian Church in Stamford, Conn., is noted for its clever use of colored light.

William Henry HARRISON

9th US President

Born: February 9, 1773
Died: April 4, 1841
Term of office: March 4, 1841—April 4, 1841
Political party: Whig

HARRISON, William Henry (1773–1841), 9th president of the US (March 4–April 4, 1841). Born on a Va. plantation and son of a former state governor, Harrison entered the army on his father's death in 1791 and fought in Indian campaigns in the Northwest Territory. He finally settled in North Bend, Ohio, and in 1800 became governor of the new Indiana Territory. In treaties with the Indians, Harrison opened up 133 650sq mi of Ohio and Ind. to white settlement. During the 1811 Indian uprising, led by TECUMSEH, Harrison's troops repulsed an Indian attack at the Battle of TIPPECANOE; he became a national hero, "Old Tippecanoe." When the War of 1812 began, he was made brigadier-general in charge of the Northwestern army, and major-general in 1813. At the war's end in 1814, he entered politics, serving in the Ohio Senate 1819–21 and in Congress 1816–19 and 1825–28. First minister to Colombia 1828–29, he retired to North Bend when Jackson took office.

In 1839 Harrison won the Whig presidential nomination at its first national convention on the strength of his military record and broad political views. He and his running mate, John Tyler, were launched by a campaign more colorful than any yet seen in the US. With the famous slogan, "Tippecanoe and Tyler, too," Harrison was put forward as a war hero and a son of the people with simple tastes. This image appealed to a country caught in a serious economic depression and he won by an overwhelming electoral vote. He appointed an able cabinet, headed by Daniel WEBSTER, and called a special session of Congress to act on the nation's financial difficulties. He delivered his inaugural address in pouring rain, however, and caught a cold which quickly turned to pneumonia. He died one month to the day after taking office.

HARRISONBURG, city in Va., seat of Rockingham Co. A trading center, it has various manufacturing industries. Pop 14 605.

HARROD, James (1742–1793), American frontiersman who in 1774 founded the first Ky. settlement at what became Harrodsburg. A member of the Va. assembly in 1779, he took part in Indian campaigns 1777–82. He mysteriously disappeared while trapping.

HARRODSBURG, city in Ky., seat of Mercer Co., 28mi SW of Lexington. It was founded in 1774 and is the state's oldest city. It is now a resort and trading center for the Blue Grass agricultural area. Pop 6 741.

HARROW, an agricultural implement for breaking up soil after plowing and cultivating top soil. The *spike-tooth harrow* consists of bars to which *tines* are attached. The tines of the *spring-tooth harrow* are flexible to resist damage by stones. The *disc harrow* uses metal discs instead of tines to break up very heavy soil, and the *chain harrow* has heavy studded chains to recondition and aerate the surface of grassland.

HARSHA (Harshavardhana), emperor of N India 606–47. A benevolent ruler and patron of Buddhism, he extended his hegemony from Gujara to Assam by war but kept his empire decentralized and diligently oversaw local administration.

HART, Sir Basil Henry Liddell. See LIDDELL HART, SIR BASIL HENRY.

HART, Lorenz Milton (1895–1943), US lyricist who collaborated with Richard RODGERS on 29 musical comedies. The most famous are *A Connecticut Yankee* (1927), *The Boys from Syracuse* (1938) and *Pal Joey* (1940).

HART, Moss (1904–1961), US dramatist and director. With George S. KAUFMAN, he wrote *You Can't Take It With You* (1936) and *The Man Who Came to Dinner* (1939). He directed the Broadway hits *My Fair Lady* (1956) and *Camelot* (1960).

HARTE, Bret (1836–1902), influential US writer. His short stories of frontier life helped create the mythology of the West. Among the stories that brought him worldwide fame are *The Luck of Roaring Camp* (1868) and *The Outcasts of Poker Flat* (1869). With success, his writing declined and he settled in Britain.

HARTEBEEST, strange-featured African ANTELOPES. Hartebeest have long faces and upright lyre-shaped horns. The name refers to two genera: the true hartebeest, *Alcelaphus*, more specialized, with exaggerated long faces, and the bastard hartebeest, *Damaliscus*, including the blesbok, bontebok and topi. Hartebeest are herd animals, grazing on the edges of floodplains.

HARTFORD, capital and largest city of Conn., on the Connecticut R. Founded in 1635, it has always been a cultural and educational center, and has many financial institutions. Its economy rests upon various industries, of which the most important are precision manufactures such as machine tools, computers, typewriters and firearms, and on its flourishing commerce. Pop 158 017.

Stowe House at Hartford, Connecticut, the home of Harriet Beecher Stowe. She was one of the authors who made Hartford something of a literary center in the late 18th and 19th centuries.

HARTFORD CONVENTION, assembly of Federalist delegates from Mass., Conn., R.I. and Vt. It met secretly from Dec. 15, 1814, to Jan. 5, 1815, and put forward seven constitutional amendments to redress New England's grievances, resulting largely from federal neglect during the WAR OF 1812. With the arrival of peace, however, opponents were able effectively to ruin the Federalist party by accusing it of attempted secession.

HARTFORD WITS, a literary circle who met in Hartford, Conn., during the last quarter of the 18th century. Mostly Yale men, they were all Federalists; their main product was political satire, typified by the *Anarchiad*, a jointly-written mock verse epic. A collection of their work, *Echo*, was published in 1807.

HARTHACANUTE. See HARDECANUTE.

HARTLEY, David (1705–1757), English physician and a founder of the school of psychology known as ASSOCIATIONISM. In his *Observations on Man* (1749), he taught that sensations were communicated to the brain via vibrations in nerve particles and that the repetition of sensations gave rise to the association of ideas in the mind.

HARTLINE, Haldan Keffer (1903–), US physiologist awarded with R. GRANIT and G. WALD the 1967 Nobel Prize for Physiology or Medicine for his work on the functioning of the nerve cells of the retina (see EYE; VISION).

HARTMANN VON AUE, late 12th-century German epic poet. His greatest works, *Erec, Gregorius, Iwein* and *Der Arme Heinrich*, set out his ethical ideals and his vision of God's infinite grace.

HARUN-AL-RASHID (c766–809), fifth ABBASID caliph of Baghdad, from 786, whose rule extended from N Africa to the Indus R in India; he exacted tribute from the Byzantine Empire. His reign marked both the height and decline of the caliphate, and is remembered in the ARABIAN NIGHTS as a golden age.

The hartebeest is still very common in many parts of Africa, roaming the grasslands in small herds. It requires very little water for survival, and is probably second only to the cheetah in running speed.

HARVARD, town in Mass., 30mi NW of Boston. Bronson ALCOTT established his Utopian colony, New Eden, here in 1844. Pop 12536.

HARVARD, John (1607–1638), American clergyman, first benefactor of Harvard College. Born in London, he emigrated to Mass. in 1637 to become Charlestown's minister. In 1638 he bequeathed half his estate and his library to the college, which was named for him in 1639.

HARVARD UNIVERSITY, founded by the General Court of Mass. in 1636, is the oldest university in the US. It has long been influenced by European patterns of education, but under the 40-year presidency of C. W. ELIOT developed a distinctive character of its own, especially in the growth of graduate schools. It now has nine faculties, administering 17 departments and nearly 200 allied institutions such as libraries, laboratories, museums and observatories.

HARVESTER ANTS, a single genus of North American ANTS, feeding on plants. Living in colonial nests often extending 1m (3.3ft) or more deep in the earth, they "harvest" great quantities of seeds and grain, storing them for consumption through the dry seasons.

HARVESTMEN, or DADDY LONG LEGS, order (Phalangiida) of ARACHNIDA, differing from SPIDERS in displaying no "waist," having a unified ellipsoidal body.

HARVEST MOON, the full moon occurring nearest to the autumnal equinox (around September 23) in the N Hemisphere. For several nights the full moon rises at about the same time (around sunset), and may be bright enough for harvesting to continue into the night. In the S Hemisphere this occurs around the spring equinox. (See EQUINOXES.)

HARVEY, city in Ill. on the Little Calumet R, 18mi S of Chicago. Its economy is based on diverse heavy industry. Pop 34636.

HARVEY, William (1578–1657), British physician who discovered the circulation of the blood. He showed that the HEART acts as a pump and that the blood circulates endlessly about the body; that there are valves in the heart and VEINS so that blood can flow in one direction only; and that the necessary pressure comes only from the lower left-hand side of the heart. His discoveries demolished the theories of GALEN that blood was consumed at the body's periphery and that the left and right sides of the heart were connected by pores. He also made important studies of the development of the EMBRYO.

HARVEY, William Hope (1851–1936), US lawyer and economics pamphleteer, under the pen-name "Coin." An ardent advocate of bimetallism and FREE SILVER, he had great influence on the 1896 campaign of William Jennings BRYAN.

HARZ MOUNTAINS, range in N Germany on the border between lower Saxony and East Germany. In medieval times it was a major mining center for various metals, but the area's economy now rests on tourism, especially for winter sports. The range's highest point is BROCKEN peak.

HASBROUCK HEIGHTS, residential borough in NE N.J., 7mi SE of Paterson. Founded 1685. Pop 13651.

HASDRUBAL (d. 207 BC), Carthaginian general in the Second PUNIC WAR. He marched from Spain in 207 BC to reinforce his brother HANNIBAL in Italy. The Romans defeated him and so deprived Hannibal of forces that might have brought him victory.

HASEK, Jaroslav (1883–1923), Czech novelist, whose *The Good Soldier Schweik* (1920–23) satirizes the WWI Austrian military machine. Schweik became the archetypical "little man," who outwits authority despite apparent stupidity.

HASHEMITE DYNASTY, Arab royal family claiming descent from the grandfather of the prophet MOHAMMED, hereditary sherifs of MECCA from the 11th century until 1919. After WWI the Hashemites FAISAL I and ABDULLAH IBN HUSSEIN became kings of IRAQ and JORDAN respectively; Abdullah's grandson HUSSEIN I is the present king of Jordan.

HASHISH, or **cannabis**, a drug produced from a resin obtained from the HEMP plant (*Cannabis sativa*), particularly from its flowers and fruits. It is a non-addictive drug whose effects range from a feeling of euphoria to fear. Hashish is mainly produced in the Middle East and India, and has been in use for many centuries, although it is still illegal in many countries. (See MARIJUANA.)

HASIDISM, Jewish pietistic movement established in 18th-century Poland by Israel ben Eliezer. Reacting against emphasis on rabbinical learning and strict observance of the law, he stressed the ecstatic, joyous element in religion. The movement became grouped around *tzadikkim*, holy men or saints. Hasidism still flourishes in Israel and New York. In Hebrew, *hasidim* means "the pious ones." It is also applied to fiercely orthodox sectarians who fought in the 2nd-century BC Maccabaean wars.

Harvard University at Cambridge, Massachusetts, founded in 1636, is the oldest institution of higher education in the United States. Prominent in the photograph are the famous Widener Library (large building, center right) and the Holyoke Center (large structure in right foreground).

HASKINS, Charles Homer (1870–1937), US historian and pioneer educationalist in graduate studies; at Harvard 1902–31. His works, notably on the Normans, were seminal in US medieval studies. He served on the US delegation to the Paris Peace Conference (1918–19).

HASMONEAN, Jewish dynasty which ruled Judea c164–63 BC. It descended from Mattathias who, with his son JUDAS MACCABAEUS, rebelled against Syria in 168 BC (see MACCABEES, BOOKS OF). From Jonathan (d. 142 BC) onwards the Hasmoneans were also high priests. The family's power, at its height under John Hyrcanus (d. 104 BC) and Alexander Jannaeus (d. 76 BC), ended with the Roman conquest of Jerusalem in 63 BC.

HASSAM, Childe (1859–1935), US painter and graphic artist. He studied in Paris, and was one of the first US artists to adopt IMPRESSIONISM, painting many New York and New England landscapes.

HASSAN II (1929–   ), king and spiritual head of Morocco since 1961. He initiated partial democratization in 1962, but has retained effective absolute power despite an abortive coup in 1971–72.

HASSEL, Odd (1897–   ), Norwegian chemist awarded with D. BARTON the 1969 Nobel Prize for Chemistry for their work on CONFORMATIONAL ANALYSIS.

HASTINGS, town in East Sussex, S England. Chief of the medieval CINQUE PORTS, it is now a popular resort. Pop 72410.

HASTINGS, city in SE Minn., on the Mississippi 20mi SE of St. Paul; seat of Dakota Co. It produces paper, clay and dairy products. Pop 12195.

HASTINGS, city in S Neb., 23mi S of Grand Island, seat of Adams Co. It manufactures farm implements and produces flour and animal feed. Pop 23580.

HASTINGS, Battle of, the prelude to the Norman conquest of England, fought between King HAROLD II and Duke William of Normandy on Oct. 14, 1066. Delayed all summer by unfavorable winds, William was finally able to cross the English Channel just when Harold was in N England defeating a Norwegian invasion. Forced marches brought Harold south with an exhausted and depleted force to meet William at Senlac (renamed Battle), near Hastings. Harold's axmen were only swept from a strong hilltop position, and Harold killed, when William, after a day's fighting, successfully managed a feigned retreat.

HASTINGS, Warren (1732–1818), first governor-general of British India (1772–85). Starting as a clerk in 1750, he rose high in the British East India Company and as governor fought corruption and banditry, but also amassed a large personal fortune. Criticized in England as an aggressive and occasionally arbitrary governor, he resigned and was impeached. Despite fierce prosecution speeches, notably by Edmund BURKE, during the celebrated trial (1788–95), Hastings was honorably acquitted.

HATCH ACTS, two unrelated acts passed by the US Congress. In 1887 William Henry Hatch successfully sponsored an act promoting scientific research in agriculture. In 1939 Senator Carl Hatch of N.M. sponsored an act to regulate political expenditure and corruption in national elections, by barring federal employees from political activity and setting limits on campaign-fund contributions and expenditures.

HATCHETFISH, name given both to a group of deep-sea marine fish and to an unrelated group of freshwater, bodied, deep-chested fish. The latter, found in South America, are able to fly, the deep chest accommodating muscles linked to specialized pectoral fins. The marine group have light-producing organs on the body.

HATFIELD-McCOY FEUD, bloody clan vendetta in the 1880s between the Hatfields of Logan Co., W. Va., and the McCoys of Pike Co., Ky. Originating during the Civil War, it erupted in 1882 over the attempted elopement of Johnse Hatfield and Rosanna McCoy.

HATHAWAY, Anne (c1556–1623), wife of William Shakespeare. Eight years his senior, she married him in 1582, bearing him three children. Her family home, "Anne Hathaway's Cottage," is at Shottery, near Stratford-upon-Avon.

HATHOR, ancient Egyptian sky goddess, generally depicted as a cow or with a cow's head. At her principal temple, at Dendera, she was worshiped as wife of the sky-god Horus; elsewhere as queen of the region of the dead, or as goddess of fertility, festivity and love. The Greeks equated her with Aphrodite.

HATRACK PLANT, *Euphorbia lactea*, a popular house plant producing candelabrum-shaped succulent stems. Family: Euphorbiaceae. (See EUPHORBIA.)

HATSHEPSUT, queen of Egypt, 18th dynasty (15th century BC). She ruled with her husband and half-brother THUTMOSE II, becoming regent to his son and then assuming the powers and titles of a pharaoh. She presided over a period of prosperity, and built the great temple of Deir el-Bahri near Thebes.

HATTERAS, Cape. See CAPE HATTERAS.

HATTIESBURG, industrial city in SE Miss., seat of Forrest Co. It has railroad shops and an oil refinery and produces chemicals and concrete. Pop 38272.

HATTUSAS. See BOĞAZKÖY.

HAUPTMANN, Gerhart (1862–1946), German author and playwright who pioneered naturalism in the German theater. His first play, *Before Dawn* (1889), dealing with social problems, won him overnight fame, and was followed—among others—by *The Weavers* (1892), a drama of working-class life. He won the Nobel Prize for Literature, 1912.

HAUSA, a people of NW Nigeria and neighboring Niger, numbering about 7 million and Muslim since the 14th century. Early in the 19th century they were mostly conquered by the FULANI, who are still dominant in Hausaland. Their language is much used in W African trade.

HAUSHOFER, Karl Ernst (1869–1946), German theoretician of geopolitics. His development of earlier theories of *Lebensraum* or "living space" influenced Hitler's ideas. Under investigation as a war criminal, he committed suicide.

HAUSSMAN, Georges-Eugène, Baron (1809–1891), French civic official (1853–70) responsible for planning and rebuilding central Paris under Napoleon III. Besides the famous boulevards, he laid out improved water and sewage systems.

HAUTERIVE, town in Saguenay county, SE Quebec, Canada; founded 1949 as the seat of the Catholic diocese of the Gulf of St. Lawrence. Pop 13181.

HAVANA, capital of Cuba, 150mi from the W tip of the island, on the Gulf of Mexico. One of the largest cities in the West Indies, it was founded by the Spanish in c1515. The U. of Havana was opened in 1728. It has an excellent harbor. An explosion on the U.S.S. *Maine* in the harbor in 1898 precipitated the SPANISH-AMERICAN WAR and Spain's withdrawal from Cuba; US forces occupied Havana 1898–1902. Tobacco from the neighboring Vuelta Abajo produced the famous Havana cigars, but the city's economy rested on gambling and tourism controlled from the US. Since Fidel CASTRO's revolution (1959), Havana has been subordinated to the general economy of Cuba. Pop 1755000.

HAVANA BROWN, cat breed created from the Chocolate Siamese in which the genetic factor producing the Siamese points did not operate. US standards now require a less "foreign" type, with oval eyes and slightly-rounded ear tips, having a short, glossy coat of chestnut brown.

HAVERILL, city in NE Mass. on the Merrimack R, manufacturing shoes and machine tools. Founded 1640. Pop 46120.

HAVERSIAN CANALS. See BONE.

HAVRE, town in Mont., 108mi NE of Great Falls, seat of Hill Co. It is a trading center for livestock and wheat. Pop 10740.

HAVRE, Le. See LE HAVRE.

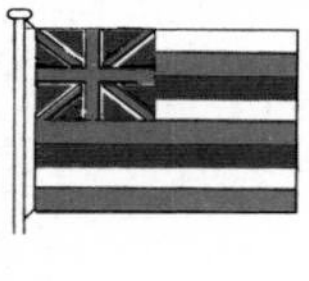

Name of state: Hawaii
Capital: Honolulu
Statehood: Aug. 21, 1959 (50th state)
Familiar name: Aloha State
Area: 6450sq mi
Population: 769913
Elevation: Highest—13796ft., Mauna Kea. Lowest—sea level, Pacific Ocean
Motto: Ua mau ke ea o ka aina i ka pono (The Life of the Land is Perpetuated in Righteousness)
State flower: Hibiscus
State bird: Né-né (Hawaiian goose)
State tree: Kukui (Candlenut)
State song: "Hawaii Ponoi" (Hawaii's Own)

HAWAII, 50th state of the US, a chain of some 130 Pacific islands, well over 1500mi long. The main islands, at the SE end of the chain and about 2400mi from the mainland, are Hawaii, Maui, Kahoolawe, Lanai, Molokai, Oahu, Kauai and Niihau. With the great naval base at Pearl Harbor, the capital Honolulu, and over 80% of the population, Oahu is the most developed.

The most southerly state of the US, Hawaii is in the tropics and of volcanic origin—MAUNA LOA, MAUNA KEA and KILAUEA, active volcanoes on Hawaii Island, still cause frequent damage. Prevailing trade winds give an equable climate with daytime temperatures of 75°–80°F. Settled by Polynesians c400–800 AD, it now has a homogeneous population of mixed descent, more than half E Asian. Remnants of the old culture, such as the *lei* (flower-necklace), the *hula* dance and the *luau* or Hawaiian feast, survive as tourist attractions. Throughout the state, school attendance is mandatory from the age of 6 to 18; the U. of Hawaii was inaugurated as such in 1920. Besides the more than 1 million tourists annually, agriculture based on pineapple and sugarcane, and military spending, are mainstays of the economy. Industry is largely devoted to food processing.

History. In 1778 Captain James Cook discovered the islands, and the arrival of the US missionaries from 1820 began the process of westernization. They introduced writing and new political concepts and opened the way to trade. Treaties (1875, 1887) freed Hawaiian sugar of duty but also gave the US Pearl Harbor as a way station. Agitation by US residents brought the fall of the monarchy in 1893 and in 1898 the US annexed the new republic. In 1908 Pearl Harbor became a US naval base and its development fed the Hawaiian economy. The Japanese attack on it (Dec. 7, 1941) brought the US into WWII, which slowed Hawaii's progress to statehood. An expanding postwar economy and resentment at taxation by the US without representation fueled agitation for admission to the Union. Statehood was granted on Aug. 21, 1959 under a constitution amended in 1968.

HAWAII (Hawaii Co.), at 4021sq mi the largest of the Hawaiian islands and the southernmost, has three great mountain masses: MAUNA KEA, MAUNA LOA and Hualalai. Cattle, sugar, coffee and tourism are the economic base.

HAWAIIAN GOOSE. See NÉ-NÉ.

HAWAIIAN TI PLANT, an evergreen shrub of the genus *Cordyline*, grown as a house plant for its white, pink, rose and green foliage. It should be grown in a sunny east or west window, or a short distance from a sunny south window and tolerates average house temperatures, suffering in artificial heat above 27°C (80°F) or below 13°C (55°F). The soil should be well watered each time the soil surface dries out. Propagation is by air-layering, taking shoot-tip cuttings or by taking cuttings of sprouts produced when dormant pieces of wood ("logs") are brought into growth. Family: Liliaceae.

HAWAII VOLCANOES NATIONAL PARK, on Hawaii Island, established 1916, has among the largest and most active volcanoes in the world. MAUNA LOA (13680ft) has the Mokuaweoweo crater on its summit, and KILAUEA crater on its E slope which is 4090ft high and over 4sq mi in area with a fiery floor called Halemaumau. Area of Park: 317sq mi.

HAW-HAW, Lord. See JOYCE, WILLIAM.

HAWKS, fast-flying, diurnal BIRDS OF PREY. The name is properly restricted to the genus *Accipiter*, though, especially in North America, it is taken as a general name for any bird of prey. True hawks are broad-winged birds of woodland or forest, the shape of the wings and the long tail enabling them to maneuver rapidly among trees. They prey mostly on small birds, approaching behind cover and making a swift dash to kill. (See also GOSHAWK.)

HAWKE, Edward, 1st Baron Hawke of Towton (1705–1781), English admiral whose victory over a French fleet in QUIBERON BAY in 1759 prevented a planned invasion of England and the reinforcement of France's Canadian province. As first sea lord (1766–71), he sent Capt. James COOK to the South Pacific.

HAWKINS, Coleman (1904–1969), US jazz virtuoso on the tenor saxophone. He established the instrument in the classic "hot" jazz of the 1920s, but his own style evolved with later developments such as "bop."

Waikiki beach, most famous of Hawaii's beaches and a paradise for surfers. In the background is Diamond Head, an extinct volcano recently saved from the plans of developers.

HAWKINS, Sir John (1532–1595). Elizabethan sea captain and, as treasurer of the navy, sponsor of reforms in ship design and gunnery which contributed to victory over the Spanish ARMADA (1588). In 1562–63 he had captained the first English slaving voyage, breaking the Spanish West Indies trade monopoly.

HAWKSBILL TURTLE, *Eretmochelys imbricata*, the second smallest marine turtle of tropical and subtropical seas. The shell is formed of strongly overlapping scutes of beautiful color—the source of the "tortoiseshell" once widely used for costume jewelry. Females emerge from the sea to nest on sandy beaches, laying up to 200 eggs.

HAWKSMOOR, Nicholas (1661–1736), English baroque architect. He achieved dramatic and massive designs, notably the Castle Howard Mausoleum; St. George's, Bloomsbury, London and the Clarendon Building, Oxford. He assisted Sir John VANBRUGH at Castle Howard and Blenheim Palace.

HAWKWEEDS, common yellow or orange flowered weeds of the family COMPOSITAE, native to North America and Europe. Some European species have become naturalized in the US.

HAWLEY-SMOOT TARIFF. See SMOOT-HAWLEY TARIFF.

HAWORTH, Sir Walter Norman (1883–1950), British chemist awarded with KARRER the 1937 Nobel Prize for Chemistry for his work on the structures of CARBOHYDRATES and VITAMIN C.

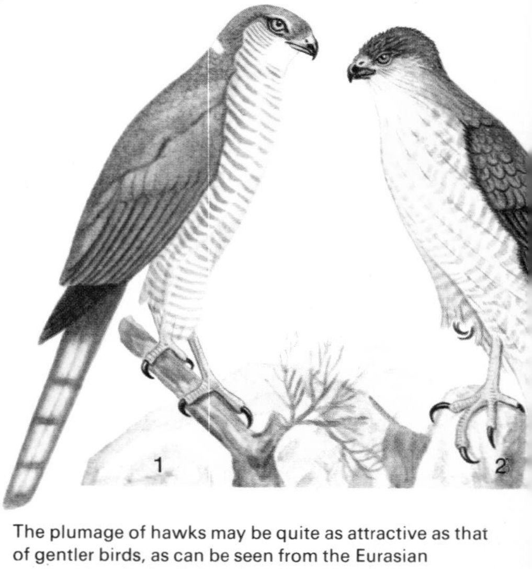

The plumage of hawks may be quite as attractive as that of gentler birds, as can be seen from the Eurasian sparrow hawk, *Accipiter nisus* (1), and Cooper's hawk, *Accipiter cooperi* (2), found in southern Canada and the United States.

HAWORTHIA, a genus of small, succulent perennials popular as greenhouse and house plants for their thick, stiff and elongate rosettes of leaves that are often striped with white, e.g., the zebra haworthia (*H. fasciata*). They grow well in light windows or under fluorescent lights and tolerate temperatures above 13°C (55°F). They should be well watered each time the soil dries out and are easily propagated by removing the small offsets produced. Family: Liliaceae.

HAWTHORNE, residential city in Cal., close to Los Angeles International Airport; important for its computer science and aerospace industries. Pop 53 304.

HAWTHORNE, a borough in N.J. 2mi NNE of Paterson. It produces hosiery, textiles, glass, paint and television tubes. Pop 19 173.

HAWTHORNE, Nathaniel (1804–1864), major US novelist and short story writer, born in Salem, Mass. At first unable to earn a living by writing, he worked at the Boston custom house. Later he was a US consul in Liverpool (1853–57). His great novels, *The Scarlet Letter* (1850) and *The House of Seven Gables* (1851), set in Puritan New England, are masterpieces of psychological portraiture and dark atmosphere. *The Marble Faun* (1860), is set in contemporary Rome. *Tanglewood Tales* (1853) is a retelling of Greek myths for children.

HAWTHORNS, thorny shrubs and trees of the genus *Crataegus*, primarily native to North America, but also found in Europe, North Africa and Asia Minor. They produce white or pink flowers and red, blue and black fruits. Family: Rosaceae.

HAY, animal feed made by drying green forage obtained from GRASSLAND and then storing it until required. GRASSES and LEGUMINOUS PLANTS such as ALFALFA are harvested for hay production. Moisture content is reduced to 50% or less mainly by drying in open fields, although some drying is carried out by special equipment. However, the latter is a very expensive process. Proper drying or curing is essential if spoilage is to be avoided.

HAY, John (Milton) (1838–1905), US statesman and author, and when young, President Lincoln's secretary. Secretary of State under McKinley and Roosevelt (1898–1905), he established US sovereignty over Hawaii and the Philippines, negotiated the HAY-PAUNCEFOTE TREATIES and the HAY-BUNAU-VARILLA TREATY which together ensured US control of the Panama Canal, and evolved the OPEN DOOR POLICY in China. His writings include *Pike County Ballads* (1871) and (with J. G. NICOLAY) *Abraham Lincoln: A History* (10 vols., 1890).

HAY-BUNAU-VARILLA TREATY, pact signed on Nov. 18, 1903 between the US and the 15-day old state of Panama, giving the US sovereignty over a 10mi wide corridor across the isthmus of Panama, in return for a guarantee of the independence of Panama. Drawn up by John Hay and Philippe Bunau-Varilla, promoter of the New Panama Canal Company, the treaty allowed the US to build a canal on payment of $10 million and a $250 000 annuity to begin nine years later. (See also PANAMA CANAL.)

HAYDN, Franz Joseph (1732–1809), Austrian composer who established the accepted classical forms of the symphony, string quartet and piano sonata. The architect of classicism, Haydn nevertheless drew inspiration from folk music in many of his works. His greatest music combines vigor, lyricism and poignancy with frequent flashes of wit. For 48 years court musician to the Esterhazy family, his huge output includes 107 symphonies, hundreds of chamber works as well as violin and piano concertos, some 25 operatic works, a number of great masses, notably the *Nelson* mass, and other great religious works, such as the oratorio *The Creation*. He visited England in the 1790s, composing the 12 "London" or "Saloman" symphonies to commissions by the impresario Salomon and winning great acclaim.

HAYEK, Friedrich August von (1899–), Vienna-born British economist (naturalized 1938). From 1931 Prof. of Economic Sciences in London U.; 1950–62 U. of Chicago, and 1962–69 U. of Freiburg. He has written prolifically on monetary theory and the history of capitalism. He shared the Nobel Prize for Economics with Gunnar MYRDAL in 1974.

HAYES, Helen (1900–), US actress, born Helen Hayes Brown. Beginning at age five, she grew to become one of America's most versatile and admired performers, associated with numerous interpretations that were often definitive and always memorable, and winner of numerous awards for stage, screen, radio and television. She married Charles MACARTHUR. A New York theater has been named for her.

Rutherford Birchard HAYES
19th US President

Born: October 4, 1822
Died: January 17, 1893
Term of office: March 5, 1877—March 3, 1881
Political party: Republican

HAYES, Rutherford Birchard (1822–1893), 19th president of the US who won office in the most bitterly contested of all presidential elections. Born in Delaware, Ohio, he graduated from Harvard Law School in 1845 to begin a successful legal career. In the Civil War he was four times wounded in action and rose to become a major general of volunteers. Elected to Congress while on active service (1865) he later won three terms as governor of Ohio (1867–75). At the Republican Convention of 1876 he won the nomination from the better known James G. BLAINE. In the election, the Democrat reform governor of New York, Samuel J. TILDEN, revived his party's fortunes to win a popular majority. But disputed results in S.C., Fla., La. and Ore. led to the formation of a special electoral commission with a Republican majority, which awarded all the disputed votes to Hayes.

President. Hayes' contribution as president has undoubtedly been underrated. Following pre-inaugural pledges to Southern Democrats for their acquiescence in the commission's decision, he recalled Federal troops from the South, thus ending 11 years of Republican military RECONSTRUCTION. Despite opposition in his own party, he appointed ex-Confederates to administration posts and began a much-needed reform of the civil service by insisting upon recruitment by competitive examination rather than political patronage. In economic affairs, although his hard money policies were modified, even overridden by Congress, he has been credited with restoring business confidence. Hayes, whose personal integrity was never impugned, refused to stand for a second term. Yet he had slowly mollified opposition resentment over the "stolen" election and he had helped to repair Republican credibility after the corruption and scandals of Grant's presidential terms. His achievements were certainly equal to those of other, better-known presidents.

HAY FEVER, common allergic disease causing RHINITIS and CONJUNCTIVITIS on exposure to allergen. The prototype is ALLERGY to grasses, but pollens of many trees, weeds and grasses (e.g., ragweed, Timothy grass) may provoke seasonal hay fever in sensitized individuals. Allergy to FUNGI or to the house-dust mite may lead to perennial rhinitis; animal fur or feathers may also provoke attacks. Susceptibility is often associated with ASTHMA, ECZEMA and ASPIRIN sensitivity in the individual or his family. Treatment consists of allergen avoidance, desensitizing INJECTIONS and cromoglycate, ANTIHISTAMINES or STEROID sprays in difficult cases.

HAY-HERRAN TREATY, agreement between the US and Colombia, signed in 1903, but refused ratification by the Colombian congress, which would have given the US rights to the Panama Canal Zone. After the refusal, US president Theodore ROOSEVELT gave aid to a revolutionary force which declared Panama independent. (See also HAY-BUNAU-VARILLA TREATY.)

HAYMARKET AFFAIR, violent confrontation between labor organizers and police in Chicago's Haymarket Square on May 4, 1886. After several workers had been killed or injured on May 3, a protest meeting was held. During the meeting a bomb was thrown at the police who intervened, and rioting started; four workers and seven policemen died. Of the eight anarchists later sentenced to death for murder, four were hanged, one committed suicide and three, in 1893, were pardoned.

HAYNE, Robert Young (1791–1839), US lawyer, politician and spokesman for the South. In a famous two-week debate in 1830 with Daniel WEBSTER, he championed states' rights and supported state NULLIFICATION of federal laws.

HAYNES, Elwood (1857–1925), US inventor who built one of the first US AUTOMOBILES (1894) and discovered several ALLOYS, including STAINLESS STEEL (patented 1919).

HAY-PAUNCEFOTE TREATY, agreement between the US and Great Britain, signed in 1901, giving the US the sole right to control and fortify the proposed Panama Canal Zone, and abrogating the CLAYTON-BULWER TREATY. Effectively the US acquired naval supremacy in the Caribbean and policing powers on the major searoute between the Atlantic and Pacific Oceans. It also brought about the American construction of the PANAMA CANAL.

HAY RIVER, river in NW Canada. The Hay rises in NE British Columbia and flows 530mi E and N through Alberta into Great Slave Lake.

HAYS, city in central Kan., seat of Ellis Co. The chief industries are flour mills and oil fields. Pop 15 396.

HAYS, Arthur Garfield (1881–1954), US lawyer, famous for his powerful defense in the SCOPES TRIAL in Tenn. (1925) and for the SACCO-VANZETTI CASE of 1927. From 1923, Hays was associated with the AMERICAN CIVIL LIBERTIES UNION.

HAYS, William Harrison (1879–1954), US politician, famous for administrating the motion-picture moral code of 1934 known as the "Hays Code." He was president of the Motion Picture Producers and Distributors of America, 1922–45.

HAYWARD, city in W Cal., 5mi E of San Francisco Bay. Industries include steel production and motor coaches. Pop 93 058.

HAYWOOD, William Dudley (1869–1928), US labor leader and principal organizer of the INDUSTRIAL WORKERS OF THE WORLD (1905). His membership in the Socialist party ended with expulsion because of his advocacy of sabotage and violence. In WWI he was convicted of sedition but escaped to Russia in 1921.

HAZEL CREST, village in NE Ill., NNW of Chicago Heights. It is a residential suburb of Chicago. Pop 10 329.

HAZEL PARK, city in SE Mich., N of Detroit, with light manufacturing industries. Pop 23 784.

HAZELS, trees and shrubs of the genus *Corylus*, family Betulaceae. They are native to North America, Europe and Asia and are cultivated for their edible nuts. **Filbert** is the name given to the nuts produced by *Corylus maxima*, which is native to SE Europe and W Asia.

HAZELWOOD, village in E Mo., a NW suburb of St. Louis. It manufactures automobile and aircraft parts, furniture and food products. Pop 14 082.

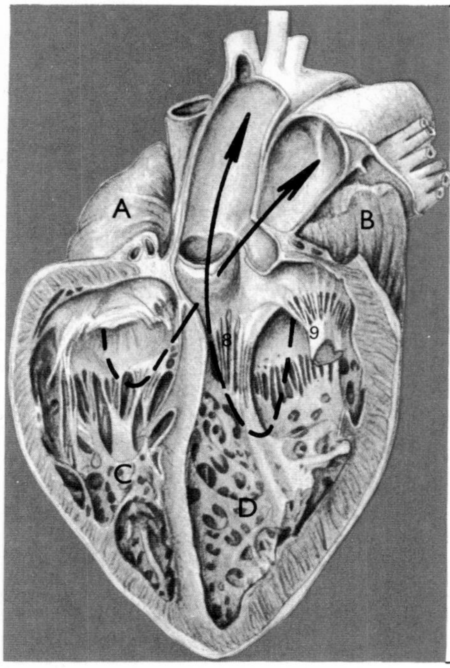

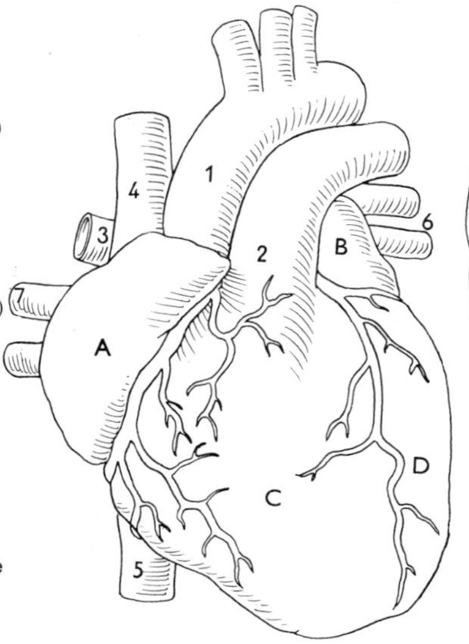

The mammalian heart and (*left*) a cross section of the same. (1) aorta; (2) left pulmonary artery; (3) right pulmonary artery; (4) superior vena cava; (5) inferior vena cava; (6) left pulmonary vein; (7) right pulmonary vein; (A) right auricle; (B) left auricle; (C) right ventricle; (D) left ventricle; (8) and (9) two of the three aortic valves; the ligaments ensure that the valves close after the blood has passed through.

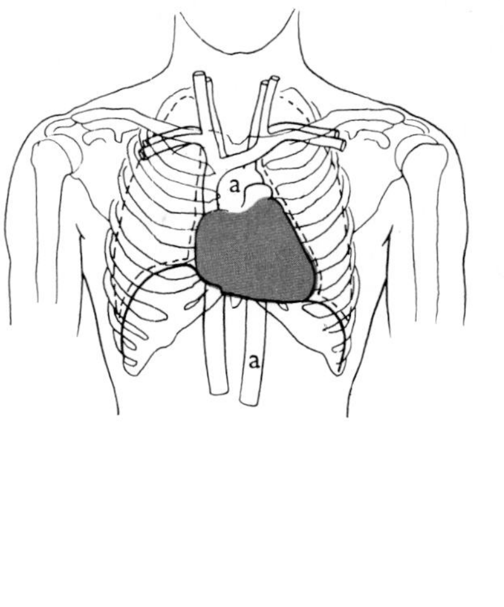

Above: The heart is located between the lungs, supported by the diaphragm. The blood is pumped from the left ventricle through the aorta (a) which runs behind the heart, through the diaphragm and into the abdominal cavity.

HAZLETON, city in E Pa., 20mi S of Wilkes-Barre, producing coal, clothing, and iron and steel goods. Pop 30429.

HAZLITT, William (1778–1830), one of England's greatest literary critics and essayists. His perceptive and sympathetic observations of culture, politics and English manners, appeared in *Characters of Shakespeare's Plays* (1817) and *Lectures on the English Comic Writers* (1819). His wit and versatility are reflected in the miscellaneous essays of *Table Talk* (1821–22) and *The Spirit of The Age* (1825).

H.D. See DOOLITTLE, HILDA.

HEADACHE, the common symptom of an ache or pain affecting the head or neck, with many possible causes including FEVER, emotional tension (with spasm of neck MUSCLES) or nasal SINUS infection. **Migraine**, due to abnormal reactivity of blood vessels, is typified by zig-zag or flashing visual sensations or tingling in part of the body, followed by an often one-sided severe throbbing headache. This may be accompanied by nausea, VOMITING and sensitivity to light. There is often a family history. **Meningeal inflammation**, as in MENINGITIS and subarachnoid HEMORRHAGE, may also cause severe headache. The headache of RAISED INTRACRANIAL PRESSURE is often worse on waking and on coughing and may be a symptom of brain TUMOR, ABSCESS or HYDROCEPHALUS. Headaches are often controlled by simple ANALGESICS, while migraine may need drugs that act on blood vessels (e.g., ERGOT derivatives).

HEADHUNTER, a warrior who severs the heads of defeated enemies either as trophies or for the magic properties of the soul they were believed to contain. Headhunting was practiced in the Balkans, Melanesia, Africa and South America well into this century.

HEAD START AND FOLLOW THROUGH, US government program, set up in 1964 by the Economic Opportunity Act to prepare "culturally deprived" children of preschool age for school, and to involve parents and local communities in the scheme. The "Head Start" program was so popular that "Follow Through" schemes for children in kindergarten were added in 1967.

HEALTH, EDUCATION AND WELFARE (HEW), executive department of the US government, created in 1953 to take overall responsibility for federal programs for public services. It now has the highest budget after Defense and covers three areas of operations: the Public Health Service, social services and education. The Public Health Service agencies are responsible for environmental controls, medical research and services, food and drug administration. The major social services agencies are the Social Security Administration and the Social and Rehabilitation Service.

HEARING. See EAR.

HEARING AID, device to amplify SOUND so as to make the best use of remaining HEARING in DEAFNESS. Sounds are picked up by a microphone receiver placed behind the EAR, amplified electronically, and transmitted to the wearer via an earphone (transducer) placed either in the ear or resting behind it. Ear trumpets are still sometimes useful.

HEARN, Lafadio (1850–1904), US writer of Irish-Greek origin. His move to Japan in 1890 and naturalization as a Japanese citizen brought about his best work: *In Ghostly Japan* (1899), *Shadowings* (1900), *Kwaidan* (1904) and *Japan: An Attempt at Interpretation* (1904).

HEARNE, Samuel (1745–1792), English explorer and fur trader. In 1770 he led an expedition which traced the Coppermine R to the Arctic Ocean. Subsequently he discovered that a short Northwest passage did not exist.

HEARST, William Randolph (1863–1951), US publisher, head of a vast newspaper empire. His early success as a newspaper publisher in "yellow journalism" was largely due to his papers' sensationalism, low prices, the introduction of color cartoons, banner headlines and Sunday supplements. In 1895 he bought the New York *Journal* and engaged in an epic circulation war with Joseph PULITZER's *World*. Both were accused of having helped to bring on the 1898 war with Spain to increase circulation. He also pursued a largely unsuccessful political career.

HEART, vital organ in the CHEST of animals, concerned with pumping the BLOOD, thus maintaining the BLOOD CIRCULATION. The evolution of the vertebrates shows a development from the simple heart found in fish to the four-chambered heart of mammals. In man, the circulation may be regarded as a figure-of-eight, with the heart at the cross-over point, but keeping the two systems separate by having two parallel sets of chambers. The pumping in the two sets, right and left, is coordinated, ensuring a balance of flow. Each set consists of an atrium, which receives blood from the LUNGS (left) or body (right), and a ventricle. The atria pump blood into the ventricles, which pump it into the lungs (right) or systemic circulation (left). The bulk of the heart consists of specialized MUSCLE fibers which contract in response to stimulation from a pacemaker region relayed via special conducting tissue. Between each atrium and ventricle are valves, the mitral (left) and tricuspid (right). Similarly, between the ventricles and their outflow tracts are aortic and pulmonary valves. The heart is lined by PERICARDIUM and receives its blood supply from the AORTA via the coronary ARTERIES. The cells in the right atrium have an inbuilt tendency to depolarize and thus to set up an electrical impulse in the conducting tissue. In **heart action** this passes to both atria, which have already filled with blood from the systemic or pulmonary veins. Blood is then pumped by atrial contraction into the ventricles, though much of it passes into the latter before the atria contract. The same electrical impulse is conducted to both ventricles and there sets up a coordinated contraction (*systole*), which leads to the forceful expulsion of blood into the aorta or pulmonary artery and to the closure of the mitral and tricuspid valves. When the contraction ceases (*diastole*), the pressure in the ventricle falls, and the aortic and pulmonary valves close. The force generated by systole is propagated into the major arteries, providing the driving force for the circulation. Heart output may be increased (e.g., in EXERCISE) through several agencies including increased rate (*tachycardia*) and force of contraction (mediated by the sympathetic NERVOUS SYSTEM and ADRENALINE), and the increased return of venous blood (effected by a muscle pumping action on the valved, collapsible VEINS). **Disorders of the heart** include: *Congenital disorders* of the structure of the chambers or valves (e.g., BLUE BABY), and disease following RHEUMATIC FEVER, leading to stenosis or incompetence of the valves, especially the mitral and aortic. These disorders may be improved by DRUG treatment but they frequently require cardiac SURGERY to correct or repair defects or to insert PROSTHETICS (e.g., artificial heart valves). **Coronary thrombosis** causes DEATH or injury to areas of heart muscle. This may lead to defects in pumping and heart failure, rhythm disorder, ANEURYSM or, rarely, cardiac rupture. *Rhythm disturbance* may follow damage to conducting tissue (where abnormal conducting or pacemaker tissue exists), in certain metabolic disorders (thyrotoxicosis—see THYROID GLAND), and in valve disease. *Bradycardia* is very slow heart rate. This may be due to disease but can be normal in fit athletes in whom it indicates increased heart efficiency. Rhythm disorders are often treated with drugs including DIGITALIS, sympathetic-nervous-system stimulants or blockers, ATROPINE, and certain agents used in local ANESTHESIA. *Heart failure*, in which inadequate pumping leads to imbalance between the two parts of the circulation or the failure of both, may be due to coronary thrombosis, cardiac muscle disease or fluid overload. It causes pulmonary EDEMA with shortness of breath on exercise or on lying flat, or peripheral edema. DIURETICS and digitalis are the cornerstone of treatment, relieving edema and increasing pump efficacy. *Infection of abnormal valves* with BACTERIA or FUNGI is a serious disease causing FEVER and other systemic manifestations including EMBOLISM, heart failure and valve destruction. Its prevention, in high-risk patients, and treatment involve careful use of selected ANTIBIOTICS. Valve replacement may also be needed. Investigation of the heart can involve the use of the ELECTROCARDIOGRAPH, chest X-RAY or cardiac CATHETER (to study ANATOMY and flow) and the study of serum ENZYME levels.

HEART ATTACK. See CORONARY THROMBOSIS.

HEARTBURN, or esophagitis, burning sensation of "indigestion" localized centrally in the upper ABDOMEN or lower CHEST. It is frequently worse after large meals or on lying flat, especially with hiatus HERNIA. Acid STOMACH contents irritate the esophageal EPITHELIUM and may lead to ULCER; relief is with ANTACIDS. Heartburn is also loosely applied to other pains in the same situation.

HEART-LUNG MACHINE. See ARTIFICIAL ORGANS.

HEART MURMUR, abnormal sound heard on listening to the CHEST over the HEART with a STETHOSCOPE. Normally there are two major heart sounds due to valve closure, separated by silence. Murmurs arise in the disease of heart valves, with narrowing (stenosis) or leakage (incompetence). Holes between chambers, valve roughening and high flow also cause murmurs.

HEART URCHINS, somewhat strangely-shaped SEA URCHINS. The characteristic heart-shaped body is covered with a dense, fur-like covering of small spines. They are burrowing animals feeding on organic matter in sand.

HEAT, the form of ENERGY that passes from one body to another owing to a TEMPERATURE difference between them; one of the basic functions in THERMODYNAMICS. The energy residing in a hot body is also loosely called heat, but is better termed internal energy, since it takes several different forms. Despite an earlier view by some philosophers that heat was a form of agitation, in the 18th century the CALORIC THEORY OF HEAT predominated, until disproved by the experiments of Sir Humphry Davy and Count RUMFORD (1798) showing that mechanical WORK could be converted to heat. James JOULE confirmed this by many ingenious experiments and found a consistent value for the **mechanical equivalent of heat** (the ratio of work done to heat produced). In the mid-18th century Joseph BLACK first clearly distinguished heat from temperature, a conceptual advance which allowed heat to be measured (see CALORIMETRY) in terms of the temperature rise of a known mass of water, the unit being the CALORIE (or the BRITISH THERMAL UNIT). In SI UNITS heat is measured, as a form of energy, in JOULES. A given mass m of any substance shows a characteristic temperature rise θ when an amount of heat Q is supplied: $Q = ms\theta$ where s is the SPECIFIC HEAT of the substance. If the substance changes its state, however, by melting, freezing, boiling or condensing, LATENT HEAT is absorbed or produced without any temperature change, the internal energy being changed by altering the molecular interrelations, not merely their degree of motion. Heat is commonly produced as required for space HEATING or to power ENGINES, by conversion of chemical energy (burning fuel—see COMBUSTION), electrical energy or nuclear energy. There are three processes by which heat flows from a hotter to a cooler body: CONDUCTION and CONVECTION, in which molecular motion is transferred, and radiation, in which INFRARED RADIATION is emitted and propagates through space. (See also BLACKBODY RADIATION.) Heat transfer may be hindered by means of thermal INSULATION. **Newton's law of cooling** states that the rate of loss of heat by a body in a draft (forced convection) is proportional to its temperature difference from its surroundings. (See also BOLOMETER; PYROMETER; REFRIGERATION; THERMOCHEMISTRY.)

HEAT DEATH, speculative theory of the final state of the UNIVERSE. If the universe is an isolated system (see THERMODYNAMICS) then its ENTROPY must tend to a maximum, at which all energy is degraded to uniform heat, everything is wholly disordered and no change is possible. In the oscillating-universe model (see COSMOLOGY) it is supposed that the entropy inequality is reversed at the universe's greatest extent, so that during contraction entropy tends to a minimum.

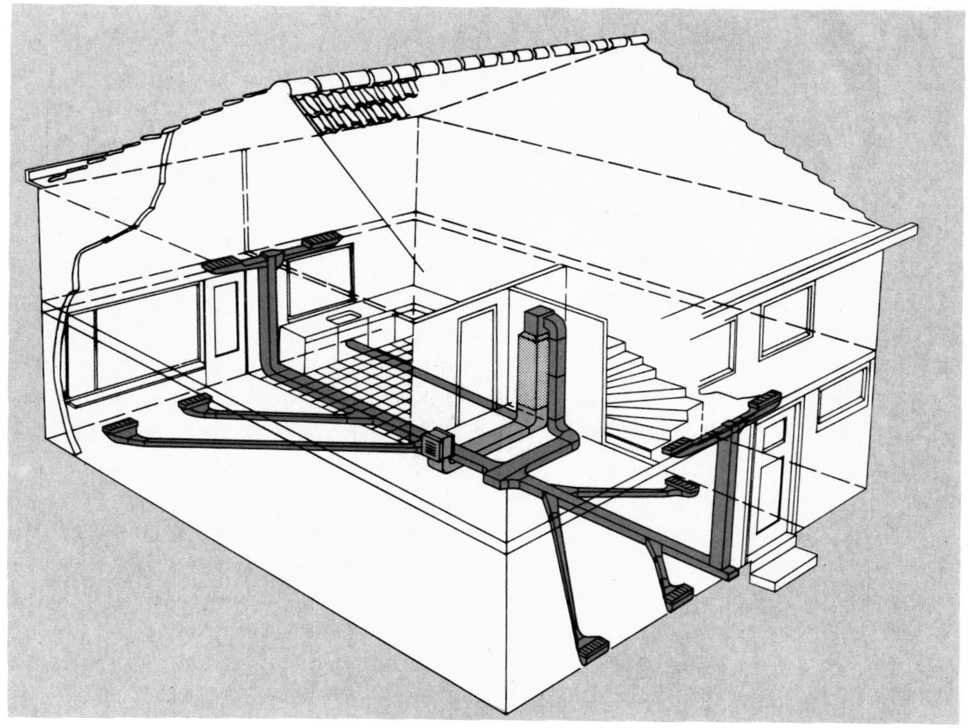

There are many different kinds of central heating in modern homes. Hot-air central heating, shown here, draws air from the outside (green pipe) which is then heated and blown down the red pipes, each of which ends in a duct in various parts of the house. The circulation of the air is completed by a return duct (blue).

HEATH, Edward Richard George (1916–), British Conservative politician, and prime minister 1970–74. He was elected to parliament in 1950, and after holding Conservative Party positions, he became Party leader in 1965. He had long advocated and eventually achieved Britain's entry into the COMMON MARKET. His administration was involved in several serious industrial disputes; for a while there was a three-day work-week.

HEATHER. See HEATHS.

HEATH HEN, the type form of the PRAIRIE CHICKEN or pinnated grouse. This species, restricted to prairies or "barrens" of the east coast of North America, was hunted to extinction in 1932.

HEATHS, low evergreen shrubs belonging to the genus *Erica*, family Ericaceae, which have persistent, bell-shaped flowers. Closely related are the **heathers**, primarily *Calluna vulgaris*, which differ from the heaths in fruit and flower structure. Both heaths and heathers are popular garden plants, many highly-colored varieties having been bred.

HEATING, the supply of heat to buildings to produce a comfortable temperature, usually between 15° and 23°C depending on one's physical activity. For centuries the chief means was an open fire of wood, charcoal or coal in a fireplace with chimney, heating by radiation and by some convection from the fireplace. But most of the heat was lost as the hot exhaust gases rose up the chimney, and the convective iron stove proved more efficient. Other local heaters used today include gas fires and electric heaters. The latter are 100% efficient (converting all the energy input to heat) but expensive to run; they work by passing a current I through a RESISTANCE R, the rate of heat output being IR^2 watts. Bar fires, with the element at the focus of a parabolic mirror, heat by radiation; other types work by convection, including underfloor electric heating. A planned heating system distributes heaters of suitable power to maintain desired temperatures throughout while making good heat loss, which is minimized by INSULATION and draftproofing. **Central heating** systems—thermostatically controlled—are now most common: from a single boiler, fired by gas, fuel oil, coal or (rarely) electricity, hot water or steam is pumped around a system of pipes and "radiators" (really convectors) in each room. Some hot-water systems are not pumped, but use large-bore pipes and gravity flow. In hot-air systems air is heated in a furnace and blown by fans through ducts to diffusers or grilles; the Roman hypocaust was an early example of underfloor hot-air central heating. (See also AIR CONDITIONING; HEAT PUMP.)

HEAT PUMP, device for transferring heat from a cold region to a hotter region by doing WORK (as required by the second law of THERMODYNAMICS). The working fluid or refrigerant is a condensible gas such as ammonia or FREON. A motor-driven compressor compresses the gas adiabatically (raising its temperature) and delivers it to a condenser coil or "radiator" in the space to be heated. As it loses heat it liquefies and passes through an expansion valve into the evaporator, a low-pressure region where the liquid evaporates, taking heat from its relatively cool environment. The gas then returns to the compressor to complete the cycle. Heat pumps are used in domestic refrigerators (see REFRIGERATION), the evaporator being inside the refrigerator, and also in AIR CONDITIONING systems for space HEATING in winter and (by reversing the pump) cooling in summer.

HEAT RASH. See PRICKLY HEAT.

HEAT SHIELD, device to prevent overheating of space capsules on re-entry to the earth's atmosphere. The craft is coated with a layer of ablative material (see ABLATION), often a plastic impregnated with quartz fibers. FRICTION with the air heats and vaporizes the outer regions. Some 80% of the heat is reradiated at the gas/liquid boundary.

HEATSTROKE. See SUNSTROKE.

HEAVEN, the celestial regions in which the heavenly bodies—sun, moon, stars and planets—exist; the abode of God, angels and the righteous after death. These two concepts have been progressively differentiated, especially since the 16th-century scientific revolution made the three-decker universe archaic. In the Old Testament, God, who dwells in heaven, also transcends it. Not until late Judaism was heaven generally regarded as the abode of the righteous; the dead were previously believed to have a shadowy existence in *sheol* (see HADES). In Christian thought, heaven is the eternal home of true believers, or the state of living in full union with Christ, which the perfected soul enters after death—or, in Roman Catholic doctrine, after PURGATORY—there "to glorify God, and to enjoy him for ever," an experience sometimes known as the beatific vision. In Islam likewise heaven is the joyful dwelling-place of faithful Muslims after death. Similar concepts are found in some other religions (see ELYSIAN FIELDS; VALHALLA). (See also ASCENSION; ESCHATOLOGY; HELL; RESURRECTION.)

HEAVES, a lung disease of horses. Symptoms include a wheezy cough, difficult breathing and dilation of the nostrils. Heaves is probably an allergic reaction to poor quality food.

HEAVISIDE, Oliver (1850–1925), British physicist and electrical engineer best known for his work in telegraphy, in course of which he developed operational calculus, a new mathematical system for dealing with changing wave-shapes. In 1902, shortly after KENNELLY, he proposed that a layer of the atmosphere was responsible for reflecting RADIO waves back to earth. This, the E layer of the IONOSPHERE, was found by APPLETON and others (1924), and is often called the **Kennelly-Heaviside Layer**, or **Heaviside Layer**.

HEAVY HYDROGEN. See DEUTERIUM; TRITIUM.

HEAVY WATER, or DEUTERIUM oxide (D_2O), occurs as 0.014% of ordinary WATER, which it closely resembles. It is used as a moderator in nuclear reactors and as a source of deuterium and its compounds. It is toxic in high concentrations. Water containing TRITIUM or heavy isotopes of oxygen (O^{17} and O^{18}) is also called heavy water. mp 3.8°C, bp 101.4°C.

HEBE, goddess of youth in Greek mythology and a cupbearer of the gods. She was the daughter of ZEUS and HERA, and wife of HERCULES.

HÉBERT, Jacques René (1757–1794), French political journalist in the French Revolution. Through his newspaper *Le Père Duchesne* he roused the extremist SANS-CULOTTES and was prominent in the REIGN OF TERROR. He was executed in March 1794.

HEBREW, the Semitic language in which the Old Testament was written and which is now the official language of Israel. The earliest extant Hebrew writings date from at least the 11th century BC, since when there has been a continuous Hebrew literature. Hebrew is now a sacred tongue and a common written language for religious Jews of all nationalities. Hebrew died out as a spoken language by the 3rd century BC. It was revived as the language of the modern Jewish nation, largely owing to Eliezer Ben-Jehudah, who compiled a Hebrew dictionary in the 19th century. Hebrew script, written from right to left, was influenced by ARAMAIC, and adopted the square letters still used in writing Hebrew.

HEBREWS, originally a contemptuous term for a group of wandering N Semitic peoples of the 2nd millennium BC, of low social standing. The name is now used especially for the early Israelites, and sometimes for all JEWS.

The mosque el-Haram in the ancient city of Hebron, a building sacred to Muslims and Jews alike—and the only one in which Muslims and Jews may be seen praying side by side. This is explained by the fact that it is here that the patriarchs Abraham, Isaac and Jacob are reputed to be buried. A substantial part of the present building was originally built by the Crusaders as a Christian church.

HEBREWS, Epistle to the, a NEW TESTAMENT book of unknown authorship, though traditionally ascribed to Paul. Addressed to Jewish converts to Christianity who were in danger of apostasy, returning to Judaism, it explains the fulfilment in Christ of the Old Testament.

HEBRIDES, or Western Islands, a group of about 500 islands off the NW coast of Scotland, fewer than 100 of them inhabited. The Outer Hebrides include Harris, Lewis, North and South Uist, Benbecula and Barra, while Skye, Mull and Iona lie among the Inner Hebrides. Apart from tourism, industries include fishing, farming, sheep-raising, distilling, quarrying and tweed-making.

HEBRON, or Al-Khalih, town in Jordan, 22mi S of Jerusalem, the reputed burial-place of ABRAHAM, ISAAC and JACOB and also once King DAVID's capital. Pop 38 300.

HECATAEUS OF MILETUS (6th–5th century BC), Greek writer, author of *Genealogia* or *Historiai*, a compendium of mythology, and *Ges periodos* or *Periegesis* (*Tour Around the World*), a book of travels.

HECATE, Greek goddess of ghosts, magic and witchcraft with the power to conjure up spirits and dreams. She is portrayed as having three heads.

HECATE STRAIT, channel off the coast of Canada between British Columbia and the Queen Charlotte Islands, 35–80mi wide. It is a ground of salmon and halibut fishing.

HECHT, Ben (1894–1964), US dramatist and novelist. After working as a journalist he collaborated with Charles MACARTHUR on the highly successful plays *The Front Page* (1928), *Twentieth Century* (1932). He also worked on the scripts of such films as *Gunga Din* (1938), *Wuthering Heights* (1939), and *Notorious* (1946).

HECKER, Isaac Thomas (1819–1888), US Roman Catholic priest, founder in 1858 of the PAULIST FATHERS, an order dedicated to the conversion of American non-Catholics. To this end Hecker lectured widely, and established the *Catholic World* and the Catholic Publication Society for the distribution of Catholic literature.

HECTARE (ha), widely used metric unit of area, equal to 10 000m² or 100 are. One hectare equals 2.471 acres.

HECTOR, prince of TROY and in the ILIAD the greatest Trojan warrior in the TROJAN WAR. Son of PRIAM and HECUBA, a favorite of APOLLO, he was brutally killed by ACHILLES. (See also HOMER.)

HECUBA, queen of TROY; in Greek mythology, wife of King PRIAM and the mother of HECTOR, PARIS, and CASSANDRA. Enslaved by Odysseus, she later avenged the murder of her son Polydorus and, as told by EURIPIDES, was turned into a howling bitch.

HEDGEHOGS, small, spine-covered insectivores of Asia, Africa and Europe. The Eurasian species is the Common hedgehog, *Erinaceus europaeus*. Nocturnal mammals, they wander about searching the ground for worms, beetles and slugs. Each spine is a modified hair about 25mm (1in) long. Hedgehogs are able to roll up for protection against predators, and become entirely enclosed by the spiny part of the skin.

A relation of the mole and the shrew, the common hedgehog (*Erinaceus europaeus*) (1), pictured here with its young, is rarely seen during the day, but scuttles about at night in search of food and, if threatened, curls up into a ball (2) pressing its head and feet against its belly so that its whole body is covered by protective spines. The tracks of its front and rear feet (3) may partially overlap owing to its peculiar mode of walking.

HEDONISM, a philosophical theory which regards pleasure as the ultimate good for man. The view of the CYRENAICS and Aristippus was that the sentient pleasure of the moment was the only good. EPICURUS thought man's aim should be a life of lasting pleasure best attained by the guidance of reason. The 19th-century theory of UTILITARIANISM, for "the greatest good of the greatest number," was a revival of hedonism. Hedonism has often been attacked, for instance by Joseph Butler who saw pleasure as a bonus when a desire is fulfilled, not as an end in itself.

HEEMSKERCK, Maarten van (1498–1574), Dutch Mannerist painter (see MANNERISM) whose religious paintings and portraits were influenced by classical antiquity and by Italian painters.

HEGEL, Georg Wilhelm Friedrich (1770–1831), German philosopher of IDEALISM who had an immense influence on 19th and 20th-century thought and history. During his life he was famous for his professorial lectures at the University of Berlin and he wrote on logic, ethics, history, religion and aesthetics. The main feature of Hegel's philosophy was the dialectical method by which an idea (*thesis*) was challenged by its opposite (*antithesis*) and the two ultimately reconciled in a third idea (*synthesis*) which subsumed both. Hegel found this method both in the workings of the mind, as a logical procedure, and in the workings of the history of the world, which to Hegel was the process of the development and realization of the World Spirit (*Weltgeist*). Hegel's chief works were *Phenomenology of the Mind* (1807), and *Philosophy of Right* (1821). His most important follower was MARX.

HEGIRA, the flight of MOHAMMED from Mecca to Medina in 622 AD, which is the year from which Muslims date their calendar.

HEIDEGGER, Martin (1889–1976), German philosopher. Influenced by KIERKEGAARD and HUSSERL, he was concerned with the problem of how man's awareness of himself as a "being" is dependent on a sense of time. His major work *Being and Time* (1927) has been fundamental in the development of existentialism, although Heidegger denied he was an existentialist. (See also EXISTENTIALISM; PHENOMENOLOGY.)

HEIDELBERG, historic city in West Germany, in Baden-Württemberg on the Neckar R. It has the oldest German university (1386), famous for its 19th-century students' duels. The city is European headquarters of the US army. Pop 123 300.

HEIDELBERG MAN. See PREHISTORIC MAN.

HEIDENSTAM, Verner von (1859–1940), Swedish lyric poet, writer and historical novelist, awarded the 1916 Nobel Prize for Literature. His best-known works are *Poems* (1895) and *New Poems* (1915).

HEIFETZ, Jascha (1901–   ), Russian-born US violinist. A child prodigy giving concerts by 1911, his virtuosity and technique have been compared with those of PAGANINI. He has transcribed many works for the violin and made many recordings.

HEINE, Heinrich (1797–1856), German romantic lyric poet and essayist. His best-known work, *Book of Songs* (1827), was influenced by German folk songs. His prose writings such as *Travel Pictures* (1827–31), although poignant, were often very satirical. His poems have been set to music by such composers as SCHUMANN, SCHUBERT and MENDELSSOHN.

HEINKEL, Ernst Heinrich (1888–1958), German aircraft designer of the first jet airplane (*He 178*) to fly, in 1939, and of rocket-propelled airplanes. After WWII he designed mass-produced motor scooters.

HEINLEIN, Robert Anson (1907–   ), US science-fiction writer, a trained physicist and engineer known for such books as *Starship Troopers* (1959) and *Stranger in a Strange Land* (1961).

HEIR, in its strict legal sense, the inheritor of the estate of a person who died intestate (without making any will). The legal term for an inheritor under a will is *legatee*. In general a person's heirs are his next of kin, though under US law some states lay down a special order of precedence.

HEISENBERG, Werner Karl (1901–1976), German mathematical physicist generally regarded as the father of QUANTUM MECHANICS, born out of his rejection of any kind of model of the ATOM and use of mathematical MATRICES to elucidate its properties. His famous UNCERTAINTY PRINCIPLE (1927) overturned traditional physics, its implications affecting areas of science far beyond the bounds of atomic physics. (See also SCHRÖDINGER.)

HEJAZ, NW province in Saudi Arabia, on the E coast of the Red Sea, the holy land of Islam. The cities of MECCA and MEDINA are the most important Muslim pilgrimage sites. Saudi Arabia annexed Hejaz in 1924.

HEKLA, volcano in SW Iceland 4 747ft high. The first recorded eruption was in 1104; the most recent in 1947. In medieval times Hekla was thought to be an entrance to Purgatory.

HEL, the goddess of the dead in Norse and early Germanic mythologies. For the Norse, Hel was also the place the goddess ruled.

HELENA, city in E Ark., seat of Phillips Co., on the Mississippi R, and scene of a Union battle victory in 1863. Pop 10 415.

HELENA, city in W central Mont., state capital and the seat of Lewis and Clark Co. Its industries are mining and the manufacture of concrete, paint and machine parts. Pop 22 730.

HELENA, Saint (c248–328?), mother of CONSTANTINE I (the Great) and the reputed discoverer of the True Cross. Eastern churches celebrate her feast day on May 21; in the West it is on Aug. 18.

HELEN OF TROY, the most beautiful of all women, according to Greek mythology. Daughter of ZEUS and LEDA, she was wife of MENELAUS king of Sparta from whom PARIS abducted her to Troy, thus provoking the TROJAN WAR. After the war she returned to Greece with Menelaus.

HELGOLAND, or Heligoland, island in the North Sea, off the Schleswig-Holstein coast, West Germany. After being in Danish and then British control, it was ceded in 1890 to the Germans for whom it was an important military base in WWI and WWII.

Two helicopters belonging to the US Navy flying on a routine mission over the Californian coast.

HELICON, mountain in Boeotia, Greece, rising to a height of 5 738ft. In Greek mythology it was sacred to APOLLO and the home of the MUSES.

HELICOPTER, exceptionally maneuverable aircraft able to take off and land vertically, hover, and fly in any horizontal direction without necessarily changing the alignment of the aircraft. Lift is provided by one or more rotors mounted above the craft and rotating horizontally about a vertical axis. Change in the speed of rotation or in the pitch (angle of attack) of all the blades at once alters the amount of lift; cyclic change in the pitch of each blade during its rotation alters the direction of thrust. Most helicopters have only a single lift rotor, and thus have also a tail-mounted vertical rotor to prevent the craft from spinning around (see TORQUE); change in the speed of this rotor is used to change the craft's heading.

Helicopter toys were known to the Chinese and in medieval Europe, but, because of problems with stability, it was not until 1939, following the success of

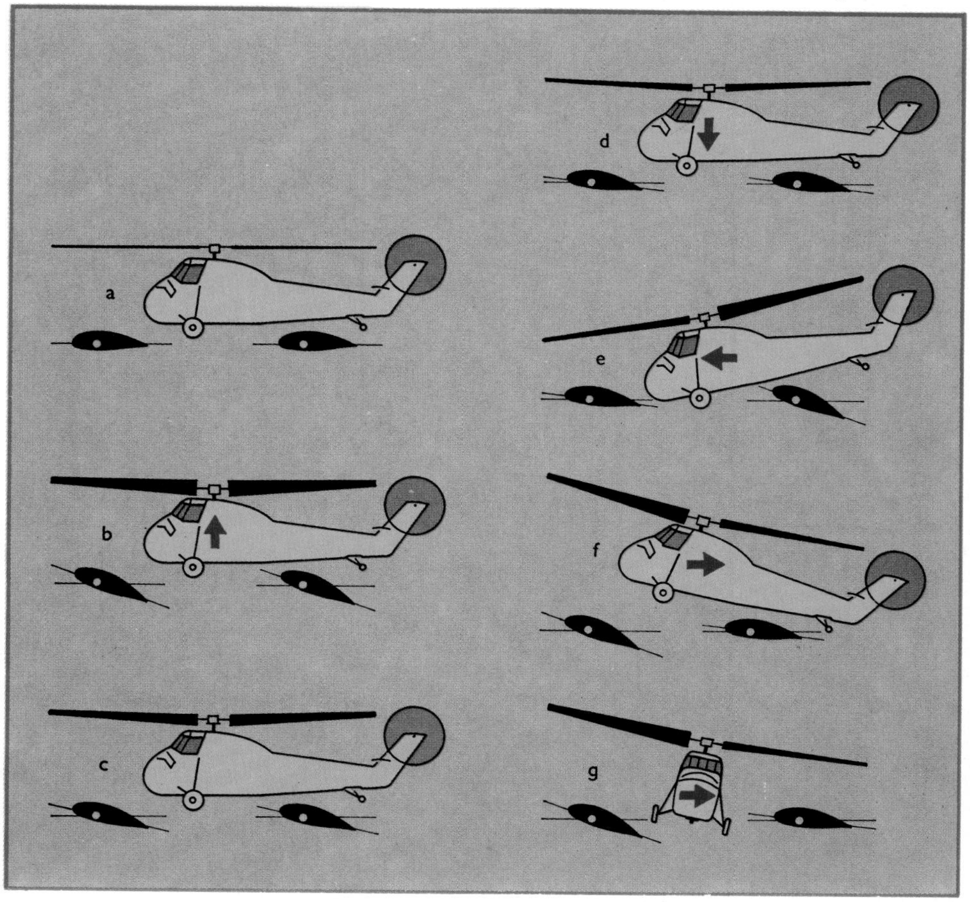

During vertical movement of a helicopter, the lift given by the rotor can be varied by changing the pitch and speed of the blades. When there is no lift, the helicopter remains on the ground (a); when the lift is greater than the weight of the helicopter, it rises (b); when it is the same, it hovers (c); when it is less, it descends (d). Horizontal movement—forward (e), backward (f) and sideways (g)—is achieved by varying the pitch of the rotor blades in such a way that they attain minimum pitch in the direction of travel selected by the pilot.

the AUTOGIRO (1923), that the first fully successful helicopter flight was achieved by SIKORSKY. (See also AERODYNAMICS; VERTICAL TAKEOFF AND LANDING AIRCRAFT.)

HELIOGABALUS, or **Elagabalus** (c205–222 AD), Roman Emperor with the imperial name Marcus Aurelius Antoninus (reigned 218–222). He outraged Rome by his corrupt homosexual favoritism and by the indecent rites offered to Elagabalus, a Syrian sun-god.

HELIOGRAPH, 19th-century instrument used for mainly military signaling, comprising essentially a mirror and a shutter to cut off the sunlight reflected from it. A further mirror permitted messages to be sent even when the sun was behind the sender. The signals could be interpreted up to 50km away.

HELIOPOLIS (city of the sun), one of the most important cities of ancient Egypt. Sited at the apex of the Nile Delta, it was the center of worship of the sun god, RA, pharaohs being known as the "sons of Ra."

HELIOPOLIS. Roman name for BAALBEK.

HELIOS, god of the sun in Greek mythology, sometimes identified with APOLLO. He was depicted driving a four-horse chariot from his palace in the E at dawn to another in the W at sunset.

HELIOSTAT, an instrument used to observe the sun. A TELESCOPE is used in conjunction with a large flat mirror which rotates so that the image of the sun appears stationary.

HELIOTROPE, popular name for half-hardy and tender annuals and shrubs of the genus *Heliotropium*, family Boraginaceae. The flowers of the common heliotrope or cherry pie (*Heliotropium arborescens*) produce a vanilla-like scent.

HELIUM (He), one of the NOBLE GASES, lighter than all other elements except hydrogen. It is a major constituent of the SUN and other STARS. The main source of helium is natural gas in Tex., Okla. and Kan. ALPHA PARTICLES are helium nuclei. Helium is lighter than air and nonflammable, so is used in balloons and airships. It is also used in breathing mixtures for deep-sea divers, as a pressurizer for the fuel tanks of liquid-fueled rockets, in helium-neon LASERS, and to form an inert atmosphere for welding. Liquid helium He^4 has two forms. Helium I, stable from 2.19K to 4.22K, is a normal liquid, used as a refrigerant (see CRYOGENICS; SUPERCONDUCTIVITY). Below 2.18K it becomes helium II, which is a superfluid with no VISCOSITY, the ability to flow as a film over the side of a vessel in which it is placed, and other strange properties explained by QUANTUM THEORY. He^3 does not form a superfluid. Solid helium can be produced only at pressures above 25atm. AW 4.0, mp 1.1K (25atm), bp 4.22K.

HELIX, the curve traced by a point P moving at a constant angle to the elements of, and on the surface of, a circular CYLINDER OR CONE: in the former case it is termed a circular helix, in the latter, a cylindroconical helix. The **Double Helix** is a nickname for DNA (see NUCLEIC ACIDS).

HELL, the abode of evil spirits (see DEMONS; DEVIL) and of the wicked after death, usually thought of as an underworld or abyss. In many ancient religions hell is merely the dark, shadowy abode of the dead—HADES or its equivalent—and the word is so used when Christ is said to have descended into hell. Zoroastrianism and many Eastern religions saw it as a place of chastisement and purification, resembling the Roman Catholic PURGATORY. In later Judaism, Christianity and Islam, hell is the place of eternal punishment of unrepentant sinners condemned at the LAST JUDGMENT. The New Testament describes hell (or GEHENNA) as a place of corruption and unquenchable fire and brimstone—images which have often been taken literally. Modern theology usually regards hell as ultimate separation from God, the confirmation of the sinner's own choice. Many Christians deny the eternity or the existence of hell (see UNIVERSALISM). (See also LIMBO.)

HELLADIC CULTURE. See AEGEAN CIVILIZATION.

HELLBENDER, *Cryptobranchus alleganiensis*, the largest SALAMANDER in North America. It is nocturnal, 450mm (18in) long, and lives strictly underwater in the eastern US. Although it possesses lungs and gills, it breathes mainly through the skin. It feeds on any smaller aquatic animals.

HELLEBORES, hardy evergreen and deciduous perennials of the genus *Helleborus*, family Ranunculaceae. Best known is *Helleborus niger*, the Christmas rose, which is cultivated for the white flowers it produces around Christmas.

HELLENISTIC AGE, the period in which Greco-Macedonian culture spread through the lands conquered by Alexander the Great. It is generally accepted to run from Alexander's death (323 BC) to the annexation of the last Hellenistic state, Egypt, by Rome (31 BC) and the death of Cleopatra VII, last of the Ptolemies (30 BC). After Alexander's death, and despite the temporary restraint imposed by Antipater, his empire was split by constant warring between rival generals eager for a share of the territory. Even after the accomplishment of the final divisions (Egypt, Syria and Mesopotamia, Macedonia, the Aetolian and Achaean Leagues in Greece, Rhodes and Pergamum), Greek remained the international language throughout most of the known world and a commercial and cultural unity held sway. The age

The famous *Winged Victory of Samothrace*, a piece of Hellenistic sculpture dating from about 185 BC and commemorating a great sea battle, was a notable exception in an age of declining artistic standards.

was marked by cosmopolitanism, sharply contrasting with the parochialism of the earlier Greek era, and by advances in the sciences (see ARCHIMEDES; ARISTARCHUS; ERATOSTHENES; EUCLID; THEOPHRASTUS). The art was powerfully naturalistic if occasionally bathetic. Traditional religious cults weakened and were superseded by others either imported from the east or increasing in influence; such as the cults of Isis, Sarapis, Cybele and Mithras. The Hellenistic age saw the emergence of Stoicism (see ZENO) and Epicureanism (see EPICURUS).

HELLESPONT, ancient name for the DARDANELLES, the strait separating Asia Minor from Europe, named for the legendary Helle, who was drowned here fleeing to Colchis with her brother Phrixus.

HELLGRAMMITE, larva of the DOBSON FLY.

HELLMAN, Lillian (1905–), US playwright, screenwriter, and autobiographer. A mordant social critic, her plays, such as *The Children's Hour* (1934), *The Little Foxes* (1939) and *Watch on the Rhine* (1941) studied the evil effects of ruthless ambition and exploitation in personal, social and political situations. Her books of reminiscences are fascinating for her portraits of famous people and events.

HELLS CANYON, gorge of the Snake R on the Ida.–Ore. boundary. At 7900ft deep it is the deepest in North America. An area of great natural beauty, it extends for 125mi and contains the Brownlee, Oxbow and Hells Canyon dams.

HELMAND RIVER, once called the Etymander, an 870mi river which rises in SW Afghanistan, flows SW and W, then N into Iran and drains into the Seistan swamps on the Iranian-Afghan border.

HELMHOLTZ, Hermann Ludwig Ferdinand von (1821–1894), German physiologist and physicist. In course of his physiological studies he formulated the law of conservation of ENERGY (1847), one of the first to do so. He was the first to measure the speed of nerve impulses (see NERVOUS SYSTEM), and invented the OPHTHALMOSCOPE (both 1850). He also made important contributions to the study of ELECTRICITY and NON-EUCLIDEAN GEOMETRY.

HELMONT, Jan Baptista van (1580–1644), Flemish chemist and physician, regarded as the father of biochemistry. He was the first to discover that there were airlike substances distinct from air, and first used the name "gas" for them.

HÉLOÏSE. See ABÉLARD, PETER.

HELOTS, Spartan slave class, natives held in serfdom to the land and occasionally to serve as soldiers. They greatly outnumbered their masters, and the punishment for any kind of revolt was immediate and savage.

HELPER, Hinton Rowan (1829–1909), US racialist author from the South. In his *The Impending Crisis in the South and How to Meet it* (1857), he attacked slavery on economic rather than moral grounds; the resulting furor in the heated atmosphere of the pre-Civil War South forced him to move to the North. He eventually committed suicide.

HELSINGØR, major commercial seaport in N Denmark. As Elsinore it is famous as the setting of *Hamlet*. Its economy rests on its port, shipbuilding, rubber manufacture and tourism. Pop 37 560.

HELSINKI, capital of Finland, situated on a rocky peninsula. Called "white city of the north" because much of it is built of local white granite, it is Finland's chief industrial center and seaport. Its main industries are shipyards, foundries, textiles and paper and machinery manufacture. Chief exports are timber, pulp and metal goods. Founded by GUSTAVUS Vasa in 1550, its Swedish name is Helsingfors. Pop 627 000.

HELVETII, Latin name of a Celtic tribe that migrated from S Germany in c200 BC to Helvetia, NW Switzerland. In the GALLIC WARS (58 BC) they tried to move into Gaul but were defeated by Julius Caesar at Bibracte (Autun). Dominated by Rome, they were conquered by the ALAMANNI in the mid-3rd century.

HELVÉTIUS, Claude Adrien (1715–1771), French philosopher and Encyclopedist whose *The Mind* (1758), considered godless, caused a furor in France. He was attacked by his fellow Encyclopedists, VOLTAIRE and ROUSSEAU, but his work later influenced UTILITARIANISM.

HEMATITE, hard, red OXIDE mineral, consisting of iron (III) oxide (α-Fe_2O_3), the chief IRON ore; also used in paints (ochre) and polishes (rouge). Hematite occurs worldwide, mainly in sedimentary rocks, though it is also formed by weathering of other iron minerals. In the US large deposits are found around

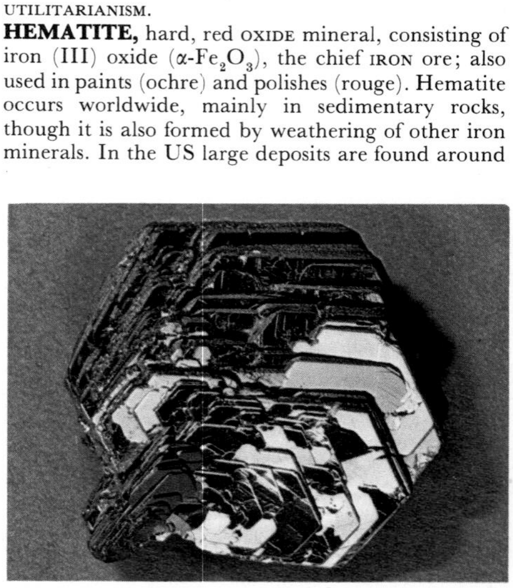

Hematite crystal layers in characteristic hexagonal formation. This specimen is steel gray, but the color ranges from red through black.

the Great Lakes. It crystallizes in the rhombohedral system, with the CORUNDUM structure.

HEMATOLOGY, branch of MEDICINE concerned with BLOOD DISEASES (e.g., ANEMIA, LEUKEMIA, CLOTTING disorder).

HEMATOMA. See BRUISE.

HEMET, city in SE Cal., 30mi S of San Bernardino. An agricultural center, it also produces metal products. Pop 12 252.

HEMICHORDATES, a group of animals related to CHORDATES and including ACORN WORMS and Pterobranchs. Small marine worms of tidal flats (Acorn worms) or deeper water (Pterobranchs), they possess many anatomical and developmental features linking them with both ECHINODERMS and chordates. (See also GRAPTOLITES.)

HEMIMORPHITE, colorless or white mineral, formerly called CALAMINE; a hydrated zinc silicate ($Zn_4Si_2O_7[OH]_2.H_2O$) of widespread occurrence, an ore of ZINC formed by alteration of other zinc minerals. It crystallizes in the orthorhombic system and exhibits PIEZOELECTRICITY.

HEMINGWAY, Ernest (1899–1961), influential US novelist and short story writer whose terse prose style was widely emulated. A friend of the American writers Gertrude STEIN and F. Scott FITZGERALD, his first major novel, *The Sun Also Rises* (1926) chronicled the postwar experiences of the "lost generation" of WWI. *A Farewell to Arms* (1929), and *For Whom the Bell Tolls* (1940) were based on his own experiences in WWI and the Spanish Civil War respectively and added greatly to his reputation as a writer. *The Old Man and the Sea* (1952) won a 1953 Pulitzer Prize and he won the Nobel Prize for Literature the next year. Increasingly depressed and ill in later years, he committed suicide.

HEMIPTERA, the largest order of external-winged insects. All have piercing and sucking mouthparts for sucking the juices from plant or animal tissues. The order consists of the HOMOPTERA and the HETEROPTERA—the true bugs.

HEMLOCK, various herbs of the parsley family, *Umbelliferae*. They produce poisonous ALKALOIDS, used in ancient Greece to put condemned prisoners to death.

HEMLOCK, popular name for evergreen CONIFERS of the genus *Tsuga* from the PINE family, Pinaceae. They are native to North America, the Himalayas and E Asia. The western hemlock (*Tsuga heterophylla*) is an important source of lumber in the US, primarily in Ore. and Wash.

HEMOCYANIN, a blue, copper-containing PROTEIN found in the BLOOD of molluscs and arthropods, especially crustacea. Its function is to carry OXYGEN from the respiratory organs to the tissues.

HEMOGLOBIN, respiratory pigment found in the BLOOD of many animals including man. It contains heme, an iron-containing molecule, and globin, a large protein, and occurs in red blood cells. The whole molecule has a high affinity for oxygen, being converted to oxyhemoglobin. In the LUNG capillaries, hemoglobin is exposed to a high oxygen concentration and oxygen is taken up. The redder blood then passes via the HEART into the systemic circulation. In the tissues the oxygen concentration is low, so oxygen is released from the ERYTHROCYTES and reduced hemoglobin returns to the lungs. Carbon monoxide has an even higher affinity for hemoglobin than oxygen and thus acts as a poison by displacing oxygen from hemoglobin, causing ANOXIA. Abnormal hemoglobin structures occur in certain races and may cause red-cell destruction and anemia. Lack of hemoglobin, regardless of cause, produces ANEMIA.

HEMOPHILIA, inherited disorder of CLOTTING in males, carried by females who do not suffer from the disease. It consists of inability to form adequate amounts of a clotting factor (VIII) essential for the conversion of soluble fibrinogen in blood to form fibrin. Prolonged bleeding from wounds or tooth extractions, HEMORRHAGE into JOINTS and MUSCLES with severe pain are important symptoms. Bleeding can be stopped by giving PLASMA concentrates rich in factor VIII and, if necessary, BLOOD TRANSFUSION. Similar diseases of both sexes are **Christmas disease** (due to lack of factor IX) and **von Willebrand's disease** (factor VIII deficiency with additional CAPILLARY defect).

HEMORRHAGE, acute loss of BLOOD from any site. Trauma to major ARTERIES, VEINS or the HEART may lead to massive hemorrhage. GASTROINTESTINAL TRACT hemorrhage is usually accompanied by loss of altered blood in vomit or feces and may lead to SHOCK; ULCERS and CANCER of the bowel are important causes. **Antepartum hemorrhage** is blood loss from the WOMB in late PREGNANCY and may rapidly threaten life of both mother and FETUS; **postpartum hemorrhage** is excessive blood loss after BIRTH due to inadequate womb contraction or retained PLACENTA. STROKE due to BRAIN hemorrhage may damage vital structures and cause COMA, while *subarachnoid bleeding* around the brain from ANEURYSM or malformation causes severe HEADACHE. FRACTURES may cause sizeable hemorrhage into soft tissues. Blood loss may be replaced by TRANSFUSION, and any blood clots may need to be removed.

HEMORRHOIDS, or **piles**, enlarged VEINS at the junction of the rectum and anus, which may bleed or come down through the anal canal, usually on defecation, and which are made worse by CONSTIPATION and straining. Sentinal pile is a SKIN tag at the anus. Bleeding from the rectum may be a sign of bowel CANCER and this may need to be ruled out before bleeding is attributed to piles.

HEMP, *Cannabis sativa*, tall herbaceous plant native to Asia, but now widely cultivated for fiber, oil and a narcotic drug called **cannabis**, HASHISH or MARIJUANA. The fibers are used in the manufacture of rope. They are separated from the rest of the plant by a process called RETTING (soaking), during which BACTERIA and FUNGI rot away all but the fibers, which are then combed out. Hemp oil obtained from the seed is used in the manufacture of PAINTS, VARNISHES and SOAPS. (See also DRUGS.)

HEMPSTEAD, historic town on Long Island, N.Y. Largely residential, it has some light industry. Pop 39 411.

HENBANE, *Hyoscyamus niger*, a poisonous, ill-smelling, biennial or annual plant native to Europe, but naturalized in the US. Dried leaves yield the narcotic drugs ATROPINE, HYOSCYAMINE and SCOPOLAMINE. Family: Solanaceae.

HENCH, Philip Showalter (1896–1965), US physician who shared with KENDALL and REICHSTEIN the 1950 Nobel Prize for Physiology or Medicine for his use of cortisone (see STEROIDS) to treat rheumatoid ARTHRITIS.

HENDAY, Anthony, 18th-century English fur trader and explorer. He joined the Hudson's Bay Co. in 1750 and traded in the Canadian interior, becoming the first European to sight the Canadian Rocky Mts.

HENDERSON, city in NW Ky., seat of Henderson Co. An agricultural and light industrial center, it was the home of John James AUDUBON. Pop 22 976.

HENDERSON, city in SE Nev. A major industrial center, most of its plants were built by the government in WWII for defense purposes. Pop 16 395.

HENDERSON, city in N.C., seat of Vance Co. Its economy rests on processing tobacco and cotton, and on manufacturing industries. Pop 13 896.

HENDERSON, city in E Tex., seat of Rusk Co. In the middle of an oil area, it has various manufacturing industries. Pop 10 187.

HENDERSON, Arthur (1863–1935), British Labour Party politician and trade unionist who held various cabinet posts 1916–17 and 1924–31. He was awarded the Nobel Peace Prize in 1934 for his work for collective security and disarmament.

HENDERSON, Fletcher (1898–1952), US jazz musician who introduced written orchestration into big band jazz. After college he began as a pianist with W. C. HANDY and accompanied such singers as Bessie Smith. In 1923 he became a bandleader, and built up his band to very high standards.

HENDERSON, Richard (1735–1785), colonial American lawyer and pioneer who began settlement in the W Tenn. area. In 1773 he established the Transylvania Co. to found a colony in Ky. and Tenn.; Daniel BOONE explored much of this region for the company.

HENDRICKS, Thomas Andrew (1819–1885), 21st vice-president of the US, under CLEVELAND. A senator 1863–69, he was governor of Ind. in 1873–77. Although sympathetic to the South, he remained loyal to the Union. He was elected Democratic vice-president in 1884, serving less than nine months.

HENEQUEN, *Agave fourcroydes*, a relative of the SISAL, which yields fibers used for making twine. Family: Agavaceae.

HENGIST AND HORSA, two brothers who apparently led a group of Saxon mercenaries invited to settle in Kent by the British king Vortigern c446 AD. Six years later they turned on him and captured Kent. Horsa was killed and Hengist became the first Anglo-Saxon king of Kent.

HENGYANG, city in S central Hunan province, China. A rail, administrative and mining center, its economy rests on processing metals and heavy manufactures. Pop 270 000.

HENLEY, William Ernest (1849–1903), British journalist, poet and critic. He began to write while recovering from the amputation of a leg, and edited various journals, most notably the *Scots Observer* from 1889. Here he published such writers as BARRIE, HARDY, KIPLING and WELLS. He edited the standard edition of BURNS and was a close friend of R. L. STEVENSON.

HENLEY-ON-THAMES, historic market town in Oxfordshire, England, famous for its Royal Regatta, a three-day series of rowing races held annually since 1839. Pop 31 744.

HENLOPEN, Cape, lies S of the entrance to Delaware Bay on the E coast of Sussex Co., Del.

HENNA, *Lawsonia inermis*, small shrub native to Asia, Australia and the Mediterranean coasts of Africa. The leaves yield a reddish dye widely used as a cosmetic among Muslims. The leaves are dried, pounded, mixed with water and applied to the skin or hair. Family: Lythraceae.

HENNEPIN, Louis (1640–1701?), Belgian Franciscan missionary and explorer. He went to Quebec (c1675) as chaplain to LA SALLE and joined his 1679 expedition. Captured but well treated by Sioux Indians, he was rescued in 1680. His exaggerated accounts of his travels were very popular.

HENRI, Robert (1865–1929), US painter and art teacher, founder of the ASHCAN SCHOOL of realistic painters. He studied and traveled in Europe 1888–1900, and taught in New York. He organized the 1908 exhibition of THE EIGHT and the 1910 Independent Artists Exhibition.

HENRIETTA MARIA (1609–1669), French princess who married King CHARLES I of England. Popular at first, she alienated public support by her Roman Catholicism and French sympathies. Her bad advice to Charles during the conflict with Parliament did much to aggravate the situation, and her continual intriguing for foreign support during the Civil War was a contributory factor to his execution.

HENRY, name of eight kings of England. **Henry I** (1068–1135), reigned 1100–35. Son of William I, he seized the English throne on the death of his brother William II and became Duke of Normandy in 1106. **Henry II** (1133–1189), reigned 1154–89, the first of the ANGEVIN kings. By marrying Eleanor, Duchess of Aquitaine, in 1152, he acquired vast lands in France. His policy of establishing royal authority in England led to Thomas à BECKET's murder. Henry made many legal and judicial reforms. **Henry III** (1207–1272), reigned 1216–72. His unpopular rule was marked by administrative and diplomatic incompetence and by the revolts of nobles who forced him to yield power to them. **Henry IV** (1366–1413), reigned 1399–1413, known as Henry of Bolingbroke, the first ruler of the House of LANCASTER. He usurped the throne after forcing Richard II to abdicate. His reign was marked by struggles with Owen GLENDOWER and Sir Henry PERCY. **Henry V** (1387–1422), reigned from 1413, son of Henry IV. He defeated the French at AGINCOURT in 1415, married Catherine of Valois and became successor to the French throne. He established civil order in England and was a great popular hero. **Henry VI** (1421–1471), reigned 1422–61 and 1470–71. A weak, unstable ruler, he was frequently dominated by factions and this led to the dynastic Wars of the ROSES. He was deposed for nine years, and

Hans Holbein the Younger's fine portrait of King Henry VIII, dating from 1540, when the king was aged 49 and had just married his fifth wife, Catherine Howard. Despite Henry's domestic troubles, his reign was distinguished by great political and social achievements.

finally murdered. **Henry VII** (1457–1509), reigned 1485–1509, the first of the TUDOR rulers. He killed Richard III in the last battle of the Wars of the ROSES and united the houses of LANCASTER and YORK by marrying Elizabeth of York. He restored order to England and Wales, and promoted efficient administration. **Henry VIII** (1491–1547), son of Henry VII, reigned 1509–47, one of the most powerful and formative rulers in British history. His religious policies led to the Act of Supremacy (1534) in which Parliament renounced papal authority and established the Church of England with the king as supreme head. He replaced feudal authority with a central system of government, albeit despotic at times, and he created a navy which was to become the basis of British power for centuries to come. His matrimonial problems arose originally from his search for a male heir; he was married successively to CATHERINE OF ARAGON, whom he divorced for Anne BOLEYN (mother of ELIZABETH I) whom he beheaded, Jane SEYMOUR (mother of Edward VI), ANNE OF CLEVES (divorced within a year), Catherine HOWARD (beheaded) and Catherine PARR, who survived him.

HENRY, name of four kings of France. **Henry I** (c1008–1060), reigned 1031–60. His rule was disturbed by feudal conflicts organized by his mother and brother. One of his chief enemies was the future William I of England. **Henry II** (1519–1559), reigned 1547–59. In 1533 he married Catherine de Médici, but he was dominated by his mistress Diane de Poitiers and his military commander, the Duc de Montmorency. A fanatic Catholic, he persecuted the HUGUENOTS and continued the war against the Holy Roman Emperor and Spain. **Henry III** (1551–1589), reigned 1574–89. He collaborated with his mother Catherine de Médici in the SAINT BARTHOLOMEW'S DAY Massacre (1572). He was dominated by the GUISE family, and his reign was unstable. He was assassinated by a Jacobin friar. **Henry IV** (1553–1610), reigned 1589–1610, king of NAVARRE 1572–1610, the first French BOURBON king. A Protestant leader of the HUGUENOTS, he converted to Roman Catholicism in 1593, granting religious freedom with the Edict of NANTES (1598). He brought unity and economic stability to France, but was assassinated by a Catholic extremist.

HENRY, name of seven kings of Germany, six of whom were also Holy Roman emperors. **Henry I** (c876–936), reigned 919–36, known as Henry the Fowler. He established Germany as a new kingdom. **Henry II** (973–1024), reigned 1002–24, emperor from 1014. By political astuteness he ensured secular and clerical support. Canonized in 1146, his feast day is July 15th. **Henry III** (1017–1056), reigned 1039–56, emperor 1046–56. During his reign the Holy Roman Empire was probably at its greatest power and unity. He carried out important papal reforms. **Henry IV** (1050–1106), reigned 1056–1105 and emperor 1084–1105. He deposed Pope Gregory VII, but Gregory excommunicated him and Henry yielded to papal authority at CANOSSA in Italy in 1077. Gregory then supported a rival king of Germany, and Henry replaced him with the antipope Clement III. He captured Rome in 1084 and was crowned emperor. After two sons rebelled against him he was forced to abdicate in favor of his son, Henry V. **Henry V** (1081–1125), reigned 1105–25, emperor 1111–25. He unified Germany and continued Henry IV's struggle against the papacy. **Henry VI** (1165–1197), reigned 1190–97 and was emperor from 1191. He was made king of Sicily in 1194; he died before being able to implement plans to invade the Holy Land. **Henry VII** (c1275–1313), reigned 1308–13, emperor from 1312. He invaded Italy in 1310 in an abortive attempt to make it the base of imperial power and he died near Siena.

HENRY (H), the SI UNIT of inductance, the inductance of a circuit in which current changing at a rate of one ampere per second induces an ELECTROMOTIVE FORCE of one volt.

HENRY, Cape, cape on the E coast of Va., on the S side of the mouth of Chesapeake Bay, opposite Cape Charles.

HENRY, Fort, fortification in NW Tenn., on the Tennessee R, captured in a joint attack by Gen. U. S. GRANT and by Andrew FOOTE in Feb. 1862. It was the first major Union victory of the Civil War.

HENRY, John, in US folk song a Negro railroad worker who won a legendary pile-driving contest against the steam engine that was to replace him, but died in the moment of victory.

HENRY, Joseph (1797–1878), US physicist best known for his electromagnetic studies. His discoveries include INDUCTION and self-induction; though in both cases FARADAY published first. He also devised a much improved ELECTROMAGNET by insulating the wire rather than the core; invented one of the first ELECTRIC MOTORS; helped MORSE and WHEATSTONE devise their telegraphs; and found SUNSPOTS to be cooler than the surrounding photosphere. The HENRY is named for him.

HENRY, O. (1862–1910), pseudonym of William Sidney Porter, US short story writer. He began writing during a short term of imprisonment, and was already popular when released. He moved to New York City in 1902, and wrote over 300 stories, collected in *The Four Million* (1906), *The Voice of the City* (1908) and many other books. A lonely and melancholy man, his last years were marred by an unhappy second marriage and alcoholism.

HENRY, Patrick (1736–1799), statesman, orator and prominent figure of the American Revolution. A lawyer, he came to public notice with his defense of the Va. legislature over a law repealed by King George II as unjust. Elected to the legislature himself in 1765, he persuaded it to reject the Stamp Act, then joined the first CONTINENTAL CONGRESS in 1774. In a speech at Va.'s second revolutionary convention in 1775, advocating war rather than negotiations, he coined the famous phrase "Give me liberty, or give me death!" He served as governor of Va. 1776–79 and 1784–86, but furiously opposed the ratification of the US CONSTITUTION in 1788.

HENRY, William (1774–1836), British chemist and physician who formulated **Henry's Law**, that, at a given temperature, the mass of a gas dissolved by a particular solvent is proportional to the pressure on it of the gas.

HENRY THE NAVIGATOR (1394–1460), Portuguese prince, third son of King John of Portugal, whose active interest inaugurated Portuguese maritime exploration and expansion overseas. He sponsored the exploration and mapping of the W coast of Africa, and his expeditions discovered the Madeiras and the Azores and rounded Cape Verde.

HENSON, Josiah (1789–1881), US slave, thought to have been the model for Uncle Tom in Harriet STOWE's book *Uncle Tom's Cabin*. He became a Methodist Episcopal preacher, and escaped to Canada in 1830 where he aided fugitive slaves and established the British-American Institute for the "colored inhabitants of Canada."

HENSON, Matthew Alexander (1866–1955), US negro Arctic explorer, who with Robert PEARY discovered the North Pole in 1909. He had already accompanied Peary to the Arctic seven times.

HENTY, George Alfred (1832–1902), English author of over 80 adventure novels for boys. They include *Out of the Pampas* (1868) and *Facing Death* (1883).

HENZE, Hans Werner (1926–), German composer known for his symphonies, concertos and operas, which include *Elegy for Young Lovers* (1961), for which W. H. AUDEN and Chester Kallman wrote the libretto.

HEPARIN. See ANTICOAGULANTS.

HEPATICAE, genus of woodland plants that flower early in the spring. They have tri-lobed leaves and white, pink, blue or purple flowers. Family: Ranunculaceae.

HEPATITIS, INFLAMMATION of the LIVER, usually due to VIRUS infection, causing nausea, loss of appetite, FEVER, malaise, JAUNDICE and abdominal pain; liver failure may result. It can occur as part of a systemic disease (e.g. YELLOW FEVER, MONONUCLEOSIS). In two forms infection is restricted to the liver: **infectious hepatitis** is an EPIDEMIC form, transmitted by feces and is of short INCUBATION; it is rarely serious or prolonged. **Serum hepatitis** is transmitted by BLOOD (e.g., used needles and syringes, TRANSFUSION), it develops more slowly but may be more severe, causing death. It is common among drug addicts; carriers may be detected by blood tests and immunization of those at risk may be helpful. Amebiasis and certain DRUGS can also cause hepatitis.

HEPBURN, Katharine (1909–), US stage and film actress. She is famous for many performances during a long career which included several films with Spencer TRACY and has won three Academy awards. Her films include *Bringing up Baby* (1938), *The Philadelphia Story* (1940), *The African Queen* (1951) and *Long Day's Journey Into Night* (1962).

HEPBURN, William Peters (1833–1916), US lawyer and congressman, known for the Hepburn Act (1906), which defined the powers of the INTERSTATE COMMERCE COMMISSION. He was for 14 years chairman of the House committee on interstate and foreign commerce.

HEPHAESTUS, Greek god of fire, the divine smith and patron of craftsmen. Son of ZEUS and HERA, he was the husband of APHRODITE. His counterpart in Roman myth was VULCAN.

HEPHTALITES. See WHITE HUNS.

HEPPLEWHITE, George (d. 1786), famous English furniture-maker and designer, influenced by Robert ADAM. In the *Cabinet-maker and Upholsterer's Guide* (1788), his furniture is characterized by elegant, fine carved forms and painted or inlaid wood.

HEPTARCHY, name for the seven kingdoms of Anglo-Saxon Britain before the 9th-century Danish conquests, comprising Kent, Sussex, Wessex, Essex, Northumbria, East Anglia and Mercia.

HEPWORTH, Barbara (1903–1975), British sculptor, and one of the most famous woman artists of the 20th century. Her abstract work, in stone and bronze, like that of Henry MOORE, is concerned with surface textures and the contrast of space and mass.

HERA, Greek goddess, queen of the Olympian gods, and sister and wife of ZEUS. The goddess of marriage and birth, she was a jealous wife who persecuted Zeus' lovers. Her sacred symbols were the cow and the peacock. The Romans identified her with Juno.

HERACLES. See HERCULES.

HERACLITUS (c540–c480 BC), Greek philosopher from Ephesus, called "the Weeping Philosopher" for his gloomy views and "the Obscure" for his cryptic style. He is known to us only through other authors. Believing in universal impermanence, and that all things (notably opposites) were interrelated, he considered fire the fundamental element of the universe.

HERAKLEION. See IRAKLION.

HERALDRY, the system of devising and granting armorial designs or insignia, and of establishing family genealogies. The designs are displayed on shields or coats of arms and identify individuals or families (in which case they are hereditary), towns, universities, military regiments and nations. The term derives from the work of the heralds of the Middle Ages who announced tournaments and became expert in identifying the armorial bearings of the participants. The practice of bearing coats of arms was adopted by the Crusaders and spread through Europe in the 12th century. The arrangement of the devices on the shields was subject to strict conventions. Coats of arms became so general in England that Richard III established the Herald's College (1483) to regulate their adoption.

HERAT, ancient historic city, in NW Afghanistan. It was on the trade route from India to Europe, and is famous for its ruins of palaces and mosques and the production of carpets. Pop 103 915.

HERB, in botany, any plant with soft aerial stems and leaves that die back at the end of the growing season to leave no persistent parts above ground. In everyday terms, herbs are plants used medicinally and to flavor food. (See COOKING; MEDICINE.)

HERBARIUM, collection of dried and preserved plant specimens systematically arranged and classified. Herbaria are valuable means of plant classification since they are built up over many years of plants from different sources and therefore show the limits of variation within species.

HERBART, Johann Friedrich (1776–1841), German philosopher and educator best remembered for his pedagogical system, now called **Herbartianism**, in which he stressed the importance of ethics (to give social direction) and psychology (to understand the mind of the pupil) acting together.

HERBERT, George (1593–1633), English poet and clergyman. His poetry, generally termed Metaphysical, deals for the most part with his own intense religious experiences, expressed in a complex but elegant, sometimes witty style. His work was first published posthumously in a collection entitled *The Temple* (1633).

HERBERT, Victor (1859–1924), Irish-American operetta composer and conductor, famous for *Babes in Toyland* (1903) and *Naughty Marietta* (1910). He also wrote two grand operas and a cello concerto.

HERBICIDE. See WEEDKILLER.

HERBIVORES, a dietary classification of the Animal Kingdom—including all animals which feed exclusively on plant materials. Preyed on by many carnivorous animals, they form the lower links of food chains.

HERBLOCK. See BLOCK, HERBERT LAWRENCE.

During excavations of the ancient Roman city of Herculaneum, this mosaic of Neptune and Amphitrite was found in the nymphaeum of a private house.

HERCULANEUM, ancient Roman city at the foot of Mt Vesuvius in Italy. Like nearby POMPEII, it was destroyed in 79 AD, by the eruption of Vesuvius which engulfed it in volcanic mud that hardened and preserved even wood and textiles. Rediscovered in 1709, it is still being excavated.

HERCULES (Heracles), Greek mythological hero famed for his strength and courage. The son of ZEUS, he performed twelve seemingly impossible labors. He killed the NEMEAN LION and the HYDRA; captured the wild boar of Mt Erymanthus and the hind of Arcadia, a deer with golden antlers; killed the man-eating birds of the Stymphalian marshes; cleaned, in one day, the AUGEAN STABLES; captured the savage bull of King MINOS of Crete and the man-eating mares of King DIOMEDES of Thrace; obtained the girdle of the Amazon queen HIPPOLYTA; seized the cattle of the monster GERYON; fetched the golden apples of the Hesperides and brought CERBERUS from the underworld.

HERCULES, a large N Hemisphere constellation containing a superb GLOBULAR CLUSTER, M13, of around 500 000 stars, and which is just visible to the naked eye.

HERCULES, Pillars of. See PILLARS OF HERCULES.

HERDER, Johann Gottfried von (1744–1803), German philosopher and literary critic in the STURM UND DRANG movement. He initiated the study of comparative folk literatures and in his *Outlines of the Philosophy of Man* (1784–91) he developed the influential concept of the evolution of human culture and the singularity of each historical epoch.

HEREDITY, the process whereby progeny resemble their parents in many features but are not, except in some microorganisms, an exact duplicate of their parents. Patterns of heredity for a long time puzzled biologists and it was not until the researches of Gregor MENDEL, an Austrian monk, that any numeric laws of heredity were discovered. Although Mendel's work was published in the mid-1860s, it went ignored by the majority of biologists until the opening of the 20th century.

Mendel showed that hereditary characteristics are passed on in units called GENES. When GAMETES (reproductive cells) are formed by MEIOSIS, the genes controlling any given characteristic "segregate" and become associated with different gametes. Thus, if the height of a pea plant is controlled by the genes T (for tallness) and t (for shortness) and pollen from a pure-breeding dwarf strain (of genotype tt) is used to fertilize ovules of a pure-breeding tall strain (of genotype TT), the resulting plants (of the "first filial"—F_1—generation), are of genotype Tt. Now the gametes of the F_1 generation contain equal numbers of genes T and t, both in the pollen and the ovules. The second filial (F_2) generation thus contains 50% of the "heterozygote" Tt, together with 25% each of the "homozygotes" TT and tt. In many cases, the heterozygote is indistinguishable from one of the homozygotes. In this case the gene that is expressed in the heterozygous condition is called a *dominant* gene; that which only manifests itself when homozygous is termed *recessive*. In the case of Mendel's peas, since T was dominant and t recessive, in the F_1 generation (100% Tt) all the plants were tall, while in the F_2 generation 75% were of the tall phenotype (i.e., the 25% TT and the 50% Tt) and 25% (the tt) of the short one.

Mendel also showed that when two or more pairs of genes segregate simultaneously the distribution of any one is independent of the distribution of the others. This work was done by crossing peas pure-breeding for round yellow seeds (*RRYY*) with peas pure-breeding for wrinkled green seeds (*rryy*). All the first-cross seeds were round yellow showing that round is dominant over wrinkled and yellow over green. The possible number of GENOTYPES is 16 but only 4 PHENOTYPES appeared: in the ratio of 9 round yellow seeds, to every 3 round green, 3 wrinkled yellow, and 1 wrinkled green. This "independent segregation" applies only to genes on different CHROMOSOMES; genes on the same chromosome are "linked" and do not segregate independently.

It is now known the genes are normally located on the chromosomes in the nucleus of the CELL. Each

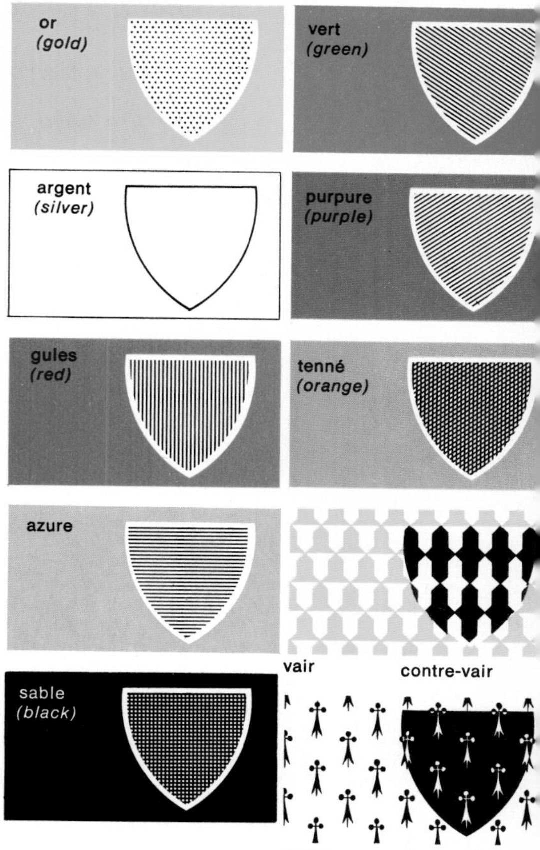

Heraldic designs flourished in the Middle Ages, although many of the actual emblems used are rather older and there is much debate about what they originally meant, beyond signifying family and rank.

chromosome carries many genes which may be transmitted together and are said to be in *coupling*. However, genes are exchanged between chromosome pairs so that RECOMBINATION occurs. Because of the occurrence of recombination the LINKAGE of genes is not complete.

In the vast majority of animals and higher plants sex is determined by a special sex chromosome which in humans is the XY chromosome. Men are XY and women XX so that all ova are X while a sperm is

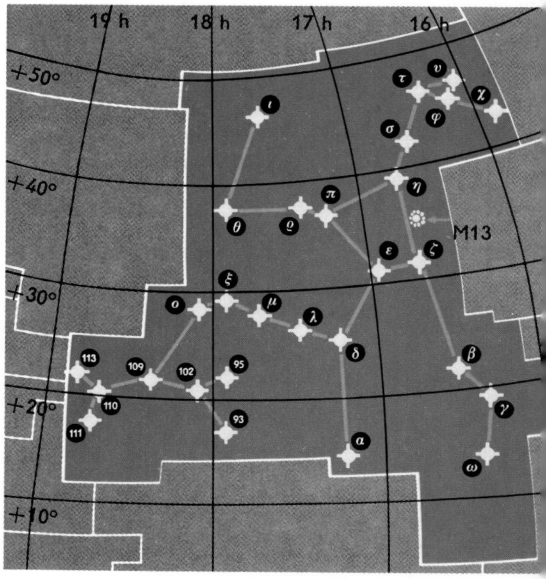

The constellation of Hercules, represented as a man kneeling. M13 is the famous globular star cluster in Hercules.

either X or Y. Therefore there should be an equal number of males and females in a population. In practise Y-bearing sperm are more successful in fertilizing ova than X, so that more boys are born than girls.

Genes not only replicate themselves to pass on genetic information and direct the synthesis of PROTEINS within individual cells, they also interact with each other both directly at the chromosomal level and indirectly through gene products. Although a particular characteristic of an organism is probably under the control of a single gene, the characteristic may be modified by a large number of other genes. For example, mice have a gene which can either slightly shorten the tail or result in early death through kidney failure, depending on the presence of other genes. Other genes exist for the sole function of suppressing the effects of another gene. The translocation of genes on chromosomes probably plays an important role in gene interaction.

In most organisms the majority of abnormal or mutant genes are recessive. But in man mutant genes tend either to be dominant or show no dominance. As humans generally avoid marrying close relatives, different combinations of genes are always being formed which give rise to the great variation seen among human beings. A reduction of variability occurs in thoroughbred animals where matings are controlled so as to select for desired constant features.

It has been estimated that throughout EVOLUTION there have been over 500 million different species of plants and animals, therefore there must have been at least 500 million different genes. Genes are composed of DNA (see NUCLEIC ACIDS) which is capable of an enormous number of variations. A sequence of 15 nucleotides composed of four different bases is capable of over 500 million alternatives. It is possible using the four different nucleotides in DNA to construct a code of 64 three-nucleotide sequences capable of indicating all the differing AMINO ACIDS (see CODON).

HEREFORD, in NW Tex., seat of Deaf Smith Co. Its economy rests on cattle, fertilizer and sugar beet. Pop 13414.

HEREWARD THE WAKE, 11th-century Anglo-Saxon hero, thane of Lincolnshire, who defied William I on the Isle of Ely 1070–71. Charles KINGSLEY's novel *Hereward the Wake* (1866) tells of his exploits.

HERKIMER, Nicholas (1728–1777), American Revolutionary soldier, brigadier general of the New York militia. He was killed at Oriskany, New York, when he was ambushed by British and Indian forces.

HERMAN, Woody (Woodrow Charles Herman; 1913–), US jazz musician and bandleader. A clarinetist, he has formed several big bands including the famous "Third Herd" in 1953.

HERMAPHRODITE, any organism in which the functions of both sexes are combined. Usually, an individual functions in only one sexual role at a time, but in a few species, e.g., earthworms, each of a pair of partners fertilizes the other during copulation. Hermaphrodite plants are usually referred to as being bisexual.

HERMES, Greek god, usually identified as the messenger of the gods, especially of his father ZEUS. He also led the souls of the dead to the underworld. Hermes was the patron of travelers and of all, including thieves, who relied on skill and cunning. He is identified with MERCURY in Roman mythology.

HERMES TRISMEGISTUS (Hermes the Thrice-greatest), Greek name for the Egyptian god Thoth. To him was ascribed the invention of writing and the authorship of the **Hermetic Writings**, books of occult wisdom which date from the 1st–4th centuries AD. They were of great importance in medieval European thought, since they were held to date from before the writings of Moses, and thus provide access to the body of primordial knowledge that had since been lost.

HERMIT, one who lives alone, to pursue an ascetic contemplative life, usually for religious reasons. Hermits were common among the early Christians of the late 3rd century and among the early FRANCISCANS.

HERMITAGE, Soviet art museum in Leningrad, one of the world's most outstanding art collections. The huge collection was begun by Empress Catherine II in the 18th century. It has art treasures from all over the world and masterpieces by Rembrandt, Picasso and Matisse.

HERMITAGE, home of President Jackson, E of Nashville, Tenn. It was built in 1819–31 in antebellum style, and is now a museum.

HERMIT CRABS, a group of crustaceans with soft bodies which occupy the empty shells of sea snails. Most members of the group occupy spiral WHELK shells and in all of them, the appendages on the right side of the abdomen are not developed. Detritus feeders, hermit crabs have well-developed pincers and two pairs of walking legs, and can withdraw into their borrowed shells if attacked. Not infrequently the shell is shared by one or more SEA-ANEMONES, commensal with the hermit crab (see COMMENSALISM).

HERMON, Mount, or Jabal ash-Shaykh mountain, the highest point (9232ft) of the Anti-Lebanon Range on the border of Lebanon and SW Syria.

HERMOSA BEACH, city in SW Cal., on the Pacific 17mi SSW of Los Angeles. It is a residential and resort community. Pop 17412.

HERMOSILLO, city in NW Mexico, capital of Sonora state, on the Sonora R 65mi from the Gulf of California. It is a commercial center for an agricultural area. Pop 206633.

HERNDON, William Henry (1818–1891), US lawyer and biographer (1889) of Abraham Lincoln. Lincoln's friend and law partner from 1843, he was faulted for his somewhat uncritical portrayal of Lincoln. Nevertheless his book is an invaluable record of the president's life.

HERNIA, protrusion of abdominal contents through the abdominal wall in the inguinal or femoral part of the groin, or through the DIAPHRAGM (**hiatus hernia**). Hernia may occur through a congenital defect or through an area of MUSCLE weakness. Bowel and omentum are commonly found in hernial sacs and if there is a tight constriction at the neck of the sac (the hernia is "strangulated"), the bowel may be obstructed or suffer GANGRENE. In hiatus hernia, part of the STOMACH lies in the CHEST. Hernia may need SURGERY to reposition the bowel and close the defect, but this is rare in hiatus hernia.

HERO AND LEANDER, Greek legend that inspired numerous authors, including SCHILLER and BYRON. Hero was priestess of Aphrodite at Sestos, and her lover, Leander, swam the Hellespont nightly to be with her. One night Hero's guiding light was blown out in a storm, and Leander was drowned. In despair Hero threw herself into the sea.

Ruins of Herod the Great's palace at Massada, Israel. Herod's mounting paranoia led to the killing of his wife's family, his wife and his own first-born son.

HEROD, family name of a dynasty in Palestine which ruled for nearly 150 years around the time of Christ. They were clients of Rome.

Herod the Great (c73–4 BC), first important ruler of the dynasty, king of Judaea from 37 BC. He strengthened his position by keeping on good terms with the Romans, including MARK ANTONY and Augustus. Although an able ruler and generous builder (especially the Temple at Jerusalem) he was hated for his ruthlessness. He was responsible for the deaths of many of his family and according to the New Testament, ordered the massacre of the Innocents.

Herod Antipas (c21 BC–39 AD), son of Herod the Great, ruler of Galilee at the time of Christ's crucifixion. He was tricked by his wife and her daughter Salome into having John the Baptist executed.

Herod Agrippa I (c10 BC–44 AD), grandson of Herod the Great, king of Judaea 41–44 AD. Helped in his career by his friendship with the Roman emperors Caligula and Claudius, he earned the support of the Jews by his adherence to Jewish tradition.

Herod Agrippa II (c27–93 AD), son of Herod Agrippa I, king of Chalcis, last important ruler of the Herodian dynasty. Lacking his father's tact in the treatment of the Jews, he contributed to their discontent, and sided with the Romans in the Jewish revolt 66–70 AD.

HERODOTUS (c484–425 BC), Greek historian, renowned as "the Father of History" for his work seeking to describe and explain the causes of the Greco-Persian wars of 499–479 BC. This involved him in a monumental survey of the whole of mankind's previous history, collected from the stories he had heard during his extensive travels. He is also famed as a geographer and ethnologist.

HEROIN, OPIUM alkaloid with narcotic ANALGESIC and euphoriant properties, a valuable DRUG in severe pain of short duration (e.g., CORONARY THROMBOSIS) and in terminal malignant disease. It is abused in DRUG ADDICTION, taken intravenously for its psychological effects and later because of physical addiction. SEPTICEMIA and hepatitis may follow unsterile INJECTIONS and early death is common.

HERONS, long-billed and long-legged wading birds of the subfamily Ardeinae, and including the EGRETS. Herons are the only birds that fly with the neck tucked back and the head between the shoulders. Gregarious at nesting time, most species disperse after breeding. Waterside or marsh birds, they feed on frogs, fish, eels, watervoles, stabbing with their heavy bills.

HERO OF ALEXANDRIA (c62 AD), or **Heron**, Greek scientist best known for inventing the **aeolipile**, a steam-powered engine that used the principle of jet propulsion, and many other complex steam- and water-powered toys. Other works ascribed to him deal with MENSURATION, optics (containing an early version of FERMAT's Principle) and MECHANICS.

HEROPHILUS (c300 BC), Alexandrian physician regarded as the father of scientific ANATOMY, and one of the first dissectors. He distinguished nerves from tendons and partially recognized their role. His work survives only through GALEN's writings.

HÉROULT, Paul Louis Toussaint (1863–1914), French metallurgist who invented at the same time as C. M. HALL the process now known as the HALL–HÉROULT PROCESS (c1886).

HERPES SIMPLEX. See COLD SORE.

HERPES ZOSTAR. See SHINGLES.

HERPETOLOGY (from the Greek *herpeton*, a creeping thing), the study of REPTILES and AMPHIBIA.

HERRICK, Robert (1591–1674), English lyric poet. Writing in the classical tradition of the Latin lyricists, he was also greatly influenced by the dramatist Ben JONSON. Most of his poems are concerned with the pleasures of nature, wine and love, and he is probably best known for the line "Gather ye rosebuds while ye may."

HERRING GULL, *Larus argentatus*, a typical, large gray-mantled GULL, of Europe and North America, nesting in large colonies on cliffs or dunes. Breeding is synchronized to minimize losses to predators, though egg-stealing and cannibalism are rife. The gulls are common scavengers of the shoreline.

HERRINGS, or clupeid fishes, a large family of important food fishes of worldwide distribution, characterized by a forward extension of the swimbladder into the skull forming two small capsules associated with the ears, and a short, deep lower jaw. Shoaling fishes, some species are found in enormous numbers: shoals of herring may be 15km (9mi) across. The herring family includes the round herrings, SHADS and MENHADEN.

HERRIOT, Édouard (1872–1957), French states-

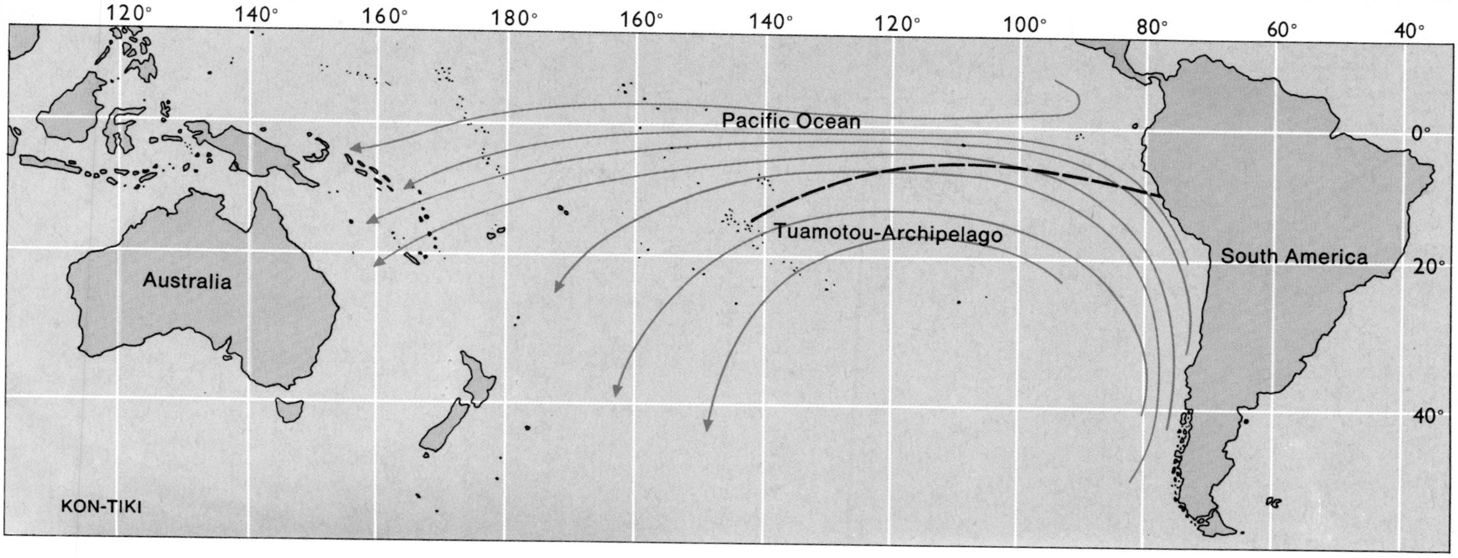

In order to show that the original settlers of Polynesia could have come from South America, Thor Heyerdahl and a number of companions set off in 1947 on a primitive balsawood raft, the *Kon-Tiki*, westward across the Pacific, relying solely on trade winds and currents (indicated here by blue arrows).

man and scholar, leader of the Radical Socialists from 1919. Mayor of Lyon from 1905, he became a senator in 1912. He was a minister, premier of France three times and president of the Chamber of Deputies. In 1942 he was imprisoned by the Germans for opposition to the Vichy government. After WWII he became president of the National Assembly, 1947–54.

HERSCHEL, family of British astronomers of German origin. **Sir Frederick William Herschel** (1738–1822) pioneered the building and use of reflecting TELESCOPES, discovered URANUS (1781), showed the sun's motion in space (1783), found that some DOUBLE STARS were in relative orbital motion (1793), and studied NEBULAE. His sister **Caroline Lucretia** (1750–1848) assisted him and herself discovered eight COMETS. His son **Sir John Frederick William Herschel** (1792–1871), with BABBAGE and Peacock helped establish Leibnitzian CALCULUS notation in Britain, was the first to use SODIUM thiosulfate (hypo) as a photographic fixer, studied POLARIZED LIGHT and made many contributions to ASTRONOMY, especially that of the S Hemisphere.

HERSEY, John Richard (1914–), US author who won a Pulitzer Prize with his first novel, *A Bell for Adano* (1944). His experiences as a war correspondent provided him with material for his books, which include *Hiroshima* (1946) and *The Wall* (1950).

HERSHEY, Alfred Day (1908–), US biologist who shared with DELBRÜCK and LURIA the 1969 Nobel Prize for Physiology or Medicine for their various researches on BACTERIOPHAGES.

HERSKOVITS, Melville Jean (1895–1963), US anthropologist. He was particularly interested in culture change and African ethnology, and in 1927 went to Northwestern University, Evanston, Ill., where he founded the first US university course in African studies.

HERTZ (Hz), SI UNIT of FREQUENCY, equal to 1 cycle per second; much used in RADIO technology.

HERTZ, Gustav Ludwig (1887–1975), German physicist who shared with J. FRANCK the 1925 Nobel Prize for Physics for their experiments showing the internal structure of the atom to be quantized, and so the value of the QUANTUM THEORY.

HERTZ, Heinrich Rudolph (1857–1894), German physicist who first broadcast and received RADIO waves (c1886). He showed also that they could be reflected and refracted (see REFLECTION; REFRACTION) much as light, and that they traveled at the same velocity though their wavelength was much longer (see ELECTROMAGNETIC RADIATION). In doing so he showed that light (and radiant heat) are, like radio waves, of electromagnetic nature.

HERTZOG, James Barry Munnik (1866–1942), South African prime minister 1924–39. Founder of the Nationalist Party (1914), he worked for separate development of Afrikaner culture and an independent republic of South Africa.

HERTZSPRUNG, Ejnar (1873–1967), Danish astronomer who showed there was a relation between a STAR's brightness and color: the resulting **Hertzsprung-Russell Diagram** (named also for Henry RUSSELL) is important throughout astronomy and cosmology. He also conceived and defined absolute MAGNITUDE; and his work on CEPHEID VARIABLES has provided a way to measure intergalactic distances.

HERZBERG, Gerhard (1904–), German-born Canadian spectroscopist, awarded the 1971 Nobel Prize for Chemistry for work on the electronic structure and geometry of molecules. In particular he pioneered the study of the spectra of FREE RADICALS.

HERZEGOVINA. See BOSNIA AND HERZEGOVINA.

HERZEN, Aleksander Ivanovich (1812–1870), Russian writer and early advocate of socialism. He was banished in 1834 for subversive activities and left Russia permanently in 1847. His writings were smuggled into Russia and did much to shape the revolutionary movement there.

HERZL, Theodore (1860–1904), Austrian writer and founder of the political Zionist movement. He worked for a Palestine homeland for the Jews in the face of mounting anti-Semitism in Europe. The fund and bank he established became essential elements in the founding of Israel.

HESIOD (8th century BC), Greek epic poet. His major works are the didactic *Theogeny*, describing the gods and heroes of Greek mythology, and *Works and Days*, which departed from the heroic tradition of Homer in dealing with the everyday life of a farmer.

HESPERIDES, in Greek mythology, the daughters of Atlas who guarded a tree bearing golden apples, planted in the "garden of the Hesperides." They were usually said to live in the W, near the Atlas Mts. Hercules stole the apples as one of his labors.

HESPERORNIS, a fossil bird of the CRETACEOUS period, evolving some 30 million years after ARCHEOPTERYX, and presenting essentially the modern bird form. Flightless diving birds with stubby tails and strong legs far back on the body, they had teeth in both jaws.

HESS, Moses (1812–1875), German journalist and socialist mentor of MARX and ENGELS, who built on the ideas of HEGEL. His most important book, *Rom und Jerusalem* (1862), advocating a homeland for the Jews, inspired later Zionist leaders.

HESS, Rudolf (1894–), German Nazi leader and Hitler's deputy, 1933–39. Depressed by his loss of influence, in 1941 he flew to Scotland to try personally to make a settlement between Germany and Britain. He was arrested, and condemned to life imprisonment for war crimes at the NUREMBERG TRIALS in 1946.

HESS, Victor Franz (1883–1964), Austrian-born US physicist who shared with C. D. ANDERSON the 1936 Nobel Prize for Physics for his discovery of COSMIC RAYS.

HESS, Walter Rudolf (1881–1973), Swiss physiologist awarded with MONIZ the 1949 Nobel Prize for Physiology or Medicine for his determination of the control exerted by certain parts of the BRAIN over the functioning of internal organs.

HESSE, West German state created by the US occupation authorities in 1945 and including most of the Prussian province of Hesse-Nassau and the state of Hesse. A fertile, hilly region, Hesse (8 150sq mi) produces grain, potatoes, fruit and wines, and is in part heavily industrialized. Chief cities are Frankfurt-am-Main, Darmstadt, Kassel, Wiesbaden.

HESSE, Hermann (1877–1962), German-born Swiss poet and novelist. The duality of man's nature, particularly with regard to the artist, is a recurrent theme in his work, with a later emphasis on symbolism and psychoanalytic insights. His novels include *Demian* (1919), *Siddhartha* (1922), *Steppenwolf* (1927) and *The Glass Bead Game* (1943). In 1946 he won the Nobel Prize for Literature.

HESSIAN FLY, a gall-midge from Germany—the one species that makes no galls. Introduced to North America in 1776 by Hessian mercenaries, it became a serious pest of American grainfields. The larva lies between the stalk and grain sheath of grasses, causing parts of the plant above it to wither.

HESSIANS, German mercenaries, mostly from Hesse-Kassel, who fought with distinction on the British side during the American REVOLUTIONARY WAR. They suffered a serious defeat at Trenton, N.J., in Dec. 1776. After the war many settled in the US and Canada.

HESTIA, in Greek religion, one of the 12 Olympians and goddess of the hearth. She had a shrine in every home and was worshiped as the guardian of the family and the state. (See also VESTA.)

HETEROCYCLIC COMPOUNDS, major class of organic compounds in which the atoms are linked to form one or more rings, at least one of which includes one or more atoms other than carbon—commonly nitrogen, oxygen or sulfur. Many such compounds are of great biochemical or industrial importance. As with ALICYCLIC COMPOUNDS, saturated heterocyclic compounds resemble their ALIPHATIC analogues except for the effect of strain in small rings. There is also a large class of heterocyclic AROMATIC COMPOUNDS, highly distinctive in properties.

HETEROTROPH. See AUTOTROPH.

HEURISTICS, an approach to problem-solving in which a formally unjustifiable solution is assumed as an aid in exploring the implications of the problem. In science, even theories which ultimately prove misconceived can be of great heuristic value in research.

HEVESEY, George Charles de (1885–1966), Hungarian-born chemist awarded the 1943 Nobel Prize for Chemistry for his work on radioactive tracers (see RADIOISOTOPES). He was also the co-discoverer of the element HAFNIUM.

HEWISH, Antony (1924–), radio astronomer, corecipient with RYLE of the 1974 Nobel physics prize, Professor of Radio Astronomy at Cambridge since 1971. He headed the team which discovered the first PULSAR (1967).

HEWITT, Abram Stevens (1822–1903), US politician and industrialist. He served as a Democratic Congressman (1874–79, 1881–86), and as mayor of New York (1887–88). A model employer, he sponsored many social reforms.

HEXAGON. See POLYGON.

HEXAHEDRON. See POLYHEDRON.

HEYDRICH, Reinhard (1904–1942), notoriously cruel German Nazi leader, deputy head of the Gestapo 1934–39, then put in charge of all security. He became known as "the Hangman," and was assassinated while acting as "protector" in Czechoslovakia (see LIDICE).

HEYERDAHL, Thor (1914–), Norwegian ethnologist famous for his expeditions to prove the feasibility of his theories of cultural diffusion, and for his books. In the **Kon-Tiki**, a primitive balsawood raft, he and his crew sailed from the W coast of South America to Polynesia, demonstrating the possibility that the Polynesians originated in South America (1947). In **Ra**, a facsimile of an ancient Egyptian papyrus reed boat, he and his cosmopolitan crew succeeded at the second attempt in sailing from Morocco to Barbados, showing the possibility that the pre-Columbian cultures of South America were influenced by Egyptian civilization (Ra I, 1969, Ra II, 1970).

HEYMANS, Corneille Jean François (1892–1968), Belgian physiologist awarded the 1938 Nobel Prize for Physiology or Medicine for discovering sensory organs, close by the carotid artery and aorta, that play a part in regulating RESPIRATION.

HEYN, Piet (1577–1629), Dutch admiral. As vice-admiral of the Dutch West India Company, he captured the Spanish treasure fleet in 1628. In 1629 he became commander-in-chief of the Dutch navy.

HEYROVSKÝ, Jaroslav (1890–1967), Czech physical chemist awarded the 1959 Nobel Prize for Chemistry for inventing the polarograph (see POLAROGRAPHY).

HEYSE, Paul Johann Ludwig von (1830–1914), German writer. Center of the traditionalist Munich circle, he was noted for his romantic short stories. He won the Nobel Prize for Literature in 1910.

HEYWARD, DuBose (1885–1940), US author, best known for his novel *Porgy* (1925), on which GERSHWIN based his opera *Porgy and Bess*. Much of his work deals with the plight of Southern negroes.

HEYWOOD, Thomas (c1574–1651), English dramatist and actor. He was a prolific writer, claiming over 200 dramas, but only about 20 have survived. Excelling at themes based on everyday life, often set in London, his best known play is *A Woman Kilde with Kindnesse* (1607).

HEZEKIAH (reigned c715–686 BC), king of Judah who instituted religious reform against pagan corruptions and asserted Judah's independence from Assyrian domination by several revolts. These were put down by SENNACHERIB, but Jerusalem was not taken.

HIALEAH, city in SE Fla., 5mi NW of Miami. It manufactures clothing and furniture, and has a famous race track. Pop 102 452.

HIAWATHA, semi-legendary American Indian chief. He founded the IROQUOIS LEAGUE (c1450) to end intertribal warfare, and has been immortalized in LONGFELLOW's *Song of Hiawatha*.

HIBBING, village in NE Minn., 75mi NW of Duluth. Originally a center for iron-ore mining, its economy now depends on a taconite industry. Pop 16 104.

HIBERNATION, a protective mechanism whereby certain animals reduce their activity and apparently sleep throughout winter. At its most developed it is a characteristic of warm-blooded animals but a comparable phenomenon, **diapause**, is found in cold-blooded forms. Diapause is a direct physiological response to cold temperatures: metabolic activity in cold-blooded animals is entirely dictated by external temperature. In hibernating animals, internal preparations, such as laying down a store of fat, begin several weeks before the onset of hibernation. Then, when temperatures drop, the animal goes to sleep. Pulse rate and breathing drop to a minimum. With metabolism reduced, the animal can live on food stored in its body till spring. Winter food supplies would not be sufficient to maintain the animal in a fully-active state. When an animal remains torpid throughout the summer, this is known as **aestivation**.

HIBERNIA, Roman name for IRELAND.

HIBISCUS, a genus of hardy and tender annuals, evergreen and deciduous shrubs and small trees, native to the tropics and subtropics. Many species are in cultivation particularly for their showy, short-lived, funnel-shaped flowers. The bark of *Hibiscus cannabinus* (gambo) produces fibers that are sometimes used as a substitute for JUTE. Family: Malvaceae.

HICCUP, brief involuntary contraction of the DIAPHRAGM that may follow dietary or alcoholic excess and rapid eating. It may also be a symptom of UREMIA, mineral disorders and brain-stem disease. Re-breathing into a paper bag or repeated swallowing are effective remedies; chlorpromazine also suppresses hiccups.

HICKOCK, Wild Bill (1837–1876), US scout and frontier law officer. During the Civil War he was a Union scout and spy. As US marshal at Hays City and Abilene, Kan. (1869–71), both lawless frontier towns, he won a reputation for marksmanship and daring which he demonstrated in 1872–73 on tour with BUFFALO BILL.

HICKORY, city in W N.C., 25mi W of Statesville. It manufactures hosiery, textiles and electronics. Pop 20 569.

HICKORY, deciduous trees of the genus *Carya* from the WALNUT family Juglandaceae, which are native to America. They produce a valuable wood and yield thin-shelled edible nuts. The most important species is PECAN (*Carya illinoensis*), but the shagbark (*C. ovata*), shellbark (*C. laciniosa*) and their hybrids are also cultivated for their nuts.

HICKORY HILLS, village in NE Ill., 15mi SW of Chicago. Pop 13 176.

HICKS, Edward (1780–1849), US primitive painter. A Quaker preacher, he is best known for his illustrations of biblical passages, including over 50 versions of *The Peaceable Kingdom*, based on Isaiah's prophecy of peace between all creatures.

HICKS, Elias (1748–1830), US Quaker preacher, one of the first advocates of the abolition of slavery in the US. His idea that beliefs could be continually revised caused a split among the Friends, and his liberal followers became known as Hicksites.

HICKS, Sir John Richard (1904–), British economist. Drummond Professor of Political Economy at Oxford University (1952–65), he was awarded the Nobel Memorial Prize for Economics (with Kenneth J. Arrow) in 1972.

HICKSVILLE, village in SE N.Y., on Long Island. It manufactures electronic and paper products. Pop 48 075.

HIDALGO, state in central Mexico, with an area of 8 103sq mi. Its economy is based on agriculture, especially maguey, and extensive mineral deposits including silver and gold.

HIDALGO Y COSTILLA, Miguel (1753–1811), Mexican revolutionary, known as "the father of Mexican independence." A village priest, when Napoleon annexed Spain he plotted independence from Spain. The plot discovered (1810), he rang his church bells and shouted the famous *grito* (cry) *de Dolores*, demanding revolution against Spain. He led a peasant revolt which after initial success was suppressed in 1811. Hidalgo was executed, but the anniversary of his *grito* (Sept. 16) is celebrated as Mexico's Independence Day.

HIDATSA INDIANS (sometimes known as the Gros Ventre), North American tribe of the Siouan language family, originating in the upper Missouri area. In the 19th century they formed one group with the neighboring MANDAN and ARIKARA, and now live on the Fort Berthold Reservation, N.D.

HIDEYOSHI, Toyotomi (1536–1598), Japanese military ruler. He rose in the army of the baron Nobunaga and after his death carried on his work of national unification. In 1585 he was appointed the emperor's chief minister, and by 1590 had won control of all Japan.

HIERARCHY, the organization of the clergy in Christian churches governed by bishops; in particular, the bishops themselves, regarded as in APOSTOLIC SUCCESSION. The Roman Catholic Church distinguishes the hierarchy of orders (see MINISTRY; ORDINATION) and the hierarchy of jurisdiction. The latter comprises the PAPACY (with derived offices such as cardinal and legate) and the episcopate (with derived offices such as vicar-general).

HIERO, name of two Greek rulers of Syracuse in Sicily. **Hiero I** (d. 467 BC), tyrant from 478, expanded Syracusan power, helped by defeating the Etruscans at Cumae (474 BC). A patron of literature, he was praised by AESCHYLUS and PINDAR in return. **Hiero II** (d. c215 BC). Tyrant from c270, he joined Carthage in opposition to Rome until forced to make a treaty with Rome in 263 BC. He pursued a public-building program, for which ARCHIMEDES was his engineer.

HIEROGLYPHICS, system of writing using pictorial characters (hieroglyphs), especially that found on Egyptian monuments. Egyptian hieroglyphics are first found from c3000 BC, their use declining during the 3rd century AD. Initially there were a fairly limited number of hieroglyphs. This was followed by a rapid expansion of the number of characters in order to reduce ambiguity, and by a further expansion around 500 BC. There were two derived cursive scripts, hieratic and demotic. **Hieratic script,** initially used only for sacred texts, coexisted with true hieroglyphics from early on until c100 AD. The less legible, more cursive **demotic script** appeared around 660 BC and disappeared around 450 AD. The writings of other ancient peoples, e.g., the Hittites and Mayas, are also termed hieroglyphics. (See also ROSETTA STONE.)

HIGASHI-OSAKA, city in Japan. It is a residential suburb of Osaka. Pop 500 173.

HIGGINSON, Thomas Wentworth (1823–1911), US pastor and abolitionist. His liberal ideas lost him his first post, and after the Fugitive Slave Act (1850) he helped runaway slaves, including Anthony BURNS. In the Civil War he was colonel of the first Negro regiment. After 1864 he turned to writing.

HIGH BLOOD PRESSURE. See BLOOD CIRCULATION.

HIGHEST COMMON FACTOR (hcf), of two or more INTEGERS, the largest integer which they share as a FACTOR. For example, the hcf of 15, 18 and 27 is 3; similarly, the hcf of 15 and 17 is 1, since 17 is a PRIME NUMBER. In ALGEBRA, the hcf of two or more algebraic expressions may be found by examination of the factors of each: hence the hcf of $9ax^2$ ($=3.3.a.x.x$) and $3a^2x$ ($=3.a.a.x$) is $3ax$. (See also LOWEST COMMON MULTIPLE.)

HIGH-FIDELITY, an adjective applicable to systems carrying a signal with very little distortion, such as a good CAMERA or RADIO transmitter, but also a generic noun ("Hi-Fi") for a wide range of domestic equipment for SOUND REPRODUCTION. The input signal may arise from a phonograph disc, in which case a high-compliance (flexibility) stylus following a groove produces a piezoelectric (see PIEZOELECTRICITY) or induced (see ELECTROMAGNETISM) voltage; from magnetic tape, on which the signal is recorded in the variations of magnetization of a ferromagnetic (see MAGNETISM) coating, produced by a finely focused ELECTROMAGNET (the recording head) and inducing a voltage in the small playback head coil; or from a radio receiver which detects the slight variations in intensity (AM) or frequency (FM) of a broadcast electromagnetic wave. The resulting voltage is amplified electronically and passed to a LOUDSPEAKER, consisting typically of a paper cone, vibrated by an electromagnet, in an enclosure which attempts to compensate for the uneven response of the cone for different directions and frequencies. The most important measures of the overall faithfulness

Section of a complex highway junction in Los Angeles, typical of large road systems all over the world. Such junctions are proving mixed blessings, speeding up normal traffic but often aggravating jams.

are the frequency response (the range of frequencies passed with intensities unchanged within a quoted tolerance), the harmonic distortion (the change in the balance of the HARMONICS of a signal—particularly a boost in the high harmonics), the hum and NOISE levels (in the absence of a signal), and the flutter and wow (fluctuations in speed of record or tape decks).

HIGH JUMP. See TRACK AND FIELD.

HIGHLAND, town in NW Ind., 25mi SE of Chicago. It is a mainly residential community. Pop 24 947.

HIGHLAND PARK, city in NE Ill., on Lake Michigan. It is a residential suburb 25mi N of Chicago. Pop 32 263.

HIGHLAND PARK, city in SE Mich., surrounded by Detroit. Its industries include a Chrysler Corporation center and a Ford tractor plant. Pop 35 444.

HIGHLAND PARK, borough in central N.J., 2mi E of New Brunswick. Although mainly residential, it has some industries and a station of the US Bureau of Mines. Pop 14 385.

HIGHLAND PARK, town in NE Tex., a residential area surrounded by Dallas. Pop 10 133.

HIGH POINT, city in N.C. It is a leading center for furniture manufacture; other industries include hosiery and machinery. Pop 63 204.

HIGH PRIEST, chief religious official in the Temple of Jerusalem and spiritual head of the ancient Israelites. He was responsible for ceremonies on the Day of Atonement and in charge of temple finances and administration. The office, first conferred on AARON by his brother Moses, was originally hereditary, and ended after the destruction of the Temple in 70 AD.

HIGH SCHOOL. See SECONDARY SCHOOLS.

HIGH SEAS, in maritime law, the sea beyond territorial waters. Since the 19th century freedom of the seas has been recognized as a rule of international law, but recently the discovery of minerals under the sea and the importance of the airspace above it have made the distinction crucial. Attempts by any state to extend their jurisdiction, for example, to protect fishing rights, should only be ratified by international agreement, but various UN conferences have failed in attempts to codify or enforce the law.

HIGHWAY, major road, often with controlled access. The term goes back to the Roman roads which were on a mound (hence "high way"), made by earth from the side ditches thrown into the center. The first roads were probably Mesopotamian, but the earliest recorded long-distance road was the Persian Royal Road stretching c1 775mi from Susa to Smyrna. The Romans were the best of the ancient road-builders, and their greatest road, the APPIAN WAY, begun 312 BC, set the standard for road-building for 2 000 years.

Until the 18th century European roads were neglected and hard to travel, but Pierre Marie Jérôme Trésaguet (1716–93) in France and John Metcalf (1777–1810) in England pioneered modern road-building. The Scots, Thomas TELFORD and John Loudon McAdam, developed lightweight road construction, and the MACADAM road relied on a compacted subgrade with a thin surface of broken stone to support the load, as opposed to the heavy Roman system.

The composition was improved in the 20th century by the addition of tar, or bitumen as a binder. The coming of the automobile and increasing loads meant that totally new requirements were introduced. It became necessary for highway systems to be integrated, so although local roads are usually still the responsibility of cities, major highways are administered on a national basis to ensure continuity and uniformity. In the US this is seen to by the Federal Highway Administration. Finances are supplied by the user, with motor-fuel taxes as the main single source of revenue. Vehicles are usually licensed on the basis of weight, and toll roads are popular in areas of high demand. In road construction the major operation is earth moving, and the soil then has to be suitably prepared to make the roadbed. The pavement, or road surface laid on the roadbed, will depend on the traffic anticipated and the nature of the ground.

First-class highways, especially designed for fast-moving traffic, are variously described as expressways, superhighways, throughways or freeways, and parkways are built in park-like country and are often landscaped. The growing numbers of automobiles and the increase in road usage demands a constant rethinking of highway policy. Compromise is often necessary to avoid conflicts with community or environmental amenities.

HIGHWAY SAFETY. See SAFETY.

HIJACKING, illegally seizing a vehicle in transit for a political or criminal purpose. The word, first used for the theft of truckloads of illegal liquor during PROHIBITION, now includes the takeover of ships, trains and planes. The first hijacking of a plane in the US was in 1961, to Cuba, and the spate of hijacking that followed, for both political and personal motives, has forced international measures.

HILARIUS, Saint (or Hilary; d. 468), pope 461–468. Successor of Pope LEO I, Hilarius carried on his policy of expanding papal control over the bishops.

HILARY OF POITIERS, Saint (c315–367 AD), doctor of the Church and bishop of Poitiers from c353. He was exiled c356 for his opposition to ARIANISM, which was supported by the emperor Constantius. After his return in 361 he wrote many books refuting the Arians.

HILBERT, David (1862–1943), German mathematician whose most important contributions were in the field of mathematical LOGIC. With the advent of the NON-EUCLIDEAN GEOMETRIES it had become clear that the axiomatic basis of EUCLID's work needed further examination. This Hilbert did, establishing a logical axiomatic system for geometry.

HILDA, Saint (614–680 AD), founder and abbess of Whitby. The poet CAEDMON was a brother there, and she made it one of the main religious centers in N England. The Synod of WHITBY (663–64) decided to accept Roman, rather than Celtic, ecclesiastical observances.

HILDEBRAND. See GREGORY VII (pope).

HILL, Ambrose Powell (1825–1865), US Confederate general, one of the outstanding leaders in the Civil War. He joined the Confederates in 1861 and his force, called the "Light Division" because of its speed in marching, came to be one of the best in the South and played a decisive role in the Battle of ANTIETAM (1862). He was killed in action at PETERSBURG.

HILL, Archibald Vivian (1886–), British physiologist who shared with MEYERHOF the 1922 Nobel Prize for Physiology or Medicine for their independent work on the biochemistry of MUSCLE contraction and relaxation.

HILL, James Jerome (1838–1916), US railroad magnate who established a continental rail system in the NW. Purchasing the St. Paul and Pacific Railroad, he extended it to the Canadian border and to the Pacific at Seattle (1893). Later, working with J. P. MORGAN, he consolidated his holdings in the Great Northern Railway Company.

HILL, Joe (born Joseph Hillstrom; 1879–1915), Swedish-American labor organizer for the INDUSTRIAL WORKERS OF THE WORLD in California. He wrote many labor songs. Tried and executed on a murder charge, his funeral was attended by about 30 000 people.

HILL, Octavia (1838–1912), English social worker, a pioneer in the struggle for better housing conditions for the urban poor. Financially supported by John RUSKIN, she set up houses for the poor, run jointly by tenants and managers.

HILL, Sir Rowland (1795–1879), English postal reformer and the founder of "penny postage" (1837). He worked for the government, 1838–64, establishing an efficient postal service.

HILLARY, Sir Edmund Percival (1919–), New Zealand explorer and mountaineer. In 1953 he and Tenzing Norkay, a Sherpa from Nepal, became the first men to reach the summit of Mount EVEREST, the world's highest mountain.

HILLEL (d. 10 AD), Jewish scholar, who was one of the great founders of rabbinic Judaism, and ethical leader of his generation. He was opposed by SHAMMAI, another teacher. His "Seven Rules" of exegesis laid the groundwork for a liberal rather than literal interpretation of scriptural law.

HILLIARD, Nicholas (c1537–1619), English miniature painter and portraitist. As court miniaturist and goldsmith to Elizabeth I, his style of "limning" was characterized by jewel-like exquisite detailing and fine drawing.

HILLMAN, Sidney (1887–1946), US labor leader. A Lithuanian immigrant, Hillman became the first president of the Amalgamated Clothing Workers of America (1914). He was a powerful supporter of industrial unions, a founder of the Congress of Industrial Organizations (CIO), and government adviser on labor relations. (See also AMERICAN FEDERATION OF LABOR.)

HILLQUIT, Morris (1869–1933), US lawyer and Socialist leader, born in Riga, Russia. He was a leader of the SOCIAL DEMOCRATIC PARTY and the SOCIALIST PARTY and defended lawyers against espionage charges. He was involved in the PROGRESSIVE PARTY.

HILLSBORO, city in NW Ore., seat of Washington Co. Its industries include lumber and farming. Pop 14 675.

HILLSDALE, borough of N.J., 9mi ENE of Paterson. It produces corn and apples. Pop 11 768.

HILLSIDE, township in NE N.J., 2mi N of Elizabeth. It manufactures insulated wire, aluminum castings and cork. Pop 21 636.

HILO, city on Hilo Bay, Hawaii, seat of Hawaii Co. It is a tourist center and exporter of sugar, coffee, fruit and orchids. Pop 26 353.

HILTON, Conrad Nicholson (1887–), US businessman who built up one of the largest hotel chains throughout the world. His first hotel was a 50-room hotel in Cisco, Tex., purchased in 1919.

HILTON, James (1900–1954), English popular novelist. His books include *Lost Horizon* (1933), and *Random Harvest* (1941), which were made into films.

HILTON, Walter (d. c1396), English mystic and writer. His *Scale of Perfection* challenged the importance of the cloistered religious life.

HIMALAYAN CAT, breed of Persian type with Siamese coloring.

The snowy peak of Mount Kanchenjunga, at over 28 000ft one of the highest peaks in the Himalayas, seen in clear weather from Sikkim.

The Hindu god Siva as Nataraja, king of dancers, a 12th- or 13th-century bronze figure from South India. This aspect of the god symbolizes the progress of creation as a continuing dance.

HIMALAYAS, the highest chain of mountains in the world, over 1 500mi long, extending from NW Pakistan and across Kashmir, N India, S Tibet, Nepal, Sikkim, Bhutan to the bend of the Tsangpo-Brahmaputra R. The Himalayas are formed by a series of parallel ranges. The Great Himalayas lie in the N, then the Lesser Himalayas, and the Outer Himalayas in the S. The average elevation is 20 000ft in the Great Himalayas, where there are 11 mountains of over 26 000ft. The Himlayas protect S and W China from the moisture-laden monsoons which strike Bhutan, Sikkim and Nepal, but this results in aridness in those parts of China. The Indus, Sutlej, Brahmaputra and Ganges rivers all rise in the mountains.

HIMEJI, city in W Honshū, Japan, 34mi WNW of Kōe. It is an industrial center for textiles and has a large Buddhist shrine. Pop 408 353.

HIMMLER, Heinrich (1900–1945), Nazi leader, police chief and politician. Head of the SS from 1929 and the GESTAPO from 1936, he was largely responsible for the CONCENTRATION CAMPS and the murder of millions of Jews and others considered undesirable to the Nazi regime in the 1930s and 1940s. He became interior minister in 1943, but fell from Hitler's favor in 1945. After the German defeat in 1945 he committed suicide.

HINAYANA, common name for Theravada, a branch of BUDDHISM in SE Asia. It claims that, by renouncing desire and the sense of his own ego, a person can subdue suffering and sorrow and gradually achieve a state of NIRVANA.

HINDEMITH, Paul (1895–1963), influential German composer and teacher. Considered a modernist because of his dissonant harmonies and counterpoint, he nevertheless embraced the classical musical forms of Bach and Mozart in a modern idiom. He viewed the composer as a craftsman who ought to write music for specific uses (*Gebrauchsmusik*). Among his many major works are the opera *Mathis der Mahler* (1938) and *Symphonic Metamorphoses* (1945).

HINDENBURG, Paul von (Paul Ludwig Hans Anton von Hindenburg und Beneckendorff; 1847–1934), German general, military hero of WWI and president of Germany (1925–34). Together with LUDENDORFF he directed the German WWI effort and military strategies. As president he was chiefly a figurehead, becoming increasingly senile. During his presidency the Nazis gradually gained popular support until HITLER became chancellor in 1933.

HINDI, the official language of India, a written form of HINDUSTANI. It is written in Devanagari script (or SANSKRIT), reading from left to right.

HINDUISM, one of the major world religions: the civilization, in all its aspects, of the Hindus, the peoples of India and the neighboring countries, with outposts elsewhere in SE Asia and Africa. A comprehensive culture embracing diverse beliefs and practices, it tolerates almost any belief, but regards none as essential. Even other religions are accepted, though not their exclusivism. Thus Hinduism has no dogma, and is almost indefinable. It had neither beginning nor founder, and has no hierarchy or source of authority. Abstract philosophies co-exist with magic, animism, pantheism, polytheism, mysticism, asceticism and cultic sexuality. Nevertheless there are some characteristics common to most Hindus. These include belief in BRAHMAN, the One that is the All, the absolute and ultimate principle which is the Self of all living things. Brahman is sometimes personified as BRAHMA, a background figure who, with SHIVA and VISHNU, forms the Trimurti, in some ways analogous to the Christian TRINITY. This element of monotheism plays almost no part in popular Hinduism, where countless gods are worshiped. Hindus have great respect for all life, many being vegetarian and revering and protecting the cow. The upper-caste class of Brahmins is respected as sacrosanct. The doctrine of TRANSMIGRATION OF SOULS in an endless cycle, under the law of KARMA, is universally believed. The three paths to escape from the cycle are duty, knowledge (sought by meditation and YOGA) and devotion to God. Hinduism has its roots in Vedism, the religion of the early Indo-Aryans who settled in

India in the late 2nd millennium BC. The authority of the VEDA is still generally recognized, though in practice the Veda is hardly known. Vedism, a chiefly ritual system, developed into BRAHMANISM, in which, from about 700 BC, philosophy developed and was enshrined in the UPANISHADS. A period of great change followed, in which the sects (as they were at first) of BUDDHISM and JAINISM arose. True Hinduism began in the 2nd century BC, marked by the BHAGAVAD-GĪTĀ (found in the epic MAHĀBHĀRATA); the cults of Vishnu and Shiva developed, becoming major sects, and were followed by the cult of SHAKTI, often associated with TANTRA, esoteric practices both ritual and sensual. Modern Hinduism has seen the rise of innumerable reform movements and sects, some influenced by Islam or Christianity. Although in present-day India traditional Hindu social structures (see CASTE SYSTEM) are weakened, Hinduism is readily adapting to modern conditions. (See also KRISHNA; RAMAKRISHNA; RAMAYANA.)

HINDU KUSH, mountain range, second highest in the world, stretching from NE Afghanistan to N Pakistan. High altitude passes cross the range as well as the recently-constructed Salang tunnel. The range's highest peak is Tirich Mir (25 260ft).

HINDUSTAN, "land of the Hindus," the Persian name for the N Indian Ganges plain between the Himalayas and the Deccan plateau.

HINDUSTANI, the most widespread language of N India, particularly of the Hindu-speaking areas. It is the spoken form of HINDI and URDU, and derives from the Prakrits (vernacular forms of classical Sanskrit). Hindustani grammar is less complex than Sanskrit in that it avoids noun inflections, gender agreement and irregular forms, and instead of prepositions it has postpositions, which explain the grammatical function of preceding words. GANDHI at the time of India's independence in 1947 wanted Hindustani to be adopted as the national Indian language, because of its simple grammar and since it can be written in Devanagari or Urdu. However, Hindi was adopted as the official language.

HINES, Earl Fatha (1905–), US jazz musician, born Earl Kenneth Hines. A member of Louis ARMSTRONG's "Hot Five" group (1948–51), he formed his own group in 1957. He is considered one of the great jazz pianists and has influenced modern jazz.

HINGHAM, town in SE Mass., on Massachusetts Bay, 11mi SE of Boston. It is primarily a summer resort. Pop 18 845.

HINNY, an infertile cross between a she-ass and a stallion. (See also MULE.)

HINSDALE, residential village in NE Ill., 17mi W of Chicago. Pop 15 918.

HINSHELWOOD, Sir Cyril Norman (1897–1967), British physical chemist awarded with SEMYONOV the 1956 Nobel Prize for Chemistry for his work on reaction rates and mechanisms (see KINETICS, CHEMICAL), especially in the reaction of hydrogen and oxygen to form WATER.

HIPPARCHUS (c130 BC), Greek scientist, the father of systematic ASTRONOMY, who compiled the first star catalog and ascribed stars MAGNITUDES, made a good estimate of the distance and size of the moon, probably first discovered PRECESSION, invented many astronomical instruments, worked on plane and SPHERICAL TRIGONOMETRY, and suggested ways of determining LATITUDE AND LONGITUDE.

HIPPOCRATES (c460–c377 BC), Greek physician generally called "the Father of Medicine" and the probable author of at least some of the **Hippocratic Collection**, some 60 or 70 books on all aspects of ancient MEDICINE. The authors probably formed a school centered around Hippocrates during his lifetime and continuing after his death. The **Hippocratic Oath**, traditionally regarded as the most valuable statement of medical ethics and good practice, probably represents the oath sworn by candidates for admission to an ancient medical guild.

HIPPODROME, ancient Greek and Roman open-air racecourse, generally U-shaped. Spectators were seated along the sides and around the curve; dignitaries watched from above the straight end. The Circus Maximus in Rome held about 250 000 people, the Hippodrome in Constantinople up to 100 000.

HIPPOLYTE, in Greek mythology, queen of the Amazons, who invaded Attica against THESEUS to rescue her sister Antiope. One labor of HERCULES was to obtain her golden belt.

HIPPOLYTUS. See PHAEDRA.

HIPPOLYTUS, Saint (c170–235 AD), scholar, martyr and anti-pope (c217–35) in opposition to Pope CALIXTUS I. His important text is *Apostolic Tradition*. His feast day is Aug. 13.

Hippopotamus agape. Its impressive tusk-like teeth, used exclusively for fighting, are razor sharp.

HIPPOPOTAMUS, *Hippopotamus amphibius*, one of the largest living terrestrial mammals, distantly related to pigs. With a massive body set on short legs, each with four toes with hoof-like nails, the hippo spends the day submerged in water, coming to land at night to graze a strip extending up to 10km (6mi) inland. Highly adapted to its daytime life in water, the hippo has its sense organs, nose, eyes and ears, on top of its head, so that they are the last parts to submerge. Indeed it rarely submerges completely, and then for up to 5min only. The Common hippopotamus is still widespread in the lakes and rivers in Africa.

HIPPO REGIUS, ancient name of ANNABA.

HIROHITO (1901–), emperor of Japan from 1926. After WWII his status dramatically changed from a god-like position to being a "symbol of the state and unity of the people," without political or sovereign power. The emperor is a distinguished marine biologist.

HIROSAKI, city in N Honshu, Japan, 23mi SW of Aomori. It is a center for silk culture, fruit and lacquer manufacture. Pop 157 603.

HIROSHIGE, Ando (1797–1858), Japanese painter and printmaker. He is famous for his sets of woodblock color prints of atmospheric landscapes of snow, rain, mist and moonlight scenes. Among his best works are *Eight Views of Lake Biwa* and *Thirty-six Views of Mount Fuji*.

HIROSHIMA, industrial city in SW Honshu, Japan, located on a bay in the Inland Sea. As a thriving industrial and commercial center, it was chosen as the target for the US atomic bomb attack of Aug. 6, 1945, which caused enormous havoc and destruction, killing over 80 000 people, and wounding 60 000. It has been largely rebuilt since 1950. Pop 541 834.

HISPANIOLA, second largest island in the West Indies, located W of Puerto Rico and E of Cuba. The island is shared between the Republic of Haiti and the Dominican Republic. There are excellent harvests of sugar, coffee and cocoa.

HISS, Alger (1904–), US public official accused of spying for Russia. Hiss was an adviser to the US State Department on economic and political affairs. In 1948 he was brought before the House Committee on Un-American Activities, and in 1950 was convicted of perjury. He served four years in prison. (See also CHAMBERS, WHITTAKER.)

HISTADRUT, Israeli labor federation which comprises 90% of organized Jewish labor. It was founded in 1920 and is a mainstay of the Israel socialist movement. It organizes most of the financial and industrial undertakings in collective and cooperative villages.

HISTAMINE, AMINE concerned with the production of INFLAMMATION, and particularly of HIVES and the allergic spasm of the BRONCHI in ASTHMA and ANAPHYLAXIS; it enhances STOMACH acid secretion and has several effects on BLOOD CIRCULATION. ANTIHISTAMINES and cromoglycate can interfere with its release; ADRENALINE counteracts its serious effects.

HISTIDINE ($C_3H_3N_2CH_2CH(NH_2)COOH$), a basic AMINO ACID found in many PROTEINS; HEMOGLOBIN contains 8.5% histidine. Man is capable of synthesizing histidine so its presence in the diet is not essential. It is the metabolic precursor of HISTAMINE.

HISTOGRAM, a graphical way of representing statistical information (see GRAPHS; STATISTICS). The data is classified, and the classes marked off along the *x*-axis (see AXES); rectangles whose bases are centered on the class midpoints, and whose heights are proportional to the frequencies in the classes, are then constructed. Similar is the **frequency polygon**, constructed by plotting the class midpoints against their respective frequencies and joining the plotted points. If it is meaningful to do so (depending on the shape of the polygon, the certainty felt that the sample is representative of the population, the way that the data has been classified, etc.) a **frequency curve** may be drawn that best "fits" the plotted points.

HISTOLOGY, the study of the microscopic ANATOMY of parts of organisms after DEATH (autopsy) or removal by SURGERY (BIOPSY). Tissue is fixed by agents that denature PROTEINS, preventing autolysis and bacterial degradation; they are stained by dyes that have particular affinity for different structures. Histology facilitates the study both of normal tissue and of DISEASED organs, or pathological tissue.

HISTOPLASMOSIS, FUNGAL disease prevalent in parts of North America and Africa, and carried by poultry, birds and bats. It may cause acute respiratory infection, a rapidly developing disseminated form, or a chronic type with FEVER, debility and specific organ involvement (especially of the LUNGS and resembling TUBERCULOSIS). Specific antifungal ANTIBIOTICS are needed for the disseminated disease.

HITACHI, coastal city in Japan, central Honshu, 83mi NE of Tokyo, important for the production of chemicals and electrical equipment. Pop 193 210.

HITCHCOCK, Alfred Joseph (1899–), English film director known for his skillful suspense and macabre humor. He has made over 50 films, including *The Thirty-Nine Steps* (1935), *The Lady Vanishes* (1938) and in Hollywood *Spellbound* (1945), *Strangers on a Train* (1951), *North by North West* (1959) and *Psycho* (1960).

HITCHCOCK, Lambert (1795–1852), US cabinetmaker who in 1818 established a furniture factory in Barkhamsted, Conn. Here he manufactured "Hitchcock chairs," which combined simplicity with elegance. They are now collector's pieces.

HITLER, Adolf (1889–1945), Austrian-born dictator of Germany 1933–45. Hitler will for a long time remain a highly controversial figure. He was without doubt an evil man, coarse and unstable by nature, but he had political genius and was one of the phenomena of the 20th century. He hardly put a foot wrong politically between 1931 and 1941, and conquered an area of Europe larger than NAPOLEON. He was the first man to understand and exploit the politics of the mass age and set up a radicalism of the right which won mass support and beat the radicals of the left on their own ground, something which earlier conservative and reactionary parties had failed to do. A powerful orator, he was one of the first to understand how to use political propaganda, including the propaganda value of violence and terror. He was indeed one of the inventors of the politics of violence from which recent decades have suffered.

The son of a customs official, he grew up near Linz, Austria. He left school at 16 and made a scanty living as a hack artist 1908–13. Drafted in WWI, he was twice awarded the Iron Cross. In 1919 he joined the small German Workers' Party, which he turned into the National Socialist Workers' (NAZI) Party. In

1923, after an abortive coup against the Bavarian government, he served nine months in prison; there he wrote *Mein Kampf*, setting out his plans for restoring greatness to Germany. He then began to make the Nazis into a national party, and by 1932, aided by unemployment and economic chaos, he made it the largest party in the country. In 1933 he became chancellor, and in 1934 secured his position by liquidating potential opponents within the party. He took full credit for the economy's recovery and prepared it for war. He paid little further attention to domestic affairs, except to intensify persecution of the Jews. After 1935 he turned increasingly to foreign affairs.

In 1936 he reoccupied the Rhineland, in 1938 annexed Austria, and in 1939 seized parts of Czechoslovakia. On September 1 his invasion of Poland began WWII. At first his conduct of the war was effective, but his invasion of Russia in 1941 was precipitate and proved disastrous. Unable to maintain two fronts, German forces lost N Africa and were pushed back on both sides after D-Day. Hitler maintained popular support despite an assassination attempt in 1944, but became increasingly ill and unbalanced. In 1945 he retreated to his Berlin bunker. After marrying his mistress, Eva BRAUN, he committed suicide with her on April 30, 1945.

HITTITES, important Indo-European people of the Middle East in the second millennium BC.

History. Of unknown origin, they appear to have first settled in southern Turkey c1900 BC; they conquered central Turkey and became a dominant power. By c1650 BC they had established a kingdom of city states (the Old Kingdom), with its capital at Hattusas (BOĞAZKÖY), just E of modern Ankara. Mursilis I overran Syria and even Babylon c1600 BC, but lost them almost at once.

The Hittite Empire proper starts with Tudhaliyas II (c1450 BC), who regained much lost territory. A period of decline followed but by the mid-14th century BC more lasting conquests were made by SUPPILULIUMAS, who finally controlled Syria as far as the Euphrates and the Lebanon, and all Anatolia. At the battle of KADESH c1285 BC the Hittites under Muwatallis drove off Egyptians under RAMSES II, but were seriously weakened. The final downfall of the Hittite empire came c1200 BC, when it was overrun and fragmented by a vast migration of uncertain origin, called by the Egyptians "peoples of the sea." Individual states continued to flourish, however, until SARGON II of Assyria captured CARCHEMISH in 715 BC.

Culture. Much of what we know about the Hittites comes from clay tablets, some written in CUNEIFORM and some in Hittite HIEROGLYPHICS, which were part of the royal archives. The main Hittite language is Indo-European in origin, though other non-Indo-European tongues were apparently also current.

The Old Kingdom was a league of city states controlled by a royal governor. Each king nominated his successor. The society was essentially feudal, consisting of nobles (the land-owning warrior caste), artisans, peasants and also slaves, who had some rights, such as owning property and marriage with free persons.

During the Hittite empire the ruler became absolute and hereditary; regarded as the representative of the weather-god, the supreme god in the polytheistic Hittite religion, he was deified at his death. The Hittite legal system was in some ways more just and liberal than the Mesopotamian and Mosaic codes. Prices were regulated, and silver pieces were used as money. The economy was based on agriculture: the main crops were wheat and barley. As well as livestock, bees were kept and horses bred for the chariotry that was the basis of the Hittite army. Copper, lead and silver were mined; iron smelting was well developed, at first for religious objects and later for military purposes. Much of Hittite architecture and art is powerful and vigorous rather than beautiful. Their surviving literature, excluding political texts, is largely religious and folkloric in nature; many epics were translated and adapted from foreign sources.

HIVES, or **urticaria,** an itchy SKIN condition characterized by the formation of weals with surrounding ERYTHEMA, and due to HISTAMINE release. It is usually provoked by ALLERGY to food (e.g., shellfish, nuts, fruits), pollens, FUNGI, DRUGS (e.g., PENICILLIN) or parasites (SCABIES, worms). But it may be symptomatic of infection, systemic disease or emotional disorder. **Dermographism** is a condition in which slight skin pressure may produce marked hives, as in the linear marks which appear after writing on the skin.

Two Hittite gods, relief carvings in stone dating from around the 8th century BC.

HOARFROST. See FROST.

HOATZIN, an unusual species of South American bird. Hoatzins live in groups in trees on the river edges of South America, feeding on leaves, flowers and fruits. Though they have large wings and tails they are poor flyers. Well adapted to life in trees, the young have articulated claws on the first two digits of the wing, and use both these and the beak for climbing.

HOBAN, James (c1762–1831), Irish-American architect. He designed the WHITE HOUSE (1792–1801) and supervised construction of the Capitol and other buildings in Washington, D.C.

HOBART, city, capital of the state of Tasmania, Australia. On the estuary of the Derwent R, it is Tasmania's main port and an expanding commercial and industrial center. Pop 52 900.

HOBART, city in NW Ind., 8mi S of Lake Michigan. It is a major residential center for the surrounding industrial area. Pop 21 485.

HOBART, Garret Augustus (1844–1899), 24th vice-president of the USA. A prominent lawyer, he served in the N.J. assembly 1872–76 and the state Senate 1876–82. Elected vice-president under McKinley in 1896, he died in Nov. 1899.

HOBBEMA, Meindert (1638–1709), Dutch landscape painter, taught by Jacob van RUISDAEL. His early atmospheric river landscapes and his later forest and road scenes, such as *The Avenue at Middelharnis* (1689), had little influence in their time but foreshadowed CONSTABLE and others.

HOBBES, Thomas (1588–1679), English political philosopher who sought to apply rational principles to the science of human nature. In both the physical and the moral sciences reasoning was to proceed from cause to effect: certain knowledge could only flow from deductive reasoning upon known principles. Hobbes' view of man was materialistic and pessimistic—men's actions were motivated solely by self-centered desires. This led Hobbes to consider that the existence of a sovereign authority in a state was the only way to guarantee its stability. *Leviathan* (1651), which gave voice to this opinion, was his most celebrated work. Hobbes saw matter in motion to be the only reality: even consciousness and thought were but the outworkings of the motion of atoms in the brain. During and after his lifetime, Hobbes was well known as a materialist and suspected as an atheist, but in the 20th century his fame as an able thinker has overshadowed his former notoriety.

HOBBS, city in SE N.M. 18mi N of Eunice. In an oil area, it is the main center of manufacture and supply for oil-field equipment. Pop 26 025.

HOBBY, Oveta Culp (1905–), US publisher, politician and public servant. Director of the Women's Army Corps, 1942–45, she became secretary of health, education and welfare under EISENHOWER 1953–55 and was editor and president of the Houston *Post* 1938–42 and from 1955.

HOBOKEN, city in NE N.J., on the Hudson R. A port and industrial center, it is linked to New York opposite by ferries and tunnels. Pop 48 441.

HOBSON, John Atkinson (1858–1940), British economist, a forerunner of KEYNES. He believed that the root cause of depression was a predominance of savings at the expense of consumption, with a resultant drop in production. He wrote many books, most notably *The Physiology of Industry* (1889).

HOCHHUTH, Rolf (1931–), controversial German playwright. His play *Soldiers* (1967) portrayed Sir Winston CHURCHILL as responsible for the murder of the Polish patriot Gen. SIKORSKI.

HO CHI MINH (1890–1969), Vietnamese political leader, president of North Vietnam from 1954 until his death. His early life is obscure until his arrival in Europe in 1914. Active in revolutionary politics, he settled in Paris in 1917, then went to study in Moscow in 1923, where he was trained as a Comintern agent. He helped organize subversion in Indochina, operating from Hong Kong. In 1941 he settled in Tonkin, China, and began to organize the Vietminh, who in 1945 proclaimed him president of Vietnam, confirming this by their crushing defeat of the French at DIEN BIEN PHU in 1954. As president of North Vietnam he trained and equipped the Vietcong forces in the VIETNAM WAR.

HOCKEY. See FIELD HOCKEY; ICE HOCKEY.

HOCKING, William Ernest (1873–1966), US religious philosopher. He was professor at Harvard 1914–43. His best-known book is *The Meaning of God in Human Experience* (1912).

HOCKNEY, David (1937–), British artist whose emphasis on figurative work and brilliant color, often using acrylic paints, brought him immediate fame. One of his most characteristic paintings, *A Bigger Splash* (1967), was also the title of a semi-autobiographical documentary film made in 1974.

HODGKIN, Alan Lloyd (1914–), British physiologist awarded with A. F. HUXLEY and J. ECCLES the 1963 Nobel Prize for Physiology or Medicine for his work with Huxley on the chemical basis of nerve impulse transmission (see NERVOUS SYSTEM).

HODGKIN, Dorothy Mary Crowfoot (1910–), British chemist awarded the 1964 Nobel Prize for Chemistry for determining the structure of VITAMIN B_{12}.

HODGKIN'S DISEASE, the most important type of LYMPHOMA or malignant proliferation of LYMPH tissue. Usually occurring in young adults, it may present with lymph node enlargement, weight loss, FEVER or malaise; the SPLEEN, LIVER; LUNGS and BRAIN may be involved. Treatment has radically improved the outlook in this disease, with cure obtained in a substantial proportion of cases; it consists of local RADIATION THERAPY or systemic intermittent CHEMOTHERAPY with a combination of agents and STEROIDS.

HODOGRAPH, the CURVE defined by the ends of the VECTORS drawn from any point 0 representing changes in the VELOCITY of a particle.

HOE, Richard March (1812–1886), US inventor who developed many machines associated with PRINTING and invented the first successful rotary printing press (c1847).

HOFEI, historic capital city of Anhwei Province, China. A rail and industrial center, it has chemical and metal industries. Pop 630 000.

HOFF, Jacobus Henricus van 't. See VAN 'T HOFF, JACOBUS HENRICUS.

HOFFA, James Riddle (1913–), US labor leader, president of the International Brotherhood of Teamsters from 1957. After an investigation, led by Robert F. KENNEDY, into his underworld links, Hoffa was convicted in 1964 of tampering with a jury over a bribery charge and jailed 1968–71. In 1975 he mysteriously disappeared.

HOFFER, Eric (1902–), self-educated US author and philosopher. A migratory worker and longshoreman until 1967, he won immediate acclaim with his first book, *The True Believer* (1951), a study of mass movements.

HOFFMAN, Ernst Theodor Amadeus (1776–1822), German romantic author, composer, man of the theater and critic. He is best remembered today for his fantastic short stories, which inspired POE and others, and an opera by OFFENBACH.

HOFFMAN, Malvina (1887–1966), US sculptress. A student of RODIN's, she is best known for the 101 figures of ethnic types executed in bronze for the Museum of Natural History, Chicago, 1930–33.

HOFFMAN ESTATES, village in NE Ill., a residential community 25mi NW of Chicago. Pop 22 238.

HOFMANN, August Wilhelm von (1818–1892), German organic chemist. While he was teaching in London, W. H. PERKIN, his pupil, prepared (1856) the first synthetic dye (see DYES AND DYEING). Hofmann returned to Germany and synthesized many new dyes, and for some 50 years thereafter Germany had the world's largest dye industry. He also discovered the **Hofmann degradation** process (see AMIDES).

HOFMANN, Hans (1880–1966), German-American artist and teacher, prominent in the ABSTRACT EXPRESSIONISM movement. His vigorous and colorful style was best characterized by *The Gate* (1959). In 1934 he opened his influential Eighth Street School in New York.

HOFMANNSTHAL, Hugo von (1874–1929), Austrian neo-romantic poet and dramatist. His early style was influenced by Stefan GEORGE and the Pre-Raphaelites. An adaptation of Sophocles' *Elektra* (1903) was made into an opera by Richard STRAUSS in 1909, beginning a long collaboration on such operas as *Der Rosenkavalier* (1911), *Ariadne auf Naxos* (1912), *Die Frau ohne Schatten* (1919) and many others. Poems, plays such as *Jedermann* (1911), and his opera librettos make him a major figure of Austrian literature.

HOFSTADTER, Robert (1915–), US physicist who shared with MÖSSBAUER the 1961 Nobel Prize for Physics for his discoveries of the structure of PROTONS and NEUTRONS.

HOGAN, a dwelling house, often communal, used by the NAVAJO Indians. The classical cone-shaped *hogan*, traditionally facing eastward, is made of logs or branches plastered with mud or clay.

HOGAN, Ben (1912–), US professional golfer. He won the US Open championship 1948, 1950, 1951 and 1953, and the Professional Golfers Association championship 1946 and 1948. He won the Masters in 1951 and 1953 and the British Open in 1953.

HOGARTH, William (1697–1764), English painter and engraver, best known for his three series of moralistic and satirical engravings, *A Harlot's Progress* (1732), *A Rake's Progress* (1735) and *Marriage à la Mode* (1745). His first success was as a portraitist. Some of his finest work, such as *Captain Thomas Coram* (1740), is in this field. A master of the early ROCOCO style, he foreshadowed later style in such works as *The Shrimp Girl* (c1760).

HOGBACK, or hog's-back, a CUESTA both of whose slopes are steep and of approximately equal gradients.

HOGFISH, *Lachnolaimus maximus*, a shore fish of the western Atlantic related to the WRASSE. The resemblance to a hog is not convincing, but hogfish may be recognized by the elongation of the first three rays of the dorsal fin. Hogfish are found feeding on mollusks near reefs.

HOGG, James (1770–1835), Scottish poet known as the "Ettrick Shepherd" for his birthplace. Among a large output *Kilmeny* (1813) and the prose story *Confessions of a Justified Sinner* (1824) have proved most enduring.

Fujiyama, woodcut by Katsushika Hokusai from his famous collection *36 Views of Mount Fuji.*

HOGG, James Stephen (1851–1906), governor of Tex. 1891–95. State attorney-general 1886–90, he established many major economic reforms, including a state railroad commission.

HOGGAR MOUNTAINS. See AHAGGAR MOUNTAINS.

HOGNOSE SNAKES, generalized and adaptable snakes which lack poison glands and eat most of their prey alive. The name derives from an upturned snout which is believed to be associated with their burrowing habits. Common in North America, they feed on amphibians, including toads. Though they will threaten an attacker, hissing and striking if disturbed, they are quite harmless. If further disturbed they may sham dead.

HOGS, or **pigs,** or **swine,** members of the hog family (Suidae), including the BABIRUSA, Wild BOAR, bushpig and WARTHOG. They are usually sociable animals, but older boars tend to be solitary. The upper or lower canines are developed in all species to form slashing tusks. Hogs live in forests or thickets, though the warthog is more commonly found in more open country, feeding on a variety of vegetable foodstuffs—grass, roots and tubers, fallen fruits and nuts—and, in addition, insects, earthworms, eggs and other animal material. The many varieties of **domestic pig** are all descended from the European boar (*Sus scrofa*). Pigs are bred primarily either for their fat (lard) or for their meat (bacon and pork). China has the largest number of domestic swine in the world; in the US they are concentrated in the corn belt.

HOHENSTAUFEN, medieval German dynasty of Swabian origin, whose members ruled Germany and the HOLY ROMAN EMPIRE. The great Hohenstaufen emperors were Conrad III, Frederick I Barbarossa, Henry VI, Frederick II and Conrad IV. Their concept of a strongly centralized empire brought them into continual conflict with the papacy, and the two powerful opposing groups: GUELPHS and GHIBELLINES.

HOHENZOLLERN, German ruling dynasty that first rose to prominence in the 12th century. In 1192 Frederick III of Zollern became the ruler of Nuremburg, and his descendants founded the Swabian and Franconian lines. From the latter were descended the electors of Brandenburg and the dukes and kings of Prussia, who ruled as emperors of Germany, 1871–1918.

HOHOKAM CULTURE, pre-Columbian North American Indian culture based along the Gila and Salt Rivers, Ariz., from c300 BC to c1400 AD. They built a complex network of irrigation canals, made various types of pottery, and built their houses over shallow pits.

HOIST. See CRANE; PULLEY.

HOKKAIDO, northernmost major island of Japan, second largest but least populated. Its aboriginal inhabitants are the AINU. Its economy rests on mining, crop agriculture and fisheries. Its main town is Sapporo.

HOKUSAI, Katsushika (1760–1849), Japanese painter, printmaker and book illustrator, greatest master of the Japanese *ukiyo-e* (popular) school. Interested in every aspect of life, Hokusai produced over 30 000 drawings, of which the most famous collections are *36 Views of Fuji* (1823–29) and *Hokusai Mangura* (1812–78).

HOLBACH, Paul Henri Dietrich, Baron d' (1723–1789), French encyclopedist and materialist philosopher, best known for *The System of Nature* (1770), published as by "J. B. Mirabeau," which included a scathing attack on religion. He translated many scientific articles for DIDEROT's *Encyclopédie*.

HOLBEIN, name of two German painters. **Hans Holbein "The Elder"** (c1465–1524), was a German Gothic painter of great distinction, best known for his many altarpieces and other church decorations, such as the Kaisheim altar (1502). His middle and later work may have been influenced by GRÜNEWALD. **Hans Holbein "The Younger"** (c1497–1543), was also a painter; a portraitist, he is generally considered the greater of the two. He appears to have lived in many European countries, and to have entered the service of Henry VIII of England, of whom he did the most famous portraits.

HOLBERG, Ludvig, Baron (1684–1754), Danish scholar and dramatist. In his youth he wandered all over Europe, studying and teaching, until he was given a lucrative post at the University of Copenhagen. With VOLTAIRE he was the leading writer of his time, producing works on law, politics, history, science, philosophy and philology, as well as his poetry and plays.

HOLBROOK, town in E Mass., a residential suburb of Boston. It has few industries except boot and shoe manufacture. Pop 11 755.

HOLDEN, town in E central Mass., formerly a center of the wool industry. Pop 12 564.

HÖLDERLIN, Johann Christian Friedrich (1770–1843), among the greatest of German lyric poets, notable for the grandeur of his images, usually deriving from classical Greek themes. Among his best-known poems are *Bread and Wine*, *The Rhine* and the *Empedocles* poems. *Hyperion* (1797–99) is a semi-autobiographical prose novel. Suffering from extreme emotional pressures, he finally went mad in 1806.

HOLDING COMPANY, a company holding a majority, or substantial minority, of the stock in another company or companies in order to control them. By *pyramiding* such companies (*subsidiaries*), that is by creating additional companies to control the stock of holding companies lower in the pyramid, it is possible for the firm at the apex to control great assets, bringing high returns for high risk. In the US this practice is restricted by law.

HOLE. See SEMICONDUCTOR.

HOLIDAY, originally *holyday*, a day commemorating an event, person or religious occasion on which people set aside their normal work to rest, celebrate or pray. Congress in 1791 transferred certain US holidays to a Monday, so that the weekend creates a three-day work break.

HOLIDAY, "Billie" (1915–1959), US jazz singer, born Eleanora Fagan. She started her career at 16, singing in dubious Harlem cafés and night spots. Her highly individual style was soon recognized, and she sang with many famous bands in the 1930s and 1940s. In later years she suffered from heroin addiction.

HOLINESS CHURCHES, group of fundamentalist Protestant churches. Their central dogma is that a state of perfection—"holiness"—may be achieved in this life through "sanctification," a religious experience similar to but following conversion.

HOLINSHED'S CHRONICLES, purported histories of England, Scotland and Ireland, largely edited by Raphael Holinshed (c1525–c1580). Colorful, imaginative and inaccurate, they provided plots for many Elizabethan dramatists, including SHAKESPEARE.

HOLLAND, former countship in the W NETHERLANDS, roughly corresponding to the present provinces of North and South Holland. Outside the Netherlands the term is frequently applied to the whole country.

HOLLAND, city in W Mich., on an inlet of Lake Michigan, settled by Dutch immigrants in 1847. In a largely agricultural area, it is famous for its annual Tulip Festival. Pop 26 337.

HOLLAND, John Philip (1840–1914), Irish-born US inventor who built the first fully successful SUBMARINE, the *Holland*, launched in 1898 and bought by the US Navy in 1900.

HOLLAND TUNNEL, second-longest underwater vehicular tunnel in the US. Its twin tubes, each 29½ft in diameter and 9 250ft long, pass beneath the Hudson R to link Jersey City, N.J., with downtown New York City. Begun in 1919, it was completed in 1927.

HOLLEY, Robert William (1922–), US biochemist who shared with NIRENBERG and KHORANA the 1968 Nobel Prize for Physiology or Medicine for his work in establishing for the first time the nucleotide structure of a NUCLEIC ACID.

HOLLIDAY, John Henry "Doc" (1852–1887), US gunman and folk hero. A dentist who went to live in Tombstone, Ariz., to cure his tuberculosis, he soon became a gambler and gunfighter. He sided with Wyatt EARP at the O.K. Corral gunfight.

HOLLISTON, industrial town in E Mass., 18mi ESE of Worcester. Pop 12 069.

HOLLY, evergreen trees of the genus *Ilex* with over 300 species and worldwide distribution. *Ilex aquifolium* is the only species native to Europe and there are many varieties with variegated leaves and red, yellow, white and black berries. There are 15 species native to North America. Family: Aquifoliaceae.

HOLLYHOCK, *Althaea rosea*, popular garden plant producing tall spikes of funnel-shaped, single and double flowers, which come in a wide range of colors including crimson, scarlet, pink and white. Many varieties are in cultivation and they can be grown as annuals, biennials or perennials. Family: Malvaceae.

HOLLYWOOD, district of Los Angeles, Cal. Its name became synonymous with the US film industry in the 1920s. Few films are now made there, but it now produces a very large percentage of US television material.

HOLLYWOOD, city on the Atlantic coast of SE Fla. It is primarily a resort center, but has some industry in the area. Pop 106 873.

HOLMES, Oliver Wendell (1809–1894), US author and physician, best known for his light essays which appeared in *Atlantic Monthly* from 1857, and in book form as *The Autocrat of the Breakfast Table* (1858) and three sequels. He taught at Harvard, 1847–82; his paper, *The Contagiousness of Puerperal Fever* (1843), is considered the first major contribution to medicine by an American.

HOLMES, Oliver Wendell, Jr. (1841–1935), US jurist, Supreme Court justice 1902–32. He is often called "the great dissenter," but this reflects the significance rather than the number of his dissenting judgments. In *Lochner v. New York* (1905) and *Hammer v. Dagenhart* (1918) he reinforced arguments for legislative checks on the economy. His dissent in *Abrams v. United States* (1919) was a powerful defense of free speech.

HOLMES, Sherlock. See DOYLE, SIR ARTHUR CONAN

HOLMIUM (Ho), element of the LANTHANUM SERIES. AW 164.9, mp 1470°C, bp 2720°C, sg 8.795 (25°C).

HOLOCENE, the later epoch of the QUATERNARY, representing the elapse from the end of the last ICE AGE up to and including the present; i.e., about the last 10 000 years. (See also GEOLOGY.)

HOLOGRAPHY, a system of recording LIGHT or other waves on a photographic plate or other medium in such a way as to allow a three-dimensional reconstruction of the scene giving rise to the waves, in which the observer can actually see round objects by moving his head. The apparently unintelligible plate, or **hologram**, records the INTERFERENCE pattern between waves reflected by the scene and a direct reference wave at an angle to it; it is viewed by illuminating it from behind and looking through rather than at it. The high spatial coherence needed prevented exploitation of the technique, originated in 1948 by D. GABOR, until the advent of LASERS. Color holograms are possible, and three-dimensional TELEVISION may ultimately be feasible.

HOLST, Gustav Theodore (1874–1934), English composer. He is best known for *The Planets* (1918), a massive symphonic suite, each piece representing a planet characterized in myth and astrology. Its popularity has overshadowed his other work, such as the opera *Savitri* (1908).

HOLY ALLIANCE, collective security agreement created at the CONGRESS OF VIENNA in 1815 by Russia, Austria and Prussia, and later joined by most other powers except Britain, Turkey and the Vatican. Its avowed aim was to conduct mutual relations according to Christian principles. It had little importance in itself, except as a symbol of reaction; revolts in Spain and Naples in the 1820s were suppressed in its name.

HOLY GHOST. See HOLY SPIRIT.

HOLY GRAIL, legendary talisman, given various forms in various versions of the tale. In his *Conte del Graal* (c1180) CHRÉTIEN DE TROYES made it the chalice from which Christ drank at the Last Supper and which was used to catch His blood on the Cross. The knight Perceval, who in the poem by WOLFRAM VON ESCHENBACH became PARSIVAL (c1210), seeks the Grail to redeem himself and others. The *Queste del Saint Graal* (c1200) linked the Grail with the ARTHURIAN LEGENDS, and was the source of MALORY'S *Morte d'Arthur* (c1470). The Grail legends have inspired such modern writers as T. H. WHITE, T. S. ELIOT and TENNYSON, and also WAGNER'S operas *Lohengrin* (1848) and *Parsifal* (1882).

HOLY INNOCENTS' DAY is celebrated on Dec. 28. According to St. MATTHEW'S Gospel (but no other source), HEROD ordered the Massacre of the Innocents—every male child of two or under—in

Some major festivals and holidays

1 January	New Year's Day
6 January	Epiphany
7 January	Christmas (Orthodox Churches)
Mid-December to Mid-January:	Ramadan (Moslem month of fasting and atonement)
	Fast-Breaking (the end of Ramadan; 1–3 Shawwal)
Late January to February:	Chinese New Year month
12 February	Abraham Lincoln's Birthday
22 February	George Washington's Birthday (3rd Monday in February)
Late February or early March:	Mardi Gras/Shrove Tuesday (the day before Lent begins)
	Purim Feast of Lots: Jewish holiday, 14 Adar I
17 March	St Patrick's Day
Mid-to-Late March or Early April:	Palm Sunday, 7 days before Easter (1st day of Holy Week)
	Maundy Thursday, 3 days before Easter
	Good Friday
	Holy Saturday
	Easter
	Pesach (Passover: Jewish holiday, 15–22 Nisan)
Late April or early May:	Ascension Day (40 days after Easter)
1 May	May Day (throughout Europe; Loyalty Day in the US)
2nd Sunday in May	Mother's Day (in US and Canada)
1st Monday preceding May 25	Victoria Day (in Canada)
30 May	Memorial Day (Decoration Day)
Late May or Early June:	Pentecost (Whitsuntide, 50 days after Easter)
	Trinity Sunday, 7 days after Pentecost
	Shavuoth (Hebrew Pentecost, Feast of Weeks; 6–7 Sivan)
3rd Sunday of June	Father's Day (US and Canada)
24 June	Midsummer Day
1 July	Canada Day (formerly Dominion Day, Canadian National holiday)
4 July	Independence Day (US national holiday)
14 July	Bastille Day (French national holiday)
Late July or Early August:	Tishe Be-Av (Feast of the 9th of Av, Jewish holiday)
1st Monday in August	Civic Holiday (Canada)
1st Monday in September	Labor Day (US and Canada)
Late September or early October:	Rosh Hashanah (Jewish New Year, 1–2 Tishri)
	Yom Kippur (Jewish Day of Atonement, 10 Tishri)
	Succoth (Jewish Feast of Tabernacles, 15–22 Tishri)
	Simhath Torah (Jewish Rejoicing of the Law, 23 Tishri)
1 October	China's National Day
2nd Monday of October	Thanksgiving (Canada)
12 October	Columbus Day (US, celebrated 2nd Monday of October)
4th Monday of October	Veterans' Day (US)
31 October	Hallowe'en
1 November	All Saints Day (All Hallows Day or Hallowmas)
2 November	All Souls Day
5 November	Guy Fawkes Day (UK)
11 November	Armistice Day (formerly Veterans' Day, US)
	Remembrance Day (Canada)
4th Monday of November	Thanksgiving (US)
Late November or early December:	Hanukkah (Feast of Lights, Jewish Holiday, 25 Kislev–2 Teveth)
25 December	Christmas Day
31 December	New Year's Eve

Bethlehem on this day, after learning from the MAJI of the birth of a Messiah.

HOLY ISLAND. See LINDISFARNE.

HOLY LEAGUE, name given to various leagues in history, but most often to the league formed in 1576 during the French Religious Wars (1562–98). Led by the powerful GUISE family and backed by the Spanish Crown, it forced Henry III to proscribe Protestantism in 1585. Henry, however, had the Duc de Guise assassinated in 1588, but was himself assassinated in 1589. It then opposed the accession of the Protestant Henry of Navarre as Henry IV, until he became a Catholic.

HOLY LOCH, a small inlet on the W shore of the Firth of Clyde in W Scotland. It is the site of a controversial US nuclear submarine base.

HOLY OF HOLIES, inner sanctum of the ancient Jewish TABERNACLE, and later of the Temple at Jerusalem. It contained the ARK OF THE COVENANT, and could be entered only by the High Priest once a year, on YOM KIPPUR, when he offered sacrifice there for his own sins and for those of the people.

HOLYOKE, industrial city on the Conneticut R, SW Mass., the main center of paper manufacture in the US. Pop 50112.

HOLY ORDERS. See ORDINATION; MINISTRY.

HOLY ROMAN EMPIRE, European empire centered in Germany which endured from medieval times until 1806. First founded by Charlemagne, it was effectively established in 962 when the pope crowned OTTO I, king of Germany, emperor at Rome. At its height in the 10th and 11th centuries, it included all the German lands, Austria, and modern W Czechoslovakia, Switzerland, the Low Countries, E France and N and central Italy. The emperor was usually the dominant German sovereign, elected by the princes and, until Maximilian I, crowned by the pope. The empire was originally seen as a universal monarchy, modeled on the Roman Empire, the temporal equivalent and ally of the papacy. From the 11th to the 13th centuries, however, it clashed continually with the papacy for European supremacy. At the Reformation a further split developed between the Catholic emperor and Protestant princes, whose sovereignty was confirmed by the Treaty of Westphalia in 1648, leaving the Emperor no more than a figurehead. The empire endured in name until Napoleon, as Emperor of the French, ceased to recognize it in 1806; Francis II of Austria then abdicated the imperial title.

HOLYROODHOUSE, palace of the Scottish kings in Edinburgh. It was begun by James I in 1504 on the site of Holyrood Abbey. Much of the present building, still a royal residence, was built for Charles II 1670–79.

HOLY SEPULCHRE (officially, Church of the Resurrection), multidenominational church in the Old City of Jerusalem, on what is traditionally the site of the tomb of Jesus. The first church was built by CONSTANTINE THE GREAT c336 AD, but it has been destroyed and rebuilt many times.

HOLY SPIRIT, or **Holy Ghost,** in Christian theology, the third Person of the TRINITY, proceeding from the Father and the Son (according to Western churches; Eastern churches reject the phrase "and the Son," Latin *filioque*). In the Old Testament the idea

Winslow Homer's *The Fox Hunt*. The peculiarly American character of his work strongly influenced other US artists of his day.

The Holy Roman Emperors

Date of Reign	Name of Emperor
	SAXON DYNASTY
962–973	Otto I
973–983	Otto II
983–1002	Otto III
1002–1024	Henry II
	SALIAN (FRANCONIAN) DYNASTY
1024–1039	Conrad II
1039–1056	Henry III
1056–1105	Henry IV
1105–1125	Henry V
1125–1137	Lothair II, Duke of Saxony
	HOHENSTAUFEN DYNASTY (and rivals)
1138–1152	Conrad III
1152–1190	Frederick I
1190–1197	Henry VI
1198–1208	Philip of Swabia
	(Otto IV, Guelph)
1208–1215	Otto IV (1208–1212: king; 1209–1215: emperor)
1212–1250	Frederick II (1212–1220: king; 1220–1250: emperor)
1237–1254	Conrad IV
1246–1247	(Henry Raspe, antiking)
1247–1256	(William, Count of Holland, antiking)
1254–1273	*INTERREGNUM*
	Richard, Earl of Cornwall and Alfonso X of Castile (rivals)
	HAPSBURG and Other Dynasties
1273–1291	Rudolf I (Hapsburg)
1292–1298	Adolf of Nassau
1298–1308	Albert I (Hapsburg)
1308–1313	Henry VII (Luxemburg)
1314–1346	Louis IV (Wittelsbach)
1346–1378	Charles IV (Luxemburg)
1378–1400	Wenceslaus (Luxemburg)
1400–1410	Rupert (Wittelsbach)
1410–1437	Sigismund (Luxemburg)
	HAPSBURG DYNASTY
1438–1439	Albert II
1440–1493	Frederick III
1493–1519	Maximilian I
1519–1558	Charles V
1558–1564	Ferdinand I
1564–1576	Maximilian II
1576–1612	Rudolf II
1612–1619	Matthias
1619–1637	Ferdinand II
1637–1657	Ferdinand III
1658–1705	Leopold I
1705–1711	Joseph I
1711–1740	Charles VI
1740–1742	*INTERREGNUM*
1742–1745	Charles VII (Wittelsbach-Hapsburg)
1745–1765	Francis I (Lorraine; husband of Maria Theresa)
	HAPSBURG-LORRAINE DYNASTY
1765–1790	Joseph II
1790–1792	Leopold II
1792–1806	Francis II

unfolds of the Spirit as God in action, both in creation and in man: the Spirit, bringing wisdom and holiness, was bestowed especially on the prophets, and was promised to indwell the MESSIAH and to characterize the coming Messianic age. The New Testament shows the Holy Spirit as empowering Jesus Christ throughout his life, and at PENTECOST descending on the apostles, filling them with power and inaugurating the Christian Church as such. The Holy Spirit is basic to the Christian life, being the agent of new (spiritual) birth, given through BAPTISM and CONFIRMATION, and producing in the Church Christian character and charismatic gifts (emphasized by PENTECOSTAL CHURCHES). By the title **Paraclete** (Greek *parakletos*) he is described as a comforter or advocate.

HOLY WATER, water blessed by a priest for use in the blessing and purification of persons, places or objects. In some Christian churches holy water is used for ritual cleansing on entering church, exorcism, consecration, etc.

HOLY WEEK, in the CHURCH YEAR, the week preceding EASTER, observed in most churches as a time of solemn devotion to the passion of Christ. From the 4th century the events of the week of the crucifixion have been liturgically re-enacted, now especially on PALM SUNDAY, MAUNDY THURSDAY, GOOD FRIDAY, Holy Saturday and Easter Day.

HOLY YEAR, in the Roman Catholic Church, proclaimed by the pope, who grants special indulgences to pilgrims who come to Rome and fulfil specified religious conditions. First observed in 1300, it has been held every 25 years since 1450.

HOMAGE, in a feudal society, a public ceremony in which the vassal made acknowledgement of allegiance to his lord and swore fealty. (See FEUDALISM.)

HOMATROPINE, short-acting ATROPINE-like DRUG used as EYE drops to dilate the pupil for eye examination.

HOME ECONOMICS, term used in education to embrace all the disciplines necessary to home maintenance: cookery, nutrition, sewing, the nature and use of textiles, household equipment and budgeting. Originally it was not considered to be a scholastic subject, but today it is a common high school elective, and about 500 colleges offer degree courses in it. In the UK it is called domestic science.

HOMEOMORPHISM. See TOPOLOGY.

HOMEOPATHY, system of treatment founded in the early 19th century by C. F. S. HAHNEMANN, based on a theory that DISEASE is cured by DRUGS whose effects mimic it and whose efficacy is increased by the use of extremely small doses, achieved by multiple dilutions.

HOMEOSTASIS, the self-regulating mechanisms whereby biological systems attempt to maintain a stable internal condition in the face of changes in the external environment. It was the 19th-century French physiologist Claude BERNARD who first realized that the internal environment of any free living organism was maintained constant within certain limits. Homeostasis is generally achieved through two types of regulating systems: on-off control and FEEDBACK control. HORMONES often play a vital role in maintaining homeostatic stability.

HOMER, Greek epic poet, probably of the 8th century BC, to whom are ascribed the ILIAD and ODYSSEY. Nothing is known of his life, nor even of the genesis of the poems. Since they were probably composed orally on traditional tales of real events in Bronze Age Mycenaean Greece, it is hard to say whether Homer actually was the author; most scholars now hold, though, that one man gave a final shape to each poem, and that it was the same man in both cases. Homer has come to represent, for many different ages and tastes, the epitome of poetry; this is still true in the 20th century, as witness his influence on POUND, KAFKA and JOYCE.

HOMER, Winslow (1836–1910), US painter, best known for his New England landscapes and sea studies, especially in watercolor, such as *Gulf Stream* (1899). Originally an illustrator, he recorded the Civil War for *Harper's Weekly*. His quasi-Impressionist paintings revolutionized the style of American painting in the 1880s and 1890s.

HOME RULE, Irish, movement to win Ireland control over its domestic affairs. The movement began in the early 1870s, and was initially peaceful despite the PHOENIX PARK MURDERS. As a result of the influence of Charles PARNELL, the Liberal Party under GLADSTONE adopted it as policy in 1886. Opposed by the Conservatives, nothing came of this; two Home Rule Bills in 1886 and 1893 foundered, and increasingly the Home Rule movement was dominated by violent radicals uninterested in constitutional solutions. A third bill was finally passed in 1914 but its implementation was postponed until after WWI. In 1916, however, extremists, fearful of losing influence, precipitated the EASTER RISING, which created lasting bitterness. LLOYD GEORGE, in 1922, finally overcame Ulster's objections by agreeing to partition. S Ireland then became completely independent as the Republic of EIRE.

HOME RULE, Municipal, partial autonomy granted by US states to some cities. This allows the cities to frame their own charters and manage their own affairs within the limits set by the state, usually in matters of taxation, finance, police and education. This move has not been altogether successful.

HOMESPUN, originally a cloth woven at home from yarns spun at home. Homespuns today are fabrics given a deliberately rough and knotty texture. The word is used figuratively to describe any person or thing which is simple or rough.

HOMESTEAD, city in SE Fla., 28mi SW of Miami, the trade center of a fruit-growing area. Pop 13 674.

HOMESTEAD ACT. See HOMESTEADING.

HOMESTEADING, the claiming and settling of federal lands under the Homestead Act (1862), which proved crucial in developing the US West. From independence, settlers in the West had complained at being charged for virgin lands which, they said, were valueless before being developed by their labor. The homestead movement, for the free distribution of such land, had won wide support by the 1830s and advocacy from such popular figures as Thomas Hart BENTON and Horace GREELEY. The 1862 act awarded land patents on 160-acre plots to individual settlers who paid a nominal registration fee, built a homestead and cultivated the land for five years. Despite much subsequent legislation there were flaws. The best lands were generally outside the provisions while loopholes left scope for bulk acquisition by railroads and speculators. Of the 250 million acres homesteaded by the 1950s, much was in large aggregates.

HOMESTEAD NATIONAL MONUMENT, established in 1939, consists of 162.73 acres of land in Gage Co., SE Nebraska. It commemorates the site of the first homestead entered under the General Homestead Act of 1862 (see HOMESTEADING).

HOMESTEAD STRIKE, bitter labor dispute (1892) between steel workers and the Carnegie Steel Company, in Homestead, Pa., a landmark in the history of the US labor movement. A clash between strikers and the company's 300 PINKERTON guards left 10 dead. The national guard were sent in and the strike was broken, but at a high cost to the union movement and to the reputations of Carnegie and President Benjamin Harrison.

HOMEWOOD, residential city in central Ala. 2mi SW of Birmingham. Pop 21 137.

HOMEWOOD, suburban village in NE Ill. 22mi S of Chicago. Pop 18 871.

HOMICIDE, the killing of a human being by another. Criminal homicide is classified as either MURDER or MANSLAUGHTER. But some homicides are excusable (occurring by accident) and others are justifiable (killing by a law officer in the line of duty or killing in self-defense or in the defense of property in certain cases).

HOMING PIGEON, a bird of the family Columbidae able to return to its loft from vast distances, and selectively crossbred to combine speed and ever greater stamina. Although the bird's navigational methods are still not fully understood, man has used the homing pigeon since ancient times, particularly to communicate over long distances. The racing of homing pigeons has been a popular sport since the 19th century. A well-trained bird may travel over 1000mi; the record flight is over 2 300mi.

HOMINY, starchy food made from Indian corn. The grains are soaked in a weak lye solution to remove the skins. After washing, the kernels are ground to produce **grits**, which may be boiled or fried.

HOMOGENIZATION, process to delay the separation of fat in milk. Milk, a rather unstable emulsion (see COLLOID), contains fat globules that tend to coalesce. In homogenization the MILK is heated to about 60°C and passed at pressure through small openings. The fatty clusters are broken up by SHEARING as they pass through the holes, by the action of pressure, and by impact with components of the homogenizer.

HOMOLOGOUS SERIES, sequence of chemical compounds which differ one from the next by a simple structural unit, and so can be given a general FORMULA. The members of a series are chemically similar, having the same FUNCTIONAL GROUPS, and their physical properties change regularly with molecular weight. Organic homologous series, such as the ALKANES, are built up by adding the methylene (CH_2) group.

HOMOLOGUE, in biology, a structure or organ that has the same evolutionary origin as an apparently different structure in another species. For instance, there is little apparent similarity between a horse's leg and the flipper of a whale, but both have similar embryonic history. (See EVOLUTION.)

HOMONYM, a word spelled the same as another but with a different meaning, as in "lead," meaning to conduct, and "lead," the metal. **Homophones** are words that sound alike but have different spellings or meanings, such as "rode" and "road."

HOMOPHONY, in music, a chordal style in which all the parts move together rather than as independent melodies. It also refers to music where one part (melody) dominates an essentially chordal accompaniment.

HOMOPTERA, a suborder of the HEMIPTERA, containing LEAFHOPPERS, CICADAS, APHIDS, SPITTLE BUGS and SCALE INSECTS. All live on the juices of plants and may injure the host plant seriously; the Homopteran group contains many serious economic pest species.

HOMO SAPIENS. See PREHISTORIC MAN; RACE.

HOMOSEXUALITY, mutual sexual attraction by members of the same sex; in women it is termed **lesbianism**. While based on physical attraction, the degree of sexual involvement is variable. It is widely regarded as acceptable social conduct between consenting adults, but the involvement of children is considered undesirable. A number of VENEREAL and other DISEASES can be transmitted by homosexual practice in males.

HOMS, commercial city in Syria, about 100mi NNE of Damascus. Strategically sited on a valley route to the Mediterranean coast, it has been important since ancient times and is now a major junction for road and rail routes and an oil pipeline. Pop 216 000.

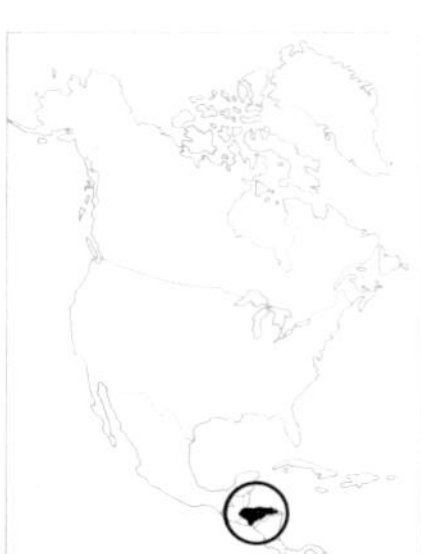

Official name: Republic of Honduras
Capital: Tegucigalpa
Area: 43 227sq mi
Population: 2 800 000
Language: Spanish, English
Religions: No official religion; Roman Catholic majority
Monetary unit(s): 1 Lempira = 100 centavos

HONDURAS, the second-largest and most mountainous Central American republic. The capital is Tegucigalpa; other towns are San Pedro Sula and La Ceiba.

Land. Mountain ranges, high open valleys and plateaus cover Honduras. The hot and humid low-lying areas are the lower reaches of the Ulúa and Chamelecón rivers, the swampy coastal plain in the NE and the narrow coastal plain on the Gulf of Fonseca. Rainfall varies from less than 40in to 120in. The terrain renders communications difficult.

People. Spanish-Indian *mestizos* compose 90% of the population; Negroes about 2%. Most people are concentrated in the rural areas of the central highlands. The prevailing language is Spanish, the religion, Catholicism. Illiteracy runs to 60%. Poverty is endemic: most Hondurans occupy poor subsistence farms. Income per capita is about $260, and the birthrate is high, 43 per thousand.

Economy. US-owned banana plantations dominate the economy, and the bulk of the population works on the land. The main exports after bananas are tobacco, coffee and timber; the mineral resources, which include silver and gold, are poorly exploited. There is little industry and poor transport facilities.

History. From the 4th to the 7th centuries AD the ancient city of Copán was a center of the civilization of the MAYAS, but when Christopher Columbus touched the Honduran coast on his 1502 voyage the country was inhabited only by semi-nomadic Indian tribes. As a Spanish colony for almost 300 years, Honduras was mostly governed from Guatemala; in 1821 it won independence from Spain to become part of the Mexican empire. Subsequently, Honduras joined the Central American federation of which the Honduran patriot Francisco Morazán was president until its dissolution in 1838. As an independent republic since that time, its history has been generally marked by conflicts, revolutions and military rule. In April 1975 General Oswaldo Lopez Arellano (proclaimed as president in 1965) was ousted following charges of accepting bribes from a US print company to reduce export levies on bananas. Colonel Juan Melour Castro became the new president.

HONDURAS, British. See BELIZE.

HONEGGER, Arthur (1892–1955), Swiss-French composer, member of the French "Les SIX" group, best known for his popular *Pacific 231* (1923) and his oratorio *King David* (1921–23).

HONEY, a sweet, sticky confection, formed of partially-digested SUGARS. NECTAR, collected from flowers by foraging worker BEES, is returned to the hive, mixed with digestive "saliva" and often a little pollen, and stored in the cells, of a wax honeycomb to act as a winter food supply for the hive. Combs, with their familiar hexagonal cells, are used for a variety of purposes in the hive, and honeycombs are not always distinct from combs of grubs. Where honey is taken from domestic hives for man's use, the beekeeper must replace the food supply by feeding sugar throughout the winter. (See BEEKEEPING.)

HONEY BADGER. See RATEL.

HONEYBEE. See BEE.

HONEYCREEPERS, a family (Coerebidae) of brightly-colored birds of the New World. Gregarious birds, they live in groups at the tops of trees feeding on NECTAR, but also on fruits and small insects. The male molts to a plumage like that of the drabber female in the nonbreeding season.

HONEYEATERS, a family (Meliphagidae) of nectar-feeding birds occurring in Australasia and the Pacific islands. Slender birds with strong feet, honeyeaters have a specialized tongue designed for extracting NECTAR from flowers; the terminal segments are split into a number of fine filaments forming a brush-like tip. In addition to nectar many species eat insects and fruits.

HONEYGUIDES, small, dull gray or brown birds of Africa and S Asia. Honeyguides are best known for their ability in finding wild bees' nests, and, if they are unable themselves to break into them, in guiding a man or honey badger to the spot. After the combs have been broken open and the honey removed, the bird consumes bee grubs and bits of wax; only two species are known for certain to show this behavior. Honeyguides, like CUCKOOS, are brood parasites.

HONEYSUCKLES, climbing, erect or prostrate shrubs of the genus *Lonicera*, native to the N Hemisphere. Many species and varieties are in cultivation for their attractive, sweet-scented tubular flowers. Family: Caprifoliaceae.

HONG KONG, British crown colony on the S China coast, consisting of mainland territories and numerous offshore islands. The island part of the city of Hong

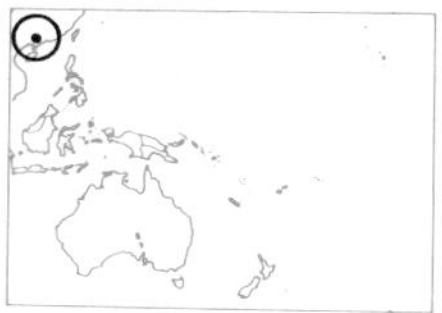

Official name: The Crown Colony of Hong Kong
Area: 403.7sq mi
Population: 4 160 000
Languages: English. Cantonese, Mandarin
Religions: Buddhist, Taoist, Christian, Muslim, Hindu
Monetary unit(s): 1 Hong Kong dollar = 100 cents

Kong (Victoria) was ceded to the British after the OPIUM WAR in 1842. Mainland Hong Kong includes Kowloon, acquired in 1860, and the New Territories (360sq mi of the colony's total area), leased to Britain for 99 years in 1898. China, while not recognizing British sovereignty, still accepts these arrangements as convenient to its international trade.

Of the rocky land surface, 75% is agriculturally valueless and a mere 14% urbanized, accommodating 90% of the population. Since the early 1900s refugees from China's political upheavals have swelled the colony's population. During Japanese wartime occupation (1941–45) the trend was briefly reversed but since then the population has almost quadrupled. Lack of land for housing has made this a critical problem. Hong Kong is virtually a free port, a center for Japanese and Western tourists, and the financial hub of SE Asia. There is much light industry, particularly textiles. The colony depends on China for most of its food and water.

HONOLULU, capital and chief seaport of Hawaii, seat of Honolulu Co. It is located on the SE coast of Oahu Island. Honolulu grew from a fishing village in 1820 to the capital of independent Hawaii, and then territorial capital when Hawaii was annexed to the US. It is important as a shipping center, for sugar and pineapple processing and as the tourist hub of Hawaii. Pop 324 871.

HONORIUS, name of four popes and one antipope. **Honorius I** (d. 638), pope from 625–638 AD. He ably administered the Church and promoted missions, but was later pronounced a heretic (681) for seeming to support MONOTHELITISM in a correspondence with the patriarch of Constantinople. **Honorius II** (d. 1072), antipope for a brief period after 1061 in opposition to Pope ALEXANDER II. **Honorius II** (d. 1130), pope from 1124–1130. In 1122 he had helped frame the Concordat of WORMS during the INVESTITURE CONTROVERSY between pope and emperor. As pope he worked to enforce it. **Honorius III** (d. 1227), pope from 1216–1227, he recognized the Dominican and Franciscan orders and also helped the young Henry III of England to secure his crown against French intervention. **Honorius IV** (c1210–1287), pope from 1285–1287. He promoted the study of Eastern languages in hopes of unity with the Orthodox Church and of proselytizing Islam.

HONORIUS, Flavius (384–423), Roman emperor of the West, the empire having been divided on the death of his father **Theodosius I** (395). Feeble and incompetent, he executed his gifted minister STILICHO for suspected treason (408) and through a fumbled negotiation hastened ALARIC's sack of Rome (410).

HONSHU, the largest island of Japan, about 89 000sq mi in area. It is Japan's prime industrial and agricultural region, containing the country's six major cities. Narrow coastal plains surround a mountainous interior of which Mt Fuji (12 388ft) is the highest peak.

HOOCH, Pieter de, or Hoogh (c1629–c1684), Dutch painter best known for his portraymals of the domestic life of the wealthy burghers of Delft, similar in style to the works of his contemporary VERMEER.

HOOD, John Bell (1831–1879), Confederate general in the American Civil War, a daring commander in the second Battle of Bull Run, the battle of Gettysburg and in the resistance to General William Sherman's drive on Atlanta (1864). Disastrously defeated at the battle of Nashville (Dec. 1864), he was relieved of his command at his own request.

HOOD, Mount, extinct volcano in the Cascade Mts, about 50mi E of Portland, Ore. The peak (11 245ft) is the center of Mount Hood National Forest, an all-season recreation area of over a million acres.

HOOD, Raymond Matthewson (1881–1934), American architect. He designed the Tribune Tower in Chicago and the Daily News building in New York in partnership with John Howells, and collaborated on the Radio City development in New York.

HOOD, Thomas (1789–1845), English comic poet, known to contemporaries for his *Comic Annuals* (1830–39, 1842). He is also remembered for his poems of protest against industrial conditions, especially "Song of the Shirt."

HOOF, a curved horny structure covering the end of the digits in UNGULATES. Since in the horse and related species the foot is effectively reduced to a single toe, the term hoof by association is applied to the whole foot.

HOOF AND MOUTH DISEASE, or foot and mouth disease, a VIRUS infection of cattle and pigs, rarely affecting domestic animals and man. Vesicles of the SKIN and mucous membranes, and FEVER are usual. It is highly contagious and EPIDEMICS require the strict limitation of stock movements and the slaughter of affected animals.

HOOKE, Robert (1635–1703), English experimental scientist whose proposal of an inverse-square law of gravitational attraction (1679) prompted NEWTON into composing the *Principia.* From 1655 Hooke was assistant to R. BOYLE but he entered into his most creative period in 1662 when he became the ROYAL SOCIETY OF LONDON's first curator of experiments. He invented the compound MICROSCOPE, the universal joint and many other useful devices. His microscopic researches were published in the beautifully illustrated *Micrographia* (1665), a work which also introduced the term "cell" to biology. He is best remembered for his enunciation in 1678 of **Hooke's Law**. This states that the deformation occurring in an elastic body under stress is proportional to the applied stress (see MATERIALS, STRENGTH OF).

HOOKER, Joseph (1814–1879), American Civil War general, called "Fighting Joe." Appointed commander of the Army of the Potomac (1863), he was defeated by General Robert E. Lee at CHANCELLORSVILLE and relieved as army commander.

HOOKER, Richard (c1554–1600), English theologian—a man of wide learning—whose eight-volume work, *Of the Laws of Ecclesiastical Polity*, in masterly English prose defended the Elizabethan religious settlement against both Roman Catholics and PURITANS. A landmark of ANGLICAN theology, it acknowledged the authority of the Bible, but gave authority to the Church and reason when Scripture was silent or unclear. Hooker's political theories, modern in tendency, influenced John LOCKE.

HOOKER, Thomas (1586–1647), early American Puritan and founder of HARTFORD, Conn. A religious exile from England, he came to Massachusetts via Holland (1633), and became minister at the New Town (now Cambridge) settlement. But conflicts with the Massachusetts leaders drove him and his congregation to Connecticut (1635–36). He wrote the FUNDAMENTAL ORDERS for the new settlements there (1639).

HOOKWORMS, intestinal PARASITES of man and his domestic animals, belonging to the nematodes (see ROUNDWORMS). The life cycle involves a free-living larval stage and direct infection of the final HOST. No intermediate host is involved. The parasitic adults are blood feeders and attack vessels in the wall of the intestine. Each worm may cause the loss of up to 0.25ml of blood a day.

HOOPA INDIANS. See HUPA INDIANS.

HOOPOE, *Upupa epops*, a pink-buff insectivorous bird with black and white stripes, widely distributed in the Old World. The name reflects the soft call. The related **Wood hoopoes** of Africa bear little similarity. Sociable, while the hoopoe is solitary, these are glossy black birds, but three species have chestnut heads. All hoopoes are insectivorous.

HOOSAC RANGE, a continuation of the Green Mountain range, in NW Mass. and SE Vt.

HOOTON, Earnest Albert (1887–1954), US physical anthropologist best remembered for his attempts to relate behavior to physical or racial type, and for books such as *Up From the Ape* (1931) and *The American Criminal* (1939).

Herbert Clark HOOVER

31st U.S. President
Born: West Branch, Iowa; August 10, 1874
Died: New York City; October 20, 1964
Term of office: March 4, 1929–March 3, 1933
Political party: Republican

HOOVER, Herbert Clark (1874–1964), 31st US president, 1929–33. Born in West Branch, Ia., he graduated as a mining engineer from Stanford U. in 1895, and managed mining operations in various parts of the world until 1914. Already a millionaire, he then became chairman of the voluntary Commission for Relief in Belgium and in 1917 was appointed US Food Administrator, responsible for increasing production and conservation of supplies. This he did with considerable success, providing large supplies for war-stricken Europe. He became secretary of commerce under Warren G. Harding in 1921. A national figure, he had already been considered as a Republican presidential nominee, but it was not until 1928 that he won the nomination. He ran on a conservative platform, proposing a program for "The New Day" to realize the country's full economic potential.

In Oct. 1929 the Wall Street crash began the Depression. In the belief that the root cause was psychological he tried to restore business confidence by cutting public expenditure and balancing the budget. He stressed the responsibility of states for relief programs and would allow the government to help only indirectly. The RECONSTRUCTION FINANCE CORPORATION was formed in 1932 and, in its first year, lent $1\frac{1}{2}$ billion to help businesses survive. In the same year, Hoover lost a great deal of popularity over his harsh handling of the BONUS MARCH. Clearly unable to cope with the economic situation, he suffered a crushing defeat by F. D. Roosevelt in the 1932 election. His foreign policy had been more successful; he had done much to assure the Latin Americn states that the US would not intervene in their affairs. The London Naval Treaty (1930) had improved European relations. He retired from public life until he helped organize European relief after WWII. He also headed two "Hoover Commissions" on the organization of the executive branch of government in 1947–49 and 1953–55. These recommended many measures to improve efficiency and management, which Congress accepted.

HOOVER, John Edgar (1895–1972), first director of the FEDERAL BUREAU OF INVESTIGATION (FBI). A lawyer in the Department of Justice 1919–29, he became director of the then Bureau of Investigation in 1924, at a time when it enjoyed a bad reputation for political corruption. Effectively ridding it of political appointees, he instituted rigorous selection and training methods. He established the world's largest fingerprint file and introduced the most up-to-date scientific criminology and research programs. Hoover held the directorship until his death at the age of 77. His prestige, so great that he could not be displaced, was seriously declining at his death, and with it that of the FBI.

HOOVER DAM, formerly Boulder Dam, on the Colorado R in Ariz. It is 726ft high and 1 244ft in length; while providing flood control and irrigation it supplies electricity to S Cal., Ariz., and Nev. and water supplies to several cities. Built 1931–35, it began operating in 1936; it was named for President Herbert Hoover.

HOP, *Humulus lupulus* and related species, tall, perennial twining vine, the female INFLORESCENCE of which is used to flavor BEER. Hops are cultivated throughout the world, the US, Germany and England being the leading producers. Family: Cannabinaceae.

HOPE, Anthony (1863–1933), pseudonym of Sir Anthony Hope Hawkins, British author of adventure romances. The most famous were *The Prisoner of Zenda* (1894) and its sequel *Rupert of Hentzau* (1898).

HOPE, Bob (1903–), stage name of Leslie Townes Hope, British-born US actor and comedian. He began in vaudeville and rose to fame with the Ziegfeld Follies and in Broadway musical comedies. Of his many films the *Road* series, beginning with *The Road to Singapore* (1940), is best known; he starred in them with Bing CROSBY and Dorothy Lamour.

HOPE, John (1868–1936), US educator and civil rights leader. Son of a black mother and white father, he could have lived as a white but threw in his lot with the black community, advocating advanced education at a time when Booker T. WASHINGTON was inclined to restrict Negro education to the purely technological. First Negro president of Morehouse College in Atlanta, Ga., in 1906, he became the first president of Atlanta U. in 1929.

HOPEWELL, independent city in SE Va., a port and industrial center. Its major manufactures are chemicals, but there are many other industries also. Pop 23 471.

HOPEWELL CULTURE, pre-Columbian culture of MOUND builders, flourishing c500 BC–c500 AD and centered in S Ohio. They appear to have had a fairly sophisticated social structure, made decorated pottery, carved stone and were skilled metallurgists.

A Hopewell burial mound in White City, Illinois, after excavation. The Hopewell people traded extensively in goods coming from as far away as the Rocky Mountains, and they seem to have enjoyed a relatively high level of social organization.

HOPI (or Moki), Pueblo Indian tribe of NE Ariz. An agricultural people, they have a complex society based on clans, lineage and matrilineal extended households. They are peaceful and deeply religious, the *kachina*, or beneficial spirit, being the center of their way of life. Around 6 000 Hopis survive today.

HOPKINS, city in E Minn., a residential suburb of Minneapolis. It is a fruit-growing center noted for its raspberries and manufactures farm machinery. Pop 13 428.

HOPKINS, Esek (1718–1802), American merchant sea-captain, commander of the Continental Navy 1775–78. In Feb. 1776, he captured New Providence, in the Bahamas, from the British.

HOPKINS, Sir Frederick Gowland (1861–1947), British biochemist who shared with EIJKMAN the 1929 Nobel Prize for Medicine or Physiology for his work showing the necessity of certain dietary elements, now identified and known as VITAMINS, for the maintenance of health.

HOPKINS, Gerard Manley (1844–1889), English poet and Jesuit priest. Largely misunderstood in his lifetime, Hopkins' work was experimental. It exploits natural speech rhythms, using what he called "sprung rhythm" rather than a syllable count, and is highly mimetic, as for example in the poem *The Windhover* and the more unconventional *Harry Ploughman*. His work was published posthumously in 1918. By the 1930s Hopkins had become a major influence on modern poetry.

HOPKINS, Harry Lloyd (1890–1946), US administrator under F. D. Roosevelt who did much to implement the NEW DEAL. He was successively administrator of the Federal Emergency Relief Administration (1933), director of the Works Project Administration (1935), secretary of commerce (1938) and US Lend-Lease administrator (1941). He was Roosevelt's aide throughout WWII, and at its close carried out important negotiations with Russia for President Truman.

HOPKINS, Johns (1795–1873), US financier and philanthropist. A Quaker, he made his fortune as a wholesale grocer. He bequeathed $7 million to endow Johns Hopkins U. and Johns Hopkins Hospital in Baltimore.

HOPKINS, Lemuel (1750–1801), US writer and physician. A member of the HARTFORD WITS, he is noted for the political verse satires characteristic of that group.

HOPKINS, Mark (1802–1887), US educator. As a Congregational minister and president of Williams College, Williamstown, Mass., where he was professor of moral and intellectual philosophy 1830–87, he was widely influential in academic life.

HOPKINS, Mark (1813–1878), US railroad tycoon, who worked as a commission merchant until 1853, when he became a partner of Collis P. HUNTINGTON, with whom he founded the Central Pacific Railroad.

HOPKINS, Samuel (1721–1803), US Congregationalist theologian and opponent of slavery. His unorthodox views, much influenced by his friend Jonathan EDWARDS, were regarded as controversial in his time.

HOPKINS, Stephen (1707–1785), a signatory of the US Declaration of Independence. A leading judge and politician of R.I., he was a determined opponent of the 1765 Stamp Act and a member of the Continental Congress 1774–76. He wrote *The Rights of the Colonies Examined* (1765).

HOPKINSON, Francis (1737–1791), American lawyer and politician, a signatory of the US Declaration of Independence, and reputed designer of the US flag. He was also a musician and author, and wrote many patriotic pamphlets, poems and satirical ballads, including *The Battle of the Kegs* (1778).

HOPKINSVILLE, city in SW Ky., seat of Christian Co. It is an important livestock and tobacco market. Pop 21 250.

HOPLITE, foot soldier making up the ranks of the infantry in the Greek armies of the 5th century and later. Each carried a large shield, spear and sword.

HOPPE, William Frederick (1887–1959), US billiards champion, winner of 51 world championships. A masterly player from the age of eight, he is regarded as the finest in the history of the game.

HOPPER, Edward (1882–1967), US painter. First recognized for his etchings, he returned to painting late in life, and became known for his quiet urban studies, usually reflecting a feeling of loneliness and alienation.

HOPPERS, term applied to various groups of invertebrates, particularly insects. The young active stages of LOCUSTS and GRASSHOPPERS are most frequently referred to in this way but the order HEMIPTERA also includes three families of jumping insects called froghoppers, TREEHOPPERS and LEAFHOPPERS. The term is used in a general sense to identify those groups of the ARTHROPODA which progress by leaping.

HOPPNER, John (1758–1810), British portraitist, much influenced by Sir Joshua REYNOLDS. Portrait painter to the Prince of Wales (1789), he was elected to the Royal Academy 1795. His portraits include studies of such eminent men as Nelson, Wellington, and Sir Walter Scott.

HOQUIAM, seaport city on Grays Harbor, W Wash. at the mouth of the Hoquiam R. It has a wide range of manufacturing industries. Pop 10 466.

HORACE (65–8 BC), Quintus Horatius Flaccus, Roman lyric poet and satirist. At first supported by the rich patron Maecenas, he later became the favored poet of AUGUSTUS. Horace's surviving work includes four books of *Odes*, two of *Satires*, two of *Epistles* and his *Epodes*. These and the *Art of Poetry* have been a profound and lasting influence on European literature.

HORATIUS (Publius Horatius Cocles), legendary Roman hero. In c508 he and two companions are said to have held the Sublician Bridge, the only remaining bridge across the Tiber, against the invading Etruscan army.

HOREHOUND, *Marrubium vulgare*, perennial herb with wrinkled leaves and small whitish flowers. The leaves were once popular as flavoring in candies and cough medicines. Also, *Ballota nigra*, the black horehound, which has a fetid odor. Family: Labiatae.

HORIZON, the apparent line where the sky meets the land or sea. At sea, its distance varies in proportion to the square ROOT of the height of the observer's eyes above sea level: if this is, say, 2m the horizon will be about 5.57km distant. The **celestial horizon** is the great circle on the CELESTIAL SPHERE at 90° from the ZENITH (the point immediately above the observer).

HORMISDAS, Saint (c450–523), pope from 514. In 519 he ended the Acacian schism (484–519) between Rome and Constantinople. In all, about 250 Eastern bishops signed the formula of Hormisdas, reaffirming the Chalcedonian condemnation of MONOPHYSITISM.

HORMONES, substances produced in living organisms to affect GROWTH, differentiation, METABOLISM, digestive function, mineral and fluid balance, and usually acting at a distance from their site of origin. Plant hormones, AUXINS and GIBBERELLINS, are particularly important in growth regulation. In animals and man, hormones are secreted by ENDOCRINE GLANDS, or analogous structures, into the BLOOD stream which carries them to their point of action. The rate of secretion, efficacy on target organs and rate of removal are all affected by numerous factors including FEEDBACK from their metabolic effects, mineral or sugar concentration in the blood, and the action of controlling hormones. The latter usually originate in the PITUITARY GLAND and those controlling the pituitary in the HYPOTHALAMUS. Important hormones include INSULIN, THYROID hormone, ADRENALINE, STEROIDS, PARATHYROID GLAND hormone, GLUCAGON, GONADOTROPHINS, ESTROGEN, PROGESTERONE, ANDROGENS, pituitary growth hormone, VASOPRESSIN, thyroid stimulating hormone, adrenocorticotrophic hormone, GASTRIN and SECRETIN.

HORN, in music, a brass wind instrument. It is derived from the primitive horns—actual animal horns—used by primitive societies. Metal was found to produce a better tone, and horns became increasingly sophisticated and complex. The principal modern horn, the French horn, is derived from hunting horns. Horns were introduced into orchestral

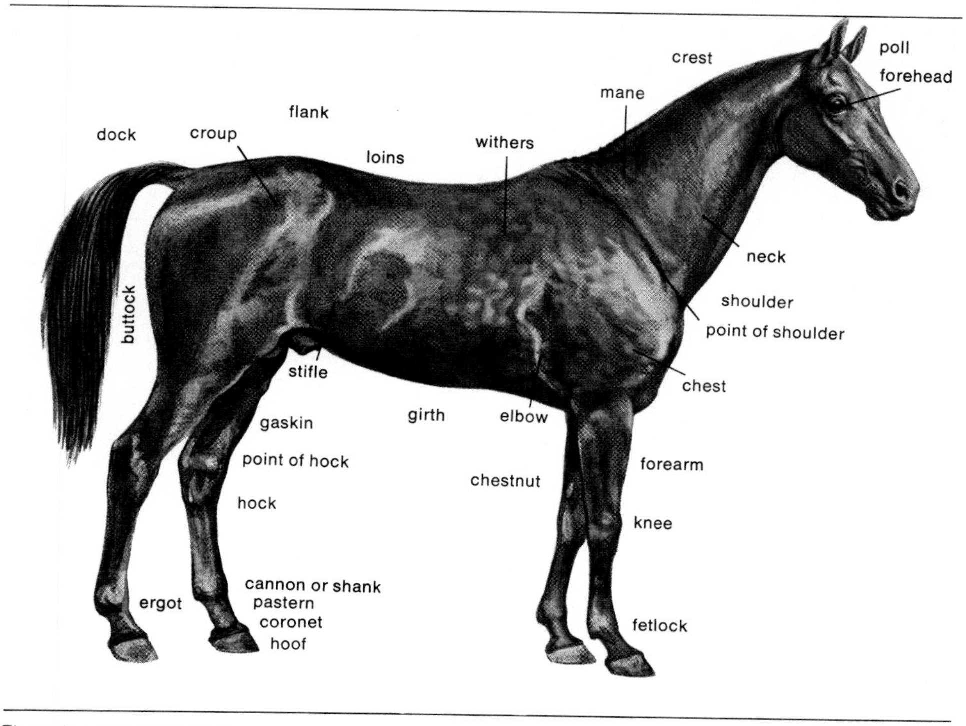

The main points of the horse.

music in the early 18th century. Valved horns were developed in the 19th century.

HORN, Cape. See CAPE HORN.

HORNBEAM, deciduous trees of the genus *Carpinus* from the BIRCH family, Betulaceae, native to North America, Europe and Asia. The American hornbeam (*Carpinus caroliniana*) produces a tough wood used to make CHARCOAL and the European hornbeam (*C. betulus*) is frequently used as hedging.

HORNBILLS, an Old World family of birds (Bucerotidae) with heavy brightly-colored bills, usually surmounted by an extra horny protruberance or casque on the upper mandible. They use these heavy bills surprisingly dexterously, plucking fruits and picking up insects or other animal food. Hornbills are divided into two main groups, the mainly terrestrial African Ground hornbills, and the arboreal species of Africa and Asia.

HORNBLENDE, group of common rock-forming minerals; dark monoclinic AMPHIBOLES of general composition $Ca_2Na(Mg, Fe, Al)_5Si_6(Si, Al)_2O_{22}(OH)_2$.

HORNBOOK, children's primer used before printed books became cheap and widely available. They were printed sheets with the alphabet, numerals, and so on, pasted to a wooden, short-handled tablet and covered with a thin transparent layer of horn for protection.

HORNED FROGS, very distinctive frogs of the genus *Ceratophrys* found in most of South America. Stocky and toad-like, they have a high-domed head and many species bear "horns"—soft extensions of the upper eyelids.

HORNED TOADS, the confusing common name of horned iguanid lizards of the genus *Phrynosoma*. Widespread in North America and Mexico, horned "toads" are small, with a very short tail, and have long hard spines on the head. They also have the odd habit of squirting thin jets of blood from the eyes—perhaps as a defense mechanism.

HORNELL, city on the Canisteo R, S N.Y. A railroad center, it has various light industries, particularly textiles. Pop 12 144.

HORNETS, large WASPS which, unlike the commoner YELLOW JACKETS which nest underground, build their nests in trees or in human dwellings. The nest is enclosed in a paper shell and consists of a series of horizontal combs. The papery material used is manufactured by the hornets by chewing woody plant matter. Hornets can inflict an extremely painful sting. Family: Vespidae.

HORNEY, Karen (1885–1952), German-born US psychoanalyst best known for her concentration on the importance of environment in character development, so rejecting many of the basic principles of FREUD's classic psychoanalytic theory, especially his stress on the LIBIDO as the root of personality and behavior (see PSYCHOANALYSIS).

HORNS, strictly, keratinous structures (see KERATIN) borne on the forehead of many UNGULATES. They show a variety of forms. Horns are usually permanent structures though the antlers of many DEER are cast and regrown annually. Horns appear occasionally to be purely ornamental, but usually they are used for defense or in intra-specific AGGRESSION. In such species horns are borne only by the males.

HORNSBY, Rogers (1896–1963), US baseball player-manager, one of the greatest right-handed batters in the game's history. His greatest successes were with the St. Louis Cardinals from 1915. He was elected to the Baseball Hall of Fame in 1942.

HORNWORTS, or horned liverworts, small group of BRYOPHYTES belonging to the class Anthocerotae. They have a very simple thallus, the cells of which contain a single chloroplast and a pyrenoid, the latter only occurring elsewhere in ALGAE.

HOROLOGY, the measurement of time, and of the construction of timepieces. See CLOCKS AND WATCHES.

HOROSCOPE. See ASTROLOGY.

HOROWITZ, Vladimir (1904–), Russian-born US virtuoso pianist. After a brilliant debut at Kiev (1922), he toured Russia and Europe (1924) and the US (1928). He became a US citizen in 1944.

HORSA. See HENGIST AND HORSA.

HORSE CHESTNUTS, trees and shrubs of the genus *Aesculus*, notably *Aesculus hippocastanum*, the common horse chestnut, which is native to Greece, but widely naturalized in temperate regions. In winter the twigs bear sticky buds and in the fall large numbers of shiny brown seeds are produced. Some North American species are called BUCKEYE. Family: Hippocastanaceae.

HORSEFLIES, biting flies, so called because they bite horses as well as other mammals, including man. Only the females bite, piercing the skin with specialized mouthparts and sucking blood. Like MOSQUITOES female horseflies require a blood-meal before laying eggs. They transmit a few diseases, but their main importance as a pest is in the pain of their bite.

HORSEHAIR worm, an adult HAIRWORM.

HORSE LATITUDES, two belts, characterized by low winds, about 30°N and S of the equator. Sailing ships bound for America carrying horses were often becalmed here: many horses died from lack of fresh water and were cast overboard. (See also TRADE WINDS.)

HORSE NETTLE, *Solanum carolinense*, a coarse, spiny, poisonous perennial weed native to North America. It has light blue or white flowers like those of the POTATO and orange-yellow berries. Family: Solanaceae.

HORSEPOWER (hp), unit of power introduced by James WATT, equivalent to 745.70 watt. Brake horsepower (bhp) is power output measured by applying a brake (usually a Prony brake) to the driving shaft. The metric horsepower, or *cheval-vapeur* (CV), originally the power required to raise a 75-kg weight through one metre in one second, is 735.5 watt.

HORSE RACING, sometimes called the sport of kings, is among the most popular spectator sports in existence. It is watched by millions of people in many different countries, but chiefly in North America, Western Europe, Australasia and South America. Its interest as a spectator sport is considerably enlarged by the practice of on- and off-course betting.

The oldest stake race in the world is the English St. Leger, first run in 1776. The world's greatest steeplechase event, the Liverpool GRAND NATIONAL, was first held in 1839. In America the most famous race is the KENTUCKY DERBY, first run in 1875. Today the three premier stake races in the US are the Derby, the Preakness Stakes and the Belmont Stakes. Besides flat racing there are also hurdling, steeplechasing, and harness events. In the latter, special trotting horses known as trotters or pacers are used.

HORSERADISH, *Armoracia rusticana*, hardy perennial of the MUSTARD family, Cruciferae. It is cultivated for its edible roots which have a pungent taste and are used grated or as a sauce in a condiment for meat dishes.

HORSES, single-toed, ungulate, herbivorous mammals. Wild horses occurred in prehistoric times over most of Eurasia. True wild horses are represented now only by Przewalski's horse (*Equus przewalskii*) of Siberia, Mongolia and western China. These live in groups of 10–15 led and protected by a stallion. Many feral strains of the domestic breeds have however become established—the famous herds of the Camargue and of Sable Island off Nova Scotia. Domestic horses (*E. caballus*) are bred in many different races and can be grouped as ponies, heavy draft horses, lightweight draft and riding horses. Barbs and Arabs, the two most popular riding horses, originated from N African stock. Thoroughbreds are descended from Arabs and both are used widely in breeding light draught and riding horses. The ponies, especially the Icelands—characterized by a "pacing" gait where both legs on the same side are lifted

A form of horse racing particularly popular in the United States and Canada is harness racing, shown here at the Montreal Hippodrome. The horses, called "trotters" or "pacers," pull a two-wheeled car.

together—are considered to be descendants of a Celtic stock of domestic horses, while heavy draft animals—Belgians, Percherons, Clydesdales, Shires and Suffolks—come from a breeding stock of central and west Europe. The fossil record of the horse family is so well documented that it provides a classic example of EVOLUTION in action. The earliest animal which can be placed in the family was *Hyracotherium*, or *Eohippus*, from the EOCENE of Europe and North America. This was a small animal the size of a fox terrier with three toes of equal size on each hindfoot and four toes on the forefeet. The development of the single-toed foot of modern horses—an adaptation to running on hard dry grassland (while the side toes represented by splint bones in the foot of the modern horse provided a flatter foot for the marshy habitat of *Eohippus*); the change in tooth pattern to allow the animal to eat grasses, a very abrasive food, and the increase in size, may be followed through a continuous series of intermediate stages through to the present day.

HORSESHOE BEND, Battle of, battle fought at Tohopeka, Ala., on March 27, 1814, in which Gen. Andrew JACKSON's forces defeated the Creek Indians led by William WEATHERFORD.

HORSESHOE CRAB. See KING CRAB.

HORSETAILS, or Sphenopsida, subdivision of the PLANT KINGDOM which reached its evolutionary peak in the CARBONIFEROUS period. Present-day sphenopsids comprise a single genus *Equisetum*, which are green, rush-like weeds found throughout the world except Australia and New Zealand.

HORST, an area that has been thrust upward between two roughly parallel FAULTS.

HORTA, Victor, Baron (1861–1947), Belgian architect and pioneer of *art nouveau*. Two of his best-known works are the *Hôtel Tassel* (1893) and the *Maison du Peuple* (1896–99), both in Brussels.

HORTHY DE NAGYBÁNYA, Miklós (1868–1957), Hungarian admiral and politician. In 1919 he headed the counter-revolutionary army which overthrew the communist and socialist coalition under Béla KUN. From 1920–44 he acted as regent, preventing Emperor Charles I from regaining his throne. He joined the Axis powers in WWII, but in 1944, after trying to make peace with Russia, was imprisoned in Germany. He was freed by US forces in 1949 and settled in Portugal.

HORTICULTURE, branch of agriculture concerned with producing fruit, flowers and vegetables. It can be divided into pomology (growing fruit), olericulture (growing vegetables) and floriculture (growing shrubs and ornamental plants). About 3% of US cropland is devoted to horticulture. It was originally practiced on a small scale, but crops such as the POTATO and TOMATO are now often grown in vast fields.

HORUS, ancient Egyptian god. Originally a sky god, depicted as a falcon or as falcon-headed, he became thought of as the son of ISIS and OSIRIS. He avenged his father's murder by defeating SET, the spirit of evil, and succeeded Osiris as king.

HOSEA, Book of, the first of the Old Testament MINOR PROPHETS. Its material originated in the prophecies of Hosea, delivered in ISRAEL in the 8th century BC. It compares God's abiding love for idolatrous Israel to Hosea's love for his prostitute wife, whom he divorced but remarried.

HOSHEA, last king of Israel (reigned c732–c723 BC). He plotted against and succeeded king Pekah. In c727 he aligned with Egypt against the Assyrians, a mistake which led to their invasion of Israel and to Hoshea's overthrow, after the fall of his capital, Samaria.

HOSPITAL, institution for the care of the sick or injured. Early hospitals and medical schools were usually attached to the temples of certain gods, for example, AESCULAPIUS and HYGEIA in Greece, and the association with religion continued; many hospices and hostels were founded by Christian religious orders, such as the KNIGHTS OF ST. JOHN. As refuges for the sick poor, hospitals tended to spread disease rather than prevent or cure it. Only in the 19th century did they improve and then they did so dramatically, as a result of Louis PASTEUR's work on germ theory, LISTER's on infection and asceptic surgery and Florence NIGHTINGALE's organization of the nursing profession. Charitable, voluntary subscription and church hospitals increased greatly in number in Europe and North America from the 18th century, while the 19th saw new government hospitals for the old, sick poor and insane.

Modern hospitals are often large, complex institutions. In most countries the majority are government-owned, but in the US only a third (mostly long-stay hospitals for the mentally ill) are government-owned. Most general hospitals in the US and over half the total are "voluntary," run by religious and other non-profit bodies. Because most charge for treatment, many people take out medical insurance. One in seven hospitals is privately run and makes a profit from fees. There are over 7 000 hospitals in the US with 1 650 000 hospital beds. Every year they admit over 30 million sick people, who stay on average just over one week. General hospitals (over 80% of hospitals) may have equipment for diagnosis (including X-rays), a pharmacy, laboratory, maternity division, operating and recovery rooms, and departments for physical and occupational therapy, for outpatients and emergencies. While larger hospitals may cover sophisticated surgery and intensive care, training of medical staff, and research, there is increased emphasis everywhere on health checks, short stays and outpatient treatment.

HOSPITALERS. See KNIGHTS OF SAINT JOHN.

HOSPITALET, city in NE Spain. It is a suburb of Barcelona, and produces steel and textiles. Pop 241 978.

HOST, an animal or plant that supports a PARASITE.

HOST (from Latin *hostia*, a sacrificial victim), the consecrated bread in the MASS, regarded as the body of Christ sacrificially offered. It is elevated to symbolize this and to exhibit it to the people for their worship.

HOTCHKISS, Benjamin Berkeley (1826–1885), US firearms inventor and manufacturer, best-known for his air-cooled, gas-operated machine gun. The American Civil War and later the Franco-Prussian war were testing grounds for many of Hotchkiss's ordnance mechanisms.

HOT LINE, direct White House–Kremlin emergency communications link, established 1963. It aims to reduce the risk of war occurring by mistake or misunderstanding. Telegraphic and radio circuits run via London, Copenhagen, Stockholm and Helsinki.

HOTMAN, François (1524–1590), French jurist and humanist scholar. He argued for French law to be less reliant on Roman models, more on native custom. His *Franco-Gallia* (1573) attacked royal absolutism.

HOT ROD, automobile with improved engine or body design, giving greater acceleration and speed. Following WWII, a cult of street racing developed in the US, consisting of acceleration races between traffic lights. In the 1950s, "drag racing" on special tracks was encouraged by police departments to try to prevent this. The term "hot rod" now includes recognized "stock" sedans and especially designed "dragsters."

HOT SPRINGS, or **thermal springs,** springs supplied by underground water heated usually by vapor from the MAGMA, and most common in recently active volcanic regions (see VOLCANISM). The water contains dissolved minerals that may form terraces around the outlet. (See also GEYSER.)

HOT SPRINGS, city in central Ark., seat of Garland Co. Principally a resort spa, it is built around the HOT SPRINGS NATIONAL PARK. Pop 35 631.

HOT SPRINGS NATIONAL PARK, in the Ouachita Mts, central Ark. It is a popular tourist and health resort noted for its 47 thermal springs. The park, created in 1921, comprises 3 535 acres.

HOTTENTOTS, people of South Africa similar to the Bushmen and Hamites. Small in stature, they have brown skins, prominent cheekbones, broad noses, coarse hair and pointed chins, and are dolichocephalic (see CEPHALIC INDEX) and commonly steatopygic (see STEATOPYGIA). Originally known to themselves as the Khoikhoin, they were nomadic herdsmen and farmers, but this way of life has largely disappeared.

HOUDINI, Harry (1874–1926), born Erich Weiss, US magician and escapologist. He was world famous for his escapes from seemingly impossible situations, as for example from a sealed chest underwater. He also pursued a campaign of exposing fake mediums and spiritualists.

HOUDON, Jean-Antoine (1741–1828), French sculptor famous for his portraits. His sitters included Catherine the Great (1773), Voltaire (1781) and Benjamin Franklin (1791). The best known of his mythological works is *Diana* (1777).

HOUMA, city in SE La., seat of Terrebonne Parish. It is an important packing and shipping center on the Intracoastal Waterway. Pop 30 992.

HOUPHOUËT-BOIGNY, Félix (1905–), president of the Ivory Coast since it gained independence (1960). In 1946 he helped found the Rassemblement Démocratique Africain (RDA), which paved the way for the independence of the French West African colonies. He was a French minister of state 1956–57.

HOUR (h), unit of time equal to 60 minutes or 3 600 seconds. In one hour, the earth rotates on its axis through 15°. The time of day at any point on earth is expressed as the number of hours and minutes that have elapsed since midnight for the time zone in which the point is situated, the time zones being fixed intervals behind or ahead of Greenwich Mean Time.

HOURGLASS, ancient instrument to measure the passage of time. A quantity of fine, dry sand is contained in a bulb constricted at its center to a narrow neck. The device is turned so that all the sand is in the upper chamber: the time taken for the sand to trickle into the lower chamber depends on the amount of sand and on the diameter of the neck. Small hourglasses are used in the home as eggtimers.

HOUSATONIC, river rising in the Berkshire Hills, W Mass., and flowing about 130mi S through Conn. into Long Island Sound, at Stratford. It is an important source of hydroelectricity for New England.

HOUSE, Edward Mandell (1858–1938), US diplomat and adviser to President Woodrow Wilson. He helped Wilson secure the 1912 Democratic nomination. In WWI, he acted for Wilson in Europe, and was responsible for arranging the peace conference and acceptance of Wilson's FOURTEEN POINTS. In 1919, his conciliatory approach during the Treaty of Versailles negotiations led to a rift with Wilson.

HOUSEFLY, *Musca domestica*, a species of fly commonly associated with man. A small gray-brown fly, it feeds by mopping up liquid or semiliquid foods with specialized mouthparts. Solid foods are predigested by expelling saliva over them. Houseflies settle on anything digestible including faeces and are greatly instrumental in the spread of disease.

HOUSE OF BURGESSES. See BURGESSES, HOUSE OF.

HOUSE OF COMMONS, lower house of the British parliament. It consists of 635 M.P.s elected by simple majority in single-member constituencies. It is the assembly to which the government is ultimately responsible; it legitimizes legislation, votes money and acts as a body in which complaints can be raised. Proceedings are regulated by the SPEAKER, and a majority of members must assent before a bill becomes law. (See also PARLIAMENT.)

HOUSE OF LORDS, upper house of the British parliament. Members consist of the Lords Temporal: hereditary peers, life peers and ex-officio law lords, and Lords Spiritual: the 2 archbishops and 24 most senior bishops. Of over 1 100 members, only about 200 attend regularly. It is the highest court of appeal and can delay the passage of a Commons bill for up to a year. (See also PARLIAMENT.)

HOUSE OF REPRESENTATIVES. See CONGRESS OF THE UNITED STATES.

HOUSING AND URBAN DEVELOPMENT, US Department of (HUD), executive department of the federal government, established 1965, to coordinate programs relating to housing problems. It took over the Housing and Home Finance Agency (HHFA). The department supervises the federal aid programs of both the Model Cities Program and the 1965 Housing and Urban Development Act. Its other programs include urban renewal and planning, mortgage insurance, housing for the elderly, low rent public housing and community facilities.

HOUSMAN, Alfred Edward (1859–1936), English poet and classical scholar. His poetry, narrow in range but at its best intensely felt and always craftsmanlike, is collected in *A Shropshire Lad* (1896), *Last Poems* (1922) and *More Poems* (1936).

HOUSSAY, Bernardo Alberto (1887–1971), Argentinian physiologist awarded (with C. and G. CORI) the 1947 Nobel Prize for Physiology or Medicine for his discovery that certain HORMONES produced by the PITUITARY GLAND were responsible for regulating the blood's sugar and insulin content.

Apollo lunar landing craft and other spacecraft at the Manned Spacecraft Center near Houston, Texas.

HOUSTON, city and seat of Harris Co. in SE Tex., third largest seaport in the US. It is situated about 25mi NW of Galveston Bay on the HOUSTON SHIP CHANNEL. Founded in 1836 and named for Sam HOUSTON, it remained relatively unimportant until 1901 when oil was discovered in the area. It is now a prosperous industrial, manufacturing and wholesale distribution center. Major industries include chemicals and petroleum refineries, and the NASA Manned Spacecraft Center (1961) has contributed to the growth of medical and technological research. Houston is a cultural center with museums, a symphony orchestra and several colleges and universities, including the U. of Houston. Pop 1 232 802.

HOUSTON, Sam (Samuel) (1793–1863), American frontiersman and politician, leader in the struggle against Mexico to create an independent Texas (1835–36). He commanded a force of fewer than 800 settlers in a decisive battle at San Jacinto (1836) and went on to become the first president of the Republic of Texas 1836–38. During a second term as president 1841–44 he worked to bring Tex. into the Union (1845). Houston served as US senator 1846–59 and was governor of Tex. 1859–61. He was deposed after refusing to support the Confederacy.

HOUSTON SHIP CHANNEL, or Houston Ship Canal, major waterway between Houston, Tex., and the Gulf of Mexico. Built 1912–14, it is 57mi long, 200ft wide and 34ft deep.

HOVENWEEP NATIONAL MONUMENT, some 505 acres in SE Ut. and SW Col., the site of a pre-Columbian Pueblo Indian settlement abandoned in about the 13th century. The area was declared a national monument in 1923.

HOVERCRAFT. See AIR-CUSHION VEHICLE.

HOVHANESS, Alan (1911–), US composer noted for his innovative use of Eastern musical materials. He is of Armenian descent, and this is evidenced in his works, among the best-known of which are *Mysterious Mountain* (1955) and *Magnificat* (1957).

HOWARD, Catherine (c1521–1542), fifth wife of King Henry VIII of England, niece of the influential Duke of Norfolk. Henry annulled his marriage to ANNE OF CLEVES (arranged by Thomas CROMWELL) and married Catherine on 28 July, 1540, the day of Cromwell's execution. But when inquiries into premarital misconduct pointed to actual adultery, Catherine's fate was soon decided. She was beheaded at the Tower of London.

HOWARD, Sir Ebenezer (1850–1928), founder of the garden-city movement in England. The ideas set out in his book *Tomorrow: A Peaceful Path to Real Reform* (1898), influenced town planning throughout the world.

HOWARD, John (1726–1790), English public official and noted reformer. Serving as high sheriff of Bedfordshire, Howard had access to Bedford jail where the conditions in which prisoners were kept appalled him. His subsequent efforts led to an act of Parliament (1774) to improve sanitation in prisons and abolish the system of discharge fees. He visited prisons throughout Britain and Europe and published *The State of Prisons in England and Wales* (1777), a study that inspired further reform.

HOWARD, Oliver Otis (1830–1909), Union general in the American Civil War and commissioner of the FREEDMEN'S BUREAU (1865–72). He helped provide ex-slaves with food, hospitals, labor contracts and schools and colleges. He was cofounder and president (1869–73) of Howard U., Washington, D.C.

HOWARD, Sidney (1891–1939), US playwright whose work is noted for its realism. He won the 1925 Pulitzer Prize with *They Knew What They Wanted* (1924). Other well-known plays include *Lucky Sam McCarver* (1925) and *The Silver Cord* (1926).

HOWE, name of an American couple who were prominent social reformers. The physician and teacher, **Samuel Gridley Howe** (1801–1876), ran a school for the blind in Boston (later the Perkins School for the Blind) where he achieved outstanding successes most notably in teaching the deaf-blind child Laura BRIDGMAN. He was also an active abolitionist and published the anti-slavery journal *Commonwealth*. His wife, the author **Julia Ward Howe** (1819–1910), is best known for her *Battle Hymn of the Republic* (1862). She was coeditor of *Commonwealth* and a campaigner for women's rights. Both she and her husband belonged to the FREE SOIL PARTY.

HOWE, name of two brothers who were British commanders in the American War of Independence. **Richard, Earl Howe** (1726–1799), commanded the British fleet in America 1776–78 but is best known for his victory over the French off Ushant (1794) as commander of the Channel Fleet. **William, 5th Viscount Howe** (1729–1814), was a commander in the British army 1775–78. He won two major victories in 1777 at BRANDYWINE and GERMANTOWN.

HOWE, Elias (1819–1867), US inventor of the first viable SEWING MACHINE (patented 1846). The early machines were sold in Britain, as in the US there was at first no interest. Later Howe fought a protracted legal battle (1849–54) to protect his patent rights from infringement in the US.

HOWELLS, William Dean (1837–1920), US author, critic and chief editor of the *Atlantic Monthly* (1872–81). He was a pioneer of American social fiction; his finest and most famous novel is *The Rise of Silas Lapham* (1885). Among those his work were Stephen CRANE and Theodore DREISER.

HOWITZER, medium-range cannon. Between a gun and a mortar in length, it fires medium-velocity shells in a curved trajectory. Howitzers are used to hit targets shielded by obstacles that normal high-velocity, low-trajectory fire cannot negotiate.

HOWLAND ISLAND, previously Worth Island, unincorporated US island covering less than 1sq mi in the central Pacific. An airstrip was built on the island in 1937 to provide a stopover between Hawaii and Australia. There is no permanent population.

HOWLER MONKEYS, several species of South American MONKEYS noted for their loud voices. Large monkeys with a thick beard on the throat, they live in groups of 15–20, and are entirely arboreal, feeding on leaves and fruits.

HOWRAH, city in E India, on the W bank of the Hooghly R, opposite Calcutta. It is a rail center with jute and shipbuilding industries. Pop 740 622.

HOXHA, Enver (1908–), Albanian leader. He helped found the Albanian Communist Party in 1941 and was the first premier of the new communist government (1944–54). A Stalinist, Hoxha successfully sought Chinese support following KHRUSHCHEV's accession in the USSR.

HOYLE, Edmond (1672–1769), English authority on card and board games, especially whist. He wrote *A Short Treatise on the Game of Whist* (1742), as well as treatises on other games, including chess and backgammon.

HOYLE, Sir Fred (1915–), British cosmologist best known for formulating with T. GOLD and H. BONDI the steady state theory (see COSMOLOGY); and for his important contributions to theories of stellar evolution, especially concerning the successive formation of the elements by nuclear FUSION in STARS. He is also well known as a science fiction writer and for popular books such as *Frontiers of Astronomy* (1955).

HRDLIČKA, Aleš (1869–1943), Bohemian-born US physical anthropologist best known for expounding the theory that the AMERINDS are of Asiatic origin, a theory still generally accepted today.

HSIANG-T'AN, or Siangtan, city in SE China, on the Siang R. It has engineering, textile and food-processing industries. Pop 281 523.

HSIUNG-NU, nomads who controlled much of Central Asia for over 500 years from the end of the 3rd century BC. They were a serious threat to China's northern border, even after the completion of the GREAT WALL OF CHINA.

HUAINAN, or Hwainan, city in E China, on the Huai R. It is a major coal mining center and has chemical and food-processing industries. Pop 500 000.

HUA KUO-FENG (c1920–), Chinese politician, Communist Party chairman from 1976. Achieving swift promotion during the Cultural Revolution, he was made premier following CHOU EN-LAI's death, and then succeeded MAO TSE-TUNG.

HUAYNA CÁPAC or Wayna Qhapaq (d. 1525), Inca emperor of Peru. He extended the empire to its farthest limits, but on his death left it to his two sons, and thus bequeathed the civil war which had only just ended when the Spanish arrived.

HUBBLE, Edwin Powell (1889–1953), US astronomer who first showed (1923) that certain NEBULAE are in fact GALAXIES outside the MILKY WAY. By examining the RED SHIFTS in their spectra, he showed that they are receding at rates proportional to their distances (see HUBBLE'S CONSTANT).

HUBBLE'S CONSTANT, ratio between the distance of a GALAXY and the rate at which it is receding from us. HUBBLE first calculated this as around 500km/s per Mpc; however, he incorrectly estimated the distances of the galaxies, and the constant has been more recently calculated to be about 75km/s per Mpc.

HUBERT, Saint (c655–727), patron saint of hunters, and of Liège and also Belgium. Hubert is reputed to have been converted after seeing a stag with a cross between its antlers. He became bishop of Maastricht (c708), later moving his diocese to Liège.

HUBLI, city in S India, incorporated with Dharwar in 1961. It is a rail and cotton-trading center. Pop 379 555.

HUCKLEBERRY, small fruit-bearing shrubs of the genus *Gaylussacia*, closely related to the BLUEBERRY and CRANBERRY. The fruit are eaten raw or used in jams and preserves. Family: Ericaceae.

HUDSON, town in NE Mass., on the Assabet R. It produces electronic equipment, plastics and chemicals. Pop 16 084.

HUDSON, residential town on the Merrimack R in N.H. Saint Anthony seminary was established here in 1956. Pop 10 638.

HUDSON, Henry (d. 1611), English navigator and explorer who gave his name to the Hudson R, Hudson Strait and Hudson Bay. After voyages for the English Muscovy Company to find a northeast passage to

China (1607 and 1608), Hudson turned to the west where, with Dutch and then once more English backing (1609 and 1610), he made his most successful voyages. He reached the river known as the Hudson in 1609 and the following year entered Hudson Strait and Hudson Bay, establishing an English claim to the area. After the bitter winter, he was set adrift by a mutinous crew and left to die.

HUDSON, William Henry (1841–1922), English author and naturalist, born in Argentina. Of his early books, romances set in the South American pampas, the best-known is *Green Mansions* (1904). He also wrote studies of bird life and books on the English countryside, such as *A Shepherd's Life* (1910).

HUDSON BAY, inland sea in N Canada, named for Henry HUDSON. Up to about 850mi long and 600mi wide, it is linked to the Atlantic by the Hudson Strait and to the Arctic Ocean by Foxe Channel. James Bay, the largest inlet, extends southwards between Ontario and Quebec provinces. Hudson Bay shipping is restricted since the bay freezes over in winter. (See also HUDSON'S BAY COMPANY.)

HUDSON RIVER, American river rising in the Adirondacks, flowing generally S for 315mi through N.Y., and emptying into the Atlantic at New York City. It was discovered in 1524, but only explored fully by Henry HUDSON in 1609. It is an important commercial waterway, being navigable by ocean ships as far upstream as Albany. A canal system links it to the Great Lakes.

HUDSON RIVER SCHOOL, group of 19th-century American landscape painters. The founders were Thomas COLE, Thomas DOUGHTY and Asher DURAND, who were especially interested in the Hudson River Valley and New England. The school later included artists who took their inspiration from other parts of the US.

HUDSON'S BAY COMPANY, mercantile corporation established by the British in 1670 for trading in the Hudson Bay region. The original intention was also to colonize the area and seek a northwest passage, but the company's major activity was fur-trading with the Indians. It played an important part during the next two centuries in opening up Canada. Although its vast lands were sold to the Dominion in 1870, it is still a major fur-trading company and one of Canada's chief business firms with holdings in metal ores, oil, gas and timber.

HUE, ancient city in central Vietnam on the Hue R. It stands about 5mi inland from the South China Sea and is a commercial and industrial center. Pop 199 893.

HUERTA, Victoriano (1854–1916), Mexican general and dictator (1913–14). After first supporting President Porfiro DÍAZ and then Francisco MADERO, he rebelled, proclaimed himself president in February 1913 and had Madero and his vice-president murdered. A combination of revolution at home and hostility from the US finally forced him into exile.

HUGGINS, Charles Brenton (1901–), Canadian-born US surgeon awarded (with F. P. ROUS) the 1966 Nobel Prize for Physiology or Medicine for his discovery that TUMORS of the male PROSTATE GLAND could be controlled by injection of female sex HORMONES, the first demonstration that CANCER might be controlled by chemical agents.

HUGH CAPET (c938–996), king of France 987–96, founder of the CAPETIAN dynasty. The son of Hugh the Great, the Duke of the Franks, he was elected king in the place of the legitimate Carolingian heir, Charles of Lower Lorraine.

HUGHES, Charles Evans (1862–1948), US jurist and statesman. He was Republican governor of New York 1906–10 and narrowly missed becoming president in 1916 when Woodrow Wilson was elected. He served as secretary of state 1921–25 and as chief justice 1930–41 during the NEW DEAL.

HUGHES, Howard Robard (1905–1976), US industrialist, aviator and film producer. President of the Hughes Aircraft Company and of the Hughes Tool Company, he was a billionaire who in his later years became an eccentric recluse.

HUGHES, John Joseph (1797–1864), Irish-born American priest, the first Roman Catholic archbishop of New York. He held controversial views, being, for example, an opponent of Abolitionism while deploring slavery.

Fort Nelson, one of the forts built by the Hudson's Bay Company for its traders and settlers. Such forts were of more use against the attacks of rival French traders than against the hostile Indians that had originally been feared. In fact the company maintained good relations with most tribes.

HUGHES, Langston (1902–1967), US poet and writer. He is best known for his portrayal of the ordinary Negro, particularly through his character Jesse B. Simple. His works include *The Weary Blues* (1926) and *Not Without Laughter* (1930).

HUGHES, Richard (1900–1976), English writer. His works include plays, poems, novels and short stories but he is best known for his novel *A High Wind in Jamaica* (1929), published in the US as *The Innocent Voyage*, and for *The Fox in the Attic* (1961), part of a projected long novel *The Human Predicament*.

HUGHES, Thomas (1822–1896), English jurist, reformer and novelist. He wrote *Tom Brown's School Days* (1857) which, through its emphasis on the Christian virtues and on athletic ability, did much to shape the popular image of the English public school.

HUGO, Victor Marie (1802–1885), major French novelist, playwright and poet, best known for his historical novel *The Hunchback of Notre Dame* (1831). Among his several important collections of verse are *Les Feuilles d'automne* (1831) and *Les Châtiments* (1853). Hugo went into exile when Napoleon III became emperor (1851), and during this period produced his famous, socially committed novel *Les Misérables* (1862). He spent his last years in France, recognized as one of his country's greatest writers and republicans.

The George Washington Bridge over the Hudson River at New York, the only bridge linking New Jersey and Manhattan. An important commercial river, the Hudson has managed to retain its great scenic beauty over much of its length.

HUGUENOTS, French Protestants, followers of John CALVIN's teaching. The Huguenot movement originated in the 16th century as part of the REFORMATION and found support among all sections of French society, despite constant and severe persecution. (See ST. BARTHOLOMEW'S DAY MASSACRE.) Some respite was provided by Henry IV's Edict of NANTES (1598) but this was revoked in 1685 and many thousands of Huguenots were forced into exile. Full civil and religious liberty was not granted to Huguenots until 1789.

Tried and True Means of recalling Heretics to the Catholic Faith, a contemporary Huguenot cartoon satirizing the revocation of the Edict of Nantes. "Means" include breaking on the wheel, flogging, the gallows, burning and being enslaved as an oarsman on a galley (visible in the background).

HUHEHOT, city in China, capital of the autonomous region of Inner Mongolia. It is an important distribution center whose major industries include flour milling and the production of textiles and agricultural machinery. Pop 700 000.

HUITZILOPOCHTLI, Aztec god of war and of the sun for whom war-prisoners were sacrificed. He was sometimes portrayed as a hummingbird or as a figure decked with hummingbird feathers. *Huitzilin* means hummingbird; warriors were believed to assume the bird's form after death.

HUIZINGA, Johan (1872–1945), Dutch historian, famous for his aesthetic, intuitive treatment of history, and a noted literary stylist. His best-known book is *The Waning of the Middle Ages* (1924).

HUKS, communist guerrillas who staged a rebellion in the Philippines (1946–54). They came near to victory in 1950 but the tide turned with the shipment of US military supplies and in 1953 the election of President Ramon MAGSAYSAY who promised land reforms.

HULA, traditional Hawaiian folk-dance. Its undulating, sensuous movements offended missionaries; despite their attempts to suppress it, it remains popular. The accompanying chants have now been influenced by Western music.

HULAGU KHAN (c1217–1265), a grandson of GENGHIS KHAN, first of the Mongol IL-KHANS of Iran. In 1256 he destroyed the ASSASSINS of N Iran; in the next year he defeated and executed the last ABBASID caliph. In 1258 he captured and sacked Baghdad. He captured Syria, but an Egyptian army drove him back to NW Iran.

HULEH, former lake, now drained for farmland, in upper Galilee, Israel. The Jordan R flows through the area, which has a nature reserve.

HULL, city and rail junction in SW Quebec, Canada, on the Ottawa R opposite OTTAWA. A center of the wood and paper industry, it has cement and meat-packing industries and also foundries. Pop 63 580.

HULL (properly Kingston-upon-Hull), seaport on the Humber R in E Yorkshire, England. An important fishing port, it handles various imports, including oil, and exports mainly manufactured goods. Pop 285 472.

HULL, Cordell (1871–1955), American statesman, secretary of state 1933–44 under ROOSEVELT. He developed the "Good Neighbor" policy in relations with South American states and helped maintain relations with the USSR in WWII. He was a Congressman 1907–21 and 1923–30 and senator 1931–33. After the war he was a major force behind US acceptance of the UN, for which he was awarded the 1945 Nobel Peace Prize.

HULL, Isaac (1773–1843), American naval officer, commander of the frigate *Constitution* ("Old Ironsides") in the War of 1812, defeating the British frigate *Guerrière*. He commanded the Pacific Squadron 1824–27 and the Mediterranean Squadron 1838–41.

HULL, William (1753–1825), American revolutionary soldier, governor of Michigan Territory 1805–12. In 1812 he was appointed brigadier-general in charge of an attack on Fort Malden, Canada. Besieged in Detroit, he surrendered to the British without resistance and was subsequently cashiered.

HULL HOUSE, one of the first US social settlement houses. Founded in Chicago in 1889 by Jane ADDAMS and Ellen Gates Starr, it provided community services and recreational facilities to a poor community.

HUMAN BODY, the physical substrate of man, *Homo sapiens*. In terms of ANATOMY, it consists of the head and neck, a trunk divided into the CHEST, ABDOMEN and PELVIS, and four limbs; two ARMS and two LEGS. The head contains (within the bony structure of the SKULL) the BRAIN, which is connected by cranial nerves to the special sense organs for VISION (EYES), hearing and balance (EARS), SMELL (NOSE), and TASTE. On the front of the head is the FACE, specialized for communication (including the special senses, and through which the VOICE emanates—see SPEECH AND SPEECH DISORDERS). The head sits at the top of the **spinal column** of VERTEBRAE, which continue through the neck, thorax and lumbar region to the sacrum and COCCYX. The spinal column is the central structural pillar of the musculoskeletal system, and that onto which the ribs, chest and abdominal walls, and pelvic bones articulate. Within the bony spinal canal is the SPINAL CORD, the downward extension of the brain concerned with relaying information to and from the body and with segmental REFLEX behavior. It is linked with the various parts of the body by the peripheral and autonomic NERVOUS SYSTEMS. The chest, abdomen and pelvis contain many vital organs comprising the various functional systems.

The **internal functions** of the human body include: the BLOOD CIRCULATION, which supplies all organs with OXYGEN and nutrients and removes waste products from them (see AORTA; ARTERIES; CAPILLARIES; HEART; VEINS; VENA CAVA); RESPIRATION, which provides oxygen for the blood and removes carbon dioxide via the LUNGS, BRONCHI and TRACHEA; the DIGESTIVE SYSTEM, which starting at the MOUTH and PHARYNX, leads into the GASTROINTESTINAL TRACT; systems for EXCRETION and METABOLISM, including particularly the LIVER, KIDNEYS and BLADDER; BLOOD, formed in the BONE MARROW and circulating throughout the body; the *lymphoreticular system*, which has a major role in IMMUNITY and blood degradation (see LYMPH; SPLEEN); sites of HORMONE secretion, or ENDOCRINE GLANDS; and the *reproductive system*, essential for the propagation of the species (including the OVARIES, FALLOPIAN TUBES, WOMB, vagina, TESTES and PENIS). The *limbs* are primarily concerned with locomotion and fine movement (see JOINTS; MUSCLES; TENDONS) and with tactile sensibility (see HANDS; TOUCH).

Hawaiian hula dancers, holding tapping sticks and wearing the traditional leaf skirts.

The whole body surface is covered with SKIN, which is a protective layer also concerned with temperature and fluid regulation, specialized for tactile sensation and bearing many HAIRS. The mucous membranes of the nose, mouth, respiratory tract and gastrointestinal tract and of exocrine GLANDS are made of surface EPITHELIUM. The thin inner layer of blood vessels (*endothelium*) is a surface which, when intact prevents the CLOTTING of the contained blood. Other TISSUES found in the body include muscle, both striated (or skeletal) and smooth (or visceral); connective tissue; ADIPOSE TISSUE; BONE; CARTILAGE, and the specialized tissues of the organs discussed above.

The basic unit of the body is the CELL. In the early stages of the development of an individual, this is a multipotential structure containing all the genetic information (in GENES on the CHROMOSOMES of its nucleus) required for the development, differentiation, growth and function of any and all the parts of the body. Each cell divides repeatedly and forms a cell line which gradually specializes into a particular aspect of body structure and PHYSIOLOGY, while suppressing its other potentialities. In this way the highly complex and subspecialized body develops, the integration and control of development being perhaps genetically inbuilt or, alternatively, controlled by hormones and the nervous system. The early development of the EMBRYO and FETUS before BIRTH continue in childhood with subtler differentiation and increase of bulk, a further growth spurt and much sexual development occurring at PUBERTY. After early adult life, the optimal function of organs begins to become impaired with the degenerative processes of AGING. Added to these are the DISEASES to which the human body is susceptible; these range from environmental influences such as trauma and infection to specific diseases such as CANCER. Disease and degeneration determine the finite quality of human life, leading to its termination in DEATH.

HUMAN ENGINEERING, or **ergonomics,** research into physical and psychological human characteristics with particular reference to the environments in and the tools with which people work, and the application of the information so received to the design of equipment, factories, etc. In fact, the techniques of human engineering are now applied to a wide range of other problems involving humans and technology; e.g. POLLUTION control.

HUMANISM, originally, the RENAISSANCE revival of the study of classical (Latin, Greek and Hebrew) literature for its own sake, rather than of medieval SCHOLASTICISM. In a broader sense it has come to mean a philosophy centered on man and human values, exalting human free will and superiority to the rest of nature; man is made the measure of all things. Renaissance thinkers such as PETRARCH began a trend towards humanism which embraced such diverse figures as BOCCACCIO, MACHIAVELLI, Thomas MORE and ERASMUS and which became the ancestor of much subsequent secular thought and literature, as well as—in another direction—of the REFORMATION. Modern humanism tends to be nontheistic (see AGNOSTICISM; ATHEISM), emphasizing the need for man to work out his own solutions to life's problems, but has a strong ethic similar to that of Christianity. Both Roman Catholic and Protestant theologians (such as Karl BARTH) have sought to show that Christian beliefs embody true humanism.

HUMANITIES, branches of learning concerned with culture, excluding the sciences. Originally the term was limited to the study of ancient Greek and Roman literature, but has been extended to include all languages, literature, religion, philosophy, history and the arts.

HUMAN RIGHTS. See DECLARATION OF HUMAN RIGHTS, UNIVERSAL.

HUMBERT (Umberto), name of two kings of Italy. **Humbert I** (1844–1900), came to the throne in 1878. Originally sharing power with a bicameral Parliament, he gradually lost power to it, a process he did not oppose. Popular for his generous aid to disaster victims, he was assassinated by anarchists. **Humbert II** (1904–   ), came to the throne in May 1946, after a hurried abdication by his father, VICTOR EMMANUEL III. On June 2, 1946, the monarchy was rejected by referendum and Humbert was exiled to Portugal.

HUMBOLDT, city in NW Tenn., 15mi NNW of Jackson. In an agricultural area, it has a major granite works. Pop 10 006.

HUMBOLDT, Friedrich Heinrich Alexander, Baron von (1769–1859), German naturalist. With the botanist **Aimé Jacques Alexandre Bonpland** (1773–1858) he traveled for five years through much of South America (1799–1804), collecting plant, animal and rock specimens and making geomagnetic and meteorologic observations. Humboldt published their data in 30 volumes over the next 23 years. In his most important work, *Kosmos* (1845–62), he sought to show a fundamental unity of all natural phenomena.

HUMBOLDT, Karl Wilhelm, Baron von (1767–1835), German philologist regarded as the father of comparative PHILOLOGY. He maintained both that the nature of language reflects the culture of which it is a product, and that man's perception of the world is governed by the language available to him.

HUMBOLDT CURRENT, or **Peru Current,** cold OCEAN CURRENT originating in the S Pacific, and flowing N along the coasts of N Chile and Peru, whose climates it moderates, before turning W to join the S EQUATORIAL CURRENT.

HUMBOLDT RIVER, 290mi-long river in N Nevada. Rising in the NE of the state, it forms the Humboldt Reservoir, which is held by Rye Patch Dam, and disappears in Humboldt Sink. Discovered in 1828, it is named for Alexander von HUMBOLDT.

HUME, David (1711–1776), Scottish Enlightenment philosopher, economist and historian, whose *Treatise of Human Nature* (1739–40) is one of the key works in the tradition of British EMPIRICISM. But it was his shorter *Enquiry Concerning Human Understanding* (1748) which prompted KANT to his most radical labors. His influential *Dialogues Concerning Natural Religion* were published posthumously in 1779, long after their composition. In EPISTEMOLOGY Hume argued that men had no *reason* to associate distinct impressions as cause and effect; if they did so, it was only because experience had shown them that this was possible. His SKEPTICISM in this respect has always been controversial. In his own day, Hume's most successful work was possibly his *History of England* (1754–63).

HUMERUS, BONE of the upper ARM, linked to the scapula and clavicle at the SHOULDER and to the radius and ulna at the elbow. Major MUSCLES are inserted into it.

HUMIDIFIER, device to maintain the air inside a building at a desirable humidity. In hot weather moisture is removed from the air by refrigeration; in cold weather it is increased by allowing water to evaporate. (See also AIR CONDITIONING; HUMIDITY.)

HUMIDITY, the amount of water vapor in the air, measured as mass of water per unit volume or mass of air, or as a percentage of the maximum amount the air would support without condensation, or indirectly via the DEW point. Saturation of the air occurs when the water vapor pressure reaches the VAPOR PRESSURE of liquid water at the TEMPERATURE concerned; this rises rapidly with temperature. The physiologically tolerable humidity level falls rapidly with temperature, as humidity inhibits cooling by EVAPORATION of sweat.

HUMMEL, Johann Nepomuk (1778–1837), Austro-Hungarian composer and pianist. A child prodigy, he studied with MOZART. After some years of European travel and study in Vienna under HAYDN, he became court conductor at Weimar in 1819, and remained there till his death. He wrote masses, ballets, operas and piano works; the latter influenced CHOPIN and SCHUMANN. His *Pianoforte School* (1828), a new fingering method, influenced subsequent keyboard techniques.

The tongue of the Ruby-throated hummingbird, and of some others, is tubular and extensible beyond the beak so that nectar may be sucked from flowers while hovering almost motionless in front of them.

HUMMINGBIRDS, an enormous family (Trochilidae) of tiny nectar-feeding birds of the New World, which take their name from the noise of their rapid wingbeats—up to 70 a second in smaller species as they hover at flowers to feed. Colorful birds, the body size in most species is 50mm (2in) or less. With their small size and fierce activity, hummingbirds must feed about once every 10–15 min. Highly adapted to flight, hummingbirds have short legs and little feet, used only for perching.

HUMORS, in ancient and medieval medicine, the four bodily fluids whose balance was required for the individual's health. They correspond to the four elements (see ARISTOTLE): *blood*:fire; *phlegm*:water; *choler* (or *yellow bile*):air; and *melancholy* (or *black bile*):earth. Excess of blood (hot and dry), for example, made one sanguine; phlegm (cold and wet), phlegmatic; etc. Cure was by enantiopathy (see ALLOPATHY), so that a fever would be treated with cold, and so forth. The idea may have originated with EMPEDOCLES in the 5th century BC, and we still retain something of it in modern words such as "choleric" and "phlegmatic."

HUMPBACK, *Megaptera novaeangliae*, a species of WHALE of some 16m (50ft) which appears to hunch its back on diving. Very similar animals to RORQUALS, humpbacks are widely distributed throughout the oceans. The head bears various nodules and the body is usually covered with large barnacles.

HUMPERDINCK, Engelbert (1854–1921), German composer. He was much influenced by WAGNER, whom he assisted at the Bayreuth Festival. He wrote several operas; only one, *Hansel and Gretel* (1893) is widely performed today, although *The Royal Children* (1910) is revived from time to time.

HUMPHREY, Doris (1895–1958), a leading choreographer in modern dance. Influenced by Ruth SAINT DENIS and Ted Shawn, under whom she studied before setting up her own school in 1928, she broke away to develop her own expressive style, based upon her theories of movement and her concept of dance as an expression of human dignity.

HUMPHREY, Hubert Horatio (1911–   ), US politician, 38th vice-president 1965–69, Democratic senator from Minn. 1948–64. His vigorous liberal policies did much to win him the vice-presidential nomination under Lyndon JOHNSON. In 1968 he received the Democratic presidential nomination, but was defeated in the 1969 elections and re-entered the Senate in 1970. He was unsuccessful in a bid for the 1972 presidential nomination.

HUMPHREYS, David (1752–1818), US revolutionary soldier and diplomat, aide-de-camp to Washington (1780) and subsequently US minister to Spain (1796–1801). A poet and satirist, he was a member of the HARTFORD WITS; he introduced Merino sheep to America and established a woollen mill.

HUMPHREYS, Joshua (1751–1838), American naval designer, first US naval constructor 1794–1801. The frigates he designed, of which the first was the *United States*, gave the US Navy an advantage in speed and maneuverability over the British.

HUMUS, the organic component of soil, decomposed plant and animal material (see PUTREFACTION). Dark brown to black, it is intimately mixed with the inorganic SOIL particles. Mainly for its good CARBON, NITROGEN, PHOSPHORUS and SULFUR content, it is of great agricultural importance.

HUNCHBACK, or kyphosis, deformity of the spine causing bent posture with or without twisting (SCOLIOSIS) and abnormal bony prominences. TUBERCULOSIS of the spine may cause sharp angulation, while congenital diseases, ankylosing spondylitis, vertebral collapse and spinal TUMORS cause smooth kyphosis.

HUNDRED DAYS, March 20–June 28, 1815, the period between NAPOLEON's return to Paris from exile on Elba and the second Bourbon restoration. Napoleon attempted in this period to reinstate himself as ruler of France on a more liberal basis; this was unacceptable to the Allies, and he had to meet their challenge at the battle of WATERLOO.

HUNDREDWEIGHT (cwt), name of two units of WEIGHT. In the US the short hundredweight of 100lb is used. The Imperial (long) hundredweight is 112lb.

HUNDRED YEARS' WAR, sporadic series of wars fought mainly between England and France 1337–1453. They originated in disputes over English possessions in France, and the claims of Edward III of England to the throne of France. In 1337 he invaded Gascony and won the battles of Sluis (1340) CRÉCY (1346) and POITIERS (1356) and seized Calais, gaining important concessions at the Treaty of Brétigny (1360). The French under Charles V regained much of their lost territory 1369–75 and attacked the English coast. Henry V of England destroyed the resulting uneasy truce when he invaded France in 1415, in pursuit of a vainglorious dream of establishing himself as monarch of Britain and France; he captured Harfleur and defeated a superior French force at AGINCOURT. At the Treaty of Troyes (1420) Henry V was recognized as heir to the French throne and from 1422 his infant son, Henry VI, ruled the dual monarchy, with John, Duke of Bedford as French regent. His able rule won French support, and only the resurgence led by JOAN OF ARC in 1429 halted English gains. Although the Dauphin was crowned Charles VII at Reims in 1429, the English position was not assailed until 1435, when PHILIP THE GOOD of Burgundy recognized Charles VII as king of France. After 1444 the English were driven back until they held only Calais (until 1558) and the Channel Islands.

One of the most appealing—and most enigmatic—figures of the Hundred Years War was Joan of Arc. This statue of her stands at Orléans, where she was captured by the English in 1428.

HUNGARIAN, or *Magyar*, one of the UGRO-FINNIC LANGUAGES in the Uralic group. It is spoken mainly in Hungary, but also by groups in Czechoslovakia, Romania and Yugoslavia. It has many loan-words from the non-Uralic tongues within it, but retains its own distinct identity. Its six dialects do not differ widely; Standard Hungarian is the speech of the Budapest area.

Official name: People's Republic of Hungary
Capital: Budapest
Area: 35 911sq mi
Population: 10 314 152
Languages: Hungarian
Religions: Roman Catholic; Protestant
Monetary unit(s): 1 Forint = 100 fillér

HUNGARY, People's Republic in central Europe, bordered by Czechoslovakia on the N, the USSR and Romania on the E, Yugoslavia on the S and Austria on the W.

Land. Most is low plain, the Kisalföld (Little Plain) in the NW and the Nagyalföld (Great Plain) in the center and E. Crossing the country are two major rivers, the Danube and Tisza, the area between the two (Cumania) being sandy plateau and reclaimed marsh. Other plains lie E of the Tisza including the Hortobagy with its dry steppes (*puszta*). In the W and SW is the more rolling Mezoföld (Middle Plain), and in the S the forested Mecsek massif. Lake Balaton (about 230sq mi) is Europe's largest natural lake. Highlands include the Bakony Forest, Vértes, Gerecse and Pilis hills, and the Carpathian foothills (Kékes, 3330ft, Hungary's highest peak).

Climate is continental. Winters are cold and summers hot and dry. Rainfall is heavier in the W and floods can occur in spring and early summer, though the E and S can have serious summer droughts.

People. Nearly all are Magyars descended from Finno-Ugrian and Asiatic Turkish stock, but there are German, Slovak, Croat, Serb and Romanian minorities. A cultured people, their distinctive language is distantly related to Finnish. About 48% of the population are urban-dwelling, the largest cities being Budapest, the capital (2039000), Miskolc, Debrecen, and Pécs.

Economy. This has expanded as a result of the "New Economic Mechanism" (inaugurated 1968). But mineral resources, including coal, oil, natural gas and iron ore are relatively poor, though bauxite is plentiful. Industrial centers include Budapest (engineering and transportation equipment) and Dunáujvaros (iron and steel). There are important electrical, chemical, food-processing and textile plants. Agriculture is collectivized. Leading crops include corn, wheat, oats, rye, potatoes, sunflowers and sugar beets. Apricots, vines, paprika and tobacco are also grown, and hogs, sheep and cattle reared.

History. The area was conquered by the Magyars under Arpád about 896 AD and Christianized in the 900s. Resistance to Turkish invasion ended with the defeat of King Lewis II at Mohács (1526), and most of the country was divided between the Ottoman Empire and Austria, the W and N coming under Hapsburg rule in 1687. A bid for independence led by Lajos Kossuth (1848) failed, but led to the Dual Monarchy (1867), the Austrian Emperor Francis Joseph I being crowned King of Hungary. After WWI, ruled by regent Admiral Horthy, Hungary came under German influence and was Nazi Germany's ally in WWII. Occupied by Russia (1945), Hungary soon turned communist (1949). An uprising against the repressive regime was crushed by Russia (1956) and a puppet government under János Kádar set up. In 1968 Hungary helped other Warsaw Pact countries crush the Dubček regime in Czechoslovakia.

HUNGER. See THIRST AND HUNGER.

HUNKERS, the conservative branch of the Democratic Party in N.Y. during the 1840s who, according to their rivals the BARNBURNERS, "hankered" or "hunkered" for power. They supported the chartering of state banks and were against antislavery agitation.

HUNS, nomadic, probably Mongolian, race who invaded SE Europe during the 4th and 5th centuries. They crossed the Volga R in c372 and attacked the Germanic Goth tribes. By 432 they had invaded the Eastern Empire. Under their great leader ATTILA, they threatened the Roman Empire, unsuccessfully invading Gaul in 451. In 452 their Italian invasion was halted at Lake Garda. After Attila's death in 453, the Hun empire gradually disintegrated.

HUNT, Leigh (James Henry Leigh Hunt; 1784–1859), English critic, journalist and poet. Hunt rubbed shoulders with the great: KEATS, SHELLEY and BYRON, but was himself something of a literary butterfly. With his brother he was imprisoned 1813–15 for an attack on the Prince Regent in their paper the *Examiner*. His best work is possibly contained in his autobiography (1850).

HUNT, Richard Morris (1828–1895), US architect. He trained and worked in Europe 1843–54, and his style in America was historically eclectic. He built the Statue of Liberty base and the 1893 Chicago Exposition administrative building.

HUNT, William Holman (1827–1910), English painter who helped to found the PRE-RAPHAELITE BROTHERHOOD. His work is noted for its brilliant coloring and accurate details. His best-known painting is *The Light of the World* (1853).

HUNTER, John (1728–1797), British anatomist and biologist who made many contributions to SURGERY, ANATOMY and PHYSIOLOGY. He is often regarded as the father of scientific surgery.

HUNTING DOG. See AFRICAN HUNTING DOG.

HUNTINGTON, city in NE Ind., seat of Huntington Co. Its economy is based on industry and limestone quarrying. Pop 16217.

HUNTINGTON, residential town and boating center in SE N.Y., on the N shore of Long Island. Pop 200172.

HUNTINGTON, city in W. Va., seat of Cabell Co. It is a large commercial and railroad center. The principal industry is mining. Pop 74315.

HUNTINGTON, name of two US railroad tycoons. **Collis Potter Huntington** (1821–1900), was chief promoter of the first railroad company in the West, the Central Pacific (1861). In 1884 he established the Southern Pacific. His nephew and heir **Henry Edwards Huntington** (1850–1927), formed an outstanding art collection and library at San Marino, Cal. It specializes in English 18th-century art and literature and is now a research center.

HUNTINGTON BEACH, coast city in SW Cal., 14mi SE of Long Beach. It has oil refineries, truck farming and metallurgical industries. Pop 115960.

HUNTINGTON PARK, city in SW Cal., 4mi S of Los Angeles. It manufactures chemicals and truck bodies. Pop 33744.

HUNTINGTON STATION, residential village in SE N.Y. on the N shore of Long Island, birthplace of Walt WHITMAN. It forms part of Huntington, N.Y. Pop 28817.

HUNTSVILLE, city in Ala., seat of Madison Co. Its industries include the manufacture of farm implements and natural gas wells. It is the site of NASA's Marshall Space Flight Center, set up in 1960. Pop 137802.

HUNTSVILLE, city in E Tex., seat of Walker Co. Its products include furniture and lumber and cotton seed oil. Pop 17610.

HUNYADI, János (c1387–1456), Hungarian leader and general. Much of his career was spent in successfully preventing the Turkish invasion of Hungary, particularly in 1441–43. His victory against the Turks in 1456 ensured Hungarian independence for a further 70 years.

HUPA INDIANS, tribe of North American Indians who, in the 19th century, were settled along the Trinity R valley in NW Cal. They belonged to the ATHABASCAN language group, and spoke Hupa. They were hunters, fishermen and gatherers. Their lands became a reservation in 1864. About 950 of the tribe survive today.

HURDY-GURDY, lute-shaped, stringed musical instrument. It has 2–4 drone strings sounded by a wheel which is rotated by means of a handle at the base of the instrument. The melody is played on one or more strings, by means of keys. Popular during the medieval period, it is still used by folk and revivalist musicians.

HURLING, an outdoor stick and ball game of Irish origin, played in Ireland and to an extent in the US. A curved broad-ended stick or *hurley* is used to drive the ball or *slitter* into the opposing side's goal. The game is played on a field, usually 150yd by 90yd, with two teams each of 15 men. The ball is made of leather and the goals are H-shaped.

Monument erected to the memory of Richard Morris Hunt in recognition of his contribution to American art and architecture.

HURON, city in E central S.D., seat of Beadle Co. It is an agricultural center with grain and stock farms. Pop 14299.

HURON, Lake, the second largest of the GREAT LAKES, covering some 23010sq mi, with Canada to the N and E, and Mich. to the S and W. It belongs to the Great Lakes–St. Lawrence Seaway navigation passage. Its principal ports are Sarnia, Owen Sound and Midland in Canada; Alpena, Port Huron and Bay City in the US.

HURON INDIANS, league of four North American Indian tribes who lived in S Ontario and in c1615 numbered some 20000. They belonged to the Iroquoian language group, and lived by agriculture. In 1650 the Iroquois virtually destroyed the league. Small numbers of Hurons remain in Quebec and in Okla.

HURRIANS, ancient people who dominated N Mesopotamia during the second millennium BC. Although conquered in the mid-14th century BC by the HITTITES they continued to exert a strong cultural influence on Mesopotamian civilization. Their language is recorded in four varieties of CUNEIFORM and seems to have an affinity with Caucasian language groups.

HURRICANE, a **tropical cyclone,** usually of great intensity. High-speed winds spiral in toward a low-pressure core of warm, calm air (the **eye**): winds of over 300km/hr have been measured. The direction of spiral is clockwise in the S Hemisphere, counterclockwise in the N (see CORIOLIS EFFECT). Hurricanes form (usually between latitudes 5° and 25°) when there is an existing convergence of air near sea level toward a center. The air ascends, losing moisture as precipitation as it does so. If this happens rapidly enough, the upper air is warmed by the water's LATENT HEAT of vaporization. This reduces the surface pressure, so accelerating air convergence. Hurricanes of the N Pacific are often called **typhoons.** (See also CYCLONE; WIND.)

HURST, city in N Tex., NE of Fort Worth. Its main industry is fruit growing. Pop 27215.

HUS, Jan (c1370–1415), Bohemian religious reformer and Czech national hero. Influenced by John WYCLIFFE, Hus attacked Church and papal abuses. He defended his ideas at the Council of CONSTANCE in 1414, where he was arrested, tried and burned at the stake as a heretic. His followers, the Hussites, demanded many reforms in the Roman Catholic Church with which they were involved in a series of wars in Bohemia in the 15th century.

HUSÁK, Gustav (1913–), premier of Czechoslovakia. Taking a pro-Moscow line after 1968, he replaced DUBČEK as secretary of the Czech Communist Party in 1969.

HUSEIN (c626–680), Shi'ite Muslim saint, grandson of MOHAMMED. He was killed by a rival claimant to the caliphate. Elaborate Shi'ite mourning rituals are conducted on Oct. 10, the anniversary of his death.

HUSEIN IBN ALI (c1854–1931), sharif of Mecca 1908–16, and king of Hejaz 1916–24. In 1916 he led the WWI Arab revolt against the Turks, and proclaimed himself king of all Arabia. Assisted by T. E. LAWRENCE, he drove the Turks from Syria, Northern Arabia and Transjordan. In 1924 IBN SAUD forced him to abdicate, and he died in exile.

HU SHIH (1891–1962), Chinese historian, philosopher and writer, a pioneer of language reform. He published work in the vernacular rather than in classical Chinese. After the communist revolution, he lived in New York and then in Taiwan.

HUSKY. See SIBERIAN HUSKY.

HUSSAR, a light-cavalry soldier. The first hussars were established in Hungary by King Matthias Corvinus in 1458 to fight against the Turks. The typical uniform included the *busby* (a fur hat), a braided jacket and a *dolman* (a loose jacket worn hanging from the left shoulder).

HUSSEIN IBN TALAL (1935–), King of Jordan since 1953. His policies are generally pro-

Western and he is a spokesman for moderation in the conflict between the Arab nations and Israel. Jordan's loss of the West Bank in the 1967 ARAB–ISRAELI WAR led to civil war in 1970 when King Hussein gained firmer control over the country.

HUSSERL, Edmund (1859–1938), Czech-born German philosopher who founded PHENOMENOLOGY. Professor at Göttingen and Freiburg universities, he was concerned by what constitutes acts of consciousness and how they relate to experience. He held that consciousness is "intentional" in that it does not exist apart from the objects of awareness.

HUSSITES. See HUS, Jan.

HUSTON, the name of two film personalities. **Walter Huston** (1884–1950), Canadian-born American actor, best known for his roles in the play, *Dodsworth* (1936), the musical comedy *Knickerbocker Holiday* (1938) and the film *The Treasure of Sierra Madre* (1947) directed by his son **John Huston** (1906–   ), Hollywood writer, then director, whose films include: *The Maltese Falcon* (1941), *The Asphalt Jungle* (1950), *The African Queen* (1951) and *Moby Dick* (1956).

HUTCHESON, Francis (1694–1746), Scottish philosopher who propounded the moral sense theory in ETHICS. He held that man has an innate faculty to distinguish between good and bad actions. His main work is *System of Moral Philosophy* (1755).

HUTCHINS, Robert Maynard (1899–   ), influential US educator, president of Chicago U. 1929–45, chancellor 1945–51. He advocated the integration and synthesis of academic disciplines. In 1959 he founded the Center for the Study of Democratic Institutions as an ideal "Community of Scholars."

HUTCHINSON, city in central Kan., seat of Reno Co. It has extensive salt mines and such industries as flour milling and oil refining. Pop 36 885.

HUTCHINSON, Anne (c1600–1643), English Puritan religious leader, one of the founders of Rhode Island. She emigrated to Mass. in 1634 where she preached that faith alone could achieve God's salvation. She opposed obedience to the strict laws of the Puritan community. In 1638 she and her followers were banished and they established a settlement on Aquidneck island (now Rhode Island). She was killed by Indians.

Contemporary engraving depicting the Boston Tea Party, precipitated largely by Thomas Hutchinson. As governor of Boston he aggravated an unstable situation by enforcing a heavy tea duty.

HUTCHINSON, Thomas (1711–1780), American colonial governor of Massachusetts, 1770–74. A political enemy of Samuel ADAMS, he opposed American independence, and enforced the STAMP ACT (1765) although considering the act unwise. In 1773 he insisted that duty be paid on tea cargoes at Boston, which led to the BOSTON TEA PARTY. In 1774 he went to England where he served George III as an adviser.

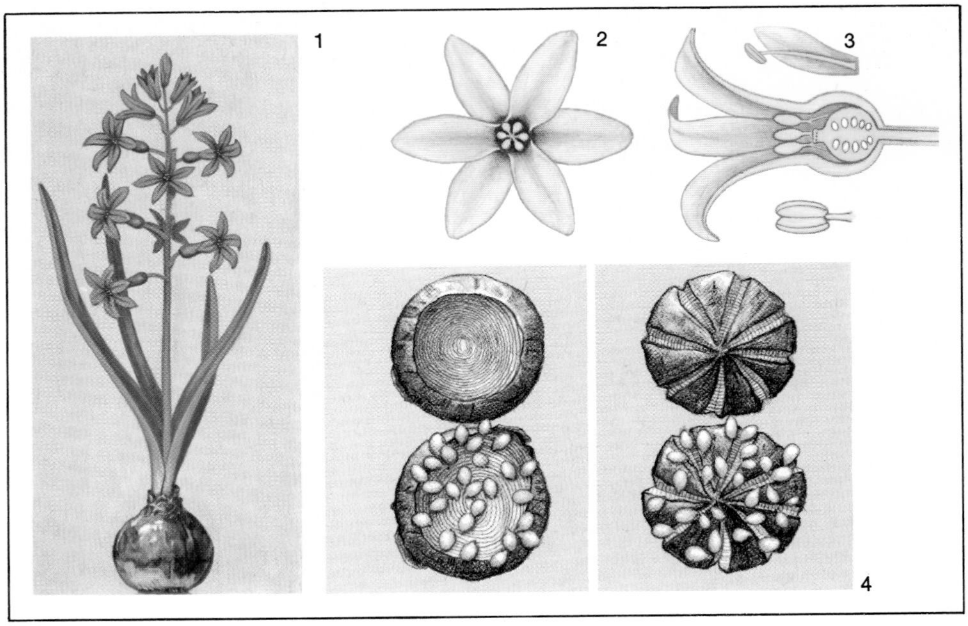

The Common hyacinth, *Hyacinthus orientalis* (1); its flower entire (2) and in section (3) with detail of stamen (*above*) and stigma (*below*). Bulbils for propagation are induced to form (4) either by scooping out the center (*left*) or cutting the surface (*right*) and replanting the old bulb.

HUTIA, large terrestrial rodents restricted to the West Indies, with one species in Venezuela. They look very like COYPU. Their continued survival is threatened by dogs and cats and by being hunted by man for food.

HUTTERITES, or Hutterian Brethren, Protestant sect found primarily in S.D., and Canada. Like the MENNONITES, they believe in common ownership of goods and are pacifists. The sect originated in 1533 as a branch of the ANABAPTISTS and takes its name from Jacob Hutter, martyred in 1536.

HUTTON, James (1726–1797), Scottish geologist who proposed, in *Theory of the Earth* (1795), that the earth's natural features result from continual processes, occurring now at the same rate as they have in the past (see UNIFORMITARIANISM). These views were little regarded until LYELL's work some decades later. (See also CATASTROPHISM.)

HUXLEY, distinguished British family. **Thomas Henry Huxley** (1825–1895) is best known for his support of DARWIN's theory of EVOLUTION, without which acceptance of the theory might have been long delayed. Most of his own contributions to paleontology and zoology (especially taxonomy), botany, geology and anthropology were related to this. He also coined the word "agnostic." His son **Leonard Huxley** (1860–1933), a distinguished man of literature, wrote *The Life and Letters of Thomas Henry Huxley* (1900). Of his children, three earned fame. **Sir Julian Sorell Huxley** (1887–1975) is best known as a biologist and ecologist. His early interests were in development and growth, genetics and embryology. Later he made important studies of bird behavior, studied evolution and wrote many popular scientific books. **Aldous Leonard Huxley** (1894–1963) was one of the 20th century's foremost novelists. Important works include *Crome Yellow* (1921), *Antic Hay* (1923) and *Point Counter Point* (1928), characterized by their wit and attitude toward lofty pretensions, and the famous *Brave New World* (1932) and *Eyeless in Gaza* (1936). After experimenting with hallucinogenic drugs he became interested in mysticism. Later works include *The Devils of Loudon* (1952), *The Doors of Perception* (1954) and *Island* (1962). **Andrew Fielding Huxley** (1917–   ) shared the 1963 Nobel Prize for Physiology or Medicine with A. L. HODGKIN and Sir J. ECCLES for his work with Hodgkin on the chemical basis of nerve impulse transmission (see NERVOUS SYSTEM).

HUYGENS, Christiaan (1629–1695), Dutch scientist who formulated a wave theory of LIGHT, first applied the PENDULUM to the regulation of CLOCKS, and discovered the surface markings of MARS and that SATURN has rings. In his optical studies he stated **Huygens' Principle**, that all points on a wave front may at any instant be considered as sources of secondary waves that, taken together, represent the wave front at any later instant.

HWANG HO. See YELLOW RIVER.

HYACINTH, popular name for bulbous plants of the genus *Hyacinthus*. Hyacinths are popular as spring garden and house plants available in a vast number of color shades. Most varieties are derived from *Hyacinthus orientalis*, which is native to Greece and Asia Minor. Family: Liliaceae.

HYANNIS, village and summer resort in SE Mass., on the S shore of Cape Cod. It is near Hyannisport, which is frequented by the Kennedy family. Pop 6 847.

HYATTSVILLE, town in S central Md., 7mi NE of Washington, of which it is a suburb. Pop 14 998.

HYBRIDIZATION. the crossing of individuals belonging to two distinct species. MULES, for example, are the result of hybridization between a horse and an ass. Hybrid offspring are often sterile, especially in animals.

HYDAPSES, Battle of the, battle on the Hydapses R in 326 BC between Alexander the Great and Porus, who ruled in what is now NE Pakistan. Alexander's attack caused Porus's elephants to plunge back into the Indian ranks. Alexander allowed Porus to continue as ruler.

HYDE, Edward. See CLARENDON, EDWARD HYDE, 1ST EARL OF.

HYDE PARK, small residential village in SE N.Y., on the Hudson R, birthplace and burial site of President F. D. Roosevelt. The Roosevelt home, adjacent to the Roosevelt Library, and the Vanderbilt home are national historic sites. Pop 2 805.

HYDERABAD, city in India, capital of Andhra Pradesh, 310mi NNW of Madras, on the Musi R. The city, founded in 1589, is famous for the Char Minar (1591) and the Old Bridge (1593). It is now a commercial center. Pop 1 612 276.

HYDERABAD, city in Pakistan 90mi ENE of Karachi. It was famous for embroidery, and now for engineering and chemical industries. Pop 834 000.

HYDRA, many-headed mythical Greek monster, which grew two heads in place of any one cut off. HERCULES killed it as one of his 12 labors.

HYDRA (the Water Monster), a large S Hemisphere constellation containing the bright star Alphard and a cluster of galaxies over 30Mpc distant.

HYDRANGEA, genus of shrubs and climbers native

to North and South America and Asia. Many species and varieties are cultivated as ornamental shrubs. The flowers are basically white, blue and pink, colors depending on the presence of aluminum in the soil and on whether the soil is basic (pink) or acid (blue). Family: Hydrangeaceae.

HYDRAS, freshwater COELENTERATA, perhaps the most familiar of the HYDROZOA. Occurring only as polyps, hydras have no medusoid, or jelly-fish, stage; they are found in ponds, lakes and streams throughout the world. The body is an elongated column with a mouth at one end surrounded by tentacles. Normally attached by the other end to the substrate, hydras can move by "looping" across a plane surface or by free-swimming. Hydras reproduce by asexual budding when food is abundant. When food is scarce, ovaries and testes develop on the column, and sexual REPRODUCTION gives rise to resistant, dormant, embryos.

HYDRATE, a compound (usually ionic) containing a definite proportion of WATER, known as water of crystallization, which may be bound as a LIGAND to the cation, to the anion, or to both. Other hydrates, with more or less water, may be formed under different conditions. Water may be lost from a hydrate spontaneously (EFFLORESCENCE) or by heating (see also DEHYDRATION), the compound becoming anhydrous. Common hydrates include COPPER (II) sulfate, $CuSO_4.5H_2O$, SODIUM carbonate, $Na_2CO_3.10H_2O$, and the ALUMS. (See also DELIQUESCENCE.)

HYDRAULIC BRAKE, a BRAKE system in which the power is transmitted by hydraulic pressure.

HYDRAULICS, application of the properties of liquids (particularly WATER), at rest and in motion, to engineering problems. Since any machine or structure that uses, controls or conserves a liquid makes use of the principles of hydraulics, the scope of this subject is very wide. It includes methods of WATER SUPPLY for consumption, IRRIGATION or navigation and the design of associated DAMS, canals and pipes; HYDROELECTRICITY, the conversion of water power to electric energy using hydraulic TURBINES; the design and construction of ditches, culverts and hydraulic jumps (a means of slowing down the flow of a stream by suddenly increasing its depth) for controlling and discharging FLOOD water, and the treatment and disposal of industrial and human waste. Hydraulics applies the principles of HYDROSTATICS and HYDRODYNAMICS and is hence a branch of FLUID MECHANICS. Any hydraulic process, such as flow of liquid through a turbine, may be described mathematically in terms of four basic equations derived from the conservation of ENERGY, MASS, MOMENTUM and the relationship between the specific FORCES and internal mechanics of the problem. In hydraulic machines which transmit energy through liquids and convert it into mechanical power, three principles of liquid behavior that have been known for centuries are applied. TORICELLI's law states that the speed of liquid flow from a hole in the side of a vessel increases with the depth of the hole below the surface of the liquid in it. PASCAL's law states that the PRESSURE (force per unit area) in an enclosed body of liquid is transmitted equally in all directions. (This law is applied directly in a **hydraulic press**, in which a force applied over a small area by a piston is transmitted through the liquid filling the system to another piston with a larger area on which a much larger force will be exerted.) BERNOULLI's law states that at any point in a tube through which liquid is flowing, if no work is done, the sum of energies due to the pressure, motion (kinetic energy) and elevation (potential energy) of the liquid is constant. Thus by increasing the cross-section of the tube and slowing the flow down, kinetic energy is converted to pressure energy. The development of pumps in the 19th century, which converted mechanical to hydraulic energy and produced greater fluid velocities and pressures than had previously been obtainable, meant that hydraulic principles could usefully be applied to operate a wide variety of machines. Self-contained hydraulic units consisting of an engine, a pump, control valves, a motor to convert hydraulic to mechanical energy, and a load were soon developed for use in industry and transportation. Hydraulics is now one of the main technologies for transmitting energy, comparing well with mechanical and electrical systems and having the advantages of being fast and accurate and good at multiplying forces. Hydraulic systems containing water, oil or special fire-resistant fluids are now used in AIRPLANE landing systems, AUTOMOBILE braking systems and many other industrial applications.

HYDRAZINE (N_2H_4), colorless liquid, a covalent HYDRIDE resembling AMMONIA, prepared by oxidizing UREA with hypochlorite in the presence of gelatin. It reacts with ALDEHYDES to form hydrazones ($RCH{=}NNH_2$); it is a weak BASE, forming hydrazonium salts. Hydrazine is a powerful reducing agent, and so is used as a rocket fuel (being oxidized by nitric acid), as well as a corrosion inhibitor in boilers. It is also used to cure rubber, and in the production of plastics, explosives and fungicides.

HYDRIDES, binary compounds of HYDROGEN and another element. They fall into three classes. **Covalent hydrides** are formed by the elements in Groups IB–VIIA of the PERIODIC TABLE, i.e., the nonmetals and some metals. They are mainly volatile, reactive compounds, though those of Groups IB and IIB, and aluminum, are nonvolatile polymers. (See the individual elements, and also BORANES; HYDROCARBONS; AMMONIA; HYDRAZINE; WATER; SULFIDES; HYDROGEN FLUORIDE; HYDROGEN CHLORIDE.) **Ionic hydrides** are formed by the ALKALI METALS and ALKALINE-EARTH METALS. They are crystalline solids containing the ion H^-, which is a very powerful BASE and reducing agent (see OXIDATION AND REDUCTION), and react violently with water to give hydrogen. **Metallic hydrides**, formed by the TRANSITION ELEMENTS (Groups IIIB–VIII), are mostly nonstoichiometric (see COMPOSITION, CHEMICAL) and electrically conducting. They resemble ALLOYS, and some have interstitial structures.

HYDROCARBONS, organic compounds composed of CARBON and HYDROGEN only. Like organic compounds in general, which are derived formally from hydrocarbons by adding FUNCTIONAL GROUPS, they are best divided into ALIPHATIC, ALICYCLIC and AROMATIC hydrocarbons; aliphatic hydrocarbons are further subdivided into ALKANES, ALKENES and ALKYNES. Some hydrocarbons, especially TERPENES, occur in plant oils, and solid, high-molecular-weight

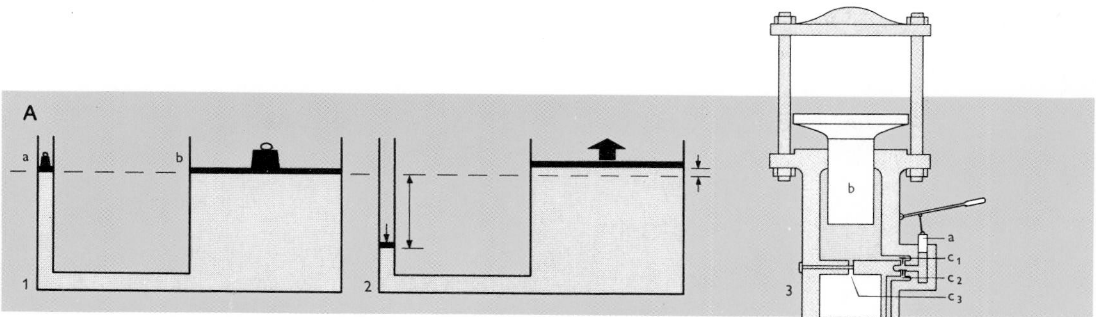

The hydraulic press (A) is based on the principle that a small force applied over a small area (1a) produces a pressure equivalent to that given by a large force applied over a large area (1b). This fact can be used to convert a small force acting over a large distance into a large force acting over a small distance (2). In an actual hydraulic press (3) the small force is applied to a small piston (a) by pressing down the handle. This is translated into a very considerable force acting upwards at the large piston (b). Valves (C_1, C_2, C_3) control the flow of fluid so that pumping the handle up and down is equivalent to moving the piston (a) through a long distance.

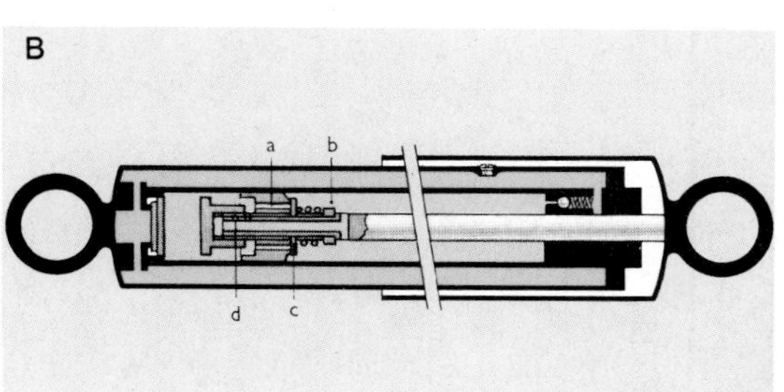

In a hydraulic shock absorber (B) a sudden shock moves the piston into the lower chamber (*left*), forcing oil through channel (a) and valve (c) into the upper chamber (b). After the shock the oil passes back through the channel in the piston rod and through small holes (d) into the lower chamber. The viscosity of the oil dampens the impact of the shock.

Fluid can be used to transmit torque or turning force (C) in the same way as air from a rotating fan will turn the blades of a second fan placed nearby (1). A basic hydraulic coupling (2) contains two sets of blades, an impeller turned by the drive shaft and a runner which turns the output shaft. A diagram of the coupling in section (3) shows the flow of fluid from the impeller (*solid arrow*) to the runner (*dashed arrow*). In a hydraulic torque converter (4) a third set of stationary or reactor blades is included. These redirect the fluid from the runner to the impeller (*dotted arrow*) giving increased torque at the output shaft.

hydrocarbons occur as BITUMEN, but by far the largest sources of all sorts of hydrocarbons are PETROLEUM, NATURAL GAS and COAL GAS. They are used as FUELS, for LUBRICATION, and as starting materials for a wide variety of industrial syntheses.

HYDROCEPHALUS, enlargement of the BRAIN ventricles with increased CEREBROSPINAL FLUID (CSF) within the SKULL. In children it causes a characteristic enlargement of the head. Brain tissue is attenuated and damaged by long-standing hydrocephalus. It may be caused by block to CSF drainage in the lower ventricles or brain stem aqueduct (e.g., by TUMOR and malformation, including those seen with SPINA BIFIDA), or by prevention of its reabsorption over the brain surface (e.g., following MENINGITIS). Apart from attention to the cause, treatment may include draining CSF into the atrium of the HEART.

HYDROCHLORIC ACID, solution of HYDROGEN CHLORIDE in water; a strong ACID of major industrial importance.

HYDROCYANIC ACID. See CYANIDES.

HYDRODYNAMICS, the branch of FLUID MECHANICS dealing with the FORCES, ENERGY and PRESSURE of FLUIDS in motion. A mathematical treatment of ideal frictionless and incompressible fluids flowing around given boundaries is coupled with an empirical approach in order to solve practical problems.

HYDROELECTRICITY, or **hydroelectric power**, the generation of ELECTRICITY using water power, is the source of about a third of the world's electricity. Although the power station must usually be sited in the mountains and the electricity transmitted over long distances, the power is still cheap since water, the fuel, is free. Moreover, running costs are low. An exciting modern development is the use in coastal regions of the ebb and flow of the tide as a source of electric power. Hydroelectric power uses a flow of water to turn a TURBINE, which itself drives a GENERATOR.

Convenient heads of water sometimes occur naturally (see WATERFALL), but more often must be created artificially by damming a river (see DAM); an added advantage is that the reservoir that forms behind the dam may be tapped for drinking or irrigation water.

The powerhouse, which contains the turbines and generators, may be at the foot of the dam or some distance away, the water then being transported in tunnels and long pipelines called **penstocks**. The turbines are of two main types: impulse (e.g., the Pelton wheel) and reaction (e.g., the Francis and Kaplan wheels). The Pelton wheel has buckets about its edge, into which jets of water are aimed, so turning the wheel. The Francis wheel has spiral vanes: water enters from the side and is discharged along the axis. The Kaplan wheel is rather like a huge propeller immersed in the water.

HYDROFOIL, a structure which, when moved rapidly through water, generates lift in exactly the same way and for the same reasons as does the AIRFOIL (see also AERODYNAMICS). It is usually mounted beneath a vessel (also called a hydrofoil). Much of a conventional boat's power is spent in overcoming the drag (resistance) of the water; as a hydrofoil vessel builds up speed, it lifts out of the water until only a small portion of it (struts, hydrofoils and PROPELLER) is in contact with the water. Thus drag is reduced to a minimum. Hydrofoils can exceed 125km/h as compared with conventional craft, whose maximum speeds rarely approach 80km/h.

HYDROGEN (H), the simplest and lightest element, a colorless, odorless gas. Hydrogen atoms make up about 90% of the UNIVERSE, and it is believed that all other elements have been produced by fusion of hydrogen (see STAR; FUSION, NUCLEAR). On earth most hydrogen occurs combined with oxygen as WATER and mineral HYDRATES, or with carbon as HYDROCARBONS (see PETROLEUM). Hydrogen is produced in the laboratory by the action of a dilute ACID on zinc or other electropositive metals. Industrially it is made by the catalytic reaction of hydrocarbons with steam, or by the WATER GAS process, or as a by-product of some ELECTROLYSIS reactions. Two-thirds of the hydrogen manufactured is used to make ammonia by the HABER

US Navy hydrofoil gunboat making a highspeed run, demonstrating its ability to rise out of the water on its foils. These allow vast speed increases, but are vulnerable in rough or shallow seas.

PROCESS. It is also used in HYDROGENATION, PETROLEUM refining, and metal smelting. METHANOL and HYDROGEN CHLORIDE are produced from hydrogen. Being flammable, it has now been largely superseded by helium for filling BALLOONS and AIRSHIPS. Hydrogen is used in oxy-hydrogen WELDING; liquid hydrogen is used as fuel in rocket engines, in BUBBLE CHAMBERS, and as a refrigerant (see CRYOGENICS). Hydrogen is fairly reactive, giving HYDRIDES with most other elements on heating, and a moderate reducing agent. It belongs in no definite group of the PERIODIC TABLE, but has some resemblance to the HALOGENS in forming the ion H^-, and to the ALKALI METALS in forming the ion H^+ (see ACIDS); it is always monovalent. (See also HYDROGENATION; HYDROGEN BONDING.) A hydrogen atom consists of one ELECTRON orbiting a nucleus of one PROTON. A hydrogen molecule is two atoms combined (H_2). In parahydrogen both the protons have the same SPIN: in orthohydrogen the protons have opposite spin. They have slightly different properties. At room temperature, hydrogen is 75% orthohydrogen, 25% parahydrogen. DEUTERIUM (H^2) and TRITIUM (H^3) are ISOTOPES of hydrogen. (See also HYDROGEN BOMB.) AW 1.008, mp −259°C, bp −253°C.

HYDROGENATION, a reaction in which hydrogen is added to a compound. Hydrogenation converts unsaturated organic compounds (see BOND, CHEMICAL) into saturated ones. Catalysts (commonly Raney nickel, palladium and platinum) are used. Hydrogenation is used to turn vegetable oils into margarine, in PETROLEUM refining, and to make many compounds.

HYDROGEN BOMB, or thermonuclear bomb, very powerful BOMB whose explosive energy is produced by nuclear FUSION of two DEUTERIUM atoms or of a deuterium and a TRITIUM atom. The extremely high temperatures required to start the fusion reaction are produced by using an ATOMIC BOMB as a fuze. Lithium-6 deuteride (Li^6D) is the explosive; neutrons produced by deuterium fusion react with the Li^6 to produce tritium. The end products are the isotopes of HELIUM He^3 and He^4. In warfare hydrogen bombs have the advantage of being far more powerful than atomic bombs, their power being measured in megatons of TNT, capable of destroying a large city. In defensive and peaceful uses they can be modified so that the radioactivity produced is minimal. Hydrogen bombs were first developed in the US (1949–52) by Edward TELLER and others, and have been tested also by the USSR, Great Britain, China and France.

HYDROGEN BONDING, the formation of a weak bond (see BOND, CHEMICAL) between a HYDROGEN atom (bound to a small electronegative atom, usually fluorine, oxygen, nitrogen or chlorine) and another such electronegative atom, in another or the same molecule. It is an electrostatic effect, but can be well described in molecular-orbital terms, especially when the three-atom system is symmetric (e.g. HF_2^-), resembling the hydrogen-bridge bonding in BORANES. Hydrogen bonding leads to anomalous physical properties due to molecular association: high melting point and boiling point, low vapor pressure, high viscosity, etc. It is important in the hydrogen halides, WATER, ICE, ALCOHOLS, OXY-ACIDS, AMMONIA, AMINES and AMIDES, and hence in vital molecules such as AMINO-ACIDS, PROTEINS and DNA.

HYDROGEN CHLORIDE (HCl), colorless acrid gas, fuming in air; a covalent HYDRIDE prepared by heating SALT with concentrated sulfuric acid or by direct combination of HYDROGEN and CHLORINE. It is unreactive when completely dry. mp −115°C, bp −85°C. **Hydrochloric acid**, a solution of hydrogen chloride in water, is a strong ACID, and reacts with active metals and bases to give chlorides (see HALIDES). It is used to make chlorine compounds and in the extraction and processing of metals. Dilute hydrochloric acid is produced in the stomach (see DIGESTIVE SYSTEM) but in excess causes gastric ULCERS. The concentrated acid is caustic. (See also AQUA REGIA.)

HYDROGEN FLUORIDE (HF), colorless liquid, fuming in air; a covalent HYDRIDE, prepared by distilling FLUORITE with concentrated sulfuric acid. Its physical properties show typical anomalies due to HYDROGEN BONDING. It is a very strong ACID, and an ionizing solvent for many inorganic and organic compounds; it is used to make FLUORINE and its compounds, especially FREON and FLUOROCARBONS. mp −83°C, bp 20°C. **Hydrofluoric acid**, a solution of hydrogen fluoride in water, is (anomalously) a weak acid, but causes very severe burns and is toxic. It dissolves silica to give fluorosilicic acid (H_2SiF_6), and so is used to etch glass.

HYDROGEN PEROXIDE. See PEROXIDES.

HYDROGEN SULFIDE. See SULFIDES.

HYDROGRAPHY, branch of hydrology dealing with bodies of water, such as oceans, lakes and rivers, on the earth's surface; and especially with the charting of their boundaries, currents, underwater contours and shipping hazards, as well as with the composition of their beds. (See also EARTH; HYDROLOGY; OCEANOGRAPHY.)

HYDROLOGIC CYCLE, the circulation of the waters of the earth between land, oceans and atmosphere. Water evaporates from the oceans into the ATMOSPHERE, where it may form CLOUDS (see also EVAPORATION). Much of this water is precipitated as RAIN back into the ocean, but much also falls on land. Of this, some is returned to the atmosphere by the TRANSPIRATION of plants, some joins rivers and is returned to the sea, some joins the GROUNDWATER and eventually reaches a sea, lake or river, and some evaporates back into the atmosphere from the surface of the land or from rivers, streams, lakes, etc. Over 97% of the earth's water is in the oceans; of the remaining fresh water, about 75% is in solid form (see GLACIER). However, although at a particular moment there is very little water in rivers, lakes and the atmosphere, the annual passage of water through them is quite high. (See also HYDROLOGY; HYDROSPHERE.)

HYDROLOGY, the branch of geophysics concerned with the HYDROSPHERE (all the waters of the EARTH), with particular reference to the HYDROLOGIC CIRCLE. The science was born in the 17th century with the work of Pierre Perrault and Edme MARIOTTE.

HYDROLYSIS, a double decomposition effected by WATER, according to the general equation

$$XY + H_2O \rightarrow XOH + YH.$$

If XY is a salt of a weak ACID or a weak BASE, the hydrolysis is reversible, and affects the pH of the solution (see BUFFER). Reactive organic compounds such as ACID CHLORIDES and ACID ANHYDRIDES are rapidly hydrolyzed by water alone, but others require acids, bases, or ENZYMES as catalysts (see also DIGESTION). Industrial hydrolysis processes include the alkaline saponification of oils and fats to glycerol and SOAP, and the acid hydrolysis of starch to glucose.

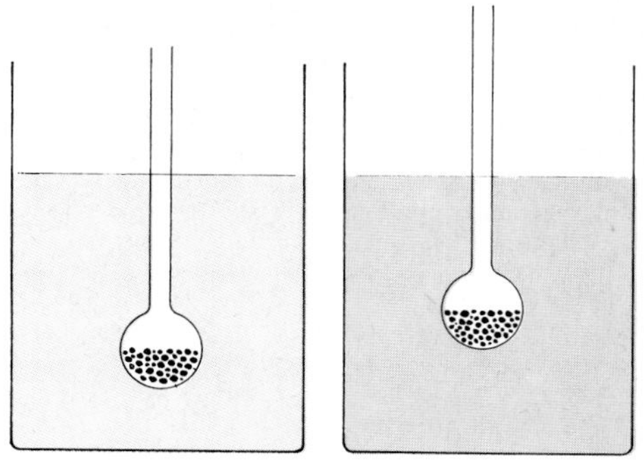

The hydrometer is used to measure the specific gravity of liquids: in a liquid of low density (*left*) the glass tube sinks more than in a liquid of greater density.

HYDROMETER, an instrument to measure the density of a liquid. In essence it consists of a closed glass tube calibrated along its stem and blown into a bulb, which is weighted, at the other. The hydrometer floats upright in the liquid to be tested: the denser the liquid, the more the instrument is buoyed up (according to ARCHIMEDES' Principle). The scale is read at the level of the liquid's surface. Though the instrument measures DENSITY directly, it is usual to calibrate the stem in terms of SPECIFIC GRAVITY, the ratio of the density of the liquid to the density of water at that temperature. Other scales are used for specific purposes.

HYDROPHOBIA. See RABIES.

HYDROPHONE, an adaptation of the MICROPHONE for use underwater. As with the microphone, the device converts SOUND (pressure) waves into electrical impulses, which are passed by cable to an external AMPLIFIER. Its prime use is in SONAR.

HYDROPHYTES, plants that are entirely submerged in water, whose upper leaves are floating, or which are entirely floating.

HYDROPLANE, or hydrofoil. See HYDROFOIL.

HYDROPLANING, or **aquaplaning,** dangerous phenomenon experienced by fast-moving cars on wet roads. A layer of water is built up between the tires and the road: since the water acts as an efficient lubricant (see LUBRICATION), the car goes out of control.

HYDROPONICS, the technique by which plants are grown without soil. It is also known as soilless culture. All the minerals required for plant growth are provided by nutrient solutions in which the roots are immersed. The technique has been highly developed as a tool in botanical research, but commercial exploitation is limited primarily because of the difficulty of aerating the water and providing support for the plants. Gravel culture has overcome these problems to some extent and is used to grow some horticultural crops.

HYDROSPHERE, all the waters of the earth, in whatever form: solid, liquid, gaseous. It thus includes the water of the ATMOSPHERE, water on the EARTH's surface (e.g., oceans, rivers, ice sheets) and GROUNDWATER. (See also HYDROGRAPHY; HYDROLOGY; LITHOSPHERE.)

HYDROSTATICS, the branch of FLUID MECHANICS dealing with FORCES and PRESSURES in stationary FLUIDS, and their effects on bodies immersed in them. The concept of FLUID PRESSURE (a normal force per unit area acting across any surface in the fluid or at its boundary) enables problems of flotation, buoyancy etc. to be treated.

HYDROTHERAPY, system of treatment by use of water, usually by treading or bathing in special pools, often supplied from mineral springs historically credited with healing properties.

HYDROXIDES, compounds containing the OH group, or the ion OH^-. Hydroxides of metals are generally BASES, and, if soluble, ionize to produce alkaline solutions (see ALKALIS) containing hydroxide ions. Nonmetals form ACID hydroxides, or OXYACIDS, which dissolve to produce hydrogen ions. Some metal hydroxides, such as zinc hydroxide, are amphoteric, that is, both basic and acidic. Hydroxides are formed by hydration of the oxide, or, if insoluble, by precipitation with an alkali. The OH^- ion acts as a LIGAND, forming hydroxo complexes. Organic compounds containing the OH group are ALCOHOLS, PHENOLS and CARBOXYLIC ACIDS.

HYDROZOA, a group of characteristically marine

coelenterates (see COELENTERATA). They are usually small and typically show an alternation of polyp and medusoid forms. The class contains both solitary and colonial forms; some of the colonies are highly complex and spectacular, with incredible polymorphism of component individuals specialized for feeding, reproduction or locomotion.

HYENAS, three species of carnivorous mammals of essentially African distribution. They are distinctive in having the shoulders considerably higher than the hindquarters and have also an unusual gait, moving both limbs on one side of the body together. All three species have massive heads with powerful jaws. Though reviled as scavengers and carrion-feeders, hyenas are active and skilful predators in their own right, hunting in packs of up to 20. Family: Hyaenidae.

HYGEIA, the Greek goddess of health, either the daughter or the wife of AESCULAPIUS, the god of medicine.

HYGINUS, Saint (d. c142) pope from c138. He is credited with establishing the hierarchy of the clergy. His feast day is Jan. 11.

HYGROMETER, device to measure HUMIDITY (the amount of water vapor the air holds). Usually, hygrometers measure relative HUMIDITY, the amount of moisture as a percentage of the SATURATION level at that temperature. The **hair hygrometer**, though of limited accuracy, is common, The length of a hair increases with increase in relative humidity. This length change is amplified by a lever and registered by a needle on a dial. Human hair is most used. The **wet and dry bulb hygrometer** (psychrometer) has two THERMOMETERS mounted side by side, the bulb of one covered by a damp cloth. Air is moved across the apparatus (e.g., by a fan) and evaporation of water from the cloth draws LATENT HEAT from the bulb. Comparison of the two temperatures, and the use of tables, gives the relative humidity. The **dewpoint hygrometer** comprises a polished container cooled until the DEW point is reached: this temperature gives a measure of relative humidity. The **electric hygrometer** measures changes in the electrical RESISTANCE of a hygroscopic (water-absorbing) strip.

HYKSOS, kings of Egypt, Asian invaders who formed the 15th and 16th dynasties. They introduced the Asian light horse and chariot, bronze weapons and the compound bow. (See also EGYPT, ANCIENT.)

The brown hyena of southern Africa enjoys a bad reputation as a cowardly scavenger which eats the carrion of others' kills. This is not entirely deserved; a hyena pack may occasionally eat carrion or finish off wounded or dying animals, but they generally live by hunting. Indeed, it is now known that lions often finish off hyena kills, and not—as was formerly thought—vice versa. Hyenas are especially notable for the enormous skull-crushing power of their jaws.

HYMEN, Greek god of marriage, usually depicted as a handsome young man carrying a lighted torch, and sometimes with a bridal veil or wreath.

HYMENOPTERA, an order of wasp-waisted insects comprising the ANTS, BEES and WASPS. The name derives from the two pairs of glassy wings linked together during flight by rows of tiny hooks.

HYMN, a sacred song in praise of gods or heroes, found in almost all cultures. The Jewish PSALMS, sung in the Temple worship, were adopted by the early Christian Church and supplemented by distinctively Christian hymns such as the CANTICLES. Greek and, later, Latin hymns became common, mostly in metrical verse. At the Reformation the REFORMED CHURCHES and the Church of England mainly used metrical psalms. But there is a continuous English hymn tradition from the 7th century, including the 16th-century CAROLS. Modern hymns were developed by Isaac WATTS, John WESLEY and many others, fostered by both the EVANGELICAL REVIVAL and the OXFORD MOVEMENT. The Lutheran churches from the beginning had many fine hymns.

HYOSCINE. See SCOPALAMINE.

HYOSCYOMINE, an ALKALOID poison found in HENBANE, BELLADONNA and JIMSON WEED. It is a major source of ATROPINE.

HYPATIA (d. 415 AD), probably the first and one of the most famous women philosophers and mathematicians. She probably occupied the chair of Neo-Platonic philosophy at Alexandria. She was murdered by a Christian mob in an Alexandrian riot.

HYPERBARIC CHAMBER, chamber built to withstand and be kept at pressures above atmospheric. The high OXYGEN pressures achieved in them may destroy the anaerobic bacteria (*Clostridia*) responsible for gas GANGRENE; SURGERY may be done in the chamber. It is also used for AEROEMBOLISM in decompression.

HYPERBOLA. See CONIC SECTIONS.

HYPERBOLIC FUNCTIONS, the FUNCTIONS that arise in hyperbolic or LOBACHEVSKIAN GEOMETRY and in the study of complex VARIABLES. They are interrelated similarly to the trigonometric functions (see TRIGONOMETRY).

Hyperbolic Functions

The base definitions for these functions are

$$\cosh x = \tfrac{1}{2}(e^{x}+e^{-x})$$
$$\text{and } \sinh x = \tfrac{1}{2}(e^{x}-e^{-x})$$

(see EXPONENTIAL). From these come

$$\text{sch} = 1/\cosh x;$$
$$\text{csch } x = 1/\sinh x;$$
$$\tanh x = \sinh x/\cosh x,$$
$$\text{and } \coth x = \cosh x/\sinh x.$$

HYPERION, a TITAN, sometimes regarded as the first sun god. According to Homer, he shipwrecked ODYSSEUS.

HYPERON. See SUBATOMIC PARTICLES.

HYPEROPIA, or hypermetropia or far- or longsightedness, a defect of VISION in which light entering the EYE from nearby objects comes to a focus behind the retina. The condition may be corrected by use of a converging spectacle LENS.

HYPERTENSION. See BLOOD CIRCULATION.

HYPERTHYROIDISM. See THYROID GLAND.

HYPNOSIS, an artificially induced mental state characterized by an individual's loss of critical powers and his consequent openness to SUGGESTION. It may be induced by an external agency or by the individual himself (**autohypnosis**). Hypnotism has been widely used in medicine (usually to induce ANALGESIA) and especially in PSYCHIATRY and PSYCHOTHERAPY. Here, the particular value of hypnosis is that, while in trance, the individual may be encouraged to recall deeply repressed memories (see MEMORY; REPRESSION) that may be the heart of, for example, a COMPLEX; once such causes have been elucidated, therapy may proceed.

Hypnosis seems to be as old as man. However, the first definite information on it comes in the late 18th century with the work of MESMER, who held that disease was the result of imbalance in the patient's "animal magnetism", and hence attempted to cure by use of magnets. In fact, some of his patients *were* cured, presumably by suggestion; and the term **mesmerism** is still sometimes used for hypnotism. Early psychotherapeutic uses include that of CHARCOT and his pupil FREUD; though Freud later rejected hypnosis and used instead his own technique, FREE ASSOCIATION. Little is known of the nature or root cause of hypnosis, and its amateur use is dangerous.

HYPO, or sodium thiosulfate. See SODIUM.

HYPOCAUST, ancient Roman heating system. Heat from fires passed through passages beneath floors and behind walls.

HYPOCHLORITES, salts containing the ClO^{-} ion derived from **hypochlorous acid**, HOCl, an unstable, weak acid. They are made by absorbing CHLORINE into an ALKALI, and are used for BLEACHING (see also BLEACHING POWDER) and as DISINFECTANTS.

HYPOCHONDRIA, or **hypochondriasis,** a PSYCHOSIS involving undue ANXIETY about real or supposed ailments, usually in the belief that these are incurable. The source of hypochondria was once thought to be the hypochondrium, the part of the ABDOMEN containing SPLEEN and LIVER.

HYPOCYCLOID, the CURVE traced by a point on the circumference of a CIRCLE that is rolling along the inside of a larger, fixed circle. (See also CYCLOID; EPICYCLOID.)

HYPODERMIC. See INJECTION; SYRINGE.

HYPOSTYLE, a large hall whose roof is supported only by columns, which are placed in rows at the perimeter and in the interior of the hall. Hypostyle halls are commonly found in ancient Egyptian and Hindu architecture.

HYPOTENUSE, the side opposite the right angle of a right-angled TRIANGLE. (See also PYTHAGORAS' THEOREM.)

HYPOTHALAMUS, central part of the base of the BRAIN, closely related to the PITUITARY GLAND. It contains vital centers for controlling the autonomic NERVOUS SYSTEM, body temperature and water and food intake. It also produces HORMONES for regulating pituitary secretion and two systemic hormones (e.g., VASOPRESSIN).

HYPOTHESIS. See SCIENTIFIC METHOD.

HYPOXEMIA, or **hypoxia.** See ANOXIA.

HYRAXES, rabbit-sized animals of Africa and S Asia, remarkable in that their closest relatives are the ELEPHANTS. There are two species of tree-hyrax and half a dozen species of rock hyrax, or dassies. They feed on plants and fruits and have rigid feeding times. The excrement which collects in the communal latrines has commercial value, containing an ingredient used in the manufacture of perfume.

HYSSOP, *Hyssopus officinalis*, a hardy perennial herb native to Mediterranean regions eastward to Central Asia. It was cultivated originally for use as a domestic medicine, but is now used as a culinary herb and as a garden ornamental. Family: Labiatae.

HYSTERECTOMY, or surgical removal of the WOMB, with or without the OVARIES and FALLOPIAN TUBES. It may be performed via either the ABDOMEN or the vagina and is most often used for fibroids, benign TUMORS of womb muscle, CANCER of the cervix or body of womb, or for diseases causing heavy MENSTRUATION. If the ovaries are preserved, HORMONE secretion remains intact, though periods cease and infertility is inevitable.

HYSTERESIS, a memory phenomenon in ferromagnetic materials (see MAGNETISM), the magnetization depending not only on the MAGNETIC FIELD applied, but also on how it was applied. In electric MOTORS, GENERATORS, and TRANSFORMERS, the refusal of the magnetization to follow the field directly often results in substantial ENERGY loss (hysteresis loss).

HYSTERIA, psychiatric disorder characterized by exaggerated responses, emotional lability with excess tears and laughter, over-activity and often overbreathing, occasionally leading to TETANY. It is often a manifestation of attention-seeking behavior. **Conversion systems** or mimicry of organic disease are often termed hysterical; the simulation of a particular disorder fulfils some psychological need in response to certain stresses and results in an unconscious gain or release from anxiety.

I

I, ninth letter of the English alphabet. It derives from a Semitic form adopted into the Greek alphabet as *iota*. The dot above the lower-case *i* was introduced in the 11th century. With the advent of printing *j* was formally distinguished from *i*.

IAPETUS, in Greek mythology, son of Uranus and Ge. He was one of the TITANS and the father of Atlas, Prometheus, Epimetheus and Menoetius.

IASI (Jassy), former capital of MOLDAVIA, NE Romania. Now an industrial city producing chemicals, antibiotics, textiles, machinery and timber. Pop 183 776.

IATROCHEMISTRY, a species of ALCHEMY which sought to find chemical treatments for disease, particularly as promoted in the 16th century by PARACELSUS and his followers. The analytic methods used in iatrochemistry were highly significant in the development of modern CHEMISTRY and the search for new remedies led to the discovery of many new chemical substances.

IBADAN, second largest city of Nigeria and capital of Western State and of Ibadan province, it is a major trading center for cocoa, palm oil, cotton, tobacco and citrus fruits. Pop 758 000.

IBAGUÉ, city in W central Colombia, at an altitude of 4300ft. It is the capital of Tolima dept. Pop 195 000.

IBÁÑEZ, Vincente Blasco. See BLASCO IBÁÑEZ, VINCENTE.

IBERIAN PENINSULA, landmass in SW Europe, occupied by Spain and Portugal; cut off from the rest of Europe by the Pyrenees Mts and separated from North Africa by the Strait of Gibraltar.

IBERIANS, a BRONZE AGE people of S and E Spain, culturally influenced by the Carthaginians and Greeks. Their sphere of influence overlapped that of the CELTS, who migrated into N and Central Spain from the 8th–6th centuries BC onward. They had a sophisticated written language and were fine potters.

IBERT, Jacques François Antoine (1890–1962), French composer of piano pieces, orchestral works, symphonic poems and operas. Among his well-known works are a cantata, *Le Poète et la Fée* (Prix de Rome, 1919), a ballet based on Oscar Wilde's *Ballad of Reading Gaol* (1922), the opera *Angélique* (1927) and the light opera for radio *Barbe-bleue* (1943).

IBERVILLE, Pierre le Moyne, Sieur d' (1661–1706), French-Canadian fur trader and explorer; founder of Louisiana. In 1699 he began exploring the mouths of the Mississippi R; he built a fort on Biloxi Bay and established a post at the site of Mobile, Ala.

IBEX, seven species of wild goats which differ from true GOATS in their flattened foreheads and usually broad-fronted horns. Always found in mountainous areas, ibex live for most of the year in separate-sexed herds, with the males only forming harems during the 7–10-day rut.

IBISES, stork-like birds of moderate size, characterized by long thin downward-curving bills. Ibises have a worldwide distribution in tropical, subtropical and temperate regions, and are usually found near fresh water, feeding on small aquatic animals. Ibises are gregarious and frequently raucous. The best known species are the Sacred ibis (*Threskiornis aethiopica*), honored in ancient Egypt, and the Scarlet ibis, *Eudocimus ruber*, a Caribbean species with scarlet plumage.

The Bald ibis (*Geronticus calvus*), rarest of the family. These birds fly in graceful formations.

IBIZA, one of the Balearic islands belonging to Spain, about 80mi E of the Spanish coast in the W Mediterranean. The island exports salt, almonds and dried fruits and is a major resort.

IBN BATTUTA (1304–1368?), greatest Arab traveler of the Middle Ages. Born in Tangier, Morocco, he spent about 25 years traveling in Africa, the Middle East, Persia, India and the Far East. His notes (the *Rihlah* or *Travels*) provide a priceless account of life in the oriental world before the rise of Europe.

IBN GABIROL, Solomon ben Judah (c1021–c1057), influential Spanish Jewish poet and neo-Platonic philosopher. His famous hymn *Keter Malkhut* (Royal Crown) concludes with a confession of sin which has been adapted for the Jewish Yom Kippur (Day of Atonement) service.

IBN KHALDUN (1332–1406), Arab historian and sociologist. The introduction to his great history of the Persians, Arabs and Berbers of North Africa contains the first attempt to interpret the pattern of history in purely secular terms of geography, sociology and allied subjects.

IBN SAUD (c1880–1953), creator of the kingdom of Saudi Arabia in 1932 and its first ruler. As a young man he set up the Ikhwan, a fanatical brotherhood of Muslims. With the Ikhwan's help in the 1920s, he conquered and united the small kingdoms which now make up SAUDI ARABIA. Saud was one of the first Arab leaders to exploit Middle East oil. (See also MUSLIMS.)

IBN-SINA. See AVICENNA.

IBO, African ethnic group of SE Nigeria which numbered about 5 million (in the 1960s). After independence (1963) they came to dominate the civil service and commerce of Nigeria. Hostilities between Ibo and other tribal groups led to the secession of BIAFRA, the Ibo homeland, in 1967. In the civil war which followed, about 2 million Ibos died in battle or from starvation.

IBSEN, Henrik Johan (1828–1906), Norwegian playwright and poet. The pioneer of modern drama, his work developed from national Romanticism (*The Vikings at Helgoland*; 1858) to the realistic and effective presentation of contemporary social problems and moral dilemmas on the stage in such plays as *A Doll's House* (1879), *Ghosts* (1881), *The Wild Duck* (1884), *Hedda Gabler* (1890). Very different, but as important to his philosophy are his verse-dramas *Brand* (1886) and *Peer Gynt* (1867).

ICARIA, Utopian society. See CABET, ÉTIENNE.

ICARUS, in Greek mythology, the son of DAEDALUS. To escape from King MINOS of Crete, he and his father attached wings to their shoulders with wax. Ignoring his father's warning, Icarus flew too close to the sun; the wax melted and he plunged to his death in the sea.

ICARUS, a small ASTEROID about 0.8km across with the shortest "year" and smallest ORBIT of all known asteroids. At perihelion it approaches to within 30Gm of the sun, closer than any other body in the solar system with the exception of some comets.

ICBM, acronym for intercontinental ballistic missile. See MISSILE.

ICE, frozen WATER: a colorless crystalline solid in which the strong, directional HYDROGEN BONDING produces a structure with much space between the molecules. Thus ice is less dense than water, and floats on it. The expansion of water on freezing may crack pipes and automobile radiators. Since dissolved substances lower the freezing point, ANTIFREEZE is used. For the same reason, seawater freezes at about −2°C (see OCEAN). Ice has a very low coefficient of FRICTION, and some fast-moving sports (ICE HOCKEY, ICE SKATING and ICEBOATING) are played on it; however, slippery, icy roads are dangerous. Ice deposited on AIRPLANE wings reduces lift. Ice is used as a refrigerant, and to cool some beverages. (See also

FROST; GLACIER; HAIL; ICE AGES; ICEBERG; ICEBREAKER; SNOW.) mp 0°C, sg 0.92 (0°C).

ICE AGES, periods when glacial ice covers large areas of the earth's surface that are not normally covered by ice. Ice ages are characterized by fluctuations of climatic conditions: a cycle of several glacial periods contains interglacial periods, perhaps of a few tens of thousands of years, when the climate may be as temperate as between ice ages. It is not known whether the earth is currently between ice ages or merely passing through an interglacial period.

There seem to have been several ice ages in the PRECAMBRIAN, and certainly a major one immediately prior to the start of the CAMBRIAN. There were a number in the PALEOZOIC, including a major ice age with a complicated cycle running through the MISSISSIPPIAN, PENNSYLVANIAN and early PERMIAN. The ice age that we know most about, however, is that of the QUATERNARY, continuing through most of the PLEISTOCENE and whose last glacial period ended about 10000 years ago, denoting the start of the HOLOCENE. (See GEOLOGY.) At their greatest, the Pleistocene glaciers covered about a third of the earth's surface, or some 45 million km^2, and may have been up to 3km thick in places. They covered most of Canada, N Europe and N Russia, N parts of what is now the US, and, in the S Hemisphere, Antarctica, parts of South America, and some other areas.

Theories about the cause of ice ages include that the SUN's energy output varies, that the earth moves with respect to its axis, that CONTINENTAL DRIFT may alter global climatic conditions, and that volcanic dust in the ATMOSPHERE could reduce the amount of solar heat received by the surface. (See EARTH; GLACIER; VOLCANO.)

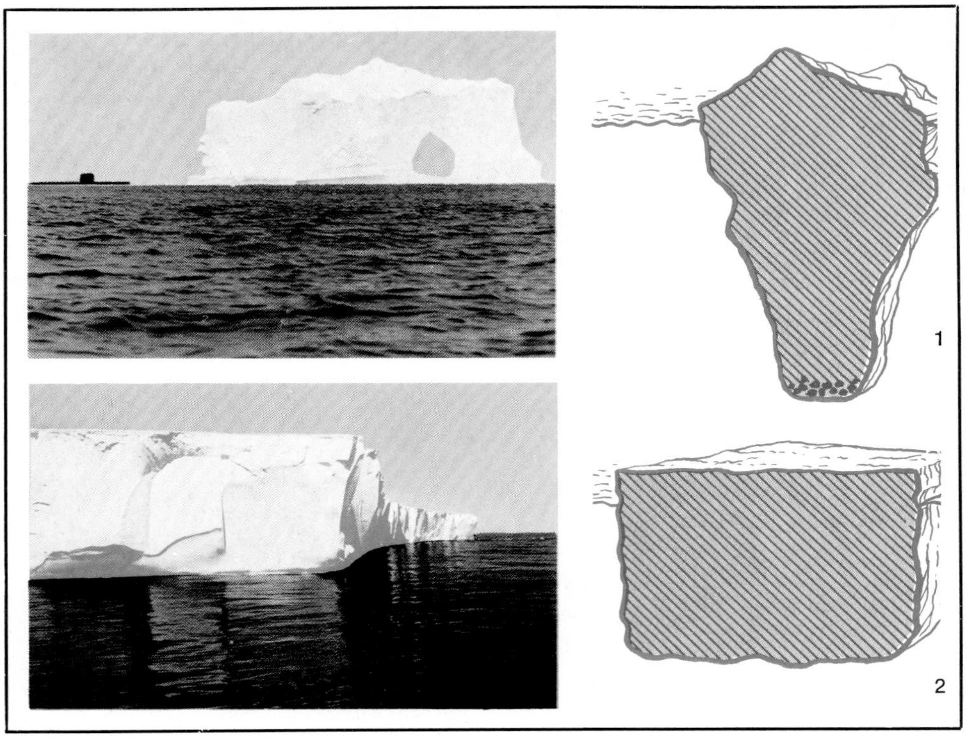

The icebergs of the Arctic and of the Antarctic differ in their general shape. Arctic icebergs (1) calve from a glacier or ice cap along a coastline and have irregular shapes. The icebergs of Antarctica (2), which break off from the ice barrier, are usually rectangular and flat-topped.

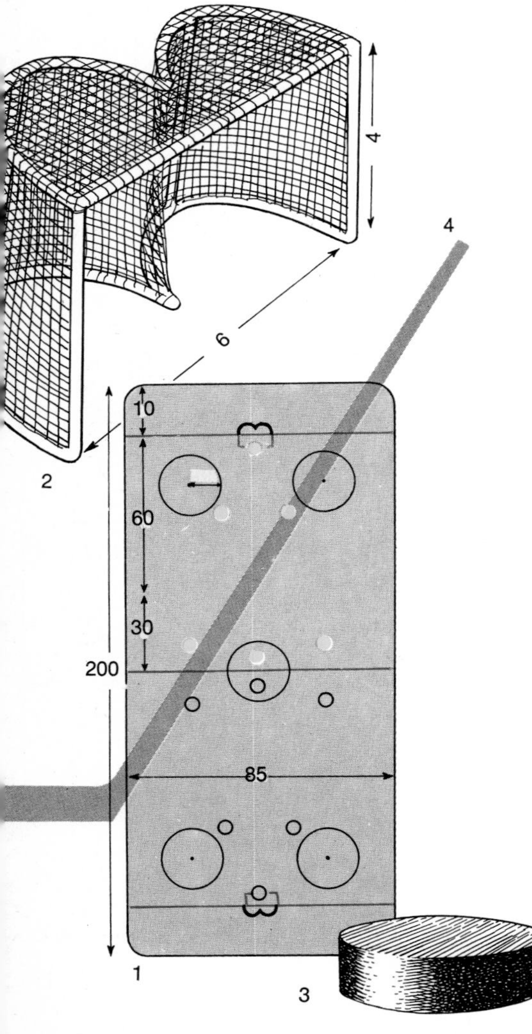

The regulation ice hockey rink (1) is surrounded by a wall about 4ft high and has a cage (2) on each goal line. The puck (3) is 3in across and 1in thick. The stick (4) may not exceed 53in in length. All dimensions in the drawing are given in feet.

ICEBERG, a large, floating mass of ice. In the S Hemisphere, the Antarctic ice sheet overflows its land support to form shelves of ice on the sea; huge pieces, as much as 200km across, break off to form icebergs. In the N Hemisphere, icebergs are generally not over 150m across. Most are "calved" from some 20 GLACIERS on Greenland's W coast. Small icebergs (growlers) may calve from larger ones. Some 75% of the height and over 85% of the mass of an iceberg lies below water. Northern icebergs usually float for some months to the Grand Banks, off Newfoundland, there melting in a few days. They endanger shipping, the most famous tragedy being the sinking of the *Titanic* (1912). The International Ice Patrol now keeps a constant watch on the area.

ICEBOATING, fast winter sport of sailing or racing iceboats. For racing purposes, boats are divided into classes by the amount of sail they carry. Iceboats have been raced at speeds over 100mph. The sport is popular in North America, Canada and N Europe.

ICEBREAKER, a ship designed to break a channel through pack ice by riding up on the ice, which breaks beneath the weight. Characteristics are: one or more powerful propellers at the stern; a very broad beam; a shallow angle of bow and stern; and armorplating to protect against impact from floating ice and resist pressure if the vessel becomes trapped. Most have an extra propeller at the bow so that they can reverse if trapped in ice.

ICECAP. See GLACIER.

ICE CREAM, popular frozen dairy food whose main constituents are sugars, milk products, water, flavorings and air. Ice cream has a high calorific value, and a very high VITAMIN A content, as well as being protein and calcium-rich. It is also a source of, in smaller quantities, iron, phosphorus, riboflavin and THIAMIN. Water ices, which contain no milk products, have been known since ancient times in Europe and Asia. Ice cream probably reached the US in the 17th century, and was first commercially manufactured by Jacob Fussel (1851). Today, the US is the world's largest producer and consumer.

ICEFISHES, antarctic fishes that appear to lack BLOOD, due to the fact that their blood contains no red cells (those which are usually responsible for carrying oxygen). Living in a stable, cold environment, these sluggish fishes seem to manage with the small amounts of oxygen that dissolve in the blood plasma.

ICE HOCKEY, modern version of field hockey played on ice. Two teams of six skaters each attempt to score goals using wooden sticks to hit a hard rubber disk (the puck) into a small cage (the opponent's goal). Ice hockey is an exciting game which places a premium on speed, strength, mobility and stamina. The game originated in Canada, where it is a national sport. Canada and the US provide teams for the North American professional organization, the National Hockey League (NHL). The International Ice Hockey Federation governs amateur groups in North America and Europe. Television has made ice hockey popular. (See also ICE SKATING.)

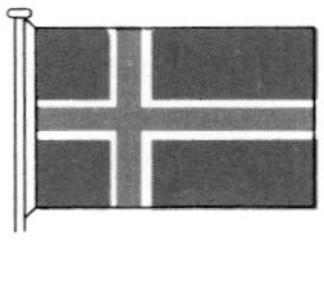

Official name: Republic of Iceland
Capital: Reykjavík
Area: 39758sq mi
Population: 210775
Languages: Icelandic
Religions: Lutheran
Monetary unit(s): 1 Króna = 100 aurar

ICELAND, island republic in the N Atlantic Ocean just touching on the Arctic Circle. Geologically young and volcanic in origin, the island is still being molded by volcanic activity. Surtsey, a new island off the S coast, first emerged from the sea in 1963, and Heimay had to be evacuated when the Helgafell volcano erupted in 1973.

Land. Iceland is mainly a high inland plateau surrounded by mountains: Hvannadalshnjúkur is the highest peak (6 952ft) and Hekla (4 747ft) is the best-known volcano. Large surface areas are covered by cooled laval flows and there are many glaciers, eroded valleys and fjords. Numerous geysers and hot springs are used for central heating and irrigation. The climate is cool and temperate, and the weather very changeable. Temperatures at Reykjavík average 30°F in Jan. and 52°F in July; rainfall averages 34in yearly at Reykjavík, but is heavier in the SE. Vegetation is mainly mosses, lichens and occasional small trees and shrubs, with some coastal grassland. Soils are thin.

People. The rapidly increasing population of Iceland lives mainly in small towns along the coast, in N valleys and the SE lowlands. The largest town is Reykjavík, the capital, chief port and cultural center. Icelanders are a homogeneous mixture of Nordic and Celtic racial stock. Their language, ICELANDIC, developed from Old Norse, and has changed little over the centuries. Iceland has a rich literary tradition of heroic medieval sagas and bardic poems which can be and are still read by the people today. Education is free and compulsory from age 7 to 15; illiteracy is practically nonexistent.

Economy. Fishing (especially cod, haddock and herring) and fish-processing are the mainstay industries and provide more than 90% of Iceland's exports. A long dispute with Great Britain over fishing rights in the North Sea led to a ruling in Great Britain's favor by the International Court of Justice (1974). This was rejected by Iceland, which plans to extend its "economic" sea limits to 200mi; an interim agreement between the two countries was in operation. There is some small scale agriculture (cattle, sheep, potatoes, turnips) and manufacturing (fertilizer, appliances, food, clothing and books). Iceland has vast resources of natural energy in her rivers, hot streams and geysers as well as important volcanic mineral potential. These natural resources are only beginning to be exploited for industrial and commercial purposes.

History. Discovered by Norsemen c870 AD, Iceland was under Norwegian rule from 1262, and under the Danes from 1380. The tradition of democratic government dates from 930 AD when the Althing, the world's oldest parliament, was established. Iceland was entirely self-governing from 1918, and became a fully independent republic in 1944.

ICELANDIC, the official language of Iceland, developed from Old Norse, which was brought to Iceland from W Norway in the 9th and 10th centuries. Although pronunciation and spelling have changed, the old grammatical structure has remained. Icelanders are still able to read their medieval literature and the SAGAS.

ICELAND MOSS, a brownish LICHEN 80 to 100mm (3 to 4in) high which grows in most of the alpine areas of the N Hemisphere, including parts of the Rockies, Appalachians and on the lava slopes and plains of Iceland. Iceland moss has been used to prepare a brown dye and as a source of a starchy food.

ICELAND SPAR. See CALCITE.

ICE PATROL, International. See ICEBERG.

ICE PLANTS, name generally applied to plants of the genus *Mesembryanthemum*, family Aizoaceae, and other leaf SUCCULENTS. Also, specifically *Mesembryanthemum crystallinum* which has glistening leaves and colorful daisy-like flowers.

ICE SKATING, movement over ice on steel blades fastened to shoe soles; a popular sport in Canada, the US and N Europe. Originally confined to frozen lakes and rivers, the sport has been widely popularized by the introduction of artificial ice rinks. Skating is not difficult, but it takes many years to become a skilled professional. Competitive ice skating is divided into figure skating and speed skating. Figure skating is really ballet on skates, demanding great body control and a feel for music. Speed skating demands strength, stamina and fitness. The first US skating club was formed in Philadelphia (1849), but only in the last 50 years has the sport achieved national and international popularity. (See also ICE HOCKEY.)

15th-century Russian icon of the Annunciation. Mary (right) spins silk for the cloth in the background which links earth and heaven (the tower behind Gabriel, left), so symbolizing Christ.

ICHIKAWA, industrial city and residential suburb of Tokyo, Japan. It produces food, leather, chemicals, metals and machine tools. Pop 261 055.

I CHING, or Book of Changes, ancient Chinese literary classic dating to c12th century BC. It consists of a set of symbols and texts for DIVINATION. There has been a revival of interest in the *I Ching* in recent years.

ICHINOMIYA, industrial town, SE Honshu, Japan. Developed from a 7th-century Shinto shrine, the town now manufactures textiles. Pop 219 274.

ICHNEUMON (*Herpestes ichneumon*), the name commonly used for a species of MONGOOSE also called the Egyptian mongoose, or Pharaoh's cat.

ICHNEUMON FLIES, parasitic wasps, members of the HYMENOPTERA, possessing a long spinelike ovipositor. They use this like a hypodermic SYRINGE in order to lay eggs inside or close to the bodies of their hosts—usually the larvae of other insects. They are very specific in the species they attack. The larva grows rapidly inside the host until it emerges from the shell of the grub or caterpillar, by that time completely consumed.

ICHTHYOLOGY (from Greek *ichthys*, fish, and *logos*, knowledge), the study of fishes. The word was first used in 1646, respectively 60 and 120 years before the study of birds and insects achieved similar scientific recognition.

ICHTHYORNIS, the earliest known type of fossil nontoothed bird. In the fossil record there is a long gap, 65m years, between the toothed ARCHAEOPTERYX, the first bird, and *Ichthyornis*, the first to display typically modern features.

ICHTHYOSAURS, extinct marine reptiles of the Jurassic and Cretaceous. Almost certainly bearing their young live, they were fish-like reptiles with a beaked snout, triangular dorsal fin, and a truly fishlike tail. Ichthyosaurs ranged from 0.3–10m (1–33ft) in length.

ICHTHYOSTEGA, a fossil amphibian of the Upper Devonian. The earliest tetrapods known, they bear many amphibian characteristics, but also retain many features reflecting their recent fish ancestry.

ICKES, Harold LeClair (1874–1952), US government official, secretary of the interior, 1933–46, and head of the Public Works Administration 1933–39. An able and responsible administrator, he was a central figure in Roosevelt's NEW DEAL.

ICON, from the Greek for image, a term used for religious images venerated in the Eastern and Russian Orthodox Churches. They also play an important part in liturgy. The Virgin Mary and Jesus were traditional icon figures; by the 7th century icon worship was an officially encouraged cult in the Byzantine Christian Church. (See BYZANTINE ART.)

ICONOCLASTIC CONTROVERSY, Christian dispute over the popular use of ICONS within the Eastern Orthodox (Byzantine) Church. With public support from Emperor Leo III (726 AD), the iconoclasts (Greek for "image breakers") prevailed, resulting in destruction of works of art and persecution of icon worshipers for idolatry and heresy. Icon veneration was officially restored in 843 AD, an event still celebrated in the Eastern Church as the Feast of Orthodoxy. (See also BYZANTINE ART.)

ICONOGRAPHY, visual representation of subjects in symbols or symbolic images, for example in early or medieval Christian art and ancient Egyptian, Greek or Aztec art. Description and analysis of iconographic imagery, symbolic relationships and meanings is a major task of modern art historians.

ICONOSCOPE, early form of TELEVISION camera tube which converts an optical image into an electrical signal. An ELECTRON beam scans a mosaic of photoemissive particles which become electrically charged depending on the amount of incident LIGHT; a signal plate produces an electric signal corresponding to this charge pattern.

ICOSAHEDRON. See POLYHEDRON.

ICTINUS (5th century BC), one of the great Greek architects of the Age of PERICLES, famous for his work on the Parthenon in Athens, the Temple of the Mysteries at Eleusis (c430 BC) and the Temple of Apollo Epicurius at Bassae. (See GREEK ART AND ARCHITECTURE; PARTHENON.)

ID, the formless collection of all parts of the mind present at birth, part of which develops to form the EGO. The id thus contains such parts of the psychic makeup as EMOTIONS and INSTINCTS. (See also PSYCHOANALYSIS; UNCONSCIOUS.)

IDA, Mount, classical name of highest mountain (8 058ft) in Crete where, according to Greek mythology, the god Zeus was reared. Also the classical name of a mountain range in NW Asia Minor near the ancient city of Troy. From Ida's highest peak the Greek gods were said to have watched the Trojan War.

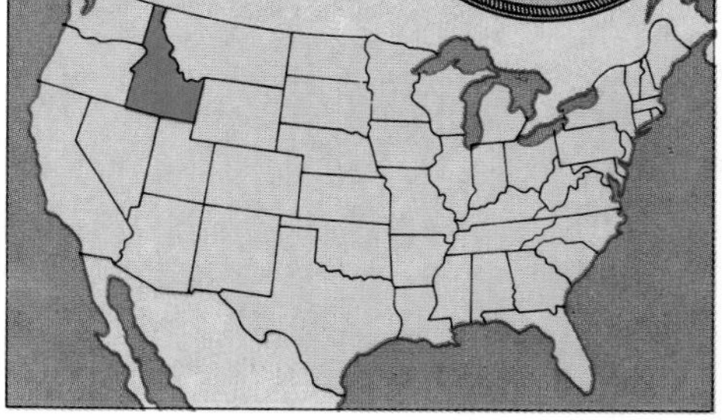

Name of state: Idaho
Capital: Boise
Statehood: July 3, 1890 (43rd state)
Familiar name: Gem State
Area: 83 557sq mi
Population: 713 008
Elevation: Highest—12 662ft., Borah Peak. Lowest—710ft, Snake River at Lewiston
Motto: Esto Perpetua (It is Forever)
State flower: Syringa (mock orange)
State bird: Mountain bluebird
State tree: Western white pine
State song: "Here We have Idaho"

IDAHO, smallest Rocky Mt state, with 83 557sq mi of some of the most rugged, unspoiled wilderness in the US.

Land. Idaho is bounded on the N by British Columbia (Canada), NE by Mont., E by Wyo., S by Ut. and Nev. and W by Ore. and Wash. The N border is only 45mi long; the S 300mi. There are 81 mountain ranges (highest peak is Mt Borah, 12 662ft), over 2 000 lakes and 10 major rivers, including the Clearwater, Salmon and Snake (a tributary of the Columbia R), which flows across the entire southern part of the state. The climate is widely varied with dry heat in the S, cold in the snow-laden Rockies and warm moist air from the Pacific in the N. Average July temperatures are 75°F–70°F; average Jan. temperatures are 30°F–16°F. Snowfall ranges from 14in (SW) to more than 200in (in the mountains). Rain varies from below 10in in the Snake R plains to 30in in the Panhandle. Evergreen forests cover two-fifths of Idaho. Wildlife is abundant, and includes elk, antelope, black bear, beaver, muskrat, game and other birds and fish.

People. Population density is the lowest in the US; 70% of all Idahoans live within about 30mi of the Snake R in the fertile agricultural areas. The people are about 98% native-born Americans with about 1% non-Caucasian residents; about 6 000 descendants of French and Spanish Basques live in metropolitan Boise. Some 100 local school districts provide free public elementary and secondary education. The U. of Idaho (at Moscow), Idaho State U. (at Pocatello), and the Mormon Ricks College (at Rexburg) are among institutions of higher education.

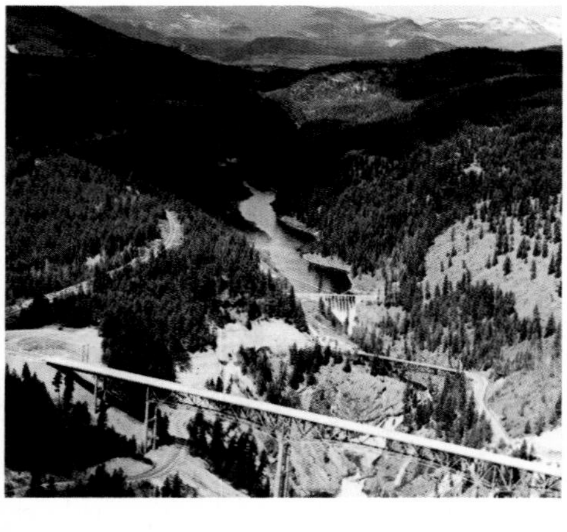

Bridges and a dam on the Moyie River in the north of Idaho, part of the state's extensive hydroelectric and irrigation system, for which the rugged and unspoiled northern country is ideal.

Economy. Farming (Idaho potatoes are famous), tourism, mining (silver, lead, gold, zinc, copper and phosphates), livestock raising, manufacturing (especially food processing) and lumbering are the state's chief sources of wealth. Tourism will probably overtake agriculture as the prime income-producing industry. Sun Valley is a famous vacation resort; other attractions include Hells Canyon (a 40mi-long gorge in the Snake R), Craters of the Moon National Monument, fish and game reserves and designated "wilderness" areas. The state has vast water resources: huge dams on the rivers provide hydroelectric power and water for irrigation. After WWII the US Atomic Energy Commission built a nuclear testing and research station in the E Snake R area.

History. Before 1800 Idaho was inhabited by American Indians. The LEWIS AND CLARK expedition crossed the area in 1805. Fur traders and missionaries arrived in the next few decades. Discovery of gold (1860) brought a rush of prospectors followed by lumbermen, farmers and ranchers. Idaho became a territory (with today's Wyo. and Mont.) in 1863; the territorial area was slowly reduced to present-day boundaries, and in 1890 Idaho became the Union's 43rd state.

IDAHO FALLS, city in SE Ida., seat of Bonneville Co., 50mi NNE of Pocatello. A shipping and agricultural center on the Snake R. Pop 35 776.

IDEA, in psychology, a loosely defined term describing any conscious (see CONSCIOUSNESS) mental event that is not stimulated by immediate PERCEPTION (e.g., a MEMORY). Some psychologists hold that idea-forming is present in perception also; e.g., when bread has just been baked, one smells an aroma and recognizes from experience that it is the aroma of new-baked bread, rather than sensing the bread directly. Others, particularly behaviorists (see BEHAVIORISM), hold that ideas do not exist but are merely reflections of other mental processes.

IDEALISM, name adopted by several schools of philosophy, all of which in some way assert the primacy of ideas, either as the sole authentic stuff of reality or as the only medium through which we can have knowledge or experience of the world. Idealisms are commonly contrasted both with the various types of REALISM and with philosophical MATERIALISM. They are often associated with methodological RATIONALISM because they usually seem to owe more to reasoning upon A PRIORI principles than to any appeal to experience. The idealism of PLATO, in which ideas were held to have an external objectivity, is unrepresentative of modern varieties, of which that of BERKELEY is archetypal. KANT and HEGEL were foremost in the German idealist tradition, while T. H. GREEN, F. H. Bradley and J. ROYCE were representative of more recent English-speaking idealists. Idealism has, however, been in eclipse in the 20th century.

IDENTIFICATION, in PSYCHOLOGY, the process of recognizing a specific MEMORY. In PSYCHOANALYSIS, the fusion of one's IDENTITY with another's either through inability to recognize one's own identity (a state common in infancy), or as a DEFENSE MECHANISM or reaction despite recognition of one's own identity.

IDENTITY, in mathematics. See ALGEBRA.

IDENTITY, or personal identity, in psychology, the individual's sense of being a distinct, continuous entity; roughly corresponding to self-awareness (see CONSCIOUSNESS). (See also EGO.)

IDEOGRAM, a written symbol which directly conveys an idea or represents a thing, rather than representing a spoken word, phrase or letter. **Logograms**, symbols that each represent an entire word, are also often called ideograms. Egyptian HIEROGLYPHICS comprised a writing system partly ideogramic, partly logogrammatic and partly phonetic. (See also WRITING, HISTORY OF.)

IDES OF MARCH, 15th day of Mar. in the ancient Roman calendar, and the day on which Julius CAESAR was assassinated in the Senate; thereafter known as an *ater dies*, black day, and hence unlucky. In the Roman calendar, the 15th of Mar., May, July or Oct. and the 13th of the other months were called the ides.

IDIOM, language, or often a popular ungrammatical phrase that cannot be literally translated, which is peculiar to a people, or an area, as in the American phrase for a deferred event, reward or payment, "take a rain check."

IDOLATRY, worship of an image or idol believed to represent a supernatural power or deity, or of a person, animal or object believed to be a god's abode. A widespread religious practice from ancient times to the present; Muslims, Jews and early Christians abjured image worship.

IDRIS I (1890–   ), king of Libya, 1951–69; chief of the powerful Muslim brotherhood, Sanusi. From Egyptian exile (1923–49), he led the struggle against the Italian occupation, and became king when Libya gained independence. He was deposed when a military junta proclaimed the Libyan Arab Republic.

IDUMAEA. See EDOM.

IDYLL, short descriptive or narrative poem, often pastoral. Popular in ancient Greece, the term was used by Tennyson for his series of poems on King Arthur, *Idylls of the King* (1859–89), but is not a definite literary form.

IEYASU TOKUGAWA (1542–1616), Japanese feudal baron (daimyo) who played a major part in the reunification of Japan during its turbulent 16th century. He founded the Tokugawa shogunate (military government) which lasted from 1603–1867 and established its center at Edo (Tokyo).

IFE, town in Western State, SW Nigeria, 54mi E of Ibadan. Formerly the capital of the YORUBA kingdom which flourished from the 12th to the 17th century. Pop 159 197.

IFNI, district of SW Morocco, 740sq mi on the Atlantic coast; a Spanish African province, 1964–69. Raising sheep, goats and camels and fishing are the prime occupations of Ifni's Berber peoples.

IGLOO, temporary winter Eskimo hut built of snow blocks, averaging 10ft in diameter, with a rounded roof and fur-lined floor below the snow line. Prefabricated houses are gradually replacing the traditional Eskimo igloos.

IGNATIUS, Loyola, Saint. See LOYOLA, SAINT IGNATIUS.

IGNATIUS OF ANTIOCH, Saint (d. c100 AD), Christian bishop of Antioch, condemned to death in TRAJAN's reign. Ignatius wrote seven letters (now precious early church documents) in which "catholic church" was first used to denote Christians everywhere and in which he tried to prove that Docetism, a doctrine which held that Christ's bodily sufferings were only "appearance," was heresy.

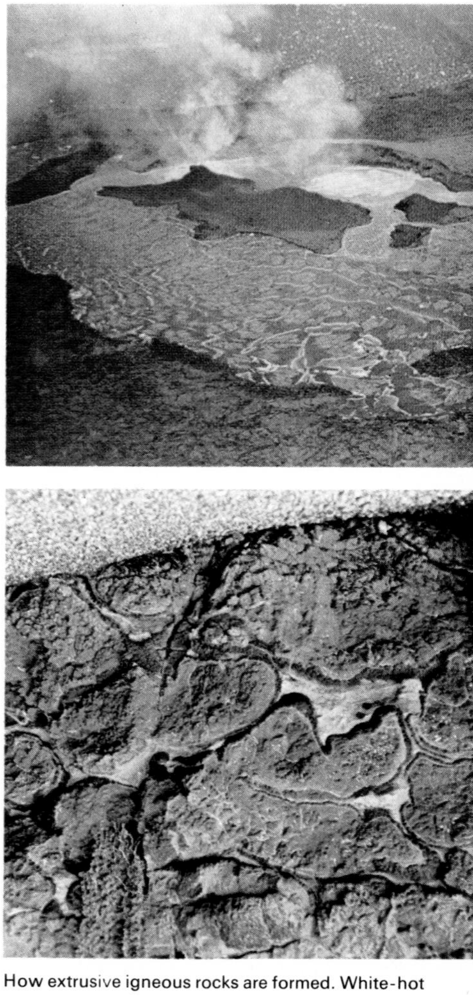

How extrusive igneous rocks are formed. White-hot magma (molten rock) is extruded from the lower depths of the Earth's crust by a volcano (*top*) and spreads over existing ground. It cools rapidly, becoming increasingly viscous and finally solidifies (*bottom*) into curving flow patterns.

IGNEOUS ROCKS, one of the three main types of rocks, those whose origin is related to heat. They crystallize from the MAGMA either at the earth's surface (extrusion) or beneath (intrusion). There are two main classes: **Volcanic rocks** are extruded (see VOLCANISM), typical examples being LAVA and PYROCLASTIC ROCKS. **Plutonic rocks** are intruded into the rocks of the EARTH's crust at depth, a typical example being GRANITE: those forming near to the surface are sometimes called **hypabyssal rocks**. Types of intrusions include BATHOLITHS, DIKES, SILLS and LACCOLITHS. As plutonic rocks cool more slowly than volcanic, they have a coarser texture, more time being allowed for crystal formation. (See also ROCKS.)

IGNIS FATUUS. See WILL-O'-THE-WISP.

IGNITION SYSTEM, the system in an INTERNAL-COMBUSTION ENGINE for igniting the fuel/air mixture In the DIESEL ENGINE the heat generated by the compression stroke is enough to ignite the fuel when it is sprayed in. In gasoline engines ignition is produced by the SPARK PLUGS whose operation is timed by the DISTRIBUTOR. The high electrical POTENTIAL is provided in automobiles by an INDUCTION COIL working off the BATTERY, and in light engines such as aircraft engines by a MAGNETO. The current in the coil's primary winding charges a CAPACITOR, without which an electric arc would burn out the breaker points when the MAGNETIC FIELD collapses. High-performance engines use TRANSISTORS to switch the current very rapidly.

IGNITRON, gas tube RECTIFIER which controls a wide range of currents, used in resistance WELDING. Current passes as an arc between the single ANODE and an electron-emitting spot formed on the surface of a MERCURY pool by a current pulse through an ignitor ELECTRODE dipping in it.

IGOR (1151–1202), Russian prince. He led a disastrous expedition into the Don steppes to try to keep the Polovtskys (CUMANS) from marauding in S and W Russia; described in the famous Russian epic poem *Tale of the Host of Igor* (c1187) and BORODIN's opera.

IGOROT, primitive people from the mountain area of northern Luzon island, Philippines; formerly head-hunting warriors. They are a varying racial mixture of Indonesian, Malay and Negrito.

IGUANAS, the largest and most elaborately marked lizards of the New World. The family (Iguanidae) includes insectivorous, carnivorous and herbivorous forms. Many species are territorial. Iguanas characteristically show ornamental scales and a dorsal fringe, and bear tubercles on the head and body. Some species have an erectile throat fan. There are two major groups: Ground iguanas and Green iguanas. All species are hunted for food, although this is greatly depleting their numbers.

IGUANODON, an enormous herbivorous DINOSAUR of the Upper Jurassic to Lower Cretaceous. Bipedal animals, iguanodons could reach 10m (33ft) in length.

IGUASSU FALLS, also Iguaçu Falls, a series of over 20 cataracts, on the Rio Iguaçu at the Brazil-Argentina border, about 16mi above the confluence of the Iguaçu and Paraná rivers. The falls (c200ft high and 2½mi wide) are a major tourist attraction.

IHS, Christian monogram derived from the first three Greek letters for the name Jesus, but later often taken to be an abbreviation for such Latin phrases as *Jesus Hominum Salvator* (Jesus, Savior of Men).

IJSSELMEER, Dutch freshwater lake formed by building a dam 19mi long across the northern part of the old Zuider Zee (completed 1932).

IKHNATON. See AKHENATON.

ÎLE-DE-FRANCE, historic name for the limestone plains area of the Paris basin, N central France—between the Oise, Aisne, Marne and Seine rivers—the traditional political power center of France.

ILEITIS, INFLAMMATION of the ileum, part of small intestine (see ENTERITIS; GASTROINTESTINAL TRACT).

ILESHA, Yoruba tribal city, Western State, SE Nigeria, 60mi NE of Ibadan. Pop 200 434.

ILEUM. See GASTROINTESTINAL TRACT.

ILF, ILYAO ARNOLDOVICH (1897–1937), real name, Ilyao Faynzilberg, Russian satirical writer and humorist who collaborated with Yevgeny PETROV on *The Twelve Chairs* (1928), *The Little Golden Calf* (1931) and *One-Storyed America* (1936).

ILIAD, ancient Greek epic poem of 24 books in hexameter verse, attributed to HOMER; internal references suggest it was composed in the mid-8th century BC. It describes a quarrel during the siege of Troy between the Greek warrior-hero Achilles and King Agamemnon which results in Achilles' brutal slaying of Hector, the Trojan warrior-prince. A companion to the ODYSSEY, the *Iliad* is one of the world's great tragic works of literature.

IL-KHANS, dynasty of Mongol origin founded by Hulagu, grandson of Genghis Khan, who took the title il-khan (il = provincial). Under their rule (1256–1353) Persia and Iraq flourished and were open to Far Eastern and Christian influences. (See ABBASIDS.)

ILLEGITIMACY, status of a child born of unmarried parents and thus not recognized as a lawful offspring. Laws and customs almost universally condemn birth outside some form of marriage, but social and legal censure varies widely according to time and place.

ILLIMANI, snow-capped Bolivian mountain (21201ft high) in the Cordillera Real, Andes Mts, 25mi SE of La Paz, the capital.

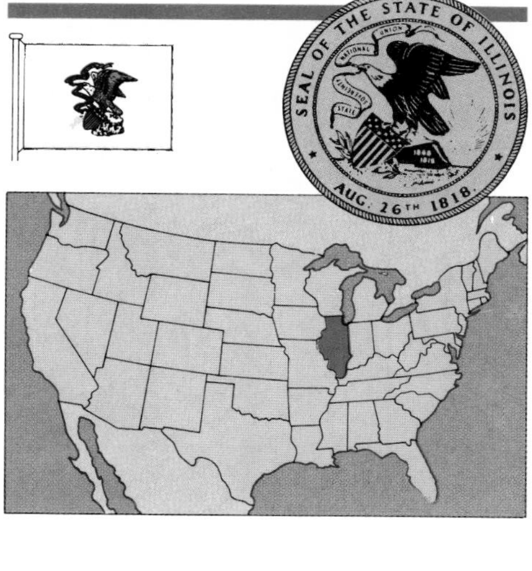

Name of state: Illinois
Capital: Springfield
Statehood: Dec. 3, 1818 (21st state)
Familiar name: Land of Lincoln, Prairie State
Area: 56 400sq mi
Population: 11 113 976
Elevation: Highest—1 241ft, Charles Mound. Lowest—269ft, Mississippi River at Cairo
Motto: State Sovereignty, National Union
State flower: Native violet
State bird: Cardinal
State tree: Oak
State song: "Illinois"

ILLINOIS, N central industrial and agricultural state, the heartland of US transportation with a vast network of railroads, highways, airways, lake and river routes. CHICAGO, its largest city, is the crossroads of America.

Land. Illinois is approximately 382mi long by 212mi wide. It is bounded in the N by Wis., in the E by its 60mi shoreline on Lake Michigan, Ind., and the Wabash R, in the SE by the Ohio R and Ken. and in the SW and W by Mo., Ia., and the Mississippi R. Flat prairies and fertile deep black soil plains cover the central and northern areas with rolling hills in the NW. Some 4 million acres of forest exist in the S, mostly in Shawnee National Forest. The climate is temperate with summers averaging 70°F (in the S) and 77°F (in the N); cold, snowy winters average 22°F (in the N) and 37°F (in the S). Rainfall averages 32–48in (N) and 48–64in (S).

Plant life is varied, with N and S tree varieties ranging from oak, white pine and hickory to cypress and tupelo gum. The state has large numbers of waterfowl, game birds, small animals and fish. Wild deer, nearly extinct by 1910, are increasing in numbers on game reserves.

People and Economy. The people are racially diversified: the first wave of settlers moved into the Ohio R valley from the E and S. They pushed the local Indians (after whom the state is named) westward by the 1820s. Since the Civil War the state has had a steady influx of blacks, primarily from the South, seeking work in industrial areas. By 1910 thousands of European immigrants had arrived, among them Germans, Austrians, Hungarians, Russians, Scandinavians, Irish and Italians.

Regionalism has always been a characteristic of Illinois; the population is divided in outlook and political attitudes between the metropolitan Chicago area and "downstate" (the smaller cities and rural areas towards the S). Four-fifths of the state's people live in urban areas; about one-third of the labor force is employed in manufacturing industries, based mainly in the Chicago area and in the East St. Louis area. A leading agricultural state, its chief products are corn, hogs, cattle and soybeans. Industry is exceptionally varied, manufacturing steel, iron, heavy machinery and household goods, producing petroleum and its byproducts; its printing, publishing and meat packing and food industries are among the largest in the US.

There is a large system of free public schools; over 100 institutions of higher learning include Northwestern U., the U. of Illinois, U. of Chicago and Illinois Institute of Technology. Unofficially named "the Land of Lincoln," the state's many tourist attractions include Abraham Lincoln's home and tomb in Springfield and a reconstruction of his earlier home in New Salem.

History. The state was first explored by JOLIET and MARQUETTE (1673) and by LASALLE (1680). By treaty, the British took the area from the French after the French and Indian Wars (1763); following the American Revolution, Illinois became part of the NORTHWEST TERRITORY (1787). In 1818 Illinois was admitted to the Union as a state. The people split over the question of states' rights and slavery at the time of the Civil War. After the war, construction of railroads aided industrial expansion. Through the later part of the 19th and early 20th centuries, Illinois was the scene of labor unrest and bitter strikes, but the result was that the state became a leader in social welfare legislation and progressive labor-employer relations. Following the 1930s depression, industrialization in "downstate" Illinois accelerated enormously and the population has grown rapidly with increasing work opportunities.

ILLINOIS INDIANS, a tribal confederation of American Indians belonging to the ALGONQUIAN linguistic group and related to Ojibwas and Miamis. Their territory originally included Ill. and parts of Ia., Wis. and Mo. After tribal wars with the IROQUOIS and other northern Indians, the few survivors moved to Kan. (1832) and later to an Okla. reservation (1867).

ILLINOIS WATERWAY, major waterway in NE Ill. linking Lake Michigan with the Mississippi R. at Grafton, Ill. It is a heavily-used bargeway consisting of the Chicago R. (its flow reversed), the canalized Des Plaines and Illinois rivers and a canal, 327mi in all.

ILLITERACY, the inability to read and write simple messages, in any language. The idea of "functional illiteracy" has spread with recognition that people need a useful working ability to read, write and do simple arithmetic in modern society. Historically, until the invention of printing, most people were illiterate. Today around 35% of the world's adults over age 15 are illiterate, the largest proportion in Africa and Asia, but ADULT EDUCATION and increasing elementary schooling are helping to decrease illiteracy

ILLUMINATI, a Latin term meaning "enlightened ones." Many varied groups and societies have claimed enlightened knowledge because of divine or supernatural power or the liberation of natural human reason. Followers of GNOSTICISM, ENLIGHTENMENT philosophers and ROSICRUCIANS are examples of illuminati.

ILLUMINATION, Manuscript, the decoration of a handwritten text with ornamental designs, letters and paintings, often using silver and gold leaf. Illumination flourished between the 5th and 16th centuries AD. The art was highly developed in the Near East, the Orient and in Christian Europe where monks and

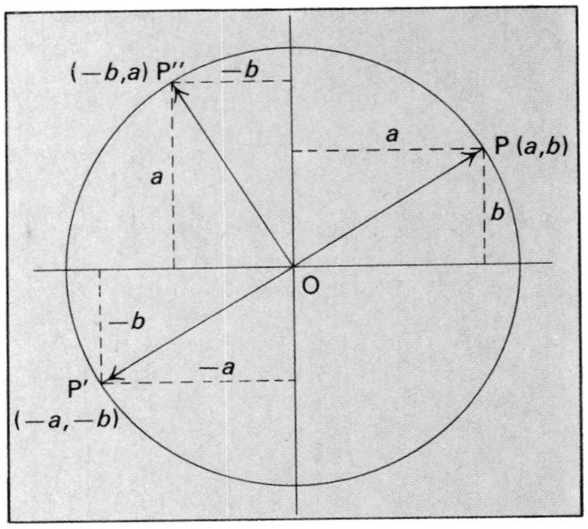

The imaginary operator j rotates the vector **OP** into **OP″**, and—on a second application—rotates **OP″** into **OP′**. In matrix notation, $\begin{pmatrix} 0 & -1 \\ 1 & 0 \end{pmatrix}\begin{pmatrix} a \\ b \end{pmatrix} = \begin{pmatrix} b \\ a \end{pmatrix}$. Thus

$$j^2 = \begin{pmatrix} 0 & -1 \\ 1 & 0 \end{pmatrix}\begin{pmatrix} 0 & -1 \\ 1 & 0 \end{pmatrix} = \begin{pmatrix} -1 & 0 \\ 0 & -1 \end{pmatrix} = -1$$

others skilled in CALLIGRAPHY and painting often devoted their lifetimes to embellishing manuscripts of all kinds, particularly religious. Among the most celebrated manuscripts are the Irish BOOK OF KELLS, the Carolingian *Utrecht Psalter* and the *Très riches heures* commissioned by Jean, duc de Berry from the LIMBOURG brothers.

ILLUSION, an erroneous perception of reality, often the result of misinterpretation by the brain of information received by the SENSES. Most commonly the sense involved is sight: one of the exploitations of optical illusion is the use by artists of PERSPECTIVE. Optical illusions may also have external causes, such as REFRACTION, as in the observation of a stick held in water (see also BROCKEN SPECTER). Examples of auditory illusions include BEATING and the apparent change in pitch of a railroad train's whistle as it passes (see DOPPLER EFFECT). Rather different classes of illusion are HALLUCINATIONS and EIDETIC IMAGES. The unconscious falsification of the MEMORY of a past experience is also termed an illusion.

ILLYRIA, an ancient country in the NW part of the Balkan peninsula. It was settled by the 10th century BC by Illyrians, an Indo-European people, who extended their influence from the Danube R to the Adriatic Sea in modern-day Yugoslavia and Albania. It became the Roman province of Illyricum (168 BC).

ILMENITE, hard, black OXIDE mineral, iron (II) titanium (IV) oxide ($FeTiO_3$), the chief ore of TITANIUM. It occurs widely in IGNEOUS ROCKS, notably in the USSR, Norway, Quebec and Wyo. It crystallizes in the rhombohedral system.

ILOILO, a province of Panay Island, Philippines. Its capital is Iloilo City (pop 209 738) the chief Philippines seaport, and its main crops are rice, sugarcane and tobacco.

ILYUSHIN, Sergei Vladimirovich (1894–   ), leading Russian aircraft designer. He created the famous Stormovik dive-bomber (1939) used in WWII and civil aircraft like the IL-62 jet passenger transport (1962).

IMAGE, Optical, a representation of an object formed in an optical instrument. Although a **virtual image** has no physical existence—light only seems to come from its apparent position—light actually comes to a focus in a **real image** and these can be made visible by using a suitable screen.

IMAGINARY NUMBERS, numbers of the form ai, where a is a REAL NUMBER and i is defined such that $i^2 = -1$. For example, $\sqrt{-16}$ is an imaginary number that can, since $\sqrt{-16} = \sqrt{-1} . \sqrt{16}$, be expressed as $4i$.

Complex numbers are SUMS of real and imaginary numbers, and are usually expressed in the form $a + bi$, *where a* and *b* are real numbers. They are frequently represented by an ARGAND DIAGRAM on a set of CARTESIAN COORDINATES, real components are plotted along the x-axis, imaginary components along the y-axis. Similarly, they may be represented in polar coordinates (see ANALYTIC GEOMETRY) in the form $r(\cos\theta + i \sin\theta)$.

In the FIELD of complex numbers, algebraic operations are carried out roughly as in the field of real numbers. Thus

$$\begin{aligned}(a+ib)+(c+id) &= (a+c)+i(b+d),\\ (a+ib)-(c+id) &= (a-c)+i(b-d),\\ (a+ib)\ .\ (c+id) &= ac+ida+ibc+i^2bd\\ &= i(da+bc)+ac-bd\\ &= (ac-bd)+i(da+bc),\\ \text{and } \frac{(a+ib)}{(c+id)} &= \frac{(a+ib)}{(c+id)} \cdot \frac{(c-id)}{(c-id)}\\ &= \frac{(ac+bd)+i(bc-ad)}{(c^2+d^2)}\\ &= \frac{(ac+bd)}{(c^2+d^2)} + \frac{(bc-ad)}{(c^2+d^2)}\end{aligned}$$

IMAGINARY OPERATOR (i-operator or **j-operator).** Consider a VECTOR **OP** where O is the origin of a set of CARTESIAN COORDINATES and P is the POINT (a, b)—see diagram. Multiplying **OP** by -1 will produce a VECTOR **OP′**; that is, will rotate **OP** through 180° such that **OP′** $= -$**OP.** Now consider a number j such that multiplying **OP** by j produces **OP″**, a vector PERPENDICULAR to **OP.** Multiplying **OP″** by j will produce **OP′**, and so in a sense $j.j$ (or $j^2) = -1$. This j is therefore imaginary, and is called the imaginary operator. The number i such that $i^2 = -1$ is fundamental in complex numbers (see IMAGINARY NUMBERS). (See also VECTOR ANALYSIS.)

IMAGISTS, a group of poets writing in the early 20th century in the US and England who rebelled against the artificiality and sentimentality of much 19th-century poetry. Free, idiomatic verse, unusual rhythms and sharp, clear imagery were characteristics of their work which was influenced by French SYMBOLISM. The movement embraced Ezra POUND, Hilda DOOLITTLE (H.D.), Amy LOWELL, D. H. LAWRENCE and James JOYCE.

IMAGO, a term referring to the adult insect emerging from a pupa in complete METAMORPHOSIS.

IMAM, in Islam, a leader (ABRAHAM is called imam in the Koran). An imam can be a caliph or ruler, a head of state, a spiritual authority (see ISMAILIS) or the official in charge of a mosque who performs religious ceremonies and leads the five daily prayers prescribed in the Koran.

IMHOTEP, ancient Egyptian architect of the Step Pyramid at Saqqara. Chief minister, priest and scribe to Pharaoh ZOSER (3rd millennium BC), Imhotep's fame spread and after his death he became a god of medicine. He is considered the first doctor known to history by name.

IMIDES, organic compounds of general formula R.CO.NH.CO.R′, obtained by reacting an AMIDE with an ACID CHLORIDE, or AMMONIA with an ACID ANHYDRIDE, and used in synthesis.

IMMACULATE CONCEPTION, Roman Catholic dogma, officially defined in 1854, that the Virgin MARY was conceived free from ORIGINAL SIN, owing to a special act of redemptive grace. It implies that Mary was always perfectly sinless.

IMMANENCE, in theology, the active presence of God within every part of the created universe. PANTHEISM holds God's immanence but denies his TRANSCENDENCE. Christianity holds both together.

IMMERSION FOOT, or **trench foot,** disease of the FEET after prolonged immersion in water, due to a combination of vasoconstriction and waterlogging. It usually starts with red, cold and numb feet, which on warming develop through EDEMA and blistering to ulceration and sometimes skin GANGRENE.

IMMIGRATION, the movement of people from one country or area of the world to another to establish a new permanent residence. People become immigrants primarily for economic, political or religious motives. MIGRATIONS in ancient times spread people throughout the world, although they tended to migrate within the same continent; Asians stayed in Asia, Africans stayed in Africa. In the first centuries AD Europe suffered successive waves of barbarian migrations from the N and E. After Columbus discovered the New World, the pattern of immigration changed and Europeans began to leave for other lands. Without modern immigration large habitable areas of the world (the USA, Canada, South America, Australia and New Zealand) would otherwise be underpopulated.

The US has received more diverse immigrant groups than any other country—about 38 million from the 1820s to 1930s, and is thus known as a "melting pot" of the world's nations. Its growth and prosperity were stimulated by great waves of immigrants in the 19th and 20th centuries. Immigration accelerated economic development by providing an abundant labor supply, while for the newcomers, America offered hope of a freer and more prosperous life. After the arrival of the original colonists and of African slaves, who accounted for 20% of the population by 1790, there was an era of "old" and

An 1880 cartoon on immigration by J. Keppler pokes gentle fun at the utopian ideals of the expanding United States in the 19th century; Uncle Sam offers refuge to a string of immigrants from every country and social class, while the demons of war and want gather in the stormclouds over Europe.

then "new" immigration. In the "old" era from 1820 to 1880 the population multiplied more than five times with the arrival of peoples from N and W Europe. In the "new" period (1880–1921) immigrants came primarily from S and E Europe.

Until WWI the US maintained more or less an open-door policy towards immigrants, but social and economic conflicts between various ethnic groups and between the older and newer immigrants led to a major policy reversal. Restrictions were placed on Chinese and Japanese and other so-called "undesirables" before WWI (see KNOW-NOTHING PARTY; GENTLEMENS AGREEMENT). In 1917 a literacy test was made compulsory for all immigrants. In 1921 and 1924 quotas were fixed which favoured immigration from N Europe, especially the UK, but which imposed an overall limit of 150000 European immigrants a year. In 1952 the MCCARRAN-WALTER ACT banned communists and other subversives, removed racial exclusions, and strengthened the quota system's ethnic and national system. A 1965 act abolished the quotas discriminating between nationalities. The criteria became professional qualifications and skills and kinship with US citizens or resident aliens. Provision, too, was made for political refugees.

Immigration elsewhere in the world has had different patterns. South America received large numbers of immigrants before the 1930s. Portuguese, Germans, Swiss, Italians and Japanese went to Brazil. The Spanish migrated to Argentina and other parts of Latin America. Since WWII an entirely new phase of immigration has taken place within Europe itself. West Indians, Asian Indians and Pakistanis have settled in the UK claiming their rights as members of the COMMONWEALTH. Since 1962, the British government has introduced new laws reducing this trend. W and N Europe have admitted large numbers of immigrants from the less developed parts of S Europe. The COMMON MARKET (EEC) requires all its member countries to allow free movement of labor across their borders. (See also EMIGRATION.)

IMMIGRATION AND NATURALIZATION SERVICE, substantially independent branch of the US Justice Department which controls entry of aliens and oversees their presence in the US. It is responsible for enforcing federal immigration, naturalization, exclusion and deportation laws.

IMMORTALITY, the life of the soul after death. This belief is found in both primitive and advanced cultures. It was important in Greek philosophy, notably that of PLATO. Immortality is a fundamental tenet of Christianity and of Islam and is generally accepted in Judaism. Their doctrines of eternal life include the RESURRECTION of the body. Hinduism, Buddhism and Jainism do not recognize individual immortality but believe souls can reach an immortal state or NIRVANA. (See also ESCHATOLOGY; HEAVEN; HELL; SPIRITUALISM.)

IMMUNITY, the system of defense in the body which gives protection against foreign materials, specifically infectious microorganisms—BACTERIA, VIRUSES, PARASITES and their products. For many DISEASES, prior exposure to the causative organism in disease itself or by VACCINATION provides acquired resistance to that organism; further infection with it is unlikely or will be less severe. This type of immunity is usually mediated by ANTIBODY AND ANTIGEN reactions and is known as **humoral immunity**. The antigens of microorganisms provoke the formation of the antibody specific to that antigen. Once formed the antibody tends to neutralize (viruses) or to bind to antigen encouraging phagocytosis and destruction (bacteria). In some diseases the development of antibodies is of value in the phase of recovery from the primary infection; once immunity has been thus primed, the easy and rapid availability of antibody protects against further infection. ALLERGY and ANAPHYLAXIS are also largely mediated by humoral immunity. A number of diseases are due to the systemic effects of **immune complexes** (antibody linked to antigen) which may arise in the appropriate response to an infection, or in serum sickness, and these especially affect the KIDNEYS, SKIN and JOINTS. In **autoimmunity** antibodies are produced to antigens of the body's own tissues for reasons that are not always clear; secondary tissue destruction may occur. The second major type of immunity is **cell-mediated immunity** (delayed type hypersensitivity); this system is mediated by lymphocytes and monocytes (including tissue macrophages). It is a reaction only occurring with certain types of infection (TUBERCULOSIS, HISTOPLASMOSIS and FUNGAL DISEASES) and in certain probable auto-immune diseases; it is also important in the immunity of TRANSPLANTS. Lymphocytes are primed by infection with the appropriate organisms or by the autoimmune or graft reaction and produce substances which affect both lymphocytes and monocytes and result in a type of INFLAMMATION with much tissue damage. The understanding of the role of immunity and its disorders in the causation and manifestations of many diseases has seen a substantial advance in recent years. This has led to the development of DRUGS and other agents which are able to interfere with abnormal or destructive immune responses. **Immune deficiency diseases**, although rare, have provided models for the separate parts of the immune system, and have led to methods of replacement of absent components of immunity. **Passive immunity** is the transfer of antibody-rich substances from an immune subject to a nonimmune subject who is susceptible to disease. It is important in infancy, where maternal antibodies protect the child until its own immune responses have matured. In certain diseases such as TETANUS and RABIES, immune serum gives valuable immediate passive protection in nonimmune subjects.

IMMUNITY, legal freedom from criminal or civil liability by reason of special status. Legislators, diplomats and heads of state have varying degrees of immunity from legal process. Criminal case witnesses are often given immunity when they testify for the state. Governments have various kinds of immunity from prosecution. (See also PRIVILEGE.)

IMPALA, *Aepyceros melampus*, one of the most abundant African antelopes. They are about 1m (39in) high and red-brown in color; males have long, black, lyre-shaped horns. Animals of the woodland edge, impala live in big herds in the dry season, breaking up into single male harems in the wetter months for breeding. Impala herds often associate with BABOONS for protection against predators.

IMPEACHMENT, a formal accusation of a crime or other serious misconduct brought against a public official by a legislature. The term sometimes includes the trial by the legislature which follows. Impeachment began in England as a way of putting officials on trial who were derelict in their duties. The impeachment of Warren HASTINGS (1785–95) was a famous English case. Under US constitutional procedure the House of Representatives has the power to impeach; the Senate tries the impeached officials. Grounds for impeachment are: "Treason, Bribery or other high Crimes and Misdemeanors," generally interpreted as being limited to demonstrably criminal acts in the US. Conviction requires a two-thirds vote of all senators present and voting, providing there is a quorum, and entails automatic removal from office. The president *pro tem* of the Senate presides. In US history Congress has impeached 13 officials and convicted four. Before Richard NIXON, the issue of presidential impeachment arose seriously only when Andrew JOHNSON was impeached in the House but acquitted in the Senate by one vote. Individual states in the US also have impeachment procedures.

IMPEDANCE, the ratio of the AC voltage applied to an electric circuit to the current it produces. It is a generalization of the concept of electric resistance (see ELECTRICITY) to include cases where the current oscillates ahead of or behind the voltage (i.e., out of PHASE with it) based on the mathematics of complex numbers. The term is also applied to the ratio between the driving force and response of other oscillatory or wave systems.

IMPERATOR, ancient Roman title given to a victorious military commander by his troops. Gaius Julius CAESAR was the first to use the title continuously, and after him the title came to denote the Roman emperor.

IMPERIAL BEACH, a city in S Cal., 10mi S of San Diego on the Mexican border and Pacific Ocean. A resort center, it is the most southwesterly city in the continental US. Pop 20244.

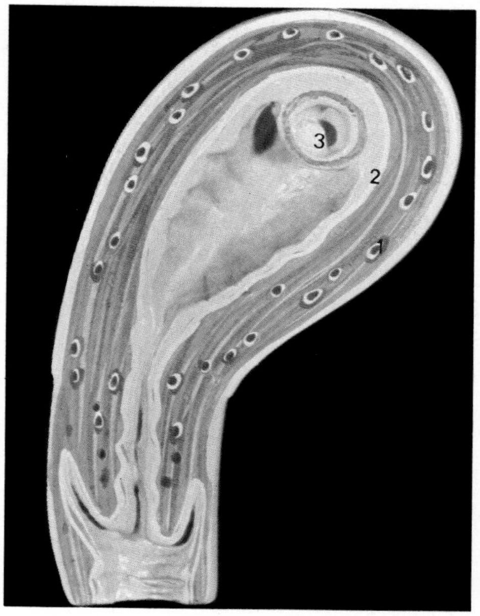

Implanted embryo in the uterus during the first month of pregnancy. (1) Muscle; (2) mucous membrane of the uterus; (3) the embryo.

IMPERIALISM, a policy of one country or people, usually "developed," extending control or influence over other territories or peoples, usually "underdeveloped" ones. There are many different kinds of imperialism—political, financial, economic, military and cultural. The justification for imperialism has been that backward countries were advanced technologically, economically and culturally by the influence of more developed nations. However, imperialist policies have also restricted individual and national freedoms and have often exploited undeveloped natural resources and native populations. (See also COLONIALISM; COLONIZATION.)

IMPERIAL VALLEY, important agricultural area in the low-lying SE Cal. desert, extending into Mexico, called the "Winter Garden" of America. Since the construction of the 80mi-long All-American irrigation canal and soil reclamation projects in the 1940s and 1950s, the valley has become a highly fertile farm region producing alfalfa, melons, tomatoes, lettuce and sugar beets. Even the January temperature averages 53°F.

IMPETIGO, superficial SKIN infection, usually of the FACE, caused by STREPTOCOCCUS or STAPHYLOCOCCUS. It starts with small vesicles which burst and leave a characteristic yellow crust. It is easily spread by fingers from a single vesicle to affect several large areas and may be transmitted to others. It is common in children and requires ANTIBIOTIC creams, and systemic PENICILLIN in some cases.

IMPLANTATION, the earliest stage of EMBRYO development in which the embryo invades the WOMB. After fertilization by SPERM, the EGG divides into a small ball of cells, whose outer layer is specialized to invade the endometrium, which is itself prepared for implantation. The interface between embryo and endometrium develops into the PLACENTA. The term is also used to refer to the placing of DRUGS, PROSTHETICS or grafts in the body in treatment of DISEASE.

IMPLIED POWERS, powers exercised by the US federal government not explicitly delegated to it by the CONSTITUTION or reserved to the individual states (see STATES' RIGHTS) or the people. This authority is implied in the so-called "elastic clause" (Article I, Section 8, Clause 18) which empowers the Congress to enact such laws as are "necessary and proper" to the execution of the government's specified powers. The doctrine of implied powers has been widely used in the areas of taxation, commerce, military and foreign policy, postal services and in the enactment of criminal laws.

Two typical paintings of Impressionism are *The Road from Louvenciennes* (1872) by Camille Pissarro and *The Café* (detail, 1877) by Auguste Renoir. The pictures were painted at the places they depict in order to keep the artist's impression fresh; but while Renoir enjoyed painting fashionable Parisians at leisure in cafés and parks, Pissarro preferred scenes of small quiet towns outside Paris. Both artists suggested form and space in their pictures by contrasts and nuances of color so that sharp clear colors in the foreground stand out from softer colors in the distance. They also favored a clear direct perspective in their paintings so that the spectator's eye is led straight into the scene.

IMPLOSION, a bursting inward, as opposed to explosion, a bursting outward. Implosion due to gravitational collapse is an important end-stage in the lives of STARS (see also BLACK HOLES). Domestic lamp bulbs implode on fracture.

IMPORTS. See INTERNATIONAL TRADE.

IMPRESSIONISM, artistic movement in France from the mid-1860s until about 1890. The Impressionist painters, who include CÉZANNE, DEGAS, MANET, MONET, PISSARRO, RENOIR and SISLEY, painted landscapes and scenes of leisure in contemporary Paris. They usually worked out-of-doors, recording the scenes before them spontaneously and directly. Their pictures were executed in bright contrasting colors in order to convey the impression of light and they emphasized the individual brushstrokes. The term "impressionist" was first used as a criticism of Monet's *Impression: Soleil levant* (*Sunrise*, 1874). The artists organized eight independent exhibitions for their pictures. The American painters CASSATT and HASSAM were influenced by the Impressionists. Impressionism also describes other art forms, notably literature which uses symbolic imagery (see RILKE) and music which expresses mood and feeling (see DEBUSSY).

IMPRESSMENT, the seizure of persons or property to place them in public service. The practice was common in many countries and the British used impressment to obtain seamen until the 19th century. Impressment of British deserters from American ships aroused public indignation in the US and was one of the causes of the WAR OF 1812.

IMPRIMATUR (Latin: let it be printed), a license to print or publish. In the Roman Catholic Church, the permission given by a bishop for the publication of a book on theology or morals.

IMPRINTING, very rapid LEARNING by a newborn creature. (See ANIMAL BEHAVIOR.)

IMPULSE, the integral (see CALCULUS) of a FORCE over an interval of time. By NEWTON's second law the impulse (a VECTOR quantity) equals the change of MOMENTUM produced by the force. It is a useful concept when a large and variable force acts for a short time, as in an impact.

INBREEDING, the breeding of individual plants or animals that are closely related. Inbreeding tends to bring together recessive GENES with, usually, deleterious effects. This is because recessive genes are often harmless in the heterozygous condition but harmful in the homozygous condition (see GENETICS). For this reason, inbreeding has long been regarded as a practice to be discouraged; in human cultures, consanguinity is frequently forbidden by law or discouraged by custom.

INCA, title of the ruler of an empire in W South America which, at the time of the Spanish conquest, occupied what is now Peru, parts of Ecuador, Chile, Bolivia and Argentina. It extended some 3 000mi from N to S, stretching back between 150 and 250mi from the narrow Pacific coastal plain into the high Andes. Communications were maintained along brilliantly engineered and extensive roads, carried over the sheer Andean gorges by fiber cable suspension bridges. Trained relay runners carried messages 150mi a day and the army had quick access to trouble spots. Restive subject tribes were resettled near Cuzco, the capital. Detailed surveys of new conquests were recorded by *quipu*, a mnemonic device using knotted cords. Writing, like draft animals and wheeled transport, was unknown, so too was monetary currency. Taxation and tribute were levied in the form of labor services. In other respects the culture was highly advanced. At sites such as MACHU PICCHU Inca architects raised some of the world's finest stone structures; precious metals from government-controlled mines were worked by supremely-skilled goldsmiths; bronze was also used; ceramic and textile design was outstanding. Agriculture was based on elaborate irrigation and hillside terracing.

The legendary founding family originated in the valley of Cuzco. By the 1430s its descendants had conquered the other peoples nearby and rapidly extended their power to its peak in the early 1500s. The Inca, believed to be a god descended from the sun, enjoyed absolute power and took a principal part in the elaborate and lengthy religious ceremonials. When PIZARRO the Spaniard landed in 1532, the empire was emerging from a civil war; his murder of Inca ATAHUALPA secured Spanish control.

INCANDESCENT LAMP. See LIGHTING.

INCANTATION, a prescribed formula used in MAGIC to invoke the aid of supernatural powers, whether good or evil. It may be chanted or spoken.

INCARNATION, embodiment of a deity as a human or animal. In Hindu belief, VISHNU has manifested himself in different incarnations or *avatara*. In Christianity the doctrine of the incarnation is that the Son of God (see TRINITY) took human nature and was born as JESUS CHRIST, who was thus fully God and fully man. This doctrine, much debated in the early Church, was finally defined at the Council of CHALCEDON 451. By the incarnation, redeemed mankind is in Christ united to God.

INCENDIARY BOMB, bomb designed to cause casualty and damage by fire. They may be made of MAGNESIUM, which burns vigorously and with great heat; be packed with THERMITE, which is scattered over a wide area by initial explosion; or contain liquid burning agents such as NAPALM which, burning, cling to people and objects. (See also FIRESTORM.)

INCENSE, aromatic substances such as FRANKINCENSE, SANDALWOOD and BALSAM, which produce a fragrant odor when burned. Incense has been widely used in religious ceremonies from earliest times.

INCENTER, the point of concurrence of the lines drawn bisecting the angles of a TRIANGLE. As this point is equidistant from the sides, it is the center of the

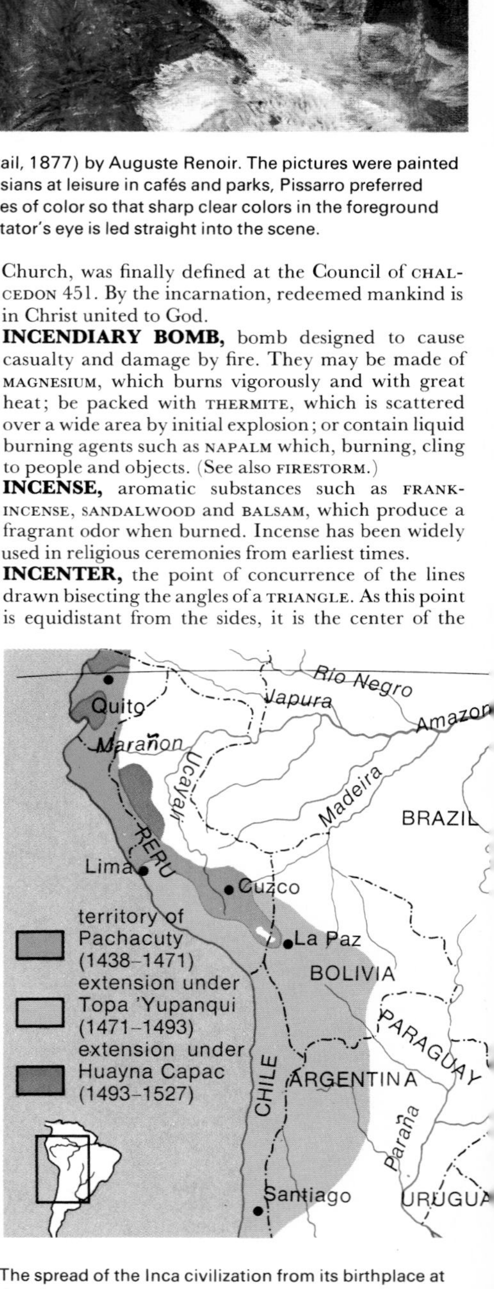

The spread of the Inca civilization from its birthplace at Cuzco in the Peruvian Andes. At the height of its power the Inca empire stretched from Ecuador south to central Chile.

circle that may be inscribed in the triangle (see INSCRIPTION).

INCEST, sexual concourse between persons to whom marriage is forbidden on grounds of kinship. The grounds vary with culture and epoch. First cousin marriage, for example, once prohibited in Christian law, is now generally permissible. Almost universally forbidden are marriages between parents and children, or between siblings, but ancient Egypt and the Incas allowed brother–sister marriages in the ruling family.

INCH (in), a unit of length in the US customary and Imperial systems. Since 1959 it has been defined exactly equal to 25.4mm.

INCHCAPE (Bell Rock), a reef in the North Sea 12mi off the Scottish coast and mostly under water. It was a hazard to shipping until a belltower was constructed there in 1811.

INCHON, industrial city of South Korea, on the Han R delta and seaport for Seoul about 20mi NE of it. In Sept. 1950, during the Korean War, a landing here by UN troops decisively checked the North Korean advance. Pop 646013.

INCH WORM. See MEASURING WORM.

INCLINED PLANE. See MACHINE.

INCLOSURE. See ENCLOSURE.

INCOME, payment accruing to an individual or company in return for labor, services or trading, or from dividends paid on stocks and rent paid on property. "Disposable personal income" is the balance remaining after tax. Income policy is the attempt to restrain rises in wages, salaries and dividends by government action. The US and Britain have initiated such policies during times of rapid inflation. A country's national income is calculated as the total wages, profits, dividends and interest accruing to its citizens and companies.

INCOME TAX, the major source of government revenue. As opposed to EXCISE taxes levied on goods, it is a direct tax on the incomes of individuals, proportionate to their wealth, or on corporations. At first imposed only to meet extraordinary expenditures such as war financing, income tax became permanent in Britain in 1874. In the US it was levied during the Civil War, but an attempt to make it a permanent federal tax was ruled unconstitutional. The 16th Amendment (1913) authorized the federal government to levy the tax and since 1919 most states have also adopted this mode of revenue raising. It is assessed on net income after allowances have been deducted for family dependents, contributions to charities and certain other expenditures. Incomes below a certain level are entirely exempt; above this the rate rises progressively from 15% (1970) to as much as 70% on earnings of $100000 or more. To lessen welfare problems, "negative" income tax has been proposed; in this system the poor receive, rather than make income-related payments. (See also TAXATION.)

INCUBATION, a method of keeping microorganisms such as BACTERIA or VIRUSES warm and in an appropriate medium to promote their growth (e.g., in identification of the organisms causing DISEASE); also, the period during which an organism is present in the body before causing DISEASE. INFECTIOUS DISEASE is contracted from a source of infective microorganisms. Once these have entered the body they divide and spread to different parts and it is some time before they cause symptoms due to local or systemic effects. This incubation period may be helpful in diagnosis and in determining length of QUARANTINE periods.

INCUBATOR, a device used for incubating microorganisms (see INCUBATION); also an enclosed cot in which a baby, particularly if premature, is placed to create an ideal protective and controllable environment. Temperature is regulated thermostatically and the possibility of infection is minimized; the air in the incubator may be enriched with controlled amounts of OXYGEN. Nursing is carried out through portholes. The use of incubators has been significant in reducing mortality in premature infants.

INCUNABULA (Latin: swaddling clothes), books printed before 1501 in the "infancy" years of typography. The known 35000 editions include the works of such printers as GUTENBERG, CAXTON and ALDUS MANUTIUS. (See also PRINTING.)

INDENTURED SERVANT, person bound to labor for a stated period, usually five to seven years. In America he had often agreed to this in return for his passage to the colonies, but many were enticed or kidnapped, and convicts were sometimes sentenced and deported to indentured labor.

INDEPENDENCE, city in SE Kansas, seat of Montgomery Co.; an important refining and oil producing area. Machinery, cement and wood products are also made. Pop 10347.

INDEPENDENCE, city in Mo., seat of Jackson Co. Its industries include plastics and farm machinery. Founded in 1827, it was the site of a Mormon colony (1831–34), and is now the world center of the Reorganized Mormon Church. Pop 111660.

INDEPENDENCE DAY (US), the Fourth of July, the principal non-religious holiday, which commemorates the adoption of the DECLARATION OF INDEPENDENCE (July 4, 1776).

INDEPENDENCE, Declaration of. See DECLARATION OF INDEPENDENCE.

INDEPENDENCE, War of. See REVOLUTIONARY WAR, AMERICAN.

INDEPENDENCE HALL, the old state house of Philadelphia, Pa., where the DECLARATION OF INDEPENDENCE was proclaimed and the Constitutional Convention of 1787 met. It now houses the LIBERTY BELL and a small museum.

INDEPENDENCE NATIONAL HISTORICAL PARK, Philadelphia, Pa., established by the federal government in 1948 to preserve the area and structures associated with the period of the Revolutionary War and the growth of the US. INDEPENDENCE HALL and many other historic buildings stand here.

INDEPENDENT TREASURY SYSTEM, US banking structure in which the treasury was isolated from the nation's banking and finance system, originally to prevent the transfer of government funds to state banks. It functioned for brief periods from 1846 but could not meet the strains of financing the Civil War. The FEDERAL RESERVE Act (1913) marked its demise.

INDETERMINACY PRINCIPLE. See UNCERTAINTY PRINCIPLE.

INDETERMINATE EQUATIONS, simultaneous EQUATIONS which for some reason have an infinite number of solutions. Examples are

$$x+y=4$$
$$2x+2y=8,$$

where the two equations are equivalent, and

$$x+y=z$$
$$\tfrac{1}{2}x+6y+3=8z,$$

where there is insufficient data.

INDEX OF FORBIDDEN BOOKS (*Index Librorum Prohibitorum*), official list of books banned by the Roman Catholic Church as being in doctrinal or moral error. A book could be removed from the Index by expurgation of offending passages, and permission could be given to read prohibited books. The Index ceased publication in 1966.

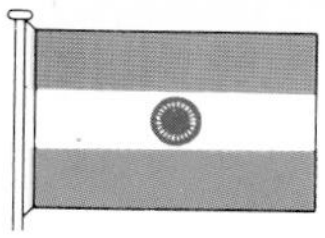

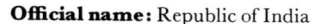

Official name: Republic of India
Capital: New Delhi
Area: 1261810sq mi
Population: 547000000
Languages: Hindi, English; fourteen other national languages
Religions: Hindu, Muslim, Christian, Sikh, Buddhist
Monetary unit(s): 1 Rupee = 100 paise

INDIA, a federal republic of 21 states, in S Asia. It occupies a land mass ranging from the Himalayas southward to Cape Cormorin on the Indian Ocean, and shares the triangular-shaped Indian subcontinent with PAKISTAN, NEPAL, BHUTAN and BANGLADESH. The world's second most populous country, India has sought development aid wherever it is offered, and follows a policy of non-alignment.

Land. The chief geographical regions of N India are the Thar Desert along the Pakistan border; the mountain valleys of KASHMIR (disputed with Pakistan); the fertile plains of the GANGES and Brahmaputra rivers; and the Himalaya Mts, with Nanda Devi (25645ft), India's highest peak. The mountains shield India from the cold winter winds of central Asia and retain the wet monsoon in summer.

The mountaintop city of Machu Picchu, an enduring testimony to Inca civilization, seen from the air. Shown here are the massive buildings of the so-called Sacred Plaza, which contained two temples and a house for the priests. As impressive as the city are the terraced fields cut into the surrounding hillside, for which topsoil must have been carried up by hand to be laid on a gravel base.

Temple complex at Somnathpur, India, built between 1050 and 1300 and still a busy center of worship. The survival of such ancient temples as places or worship and not mere museums testifies to the enduring importance of Hinduism in Indian daily life.

The Deccan plateau, bordered by the Western and Eastern Ghats mountain ranges, occupies most of S India. Here rivers flow sluggishly to the Eastern Ghats, then descend through broad valleys to the Bay of Bengal. The rich volcanic soil is used mainly for cotton-growing, though there are important mineral deposits. Most of the country has a tropical MONSOON climate, temperatures reaching 120°F in the hot season on the Northern Plains and, in the cool season, falling below freezing point in the mountains. The monsoon rains are especially heavy on the Western Ghats and in NE India and some places average more than 426in of rain a year.

People. In 1971, India's population was over 547 million; despite birth control programs it is still rapidly expanding. The ethnic composition is complex, but there is a basic division between the light-skinned INDO-ARYANS in the N and the darker DRAVIDIANS in the S. About 80% of the population lives in villages, though the towns are growing fast, the chief cities being the seaports of BOMBAY, CALCUTTA and MADRAS and the capital NEW DELHI. The dominant religion is HINDUISM which, through its CASTE system, profoundly affects the nation's social structures. Most Indians live on the poverty line in crowded slums or primitive villages, eating a mainly vegetarian diet.

Economy. India is an importer of food and industrial goods and an exporter of raw materials. Rice, beans, peas, tea, sugarcane, jute, pepper and timber are the main agricultural products, since the Indian economy is primarily agricultural. Output, however, is relatively low. Improvements are being sought by irrigation, land reclamation projects and the introduction of improved strains of crops and fertilizers. There are iron and steel mills, electronic and engineering plants, but about 45% of the industrial manpower works in the jute, cotton and other textile mills. Mineral resources include gold and oil, iron ore, coal and mica, but are poorly exploited. Energy requirements are supplemented by hydroelectric plants and India's first atomic power station, at Tarapur, came into operation in 1969.

History. The INDUS VALLEY CIVILIZATION, in modern Pakistan, was the first great culture on the subcontinent. It succumbed c1500 BC to Aryan peoples invading through the NW mountain passes; they brought the SANSKRIT language, and Hinduism to India. The MAURYA EMPIRE and GUPTA dynasties represented high points of Buddhist and Hindu rule, but India was never united and from the 10th century AD, Muslim invaders added to the warring states. In the 14th century the Delhi Muslim sultanate and the Hindu kingdom of Vijayanagar in the S were dominant; in the 1520s the Muslim empire of the MOGULS was founded. Europeans also began to settle and in the 18th century English and French interests contested for control of the by then moribund empire. Victory went to the British EAST INDIA COMPANY whose first governor-general of India was Warren HASTINGS (1774). After the **Sepoy Rebellion** (1857–58), the British government took over rule of much of the country and the remaining independent princes, both Muslim and Hindu, recognized British paramountcy. The British did nothing to weaken religious rivalries but did give the subcontinent a unified code of law, a single administrative language and the world's greatest railroad network. In 1885, the Indian National CONGRESS PARTY was set up; under GANDHI and NEHRU it led the movement for independence. JINNAH led the MUSLIM LEAGUE urging partition into India and Pakistan on religious grounds. Many thousands died in fierce communal riots following partition in 1947.

India achieved sovereign status in 1948. The constitution (1949) provided for a bicameral democratically-elected parliament and a cabinet government with prime minister and a president. Congress has been the ruling party, first under Nehru and (since 1966) under his daughter Mrs. Indira GANDHI. Domestic politics have been concerned with the vast problem of food supply, the drive towards large-scale industrialization, the mitigation of the worst injustices of the caste system and, since the late 1960s, tension between the central and provincial governments. Foreign policy was long overshadowed by the dispute with Pakistan over Kashmir, which flared into war in 1965. A frontier war in 1962 also emphasized the strained relations between India and China. In 1975 Mrs. Gandhi, convicted of irregularities in an election, declared a state of emergency, jailed her opponents and began to rule by decree. SIKKIM became an Indian state in 1975.

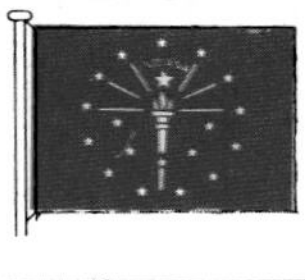

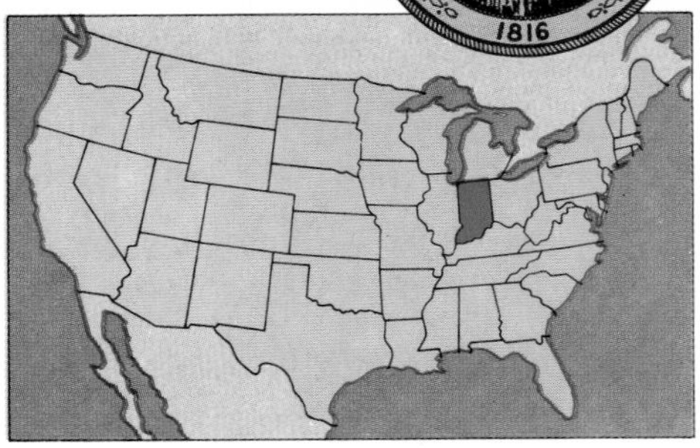

Name of state: Indiana
Capital: Indianapolis
Statehood: Dec. 11, 1816 (19th state)
Familiar name: Hoosier State
Area: 36 291sq mi
Population: 5 193 669
Elevation: Highest—1 257ft, Wayne County. Lowest—320ft, Ohio River in Posey County
Motto: The Crossroads of America
State flower: Peony
State bird: Cardinal
State tree: Tulip Tree (yellow poplar)
State song: "On the Banks of the Wabash"

INDIANA, smallest Midwest state of the US, known as the "Hoosier State." Created from the NORTHWEST TERRITORY, it is bounded to the N by Mich. and Lake Michigan, on the E by Ohio, on the S by the Ohio R, which forms the border with Ky., and on the W by Ill.

Land. There are three main regions in Indiana. In the N are the Great Lakes Plains, in the center the Till Plains, and to the S the Southern Hills and Lowlands. Glacial cover created many small lakes and left rich soil in the N and center. Main rivers are the Wabash, Kankakee and Maumee. The climate is humid, with summer temperatures from 65°F to 90°F typical; in winter they can be as low as 27°F, with heavy snow in the N.

People. Indiana's population swelled after statehood, driving out the Indians by about 1840. Since WWI it has become increasingly urbanized with the growth of industry. The Negro minority has become increasingly significant, especially in urban areas. Under the constitution of 1851 the bicameral legislature is headed by a governor and lieutenant-governor elected for four-year terms. The 1816 constitution was the first to specifically provide free public education; the state now has two state universities and many private institutions.

Economy. Before WWI the state's economy rested on agriculture, but it then expanded until today it is among the top ten industrial states. Its largest industry is steel and other metal production, particularly in the Lake Michigan area, which also has major oil refineries. Second largest is the electrical industry. The cities, especially Indianapolis, are manufacturing centers, making machinery, chemicals, furniture and foodstuffs. Agriculture remains important, however; the major crops are corn and soybeans, the most important livestock hogs, cattle and poultry.

History. Algonkin, Iroquois and Delaware Indians occupied the area when French fur traders explored it in the 17th century. After the FRENCH AND INDIAN WARS, the area passed to the British and to the US after the Revolution. In 1800 it became a territory, with William Henry HARRISON as governor. Initial Indian resistance to white settlement ended after the battle of FALLEN TIMBERS, but revived under the Shawnee chief TECUMSEH until the battle of TIPPECANOE. In 1816 Indiana became a state, although its settlements were too isolated to form a coherent political body until about 1850. In the Civil War it supported the Union, but despite this and the growth of industrialization it remained a rural and reactionary state, in the 1920s a center of the KU KLUX KLAN. Social advances, however, have come in the wake of industrialization and consequent prosperity.

INDIAN AFFAIRS, Bureau of, US federal agency, part of the Department of the Interior, set up in 1824 to safeguard the welfare of American Indians. It acts as trustee for tribal lands and funds, supervises the reservations and provides welfare and education facilities.

INDIANAPOLIS, city in central Ind., state capital and seat of Marion Co. Situated on the White R, the city is the market center for a rich agricultural region. The economy rests on its manufacturing industries; among the largest are airplane and truck engines, and meat-packing. The city is famous for the annual "Indy 500" motor race. Pop 745 739.

INDIAN ART AND ARCHITECTURE. The classical tradition begins after the fall of the INDUS VALLEY CIVILIZATION, c1500 BC and the establishment of the Indo-Aryan culture based on HINDUISM. The naturalistic Aryan pantheon assimilated local deities and concepts to produce a complex system, celebrated in the sacred Hindu texts called VEDAS. Statues, paintings and temples, often lavishly embellished with sculpture, both symbolize and embody the gods and their attributes or powers. Cosmic symbols and a profuse, intricate language of imagery in form and gesture, present the divine aspects of meditation, courage, mercy, erotic love, war, death and life. The spread of BUDDHISM under ASOKA (d. 232 BC) brought a new emphasis. In architecture, the stupa was a round, brick- or stone-faced earth mound, containing a relic or tomb and surrounded by a square stone railing. Painting and sculpture, notably in the AJANTA caves and the art of

Indian miniature, depicting scenes from the life of the Hindu god Krishna (traditionally shown as blueskinned). From the Rajasthan area, it dates from the 18th or 19th century.

Gandhara (influenced by Hellenism), portray episodes in the physical and spiritual life of the Buddha. The golden age of Indian culture came during the GUPTA DYNASTY (320–c500 AD). Resurgent Hinduism soon adapted the Buddhist cella and porch temples to the classic porch, pillared hall and cella of the Hindu temple, often surmounted by massive conical spires, as at Khajuraho (c1000 AD). In the 13th century S India perfected the Dravidian pyramidal temple and produced superb bronze sculptures such as the famous dancing Siva. Indian Muslim art reached its peak under the MOGULS (see also TAJ MAHAL).

INDIAN CLAIMS COMMISSION, independent federal agency, set up in 1946 to decide on all Indian claims of unjust land dealings by the government. More than $200 million has already been awarded. The commission's decisions may be appealed against in the Court of Claims.

INDIAN MALLOW, *Abutilon avicennae*, an annual herb native to the tropics. It is cultivated in China and yields a fiber called China jute that is used for making ropes, cords and coarse fabrics.

INDIAN MUTINY. See SEPOY REBELLION.

INDIAN OCEAN, at about 28 350 000sq mi the world's third largest ocean. It is bounded by Antarctica to the S, Africa to the W, and Australia and Indonesia to the E. The Indian subcontinent divides the N part of the ocean into two great arms, the Arabian Sea to the W and the Bay of Bengal to the E. Largest of its many islands are Madagascar and Ceylon; others include Zanzibar, Mauritius and the Seychelles. Major inflowing rivers include the Limpopo, Zambezi, Ganges and Indus. The deepest recorded point is in the Java or Sunda Trench (24 390ft).

INDIAN PAINT BRUSHES, colorful herbs of the genus *Castilleja*, family Scrophulariaceae, that are native to western North America. The flowers are small and colorless, but are surrounded by large red, yellow, orange or white modified leaves called bracts. They are parasitic on the roots of other plants.

INDIAN PIPES, colorless, saprophytic herbs of the genus *Monotropa*, found growing in moist woods in temperate North America and parts of Asia. Specifically, *Monotropa uniflora* which is a waxy-white plant saprophytic on fallen leaves but sometimes parasitic on roots. Family: Monotropaceae.

INDIAN RIVER, 165mi lagoon in E Fla., off the coast from Brevard Co. to St. Martin Co. The lagoon has a number of resorts and its valley is noted for its citrus fruits.

INDIANS, Central and South American, are like their counterparts in the N believed to be of Asiatic origin. (See INDIANS, NORTH AMERICAN.) The major Indian groups in Central and N South America at the beginning of the European conquest (16th century) included the CARIBS, ARAWAKS, AZTECS, MAYAS and the INCAS. The Maya civilization had reached its zenith some 700 years before, but the Inca and Aztec were at their peak. The three cultures had developed complex political and religious structures, built great temples, roads and bridges and achieved sophisticated astronomical and calendrical calculations, yet writing was rudimentary and wheeled transport unknown. The cultures were overthrown and millions of Indians killed by warfare and disease during the 16th-century Spanish conquest. The Spanish government proclaimed the Indians to be subjects and not slaves, but the settler community treated them as chattels and subjected them to forced labor. The situation was little better in Portuguese Brazil, though Jesuit-run plantations here and elsewhere treated their Indians humanely. Where they were able, Indians withdrew physically and psychologically from European culture. South American independence in the 19th century did little to improve their status. Atrocities committed against them by rubber barons in the early 20th century brought a degree of government protection. In Mexico Indian influence in the 1916 revolution, the restitution of certain Indian property rights and some integration between Indian and European cultures greatly improved Mexican Indians' standing today.

In South America it is variable, however, for cultural more than racial reasons. Indian tribal values lay more emphasis on the communal good and the sanctity of the soil; they cannot be easily integrated into a money economy. There is still a good deal of exploitation and maltreatment of remote tribes, often by government officials; they are still sometimes brutally driven off their lands, or simply massacred.

INDIANS, North American, aboriginal inhabitants of North America. It is generally believed that their ancestors migrated from Asia c25 000 years ago across a land bridge (now the Bering Strait) between Siberia and Alaska. An alternative theory, less popular, suggests that they evolved on the American continent. It is certain that by 6000 BC they inhabited the whole continent. By the time of the European incursion,

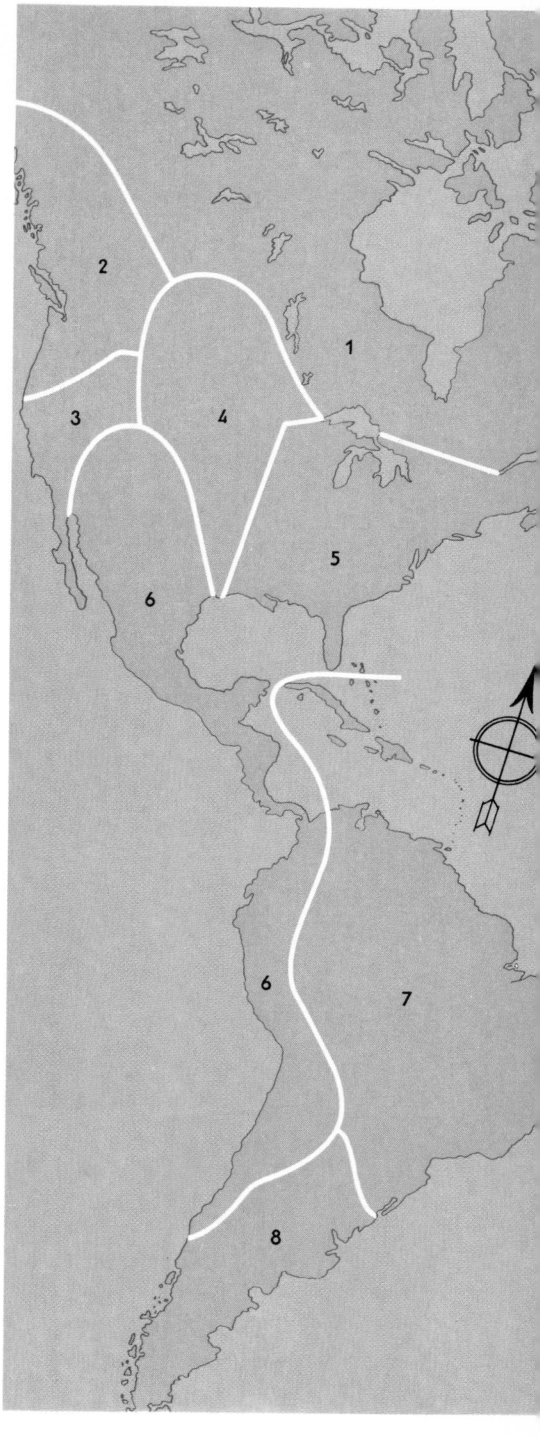

Map showing the broad divisions of Indian cultures in North and South America, according to their different staple foods and means of cultivation, and some of the major tribes in each area.

(1) Caribou area: Algonquins, Chipeywans, Cree, Fox, Winnebage.

(2) Salmon area: Chinooks, Tlingits, Haida, Kwakiutl, Nootka.

(3) Wild seed area: Kotsimi, Seri, Shoshone, Waikuru.

(4) Buffalo area: Arapaho, Blackfoot, Cheyenne, Comanche, Pawnee, Sioux.

(5) Corn area: Cherokee, Chickasaw, Creek, Huron, Iroquois.

(6) Intensive farming area: Apache, Chibcha, Hopi, Toltecs, Mayas, Incas, Aztecs.

(7) Manioc area: Bacahiri, Cayapo. Guato, Mundrucu, Siriono.

(8) Guanaco area: Albipone, Charrua, Ona, Puelches, Tehuelches.

American Indians

A profusion of different cultures

The prevailing view of the North American Indian, sedulously propagated by the film industry and other media, is of the romantic western warrior of the 19th century, the fearless befeathered horseman of the Great Plains, his latest scalp dangling from his side, who wages a gallant but hopeless battle against the encroaching white man.

In actuality the New World demonstrated an immense variety of Indian cultures, from the sophisticated theocracy of the Maya to the primitive "diggers" of California; and the Plains Indian culture itself was a fragile creation of very recent times, its brief but glorious eruption in the 19th century only made possible by the introduction of the white man's horse. Even without the depredations of the westward-moving settlers, the Plains culture would have collapsed through over-population and the inevitable extermination of the buffalo herds. And as for scalping, it was anything but a widespread practice before the advent of the European. Its spread was primarily encouraged by colonial administrators who offered rewards for dead Indians. A scalp was a more convenient and less grisly proof of death than the whole head.

An equally deep-seated myth about the origin of the North American Indian has us believe that all the earliest settlers of the two American continents flooded across from Siberia on a convenient land bridge where the Bering Strait is today. Probably there were land bridges at the Bering Strait two times in recent geological history—between 28 000 and about 26 000 years ago, and between 20 000 and 10 000 to 12 000 years ago—and migrants could have crossed at either time. But modern scholars have worked out a more reasonable and flexible theory: constant small migrations could also have taken place at other times by boat or raft across the Straits (with a flow of water much lower than at present) or the journey could have been made on snowshoes across the ice in winter. Radiocarbon dates from the recently discovered site of Old Crow in Alaska suggest that the initial settlements were probably made about 28 000 BC, and the settlers would have found a congenial environment, with plants and animals similar to those they had known in Siberia. Their sophisticated tools, made by methods long worked out in Asia, would have sufficed for the gathering, fishing and the hunting of camels, elephants and mammals they practiced.

Probably very few families made the actual crossing from Siberia. This is suggested by the genetic structure of the American Indian today, which shows predominantly blood group O alone, whereas in Asia all three blood groups—O, A and B—occur. If by pure chance a group of families among whom the hereditary gene for O was most common actually made the principal crossing, their descendants would also be marked by this genetic trait. But how could all the Indians of the two continents be descended from such a handful of emigrants? In modern theory, this is possible, given a favorable environment such as the settlers first met in Alaska. Over hundreds of years there would have been a population explosion leading to a gradual spread southward when glacial conditions made it possible. By 10 000 BC prehistoric hunters were to be found in all parts of the Western Hemisphere—and almost all of them were native born.

The Eskimo is not generally considered an Amerindian since his genetic structure differs markedly from that of the American Indian. It is likely that the Eskimo was a product of another, later migration from Asia, perhaps across the Bering Strait land bridge of about 10 000 years ago, though some believe he may have crossed as late as about 2000 BC. That Eskimos have all three blood groups indicates that their migration from Asia was not connected with the earlier one, and that they are closely related to the natives of Siberia.

The distinctive culture areas of North America did not begin to emerge until about 6000 BC when a few of the hunter-gatherers began to practice agriculture. The Archaic Culture area stretched from Texas to Canada inland from the east coast, while the Desert Culture area covered the southwest, and along the northwest coast were the Pacific subcultures. These areas were to produce the most advanced cultures of North America in the late prehistoric period just before the coming of the white man. It is very difficult to make any general survey of North American Indian cultures in their prime, partly because so many of these cultures were altered or upset in the 19th century through European influences, and because of the extreme variety and complexity of cultures and subcultures. In North America in excess of 500 languages, some as different from each other as Chinese and English, were spoken (though they have now been grouped into five main divisions).

In a thin belt stretching from the Tlingit of southern Alaska in the north to the Hupa and Yoruk of California in the south, a number of tribes were found, known under the collective rubric "the Northwest Coast Indians." Inhabiting what was once, for many of the tribes, a land of comparative plenty, these Indians gained a living primarily from the streams, woods and sea. Because of the widely various means by which they culled an amazing assortment of foodstuffs from these areas, they changed their diet and habits frequently throughout the year. Yet they were never as nomadic or as changeable as one might have expected. They were organized for the most part into chiefdoms, and it was therefore possible for a glut of food enjoyed by one section to be partly redistributed to others less fortunate. At a later date, of course, when the situation was reversed, the latter would provide, indirectly, for the former.

These societies are probably best known for a remarkable mechanism in which wealth was redistributed. Not just salmon and berries, either, but all forms of

Unlike the majority of American Indians the Pueblo tribes of Arizona and New Mexico were living in permanent dwellings, made of adobe, mud or stone, before the advent of the white man. They also had a complex social structure, and were essentially peaceful farmers.

there appear to have been about 900 000 Indians N of the Rio Grande. European weapons, diseases and destruction of natural resources took their toll, however, and the Indian population declined rapidly. The Indians had hundreds of peoples and nations, with as many languages. These may be divided into six broad culture areas: Eastern Woodlands, Plains, Southwest, Plateau, Northwest Coast and North or Sub-Arctic; the ESKIMOS are treated separately.

Eastern Woodlands. Early inhabitants of this region, the eastern US and SE Canada, were the Mound Builders (see MOUNDS) of the Mississippi Valley. Later tribes in the area belonged to the great ALGONQUIAN and IROQUOIAN linguistic families; they included Cherokee, Chickasaw, Powhatan, Shawnee, Choctaw, Creek and Natchez. In the SE the SEMINOLE were the dominant tribe. The Eastern Woodland tribes, notably the IROQUOIS confederacy, had effective political structures which were strengthened when the colonists appeared. Their main occupations were farming, tribal warfare and religious ceremonial.

Plains. The vast Plains area lay between the Mississippi R and the Rocky Mts. It was uninhabited until the 1600s, when the introduction of horses and guns by settlers made it possible for tribes to live as nomadic buffalo hunters. These included the Apache, Cheyenne, Sioux, Comanche, Blackfoot and Arapaho. The buffalo herds supplied food, fuel, bone utensils and skin for shelter and clothing. Status was achieved by success in warfare, often in defense of hunting grounds. The Plains Indians maintained a long resistance to white encroachment with skill and courage.

Southwest. The original inhabitants of the area,

wealth changed hands in the institution known as the potlatch. The potlatch was a form of competitive feast-giving. A chief, representing his people, would invite their rivals to a feast at which the aim was to provide the most lavish hospitality possible, in terms of food available and presents given—even, in later years, of material wealth destroyed. The recipients of this feast were then under an obligation to return the honor, desperately trying to match or outdo their competitors. The emphasis on honor and personal status was of primary importance in these societies, to an extent which may often seem excessive to us but is in fact paralleled by features of our own society such as visits of foreign heads of state, or the Olympic Games and, in general, conspicuous material consumption.

In complete contrast to these comparatively wealthy and highly status-oriented Indians of the Northwest coast are those tribes known to early settlers as "Digger Indians." Occupying an area on the edge of the Great Plains, around the Great Salt Lake, lived such tribes as the Shoshone, the Nez Percé and the Salish. These tribes, in historic times, had a reasonably sophisticated material culture, but without pottery, though they had baskets; also covered semi-subterranean pits for a winter home and either mat- or rush-covered tents or brush shelters in summer. They lived off salmon, occasional deer, berries and roots, the last being collected with the aid of the handled digging-stick whose use led to their early name. Correlate with the nomadism necessitated by their food supply, which was extremely unreliable, the social organization of these people was almost entirely that of the nuclear family group, although cooperation between groups for specific purposes was not infrequent. Living where they did, they were among those drawn into the Plains Indian culture with the advent of the horse, thereby losing most of their original distinguishing characteristics.

The League of the Iroquois among northeastern tribes is famous in American history for its supposed early democracy. In fact the League was by no means as close to our conception of democracy as is often suggested. Nevertheless it deserves a place in history for the fine political organization it was. Although the United Nations may be a closer parallel to the Council of Sachems than is the Federal Government, still the Council represented a surprising confederation of tribes, for such alliances are rare between tribal groups. First appearances might suggest that the Council was composed of democratically-elected members, but in fact membership was restricted to men from certain matrilineages, the actual representatives being selected from among those eligible by the women of the lineage. Furthermore, all decisions had to be unanimous, and discussion and persuasion went on between tribal blocs until agreement was reached. The Council had no control at all over intratribal matters but functioned rather to allay disputes and foster cooperation between tribes. This common external policy was one of the main contributory factors which allowed the Iroquois to conquer many of their neighbours, e.g. the Algonquins. But it should not be forgotten that such systematic conquests would not have been possible without the sedentary life of the Iroquois tribes. Based on intensive agriculture, primarily of corn, squash and beans, their economy allowed of a certain amount of specialization: masked secret societies, the construction of stockaded villages, and a number of other elaborations, many of which gave them advantages over their nomadic neighbors.

Many of the most famous tribes of North American Indians, such as the Cheyenne and the Arapaho, lived in the area known as the Great Plains, ranging from Canada in the north to Texas in the south, from Iowa in the east to Utah in the west. The economy of these people was strongly dependent on the nomadic buffalo herds of the plains. Although they also fished, and collected roots and berries as well as hunting smaller animals like deer and rabbit, the Plains Indians devoted a large part of their energy to hunting buffalo. In the horseless days of the stone arrowhead, whose power of penetration was in no way comparable with that of the metal head, the killing of the animal on the run was extremely difficult, usually requiring a number of shots from close range, which put the hunters in great danger. A more productive form of slaughter, though one which still required skill, courage and labor, was the channeled stampeding of a herd over a cliff or ridge, usually into a pen. Within the pen, those animals not killed by the fall or under the hooves of other maddened beasts could be finished off at short range and small risk with clubs and arrows.

The horse, the metal arrowhead and the gun all made the hunting of buffalo a far easier and safer pursuit. On the other hand, of course, these innovations also enabled a far greater number of Indians to live in this manner, and the influx of Indians to the plains, coupled with the systematic destruction of the herds by settlers (often with the express aim of ruining the Indians' subsistence) eventually reduced the once massive herds to near-extinction. An idea of the extent to which the Plains Indian lived off the buffalo can be reached if we recall that from it he derived not only much of his food (both fresh and preserved), but also his clothing, his housing (the famous teepee) and many other elements of his material culture such as bone tools and ornaments. With the buffalo beginning to die out by the second half of the 19th century, the Plains Indian was doomed to a similar fate.

Perhaps the highest level of general culture reached by any of the Indian groups of North America proper was that of the Pueblo Indians. The Pueblo group, which includes the Zuñi and Hopi, and his affiliations with tribes like the Apache and the Navajo, principally inhabited parts of Arizona and New Mexico. The Pueblo Indians were—and still are—characterized primarily by their adobe houses clustered into villages ("pueblo" is Spanish for village), their highly developed agriculture and their elaborate religious system. Their material culture was well developed, with loom-weaving, decorated pottery and the domestication of the turkey. Almost unique among North American tribes was the custom that the men worked at the cultivation of the staple crop, corn. The villages, with their picturesque and piled-up appearance, were based on the tribal form of organization which structured the whole society. The cohesion of both tribe and village was largely a product of the complicated religious system and ritualism running through the entire society—perhaps half of a Zuñi's waking hours were engaged by religious observances. Although their numbers have diminished greatly since their first contact with the Spaniards, the Pueblo Indians probably maintain more of their original cultural traits than any other Indian group.

Aboriginal Indian culture was immensely rich and varied. The survey above hardly begins to plot the diversity of North American life, and there are of course many other very different groups in Central and South America. Nowadays the Indians have begun to lose their identity, despite the tenacity of groups like the Pueblo Indians, either by impoverishment on reservations or by being sucked into modern life. Various recent attempts have been made, by both Indians and whites, to ameliorate the situation, but they may well have come too late.

Major cultural groups of North American Indians

Name of Group	Location	Major Tribes
Eastern Woodlands (early inhabitants: The Mound Builders)	southeastern Canada, eastern US	Cherokee, Chickasaw, Powhatan, Shawnee, Choctaw, Creek, Natchez Iroquois Nation: Cayuga, Onondaga, Oneida, Mohawk, Seneca Seminole
Plains (buffalo-hunting nomadic tribes)	the area between the Mississippi R and the Rocky Mountains	Apache, Cheyenne, Sioux, Comanche, Blackfoot, Arapaho
Southwest (early inhabitants: The Basket Makers)	the area that includes Arizona, New Mexico, southern Colorado, southern Utah	Apache, Navaho Eastern Pueblos: Taos, Santa Clara, San Ildefonso, Santo Domingo, Isleta Western Pueblos: Hopi, Zuñi, Acoma
California-Intermountain (mainly food gathering tribes, sometimes called Diggers)	much of California and the Great Basin between the Rocky Mountains and the Sierra Nevada	Great Basin Tribes: Kutenai, Nez Percé, Flathead California Tribes: Midu, Wintun, Miwok, Pomo, Yokut
Northwest Coast	Pacific coast from southern Alaska to northern California	Chinook, Haidu, Tlingit, Kwakiutl, Nootka, Tshimshian, Yurok
North	Newfoundland to Alaska	Algonquian speakers (east of Hudson Bay): Saulteaux, Cree, Montagnai, Naskapi Athapaskan speakers (west of Hudson Bay): tribes of many small nomadic bands in this subarctic forest zone

what is now Ariz., N.M., S Col. and S Ut., included a group called the BASKET MAKERS (100–700 AD), who may have been the ancestors of the PUEBLO INDIANS. The peace-loving Pueblo peoples depended on agriculture for food, while their neighbors, tribes of the Apache and Navaho, relied on hunting and marauding. The Apaches were seminomadic, whereas the Navaho lived, and still live, in wooden HOGANS. Today there are about 200 000 sheep-farming Navaho on their reservation in Ariz., the largest existing Indian group.

California-Intermountain. This plateau region included most of what is now Cal. and the Great Basin between the Rocky Mts and the Sierra Nevada Ranges. Food was plentiful in the W part, and most tribes lived simply by gathering. Their culture was not sophisticated and there was little warfare. The dietary staple was acorn flour; rabbits, deer, elk and caribou were hunted and in the N fish.

Northwest Coast. The tribes of this group, notably the HAIDA, KWAKIUTL and NOOTKA, lived along the Pacific coast from S Alaska to N Cal. The area was rich in food, principally fish, freeing the tribes to develop an elaborate and sophisticated culture. Art, particularly carving, was complex and developed; it still flourishes today, often commanding high prices. Social status was based on the surplus wealth available, mainly through the POTLATCH ceremony, in which office or status was gained by the distribution or destruction of wealth. The N tribes retain much of their culture today.

North. The peoples of the sparse region from Newfoundland to Alaska belonged to the ATHABASCAN language group in the W and the ALGONQUIAN group

Language groups of North American Indians

Group	Location
Athapascan	Alaska and west Canada, south Ore. and north Cal.
	southwest US and north Mexico
Muskogean	southeast US
Siouan	Great Plains, southeast US
Caddoan	southern Plains to the Gulf of Mexico
Algonquian	Newfoundland to B.C. Hudson Bay to Tenn.
Iroquoian	southeast US, the Great Lakes and the St Lawrence River

around Hudson Bay. Warfare played small part in their seminomadic life styles; too much energy went into the search for food.

Religion. Most Indian religion, even the fasts and self-mortification of the Plains Indian SUN DANCE, reveals a deep-felt communion with nature and a belief in a divine power. Individuals and kin groups of many tribes had spiritual ties with particular "totem" birds and animals. Shamans often organized in tribal societies, performed sacred ritual and treated the sick. The 1880s saw the tragic rise and fall of the last new Indian religion, the millenarian GHOST DANCE.

Indians in the US. The paternalistic attitudes of the first English colonists did not stop their encroachment on Indian lands (see INDIAN WARS). Indians were caught up in British and French rivalry in the FRENCH AND INDIAN WARS. Unscrupulous land speculators hardened mistrust. With the NORTHWEST ORDINANCE (1787) the newly independent US, in need of Indian support, proclaimed a policy of peaceful coexistence, yet with new expansion hostilities increased. The Indian Removal Act of 1830 (see INDIAN TERRITORY) was followed from 1850 by campaigns against Plains Indians which ended in GERONIMO's surrender in 1886. In 1871 Congress ceased to recognize the Indian nations' independent rights; the Dawes Act (1887), by breaking up tribal land into individual grants deprived the Indians of around 86 million acres, more than half their territory. A decline in the Indian population due to disease, war and starvation led to a belief that Indians were "naturally" dying out by natural selection; no long-term provision was therefore made for them. Reform began with the Indian Reorganization Act of 1934, aimed at increasing Indian autonomy and improving their economic position; it restored some lands. Other reforms followed, but poverty, poor education and unemployment are still a terrible problem on the reservations where the majority of the 790000 US Indians still live. However, there is now a strong revival of Indian culture and an increasing awareness of their political and social identity. Although occasionally expressed in pointless violence this, combined with respect for the Indian philosophy of life.

INDIAN SUMMER, period of unusually warm, sunny weather often occurring in the late fall in the central and eastern US. It is caused by a warm anticyclone stabilized by a strong temperature inversion, hindering vertical air motions. Thus days are hazy and nights cold.

INDIAN TERRITORY, region W of Ark. into which the FIVE CIVILIZED TRIBES were forcibly moved under the 1830 Indian Removal Act. In 1866 they were penalized for supporting the South in the Civil War by having other tribes resettled in the W part of this territory. Massive white settlement of other portions after 1889 led to disorder and the collapse of tribal government; by 1906 whites outnumbered Indians six to one, and the territory was incorporated into the state of Okla.

INDIAN TOBACCO, *Lobelia inflata*, herb native to North America which yields a poisonous substance called lobeline that has properties similar to those of NICOTINE. A medicinal tincture produced from lobeline is used to treat ASTHMA and chronic BRONCHITIS. Family: Lobeliaceae. (See also LOBELIA.)

INDIAN WARS, the continuing struggle between the North American Indians and white colonizers from the earliest colonial times to the late 19th century. The first permanent English settlement was established at JAMESTOWN, Va., in 1607; despite peaceful trade with the Indians under POWHATAN, hostilities began in 1622 and by 1644 the Indians had been crushed. In New England, early relations between Puritan settlers and local Indians were good; but in 1636 war broke out with the PEQUOT tribe, resulting in their massacre. With the end of KING PHILIPS WAR in 1678 Indian resistance in New England was broken.

The FRENCH AND INDIAN WARS (1689–1763) involved the NE tribes in constantly shifting alliances. In the long struggle for possession of North America both France and Britain offered guns and liquor to win Indian allies. In 1763 the tribal alliance headed by PONTIAC resulted in British recognition of Indian territorial and hunting rights. This was ignored and flouted by the colonists and corrupt officials.

With the Revolutionary War in 1775 the colonists needed Indian allegiances, and trade regulations were introduced to protect the Indians from exploitation. Trade and land companies continued to cheat the Indians, however, provoking uprisings which government troops were sent in to crush. In 1811 an alliance of southern and western tribes under the SHAWNEE chieftain TECUMSEH was defeated at the Tippecanoe R by William Henry HARRISON; Tecumseh's death in 1813, after an abortive alliance with the British in the WAR OF 1812, virtually ended Indian resistance in this area. The SEMINOLE in Fla., however, continued hostilities until 1816. In 1830 the Indian Removal Act, passed by President JACKSON, authorized the transfer of SE tribes to land W of the Mississippi. Indian resistance was met by illegal force; Jackson even ignored a Supreme Court order upholding the land rights of the CHEROKEES.

In 1855, the defeated NEZ PERCÉ tribes were given land in the NW states, but when gold was found in the area they were again forced to move. Chief JOSEPH led an unsuccessful revolt against this in 1877. The Cal. GOLD RUSH also led to the overrunning of Indian lands and to the deaths of thousands of Indians 1848–58. The second half of the 19th century saw the final suppression of the Indians. The NAVAHO, holding the land between the Rio Grande and Cal., were defeated by Kit CARSON in 1863 and transferred to NW Ariz. After the Civil War attempts were made to restrict the Apaches, though COCHISE and others resisted; their last war chief, GERONIMO, surrendered in 1886. In 1871 the government ceased to recognize Indian tribes as independent nations.

The Great Plains, home of the SIOUX, APACHE and CHEYENNE, were subdued 1870–90 by a combination of military force and the depletion of buffalo herds. The Indian victory at the battle of LITTLE BIGHORN only hastened their defeat; it was marked by the surrender of CRAZY HORSE in 1877, and the suppression of the GHOST DANCE in 1890.

INDIA PAPER, thin but tough paper, developed in China and Japan, used for lightweight editions of large books such as the Bible. An absorbent variety is used to take the best proofs of engravings.

INDICATOR, substance which indicates when the concentration of a chemical species has passed a certain threshold value, by a change of color, turbidity or fluorescence. They are generally used to find the end-point of a TITRATION. The indicator is a substance existing in two visibly different forms in an EQUILIBRIUM that is the same kind as that of the reaction being followed. Thus, to follow an acid-base titration, a conjugate ACID-base system is used as indicator which changes color over a narrow range of pH corresponding to the end-point. (For this to happen, the equilibrium constant K of the indicator must approximately equal the hydrogen-ion concentration at the end-point.) A **universal indicator** is a mixture of indicators which changes color continuously over a wide pH range, used as a quick guide to acidity. To follow an OXIDATION-reduction reaction, an indicator is used which exists reversibly in an oxidized or reduced state, its oxidation potential being about the same as that of the reaction. For a precipitation or complexing reaction, an indicator is used which itself forms a colored precipitate or complex with excess added reagent. A good indicator must be visible at such low concentrations that it does not interfere with the reaction.

INDICES, the small numbers written as superscripts following a number or term to indicate the POWER to which it is to be raised. (See also EXPONENT.)

INDICTMENT, in US law a written accusation by a grand jury, presented to a court trying the accused. Under the 5th Amendment to the Constitution all capital crimes must be tried by indictment, but some states waive or abandon the procedure.

INDIGESTION. See DYSPEPSIA.

INDIGO, a blue dye obtained from LEGUMINOUS PLANTS of the genus *Indigofera*. The dye is produced by natural acidation of a solution containing pieces of the plants. Cultivation of indigo plants was once carried out on a large scale in India, but cheap synthetic indigo is now mainly used. Family: Leguminosae.

INDIGO BUNTING, a pyrrhuxoline bunting of North America. The male is brilliant iridescent blue

Little Bighorn, one of the last battles of the Indian wars, as seen in a contemporary lithograph by Feodor Fuchs. It was the last victory of the Cheyenne-Sioux alliance, and in reality only hastened its end. It aroused massive anti-Indian feeling in the East, and magnified the rather dubious character of General George Custer into a heroic martyr; the viewpoint of the artist is made quite clear here, as a heroic Custer strikes out at Indians portrayed as scowling savages. In actual fact Custer seems to have been a less than competent and overambitious commander.

Plowing a rice paddy in Indonesia. Rice is one of the main staples of the country's enormous population, and a large part of the agricultural land is devoted to its cultivation. Since it requires so much water to grow the fields are constructed to retain water.

with a dark crown, the females and immatures, plain brown. The song is long and varied with most phrases paired. This species is a social migrant.

INDIO, city in SE Cal., ESE of Palm Springs. It is a tourist resort in an agricultural area. Pop 14459.

INDIUM (In), rare metal, very soft and silvery-white, in Group IIIA of the PERIODIC TABLE, resembling ALUMINUM. It is prepared from flue dust residues of zinc processing. Indium forms trivalent compounds and some monovalent ones. It is used in solders, low-melting-point alloys, germanium TRANSISTORS, glass-seals, bearing alloys, and (combined with Group VA elements) in SEMICONDUCTORS. AW 114.8, mp 157°C, bp 2080°C, sg 7.31 (20°C).

INDO-ARYAN LANGUAGES, group of languages of the family of INDO-EUROPEAN LANGUAGES, spoken on the Indian subcontinent. The oldest known is SANSKRIT, from which the others are directly or indirectly descended. Most widely spoken today are Hindi-Urdu, Bengali, Marathi, Punjabi, Gujarati, Oriya, Bihari and Rajasthani. Romany, the language of the gypsies, is known to be descended from an Indo-Aryan original.

INDOCHINA, political term for that area of geographical Indochina (peninsular SE Asia between China and India) which was formerly French Indochina, later divided into North and South VIETNAM, LAOS and CAMBODIA. The area contains two densely-peopled, rice-rich deltas (Red R in the N, Mekong R in the S) separated by Annamite China. Thais, Laos and Annamese (Vietnamese) settled Indochina from the N. From the second century AD, many states and cultures, affected by India and China, rose and fell there, including FUNAN, the KHMER EMPIRE, CHAMPA and ANNAM. European penetration began in the 16th century; France concluded a treaty with Annam in 1787, annexed COCHIN CHINA in 1862 and by 1900 had welded separate states into the single political unit of French Indochina. WWII and militant nationalism destroyed France's authority and in 1949 Cambodia and Laos gained independence. The communist Vietminh drove the French out of Vietnam; the US continued France's anti-communist role in the long VIETNAM WAR, but by 1976 Indochina was effectively under communist control.

INDO-EUROPEAN LANGUAGES, one of the most important language families, spoken throughout most of Europe and much of Asia, and descended from a hypothetical common ancestor, Proto-Indo-European, extant more than 5000 years ago. There are two main branches, Eastern, with six main groups, and Western, with four. The Eastern branch includes the extinct Anatolian and Tocharian groups, as well as Albanian, Armenian, Balto-Slavic and Indo- Iranian (with its important sub-group, the INDO-ARYAN LANGUAGES). The Western branch includes Celtic, Greek, Romance or Italic (Latin and the languages derived from it) and Teutonic or Germanic (one of which is English). Until the beginning of the 20th century it was thought that SANSKRIT inscriptions represented the oldest written form of any of the family; however, both ancient Hittite and Linear B (see MINOAN LINEAR SCRIPTS), which have since been deciphered, are older. (See also LANGUAGE.)

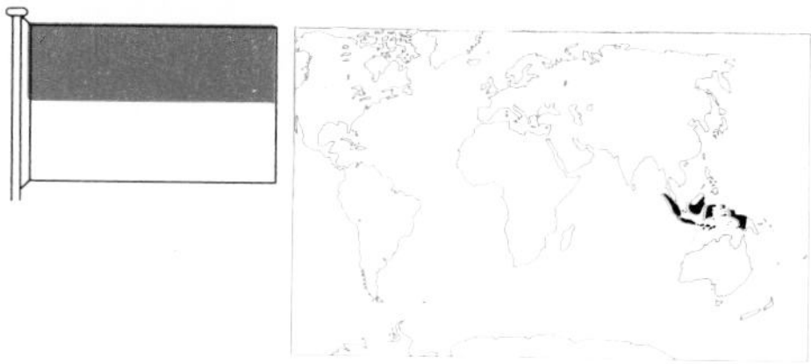

Official name: Republic of Indonesia
Capital: Jakarta
Area: 575450sq mi
Population: 119232499
Languages: Bahasa Indonesia
Religions: Muslim, Christian, Buddhist
Monetary unit(s): 1 Rupiah = 100 sen

INDONESIA, republic in SE Asia, occupying most of the enormous Malay Archipelago.

Land. Indonesia consists of more than 13000 islands and islets strung out along the equator from Sumatra to New Guinea. There are three main island groups: the Greater Sunda Islands, including JAWA, SUMATERA, Indonesian Borneo (KALIMANTAN) and SULAWESI; the Lesser Sunda Islands, including BALI, FLORES, Lombok, Sumba, Sumbawa and Indonesian Timor; and the MOLUCCAS (Maluku), including Ambon, Aru Island, Banda Islands, Buru, Ceram, Halmahera and the Tanimbar Islands. Indonesia also has West Irian (W New Guinea). The islands are mountainous and volcanic (many actively so), with tropical rain forests nourished by a hot, wet equatorial climate. There is abundant wild life, including many marsupials and the KOMODO DRAGON.

People. Two-thirds of the population lives on Jawa, site of the capital and chief port Jakarta. The population can be broadly divided into Malays and Papuans, with Chinese, Arabs and others; over 250 languages are spoken. Education is compulsory and most Indonesians are literate. There are more than 50 universities and technological institutes.

Economy. Some 80% of the population are farmers, producing rice, coconuts, cassava, corn, peanuts, sweet potatoes, spices, and coffee and raising cattle, goats and hogs and chickens. Forest products include hardwoods, rubber, palm oil, quinine and kapok. The economy rests largely on agriculture, forestry and fisheries, but mineral resources are being increasingly exploited. Coal, bauxite, copper, manganese, nickel and precious metals are mined. Indonesia's most important products are oil, its chief export, and tin, of which it is one of the world's major producers. In general raw materials are exported and manufactured goods imported; most native manufacturing is light, and centered on Jawa. The multitude of islands, most of them rugged and mountainous, hinder transportation; air links are important.

History. Primitive man existed on Jawa c1 million years ago. Civilization grew under Indian influence after the 4th century AD; several kingdoms flourished from the 12th to 14th centuries. Islam spread swiftly in the 15th century. European impact began in 1511 when the Portuguese captured Malacca. But Portugal eventually kept only E Timor, losing control to the competing English and Dutch. The victorious Dutch EAST INDIA COMPANY founded Batavia (Jakarta) in 1619 and dominated the so-called Dutch East Indies until the Netherlands assumed control in 1798. Britain occupied the islands (1811–16) during the Napoleonic Wars, then returned them to the Dutch, who greatly expanded cash-crop exports during the 19th century. Nationalist movements emerged in the early 1900s, and after Indonesia's occupation by Japanese forces in WWII (1942–45), SUKARNO proclaimed Indonesia an independent republic; the Dutch were forced to grant independence in 1949. President Sukarno's dictatorial, anti-Western regime and extravagant spending damaged the economy; General SUHARTO deposed Sukarno in 1968. He severed links with communist China and restored relations with the West. He sought to stabilize the economy, and in 1971 held the first free elections since 1955; they gave him powerful support.

INDORE, largest city of Madhya Pradesh State in W central India. A commercial center, it has important cotton and engineering industries. Pop 494664.

INDRA, Hindu war deity, head of the Vedic pantheon (see VEDA). To modern Hindus he is the guardian of the eastern quarter of the compass.

INDRI, a gray and black LEMUR with a short tail, the largest of the lemurs of Madagascar. Indris live in small social groups of 2–4 adults feeding on leaves, buds and flowers. They are noted for their eerie call, probably a territorial proclamation.

INDUCTANCE (self), the ratio of the voltage induced in an electric circuit (see INDUCTION, ELECTROMAGNETIC) to the rate of change of the current in it. It depends on the circuit geometry, being large for coils and small for extended circuits, and is greatly increased by the presence of ferromagnetic materials (see MAGNETISM). Voltages induced by currents in a different circuit are measured in terms of **mutual inductance**. Inductors have an IMPEDANCE to AC currents proportional to the current, and are widely used in electronics. The SI unit of inductance is the HENRY (H).

INDUCTION, in philosophy, the process of reasoning from particular instances to general propositions.

INDUCTION, Electromagnetic, the phenomenon in which an ELECTRIC FIELD is generated in an electric circuit when the number of MAGNETIC FIELD lines passing through the circuit changes, independently discovered by M. FARADAY and J. HENRY. The voltage induced is proportional to the rate of the change of the field, and large voltages can be produced by switching off quite small magnetic fields suddenly. Frequently, the magnetic field is itself generated by an electric current in a coil, in which case the voltage induced is proportional to the rate of change of the current (see INDUCTANCE).

The principle finds numerous applications in electric GENERATORS and MOTORS, TRANSFORMERS, MICROPHONES, and engine ignition systems (see INDUCTION COIL, MAGNETO). In the less familiar technique of **induction heating**, widely used in metal working, an object is heated by currents created in it by the voltage induced by a high-frequency current in a nearby coil; as the coil field will pass through insulators without heating them, the principle can be applied to produce "cold hob" electric stoves.

INDUCTION COIL, a device generating very high voltages, usually for sparking, and particularly in engine IGNITION SYSTEMS. A large secondary and small primary coil are wound together on a ferromagnetic (see MAGNETISM) core. When a low current in the primary is interrupted by a switch, the rapid change induces (see INDUCTION) a large voltage in the secondary. In a variant producing high-frequency AC voltage pulses, the primary current switches itself on and off through a relay, much as in an electric BELL mechanism.

INDUCTION HARDENING, the use of electromagnetic INDUCTION to heat metals rapidly in order to harden them (see METALLURGY; STEEL). A very high-frequency current is passed through an induction coil surrounding the workpiece.

INDUCTION MOTOR, an alternating-current electric MOTOR in which the current in the moving part is induced (see INDUCTION) rather than supplied via slip-ring contacts. Also called an asynchronous motor, it is the commonest motor in domestic and industrial use.

INDULGENCE, in the Roman Catholic Church, a remission of the temporal punishment (on earth or in PURGATORY) that remains due for sin even after confession, absolution and doing penance. In consideration of prayers and good works, the Church may grant plenary (full) or partial indulgences by administering the merits of Christ and the saints. Sale of indulgences was denounced by the Protestant reformers, and the abuse was abolished by the Council of TRENT.

INDUS, longest river of SW Asia, rising in the Himalayas of W Tibet and flowing 1800mi through Kashmir and Pakistan to its 75mi-long delta on the N Arabian Sea. Cradle of the ancient INDUS VALLEY CIVILIZATION, it is now an important source of hydroelectric power and irrigation.

INDUSTRIAL DESIGN, expression of the special relationship between the artist, the consumer and the manufacturer in an industrial society. Many of the goods produced by early industrialism were ugly and shoddy. William MORRIS and his followers tried to inspire the rebirth of craftsmanship. In the 1920s BAUHAUS designers and others proved that mass-produced articles could be aesthetically attractive as well as functional. The Society of Industrial Artists in Britain and the American Society of Industrial Designers and Industrial Designers Institute in the US have gained recognition for industrial design as an independent profession.

INDUSTRIAL PSYCHOLOGY, or **occupational psychology,** the study of the mental responses and attitudes of people at work, particularly in their relations with each other, with the organization, and with the devices which they operate. Its purpose is to increase efficiency and provide conditions in which people derive maximum satisfaction from their work. Industrial psychologists use personality tests to determine workers' aptitudes, and contribute to the design of machines and factories. (See also AUTOMATION; HUMAN ENGINEERING; MECHANIZATION AND AUTOMATION; PSYCHOLOGY.)

INDUSTRIAL RELATIONS, the conduct of relations between organized labor and management, and the relations between individual workers and their immediate supervisors. Wage rates, work conditions and productivity are among potential sources of conflict between the two sides. Unresolved conflicts can result in strikes and lockouts that cut output and profits and thus harm employees and employer alike. In the US the federal government helps to settle major industrial disputes, the Labor Relations Board serving as adjudicator. US Industrial relations are largely governed by the WAGNER ACT of 1935 and the TAFT-HARTLEY ACT of 1947. (See also ARBITRATION; LABOR; UNIONS.)

INDUSTRIAL REVOLUTION, in a country's history a period of rapid transition from an agrarian to an industrial society; specifically, the prototype of such periods, the late 18th and early 19th centuries in the UK. This period saw Britain transformed from a predominantly agricultural society into the world's first industrial nation. In the 18th century, British expansionism, inventiveness, economic sophistication and natural resources combined to provide unique opportunities for building business fortunes. The growth of capitalism developed the FACTORY system to harness new inventions that cheaply mass-produced textiles to exploit the expanding world market for British cloth. Key inventions in textile production included KAY's flying shuttle, HARGREAVES' spinning jenny, ARKWRIGHT's water frame and CARTWRIGHT's powered loom. In 1709 Abraham DARBY had learned to smelt iron with coke; in 1781, James WATT patented a steam engine producing rotary motion. Soon many factories were using steam-powered iron machinery. Canals and, from the 1830s, railroads and steamships provided a transportation network linking new industrial cities with sources of supply and markets. The urban masses were supported by increasingly efficient agriculture, due to scientific advances and the stimuus to self-sufficiency of the NAPOLEONIC WARS. Largely through improvements in food supply, sanitation and medicine Britain's population rose from under 7 million in 1750 to over 20 million in 1850, creating both an increased labor force and escalating consumer demand. Factory workers endured appalling conditions before legislation brought improvements. The wealth they had created, however, made possible a more general prosperity.

INDUSTRIAL UNION. See UNIONS.

INDUSTRIAL WORKERS OF THE WORLD (IWW), American labor organization, founded 1905 by revolutionary socialists to radicalize the labor movement. It reached its greatest influence 1912–17, with a policy of confrontation, often violent; at its peak it had almost 100 000 members. Unlike the American Federation of Labor (AFL) it aimed not at improving labor conditions but at revolution. It lost support by attempting to exploit WWI; its strikes were considered treasonable. IWW leaders were imprisoned and the movement almost wholly suppressed.

INDUS VALLEY CIVILIZATION, centered round the Indus R in India and Pakistan, the earliest known urban culture of the Indian subcontinent. Superimposed on earlier stone- and bronze-using (see STONE AGE; BRONZE AGE) cultures dating from c4000 BC, the Indus Valley civilization, centered around HARAPPA and MOHENJO-DARO, lasted from c2500 to c1750 BC. About 100 of its towns and villages, some with fortified citadels, have been identified.

INDY, Vincent d'. See D'INDY, VINCENT.

INEQUALITIES, statements that two quantities are not equal (see EQUALITY), specifically statements as to which is the larger. The relationships are written $>$ (greater than) and $<$ (less than); and these may be coupled with the symbol of equality, as $\geqslant$ (greater than or equal to) and $\leqslant$ (less than or equal to). (See also ALGEBRA.)

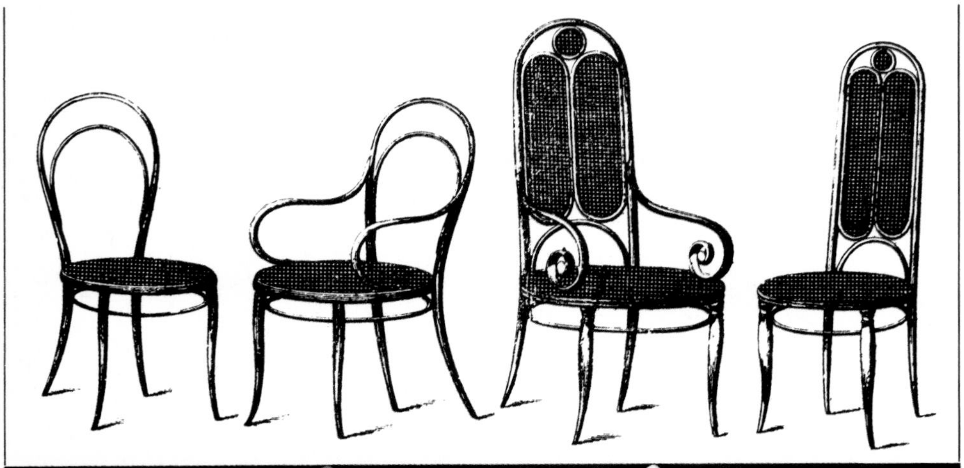

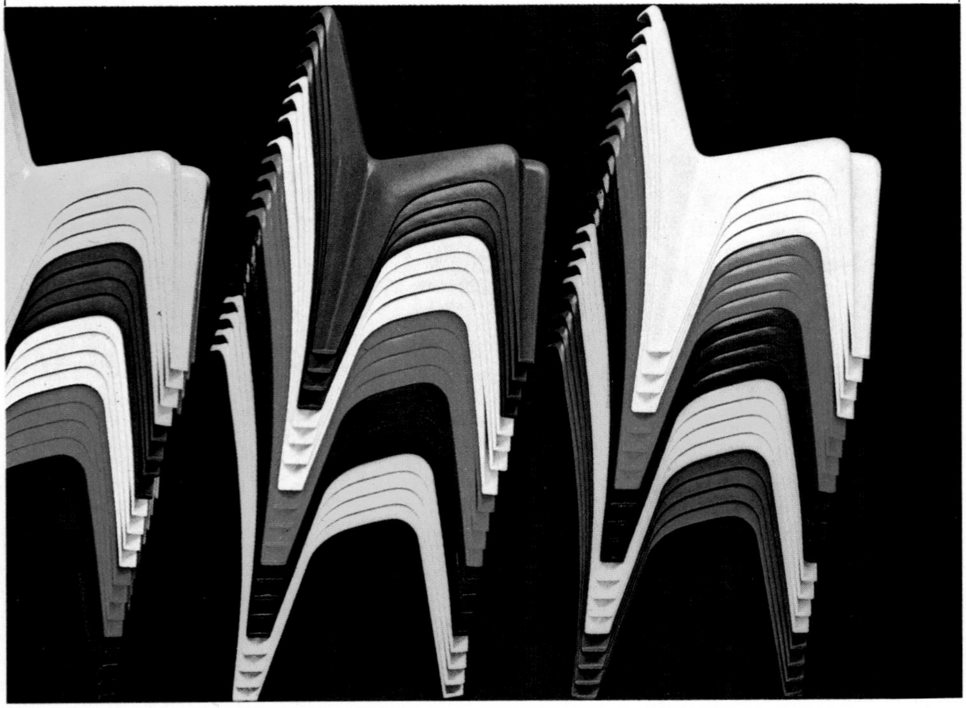

Above: These elegant chairs are an early example of industrial design, produced by Michael Thonet (1796–1871) in an attempt to allow standardization for production purposes without sacrificing appearance. *Below:* A modern attempt to do the same, stacking chairs from about 1970; they were among the earliest examples of furniture molded from one piece of plastic.

INERT GASES, former name for the noble gases.

INERTIA, property of all matter, representing its resistance to any alteration of its state of motion. The mass of a body is a quantitative measure of its inertia; a heavy body has more inertia than a lighter one and needs a greater force to set it in motion. Newton's laws of motion and his principle on relativity depend on the concept of inertia. In Einstein's theory of relativity, the inertial properties of matter are interrelated with its total energy content.

INERTIAL GUIDANCE, an automatic navigational apparatus carried in guided missiles, airplanes, ships and submarines, which depends on the forces of inertia for sensing changes in the magnitude and direction of the vehicle's motion. Accelerometers are mounted on gyrostabilized platforms to isolate them from the vehicle's angular motion; by measuring the forces needed to keep a suspended mass stationary with respect to the moving vehicle, they sense changes in its motion and gravitational fields. The orientations of the accelerometers are found from reference directions provided by gyroscopes. A computer calculates velocities or distances from the instrument signals and can compare these with stored data. The accuracy of the system is improved by a method of feedback called Schuler tuning.

INFALLIBILITY, Papal. See papacy.

INFANCY. See childhood.

INFANTILE PARALYSIS. See poliomyelitis.

INFANTILE SEXUALITY, general term embracing those aspects of sexuality (see sex) exhibited by most children less than about five years old. They do not in general persist into adulthood, though the adult may suffer from a complex caused by guilt concerning them. (See also oedipus complex.)

INFANTRY, body of soldiers who fight on foot using light weaponry, such as rifles, machine guns, bazookas, mortars and grenades. Despite the mechanization of warfare, infantry units still form the largest combat branch of most armies. In the US army an infantry division consists of about 15000 infantrymen and normally comprises eight infantry battalions and two supporting armored battalions equipped with tanks and heavy weapons.

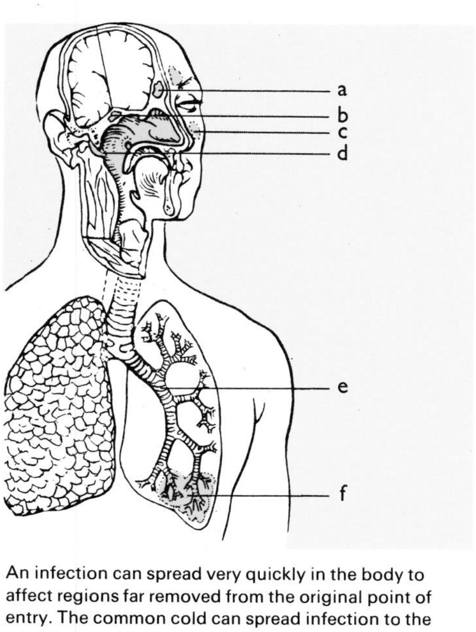

An infection can spread very quickly in the body to affect regions far removed from the original point of entry. The common cold can spread infection to the frontal sinus (a), the sphenoid (b), the maxillary sinuses (c), the Eustachian tube and middle ear (d), or even into the bronchial network (e), creating local center of infection in the tissue of the lungs (f).

INFECTIOUS DISEASES, diseases caused by any microorganism, but particularly viral and bacterial diseases and parasitic diseases, in which the causative agent may be transferred from one person to another (directly or indirectly). Knowledge of the stages at which a particular disease is liable to infect others and of its route (via skin scales, cough particles, clothing, urine, feces, saliva, or by insects, particularly mosquitos and ticks) helps physicians to limit the spread of diseases in epidemics.

INFERIORITY COMPLEX, term used by adler and now mainly by psychoanalysts to describe the complex of fears and emotions arising out of feelings of inferiority or inadequacy, particularly those concerned with (usually imagined) inferiority of the sexual organs. (See superiority complex.)

INFINITESIMAL, originally, an infinitely small quantity, smaller than any finite quantity. The term is now applied to a part of a quantity whose magnitude is vanishingly small in terms of that of the quantity itself; and hence to that part of a function which is vanishingly small for all values of the variable, as in $f(x)=x+10^{-10}x$. Calculus has sometimes been called **infinitesimal calculus.**

INFINITIVE, that form of a verb often used as a noun and requiring neither subject nor object. In English the infinitive is usually preceded by "to," as in "to be." (See also verb.)

INFINITY (∞)**,** a quantity greater than any finite quantity. In modern mathematics infinity is viewed in two ways. In one, the word infinity has a definite meaning; and with transfinite cardinal numbers, for example, it may have a plurality of meanings. In the other, infinity is seen as a limit: to say that parallel lines intersect at infinity, for example, means merely that the point of intersection of two lines may be made to recede indefinitely by making the lines more and more nearly parallel. Similarly, in $f(x)=1/x$, it is meaningful to say that $f(x)$ tends to infinity as x tends to zero (see calculus); again, the sequence $1, 2, 3, \ldots, n$, tends to infinity since, however large n is chosen, there is an $(n+1)$ greater than it. (See also series.)

INFLAMMATION, the complex of reactions established in body tissues in response to injury and infection. It is typified by redness, heat, swelling and pain in the affected part. The first change is in the capillaries, which dilate, causing erythema, and become more permeable to cells and plasma (leading to edema). White blood cells accumulate on the capillary walls and pass into affected tissues; foreign bodies, dead tissue and bacteria are taken up and destroyed by phagocytosis and enzyme action. Active substances produced by white cells encourage increased blood flow and white cell migration into the tissues. Lymph drainage is important in removing edema fluid and tissue debris. Antibody and antigen reactions, allergy and other types of immunity are concerned with the initiation and perpetuation of inflammation. Inflammatory diseases comprise viral and bacterial disease, parasitic disease and disorders in which the inflammatory response is activated inappropriately (e.g., by autoimmunity) causing tissue damage.

INFLATION, economic phenomenon characterized by rising prices of goods and services which result in the diminished purchasing power of a given nominal sum of money. It is the opposite of deflation, where prices and costs are falling. Inflation is usually measured by an index that reflects price changes of a selected list or "market basket" of goods and services commonly purchased by households and which indicates the cost of living. Inflation is generally considered unfavorable because (1) it may lead to undesirable redistribution of real income where people with fixed incomes or whose money income rises slower than the rate of inflation suffer a loss in their purchasing power; (2) unless interest rates rise, saving is discouraged as the sum saved falls in value over time; (where alternative forms of saving exist that would compensate for the falling value of money, inflation affects the pattern and direction of savings rather than the amount); (3) higher prices and costs make a nation's exports less competitive in the international market, thus adversely affecting domestic production, employment and the balance of payments. The two principal theories on the causes of inflation are the Cost-Push theory, which explains inflation as stemming from higher costs of production leading to higher prices, and the Demand-Pull theory which attributes inflation to excessive aggregate demand caused by an excess volume of money relative to available supply of goods and services, driving up prices. Remedies for inflation depend on which of these two theories is accepted. Demand-Pull theorists advocate use of fiscal and monetary policies (control over money supply) to restrain aggregate demand. Cost-Push theorists, by contrast, would either allow unemployment to rise or would intervene in wage negotiations to curtail inflationary wage claims.

INFLECTION, a change in the tone, pitch or volume of the voice; and in linguistics more importantly a change in the form of a word for grammatical reasons. In modern English, inflections are usually suffixes: "to kick," "kicks" and "kicked." As syntax increases in importance in a language, inflections become less frequent. (See also grammar; linguistics.)

INFLECTION, Point of, a point on a curve at which the direction of curvature changes. At such a point the *second* derivative of the curve's function has a value of zero, its value changing from negative to positive, or *vice versa*, between the two points immediately adjacent on each side. (See also extremum.)

INFLORESCENCE, term applied to the conspicuous clusters of flowers that are produced by many angiosperms. There are several types of inflorescence, the forms of which vary according to the arrangement of individual flowers. In the type of inflorescence known as a **raceme** the flowers are attached to the main flower axis by short stalks, or pedicels, of equal length, for example the hyacinth, while in the spike there are no pedicels and the flowers are directly attached to the main axis, for example the gladiolus. Plants such as lilac and oats have an inflorescence similar to a raceme, but the pedicels bear more than one flower. This formation is called a panicle. In the corymb, the pedicels are of unequal length so that the inflorescence has a flat-topped appearance, for example hawthorn. In some plants, particularly those of the family compositae, all the flowers are bunched on a flat disk, this arrangement being known as a head. In the simple umbel the pedicels appear to arise from a central point, while in the compound umbel several simple umbels are borne on a single stalk or ray and each inflorescence comprises a number of rays growing from the tip of the main axis. A simple umbel is produced by the milkweed and most members of the carrot family (Umbelliferae) produce compound umbels.

INFLUENZA, grippe, or **'flu,** a group of viral diseases causing mild respiratory symptoms, fever, malaise, muscle pains and headache, and often occurring in rapidly spreading epidemics. Gastrointestinal tract symptoms may also occur. Rarely, it may cause a severe viral pneumonia. A characteristic of influenza viruses is their property of changing their antigenic nature frequently, so that immunity following a previous attack ceases to be effective. This also limits the usefulness of influenza vaccination.

INFORMATION RETRIEVAL, a branch of technology of ever-increasing importance as man attempts to cope with the "information explosion." To store and have reference to the vast amount of printed matter produced annually is impossible for most libraries. The problem can be solved by microphotography. Pages are photographed at a reduction (typically to about $\frac{1}{20}$ and stored on 35mm or 16mm film (microfilm), on transparent cards measuring about 100×150mm (microfiches) or as positive prints on slightly smaller cards (microcards). Videotape is also used. Reference may be manual or by machine, usually computer. The information must be classified so that the user may gain rapid access *either* to a particular book or paper *or* to all the relevant material on a particular subject.

In computers, information retrieval involves a reverse of those operations used for data storage. The operator inserts a classification which the computer matches with the classification in its memory.

INFORMATION THEORY, or communication theory, a mathematical discipline that aims at maximizing the information that can be conveyed by communications systems, at the same time as minimizing the errors that arise in the course of transmission. The information content of a message is

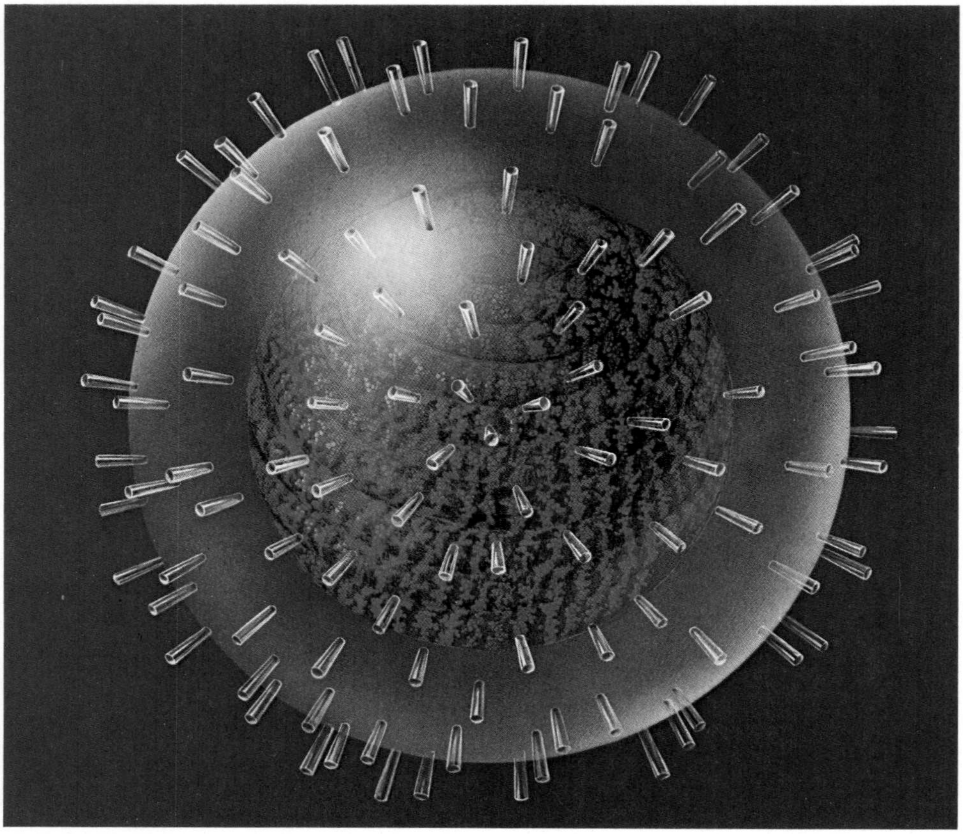

Reconstruction of one of the many influenza viruses, based on electron-microscope photographs.

conventionally quantified in terms of "bits" (*b*inary dig*its*). Each BIT represents a simple alternative—in terms of a message, a yes-or-no; in terms of the components in an electrical circuit, that a switch is opened or closed. Mathematically, the bit is usually represented as a 0-or-1. Complex messages can be represented as series of bit alternatives. Five bits of information only are needed to specify any letter of the alphabet, given an appropriate code. Thus able to quantify "information," information theory employs statistical methods to analyze practical communications problems. The errors that arise in the transmission of signals, often termed NOISE, can be minimized by the incorporation of **redundancy**. Here more bits of information than are strictly necessary to encode a message are transmitted, so that if some are altered in transmission, there is still enough information to allow the signal to be correctly interpreted. Clearly, the handling of redundant information costs something in reduced speed of or capacity for transmission, but the reduction in message errors compensates for this loss. Information theoreticians often point to an analogy between the thermodynamic concept of ENTROPY and the degree of misinformation in a signal.

INFRARED RADIATION, ELECTROMAGNETIC RADIATION of wavelength between 780nm and 1mm, strongly radiated by hot objects and also termed heat radiation. Detected using PHOTOELECTRIC CELLS, BOLOMETERS and photographically, it finds many uses—in the home for heating and cooking and in medicine in the treatment of muscle and skin conditions. Infrared absorption SPECTROSCOPY is an important analytical tool in organic chemistry. Military applications (including missile-detection and guidance systems and night-vision apparatus) and infrared PHOTOGRAPHY (often FALSE-COLOR PHOTOGRAPHY) exploit the **infrared window**, the spectral band between 7.5 and 11μm in which the ATMOSPHERE is transparent. This and the high infrared reflectivity of foliage give infrared photographs their striking, often dramatic clarity, even when exposed under misty conditions.

INFRASTRUCTURE, the foundations underpinning an organization or enterprise. In a national economy these may include installations for extracting, transporting and processing essential raw materials, also the means of training the labor force and building the equipment needed.

INFUSORIA, a term originally applied to any of the miscellaneous microorganisms associated with infusions of decomposing organic matter, but later restricted to a single protozoan assemblage containing the Ciliates and Suctorians. The term is not now in taxonomic use.

INGE, William (1913–1973), US playwright, noted for psychological studies of life in small Midwest towns, in such plays as *Come Back, Little Sheba* (1950), *Picnic* (1953) which won a Pulitzer Prize, *Bus Stop* (1955) and *A Loss of Roses* (1959).

INGERSOLL, Jared (1749–1822), US statesman and jurist. As delegate from Pa. to the Constitutional Convention (1787) he was a signer of the Constitution. Attorney-general of Pa. 1790–99 and 1811–17, he was Federalist vice-presidential nominee in 1812.

INGERSOLL, Robert Green (1833–1899), US lawyer, writer and politician. Known for his lectures and publications advocating agnosticism, he became famous for his forceful speech in favor of James G. BLAINE at the 1876 Republican convention.

INGLEWOOD, city in S Cal., site of Los Angeles International Airport. Mainly residential, it has metal, plastics and furniture industries. Pop 89 985.

INGRES, Jean Auguste Dominique (1780–1867), French Neoclassical painter, renowned for his mastery of line. *The Vow of Louis XIII* (1824) won him acclaim as the foremost classicist of his time but today he is better known for portraits and nude studies such as the *Odalisque* (1814). He was a determined opponent of the Romantic movement.

INHERITANCE TAX, levy or assessment on property bequeathed by a deceased person to a specific legatee. It thus differs from estate tax, levied on a deceased person's estate as a whole. In the US most states levy both estate and inheritance taxes; since 1916 the federal government has levied only estate tax.

INHIBITION, the action of a mental process or function in restraining the expression of another mental process or function; e.g., fear of social condemnation inhibiting fulfilment of sexual desire. Most often the EGO or SUPEREGO inhibits instinctual behavior (see INSTINCT). (See also REPRESSION.)

INHIBITION, in biochemistry. See ENZYMES.

INITIAL TEACHING ALPHABET (i.t.a.) alphabet of 44 phonetic symbols designed to teach elementary reading of English by relating the spelling of a word to the pronounced sounds (*phonemes*) that make it up. Devised by Sir James Pitman, it was experimentally introduced in Britain in 1960, in the US in 1963.

INITIATIVE, REFERENDUM AND RECALL, methods by which a country's citizens may directly intervene to influence government policy between elections. Initiative, provided for in most US states, is a procedure whereby a new law is proposed in a petition then submitted to a vote by legislature or electorate or both. Laws so passed are generally not subject to veto. Referendum allows citizens a direct vote on proposed laws and policies. A referendum may be demanded by petition, but in most US states it is mandatory for measures such as constitutional amendments and bond issues. Recall, adopted by many cities and some states, provides for the removal of an elected official by calling a special election. Such an election must usually be demanded in a petition whose signers number at least 25% of the votes originally received by the official. Recall has rarely succeeded at state level.

INJECTION, the administration of a substance, usually a DRUG or vaccine, by SYRINGE and needle which allows the SKIN to be broached and the substance to be delivered intradermally, subcutaneously, intramuscularly, intravenously, intra-arterially or into body organs or cavities. This bypasses the GASTROINTESTINAL TRACT which may be ineffective, slow or unreliable, or may destroy the agent. VACCINATION, desensitization for ALLERGY, drugs for seriously ill or VOMITING patients and INSULIN for DIABETICS are almost always given by injection.

INJECTION MOLDING, technique used in forming thermoplastic materials. The hot, plastic material is forced into a chilled (usually by water) mold, in which it sets. (See also PLASTICS.)

INJUNCTION, formal court order prohibiting or, more rarely, commanding some particular act. It may be temporary, pending some further ruling, or permanent, embodying a court's decision. Violation of either variety may be punished as contempt of court. Injunctions are generally granted at the court's discretion, provided there is a real threat to the complainant's right.

INK, liquid or paste, containing DYES or PIGMENTS, used for writing or PRINTING. Writing inks date from the mid-3rd millennium BC in China and Egypt. The most common today is blue-black permanent ink, made by dissolving GALLIC ACID, IRON (II) sulfate and TARTARIC ACID in water. Since the blue-black color is produced only when the ink dries, a dye is usually added to color the ink during writing. In ballpoint inks, dyes are dissolved in GLYCOLS and other liquids, and wetting agents are added. Black, waterproof India ink is a suspension of CARBON particles stabilized by GELATIN, glue etc. Carbon black is also the pigment used in black printing ink. Printing inks—diverse in their composition and uses—are viscous pastes made by grinding pigments with varnishes or petroleum solvents, and contain various additives for printability and drying speeds.

INKBERRY, evergreen winterberry, bearbush or Appalachian tree, *Ilex glabra*, an evergreen shrub of the HOLLY family, Aquifoliaceae, which is native to North America. It seldom grows above 2m (6.6ft) and produces small white flowers followed by black berries.

INKBLOT TEST, or **Rorschach Test.** See RORSCHACH, H.

INKSTER, residential village in SE Mich., a suburb of Dearborn. Pop 38 595.

INLAND SEA (*Seto-nakai*), in Japan, a narrow sea 3 500sq mi in area between the islands of Honshu, Kyushu and Shikoku, joined to the outer sea by four straits. It has some 300 islands. An important commercial waterway and fishing ground, it is also the site of the Inland Sea National Park.

INLAND WATERWAY, navigable stretch of inland water used for transport and often for recreation. Rivers, lakes and CANALS were of crucual importance before the development of railroads and reliable highways, and many still play a vital role in the low-cost transportation of bulky raw materials and manufactured products. In the US, inland waterways, excluding the Great Lakes, account for some 10% of the total movement of commercial goods. (See also INTRACOASTAL WATERWAY; SAINT LAWRENCE SEAWAY.)

INLAY, the decorative setting of materials flush into the surface of an object of contrasting kind or color, as for example in DAMASCENING, INTARSIA and MOSAIC.

INNER MONGOLIA, autonomous region in N China, 455 000sq mi in area. Its NW area is part of the Gobi desert, bordering the Mongolian People's Republic; the rest is steppe plateau. The economy is mainly agricultural.

INNES, George (1825–1894), US landscape painter. His best-known work, such as *The Lackawanna Valley* (1855), shows the influence of COROT and the BARBIZON SCHOOL. His later work, such as *The Home of the Heron* (1893) is less realistic and more atmospheric.

INNOCENT, name of 13 popes. **Saint Innocent I** (d. 417), was pope from 401. He championed papal supremacy, but failed to prevent the sack of Rome by ALARIC in 410. **Innocent II** (d. 1143), was elected pope in 1130 by a minority. He spent the rest of his reign in refuge from the majority's choice, ANACLETUS II. **Innocent III** (c1161–1216), was pope from 1198. Under him the medieval papacy reached the summit of its power and influence. In an assertion of temporal power he forced King John of England to become his vassal and had Emperor Otto deposed in favor of Frederick II. He initiated the Fourth Crusade (1202) and supported the crusade against the ALBIGENSIANS (1208). He presided over the Fourth Lateran Council (1215), culmination of the entire medieval papacy. **Innocent IV** (c1190–1254), was pope from 1243. He clashed with Emperor Frederick II over the temporal power of the papacy, and was forced to flee to Lyons, France, until Frederick's death. He worked for the unification of the Christian churches. **Innocent V** (c1224–1276), pope in 1276, was the first Dominican pope. **Innocent VI** (d. 1362), pope from 1352, reigned from Avignon. **Innocent VII** (1336–1406), pope from 1404, vainly tried to heal the GREAT SCHISM. Unrest in Rome obliged him to flee to Viterbo. **Innocent VIII** (1432–1492), pope from 1484, was worldly and unscrupulous. He fomented the

Pope Innocent X, a detail from the famous portrait by Velasquez (1650).

witchcraft hysteria and meddled in Italian politics. For a fee he kept the brother and rival of Sultan BAYAZID II imprisoned. **Innocent IX** (1519–1591), was pope for two months in 1591. **Innocent X** (1574–1655), pope from 1644, was weak, ineffectual and much given to nepotism. He was dominated by his ambitious sister-in-law, and at her instigation dispossessed the BARBERINI family. **Innocent XI** (1611–1689), was pope from 1676. An opponent of QUIETISM, he favored toleration of Protestantism, and over this and the issue of papal power clashed with Louis XIV of France. **Innocent XII** (1615–1700), was pope from 1691. A stern reformer, he abolished nepotism and was renowned for his piety and charity. **Innocent XIII** (1655–1724), was pope from 1721. He bestowed Naples and Sicily on their de facto possessor, the Emperor Charles VI, and recognized the claims of James, the Old Pretender, to the British throne in the hope of a Catholic revival there.

INNOCENTS, Holy. See HOLY INNOCENTS' DAY.

INN RIVER, river about 320mi long which rises in E Switzerland and joins the Danube at Passau. For some of its length it forms part of the border between Austria and Germany. It has hydroelectric plants.

INNSBRUCK, capital of Tyrol province, Austria, situated on the Inn R between steep Alpine ranges. An important medieval trading post (chartered 1233), its fine historic buildings make it a popular tourist center. Pop 115 293.

INNS OF COURT, the four legal societies in London which, since the Middle Ages, have controlled admissions to the English bar. They are Lincoln's Inn, Gray's Inn, the Inner Temple and the Middle Temple.

INOCULATION, the INJECTION or introduction of microorganisms or their products into living TISSUES or culture mediums. It is used in man to establish antibody formation and IMMUNITY in VACCINATION.

INÖNÜ, Ismet (1884–   ), Turkish statesman, twice prime minister between 1923 and 1937, and second president of Turkey (1938–50). Militarily and politically second in command to ATATURK, he helped found the republic. In 1950 he held free elections, his own party being defeated. Following the military coup of 1960, he won further terms as premier (1961–65).

INORGANIC CHEMISTRY, major branch of CHEMISTRY comprising the study of all the elements and their compounds, except carbon compounds containing hydrogen (see ORGANIC CHEMISTRY). The elements are classified according to the PERIODIC TABLE. Classical inorganic chemistry is largely descriptive, synthetic and analytical; modern theoretical inorganic chemistry is hard to distinguish from PHYSICAL CHEMISTRY.

INPUT-OUTPUT ANALYSIS, a technique of economics which quantifies the interdependence of the productive sectors and units of an economy. By showing how given products function not only as units of consumption, but also in the production of further goods, input-output tables assist the planning of production or consumption goals.

INQUEST, a formal legal inquiry to ascertain a certain fact, generally the circumstances and medical cause of a sudden or unexplained death; such an investigation is conducted by a coroner, assisted by a jury. An inquest may also determine damages in certain cases.

INQUISITION, a medieval agency of the Roman Catholic Church to combat heresy, first made official in 1231, when Pope Gregory IX appointed a commission of Dominicans to investigate heresy among the ALBIGENSIANS of S France. It aimed to save the heretic's soul, but a refusal to recant was punished by fines, penance or imprisonment, and often by confiscation of land by the secular authorities. Later the penalty was death by burning. Torture, condemned by former popes, was permitted in heresy trials by Innocent IV (d. 1254). The accused was not told the name of his accusers but could name his known enemies so that their hostile testimony might be discounted. Often the Inquisition was an object of political manipulation. In 1542 it was reconstituted to counter Protestantism in Italy; its modern descendant is the Congregation of the Doctrine of the Faith.

The Spanish Inquisition, founded in 1478 by Ferdinand V and Isabella, was a branch of government and was distinct from the papal institution. Its first commission was to investigate Jews who had publicly embraced Christianity but secretly held to

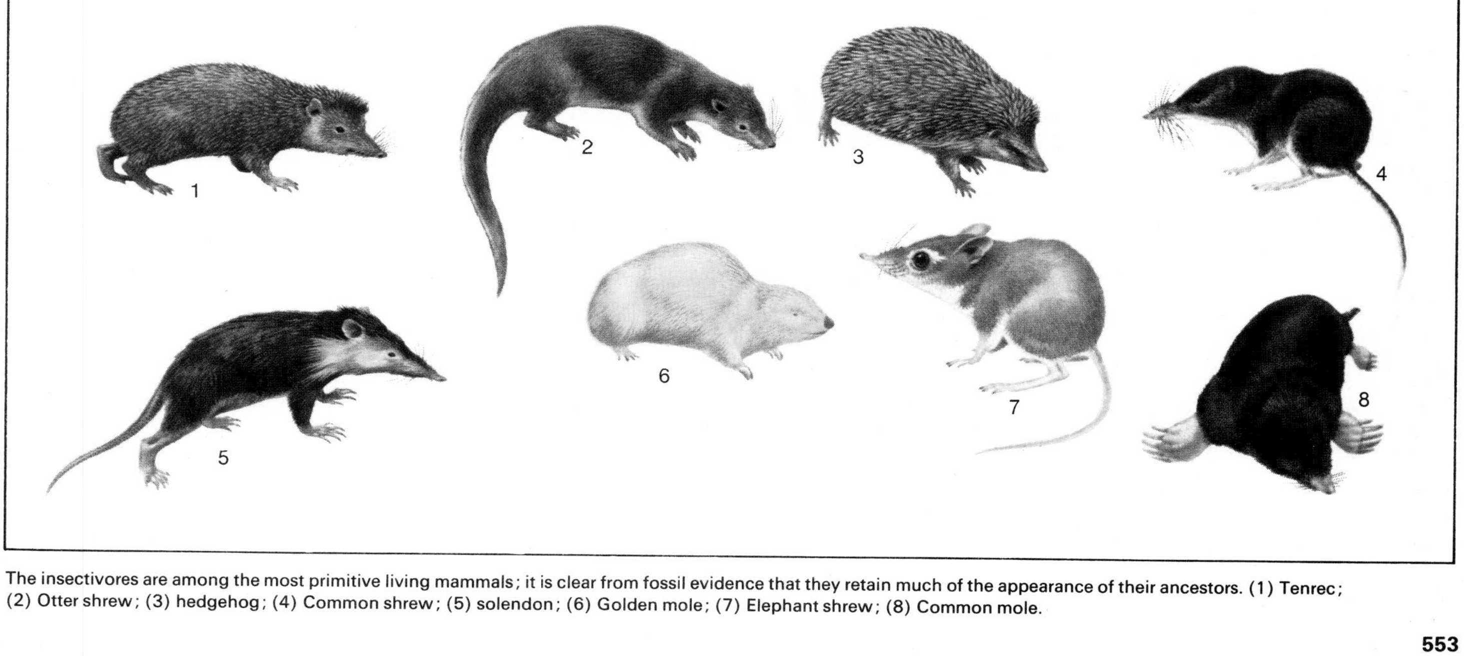

The insectivores are among the most primitive living mammals; it is clear from fossil evidence that they retain much of the appearance of their ancestors. (1) Tenrec; (2) Otter shrew; (3) hedgehog; (4) Common shrew; (5) solendon; (6) Golden mole; (7) Elephant shrew; (8) Common mole.

Judaism. Under the grand inquisitor TORQUEMADA, it became an agency of official terror—even St. Ignatius Loyola was investigated. It was extended to Portugal and South America and not dissolved until 1820.

INSANITY, term descriptive of an individual's mental state employed in legal and popular usage. In psychology and psychoanalysis, the term is considered a loose synonym for PSYCHOSIS.

INSCRIPTION, in plane GEOMETRY, the construction of a CIRCLE such that each side of a POLYGON is a tangent to it (see TANGENT OF A CURVE). An inscribed ANGLE is one whose sides are chords of a circle and whose vertex lies on the circle. In three dimensions, inscription implies the construction of a sphere such that every side of a regular POLYHEDRON is a tangent plane to it. (See also CIRCUMSCRIPTION.)

INSECTICIDE, any substance toxic to INSECTS and used to control them in situations where they cause economic damage or endanger the health of man and his domestic animals. There are three main types: **stomach insecticides**, which are ingested by the insect with their food; **contact insecticides**, which penetrate the cuticle, and **fumigant insecticides**, which are inhaled. Stomach insecticides are often used to control chewing insects like CATERPILLARS and sucking insects like APHIDS. They may be applied to the plant prior to attack and remain active in or on the plant for a considerable time. They must be used with considerable caution on food plants or animal forage. Examples include ARSENIC compounds which remain on the leaf, and organic compounds which are absorbed by the plant and transported to all its parts (systemic insecticides). Contact insecticides include the plant products NICOTINE, derris and PYRETHRUM, which are quickly broken down, and the synthetic compounds such as DDT (and other chlorinated HYDROCARBONS, organophosphates (malathion, parathion) and carbamates. Polychlorinated biphenyls (PCBs) are added to some insecticides to increase their effectiveness and persistance. Highly persistent insecticides may be concentrated in food chains and exert harmful effects on other animals such as birds and fish (see ECOLOGY).

INSECTIVORA, an order of small insectivorous MAMMALS, regarded as the most primitive group of placental mammals, having diverged little from the ancestral form. The skull is generally long and narrow, with a primitively large complement of unspecialized teeth in the jaw. Ears and eyes are small and often hidden in fur or skin. The group includes SHREWS, HEDGEHOGS, TENRECS, and MOLES.

INSECTIVOROUS PLANTS, or **carnivorous plants**, specialized plants whose leaves are adapted to trap and digest insects, which supplement their food supply. They normally live in boggy habitats or as EPIPHYTES. The insects may be caught in vase-like traps (see PITCHER PLANT), by leaves that spring shut (see VENUS' FLY TRAP), by a trapdoor (see BLADDERWORT) or on sticky leaves (see SUNDEW). The captured insects are broken down by ENZYMES secreted from the plants and the products absorbed.

INSECTS, animals having an external skeleton of chitin, characterized by having the body divided into three distinct sections: head, thorax and abdomen. The thorax typically bears two pairs of wings and three pairs of legs. This last is the most diagnostic feature and gives them their alternative name: Hexapoda. The insects are by far the most diverse class of invertebrates, and many are highly specialized. In terms of numbers they are undoubtedly the most successful group in the ANIMAL KINGDOM: the number of species alone exceeds that of all other groups of animals combined. The head bears the mouth, complex mouthparts, the antennae and eyes. The mouthparts above all reflect the diversity of the group. Although they are composed of the same six basic structures in all species, the mouthparts show incredible modifications to specialized modes of feeding. Primitively distinct, heavy, serrated structures for chewing and crushing in the COCKROACH, they form piercing stylets in MOSQUITOES and APHIDS, with animal or plant juices drawn up a central groove. The long, coiled proboscis of BUTTERFLIES and MOTHS, adapted for sucking NECTAR, is also a tube—but one formed from the modification of different mouthparts.

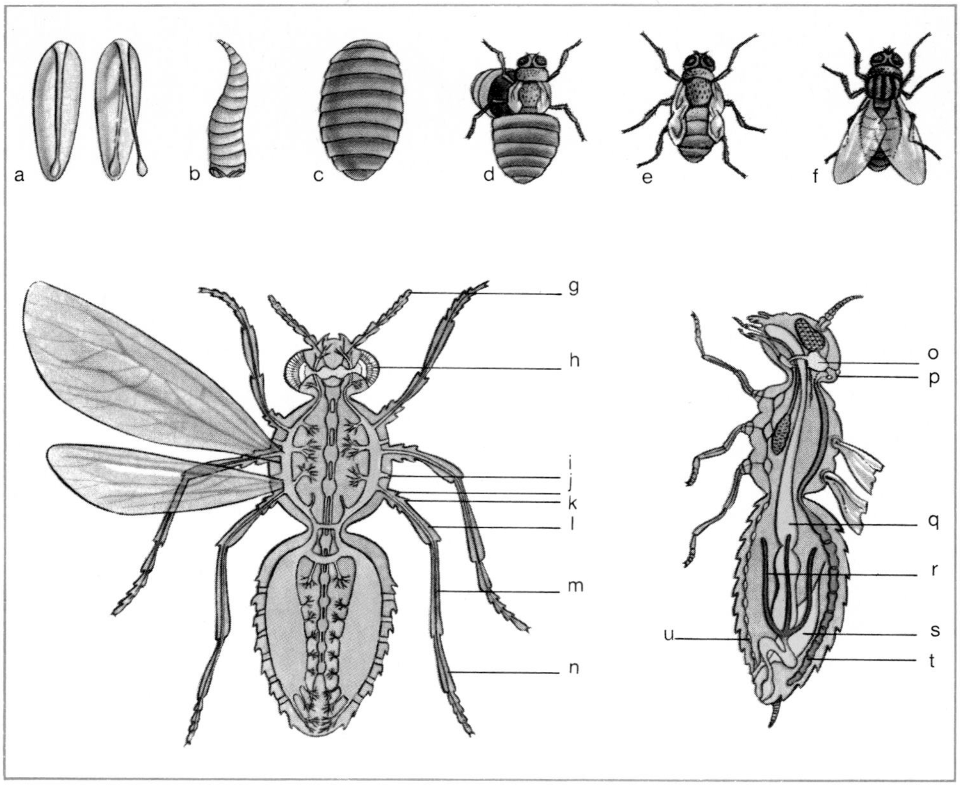

Insect metamorphosis is one of the most remarkable of natural phenomena. The metamorphosis of a fly (*top*) begins with an egg (a), from which the larva hatches (b). The pupa stage (c) appears dormant, but within the puparium important changes are taking place under the influence of the hormones. The immature fly (d) creeps out of the puparium already equipped with legs and eyes but with rudimentary wings (e) and finally reaches the adult stage, called the imago (f). Insects display all the characteristics of their phylum, Arthropoda: a skin covered with a hard layer (cuticula), which also serves as an exoskeleton; a body which is clearly segmented; and jointed appendages. The body is divided into a head, thorax and abdomen. The head has a pair of jointed antennae (g), in which the sense of smell is located, and three pairs of legs and two pairs of wings. Each leg consists of a number of segments, namely, the coxa (j), trochanter (k), femur (l), tibia (m) and tarsus with five segments (n). On the sides of the head are large compound eyes composed of many facets (h), and on the forehead there are generally three simple eyes or ocelli (p). The respiratory organs consist of a system of air tubes (tracheae), the finest branches of which penetrate to all the

In WASPS and BEES some of the mouthparts have formed a tube for drawing up nectar, while others have retained their chewing form, for handling wax and pollen. The thorax also reflects the great diversity of the insects. Though typically of three segments each bearing a pair of legs, and the last two segments each with a pair of wings, wings are absent in some primitive forms (the Apterygota) and modified in others. In the BEETLES, and other groups, one pair of wings loses its flight function and forms a protective case for the other, flying wings. In the FLIES the second pair of wings are modified as balancing organs. Insects have highly-developed sense organs: on the head are COMPOUND EYES and antennae, which are covered with little "hairs" sensitive to the chemical stimuli of smell and taste. Little hairs over the body are sensitive to touch and smell. The life history of insects always involves a larval stage. As the LARVA grows, it passes through a series of molts before it reaches the adult stage, each time shedding the existing, rigid EXOSKELETON, after laying down another, larger one within. The new cuticle is at first soft and can be extended. It hardens on contact with air. Larvae are of two types: those which, with each succeeding molt not only increase in size, but also show a progressive development of adult features; and those which remain totally unlike the adult during growth, but pass through a resting stage or PUPA, when the internal and external structures are completely reorganized to form the adult insect (see METAMORPHOSIS).

INSIDE PASSAGE, shipping route, some 950mi long, sheltered by a chain of islands along the W coast of North America. Its main ports are Seattle, Wash., Vancouver and Juneau and Skagway in Alaska.

INSIGHT, as a technical term in psychology, means an awareness of one's own mental condition, or the grasp of a principle behind a problem without apparent use of logical processes. Insight learning is direct, bypassing the process of trial and error.

INSIGNIA, Military, device worn by members of the armed forces to denote rank, branch of service, special duties or qualifications. US army and air force officers wear shoulder loops, with stars or bars, while enlisted personnel have cloth chevrons. Specialists wear an eagle device and members of regiments wear enameled shields with a coat of arms. Naval officers wear gold insignia on their sleeves and shoulder-boards. Rank and unit are also indicated by badges on caps.

INSTALLMENT PLAN, system of credit trading mostly used for durable consumer goods but also for services. An initial deposit is generally required, the balance being paid in a series of installments: part purchase price, part interest, insurance and financing charges. The goods remain the vendor's property until the scheduled payments are completed and may be repossessed in case of default. Originating in Paris in the 1850s, it is now an integral part of Western economies. The transaction is now generally handled on behalf of the retailer by specialist finance houses.

INSTINCT, a phenomenon whose effects can be observed in animals and man, but whose precise nature is little understood. In general one can say that instinctive behavior comprises those fixed reactions to external stimuli that have not been consciously learned (see ANIMAL BEHAVIOR). In fact, such behavior seems to stem from a complex of hereditary and environmental factors (see ENVIRONMENT; HEREDITY), since animals placed from birth in artificial environments display some, but not all, instinctive reactions characteristic of their species. It has been

tissues. The openings (spiracles) of this system (i) are equipped with muscular rings which keep them closed as long as the animal is not active and needs only a small amount of oxygen; thus gas exchange and water loss are minimized. The internal organs of an insect are located primarily in the abdomen. Nearest the back lies the tube-like heart (t), which consists of a number of segments separated by valves. Toward the front, it passes over into the aorta, the only part of the blood-vessel system that has its own wall: everywhere else the blood flows freely among the organs. In the middle is the intestinal canal (q), consisting of the fore-gut, mid-gut and hind-gut. The long, tubular excretory organs (r) arise at the division between mid- and hind-gut. The abdomen also contains the reproductive organs, such as the ovary (s). The nervous system consists of the brain (o) and the abdominal nerve cord (u), along which are strung clusters of nerve cell bodies called ganglia. *Above:* head of a horsefly showing the remarkable color patterns typical of the compound eyes of this family (Tabanidae).

further suggested that EMBRYOS may have some LEARNING ability; i.e., that some learning before birth is possible. Numbered among the instincts are the sex drive, AGGRESSION, TERRITORIALITY and the food urge; but much debate surrounds such classification. In psychology, "instinct" (sometimes called **drive**) has a similar meaning, with special emphasis on the response as a complex one (see REFLEX). Frustration of, or conflict between, instincts engenders NEUROSES. FREUD suggested the existence of two fundamental instincts: the life instinct, rather akin to the LIBIDO; and its opposite, the death instinct.

INSTITUTE FOR ADVANCED STUDY, research center in Princeton, N.J., founded for graduate study in various fields. It has long specialized in the physical sciences and social studies. It was opened in 1933 and one of its first members was Albert Einstein.

INSTRUMENTALISM, or experimentalism, in philosophy, the development of PRAGMATISM promoted by John DEWEY. It is based on the contention that ideas are validated solely by their usefulness in solving problems.

INSTRUMENT LANDING SYSTEM (ILS), radio system used in conditions of poor visibility to guide aircraft towards runways. Two RADIO transmitters are used, each producing two beams which overlap at a slight angle. The **localizer**, at the far end of the runway, transmits in a horizontal plane; the **glide slope**, at the near end of the runway, does so vertically, the overlap sloping up from the runway at an angle of about 3°. Instruments in the pilot's cockpit indicate deviations from the "cone" of the two overlaps, so guiding him into the point where direct observation of the runway is possible.

INSTRUMENTS, Scientific, devices used for measurement and hence for scientific investigation and control (see also MECHANIZATION AND AUTOMATION). They extend the observing faculties of the human senses, providing accuracy and a greater range. They can also detect and measure phenomena such as X rays which man cannot sense. Early instruments, used mainly in the fields of astronomy, navigation and surveying, measured the basic quantities of mass, length, time and direction (see ASTROLABE; BALANCE; CLOCKS AND WATCHES; COMPASS). With the rise of modern science came several instruments including the MICROMETER, MICROSCOPE, TELESCOPE and THERMOMETER. During the Industrial Revolution and after were invented instruments too many to mention; and today in science, industry and even the home there are a host of instruments to measure every conceivable quantity. A few simple instruments, such as the ruler or balance, work by direct comparison, but most are **transducers**, representing the quantity measured by another sensible quantity (usually the position of a pointer on a scale). All instruments require initial CALIBRATION against a known or calculable standard. In general, an instrument interacts with the measured phenomenon, and the resultant change in its state is amplified if necessary, displayed by means of a pointer, pen, light beam, oscilloscope etc., and recorded, usually on chart paper or by photography. Although precision instruments are designed for high accuracy, inevitably errors are introduced: amplification produces NOISE, the slowness of the instrument's response results in lag and damping, and the intrinsic nature of the response may be defective owing to hysteresis or drift; moreover, the observer may misread the scale because of PARALLAX or INTERPOLATION errors. Most fundamental of all, the act of measuring a system may significantly alter the state of the system (see also UNCERTAINTY PRINCIPLE).

INSULAR CASES, decisions by the US Supreme Court in 1900–01 defining the legal status of Puerto Rico, under US sovereignty since 1899. The cases established that US sovereignty does not of itself confer full constitutional rights.

INSULATION, Electric, the containment of electric currents or voltage by materials (insulators) that offer a high resistance to current flow, will withstand high voltages without breaking down, and will not deteriorate with age. Resistance to sunlight, rain, flame or abrasion may also be important. The electrical resistance of insulators usually falls with temperature (paper and asbestos being exceptions) and if chemical impurities are present. The mechanical properties desired vary with the application: cables require flexible coatings, such as polyvinyl chloride, while glass or porcelain are used for rigid mountings, such as the insulators used to support power cables. In general, good thermal insulators are also good electrical ones.

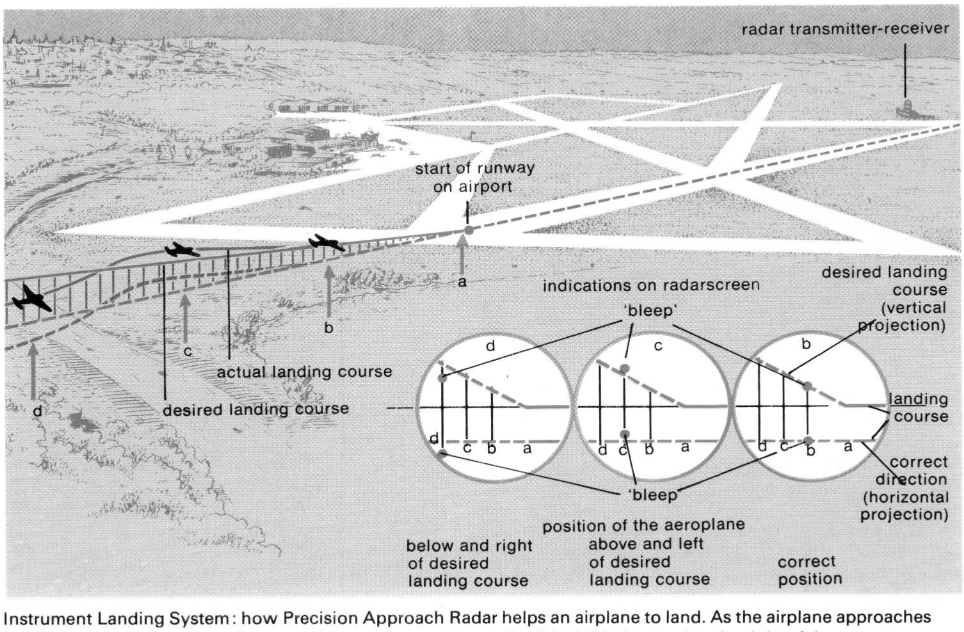

Instrument Landing System: how Precision Approach Radar helps an airplane to land. As the airplane approaches the runway, the flight controller can tell from his radar screen that it is (d) below and to the right of the correct approach path; (c) above it and to its left, and (b) on course for a smooth touchdown at (a).

INSULATION, Thermal, the reduction of transfer of heat from a hot area to a cold. Thermal insulation is used for three distinct purposes: to keep something hot; to keep something cold; and to maintain something at a roughly steady temperature. HEAT is transferred in three ways, CONDUCTION, CONVECTION and RADIATION. The VACUUM BOTTLE thus uses three different techniques to reduce heat transfer: a vacuum between the walls to combat conduction and convection; silvered walls to minimize the transmission of radiant heat from one wall and maximize its reflection from the other; and supports for the inner bottle made of CORK, a poor thermal conductor. (See also FIREBRICK; POLYSTYRENE; REFRACTORY.)

INSULIN, HORMONE important in METABOLISM, produced by the islets of Langerhans in the PANCREAS, which act as an ENDOCRINE GLAND. Insulin is the only hormone which reduces the level of SUGAR in the BLOOD and is secreted in response to a rise in blood sugar (e.g., after meals, or in conditions of stress); the sugar is converted into GLYCOGEN in the cells of MUSCLE and the LIVER under the influence of insulin. Absence or a relative failure in secretion of insulin occurs in DIABETES, in which blood sugar levels are high and in which sugar overflows into the urine. The isolation of insulin as a pancreatic extract by F. G. BANTING and C. H. BEST in 1921 was a milestone in medical and scientific history. It is a PROTEIN made up of fifty AMINO ACIDS as two peptide chains linked by sulfur bridges. Because it is destroyed in the GASTROINTESTINAL TRACT, it has to be taken by subcutaneous INJECTION in diabetics with severe insulin lack. Its use in diabetics has revolutionized treatment of this disease; the aim in its administration is to be as close to natural secretion patterns as possible. If insufficient insulin is taken, diabetic COMA may result, while in excess hypoglycemia supervenes; both require prompt medical treatment.

INSULL, Samuel (1859–1938), English-born US financier. Secretary to Thomas Edison in the 1880s, he became head of the Chicago Edison Co and built a huge conglomerate supplying electricity throughout Ill. and other states. It collapsed in 1932. Later tried for fraud, he was acquitted.

INSURANCE, method of financial protection by which one party undertakes to indemnify another against certain forms of loss. An insurance company pools the payments for this service and invests them to earn further funds. Each insured person pays a relatively small amount, the *premium*, for a stated period of cover. In return the company will, subject to an assessment of his claim, reimburse him for loss caused by an event covered in the policy. Forms of insurance have existed since the earliest civilizations. Modern insurance began with the medieval GUILDS, which sometimes insured members against trade losses. The specialized fields of fire and maritime insurance (see LLOYDS OF LONDON) developed in the 17th and 18th centuries. The development of PROBABILITY theory allowed the statistical likelihood of damage to be calculated, making insurance as a business possible.

INSURGENTS, in the US Republican party a group of senators and representatives who in 1909–10 rebelled against the leadership of William H. TAFT and the domination of House speaker Joseph G. CANNON. Many subsequently joined the breakaway PROGRESSIVE PARTY.

INTAGLIO, decorative design cut concave into the surface of stone or other materials such as semi-precious stones or metal. The term also describes various engraving and printing processes such as etching, where the design is cut into a metal plate and then printed.

INTARSIA, or *tarsia*, form of wood INLAY, also in other materials such as metal or ivory. It is specifically applied to a style, probably Eastern-influenced, developed in 13th-century Siena, Italy.

INTEGERS, the set (see SET THEORY) of whole numbers, including ZERO and negative whole numbers. (See also NATURAL NUMBERS; RATIONAL NUMBERS; TRANSFINITE CARDINAL NUMBER.)

INTEGRAL DOMAIN. See FIELD.

INTEGRATED CIRCUIT, a single structure in which a large number of individual electronic components are assembled. (See ELECTRONICS.)

The development of human intelligence: a graph showing how, according to some psychiatrists, general intelligence typically grows and declines in the course of a lifetime. Age is shown along the horizontal axis; the scale along the vertical axis is arbitrary.

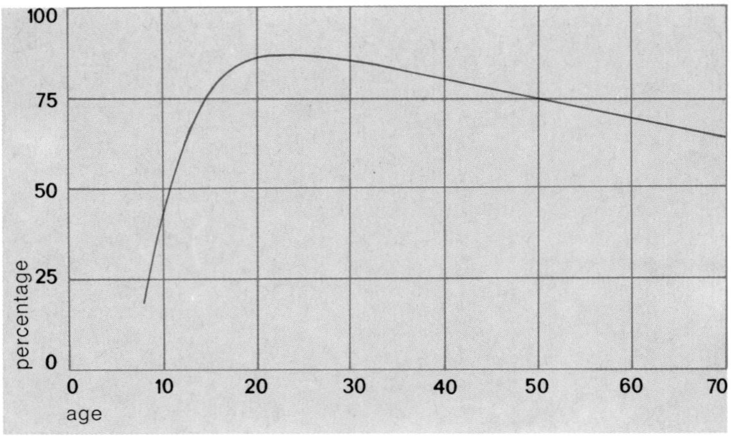

INTEGRATION. See CALCULUS.

INTEGRATION, Racial, the right to equal access for people of all races to such facilities as schools, churches, housing and public accommodations. It became an issue of public importance in the US after the Civil War and the passage of the 13th, 14th and 15th Amendments to the Constitution, 1864–70, which declared the Negro free and equal, and the Civil Rights Act of 1866. Although slavery was ended as a legal institution state laws were passed during the reaction against RECONSTRUCTION to enforce the physical segregation of blacks and whites. Tennessee adopted the first "Jim Crow" law in 1875, segregating public transportation. In 1896 the Supreme Court attempted a compromise in a guideline ruling for legally segregated facilities—"separate but equal"—following which segregation laws proliferated. In the North segregation in housing created the black slum ghettos; while less common than in the South it still continued in factories, unions and restaurants. In 1910 the NATIONAL ASSOCIATION FOR THE ADVANCEMENT OF COLORED PEOPLE (NAACP) was founded in New York, followed by the National URBAN LEAGUE in 1911. Several activist groups were formed after WWI, such as Marcus GARVEY's Universal Negro Improvement Association (UNIA) and the CONGRESS OF RACIAL EQUALITY (CORE). The NAACP won its greatest legal victories in 1954 and 1955, when the Supreme Court outlawed segregation in the public schools and ordered that integration be implemented "with all deliberate speed." Non-violent crusades were organized, but the violence and rioting advocated by extremist groups such as the BLACK PANTHER PARTY inflamed the situation in the 1960s. In the 1970s integration was more generally accepted. This, combined with the desire of many blacks for a culture of their own rather than entry into a white one, defused the issue to some extent. In Boston, Mass., and elsewhere, however, there was serious unrest over "bussing," designed to end school segregation. (See also CIVIL RIGHTS AND LIBERTIES; OPEN HOUSING.)

Italian coffer, exquisitely decorated by means of intarsia. Although skilled European craftsmen produced many magnificent examples of occidental design, the finest pieces, like that shown here, employ traditional eastern designs; particularly evident are the geometric swirls and intricately conceived floral borders characteristic of Islamic art.

INTELLIGENCE, the general ability to solve problems. The ability to solve specific problems only may arise as a result of INSTINCT or through experience, neither of which can be regarded as contributing to intelligence; though intelligence affects the ability of the individual to apply experience to problem-solving.

By far the most intelligent animal on this planet is man. For this reason, among others, most investigations of intelligence have been carried out in human beings. Intelligence tests are structured upon seven main bases: numerical ability (the speed and accuracy with which the individual can solve problems of simple arithmetic); verbal fluency; verbal meaning (the ability to understand words); the ability to remember; speed of perception and, most importantly, the ability to reason. Such tests are of considerable use, though their limitations must be recognized: they are of little value in comparisons between ethnic groups, or even between social classes, since in both cases environment plays a very large part in an individual's performance. Moreover, their accuracy in measuring IQs outside the normal limits is suspect. Such qualms have led to a definition of human intelligence as "that which can be measured by intelligence tests" (see also IQ; PSYCHOLOGICAL TESTS).

Throughout the animal kingdom, there is a good correlation between the intelligence of an animal and the size of its brain relative to that of its body. There is an even better one when the surface area of the BRAIN is considered: the higher mammals have a more convoluted cortex (outer layer) than do the lower. After man, the most intelligent animal is the DOLPHIN. Perhaps surprisingly, ANTS show an ability to solve mazes that compares with that of some mammals.

The ways in which animals solve problems are a useful pointer to their intelligence. The two important ways are trial-and-error, which is a LEARNING process dependent upon intelligence, and insight. This latter is displayed only by the higher animals.

The evolution of intelligence is unclear, though obviously it has had a profound effect on the emergence of man as earth's dominant animal. Equally obviously, intelligence is a considerable aid to species survival. Much effort has been used in recent years to examine how much of an individual's intelligence is determined by hereditary factors, how much by environmental factors. Although results have not been conclusive, it would seem that over half the difference in intelligence between people is determined by inheritance, the remainder by early environmental conditions (see also HEREDITY). (See also MEMORY; MENTAL RETARDATION; MIND.)

INTELLIGENCE QUOTIENT. See IQ.

INTELLIGENCE SERVICE, department of government directing espionage abroad and countering it at home. Under Elizabeth I of England Sir Francis WALSINGHAM set up one of the first professional intelligence networks in the West. In France networks were first set up by Cardinal RICHELIEU in the 17th century and by Joseph FOUCHÉ under Napoleon I. In Britain MI-6, for intelligence abroad and MI-5, for counterintelligence, developed before WWII, in which they reached their peak. The US intelligence service was then largely organized by the OFFICE OF STRATEGIC SERVICES. It was given its present form in 1947 with the creation of the CENTRAL INTELLIGENCE AGENCY (CIA), which coordinates the espionage of all government departments and agencies. In Russia the *Oprichnina* of Ivan IV (1565) was the first of various ruthless espionage and secret police organizations, which changed little under the tsars or the Soviet government. They evolved into the KGB, which even has its own armed forces (formerly with nuclear weapons); it controls espionage abroad and state security at home.

INTELLIGENCE TEST. See PSYCHOLOGICAL TESTS.

INTERCEPT, in mathematics the point at which a CURVE or straight LINE intersects the x, y or z axis of a coordinate system (see ANALYTIC GEOMETRY). The parabola (see CONIC SECTIONS) $y = x^2 - 4$, for example has a y-intercept at -4 and x-intercepts at $+2$ and -2. The term is also used to refer to the portion of a line lying between two other lines or planes that intersect it.

INTERCHANGEABLE PARTS, manufacturing technique using a jig to produce identical parts, pioneered in the US by Eli WHITNEY in musket manufacture (1798). By facilitating MASS PRODUCTION it advanced the INDUSTRIAL REVOLUTION and the decline of artisan manufacture.

INTERDICT, in the Roman Catholic Church, a rarely-used sanction against territories; it withholds certain sacraments from their inhabitants. In Roman and civil law it is a remedy granted against a breach of law for which there is no other remedy.

INTEREST, money paid for the use of money loaned. It is generally expressed as a percentage of the principal (sum loaned) per period (usually per year or per month). In "simple" interest, where the principal does not change, the interest can be calculated by the formula $I = prt$, where I is interest, p is principal (the amount borrowed), r the rate of interest and t the time. "Compound" interest is added periodically to the principal; interest is subsequently paid on the resulting compound total. The formula for this is $S = p\,(1 + r/k)^n$ where S is the final amount, p and r are as before, k is the time interval between compounding and n is the number of times the interest is compounded.

Medieval Christian law forbade the taking of interest on moral grounds as "usury," but Jewish businessmen were freely used as bankers; in the face of this the Church was eventually forced to relax its attitude. Today, interest rates, by determining the availability of money, are an important factor in the economy; US bank and savings loan society interest rates are government regulated.

INTERFERENCE, the interaction of two or more similar or related WAVE MOTIONS establishing a new pattern in the AMPLITUDE of the waves. It occurs in all wave phenomena including SOUND, LIGHT and water waves. In most cases the resulting amplitude at a point is found by adding together the amplitudes of the individual interfering waves at that point. Interference patterns can only result if the interfering waves are of related wavelength and exhibit a definite PHASE relationship.

Optical interference. Light from ordinary sources is "incoherent"—there is no definite relationship between the phases of the waves associated with different PHOTONS. Until recently the only way to demonstrate optical interference was to use light from a single source which had been divided and led to the interference zone along paths of differing length, thus ensuring that the interfering beams were coherent at least with each other. In this way Thomas YOUNG in 1801 first demonstrated optical interference, showing, because interference effects cannot be explained on either ray or particle models, that light was indeed to be regarded as a wave phenomenon. Young passed light from a single pinhole source through two parallel slits in an opaque screen and found that interference fringes—alternate bands of light and dark—were formed on another screen placed beyond the slits. The bright bands resulted from the constructive interference of the two beams, the wave amplitude of each reinforcing the other; the dark bands, destructive interference, the amplitude of one wave effectively canceling the effect of that of the other. Newton's rings, colored fringes seen in thin transparent films, are a similar interference effect. In recent years LASERS (which produce coherent light—radiation having a uniform and controllable phase structure) have enabled physicists to produce optical interference effects much more easily, an important application being HOLOGRAPHY. (See also INTERFEROMETER.)

INTERFERENCE, Radio, unwelcome additions to a desired signal in RADIO and TELEVISION receivers and TELEPHONE circuits, often arising in nearby power circuits or other electrical appliances.

INTERFEROMETER, any instrument employing INTERFERENCE effects used: for measuring the wavelengths of LIGHT, RADIO, SOUND or other wave phenomena; for measuring the refractive index (see REFRACTION) of gases (Rayleigh interferometer); for measuring very small distances using radiation of known wavelength, or, in ACOUSTICS and RADIO ASTRONOMY, for determining the direction of an energy source. In most interferometers the beam of incoming radiation is divided in two, led along paths of different but accurately adjustable lengths and then recombined to give an interference pattern. Perhaps the best known optical instrument is the Michelson interferometer devised in 1881 for the MICHELSON-MORLEY EXPERIMENT. More accurate for wavelength measurements is the Fabry-Perot interferometer in which the radiation is recombined after multiple partial reflections between parallel lightly-silvered glass plates.

INTERFERON, substance produced by living tissues following infection with VIRUSES, BACTERIA etc., which interferes with the growth of any organism. It is responsible for a transient and mild degree of nonspecific IMMUNITY following infection.

INTER-GOVERNMENTAL MARITIME CONSULTATIVE ORGANIZATION (IMCO), specialized UN agency operational from 1958 (though provided for in 1948). It promotes cooperation on technical aspects of international shipping, especially safety at sea, and arranges maritime conferences and conventions. It is headed by an assembly, for policy decisions, and a governing council.

INTERHALOGENS, group of binary compounds of the HALOGENS with each other, of general formula XX'_n where X' is the more electronegative halogen, and $n = 1, 3, 5$ or 7. They are volatile, covalent, reactive substances. Bromine (III) fluoride (BrF_3) is a very powerful fluoridating agent, and a good solvent for fluorine compounds. Polyhalide salts, containing ions XX'^{-}_{n+1}, are formed by reacting halogens or interhalogens with HALIDES.

INTERIOR, US Department of the, executive branch of the federal government, headed by the secretary of the interior. Founded in 1849, its original task was to administer the census and Indian affairs, and to regulate the exploitation of natural resources. In recent years, however, it has been increasingly exercised by the need for conservation of resources and protection of the environment. Today it has five major areas of responsibility, each in the charge of an assistant secretary. These are Fish, Wildlife, Parks and Marine Resources; Mineral Resources; Water and Power Development; Water Quality and Research, and Public Land Management, which as well as agencies responsible for federally owned lands includes the Office of the Territories, which administers US territories and trust territories, and the Bureau of INDIAN AFFAIRS.

INTERIOR ANGLES, the angles within a POLYGON formed by its adjacent sides.

INTERLOCKING DIRECTORATE, system of corporate management in which the boards of different companies have directors in common. This tends towards greater cooperation and efficiency, but may lead to monopolistic practices; it is therefore limited by ANTITRUST LEGISLATION.

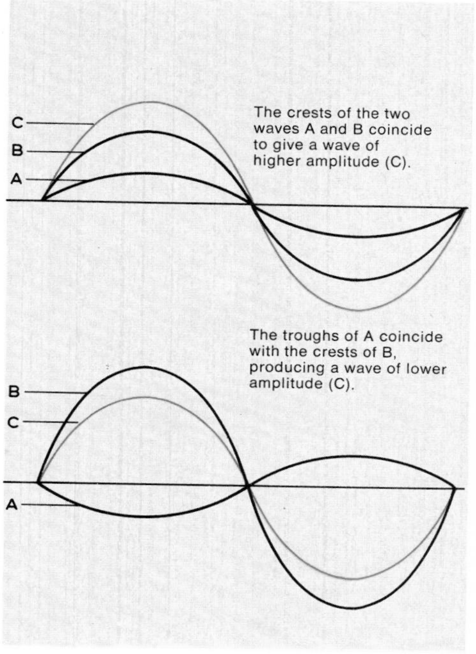

C
B
A
The crests of the two waves A and B coincide to give a wave of higher amplitude (C).
B
C
A
The troughs of A coincide with the crests of B, producing a wave of lower amplitude (C).

Interference phenomena are shown by all wave motions, including light and sound. This is exemplified by superimposing two waves of the same frequency. If the crests of these two coincide, they reinforce each other, producing a resultant wave of higher amplitude. If the crests of one coincide with the troughs of the other, the opposite effect is achieved and the resultant wave has lower amplitude.

INTERLUDES, medieval comic plays derived from the lighter pieces staged in the intervals of MORALITY PLAYS, or during banquets. Later interludes, seriocomic in form, were ancestors of the Elizabethan drama.

INTERNAL-COMBUSTION ENGINE, type of ENGINE—the commonest now used—in which the fuel is burned inside the engine and the expansion of the combustion gases is used to provide the power. Because of their potential light weight, efficiency and convenience, internal-combustion engines largely superseded STEAM ENGINES in the early 20th century. They are used industrially and for all kinds of transport, notably to power AUTOMOBILES. There are three classes of internal-combustion engine: RECIPROCATING ENGINES, which include the **gasoline engine**, the DIESEL ENGINE and the FREE-PISTON ENGINE; rotary engines, including the GAS TURBINE, the turbojet (see JET PROPULSION) and the WANKEL ENGINE; and ROCKET engines and non-turbine jet engines, working by reaction. Although originally coal gas and even powdered coal were used as fuel, now almost all fuels used are PETROLEUM products: diesel oil, GASOLINE, BOTTLED GAS and NATURAL GAS. The first working (though not usable) internal-combustion engine was a piston engine made by HUYGENS (1680) that burned gunpowder. In 1794 Robert Street patented a practicable though inefficient engine into which the air had to be pumped by hand. In 1876 N. A. OTTO built the first four-stroke engine, using the principles stated earlier by Alphonse Beau de Rochas. The cycle is (1) intake of fuel/air mixture; (2) compression of mixture; (3) ignition (see IGNITION SYSTEM) and expansion of burned gases; (4) expulsion of gases as exhaust. Only the third stroke is powered, but the engine is highly efficient, and modern gasoline engines are basically the same. Generally four, six or eight cylinders are linked to provide balanced power. The engine is cooled by water circulating through pipes or by air from a fan. The fuel/air mixture is produced in the CARBURETOR; greater power is given by **supercharging**, by which the proportion of air and the initial pressure of the mixture are increased. The two-stroke engine, giving greater power for a given size, but less efficient in fuel use, does not usually have valves, but an inlet and an exhaust port in the cylinder, blocked and uncovered in turn by the piston. At the end of the powered stroke, the piston drives fresh fuel mixture from the crankcase into the cylinder, pushing out the exhaust gases. The EFFICIENCY of an internal-combustion engine increases with the COMPRESSION RATIO; if this is too high, however, "knocking" occurs due to irregular burning and detonations. It is avoided by using fuel of high OCTANE number, and by using ANTIKNOCK ADDITIVES. (See also AIR POLLUTION.)

INTERNAL REVENUE SERVICE (IRS), agency of the US Department of the Treasury. Created by Congress in 1789, it assesses and collects domestic or "internal" taxes. These include federal taxes on goods and services, income taxes and corporate taxes, as well as gift and estate taxes. The service is headed by a commissioner of internal revenue appointed by the president. Its headquarters are in Washington, D.C., and it has seven regional and 58 district offices.

INTERNATIONAL, The, anthem of international COMMUNISM. The words were written in 1871 by Eugène POTTIER and set to music in 1888 by Pierre Degeyter.

INTERNATIONAL, The, common name of a number of socialist-communist revolutionary organizations. Three of these have had historical significance. The First International, officially the International Working Men's Association, was formed under the leadership of Karl MARX in London in 1864 with the aim of uniting workers of all nations to realize the ideals of the *Communist Manifesto*. Divisions grew up between reformers and violent revolutionaries; these became increasingly bitter, culminating in the expulsion of the faction led by Mikhail BAKUNIN after a leadership struggle in 1872. The association broke up in 1876. The Second, commonly called the Socialist, International was founded in Paris in 1889 by a group of socialist parties who later made their headquarters in Brussels. The leading social democratic parties, including those of Germany and Russia were represented. Among representatives were Jean JAURÈS, Ramsay MACDONALD, LENIN and TROTSKY. It influenced international labor affairs until WWI, when it broke up. The Third or Communist International, generally known as the Comintern, was founded by Lenin, following his seizure of power in Russia in 1919, in an attempt to win the leadership of world socialism; ZINOVIEV was its first president. Soviet-dominated from the outset, it aimed, in the 1920s, to foment world revolution. In the 1930s, under STALIN, it sought contacts with less extreme left-wing groups abroad, to assuage foreign hostility. Stalin dissolved it in 1943 as a wartime conciliatory gesture to the Allies.

The Palace of Peace in The Hague, since 1946 the seat of the International Court of Justice. The building was originally designed by the French architect Cordonnier but finally built by V. A. G. van der Steur, who modified the plans considerably. It was completed by 1913.

INTERNATIONAL AIR TRANSPORT ASSOCIATION (IATA), cooperative organization of airlines from 84 countries founded in 1945 to succeed the International Air Traffic Association. It seeks to regulate fares over standard routes and deal with traffic, scheduling and safety problems.

INTERNATIONAL ATOMIC ENERGY AGENCY (IAEA), intergovernmental agency closely related to the UN. Established in 1957, it promotes and conducts research into peaceful uses of atomic energy and seeks to ensure adequate safety standards. It is particularly concerned that agency assistance should not be used for military purposes.

INTERNATIONAL BANK FOR RECONSTRUCTION AND DEVELOPMENT. See WORLD BANK.

INTERNATIONAL BUREAU OF WEIGHTS AND MEASURES, international agency founded in Paris in 1875 to unify and standardize systems of measurement.

INTERNATIONAL CIVIL AVIATION ORGANIZATION (ICAO), UN agency seeking to foster and coordinate cooperation among the world's airlines.

INTERNATIONAL COURT OF JUSTICE, highest judicial organ of the UN, founded in 1946 to provide a peaceful means of settling international disputes according to the principles of INTERNATIONAL LAW. Like its predecessor under the LEAGUE OF NATIONS, the World Court, it sits at the Hague. In practice its authority is limited by frequent refusals to accept its decisions.

INTERNATIONAL CRIMINAL POLICE ORGANIZATION. See INTERPOL.

INTERNATIONAL DATE LINE. See DATE LINE, INTERNATIONAL.

INTERNATIONAL DEVELOPMENT ASSOCIATION (IDA), organization affiliated to the WORLD BANK. It was established in 1960 to make loans for development projects to member countries on less economically burdensome terms than World Bank loans; a service charge is substituted for interest.

INTERNATIONAL FINANCE CORPORATION (IFC), an agency of the UN and an affiliate of the World Bank, established in 1956 to promote and finance economic development through private enterprise in member countries.

INTERNATIONAL GEOPHYSICAL YEAR (IGY), period from July 1, 1957 to Jan. 1, 1959, devoted to international geophysical research. Organized by a committee of the International Council of Scientific Unions, it involved some 70 nations. The period was chosen as one of intense sunspot activity.

INTERNATIONAL LABOR ORGANIZATION (ILO), UN agency with headquarters in Geneva, formed in 1919 to develop and improve working conditions worldwide. In 1934 the US joined; in 1946 the organization became affiliated to the UN.

INTERNATIONAL LADIES' GARMENT WORKERS' UNION, AFL-CIO union in the US women's and children's clothing industry. It was founded in 1900 by AMERICAN FEDERATION OF LABOR charter. Strikes in New York 1909–10 led to Louis BRANDEIS' Protocol of Peace, which set a pattern for Labor-management cooperation. Under David DUBINSKY (president 1932–66) the ILGWU grew fast in the 1930s, was active in the AFL-CIO debate and pioneered union welfare schemes. Its membership is about 450000.

INTERNATIONAL LAW, body of laws assumed to be binding between nations by virtue of their general acceptance. Although customary rules on maritime matters and on ambassadorial immunity had existed for a long time before, the real beginnings of international law lay in attempts to humanize the conduct of war. The seminal work of Hugo GROTIUS, *On the Law of War and Peace* (1625), was one such, but he also formulated several important principles, including a legal basis for the sovereignty of states. The works of Grotius and his successors were widely acclaimed but never officially accepted; however, legal rules were increasingly incorporated into international agreements such as the Congress of VIENNA and the constitution of the UNITED NATIONS. International laws may arise through multilateral or bilateral agreements, as with the GENEVA CONVENTION, or simply by long-established custom, as with a large part of MARITIME LAW. In some cases, as with the war crimes rulings of the NUREMBERG TRIALS, they may be said to arise retrospectively. Because few nations are willing to relinquish any sovereignty, the law lacks a true legislative body and an effective executive to enforce it. The INTERNATIONAL COURT OF JUSTICE is the international judicial body; the UN, in the process of compiling an international legal code, is the nearest thing to a legislature, but all these bodies are limited by the willingness of states to accept their decisions, as was the LEAGUE OF NATIONS in the 1930s. These difficulties have led some theorists to deny international law true legal status, but this is an extreme view; the need for international rules is widely recognized, as shown by the increasing tendency to anticipate matters such as space exploration and exploitation of seabed resources and to attempt to develop international rules to regulate them.

INTERNATIONAL MONETARY FUND (IMF), international organization, affiliated to the UN, existing to develop international monetary cooperation, in particular to stabilize exchange rates by providing international credit. Members cannot make changes greater than 10% in the exchange rate of their national currency without consulting the Fund. Established by the BRETTON WOODS CONFERENCE, it began operating in 1947. Operating funds are subscribed by its member governments; the Group of Ten (US, UK, Belgium, Canada, France, West Germany, Italy, Japan, Netherlands and Sweden) are pledged to lend further funds if necessary. (See also WORLD BANK.)

INTERNATIONAL RED CROSS. See RED CROSS.

INTERNATIONAL RELATIONS, relationships between nations, through politics, treaties, military confrontation or cooperation, economics or culture. Peacetime contact is generally maintained through DIPLOMACY; each nation maintains embassies in other countries it recognizes as nations. Even when states do not maintain mutual embassies, however, they may find it desirable to keep contacts open, often through the offices of a third nation. The other primary link is through membership of international organizations, either for global politics as with the UNITED NATIONS, defense as with NATO or the WARSAW PACT, or simply mutual convenience, as with the UNIVERSAL POSTAL UNION. From 1946 on international relations were dominated by the concept of the COLD WAR, in which the complications of world diplomacy were reduced to an oversimplified model of an ideological contest between two global antagonists, the communist and capitalist systems as exemplified by the US and USSR. In the 1960s the rise of the Third World countries negated this simple division, though many of these took one or the other side. In the 1970s relations between the US and USSR improved, largely through trade and nuclear limitation agreements and also because of the rise of China as a rival superpower. The endurance and value of the resulting detente, however, remained in dispute. (See also INTERNATIONAL LAW; INTERNATIONAL TRADE.)

INTERNATIONAL STYLE, architectural style, best defined in its widest sense as the dominant trend in large-scale buildings in industrialized countries since the 1920s. It emphasizes a clean functionalism, open space with large areas of glass, and reinforced concrete construction. Among pioneering exponents were Walter GROPIUS, MIES VAN DER ROHE, LE CORBUSIER, Piet NERVI and in the US Philip C. JOHNSON and R. I. NEUTRA.

INTERNATIONAL SYSTEM OF UNITS. See SI UNITS.

INTERNATIONAL TRADE, or world trade, the exchange of goods and services between nations. Since the 18th century it has become a vital element in world prosperity. One reason for this is that it is generally thought more profitable for countries to specialize in making those things in which such factors as natural resources, climatic conditions, availability of raw materials, a skilled labor force or low labor costs give them a special advantage. This is known as the international division of labor. Some countries, such as the UK, rely largely on exports; US exports amount to 15% of the world total, but are less vital to its economy.

Even in prehistoric times the amber route carried trade between tribes thousands of miles apart. The ancient Greeks, Romans and Phoenicians were active traders. Chinese merchants penetrated most of Asia, and Arabs operated trade routes on the Indian Ocean and in Africa. Most explorers before the 20th century sought to open trade routes. Early trade was largely in goods yielding high prices on small amounts because of the difficulty of transportation. Only with modern transport did international trade become economically vital.

There are two schools of thought on the status of international trade. PROTECTIONISM believes that restriction of imports is necessary to allow home industries to develop. Arguing that if everyone did this there would be no trade, the FREE TRADE school seeks to restrict trade as little as possible, so reducing prices and raising quality by competition. Protectionism raises the cost of living by not allowing cheaper foreign products to enter the market, but it can help establish an indigenous industry, which may be important for national security reasons by ensuring independence from foreign suppliers in times of war and as a factor in reducing home unemployment. The import TARIFF, moreover, is an easy way of raising government revenues.

The financing of world trade relies on the foreign exchange market where an importer can buy the necessary currency to pay his foreign supplier. Most countries keep a record of their BALANCE OF PAYMENTS with foreign trading partners; a large surplus or deficit in this is often a good economic indicator.

After WWII efforts were made to promote free trade throughout the world. In 1948 the US and 23 other nations made an agreement within the framework of the UN known as the GENERAL AGREEMENT ON TARIFFS AND TRADE (GATT). In 1962 Congress passed the Trade Expansion Act, enabling President Kennedy to lower or remove tariffs affecting the European COMMON MARKET countries. Subsequently, a series of tariff reductions have been negotiated under what is known as the "Kennedy Round." The Common Market had as its main aim free trade between its members, but it also created a system of common external tariffs in agriculture, a source of continual controversy. (See also EFTA; COMECON.)

One of the biggest unsolved problems of international trade is the balance between industrialized and developing countries of the Third World. Since they export mainly food and raw materials, which rise only slowly in price, and import manufactured goods, their expansion is much slower than that of rich countries.

INTERNATIONAL TELECOMMUNICATIONS (ITU), UN agency founded in 1934, which allocates radio frequencies and organizes international regulations governing radio, telegraph, telephone and space-radio communications.

INTERPOL, contraction of the International Criminal Police Organization, established in 1923. Its headquarters are now in Paris. It is a clearing house for police information and specializes in the detection of counterfeiting, smuggling and trafficking in narcotics.

INTERPOLATION AND EXTRAPOLATION, techniques used in mathematical ANALYSIS to estimate undetermined values of a dependent VARIABLE, a number of values of which, corresponding to determined values of an independent variable, are known. This is done by finding a FUNCTION $f(x)$ of the independent variable x such that, for any value, x_a, the known corresponding value y_a of the dependent variable y closely approximates to the value $f(x_a)$. In interpolation it is then assumed that, within the range covered by the known values of the variables, $y=f(x)$ for all intermediate values of x and y. In extrapolation, one assumes this relationship to hold outside the range of known values—a rather less justifiable assumption. The simplest (and most commonly used) technique is that of drawing the best straight LINE or CURVE through a set of points on a graph, and assuming that it represents a genuine relationship between the two variables in question (see also LEAST SQUARES). Others include use of partial DIFFERENCE EQUATIONS.

INTERSECTION, in plane GEOMETRY, the crossing of two LINES or CURVES at a point known as the point of intersection. In terms of ANALYTIC GEOMETRY, if two lines have equations $y=f(x)$ and $y=g(x)$ where $f(x)$ and $g(x)$ are FUNCTIONS of x, their points of intersection are given by those values of x for which $f(x)=g(x)$. For example, the line $y=2x$ intersects the curve $y=x^2$ in two points whose coordinates are given by solution of the EQUATION $2x=x^2$; this has two roots (see ROOTS OF AN EQUATION), 0 and 2, and hence the points of intersection are (0,0) and (2,4). Should the equation $f(x)=g(x)$ have roots that are not unique (i.e., two or more are equal), then the curves are tangential (see TANGENT OF A CURVE) at the point or points defined by the equal roots. (See also SET THEORY.)

INTERSTATE COMMERCE, commercial transactions that cross state boundaries or concern more than one state. By Article I, section 8 of the US Constitution, Congress is empowered to regulate commerce among foreign nations and the various states. The Interstate Commerce Act of 1887 created the INTERSTATE COMMERCE COMMISSION (ICC), to prevent discriminatory practices in interstate transportation. In 1914 Congress created the FEDERAL TRADE COMMISSION, and since then other similar agencies have been established: the Civil Aeronautics Board, the Federal Aviation Administration, the Federal Communications Commission and the Federal Power Commission. The Civil Rights Act of 1964, forbidding racial discrimination in public accommodation, was also based on the widespread powers of Congress over interstate commerce.

INTERSTATE COMMERCE COMMISSION (ICC), independent US government agency which regulates all surface transportation of passengers and freight across state lines. It has 11 commissioners appointed by the president for seven-year terms. Established by the Federal government in 1887, it had hardly any authority to enforce its decisions or to set rates until strengthened by a series of legislative enactments in the 20th century. These extended its authority to all pipeline systems except water and natural gas. In 1961, following months of demonstration, conflict and litigation over racial segregation on buses in Ala. and Miss., the ICC formally banned such discrimination on interstate transportation.

INTERSTELLAR MATTER, thinly dispersed matter, in the form of gas and dust, between the stars, detectable through its light-absorbing effects. Thicker clouds are seen as NEBULAS. There is in the arms of the MILKY WAY almost as much interstellar as stellar matter. It is thought that STARS form out of interstellar matter.

INTERVAL, in music, the PITCH difference between two notes, an *n*th being the interval between do and the note $(n+1)$ tones above.

INTESTINE. See GASTROINTESTINAL TRACT.

INTOLERABLE ACTS, also known as Coercive Acts, five acts of the British Parliament passed in 1774 to penalize dissidents in Mass. The Boston Port Act closed the harbor in default of compensation for the BOSTON TEA PARTY. The Massachusetts Bay Regulating Act suspended many of the colony's original rights. The Impartial Administration of Justice Act ordained that British officials accused of crimes within the colonies should be tried in other colonies or in England. The Quartering Act required colonists to shelter and feed British troops. The QUEBEC ACT extended Quebec's boundary S to the Ohio R. These strong measures were widely protested throughout the colonies and led to the calling of the First Continental Congress and hence the REVOLUTIONARY WAR.

INTOXICATION, state in which a person is overtly affected by excess of a DRUG or poison. It is often used to describe the psychological effects of drugs and particularly ALCOHOL, in which behavior may become disinhibited, facile, morose or aggressive and in which judgment is impaired. Late stages of intoxication affecting the BRAIN include stupor and COMA. Ingestion of very large amounts of water causes water intoxication and may lead to coma and death. POISONING with TOXINS and drugs may cause intoxication of other organs (e.g., HEART with DIGITALIS overdosage).

INTRACOASTAL WATERWAY. See ATLANTIC INTRACOASTAL WATERWAY; GULF INTRACOASTAL WATERWAY.

INTRAVENOUS FEEDING, method of supplying nutrients essential for growth or maintenance of body mass when the GASTROINTESTINAL TRACT is unable to provide adequate nutrition in certain DISEASES of the gut and following SURGERY.

INTROVERSION AND EXTRAVERSION, terms coined by JUNG for two opposite character traits. Introverts are shy, introspective, "ingoing"; extraverts sociable, little concerned with their own inner thoughts and feelings, "outgoing." We all display both traits, one or other dominating at different times: Jung suggested that conflict between them was a cause of NEUROSIS. The terms are little used in modern psychology, though introversion is sometimes used to describe the withdrawal characteristic of SCHIZOPHRENIA.

INUVIK, settlement in Northwest Territories, Canada. It was founded in 1954–62 on the Mackenzie R as a new and model site for AKLAVIK. Pop 2 669.

INVAR, an ALLOY composed of 64% iron, 36% nickel and a trace of carbon. Having a very small coefficient of thermal EXPANSION, it is used for pendulums, tuning-forks, measuring devices and other components whose dimensions must be independent of temperature.

INVENTION, the act of devising an original process or device which facilitates or makes possible what was previously more difficult or impossible; also, such a process or device. Inventiveness is one of man's most valuable characteristics. Some of his earliest inventions—the stone ax, painting, wood and ivory carving—are shrouded in the mists of prehistory. But, although invention continued at a steady rate throughout the ancient and medieval periods, most of the inventions that have created the modern world date from 1500 AD at the earliest and the majority belong to the 20th century. If the 19th century was the age of the independent inventor, individually patenting (legally protecting) and marketing his invention, Thomas EDISON pointed the way to a later era in 1876 when he opened his first "invention factory." Today the majority of inventions flow from industrial research laboratories and the costly *development* of a new product is as important as the *research* which produces the basic idea for it: invention has become an industrial activity. The relations of science and invention have often been disputed; on balance it seems fair to admit that benefits have flowed in both directions.

INVER GROVE HEIGHTS, residential village in SE Minn., a suburb of St. Paul. Pop 12 148.

INVERSE, of a number a, the number b such that $a*b=e$, where * is an algebraic operation and e is the identity element relative to the operation * of the set (see SET THEORY) of which a and b are members. For example, 1 is the identity element of the set of REAL NUMBERS relative to multiplication: hence if $a.b=1$, a is the inverse of b, b the inverse of a, relative to the multiplication of real numbers. (Moreover, a and b are RECIPROCALS in this case.)

Inverse operation. If two operations negate each other, they are termed inverse operations. For example, since $a+b-b=a$, ADDITION and SUBTRACTION are inverse operations.

Inverse of a proposition. For a proposition $h \rightarrow c$ (read "h implies c"), the proposition not-$h \rightarrow c$ is described as its inverse.

Inverse function. For a FUNCTION $f(x)$, the function $g(x)$ such that $f(a)=b$ implies that $g(b)=a$ is described as the inverse of $f(x)$. In practice, the inverse function of $f(x)$ is written $f^{-1}(x)$. For example, the inverse of $f(x)=ax+b$ is $f^{-1}(x)=(x-b)/a$, since $f^{-1}(ax+b)=(ax+b-b)/a=ax/a=x$.

Inverse Trigonometric function. For a function of the form $y=\sin x$, the function of the form $x=\sin^{-1}y$ (read as "x is the angle whose sine is y") is described as its inverse. This may also be written as $x=\arcsin y$. (See TRIGONOMETRY.)

INVERSE SQUARE LAW, relationship according to which the intensity of a spherical wave (see WAVE MOTION) varies inversely (see INVERSE VARIATION) with

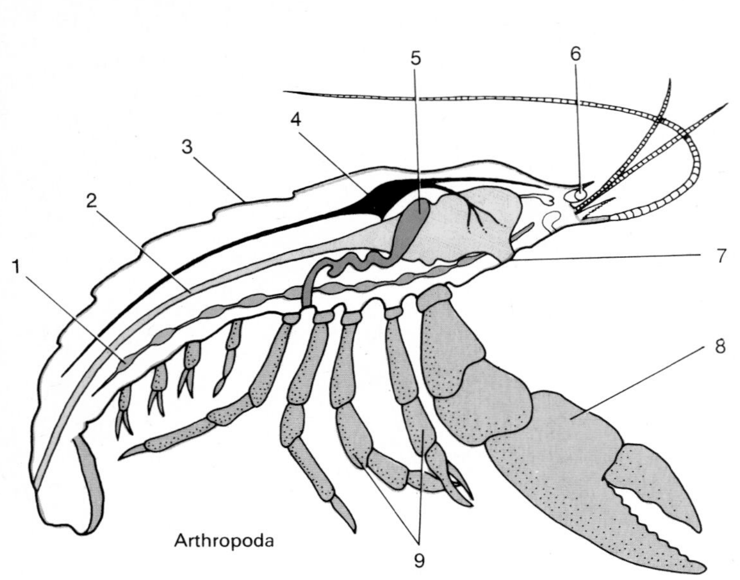

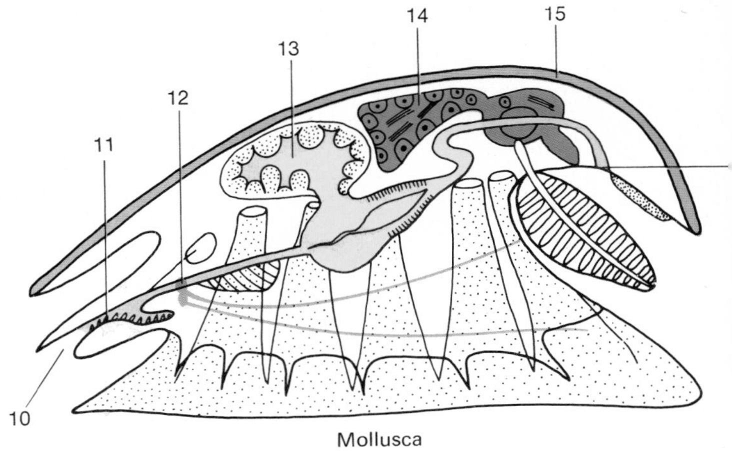

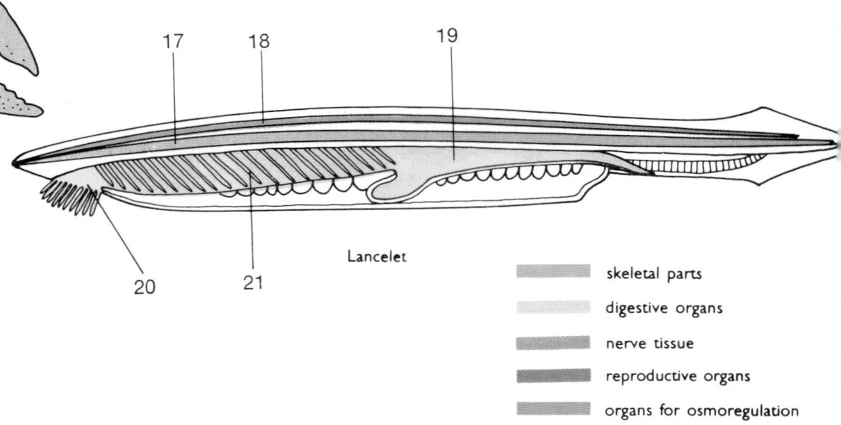

Over 95% of animal species are invertebrates, and they differ from each other quite as much as they differ from vertebrates. Here are diagrams of three representatives of the major invertebrate groups, indicating their basic structures: (1) nerve cord; (2) alimentary canal; (3) exoskeleton of chitin; (4) heart; (5) gonad; (6) eye; (7) mouth; (8) claw; (9) jointed limbs; (10) mouth; (11) radula; (12) cerebral ganglia; (13) digestive gland; (14) gonad; (15) shell; (16) anus; (17) notochord; (18) nerve cord; (19) intestine; (20) tentacles; (21) branchial basket.

the square of its distance from the source. The law applies only where the source is small compared with the distance and the medium is unbounded, homogeneous, isotropic and nondissipative.

INVERSE VARIATION, a relationship between two variables in which increase in value of one implies decrease in value of the other; e.g.

$$y = \frac{k}{x}$$

where k is a constant. y may vary with the reciprocal or a power of x, as in the inverse square law. The idea is of particular interest in statistics; as in, for example, a case where the consumption of alcohol might vary inversely with the level of taxation on it.

INVERSION, Temperature, a condition of the lower part of the atmosphere in which temperature increases with increase in height above the surface. Normally, temperature decreases upward through most of the atmosphere, but certain atmospheric disturbances (e.g., a front) can create inversions. The condition occurs also on cold nights. Inversions sometimes aggravate air pollution, as the cooler air trapped near the surface cannot rise and so carry away the pollutants.

INVERTEBRATES, animals without backbones, a miscellaneous collection of groups from single-celled protozoa to highly-specialized insects and spiders. Apart from the universal lack of an internal backbone of vertebrae, many of these groups have little in common.

INVERTER. See computer.

INVESTITURE CONTROVERSY, conflict between European rulers and the papacy in the 11th and 12th centuries. Originally a dispute about the appointment of bishops and abbots, it became a power struggle between church and state. In England a compromise was reached in 1107; in Germany the issue was resolved in 1122 by the Concordat of worms.

INVESTMENT, the productive employment of resources (*capital*) or the transformation of savings into active wealth (*capital formation*), also the use of funds to obtain dividends, for example, from corporate stock or government bonds.

Investment is now one of the prime areas of concern for governments seeking to influence or control the progress of their economies. Planned investment in modern industry is achieved through an elaborate system of institutions and intermediaries including stock markets, investment banks, industrial finance corporations and commercial banks. This system enables individual investors to handle their assets easily and to choose the degree of risk they are willing to take.

Foreign investment can take two forms: *portfolio* investment, the purchase of the stock of foreign corporations, and *direct* investment, the establishment or expansion of an investor-controlled corporation in a foreign country. (See also banking; capital; economics; stocks and stock market.)

INVESTMENT BANKING, system of banking that enables companies—and sometimes countries—to raise capital by selling stocks and bonds to investors. Investment bankers arrange to try and sell these securities to insurance companies, pension funds, commercial banks and members of the investing public. They receive a commission for their efforts which ranges from 1% to 6%. In addition they try to sell the securities for a higher price than they pay the issuing company. This difference represents their profit.

INVISIBLE INK, an ink, used for secret communication, that is colorless when written but that can be developed by heat or chemical reaction. For example, potassium hexacyanoferrate(II) ink can be developed by an iron(III) salt, giving prussian blue. Fluorescent inks fluoresce in ultraviolet light.

IO, in Greek myth, girl loved by zeus, who changed her into a heifer to protect her from the anger of his wife hera. Persecuted by a gadfly sent by Hera, Io wandered to the Ionian Sea (named for her) and crossed the Bosporus (which means "ox-ford") and finally reached Egypt where, transformed back into human form, she bore a son.

IODINE (I), the least reactive of the halogens, forming black lustrous crystals which readily sublime to pungent violet vapor. Most iodine is produced from calcium iodate ($Ca[IO_3]_2$), found in chile saltpeter. In the US, much is recovered from oil-well brine, which contains sodium iodide (NaI). Chemically it resembles bromine closely, but has a greater tendency to covalency and positive oxidation states. It is large enough to form 6-coordinate oxy-anions. Most plants (especially seaweeds) contain traces of iodine; in the higher animals it is a constituent of the thryoxine hormone secreted by the thyroid gland. Iodine deficiency can cause goiter. Iodine and its compounds are used as antiseptics, fungicides and in the production of dyes. The radioisotope I^{131} is used as a tracer and to treat goiter. Silver iodide, being light-sensitive, is used in photography. (See also halides.) AW 126.9, mp 113.5°C, bp 184°C, sg 4.93 (20°C).

ION, an atom or group of atoms that has become electrically charged by gain or loss of negatively-charged electrons. In general, ions formed from metals are positive (cations), those from nonmetals negative (anions). Compound ions are usually anions derived from oxyacids, e.g., sulfate SO_4^{2-}. Crystals of ionic compounds consist of negative and positive ions arranged alternately in the lattice and held together by electrical attraction (see bond, chemical). Many covalent compounds undergo ionic dissociation in solution. Ions may be formed in gases by radiation or electrical discharge, and occur in the ionosphere (see also atmosphere). At very high temperatures gases form plasma, consisting of ions and free electrons. In solution, many simple ions combine with ligands to give complex ions, including hydrates. (See electrolysis; ion exchange; ionization chamber; ionization potential; ion propulsion; zwitterion.)

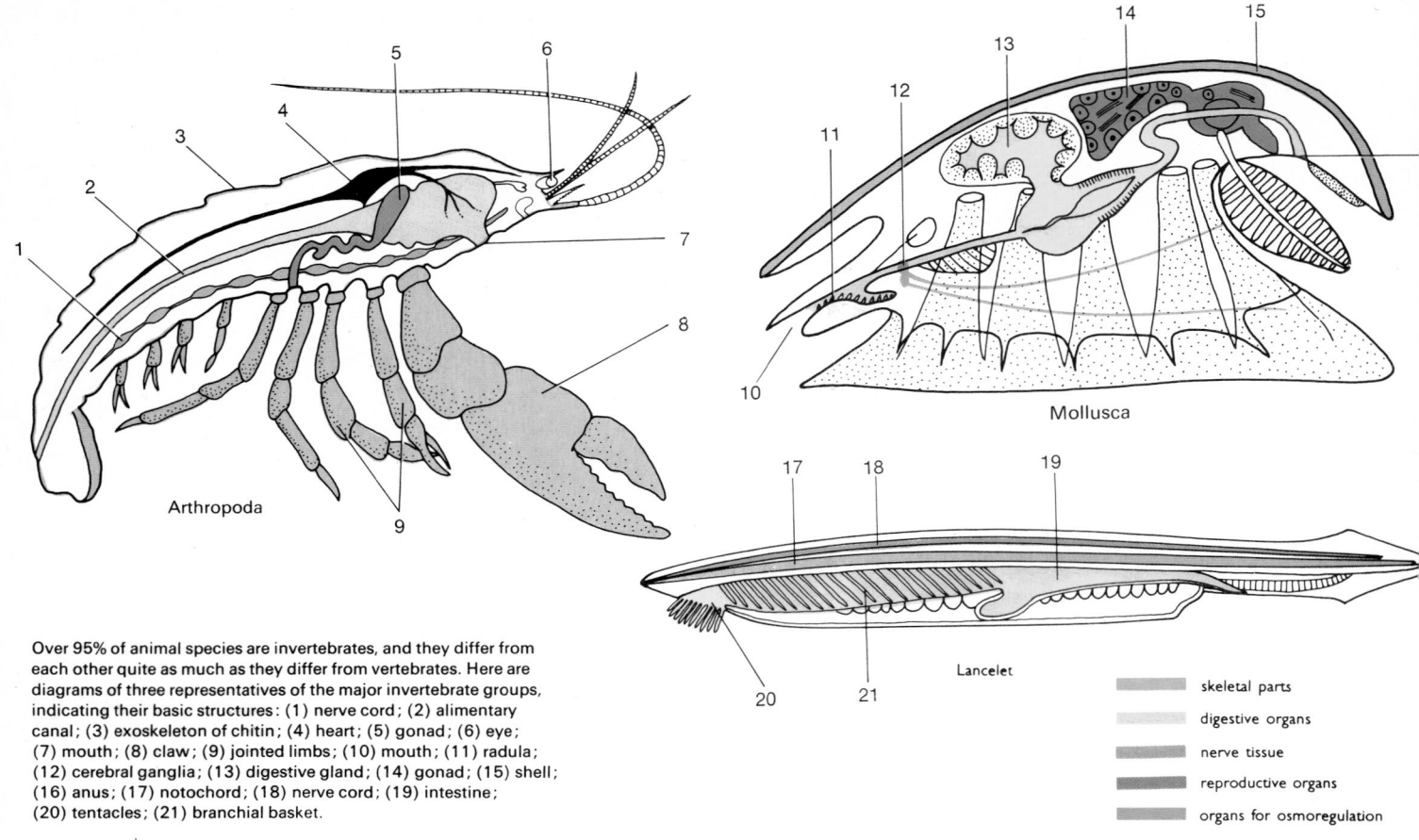

IONA, island in the Inner Hebrides, off the W coast of Scotland. It is famous as the site of Saint columba's monastery, founded in 563. There is only a very small permanent population; the chief source of income is agriculture and tourism. Members of the Iona religious community (founded in 1938) spend part of each year on the island.

ION COUNTER. See GEIGER COUNTER; SCINTILLATION COUNTER.

IONESCO, Eugène (1912–), Rumanian-born French playwright, a leading figure in the so-called theater of the absurd. Among his best-known works are *The Bald Soprano* (1950), *Rhinoceros* (1959) and *Exit the King* (1962).

ION EXCHANGE, chemical reaction in which IONS in a solution are replaced by others of like charge. An insoluble solid is used that has an open, netlike molecular structure: a ZEOLITE, or a synthetic organic polymer called an **ion-exchange resin**, whose composition and properties can be tailored for the use required. The solid has attached anionic groups, which are neutralized by small mobile cations in the interstices. It is these cations which are exchanged for others when a solution is passed through. The principle of anion exchange is similar. Ion exchange is used for softening HARD WATER, purifying sugar, and concentrating ores of uranium and the NOBLE METALS. Ion-exchange CHROMATOGRAPHY is used to separate the RARE EARTHS, and in chemical ANALYSIS.

IONIAN ISLANDS, group of islands off the SW mainland of Greece, chief of which are Cephalonia, Cerigo, Corfu, Ithaca, Leukas, Paxos and Zante. A Byzantine province in the 10th century, the islands passed through periods of Venetian, French, Russian and British control before becoming part of Greece in 1864. Exports include wine, cotton, olives and fish.

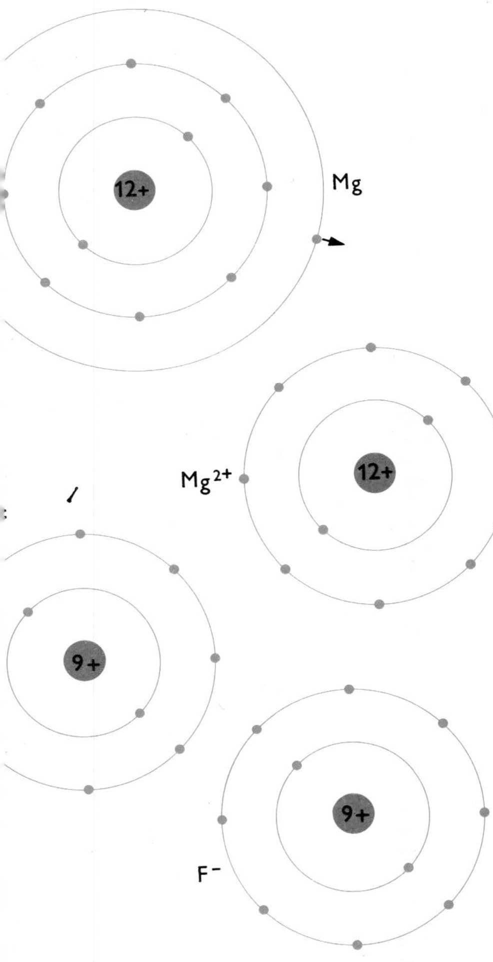

An ion is an electrically charged atom. An electrically neutral atom has an equal number of protons (positive) and electrons (negative), like the magnesium atom (Mg) depicted schematically here. It becomes a positively charged ion (or cation) when it loses two electrons. If an atom gains an electron it becomes a negative ion (or anion), like the atom of fluorine (F) here.

IONIANS, ancient Greek people, who colonized the W coast of Asia Minor that became known as Ionia. They are said to have been driven from the mainland by invading DORIANS. The Ionians made a major contribution to classical Greek poetry and philosophy.

IONIAN SEA, arm of the Mediterranean Sea, between SE Italy and W Greece. It is connected to the Adriatic by the Strait of Otranto and the Tyrrhenian Sea by the Strait of Messina.

IONIZATION CHAMBER, instrument for measuring the amount of ionization created in it by radiation such as ALPHA PARTICLES, BETA RAYS, GAMMA RAYS or X RAYS. A gas-filled chamber contains two ELECTRODES with a variable POTENTIAL difference between them. The IONS produced move towards the oppositely charged electrode, forming an electric current which is a measure of the amount of incoming radiation.

IONIZATION POTENTIAL, the ENERGY needed to remove an ELECTRON from the ground state of a given type of ATOM to infinity. It increases for removal of successive electrons, which are bound by the atom's positive charge. Ionization potentials can be determined by SPECTROSCOPY.

ION MICROSCOPE. See FIELD-ION MICROSCOPE.

IONOSPHERE, the zone of the earth's ATMOSPHERE extending outward from about 75km above the surface in which most atoms and molecules exist as electrically charged IONS. The high degree of ionization is maintained through the continual ABSORBTION of high-energy solar radiation. Several distinct ionized layers, known as the D, E, F_1, F_2 and G layers, are distinguished. These are somewhat variable, the D layer disappearing and the F_1, F_2 layers merging at night. Since the free ELECTRONS in these layers strongly reflect RADIO waves, the ionosphere is of great importance for long-distance radio communications.

ION PROPULSION, or **ion drive,** drive proposed for spacecraft on interstellar or longer interplanetary trips. The vaporized propellant (liquid CESIUM or MERCURY) is passed through an ionizer, which strips each atom of an ELECTRON. The positive IONS so formed are accelerated rearward by an ELECTRIC FIELD. The resultant thrust is low, but in the near-vacuum of space may be used to build up huge velocities by constant acceleration over a long period of time. The drive has been tested in orbit around the earth.

IOU, abbreviation of "I Owe You." It is used on documents declaring that the signatory owes a stated sum of money which he undertakes to repay. The right to collect the debt can be passed on to a third party.

IOWA, state in the midwestern US. It lies between the Mississippi and Missouri rivers, which have contributed to its development, as routes first for exploration and then commerce. Iowa consists of a gently rolling plain, sloping towards the SE, about two-thirds of which lies at 800–1 400ft. It is crossed by several large rivers, tributaries of the Mississippi and the Missouri. From 85% to 90% of the state's area is suitable for cultivation, and about one-fourth of all the finest agricultural land in the US is found in Iowa.

People. The first settlers came to Iowa from the states in the E and S, but from the 1840s many Europeans, particularly those with farming experience, joined them. Now 80% of residents are Iowa-born. The 1970 census showed a 1.2% population increase, compared with a national average of 13%. This is chiefly due to the fact that the number of farm-workers has been reduced by mechanization while local industry has not created sufficient replacement jobs.

Economy. The state's income from agriculture is the nation's highest, and its total agricultural income is second only to that of Cal. Cattle and hogs are the most important livestock, and the major crops are corn and soybeans. After the sharp decline in farm prices in the 1930s, Iowa began a drive to diversify its economy. Industrial plants used to be chiefly related to agriculture, with food processing the most

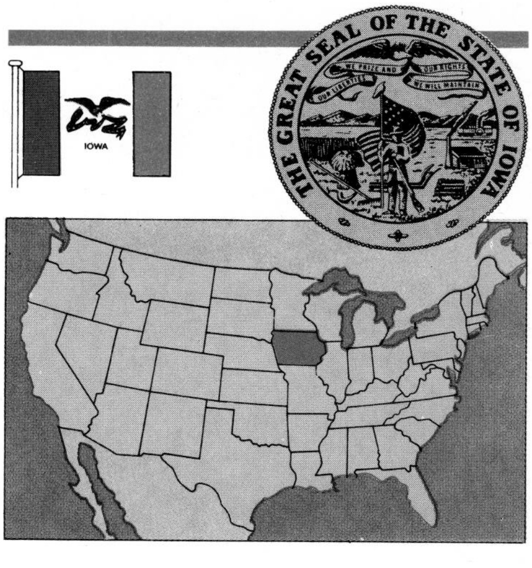

Name of state: Iowa
Capital: Des Moines
Statehood: Dec. 28, 1846 (29th state)
Familiar name: Hawkeye State
Area: 56 290sq mi
Population: 2 852 041
Elevation: Highest– 1 675ft, Ocheyedan Mound. Lowest— 480ft, Mississippi River in Lee County
Motto: Our Liberties We Prize and Our Rights We Will Maintain
State flower: Wild Rose
State bird: Eastern Goldfinch
State tree: Oak
State song: "The Song of Iowa"

important, but chemicals and electrical machinery have begun to gain in importance. Mineral production is relatively small, but the state is one of the nation's leading producers of gypsum. A high railroad mileage and a good rural road system have contributed to the growth of industry.

History. French explorers entered the region in 1673, and by 1682 France had claimed the area, naming it Louisiana for the French king. The territory W of the Mississippi was ceded to Spain (1762–1800), but in 1803 France sold the area to the US under the LOUISIANA PURCHASE. From 1804 to the early 1830s it was Indian land, not open to legal settlement; by 1851 the entire area had been opened to settlers. The Territory of Iowa was created in 1838, and it became the 29th state of the US in 1846. In 1857 a second constitution was adopted and the state capital established at Des Moines.

IOWA CITY, city in Ia., seat of Johnson Co. It has various manufacturing industries, but centers around the U. of Iowa. Pop 46 850.

IOWA INDIANS, Siouan-speaking tribe of North American Indians. Farmers and buffalo-hunters, they lived in what is now Iowa. Today they are scattered through Neb., Kan, and Okla.

IOWA RIVER, rises in Hancock Co., in central N Ia., and flows about 290mi SE to join the Mississippi R.

IPECAC, a drug produced from the dried stems and roots of *Cephalaelis ipecacuanha* and *C. acuminala*, plants native to South America, but also cultivated in Malaysia. The drug is used as an emetic and to treat amebic dysentery, its medicinal properties being due to the ALKALOIDS, emetine cephaeline and psychtrine.

IPHIGENIA, in Greek mythology, daughter of AGAMEMNON and CLYTEMNESTRA. During the TROJAN WAR the goddess ARTEMIS requested the sacrifice of Iphigenia. In one version she consented to die for the glory of Greece, in another Artemis put a stag in Iphigenia's place at the very last moment and had her carried off to the land of Tauris. Both versions are treated by the classical Greek dramatist EURIPIDES.

I-PIN, city in S central China. An administrative and commercial center, it stands on the Yangtze R. Among its industries are paper milling and food processing. Pop 275 000.

IPOH, city in N Malaysia, capital of Perak state. It is the commercial center of the Kinta Valley tin-mining region. Pop 247 969.

IPPOLITOV-IVANOV, Mikhail Mikhailovich (1859–1935), Russian composer and conductor. His work, which includes orchestral pieces, chamber music and operas, bridges Russian pre-revolutionary and post-revolutionary music.

IPSWICH, residential town in NE Mass. It has some light industry, and produces electronic goods, machine parts and processed foods. Pop 10 750.

IQ (*I*ntelligence *Q*uotient), a measure of an individual's INTELLIGENCE. If the intelligences of a large number of people are measured—by any valid means—the result will be very close to a NORMAL DISTRIBUTION. The mean (see MEAN, MEDIAN and MODE) intelligence can be defined as 100; and a person with that intelligence is said to have an IQ of 100. Using this basic, the IQ of an individual can be calculated from

$$IQ = 100 + \frac{16}{\mu}(x - \bar{x}),$$

where $\bar{x}$ is the mean score for individuals of the subject's age, μ is the STANDARD DEVIATION of the distribution of those scores, and x is his own score. (See also PSYCHOLOGICAL TESTS.)

IQBAL, Sir Muhammad (1873–1938), Indian Muslim poet, philosopher and politician. He was president of the Muslim League in 1930 and is considered one of the spiritual founders of Pakistan.

IQUITOS, city and inland port in NE Peru, capital of Loreto department. It stands on the Amazon R, some 2 300mi from the Atlantic, and is the commercial and cultural center of Peru's Amazon territory. Pop 74 000.

IRAKLION, or Candia, city in N Crete, capital of Herakleion department. It is an important seaport and exporting center. Pop 77 783.

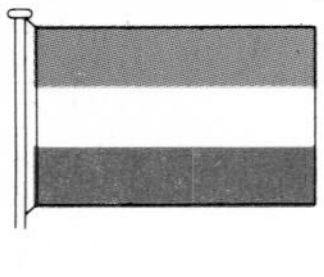

Official name: Iran
Capital: Teheran
Area: 634 000sq mi
Population: 30 159 000
Languages: Persian (Farsi); Kurdish; Luri; Turkic; Arabic
Religions: Muslim
Monetary unit(s): 1 Rial = 100 dinars

IRAN, known as Persia until 1935, a kingdom in SW Asia, a major oil-exporting country. It is bordered by the USSR and the Caspian Sea in the N, Afghanistan and Pakistan in the E and by Turkey and Iraq in the W. The Persian Gulf and the Gulf of Oman lie to the S.

Most of the country is above 1 500ft, with an interior plateau of desert which contains a salt waste about 200mi long and half as wide. The climate ranges from subtropical to subpolar. About 11% of the land is forested.

People. Iran is multi-lingual and culturally diverse. The Kurds are an independent and nomadic people living in the W mountains, where about 350 000 Lurs, thought to be aboriginal Persians also live. There are Armenians, who are primarily concerned with commerce and live in big cities, and groups of Turks and Jews. About 45% speak Persian, and although the Turkish groups are small, about 26% of Iranians

Arid, rock-strewn wastes like this are common in Iran owing to the hot, dry climate that obtains over most of the country. Yet people manage to live in these inhospitable regions, irrigating the land when they can and cultivating such crops as will grow.

speak Turkish—there was a long period of Turkish rule in the N.

Economy. In the early 1970s Iran's growth rate was one of the highest in the developing countries. Agriculture is important, employing half the economically active population. Crops include cereals, cotton, tobacco and olives. In the early 1970s Iran was the world's fourth largest producer of oil. Natural gas was becoming important, though Iran's other mineral resources, including coal, chromium, lead and copper, were largely undeveloped. Since 1954 the government has instituted a major drive for self-sufficiency, and by the 1970s manufactures included machine tools, textiles and automobiles.

History. Iran's history before 650 AD is treated under the entry on Ancient PERSIA. In 1055 Iran was invaded by the Turks, who in turn were overthrown by the Mongol leader GENGHIS KHAN in 1219. Between 1381 and 1404 there were frequent attacks by TAMERLANE, and it was not until 1501 that the Safavid dynasty, which ruled until 1736, was established, making Iran into a national state. There followed the rule of NADIR SHAH, and then, after 50 years of rival factions, the Kajar dynasty was established in 1795 and ruled until 1925. During this time Iran was dominated politically and economically by the great powers, especially Britain and Russia. After WWI Reza Khan, an army officer, overthrew the Shah and as REZA SHAH PAHLAVI founded the Pahlavi dynasty. Iran joined WWII against Germany in 1943 and in return was promised aid by Britain, the USSR and the US. Iran succeeded in maintaining its independence and in 1951 the oil industry was nationalized. Its internal political stability and success in maintaining good relations with both Western and Soviet countries have contributed to its recent advance.

IRAPUATO, city in N central Mexico on the Irapuato R. It is a communications center in an agricultural and mining region. Pop 138 522.

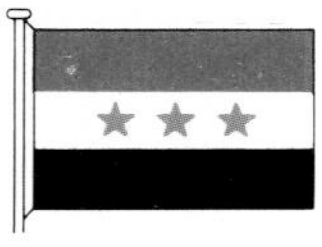

Official name: Republic of Iraq
Capital: Baghdad
Area: 169 240sq mi
Population: 10 070 000
Languages: Arabic
Religions: Muslim; Christian
Monetary unit(s): 1 Iraqi dinar = 1 000 fils

IRAQ, independent Arab republic in SW Asia, a major oil-producing state. It is bounded by Turkey in the N, Iran in the E, and Syria and Jordan in the W. The S border is with Kuwait, the Persian Gulf and Saudi Arabia.

Iraq consists of a largely level region between the Tigris and Euphrates rivers. There are two climatic regions, a hot arid lowland in the W and SW and a damper area in the NE where rain is sufficient for crops. In the N and E there is steppe vegetation with bushes and thorns, but the S and W support only salt-resistant shrubs.

People. Arabs and Kurds (less than 20%) are the main occupants of Iraq. The Arabs occupy most of the center and the W, and the Kurds, akin to the Iranians, live in the N and E. Minorities include small groups of Iranians and Turkomans and a Christian minority. Living standards and literacy levels are generally low, though with the development of oil resources social advances are gradually taking place.

Economy. Since the 1920s an almost wholly agricultural economy has been transformed by the oil industry, so that Iraq now produces 6% of the world's oil. Oil from the Zubayr field (near Basra) is shipped by tanker through the Persian Gulf, and there is an overland pipeline to the Mediterranean from the Kirkuk oilfield. Until 1961 the industry was monopolized by the Iraq Petroleum Company, largely British owned, but the government then took over much of I.P.C.'s holdings and the industry was nationalized in 1972. Other industries include the production of electronic equipment, textiles, cement, fertilizers, light machinery and refined sugar. Air and road transport are becoming increasingly important.

History. For the history of the region before the 7th century see under the entries ASSYRIA, BABYLONIA and MESOPOTAMIA. When the Arabs settled in the area now known as Iraq in the 7th century AD, they brought about a cultural and scientific revival. Baghdad became the capital of the ABBASID caliphate. After the Mongol invasion in the 13th century the country was impoverished and continuing political instability prevented its rebuilding. Iraq's modern history begins in 1914, with the British invasion during WWI. It was not until 1932, after years of violence and unrest, that the British were prepared to pull out. Unrest continued, particularly over Kurdish demands for self-government. In 1945 Iraq joined the ARAB LEAGUE but then in 1955 joined the Baghdad Pact (see CENTRAL TREATY ORGANIZATION). Conflict with the Kurds erupted in 1962 and continued into the 1970s. By 1975 Iraq had aligned with the USSR, which now provides considerable technical aid.

IREDELL, James (1751–1799), English-born American jurist, a Supreme Court justice 1790–99. His decision in the case Chisholm v. Georgia (1793) denying the court's right to hear a suit brought against a state by a citizen from another state was later endorsed by the 11th Amendment.

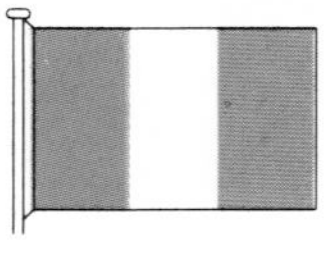

Official name: Irish Republic
Capital: Dublin
Area: 26 599sq mi
Population: 2 978 248
Languages: Irish, English
Religions: Roman Catholic, Protestant
Monetary unit(s): 1 pound = 100 new pence

IRELAND, Republic of, or Eire, independent country in the British Isles occupying all of the island of Ireland except the NE (see IRELAND, NORTHERN).

The ruins of this ancient cathedral, typical of the finest Irish Romanesque architecture, stand on the Rock of Cashel which rises above the small town of Cashel, southern Tipperary, in the Irish Republic.

Land. The chief physical feature is the broad central limestone plain; seldom rising above 400ft, it is marked by numerous *loughs* (lakes) and large peat bogs. Rimming the plain are groups of hills and mountains, the most extensive being the Wicklow Mts in the E. The country's highest peak, Carrantuohill (3414ft), rises in Macgillycuddy's Reeks in the SW near the beautiful Lakes of Killarney. The chief river is the Shannon (240mi), longest in the British Isles; like the Erne R it is harnessed for hydroelectric power. The long Shannon estuary is one of many inlets of the much-indented W coast, which is fringed by many islands. The climate is mild and damp, with annual rainfall ranging from 30–40in in the lowlands to over 60in in the W uplands. This has helped create the lush green pastures which have made Ireland "the Emerald Isle." Rainfall and high winds are more frequent in the W and N than in the sunnier E.

People. The population today is less than half of what it was in 1841, due to persistent emigration. It is concentrated mainly in or near the cities, the largest of which are Dublin, the capital, Cork and Limerick. The Irish are a Celtic people; since 1922 the government has encouraged the revival of Gaelic, their ancient language. St. Patrick converted the Irish to Christianity in the 5th century and today about 95% of the people are Roman Catholics.

Economy. It is based mainly on small mixed farms rearing cattle or engaged in dairying (especially in the S), with barley, wheat, oats, potatoes, turnips and sugar beets as the chief arable crops. Ireland is relatively poor in minerals, but some coal is mined, along with recently-discovered deposits of lead, zinc, copper and silver. Peat from the bogs is a valuable fuel, used mainly for electricity generation. Industries include food-processing, distilling, brewing, tobacco products, textiles, clothing and small-scale engineering. Foreign manufacturers, mainly W German and Japanese, have been encouraged to set up export-oriented plants, and tourism is important.

History. In the 4th century BC the GAELS evolved a Celtic civilization which in its full flowering, after St. PATRICK introduced Christianity in the 5th century, produced superb works of art (see BOOK OF KELLS) and sent religious and cultural missionaries to the rest of Europe (see CAROLINGIAN REVIVAL). It was destroyed by the VIKINGS (though they were defeated by BRIAN BORU in 1041). In 1166 the Anglo-Normans invaded Ireland and thereafter the English tried constantly to assert their authority over the native Irish and the settlers, now largely assimilated with them. The Tudors and Stuarts promoted English and Scottish settlement (see ULSTER), and mercilessly tried to anglicize the country in wars constantly embittered by religious differences, until Oliver CROMWELL's pacification. Roman Catholic gentry fled when Protestant ascendency was confirmed by WILLIAM III's victory at the Boyne (1690). In the Rebellion of 1798 the Irish peasantry, roused by such patriots as Wolfe TONE, rebelled, but were ruthlessly suppressed. The Act of Union (1801) ended parliamentary independence from England; nevertheless, despite the POTATO FAMINE and FENIAN violence, a measure of independence by constitutional means was slowly attained through agitation for Catholic Emancipation and the emergence of leaders like O'CONNELL and J. S. PARNELL. One result was the cultural CELTIC REVIVAL of the 1890s. The failure of HOME RULE led to the bitter EASTER RISING (1916), and the armed struggle after WWI resulted in Britain's grant of dominion status to the IRISH FREE STATE (1921), but the civil war was continued on a terrorist basis by the IRISH REPUBLICAN ARMY until 1923. Eamonn DE VALERA, in power from 1932, broke with the British Crown and renamed the country Eire (1937). In 1949 it left the British Commonwealth as the Republic of Ireland. In the 1960s the six counties of Ulster which still wished to remain part of the UK were the scene of renewed IRA terrorism. In 1973 the then government of Eire recognized Northern Ireland as part of the UK. In 1976 stronger measures were taken against the IRA.

IRELAND, Northern, comprises the six counties of Ulster in NE Ireland. Since 1922 it has been a province of the UK. Covering 5462sq mi, it has a predominantly Protestant population with a Roman Catholic minority swelled in recent years to around 30%. The largest towns are the capital, Belfast and Londonderry. Major industries include engineering and shipbuilding, textiles (man-made fibers and linen) and electronics,

History. The Ulster counties, predominantly Protestant, chose to remain British after partition in 1921 and maintained this resolve despite occasional outbreaks of terrorism by the IRISH REPUBLICAN ARMY. Discrimination against the growing Catholic minority in politics led them to form a civil rights movement (1968), which was used to justify renewed IRA terrorism. The resulting violence and civil unrest led the UK) government to suspend the Northern Ireland Parliament at Stormont (1972) and assume direct rule of the province. A multilateral Council of Ireland (1973) failed to solve the problem. Though a new Northern Ireland Assembly was elected (1975) in an effort to promote power-sharing, neither Catholic nor Protestant extremists accepted it; violence by both sides continued.

IRELAND, John (1838–1918), Irish-American Roman Catholic prelate, first archbishop of St. Paul, Minn. He was known for his liberal ideas, especially on the importance of integrating immigrant parishes into the US Church.

IRENAEUS, Saint (c130–202), major theologian of his time. Bishop of Lugdunum (now Lyons, France), from 177, he opposed GNOSTICISM in his work *Against Heretics* (c180) and in so doing reinforced episcopal authority.

IRETON, Henry (1611–1651), English Parliamentary general and statesman, from 1616 son-in-law of Oliver CROMWELL. Of moderate outlook, he unsuccessfully attempted to arrange a compromise between the army, Parliament and the king. From 1649 he was Cromwell's deputy in Ireland.

IRGUN ZVAI LEUMI (Hebrew: National Military Organization), irregular Zionist military force founded in 1935 as an arm of the extremist Revisionist Party; it used violent terrorism, including the murder of hostages, against Arabs and British. In 1947 Irgun split over the massacre of an Arab village; in 1948 it disbanded, although members formed the *Herut* political party.

IRIDESCENCE, production of colors of varied hue by INTERFERENCE of light reflected from front and back of thin films (as in soap bubbles) or from faults and boundaries within crystalline solids such as mica or opal. The colors of mother-of-pearl and some insects are due to iridescence.

RIDIUM (Ir), hard, white metal in the PLATINUM GROUP, the most resistant element to corrosion at room temperature. AW 192.2, mp 2410°C, bp 4527°C, sg 22.4 (20°C).

IRIS, in Greek mythology, goddess of the rainbow, usually portrayed with wings and a herald's staff.

IRIS, the pigmented diaphragm forming the aperture of the vertebrate EYE.

IRISES, perennial rhizomatous or bulbous herbaceous plants of the genus *Iris*, family Iridaceae, which are native to the N Hemisphere. The leaves are sword-like and the petals are arranged in multiples of three. Irises are widely cultivated as garden ornamentals and numerous varieties and hybrids are available.

IRISH ELK, an extinct DEER related to the modern European ELK and the MOOSE of North America. It had palmated antlers up to 3.4m (11ft) across, and stood 2m (6.6ft) tall.

IRISH FREE STATE, the forerunner of the Republic of IRELAND, constituted by the Irish Free State (Agreement) Act, 1922, as a British dominion under a governor general, representing the monarch. The first president of the executive council (1922–32) was W. T. Cosgrave.

IRISH LANGUAGE. See CELTIC LANGUAGES; GAELIC.

IRISH LITERARY REVIVAL. See CELTIC RENAISSANCE.

IRISH LITERATURE. See GAELIC LITERATURE.

IRISH MOSS, popular name for the red alga *Chondrus crispus* and related ALGAE, which are found growing on the rocky Atlantic coasts of Europe and North America. A gelatinous substance called carrageenin is extracted from Irish moss and used in the food and pharmaceutical industry as an emulsifying and suspending agent.

IRISH REPUBLICAN ARMY (IRA), illegal paramilitary force formed 1916–20; its political wing is the SINN FEIN. The granting of home rule to Eire as the IRISH FREE STATE split the IRA, the "Irregulars" continuing terrorism and sabotage in the S until 1923. There were further outbreaks in Northern Ireland and Britain in the 1930s, 1940s and 1950s. In 1969 the IRA split into the Marxist-oriented "officials" and the nationalist "Provisionals," who rely on Irish-American financial aid. The Provisionals launched a campaign of often indiscriminate bombings and assassinations, which spread to Britain 1972–73.

IRISH SEA, arm of the Atlantic, separating Ireland from England. Connected to the Atlantic by the North Channel to the NW and St. George's Channel to the S, it is about 130mi across.

IRISH SETTER, an exuberant red working dog, oldest of the setter family. It has a narrow head, long feathery body and tail. An elegant and gentle dog, it is used extensively as a game dog and retriever in both England and the US.

IRISH TERRIER, a red or red-gold dog of about 0.45m (18in) descended from the ancient terrier-type known as Madadh. Though popular as a pet, it is a working strain, used for flushing and killing vermin.

IRISH WATER SPANIEL, a distinctive working dog, especially bred for working in water as a duck-dog. It has a liver-colored coat with dense tight curls over the whole body except for the face.

IRISH WOLFHOUND, a dog originally used, as its name suggests, for wolf or elk-hunting. The dogs are at least 790mm (31in) high and weigh a minimum of 55kg (120lb). They have a rough hard coat, gray or brown in color.

IRKUTSK, city in the E central Russian SFSR, a major industrial center of Siberia at the confluence of the Angara and Irkut rivers. Pop 451 000.

IRON (Fe), silvery-gray, soft, ferromagnetic (see MAGNETISM) metal in Group VIII of the PERIODIC TABLE; a TRANSITION ELEMENT. Metallic iron is the main constituent of the earth's core (see EARTH), but is rare in the crust; it is found in meteorites (see METEORS). Combined iron is found as HEMATITE, MAGNETITE, LIMONITE, SIDERITE, GOETHITE, TACONITE, CHROMITE and PYRITE. It is extracted by smelting oxide ores in a BLAST FURNACE to produce PIG IRON which may be refined to produce CAST IRON or WROUGHT IRON, or converted to STEEL in the OPEN-HEARTH PROCESS or the BESSEMER PROCESS. Many other iron ALLOYS are used for particular applications. Pure iron is very little used; it is chemically reactive, and oxidizes to RUST in moist air. It has four allotropes (see ALLOTROPY). The stable oxidation states of iron are +2 (ferrous) and +3 (ferric), though +4 and +6 states are known. The ferrous ion (Fe^{2+}) is pale green in aqueous solution; it is a mild reducing agent, and does not readily form LIGAND complexes. **Iron(II) Sulfate** ($FeSO_4.7H_2O$), or **green vitriol**, or **copperas**, green crystalline solid, made by treating iron ore with sulfuric acid, used in tanning, in medicine to treat iron deficiency, and to make ink, fertilizers, pesticides and other iron compounds. mp 64°C. The ferric ion (Fe^{3+}) is yellow in aqueous solution; it resembles the ALUMINUM ion, being acidic and forming stable LIGAND complexes, especially with CYANIDES (see PRUSSIAN BLUE). **Iron(III) Oxide** (Fe_2O_3), red-brown powder used as a pigment and as jewelers' rouge (see ABRASIVES); occurs naturally as HEMATITE. mp 1565°C. (See also ALUM; SANDWICH COMPOUNDS.) In the human body, iron is a constituent of HEMOGLOBIN and the CYTOCHROMES. Iron deficiency causes ANEMIA. AW 55.8, mp 1535°C, bp 2750°C, sg 7.874 (20°C).

IRON AGE, the stage of man's material cultural development, following the STONE AGE and BRONZE AGE, during which iron is generally used for weapons and tools. Though used ornamentally as early as 4000 BC in Egypt and Mesopotamia, iron's difficulty of working precluded its general use until efficient techniques were developed in Armenia, c1500 BC. By c500 BC the use of iron was dominant throughout the known world, and by c300 BC the Chinese were using cast iron. Some cultures, as those in America and Australia, are said never to have had an iron age.

IRONCLADS, the first armored warships, wooden-hulled ships with iron plate armor, developed by the French and British in the CRIMEAN WAR. The first engagement between ironclads came in the US Civil War, involving the famous MONITOR. Iron-hulled ships superseded ironclads in the 1890s.

IRON CURTAIN, term for the self-imposed exclusion of the communist countries, especially during the Stalinist era. The term was popularized by Sir Winston CHURCHILL in a speech at Fulton, Mo., on March 5, 1946.

IRON GATE, at 2 600ft the deepest gorge in Europe, 2mi long. It lies on the Danube R at the Romania-Yugoslavia border; the two countries run a joint hydroelectric project in the gorge.

IRON GUARD, Romanian Fascist party 1927–41; largely modelled on the Nazi party, it won 16% of the vote in the 1937 elections but in 1938 was dissolved by King Carol II. Revived in 1940, it was broken up following an abortive coup.

IRON LUNG. See ARTIFICIAL ORGANS.

IRON MASK, Man in the, political prisoner of unknown identity, imprisoned by the French first in Italy and then in the BASTILLE from 1698 until his death in 1704. He was named for the mask (in fact of black velvet) which he always wore.

IRONTON, industrial city in S Ohio, seat of Lawrence Co. A major iron center until after the Civil War, it now has a large chemical industry. Pop 15 030.

IRONWOOD, trees that produce very hard and heavy wood. Also, the general name given to the wood, which is difficult to cut and is used as a fuel, for fence posts and tool handles.

IROQUOIAN, family of languages spoken by North American Indians chiefly in what is now N N.Y. The languages of the first five confederated IROQUOIS tribes and Wyandot, the Huron language, are the most closely related. The two southern languages are Tuscarora and Cherokee.

IROQUOIS, North American Indian tribes of the IROQUOIAN linguistic family, members of the Iroquois League. This political union of the Mohawk, Oneida, Onondaga, Cayuga and Seneca tribes was founded in the 16th century by the Onondaga chief HIAWATHA and Dekanawida, formerly a Huron. Villages and tribes were sometimes adopted into the League, as with the Tuscarora in 1722. Hunters and farmers, the Iroquois tribes lived in stockaded villages of *longhouses*; families were matrilineal, and belonged to an inter-tribal clan system. In the 1600s they were supplied with firearms and metal weapons by the Dutch, and became supreme in the NE. During the FRENCH AND INDIAN WARS the Iroquois supported the British, but the league split over the REVOLUTIONARY WAR.

IRRADIATION, exposure of a sample to RADIATION, usually for a definite purpose. Biological and pharmaceutical materials may have their properties altered by exposure to ULTRAVIOLET RADIATION; X RAYS are widely used in medicine and industry. Materials may be irradiated directly with radiation of a given type and ENERGY by placing them in a particle ACCELERATOR or NUCLEAR REACTOR, but it is often more practical to use the radiation from manufactured radioactive ISOTOPES to change their physical and chemical properties as required. Neutrons and GAMMA RAYS are used to sterilize foodstuffs and control the reproduction of insect pests.

IRRATIONAL NUMBERS, those REAL NUMBERS that cannot be expressed as the RATIO of two INTEGERS (see RATIONAL NUMBERS). Common examples include π (see PI), e (see EXPONENTIAL) and $\sqrt{2}$ (see ROOT).

IRRAWADDY RIVER, main waterway of Burma, formed by the confluence of the Mali and Nmai rivers. It flows S for about 1 350mi to empty into the Bay of Bengal. Its delta is one of the world's richest rice-growing areas.

IRREDENTISM (from *Italia irredenta*: unredeemed Italy), Italian nationalist movement begun after unification (1866) to acquire Italian-speaking lands still under foreign rule, an end achieved after WWI. The term is now used for any movement attempting to free territory from foreign control.

IRRIGATION, artificial application of water to soil to promote plant growth. Irrigation is vital for agricultural land with inadequate rainfall. The practice dates back at least to the canals and reservoirs of ancient Egypt. Today over 320 million acres of farmland throughout the world are irrigated, notably in the US, India, Pakistan, China, Australia, Egypt and the USSR. There are three main irrigation techniques: **surface irrigation**, in which the soil surface is moistened or flooded by water flowing through furrows or tubes; **sprinkler irrigation**, in which water is sprayed on the land from above; and **subirrigation**, in which underground pipes supply water to roots. The amount of water needed for a particular project is called the **duty of water**, expressed as the number of acres irrigated by 1cu ft of water per second.

IRRITABILITY, in biology and psychology, the ability to be affected by external stimuli (see PERCEPTION). (See also ANIMAL BEHAVIOR.)

IRTYSH RIVER, main tributary of the Ob R in W central Asia. Rising in glaciers of the Altai Mts of China, it flows 2 760mi W to Lake Zaisan, then NW to Siberia.

IRVING, city in NE Tex., a W suburb of Dallas. It

During the Middle Ages the Irish wolfhound was an exceedingly popular hunting dog but by the end of the 19th century very few remained. Since then it has been crossbred with the Deerhound and its gentle, obedient nature has made it once again the object of much affection in many homes.

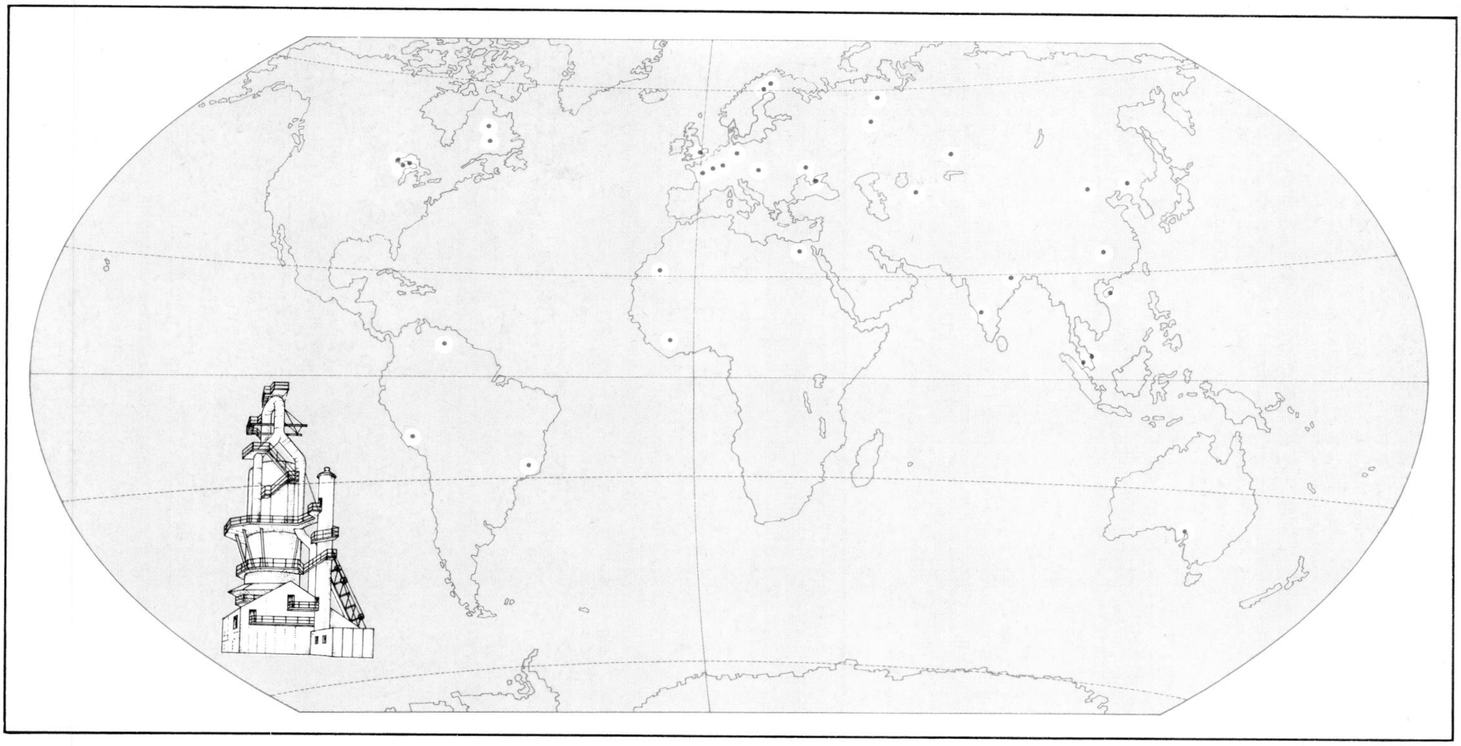

Map showing the major iron mining areas of the world. The inset drawing is of a typical smelting furnace.

has manufacturing industries and is the home of Dallas U. Pop 97 260.

IRVING, Edward (1792–1834), Scottish clergyman who helped to found the CATHOLIC APOSTOLIC CHURCH. He preached the imminence of Christ's second coming and was excommunicated and deposed by the Church of Scotland for maintaining "the sinfulness of Christ's humanity."

IRVING, Sir Henry (1838–1905), stage name of John Henry Brodribb, greatest British actor and actor-manager of his day. At the Lyceum Theater, London, 1878–1902, he staged spectacular Shakespeare productions, often with Ellen TERRY as his leading lady.

IRVING, Washington (1783–1859), first US writer to achieve international acclaim. Born in N.Y., he became a casual writer and publisher; he went to Europe in 1815 on business and remained there until 1832. His most famous stories, *Rip Van Winkle* and *The Legend of Sleepy Hollow*, appeared in *The Sketch Book of Geoffrey Crayon* (1820). None of his later works approached the success of this collection. He served as minister to Spain 1842–46, but spent the rest of his life at Tarrytown, N.Y., near the setting of many of his tales.

IRVINGTON, town in NE N.J., an industrial suburb of Newark producing mainly textiles and metal products. Pop 59 473.

ISAAC, in the Old Testament, second of the Hebrew patriarchs. Son of Abraham and Sarah, he was spared at the last moment from being sacrificed as proof of his father's faith. He married REBECCA and fathered ESAU and JACOB, who cheated Esau out of Isaac's last blessing.

ISAAC, name of two Byzantine emperors. **Isaac I Comnenus** (c1005–1061), was emperor 1057–59. An army commander, he deposed Michael VI. He reduced church power and confiscated some of its property. In 1059 he led a campaign against the Hungarians, but abdicated due to illness. **Isaac II Angelus** (c1155–1204), was emperor 1185–95 and 1203–04. Proclaimed emperor during an insurrection in Constantinople he was deposed and blinded by his brother Alexis III during a campaign against the Bulgarians in 1195. Restored in 1203 with his son Alexius IV, he was deposed in 1204 by Alexius V.

The regular irrigation of vast tracts of land in the northwestern United States with the waters of Lake Roosevelt is made possible by controlling the flow from the Grand Coulee dam, shown here.

ISAAK, Heinrich (c1450–1517), major Flemish composer. He served Lorenzo de MEDICI and Emperor MAXIMILIAN I. The bulk of his work was church music, particularly masses, but he also wrote many German and Italian secular songs.

ISABELLA, name of two queens of Spain. **Isabella I** (1451–1504), was queen of Castile from 1474 and of Aragon from 1481 by marriage to the future Ferdinand II of Aragon (1469). The marriage unified Christian Spain; royal power was strengthened and the INQUISITION reestablished, Isabella supporting its call for the expulsion of Spanish Jews. She financed COLUMBUS' expedition in 1492. She helped direct the conquest of Moorish Granada. **Isabella II** (1830–1904), was queen of Spain 1833–68, under a regency until 1843. Her succession was disputed by the Carlists, provoking civil war 1833–39; after the regency was ended by a revolt her personal rule proved arbitory and ineffectual. Promiscuous and irresponsible, she was ousted in 1868 and abdicated in 1870.

ISAIAH, great Hebrew prophet of the 8th century BC, for whom the Old Testament Book of Isaiah is named; probably only the first 36 chapters represent his teachings, the remainder (often known as Deutero—and Trito—Isaiah) being additions by his followers. Isaiah condemns the decadence of Judah, foretelling coming disaster; he warns against trusting in foreign alliances rather than in God and heralds the Messiah.

ISFAHAN (Esfahan), historic city in W central Iran, its capital 1598–1722 under the Safavid dynasty. Many great buildings date from this period; the city became a center of arts and crafts, especially in textiles and the world-famous Isfahan carpets. Pop 520 000.

ISHERWOOD, Christopher William Bradshaw (1904–   ), English-born novelist and playwright who settled in the US in 1939. His best-known novels are *Mr. Norris Changes Trains* (1935) and *Goodbye to*

Berlin (1939), set in the decaying Germany of the 1930s. He collaborated with W. H. AUDEN on three plays, the best-known being *The Ascent of F-6* (1936).

ISHII, Viscount Kikujiro (1866–1945), influential Japanese diplomat, ambassador to France 1912–15 and 1920–27. He negotiated the GENTLEMAN'S AGREEMENT and the LANSING-ISHII AGREEMENT with the US. He opposed Japan's alliance with the Axis powers in WWII, favoring the Allies, but was killed in a US air raid.

ISHMAEL, in the Old Testament, son of Abraham and his concubine Hagar. After ISAAC's birth, Abraham's wife Sarah drove Hagar and Ishmael into the desert, but he survived to father 12 sons. These founded a "great nation," the Ishmaelite Arab tribes.

ISHTAR, fertility goddess of Babylonia and Assyria; she became an ambiguous mother-goddess in the Middle East, personifying both fertility and love and also lust, war and death. (See also ASTARTE.)

ISINGLASS, white form of GELATIN, made from dried membranes of swim bladders of fish. It is used as an adhesive, a fabric size, and an additive to clarify wines, beer and vinegar. For the mineral isinglass, see MUSCOVITE.

ISIS, in ancient Egyptian mythology the dominant mother goddess, protectress of living and dead. Sister and wife of OSIRIS, she temporarily restored him to life after his murder and dismembering by SET, and so conceived HORUS. Her cult spread from Lower Egypt throughout the Roman world as one of the MYSTERIES.

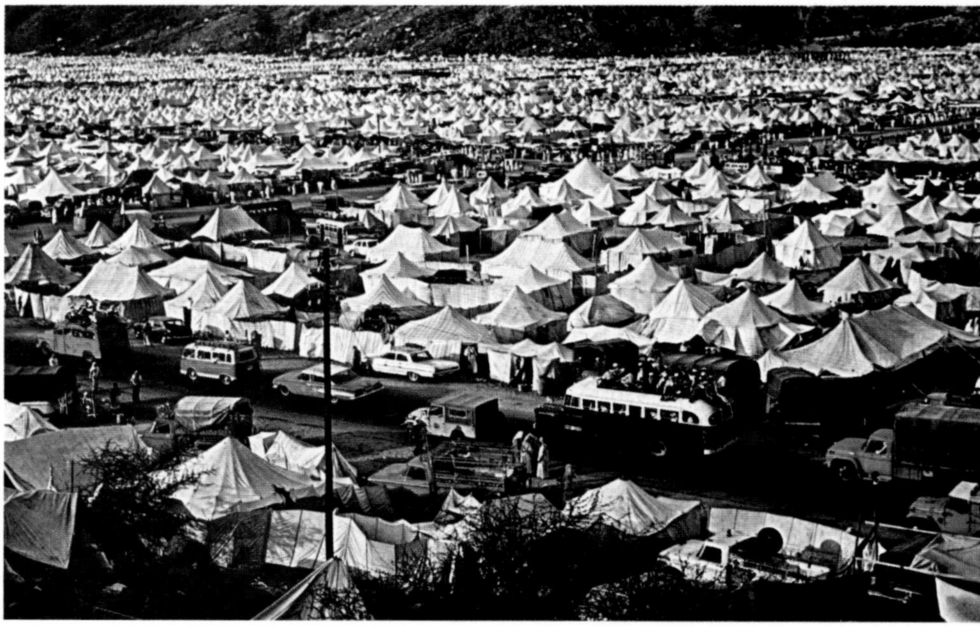

All Muslims aspire to visit the holy city of Mecca once in their lifetime, to assure themselves of a place in paradise; those that manage the journey camp here in this sea of tents on the Plain of Arafat, just outside the gates of Islam's spiritual center, where no infidel is allowed to enter.

ISLAM (Arabic: Submission to God), major world religion, founded by Mohammed in the 7th century AD; a monotheistic faith, it incorporates elements of Judaic and Christian belief. Today there are more than 400 million MUSLIMS ("ones who submit"), mainly in the Arab countries and SW Asia, and in N and E Africa, Turkey, Iran, Afghanistan, Pakistan, India, SE Asia and the USSR. The Prophet MOHAMMED was a merchant of Mecca in the early 7th century; on his journeys he came into contact with Jews and Christians. Inspired by a vision of the archangel Gabriel, he began to preach the worship of the one true God (Arabic: *Allah*), and to denounce idolatry. In his lifetime Mecca was converted to Islam. In the century after his death (632 AD) Muslim armies forged an Arab Empire extending from Spain to India.

Teachings. The KORAN, the holy book of Islam, sets forth the fundamental tenets of Islam as revealed by God to Mohammed. These include the five basic duties of Muslims and also rules for their social and moral behavior. Muslims also study the prophet's teachings, or *Sunna*, collected in the *Hadith* ("traditions"). A legal system, the *Shari'a*, based on the Koran and the Sunna, has been the law of many Muslim countries.

Worship. Public worship takes place in MOSQUES; these are often highly decorated in abstract patterns, because representational art is forbidden as idolatrous. (See ISLAMIC ART AND ARCHITECTURE.) Before entering a mosque, Muslims must ritually cleanse themselves. Special services are held at midday on Friday. Devout Muslims must pray five times daily, facing in the direction of Mecca. Islam has no priests as such; worship is led by a lay leader, the *imam*. A *muezzin* calls the faithful to prayer from a rooftop or MINARET. Other leaders in Muslim communities include the *ulema*, experts on the *Shari'a*, who give guidance and may even decide legal disputes.

ISLAMABAD, newly-built capital of Pakistan, 8mi NE of Rawalpindi. Begun in 1961, it is largely a governmental and administrative center, but also houses educational, scientific and cultural institutions. Pop 250 000.

ISLAMIC ART AND ARCHITECTURE, art that grew out of the Islamic way of life. Because there was no strong tradition of Arab art, it adapted the Byzantine, Sassanian and Coptic styles of Muslim-dominated lands. Arab influence added a sense of visual rhythm and an interest in astronomy and mathematics. Interpretations of the Prophet's sayings, however, forbade portrayals of people or animals either in religious art or altogether. Figures appeared in the book illustration and miniature work at which Persian and Indian artists excelled, and (in Persia only) in the decoration of some mosques. In general, however, designs relied on abstract and mathematical forms, and also calligraphic Koran texts; often every available piece of a building may be so decorated.

Early examples of Islamic architecture are the KAABA and the Dome of the Rock in Jerusalem. The dominant style of MOSQUE, with a minaret tower, was introduced under the Omayyad dynasty. A characteristic feature of Islamic buildings is the arch, in horseshoe, trefoil and zigzag forms. The greatest Muslim mausoleum is the TAJ MAHAL. The Moorish ALHAMBRA in Granada, Spain, is the most famous palace in the Islamic style. In craftwork there is also a distinctive Islamic tradition; as well as the famous rugs and textiles the Islamic world developed beautiful pottery, including luster-glazed ceramics, and metalwork, inventing DAMASCENING.

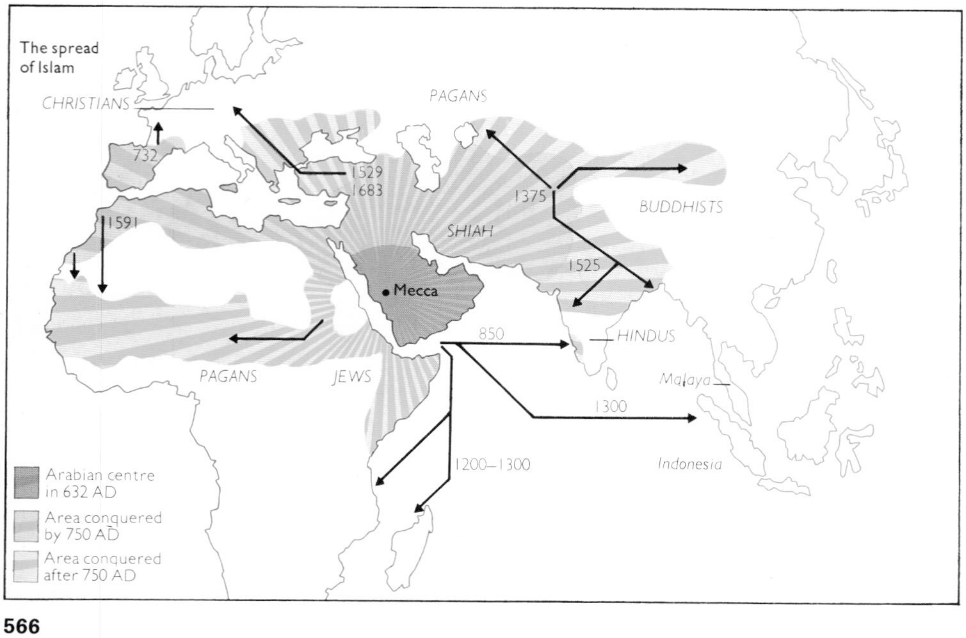

ISLAND, comparatively small land area entirely surrounded by water, a result of the buildup of the cone of a submarine VOLCANO, EROSION by the sea or GLACIERS of parts of coastal regions, DIASTROPHISM or other process. **Island arcs** are curving chains of islands. They are often associated with EARTHQUAKE activity, and often have deep OCEAN trenches on the convex sides. (See also ATOLL; CORAL; PLATE TECTONICS.)

ISLE OF MAN. See MAN, ISLE OF.

ISLE OF PINES, island in the Caribbean Sea off SW Cuba, to which it belongs. Its economy rests largely upon fishing and agriculture, and it houses a major prison.

ISLE OF WIGHT. See WIGHT, ISLE OF.

ISLE ROYALE NATIONAL PARK, wildlife reserve, established in 1931, comprising more than 200 islands in NW Lake Superior, N Mich. Isle Royale itself (229sq mi) is the site of Precolumbian Indian copper mines; its wildlife includes moose, timber wolves and diverse bird life.

ISLETS OF LANGERHANS. See INSULIN; PANCREAS.

ISMAILIS, Muslim SHI'ITE sect sometimes known as Seveners because they venerated the religious leader Ismail (d. 760) as the seventh IMAM. Among branches of the Ismaili faith were the ASSASSIN sects of Iran and Syria. The Ismaili spiritual leader today is the AGA KHAN.

ISMAIL PASHA (1830–1895), Ottoman viceroy of Egypt 1863–79. He extended Egyptian rule in the

Sudan. In Egypt he improved administration, education and communications, opening the Suez Canal in 1869. Huge debts resulted from his schemes and he was dismissed by the Ottoman sultan in 1879.

ISOBAR, line drawn on a meteorological map joining points which are, at a given moment in time, experiencing the same air pressure (see ATMOSPHERE).

ISOCRATES (436–338 BC), Athenian orator who founded a celebrated school of RHETORIC there. His vision of a Greece united to invade Persia influenced ALEXANDER THE GREAT.

ISOLATIONISM, national policy of avoiding entanglement in foreign affairs, a recurrent phenomenon in US history. In 1823 the MONROE DOCTRINE tried to exclude European powers from the Americas. The US entered WWI reluctantly, stayed out of the League of Nations it helped create and entered WWII only when attacked. Thereafter it joined the UN and international defense pacts (NATO, SEATO), but having found a military presence in Indochina costly and ineffectual, developed a renewed isolationist tendency.

ISOMERISM, in nuclear physics, the existence of metastable states of an atomic nucleus (see ATOM), having the same atomic number and mass number as the ground state, but higher energy. Nuclear isomers are formed by bombardment or in a radioactive decay chain (see RADIOACTIVITY). They usually have very short HALF-LIVES and decay by emitting GAMMA RAYS.

ISOMERS, chemical compounds having identical chemical COMPOSITION and molecular FORMULA, but differing in the arrangement of atoms in their molecules, and having different properties. The two chief types are STEREOISOMERS, which have the same structural formula, and **structural isomers**, which have different structural formulas. The latter may be subdivided into positional isomers, which have the same FUNCTIONAL GROUPS occupying different positions on the carbon skeleton; and functional isomers, which have different functional groups. (See also CRACKING; TAUTOMERISM.)

ISOMETRICS, exercises in which MUSCLES are contracted against resistance, but without movement at JOINTS; the muscles remain at the same length but their tension is increased. It is used in some systems of physical training and in PHYSIOTHERAPY.

Epitome of elegance and harmony, the facade of the Great Mosque at Cordova built by Caliph al-Hakam II (961–976). During the 10th century Cordova steadily increased its power and became a capital rivaling the splendor of Baghdad.

ISOMORPHISM, the formation by different compounds or MINERALS of CRYSTALS having closely similar external forms and lattice structure. Isomorphous compounds have similar chemical composition—ions of similar size, charge, and electrical polarizability being substituted for each other—and form mixed crystals.

ISONZO RIVER, river rising in NW Yugoslavia and flowing 84mi S to the Gulf of Trieste in NE Italy. The Isonzo Valley was the scene of fierce battles in WWI. (See CAPORETTO, BATTLE OF.)

ISOPODA, a distinct order of CRUSTACEA which includes WOODLICE and GRIBBLES. Typically flattened from above downward, the body is generally oval and shield-like. Though the most familiar forms are the terrestrial ones, isopods are for the most part marine animals.

ISOPRENE, or 2-methyl-1,3-butadiene, derivative of 1,3-BUTADIENE, a conjugated diene (see ALKENES; DIELS-ALDER REACTION; RESONANCE). Isoprene is a colorless liquid made by destructive distillation of rubber or from PETROLEUM, and used to make synthetic RUBBER. It is the basic unit of plant products including CAROTENOIDS, STEROLS and TERPENES.

ISOPTERA, the order of INSECTS containing the TERMITES. Biologically they are remarkable for their highly-developed social organization, and different iation into functionally distinct "castes."

ISOSTASY, the theoretical tendency of the earth's crust to maintain equilibrium as it floats on the MANTLE; assumed to result from flows of the dense plastic SIMA in the lower crust in response to local changes in the pressure on it of the lighter SIAL above. Local differences in the proportion of sima to sial thus maintain an equal weight of crust all around the EARTH.

ISOTHERM, line drawn on a meteorological map joining points that are, at a given moment in time, experiencing the same temperature. (See METEOROLOGY.)

ISOTOPES, ATOMS of a chemical ELEMENT which have the same number of PROTONS in the nucleus, but different numbers of NEUTRONS, i.e., having the same atomic number but different MASS NUMBER. Isotopes of an element have identical chemical and physical properties (except those determined by atomic mass). Most elements have several stable isotopes, being found in nature as mixtures. The natural proportions of the isotopes are expressed in the form of an **abundance ratio**. Because some isotopes have particular properties (e.g., 0.015% of HYDROGEN atoms have two neutrons and combine with oxygen to form HEAVY WATER, used in NUCLEAR REACTORS), mass-dependent methods of separating these out have been devised. These include MASS SPECTROSCOPY, DIFFUSION, DISTILLATION and ELECTROLYSIS. A few elements have natural radioactive isotopes (RADIOISOTOPES) and others of these can be made by exposing stable isotopes to RADIATION in a reactor. These are widely used therapeutically and industrially; their radiation may be employed directly, or the way in which it is scattered or absorbed by objects can be measured. They are useful as tracers of a process, since they may be detected in very small amounts and behave virtually identically to other atoms of the same element. They may also be used to "label" particular atoms in complex molecules, in attempts to work out chemical reaction mechanisms.

ISOTROPY, property exhibited by a medium in which physical properties are independent of direction. Most liquids and materials composed of small randomly oriented crystals are isotropic in all properties, while crystalline materials are, in general, anisotropic.

ISRAEL, Jewish republic on the E extremity of the Mediterranean. Founded in 1948, it is surrounded on its landward sides by Arab countries whose declared policy is to eliminate Israel. Although small in itself Israel controls large territories captured from Egypt, Syria and Jordan in various wars; these are the subject of continual international controversy.

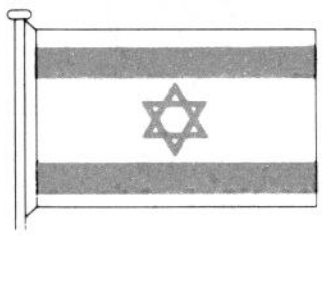

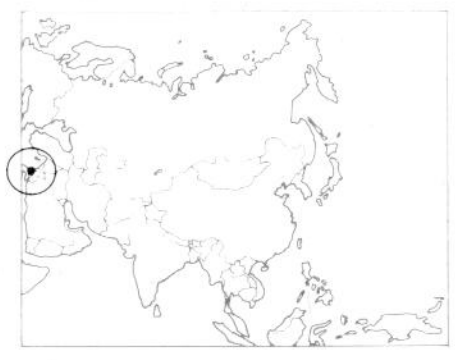

Official name: State of Israel
Capital: Jerusalem
Area: 7 993sq mi
Population: 3 164 000
Languages: Hebrew, Arabic
Religions: Judaism, Muslim, Christian
Monetary unit(s): 1 Israeli pound = 100 agorot

Land. Israel has a long straight Mediterranean coastline, and to the S access to the Red Sea from the port of Eilat through the Straits of Tiran. There are three main regions, the mountainous but fertile Galilee area in the N, the more fertile coastal plain in the W and in the S the Negev Desert, barren but with important mineral resources. In the E a depression contains the Huleh Valley, Sea of Galilee and Jordan R. Summers are hot and dry, winters mild; rainfall (mainly in winter) varies from 40in in the N to almost nil in the S. Because much of Israel's potential farmland lacks water supplies a vast irrigation program has been put into operation; huge areas of formerly barren land are now productive. Available water resources, however, are already almost fully exploited.

People. Most Israelis are Jews, and most of these are immigrants, notably from central and western Europe, the Middle East, N Africa and the USSR. Minorities include Christian and Muslim Arabs, DRUSES, CIRCASSIANS and SAMARITANS. The official language is HEBREW, but Arabic is also important and English, French, German and Yiddish are widely spoken. Elementary schooling is free and compulsory and there are seven centers of higher learning. Most of the population is urban, especially in Tel Aviv, Jaffa, Haifa and Jerusalem, but there are numerous *Kibbutzim*, agrarian communal settlements.

Economy. Heavy defense expenditure, immigration and limited natural resources have produced an unstable economy; assistance has come from American aid, German reparation and Jews abroad. Many immigrants bring technical and administrative skills. Land reclamation and irrigation have nearly trebled the cultivated area since 1955 and the country produces most of its own food. Major crops include citrus fruit, grains, olives, melons, grapes. Mineral resources include copper, gypsum, iron, natural gas, oil and phosphates; potash, magnesium and bromine come from the Dead Sea. Thermal and nuclear power stations provide electricity. Light industry is developing, and manufactures include chemicals, textiles and paper. Citrus fruits, diamonds, chemicals and textiles are major exports. Tourism, despite war and terrorism, is a growing industry.

History. (For the early history of the Jews in Palestine see JEWS; PALESTINE.) In 1947 the UN voted to divide Palestine (then under British mandate) into Jewish and Arab states. After the subsequent British withdrawal, Palestine Arabs and Arab troops from neighboring countries immediately tried to eradicate Israel by force, but the Israelis defeated them, capturing almost all Palestine. Arab refugees, maintained by the Arab countries in camps near Israel's borders, are a continuing social and political problem; also, refugee camps have proved a fruitful recruiting area and cover for Arab terrorists. When Egypt nationalized the SUEZ CANAL in 1956 it closed it to Israeli shipping; Israeli troops then overran Gaza and Sinai, winning the right of passage from Eilat to the Red Sea. In the Six-Day War (1967) Israel acquired large tracts of its neighbors' territories; these it refused to return without a firm peace settlement. It lost some of these in the Yom Kippur War (1973), but relations with Egypt have improved, largely due to US pressure and the strain of war on both countries'

One of Israel's most honored national monuments, the natural rock fortress of Masada on the western side of the Dead Sea. Captured by Jewish Zealots, it was the site of their last stand against the Romans in 73 AD; the garrison committed mass suicide rather than surrender.

economies; Israel in particular was suffering serious inflation in the early 1970s. (See ARAB-ISRAELI WARS.)

ISRAEL, Kingdom of, Hebrew kingdom, first as united under Saul, David and Solomon c1020 BC–922 BC, and then the breakaway state in the N founded by JEROBOAM I in the territory of the 10 tribes. In 722 BC this was overrun by the Assyrians; the tribes were apparently killed, enslaved or scattered. (See also TWELVE TRIBES OF ISRAEL.)

ISSUS, Battle of, important victory of ALEXANDER THE GREAT over DARIUS III of Persia near the Gulf of Issus (now Iskenderun in Turkey), 333 BC.

ISTANBUL, largest city in Turkey, divided by the Bosporus. Until 1930 its official name was Constantinople, of which Istanbul was originally a contraction. Built on the site of a former Greek town, BYZANTIUM, in 330 AD by CONSTANTINE I, it became the capital of the BYZANTINE EMPIRE; it reached its cultural height under JUSTINIAN I in the 6th century. The city was taken and sacked by the Fourth Crusade in 1204; after years of decay it was taken by the Ottoman Turks in 1453, and was rebuilt as the Turkish capital, which it remained until 1923. It is still the economic and cultural heart of Turkey, a port, transport hub and manufacturing center. It was the Ottoman capital until replaced by Ankara, 1923. Pop 2 247 630.

ISTHMIAN GAMES, in ancient Greece, Panhellenic athletics contests held in honor of Poseidon on the Isthmus of Corinth, in the 2nd and 4th years of each Olympiad. Established 6th century BC.

ISTHMUS, narrow strip of land joining two large landmasses, or a peninsula to the mainland. Best known is the Panama Isthmus. (See also STRAIT.)

ISTRIA, mountainous peninsula in NW Yugoslavia, on the N Adriatic Sea. It became part of Yugoslavia in 1947. Its population's chief occupations are fruit growing, fishing and mining.

ITALIAN, one of the ROMANCE LANGUAGES, spoken in Italy and in parts of Switzerland, France and Yugoslavia. It derives from colloquial LATIN. The Tuscan dialect established as a literary language by Dante, Petrarch and Boccaccio became the foundation of modern Italian. Since the Renaissance, words from other Romance languages have been added. There are regional dialects.

ITALIAN GREYHOUND, a breed of dog that is almost a miniature whippet. Only 250mm (10in) high, the dog has a racy, tucked-up body, long, fine-boned legs and a tapering tail. It has a characteristic high-stepping gait.

ITALO-ETHIOPIAN WAR (1935–36), Fascist Italy's conquest of Ethiopia, launched from Italian-held Eritrea and Somalia. Refusing to accept the League of Nations proposals for settling border disputes, Mussolini used planes, guns and poison gas to overwhelm the ill-equipped Ethiopians, and to forge a new empire. Too weak to halt aggression, the League merely voted economic sanctions against Italy, which simply left the League.

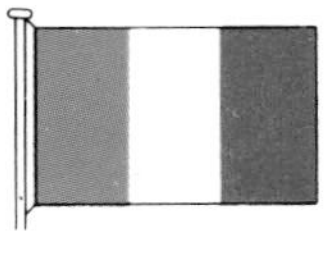

Official name: Republic of Italy
Capital: Rome
Area: 116 303sq mi
Population: 54 134 846
Languages: Italian
Religions: Roman Catholic
Monetary unit(s): 1 lire = 100 centesimi

ITALY, republic in S Europe comprising a long, narrow peninsula and nearby Sicily, Sardinia and smaller Mediterranean islands. Italy is a land of great natural beauty, with an immensely rich historical and artistic heritage. It made a phenomenal economic recovery after the destruction of WWII.

Italy is predominantly mountainous. In the N is the great curve of the Alps, while the Apennine chain forms the peninsula's spine. Between the two lies the N plain containing the Po R—Italy's largest natural waterway, flowing E to the Adriatic Sea. The Arno and Tiber flow W from the Apennines, respectively to the Ligurian and Tyrrhenian seas. Except in the cooler, wetter mountains, summers are hot and dry, winters mild and rainy. Forest and scrub clothes much of the mountains; the lowlands are largely cultivated. Bears, chamois, deer and wolves still roam remote highlands.

People. People of short, dark, Mediterranean stock predominate in the S; in the N are taller, fair-haired peoples of Celtic and Alpine origin. Italy is densely populated, with the highest concentrations in the industrial cities of the N, the Po Valley, Rome and Naples. About half the population is urban. Rural poor from the underdeveloped S migrate to the N and abroad. Italian is the official language, but French and German are spoken respectively in the extreme NW and N. Over 90% of Italians profess Roman Catholicism. Education is free and compulsory for ages 6–14 and more than 40 cities and towns have university centers.

Economy. Foreign aid and founder membership of the European Common Market vastly boosted Italy's postwar economy before the 1973–74 oil crisis damaged it. Increased industrial output (steel, chemicals, automobiles, typewriters, machinery, textiles and shoes) enriched the N, but a faltering agriculture kept the S poor. The main farm products are grapes, citrus fruits, olives, grains, vegetables and cattle. Mineral resources are limited, but Italy has hydroelectric power, natural gas and oil. There are also nuclear power stations. Tourism helps the trade balance. Italy has an advanced system of roads and railroads.

History. The Romans—a Latin people of central Italy—held most of the peninsula by 200 BC, absorbing the ETRUSCAN CIVILIZATION in the N and Greek colonies (dating from the 8th century BC) in the S. (See ROME, ANCIENT.) In the 5th–6th centuries AD, barbarian tribes (VISIGOTHS; OSTROGOTHS and LOMBARDS) overran Italy, forming Germanic kingdoms. These kingdoms were disputed by the Byzantine Empire, whose lands in Italy became the core of the PAPAL STATES. Italy was to remain divided for over 1000 years, although nominally part of Charlemagne's empire from 774 and part of the Holy Roman Empire from 962.

In the Middle Ages the S came under Norman rule (see NAPLES, KINGDOM OF). Powerful rival city-states (see GUELPHS AND GHIBELLINES) emerged in the center and N, from the late Middle Ages under the MEDICI and other dynasties. Italy pioneered the RENAISSANCE, but Spain (from the late 1400s) and Austria (from the early 1700s) controlled much of the land until the RISORGIMENTO culminated in independence under Victor Emmanuel II (1861). Italy gained Eritrea, Italian Somaliland and Libya in Africa, and fought alongside the Allies in WWI. In 1922 the Fascist dictator Benito MUSSOLINI seized power, later conquering Ethiopia and siding with Nazi Germany in WWII. Defeated Italy emerged from the war as a republic shorn of its overseas colonies and firmly allied with the West.

ITASCA, Lake, small lake in a NW Minn. swamp region, identified in 1832 as the source of the Mississippi R. Now part of the Itasca State Park.

ITHACA, one of the Ionian islands off W Greece, identified by Homer as the home of ODYSSEUS. Area: 37sq mi. Main products: wine, olive oil and currants.

ITHACA, city in S central N.Y. on Cayuga Lake, seat of Tompkins Co. and home of Cornell U. It has various light industries. Pop 26 226.

I-THOU RELATIONSHIP, Jewish philosopher Martin BUBER's philosophy of dialogue, set forth in his book *I and Thou* (1923). He conceived of relations between God and man, and man and man, as mutual and direct. The "I-Thou" relationship is opposed to the "I-It" relationship between people and objects.

ITURBIDE, Agustín de (1783–1824), Mexican revolutionary, emperor of Mexico 1822–23. A royalist officer, he united the revolutionaries with his Plan of Iguala (1821), which proclaimed Mexican independence. Exploiting political divisions, he became emperor of independent Mexico. But opposition

Above: The Tiber valley in Middle Italy. *Above right:* One of the many seaside resorts along the northwest coast of Italy. The growth of palm trees is a sign of the mild climate here. *Below right:* In Italy we find many remnants from ancient culture. Here is shown the Greek theater of Syracuse (Sicily), built in 500 BC; later restored by the Romans.

to his capricious rule brought abdication, exile and (on his return) execution.

IVAN, name of six Russian rulers. **Ivan I Kalita** (c1304–1340), was grand prince of Moscow 1328–40. **Ivan II Krasnyi** (1326–1359), was grand prince of Moscow 1353–59. **Ivan III the Great** (1440–1505), was grand prince of Moscow 1462–1505. He paved the way for a unified Russia by annexing land, repelling the Tatars, strengthening central authority over the Church and nobility, and revising the law code. **Ivan IV the Terrible** (1530–1584), was grand prince from 1533 and the first tsar of Russia 1547–84. He annexed Siberia, consolidated control of the Volga R, and established diplomatic and trading relations with Europe. He strengthened the law and administration, but was notoriously cruel. **Ivan V** (1666–1696), was co-tsar (with Peter I) 1682–96. **Ivan VI** (1740–1764), was tsar 1740–41.

IVANOVO, industrial city in the USSR, in the Russian SFSR, 145mi NE of Moscow. It manufactures textiles, machinery and dyes. Pop 434 000.

IVES, Burl (1909–), US folk singer and actor. He is known for his revivals of traditional American folk songs, and has acted in theater and films.

IVES, Charles Edward (1874–1954), US composer, a major 20th-century innovator. His music (mostly pre-1915) incorporated popular songs and hymn tunes, and exploits dissonance, polytonality and polymetric construction. Ignored by his contemporaries, he influenced later composers. His best-known works include *Three Places in New England* (1903–14) and the *Second (Concord) Piano Sonata* (1909–15). His *Third Symphony* (1904–11) won a 1947 Pulitzer Prize.

IVES, James Merritt. See CURRIER AND IVES.

IVIZA. See IBIZA.

IVORY, hard white substance obtained from the tusks of ELEPHANTS, HIPPOPOTAMUSES, WALRUSES and NARWHALS. It is no more than a thickened form of dental enamel, yet carved ivory has been greatly prized—and priced—for centuries. Elephant ivory is the most sought-after, due to its greater length and finer grain; the poaching of elephants for their tusks threatens their existence in Africa. A vegetable ivory is also produced, from the nuts of the DOUM PALM.

IVORY COAST, one of the most prosperous West African republics, located on the N coast of the Gulf of Guinea and bordering Liberia, Guinea, Mali, Upper Volta and Ghana.

One-third of the country is covered by dense rain forest, with a grassy and wooded plateau to the N and mountains to the NW. The climate is hot and rainy in the S, drier and cooler in the N. Wildlife includes African big game animals.

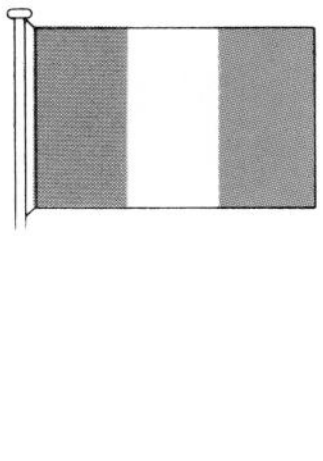

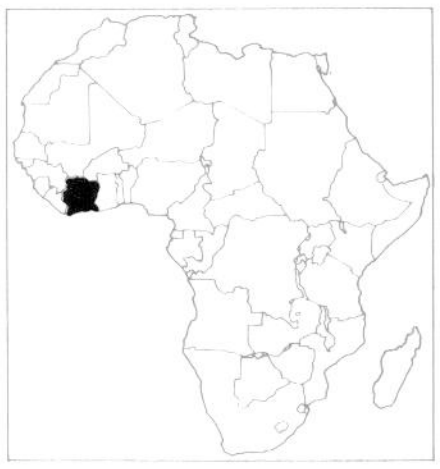

Official name: Republic of Ivory Coast
Capital: Abidjan
Area: 124 502sq mi
Population: 4 420 000
Languages: French, Dioula
Religions: Animist, Muslim, Roman Catholic
Monetary unit(s): 1 CFA franc = 100 centimes

People. There are some 60 tribal groups and about 15 000 foreigners—mainly French. Over 20% of the population is urban. Tribal languages and animist faiths predominate. Some two-fifths of the population is aged under 15, and spending on basic education is relatively high. There is a university at Abidjan.

Economy. Farming, forestry and fisheries provide most of the gross national product. Major cash crops are cotton, coffee and cocoa. Palm-oil, pineapples and bananas are also exported, as are hardwoods including mahogany, iroko, satinwood and teak. Diamonds and manganese are mined. An expanding manufacturing industry produces palm-oil, instant coffee, fruit juices and textiles. Trade is chiefly with European Common Market countries and the US. Exports usually exceed imports in value.

History. In the 16th century the Portuguese traded in slaves and ivory along the coast. In the 18th century Ashanti peoples entered the region, while French trade and missionary activity increased in the E. France began systematic occupation in 1870, declaring a protectorate in 1893. A railroad built in 1903 made the Ivory Coast potentially the most prosperous colony in FRENCH WEST AFRICA. In 1946 Félix HOUPHOUËT-BOIGNY founded an all-African political party. He became president of the Ivory Coast upon independence (1960). His government's policies encouraged foreign investment, exploited natural resources and raised living standards.

IVORY-NUT PALM, *Phytelephas macrocarpa*, tree of tropical America, the hard white seeds of which yield vegetable ivory which is used to make buttons and for carving. Family: Palmae.

IVY, hardy, evergreen climbers of the genus *Hedera*, family Araliaceae. In the juvenile stage the plants have lobed leaves and numerous aerial roots, while in the adult or arborescent stage the leaves are entire, there are no aerial roots and flowers and fruits are produced. The English ivy (*H. helix*) is a popular house plant, coming in a number of dwarf, climbing and variegated varieties. Indoors, they should be grown in bright positions, although they survive for a long time under artificial light. They grow best at temperatures between 16°C and 21°C (60°F and 70°F) and the soil should be kept evenly moist. Propagation is by shoot tip cuttings. Several other plants which have ivy-like leaves are also called ivy, for example GROUND IVY (*Glectoma hederacea*), Boston or GRAPE IVY (Cissus) and German ivy (*Senecio milkanoides*), the latter being a popular house plant requiring similar cultural practices to English ivy although it is less tolerant of low light intensities. The red ivy (*Hemigraphis*) is so-named because of its trailing habit, but apart from this is quite unlike and unrelated to English ivy. Red ivy is also a popular house plant grown mainly for its ornamental foliage that is maroon or burgundy colored. It should be grown in a bright window avoiding strong sunlight, at average house temperatures and should be watered often enough to keep the soil evenly moist.

IWAKI, city in Japan on E Honshu Island, about 110mi NNE of Tokyo. Pop 327 164.

IWO, city in SW Nigeria, near Ibadan, on the Lagos-Kano railroad. Its economy is mainly agricultural. Pop 192 000.

A statue of soldiers raising the American flag commemorates the conquest of the island of Iwo Jima, a major Japanese airbase during WWII. American losses were particularly heavy.

IWO JIMA, Japanese island in the NW Pacific, scene of a fierce battle in WWII. Largest of the Volcano Islands (about 8sq mi), it was annexed by Japan in 1891 and captured by US marines in Feb.–March 1945 at the cost of over 21 000 US casualties. US administration ended in 1968.

IWW. See INDUSTRIAL WORKERS OF THE WORLD.

IXION, in Greek mythology, king of the Lapiths. He attempted to rape HERA; ZEUS substituted a cloud in her shape, and on this Ixion engendered the CENTAURS. As punishment he was chained to a burning wheel which rotates eternally in TARTARUS.

IZHEVSK, town in the USSR, in the Russian SFSR, capital of the Udmurt autonomous republic. Its chief industries are metallurgy, sawmilling and food processing. Pop 456 000.

IZMIR (formerly Smyrna), city in W Turkey on the Gulf of Izmir, capital of Izmir province. Founded by the Greeks, it became successively part of the Roman, Byzantine and Ottoman empires. Turkey's third-largest city and chief Asian port, it exports figs, raisins, olives, wheat, opium, tobacco, carpets and silk. Pop 521 000.

IZTACCÍHUATL ("white woman"), dormant volcano in central Mexico, SE of Mexico City. It is 17 343ft high with three snowy summits but no crater.

J

J, tenth letter of the English alphabet, a variant of the letter *i*, from which it became formally distinguished with the advent of printing. It has a *y* sound in most European languages but French influence has given it a *dzh* sound in modern English.

***j*-OPERATOR.** See IMAGINARY OPERATOR.

JABALPUR, city in central India, in Madhya Pradesh state. It is a major commercial and industrial center, and also a major military headquarters. Pop 425 122.

JABIR, or Abu-Musa-Jabir-ibn-Haiyan, or (Latin) **Geber**, 9th-century Arab alchemist to whom the authorship of the "Jabir corpus" of writings was formerly ascribed. The early Jabir writings contained many novel contributions to the theory of ALCHEMY.

JABIRUS, large, stork-like birds. Used as a common name for some of the "true" STORKS, the word is more properly restricted to the "storks" of America. The group includes the Jabiru, *Jabiru mycteria*, at 1.4m (4.6ft) long, one of the largest of American flying birds.

JABORANDI, popular name for several South American trees of the genus *Pilocarpus*, the leaves of which yield an ALKALOID called pilocarpine which is used medicinally to treat ASTHMA and DIABETES and in large doses as an EMETIC. Family: Rutaceae.

JACAMARS, a family, Galbulidae, of tropical American birds resembling the BEE-EATERS of the Old World. Small, brightly-colored insectivorous birds with long beaks, they are quiet and nonsocial. The legs are short with toes arranged two forward, two backward.

JACANAS, or lily-trotters, a small family (Jacanidae) of wading birds. With seven species distributed over America, Africa and Australasia, jacanas form a surprisingly uniform group of crake-like birds inhabiting the fringes of lakes and rivers, feeding on a variety of invertebrates and seeds. The long toes of the foot enable them to walk nimbly out over lily leaves and floating vegetation in search of food.

JACARANDA, genus of trees native to tropical America which produce colorful clusters of blue or violet flowers. The wood of some species is used for construction work and carpentry. Family: Bignoniaceae.

JACKALS, carnivorous mammals closely related to DOGS and wolves. The four species are distributed throughout Africa and S Asia. All are extreme opportunists—although often considered to be primarily scavengers, they will also hunt and kill birds, hares, mice and insects. Small packs may be formed temporarily, but they are usually solitary animals.

JACKDAW, *Corvus monedula*, a social member of the CROW family, black with a gray hood, found through much of Europe and W Asia. Highly intelligent birds, they live in colonies with a complex social structure.

JACK FROST, personification of winter, depicted as an imp who paints the world with frost at night. The name may derive from minor Norse divinities called *Jokul* (icicle) and *Frosti* (frost).

JACK-IN-THE-PULPIT, or **Indian turnip** *Arisaema triphyllum*, a North American wild flower. The small flowers are clustered on a spadix and surrounded by a spathe (see ARUM). The dried tubers are eaten locally, used in the preparation of cosmetics and have medicinal uses in the treatment of ASTHMA, BRONCHITIS and WHOOPING COUGH. Family: Araceae.

JACK O'LANTERN. See WILL-O'-THE-WISP.

JACK RABBITS, true HARES of the genus *Lepus*. All seven species are found in Central and W North America. Jack rabbits have enormously large ears functional in body temperature control. Found in open, comparatively arid plains they actually flourish in drought-stricken, overgrazed areas. Among the most abundant of American LAGOMORPHA, they constitute a considerable pest in agricultural areas.

JACKS, name commonly used in the US for fish of the family *Carangidae*, also known as MACKERELS.

JACKSON, city in S Mich., seat of Jackson Co., on Grand R. Named for Andrew JACKSON, it was the birthplace of the REPUBLICAN PARTY. It has diverse manufacturing industries, especially automobile and aircraft parts. Pop 45 484.

JACKSON, capital city of Miss. and a seat of Hinds Co., on Pearl R. It was devastated during the Civil War, but is now a major manufacturing and transport center. Site of several colleges, it holds an annual Arts Festival. Pop 153 968.

JACKSON, city in W Tenn., seat of Madison Co. Trade center of an agricultural area; also a medical, financial and educational center. Pop 39 996.

JACKSON, Andrew (1767–1845), seventh president of the US. The first from W of the Alleghenies, he

A young American jacana (*Jacana spinosa*) with the long toes which it develops at an early age to enable it to walk over water lilies and other floating plants in its natural habitat. This species is generally found between Argentina and Mexico.

Andrew JACKSON

7th US President

Born: March 15, 1767
Died: June 8, 1845
Term of office: March 4, 1829–March 3, 1837
Political party: Democratic

was a self-made statesman championing the common man against monopoly and privilege.

Born in a log cabin in the Waxhaw settlement, S.C., Jackson had a minimal education; he joined the militia at 13 and was briefly captured by the British in 1781. He decided to study law, was admitted to the N.C. bar in 1787 and began his political career in 1796 as a member of the Tenn. constitutional convention. He became the first congressman from Tenn. 1796–97, senator from Tenn. 1797–98 and a superior court judge in Nashville 1798–1804. In the WAR OF 1812 he became a national hero as commander of the Tenn. militia; at the Battle of Horseshoe Bend he forced the Creek Indians to yield 23 million acres, opening much of the South for settlement. In 1815 he led a decisive victory over the British at the battle of NEW ORLEANS. Jackson's rough personality and leadership earned him the epithet "Old Hickory." As commander of the US army in the South he campaigned against the SEMINOLE Indians, entering and raiding Spanish-owned Florida; this accelerated the sale of Florida to the US (1819). Military governor of the Florida Territory in 1821, he was reelected to the US Senate from Tenn. in 1823. A presidential candidate in 1824, Jackson received the most electoral votes but no overall majority, and the House of Representatives chose runner-up John Quincy Adams. Jackson considered this a "corrupt bargain"; bitter personal attacks disfigured the campaign for the 1828 election, which Jackson resoundingly won.

Inaugurated in 1829, he attempted to root out corruption in the bureaucracy by dismissing over 2000 government employees and appointing his poliical supporters in their place; he thus created the SPOILS SYSTEM. He also built up a KITCHEN CABINET of personal advisers. Opposition to his powerful executive control eventually produced the Whig Party, revitalizing the two-party system. In 1832 Jackson vetoed a bill to recharter the BANK OF THE UNITED STATES, denouncing the bank as an unconstitutional monopoly. Making the bank a presidential campaign issue, Jackson easily defeated Henry CLAY and won reelection in 1832. Later that year Jackson prepared to send troops to S.C. to prevent secession, after it had rejected federal tariff laws. The president paid off the national debt in 1835 and his SPECIE CIRCULAR (1836) helped halt land speculation. In 1837 Jackson retired to the Hermitage, his estate near Nashville. He had helped found the modern Democratic Party, strengthened respect for democratic government, and established the role of the president as a popular leader.

JACKSON, Helen (Maria) Hunt (1831–1885), US author who publicized the mistreatment of Indians. *A Century of Dishonor* (1881) condemned governmental malpractice; the novel *Ramona* (1884) described the plight of California's mission Indians.

JACKSON, Henry Martin (1912–), US politician, Democratic senator from Washington from 1952; he was a congressman 1940–52. A leading liberal, he was chairman of the committee on interior and insular affairs from 1963. In 1972 he sought Democratic presidential nomination.

JACKSON, Joseph Jefferson (1888–1951), US baseball player. With a lifetime batting average of .356, "Shoeless Joe" was one of eight Chicago players barred from baseball after the 1919 BLACK SOX SCANDAL.

JACKSON, Mahalia (1911–1972), US black gospel singer with a powerful and expressive contralto voice; her concerts and recordings gained worldwide recognition for Negro religious music. In the 1960s she was active in the civil rights movement.

JACKSON, Robert Houghwout (1892–1954), US Supreme Court justice from 1941, chief US prosecutor in the NUREMBERG TRIALS. A supporter of the NEW DEAL, he served as solicitor general 1938–40 and attorney general 1940–41.

JACKSON, Sheldon (1834–1909), US Presbyterian missionary and educator. After founding many schools and churches in Western states 1859–83 he became Alaska's first federal superintendent of public instruction; he did much to help the Eskimos there, including the founding of schools and the introduction of reindeer from Europe.

JACKSON, Shirley (1919–1965), US author. Her best-known works, such as *The Haunting of Hill House* (1959) and the short story *The Lottery* (1948), blend Gothic horror with psychological insight. Autobiographical works such as *Raising Demons* (1957) are in a contrastingly humorous vein.

JACKSON, Thomas Jonathan "Stonewall" (1824–1863), brilliant Confederate general, one of America's greatest commanders. After service in the MEXICAN WAR he was given command of a regiment at the outbreak of the Civil War. As a brigadier-general at the First Battle of BULL RUN, 1861, he was nicknamed "Stonewall" for his stand against Union troops. After his bold tactics in the 1862 Shenandoah Valley campaign he fought brilliantly at the battles of Richmond, the Seven Days' Battles, Cedar Mt, the Second Battle of Bull Run, Antietam and Fredericksburg. At CHANCELLORSVILLE he was accidentally mortally wounded by his own troops.

JACKSON HOLE, fertile valley in NW Wyo, in GRAND TETON NATIONAL PARK. Once a major hunting area for moose, deer and elk, it is now a wildlife range.

JACKSONVILLE, city in central Ark. A manufacturing center, its economy has been expanded by air force and missile bases in the area. Pop 19832.

JACKSONVILLE, city in NE Fla., seat of Duval Co., most of which it annexed in 1968. It now has the largest area of any US city. On the St. John's R, it is a principal seaport and a major commercial and manufacturing center of the South. It has many colleges and cultural facilities. Pop 528865.

JACKSONVILLE, city in W central Ill., seat of Morgan Co. The trade center of a crop-growing area, it has light industries and three colleges. Pop 20553.

JACKSONVILLE, city in SE N.C., seat of Onslow Co. In an agricultural area, it is a popular summer resort. Pop 16021.

JACKSONVILLE BEACH, city adjoining Jacksonville, NE Fla., primarily a residential resort. Pop 13326.

JACOB, in the Old Testament, son of ISAAC and REBECCA, progenitor of the Israelites. He fled after tricking his elder brother Esau out of his birthright; he settled in Mesopotamia, where he married, then returned to Canaan. In a vision he wrestled with and overcame an angel, and was honored with the name Israel. In a time of famine he migrated to Egypt, where he died, living with his favorite son JOSEPH.

JACOB, François (1920–), French biologist who shared with MONOD and LWOFF the 1965 Nobel Prize for Physiology or Medicine for his work with Monod on regulatory GENE action in BACTERIA.

Tranquil wooded setting of the Hermitage, Andrew Jackson's home, in Nashville, Tennessee. The original building, dating from 1809, was partly destroyed by fire in 1834 and rebuilt three years later in the Neoclassical Georgian style.

JACOB, Max (1876–1944), French surrealist poet, whose work is characterized by verbal clowning, fantasy and mysticism. Born Jewish, he became a Roman Catholic in 1915. His most famous collection of poems among a large output is *Dice Box* (1917). He died in Drancy concentration camp, near Paris.

JACOBEAN STYLE, English Renaissance architectural and furniture style fashionable around the reign of James I (1603–25). It combined elements of the late PERPENDICULAR STYLE with free use of classical motifs. Many college buildings at Oxford and Cambridge are in this style.

JACOBINS, powerful political clubs during the FRENCH REVOLUTION, named for the former Jacobin (Dominican) convent where the leaders met. Originally middle-class, they became increasingly radical advocates of terrorism. After they seized power in 1793 the extremists, led by ROBESPIERRE, instituted the REIGN OF TERROR. In the THERMIDOR reaction the clubs were suppressed, to revive under the Directory and be finally put down by NAPOLEON.

JACOBITE CHURCH, or Syrian Orthodox Church, Christian church of Syria, India and Iraq. One of the MONOPHYSITE CHURCHES, it was founded in 6th century Syria by Jacobus Baradaeus. Its head is the patriarch of Antioch, who now resides at Damascus, and its ritual language is Syriac. An offshoot of the Jacobites is the Syrian Catholic Church, one of the UNIATE CHURCHES.

JACOBITES, supporters of that branch of the House of Stuart exiled by the GLORIOUS REVOLUTION of 1688; a large number were Highland Scots. Jacobites sought to regain the English throne for JAMES II and his descendants, notably James Edward Stuart (1699–1766), "The Old Pretender," and CHARLES EDWARD STUART, "Bonnie Prince Charlie." After rebellions in 1715, 1719 and 1745 they were effectively crushed at the battle of CULLODEN MOOR (1746).

JACOBS, W. W. (William Wymark Jacobs; 1863–1943), English author, mainly of short stories centered around the dock areas in which he was brought up, collected in *Many Cargoes* (1896) and many other volumes. His best-known story is the horror story *The Monkey's Paw* (1902).

JACOBSEN, Arne (1920–1971), Danish architect and industrial designer famous for his clean and functional style. Major works include the Bellabista Housing Estate and the SAS Building in Copenhagen, and also St. Catherine's College, Oxford.

JACOBSEN, Jens Peter (1847–1885), major Danish writer, known for his early Romantic poetry and his translation of DARWIN's works. He later turned to naturalism in the novels *Marie Grubbe* (1876) and *Niels Lyhne* (1880), developing a rich style despite suffering from serious tuberculosis after 1873.

JACOB'S LADDER, *Polemonium coeruleum*, blue- and white-flowered plants native to Eurasia and naturalized in North America. They are also cultivated as a garden plant. The arrangement of the leaves on the stem resembles the rungs of a ladder. Family: Polemoniaceae.

JACQUARD, Joseph Marie (1752–1834), French inventor of the **Jacquard loom** (completed 1801), which could weave complex patterns according to instructions coded on punched cards (a technique adopted by BABBAGE for his calculator and still used for COMPUTERS). Modern looms are still based on Jacquard's principles. (See also WEAVING.)

JACQUERIE, peasant revolt in NE France in 1358, named for "Jacques Bonhomme," the popular nickname for peasants. A reaction against the hardships of the HUNDRED YEARS' WAR, famine and oppression, it was savagely crushed by baronial armies.

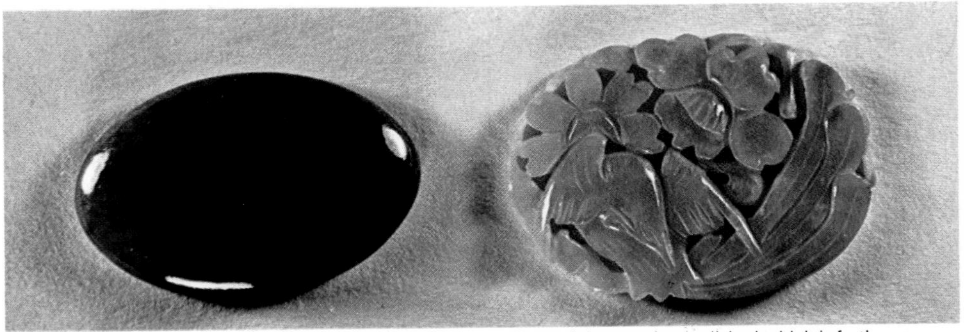

Jade is found in a variety of different colors and has an extraordinary richness when polished which is further enhanced by skilled carving. The Chinese, who have produced the finest examples of the art, traditionally regarded the qualities of jade as symbolic of the virtues.

JADE, either of two tough, hard minerals with a compact interlocking grain structure, commonly green but also found as white, mauve, red-brown or yellow; used as a GEM stone to make carved jewelry and ornaments. Jade carving in China dates from the 1st millennium BC, but the finest examples are late 18th century AD. **Nephrite**, the commoner form of jade, is an AMPHIBOLE, a combination of tremolite and actinolite, occurring in China, the USSR, New Zealand and the western US. **Jadeite**, rarer than nephrite and prized for its more intense color and translucence, is a sodium aluminum PYROXENE, found chiefly in upper Burma.

JADE PLANT, *Crassula argentea*, a succulent evergreen plant that produces light to golden-green leaves with coppery-red margins and clusters of star-shaped white flowers in winter and spring. It is a popular ornamental plant that can be grown outside during the summer in warm regions, but must be brought indoors during the winter, when it should be placed in a sunny window. It fails to thrive at temperatures above 27°C (80°F) or below 10°C (50°F), and should be watered well when the soil surface dries out. Propagation is by leaf or shoot tip cuttings. Family: Crassulaceae.

JAEGERS, North American name for three of the four species of SKUA, Stercorariidae: the Long-tailed; Pomarine, and Arctic or Parasitic Skuas. Jaegers are hawk-like birds, best known for their piratical attacks on other birds, forcing them to disgorge their food.

JAFFA, (formerly Joppa), ancient port city on the Mediterranean coast of Israel. Dating from at least the 15th century BC, it became an Arab city until taken over by Israel in 1948; it was incorporated into TEL AVIV in 1949.

JAFFNA, city in N Sri Lanka, on the Jaffna Peninsula. Former capital of a Tamil kingdom, it is one of the country's largest cities and is a trading center for the area's agricultural produce. It is also a fishing port. Pop 107 663.

JAGIELLO, ruling family of Poland, Lithuania, Bohemia and Hungary in the 14th–16th centuries. It was named for its founder, Jagiello, grand duke of Lithuania who became king of Poland in 1386. His son **Vladislav III** also became king of Hungary (1440); Vladislav's son **Casimir IV** (reigned 1447–92) was able to make his own sons kings of Bohemia (1471) and Hungary (1490). In the reign of another son, **Sigismund the Old** (reigned 1506–48) Poland had its "Golden Age"; his son **Sigismund Augustus** (reigned 1548–72) united Poland and Lithuania, but left no heirs, ending the dynasty.

JAGUAR, *Panthera onca*, the only true "big cat" of the American continent. The coat bears black spots arranged in rosettes on a background varying from almost white and buff, through black, where the rosettes appear only as a variation in texture. It lives in thick cover in forests or swamps and although an accomplished swimmer, hunts mostly on the ground or in trees.

JAGUARUNDI, *Felis yagouaroundi*, a small cat of the Americas, in many ways approaching the general form of mustelids (e.g., WEASELS and OTTERS), the body and head being elongated. It is a nocturnal animal never found far from water, though its prey includes both small mammals and game birds.

JAHN, Friedrich Ludwig (1778–1852), German educator and soldier, a pioneer of gymnastics. In 1811 he founded the *Turnvereinen* (German: gymnastics clubs) to promote physical fitness and a romantic German nationalism.

JAI ALAI, very fast ball game, similar to SQUASH, popular in parts of the US, Cuba, Mexico and Spain, where it is called *pelota*. It is played in a three-walled court; each player has a wicker racket (*cesta*) strapped to his wrist. With this he tries to bounce a small hard rubber ball off a wall, beyond his opponent's reach.

JAINISM, philosophy and religion—an offshoot of HINDUISM—largely confined to India, with 2 million adherents. It was founded alongside BUDDHISM, which it resembles, in about the 6th century BC by Mahavira, an ascetic saint who taught the doctrine of *ahimsa* or non-injury to all living creatures. Jains do not believe in a creator God but see in the universe two independent eternal categories: "Life" and "Non-life" (see DUALISM), maintaining that man can reach perfection only through ascetic, charitable and monastic discipline.

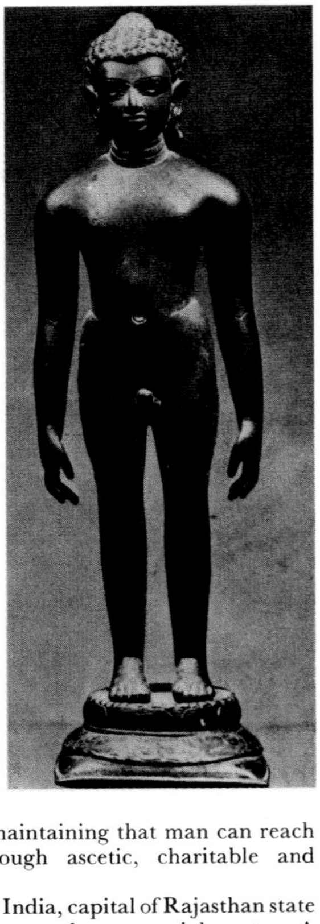

Bronze statuette of Jaina the Redeemer, dating from the 8th century AD. Total nakedness symbolizes purity in Jain sculpture, which otherwise closely resembles Buddhist works in most respects.

JAIPUR, city in NW India, capital of Rajasthan state and a major transport and commercial center. A beautiful city, it was laid out in the 18th century on an unusual rectangular pattern; among its many historic buildings is an open-air observatory. Pop 613 144.

JAKARTA (formerly Batavia), capital and largest city of Indonesia, in NW Jawa. It is the country's commercial, transport and manufacturing center, manufacturing automobiles, textiles, chemicals and iron products, and processing lumber and food. Much of Indonesia's external trade passes through the port. The city is also the administrative center and the home of the University of Indonesia. It grew out of the Dutch East India company settlement of Batavia (1614–19) and became British 1811–14. With independence it was renamed Djakarta, now officially spelled Jakarta. Pop 4 576 000.

JAKOBSON, Roman (1896–), Russian-born US linguist and philologist best known for his pioneering studies of the Slavic languages.

JALAPA, city in Mexico, capital of Veracruz state on the E slope of the Sierre Madre Mts, at about 4 500ft. A beauty spot, it is a market center for local produce, including tobacco, coffee and sugar. Pop 127 000.

JALISCO, state in SW Mexico occupying 30 941sq mi between the tropical Pacific coast and the Sierra Madre Mts. The capital is Guadalajara. It is a major agricultural area, but also has silver, gold and other mineral mines.

JAM. See JELLY AND JAM.

JAMAICA, island republic in the Caribbean. The body of the island is a limestone plateau with an E–W backbone of mountains and volcanic hills. The climate is tropical, with heavy rainfall, and the lush vegetation reflects this. The majority of Jamaicans are of African descent, but there are East Indians, Chinese and Europeans also. High population and birthrate causes serious problems. The economy is largely agricultural, relying on sugar processing for its major industry. Bauxite and gypsum mining has become important, as has tourism.

Official Name: Jamaica
Capital: Kingston
Area: 4411 sq mi
Population: 1 861 300
Languages: English
Religions: Protestant, Roman Catholic
Monetary Unit(s): 1 Jamaican dollar = 100 cents

Discovered by Columbus in 1494, Jamaica was a Spanish settlement until captured by the British in 1655. The original ARAWAK INDIANS had been wiped out and the British, under such governors as Sir Henry MORGAN, accelerated the importation of Negro slaves to man the sugar industry. After the abolition of slavery in 1834 the sugar industry declined and poverty, unemployment and overpopulation led to serious unrest in the 19th and early 20th centuries. Crop diversification and reforms improved conditions. Full internal self-government came in 1959, within the WEST INDIES ASSOCIATION, and full independence as a member of the British Commonwealth in 1962.

JAMES, name of two saints, both Apostles. **St. James the Greater** (d. c43 AD), son of Zebedee and brother of St. John, was killed by Herod Agrippa I. There is a famous shrine to him at SANTIAGO DE COMPOSTELLA. **St. James the Less** (1st century AD) was possibly the son of Alphaeus and Mary.

JAMES, name of two kings of ARAGON. **James I the Conqueror** (1208–76), king from 1213, won the Balearic Islands (1235) and Valencia (1238) from the Moors. His son James (1243–1311) was first king of MAJORCA from 1276. **James II** (d. 1327), king of Aragon 1291–1327 and of SICILY 1286–95, succeeding his father PETER III there.

JAMES, name of two kings of England and Scotland. **James I and VI** (1566–1625), was king of Scotland from 1567, after his mother MARY QUEEN OF SCOTS was forced to abdicate, and king of England from 1603. James gained control over the nobles who sought to dominate him in 1583. Anxious to be Elizabeth I's heir, he condoned her execution of his mother. Early popularity in England, reinforced when he escaped the GUNPOWDER PLOT, waned as James sought autocratic control over Parliament, bolstered by his belief in the DIVINE RIGHT OF KINGS. His extravagance and dubious personal life alienated many, as did the execution of Sir Walter RALEIGH, part of a pro-Spanish policy. He was, however, scholarly and in some ways progressive. He established a large Presbyterian settlement in IRELAND and encouraged the first English colonies in America. He wrote the treatise on government *Basilikon Doron* and commissioned the Authorized Version of the Bible (1611). **James II** (1633–1701), reigned 1685–88. Although able, he sought to disregard Parliament and alienated many by his attempt to introduce toleration of Roman Catholicism. It was suspected—perhaps correctly—that he intended to make it the state religion. His Dutch son-in-law William of Orange was invited to invade Britain, deposing James in the GLORIOUS REVOLUTION. James' forces were driven out of Ireland also at the battle of the BOYNE.

JAMES, name of seven Stuart kings of Scotland. **James I** (1394–1437), technically reigned from 1406, but was a prisoner in England 1406–24. There he wrote his great poem *The Kingis Quair* (1424), of his captivity and romance with Joan Beaufort, whom he married. A capable and energetic ruler, he suppressed a turbulent aristocracy; he was assassinated during an abortive aristocratic revolt. **James II** (1430–1460), reigned from 1449. **James III** (1451–1488), reigned from 1469. **James IV** (1473–1513), king from 1488, was the great Renaissance king of Scotland. He reformed law and administration, and extended royal authority; he built a powerful navy. A patron of arts and sciences, he married Margaret, daughter of Henry VII of England. He was killed at the battle of FLODDEN FIELD. **James V** (1512–1542), was king from 1513, but reigned 1528–42, during the beginnings of the REFORMATION. He supported Catholicism for financial and political reasons. His daughter by his wife MARY OF GUISE was MARY QUEEN OF SCOTS. He died soon after his army was defeated by the English at Solway Moss. (For James VI and James VII of Scotland, see JAMES, two kings of England and Scotland.)

Open-cast bauxite mine in Jamaica. Mining of bauxite, the island's most important natural resource, has expanded rapidly in recent years.

JAMES, Epistle of, 20th book of the NEW TESTAMENT, traditionally attributed to St. James, kinsman of Jesus and first bishop of Jerusalem. One of the Catholic (general) Epistles, it is primarily a homily on Christian ethics.

JAMES, Henry (1843–1916), British-American novelist and critic, brother of William JAMES. He settled in London (1876) and became a British citizen in 1915. A recurring theme in his work is the corruption of innocence, particularly in the contrast between sophisticated and corrupt Europe and brash, innocent US society. His most famous works, distinguished by subtle characterization and a precise but often laborious style, include *The American* (1877), *Daisy Miller* (1878), *The Portrait of a Lady* (1881), *The Turn of the Screw* (1898) and *The Golden Bowl* (1909).

JAMES, Jesse Woodson (1847–1882), US outlaw. A member of William QUANTRILL's raiders in the Civil War, he and his brother Frank led the "James Gang" 1866–79, robbing banks and trains from Ark. to Col. and Tex. Living as an ordinary citizen in St. Joseph, Mo., he was murdered for reward by gang member Robert Ford.

JAMES, William (1842–1910), US philosopher and psychologist, the originator of the doctrine of PRAGMATISM. Intermittently dogged by ill-health, his first major contribution was *The Principles of Psychology* (1890). Turning his attention to questions of religion, he published in 1902 his Gifford Lectures, *The Varieties of Religious Experience*, which has remained his best-known work.

JAMES BAY, 300mi arm of Hudson Bay, Canada, named for Sir Thomas James who explored much of it in 1631.

JAMES RIVER, rising in central N.D., flows over 700mi S into S.D., joining the Missouri R at Yankton. At Jameston, N.D., it forms the Jamestown reservoir.

JAMES RIVER, in Va., rises in the Allegheny Mts at the union of the Jackson and Cowpasture rivers and flows about 340mi E and SE to Chesapeake Bay. It is navigable for about 150mi to Richmond.

JAMESON, Sir Leander Starr (1853–1917), British colonial administrator in Southern Africa. In 1895, at the instigation of Cecil RHODES, he led the illegal and disastrous **Jameson Raid** into the Boer colony of Transvaal to support a rebellion intended to form a South African federation.

JAMESTOWN, city in W N.Y., on Lake Chautauqua. Commercial center of the surrounding agricultural area, its industries are food processing and furniture manufacture. Pop 39 975.

JAMESTOWN, city in N.D., seat of Stutsman Co. on the James R. It is a railroad and trade center for an agricultural area. Pop 15 385.

JAMESTOWN, former village in SE Va. on the James R, the first permanent English settlement in North America. Founded in 1607 by colonists from the LONDON COMPANY led by John SMITH, it was named for King James I. Lord DE LA WARR reinforced it in 1610 and John ROLFE introduced tobacco cultivation in 1612. In 1619 the House of Burgesses, the first representative government of the colonies, met here. It is now part of Colonial National Historical Park.

JAMMU AND KASHMIR. See KASHMIR.

JAMNAGAR, city in W central India, on the Gulf of Kutch. Famous for its silk, cotton and other textiles, and for dye work and embroidery, it has major naval and aeronautic schools. Pop 214 853.

JANÁČEK, Leoš (1854–1928), major Czech composer and collector of Moravian folk music, best known for the *Sinfonietta* (1926) and the opera *Jenufa* (1904). Other operas include *Mr Brouček* (1920), *Katya Kabanova* (1921), *The Cunning Little Vixen* (1924), *The Makropoulos Case* (1926), and *From the House of the Dead* (1928). First professor of composition at Prague Conservatory (1919), he wrote many songs, chamber and choral works, especially the *Glagolitic Mass* (1926).

JANESVILLE, city in S central Wis., seat of Rock Co. on the Rock R. Its economy rests on manufacturing and farming. Pop 46 426.

JANET, Pierre Marie Félix (1859–1947), French psychologist and neurologist, best known for his studies of HYSTERIA and NEUROSIS, who played an important role in reconciling the theories of psychology and the practice of clinical treatment of mental disease.

JANISSARIES (Janizaries), elite Turkish infantry of the 14th–19th centuries, conscripted from prisoners of war and Christian children abducted and reared as fanatical Muslims. From c1600 Turks gradually infiltrated the highly privileged corps, which became increasingly corrupt. Unruly and rebellious, it was massacred by order of Sultan MAHMUD II in 1826.

JANSEN, Cornelius. See JANSENISM.

JANSENISM, French and Flemish Roman Catholic reform movement, based on the ideas of the Flemish theologian Cornelius Jansen (1585–1638) and centering on the convent of PORT-ROYAL. Jansen stressed St. Augustine's teaching of redemption by divine grace and also accepted PREDESTINATION; opponents charged his followers with CALVINISM. Cultivated at first by French statesmen because it opposed the Catholic establishment, Jansenism and its prominent leaders, Antoine ARNAULD and Blaise PASCAL, were condemned by Pope INNOCENT. In the 18th century persecution in France, especially under Louis XIV, drove much of the movement into the Netherlands, where there are still Jansenist bishops (now OLD CATHOLICS). In France it survived mainly as a school of thought within the church.

JANSSEN, Zacharias (c1600), Dutch spectacle-maker credited with inventing the compound MICROSCOPE (1590).

JANUARY, first month of the year in the Julian calendar, named for the god JANUS.

JANUS, exclusively Roman deity, protector of doorways and gates and the god of beginnings. His image is a double-faced head looking in opposite directions. Originally he may have been a solar god.

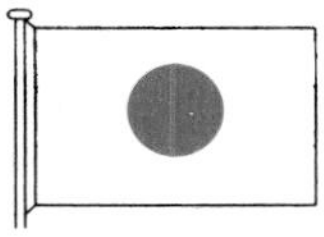

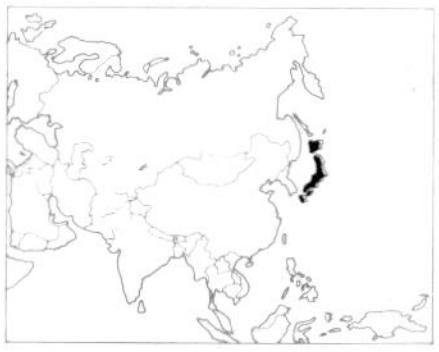

Official Name: Japan
Capital: Tokyo
Area: 142 726.5sq mi
Population: 108 430 000
Languages: Japanese
Religions: Shinto, Buddhism
Monetary Unit(s): 1 Yen = 100 sen = 1000 rin

JAPAN (Nippon), an island country off the E Asian coast, now a leading industrial superpower.

Land. The Japanese archipelago, about 2 000mi long, comprises some 3 500 islands. The four major islands are HOKKAIDO, HONSHU, SHIKOKU and KYUSHU. Around 80% of the country is mountainous, and there are more than 190 active volcanoes; earth tremors and quakes are frequent. Many of the fast-flowing rivers are harnessed for hydroelectric power. Lowland is scarce, consisting mainly of coastal plains, including the 5 000sq mi Kanto plain on Honshu. About 70% of the land is forested, only 16% cultivable. The monsoonal climate is moderated by latitude and the sea. Winters are very cold, summers hot and humid with frequent typhoons. Rainfall is high and winter snowfall heavy.

People. The Japanese are basically a Mongoloid race. Japan is the world's most densely populated country in terms of arable land per person. Most Japanese live in the nonmountainous areas and more than 66% in cities like Tokyo, the capital, Osaka and

Japan

Miracle of economic growth

Japan is the most prosperous country in Asia. The average annual per capita income exceeds $3 000, and distress and poverty, though evident in the poorer sections of large cities like Tokyo and Osaka, are on nothing like the scale common in some other parts of Asia. More than two decades of ultra-rapid economic growth have won Japan third place in the world league of industrial superpowers and have dramatically changed the life-style of many Japanese.

A large proportion of Japanese now regard themselves as middle class. With the rise to prosperity they have found it possible not only to set aside the customary 20% of their earnings as savings, but also to fill their small homes with the consumer durables that go with this classification. *Rejah* (leisure activities) has become a national obsession. Each year has brought some new activity into fashion and clever promotion has made the sports-goods industry big business. Although traditional sports like *Sumo* (Japanese wrestling), *Judo* and *Kendo* still have large followings, the number-one spectator sport is baseball. Most large corporations give their workers 21 days annual vacation. This has customarily been taken four or five days at a time, especially in summer when the popular resorts are packed to capacity. Now, however, the trend is foreign travel, in the form of package tours to South Korea and other countries. By 1980 more than 3 000 000 Japanese could be visiting Europe annually. In spite of serious current economic problems Japan's wealth seems likely to continue to grow.

Japan lives by importing raw materials and exporting manufactured goods. Her own natural resources are very limited, and in her characteristically aggressive search for both raw materials and markets she has sometimes provoked the resentment of the US and the European Common Market countries. Among her leading products are steel, ships, chemicals, automobiles, motorcycles and precision-made engineering products. Automobiles, motorcycles, electronic equipment and sophisticated high-grade consumer goods such as radios, cameras and watches are exported all over the world. The penetration and domination of many of the world's markets by Japanese goods is a remarkable economic achievement. Technologically inventive and always alert to adopt foreign techniques and expertise, and with labor abundant and cheap, the Japanese have been able to compete strongly against other manufacturing nations.

A feature of the industrial set-up is "industrial dualism," the division of industry into a small number of very large corporations and a multitude of small companies. More than 50% of the total number of industrial establishments are companies with fewer than five workers each. The large family corporations (*Zaibatsu*) came to dominate the industrial scene in the 1920s. Controling "the major part of industry, mining, finance and commerce, and in a large part, the livelihood of the people of Japan," they were branded after WWII for organizing and participating in the war "in concert with the Japanese military" (*US Initial Post-surrender Policy for Japan*, 1945). Attempts to break their stranglehold were not successful and mammoth concerns like Mitsubishi and Mitsui continue to thrive. Mitsubishi alone, Japan's largest corporation, with its 44 major companies and 1 300 associated firms, provides a livelihood for about 25% of the country's workforce, and its products earn more than $45 000 million annually. Other large corporations include Narubeni, C. Itoh, Sumitomo and Nissho-Iwai.

The Japanese tend to be group conformists, and many young workers, upon graduation, enter a large corporation with the intention of remaining its employee until retirement. Such a job is a matter of pride; dismissal is a deeply-felt personal disgrace which has sometimes been followed by suicide.

The large corporations are paternalistic to their employees, whose wives and children are regarded as members of the company "family." They provide a wide range of welfare, medical, housing, educational and other benefits. A typical corporation man, who may well wear the company badge, and perhaps a company suit, and who will loyally sing the company song, may receive a small gift when one of his children begins school or marries, and a condolence gift of "incense money" when a death occurs in his family. He may also receive "special cash earnings" in addition to his usual salary or wage. The company also contributes to his social life and *rejah* and may reward faithful long service with a free package-tour vacation. Retirement is marked by a gratuity usually based on length of service, status and final salary, and some corporations also have contributory pension schemes. In this lifelong commitment, the employee gains most from diligence and "cooperativeness." There is little place for individualism.

Japan does not have labor unions representing each trade or industry. Each plant within a corporation has its own wage-negotiating union which is also represented in a federated union covering the whole corporation. Most trade unions are affiliated to a national federation such as Sohyo (General Council of Trade Unions), a militant Marxist organization which mainly represents public

Yokohama. Massive social upheavals since WWII have combined with overcrowding and a hectic industrial society to cause social tensions and political instability. The population includes about 15 000 aboriginal AINUS and more than 737 000 foreigners, mostly Koreans. The literacy rate is the highest in Asia. Buddhism and Shintoism are the chief religions, but Japanese thought has also been greatly influenced by Confucianism.

Economy. Since 1945 Japan has become a leading industrial power, with a record annual real growth rate (since 1955) of more than 10%. Products range from ships and automobiles to electronic equipment, cameras and textiles for world markets, notably the US. Imports include coal, petroleum and industrial raw materials; Japan has few mineral resources. Agriculture, once the mainstay, continues to decline; rice is still the chief crop. Because of inaccessibility, only 27% of Japan's forests are commercially exploited. It has extensive fisheries, including a controversially large whaling fleet.

History. Artifacts dating from at least 4000 BC have been found in Japan. Asiatic invaders drove the aboriginal Ainus into the extreme N. The first Japanese state was ruled by the Yamato clan, from whom the present imperial house supposedly descends.

Japan was subject to powerful cultural influences from China through Korea. Rice cultivation had been introduced from China c250 BC and Buddhism from Korea (c538 AD). Under the Taika Reforms (646–702 AD) the Chinese ideographic script (somewhat adapted to Japanese) and T'ANG DYNASTY administrative system was adopted. Clan chiefs became imperial officials and land became the property of the emperor, who distributed it according to rank. The powerful FUJIWARA family tried to maintain strong government centered on a figurehead emperor, and were dominant from the 9th to the 12th century; theirs was a classical age in art and literature.

In 1192 YORITOMO Minamoto seized power as SHOGUN (military dictator). Successive *shoguns* ruled absolutely with the emperors relegated to purely ritual functions. Power was based on a vassal class of warrior knights, SAMURAI. Feudal warfare (1300–1573) saw the rise of powerful lords, often free

Geishas are trained from an early age in the art of pleasing a man socially, with conversation, food, tea and anything he may require to make him relax and feel at ease in her company.

of *shogun* rule. In 1543 the Portuguese visited Japan and other European traders followed; Christianity, introduced by St. Francis Xavier (1549) became involved with politics and was banned in 1614, with savage persecution. A policy of isolation (*sakoku*) closed Japan to all foreigners except a few Dutch and Chinese traders until 1853–54, when US Commander Matthew PERRY negotiated a trade treaty. Similar treaties with Britain, France, the Netherlands and Russia followed. The shogunate collapsed in 1867 and under Emperor MEIJI (1867–1912) Tokyo became the capital; a program of westernization began. A new constitution (1889) established a parliamentary system under the divine emperor, and finance, industry and trade were developed by the *zaibatsu*, powerful family corporations.

Japan's spectacular victories over Russia and China (see RUSSO-JAPANESE WAR and SINO-JAPANESE WARS) won her recognition as a world power, as did her support of the Allies in WWI. In the 1930s a militarist regime took power after an economic crisis; Japan then built a large Asian colonial empire. The regime increasingly favored Nazi Germany, signing an Anti-Comintern Pact in 1936. Japan entered WWII with the surprise attack on PEARL HARBOR in 1941; war brought economic ruin and finally nuclear devastation at HIROSHIMA and NAGASAKI. Following the Japanese surrender (1945), Japan was occupied by US troops. A new democratic constitution was introduced (1947) and full sovereignty and independence restored by the San Francisco Peace Treaty (1951). With US aid the economy was rebuilt, making Japan a vast industrial giant but bringing severe social problems. Japan was admitted to the UN in 1956. The economic boom slowed considerably in the middle 1970s.

JAPAN, Sea of, part of W Pacific Ocean, bounded on the E by Japan and on the W by the Soviet Union and service unions whose members are forbidden by law to strike, and Domei (Confederation of Labor), which mainly represents unions in the private sector whose members have the right to strike.

The tendency now is for union militancy to increase. The paternal image of the big industrialists was tarnished by exposure of their speculative practices and enormous profits by a Japanese House of Representatives investigating committee. The image was further tarnished by the resignation of the prime minister in 1974 against a background of serious allegations about his financial dealings. In 1976 further revelations about commercial bribery by the US Lockheed Corporation caused a major political scandal.

The oil crisis of 1973 was a severe shock to the economy. Japan has to import about 80% of her oil and most of this customarily comes from the Middle East. In 1974, when the import volume had been cut by nearly 4%, the cost amounted to more than $18.8 million which led to a deficit of over $6.8 million in the overall balance of trade. Japan was also hit by the world trade recession. To the accompaniment of lay-offs, "voluntary" resignations and early retirement, production fell and the postwar growth miracle seemed over with Japan heading for disaster. By 1975 rigid anti-inflation measures had reduced the annual rate of inflation from over 25% to about 20%. But unemployment stood around the million mark, bankruptcies averaged 1 200 monthly and the consumer price index remained intolerably high (Japan has the highest cost of living in the world).

Most Japanese economists were prepared for a minus growth rate by spring 1975. In fact an estimated 2.6% growth was achieved in that year, and many experts in the outside world, mindful of Japanese toughness and resilience, expect rapid recovery with Japan "setting a standard for the world in economic performance" in the 1980s. According to the Japan Economic Research Center, output per head in Japan in 1985 will reach $24 000, compared with $14 000 in the US. But it has also been argued that if Japan were to return to the former growth rate of more than 10% annually, she would require by 1985 25% of the world's oil, 50% of its iron ore and all of its nickel and copper—which is not a practical proposition, if only in terms of maintaining friendly relations with other countries.

The Japanese have realized how much depends on maintaining such good relations with other countries, and on promoting development projects which are not aimed merely at providing new outlets for Japanese-manufactured goods. The energy crisis led Japan to "reconsider" her customary pro-Israel stance in favor of an understanding with the Arab countries. Iran and other oil-exporting countries were courted; also China, whose Taching oil field is expected to provide Japan with up to 50 000 000 tons of crude oil annually by 1978. Japan is also helping the development of the Brazilian steel industry and may eventually be a customer for its products. Her "resources diplomacy" with Russia led to agreements in 1974–75 on the joint development of oil, natural gas and other resources in Siberia, representing an investment by Japan of several billion dollars. In seeking to ensure supplies of raw materials, Japan has become the foremost trading partner of Australia, buying 40% of that country's coal, more than 70% of her iron ore, nearly 40% of her wool clip and about 15% of her beef. Japan, therefore, continues to vie with other industrial nations in winning the favor of countries which have raw materials to export, at a time when certain such materials are becoming scarce.

Agriculture continues to decline. It is the older, retired members of the rural families who keep the farms going while the farmers, and their adult sons and daughters, work during the week in factories and offices. By 1973 nearly 84% of all farm families were working on this basis. Agriculture is government-subsidized and rice, the chief crop, is grown in such quantities that overproduction is a problem and farmers are being encouraged to diversify.

Traditionally rice has provided 40% of the protein in the Japanese diet; the average pre-WWII Japanese ate more than 330lb of rice annually. The Japanese are also great fish-eaters, with a per capita consumption four times the world average. Japan is second only to Peru as a fishing nation, her catch reaching a record 10.2 million tons in 1972.

As from 1955 the population has been increasing at a rate of about 1 000 000 yearly and is expected to total 132 000 000 by the year 2000. More than 66% of the present population is concentrated in the cities and depopulation of the countryside is continuing. Land shortage and soaring construction costs hinder proper urban planning. One result of the acute land shortage has been the construction of big underground shopping centers in the large cities and of multistory buildings in central Toyko. Some of the latter have more than 30 floors, but are nevertheless pronounced earthquake-proof. Japan averages more than 1 000 earth tremors every year and can expect a major earthquake about once every five years.

The Japanese are deeply concerned about environmental pollution and about the social problems arising from rapid urbanization. Government action has had some effect, but hopes for a pollution-free Japan have still to be realized. There is a growing demand for greater official investment in the public sector so that urgent social problems can be solved. There is a desperate need for the restructuring of industry and the dispersal of its heavy concentration along the Pacific coast. But all this will take time.

Isolation, of great significance throughout Japanese history, goes a long way to explain the present ethnic and linguistic uniformity of the country. Although economic necessity has brought Japan closer to China and Russia, the Japanese remain grateful that the sea separates them from these two powerful neighbors. Westernization was accelerated by the postwar occupation, but it is difficult to decide how deeply it has penetrated.

Protected by her defense treaties with the US, and pledged by the 1947 Constitution not to maintain "land, sea and air forces or other war potential," Japan spends less than 0.9% of her gross national product on defense. From 1950, however, the Japanese—despite the Constitution—have been encouraged to build up "self-defense forces" and to manufacture various armaments including military aircraft, warships and guided missiles. But with still-vivid memories of WWII, many Japanese stand firmly opposed to military revivalism in any form.

Relatively inexpensive, mass-produced Japanese products, such as these automobiles, have radically altered world trade patterns since WWII.

Korea. About 389 100sq mi in area, its maximum depth is 12 276ft. It helps moderate the climate of Japan and is a major fishing area.

JAPAN CURRENT, or **Kuroshio,** warm strong ocean current running NE along the SE Japanese coast. In summer, some splits off eventually to reach the Sea of Japan: most, however, turns E past the Aleutians to form the NORTH PACIFIC CURRENT.

JAPANESE, language probably related to the ALTAIC group. Written Japanese originally used only adapted Chinese characters (*kanji*) despite their unsuitability; in the 8th century phonetic characters (*kana*) were added. Since 1945 both types have been simplified, their number reduced and romanized writing introduced.

JAPANESE ART AND ARCHITECTURE, has been influenced by China, Korea and India, particularly through Buddhism from the 6th and 7th centuries. Japanese Buddhist temple architecture is subtler than Chinese in proportion and decoration. Early Buddhist sculpture reflects the Chinese Wei and T'ang styles (3rd–9th centuries), but tends toward naturalism and clear proportioning. Colored wall paintings on temple interiors show Indian influence.

In the FUJIWARA period (886–1160) fortified castles and palaces with moats and massive walls were built. Wood was the major temple and domestic building material. Domestic interior design is based on multiples of the *tatami*, a straw mat 3ft wide by 6ft long. Houses are built on wooden frames with sliding interior walls and doors opening onto a landscaped garden. Historical and landscape painting (*Yamato-e*) decorated palace walls and screens. Hand scrolls (*makimono*) were a popular medium. The Chinese-derived black and white *Sumi* style, inspired by ZEN, was exemplified by SESSHU (1420–1506). In the 16th century *ukiyo-e*, subjects from everyday life, was perfected in block prints (see UTAMARO, HOKUSAI, HIROSHIGE). Little regarded in Japan, these popular prints influenced late 19th century European art. Modern Japanese art has often been an uneasy compromise with Western influence.

JAPANESE BEETLE, *Popillia japonica*, a pest beetle in the family *Scarabeidae*. The grubs feed on the roots of grasses, especially in lawns. Adults feed on almost all kinds of green vegetation, flowers and fruits. Trees and shrubs may be severely defoliated. Introduced to N.J. about 1916, the adults have a shiny bronze-green head and deep tan wing covers. They are about 13mm (0.5in) long.

JAPANESE SPANIEL, variety of toy spaniel, standing 9–12in high and weighing up to 7lb. The long thick coat is white with red or black markings. The neck is short, head large and muzzle short.

JAPANNING, a means of varnishing articles of wood, metal or glass in imitation of Japanese lacquerwork. The varnish is usually resin-based with

The shining five-storey donjon of the castle at Himeji, on the Japanese island of Honshu, was built in 1609 and came to be known as the "Castle of the White Heron" because of the white walls surrounding it.

a variety of pigments; it is applied in successive layers which are heat-dried.

JAPURA RIVER, river rising in the Colombian Andes as the Caqueta and flowing 1 300mi ESE into Brazil, entering the Amazon through a network of streams.

JACQUES-DALCROZE, Émile (1865–1950), Swiss composer and educator, best known for his invention of EURHYTHMICS as a teaching aid for musicians.

JARRELL, Randall (1914–1965), US poet and influential critic. His poetry is emotional and often pervaded with a sense of tragedy and alienation; best-known collections are *Blood for a Stranger* (1942) and *Losses* (1948). *Poetry and the Age* (1953) is the first of three collections of his criticism.

JARRY, Alfred (1873–1907), eccentric French poet and dramatist whose *Ubu* plays (1896–1902) anticipated SURREALISM, DADA and the Theate of the Absurd. Brilliant but disordered, Jarry became an alcoholic while still young. The revoltingly gross, comic but sinister Ubu embodies his view of the bourgeoisie.

JARVIS ISLAND, one of the Line Islands in the central Pacific, 1.74sq mi in area. It was worked for guano by the US 1857–79, annexed by Britain in 1889 and by the US in 1935.

JASMINE, popular name for deciduous and evergreen shrubs and climbers of the genus *Jasminium*, producing clusters of tubular flowers that are often strongly fragrant. Several species can be grown outdoors either as ground cover on rock gardens or trailing against walls and fences. *Jasminium sambac*, and the closely related *Osmanthus fragrans* (sweet olive), make excellent house plants requiring a sunny position during the winter but avoiding direct sun in the summer. Indoors, daytime temperature should be about 21°C (70°F) dropping to 17°C (63°F) at night. They require sufficient watering to keep the soil evenly moist, avoiding extremes of wetness or dryness. They are propagated from shoot cuttings. Family: Olaceae.

JASON, in Greek myth the leader of the ARGONAUTS on the quest for the GOLDEN FLEECE. He gained it with the aid of the sorceress MEDEA, whom he married and later deserted. In old age he was killed when the prow of his ship, the *Argo*, fell on him.

Jasper: rough, and cut and polished,

JASPER, city in NW central Ala., seat of Walker Co. It has coal mining and processes cotton and timber. Pop 10 798.

JASPER, common variety of CHALCEDONY containing admixed HEMATITE or GOETHITE, normally red, brown or yellowish, often with banding and spotting. Good grades are used for semiprecious GEM stones.

JASPER NATIONAL PARK, area covering 4 200sq mi in the E Rocky Mountains in SW Alberta, Canada. Established in 1907, it is a game reserve and scenic area with glaciers and hot springs.

JASPERS, Karl Theodor (1883–1969), German philosopher, noted for his steadfast opposition to National Socialism and his acute yet controversial analyses of the state of German society. Early work in psychopathology led him into the Heidelberg philosophical faculty in 1913. He there became one of Germany's foremost exponents of EXISTENTIALISM.

JASSY. See IASI.

The North American Blue jay, with its splendid plumage and nimble flight, bears little resemblance to other members of the crow family. Among other birds it is not very popular as it will often eat their eggs and nestlings.

JAUNDICE, yellow color of the SKIN and sclera of the EYE caused by excess bilirubin pigment in the BLOOD. HEMOGLOBIN is broken down to form bilirubin which is excreted by the LIVER in the BILE. If blood is broken down more rapidly than normal (hemolysis), the liver may not be able to remove the abnormal amount of bilirubin fast enough. Jaundice occurs with liver damage (HEPATITIS, late CIRRHOSIS) and when the bile ducts leading from the liver to the DUODENUM are obstructed by stones from the GALL BLADDER or by CANCER of the PANCREAS or bile ducts.

JAURÈS, Jean (1859–1914), French pacifist politician, one of the founders of the French Socialist Party (1905). He was a member of the Chamber of Deputies 1885–88 and 1893–98; in 1904 he founded the socialist journal *Humanité*. Jaurès, who opposed war with Germany in 1914, was assassinated by a fanatic.

JAVA. See JAWA.

JAVA MAN. See PREHISTORIC MAN.

JAVA SEA, a shallow part of the Pacific Ocean, about 120 000sq mi in area. It is bounded by Jawa on the S, Sumatra on the W and Kalimantan on the N, and merges in the E with the Flores Sea.

JAVA SEA, Battle of the, WWII naval engagement in Feb. 1942 in which the Allies were seriously defeated by the Japanese fleet. The defeat left Jawa vulnerable to Japanese occupation.

JAVARI, river in NW South America. It flows NE for about 550mi and forms a large part of the Peru–Brazil frontier. Navigable only by light craft, it drains into the Amazon near Benjamin Constant.

JAVELIN. See TRACK AND FIELD.

JAVITS, Jacob Koppel (1904–), US lawyer and politician. He was a Republican congressman 1946–54, New York attorney-general 1955–57; and senator from N.Y., from 1957. In the Senate he became known for his liberal views on social issues.

JAWA (Java), island in SE Asia, part of Indonesia. It contains Indonesia's capital, Jakarta, and two-thirds of the population. Major towns are Surabaja, Bandung, Semarang and Surakarta. The island is traversed by a volcanic mountain chain; there is a fertile tropical plain on the N coast. The climate is warm and humid with heavy rainfall. Jawa exports rubber, coffee, tea, sugar and quinine, and is famous for its silverwork and batik textiles. Timber, coal, oil and other mineral resources are also exploited.

JAWFISHES, small, rather elongated marine fishes with enormous mouths. Some species have a backward extension of the upper jaw. They live in shallow waters in the Pacific region, constructing elaborate burrows with a roomy end-chamber lined with pieces of rock and coral.

JAWLENSKI, Alexei von (1864–1941), Russian artist who in 1896 left the Imperial Guard and went to Munich to study painting. He was influenced by the work of Van Gogh, Cézanne and Matisse (whom he met) and in 1905–13 by FAUVISM. He is particularly noted for his series of human faces (post-1918).

JAWLESS FISHES, primitive fishes now represented solely by the LAMPREYS and HAGFISHES. See AGNATHA.

JAY, John (1745–1829), American statesman. An attorney, he drafted the N.Y. state constitution in 1777. In 1778 he was elected president of the Continental Congress and in 1779 first minister to Spain. In 1782, with Benjamin FRANKLIN and John ADAMS, he negotiated peace with Britain, resulting in the Treaty of PARIS (1783). As secretary for foreign affairs 1784–89 he supported the new Constitution, believing in the need for a strong central government. He was the first Chief Justice of the Supreme Court 1789–95. In 1794 he negotiated the unpopular JAY TREATY. A conservative member of the FEDERALIST PARTY, he served as governor of N.Y. 1795–1801.

JAYS, a diverse group of birds in the crow family, Corvidae, many of which are brightly-colored, with screeching, raucous voices. Adaptable and omnivorous, they have evolved to fill a variety of ecological roles and habitats. The original bearer of the name is the European jay, *Garrulus glandarius*, found in the woodlands of most of Europe and Asia, a striking bird with a pinkish body, black, white and blue wings and a white rump. There are in addition some 30 species of New World jays.

JAY TREATY, agreement between the US and Britain negotiated by John JAY, 1794. The British held forts in US territory and were inciting Indians against American settlers. Some American ships trading with the French were being seized and American seamen impressed. The Jay Treaty provided for British evacuation of NW forts, compensation for confiscated shipping, American repayment to Britain of prewar debts and limited trading concessions to the US. No mention was made of impressment, incitement of the Indians or compensation for abducted slaves. The treaty, considered a capitulation to the British, made Jay and the FEDERALIST PARTY unpopular. It led France to break its alliance with America and pursue an undeclared naval war (1798–1800), but it averted a potentially crippling war with Britain.

JAYHAWKERS, guerrilla fighters who championed Kansas' entry into the Union as a free state before the Civil War. A contemptuous nickname, it was applied to unionist guerrillas generally during the Civil War, and to the Seventh Kansas Cavalry, made up of former guerrillas.

JAZZ, form of music which grew out of Southern US Negro culture. Rhythmically complex, with a strong emphasis on syncopation, it is often highly improvisatory. Jazz may be said to have been born in the work songs, laments and spirituals of slaves and Southern Negro communities and to derive ultimately from African music. It was popularized by street bands that played for special occasions, particularly in New Orleans. By the 1900s such early forms as Stomp and RAGTIME had developed, and the BLUES had begun to evolve.

In the 1920s jazz moved north with the Negro populations to the cities, notably Chicago and New York. With increasing musical sophistication new styles developed, and jazz found a wider audience through radio and phonograph. Big bands developed a commercialized jazz called Swing in the 1930s and 1940s. In early 1940s Negro musicians pioneered a vivid new style, BOP. "West Coast" and "cool" styles appeared in the 1950s and 1960s, which saw the development of "free form" jazz.

Among early jazz musicians were Joe "King" OLIVER, Sidney BECHET, Ferdinand "Jelly Roll" MORTON, Louis ARMSTRONG, Thomas "Fats" WALLER and Leon "Bix" BEIDERBECKE. Edward "Duke" ELLINGTON and William "Count" BASIE led bands of the 1930s and 1940s and Glenn MILLER and Benny GOODMAN dominated the Swing era. Bessie SMITH and Eleanor "Billie" HOLIDAY are considered two of the greatest jazz singers. Among more modern artists are Lester YOUNG, Charlie PARKER, Dizzy GILLESPIE, Miles DAVIS, John COLTRANE and the "free-form" pioneers Ornette COLEMAN and Cecil Taylor.

JEAN PAUL. See RICHTER, JEAN PAUL FRIEDRICH.

JEANNETTE, city in SW Pa., against the Allegheny Mts. Its economy rests on light manufacturing, particularly of glass. Pop 15 209.

JEANS, Sir James Hopwood (1877–1946), British physicist and mathematician best known for his contributions to astronomy and for his popular science books. He played a valuable role in proving the invalidity of the NEBULAR HYPOTHESIS, but his own theory of the formation of the SOLAR SYSTEM, that the planets were "drawn out" of the sun by a star passing close by, has now in turn been largely discarded.

JEFFERS, (John) Robinson (1887–1962), American poet. His powerful poetry is violently disillusioned, seeing man as a mere doomed animal and glorifying nature. *Tamar and Other Poems* (1924) is his best-known collection, but his chief success was a searing adaptation of EURIPEDES' *Medea* (1946).

JEFFERSON, Fort. See FORT JEFFERSON NATIONAL MONUMENT.

JEFFERSON, Joseph (1829–1905), US actor most famous in the role of Rip van Winkle. Already a successful actor, he created this role in London in 1865 and played it regularly for the rest of his life.

JEFFERSON, Thomas (1743–1826), third president of the US. The son of a Va. planter, he was admitted to the bar in 1767. He entered politics in 1769 as a member of the Va. House of Burgesses. In reply to the INTOLERABLE ACTS of 1774 he wrote *A Summary View of the Rights of British America*, in which he entirely denied Britain any right of government in the colonies. In 1775 he was a delegate to the second Continental Congress. In 1776, as leading member of a five-man committee, he wrote most of the DECLARATION OF INDEPENDENCE.

Jefferson was governor of Va. 1779–81 and after a short retirement was elected to Congress. In 1785 he succeeded Benjamin FRANKLIN as minister to France and secured trade concessions for the US there. From 1789 to 1793 he was secretary of state under Washington. Two parties, the Democratic-Republicans and the Federalists, formed respectively around Jefferson—who believed in agrarian egalitarianism based on the rationality of man—and Alexander HAMILTON, secretary of the treasury, who favored a strong

Thomas JEFFERSON

3rd US President

Born: April 13, 1743
Died: July 4, 1826
Term of office: March 4, 1801–March 3, 1809
Political party: Democratic-Republican

central government led by a wealthy and able aristocracy.

In 1796 Jefferson ran as presidential candidate against the Federalist John ADAMS. Though he received the larger popular vote he lost by three electoral votes and became vice-president. During this time he wrote a *Manual of Parliamentary Practice*, and, with James MADISON, the KENTUCKY AND VIRGINIA RESOLUTIONS, protesting against the Federalists' ALIEN AND SEDITION ACTS which restricted freedom of speech and the press. From these resolutions there evolved the doctrines of STATES' RIGHTS and NULLIFICATION.

In 1800 Jefferson ran against Adams again and, gaining the same number of electoral votes as his opponent Aaron BURR, was chosen president by Congress. His administration was notable in foreign affairs and domestic expansion. He negotiated the LOUISIANA PURCHASE in 1803 and sent out the LEWIS AND CLARK EXPEDITION. He balanced the budget and reduced the national debt.

He was reelected in 1804 and during his second term tried to maintain US neutrality during the Napoleonic wars. He attempted to combat the seizure of ships and impressment of seamen with the EMBARGO ACT of 1807, prohibiting American export, but this damaged American agricultural and commercial interests and violated his principle of individual liberty. He repealed it in 1809, and in that year retired to his home, MONTICELLO. A noted scholar, he founded the U. of Virginia (1819–25).

A jazz festival in New Orleans, the city which, more than any other, is regarded as the home of jazz. It was street bands like the one seen here that made this music popular in the early 1900s.

JEFFERSON CITY, capital city of Mo. and seat of Cole Co., on the Missouri R. A trading center, its major industries include printing and publishing and the manufacture of shoes, clothing and electrical appliances. Pop 32 407.

JEFFERSON HEIGHTS, urban community in SW La., largely a residential suburb of New Orleans. Pop 16 489.

The Jefferson Memorial, one of Washington's most impressive buildings, constructed in honor of America's third president, 200 years after his birth.

JEFFERSON MEMORIAL, monument in Washington, D.C., dedicated in 1943 to the memory of Thomas Jefferson. A white marble structure in classical style, it was designed by John Russell Pope and contains a statue of Jefferson by Rudulph Evans.

JEFFERSON TERRITORY, area comprising what is now Col. and parts of Ut., Neb. and Kan. It was designated a territory by a constitution ratified in 1859; a provisional government was formed and a legislature elected. However, because of controversy over the issue of slavery Congress did not recognize it. In 1861 it became the territory of Colorado.

JEFFERSONVILLE, city in S Ind. and seat of Clark Co., on the Ohio R. A river port, it has shipyards and manufactures cement and building materials. Pop 20 008.

JEFFRIES, James J. (1875–1953), US heavyweight boxer who won the championship from Bob Fitzsimmons in 1899. He retired undefeated in 1905; returning to the ring in 1910 he was defeated by Jack Johnson.

JEHAN, Shah. See SHAH JEHAN.

JEHANGIR (1569–1627), emperor of India from 1605, who consolidated and expanded the MOGUL EMPIRE. Known as a just ruler and patron of the arts, he established trade agreements with the British in return for naval protection.

JEHOAHAZ, name of two kings of Israel and of Judah. **Jehoahaz, king of Israel**, ruled c814–c798 BC, a period during which Israel was weak and insignificant. **Jehoahaz, king of Judah**, ruled c608 BC, succeeding his father Josiah, but the Pharaoh Necho deposed him and exiled him to Egypt, replacing him with his brother Jehoiakim.

JEHOASH (Joash), name of two kings of Israel and of Judah. **Jehoash, king of Israel** (c798–782 BC), son of Jehoahaz. He fought successfully against Damascus and conquered Amaziah of Judah. **Jehoash, king of Judah**, ruled c835–c796. Saved by his uncle Jehoida when his grandmother seized power and murdered his father, he was dominated by him throughout his reign.

JEHOIACHIN, king of Judah c597 BC. He succeeded his father Jehoiakim but was taken with 10 000 of his subjects by NEBUCHADNEZZAR to Babylon (c597 BC) and not released until the latter's death 40 years later. (See BABYLONIAN CAPTIVITY.)

JEHOIAKIM, king of Judah c608–c597, son of Josiah. He was set up by the Pharaoh Necho in place of his brother Jehoahaz. Contrary to the advice of JEREMIAH, he rebelled against Babylon and died during the resulting siege of Jerusalem.

JEHORAM, name of two kings of Israel and of Judah. **Jehoram, king of Israel**, c852–c841, son of AHAB. He succeeded his brother Ahaziah. After brutally quelling a Moabite revolt he was killed during the revolt of JEHU. **Jehoram, king of Judah**, c853–c842, son of Jehosaphat, married Athalia and was succeeded by Ahaziah. Remembered as an idolator, he was repeatedly denounced by ELIJAH.

JEHOSAPHAT, fourth king of Judah, c872–c848 BC, son of Asa. A good and conscientious king, his attempts to revive former power met with little success. He maintained good relations with his neighbors and allied with the former rival, Israel.

JEHOVAH, variant of the Old Testament personal name for God. The sacred name YHWH, probably pronounced "Yahweh," was not used by the Jews after about 300 BC for fear of blaspheming. Hence in reading the Hebrew Bible *Adonai* (Lord) was substituted. Medieval translators combined the consonants of one name with the vowels of the other, arriving at "Jehovah."

JEHOVAH'S WITNESSES, religious movement founded in 1872 by Charles Taze Russell in Pittsburgh, Pa. There is no formal church organization. Their central doctrine is that the Second Coming is at hand; they avoid participation in secular government which they see as diabolically inspired. Over a million members proselytize by house-to-house calls and through publications such as *The Watchtower* and *Awake*, issued by the Watchtower Bible and Tract Society.

JEHU, king of Israel, reigned c842–815 BC. An army commander proverbial for his wild chariot-driving, he overthrew and succeeded King JEHORAM at the prophet ELISHA's instigation. He destroyed the cult of BAAL and put to death its followers, including Queen JEZEBEL.

JELLICOE, Sir John Rushworth, 1st Earl Jellicoe (1859–1935), British admiral, commander of the British fleet at the battle of Jutland in 1916. He was governor-general of New Zealand 1920–24.

JELLY AND JAM, sweet foods made by heating fruit juice (jelly) or crushed or chopped fruit (jam) with sugar. They set because of the PECTIN, present in all fruits: in some cases, extra pectin and CITRIC ACID must be added. **Marmalades** contain peel as well as pulp; **preserves** contain whole fruits.

JELLYFISH, familiar marine cnidarians (see CNIDARIA) with a pulsating "jelly" bell and trailing tentacles. Many cnidarian classes display ALTERNATION OF GENERATIONS, where a single species may be represented by a polyp form, usually asexual, and a medusoid, sexually reproductive stage. These medusoid forms are frequently referred to as jellyfish. The true jellyfish all belong to the class Scyphozoa, where the medusa is the dominant phase and the polyp or hydroid is reduced or absent. Jellyfish are radially symmetrical. Rings of muscle around the margin of the bell contract to expel water and propel the jellyfish forward.

JEMAPPES, Battle of, battle of the French Revolution on Nov. 6, 1792. The French Republican Army, led by DUMOURIEZ, won its first victory over Austrian forces and dominated Belgium.

JENA, city on the Salle R in East Germany. Napoleon defeated the Prussian army here in 1806. The original site of the Zeiss optical and precision instrument firm, it has long been a center of the optical industries. Pop 88 346.

JENGHIZ KHAN. See GENGHIS KHAN.

JENKINS' EAR, War of, a conflict between England and Spain, 1739–41. The allegation by ship's master Robert Jenkins that a Spanish coast guard in the West Indies had cut off his ear while pillaging his ship was exploited to foment popular anger in England.

JENNER, Edward (1749–1823), British pioneer of VACCINATION. He examined in detail the country maxim that dairymaids who had had COWPOX would not contract SMALLPOX: in 1796 he inoculated a small boy with cowpox and found that this rendered the boy immune from smallpox.

JENNEY, William Le Baron (1832–1907), US engineer and architect, whose innovative building techniques were of great importance in the development of the skyscraper. He developed the idea of using internal metal frames and was the first architect to utilize steel as a structural material.

JENNINGS, city in SW La., seat of Jefferson Davis Parish. The economy is based on gas, oil, rice, truck agriculture and shipbuilding. Pop 11 783.

JENNINGS, city and residential suburb in E Mo., 4mi N of St. Louis. Pop 19 379.

JENSEN, Johannes Hans Daniel (1907–), German physicist who shared with M. G. MAYER and E. H. WIGNER the 1963 Nobel Prize for Physics for his suggestion (independent of Mayer's) that the PROTONS and NEUTRONS of the atomic nucleus are arranged in concentric shells.

JENSEN, Johannes Vilhelm (1873–1950), Danish winner of the 1944 Nobel Prize for Literature. His main works are a series of more than 100 tales entitled *Myths* (1907–44) and a six-volume novel cycle on the rise of Man, *The Long Journey* (1908–22).

JEOPARDY. See DOUBLE JEOPARDY.

JERASH, small town in Jordan, site of ancient Gerasa, one of the Decapolis cities settled by Greeks following the conquests of ALEXANDER THE GREAT. Extensive ruins still survive.

JERBOAS, small desert rodents forming the family Dipodidae, found from central Asia to the Sahara. They progress by jumping on their very long hindlegs and feet, not unlike the KANGAROO RATS of North America. The tail is always very long, sometimes more than twice the length of the body, and ends in a tassel of hairs. Jerboas are nocturnal animals, spending the day in burrows, out of the heat of the sun.

JEREMIAH (c650–c570 BC), prophet of Judah, and the primary author of the Old Testament Book of Jeremiah, a collection of his oracles. He prophesied the subjugation of Judah by Babylon and the destruction of Jerusalem and the Temple, and called for submission to the conquerors as God's agents in punishing idolatry. He was distressed by his message, but endured imprisonment for treason and threats to his life.

JEREZ DE LA FRONTERA, historic city in SW Spain, 13mi NE of Cadiz. A trade center noted especially for its sherry (a corruption of "Jerez") it is also famous for breeding horses. Pop 149 867.

JERICHO, village in Jordan, 14mi ENE of Jerusalem, built 825ft below sea level. Dating possibly from 9000 BC, it was captured from the Canaanites by Joshua in 1400 BC. It has regularly been destroyed and rebuilt; HEROD the Great built a Jericho 1mi S of the Old Testament city. In 1967 it was occupied by Israel. Pop 6 829.

JERICHO, urban residential community in SE N.Y., on Long Island. It has a beverages industry. Pop 14 010.

JEROBOAM, the name of two kings of Israel. **Jeroboam I** was the first king of the N kingdom of Israel, 933–912 BC. He led the revolt against REHOBOAM and separated the kingdom of Israel from that of Judah. He founded new shrines in the N, away from Jerusalem, for which the Bible criticizes him as an idolator. The reign of **Jeroboam II**, c782–741 BC, was marked by great prosperity and social injustice, and AMOS and HOSEA made their prophecies.

JEROME, Saint (Sophronius Eusebius Hieronymus; c347–c420), biblical scholar, one of the first theologians to be called a Doctor of the Christian Church. After being educated in classical studies he fled to the desert as a hermit in 375 to devote himself to prayer. He was subsequently papal secretary and translated the Old Testament into Latin (see VULGATE) and wrote New Testament commentaries.

JEROME, Jerome Klapka (1859–1927), English humorist and playwright, who wrote the classic comic novel *Three Men in a Boat* (1889), a work cherished for its broad humor and sentimentality.

JEROME OF PRAGUE (c1380–1416), Bohemian religious reformer and companion of Jan HUS. Because of his proposals for reformed liturgy and his attacks on the church he was burnt as a heretic.

JERSEY, largest bailiwick of the British CHANNEL ISLANDS, 44.87sq mi in area. Its main industries are tourism and agriculture. It is a British Crown dependency, but the official language is French. The port and capital is St. Helier.

JERSEY CITY, city in NE N.J., seat of Hudson Co., a major transportation center. Its industries include freight shipping, oil refining, chemicals and consumer products. Its large stockyards supply the meatpacking industry. Pop 260 545.

JERUSALEM, capital of Israel, and holy city for Jews, Christians and Muslims. The city stands on a ridge at an altitude of 2 500ft, W of the Dead Sea and 35mi from the Mediterranean. It retains many grandiose shrines and the cobbled streets of the Old City.

The city dates from possibly the 4th millenium BC. In c1000 BC King DAVID captured the city from the Jebusites and made it his capital. The great Temple was built by his son SOLOMON c970 BC. David's dynasty was ended by the invasion of King NEBUCHADNEZZAR in 586 BC, who sacked the Temple and deported most of the Jews to Babylon. The Jews were allowed to return by CYRUS II of Persia, and the Temple was rebuilt. Jerusalem subsequently became part of Syria, but in 165 BC JUDAS MACCABEUS freed the city and it was ruled by the HASMONEAN dynasty. From 37 BC the HEROD family led the state under the aegis of the Roman Empire. The Jewish revolts, in 66 AD and 132 AD led to the destruction of the Temple and complete subjugation to the Romans until the 4th century, when Christianity became the religion of the Byzantine Roman Empire.

The city was captured by the Persian king KHOSRAU II in 614, from whom it passed to the religiously tolerant rule of the Muslim Omar. In 1099 the knights of the First Crusade took Jerusalem and set up the Latin Kingdom of Jerusalem. However in 1187 the Muslims under SALADIN recaptured the city. The

The original site of the biblical city of Jericho is believed to be at Tel-es-Soeltan, which lies to the west of the present-day village. This 30-ft tower, dating from 6000 or 5500 BC, was unearthed during recent excavations.

The magnificent Dome of the Rock, or Omar Mosque, in Jerusalem.
Some of the surrounding structures date from the time of their builder, Herod the Great. Much of the Old City has changed little over the centuries.

MAMELUKES and then the Ottoman emperor SULEIMAN I restored Jerusalem. The city declined as a religious and economic center from the 16th to the 19th century. It was conquered by the British in 1917 and became the capital of Palestine. The 1947 UN resolution made it an international city, but in the 1948 Arab–Israeli conflict it was divided, the Old City being under Jordanese administration, and the New City becoming the capital of Israel. In the 1967 ARAB-ISRAELI WAR, Israel took the Old City and all Jerusalem was placed under unified administration.

Armenian, Christian, Jewish and Muslim communities each now occupy a quarter of the Old City. Tourism and religious activity dominate life in Jerusalem. Pop 304 500.

JERUSALEM ARTICHOKE, *Helianthus tuberosus*, a hardy perennial cultivated for its edible tubers, which have white flesh under a knobbly purple skin. The plant may grow up to 3.7m (12.1ft) in height and thrives in sunny positions on well-drained soil. Family: COMPOSITAE.

JERUSALEM CHERRY, *Solanum pseudocapsicum*, a popular house plant grown mainly for its attractive red berries which last for several months. Ideally it should be grown in a sunny window at average house temperatures, although it fails to thrive below 13°C (55°F). The soil should be kept evenly moist and the plants misted often. Jerusalem cherry is propagated from seeds germinated in the spring. Family: Solanaceae.

JESPERSON, Jens Otto Harry (1860–1943), Danish philologist and educator best known for his studies of English GRAMMAR and for devising the international language **Novial** (c1928).

JESSE, according to the Bible, the father of King DAVID, and as such the first in the genealogy of Jesus Christ. The "tree of Jesse," is often used in illustration to depict the line of descent of Christ.

JESUIT RELATIONS, reports sent by French Jesuit missionaries in North America between 1632 and 1673. They are valuable records of French exploration and accounts of Indian tribes before the arrival of settlers.

JESUITS, name given to members of the Society of Jesus, an order of the Roman Catholic Church dedicated to foreign missions, education and studies in the humanities and sciences. Jesuit life is regulated by the constitutions written by the founder of the Society, St. Ignatius LOYOLA. Vows of obedience, poverty, chastity and obedience to the pope are taken, and training may last up to 15 years. After its foundation in 1540 the Society undertook notable missions in the Far East under St. FRANCIS XAVIER, and in Europe as part of the Counter-Reformation. Their influence and power eventually led to their expulsion from many countries, and in 1773 Pope CLEMENT XIV dissolved the Society, but it was restored in 1814. Today there are about 31 000 Jesuits.

JESUS CHRIST, or Jesus of Nazareth (c6 BC–c30 AD), the founder of CHRISTIANITY. The four GOSPELS, embodying early Christian tradition, are the primary sources for his life. Born in Bethlehem, Judaea, to MARY (see VIRGIN BIRTH), Jesus grew up with his parents in Nazareth in Galilee. Little is known of his life before he began his public ministry at the age of about 33; this was inaugurated when he was baptized in the Jordan R by JOHN the Baptist. For the next three years he journeyed, mainly in Galilee, gathering a band of disciples, in particular the 12 APOSTLES, teaching and training them, preaching to large crowds and healing the physically and mentally ill. His homely parables are memorable teaching aids; the MIRACLES, few but significant, had the same function. The chief theme of Jesus' teaching was the imminent coming of the Kingdom of God and his own central role as the agent of God, bringing redemption and requiring commitment. He disavowed the popular wish for a political Messiah (see ZEALOTS), but made claims in which he transformed the traditional idea of the MESSIAH; toward the end of the three years, as he and his disciples traveled to Jerusalem, he introduced teaching about his coming humiliation, suffering and death. Appealing throughout to the Old Testament, he antagonized the Scribes and Pharisees by denouncing their legalism. In the last week of his life he entered Jerusalem and taught there; after the LAST SUPPER he was betrayed by JUDAS ISCARIOT and arrested in the garden of GETHSEMANE. The Jewish authorities handed him over to the Roman governor, Pontius Pilate, who had him executed by CRUCIFIXION. Two days later his tomb was found to be empty, and many recognizable appearances of Jesus to his disciples convinced them of his RESURRECTION. According to the Acts of the Apostles, 40 days later he ascended to heaven (see ASCENSION). The early Church soon crystallized its beliefs about Jesus, accepting him as Messiah, Lord and Son of God (see also INCARNATION; TRINITY), and as the Savior who by dying redeemed mankind (see ATONEMENT). Muslims believe Jesus to have been the greatest prophet before Mohammed, but deny his deity.

JET, compact, hard variety of lignite COAL, deep black and polishable, mined at Whitby, England, and used as a GEM material.

JET PROPULSION, the propulsion of a vehicle by expelling a fluid jet backward, whose MOMENTUM produces a reaction that imparts an equal forward momentum to the vehicle, according to NEWTON's third law of motion. The squid uses a form of jet propulsion. Jet-propelled boats, using water for the jet, have been built, and air jets have been used to power cars, but by far the chief use is to power AIRPLANES and ROCKETS, since to attain high speeds, jet propulsion is essential. The first jet engine was designed and built by Sir Frank WHITTLE (1937), but the first jet-engine aircraft to fly was German (Aug. 1939). Jet engines are INTERNAL-COMBUSTION ENGINES. The **turbojet** is the commonest form. Air enters the inlet diffuser and is compressed in the air compressor, a multistage device having sets of rapidly rotating fan blades. It then enters the combustion chamber, where the fuel (a kerosine/gasoline mixture) is injected and ignited, and the hot, expanding exhaust gases pass through a TURBINE that drives the compressor and engine accessories. The gases, sometimes heated further in an AFTERBURNER, are expelled through the jet nozzle to provide the thrust. The nozzle converges for subsonic flight, but for supersonic flight one that converges and then diverges is needed. The fanjet or turbofan engine uses some of the turbine power to drive a propeller fan in a cowling, for more efficient subsonic propulsion; the **turboprop**, similar in principle, gains its thrust chiefly from the propeller.

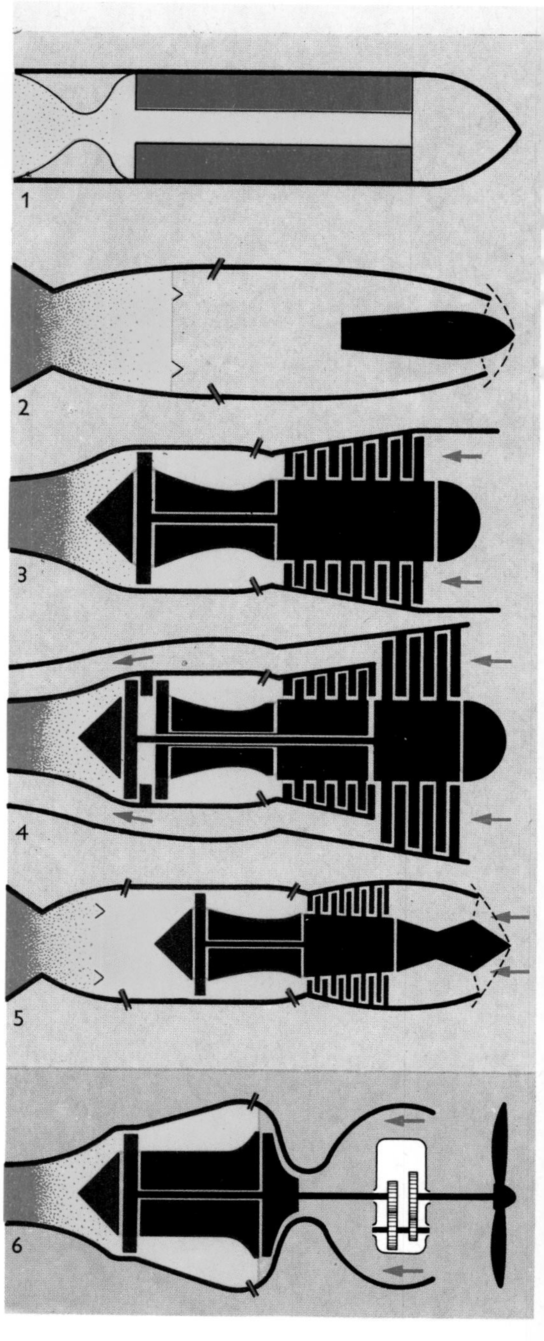

The rocket (1) uses the principle of jet propulsion, but carries its own oxygen. In a ramjet (2), the velocity of the incoming air is reduced, causing its pressure to increase. Fuel is then burned in the compressed air and the subsequent explosion of hot gases creates thrust. A turbojet (3) employs a compressor to force air into the combustor. The compressor is driven by a turbine which is set in motion by the gas flow. In a turbofan or bypass turbojet (4), part of the incoming air bypasses the combustor and is mixed with exhaust gases, improving thrust and reducing engine noise. A turbojet with afterburner (5) accelerates the exhaust gases by mixing them with additional fuel. In the turboprop or propjet (6) the compressor-turbine shaft is extended in front of the engine and fitted with a conventional propeller.

The **ramjet** is the simplest air-breathing jet engine, having neither compressor nor turbine. When accelerated to supersonic speeds by an auxiliary rocket or turbojet engine, the inlet diffuser "rams" the air and compresses it; after combustion the exhaust gases are expelled directly. Ramjets are used chiefly in guided missiles.

JETSAM. See FLOTSAM, JETSAM AND LAGAN.

JET STREAM, a narrow band of very fast E-flowing winds, stronger in winter than in summer, found around the level of the tropopause (see ATMOSPHERE). Speeds average about 60km/h in summer, about 125km/h in winter, though over 300km/h has been recorded. (See also METEOROLOGY; WIND.)

JETTY. See BREAKWATER.

JEVONS, William Stanley (1835–1882), English economist and logician. In 1862 he introduced the marginal utility theory of value, stating that value was determined by utility. His most famous work was *Theory of Political Economy* (1871).

JEWEL CAVE NATIONAL MONUMENT, series of small subterranean chambers, located in SW S.D., which are lined with jewel-like calcite crystals. The caves cover about 1275 acres. The monument was established in 1908.

JEWELS. See GEMS.

JEWELWEEDS, many species of the genus *Impatiens*, but principally *Impatiens biflora* and *I. pallida* which are found in moist, shady habitats in North America. Flowers are orange-yellow or yellow, flecked with brown or red. Family: Balsaminaceae.

JEWETT, Sarah Orne (1849–1909), US novelist and writer of realistic short-stories based on small-town life in upper New England. Her best-known work is *The Country of the Pointed Firs* (1896).

JEWISH AGENCY, international Zionist organization founded in 1929 by Chaim WEIZMANN to help Jewish immigrants settle in Palestine. After WWII it represented the Jewish cause in the negotiations for the foundation of Israel.

JEWISH AUTONOMOUS OBLAST. See BIROBDZHAN.

The Rabbi is traditionally the central figure in the Jewish community; this picture by Chagall shows him holding the Torah scrolls, the Jewish holy scriptures, embossed with the Star of David, an emblem of the faith and a symbol of great mystical significance.

JEWS, a people who share common racial origins, history and culture and who date from at least 1500 BC. It is nevertheless very difficult to define what constitutes Jewishness. In Israel there are Jews from many origins and races, but most Jews in Israel are not observant or practicing religious Jews.

According to the Old Testament the history of the Jewish people begins with ABRAHAM, who led his family from Mesopotamia to Canaan. The Egyptians reduced the Israelites to captivity, until MOSES led his people into the wilderness of Sinai. After 40 years of wandering the tribes reached and conquered Canaan. External threats forced the 12 tribes to unite under SAUL, whose successor, King DAVID, brought peace and prosperity to the country. Under the rule of David's grandson, JEROBOAM, however, the northern 10 tribes seceded to form the kingdom of Israel. Israel was defeated in 721 BC by the Assyrians and these tribes lost their identity in captivity. The southern kingdom, Judah, was defeated by the Babylonians in 586 BC and the people were sent into exile in Babylon, where they later introduced the SYNAGOGUE as a place of study and prayer. Babylon was conquered by the Persian CYRUS THE GREAT in 538 BC; he allowed the Jews to return to Judah. Their later conquest by ALEXANDER THE GREAT meant a gradual imposition of Greek culture, until a rebellion under JUDAS MACCABAEUS in 165 BC led to the foundation of the HASMONEAN dynasty. The religious strife and disagreement between the SADDUCEES, PHARISEES and such sects as the ESSENES brought about Roman intervention in 53 BC when POMPEY's legions entered Jerusalem and Palestine became a Roman province. In c33 AD Jesus was executed because he was regarded as a threat to the security of the Roman rule. A Jewish revolt in 66 led to the destruction of Jerusalem by the Romans; after a further revolt in 131 led by BAR COCHBA the Jewish state was completely crushed by the Romans, Judah was renamed Syria Palestina, and Jews were forbidden to enter Jerusalem. Fearing the loss of their religion, Jewish scholars and rabbis codified the oral law into the MISHNAH and the TALMUD.

Many Jews moved to Western Europe and their culture flourished, particularly in Spain. However the CRUSADES led to widespread suppression of the Jews and throughout Western Europe there were laws confining them to GHETTOS, excluding them from most trades and professions other than that of money-lending, and barring them from owning land. From the end of the 13th century they were in turn banished from England, France and from Spain where they were persecuted by the INQUISITION. By the end of the Middle Ages only small parts of Germany and Italy still allowed Jews within their borders. Many of the exiles perished; some of the descendants of the Spanish Jews, the SEPHARDIM, settled in the Ottoman Empire, while others, the MARRANOS, reestablished Jewish communities in England, France and the Netherlands in the 17th century. In 1654, twenty-three Dutch Jews founded the first Jewish congregation at New Amsterdam (New York). The descendants of German Jews, the ASHKENAZIM, took refuge in E Europe, in Poland and Lithuania, but many found themselves trapped in ghettos and persecuted by the Russians. Some adopted HASIDISM, a form of religious mysticism.

In Western Europe tolerance for the Jews increased after the French Revolution, and Jewish communities grew. Nevertheless there was considerable opposition to the Jewish race and religion, as manifested by the DREYFUS AFFAIR in France. Between 1880 and 1922 harsh conditions in E Europe and the Russian POGROMS brought about both a massive Jewish emigration from E Europe, especially to the US, and the modern movement of ZIONISM led by Theodore HERZL and Chaim WEIZMANN who hoped to reestablish a state of Jewry in Palestine. In Palestine most new Jewish immigrants from Europe settled on the land. The 1917 BALFOUR DECLARATION guaranteed "a national home for the Jewish people" in Palestine but increasing Jewish settlement aroused the hostility of the Arab inhabitants whose own national aspirations were beginning to awaken.

From the 1930s NAZISM brought virulent ANTI-SEMITISM in Germany and before the outbreak of WWII the Nazis were systematically murdering European Jews, and by 1945 they had exterminated over six million. Many Jews moved to Palestine after the war and world reaction to the WWII catastrophes led to the establishment of the state of ISRAEL in 1948. Its presence, however, has resulted in continuous hostility and warfare between Israel and other Arab countries. (See ARAB-ISRAELI WARS.) The majority of Jews now live in Israel, in the US, and in Russia where their cultural and religious life is seriously restricted.

JEW'S HARP, small musical instrument. The mouth cavity acts as a sound-box for a vibrating metal strip attached to a metal frame which is held between the teeth.

JEZEBEL, Phoenician princess, wife of King AHAB of Israel, notorious in the Old Testament for introducing the worship of BAAL into Palestine and for murdering many of JEHOVAH's prophets. She was opposed by the prophet ELIJAH and murdered by JEHU. Her name denotes a wicked woman or harlot.

JHELUM RIVER, river in India and Pakistan, a major source of irrigation for the Punjab, particularly at the Mangla Dam which provides hydroelectric power. It is about 450mi long.

JIDDA, seaport in Saudi Arabia on the Red Sea, 46mi W of Mecca, for which it is the chief port. It was Turkish until taken by the British in 1916, and then part of HEJAZ until 1925. Pop 194 000.

JIG, lively dance of English origin popular throughout the British Isles, particularly in Ireland, from the 16th-century. In France it became the stately *gigue*; the form was used by such composers as J. S. BACH and HANDEL.

JIGGER. See CHIGGER.

JIHAD, a religious duty imposed upon the Muslims in order to extend ISLAM, synonymous with holy war. It once meant a physical struggle, but is now considered a purely spiritual one.

JIM CROW, name for a system of laws and customs in the Southern US to segregate Negroes from white society. The name comes from a minstrel song. The laws dated from the 1880s and applied to schools, transportation, theaters and parks. After the mid-1950s Supreme Court rulings overturned the legislation. (See CIVIL RIGHTS AND LIBERTIES; INTEGRATION.)

JIMÉNEZ, Juan Ramón (1881–1958), major Spanish poet. At first influenced by SYMBOLISM, in *Diary of a Poet and the Sea* (1917) he developed a free, direct style of his own, *poesía desnuda* (Spanish: naked poetry). After the Spanish Civil War he moved to Puerto Rico. He received the Nobel Prize for Literature in 1956.

JIMÉNEZ, Marcos Pérez. See PÉREZ-JIMÉNEZ, Marcos.

JIMÉNEZ DE QUESADA, Gonzalo (c1500–1579), Spanish conquistador who claimed the Colombia area for Spain as New Granada. He settled there, doing much to improve the colonists' lot. He led a disastrous expedition in search of ELDORADO 1569–71.

JIMSON WEED, or thorn apple, *Datura stramonium*, poisonous annual plant common in warm-temperate regions. It yields an ALKALOID poison called HYOSCYOMINE, which is a major source of ATROPINE.

JINGOISM, attitude of blustering patriotic belligerence, derived from the expression "By jingo!" in a popular song urging British intervention in the 1878 Russo–Turkish War.

JINNAH, Mahomed Ali (1876–1948), Indian Muslim lawyer and statesman, founder of Pakistan. At first a member of the Indian CONGRESS PARTY, he resigned in 1921 because of its Hindus bias. From 1934 head of the MUSLIM LEAGUE, he campaigned for Muslim rights in an independent state, and in 1947 became Pakistan's first head of state.

JINNI. See GENIE.

JIVARO, Indian tribe in E Ecuador, notorious for their practice of shrinking heads taken as battle trophies. Warlike and proudly independent, they live by hunting and growing forest crops. Around 20 000 survive today.

JOAN OF ARC, Saint (c1412–1431), French heroine of the HUNDRED YEARS' WAR, a peasant girl from Domrémy, Lorraine, who heard "voices" telling her to liberate France from the English. Given command of a small force by the Dauphin Charles, she inspired it to victory at Orléans and in the surrounding region in 1429. She stood beside the Dauphin when he was crowned Charles VII that year, but failed to relieve

When Joan of Arc was tried in 1429 the clerk who recorded the trial sketched her in the margin of the transcription of the "Conseil du Parlement."

besieged Paris because he denied her adequate forces. Captured at Compiègne (1430), she was tried for heresy by French clerics who sympathized with the English, and burnt at the stake. The verdict was reversed in 1456 and she was canonized in 1920.

JOAN, THE FAIR MAID OF KENT (1328–1385), granddaughter of Edward I, became by her second husband, Edward the Black Prince, mother of Richard II. In 1378 she intervened on behalf of John WYCLIF.

JOÃO PESSOA, port city in NE Brazil, capital of Paraiba state on the Paraiba R. An industrial center, it ships cotton, sugar and minerals. Pop 197 398.

JOB, 18th book of the OLD TESTAMENT. It seeks to show that suffering need not be God's penalty for sin. God permits Satan to torment the virtuous Job with the loss of family, wealth and health. Finding small comfort in wife and friends, Job is bitterly questioning but remains faithful, and is restored to good fortune in old age.

JOB'S-TEARS, *Coix lacryma-jobi*, tall grass native to tropical Asia. The hard, shining seeds are used as beads, may be ground into flour or made into a tea. The foliage is used as livestock feed. Family: Graminae.

JOCASTA. See OEDIPUS.

JODHPUR, walled city in Rajasthan state, NW India. A former princely capital, its fortress and palaces are now museums. A textile center, it has electrical and other industries. Pop 318 894.

JODL, Alfred (1890–1946), German soldier, chief of operations staff in WWII. He signed the surrender at Rheims, May 7, 1945. Convicted of war crimes at the NUREMBERG TRIALS, he was executed.

JODRELL BANK EXPERIMENTAL STATION, England, radio astronomy observatory pioneered by Alfred Charles Bernard Lovell (1913–), and including one of the largest steerable RADIO TELESCOPES ("dish" 250ft (76.2m) across) (1957).

JOEL, second book of the Minor Prophets in the OLD TESTAMENT. Messianic in nature, it forecasts the Day of the Lord in apocalyptic terms. Its prophecy of the outpouring of the Spirit upon all flesh is regarded by the Christian Church as fulfilled at PENTECOST.

JOFFRE, Joseph-Jacques-Césaire (1852–1931), commander-in-chief of the French army 1914–16. He underestimated German power at the start of WWI, but shared with GALLIENI credit for the victory on the MARNE. After the mismanagement of VERDUN he resigned, but was immediately made a marshal of France.

JOFFREY, Robert (1930–), US dancer and choreographer. He founded the American Ballet Center and the Robert Joffrey Ballet 1953–54, and in 1965 the City Center Joffrey Ballet in New York.

JOGJAKARTA, city in S Jawa, capital of Indonesia 1945–50. A traditional cultural and religious center, it is a commercial, administrative and tourist center also. Pop 342 267.

JOGUES, Saint Isaac (1607–1646), French Jesuit missionary to the Huron Indians of Quebec. Sent to negotiate with the Mohawks, he was accused of witchcraft and killed. Canonized in 1930, his feast day, Sept. 26, is shared with other American martyrs.

JOHANN BEN ZAKKAI, Jewish PHARISEE who, after the destruction of the Temple by Rome in 70 AD, founded the academy at JAMNIA (Yibna), thus ensuring the survival of Judaism.

JOHANNESBURG, city in South Africa, one of the largest in Africa and the country's economic center. It was founded in 1886 as a gold-mining camp; its economy still rests on gold and diamonds, but there is also a wide range of industries. It is the site of Witwatersrand University. Pop 654 682.

JOHN, Saint (called the Evangelist or the Divine), son of Zebedee and brother of James, is usually thought to be the author of three New Testament Epistles and possibly the fourth GOSPEL.

JOHN, Saint (d. c30 AD), called John the Baptist, the preacher who proclaimed the coming of Christ and urged repentance, baptizing his followers in the Jordan R. He denounced HEROD Antipas for marrying Herodias, wife of Herod's brother, and was beheaded at her instigation. (See also SALOME.)

JOHN, name of 22 popes and 2 antipopes. **Saint John I** (d. 526) pope from 523, was sent to Constantinople by THEODORIC to win toleration for ARIANISM from the emperor; Theodoric imprisoned him when he failed. **John II** (d. 535) reigned from 533. **John III** (d. 574) reigned from 561. **John IV** (d. 642) reigned from 640. **John V** (d. 686) reigned from 685. **John VI** (d. 705) reigned from 701. **John VII** (d. 707) reigned from 705. **John VIII** (d. 882) reigned from 872. He sought political power for the papacy, intervening, with mixed success, in the rivalries of the CAROLINGIAN imperial house and excommunicating his opponent FORMOSUS. In 877 he had to bribe SARACEN raiders to spare Rome. He resolved a dispute with the Eastern Church by recognizing PHOTIUS as patriarch of Constantinople in 879. He was assassinated by a household conspiracy. **John IX** (d. 900) reigned from 898. **John X** (d. 928) reigned from 914. His army defeated the Saracens in 915. He was assassinated by order of the senatrix Marozia. **John XI** (c910–936) reigned from 931. A figurehead for his mother Marozia, he was imprisoned when she was deposed by her other son Alberic II of Spoleto. **John XII** (c937–964), Alberic's son, reigned from 955. Dissolute and corrupt, he crowned OTTO I emperor in 962. In 963 he clashed with Otto, and was deposed. **John XIII** (d. 972) reigned from 965. A good and pious man, he was protected by OTTO II. **John XIV** (d. 984) was appointed by Otto II in 983, but was deposed and murdered by the antipope BONIFACE VII when Otto died. **John XV** (d. 996) reigned from 985. He was a corrupt appointee of the Crescentius family. **John XVI** (d. 1013) an antipope, reigned 997–98. An ally of the Crescentii, he was deposed, blinded and imprisoned by OTTO III. **John XVII** (d. 1003) reigned for five months in 1003. **John XVIII** (d. 1009) reigned from 1003, like his predecessors a puppet of the Crescentii. **John XIX** (d. 1032) reigned from 1024. He was a layman until consecrated. There appears to have been no **John XX**; this may have been a purely chronological error or may reflect some forgotten pope or antipope. **John XXI** (c1215–1277) reigned from 1276. A Portuguese, he was a notable scholar, author of treatises on logic, medicine and the soul. He was killed by a collapsing ceiling at Viterbo. **John XXII** (c1249–1334) reigned from 1316. The second pope at Avignon, he filled the college with French cardinals. A skilful administrator, he lost popularity for his persecution of the Spiritual FRANCISCANS, who sought to observe a strict rule of evangelical poverty. He contested the election of Emperor LOUIS IV; Louis attempted to have him declared a heretic, but John imprisoned the antipope Louis appointed, NICHOLAS V. **John XXIII** was first taken as a name by Baldassare Cossa (d. 1419) schismatic antipope 1410–15. He promoted the council of PISA (1408) to end the Great SCHISM. Elected pope by the Pisa cardinals, he defended Rome against his rival GREGORY XII. Prompted by Emperor Sigismund, he convened the Council of CONSTANCE. At this he agreed to abdicate if his two rivals did, but reneged; the Council deposed all three. Cossa was made a cardinal-bishop in 1419. The name **John XXIII** was therefore taken by Angelo Giuseppe Roncalli (1881–1963), who reigned from 1958. Of peasant stock, he was an army chaplain in WWI. He was made a titular archbishop in the Vatican diplomatic corps 1925–35 and nuncio 1925–53, serving in Turkey, the Balkans and France; in this post he won great popularity. Made cardinal in 1953, he was elected pope, in 1958. He revolutionized the Church, promoting cooperation with other Christian churches and other religions in the face of world problems; the encyclicals *Mater et Magister* (1961) advocated social reform in underdeveloped areas of the world. In 1962 he called the influential Second VATICAN COUNCIL.

JOHN, name of eight Byzantine emperors. **John I Tzimisces** (c925–976), reigned from 969, when he overthrew Nicephorus II. He subdued the Balkans in 971; he died after a successful domination of Syria 969–75. **John II Comenus** (1088–1143), reigned from 1118. An austere and efficient ruler-soldier, he checked the expansionist Norman king of Sicily and won victories in the Balkans and against the Turks and Armenians in Anatolia. He died while campaigning against Antioch. **John III** (1193–1254) reigned in Nicaea from 1222. **John IV** (1250–1261?) reigned as a minor in Nicaea. **John V Palaeologus** (1332–1391) reigned from 1341. **John VI Cantacuzenus** (1292–1383) reigned 1347–54. **John VII Palaeologus** (1360–1410?) reigned briefly in 1390. **John VIII Palaeologus** (1392–1448), reigned from 1425 over the last fragments of the BYZANTINE EMPIRE, making desperate appeals for Western help against the Turks; these were not answered.

JOHN, name of two kings of Castile and León. **John I** (1358–1390), king from 1379, resisted JOHN OF GAUNT's claims to Castile. His attempt to annex Portugal was defeated at ALJUBARROTA (1385). **John II** (1405–1454), king from 1406, reigned from 1419.

JOHN (1167–1216), king of England from 1199. Youngest son of HENRY II, he succeeded his brother Richard I. John refused to accept a papal nominee as archbishop of Canterbury, and so was excommunicated in 1209; he faced invasion by Philip II of France, to whom he had lost England's French possessions. Expensive military provisions had alienated the barons, already curbed by Henry II; in 1215 they rose in revolt and forced John to sign the MAGNA CARTA, confirming their feudal rights. John later repudiated it and waged a new war against the barons, who summoned French support. John died while the issue was still in doubt.

JOHN, name of two kings of France. **John I the Posthumous** (c1316) lived only five days, being succeeded by his uncle Philip IV. **John II the Good** (1319–1364), reigned from 1350. Inept and unpopular, he was captured by the English at POITIERS (1356) and released for ransom and hostages in 1360. When a hostage escaped John honorably returned to captivity until his death.

JOHN, name of two kings of Hungary. **John I Zapolya** (1487–1540), reigned from 1526. Governor of Transylvania 1511–26, he failed to assist King Louis II at the battle of MOHACS; Louis was killed and John succeeded him. In 1529 John recognized Turkish overlordship for support against his rival Ferdinand. **John II** (1540–71), son of John I, reigned 1540–62. In John's infancy the Turks occupied his capital, Buda (1541). Their treaty with Austria (1562) divided HUNGARY into three, leaving John prince of Transylvania.

JOHN, name of three kings of Poland. **John I Albert** (1459–1501), reigned from 1492. **John II Casimir** (1609–1672), reigned 1648–68, a period known as "the Deluge" in which much territory was lost to Sweden, Khotin, Prussia and Russia. **John III Sobieski** (1629–1696), reigned from 1674. His defeat of the Turkish army at Khotin (1673) showed him to be a brilliant soldier, likely to recover much of

Poland's territory. In 1683 he drove away the Turkish army that was besieging Vienna and threatening W Europe, but his further campaigns 1684–91 were inconclusive.

JOHN, name of six kings of Portugal. **John I the Great** (1357–1433), reigned from 1385. Illegitimate son of Pedro I, he was elected king after a popular revolt. He assured Portuguese independence with the great victory over the Castilians at ALJUBAROTTA. **John II the Perfect** (1455–1495) reigned from 1481. A cultured and astute Renaissance ruler, he subdued the nobility. A patron of explorers such as Bartholomew DIAZ, he refused aid to COLUMBUS. By the treaty of TORDESILLAS (1494) he and Spain divided the non-Christian world between themselves. **John III** (1502–1557) "the Fortunate" reigned from 1521, at the height of the empire. In 1536 he established the Inquisition in Portugal. **John IV** (1604–56), reigned from 1640. Duke of Braganza, he was put on to the throne by the revolution that deposed Philip IV. His daughter married Charles II of England (1662). **John V the Magnanimous** (1689–1750), reigned from 1706. **John VI** (1769–1826), regent from 1799 for his mother, reigned from 1816. In 1807 he and the royal family fled to Brazil before NAPOLEON's invasion, returning only in 1821. In 1825 John recognized BRAZIL's independence.

JOHN, Augustus Edwin (1878–1961), leading British painter, famous for his portraits of contemporary celebrities such as George Bernard SHAW, Dylan THOMAS and James JOYCE. He is noted for his vigorous use of rich color and his excellent draughtsmanship.

JOHN, Epistles of, three NEW TESTAMENT epistles ascribed to St. John the Apostle. The first and longest seeks to strengthen Christians by giving the signs of the faith; the second attacks gnostic denials of Christ's incarnation; the third urges an obstinate church leader to receive genuine missionaries.

JOHN, Gospel of, the fourth GOSPEL in the New Testament, written c100 AD and traditionally ascribed to St. John the Apostle. Based on a series of long discourses by Jesus, it has little in common with the SYNOPTIC GOSPELS; it emphasizes Jesus' deity, and is spiritual and theological in tone. (See also LOGOS.)

JOHN BIRCH SOCIETY, US organization founded in 1958 by businessman Robert Welch. Named for a US officer murdered by the communist Chinese in 1945, it seeks to combat the spread of communist influence in the US, urging abandonment of welfare legislation and withdrawal from the UN.

JOHN BOSCO, Saint. See BOSCO, SAINT JOHN.

JOHN BULL, personification, favorable or otherwise, of the typical Englishman, usually portrayed as a burly good-natured farmer or tradesman wearing a Union Jack waistcoat. The name derives from a satire by John ARBUTHNOT.

JOHN CAPISTRAN, Saint. See CAPISTRANO, SAINT GIOVANNI DI.

JOHN CHRYSOSTOM, Saint. See CHRYSOSTOM, SAINT JOHN.

JOHN DORY, *Zeus faber*, an oval compressed fish found in temperate oceans. The rays of the anterior dorsal fin are elongated into filaments and the jaws are protrusible. John dories occur at moderate depths and feed on herrings, pilchards and sand-eels.

JOHN HENRY. See HENRY, JOHN.

JOHNNY APPLESEED. See APPLESEED, JOHNNY.

JOHN OF AUSTRIA (1547–1578), Spanish military commander, illegitimate son of Emperor Charles V. Noted for his skill and gallantry, he commanded the Christian fleet at LEPANTO (1571) and conquered Tunis (1573). Governor-general of the Spanish Netherlands 1576–78, he fought the rebellion of WILLIAM THE SILENT.

JOHN OF DAMASCUS, Saint (c675–749), Orthodox Syrian theological writer and antagonist of ICONOCLASM. He resigned an inherited post under the Saracen caliph to become a monk.

JOHN OF GAUNT (1340–1399), fourth son of Edward III, became duke of Lancaster in 1362. Born at Ghent (hence "Gaunt"), he was a commander in France 1367–74, during the HUNDRED YEARS' WAR. From 1371 he ruled England for his senile father and young nephew RICHARD II; his economic policies and alliance with John WYCLIF made him unpopular in many quarters, as did his unsuccessful campaigns to claim the Castilian throne 1369–73. His eldest son became HENRY IV.

JOHN OF GOD, Saint (1495–1550), Portuguese founder of the order of Brothers Hospitallers. A former soldier, he was converted to religion by John of Avila; he founded the order's first hospital in 1537.

JOHN OF LANCASTER (1389–1435), duke of Bedford, brother of Henry V. As his regent John ruled Normandy, driving back the French king Charles VII until 1429, when JOAN OF ARC appeared, and 1433, when his ally Philip of Burgundy defected.

JOHN OF LEIDEN, or Jan Beuckelzoon (1509–1536), Dutch innkeeper who became leader of the ANABAPTISTS in Münster and in 1534 set up a brutally corrupt theocracy, the "Kingdom of Zion" with himself as king, in which private ownership was abolished. In 1535 the bishop of Münster crushed the revolt; John was tortured and executed.

JOHN OF NEPOMUK, Saint (d. 1393), patron saint of the Czechs. He was tortured and later murdered by King Wenceslas IV for opposing his intervention in church affairs.

JOHN OF SALISBURY (c1110–1180), English churchman and leading SCHOLASTIC philosopher. Friend and secretary to Archbishop Thomas à Becket he shared his exile 1163–70. John, who studied under Peter ABELARD, was a principal theorist of REALISM.

JOHN OF THE CROSS, Saint (1542–1591), Spanish poet and mystic, founder of a reformed Carmelite order. Influenced by St. TERESA OF AVILA, he is remembered for poems such as *The Dark Night of the Soul*. Canonized in 1726, he was made a CHURCH DOCTOR in 1926.

JOHNS, Jasper (1930–), US painter, a leading exponent of POP ART in such works as *Flag* (1958), a copy of the US flag, and *Painted Bronze* (1960) two cast beer cans.

Andrew JOHNSON

17th US President

Born: December 29, 1808 **Died:** July 31, 1875
Term of office: April 15, 1865–March 3, 1869
Political party: Democratic (elected on the "National Union" ticket with Republican Abraham Lincoln)

JOHNSON, Andrew (1808–1875), 17th President of the US. He was born in Raleigh, N.C., of a poor family and at 10 apprenticed to a tailor. In 1826 he moved to Greenville, Tenn., where in 1827 he married Eliza McCardle; she taught him writing and arithmetic. He took an active part in public life, and after becoming mayor was elected to the Tenn. House of Representatives and then the state Senate. A Democrat, he served 10 years as a US congressman. Governor of Tenn. 1853–57, he was then elected to the Senate. Though supporting some measures by the pro-slavery South he introduced a HOMESTEADING bill which was opposed by slave owners and most Southern congressmen. After Lincoln became president in 1860, Tenn. seceded; Johnson, the only Southern senator not to join the Confederate cause, was made military governor of Tenn., establishing a working basis for civilian rule. In 1865 he was elected vice-president, but six weeks later became president when Lincoln was assassinated. He inherited the problems of RECONSTRUCTION. On May 29, 1865, with Congress adjourned, he issued a proclamation of amnesty, allowing Southern states the right to adopt new constitutions and elect governments. His policy offended radical Republicans because it threatened their absolute control of Congress and robbed them of the chance of holding office in the South. In a mid-term election characterized by a vicious and emotive campaign by Johnson's opponents, they were returned with a two-thirds majority. On March 2, 1867 the first radical reconstruction act was passed. To further restrict Johnson Congress passed, over his veto, the Tenure of Office Act, forbidding the dismissal of certain federal officeholders. Despite this he dismissed the secretary of war, Edwin Stanton, and in March 1868 Johnson was impeached. The vindictiveness of the radical attack won him sympathy and he escaped conviction by one vote. He failed to capture the Democratic nomination, and attempts to reenter Congress failed until he was elected senator from Tenn. in 1874. He served a short session in 1875 and died of a stroke soon after.

JOHNSON, Charles Spurgeon (1893–1956), US Negro educator, sociologist and first black president of Fisk University, Tenn. (1946–56). After research work for race relations organizations he helped reorganize the Japanese educational system after WWII and was US delegate to UNESCO.

JOHNSON, Hiram Warren (1866–1945), US statesman. As a prosecuting attorney in San Francisco he successfully prosecuted corrupt political bosses (1908); he became governor of Cal. 1911–17. A senator from 1917, he was a hard-line isolationist, opposing US membership of the League of Nations and any war preparations.

JOHNSON, Hugh Samuel (1882–1942), US army officer and administrator. In WWI he developed and administered the selective draft system. He was administrator of the NATIONAL RECOVERY ADMINISTRATION 1933–34.

JOHNSON, Jack (1878–1946), US boxer, in 1908 first Negro to win the world heavyweight championship. Unpopular with the white boxing world, he jumped bail on serious charges and fled abroad (1912). He lost the title to Jess Willard in Havana in 1915.

JOHNSON, James Weldon (1871–1938), US black poet and statesman. US consul in Venezuela and Nicaragua (1906–12) and secretary of the NATIONAL ASSOCIATION FOR THE ADVANCEMENT OF COLORED PEOPLE 1916–30. He wrote *God's Trombones* (1927), a collection of verse sermons and edited *The Book of American Negro Poetry* (1922).

JOHNSON, John Harold (1918–), leading US Negro publisher of the popular Negro magazines *Ebony*, *Tan*, *Jet* and *Black World* and many books. He is also president of the major black-run insurance company, and has served on many government committees.

JOHNSON, John Rosamond (1873–1954), US Negro composer and singer. He wrote the music for *Lift Every Voice and Sing* to words by his brother James Weldon JOHNSON.

JOHNSON, Lyndon Baines (1908–1973), 36th President of the US. He became chief executive on Nov. 22, 1963, after the assassination of John F. KENNEDY.

Johnson was born on a farm near Stonewall, SW Tex., of a prominent local family. He did not go to college until 1927, and taught after graduating in 1930. In 1931 he became secretary to the Republican congressman Richard Kleberg. In 1934 he married Claudia Alta Taylor, nicknamed "Lady Bird." He was Texan administrator of the NEW DEAL National Youth Administration 1935–37, and was elected to

Lyndon Baines JOHNSON
36th US President

Born: August 27, 1908
Died: January 22, 1973
Term of Office: November 22, 1963–January 20, 1969
Political Party: Democratic

Congress as a Democratic New Deal supporter 1937–48, with a period of naval service 1941–42; he served on the House Naval and later Armed Services Committees. Elected to the Senate in 1948, he became the youngest majority leader in its history when the Democrats regained control in 1954. He used his influence and mastery of procedure to secure a unanimous Democratic condemnation of Senator J. R. McCARTHY and passage of important CIVIL RIGHTS bills. After losing the presidential nomination in 1960 Johnson became vice-president under John F. Kennedy, despite prior disagreements. He influenced committee decisions on space projects and civil rights and traveled abroad as a kind of roving ambassador, but remained in the background politically.

After Kennedy's assassination Johnson quickly and capably assumed his presidential responsibilities. With the same cabinet and presidential staff he implemented the faltering Kennedy tax reform and civil rights programs, as well as a massive anti-poverty program of his own. Winning a landslide victory in 1964, with Hubert HUMPHREY as vice-president, Johnson pushed through extensive liberal legislation to build the "Great Society," including the MEDICARE PROGRAM and the Voting Rights Act. He equally vigorously extended Kennedy's policy of US involvement in the VIETNAM WAR, despite mounting hostility from sections of the public. Campus demonstrations and general civil unrest caused three years of turbulence rarely equalled in US history. On Mar. 31 1968, Johnson announced that he would neither seek nor accept renomination, and retired to his home in Tex., where early in 1973 he suffered a fatal heart attack.

JOHNSON, Philip Cortelyou (1906–), US architect, a major exponent of the INTERNATIONAL STYLE. His "Glass House" (1949) at New Canaan, Conn., won him international recognition. In the 1950s he worked with MIES VAN DER ROHE on the Seagram Building, New York. His later work has become less severely functional.

JOHNSON, Reverdy (1796–1876), US statesman and lawyer, senator from Md., 1845–49 and 1863–68, attorney-general 1849–50 and minister to the UK 1868–69. An opponent of slavery, he helped keep Md. from seceding in the Civil War; in 1857, however, he was defense counsel in the DRED SCOTT CASE.

JOHNSON, Richard Mentor (1780–1850), ninth US vice-president, in the Democratic administration of Martin VAN BUREN. Chosen by the Senate after a tied vote, he served until 1841, when growing unpopularity lost him the backing of the Democratic convention and the subsequent election.

JOHNSON, Samuel (1709–84), English man of letters, poet, critic, essayist and lexicographer. After failing as a schoolmaster he supported himself in London by journalism and hack writing. He published the poems *London* (1738) and *The Vanity of Human Wishes* (1749). From 1746 to 1755 he prepared his pioneering *Dictionary of the English Language* (1755), an idiosyncratic but brilliant work which won him a wide reputation. The satirical *Rasselas* (1759) was produced as a quick moneyspinner. In 1763 he met James BOSWELL, his biographer, who recorded much of Johnson's fiery but polished conversation. The critical works, particularly the edition of Shakespeare (1765) and *Lives of the Most Eminent English Poets* (1781) combine excellent writing and insight with often eccentric judgments.

JOHNSON, Thomas Loftin (1854–1911), US municipal reformer, an Indianapolis businessman who made a fortune from streetcar investments. Democratic congressman 1891–95, he advocated single tax and public ownership of public utilities. Mayor of Cleveland 1901–10, he introduced many reforms.

JOHNSON, Walter Perry (1887–1946), US baseball pitcher famous for his speed. With the Washington Senators 1907–27 he won 414 games and in 1913 pitched 56 consecutive scoreless innings. In 1936 he became the first player elected to the Baseball Hall of Fame.

JOHNSON, Sir William (1715–1774), British superintendent of Indian affairs in North America. His just and honest conduct kept the IROQUOIS tribes, into which he was adopted, on the British side in the FRENCH AND INDIAN WAR. He commanded the victorious colonial forces at the battle of Lake George.

JOHNSON CITY, industrial village in S N.Y., with Binghampton and Endicott one of the Triple Cities. Built up around a large footwear factory, it now has other heavy industry also. Pop 18 025.

JOHNSON CITY, city in Tenn. In an agricultural area, it is a hardwood center with iron foundries and other industries. Pop 33 770.

JOHNSON GRASS, *Sorghum halepense*, a subtropical grass cultivated as cattle feed in many areas of the world, but classified as a weed in the southern US. Family: Graminae.

JOHNSTON, industrial town of R.I., 5mi SW of Providence. It has granite quarries and manufactures metal goods and machinery. Pop 22 037.

JOHNSTON, Albert Sydney (1803–1862), brilliant Confederate general, secretary of war for the Texas Republic 1838–40. Confederate second-in-command, he was driven back by superior forces on the Mississippi-Allegheny front. His daring strategy almost won the battle of SHILOH, but he was mortally wounded in the first day's fighting.

JOHNSTON, Joseph Eggleston (1807–1901), Confederate general, credited with the victory at BULL RUN in 1861. Wounded at FAIR OAKS, he was replaced after a feud with Jefferson DAVIS in 1863; he returned to command in 1865 but had to surrender to SHERMAN after two months.

JOHNSTON ISLAND, lies in the central Pacific over 700mi SW of Honolulu. Named for its English discoverer, Captain C. J. Johnston (1807), it was annexed by the US for its guano deposits (1858). A naval base and nuclear testing site 1941–62, it is now a bird sanctuary.

JOHNSTOWN, manufacturing city in E N.Y., seat of Fulton Co. Settled by Scottish glovers c1760, it is still a glove-manufacturing center and has diverse industries. Pop 10 045.

JOHNSTOWN, industrial city in SW Penn., 76mi E of Pittsburgh on the Conemaugh R. In an iron ore region, its economy rests upon a massive iron and steel industry and on other heavy manufacturing. Often flooded, it was devastated by flood in 1889 and 1936. Pop 42 476.

JOINT, specialized surface between BONES allowing movement of one on the other. Major joints, especially of limbs, are **synovial joints** which are lined by synovial membrane and CARTILAGE and surrounded by a fibrous capsule; they contain SYNOVIAL FLUID, which lubricates the joint surfaces. Parts of the capsule (e.g., in the ankle) or overlying TENDONS (e.g., in the knee) form LIGAMENTS important in joint stability, though at some joints (e.g., the SHOULDER) resting activity in MUSCLES ensures stability, while in others (e.g., the hip) it is due to the shape of the bony surfaces. **Fibrous** and **cartilaginous joints** between bones are relatively fixed except under special circumstances (e.g., the widening of the symphysis pubis in PREGNANCY). Joint disease causes ARTHRITIS, with pain, limitation of movement and sometimes increase in fluid.

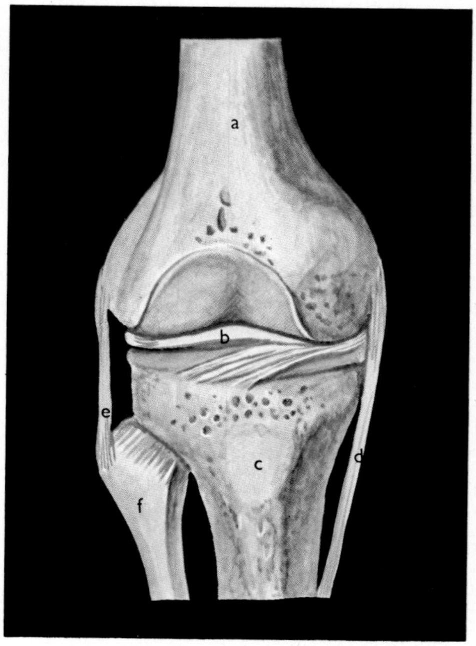

Posterior view of an exposed knee joint: (a) femur; (b) articulation surfaces and space of the joint; (c) tibia; (d) and (e) ligaments; (f) fibula.

JOINT CHIEFS OF STAFF, US committee of military advisers to the president, the NATIONAL SECURITY COUNCIL and the secretary of defense. Set up in 1942, its members are the Army, Navy and Air Force chiefs of staff and a chairman. The Marine Corps commandant may be called upon to assist.

JOINT STOCK COMPANY, form of business enterprise in which capital is divided into small shares; profits are divided in proportion to the number of shares held. The parties are severally liable for the company's debts. Misuses of this form led to the development of the statutory CORPORATION.

JOINT TENANCY, holding of real property by two or more persons where each has an equal interest in the whole. Each joint tenant has a right of ownership; when one dies the others own the whole estate, and the last survivor owns it entirely himself.

JOINTWORM, name given the larvae of certain North American WASPS. These larvae are a pest of the wheat stem.

JOINVILLE, Jean, sire de (c1224–1317), French soldier whose *Histoire de saint-Louis* (c1309) is a moving account of the Seventh CRUSADE, its leader Louis IX and the frank and amiable author. He refused to join Louis' fatal crusade to Tunis (1270).

JÓKAI, Mór (1825–1904), Hungarian novelist. His best known works are *Transylvania's Golden Age* (1882) and *A Hungarian Nabob* (1854). A leading political figure, he was a member of the national assembly from 1861 and was elected to the upper house in 1897.

JOLIET, city in Ill., seat of Will Co., an industrial center served by railroad and canal. Pop 80 373.

JOLIET, Louis (c1645–c1700), French-Canadian explorer who with Father MARQUETTE, led the first expedition down the Mississippi R. In 1672–73 they reached its confluence with the Arkansas R, but turned back when they found it led not to the Pacific but into the Spanish-held Gulf of Mexico.

JOLIETTE, city in Quebec, Canada. After 1935 it became a major tobacco center; it has many other industries including textile manufacture. Pop 20 127.

JOLIOT-CURIE, Irène (1897–1956), French physicist, the daughter of Pierre and Marie CURIE. She and her husband, **Jean Frédéric Joliot** (1900–1958), shared the 1935 Nobel Prize for Chemistry for their discovery of artificial RADIOACTIVITY. Both later played a major part in the formation of the French atomic energy commission but, because of their communism, were removed from positions of responsibility there (Frédéric 1950, Iréne 1951). Like her mother, Irène died from LEUKEMIA as a result of prolonged exposure to radioactive materials.

JOLSON, Al (1886–1950), Russian-born US singer, blackface comedian and songwriter, famous for sentimental songs such as *Mammy* and *Sonny Boy*. After various Broadway musicals and talking pictures he appeared in *The Jazz Singer* (1927), first full length talking picture.

JONAH, Book of, fifth book of the MINOR PROPHETS, unique in its entirely narrative form. Jonah is portrayed as so intolerant of Gentiles that he disobeys God's command to convert the city of Nineveh. Thwarted in the "great fish" episode, he obeys God but, still resentful, has the necessity of mercy demonstrated to him.

JONES, Alfred Ernest (1897–1958), British psychoanalyst who played a major role in gaining recognition for PSYCHOANALYSIS in Britain and North America.

JONES, Bobby (Robert Tyre Jones; 1902–1971), US amateur golfer, only man to have won both the US amateur and open championships—the "Grand Slam"—in the same year (1930).

JONES, Casey (John Luther Jones; 1863–1900), US railroad engineer and folk hero who drove the Cannon Ball express from Memphis, Tenn. to Canton, Miss. When it collided with a freight train on April 30, 1900, Jones stayed in the cab to apply the brakes. He was killed, but saved the passengers and crew.

JONES, David (1895–1975), English writer and artist. *In Parenthesis* (1937) is an evocation in prose and FREE VERSE of his WWI experiences. The religious poem *Anathemata* (1952), based on the Roman Catholic mass, is a mystical synthesis of mythical and historical elements.

JONES, Inigo (1573–1652), English architect who introduced the classical style to England. While staying in Italy he had been influenced by the works of PALLADIO. Surveyor of the King's Works 1615–44, his masterpieces include the Queen's House at Greenwich, Whitehall Banqueting Hall and St. Paul's Church, Covent Garden. His sets and costumes for court MASQUES greatly influenced subsequent stage design.

JONES, James (1921–), US novelist. His first book, *From Here to Eternity* (1951) portrayed the degradation of army life on the eve of WWII. Other works include *Some Came Running* (1957), *The Pistol* (1959) and *The Thin Red Line* (1962).

JONES, John Paul (1747–1792), US naval hero, born John Paul in Kirkudbrightshire, Scotland. Serving at first in British ships, he killed one of his crew (1773) and deserted to America. In the Revolution he joined the Continental navy, taking command of the *Alfred* in 1775, in 1776 the *Providence*, and in 1777 the *Ranger*. His successes against British Atlantic shipping won him command of the French-donated *Bon Homme Richard* (1779). After petty raiding around the Scottish and Irish coasts he attacked a convoy escorted by the British ship *Serapis*. In a fierce battle the *Richard* was irreparably damaged, but Jones refused to surrender with the famous words "I have not yet begun to fight!" He managed to capture the *Serapis* as the *Richard* sank. Service in the Russian navy 1788–89 left him physically and mentally broken, and he died in Paris.

JONES, LeRoi (1934–), US black author whose plays, especially *Dutchman* (1964), express the revulsion of a black man at white society. Active in black politics, he is now known as Imamu Baraka.

JONES, Samuel Milton "Golden Rule" (1846–1904), Welsh-born US businessman, an advocate of good management relations and a political reformer. Mayor of Toledo 1897–1904, he stood independently when political factions tried to remove him; he introduced many labor reforms for city employees.

JONESBORO, city in Ark., seat of Craighead Co. Formerly a lumbering center, its economy now rests on agricultural trading and diverse industries. Pop 27 050.

JONESBORO, Battle of, fought at Jonesboro, W Ga., S of Atlanta. A tactical victory for Union forces under Gen. SHERMAN, it opened their way to Atlanta.

JONGKIND, Johann Barthold (1819–1891), Dutch painter, a precursor of IMPRESSIONISM. Resident in France from 1846, he met COROT there and painted in Normandy with Boudin. His landscapes and seascapes continued the Dutch tradition with a new exploration of light and atmospheric effects, a major influence on MONET.

JONSON, Ben (1572–1637), English dramatist and lyric poet. He served in the Dutch wars in the 1590s, returning to London to act and write for the stage. *Every Man in his Humour* (1598) established him as a playwright. His tragedies *Sejanus* (1603) and *Catiline* (1611) are still admired, but it is the comedies that are most often performed, especially *Volpone* (1606) and *The Alchemist* (1610); both of these are sardonic depictions of human gullibility before the lure of gold. Under James I Jonson and Inigo JONES collaborated on masques for the court, but he fell from favor under Charles I.

JOPLIN, city in SW Mo. An industrial center, it is the shipping point for the surrounding agricultural area. Pop 39 256.

JOPLIN, Scott (1868–1917), US black composer who in lyrical and elegant pieces such as *Maple Leaf Rag* (1899) sought to establish RAGTIME as serious music. When ambitious ventures such as the opera *Treemonisha* (1911) failed, Joplin declined into mental illness. In the 1970s his works enjoyed a great revival.

JORDAENS, Jacob (1593–1678), Flemish baroque painter. Influenced by RUBENS, with whom he studied, he painted religious and allegorical scenes, genre works and portraits in a vigorous if occasionally crude style. Among his best-known works is *The King Drinks* (1638).

Official Name: The Hashemite Kingdom of Jordan
Capital: Amman
Area: 37 730sq mi
Population: 2 467 000
Languages: Arabic
Religions: Muslim (Sunni), Christian
Monetary Unit(s): 1 Jordanian dinar = 1000 fils

JORDAN, Arab HASHEMITE monarchy in the Middle East, bordered to the E by Saudi Arabia, the N by Syria and Iraq, and the W by Israel.

Land. Jordan is bisected by the GREAT RIFT VALLEY and the JORDAN R. The E region has 94% of the land area but under 50% of the population, being largely desert rising to greener highlands. In the SW is the capital, Amman, and the only port, Aqaba. The W area, known as the West Bank, is smaller but much more fertile, especially in the N. The climate ranges from Mediterranean in the highlands to subtropical in the Jordan valley; the desert is Saharan, with minimal rainfall.

People and Economy. The population is mainly Arab, but there is a wide cultural gulf between the nomadic BEDOUIN of the E region and the Palestinians (including some 600 000 refugees from Israel) of the West Bank. About 90% of the people are Sunni Muslims, the remainder Christians. Government is by two-chamber parliament and a premier responsible to the king, the effective ruler. Jordan's economy is largely agricultural; before the 1967 war with Israel tourism and light industry (mostly on the West Bank) were also important. Israeli occupation reduced Jordan to relying on aid from oil-rich Kuwait, Libya and Saudi Arabia.

History. In biblical times the West Bank was settled by the Israelites, the E region by their enemies the AMMONITES, MOAB and EDOM. This region later became the NABATEAN empire, its capital at PETRA. Later ruled by Rome and Byzantium, it was conquered by the Arabs in the 7th century. Part of the OTTOMAN EMPIRE from 1516 until the 20th century, it was liberated in WWI by British and Hashemite Arab forces (see FAISAL I.; LAWRENCE, T. E). In 1923 it was made into the British-supervised state of Transjordan, ruled by the Emir ABDULLAH. Its army, the Arab Legion, was trained by British officers led by Sir John GLUBB. In 1946 Transjordan won full self-government as Jordan, Abdullah becoming king; in 1948 the Arab Legion conquered the West Bank. In 1951 Abdullah, who had made a truce with Israel, was assassinated; his grandson HUSSEIN I became king in 1952. Jordan was often threatened by Egyptian policies until 1967, when a mutual defence agreement was signed. Jordan's subsequent involvement in the Six-Day War cost her the West Bank, occupied by Israel. In 1970 the growing power of the Palestine guerrillas in Jordan led to a short civil war in which they were defeated. In 1975 Hussein ceded control of the West Bank to the PALESTINE LIBERATION ORGANIZATION.

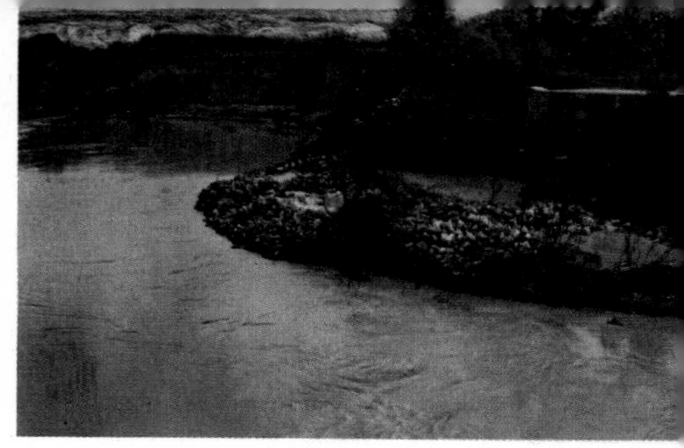

The Jordan River, the largest river in the Holy Land, has played a key role in the histories of many peoples for thousands of years. On this spot, according to tradition, St John the Baptist baptized Jesus.

JORDAN, David Starr (1851–1931), US naturalist and authority on fishes best known for his many books and for his pacifist activities.

JORDAN RIVER, starts from a confluence in the Hula basin and flows about 200mi S through the Sea of Galilee and the Ghor valley to the Dead Sea. Honored in the Christian, Muslim and Jewish religions, it formed the truce line between Israel and Jordan after 1967.

JORURI, in Japan a style of declamation to music, usually accompanying *bunraku* (puppet drama). It was elevated to a literary form in the 17th century by the dramatist Chikamatsu Monzaemon.

JOSEPH, Saint, husband of Mary, mother of Jesus. A carpenter, he was a descendant of David. Warned by God, he took Mary and the infant Jesus into Egypt to escape the wrath of Herod. He is honored as patron saint of the Roman Catholic Church.

JOSEPH, Jewish patriarch, favorite son of JACOB. His jealous brothers sold him into slavery in Egypt. There he won favor with Pharaoh by correctly interpreting premonitory dreams, and was eventually made chief minister. He forgave his brothers and rescued the family from famine.

JOSEPH, name of two Holy Roman Emperors. **Joseph I** (1678–1711), reigned from 1705, during the War of the SPANISH SUCCESSION and a Hungarian revolt led by Francis RAKOCZY. **Joseph II** (1741–1790), reigned from 1765, but until 1780 with his mother, MARIA THERESA. When she died he began to institute a massive social reform program on ENLIGHTENMENT principles, abolishing serfdom and attacking feudal class and property systems. His religious, administrative, and language reforms made him unpopular in

Austria and caused revolts abroad. His attempt at enlightened despotism was hindered by his tactless autocracy, and few of his reforms survived him.

JOSEPH, Father (François Leclerc de Tremblay; 1577–1638), called the "Grey Eminence," French Capuchin friar, agent of Cardinal RICHELIEU. A mystic who sought the reestablishment of Roman Catholicism in Europe, he was nevertheless a skillful negotiator employed on delicate diplomatic matters.

JOSEPH, Chief (c1840–1904), Nez Percé Indian chief. In 1877, faced with forcible resettlement under a basically fraudulent treaty, he led his people in a mass flight from their Oregon lands to Canada. The Nez Percé were defeated only 30mi from the frontier; Joseph won popular sympathy for his heroic and brilliant resistance.

JOSÉPHINE. See BEAUHARNAIS, JOSÉPHINE DE.

JOSEPH OF ARIMATHEA, Saint, rich Jew who gave Christ burial in his own tomb. Improbable legend makes him founder of the first English church at GLASTONBURY, where he is supposed to have traveled with the HOLY GRAIL.

JOSEPHSON, Brian David (1940–), British physicist awarded, with I. GIAEVER and L. ESAKI, the 1973 Nobel Prize for Physics for his discovery of the **Josephson Effect**, the passage of ELECTRICITY through an insulator between two superconductors (see SUPERCONDUCTIVITY). Pairs of ELECTRONS form in the superconductors and tunnel (see WAVE MECHANICS) through the insulating layer.

JOSEPHUS, Flavius (c37–100 AD), Jewish historian, governor of Galilee in the Roman–Jewish War of 66 AD. He later took Roman citizenship. His *History of the Jewish War* (c79 AD) and histories of the Jews are masterpieces of Jewish literature.

JOSHUA, sixth book of the OLD TESTAMENT. It describes the conquest of CANAAN by the Israelites under Joshua, associate of and successor to MOSES, and its division among the TWELVE TRIBES OF ISRAEL.

JOSHUA TREE, or tree yucca, *Yucca brevifolia*, a much-branched tree native to desert regions of the western US. It was so-named by the Mormons who believed its outstretched branches once directed them out of the Utah desert. Family: Liliaceae.

JOSHUA TREE NATIONAL MONUMENT, in S Cal., covers 558 200 acres of the Mojave and Colorado deserts. Established in 1936, it has a wide variety of desert fauna and flora, notably Joshua trees, granite and quartz formations.

JOSIAH, king of Judah c640–c609 BC. A just ruler, he reformed religion, using a book of law (perhaps DEUTERONOMY) discovered in the Temple; he sought to center worship at Jerusalem. Later in his reign he faced growing threats from Assyria and Egypt; he was killed in battle with the Egyptians at MEGIDDO.

JOSQUIN DES PRÉS (c1450–1521), major Flemish composer. He traveled widely in Europe; much of his work was done in Italy. Technically brilliant, his music ranges from the almost mystical fervor in his 20 masses and 90 motets to the gaiety and elegance of his secular songs. His music has enjoyed a revival since the 1950s.

JOTHAM (d. c735 BC), king of Judah, a contemporary of ISAIAH. He is remembered for his defeat of the AMMONITES.

JOTUNHEIM MOUNTAINS, range in S central Norway, the highest in Scandinavia. Largely desolate, the mountains are named for the giants supposed to inhabit them.

JOUHAUX, Leon (1879–1954), French labor leader. A socialist, he fought communism in the unions at home and internationally and wrote on labor topics and disarmament. He won the 1951 Nobel Peace Prize.

JOULE (J), the SI UNIT of ENERGY, defined as the WORK done when a FORCE of one NEWTON acts through the distance of one metre. Also equivalent to the energy dissipated by one WATT in one second, it equals 10^7 erg in CGS UNITS.

JOULE, James Prescott (1818–1889), British physicist who showed that HEAT energy and mechanical energy are equivalent and hinted at the law of conservation of ENERGY. From 1852 he and Thomson (later Lord KELVIN) performed a series of experiments in THERMODYNAMICS, especially on the Joule–Thomson effect (see CRYOGENICS). The JOULE (unit) is named for him. (See also JOULE'S LAW.)

JOULE'S LAW, law derived by J. P. JOULE that the heat evolved in a given time by passage of electricity through a conductor is proportional to the RESISTANCE of the conductor times the square of the electrical intensity. We now write it $H=I^2R$, where H is the rate of generation of heat in WATTS, I the current in AMPERES and R the resistance in OHMS.

JOVE, derivative form of Jupiter, Roman god identified with ZEUS.

JOVIAN (c331–364 AD), Roman emperor from 363. On campaign in Persia with the emperor JULIAN, he was made emperor by the army when Julian was killed. He ended Roman involvement in Persia and reversed Julian's anti-Christian policies.

JOWETT, Benjamin (1817–1893), English classical scholar, master of Balliol College, Oxford from 1870 and vice-chancellor of Oxford University, 1882–86. His translations of PLATO's *Dialogues* (1871) and *Republic* (1844) are literary and scholastic masterpieces.

Caricature of the controversial novelist James Joyce, whose experimental, idiosyncratic writings contributed significantly to the development of modern prose fiction. The censorship of his novel *Ulysses* publicized the sexual frankness of his work.

JOYCE, James Augustine Aloysius (1882–1941), Irish novelist and poet whose novel *Ulysses* (1922) is a seminal work of 20th-century literature. Within the framework of Homeric myth he dissects his characters' thoughts and actions in the course of a single day through STREAM OF CONSCIOUSNESS techniques and the creation of an allusive private language. This he developed in *Finnegan's Wake* (1939), a complex cyclical exploration of dream consciousness. Dublin, where Joyce grew up, is central to his writing (as in *Dubliners*, (1914), and the autobiographical *Portrait of the Artist as a Young Man*, (1916), but from 1904 he lived abroad, in Paris, Trieste (where he encouraged SVEVO) and Zurich, where he died. (For the *Ulysses* case see PORNOGRAPHY.)

JOYCE, William (1906–1946), US-born Nazi propagandist, named "Lord Haw-Haw" for the affected and sneering tone he adopted in broadcasts to Britain in WWII. Captured in 1945, he was hanged for treason.

JUAN CARLOS (1938–), king of Spain from Nov. 1975, after the death of Gen. FRANCO. Educated as Franco's successor, he was so named in 1969 in preference to his father Don Juan, son of ALFONSO XIII; in 1971 he was empowered to deputize as head of state. In 1962 he married Princess Sophia of Greece, by whom he had three children.

JUAN DE FUCA, Strait of, runs for about 100mi between the Wash. Coast and Vancouver Island, British Columbia, forming the principal shipping route from Vancouver and Seattle to the Pacific.

JUAN FERNANDEZ ISLANDS, three S Pacific islands, 400mi W of Chile, which used them as a penal colony in the 19th century. Alexander SELKIRK was marooned on one of the islands.

JUANA INÉS DE LA CRUZ (1651–1695), Mexican Spanish poet and scholar. As a girl she left court to become a nun. Criticized for her "unwomanly" studies, she defended women's education in a vigorous letter to her bishop (1691). Her lyric poetry, especially sonnets, is among the finest in Spanish. She died nursing epidemic victims in Mexico City.

JUAREZ, city in N Mexico, on the Rio Grande opposite El Paso, Tex. Named for Benito JUAREZ, it is the major border point and shipping center between Mexico and the US. There is also a major cotton industry. Pop 436 059.

JUAREZ, Benito Pablo (1806–1872), Mexican national hero, effective ruler from 1861. Of Indian descent, he was imprisoned and exiled as a liberal 1853–55, when he was made justice minister in the administration that ousted SANTA ANNA (1855). His reforms attacked privilege in the Church and the army, precipitating civil war 1855–61. In 1861 he was elected president. The French incursion under MAXIMILIAN 1864–67 forced him to conduct a guerrilla campaign, which he won with US backing. His second presidency, 1871–72, was marred by factionalism and corruption.

JUBILEE, ancient Hebrew year of amnesty, recurring every 50th year; slaves were freed and debts remitted. Also a Roman Catholic HOLY YEAR.

JUDAEA, Greco-Roman name for S Palestine, occupied by the kingdom of Judah till 586 BC. It was then a province of the Greek Seleucid kings and the Roman empire.

JUDAH, in the Old Testament fourth son of JACOB, the spokesman for his brothers before JOSEPH. Ancestor of the tribe of Judah, he settled in S Palestine after the EXODUS, his tribe becoming part of the kingdom of JUDAH.

JUDAH, Kingdom of, territory in S Palestine, held by the tribes of Judah and Benjamin, after the break-up of SOLOMON's kingdom under REHOBOAM, c931 BC. The house of David ruled Judah until the destruction of Jerusalem in 587 BC.

JUDAH HA-LEVI (c1075–1141), Jewish rabbi, philosopher and poet who lived and worked in Muslim Spain. His *Sefer ha-Kuzari* is a great expression of Hebrew philosophy. He died in Egypt on his way to the Holy Land.

JUDAH HA-NASI (Hebrew: prince), rabbi, president of the SANHEDRIN, who codified the Mishnah (see TALMUD) in the 2nd century AD.

JUDAISM, the religion of the Jews, the most ancient of the world's surviving monotheistic religions and as such deeply influential on CHRISTIANITY and ISLAM. It sees the world as the creation of a living god and the Jews as his chosen people. Central is the idea of the COVENANT made between God and Abraham, ancestor of the Jews. This was sealed and is commemorated by the ceremony of male CIRCUMCISION; it was reaffirmed at the time of the EXODUS by the PESACH of Passover. Abraham bound himself and his descendants to carry the message of one God to the world in return for His protection. The relationship between God and His chosen people is the great theme of the Hebrew Bible.

Its first five books, the PENTATEUCH, constituted the TORAH, or law, which is the foundation of the religion. It contains a history of the Jews until the death of MOSES, the Ten Commandments and a corpus of ritual and ethical precepts. The Torah is supplemented by a body of oral traditions and interpretations and instructions, set down in the 1st century and known as the Mishnah. With a commentary on it, known as the Gemara, it is part of the TALMUD. Yet doctrinally

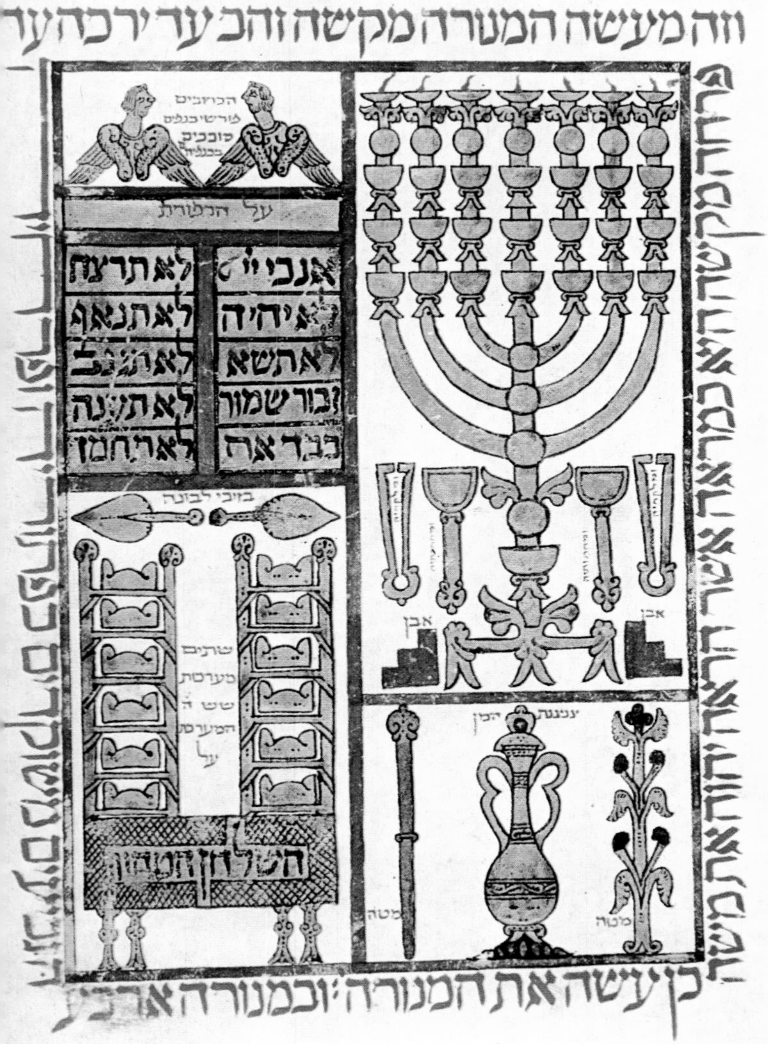

Illustration from a medieval Judaic manuscript of the Torah, showing the furnishings of the Tabernacle. Above left: the Ark of the Covenant, surmounted by two cherubim and containing the tablets of the Ten Commandments. Below left: the table with the shewbread. Above right: the menorah, a seven-armed candlestick. Below right: the staves of Moses and Aaron, and jar of manna.

Judaism is not a dogmatic religion. No analytical statement of the nature of God exists, the concept of the afterlife is undefined, and there is no formal creed.

The faith was many times in danger of destruction by conquest or corruption from within. Its survival was, often, due to great kings, but principally to great spiritual leaders (among whom Moses ranks almost as a second founder), great PROPHETS and great scholars. Until the conquest of Jerusalem by Babylon in 586 BC the Temple built by SOLOMON was the great religious center. Its destruction and the dispersion of Jewish communities through the ancient world made the SYNAGOGUE, or local meeting increasingly important. Judaism survived the catastrophic destruction of the second Temple and depopulation of Jerusalem by Romans in 70 AD, thanks largely to JOHANAN BEN ZAKKAI. His emphasis on the Torah, with the consolidation of the synagogue, provided Judaism with the intellectual and community strongholds in which to withstand the persecution of ensuing centuries. Also important was the ancient concept of the MESSIAH, a descendant of the house of David to be sent by God to restore and rule a triumphant Israel, and the strict observance of Judaic rituals and customs. (See BAR MITZVAH; KOSHER.) An important festival is the weekly SABBATH; others are ROSH HASHANAH, YOM KIPPUR, SHAVUOT, HANNUKAH, TISHAH B'AV.

Modern Western Judaism has three main branches; Orthodoxy; Reform Judaism which largely rejects the Talmudic tradition; and Conservative Judaism, an evolutionary system which retains much tradition but believes the faith can coexist with foreign elements while retaining its independence.

JUDAS ISCARIOT (d. c30 AD), the APOSTLE who betrayed Jesus. For 30 pieces of silver he identified Jesus to the soldiers at GETHSEMANE by a kiss of greeting. According to MATTHEW he later repented and hanged himself.

JUDAS MACCABEUS (d. 160 BC), Jewish leader of the HASMONEAN dynasty. He defeated Antiochus IV, a SELEUCID king seeking to force paganism on the Jews, and in 165 BC reconsecrated the Temple. This event is commemorated by the festival of HANNUKAH.

JUDAS TREE, small trees and shrubs of the genus *Cercis*, which are native to Eurasia and North America. Several species are also called **redbud**. So-named because JUDAS ISCARIOT is reputed to have hanged himself from a tree of this type. Family: Leguminosae.

JUDDAH. See JIDDAH.

JUDE, Saint, (or Judas) one of the APOSTLES, possible author of the New Testament Epistle of Jude, which combats heresy. Jude is an anglicized form of Judas, to distinguish him from JUDAS ISCARIOT.

JUDGE, public officer who presides over a court, and enters judgment in the cases it hears; he may decide the case on his own or rely on the verdict of a JURY. He will in any case advise on and decide any points of law which arise. (See also JUDICIARY; LEGAL PROFESSION.)

JUDGE ADVOCATE GENERAL, chief legal officer of a military establishment. In the US there is a judge advocate general for each of the armed services. He presides over court-martials, military commissions and courts of inquiry.

JUDGES, seventh book of the OLD TESTAMENT. It recounts the exploits of military leaders, known as "judges," between the time of Joshua and the birth of Samuel. Israel's successive apostasies from God are punished by enemy oppression, until God sends a judge to deliver the people. The main judges are Barak, DEBORAH, GIDEON, Abimelech, Jephthah and SAMSON.

JUDICIAL REVIEW. See SUPREME COURT OF THE UNITED STATES; UNITED STATES CONSTITUTION.

JUDICIARY, body of public officials, usually called JUDGES or magistrates, whose task it is to interpret the laws of a state made by its LEGISLATURE and executed by its EXECUTIVE (see SEPARATION OF POWERS). The US federal judicial system was established by the Judiciary Act, passed by Congress Sept. 24, 1789. It set up the federal COURTS and defined their powers, procedures and jurisdiction. Under COMMON LAW systems such as exist in the US and UK the rules of precedent give the judiciary such wide powers that they are often said to help make as well as interpret the law. (See also LEGAL PROFESSION.)

JUDITH, book of the Old Testament APOCRYPHA. During an Assyrian invasion a young Jewish widow, Judith, seduces the Assyrian general Holofernes in order to murder him. She shows his head to the Jewish army, which routs its leaderless enemy.

JUDO, a form of unarmed combat, a sport developed by Jigoro Kano in 1882 as a less violent form of Japanese *jujitsu*. It uses grappling and throwing holds, combined with a skillful use of balance and timing, to turn an opponent's strength against him; judo can thus enable a weaker person to overcome a stronger. Colored belts, ranging from white for beginners to black for experts, denote proficiency grades. Introduced into the US in 1902, it has been regulated by the Amateur Athletic Union since 1952, and has featured in the OLYMPIC GAMES since 1964.

JUDSON, Adoniram (1788–1850), US Baptist missionary to Burma, from 1813 a founder of US overseas missionary work. He translated the Bible into Burmese (1849) and wrote a Burmese–English dictionary.

JUDSON, Edward Zane Carroll. See BUNTLINE, NED.

JUGENDSTIL, German ART NOUVEAU style c1890–c1910. Centering particularly on Munich and Vienna, it was named for the magazine *Die Jugend* (Youth). Among major exponents was Henry VAN DER VELDE.

JUGGERNAUT (from Sanskrit *Jagannatha*, lord of the world), cult at Puri, Orissa, in India. The idol is carried in procession on a massive wagon once a year; the legend of devotees sacrificing themselves beneath its wheels appears to result from accidental crushings.

Among the greatest achievements of Jugendstil was to make the poster a work of art. This one by Alphons Mucha, announcing an 1897 exhibition of his work, typifies the style.

JUGOSLAVIA. See YUGOSLAVIA.
JUGULAR VEINS, a pair of veins on each side of the neck which collect venous blood from the BRAIN (internal jugular vein) and the rest of the head (external jugular vein). Their proximity to the surface makes them liable to trauma with HEMORRHAGE and AEROEMBOLISM.
JUGURTHA (c156–104 BC), king of Numidia from 118 BC. He was not hostile to Rome but lost its support through irresponsible murders. He defeated Roman invasions in favor of his rival Adherbal, but was captured in 106 BC and murdered at Rome.
JUIZ DE FORA, city in Minas Gerais state, Brazil, a major manufacturing center in an agricultural area. Pop 238052.
JUJITSU. See JUDO.
JUJUBE, *Ziziphus jujuba*, shrub or small tree native to Asia and cultivated for its edible fruits. Extracts from the fruits are used in bronchial pastilles. Family: Rhamnaceae.
JULIAN, George Washington (1817–1899), US abolitionist politician, a FREE SOIL PARTY founder and congressman 1849–51, and in 1852 its vice-presidential nominee. A Republican congressman 1861–71, he supported RECONSTRUCTION and the impeachment of Andrew JOHNSON, and also women's rights.
JULIANA (1909–), queen of the Netherlands from 1948, since the abdication of her mother Queen Wilhelmina. In 1937 she married Prince Bernhard of Lippe-Biesterfeld; they have four daughters.
JULIAN ALPS, eastern range of the Alps in NE Italy and NW Yugoslavia. Its highest peak is Mt Triglav (9395ft).
JULIAN CALENDAR. See CALENDAR.
JULIAN OF NORWICH (or Juliana; c1342–after 1416), English mystic. She lived as an ANCHORITE and in 1373 received a series of ecstatic visions, which she described 20 years later in *The Sixteen Revelations of Divine Love*, the fruit of her meditations.
JULIAN THE APOSTATE (c331–363 AD), Roman emperor from 361, proclaimed by the army he commanded. He greatly reduced taxes by cutting court expenditure and corruption. He attempted to restore paganism, but did not persecute Christians. In 363 he was killed in battle with the Persians.
JULIUS, name of three popes. **Saint Julius I** (d. 352), reigned from 337. An opponent of ARIANISM, he convened the council of Sardica which endorsed the Council of NICAEA's stand. **Julius II** (1443–1513), reigned from 1503. As Cardinal Giuliano della Rovere he dominated INNOCENT VIII but went into exile 1492–1503 when his bitter enemy Rodrigo Borgia became pope as ALEXANDER VI. As pope, Julius commanded the armies that reconquered the papal states, and led the HOLY LEAGUE against France (1510). The Fifth LATERAN Council, which he assembled, criticized the French Church and attacked Church corruption. Patron of RAPHAEL, MICHELANGELO and BRAMANTE, he laid the foundation stone of the new SAINT PETER'S BASILICA. **Julius III** (1487–1555), reigned from 1550.
JULIUS CAESAR. See CAESAR, GAIUS JULIUS.
JULLUNDUR, city in N India, capital of Punjab state 1947–53. Its economy now rests on manufacturing, particularly flour and silk. Pop 296103.
JULY, the seventh month of the year, named for Julius Caesar, who reorganized the CALENDAR. It has 31 days.
JULY REVOLUTION, popular rising in France, July 26–30, 1830, against the reactionary aims of King Charles X. Middle-class opposition was aroused when the ultraroyalist POLIGNAC ministry published the July Ordinances, which suspended freedom of the press, dissolved the Chamber and reduced the small electorate by 75%. Rioting broke out on July 27, and by July 29 most of Paris was in insurgent hands; on July 30 Charles repealed the Ordinances, but was forced to abdicate. His cousin the duke of Orleans became king as LOUIS PHILIPPE.
JUMNA RIVER, (or Yamuna), rises in the Himalaya Mts, N India and flows about 860mi SE to join the Ganges at ALLAHABAD. The river irrigates most of Uttar Pradesh and Punjab states.
JUMPING BEAN, the seeds of various Mexican shrubs, principally those of the genus *Sebastiania*, which contain the larvae of the moth *Carpocapsa saltitans*, movement of which cause the seeds to "jump."

The founder of analytical psychology, Karl Gustav Jung, who increasingly explained behavior in terms of introversion and extraversion, and was also responsible for developing such concepts as "persona," "anima" and "collective unconscious."

JUMPING MICE, a family of mice with elongated hindlegs and long, partially prehensile tails. The family includes the true jumping mice, Zapodidae, of North America and Asia, and the Birch mice of Europe and Asia. They feed on grasses, insects and berries and build spherical nests of grass on the ground or in small bushes.
JUMPING SPIDERS, short-legged hunting spiders of the family Salticidae. Though most numerous in the tropics, a few species are found in temperate regions. Salticids have enormously well-developed eyes which provide a clear image of distant objects. They leap upon their prey with their hindlegs and seize it with the frontlegs.
JUMPING HARE, or Spring hare, *Pedetes capensis*, a rodent found in the short-grass plains of E or southern Africa. A large, burrowing animal unrelated to true hares, it measures up to 380mm (15in) with a bushy tail of equal length. Bipedal, with long hindlegs and feet, they emerge at night from their complex burrows to feed on bulbs and rhizomes.
JUNCOS, certain North American species of finch-like birds related to BUNTINGS. Often found in very large flocks, they are gray-brown seed-eating birds with light bills, gray or black hoods, and white outer tail feathers.
JUNCTION CITY, city in Kan., seat of Geary Co., at the junction of the Republican and Smoky Hill rivers. Pop 19018.
JUNE, sixth month of the year, named for the Roman goddess Juno; it has 30 days.
JUNE BEETLES, or **May bugs,** a group of scarabaeid beetles similar to JAPANESE BEETLES, whose larvae are pests in soil and lawns, feeding on grass roots. The adults feed on foliage.
JUNE DAYS, phase in the February Revolution in France, June 23–26, 1848. The unemployed of Paris rose in riot when the insensitive provisional government abolished the national workshops (a primitive dole system). Gen. CAVAIGNAC suppressed the rioting with great savagery.
JUNEAU, capital city of Alaska, sited in the Panhandle area. Its icefree harbor and its airport make it a trade center; lumbering and fishing are also important, as is tourism. Mt Juneau and Mt Roberts overlook the city. Pop 13556.
JUNG, Carl Gustav (1875–1961), Swiss psychiatrist who founded analytical psychology. He studied PSYCHIATRY at Basel University, his postgraduate studies being of PARAPSYCHOLOGY. After working with BLEULER and JANET, he met FREUD (1907), whom he followed for some years. But he disagreed with, particularly, Freud's belief in the purely sexual nature of the LIBIDO, and in 1913 broke away completely. In *Psychological Types* (1921) he expounded his views on INTROVERSION AND EXTRAVERSION. Later he investigated anthropology and the occult to form the idea of ARCHETYPES, the universal symbols present in the COLLECTIVE UNCONSCIOUS. (See also ANIMA AND ANIMUS; PERSONA; PSYCHOANALYSIS; PSYCHOLOGY.)
JUNGER, Ernst (1895–), German writer whose earlier works, such as *Storm of Steel* (1920), glorified war as a purifying factor in a corrupt society. He opposed Hitler and WWII, however, and later works such as *On The Marble Cliffs* (1939) call for a unifying peace.
JUNGFRAU, mountain in the Bernese Alps, S central Switzerland, 13642ft high. A railroad runs up to the Jungfraujoch, the mountain's saddle, at about 11000ft.
JUNGLE. See FORESTS.
JUNGLEFOWL, ancestors of the domestic fowl, and closely resembling the domestic CHICKEN. They are found all over Asia and Malaysia, and inhabit a wide variety of habitats. They feed chiefly on seeds and shoots but also eat insects. During the breeding season they consort in family parties; in winter they congregate into larger flocks.
JUNIOR COLLEGE, US educational institution providing two-year courses for students who do not wish a full college career. Since the late 19th century more than 1000 have been opened; Canada now has around 100 similar colleges.

Founded in 1880 during a gold-rush, Juneau has been Alaska's capital since 1900 and is now a thriving ice-free port serving the rich mineral mining industries of the surrounding mountains and the adjacent lumber and sawmilling plants.

JUNIPERS, evergreen trees and shrubs of the genus *Juniperus*, family Cupressaceae. Young plants have needle-shaped leaves, while those of older plants are scale-like. Some junipers are called CEDARS, e.g., the American eastern red cedar (*Juniperus virgiana*), the wood of which is used for clothes chests, fencing and telegraph poles. Several species and their hybrids are cultivated as garden ornamentals.
JUNK, variety of ship used in the Far East for centuries. The hull is wooden and flat-bottomed; the sails are of bamboo-stiffened matting or linen. Trading junks are about 30ft long but others, such as Chinese war junks, were much larger.
JUNKER, Prussian landowner of the middle aristocracy. The junkers were powerful in the Prussian bureaucracy and army from the 17th century. In the 19th century the name was applied to German aristocratic conservatives generally.
JUNKERS, Hugo (1859–1935), German airplane engineer. He built the first internally-braced cantilever monoplane in 1915. Junkers founded one of the early airlines and developed widely-used passenger planes.
JUNO. See HERA.
JUPITER. See ZEUS.
JUPITER, the largest and most massive planet in the

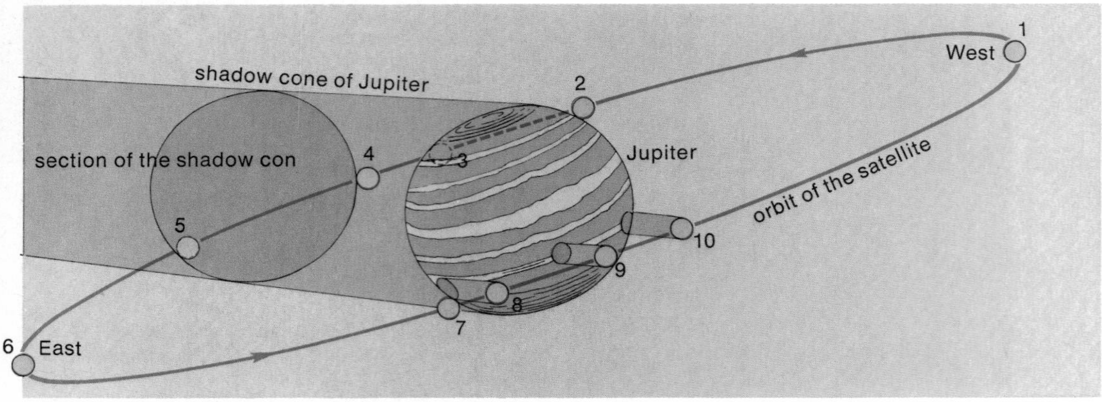

Jupiter has thirteen known satellites which orbit the planet in such a way that they seem to us to move to and fro along a straight line. At positions 1 and 6 the moon reaches the farthest eastern and western elongation and seems farthest away from the planet, while between 2 and 5 it disappears entirely, eclipsed by the planet itself and the shadow of the planet. When it moves in front of Jupiter, it casts its own shadow on the planet (7–10).

solar system (diameter about 143Mm, mass 317.8 times that of earth), fifth from the sun. Jupiter is larger than all the other planets combined and, with a mean solar distance of 5.20AU and a "year" of 11.86 earth-years, is the greatest contributor to the solar system's angular MOMENTUM. Its atmosphere consists mainly of METHANE, AMMONIA and HYDROGEN. Its disk is marked by prominent cloud-belts paralleling its equator, these being occasionally interrupted by turbulences and particularly the **Great Red Spot**, an elliptical area 40Mm long and 13Mm wide: unlike most other features of Jupiter's disk, which have a lifetime of a few days, it has been observed for about 150 years. Another long-term feature, the **South Tropical Disturbance**, was first observed in 1901 and disappeared in 1939. The nature of these features is not yet known. Jupiter's day is about 9.92h and this high rotational velocity causes a visible flattening of the poles: the equatorial diameter is some 7% greater than the polar diameter. Jupiter has 13 moons, the two largest of which, Callisto and Ganymede, are larger than MERCURY: Io has an atmosphere. Jupiter radiates energy, possibly because of nuclear reactions in its core or a gravitational contraction of the planet.

JURA MOUNTAINS, range in W Europe. It runs from the Rhône R to the Rhine R on the Swiss–German border, a series of heavily forested ridges crossed by gorges and with fertile valleys. The highest peak is Crêt de la Neige (5 652ft).

JURASSIC, the middle period of the MESOZOIC era, lasting from about 190 to 135 million years ago. (See also GEOLOGY.)

JURISPRUDENCE. See LAW.

JURUA RIVER, rises in the Peruvian Andes and flows around 1 500mi NE through Brazil to join the Amazon R near Forte Boa.

JURY, in COMMON LAW, body of people responsible for deciding points of fact in legal proceedings such as inquests and trials. The jury, probably a product of the Norman practice of calling character witnesses, was adopted from English law into the US system; the 6th and 7th Amendments to the Constitution provide for jury trial in most criminal and civil cases. A grand jury of 12–13 persons hears evidence in a criminal case to decide whether it should go for trial; a petty (small) jury of 12 persons sits at the trial proper. Its members may be challenged by counsel for either party on various grounds. The jury system reflects community standards in the law, but may for this reason produce biased or unjust decisions. Many legal systems have little or no equivalent of the jury.

JUSTICE, US Department of, federal executive department created by Congress in 1870. Headed by the ATTORNEY GENERAL, it comprises eight divisions, three bureaus and two boards whose functions are to enforce federal laws, administer federal prisons and supervise district attorneys and marshals; it also represents the federal government in legal matters and legally advises the president.

JUSTICE OF THE PEACE, local magistrate in England and the US; in most states they are elected. Once powerful royal justices, they now have jurisdiction over minor criminal and civil cases, and civil duties such as marriages and warrants.

JUSTIFICATION BY FAITH, Pauline doctrine that justification is given freely by God on the grounds of Christ's ATONEMENT and by imputation of his righteousness. Justification is God's declaration that a person is righteous. The sinner is justified through believing in Jesus Christ, not by his own works. The Reformers, especially LUTHER, emphasized the doctrine in opposition to the popular medieval Roman Catholic belief in justification by works. It is no longer controversial.

JUSTINIAN I (483–565), Byzantine emperor 527–565, the last to rule in the West. His generals BELISARIUS and NARSES reconquered Italy and North Africa 533–534. Justinian's attempts to impose heavy taxation and religious Orthodoxy on the diverse peoples and sects of the empire, especially the MONOPHYSITES, caused periodic unrest. In 532 political rivalries in the capital caused the Nika riots, quelled only by the decisiveness of the empress THEODORA. Justinian commissioned the great *Digest* of Roman law (see CORPUS JURIS CIVILIS) and built such great churches as HAGIA SOPHIA and SAN VITALE.

JUSTINIAN CODE. See CORPUS JURIS CIVILIS.

JUSTIN MARTYR, Saint (c100–165), Christian theologian who conducted a school of Christian studies in Rome; he was martyred under Marcus Aurelius. His *Apology* defended Christianity against charges of impiety and sedition.

JUTE, the fibers produced from the annual herbs *Corchorus capsularis* and *C. olitorius*, which are cultivated in India and Bangladesh. The stems are soaked in water (retted) until the fibers can be separated and then spun into yarn that is used for sacking. Family: Tiliaceae.

JUTES, Germanic people who originated in Scandinavia, probably in Jutland. With the ANGLES and SAXONS they invaded Britain in the 5th century AD, settling in S and SE England. Their national identity was soon lost, although some cultural influence seems to have survived in Kent.

JUTLAND, peninsula in NW Europe, comprising continental Denmark and N Schleswig-Holstein state, West Germany. The name is usually applied only to the Danish territory.

JUTLAND, Battle of, only major naval battle in WWI, fought between the British and German fleets off the coast of Jutland on May 31, 1916, for domination of the North Sea. The British fleet under Admiral JELLICOE lost more ships but won a tactical victory.

JUVENAL, (c60–130 AD), Roman poet whose 16 *Satires* (100–128 AD) are scathing attacks on the corruption of social and political life in Rome, which he contrasts with older standards. Many of his epigrammatic sayings—for example, "A sound mind in a sound body"—have passed into everyday use.

JUVENILE COURT, a court dealing with young offenders. Because a child is not regarded as bearing legal responsibility for his actions most juvenile courts seek to rehabilitate rather than punish. The first US juvenile court was established in Ill. in 1899; they are now found in every state. Their proceedings are less formal than those of adult courts and they can deprive a minor of such civil rights as the right to remain silent, in order to achieve greater flexibility. The juvenile court has wide discretionary powers and may even remove a child from its parents if the home environment seems harmful.

JUVENILE DELINQUENCY, term for crime committed by minors. Illegal activity by juveniles appears to be increasing throughout the world, although it may be that it is simply attracting more attention. In the US 50% of those arrested for theft are under eighteen years of age. Personal factors such as poor health, environmental factors such as cultural deprivation and the general emotional crises of adolescence are all seen as contributing to juvenile delinquency. Young offenders in the US are dealt with in JUVENILE COURTS. Often their sentences may depend on reports from a social worker, psychiatrist or welfare worker, the policy being to "cure" rather than supress criminal tendencies, but in extreme cases offenders may be sent to corrective institutions.

JUVENILE HORMONE, or **neotenin,** an insect hormone which maintains the presence of juvenile features in the LARVA. In its absence, adult features appear on molting. It is also involved in normal egg production by female insects. In years to come it may find application in insect control by preventing the emergence of adults.

Although none of the original medallions of Justinian the Great survived, some of the molds for them did. This example was cast from one such mold and is thus in mint condition.

K

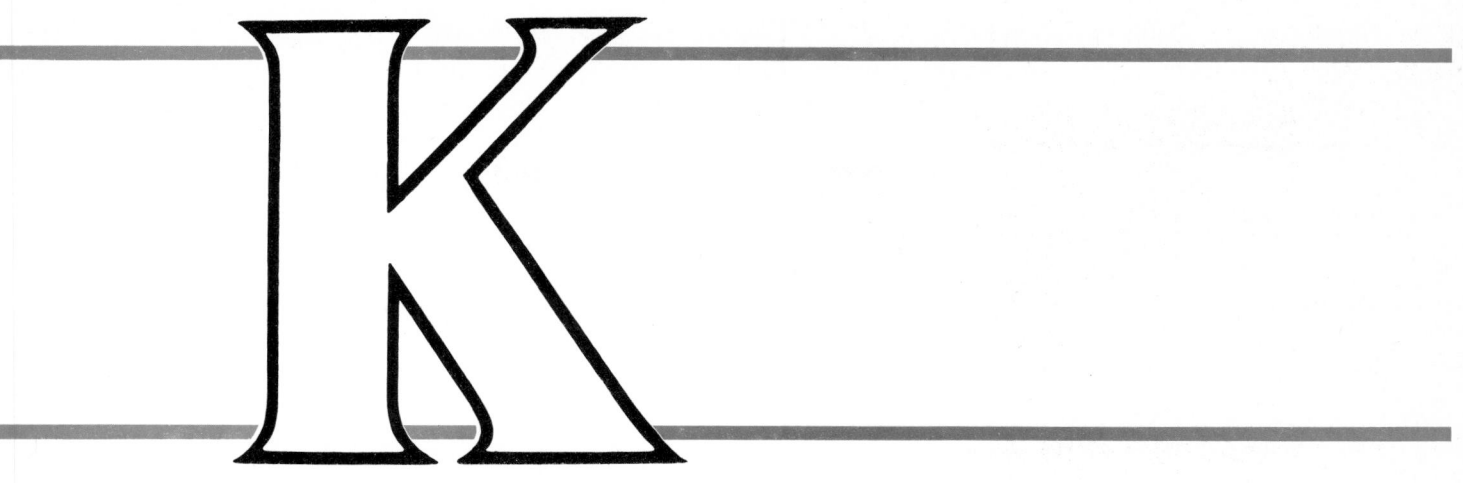

K, the 11th letter of the English alphabet, from the Semitic *kaph*, representing the palm of the hand, and the ancient Greek *kappa*. K stands for *King* in chess.
K2 (also, unofficially, Mt Godwin Austen or Dapsang), at 28 250ft the world's second highest peak after Mt Everest. Situated in the Karakoram Range in N Kashmir, it was first climbed in 1954.
KAABA, most sacred shrine of ISLAM, in the courtyard of the Great Mosque at Mecca, Saudi Arabia. Pilgrims must circle the flat-roofed Kaaba seven times and at its E corner kiss the Black Stone, which is said to have been given to Adam on his fall from paradise.

The Kaaba at Mecca, surrounded by pilgrims. This enigmatic structure seems originally to have been a pre-Islamic shrine attributed to Abraham. By Mohammed's time it was filled with idols, which he ordered removed when restoring the monotheistic faith for which he believed it had been intended.

KABALEVSKY, Dmitri (1904–), Russian composer and critic. His work includes symphonies, ballet, chamber music and operas such as *Colas Breugnon* (1938) and *The Taras Family* (1949).
KABUKI, traditional Japanese popular theater which developed in the 17th century in contrast to the aristocratic NOH theater. A blending of dance, song and mime, the kabuki dramatized both traditional stories and contemporary events in a stylized but exuberant fashion. It remains popular today and has influenced much Western theatrical thought.
KABUL, capital and largest city of Afghanistan, lying in a high valley (5 900ft) on both banks of the Kabul R. The city is now a commercial and manufacturing center with cement and textile industries. Pop 318 094.
KÁDÁR, János (1912–), Hungarian politician, premier in 1956–58 and 1961–65 and first secretary of the Socialist Workers' Party. As leader of the counter-revolutionaries during the 1956 anti-Soviet uprising, he had many rebel leaders executed.
KADDISH, Jewish doxology or hymn of praise in HEBREW. It has various forms and uses, but is best known as a prayer for the dead.
KADESH, ancient Syrian city which flourished in the 2nd millennium BC. In 1299 BC it was the scene of a battle between the Egyptians under RAMSES II and the Hittites under Muwatallis, resulting in a historic truce between them.
KAFFIR (CAFER) CAT, or **African Wild Cat,** *Felis lybica*, the ancestor of the domestic CAT. They inhabit steppe, bush regions and savannas in Asia and Africa. Small and slender with narrow heads, they are yellowish-gray in color, with the back always darker than the belly and flanks.
KAFIR, several varieties of grain SORGHUM that are grown in tropical and subtropical climates, including the US. The ground grain is used to make bread and the green parts are used as forage.
KAFKA, Franz (1883–1924), German-language writer born in Prague of Jewish parents. Most of Kafka's stories confront his protagonists with nightmarish situations which they cannot resolve or escape from. They reflect his profound sense of alienation, and his inhibitions and shortcomings, particularly in relation to the powerful figure of his father. Kafka died of tuberculosis at age 40. His friend and executor Max BROD ignored his instructions to destroy all his work, and subsequently published Kafka's many short stories and his novels *The Trial* (1925), *The Castle* (1926) and *America* (1927).
KAGOSHIMA, capital city of Kagoshima prefecture on S coast of Kyushu, Japan. A seaport city, it is the manufacturing center of Satsuma porcelain. Pop 403 340.
KAHN, Louis Isadore (1901–1974), US architect, noted for his work on housing projects and university buildings, particularly the Richards Medical Research Laboratories at the U. of Pennsylvania, where he was a professor.
KAHN, Otto Hermann (1867–1934), German-born US banker and patron of the arts. As a member of the New York Metropolitan Opera Company board he instituted many reforms, and appointed TOSCANINI as principal conductor.
K'AI-FENG, historic city in N Honan province, E China. From 907–960 AD it was the imperial capital of the Five Dynasties. Pop 318 000.
KAISER, title, derived from Latin *Caesar*, sometimes used by rulers of the HOLY ROMAN EMPIRE (800–1806) and the German Empire (1871–1918).
KAISER, Henry John (1882–1967), US industrialist, founder of the Kaiser-Frazer Corporation. He contributed greatly to the Allied war effort in WWII by his development of faster production techniques for ships, aircraft and military vehicles, especially the famous "jeep."
KAKAPO, *Strigops habroptilus*, a strange nocturnal New Zealand parrot, feeding on the leaves of tussock plants, berries and nectar. Fibrous material is not swallowed, but chewed to extract the juices and then rejected. Almost flightless, the kakapo runs along well-defined paths through the forests.
KALA-AZAR. See LEISHMANIASIS.
KA LAE (South Cape), cape on the southernmost extremity of Hawaii, site of a US missile tracking station.

Bushmen in the Kalahari Desert, the only human inhabitants of this arid area. The rows of black lines on their faces are tribal markings.

KALAHARI DESERT, arid plain of some 100 000 sq mi in S Africa. It lies mainly in Botswana but extends into SW Africa and South Africa. Though not a true desert, the region has low annual rainfall and only seasonal pasture for sheep. It is inhabited only by Bushmen. There is a wide variety of game.

KALAMAZOO, city in Mich., lying NE of Chicago, on the Kalamazoo R. Its varied industries include paper, pharmaceuticals, taxicabs, musical instruments and fruit. Pop 85 555.

KALANCHOE, a genus of succulent perennial plants widely grown as house and greenhouse plants for their ornamental foliage and clusters of tubular flowers. Kalanchoes tolerate a great deal of neglect, but grow best when placed in a sunny position where the temperature does not fall below 13°C (55°F). They should be watered whenever the soil surface dries out; they are propagated either from seeds or by taking stem and leaf cuttings. Family: Crassulaceae.

KALB, Johann. See DE KALB, JOHANN.

KALE, *Brassica oleracea*, a form of CABBAGE that is used as winter feed for cattle and as a winter green vegetable. Family: Cruciferae.

KALEDIN, Alexei Maximovich (1861–1918), Russian general, elected leader of the Cossack armies in 1917 and head of the Don Cossack government after the Bolshevik revolution. Forced to withdraw from his capital, Taganrog, by a Bolshevik army, he resigned and shot himself.

KALEIDOSCOPE, a cylindrical device patented in 1817, now a popular toy, in which two plane mirrors, set at an angle of 60° or 90°, multiply the images of objects placed between them into a symmetrical pattern.

KALEVALA ("Land of Heroes"), Finnish national epic. Compiled from traditional material by Elias Lönnrot (1802–1884), it tells of the exploits of the legendary Finnish warrior-magicians. It was first published in 1835, and in an expanded version in 1849. LONGFELLOW's *Hiawatha* and much of the music of SIBELIUS, were inspired by it.

KALGAN (Ch'ang-chia-k'ou), city in Hopeh province, N China. A city of strategic and commercial importance under the Ming and Manchu dynasties, it is now a textile center. Pop 750 000.

KALI (Hindi: black mother), Hindu goddess of fearsome aspect, associated with the god SHIVA (her husband) in his role as destroyer of evil by death and disease, and once propitiated with blood sacrifice. (See also THUGS.)

KALIMANTAN, the Indonesian section of Borneo, excluding Malaysian North Borneo, Sarawak and the sultanate of Brunei. The name is used by the Indonesians to denote the entire island.

KALININ, Mikhail Ivanovich (1875–1946), Russian revolutionary leader. A loyal Stalinist, Kalinin was chairman of the central executive (now the presidium) from 1919 and a member of the Politburo from 1925.

KALININGRAD (Königsberg), Baltic port and industrial center. Formerly German, the city was ceded to the USSR in 1945. Pop 297 000.

KALISPELL, city, in NW Mont., seat of Flathead Co. A tourist resort, it also has lumber mills and an aluminum plant. Pop 10 256.

KALM, Peter (1716–1779), Swedish botanist best known for his survey of North American natural history. His results were published between 1753 and 1761.

KALMAR UNION, treaty whereby Denmark, Norway and Sweden were united under Margaret of Denmark and her heirs. It was signed at the Swedish port of Kalmar (1397), which became the Union's political center. The Union endured until 1523.

KALMUCKS, a Mongol people who now inhabit parts of W China and the USSR, especially the Kalmuck SSR along the Volga R. Exiled by the Soviet government in 1945, they were returned to their lands in 1957. Famous as horsemen and soldiers, they are traditionally nomadic, but many have now turned to agriculture and settled down.

KAMAKURA, town in Karnagawa prefecture, SE Honshu, Japan, about 10mi S of Yokohama. It was the seat of government from 1192, but declined with the rise to power of Tokyo in 1603. Today it is a dormitory and resort town. Pop 139 249.

KAMA RIVER, river in E European Russia, chief tributary of the Volga R. Some 1 260mi long, it rises in the central Urals and joins the Volga about 40mi S of Kazan. It is navigable for about 1000mi.

KAMCHATKA PENINSULA, land area and oblast

The bright colors and the hardy nature of the kalanchoe, here growing wild, make it one of the most popular and easily looked-after house plants.

in the USSR which extends about 750mi S from NE Siberia to separate the Sea of Okhotsk from the Bering Sea. Largely tundra and pine forest, it has Siberia's highest peak, Klyuchevskaya Sopka (15 584ft).

KAMEHAMEHA I (c1738–1819), Hawaiian monarch from 1790, a benevolent despot who united the islands (1810). He encouraged foreign contact and trade, but always sought to preserve the independence of his country and its people.

KAMENEV, Lev Borisovich (1883–1936), Russian politician, an associate of Lenin in exile. As president of the Moscow Soviet 1918–26, he sided with his brother-in-law TROTSKY and with ZINOVIEV against Stalin after Lenin's death (1924). Stalin used the murder of Sergei KIROV as a pretext for arresting Kamenev; he was executed after a "show trial."

KAMERLINGH-ONNES, Heike (1853–1926), Dutch physicist awarded the 1913 Nobel Prize for Physics for his work on low-temperature physics (see CRYOGENICS). He discovered SUPERCONDUCTIVITY and was the first to liquefy HELIUM (1908).

KAMIKAZE ("Divine Wind"), Japanese force of suicide pilots in WWII. Inspired by the ancient SAMURAI code of patriotic self-sacrifice, they deliberately crashed bomb-bearing planes onto Allied ships and installations. They inflicted particularly heavy damage at Okinawa.

KAMLOOPS, resort city in S British Columbia, Canada, 160mi NE of Vancouver. It is also a mining and lumbering supply center. Pop 26 168.

KAMPUCHEA. See CAMBODIA.

KANAWHA RIVER, chief river of W. Va., formed by the confluence of the New R and Gauley R. Navigable over its 97mi length, the Kanawha flows NW to join the Ohio R at Point Pleasant.

KANAZAWA, chief city on the W coast of Honshu, Japan. Once a feudal capital, it is now noted for its porcelain and textiles. Pop 361 379.

KANCHENJUNGA, the world's third highest mountain, part of the Himalayas, on the boundary between Nepal and Sikkim. First climbed in 1955, its main peak is 28 146ft high.

KANDAHAR, second largest city of Afghanistan, situated on the Arghandeb R plain. Said to have been founded by Alexander the Great, it is now Afghanistan's most important agricultural trading center. Pop 130 212.

KADINSKY, Wassily (1866–1944), Russian painter, widely regarded as one of the fathers of ABSTRACT ART. A founder of the BLAUE REITER group of artists (1912), he taught at the BAUHAUS design school (1922–33). His works, largely abstract, are characterized by their dynamic color and style.

KANDY, town in Sri Lanka, on Mahaweli R, 60mi ENE of Colombo. The last capital of the ancient kings of Ceylon, Kandy is the site of the world's most sacred Buddhist temple. Pop 93 602.

KANE, Elisha Kent (1820–1857), US Arctic explorer and physician who led an expedition to find Sir John FRANKLIN and establish whether there was an open sea around the North Pole. He found neither but carried out much pioneering Arctic research.

KANEOHE, city on Oahu Island, Hawaii. It is the site of a missile tracking station. Pop 29 903.

KANGAROO COURT, mock court set up to give a semblance of legality to illegal proceedings. The name referred to summary trials by US frontier judges who "hopped" from place to place, but is now used of any illegal court, such as those of the IRISH REPUBLICAN ARMY and the KU KLUX KLAN.

KANGAROO RATS, or Rat Kangaroos, small members of the kangaroo family with a long tail and bipedal locomotion. True marsupials, unlike other jumping rats, kangaroos rats are nest-building KANGAROOS weighing 0.25–3kg (0.6–6.6lb). There are five species. The name Kangaroo rat is also applied to certain jerboa-like North American rodents of the genus *Dipodomys*.

Gray kangaroos drinking at a waterhole. Largest of 50 species, they may grow to 6ft in height, with a 4ft tail, and generally live in open forest, feeding on roots and leaves.

KANGAROOS, MARSUPIAL mammals with large hind feet, strong hindlimbs and a tail. Normally quadrupedal, they rise to a bipedal stance when moving quickly, progressing in huge leaps. The tail in true kangaroos is heavily built and serves to balance the body in bipedal locomotion. It may also be used as a prop during fighting when a kangaroo can kick with both hindfeet together. Female kangaroos have a pouch containing the teats, in which the young, born singly and at a very "premature" stage, are raised. Kangaroos are herbivorous; the alimentary canal shows strong similarities to the stomach of placental, ruminant mammals. A diverse group, kangaroos include true kangaroos, WALLABIES, Tree kangaroos and Rat kangaroos or KANGAROO RATS.

KANGAROO VINE, *Cissus antarctica*, a woody

Arrows, by Wassily Kandinsky. The hard lines and geometrical construction are typical of his later work, much influenced by the Bauhaus school.

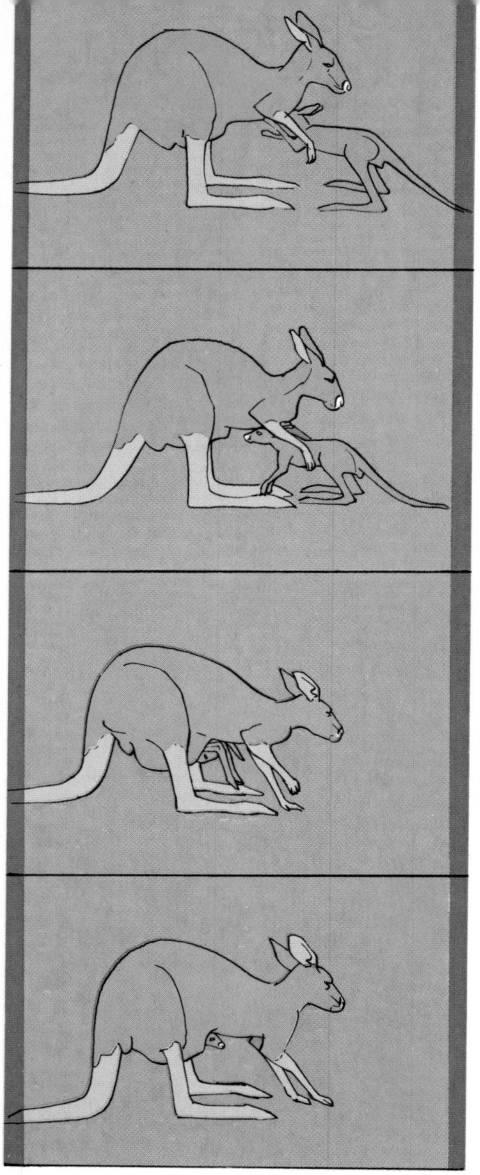

Seven-month-old red kangaroo reentering the pouch, in which it has lived since birth. Sliding its head under the mother's body, it feels for the pouch opening. It then grasps the sides of the pouch, puts its head in and, while the mother patiently waits, pushes with its hind feet on the ground. Having drawn its legs in after it, it turns around to have only its head protruding.

evergreen climber, native to Australia; widely grown as a house plant for its shiny dark-green leaves. It should be grown in a sunny window, but avoiding direct sun in summer. The temperature should be maintained between 13°C and 21°C (55°F and 70°F). The soil should be kept evenly moist. The Kangaroo vine is extremely easy to propagate by taking stem cuttings. Family: Vitaceae.

KANISHKA, king of N India and Afghanistan in the 2nd century AD. He is chiefly remembered as a patron of BUDDHISM. His encouragement of trade with China and the Roman Empire led to extensive, two-way cultural exchange.

KANKAKEE, city in NE Ill., 32mi SSE of Joliet. A light industrial center, it also ships grain and livestock. Pop 30 944.

KANNAPOLIS, town in S central N.C. It has a flourishing textile industry. Pop 36 293.

KANO, capital city of Kano state in N central Nigeria, 500mi NE of Lagos. Its varied industries include oil, steel, concrete, meat and textiles. Pop 366 211.

KANPUR (Cawnpore), largest city of Uttar Pradesh state, India, on the Ganges R, 245mi SE of Delhi. The scene of a massacre of British soldiers and civilians during the SEPOY REBELLION, it is now a major industrial center. Pop 1 151 975.

KANSA INDIANS, or Kansas, a Plains tribe who lived in what is now E Kan. by the Kansas R. In 1873 they were moved to a reservation in Okla. There they were decimated by disease; very few remain today.

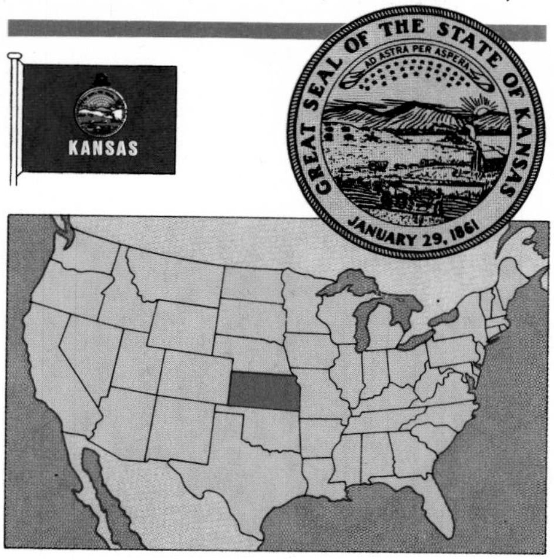

Name of state: Kansas
Capital: Topeka
Statehood: Jan. 29, 1861 (34th state)
Familiar name: Sunflower State
Area: 82 264sq mi
Population: 2 249 071
Elevation: Highest—4 039ft., Mt. Sunflower. Lowest—680ft., Verdigris River in Montgomery County
Motto: Ad Astra per Aspera (To the Stars through Difficulties)
State flower: Sunflower
State bird: Western meadowlark
State tree: Cottonwood
State song: "Home on the Range"

KANSAS, the 34th state of the US, situated midway between the Atlantic and Pacific Oceans. Its name derived from the Kansas or KANSA INDIANS, earliest inhabitants of the area.

Kansas is not all prairie, as is sometimes thought, but rises from under 700ft in the SE to over 4 000ft in the NW, with many rolling hills. Its soils are generally dark, fertile loam, irrigated by a system of over 100 artificial lakes. The two major river systems are the Kansas and the Arkansas, with their tributaries. Kansas has cold winters and warm to hot summers, the average temperatures ranging from 32°F in Jan. to 70°F in July. Rainfall averages about 40in in the SE and under 18in in the W.

People and Economy. The population is concentrated in the E of the state and, reflecting the change from a farm to a mixed farm-factory economy, nearly two-thirds live in urban areas.

Since WWII manufacturing has developed rapidly and is now the state's chief money earner. Kansas is the nation's largest wheat producer, and livestock, dairy products and poultry account for over half the agricultural income. Petroleum makes up over 50% of the value of mineral production, and the state is the nation's principal source of helium.

A state board of education heads the Kansas public school system. School attendance is compulsory between 7 and 16, and 24 universities and senior colleges cater for further education. Kansas is still governed under its original constitution of 1859. The legislature now has a Senate of 40 members and a House of Representatives, comprising 125 members.

History. The Kansas area remained in European hands for some time, but in 1803 the US acquired most of Kansas under the LOUISIANA PURCHASE and used the region for Indian resettlement from the E. The cutting of the SANTA FE TRAIL (1821) and the OREGON TRAIL (1830) led to the first permanent white settlements. In 1854 the KANSAS-NEBRASKA ACT made the territory the focus of the growing slavery problem, a dispute which resulted in virtual civil war. Anti-slavery forces finally gained control and in 1861 Kansas achieved statehood. After the Civil War came rapid settlement and economic expansion, aided by railroad construction and cattle ranching in the W; mineral exploitation in WWI and growth in manufacturing industries after WWII gave Kansas a solid industrial, agricultural and mining economy.

KANSAS CITY, industrial city, seat of Wyandotte Co., in E Kan. It is situated at the confluence of the Missouri and Kansas rivers opposite Kansas City, Mo. Pop 168 213.

KANSAS CITY, city in W Mo., opposite Kansas City, Kan. It was founded in 1833 and became the eastern terminus of the Santa Fe trail. It is an important port of entry and industrial center and has extensive stockyards. Pop 507 187.

KANSAS-NEBRASKA ACT, bill passed by Congress in 1854 which upset the balance of power between slave and free states and helped bring on the Civil War. It established Kansas and Nebraska with a provision that each territory, and subsequent ones, could decide for itself whether or not to introduce slavery. Settlers were poured in by both North and South in an attempt to establish control. The act upset the MISSOURI COMPROMISE (1820–21) and led to the formation of the REPUBLICAN PARTY.

KANT, Immanuel (1724–1804), German philosopher, one of the world's greatest thinkers. He was born and lived in Königsberg (Kaliningrad). The starting point for Kant's "critical" philosophy was the work of David HUME, who awakened Kant from his "dogmatic slumber" and led him to make his "Copernican revolution in philosophy." This consisted of the radical view found in *Critique of Pure Reason* (1781) that objective reality (the phenomenal world) can be known only because the mind imposes the forms of its own intuitions—time and space—upon it. Things that cannot be perceived in experience (noumena) cannot be known, but as Kant says in *Critique of Practical Reason* (1788) their existence must be presumed in order to provide for man's free will (see ETHICS). In his third major work, *Critique of Judgment* (1790) he makes aesthetic and teleological judgments serve to mediate between the sensible and intelligible worlds which he divided sharply in the first two *Critiques*.

KAO-HSIUNG, city and chief port in S Taiwan. It has a wide range of industries and is a major naval base. Pop 845 900.

KAOLIN, or **china clay**, soft, white CLAY composed chiefly of KAOLINITE, and mined in England, France, Saxony, Czechoslovakia, China and the S US. It is used for filling and coating paper, filling rubber and paints, and for making POTTERY AND PORCELAIN.

KAOLINITE, prototypical member of the kaolinite group of CLAY minerals. It consists of hexagonal flakes of composition $Si_4Al_4O_{10}(OH)_8$. It is formed by alteration of other clays or FELDSPAR.

KAPITZA, Peter Leonidovich (1894–), Russian physicist best known for his work on low-temperature physics (see CRYOGENICS), especially his discovery of the SUPERFLUIDITY of HELIUM II.

KAPOK, water-resistant fibers obtained from the seeds of the silk-cotton or kapok tree (*Ceiba pentandra*). The tree is native to tropical America but is naturalized in many parts of the world and extensively cultivated in the Far East, particularly in Indonesia. Kapok is used in the manufacture of mattresses, life-preservers and insulation materials, but its importance has diminished since the advent of man-made fibers. Family: Bombacaceae.

KAPP, Wolfgang (1868–1922), German politician who led a rightist putsch against the WEIMAR REPUBLIC. In March, 1920, he took Berlin with the intention of restoring the monarchy but a socialist-staged general strike brought him down.

KAPUSKASING, town on the Kapuskasing R in Ontario, Canada. It produces pulp and paper and has an agricultural research establishment nearby. Pop 12 834.

KARACHI, former capital (1947–59) and largest city of Pakistan. The country's major port and industrial center, it stands on the Arabian Sea near the Indus Delta in Sind province, of which it is the capital. Pop 3 469 000.

KARAGANDA, city and capital of Karaganda oblast in Kazakhstan, USSR. It is the center of a huge coalmining area and produces iron and steel. Pop 522 000.

KARAITES, Jewish sect which arose in 8th-century Persia. It venerated the Torah as the written word of God himself, to the total exclusion of the recorded oral traditions of the Talmud, and practiced extreme asceticism. A group survives in modern Israel.

KARAJAN, Herbert von (1908–), Austrian conductor. He directed the Berlin State Opera 1938–45; the Vienna State Opera 1954–64 and concurrently from 1954 the Berlin Philharmonic Orchestra.

KARAKORAM RANGE, mountain chain in N Kashmir, extending for some 300mi between India, China and Tibet. Among its 60 or so peaks, it has the world's second highest mountain, K2 (28 250ft).

KARAKORUM, ancient capital of Genghis Khan's empire. Its ruins stand in what is now the Mongolian People's Republic, on the Orhon R. Established early in the 13th century, it had fallen into decay by the 16th century. Marco POLO visited here in around 1275.

KARAKUL SHEEP, a broadtail breed native to central Asia. Grown animals have a narrow body and coarse wiry brown coat but the newborn have a glossy black coat of tight curls. Lambs are bred (in the US mainly in Texas) for this pelt called karakul, broadtail, krimmer, astrakhan or Persian lamb.

KARAMANLIS, Constantine (1907–), Greek statesman who in 1974 returned to national acclaim as prime minister and leader of the New Democratic Party after the overthrow of the Colonels' junta (1967–74). A lawyer, Karamanlis held several ministries 1946–55 and was premier 1955–63, apart from March–May 1958 and Sept.–Nov. 1961.

KARAMZIN, Nikolai Mikhailovich (1766–1826), Russian writer and noted prose stylist. His *Letters of a Russian Traveller* (1792) introduced to Russia the style of sentimental sensibility developed by J. J. ROUSSEAU and Laurence STERNE. As court historian to Alexander I, he wrote an 11-volume history of Russia.

KARA SEA, an arm of the Arctic Ocean off N Siberia. Though frozen much of the year its routes have become important with the discovery of oil and gas at Ob-Yenisey.

KARAT. See CARAT.

KARATE, unarmed combat and sport, originating in ancient China, popularized throughout the world by the Japanese. Calloused skin pads are developed on hands, knees, elbows and feet which are used to deliver blows against vulnerable pressure points on the body. (See also JUDO.)

KARBALA, city in central Iraq, capital of Karbala province. It is a trade center and a holy city for Muslims of the Shi'ite sect, containing the tomb of HUSAIN. Pop 107 496.

KARELIA, Soviet republic on Russia's border with Finland. Vast lakes and pine forests maintain lumbering and fishing, and there are mineral deposits. E Karelia has belonged to Russia since 1721 and the W, formerly Finnish, since 1940. The native Karelian language belongs to the Finno-Ugric family.

KARELIAN ISTHMUS, narrow land bridge (25–70mi wide) between Lake Ladoga and the Gulf of Finland, linking the USSR and Finland. During WWII the MANNERHEIM line was located here.

KARIBA DAM, on the Zambezi R between Zambia and Rhodesia. A major hydroelectric project supplying Zambia and Rhodesia, it is one of the world's largest dams, being about 420ft high and 2 000ft long. The dam was completed in 1959. Its reservoir, Lake Kariba, stretches about 180mi back up the Kariba Gorge.

KARLFELDT, Erik Axel (1864–1931), Swedish lyric poet of rustic themes. As permanent secretary of the Nobel Committee, he refused the Prize for Literature (1918; awarded posthumously 1931.)

KARL-MARX-STADT, formerly Chemnitz, industrial city of East Germany, capital of Karl-Marx-Stadt district. An historic textile center, it now also produces machinery, chemicals and optical instruments. Pop 299 312.

KARLOFF, Boris (1887–1969), stage name of William Henry Pratt, British actor who rose to fame with his sympathetic portrayal of the Monster in the film *Frankenstein* (1930). He infused villainous roles with a subtly understated sense of evil.

KARLOVY VARY, health spa in Czechoslovakia, famous for its mineral springs. It was founded as Karlsbad by Emperor Charles IV in the 1340s. It is noted for its glass and ceramics. Pop 43 708.

KARLOWITZ, Treaty of, compact concluded in 1699 after the 1683–97 Ottoman Turkish wars in Europe. By the treaty, the Turks ceded most of their Hungarian gains to Austria, and other territories to Poland and Venice.

KARLSBAD. See KARLOVY VARY.

KARLSRUHE, city in Baden-Württemberg, seat of West Germany's federal judicial and constitutional courts. It is a transportation center linked by canal to the Rhine and has manufacturing industries. Pop 259 245.

KARMA, Sanskrit term denoting the inevitable effect of man's actions on his destiny in successive lives, central to Buddhist and Hindu thought. (See also TRANSMIGRATION OF SOULS.

KÁRMÁN, Theodore von (1881–1963), Hungarian-born US aeronautics engineer best known for his mathematical approach to problems in aeronautics (especially in jet engineering) and astronautics.

Pillared main hall of the 18th-dynasty temple of Amon at Karnak, one of the largest religious complexes ever built. Many other shrines and smaller temples were added to this magnificent building during later periods.

KARNAK, village E of LUXOR, on the Nile in Central Egypt, part of ancient Thebes. It is the site of the famous temple of AMON, perhaps the finest example of ancient Egyptian religious architecture.

KARO, Joseph ben Ephraim. See CARO, JOSEPH BEN EPHRAIM.

KARRER, Paul (1889–1971), Russian-born Swiss chemist awarded with W. N. HAWORTH the 1937 Nobel Prize for Chemistry for his work on the CAROTENOIDS and flavins, and on VITAMINS A and B_2.

KARSH, Yosuf (1908–), Turkish-Armenian born Canadian portrait photographer, whose company used the professional name Karsh of Ottawa. In 1935 he was appointed the Canadian government's official photographer.

KARST (from the Karst region of Yugoslavia), a LIMESTONE topography, typically including collapsed caverns, SINK HOLES where streams disappear underground, and areas of bare "limestone pavement." (For diagram, see GEOMORPHOLOGY.)

KARYOTYPE, the characteristic CHROMOSOMES of an individual organism or cell-line arranged in a systematized form and obtained by microscopic examination of CELLS during MEIOSIS. The chromosomes are numbered by pairs and grouped by their appearance in descending order of size.

KASAI RIVER, southern tributary of the Congo R. About 1 100mi long, it is navigable for about 475mi and is an important trade route. It rises in Angola and forms part of the Angola-Zaire border.

KASAVUBU, Joseph (c1915–1969), African politician, first president of the Republic of Congo (now Zaire) 1960–65. He ousted Premier Patrice LUMUMBA but was himself supplanted (1965) by Col. Joseph MOBUTU.

KASHMIR, territory administered by India (Jammu and Kashmir) and Pakistan (Azad Kashmir), bordered by those countries and by Afghanistan and China. Ever since Indian partition in 1947 the territory, which was formerly one of India's largest princely states, has been a cause of conflict between India and Pakistan, with some interference from China 1959–63, cease-fire lines being drawn and redrawn repeatedly. An agreement in 1972 confirmed the positions held by both sides at the end of the 1971 war. The Jhelum R forms the rich and scenically beautiful Vale of Kashmir. The region is mainly agricultural but also produces timber, medicines, silk, carpets and perfume oil. The chief cities are Srinagar (Jammu) and Muzaffarabad (Azad).

KASKASKIA, historic settlement, now almost uninhabited, on Kaskaskia Island in the Mississippi R, SE Ill. It was Illinois Territory capital (1809–18) and state capital (1818–20). Persistent flooding restricted further development.

KASSEL, city in West Germany on the Fulda R. Now a major industrial center, producing machinery, textiles, chemicals and automobiles, it served as the capital of Westphalia (1807–13). Pop 214 156.

KASSITES, conquerors, in the 18th century BC, of Babylonia. Originally from the Iranian plateau and probably of Indo-European stock, they held the region for some six centuries.

KASTLER, Alfred (1902–), French physicist awarded the 1966 Nobel Prize for Physics for his work on the structure of the ATOM, work which led eventually to the development of the LASER.

KATANGA. See SHABA.

KATAYEV, Valentin Petrovich (1897–), Russian novelist and playwright. Among his best-known works are the novels *The Embezzlers* (1927), *Lonely White Sail* (1936), *The Small Farm in the Steppe* (1956) and the farce *Squaring the Circle* (1928).

KATHAKALI, classical Hindu dance drama of SW India. The male dancers enact a mime characterized by vigorous and stylized movements and gestures to the chanting of traditional stories from such sources as the Mahabharata.

KATMAI NATIONAL MONUMENT, volcanic region of 2 792 137 acres on the Alaska Peninsula. It contains the Valley of Ten Thousand Smokes, formed in 1912 when the Katmai volcano erupted. The Katmai crater is one of the largest in the world. The monument was established in 1918.

KATMANDU, capital of Nepal, in a high valley of the E Himalayas. It stands on an ancient route from India to Tibet and China and remains an important transportation center. Pop 332 982.

Hindu temple to the god Shiva in the ancient city of Bhadgaon in the Katmandu valley, Nepal. Tibetan Buddhism and Hinduism coexist in the country; their intermingling is visible in the architecture.

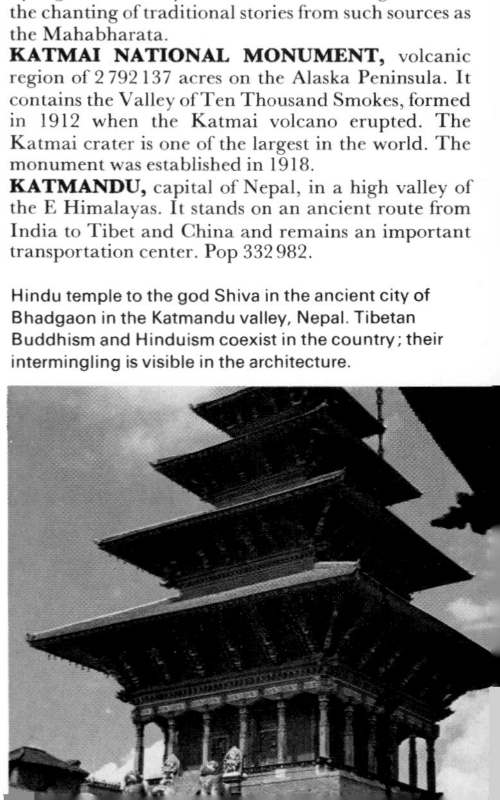

KATOWICE, industrial city and major mining center, capital of Poland's Katowice province. The city has belonged to Poland since 1921. Pop 303 264.

KATTEGAT, strait between Denmark and Sweden, linked by the Skagerrak to the North Sea and in the E to the Baltic. It is about 140mi long and 40–100mi wide.

KATYDID, North American name for bush crickets, jumping insects related to the true CRICKETS. Superficially similar in appearance to other GRASSHOPPERS, they have very long, thread-like antennae. Most bushcrickets tend to be nocturnal. Some species achieve outbreaks of pest proportions, like those of LOCUSTS.

KATYN FOREST, site in the USSR of a massacre of some 4 250 Polish officers in WWII. The mass grave was reported in 1943 by the Germans, who accused the Russians, who in their turn accused the Germans. Stalin refused a Red Cross enquiry; the Polish government in exile in London took this as an admission of Russian guilt.

KATZ, Sir Bernard (1911–), German-born British biophysicist who shared with AXELROD and von EULER the 1970 Nobel Prize for Physiology or Medicine for their independent work on the chemistry of the transmission of nerve impulses.

KAUAI, Hawaiian island NW of Oahu. In geological terms this mountainous island is the oldest of the Hawaiian group. It has several rivers and its fertile plains and valleys produce rice, sugar and pineapples.

KAUFFMANN, (Maria Ann) Angelica (1741–1807), Swiss artist. She worked in England in 1766–81 and was a friend of Sir Joshua REYNOLDS. She is noted for her portraits but is best remembered as a designer for Robert and James ADAM.

KAUFMAN, George Simon (1889–1961), US dramatist who collaborated on several successful plays noted for their dry satirical humor. Among his works are, with Marc Connelly, *Beggar on Horseback* (1924); and with Moss Hart *You Can't Take it With You* (1936). He won Pulitzer prizes in 1932 and 1937.

KAUKAUNA, city in E Wis. A dairying center, it also produces precision tools and paper and has some stone quarrying. Pop 11 292.

KAUNAS, port and industrial city in the Lithuanian republic of the USSR at the confluence of the Neris and Neman rivers. In the Middle Ages it was an outpost of Lithuania against the Teutonic knights. Pop 284 000.

KAUNDA, Kenneth David (1924–), first president of Zambia, from 1964. From 1953 he worked ardently for African rule in the then British colony of N Rhodesia, suffering exile and imprisonment. Released in 1960, he headed the new United National Independence Party. Kaunda has maintained a hard line against white Rhodesia.

KAUTSKY, Karl Johann (1854–1938), German Marxist. Influenced by Eduard BERNSTEIN, and a friend of ENGELS, he was a great popularizer of MARXISM. After the revolution in Russia (1917) he became a staunch opponent of BOLSHEVISM

KAVAFIS, Konstantinos Petrou, or Constantine Cavafy (1863–1933), Greek poet. He spent most of his life in his native Alexandria. His ironic poetry, of great breadth and dramatic power, has proved widely influential since his death.

KAWABATA, Yasunari (1899–1972), Japanese novelist. He is noted for his impressionistic, lyrical style and a preoccupation with loneliness and death; he finally committed suicide. One of his best-known works is *Snow Country* (1947). He was awarded the 1968 Nobel Prize for Literature.

KAWAGUCHI, city in SE Honshu, Japan, N of Tokyo. Industries include metal casting and textile manufacture. Pop 305 886.

KAWASAKI, Japanese seaport on the W coast of Tokyo Bay. Industries include shipbuilding, chemicals and oil refining. Pop 973 486.

KAY, John (1704–c1764), British inventor of the flying shuttle (patented 1733), which greatly increased the speed of WEAVING while reducing the number of workers required.

KAYAK, Eskimo word for a one-man canoe originally made of a wooden or bone frame covered in sealskin. The term is now applied to modern canoes of similar design. Often made of plastics, they may be between 8ft and 14ft in length and are popular as sports boats.

KAYE, Danny (1913–), US comedian and entertainer. His best-known films are *The Secret Life of Walter Mitty* (1946), and *Hans Christian Anderson* (1952). A favorite with children, he was active as a fund-raiser for the UN Children's Fund.

KAZAKHSTAN, constituent republic of the USSR. In central Asia, it runs from the Caspian Sea in the W to the Chinese frontier in the E. Over 50% of the population is Russian and Ukrainian, the Kazakhs forming nearly 30%. Rich in coal, tungsten, oil, copper, lead, manganese and zinc, it is one of Russia's leading industrial and agricultural areas, providing various grain crops.

KAZAN, historic Russian port on the Volga R, capital of the Tatar SSR. Founded in the late 13th century, it is an important commercial, industrial and cultural center. Pop 869 000.

KAZAN, Elia (1909–), Turkish-born US film and stage director best known for realistic films on social issues, such as *On the Waterfront* (1954). Among his many other films are *A Streetcar Named Desire* (1951) and *Viva Zapata!* (1952). He wrote and directed *The Arrangement* (1967) and *The Assassins* (1972).

KAZANTZAKIS, Nikos (1883?–1957), prolific Greek writer and statesman, minister of public welfare 1919–27 and minister of state 1945–46. Among his known works are *Christ Recrucified* (1938), *The Odyssey, a Modern Sequel* (1938) and *Zorba the Greek* (1946).

KAZIN, Alfred (1915–), influential US critic. His book *On Native Grounds* (1942), was a major study of contemporary US prose literature. This and later work, such as *The Ambassador* (1969), are concerned also with the historical development of US culture.

KEA, *Nestor notabilis*, a primitive mountain parrot now found only in the South Island of New Zealand. It has a long, slightly curved beak, and a hairlike fringe to the tongue. Keas are social birds, feeding on berries, shoots and carrion. They are also suspected of attacking live sheep.

KEAN, Edmund (1787–1833), leading English actor of his time. His greatest roles were in Shakespearian tragedy, notably as Othello, to which he introduced a dynamic naturalistic style.

KEARNEY, Denis (1847–1907), Irish-born US labor agitator. He organized San Francisco workers against Chinese immigrant labor, provoking riots in 1877. His Workingmen's Party forced through a new Cal. constitution by dubious means, but collapsed after financing a European tour for Kearney.

KEARNS, unincorporated urban community in N Ut., in an agricultural area SW of Salt Lake City. Its economy rests on dairy products and sugar beet. Pop 17 071.

KEARNY, town on Newark Bay in NE N.J. It produces bricks, tiles, textiles, chemicals and electronic equipment. Pop 37 585.

KEARNY, Philip (1814–1862), US general who served in Algeria, in Mexico (where he lost an arm) and in Italy. In the Civil War he commanded the 1st New Jersey Brigade as brigadier-general of Union volunteers. Noted for his bravery, he was killed in a skirmish at Chantilly.

KEARNY, Stephen Watts (1794–1848), US general. During the MEXICAN WAR (1846–48) he conquered N.M. by diplomacy, persuading the more powerful Mexican force to withdraw peacefully. He subdued Cal. also, despite conflict with fellow-officers Robert STOCKTON and John FRÉMONT. Governor of Vera Cruz and of Mexico City in 1848, he died there of yellow fever.

Statue of General Stephen Kearny, marking his grave in Arlington Cemetery, Washington, D.C.

KEARSARGE, The, US warship (1031 tons) built during the Civil War. It sank the Confederate ship *Alabama* on June 14, 1864, off Cherbourg, France. The *Kearsarge* sank in the Caribbean on Feb. 2, 1894.

KEATON, (Joseph Frank) Buster (1895–1966), US silent film comedian. In such films as *The Navigator* (1924) and *The General* (1926) he created the character of an innocent in conflict with malevolent machinery. His apparently deadpan face had in fact a very subtle range of expressions.

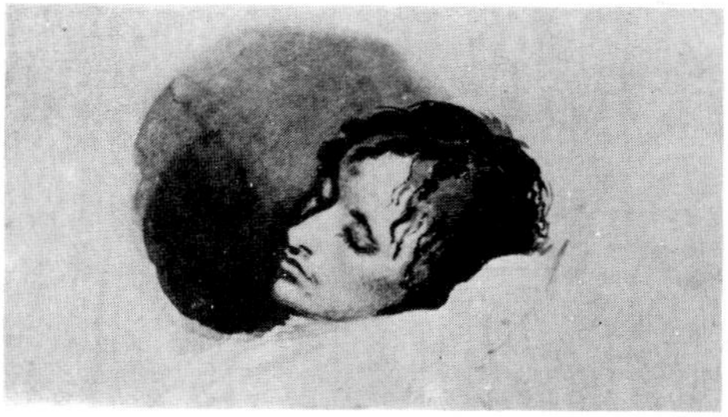

The poet John Keats on his deathbed in Rome, a sketch by his friend and companion on the journey Joseph Severn. Keats was buried in Rome's Protestant cemetery, and Severn was later buried there alongside him.

KEATS, John (1795–1821), one of the greatest English Romantic poets. He gave up medicine in 1816 to devote himself to poetry. His earlier poems and the Spenserian epic *Endymion* (1817) attracted little attention except politically motivated abuse. During 1817 his brother Tom died of tuberculosis, and his own health suffered after a long walking tour. The epic *Hyperion*, the ballad *La Belle Dame sans Merci* and *The Eve of St. Agnes* were written at this time. A developing romance with Fanny Brawne was offset by serious financial troubles caused by his guardian. In May 1819 he wrote the four odes—*To a Nightingale*, *On a Grecian Urn*, *On Melancholy*, and *On Indolence*. *Lamia* and *To Autumn*, effectively his last work, followed later that summer. In Jan. 1820 he developed definite tuberculosis symptoms. Taken to winter in Italy, he died in Rome, where he is buried.

KEDIRI, historic capital of the Kediri region in East Jawa, Indonesia, on the Brantas R. It processes and exports sugar, cotton and coffee. Pop 158 918.

KEELING ISLANDS. See COCOS AND KEELING ISLANDS.

KEENE, city in SW N.H., seat of Chester Co. In an agricultural area, it has various industries and is a market center and summer resort. Pop 20 467.

The keeshond was introduced to America from the Netherlands. Its disciplined yet affable nature makes it a popular pet and an excellent guard dog.

KEESHOND (or Dutch barge dog), small dog up to 18in long and weighing up to 36lb, related to the SPITZ and POMERANIAN, with a long thick coat, plumed tail and pointed face. It was the mascot and symbol of the 18th-century Patriot's Party of Holland.

KEEWATIN DISTRICT, SE area of the NORTHWEST TERRITORIES, Canada, including the mainland and islands of the Hudson and James Bays. The district is rocky and within the permafrost zone.

KEFAUVER, Carey Estes (1903–1963), US Democratic senator from Tenn., who in 1950 headed the Senate committee investigating organized crime. From this he drew his book *Crime in America* (1951). He was Democratic vice-presidential nominee in 1956 under Adlai STEVENSON.

KEFLAVIK, fishing port on Faxa Bay in SW Iceland. It is the site of a major international airport and a NATO airbase. Pop 5663.

KEITEL, Wilhelm (1882–1946), German field-marshal, head of the armed forces high command during WWII. A man of little ability or experience, he was primarily Hitler's puppet. He was convicted at NUREMBERG of violations of international law and executed.

KEKKONEN, Urho Kaleva (1900–   ), Finnish statesman, leader of the Agrarian Party. President for three terms from 1956, he was sworn in for a further term by a special act of the Finnish Diet in Jan. 1973.

KEKULÉ VON STRADONITZ, Friedrich August (1829–1896), German chemist regarded as the father of modern ORGANIC CHEMISTRY. At the same time as **Archibald Scott Couper** (1831–1892) he recognized the quadrivalency of CARBON and its ability to form long chains. With his later inference of the structure of BENZENE (the "benzene ring"), structural organic chemistry was born.

KELLER, Gottfried (1819–1890), German-speaking Swiss author, best known for his autobiographical novel *Green Henry* (1854–55), the story of a naïve young man who, after failing as an artist, finds satisfaction as a public official.

KELLER, Helen Adams (1880–1968), US author and lecturer. Born blind, deaf and dumb, she became famous for her triumph over her disabilities. Taught by Anne SULLIVAN from 1887, she learned to read, write and speak, and graduated from Radliffe College, Cambridge, Mass., with honors in 1904. Her books include *The Story of My Life* (1903) and *Helen Keller's Journal* (1938).

KELLEY, Florence (1859–1932), US social reformer and lawyer. A campaigner for labor legislation to protect women and children, she was director of the National Consumer's League from 1899.

KELLOGG, Frank Billings (1856–1937), US diplomat, senator 1917–23 and ambassador to Britain 1923–25. His most important achievement was the KELLOGG-BRIAND PACT of 1928. A judge of the Permanent Court of International Justice 1930–35, he was awarded the 1929 Nobel Peace Prize.

KELLOGG, Will Keith (1860–1951), US industrialist and philanthropist. He made his fortune through the breakfast cereal industry he established in 1906 at Battle Creek, Mich., originally to manufacture the cornflakes developed as a health food by his physician brother.

KELLOGG-BRIAND PACT, agreement signed on Aug. 27, 1928, by 15 nations (later observed by 64 others) renouncing "war as an instrument of national policy." Conceived by Aristide BRIAND of France and F. B. KELLOGG of the US, it left many loopholes, and ultimately proved ineffectual.

KELLS, Book of. See BOOK OF KELLS.

KELLY, Grace (1929–   ), US film and stage actress, Oscar winner for *Country Girl* (1954). After such films as *The Swan* (1956) and *High Society* (1956), she married Prince Ranier III of Monaco.

KELLY, Ned (1855–80), Australian outlaw, robber and murderer, famous for the crude armor he wore. Kelly was captured and hanged after an attempt to take over a small town. The body of myth around him has no basis in truth.

KELLY, William (1811–1888), US inventor, simultaneously with Sir Henry BESSEMER, of the steelmaking process now known as the BESSEMER PROCESS.

KELMSCOTT PRESS, press set up by William MORRIS in 1890 in an attempt to revive the craft of book production in the face of current low standards. Producing only 18 000 copies of 52 books in its eight-year life, it used a pseudo-medieval style heavily influenced by the Pre-Raphaelites.

KELOWNA, city in S British Columbia, Canada, on the shore of Lake Okanagan. In a fruit-growing area, it has canneries and sawmills and also makes wine. Pop 19 089.

KELP, general name for brown SEAWEEDS (ALGAE) of the order Laminariales. Some (e.g. *Macrocystis* sp and *Nereocystis* sp) grow up to 30m (100ft) long. Kelps are common in cooler seas throughout the world. In many regions, kelps are harvested and used for fertilizer and cattle feed. Some are used for human consumption. In the past, kelps were major sources of IODINE and POTASH.

KELSO, city, seat of Cowlitz Co., SW Wash. The economy rests on timber, fishing and agriculture. Pop 10 296.

KELVIN (K), the SI UNIT of thermodynamic TEMPERATURE, defined as 1/273.16 of the thermodynamic temperature of the triple point of WATER. It is used both as a unit of temperature difference (when the centigrade degree is defined equal to it) and for expressing ABSOLUTE temperatures (in kelvins above ABSOLUTE ZERO). Temperatures expressed in degrees Celsius equal temperatures expressed in kelvins less 273.15. The older terms "degree Kelvin" and "Kelvin scale" are obsolete.

KELVIN, William Thomson, 1st Baron (1824–1907), British physicist who made important contributions to many branches of physics. In attempting to reconcile CARNOT's theory of heat engines and JOULE's mechanical theory of HEAT he both formulated (independently of CLAUSIUS) the 2nd Law of THERMODYNAMICS and introduced the ABSOLUTE temperature scale, the unit of which is called KELVIN for him. His and FARADAY's work on ELECTROMAGNETISM gave rise to the theory of the electromagnetic field, and his papers, with those of Faraday, strongly influenced J. Clerk MAXWELL's work on the electromagnetic theory of LIGHT (though Kelvin himself rejected Maxwell's over-abstract theory). His work on wire-telegraphic signaling played an essential part in the successful laying of the first ATLANTIC CABLE.

KELVIN SCALE. See ABSOLUTE ZERO; TEMPERATURE.

KEMAL ATATURK. See ATATURK, KEMAL.

KEMEROVO, city, capital of Kemerovo region in the Russian SFSR. It is a major coal mining center and produces chemicals. Pop 385 000.

KENDALL, Amos (1789–1869), US journalist and politician. Coeditor of the *Argus of Western America* (1816–29), he became a member of the "Kitchen Cabinet" of President Jackson who made him postmaster general in 1835. He later promoted Samuel MORSE's telegraph service.

KENDALL, Edward Calvin (1886–1972), US biochemist awarded with HENCH and REICHSTEIN the 1950 Nobel Prize for Physiology or Medicine for his work on the corticoids and isolation of cortisone (see STEROIDS), applied by Hench to the treatment of rheumatoid ARTHRITIS.

KENDREW, John Cowdery (1917–   ), British biochemist awarded with PERUTZ the 1962 Nobel Prize for Chemistry for his first determining the structure of a globular PROTEIN (myoglobin).

KENILWORTH, historic town in Warwickshire, England, centered around the ruined castle of Kenilworth. Originally Norman, the castle was granted by Elizabeth I to the Earl of Leicester, and was destroyed in the Civil War. Pop 20 121.

KENMORE, residential village on the Niagara R in W N.Y. Pop 20 980.

KENNAN, George Frost (1904–   ), US diplomat, one of the main authors of the US postwar policy of "containment" of Russian expansionism. Ambassador to the USSR 1952 and Yugoslavia in 1961–63, he wrote *Russia Leaves the War* (1956), for which he received the Pulitzer Prize, and *Memoirs, 1925–1950* (1967–72).

KENNEBEC RIVER, flows 150mi S from Moosehead Lake, Me., to the Atlantic NE of Brunswick.

John Fitzgerald KENNEDY
35th US President

Born: May 29, 1917
Died: November 22, 1963
Term of office: January 20, 1961–November 22, 1963
Political party: Democratic

KENNEDY, Cape. See CANAVERAL, CAPE.

KENNEDY, Edward Moore (1932–   ), US Democratic politician. He was elected to his brother John F. Kennedy's vacant Senate seat in 1962. His hopes for Democratic presidential nomination received a setback in 1969, when a car he was driving crashed into a creek on Chappaquiddick, killing his female companion. He withdrew from presidential politics but remained active in the Senate.

KENNEDY, Jacqueline Bouvier. See ONASSIS, JACQUELINE BOUVIER KENNEDY.

KENNEDY, John Fitzgerald (1917–1963), 35th president of the US, was the youngest man to be elected president and the fourth president to be assassinated. The second son of Joseph P. KENNEDY, he was brought up in Boston and New York. Popular but undistinguished at school, he was overshadowed by his older brother Joseph Jr., upon whom their father's ambitions focused. In his senior year at Harvard in 1939, however, his thesis on British policies leading to the MUNICH PACT was well-received and published as *Why England Slept* (1940). He joined the US Navy in 1941; when his torpedo boat was sunk by the Japanese in 1943 he led survivors to safety, himself towing an injured man three miles through rough seas. His already bad health was seriously weakened by a back injury and malaria, and he was discharged in 1945 with the Purple Heart and the Navy and Marine Corps medal. His brother Joseph had been killed in 1944 and the family ambition now rested on him. In 1952 he became junior senator for Mass., taking a position on the moderate right. In 1953 he married Jacqueline Bouvier (see ONASSIS, JACQUELINE). While convalescing after operations on his injured back he wrote *Profiles in Courage* (1956); a study of US statesmen who put national interest before party, it won the Pulitzer Prize for biography in 1957. By 1957 he was becoming known for his liberal views on race, social and foreign issues.

Narrowly missing the 1956 vice-presidential nomination, in 1960 he was nominated as Democratic presidential candidate, running with Lyndon B. Johnson, and defeated Richard M. Nixon in the election. The abortive BAY OF PIGS invasion of Cuba in 1961 rocked the new administration, but the action was supported by both parties. More serious was the

Seconds after the assassination of President John F. Kennedy on November 22, 1963, in Dallas, Texas, a secret serviceman leaps on the back of the presidential car as shocked bystanders run forward. Although the entire sequence of events was filmed, what actually happened is still hotly debated.

growing confrontation with the USSR under Khrushchev over West Berlin. Kennedy met the Russian challenge with equal obstinacy and the crisis was gradually defused, despite the construction of the BERLIN WALL. A more serious confrontation threatened in Oct., 1962, when aerial reconnaissance revealed Russian missile bases under construction in Cuba. Kennedy immediately imposed a quarantine on all weapons shipments to Cuba, threatening to search and turn back any such consignments. After a week of tense confrontation the USSR capitulated, a considerable victory for Kennedy, as was his part in persuading the USSR to sign a limited nuclear test-ban treaty, a significant check to COLD WAR policies. A massive foreign aid program for Latin America and his support of the European COMMON MARKET won him considerable support abroad. At the height of his popularity he was shot dead by Lee Harvey OSWALD in a motorcade through Dallas, Tex. Theories of a conspiracy are unsupported by evidence.

KENNEDY, Joseph Patrick (1888–1969), US businessman and diplomat. Having amassed a fortune in banking, the stock market and other areas in the 1920s, he was active in government and served as US ambassador to Britain 1937–40. His sons John Fitzgerald and Robert Francis were both assassinated in high office; his fourth son, Edward, continued to represent the family in politics.

KENNEDY, Robert Francis (1925–1968). Younger brother of John F. KENNEDY, he served as US attorney general 1961–64 and was senator for New York from 1965. After his brother's death, he became a popular leader of the liberal wing of the Democratic Party and ran as presidential candidate in 1968. On June 4, 1968, the evening of his victory in the Cal. primary, he was assassinated by Sirhan SIRHAN.

KENNELLY, Arthur Edwin (1861–1939), US electrical engineer who, independently of HEAVISIDE, proposed the existence of that layer of the IONOSPHERE (the E layer) now often called the Kennelly-Heaviside Layer.

KENNER, city on the Mississippi R in SE La., W of New Orleans. Both residential and industrial, its main manufactures are wood products. Pop 29 858.

KENNESAW MOUNTAIN, Battle of, fought in the Civil War near Atlanta, Ga., on June 27, 1864. Union troops under Gen. William SHERMAN made a frontal attack on Confederate positions but were repulsed with heavy losses. They forced a Confederate withdrawal by outflanking.

KENNETH I MACALPIN (d. 858 AD), traditionally the first king of a united kingdom of Picts and the Scots of Dalriada, called Alba, in Scotland. He ruled N of a line between the Forth and the Clyde.

KENNEWICK, residential city and port on the Columbia R in an agricultural region of S Wash. The Hanford Atomic Project is nearby. Pop 15 212.

KENNY, Sister Elizabeth (1886–1952), Australian nurse best known for developing the treatment of infantile paralysis (see POLIOMYELITIS) by stimulating and reeducating the muscles affected.

KENOGAMI, city in S Quebec, Canada, on the Saguenay R. It has pulp and paper mills. Pop 10 970.

KENORA, town in W Ontario, Canada. Its industries include lumber, pulp, paper and flour mills and it is a base for fishing and hunting. Pop 10 952.

KENOSHA, city in SE Wis., seat of Kenosha Co., Lake Michigan. Among its manufactures are clothing, automobiles and electronic equipment. Pop 78 805.

KENSETT, John Frederick (1816–1872), US landscape painter identified with the HUDSON RIVER SCHOOL. He was trained as an engraver, and his paintings preserve the engraver's detailed clarity, with subtle color gradations.

KENSINGTON RUNE STONE, found in 1898 on a farm near Kensington, Minn. Inscribed in RUNES dated 1362 is an account of Norse exploration of the Great Lakes of North America. The stone is in a special museum in Alexandria, Minn., but most scholars now think it to be a forgery.

KENT, industrial city in NE Ohio, on the Cuyahoga R. Its manufactures include buses and machinery. Kent State U. is located here. Pop 28 183.

KENT, city in W central Wash. It is a processing center for a farming area and manufactures furniture, chemicals and aircraft parts. Pop 16 275.

KENT, James (1763–1847), American jurist. He was the first professor of law at Columbia College 1794–98 and chief judge of the Supreme Court (1804). As chancellor of the N.Y. court of chancery (1814–23) he revived EQUITY jurisdiction in US law. He wrote the monumental *Commentaries on American Law* (1826–30).

KENT, Rockwell (1882–1971), US writer and artist. He is best known for his illustrations of popular classics and his own works, which include *Wilderness* (1921) and *This is My Own* (1940).

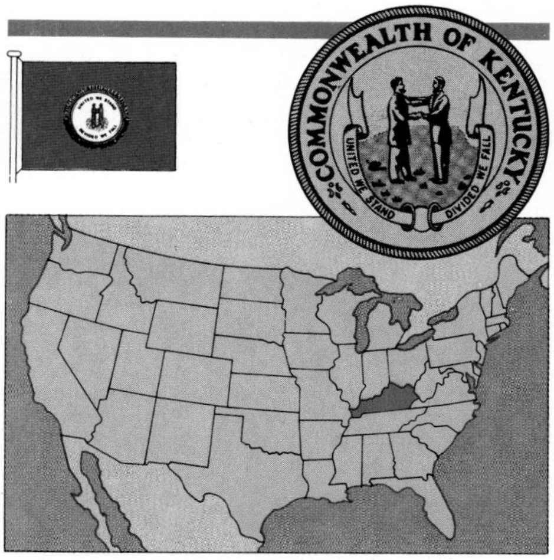

Name of state: Kentucky
Capital: Frankfort
Statehood: June 1, 1792 (15th state)
Familiar name: Bluegrass State
Area: 39 650sq mi
Population: 3 219 311
Elevation: Highest—4 145ft, Black Mountain. Lowest—257ft, Mississippi River in Fulton County
Motto: United We Stand, Divided We Fall
State flower: Golden Rod
State bird: Kentucky cardinal
State tree: Tulip poplar
State song: "My Old Kentucky Home"

KENTUCKY, southern central state of the US, known as the Bluegrass state. It is roughly triangular in shape and may be divided into three regions. In the west, the land slopes down to the Jackson Purchase Area, including swampland flanking the Mississippi R. The Interior Low Plateau consists of the W coalfield and the gently rolling Bluegrass Region, where there are rich soils and where the largest cities and major industries are also situated. The blue blossoms of the grasses around Lexington, in this region, have given Kentucky its nickname. The third

Tobacco plantation in Kentucky. Tobacco is the state's leading crop and a mainstay of its economy, since the cigarette industry is a major employer. The main tobacco-growing regions are between the Green and Cumberland rivers.

land region, the Appalachian Plateau, is a mountainous area of narrow valleys, in which the CUMBERLAND GAP is one of the few natural passes to the West. The most important rivers are the Ohio and the Tennessee, dammed at Gilbertsville to create KENTUCKY LAKE. Kentucky has a mild climate with warm summers and cool winters.

People and Economy. The majority of Kentuckians now live in urban areas, the drift to the cities having been considerable through the past 50 years. Frankfort, Louisville and Lexington are the chief cities. Industry is concentrated along the Ohio R and the chief products are foodstuffs, machinery, and cigarettes, of which Kentucky produces one quarter of the US total. Other important products are burley tobacco, coal, gas, oil, livestock, grains and bourbon whiskey. Kentucky, home of the world-famous KENTUCKY DERBY, ranks first in the US in thoroughbred racehorse breeding.

History. The first permanent settlement was established by James HARROD in 1774 after Daniel BOONE's expeditions over the Appalachians 1769–71. After the Revolutionary War, new settlers flowed in. In 1792 a constitution for the Commonwealth of Kentucky was adopted and in the same year Kentucky became the 15th state in the Union. On the eve of the Civil War, Kentucky had vast tobacco plantations worked by Negro slaves, but as much of the land was occupied by small farmers raising corn and hogs, the state was divided during the war. The legislature declared allegiance to the Union although 35 000 men enlisted in the Confederate armies.

After the war, burley tobacco became the mainstay of Kentucky's agriculture, though the new railroads opened up the coalfields of the Appalachians. Following the depression years of the 1930s, WWII brought economic recovery and since then industrial expansion has continued. Despite general prosperity, however, pockets of poverty still exist, notably in the E coalmining regions of the Appalachians.

KENTUCKY AND VIRGINIA RESOLUTIONS, passed by the legislatures of Ky. and Va. in 1798 and 1799, after the Federalist-controlled Congress had passed the ALIEN AND SEDITION ACTS. The Kentucky Resolutions, drafted by Thomas Jefferson, claimed that the federal government was the result of a compact between the states. If it assumed powers not specifically delegated to it, the states could declare any acts under these powers unconstitutional. The Virginia resolutions, drafted by James MADISON, declared the same theory in milder form. The resolutions were concerned principally with individual civil liberties, but John CALHOUN and other Southern leaders used them as the basis for the doctrines of NULLIFICATION and SECESSION.

KENTUCKY DERBY, famous US horserace. It is an annual classic for three-year-olds run over a course of 1¼mi at Churchill Downs, Louisville, Ky. It was founded in 1875 by Col. M. Lewis Clark. (See also HORSE RACING.)

KENTUCKY LAKE, one of the world's largest man-made lakes, created when the Tennessee R was dammed in 1944. It covers 247sq mi in Ky. and Tenn., and serves as a reservoir and recreation area.

KENTUCKY RIVER, formed by the confluence of three streams at Beattyville, Ky., near the Cumberland Mts. It flows NW for about 250mi through the Bluegrass Region and empties into the Ohio R at Carrollton, Ky. It is navigable as far as Heidelberg.

KENTWOOD, city in W Mich., 8mi S of Grand Rapids. Pop 20 310.

KENYA, East African republic, bounded by the Sudan, Ethiopia, Somalia, Uganda and Tanzania, famous for its national parks and game reserves. The country straddles the equator and has four main regions: the narrow fertile coastal strip, with rain forests and mango swamps; the vast dry scrubland pastures of the Niyika, crossed by Kenya's two chief rivers, the Tana and the Athi; the highlands, cut by the Great Rift Valley, where Mt Kenya (17 058ft) and Mt Elgon (14 178ft) stand and where the rich volcanic soil, moderate temperatures and ample rainfall provide most farm crops; the western (Nyanza) plateau, stretching to Lake Victoria, an area of farmlands, forests and grasslands.

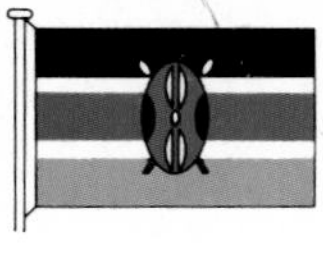

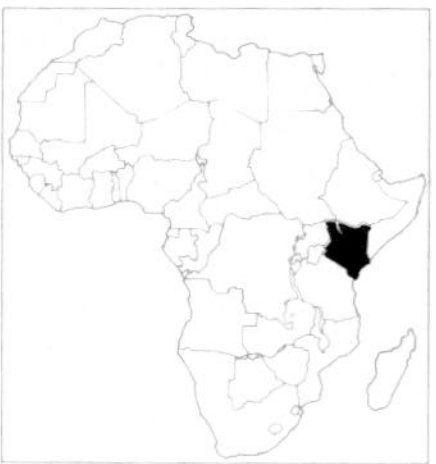

Official name: Kenya
Capital: Nairobi
Area: 224 960sq mi
Population: 11 694 000
Languages: English, Swahili, Kikuyu, Luo widely spoken
Religions: Animist, Christian, Muslim, Hindu
Monetary unit(s): 1 Kenya shilling = 100 cents

People and Economy. More than 95% of the population is African. There are also Indian, Arab and European communities. Chief among the many African tribal groups are the KIKUYU. More than eight million Kenyans live in the SW, mainly in the highlands where Nairobi, the capital and largest city, is situated. Agriculture is the major occupation with tea, coffee, timber, fruit and vegetables the main exports. There are few mineral resources but oil is being prospected and deposits of lead and silver have recently been found. Hides and wool are produced for export and for domestic use. Manufacturing industries grew up after WWII, and in the 1960s construction and food-processing boomed. Tourism is important, providing more than 2% of the national income.

History. Until 1887 the coast was under Arab control; the British then opened the interior with imported Indian labor and encouraged European settlement. In 1944 the first African nationalist party was set up, Jomo KENYATTA becoming its leader in 1947. Discontent led to the formation of the MAU MAU terrorist organization. Pacified by reforms, Kenya gained independence in 1963, becoming a republic in 1964 under Kenyatta's presidency.

KENYA, Mount, extinct volcano in central Kenya, E Africa, on the E of the Great Rift Valley. At 17 058ft it is Africa's second highest mountain. The summit was first reached in 1899.

KENYATTA, Jomo (1893?–), African politician, Kenya's first president, from 1964. His early political career was concerned with Kikuyu rights. In 1953 he was imprisoned on charges of leading the MAU MAU. His release came in 1961 following pressure from African nationalists. Kenyatta was one of the most influential of the early African nationalist leaders.

KEOKUK, city in SE Iowa, seat of Lee Co. Manufactures include corn and oats products, and shoes. It has big commercial fisheries. Pop 14 631.

Village in south Kenya. Only about 10% of the population live in urban areas, and of the rural remainder a large percentage is nomadic, wandering over the arid and thinly inhabited plains in search of new grazing.

KEOKUK (c1780–1848), American Indian chief of the Sauk tribe. In the WAR OF 1812, when Black Hawk, then leader of the tribe, supported the British, he remained on the American side. He became leader after the BLACK HAWK WAR (1832).

KEPLER, Johannes (1571–1630), German astronomer who, using BRAHE's superbly accurate observations of the planets, advanced COPERNICUS' heliocentric model of the SOLAR SYSTEM in showing that the planets followed elliptical paths. His three laws (see KEPLER'S LAWS) were later the template about which NEWTON formulated his theory of GRAVITATION. Kepler also did important work in optics, discovering a fair approximation for the law of REFRACTION.

KEPLER'S LAWS, three laws formulated by Johannes KEPLER to describe the motions of the planets in the solar system. (**1**) Each planet orbits the sun in an ELLIPSE of which the sun is at one focus. (**2**) The line between a planet and the sun sweeps out equal areas in equal times: hence the planet moves faster when closer to the sun than it does when farther away. (**3**) The square of the time taken by a planet to ORBIT the sun is proportional to the cube of its mean distance from the sun.

KERATIN, a fibrous insoluble PROTEIN high in sulfur, found in the skin of vertebrates where it forms the major component of hair, feathers, nails, claws and hooves.

KERBELA. See KARBALA.

KERENSKY, Alexander Feodorovich (1881–1970), Russian moderate revolutionary leader and head of the provisional government July to Oct. 1917. Overthrown in the Bolshevik Revolution (October 1917), he emigrated to Western Europe and in 1940 went to the US. His books include *The Catastrophe* (1927) and *The Kerensky Memoirs* (1966).

KERGUELEN ISLANDS, archipelago in the S Indian Ocean, belonging to France since 1893. The largest is Kerguelen Island, which is mainly glacial in the interior; there are about 300 other small islands.

KERKYRA. See CORFU.

KERMADEC ISLANDS, volcanic group of about 13sq mi in the S Pacific. It was annexed by New Zealand in 1887.

KERMAN, city in SE Iran, capital of Kerman province. It manufactures shawls and is the largest carpet-exporting center in Iran. Pop 88 000.

KERMES, a genus of hemipterous insects common in North America and Europe. Large numbers are found in crevices in oak bark where they produce an abundant flow of mucus. In the Mediterranean one species forms galls on the leaves of oak trees. The dried bodies of the females constitute a purplish-red dye also known as kermes.

KERN, Jerome David (1885–1945), US composer. His most famous work is the score of *Show Boat* (1927) which includes the song "Ol' Man River." Among his classic songs are "Smoke Gets in Your Eyes" and "The Song is You."

KERNER COMMISSION, appointed by President L. B. Johnson in 1967 to investigate the causes of the race riots of the mid-1960s. The commission, headed by Gov. Otto Kerner of Ill., put most of the blame on "white racism." It concluded that the US was moving towards two societies, one black and one white—"separate but unequal." It suggested improvements in schools and housing and better police protection for residents of black ghettoes.

KERNITE, a mineral form of hydrated sodium tetraborate ($Na_2B_4O_7.4H_2O$), found associated with BORAX in Kern Co., Cal. It forms colorless monoclinic crystals, and occurs as veins in clay shale beds. Kernite is a major source of BORON.

KEROSINE, or paraffin oil, a mixture of volatile HYDROCARBONS having 10 to 16 carbon atoms per molecule, used as a FUEL for jet engines (see JET PROPULSION), for heating and lighting and as a solvent and paint thinner. Although it can be derived from oil, coal and tar, most is produced from PETROLEUM by refining and CRACKING. Kerosine boils between 150°C and 300°C.

KEROUAC, Jack (1922–1969), US novelist. His best-known book is *On the Road* (1957), describing his life of freedom from conventional middle-class ties

Parent Common kestrel bringing a small mammal as food to the young at the nest. As is usual, this is the abandoned nest of some other large bird, possibly a crow.

and values. He was a leading figure of the BEAT GENERATION.

KERRVILLE, city in S central Tex., seat of Kerr Co. It is a popular tourist resort and a market center for wool and mohair. Pop 12 672.

KERRY BLUE TERRIER, hunting and herding dog originating in Co. Kerry, Ireland. It is a versatile and hard-working dog with high intelligence, and has a soft wavy coat of varying shades of gray-blue.

KERYGMA (Greek: preaching), the proclamation in Christian apologetics—especially the apostolic proclamation of the GOSPEL of Jesus Christ—contrasted with the teaching or **didache** (Greek: teaching) given to candidates for baptism or confirmation, often by means of a CATECHISM. There is now renewed emphasis on the kerygma as the basis for conversion and it is thus central to existential theology.

KESSELRING, Albert (1885–1960), German field marshal of WWII. He became commander in chief in Italy (1943) and in the West (1945). He was convicted of war crimes (1947) and sentenced to life imprisonment, but was released in 1952.

KESTRELS, a distinctive group of FALCONS which persistently hover for ground prey, rather than taking birds or insects in flight. They are small red-brown falcons, males often distinguished by a gray head.

KETONES, class of organic compounds of general formula RR′CO, containing a carbonyl group, but less reactive than ALDEHYDES, which in some ways they resemble. They are used as solvents and in industrial synthesis. The simplest and most important is ACETONE (see also CAMPHOR). Ketones are formed by dehydrogenation or oxidation of secondary ALCOHOLS, FRIEDEL-CRAFTS acylation of aromatic compounds, and by other methods. They may be reduced by hydrogen or metal HYDRIDES to secondary alcohols, and undergo addition and condensation reactions with NUCLEOPHILES (see also OXIMES). The presence of α-hydrogen yields greater reactivity because of keto-enol TAUTOMERISM.

KETOSIS, metabolic state in which breakdown of body FATS leads to the production of KETONE bodies (β-hydroxybutyrate and acetoacetate). These break down to ACETONE, which may be smelled in the breath. Ketosis occurs in diabetic coma where INSULIN lack alters the pattern of fat and glucose METABOLISM. It is also seen in starvation.

KETTERING, city in SW Ohio. It is a residential suburb S of Dayton; manufactures include electric motors and aircraft accessories. Pop 71 864.

KETTERING, Charles Franklin (1876–1958), US inventor of the first electric cash register and the electric self-starter, who made many significant contributions to AUTOMOBILE technology.

KETTLEDRUM. See TIMPANI.

KETTLEHOLE, a depression in an area covered by glacial drift, formed where a mass of ice, submerged in the DRIFT, has melted. Kettle lakes are water-filled kettleholes. (See also GLACIER.)

KEUKA LAKE, in W N.Y. It is about 18mi long and half to 2mi wide and drains into Lake Seneca from its N end. (See FINGER LAKES.)

KEWANEE, city in NW Ill. Its economy is based on agriculture, especially hogs, and manufacturing (farm equipment and boilers). Pop 15 762.

KEWEENAW PENINSULA, in extreme N of Mich., projecting into Lake Superior. It is crossed by the Keweenaw Waterway through Portage Lake. Formerly a copper-mining area, it is now a resort region.

KEY, in music, the prescribed system of tones forming a major or minor scale, often used synonymously with TONALITY. It includes all the tones in the scale, and the chords built upon them, and receives its name from the lowest note of the scale to which it belongs. Thus the key of C Major has C as its principal note. In musical notation the key of a piece of music is shown at the beginning by the key signature, composed of the sharps and flats necessary for that particular key.

KEY. See LOCKS AND KEYS.

KEY, Francis Scott (1779–1843), American lawyer, author of the STAR-SPANGLED BANNER. He wrote it after witnessing the night bombardment of Fort McHenry by the British in September 1814. It became the national anthem of the US by act of Congress (1931).

KEYBOARD INSTRUMENTS, musical instruments played by depressing a row of levers called keys. The organ has keyboards for both hands and feet but the term usually refers to instruments like the harpsichord and piano which have a keyboard consisting of long keys covered with ivory, and short keys covered with ebony, which when pressed by the fingers hit or pluck a string to produce a note.

KEY LARGO, island S of Miami off the coast of Fla. About 30mi long, it is the largest of the FLORIDA KEYS.

KEYNES, John Maynard, 1st Baron of Tilton (1883–1946), British economist at Cambridge University, the most important figure in the development of modern economics. He resigned in protest as treasury representative at the VERSAILLES PEACE CONFERENCE, stating his objections to the possible outcome of the treaty in *The Economic Consequences of the Peace* (1919). His chief work, *The General Theory of Employment, Interest, and Money* (1936), formed the basis of the "new" or Keynesian economics. It argued against the traditional idea that the economy was best left to run itself and showed how government policies could maintain high levels of economic activity and employment. He attended the BRETTON WOODS CONFERENCE. Keynes was a prominent member of the BLOOMSBURY GROUP. (See also ECONOMICS.)

KEYSTONE. See ARCH.

KEY WEST, southernmost city of mainland US, on Key West Island, Fla., seat of Monroe Co. A winter resort and US naval station, it is a fishing center and makes cigars. Pop 29 312.

KHABAROVSK, chief industrial city of Siberia, USSR, on the Amur R. Industries include shipbuilding, heavy engineering, oil refining, furs, timber and chemicals. Pop 462 000.

KHACHATURIAN, Aram Ilich (1903–), Soviet-Armenian composer, greatly influenced by folk music of Armenia and other Soviet nationalities. He is famous for the *Violin Concerto* (1940) and the "Saber Dance" in his ballet *Gayane* (1942).

KHAFRE (or Chephren), Egyptian pharaoh of the 4th dynasty who reigned late in the 26th century BC. He built the second pyramid at GIZA, smaller only than that of his father KHUFU (Cheops).

KHALID IBN ABDUL-AZIZ (1912–), King of Saudi Arabia. Appointed as Crown Prince in 1965, he acceded to the throne in 1975 on the death of his brother FAISAL.

KHARKOV, sixth largest city of the USSR and a major industrial, railroad and cultural center in the Ukraine. It is important for heavy engineering and agricultural machinery. Pop 1 280 000.

KHARTOUM, capital of Sudan, at the junction of the White and Blue Niles, a cotton trading center linked by rail and river to Egypt and Port Sudan. General GORDON was killed here in 1885 defending the city against the MAHDI. Pop 648 000.

KHAYYAM, Omar. See OMAR KHAYYAM.

KHAZARS, a Turkic people whose empire in S Russia and the Caucasus controlled trade between the N Slavs, Byzantium and the Far East from c550 until the Byzantines and Russians overwhelmed it (969–1030). The king and nobility adopted Judaism c740.

KHEMELNITSKY, Bohdan. See CHMIELNICKI, BOHDAN.

KHIVA, oasis town in Uzbek, USSR, manufacturing carpets and textiles. It was the capital of the Uzbek Muslim Khiva Khanate, c1512–1873, which then became a Russian protectorate. Pop 24 000.

KHMER EMPIRE, ancient Cambodian empire dating from the 6th century, which at its acme under the Angkors occupied much of modern Laos, Thailand and South Vietnam. The capital, Angkor Thom, and the Hindu temple of Angkor Wat (12th century) were architectural masterpieces. After the empire fell to the Thais in 1434 the court moved to Phnom Penh. (See also ANGKOR.)

KHMER REPUBLIC. See CAMBODIA.

KHORANA, Har Gobind (1922–), Indian-born US biochemist who shared with HOLLEY and NIRENBERG the 1968 Nobel Prize for Physiology or Medicine for his major contributions toward deciphering the genetic code (see GENETICS).

KHORSABAD, village in N Iraq near the Tigris R, site of the ancient Assyrian city of Dur Sharrukin built in the 8th century BC by SARGON II.

KHOSRU (or Chosroes), name of two Persian kings of the SASSANIAN dynasty. **Khosru I**, a strong and able despot (ruled 531–79 AD), extended the size and power of Persia in wars with Byzantium. **Khosru II**, grandson of Khosru I, ruled 590–628. Before his death, the Byzantines regained his conquests of Syria, Jerusalem and Egypt.

KHRUSHCHEV, Nikita Sergeyevitch (1894–1971), Ukrainian-born Soviet statesman and premier of the USSR, 1958–64. He rose in the communist hierarchy to membership of the Praesidium (1952). On STALIN's death he succeeded him as party secretary, but at the 20th Party Congress (1956) denounced STALINISM. He ousted the other members of the "collective leadership" to assume sole power (1958). His rule saw the launching of SPUTNIK, the break with China and a rapprochement with the West, but the failure of his farm policy and loss of face in the Cuban missile crisis led to his fall.

KHUFU (or Cheops), Egyptian pharaoh of the 4th dynasty, reigned 23 years, early 26th century BC. He built the great pyramid at GIZA, the largest single structure ever erected.

KHWARIZMI, Muhammad ibn-Musa al-, or al-Khwarizmi, 9th-century Arab mathematician. The title of his treatise on the solution of many basic mathematical problems contained the word *al-jabr*, from which comes the modern English term, ALGEBRA.

KHYBER PASS, mountain pass on the Pakistan border between PESHAWAR and KABUL, Afghanistan, historically crucial for the control of India, now a strategic military road and railroad. It is about 28mi long.

KIANG, the Tibetan subspecies of the Asiatic wild ass, *Equus hemionus*. Tallest of the wild asses, 1.4m (4.3ft) at the shoulder, it is pale chestnut in color.

KIBBUTZ, type of cooperative farming settlement in Israel jointly owning or leasing land. All work, economic and municipal activities are done communally. Kibbutzim provide food, accommodation, nursery and elementary education. They began in Israel in the early 20th century, which now has over 230 with a total population of over 80 600.

KICKAPOO INDIANS, Algonquian-speaking tribe living in SW Wisconsin in the 17th century and moving to central Illinois after 1769. They were formidable warriors, fighting against the US in the Revolutionary and 1812 wars. Ceding their Ill. land to the US in 1819, most went to Kan. or Mo., but later many to Mexico and Okla. Today only 800 Kickapoo remain.

KIDD, William (c1645–1701), famous British pirate. Settling in New York, he was employed in 1696 by the British governor there to privateer against French ships in KING WILLIAM'S WAR. He later plundered the British in the Indian Ocean and was hanged in London for murder and piracy.

KIDDUSH, Jewish prayer recited in Hebrew on the Sabbath evening and most holy days; it is said over a cup of wine to express gratitude to God for his law.

KIDNAPPING, unlawful abduction and detention of a human being, usually in order to obtain a ransom or concession in return for his release. Kidnapping was made a federal offence after the LINDBERGH case in 1932. Recently revolutionary groups have kidnapped ambassadors and businessmen to gain the release of political detainees.

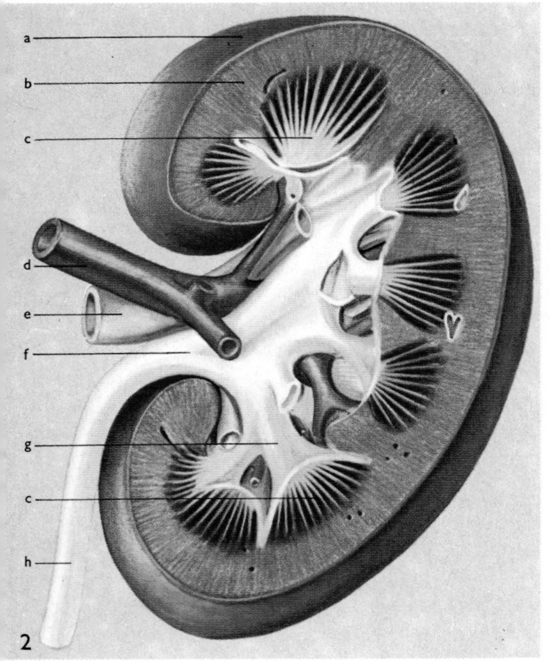

Section through a kidney. Under its protective capsule (a) is the renal cortex (b). The rounded projections called pyramids (c) empty into the renal calyxes (g) of the renal pelvis (f), where the urine from the collecting tubules is gathered. This is then drained off to the bladder through the ureter (h), which lies close to the renal artery (d) and the renal vein (e).

KIDNEYS, two organs concerned with the excretion of waste products in the urine and the balance of salt and water in the body. They lie behind the peritoneal cavity of the ABDOMEN and excrete urine via the ureters, thin tubes passing into the PELVIS to enter the BLADDER. The basic functional unit of the kidney is the *nephron*, consisting of a glomerulus and a system of tubules; these feed into collecting ducts, which drain into the renal pelvis and ureter. BLOOD is filtered in the glomerulus so that low-molecular-weight substances, minerals and water pass into the tubules; here most of the water, sugar and minerals are reabsorbed, leaving behind wastes such as urea in a small volume of salt and water. Tubules and collecting ducts are concerned with the regulation of salt and water reabsorption, which is partly controlled by two HORMONES, VASOPRESSIN and aldosterone). Some substances are actively secreted into the urine by the tubules and the kidney is the route of excretion of many DRUGS. Hormones concerned with ERYTHROCYTE formation and regulation of aldosterone are formed in the kidneys, which also take part in protein METABOLISM. DISEASES affecting the kidney may result in acute NEPHRITIS, including BRIGHT'S DISEASE, the nephrotic syndrome (EDEMA, heavy protein loss in the urine and low plasma albumin) or acute or chronic renal failure. In acute renal failure, nephrons rapidly cease to function, often after prolonged SHOCK, SEPTICEMIA, etc. They may, however, recover. In chronic renal failure, the number of effective nephrons is gradually and irreversibly reduced so that they are unable to excrete all body wastes. Nephron failure causes UREMIA. Disease of the kidneys frequently causes hypertension (see BLOOD CIRCULATION). Advanced renal failure may need treatment with DIETARY FOODS, dialysis and renal TRANSPLANT.

KIDRON, biblical valley and stream in Jordan, E of Jerusalem and in the region occupied by Israel in 1967.

KIEL, port on the Baltic Sea, West Germany, chief German naval base 1871–1945, whose industries are shipbuilding and engineering. Pop 271 719.

KIEL CANAL, German canal 61mi long from the Elbe R mouth to Holtenau near Kiel. It opened in 1895 and as a major commercial-naval canal cut 300mi off the sea route between the North and Baltic Seas. After WWI it was internationalized until 1936.

KIERKEGAARD, Sören Aabye (1813–1855), Danish religious philosopher, precursor of EXISTENTIALISM. Opposing HEGEL, he believed instead that man has free will and can pass from the aesthetic (or material) to the ethical point of view and finally, through "a leap of faith," to the religious. His attack on systematic philosophy and rational religion was ignored in the 19th century but has influenced 20th-century Protestant theology and much modern literature and psychology. His main works are *Either/Or* (1843) and *Philosophical Fragments* (1844).

KIESELGUHR, or diatomaceous earth, a fine, porous, chalklike material (amorphous SILICA) formed by the accumulation on ocean floors of the shells of DIATOMS. It is used as an abrasive, a filter and an absorbent, especially in DYNAMITE.

KIESINGER, Kurt Georg (1904–), West German Christian Democrat politician, chancellor of the Federal Republic 1966–69. He governed in coalition with the Social Democrats, and generally pursued the West-oriented policies of his predecessors ADENAUER and ERHARD, with particular emphasis on Franco-German relations.

KIEV, third largest city in the USSR and capital of the Ukraine, on the Dnieper R. Known in Russia as "the mother of cities," it was founded before the 9th century and was the seat of the Russian Orthodox Church from 988. Much of Kiev (more than 40%) was destroyed in WWII, but after extensive reconstruction it is now a flourishing industrial, communications and cultural center. Pop 1 764 000.

KIGALI, capital of Rwanda in E central Africa. It is a center of the tin mining industry and trades in coffee, cattle and hides. Pop 60 000.

KIKUYU, agricultural Bantu-speaking tribe, one of the largest groups in Kenya, living N of Nairobi. Racial and tribal tensions led to "Mau-Mau," a Kikuyu nationalist uprising against European colonialists in the late 1940s and 1950s.

KILAUEA, world's largest active volcano, located on SE Hawaii island, Hawaii. Its elevation is 4 090ft, and it is 2mi wide, 3mi long and over 700ft deep. Kilauea last erupted in 1968.

KILIMANJARO, Africa's highest mountain, in NE Tanzania, near the Kenyan border. It is an extinct volcano and its highest peak, Kibo, reaches 19 340ft and is snow-capped.

KILLDEER, a noisy North American PLOVER, *Charadrius vociferus*. Taking its name from its repeated call, it is a largely insectivorous farmland bird, brown above, white beneath and with two black breast bands.

KILLEEN, city in central Tex., N of Austin, the site of an army camp and concrete industry. Pop 35 507.

KILLER WHALE, or **Grampus,** *Orcinus orca*, a true DOLPHIN, but lacking a beak. Fast and voracious predators, they eat dolphins, porpoises, seals and fish. They may hunt in small groups or form packs of 40 or more, driving their prey into shallow water where escape is impossible. Huge animals, average length about 6m (20ft), Killer whales are found throughout the world.

KILLIFISHES, also known as topminnows or toothcarps, the most diverse family of toothed carp, divided into Cyprinodonts of North America, Mediterranean and W Asia, and Fundulids, of South America, Africa and Asia. Today mainly freshwater species, some retain the ability to withstand water of great salinity. While New World species feed primarily on plants, the Old World forms are predators.

KILLINGLY, town in NE Conn. on the Quinebaug R., close to R.I. It was settled c1700 and has light manufacturing industries. Pop 13 573.

KILMER, Joyce (1886–1918), US poet remembered for his sentimental poem *Trees* (1913). He was killed in WWI.

KILN, a FURNACE used for firing CERAMICS. The best known type is the **rotary kiln**, used chiefly for CEMENT: the burners are at the lower end of a slowly rotating cylinder, perhaps 100m long, which is at a slight angle to the horizontal. Material is placed in the upper end and slowly falls to the lower, where it is removed. In **tunnel kilns** the burners are at the center of a tunnel through which slowly pass cars loaded with material. (See also POTTERY AND PORCELAIN.)

KILO- (k), the SI prefix multiplying a unit one-thousandfold. Examples include kilohertz (kHz), kilometre (km), kiloton and kilowatt (kW). (See SI UNITS.)

KILOGRAM (kg), the base unit of MASS in SI UNITS, defined as the mass of a platinum-iridium prototype kept under carefully controlled conditions at the International Bureau of Weights and Measures, near Paris, France.

KILOWATT-HOUR (kWh), the commercial unit of electrical ENERGY, being the energy dissipated by a one-kilowatt device in one hour.

KIMBERLEY, city in N Cape Province, South Africa, probably the world's most important diamond center, though Kimberley mine no longer yields diamonds. Pop 104 000.

KIMBERLITE, basic IGNEOUS ROCK, often altered and fragmented, which contains DIAMONDS formed *in situ*. It consists of OLIVINE with MICA, SERPENTINE, CALCITE and other minerals. Its chief occurrence is as pipes and DIKES at Kimberley, South Africa.

KIM IL SUNG (1912–), statesman and president of North Korea from 1972. He led the Korean People's Revolutionary Army against the Japanese in the 1930s. After WWII he set up the North Korean communist government and was prime minister 1948–72.

KINDERGARTEN, school for children aged 4–6, conceived by FROEBEL in 1837. The school aims to develop a child's self-expression and sociability through games, play and creative activities. One of the first American schools was opened in 1860 by Elizabeth PEABODY. Over 50% of children aged five in the US are enrolled in kindergartens.

KINEMATICS, the branch of MECHANICS concerned with describing the motions of objects without consideration of the forces causing those motions. It thus deals with quantities such as distance, time, VELOCITY and ACCELERATION. With KINETICS it makes up DYNAMICS.

KINESIS, an animal's random movement made in response to a stimulus. The animal tends to spend most time in regions where the stimulus is least (or most). **Taxis** is directed movement, away from or towards a directional stimulus.

KINETIC ART, style of art concerned with movement. There are several forms: OP ART involving dynamic optical effects; mobiles whose structure

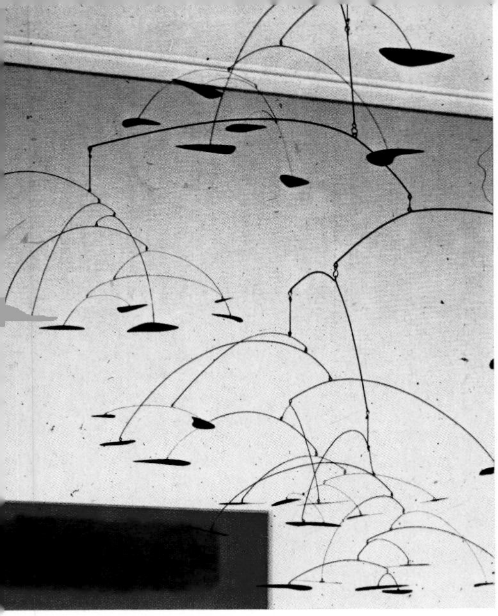

Kinetic art derives its name from the Greek *kinetos*, "moving." The motion may be merely apparent or it may be real, as in this mobile by American sculptor Alexander Calder (1898-1976). The play of air currents creates graceful and fluid patterns.

moves randomly and unaided; and works which are mechanically powered and use lights, water or electromagnets. The style first evolved about 1910.

KINETIC ENERGY. See ENERGY.

KINETICS, the branch of applied MATHEMATICS concerned with the effects of FORCES on the motions of objects (see also KINEMATICS).

KINETICS, Chemical, branch of PHYSICAL CHEMISTRY dealing with reaction rates and mechanisms. In a chemical system, several reactions may be possible according to THERMODYNAMICS, but in practice the fastest reaction predominates, not necessarily the most energetically favored. The reaction rate—the rate at which the concentration of one reactant decreases—is normally proportional to a certain POWER of the concentrations of the reactants, the sum of the exponents being called the *reaction order*. Thus for the reaction $A+B \rightarrow C+D$ it may be found that the rate is given by

$$\frac{d[A]}{dt} = k[A]^2[B]$$

(see CALCULUS; EQUILIBRIUM, CHEMICAL): such a reaction is third order overall (second order in A, first order in B). The *rate constant*, k, depends exponentially (see EXPONENT) on the absolute TEMPERATURE (so that at room temperature most reactions double in rate for a 10K rise in temperature) and on the ACTIVATION ENERGY. CATALYSIS speeds up a reaction by providing an alternative mechanism with lower activation energy. Reaction rates are studied by measuring concentration as a function of time, regular or continuous chemical ANALYSIS being used. (See also FLASH PHOTOLYSIS.)

KINETIC THEORY, widely used statistical theory based on the idea that matter is made up of randomly moving ATOMS or MOLECULES whose kinetic ENERGY increases with TEMPERATURE. It is closely related to statistical mechanics, and predicts macroscopic properties of solids, liquids and gases from motions of individual particles using MECHANICS and PROBABILITY theory. Gases are particularly suited to treatment by kinetic theory, and useful laws connecting their pressure, temperature, density, diffusion and other properties have been deduced with its aid.

KING, Billie Jean Moffitt (1943–   ), US tennis player, a prominent figure in the international game, whose efforts have done much to improve the lot of women in tennis. She took her sixth Wimbledon women's singles title in 1975, and was US women's winner 1971 and 1972.

KING, Ernest Joseph (1878–1956), US admiral, the only officer who was both commander of the US fleet and naval operations chief in WWII. His stress on the superiority of aircraft carriers to battleships led to Japan's naval defeat.

KING, Martin Luther, Jr. (1929–1968), American Negro clergyman and civil rights leader, recipient of the 1964 Nobel Peace Prize for his work for racial equality in the US. Born in Atlanta, Ga., King organized the boycott of the Montgomery, Ala. transit company in 1955 to force desegregation of the buses. Under his leadership in the late 1950s and 1960s civil disobedience and non-violent tactics, like the Washington March of 250000 people in 1963, brought about the Civil Rights Act and Voting Rights Act in 1965. Black militants challenged his methods in 1965 but in 1966 he extended his campaign to slum conditions in the N cities of the US and set up the Poor People's Campaign in 1968. He was less successful in this area since the Vietnam War distracted national attention from the civil and urban rights issues. He was assassinated in Memphis, Tenn. (See also CIVIL RIGHTS AND LIBERTIES.)

KING, Rufus (1755–1827), NY senator who helped frame the CONSTITUTION. He was the federalist candidate for the presidency in 1816 and was twice minister to England.

KING, William (1768–1827), American statesman, who assisted in separating Me. from Mass. and was Me.'s first governor in 1820–21.

KING, William Lyon Mackenzie (1874–1950), Canadian statesman, three times Liberal prime minister. In his first term, 1921–26, he established Canada's right to act independently in international affairs; in his second, 1926–30, he introduced old age pensions—Canada's first national social security scheme; and in his third, 1935–48, he united Canada as the "arsenal of democracy" in WWII making the national economy a federal responsibility.

KING, William Rufus Devane (1786–1853), 13th US vice-president in 1852 but could not serve due to ill-health. He was Ala. senator, 1819–44 and 1848–53 and as minister to France, 1844–48, prevented France and England hindering US annexation of Tex.

KINGBIRDS, certain species of the North American family of tyrant-flycatchers. Dark-backed, white or yellow-bellied birds, they are aggressive hunters with the typical flycatcher habit of darting out from an upright perch to snatch insects.

KING CRABS, or **Horseshoe crabs,** large marine arthropods closely related to the extinct Water scorpions. They have remained virtually unchanged over 300m years. The upper surface of the body is covered by a hemispherical, scoop-shaped carapace, whose edges, on the abdomen, are fringed with short movable spines and which ends in a long tail spine. King crabs live in shallow coastal waters, preying on worms and mollusks.

KINGDOM. See TAXONOMY.

KINGDOM OF GOD, or **Kingdom of Heaven,** the exercise by God of his sovereign rule. It was the central theme of JESUS CHRIST's teaching; introduced by Jesus himself, and now present though hidden, the kingdom was to grow and would be revealed in future glory (see ESCHATOLOGY; SECOND COMING); only the godly would enter it. From St. Augustine's time the kingdom was identified with the Church.

KINGFISHERS, a family, Alcedinidae, found worldwide, of brightly-colored fish-eating birds of rivers, lakes and streams. When hunting, the bird watches from a perch until prey is sighted, then dives arrowlike into the water to take the fish. Certain African species do not frequent water, and are insectivorous.

KING GEORGE'S WAR. See FRENCH AND INDIAN WARS.

KINGLETS, small warbler-like birds of North America, related to the European goldcrest. There are two species, the crowned kinglet, *Regulus sapatra*, and the Ruby-crowned kinglet, *R. calendula.*

KING PHILIP'S WAR (1675–76), last Indian resistance to the whites in S New England. In 1675, the Plymouth colony executed three Indians for an alleged murder. Metacom, a WAMPANOAG chief also called "King Philip," led an alliance of tribes in fierce guerrilla raids. The whites replied in kind and Metacom was killed when his secret refuge was betrayed. The colonists then drove most of the Indians from S New England.

KINGS, Books of, two books of the OLD TESTAMENT (one book in Hebrew), numbered as 1 and 2 Kings by Protestants, but as 3 and 4 Kings by Roman Catholics (see SAMUEL, BOOKS OF). Related to DEUTERONOMY and religious in aim, they cover Israelite history from the reign of Solomon through the period of the two kingdoms of Israel and Judah to the destruction of Judah by the Babylonians.

KINGS CANYON NATIONAL PARK, area of about 460330 acres in the Sierra Nevada, S central Cal., established as a national park in 1940. The canyon is formed by the Kings R and is noted for its surrounding snow-covered peaks and rich wildlife.

KING'S EVIL. See SCROFULA.

KINGSLEY, Charles (1819–1875), English writer and clergyman and an ardent advocate of social reform. His early novel, *Alton Locke* (1850) is a sympathetic study of working class life. He also wrote historical novels, notably *Westward Ho!* (1855) and the famous children's fantasy *The Water Babies* (1863).

KINGSLEY, Sidney (1906–   ), US playwright noted for his treatment of social problems. His first play, *Men in White* (1933), won a Pulitzer Prize.

KING'S MOUNTAIN, Battle of, battle in the REVOLUTIONARY WAR in Oct. 1780 at King's Mt on the borders of N.C. and S.C. Some 900 American sharpshooters defeated a larger British force, checking CORNWALLIS in his Carolina campaign.

KING SNAKES, North American, nonvenomous snakes of the genus *Lampropeltis*, that range from a little over 600mm (2ft) to 1.8m (6ft). King snakes are constrictors whose food includes not only small mammals and lizards, but other smaller snakes, including RATTLESNAKES, to whose poisons they are immune.

KINGSPORT, industrial city in NE Tenn., on the Holston R. It produces books, chemicals, plastics, glass and leather. Pop 31938.

KINGSTON, city in SE Ontario, Canada, seat of Frontenac Co. On Lake Ontario, at the head of the St. Lawrence R, it is an important inland port with heavy engineering industries. Pop 61870.

KINGSTON, capital and chief port of Jamaica, situated on the SE coast. It has a fine natural harbor and is the island's main commercial and tourist center. Pop 111879.

KINGSTON, city, seat of Ulster Co., N.Y., on the Hudson R. In 1777 it served as N.Y.'s first capital, but was burnt down by the British in the same year. Pop 25544.

KINGSVILLE, city in S Tex. seat of Kleberg Co. It is a center for cattle breeding and for petrochemical and gas industries. Pop 28915.

KING WILLIAM'S WAR. See FRENCH AND INDIAN WARS.

KININS, plant HORMONES which affect GROWTH and are used to preserve cut flowers; also, in animals, PEPTIDES released by ENZYME action which cause contraction of smooth muscle and elevate blood pressure, thus playing an important role in INFLAMMATION and SHOCK.

KINKAJOU, or **Honey bear,** *Potos flavus*, a South American RACCOON which is almost exclusively arboreal. A long, low-bodied animal, it uses its heavy prehensile tail as a fifth grip when moving through the trees in search of food. They are solitary, nocturnal animals, except during the breeding season, and feed on fruit, insects and even bird nestlings.

KINO, Eusebio Francisco (c1644–1711), Italian Jesuit missionary who explored Lower Cal. (1683–85) and into Ariz. from 1689. He established stock ranches at his missions. His map (1705) remained the basis of maps of the SW and of NW Mexico for a century.

KINORHYNCHS, a class of small worm-like creatures related to nematodes (see ROUNDWORMS). Segmented invertebrates, they are bristly animals less than 1mm (0.04in) long. They burrow in the mud of coastal waters feeding on organic detritus.

KINSEY, Alfred Charles (1894–1956), US zoologist best known for his statistical studies of human sexual behavior, published as *Sexual Behavior in the Human Male* (1948) and *Sexual Behavior in the Human Female* (1953).

KINSHASA, formerly Leopoldville, capital and largest city of Zaire, 350mi inland on the Congo R opposite BRAZZAVILLE. It is an important commercial and shipping center. Pop 1 323 039.

KINSTON, city in E N.C., seat of Lenoir Co. It is a cotton and truck farming center, and has lumber, yarn and fertilizer industries. Pop 23 020.

KIOWA INDIANS, tribe of the S Great Plains. A warlike nomadic people, they were settled in Okla. in 1868. A serious Kiowan uprising was put down in 1874. The Kiowas were followers of SUN DANCE and GHOST DANCE cults.

KIPLING, Rudyard (1865–1936), English writer, born in India. Kipling is perhaps now most admired for his short stories about Anglo-Indian life, as in the collection *Plain Tales from the Hills* (1888), and for his verse, including such pieces as *Mandalay* and *Gunga Din*, while his children's stories, among them *Kim* (1901) and the *Just So Stories* (1902), are perennial favorites. After an English education he worked as a journalist in India 1882–89. He lived in Vt. 1892–96 and in England from 1900. Kipling was enormously popular in his day. He was the first English winner of the Nobel Prize for Literature (1907).

KIRBY-SMITH, Edmund (1824–1893), Civil War general, the last Confederate commander to surrender, May 26, 1865. A major in the US army, he joined the Confederacy when Fla., his native state, entered the war. He was commander of the Trans-Mississippi Dept. 1863–65.

KIRCHNER, Ernst Ludwig (1880–1938), German expressionist painter, co-founder of the Brücke (Bridge) movement (1905–13). He is noted for his expressive woodcuts and, in his painting, for his vigorous use of color and form. His work condemned by the Nazis, Kirchner committed suicide.

KIRCHHOFF, Gustav Robert (1824–1887), German physicist best known for his work on electrical conduction, showing that current passes through a conductor at the speed of light, and deriving KIRCHHOFF'S LAWS. With BUNSEN he pioneered spectrum analysis (see SPECTROSCOPY), which he applied to the solar spectrum, identifying several elements and explaining the FRAUNHOFER LINES.

KIRCHHOFF'S LAWS, two laws governing electric circuits involving Ohm's-law conductors and sources of electromotive force, stated by G. R. KIRCHHOFF. They assert that the sums of outgoing and incoming currents at any junction in the circuit must be equal, and that the sum of the current-resistance products around any closed path must equal the total electromotive force in it.

KIRGIZIA, constituent republic of the USSR. The Kirgiz SSR covers 76 640sq mi of central Asia between China and Kazakhstan, and is very mountainous. The Kirgiz, a Turkish-speaking Muslim people, form 40% of the population. The republic is famous for its sheep; the chief crops are wheat, corn, cotton, sugar beet, tobacco and fruit. Industries include food processing, engineering and sawmilling.

KIRIN, historic city of NE China, on the Sungari R, a great industrial center. It has major chemical plants and is an important port and railroad junction. Pop 1 200 000.

KIRKLAND, Samuel (1741–1808), US Congregationalist missionary to the IROQUOIS Indians. He helped secure their neutrality during the Revolutionary War and later worked for their welfare, founding a college in N.Y. for joint white-Indian education (1793).

KIRKSVILLE, city in N Mo., seat of Adair Co. It is a coal-mining and dairying center with shoe and electrical appliance industries. Pop 15 860.

KIRKWOOD, city in E Mo., SW of St. Louis, of which it is a commercial and residential suburb. Pop 31 769.

KIROV, industrial city, capital of Kirov state, in Russian SFSR. Its products include heavy machinery, lumber and leather. It is also a cultural center with several research institutes. Pop 332 000.

KIROV, Sergei Mironovich (1886–1934), Russian revolutionary leader, one of Stalin's chief aides. He was assassinated, probably on the instruction of Stalin, who used his death for an excuse for a wave of purges.

KIRSCH, a colorless liqueur distilled in parts of France, Germany and Switzerland, from the fermented stones and pulp of black cherries.

KIRSTEIN, Lincoln (1907–   ), US ballet promoter who with George BALANCHINE, established the School of American Ballet in New York in 1934. He has written several books on ballet.

KISANGANI, formerly Stanleyville, city in NE Zaire. On the Congo R, it is a port and commercial and industrial center. Pop 230 000.

KISH, ancient Mesopotamian city, about 55mi S of Baghdad, Iraq. It was the capital of SUMER before 3000 BC and remained important until SASSANIAN times. A vast temple built by Nebuchadnezzar and Nabonidus has been excavated here.

KISHINEV, capital of Russia's Moldavian SSR. A center of light industry, the city, which stands on a tributary of the Dneister R, also exports wine and tobacco. Pop 357 000.

KISKA, largest island of the Rat group in the W Aleutian Islands. It was seized by the Japanese in June 1942, but reoccupied by the US and Canada on Aug. 15, 1943.

KISSINGER, Henry Alfred (1923–   ), German-born US adviser on foreign affairs and one of the most influential men in government. He was professor at Harvard when his book *Nuclear Weapons and Foreign Policy* (1957) brought him international recognition. Kissinger served as special assistant for national security affairs (1969) and secretary of state (1973) to President Nixon, continuing under President Ford. He was instrumental in initiating the STRATEGIC ARMS LIMITATION TALKS on disarmament (1969), in ending US involvement in Vietnam and opening US policies toward China. In 1974–75 he made major peace initiatives in the Middle East and in 1976, in southern Africa. He received the Nobel Peace Prize in 1973.

KITAKYŪSHŪ, city in N Kyushu, Japan. It is a major center for heavy industry including shipbuilding, iron and steel, glass and machinery. Pop 1 042 321.

KITASATO, Shibasaburo (1852–1931), Japanese bacteriologist who discovered, independently of YERSIN, the PLAGUE bacillus; and with BEHRING discovered that graded injections of toxins could be used for immunization (see ANTITOXINS).

KITCHEN CABINET, popular name for an unofficial body of advisers to President Andrew Jackson (1829–31). It included politicians, editors and government officials.

KITCHENER, city in Ontario, Canada, seat of Waterloo Co., in Grand River Valley. It is a major industrial center, producing textiles, leather, paper, electrical goods and tires. Pop 109 954.

KITCHENER, Horatio Herbert, Earl (1850–1916), British field marshal, secretary of state for war in WWI. In the Sudan in 1898, he defeated the MAHDI at Omdurman and retook Khartoum. He was commander in chief in the Boer War, 1900–02, and in India to 1909. At the outbreak of WWI he foresaw a long war and his appeals raised thousands of patriotic volunteers. He died when a ship taking him to Russia hit a mine and sank.

KITCHEN MIDDEN, or **Shell Mound,** refuse heap of usually STONE AGE origin in which, among bones, shells, etc., archaeologists may find potsherds and implements of stone, horn and bone. They are 1–3m high, 40–70m wide and up to 400m long.

KITE, recreational AIRCRAFT consisting of a light frame covered with thin fabric (e.g. paper) and tethered to a long line. Kites fly in the wind by AERODYNAMIC lift. Originating in the ancient Far East, kite flying has long been a popular sport, and has been used for meteorological observations.

KITE, in GEOMETRY, a QUADRILATERAL with two pairs of equal adjacent sides.

KITES, a diverse assemblage of BIRDS OF PREY, worldwide in distribution but especially developed in America and Australia. The name is properly restricted to Old World Fork-tailed kites of the genus *Milvus* but it is also used for 25 other species. Most kites are mainly or entirely insectivorous. A few species are scavengers: the Black and Red kites of Europe were formerly common scavengers of city streets.

KITHARA, ancient stringed instrument, a form of LYRE used by the Greek bards to accompany songs and epic poems. It usually had seven strings and was played with a plectrum.

KITIMAT, seaport and aluminum smelting center in W British Columbia, Canada, at the head of Douglas Channel. Pop 11 803.

KITTERY, town in SW Me., opposite Portsmouth, N.H., at the mouth of the Piscataqua R. Portsmouth Navy Yard was established here in 1806. Pop 11 028.

KITTIWAKE, *Rissa tridactyla*, a lightly-built GULL of the open sea, with yellow bill and black legs. Usually solitary, they form colonies to breed, nesting on precipitous cliff ledges on rocky coasts. Kittiwakes show many adaptations to this cliff-nesting habit making them divergent from other gulls.

KITT PEAK NATIONAL OBSERVATORY, sited on the Papago Indian reservation in Ariz., was opened in 1960. Its main telescopes are the McMath 60in solar tower telescope, the world's largest of its type, and the Mayall 158in reflector, built in 1973.

KITTY HAWK, peninsula in N.C., scene of the first power-driven flight, Dec. 17, 1903. The flight, by the WRIGHT BROTHERS, lasted 12 seconds, and is commemorated by a monument on Kill Devil Hill.

KIVA, secret underground ceremonial chamber of the PUEBLO INDIANS. Generally round, 15ft across (though sometimes much larger), it has a central fireplace, an altar and a *sipapu* or symbolic hole leading to the spirit world.

KIWANIS INTERNATIONAL, US services association, founded 1915 to promote the Golden Rule, higher standards in business and participation in community affairs. It sponsors the Key Club International for high school boys and Circle K International for college men.

KIWI, the genus *Apteryx*, three species of flightless New Zealand birds about 460mm (18in) high, lacking a tail and, unlike most flightless birds, even lacking visible wings. The feathers are gray-brown and hair-like in texture. The long slender bill is adapted for probing into soil as they feed at night on worms, insects and berries. Birds of damp forests, they are extremely shy and rarely seen.

KLAMATH FALLS, lumber and farming city in S Ore., seat of Klamath Co. It stands at the S end of Upper Klamath Lake. Pop 15 775.

KLAMATH INDIANS, North American Indians of SE Ore. and N Cal., neighbors of the MODOC INDIANS with whom they share a reservation around Upper Klamath Lake, established in 1864.

KLAMATH MOUNTAINS, mountain range of the Pacific Coast Ranges in SW Ore. and NW Cal. It has peaks and ridges reaching 9 000ft.

KLAMATH RIVER, flows from Lake Ewauna, Ore., 250mi SW to the Pacific at Requa, Cal. It provides irrigation and hydroelectricity.

KLAPROTH, Martin Heinrich (1743–1817), German chemist noted for his pioneering work in

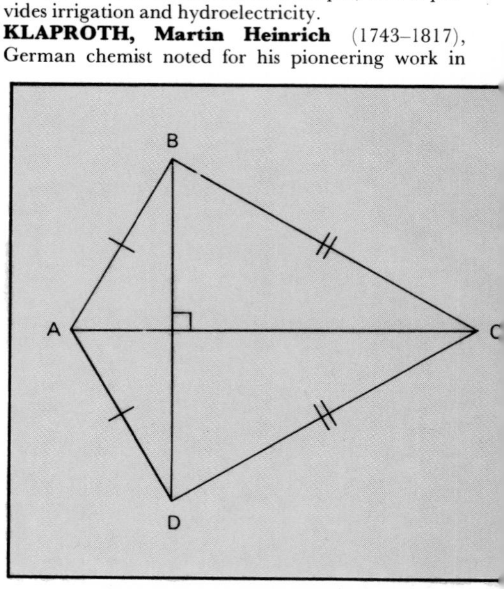

The kite, in geometry. Side AB = AD and BC = CD, and diagonals AC and BD intersect at right angles.

chemical ANALYSIS. He discovered the elements ZIRCONIUM (1789) and URANIUM (in fact, uranium oxide: 1789), and rediscovered and named TITANIUM (1795).

KLEBS, Edwin (1834–1913), German pathologist and bacteriologist whose work permitted LÖFFLER to isolate the DIPHTHERIA bacillus (1884), often now called the Klebs-Löffler bacillus.

KLEE, Paul (1879–1940), Swiss painter and graphic artist. In Munich, from 1906, he exhibited with the BLAUE REITER group, and developed a subtle color sense. In 1920–31 he taught at the BAUHAUS, publishing an important textbook on painting. Sensitive line, color and texture are combined in Klee's varied paintings with wit and fantasy.

KLEIN, Christian Felix (1849–1925), German geometer whose application of GROUP theory to the unification of mathematics was particularly important in the development of modern GEOMETRY.

KLEIN, Melanie (1882–1960), Austrian-born psychoanalyst whose development of a psychoanalytic therapy for small children radically affected techniques of child psychiatry and theories of child psychology.

KLEIN BOTTLE, a topological space (see TOPOLOGY) of interest in that it has only one side. Consider a hollow CYLINDER made of some flexible material. If one end is bent toward the other, passed through the side of the cylinder and then joined to the other end, the result is a figure which has no "inside." The figure cannot be constructed in Euclidean space (see EUCLIDEAN GEOMETRY); however, if it were correctly cut in two, the result would be two MÖBIUS STRIPS.

KLEIST (Bernd) Heinrich (Wilhelm) von (1777–1811), German dramatist and writer of novellas, known for his power and psychological insight. His works include the plays *Penthesilea* (1808) and *Prince Friedrich of Homburg* (1821), and the NOVELLEN *Michael Kohlhaas* and *The Marquise of O* (1810–11).

KLEMPERER, Otto (1885–1973), German conductor. As director of the Kroll opera house, Berlin (1927–33) he introduced many modern works and new interpretations of classics. After a period of crippling illness he revived his career from 1947, notably as an interpreter of BEETHOVEN and MAHLER.

KLENZE, Leo von (1784–1864), Bavarian court architect from 1816 and designer of Munich's Greek revival and Renaissance-style public buildings. He also designed the Hermitage museum, Leningrad.

KLEPTOMANIA, an individual's obsessive (see OBSESSION) urge, usually the result of internal conflict (see COMPLEX; NEUROSIS) and often linked with sexual perversion, to steal objects which, in general, he does not actually wish to possess. Most children pass through a kleptomaniac phase.

KLIKITAT INDIANS, Shahaptian tribe noted for their sophisticated trading methods. They lived in Klikitat and Skamania counties, Wash., until resettled in 1855 on the Yakima reservation.

KLIMT, Gustav (1862–1918), Austrian painter and designer, a leader of the Vienna SEZESSION (1897). His interior designs, as for the Palais Stoclet, Brussels, and in Vienna, influenced JUGENDSTIL. His paintings often center on large areas of mosaic patterns.

KLINE, Franz Joseph (1910–1962), US abstract expressionist painter. His huge, stark, black-and-white compositions influenced the "calligraphic" style of the 1950s New York school. Later, Kline reintroduced color into his works.

KLIPSPRINGER, *Oreotragus oreotragus*, a small African ANTELOPE related to the DIK-DIKS. True dwarf antelopes, klipspringers have tall, truncated hooves and pithy, protective fur, both adaptations to its mountainous habitat.

KLONDIKE, subarctic region S of the Klondike R in the W central Yukon, site of the gold rush of 1896. By 1900 $22 million was being panned annually, but the creeks were quickly worked out. Working in more inaccessible reaches ceased in 1966.

KLOPSTOCK, Friedrich Gottlieb (1724–1803), German poet. His *Der Messias* (1749–73), on Christ's salvation of mankind, an epic modelled on Milton and Homer, freed German poetry from the conventions of French classicism. He wrote some fine *Odes*.

KNAPWEED, *Centaurea nigra*, and related species, common herbs of meadowland in Europe and naturalized in North America. The flowers are blue or purple and thistle-like. A tonic can be prepared from the leaves. Family: COMPOSITAE.

KNEE. See LEG.

KNELLER, Sir Godfrey (1646–1723), German-born English portrait painter, a court painter from 1688. He founded the first English painting academy (1711); his finest works are the 42 *Kit Cat* portraits.

KNESSET, the single-chamber legislature of Israel, which also elects the president of the republic. Its 120 members are elected for a four-year term by secret ballot and universal suffrage.

KNIFEFISH, three families of South American freshwater fishes related to the Electric eel. They have an eel-like body with a long anal fin and swim by undulations of the body and fin. Like the electric eel, they have electric organs along the flanks which they use like radar for locating objects.

KNIGHTHOOD. See CHIVALRY; FEUDALISM.

KNIGHTS OF COLUMBUS, US organization for Roman Catholic men, started in 1882 in Conn. It sponsors deserving causes and disseminates religious information to its members, who number over a million.

KNIGHTS OF LABOR, early US labor group, precursor of the American Federation of Labor. Founded in 1869 to organize all workers in one union, it led successful strikes in 1884–86, but declined after the HAYMARKET AFFAIR.

KNIGHTS OF PYTHIAS, US social and charitable organization founded 1864. It has over 3 000 lodges and several auxiliary organizations.

KNIGHTS OF SAINT JOHN (officially, Order of the Hospital of St. John of Jerusalem; also known as Hospitalers, Knights of Rhodes, and Knights of Malta), religious order founded by papal charter (1113) to tend sick pilgrims in the Holy Land. It became a military order as well c1140, and after the fall of Jerusalem was based successively on Cyprus (1291), Rhodes (1309) and Malta (1530) to provide a defence against Muslim seapower. Expelled from Malta by Napoleon in 1798, the Knights have been established at Rome since 1834 in their original humanitarian role.

KNIGHTS OF THE GOLDEN CIRCLE, semimilitary US secret society organized in the Midwest states during the Civil War to set up proslavery colonies in Mexico, to help the South against the North. It merged with the Order of American Knights, later the Sons of Liberty, and disbanded in the 1860s.

KNIGHTS OF THE WHITE CAMELIA, southern US secret society to sustain white supremacy after the Civil War. It was dissolved in the 1870s.

KNIGHTS TEMPLAR, Christian military order founded c1118, with its headquarters on the site of Solomon's Temple in Jerusalem, to protect pilgrims. It provided elite troops for the kingdom of Jerusalem. Its immense riches from endowments and banking excited the greed of Philip IV of France, who (1307–14) confiscated its property, forced the pope to suppress the order and executed the Grand Master and other knights. What remained of its possessions in France and elsewhere were transferred to the KNIGHTS OF ST. JOHN.

KNITTING, production of fabric by using needles to interlock yarn or thread in a series of connected loops. The basic handknitting stitches are plain (or jersey) and purl. It was practiced in North Africa in the 3rd century BC and was taken to Europe by Arab traders. In the Middle Ages there were knitting guilds. The first knitting machine was invented by William Lee in England in 1589.

KNOSSOS, ancient city near Candia on the N coast of Crete, center of the MINOAN CIVILIZATION. Excavations by Sir Arthur Evans revealed settlements from the 3rd millennium and the great 2nd-millennium palace, now partly restored. Associated with the mythological King MINOS, it comprises more than five acres of halls, ceremonial rooms and staircases. It has magnificent fresco decorations, advanced sanitation and every amenity of luxury. Fire destroyed it c1400 BC.

KNOT (kn), unit of speed used at sea, defined as one nautical mile per hour. The international knot (1852m/h) used in the US differs slightly from the UK knot (6080ft/h). The name comes from the old practice of measuring speed at sea by counting the number of knots in a knotted line payed out over the stern in a given time.

Portrait of Gaia, painted by Paul Klee in 1939. Like much of his work, it has a childlike wit and charm that soften the impact of his innovative technique. He was in fact one of the major theorists of 20th-century art.

KNOTGRASS, or knotweed, popular name for several plants of the genus *Polygonum. Polygonum aviculare* is a small prostrate herb common on cultivated and waste ground. Family: Polygonaceae.

KNOW-NOTHING PARTY, US political party formed to restrict immigration and exclude naturalized citizens and Roman Catholics from politics. It won success in the 1854 election as the American Party, but split irremediably in 1856 over the slavery issue. Its name came from its members' habit of saying they "knew nothing" of the movement.

KNOX, Frank (1874–1944), US journalist, publisher of the *Chicago Daily News* from 1931 and, as President Roosevelt's secretary of the navy in WWII, responsible for building the US two-ocean navy.

KNOX, Henry (1750–1806), US general and secretary of war under his friend Washington. He was artillery commander at Bunker Hill, Yorktown and other important battles of the Revolution. He proposed the establishment of the West Point military academy.

KNOX, John (c1514–1572), Scottish Protestant Reformation leader, preacher and chronicler of the Scottish Reformation. A converted Roman Catholic priest, Knox was active in the English Reformation, but fled in 1554 from the Roman Catholic regime of Queen Mary I to Geneva, where he was a follower of CALVIN. He returned to Scotland in 1559 ardently preaching Protestantism. When it became the state religion (1560) Knox gained great political influence, opposing Mary Queen of Scots. His fiery prose includes a history of the Reformation in Scotland and the *First Blast of the Trumpet against the Monstrous Regiment of Women* (1556–58). He also wrote the *Book of Common Order*, which regulated Scottish worship.

KNOX, Philander Chase (1853–1921), US lawyer and attorney general under presidents McKinley and Theodore Roosevelt. A well-known corporation lawyer, he became a senator in 1904 and secretary of state under Taft in 1909. He opposed the Versailles Treaty and the League of Nations.

KNOXVILLE, city in E Tenn., founded 1785 and named for Henry Knox. A tobacco auction center, it makes textiles, chemicals and food products. The U. of Tennessee is here. Pop 174 587.

KOALA, *Phascolarctos cinereus*, a large, arboreal, superficially bear-like MARSUPIAL of eastern Australia. It feeds on the foliage of *Eucalyptus* and a few other trees. Alone among the marsupials but for the WOMBATS, koalas have a true allantoic placenta, though the young are brooded in a marsupial pouch. The koala has been considered an endangered species but is now increasing in numbers again.

KOBARID. See CAPORETTO.

KOBE, Japan's second deepwater port (after Yokohama) on the S of Honshu Island 18mi W of Osaka. It is an important commercial center, with its own heavy industry and coastal trade in addition. It is also a cultural center. Pop 1 288 937.

KØBENHAVN. See COPENHAGEN.

KOBLENZ (Coblenz), historic city in W West Germany at the confluence of the Rhine and Moselle Rivers. Long a commercial center, it has many industries and is an important Rhine port. It is a cultural and educational center, with many historic buildings such as the great Ehrenbreitstein fortress and many churches. It is a center for tourism and the wine trade. Pop 119 434.

KOCH, Robert (1843–1910), German medical scientist regarded as a father of BACTERIOLOGY, awarded the 1905 Nobel Prize for Physiology or Medicine for his work. He isolated the ANTHRAX bacillus and showed it to be the sole cause of the disease; devised important new methods of obtaining pure cultures; and discovered the bacilli responsible for TUBERCULOSIS (1882) and CHOLERA (1883).

KÖCHEL, Ludwig von (1800–1877), Austrian musicologist (and also scientist), whose 1862 catalogue of Mozart's compositions, though revised, is still standard. The works are usually identified with a "K" number.

KOCHER, Emil Theodor (1841–1917), Swiss surgeon awarded the 1909 Nobel Prize for Physiology or Medicine for his discovery of the relation between the THYROID GLAND and CRETINISM.

KODÁLY, Zoltán (1882–1967), Hungarian composer and, with BARTÓK, an ardent researcher of Hungarian folk music. Folk influences are evident in such works as the cantata *Psalmus Hungaricus* (1923), the opera *Háry János* (1925–26) and the orchestral *Peacock Variations* (1938–39).

KODIAK, island S of Alaska, site of Kodiak National Wildlife Refuge, home of the Kodiak bear. Fishing and fish canning are the chief industries of Kodiak, the capital. Pop 6 357.

KOESTLER, Arthur (1905–), Hungarian-born British writer. His novel *Darkness at Noon* (1940), based on his own experience in a Spanish death cell, analyzed the psychology of victims of Stalin's 1930s purges. Many later works on philosophical and scientific subjects include *The Sleepwalkers* (1964) and *The Case of the Midwife Toad* (1971).

KOFFKA, Kurt (1886–1941), German-born US psychologist who, with KÖHLER and WERTHEIMER, was responsible for the birth of GESTALT PSYCHOLOGY.

KOFU, capital of the Yamanashi prefecture of S Honshu, Japan, 65mi W of Tokyo. It trades in silk and is a tourist center. Pop 182 669.

KOHLER, Wolfgang (1887–1967), German-born US psychologist who, with KOFFKA and WERTHEIMER, was responsible for the birth of GESTALT PSYCHOLOGY.

KOHLRABI, a form of CABBAGE (*Brassica oleracea*) which produces a turnip-shaped edible stem. Family: Cruciferae.

KOKOMO, industrial city of Ind., seat of Howard Co. 50mi N of Indianapolis. It produces glass, tools, auto parts and plastics. Pop 44 042.

KOKOSCHKA, Oskar (1886–), Austrian painter and writer, a naturalized British subject from 1947, a leader of German EXPRESSIONISM. He is known for psychologically acute portraits such as *The Tempest* (1914), a self-portrait with Alma Mahler, and for lyric landscapes and townscapes.

KOLA, *Cola acuminata* and *C. nitida*, trees native to tropical W Africa. They produce edible nuts that contain CAFFEINE. The nuts are an important food for local populations. They are also exported for use in manufacture of soft drinks. Family: Sterculiaceae.

KOLA PENINSULA, projects E on the NW coast of the USSR between the White Sea and Barents Sea. This 40 000sq mi area, mostly granite, is mineral-rich. Its chief city is Murmansk.

KOLAR GOLD FIELDS, city in SE Mysore, India. Gold has been mined here since 1881. Pop 76 143.

KOLCHAK, Alexander Vasilievich (1873–1920), Russian admiral, leader of the White Russian forces 1918–20. He took power in Omsk in 1918, proclaiming himself head of state. Defeated by the Red Army and overthrown after his move to Irkutsk in 1919, he was finally executed by the Bolsheviks.

KÖLN. See COLOGNE.

KOL NIDRE, opening words, and hence name, of the Jewish prayer of repentance and absolution at the start of the synagogue service on the eve of YOM KIPPUR.

KOLYMA RIVER, 1 110mi long river in NE USSR, rising in the Kolyma Mts in Khabarovsk Krai and flowing into the Arctic. It yields gold.

KOMANDORSKI ISLANDS, E of Kamchatka Peninsula in the SW Bering Sea, USSR. Bering and Medny are the chief islands. There is a radio and naval station at Nikolskoye.

KOMODO DRAGON, *Varanus komodoensis*, a monitor lizard found on the island of Komodo, east of Jawa, reaching at least 3m (10ft) in length. Like snakes, MONITORS can dislocate the jaw hinge to engulf large prey, but Komodo dragons are mainly carrion feeders.

KOMONDOR, herding dog and watchdog from Hungary, white with a long shaggy coat, weighing about 75lb and 24in high. It is listed by the US Kennel Club in its "working" category.

KOMSOMOL, Soviet political youth organization open to all between 14 and 28 years. Founded in 1918, it has gone through military, economic and political phases, but its constant goal is obedience to Communist Party policies.

KOMSOMOLSK-NA-AMURE, industrial city in S Khabarovsk Krai, USSR, on the Amur R. Founded 1932. Pop 218 000.

KONAKRI. See CONAKRY.

KONEV, Ivan Stepanovich (1897–1973), USSR field marshal of WWII, who drove the Germans from the Ukraine, captured Prague and took part in the fall of Berlin. He headed the Warsaw Pact armies 1955–60.

KÖNIGSBERG. See KALININGRAD.

KONOYE, Prince Fumimaro (1891–1945), Japanese premier 1937–39 and 1940–41. A moderate, he appeased the military extremists and so furthered expansionism. He killed himself when listed for trial as a war criminal.

KON-TIKI. See HEYERDAHL, THOR.

KONYA, city in Turkey, 145mi S of Ankara. Continuously settled since the 3rd millennium, as Iconium it was an important Greek city. From the 1080s capital of the Selchuk sultanate of Rum, it became a major Turkish cultural center, famed for its mosque of the whirling Dervishes. It produces fruit, sugar and grain. Pop 201 000.

KOOKABURRA, or **Laughing Jackass,** *Dacelo gigas*, the largest Australian KINGFISHER, named for the wild, laughing cry it makes from its roost at dawn and dusk. Kookaburras feed on snakes and lizards, but may also rob farmyards of ducklings and chickens.

KOOTENAY INDIANS. See KUTENAI INDIANS.

KOOTENAY NATIONAL PARK, in SE British Columbia, Canada, established in 1920. Part of the ROCKY MOUNTAINS, its 543sq mi contain hot springs and spectacular peaks and canyons.

KOOTENAY RIVER, spelled Kootenai in the US, 407mi long river flowing S from the Rocky Mts through Kootenay Park, into NW Mont. and Ida. It then returns N into Canada, flows through Kootenay Lake and joins the Columbia R.

KOPEISK, coalmining town in W Siberian USSR, 7mi SE of Chelyabinsk. Pop 156 000.

KORAN, sacred scripture of the religion of ISLAM, regarded by Muslims as God's actual words revealed to the prophet MOHAMMED in the 7th century AD. A canonical text was established in 651–52 AD, and Arabic itself was molded and preserved by its highly-

The first two chapters of the Koran in a superbly illuminated manuscript. Muslims believe that the words are those of God Himself, as conveyed to the Prophet Mohammed by the angel Gabriel, and for a long time considered it sacreligious to translate or print them.

charged, poetic language. Comprising laws, moral precepts and narrative, the Koran is divided into 114 *suras* or chapters, arranged according to length from the longest to the shortest except for the brief opening prayer. The Koran demands total surrender to the will of Allah (God), and stresses Allah's compassion and mercy. It contains much in common with the Judeo-Christian tradition, and indeed all Christians and Jews are regarded as believers since they accept the existence of one God. Today there is a greater emphasis on the spirit rather than the letter of Koranic laws which govern, for instance, moral behavior and social life. The Koran remains, however, the inspiration and guide for millions of Muslims and is the supreme authority of the Islamic tradition.

KORAT, breed of cat from Thailand (Korat Plateau) with low-lying body, heart-shaped face and large ears. Its smooth, close coat is an even, silvery blue and in the adult the eyes are green-gold.

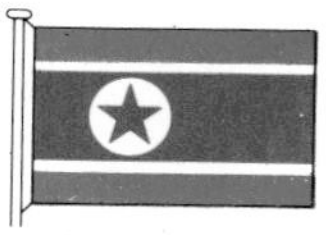

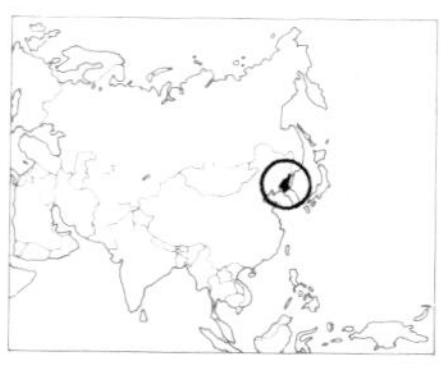

Official name: Democratic People's Republic of Korea
Capital: Pyongyang
Area: 47 225sq mi
Population: 14 281 000
Language: Korean
Religions: No official religion
Monetary unit(s): 1 Won = 100 jun

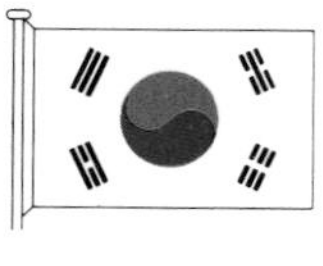

Official name: Republic of Korea
Capital: Seoul
Area: 38 452sq mi
Population: 33 524 000
Language: Korean
Religions: Buddhism, Confucianism, Christianity, Shamanism, Chondokyo
Monetary unit(s): 1 Won = 10 hwan

KOREA, 600mi-long peninsula of E Asia, separating the Yellow Sea from the Sea of Japan. It is bounded N by China and the USSR, and S by Korea Strait. Korea is two countries: the communist Democratic People's Republic (North Korea) and the Republic of Korea (South Korea). The division, which runs along 38°N, was made in 1945 and formalized in 1948. Korea is mostly mountainous, with coastal plains in the W. Most rivers flow W and S from the mountains to the Yellow Sea. The climate is varied and includes extremes of cold and humidity.

People. South Korea, though smaller, has more than twice the population of North Korea. The Koreans are mostly agricultural workers, and less than a third of the people live in towns. In the North, as in other communist countries, religious belief is discouraged. In the South, Buddhism, Confucianism and Christianity coexist.

Economy. Agricultural crops are still of primary importance in Korea, but in the 1960s rapid industrial expansion, facilitated by foreign aid, profoundly altered the economy of both North and South. The north especially is now highly industrialized, and produces large quantities of iron and steel. Farming is cooperative and mechanized. The North also has the dominant share of the country's mineral wealth. The South has widely mixed industry including plywood, chemicals and textiles.

History. After more than 1000 years of Chinese settlements among the Korean tribes, the first of several native kingdoms arose, in the N, c100 AD. Korea was not united until the 7th century. Most of its early civilization was destroyed by the Mongol invasions of the 13th century; but with the establishment (1392) of the Yi dynasty, Korea entered an age of stability and outstanding cultural achievement which included the first known printing with moveable metal type. In 1592 Japan invaded the peninsula, followed soon after by the Manchu. Korea became a Chinese vassal state, entirely cut off from the world. Commercial contact with Japan in the late 1800s foreshadowed Japan's annexation of Korea in 1910. After Japan's 1945 capitulation in WWII Korea was divided into a Russian zone of occupation in the N and a US zone in the S. Negotiations to unite the country failed, and in 1948 separate regimes were established. The North became a communist state under the former guerrilla leader, KIM IL SUNG. Elections in the South produced a republic under Syngman RHEE. On June 25, 1950, the communists of the North invaded South Korea, thus beginning the KOREAN WAR. The heavy fighting was eventually stopped (July 1953) by an armistice. In the South, Syngman Rhee's increasingly autocratic and corrupt regime was displaced (1960). A military coup in 1961 brought General PARK Chung Hee to power. President under a new constitution since 1963, he gained wider powers and the right to unlimited terms of office in 1972.

KOREAN, language spoken by the Korean people, numbering about 47 million. Of uncertain origin, Korean is considered by some to belong to the ALTAIC LANGUAGES. The official script has a simple phonetic alphabet called *hankul*, with 11 vowels and 14 consonants.

KOREAN WAR (1950–1953), a conflict between forces of the United Nations (primarily the US and South Korea) on one side and forces of North Korea and (later) communist China on the other. KOREA had been divided along latitude 38°N in 1945, Russia becoming the occupying force N of this line, and the US S of it. The war began when, having attempted to topple the government of the south by indirect means, North Korea launched a surprise invasion. UN forces were sent to assist South Korea under General Douglas MACARTHUR. By July the UN forces had been pushed SE to a small area around Pusan, but MacArthur's surprise landing at Inchon, near the captured capital Seoul, altered the complexion of the war. The UN forces destroyed the North Korean army in the south, retook Seoul, and advanced into North Korea. By November 1950 they were approaching the Yalu R on the Chinese border. At this point nearly 300 000 Chinese troops went into action and there was another major reversal as the UN forces were beaten back into South Korea. They recovered, and the fighting moved back and forth over the 38th parallel. MacArthur, urging a direct attack on China herself, was replaced in April 1951 by General RIDGWAY. Two years of negotiations, begun in July, achieved only an armistice (signed at Panmunjom on July 27, 1953). By then the communists had suffered about 2 000 000 casualties and the UN nearly 1 500 000. A peace treaty has never been signed and Korea remains divided as before.

KORIYAMA, city in N central Honshu, Japan, 25mi S of Fukushima. It is an important commercial center with large-scale light industry. Pop 241 673.

KORNBERG, Arthur (1918–), US biochemist awarded with OCHOA the 1959 Nobel Prize for Physiology or Medicine for discovering an ENZYME (DNA polymerase) that could produce from a mixture of NUCLEOTIDES exact replicas of DNA molecules. He thus extended Ochoa's related work.

KORNILOV, Lavr Georgeyevich (1870–1918), Russian general placed in command of the armies after the February Revolution of 1917. His efforts to restore military discipline led KERENSKY to suspect him of planning an army takeover. Imprisoned, he escaped to lead the anti-Bolsheviks after the October Revolution and died in battle.

KORSAKOV'S PSYCHOSIS, or **Korsakov Syndrome,** a condition of AMNESIA, unaccompanied by DEMENTIA, observed particularly among alcoholics (see ALCOHOLISM), but also among sufferers from localized BRAIN damage. It is named for the Russian neurologist S. S. Korsakov (1854–1900).

KORZYBSKI, Alfred Habdank Skarbek (1879–1950), Polish-born US scientist who formulated the philosophical linguistic system, General SEMANTICS.

KOS, island in the Aegean Sea, SE Greece, one of the DODECANESE. HIPPOCRATES was born and founded a medical school there. The island has a temple of AESCULAPIUS. The main town is Kos on the NE coast.

KOSCIUSKO, Thaddeus (1746–1817), Polish soldier and patriot who fought as a volunteer in the American Revolution. As colonel of engineers he helped build defense works at Saratoga and West Point. He was given US citizenship and made brigadier general. Returning to Poland in 1784, he instigated and led (1794) an unsuccessful fight for independence and unification. He died in exile in Switzerland.

KOSCIUSKO, Mount, the highest mountain (7 316ft) in Australia, SE New South Wales, in the Australian Alps.

KOSHER, Hebrew word meaning "proper" or "fit" used especially of food prepared according to Orthodox dietary and religious laws. Forbidden are pork, horseflesh, parts of beef and lamb, and shellfish. All meat and poultry must be killed by a Jew trained in the prescribed ritual, and soaked or salted to remove all blood. Milk and its products must not be eaten with meat.

KOSSEL, Albrecht (1853–1927), German biochemist awarded the 1910 Nobel Prize for Physiology or Medicine for his work on PROTEINS and NUCLEIC ACIDS. His main contribution was to show that "nuclein" from cellular sources was not one substance but comprised of a protein and a nonprotein (nucleic acid) component.

KOSSUTH, Lajos (1802–1894), Hungarian patriot and statesman who campaigned against Austrian rule and led the Hungarian revolution of 1848–49. A minister in the government which was set up in April 1848, he engineered Hungary's declaration of independence as a republic the following year, and became president. Austria, with the aid of Russian troops, forced a surrender, and Kossuth fled. Received as a hero in the US and England, where he lived many years, he died in Italy.

KOSTROMA, city in E European USSR, at the confluence of the Volga and Kostroma rivers. The administrative center of Kostroma Oblast, it is also important for the production of flax and linen. Pop 223 000.

KOSYGIN, Aleksei Nikolaevich (1904–), Soviet prime minister, elected 1964. He joined the Communist Party in 1927, and by 1939, with much industrial–managerial experience behind him, was on the Central Committee. In 1948 he was made a full Politburo member and in 1960 became first deputy to Khrushchev whom he succeeded.

KOTAH, city in NW India, capital of Kotah district, Rajasthan state. An industrial and communications center, Kotah is also noted for its temples and palaces. Pop 213 005.

KOTZEBUE, Otto von (1787–1846), Russian explorer who circumnavigated the world 1803–06, 1815–18, and 1823–26. He discovered many Pacific islands and explored much of the Alaskan coast. Kotzebue Sound is named for him.

KOUCHIBOUGUAC NATIONAL PARK, in E New Brunswick, Canada, established in 1969. Situated on Kouchibouguac Bay, its 87sq mi include fine camping sites.

KOUFAX, Sandy (Sanford Koufax; 1935–), US left-handed baseball pitcher who played with the Dodgers in Brooklyn and Los Angeles (1955–66). He made many pitching records and was the only major leaguer to pitch four no-hit games.

KOUMISS. See KUMISS.

KOUPREY, *Bos sauveli*, a species of wild ox confined to a small area of Cambodia. Bulls reach 1.9m (6.2ft) tall and are black, with white stockings and an enormous dewlap between the forelegs. Cows are smaller and gray-brown. Koupreys live in open parkland forming small herds which, except during the rut, are single-sexed.

KOUSSEVITSKY, Serge (1874–1951), Russian-US conductor. He left Russia in 1920 and settled in the US as conductor of the Boston Symphony Orchestra (1924–49). In 1940 he established the Berkshire Music Center. He is remembered as a champion of contemporary composers.

The people of the Korat plateau in Thailand call the Korat the Si-Sawat, or cat of good fortune, and regard it as an honor to receive one as a gift.

KOVALEVSKI, Sonya (1850–1891), Russian mathematician and novelist who made important contributions to the theory of DIFFERENTIAL EQUATIONS. Her brother-in-law, **Alexandr Onufrievich Kovalevski** (1840–1901) did pioneering work in EMBRYOLOGY.

KOVNO. See KAUNAS.

KOWLOON, industrial and commercial area of HONG KONG. On the Kowloon Peninsula facing Hong Kong Island, it was ceded to Britain in 1860 by China. Pop 715 440.

KOZHIKODE. See CALICUT.

KRAFFT-EBING, Richard, Baron von (1840–1902), German psychologist best known for his work on the psychology of SEX. He also showed there was a relation between SYPHILIS and general PARALYSIS.

KRAKATOA, volcanic island in the Sunda Strait, Indonesia. The eruption of Aug. 1883, one of the most violent ever known, destroyed most of the island, caused a tidal wave killing 36 000 people in neighboring Jawa and Sumatera, and threw debris as far as Madagascar.

KRAKÓW, or Cracow, city in S Poland on the Vistula R, administrative center of Kraków province. Capital of Poland from 1320 to 1609, the city has much outstanding architecture, including that of Jagiellonian U. (founded 1364). Still today a center of culture and learning, modern Krákow is also a major industrial city. Notable products are iron, steel, machinery and chemicals. Pop 583 000.

KRASNOYARSK, city in W Siberian USSR, administrative center of Krasnoyarsk territory, on the Yenisei R. It is a world leader in hydroelectric power. Varied and large-scale industries include aluminum and heavy machinery. Pop 688 000.

KRAUS, Karl (1874–1936), Austrian critic and poet, a master of language sometimes deemed the equal of Juvenal and Swift. Much of his satire of contemporary society appeared in his periodical *Die Fackel*. His works include nine volumes of poetry and the drama *The Last Days of Mankind* (1919).

KREBS, Sir Hans Adolf (1900–), German-born British biochemist awarded (with LIPMANN) the 1953 Nobel Prize for Physiology or Medicine for his discovery of the CITRIC ACID CYCLE, or "Krebs cycle."

KREFELD, city in W West Germany, on the Rhine R, 19mi WSW of Essen. Manufactures include textiles and machinery. Pop 222 250.

KREISLER, Fritz (1875–1962), world-renowned Austrian-US violinist of great brilliance and elegance of style. His compositions included musical forgeries of various 17th and 18th century composers, which he later admitted were his own. He lived in the US from 1943.

KREMLIN, medieval fortified center of a Russian city, especially that of MOSCOW. The Moscow Kremlin's great wall, built in the 15th century, encloses magnificent palaces and churches from the time of the tsars. The Kremlin is the administrative and political center of the Soviet Union.

KRENEK, Ernst (1900–), Austrian-US composer of the jazz opera *Johnny Strikes Up* (1926), and of TWELVE TONE MUSIC such as the *Fourth Symphony* (1947). He moved to the US in 1938.

KREUGER, Ivar (1880–1932), Swedish international financier who attempted to control world production of matches with his Swedish Match Co. His empire collapsed with the 1929 stock market crash. Facing prosecution for fraud, Kreuger killed himself.

KRISHNA, or **Govinda** or **Gopala,** major deity in later Hinduism, depicted as a blue-skinned, sportive youth generally playing the flute; he is worshiped as an incarnation of VISHNU. He is the hero of the MAHABHARATA; his teachings, related in the BHAGAVAD-GĪTĀ, advocate selfless action.

KRISHNAMURTI, Jiddu (1895–), Hindu religious thinker and teacher. His meeting (1909) with Annie BESANT led to claims that he was the reincarnation of Buddha, which he later denied. Since 1969 he has led the Krishnamurti Foundation in Cal.

KRIVOY ROG, city in the USSR, SE central Ukraine, 80mi SW of Dnepropetrovsk. It is a center for heavy industry within a major iron and coal mining area. Pop 600 000.

KROEBER, Alfred Louis (1876–1960), US anthropologist who made contributions to many aspects of cultural ANTHROPOLOGY and ARCHAEOLOGY, particularly with reference to the AMERINDS.

KROGH, Schack August Steenberg (1874–1949), Danish physiologist awarded the 1920 Nobel Prize for Physiology or Medicine for his discovery that CAPILLARIES contract and expand so as to vary the amount of BLOOD-oxygen supplied to parts of the body in accordance with their requirements.

KRONSTADT, fortress and naval base in the USSR, on Kotlin Island in the Gulf of Finland. For most of the 18th and 19th centuries it was of primary importance, both as port and as garrison, to the then Russian capital of St. Petersburg (present-day Leningrad). The scene of several mutinies (the last, in 1921, against the Soviets) it also played a significant part in WWII.

KROPOTKIN, Peter Alexeyevich, Prince (1842–1921), Russian theorist of ANARCHISM whose writings, especially *Mutual Aid* (1902), won international respect. An established geographer, he abandoned (1871) career and social position to pursue revolutionary activities. Imprisoned (1874) in Russia, he escaped to Europe, where after a further spell of imprisonment in France (1883–86) he lived in England and devoted himself to studying, writing and lecturing. He returned to Russia in 1917, but denounced the October (Bolshevik) Revolution and lived in retirement until his death.

KRUGER, Paul (Stephanus Johannes Paulus Kruger; 1825–1904), South African Boer leader. He opposed the annexation (1877) of the Transvaal by the British and played a leading part in the Boer rebellion of 1880. Elected president of the new self-governing Transvaal Republic (1883), he attempted to extend the frontiers of Transvaal territory, and his pursuit of anti-British policies ultimately led to the second BOER WAR (1899–1902). In 1900 he went to Europe and sought vainly for support for the Boers. He died in Switzerland.

KRUGER NATIONAL PARK, game reserve in South Africa, NE Transvaal Province. Founded by Paul KRUGER in 1898, it was expanded and established as a national park in 1926. Its 8 000sq mi contain almost all native species of wildlife.

KRUPA, Gene (1909–1973), US jazz musician and outstanding virtuoso drummer. He played with Chicago bands until 1935, when he joined the Benny Goodman orchestra. He had his own band from 1938 to 1951.

KRUPP, family of German industrialists famous as armaments makers and long associated with German militarism. The Essen firm was founded in 1811 by **Friedrich Krupp** (1787–1826) with a small steel casting factory, and under his son **Alfred** (1812–1887), became the largest cast steel enterprise in the world. It played a key role in the Franco-Prussian War, WWI and WWII. The Krupps clung to family ownership and opposed unionism. After WWII, **Alfred Krupp von Bohlen und Halbach** (1907–1967), head of the firm from 1943, was imprisoned (1948–51) for war crimes. The company, reorganized but retaining much of its holdings, now concentrates on heavy industrial equipment.

KRUPSKAYA, Nadezhda Konstantinovna (1869–1939), Soviet revolutionary and educationist. She married LENIN in 1898 while both were exiled in Siberia, thereafter sharing his life in Europe and his return (1917) to Russia. An opponent of Stalin, she lost her considerable influence in the Communist Party after Lenin's death.

KRUTCH, Joseph Wood (1893–1970), US literary critic, social critic and naturalist, author of many books in all three fields. An early environmentalist, he began to concentrate on nature studies when he moved to Arizona in 1950. His subsequent books include *The Great Chain of Life* (1957).

KRYLOV, Ivan Andreyevich (1769–1844), Russian author of nine books of fables (from 1809) which have become popular classics of satire. Influenced by or adopted from AESOP and LA FONTAINE, they are nonetheless typically Russian in spirit.

KRYPTON (Kr), one of the NOBLE GASES, used to fill high-wattage electric light bulbs, flash lamps and electric-arc lamps. It combines with fluorine in an electric discharge to give krypton (II) fluoride (KrF_2), a highly reactive, colorless crystalline solid, which decomposes slowly at 20°C and is hydrolyzed by water. Other compounds have been claimed. AW 83.8, mp −157°C, bp −152°C.

KUALA LUMPUR, capital and largest city of Malaysia, on the S Malay Peninsula, in Selangor state. It is Malaysia's commercial, transportation, cultural and educational center. Founded in 1857, the city owed much of its subsequent rapid growth to the local abundance of tin and rubber. Pop 451 278.

KUBAN RIVER, river in the USSR, rising in the Caucasus Mts and flowing NW to the Sea of Azov.

KUBELIK, (Jeronym) Rafael (1914–), Czech conductor and composer. He was principal conductor of the Chicago Symphony Orchestra (1950–53) and musical director of the Royal Opera, Covent Garden.

KUBITSCHEK, Juscelino (1902–), president of Brazil 1955–60. He encouraged scientific and industrial progress, but economic problems followed the building of the new capital BRASILIA. In 1964 he was accused of corruption and went into exile for some years.

KUBLAI KHAN (c1216–1294), Mongol emperor from 1259, founder of the Mongol Yüan dynasty of China and grandson of GENGHIS KHAN. By 1279, the last resistance of the Chinese SUNG dynasty crushed, his empire reached from the Pacific to the Volga R and into Poland. Under his skilled and tolerant rule China flourished both economically and culturally. His new capital Cambuluc, described by MARCO POLO, became the nucleus of modern Peking.

KUBRICK, Stanley (1928–), US film director noted for his technical brilliance and thematic daring. His films include *Lolita* (1962), *Dr. Strangelove* (1964), *2001: A Space Odyssey* (1968) and *A Clockwork Orange* (1971).

KUDU, two species of large African ANTELOPE related to bushbucks and NYALA. Dark brown with white stripes on the back and flanks, the males have spiral horns reaching up to 1m (39in) long in the Greater kudu, *Tragelaphus strepsiceros*. Animals of bush and dense scrub, kudu associate in one-male harems.

KUDZU, *Pueraria thunbergiana*, a vine native to Japan and China and cultivated as a forage crop. It has tuberous roots that are eaten as a vegetable or used in the manufacture of Japanese arrowroot. The stem is a source of fiber. Family: Leguminosae.

KUEI-YANG, city in S China, capital of Kweichow province. It is a major center for transportation and heavy industry. Pop 1 500 000.

KUHN, Fritz (1896–1951), German-born US leader of the GERMAN-AMERICAN BUND, an American pro-Nazi organization of the 1930s. Prosecuted for larceny and forgery in 1939, he was deported.

KUHN, Richard (1900–1967), German chemist awarded the 1938 Nobel Prize for Chemistry for his work on the CAROTENOIDS and VITAMINS.

KUK'AI-CHIH (c344–406 AD), reputedly the first great Chinese painter, noted for his portraits and landscapes. They are known only from ancient writings and from paintings thought to be copies. Of these last the most famous is *The Admonitions of the Instructress to the Palace Ladies* (7th century).

KU KLUX KLAN, secret organization originally begun (1866) to conduct a campaign of terror against newly enfranchized Negroes. Founded by Confederate veterans, it spread from Tenn. throughout the South. Its members adopted an arcane hierarchy and dressed in hoods and white sheets to play on their victims' belief in vengeful ghosts. Its emblem was a fiery cross. It was officially disbanded in 1869, although many members remained active throughout RECONSTRUCTION and beyond. The second Klan, organized in 1915, extended its hostilities to Jews, Catholics, pacifists, the foreign born, radicals and labor unions. A membership of nearly 5 000 000 was claimed in the 1920s. Officially disbanded once more in 1944, the Klan again revived in the 1950s and 1960s as a response to desegregation.

KULAKS, term for the historical class of prosperous peasants in Russia: those, e.g., who owned large farms and could employ labor. Stalin designated the Kulaks an anachronism in a state-planned economy; they were dispossessed (1929–34) and deported en masse to labor camps.

KUMAMOTO, city in W Kyushu, Japan, on the Shira R. An agricultural trading center, it has food-processing and textile plants. Pop 440 020.

KUMASI, city in Ghana, capital of Ashanti region, and seat of the ASHANTI kings. It is a major cultural and trading center. Pop 234 274.

KUMISS, or koumiss, a fermented liquor prepared from mares' milk by the Tartars of central Asia.

KÜMMEL, alcoholic drink of the liqueur type, produced by flavoring spirit with cumin and caraway seeds. It is made in the Baltic states.

KUMQUAT, evergreen shrubs and trees of the genus *Fortunella*, which is closely related to the ORANGE and LEMON. Kumquat fruit are oval-shaped, orange-yellow with a juicy pulp and edible spongy skin. They are normally used in candies and preserves. Family: Rutaceae.

KUN, Béla (1886–c1939), Hungarian politician and communist premier of Hungary for four months in 1919. Forced to flee by counterrevolutionists, Kun settled in Moscow, returning briefly to Hungary in 1928 to attempt another revolution. He was liquidated in Russia during the 1930s purges.

KUNLUN MOUNTAINS, great chain of mountain ranges in China, on the N extremity of the Tibetan plateau, extending E -W for over 1000mi. The highest peak is Ulugh Mus Tagh (25 340ft).

KUNMING, city in S China, capital of Yunnan province. It is a major transport and commercial center, with large-scale mixed industry. Educational facilities are outstanding. Pop 1 700 000.

KUOMINTANG (Chinese: National People's Party), political party of CHINA founded (1912) by SUN YAT̂SEN to stand for an independent Chinese republic with a moderate socialist reform program. In 1924 Sun's "Three People's Principles" (nationalism, democracy and work for all) were accepted by a coalition that included the communists. After Sun's death (1925) CHIANG KAI-SHEK took over the leadership and in 1927 expelled the communists. Most of China was under Kuomintang rule until 1947, but corruption and galloping inflation hastened communist victory (1949). The Kuomintang survives in TAIWAN.

KUPRIN, Alexander Ivanovitch (1870–1938), Russian author of outstanding novels and short stories in the realist vein, such as *The Pit* (1909) which deals with prostitution. After the Revolution Kuprin emigrated to France but returned to the USSR in 1937.

KURA RIVER, major river of the S European USSR. It rises in NE Turkey and flows 941mi N through Georgia and ESE through Azerbaijan to the Caspian Sea. It provides hydroelectricity and irrigation.

KURASHIKI, city in Japan, Honshu Island, on the Takahashi R. Now chiefly a cultural center, it has a long-established textile industry. Pop 339 799.

KURCHATOV, Igor Vasilevich (1903–), Russian nuclear physicist largely responsible for the development of Soviet nuclear armaments and for the first Soviet nuclear power station. The Soviets have named RUTHERFORDIUM *kurchatovium* for him.

KURCHATOVIUM. See RUTHERFORDIUM.

KURDISTAN, non-political region of about 74 000sq mi inhabited by KURDS. It lies chiefly in E Turkey but includes parts of NW Iran, NE Iraq, and Soviet Armenia.

KURDS, people of KURDISTAN in W Asia, estimated to number about 8 000 000. Traditionally nomadic, most Kurds today are settled farmers. Almost all are Muslims. Kurds have fought vigorously against various rulers for an independent Kurdistan. In Iraq the 1960s and 1970s saw much warfare between the Kurds and Iraqi troops over the issue of self-government.

KURE, city and port in Japan, SW Honshu Island. Kure has a naval base and its industry is led by shipbuilding. Pop 234 184.

KURIL ISLANDS, USSR, chain of 56 volcanic islands, stretching from the Kamchatka Peninsula of Siberia to Hokkaido Island, Japan. Sparsely inhabited, the islands are the subject of a territorial dispute between Japan and the USSR.

KUROSAWA, Akira (1910–), Japanese movie director whose outstanding talent and originality has been internationally recognized. His films include *Rashomon* (1950), the widely-distributed epic *Seven Samurai* (1954) and *Throne of Blood* (1957), a Japanese interpretation of *Macbeth*.

KURSK, city in central European USSR, administrative center of Kursk region. A major railroad junction, it has varied industries led by food-processing. Pop 284 000.

KUSCH, Polykarp (1911–), German physicist who shared with W. E. LAMB the 1955 Nobel Prize for Physics for showing that the ELECTRON had a magnetic moment (see MAGNETISM) greater than that theoretically calculated. This result inspired radical changes in nuclear theory.

KUSH. See CUSH, KINGDOM OF.

KUSHANS, central Asian people that conquered N India in the 1st century AD. The greatest ruler of the Kushan dynasty was Kanishka (c78–101 AD) under whom Buddhist literature and scholarship flourished, and Greek and Roman cultural influence was strong. The empire declined in the 3rd century AD.

KUSHIRO, city and port in Japan, SE Hokkaido Island. Fish, lumber and coal supply processing industries and exports. Pop 191 946.

KUTCHIN INDIANS, Athabaskan-speaking North American Indians inhabiting E Alaska and the Yukon valley. Traditionally warriors and hunters, they were strongly influenced by their Eskimo neighbors. By 1970 the Kutchin numbered about 1 100.

KUTENAI INDIANS, North American Indians of uncertain linguistic stock who inhabited N Ida., NW Mont. and SE British Columbia. They were skilled in hunting, fishing and war. By 1970 they numbered about 1000.

KUTUZOV, Mikhail Illarionovich, Prince (1745–1813), Russian field marshal in charge of the forces opposing NAPOLEON I's invasion of Russia in 1812. After a heavy defeat at BORODINO Kutuzov successfully adopted evasive tactics, then hounded Napoleon during the retreat from Moscow.

KUVASZ, Hungarian breed of sheep dog and watchdog standing about 26in high, with a thick white coat. It is thought to be Tibetan in origin.

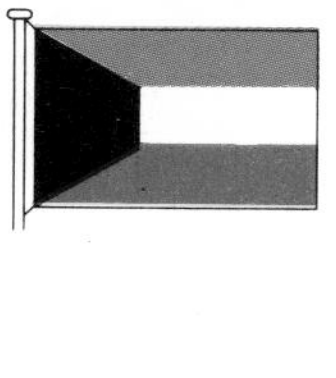

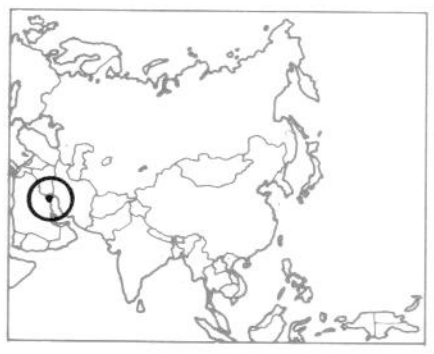

Official name: Kuwait
Capital: Kuwait
Area: 9 375sq mi
Population: 831 000
Languages: Arabic, English
Religions: Muslim, Christian
Monetary unit(s): 1 Kuwait dinar = 1000 fils

KUWAIT, independent Arab state on the NW coast of the Persian Gulf, bounded S by Saudi Arabia and N and W by Iraq. The country is nearly all desert and the bulk of the population lives in the cities, chief of which is Kuwait, the capital and major port. A major oil-producer since the 1940s, Kuwait is now a leading economic power with an estimated 20% of the world's oil reserves. Oil revenues finance free education and medical care for all, housing, power stations and water supplies, as well as providing Kuwait with the highest per capita income in the world. Since its foundation in the 18th century, Kuwait has been ruled by the al-Sabah dynasty. Even when a part of the Ottoman Empire, Kuwait retained independence, relying upon the port of Kuwait as its main source of income. A British protectorate from 1899 to 1961, Kuwait has successfully resisted territorial claims from both Saudi Arabia and Iraq. It is now an influential member of the ARAB LEAGUE.

The Heian Shrine, one of some 200 Shinto shrines in Kyoto, Japan. Built in 1895, it is a copy of a former imperial palace dating from 894 AD.

KUYBYSHEV, city in E central European USSR, named Samara until 1935. A river port on the Volga R, it is a major center of commercial and heavy industry, including oil refining. Pop 1 047 000.

KUZNETS, Simon Smith (1901–), Russian-born US economist. He pioneered development of a conceptual basis for national income accounts in the US, for which he won the Nobel Prize for Economics in 1971. He is noted for studies of structural changes in economic development and growth of nations. Since 1960, he has been a professor of economics at Harvard U.

KUZNETSK BASIN, region of about 10 000sq mi in the W Siberian USSR containing coalfields with estimated reserves of at least 299 billion tons. Massive iron and steel works are located there, notably at NOVOKUZNETSK.

KWAJALEIN, largest of the MARSHALL ISLANDS, W central Pacific Ocean. A coral atoll, it comprises 97 islets encircling a lagoon of 655sq mi. A US military base is located there.

KWAKIUTL INDIANS, North American Indians of Wakashan linguistic stock, native to Vancouver Island and coastal British Columbia, Canada. Skilled in fishing and crafts, they had a strictly hierarchical society in which the POTLACH ceremony played a significant part. In 1970 the Kwakiutl numbered about 1 500.

KWANGJU, city in SW South Korea, capital of South Cholla province. It is a commercial and cultural center. Manufactures include automobiles and textiles. Pop 502 753.

KWASHIORKOR, PROTEIN malnutrition simultaneous with the maintenance of relatively adequate calorie intake. In affected children it causes EDEMA, SKIN and HAIR changes, loss of appetite, DIARRHEA, LIVER disturbance and apathy. Its name derives from its occurrence in children rejected from the breast at the birth of the next sibling. Treatment involves rehydration, treatment of infection and a balanced diet with adequate protein.

KYD, Thomas (1558–1594), English dramatist, whose *The Spanish Tragedy* (c1586) was a prototype of the Elizabethan and Jacobean revenge tragedy. The work is partly modeled on Seneca but is both more lurid and more psychologically acute. Kyd may have written a version of the Hamlet story.

KYFFAÜSER, small range of hills in W East Germany, Halle district. According to legend FREDERICK I sleeps under the hills but will one day waken to lead the German people.

KYOTO, city in Japan, Honshu Island, about 25mi NE of Osaka. The national capital from its foundation in 794 AD until supplanted by Tokyo in 1868, Kyoto is rich in architectural relics and art treasures. Still today a cultural and religious center, it also has leading educational establishments and large-scale mixed industry. Pop 1 418 933.

KYTHERA, southernmost of the IONIAN ISLANDS of Greece, off the SE coast of the Peloponnesus. In ancient times the island had a temple of APHRODITE, who was said to have risen from the sea there.

KYUSHU, most southerly of the four major islands which make up JAPAN. Area 16 205sq mi.

KYZYL-KUM (Turkish: red sand), desert of Soviet Central Asia, SE of the Aral Sea and covering some 115 000sq mi of Kazakhstan and Uzbekistan. Some parts have been irrigated to produce cotton, rice and wheat.

L

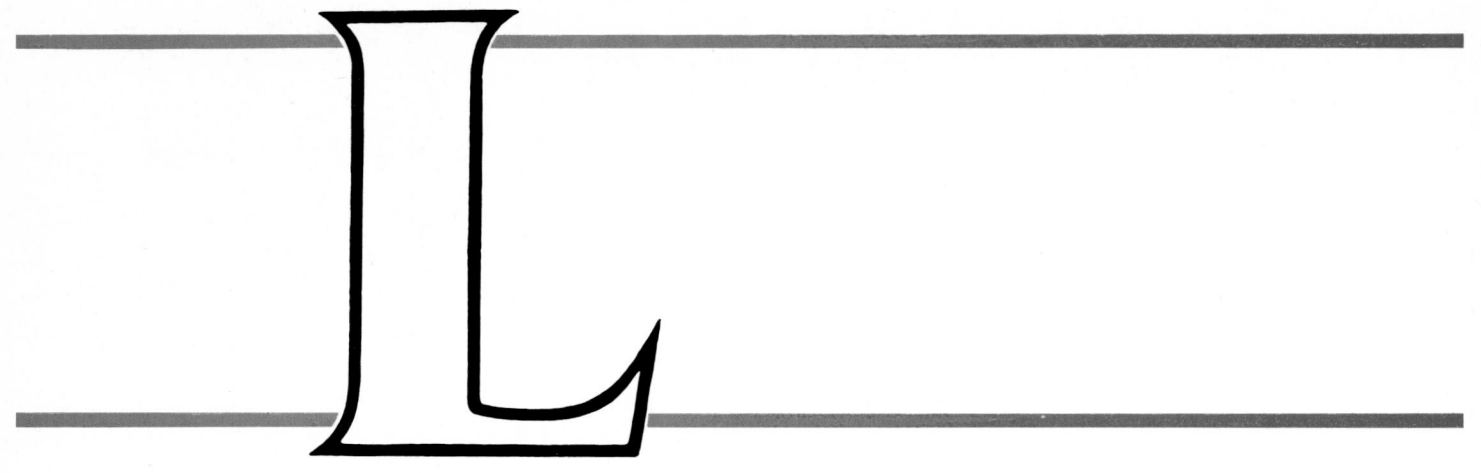

L, the 12th letter of the English alphabet, derived from the Semitic *lamedh* and the Greek *lambda*. In Roman numerals, L represents 50. The symbol £, a form of L, is an abbreviation of the Latin *libra*, a pound in weight.

LABOR, the act of physical work or the social group that does it, namely the LABOR FORCE; also an economic term applied to any kind of service that commands an economic return. The economic concept of labor was developed in the mid-18th century by Adam SMITH, and later by MALTHUS and above all by MARX in his LABOR THEORY OF VALUE.

In ancient civilizations manual laborers were generally slaves (see SLAVERY). In medieval Europe agriculture was carried on by SERFS while other productive processes came to be controlled by master craftsmen, who formed GUILDS largely consisting of journeymen. Apprentices were used for simple preparatory operations. Such distribution of production tasks is found even in primitive economies, but it was the mechanization of the INDUSTRIAL REVOLUTION that made division of labor fundamental. This breaks down a given production process into as many simple, repetitive functions as possible, to minimize time-consuming skill and judgment. The immediate result was improved productivity, but also the degradation of work from a potentially creative act to a tedious chore. At the same time, regular hours were needed to get maximum output from machinery, and, because of the fluctuating demand patterns of a growth economy, labor had to be available or dismissable at will. The notion of "free labor" evolved. This replaced the master-servant relationship with a simple implied contract in which the wages, paid only for work done, became full quittance for the laborer's service. The day-laborer, the exception in early civilizations, became the norm. The labor contract released the employer from even notional responsibility for the laborer, but gave the laborer a highly limited freedom to contract where he would.

The original home of the Labrador retriever was Newfoundland, from where it was taken to Europe early in the 19th century. Its gentleness and intelligence make it an excellent guide dog for the blind, as well as an ideal family pet.

Labor UNIONS grew from employees' determination to force employers to observe the labor contract, to acknowledge obligations of humanity in terms of pay and working conditions, and then to improve these terms and conditions. Working hours have diminished from about 70 hours per week (c1800) to the present standards of 40 or 48 hours. In many countries organized labor has come to be represented by political parties. (See also CAPITAL; CHILD LABOR; INDENTURED SERVANT; MASS PRODUCTION; TIME AND MOTION.)

LABOR, US Department of, federal department, independent since 1913, responsible for US workers' welfare. Headed by the secretary of labor, a cabinet member, it is concerned with the enforcement of federal laws regulating hours, wages and safety measures; it collects and issues industrial statistics; it administers job-training programs and provides information in labor disputes. It has several specialized divisions.

LABOR DAY, official holiday in the US and Canada since 1894, held on the first Monday in September. In socialist countries and most others, labor is honored on MAY DAY.

LABOR FORCE, that section of the population which is employed or capable of employment. In the US in 1970 the labor force formed over 30% of the population between 14 and 65, excluding housewives and students.

LABOR-MANAGEMENT RELATIONS ACT. See TAFT-HARTLEY ACT.

LABOR-MANAGEMENT REPORTING AND DISCLOSURE ACT. See LANDRUM-GRIFFIN ACT.

LABOR THEORY OF VALUE, economic theory propounded by David RICARDO and others, which became a central thesis of Karl MARX's analysis of capitalism. The value of a product is defined in terms of the amount of labor required to manufacture it. This concept has had influence on non-Marxian economics; its prime Marxian corollary is that the value of the products the laborer can buy with his wages is less than that of those he produces. The differential, or **surplus value**, makes the profit of the capitalist.

LABOR UNIONS. See UNIONS.

LABOUR PARTY, British, political party founded in 1900 by trade unions and socialist groups—the Independent Labour Party (1893) and the FABIAN SOCIETY—with Keir HARDIE its first leader. It gained nationwide support after WWI, first coming to power under Ramsay MACDONALD in 1924. His second administration, 1929–31, ended in coalition with the Conservatives, division within the party and electoral defeat. The first effective socialist program was implemented by the Labour government of Clement ATTLEE (1945–51): Aneurin BEVAN instituted the National Health Service, and the Bank of England and major industries were nationalized. Attlee was followed as leader by Hugh GAITSKELL who was succeeded at his death (1963) by Harold WILSON. Prime minister in four Labour governments, he was succeeded by James Callaghan in 1976.

LABRADOR. See NEWFOUNDLAND.

LABRADOR CURRENT, cold ocean current originating in the Davis Strait. Bearing ICEBERGS, it flows S down the W side of the Labrador Sea to meet the GULF STREAM. (See also OCEAN CURRENTS.)

LABRADORITE, variety of plagioclase FELDSPAR, consisting of ALBITE and ANORTHITE, commonly occurring in BASALT and GABBRO. Gray to black in color, it often shows red, blue or green iridescence, and hence is used as a GEM stone and for building.

LABRADOR RETRIEVER, sporting dog, about 2ft high and 65lb in weight, with a square muzzle, broad head and short straight fur, black or golden in color. It is used to hunt waterfowl and other game birds.

LABRADOR TEA, *Ledum groenlandicum*, small evergreen shrub of the HEATH family (Ericaceae). It grows in marshy ground in the northern US and Canada. The crushed leaves have been used as a TEA substitute.

LA BREA TAR PITS, asphalt bog in Hancock Park, Los Angeles, containing skeletons of prehistoric animals, including mammoths, saber-toothed tigers and giant sloths, preserved by the tar.

LA BRUYÈRE, Jean de (1645–1696), French moralist. His *Les Caractères* (1688) is partly a translation of THEOPHRASTUS, but mostly his satirical impressions of contemporary society.

LABURNUM, genus of trees and shrubs of the PEA family (Leguminosae) widely cultivated in the US and Europe for their decorative yellow flowers. Its wood is hard and valued for cabinet-making. All parts of the plant are poisonous, particularly the seeds.

LABYRINTH, or **maze,** complex, tortuous system of rooms and passages intended to perplex strangers trying to find their way in or out. The legendary labyrinth at Knossos, Crete, was built by DAEDALUS for King MINOS, to house the MINOTAUR. Hedges are often used to form garden mazes. (See also MAZE.)

LABYRINTHODONTIA, a group of fossil AMPHIBIA totally unlike the specialized amphibia living today. Many were very large and it is probable that all had bony scales in the skin. Though seemingly very reptilian, they are classed with the amphibia because they did not lay terrestrial amniote eggs. The Labyrinthodontia were probably the ancestors of modern reptiles.

LAC. See SHELLAC.

LA CANADA-FLINTRIDGE, unincorporated residential town in S Cal., NW of Pasadena. Pop 18 338.

LACCADIVE, MINICOY AND AMINDIVI ISLANDS, renamed the Lakshadweep Islands (1974), group of 26 islands (10 inhabited) in the Arabian Sea off SW India, a Union Territory administered by India. Their economy rests on copra, bananas and fishing. Pop 31 798.

LACCOLITH, a dome-like intrusion of igneous rock, usually arching the overlying strata and with an approximately flat floor. **Phacoliths** are similar but lens-shaped, with a concave side facing downward and a convex side facing upward.

LACE, fine openwork decorative fabric made by braiding, looping, knotting or twisting thread, usually linen or cotton, sometimes silver and gold. Before 19th-century mechanization, it was handmade either by needlepoint or with bobbins. Lace was developed in 16th-century Italy and Flanders and became highly popular. Some towns, such as Brussels, gave their names to their particular styles of lace. (See also CROCHET; NEEDLEWORK.)

LACERTID LIZARDS, LIZARDS of the Old World distinguished by the presence of bony plates (osteoderms) on the surface of the skull, and by an aperture in the skull roof through which the PINEAL BODY projects.

LACEWINGS, insects of the order Neuroptera, with veined membranous wings. The larvae are predatory on APHIDS.

LACHESIS. See FATES.

LACHINE, city in S Quebec, 8mi SW of Montreal. It produces iron, steel and heavy machinery, and is a terminal of the Lachine Canal. Pop 44423.

LACKAWANNA, city in W N.Y. on Lake Erie 5mi S of Buffalo. It is a major steel center, and has a famous Roman Catholic basilica. Pop 28657.

LACKAWANNA RIVER, river that rises in NE Pa. and flows about 50mi SW to join the Susquehanna R near Pittston. Anthracite was once mined in the area.

LACLOS, Pierre Ambroise François Choderlos de (1741–1803), French army officer and writer, best known for his novel *Les Liaisons Dangereuses* (1782), which cynically recounts the callous maneuvers of two seducers. He served as a general under Napoleon.

LACONIA, in ancient Greece, SE region of the PELOPONNESUS, bounded by Arcadia, Argolis and Messenia. Its capital, SPARTA, stood in the central Lacedaemon plain. Modern Laconia is a department of Greece.

LACONIA, city in central N.H. 22mi N of Concord; seat of Belknap Co. It manufactures machinery and textiles, and is a popular resort. Pop 14888.

LA CORUÑA (Corunna), seaport in NW Spain, capital of La Coruña province, Galicia. Inhabited from Roman times, it has always been a major Spanish trading and fishing port; from it sailed the Spanish ARMADA. Pop 189654.

LACQUERWARE, articles treated with **lacquer**, a colored, usually opaque VARNISH. The process originated in the Far East some 2000 years ago, the sap of the sumac tree *Rhus vernicifera* being used as varnish. The basis of much lacquerwork is SHELLAC. Many layers of varnish were applied to form a hard bright surface suitable for decorative painting. The process of JAPANNING arose in imitation of oriental lacquerware. Modern synthetic lacquers are widely used for protective coating.

LA CROSSE, city in W Wis., seat of La Crosse Co. It produces air conditioning systems and clothing, and is the site of Wisconsin State U. Pop 51153.

LACROSSE, team game derived by French settlers from the North American Indians' game of baggataway, and now the national game of Canada. It is played with a stick called a cross having a net at one end, and a hard rubber ball. The cross is used to catch, throw and carry the ball with the aim of sending it into the opposing goal. In men's lacrosse, played in Canada, the US and the UK, each team has 10 members. Women's lacrosse is usually played 12 a side.

LACTATION, the production of MILK by female mammals. Shortly before the birth of her young, hormonal changes in the mother result in increased development of the mammary glands and teats. Glandular cells in the body of the mammaries secrete milk which is released to the young when the teats are stimulated. Lactation and the feeding of young on milk are characteristic of the MAMMALS.

LACTIC ACID (CH_3.CHOH.COOH), hydroxypropionic acid, a syrupy odorless liquid produced by the action of lactic-acid bacteria on MILK. It is responsible for the flavor of plain YOGHURT. MUSCLE tissue which is being vigorously exercised is unable to obtain sufficient OXYGEN from the blood to supply the ENERGY it needs. Under these conditions additional energy can be obtained by the reduction of GLUCOSE to lactate. This lactate tends to build up in the muscle and is probably responsible for the CRAMPS which are experienced in vigorous EXERCISE.

LACTOSE ($C_{12}H_{22}O_{11}$), or "milk sugar," a disaccharide SUGAR forming about 4.5% of MILK. It yields GLUCOSE and galactose with the ENZYME lactase.

LADAKH, E district of KASHMIR, astride the Ladakh Mts, on the Tibetan border. It covers about 45750sq mi (118500sq km). In 1949 it was divided between India and Pakistan, and in 1962 China occupied the NE section.

LADINO, or Judeo-Spanish, language of Jewish communities in the Balkans, Near East and N Africa brought by 15th-century Spanish refugees (see SEPHARDIM). It is an archaic form of Spanish, written in Hebrew characters. The term Ladino is also used for a Spanish–American culture type in central America.

LADISLAS I, Saint (1040–1095), or László I, king of Hungary from 1077. He annexed CROATIA and conquered the CUMANS, enforcing their conversion to Christianity. He died while preparing to go on the first Crusade. He was traditionally honored as the embodiment of chivalry.

LADYBUGS, or **ladybirds,** small brightly-colored beetles with 5000 species of worldwide distribution. In length 2.5–7.5mm (0.1–0.3in), they are harlequin-patterned insects with, commonly, black spots on a red background or yellow spots on black. The colors are borne on the wingcases, modified forewings covering the true flying wings. Ladybugs and their larvae feed on plant aphids and have considerable economic value in controlling pest populations.

LADY DAY, March 25, feast of the ANNUNCIATION. It is an English **quarter-day**, when traditionally rents were paid and leases contracted. Old Lady Day, April 6, begins the English fiscal year.

LADYSMITH, town in W Natal, South Africa, 160mi NW of Durban. It is a rail junction and market center for a dairy and stock area. The Boers besieged it for four months 1899–1900 (see BOER WAR). Pop 28554.

LADY'S SLIPPER, popular name for plants of the genus *Cypripedium*, which belongs to the ORCHID family (Orchidaceae). Solitary flowers resembling a slipper are produced on each stem. The genus is native to north-temperate and tropical regions of Eurasia and the Americas.

LAERTIUS, Diogenes. See DIOGENES LAERTIUS.

LA FARGE, John (1835–1910), influential US artist noted for his fine mural painting and stained glass, chiefly executed for churches, e.g. the mural "Ascension" in the Church of the Ascension, New York.

LA FARGE, Oliver Hazard Perry (1901–1963), US writer and anthropologist who used his archaeological work in Ariz. and central America as background for his books. His novel of Navaho life, *Laughing Boy*, won a Pulitzer Prize in 1929.

LAFAYETTE, residential town in NW Cal. E of Berkeley. It was settled in 1848. Pop 20484.

LAFAYETTE, city in W central Ind. 64mi NW of Indianapolis, seat of Tippecanoe Co. It produces aluminum and rubber goods and is the site of Purdue University. Pop 44955.

LAFAYETTE, city in S central La., 55mi SW of Baton Rouge, seat of Lafayette parish. It is a shipping center for a region producing sugar, cotton and oil. Pop 68908.

LAFAYETTE, Marie Joseph Paul Yves Roch Gilbert du Motier, Marquis de (1757–1834), French soldier and statesman who fought in the American Revolution and worked for French–American alliance. He came to America 1777, joined Washington's staff as major general and fought in the campaigns of 1777–78 and at Yorktown (1781). On a visit to France (1779) he persuaded Louis XVI to send troops and a fleet to aid the colonists. In the French Revolution he supported the bourgeoisie, helped set up the National Assembly, drafted the Declaration of the Rights of Man, and commanded the National Guard, but fell from power after ordering his troops (July 1791) to fire on the populace. In 1824 he revisited the US, hailed as a hero. He was one of the leaders of the JULY REVOLUTION (1830).

LA FAYETTE, Marie Madeleine Pioche de la Vergne, Comtesse de (1634–1693), French writer and pioneer of the novel of character. She is especially noted for *The Princess of Clèves* (1678).

LAFAYETTE ESCADRILLE, in WWI a flight of US volunteer airmen with the French air service. In 1918 they became the US 103rd Pursuit Squadron.

Typical coastal lagoon (*right*), separated from the sea by a barrier beach thrown up by wave action.

LAFFITTE, Jean (c1780–1825?), also **Lafitte**, French pirate and smuggler who attacked Spanish ships S of New Orleans. He and his men received a pardon from President Madison in return for aiding Andrew Jackson against the British in 1815, but later went back to piracy. When he attacked US ships (1820) the navy sailed against him, and he set out in his favorite ship the *Pride*, never to be seen again.

LA FOLLETTE, Robert Marion, Sr. (1855–1925), US statesman and reform legislator. He served in the House of Representatives 1885–91. He became Wis. governor (1901–06), supported by progressive Republicans, and initiated the "Wisconsin idea" reform program, proposing direct primaries and a state civil service. He served as senator (1906–25), founded the PROGRESSIVE PARTY, opposed US entry to WWI and the League of Nations, and ran for president 1924.

His son **Robert Marion La Follette, Jr.** (1895–1953), was senator 1925–47, and another son, **Philip Fox La Follette** (1897–1965), was twice governor of Wis.

LA FONTAINE, Henri Marie (1854–1943), Belgian international lawyer and statesman; president of the International Peace Bureau (1907–43) and winner of the Nobel Peace Prize in 1913.

LA FONTAINE, Jean de (1621–1695), French writer, remembered especially for his *Fables* (1668–94), moral tales drawn from AESOP and oriental sources which he used to comment satirically on contemporary society; and for his humorous, bawdy *Tales* (1664–66).

LAFONTAINE, Sir Louis Hippolyte (1807–1864), Canadian statesman and judge. Leader of the French Canadians from 1837 and joint prime minister with Robert BALDWIN in 1842–43 and of the "great ministry" 1848–51 (its legislation included the Rebellion Losses Bill), he was chief justice of Lower Canada from 1853.

LAGERKVIST, Pär Fabian (1891–1974), Swedish poet, novelist and dramatist, winner of the 1951 Nobel Prize for Literature. He was much disturbed by WWI and later also protested against fascism. His works, which include *Barabbas* (1950), explore the problem of good and evil in man.

LAGERLÖF, Selma Ottiliana Lovisa (1858–1940), Swedish novelist, the first woman to win a Nobel Prize for Literature (1909). Her works, rooted in legend and the folklore of her native Värmland, include *Gösta Berlings Saga* (1891).

LAGOMORPHA, an order consisting of two families—the Leporidae, HARES and RABBITS, and the Ochotonidae, PIKAS. Characteristic of the order are the long incisors which grow continuously to counteract wear due to feeding on abrasive vegetation, grasses, leaves and bark. To make better use of this indigestible material, lagomorphs habitually reingest their feces to reprocess them.

LAGOON, stretch of water separated from the sea by a bank or reef, a common phenomenon in CORAL reef areas (see also ATOLL). A lagoon may also be formed when the sea throws up a barrier beach at high tide. **Haffs** are lagoons created by a sandy spit at a river mouth.

LAGOS, capital and chief port of Nigeria, and capital of Lagos State, on the Bight of Benin. The city takes up four islands and part of the mainland. It produces textiles and metal goods, and exports palm products, groundnuts and cocoa. It houses Lagos U. Pop 943 000.

LA GRANGE, city in W Ga. 41mi N of Columbus, seat of Troupe Co. Its products include textiles and pulpwood. Pop 23 301.

LA GRANGE, village in NE Ill. 13mi W of Chicago. It has some light industry; there are limestone quarries nearby. Pop 16 773.

LAGRANGE, Joseph Louis (1736–1813), French mathematician who made important contributions to CALCULUS, DIFFERENTIAL EQUATIONS and especially the application of techniques of ANALYSIS to MECHANICS. He worked also on celestial mechanics, in particular explaining the MOON's libration.

LA GRANGE PARK, village in NE Ill., just N of La Grange. It is residential with some light industry. Pop 15 626.

LA GUARDIA, Fiorello Henry (1882–1947), US statesman and reforming mayor of New York. A Progressive member of Congress 1916–17 and 1923–33, he supported liberalizing and pro-labor measures, including the Norris–La Guardia Act forbidding the use of injunctions in labor disputes. As mayor 1933–45 he instituted major reforms in New York and fought corruption.

LAGUNA BEACH, city in S Cal., on the Pacific coast. It is a resort noted for its scenery and its art colony. Pop 14 550.

LA HABRA, city in S Cal., a SE suburb of Los Angeles. It is the commercial center of a fruit-growing area, and has some light industry. Pop 41 350.

LAHONTAN, Lake, lake of the mid-Pleistocene once extending over much of NW Nev. and parts of NE Cal. Remnants of it include Carson Sink, Pyramid Lake, Walker Lake and Winnemucca Lake.

LAHORE, city and ancient cultural center in E central Pakistan, a former MOGUL capital. Its celebrated Mogul architecture includes the Shalimar gardens and the Palace of Jahangir. Modern Lahore is a commercial and marketing center with numerous manufacturing industries. Pop 2 148 000.

LAIBACH, German name for LJUBLJANA.

LAIBACH, Congress of, held in 1821 by the HOLY ALLIANCE powers, with observers from France and Great Britain. It sanctioned the use of the Austrian army to quell the liberal revolutions in Naples and Piedmont, and marked the growing breach between Great Britain and the Holy Alliance.

LAISSEZ-FAIRE (French: let things alone), doctrine which opposes state intervention in economic affairs. First enunciated by the French PHYSIOCRATS in the 18th century as a reaction against MERCANTILISM, the idea was taken up by Adam SMITH and became a cornerstone of classical economics.

LAKE. See RIVERS AND LAKES.

LAKE CHARLES, city and inland port in SW La. It is a shipping center for rice, timber, chemicals and petroleum, and has petrochemical and other industries. Pop 77 998.

LAKE CITY, city in N Fla., seat of Columbia Co. It is the center of a farming region producing tobacco and lumber. Pop 10 575.

LAKE DISTRICT, region in NW England, since 1951 a national park. It contains the highest mountain in England (Scafell Pike, 3 210ft) and 15 lakes including Windermere, Ullswater and Derwentwater. Its scenic beauty has made it a popular walking and tourist area. (See also LAKE POETS.)

LAKE DWELLING, dwelling built on stilts or piles in the waters of a lake. In parts of Europe can be found STONE AGE and BRONZE AGE lake dwellings, and in some parts of the world they are still built. **Crannogs**, strongholds built on artificial islands, were built in Ireland, Scotland and England from the Late Stone Age until the Middle Ages.

LAKE ERIE, Battle of. See ERIE, BATTLE OF LAKE.

LAKE FOREST, city in NE Ill., on Lake Michigan.

Tibetan Lamaist prayer wheels set into the wall of a temple. These are all inscribed with important mantras or ritual prayers, and are turned by hand during the recitation of sacred scriptures from Lamaist texts. The monk holds a smaller wheel in his hand.

It is a residential suburb of Chicago. Pop 15 654.

LAKE HERRINGS, whitefish related to SALMON, which are found in the deeper lakes of Europe and North America. Shoaling fish, they feed on small insect larvae, crustacea and young fishes.

LAKEHURST, borough in E N.J. It is the site of a US naval air station which was an airship base 1923–62. In 1937 the zeppelin *Hindenburg* caught fire there with the loss of 36 lives. Pop 2 641.

LAKE JACKSON, residential city in SE Tex., near the Gulf of Mexico, 50mi S of Houston. Pop 13 376.

LAKELAND, city in central Fla., 32mi E of Tampa. It is a winter resort and center for the local citrus fruit industry. Pop 41 550.

LAKELAND TERRIER, small hunting dog originally bred in the LAKE DISTRICT of England, principally to hunt foxes. Usually black and tan in color, it has a short body and wiry coat, and stands about 14in high at the shoulder. It is a popular pet.

LAKE OF THE WOODS. See WOODS, LAKE OF THE.

LAKE OSWEGO, city in NW Ore. An early iron town, it is now a suburb of Portland. Pop 14 573.

LAKE POETS, name given to the English poets WORDSWORTH, COLERIDGE and SOUTHEY, who lived in the LAKE DISTRICT for a time and were described by the critic Jeffrey as constituting the "Lake school of poetry." Although all three were friends, they do not really form a group, for Southey's style differed widely from the others'.

LAKEVIEW, town in S central Mich. It is a suburb S of Battle Creek. Pop 11 391.

LAKEWOOD, city in S Cal., NE of Long Beach. It is residential, with some manufactures. Pop 82 973.

LAKEWOOD, city in N central Col. It is a residential suburb of Denver. Pop 92 787.

LAKEWOOD, township in E N.J. near the Atlantic coast. The site of an early ironworks, it is now a resort in a forest and lake area. Pop 17 874.

LAKEWOOD, city in NE Ohio W of Cleveland on Lake Erie. Largely residential, it has a variety of light industries. Pop 70 173.

LAKE WORTH, city in SE Fla. on Lake Worth, a lagoon 6mi S of West Palm Beach. It is a popular water resort. Pop 23 714.

LAKSHADWEEP ISLANDS. See LACCADIVE, MINICOY AND AMINDIVI ISLANDS.

LAKSHMI, or Shri, Hindu goddess of prosperity. The consort of VISHNU, the Preserver, she is supposed to have risen from the sea. She is considered to be benevolent and beautiful and her worship in India is widespread.

LALANDE, Saint Jean (d. 1646), French Jesuit missionary to Canada and N.Y. With Father Isaac JOGUES, he was killed by the Mohawk Indians, and canonized in 1930 as a North American Jesuit martyr.

LALANDE, Michel Richard de (1657–1726), French composer. Organist to four Paris churches in his youth, he became director of all sacred music at the court of Louis XIV. He is remembered for his 42 motets for chorus and orchestra.

LALEMANT, Saint Gabriel (1610–1649), French Jesuit missionary to North America, killed by Iroquois Indians while on a mission to the Huron. He was one of the North American Jesuit martyrs canonized in 1930.

LALO, Édouard (1823–1892), French composer. A fine orchestrator, he is remembered for his *Symphonie espagnole* (1875) for violin and orchestra, the ballet *Nanouma* (1882) and the opera *Le roi d'Ys* (1888).

LAMAISM, popular term for Tibetan BUDDHISM (Mahayana), a distinctive form that evolved from the 7th century AD; it incorporated strict intellectual disciplines, demon-worship, YOGA and ritual, and large monastic orders as well as the shamanistic features of the old folk-religion. Spiritual and temporal power combined in the DALAI LAMA and PANCHEN LAMA, and the continuity provided by reincarnating Lamas created an intensely religious society which remained unchanged until the Chinese invasion (1959). Like Hinduism, it used innumerable deities with consorts and families to represent symbolically the inner life. It survives in Bhutan, Sikkim, S Siberia and Mongolia.

LA MANCHA, a dry plateau in S central Spain, about 2 000ft high, covering the area S of Madrid as far as the Sierra Morena. Wine grapes and cereals are grown there, and it is famed as the setting for the exploits of CERVANTES' Don Quixote.

LAMANITES, in MORMON belief the ancestors of the American Indians. They are supposed to be part of an Israelite migration to America c600 BC, who broke away under Laman to become nomads.

LAMAR, Lucius Quintus Cincinnatus (1825–1893), US statesman and judge. He drafted the Mississippi ordinance of secession in 1861, but after the Civil War promoted friendship between North and South. He was secretary of the interior 1885–88.

LAMAR, Mirabeau Buonaparte (1798–1859), vice-president (1836–38) and president (1838–41) of the Republic of Texas. While in office he resisted union with the US, though he later supported it. He set up a system of public education in Texas.

LAMARCK, Jean Baptiste Pierre Antoine de Monet, Chevalier de (1744–1829), French biologist who did pioneering work on taxonomy (especially that of the INVERTEBRATES) which led him to formulate an early theory of EVOLUTION. Where DARWIN was to propose NATURAL SELECTION as a mechanism for evolutionary change, Lamarck felt that organisms could develop new organs in response to their need for them, and that ACQUIRED CHARACTERISTICS could be inherited.

LA MARQUE, city in SE Tex. It is a residential suburb for Texas City and an important railroad junction. Pop 16 131.

LAMARTINE, Alphonse Marie Louis de (1790–1869), French poet and statesman, briefly head of government after the 1848 revolution (see REVOLUTIONS OF 1848). His collection *Poetic Meditations* (1820) was a landmark of French Romantic literature; lyric evocations of love and nature are underlaid by gentle melancholy and religious feeling.

LAMB, Lady Caroline (1785–1828), wife of 2nd Viscount MELBOURNE, notorious for her passionate affair with Lord BYRON. She wrote several minor novels, including *Glenarvon* (1816) which contains a caricature of Byron. She was famed for her unconventionality and impetuosity.

LAMB, Charles (1775–1834), English essayist and critic. With his sister Mary he wrote *Tales from Shakespear* (1807) for children. His famous *Essays of Elia* (1823, 1833) contain personal comments on many subjects written with humor and brilliance. He helped revive interest in Elizabethan drama with *Specimens of English Dramatic Poets* (1808).

LAMB, Willis Eugene, Jr. (1913–), US physicist who shared with KUSCH the 1955 Nobel Prize for Physics for his examinations of the hydrogen spectrum. He devised new techniques whereby he was able to show that the positions of certain lines differed from the theoretical predictions, thus necessitating a revision of atomic theory.

LAMBARÉNÉ, village in the W Gabon Republic on the Ogooué R, famed for the mission hospital run by Albert SCHWEITZER.

LAMBERT (L), in PHOTOMETRY, a former unit of LUMINANCE, being that of a uniformly diffusing surface reflecting or emitting 1 lumen per cm^2.

LAME DUCK AMENDMENT, 20th amendment to the US Constitution, passed in 1933, providing for a new Congress to start work on Jan. 3 after an election, as opposed to the previous date of March 4. It abolished "lame duck" legislative sessions including congressmen who had not been re-elected.

LAMENTATIONS, book of the OLD TESTAMENT, traditionally ascribed to Jeremiah, though this is disputed by modern scholars. It consists of a series of five poems in dirge meter (the first four are acrostics) lamenting the fall of Jerusalem at the hands of the Babylonians (586 BC).

LA MESA, city in S Cal. It is a residential suburb of San Diego and a retail trade center for a fruit-growing area. Pop 39 178.

LAMESA, city in NW Tex., seat of Dawson Co. It is a processing and distribution center for cotton, cattle and grain from the surrounding area. Pop 12 438.

LA METTRIE, Julien Offray de (1709–1751), French physician and philosopher who took the idea of "man as machine" to its extreme. He held that all mental phenomena resulted from organic changes in the NERVOUS SYSTEM.

LAMINATES, components where several laminae (thin sheets) of different substances are bonded together with RESINS. Laminated plastics comprise layers of cloth, paper, plastic, etc., impregnated with synthetic resin, bonded together by heat and pressure. Laminated glass is used in auto and airplane windows and as bulletproof glass; and laminated woods for many purposes (see also VENEER).

LA MIRADA, city in S Cal., 18mi SE of Los Angeles. In an area of olive and citrus fruit cultivation, it is now a residential city with some light industry. Pop 30 808.

LÄMMERGEIER, or **Bearded vulture,** *Gypaetus barbatus*, a carrion-feeding VULTURE of Asia, Africa and S Europe. It lives on rocky cliffs and is known to obtain part of its food by dropping large bones, or even tortoises, onto rocks to break them open.

LAMP. See LIGHTING.

LAMPREYS, one of the two remaining groups of jawless fishes, AGNATHA, found both in freshwater and in the sea. The body is eel-like and there is a round, sucking mouth with horny teeth with which they rasp away at their prey. Many species are parasitic when adult, feeding on the flesh of living fishes. The blind, worm-like, filter-feeding larva or ammocoete, is totally unlike the adult, and lives only in freshwater. Sea lampreys migrate into fresh waters to breed.

LAMP SHELLS, marine animals closely resembling bivalve MOLLUSKS, but forming their own phylum, Brachiopoda. The upper, smaller valve of the shell fits into a larger, lower one, giving the resemblance to an ancient Roman oil lamp. A ciliated lophophore draws a feeding current from which organic matter is removed into the partially opened shells.

LAMPEDUSA, Giuseppe di (1896–1957), Italian novelist. A Sicilian prince, he won critical and popular acclaim with *The Leopard*, posthumously published in 1958.

LANAI, island which makes up part of Hawaii. Covering 141sq mi, it lies W of Maui and is extensively planted with pineapples.

LANCASTER, unincorporated city in S Cal., in an irrigated area of the W Mojave Desert. It has electronics and aerospace industries connected with the nearby Edwards Air Force base. Pop 30 948.

LANCASTER, village in W N.Y., 11mi E of Buffalo. It is a residential suburb of Buffalo and has lumber mills and stone quarries. Pop 13 365.

LANCASTER, city in S Ohio, seat of Fairfield Co. It is the trade center for a farm region and produces glassware, machinery and shoes. Pop 32 911.

LANCASTER, city in SE Pa., seat of Lancaster Co. Once the state capital, it remains an important trade and industrial center, producing watches, linoleum, machinery and metal goods, and has a large cattle market. Pop 57 690.

LANCASTER, city in N Tex. S of Dallas, in a farm region. Pop 10 522.

LANCASTER, House of, English royal family which produced the kings HENRY IV, HENRY V and HENRY VI. Edmund Crouchback, second son of HENRY III, was first earl of Lancaster (1267); his son Thomas (d. 1322) led baronial opposition to EDWARD II. JOHN OF GAUNT became duke of Lancaster by marriage in 1362, and his son became HENRY IV in 1399. The Lancastrians were deposed by the house of YORK during the WARS OF THE ROSES, but the heir to their claims, Henry TUDOR, reestablished the line in 1485 as HENRY VII.

LANCASTER SOUND, arm of Baffin Bay in NW Territories, Canada. It runs W between Devon Island and Baffin Island towards the Beaufort Sea.

LANCELET, fish-like animal also called AMPHIOXUS.

LANCELOT, Sir (Lancelot of the Lake), the bravest knight of King ARTHUR's court. He glimpsed the HOLY GRAIL and was father of the perfect knight, Sir GALAHAD. But his adulterous love of GUINEVERE, Arthur's queen, broke the fellowship of the Round Table.

LANCHOW, capital of Kansu province, W China. An ancient city, it has now become a communications and industrial center, with a major oil refinery and chemical and manufacturing industries. Pop 1 200 000.

LAND, Edwin Herbert (b. 1909), US physicist and inventor of Polaroid, a cheap and adaptable means of polarizing light (1932), and the POLAROID LAND CAMERA (1947). In 1937 he set up the Polaroid Corporation to manufacture scientific instruments and antiglare sunglasses incorporating Polaroid.

LANDAU, Lev Davidovich (1908–1968), Soviet physicist who made important contributions in many fields of modern physics. His work on CRYOGENICS was rewarded by the 1962 Nobel Prize for Physics for his development of the theory of liquid HELIUM and his predictions of the behavior of liquid He^3.

LAND CRABS, a term applied to any large decapod crustaceans which have adapted to a terrestrial way of life, particularly Land crabs of W Africa and the West Indies, and the Robber crab of the Pacific Islands. All breathe air and return to the sea to lay their eggs.

LAND-GRANT COLLEGES, US colleges set up with the proceeds of land sales. By the Morrill Act of 1862 Congress granted the states federal lands to be sold to establish agricultural and mechanical arts colleges. There are some 70 land-grant colleges in existence today, including many state universities.

LANDING CRAFT, naval vessel used for landing troops and equipment on beaches. The most common US types are the LST (landing ship, tank), capable of transporting heavy vehicles for long voyages; the LCVP (landing craft, vehicle and personnel) for transporting 36 men and their arms from ship to shore; the LCM (landing craft, mechanized); and the all-purpose LCU (landing craft, utility).

LANDIS, Kenesaw Mountain (1866–1944), US judge and baseball commissioner. A well-known judge, he was appointed the first baseball commissioner in 1920 after the "Black Sox" bribery scandal and ruled the game with uncompromising integrity until his death.

LÄNDLER, lively Austrian and Bavarian folk dance, in 3/4 time. Becoming fashionable in 18th-century Vienna, it evolved into the WALTZ.

LANDON, Alfred Mossman (1887–), governor of Kan. and Republican presidential candidate in 1936, when he lost to Franklin D. ROOSEVELT.

LANDOR, Walter Savage (1775–1864), English poet and prose writer. He wrote epics, dramatic fragments, lyrics and epigrams, but is best known for his *Imaginary Conversations* (1824–53), a series of 150 stylish and amusing dialogues between notable characters from different ages.

LANDOWSKA, Wanda (1877–1959), Polish harpsichord virtuoso, largely responsible for the modern revival of the harpsichord. Living in Paris 1900–40, and then in the US, she was famous as a performer, teacher and authority on early music.

LAND RECLAMATION, the transformation of useless land into productive land, usually for agricultural purposes. The major techniques are irrigation, drainage, fertilization and desalination (see DESALINATION; DRAINAGE; FERTILIZERS; IRRIGATION). The most spectacular examples of land drainage are those where land has been reclaimed from the sea. Best known is that of the Netherlands, where about 8 000km^2 of land have been reclaimed, mainly in the 20th century. (See also CONSERVATION; DRY FARMING; SOIL EROSION.)

LANDRUM-GRIFFIN ACT, labor relations act passed by the US Congress in 1959. It sought to end corruption in the labor unions, in particular by controlling the use of union funds, regulating pickets and ensuring freedom of speech and elections by secret ballot.

LANDSCAPE ARCHITECTURE, the art of modifying land areas to make them more attractive, useful and enjoyable. Highly developed in the ancient civilizations—in China and Japan it had symbolic significance—the art was neglected in Europe after the fall of Rome, but was revived in Renaissance Italy and spread through Europe. The French stress on geometric formality, as at VERSAILLES, was superseded in early 18th-century England by picturesque and dramatic, yet apparently natural hills and lakes and vistas, often over large areas; this style shaped the US tradition. Today landscaping is used in parks, highways and other public amenities. (See also BROWN, CAPABILITY; OLMSTEAD, FREDERICK LAW; REPTON, HUMPHREY.)

LANDSEER, Sir Edwin Henry (1802–1873), English artist whose sentimental animal paintings, such as *The Monarch of the Glen* (1851), were enormously popular and frequently reproduced as engravings. He also modeled the lions around Nelson's Column in Trafalgar Square, London.

LANDSTEINER, Karl (1868–1943), Austrian-born US pathologist awarded the 1930 Nobel Prize for Physiology or Medicine for discovering the major BLOOD groups and developing the ABO system of blood typing.

LANFRANC (d. 1089), Italian churchman, chief

A truck comes ashore from USS Newport, an LST-type landing craft. This is one of the larger types of landing craft and is able to ferry tanks and bulldozers across an ocean before landing them.

advisor to WILLIAM THE CONQUEROR and from 1070 archbishop of Canterbury. He appointed reforming Norman bishops, enforced clerical celibacy and strengthened the monasteries. As a scholar he helped shape the doctrine of TRANSUBSTANTIATION.

LANG, Fritz (1890–1976), Austrian film director, one of the masters of EXPRESSIONISM in the silent film. *Metropolis* (1926) was a bleak futuristic drama; in the *Doctor Mabuse* films (1922, 1933, 1960) and above all *M* (1933), about a child murderer, Lang explored the psychology of evil. He left Germany in 1936, and his Hollywood films include the social drama *Fury* (1936), westerns, *Clash by Night* (1952) and *Beyond a Reasonable Doubt* (1956).

LANGDELL, Christopher Columbus (1826–1906), US lawyer and educator. Dean of Harvard law school 1875–95, he instituted the teaching of law by case histories, which has since been universally adopted.

LANGDON, Harry, one of the great comedians of the silent screen. An obscure US vaudeville performer, he shot to fame with such films as *Tramp, Tramp, Tramp* (1926), *The Strong Man* (1926) and *Long Pants* (1927), in which he played an innocent, stupid but lovable character.

LANGDON, John (1741–1819), US merchant who gave his fortune to help finance the REVOLUTIONARY WAR. He served in the CONTINENTAL CONGRESS (1775–76, 1783–84), signed the Constitution (1787), was a US senator (1789–1801) and governor of N.H. (1805–9, 1810–12).

LANGE, Christian Louis (1869–1938), Norwegian pacifist and international statesman. He was secretary of the Interparliamentary Union (1909–33) and a delegate to the League of Nations. He shared the 1921 Nobel Peace Prize.

LANGE, Dorothea (1895–1965), US documentary photographer. Her powerful, stark pictures of Depression victims, migrant workers and the rural poor created a profound impression and greatly influenced subsequent photojournalistic technique. In 1939 she published *American Exodus: A Record of Human Erosion.*

LANGER, Susanne Knauth (1895–   ), US philosopher whose *Philosophy in a New Key* (1942) propounded for the nondiscursive symbolism of art a meaning and significance equal to that of the discursive symbolism of language and science. Other works include *Mind: An Essay on Human Feeling* (2 vols., 1967, 1972).

LANGLADE, Charles Michel de (1729–1800), Canadian soldier and pioneer settler. Half Indian, he fought against the British in the FRENCH AND INDIAN WAR (1755–59), but later supported them in the REVOLUTIONARY WAR. In retirement at Green Bay, Wis., he became known as the father of Wisconsin.

LANGLAND, William (c1332–c1400), presumed poet of *The Vision of Piers Plowman*, a religious allegory representing a dream-vision of the Christian life and one of the finest examples of Middle English alliterative verse.

LANGLEY, Samuel Pierpont (1834–1906), US astronomer, physicist, meteorologist and inventor of the BOLOMETER (1878) and of an early heavier-than-air flying machine. His most important work was investigating the sun's role in bringing about meteorological phenomena.

LANGMUIR, Irving (1881–1957), US physical chemist awarded the 1932 Nobel Prize for Chemistry for his work on thin films on solid and liquid surfaces (particularly oil on water), which gave rise to the new science of surface chemistry.

LANGOUSTE, or crawfish, *Palinurus vulgaris*, a Spiny lobster up to 250mm (10in) long with small claws, living offshore in the eastern Atlantic. It is famous as a

Some major living families of languages

The relationship of several languages, such as AINU (the tongue of a mysterious white race of northern Japan) and the HYPERBOREAN TONGUES of northeast Siberia, is still unclear to linguists.

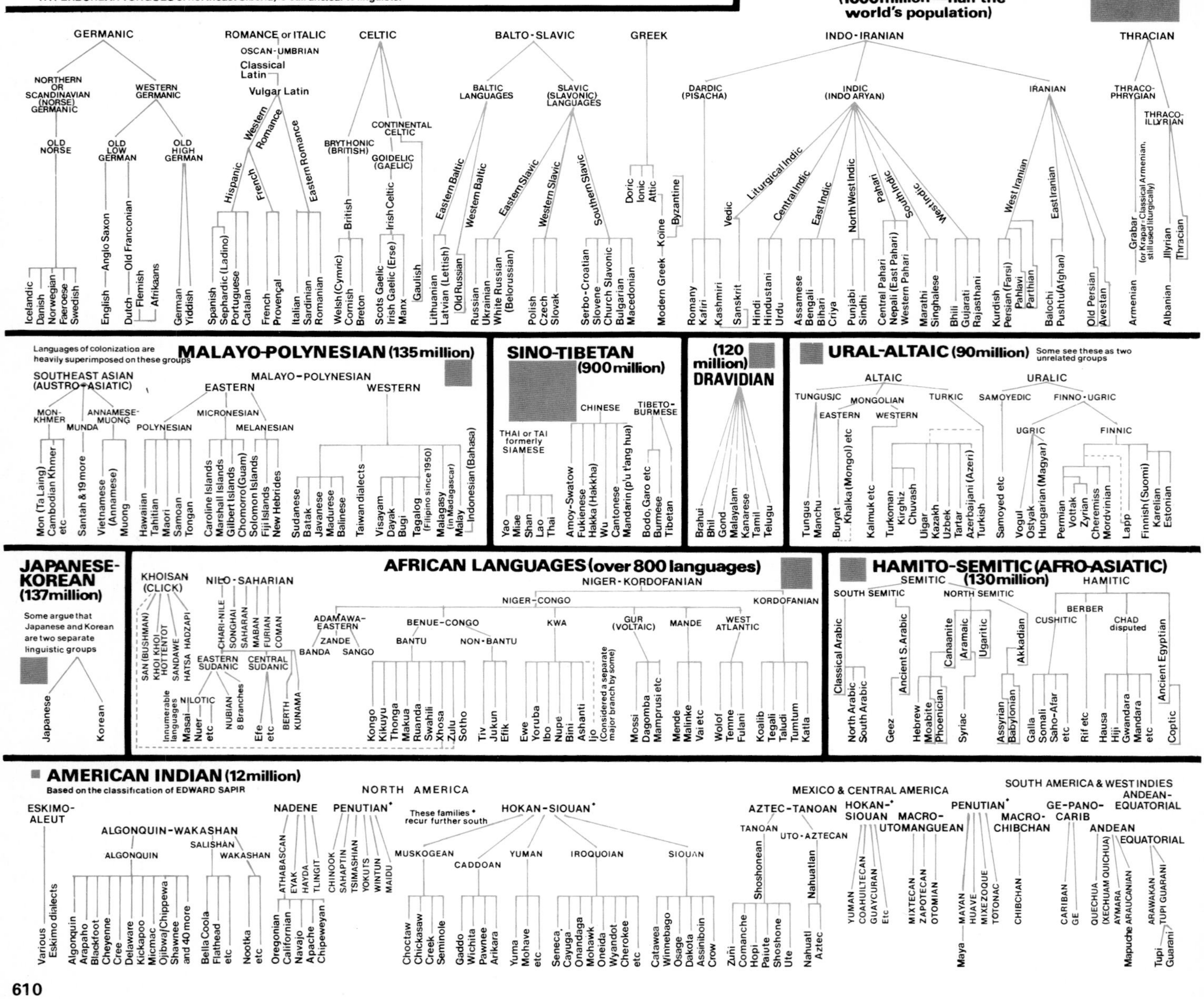

culinary delicacy, and has a remarkable larva, flat, paper-thin and as transparent as glass.

LANGTON, Stephen (c1155–1228), English cardinal, whose appointment as archbishop of Canterbury (1207) led to a quarrel between Pope INNOCENT III and King JOHN. Despite a papal INTERDICT, John kept him out of his see until 1213. Langton led baronial opposition to the king, and his is the first signature on MAGNA CARTA. He was a distinguished theologian, noted for his Old Testament commentaries, and helped to develop English canon law and the autonomy of the English Church.

LANGTRY, Lillie (1853–1929), British actress, known as the "Jersey Lily." A famous beauty, she was a mistress of King EDWARD VII.

LANGUAGE, the spoken or written means by which man expresses himself and communicates with others. The word "language" comes from the Latin *lingua*, tongue, demonstrating that speech is the primary form of language and writing the secondary. Language comprises a set of sounds that symbolize the content of the message to be conveyed. It is, on this planet, peculiar to man, constituting as it does a formal system with rules whereby complex messages can be built up out of simple components (see GRAMMAR). Languages are the products of their cultures, arising from the cooperative effort required by societies. There are some 3000 different languages spoken today, added to which are many more regional dialects. Languages may be classified into families, groups and subgroups. To us the most important language family is the Indo-European, to which many Asian and most European languages (including English) belong. Other important families are the Hamito-Semitic, Altaic, Sino-Tibetan, Austro-Asiatic and Dravidian, among others. (See also ETYMOLOGY; LINGUISTICS; PHILOLOGY; PRONUNCIATION; SEMANTICS; SEMIOLOGY; SHORTHAND; SIGN LANGUAGE; WRITING, HISTORY OF.)

LANGUEDOC, historic region of S France, W of the Rhône R. Montpellier and Nîmes are the main cities, and the chief product wine. Its name comes from *langue d'oc*, the language of the PROVENÇAL culture. Languedoc was the center of the ALBIGENSIAN heresy, and later of French Protestantism.

LANGURS, leaf-eating monkeys of Asia, related to the African colobus. They are a heterogeneous grouping of three main genera, *Presbytis*, *Nasalis* and *Pygathrix*. Open country species live in bisexual troops of up to 20 members. Among forest-living langurs, single-male harem groups seem to be the rule.

LANIER, Sidney (1842–1881), US poet and musician. A Southerner who fought in the Civil War (recalled in his novel *Tiger-Lilies*, 1867), he practiced law, and became a professional flutist. After publication of his *Poems* (1877) he became a lecturer at Johns Hopkins U.

LANOLIN, soft, yellow-white unctuous solid, a hydrated grease or wax from sheep's wool. It is a mixture of CHOLESTEROL and its ESTERS of FATTY ACIDS, and is used as a base for ointments and cosmetics.

LANSBURY, George (1859–1940), British leader of the Labour Party 1931–35. He helped found the pro-labor *Daily Herald* and edited it 1912–22. He became party leader after being commissioner of works in the 1929–31 Labour government.

LANSDOWNE, borough in SE Pa. It is a suburb of Philadelphia, with some light industry. Pop 14090.

LANSING, village in NE Ill., a suburb of Chicago. Pop 25805.

LANSING, state capital of Mich., at the junction of Grand R and Cedar R. It is a transportation and commercial center, with an important automobile industry. Pop 131546.

LANSING, Robert (1864–1928), US international lawyer and statesman. He founded the *American Journal of International Law* (1907), and as secretary of state (1915–20) he concluded the LANSING-ISHII agreement with Japan, 1917.

LANSING-ISHII AGREEMENT, signed by Robert LANSING for the US and Kikujiro Ishii for Japan, Nov. 1917. It reaffirmed the OPEN DOOR POLICY towards China, while recognizing Japan's imperial interests.

LANTANA, a genus of evergreen shrubs of which *Lantana montevidensis* and *L. camara* are cultivated as container plants outdoors and as house plants for the domed heads of colorful tubular flowers they produce. They can tolerate the full sun of a south-facing window and should be grown between 13°C and 21°C (55°F and 70°F). In spring and summer, the soil should be kept evenly moist, but in other seasons it should be allowed to dry out more before watering. Lantanas are propagated from seeds or by taking shoot tip cuttings. Family: Verbenaceae.

LANTERNFISH, a large family, Myctophidae, of small marine fishes whose bodies are covered in small luminous spots. Most live in deep water but come to the surface at night.

LANTHANIDES, the 14 elements with atomic numbers (see ATOM) 58–71, immediately following LANTHANUM in the PERIODIC TABLE. They comprise CERIUM, PRASEODYMIUM, NEODYMIUM, PROMETHIUM, SAMARIUM, EUROPIUM, GADOLINIUM, TERBIUM, DYSPROSIUM, HOLMIUM, ERBIUM, THULIUM, YTTERBIUM and LUTETIUM. (See also LANTHANUM SERIES.)

LANTHANUM (La), the second most abundant of the RARE EARTHS, and the prototypical member of the LANTHANUM SERIES. AW 138.9, mp 921°C, bp 3457°C, sg 6.145 (25°C).

LANTHANUM SERIES, the 15 elements with atomic numbers (see ATOM) 57–71, comprising LANTHANUM and the LANTHANIDES (see PERIODIC TABLE). Their electronic structures are very similar, differing only in inner ORBITALS; hence their properties are very similar. This also produces a decrease (the *lanthanide contraction*) in ionic radii through the series, so that the third-row TRANSITION ELEMENTS following the lanthanum series have ionic radii almost identical to those of their analogues in the second row, and hence have similar properties. The lanthanum series elements are all reactive metals resembling SCANDIUM, forming trivalent salts and LIGAND complexes. Cerium, praseodymium and terbium also form tetravalent compounds, and europium, ytterbium and samarium form divalent ones. All form divalent ionic hydrides and sulfides. (See also RARE EARTHS.)

LAOCOÖN, in Greek mythology, Trojan priest of Apollo who warned the Trojans not to drag the Greeks' wooden horse into their city (see TROJAN WAR). This interference in their schemes angered the gods, and he and his sons were killed by sea serpents. A famous sculpture of their death struggle, made in Rhodes c50 BC, is now in Rome.

LAOMEDON, legendary king of TROY, who refused to pay HERCULES for killing a monster sent by the gods to ravage his kingdom as a punishment for failing in his obligations to them. Hercules killed Laomedon and all his sons except PRIAM.

LAOS, landlocked republic of SE Asia, bordered by China to the N, Vietnam to the E, Cambodia to the S and Thailand and Burma to the W.

Land. Laos is dominated by mountain chains and plateaus, cut by deep, narrow valleys, covered by forests interspersed with grassland. In the S, limestone plateaus slope W to rice plains along the Mekong R, which forms the border with Burma and most of the border with Thailand and is for 300mi the main transport route of Laos. The wet season of the monsoon climate is from May to Oct., while Nov. to April is a time of near drought. Average temperature in the valleys is above 70°F. Animal life includes elephants, used for lumbering, draft buffalo, tigers and many kinds of lizard and butterfly.

People. The Lao, by far the largest ethnic group, are a Thai people; Hinayana (Theravada) Buddhism is the religion of their chiefly valley communities. Animist cults predominate among the mountain peoples, the Meo and Yao (in the N) and Kha (S). In the Mekong towns Chinese and Vietnamese traders are important minorities.

Economy. Laos has few manufactures (some silk and silver products). Apart from tin (central Laos) and timber (teak from the largely unexploited N forests), probably the main export is from the opium poppies grown in the N. In the valleys in the center and S rice is the chief crop though tobacco, cotton, tea and coffee are also grown. There are some hydroelectric and irrigation schemes and, in the NW, unexploited iron deposits.

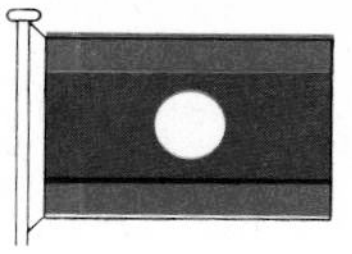

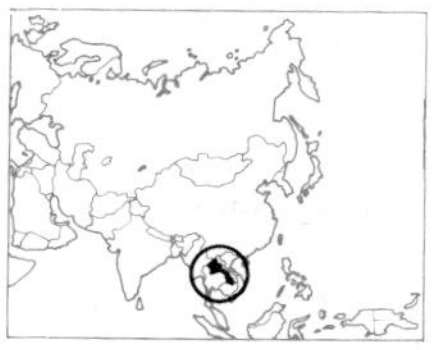

Official name: People's Democratic Republic of Laos
Capital: Vientiane
Area: 91428sq mi
Population: 3106000
Languages: Lao; French widely used
Religions: Buddhist, Animist
Monetary unit(s): 1 Kip = 10 bi = 100 at

History. Part of the KHMER EMPIRE, the territory was settled from the 10th to 13th centuries by Thai Lao, forced out of Yünnan, S China. By the 17th century a powerful Lao kingdom, based on Khmer culture and Buddhism, had emerged; but in the early 1700s it split between Luang Prabang in the N and Vientiane in the S. Civil wars invited foreign dominance, notably from Siam, but in 1893 France established hegemony. After WWII national insurgency led by the communist PATHET LAO with Vietnamese support won independence in 1954. In 1959 renewed civil war between the neutralist premier Souvanna Phouma and right- and left-wing rivals brought intervention from the great powers. A coalition government was formed in 1973. In May 1975 the right-wing was toppled in an almost bloodless coup; in Dec. 1975 the king abdicated, the country becoming a republic under the Pathet Lao.

LAO-TSE, or Lao-Tsu ("Old Master"), Chinese philosopher of the 6th century BC, said to be the founder of TAOISM and the author of *Tao Te Ching*. His actual existence is uncertain, but he was allegedly a librarian at the Chou court.

LA PAZ, largest city and administrative capital of Bolivia (the legal capital is Sucre). Founded in 1548 by the CONQUISTADORS, it is located in the La Paz river valley, some 12000ft above sea level, the world's highest capital. Local products include cement, glass, textiles and consumer goods. Pop 850000.

LAPIDARY. See GEMS.

LAPIS LAZULI, deep blue METAMORPHIC ROCK, found in crystalline LIMESTONE, and consisting of LAZURITE mixed with other silicates, CALCITE and PYRITE. It chiefly occurs in Afghanistan and Chile, and has long been valued as a GEM stone and as the source of the pigment ultramarine.

LAPLACE, Pierre Simon, Marquis de (1749–1827), French scientist known for his work on celestial mechanics, especially for his NEBULAR HYPOTHESIS; for his many fundamental contributions to mathematics, and for his PROBABILITY studies.

LAPLAND, region in the extreme N of Europe, the homeland of the LAPPS. Within the Arctic Circle, it embraces parts of Norway, Sweden, Finland and Russia, with an area of about 150000sq mi. It has tundra vegetation and rich mineral deposits.

LA PLATA, capital of Buenos Aires province, E Argentina. It is an important port and a petroleum-refining and meat-packing center, with diverse manufacturing industries. Pop 408300.

LA PLATA, Rio de. See RIO DE LA PLATA.

LA PORTE, industrial city in NW Ind., seat of La Porte Co. The world's first automatic telephone exchange was opened there in 1892. Pop 22140.

LAPPS, a people of N Europe who speak a Finno-Ugric language and may have come originally from central Asia. They number about 30000 and live mostly in N Norway. Many are nomads who live off their wandering reindeer herds; others engage in fishing, hunting, forestry and agriculture, and live in settled communities.

LAPTEV SEA, a part of the Arctic Ocean between the Taymyr peninsula and the New Siberian Islands.

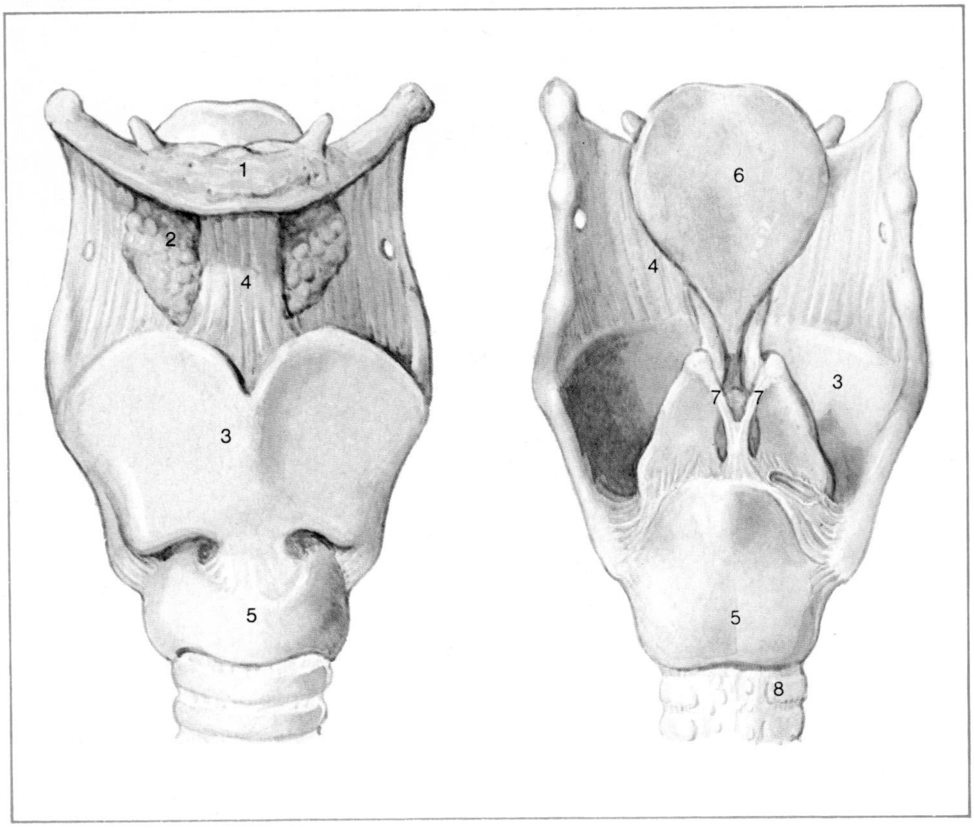

The larynx viewed from the front (*left*) and from the back (*right*). (1) Hyoid bone; (2) thyroid gland; (3) thyroid cartilage; (4) hypothyroid membrane; (5) cricoid cartilage; (6) epiglottis; (7) vocal chords; (8) ringed trachea.

It is a shallow sea and frozen for most of the year.

LA PUENTE, city in S Cal. It is a residential suburb of Los Angeles. Pop 31 092.

LAPWINGS, a genus, *Vanellus*, of PLOVERS, usually occurring on grass plains or pastures. Unlike other plovers many lapwings possess either crest or wattles. Strongly patterned but cryptic birds with worldwide distribution, they are characterized by their peevish call.

LARAMIE, city in SE Wyo., seat of Albany Co. It is a commercial and tourist center in a lumber and stock-raising region. Pop 23 143.

LARCENY, legal term for the unlawful misappropriation of property of another person, without his consent and with intent to deprive him of it. In the US, definition and penalties differ from state to state. There is usually a distinction, based on the value of the goods, between grand larceny, a FELONY, and petty larceny, a MISDEMEANOR. Larceny is a form of THEFT.

LARCH, common name for deciduous CONIFERS of the genus *Larix* from the PINE family (Pinaceae). They are native to cool-temperate and subarctic regions of the N Hemisphere. The European larch (*Larix decidua*) produces a fine-textured wood used for boat-making and fencing. It is also a source of TURPENTINE and is used for reforestation in Britain and the US.

LARDNER, "Ring" (Ringgold Wilmer Lardner; 1885–1933), US sports journalist and short-story writer. Stories in racy sports idiom, as in *You Know Me, Al* (1916), satirize vulgarity and greed in US life and the success cult. With G. S. Kaufman, he wrote the comedy *June Moon* (1929).

LAREDO, city in S Tex. on the Rio Grande, seat of Webb Co. A Spanish settlement 1755, it retains a Mexican flavor. It is a trading center for a farming and oil-producing region. Pop 69 024.

LARES AND PENATES, in ancient Rome, household guardian gods, originally spirits of fields and crossroads. The *lares* became, in the main, deified ancestor figures; the *penates* were seen as personified natural powers bringing prosperity. But the names were generally interchangeable.

LARGO (Italian: broad), musical term indicating a stately, dignified performance. **Larghetto**, the diminutive, denotes a somewhat more sprightly style. Handel's *Largo* is a popular name for an arrangement from an aria in his opera *Serse*.

LARK BUNTING, *Calamospiza melanocorys*, a gregarious bunting of North America, common in short grass prairies where it feeds on seeds and insects. The name derives from the long and varied, lark-like song, often given in flight.

LARKS, small terrestrial songbirds of Europe, Asia, India and Africa, forming the family, Alaudidae. Streaked brown birds, they feed on insects and seeds, walking or running at great speed along the ground. Larks are renowned for their beautiful songs, usually delivered on the wing.

LARKSPUR, city in W Cal., residential suburb of San Francisco. Pop 10 487.

LARKSPURS, herbaceous plants of the genus *Delphinium*, many of which are cultivated as annuals. Perennial varieties, normally referred to as DELPHINIUMS, have been developed from the garland larkspur (*Delphinium cheilanthum*) and the rocket larkspur (*D. ajacis*). Larkspur flowers are borne on long terminal clusters and come in a number of shades of red, yellow and purple, as well as white. Family: Ranunculaceae.

LA ROCHEFOUCAULD, François, Duc de (1613–1680), French writer known for his *Memoirs* of the FRONDE, and his *Maxims* (1665), a collection of more than 500 moral reflections and epigrams, generally paradoxical, often pessimistic, usually acute.

LA ROCHELLE, historic fishing port of W France. Founded in the 12th century, it was a HUGUENOT refuge and stronghold after the massacre of SAINT BARTHOLOMEW'S DAY (1572). Pop 72 075.

LARVA, a pre-adult stage in the life history of many animals, differing structurally from the adult in more than merely sexual immaturity. The possession of a larva usually enables a species to exploit a different food source from that used by the adult. Again, it may be important in dispersing individuals to new areas, or, in many parasites, as an infective phase. The larva undergoes a change of structure to adult form known as METAMORPHOSIS.

LARYNGITIS, or INFLAMMATION of LARYNX, usually due to either VIRUS or bacterial infection or chronic VOICE abuse, and leading to hoarseness or loss of voice.

LARYNX, specialized part of the respiratory tract used in VOICE production (see SPEECH AND SPEECH DISORDERS). It lies above the TRACHEA in the neck, forming the Adam's apple, and consists of several CARTILAGE components linked by small MUSCLES. Two folds, or *vocal cords*, lie above the trachea and may be pulled across the airway so as to regulate and intermittently occlude air flow. It is the movement and vibration of these that produce voice.

LA SALLE, city in S Quebec, Canada, on the S shore of Montreal Island, a residential suburb of Montreal with various light industries. It was first settled by the Sieur de LA SALLE 1668. Pop 72 912.

LA SALLE, industrial city in N Ill. 13mi W of Ottawa, associated with Peru and Oglesby. Pop 10 736.

LA SALLE, Saint Jean Baptiste de. See JEAN BAPTISTE DE LA SALLE, SAINT.

LA SALLE, René Robert Cavelier, Sieur de (1643–1687), French explorer and fur trader in North America, who claimed the Louisiana territory for France. In Canada from 1666, he commanded Fort Frontenac, sailed across Lake Michigan (1679) and explored the Illinois R and followed the Mississippi R to its mouth on the Gulf of Mexico. In 1684, sailing to plant a colony there, his fleet was wrecked by storms and Spanish raiders. He was killed by a mutinous crew.

LA SCALA, world-famous opera house in Milan, Italy. Built 1776–78, it can seat 3600. TOSCANINI was its artistic director 1898–1907, 1921–31.

LAS CASAS, Bartolomé de (1474–1566), Spanish missionary in the West Indies, South and central America. He exposed the oppression of the Indians, notably the forced labor of the ENCOMIENDA system, persuaded Madrid to enact the New Laws for Indian welfare (1542) and in his monumental *History of the Indies* recorded data valuable to modern anthropology.

LASCAUX CAVE, cave near Montignac, France, containing many outstanding examples of AURIGNACIAN cave paintings. Opened to the public in 1940, deterioration of the paintings led to its being closed in 1963. (See also ALTAMIRA.)

LAS CRUCES, city in S N.M. near the Rio Grande, seat of Dona Ana Co. The name comes from a massacre (1830) by Apache Indians; today the White Sands Missile Range is in the region, near where the first atomic bomb was tested. Pop 37 857.

LASER, a device producing an intense beam of parallel LIGHT with a precisely defined wavelength. The name is an acronym for "*l*ight *a*mplification by *s*timulated *e*mission of *r*adiation," and the device is in fact a MASER operating as an oscillator at visible wavelengths.

The light produced by lasers is very different from that produced by conventional sources. In the latter, all the source atoms radiate independently in all directions, whereas in lasers they radiate in step with each other and in the same direction, producing **coherent light.** Such beams spread very little as they travel, and provide very high capacity communication links. They can be focused into small intense spots, and have been used for cutting and WELDING—notably for refixing detached retinas in the human EYE. Lasers also find application in distance measurement by INTERFERENCE methods, in SPECTROSCOPY and in HOLOGRAPHY.

The principles of laser operation are described under MASER. The active material is enclosed between a pair of parallel MIRRORS, one of them half-silvered; light traveling along the axis is reflected to and fro and builds up rapidly by the stimulated emission process, passing out eventually through the half-silvered mirror, while light in other directions is rapidly lost from the laser.

In pulsed operation, one of the end mirrors is concealed by a shutter, allowing a much higher level of pumping than usual; opening the shutter causes a very intense pulse of light to be produced—up to 100MW for 30ns—while other pulsing techniques can achieve 10^{13} W in picosecond pulses.

Among the common laser types are ruby lasers

(optically pumped, with the polished crystal ends serving as mirrors), liquid lasers (with RARE EARTH ions or organic dyes in solution), gas lasers (an electric discharge providing the high proportion of excited states), and the very small SEMICONDUCTOR lasers (based on electron-hole recombination).

LASKER, Emanuel (1868–1941), German mathematician and chess master. World chess champion from 1894 until defeated by CAPABLANCA (1921), he was one of the greatest players ever, especially in closed positions.

LASKI, Harold Joseph (1893–1950), English political theorist, economist and author, active in the FABIAN SOCIETY and the Labour Party. From 1920 he lectured at the London School of Economics and was a visiting lecturer in many countries. In the 1930s he moved from political pluralism to Marxism. His books include *Democracy in Crisis* (1933) and *Liberty in the Modern State* (1948).

LAS PALMAS, capital of Las Palmas province, Spain, on the island of Gran Canaria. Largest city and chief port of the Canary Islands; a major tourist resort. Pop 287 038.

LA SPEZIA, capital of La Spezia province in NW Italy, a major port and naval base on the Ligurian coast. It was rebuilt after almost total destruction in WWII. Pop 128 413.

LASSALLE, Ferdinand (1825–1864), German socialist and lawyer, co-founder (1863) of the General German Workers' Association, later the Social Democratic Party, the first labor party in Germany. A Hegelian influenced by Marx's economic theories, he nevertheless favored state action, not revolution, as the way to socialism.

LASSEN PEAK, the only active volcano in the continental US, the latest eruption being 1921. It stands 10 457ft high in Lassen Volcanic National Park, NE Cal.

LASSUS, Roland de, or **Orlando di Lasso** (c1530–1594), Flemish Renaissance composer. He was choirmaster at St. John Lateran, Rome, and from 1556 director of music at the ducal court at Munich. His vast and varied output includes religious motets, secular chansons and the great *Penitential Psalms of David* (1584). His expressive integration of music and text anticipated the BAROQUE.

LAST JUDGMENT, in Christian theology, the judgment of all men by God at the end of the world. According to the New Testament, at Christ's SECOND COMING the dead will be raised (see RESURRECTION) and, with those then living, assembled before God to be judged by what they have done: the unrighteous thrown into HELL with Satan, the righteous admitted to HEAVEN. (See also ESCHATOLOGY; PURGATORY.)

LAST SUPPER, the final PASSOVER meal held by Jesus and his disciples in Jerusalem before his crucifixion. In it he distributed bread and wine to them, inaugurating the Christian sacrament of Holy COMMUNION. A popular subject in art, the best known is Leonardo da Vinci's fresco in Milan.

LAS VEGAS, city in SE Nev., seat of Clark Co.; world-renowned for "The Strip" with its casinos (state-legalized gambling), luxury hotels, bars, and night clubs. The city is also a mining and cattle-farming center. There are artesian springs nearby. Pop 125 787.

LAS VEGAS, city in N central N.M., seat of San Miguel Co., on the Gallinas R. It is the site of N.M. Highlands U. Pop 13 835.

LATAKIA, chief port of Syria and capital of the governorate of Latakia, a separate French state 1922–26. Founded by the Phoenicians, it was rebuilt by Seleucus I (c290 BC). It is famous for its tobacco. Pop 126 000.

LATENCY PERIOD, in psychoanalysis, the stage in human development starting around the age of five and ending at PUBERTY, marking the transition to adult from INFANTILE SEXUALITY.

LA TÈNE, late IRON AGE culture of European CELTS, named for the site of the same name at the E end of Lake Neuchâtel, Switzerland. Originating c450 BC, when the Celts came into contact with Greco-Etruscan influences, it died out c50 AD as the Celts became subservient to Rome. La Tène ornaments are decorated with round, S-shaped and spiral patterns.

A laser beam penetrating a ruby plate 0.5mm thick, photographed using light from the beam itself.

LATENT HEAT, the quantity of HEAT absorbed or released by a substance in an isothermal change of state, such as FUSION or vaporization. The temperature of a heated lump of ice will increase to 0°C and then remain at this temperature until all the ice has melted to water before again rising. The heat energy absorbed at 0°C overcomes the intermolecular forces in the ordered ice structure and increases the kinetic ENERGY of the water molecules.

LATERAL LINE, a system of sensory cells embedded in pits or canals along the side of the body in fish and tailed amphibians. These organs probably detect the low-frequency vibrations in water which come from the movement of prey and shoaling companions. It is also possible that water movements set up by the animal itself and reflected off distant objects may be detected in a form of echo-location.

LATERAN, district of SE Rome, given to the church by Emperor Constantine I in 311. The Lateran palace—the papal residence until 1309—was rebuilt in the 16th century. The basilica of St. John Lateran is the cathedral church of the pope as bishop of Rome. Of the five Lateran ECUMENICAL COUNCILS the fourth, convened by INNOCENT III, was of major importance.

LATERAN TREATY, concordat between the papacy and the government of Italy, signed 1929 in the Lateran palace and confirmed by the 1948 Italian constitution. It established Roman Catholicism as Italy's state religion and VATICAN CITY as an independent sovereign state.

LATERITE, residual red CLAY soil, usually soft and porous, consisting mainly of hydrated oxides of iron and aluminum. (Some is used as IRON ore.) It is formed from various iron-containing parent rocks by a process known as *laterization*: secular weathering with powerful leaching out of silica, alkalis and alkaline earths, under oxidizing conditions. A tropical climate with heavy seasonal rainfall and good drainage is required.

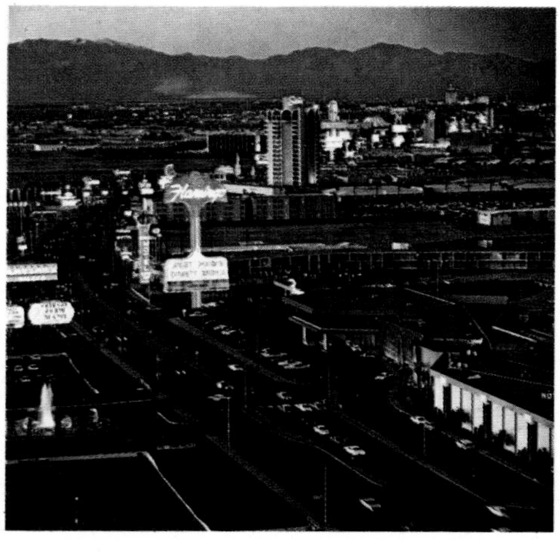

The glare of neon on The Strip advertises various pleasures of Las Vegas. Legalized gambling has turned the city into a boom town dedicated to high stakes and fast living; casino interiors are without clocks, so that the passage of time need not disturb the dedicated gambler.

LATEX. See RUBBER.

LATHE, MACHINE TOOL used to shape components whose cross-sections are circular, but whose diameter usually varies along their length. Typically, the workpiece is held in a stock or lathe bed, and supported and rotated by components at each end, the *headstock* and *tailstock*. Cutting tools are introduced from the side to shape the part. In a screw-cutting lathe, the tool is moved along the piece to produce a thread of given depth and pitch (see BOLTS AND SCREWS). Modern lathes may hold several workpieces and use several cutting tools.

LATHROP, Julia Clifford (1858–1932), US social worker, founder of the first US juvenile court (1899) and first head of the Children's Bureau of the Department of Labor (1912–21).

LATIMER, Hugh (c1490–1555), English Protestant martyr and REFORMATION leader. He defended Henry VIII's divorce from Katharine of Aragon, and was made bishop of Worcester 1535, but resigned 1539 in protest against the king's Six Articles. With Nicholas Ridley, he was burned at Oxford as a heretic, by order of the Roman Catholic Mary I.

LATIN, INDO-EUROPEAN LANGUAGE of the Italic group, the language of ancient Rome and the ancestor of the ROMANCE languages. Originating in LATIUM c8th century BC, Latin spread with Roman conquests throughout the Empire, differentiating into vulgar Latin and classical (literary) Latin. It is a logical and highly inflected language that has furnished scientific and legal terminology and is still used in the Roman Catholic Church. It was the international language of scholarship and diplomacy until the 18th century. About half all English words are Latin in origin, many derived through Old French.

LATIN AMERICA, traditionally, those parts of CENTRAL and SOUTH AMERICA and the WEST INDIES where Spanish or Portuguese is the national language. Today the term sometimes includes all countries in these regions.

LATITUDE AND LONGITUDE, the coordinate system used to locate points on the earth's surface. **Longitude** "lines" are circles passing through the poles whose centers are at the center of the earth; they divide the earth rather like an orange into segments. Longitudes are measured 0°–180°E and W from the line of the GREENWICH OBSERVATORY. Assuming the EARTH to be a sphere, we can think of the **latitude** of a point as the ANGLE between a line from the center of the earth to the point and a line from the center to the equator at the same longitude. Each pole, then, has a latitude of 90°, and so latitude is measured from 0° to

Latin America

Movement toward increased cooperation

In a modern context it may seem an oversimplification to define Latin America on a linguistic basis. To group together the countries of Central and South America where Romance languages (Spanish, Portuguese and French) are spoken emphasizes important common aspects of the past but accords insufficient recognition to present realities. That is why many people, with an eye to geography, politics and trade, prefer to treat Latin America as comprising all the countries of Central and South America and the West Indies, ignoring the fact that English is the language of Belize, Guyana and many Caribbean countries, and Dutch the official language of Surinam and the Netherlands Antilles. The reality is that this vast region contains a great diversity of people and countries, many of which have strong historical and cultural ties. They are still divided over many issues, but united on some and moving toward agreement on others.

When Christopher Columbus discovered San Salvador (or Watlings) Island, Cuba and Haiti (1492) and probed southward to the Orinoco R (1498), Latin America was inhabited by scattered Indian communities. The three main continental civilizations were the Aztec (Mexico), the Maya (Guatemala and Yucatan), and—greatest of all—the Inca (highlands of Ecuador, Peru, Bolivia and N Chile). In the 1500s these were overcome by the Spanish under Hernando Cortés, Francisco Pizarro and other conquistadors. Greedy for gold and silver, they were no less fanatical in their determination to Christianize the Indians, the condition upon which popes gave the colonization their blessing. Eastern South America had been earmarked for Portugal by the treaty of Tordesillas (1494) and there, in the 1530s, the Portuguese began creating their own colony, which they called Brazil. They were the first in South America to grow an export crop, sugar, and when Indian labor proved unequal to the task of cultivating the plantations, the Portuguese imported Negro slaves from Africa.

The period of colonial rule by the two Iberian powers lasted about 300 years. The administrative divisions established by Spain, the viceroyalties, the later *audiencias* (area courts of law) and the captaincies-general, influenced the extent and identities of countries like Venezuela, Colombia, Ecuador, Bolivia and Chile when independence came. The Roman Catholic church was everywhere. Perhaps the most influential clerics in Latin America were the Jesuits, who in the 1600s colonized what later became part of eastern Paraguay; they were finally expelled in 1767 by Spain's Charles II, who feared their growing power. A pyramidal social pattern emerged with the *peninsulares* (those born in Spain or Portugal) at the apex, followed by the *criollos* or Creoles (whites born in Latin America), the *mestizos* of mixed European-Indian stock and finally the Indians and imported Negroes.

It was conflict between Creoles and *peninsulares* which culminated in the wars of independence in the early 1800s, when leaders such as José de San Martín, Simón Bolívar and Bernardo O'Higgins overthrew Spanish rule. In both Central and South America the difficult terrain between the chief centers of Spanish power had encouraged the growth of regional loyalties and identities. When the empire fell, therefore, attempts at overall political unity met with little success and a pattern of individual, independent republics emerged. The people of Brazil, held by Portugal on a much lighter rein than that favored by Spain, had already developed a sense of unity and pride of achievement. Brazil remained united and even continued as a monarchy until 1889, when a republic was proclaimed.

Today the peoples of Latin America range from the half-forgotten Indian tribes of the Amazon basin whose survival is threatened by the new roads and settlements being hacked out of the rain forest, to the populations of fast-growing modern cities like São Paulo. Mexico, though about 60% *mestizo*, has ethnic variations ranging from pure Indian to pure white, and its Indian population belongs to more than 50 different linguistic groups. Colombia is also chiefly *mestizo*, but has pure Negro communities along the coast and pure Indians in the highlands and the east. Most West Indians are of Negro or mixed-Negro descent. Creoles predominate in Argentina and Uruguay, and in parts of Chile and Brazil, where racial intermingling, say the Brazilians, is helping develop the world's first "cosmic race." Paraguay is presominantly *mestizo*, but about 50% of the population speaks only Guaraní Indian.

Life for most Latin Americans is hard. Many Latin American countries are dominated by a wealthy minority; and all too often where there is wealth there is also abject poverty, for both the peasants and the slum-dwellers of the great cities. In some republics the colonial social structure still prevails, with power, wealth and privilege concentrated in the landowners, the church and the army at the expense of the poorly-paid and undernourished peasants. In others, economic development and population growth have led to the emergence of an increasingly articulate middle class, active in government, industry and commerce.

Education has been a low priority in many countries, hampered by serious lack of teachers, schools and money. Inevitably it made progress in the fast-expanding cities, where private and public education reflect middle-class interests. A universal problem is how to extend education to the illiterate people of the rural areas and remote highlands. Mexico began by sending out teams of teachers in 1923 and since that time other countries have attempted various similar projects. But even such ambitious efforts as Brazil's nationwide "reading drive" (1971) have failed to make the necessary impact on rural illiteracy and it is often only the

90° N and S of the EQUATOR, latitude "lines" being circles parallel to the equator that get progressively smaller towards the poles. (See CELESTIAL SPHERE.)

LATIUM, historic region of Italy, "the cradle of the Roman people," extending from the Tiber R to the Alban Hills; now part of the W coast region of Latium, or Lazio. This includes the provinces of Rome, Frosinone, Latina, Rieti and Viterbo.

LA TOUR, Georges de (1593–1652), French painter of religious and genre subjects. Renowned in his lifetime, he was virtually forgotten until 1915. Influenced indirectly by CARAVAGGIO, his lighting effects exploit indirect sources and candlelight, with simple forms and warm colors. (See also CHIAROSCURO.)

LATROBE, industrial borough in SW Pa., the official birthplace of professional FOOTBALL (1895). Pop 11 749.

LATROBE, Benjamin Henry (1764–1820), English-born US architect and engineer. His work includes the S wing of the Capitol in Washington and Baltimore Roman Catholic cathedral. A pioneer of the Classical revival, he was the first major professional architect in the US.

LATTER-DAY SAINTS, Church of Jesus Christ of. See MORMONS.

LATTER-DAY SAINTS, Reorganized Church of Jesus Christ of, sect which split from the main body of MORMONS when Brigham Young became leader at the death of Joseph Smith. They chose Smith's son as their leader, becoming formally organized in 1852. They follow the main Mormon beliefs but admit blacks as priests. The headquarters are at Independence, Mo.

LATTICE, in ALGEBRA, a partially ordered set S in which, for any pair of elements a and b, there is in S a least element which is greater than both a and b, and a greatest element which is less than both a and b: for example, the set of REAL NUMBERS forms a lattice. (See also SET THEORY.)

LATTICE, infinite three-dimensional periodic array of points in space, each point being surrounded in an identical way by its neighbors. An assembly of ATOMS placed in the same way at each lattice point makes up a CRYSTAL structure. (See also BRAVAIS LATTICES.)

LA TUQUE, resort town in S Quebec, Canada, on the Saint-Maurice R. Its economy rests on lumber and a hydroelectric power station. Pop 13 099.

LATUS RECTUM, a LINE drawn PERPENDICULAR to the major axis of an ellipse (see CONIC SECTIONS), bounded at either end by the ellipse, and passing through one of the foci.

LATVIA, a republic of the USSR, bordering on the Baltic Sea, between Estonia and Lithuania; its capital is RIGA. It is a lowland country, covering some 24 600sq mi, with a moderate continental climate. Nearly a third of the people are Russians but the majority are Letts, an ancient Baltic people. Dairying and lumbering are still important but there are highly developed industries, including steel, shipbuilding, engineering, textiles, cement and fertilizers. Christianized by the German Livonian Knights in the 13th century, Latvia was ruled by Poles, Swedes and, from the 18th century, Russians. From 1920 to 1940, when it was reabsorbed in Russia, it enjoyed a precarious independence.

LATVIAN LANGUAGE. See LETTISH.

LAUD, William (1573–1645), archbishop of Canterbury from 1633 and a chief advisor of CHARLES I. He enforced High Church beliefs and ritual, and his authoritarianism and persecution of English Puritans and Scottish Presbyterians provoked parliamentary impeachment (1640). He was executed for treason.

LAUDANUM, or tincture of opium, an extract of OPIUM in alcohol formerly much used in medicine.

LAUDERDALE LAKES, city in SE Fla., a residential suburb of Fort Lauderdale. Pop 10 577.

LAUE, Max Theodor Felix von (1879–1960), German physicist awarded the 1914 Nobel Prize for Physics for his prediction (and, with others, subsequent experimental confirmation) that X rays can be diffracted by crystals (see X-RAY DIFFRACTION).

LAUGHING GAS, or nitrous oxide. See NITROGEN.

LAUGHING JACKASS. See KOOKABURRA.

LAUGHTON, Charles (1899–1962), English-born actor, a US citizen from 1950. Films include the award-winning *The Private Life of Henry VIII* (1933) and *The Hunchback of Notre Dame* (1939). He directed *Night of the Hunter* (1955).

LAUNCELOT. See LANCELOT.

LAURASIA, ancient N-Hemisphere supercontinent formed, with Gondwanaland to the S, after the splitting of Pangaea (see CONTINENTAL DRIFT; GONDWANALAND; PANGAEA). It appears to have comprised present Europe, North America and N Asia.

LAUREL, town in W central Md., horse-racing center and residential suburb midway between Baltimore and Washington, D.C. Pop 10 525.

LAUREL, city in SE Miss., seat of Jones Co., with oil-refining and lumber industries. Pop 24 125.

LAUREL, common name for a number of unrelated evergreen shrubs and small trees. The bay laurel church which provides any form of schooling for the under-privileged, including the Indians.

All this has not prevented the development in much of Latin America of a rich and varied culture, ranging from lively folk traditions in music and song to distinctive modern architecture and personalities of world stature in many of the arts.

Despite the idealism which helped frame the constitutions in the early years of independence, Latin America was not slow in establishing a reputation for political instability. Most of its peoples were politically inexperienced. Conflicts occurred between church and state, intellectuals and landowners, while the peasants, the great mass of the population, remained unorganized and apathetic in rural isolation. In the 19th century the landowning *caudillo*, or warlord, often wielded great power, but distinct conservative church-landlord and liberal intellectual groupings emerged in most countries. Many countries experienced a long series of dictatorships and abrupt changes of regime.

The 20th century has seen the emergence of organized labor as an important political force in many countries, though it is split both nationally and internationally between communist, social-democratic, Peronist and Catholic confederations. Most political parties are pragmatic radicals or Christian democrats, but there are also nationalist, socialist and pro-Russian and pro-Peking communist parties. Political instability is manifest in the proliferation of armed groups like the Trotskyite People's Revolution Army and the Anti-Communist Alliance of Argentina. Faced with deadlock and the absence of a Christian-democratic or social-democratic consensus, the military have often stepped in. Even countries with a tradition of constitutional democracy have not been immune, a recent example being Chile, where the communist government of President Allende was overthrown by a military coup in 1973. Apart from the military regimes in the S, most Latin American countries have what is best described as a centralized presidential system of government.

Despite—or perhaps because of—their troubled internal politics, Latin American countries increasingly recognize the need and potential for mutual cooperation in political and economic fields. Liberation from Spain and Portugal in the 1800s was not merely political. It was also economic. The need to build up new national economies and trading patterns presented many problems. Capital from Europe and the US helped finance new ports, railroads and highways; immigrants began to pour in. In South America many of these newcomers established themselves in the towns, but the majority found work in agricultural undertakings.

Agriculture has always been of prime importance. Long before the Europeans came, the Indians had discovered and domesticated many valuable food plants such as corn, potatoes, beans, tomatoes, sweet potatoes, cacao and manioc. The Europeans developed plantation crops like sugar and coffee, exploited the hardwoods and rubber of the forests, and created the great cattle ranches of the pampas.

Before WWI the US had increasingly intervened in the politics of Caribbean and Central American countries, with both "dollar diplomacy" and the Marines. The 1930s saw Roosevelt's "Good Neighbor" reinterpretation of the Monroe Doctrine. But the interwar years also revealed the often exploitive nature of foreign investment in, for example, mining, and WWII again demonstrated Latin American dependence on outside steel and machinery supplies. A new economic nationalism emerged, seeking the development of manufacturing industries in Latin America.

Today a number of Latin American countries still rely for 50% or more of their foreign currency earnings, and for 25%–35% of their gross national production, on export crops like sugar (Dominican Republic), coffee (Brazil, Colombia, Costa Rica, El Salvador and Guatemala) and bananas (Ecuador). These crops are highly vulnerable to world price fluctuations. Attempts to diversify and to introduce improved methods have met with uneven success. The same dependence on one principal export besets the mineral-exporting countries, Chile (copper), Bolivia (tin) and Venezuela (oil). Uruguay depends similarly on her wool exports. As a result, efforts at establishing an independent industrial base in the period after WWII have often still had to rely on foreign investors such as multinational corporations. Many Latin Americans are suspicious of foreign aid, especially from the superpowers, that might have political strings attached. Many countries have favored loans from international agencies such as the International Bank for Reconstruction and Development.

A major development in recent years has been the move towards intraregional economic cooperation: only 5%–10% of foreign trade takes place between Latin American countries themselves. Trade with the US and Europe accounts for most of the rest. The Central American Common Market was established in 1957, the looser Latin American Free Trade Association in 1960, and the Andean Group in 1969. By the 1974 Declaration of Guyana, Venezuela pledged large-scale financial aid to six poorer countries to the N: Costa Rica, El Salvador, Guatemala, Honduras, Nicaragua and Panama.

Political cooperation independent of the US has followed. Cuba, outlawed from the Organization of American States in 1962 and subject to diplomatic and trade sanctions, proposed (1973) a new Latin American regional organization from which the US would be excluded, but which would include the English-speaking countries of the region. Many Latin American countries reestablished formal relations with the Cuban government.

The Declaration of Ayacucho signed in Dec. 1974 by Argentina, Bolivia, Colombia, Cuba, Ecuador, Panama, Peru and Venezuela, condemned the "economic dependence imposed on the continent" and the survival of colonies in the region ("a threat to peace"). The signatory countries pledged themselves to the peaceful settlement of disputes, arms limitation and economic cooperation. Latin-American nationalism was defined as "the awareness of the peoples of their true personality . . . the result of cross-breeding, the fusion of cultures and common historical, social and economic backgrounds."

By early 1975 there was also talk of reconstructing the OAS and US opinion seemed prepared for an easing of relations with Cuba; US secretary of state Dr. Henry Kissinger was looking to a "new dialogue" with Latin America. Such developments were seriously jeopardized in 1975 by the Russian-backed Cuban military intervention in Angola and by Latin American opposition to the US Trade Act. However, following exchanges between many countries, in which Venezuela and Mexico played a prominent role, a new Latin American Economic System (SELA) agreement was signed in Oct.–Nov. 1975 by representatives of all the countries in wider Latin America except the Bahamas.

(*Laurus nobilis*) is probably the classical laurel and is native to Mediterranean regions. Its leaves are used for flavoring fish and other dishes. The common or cherry laurel (*Prunus laurocerasus*) produces white flowers followed by black fruit and is frequently used for hedging.

LAUREL AND HARDY, famous Hollywood comedy team. The English-born **Stan Laurel** (Arthur Stanley Jefferson; 1890–1965) and the American **Oliver Hardy** (1892–1957), thin man and fat man, simpleton and pompous heavy, made over 200 films between 1927 and 1945 in a style, shaped by Laurel, which ranged from slapstick to slow-paced comedy of situation and audience anticipation.

LAURENS, city in NW S.C., seat of Laurens Co., where three battles were fought in the Revolutionary War. Its economy rests on farming, textiles and glass. Pop 10 298.

LAURENS, Henry (1724–1792), American statesman, a trader and planter in S.C. before the Revolution. He was president of the Continental Congress 1777–78. Captured at sea by the British in 1780 but released in 1781, he was then appointed one of the American peace negotiators in Paris.

LAURENTIAN MOUNTAINS, or Laurentides, range in S Quebec, Canada. One of the oldest in the world; it rises almost 4 000ft. Heavily forested, the area's economy rests on wood and the tourist industry.

LAURIER, Sir Wilfrid (1841–1919), first French-Canadian Prime Minister of Canada 1896–1911. Leader of the federal Liberal party 1887–1919, he encouraged provincial autonomy while seeking to unite the country. Many of his attempts to better the rights of French-Canadians, particularly in education, met with little success. Defeated in the 1911 election, he was supported by Quebec and rejected by the rest of Canada in the 1917 election, a divisive result he worked against.

LAUSANNE, capital city of Vaud canton, W Switzerland, on the N shore of Lake Geneva. The cultural center of French Switzerland, the town has many historic buildings, including the cathedral of Notre-Dame (1275). Pop 137 383.

LAVA, both molten ROCK rising to the earth's surface through VOLCANOES and other fissures, and the same after solidification. Originating in the MAGMA deep below the surface, most lavas (e.g., BASALT) are basic and flow freely for considerable distances. The acidic, SILICA-rich lavas such as RHYOLITE are much stiffer. Basic lavas solidify in a variety of forms, the commonest being *aa* (Hawaiian, rough) or block lava, forming irregular jagged blocks, and *pahoehoe* (Hawaiian, satiny) or ropy lava, solidifying in ropelike strands. Pillow lava, with rounded surfaces, has solidified under water, and slowly-cooled basalt may form hexagonal columns.

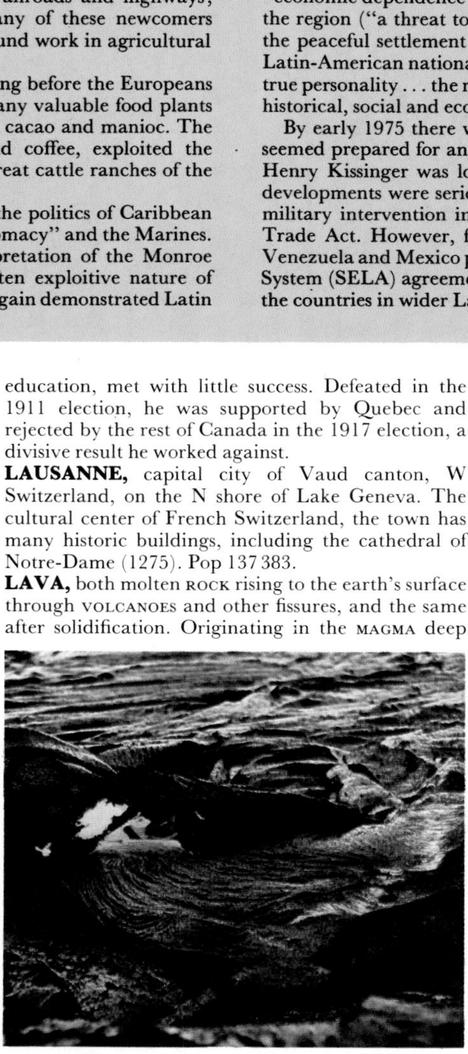

Lava of the *pahoehoe* type. As it cools, its surface is wrinkled into ropelike strands by the movement of liquid lava underneath.

LAVA BEDS NATIONAL MONUMENT, 72sq mi recently formed volcanic region in N Cal. It has many strange and often unique lava formations; some caves contain Indian pictographs and frozen streams. The area was the main battlefield of the MODOC INDIAN War (1872–73).

LAVAL, city in Quebec province, Canada. An amalgam of six cities and seven towns created as a planned industrial center in 1965, it covers the whole of Jesus Island. Pop 228 010.

LAVAL, François de Montmorency (1623–1708), vicar-apostolic of New France (1659) and first bishop of Quebec, Canada from 1674. He frequently clashed with the administrators of New France, bitterly opposing the profitable liquor trade with the Indians. He retired in 1684 to the Quebec Seminary (now Laval U.) founded by him in 1663.

LAVAL, Pierre (1883–1945), French politician who collaborated with the Germans in WWII. A socialist and pacifist, he served three unsuccessful terms as premier 1931–32, 1932 and 1935–36. Believing that Nazi victory was inevitable, he allowed himself to be installed as a Nazi puppet premier 1942–44. He fled abroad, returned for trial (1945) and was executed.

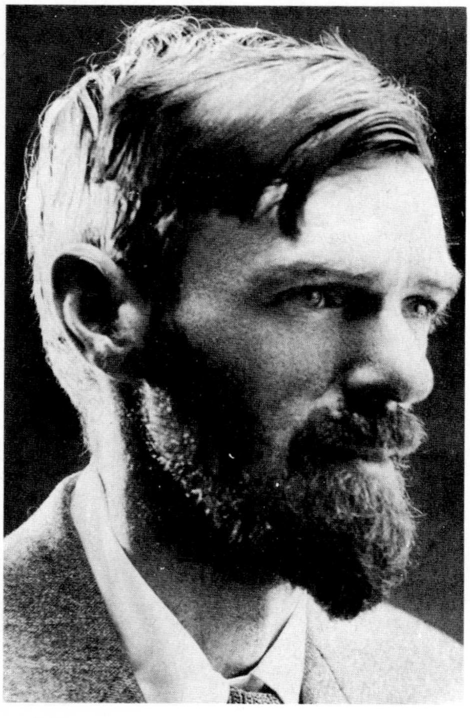

The novelist D. H. Lawrence, a passionate critic of modern industrial society and of contemporary attitudes toward sex and the emotions.

LAVENDER, hardy evergreen shrubs of the genus *Lavendula,* from the MINT family, Labiatae. The plants produce spikes of fragrant purple and violet flowers which are often dried and used to scent wardrobes and closets. The name is most commonly applied to the old English lavender (*Lavendula spica*). *L. dentata* (fernleaf lavender) is often cultivated as a house plant, growing best at average house temperatures in a sunny window. The soil should be kept evenly moist and the foliage misted often. Propagation is by stem cuttings. Other species grown indoors include *L. multifida* and *L. stoechas*.

LAVERAN, Charles Louis Alphonse (1845–1922), French physician awarded the 1907 Nobel Prize for Physiology or Medicine for his discovery of the MALARIA parasite, a protozoan of the genus *Plasmodium*. (See also PARASITE.)

LA VÉRENDRYE, Pierre Gaultier de Varennes, Sieur de (1685–1749), French-Canadian explorer and fur trader. He founded a trail of important fur-trading posts as far as Mo. in his unsuccessful efforts to find an overland route to the Pacific.

LA VERNE, city in SW Cal., 25mi E of Los Angeles, in a citrus fruit-growing area. Pop 12 965.

LAVOISIER, Antoine Laurent (1743–1794), French scientist who was foremost in the establishment of modern CHEMISTRY. He applied gravimetric methods to the process of COMBUSTION, showing that when substances burned, they combined with a component in the air (1772). Learning from J. PRIESTLEY of his "dephlogisticated air" (1774), he recognized that it was with this that substances combined in burning. In 1779 he renamed the gas *oxygène*, because he believed it was a component in all acids. Then, having discovered the nature of the components in water, he commenced his attack on the PHLOGISTON theory, proposing a new chemical nomenclature (1787), and publishing his epoch-making *Elementary Treatise of Chemistry* (1789). In the years before his tragic death on the guillotine, he also investigated the chemistry of RESPIRATION, demonstrating its analogy with combustion.

LAW, body of rules governing the relationship between the members of a community and between the individual and the state. In England, the British Commonwealth and the US the law is based upon statute law, laws enacted by legislative bodies such as Congress, and upon COMMON LAW, the body of law created by custom and adherence to rules derived from previous judgments. This also covers the body of law created by EQUITY. The other main system, CIVIL LAW, derives from the laws of ancient Rome and relies not on precedent but on a code of rules established and modified only by statute. This is the dominant system in most of Europe and in many other countries of the world. In fact the division is not absolute. Many areas of the common law are codified by statute for convenience; there is often unofficial but very real reliance on previous decisions in civil law countries.

All major bodies of law break down into two divisions, public law and private law (often called civil law also). Public law governs matters which concern the state. Criminal law is public because a crime is an offense against the state; other kinds of public law are ADMINISTRATIVE LAW, INTERNATIONAL LAW and CONSTITUTIONAL LAW. Private law governs the relationship between individuals (including corporate bodies such as companies) in such matters as CONTRACT, and the law of TORT; this covers damaging acts done by one individual to another which are not necessarily crimes.

History of law. The first legal system of which we have any detailed knowledge is that of the Babylonian King HAMMURABI in c1700 BC, a complex code linking crime with punishment and regulating the conduct of everyday affairs. Like the Hebrew Mosaic Law it treated law as a divine ordinance; the ancient Greeks were probably the first to regard law as made by man for his own benefit. Roman law was based on the Twelve Tables, compiled c451–450 BC; it developed a complex equity system when these became outdated. The emperor JUSTINIAN produced the last definitive code in an attempt to clear up resulting difficulties. Much medieval law was based on Church law, although an independent system arose quite early in England. This grew into the common law and spread outwards with the growth of the British Empire. Napoleon revised Roman law as the basis for his CODE NAPOLÉON, the model for most subsequent civil law codes. US law grew out of the common law, but has been much modified in the federal system. (See also LEGAL PROFESSION.)

LAW, Andrew Bonar (1858–1923), Canadian-born Scottish politician. He succeeded BALFOUR as leader of the Conservative Party in 1911. Colonial secretary in the 1915 war cabinet, he was chancellor of the exchequer under LLOYD GEORGE 1916–18 and prime minister 1922–23.

LAW, John (1671–1729), pioneering Scottish financier. After the success of a private bank he established in Paris in 1716 he founded his Mississippi Company, winning a monopoly of La. commerce; it later bought up the French East India Co. His bank became the state bank and he was made controller-general of France. Lacking experience of inflation, he created a boom by issuing unredeemable paper money. Ruined in the resulting collapse, he had to leave France and died in poverty.

LAWN BOWLING. See BOWLS, LAWN.

LAWNDALE, residential suburb city of Los Angeles in Los Angeles Co., S Cal. It has a major aircraft industry nearby. Pop 24 825.

LAWRENCE, city in central Ind., 9mi N of Indianapolis, of which it is a suburb. The main industry is electronics. Pop 16 646.

LAWRENCE, city in NE Kan., seat of Douglas Co., on the Kansas R. It houses Kansas U and Haskell Institute, a large Indian college. Stronghold of the free-state abolitionist movement, it was razed in 1863 by William QUANTRILL. Pop 45 698.

LAWRENCE, industrial city, one of three seats of Essex Co., NE Mass. A historic manufacturing and trading center, it is famous for textiles but has many other industries. Pop 66 915.

LAWRENCE, Saint, Roman deacon martyred c258, during the persecution of the emperor Valerian, by being roasted on a gridiron. His feast day is Aug. 10.

LAWRENCE, David Herbert (1885–1930), major English author. He combined a vivid prose style with a solid background of ideas and intense human insight. Stressing the supremacy of instinct and emotion over reason in human relationships, he advocated absolute sexual candor; his novel *Lady Chatterley's Lover* (1928) is known for this to the exclusion of its other themes. Perhaps his best works are *The Rainbow* (1915) and *Women in Love* (1920). From a working-class background (reflected in *Sons and Lovers*, 1913), he was for some years a teacher. He died of pleurisy at Vence in France.

LAWRENCE, Ernest Orlando (1901–1958), US physicist awarded the 1939 Nobel Prize for Physics for his invention of the CYCLOTRON (1929; the first successful model was built in 1931).

LAWRENCE, Gertrude (1898–1952), versatile and sophisticated English actress and singer. Her first great success was in her friend Noel COWARD's *Private Lives* (1930). Famous in London and on Broadway, her last appearance was in *The King and I* (1951).

LAWRENCE, James (1781–1813), US naval officer, captain of the frigate *Chesapeake*, sunk by the British frigate *Shannon* off Boston in 1813. He was mortally wounded; his dying words "Don't give up the ship!" have become proverbial.

LAWRENCE, Sir Thomas (1769–1830), English painter, the most fashionable portraitist of his time. President of the Royal Academy from 1820, he never had the success he wished for as a history painter. His style is richly colorful, fluid and vigorous, but occasionally careless.

LAWRENCE, Thomas Edward (1888–1935), English scholar, writer and soldier, legendary guerrilla fighter with the Arabs against the Turks in WWI. As a British Intelligence officer he carried out with Prince FAISAL a successful guerrilla campaign against Turkish rail supply lines, and was with the Arab forces that captured Damascus in 1918. In *The Seven Pillars of Wisdom* (1926) he described his wartime experiences and his personal philosophy. A neurotic, lonely man, he joined the Royal Air Force and Royal Tank Corps under assumed names 1923–25 and again 1925–35. He was killed in a motorcycle crash.

T. E. Lawrence, better known as Lawrence of Arabia. Before WWI he acquired extensive first-hand knowledge of Middle Eastern affairs while pursuing archaeological interests in the area.

LAWRENCIUM (Lr), a TRANSURANIUM ELEMENT; the final member of the ACTINIDE series, prepared by bombardment of lighter actinides. The most stable isotope, Lr^{256}, has a half-life of only 35s.

LAWSON, Ernest (1873–1939), US Impressionist painter; one of the EIGHT, he exhibited at their controversial Armory Show. Seeking a greater degree of naturalism, he specialized in serene landscapes, often in glowing colors, such as *Winter* (1914) and *High Bridge* (1939).

LAWTON, city, seat of Comanche Co., SW Okla. A trade center for the surrounding farming area, it manufactures food products, mobile homes and concrete products. Pop 74 470.

LAWYER. See LEGAL PROFESSION.

LAXATIVE, DRUG or DIETETIC FOOD taken to promote bowel action and to treat CONSTIPATION. They may act as irritants (cascara, senna, phenolphthalein, castor oil), softeners (mineral oil), or bulk agents (bran, methylcellulose and magnesium sulfate—Epsom salts). Laxative abuse may cause GASTROINTENSTINAL TRACT disorders, POTASSIUM deficiency and LUNG disease.

LAXNESS, Halldor Kiljan (1902–), Iceland's greatest modern writer. He became famous with his novel *Salka Valka* (1931–32). This and later books such as *The Atom Station* (1945) are harsh but compassionate descriptions of Icelandic rural life and post-WWII problems. He was awarded the Nobel Prize for Literature in 1955.

LAYAMON, English poet (apparently a priest) author of the *Brut* (c1200), a fictional history of England. In about 16000 alliterative lines Layamon incorporates much legendary matter, including the ARTHURIAN LEGENDS in an early form; it was the source of Shakespeare's *King Lear* and *Cymbeline*.

LAYARD, Sir Austen Henry (1817–1894), British archaeologist known for his excavations of Assyrian and Babylonian remains, and especially for his confirmation of the site of Nineveh.

LAYING ON OF HANDS, ritual act of blessing, derived from Judaism and adopted by Christianity to signify the bestowal of the Holy Spirit. Much used in the early Church, it is maintained today in the rites of confirmation, ordination and EXTREME UNCTION.

LAYTON, city in N Ut., N of Salt Lake City. An agricultural center, its main industry is sugar refining. Pop 13063.

LAZARUS, in the New Testament, a man of Bethany brought back from the dead by Jesus (John 11 and 12). Lazarus is also the name of the beggar at the rich man's gate in the parable (Luke 16:19–25).

LAZARUS, Emma (1849–1887), US poet best known for the sonnet *The New Colossus* engraved at the base of the Statue of Liberty. Of a Sephardic Jewish family, she based much of her work on Jewish culture and supported Jewish nationalism.

LAZEAR, Jesse William (1866–1900), US physician, a member of W. REED's commission investigating C. FINLAY's theory that YELLOW FEVER is spread by the MOSQUITO. Lazear's death five days after a mosquito bite was a tragic demonstration of the truth of the theory.

LAZURITE ($Na_4Al_3Si_3O_{12}S$), sulfur-bearing feldspathoid SILICATE mineral, forming deep blue granular masses; the chief constituent of LAPIS LAZULI.

LEACHING, the process whereby water, as it percolates through the soil, dissolves out various mineral salts. RAIN water is slightly acidic, because of dissolved CARBON dioxide from the ATMOSPHERE, and thus important in the leaching of SOILS.

LEACOCK, Stephen Butler (1869–1944), Canadian political scientist and humorist. Head of Economics and Political Science at McGill U., Montreal, 1908–36, he wrote 57 books, the majority humorous. *Literary Lapses* (1910), his first, was made an immediate success by its dry, observant and witty style.

LEAD (Pb), soft, bluish-gray metal in Group IVA of the PERIODIC TABLE, occurring as GALENA, and also as CERUSSITE and anglesite (lead sulfate). The sulfide ore is converted to the oxide by roasting, then smelted with coke. Lead dissolves in dilute nitric acid, but is otherwise resistant to corrosion, because of a protective surface layer of the oxide, sulfate etc. It is used in roofing, water pipes, coverings for electric cables, RADIATION shields, ammunition, storage BATTERIES, and alloys, including solder (see SOLDERING), PEWTER, BABBITT METAL and type metal. Lead and its compounds are toxic (see LEAD POISONING). AW 207.2, mp 327.5°C, bp 1740°C, sg 11.35 (20°C).

Lead forms two series of salts; the lead(II) compounds are more stable than the lead(IV) compounds. **Lead(II) Oxide** (PbO), or **Litharge**, yellow crystalline solid, made by oxidizing lead; used in lead-acid storage batteries, glass and glazes. mp 888°C. **Lead(IV) Oxide** (PbO_2), brown crystalline solid, a powerful oxidizing agent used in matches, fireworks, and dyes; it decomposes at 290°C. **Trilead Tetroxide** (Pb_3O_4), or **Red Lead**, orange-red powder, made by oxidizing litharge, used in paints, inks, glazes and magnets. **Lead Tetraethyl** ($Pb[C_2H_5]_4$), colorless liquid, made by reacting a lead/sodium alloy with ethyl chloride. It is used as an ANTIKNOCK ADDITIVE TO GASOLINE.

LEADBELLY. See LEDBETTER, HUDDIE.

LEAD-CHAMBER PROCESS, process for manufacturing SULFURIC ACID, now largely superseded by the CONTACT PROCESS.

LEAD POISONING, DISEASE caused by excessive LEAD levels in TISSUES and BLOOD. It may be taken in through the industrial use of lead, through AIR POLLUTION due to lead-containing fuels or, in children, through eating old paint. BRAIN disturbance with COMA or CONVULSIONS, peripheral NEURITIS, ANEMIA and abdominal COLIC are important effects. Chelating agents (see CHELATE) are used in treatment but preventitive measures in the community are essential.

LEADVILLE, city, seat of Lake Co., central Col. In a heavily forested area of the Rocky Mts., it is a major national mining center for various metals and minerals such as gold, silver, lead, zinc, molybdenum and manganese. Pop 4314.

LEADWORT, evergreen shrubs and climbers of the genus *Plumbago* which produce clusters of blue, white or red flowers. The roots are poisonous and extracts from some species have been used to treat toothache. Family: Plumbaginaceae.

LEAF, green outgrowth from the stems of higher plants and the main site of PHOTOSYNTHESIS. The form of leaves varies from species to species but the basic features are similar. Each leaf consists of a flat blade or lamina, attached to the main stem by a leaf stalk or petiole. Leaf-like stipules may be found at the base of the petiole. The green coloration is produced by CHLOROPHYLL which is sited in the CHLOROPLASTS. Most leaves are covered by a waterproof covering or cuticle. Gaseous exchange takes place through small openings called STOMATA, through which water vapor also passes (see TRANSPIRATION). The blade of the leaf is strengthened by veins which contain the vascular tissue that is responsible for conducting water around the plant and also the substances essential for METABOLISM.

In some plants the leaves are adapted to catch insects (see INSECTIVOROUS PLANTS), while in others they are modified to reduce water loss (see SUCCULENTS; XEROPHYTE). Leaves produced immediately below the FLOWERS are called bracts and in some species, e.g., POINSETTIA, they are more highly colored than the flowers.

LEAF-CUTTING ANTS, or **Parasol ants**, a group of tropical ants which culture fungus gardens on beds of macerated leaves deep in their underground nests. The worker ants strip nearby trees of leaves and may be a serious agricultural pest, and the young are fed on bromatia—bodies produced by the fungus only in this underground situation.

LEAF FISHES, a family, Nandidae, of tropical freshwater fishes of South America, W Africa and southeast Asia, the members of which to a greater or lesser extent resemble floating leaves drifting with the water current in order to approach the small fishes on which they feed.

LEAFHOPPERS, insects closely related to SPITTLE BUGS and APHIDS. Hemipterans, they feed on leaves by sucking the sap, and may be instrumental in transmitting virus diseases from one plant to another. As such they are important agricultural pests.

LEAF INSECTS, the name given to some large, tropical insects, mostly Phasmidae, which have the body flattened and wings expanded to look like leaves. They are usually green or brown with wing veins emphasized to resemble the veins of a leaf.

LEAGUE CITY, city in SE Tex., 25mi NW of Galveston. It lies in a truck-farming and oil area. Pop 10818.

LEAGUE OF NATIONS (1920–46), the first major international association of countries; a total of 63 states were members, although not all simultaneously. In WWI Allied leaders, particularly President WILSON, became convinced of the need for an international organization to resolve conflicts peacefully and avert another devastating war. The charter of the proposed League of Nations was incorporated in the Treaty of VERSAILLES. Ironically, however, Wilson was unable to persuade the US Senate to ratify the Treaty and thus join the League; this may have been the League's greatest weakness. The Covenant embodied the principles of collective security against an aggressor, arbitration of international disputes, disarmament and open diplomacy.

Established at Geneva, Switzerland, the League grew during the 1920s, taking in many new members, but it never had much influence. It could do little to stop the Italian invasion of Corfu in 1923 or the CHACO WAR. It did no more than investigate and protest the Japanese invasion of Manchuria in 1931. Its failure to take decisive action against Italy over the invasion of Ethiopia in 1934 was the final blow to its prestige; WWII proved it a failure. Its subsidiary organizations, however, such as the INTERNATIONAL LABOR ORGANIZATION and the INTERNATIONAL COURT OF JUSTICE, have endured, as have the public health bodies it created.

LEAGUE OF WOMEN VOTERS, nonpartisan organization with over 160000 members in the US and Puerto Rico, founded in 1920 by members of the National American Women Suffrage Association (see WOMEN'S RIGHTS). Apart from political education for its members, the league studies and campaigns on economic and social issues such as equal opportunity in education. It does not sponsor electoral candidates or political parties.

LEAHY, William Daniel (1875–1959), US admiral and diplomat. Chief of Naval Operations 1937–39, he was made governor of Puerto Rico after his retirement. From December 1940 to 1942 he was US ambassador to Vichy France and chief of staff to Presidents ROOSEVELT and TRUMAN 1942–49.

LEAKEY, Louis Seymour Bazett (1903–1972), British archaeologist and anthropologist best known for his findings of human FOSSILS, especially in the region of Olduvai Gorge, Tanzania, and for his (sometimes controversial) views on their significance.

LEAMINGTON, town in Canada, in SE Ontario, on Lake Erie. It is a food-processing center, resort and lake port. Pop 10589.

LEANDER. See HERO AND LEANDER.

LEANING TOWER OF PISA, white marble bell tower or *campanile* in Pisa, Italy. Building was started in 1174, reputedly by Bonanno Pisano, but the foundations were unsound and the 184.5ft tower had

The Leaning Tower of Pisa. Its original shallow foundations are no wider than the visible structure.

already begun to lean by the time of its completion in the 14th century. It now tilts more than 17ft from the perpendicular.

LEAP YEAR. See CALENDAR.

LEAR, Edward (1812–1888), English artist, traveler and versifier, best known for his LIMERICKS and nonsense rhymes. *The Owl and the Pussy-Cat* is a famous example. His landscapes and illustrated journals are highly regarded.

LEARNING. Almost everything that we do derives from learning. If it were not for early school learning you would be able neither to read these words nor to understand them. The concepts of learning and MEMORY are clearly closely related, though learning is usually considered to be the result of practice, and there is usually considered to be a particular stimulus that encourages such practice. The simplest learned response is the conditioned REFLEX. The most powerful learning stimulus is the satisfaction of instinctive drives (see INSTINCT). For example, a dog might learn that if he sits up and "begs" he will be fed by his owner. Here the stimulus is positive, in that the result of his response is a reward, rather than negative, where the correct response earns only escape from punishment: positive stimuli are more effective encouragements to learning than are negative. All animals display the ability to learn, and even some of the most primitive have the ability to become bored with the tests of experimenters (where the reward is not an adequate stimulus). In humans, learning ability depends to a great extent on INTELLIGENCE, though social and environmental factors clearly play a part. (See also CONDITIONING; HABIT; IMPRINTING.)

LEASE, an agreement whereby the owner of a property permits its habitation or use by a tenant for an agreed period, usually in exchange for a fixed rental. A lease may be contracted for a specified term of months or years—often 99 years—or for life.

LEASE, Mary Elizabeth (1853–1933), US barrister, better known as an agrarian protester and temperance advocate. An active supporter of POPULISM in the 1890s, she earned the nickname Mary "Yellin'" Lease, urging farmers to "raise less corn and more hell."

LEASIDE, town in Canada, in SE Ontario. An industrial and residential suburb NE of Toronto. Pop 21 250.

LEAST SQUARES, technique, widely used in science, for finding the curve which best fits a set of experimental results by minimizing the sum of the squares of the differences between the results and the corresponding points on the curve.

LEATHER, animal hide or skin that has been treated by TANNING to preserve it from decay and to make it strong, supple, water-resistant and attractive in appearance. The skins are typically preserved temporarily by soaking in brine and kept in cold storage. They are washed and soaked in an alkaline solution, and then scraped to remove the hair. Rapidly rotating blades remove residual fat and flesh. The hides are then neutralized and softened by soaking in pancreatic enzymes, and pickled in dilute acid to make them ready for TANNING. The tanned leather is finished by being squeezed to remove excess liquid, lubricated with oil, slowly dried, and impregnated with resins. It is commonly dyed, and a shiny surface is produced by compression. Most leather is made from the hide of sheep, cows, calves, goats, kids and pigs; and for exotic products from the skins of crocodiles, sharks and snakes. Leather is used to make shoes, gloves, coats and other garments, upholstery, bags and luggage, wallets, transmission belts, etc. and to bind books. Chamois leather, for cleaning, is now made from sheepskin. (See also SUEDE).

LEATHERBACK, or **Leathery turtle,** *Dermochelys coriacea*, the largest of the marine TURTLES. It has a CARAPACE of dermal bones which are free and not fused to the vertebrae and ribs as in other turtles. The skin has thus the appearance of brown leather.

LEATHERWOOD, *Dirca palustris*, a North American shrub with tough but pliable stems and yellow flowers that appear before the leaves. Fiber produced from the bark was once used by local Indians. Family: Thymelaeaceae.

LEAVEN, substance used to make DOUGH rise during baking by producing gases which expand to make the food light and porous. YEAST produces CARBON dioxide by FERMENTATION; BAKING POWDER and SODIUM bicarbonate produce carbon dioxide by chemical reaction. Air may be introduced by vigorous whipping.

LEAVENWORTH, city in NE Kan., seat of Leavenworth Co., on the Missouri R. The oldest city in Kan. (incorporated 1855), it is an industrial and railroad center. Fort Leavenworth is a US army reservation with federal and military prisons. Pop 25 147.

LEAVIS, F. R. (Frank Raymond Leavis; 1895–), influential English literary critic and lecturer. Leavis judged works by their moral standpoint and condemned low standards in modern culture. He edited the quarterly review *Scrutiny* 1932–53 and wrote *New Bearings in English Poetry* (1932), *The Great Tradition* (1948) and *The Common Pursuit* (1952).

LEAWOOD, city in NE Kan., S of Kansas City. It is an agricultural center. Pop 10 349.

LEBANON, Mediterranean republic in SW Asia, a small Arab state bordered by Syria and Israel. The four main regions, paralleling the sea, are the flat, fertile, coastal strip; the Lebanon Mountains; the narrow, fertile Bekaa (Biqa) Valley and the Anti-Lebanon Mountains. Lebanon has more rain and a more moderate climate than its neighbors. Only a few groves of cedars remain on the once-forested mountains.

People. Lebanon is an Arab state, but about half of the people are Christian, mainly MARONITE. Most of the remainder are SUNNITES, though the DRUSES, a small Muslim sect, are historically of great importance. A convention has been established whereby the president is a Maronite, the prime minister a Sunnite and the speaker in the unicameral chamber of deputies a SHI'ITE Muslim. Other offices are allocated to various religious groups according to a fixed scheme.

The level of education is relatively high. There are four universities, including the American University in Beirut (1866) which has an international reputation.

Economy. Agriculture occupies half the population, and consumer goods are produced, but national prosperity stems largely from tourism, international banking and transshipment of goods. The capital and chief seaport, BEIRUT, the most cosmopolitan city in the Middle East, is a major center for the reexportation of goods and for shipping and refining Iraqi oil.

History. The site of ancient PHOENICIA, Lebanon is a land of great antiquity and resilience. Although engulfed by successive invaders—Greek, Roman, Arab and Turkish—it invariably preserved some degree of autonomy. Lebanon was an early refuge for persecuted religious groups, especially Christians, whose influence was entrenched during the CRUSADES. Freed from Turkish rule after WWI, the country passed into French hands, becoming effectively independent in 1943. It has tried to steer a course of non-involvement in the Arab-Israeli conflict. In 1975 violence erupted in the Lebanon as the right-wing Christian Phalangists and left-wing Muslim militias fought in the streets of Beirut. Despite numerous abortive ceasefires, the fighting continued into 1976.

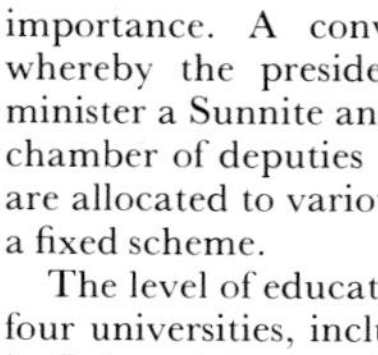

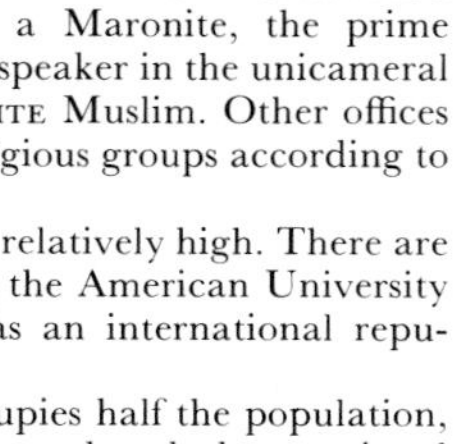

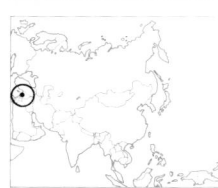

Official name: Lebanon
Capital: Beirut
Area: 4 015sq mi
Population: 2 700 000
Languages: Arabic; French and English widely used
Religions: Muslim, Christian
Monetary unit(s): 1 Lebanese pound = 100 piastres

LEBANON, city in SE Pa., seat of Lebanon Co. It produces steel, textiles, chemicals and electrical products. Pop 28 572.

LEBANON, city in N central Tenn., seat of Wilson Co. A manufacturing center, it serves an agricultural area. Pop 12 492.

LEBLANC, Nicolas (1742–1806), French chemist who invented the **Leblanc process** for obtaining alkali (SODIUM sulfate) from common SALT. The salt was treated with SULFURIC ACID to give sodium sulfate, which was then heated with CHALK and CHARCOAL to give a "black ash" from which the sodium carbonate could be washed with water. The process was supplanted late in the 19th century by the SOLVAY PROCESS.

LE BRUN, Charles (1619–1690), French artist, "first painter" to Louis XIV and virtual dictator of the arts in France 1662–83. He directed the GOBELIN tapestry works and decorated the Palace of Versailles.

LE CHATELIER, Henri Louis (1850–1936), French chemist best known for formulating **Le Chatelier's principle** (1888), that if a change occurs in one of the conditions of a system initially in equilibrium, the system will adjust, tending to nullify the change and return to equilibrium.

LECLANCHÉ CELL. See BATTERY.

LECLERC, Jacques Philippe (1902–1947), name assumed by Jacques Philippe, Vicomte de Hauteclocque, WWII Free French commander. He led his forces from French Equatorial Africa 1 500mi across the Sahara to Tunisia 1942–43. In 1944 he received the surrender of Paris.

LECOMPTON CONSTITUTION, proslavery state constitution approved at Lecompton, Kan., 1857. Overwhelmingly rejected by referendum in 1858, and replaced by the antislavery Wyandotte Constitution, 1859, it helped to delay the admission of Kan. into the Union until 1861.

LECONTE DE LISLE, Charles Marie René (1818–1894), French poet and translator of classical verse. Established by his *Poésies barbares* (1862) as chief among the PARNASSIANS, he succeeded Victor HUGO at the Académie Française (1886).

LE CORBUSIER (1887–1965), professional name of Charles-Edouard Jeanneret: Swiss-born, French-trained architect, a founder of the INTERNATIONAL STYLE. His austere, rectangular designs made in the 1920s and 1930s reflected his view of a house as a "machine to live in." Later influential designs (featuring reinforced concrete) included apartments at Marseilles, a chapel at Ronchamp and CHANDIGARH.

LEDA, in Greek mythology, mother of CLYTEMNESTRA, CASTOR AND POLLUX and HELEN OF TROY. In most versions of the myth Clytemnestra and Castor fathered by the Spartan king Tyndareus, and the others by ZEUS, who appeared to Leda as a white swan.

LEDBETTER, Huddie ("Leadbelly"; c1888–1949), US Negro blues and folk singer and guitarist, born in La. His repertoire and powerful singing style impressed the folk historian and archivist John Avery LOMAX, who became his patron. Leadbelly sang in New York nightclubs in the 1940s.

LEDERBERG, Joshua (1925–), US geneticist awarded with G. W. BEADLE and E. L. TATUM the 1958 Nobel Prize for Physiology or Medicine for his work on bacterial genetics. With Tatum, he showed that the offspring of different mutants of *Escherichia coli* had genes recombined from those of the original generation, thus establishing the sexuality of *E. coli*. Later he showed that genetic information could be carried between *Salmonella* by certain bacterial viruses. (See also BACTERIA; GENETICS; VIRUS.)

LEDOUX, Claude Nicolas (1736–1806), unconventional French architect who proposed an ideal city in *Architecture* (1804), and houses shaped as spheres and pyramids. His completed designs included private mansions, a factory and offices.

LEDYARD, town in SE Conn., 7mi NE of New London, site of Fort Decatur. It is an agricultural center and also manufactures plastics. Pop 14 837.

The Custis–Lee mansion, home of Robert E. Lee, stands in what is now Arlington National Cemetery, Va.; it overlooks the grave of John F. Kennedy.

LEE, Ann (1736–1784), English-born religious mystic, founder of the SHAKERS in North America. Imprisoned in 1770 for street-preaching, in 1774 she emigrated to America, founding the first Shaker colony near Albany, N.Y., in 1776.

LEE, Arthur (1740–1792), American diplomat who sought aid in Europe 1776–79 as an agent of the CONTINENTAL CONGRESS. He made little headway in Spain and Berlin and quarreled with fellow commissioners Silas DEANE and Benjamin FRANKLIN. But in 1778 all three signed treaties with France.

LEE, Charles (1731–1782), American major general in the Revolutionary War. He refused orders from George Washington (1776), planned betrayal while in British captivity (1776–78), and retreated at the Battle of MONMOUTH (1778), robbing Washington of a victory. He was court-martialed, deprived of his command and later dismissed.

LEE, Henry ("Light Horse Harry"; 1756–1818), dashing American cavalry officer in the Revolutionary War, highly praised by George Washington. He was governor of Va. 1791–94 and a representative in Congress 1799–1801. Civil War general Robert E. LEE was his son.

LEE, Ivy Ledbetter (1877–1934), US pioneer in public relations. In 1906 he persuaded coal-mine owners criticized during a strike to make him their press representative, and later gained an impressive array of big-business clients.

LEE, Richard Henry (1732–1794), American Revolutionary statesman from Va., member of the CONTINENTAL CONGRESS 1774–79, 1784–87, president 1784–85. On June 7, 1776, he introduced the motion that led to the DECLARATION OF INDEPENDENCE. He opposed ratification of the US Constitution, fearing its effects on states' rights. As a US senator from Va., 1789–92, he helped secure adoption of the BILL OF RIGHTS.

LEE, Robert E. (Edward) (1807–1870), American general who commanded the Confederate armies in the American Civil War. Son of Henry LEE, he was born at Stratford, Va., graduated from WEST POINT (1829) and served brilliantly as a field engineer in the MEXICAN WAR 1846–48. He was superintendent of West Point 1852–55, and in 1859 arrested John BROWN at HARPERS FERRY. Lee opposed slavery and secession, but from loyalty to his native Va., declined Lincoln's offer of command of the Union armies in 1861 and reluctantly accepted a Confederate post. He became a full general in May 1861 and a year later gained command of the Army of Northern Virginia. His first great success was the defense of Richmond in the SEVEN DAYS' BATTLE (June 26–July 2, 1862). After the Confederate victory at the second Battle of BULL RUN, Lee invaded Maryland but was halted at ANTIETAM. Victory at CHANCELLORSVILLE encouraged a further offensive into Pa., but he was turned back at the Battle of GETTYSBURG. Lee finally surrendered to Ulysses S. GRANT at APPOMATTOX COURT HOUSE on April 9, 1865. Universally respected for his personal qualities and brilliant generalship, he ended his days as a college president.

LEE, Tsung Dao (1926–), Chinese-born US physicist who shared with YANG the 1957 Nobel Prize for Physics for their investigations of examples of the principle of PARITY being violated, which led to significant improvements in our understanding of SUBATOMIC PARTICLES.

LEECHES, annelid worms, segmented, with a prominent attachment sucker at the posterior end and another sucker around the mouth. Leeches are hermaphrodite. Freshwater or semiterrestrial animals, they feed by sucking the blood or other body fluids of mammals, small invertebrates, worms, insect larvae or snails. The crop is capable of great distention to enable large meals to be taken as occasion permits, for, with many species, meals are available only at intervals, and then only by chance. A fully-grown Medicinal leech can survive for a whole year on a single blood meal.

LEEDS, city in England in the Co. of West Yorkshire, on the Aire R. It is a major commercial and industrial center, producing textiles, machinery, chemicals and metal goods, and is the home of Leeds U. Pop 499 000.

LEEK, *Allium porrum*, vegetable related to the ONION and cultivated as an annual for use in the fall and winter. The edible portion consists of a mass of tightly packed, succulent leaf bases. Family: Alliaceae.

LEE KUAN YEW (1923–), prime minister of the Republic of Singapore, since its secession from Malaysia in 1965. After training as a lawyer in England, where he was called to the bar, he returned to Singapore and became leader of the People's Action Party (PAP)—since 1968 the only official party.

LEE'S SUMMIT, city in W Mo., 18mi SE of Kansas City. It is an agricultural center and has a meat processing industry. Pop 16 230.

LEEUWENHOEK, Anton van (1632–1723), Dutch microscopist who made important observations of CAPILLARIES, red BLOOD corpuscles and SPERM cells, and who is best known for being the first to observe BACTERIA and PROTOZOA (1674–6), which he called "very little animalcules."

LEEWARD ISLANDS, chain of about 15 islands and many islets in the West Indies, northernmost group of the Lesser Antilles. They include Antigua and St. Kitts-Nevis-Anguilla (associated states of Britain); Montserrat and the British Virgin Islands (British colonies); St. Eustatius, Saba and S St. Martin (Dutch); Guadeloupe and dependencies (French); and the Virgin Islands of the US.

LEFT-HANDEDNESS. See HANDEDNESS.

LEG, in man, the lower limb, which is attached to the trunk at the PELVIS by the hip joint. Its major bones are the femur, passing from the hip to the knee, and the tibia and fibula, which pass from the knee to the ankle JOINT, where the leg articulates with the FOOT. The legs are concerned with maintenance of posture, walking, running and jumping. The powerful MUSCLES of the buttock, pelvis and thigh act about the hip and knee joints, while calf muscles act via the ACHILLES TENDON across the ankle on the foot.

LEGAL AID, free or subsidized professional legal help for those who need but cannot afford it. In the US, such help is provided through legal aid societies including charitable corporations and tax-supported bureaus, with salaried lawyers or volunteers from private practice. In the criminal courts, aid is provided by tax-supported defender offices known as public defenders.

LEGAL PROFESSION, body of people concerned with the interpretation and application of the law. The first law school in the US was started at Harvard U. in 1817. Students wishing to qualify as attorneys must usually complete at least two years of college, graduate from law school and pass a state bar examination. Since requirements vary from state to state, a lawyer may usually practice only in the state in which he qualified. There are different types of legal careers. Lawyers may enter private practice, where they will advise individuals or firms on matters ranging from criminal defense to divorce, income tax, wills, contracts, trusts, mortgages and claims for injury. Then there are law-firms that specialize in corporation law, and advise clients on such matters as labor laws, antitrust laws, tax laws and corporate organization and finance. Large corporations often possess their own legal department. State and federal governments employ lawyers as city attorneys, judges, prosecutors and in LEGAL AID organizations. Most lawyers belong to a professional legal association, the largest of which is the AMERICAN BAR ASSOCIATION. Many states have their own bar association. The other main branch of the legal profession is the bench. A JUDGE is a member of the bench just as a lawyer is a member of the bar. Judges serve at all levels from district and municipal courts to the Supreme Court. Federal judges are appointed by the president with the Senate's advice and consent and may only be removed by impeachment. State judges are elected and serve for a given number of years. The legal profession in England differs chiefly in retaining the official separation of barrister and solicitor. (See also JUDICIARY.)

LEGAL TENDER, currency which the law requires creditors to accept in payment of debts. Since 1933 all coins and currencies in the US, except those that have since been withdrawn, have been legal tender for all amounts.

LEGAL TENDER CASES, US Supreme Court cases which tested Congress' constitutional right to make US notes LEGAL TENDER. The ruling in *Hepburn v. Griswold* (1870) implied that greenbacks were not legal tender. This ruling was reversed in *Knox v. Lee* (1871) and *Juillard v. Greenman* (1884).

LEGATE, a papal ambassador. He may be one of

Frontal view of dissected leg. (1) Outer broad femoral muscle (*musculus vastus lateralis*); (2) straight femoral muscle (*musculus rectus femoris*); (3) tailor's muscle (*musculus sartorius*); (4) iliopsoas muscle (*musculus iliopsoas*); (5) pubic comb-like muscle (*musculus pectineus*); (6) nerves (yellow), artery (red) and veins (blue) of the femur (*nervus, arteria* and *vena femoralis*); (7) knee cap (*patella*); (8) long toe stretcher (*musculus extensor digitorum longus*); (9) anterior tibial muscle (*musculus tibialis anterior*); (10) superficial lower leg artery and nerve.

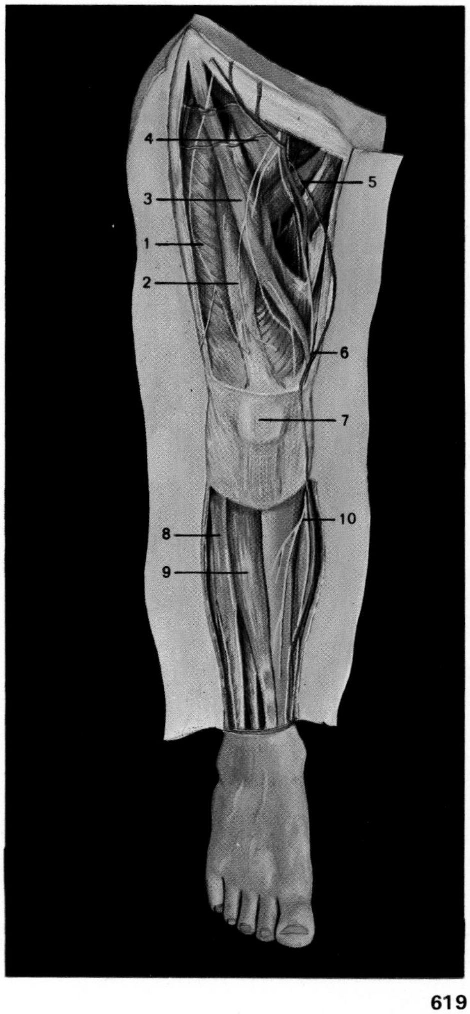

The Steppe lemming, pictured here in its summer coat, is found in most areas of the northern forests and tundras. During the winter it lives under the snow and its coat turns white.

three kinds: a *legatus a latere* who is appointed for a particular assignment, a NUNCIO who has the status of an ordinary ambassador from a secular state, and an Apostolic Delegate whose status is ecclesiastical only.

LEGENDRE, Adrien Marie (1752–1833), French mathematician best known for his work on elliptic integrals; for first publishing the method of LEAST SQUARES (1806); and for deriving the Legendre functions, which find many applications in physics.

LÉGER, Alexis Saint-Léger. See PERSE, SAINT-JOHN.

LÉGER, Fernand (1881–1955), French painter. A Cubist, he used strong colors and geometrical shapes and introduced such objects as cogwheels and pistons. His preoccupation with the machine age may be seen in such paintings as *The City* (1919). He designed huge murals for the UN in New York. (See also CUBISM).

LEGHORN (Italian: Livorno), city and port in N central Italy, on the Ligurian Sea. It is a major trading and manufacturing center. Industries include shipbuilding, chemicals, oil and metal refining, tools and electrical products. Pop 173 774.

LEGION, main fighting unit in the Roman army, of 3 000 to 6 000 men, divided into *cohorts* of about 500 men.

LEGION OF HONOR, a French order created by Napoleon Bonaparte in 1802 to reward distinguished service in military or civil life.

LEGISLATURE, representative assembly empowered to enact, revise or repeal the laws or statutes of a community. The earliest modern legislatures were the British Parliament and the French States-General, which were forerunners of the contemporary bicameral system of upper and lower houses. In the US the two chambers are the Senate and the House of Representatives which together are called Congress. In most bicameral systems both chambers must usually approve a bill before it becomes law. Under a parliamentary system, such as Britain's or Canada's, a government can only remain in power if it retains a majority in the main legislative chamber. Under the US system, the president stays in office for his term even if he lacks a majority in the legislature. (See CONGRESS OF THE US.)

LEGUME, or pod, multiseeded dry fruit that liberates its seeds by splitting along two margins, in for example the BEAN and PEA. (See also FOLLICLE.)

LEGUMINOUS PLANTS, general name for plants of the PEA family (Leguminosae) the fruit of which are called LEGUMES (pods). In terms of number of species, this family is second in size only to the COMPOSITAE. There are many economically important species including ACACIA, ALFALFA, BEAN, LENTIL, PEA and SOYBEAN. The roots of leguminous plants produce nodules containing nitrogen-fixing bacteria (see NITROGEN FIXATION; PULSES.)

LEHÁR, Franz (1870–1948), Hungarian composer famous for Viennese-style light opera. His most successful work was the melodious operetta *The Merry Widow* (1905).

LE HAVRE, seaport in N France, on the Seine estuary. Second only to Marseille as a French commercial port, it is also an industrial center with oil-refineries. Pop 207 100.

LEHIGH RIVER, river rising in NE Pa. and flowing about 100mi mainly SE to join the Delaware R at Easton. The Lehigh Valley is an important coal-mining and industrial region.

LEHMAN, Herbert Henry (1878–1963), US statesman. As Democratic governor of New York (1932–42) he supported widespread social legislation. Later he was director (1943–46) of the United Nations Relief and Rehabilitation Administration, and a leading liberal senator (1949–56) and opponent of Joseph MCCARTHY.

LEHMAN CAVES NATIONAL MONUMENT, 640 acres of limestone caverns in E Nev., established as a national monument in 1922.

LEIBNIZ, Gottfried Wilhelm von (1646–1716), German philosopher, historian, jurist, geologist and mathematician, codiscoverer of the CALCULUS and author of the theory of monads. His discovery of the calculus was independent of though later than that of NEWTON, yet it is the Leibnizian form which predominates today. He devised a calculating machine and a symbolic mathematical logic. By theologians he is remembered for his theodicy (analysis of the problem of evil) which, together with his philosophical speculations, helped mold the mind of the Enlightenment.

LEICESTER, city in central England, the county town of Leicestershire and site of Leicester U. Products include clothing and footwear. There are ruins of a Norman castle. Pop 283 549.

LEICESTER, Robert Dudley, Earl of (c1532–1588), favorite and one-time suitor of Elizabeth I of England. Although his political and military performances were poor and his reputation was marred by suspicions of treason, wife-murder and bigamy, he wielded great power and was made a privy councillor and army commander.

LEIDEN, or Leyden, city in the W Netherlands, at the confluence of the Old Rhine and New Rhine rivers. It has mixed industries among which textiles have been important since the 1300s and printing since the establishment (c1581) of the house of ELZEVIER. It is the home of Leiden U. Pop 100 135.

LEIF ERICSON. See ERICSON, LEIF.

LEIPZIG, city in S central East Germany, capital of Leipzig District. A major cultural, commercial and manufacturing center, it has fine medieval and renaissance architecture. Karl Marx U. (formerly Leipzig U.) is there. Pop 584 365.

LEISHMANIASIS, or **Kala-azar,** a chronic tropical DISEASE, particularly of the young, caused by protozoa and carried by sandflies; it causes FEVER, systemic disturbance, ANEMIA, enlargement of the SPLEEN and LIVER and susceptibility to infection. It also causes a chronic SKIN condition (oriental sore) with ulceration and crusting, which may also affect mucous membranes of the MOUTH, NOSE and PHARYNX. Specific treatment is with antimony compounds.

LEISLER, Jacob (1640–1691), German-born Protestant political leader who seized control of colonial New York in the confusion following the deposition (1688) of JAMES II of England. He was supported by those who feared invasion from Catholic French Canada. On arrival (1691) of the new authorized governor, Henry Slaughter, Leisler was forced to surrender and executed for treason.

LEITMOTIV (German: leading theme), recurring melodic phrase with extra-musical associations such as a particular idea or person, as in the operas of WAGNER. In a wider sense, the leitmotiv may refer to any musical phrase which is repeated and developed.

LELOIR, Luis Federico (1906–   ), Argentinian biochemist who won the 1970 Nobel Prize for Chemistry for his discovery of the existence and biological significance of the sugar NUCLEOTIDES.

LELY, Sir Peter (1618–1680), Dutch-English portrait painter, born Pieter van der Faes. He moved to England in 1641 and became court painter to Charles I and Charles II. His works include portrait series of court beauties and English admirals.

LEMAÎTRE, Georges Édouard (1894–1966), Belgian physicist who first proposed the "big bang" model of the universe, explaining the RED SHIFTS of the galaxies as due to recession (see DOPPLER EFFECT), thereby inferring that the universe is expanding. The theory holds that the origins of the universe lie in the explosion of a primeval atom, the "cosmic egg." (See also COSMOLOGY.)

LE MANS, city in NW France, capital of Sarthe dept. A market and manufacturing center, it is famous for its annual 24-hour automobile race. Pop 149 100.

LEMAY, Curtis Emerson (1906–   ), US airforce commander under whom the first atomic bombs were dropped on Japan in 1945. He was in charge of US planes in the 1948 airlift to besieged Berlin, and headed Strategic Air Command (1948–61).

LEMMA, in logic and particularly in mathematics, a subsidiary THEOREM either proved or assumed to be true during the proof of a more major theorem.

LEMMINGS, small rodents, 75–150mm (3–6in) long, closely related to voles. They are the characteristic rodents of the arctic tundra and are well adapted to severe conditions. Like many small mammals of simple ecological systems lemmings show periodic fluctuations in numbers with a periodicity of 3–4 years. These result in spectacular mass migrations whereby surplus animals in a high population area emigrate to find new ranges.

LEMNISCATE OF BERNOULLI. See CASSINI OVALS.

LEMNITZER, Lyman Louis (1899–   ), US army officer, Supreme Allied Commander of NATO (1963–69). He fought in the Korean War and became commander in chief of UN forces there (1955–57).

LEMON, *Citrus limon*, a small evergreen tree which produces the popular, sour, yellow fruits that are rich in VITAMIN C. The fruits also contain an oil that is used

In his study at the Kremlin, Vladimir Ilyich Lenin, architect of both the Russian Revolution and the Soviet state. Lenin was unsure even in 1917 that he would see any revolutionary change in Russia in his lifetime, but by the end of that year was effective dictator of the country.

The St. Nicholas Military-Naval Cathedral in Leningrad, one of the city's greatest Russian Baroque buildings, was designed by Chevakinsky in the mid-18th century.

in cooking and the manufacture of perfume. The US and Italy are the chief producers of lemon fruit. Family: Rutaceae.

LEMON GROVE, unincorporated urban community in S Cal., E of San Diego. It is a residential and agricultural area. Pop 19 690.

LEMONNIER, Pierre Charles (1715–1799), French astronomer best known for his lunar observations and for introducing to France more sophisticated British techniques and instruments.

LEMOYNE, Charles, Sieur de Longueuil (1628–1685), French Canadian colonial administrator who founded the city of Longueuil. He went to Canada in 1641 and was first of a famous French-Canadian family.

LEMURS, cat-sized primates found on Madagascar and small islands nearby, related to primitive ancestors of the whole primate group of monkeys and apes. They are nocturnal and strictly arboreal, feeding on insects, fruit, even small mammals. The family Lemuridae includes two subfamilies: the Cheirogaleinae or Mouse lemurs, and the Lemurinae, true lemurs.

LENARD, Philipp Eduard Anton (1862–1947), Hungarian-born German physicist awarded the 1905 Nobel Prize for Physics for his investigations of COSMIC RAYS, during which he showed that the ATOM is mainly empty space. He also made pioneering studies of the PHOTOELECTRIC EFFECT, showing that cathode rays are generated thereby.

LENA RIVER, river in the USSR, E Siberia. It rises in the Baikal Mts and flows NE and N for 2 653mi to a delta 250mi wide on the Laptev Sea. It is navigable for about 2 000mi from its mouth.

LENAU, Nikolaus (1802–1850), pseudonym of the Austrian poet Nikolaus Franz Niembsch von Strehlenau, a leading German-language Romantic poet. His work (e.g. *Faust*, 1836) displays a strong lyric gift and a profound sense of melancholy.

LENCLOS, Ninon de (Anne de Lanclos; 1620–1705), French courtesan. Noted for wit and beauty, she cultivated intellectual and artistic friends who included La Rochefoucauld and Molière.

LEND-LEASE, program by which the US sent aid to the Allies in WWII, during and after neutrality. President Roosevelt initiated the program in 1941 to help countries "resisting aggression." Total aid exceeded 50 billion dollars and not only bolstered Allied defense but developed the US war industries and helped mobilize public opinion.

L'ENFANT, Pierre Charles (1754–1825), French-American engineer and architect who fought in the Revolutionary War and was commissioned (1791) to plan Washington, D.C. Because of opposition his plans were shelved and L'Enfant was long dead when they were revived to become (1901) the basis for the development of the city. L'Enfant also designed Federal Hall in New York City.

LENGTH, in GEOMETRY, the first DIMENSION. The length of a straight LINE is given by the difference in the spatial coordinates of its end-points; it is customary to measure this distance along the line. The length of a CURVE is measured along it similarly, coordinates being determined by a moving TRIHEDRON. (For units of length see METRIC UNITS; SI UNITS; WEIGHTS AND MEASURES.)

LENIN, Vladimir Ilyich (1870–1924), Russian revolutionary, founder of the Bolshevik (later Communist) Party, leader of the Bolshevik Revolution of 1917 and founder of the Soviet state. Born Vladimir Ilyich Ulyanov, Lenin became a revolutionary after his elder brother was executed (1887) for participating in a plot to assassinate the tsar. By then a follower of Karl MARX, Lenin was exiled to Siberia (1887–90) for his activities and on his release he went to W Europe. In 1902 he published his famous pamphlet *What is to be Done?* arguing that only professional revolutionaries trained to lead a proletarian-peasant rising could bring Marxist socialism to Russia. Subsequent factional disputes between proponents of Lenin's BOLSHEVISM and the less radical MENSHEVIKS were interrupted only by the abortive Russian revolution of 1905, when Lenin and his fellow Marxists returned briefly to Russia. Lenin's confidence in the imminence of revolution was profoundly shaken by the rush of the socialist parties of Europe to support their own governments at the outbreak of WWI, and news of the 1917 RUSSIAN REVOLUTION, when it came, was sudden and unexpected. Lenin returned at once to Russia with German aid and within six months the Bolsheviks controlled the state. Against overwhelming odds, and at the massive cost of the German-Russian treaty of BREST-LITOVSK, Lenin maintained and consolidated power. The history of his remaining years is that of the birth of Soviet RUSSIA herself.

Lenin influenced COMMUNISM more than anyone else except Karl Marx. He adapted Marxist theory to the realities of Russia's backward economy but displayed his continuing hope of world-wide socialist revolution by founding the COMINTERN. Before his death from a series of strokes he warned against STALIN's growing ambition for power.

LENINGRAD, second largest city and chief port of the USSR, on the Gulf of Finland, capital of Leningrad Oblast and former Russian capital (as St. Petersburg 1712–1914, Petrograd 1914–18). Founded (1703) by Peter the Great and linked by its port with W Europe, it rapidly became a cultural and commercial center. Industrial expansion during the 19th century was followed by a temporary decline during WWI and the RUSSIAN REVOLUTION. The city was renamed for Lenin in 1924. There was great destruction and loss of life in the German siege (1941–44) during WWII, since when Leningrad has been restored and enlarged. Today industries include heavy engineering, shipbuilding, chemicals and textiles. The city has a university, outstanding libraries and art galleries, museums and palaces. Pop 3 950 000.

LENOIR, town in W N.C., seat of Caldwell Co. It is a summer resort in the Blue Ridge foothills, with furniture and textile industries. Pop 14 705.

LENOIR, Jean Joseph Étienne (1822–1900), Belgian-French inventor of the first practical INTERNAL COMBUSTION ENGINE (patented 1860). In 1862 he used it to power an automobile.

LE NÔTRE, André (1613–1700), French landscape architect who dominated European garden design for many years. His strictly geometrical creations, including the gardens of VERSAILLES, featured splendid vistas and radiating paths.

LENOX, town in W Mass., 7mi S of Pittsfield. A well-known resort, it boasts the Boston Symphony Orchestra (at Tanglewood) during summers. The Berkshire Music Festival is held there. Pop 5 804.

LENS, Optical, a piece of transparent material having at least one curved surface and which is used to focus light radiation in CAMERAS, GLASSES, MICROSCOPES, TELESCOPES and other optical instruments. The typical thin lens is formed from a glass

A series of photographs taken from the same spot but with lenses of increasing focal length, shown in millimetres.

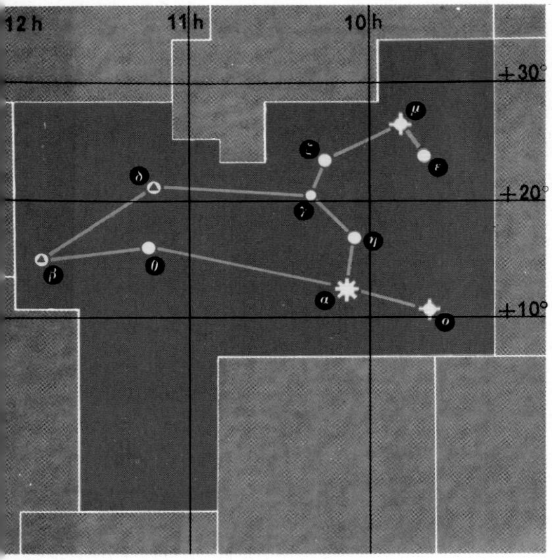

Leo (the Lion), a large bright constellation in the Northern Hemisphere of the sky, is the fifth sign of the zodiac.

disk, though crystalline minerals and molded plastics are also used and, as with spectacle lenses, shapes other than circular are quite common.

The principal axis of a lens is the imaginary perpendicular to its surface at its center. Lenses which are thicker in the middle than at the edges focus a parallel beam of light traveling along the principal axis at the principal focus, a point on the axis on the far side of the lens from the light source. Such lenses are converging lenses. The distance between the principal focus and the center of the lens is known as the focal length of the lens; its focal power is the reciprocal of its focal length and is expressed in dioptres (m^{-1}).

A lens thicker at its edges than in the middle spreads out a parallel beam of light passing through along its principal axis as if it were radiating from a virtual focus one focal length out from the lens center on the same side as the source. Such a lens is a diverging lens.

Lens surfaces may be either inward curving (concave), outward bulging (convex) or flat (plane) and it is the combination of the properties of the two surfaces which determines the focal power of the lens. In general, IMAGES of objects produced using single thin lenses suffer from various defects including spherical and chromatic aberration (see ABERRATION, OPTICAL), coma (in which peripheral images of points are distorted into pear-shaped spots) and astigmatism. The effects of these are minimized by designing compound lenses in which simple lenses of different shapes and refractive indexes (see REFRACTION) are combined. ACHROMATIC LENSES reduce chromatic aberration; aplanatic lenses reduce this and coma, and anastigmatic lenses combat astigmatism. (See also CONTACT LENS; LIGHT.)

LENT, period of 40 days dedicated by Christians to penitential prayer and FASTING as a preparation for EASTER. In the West it begins on ASH WEDNESDAY. (See CHURCH YEAR.)

LENTIL, *Lens culinaris,* a small LEGUMINOUS PLANT widely cultivated in warm climates for its protein-rich seeds, used to make soups. The foliage is used as a fodder crop. Family: Leguminosae.

LENZ'S LAW, of electromagnetic INDUCTION, states that the ELECTROMOTIVE FORCE (emf) induced in a circuit is such as to oppose the flux change giving rise to it.

LEO, name of 13 popes. **Leo I, Saint** (d. 461), called "the Great," reigned 440–461. He suppressed heresy and established his authority in both the West and the East. He persuaded the barbarian leaders ATTILA (in 452) and GENSERIC (in 455) not to destroy Rome. **Leo II, Saint** (d. 683), reigned 681–683. He condemned MONOTHELETISM. **Leo III, Saint** (d. 816), reigned 795–816. He crowned CHARLEMAGNE "Emperor of the Romans" in Rome on Christmas Day, 800, thus allying church and state. **Leo IV, Saint** (d. 855), reigned 847–855. He fortified Rome against Muslim attack, creating the so-called Leonine City. **Leo V** (d. 903), reigned July–Sept., 903. **Leo VI** (d. 928), reigned May–Dec., 928. **Leo VII** (d. 939), reigned 936–939. **Leo VIII** (d. 965), reigned 963–965. **Leo IX, Saint** (1002–1054) reigned 1049–54. He fought against SIMONY, and vigorously enjoined clerical celibacy. The GREAT SCHISM began in his reign. **Leo X** (1475–1521), reigned 1513–21. A MEDICI, he made Rome a center of the arts and literature, and raised money for rebuilding St. Peter's by the sale of indulgences—a practice attacked by Martin LUTHER at the start of the REFORMATION. **Leo XI** (1535–1605), reigned in April 1605. **Leo XII** (1760–1829), reigned 1823–29. A reactionary in domestic affairs, he recognized diocesan changes in newly independent nations of Latin America. **Leo XIII** (1810–1903), reigned 1878–1903. He worked to reconcile Roman Catholicism with science and liberalism, and generally applied Christian principles to the religious and social questions of his time. His famous encyclical *Rerum Novarum* (1891) on the condition of the working classes, strengthened Roman Catholicism's links with the working-class movement and helped counter ANTICLERICALISM at home and abroad.

LEO, name of six Byzantine emperors. **Leo I** (d. 474), reigned from 457. He sent an expedition against the VANDALS of N Africa which ended in disaster (468). His infant grandson **Leo II** survived him by a few months. **Leo III,** the Isaurian (c680–741) was elected emperor in 717, defeated the Arabs (718 and 740), reorganized imperial administration and initiated the ICONOCLASTIC CONTROVERSY. His grandson, **Leo IV** (749–780), ruled from 775. **Leo V,** the Armenian (d. 820), ruled from 813. **Leo VI,** the Wise (862?–912), ruled from 886 and codified Byzantine law.

LEO (the Lion), a constellation on the ECLIPTIC and fifth sign of the ZODIAC. It contains the bright star REGULUS (apparent magnitude +1.35). Leo gives its name to the annual Leonid METEOR shower.

LEO AFRICANUS (c1465–1550), latinized name of the Moorish traveler Al-Hassan ibn Muhammad. Returning from one of many journeys to Africa, he was captured by pirates and converted to Christianity by Pope Leo X. In Rome he wrote a *Description of Africa* (1526), long a major source of European knowledge of Islam and North Africa.

LEÓN, medieval kingdom of NW Spain, today a region which includes the provinces of León, Salamanca and Zamora. Forged in the 10th century by the rulers of ASTURIAS, the kingdom for a while spearheaded the Christian reconquest of Spain from the Moors. It was permanently joined to Castile in 1230.

LEÓN, municipality in central Mexico, 200mi NW of Mexico City. Founded in 1576, it is now a major commercial and industrial center. Pop 453 976.

LEÓN, Juan Ponce de. See PONCE DE LEÓN, JUAN.

LEONARDO DA VINCI (1452–1519), Italian RENAISSANCE painter, sculptor, architect, engineer and naturalist. Born in Vinci, Tuscany, the illegitimate son of a notary, he studied painting with VERROCCHIO in Florence. He worked at SFORZA's court in Milan as an architect, military engineer, inventor, theatrical designer, sculptor, musician, scientist, art theorist and painter. His *Last Supper* (c1495) was noted for its innovatory composition and variety of gesture. He said that painting should express the laws of light and space and of sciences like anatomy, botany and geology, and this he attempted in *Virgin of the Rocks* (c1506). He made thousands of sketches and notes on the causes of natural sciences; his growing sense of awe of the world is reflected in *Mona Lisa* (c1514). In Rome, 1513–16, he was preoccupied by the dynamic movement to be found in nature. He spent his last years at the French court of FRANCIS I, venerated as a genius.

LEONARDO OF PISA. See FIBONACCI, LEONARDO.

LEONCAVALLO, Ruggiero (1858–1919), Italian opera composer. He wrote many operas, of which only the melodramatic *I Pagliacci* (The Clowns, 1892) is now widely known.

LEONIDAS (d. 480 BC), king of Sparta who, with 300 Spartans and about 1 000 other Greeks died heroically defending the pass of THERMOPYLAE against the huge invading Persian army of XERXES.

LEONOV, Leonid Maksimovich (1899–   ), Russian novelist and dramatist who treats psychological and moral themes in a Soviet setting. His works include the novel *The Thief* (1927), and the play *Invasion* (1942).

LEONTIEF, Wassily (1906–   ), Russian-born US economist, who developed the techniques of INPUT-OUTPUT ANALYSIS. He came to New York in 1931 and subsequently worked at Harvard U. and New York U. In 1973 he won the Nobel Memorial Prize for Economics.

LEOPARD, *Panthera pardus,* a big cat similar to the JAGUAR, with a yellow coat marked with black rosettes. Found in a variety of habitats across Africa and Asia, they are agile cats which rely when hunting on their power to spring quickly. The leopard is well known for its habit of dragging its kill up into a tree out of the reach of jackals and hyenas. The kill may weigh more than the leopard itself.

LEOPARDI, Giacomo, Count (1798–1837), Italian poet and philosopher, one of the foremost writers of his time. Acutely unhappy almost all his life, he expressed himself most fully in his brilliant, supple, lyric poetry of which the major volume is *Songs* (1836). *Moral Essays* (1827) reveals his bleak philosophy.

LEOPARD PLANT, an attractive house plant of the genus *Ligularia* which produces rounded leaves variegated with golden-yellow to cream spots and yellow daisy-like flowers. It grows well at temperatures between 10°C and 21°C (50°F and 70°F), in a fairly light position, avoiding direct sun in summer. The soil should be kept evenly moist, avoiding extremes of wetness or dryness, and the foliage benefits from frequent misting. Propagation is achieved by dividing the plants, preferably in spring or summer. Family: COMPOSITAE.

LEOPARD SEAL, *Hydrurga leptonyx,* a large penguin-eating seal found around the fringes of the Antarctic ice pack.

LEOPOLD, name of two Holy Roman emperors. **Leopold I** (1640–1705), emperor from 1658, was also king of Hungary from 1655, and of Bohemia from 1656. A Hapsburg, he was involved for most of his reign in wars with France and Turkey which left Austria considerably strengthened. (See AUGSBURG, WAR OF THE LEAGUE OF; SPANISH SUCCESSION, WAR OF THE.) **Leopold II** (1747–1792), emperor from 1790, was king of Bohemia and Hungary from 1790, and grand duke of Tuscany 1765–90. A reformist at home, he reacted to revolutionary France by pledging (1791) his support for the monarchy.

LEOPOLD, name of three kings of Belgium. **Leopold I** (1790–1865), a Saxe-Coburg, was elected king by the Belgians in June 1831. He did much to create national unity and carried out some reforms. He was the uncle of England's Queen Victoria. **Leopold II** (1835–1909), his son, reigned from 1865. He promoted exploration in Africa and in 1885 established the Congo Free State (see ZAÏRE), which he exploited for personal gain until it was taken over by the Belgian government in 1908. There was great commercial and industrial growth in Belgium during his reign. **Leopold III** (1901–   ), reigned 1934–51. He lost popularity by ordering surrender to the Nazis in 1940, and was compelled to abdicate in favor of his son BAUDOUIN I.

LEOPOLDVILLE. See KINSHASA.

LEPANTO, Battle of, Christian naval victory over the Muslim Turks, Oct. 7, 1571. JOHN OF AUSTRIA led combined Spanish, Venetian and papal fleets which crushed the Turkish fleet in the Gulf of Patras near Lepanto, Greece. The battle somewhat moderated the power of the OTTOMAN EMPIRE.

LEPIDOPTERA, the insect order that includes the BUTTERFLIES and MOTHS. Their bodies and wings are covered with minute scales of chitin often pigmented to produce the colors and patterns characteristic of these insects. The mouthparts of the adults are formed into a *proboscis,* a tube for sucking up liquid such as the NECTAR from flowers. The life history includes the egg, a LARVA OR CATERPILLAR, a PUPA OR CHRYSALIS and the usually winged adult. The caterpillar is totally different in structure and habit from the adult, feeding with chewing mouthparts on a variety of vegetable materials, completely separated ecologically from the adult. Caterpillars feed voraciously and those of many species are agricultural pests. In the chrysalis, a resting stage, the structure of the adult insect is organized (see METAMORPHOSIS).

LEPIDUS, Marcus Aemilius (d. 13 BC), Roman politician who supported Julius CAESAR against POMPEY and was consul in 46 BC. He joined Mark Antony and Octavian (later AUGUSTUS in the Second TRIUMVIRATE in 43 BC, but was forced into obscurity (36 BC) after trying to topple Octavian.

LEPRECHAUN, in Irish folklore, mischievous fairy usually depicted as a little old man. Traditionally each leprechaun has buried a crock (pot) of gold which it can be forced to reveal.

LEPROSY, or **Hansen's disease**, chronic disease caused by a mycobacterium and virtually restricted to tropical zones. It leads to SKIN nodules with loss of pigmentation, mucous membrane lesions in NOSE and PHARYNX, and NEURITIS with nerve thickening, loss of pain sensation and patchy weakness, often involving FACE and intrinsic HAND muscles. Diagnosis is by demonstrating the organisms in stained scrapings or by skin or nerve BIOPSY. The type of disease caused depends on the number of bacteria encountered and basic resistance to the disease. Treatment is with sulfones (Dapsone).

LEPTIS MAGNA, ancient seaport in North Africa, in what is now NW Libya. Settled by Carthage in the 6th century BC, it became a Roman colony c100 AD. It has notable ruins of Roman Africa.

LEPTON. See SUBATOMIC PARTICLES.

LERMONTOV, Mikhail Yurevich (1814–1841), Russian poet and novelist. Initially influenced by BYRON, he wrote outstandingly fine lyric and narrative poetry. His prose masterpiece is the novel *A Hero of our Time* (1840), an early example of psychological realism. He died in a duel.

LERNER, Alan Jay (1918–   ), US playwright and lyricist. With Frederick LOEWE he created such famous musicals as *Brigadoon* (1947), *Paint Your Wagon* (1951) and *My Fair Lady* (1956).

LE SAGE, Alain René (1668–1747), French novelist and dramatist. His picaresque masterpiece *Gil Blas* (1715–35) greatly influenced the development of the realistic novel in France. It is a witty satirical account of all levels of French society.

LESBIANISM. See HOMOSEXUALITY.

LESBOS, or Mytilene, Greek island in the E Aegean Sea, about 10mi from the coast of Turkey. Some 630sq mi in area, it is fertile, forested and mountainous, and produces olives, wheat, grapes and citrus fruits. Its capital and chief port is Mytilene. Lesbos was the home of the poets SAPPHO and ALCAEUS. Pop 86 337.

LESKOV, Nikolai Semyonovich (1831–1895), Russian novelist and short story writer. A master of narrative, he drew on his own varied experience of Russian life to write such stories as the famous *Lady Macbeth of the Mzinsk District* (1865).

LESOTHO (formerly Basutoland), landlocked kingdom in S Africa. It is a black African nation surrounded by, and economically dependent on, the white supremacist Republic of South Africa. Part of the great plateau of S Africa, Lesotho lies mainly between 8 000ft and 11 000ft. In the E and N is the Drakensberg mountain range. The chief rivers are the Orange R and its tributaries. Annual rainfall averages under 30in and temperatures vary seasonally from 93°F to 30°F. Sparsely forested, Lesotho is mainly dry grassland, often severely eroded. The Basuto are chiefly rural. Education is mainly in the hands of missionaries; there is a literacy rate of about 50% and some 70% are Christian. An agricultural country, Lesotho is heavily dependent on livestock and food crops such as wheat and maize. The sole mineral resource is diamonds. Over 10% of the population work in the mines of South Africa. The nation was established c1820 by Chief Moshesh, who secured British protection from Boer encroachment. As Basutoland, it was under British rule from 1884, gaining independence in 1966.

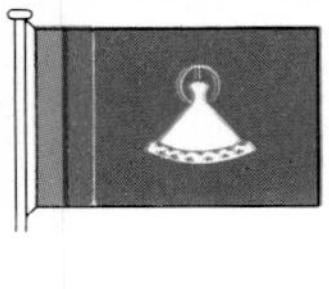

Official name: Kingdom of Lesotho
Capital: Maseru
Area: 11 716sq mi
Population: 1 043 000
Languages: Sesotho, English
Religions: Christian
Monetary unit(s): 1 Rand = 100 cents

LESPEDEZA, genus of LEGUMINOUS PLANTS grown for forage and green manure, chiefly in the US. Some are cultivated as garden plants. They are native to E Asia and North America. Family: Leguminosae.

LESSEPS, Ferdinand Marie, Vicomte de (1805–1894), French diplomat whose idea for a canal to cross the isthmus of Suez resulted in the SUEZ CANAL. Lesseps supervised the building of it (1859–69) himself. His later plans for a Panama canal failed.

LESSING, Gotthold Ephraim (1729–1781), German playwright, critic and philosopher, founder of a new national literature. He rejected French classicism and pioneered German bourgeois tragedy with *Miss Sara Sampson* (1755). He also wrote the influential comedy *Minna von Barnhelm* (1767), the prose tragedy *Emilia Galotti* (1772) and the dramatic poem *Nathan the Wise* (1779). The treatise *Laokoön* (1766) critically contrasted the natures of poetry and painting.

LE SUEUR, Pierre Charles (c1657–1705), French trader and explorer of North America, who traveled the Mississippi and Minnesota rivers and the shores of Lake Superior. He went to Canada about 1679 as an Indian trader.

LETHAL CHAMBER. See GAS CHAMBER.

LETHBRIDGE, city in Canada, S Alberta, 110mi SSE of Calgary. A center of trading and mixed industry, it is also the home of Lethbridge U. Pop 41 217.

LETHE, in Greek and Roman mythology, the river of oblivion from which the dead drank before they entered HADES.

LETTER OF CREDIT, document used in international trade to assure an exporter that he will be paid for his goods. The importer's bank arranges a letter of credit (guaranteeing payment) with a bank in this country where he is buying goods. The same system allows travelers abroad to draw sums of money guaranteed by their own banks.

LETTER OF MARQUE, government commission authorizing a shipowner to use his vessel as a private warship or PRIVATEER.

LETTISH, or Latvian, language spoken by some 2 000 000 people, chiefly in LATVIA. One of the Baltic groups of Indo-European languages, Lettish preserves many archaic features, and has changed little since books were first printed in it in the 16th century.

LETTRE DE CACHET, in pre-Revolutionary France, a command sent under the king's seal (*cachet*). *Lettres de cachets* were often used as warrants to public officers and even private persons, authorizing the arrest and imprisonment of individuals. The system led to many abuses.

LETTUCE, *Lactuca sativa*, popular salad plant that has been cultivated since the times of ancient Greece. There are a number of types in cultivation including asparagus forms with narrow leaves and a succulent stem, head or cabbage forms with compact heads, cos forms with an oblong loose head and leaf or curled forms with oak-leaf-shaped leaves. Family: COMPOSITAE.

LEUCIPPUS (5th century BC), Greek philosopher who, according to ARISTOTLE, originated the theory that matter is made up of indivisible, infinitely small atoms (see ATOMISM). His pupil DEMOCRITUS further developed the theory.

Leptis Magna, birthplace of the Roman emperor Septimus Severus, flourished as a major city and seaport in Roman Africa during his reign (193–211). He was responsible for the construction of many of the public buildings of this time, among them the magnificent basilica pictured here, completed in 216 by his son Caracalla.

LEUCTRA, Battle of, battle in 371 BC that made Thebes supreme in Greece. The Thebans under EPAMINONDAS crushed the numerically superior Spartans by using brilliant innovatory tactics.

LEUKEMIA, malignant proliferation of white blood cells in BLOOD OF BONE MARROW. It may be divided into acute and chronic forms for both granulocytes and lymphocytes. In acute forms, primitive cells predominate and progression is rapid with ANEMIA, bruising and infection. Acute lymphocytic leukemia is commonest in young children. Chronic forms present in adult life with mild systemic symptoms, susceptibility to infection and enlarged LYMPH nodes (lymphatic) or SPLEEN and LIVER (granulocytic). Cancer CHEMOTHERAPY and ANTIBIOTICS have greatly improved survival prospects.

LEUKOCYTES. See BLOOD.

LEUTZE, Emanuel (1816–1868), US historical painter. His large-scale, patriotic works include *Westward the Course of Empire Takes its Way* and *Washington Crossing the Delaware.*

LEVANT, the E Mediterranean countries, from Turkey to Egypt (inclusive), so named from the French *lever* (to rise), Levant implying lands of the sunrise, that is, of the east.

LEVEE. See FLOODS AND FLOOD CONTROL.

LEVEL, or **spirit level**, device used to determine whether a surface is level or not. Usually it is a glass tube, curved upward at the center, almost filled with alcohol or ether, leaving a bubble of vapor. This bubble floats to the highest point of the tube which is, when the level is on a perfectly horizontal surface, the center.

LEVELLAND, city in NW Texas, seat of Hockley Co. It refines petroleum and handles and processes cotton, fruit, grain and vegetables. Pop 11 445.

LEVELLERS, radical reformers of the English Civil War and Commonwealth period. Their leader, John LILBURNE, advocated a republic, economic reforms and political and religious equality. Oliver Cromwell, to whom they were bitterly opposed, broke their power.

LEVER, the simplest MACHINE, a rigid beam pivoted at a *fulcrum* so that an *effort* acting at one point of the beam may be used to shift a *load* acting at another point on the beam. There are three classes of lever: those with the fulcrum between the effort and the load; those with the load between the fulcrum and the effort, and those with the effort between the fulcrum and the load. The part of the beam between the load and the fulcrum is the load arm; that between the effort and the fulcrum, the effort arm. The effort multiplied by the length of the effort arm equals the load multiplied by the length of the load arm: a load of 50kg, 5m from the fulcrum, may be moved by any effort 10m from the fulcrum greater than 25kg (the longer the effort arm, the less effort required). Load divided by effort gives the mechanical advantage; in this case 2. A first-class lever (e.g., a crowbar) has a mechanical advantage greater, less than or equal to 1; a second-class (e.g., a wheelbarrow), always more than 1; a third-class (e.g., the human arm), always less than 1. (See also ARCHIMEDES; MECHANICS; MOMENT.)

LEVERRIER, Urbain Jean Joseph (1811–1877), French astronomer whose calculations enabled **Johann Gottfried Galle** (1812–1910) to discover the planet NEPTUNE (1846). (See also ADAMS, J. C.)

LEVIATHAN, in the Bible, the name of a primordial monster, or, as in the Book of Job, a sea monster, perhaps a whale. The name is commonly used for anything massive, particularly ships. It was used by HOBBES as an allegorical title for the state.

LEVINE, Jack (1915–), US satirical painter. Believing that art must have some social significance, he rejects abstract art in favor of a satirically distorted socialist realism seen in such works as *Feast of Pure Reason* (1937), *Welcome Home* (1946) and *Gangster Funeral* (1953).

LÉVIS, city in SE Quebec, Canada, on the St. Lawrence R opposite Quebec. Its economy rests on port facilities and lumber shipping. Pop 16 597.

LÉVIS, François Gaston, Duc de (1720–1787), French military commander of Canada. He defeated the British at Ste-Foy in April, 1760, and besieged Quebec. The arrival of British reinforcements forced him to surrender in September, 1760. He returned to Europe and was made a marshal of France in 1783 and Duc in 1784.

LÉVI-STRAUSS, Claude (1908–), Belgian-born French social anthropologist, best known for his advocacy of *structuralism*, an analytical system whereby different cultural patterns may be related such that the universal logical substructure underlying them may be elicited.

LEVITES, in ancient Israel, the tribe descended from Levi, son of Jacob. As priestly auxiliaries the care of the Ark and the Sanctuary was their special responsibility, and in Jerusalem they had hereditary duties at the Temple and were later teachers of the Law.

LEVITICUS, in the Old Testament, third of the five books of the PENTATEUCH. It is essentially a collection of liturgical and ceremonial laws.

LEVITTOWN, village on Long Island in SE N.Y., 10mi E of New York City. A planned residential community for WWII veterans, it has no industry. Pop 65 440.

LEWIN, Kurt (1890–1947), Prussian-born US psychologist, an early member of the GESTALT PSYCHOLOGY school, best known for his development of the concept of GROUP dynamics, especially field theory.

LEWIS, Cecil Day (1904–1972), English poet and critic, POET LAUREATE from 1968. *The Magnetic Mountain* (1933) is his best known work from the 1930s, but his style matured fully after 1945. He wrote novels under his own name and detective novels as "Nicholas Blake."

LEWIS, C.S. (Clive Staples Lewis; 1898–1963), British author, literary scholar and Christian apologist. Of more than 40 books his best-known is *The Screwtape Letters* (1942), a diabolical view of humanity. *The Allegory of Love* (1936), his major critical work, was a study of love in medieval literature. He also wrote a well-known science-fiction trilogy and the *Narnia* fantasies for children.

LEWIS, Gilbert Newton (1875–1946), US chemist who suggested that covalent bonding consisted of the sharing of valence-electron pairs. His theory of ACIDS and bases involved seeing acids (Lewis acids) as substances which are able to accept electron pairs from bases which are electron-pair donating species (Lewis bases). In 1933, Lewis became the first to prepare HEAVY WATER (D_2O).

LEWIS, Isaac Newton (1859–1931), US inventor of the Lewis MACHINE GUN (patented 1911), which could fire 600 rounds per minute and had the advantage of being light. Because of its low recoil it was much used as an airplane armament.

LEWIS, John Llewellyn (1880–1969), colorful US labor leader, president of the United Mine Workers of America 1920–60. He organized the Congress of Industrial Organizations in 1935 as a rival to the AMERICAN FEDERATION OF LABOR, beginning a bitter rivalry; he resigned as president of CIO in 1940.

LEWIS, Matthew Gregory, "Monk" (1775–1818), English poet, dramatist and novelist, best known for the Gothic romance *Ambrosio, or The Monk* (1796), which blended natural and supernatural horror with perverse sexuality. A member of Parliament 1796–1802, he sought humanitarian reforms of slavery in the West Indies.

LEWIS, Meriwether (1774–1809), American explorer and commander of the LEWIS AND CLARK EXPEDITION, which penetrated to the NW Pacific coast 1804–06. In 1808 he became governor of the Louisiana Territory, but was badly affected by the pressures of the post. En route for Washington, he was found dead at a lonely inn in Tenn., either by murder or suicide.

LEWIS, Sinclair (1885–1951), US novelist, best known for five novels satirizing small-town life in the Middle West, an environment in which he himself grew up and only escaped from at college. *Main Street* (1920) was his first major success. *Babbitt* (1922), a satire on the provincial small businessman, is perhaps his best-known book. He refused a Pulitzer Prize for *Arrowsmith* (1925); it was followed by *Elmer Gantry* (1927) and *Dodsworth* (1929). In 1930 he became the first American to win the Nobel Prize for Literature, but his work declined thereafter.

LEWIS, Wyndham (1882–1957), controversial English painter, critic and writer, the founder of VORTICISM. He is best known for his savage satirical novel *The Apes of God* (1930).

LEWIS AND CLARK EXPEDITION, first overland American expedition to the NW Pacific coast under the command of Meriwether LEWIS and William CLARK, with Sacagawea, the Indian wife of an expedition member, acting as interpreter and guide. Setting out from St. Louis in May, 1804, the expedition pushed westwards through the Rockies, reaching the Pacific Ocean at the mouth of the Columbia R in Nov., 1805. They returned to St. Louis in Sept., 1806.

The expedition was despatched by President Jefferson to explore the newly-purchased Louisiana Territory which expanded America's borders to the Continental Divide. It caught the popular imagination and played a major part in establishing the view that it was the "Manifest Destiny" of the US to expand to the Pacific Ocean.

LEWISTON, city in NW Ida., seat of Nez Perce Co. Originally a mining town, its economy is now based on agriculture and the timber industry. Pop 26 068.

LEWISTON, city on the Androscoggin R in SW Me. A major textile center drawing power from two hydroelectric dams, it has acquired other industries, largely since 1957. Pop 41 779.

LEWISTOWN, borough in central Pa., seat of Mifflin Co. Originally an iron-manufacturing center, its economy now rests on mining, dairy agriculture and various manufactures. Pop 11 098.

LEXINGTON, city in N central Ky., seat of Fayette Co. A horse-breeding and tobacco center, it is a market and manufacturing town in a rich agricultural area. It is the site of the historic Transylvania U. Pop 108 137.

LEXINGTON, town in E Mass., a residential suburb of Boston. Settled in 1640, it was the site of the first engagement of the American Revolution (see LEXINGTON, BATTLE OF). Pop 31 886.

LEXINGTON, city in central N.C., seat of Davidson Co. In an agricultural area, it has a range of light manufactures. Pop 17 205.

LEXINGTON, Battle of, first engagement of the American REVOLUTIONARY WAR on April 19, 1775. A force of around 700 British troops marching to destroy illegal military stores at Concord, Mass., were met at Lexington by 70 MINUTEMEN. These obeyed an order to disperse, but one fired a shot which was returned by a volley, killing eight Americans and wounding ten. The British marched on unopposed, but were turned back at the battle of CONCORD.

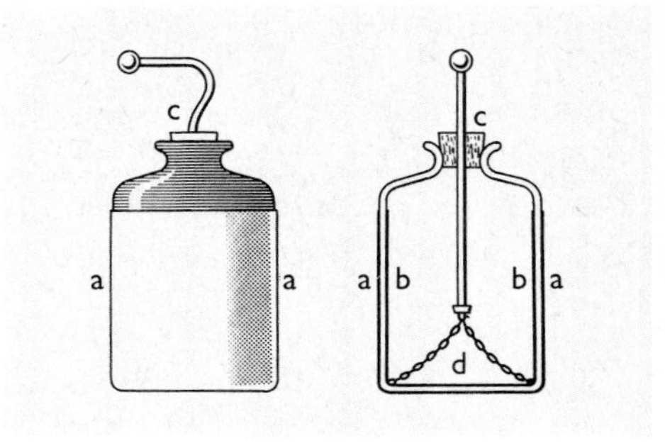

A Leyden jar, with outside layer of foil (a), inside layer (b), insulating cap and brass rod (c), and chain connecting rod with inner surface of jar (d). When the rod is connected to a source of electricity, it charges the inner layer of foil, which in turn induces an opposite charge in the outer layer. Connecting the two layers then creates a spark.

LEYDEN JAR, the simplest and earliest form of CAPACITOR, a device for storing electric charge. It comprises a glass jar coated inside and outside with unconnected metal foils, and a conducting rod which passes through the jar's insulated stopper to connect with the inner foil. The jar is usually charged from an ELECTROSTATIC GENERATOR. The device is now little used outside the classroom.

LEYTE, fertile mountainous island in the Philippines, scene of a major landing by US forces in the WWII Philippines campaign. In area it is 2 785sq mi, rising to a maximum height of 4 400ft; the coastal areas are largely plains. The economy rests on rice and corn and various cash crops, although manganese deposits are also exploited.

LEYTE GULF, Battle of, a major air-sea battle off Leyte Island in the Philippines on Oct. 25–26, 1944, in which the Japanese were decisively defeated in an attempt to decoy the US 3rd Fleet N and attack the landing on Leyte it was protecting.

LHASA, former capital of Tibet, now capital of the Tibetan Autonomous Region of China. Western visitors were discouraged before the 20th century, and Lhasa became known as the "Forbidden City." Centered around a massive Buddhist temple, it is dominated by the Potala, former citadel of the DALAI LAMA, on a 400ft hillside above the city. It was a trading center before it was occupied by the communist Chinese in 1951. Most of the former inhabitants have been resettled and the population is now substantially Chinese. Pop 175 000.

LHASA APSO, small Tibetan breed of long-haired dog. Standing up to 10in high at the shoulder, it has a long, fine coat in colors varying from white through yellow and brown shades to gray and black.

LIADOV, Anatol Konstantinovich (1855–1914), minor Russian composer, best known for his delicate and graceful piano works. His orchestral works are fewer; the most famous are the symphonic poems *Eight Russian Folk Songs* and *Kikimora* (after 1900, based on material for an unfinished opera).

LIANA, *Bignonia unguis-cati*, a woody vine native to the tropical rain forests of Middle and South America, where they grow to the tops of trees to form a dense canopy. The stems are used locally to make ropes. Family: Bignoniaceae.

LIAQUAT ALI KHAN. See ALI KHAN, LIAQUAT.

LIARD RIVER, rises in SE Yukon, NW Canada, and flows 755mi SE and NE to join the Mackenzie R at Fort Simpson in the Northwest Territories.

LIBBY, Willard Frank (1908–), US chemist awarded the 1960 Nobel Prize for Chemistry for discovering the technique of RADIOCARBON DATING (1947).

LIBBY PRISON, notorious Confederate prison for Union officers in Richmond, Va., 1863–64. A converted warehouse, it lacked heat, ventilation and sufficient sanitation. Up to 1 200 prisoners were confined there, and when food supplies became inadequate many died in the bad conditions.

LIBEL, a false and malicious statement in writing or other durable form (such as on film), tending to injure the reputation of a living person, or, in criminal libel, blacken the memory of the dead. It is not enough in defense to prove that the statement was true; it must have been made from good motives also, without malice. An alternative defense is that the statement was made in a privileged situation, being a situation in which it is held to be socially desirable that a frank statement be made.

LIBERAL, city in SW Kan., seat of Seward Co. In an agricultural area, it also has many oil and natural gas fields about it. Pop 13 489.

LIBERAL ARTS, term now applied to college curriculums covering such subjects as languages, philosophy, history, literature and pure science, when these are studied as the basis of a general or liberal education, and not as professional or vocational skills. (See also SEVEN LIBERAL ARTS.)

LIBERALISM, a political philosophy that stresses individual liberty, freedom and equality of opportunity. Liberalism tends to place its faith in progress. Classical liberalism developed in Europe in the 18th century, characterized by a rational critique of traditional institutions and a distrust of state power over individuals and interference in the economy (see LAISSEZ-FAIRE). Modern liberalism accepts state interference in the economy, but is still very concerned with social issues such as civil rights and equality of opportunity. In the US, although not many call themselves outright liberals, a degree of liberalism has been the dominant creed of both major political parties.

LIBERAL PARTY, British, a political party, powerful from about 1832 to 1922. With its origins in the traditional Whig Party, the Liberal Party was associated with such policies as free trade, LAISSEZ-FAIRE economics, religious liberty and anti-imperialism. Under great leaders like GLADSTONE, ASQUITH and LLOYD GEORGE, the Liberal Party enjoyed a golden age, but it was unable to adjust to the rise of socialism, and was replaced in the 1920s by the Labour Party as the chief opposition to the Conservative Party. Where no party has a clear majority, however, the Liberals could still hold the balance of power.

LIBERAL PARTY, Canadian, dating from Confederation (1857), it has been one of the two main political parties ever since. It has always been a party of the center, but has been more sympathetic to French minority interests than the Conservatives. In April, 1968, Pierre TRUDEAU became leader of the Liberal Party and prime minister of Canada, succeeding Lester B. PEARSON.

LIBERAL PARTY, New York, minor US political party in N.Y., founded in 1944. The party has put up its own candidates in state elections, but has generally supported the Democrats in presidential elections.

LIBERAL REPUBLICAN PARTY, a party formed during the administration of President U. S. GRANT, seeking reconciliation with the South and action against corruption in government and public service. In 1872 the Liberal Republicans nominated Horace GREELEY for president, but when he was soundly defeated the party effectively broke up.

LIBERIA, oldest black republic in Africa. It lies on the W coast, and has a land area only slightly larger than that of Ohio. Beyond a narrow coastal plain it consists of tropical rain forests, with mountainous plateaus in the interior. The climate is hot and humid, with an average temperature of 80°F, and up to 150in of rain a year.

People. Liberia was founded by US philanthropists who created the state early in the 19th century as a home for freed American slaves. Today the country is dominated by the descendants of these slaves, who are Christian, English speaking and generally live in the coastal urban areas. However, indigenous Africans, practising animist religions and speaking tribal languages, make up 90% of the population. Most of these are poor subsistence farmers, and almost all are illiterate; only 10% of school age children are enrolled. The capital, Monrovia, is located on the coast.

Economy. The Liberian economy is still under-

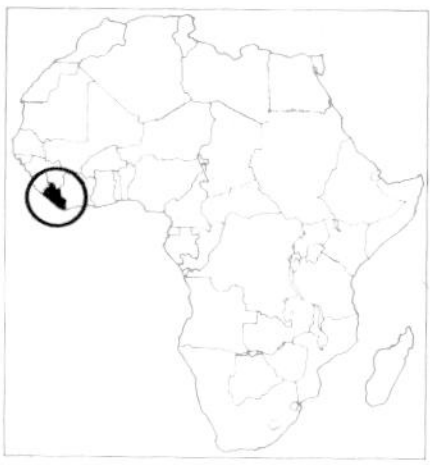

Official name: Republic of Liberia
Capital: Monrovia
Area: 43 700sq mi
Population: 1 571 000
Languages: English; tribal
Religions: Protestant, Roman Catholic; Muslim; Animist
Monetary unit(s): 1 Liberian dollar = 100 cents

developed. Its main industries are rubber plantations, established in the 1920s, and the mining of iron ore, dating from the 1950s. Both of these have been run and maintained by US firms. Apart from iron ore and rubber, Liberia exports several crops including coffee, sugarcane, bananas and cocoa. Valuable foreign-exchange is also earned by registering foreign ships under extremely lax rules; this practice has made the Liberian merchant navy appear to be one of the world's largest.

History. The first repatriated slaves arrived from the US in 1822 under the aegis of the AMERICAN COLONIZATION SOCIETY. In 1847 independence was declared, and since then the Americo-Liberians (the descendants of the repatriated slaves) have dominated the country. Indeed, in 1931 a League of Nations investigation confirmed charges that slave trading was being carried on in Liberia with the knowledge of the government. Since 1877 the True Whig party has won every election, especially under President W. V. S. TUBMAN (1944–71). On his death in 1971 W. R. Tolbert became president, promising many reforms which have had little or no effect so far.

LIBERTY, city in NW Mo., NE of Kansas City, seat of Clay Co. It is the trading center of an agricultural area. Pop 13 704.

The Statue of Liberty, facing the main entrance channel of New York Harbor, has for over a century symbolized the hopes of the New World and extended a welcome to millions of immigrants who have landed at New York.

LIBERTY, Statue of, or in full, *Liberty Enlightening the World*, a 300ft bronze female figure on Liberty Island in New York Harbor. The statue, designed by Frédéric BARTHOLDI, was given to the US by France on the 100th anniversary of US independence.

LIBERTY BELL, famous American bell housed in Independence Hall, Philadelphia. It was cast in London and arrived in America in 1752. It rang on many historic occasions, including the announcement of the Declaration of Independence on July 8, 1776; having been twice recast, it reputedly cracked while tolling for the funeral of Chief Justice John Marshall in 1835.

LIBERTY ISLAND, in New York Harbor, island on which the Statue of Liberty stands. Formerly called Bedloe's Island, it has an area of about 11 acres.

LIBERTY LEAGUE, a political organization active 1934–40, made up of conservative Republicans and Democrats. It opposed Roosevelt's NEW DEAL policies, but lost influence after his reelection in 1936.

LIBERTY PARTY, antislavery political party founded in 1839 by J. G. BIRNEY and other abolitionists. In 1840 and 1844 it put up presidential candidates, but in 1848 the party united with other groups to form the FREE SOIL PARTY.

LIBERTYVILLE, village in NE Ill., with some light industry. Pop 11 684.

LIBIDO, originally and still popularly, the sexuality or general SEX drive of the individual. In PSYCHOANALYSIS, following FREUD, the libido, with its source in the ID, is a type of mental energy (though it may, as in sexuality, generate physiological energy or activity) responsible for all human constructive action.

LIBRA (the Scales), an average size constellation on the ECLIPTIC, the seventh sign of the ZODIAC.

LIBRARY. The earliest libraries were kept by the ancient peoples of Mesopotamia; inscribed clay tablets have been found going back to about 3500 BC.

The Library of Congress in Washington is now the largest library in the world, with one of the most important research collections. The main building, seen here with its elegant facade, dates from 1897. Additional space is afforded by an annex and twelve other buildings.

The Liberty Bell was moved from the bell tower into the main building of Independence Hall, Philadelphia, after a crack appeared. During the Bicentennial celebrations in July 1976, Queen Elizabeth II of Great Britain presented the city with a new bell, cast in the same foundry as the original.

The most famous library of the ancient world was begun at Alexandria by Ptolemy I Soter (305–283 BC) and destroyed in various fires. The Roman Empire had many libraries, but during the Dark Ages the Church alone kept the library tradition alive in Europe. The Renaissance saw the formation of many new libraries such as the Vatican Library (1447), and the growth of libraries was further stimulated by the invention of printing in the 15th century. The Bodleian Library, Oxford, dates from 1602, but it was the 18th century that saw the formation of many of the great national libraries: the British Museum Library (1753), Italy's National Central Library at Florence (1741), and Russia's Saltykov-Shchedrin Library in Leningrad.

The United States. The oldest library in the USA originated in the 320 books bequeathed by John HARVARD (1638), Harvard U.'s chief benefactor. The present LIBRARY OF CONGRESS originated in 1815 in a purchase of JEFFERSON's personal library by Congress. The first tax-supported public library was established in New Hampshire in 1833. The American Library Association was founded in 1876. An important figure in library history is Melvil DEWEY whose decimal classification system has now been adopted in many countries. In the late 19th century great industrialists such as Andrew CARNEGIE were often benefactors of libraries. In the 20th century the public library system has been extended and consolidated. There are many types of libraries, ranging from the great university research libraries to school libraries, business libraries and area public libraries. (See also INFORMATION RETRIEVAL.)

LIBRARY OF CONGRESS, national library of the US, located to the E of the Capitol in Washington, D.C. Originally established by Congress in 1800, and re-established 1815 after destruction in the WAR OF 1812, it now contains more than 58 million items, including over 14 million books and pamphlets. Since 1870 the library has been entitled to two free copies of all material copyrighted in the US. The library's catalog, the National Union Catalog, lists books in libraries all over the US and Canada.

LIBRATION. See MOON.

LIBRETTO, term for the text of an opera or oratorio, from the Italian for "small books." Among prominent librettists have been METASTASIO, DA PONTE, HOFMANNSTHAL and AUDEN. A few composers, such as WAGNER and BERLIOZ, wrote their own librettos.

LIBREVILLE, capital city of Gabon at the mouth of the Galou R on the W coast of Africa. A port city, it exports timber, cacao and palm oil; its economy rests on timber and fishing, and a small tourist industry. Pop 55 000.

LIBYA, independent republic in North Africa, a historic state once an important part of the Roman empire. Most of the country is in the Sahara Desert, although there is a fertile strip along the Mediterranean coast, with an average rainfall of 10in and a warm Mediterranean climate.

People. The population is predominantly Arab, but there are many Berbers of Hamitic stock, with a strong negroid strain. They live by small-crop, primitive farming along the Mediterranean coast and in the desert to the S. There are also Bedouins and Tuaregs in the Sahara regions. Only about 25% of the total population live in urban areas, the largest of which is the capital, Tripoli, located on the coast. Educationally Libya is backward; 60% of Libyans still cannot read or write. There have however been great educational advances in recent years, largely resulting from the wealth created by foreign oil companies and oil revenues. Education is free to college level.

Economy. In 1959 the discovery of vast petroleum reserves in the desert revolutionized the economy. New homes, power stations, roads, schools and hospitals have been built, and in recent years per capita income has increased tenfold. Though the economy now depends on the export of crude oil, agriculture is still of great importance. In the coastal area cereals, oranges, olives, almonds and groundnuts are grown. Dates are plentiful in the desert oases. Libya consumes much of her agricultural produce, and is a net importer of foodstuffs.

History. Because of Libya's strategic position on the Mediterranean coast, it has been occupied by many foreign powers throughout its history—the ancient Greeks, Egyptians, Romans, Arabs and Ottoman Turks controlled the country successively. In 1912 Italy annexed Libya and introduced many modern amenities. In WWII Libya was an Axis military base and the scene of desert fighting between the Axis powers and the British. In 1951 the UN declared Libya an independent sovereign state under the rule of King Idris I. He was overthrown on Sept. 1, 1969, by a military coup led by Colonel Muammar al-Qaddafi who proclaimed Libya a republic; it is in effect an Islamic military dictatorship. Qaddafi has greatly increased oil revenues through a series of price increases and nationalizations. Driven by a fervent desire for Arab unity, he has attempted to unite Libya with Egypt (1973) and Tunisia (1974), but has been rebuffed. He has made Libya a refuge for anti-Israel terrorists and threatened to use the vast oil revenues to harass countries supporting Israel.

Official name: Libyan Arab Republic
Capital: Tripoli
Area: 679 358sq mi
Population: 2 010 000
Languages: Arabic; English and Italian used
Religions: Muslim
Monetary unit(s): 1 Libyan dinar = 1000 dirhams

LICE, wingless parasitic insects of two orders: Mallophaga, Bird lice or Biting lice, and Anoplura, Mammalian or Sucking lice. Dorsoventrally flattened with a broad, clearly-segmented abdomen, lice are well-adapted to moving between hair or feathers, and are usually host-specific. Bird lice feed with chewing mouthparts on feather fragments or dead skin, occasionally biting through the skin for blood. Mammalian lice feed purely on blood obtained with needle-like sucking mouthparts. The human lice are instrumental in the spread of several diseases.

LICHEN, name given to plants that are in fact an association between FUNGI and ALGAE. The fungus prevents the alga from drying-out, while the alga probably provides assistance to the fungus in mineral absorption. This relationship is a form of SYMBIOSIS. Lichens occur on the bark of trees, rotting wood, rock and soil. They are particularly important because they are primary colonizers of bare rock.

LICK OBSERVATORY, astronomical observatory, opened in 1888, on Mt Hamilton, Cal. Financed by James Lick (1796–1876), it was turned over by him to the U. of California. Among its six major telescopes are the second largest refracting telescope in the world (36in) and a 120in reflecting telescope.

LICORICE, *Glycyrrhiza glabra*, LEGUMINOUS PLANT primarily cultivated in Mediterranean regions for the licorice of commerce which is extracted from its roots.

LICTORS, in ancient Rome, attendants of magistrates and other high officials. Originally a constabulary, they bore the FASCES, a symbol of authority, before their masters in processions.

LIDDELL HART, Basil Henry (1895–1970), English military authority and writer. Among his works is the redrafted *British Infantry Training Manual* (1920). An advocate of tank warfare, he put forward a strategy developed by General GUDERIAN into the Nazi BLITZKRIEG; his far-seeing ideas were not accepted by the British army in his time.

LIDICE, Czech village, about 16mi NW of Prague, destroyed by the Gestapo in 1942 as a reprisal for the assassination of Reinhard HEYDRICH, the Nazi governor of Bohemia. A new village has been built near the site, which is now a national memorial.

LIDO, resort town at N end of Lido Island outside the Lagoon of Venice, NE Italy.

LIE, Trygve Halvdan (1896–1968), Norwegian statesman, first secretary-general of the United Nations 1946–53. He believed in the UN as an effective peace agency, and incurred Russian hostility by his support for UN action in Korea. He resigned in 1953 to ease the tension over Korea. Returning to Norway, he served in ministerial and ambassadorial posts, and as governor of Oslo.

LIEBER, Francis (1798–1872), German political philosopher whose liberal views and activities forced him to flee from Berlin to the US, in 1827. Professor of history and political economy at South Carolina College 1835–57 and at Columbia U. from 1857, he founded the *Encyclopedia Americana* (1829–33) and was its first editor.

LIEBERMANN, Max (1847–1935), German painter of the Impressionist and Realist schools. Heavily influenced by Courbet and Millet, his GENRE paintings of peasant life, such as *Potato Harvest* (1875) and *Beach at Scheveningen* (1908), are nonetheless German in style.

LIEBIG, Baron Justus von (1803–1873), German chemist who with WÖHLER proposed the radical theory of organic structure. This suggested that groups of atoms such as the benzoyl radical (C_6H_5CO–), now known as the benzoyl group (see BENZOIC ACID), remained unchanged in many chemical reactions. He also developed methods for organic quantitative analysis and was one of the first to propose the use of mineral fertilizers for feeding plants. (See also MIRROR.)

LIEBKNECHT, Karl (1871–1919), German socialist leader, one of the founders of the German Communist Party. He was mainly known as a campaigner against militarism. With Rosa LUXEMBURG he took part in the SPARTACUS LEAGUE's abortive uprising in 1919, after which he was arrested and shot.

LIECHTENSTEIN, tiny European principality in the mountains, between Switzerland and Austria. The population is mainly of Austrian origin. Agriculture is the chief occupation with corn, fruit, wine and dairy goods the main products. Precision instruments are exported. The mild climate and attractive scenery make Vaduz, the capital, a thriving tourist center. A former member of various confederations, Liechtenstein became independent in 1866. It was neutral in both world wars, and is now closely linked with Switzerland, its major market.

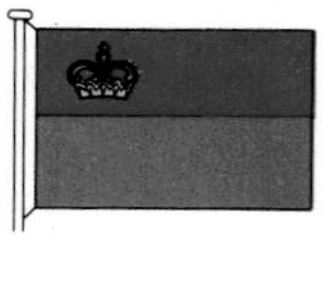

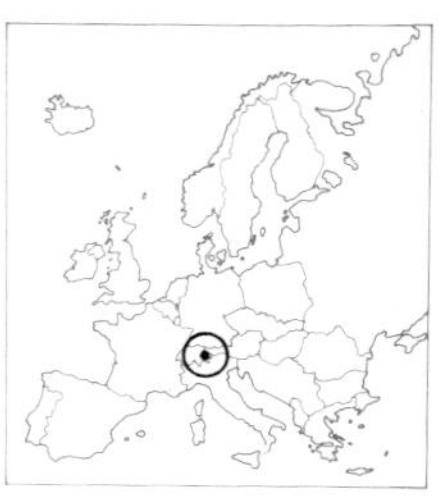

Official name: Principality of Liechtenstein
Capital: Vaduz
Area: 61.8sq mi
Population: 22 300
Languages: German
Religions: Roman Catholic
Monetary unit(s): 1 Swiss franc = 100 rappen

LIEDER. See SONG.

LIE DETECTOR, or **polygraph**, device which gives an indication of whether or not an individual is lying. Though much used in criminal investigation, its results are not admissible as legal evidence. Its use is based on the assumption that lying produces emotional, and hence physiological (see EMOTION), reactions in the individual. It usually measures changes in BLOOD pressure, PULSE rate and RESPIRATION; sometimes also muscular movements

Life

Piecing together the preconditions

Despite its diversity, living matter is characterized by an astonishing biochemical uniformity. All known forms of life have two features in common: they have a cellular structure, in which the cells are bounded by membranes; and they are composed of two kinds of macro-molecule, nucleic acids and proteins. The combination of all these features is a certain indication of life, quite apart from the consideration of function. It is thus possible to define "life" without having to define the difference between "living" and "dead."

Most theories for the origin of life presuppose that life has evolved from simpler organic entities. The investigation of the origin of life seeks to differentiate true life from some prebiological entity that was its precursor, and which may be called "protolife." The most direct evidence for the origin of life would be the discovery of protolife among the early fossils.

Early Precambrian fossils are found in two situations. Macroscopic fossils are found in the form of stromatolites, formed in dolomite or limestone, and interpreted as blue-green algal reefs. Microscopic fossils of two kinds, filaments and spheres, of diameters in the range 10–20 microns are found in cherts.

The oldest stromatolites occur in the Bulawayan Formation and have been dated at 2 900 million years. The oldest cherts with microfossils are from the Onverwacht Formation and are over 3 300 million years old. The stromatolites are universally regarded as the remains of true life. The earlier microscopic fossils may well also represent the remains of blue-green algae; but it is perfectly probable that they represent some form of primitive protolife.

The oldest known rocks bear a metamorphic imprint dated at 3 760 million years, and are therefore considerably older than the Onverwacht fossils. These rocks include metamorphosed water-laid sediments, some of which have been claimed as derived from biological sources. There are three kinds of such rock: marbles claimed as metamorphosed stromatolites; graphitic schists, claimed as metamorphosed oil-shales; and quartz magnetites claimed as banded ironstones, which are in turn postulated as oxygen receptors for photosynthetic organisms. If these claims are admitted, life cannot have originated after about 4 000 million years ago. As the age of the earth is supposed to be only about 4 600 million years, the origin of life must have been a very early event in the earth's history.

Experimental evidence has shown that some kinds of protolife could form even before the planets themselves in the solar nebula. It could also form within planetary atmospheres, and on the land-surface of planets in a volcanic environment.

Experiments designed to test the hypothesis that organic synthesis could occur in the solar nebula have been mounted by E. Anders and his collaborators from Chicago. He has shown that a Fischer-Tropsch-like synthesis occurs when gases containing hydrogen, methane and ammonia are heated in the presence of powdered refractory catalysts. The organic products include most of those found in carbonaceous meteorites, which are therefore postulated by Anders as having formed in this way. Notable among such products are amino acids, which have been found as racemic mixtures in several carbonaceous chondrites and which, if polymerized, could give rise to proteins. Biologically produced amino acids are never racemic when fresh, so these must be indigenous to the meteorite. Carbonaceous meteorites also contain organic spheres, and mineral grains coated with organic sheaths, that have been likened to "protocells."

Experiments designed to test the hypothesis that organic synthesis can occur in primitive planetary atmospheres have been mounted by several biologists and exobiologists. An electric spark (designed to simulate lightning) is passed through a gas mixture which is kept circulating through hot water. Amino acids and other organic compounds have been identified among the products, and it has since been shown that cell-like bodies are also produced among the insoluble organic products.

Experiments designed to show that polymerization of organic compounds produced in these ways can occur in certain environments have also been mounted, by Sidney Fox of Miami. He has shown that if solutions of amino acids are evaporated on a bed of hot lava, and subsequently heated to the point of fusion before quenching with cold water, cell-like structures are produced which possess a double-layered membrane. Some degree of polymerization has occurred, and they are referred to as "proteinoid microspheres." They can be manipulated in certain ways (e.g., by changing the acidity of the solution) so that they grow and divide.

These experiments suggest that life could have originated in any one of three environments. The first suggestion is that some form of protolife, synthesized in the solar nebula, infected the atmosphere of the primitive earth and subsequently invaded a primeval broth, where it evolved into life.

The second alternative is that protolife formed in the atmosphere of the primitive earth as the result of thunderstorms. This protolife was washed into the sea, which became the primeval broth that gave rise to true life. Objections have been raised that such a broth would be incredibly dilute, but others have suggested that one form of protolife could have been oil, with the consequent production of an oil slick which would float on the seas and thus embody its own concentrating device.

The third possible environment would be a volcano in its later eruptive stages. Thunderstorms would occur during the eruptions, which would provide gases rich in carbons. Amino acids and other simple organic compounds would be washed down on to hot lava, and subjected to the processes invoked by Fox. Later the combined effects of heat and water produce sugars and polynucleotides, which could invade the proteinoid microspheres and produce the first living organisms.

Convincing evidence in support of these theories is not easy to come by. Some Russian observers claim to have recognized racemic mixtures of amino acids among the products of volcanoes, but these observations remain to be confirmed.

The most speculative hypothesis of all is the celebrated "bootstraps" theory, that a visitor from elsewhere arrived on the earth, walked around for a while, and then left. However, microorganisms that were brushed off his boots contaminated the surface of the planet, and it was these that evolved toward modern terrestrial life. Of course, this theory begs the question—what did the spacemen evolve from?—and is unprovable. Nonetheless, some scientists bear it in mind as a remote possibility.

Early stages in the production of protolife could still occur on earth, although later stages are not likely to survive biological attack from contemporary life. Hydrothermal environments have been explored with such a possibility in view, and it has been claimed that oil and bitumen found associated with hydrothermal mineral veins are non-biological products. It has also been claimed that hydrocarbon globules found in fluid incisions within vein-quartz may similarly be non-biological in origin, and these may contain associated proteinoid microspheres. Others believe that all these products are the result of contamination by biological products.

and PERSPIRATION. Success varies with the individual.

LIÈGE, historic Flemish city in Belgium, capital of Liège province. It is a port on the Meuse R, and dates from the 8th century. There is an important steel industry, founded by the English in the early 19th century. Zinc and chemicals are also produced; small-arms are a major manufacture. Pop 147 277.

LIEN, the legal right of a creditor to hold or claim the property of another person as security for payment of a debt. In general the holder of a lien may not sell the property unless authorized to do so by a court.

LIEUTENANT GOVERNOR, US official, ranking second to the governor of a state, elected in the same manner and for the same term of office. He may well be of an opposing party. Thirty-nine states have a lieutenant governor, and in 37 of them he presides over the state senate. He may act for the governor in his absence and succeed to the governorship if the office becomes vacant.

LIFE, the property whereby things live. Despite the vast knowledge that has been gained about life and the forms of life, the term still lacks any generally accepted definition. Indeed, biologists tend to define it in terms that apply only to their own specialisms. Physiologists regard as living any system capable of eating, metabolizing, excreting, breathing, moving, growing, reproducing and able to respond to external stimuli. Metabolically, life is a property of any object which is surrounded by a definite boundary and capable of exchanging materials with its surroundings. Biochemically, life subsists in cellular systems containing both NUCLEIC ACIDS and PROTEINS. For the geneticist, life belongs to systems able to perform complex transformations of organic molecules and to construct from raw materials copies of themselves which are more or less identical, although in the long term capable of EVOLUTION by natural selection. In terms of THERMODYNAMICS, it has been said that life is exhibited by localized regions where net order is increasing (or net ENTROPY decreasing). But the scientist has no monopoly over the use of the term, and for poets, philosophers and artists, it carries another myriad significations.

Life on Earth is manifest in an incredible variety of forms—over 1 million species of animals and 350 000 species of plants. Yet, despite superficial differences, all organisms are closely related. The form and matter of all life on earth is essentially identical, and this implies that all living organisms shared a common ancestor and that life on earth has originated only once.

LIFE CYCLE, the series of stages through which an individual organism passes in its progression through life. It may be simple, as in VERTEBRATES—from the union of the GAMETES in FERTILIZATION to the DEATH of the organism—or rather more complex, as in types exhibiting ALTERNATION OF GENERATIONS.

LIFE SAVING, rescue of persons in difficulty at sea. Rescue services as such were first introduced in England in the 18th century. In the US the Humane Society of Mass. built huts to harbor shipwreck victims, and later supplied lifeboats manned by volunteers. After 1848 the government began increasingly to organize the lifesaving services; from 1871 it was reorganized by Sumner Kimball, who headed the US lifesaving service until it was

The historic Beavertail lighthouse at Jamestown, Rhode Island, was constructed some time before 1750. It is the oldest lighthouse still in operation in America.

incorporated into the Coast Guard service in 1915. The greatest advances in lifesaving came about during and after WWII. Today there is a whole technology ranging from inflatable life-rafts to search helicopters. Most popular US beaches and pools have at least one lifeguard to rescue swimmers in difficulty.

LIFT. See elevator.

LIGAMENT, specialized fibrous thickening of a joint capsule, providing tensile strength against forces tending to force the joint beyond its normal range. Sudden distraction or twisting forces may cause ligamentous strain or tears (sprain). External joint support encourages its healing.

LIGAND, an ion or molecule linked to a central metal ion by a coordinate bond (see bond, chemical) to form a so-called **complex compound**. Almost any ion or molecule that can act as a base, having an atom able to donate an electron-pair, may act as a ligand—common examples include NH_3, H_2O, Cl^-, OH^-, SO_4^{2-}, CO, NO^+, H^-, $C_5H_5^-$, CH_3COO^-. The complex formed may be cationic, uncharged or anionic. The *coordination number* of the central ion in the complex is the number of ligand-to-ion bonds; this equals the number of ligands unless they are polydentate—having more than one donating atom—when they may occupy more than one coordination site forming a chelate complex. Coordination numbers of 2 to 10 are known, but 6 (octahedral) and 4 (tetrahedral or square planar) are commonest. Many complexes with more than one kind of ligand have stereoisomers. Complexes vary greatly in their lability, i.e., the rapidity with which the ligands are replaced by others: they are described as labile or inert. The bonding in complexes has been described by several theories: crystal field theory considers the effect that the electrostatic field due to the ligands has on the energies of the central ion *d*-orbitals; ligand field theory includes the mixing of ligand and ion orbitals.

LIGHT, electromagnetic radiation to which the human eye is sensitive. Light radiations occupy the small portion of the electromagnetic spectrum lying between wavelengths 400nm and 770nm. The eye recognizes light of different wavelengths as being of different colors, the shorter wavelengths forming the blue end of the (visible) spectrum, the longer the red. The term light is also applied to radiations of wavelengths just outside the visible spectrum, those of energies greater than that of visible light being called ultraviolet light, those of lower energies, infrared. (See ultraviolet radiation; infrared radiation.) White light is a mixture of radiations from all parts of the visible spectrum, typified by the blackbody radiation reaching the earth from the sun. Bodies which do not themselves emit light are seen by the light they reflect or transmit. In passing through a body or on reflection from its surface, particular wavelengths may be abstracted from white light, the body consequently displaying the colors which remain. Objects which reflect no visible light at all appear black.

For many years the nature of light aroused controversy among physicists. Although Huygens had demonstrated that reflection and refraction could be explained in terms of waves—a disturbance in the medium—Newton preferred to think of light as composed of material corpuscles (particles). Young's interference experiments reestablished the wave hypothesis and Fresnel gave it a rigorous mathematical basis. At the beginning of the 20th century, the nature of light was again debated as Planck and Einstein proposed explanations of blackbody radiation and the photoelectric effect respectively which assumed that light carried energy in discrete quanta (see photon). Today physicists explain optical phenomena in terms either of waves (reflection, refraction, diffraction, interference, polarization—see polarized light—and scattering) or quanta (blackbody radiation, photoelectric emission and the interaction of light with substantial matter) as is most convenient in each case (see also wave motion; quantum theory).

Light from the sun is the principal source of energy on earth, being absorbed by plants in photosynthesis. Many other chemical reactions involve light (see chemiluminescence; photochemistry; photography) though few artificial light sources are chemical in nature (but see flashbulb). Most light sources employ radiation emitted from bodies which have become hot or have been otherwise energetically excited (see energy level; laser; lighting; luminescence). Light can be converted into electricity using the photoelectric cell. Light used for illumination is the subject of the science of photometry. (See also optics.)

LIGHTHOUSE, tower with a light at its head, erected on or near the coast, or on a rock in the sea, as a warning to ships. One of the earliest lighthouses was on the Pharos peninsula at Alexandria, built in the 3rd century BC, and one of the "Seven Wonders of the World." In modern lighthouses, the lantern usually consists of a massive electric light with an elaborate optical system, producing intense beams which sweep the horizon. Radio signals may be transmitted, and foghorns are sometimes used. Where conditions make it difficult to build a lighthouse, an anchored lightship may be used. Most lighthouses are operated by small teams of men who may live isolated in the lighthouse for weeks at a time.

LIGHTING, Artificial, the illumination of sectors of man's physical environment in the absence of natural light. In the course of evolution, eyes sensitive to the solar radiation penetrating the earth's atmosphere to the surface developed in many of the planet's animals. Man's eyes are thus sensitive to light of these same wavelengths, so artificial light sources must be designed to produce radiations having an intensity spectrum similar to that of natural sunlight.

Oil lamps, brushwood torches and candles formed man's earliest means of artificial lighting, developments leading towards the kerosene lamp of the late 19th century (see also argand burner). Gas lighting dates from 1792 when the British engineer William Murdock used coal gas to light his Cornish home. The modern portable camping lamp burns butane gas to heat an incandescent mantle.

In the 20th century the industrialized nations have come to use electricity for most lighting purposes because it offers an instant source of bright, clean, fume-free light. One of the earliest electrical lighting sources was the arc lamp which utilizes the flame

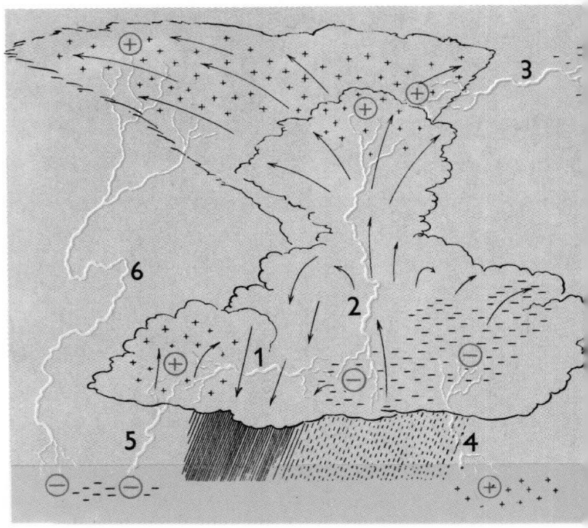

Lightning occurs when electrical charge separation occurs in thunderstorms, creating some regions with overall positive charge (+) and others with predominantly negative charge (−). Six types of lightning are indicated on the diagram, numbered (1), the most frequent, through (6), the least common. Air currents in the cloud are indicated by black arrows.

arcing between two pointed carbon electrodes maintained with a moderate voltage between them. Successful incandescent filament lamps date from 1879 when Sir Joseph William Swan and Edison demonstrated lamps in which a carbon filament enclosed in an evacuated glass bulb was heated electrically until it glowed. After 1913 these gave way to lamps having tungsten filaments, coiled to improve efficiency (from 1918), and filled with an unreactive gas such as nitrogen. In 1937 efficiency was further improved by coiling the coiled filament (coiled-coil lamp). A more recent development is the tungsten-halogen lamp (an early type of which was the quartz-iodine lamp) in which efficiency is improved and life extended by filling the bulb with a halogen with which tungsten evaporating from the filament can combine, preventing deposition of the metal on the envelope (which is sometimes made of quartz). Because discharge lamps (in which a glow discharge is set up in mercury or sodium vapor—glowing blue-green and yellow respectively) do not produce light in all parts of the solar spectrum they find their greatest use in highway rather than domestic lighting. More recent high-pressure sodium lamps, however, offer a fuller light spectrum. Cold-discharge tubes containing neon (glowing red) or argon (glowing blue) are contorted into exotic shapes for use in advertising signs. Fluorescent lamps produce light similar to sunlight by using a phosphor coating on the inside of the tube to convert ultraviolet light produced in a mercury-vapor discharge. Although they require more complex circuitry than filament lamps, they are much more efficient and last longer. Other light sources such as light-emitting diodes (LEDs—see semiconductors) and electroluminescent panels find use in instrument display panels. (See also fireworks; flashbulb; photometry.)

LIGHT METER, a device for measuring light levels, particularly in photography where they are often coupled directly to the exposure controls of a camera. Most light meters employ either photovoltaic cells (e.g., selenium type) or photoconductive detectors (e.g., cadmium sulfide—"CdS"—type).

LIGHTNING, a discharge of atmospheric electricity resulting in a flash of light in the sky. Most occur between two parts of a single cloud, some between cloud and ground, and a few between one cloud and another. Flashes range from a few km to about 150km in length, and typically have an energy of around 300kWh and an electromotive force around 100MV.

Cloud-to-ground lightning usually appears forked. A relatively faint light moves towards the ground at about 125km/s in steps, often branching or forking. As this first pulse (leader stroke) nears the ground, electrical discharges (streamers) arise from terrestrial objects; where a streamer meets the leader stroke a brilliant, high-current flash (return stroke) travels up along the ionized (see ION) path created by the leader stroke at about 100Mm/s (nearly $\frac{1}{3}$ the speed of light). Several exchanges along this same path may occur. If strong wind moves the ionized path, **ribbon lightning** results.

Sheet lightning occurs when a cloud either is illuminated from within or reflects a flash from outside, in the latter case often being called **heat lightning** (often seen on the horizon at the end of a hot day). **Ball lightning**, a small luminous ball near the ground, often vanishing with an explosion, and **bead lightning**, the appearance of luminous "beads" along the channel of a stroke, are rare.

Lightning results from a buildup of opposed electric charges in, usually, a cumulonimbus CLOUD, negative near the ground and positive on high (see ELECTRICITY). There are several theories which purport to explain this buildup. Understanding lightning might help us probe the very roots of life, for lightning was probably significant in the formation of those organic chemicals that were to be the building blocks of life. (See also SAINT ELMO'S FIRE; THUNDER.)

LIGHTNING BUG, alternative name for the FIREFLIES.

LIGHTNING ROD, or **lightning conductor**, safety device on buildings, etc., as protection from the destructive effects of LIGHTNING. One end of a strip of conducting metal (e.g., COPPER) is earthed, the other mounted high on the building; any discharge thus passes directly to the ground.

LIGHTSHIP. See LIGHTHOUSE.

LIGHT YEAR, in astronomy, a unit of distance equal to the distance traveled by light in a vacuum in one sidereal year, equal to 9461Tm (about 6 million million miles). The unit has largely been replaced by the PARSEC (1 ly = 0.3069pc).

LIGNIN, complex CARBOHYDRATE which gives strength and rigidity to the woody tissue of plants and which may account for from 25% to 30% of the WOOD of some trees. In making PAPER the lignin must be separated from the CELLULOSE.

LIGNITE, or brown coal. See COAL.

LIGNUM VITAE, *Guaiacum officinale* and *G. sanctum*, trees native to tropical America which produce hard, heavy wood that sinks in water and is used for furniture and tool handles. The gum extracted from the wood was reputed to have many medicinal properties from which the name lignum vitae was derived. Family: Zygophyllaceae.

LIGUORI, Saint Alphonsus. See ALPHONSUS LIGUORI, Saint.

LIGURIA, crescent-shaped region of NW Italy, sweeping around the Mediterranean coast from Tuscany to the French border. It is mountainous except for the sheltered coastal resorts of the Italian RIVIERA. Products include vines, olives and citrus fruit, and industry, centered on Genoa, Savona and La Spezia, includes shipbuilding, chemicals and textiles.

LIGURIAN SEA, part of the Mediterranean enclosed by the Italian Riviera to the N, Tuscany to the E and Corsica to the S, including the Gulf of Genoa.

LI HUNG-CHANG (1823–1901), Chinese general and westernizing statesman. He helped crush the TAIPING REBELLION (1850–64). As governor general of the capital province, Chihli (1870–95), he tried to modernize the army and introduce western industries, and was virtually in charge of conducting China's relations with the West.

LILAC, shrubs and small trees of the genus *Syringa*, which are native to E Europe and Asia and now widely grown as ornamentals for their sweet-scented flowers. Family: Oleaceae.

LILBURNE, John (c1614–1657), English pamphleteer and leader of the LEVELLERS. Imprisoned 1638–40, he became a commander in the CIVIL WAR (1640–45), but was then persecuted, spending much time in prison or exile. He remained popular, however, and was twice (1649, 1653) acquitted of treason by a London jury.

LILIENTHAL, David Eli (1899–), US lawyer and government official. He was a director (1933) and chairman (1941–46) of the TENNESSEE VALLEY AUTHORITY. As chairman (1946–50) of the ATOMIC ENERGY AUTHORITY, he championed civilian control of atomic energy.

LILIENTHAL, Otto (1848–1896), German pioneer of aeronautics, credited with being the first to use curved, rather than flat, wings, as well as first to discover several other principles of AERODYNAMICS. He made over 2000 glider flights, dying from injuries received when one of his gliders crashed. (See also FLIGHT, HISTORY OF.)

LILITH, female demon of Jewish folklore (from the Assyrian demon Lilit, "night monster"), killer of children and legendary first wife of Adam.

LILIUOKALANI (1838–1917), queen of Hawaii, who reigned 1891–93. She succeeded her brother King Kalakaua. When she tried to assert her royal powers, Americans living in Hawaii fostered a revolt in which she lost her throne. She wrote the well-known farewell song "Aloha Oe."

LILLE, city and important industrial center in N France. Traditional home of the French textile industry, since WWII it has become the hub of a vast industrial conurbation. Industries include iron and steel, machinery, chemicals and food processing. Pop 189300.

LILY, bulbous plants of the genus *Lilium*, many hybrids and varieties of which are in cultivation. Many other flowers that resemble lilies are given this name, but true lilies have six petals and six stamens. Most lilies are easy to grow, but some require specialist cultivation. Family: Liliaceae.

LILY-OF-THE-VALLEY, *Convallaria majalis*, a woodland plant native to Eurasia and North America, now widely cultivated in gardens. It produces sweet-scented white, bell-shaped flowers that are borne in clusters from a long stalk. It is not a true LILY. Family: Liliaceae.

LILY-TURF, perennial plants with grass-like, variegated leaves and lily-like flowers, which are often used outdoors for ground cover, but which can be grown indoors out of direct sun and at cool temper atures. *Ophiopogon intermedius argenteo-marginatus* and various species of the genus *Liriope* are known as lily-turf. They are propagated either from seeds or by division of the plants. Family: Liliaceae.

LIMA, historic capital and largest city of Peru, about 8mi inland from the port of Callao. Founded 1535, Lima was the chief residence of the Spanish viceroys. Earthquakes in 1687 and 1746 destroyed most of the city, but it still retains its old character. Rapidly expanding, Lima has many industries, including textiles, chemicals, oil refining and food processing. Pop 2673400.

The delicately speckled tiger lily is widely cultivated as a decorative plant. It is not difficult to grow, but needs special soil conditions, particularly a degree of acidity.

LIMA, city in NW Ohio, seat of Allen Co. Formerly a center of oil production, it now has numerous manufacturing industries. Pop 53734.

LIMA BEAN, *Phaseolus lunatus*, LEGUMINOUS PLANT native to Middle America and widely cultivated particularly in W Africa and the US for its edible seeds. (See also BEAN.) Family: Leguminosae.

LIMAÇON, the GRAPH, in polar coordinates (see ANALYTIC GEOMETRY) of the FUNCTION $r = a\cos\theta - 1$ where a is a constant. (See also TRIGONOMETRY.) The light reflected by the inner walls of a cup delineates a limaçon upon the surface of the liquid within.

LIMBO, in Roman Catholic theology, the abode of those excluded from HEAVEN but not punished in HELL or PURGATORY. The Old Testament saints were in limbo until Christ's coming; the unbaptized who die in infancy remain there for ever. Limbo's existence is not an officially-defined dogma.

LIMBOURG, Pol de (d. 1416?), Flemish manuscript illuminator, one of three brothers who after 1404 worked for the Burgundian duc de Berry. Their renowned devotional book of hours, the *Très riches heures du duc de Berry*, shows courtly life and landscape in brilliant detail and dazzling color. (See also ILLUMINATION, MANUSCRIPT.)

LIME, or calcium oxide or hydroxide. See CALCIUM.

LIME, a CITRUS tree (*Citrus aurantifolia*) that produces fruit resembling a small green ORANGE. They are widely grown in tropical and subtropical regions of the world. The fruit is very rich in VITAMIN C and was once important in preventing outbreaks of SCURVY on long sea voyages. It should not be confused with the LINDEN tree which is also called lime. Family: Rutaceae.

LIMERICK, Irish Atlantic port on Shannon R estuary. Its name is given to a five-line comic verse form, rhyming AABBA, popularized by Edward LEAR. Pop 57137.

LIMESTONE, town in NW Me., 18mi NNE of Presque Isle. Pop 10360.

LIMESTONE, sedimentary rock consisting mainly of calcium carbonate (see CALCIUM), in the forms of CALCITE and aragonite. Some limestones, such as CHALK, are soft but others are hard enough for use in building. Limestone may be formed inorganically (oolites) by evaporation of seawater or freshwater containing calcium carbonate, or organically from the shells of mollusks or skeletons of coral piled up on sea beds and compressed. In such limestone fossils usually abound.

LIMITATIONS, Statutes of, laws which limit the effective duration at law of justifiable legal claims by specifying a time limit after which proceedings can no longer be instituted. The limit may range from a few months to as long as 30 years, according to country and type of offence.

LIMITS. The limit of a SEQUENCE is a fixed number towards which the terms tend. This number may or may not be a member of the sequence. Similarly, the limit of a FUNCTION $y = f(x)$ is the value which $f(x)$ approaches as x tends to a particular value. The limit may or may not be a value of $f(x)$ (see ASYMPTOTE). The limit point of a point set (or CURVE) is a POINT such that, no matter how small a distance from it is chosen, there is a member of the set closer to it. Limit points may or may not be members of the set.

LIMNOLOGY, a branch of BIOLOGY that deals with the study of freshwater habitats and the PLANTS and ANIMALS within these habitats.

LIMOGES, city of S central France, on the Vienne R. Renowned from the 13th to the 17th century for its enamels (see ENAMELING), since the 18th century it has been an important porcelain manufacturing center. Other industries include shoes and textiles. Pop 135197.

LIMONITE, a dark brown, amorphous OXIDE mineral consisting of hydrated iron(III) oxide ($FeO[OH].nH_2O$). A major IRON ore of widespread occurrence, often with GOETHITE, it is formed by alteration of other iron minerals.

LIMPET, name applied to any sedentary MOLLUSK with a conical or flattened shell, though originally reserved for species of *Patella*, European limpets. They are herbivorous mollusks of intertidal regions which browse on algae when covered by the tide. All have a special "home" on their rock, and minor irregularities of the rock surface are accommodated by differential shell-growth so that the shell fits the surface of the rock exactly. Other limpets include the Slipper limpets and Keyhole limpets. The Slipper limpets are communal animals living in chains one attached to the back of another. Like most *Patella* species, slipper limpets undergo a sex reversal during their life.

LIMPKIN, a long-legged wading bird of marshes and floods of North America. Related to crakes and rails, it is the only species of the family Aramidae. It is 585–710mm (23–28in) long, olive brown with white streaks, and feeds on water snails which it shells before swallowing.

LIMPOPO RIVER, or Crocodile R, some 1100mi long, rising in South Africa, and flowing in a great arc N, E and then SE through Mozambique to the Indian Ocean. It forms South Africa's NW frontier with Botswana and its N frontier with Rhodesia.

LINCOLN, county town of Lincolnshire, E England. A Roman town, and an important medieval city with a fine cathedral, it is now a transportation center with varied industries, including heavy machinery. Pop 74207.

LINCOLN, city in central Ill., seat of Logan Co., named for Abraham LINCOLN. It is an agricultural trading center with some light industry. Pop 17582.

LINCOLN, capital of Neb., named for Abraham LINCOLN. A transportation hub and a commercial and industrial city, it is also a trade center for livestock and grain. Pop 149518.

LINCOLN, unincorporated residential town in N central Ohio. Pop 11215.

LINCOLN, town in NE R.I. A former textile center, it has some light manufacturing industry. Pop 16182.

LINCOLN, Abraham (1809–1865), 16th president of the US who, while leading the North in the Civil War, preserved the Union which he saw as a bastion of democratic government. By his EMANCIPATION PROCLAMATION in 1863, he prepared the abolition of slavery in the US. He was not free from faults and vacillations, but his patience, fortitude and fierce devotion to the Union made him one of America's greatest presidents.

Lincoln was born in a log cabin in backwoods Ky., and raised in poverty. His father Thomas, and stepmother, Sarah Bush Johnston Lincoln, were barely literate. In 1831 Abraham set up house in New Salem, Ill., and taught himself law in his spare time, eventually becoming one of the leading lawyers in the state. From 1834 to 1841 he served in the Ill. state legislature. He retained something of his rough frontier manner, even after a well-connected marriage, in 1842, to Mary Todd.

Abraham LINCOLN

16th US President

Born: February 12, 1809
Died: April 15, 1865
Term of office: March 4, 1861–April 15, 1865
Political party: Republican

The fountain in New York's Lincoln Center for the Performing Arts, and behind it the graceful yet imposing frontage of the new Metropolitan Opera House. Designed by Wallace K. Harrison, the opera house—the "New Met"—cost $45700000, and was opened in 1966.

Lincoln entered the House of Representatives in 1847 as a Whig, but his opposition to the MEXICAN WAR lost him his seat in 1849. Returning to politics in 1854 he took his stand on slavery. Though not an abolitionist, he opposed the KANSAS-NEBRASKA ACT of Senator Stephen DOUGLAS, which by repealing part of the MISSOURI COMPROMISE seemed likely to introduce slavery into the new Western territories. Lincoln's speeches against slavery in 1854 aligned him with the new REPUBLICAN PARTY, which he joined in 1856. In 1858 he contested a senate seat with Douglas, challenging him in a series of historic debates in which, though he lost the election, Lincoln emerged as an orator of national stature. In 1860 he was nominated as a compromise presidential candidate, winning against a split Democratic vote.

Before he took office as president seven Southern states had already seceded from the Union. Determined to hold FORT SUMTER in S.C. for the Union, Lincoln ordered supplies to its beleaguered garrison. War broke out on April 12, 1861 (see CIVIL WAR, AMERICAN). At first the North suffered numerous reverses, but Lincoln built up the army, blockaded southern ports and personally directed strategy as commander in chief until, in March 1864, he gave Ulysses S. GRANT command of the armies in the field. Grant and gifted subordinates like William T. SHERMAN carried out Lincoln's grand strategy of multiple coordinated offensives against the numerically inferior South. In the continuing debate on slavery, Lincoln put the Union before abolition, but in response to increasing demands made the EMANCIPATION PROCLAMATION on Jan. 1, 1863. It was to be followed by the 13th Amendment to the CONSTITUTION, sponsored by Lincoln.

The tide turned, with Grant's victory at VICKSBURG and LEE's defeat at GETTYSBURG (1863) where Lincoln made his famous address. In 1864 came the victories of the SHENANDOAH VALLEY, ATLANTA and MOBILE BAY, and Lincoln, who had lost some political ground, was reelected. In his second inaugural address in March, 1865, he made plain his lenient intentions towards the South. Within four weeks Grant took Richmond, and on April 9 Lee surrendered. Five days later Lincoln was shot in his box at the theater by John Wilkes BOOTH, and died early on April 15.

LINCOLN, Benjamin (1733–1810), American officer in the REVOLUTIONARY WAR. Made commander of the South (1778), he was forced to surrender Charleston in 1780. He became secretary of war 1781–83, and in 1787 suppressed SHAYS' REBELLION.

LINCOLN, Robert Todd (1843–1926), son of Abraham Lincoln. Having served on GRANT's staff in the Civil War, he became a corporation lawyer, and was US secretary of war (1881–85), and minister to Great Britain (1889–93).

LINCOLN CENTER FOR THE PERFORMING ARTS, in New York City, a complex of buildings, designed by leading modern architects, to accommodate such cultural organizations as the New York Philharmonic Orchestra, Metropolitan Opera, theaters, and a library of the performing arts.

LINCOLN MEMORIAL, marble memorial to Abraham Lincoln at the end of the Mall in Washington, D.C., dedicated in 1922. Its 36 Doric columns represent the states of the Union when Lincoln was president. The great hall contains a huge statue of Lincoln by Daniel Chester FRENCH.

The Lincoln Memorial, at the end of the Mall in Washington, D.C. This imposing Neoclassical building in marble was dedicated to Abraham Lincoln in 1922; today it serves as a popular rallying point for demonstrations in the capital.

LINCOLN PARK, city in SE Mich. It is a residential suburb 9mi SW of Detroit. Pop 52984.

LINCOLN TUNNEL, road tunnel, 8216ft long, under the Hudson R from Manhattan Island, New York City, to Weehawken, New Jersey. The first tube was opened in 1937; the second and third in 1945 and 1957.

LINCOLNWOOD, village in NE Ill. It is a residential suburb of Chicago. Pop 12929.

LIND, Jenny (1820–1887), Swedish soprano, the "Swedish Nightingale." With a voice of exceptional flexibility and clarity, she had brilliant success in opera, and after 1849 in oratorio and concert recitals.

LINDBERGH, Charles Augustus (1902–1974), US aviator who made the first solo nonstop flight across the Atlantic, in 33½ hours, on May 20, 1927, in "The Spirit of St. Louis." A hero overnight, he became an airline consultant and made many goodwill flights. The kidnapping and murder of his son in 1932 led to a federal law on kidnapping, popularly known as the Lindbergh Act. Criticized for his pro-German, isolationist stance 1938–41, he later flew 50 combat missions in WWII. His autobiography, *The Spirit of Saint Louis* (1953), won a Pulitzer Prize.

LINDEN, city in NE N.J. Manufactures include chemicals, petroleum products and machinery, including automobiles. Pop 41409.

LINDEN, tall deciduous tree of the genus *Tilia* producing heart-shaped, toothed leaves and sweet-scented flowers. The wood is very fibrous and used for carvings and making paper and ropes. Several species are called BASSWOOD (e.g., *Tilia americana*) while *T. cordata* is often called lime, although it is not related to the citrus LIME. Family: Tiliaceae.

LINDENHURST, village on Long Island, SE N.Y. It is mainly residential, with some manufacturing industry, including paper and chemicals. Pop 28338.

LINDENWOLD, borough in SW N.J. Industries include plastics and meat-packing. Pop 12199.

LINDISFARNE or **Holy Island**, off the coast of NE England, the earliest center of Celtic Christianity in England. Settled by St. AIDAN in 635 AD, it became a bishopric until the Danish invasions in 875. The *Lindisfarne Gospels*, a famous illuminated manuscript, was created here c700.

LINDSAY, town in SE Ontario, Canada, on the Scugog R. It is a market and processing center for lumber, grain and cattle. Pop 12746.

LINDSAY, Howard (1889–1968), US playwright,

producer and actor. With Russel Crouse he wrote *State of the Union* (1945), which won a Pulitzer Prize, and scripts for *Call Me Madam* (1950) and *The Sound of Music* (1959).

LINDSAY, John Vliet (1921–), US politician. Elected to Congress 1958, he was mayor of New York City 1966–74, the first Republican to win the office in 21 years. A liberal reformer, in 1971 he became a Democrat.

LINDSAY, (Nicholas) Vachel (1879–1931), US poet of rhythmic, ballad-like verse designed to be read out loud. Among the best known are "The Congo" (1914) and "Abraham Lincoln Walks at Midnight" (1914).

LINDSEY, Benjamin Barr (1869–1943), US judge and social reformer. As a juvenile court judge in Denver 1900–27, he helped mold the US juvenile court system. He also held controversial views on marriage and divorce.

LINE, a CURVE. In general the term is used to denote a straight line; i.e., one whose equation is of the type $y = ax + b$, where a and b are constants (see ANALYTIC GEOMETRY). A straight line has only one DIMENSION, length, may be infinite in extent, and is the shortest distance between any two points. (See also LINEAR RELATIONSHIP.)

LINEAR ACCELERATOR. See ACCELERATORS, PARTICLE.

LINEAR MOTOR, a form of induction motor first built by WHEATSTONE (1845). It comprises a series of ELECTROMAGNETS, current being passed through each along the line in turn, so that a moving component (usually of ALUMINUM) is drawn along the line. (See also INDUCTION MOTOR.)

LINEAR PROGRAMMING, an application of ALGEBRA and CALCULUS to, usually, commercial problems involving a number of unrelated VARIABLES, in order to provide an optimum result. Each of the variables is expressed in the form of a line FUNCTION within specified LIMITS or constraints. The overall most favorable result is then found, usually by COMPUTER. (See also OPERATIONS RESEARCH.)

LINEAR RELATIONSHIP, a relationship between two VARIABLES such that, if one is plotted as a FUNCTION of the other (see ANALYTIC GEOMETRY), the result is a straight LINE. A linear relationship can be said to exist between x and y in the EQUATION $y = ax + b$ (a and b CONSTANTS).

LINE INTEGRAL, the integral (see CALCULUS) along a directed CURVE of any FUNCTION that is continuous and single-valued along that curve.

LINE ISLANDS, central Pacific archipelago straddling the equator, partly UK and partly US territory. CHRISTMAS ISLAND, the site of nuclear tests, and Fanning Island are inhabited.

LINEN, yarn and fabric manufactured from the fibers of the FLAX plant. The stems of the flax plant must first be softened by soaking in water (retting). Next, the fibers are separated from the woody core in a "scutching" mill. The short fibers (tow) are combed out from the long fibers (line) in the "hackling" mills. The tow is finally spun into yarn.

LINGONBERRY, fruit of a small Eurasian shrub (*Vaccinum vitis-idaea vitis-idaea*), which is closely related to the CRANBERRY. Family: Ericaceae.

LINGUA FRANCA, auxiliary, usually hybrid language used between people of different tongues. Examples are PIDGIN English, SWAHILI and the CHINOOK language. The original *lingua franca* developed among the medieval traders in the Mediterranean. A language used in diplomacy, such as French, may also be called a lingua franca.

LINGUISTICS, the scientific study of spoken language. Different branches of linguistics deal with the development of languages over time; the structures of languages (see GRAMMAR); the description of different languages at a particular time; the physical and mental factors involved in the production of speech and use of language, and the study of meaning (see SEMANTICS). *Applied linguistcs* makes use of the discoveries of other areas of linguistics to deal with practical problems, in particular language teaching and the deduction of information about a culture, past or present, from the language that it uses (see ANTHROPOLOGY; PHILOLOGY). (See also ETYMOLOGY; LANGUAGE; PHONETICS; SIGN LANGUAGE; WRITING, HISTORY OF.)

A group of lionesses prowling sedately across the African savanna in Tanganyika in search of prey. The males, although more powerful, generally leave hunting to their mates.

LINK, Edwin Albert (1904–), US aviation executive, and inventor of the Link trainer, a flight simulator which enables pilots to do much of their basic training on the ground. He founded the Link Aeronautical Corporation and Link Aviation Inc.

LINKAGE, the occurrence together on the same CHROMOSOME of two or more GENES. Linked genes are normally transmitted together from generation to generation. These genes are said to be in *coupling*. Examples of genes linked to the male sex chromosome include red-green COLOR BLINDNESS and HEMOPHILIA.

LINNAEUS, Carolus (1707–1778), later **Carl von Linné**, Swedish botanist and physician, the father of TAXONOMY, who brought system to the naming of living things. His classification of plants was based on their sexual organs (he was the first to use the symbols ♂ and ♀ in their modern sense), an artificiality dropped by later workers; but many of his principles and taxonomic names are still used today.

LINNET, *Acanthis cannabina*, a small finch of Europe and W Asia, associated with agricultural areas and waste land where it feeds on weed seeds. The name is also applied to other finches: the European greenfinch and North American siskin being referred to as Green linnet and Pine linnet.

LINOLEUM, a durable floor-covering material. Linoleum cement (oxidized linseed oil with various RESINS) is mixed with fillers (e.g., wood flour) and coloring elements, the whole having a foundation of, usually, burlap (hessian).

LINOTYPE, technique of letterpress printing in which characters are cast from molten type-metal (see ALLOY) a line at a time. Keying by the operator assembles the matrices (molds) for the characters in the correct order, wedge-shaped space bands being placed between the words: when the line is nearly full, pressure is applied to these so that they force apart the words and justify the line (align the right-hand margin). The slug of type is cast from the completed line. If a single character is wrong, the whole line must be recast. (See also MONOTYPE.)

LIN PIAO (1907–1971), Chinese communist general and statesman. He was a leader in the LONG MARCH (1934–35) and, by his capture of Manchuria in 1948, crucial in the final defeat of CHIANG KAI-SHEK. Minister of defense from 1959, he was a leader of the "Cultural Revolution" (1965–69). In 1969 he was designated the successor of MAO TSE-TUNG. He was killed in an air crash, and the Chinese press later reported that he had been escaping to Russia after an abortive coup.

LINSANGS, *Prionodon spp.*, two species of the Viverridae, a family including MONGOOSES, CIVETS and GENETS. Exclusively Asian, they are solitary and nocturnal "cats" hunting lizards, small mammals, birds and insects.

LINSEED OIL, mixture of fatty acids (see CARBOXYLIC ACIDS) extracted from the seeds of a variety of FLAX. It is used in varnish and oil paints because of the quick-drying durable finish produced. It is also used to manufacture oil cloth, linoleum and printing ink. Leading producers of linseed oil are the US, USSR and Argentina.

LINTON, Ralph (1893–1953), US anthropologist best known for the eclecticism of his studies in cultural ANTHROPOLOGY, as expressed in *The Study of Man* (1936) and *The Tree of Culture* (1955).

LINUS, Saint (perhaps martyred c76 AD), according to tradition the immediate successor of St. Peter as bishop of Rome.

LIN YUTANG (1895–1976), Chinese author and translator who promoted Western understanding of China in such books as *My Country and My People* (1935), and the novel *Moment in Peking* (1939). After 1935 he lived in the US.

LINZ, city, capital of Upper Austria and a port on the Danube R. A historic city with much fine architecture, it now manufactures steel (the LINZ-DONAWITZ PROCESS originated here), machinery and electrical equipment. Pop 202 900.

LINZ-DONAWITZ PROCESS, or Basic Oxygen Process, major variant of the BESSEMER PROCESS for making STEEL, developed in Linz and Donawitz, Austria (1952) and popular in North America for its low cost. The basic-lined converter has no tuyères; a stream of pure oxygen is blown through a lance onto the surface of the molten pig iron (low in phosphorus) mixed with scrap.

LION, *Panthera leo*, one of the largest of the big cats, distributed through Africa and Asia. They live in family groups loosely associated into large social units or prides, which share a range. Lionesses usually kill for the pride, though the big-maned males are well able to kill for themselves, and frequently do so—particularly those in bachelor groups of immature males. Amazingly powerful animals, they are characteristic of bush or veld, killing zebra, wildebeest, even buffalo by dragging on the neck, bringing the prey to the ground and breaking its neck. The roar of a male lion is a territorial proclamation.

LIONFISH, or **turkeyfish**, *Pterois volitans*, a colorfully striped and dangerous scorpionfish of the Indo-Pacific. When threatened, it erects the long spines that extend from its pectoral and dorsal fins. These spines contain a poison painful even to humans.

LIONS CLUBS, International Association of, or **Lions International**, organization of business and professional men dedicated to community service, founded in Chicago in 1917. Today there are some 25 000 clubs with a total membership of nearly 1 million in over 140 countries.

LIPARI ISLANDS, group of Italian volcanic islands in the Tyrrhenian Sea N of Sicily. They include Stromboli (an active volcano), Salina, Vulcano and Lipari. Their economy depends on fishing, tourism, wine and pumice stone.

Lipchitz' sculpture was strongly influenced by Cubism, and later by Expressionism and his study of primitive art. These influences are visible in this bronze, *Mother and Child II* (1941–45), now in the Museum of Modern Art, New York.

LIPASE, an enzyme which splits fats into CARBOXYLIC ACIDS and GLYCEROL. As the fat is normally water insoluble, lipases act relatively slowly on the surface of a fat globule. They occur widely in oil seeds and are involved in GERMINATION.

LIPCHITZ, Jacques (1891–1973), Russian-born sculptor whose early works in Paris were constituted by places and volumes, as in CUBISM. From 1925 he produced a series he called "transparents," in which, as in the *Harpist* (1928), contour was emphasized. His later work was more romantic and metaphorical.

LIPETSK, city in the USSR, about 200mi SSE of Moscow. It is an iron and steel-producing center, with chemical, cement and food-processing industries. Pop 290 000.

LIPIDS, a diverse group of organic compounds found in plants, animals and microorganisms and characterized by their solubility in nonpolar organic solvents such as ETHER, CHLOROFORM and ETHANOL. Lipids include many heterogeneous substances and unlike PROTEINS and CARBOHYDRATES have no characteristic type of building block. They are classified into FATS, phospholipids, WAXES, STEROIDS, TERPENES and other types, according to their products on HYDROLYSIS. Most commonly, these are fatty acids, particularly those having an even number of carbon atoms. Other components found in many lipids include GLYCEROL, choline and derivatives of ISOPRENE. Phospholipids contain PHOSPHORUS, most commonly in the form of phosphoric acid. They are found especially in brain and nervous tissue as cephalins and in egg yolk as lecithin. Phospholipids are good emulsifiers and detergents, hence the use of egg yolk in mayonnaise. Waxes are ESTERS of fatty acids with alcohols other than glycerol and include whale oil and beeswax. Terpenes are a wide range of compounds having usually distinctive fragrances obtained from plants such as pine trees (TURPENTINE), citrus fruits (limonene) and geraniums. They have a wide application in cosmetics, toiletries and medicines.

LIPMANN, Fritz Albert (1899–), German-born US biochemist who shared with KREBS the 1953 Nobel Prize for Physiology or Medicine for his discovery in 1947 of coenzyme A (see ENZYMES).

LI PO (Li Tai-po; 701–762 AD), regarded as one of China's greatest lyric poets. He was a prolific writer, and produced graceful verses using very simple language. His love of wine was a frequent theme.

LIPPI, name of two Italian early RENAISSANCE painters in Florence. **Fra Filippo Lippi** (c1406–1469) was influenced by MASACCIO, DONATELLO and by Flemish painting. His frescoes in Prato cathedral have a prettiness derived from Fra ANGELICO. **Filippino Lippi** (c1457–1504), his son, influenced by BOTTICELLI, painted the brilliantly-detailed *Adoration of the Magi* (1496).

LIPPMANN, Gabriel (1845–1921), French physicist awarded the 1908 Nobel Prize for Physics for inventing (c1891) the first system of color PHOTOGRAPHY. His process required long exposures, and thus is now obsolete. He also invented the coelostat, and predicted PIEZOELECTRICITY.

LIPPMANN, Walter (1889–1974), influential US political columnist and foreign affairs analyst. His column, "Today and Tomorrow," first appeared in the *New York Herald-Tribune* in 1931, and eventually won two Pulitzer prizes (1958, 1962). Books include *Public Opinion* (1922) and *The Good Society* (1937).

LIPSTICK VINE, a perennial trailing plant of the genus *Aeschyanthus* grown indoors for its profusion of foliage and attractive orange-red flowers that are borne on brownish stalks resembling lipsticks. Lipstick vines grow best in bright indirect light, but fail to thrive at temperatures below 13°C (55°F); the soil should be kept evenly moist. They are propagated by means of shoot tip cuttings. Family: Gesnariaceae.

LIQUEFIED PETROLEUM GAS (LPG). See BOTTLED GAS.

LIQUID, one of matter's three states, the others being SOLID and GAS. Liquids take the shape of their container, but have a fixed volume at a particular temperature and are virtually incompressible (see COHESION). Nearly all substances adopt the liquid state under suitable conditions of temperature and pressure. (See also FLUID; KINETIC THEORY; VAPOR.)

LIQUOR. See ALCOHOLIC BEVERAGES.

LISBON, capital and largest city of Portugal, on the Tagus R estuary. Its fine harbor handles the bulk of the country's foreign trade. Reconquered from the Moors in 1147, Lisbon became the capital c1260. Much of the city was rebuilt after the disastrous earthquake of 1755. Industries include steelmaking, petroleum refining, textiles, chemicals, paper and metal products. Pop 782 266.

LISSAJOUS' FIGURES, or **Bowditch curves**, plane CURVES traced by a POINT moving in two SIMPLE HARMONIC MOTIONS that are at right angles to each other. They can most easily be formed by supplying different alternating voltages (see ELECTRICITY) to the *x*- and *y*-deflection plates of an OSCILLOSCOPE. Only if the frequencies are commensurable will a true Lissajous figure (i.e., a closed curve) be formed.

LISSITSKY, El (1890–1941), Russian abstract painter, designer and architect, proponent of CONSTRUCTIVISM and SUPREMATISM. His series of paintings and drawings, *Proun*, applied geometric forms to art and architecture.

LIST, Friedrich (1789–1846), German-US economist and author of *The National System of Political Economy* (1841). Exiled in 1825 for his liberalism, in 1832 he returned to Germany as US consul at Leipzig. He argued for a German customs union, but advocated tariffs to protect developing industries.

LISTER, Joseph Lister, 1st Baron (1827–1912), British surgeon who pioneered antiseptic SURGERY, perhaps the greatest single advance in modern medicine. PASTEUR had shown that microscopic organisms are responsible for PUTREFACTION, but his STERILIZATION techniques were unsuitable for surgical use. Lister experimented and, by 1865, succeeded by using carbolic acid (see PHENOL).

LISTON, Charles "Sonny" (c1932–1970), heavyweight boxing champion of the world 1962–64. He won the title by beating Floyd PATTERSON, but lost it to Cassius Clay (now Muhammad ALI) in 1964.

LISZT, Franz (1811–1886), Hungarian Romantic composer and virtuoso pianist who revolutionized keyboard technique and became a public idol. He was director of music at Weimar 1843–61, and then lived in Rome where he took minor holy orders in 1865. His highly programmatic music includes 13 symphonic poems, a form he invented; program symphonies such as *Faust* (1854); the great B minor piano sonata (1853); *Transcendental Studies* for piano (1852) and 20 *Hungarian Rhapsodies*. His daughter Cosima married WAGNER.

LITCHFIELD, township in W Conn., a supply point for American troops in the REVOLUTIONARY WAR. It was the site of the country's first law school (1784) and birthplace of Harriet Beecher STOWE. Pop 7 399.

LITCHI. See LYCHEE.

LITERATURE, in its widest sense the accumulation of the world's written culture, but more usually applied to particular forms of writing distinguished for their aesthetic, emotional and intellectual qualities, such as POETRY, drama (see THEATER) or the NOVEL. For the many different literary forms see under BALLAD, BLANK VERSE, COMEDY, ELEGY, EPIC etc. See also AMERICAN LITERATURE (special feature); ENGLISH LITERATURE.

LITHARGE, or lead(II) oxide. See LEAD.

LITHIUM (Li), a white metallic element somewhat harder and less reactive than the other ALKALI METALS. Physically and chemically, lithium also resembles the ALKALINE EARTH METALS. It is the lightest element which is a solid at room temperature. It is made by ELECTROLYSIS of fused lithium chloride. Lithium metal is used in heat transfer because of its high specific heat; the isotope Li^6 is important in thermonuclear processes. Lithium stearate is an additive to lubricating greases. AW 6.9, mp 180°C, bp 1347°C, sg 0.534 (20°C).

LITHOGRAPHY. See PRINTING.

LITHOSPHERE, the rocks of the earth, as contrasted with the ATMOSPHERE and HYDROSPHERE. Today, use of the term is often restricted to reference to the upper part of the earth's crust. (See EARTH.)

LITHUANIA, constituent republic of the USSR, bounded N by Latvia, E by Belorussia, S by Poland and W by the Baltic. The country is mainly flat with many lakes and forests, and is drained by the Neman R. The climate is generally mild and humid in summer, cold in winter. The population is 80% LITHUANIAN-speaking.

Agriculture, the basic economic resource occupying half the population, is collectivized. The chief cities and industrial centers are Vilnius, the capital, Kaunas and Klaipeda, the main port. Roman Catholicism is the traditional religion.

Fourteenth-century Lithuania, comprising Belorussia and parts of the Ukraine and Russia, was central Europe's most powerful state. In 1386 Lithuania and Poland were united under Grand Duke JAGIELLO. In 18th-century partitions of Poland Lithuania became a Russian province. From 1918 to 1940, when it was reabsorbed by Russia, it had an independent, near fascist, regime. Pop 3 129 000.

LITHUANIAN, the most ancient of the BALTIC LANGUAGES and the official language of Lithuania. It has a modified Latin alphabet, and has been a literary language since the 16th century, experiencing a revival in the 19th. Its literary traditions are rich in folklore.

LITMUS, mixture of colored compounds, extracted from LICHENS, used as an acid-base INDICATOR.

LITRE (l), a metric unit of volume, originally defined as that of 1kg of water at the temperature of its maximum density (= 1.000 028dm^3), but redefined in 1964 as exactly equal to one cubic decimetre (= 1dm^3). The litre is not recommended for use alongside SI UNITS.

LITTLE AMERICA, US Antarctic base on the Ross Ice Shelf S of Whale Bay. It was first set up by Richard E. BYRD in 1928, and used by him on his subsequent expeditions.

LITTLE BIGHORN, Battle of, in SE Mont. on June 25, 1876, known as "Custer's last stand." General George A. CUSTER was killed and his troops annihilated by Cheyenne and Sioux Indians led by chiefs SITTING BULL and CRAZY HORSE.

LITTLE DIPPER (Ursa Minor, the Little Bear), N Hemisphere circumpolar constellation containing POLARIS, the N polestar.

LITTLE ENTENTE, political, economic and military alliances formed in 1920–21 between Yugoslavia, Czechoslovakia and Romania, backed by France. The entente began to weaken in the 1930s, and finally collapsed in 1938 with the German annexation of Czechoslovakia.

LITTLE FALLS, township in N N.J., on the Passaic R 5mi SW of Paterson. Pop 11 727.

LITTLE LEAGUE BASEBALL, junior baseball organization for teams aged 8–12 years, founded in 1939. The playing area is two-thirds full size, and six rather than nine innings are played; there is a World Series and over 7 500 member leagues.

LITTLE ROCK, capital and principal commercial and manufacturing city of Ark., on the Arkansas R. It achieved notoriety in 1957 when federal troops were sent in to enforce INTEGRATION at the Central High School after Governor Faubus had ordered the state militia to stop black pupils entering. Pop 132 483.

LITTLETON, town in NE Col., seat of Arapahoe Co. A suburb of Denver, it manufactures trucks and precision instruments. Pop 26 466.

LITTLE TURTLE (c1752–1812), Miami Indian chief, orator and warrior. He won resounding victories against the whites in 1790 and 1791, but shared in the defeat of FALLEN TIMBERS, and in 1795 ceded Indian lands in the Ohio valley to the US.

LITTORAL FAUNA, term applied to animals which live on the seashore (the littoral or intertidal zone). They comprise a special assemblage which are uniquely adapted to being alternately covered and uncovered by the tide. On any one shore the organisms are "zoned," changing from animals adapted to aquatic conditions in the lower regions, to often closely related semiterrestrial species higher up.

LITURGY, services of public worship, especially in Christianity and Judaism; often applied specifically to Holy COMMUNION (the chief worship service) and to the texts that prescribe the order of services, such as the BREVIARY or the BOOK OF COMMON PRAYER. The 20th-century **Liturgical Movement** in most churches has emphasized reform of the liturgy, use of the vernacular, and lay participation.

LITVINOV, Maxim Maximovich (1876–1951), Russian revolutionary and commissar for foreign affairs from 1930–39. He maintained a policy of cooperation with the West, negotiating US recognition of the USSR in 1933 and taking Russia into the League of Nations in 1934. From 1941–43 he was ambassador to the US.

LIUTPRAND (c690–744), king during whose reign (712–44) Lombardy reached the height of her power. He introduced sweeping domestic reforms to curb the bishops and nobles and won Spoleto and Benevento from Byzantine rule.

LIU SHAO-CHI (1898–1973?), Chinese communist leader, who succeeded MAO TSE-TUNG as chairman of the Chinese People's Republic (1959) and came to be seen as his heir. But in 1968 he was publicly denounced and dismissed. He died in mysterious circumstances, reportedly in an air crash near the Russian border.

LIVER, the large organ lying on the right of the ABDOMEN beneath the DIAPHRAGM and concerned with many aspects of METABOLISM. It consists of a homogeneous mass of cells arranged round blood vessels and bile ducts. Nutrients absorbed in the GASTROINTESTINAL TRACT pass via the portal VEINS to the liver and many are taken up by it; they are converted into forms (e.g., GLYCOGEN) suitable for storage and release when required. PROTEINS, including ENZYMES, PLASMA proteins and CLOTTING factors, are synthesized from amino acids. The liver converts protein breakdown-products into urea and detoxifies or excretes other substances (including drugs) in the blood. Bilirubin, the HEMOGLOBIN break-down product is excreted in the BILE; this also contains bile salts, made in the liver from CHOLESTEROL and needed for the DIGESTIVE SYSTEM.

Diseases of the liver include CIRRHOSIS and HEPATITIS, while abnormal function is manifested as JAUNDICE, EDEMA, ascites (excessive peritoneal fluid), and a variety of BRAIN and NERVOUS SYSTEM disturbances including DELIRIUM and COMA. Chronic liver disease leads to SKIN abnormalities, a bleeding tendency and alterations in routes of BLOOD CIRCULATION, which may in turn lead to HEMORRHAGE. Hepatitis may be caused by VIRUSES (e.g., infectious and serum hepatitis); their high infectivity has made them a hazard in hospital dialysis units. Many drugs may damage the liver, causing disease similar to hepatitis, and both drugs and severe hepatitis can cause acute liver failure.

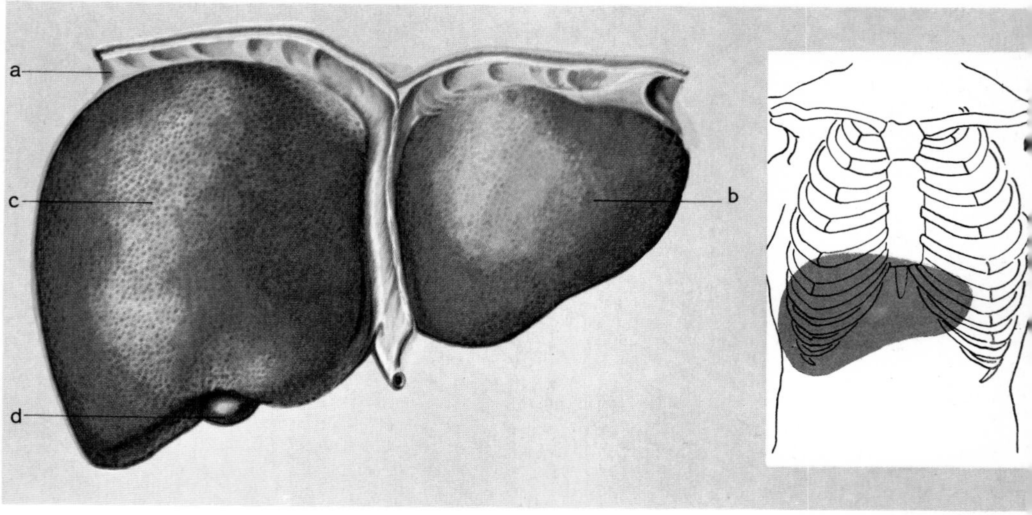

The liver, seen here from the front, lies just below the diaphragm (a) at the top of the abdominal cavity. On the lower surface of the liver, between the left and right lobes (b and c), is the gall bladder (d). This acts as a reservoir for the bile produced by the liver.

LIVER FLUKES. See FLUKES.

LIVERPOOL, industrial city and second largest port in Britain, on the Mersey R, 3mi from the Irish Sea. The borough was chartered in 1207; in the 18th century it was a major slave-trading port. Its extensive docks are now among Europe's finest. Pop 589 000.

LIVERWORTS, primitive prostrate plants growing in moist habitats and occasionally in water. They form the class Hepaticae of the division BRYOPHYTA, which also includes the MOSSES and HORNWORTS. The most familiar types have a flat, lobed thallus attached to the ground by root-like rhizoids. Other types have a thallus bearing leaf-like expansions.

LIVESTOCK. See ANIMAL HUSBANDRY; CATTLE.

LIVINGSTON, township in NE N.J. It is a center for dairy, poultry, and truck farming. Pop 30 127.

LIVINGSTON, Robert R. (1746–1813), US statesman. He was a delegate at the CONTINENTAL CONGRESS and assisted in drafting the DECLARATION OF INDEPENDENCE. In 1777 he helped draft the N.Y. state constitution. As chancellor of N.Y. state 1777–1801, he administered the presidential oath of office to George Washington. In 1801–04 he negotiated the LOUISIANA PURCHASE. The Livingston family was prominent in N.Y. and national affairs 1680–1823.

LIVINGSTONE, David (1813–1873), Scottish missionary and explorer in Africa, from 1841. He discovered the Zambesi R in 1851 and explored it in three remarkable journeys (1852–56, 1858–63, 1866–73). In 1855 he reached the waterfall he was to name as Victoria Falls. His historic meeting with the New York journalist Henry Morton STANLEY took place in 1871. Livingstone was a sworn enemy of the slave trade. He died in central Africa; his body was carried to the coast by two African followers.

LIVING STONES, stoneface or pebble plants, unusual stone-like succulent plants of the genus *Lithops*. Their markings closely resemble the stones of their native desert habitat. The yellow or white daisy-like flowers are produced from a fissure on the top of the body. Indoors they should be grown in a sunny window, keeping the temperature between 13°C and 21°C (55°F and 70°F). They should be well watered whenever the surface soil becomes dry. They are propagated either by sowing seeds or (in the case of clump-forming types) by dividing the plants. Family: Aizoaceae.

LIVONIA, or Livland, historic Baltic territory comprising parts of Latvia and Estonia in the USSR. It was conquered and Christianized in the 13th century by the Livonian Knights, a group affiliated to the TEUTONIC KNIGHTS.

LIVONIA, city in SE Mich., a suburb of Detroit. It produces automobile bodies and parts, and paint. Pop 110 109.

LIVORNO. See LEGHORN.

LIVY, or Titus Livius (c59 BC–17 AD), important Roman historian. Of his 142-book *History of Rome* 35 books survive, with fragments and an outline of the rest. This work, which set out to praise the ancient republican virtues, won the approval of AUGUSTUS.

LIZARD FISHES, marine fishes of the family Synodontidae. They have long, cylindrical bodies, lizard-like heads and large mouths. They spend most of their time lying on the bottom, supporting the body at an angle on large pelvic fins.

LIZARDS, a diverse group of REPTILES, placed with SNAKES and amphisbaenids in the order Squatama. Lizards usually possess well-developed limbs, though these are reduced or absent in some species. In some families the tail vertebrae have a predetermined plane of fracture where the tail can be cast if seized by a predator. The missing portion of tail can usually be regenerated. The various groups are adapted to a wide variety of environments, and lizards are found even in dry or desert conditions. A number of African species of lacertid lizards live in tropical forest where they climb among trees. Some of these have flattened flaps of skin which can be stretched between hind and fore limbs, permitting the lizard to glide down from tree to tree. Lizards are typically insectivorous though some will take eggs or small mammals. The group includes GECKOES, CHAMELEONS, SKINKS, true LACERTID LIZARDS and MONITORS.

LJUBLJANA, capital city of Slovenia republic,

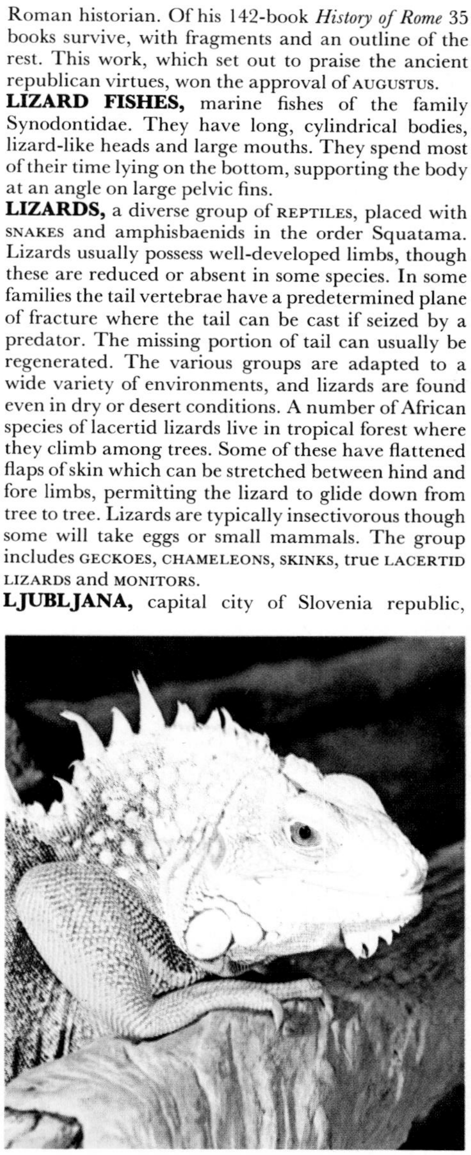

Head of the common Iguana, looking like a miniature dragon. Iguanas are the commonest lizard family in the tropical areas of the Americas, and many grow up to 6ft in length.

Yugoslavia. An ancient city with many fine old buildings, it is also an important commercial and industrial center. Among its chief products are textiles, machinery and tobacco. Pop 258 000.

LLAMA, domestic form of a *Lama* species, the generic name for humpless New World camellids including the llama and ALPACA, with the wild GUANACO and VICUNA. It has thick fleece which may be used for wool, and is the principal beast of burden of Indians from Peru to Chile, thriving at altitudes of 2 300–4 000m (7 500–13 000ft).

One of the oldest domesticated animals in the world, the llama is a relative of the camel found in the higher Andes in South America, where it is used as a pack animal. It also provides wool and meat, dung for fuel, and fat for candles.

LLANO ESTACADO, or Staked Plain, some 35 000sq mi in the S Great Plains in NW Okla., W Tex. and E N.M. It is used for cattle grazing and has oil and natural gas deposits.

LLANOS (Spanish: plains), a vast area in the Orinoco R basin in E Colombia and Venezuela. It comprises about 200 000sq mi of grassland and is used for raising livestock.

LLOYD, Harold Clayton (1894–1971), US comedian of the silent screen. He is famous for his role as the timid little man in glasses and straw hat, forever teetering over disaster only to be saved at the last moment. Among his best-known films are *Safety Last* (1923), *The Kid Brother* (1927) and *Feet First* (1930).

LLOYD, Henry Demarest (1847–1903), US reforming journalist or MUCKRAKER. He exposed the sharp practices of big business, notably in *Wealth Against Commonwealth* (1894), a history of the Standard Oil Company.

LLOYD GEORGE, David, 1st Earl of Dwyfor (1863–1945), Welsh statesman, British prime minister from 1916–22, one of Britain's greatest war leaders and a brilliant orator. He was elected a Liberal member of Parliament in 1890 and served the same Welsh constituency for 54 years. As chancellor of the exchequer he forced through the so-called "people's budget" 1910–11, virtually founding British welfare legislation. The budget was at first rejected by the House or Lords, an incident which led to effective curtailment of their power of veto. In WWI, Lloyd George became successively minister of munitions, minister of war, and in 1916 prime minister of a coalition government. He was one of "the Big Four" at the Paris Peace Conference, 1919. His later policies, particularly over Ireland, lost him support; he was forced to resign in 1922. In the 1930s he opposed policies of appeasement towards Nazi Germany.

LLOYD'S OF LONDON, the world's largest marine insurance association, also involved in other types of insurance. Risks are assured by individual "underwriters," grouped in some 300 "syndicates." The underwriters assume unlimited personal liability for their portion of any given claim.

LOACHES, fishes related to CARPS, living in the fresh waters of Asia and Europe. Most species have barbels around the mouth. The swimbladder is reduced and encased in bone. Loaches are bottom-living fishes, many being nocturnal in habit.

LOAM, soil comprised of about 30%–50% SAND particles, 30%–50% SILT particles, and less than 20% CLAY particles. (See SOIL.)

LOBACHEVSKI, Nikolai Ivanovich (1792–1856), Russian mathematician who, independently of BOLYAI, developed the first NON-EUCLIDEAN GEOMETRY, hyperbolic or LOBACHEVSKIAN GEOMETRY, publishing his developments from 1826 onward.

LOBACHEVSKIAN GEOMETRY, or **hyperbolic geometry**, the branch of NON-EUCLIDEAN GEOMETRY based on the hypothesis that for any point P not lying on a line L, there are at least two lines that can be drawn through P parallel to L.

LOBBYING, the attempt to influence legislation by personal persuasion and propaganda outside official hearings or channels. Corporations, professions and trade associations maintain expensive operations to this end. Lobbying abuses are controlled in the US by the Regulation of Lobbying Act (1946).

LOBELIA, genus of mainly annual and perennial herbs and shrubs native to many temperate and warm regions of the world. However, tree lobelias grow up to 5m (16ft) and are found in mountainous regions of tropical Africa. All have tubular flowers with a broad, lobed lip. Some species yield a poisonous ALKALOID called lobeline, which has properties similar to NICOTINE. Family: Campanulaceae.

LOBOTOMY, operation in which the FRONTAL LOBES are separated from the rest of the BRAIN, used in the past as treatment for refractory DEPRESSION. It leads to a characteristically disinhibited type of behavior and is now rarely used.

LOBSTERS, large marine decapod crustaceans with the first pair of legs bearing enormous claws. True lobsters, genus *Homarus*, are animals of shallow water living among rocks in crannies feeding on carrion, small crabs and worms. The two large claws differ in both structure and function, one of them always adapted for crushing, the other adapted as a fine picking or scraping claw. The dark blue pigment of the living lobster is a complex compound broken down by heat to the familiar red.

LOCAL OPTION, in the US, the legal right of a community or a state to vote to accept or reject certain laws. It usually applies to decisions as to whether, when or how liquor can be served or sold.

LOCARNO TREATIES, a series of pacts drawn up in Locarno, Switzerland, in 1925, among seven European nations, guaranteeing existing borders in E and W Europe. They also established arbitration procedures to solve disputes, notably between France and Germany, the latter being treated as an equal among the European powers for the first time since WWI. The "spirit of Locarno" died in 1936 when Germany denounced the pacts and occupied the Rhineland.

LOCATION THEORY, a topic in urban and regional economics and economic geography, which seeks to explain the geographical distribution of economic activities. Given assumptions of perfect competition and profit maximization, for example, a firm would locate where production costs (e.g. of raw materials) and transport costs (e.g. proximity to market) would be minimized.

LOCH LOMOND. See LOMOND, LOCH.

LOCH NESS. See NESS, LOCH.

LOCHNER, Stephan (c1400–1451), German painter of the Cologne school. His most famous work is the triptych altarpiece (1440s) in Cologne Cathedral, in which the central panel depicts the Adoration of the Magi.

LOCHNER V NEW YORK (1905), a landmark in US economic legislation. The Supreme Court justices invalidated the 10-hour limit on the working day of bakers. Oliver Wendell HOLMES fiercely opposed the decision.

LOCK. See CANALS.

LOCKE, David Ross (1833–1888), US journalist editor of the Toledo *Blade* from 1865. An ardent Unionist, his sharply satirical anti-South letters first published in the Findlay, Ohio, *Jeffersonian* under the name Petroleum Vesuvius Nasby were widely read during the Civil War.

LOCKE, John (1632–1704), English empiricist philosopher whose writings helped initiate the European Enlightenment. His *Essay Concerning Human Understanding* (1690) is one of the highlights of English philosophy. In it he adopted a nominalist view of language, yet believed that our ideas of things, inasmuch as they reflected real essences—the properties of the insensible corpuscles of matter—were founded upon and could be checked against experience. His *A Letter Concerning Toleration* (1689) and *The Reasonableness of Christianity* (1695) were seminal for the British religious thought of the 18th century.

LOCK HAVEN, city and seat of Clinton Co., Pa., on the W branch of the Susquehanna R. It manufactures light aircraft. Pop 11 427.

LOCKJAW. See TETANUS.

LOCKOUT, in labor disputes, the closure of a plant or factory by the employer, or the dismissal of all employees and selective reemployment to exclude activist labor leaders. If such action violates an existing agreement, US courts may judge it illegal.

LOCKPORT, manufacturing city in N.Y., seat of Niagara Co., It is situated 20mi ENE of Niagara Falls, on the New York State Barge Canal. Pop 25 399.

LOCKS AND KEYS. The earliest known mechanical lock is from ancient Egypt, c2000 BC. The bolt was hollow, with a number of holes bored in its top; one of the bolt staples held a number of wooden pegs which fell into the holes in the bolt, holding it in place. The key could be fitted into the bolt; it had spikes in the same pattern as the holes, and thus could lift the pegs clear. The ancient Greeks situated their locks on the inside of the door, access being achieved *via* a keyhole to whose shape the key conformed. The Romans improved the Egyptian design by having pegs of different shapes and using springs to drive the pegs home; and invented the **warded lock**, whose key must be slotted to clear wards, obstacles projecting from the back of the lock. Early portable locks, and later padlocks, also used this principle. The modern *lever-tumbler lock* was invented by Robert Barron (1778): levers fit into a slot in the bolt patterned such that each lever must be raised a different distance by the key to free the bolt. Jeremiah Chubb added another lever to jam the lock if the wrong key were tried (1818). The *Bramah lock*, invented by Joseph BRAMAH (1784), has a cylindrical key slotted to push down sprung slides, each of which must be depressed a different distance to clear an obstacle. Most domestic locks are now *Yale locks*, invented by Linus YALE (1861). An inner cylindrical plug has holes into which sprung drivers press pins of different lengths. The key is patterned to raise each pin so that its top is flush with the cylinder, which can then turn. Modern safes have combination locks and time devices so that they can only be opened at certain times.

LOCKWOOD, Belva Ann Bennett (1830–1917), US lawyer and suffragette. She won the right for women lawyers to plead before the Supreme Court (1879) and gained equal property rights and equal guardianship of their children for women in the District of Columbia.

LOCOFOCOS, trade name of a phosphorus friction match invented in the US about 1830. The name was used derisively in 1835 to describe the volatile radical wing of the New York Democratic Party.

LOCOMOTION, the means by which animals move from point to point—crawling or running over hard surfaces; burrowing in sand or soil; flying and swimming. Animals which can move are termed *motile*, contrasted with those which cannot, which are *sessile*. There are two anatomical features of the vast majority of animals that make locomotion possible: a skeletal system, and a muscle system. The skeletal system is frequently composed of chitin (see CARAPACE), CARTILAGE or BONE and provides mechanical levers which are operated by MUSCLES. Soft-bodied animals employ a hydrostatic skeleton composed of water-filled cavities that are distorted by muscular walls to produce movement (see also AMOEBA).

Among VERTEBRATES there are many variations of the basic locomotor organ, the limb. In birds and bats it has been modified to form a wing, while in various groups, notably snakes, the limbs are lost and the

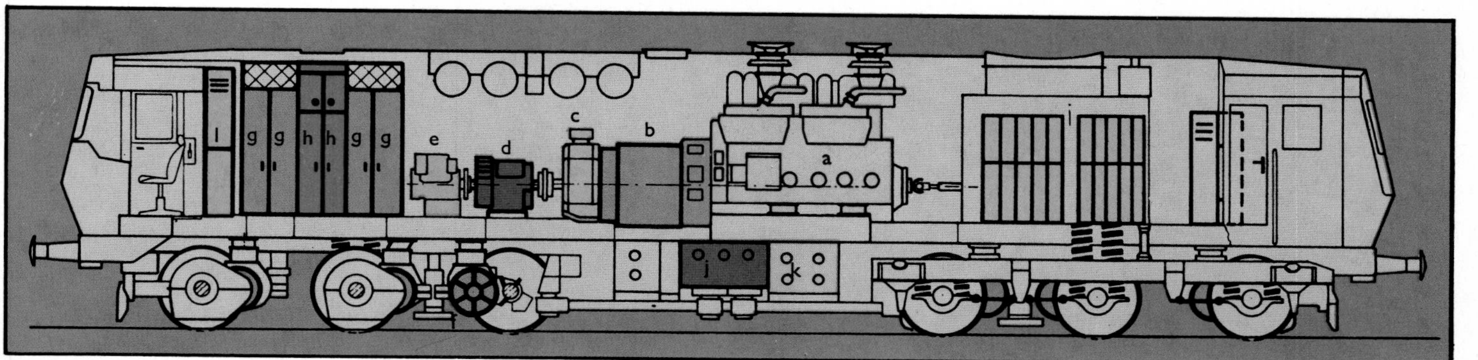

Diagram of a diesel-electric locomotive, showing (a) diesel engine; (b) generator; (c) generator blower; (d) starting motor; (e) air compressor; (f) asynchronous traction motor; (g) rectifier and rotary converter (transformer); (h) resistors for regenerative braking mechanism; (i) radiator for the diesel motor; (j) storage batteries; (k) fuel tank and supplementary electronic equipment.

animal moves by undulations of the body. In aquatic animals, the tail is the most important organ of locomotion, the main function of the fins being steering and stabilization.

LOCOMOTIVE, originally locomotive engine, power unit used to haul railroad trains. The earliest development of the railroad locomotive took place in the UK, where R. TREVITHICK built his first engine c1804. R. STEPHENSON's famous *Rocket* of 1829 proved that locomotive engines were far superior to stationary ones and provided a design that was archetypal for the remainder of the steam era. Locomotives were first built in the US c1830. These pioneered many new design features including the leading truck, a set of wheels preceding the main driving wheels, guiding the locomotives over the usually lightly-constructed American tracks. For most of the rest of the 19th century, locomotives of the "American" type (4-4-0) were standard on US passenger trains, though towards the end of the century, progressively larger types came to be built. Although electric locomotives have been in service in the US since 1895, the high capital cost of converting tracks to electric transmission have prevented their widespread adoption. Since the 1950s, however, most US locomotives have been built with DIESEL ENGINES. Usually the axles are driven by electric motors mounted on the trucks, the main diesel engine driving a generator which supplies power to the motors (diesel-electric transmission). Elsewhere in the world, particularly in Europe, much greater use is made of electric traction, the locomotives usually collecting power from overhead cables via a PANTOGRAPH. Although some GAS-TURBINE locomotives are in service in the US, this and other novel power sources do not seem to be making much headway at present.

LOCOWEED, poisonous LEGUMINOUS PLANTS of the genera *Astragalus* and *Oxytropis*, which are native to dry regions of the W and SW US. Poisoning causes livestock to become stuporous and stagger, a disease commonly known as locoism.

LOCUST, a name restricted to about 50 species of tropical GRASSHOPPERS which have a swarming, gregarious stage in the life cycle. In the arid regions where they occur they have become opportunists, breeding in large numbers where conditions are suitable, then flying in huge swarms to wherever food may be abundant. Here they can rapidly effect an agricultural disaster. They lay their eggs in bare earth just after rain. The young hoppers which hatch thus have new vegetation on which to feed when they emerge. Then they form into bands which march across the country eating the leaves of grasses, herbs and bushes as they go. Once they fledge, a swarm of Desert locusts can cover 50km (30mi) a day, on a front 50km wide, devastating the vegetation as it proceeds.

LOCUST TREE, deciduous, leguminous trees and shrubs of the genus *Roinia*, which are native to Middle and North America. Black locust *Robinia pseudacacia* produces hard heavy wood used for general construction and as fuel. Family: Leguminosae.

LOD, or Lydda, city in Israel 23mi NW of Jerusalem, a major railroad junction. Nearby is Israel's main international airport. A biblical town, it is the reputed birthplace of St. George. Pop 30 500.

LODESTONE. See MAGNETITE.

LODGE, name of two US statesmen. **Henry Cabot Lodge** (1850–1924), senator from Mass. 1893–1924, known for his successful opposition to US membership of the LEAGUE OF NATIONS, which he felt threatened US sovereignty. Instructor in American history at Harvard 1876–79, he was a prominent historian even during his Senate career. His grandson, the diplomat **Henry Cabot Lodge** (1902–), was a Republican senator 1937–44 and 1947–52, when he lost his seat to John F. KENNEDY. In 1960 he was Richard Nixon's vice-presidential candidate. He served as ambassador to the UN 1953–60 and ambassador to South Vietman 1963–64 and 1965–67. As ambassador to West Germany 1968–69, he was chief negotiator at the Vietnam peace talks in Paris.

LODGE, Sir Oliver Joseph (1851–1940), British physicist best known for his work on the propagation of ELECTROMAGNETIC RADIATION, devising an early instrument (the coherer) for detecting it. He also did important work on PARAPSYCHOLOGY.

LODI, city in central Cal. A wine-producing center, it packs and ships fruit, cereals and other agricultural produce. It has some light industry. Pop 28 691.

LODI, industrial borough in NE N.J. It produces textiles, dyes and paints, chemicals and electrical equipment. Pop 25 213.

ŁÓDŹ, capital city of Łódź province, Poland. An industrial center, particularly for textiles, since 1839, it became Polish in 1919. Pop 761 800.

LOEB, Jacques (1859–1924), German-born US biologist best known for his work on PARTHENOGENESIS, especially his induction of artificial parthenogenesis in sea urchins' and frogs' eggs, thereby highlighting the biochemical nature of FERTILIZATION.

LOESS, fine-grained, wind-deposited SILT found worldwide in deposits up up to 50m thick. Its main components are QUARTZ, FELDSPAR and CALCITE. Extremely porous, it forms highly fertile topsoil, often CHERNOZEM. It is able to stand intact in cliffs.

LOEWE, Frederick (1904–), Austrian-born US composer of musical plays, usually to lyrics by Alan Jay LERNER. After *Brigadoon* (1947) and *Paint Your Wagon* (1951), their major successes were *My Fair Lady* (1956) and *Camelot* (1960).

LOEWI, Otto (1873–1961), German-born US pharmacologist awarded (with Sir Henry DALE) the 1936 Nobel Prize for Physiology or Medicine for his work showing the chemical nature of nerve impulse transmission. (See NERVOUS SYSTEM.)

LOEWY, Raymond Fernand (1893–), French-born US industrial designer famous for his pioneering automobile designs, which were both functional and visually attractive. His firm designed many hundreds of different products, from refrigerators to passenger ships.

LÖFFLER, Friedrich August Johannes (1852–1915), German bacteriologist who first isolated the DIPHTHERIA bacillus (1884), which had first been observed by KREBS the previous year. He also discovered the causative organism of GLANDERS; and, with others, showed that HOOF-AND-MOUTH DISEASE is caused by a VIRUS, developing a SERUM against it.

LOFOTEN ISLANDS, chain of islands and islets off the NW coast of Norway, noted for their cod fisheries. Their chief port is Svolvaer. The Maelstrom whirlpool is S of Moskenesφy, a moderate-sized island towards the SW of the group.

LOFTING, Hugh (1886–1947), English-born US author and illustrator of the famous *Dr. Dolittle* stories, begun in letters to his children. *The Voyages of Dr. Dolittle* (1922), the second in the series, won him the Newbery medal in 1923.

LOG, device to measure the speed of a ship. The oldest type was essentially a float to which was attached a line knotted at regular intervals: the number of knots paid out as the ship sailed for a timed period gave the speed (see KNOT). Nowadays, smaller boats use a device like a propeller whose rate of rotation as it is dragged through the water gives a measure of the speed. Larger ships use a pitometer, a PITOT TUBE with one hole facing forward, one sideways, the water PRESSURE difference indicating the speed.

LOGAN, city in N Ut., seat of Cache Co. Its economy rests on processing the produce of the surrounding agricultural area. Utah State U. is situated here. Pop 22 333.

LOGAN, James John (1725–1780), or Tah-Gah-Jute, prominent Cayuga Indian. Originally a friend of white men, he took the name of a white friend. During an attempt by John DUNMORE to seize the Ohio area Logan's family was massacred, which made him an impassioned foe of the white man.

LOGAN, John Alexander (1826–1886), US politician. A member of the House of Representatives 1858–62 and 1866–71, he tended to oppose ABOLITIONISM but championed the North and served with distinction in the Civil War, rising to the rank of brigadier-general. He was senator from Ill. 1871–77 and from 1879. Founder (and three times president) of the GRAND ARMY OF THE REPUBLIC, he led the movement that established Memorial Day (May 30).

LOGAN, Joshua (1908–), US theater and film director, producer and writer. Among his many stage productions were *Mister Roberts* (1948) and the Pulitzer Prize-winning musical *South Pacific* (1949), filmed in 1957.

LOGAN, Mount, peak in the St. Elias range in the SW Yukon Territory, Canada, near Alaska. At 19 850ft it is the highest mountain in Canada and the second highest in North America.

LOGANBERRY, *Rubus loganobaccus*, climbing perennial similar to the BLACKBERRY, but which produces fruit similar in color to the RASPBERRY. It is thought to have originated as a cross between the blackberry and raspberry. Family: Rosaceae.

LOGANSPORT, city in N central Ind., seat of Cass Co. Trading center of an agricultural area, it has many industries. Pop 19 255.

LOGARITHMS, a method of computation using EXPONENTS. A logarithm is the power (see ALGEBRA) to which one number, the base, must be raised in order to obtain another number. For example, since $10^2 = 100$, $\log_{10} 100 = 2$ (read as "log to the base 10 of 100 equals 2"). The most common bases for logarithms are 10 (common logarithms) and the EXPONENTIAL, e (natural logarithms).

Since $a^0 = 1$ for any a, $\log 1 = 0$ for all bases. In

The log cabin, quickly and soundly built from the forest around and the mud it grew in, was the commonest frontier home. Many of America's greatest citizens, such as Andrew Jackson and Abraham Lincoln, began life in a dwelling of this sort.

order to multiply two numbers together, one uses the fact that $a^x . a^y = a^{x+y}$, and hence $\log (x.y) = \log x + \log y$. We therefore look up the values of $\log x$ and $\log y$ in logarithmic tables, add these values, and then use the tables again to find the number whose logarithm is equal to the result of the addition. Similarly, since $\frac{a^x}{a^y} = a^{x-y}$, $\log\left(\frac{x}{y}\right) = \log x - \log y$; and since $(a^x)^y = a^{xy}$, $\log x^y = y . \log x$. $\mathrm{Log}_x\, x = 1$ since $x^1 = x$. The antilogarithm of a number x is the number whose logarithm is x; that is, if $\log y = x$, then y is the antilogarithm of x. A *logarithmic curve* is the plotting of a FUNCTION of the form $f(x) = \log x$.

LOG CABIN, primitive dwelling erected by early settlers in North America. It was built from logs, stripped of their bark and branches, laid horizontally and notched at each end to overlap and interlock at the corners. No nails were necessary, and few tools. Gaps between the logs were filled with clay or mud. It was usually roofed with branches or bark; in later versions, with shingles or slate.

LOGGERHEAD TURTLE, *Caretta caretta*, a marine TURTLE found in all tropical and subtropical seas. Only 1m (39in) long, it is entirely adapted for swimming. Its flippers are clawless. It is carnivorous, feeding on fishes, mollusks and crustaceans.

LOGIC, the branch of PHILOSOPHY concerned with analyzing the rules that govern correct and incorrect reasoning, or inference. It was created by ARISTOTLE, who analyzed terms and propositions and in his *Prior Analytics* set out systematically the various forms of the SYLLOGISM; this work has remained an important part of logic ever since. Aristotle's other great achievement was the use of symbols to expose the form of an argument independently of its content. Thus a typical Aristotelian syllogism might be: all A is B; all B is C; therefore all A is C. This formalization of arguments is fundamental to all logic.

Aristotle's pupil THEOPHRASTUS developed syllogistic logic, and some of the STOICS used symbols to represent not single terms but whole propositions, but apart from this there were no significant developments in later antiquity or the early Middle Ages, although logic (dialectic) was part of the TRIVIUM. From the 12th century onward there was great revival of interest in logic: Latin translations of Aristotle's logical works (collectively called the *Organon*) were intently studied, and a kind of program emerged, which was based on Aristotle and included much that would nowadays be regarded as GRAMMAR, EPISTEMOLOGY and linguistic analysis. It was a great age of commentaries and compendiums, with much refinement and minute analysis (see SCHOLASTICISM) but little original work. Among the most important medieval logicians were WILLIAM OF OCKHAM, Albert of Saxony and Jean BURIDAN. After the Renaissance an anti-Aristotelian reaction set in, and logic was given a new turn by Petrus RAMUS and by Francis BACON's prescription that induction (and not deduction) should be the method of the new science. In the work of George BOOLE and Gottlob FREGE the 19th century saw a vast extension in the scope and power of logic. In particular, logic became as bound up with mathematics as it was with philosophy. Logicians became interested in whether particular logical systems were either consistent or complete. (A consistent logic is one in which contradictory propositions cannot be validly derived). The climax of 20th-century logic came in the early 1930s when Kurt GÖDEL demonstrated both the completeness of Frege's first-order logic and that no higher-order logic could be both consistent and complete.

LOGICAL POSITIVISM, the doctrines of the "Vienna Circle," a group of philosophers founded by M. SCHLICK. At the heart of logical positivism was the assertion that apparently factual statements that were not sanctioned by logical or mathematical convention were meaningful only if they could conceivably be empirically verified. Thus only mathematics, logic and science were deemed meaningful; ethics, metaphysics and religion were considered worthless. The influence of logical positivism evaporated after WWII.

LOGISTICS, movement and maintenance of military forces, and specifically noncombatant activities that support military operations, including administration, transport, engineering, supplies and medical services. There was little need of such organization when armies lived off the land, but it is an important and costly part of modern warfare, with all its demands on equipment and munitions. In WWII one half of the US Army was supporting the half engaged in actual combat.

LOGOGRAM. See IDEOGRAM.

LOGOS (Greek: word, reason), term used in Greek philosophy to describe the divine reason and will that was seen to be implicit in the order of the universe. It was adopted in later Judaism (notably by PHILO) and used by Christian writers to define the role of Jesus Christ as the "Word of God" made flesh, the active will of God and an embodied revelation of it to mankind.

LOGROLLING, derogatory term for the political practice of supporting another's cause on the understanding that the favor will be returned in some future legislation. It often occurs when local finance appropriations are being voted.

LOGROLLING. See BIRLING.

LOGWOOD, *Haematoxylon campechianum*, a tropical American tree from which is produced a blood-red dye used in the fabric and leather industries. Family: Leguminosae.

LOHENGRIN, in German myth, a knight sworn to the service of the HOLY GRAIL. The son of PARSIFAL, he was allowed to champion and marry a mortal princess but when she forced him to reveal his identity he sailed away forever in his swan-drawn boat. The legend is most fully treated in the 13th-century epic *Lohengrin*, an anonymous continuation of WOLFRAM VON ESCHENBACH's *Parzival*, and in WAGNER's opera based on it (1848).

LOIRE RIVER, at 627mi the longest river of France. It rises in the Cévennes mountains and flows NW to Orléans, then SW to the ports of Nantes and Saint-Nazaire to empty into the Bay of Biscay. It drains an area of 44 000sq mi, more than a fifth of all France. Canals link the Loire with the Saône, Rhône and Seine rivers.

LOKI, in Teutonic myth a cunning and malicious trickster-god of fire. A companion of ODIN and THOR, he both assists and hampers them. For causing BALDER's death he was bound to a rock beneath a venom-dripping serpent.

LOLLARDS ("idlers" or "babblers"), derisory name given to the 14th-century followers of the English religious reformer John WYCLIFFE. Wandering preachers, the Lollards sought to base their beliefs solely on the Bible and simple worship, rejecting the organized Church altogether. Although considered to have declined during the 15th century, Lollard beliefs were linked with radical social unrest and remained as underground influences on later movements.

LOMAS DE ZAMORA, city in NE Buenos Aires province, E central Argentina, a suburb of Greater Buenos Aires. It has become a major industrial center, with electrical, chemical and cement industries. Pop 410 806.

LOMAX, John Avery (1867–1948), pioneering US folk musicologist. His collections of American folksongs include *Cowboy Songs and other Frontier Ballads* (1910) and *Our Singing Country* (1938).

LOMBARD, residential village in Ill., a suburb of Chicago. In a dairying area, it also has a plastics industry. Pop 35 977.

LOMBARD, Peter (c1100–1160), Italian theologian, Archbishop of Paris from 1158. He is best known for his four *Books of Sentences*, written as source material for theological students and drawing on both biblical and patristic texts and on his contemporaries.

LOMBARDS, Germanic people who moved down from NW Germany in the 4th century AD towards Italy; in 568 they crossed the Alps and conquered most of N Italy, dividing it into dukedoms until 584, when they united into a kingdom against the threat of Frankish invasion. The kingdom reached its height under LIUTPRAND in the 8th century, but was soon overrun by the Franks c770.

LOMBARDY, region of N Italy, once a kingdom of the Lombards, for whom it is named. The country's main industrial and commercial region, it also has efficient and prosperous agriculture. Its capital, Milan, is a major transport hub and commercial center. In area Lombardy is 9 202sq mi and has about 16% of Italy's total population.

LOMBROSO, Cesare (1836–1909), Italian physician who pioneered scientific criminology. His view that criminals were throwbacks to earlier evolutionary stages (see ATAVISM) has now been generally discarded. In retrospect his most valuable work is seen to have been his defense of the rehabilitation and more humane treatment of criminals.

LOMÉ, capital city of Togo, in W Africa. An important industrial, commercial and administrative center, it has been made into a modern seaport since the 1960s and now handles most of the country's trade. Pop 83 845.

LOMITA, residential city in SW Cal. It is a suburb of Los Angeles. Pop 19 784.

LOMOND, Loch, Scotland's largest lake, lies at the S extremity of the Highlands. About 24mi long, it is flanked by the Grampian Mts to the NE, and is famous throughout the world for the beauty of its scenery.

LOMONOSOV, Mikhail Vasilievich (1711–1765), Russian scientist and man of letters, best known for his corpuscular theory of matter, in course of developing which he made an early statement of the KINETIC THEORY.

LOMPOC, city in SW Cal. Its economy rests on the Vandenburg Air Force Base complex, on local oilfields and on truck farming. Pop 25 284.

LONDON, industrial city in SE Ontario, Canada, seat of Middlesex Co., on the Thames R. Its port is Port Stanley on Lake Erie. Pop 221 430.

LONDON, capital of the UK and third largest city in the world. Divided into 33 boroughs, Greater London now covers over 650sq mi along both banks of the Thames R in SE England, including all the historic city and county of London. The national center of government, trade, commerce, shipping, finance and industry, it is also one of the cultural centers of the world.

The Port of London handles over 33% of UK trade. London is also an important industrial region in its own right, with various manufacturing industries. Many of the most important financial and business institutions such as the BANK OF ENGLAND, the Stock Exchange and LLOYD'S OF LONDON, as well as many banking and shipping concerns, are concentrated in the single square mile known as the City; the ancient nucleus of London, it has its own Lord Mayor and corporation. To the W of it is the legal area, with the Law Courts and the INNS OF COURT, and the governmental area centered on the HOUSE OF COMMONS and HOUSE OF LORDS at Westminster.

London is also a historic city with many beautiful buildings: the TOWER OF LONDON, WESTMINSTER ABBEY and BUCKINGHAM PALACE are major tourist attractions. Home of universities, colleges and some of the world's greatest museums and libraries, it also has a flourishing night life and many cinemas. London's art galleries, concert halls, theaters and opera houses are world-famous. Distant areas of London are linked by the complex and highly efficient subway system known as the Underground. Pop 7 379 014.

LONDON, Jack (1876–1916), US writer of novels and short stories, many set during the Yukon GOLD RUSH, that treat the struggles of men and animals to survive as romantic conflicts with nature. The best examples are *The Call of the Wild* (1903), *White Fang* (1906) and *Burning Daylight* (1910), but perhaps his finest work is the autobiographical novel *Martin Eden* (1909).

LONDON, Treaties of, many important international treaties signed in London during the 19th and 20th centuries. The most important are dealt with here. In the Treaty of 1827 Great Britain, France and Russia supported Greek independence in her struggle against Turkey. The Treaty of 1913 ended the First Balkan War (1912) but led to the Second (1913). Defeated, Turkey lost Macedonia, Crete and most of Thrace to Greece, Serbia and Bulgaria. The Treaty of 1915, signed secretly by Great Britain, France, Russia and Italy, promised Italy the South Tyrol, Istria, Gorizia and north Dalmatia if she entered WWI against Germany. The Treaty of 1930 (London Naval Treaty) was signed by the US, Great Britain, France, Italy and Japan; it imposed limits on naval armaments and regulated submarine warfare.

LONDON BRIDGE, actually a historical succession of bridges in London, for centuries the only bridge in the whole area. The first stone bridge, built c1176–1209, had many buildings along it, including a chapel and defensive towers. Rebuilt many times, it was demolished and replaced in the 1820s by New London Bridge. It was again replaced in the 1960s, when its facing was sold and shipped to Lake Havasee, Ariz., where it was rebuilt as a tourist attraction.

LONDON COMPANY, joint stock company chartered by James I in 1606 to found an English colony on the Atlantic coast of North America. It settled Jamestown, Va., but was never a success; in 1624 the charter was canceled, its interests vested in the Crown, and Jamestown became a royal colony.

LONDONDERRY, or **Derry**, seaport in Northern Ireland, on the Royle R. It has a traditional shirtmaking industry, and some light manufacturing industries. Since 1968 it has been a center of violent conflict between Protestants and Roman Catholics (see IRELAND, NORTHERN). Pop 51 617.

LONDRINA, city in SE Brazil, 280mi W of São Paulo. Industries include the processing of coffee, cotton, fruit and meat. Pop 156 670.

LONG, Crawford Williamson (1815–1878), US physician who first discovered the surgical use of diethyl ETHER as an ANESTHETIC (1842). His discovery followed an observation that students under the influence of ether at a party felt no pain when bruising or otherwise injuring themselves.

LONG, Huey Pierce (1893–1935), US political leader of La., called the "Kingfish." He entered the state administration in 1918. Governor after a landslide victory in 1928, he put through economic and social reforms, but virtually suspended the democratic process and ruthlessly used his powers of patronage to create what some saw as a semi-fascist system of state government. A US senator from 1931, he attacked President Roosevelt's NEW DEAL policies, advocating his own "share-the-wealth" program and openly proclaiming his presidential ambitions. He was assassinated at Baton Rouge by Dr. Karl Weiss. The "Long machine" dominated La. politics for a generation.

LONG, Stephen Harriman (1784–1864), US explorer, army engineer and surveyor. He explored the Rocky Mts, where Long's Peak is named for him, the upper Mississippi R and the Minnesota R. He also surveyed for the Baltimore and Ohio railroad.

LONG BEACH, city and resort in Cal., S of Los Angeles. It is a major fishing port and a naval base. Industries include oil refining, aircraft, automobiles and chemicals. Pop 358 633.

LONG BEACH CITY, city on the S shore of Long Island, N.Y. It is a residential suburb and beach resort. Pop 33 127.

LONGBOW, a large bow, generally made of yew and about six feet long, probably first used in Wales in the late 13th century. It was used with great effect by the English in the HUNDRED YEARS' WAR and challenged the supremacy of the CROSSBOW until both were superseded with the advent of firearms.

LONG BRANCH, coastal city in E central N.J. A popular resort from the early 1800s and a summer residence of several presidents, it also has textile and electronics industries. Pop 31 774.

LONGFELLOW, Henry Wadsworth (1807–1882), the most popular US poet of his age. A contemporary of HAWTHORNE at Bowdoin College, he became a professor there and then at Harvard (1836–54). His principal works were *Ballads and Other Poems* (1841) and the narrative poems *Evangeline* (1847), *The Golden Legend* (1851), *The Courtship of Miles Standish* (1858) and above all *The Song of Hiawatha* (1855), which created romantic American legends. Famous individual poems are "The Wreck of the Hesperus" and "Excelsior."

LONGHI, Pietro (1702–1785), Venetian painter best known for his small-scale GENRE works of Venetian life, like *The Exhibition of a Rhinoceros* (1750), or of upper-class Venetian activities, like *The Family Concert*.

LONGHORN CATTLE, a Mexican breed of cattle with Spanish blood. It became the basic stock of the US ranch herds during the 19th century. They are known as strong and hardy animals; however they have nearly been bred out of existence in favor of meatier types.

LONGHOUSE, a combined dwelling and council house of the Iroquois Indians. It could be over 300ft long, and housed many families either side of a central fireplace. The longhouse played a central role in the social organization of the Iroquois.

LONGINUS, putative author of a Greek treatise on literary style, *On the Sublime*, probably written in the 1st century AD, which discusses the elevated or "sublime" style of writing. Translated into French (1674), it became very influential in Europe.

LONG ISLAND, island off the SE coast of N.Y., extending E from the mouth of the Hudson R. It is about 118mi long and 12–23mi wide, and covers an area of 1 723sq mi. Brooklyn and Queens Co. at the W end are part of New York City, and many residents of the island work there. Nassau Co. and Suffolk Co., formerly predominantly agricultural, now have much residential and light industrial development. Its beaches and bays make it a popular resort and fishing center.

LONG ISLAND, Battle of, Aug. 1776, an opening engagement of the American REVOLUTIONARY WAR. Five months after the British evacuated Boston, General Sir William HOWE landed troops on Long Island and drove WASHINGTON's defending army back to Brooklyn Heights. After a few days' siege, the American troops were successfully evacuated.

LONG ISLAND SOUND, an arm of the Atlantic, more than 90mi long, separating Long Island, N.Y., from Conn. A busy shipping route, it is also a popular fishing and boating area.

LONGITUDE. See LATITUDE AND LONGITUDE.

LONG JUMP. See TRACK AND FIELD.

LONG MARCH, 1934–35, the epic march of the Chinese communists, from Kiangsi in the SE to Shensi in the extreme NW, which saved the movement from extermination by the Nationalist (Kuomintang) forces of CHIANG KAI-SHEK. The communists were surrounded by the Kuomintang. Led by MAO TSE-TUNG, CHOU EN-LAI and LIN-PIAO, the Red Army of some 100 000 broke the trap to begin a 6 000mi trek which took them over 18 mountain ranges and 24 rivers under constant air and land attack by Kuomintang troops and local warlords. Thousands were killed but the heroism and determination of the survivors made the Long March the founding legend of Revolutionary China.

LONGMEADOW, town in S central Mass. on the Connecticut R. It is a residential suburb of Springfield. Pop 15 630.

LONGMONT, city in N central Col., 30mi N of Denver. It produces beet and is near silver and gold mines. Pop 23 209.

LONG PARLIAMENT, English legislative assembly that met between 1640 and 1660. Convened by CHARLES I, it immediately tried to check his power. The conflict culminated in the attempted arrest of John PYM, and the CIVIL WAR (1642), during which the parliament remained in session. In 1648 it was "purged" (see RUMP PARLIAMENT), and in 1653 abolished altogether under the PROTECTORATE. It was briefly reconvened in 1660 prior to the RESTORATION.

LONGSPURS, gregarious, sparrow-like, ground birds of America, occurring in open fields and tundra. They are related to SNOW BUNTINGS.

LONGSTREET, Augustus Baldwin (1790–1870), US lawyer, clergyman and educationist, remembered for the light-hearted, sketches *Georgia Scenes* (1835).

Overlooking London's River Thames is the Palace of Westminster, which contains the Houses of Parliament. Its clocktower holds the famous bell *Big Ben*, the sound of whose chimes has come to epitomize this great city.

LONGSTREET, James (1821–1904), Confederate general in the US CIVIL WAR, who fought many important battles in Va. His delay in attack at GETTYSBURG (1863), where he was second in command, is generally thought to have lost the battle. He fought in the Battle of the WILDERNESS and in the last defense of Richmond.

LONGUEUIL, city in Quebec province, Canada. It is a residential suburb of Montreal on the E side of the St. Lawrence R. Pop 97 590.

LONGVIEW, city in NE Tex., seat of Gregg Co. It has oil wells and refineries, and some manufacturing industry. Pop 45 547.

LONGVIEW, city in SW Wash., at the confluence of the Columbia and Cowlitz rivers. Founded as a lumber town, it is a port with wood-pulp, paper and aluminum as its principal manufactures. Pop 28 373.

LOOKOUT, Cape. See CAPE LOOKOUT NATIONAL SEASHORE.

LOOKOUT MOUNTAIN, Battle of, 1863, also called the "Battle above the Clouds," a Union victory in the CIVIL WAR. The Confederates were swept from the ridge of Lookout Mt, near Chattanooga, by General HOOKER.

LOOM. See WEAVING.

LOONS, or **Divers**, genus *Gavia*, large swimming birds of open water. Long-bodied, with legs set well back on the body, they dive and swim expertly under water. An eerie, laughing call gives the birds their name. The four species are widely distributed in more northerly lakes in America.

LOOSESTRIFE, common name for plants of the family Lythraceae and for some genera of the family Primulaceae, notably *Lysimachia* and *Steironema*. Best known is the purple loosestrife (*Lythrum salicaria*) with conspicuous spikes of rose-colored flowers.

LOPE DE VEGA. See VEGA, LOPE DE.

LÓPEZ MATEOS, Adolfo (1910–1969), president of Mexico (1958–64) after being a successful minister of labor (1952–58). His presidency was characterized by agrarian reform and a vast industrialization program.

LOP NOR, or **Lo-pu po,** salt marsh area in the Tarim R basin, SE Sinkiang, China. The region has been used as a testing ground for China's nuclear weapons since 1964.

LOQUAT, *Eriobotrya japonica*, small evergreen, ornamental tree, extensively grown in Asia and subtropical America. It is also cultivated for its edible, yellowish plum-like fruit. Family: Rosaceae.

LORAIN, city in N Ohio, on Lake Erie 20mi W of Cleveland. It is an ore-shipping port and has shipbuilding, steel and heavy manufacturing industries. Pop 78 185.

LORAN (*lo*ng *ra*nge *n*avigation), a NAVIGATION system in which an aircraft pilot may determine his position by comparing the arrival times of pulses from two pairs of RADIO transmitters. Each pair gives him enough information to draw a line of possible positions on a map, the intersection of the two lines marking his true position.

LORCA, Frederico García (1898–1936), celebrated Spanish poet and dramatist inspired by his native Andalusia and by gypsy folklore. He made his reputation with *Gypsy Ballads* (1928) and surrealism influenced *Poet in New York* (published 1940), but he returned to folk themes in the plays *Blood Wedding* (1933), *Yerma* (1935) and *The House of Bernarda Alba* (1936). He was also a talented musician and theater director. He was murdered by the Nationalists in the Civil War.

LORD'S PRAYER, the chief Christian PRAYER, taught by Christ to his disciples and prominent in all Christian worship. Addressed to God the Father, it contains seven petitions, the first three for God's glory, the last four for man's bodily and spiritual needs. The closing doxology ("For thine is the kingdom" etc.) is a very early addition.

LORELEI, rock on the Rhine R in Germany, between Koblenz and Bingen. It rises some 430ft above a point where the river narrows. The legend of its river maiden who lured boatmen to their death by her singing is the subject of HEINE's famous poem, "Die Lorelei."

LOREN, Sophia (1934–   ), Italian screen actress whose combination of statuesque beauty and real dramatic ability has won her international acclaim, including an Academy Award for her performance in *Two Women* (1961). She is married to producer Carlo Ponti.

LORENTZ, Hendrik Antoon (1853–1928), Dutch physicist awarded with P. Zeeman the 1902 Nobel Prize for Physics for his prediction of the ZEEMAN effect. Basing his work on J. Clerk MAXWELL's equations, he explained the REFLECTION and REFRACTION of light; and proposed his *electron theory*, that LIGHT occurred through motion of electrons in a stationary electromagnetic ETHER. Thus the wavelength should change under the influence of a powerful magnetic field; and this was experimentally shown by Zeeman (1896).

But the theory was inconsistent with the results of the MICHELSON-MORLEY EXPERIMENT, and so Lorentz introduced the idea of "local time," that the rate of time's passage differed from place to place; and, incorporating this with the proposal of **George Francis Fitzgerald** (1851–1901) that the length of a moving body decreases in the direction of motion (the Fitzgerald contraction), he derived the *Lorentz transformation*, a mathematical statement which describes the changes in length, time and mass of a moving body. His work, with Fitzgerald's, laid the foundations for EINSTEIN's Special Theory of RELATIVITY.

LORENZ, Konrad (1903–   ), Austrian zoologist and writer, the father of ETHOLOGY, awarded for his work the 1973 Nobel Prize for Physiology or Medicine with FRISCH and TINBERGEN. He is best known for his studies of bird behavior and of human and animal AGGRESSION. His best known books are *King Solomon's Ring* (1952) and *On Aggression* (1966).

LORENTZ, Pare (1905–   ), US film critic and director, who founded and ran a government documentary film unit, 1935–41. *The Plow That Broke The Plains* (1936), on the creation of the DUST BOWL, and *The River* (1937), on the TENNESSEE VALLEY AUTHORITY, were classic and influential documentaries.

LORENZETTI, name of two Sienese painters influenced by GIOTTO. **Ambrogio** (c1290–1348), is best known for the fresco cycle *Good and Bad Government* (c1338–48) in Siena. His brother **Pietro** (c1280–1348), painted the *Passion* cycle in the Orsini Chapel, Assisi.

LORENZO DI CREDI (c1456–1537), Florentine painter, a pupil of VERROCHIO. His paintings, such as the *Virgin and Child* tondo, resemble LEONARDO DA VINCI's early work.

LORENZO MONACO (Piero di Giovanni; c1370–c1422), Italian painter. Born in Siena, he became a Camaldolensian monk in Florence in 1391. He is known as a manuscript illuminator and a painter of altarpieces.

LORETO, town and place of pilgrimage in central Italy. Its famous shrine is the *Santa Casa*, the Sacred House of the Virgin Mary miraculously transported from Nazareth by Angels. Pop 9 530.

LORIES, a group of about 65 species of PARROT, all of which have a brush-like tip to the tongue as an adaptation to feeding on nectar and pollen, though some larger species also eat fruit. Lories are brilliantly-colored, noisy, gregarious birds.

LORISES, nocturnal mammals of Asia, related to LEMURS, with large, forward-oriented eyes and well-developed, grasping hands. Neither of the two species, the Slender loris and the Slow loris, has a tail long enough to show through the fur. Both are omnivorous, eating insects, fruit, leaves, birds' eggs, lizards and small mammals.

LORRAINE. See ALSACE-LORRAINE.

LORRAINE, Claude. See CLAUDE LORRAINE.

LOS ALAMITOS, village in S Cal., 6mi ENE of Long Beach, in a fruit-growing area. A US naval air station is nearby. Pop 11 346.

LOS ALAMOS, town in N.M., 25mi NW of Sante Fe. It grew up around the scientific laboratory (1943) where the world's first atomic and hydrogen bombs were developed. Pop 11 310.

LOS ALTOS, residential city in W Cal., in the foothills of the Santa Cruz Mts. Pop 24 956.

LOS ANGELES, city in S Cal., third largest in the US. It is a sprawling city of some 464sq mi dominated by freeways and the automobile, and the center of a metropolitan area with a population of over 7 million. Situated between sea and mountains, it has no extremes of temperature, which average 55°F in January and 73°F in July. It is the third largest industrial center in the US, producing among other things aircraft, electrical equipment, automobiles, glass, furniture, rubber, canned fish and refined oils (but industrialization has made smog a serious problem). It is the world capital of the motion-picture and television industry (see HOLLYWOOD) and also a distribution and commercial center for the nearby mining regions, oilfields and rich farm areas. Its port, San Pedro, handles more tonnage than any other US Pacific port, and accommodates a large fishing fleet. Tourism is another source of wealth. The city is dominated by fine buildings, including a number by Frank Lloyd WRIGHT. It has several museums, many fine churches and libraries, and four universities. Taken from the Mexicans in 1846, it was incorporated in 1850. It was linked with the transcontinental railroad system in the 1870s and 1880s. Oil was discovered in the region in the 1890s. Pop 2 809 596.

LOS GATOS, city in W Cal., 8mi SW of San Jose, notable for its wine. Pop 23 735.

LOST COLONY, an English settlement (1587) on Roanoke Island off the coast of N.C., which disappeared without trace. It was founded by 117 settlers led by John White, sponsored by Sir Walter RALEIGH. Supplies ran out and White visited England for help. When he returned in 1590, the colony had disappeared, possibly having been wiped out by hostile Indians.

LOST GENERATION, a term for the US writers of the post-WWI generation, coined in a remark by Gertrude STEIN to Ernest HEMINGWAY. Besides him they included Scott FITZGERALD, John DOS PASSOS, E. E. CUMMINGS and others. Their ideals shattered by the war, they felt alienated from the materialism of America in the 1920s, and many lived bohemian expatriate lives in Paris.

LOT, in the Old Testament, ABRAHAM's nephew whose wife was turned to a pillar of salt when, in spite of being warned not to, she looked back while fleeing from the destruction of SODOM.

LOTTO, Lorenzo (c1480–1556), Italian painter influenced by RAPHAEL and the Venetians, notably, TITIAN. He painted portraits, landscapes and mystical and religious subjects which became, as in *St. Anthony giving Alms* (1542), increasingly direct and moving in style.

LOTUS, popular name for a number of unrelated species of plants. The Egyptian lotus, the sacred lotus and American lotus are all species of WATER LILY. The lotus fruits of the Greeks are produced by *Zizyphus lotus*. The genus *Lotus* of the family Leguminosae comprises herbs and shrubs with pea-like, normally yellow flowers.

LOTUS-EATERS, mentioned in Homer's *Odyssey*, the legendary inhabitants of the N coast of Africa. They lived on the fruit and flowers of the lotus tree which drugged them into happy forgetfulness. TENNYSON wrote a famous poem with this title.

LOUDSPEAKER, or **speaker,** device to convert electrical impulses into sound. It commonly comprises a rigid conical diaphragm attached to a coil held such that it may move backward and forward; within the cylinder of the coil is a fixed permanent magnet. Changes in the current supplied to the coil alter its magnetic field so that it, and the cone, vibrate to produce the compression waves that are SOUND. (See also AMPLIFIER; ELECTRICITY; ELECTROMAGNETISM; MAGNETISM.) HIGH FIDELITY sets use two or more loudspeakers of different sizes for more accurate reproduction.

LOUIS, name of 18 kings of France. **Louis I** (778–840), Holy Roman Emperor 814–40, known as "the Pious." He was the third son of CHARLEMAGNE. He divided the empire among his sons, thereby contributing to its fragmentation, but laying the foundations of the state of France. **Louis II** (846–879), reigned 877–79. **Louis III** (c863–882), reigned 879–82. As king of N France he defeated

Norman invaders. **Louis IV** (c921–954), reigned 936–54. He was called "Transmarinus" because of his childhood exile in England. **Louis V** (c966–987), reigned 986–87. The last Carolingian ruler of France, he was known as "the Sluggard." **Louis VI** (1081–1137), reigned 1108–37. He subdued the robber barons around Paris, granted privileges to the towns and aided the Church. He engaged in war against Henry I of England (1104–13 and 1116–20). **Louis VII** (c1120–1180), reigned 1137–80. He joined the second Crusade (1147–49) in defiance of a papal interdict. From 1157 onwards, Louis was at war with Henry II of England who had married Louis' former wife, Eleanor of Aquitaine. **Louis VIII** (1187–1226), reigned 1223–26. Nicknamed "the Lion," he was a great soldier and was at first successful in his attempts to aid the barons rebelling against King John of England. **Louis IX, Saint** (1214–1270), reigned 1226–70. He repelled an invasion by Henry III of England (1242), and led the sixth Crusade (1248), but was defeated and captured in Egypt and had to be ransomed. In 1270 he led another crusade, but died of plague after reaching N Africa. A just ruler, he was regarded as an ideal Christian king and was canonized in 1297. His feast day is Aug. 25. **Louis X** (1289–1316), reigned 1314–16, a period in which the nobility reasserted their strength. **Louis XI** (1423–1483), reigned 1461–83. A cruel and unscrupulous king, he had plotted against his father for the throne, but unified most of France. **Louis XII** (1462–1515), reigned 1498–1515. Nicknamed "Father of the People," he was a popular ruler who inaugurated reforms in finance and justice and was ambitious for territorial gains. **Louis XIII** (1601–1643), reigned 1610–43. A weak king, he was greatly influenced by his chief minister Cardinal RICHELIEU. **Louis XIV** (1638–1715), reigned 1643–1715, known as "Louis the Great" and "the Sun King." The archetypal absolute monarch, he built the great palace at VERSAILLES. "The state is myself," he is said to have declared. His able ministers, MAZARIN and COLBERT, strengthened France with their financial reforms. But Louis squandered money in such escapades as the War of DEVOLUTION (1667–68) and the War of the SPANISH SUCCESSION (1701–13), which broke the military power of France. **Louis XV** (1710–1774), reigned 1715–74, nicknamed "the Well-Beloved." He was influenced by Cardinal Fleury until the cardinal's death in 1743. A weak king dependent on mistresses (especially Madame de POMPADOUR) his involvement in foreign wars ran up enormous debts. **Louis XVI** (1754–1793), reigned 1774–92. Although he accepted the advice of his ministers TURGOT and NECKER on the need for social and political reform, Louis was not strong enough to overcome the opposition of his court and his queen, MARIE ANTOINETTE. This led to the outbreak of the FRENCH REVOLUTION in 1789 with the formation of the National Assembly and the storming of the Bastille. In 1791 Louis attempted to escape but was brought back to Paris and guillotined on Jan. 21, 1793. **Louis XVII** (1785–1795), son of Louis XVI, king in name only. He was imprisoned in 1793 and was reported dead in 1795. **Louis XVIII** (1755–1824), brother of Louis XVI. He escaped from France in 1791. For more than 20 years he remained in exile, but after the final defeat of Napoleon in the Battle of WATERLOO (1815), he became firmly established. He proclaimed a liberal constitution, but on his death the reactionary Ultraroyalists gained control under Charles X.

LOUIS, Joe (1914–), known as the "Brown Bomber," heavyweight boxing champion of the world 1937–49. Louis, who defended his title 25 times, was only ever beaten three times, finally by Rocky MARCIANO.

LOUISBOURG, town in NE Nova Scotia, Canada, on the Atlantic. A French fortress, it was captured by the American colonials in 1745, restored to France in 1748, but taken by the English in 1758. The remains of the fortress are now part of a National Historic Park and Louisbourg is a port for coal-shipping and fishing. Pop 1 578.

LOUISE, Lake, in Banff National Park, SW Alberta, Canada. It is sheltered by the Rockies and is a popular tourist center.

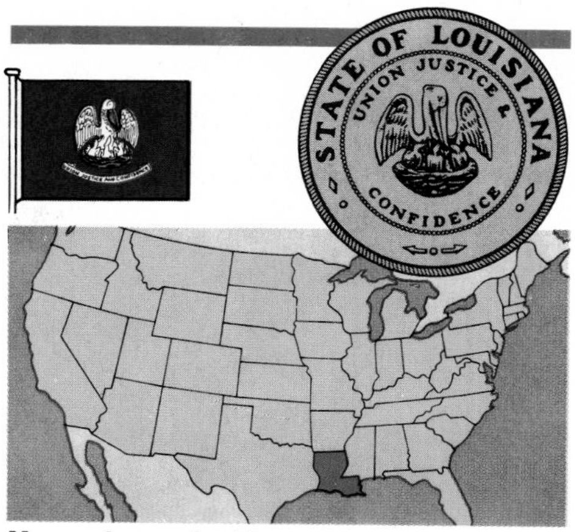

Name of state: Louisiana
Capital: Baton Rouge
Statehood: April 30, 1812 (18th state)
Familiar name: Pelican State
Area: 48 523sq mi
Population: 3 643 180
Elevation: Highest—535ft, Driskill Mountain. Lowest—5ft below sea level, at New Orleans
Motto: Union, Justice and Confidence
State flower: Magnolia
State bird: Brown pelican
State tree: Bald Cypress
State song: "Song of Louisiana"

LOUISIANA, or the "Pelican State," a Southern state on the Gulf of Mexico, at the mouth of the Mississippi R. Louisiana can be divided into three geographical regions: the E and W Gulf coastal plains, and between them the Mississippi alluvial plain. The two coastal plains are mainly composed of rolling hills and prairie. The flat and fertile alluvial plain, averaging a width of 50mi, extends into the Mississippi delta which covers about a third of the state's land area. Louisiana has long, hot and humid summers, and brief cool winters.

People. About two-thirds of Louisiana's population live in urban areas. The capital is Baton Rouge, but the port of New Orleans is the largest city. The N of the state is a Protestant Anglo-Saxon area, but the people of the S are descended from French and Spanish settlers, and this has clearly influenced architecture, the legal system and cooking.

Economy. About 15% of the workforce is employed in agriculture, yet Louisiana is the nation's leading producer of rice and sweet potatoes. Livestock and dairy products are of importance, as are soybeans, cotton, corn and sugarcane. Louisiana is second only to Tex. in the production of petroleum; natural gas, sulfur and salt are also produced. The most important industries are chemicals, foodstuffs, paper and paper products and aerospace. Tourism is also important.

History. In the 18th century, Louisiana was controlled by the French and the Spanish, but in 1803 the state was sold to the US as part of the LOUISIANA PURCHASE. Louisiana was admitted to the Union in 1812 and quickly prospered. Her population increased almost tenfold between 1812 and the Civil War; but at the outbreak of the war, half the population was composed of slaves. The pre-Civil War period saw the heyday of the great Mississippi steamboats. However, Louisiana's prosperity was checked by the Civil War and the harsh policies of RECONSTRUCTION. The discovery of oil and natural gas early in the 20th century brought new investment to Louisiana, but she suffered greatly in the DEPRESSION. Since WWII, Louisiana has experienced rapid industrialization, but she still has one of the nation's lowest per capita incomes.

LOUISIANA PURCHASE, the huge territory purchased by the US from France in 1803. It stretched from the Mississippi R to the Rockies, and from the Canadian border to the Gulf of Mexico, some 828 000sq mi. Its acquisition more than doubled the area of what was then the US.

From 1762 the old French province of Louisiana, roughly where Louisiana is today, had been held by Spain. In 1800 Napoleon persuaded the Spanish to return the province to France. President Jefferson received reports of this with alarm, realizing that Napoleon hoped to establish an empire in North America. Jefferson instructed Livingston and Monroe to purchase New Orleans and other strategic parts of the Louisiana province from France. Much to their surprise, Napoleon, who was expecting renewed war with England, in April 1803 offered to sell the huge Louisiana Territory to the US, and the envoys quickly accepted the offer for a total price of $15 million. The Purchase had greatly exceeded Jefferson's instructions, and there was some opposition from US businessmen, but most Americans saw the doubling of their territory as a triumph.

LOUIS PHILIPPE (1773–1850), king of the French 1830–48. Exiled from France in 1793, he traveled in Europe and the US until 1815, when he was accepted as a compromise candidate for the crown. As king from 1830 he was unwilling to extend the voting franchise, and the revolution of Feb., 1848, led to his abdication.

LOUISVILLE, largest city in Ky., and seat of Jefferson Co., on the Ohio R. It is a major river port, producing tobacco, whiskey, gin, clothing, food products and automobiles. Pop 361 958.

LOURDES, center of Roman Catholic pilgrimage, in SW France where, in 1858, the Virgin is said to have appeared to a 14-year-old peasant girl, now St. BERNADETTE. Lourdes is visited by some three million pilgrims annually. Pop 18 310.

LOURENÇO MARQUES, now **Maputo,** capital, largest city and chief port of the former Portuguese colony of Mozambique in SE Africa. Chief among its exports are coal, agricultural goods and lumber. The name was briefly changed to Can Phumo in 1975. Pop 383 775.

LOUSE. See LICE.

L'OUVERTURE, Toussaint. See TOUSSAINT L'OUVERTURE.

LOUVRE, historic palace in Paris, mostly built during the reign of LOUIS XIV. Now one of the world's largest and most famous art museums, its treasures include paintings by Rembrandt, Rubens, Titian and Leonardo da Vinci.

LOVAGE, *Levisticum officinale*, perennial herb native to S Europe and cultivated for its seeds, which have an aromatic odor and are used to flavor foods and confectionary. Family: Umbelliferae.

LOVEBIRDS, eight or nine species in a genus of African PARROTS, *Agapornis*, so-called because of their close pair-bond and the frequency with which paired birds preen each other.

LOVEJOY, surname of two American brothers, both dedicated advocates of ABOLITIONISM. **Elijah Parish Lovejoy** (1802–1837) published newspapers in St. Louis and in Alton, Ill., advocating abolitionism. He was killed while defending his press from a mob. **Owen Lovejoy** (1811–1864), pastor, and later abolitionist leader in Illinois. A supporter of Abraham Lincoln, he was elected to Congress in 1856 and constantly denounced slavery there.

LOVELACE, Richard (1618–1657?), English Royalist soldier and one of the CAVALIER POETS. His poems, in two volumes, entitled *Lucasta*, were published in 1649 and 1660. They are noted at their best for a fine melodic line.

LOVELAND, town in N Col., on the Big Thompson R. It is a processing center for agricultural produce. Pop 16 220.

LOVELL, James Arthur, Jr. (1928–), US astronaut. He first flew in Gemini 7 (1965) and Gemini 12 (1966) before joining Apollo 8 (1968), the first manned flight around the moon. In 1970 he commanded the nearly disastrous Apollo 13, when an explosion in the spacecraft prevented a moon landing.

LOVES PARK, city in N Ill. on Rock R. It is a residential area NE of Rockford. Pop 12 390.

LOW, Juliette Gordon (1860–1927), founder of the Girl Scouts in the US. She organized the first troop in her home town, Savannah, Ga., in 1912. By the time of her death there were 140 000 Girl Scouts in the US.

LOW, Seth (1850–1916), US politician and educator. Born in Brooklyn, N.Y., he was president of Columbia College 1889–1901, and mayor of New York from 1901–03.

LOW COUNTRIES. See BELGIUM; NETHERLANDS; LUXEMBOURG.

LOWELL, industrial city in Mass., 24mi NW of Boston, named for Francis Cabot LOWELL. It was once a major textile center. Pop 94 239.

LOWELL, Amy (1874–1925), US critic and poet of the IMAGIST school. Her collections of verse include *Sword Blades and Poppy Seed* (1914), *Men, Women and Ghosts* (1916) and *Can Grande's Castle* (1918).

LOWELL, Francis Cabot (1775–1817), US cotton manufacturer. In 1812 he founded the Boston Manufacturing Company—the first mill in the US to convert raw cotton into the finished cloth in a single plant.

LOWELL, James Russell (1819–1891), US poet, editor, essayist and diplomat. His best poems, including the famous *Vision of Sir Launfal* (1848), were written before his wife's death in 1853. His reputation as a political satirist was made by the witty *Bigelow Papers* (1848 and 1867). In 1855 he became professor of modern languages at Harvard, and was minister to England 1877–85.

LOWELL, Percival (1855–1916), US astronomer and writer who predicted the existence of and initiated the search for PLUTO; but who is best known for his championing the theory (now discarded) that the "canals" of MARS were signs of an irrigation system built by an intelligent race.

LOWELL, Robert (1917–   ), US poet and playwright. For his collection *Lord Weary's Castle* (1946) he won the Pulitzer Prize. Later books, *The Mills of the Kavanaughs* (1951), the autobiographical *Life Studies* (1959) and *For the Union Dead* (1964), established his reputation as a major poet. His dramatic trilogy *The Old Glory* was published in 1965. His versions of Greek tragedy and various European poets have brought him acclaim as a translator.

LOWER CALIFORNIA. See BAJA CALIFORNIA.

LOWER MERION, town NW of Philadelphia, SE Pa. Pop 63 470.

LOWER SOUTHAMPTON, town NE of Philadelphia, SE Pa. Pop 17 578.

LOWEST COMMON MULTIPLE (LCM), in ARITHMETIC, the lowest number of which two or more positive whole numbers are FACTORS.

LOWRY, Malcolm (1909–1957), English novelist and poet. While living on the coast of British Columbia (1940–54) he published his greatest work *Under the Volcano* (1947) concerned in part with the problem of alcoholism, which eventually proved fatal to the author.

LOYALTY ISLANDS, dependency of French New Caledonia, SW Pacific. A chain of islands 60mi E of New Caledonia, they produce coconuts, fruit and vegetables and export copra.

LO-YANG, city in E central China. Once the capital for several dynasties, it is now a center for agriculture, commerce and coal mining. Pop 750 000.

LOYOLA, Saint Ignatius of (1491–1556), Spanish founder of the Society of Jesus (see JESUITS). Having spent his youth as a Basque nobleman and soldier, Loyola became converted to the life of God in 1521 while recovering from a serious wound. He wrote the famous *Spiritual Exercises* (begun 1522–23), and later went to Paris where, with St. FRANCIS XAVIER, he formed the Society of Jesus (1534). Loyola was its first general, and the author of its *Constitutions* (1547–50).

LSD, lysergic acid diethylamide, a HALLUCINOGENIC DRUG based on ERGOT alkaloids. It may lead to psychotic reaction and bizarre behavior.

LUANDA, formerly Sao Paulo de Luanda, seaport and capital of Angola, SW Africa. It has food-processing industries and among its exports are coffee and palm products. Pop 475 328.

LUANG PRABANG, state and town in N Laos. The town, on the left bank of the Mekong R, was once the capital of the Laotian kings. It is a trading center for rubber, teak and rice. Pop 25 000.

LUBBOCK, city and seat of Lubbock Co., NW Tex. It is an agricultural center and major cotton market. Pop 149 101.

LÜBECK, seaport of Schleswig-Holstein, West Germany. An important commercial center in the Middle Ages, Lübeck became the headquarters of the HANSEATIC LEAGUE. Today it has large shipyards and foundries, and makes machinery and textiles. Pop 239 339.

LUBITSCH, Ernst (1892–1947), German film director, noted chiefly for the sophisticated comedies he made after his emigration to Hollywood in 1923. Among his known films are *Forbidden Paradise* (1924), *Ninotchka* (1939), *The Merry Widow* (1939), and *That Uncertain Feeling* (1941).

LUBLIN, historic city in SE Poland, on the Bystrzyca R. An important trade center since the 13th century, it is now a manufacturing town and a transport hub. Pop 239 000.

LUBRICATION, the introduction of a thin film of lubricant—usually a semiviscous fluid—between two surfaces moving relative to each other, in order to minimize FRICTION and abrasive wear. In particular, BEARINGS are lubricated in engines and other machinery. Liquid lubricants are most common, usually PETROLEUM fractions, being cheap, easy to introduce, and good at cooling the parts. The VISCOSITY is tailored to the load, being made high enough to maintain the film yet not so high that power is lost. Multigrade oils cover a range of viscosity. The viscosity index represents the constancy of the viscosity over the usual temperature range—a desirable feature. Synthetic oils, including SILICONES, are used for high-temperature and other special applications. **Greases**—normally oils thickened with soaps, fats or waxes—are preferred where the lubricant has to stay in place without being sealed in. Solid lubricants, usually applied with a binder, are soft, layered solids including graphite, molybdenite, talc and boron nitride. TEFLON, with its uniquely low coefficient of friction, is used for self-lubricating bearings. Rarely air or another gas is used as a lubricant. Additives to liquid lubricants include antioxidants, detergents, pour-point depressants (increasing low-temperature fluidity), and polymers to improve the viscosity index.

LUBUMBASHI (formerly Elizabethville), city in SE Zaire, capital of the Shaba region. Originally a mining center, it now has many other industries. It has a Roman Catholic cathedral and several educational institutions. Pop 318 000.

LUCAN (39–54 AD), Marcus Annaeus Lucanus, Roman poet best known for his *Bellum Civile* (or, incorrectly, *Pharsalia*), an epic poem on the clash between Julius Caesar and Pompey. He was a protégé of Nero's but eventually aroused the latter's jealousy. Lucan joined the Pisonian conspiracy against Nero and when this failed, committed suicide.

LUCAS VAN LEYDEN (c1494–1533), foremost Dutch painter of his day. A noted engraver and printmaker, he was as highly regarded as his acquaintance DÜRER. He painted biblical themes, such as *Lot and His Daughters* (c1509); some of his work foreshadows that of the great GENRE painters.

LUCCA, historic city in N Italy, capital of Lucca province, Tuscany. A silk-manufacturing center since the 11th century, it is a major industrial and commercial center in a rich agricultural region. Pop 90 889.

LUCE, Clare Boothe (1903–   ), US dramatist, editor and politician. She worked for *Vogue* magazine and was managing editor of *Vanity Fair* 1933–34, marrying Henry LUCE in 1935. Her play *The Women* (1936), was the first of several successes. She served in Congress 1943–47 and was appointed US ambassador to Italy 1953–56, the first American woman to hold high diplomatic office. Named ambassador to Brazil, in 1959, she resigned when the appointment was attacked in the Senate.

LUCE, Henry Robinson (1898–1967), US editor and publisher of *Time*, which he founded with Briton Hadden in 1923. He also produced *Fortune* (1930), *Life* (1936) and *Sports Illustrated* (1954), as well as many books, radio series and newsreels.

LUCERNE. See ALFALFA.

LUCERNE (or Luzern), historic capital city of Lucerne canton, on the NW shore of Lake Lucerne in central Switzerland. It is a major resort center, serves a rich dairying area and also has some light industries. Pop 69 879.

LUCIAN (c125–c190 AD), Syrian-Greek satirist. Among his best-known works are *Dialogues of the Gods*, a parody of mythology; *Dialogues of the Dead*, a biting satire on human vanities; and the *True History*, a lampoon of fantastic travellers' tales, which influenced RABELAIS and Jonathan SWIFT.

LUCIFER (Latin: light-bearer), in classical mythology, the morning star (the planet Venus). The word was used to translate "day star" in Isaiah 14:12—an epithet of the king of Babylon. Early biblical interpreters subsequently took it as the name of Satan before his fall from heaven.

LUCIFER, an early type of MATCH made by Samuel Jones of London (c1830).

LUCITE (**Perspex** or **Plexiglass**), extremely tough, light, very transparent thermoplastic used for auto and aircraft windshields, contact lenses, watchglasses, etc. It is composed of polymethylmethacrylate. (See also PLASTIC.)

LUCIUS, name of three popes. **Lucius I,** pope for eight months (253–254 AD). **Lucius II**, pope from March 1144 to Feb. 1145. His rule was marked by conflict in Rome over the temporal authority of the papacy; he was killed in battle. **Lucius III**, pope 1181–1185. Forced into exile by Roman politics, he was supported by the Emperor Frederick I Barbarossa, and presided over a great synod at Verona in 1184.

LUCKNOW, historic city in N India, capital of Uttar Pradesh state. A market center with many industries, it is the administrative headquarters for the area. Lucknow is an important cultural center and has much notable architecture. Pop 750 512.

LUCRETIA, in Roman myth the virtuous wife of Lucius Tarquinius Collatinus. In c509 BC she killed herself after being raped by Sextus Tarquinius, son of the Etruscan king of Rome. This resulted in the expulsion of the Tarquins from Rome. Her story inspired Shakespeare's *Rape of Lucrece*.

LUCRETIUS (c95–55 BC), Roman poet, the author of *De rerum natura*, and the last and greatest classical exponent of ATOMISM. His description of atoms in the void and his vision of the progress of man suffered undeserved neglect on account of his antireligious reputation.

LUDDITES, bands of English textile workers who destroyed labor-saving textile machinery in the early 19th century. They were protesting against unemployment and low wages which resulted wherever the new machinery was introduced and also against the poor quality of goods produced on the machines. Repressive government measures and an improving economic climate combined to end the rioting by 1816.

LUDENDORFF, Erich (1865–1937), German general who with Hindenburg did much to defeat the invading Russian armies in WWI, particularly at TANNENBERG. He was responsible for much German policy 1917–18 and for the request of an armistice in 1918. After the war he led a nationalist movement; he took part in Hitler's abortive coup in Munich in 1923, but severed relations with him soon after.

LUDLOW, town in S central Mass. Formerly a milling town, it is now a manufacturing center producing printed products, metal and plastics. Pop 17 580.

LUDLOW, Roger (1590–c1664), English colonizer and Puritan politician. A director of the MASSACHUSETTS BAY COMPANY, he became colonial deputy governor in 1634. In 1635 he headed colonizing projects in the Conn. area and wrote the FUNDAMENTAL ORDERS, its first legal code. He returned to England in 1654.

LUDWIGSHAFEN, commercial and industrial city on the W bank of the Rhine in the SE Rhineland-Palatinate, West Germany. Pop 174 698.

LUFKIN, city in E Tex. and seat of Angelina Co., A lumbering center, it is in an oil and gas area and has mixed agriculture. Pop 23 049.

LUFTWAFFE (German: air arm), title of the German air force. Formed in 1935 under Hitler, it was commanded by Herman GOERING during WWII.

LUGANO, Lake, lies in the foothills of the Alps between lakes Maggiore and Como, Italy. Around 22mi long by 2mi wide, it extends into Switzerland.

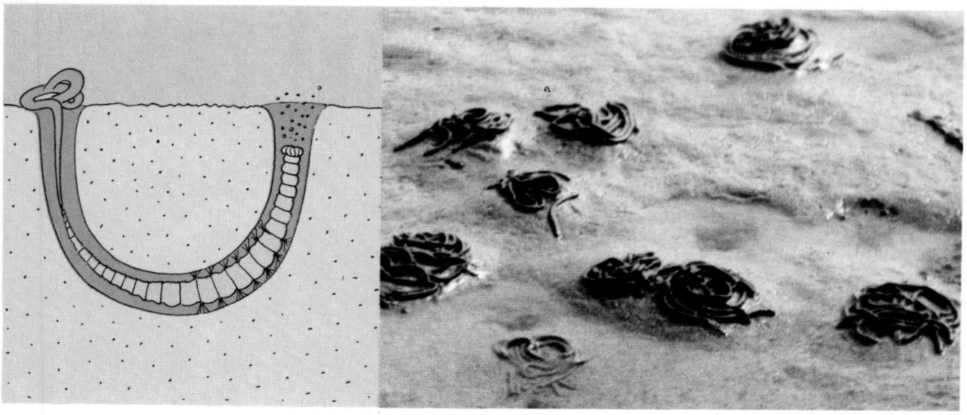

How the lugworm's characteristic cast is formed. The worm eats sand, digests the minute food particles it contains and excretes what is left into coiling casts on the surface.

LUGARD, Frederick John Dealtry Lugard, 1st Baron (1858–1945), British soldier and colonial governor. He was instrumental in negotiating treaties with the natives of W and S Nigeria and served as high commissioner for N Nigeria 1900–06. He pioneered administration by indirect rule through traditional tribal institutions. Lugard was governor of Hong Kong 1907–12, and governor of a unified Nigeria 1912–19.

LUGWORMS, large polychaete worms of the genus *Arenicola* and allied genera, whose coiled casts are a familiar sight on sandy shores. Tube-dwelling worms, they have a fat, cylindrical body and reduced appendages. They form a U-shaped burrow in the sand, eating the sand and extracting organic material from it, then backing up the tube to defecate.

LUKACS Gyorgy (1885–1971), Hungarian-born leading Marxist literary critic. He was made professor of aesthetics at Budapest U. in 1945. After the 1956 Hungarian uprising, Lukacs fell from political favor. Among his major works are *Studies in European Realism* (1946) and *The Historical Novel* (1955).

LUKE, Saint, by tradition the author of the third GOSPEL and its sequel, the Acts of the Apostles. Luke was a Gentile and worked as a physician, probably in Antioch. He was influenced by his friend, St. Paul, whom he accompanied on his missionary journeys. The Gospel, written for Gentiles, claims to be based on eyewitness accounts.

LUKS, George Benjamin (1867–1933), US realist painter, one of the ASHCAN SCHOOL. Primarily a painter of figures, his bold and vigorous style in such works as *The Wrestlers* (1905) may have owed something to his work as a cartoonist.

LULLY, Jean-Baptiste (1632–1687), Italian-born French composer who became Louis XIV's favorite musician. He wrote much stage music, for MOLIÈRE among others, and his operas, particularly *Alceste* (1674) and *Armide* (1686), founded a French operatic tradition.

LUMBAGO, popular term for low back pain or lumbar back ache. It may be of various origins including chronic ligamentous strain, SLIPPED DISK (sometimes with SCIATICA), certain types of ARTHRITIS affecting the spine and congenital disease of the spine. Diagnosis and treatment may be difficult.

LUMBER, cut wood, especially when prepared for use ("dressed"). Lumbering, the extraction of timber from the forest, is a major industry in the US, which still has vast natural forests. In world timber production, the USSR is first, followed by the US, Japan, and Canada. The demand for lumber is vast; it takes as many as 20 trees to make a ton of paper and the annual US paper production exceeds 35 million tons. The forests would soon be depleted without modern conservation and reforestation programs.

Trees used for lumber are classed as either softwoods or hardwoods. Softwoods, which thrive in cold regions, are the evergreen conifers such as fir, pine, cedar and spruce. Hardwoods, which thrive in temperate regions, include the deciduous trees like oak, birch, aspen and beech. The softwoods, used in building, make up 75% of the US timber market.

In the vast softwood forests of the US lumbering has become a mechanized industry, using power saws to fell and cut to size the trees, and tractors or tractor winches to drag logs to a central clearing by cable. Since forests are often located in inaccessible regions, new roads and new railroads may have to be built to transport the logs. Logs are often floated down mountain streams to broader rivers and lakes on whose banks sawmills are often located. Great masses of logs can be towed by tug down river, inside huge floating collars or booms. Once at the mill they may be stored until needed in a huge log pond, or millpond, protected by the water from fire and disease. After sorting, the logs are fed onto a conveyor belt and into the mill. Each log is clamped to a carriage and fed back and forth against a vertical bandsaw. The boards then pass to an edger, to remove the bark, and a trimmer which cuts them to standard lengths. Other legs are cut into sheets or veneer, for plywood. The newly-cut wood, still green with moisture, is then seasoned (dried) before it is used commercially. (See FORESTRY; PAPER; TREE.)

Lumber in log booms floats in the millpond of a sawmill at Nanaimo, British Columbia. The water protects the logs from fire and disease.

LUMBERTON, city in S N.C., seat of Robeson Co., on the Lumber R. Pop 16961.

LUMEN (lm), SI UNIT of luminous flux (see PHOTOMETRY).

LUMIÈRE, Louis (1864–1948), French pioneer of motion PHOTOGRAPHY who, with his brother Auguste (1862–1954), invented an early motion-picture system (patented 1895), the *cinématographe*; and made what is regarded as the first movie (1895).

LUMINANCE, in PHOTOMETRY, the brightness of an extended surface. In SI UNITS luminance is measured in CANDELAS per square metre but older units include the APOSTILB, the LAMBERT and the STILB.

LUMINESCENCE, the nonthermal emission of ELECTROMAGNETIC RADIATION, particularly LIGHT, from a PHOSPHOR. Including both fluorescence and phosphorescence (distinguished according to how long emission persists after excitation has ceased, in fluorescence emission ceasing within 10ns but continuing much longer in phosphorescence), particular types of luminescence are named for the mode of excitation. Thus in photoluminescence, X-ray PHOTONS are absorbed by the phosphor and lower-energy radiations emitted; in CHEMILUMINESCENCE the energy source is a chemical reaction; cathodoluminescence is energized by cathode rays (ELECTRONS), and BIOLUMINESCENCE occurs in certain biochemical reactions. (See also ELECTROLUMINESCENCE.)

LUMPFISHES, or **Lumpsuckers**, a family of marine, bottom-living fishes with warty lumps on the body, and a ventral sucking disk. Females produce a large mass of eggs in a loose ball above the low water mark. These are guarded by the male, even when exposed at low tide.

LUMPY JAW, common name for actinomycosis in cattle, a disease caused by infection with the ACTINOMYCETE, *Actinomyces bovis*. Actinomycosis also affects swine and, occasionally, man.

LUMUMBA, Patrice Emergy (1925–1961), first prime minister of the Republic of the Congo (Zaire). He negotiated independence from Belgium (1960). Soon after, the army mutinied and Katanga seceded. Following his dismissal by President Joseph Kasavubu in Sept. 1960, he was arrested by General Joseph Mobutu and killed in mysterious circumstances some time later.

LUNAR SOCIETY OF BIRMINGHAM, the most illustrious of the British provincial scientific societies of the late 18th century. Its members included the industrialists Matthew BOULTON and Josiah WEDGWOOD, the physician Erasmus DARWIN and the chemist and theologian, Joseph PRIESTLEY.

LUNDY, Benjamin (1789–1839), American abolitionist who gave up his business to devote his life to antislavery activities. Lundy founded the abolitionist Union Humane Society (1815) and published several antislavery periodicals.

LUNDY'S LANE, Battle of, fought during the War of 1812 in Canada near Niagara Falls (July 25, 1814). It halted the US advance into Canada at Fort Erie, but despite heavy casualties it was otherwise inconclusive.

LUNGFISHES, primitive bony fishes that were worldwide in distribution in DEVONIAN and TRIASSIC times, but are now restricted to South America, Africa and Australia. They are characterized by the presence of true LUNGS, used for breathing air, though in well-oxygenated water they may use their GILLS for breathing. Pectoral and pelvic fins are reduced to fleshy feelers, and the tail is replaced by the union of the upper and lower halves of the median fin.

LUNGS, in vertebrates, the (usually) two largely air-filled organs in the CHEST concerned with RESPIRATION. the absorption of OXYGEN from and

The human lungs: (1) right superior lobe; (2) aorta; (3) trachea; (4) left superior lobe; (5) pulmonary artery; (6) diaphragm; (7) right inferior lobe; (8) middle lobe; (9) heart; (10) left inferior lobe.

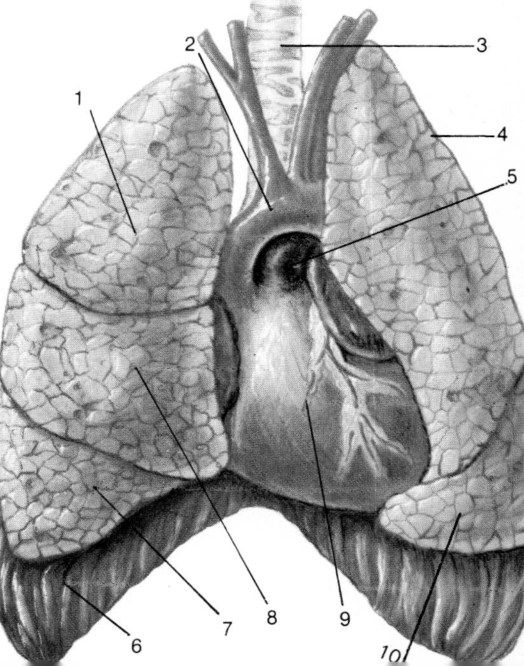

release of carbon dioxide into atmospheric air. In man, the right lung has three lobes and the left, two. Their surfaces are separated from the chest wall by two layers of *pleura*, with a little fluid between them; this allows free movement of the lungs and enables the forces of expansion of the chest wall and DIAPHRAGM to fill them with air. Air is drawn into the TRACHEA via MOUTH or NOSE; the trachea divides into the BRONCHI which divide repeatedly until the terminal airsacs or *alveoli* are reached. In the alveoli, air is brought into close contact with unoxygenated BLOOD in lung CAPILLARIES; the BLOOD CIRCULATION through these comes from the right ventricle and returns to the left atrium of the HEART. Disorders of ventilation or of perfusion with blood leads to abnormalities in blood levels of carbon dioxide and oxygen. Lung DISEASES include ASTHMA, BRONCHITIS, PNEUMONIA, PLEURISY, PNEUMOTHORAX, PNEUMOCONIOSIS, EMBOLISM, CANCER and TUBERCULOSIS; lungs may also be involved in several systemic diseases (e.g., sarcoidosis, LUPUS ERYTHEMATOSUS). Symptoms of lung disease include COUGH, sputum, blood in the sputum, shortness of breath and wheeze. Sudden failure of breathing requires prompt ARTIFICIAL RESPIRATION. Chest X RAY and estimations of blood gas levels and of various lung volumes aid diagnosis.

LUNT AND FONTANNE, famous US acting couple. Alfred Lunt (1893–) and Lynn Fontanne (c1887–) married in 1922 and co-starred in plays in Europe and the US for nearly 40 years. Best known for sophisticated comedies such as COWARD's *Design for Living* (1933), they also appeared in classics such as *The Taming of The Shrew* in 1935, and in modern works, mostly DÜRRENMATT's *The Visit*, with which they opened their own theater in 1958.

LUPINE, annual and perennial plants of the genus *Lupinus*, which are native to North and South America and the Mediterranean region. They have pea-like flowers clustered around a tall stem. Many hybrids and varieties are in cultivation. The seeds and leaves are toxic to animals. Family: Leguminosae.

LUPUS ERYTHEMATOSUS (LE), a rare systemic disorder affecting mainly young women and causing a characteristic SKIN rash with butterfly distribution over the face. It also causes LUNG, KIDNEY and BLOOD disease, largely due to abnormal IMMUNITY directed against substances in cell nuclei. Treatment is with STEROIDS and immunosuppressives.

LUPUS VULGARIS, TUBERCULOSIS of the SKIN.

LURAY CAVERNS, enormous limestone caves near Luray in Page Co., Va., discovered in 1878. Massive caverns and strange rock formations make the area a great tourist attraction.

LURIA, Salvador Edward (1912–), Italian-born US biologist who shared with DELBRÜCK and HERSHEY the 1969 Nobel Prize for Physiology or Medicine for research on BACTERIOPHAGES.

LUSAKA, capital city of Zambia. An administrative center, it has manufacturing industries (notably cement) and an international airport but its economy rests on agriculture. Pop 238 200.

LUSITANIA, province of the Roman Empire on the Iberian peninsula. It occupied what is now central Portugal and part of present-day W Spain. It was named for the Lusitani, a federation of Celtic peoples who put up spirited resistance to the Romans during the 2nd century BC.

LUSITANIA, British transatlantic liner torpedoed by a German U-boat off the Irish coast in 1915, on the pretext that it was carrying munitions. Around 1 195 civilians were killed, including 128 Americans. The incident helped bring the US into WWI.

LUTE, fretted stringed instrument related to the guitar, played by plucking the strings with the fingers. It was perhaps the most popular single instrument between 1400 and 1700, both for solo playing and as accompaniment to songs and madrigals; the great 16th-century composer DOWLAND wrote mostly for the lute.

LUTEINIZING HORMONE (LH), a pituitary-gland GONADOTROPHIN which in female mammals (including humans) causes release of EGGS from mature FOLLICLES and promotes the secretion of PROGESTERONE. In males it stimulates testicular ANDROGEN formation. Variations in LH secretion are involved in the onset of PUBERTY and in the menstrual cycle.

LUTEOTROPHIC HORMONE. See PROLACTIN.

LUTETIUM (Lu), the final member of the LANTHANUM SERIES. AW 175.0, mp 1663°C, bp 3315°C, sg 9.840 (25°C).

LUTHER, Martin (1483–1546), German REFORMATION leader and founder of LUTHERANISM. Following a religious experience he became an Augustinian friar, was ordained 1507, and visited Rome (1510), where he was shocked by the worldliness of the papal court. While professor of Scripture at Wittenberg U. (from 1512) he wrestled with the problem of personal salvation, concluding that it comes from the unmerited grace of God, available through faith alone (see JUSTIFICATION BY FAITH). When Johann TETZEL toured Saxony 1517 selling papal INDULGENCES, Luther denounced the practice in his historic 95 Theses, for which he was fiercely attacked, especially by Johann ECK. In 1520 he published *To the Christian Nobility of the German Nation*. It denied the pope's final authority to determine the interpretation of Scripture, declaring instead the priesthood of all believers; and it rejected papal claims to political authority, arguing for national churches governed by secular rulers. Luther denied the special spiritual authority of priests, advocated clerical marriage and denied the doctrine of TRANSUBSTANTIATION, adhering to CONSUBSTANTIATION. In Dec. 1520 he publicly burned a papal bull of condemnation and a copy of the canon law; he was excommunicated 1521. Summoned by Emperor Charles V to renounce his heresies at the Diet of WORMS (1521), he refused, traditionally with the words, "Here I stand: I can do no other." He was outlawed but, protected by Frederick III of Saxony, he retired to the WARTBURG castle. There, in six months, he translated the New Testament into German and began work on the Old. His hymns have been translated into many languages, and he wrote two catechisms (1529), the basis of Lutheranism. Against ERASMUS he wrote *The Bondage of the Will* (1525). He directed the reform movement from Wittenberg, aiming to moderate more extreme elements (see ANABAPTISTS), and opposed the PEASANTS' WAR, condoning princely repression of the revolt. In 1525 he married a former nun; they had six children.

LUTHERAN CHURCH, American, a US Lutheran church of some $2\frac{1}{2}$ million members formed by the merger of three churches (1961). Its headquarters are at Minneapolis, Minn.

LUTHERAN CHURCHES, the churches adhering to LUTHERANISM and springing from the German REFORMATION. From the beginning they were state churches ruled by the local princes; national Lutheran churches also formed in the Scandinavian countries. (See also THIRTY YEARS' WAR.) In 1817 Frederick William III of Prussia enforced union between the Prussian Lutheran and Reformed Churches, provoking the first of several schisms to form free Lutheran churches. A united German Lutheran Church was formed in 1949. Lutheran migrants to the US and Canada formed numerous churches now merged into three: the American LUTHERAN CHURCH, the LUTHERAN CHURCH IN AMERICA and the LUTHERAN CHURCH—MISSOURI SYNOD. The Lutheran World Federation has about 53 million members. Lutherans have played a major formative role in modern theology.

LUTHERAN CHURCH IN AMERICA, the largest Lutheran community in North America, formed by the merger of four churches in 1963. Its headquarters are in New York City. Its 33 synods and more than 3 million members are governed by a president, elected for four years.

LUTHERAN CHURCH—MISSOURI SYNOD, a US Lutheran church of some 3 million members with headquarters in St. Louis, Mo. Established in 1847 by German immigrants, it is doctrinally conservative. Local congregations enjoy wide autonomy.

LUTHERANISM, Protestant doctrinal system based on the teachings of Martin LUTHER. It regards the Bible as the only source of doctrine; stresses JUSTIFICATION BY FAITH alone; and recognizes only two SACRAMENTS: baptism and Holy Communion (see also CONSUBSTANTIATION). Luther's two catechisms (1529) and the AUGSBURG CONFESSION (1530) were collected with other basic standards in the *Book of Concord* (1580), consolidating Lutheranism against both Roman Catholicism and CALVINISM. (See also PIETISM.)

LUTHERVILLE-TIMONIUM, residential urban area in Md. It manufactures vehicle bodies. Pop 24 055.

LUTHULI, Albert John (1898–1967), Rhodesian-born Christian leader in South Africa, an unyielding opponent of APARTHEID. A Zulu chief, he was elected president of the AFRICAN NATIONAL CONGRESS (1952). In 1959 he was confined to his village by the South African government. He won the 1960 Nobel Peace Prize.

LÜTZEN, Battle of (1632), engagement at Lützen, SW of Leipzig, Germany, in the THIRTY YEARS' WAR; a brilliant victory over the imperial army of WALLENSTEIN by King GUSTAVUS II of Sweden, who was, however, killed in the battle.

LUX (lx), SI UNIT of illuminance (see PHOTOMETRY).

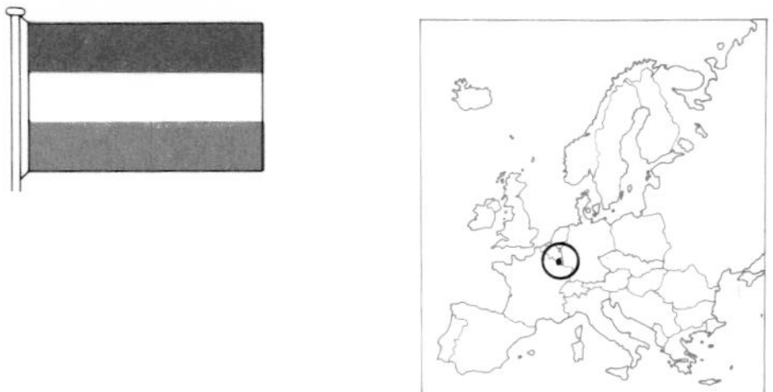

Official name: The Grand Duchy of Luxembourg
Capital: Luxembourg
Area: 999sq mi
Population: 348 200
Languages: Letzeburgesch; French, German and English widely used
Religions: Roman Catholic
Monetary unit(s): 1 Franc = 100 centimes

LUXEMBOURG, Grand Duchy of, constitutional monarchy of W Europe, bounded by West Germany, Belgium and France. It is about 55mi long and 35mi wide. Luxembourg extends into the rugged ARDENNES upland in the N; the agriculturally fertile "Good Country" is in the S lowlands; the SE region along the Moselle R produces wine and fruit. The industrial SW, rich in iron ore, provides the bulk of the national income. Agriculture and tourism are other major industries. The people, chiefly Roman Catholic, speak French, German and Letzeburgesch, the local dialect. Formerly including the Luxembourg province of Belgium, the country was a major duchy of the medieval empire; a Hapsburg possession 1482–1797; a subject of dispute between France and Germany in the 19th century and fully autonomous from 1867. The ruling house of Nassau came to the throne in 1890. Luxembourg formed an economic union with Belgium in 1922; it is a member of NATO and since the 1950s a member of BENELUX and the COMMON MARKET.

LUXEMBOURG, capital city of the Grand Duchy of Luxembourg and an administrative center of the COMMON MARKET. The old town stands on steep cliffs above the Alzette R. The fortress was a military stronghold from the 10th century until dismantled 1867. Pop 76 143.

LUXEMBURG, Rosa (1871?–1919), Polish-born German Marxist revolutionary, cofounder with Karl LIEBKNECHT of the SPARTACUS LEAGUE, Germany's first communist party. In the 1918 Berlin revolution she edited their journal, *Red Flag*. She and Liebknecht were arrested and murdered in 1919.

LUXOR, city in Upper Egypt on the E bank of the Nile R on part of the site of the ancient city of THEBES (see also KARNAK). Its famous temple of Amon, built by AMENHOTEP III, is 623ft long and has a colonnade and hall of hypostyle columns. Pop 84 600.

LUZERN. See LUCERNE.

LUZON, the main island of the PHILIPPINES. It is mountainous and produces gold, chromite, iron, coconuts, hemp, rice and lumber. The chief cities are Manila, the republic's seat of government, and Quezon City, the official capital.

LVOV, industrial city and transportation center in the W Ukraine, USSR. A historic university city and cultural center, its industries include machinery, textiles and oil refining. Pop 553 000.

LVOV, Prince Georgi Yevgenyevich (1861–1925), Russian liberal statesman, prime minister of the first provisional government 1917 (see RUSSIAN REVOLUTION). After the Bolshevik Revolution he fled to Paris.

LWOFF, André Michael (1902–), French microbiologist awarded with F. JACOB and J. MONOD the 1965 Nobel Prize for Physiology or Medicine for his work on lysogeny, a process of genetic interaction between BACTERIOPHAGES and BACTERIA.

LYALLPUR, city in the Punjab, Pakistan, 75mi SW of Lahore. A commercial center noted for its grain market, textiles and machinery. Pop 820 000.

LYCANTHROPY (from Greek *lykanthrōpos*, werewolf), in popular tradition, the assumption by a man of a wolf's form. In psychology, the belief by an individual that he can become a wild animal. The classic study is FREUD's of "The Wolfman."

LYCEUM, school outside Athens, in a grove dedicated to Apollo Lyceus, where ARISTOTLE taught. (See also PERIPATETIC SCHOOL.)

LYCEUM MOVEMENT, US associations for popular ADULT EDUCATION, influential in the 19th century. The first was founded by Josiah Holbrook in 1826 in Millbury, Mass. (See also CHAUTAUQUA MOVEMENT.)

LYCHEE, or **Litchi**, *Litchi chinensis*, tree native to S China, but now widely cultivated for its fruit, which is eaten fresh, canned or dried. Family: Sapindaceae.

LYDDA. See LOD.

LYDIA, ancient kingdom of W Asia Minor, of legendary wealth. The Lydians invented metal coins in the 7th century BC. During the 6th century BC its magnificent capital, Sardis, was the cultural center of a growing empire. Its zenith came under CROESUS, but he was defeated c546 BC by Cyrus of Persia.

LYE, any strong caustic ALKALI, especially POTASSIUM or SODIUM hydroxide.

LYELL, Sir Charles (1797–1875), British geologist and writer whose most important work was the promotion of geological UNIFORMITARIANISM (originally developed by James HUTTON) as an alternative to the CATASTROPHISM of CUVIER and others. The prime expression of these views came in his *Principles of Geology* (1830–33). His other works included the *Elements of Geology* (1838), and *Geological Evidence of the Antiquity of Man* (1863). Here he expressed guarded support for DARWIN's theory of evolution.

LYLY, John (c1554–1606), English author best known for his *Euphues* (part I, 1578; II, 1580), a prose romance in a highly artificial and allusive style (see EUPHUISM). Lyly also wrote elegant comedies on classical themes, and was influential on other Elizabethan playwrights.

LYMPH, fluid which drains from extracellular fluid via lymph vessels and nodes (glands). Important node sites are the neck, axilla, groin, CHEST and ABDOMEN. Fine ducts carry lymph to the nodes, which are filled with lymphocytes and reticulum cells. These act as a filter, particularly for infected debris or PUS and for CANCER cells, which often spread by lymph. The lymphocytes are also concerned with development of IMMUNITY. From nodes, lymph may drain to other nodes or directly into the major thoracic duct which returns it to the BLOOD. Specialized lymph ducts or lacteals carry FAT absorbed in the GASTROINTESTINAL TRACT to the thoracic duct. In addition, there are several areas of lymphoid tissue at the portals of the body as a primary defense against infection (TONSILS, ADENOIDS, Peyer's patches in the gut). Lymph node enlargement may be due to INFLAMMATION following DISEASE in the territory drained (SKIN, PHARYNX), or to development of an ABSCESS in the node (STAPHYLOCOCCUS, TUBERCULOSIS) due to INFECTIOUS DISEASE, secondary spread of cancer and the development of LYMPHOMA or LEUKEMIA. BIOPSY is valuable in diagnosis.

LYMPHOMA, malignant proliferation of LYMPH tissue, usually in the lymph nodes, SPLEEN or GASTROINTESTINAL TRACT. The prototype is HODGKIN'S DISEASE, but a number of other forms occur with varying HISTOLOGY and behavior. Cancer CHEMOTHERAPY and RADIATION THERAPY have much to offer in these disorders.

LYNBROOK, residential village in SE N.Y., a suburb of New York City on Long Island. Pop 23 776.

LYNCHBURG, city in Va., on the James R in the foothills of the Blue Ridge Mts. A manufacturing center, it is also the seat of several colleges.

LYNCHING, illegal "execution" conducted by a self-appointed body, or a killing by mob violence; probably named for Charles Lynch, a Va. magistrate who in 1780 dispensed summary justice to Tory conspirators. Vigilante bodies in pioneer communities sometimes authorized lynchings. Lynchings in this century have occurred mainly in the South, often instigated by the KU KLUX KLAN; always rare, the practice seems to have died out.

LYNDHURST, city in NE Ohio, a residential suburb of Cleveland. Pop 19 749.

LYNEN, Feodor (1911–), German biochemist who shared with K. E. BLOCH the 1964 Nobel Prize for Physiology or Medicine for their independent work on the metabolism of CHOLESTEROL and the fatty acids.

LYNN, city in NE Mass. Incorporated as a town in 1631, it was the site of the first American ironworks and is still an industrial center. Pop 90 294.

LYNN CANAL, SE Alaska, a narrow fjord 90mi long leading N from Juneau. It is an important route to the Klondike region, used in the GOLD RUSH.

LYNNFIELD, residential town in NE Mass. Pop 10 826.

LYNNWOOD, city in Wash. on Puget Sound. Industries include prefabricated houses. Pop 16 919.

LYNWOOD, city in Cal. just S of Los Angeles. It is residential with various light industries. Pop 43 353.

LYNXES, bobtailed members of the CAT family, of both Old and New Worlds. Tawny yellow cats, lynxes live in forests, especially of pine, leading solitary lives, hunting by night for small deer, badgers, hares, rabbits and small rodents—as well as occasionally raiding domestic stock.

LYON, or Lyons, major city in E central France at the confluence of the Rhône R and the Saône; capital of the Rhône department. Founded by the Romans and long famed for its silk, it now also produces rayon, nylon, pharmaceuticals, trucks and electrical appliances. Pop 527 890.

LYON, Mary (1797–1849), US pioneer of women's higher education. A teacher from the age of 17, she was founder and first president of Mount Holyoke Female Seminary (1837), South Hadley, Mass.

Lyra, "the harp" or "lyre", is a small but prominent constellation in the Northern sky containing the bright star Vega (α). Around April 21, the Lyrid meteors may be seen radiating from the constellation at the rate of about 10 an hour.

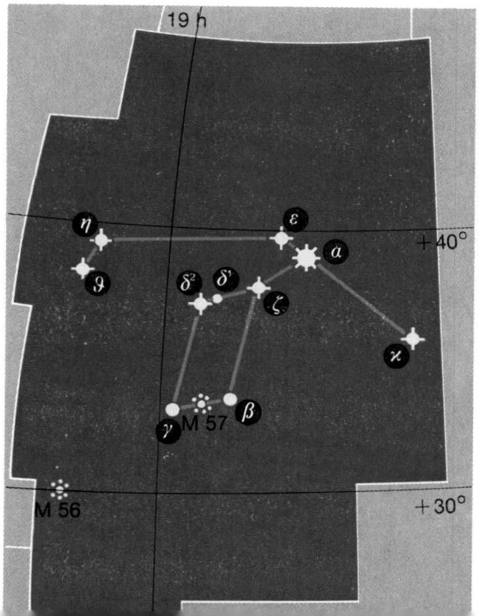

Lynx with its prey. A ferocious hunter whose existence is now threatened as its woodland habitat is increasingly disturbed, the lynx is also hunted for its fur and as a dangerous predator.

LYON, Matthew (1750–1822), Irish-born American pioneer and politician. He fought in the American Revolutionary War. In 1797 he was elected to the House of Representatives. A voluble anti-Federalist, he was convicted of sedition (1798) for criticizing President Adams. (See ALIEN AND SEDITION ACTS.)

LYONS, village in NE Ill., 8mi W of Chicago. It stands at an old portage used by early explorers and the Indians. Pop 11 124.

LYRA (the Lyre), a medium-sized N Hemisphere constellation containing VEGA and the Ring Nebula (M57), the relic of a stellar explosion 1.66kpc from the earth.

LYRE, STRINGED INSTRUMENT originating in ancient Greece and the FERTILE CRESCENT. The strings, usually plucked, stretch between the body and a crossbar joining two arms. (See also KITHARA.)

LYREBIRDS, Australian birds, genus *Menura*, with remarkable powers of vocal mimicry, and characterized by the male's lyre-shaped tail, erected and held over the back in courtship and territorial display. Males occupy territories during the breeding season, displaying in the early morning from special mounds, singing and quivering the tail.

LYRIC POETRY, originally poetry sung to the accompaniment of the LYRE. It now denotes any poem, usually short, such as the SONNET, expressing strongly felt personal emotion. Lyric poetry is particularly associated with the ROMANTICS, such as KEATS, SHELLEY and WORDSWORTH.

LYSANDER (d. 395 BC), Spartan admiral and statesman. In the PELOPONNESIAN WAR he enlarged the Spartan fleet, crushed Athenian sea power and entered Athens in triumph, 404 BC. He set up the government of the THIRTY TYRANTS there.

LYSENKO, Trofim Denisovich (1898–1976), Soviet agronomist whose antipathy for GENETICS and position of power under the Stalin regime led to the stifling of any progress in Soviet biological studies for 25 years or more. Refusing on ideological grounds to believe in GENES, he adopted a peculiar form of Lamarckism (see LAMARCK; MICHURIN), and forced other Soviet scientists to support his views. He was removed from power in 1964.

LYSIAS (c459–c380 BC), Athenian orator noted for clarity and elegance of style. Exiled under the THIRTY TYRANTS, he helped restore democracy and impeached the tyrant Eratosthenes. Some 35 of his speeches survive.

LYSOSOME, a small particle found in the cytoplasm of many living CELLS consisting of granules of ENZYMES surrounded by a lipoprotein membrane. The enzymes are inactive until released into the cytoplasm. This happens when the cells are damaged, the enzymes helping to destroy invading bacteria.

LYTTON, Edward George Earle Lytton Bulwer-Lytton, 1st Baron. See BULWER-LYTTON.

M

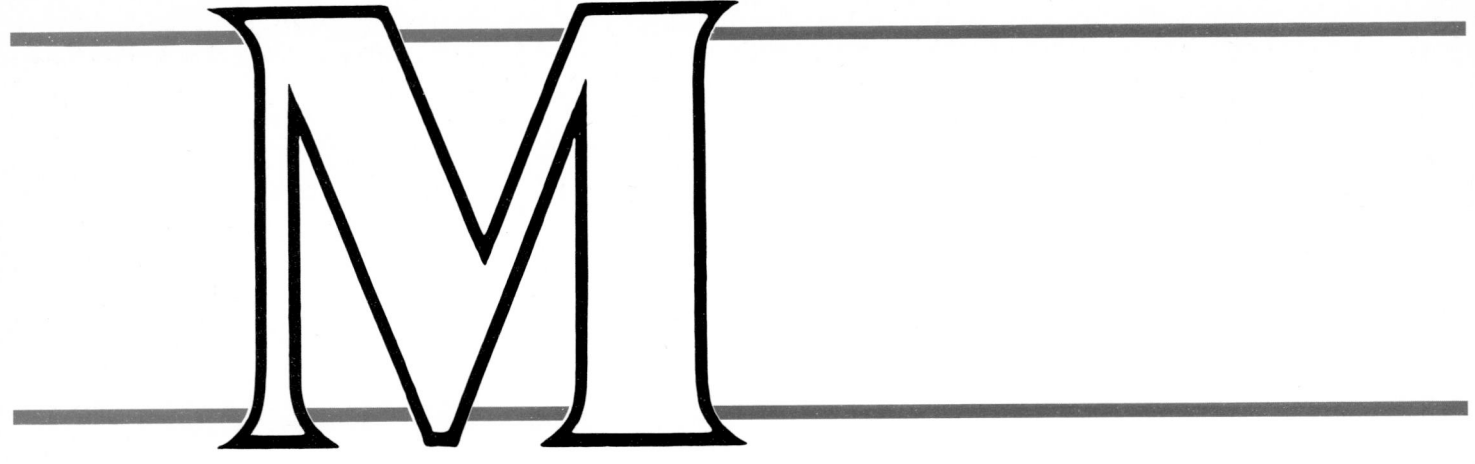

M, 13th letter of the English ALPHABET. It corresponds to the Semitic letter *mem* and the Greek *mu*. It represents a labial nasal sound.

MABUSE, Jan de (c1478–1532), Flemish painter, born Jan Gossaert. He visited Italy in 1508 (the first of many Netherlandish painters to do so) and his work developed an Italianate style. One of his best known paintings is *Danaë*.

MACADAM, road-building system devised by the Scots engineer **John Loudon McAdam** (1756–1836). The soil beneath the road, rather than foundations, takes the load, the road being waterproof and well-drained to keep this soil dry. For modern highways a first layer of larger rocks is laid, then smaller rocks and gravel, the whole being bound with, usually, ASPHALT or TAR.

MACADEMIA, the generic and common name for the edible seeds of two trees (*Macademia ternifolia* and *M. tetraphylla*) which are also known as Australian nuts or Queensland nuts. The kernels are roasted and are used in exotic foods. Family: Proteaceae.

McADOO, William Gibbs (1863–1941), US lawyer and politician. He was secretary of the treasury (1913–18), US director general of railways (1917–19), first chairman of the Federal Reserve Board, which he helped institute (1913) and manager of the government financing of WWI. He served as US senator from California 1932–39.

McALESTER, city in SE Okla., seat of Pittsburg Co. It is the processing and distribution center for an agricultural region, and manufactures clothing and transport machinery. Pop 18802.

McALLEN, city in S Tex., on the Rio Grande. It has oil refineries and processes citrus fruits and vegetables. Pop 37636.

McALLISTER, Samuel Ward (1827–1895), US society leader. In 1892 he claimed that there were "only about 400 people in New York society," and his phrase the "Four Hundred" passed into American idiom. He wrote *Society as I Have Found It* (1890).

General Douglas MacArthur signs the acceptance of Japanese surrender aboard the U.S.S. *Missouri* on September 1, 1945. He was to be instrumental in the postwar reconstruction of Japan.

MACAO, Portuguese colony in SE China, on the estuary of the Canton (Pearl) R. The colony comprises the peninsula of Macao, and the two small islands of Taipa and Colôane. The chief town, Macao, is a popular resort and gambling center with a major commercial port. Fishing is the most important industry.

MACAPAGAL, Diosdado (1911–), Liberal President of the Philippines (1962–65). His attempts at reform were hampered by minority support in the government, and he lost the 1965 election to Ferdinand MARCOS.

MACAQUES, the common, omnivorous MONKEYS of Asia, related to BABOONS and occupying much the same ecological position. Some are terrestrial, others at least partly arboreal. Macaques form large troops of 30 to 60 in which dominance ranking is quite marked. There is even a strict ranking of troops within any area. Macaques, which include Rhesus and Pig-tailed monkeys, are distinguished by pronounced brow ridges.

MacARTHUR, Charles (1895–1956), US playwright who won a Pulitzer Prize for *The Front Page* (1928), written with Ben HECHT. They also collaborated on *Twentieth Century* (1933), *Swan Song* (1946) and the screen play *The Scoundrel* (1935).

MacARTHUR, Douglas (1880–1964), US general and hero of WWII. He organized the 42nd (Rainbow) Division in WWI, and was superintendent of West Point (1919–22). In 1930 he became chief of staff of the US army, the youngest man ever to hold the post, and was promoted to general. He retired from the army in 1937, but was recalled in 1941 as commander of US army forces in the Far East. In 1942 he became supreme commander of the Southwest Pacific Area and in 1944 general of the army. Signatory of the Japanese surrender, he led the reconstruction of Japan as Allied supreme commander (1945–54). When the KOREAN WAR broke out (1950) he was selected commander of the UN forces sent to aid South Korea. His unwillingness to obey President TRUMAN's orders to restrict the war to Korea led to his dismissal the following year.

MACASSAR. See MAKASSAR.

MACAULAY, Dame Rose (1881–1958), English author who won recognition as a social satirist with such novels as *Told by an Idiot* (1923) and *Staying with Relatives* (1930). Her works include outstanding travel books, poems and literary criticism.

MACAULAY, Thomas Babington (1800–1859), English historian and essayist. He sacrificed a flourishing political career to undertake his *History of England* (5 vols, 1849–61), but he died before completing it. Its clarity and readability made it an immediate success. Like the *History*, his *Essays* display great range and brilliance, together with supreme confidence of judgment.

McAULIFFE, Anthony Clement (1898–), US army general, acting commander of the 101st Airborne division and other troops in December 1944 during the BATTLE OF THE BULGE. He played a significant part in the defense of Bastogne, contributing directly to the final defeat of the Germans.

MACAWS, 15 species of large, gaudy PARROTS of the New World. The bill is extremely large and very strong. Being articulated with the skull, it is movable and is used for climbing as well as for feeding. They are forest birds, feeding on a variety of fruits.

MACBETH (d. 1057), king of Scotland, formerly chief of the province of Moray, who killed King Duncan in battle (1040) and took the throne. SHAKESPEARE's famous tragedy *Macbeth*, based on Holinshed's *Chronicles*, gives a historically inaccurate picture of him as a villainous usurper.

MACCABEES, Books of, two books of the Old Testament APOCRYPHA which tell the story of the Maccabees or HASMONEANS, Jewish rulers of the 2nd and 1st centuries BC who fought for the independence of Judea from Syria. 1 Maccabees, a prime historical source, was written c100 BC. 2 Maccabees is a devotional work of low historical value, written before 70 AD. Two other books, 3 and 4 Maccabees, are among the PSEUDEPIGRAPHA.

McCARRAN, Patrick Anthony (1876–1954), US Democratic senator from Nevada (1933–54). He sponsored two controversial measures, the McCarran-Wood Act (1950), requiring the registration of all communists, and the McCarran-Walter Act (1952), which tightened controls over aliens and immigrants.

McCARTHY, Charles (1873–1921), US public official. He organized (1901) and subsequently directed the first official legislative reference library and bill drafting bureau in the US in Madison, Wis.

McCARTHY, Eugene Joseph (1916–), US Democratic senator from Minn. (1959–71). A consistent opponent of the VIETNAM WAR, he campaigned for the presidential nomination in 1968 and attracted considerable initial support. He lost the nomination to Hubert HUMPHREY, but his campaign consolidated public opposition to the war.

McCARTHY, Joseph Raymond (1908–1957), US Republican senator from Wis. (1947–57) who created the "McCarthy era" in the mid-1950s through his sensational investigations into alleged communist subversion of American life. These investigations were first made (1950) into federal departments, then into the army and among prominent civilians. **McCarthyism** became a word for charges made without proof and accompanied by publicity. After the Republicans lost control of the Senate in 1954, McCarthy was formally censured by fellow senators.

McCARTHY, Mary (1912–), US writer, best known for her satirical novel *The Group* (1963), about the lives of a generation of Vassar graduates. Her nonfiction works include the influential *Vietnam* (1967).

McCLELLAN, George Brinton (1826–1885), controversial Union general in the American Civil War. In 1861 he was given command of the Army of the Potomac, and later that year the supreme command. His hesitation in taking the offensive, and his failure to take Richmond and to follow up his success at the Battle of ANTIETAM, brought his dismissal in 1862. In 1864 he ran unsuccessfully for the presidency against Abraham LINCOLN.

McCLOSKEY, John (1810–1885), US Roman Catholic prelate. He became archbishop of New York (1864) and was created the first US cardinal (1875). He was responsible for the completion of St. Patrick's Cathedral in New York City.

McCLURE, Sir Robert (1807–1873), British arctic explorer and naval officer. On a search (1850–53) in the Arctic Archipelago for Sir John FRANKLIN, he discovered McClure Strait and became the first to prove the existence of the NORTHWEST PASSAGE.

McCLURE, Samuel Sidney (1857–1949), US editor and publisher who founded (1884) the first US newspaper syndicate. *McClure's Magazine*, of which he was founder (1893) and editor, presented many famous writers to the American public.

McCOLLUM, Elmer Verner (1879–1967), US biochemist who is credited with the discovery of fat-soluble VITAMINS A and B (1913), and who contributed to the discovery of vitamins D and E.

McCOMB, city in SW Miss. It is a trading and shipping center for a timber and agricultural region. Pop 11 969.

McCONE, John Alex (1902–), US government official, director of the CENTRAL INTELLIGENCE AGENCY (1961–65). He was chairman of the Atomic Energy Commission (1958–60) and succeeded Allen DULLES at the CIA after the unsuccessful BAY OF PIGS landing in Cuba.

McCORMACK, John (1884–1945), Irish-American tenor. He began his operatic career in London, first appearing in the US in 1909. He gained his greatest popularity as a concert singer, especially of Irish songs.

McCORMACK, John William (1891–), US Democratic Congressman. A member of the House of Representatives from 1928, he served as deputy speaker for 21 years and was speaker from 1962 to 1970.

McCORMICK, Cyrus Hall (1809–1884), US inventor and industrialist who invented an early mechanical REAPER (patented 1834), the first models appearing under license from 1841 onward.

McCORMICK, Robert Rutherford (1880–1955), US newspaper publisher who became sole owner of the Chicago *Tribune* after WWI. Pursuing an extreme right-wing policy, it won the largest circulation of any paper in the Midwest.

McCRAE, John (1872–1918), Canadian physician and poet of WWI, famous for his poem "In Flanders Fields," which was written under fire. It was first published in *Punch* in December 1915.

McCULLERS, Carson (1917–1967), US novelist. Her novels, set in her native South, deal with the problems of human isolation. Her best known book is *The Member of the Wedding* (1946).

McCULLOCH, John Ramsay (1789–1864), Scottish economist and statistician. His best known work was *The Principles of Political Economy* (1825), which helped to spread the ideas of his friend David RICARDO.

McCULLOCH v. MARYLAND, case before the US Supreme Court in 1819 in which it was ruled that Congress has implied powers other than those specifically granted by the Constitution. The case involved the Baltimore branch of the US bank which refused to pay a tax imposed by Maryland. The court ruled that the tax was unconstitutional as it interfered with an arm of the Federal government.

MacDIARMID, Hugh (1892–), Scottish poet, born Christopher Murray Grieve. Founder of the Scottish Nationalist Party, he gave fresh impetus to Scottish literature. He is best known for the long rhapsodic poem *A Drunk Man Looks at the Thistle* (1926).

McDONALD, David John (1902–), US union leader. President of the United Steelworkers, he was a key figure in the 1955 merger between the American Federation of Labor and the Congress of Industrial Organizations.

MacDONALD, James Ramsay (1866–1937), British statesman who was the chief founder of Britain's Labour Party (1900) and prime minister of the first and second labour governments (Jan.–Oct. 1924 and 1929–35). He lost most of his party's confidence when in 1931 he formed a national coalition to deal with the Depression.

MACDONALD, Sir John Alexander (1815–1891), Canadian statesman, first premier of the Dominion of Canada. Elected to the Ontario legislature in 1844, he became premier in 1857 as head of a Conservative coalition which was joined (1864) by George BROWN and others. He led subsequent negotiations which resulted (1867) in the confederation of Canada. The PACIFIC SCANDAL (1873) caused his government's resignation, but he was again premier from 1878 until his death.

MACDONOUGH, Thomas (1783–1825), US naval officer who defeated the British at the decisive Battle of PLATTSBURGH (1814) during the War of 1812. His victory saved New York and Vermont from invasion.

McDOUGALL, William (1871–1938), British psychologist best known for his fusion of the disciplines of PSYCHOLOGY and ANTHROPOLOGY in order to obtain a better understanding of the roots of social behavior. He also conducted important researches into PARAPSYCHOLOGY.

MacDOWELL, Edward Alexander (1861–1908), US composer and pianist. He is most remembered for his lyrical piano works and for the orchestral *Indian Suite* (1897). His wife founded the MACDOWELL Colony in Peterborough, N.H., a retreat for creative artists.

McDOWELL, Ephraim (1771–1830), US surgeon who performed the first successful ovariotomy (1809) to remove an ovarian TUMOR, as well as a number of other pioneering abdominal operations.

MACE, a weapon with a weighted iron or steel head used like a club which became a symbol of authority and is still used in many ceremonial rituals. Mace is also a SPICE made from the NUTMEG.

MACEDONIA, mountainous region of SE Europe, the ancient Macedon. It extends from the NW Aegean coast into the central Balkan peninsula. Divided among GREECE, YUGOSLAVIA and BULGARIA, it covers 25 636sq mi. Ethnically it is very mixed, but there are mainly Slavs in the N and Greeks in the S. The region is primarily agricultural, with tobacco, grains and cotton the chief crops. One of the great powers of the ancient world under ALEXANDER THE GREAT, Macedonia was later ruled by Romans, Byzantines, Bulgars and Serbs. From 1389 to 1912 it was part of the OTTOMAN EMPIRE. The present boundaries derive from the BALKAN WARS (1912–13).

MACE GAS. See TEAR GAS.

MACEIÓ, city and port in NE Brazil, capital of Alagoas state. Industries include textile mills and sugar refineries and distilleries. Sugar, cotton and rum are exported. Pop 263 583.

McGILLIVRAY, Alexander (c1759–1793), American chief of the Creek tribe. The son of a Scottish merchant and half-Creek mother, he joined the Creeks as a trader. During the Revolution he became chief of the tribe, siding with the British. Afterwards he protected Creek territory by entering into an alliance with the Spanish in Florida and Louisiana.

McGOVERN, George Stanley (1922–), US Senator from S.D. from 1962, and the 1972 Democratic presidential candidate. A leading advocate of an end to the Vietnam War, he campaigned for a broad program of social and political reforms. He attracted initially substantial support from liberals, but with serious party divisions his campaign went badly and Richard NIXON won with a record 61% of the popular vote.

McGRAW, John Joseph (1873–1934), US professional baseball player and manager. A star third baseman for the Baltimore Orioles, he became manager of Baltimore's American League team (1901). He went to the New York Giants as manager in 1902 and by his retirement in 1932 his team had won ten league championships and three world series.

McGUFFEY, William Holmes (1800–1873), US educator. His series of six *Eclectic Readers* (1836–57) sold an estimated 122 million copies. Almost universal readers for elementary schools in the Middle West and South, they had an immense influence on public education.

MACH, Ernst (1838–1916), Austrian physicist and philosopher whose name is commemorated in MACH NUMBERS. His greatest influence was in philosophy where he rejected from science all concepts which could not be validated by experience. This freed EINSTEIN from the absoluteness of Newtonian space-time (and thus helped him toward his theory of RELATIVITY) and helped inform the LOGICAL POSITIVISM of the Vienna Circle.

MACHADO Y MORALES, Gerardo (1871–1939), president of Cuba (1925–33). His rule began with a program of reforms, but became increasingly despotic and repressive until he was forced into exile.

MACHAUT, Guillaume de (c1300–1377), French poet and composer. He was a leading figure in the 14th-century Ars Nova ("new art") school of music, which developed many new forms. His Mass for four voices was the first complete polyphonic setting by a single composer.

McHENRY, FORT. See FORT MCHENRY NATIONAL MONUMENT AND HISTORIC SHRINE.

MACHETE, broad heavy knife, usually with a curved blade. It is used in Central and South America and the West Indies as a tool and as a weapon.

MACHIAVELLI, Niccolò (1469–1527), Florentine statesman and political theorist. He served the Republic of Florence, and was its emissary on several occasions. When the MEDICI family returned to power in 1512 he was imprisoned; on his release he devoted himself principally to writing. Despite his belief in political morality and his undoubted love of liberty, as revealed in his *Discourses on Livy* (1531), his master work, *The Prince* (1532; written 1513), describes the amoral and unscrupulous political calculation by which an "ideal" prince maintains his power. It is often seen as a cynical guide to power politics, although Machiavelli's motives in writing it are much debated. He also wrote a brilliant *History of Florence* (1532).

MACHINE, a device that performs useful work by transmitting, modifying or transforming motion, forces and energy. There are three basic machines, the inclined plane, the lever, and the wheel and axle: from these, and adaptations of these, are built up all true machines, no matter how complex they may appear. There are two essential properties of all machines: *mechanical advantage*, which is the ratio load/effort, and *efficiency*, the ratio of actual performance to theoretical performance. Mechanical advantage can be less than, equal to or greater than 1; while efficiency, owing to such losses as FRICTION, is always less than 100% (otherwise a PERPETUAL MOTION machine would be possible). (See also EFFICIENCY; ENERGY; FORCE; LEVER; WHEEL; WORK.)

Simple machines derived from the three basic elements include: from the inclined plane, the *wedge* (effort at the top being translated to force at the sides), and the *screw*, (an inclined plane in spiral form); from the lever, the wrench or spanner (the BALANCE also uses the principle of the lever), and from the wheel and axle, the PULLEY, (which can also be viewed as a type of lever). (See also BOLTS AND SCREWS; ENGINE; PUMP.)

MACHINE GUN, a GUN that can fire a number of rounds in rapid succession, a weapon that has changed the face of war in our century. Such guns are known from as early as the 14th century, and LEONARDO DA VINCI produced designs for several. These early guns were little more than a number of single guns arranged so that they could be set off by a single spark. James Puckle patented (1718) the precursor of the modern machine gun: it had a single barrel and a rotating stock holding square bullets: it fired about 9 rounds/min. FLINTLOCK was discarded with the invention of the percussion cap (c1816), and firing reliability much increased. By 1862 GATLING had developed a single-barreled machine gun, used in the Civil War, and later a multi-barreled gun that fired 3 000 rounds/min. MAXIM devised the first fully automatic machine gun around 1884; closely followed by John BROWNING, many of whose designs are in use today.

Three power sources are tapped to operate modern guns: the pressure of the expanding gases in the barrel; the recoil of the bolt and barrel; and the

Part of the ancient Inca city of Machu Picchu.

sprung return of a barrel that has recoiled. (See also AMMUNITION; FIREARMS.)
MACHINE TOOLS, nonportable, power-driven tools used industrially for working metal components to tolerances far finer than those obtainable manually. The fundamental processes used are cutting and grinding, individual machines being designed for boring, broaching, drilling (see DRILLS), milling, planing and sawing. Essentially a machine tool consists of a jig to hold both the cutting tool and the workpiece, and a mechanism to allow these to be moved relative to each other in a controlled fashion. A typical example is the LATHE. Auxiliary functions facilitate the cooling and lubrication of the tool and workpiece while work is in progress using a cutting fluid. The rate at which any piece can be worked depends on the material being worked and the composition of the cutting point. High-speed STEEL, TUNGSTEN carbide and CORUNDUM are favored materials for cutting edges. Where several operations have to be performed on a single workpiece, time can be saved by using multiple-function tools such as the turret lathe, particularly if numerically rather than manually controlled. Modern industry would be inconceivable without machine tools. It was only when these began to be developed in the late 18th century that it became possible to manufacture interchangeable parts and thus initiate MASS PRODUCTION.
MACH NUMBER, ratio of the speed of an object or fluid to the local speed of SOUND, which is temperature dependent. Speeds are subsonic or supersonic depending on whether the mach number is less than or greater than one.
MACHU PICCHU, ancient (15th-century?) Inca city in Peru, an impressive ruin dramatically situated on a high ridge of the Andes. It was discovered in 1911 by the American explorer Hiram BINGHAM.
MACINTOSH, Charles (1766–1843), Scots chemist who invented the waterproof fabric eventually known as **mackintosh** (1823), a layer of RUBBER dissolved in naphtha sandwiched between two layers of cloth. Quality was much improved with the advent of vulcanized rubber (patented 1844 by GOODYEAR).
MACK, Connie (1862–1956), famous US baseball player and manager. As owner and manager of the Philadelphia Athletics from 1901 to 1950, he led his team to victory in five world series.
McKAY, Claude (1890–1948), US Negro poet and novelist. His was the first and most militant voice of the New York Negro movement in the 1920s. His works include *Harlem Shadows* (1922) and the novel *Home to Harlem* (1927).
McKAY, Donald (1810–1880), US naval architect, master builder of clipper ships. His *Great Republic* (1853) was at 4 555 tons the biggest clipper ever built. The use of steam brought a decline in business that forced him to close his yards in 1855.
McKEESPORT, industrial city 10mi SE of Pittsburgh, Pa., and a center of the local steel industry. Pop 37 977.
MacKEES ROCKS, borough in SW Pa. Situated on the Ohio R, it is part of the Pittsburgh iron and steel industrial complex. Pop 11 901.
MACKENZIE, District of, district of the NORTHWEST TERRITORIES of Canada, bounded to the N by the Arctic Ocean and the W by the Yukon Territory. It is rich in minerals: goldmining is centered on Yellowknife, and uranium is mined on Great Bear Lake. Area 527 460sq. mi.
MACKENZIE, Sir Alexander (c1764–1820), Canadian fur trader and explorer, the first white man to cross the northern part of North America to the Pacific. Born in Scotland, he emigrated to Canada and in 1789 made an expedition down the MACKENZIE RIVER (named for him). In 1793 he crossed the Rockies to the Pacific coast.
MACKENZIE, Alexander (1822–1892), Canadian statesman. Born in Scotland, he went to Canada in 1842, entering the legislative assembly in 1861, having worked his way up to the editorship of a Liberal paper. From 1873 until 1878 he was Canada's first Liberal prime minister.
MACKENZIE, William Lyon (1795–1861), Canadian journalist, radical politician and leader of the December revolution (1837), an unsuccessful attempt to achieve self-government in Canada. He fled to the US, and returning in 1849, was reelected to Parliament in 1851.
MACKENZIE RIVER, in NW Canada, flowing from Great Slave Lake to the Arctic Ocean. The Mackenzie itself is 1 120mi in length, the total length of the system about 2 500mi, the second largest in North America. It is named for Sir Alexander MACKENZIE.
MACKERELS, small, streamlined fishes with pointed jaws and a tapered body, found on both sides of the N Atlantic. They are pelagic fishes forming enormous shoals during the summer and feeding on small crustaceans and other fish. In winter the shoals disband and move into deeper water where the fish remain in a state approaching HIBERNATION. Family: Scombridae.
MACKEREL SHARKS, or **Mako sharks**, large, fast-swimming fishes found in all warm seas. Streamlined SHARKS which may reach 4m (13ft) in length, they are renowned as game fishes, when they make gigantic leaps from the water. Family: Isuridae.
McKIM, Charles Follen (1847–1909), US architect, founder of his own firm (1878) and of the American Academy in Rome. His best-known projects, such as the University Club in New York City (1900), are in neoclassical style.
MACKINAC, Straits of, channel separating Upper and Lower Michigan. It connects lakes Huron and Michigan and is spanned by the MACKINAC BRIDGE from Mackinaw City to St. Ignace.
MACKINAC BRIDGE, 7 400ft long, connects Upper and Lower Michigan. It is one of the longest suspension bridges in the world, with a main span of 3 800ft.
MACKINAC ISLAND, summer resort in the Straits of Mackinac, Mich. It was a center of John Jacob Astor's fur-trading empire in the mid-19th century, and since 1895 has been a state park. It is thickly wooded, and automobiles are banned.
MACKINDER, Sir Halford John (1861–1947), British political geographer influential in establishing geography as an academic discipline in English universities. In 1904 he propounded an important thesis of the "heartland" of Eurasia as a new "geographical pivot of history."
McKINLEY, Mount, highest peak (20 320ft) in North America. Part of the McKinley National Park in S central Alaska, much of it is covered by permanent snowfields and glaciers. It was first climbed in 1913.
McKINLEY, William (1843–1901), 25th president of the US. The son of a small ironfounder in Niles, Ohio, he enlisted as a private in the 23rd Ohio Volunteers at the outbreak of the CIVIL WAR, at the age of 18. By the end of the war he had reached the rank of brevet major. He then studied law in Albany, N.Y., and set up practice in Canton, Ohio, where, in 1871, he married Ida Saxton. Although she became a chronic invalid after the early deaths of their two daughters, the marriage was a happy one.

McKinley was elected to Congress as a Republican in 1876 and stayed there, except for one term, until 1891. He sponsored the Tariff Act of 1890, which set record-high protective duties. This unpopular measure contributed to his defeat in the 1890 congressional elections. He had, however, attracted the backing of the wealthy Cleveland irondealer, Marcus Alonzo HANNA, with whose help he was elected governor of Ohio in 1891, and again in 1893. Again with Hanna's backing, he was chosen Republican presidential candidate in 1896. His Democratic opponent, William Jennings BRYAN, had early successes with his chosen issue of FREE SILVER, but with the help of $3.5 million that Hanna collected, McKinley's "front porch" campaign was effective enough to gain him a decisive victory.

Immediately after his inauguration he called a special session of Congress, which raised duties still higher, though without the reciprocal measures that McKinley wanted. The Gold Standard Act of 1899 killed Free Silver. With prosperity rising at home, he turned his attention to foreign affairs. The SPANISH-AMERICAN WAR over Spanish outrages in Cuba was followed by a revolt against American rule in the Philippine Islands, and in 1899 the "Open Door" policy on trade with China was introduced. Reelected in 1900, McKinley was assassinated in 1901 by the anarchist Leon CZOLGOSZ. He had presided over a period characterized by rapidly growing prosperity and the emergence of the US as a world power.

William McKINLEY
25th US President

Born: January 29, 1843
Died: September 14, 1901
Term of office: March 4, 1897–September 14, 1901
Political party: Republican

McKINNEY, city in N Tex., seat of Collin Co. It is a trade and processing center for the rich agricultural lands NNE of Dallas. Pop 15 193.
MACKINTOSH, Charles Rennie (1868–1928), Scottish architect and designer, a pioneer of ART NOUVEAU. He is best known for designing The Cranston tearooms in Glasgow (1896–1904) and the Glasgow School of Art (1896–1909).
McKISSICK, Floyd Bixler (1922–), US Negro lawyer and exponent of black power. He won national fame as counsel for the CONGRESS OF RACIAL EQUALITY, later becoming its director (1966–68).
MacLEISH, Archibald (1892–), US poet and playwright. *Conquistador* (1932), a narrative poem on the conquest of Mexico, *Collected Poems* (1952), containing his best lyrical verse, and *J.B.* (1958), a verse drama based on Job, all won Pulitzer prizes. Cultural adviser to President ROOSEVELT, he was Librarian of Congress 1939–44.
MACLEOD, John James Rickard (1876–1935), British-born physiologist who shared with Sir F. G.

BANTING the 1923 Nobel Prize for Physiology or Medicine for his role in the isolation of INSULIN. Macleod provided laboratory facilities and a degree of direction for Banting and his collaborator, C. H. BEST, who did not share in the award.

McLOUGHLIN, JOHN (1784–1857), Canadian fur trader and physician, known as the "Father of Oregon." He represented the HUDSON BAY COMPANY along the Columbia R, and in 1825 built Fort Vancouver (now Vancouver, Wash.).

McLUHAN, (Herbert) Marshall (1911–), Canadian professor of humanities and mass communications specialist, best known for his book *Understanding Media* (1964), which contains the famous phrase "the medium is the message"; that is, the content of communication is determined by its means, with the implication that modern mass communications technology, particularly television, is transforming our way of thinking and perceiving.

MACLURE, William (1763–1840), British-born US geologist regarded as the father of American geology for his monumental *Observations on the Geology of the United States* (1809), which was accompanied by a geological map.

MacMAHON, Marie Edmé Patrice Maurice de (1808–1893), marshal of France and president of the French Republic (1873–79). A successful army officer, he became governor general of Algeria (1864–70). In 1871 he suppressed the PARIS COMMUNE. His conservative, royalist views led to conflict with the republican majority in parliament, and he was finally obliged to resign the presidency.

MacMILLAN, Donald Baxter (1874–1970), US explorer of the Arctic. His first expedition was with Commander Robert PEARY in 1908. In all he undertook 31 Arctic expeditions, and made many scientifically valuable contributions to knowledge of the region.

McMILLAN, Edwin Mattison (1907–), US nuclear physicist who shared with SEABORG the 1951 Nobel Prize for Chemistry for his discovery of the first TRANSURANIUM ELEMENT, number 93, NEPTUNIUM (1940). Independently, he and the Soviet physicist **Vladimir Veksler** (1907–1966) developed the SYNCHROTRON, for which they shared the 1963 Atoms for Peace award.

MACMILLAN, (Maurice) Harold (1894–), British statesman and Conservative prime minister from 1957 to 1963. He entered Parliament in 1924, and was an opponent of APPEASEMENT. Having served in ministerial posts in WWII and the 1950s, he became prime minister after the SUEZ affair. He restored Anglo-US relations, tried to take Britain into the COMMON MARKET and presided over an economic boom, which, however, was already over when he resigned in ill health.

McMINNVILLE, city in NW Ore., seat of Yamhill Co. It is a trade and processing center for lumber and dairy products. Pop 10125.

McMINNVILLE, manufacturing town in central Tenn., seat of Warren Co. It is a center for agriculture and dairy products. Pop 10662.

McMURDO SOUND, inlet of the Ross Sea in Antarctica, between Ross Island and Victoria Land. It was discovered in 1841 by Sir James Clark ROSS.

McNAMARA, Robert Strange (1916–), secretary of defense under presidents KENNEDY and JOHNSON (1961–68), who played an important part in the shaping of US defense policy. Before this he had been president of the Ford Motor Company, and in 1968 he became president of the World Bank.

McNARY DAM, dam on the Columbia R, between Wash. and Ore. Built 1947–56, it provides hydroelectric power and irrigation. It is 183ft high and 7265ft long.

MacNIECE, Louis (1907–1963), British poet, born in Northern Ireland. His low-keyed, socially committed poetry links him with the "Oxford Group" of the 1930s, which included W. H. AUDEN and Stephen SPENDER. His *Collected Poems 1925–1940* appeared in 1940.

MACOMB, city in W Ill., seat of McDonough Co. It is an industrial city and trading center in an agricultural and coalmining area. Pop 19643.

MACON, city in central Ga., seat of Bibb Co. It is a commercial and trade center for agricultural products and has some light industry, including bricks and ceramics. Pop 122423.

MACON, Nathaniel (1758–1837), US politician, member of the House of Representatives (1791–1815) and of the Senate (1815–28). A Jeffersonian individualist, he consistently championed states' rights and opposed federal measures. (See also MACON'S BILL NO. 2.)

MACON'S BILL NO. 2, US bill passed in 1810, forbidding French and British warships to enter US waters, but permitting trade with those countries (see NONINTERCOURSE ACT). Nathaniel MACON, chairman of the Foreign Relations Committee which originated the bill, in fact opposed it in its revised form.

McPHERSON, city in central Kan., seat of McPherson Co. Industries include flour milling and oil refining. Pop 10851.

McPHERSON, Aimee Semple (1890–1944), US evangelist, famed for her flamboyant preaching. She worked as a missionary in China, then returned to the US to become an itinerant preacher and faith-healer, eventually founding the Foursquare Gospel Church in Los Angeles. She was married three times, and involved in numerous legal actions.

MACPHERSON, James (1736–1796), Scottish poet and member of Parliament from 1780, famous for his purported translations of the Gaelic bard OSSIAN, published 1760–75. Disputed by Samuel JOHNSON and others, they appear to have been Macpherson's own work, loosely based on contemporary Gaelic verse.

MACRAMÉ (from Turkish *maqrama*, towel fringing), the craft of knotting cord or rope. It spread from the Middle East through Europe, was practiced by sailors and was an English court pastime in the reign of William III (1689–1702). It was much used for the ornate decorations of 19th-century homes.

McREYNOLDS, James Clark (1862–1946), US attorney general 1913–14 and associate justice of the Supreme Court 1914–41. President F. D. ROOSEVELT opposed his attempts to invalidate NEW DEAL legislation.

MACROECONOMICS, the study of aggregates in the national economy, as opposed to that part of economics concerned with the constituent elements, MICROECONOMICS. Macroeconomics studies key economic quantities (such as National Income, SAVINGS, INVESTMENT and BALANCE OF PAYMENTS), the factors determining them and the relationships between them.

MACROPHAGE. See RETICULO-ENDOTHELIAL SYSTEM.

MACSWINEY, Terence James (1880–1920), Irish patriot and mayor of Cork, an organizer of the Easter Rising of 1916. He was gaoled for sedition in 1920; his death on hunger strike provoked fierce anti-British feeling.

MADAGASCAR, formerly **Malagasy Republic**, Democratic Republic in the Indian Ocean comprising Madagascar and small nearby islands.

Land. It is separated from the SE African mainland by the Mozambique Channel. The island has rugged central highlands and fertile low-lying coastal plains. The highlands have several extinct volcanoes and mountain groups which rise to over 9000ft. They have a pleasantly cool, and occasionally cold, climate. The coastal plains tend to be hot and humid, with luxuriant tropical vegetation. Soil erosion is a serious problem, and destructive hurricanes may occur between December and April.

People. The island's population includes some French, Indians and Chinese. But the people can be broadly divided into two groups: those of Indonesian-Polynesian descent, living mainly in the highlands, and those of African Negro descent (*côtiers*), living mainly in the coastal regions. Over 90% of the people live in rural areas and the main cities are Tananarive, the capital, Antsirabe, Diégo-Suarez, Majunga and Tuléar.

Economy. The island is predominantly farming and stock-raising country. Important crops are rice, cassava, coffee, sugar and bananas. Graphite, mica, phosphates, chromite and ilmenite are mined, and mineral products, textiles and foodstuffs are the main export. Industries include oil refining, vehicle assembly, plastics, textiles, rubber products and paper.

History. Portuguese, French and English rivalry for control of Madagascar ended in French invasion and

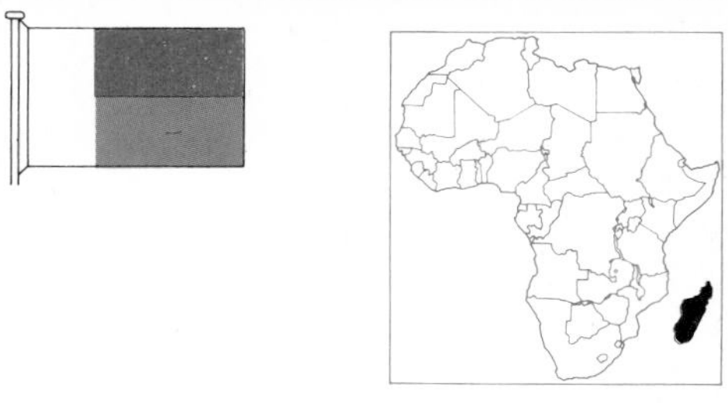

Official name: Democratic Republic of Madagascar
Capital: Tananarive
Area: 229233sq mi
Population: 7655134
Languages: Malagasy, French. Hova spoken
Religions: Christian, Muslim, Animist
Monetary unit(s): 1 Malagasy franc (FMG) = 100 centimes

annexation (1885–1905). In 1947, a revolt against French rule was crushed, but in 1958 the island gained self-government within the French community as the Malagasy Republic. It achieved full independence in 1960 under President Tsiranana. In May 1972 he handed over power to General Ramanantsoa, who in 1975 was replaced by Commander Didier Ratsiraka.

MADARIAGA, Salvador de (1886–), Spanish diplomat and writer. A liberal historian and political philosopher, he settled in England after the Spanish Civil War. His works include *The Genius of Spain* (1923) and *Victors, Beware* (1946).

MADDER, plants of the genus *Rubia* which yield the red dye ALIZARIN. The dye has been used since earliest times, but has now been replaced by synthetically produced analine. Family: Rubiaceae.

MADEIRA, archipelago in the N Atlantic some 360mi W of Morocco, constituting the Funchal district of Portugal. Madeira, the largest island, is mountainous; settlement, including the capital Funchal, is largely on the coast. The islands produce sugarcane, bananas and the famous Madeira wine. Their scenic beauty and warm climate make them a year-round tourist resort.

MADEIRA RIVER, S tributary of the Amazon, formed at the N border of Bolivia by the confluence of the Beni and Mamore. It then flows some 900mi NE through Brazil, joining the Amazon below Manaus; it is navigable for 600mi.

MADERA, city in central Cal., seat of Madera Co. A wine center, it has many other industries, notably olive-growing and lumber. Pop 16044.

MADERNO, Carlo (1556–1629), Italian architect of the early BAROQUE. Chief architect of St. Peter's, Rome, from 1603, he designed the nave and facade. He designed the church of Sta. Maria della Vittoria (1620) and began the Palazzo Barberini for URBAN V in 1625.

MADERO, Francisco Indalecio (1873–1913), president of Mexico 1911–13. A democratic idealist, he opposed Porfirio DIAZ in the 1910 election and was imprisoned. He escaped to Tex. and there declared a revolution; joined by Francisco VILLA and ZAPATA, he deposed Diaz in 1911 and was elected president. His administration was marred by his own ineptitude, and division and corruption among his followers. In the face of widespread revolt he was deposed and murdered by Gen. Victoriano HUERTA.

MADISON, city in SE Ind., seat of Jefferson Co. on the Ohio R. A major tobacco trading center, it has various manufacturing industries. Pop 13081.

MADISON, borough in NE N.J. Now a residential suburb, it was settled in 1685 and named Bottle Hill until 1834. Pop 16710.

MADISON, capital city of Wis. and seat of Dane Co. A commercial and administrative center, its main manufactures are meat and dairy products. It is the site of U. of Wisconsin. Pop 172 007.

MADISON, Dolley Payne (1768–1849), wife of James MADISON from 1794. Of Quaker family, she was the widow of John Todd. She was known as a charming and lavish hostess.

MADISON, James (1751–1836), 4th president of the US 1809–17. Born at Port Conway, Va., he graduated from the College of New Jersey (Princeton U.) in 1771. In 1776 he helped draft Va.'s constitution and served in the CONTINENTAL CONGRESS 1780–83. He pressed the need for a stronger central government than was possible under the ARTICLES OF CONFEDERATION. In the Va. house of delegates 1784–86 he advocated federal unity; he promoted the ANNAPOLIS CONVENTION which led in turn to the Federal Constitutional Convention (1787). He submitted a series of proposals to it, the general framework of which is reflected in the US CONSTITUTION adopted by the Convention. This and his skillful conduct in the debates has earned him the title of "father of the Constitution." He was one of the authors of the FEDERALIST PAPERS. As a congressman 1789–97 he advocated the BILL OF RIGHTS.

An influential secretary of state under JEFFERSON 1801–08, he was chosen by Jefferson as his successor. As president himself from 1809 Madison took a firm grip on affairs, writing all major state papers in the first two years. In foreign affairs, he sought to free US shipping of the trade restraints imposed by Britain and France in the NAPOLEONIC WARS. Trusting dubious French assurances, Madison imposed an embargo on trade with Britain in 1810. This and a popular desire to conquer Canada provoked the WAR OF 1812 in

James MADISON
4th US President
Born: March 16, 1751
Died: June 28, 1836
Term of office: March 4, 1809–March 3, 1917
Political party: Democratic Republican

which Madison's prestige suffered, especially after the burning of the White House by the British in 1814. After the war Madison presided over a period of new prosperity and expansion. He retired in 1817 to his Va. plantation Montpelier. Rector of the University of Virginia. from 1826, he became interested in the abolition of slavery.

MADISON HEIGHTS, city in SE Mich., an industrial suburb of Detroit. Steel processing and auto and aircraft parts are the main industry. Pop 38 599.

MADISON SQUARE GARDEN, world-famous indoor sports, entertainment and convention center in New York City. The first Garden was built on the site of a railroad terminal at Madison Square; the second Garden was at 49th Street and Eighth Avenue (1925). A new Madison Square Garden center was built 1964–69 on the site of the old Pennsylvania Station. It includes a 20 000-seat arena and a 5 200-seat forum.

MADISONVILLE, city in W K., seat of Hopkins Co. A coal-mining center, its other main industry is food processing. Pop 15 332.

MADONNA (Italian: my Lady), name given to the Virgin Mary, especially as depicted in works of art. The Madonna is often shown with the infant Jesus or, in the PIETA, mourning over his body taken down from the Cross.

MADONNA LILY, *Lilium candidum*, common white garden lily known as the plant of purity and antiquity. The flowers yield an oil that is used in perfumery. Family: Liliaceae.

MADRAS, city in SE India, capital of Tamil Nadu state on the Bay of Bengal. India's third largest port, it has large textile, chemical and tanning industries. Based on a British settlement, Madras is now a cultural center, site of Madras U. Pop 2 470 288.

MADRID, capital of Spain and of Madrid Province, on the Manzanares R in New Castile. A 10th-century Moorish fortress captured by Castile in 1083, it was made the capital by PHILIP II (1561). Now Spain's administrative and financial headquarters, it has a wide range of industries. A cultural center, its landmarks include the Prado art gallery, the royal palace and the university city. Pop 3 146 071.

MADRIGAL, part song for two or more voices. Originating in 14th-century Italy, it reached the height of its popularity in the 16th century, through the works of MONTEVERDI and GESUALDO. Thomas MORLEY and others developed a distinctive English form.

MADRONA, *Arbutus menziesii*, tree or shrub of the heath family, Ericacaea. It is an evergreen which produces white flowers and red berries. It grows in the Pacific regions of the US and in Mexico. TANNINS produced from the bark are used in the tanning industry and the wood for furniture.

MADTOMS, North American catfishes of the Horned pout family. All have a poison gland at the base of the pectoral fin, making them dangerous to handle. The family, Ictaluridae, includes some blind, cave-dwelling forms.

MADURAI, city in S India, in Tamil Nadu state. Capital of the Padya kingdom from the 5th to the 11th centuries BC, it is famous for its historic temples. It is now a textile, tea and coffee center. Pop 548 298.

MAEANDER, ancient Greek name for the Büyük Menderes R in Turkey, from whose winding course the word "meander" derives. It rises in W Turkey and flows about 250mi W to the Aegean Sea.

MAEBASHI, historic castle city in Japan, on central Honshu. It is now a silk manufacturing center. Pop 233 632.

MAECENAS, Gaius (d. 8 BC), Roman statesman famous as the patron of HORACE, VERGIL and PROPERTIUS. Friend, adviser and agent of the emperor AUGUSTUS, he was criticized by SENECA for his extravagance. His name has come to symbolize patronage.

MAELSTROM, tidal whirlpool, more than 2mi wide, off Moskenesøy Island in the Lofoten Islands, NW Norway.

MAENADS, in Greek mythology, female devotees of DIONYSUS. Also called *bacchantes* (for Bacchus, Dionysus' other name), they were known for their ecstatic frenzies.

MAETERLINCK, Maurice (1862–1949), Belgian poet and playwright. His early work was influenced by SYMBOLISM; he is best known for the tragedy *Peléas and Mélisande* (1892), set as an opera by DEBUSSY, and the dramatic fable *The Blue Bird* (1908). He was awarded the Nobel Prize for Literature in 1911.

MAFEKING, town in N South Africa, in Cape Province, a cattle and dairy-farming center. In the BOER WAR a British garrison under Lord BADEN-POWELL was besieged there for 217 days. Pop 6 900.

MAFIA, Italian-American criminal organization. Its name derives from 19th-century Sicilian bandits who dominated the peasantry through terrorism and the tradition of the VENDETTA. Despite repression by successive governments, including MUSSOLINI, the Mafia remains very powerful in Italy. *Mafiosi* emigrated to the US and set up sophisticated criminal bodies there, organized in "families." These prospered during PROHIBITION, and diversified from bootlegging into gambling, narcotics, vice, labor unions and more recently into some legitimate business. In the 1950s and 1960s attention was drawn to the Mafia by the fruitless trial of 60 of its leaders, caught in conference at Apalachin, N.Y., in 1957, and the disclosures of former *mafioso* Joseph Valachi. *Mafiosi* may refer to the organization as *Cosa Nostra* (Italian: our affair) but usually deny its existence.

MAGDALA, in the Bible a village on the W shore of the sea of Galilee, home of St. Mary Magdalene. It was probably present-day Majdol, N of Tiberias.

MAGDALENA RIVER, in Colombia, rises in the Cordillera Central and flows about 956mi N to the Caribbean Sea at Barranquilla. Discovered in 1501, it is the country's principal waterway.

MAGDALENIAN, upper-Paleolithic culture named for La Madeleine cave, Dordogne, France, noted for the quality of its painting and bone engraving (see also ALTAMIRA; STONE AGE.)

MAGDALEN ISLANDS, island group, part of Quebec, Canada, in the Gulf of St. Lawrence. There are nine main islands, covering about 88sq mi of land. The economy rests largely on fishing and sealing.

MAGDEBURG, city of East Germany, a major inland port and industrial center on the Elbe R. Founded in the 9th century, it became one of the leaders of the HANSEATIC LEAGUE. Razed during the THIRTY YEARS WAR, it became a duchy in Brandenburg in 1648. Many historic buildings survive despite WWII bombings. Pop 270 692.

MAGELLAN, Ferdinand (c1480–1521), Portuguese navigator who commanded the first expedition to sail around the world. Accused of peculation during his service in the Portuguese Indian army, he fell from favor at court and so sought Spanish backing for his proposed voyage in search of a western route to the Spice Islands or East Indies, then believed to be only a few hundred miles beyond America. Financed by Charles I, Magellan sailed from Sanlucar de Barrameda with five ships on Sept. 20, 1519. In Jan. 1520 he discovered the Rio de la Plata and sailed S to Patagonia, where Magellan had to put down a mutiny. Then with only three ships, he sailed to the Pacific through the straits now named for him. For two months no land was sighted and the expedition was near starvation; in March 1521 they reached Guam, and in April the Philippines. Magellan was killed in a skirmish with natives there on April 27. Only one ship, the *Victoria*, under Juan del CANO, returned to Spain, having sailed around the world. Although he did not survive the journey, Magellan was undoubtedly responsible for its success.

MAGELLAN, Strait of, separates mainland South America from Tierra del Fuego and islands to the S. Around 330mi long, it is named for MAGELLAN.

MAGELLANIC CLOUDS, two irregular GALAXIES that orbit the MILKY WAY, visible in S skies. The Large Magellanic Cloud (Nubecula Major), about 4.5kpc in diameter, has a well marked axis suggesting that it may be an embryonic spiral galaxy. The Small Magellanic Cloud (Nubecula Minor) is about 3kpc across. Both are rich in CEPHEID VARIABLES and about 46kpc from the earth.

MAGENDIE, François (1783–1855), French physiologist, regarded as the father of experimental PHARMACOLOGY. He introduced the medical use of several DRUGS (e.g., MORPHINE); and first proved that in a spinal nerve (see NERVOUS SYSTEM; SPINAL CORD) the ventral (anterior) root has a motor function and the dorsal (posterior) root a sensory function.

MAGENTA, manufacturing town in N Italy. The banks of the nearby Ticino R were the site of a French victory over the Austrians in 1859. Pop 23 690.

MAGGIORE, Lake, formed by the Ticino R in the foothills of the Alps, lies partly in Switzerland and partly in Italy, in Piedmont and Lombardy. At 82sq mi it is the second largest lake in Italy and is a famous beauty spot.

MAGGOTS, the legless GRUBS or LARVAE of HOUSEFLIES and their relatives. They are generally soft, pale and segmented, with a pointed head end and blunt posterior.

MAGHREB (Arabic: the west), used to designate the NW African Islamic states of Algeria, Libya, Morocco and Tunisia.

MAGI, Persian priestly caste or tribe. Little is known of them beyond their reputation for wisdom and supernatural powers: *magic* is named for them. Zoroaster was probably a Magus; the Magi headed

ZOROASTRIANISM, and it may have been based upon their original religion.

MAGIC, Primitive, the prescientific belief that an individual, by use of a ritual or spoken formula, may achieve a result that would otherwise be beyond his, or human, powers. Should the magic fail to work, this is assumed to be due to deviations from the correct formula. FRAZER classified magic under two main heads, imitative and contagious. In **imitative magic** the magician acts upon or produces a likeness of his desired object: rainmakers may light fires, the smoke of which resembles rainclouds; voodoo practitioners stick pins in wax models of their intended victims. In **contagious magic** it is assumed that two objects once close together remain related even after separation: the magician may act upon hair clippings in an attempt to injure their former owner. Magic is crucial to many primitive societies, most tribes having at least an equivalent to a medicine man (see SHAMANISM) who is believed to be able to provide them with extra defense against hostile tribes or evil spirits. (See also AMULET; FETISH.)

MAGIC LANTERN, forerunner of the slide projector. Light shone through a slide (often a simple scene painted on glass) to a LENS, which cast a magnified picture on the screen.

MAGIC SQUARE, square array of numbers such that the sums along each row, column and diagonal are equal; e.g.:

6	7	2
1	5	9
8	3	4

MAGINOT LINE, massive French fortifications system, built 1930–34 between the Swiss and Belgian borders. Named for war minister André Maginot (1877–1932), it consisted of linked underground fortresses. Obsolete before it was completed, it was easily bypassed by the German mobile advance in WWII.

MAGMA, molten material formed in the upper mantle or crust of the EARTH, composed of a mixture of various complex SILICATES in which are dissolved various gaseous materials, including WATER. On cooling magma forms IGNEOUS ROCKS, though any gaseous constituents are usually lost during the solidification. Magma extruded to the surface forms LAVA. The term is loosely applied to other fluid substances (e.g., molten salt) in the earth's crust. (See also HOT SPRINGS; VOLCANISM.)

MAGNA CARTA (Latin: great charter), major British constitutional charter forced on King JOHN I by a baronial alliance at Runnymede in June 1215. The barons rebelled because of John's heavy taxation to finance wars and his exclusion of them from government. He sought to repudiate the charter but died soon after. It falls into 63 clauses, designed to prevent royal restriction of baronial privilege and feudal rights. It also safeguarded church and municipal rights and privileges. Altered forms of it were issued on John's death in 1216, in 1217 and 1225. In fact a reactionary measure, its vagueness allowed many later commentators to find in it the roots of whatever civil rights they wished to defend, such as HABEAS CORPUS and JURY trial. It did, however, pave the way for constitutional monarchy by implicitly recognizing that a king may be bound by laws enforceable by his subjects.

MAGNA GRAECIA, coastal area of Italy S of the Bay of Naples and the Gulf of Taranto colonized by Greece in the 8th century BC. The philosophers PARMENIDES and PYTHAGORAS came from cities of Magna Graecia. The colonies declined after 500 BC.

MAGNESIA, or magnesium oxide. See MAGNESIUM.

MAGNESITE, mineral form of magnesium carbonate ($MgCO_3$), found in the US, Austria and Manchuria. It forms hexagonal crystals, usually massive and white. Magnesite is mainly used for lining furnaces, since it decomposes to give magnesium oxide (see MAGNESIUM) on heating.

MAGNESIUM (Mg), a reactive, silvery-white ALKALINE-EARTH METAL, the eighth most abundant element. Its chief ores are dolomite, brucite and magnesite. It is also found in many other minerals and in large quantities in the sea. Magnesium is light but strong, and forms useful alloys with aluminum and other metals. Magnesium is manufactured, either by

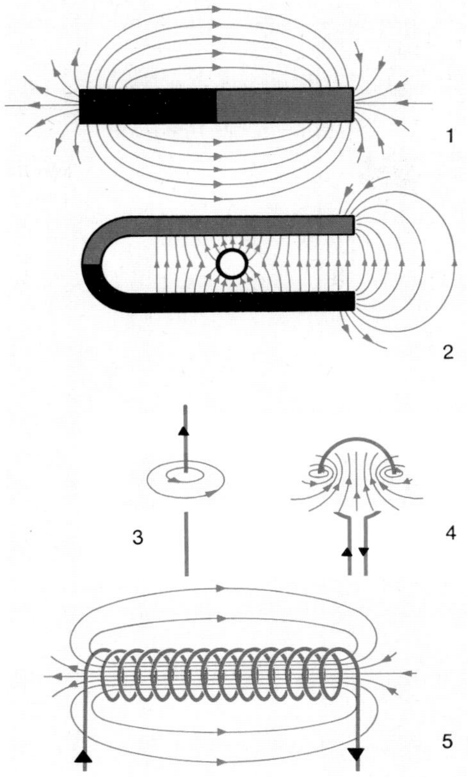

The lines of force of the magnetic field associated with a bar magnet (1) can be demonstrated by sprinkling iron filings on to a piece of paper over the magnet. An iron ring placed between the arms of a horseshoe magnet (2) will deflect the otherwise straight lines of force. A wire carrying an electric current also produces a magnetic field (3–4), which increases in strength if the current and the number of turns are augmented. Figure (5) represents a simple electromagnet; it loses its magnetism when the current is switched off.

the ELECTROLYSIS of fused magnesium chloride, or by the silicothermic process, in which mixed oxides, formed by the calcination of dolomite, are reduced at high temperature with ferrosilicon, forming magnesium crystals. When heated in air, divided magnesium burns readily with a dazzling white flame: hence its use in FLASHBULBS and flares. It is also used as a powerful reducing agent in the preparation of many other metals. AW 24.3, mp 649°C, bp 1090°C, sg 1.738 (20°C).

Magnesium Hydroxide ($Mg(OH)_2$), occurs naturally as colorless hexagonal plates of brucite. It is formed as a gelatinous precipitate when ALKALI is added to magnesium salts. It is a BASE and loses water when heated to 350°C. (See also MILK OF MAGNESIA.)

Magnesium Oxide (MgO), or **Magnesia**, is a white crystalline solid and also a BASE. Being highly refractory, it is used in furnace linings. When mixed with magnesium chloride solution, magnesia forms a durable cement used as a stucco finish on buildings.

Magnesium Sulfate ($MgSO_4$), or EPSOM SALTS, is a colorless crystalline solid. The aqueous solution is used as a purgative.

MAGNET. See MAGNETISM.

MAGNETIC FIELD, what is said to exist where electric charges (see ELECTRICITY) experience a FORCE proportional to their VELOCITY but at right angles to it, or where magnetic dipoles (see MAGNETISM) experience a torque. The field is defined in the direction of zero torque, with a strength equal to the torque on a unit dipole at right angles to the field. Magnetic fields originate at magnetic dipoles or electric currents.

MAGNETIC LENS, a device using a MAGNETIC FIELD to focus a beam of charged particles. The field is produced between two annular pole pieces around the beam driven by an ELECTROMAGNET. Its imaging properties were first studied by Hans Busch in 1926.

MAGNETIC STORM, an occasional disturbance in the earth's MAGNETIC FIELD, correlated with SUNSPOT activity. A high energy PLASMA ejected from a solar flare sets up large currents in the MAGNETOSPHERE on reaching the earth, causing a rapid rise of around 0.2% in the magnetic field at the surface. The plasma subsequently moves around the earth, often accompanied by auroral displays, while the field drops to about 0.5% below its normal value, recovering over several days.

MAGNETISM, the phenomena associated with "magnetic dipoles," commonly encountered in the properties of the familiar horseshoe (permanent) magnet and applied in a multitude of magnetic devices.

Man first learned of magnetism through the properties of the *lodestone*, a shaped piece of MAGNETITE that had the property of aligning itself in a roughly north-south direction. Eventually he found how to use a lodestone to magnetize a steel bar, thus making an artificial **permanent magnet**. The power of a magnet was discovered to be concentrated in two "poles," one of which always sought the north, and was called a north-seeking pole, or north pole, the other being a south-seeking pole, or south pole. It was early learned that, given two permanent magnets, the unlike poles were attracted to each other and the like poles repelled each other. Furthermore, dividing a magnet in two never resulted in the isolation of an individual pole, but only in the creation of two shorter two-poled magnets. Again, it was found that magnetic poles attracted or repelled each other according to an inverse-square law. The explanation of these properties in terms of magnetic "lines of force" was an early achievement of the science of magnetostatics.

Today, physicists explain magnetism in terms of *magnetic dipoles*. Magnetic dipole moment is an intrinsic property of fundamental particles. ELECTRONS, for example, have a moment of 0.928×10^{-23} $A.m^2$ parallel or antiparallel to the direction of observation. The forces between magnetic dipoles are identical to those between electric dipoles (see ELECTRICITY). This leads scientists often to regard the dipoles as consisting of two magnetic charges of opposite type, the poles of traditional theory. But unlike electric charges, magnetic poles are believed never to be found in isolation.

In **ferromagnetic materials** such as IRON and COBALT, spontaneous dipole alignment over relatively large regions known as *magnetic domains* occurs. Magnetization in such materials involves a change in the relative size of domains aligned in different directions, and can multiply the effect of the magnetizing field a thousand times. Other materials show much weaker, nonpermanent magnetic properties (see DIAMAGNETISM, PARAMAGNETISM).

Magnetism is intimately associated with electricity (see ELECTROMAGNETISM). Electric currents generate MAGNETIC FIELDS circulating around themselves— the EARTH's magnetic field is maintained by large currents in its liquid core—and small current loops behave like magnetic dipoles with a moment given by the product of the loop current and area.

MAGNETISM, Terrestrial. See EARTH.

MAGNETITE, hard, black OXIDE mineral of composition Fe_3O_4. As an IRON ore of widespread occurrence in igneous rocks, it is second only in importance to HEMATITE. Magnetite has the inverse SPINEL structure. It is strongly ferromagnetic (see MAGNETISM) and was used in the ancient world as a COMPASS, under the name *lodestone*.

MAGNETO, a simple electrical AC GENERATOR based on a rotating permanent magnet which induces (see ELECTROMAGNETISM) a current in a coil. It is the basis of an IGNITION SYSTEM used in INTERNAL-COMBUSTION ENGINES without BATTERIES, the spark voltage being induced as usual in a large secondary coil when the current in a primary coil is interrupted, but the primary current being itself induced by the rotating magnet rather than being drawn from a battery.

MAGNETOHYDRODYNAMICS (MHD), the DYNAMICS of conducting fluids such as liquid metals or

PLASMAS, in ELECTRIC and MAGNETIC FIELDS. It is a macroscopic form of ELECTRODYNAMICS, deriving from fluid dynamics such concepts as magnetic pressure and magnetic viscosity. Its equations often defy exact solution. The most important applications are in magnetohydrodynamic GENERATORS and controlled nuclear FUSION processes. The extremely hot plasma produced by the fusion is contained by strong circulating magnetic fields; various designs are possible, the stability of each being the paramount consideration.

MAGNETOMETER, a device measuring MAGNETIC FIELD strength. Various types exist, exploiting, for instance, the oscillation rate of a small, freely suspended bar magnet or the deflection of a magnet against its suspension or a reference field. Sensitive magnetometers used in space research include the proton precession magnetometer and the helium magnetometer.

MAGNETOSPHERE, term applied to the region of the ATMOSPHERE containing the VAN ALLEN RADIATION BELTS.

MAGNETOSTRICTION, the interaction between the physical dimensions of a ferromagnetic specimen and its magnetization. A long iron rod, for example, contracts slightly in a MAGNETIC FIELD. Magnetization by mechanical strain is exploited in high-frequency vibration detectors.

MAGNIFICAT, biblical song of thanksgiving by the Virgin Mary (Luke 1:46–55), used as a CANTICLE in the liturgy of most Christian churches.

MAGNIFYING GLASS, or simple MICROSCOPE, a converging LENS used to form an enlarged image of an object. In normal use, the object is held within the focal length of the lens and an enlarged, upright virtual IMAGE is seen through the lens. A magnifying glass can also be used to form a real but inverted image of an object if the object is placed outside the focal length of the lens. A large converging lens can also be used as a **burning glass**, focusing light and heat from the sun.

MAGNITOGORSK, city in SW Chelyabinsk oblast, USSR. It is a major center of heavy industry, built to exploit the vast local ore deposits. Pop 364 000.

MAGNITUDE, Stellar, a measure of a star's brightness. The foundations of the system were laid by HIPPARCHUS (c120 BC), who divided stars into six categories, from 1 to 6 in order of decreasing brightness. Later the system was extended to include fainter stars which could be seen only by telescope, and brighter stars, which were assigned negative magnitudes (e.g., Sirius, –1.5). Five magnitudes were defined as a 100-times increase in brightness. These *apparent magnitudes* depend greatly on the distances from us of the stars. *Absolute magnitude* is defined as the apparent magnitude a star would have were it at a distance of 10pc from us: Sirius then has magnitude +1.4. Absolute magnitudes clearly tell us far more than do apparent magnitudes. Stars are also assigned red, infrared, bolometric and photographic magnitude.

MAGNOLIA, city and seat of Columbia Co., SW Ark. There are rich oil and gas deposits nearby. Pop 11 303.

MAGNOLIA, a genus of hardy and half-hardy deciduous and evergreen ornamental shrubs and trees. The species are native to eastern North America, East Asia and the Himalayas. The TULIP TREE is a near relative. Family: Magnoliaceae.

MAGOG, industrial city in S Quebec, Canada. It is a resort center at the N end of Lake Memphremagog. Pop 13 280.

MAGOG. See GOG AND MAGOG.

MAGPIES, birds of the crow family, Corvidae, most of which are brightly-colored or strikingly pied in black and white. Omnivorous and opportunistic, magpies feed on insects, carrion, birds' eggs and chicks. They are a successful group distributed through America, Europe and Asia.

MAGRITTE, René (1898–1967), Belgian Surrealist painter. He was an adherent of SURREALISM from about 1925, developing a style which often juxtaposed realistically portrayed subjects in a deeply disconcerting manner.

MAGSAYSAY, Ramon (1907–1957), president of the Philippines 1953–57. In WWII he led anti-Japanese guerrillas on Luzon. As defense secretary 1950–53, he defeated the Hukbalahap (Huk) communist guerrillas.

MAGUEY, common name for several plants of the genus *Agave*, which are native to South America and S North America. They are the source of several drinks in Mexico, including mescal and PULQUE. Family: Agavaceae.

MAGYARS, speakers of the Hungarian language. A nomadic warrior people, originally from the Urals, they entered central Europe in the 9th century and settled in the region which is now Hungary. The Magyar language belongs to the Ugro-Finnic linguistic group. (See also HUNGARY.)

MAHĀBHĀRATA, great Hindu epic poem, comprising some 110 000 32-syllable couplets, perhaps basically written before 500 BC, though with many later passages. It concerns the lengthy feud between two related tribes, the Pandavas and the Kauravas, and has as its central episode the BHAGAVAD-GĪTĀ; a later insertion. There are numerous editorial passages on mythology, religion, philosophy and morals.

MAHAN, Alfred Thayer (1840–1914), US naval officer and historian. His works on the historical significance of sea power are classics in their field. They include *The Influence of Sea Power upon History, 1660–1783* (1890) and *The Influence of Sea Power upon the French Revolution and Empire, 1793–1812* (1892). His work stimulated worldwide naval expansion.

MAHĀYĀNA (Sanskrit: Great Vehicle), school of BUDDHISM founded c200 BC; its teachings were aimed more at a spiritual elite (i.e. those who aspired to Buddhahood or enlightenment) than those of the Hinayana (Lesser Vehicle), a rival school.

MAHDĪ (Arabic: the guided one), the prophet or savior who Muslims believe will bring peace and justice to the world. One of the most notable claimants was 'Ubayd Allah (reigned 909–34), founder of the Egyptian Fatimid dynasty. Another was Muhammad Ahmad (d. 1885), who raised a revolt against Egyptian rule in the Sudan and fought the British 1883–85.

MAHICAN INDIANS. See MOHICAN INDIANS.

MAH-JONGG, Chinese game for four people played with ivory or plastic tiles. It was very popular in Europe and the US in the early 20th century.

MAHLER, Gustav (1860–1911), Austrian composer and conductor. He wrote nine symphonies (a tenth was unfinished) and a number of song cycles. The symphonies are a culmination of 19th-century Romanticism, but their startling harmonic and orchestral effects link them with early 20th-century works. Among other positions, Mahler was director of the Imperial Opera in Vienna 1897–1907.

MAHMUD, name of two Ottoman sultans. **Mahmud I** (1696–1754), reigned 1730–54. His armies fought a war against Austria and Russia 1736–39, resulting in the restoration of Belgrade to Turkey. **Mahmud II** (1785–1839), reigned 1808–39. During his rule Greece revolted (1821) and gained independence in 1830. Russia declared war on his empire in 1828 and forced the Treaty of Adrianople in 1829.

MAHMUD OF GHAZNI (971–1030), Afghan conqueror, who ruled Ghazni and Khorasan from 998. A devout Muslim, he invaded India many times, destroying Hindu temples and bringing the Punjab and Kashmir into his empire. He led a new era of Islamic dominance.

MAHOGANY, a number of trees growing in the tropics which yield a valuable fine-grained hardwood used in cabinet making. The term includes true mahoganies of the genus *Swietenia* and several trees of other genera which are marketed as mahogany. Family: Meliaceae.

MAHRATTĀ, or Marāthā, central Indian Hindu warrior people. Their empire was founded by Sivaji in 1674; it dominated India for about 150 years, following the MOGUL empire, but by the mid-19th century the British had completely broken its power.

MAIDENHAIR FERN, common name for about 200 species of fern of the genus *Adiantum*. They are mainly native to tropical America, with a few temperate species. These dainty plants are popular greenhouse ornamentals.

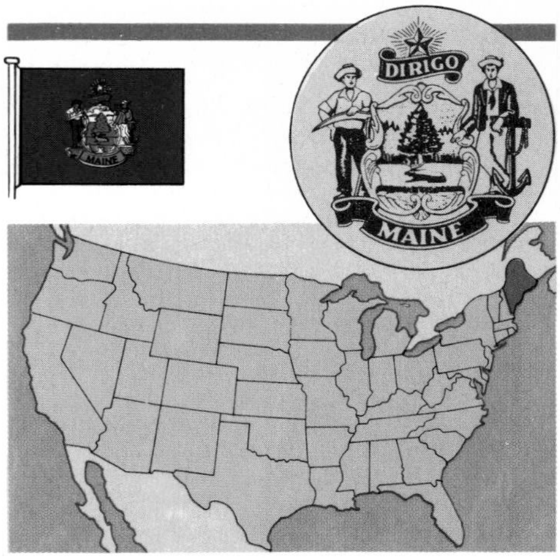

Name of state: Maine
Capital: Augusta
Statehood: March 15, 1820 (23rd state)
Familiar name: Pine Tree State
Area: 33 215sq mi
Population: 993 663
Elevation: Highest—5 268ft, Mount Katahdin. Lowest—sea level, Atlantic Ocean
Motto: Dirigo (I direct)
State flower: White-pine cone and tassel
State bird: Chickadee
State tree: White pine
State song: "State of Maine Song"

The topography of Maine is largely the result of glaciation during a succession of ice ages.

MAIDENHAIR TREE. See GINKGO.

MAIDU INDIANS, aboriginal Indians of N Cal. They lived mainly in the Sacramento Valley and the Sierra Nevada Mountains. The Maidus are part of the Penutian linguistic family. Today they number fewer than 200.

MAILER, Norman (1923–), US novelist and journalist. After the great success of his first novel, *The Naked and the Dead* (1948), he became a trenchant critic of the American way of life. He developed an amalgam of journalism, fiction and autobiography, first evident in his collection *Advertisements for Myself* (1959). He shared a 1969 Pulitzer Prize for *The Armies of the Night* (1968), an account of the 1967 Washington peace march.

MAILLOL, Aristide (1861–1944), French sculptor and painter. His chief subject was the female nude, which he sculpted in monumental, static forms that represent a revival of Classical ideals. In the early 1900s he was linked with the NABIS, as a painter; but when he was nearly 40 years old he took up sculpture.

MAIMONIDES, Moses (1135–1204), Moses ben Maimon, or Rambam, the foremost medieval Jewish philosopher. He was born in Muslim Spain, but persecution drove his family to leave the country. They eventually settled near Cairo in Egypt, where Maimonides became renowned as court physician to Saladin. Two of his major works were the *Mishneh*

Torah (1180), a codification of Jewish doctrine, and *Guide to the Perplexed* (1190), in which he attempted to interpret Jewish tradition in Aristotelian terms. His work influenced many Jewish and Christian thinkers.

MAINE, the northeasternmost state of the US. Some 80% of the state is forested and much of its economy is based on wood and wood products. The scenic forests, lakes, hills, rivers and coastal regions make tourism an important industry, bringing in about $450 million every year. But the most important branch of Maine's economy is manufacturing. This employs 35% of the labor force and accounts for an income of about $750–800 million each year. However, the state's isolated location and sparse population have kept it relatively free of pollution and urban blight.

There are three distinct land regions in the state—the Seaboard (coastal) Lowlands, the New England Upland running SW–NE and the White Mountain region in the NW.

History. In the 1600s the Algonquin Indians who inhabited the region offered little resistance to the establishment of the first white settlements on the coast and along the navigable rivers. But Maine was the scene of many conflicts during the FRENCH AND INDIAN WARS. Maine came under English control after the Treaty of Paris in 1763. Settlement began to increase, but remained low in comparison with other states until the 19th century.

Maine's soldiers played an active part in the Revolutionary War and the first naval engagement of the war took place off the state's coast, near Machias. In 1775 the British burned the town of Falmouth (now Portland). During the WAR OF 1812 the British easily captured and held the eastern portion of the state.

Maine was admitted to the Union as a free state in 1820, as part of the MISSOURI COMPROMISE. A leading issue in the first years of statehood was the boundary dispute with New Brunswick which had been simmering since the end of the Revolutionary War. The conflict finally led to the AROOSTOOK WAR of 1839. The boundary was later permanently set by the WEBSTER-ASHBURTON TREATY of 1842.

Maine is still governed under its original 1819 constitution. There is a complex local government system based on towns (townships), cities, counties and plantations (small incorporated areas). The state's 21 cities operate under charters from the legislature.

MAINE, US battleship, sent to protect US citizens and property in Cuba, which mysteriously blew up in Havana harbor on Feb. 15, 1898, with a loss of 260 men. The incident helped spark off the SPANISH-AMERICAN WAR.

MAINE COON CAT, US breed probably produced by crosses between domestic type cats and long-haired cats brought home by seamen from the orient, *not* by matings between racoons and cats as is sometimes said (such coupling is biologically impossible). Large and of any color or pattern, they have a longer legged look than the Persian with a more tapering head, larger ears and large, slightly slanting eyes. Their fur is easier to keep in condition than the Persian's.

MAIN RIVER, rises in the Fichtelgebirge in N Bavaria and flows W into the Rhine R opposite Mainz. About 240mi of its 325mi length are navigable.

MAINTENON, Françoise d'Aubigné, Marquise de (1635–1719), second wife of Louis XIV of France. After the death of her first husband (1660), she became governess to the sons of Louis and his mistress Mme de Montespan. She replaced the latter in Louis' affections and, on the death of the queen, married him.

MAINZ, or Mayence, capital of Rhineland-Palatinate state, West Germany. It is a manufacturing and commercial city on the Rhine R and the center of the Rhenish wine industry. Pop 172 195.

MAISONNEUVE, Paul de Chomedy, Sieur de (1612–1676), founder and first governor of Montreal, Canada, 1642–63. An ex-soldier, he was sent to Canada as a missionary and leader of a small French colonial group.

MAISTRE, Joseph Marie, Comte de (1753–1821), French philosopher, author and founder of the Ultramontanist movement. A staunch conservative, he believed papal and royal power should be absolute and was an inveterate opponent of the French Revolution.

MAITLAND, Frederic William (1850–1906), English jurist and legal historian. He was particularly concerned with early English law and founded the Selden Society (1887). Notable among his works is *The History of English Law before the Time of Edward I* (1895), written with Sir Frederick Pollock.

MAIZE. See CORN.

MAJOLICA, maiolica, or faience, a simple Italian earthenware pottery coated with tin-glaze and covered with painted decoration. It was perfected in 15th and 16th century Italy, being based on original Spanish earthenware (from Majorca—hence the name).

MAJORCA, or Mallorca, largest of the Balearic Islands of Baleares province, Spain. Majorca lies in the W Mediterranean, 115mi E of the Spanish coast. It is a major tourist center with many resorts, including its capital, Palma.

MAKAH INDANS, Amerindian tribe living in the area of Cape Flattery, Puget Sound, Wash. In 1855 they ceded their lands (between Flattery Rocks and the Hoko R) to the US government. The Makah are the southernmost of the Wakashan linguistic group, which includes the NOOKTA INDIANS.

MAKARIOS III, Archbishop (1913–), born Michael Christodoulos Mouskos, the first president of independent Cyprus (from 1959), archbishop and primate of the Cypriot Orthodox Church since 1950. During British rule he led the movement for *enosis* (union with Greece). He had links with the EOKA terrorist group and was exiled by the British 1956–57. He fled temporarily during the political disturbances of 1974.

MAKASAR, or Macassar, seaport and capital of South Sulawesi province, SW Celebes Island, Indonesia. It was an important 18th-century Dutch port, and is now a major transportation center. Pop 384 159.

MAKASSAR STRAIT, channel between E Borneo and Celebes, W Indonesia. It links the Celebes Sea in the N with the Java Sea in the S and is about 500mi long.

MAKEMIE, Francis (c1658–1708), colonial clergyman and father of American Presbyterianism. Born in Ireland, he was an evangelist in America during 1683–98. He then settled in E Va. (1699) and founded the first American presbytery, in Philadelphia (1706).

MALABAR CHRISTIANS, or St. Thomas Christians, a group mostly found in Kerala state, SW India. Considered heretics by the Portuguese, though traditionally aligned with Rome since the 6th century, they broke with Rome in 1653. The majority reverted to Catholicism in 1661 but some joined the Syrian Orthodox Church.

MALABAR COAST, coastal region of SW India, from Goa to Cape Comorin peninsula. The principal industries are fishing and rice growing. In the 16th century it was an important Portuguese trading area.

MALACCA, or Melaka, port and capital city of Malacca, a state of Malaysia, SE Asia. It is a trade center for rice and rubber. It was ruled by the Portuguese from 1511, who made it the center of the East Indian spice trade, by the Dutch, 1641–1824, and then by the British until Malaysian Independence, 1957. Pop 86 357.

MALACCA, Strait of, channel about 500mi long between the S Malay Peninsula and Sumatra. It connects the Indian Ocean and South China Sea.

MALACHI, Book of (Hebrew: my messenger), the 12th of the Old Testament MINOR PROPHETS. Written anonymously about the 5th century BC, it prophesies judgment for insincerity and negligence in religion at the coming of the MESSIAH.

MALACHITE, a green mineral consisting of basic copper (II) carbonate ($Cu_2CO_3[OH]_2$). It is of widespread occurrence, usually with AZURITE, and is formed by weathering of other copper minerals. A minor ore of COPPER, it is used for ornamental stone and GEMS.

MALACHY, Saint (1095–1148), Irish churchman and Archbishop of Armagh c1136. He restored clerical discipline and hierarchy in Ireland. Assisted by Saint BERNARD OF CLAIRVAUX, he introduced the order of the CISTERCIANS into Ireland. Feast day Nov. 3.

MÁLAGA, seaport city and popular resort in S Spain. Dating from Phoenician times, it is now also a commercial and manufacturing center. Pop 374 452.

MALAGASY REPUBLIC. See MADAGASCAR.

MALAMUD, Bernard (1914–), US novelist and short story writer. He won the Pulitzer Prize for his novel *The Fixer* (1966). Malamud's work deals mainly with Jewish life and traditions in the US. The heroes of his books are often humble, solitary individuals.

MALAMUTE. See ALASKAN MALAMUTE.

MALAN, Daniel François (1874–1959), South African politician. He founded the Purified Nationalist Party (1934) and was prime minister of South Africa (1948–54). He was a dedicated believer in APARTHEID.

MALARIA, tropical PARASITIC DISEASE causing malaise and intermittent FEVER and sweating, either on alternate days or every third day; bouts often reoccur over many years. One form, cerebral malaria, develops rapidly with ENCEPHALITIS, COMA and SHOCK. Malaria is due to infection with *Plasmodium* carried by mosquitos of the genus *Anopheles* from the BLOOD of infected persons. The cyclic fever is due to the parasite's life cycle in the blood and LIVER; diagnosis is by examination of blood. QUININE and its derivatives, especially CHLOROQUINE and primaquine, are used both in prevention and treatment but other chemotherapy (ATABRINE, pyrimethamine) may also be used. Mosquito control, primarily by destroying their breeding places (swamps and pools), provides the best method of combating the disease.

MALATESTA, Italian family, rulers of Rimini from the 13th to 16th century. The court of **Sigismondo Malatesta** (1417–1468), was a center of Renaissance culture. In 1500 the Malatesta fled when Cesare BORGIA advanced on the town.

MALAWI, formerly Nyasaland, a republic in E central Africa. High plateaus, 2 500ft–4 500ft in elevation, comprise much of the country, and over 20% of the area is occupied by Lake Nyasa (or Malawi), lying in the GREAT RIFT VALLEY. The valley climate is hot; that of the Highlands moderate. Most of the population are Bantu-speaking Africans, and 90% live in villages. The largest towns are Blantyre, Lilongwe, the capital, and Zomba. Malawi has no significant mineral deposits and the economy is based on agriculture, particularly the growth of tea, tobacco and cotton, which are all exported. There is light industry at Blantyre and Lilongwe and bauxite deposits on Mt Mulanje. Road and rail networks link Malawi with Mozambique, and Blantyre has an international airport.

History. In 1859 the Scottish missionary David LIVINGSTONE visited the area. Missions were later set up and the Arab slave trade suppressed. In 1891 a British protectorate of Nyasaland was formed,

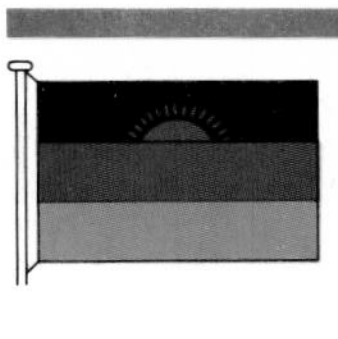

Official name: Republic of Malawi
Capital: Lilongwe
Area: 36 350sq mi
Population: 4 549 000
Languages: English; Bantu languages, Swahili
Religions: Christian, Muslim, Animist
Montetary unit(s): 1
Kwacha = 100 tambala

becoming the British Central Africa Protectorate in 1893. In 1907 the name reverted to Nyasaland. From 1953–63 the country was part of the Federation of Rhodesia and Nyasaland. In 1964 it became the independent state of Malawi, remaining within the British Commonwealth, and Dr. Hastings BANDA became premier. It was made a republic in 1966 with Banda as president. He follows an independent foreign policy maintaining ties with South Africa.

MALAWI, Lake. See NYASA, LAKE.

MALAY, general term for a group of about 100 million people who live on the Malay Peninsula and on islands of the Philippines and Indonesia. They are a short, brown-skinned, Mongoloid people. They probably emigrated originally from central Asia. By the 2nd century AD, the powerful Malay kingdom of Srivijaya ruled in Sumatra, Indonesia.

MALAY ARCHIPELAGO, formerly the East Indies, the world's largest group of islands, off the coast of SE Asia, between the Indian and Pacific Oceans. They include all the Indonesian and Philippine islands and New Guinea.

MALAYO-POLYNESIAN LANGUAGES, or **Austronesian Languages**, family of some 500 languages found throughout the Central and S Pacific (except New Guinea and Australia, but including New Zealand) and especially in Malaysia and the Indonesian islands. There are two main groups, Oceanic to the E and Indonesian to the W.

MALAY PENINSULA, the southernmost peninsula in Asia, comprising West Malaysia and SW Thailand. Over half the area is tropical rain forest and a mountain range runs from N to S. It is one of the world's richest producers of rubber and tin.

MALAYSIA, independent federation in Southeast Asia, comprising West Malaysia on the Malay Peninsula and, 400mi away across the South China Sea, East Malaysia, formed by Sabah and Sarawak in Borneo.

Land. The landscape of Malaya (West Malaysia) is mainly mountainous (rising to over 7000ft) with narrow coastal plains and lush equatorial forests. The climate is hot and very humid. Sarawak and Sabah also have large areas of rain forest. Many rivers flow from central Borneo to the coastal swamps. Malaysia's highest mountain, Mt Kinabalu (13455ft) is on Sabah.

People. The predominantly rural population is over 40% Malay, under 40% Chinese and 10% Indian and Pakistani. Whereas in West Malaysia the population comprises 50% Malay and 33% Chinese, in East Malaysia the Chinese and Ibans together form over 60% and the Malays under 20%. The largest cities are Kuala Lumpur, the capital, Penang (George Town) and Ipoh, in the W, and Kota Kinabalu in Sabah, and Kuching in Sarawak. Government is by constitutional monarchy, a paramount ruler being elected for five-year terms.

Economy. Malaysia has rich natural resources. It is one of the world's leading producers of natural rubber and tin. The forests also provide valuable timber, palm oil and coconuts. Rice is the chief food crop, and bananas, yams, tea and tobacco are also grown. Malaysia produces petroleum, iron ore, bauxite, coal and gold. The principal exports are rubber, tin, iron ore, palm oil and timber.

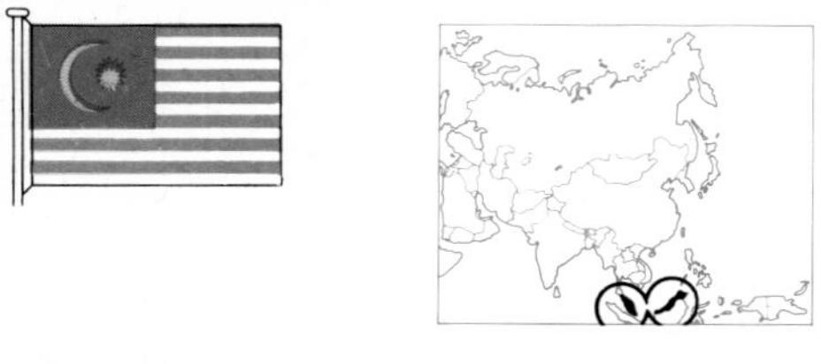

Official name: Federation of Malaysia
Capital: Kuala Lumpur
Area: 127581sq mi
Population: 12324000
Languages: Malay; English, Chinese
Religions: Muslim
Monetary units(s): 1 Malaysian dollar = 100 cents

History. In the 9th century Malaya was the seat of the Buddhist Srivijava empire. The Portuguese took Malacca in 1511. The British formed the East India Company in Penang in 1592, and in 1826 united Penang, Singapore and Malacca into the Straits Settlement. Between 1888 and 1909 the British established many protectorates in Malaya and Borneo. After the WWII Japanese occupation (1941–45), Malaya was reorganized as the Federation of Malaya (1948), gaining independence within the British Commonwealth (1957). In 1963 the union of Malaya with Singapore, Sarawak and Sabah formed the Federation of Malaysia. Indonesia waged guerrilla warfare against the Federation during 1963–65. In 1965 Singapore seceded to become an independent republic. Parliament was suspended for 22 months in 1969 after racial riots broke out between Malays and Chinese in West Malaysia. Abdul Razak, premier of the National Front coalition government from 1974 until his death in 1976, was succeeded by his deputy Datuk Hussein Onn.

MALCOLM X (Malcolm Little; 1925–1965), US black radical leader. While in prison 1946–52, he was converted to the BLACK MUSLIMS. In 1964 he formed the rival Organization of Afro-American Unity, pleading for racial brotherhood instead of separation. He was assassinated at an OAAU meeting in New York City.

MALDEN, city in Mass., on the Malden R. It is a residential and manufacturing suburb of Boston. Pop 56127.

MALDIVES, Republic of, formerly the Maldive Islands, a group of 19 coral atolls in the Indian Ocean. They lie about 400mi SW of Ceylon and comprise some 2000 islands, of which about 220 are inhabited. The people are Muslims and their language, Maldivian, is related to Old Sinhalese. The capital, Malé, lies on the island of the same name. The chief industry is fishing. The Islands were under British protection 1887–1965, becoming independent in 1965, and a republic in 1968.

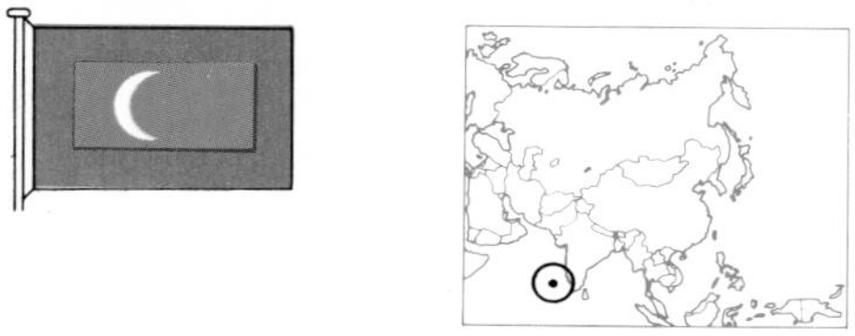

Official name: Republic of Maldives
Capital: Malé
Area: 115sq mi
Population: 118818
Languages: Divehi (Maldivian)
Religions: Muslim
Monetary unit(s): Maldivian rupee

MALEBRANCHE, Nicolas (1638–1715), French philosopher, scientist and Roman Catholic priest. In both philosophy and science he was much influenced by the thought of DESCARTES, in the former field attempting to reconcile Cartesian philosophy with that of St. Augustine, in the latter field researching LIGHT, VISION and the CALCULUS.

MALENKOV, Georgy Maksimilianovich (1902 –   ), Soviet premier 1953–55, after STALIN's death. Malenkov was replaced in 1955, then expelled from the PRESIDIUM (1957), accused of forming an "anti-party" group, and from the Party in 1961.

MALEVICH, Kasimir (1878–1935), Russian painter, a pioneer of ABSTRACT ART. In 1913 he began painting works based on geometric shapes and in 1915 published a manifesto to propagate SUPREMATISM. Among his works is *White Square on White Ground*, 1918.

MALHERBE, François de (1555–1628), French court poet to Henry IV and Louis XIII. A critic of the classical style of the PLÉIADE poets, he emphasized the importance of French classic language and of a precise form of writing.

MALI, landlocked republic in West Africa. The great Niger R flows across S Mali, and its channels and marshy lakes form an "inland delta" suitable for rice and cotton growing. Without irrigation from the Niger and Senegal Rivers agriculture would be impossible.

Land and People. Middle Mali is arid, with shrub, thorn and acacia. The NE and SW regions are mountainous. Mali has many ethnic groups: negroid farming peoples in the S like the Bambara and Malinké, the Peuls (Fulani) in the Niger Valley and white nomadic pastoralists, the Tuareg, Moors and Arabs in the N. The capital and largest town is Bamako in the S on the Niger R.

Economy. Mali is a predominantly farming and pastoral country. In the S, corn, cotton, millet, rice and sorghum are important crops. In the central plain vast numbers of cattle, goats and sheep are reared. There is little industry apart from food processing and handicraft production. The country's mineral riches are as yet hardly exploited.

History. In the 14th century the MALI EMPIRE was at its height and, as late as 1507, TIMBUKTU was still a flourishing cultural center. By the mid-17th century Mali had crumbled under external attacks and internal rivalries. In 1896 the area came under French rule, and in 1904 became the French Sudan. In 1958 the colony accepted autonomy within the French community. During 1959–60, with Senegal, it composed the Sudanese Republic. In 1960 Mali became fully independent under President Keita. In 1968 a military coup gave power to the National Liberation Committee.

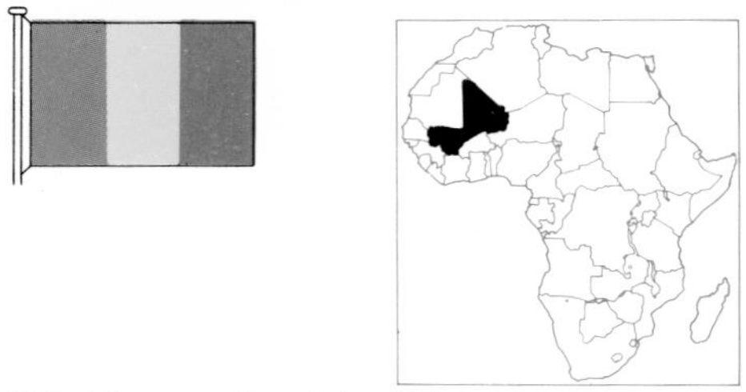

Official name: Republic of Mali
Capital: Bamako
Area: 478767sq mi
Population: : 5300000
Languages: French; Tribal languages
Religions: Muslim, Animist
Monetary unit(s): Mali franc = 100 centimes

MALIC ACID (HOOC.CH_2.CHOH.COOH), dibasic acid found in the juice of unripe apples and some other fruits. mp 133°C.

MALI EMPIRE, greatest of the Sudanese empires of Africa. Founded in the 13th century, it reached its height under Mansa Musa who reigned c1312–37. He and his successors were devout Muslims. The towns of Mali and TIMBUKTU became centers both of the caravan trade and of Islamic culture. The empire declined in the 15th century, mainly because of SONGHAI expansion.

MALIGNANCY. See CANCER.

MALINOIS (Mechelaar), Belgian drover's dog, similar to the Belgian Sheepdog (Groenendael) but with a short, dense coat and longer on the neck and tail. It stands 24in high. Its fawn coat has black tips and a black mask is preferred.

MALINOWSKI, Bronislaw Kasper (1884–1942), Polish-born British anthropologist, generally accepted as the founder of social ANTHROPOLOGY. In his functional theory all the mores, customs or beliefs of a society perform a vital function in it. From 1927 to 1938 he was a professor at London University; from 1939 until his death, a professor at Yale.

MALLARD, *Anas platyrhynchos*, the Wild duck found in large numbers throughout North America, Europe and Asia. The male, or *drake*, is a striking bird with green head, purple breast and gray body, and with the four central tail feathers curled distinctively upward. Out of the breeding season, it molts to a speckled brown plumage like that of the female.

MALLARMÉ, Stéphane (1842–1898), French

Symbolist poet (see SYMBOLISM). He held that the subject of poetry should be the ideal world which language would suggest or evoke, but not describe. Although the syntactical and grammatical structure of his poems are difficult, he had considerable influence on French poetry. His works include *The Afternoon of a Faun* 1876, which inspired DEBUSSY and *A Throw of the Dice will never eliminate Chance*, 1897.

MALLEABILITY, the property of metals and alloys to be deformed by beating, rolling, etc., without breaking. GOLD is the most malleable of metals, and can be beaten into almost any shape. Malleability is not equivalent to DUCTILITY, the ability to be drawn out without breaking: LEAD is malleable but not ductile.

MALLORCA. See MAJORCA.

MALLORY, Stephen Russell (c1813–1873), US senator (1851–61) and Confederate secretary of the navy (1861–65). He was the architect of Confederate naval strategy and urged the construction of ironclad ships to break the Union blockade.

MALLOW, common name for hardy annual, biennial and perennial plants of the genera *Hibiscus* and *Malva,* family Malvaceae. There are about 30 species of true mallows native to temperate regions of the Old World, some of which are in cultivation. Several have become naturalized in North America.

MALMÖ, historic seaport city in SW Sweden. It is the third largest Swedish city and a transportation hub, and has textile and shipbuilding industries. Pop 262 260.

MALNUTRITION, inadequate nutrition, especially in children, which may involve all parts of diet (marasmus), or may be predominantly of PROTEINS (KWASHIORKOR) or VITAMINS (PELLAGRA, BERIBERI, SCURVY). In *marasmus*, essential factors for METABOLISM are derived from the breakdown of body TISSUES; extreme wasting and growth failure result. In adults, starvation is less rapid in onset, as the demands of growth are absent, but similar metabolic changes occur.

MALORY, Sir Thomas (d. 1471), English writer and adventurer, author of *The Book of King Arthur and His Noble Knights of the Round Table*, which CAXTON published as *Morte d'Arthur*, 1485. Much of the work is based on French versions of the ARTHURIAN LEGENDS.

MALPIGHI, Marcello (1628–1694), Italian physician and biologist, the father of microscopic ANATOMY, discoverer of the CAPILLARIES (1661), and a pioneer in several fields of medicine and biology.

MALPRACTICE, wrongful or improper practice of a profession, such as accountancy, law or medicine, by a qualified member. A professional governing body such as the AMERICAN MEDICAL ASSOCIATION may discipline an offender, who may also be liable to civil suit and criminal prosecution.

MALRAUX, André (1901–1976), French writer, critic and politician. He fought in China, in the Spanish CIVIL WAR and in the resistance in WWII. He was minister of information 1945–46 and 1958, and of culture 1955–69. His novels *Man's Fate* (1933) and *Hope* (1938) reflect his experiences in China and Spain; nonfiction works such as *The Voices of Silence* (1951) and *The Metamorphosis of the Gods* (1960) are concerned with art and civilization.

MALT, the product made from any cereal grain by steeping it in water, germinating and then drying it. This activates dormant ENZYMES such as DIASTASE, which converts the kernel STARCH to MALTOSE. Malt is used as a source of enzymes and flavoring.

MALTA, independent country strategically placed in the central Mediterranean. It comprises the islands of Malta, Gozo, Comino and two uninhabited islets.

Malta has almost no natural resources. Some light industry was developed in the 1960s, but the country is dependent on agriculture, tourism and the rental of its naval dockyard, at present leased to NATO.

Inhabited since the 4th millennium BC, Malta was visited by Phoenicians, Greeks and Carthaginians before succumbing to Roman control in 218 BC. In c60 AD St. Paul was shipwrecked on Malta. In 1530, after occupation by the Arabs, Normans and Spaniards, the islands were granted to the KNIGHTS OF SAINT JOHN. The Knights defeated the Turks in the Great Siege of 1565 and built Valletta. In 1798 they were briefly ousted by the French and in 1814 the British took over the islands. In 1942 Malta was awarded the British George Cross for the courage of its people under siege and bombardment in WWII. In 1964 the country became independent within the British Commonwealth.

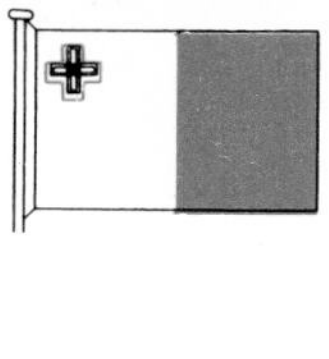

Official name: Malta
Capital: Valletta
Area: 121.8sq mi
Population: 322 070
Languages: Maltese, English. Italian widely spoken
Religions: Roman Catholic
Monetary unit(s): 1 Pound (M) = 100 cents

MALTESE, Semitic language of the inhabitants of Malta. Punic-Arabic in origin, it contains elements of several other Mediterranean languages.

MALTESE DOG, the oldest known breed of lapdog, sometimes wrongly called the Maltese terrier. Its straight, white, silky coat reaches almost to the ground. The dog's short tail is doubled into the coat along the back.

MALTHUS, Thomas Robert (1766–1834), English clergyman best known for his *Essay on the Principle of Population* (1798; second, larger edition, 1803). In this he argued that the population of a region would always grow until checked by famine, pestilence or war. Even if agricultural production were improved, the only result would be an increase in population and the lot of the people would be no better. Although this pessimistic view held down the provision of poor relief in England for many decades, it also provided both C. DARWIN and A. R. WALLACE with a vital clue in the formulation of their theory of EVOLUTION by natural selection.

MALTOSE ($C_{12}H_{22}O_{11}.H_2O$), or "malt sugar," disaccharide SUGAR, produced by the action of DIASTASE on STARCH and yielding GLUCOSE with the ENZYME maltase.

MALVERNE, village in SE N.Y. Situated on Long Island, it is a residential suburb of New York City. Pop 10 036.

MALVERN HILL, Battle of (July 1, 1862), last of the Seven Days' Battles in Union Gen. McClellan's Peninsular Campaign. Nine Union brigades successfully repulsed a series of attacks by 16 Confederate brigades near Richmond, Va.

MAMARONECK, residential village on Long Island Sound, SE N.Y. It is a yachting center and light industrial suburb of New York City. Pop 18 909.

MAMBAS, large, slender snakes of the genus *Dendroaspis*, restricted to parts of Africa. With hollow poison fangs in the upper jaw they are among the world's most dangerous snakes. The venom is a potent nerve poison. Three species are arboreal and feed on lizards, birds and their eggs. The fourth, the Black mamba, inhabits dry savannas and feeds largely on small mammals.

MAMELUKES, or Mamlūks, originally non-Arab slaves forming the personal bodyguard of the Egyptian caliphs and sultans. In 1250 the Mamelukes overthrew the sultanate and ruled until defeated by the Ottomans (1517). They then became an important part of the Turkish army. But in 1811 the Egyptian pasha Muhammad Ali ordered a massacre of all Mamelukes. A very few escaped to Lower Nubia, but soon dispersed.

MAMMALS, a class of VERTEBRATES distinguished by the possession of mammary glands in the female for suckling the young, and of body hair. Living mammals are divided into MONOTREMES, egg-laying mammals; MARSUPIALS, pouched mammals that bear their young in an undeveloped state, and PLACENTAL MAMMALS that nourish the young in the uterus with a PLACENTA. Monotremes, ECHIDNAS and the duck-billed PLATYPUS are a very divergent group with many reptilian characters. Placental mammals and marsupials show closer affinities. Mammals evolved from Synapsid reptiles; these diverged early from the main reptilian stem and have no living representatives. Thus the actual origin of mammals is a matter for speculation. Certainly many groups of late synapsids independently developed mammal-like characters, and it is probable that more than one group crossed the "mammal line," i.e., that mammals are of polyphyletic origin.

MAMMARY GLANDS. See BREASTS; LACTATION.

MAMMILLARIA, a genus of globular or cylindrical CACTI that are widely grown as house plants for their colorful bell-shaped flowers and attractive arrangements of spines. The plant blooms if kept nearly dry in winter at a temperature of 7°C to 13°C (45°F to 55°F). Family: Cactaceae.

MAMMOTH, a name that properly applies to only one species of large hairy elephant, the Woolly mammoth, *Elephas primigenius*, which lived in the late Pliocene, but is now used for a whole group of large, extinct ELEPHANTS. These resembled modern forms but were covered with reddish hair and bore tusks far longer than any of today.

MAMMOTH CAVE, limestone cavern about 85mi SW of Louisville, Ky., containing a series of vast subterranean chambers. It includes lakes, rivers, stalactites, stalagmites and formations of gypsum crystals. The mummified body of a pre-Columbian man has been found there. It is part of Mammoth Cave National Park.

MAN, *Homo sapiens*, the most widespread, numerous, and reputedly the most intelligent (see INTELLIGENCE) of the PRIMATES. For man's evolutionary history see PREHISTORIC MAN; for the varieties of man see RACE, and for his earliest social development see PRIMITIVE MAN.

MAN, Isle of, island in the Irish Sea off the NW coast of England. It is a British dependency with its own legislature (Court of Tynwald) and representative assembly (House of Keys). Tourism is the main industry. The Manx language is now virtually extinct. Pop 56 289.

MANA, a concept found among the more sophisticated Polynesian and Melanesian societies. Mana is the possession of supernatural power by a person or inanimate object, and epitomizes a pre-animistic stage in the evolution of religious thought.

MANAGUA, capital of Nicaragua and of the Managua department. It is the country's largest city and chief commercial center. It suffered serious earthquakes in 1931 and 1972. Pop 398 514.

MANAGUA, Lake, in W Nicaragua, the country's second-largest lake. It drains S, through the Tipitapa R, into the larger Lake Nicaragua. Lake Managua is 38mi from E to W and 575sq mi in area.

MANAKINS, small New World birds of the family Pipridae, with short bills and short wings. Confined to Middle and South America, they live in dark forests feeding on berries, which they snap off in flight, and insects. Males are usually brightly-colored and have a complicated courtship display.

MANAMA, or Al-Manāmah, capital of Bahrain on the Persian Gulf. It is the country's chief port and commercial and financial center. Pop 89 112.

MANASSAS. See BULL RUN, BATTLES OF.

MANASSEH, king of Judah (reigned 687–642 BC). He ascended the throne when he was 12. Under Assyrian influence, he enforced idolatrous practices. The Apocryphal Prayer of Manasseh is traditionally attributed to him.

MANASSEH, one of the 12 tribes of Israel. Together with the tribe of Ephraim, it composed the house of Joseph. Among prominent Manasseh leaders were Gideon and Jephthah.

MANATEES, large and fully-aquatic herbivorous mammals of tropical and subtropical Atlantic coasts

(A) Skeleton of a typical mammal, the rat. (1) skull; (2) shoulderblade; (3) humerus; (4) radius and ulna; (5) tarsal bones; (6) spinal column; (7) ribs; (8) sternum; (9) pelvis; (10) thighbone; (11) tibia; (12) fibula; (13) rear tarsal bones. (B) Internal organs of the rat. (1) aorta (red); (2) heart; (3) lungs; (4) diaphragm; (5) liver; (6) stomach; (7) kidney; (8) spleen; (9) large intestine; (10) bladder. (C) Commonest varieties of mammalian foot. (1) plantigrade foot (bear), standing on the sole of the foot; (2) digitigrade (lion), standing on the toes; (3) ungulate (cow), standing on a hoof. Bones of the foot are shown in black. (D) How cushioning pads protect the feet of various mammals. Most predators have pads at toe and sole (1); in ungulates there is a shock-absorbent cushion above the hoof (2); the elephant has an elastic cushion on the sole of the foot (3).

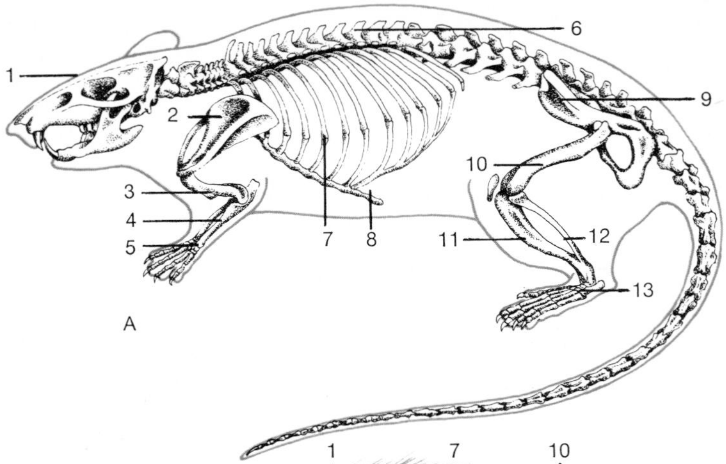

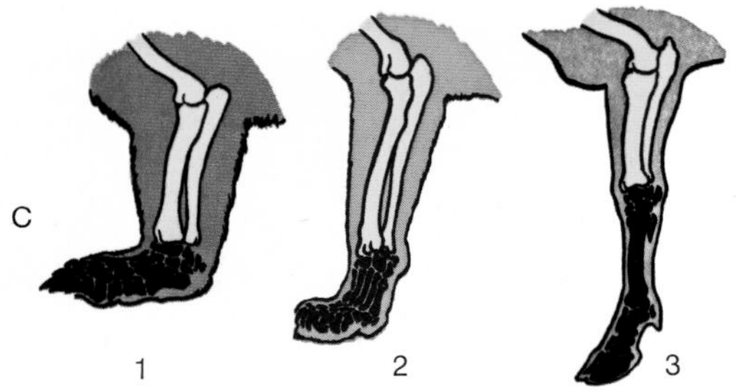

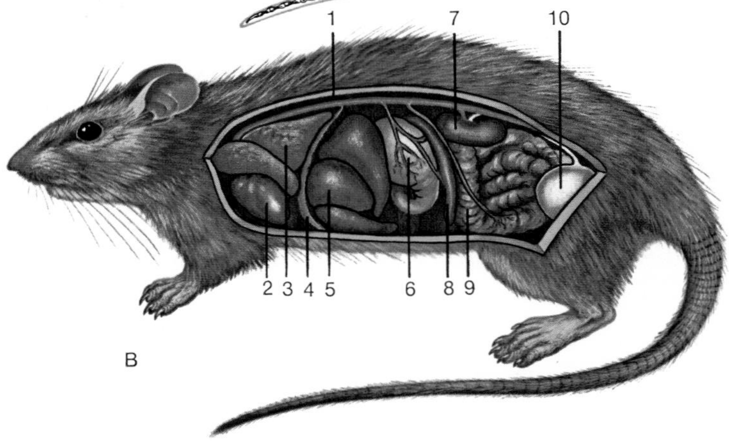

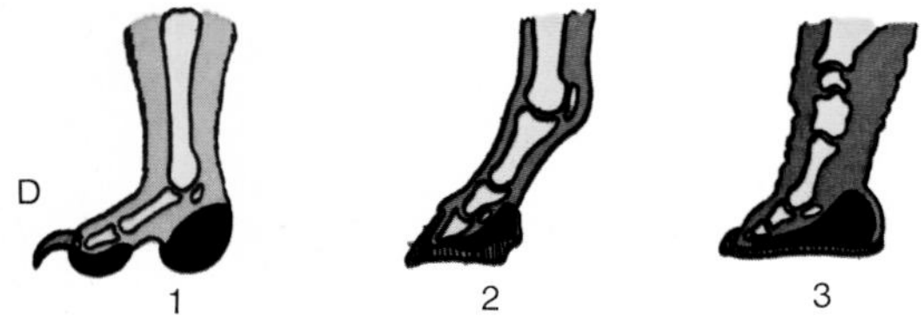

Some mammals, such as the camel (1) have been domesticated by man; others such as the African black rhinoceros (2) have been brought to the edge of extinction by him. Some mammals, such as the seal (3), have taken to an aquatic existence; others, such as the Asian Small-clawed otter (4) are more or less amphibious. The chimpanzee (5) and the other apes are the most intelligent mammals, with the possible exception of dolphins—and of course man.

1

2

3

4

5

and large rivers. With the DUGONGS they are the only living sea-cows (order: Sirenia). Heavily-built and torpedo-shaped, they have powerful rounded tails which are flattened horizontally. The forelimbs are small and hindlimbs completely absent; the tail provides all propulsion.

MANAUS, or Manáos, trading and commercial center and capital of Amazonas state, NW Brazil. It lies on the Rio Negro, 7mi above its junction with the Amazon R, but is accessible to oceangoing ships. Pop 303 155.

MANCHESTER, industrial city in NW England. A major commercial and transportation center, lying on the Irwell R, Manchester became famous for cotton in the 19th century. It is also an important seaport made accessible to oceangoing traffic by the Manchester Ship Canal. It is the home of the Hallé Orchestra. Pop 531 000.

MANCHESTER, manufacturing town in central Conn. The surrounding district produces fruit, vegetables and tobacco. Pop 47 994.

MANCHESTER, industrial city in S N.H. It lies on the Merrimack R and power is supplied by nearby Amoskeag Falls. Incorporated as Derryfield in 1751, it was renamed in 1810. Pop 87 754.

MANCHESTER SCHOOL, a group of English businessmen and members of Parliament, c1820–1860, mostly from Manchester, who advocated worldwide free trade. They were led by John BRIGHT and Richard COBDEN. In 1839 Cobden formed the Anti-Corn-Law League, which brought about the repeal of the corn laws in 1846.

MANCHESTER SHIP CANAL, NW England, connects the Mersey R estuary with Manchester. It made the city accessible to oceangoing traffic and allowed the expansion of Manchester's textile industry. The canal was built 1887–94.

MANCHESTER TERRIER, dog originally bred near Manchester, England, for rat-killing and rabbit-coursing. Developed from the whippet, it has a short, glossy black coat and tan head.

MANCHINEEL, *Hippomane mancinella*, a poisonous tree of the American tropics. Its poisonous milky sap contains oil of euphorbia which can cause DERMATITIS. The wood is used for cabinet making. Family: Euphorbiaceae.

MANCHUKUO, or Manchutikuo, former E Asia state (1932–45). It was set up by the Japanese as a puppet republic within conquered Manchuria. In 1934 it was made an empire, with the Manchu emperor P'u-yi as nominal ruler. Its capital was Hsinking (now Ch'ang-ch'un).

MANCHURIA, or Manchow, a region of NE China comprising Heilungkiang, Kirin and Liaoning provinces. It is an important agricultural and industrial area.

Historically, Manchuria was the home of the MANCHUS. They tried to limit Chinese settlement in the area, but this steadily increased, especially after 1900. In the 1890s Russia had declared an interest in the province; but Russia's defeat in the 1904–05 Russo-Japanese War brought Japanese domination, first of S Manchuria, then, in 1932, of the whole country. The puppet state of MANCHUKUO was created. In 1945 Russian and Chinese communist forces occupied the country and in 1950 Russia recognized it as part of the Chinese People's Republic. In 1954 the W part of the country became part of the Inner Mongolia Autonomous Region, and the remainder became present-day Manchuria.

MANCHUS, a Manchurian people who conquered China and formed the Ta Ch'ing dynasty (1644–1912). They originated from the Jurchen tribe of the TUNGUS and were originally a nomadic, pastoral people. The Manchus have now been racially and culturally absorbed by the Chinese and their language is virtually extinct.

MANCO CAPAC, name of two Inca rulers. **Manco Capac I** was the legendary 13th-century founder of the Inca dynasty. **Manco Capac II** (c1500–1544) was the last of the Inca rulers. He led a revolt against the Spanish and sacked Cuzco city (1536), but was later forced to withdraw.

MANDALAY, capital of the Mandalay division and district, N Burma. It is a Buddhist center, and a trade point with air, railroad and river connections. Mandalay was the last capital of the kingdom of Burma. Pop 375 000.

MANDAMUS, an order issued by a court, requiring a person, official or body to perform a legal duty. A mandamus can compel a lower court to hear a case within its jurisdiction.

MANDAN, city and seat of Morton Co., central N.D. It is a market for the surrounding wheat-growing and stock-rearing area. Pop 11 093.

MANDAN INDIANS, Indian tribe of the upper Missouri valley. Of Siouan linguistic stock, they inhabited what is now N.D. The tribe was almost wiped out by smallpox in the early 19th century. About 300 pure Mandans survive on the Fort Berthold Reservation, N.D.

MANDARIN, name of nine grades of important civil servant or military official in imperial China. Mandarin Chinese, formerly an upper-class language, is now the official national language of China, though many dialects still exist.

MANDARIN DUCK, *Aix galericulata*, a DUCK of wooded inland waters of Africa and Asia, introduced as ornamental fowl elsewhere. The female is drab brownish-gray, but the male is brightly-colored with upstanding orange "sails" on the closed wings, a drooping crest and chestnut sidewhiskers.

MANDATE, the authority to administer a territory, granted under Article 22 of the Covenant of the LEAGUE OF NATIONS. This "caretaker" system was devised to administer former Turkish territories and German colonies after WWI. With the formation of the UN, the mandate system was replaced by the TRUST TERRITORY system.

MANDELSTAM, Osip Emilievich (1891–1938?), Russian poet, at first a member of the neoclassicist Acmeist school. He was arrested in 1934 and exiled until 1937. Rearrested in 1938, he reportedly died soon afterwards in a Siberian prison.

MANDEVILLE, Sir John (active 1350), putative author of *Mandeville's Travels*. Most of the book is drawn from previous works, including those of Vincent de Beauvais, William of Boldensele and Odoric of Pordenone. Mandeville's real identity is unknown.

MANDOLIN, stringed instrument of the lute family. It has a pear-shaped body and a fretted neck. The Neopolitan mandolin has four pairs of strings; the Milanese five or six.

MANDRAKE, *Mandragora officinarum*, perennial plant with purplish to white flowers, of the POTATO family, Solanaceae. In medieval Europe, the thin stalk and forked root were associated with the human form. The mandrake was said to scream when pulled from the soil. Its poisonous root has been used as an emetic, purgative and pain-killer. In North America, the May apple (*Podophyllum peltatum*) is called mandrake.

MANDRILL, *Papio sphinx*, a large, forest-living BABOON of the West African coast, dark brown with white cheek fringes. The face is brilliantly-colored with a red nose, and blue ridges on either side. The male has a red penis and blue scrotum.

MANEATER SHARKS, several species of SHARKS notorious for alleged attacks on humans, particularly the Great White shark, the Blue shark, the Tiger shark and the Makos or MACKEREL SHARKS. Attacks on man are in fact extremely rare.

MANED WOLF, *Chrysocyon brachyurus*, one of the most striking of all canids, found throughout the plains regions of South America. Solitary animals with thin muzzles, narrow chests and long legs, they are adapted for moving through and seeing over the long pampas grass. They are not fast runners, but pounce on prey.

MANET, Édouard (1832–1883), French painter. Though partly influenced by GOYA and VELÁZQUEZ, his work introduced a new pictorial language, and was often severely criticized by the artistic establishment. His paintings *Olympia* and *Le Déjeuner sur l'Herbe* (both 1863) were thought scandalously bold. He strongly influenced the Impressionists, though he refused to exhibit with them.

MANFRED (c1232–1266), illegitimate son of Holy Roman Emperor Frederick II. On Frederick's death (1250) Manfred took over as regent of Italy. In 1258, with Saracen aid, he was crowned king of the Two Sicilies. Later, popes Urban IV and Clement IV called on Charles I of Anjou for aid to defend the empire, and Manfred was killed in battle.

Swampy mangrove forests with their tangles of roots are common coastal features in the warmer areas of the world. A whole ecological system of animal and plant life has developed in them.

MANGABEYS, Old World MONKEYS closely related to BABOONS but with shorter faces and long tails. Robust monkeys, they are essentially arboreal, forest baboons. They form tight-knit troops with well-developed social patterns.

MANGALORE, city in SW Mysore state, S India. It is a seaport and export center on the Malabar Coast. Pop 214 093.

MANGANESE (Mn), hard, grayish metal in Group VIIB of the PERIODIC TABLE; a TRANSITION ELEMENT. It occurs naturally as PYROLUSITE and MANGANITE. Elementary manganese is obtained by the reduction of manganese (IV) oxide with aluminum in a furnace, or by ELECTROLYSIS. When smelted with iron ore, manganese ore gives the alloys SPIEGELEISEN and ferromanganese, widely used in STEEL production. Manganese also forms useful ALLOYS with some nonferrous metals. Manganese is fairly reactive, resembling IRON chemically. Its main oxidation states are +2, +3, +4, +6 and +7. **Manganese (IV) oxide** (MnO_2), a black crystalline solid, is widely used as an oxidizing agent and as a depolarizer in electric dry cells. **Permanganate** (MnO_4^-) is used in nickel refining and tanning, and as a bleach, disinfectant and powerful oxidizing agent. **Manganese (II) sulfate** ($MnSO_4$) is a component of some fertilizers. AW 54.9, mp 1244°C, bp 1962°C, sg 7.20 (20°C).

MANGANITE, a black mineral consisting of hydrated manganese (III) oxide (MnO[OH]); an ore of MANGANESE, found in W Europe, Mich. and Cal. It occurs as bundles of prismatic crystals, and alters to PYROLUSITE.

MANGE, INFECTIOUS DISEASE of domestic animals, caused by mites in the fur and leading to itching and irritability.

MANGEL-WURZEL, or **mangold**, root crop belonging to the species *Beta vulgaris*, other varieties of which include SUGAR BEET and SWISS CHARD. The roots have a high sugar content and are used as a livestock feed in Europe and North America. Family: Chenopodiaceae.

MANGO, large tropical evergreen trees and their fruit, from the genus *Mangifera*. The tree is grown commercially in SE Asia, Cal. and Fla. The juicy, oval stone-fruit is either eaten raw or used in preserves. Family: Anacardiaceae.

MANGOSTEEN, *Garcinia mangostana*, a small evergreen tree native to Malaysia and the E Indies. Some mangosteens are cultivated in the W Indies, Middle America and Hawaii. The term also denotes the purple, juicy, white-pulp fruit. Family: Guttiferae.

MANGROVE, shrubs and small trees of the genera *Rhizophora* and *Avicennia*, which are native to tropical and subtropical coasts, estuaries and swamps. The seeds germinate in the fruit to produce a long root, which embeds in the mud when the fruit falls.

Dwarfed by the concrete giants of the Manhattan skyline, the trees of Central Park still thrive, providing New York with much-needed greenery.

Mangrove trees produce masses of aerial adventitious roots, which result in the mass of tangled vegetation typical of mangrove swamps. The mangrove's bark is rich in TANNIN.

MANHATTAN, borough of NEW YORK CITY, co-extensive with New York Co., N.Y. Consisting largely of Manhattan Island, it contains the main financial, commercial and cultural centers of New York City. Pop 1 539 233.

MANHATTAN, city and seat of Riley Co., NE Kan., on the Kansas R. It is an agricultural trading and distribution center. Pop 27 575.

MANHATTAN BEACH, manufacturing city and resort in SW Cal., on the Pacific coast. It has an electronics industry and makes aircraft parts. Pop 35 352.

MANHATTAN PROJECT, US project to develop an explosive device working by nuclear FISSION. It was established in Aug. 1942, and research conducted at Chicago, California and Columbia universities, as well as at Los Alamos, N.M., and other centers. By Dec. 1942 a team headed by FERMI initiated the first self-sustaining nuclear CHAIN REACTION. On July 16, 1945 the first ATOMIC BOMB was detonated near Alamogordo, N.M., and similar bombs were the following month dropped on Hiroshima (Aug. 6) and Nagasaki (Aug. 9). (See also NUCLEAR WARFARE.)

MANIA, a PSYCHOSIS characterized by high elation, excitement and acceleration of physiological as well as mental processes. **Homicidal mania** is characterized by an uncontrollable urge to kill.

MANIC-DEPRESSIVE PSYCHOSIS, a PSYCHOSIS characterized by alternating periods of deep depression and MANIA. Periods of sanity may intervene.

MANICHAEISM, religion founded by **Mani** (c216–c276 AD), a Persian sage. He preached it from c240 and claimed to be the Paraclete (intercessor) promised by Christ. Mani borrowed ideas from BUDDHISM, CHRISTIANITY, GNOSTICISM, Mithraism and ZOROASTRIANISM. A form of DUALISM, Manichaeism contained an elaborate cosmic mythology of salvation. Man was created by Satan, but had particles of divine light in him, which had to be released. In the Middle Ages, Manichee doctrines revived in the BOGOMILS and CATHARI. Manichaeism survived in Fukien, China, until the 13th century.

MANIFEST DESTINY, a phrase coined in 1845. It implied divine sanction for the US "to overspread the continent allotted by Providence for the free development of our multiplying millions." The concept was used to justify most US territorial gains.

MANILA, city on the E shore of Manila Bay in SW Luzon, Philippines. It is the commercial, industrial and cultural center and chief port of the islands. Manila was occupied by the Japanese 1942–45 and almost completely rebuilt after the war. It is the country's seat of government, though not its capital. Pop 1 377 000.

MANILA BAY, Battle of (May 1, 1898), an important naval battle early in the SPANISH-AMERICAN WAR. US Commodore George DEWEY's squadron completely destroyed a Spanish fleet, with almost no US losses. The victory made Dewey a national hero.

MANILA HEMP, or **abaca**, a hard fiber obtained from the leaf stalks of several tropical tree species including *Musa textilis*, of the BANANA family Musaceae. The Philippines provide 95% of the world's output. (See also HEMP.)

MANIN, Daniele (1804–1857), Italian patriot and politician. Arrested as an activist by the Austrians in 1848, he was freed in the same year during the revolution. He headed the Venetian Republic and led the city against the four-month Austrian siege (1849). When Venice fell he went into exile in Paris.

MANIOC. See CASSAVA.

MANITOBA, easternmost of central Canada's "prairie" provinces." Manitoba comprises four regions. The Saskatchewan Plain is a rich farming area. The Manitoba Lowland is a region of forests, lakes and swamps. Both are part of the W Interior Plains. The Hudson Bay Lowland is a flat, thinly populated plain extending 50–100mi inland from the bay's S shore. The fourth region is an area of lakes, rivers, forests, muskeg (sphagnum bog) and mineral-rich rock; it covers 60% of Manitoba and is part of the vast Canadian Shield area. About 60% of the province is forested and about 15% is covered by rivers and over 100 000 lakes.

With agriculture, minerals, forests, fisheries and expanding manufacturing industries, Manitoba has a more diversified economy than the other prairie provinces. Manitoba's largest industry is manufacturing, centered on metropolitan Winnipeg, Virden and St. Boniface. The largest section of this industry produces processed foods and beverages. But agriculture remains a large industry. Winnipeg is Canada's leading grain market and large quantities of wheat are exported. In many parts of the province beef cattle are raised, and dairy farming is especially important in the Manitoba Lowland along the Red R valley.

Manitoba's first white settlers were fur traders of the HUDSON'S BAY COMPANY (1670) and the NORTH WEST COMPANY (1783). There was intermarriage with native Indian women, the offspring being called Métis. In 1812 Thomas Douglas founded the first farming settlement along the Red R. The Métis rebelled against this interference with the fur trade, but by 1821 peace was restored. When the Dominion of Canada gained Manitoba from the Hudson's Bay Company in 1869, the Métis again rebelled (under Louis RIEL). They were afraid of losing their lands to British-Canadian settlers. Their rights were respected in the 1870 Manitoba Act, but waves of immigrants did come from Britain, Scandinavia and Central Europe. Today over half Manitoba's total population lives in the Winnipeg metropolitan area.

Name of province:
Manitoba
Joined confederation:
July 15, 1870
Capital:
Winnipeg
Area:
251 000sq mi
Population:
988 247

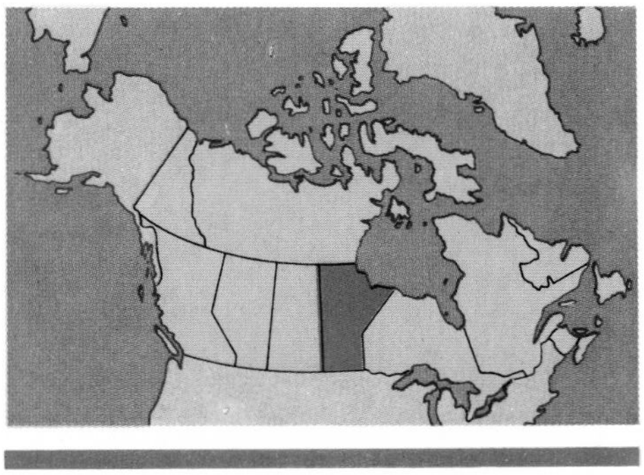

MANITOBA, Lake, lake covering 1 817sq mi in S Manitoba province, Canada. With lakes Winnipeg and Winnipegosis, it is one of the Manitoba Great Lakes.

MANITOU (Indian: Great Spirit), in several North American Indian tribes, the term for a presiding religious spirit. The manitou could be good or evil and could inhabit a fetish, amulet or any object of awe.

MANITOULIN ISLANDS, a group of islands in Lake Huron, S Ontario, Canada. The chief islands are Grand Manitoulin and Cockburn (or Little Manitoulin). Also included is Drummond Island, part of NE Mich.

MANITOWOC, commercial and industrial city, port of entry and seat of Manitowoc Co., E Wis. It lies on Lake Michigan. Pop 33 430.

MANIZALES, capital of Caldas department, central Colombia. It is a trading center for the surrounding coffee growing area. Pop 307 000.

MANKATO, manufacturing city and seat of Blue Earth Co., S Minn. It lies on the Minnesota R in a livestock, grain and dairy area. Pop 30 895.

MANN, Horace (1796–1859), US educator, lawyer and politician. He served in the Mass. house of representatives (1827–33), and was state senator (1835–37), secretary of the state board of education (1837–48) and US congressman (1848–53). Mann, who published 12 annual reports (1837–48) promoting public education for all children, greatly raised educational standards in Mass.

MANN, James Robert (1856–1922), US lawyer and congressman. Two important pieces of legislaton are associated with him. The Mann Act, known also as the White Slave Traffic Act (1910), prohibited interstate transportation of women for immoral purposes. The Mann-Elkins Act (1910) placed railroad charges under the jurisdiction of the INTERSTATE COMMERCE COMMISSION.

MANN, Thomas (1875–1955), German novelist, essayist and winner of the 1929 Nobel Prize for Literature. He left Germany (1933), settled in the US (1938) and became a US citizen (1944). His works include *Buddenbrooks* (1901), *Death in Venice* (1912), *The Magic Mountain* (1924) and *Joseph and His Brothers* (4 novels; 1933–43). His literary themes are often concerned with the effects of a changing world on people's inner thoughts and lives; with death in the midst of life; and with the artist's isolation.

MANNA, in the Bible, the food that fell from heaven and miraculously sustained the Israelites during their 40 years in the wilderness. Described as small white honey-flavored flakes, it may have been *Lecanora esculenta*, lichen carried by the wind; or an edible resin formed by scale insects feeding on tamarisk trees.

MANNED SPACECRAFT CENTER. See NATIONAL AERONAUTICS AND SPACE ADMINISTRATION.

MANNERHEIM, Baron Carl Gustaf Emil von (1867–1951), Finnish soldier and statesman. He successfully led the Finnish nationalists against the Russo-Finnish communists in 1918. He also led the Finnish forces in the RUSSO-FINNISH WAR (1939–40), holding the "Mannerheim Line" defenses on the Karelian Isthmus. He was president of Finland 1944–46.

MANNERISM, the artistic and architectural style between the RENAISSANCE and the BAROQUE. It was developed in Bologna, Florence and Rome during the early 16th century and flourished until the century's end. Marked by strained (though apparently executed with great facility) human postures and crowded compositions, the style was a reaction against the Renaissance's classical principles. Mannerists included PARMIGIANINO and PONTORMO.

MANNHEIM, commercial and manufacturing city in Baden-Württemberg, West Germany. It is a port at the confluence of the Rhine and Neckar rivers and produces steel and chemicals. Pop 330 900.

MANNHEIM, Karl (1893–1947), Hungarian-born sociologist. His *Man and Society in an Age of Reconstruction* (1940) stressed the importance of science in sociological change. He taught in Britain at London U., from 1933.

MANNING, Henry Edward (1808–1892), English cardinal. He was an Anglican priest 1833–50 and a member of the OXFORD MOVEMENT. In 1851 he entered the Roman Catholic Church and in 1865 became archbishop of Westminster, being made a cardinal in 1875. He founded the League of the Cross temperance movement and mediated in the 1889 London dock strike.

MANOLETE (1917–1947), famous Spanish bullfighter. He was recognized as a true professional at Seville (1939) and remained the world's leading matador until fatally gored.

MANOMETER, device, usually consisting of a double-legged liquid column in a glass or metal tube, for determining the difference between two fluid pressures. In a simple U-tube manometer, the mercury (or other low-vapor-pressure liquid) rises in the lower pressure side and drops in the other, the difference in heights being measured on a suitably calibrated scale. Sensitivity is increased by inclining the tube or giving the legs different cross-sections.

MANSART, Nicolas François, or Mansard (1598–1666), French architect who popularized, but did not invent, the high-pitched mansard roof. He helped initiate the purity of the French classical style of architecture.

MANSFIELD, agricultural and manufacturing town in N Conn. It was the site of the first US silk mill (1810). Pop 19 994.

MANSFIELD, industrial city and seat of Richland Co., central Ohio. Chief among its products are automobile bodies, rubber goods and electrical equipment. Pop 77 599.

MANSFIELD, Katherine (1888–1923), born Kathleen Mansfield Beauchamp, New Zealand-born British short story writer, poet and essayist. The short stories collected in *The Garden Party* (1922) are among her finest mature work.

MANSFIELD, Michael ("Mike") Joseph (1903–), US Democratic senator and Senate majority leader from 1961. In 1964 he suggested the neutralization of both N and S Vietnam.

MANSFIELD, Mount, at 4 393ft, the highest peak in the Green Mts and in Vt.

MANSHIP, Paul (1885–1966), US sculptor. He is best known for his interpretations of classical mythological subjects, among which is his statue of *Prometheus* (1934) at the Rockefeller Center, New York.

MANSLAUGHTER, in US criminal law, the unlawful but unpremeditated killing of another human being. In some states a distinction is made between *voluntary manslaughter*, where injury was intended, and *involuntary manslaughter*, where there was no such intent.

MANSON, Sir Patrick (1844–1922), British medical scientist known for his pioneering researches in TROPICAL MEDICINE, especially for his naming the MOSQUITO as the transmitter of FILARIASIS and MALARIA. (See also ROSS, SIR RONALD.)

MANSŪRA, El. See AL-MANSŪRA.

MANTA RAYS, or Devil rays, huge marine RAYS up to 6m (20ft) long, which have abandoned life on the bottom for a pelagic existence, using their pectoral fins to "fly" through the water. The mouth and gills have become adapted for taking in vast amounts of water and straining out the PLANKTON.

MANTEGNA, Andrea (c1431–1506), Italian painter and engraver. He was a member of the Paduan school, acclaimed for his mastery of anatomy and illusionistic perspective. Among his most famous works are the cartoons of the *Triumph of Caesar* (c1495). His frescoes in the Eremitani church, Padua (1448–57), were almost totally destroyed by bombing in 1944.

MANTINEA, Battles of. In 418 BC the Argives, Athenians and Mantineans were defeated by the Spartans. In 362 BC the Thebans under Epaminondas defeated the Spartans. In 207 BC the Achaean League under Philopoemen defeated the Spartans.

MANTISES, long, narrow, carnivorous insects usually found in the tropics. Most species are well-camouflaged as leaves or twigs. Mantids feed on other insects and sit motionless waiting for prey to approach within striking distance when the long front legs are shot out at great speed to catch it. Many sit "praying" with forelegs raised and clasped together when awaiting prey. The female usually devours the male after mating.

MANTIS FLIES, a genus of neuropteran insects closely resembling MANTISES: the forelegs have been modified for the capture of prey in an identical manner. While the adults are active predators, the larvae are parasitic on spiders' eggs. The newly-hatched larva can move freely but when it encounters a spider cocoon it molts to take on an unsegmented maggot-like form.

MANTLE, the layer of the earth lying between the crust and the core. (See EARTH.)

MANTLE, Mickey Charles (1931–), US baseball player with the New York Yankees; they signed him for $1000 in 1949. He is a switch hitter (both right- and left-handed) and won the 1956 Triple Crown in batting.

MANTRA, in HINDUISM and BUDDHISM, sacred utterance believed to possess supernatural power. The constant repetition of *mantras* is used to concentrate the mind on an object of meditation, e.g. the syllable OM, said to evoke the entire VEDA.

MANTUA, or Mantova, manufacturing commune and capital city of Mantova province, Lombardy, N Italy, on the Mincio R. It processes farm produce. Pop 67 151.

MANU (from Sanskrit *man-*, to think), in Indian mythology, the ancestor of the human race, also the name used by the author or authors of the Hindu sacred book *The Code of Manu*.

MANURE, animal or plant material applied to soil to increase its fertility (see FERTILIZERS). **Animal manure** is composed essentially of animal wastes together with some plant material, such as straw. It supplies NITROGEN, potash (see POTASSIUM) and PHOSPHATES, as well as smaller quantities of COPPER, IRON and other micronutrients (see also NITROGEN CYCLE). **Green manure** consists of growing plants, usually LEGUMINOUS PLANTS, plowed directly into the soil. **Compost** comprises plant and sometimes animal material allowed to rot (see PUTREFACTION) before application to the soil: composts are usually reinforced with nitrogen and phosphorus. (See also CARBON CYCLE; FERTILIZERS; GUANO; HUMUS; SOIL.)

MANUTIUS, Aldus. See ALDUS MANUTIUS.

MANVILLE, manufacturing borough in central N.J., the scene of several skirmishes in the Revolutionary War. Pop 13 029.

MANX, Celtic dialect of the Isle of Man. See CELTIC LANGUAGES.

MANX CAT, breed of cat with no tail, popularly believed to come from the Isle of Man (hence Manx) but a widely distributed mutation. In addition to its rounded rump, which should show no vestige of tail, it has a special double coat and long hind legs. The mutation causing taillessness affects the whole spine and continuous breeding of Manx to Manx can produce other abnormalities and dead births.

MANZANITA, common name applied to many species of the genus *Arctostaphylos*. They range from trailing shrubs to small trees. Most are native to the western US. They have small, urn-shaped, pink or white flowers and a reddish brown fruit. Family: Ericaeae.

MANZIKERT, Battle of (1071), historic battle at Manzikert in E Turkey. Turkish leader Alp Arslan captured the Emperor Romanus IV, defeated his largely mercenary army and effectively crushed the Byzantine Empire's power in Asia Minor. The consequent blocking of pilgrim routes to the Holy Land by the Seljuk Turks was a direct cause of the CRUSADES.

MANZONI, Alessandro Francesco Tommaso Antonio (1785–1873), Italian novelist and poet. He was a leading figure in the Romantic movement and his novel *The Betrothed* (1825–27) influenced many later writers. Manzoni's death inspired VERDI's *Requiem* (1874).

MANZU, Giacomo (1908–), Italian sculptor. His works include the great bronze doors of St. Peter's, Rome (consecrated 1964).

MAORIS, the pre-European inhabitants of New Zealand. They are a Polynesian people who migrated to New Zealand c1200–1400 AD. When the first Europeans arrived, the Maoris were a well-organized Neolithic tribal society. Some of their tribes fought the British in the Maori Wars of the 1860s. The Maoris have full political rights, and intermarriage with whites is widespread. (See also NEW ZEALAND.)

MAO TSE-TUNG (1893–1976), Chinese communist leader, a founder of the People's Republic of China. Son of an educated peasant in Shao-shan, Hunan province, he became interested in various political creeds, including anarchism; in 1921 he joined the newly-founded Shanghai Communist Party, and in 1927 led the Autumn Harvest uprising. This was crushed by the local KUOMINTANG militia, and Mao fled to the mountains. There he built up the Red Army, and in 1931 proclaimed a republic in Kiangsi. Surrounded by Kuomintang forces in 1934, the army was forced to embark on the famous LONG MARCH to Yenan, Shensi. The appalling rigors of the march united the communists behind Mao, and he was elected chairman. In 1937 an uneasy alliance was made with the Kuomintang under CHIANG KAI-SHEK against the Japanese; after WWII Mao's forces drove the Kuomintang to Taiwan. Mao then became chairman of the new People's Republic. During the 1950s and 1960s he steered China ideologically further away from the USSR. In 1966 he launched the "Cultural Revolution" to clear the party of "revisionists." In the 1970s Mao appeared to favor a degree of detente with the West, especially Europe. From 1974 age and ill-health forced him increasingly to withdraw from public life. It is uncertain how much influence his wife CHIANG CH'ING had on his rule. (See also CHINA.)

MAP, diagram representing the layout of features on the earth's surface or part of it. Maps have many uses, including routefinding; marine or aerial NAVIGATION (such maps are called *charts*); administrative, political and legal definition, and scientific study. **Cartography**, or mapmaking, is thus an important and an exact art. The techniques of SURVEYING and GEODESY are used to obtain the positional data to be represented. Since the EARTH is roughly spheroidal—the GEOID being taken as the reference level—and since the surface of a sphere cannot be flattened without distortion, no plane map can perfectly represent its original, the distortion becoming worse the larger the area. But spherical maps or *globes* are impractical for large-scale work. Thus plane maps use various **projections**, geometrical algorithms for transforming the spherical coordinates into plane ones. The choice of projection depends on the purpose of the map; one may aim for correct size or correct shape, but not both at once: a suitable compromise is generally reached. Projections fall into three main classes: *Cylindrical projections* are obtained by projection from the earth's axis onto a cylinder touching the equator. MERCATOR's Projection from the center of the earth is a well-known example: its graticule (net of parallels and meridians) takes the form of a rectangular grid with the scale increasing toward the poles, which are infinitely distant; straight lines represent RHUMB LINES. *Conic projections*, best suited to middle latitudes, are obtained by projection onto a cone that caps the earth, touching a given parallel. *Azimuthal projections* are from a single point onto a plane. The *gnomonic* projection, having the point at the center of the earth, represents GREAT CIRCLE ROUTES by straight lines. The *orthographic* projection has the point at infinity, the projective rays being parallel; distortion is great, but the map looks like the globe. These geometric projections are now seldom used as such, but are modified to give correct relative areas, distances or shapes. The *scale* of a map (assuming it to be constant) is the ratio of a distance on the map to the distance that it represents on the earth's surface. It may be expressed directly as the ratio or representative fraction (1:63 360), as a unit ratio (1in to 1mi), or by a graphic graduated scale. Maps use standard symbols and colors to show features, giving the maximum information clearly. Types of map include physical, political, economic, demographic, historical, geological and meteorological maps; there are also star maps (see CELESTIAL SPHERE).

Maps have been drawn from earliest times, but until the Middle Ages most were little more than sketch maps based on impressions and guesswork, except for those of the Greek geographers, notably PTOLEMY of Alexandria. In the 14th century, Mediterranean sea charts were in use which were remarkably accurate, owing to the introduction of the COMPASS and good estimates of distances sailed. The great voyages of discovery, the rediscovery of Ptolemy's map, and accurate surveying in the Low Countries revolutionized cartography in the 16th and 17th centuries, the work of Gerardus MERCATOR and Abraham Ortelius (who produced the first modern atlas) being well-known. Louis XIV promoted a national survey of France, the British Ordnance Survey (1791) followed suit, and in the 19th century most civilized countries produced extensive maps. The US Geological Survey began in 1879. The International Map of the World (IMW), comprising about 1 000 sheets at a scale of 1 : 1 000 000, was started in 1913 but is yet to be completed.

MAPLE, common name for trees of the genus *Acer*, which are found throughout the N Hemisphere. The wood is hard and suitable for making furniture. The foliage of some species is noted for the red and orange colors produced in the fall. Maples are often grown as ornamental garden trees. The North American sugar maple (*Acer saccharum*) is tapped to produce MAPLE SYRUP. Family: Aceraceae. **Flowering maples** are not related to the true maples, but belong to the genus *Abutilon*, family Malvaceae. They have maple-like leaves and produce funnel-shaped, droopy flowers. They are often grown as house plants, requiring a sunny position in winter, less so in summer; the temperature should drop from about 21°C (70°F) in the daytime to about 17°C (63°F) at night. The soil should be kept evenly moist, particularly avoiding extreme dryness which causes leaf and flower-bud drop. Propagation is by shoot tip cuttings.

MAPLE HEIGHTS, city in NE Ohio, a residential suburb of Cleveland. Pop 34 093.

MAPLE SHADE, village in SW N.J., a manufacturing center in an agricultural region. Pop 16 464.

Tapping a sugar maple in New Hampshire for the sap which will become the delicious maple syrup. Sugar maples are found all over the NE US and Canada, which has adopted the maple leaf as the emblem on its flag.

MAPLE SYRUP, crop produced solely in North America and obtained from the sap (sweet water) of the sugar MAPLE (*Acer saccharum*). Up to 50 litres of sap are required to produce one litre of syrup; the flavor and coloring are imparted to the syrup as the sap is concentrated by evaporation.

MAPLE SYRUP URINE DISEASE, hereditary disorder in which the metabolism of certain AMINO ACIDS is defective, and hence the urine has an odor like that of maple syrup.

MAPLEWOOD, village in E Minn., a residential suburb of St. Paul. Pop 25 222.

MAPLEWOOD, residential city in E central Mo., 7mi W of St. Louis. Pop 12 785.

MAPLEWOOD, township in NE N.J. A residential suburb of Newark and New York, it has some manufacturing industries. Pop 24 932.

MAPPING, the assignment to each element *a* in a set *A* (see SET THEORY) of at least one element *b* in a set *B* according to a rule, *f*. This is written $f\!:\!A \rightarrow B$. In a single-valued or one-to-one mapping each element *a* is assigned a single, unique element *b*. In many cases, the term mapping is considered synonymous with FUNCTION.

MAPUTO, port and capital of the MOZAMBIQUE Republic formerly known as LOURENÇO MARQUES. The name was briefly changed to Can Phumo upon independence (1975).

MAQUIS, French underground resistance movement in WWII, named for the undergrowth along the Mediterranean coast in which bandits often hid. The Maquis grew out of refugees from a forced-labor draft ordered by the VICHY regime in 1943. Its activities continued until 1944, when it was incorporated into the French Forces of the Interior.

MARABOU, *Leptoptilos crumeniferus*, a large species of African STORK with massive bill, almost featherless head and neck and long pouch of pink skin dangling from the throat, blown up in courtship display. They feed on carrion and also prey on small mammals. The **Adjutant stork**, *L. dubius*, of S Asia, is similar.

MARACAIBO, capital city of Zulia state, Venezuela, a seaport on the Gulf of Venezuela. It is one of the continent's major oil centers, with a flourishing petrochemical industry. Pop 650 002.

MARACAIBO, Lake, in NW Venezuela, a 5 000sq mi expanse of water, linked to the Gulf of Venezuela by a narrow channel. The lake is among the world's richest oil-producing regions and is also a waterway for local agricultural products.

MARACAY, city in N Venezuela, capital of Aragua state. It was the country's effective capital under the dictator Juan GOMEZ. It is the fifth largest city in Venezuela and a major industrial center. Pop 255 134.

MARAJÓ, island covering 15 500sq mi in the Amazon Delta, in NE Brazil. It is an agricultural area producing mainly livestock. The chief city is Soure, a resort on the Atlantic coast.

MARANHÃO, state in NE Brazil. The capital and only major port is São Luis, on Maranhão Island. The country is largely tropical rain forest, though fertile river valleys permit agriculture.

MARAÑON RIVER, rises in the Andes Mts in Peru and flows 1000mi NW and E to N Peru, joining the Ucayali R below Iquitos to form the Amazon R.

MARANTA, a genus of evergreen perennial plants grown in houses and greenhouses for their ornamental foliage. *Maranta leuconeura kerchoveana* is also called the Rabbit-track plant because of the dark green patterns formed on the pale green leaves. *M.l. massangeana* has dark green leaves with pale margins and red-tinged veins. It is also known as Cathedral windows because of the leaf patterns revealed when it is held up to the light. Both these species are also called Prayer plants because the leaves fold together at night like praying hands. Marantas grow best in bright, north-facing windows (or under fluorescent light), at a temperature not below 13°C (55°F). The soil should be kept evenly moist and the leaves showered with water at least once a month. Propagation is achieved by dividing the roots or taking stem cuttings. Family: Marantaceae.

MARAT, Jean Paul (1743–1793), French Revolutionary politician and demagogue. A doctor and journalist, he was elected to the National Convention in 1792, and came to lead the radical faction. Chief instigator of the September Massacre (1792) at which over 1 000 died, he was an active supporter of the REIGN OF TERROR. Marat was murdered in his bath by Charlotte CORDAY.

MARATHAS. See MAHRATTĀ.

MARATHON, famous plain in Greece, about 25mi NE of Athens, where in 490 BC MILTIADES led an Athenian force of about 11 000 to victory over 20 000 Persians led by DARIUS I. Fearing Athens might surrender prematurely to the Persian fleet, Miltiades sent the runner Pheidippides to report the victory. On reaching Athens, he delivered the message, collapsed and died. The modern OLYMPIC GAMES marathon race commemorates this incident.

MARBLE, metamorphic rocks formed by recrystallization of CALCITE or DOLOMITE. The finest Italian marble is pure white calcite and has been prized by sculptors throughout history. Many types of marble contain impurities causing discoloration.

MARBLE CANYON NATIONAL MONUMENT, section of the Colorado R gorge in N Ariz., often regarded as a continuation of the Grand Canyon. An area of 26 000 acres was declared a national monument in 1969.

MARBLEHEAD, historic town in NE Mass. It is now a residential suburb of Boston and a popular yachting and fishing resort. Pop 21 295.

MARBURY v. MADISON, historic US Supreme Court decision. In 1803, William Marbury sued James Madison, then secretary of state, for failure to deliver a commission given by the previous administration. Chief Justice John Marshall held the act upon which Marbury relied to be unconstitutional, thus establishing the judicial right to review the constitutionality of legislation.

MARC, Franz (1880–1916), German expressionist painter, with KANDINSKY a cofounder of the BLAUE REITER group. His work is characterized by vigorous lines and a vivid and symbolic use of color.

MARCEAU, Marcel (1923–), perhaps the greatest living mime. Born in France, he studied drama in Paris, rising to fame with a brief mime role in the film *Les Enfants du paradis* (1947). In that year he created his most famous characterization, the white-faced Chaplinesque clown, Bip. He became world-famous with stage appearances in the 1950s.

MARCEL, Gabriel (1889–1973), French philosopher and dramatist, perhaps the first French existentialist. His philosophy considers human experience from the point of view of the private individual and of the individual in the community.

MARCELLINUS, Saint (d. 304), pope from 296. Towards the end of his reign, under the persecutions of DIOCLETIAN, he appears to have become an apostate, but according to some histories he repented and was martyred. His feast day is April 26.

MARCELLUS, name of two popes. **Saint Marcellus I** (d. c309), pope c308–c309, was banished from Rome after his harsh penances imposed on apostates under DIOCLETIAN led to rioting. **Marcellus II** (1501–1555), pope in 1555, was a renowned humanist and antiquarian. He had presided at the Council of TRENT in 1545.

MARCH, third month of the Gregorian CALENDAR. It corresponds to the Roman month Martius (after Mars, god of war), first month of the Roman calendar until 153 BC, when Jan. 1 was made New Year's Day. March has 31 days; the spring equinox occurs on March 21.

MARCHE (The Marches), region composed of four provinces in E central Italy, bordering the Adriatic Sea. Dominated by feudal overlords before the 14th century, it was taken over by the Papal States in the 15th century and became part of the kingdom of Italy in 1860. The economy is primarily agricultural, producing wheat, corn, livestock and wine; livestock are raised, and fishing is important on the coast.

MARCH TO THE SEA. See SHERMAN, WILLIAM TECUMSEH.

MARCIANO, Rocky (1923–1969), US boxer, world heavyweight champion 1952–56, when he retired undefeated. Born Rocco Marchegiane, Marciano fought 49 bouts in 9 years, winning by knockout in 43 bouts. He was killed in an aircrash.

MARCION (d. c160 AD), founder of a heretical Christian sect. He joined the church in Rome c140 but was excommunicated in 144. Influenced by GNOSTICISM, he taught that there were two rival Gods: one, the tyrannical creator and lawgiver of the Old Testament; the other, the unknown God of love and mercy who sent Jesus to purchase salvation from the creator God. Marcion rejected the Old Testament wholly, and of the New Testament accepted only expurgated versions of Luke's Gospel and 10 of St. Paul's Letters. This forced the orthodox Church to fix its canon of Scripture. Marcionism spread widely but by the end of the 3rd century had mostly been absorbed by MANICHAEISM.

MARCONI, Guglielmo (1874–1937), Italian-born inventor and physicist, awarded (with K. F. BRAUN) the 1909 Nobel Prize for Physics for his achievements. On learning of Hertzian (RADIO) waves in 1894, he set to work to devise a wireless TELEGRAPH. By the following year he could transmit and receive signals at distances of about 2km. He went to the UK to make further developments, and in 1899 succeeded in sending a signal across the English Channel. On Dec. 12, 1901 in St. John's, Newfoundland, he successfully received a signal sent from Poldhu, Cornwall, thus heralding the dawn of transatlantic radio communication.

MARCOS, Ferdinand Edralin (1917–), president of the Philippines since 1966, reelected in 1969. A lawyer and war hero, he gave the country considerable progress in agriculture, industry and education. He declared martial law in 1971, after a bomb attack on a political rally and in 1972 introduced emergency powers under a new constitution.

MARCUS, Saint, pope c337–40, is believed to have established the right of bishops of the city of Ostia to consecrate new popes. His feast day is Oct. 7.

MARCUS AURELIUS (121–180 AD), one of the greatest of Roman emperors. Adopted at 17 by ANTONINUS PIUS, he succeeded him as emperor in 161 AD, after a distinguished career in public service. During this he wrote his famous *Meditations*, his personal philosophy; he was one of the major exponents of STOICISM. His reign was marred by plague, rebellion, barbarian attacks along the Rhine and Danube, and his own savage persecution of Christians, to whom he had taken a dislike strange in so humane a man. His government was otherwise noted for social reform, justice and generosity.

MARCUSE, Herbert (1898–), German-born US political philosopher. According to Marcuse modern society is automatically repressive and requires violent revolution as the first step towards a Utopian society. He became something of a cult figure in the US in the 1960s.

MARCY, Mount, at 5 344ft the highest peak in N.Y., situated in the Adirondack Mts near Lake Placid. First climbed in 1837, it was named for W. L. MARCY.

MARCY, William Learned (1786–1857), US statesman. After training as a lawyer and serving in the WAR OF 1812, Marcy entered politics, holding high state offices under the patronage of Martin VAN BUREN and supporting him as a senator 1831–33. Governor of N.Y. 1833–38, he was secretary for war 1845–49, during the Mexican War. He was a particularly successful secretary of state 1853–57, concluding the GADSDEN PURCHASE and settling many other international problems.

MAR DEL PLATA, coastal city in Argentina, the country's main resort. It also has building and fishing industries and is a transport center. Pop 298 979.

MARDI GRAS, (literally "fat Tuesday"), festivities on Shrove Tuesday, the last day of carnival before the start of Lent. Celebrated as a holiday in various Catholic countries, it was introduced into the US by French settlers and is now observed in many states, most particularly in New Orleans.

MARDUK (Merodach or Baal in the Old Testament), chief god of Babylon. A legendary hero who attained supreme power by slaying Tiamat, the master of chaos, he was usually referred to as Bel (lord), which the Hebrews translated as Baal. (See BABYLONIA AND ASSYRIA.)

MARENGO, Battle of, major victory of Napoleon's second Italian campaign, against Austrian troops on the Marengo plain near Alessandria, Lombardy, on June 14, 1800. It gave Napoleon control of much of N Italy.

MARE'S TAIL, aquatic plants of the genus *Hippuris*, notably *Hippuris vulgaris* which is found in arctic and temperate climates. The plants have an erect stem bearing a dense whorl of leaves. They are cultivated in water gardens. Family: Hippuridaceae.

MARGARET, Saint (3rd century?), virgin martyr of Antioch. The account of her martyrdom is exaggerated and it is doubtful whether she ever existed. Her feast day, formerly July 2, was removed from the calendar in 1969.

MARGARET OF ANJOU (1429–1482), French queen consort of HENRY VI of England from 1445. Her attempt at autocratic rule through the ineffectual king was one of the causes of the WARS OF THE ROSES. Margaret was imprisoned 1471–76 by Edward IV, who had Henry and her son murdered. Ransomed by Louis XI, she returned to France.

MARGARET OF AUSTRIA (1480–1530), daughter of Emperor Maximilian I of Austria and regent of the Netherlands 1507–15 and 1518–20. Adopting a pro-English policy, she avoided war with France for as long as possible and negotiated the peace of Cambrai in 1529.

MARGARET OF NAVARRE (1492–1549), sister of Francis I of France and queen consort of Henry II of Navarre, was a patron of the arts and of religious reformers. She was an author and poet; her best-known work is *Heptaméron* (published 1558).

MARGARET OF PARMA (1522–1586), natural daughter of Charles V, regent of the Netherlands 1559–67. A benevolent ruler, she attempted to quell growing resistance to Spanish rule. Although a capable ruler, she had to stand down to the brutal duke of ALVA in 1567, but returned to head the civil administration 1580–83.

MARGARET OF SCOTLAND, Saint (c1045–1093), queen consort of Malcolm III of Scotland. She did much to implement the Gregorian reform of the Church and improved relations with England. She died during a siege of Edinburgh castle, where her chapel still stands. Canonized in 1250, her feast day is on June 10.

MARGARET OF VALOIS (1553–1615), queen consort of Navarre and queen of France by a political marriage to Henry of Navarre in 1572. Daughter of Henry II and Catherine de Médicis, she agreed to the dissolution of the marriage in 1600 but retained her royal title. Known as "Queen Margot," she had a remarkable succession of lovers and was a patron of the arts and an author. Her *Memoirs* (published 1842) are a vigorous account of France in her lifetime.

MARGARET TUDOR (1489–1541), daughter of Henry VII of England, queen of Scotland by marriage to James IV in 1503. Continually involved in intrigues, she became regent after James' death in 1513, but was displaced and discredited by treasonable dealing with her brother Henry VIII.

MARGARINE, a spread high in food value, prepared from vegetable or animal fats together with milk products, preservatives, emulsifiers, butter and salt. It was first developed in the late 1860s by the French chemist Hippolyte Mège-Mouriès, inspired by a competition launched by Napoleon III to find a cheap BUTTER substitute. The fats used were, early on, primarily animal, with whale oil being particularly popular in Europe, but recently vegetable oils (especially soybean and corn) have been used almost exclusively.

MARGATE CITY, coastal city in SE N.J., 5mi WSW of Atlantic City. Pop 10 576.

MARGAY, *Felis Wiedii*, a small cat related to the OCELOT, found in South America. It is a forest animal, an excellent climber running up and down trees headfirst in pursuit of its prey: rats, squirrels, monkeys and birds.

MARGINAL UTILITY. In classical economics utility is defined as the psychological satisfaction derived from consuming a particular good or service, whose demand was therefore explained by the amount of utility it afforded. Total utility increases as more of the given good is consumed, and the amount of extra utility derived by consuming each additional unit is called marginal utility.

MARGRETHE, two queens of Denmark. **Margrethe I** (1353–1412), often called Margaret, was the daughter of Waldemar IV of Denmark. Married to Haakon VI of Norway in 1363, she inherited that throne on the death of her son Olaf in 1387. Gaining the Swedish throne by conquest in 1389, she sought to unite the three countries in the KALMAR UNION. **Margrethe II** (1940–), queen of Denmark since 1972, was the first queen to take the Danish throne in her own right. She married Count Henri de Laborde de Monpezat, now Prince Henrik, in 1967.

MARIANA ISLANDS, group of islands in the W Pacific. Lying 1 500mi E of the Philippines, their total area is 184sq mi. Discovered by MAGELLAN in 1521, they were named the Ladrones (Thieves) Islands until renamed in 1668 by Jesuit missionaries. After WWI they were under a Japanese mandate until seized by the US in WWII. The majority of the population lives on the largest and southernmost island, Guam, a US outlying territory. The group's economy rests on subsistence agriculture, copra export and government and military installations. The Marianas are part of the UN Trust Territory of the Pacific Islands.

MARIANAO, city in La Habana province, W central Cuba. Founded in 1726, it has become Havana's main residential suburb, with exclusive estates and casinos. Pop 368 747.

MARIANA TRENCH, world's deepest discovered submarine trench, in the W North Pacific E of the Mariana Islands. More than 1 500mi long, it averages over 40mi in width and has maximum known depths of 36 201ft.

MARIA THERESA (1717–1780), Empress, archduchess of Austria, Queen of Hungary and of Bohemia and wife of the Holy Roman Emperor Francis I, one of the most able of Hapsburg rulers. Despite the PRAGMATIC SANCTION, its signatories launched the War of the AUSTRIAN SUCCESSION against her as soon as she succeeded her father in 1740. This lost Silesia to Prussia; she allied with France in the SEVEN YEARS WAR against Prussia, but was defeated. A capable ruler, she introduced administrative and fiscal reforms and maintained a strong army. Married to Francis of Lorraine in 1736, she arranged his election as emperor.

MARICOPA INDIANS, American Indian tribe of the Yuman linguistic group. Driven from the Lower Colorado R area by intertribal rivalry, they now live on the Gila and Salt R reservations in Ariz. with the Pima tribe. They united with the Pima to drive off the invading Yuma in a great battle in 1857.

MARIE ANTOINETTE (1755–1793), queen of France from 1774. Daughter of Maria Theresa and the Emperor Francis I, she married the Dauphin in 1770 and became queen on his accession as Louis XVI. Youthful extravagances made her many enemies, as did her unwitting involvement in a confidence trick perpetrated on the Cardinal de Rohan. When the French Revolution broke out she advised the attempted escape of the royal family which ended with its capture at Varennes. Imprisoned with Louis, she was guillotined nine months after him, in Oct. 1793.

MARIE DE MÉDICIS. See MEDICI.

MARIE LOUISE (1791–1847), empress of France. Eldest daughter of Francis I of Austria, she married Napoleon after he divorced Josephine, and was the mother of Napoleon II. She was never popular in France. After Napoleon was exiled in 1814 she became duchess of Parma.

MARIETTA, city in Ga., seat of Cobb Co. Its many industries include processing locally-quarried marble. Pop 27 216.

MARIETTA, city in Ohio, seat of Washington Co. It has many industries and ships fruit and vegetables grown in the area. Pop 16 861.

MARIGNANO, Battle of, victory of a French and Venetian army over Swiss mercenaries defending Milan on Sept. 13–14, 1515, during Francis I of France's first Italian campaign; it won him the Duchy of Milan.

MARIGOLD, popular name for many plants of the family COMPOSITAE, notably the African marigold (*Tagetes erecta*), the French marigold (*T. patula*), the pot marigold (*Calendula officinalis*) and the corn marigold (*Chrysanthemum segetum*). Many varieties of these species are in cultivation.

MARIJUANA, term applied to any part of the HEMP plant (*Cannabis sativa*) or extract from it. The intoxicating drug obtained from the flowering tops is also called **cannabis** or HASHISH. This drug is usually smoked in cigarettes or pipes, but can also be sniffed or taken as food. It is mainly used for the mild euphoria it produces, although other symptoms include loss of muscular coordination, increased heart beat, drowsiness and hallucination. Its use, the subject of much medical and social debate, is widespread throughout the world.

MARIMBA, musical instrument, found in many primitive cultures, made of tuned bars of hardwood suspended over resonators. The modern marimba is made with metal bars, resembling the XYLOPHONE.

MARIN, John (1870–1953), US painter and print maker best known for his expressionistic watercolors (influenced by CÉZANNE and the German Expressionists) of Manhattan and the Maine coast, such as *Singer Building* (1921) and *Maine Islands* (1922).

MARINE, soldier trained for combined sea and land operations, and now air operations also. While the concept is old, its modern development stems from the British Royal Marines and the Dutch Koninklijke Corps Mariniers, founded in 1664 and 1665 respectively. (See also MARINE CORPS, UNITED STATES.)

MARINE BIOLOGY, the study of the flora and fauna in the sea, from the smallest PLANKTON to massive WHALES. It includes the study of the complex interrelationships between marine organisms that make up the food chains (see ECOLOGY) of the sea. It has become apparent in recent years that if the sea is to remain a major and increasing source of food for man, CONSERVATION measures must be taken, particularly to retain adequate stocks of breeding fish. POLLUTION must also be controlled.

MARINE CORPS, United States, armed service within the Department of the Navy providing troops trained for land, sea and air operations. The Corps was founded by the Continental Congress in 1775 and established by act of Congress on July 11, 1798. It has served in the REVOLUTIONARY WAR, the naval war with France 1798–1801, the war with Tripoli 1801–05 and all subsequent major conflicts in which the US has been involved. Nearly 79 000 Marines served in WWI; they played a major role in the Pacific theater in WWII, first with their heroic stands at Wake, Guam, Bataan, Corregidor and Midway, and later the assault at Guadalcanal and the Pacific campaign. Over 475 000 Marines fought in WWII. Subsequently the Corps has fought in Korea, preserved order in the Lebanon in 1958, and ended fighting in the Dominican Republic in 1965. In Vietnam they developed a whole new technique of riverine warfare. The Marine Corps has made in all over 300 landings on enemy territory.

MARINER PROGRAM, US unmanned space probes which have made close "fly-by" observations of VENUS, MARS and MERCURY. Mariner 9 orbited Mars 1971–72, sending back a detailed surface survey. Mariner 10 flew by Venus in 1974, and took the first pictures of Mercury's surface during three fly-bys 1974–75.

MARINETTE, port city in NE Wis., seat of Marinette Co., at the mouth of the Menominee R on Green Bay, Lake Michigan. Originally a fur-trading and later logging center, it has various industries. Pop 12 696.

MARINETTI, Filippo Tommaso (1876–1944), Italian writer, progenitor of FUTURISM. His *Manifesto* (1909), published in *Le Figaro* in Paris, called for the abandonment of art of the past and the creation of a new art based on continual revolution and change. He came to support Fascism as the best means of revolution.

Mariner 9 orbited Mars in 1971, sending back over 7000 pictures. At center is the parabolic reflector of the directional antenna (green). Below is the instrument package, and on top the retro-rocket and another antenna. Four solar cell panels (purple) extend from the hull, to provide the craft's power supply.

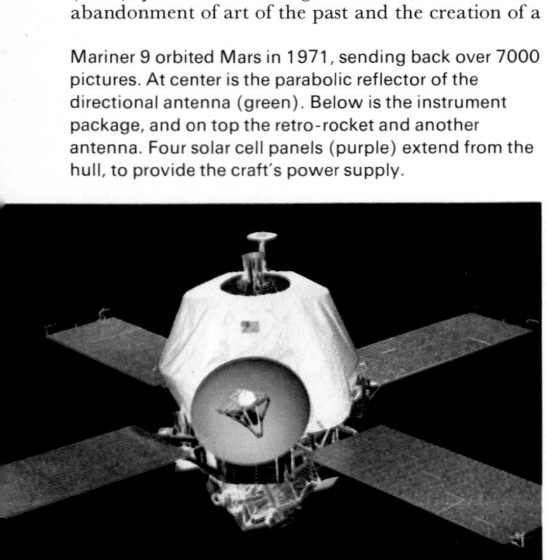

MARION, city in S central Ill., seat of Williamson Co., named for Francis MARION. The city's economy rests on agriculture and the area's coal mines. Pop 11 724.

MARION, city in E central Ind., seat of Grant Co. Originally an oil and gas center, it is now a commercial and manufacturing city. Pop 39 607.

MARION, city in E Ia., seat of Linn Co. until 1922. It is a rail center with various manufacturing industries. Pop 18 028.

MARION, city in Ohio, seat of Marion Co. It is the industrial and railroad center of an agricultural area, specializing in heavy machinery manufacture. Pop 38 646.

MARION, Francis (c1732–1795), guerrilla leader in the REVOLUTIONARY WAR. Commander of S.C. troops, he fought at Charleston in 1776. In 1780 he and his men were forced to take refuge in the swamps, from which they waged a ceaseless guerrilla warfare on Loyalist farms and on British troops, who nicknamed Marion "the Swamp Fox." He served in the state senate 1782–90, and on the state constitutional convention.

MARIONETTE. See PUPPET.

MARIOTTE, Edmé (1620–1684), French physicist who independently discovered BOYLE'S LAW (Mariotte's law) and also discovered the blind spot of the EYE (1660).

MARIPOSA LILY, common name for perennial lilies of the genus *Calochortus* which are native to western North America. They bear white, yellow, lilac or bluish flowers and have long narrow leaves. Family: Liliaceae. (See also LILY.)

MARISTS, a number of religious congregations of the Roman Catholic Church, centered around the Marist Fathers (Society of Mary), a society founded in 1822 to undertake ministerial duties and propagate the virtues of the Virgin Mary. It has many foreign missions.

MARITAIN, Jacques (1882–1973), leading French Neo-Thomist philosopher. He turned to the study of THOMISM after his conversion to Catholicism in 1906. Professor of modern Philosophy at the Catholic Institute, Paris, 1914–39, he was French ambassador to the Vatican 1945–48 and a professor at Princeton U. 1948–60.

MARITIME ADMINISTRATION, US federal agency administered by the Department of Commerce, established in 1950 to foster the development of the US merchant marine. It is responsible for administering shipbuilding, shipping, port development and other programs in this field; it maintains a reserve fleet and shipyards, and operates the US Merchant Marine Academy at Kings Point, N.Y.

MARITIME LAW, body of law, based on custom, court decisions and statutes, seeking to regulate all aspects of shipping and ocean commerce such as insurance, salvage and contracts for carriage of goods by sea. It is international to the extent that firm general principles exist, but these have no legal force except as they are incorporated by individual countries into their own legal systems; they are often modified in the process. Many derive from decisions of medieval maritime courts. In the US maritime law is administered by the federal district courts.

MARITIME PROVINCES, NEW BRUNSWICK, NOVA SCOTIA and PRINCE EDWARD ISLAND, on the Atlantic coast and Gulf of St. Lawrence in Canada. Formerly the French colony of Acadia, they were ceded to Britain by the treaty of UTRECHT and were separately administered until Canadian confederation in 1867.

MARIUS, Gaius (157–86 BC), Roman general and politician. After successes in the field he was elected consul seven times. In 88 BC he was defeated in a civil war by his rival SULLA. He returned from exile in 86 BC and massacred his opponents but died soon after.

MARIVAUX, Pierre Carlet de Chamblain de (1688–1763), French playwright and novelist, best known for his witty comedies. Sparkling dialogue is still termed *marivaudage*. His most famous works are the comedy *A Game of Love and Chance* (1730) and the novel *The Parvenu Peasant* (1735–36).

MARJORAM, hardy perennial herbs, the leaves of which are used for flavoring. Sweet marjoram (*Origanum hotensis*) and pot marjoram (*O. onites*) are widely cultivated and wild marjoram or **oregano** (*O. vulgare*) is a common plant in Europe and Asia and naturalized in the US. Family: Labiatae.

MARK, Saint (John Mark; flourished 1st century AD), Christian evangelist, traditional author of the second GOSPEL, deriving information from St. Peter in Rome. The Gospel is the earliest and simplest and was a source for the other SYNOPTIC GOSPELS. Mark accompanied Barnabas (his cousin) and Paul on their missionary journeys.

MARKHAM, village in NE Ill., a residential suburb to the S of Chicago. Pop 15 987.

MARKHAM, town in SE Ontario, Canada, on the Rouge R., settled in 1794 by German emigrants from N.Y., USA. Its economy now rests on processing the area's agricultural produce. Pop 36 684.

MARKHAM, (Charles Edward Anson) Edwin (1852–1940), US poet and lecturer whose poem of social protest, *The Man with the Hoe* (1899), based on a painting by MILLET, brought him a fortune and worldwide acclaim.

MARKHOR, *Capra falconeri*, a species of wild GOAT of eastern Asia and USSR, with compressed spiral horns. Both sexes have long, silky coats of gray-brown color. Males tend to live apart from the herds of females and young except during the rut.

MARKOVA, Dame Alicia (1910–), leading British ballerina, born Lilian Alicia Marks. Having appeared with most of the world's major companies, she founded her own with Anton DOLIN, 1935–38. This grew into the London Festival Ballet, which they headed 1944–52. She retired in 1963 and became director of the Metropolitan Opera Ballet.

MARK TWAIN. See TWAIN, MARK.

MARL, natural mixture of clay and calcium carbonate ($CaCO_3$: see CALCIUM; CLAY). If the former predominates, it is a mudstone; if the latter, it is termed calcareous. Greensand marls contain hardly any $CaCO_3$ (see also GLAUCONITE). Marls are used as SOIL conditioners and in making portland CEMENT.

MARLBOROUGH, city in E central Mass. It became a town in 1660 and now has various industries. Pop 27 936.

MARLBOROUGH, John Churchill, 1st Duke of (1650–1722), British soldier and statesman, one of the country's greatest generals. He helped suppress MONMOUTH'S rebellion for James II, but transferred his allegiance to William of Orange in 1688 and was made an earl and a member of the Privy Council. His wife was Sarah Jennings, a friend and attendant of Princess (later Queen) Anne; together they had great influence with the queen. After her accession in 1702 Marlborough commanded English, Dutch and German forces in the war of the SPANISH SUCCESSION. In 1704 he won a great victory over the French at BLENHEIM; a palace of that name was built for him at the queen's expense. Further victories followed at Ramillies (1706), Oudenarde (1708) and Malplaquet (1709). His wife fell from favor with the Queen in 1711 and Marlborough was dismissed; in 1714, however, he was restored to favor by George I.

MARLINS, large, tropical, oceanic fishes related to the sailfish and swordfish. The long bony snout is an effective weapon but it is probable that its evolution was determined chiefly by the hydrodynamics of fast swimming. The rest of the body is certainly adapted for this, the streamlined shape and great strength of the vertebral column, particularly in the tail, makes these fishes extremely rapid swimmers.

MARLOWE, Christopher (1564–1593), English poet and dramatist, a major influence on Shakespeare. He developed the use of dramatic blank verse in a rhetorically rich and splendid language. In *Dr. Faustus* (c1589) he developed a new concept of tragedy, the struggle of a great personality doomed to inevitable failure by its own limitations. In *Tamburlaine* (c1587) he treated a heroic theme without the depth of characterization that appears in his most mature work, *Edward II* (c1592). Often accused of homosexuality, atheism and of being a government spy, he was stabbed to death in a tavern brawl.

MARMARA, Sea of, inland sea, the classical *Pro-*

pontis, lying between Asiatic and European Turkey. Linked to the Mediterranean by the Dardanelles and to the Black Sea by the Bosporus, it is 175mi long and 50mi wide at its widest.

MARMOSETS, a family of New-World MONKEYS, the Callitricidae. All are extremely small, living in tropical forests, keeping to the larger branches where their claws provide a firm hold. Marmosets live in territorial family groups. They eat insects, leaves and fruits. They are fairly primitive monkeys with small brains, peculiar in possessing tactile hairs on the wrists.

MARMOTS, ground-living, burrowing rodents forming a distinct genus, *Marmota*, or GROUND SQUIRRELS. Marmots are found throughout the northern temperate region in open country. Only one species, the WOODCHUCK, lives in woodland. Sociable animals, marmots live in colonies in deep burrows. They are diurnal, feeding on green vegetation and never moving far from the burrow entrance, into which they dart if endangered.

MARNE, Battles of the, two WWI battles fought in the Marne R area of France. In the first, in Sept. 1914, the German advance on Paris was halted by an Allied offensive. The second, in July 1918, countered the last German offensive of the war.

MARNE RIVER, chief tributary of the Seine R in France. About 325mi in length, it rises on the Langres plateau, flowing NW to Épernay and from there W to join the Seine at Charenton. It is navigable for about 220mi, much of which has been canalized.

MARONITES, a sect of eastern Christians who in the 7th century espoused MONOTHELETISM. In the 12th century they became affiliated with the Roman Catholic Church (see UNIATE CHURCHES). Although some Maronites have settled in Cyprus, Syria and Egypt, their largest community is still in the Lebanon, where their immediate spiritual head under the pope, the Maronite patriarch, also resides.

MARPLE, town in SE Pa., a suburb of Chester. Pop 25 040.

MARPRELATE, Martin, pseudonym of a Puritan author or authors of a series of scurrilous, satirical tracts attacking the episcopacy of the Church of England, published 1588–89. The controversy provoked the formulation of the "divine right" of episcopacy in Anglican apologetics.

MARQUAND, John Phillips (1893–1960), US novelist best known for his detective stories centered around the Japanese agent Mr. Moto, and for his gentle satires of New England society, such as *The Late George Apley* (1937), for which he won a 1938 Pulitzer Prize, and *Point of No Return* (1949).

MARQUE, Letters of. See LETTER OF MARQUE.

MARQUESAS ISLANDS, two clusters of mountainous and volcanic islands in the S Pacific, 740mi NE of Tahiti. Their total area is about 492sq mi; the largest islands are Hiba Oa and Nuku Hiva. The S group was discovered by the Spanish in 1595; both were annexed by France in 1842. The islands are fertile, producing breadfruit, coffee, vanilla and copra for export.

MARQUETTE, city in Mich. on Lake Superior, seat of Marquette Co. Named for Jacques MARQUETTE, it was originally an important industrial port; its economy now rests on a wide variety of industries. It is a cathedral city, and houses Northern Michigan U. Pop 21 967.

MARQUETTE, Jacques (1637–1675), French Jesuit missionary and explorer. With Louis JOLIET he left St. Ignace mission, Mich., in 1673 on a search for the mouth of the Mississippi. They traced its course as far as the mouth of the Arkansas R and learned that it entered the Gulf of Mexico. In 1674 Marquette went back to Ill. to found a mission among Indians who had befriended him, but his health deteriorated. He died on the E shore of Lake Michigan while returning to St. Ignace.

MARQUIS, title of nobility, in England higher than an earl and lower than a duke; in Europe it ranks between a count and a duke. In England it is usually spelt "marquess," and the female form is "marchioness."

MARQUIS, Don (Donald Robert Perry; 1878–1937), US literary journalist, poet and playwright, best known as the creator of "archy," a poet reincarnated as a cockroach, and his friend "mehitabel," a disreputable cat, who appeared in Marquis' columns in the *New York Sun* 1912–22 and *Tribune* 1922–25, and in subsequent books.

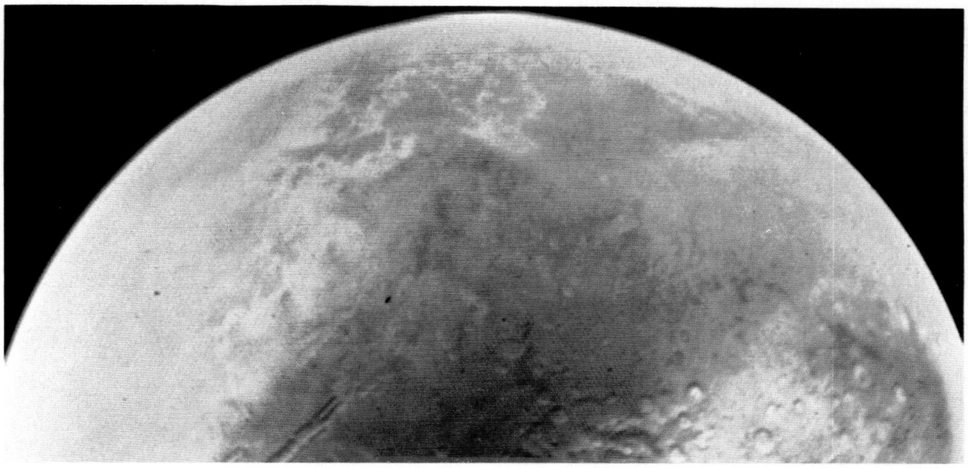

Mars, seen from the south by the Viking 1 probe in June 1976. Visible is the huge Valle Marineres canyon, running just south of and parallel to the equator.

MARRAKESH, chief city of S Morocco, lying in the fertile Haouz plain near the Atlas Mts. Founded c1062 by the Berbers, it is now a commercial and tourist center with many industries. Pop 332 741.

MARRANOS, derogatory term for Portuguese and Spanish Jews who were baptized to escape persecution in the 14th century; most continued to practice Judaism in secret. With the expulsion of the Jews and the establishment of the INQUISITION in the late 15th century, most fled abroad and the remainder died out, except in Portugal and the Balearic Islands.

MARRIAGE, durable union between man and woman for the purpose of cohabitation and usually also for raising children. In the broadest sense it is not an exclusively human institution; some animal pair bonds may endure for life. Most human marriages are at least intended to last for life, but most societies have some provision for DIVORCE, ranging from the easy to the almost impossible. The modern trend is towards **monogamy,** union between one man and one woman only. Many societies still permit POLYGAMY, but it is increasingly frowned upon. Forms of group and communal marriage have been tried from time to time, though with little success or social acceptance.

Marriage is in some senses a contract, often involving property and in some societies a DOWRY or a bride-price. In US law today marriage creates special ownership rights in marital property. It is, however, still also a religious matter in many countries; marriage is a minor sacrament of the Roman Catholic Church.

Most societies limit marriage in certain ways. It is forbidden in most countries between partners who have too close a blood relationship, or **consanguinity,** though the degree permissible varies widely between countries, religions and even between US states. On US COMMON LAW a purported marriage involving BIGAMY is void; other conditions, such as non-consummation, render marriage void or voidable, generally through the courts. A marriage is also void if not carried out in the prescribed legal form, although in some states common-law marriage may arise after long cohabitation without any formality. Marriages in the US are performed either by civil authority or by a religious ceremony with civil authorization; the ceremonies of most denominations are so authorized in most states. In general a marriage valid in one state is recognized in the others. Some states require a waiting period, and some religions require BANNS to be posted.

MARROW, Bone, the material in the center of BONES, in which ERYTHROCYTES, white blood cells and platelets are made. Mature cells only are released unless the marrow is diseased, as in LEUKEMIA, secondary CANCER or in serious infections. Bone marrow aspiration or BIOPSY is often valuable in diagnosis.

MARS, the fourth planet from the sun with a mean solar distance of 228Gm (about 1.52AU) and a "year" of 687 days. During the Martian day of about 24.62h the highest temperature at the equator is about 30°C, the lowest just before dawn being about −100°C. Mars has a mean diameter of 6 750km, with a small degree of polar flattening, and at its closest to earth (see CONJUNCTION) is some 56Gm distant. Its tenuous atmosphere is believed to consist mainly of carbon dioxide, nitrogen and NOBLE GASES, and the distinctive Martian polar caps are thought to be composed of frozen carbon dioxide and ice.

Telescopically, Mars appears as an ocher-red disk marked by extensive dark areas: these latter have in the past been erroneously termed *maria* (seas). Several observers have reported sighting networks of straight lines on the Martian surface—the famous canals—although observations with large telescopes and the photographs sent back by the probes of the MARINER PROGRAM show no signs of these. Mars is spotted with craters, rather as is the MOON. It is not yet known if Mars can support life as we know it. Mars has two moons, PHOBOS and DEIMOS.

MARS, in Roman mythology, the god of war, identified with the Greek Ares. Mars was son of Jupiter and father of ROMULUS, founder of Rome. He was worshiped in March (named for him) and October at his altar on the Campus Martius (Latin: Plain of Mars).

MARSEILLAISE, French national anthem composed in 1792 by Claude Rouget de Lisle, a Revolutionary engineer captain. Named for its popularity with the Marseilles soldiers, it was banned by NAPOLEON I, LOUIS XVIII and NAPOLEON III until 1879.

MARSEILLES, city in SE France, its chief Mediterranean seaport and a major industrial center. It was originally the Greek settlement of Massilia, annexed by Rome in 49 BC. The city's recent expansion began with the conquest of Algeria and the opening of the SUEZ CANAL in the 19th century. It has a wide range of industries; its port handles around 25% of French maritime trade. Pop 889 029.

MARSH. See SWAMP.

MARSH, Reginald (1898–1954), US painter. A newspaper illustrator, he later turned to the realistic depiction of New York City life in egg TEMPERA paintings such as *Twenty-Cent Movie* (1936).

MARSHALL, city in N central Mo., seat of Saline Co. In an agricultural area, it has a footwear factory and processes local products. Pop 12 051.

MARSHALL, city in NE Tex., seat of Harrison Co. The surrounding area is mainly agricultural, but has major oil deposits. The city has oil refineries and a petrochemical industry. Pop 22 937.

MARSHALL, Alfred (1842–1924), British economist, professor of political economy at Cambridge 1885–1908. His *Principles of Economics* (1890) systematized economic thought up to that time, and was the standard text for many years. Through his work on cost and value Marshall developed a viable concept of MARGINAL UTILITY.

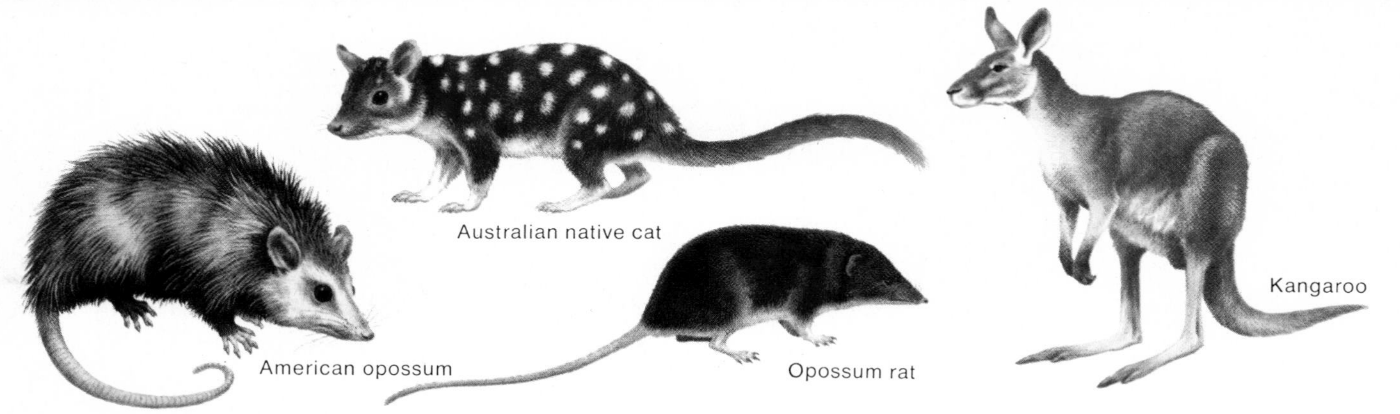

Some typical marsupials. Once widespread, this ancient family is now found only in the Americas (mainly South), New Guinea and Australia.

MARSHALL, George Catlett (1880–1959), US general and statesman. As chief of staff 1939–45 he influenced Allied strategy in WWII. Special ambassador to China in 1945, he was then made secretary of state (1947–49) by President TRUMAN. He introduced the European Recovery Program, or MARSHALL PLAN. He was active in the creation of the NORTH ATLANTIC TREATY ORGANIZATION, serving as US secretary of defense 1950–51. He was awarded the 1955 Nobel Peace Prize.

MARSHALL, John (1755–1835), fourth chief justice of the US, known as the "Great Chief Justice." He established the modern status of the SUPREME COURT. Born in Va., he served in the REVOLUTIONARY WAR, studied law and was elected to the Va. legislature in 1782. A staunch Federalist, he supported acceptance of the Constitution. He declined ministerial posts but became one of the US negotiators who resolved the XYZ AFFAIR. Elected to Congress 1799, he was made secretary of state by President ADAMS 1800–01; in 1802 he became chief justice. He labored to increase the then scant power and prestige of the Sureme Court. In MARBURY V. MADISON he established its power to review a law and if necessary declare it unconstitutional. An opponent of STATES' RIGHTS, he established in MCULLOCH V. MARYLAND and GIBBONS V. OGDEN (and incidentally in the DARTMOUTH COLLEGE CASE) the superiority of federal authority under the Constitution. In 1807 he presided over the treason trial of Aaron BURR.

MARSHALL, Thomas Riley (1854–1925), 28th vice-president of the US. A lawyer, he was governor of Ind. 1909–13, and a popular vice-president under Woodrow WILSON 1913–16 and 1916–21.

MARSHALL, Thurgood (1908–), US judge, first black member of the US SUPREME COURT. Chief counsel for the NATIONAL ASSOCIATION FOR THE ADVANCEMENT OF COLORED PEOPLE 1938–61 and solicitor general 1965–67, he was appointed to the Supreme Court by President JOHNSON in 1967.

MARSHALL ISLANDS, archipelago in the W central Pacific, consisting of the Ralik and Ratal chains of islands and atolls; total land area is about 70sq mi. Japan seized the islands from nominal German possession in 1914; in 1947 they became part of the US Trust Territory of the PACIFIC ISLANDS. The population is mainly Micronesian; the economy rests on cocoa, copra, sugar and coffee.

MARSHALL PLAN, the European Recovery Program 1947–52, named for its originator, US Secretary of State George C. MARSHALL. In general it succeeded in its design, which was to help Europe's economic recovery after WWII and so check Eastern bloc communist influence. Material and financial aid amounting to almost 13 billion dollars was sent to the 17 European countries who formed the Organization for European Economic Cooperation. The plan was administered by the US Economic Cooperation Administration, headed by Paul G. Hoffmann.

MARSHALLTOWN, city in central Ia., on the Iowa R. It is a manufacturing city and a trade and rail shipping center for the surrounding agricultural area. Pop 26 219.

MARSH CROCODILE. See MUGGER.

MARSH DEER, *Blastocerus dichotomus*, the largest of the South American DEER. A deep red deer with antlers of eight to ten points, this is, as its name suggests, an animal of marshy ground.

MARSHFIELD, city in SE Mass., a resort on the Atlantic coast. Pop 15 223.

MARSHFIELD, city in central Wis., a manufacturing center in a dairying area. Pop 15 169.

MARSH GAS. See METHANE.

MARSH MARIGOLD. See COWSLIP.

MARSH WARBLER, *Acrocephalus palustris*, a WARBLER with eastern European and Asian distribution which is found in dense vegetation or reed beds, usually near water. It is distinguished from the Reed warbler by its beautiful song.

MARSILIUS OF PADUA (c1275–1343), Italian political philosopher whose *Defensor pacis* (Latin: defender of peace; 1324) denied the Church's temporal power and proposed its subjugation to the sovereign, who ruled by popular mandate. He was protected from papal attacks by his patron, Emperor LOUIS IV.

MARSTON, John (1576–1634), English playwright best known for his tragicomedy *The Malcontent* (1604) and his rivalry with Ben JONSON. Both were imprisoned for offending JAMES I in their collaboration *Eastward Ho!* (1605). Marston was ordained 1609.

MARSUPIALS, MAMMALS with a double womb, giving birth to incompletely developed young which continue development attached to the mother's teats. Differences in the reproductive system are the only infallible way of separating marsupials from true mammals: in marsupials the urinary ducts from the kidneys separate the developing sex ducts, so that in the female both uterus and vagina are double structures. In the male, the urinary ducts lie between the sperm ducts; in PLACENTAL MAMMALS, they lie outside them. The pouch, or marsupium, is not an exclusive or even universal feature of the group. Marsupials are at their most developed in Australia, where, in the absence of placental mammals, they achieved great diversity of form. In addition, there remain a number of groups in the Americas.

MARSYAS, in Greek mythology, a satyr who learned to play the first flute, invented by ATHENA. He challenged APOLLO, who played the lyre, to a contest judged by the MUSES. Marsyas lost and Apollo flayed him.

MARTEL, Charles. See CHARLES MARTEL.

MARTENS, cat-sized members of the WEASEL family widely distributed in North America and Eurasia. Dark-furred animals with a white or yellow bib, they have triangular heads and large rounded ears. Arboreal predators, they are agile tree climbers.

MARTHA, in the GOSPEL a friend of Jesus, sister of Lazarus and Mary of Bethany. Martha, a busy housewife, has come to symbolize the active Christian life and Mary the contemplative.

MARTHA'S VINEYARD, island off the coast of SE Mass. About 100sq mi in area, it is separated from Cape Cod by Vineyard Sound. Discovered and named by Bartholomew Gosnold (1602), it was settled c1632. A major whaling center in the 18th and 19th centuries, it is now a popular summer resort.

MARTI, José Julian (1853–1895), major Cuban poet and hero of the anti-Spanish independence movement. He founded the Cuban Revolutionary Party in the US 1881–95. His best known poems appear in *Ismaelillo* (1882), *Versos libres* (1913) and *Versos sencilles* (1891). A leader of the 1895 independence campaign, Marti was killed at the battle of Dos Rios.

MARTIAL (Marcus Valerius Martialis; c40–c104 AD), Spanish-born Latin epigrammatic poet. He lived in Rome 64–98 AD, and was favored by emperors TITUS and DOMITIAN and befriended by PLINY the Younger, JUVENAL and QUINTILIAN. Martial wrote in all 15 books of EPIGRAMS.

MARTIAL LAW, temporary superimposition of military on domestic civil government, usually in wartime or other national emergency. The army takes over executive and judicial functions, and civil rights such as HABEAS CORPUS may be suspended. When an invading army assumes control of a country it is said to act not under martial law but as a military government; law applying only to those in military service is not martial but military.

MARTIN, name of three popes. **Saint Martin I** (d. 655), reigned 649–55. He offended the Byzantine emperor Constans by condemning MONOTHELETISM, and was imprisoned and exiled. **Martin IV** (d. 1285), was so-called because of a numbering error, being in fact Martin II; he reigned 1281–85. **Martin V** (1368–1431), reigned 1417–31. His election ended the GREAT SCHISM; he arrived at Rome in 1420 and began rebuilding the power of the papacy. He condemned the Conciliar theory.

MARTIN, Archer John Porter (1910–), British biochemist awarded with R. L. M. SYNGE the 1952 Nobel Prize for Chemistry for their development of paper CHROMATOGRAPHY, a biochemical tool of great medical importance. He later helped perfect gas chromatography.

MARTIN, Glenn Luther (1886–1955), pioneering US aircraft designer and manufacturer. A former barnstorming flyer, he developed various military designs after WWI, one of which became the famous B-26 bomber. Many of his other planes and flying boats were used in WWII.

MARTIN, Joseph William, Jr. (1884–1968), US politician, speaker of the House of Representatives 1947–49 and 1953–55. A newspaper owner, he was elected Republican congressman from Mass. 1925–67 after service in the state legislature. He chaired every party national convention 1940–56, and was minority leader of the house 1939–59, except when speaker.

MARTIN, Mary (1913–), US musical comedy star, famous for her stage appearances in *One Touch of Venus* (1945), *South Pacific* (1949) and *The Sound of Music* (1959).

MARTIN. Pierre Émile (1824–1915), French engineer who developed the open-hearth smelting process now known as the Siemens-Martin process (1864–65). (See OPEN-HEARTH PROCESS; SIEMENS.)

MARTIN DU GARD, Roger (1881–1958), French novelist known for his objective but somber exploration of human relationships and the large backgrounds in which he sets them. In *Jean Barois* (1913) it is the DREYFUS AFFAIR; in *The Thibaults* (1922–40) it is WWI. In 1937 he won the Nobel Prize for Literature.

MARTINEZ, city in W Cal., seat of Contra Costa Co. A port and industrial center, it has oil refineries and produces metals and chemicals. Pop 16 506.

MARTINI, Simone (c1284–1344), Italian painter of the Sienese school. Influenced by DUCCIO and the French Gothic, he painted many altarpieces and chapel decorations. His portraits, such as one of Laura for his friend PETRARCH, introduced secular themes into Sienese art.

MARTINIQUE, island in the Windward group in the West Indies, an overseas department of France 1946. Discovered by COLUMBUS c1502, it was colonized by France as a sugar-growing center after 1635; slave-labor was used until 1848, and much of the present population is of African descent. The economy still rests on sugar, and also rum, fruit and tourism. The island is volcanic, and so is rugged and mountainous but very fertile. Its main town is Fort-de-France.
MARTIN OF TOURS, Saint (d. 397), patron saint of France. Son of a pagan, he served in the Roman army but after a vision of Christ sought a religious life. Bishop of Tours from c372, he encouraged monasticism and opposed execution of heretics.
MARTINS, certain birds of the SWALLOW family, Hirundinidae. There is no biological difference between swallows and martins, the common names having been somewhat arbitrarily applied.
MARTINSBURG, city in E W.Va., seat of Berkeley Co. An early rail center, it is now a manufacturing center in a fruit-growing area. Pop 14 626.
MARTIN'S FERRY, city in E Ohio on the Ohio R. Coal deposits in the area have made it a major industrial center and river port. Pop 10 757.
MARTINSVILLE, city in S Va., seat of Henry Co. It has various industries, including furniture and textile manufacture. Pop 19 653.
MARTINŮ, Bohuslav (1890–1959), Czech composer who lived in Paris 1923–40, and the US 1940–46. Although incorporating Czech folk themes, his highly individual work is usually neoclassical in style, as in the ballet *Istar* (1922) and the powerful *Double Concerto* (1940).
MARTIN v. HUNTER'S LESSEE, case decided by the US SUPREME COURT in 1816, in which Va.'s attempt to confiscate British-owned land was held to be overridden by treaties made by the federal government with Britain. The decision established the Supreme Court's power to review state court decisions.
MARTYR (from Greek *martus*: a witness), a person who willingly gives his life or makes great sacrifices for his faith or convictions. The first Christian martyr was St. STEPHEN. The early martyrs were greatly revered.
MARVELL, Andrew (1621–1678), English METAPHYSICAL POET. Assistant to John MILTON from 1657, he was a member of Parliament from 1659. A Puritan, he was known as a wit and satirist, but is today best remembered for his lyric poetry such as "To his Coy Mistress" and "The Garden."
MARX, Karl Heinrich (1818–1883), German philosopher and social and economic theorist, the most important of socialist thinkers. Born at Trier of Jewish parents, Marx studied at Bonn and Berlin. When the Cologne newspaper he edited was suppressed (1843), he moved with his wife Jenny von Westphalen to Paris, Brussels and London, where he spent most of his life in great poverty.

With Friedrich ENGELS, his lifelong friend and collaborator, Marx published the COMMUNIST MANIFESTO (1848) on the eve of the REVOLUTIONS OF 1848. It summarizes Marx's social philosophy. In London Marx cofounded (1864) and led the International Workingmen's Association (First INTERNATIONAL). But most of his energy went into his writing, of which *Capital* (3 volumes: 1867, 1885, 1894) is the most important.

In developing DIALECTICAL MATERIALISM, Marx adapted HEGEL's dialectic to his own economic interpretation of history. Ethics, politics and religion are the products of socioeconomic relations. Accepting the LABOR THEORY OF VALUE of RICARDO, Marx argued that the surplus value, or profit, extracted by the capitalist from his workforce would in time inevitably decline. CAPITALISM, the inevitable successor to FEUDALISM, would in turn inevitably be replaced by SOCIALISM and eventually COMMUNISM. The class war between the capitalist and the worker he exploits would end in the overthrow of capitalism. (See MARXISM.)
MARX BROTHERS, Groucho, Harpo and Chico, famous US film and radio comedy team. The original team consisted of **Chico** (Leonard; 1891–1961), **Groucho** (Julius; 1895–), **Gummo** (Milton; 1894–), **Harpo** (Arthur; 1893–1964) and **Zeppo** (Herbert; 1901–). In films such as *Animal Crackers* (1930), *Duck Soup* (1933) and *A Night at the Opera* (1935) they established their blend of wisecracking verbal routines and frenetic slapstick.
MARXISM, the foundation philosophy of modern COMMUNISM, originating in the work of Karl MARX and Friedrich ENGELS. Three basic concepts are: that productive labor is the fundamental attribute of human nature; that the structure of any society is determined by its economic means of production; and that societies evolve by a series of crises caused by internal contradictions, analyzable by DIALECTICAL MATERIALISM. Marx held that 19th-century industrial CAPITALISM, the latest stage of the historical process, had arisen from FEUDALISM by class struggle between the aristocracy and the rising bourgeois capitalist class. Dialectical materialism predicted conflict between these capitalists and the working class, or PROLETARIAT, on which the new industrialism depended. The triumphant dictatorship of the proletariat, an idea further developed by LENIN, would give way to a classless, stateless communist society where all would be equal, contributing according to their abilities and receiving according to their needs. A key concept of Marxist economics is the LABOR THEORY OF VALUE, that value is created by labor and profit is surplus value creamed off by the capitalist. The fact that he owns the means of production makes this exploitation possible. It also means that the worker cannot own the product of his labor and thus suffers ALIENATION from part of his own humanity and the social system. Marx believed capitalism would be swept away by the last of a catastrophic series of crises. Among numerous later Marxist theorists are Karl KAUTSKY and Rosa LUXEMBURG. In *The Accumulation of Capital* (1913), Luxemburg argued that capitalism was able to adapt and survive by exploitation of its colonial empires. In Russia STALIN proclaimed Marxism-Leninism, an active philosophy of society in forced evolutionary conflict. In China MAO TSE-TUNG adapted Marxism to an agricultural peasant situation. Yugoslavia's TITO gave Marxism a nationalist bias, still more marked in the thinking of Fidel CASTRO of Cuba. Western economists, sociologists and historians have been widely influenced by Marxism.
MARY, the mother of JESUS CHRIST, also called the Blessed Virgin. The chief events of her life related in the Gospels are her betrothal to JOSEPH; the ANNUNCIATION of Christ's birth; her visit to her cousin Elizabeth, mother of John the Baptist; the birth of Christ, and her witnessing his crucifixion. In the Roman Catholic Church Mary is accorded a special degree of veneration, called hyperdulia, superior to that given to other saints, and is regarded as mediatrix of all graces and coredemptress. Roman Catholic doctrine holds she was born free from sin, remained always a virgin, and was assumed bodily into heaven (see IMMACULATE CONCEPTION; ASSUMPTION OF THE VIRGIN.)
MARY, name of two English queens. **Mary I** (1516–1558), daughter of HENRY VIII and Catherine of Aragon, succeeded EDWARD VI in 1553. She tried to restore Roman Catholicism in England. Some 300 Protestants were burnt as heretics—a persecution unparalleled in England, which earned her the name of "bloody Mary." Her unpopular alliance with and marriage to PHILIP II of Spain (1554), led to war with France and the loss of Calais (1558). **Mary II** (1662–1694), was the Protestant daughter of JAMES II and wife of her cousin WILLIAM III. She was proclaimed joint sovereign with him in 1689.
MARYKNOLL FATHERS, popular name for the Catholic Foreign Mission Society of America. It was founded in 1911 with headquarters at Maryknoll, N.Y. It has sent missions to Asia, Latin America and the Pacific Islands.
MARYLAND, Atlantic coast state of the US, one of the 13 Colonies (see UNITED STATES), bounded by Pa. to the N, Del. to the NE, Va. and Washington D.C. to the S and W. Va. to the W. There are three major regions: the Atlantic coastal plain in the E, the Piedmont-Blue Ridge region in the center, and the Appalachian-Allegheny Mts in the W. The Potomac R, forming the state's W border, flows into

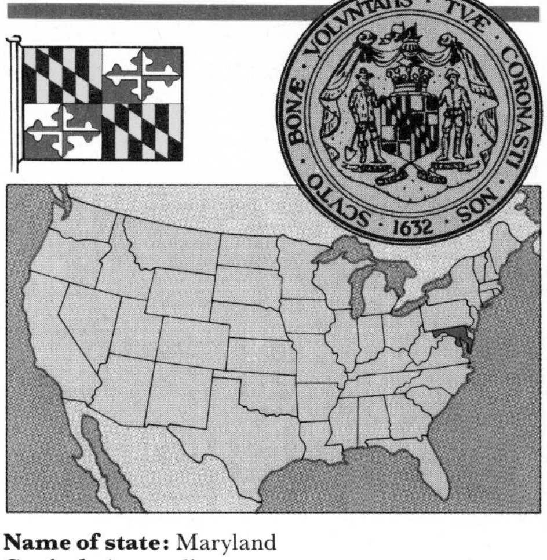

Name of state: Maryland
Capital: Annapolis
Statehood: April 28, 1788 (7th state)
Familiar name: Old Line State, Free State
Area: 10 577sq mi
Population: 3 922 399
Elevation: Highest—3 360ft., Backbone Mountain. Lowest—sea level, Atlantic Ocean
Motto: Fatti Maschii, Parole Femine (Manly deeds, womanly words)
State flower: Black-eyed susan
State bird: Baltimore oriole
State tree: White oak
State song: "Maryland, My Maryland"

CHESAPEAKE BAY which divides Md. from N to S. Much of the state is covered by forests, including 12 state forests. The average annual temperature is 53°F.

Md. has 20 universities and a US naval academy. Its population is heavily urban. A diversified economy is dominated by shipbuilding and the manufacture of iron and steel, transportation equipment and electrical machinery. There are also large livestock, horsebreeding and fishing industries.

Md. was first explored by John Smith in 1608. In 1632 George CALVERT, Lord Baltimore, was granted the territory and founded a colony named for Henrietta Maria, wife of Charles I of England. The colony's initial religious freedom was eroded by the Puritans' ascendancy. In 1763 the MASON-DIXON line set the boundary between Md. and Pa. Staunchly anti-loyalist during the War of Independence, Md. was the seventh state to ratify the US Constitution (1788). In 1790–91 it ceded a tract of land along the Potomac R for the new national capital, Washington D.C. In the 19th century an extensive transportation system was constructed and Baltimore became the shipbuilding center of the nation. Although locally divided, Md. remained in the Union during the Civil War. The opening, 1952, of the Chesapeake Bay bridge quickened industrialism on the Eastern Shore. Md.'s historic sites include Fort McHenry (see WAR OF 1812), the state house in Annapolis and the ANTIETAM National Battlefield site.
MARY MAGDALENE, Saint, in the New Testament, the woman of MAGDALA from whom Jesus cast out seven demons (Luke 8:2). She became his devoted follower and was present at his death and burial. Mary was the first person to see the risen Jesus.
MARY OF BURGUNDY (1457–1482), daughter and heir of CHARLES THE BOLD of Burgundy, wife of Maximilian of Austria, later Holy Roman Emperor MAXIMILIAN I. Her marriage (1477) was critical in European history, eventually bringing the Netherlands, Artois and Franche-Comté to the imperial HAPSBURG house.
MARY OF GUISE (1515–1560), French queen of JAMES V of Scotland, mother of MARY QUEEN OF SCOTS and regent (1554–60). Her aggressive Roman Catholicism and pro-French policies provoked rebellion and hastened the Protestant Reformation in Scotland.

MARY OF MODENA (1658–1718), Italian queen consort of JAMES II of England, mistrusted for her friendship with France and her Roman Catholicism. The birth of her son (1688), a Catholic heir to the Throne, was the overt precipitant of the GLORIOUS REVOLUTION. Mary fled to France with her son.

MARY OF TECK (1867–1953), queen consort of GEORGE V of England. With her husband she raised the prestige of the monarchy by devotion to duty and by her many philanthropic activities.

MARY QUEEN OF SCOTS (1542–1587), queen of Scotland (1542–67), daughter of JAMES V (d. 1542) and MARY OF GUISE. Brought up in France, she married (1558) the Dauphin, king as FRANCIS II (d. 1560). Returning to Scotland (1561) she married (1565) Lord DARNLEY. In 1566 he murdered her favorite David Rizzio, but was himself later murdered, supposedly by the Earl of BOTHWELL, whom Mary married. Public outrage and Presbyterian opposition forced her abdication and in 1568 she fled to England. Mary, heir presumptive of ELIZABETH I and a Roman Catholic, soon became the natural focus of plots against the English throne. Parliament demanded her death, but it was only in 1587, after the BABINGTON plot, that Elizabeth reluctantly agreed. Mary's trial and execution at Fotheringay castle inspired SCHILLER's tragedy *Maria Stuart.*

MARYVILLE, city in E Tenn., seat of Blount Co., near the Great Smoky Mts National Park. Its industries are led by aluminum products. Pop 13 808.

MASACCIO (Tommaso Guidi; 1401–1428), Florentine painter of the RENAISSANCE, one of the great innovators of western art. He was possibly a pupil of MASOLINO. By taut line, austere composition, and inspired use of light Masaccio created expressive monumental paintings, notably in the Brancacci chapel, S. Maria del Carmine, Florence.

MASADA, rock fortress near the SE coast of the Dead Sea, Israel, the historic scene of Jewish national heroism. The castle-palace complex, built largely by Herod the Great, was siezed from Roman occupation by Jewish ZEALOTS in 66 AD. A two-year siege, 72–73, was needed to recover it but the garrison committed suicide rather than surrender. The site has been excavated and restored.

MASAI, a people of E Africa who speak the Masai language of the Sudanic group. The nomadic pastoral Masai of Kenya, the largest Masai tribe, practice polygyny and organize their society on a system of male age sets, graded from junior warrior up to tribal elder. They subsist almost entirely on livestock.

MASARYK, name of two Czechoslovakian statesmen. **Tomas Garrigue Masaryk** (1850–1937), was chief founder and first president of Czechoslovakia (1918–35). Professor of philosophy at Prague from 1882, he was a fervent nationalist. During WWI he lobbied western statesmen for Czech independence and helped delimit the frontiers of the new state. His son **Jan Garrigue Masaryk** (1886–1948) was foreign minister of the Czech government in exile in London in WWII, broadcasting to his German-occupied country. He continued as foreign minister in the restored government (1945). Soon after the communist coup (1948) he was said to have committed suicide.

MASAGNI, Pietro (1863–1945), Italian opera composer of the *verismo* (realist) school, known for the one-act *Cavalleria Rusticana* (1890). In 1929 he became musical director of La Scala, Milan.

MASEFIELD, John (1878–1967), English poet, novelist and playwright. As a youth he served on a windjammer ship, and love of the sea pervades his poems. He won fame with such long narrative poems as *The Everlasting Mercy* (1911), *Dauber* (1913) and *Reynard the Fox* (1919). In 1930 he became POET LAUREATE.

MASER, a device used as a MICROWAVE oscillator or amplifier, the name being an acronym for "*m*icrowave (or *m*olecular) *a*mplification by *s*timulated *e*mission of *r*adiation." As OSCILLATORS they form the basis of extremely accurate ATOMIC CLOCKS; as AMPLIFIERS they can detect feebler signals than any other kind, and are used to measure signals from outer space.

ATOMS and MOLECULES can exist in various states with different energies; changes from one ENERGY LEVEL to another are accompanied by the emission or absorption of ELECTROMAGNETIC RADIATION of a particular frequency. Maser action is based on the fact that irradiation at the frequency concerned stimulates the process. If more atoms are in the higher energy (excited) state than in the lower state, incident waves cause more emission than absorption, resulting in amplification of the original wave.

The main difficulty is one of maintaining this arrangement of the states, as the EQUILIBRIUM configuration involves more atoms being in the lower than in the excited state. In the AMMONIA gas maser, molecules in the lower state are removed physically through their different response to an ELECTRIC FIELD, while in solid-state masers, often operated at low temperatures, a higher frequency "pumping" wave raises atoms into the excited state from some state not involved in the maser action.

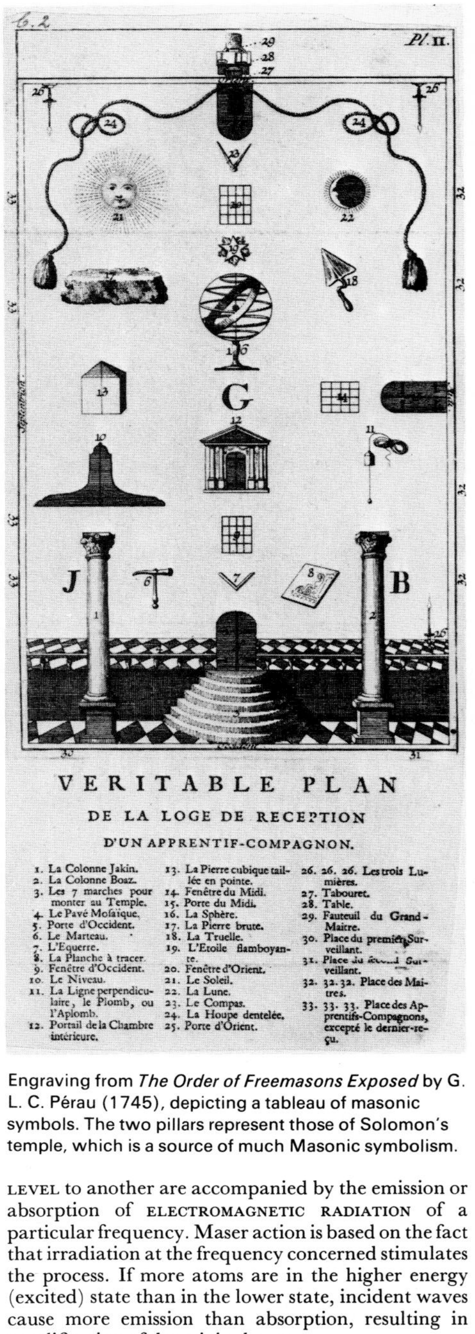

Engraving from *The Order of Freemasons Exposed* by G. L. C. Pérau (1745), depicting a tableau of masonic symbols. The two pillars represent those of Solomon's temple, which is a source of much Masonic symbolism.

MASERU, capital of Lesotho, near the NW border with South Africa. It is Lesotho's administrative, commercial and communications center. Pop 20 000.

MASOCHISM, mental state in which the individual gains erotic pleasure from experiencing PAIN. In PSYCHOANALYSIS, analogously, masochism describes the unconscious desire to bring humiliation upon oneself, and may again have an erotic basis. In **sadomasochism**, the individual is both sadistic (see SADISM) and masochistic, perhaps inflicting pain on himself.

MASOLINO (1383–1447?), Florentine painter, born Tommaso di Cristoforo. His decorative Gothic style was modified to greater realism under the influence of MASACCIO (possibly his pupil), with whom he executed notable frescoes in the Brancacci chapel, Florence.

MASON, George (1725–1792), American statesman who helped draft the US constitution but refused to sign it because of its compromise on slavery and other issues. His Va. declaration of rights became the basis for the BILL OF RIGHTS. Much of the Va. constitution was also his work.

MASON, John (1586–1635), English colonist in America. He founded N.H. on lands granted him between the Merrimack R and the Piscataqua R, mapped the Newfoundland coast and was vice-admiral of New England, 1635.

MASON, John Young (1799–1859), US statesman, judge and diplomat. He was a cabinet member (1844–46) and from 1853 was minister to France. He helped draft the OSTEND MANIFESTO (1854).

MASON, Lowell (1792–1872), US music-teacher and composer of more than 1 000 hymns. He founded the Boston Academy of Music (1832).

MASON AND SLIDELL, two Confederate statesmen, **James Murray Mason** (1798–1871), and **John Slidell** (1793–1871), sent to obtain help for the South from Britain and France respectively in 1861. Their interception by a US ship led to the TRENT AFFAIR.

MASON CITY, city in N central Iowa, seat of Cerro Gordo Co. It is the center for a large agricultural region and has related industries. Pop 30 379.

MASON-DIXON LINE, the S boundary of Pa., surveyed by two English astronomers, Charles Mason and Jeremiah Dixon, in the 1760s. It settled a dispute between the proprietary families of Pa. and Md. In 1779 it was extended westward to become the boundary between Va. and Pa. Up to the Civil War the line was popularly taken as the boundary between free and slave states.

MASONRY, or **Freemasonry,** common name for the practices of the order of Free and Accepted Masons, one of the world's largest and oldest fraternal organizations. Members participate in elaborate, secret rituals and are dedicated to the promotion of brotherhood and morality. Membership, of which there are several grades, is restricted to men and allegiance to some form of religious belief is required. Modern Masonry emerged with the Grand Lodge of England, founded in 1717, though masons trace their ancestry to the craft associations or "lodges" of medieval stone masons. The first US lodge was founded in Philadelphia, Pa. in 1730. The basic organization of Masonry is the blue lodge. In the US each state has a grand lodge and grand master, who presides over all the blue lodges in the state. There are associated organizations for women, boys and girls. The world-wide membership is more than six million.

MASORETIC TEXT, text of the Hebrew BIBLE with annotations mostly in Aramaic made from the 6th to the 10th centuries AD by Jewish scholars called Masoretes. They checked each word and letter, and produced the standard text, adding vowel points and accents (see HEBREW).

MASQUE, or **mask,** a dramatic entertainment popular at the early 17th-century English court. It concentrated on spectacle rather than plot. Members of the aristocracy often took part with the actors and masks were generally worn (hence the name). Ben JONSON was the most famous masque writer and Inigo JONES designed many of the lavish sets.

MASS, a measure of the linear INERTIA of a body, i.e., of the extent to which it resists ACCELERATION when a FORCE is applied to it. Alternatively, mass can be thought of as a measure of the amount of MATTER in a body. The validity of this view seems to receive corroboration when one remembers that bodies of equal inertial mass have identical WEIGHTS in a given gravitational field. But the exact equivalence of inertial mass and gravitational mass is only a theoretical assumption, albeit one strongly supported by experimental evidence. According to EINSTEIN's special theory of RELATIVITY, the mass of a body is increased if it gains ENERGY; according to the famous Einstein equation: $\Delta m = \Delta E/c^2$ where Δm is the change in mass due to the energy change ΔE, and c is the electromagnetic constant. It is an important property of nature that in an isolated system mass-energy is conserved. The international standard of mass is the international prototype KILOGRAM.

MASS, term for the celebration of Holy COMMUNION in the Roman Catholic Church and in Anglo-Catholic churches, derived from the final words of the Latin rite: *Ite, missa est* (Go, you are dismissed). Roman Catholics believe that the bread (HOST) and the wine become Christ's body and blood (see TRANSUBSTANTIATION), which are offered as a sacrifice to God. The priest both drinks the wine and eats the wafer; the laity are permitted only the latter. The text consists of the "ordinary," spoken or sung at every celebration, and the "proper," sections which change according to the day (Gospel, including Collect and Epistle) or occasion—for example the REQUIEM mass has its own proper. In high mass, celebrated with priest, deacon and choir, the text is sung to plainchant with choral responses. The ordinary comprises the Kyrie, Gloria, Creed, Sanctus and Benedictus, Agnus Dei, and the Missa est. Medieval choral settings of it are the first great masterpieces of western music; it remained a major musical form into the 20th century. Low mass, said by a single priest, is the basic Roman Catholic service. In 1965 the Vatican sanctioned the use of vernacular languages in place of Latin.

MASSACHUSETTS, US Atlantic coast state, one of the 13 colonies (see UNITED STATES), the leading state of NEW ENGLAND. Mass. is small and densely populated; the coastal plain supports the majority of the population and the principal industries.

Central Mass. consists of a hilly region separated from the more rugged Berkshire Hills and Taconic Mts in the W by the Connecticut R valley. The climate is humid and the hillier regions in the W are colder than the eastern plains. Average annual rainfall is about 43in.

People. Mass. has the third highest population density in the nation. BOSTON is the seat of government. The executive is headed by a governor and a nine member governor's council. The state legislature is the general court of the Commonwealth of Mass. and the principal court is the supreme judicial court. Mass.'s public school system dating from the 1630s is the oldest in the nation, and its universities and colleges, including HARVARD UNIVERSITY and MASSACHUSETTS INSTITUTE OF TECHNOLOGY, rank among the world's foremost.

Economy. Industries include electrical and non-electrical machinery, fabricated metal products, foodstuffs, textiles and leather products. Agriculture, fishing and mining are now minor branches of the state's economy. Electronics industries serving communications and space research and development became of major importance in the 1950s and 1960s.

History. The first permanent colony in Mass. was founded by the PILGRIM FATHERS in 1620. (See also MAYFLOWER; MAYFLOWER COMPACT.) In 1629 a group of English Puritans was granted a charter (see MASSACHUSETTS BAY COMPANY), and the following year they established a settlement at Boston. The colony, the "Bible Commonwealth," remained a Puritan theocracy until its original charter was revoked by the English crown in 1684. (See also SALEM.)

The expansion of white settlement aroused Indian resistance, culminating in KING PHILIP'S WAR (1675–76). Mass. played a major role in the events leading up to the American Revolution (see BOSTON MASSACRE; BOSTON TEA PARTY). The depression which followed the revolution fell most heavily on the farmers and led to SHAY'S REBELLION in 1786, which influenced the state's leaders to ratify the Federal Constitution. As farmers moved West in the 19th century, shipbuilding and whaling became leading industries, but by the end of the century manufacturing was the basis of the state's economy. Mass. played a leading role in abolitionism, under such leaders as William Lloyd GARRISON and Wendell PHILLIPS. Between the Civil War and WWI, thousands of European immigrants, notably Irish, came to Mass. The state is rich in cultural facilities, historic sites and magnificent vacation areas.

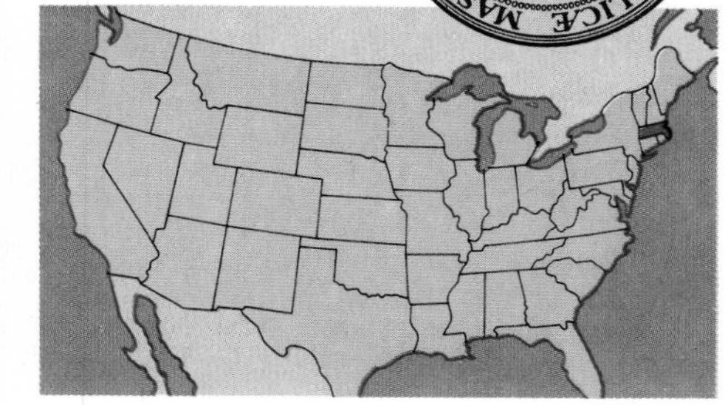

Name of state: Massachusetts
Capital: Boston
Statehood: Feb. 6, 1788
Familiar name: Bay State
Area: 8257sq mi
Population: 5689170
Elevation: Highest—3491ft., Mount Greylock. Lowest—sea level, Atlantic Ocean
Motto: Ense petit placidam sub libertate quietem (By the sword we seek peace, but peace only under liberty)
State flower: Mayflower
State bird: Chickadee
State tree: American elm
State song: "Hail Massachusetts"

MASSACHUSETTS BAY COMPANY, joint stock company set up by royal charter in 1629 and styled the "Governor and Company of the Massachusetts Bay in New England." This gave the company self-government subject only to the king; the charter effectively became the constitution of the colony. In 1630 almost 1000 immigrants landed in Mass., led by John WINTHROP, who became the first governor. The franchise was then restricted to Puritan "freemen" and the colony became an independent Calvinistic theocracy; it coined its own money and restricted freedom of worship. As a result the charter was revoked in 1684 and in 1686 the Dominion of New England was established with a royal governor.

MASSACHUSETTS INSTITUTE OF TECHNOLOGY (MIT), independent educational institution in Cambridge, Mass., founded in 1861. It awards undergraduate and graduate degrees in a wide variety of scientific subjects and in the humanities at undergraduate level. It enjoys a world-wide reputation for scientific research.

MASSAPEQUA PARK, residential village in the town of Oyster Bay, Long Island, N.Y. Pop 22112.

MASSASOIT, or Ousamequin (d. 1661), powerful Wampanoag Indian chief who signed a treaty with the PILGRIM FATHERS of Plymouth in 1621. He befriended the Plymouth colony, teaching the settlers much that they needed to know to survive. When he fell ill in 1623, the Pilgrims nursed him back to health, and he kept up friendly relations until his death.

MASSENA, village and township in N N.Y., on the St. Lawrence Seaway, the headquarters of Seaway Development. An aluminum production center, it is linked to Cornwall, Ontario by a bridge. Pop 16821.

MASSENET, Jules Émile Frédéric (1842–1912), French composer, best known for his operas *Manon* (1884), *Esclarmonde* (1889) and *Thaïs* (1894). He also wrote oratorios and stage music, and over 200 songs. He was a very influential teacher of composition at the Paris Conservatory from 1878.

MASSEY, Charles Vincent (1887–1967), Canadian diplomat, first Canadian-born governor general of Canada 1952–59. A Liberal minister under Mackenzie King in 1925, he was first Canadian minister to the US 1926–30. From 1935–46 he was Canadian high commissioner in the UK.

MASSIF, plateau-like upland area, with abrupt margins and often complex geologic structure. The term is most often applied to the Massif Central, France. (See also MOUNTAIN.)

MASSIF CENTRAL, mountainous upland plateau in S central France covering about 35000sq mi, one sixth of the country. It has a wide variety of agriculture and industry, mining being important.

MASSILLON, city on the Tuscarawas R in NE Ohio. Originally a wheat center, it is now a shipping town with diverse industries. Pop 32539.

MASSINE, Léonide (1896–), Russian-born US dancer and choreographer. He made his early career with the DIAGHILEV company, and was choreographer, dancer and director of the Ballet Russe de Monte Carlo 1932–41; he has worked with many of the world's great companies.

MASSINGER, Philip (1583–1640), English dramatist best known for satirical comedies such as *A New Way to Pay Old Debts* (1626?) and romantic tragedies such as *The Duke of Milan* (1621–22). He wrote many works in collaboration with others such as DEKKER and John FLETCHER.

MASS NUMBER (*A*), the total number of nucleons (PROTONS and NEUTRONS) in the nucleus of an ATOM, written as a number following its name after a hyphen (e.g., oxygen-16), or as a superscript following its chemical symbol (e.g., O^{16}).

MASSON, André (1896–), French painter and graphic artist. Influenced by SURREALISM, he developed a style of drawing ("automatic drawing") intended to be spontaneous and without conscious intent to portray a specific subject.

MASS PRODUCTION, the production of large numbers of identical objects, usually by use of mechanization. The root of mass production is the assembly line, essentially a conveyer belt which transports the product so that each worker may perform a single function on it (e.g., add a component). The advantages of mass production are cheapness and speed; the disadvantages are the lack of job satisfaction for the workers and the resultant sociological problems.

MASS SPECTROSCOPY, spectroscopic technique in which electric and magnetic fields are used to deflect moving charged particles according to their mass, employed for chemical ANALYSIS, separation, ISOTOPE determination or finding impurities. The apparatus for obtaining a mass spectrum (i.e., a number of "lines" of distinct charge-to-mass ratio obtained from the beam of charged particles) is known as a mass spectrometer or mass spectrograph, depending on whether the lines are detected electrically or on a photographic plate. In essence, it consists of an ion source, a vacuum chamber, a deflecting field and a collector. By altering the accelerating voltage and deflecting field, particles of a given mass can be focused to pass together through the collecting slit.

MASSYS, Quentin. See MATSYS, QUENTIN.

MASTABA, ancient Egyptian rectangular stone tomb. Its sloping sides supported a flat roof. It usually had three chambers; in the third, entered by a vertical shaft, the mummy was sealed off.

MASTECTOMY, removal of a BREAST including the skin and nipple; LYMPH nodes from the armpit and some CHEST wall muscles may also be excised. Mastectomy, often with RADIATION THERAPY, is used for breast CANCER.

MASTERS, Edgar Lee (1869–1950), US poet, novelist, biographer and playwright whose best known work is *Spoon River Anthology* (1915), the life of a small town seen through the epitaphs of its inhabitants. He also wrote critical biographies of Lincoln and Mark Twain, and several novels.

MASTERSINGER. See MEISTERSINGER.

MASTERSON, William Barclay "Bat" (1853–1921), US frontiersman. Son of a farmer, he was a professional gambler and law officer in early life; he is most famous as Wyatt EARP's assistant at Tombstone, Ariz. in 1880. In 1902 he became a sports journalist in New York.

MASTIC, resinous exudate obtained from the lentisk pistache (*Pistacia lentiscus*), which is an evergreen shrub native to the Mediterranean region. Mastic was used by the ancient Egyptians for embalming and is now used in varnish, as a theatrical fixative and for temporary teeth fillings.

MASTIFF, large and powerful English breed of dog, now much used as guard dogs although usually gentle by nature. Their short coat is usually fawn or fawn and black. They have blunt muzzles and drooping ears, both dark, and can be up to 30in tall and weigh up to 185 pounds.

The mastiff, the oldest surviving English breed of dog, is also one of the world's most ancient breeds. Its keen intelligence and strength make it an excellent guard dog.

MASTODONS, ELEPHANTS intermediate between the earliest elephant types and those of today. In North America, mastodons survived alongside the elephants into postglacial times. *Mastodon americanus* even outlived elephants in this part of the world.

MASTOID, air spaces lined by MUCOUS MEMBRANE lying behind the middle EAR and connected with it; they are situated in the bony protruberance behind the ear. Mastoid infection may follow middle ear infection; block to its drainage by INFLAMMATION and PUS may make eradication difficult. ANTIBIOTICS have reduced its incidence and SURGERY to clear or remove the air spaces is now infrequent.

MATA HARI (1876–1917), pseudonym of Margaretha Zelle, Dutch-born dancer, courtesan and spy. Having lived in Indonesia, she appeared as Mata Hari in Paris in 1905; her Oriental erotic dances soon made her world famous. She became the mistress of many French officials, and began to spy for Germany before and during WWI, for which she was tried and executed.

MATAMOROS, city in N Mexico on the S bank of the Rio Grande R. Lying across from Brownsville, Tex., it is one of Mexico's major ports and a manufacturing and commercial center. Pop 182 881.

MATANE, town in E Quebec, Canada, on the S bank of the St. Lawrence R. Its economy rests on the wood industry, agriculture, fishing and tourism. Pop 11 841.

MATANUSKA VALLEY, farm region around the Matanuska R in S central Alaska NE of Anchorage. In 1935 the federal government resettled here 208 families from the Middle West whose lands had been badly hit by drought.

MATANZAS, Fort. See FORT MATANZAS NATIONAL MONUMENT.

MATAPAN, Cape, promontory in S Greece. The British defeated the Italians in an important sea battle off the Cape during WWII.

MATCH, short splint of wood or cardboard having a head that can be ignited by friction, used to kindle fire (see COMBUSTION). Early matches were complex, unreliable and somewhat dangerous (e.g., dipping a match treated with potassium chlorate and sugar into a bottle of concentrated sulfuric acid). Friction matches of the modern type were first produced in 1827, containing antimony (III) sulfide and potassium chlorate. Soon white PHOSPHORUS was introduced for strike-anywhere matches. This, however, caused the disease "phossy jaw" in match-factory workers, and was banned from about 1900, being replaced by phosphorus sesquisulfide (P_4S_3) and potassium chlorate, with iron (III) oxide, ground glass and glue. Safety matches have in the head potassium chlorate, manganese (IV) oxide, sulfur, iron oxide, ground glass and glue. They ignite only when struck on the mixture on the side of the box, which consists of red phosphorus, antimony (III) sulfide and an abrasive. The matchstick is coated with paraffin wax to give a better flame.

MATÉ, or **Yerba maté,** or Paraguay tea, the dried leaves of an evergreen tree (*Ilex paraguariensis*) which is native to Paraguay and Brazil. Maté is used to produce a tea which contains small amounts of CAFFEINE. Family: Aquifoliaceae.

MATERIALISM, in philosophy, as opposed to IDEALISM, any view asserting the ontologic primacy of MATTER; in psychology, any theory denying the existence of MIND, seeing mental phenomena to be the mere outworking of purely physico-mechanical processes in the BRAIN; in the philosophy of religion, any synthesis denying the existence of an immortal soul in man. The earliest thoroughgoing materialists were the classical ATOMISTS, in particular DEMOCRITUS and LUCRETIUS. The growth of modern science brought a revival of materialism, which many have argued is a prerequisite for scientific thought, particularly in the field of psychology. Other philosophers, however, have argued against this view, recognizing the arbitrariness of the materialist hypothesis.

MATERIALS, Strength of, a branch of MECHANICS concerned with the behavior of materials when subjected to loads. When force is applied to an object there is a tendency for it to deform: the internal forces resulting from the applied force are called stresses; the deformations are called strains.

Stress. The four main types of stress are: shearing (e.g., the forces set up in a rivet joining two plates that are pulling in opposite directions); bending; tension and compression (which tend to elongate or shorten the member), and torsion (twisting). When we analyze a structure, we are concerned with the stresses that each component is called upon to resist, and its ability to do so without undue strain.

Strain. Materials deform in different ways under load. Basic properties include ELASTICITY, where a material regains its original dimensions when load is removed; plasticity, where the deformation is permanent; brittleness, where deformation is negligible before fracture, and creep, deformation under a constant load over a period of time. (See also DUCTILITY; HARDNESS; MALLEABILITY.) Within limits, elastic materials deform in proportion to the stress; i.e., $\frac{\text{stress}}{\text{strain}} = \text{a constant}$ (Hooke's Law). The value of the constant depends on the material and on the type of stress. For tensile and compressive forces it is called Young's modulus, E (see YOUNG, Thomas); for SHEARING forces, the shear modulus, S; and, for forces affecting the VOLUME of the object, the bulk modulus, B. There comes a point (the elastic limit), however, when further stress results in a permanent deformation. (See also TENSILE STRENGTH.)

MATHEMATICAL LOGIC, or symbolic logic. See BOOLE, GEORGE; LOGIC.

MATHEMATICAL MODELS, physical objects used to represent mathematical abstractions; or, more frequently, mathematical constructions (formulae, FUNCTIONS, GRAPHS, etc.) used to represent physical phenomena. Such models occur throughout applied mathematics and physics, their greatest value being heuristic; i.e., the model may suggest the existence of unsuspected properties in the phenomenon.

MATHEMATICS, commonly abbreviated to Maths or Math, the fundamental, interdisciplinary tool of all science. It can be divided into two main classes, pure and applied mathematics, though there are many cases of overlap between these. Pure mathematics has as its basis the abstract study of quantity, and thus includes the sciences of NUMBER— ARITHMETIC and its broader realization, ALGEBRA—as well as the subjects described collectively as GEOMETRY (e.g., ANALYTIC GEOMETRY, EUCLIDEAN GEOMETRY, MENSURATION, NON-EUCLIDEAN GEOMETRY, TRIGONOMETRY and sometimes TOPOLOGY) and their extensions, the subjects described collectively as ANALYSIS (particularly CALCULUS and some aspects of Analytic Geometry and VECTOR ANALYSIS). In modern mathematics, many of these subjects are treated in terms of SET THEORY. Applied mathematics deals with the applications of this abstract science. It thus has particulary close associations with PHYSICS and ENGINEERING. Specific subjects that come under its aegis are boolean algebra (an application of Set Theory to LOGIC—see BOOLE, GEORGE); GAME THEORY; INFORMATION THEORY; PROBABILITY; STATISTICS, and VECTOR ANALYSIS.

MATHER, family of American colonial divines. **Richard Mather** (1596–1669) emigrated to Mass. in 1635 and there became an influential preacher. A coauthor of the BAY PSALM BOOK, he wrote the *Platform of Church Discipline* (1649), the basic creed of Massachusetts Congregationalism. **Increase Mather** (1639–1723), son of Richard, was president of Harvard 1685–1701. A renowned preacher and scholar, he helped negotiate the colony's new charter with William III in 1692. In that year he also intervened to mitigate the witchcraft persecution. **Cotton Mather** (1663–1728), son of Increase, was also a famous preacher and scholar; his early work contributed to the witchcraft trials, which he always defended in part. His *Magnalia Christi Americana* (1702) is a brilliant religious history of the colonies. He helped found Yale U.; his wide scientific interests made him the first native American to be elected to the Royal Society of London.

MATHEWSON, Christopher "Christy" (1880–1925), US baseball player, one of the most successful of pitchers. During a 17-year career he won 373 games while losing 188 and set the National League strikeout record of 2 499. He pitched three shutouts in six days against the Philadelphia Athletics in 1905. Gassed in WWI, he died of tuberculosis.

MATILDA, or **Maud** (1102–1167), queen of England and Holy Roman Empress until the death of her husband the Emperor Henry V in 1125. Her claim to the English throne was recognized in 1127, but countered successfully by Stephen of Blois in 1135. Her eldest son, however, became HENRY II in 1154.

MATING RITUALS. In most animal species the close approach of one individual to another is an aggressive action. Yet, for reproductive purposes such a male–female approach must be made. Thus complicated behavior patterns have evolved from a combination of submissive gestures and ritualized DISPLACEMENT ACTIVITIES, to appease the sexual partner. In many cases these rituals also involve the development of morphological display characters. Mating rituals may also serve as an isolating mechanism to ensure that mating is with another member of the same species.

MATISSE, Henri Émile Benôit (1869–1954), French painter, one of the most important artists of the 20th century. He studied under MOREAU and was much influenced by IMPRESSIONISM. The brilliance of color in such paintings as *Woman with a Hat* (1905) and *Joy of Life* (1906) caused the style of his circle to be dubbed FAUVISM. He visited and exhibited in the USSR and US, and in 1917 settled in Nice, France. A prolific painter, he also produced lithographs, etchings, designs, illustrations and much sculpture. He himself considered the decor of the Dominican Nunnery chapel at Vence, France, his masterpiece.

MATO GROSSO, state in Brazil, bordering Bolivia and Paraguay. Its area is 484 486sq mi, of which the N is dense rain forest and the S a damp plain. The economy rests on agriculture; there are extensive but little-exploited mineral resources.

MATRICES, arrays of numbers (such as the COEFFICIENTS of a set of simultaneous linear EQUATIONS) of the form

$$\begin{matrix} a_{11} & a_{12} & \cdots & a_{1n} \\ a_{21} & a_{22} & \cdots & a_{2n} \\ \cdot & \cdot & \cdots & \cdot \\ a_{m1} & a_{m2} & \cdots & a_{mn} \end{matrix} = \mathbf{A}.$$

A is described as an $m \times n$ matrix over F, where F is a FIELD, without characteristic, to which all the mn elements of **A** belong. **A** is made up of m 1 $\times n$ matrices (row vectors) and $nm \times 1$ matrices (column vectors).

Addition: If two matrices **A** and **B** of F are both $m \times n$, the result of their ADDITION is defined to be the

$m \times n$ matrix of which a typical element is $(a_{ij} + b_{ij})$. Their addition is thus commutative and associative (see ALGEBRA). Moreover, the set of $m \times n$ matrices of F forms an ABELIAN GROUP under addition since it has an identity element (see GROUPS), **O**, the zero matrix whose elements are all ZERO, since $\mathbf{A} + \mathbf{O} = \mathbf{A}$ for all **A**; and since every **A** has an INVERSE $-\mathbf{A}$, whose typical element is $(-a_{ij})$, such that $\mathbf{A} + (-\mathbf{A}) = \mathbf{O}$.

Multiplication: If l is an element of F, the product $l\mathbf{A}$ is defined as the matrix whose typical element is la_{ij}. Multiplication of one matrix by another is possible only if the first has the same number of columns as the second has rows. If **A** is an $m \times n$ matrix and **B** an $n \times p$ matrix then their product **AB** is an $m \times p$ matrix with typical element

$$a_{i1}b_{1j} + a_{i2}b_{2j} + \quad . \quad . \quad . \quad + a_{in}b_{nj}.$$

Notice that, in this case, **BA** does not exist unless $p = m$ since otherwise **B** does not have the same number of columns as **A** has rows.

Transposition and Symmetry. The transpose of an $m \times n$ matrix **A** is an $n \times m$ matrix **A′**, obtained by setting the row vectors of **A** as the column vectors of **A′**, the column vectors of **A** as the row vectors of **A′**. Some basic results emerge:

$$(\mathbf{A}')' = \mathbf{A},$$
$$(\mathbf{AB})' = \mathbf{B}'\mathbf{A}',$$
and $$(k\mathbf{A} + l\mathbf{B})' = k\mathbf{A}' + l\mathbf{B}',$$

where k, l, are elements of F. A matrix **A** is termed symmetric when $\mathbf{A} = \mathbf{A}'$ and skew-symmetric when $\mathbf{A} = -\mathbf{A}'$: of course, only matrices where $n = m$ can be symmetric or skew-symmetric. For symmetry the element a_{ij} in **A** must equal a_{ji} for all i, j; for skew-symmetry $a_{ij} + a_{ji} = 0$ for all i, j. (See also DETERMINANT.)

MATSUDO, city in Honshu, Japan, a suburb of Tokyo. In part residential, it has some heavy industry also. Pop 253 591.

MATSU ISLAND, island in the E China Sea off mainland China. Occupied by the Nationalist Chinese in 1944, it was attacked by the communists in 1958 provoking a major diplomatic incident.

MATSUMOTO, historic city in central Honshu, Japan. A tourist center in an isolated agricultural area, it has various industries, including silk. Pop 162 931.

MATSUO BASHO, pseudonym of Matsuo Munefusa (1644–1694), the greatest Japanese exponent of HAIKU poetry. A follower of ZEN, he introduced this philosophy into the formerly trivial *haiku* form, with compact and delicate imagery. He is also remembered for his *renga* verses and his accounts of travels.

MATSUOKA, Yosuke (1880–1946), Japanese businessman and statesman, educated in the US. He was an extreme nationalist; he headed the delegation to the LEAGUE OF NATIONS that walked out in 1932. Foreign minister 1940–41, he brought about the Tripartite Pact with the Axis powers in 1940. He died before his impending trial as a war criminal.

MATSUYAMA, port city on NW coast of Shikoku Island, Japan. Located in a rich agricultural plain, it has many industries; it has been drastically replanned and rebuilt since WWII. Pop 322 902.

MATSYS, Quentin (c1466–1530), Flemish painter. Influenced by LEONARDO DA VINCI and the Italian Renaissance, he is best known for portraits, genre scenes and religious works, particularly the *Holy Kinship* and *Pieta* triptych altarpieces (1509 and 1511 respectively).

MATTATHIAS (d. c166 BC), Jewish priest from Modin, near Jerusalem. With his five sons he waged a guerrilla war against the Syrian ruler Antiochus IV. (See also HASMONEANS.)

MATTER, material substance, that which has extension in space and time. All material bodies have inherent INERTIA, measured quantitatively by their MASS, and exert gravitational attraction on other such bodies. Matter may also be considered as a specialized form of ENERGY. There are three physical states of matter: solid, liquid and gas. An ideal solid tends to return to its original shape after forces applied to it are removed. Solids are either crystalline or amorphous; most melt and become liquids when heated. Liquids and gases are both FLUIDS: liquids are only slightly compressible but gases are easily compressed. On the molecular scale, the state of matter is a balance between attractive intermolecular forces and the disordering thermal motion of the molecules. When the former predominate, MOLECULES vibrate about fixed positions in a solid crystal LATTICE. At higher temperatures, the random thermal motion of the molecules predominates, giving a featureless gas structure. The short-range intermolecular order of a liquid is an intermediate state between solid and gas.

MATTERHORN (French: Mont Cervin; Italian: Monte Cervino), 14 691ft high mountain in the Alps on the Swiss-Italian frontier. It was first climbed by Edward WHYMPER in 1865.

MATTHEW, Saint, or Levi, one of the twelve APOSTLES, traditionally the author of the first GOSPEL. He was a tax-collector before Jesus called him; little more is known of him. The gospel, the fullest of the four, was written probably c80 AD for Jewish Christians. By many Old Testament quotes it shows Jesus as the promised MESSIAH. (See also SYNOPTIC GOSPELS.)

MATTHIAS, Saint, APOSTLE chosen by lot to replace JUDAS ISCARIOT (Acts 1:21–26). Little otherwise is known of him.

MATTHIAS CORVINUS (c1443–1490), elected king of Hungary in 1458, son of the soldier Janos HUNYADI. In a successful reign he defended himself against the Turks and against the Emperor Frederick III, his rival. A patron of arts and learning, he made his capital at Buda famous throughout Europe.

MATTOON, city in E central Ill. A railroad junction, it is an oil center with light manufacturing industries. Pop 19 681.

MATZAH, Hebrew name for unleavened bread traditionally eaten at the PASSOVER feast and used in Jewish cooking.

MAUGHAM, William Somerset (1874–1965), British author. After qualifying as a medical student he became a successful playwright and novelist; in WWI he served as a secret agent. His plays are no longer popular, and his fame rests on his many short stories and four of his novels, *Of Human Bondage* (1915), *The Moon and Sixpence* (1919), inspired by the life of GAUGUIN, *Cakes and Ale* (1930), and *The Razor's Edge* (1944). These reveal a cynical but sometimes compassionate view of humanity.

MAUI, second largest island in Hawaii state, 728sq mi in area. It was built up by two volcanoes, Puu Kukui and HALEAKALA. The island's economy rests mainly on sugar and fruit plantations.

MAULDIN, Bill (William Henry-Mauldin; 1921–   ), US cartoonist who rose to fame with his sympathetic caricatures of G.I. life in WWII. After 1945 he became a political cartoonist well known for his biting but sensitive wit. He was awarded two Pulitzer prizes in 1945 and 1958.

MAU MAU, Kenyan Kikuyu terrorist organization whose main aim was to expel the British. Organized on the lines of a cult or secret society, the Mau Mau ran a campaign of murder and sabotage 1952–60, although the movement was contained with the minimum of bloodshed after 1956. In all, however, 100 Europeans and 11 000 rebels had been killed; 20 000 were detained, among them Jomo KENYATTA. The Mau Mau also murdered at least 2 000 Africans who were from other tribes or were reluctant to join the organization.

MAUNA KEA (white mountain), dormant snow-capped volcano in N central Hawaii island, Hawaii. At 13 796ft it is the world's highest island peak.

MAUNA LOA (long mountain), highly active volcano in the HAWAII VOLCANOES NATIONAL PARK, which erupts about once every 3.5 years. It is 13 680ft in height and has several other large craters on its SW slope.

MAUNDY THURSDAY, the Thursday before EASTER (see HOLY WEEK), commemorating Christ's washing of his disciples' feet and institution of the Holy COMMUNION at the LAST SUPPER. The English monarch distributes special "Maundy money" to poor persons on this day.

MAUPASSANT, (Henri René Albert) Guy de (1850–1893), French short-story writer and novelist. A pupil of FLAUBERT, from 1880 to 1891 he produced some 300 short stories of outstanding quality, which excel in the unsentimental portrayal of the less attractive aspects of life and human nature. His direct style, pessimism and NATURALISM are seen at their best in "Boule de suif" (1880) and "The House of Madame Tellier" (1881).

The massive portrait of St Matthew dominating the entrance to the Roman Catholic Cathedral of St Matthew in Washington, D.C.

MAUPERTUIS, Pierre Louis Moreau de (1698–1759), French mathematician and astronomer who showed the EARTH to be flattened at the poles (1738), and who formulated the *principle of least action*, which assumes that, in nature, phenomena such as the motion of bodies occur with maximum economy.

MAURIAC, François (1885–1970), French writer whose novels of middle-class life concern man's vulnerability to sin and evil; they reflect his deeply-held Roman Catholic faith. In 1952 he won the Nobel Prize for literature. His works include *A Kiss for the Leper* (1922), *Génitrix* (1923), *The Desert of Love* (1925), *Thérèse Desqueyroux* (1927) and *Viper's Tangle* (1932).

MAURICE OF NASSAU (1567–1625), Prince of Orange from 1618, Dutch statesman and military leader. A son of WILLIAM THE SILENT, he conducted a successful war against Spanish rule, and was an architect of the emerging Dutch republic. He was virtually ruler of the Netherlands, executing his former ally OLDENBARNEVELDT in 1619, and establishing the supremacy of the house of ORANGE.

MAURITANIA, Islamic republic on the NW coast of Africa, bounded by Western Sahara on the NW, Algeria NE, Mali E and S and Senegal SW. The interior is largely desert and rocky plateau at an average height of 500ft. The climate is hot, with average rainfall less than 4in except in the fertile Senegal R valley in the S, where it rises to 24in. Moors of Arab-Berber descent, mostly nomadic herdsmen, form some 80% of the population; FULANI form about 13% and Negro groups such as the Soninke, Bambara and Wolof make up the remainder. Nouakchott, the capital and largest town, has a population of 37 000.

Basic crops, grown in the S, are millet, dates, maize and beans; sheep, goats, cattle and camels are raised. There are large iron ore and copper deposits and oil has been discovered. Mauritania exports iron ore, livestock and dates.

In the 11th century the Ghanaian empire, to which most of Mauritania then belonged, was shattered by invading nomad Berbers of the Almoravid group (see ALMOHAD AND ALMORAVID). In the 13th century S Mauritania fell to the MALI EMPIRE and Islam was firmly established. The Portuguese probed the coast in the 15th century, inland penetration coming with

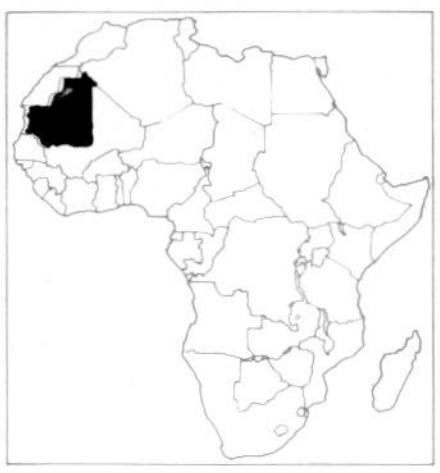

Official name: Republic of Mauritania
Capital: Nouakchott
Area: 397 956sq mi
Population: 1 200 000
Languages: Arabic, French
Religions: Muslim
Monetary unit(s): 1 CFA franc = 100 centimes

the French only in the 19th century. A French colony by 1921, Mauritania left the FRENCH COMMUNITY at full independence in 1960.

MAURITIUS, island republic of the British Commonwealth, 500mi E of the island of Madagascar in the Indian Ocean, comprising the islands of Mauritius and Rodriguez and associated archipelagos. Its warm and humid climate has average temperatures of 79°F from Nov. to April and 72°F in winter. The wet season, Dec. to March, is a time of dangerous cyclones.

Indians, descended from indentured laborers brought in to work the sugar plantations, form some 70% of the population; Europeans, Creoles, Africans and some Chinese constitute the remainder. Rapid population increase, coupled with unemployment and ethnic rivalries, has exacerbated political problems. The capital, Port Louis, is the chief port and sugar the main export crop, others including tobacco and tea.

Formerly uninhabited, Mauritius was settled by the Portuguese in the early 1500s but then abandoned. After a period of Dutch occupation in the 17th century, the French settled the island in 1715, founding the sugar industry. The British took Mauritius during the Napoleonic wars (1810), initiated moves to representative government in the late 19th century and granted independence in 1968.

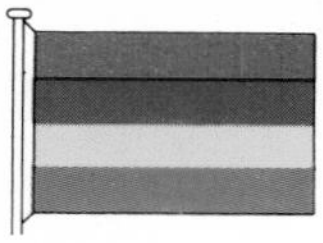

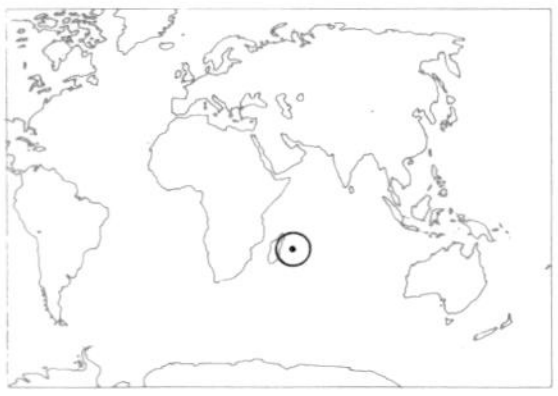

Official name: Mauritius
Capital: Port Louis
Area: 720sq mi
Population: 833 977
Languages: English, French, Creole
Religions: Hindu, Christian, Muslim
Monetary unit(s): 1 Mauritian rupee = 100 cents

MAUROIS, André (born Émile Herzog; 1885–1967), French novelist and biographer, notably of Shelley (1923), Byron (1930), George Sand (1952) and Proust (1949). His first success was *The Silence of Colonel Bramble* (1918), a humorous study of the English, and his novels include *Climats* (1929).

MAURY, Matthew Fontaine (1806–1873), US naval officer, head of the Depot of Charts and Instruments, 1842–61. His profile of the bed of the Atlantic and his *Physical Geography of the Sea* (1855) helped pioneer the science of oceanography.

MAURYA, Indian imperial dynasty ruling c325–c183 BC, founded by CHANDRAGUPTA Maurya, with its capital near modern Patna. His grandson ASOKA (d. 232) ruled almost the whole subcontinent and made Buddhism the state religion. Mauryan art, influenced by Greek and Persian styles, marks a great flowering of Indian Buddhist culture.

MAUSOLEUM, large sepulchral monument, named for the tomb of Mausolus of Caria (built c352 BC) at Halicarnassus in Asia Minor, one of the SEVEN WONDERS OF THE WORLD. About 100ft square and 150ft high, it had superb sculptures, some preserved in the British Museum. Other mausoleums are the TAJ MAHAL and Lenin's tomb in Moscow.

MAUVE, or mauveine, the first synthetic DYE, made by William PERKIN (1856).

MAWSON, Sir Douglas (1882–1958), Australian explorer and geologist. A member of SHACKLETON's 1907–09 Antarctic expedition, Mawson later led the 1911–14 Australian Antarctic Expedition. He was professor of geology at Adelaide University from 1920.

MAXENTIUS, Marcus Aurelius Valerius (d. 312 AD), Roman emperor 306–12. Recognized in Italy, he was opposed by CONSTANTINE I who defeated and killed him at the Battle of the Milvian Bridge.

MAXIM, US family of inventors, best known for work on FIREARMS and EXPLOSIVES. **Sir Hiram Stevens Maxim** (1840–1916), invented the Maxim MACHINE GUN (c1884) and contributed to the development of CORDITE. He patented hundreds of other inventions. His brother **Hudson Maxim** (1853–1927), a chemist, developed explosives much used in WWII, and notably the high explosive maximite. Sir Hiram's son **Hiram Percy Maxim** (1869–1936), invented the Maxim silencer for firearms and the Maxim MUFFLER for automobiles.

MAXIMILIAN, name of two Hapsburg Holy Roman emperors. **Maximilian I** (1459–1519), reigned from 1493. He married first MARY OF BURGUNDY (1477) and then a Milanese princess, and arranged other family marriages that brought the Hapsburgs much of Burgundy, the Netherlands, Hungary, Bohemia and Spain. He reorganized imperial administration and set up a supreme court of justice, but had to recognize Switzerland's independence (1499), and failed to hold Milan. Loans from the FUGGER bank supported his finances, which were severely strained by continual warfare in support of his dynastic ambitions. **Maximilian II** (1527–1576), emperor from 1564, was king of Bohemia from 1549 and of Hungary from 1563. A humanist, he adopted a policy of religious toleration which brought a respite from the struggles of the REFORMATION.

MAXIMILIAN (1832–1867), Austrian archduke and emperor of Mexico from 1864. Liberal and idealistic, he was offered the throne as a result of NAPOLEON III's imperial intrigues. He believed the Mexicans would welcome him, and attempted to rule liberally and benevolently, but found French troops essential against popular support for President JUAREZ. After US pressure had secured his recall he was defeated by Juarez's forces and executed.

MAXWELL, James Clerk (1831–1879), British physicist whose contributions to science have been compared to those of Newton and Einstein. His most important work was in ELECTROMAGNETISM (he pointed to the electromagnetic nature of LIGHT) and THERMODYNAMICS. Most important of all was his derivation of the equations that bear his name, four equations that together describe in terms of the relevant VECTOR quantities the interrelation between electric and magnetic fields in a particular space. (See also ELECTROMAGNETIC RADIATION.)

MAY, fifth month of the year, with 31 days. The name is perhaps derived from Maia, the Roman goddess of growth. (See also MAY DAY.)

MAY, Cape. See CAPE MAY.

MAYAGÜEZ, seaport in W Puerto Rico, exporting sugar, coffee and fruit. Famed for its embroidery, it also has some manufacturing industry. Pop 68 872.

MAYAGUEZ INCIDENT, May 1975. The US ship *Mayaguez* was intercepted and searched for arms by Cambodian gunboats. President FORD ordered in the Air Force and Marines who bombed the ship and rescued the crew.

MAYAKOVSKY, Vladimir Vladimirovich (1893–1930), Soviet futurist poet and playwright whose powerful, declamatory verse, innovative in rhythm and diction, expresses his sense of being a new man in a revolutionary epoch. Notable works are the elegiac lament *Lenin* (1924), *Very Good!* (1927) on a decade of Soviet successes and the play *The Bedbug* (1928), satirizing Soviet bureaucracy. He committed suicide.

MAYAS, American Indians whose brilliant civilization in central America was at its height c300–c900 AD. The Maya confederation covered the Yucatán peninsula, E Chiapas state in Mexico, most of Guatemala and the W parts of El Salvador and Honduras. They were a farming people of the rain forests and grew corn, cassava, cotton, beans and sweet potatoes and kept bees for wax and honey. The hierarchy of priest-nobles under a hereditary chief had an involved, hieroglyphic form of writing, still undeciphered, and a remarkable knowledge of mathematics, astronomy and chronology. The priests devised two calendars: a 365-day civil year astronomically more accurate than the western Gregorian CALENDAR and a sacred year of 260 days. Mayan art comprises fine sculpture in the round and relief, painted frescoes and manuscripts, ceramics and magnificent architecture. The chief features of their great cities was the lofty stone pyramid, topped by a

Residential quadrangle at Uxmal, a late Classic Maya site. The buildings undoubtedly housed the priests and officials who served at this typical semi-religious, semi-administrative ceremonial center.

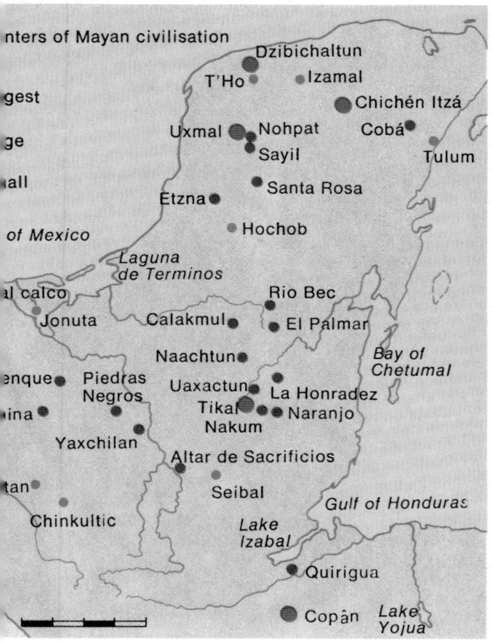

temple. By 900 AD their main centers, such as Palenque, Peidras and Copán, were abandoned to the jungle for reasons unknown. A "post-classical" tradition, under TOLTEC influence, sprang up in new centers, notably Chichén Itzá, but in the early 1500s the whole region came under Spanish rule.

MAY BUGS. See JUNE BEETLE.

MAY DAY, spring festival on May 1. Traces of its pagan origins survive in the decorated maypoles and May queens of England. Declared a socialist labor festival by the Second INTERNATIONAL in 1889, it is celebrated, particularly in communist countries, by parades and demonstrations.

MAYER, Julius Robert von (1814–1878), German physician and physicist who contributed to the formulation of the law of conservation of ENERGY.

MAYER, Louis Burt (1885–1957), Russian-born US motion picture producer and tycoon. As head of the Metro-Goldwyn-Mayer Corporation, MGM (1924–51), he "discovered" such stars as Greta Garbo, Joan Crawford, Rudolf Valentino and Clark Gable.

MAYER, Maria Goeppert (1906–1972), German-born US physicist awarded, with J. H. D. JENSEN and E. P. WIGNER, the 1963 Nobel Prize for Physics for her proposal (independent of Jensen's) that the PROTONS and NEUTRONS of the atomic nucleus are arranged in concentric shells.

MAYERLING. See RUDOLPH.

MAYFIELD, city in SW Ky., seat of Graves Co. It is a market center for tobacco and grain, and has some light industry. Pop 10 724.

MAYFIELD HEIGHTS, city in NE Ohio, a residential suburb of Cleveland. Pop 22 139.

MAYFLOWER, the ship that carried the PILGRIM FATHERS to America in 1620, leaving Plymouth, England, on Sept. 21 and reaching Provincetown, Mass., on Nov. 21; the Pilgrims sailed on to settle what is now PLYMOUTH, Mass., after signing the MAYFLOWER COMPACT. A two-decker, probably some 90ft long and weighing about 180 tons, the ship has not survived but an English-built replica, *Mayflower II*, sailed the Atlantic in 1957 and is now at Plymouth, Mass.

MAYFLOWER COMPACT, agreement signed by 41 of the PILGRIM FATHERS on Nov. 21, 1620. Having landed outside any civil jurisdiction, and fearing that their group might split up, they undertook to form a "civil body politic" and to "frame just and equal laws." The compact became the basis of the government of the colony of Plymouth.

MAYFLIES, the order Ephemeroptera, aquatic INSECTS of river banks and lake margins, whose adults are supposed to live only for a single day. The larvae are completely aquatic detritus-feeders characterized by three "bristle-tails." Rising to the surface, the NYMPH goes through two molts to produce the adult: from the first molt an insect emerges with fully-developed wings and adult form; this molts again almost immediately and emerges as the fully-active adult. The double molt is unique among insects.

MAYHEM, in English and US law, maiming or physical disablement caused by intent or in consequence of severe battery (see ASSAULT). The victim can sue for damages.

MAYHEW, Henry (1812–1887), British journalist, miscellaneous writer, social commentator and a founder of the magazine *Punch* (1841). His 4-volume *London Labour and the London Poor* (1851–62), a sympathetic and penetrating study, is an invaluable source of social history.

MAYHEW, Jonathan (1720–1766), liberal American clergyman, pastor of Boston's West Church from 1747. Outspoken in opposition to religious dogmatism and authoritarianism, and in defense of civil liberties, he clashed with the British Society for the Propagation of the Gospel, and was accused (unjustly) of instigating the STAMP ACT riots of 1765.

MAYO, George Elton (1880–1949), Australian pioneer of industrial sociology and psychology. Teaching at the Harvard Graduate School of Business Administration (1926–47), he organized a classic study of labor-management relations at the Western Electric Co. (1927).

MAYO, distinguished US family of surgeons. **William Worrall Mayo** (1819–1911), founded St. Mary's Hospital, Rochester, Minn. (1889), which was to become the famous Mayo Clinic. His sons, **William James Mayo** (1861–1939) and **Charles Horace Mayo** (1865–1939), traveled to many countries both to discover new surgical techniques and to attract foreign surgeons to the Clinic; in 1915 they set up the Mayo Foundation for Medical Education and Research. Charles' son, **Charles William Mayo** (1898–1968), was also a distinguished surgeon.

MAYO CLINIC, one of the world's largest medical centers, founded in 1889 at Rochester, Minn., as a voluntary association of physicians. It developed from an emergency hospital set up by Dr. William W. MAYO to help cyclone victims. The Clinic treats about 175 000 patients a year and is financed by the Mayo Foundation.

MAYOR, the highest official of city government. In the US and many European countries the mayor is an active administrative and executive officer, and in France he is also an agent of the central government. In the UK the office is now primarily ceremonial. Nowadays mayors are nearly always elected, not appointed.

MAYS, Willie Howard Jr. (1931–), baseball player who joined the New York Giants in 1951. A great hitter and spectacular outfield player, he won four National League home run titles and two Most Valuable Player awards, before retiring in 1973.

MA YÜAN (c1160–c1225), Chinese SUNG period artist, one of China's greatest landscape painters. He was noted for his spare and dramatically asymmetrical compositions.

MAYWOOD, city in S Cal. It is an industrial and residential suburb SE of Los Angeles. Pop 16 996.

MAYWOOD, village in NE Ill., a suburb of Chicago. Noted for the Maywood Park Harness Race Track, it has food processing and light manufacturing industries. Pop 30 036.

MAYWOOD, borough in NE N.J. It is a residential suburb 12mi W of New York City, and has chemical and pharmaceutical industries. Pop 11 087.

MAZARIN, Jules (1602–1661), Italian-born French statesman and cardinal who strengthened the French monarchy and by successful diplomacy increased France's influence abroad. After the deaths of RICHELIEU (1642) and LOUIS XIII (1643), he became the trusted chief minister of the regent, ANNE OF AUSTRIA, and educator of her son, the future LOUIS XIV. His policy of centralized power and his imposition of taxes provoked the revolts known as the FRONDE (1648–53), which he eventually crushed decisively. In foreign policy he gained favorable terms in the treaties that ended the THIRTY YEARS' WAR (1648) and the war with Spain (1659). He amassed a huge fortune, and was a patron of the arts.

MAZATLÁN, city on the Pacific coast of Mexico. It is a seaport and industrial and commercial center, and also a tourist resort. Pop 171 835.

MAZE, a prime tool of animal psychology studies. The animal is introduced at the "start" position and must solve the maze to reach an incentive, usually food. There are two distinct aims in the use of mazes: to examine the animal's learning ability; or to test its intelligence and/or senses. Mazes may be very simple: some have no more than a single straight passage. (See also LABYRINTH.)

MAZEPA, Ivan Stepanovich (c1640–1709), Cossack *hetman* (chief) who vainly aided CHARLES XII of Sweden against PETER THE GREAT, hoping to win independence for his native Ukraine. BYRON's *Mazeppa* immortalizes a youthful incident in which he is said to have been tied to a wild horse by a jealous Polish nobleman.

MAZURKA, a type of Polish folk dance, made famous through many piano pieces by CHOPIN.

MAZZINI, Giuseppe (1805–1872), Italian patriot and a leading propagandist of the RISORGIMENTO. A member of the CARBONARI, he was exiled in 1831, formed the "Young Italy" societies, and from France, Switzerland and England promoted his ideal of a united, democratic Italy. In 1849 he became a leader of the short-lived republic of Rome, but was soon in exile again, continuing his revolutionary propaganda and organizing abortive uprisings. His relations with the moderate CAVOUR were strained, and the actual unification of Italy, in which he took little part, fell short of his popular republican ideals.

MBABANE, the capital of Swaziland, SE Africa, 93mi WSW of Maputo. It is a commercial and administrative center, with no significant industry. Pop (est.) 17 850.

MBOYA, Tom (1930–1969), Kenyan political leader. General secretary of the Kenya Federation of Labor (1953–63), and a member of the colonial legislative assembly (1957), he played a key role in securing Kenya's independence. Economics minister from 1964, he was established as a likely successor to KENYATTA, and his assassination led to rioting and political tension.

MEAD, George Herbert (1863–1931), US social psychologist and philosopher. Initially influenced by HEGEL, he then moved toward PRAGMATISM. He attempted to explain social psychology in terms of the evolution of the self, and through analyses of spoken language.

MEAD, Lake, on the Colorado R, 25mi E of Las Vegas, formed by the HOOVER DAM. It is 115mi long and 8mi at its widest, and is the largest artificial reservoir in the US. It provides hydroelectric power and irrigation.

MEAD, Margaret (1901–), US cultural anthropologist best known for books such as *Coming of Age in Samoa* (1928), *Growing Up in New Guinea* (1930), *The Mountain Arapesh* (3 vols., 1938–49), and *Male and Female* (1949). A first autobiography, *Blackberry Winter*, appeared in 1972.

MEADE, George Gordon (1815–1872), Union general in the US CIVIL WAR who, as commander of the Army of the Potomac, won the Battle of GETTYSBURG. Promoted to brigadier-general, he commanded his army under U. S. GRANT in the 1864 WILDERNESS campaign.

MEADOW BEAUTY, popular name for several North American plants of the genus *Rhexia*. Best known is *Rhexia virginica*, or deer grass, which grows in sandy marshes. Family: Melastomaceae.

MEADOWLARKS, medium-sized perching birds of the New World. They are ground-dwelling birds of open country, feeding mainly on insects. They jab the bill into knotted vegetation, then open it so that any insects present will be exposed. The eyes are placed so that the bird can look between the open mandibles.

MEADOW RUE, common name for species of the genus *Thalictrum*, notably *Thalictrum aquifolium*, which is native to Europe and N Asia. Some species are grown as garden ornamentals. Family: Ranunculaceae.

MEADOW SAFFRON, *Colchicum autumnale*, CROCUS-like ornamental plants that produce lilac-colored flowers in the autumn. The CORMS and seeds contain a toxic ALKALOID, COLCHICINE. Family: Liliaceae.

MEADOWSWEET, common name for a number of plants that produce fragment clusters of small white flowers. The North American species (*Spiraea alba* and *S. latifolia*) are shrubs, while the European meadowsweet (*Filipendula ulmaria*) is a perennial herb characteristic of damp habitats. Family: Rosaceae.

MEADVILLE, city in NW Pa., seat of Crawford Co. Manufactures include zippers, yarns, machinery and metal goods. Pop 16573.

MEALY BUGS, a large family, Pseudococcidae, of SCALE INSECTS, whose adults are covered with a waxy secretion of mealy or cottony texture. Members of the HOMOPTERA, they are important agricultural pests.

MEAN, MEDIAN AND MODE, three terms concerned with different types of averaging processes. An average, in the simplest arithmetical sense, of n terms is the SUM of those terms divided by n. Hence the average of 4, 6 and 9 is $\frac{19}{3}$ or 6.333 . . . . The average value A of a FUNCTION between $x = a$ and $x = b$ is defined as the AREA under the curve of the function (see CALCULUS) divided by $(b - a)$:

$$A = \frac{\int_a^b f(x)\,dx}{b-a}$$

Mean. The simple arithmetical average described above is an arithmetic mean (see also PROGRESSION). The geometric mean of n numbers is defined as the nth ROOT of their PRODUCT. The geometric mean of 4, 6 and 9 is thus $\sqrt[3]{4\times6\times9} = \sqrt[3]{216} = 6$. That of x and y is $\sqrt{xy}$. The geometric mean of a set of positive terms is always less than their arithmetic mean.

Median and Mode. In STATISTICS, ranking all the observations of a sample in increasing order of frequency, the frequency of the middle observation (or, if there is an even number of observations, the arithmetic mean of the two middle observations), is described as the median. The observation with the highest frequency is termed the mode: should a sample contain two (or three) observations of equal frequency greater than that of any of the other observations, it is termed bimodal (or trimodal).

MEANY, George (1894–), US labor leader, president since 1955 of the AMERICAN FEDERATION OF LABOR AND CONGRESS OF INDUSTRIAL ORGANZATIONS (AFL-CIO). He was president of the N.Y. state Federation of Labor (1934) and secretary-treasurer (1939) and president (1952) of the AFL.

MEASLES, common INFECTIOUS DISEASE, caused by a VIRUS. It involves a characteristic sequence of FEVER, HEADACHE and malaise followed by CONJUNCTIVITIS and RHINITIS, and then the development of a typical rash, with blotchy ERYTHEMA affecting the SKIN of the FACE, trunk and limbs. COUGH may indicate infections in small BRONCHI and this may progress to virus PNEUMONIA. Secondary bacterial infection may lead to middle EAR infection or pneumonia. ENCEPHALITIS is seen in a small but significant number of cases and is a major justification for VACCINATION against this common childhood disease. Recently, an abnormal and delayed IMMUNITY to measles virus has been associated with a number of BRAIN diseases, including MULTIPLE SCLEROSIS.

MEASURE. See WEIGHTS AND MEASURES.

MEASURING INSTRUMENTS. See INSTRUMENTS, SCIENTIFIC.

MEASURING WORMS, or **Inch worms** or **loopers**, larvae of a family of MOTHS, Geometridae, which have prolegs only at the very front and very end of the abdomen. They therefore progress in a series of looping movements, as if "measuring out" distances. A few species occur in large numbers and may do extensive damage to foliage.

MEAT, the flesh of any animal, in common use usually restricted to the edible portions of cattle (beef and veal), sheep (lamb) and swine (pork), and less commonly applied to those of the rabbit, horse, goat and deer (venison). Meat consists of skeletal MUSCLE, connective TISSUE, FAT and BONE; the amount of connective tissue determines the toughness of the meat. Meat is an extremely important foodstuff. A daily intake of 100g (3½oz) provides 45% of daily PROTEIN, 36% of daily iron and important amounts of B VITAMINS, but only 9% of daily energy. Meat protein is particularly valuable as it supplies eight of the AMINO ACIDS which human beings cannot make for themselves. The meat-packing industry employs about 350000 people in the US.

MECCA, Arabic Makka, chief city of the Hejaz region of Saudi Arabia, birthplace of MUHAMMAD and the most holy city of ISLAM. The courtyard of the great Haram mosque encloses the sacred shrine, the KAABA; nearby is the holy Zem-Zem well. Pilgrimage to Mecca, the *hajj*, is a duty for all Muslims able to perform it. The economy of Mecca depends on the pilgrims. Pop 250000.

MECHANICAL DRAWING, or engineering drawing, the representation of a component or structure in such a way that it can be formed or assembled by someone else without error or misunderstanding. To this end, various projections are used—isometric and orthographic being the most important (see DESCRIPTIVE GEOMETRY; PROJECTIVE GEOMETRY). A person who executes mechanical drawings is a draftsman. (See also PERSPECTIVE.)

MECHANICS, the branch of applied mathematics dealing with the actions of forces on bodies. There are three branches: kinematics, which deals with relationships between distance, time, velocity and acceleration; dynamics, dealing with the way forces produce motion, and statics, dealing with the forces acting on a motionless body.

Kinematics. In kinematics we deal with distance and time, which are SCALAR quantities, and with VELOCITY and ACCELERATION, which are VECTOR quantities. Velocity is the rate of change of position of a body in a particular direction with respect to time: it thus has both magnitude and direction. Its magnitude is the scalar quantity speed (S), related to distance (s) and time (t) by the equation $S = s/t$; similarly velocity ($\mathbf{v}$) is related to distance and time by $\mathbf{v} = ds/dt$ (see CALCULUS). Acceleration is rate of change of velocity with respect to time: $\mathbf{a} = d\mathbf{v}/dt = d^2s/dt^2$. Thus, if velocity is measured in km/s, acceleration is measured in km/s^2.

Often we have to consider the combination of velocities in different directions. Consider a ship sailing due E at velocity $\mathbf{x}$, and carried N by a current with velocity $\mathbf{y}$. The resultant velocity $\mathbf{z}$ can be found by using a diagram where the arrows represent the velocities in both magnitude and direction or by TRIGONOMETRY. Velocities can be resolved in a similar way (by resolving we mean simply finding its components in different directions).

Dynamics is based on NEWTON's three laws of motion: that a body continues in its state of motion unless compelled by a force to act otherwise; that the rate of change of motion (acceleration) is proportional to the applied force and occurs in the direction of the force, and that every action is opposed by an equal and opposite reaction. The first gives an idea of INERTIA, which is proportional to the MASS and opposes the change of motion: combining the first with the second, we find that $\mathbf{F} \propto m\mathbf{a}$, where $\mathbf{F}$ is the force, m the mass of the body and $\mathbf{a}$ the acceleration produced by the FORCE. In practice we choose units such that $\mathbf{F} = m\mathbf{a}$. (See also MOMENTUM.)

Newton suggested that gravitational attraction existed between all bodies, and proposed a law to describe this: if two bodies, masses m_1 and m_2 are separated by distance d, the force of attraction, $\mathbf{F}$, between them is given by $\mathbf{F} = G(m_1m_2)/d^2$, where G is the universal gravitational constant (see GRAVITATION). Near the surface of the earth we find for a body of mass m that $\mathbf{F} \propto m$ (G and the mass of the earth are constant and the distance from the surface to the center is approximately so). We usually set $\mathbf{F} = m\mathbf{g}$ where $\mathbf{g}$ is another constant, the ACCELERATION due to gravity (usually denoted g although it is a vector).

Statics. We can combine forces much as we do velocities. If forces $\mathbf{P}_1$ and $\mathbf{P}_2$, with resultant $\mathbf{R}$, act at a point, there must be a third force, $\mathbf{P}_3$, equal and opposite to $\mathbf{R}$, for equilibrium. We can combine forces similarly over more complex structures. For a bridge whose weight (w) acts as a downward force $\mathbf{W}$ at the center, the upward reactions $\mathbf{R}_1$ and $\mathbf{R}_2$ at the piers must be such that $\mathbf{R}_1 + \mathbf{R}_2 = -\mathbf{W}$ for it to be in EQUILIBRIUM. Similarly, we examine the members of the bridge to determine the stresses acting on each (see MATERIALS, STRENGTH OF; VECTOR ANALYSIS).

MECHANICSVILLE, Battle of, also called the Battle of Beaver Dam Creek, June 26, 1862, one of the SEVEN DAYS' BATTLES in the US CIVIL WAR. The Confederate force of A. P. Hill was defeated some 7mi NE of Richmond, Va.

MECHANIZATION AND AUTOMATION, the use of machines wholly or partly to replace human labor. The two words are often used synonymously, but it is of value to distinguish mechanization as requiring human aid, automation as self-controlling.

The most familiar automated device is the domestic THERMOSTAT. This is set to switch off the heating circuit if room temperature exceeds a certain value, to switch it on if the temperature falls below a certain value. Once set, no further human attention is required: a machine is in full control of a machine.

The thermostat is a sensing element; the information it detects is fed back to the production mechanism (the heater), which adjusts accordingly. All automated processes work on this principle. In fact, fully automated processes are still rare: most often the role of sensing element will be taken over by a human being, who will check the accuracy of the machine and adjust it if needed.

The most versatile devices we have are COMPUTERS: very often, the complexity of their physical construction is more than matched by that of the network of subprograms which they contain. Data can be fed in automatically or by human operators and the computer can be programmed to respond in many ways: to present information; adjust and control other machines, or even to take decisions. Computerized automation plays a larger role in our lives than most of us realize: airline and theater agents often book seat reservations with a computer, not a staffed box office; food manufacture is often automatically controlled from raw materials to packaged product; atomic energy is controlled automatically where radiation prohibits the presence of humans, possible leaks or even explosions being forestalled by machine; the justification of the columns of this book has been performed by a fully automated process. In addition, man would not have reached the moon had it not been for computerized automation.

Since mechanization and automation emerged in the "Second Industrial Revolution," they have been associated with all kinds of sociological problems and upheavals. And this is more than ever true today. Long-term benefits to the human race have to be balanced against short-term evils such as unemployment and its attendant human sufferings. (See also LINEAR PROGRAMMING; MASS PRODUCTION; MACHINE TOOLS; SERVOMECHANISM.)

MECHNIKOV, Ilya. See METCHNIKOFF, ÉLIE.

MECKLENBURG DECLARATION OF INDEPENDENCE, resolution allegedly passed on May 20, 1775, by citizens of Mecklenburg Co., N.C., declaring their independence of Britain. Evidence exists for anti-British resolutions later that month, but not for one on May 20; historians have long argued for and against N.C.'s tradition on the matter.

MECOPTERA, the Scorpion-flies, an order of insects which are mostly carnivorous. The males have bulbous genitals, carried above the body like a scorpion's sting.

MEDAN, city in NE Sumatra, Indonesia, capital of North Sumatra province. It is a trade and transportation center for tobacco, rubber, tea, coffee and palm-oil, and has some manufacturing industry. Pop 635562.

MEDAWAR, Sir Peter Brian (1915–), British zoologist who shared with F. M. BURNET the 1960 Nobel Prize for Physiology or Medicine for their work on immunological tolerance. Inspired by Burnet's ideas, Medawar showed that if fetal mice were injected with cells from eventual donors, skin grafts made onto them later from those donors would "take," thus showing the possibility of acquired tolerance and hence, ultimately, organ TRANSPLANTS.

MEDEA, in Greek mythology, princess of Colchis, whose sorcery helped JASON steal the Golden Fleece. They married, but when he left her for Creusa of Corinth, she killed Creusa and her own children by

Jason in revenge. She is the subject of a play by EURIPIDES.

MEDELLÍN, city in W central Colombia. It is Colombia's chief industrial city, producing textiles, steel, chemicals and machinery. Gold is mined nearby. It is also a cultural and educational center. Pop 1 208 000.

MEDES, ancient INDO-EUROPEAN people of W Asia. Originally nomadic warrior herdsmen, they settled Media (in modern NW Iran) c900 BC. They controlled PERSIA by 700 BC, and in 612 BC, in alliance with Babylon, destroyed the Assyrian empire (see BABYLONIA AND ASSYRIA). c550 BC CYRUS THE GREAT captured Ecbatana, the Median capital, and made Media a Persian province.

MEDFORD, city in NE Mass. It is a residential suburb N of Boston, with some manufacturing industry. Pop 64 397.

MEDFORD, city in SW Ore., seat of Jackson Co. A resort center, it also serves a farming and lumber region. Pop 28 454.

MEDIAN. See MEAN, MEDIAN AND MODE.

MEDIATION. See ARBITRATION.

MEDICAID, US government-financed system of medical aid to people under 65 years old of low income, introduced alongside the MEDICARE legislation in 1965. The federal government pays from 50% to 83% of the costs for anyone eligible, as determined by each state separately.

MEDICARE, US government-financed system of medical and hospital insurance for people aged 65 and over. It was set up in 1965 by legislation keenly supported by President Johnson. It was opposed by the American Medical Association who objected on principle to possible government intervention, although the cost of private treatment had risen beyond the means of most older people.

MEDICI, Italian family of bankers, princes and patrons of the arts who controlled Florence almost continually from the 1420s to 1737, and provided cardinals, popes LEO X, CLEMENT VII and LEO XI and two queens of France. The French spelling of the name is Médicis.

The foundations of the family's power were laid by **Giovanni di Bicci de' Medici** (1360–1429). His son **Cosimo de' Medici** (1389–1464), was effectively ruler of Florence from 1434 and was voted "Father of the Country" after his death. He founded the great Laurentian Library and patronized such artists as DONATELLO and GHIBERTI. His grandson **Lorenzo** (1449–1492), called "the Magnificent," was Italy's most brilliant Renaissance prince. Himself a fine poet, he patronized BOTTICELLI, GHIRLANDAIO, the young MICHELANGELO and many other artists. His son **Piero** (1471–1503), was expelled from Florence (1494) by a popular rising led by SAVONAROLA. The family were restored in 1512; **Lorenzo** (1492–1519), ruled from 1513 under the guidance of his uncle **Giovanni** (1475–1521), who as Pope Leo X was a magnificent patron of the arts in Rome. The ruthless **Cosimo I** (1519–1574), doubled Florentine territory and power and was created grand duke of Tuscany in 1569. The later Medicis were less distinguished, and the line died out with **Gian Gastone** (1671–1737).

Catherine de Médicis (1519–1589), wife of HENRY II of France, was regent from 1560 for her second son CHARLES IX, and helped plan the SAINT BARTHOLOMEW'S DAY MASSACRE. **Marie de Médicis** (1573–1642), second wife of HENRY IV of France (1600), was powerful regent for her son LOUIS XIII (1610–17), but was forced into exile (1630) by Cardinal RICHELIEU.

MEDICINE, the art and science of healing. Within the last 150 years or so medicine has become dominated by scientific principles. Prior to this, healing was mainly a matter of tradition and magic. Many of these prescientific attitudes have persisted to the present day.

The earliest evidence of medical practice is seen in Neolithic (see STONE AGE) skulls in which holes have been bored, presumably to let evil spirits out, a practice called trepanning (see TREPHINE). Treatment in primitive cultures was either empirical or magical. Empirical treatment included bloodletting, dieting, primitive surgery and the administration of numerous potions, lotions and herbal remedies (some used in modern medicines). For serious ailments, magical treatment, involving propitiation of the gods, special rituals or the provision of charms, was performed by the medicine man or witch doctor, who was usually both doctor and priest (see SHAMANISM). Exorcism, the casting out of devils, and FAITH HEALING are still practiced in modern societies. ACUPUNCTURE and OSTEOPATHY, both being ancient and empirical, are also practiced today.

Detail from Giorgio Vasari's portrait of the famous Medici family's most illustrious member, Lorenzo, called "the Magnificent." One of the great figures of the Italian Renaissance, he was not only a skilled statesman and lavish patron of the arts but was himself a writer and poet of talent and imagination.

The growth of scientific medicine began with the Greek philosophy of nature. The great Greek physician HIPPOCRATES, with whose name is associated the Hippocratic oath which codifies the physician's ideals of humanity and service, has justly been called the father of medicine. Galen of Pergamum, the encyclopedist of classical medicine, clearly distinguished ANATOMY from PHYSIOLOGY. Medieval medicine was basically a corrupted Galenism. The 16th century saw the dawn of modern medicine. Men such as FABRICIUS, VESALIUS and William HARVEY revived the critical, observational approach to medical research. Perhaps the most far-reaching advances since then have been in preventive medicine, anesthesia and drug therapy. Preventive medicine was attempted in medieval times when ships arriving in Europe during the Black Death were "quarantined" for 40 days. More recent major milestones have been Edward JENNER's work on VACCINATION and the "germ theory of disease" proposed by Louis PASTEUR and developed by Robert KOCH. ANAESTHESIA and ASEPSIS (see LISTER, JOSEPH) made possible great advances in SURGERY. Crawford LONG and James SIMPSON were both pioneers of their use. Drug therapy originated with herbal remedies, but perhaps the two most important discoveries in this field both came in the 20th century: that of INSULIN by Frederick BANTING and Charles BEST, and that of PENICILLIN by Alexander FLEMING. (See also ANIBIOTICS; CHEMOTHERAPY; DRUGS; SULFA DRUGS.)

Medical training to high set standards is used to protect society against charlatans and is usually undertaken in universities and hospitals. Since the progress of medical knowledge is very rapid, doctors today undergo continual retraining to keep them up to date. Socialized medicine, under the name MEDICARE, was set up in the US in 1965 and helps to pay the costs of medical care. However, several other countries have more comprehensive programs of socialized medicine.

The success of medicine in preventing disease is largely responsible for today's population explosion. This has stimulated an extensive re-examination of traditional attitudes to medical ethics, particularly in the areas of CONTRACEPTION, ABORTION and EUTHANASIA. (See also DISEASE.)

MEDICINE BOW MOUNTAINS, range of the Rocky Mts, straddling the Col.-Wyo. border NW of Denver, mostly within Medicine Bow National Forest. Medicine Bow Peak, the highest, is 12 013ft high.

MEDICINE HAT, city in SE Alberta, Canada. Its economy depends on ranching and the exploitation of one of the world's largest natural gas fields. Pop 26 518.

MEDICINE MAN. See SHAMANISM.

MEDILL, Joseph (1823–1899), Canadian-born US editor and publisher of the *Chicago Tribune*, and a founder of the REPUBLICAN PARTY. A strong emancipationist and admirer of Lincoln, he was elected mayor of Chicago in 1871.

MEDINA, holy Muslim city and place of pilgrimage in Hejaz, Saudi Arabia, 210mi N of Mecca. The prophet Mohammed came to Medina after his HEGIRA (flight) from Mecca (622 AD), and the chief mosque contains his tomb. A walled city, Medina stands in a fertile oasis noted for its dates, grains and vegetables. Pop 100 000.

MEDINA, city and Medina Co. seat, N Ohio, 18mi WNW of Akron, mainly providing services for a farm area. Pop 10 913.

MEDITERRANEAN FRUIT FLY, *Ceratitis capitata*, a serious pest of fruit in Africa, Australia and South America, attacking, in particular, peaches, apricots and citrus fruits. The larvae completely destroy the fruits and whole harvests may be lost. The maggots are capable of prodigious leaps of about 100mm (4in) high and over distances of 200mm (8in).

MEDITERRANEAN SEA, intercontinental sea between Europe, Asia and Africa, connected to the Atlantic Ocean in the west by the Strait of Gibraltar and to the Black Sea by the Dardanelles and Bosporus. The man-made Suez Canal provides the link with the Indian Ocean via the Red Sea. Peninsular Italy, Sicily, Malta, Pantelleria and Tunisia's Cape Bon mark the dividing narrows between the eastern and western basins. The many islands of the western basin include Sicily, Sardinia, Elba, Corsica and the Balearics. Crete, Cyprus, Rhodes and the numerous Aegean islands are contained in the eastern basin. Geologically, the Mediterranean is a relic of Tethys, an ocean which separated Eurasia from Africa 200

Medicine

Our helpful parasites

How many living creatures enter a room when you come in? The question might have been resented by a clean and healthy citizen of a few generations back. Confident of his freedom from fleas, lice, worms and suchlike, he might have replied indignantly that *he* did not carry parasites. He would have been far from the truth. It is technically impossible to conduct an accurate census of the inhabitants of our bodies. However, each human being living on the surface of this planet has some hundreds of microorganisms (bacteria, some fungi and probably some mites, which are animals) living on or in his skin; and for each one of these surface residents there are another hundred or so (mainly bacteria) living within us, mostly in our intestines. The correct answer to the question is that something like 10^{14} (one hundred million million) living creatures enter the room.

Such figures, if unfamiliar, may be startling—even horrifying. "Microbe," "germ" and "parasite" are heavily loaded words, frequently terms of abuse. This reflects a widespread misconception about microorganisms. Since microbiology developed largely as a medical subject, preoccupied with finding the causes of infectious diseases, it has given us a picture of the microbial world about as fair as the concept of a human community we might derive from police records. In most microbiological research, a bacterium, virus or some other microorganism turns out to be the villain, whereas little is said about the uncountable millions of innocent and even useful microbial citizens with no criminal record. So we have come to think of microorganisms as bad, to be avoided or to be killed with the latest all-powerful disinfectant.

Louis Pasteur, the great founding father of microbiology, knew better than this. In 1861 he wrote: "If microscopic beings were to disappear from our globe, the surface of the earth would be encumbered with dead organic matter and corpses of all kinds, animal and vegetable . . . Without them, life would become impossible because death would be incomplete." For such organisms, which break down dead organic matter into raw materials for use by succeeding generations of living creatures, microbiologists use the name *saprophytes*. It is on their activities that the gardener depends when he makes compost, and on a larger scale, as Pasteur indicated, we are totally dependent on them for our physical existence; but they do not qualify for further discussion in this article because they are not parasites (with arguable exceptions, such as the bacteria which live on and break down food residues between our teeth or in our intestines).

Parasites are creatures that derive some or all of their vital needs from other (usually larger) living creatures known as their hosts. Our parasites can be classified according to their effects on us. Those which cause diseases, the *pathogens*, are only a tiny minority but receive most of the publicity. The vast "silent majority" are either *commensals* (literally, those sharing the same table) which derive nourishment from us but give us nothing in return, or *symbionts* which live in a mutually beneficial relationship with us—if you like, either non-paying or paying guests. It is with the last group that this article is concerned, but we must not be misled by our terminology, which oversimplifies a complex and often poorly understood situation. Because a particular type of organism is known to be capable of causing disease, a potential pathogen, that does not mean that it cannot lead a commensal or symbiotic existence; indeed, most of them do so most of the time, just as most criminals spend most of their lives in other activities than crime. Furthermore, the use of the labels commensal and symbiont is at least as much a comment on the state of our knowledge of the organisms as it is upon their actual ways of life: we call them commensals when we have not discovered whether and how they pay the rent. Furthermore, when we have described the relationship of a parasite to its human host, we have dealt with only one facet of its complex social life. Its relationship with its many and varied microbial neighbors may be at least as important to it, and far harder for us to unravel.

Symbionts are much more difficult to identify than pathogens. When a scientist is on the tracks of a pathogen, he has something reasonably well defined to investigate—an abnormality called a disease. If in association with this abnormality he can consistently detect the presence of an abnormal organism, or of a normal organism in abnormal numbers or in an abnormal site, he is usually well on the way to finding the causative organism (though sometimes the scientist will find that the presence of the organism is an effect of the disease rather than its cause). If he can cultivate the suspect organism in the laboratory and then use it to reproduce the disease in experimental animals or in human volunteers, the chase is over. But spotting a symbiont at work is another matter. The scientist must start from a normal situation, analyze it, decide which component to study, and then try to associate with that component one particular organism or group of organisms from among the plethora of promising candidates included in the "normal flora" of the relevant part of the host's body. Usually the ecosystem is so complex that the scientist has little hope of understanding it until he can take it to pieces—and in doing that he may produce serious distortions of the effects he is trying to study.

The symbiotic activities of some of our resident organisms have been elucidated by finding out what they can do in the test tube or the culture plate, away from the host. Here the scientist can give them appropriate conditions and *substrates* (living bases) and look for activities and products that might be useful to their usual hosts. However, this method has severe limitations. If we study one type of organism on its own in "pure culture" we may be debarred from detecting potentially useful activities that depend on interplay with other microbial species or strains, just as an observer from outer space would have difficulty in discovering the value of a rowing cox studied in an otherwise empty boat. On the other hand, if we study mixed cultures, their interactions with one another may be too complex for us to analyze. Such work, therefore, has proceeded slowly.

Another source of information over the last 40 years has been the study of "germ-free" animals, born by caesarian section and brought up in sterile conditions. Such animals have special dietary needs and other special problems, and in some cases it has been possible to correct an abnormality by allowing the animal to develop known microbial populations. General principles about symbiosis between microorganisms and their animal hosts have been established in this way, but detailed conclusions about the activities and value of our own microbial parasites cannot be drawn from such animal experiments; it is of course

million years ago. Its name, given by the Romans, reflects its central position and importance in the ancient world. The limited access from the Atlantic and the confined entries to both the Black and Red seas, made it through history a natural theater of naval and maritime power.

MEDLAR, *Mespilus germanica*, small deciduous tree belonging to the ROSE family (Rosaceae) and indigenous to parts of Europe and Asia. It is cultivated for its small, brown, apple-like fruit, which are extremely acid when first picked, but become palatable after a few weeks.

MÉDOC, wine-growing district NW of Bordeaux, in the department of Gironde, France. Its vineyards produce some of the most famous of French wines, including Château Lafite and Château Latour.

MEDUSA, one of the two basic forms shown by many of the CNIDARIA. Medusae are usually free-swimming sexually reproductive forms. (See JELLYFISH.)

MEDUSA, in Greek mythology, most celebrated of the GORGON sisters, the very sight of whom turned men to stone. Medusa was eventually decapitated by PERSEUS, who avoided her fatal gaze by looking at her reflection in his bronze shield.

MEERKAT, or **Suricate**, a small mongoose confined to southern Africa that has developed separately from other species. They live in colonies in burrows in sandy areas, feeding on insects, lizards and mammals. They do not forage far; when local food supplies are exhausted the whole colony migrates in search of new feeding grounds.

MEERSCHAUM, or **sepiolite**, fibrous CLAY mineral, light and porous, consisting of hydrated magnesium silicate. Chiefly occurring in Turkey, it is used to make tobacco pipes.

MEERUT, city in N India, capital of Meerut Division in Uttar Pradesh state. The first SEPOY REBELLION began here, May 1857. Today the city is a fast-growing industrial center. Pop 271 325.

MEG-, mega- (M), SI prefix multiplying a unit one-millionfold. Examples include the megahertz (MHz), megametre (Mm) and megohm (MΩ). One megagram is one tonne (t). (See SI UNITS.)

MEGALITHIC MONUMENTS, large, usually undressed stone monuments found principally in Europe but also in many other parts of the world, believed to date usually from the late STONE AGE and early BRONZE AGE. They are of four main types: the **menhir** (from Breton *hir*, long, and *men*, stone) or single standing stone; the **stone circle**, or circles, as exemplified by STONEHENGE; the chamber or room, usually associated with a tomb, the most ancient of which is the DOLMEN; and the **alignment**, or row of stones, such as those at CARNAC.

MEGALOSAURUS, a genus of giant carnivorous DINOSAURS of the Jurassic. Fossil remains are fragmentary and apart from the fact that they were bipedal nothing is known of this group.

MEGAPHONE, device to amplify the sound of a voice. It amplifies the sound because of its shape (a hollow cone of metal or plastic), and increases the effective sound power by concentrating the sound in a single direction. Electric megaphones combine a MICROPHONE, AMPLIFIER and LOUDSPEAKER.

MEGAPODES. See MOUNDBIRDS.

MEGARON, archaeological term for the main inner room or hall of a house in the AEGEAN CIVILIZATIONS, characteristically entered through a short porch at one end.

MEGATHERIUM. See GROUND SLOTHS.

MEGATON, unit descriptive of the explosive power of the HYDROGEN BOMB. Each megaton represents the equivalent explosive power of one million tons of TNT.

MEGIDDO, ancient fortified city 15mi S of Haifa, Israel, overlooking the plain of Esdraelon. Excavations have shown that it was inhabited c4000–450 BC. The city was the scene of many battles: the eschatological ARMAGEDDON was named for it.

MEGILLOTH, five Jewish sacred scrolls grouped together in the Hagiographa of the Hebrew not possible to make comparable observations on human beings, except as occasional by-products of highly abnormal situations.

Our most direct information on this subject has come as a result of the use of antibiotics and other antibacterial drugs in medicine. These drugs are very far from being precision tools for the elimination of pathogens. Even those with the narrowest ranges of antimicrobial activity will kill or inhibit many species besides those at which they are directed, they have no means of discriminating between "good" and "bad" germs. Increasingly in recent years it has been recognized that some of the undesirable side effects of antimicrobial drug treatment can be attributed to disappearance of elements of the host's normal microbial population, and are reversed when these elements reappear. It is indeed the increasing use of powerful antimicrobials which has drawn scientists' attention to our symbionts and has made it necessary for us to understand them better. When there was little scientists could do which interfered with them or prevented them going about their normal business, we could afford to be ignorant of them. Now that they are liable to be mown down by indiscriminate weapons directed at real or hypothetical pathogens, we are learning to value them and to treat them with more respect.

Some early bacteriologists thought that the vast numbers of bacteria in our intestines were an essential part of our mechanism for digesting food. Ruminant animals do in fact depend on bacteria in the rumen (the first compartment of the stomach) for digestion of cellulose and other polysaccharides; similarly rabbits and some other herbivores are indebted to their cecal bacteria; but it seems that man, in common with many animal species, manages most of his digestive processes without bacterial assistance. However, our intestinal organisms do synthesize vitamin K and other vitamins for us, and they do an important job in the conservation of bile salts; these salts are excreted in the bile in conjugated, or compound, form, carry out their digestive functions in the small intestine, and then further down the intestine are broken down by the action of bacteria and so made available for reabsorption into the bloodstream and return to the liver for reuse. There are hints, largely from animal experiments, about other ways in which intestinal bacteria help our digestive functions and nutrition, and there is doubtless a great deal more to be discovered on these subjects.

However, the main contribution to our wellbeing made by our resident microbial populations is almost certainly in the realm of defense against potential pathogens. In descriptions of the body's defenses we usually read about its mechanical defenses, such as its relatively impermeable covering of skin; its chemical defenses, such as tears and gastric juice; its cellular defenses, the white blood cells and other phagocytes which ingest and destroy invaders; and its humoral defenses, the antibodies which react with particular organisms and in various ways assist their elimination. Seldom do we read about the body's bacterial defenses and the ways in which its normal population of microbial residents makes it hard for potential pathogens to establish adequate bridgeheads for invasion.

We are familiar these days with the problems of chemical pollution of the environment, such as the elimination of fish from rivers and lakes by factory effluents. The activities of some of our symbionts are rather like this, with the important difference that the effects of their "pollution" are beneficial to us, not harmful. The best-known example of bacterial contribution to the chemical defenses of the body is found in the genital tract of the healthy woman of childbearing age, which is in large measure protected against infection by the acidity of the vaginal secretion. The cells lining the vagina provide glycogen, used by bacteria called lactobacilli for their own purposes; in doing this the lactobacilli produce a concentration of lactic acid higher than most other microorganisms can tolerate. Similarly, the microbial population of human skin is restricted to a rather small number of species, and many potential pathogens are unable to survive there for more than a short while, because of the concentrations of fatty acids found there; these fatty acids are themselves produced by the action of some of the normal residents on glyceride compounds in the secretions of skin glands. Other examples of resident bacteria producing substances with rather generalized antimicrobial activity have been shown to occur in the mouth; for example, normal mouth streptococci can form hydrogen peroxide, a substance which in higher concentrations is used medically as a wound disinfectant.

Lactic acid, fatty acids and hydrogen peroxide are examples of substances produced by our resident bacteria and effective against wide ranges of microorganisms, most of which are unrelated to the producers. Rather different are the antibiotic-like substances (*bacteriocins* is one name for some of them) produced by some of our normal residents in the laboratory, and probably also in their natural habitat; these are much more selective in their action and in many cases are active mainly against organisms closely related to their producers. It is probably by such means that some strains of harmless skin staphylococci protect us against the pathogenic staphylococci which cause boils and many other forms of skin sepsis.

The exhaustion of essential materials is another way in which our normal parasites can make things difficult for potentially harmful organisms. It is probable that some of our normal throat streptococci discourage in this way the growth of those other streptococci which are the commonest cause of sore throats and tonsillitis. In the intestine, any available oxygen is used up by the enormous bacterial populations. Consequently, only those organisms which do not need oxygen can thrive there, and some oxygen-requiring organisms which might make a nuisance of themselves in the intestine are normally excluded.

These and other mechanisms, some understood at least in part and others not yet discovered, combine to preserve the balance of our microbial populations. Like our other forms of defense against infection, the bacterial defenses are not impregnable and are overwhelmed from time to time, but without them we should succumb far more often. We are now able to make defeat of infections more likely by using antibacterial drugs. Penicillin is a remarkably useful means of treating certain bacterial infections, and when given in modest dosage it does little to upset our normal bacterial populations; but when it is given in very large amounts (for which there are sometimes good reasons) it can so disturb the balance of power in the mouth, the throat, the vagina and elsewhere that unpleasant local infections can occur. The organisms responsible for these are commonly yeasts or intestinal bacteria that have been released from the restraints normally imposed on them by penicillin-sensitive bacteria. Antibiotics with wider ranges of action than penicillin can cause even greater havoc, for example by largely depopulating the intestine and leaving it at the mercy of staphylococci which in such circumstances can cause severe enteritis.

In addition to this help to invading pathogens, antibiotic treatment can also sometimes hinder eviction of pathogens by the normal inhabitants. This is probably the reason why antibiotic treatment tends to lengthen rather than shorten the period during which people who have had salmonella gastroenteritis continue to carry and excrete the salmonellae: the main impact of the treatment falls not on the salmonellae bacteria but on the normal inhabitants which, left to themselves, could have handled the situation more efficiently.

Conservation of our terrestrial environment has rightly received an increasing amount of attention and publicity in recent years, and we know that it is vitally important to the future of mankind. A balanced view of the microorganisms in the human body shows that conservation of our personal microbial environment can also be vitally important.

scriptures. They are read at certain festivals and consist of the Song of Solomon, Ruth, Lamentations, Ecclesiastes and Esther.

MEHMET ALI (or Mohammed Ali; c1769–1849), an Albanian soldier who in 1806 became pasha (governor) of the Turkish province of Egypt and founder of the dynasty which ruled until 1952. He extended Egypt's borders and improved the economy. His power rivaled that of his overlord, the Sultan of Turkey.

MEIGHEN, Arthur (1874–1960), Canadian statesman who became Conservative prime minister in 1920. In 1921 he opposed renewal of the Anglo-Japanese alliance, and resigned after the Conservatives were defeated in the general election. Prime minister again in June 1926, he resigned three months later. In 1932 he was elected to the Senate.

MEIJI. See MUTSUHITO.

MEININGEN PLAYERS, German theatrical company, whose European tours (1874–90) had a profound influence on the development of modern theater. The company's founder, George II, Duke of Saxe-Meiningen, introduced many technical innovations and was himself the prototype director.

MEIN KAMPF. See HITLER, ADOLF; NAZISM.

MEIOSIS, a special mechanism of CELL division which results in the formation of a HAPLOID cell which is normally a GAMETE. Meiosis is similar in all plant and animal cells; there are two divisions of the nucleus in the course of which the CHROMOSOMES divide once so that 1 DIPLOID cell gives 4 haploid daughter cells. Meiosis, which is often the occasion of genes "crossing over," is at the heart of genetic segregation.

MEIR, Golda (1898–   ), Israeli leader, prime minister of Israel 1969–74. Born Golda Mabovitch in Kiev, USSR, she was raised in the US and emigrated to Palestine in 1921. She was a prominent figure in the establishment of the State of Israel (1948). Elected to the KNESSET in 1949, she became foreign minister in 1956 and in 1966 was elected general secretary to the dominant Mapai party, later the Israel Labor Party (1968). In 1969 she succeeded Levi Eshkol as premier and formed a broad coalition government. She visited Washington on three occasions to strengthen US support and in 1973 helped Israel to fight off a surprise Egyptian-Syrian attack. In 1974 Mrs. Meir resigned her premiership and was succeeded by General Itzhak Rabin.

MEISTERSINGER, a coveted title taken by poets and singers belonging to certain 15th-century German guilds, who had perfected their art in accordance with an elaborate set of rules and traditions.

MEITNER, Lise (1878–1968), Austrian physicist who worked with Otto HAHN to discover PROTACTINIUM. Following their experiments bombarding URANIUM with NEUTRONS, Meitner collaborated with her nephew, **Otto Robert Frisch** (1904–   ), to discover nuclear FISSION and predict the CHAIN REACTION.

MEKNES, city in Morocco, capital of Meknes province, 36mi WSW of Fez. Founded in the 10th century, it is a commercial center for the agricultural products of the surrounding region. Pop 248 000.

MEKONG RIVER, one of the chief rivers of SE Asia. Rising in the Tibetan highlands, it flows 2 600mi southward through the Yunnan province of China and Laos, along the Thailand border and through Cambodia to its wide fertile delta in S Vietnam, on the South China Sea. The lower 340mi can accommodate medium-sized vessels and PHNOM-PENH is an important port.

MELANCHTHON, Philipp (1497–1560), German scholar and humanist, second to LUTHER in initiating and leading the Protestant REFORMATION in Germany. His *Loci communes* (1521), a systematic statement of Lutheran beliefs, was the first great Protestant work on religious doctrine; and his *Augsburg Confession* (1530) was one of the principal statements of faith in the Lutheran Church.

MELANESIA, one of three main ethnographic

The thriving metropolis of modern Melbourne, a far cry from the small settlement founded here in 1837. Part of its modern harbor complex can be seen in the background.

divisions of the Pacific islands, the other two being MICRONESIA and POLYNESIA. (See also OCEANIA.)

MELANIN, black pigment which lies in various SKIN layers and is responsible for skin color, including the racial variation. It is concentrated in MOLES and FRECKLES. The distribution in the skin determines skin coloring and is altered by light and certain HORMONES.

MELANISM, an excessive development of the dark pigment, MELANIN, in an animal, as in the panther, a black variety of LEOPARD. Animals without any pigmentation are termed ALBINO.

MELBA, Dame Nellie (1861–1931), Australian soprano, born Helen Porter Mitchell. For almost 40 years (1887–1926) hers was one of the most celebrated coloratura voices on the operatic stage. She made her debut as Gilda in Verdi's *Rigoletto* in Brussels in 1887.

MELBOURNE, second largest city in Australia and state capital of Victoria, on the Yarra R. Founded by settlers in 1835, the city is now one of the nation's chief ports and ranks with Sydney as a major industrial center. It leads in the manufacture of textiles, leather goods and aircraft construction, and oil refineries have been built. Pop 2 389 000.

MELBOURNE, city in E Fla., on the Indian R, SE of Orlando. It is a sporting resort and fruit center and is involved in the aerospace industry. Pop 40 236.

MELBOURNE, William Lamb, 2nd Viscount (1779–1848), British statesman. A member of the House of Commons from 1806, he served as chief secretary to Ireland 1827–1828, entered the House of Lords (1829) and as home secretary (1830–34) suppressed agrarian unrest. He became prime minister briefly in 1834 and again 1835–41, when he instructed the young Queen Victoria in her duties.

MELCHIOR, Lauritz (1890–1973), Danish-American tenor. He was originally a baritone, but achieved fame as a Wagnerian tenor—notably in the role of SIEGFRIED—and appeared frequently at BAYREUTH.

MELEAGER, in Greek mythology, warrior son of King Oeneus of Calydon and slayer of the CALYDONIAN BOAR. The earliest account is found in the *Iliad*.

MÉLIÈS, Georges (1861–1938), French movie pioneer, a Paris theater owner and stage illusionist. Impressed by the LUMIÈRE cinematograph, he invented his own camera and mastered its trick possibilities.

MELILLA, military enclave held by Spain on the Mediterranean coast of Morocco since 1497. It was the scene of the revolt that sparked off the SPANISH CIVIL WAR (1936). It exports iron ore. Pop 60 843.

MELLON, Andrew William (1855–1937), US financier and industrialist who was an outstandingly able US treasury secretary (1921–31) under three presidents, reducing the national debt by some nine billion dollars. He was US ambassador to Britain (1932–33). A multimillionaire himself, he founded the Mellon Institute of Industrial Research. His vast art collection formed the basis of the NATIONAL GALLERY OF ART.

MELODRAMA, originally a dramatic recitation interrupted for effect by music, but now associated with the sentimental drama, popular in the 19th century, with plots revolving around a series of improbable and sensational incidents, ending in the triumph of virtue.

MELON, *Cucumis melo*, a vine of the gourd family Cucurbitaceae, cultivated for its juicy sweet-flavored fruits. It is a native to Africa and Asia but is now cultivated in most hot, dry climates. The main types of melon are the canteloupes, the honeydew and the casba. Closely related is the **watermelon** (*Citrullus vulgaris*) which is also native to Africa, but now widely cultivated.

MELOS, one of the CYCLADES islands in the Aegean Sea. About 60sq mi in extent and mountainous, it was important in early times as a source of obsidian. Much excavated, the principal city of the same name yielded the VENUS DE MILO. Pop 4 910.

MELPOMENE, Muse of Tragedy. See MUSES.

MELROSE, city in Middlesex Co., NE Mass., 7mi N of Boston. Primarily a residential suburb of Boston, manufactures include machine tools and electronics equipment. Pop 33 810.

MELROSE PARK, industrial and residential village W of Chicago, Ill. Manufactures include heavy automotive and electronics equipment. Pop 22 706.

MELTING POINT, the temperature at which FUSION occurs, so that a solid and the corresponding liquid are at equilibrium (see PHASE EQUILIBRIUM). For pure compounds it has a precise value equal to the FREEZING POINT.

MELTING POT. See IMMIGRATION.

MELVILLE, Andrew (1545–1622), Scottish educational and religious reformer. Influenced abroad by Theodore BEZA, he returned in 1574 to Scotland where he did much to reorganize the universities, and was chiefly responsible, after John KNOX, for the PRESBYTERIAN organization of the Scottish Church.

MELVILLE, George Wallace (1841–1912), US arctic explorer and naval engineer. Heroic survivor of George DE LONG's expedition (1879) and rescuer of Adolphus GREELY's expedition (1884), he related these adventures in his *In The Lena Delta* (1885). In 1887 he became chief of engineers in the US Navy.

MELVILLE, Herman (1819–1891), one of the greatest of US writers. His world reputation rests mainly on the masterpiece, *Moby-Dick* (1851), and the short novel *Billy Budd*, published posthumously (1924). His whaling and other voyages provided material for several of his earlier, very popular books. *Typee* (1846), his first, was based on his adventures after jumping ship in the Marquesas Islands. *Moby-Dick* is a deeply symbolic work, combining allegory with adventure. Too profound and complex for its audience, the novel was not successful and subsequent books did not recapture his former popularity. It was not until the 1920s that his great talent was fully recognized.

MELVILLE, Lake, 120mi long saltwater lake on the Labrador coast of Newfoundland, Canada, linked with the Atlantic through Hamilton Inlet. A major airbase is on Goose Bay.

MELVILLE PENINSULA, part of Canada's Northwest Territories. Lying to the N of Hudson Bay, it is some 250mi long and is joined to the mainland by the Rae Isthmus.

MELVINDALE, city, residential suburb 8mi WSW of Detroit, Mich. Pop 13 862.

MEMBRANES, layers that form part of the surface of CELLS and which enclose organelles within the cells of all animals and plants. The membranes of the cell wall function to allow some substances into the cell; to exclude others, and actively to transport others into the cell even though the direction of movement may be against existing concentration gradients. Membranes are composed of layers of LIPID or FAT molecules which sandwich a layer of PROTEIN molecules. The protein layer is double but appears as a single layer when viewed under the ELECTRON MICROSCOPE. Thus most membranes appear to be triple-layered, although some appear to be composed of a single layer. Triple-layered membranes are normally 5–10nm thick.

MEMEL. See KLAIPEDA.

MEMEL RIVER. See NEMAN RIVER.

MEMLING, Hans (c1440–1494), Flemish painter famous for his portraits and religious works, among which the paneled *Shrine of St. Ursula* (c1489) is one of the most famous. He worked in Bruges, Belgium, and was probably a pupil of Roger VAN DER WEYDEN.

MEMNON, in Greek mythology, son of Tithonus and Eos and king of Ethiopia. In post-Homeric legends he aids his uncle PRIAM in the Trojan War, is killed by Achilles, but is granted by ZEUS a new lease of life in Egypt. The Greeks gave his name to the great "singing" statue of AMENHOTEP III, at Thebes.

MEMORIAL DAY, or Decoration Day, a US holiday, honoring the dead of all wars, observed on the last Monday in May. Traditionally, Memorial Day originated in the South after the Civil War when the graves of both Confederate and Union soldiers were decorated.

MEMORY, the sum of the mental processes that result in the modification of an individual's behavior in the light of previous experience. There are several different types of memory. In rote memory, one of the least efficient ways of storing information, data is learned by rote and repeated verbatim. Logical memory is far more efficient: only the salient data are stored, and each may be used in its original or in a different context. Mnemonics, which assist rote memory, superimpose what is in effect an artificial logical structure on not necessarily related data. (See also EIDETIC IMAGE.) Testing of the efficiency of memory may be by recall (e.g., remembering a string of unrelated syllables); recognition (as in a multiple-choice test, where the candidate recognizes the correct answer among alternatives); and relearning, in which comparison is made between the time taken by an individual to commit certain data to memory, and the time taken to recommit it to memory after a delay. Though recent studies of certain COMPUTER functions have thrown light on some of the workings of memory (see also CYBERNETICS), little is known of its exact physiological basis. It appears, however, that chemical changes in the brain, particularly in the composition of RNA (see NUCLEIC ACIDS), alter the electrical pathways there. Moreover, it seems that some form of initial learning takes place in the NERVOUS SYSTEM before data are stored permanently in the BRAIN. (See also ELECTROENCEPHALOGRAPH; INTELLIGENCE; LEARNING.)

MEMPHIS, capital of the Old Kingdom of ancient Egypt until c2200 BC. Probably founded by MENES, the first king of a united Upper and Lower Egypt, c3100 BC, the city stood on the W bank of the Nile some 15mi S of modern Cairo. Excavations have revealed the temple of Ptah, god of the city, and the two massive statues of RAMSES II.

MEMPHIS, largest city and chief port of Tenn., seat of Shelby Co., on the Mississippi R in the SW corner of the state. It is an important market for cotton, lumber and livestock and its manufactures include cottonseed products, textiles, farm machinery and paper. Pop 623 530.

MEMPHREMAGOG, Lake, narrow lake about 30mi long, extending from Newport in N Vt. to Magog in S Quebec where there is a small hydroelectric development.

MENAHEM, king of Israel c749–737 BC. He seized the throne after Zechariah's death, ruled cruelly and paid tribute to Assyria—events recounted in the Old Testament (2 Kings 15:14–22).

MENANDER (c342–c291 BC), leading Greek writer of New Comedy. Out of over 100 plays, only *Dyscolos* (The Grouch) survives complete, though there are adaptations by PLAUTUS and TERENCE. His plots are based on love-affairs and he is noted for his elegant style and deft characterization. He won eight prizes at Athenian festivals.

MENASHA, city in E Wis., on Lake Winnebago. It is a summer resort, with important paper-making and printing industries. Pop 14905.

MENCIUS (c370–c290 BC), Chinese philosopher, a follower of CONFUCIUS. He held that man is naturally good and that the principles of true moral conduct are inborn. He was a champion of the ordinary people and exhorted rulers to treat their subjects well.

MENCKEN, Henry Louis (1880–1956), US journalist and author, caustic critic of American society and literature. He wrote for the *Baltimore Sun* and founded and edited the *American Mercury* (1924). His collected essays appeared in *Prejudices* (1919–27), and he wrote an authoritative study, *The American Language* (1919).

MENDEL, Gregor Johann (1822–1884), Austrian botanist and Augustinian monk who laid the foundations of the science of GENETICS. He found that self-pollinated dwarf pea plants bred true, but that under the same circumstances only about a third of tall pea plants did so, the remainder producing tall or dwarf pea plants in a ratio about 3:1. Next he cross-bred tall and dwarf plants and found this without exception resulted in a tall plant, but one that did not breed true. Thus, in this plant, both tall and dwarf characteristics were present. He had found a mechanism justifying DARWIN's theory of EVOLUTION by NATURAL SELECTION; but contemporary lack of interest and his later, unsuccessful experiments with the hawkweeds discouraged him from carrying this further. It was not until 1900, when H. de VRIES and others found his published results, that the import ance of his work was realized. (See also HEREDITY; POLLINATION.)

MENDELEVIUM (Md), a TRANSURANIUM ELEMENT in the ACTINIDE series, first made by bombarding einsteinium-253 with ALPHA PARTICLES.

MENDELEYEV, Dmitri Ivanovich (1834–1907), Russian chemist who formulated the Periodic Law, that the properties of elements vary periodically with increasing atomic weight, and so drew up the PERIODIC TABLE (1869). (See also MEYER, J. L.)

MENDELSOHN, Erich (1887–1953), German-born expressionist architect, designing "sculptured" and functional buildings, notably the Einstein Tower, Potsdam (1921). He worked in England 1933–37, Palestine 1937–41 and the US, where he was naturalized.

MENDELSSOHN(-BARTHOLDY), (Jacob Ludwig) Felix (1809–1847), German Romantic com poser. He wrote his masterly *Overture to A Midsummer Night's Dream* when only 17. Other works include his *Hebrides Overture* (also known as "Fingal's Cave"), *Italian Symphony* (no. 4), Violin Concerto, chamber music and the oratorio *Elijah*. He was also a celebrated conductor, notably of the Leipzig Gewandhaus orchestra, and revived interest in BACH's music.

MENDELSSOHN, Moses (1729–1786), Jewish philosopher, a leading figure of the Enlightenment in Prussia and a promoter of Jewish assimilation into German culture. He was the model for the hero of LESSING's play *Nathan the Wise*, and a grandfather of the famous composer.

MENDÈS-FRANCE, Pierre (1907–), French statesman. As center-left prime minister (1954–55), he ended France's war in Indochina and kept France out of a projected European Defense Community. He granted Tunisia internal self-government, but was defeated over his liberal Algerian policy.

MENDOZA, city in W Argentina, capital of Mendoza Province. It is the center of an irrigated wine producing and fruit and vegetable growing area. Pop 118568.

MENELAUS, in Greek mythology, king of Sparta, brother of AGAMEMNON and husband of HELEN OF TROY. When PARIS abducted Helen, Menelaus persuaded the Greeks to join him in the TROJAN WAR, after which he was reconciled with Helen.

MENELIK II (1844–1913), emperor of Ethiopia from 1889, founder of the modern Ethiopian nation. He unified Ethiopia and doubled its territory, crushed invading Italian forces at ADWA (1896) and instituted reforms and modernization.

MENÉNDEZ DE AVILÉS, Pedro (1519–1574), Spanish adventurer and conquistador who founded St. Augustine, Fla., oldest city in the US. Authorized by Philip II of Spain to start a Spanish colony in Florida and end French HUGUENOT influence there, in 1565 he built a fort on St. Augustine Bay and destroyed the rival French colony, Fort Caroline.

MENES (flourished c3100 BC), traditional name of the founder of the 1st dynasty in ancient Egypt. He is identified by some modern scholars with King Narmer, and is said to have united N and S Egypt and to have founded Memphis.

MENHADEN, herring-like fishes related to SHADS, found in enormous shoals along the coasts of the W Atlantic and distinguished by a double row of ridge-like scales along the back. The species is used commercially for food, but more extensively for oil.

MENHIR. See MEGALITHIC MONUMENTS.

MÈNIÈRE'S DISEASE, disorder of the cochlea and labyrinth of the EAR, causing brief acute episodes of VERTIGO, with nausea or VOMITING, ringing in the ears and DEAFNESS. Ultimately permanent deafness ensues and vertigo lessens. It is a disorder of inner-ear fluid and each episode causes some destruction of receptor cells. Drugs can reduce the vertigo.

MENINGITIS, INFLAMMATION of the meninges (see BRAIN) caused by BACTERIA (e.g., meningococcus, pneumococcus, hemophilus) or VIRUSES. **Bacterial meningitis** is of abrupt onset with HEADACHE, vomiting, FEVER, neck stiffness and avoidance of light. Early and appropriate ANTIBIOTIC treatment is essential as permanent damage may occur in some cases, especially in children. **Viral meningitis** is a milder illness with similar signs in a less ill person; symptomatic measures only are required. **Tuberculous meningitis** is an insidious chronic type which responds slowly to antituberculous drugs. Some FUNGI, unusual bacteria and syphilis (see VENEREAL DISEASES) may also cause varieties of meningitis.

A monumental menorah with carvings depicting scenes from Jewish history, a gift from the British government to the state of Israel at its foundation. The seven-branched candelabrum is one of the great symbols of Judaism. Among other things, it signifies the seven days of creation.

MENLO PARK, residential city in W Cal., 23mi SE of San Francisco. Pop 26906.

MENLO PARK, unincorporated community in NW N.J., 5mi NW of Perth Amboy. The Edison Memorial Tower marks the site of the laboratory where EDISON invented the incandescent electric bulb.

MENNINGER, Karl Augustus (1893–), US psychiatrist who, with his brother **William Claire Menninger** (1899–1966) and father **Charles Frederick Menninger** (1862–1953), set up the Menninger Foundation (1941), a nonprofit organization dedicated to the furtherance of psychiatric research.

MENNONITES, Protestant sect originating among the ANABAPTISTS of Zurich, Switzerland. They became influential particularly in the Netherlands, and are named for the Dutch reformer Menno SIMONS. They base their faith solely on the Bible, believe in separation of Church and State, pacifism, and baptism only for adults renouncing sin. Despite persecution, the sect spread and now totals about 550000 with some 89000 members in Canada and 208000 in the US. They are known for the strict simplicity of their life and worship. (See also AMISH; HUTTERITES.)

MENOMINEE, city in N Mich., on Lake Michigan, seat of Menominee Co. It is a summer resort and manufactures wood products, machinery and electrical equipment. Pop 10748.

MENOMINEE INDIANS, North American Indian tribe of the ALGONQUIAN linguistic group. Most lived in upper Mich. and Wis., along the W shore of Green Bay, gathering wild rice (*Menominee* means "wild rice people"). In 1854 they were settled on a reservation on the Wolf and Oconto rivers in Wis., now a county, where their descendants (about 4000) still live.

MENOMONEE FALLS, village in SE Wis., NNW of Milwaukee. It is the center of a dairy farming area and has some light industry. Pop 31697.

MENOMONIE, city in W Wis., seat of Dunn Co. Once an important lumber town, it is now a trade and marketing center for a rich agricultural area. Pop 11275.

MENOPAUSE. See MENSTRUATION.

MENORAH, candelabrum used in Jewish worship, a symbol of Judaism. It symbolizes the Tree of Life, and its seven branches may be said to represent light, justice, peace, truth, benevolence, brotherly love and harmony. The special candelabrum used in celebrating HANUKKAH is also called a menorah.

The impressive skyline of Memphis, Tennessee, sited on the rising bluffs of the Mississippi River's east bank. Just visible is the famous King Cotton hotel, named for the trade which brought the city prosperity.

MENORCA. See MINORCA.

MENOTTI, Gian Carlo (1911–), Italian-born US composer of dramatically powerful operas with his own librettos, and founder (1958) of the Two Worlds festival at Spoleto, Italy. His works include *The Medium* (1946) and the television opera *Amahl and the Night Visitors* (1951). *The Consul* (1950) and *The Saint of Bleecker Street* (1954) won Pulitzer prizes.

MENSHEVIKS, minority group in the Russian Social Democratic Workers' Party, opposed to the Bolsheviks, the majority group led by LENIN (see BOLSHEVISM). Unlike Lenin, the Menshevik theoretician Georgi PLEKHANOV favored mass membership and thought a spell of bourgeois rule must precede communism. Led by L. Martov, the Mensheviks emerged in 1903, backed KERENSKY's government and opposed the Bolshevik seizure of power. By 1921 they had been eliminated.

MENSTRUATION, specifically the monthly loss of BLOOD (period), representing shedding of WOMB endometrium, in women of reproductive age; in general, the whole monthly cycle of hormone, structural and functional changes in such women, punctuated by menstrual blood loss. After each period, the womb-lining endometrium starts to proliferate and thicken under the influence of GONADOTROPHINS (FOLLICLE STIMULATING HORMONE) and ESTROGENS. In midcycle a burst of LUTEINIZING HORMONE secretion, initiated by the HYPOTHALAMUS, causes release of an egg from an ovarian follicle (*ovulation*). More PROGESTERONE is then secreted and the endometrium is prepared for IMPLANTATION of a fertilized egg. If the egg is not fertilized, PREGNANCY does not ensue and blood-vessel changes occur leading to the shedding of the endometrium and some blood; these are lost through the vagina for several days, sometimes with pain or COLIC. The cycle then restarts. During the menstrual cycle, changes in the BREASTS, body temperature, fluid balance and mood occur, the manifestations varying from person to person. Cyclic patterns are established at PUBERTY (*menarche*) and end in middle life (age 45–50) at the *menopause*, the "change of life." Disorders of menstruation include heavy, irregular or missed periods; bleeding between periods or after the menopause, and excessively painful periods. They are studied in GYNECOLOGY.

MENSURATION, the branch of GEOMETRY dealing with the measurement of LENGTH, AREA and VOLUME. The base of all such measurements is length, since the areas and volumes of geometric figures can be calculated from suitable length measurements. The area of a rectangle is bh, where b is the length of one side (the base) and h that of the other (the height) (see QUADRILATERAL). It is easy to show that this formula holds also for the parallelogram, if h stands for the altitude (the PERPENDICULAR distance from one side to that facing it) rather than for the height; from this can be found the formula for the area of a TRIANGLE (which can be thought of as half a parallelogram), $\frac{1}{2}bh$; and those for other POLYGONS.

The area and circumference of a CIRCLE, which can be considered as a regular polygon with an infinite number of infinitely small sides, are πr^2 and $2\pi r$ respectively, where π is a constant (see PI) and r is the radius. The area of an ellipse (see CONIC SECTIONS) is given by πab where a is the semi-major and b the semi-minor axis; the circumference of an ellipse cannot be expressed in algebraic terms.

From this information, it is fairly easy to determine formulae for the volumes of regular solids, such as the POLYHEDRON; CONE; CYLINDER; ELLIPSOID; PYRAMID, and SPHERE. The areas of irregular plane shapes can be approximated by considering a large number of extremely small strips, each being almost trapezoidal, formed in them by the construction of a large number of parallel chords; the same principle can be applied to finding the approximate volumes of irregular solids: this process is akin to integral CALCULUS.

MENTAL ILLNESS, or psychiatric DISEASE, disorders characterized by abnormal function of the higher centers of the BRAIN responsible for thought, perception, mood and behavior, in which organic disease has been eliminated as a possible cause. The borderline between disease and the range of normal variability is indistinct and may be determined by cultural factors. Crime may result from mental disease, but modern Western society is careful to eliminate it as far as possible before subjecting a criminal to justice. However, in certain repressive regimes, political or ideological nonconformity can be grounds for admission to mental hospital. Mental disease has been recognized since ancient times and both HIPPOCRATES and GALEN evolved theories as to its origins; but in many cultures, over the centuries, madness has been equated with possession by evil spirits and sufferers were often treated as witches. In the 15th century, PARACELSUS proposed that the moon determined the behavior of mad people (hence "lunacy"), while in the 18th century MESMER favored the role of animal magnetism (from which HYPNOSIS is derived). The first humane *asylum* for the mentally ill was founded in Paris by PINEL (1795). Originally only socially intolerable cases were admitted to such hospitals, but today voluntary admission is more common. The *Viennese school* of psychology, in particular Sigmund FREUD and his pupils, emphasized the importance of past, especially childhood experiences, sexual attitudes and other functional factors. Behavior therapy, PSYCHOANALYSIS and PSYCHOTHERAPY derive from this school. On the other hand, the influence of subtle organic factors (e.g., brain biochemistry) favored by others; this led to using LOBOTOMY, SHOCK THERAPY and DRUGS.

Mental illness may be classified into PSYCHOSIS, NEUROSIS and personality disorder. **Schizophrenia** is a psychosis causing disturbance of thought and perception in which mood is characteristically flat and behavior withdrawn. Features include: auditory hallucinations; delusions of person ("I'm the King of Spain"), of surroundings and other people (e.g., suspicion of conspiracy in PARANOIA); blocking, insertion and broadcasting of thought, and knight's-move thinking, or nonlogical sequence of ideas. Conversation lacks substance and may be in riddles and neologisms; speech or behavior may be imitative, stereotyped, repetitive or negative. Phenothiazine drugs, especially chlorpromazine and long-acting analogues, are particularly valuable in schizophrenia. In **affective psychoses**, disturbance of mood is the primary disorder. Subjects usually exhibit DEPRESSION with loss of drive and inconsolably low mood, either in response to situation (exogenous) or for no apparent reason (endogenous). Loss of appetite, CONSTIPATION and characteristic sleep disturbance also commonly occur. ANTIDEPRESSANTS and SHOCK THERAPY are valuable, but psychotherapy may also be needed. In hypnomania or MANIA, excitability, restlessness, euphoria, ceaseless talk, flight of ideas and loss of social inhibitions occur. Financial, sexual and alcohol excesses may result. Chlorpromazine, haloperidol and lithium are effective. **Neuroses** include ANXIETY, pathological exaggeration of a physiological response. This may coexist with depression but responds to benzodiazepines (Valium) and psychotherapy. Obsessional and compulsive neuroses, manifested by extreme habits, rituals and fixations (which may be recognized as irrational); PHOBIAS, excessive and inappropriate fears of objects or situations (e.g. AGORAPHOBIA), and HYSTERIA are helped by behavior therapy. Psychopathy is a specific disorder of personality characterized by failure to learn from experience. Irresponsibility, inconsiderateness and lack of foresight result, and may lead to crime. Other **personality disorders** are exhibited by a variety of people, often with unstable backgrounds, who seem unable to cope with the realities of everyday adult life; attempted suicide is a common gesture. In sexual disorders with antisocial or perverse sexual fixations, behavior therapy may be of value. (See also ALCOHOLISM; ANOREXIA NERVOSA; DRUG ADDICTION.)

MENTAL RETARDATION, low intellectual capacity arising, not from MENTAL ILLNESS, but from impairment of the normal development of the BRAIN and NERVOUS SYSTEM. Causes include genetic defect (as in MONGOLISM); infection of the EMBRYO or FETUS; HYDROCEPHALUS or inherited metabolic defects (e.g., CRETINISM), and injury at BIRTH including cerebral HEMORRHAGE and fetal ASPHYXIA. Disease in infancy such as ENCEPHALITIS may cause mental retardation in children with normal previous development. Retardation is initially recognized by slowness to develop normal patterns of social and learning behavior and confirmed through intelligence measurements. It is most important that affected children should receive adequate social contact and education, for their development is truly retarded and not arrested. In particular, special schooling may help them to achieve a degree of learning and social competence.

MENTHOL, or 3-hydroxy-*p*-menthane, a TERPENE alcohol, an ALICYCLIC COMPOUND. It is a white crystalline solid with a pungent odor and mint flavor, having a cooling, soothing effect on the throat and nasal passages, and used in medications, cosmetics, cigarettes and flavorings. Menthol is extracted from peppermint oil or synthesized.

MENTOR, residential city in NE Ohio, near Lake Erie, 24mi NE of Cleveland. Pop 36 912.

MENUHIN, Yehudi (1916–), US violinist and conductor. He made his concert debut at seven, played to Allied forces in WWII, and later to raise cash for war victims. He has revived forgotten masterpieces, aroused interest in Eastern music and directed festivals. In 1963 he opened a school for musically gifted children in England.

MENZIES, Sir Robert Gordon (1894–), Australian statesman, prime minister 1939–41, 1949–66. He was attorney general 1935–39 and leader of the opposition 1943–48. As leader of the Liberal-Country Party coalition 1949–66, he pursued a conservative anti-communist policy, and encouraged rapid industrial growth.

MEO (Miao), a non-Chinese people of SW China, N Laos, Vietnam and Thailand. They live in mountain villages and practice shifting cultivation. Many groups raise opium as a cash crop. Numbering about 2 500 500, they have virtually no political organization, and minimal contact with governments and other peoples.

MEPHISTOPHELES, in medieval legend, the devil to whom FAUST sold his soul. He is primarily a literary creation, and appears in the famous plays by MARLOWE and GOETHE.

MEQUON, city in Wis. It is an industrial and residential suburb of Milwaukee. Pop 12 150.

MERBROMIN, or mercurochrome, mercurial salt formerly used for disinfection. It acts by interfering with SULFUR bridges in microorganism PROTEINS.

MECANTILISM, in economic history, theories prevailing in 16th- to 18th-century W Europe, reflecting the increased importance of the merchant. Mercantilists favored TARIFFS to secure a favorable INTERNATIONAL TRADE balance and maintain reserves of precious metals, considered essential to a nation's wealth. Their PROTECTIONISM was succeeded by the FREE TRADE arguments of the French PHYSIOCRATS.

MERCATOR, Gerardus (1512–1594), Flemish cartographer and calligrapher, best known for Mercator's Projection (see MAP), which he first used in 1569 for a world map. The PROJECTION is from a point at the center of the earth through the surface of the globe onto a cylinder that touches the earth around the equator.

MERCED, city in central Cal., seat of Merced Co. It is a tourist center and a market for farm produce, and has an Air Force base nearby. Pop 22 670.

MERCENARY, freelance professional soldier. Mercenaries were known in ancient Greece. They were important in the Middle Ages and Renaissance; English and Flemish mercenaries fought in the HUNDRED YEARS WAR, Swiss soldiers served many rulers, so-called *Landsknechte* worked for German princes and CONDOTTIERI helped Italian city states. Modern mercenaries include white soldiers used by and against new African governments.

MERCER, Hugh (c1725–1777), Scottish-born American brigadier-general. In the REVOLUTIONARY WAR he retreated with Washington through New Jersey, helped win the Battle of TRENTON, and was mortally wounded at Princeton. He had earlier survived CULLODEN MOOR (1746) and the ambush that killed BRADDOCK (1755).

MERCER ISLAND, city in W central Wash., an island on Lake Washington. It is a residential suburb of Seattle, 4mi E of the city. Pop 19 047.

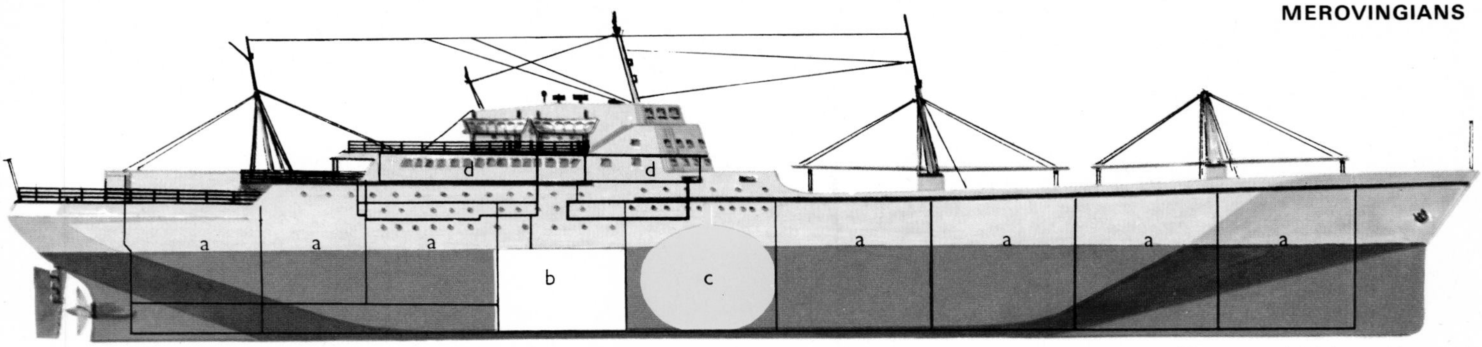

The first nuclear-powered merchant ship, the USS *Savannah* (named for the first US steamship to cross the Atlantic) was launched in 1959. The reactor (c) is housed in a steel cylinder enclosed by a lead-concrete shield weighing 2 000 tons. (a) Holds; (b) engine room; (c) reactor area; (d) passenger cabins.

MERCERIZING, technique patented in 1850 by John Mercer (1791–1866) for making textiles take DYE more readily and show more brilliant colors (see TEXTILES). The yarn or cloth (usually under tension to reduce shrinkage) is steeped in a concentrated caustic soda (see SODIUM) solution.

MERCHANT SHIPPING, non-military sea transportation. Until the Industrial Revolution most ships were small and carried cargoes of high-value goods like gold, silks and spices. Today huge tonnages of foods, coal, ores, machinery and petroleum travel in vast merchant vessels. Without this traffic industry would run down and millions would starve. Since 1800, merchant ships have enormously increased in speed, size and number. In 1819 the first US steamship to cross the Atlantic, the *Savannah*, took 29 days. In 1952 the *United States* crossed in 3 days. In 1847 the *Washington* displaced 1 720 tons and was then a large ship. The modern Japanese-built oil tanker, *Globtik London*, is 483939 dwt (dwt = deadweight tons, measured by the weight of cargo a ship can carry) and 1 243ft long. In 1886 the world's merchant fleets totaled 21 million gross tons (1 gross ton = 100cu ft of ship space), half of which was under sail. In 1973, the world's merchant fleets totaled 290 million gross tons shared out among some 60000 vessels. Patterns of ownership have also changed. Britain owned half of the world's cargo ships a century ago. In 1973 the flags of Liberia, Japan, Britain, Norway, Greece, the USSR and the US (in that order) led the list of tonnages. (For tax purposes, many American and Greek-owned vessels are registered under Liberian and Panamanian flags of convenience.)

Types of Ships. The main types of merchant ship are the tramps that roam the world picking up cargoes and sailing where required, and liners that travel fixed routes on regular schedules. Passenger liner traffic has declined in competition with air travel, but the growth in cargo traffic has produced today's supertankers and bulk carriers that have led to big new port developments. (See also HARBOR.) The latest advance in cargo transport is the container ship carrying huge rectangular containers preloaded with assorted cargo. (See also SHIPS AND SHIPPING.)

MERCIA, kingdom founded by the ANGLES in the W Midlands of England. Lasting from the early 7th century to the mid-9th century, under rulers like PENDA (d. 654) and OFFA (d. 796) it came to dominate all central England. It declined in the 9th century, and by 900 had been partitioned between the invading Danes and the kingdom of WESSEX.

MERCUROCHROME See MERBROMIN.

MERCURY (Hg), or **quicksilver**, silvery-white liquid metal in Group IIB of the PERIODIC TABLE; an anomalous TRANSITION ELEMENT. It occurs as CINNABAR, calomel and rarely as the metal, which has been known from ancient times. It is extracted by roasting cinnabar in air and condensing the mercury vapor. Mercury is fairly inert, tarnishing only slowly in moist air, and soluble in oxidizing acids only; it is readily attacked by the HALOGENS and sulfur. It forms Hg^{2+} and some Hg_2^{2+} compounds, and many important ORGANOMETALLIC COMPOUNDS. Mercury and its compounds are highly toxic. The metal is used to form AMALGAMS; for electrodes, and in barometers, thermometers, diffusion PUMPS, and mercury-vapor lamps (see LIGHTING, ARTIFICIAL). Various mercury compounds are used as pharmaceuticals. AW 200.6, mp −39°C, bp 357°C, sg 13.546 (20°C). **Mercury (II) cyanate** ($Hg[ONC]_2$), or **mercury fulminate**, is a white crystalline solid, sensitive to percussion, and used as a detonator. **Mercury(II) chloride** ($HgCl_2$), or **corrosive sublimate**, is a colorless crystalline solid prepared by direct synthesis. Although highly toxic, it is used in dilute solution as an ANTISEPTIC, and also as a fungicide and a polymerization catalyst. mp 276°C, bp 302°C. **Mercury(I) chloride** (Hg_2Cl_2), or **calomel**, is a white rhombic crystalline solid, found in nature. It is used in ointments and formerly found use as a LAXATIVE. A calomel/mercury cell with potassium chloride electrolyte (the Weston cell) is used to provide a standard ELECTROMOTIVE FORCE. mp 303°C, bp 384°C.

MERCURY, Roman god of merchandise and messenger of the gods, identified by the Romans with the Greek god HERMES. His festival was held in May and his temple was on the Aventine Hill.

MERCURY, the planet closest to the sun with a mean solar distance of 58Gm. Its highly eccentric ORBIT brings it within 46Gm of the sun at perihelion and takes it 70Gm from the sun at aphelion. Its diameter is about 4 870km, its mass about 0.054 that of the earth. It goes around the sun in just under 88 days and rotates on its axis in about 59 days. The successful prediction by Albert EINSTEIN that Mercury's orbit would be found to advance by 43″ per century is usually regarded as a confirmation of the General Theory of RELATIVITY. Night surface temperature is thought to be about 110K, midday equatorial temperature over 600K. The planet's average density (5.2 grams per cubic centimeter) indicates a high proportion of heavy elements in its interior. Mercury has little or no atmosphere and no known moons.

MERCURY POISONING, the cause of acute GASTROINTESTINAL TRACT and KIDNEY disease if mercury(II) salts are ingested. A chronic form, often from vapor inhalation, causes BRAIN changes with tremor, ataxia, irritability and social withdrawal. The mental changes ensuing from the former use of mercury in making felt hats led to the phrase "mad as a hatter." Organic mercury from fish (e.g., tuna) living in contaminated water, or from cereals treated with antifungal agents may cause ataxia, swallowing difficulty, abnormalities of VISION and COMA. Nephrotic syndrome of the kidneys may also be seen. Treatment is with dimercaprol, a chelating agent (see CHELATE).

MERCURY PROGRAM, first US manned space flights 1960–63, using the one-man Mercury capsule. In 1961 Alan SHEPARD and Virgil GRISSOM were launched on suborbital flights by the Redstone carrier missile. In 1962 John GLENN made the first US orbital flight, followed by M. Scott Carpenter, Walter SCHIRRA and Leroy COOPER; orbital missions were launched by Atlas carriers. (See also SPACE EXPLORATION.)

MERCY, Sisters of, Roman Catholic congregation, founded in Ireland in 1831 by Catherine McAulay and established in the US by Mary Xavier Warde in 1843. Today there are more than 25 000 sisters, half of this number in the US, where they run colleges, schools and hospitals.

MERCY KILLING. See EUTHANASIA.

MEREDITH, George (1828–1909), English novelist and poet. His best-known novel is the tragicomic *Ordeal of Richard Feverel* (1859). The sonnet sequence *Modern Love* (1862) grew out of the breakdown of his marriage. Other well-known works are *The Egoist* (1879) and *Diana of the Crossways* (1885).

MEREDITH, James Howard (1933–), US civil rights worker and lecturer. In 1962 he became the first Negro to enter Mississippi U., in the face of threats and rioting.

MEREZHKOVSKI, Dmitri Sergeyevich (1865–1941), influential Russian author and critic. A mystic, he saw life and literature as divided between seers of the flesh and of the spirit. An opponent of both tsarism and bolshevism, he emigrated after the Revolution.

MERGANSERS, various species of salt-water diving ducks characterized by a long slim bill, serrated for gripping their prey (small fish). There are six species, genus *Mergus*, the best-known of which are perhaps the Red-breasted and American mergansers.

MERGENTHALER, Ottmar (1854–1899), German-born US inventor of the first linotype PRINTING machine (1884), first put to commercial use in 1886.

MERGER, joining of two or more companies to make one large corporation, often dominated by the management of the larger or more prosperous company. Pooling resources can cut production costs but may allow monopolies and restrictive practices. In the US therefore, mergers are subject to government review under ANTITRUST LEGISLATION.

MÉRIDA, city in SE Mexico, capital of Yucatan State. Its economy rests largely on sisal grown in the region, and on tourism. Pop 253856.

MÉRIDA, town in SW Spain. Capital of Roman LUSITANIA, it has extensive Roman ruins. Its economy rests on light manufacturing. Pop 40059.

MERIDEN, city in S Conn., 17mi NE of New Haven. Settled in 1661, it has had a large silver industry since the 18th century, and now has other manufacturing industries also. Pop 55959.

MERIDIAN, city in E Miss., seat of Lauderdale Co. It is a transport hub and a major industrial and commercial center in an agricultural area. Pop 45083.

MERIDIAN, on the celestial sphere, the great circle passing through the celestial poles and the observer's ZENITH. It cuts his HORIZON N and S. (See also CELESTIAL SPHERE; TRANSIT.) The term is used also for a line of terrestrial longitude.

MÉRIMÉE, Prosper (1803–1870), French author, historian, archaeologist and linguit. He is best known for short stories such as *Mateo Falcone* (1829) and the romance *Carmen* (1847), source of BIZET's opera.

MERIT SYSTEM, system of appointing public service employees on an open competitive basis. In US federal government it began replacing the SPOILS SYSTEM after the PENDLETON ACT of 1883, which set up a Civil Service Commission.

MERMAID, mythical seacreature, a beautiful woman with the tail of a fish. Like SIRENS, they were reputed to lure men to their deaths. In some legends mermaids assumed human shape and married mortals.

MERÖE, ruined city on the Nile R in NE Sudan, capital of the kingdom of CUSH c590 BC–c350 AD and a major early ironworking center. Among surviving ruins are palaces, temples and pyramids.

MEROVINGIANS, dynasty of Frankish kings 428–751. They were named for the fifth century king

One of Mesa Verde National Park's ruined pueblos, sheltered by an overhanging rock face. It was built by the Anasazi, an advanced tribe of agrarian Indians, over a thousand years ago.

Merovech; his grandson CLOVIS I first united much of France. The kingdom was later partitioned, but enlarged and reunited (613) under Clotaire II. The Merovingians governed through the remnants of the old Roman administration and established Catholic Christianity. After DAGOBERT I in the 7th century the kings became known as *rois-fainéants* (do-nothings) and power passed to the mayors of the palace, nominally high officials; the last of these, PEPIN THE SHORT, deposed the last Merovingian, Childeric III. (See also AUSTRASIA; NEUSTRIA.)

MERRIAM, city in E Kan., a SW suburb of Kansas City. Pop 10851.

MERRICK, unincorporated urban community in SE N.Y., on Long Island. Pop 25904.

MERRIMACK. See MONITOR AND MERRIMACK.

MERRIMACK RIVER, about 110mi long, is formed by the confluence of the Pemigewasset and Winnepesaukee rivers at Franklin, N.H. It flows S through N.H. and NE through Mass. into the Atlantic. Its many waterfalls have provided power for textile mills and now power hydroelectric schemes.

MERRYMOUNT. See MORTON, THOMAS.

MERSEY, river in NW England. Created by the confluence of the Etheron and Goyt rivers at Stockport, it flows 70mi W through Greater Manchester and Cheshire, partly as the MANCHESTER SHIP CANAL, to the Irish Sea at Liverpool.

MERTON, Thomas (1915–1968), or Father M. Louis, US religious writer of poetry, meditative works and the autobiography *The Seven Storey Mountain* (1948). Converted to Roman Catholicism, he became a Trappist monk (1941) and later a priest.

MESA, Mormon-founded city in SW Ariz. 15mi E of Phoenix. A winter resort in a fruit-growing area, its industries include aircraft and electronics manufacture. Pop 62853.

MESA (Spanish, table; from Latin *mensa*), steep-sided, flat-topped area formed beneath a horizontal cap of hard rock where the surrounding softer rock has been worn away. Further EROSION of the sides produces a smaller hill, or **butte**.

MESABI RANGE, hills in NE Minn., NW of Lake Superior from Babbitt to Grand Rapids; highest point is 2000ft. The range is famous for its vast iron ore deposits, lying near the surface. They have been mined since the 1890s.

MESA VERDE NATIONAL PARK, area of 52074 acres in SW Col., established in 1906. It contains extensive pueblo ruins built by the CLIFF DWELLERS over 1300 years ago, and much distinctive wild life.

MESCALINE, HALLUCINOGENIC DRUG, derived from a Mexican cactus, whose use dates back to ancient times when "peyote buttons" were used in religious ceremonies among American Indians. The hallucinations experienced during its use were among the first to be described (by Aldous HUXLEY) and resemble those of LSD.

MESENTERY, the membranous fold in which the GASTROINTESTINAL TRACT is slung from the back wall of the ABDOMEN so that it lies relatively free and mobile in the peritoneal cavity. It consists of a double layer of peritoneum and within it lie the BLOOD vessels and LYMPH nodes and vessels of the gut.

MESHED (Mashdad), city in NE Iran, capital of Khorasan province. In a rich farming area, it has been an important trading city and a shrine of Shi'ite Muslim pilgrimage since the 8th century; in the 18th century it was capital of Persia.

MESMER, Franz Anton (1734–1815), German physician, controversy over whose unusual techniques and theories sparked in CHARCOT and others an interest in the possibilities of using "animal magnetism" (or mesmerism, i.e., HYPNOSIS) for psychotherapy.

MESOLITHIC AGE. See STONE AGE.

MESONS. See SUBATOMIC PARTICLES.

MESOPHYTE, any plant that grows in conditions where the water supply is neither scanty nor abundant. Mesophytes have flat, expanded leaves. (See also HYDROPHYTE; XEROPHYTE.)

MESOPOTAMIA (Greek: between the rivers), ancient region between the Tigris and Euphrates rivers in SW Asia, home of many early civilizations. (See also FERTILE CRESCENT.) Most of it lies in Iraq, between the Armenian and Kurdish Mts in the N and the Persian Gulf in the S; the N is mainly grassy, rolling plateau; the S is a sandy plain leading to marshes. Since ancient times the rivers have been used to irrigate the area, most notably under ABBASIDE rule (749–1285 AD), but the ancient systems degenerated under Mongol invasion and OTTOMAN rule, and were not replaced until the 20th century. Neolithic farming peoples were settling Mesopotamia by 6000 BC followed by the Tell Halaf and al'Ubaid cultures after 4000 BC. By 3000 BC the SUMERIANS had created a civilization of independent city-states in the S. From c3000–625 BC Mesopotamia was successively dominated by SUMER, AKKAD, the Sumerian dynasty of UR, the empires of BABYLONIA AND ASSYRIA and CHALDEA. In 539 BC the Persian Empire absorbed Mesopotamia; in 331 BC it was conquered by Alexander the Great. It then came under Roman, Byzantine and Arab rule. The Abbaside caliphs made BAGHDAD their capital in 762 AD, but prosperity collapsed with the Mongol invasion of 1289. Mesopotamia was under Ottoman rule 1638–1918, when it was largely incorporated into IRAQ.

MESOSPHERE, the atmospheric zone immediately above the stratosphere, marked by a TEMPERATURE maximum (about 10°C) between ALTITUDES 48km and 53km. (See ATMOSPHERE.)

MESOZOA, a group of simple parasitic animals whose taxonomic position poses great problems. They may be the missing link between PROTOZOA and METAZOA. However, they may equally be derived from a more complex group, secondarily simplified as a consequence of their parasitic way of life.

MEZOZOIC, the middle era of the PHANEROZOIC, lasting from 225 until 65 million years ago. It has three periods: the TRIASSIC, JURASSIC and CRETACEOUS. (See GEOLOGY.)

MESQUITE, tough shrubs of the genus *Prosopis*, which are native to South America and the southwestern US. Closely related is the screw bean mesquite (*Strombocarpa odorata*) which occurs from Tex. to Calif. and Mexico. The roots of these plants may penetrate 22m (70ft) underground. The wood and gum from the stem have limited commercial value. Family: Leguminosae.

MESQUITE, city in NE Tex., an E residential and industrial suburb of Dallas. It is a center for local amenities industries. Pop 55131.

MESSERSCHMITT, Wilhelm "Willy" (1898–), German pioneer aircraft designer famous for his fast monoplane fighters used in WWII. They included the Me-109 (1934) and the Me-262, the first jet plane used in war (1944).

MESSIAEN, Olivier Eugène Prosper Charles (1908–), influential French composer and organist. His music is extremely personal, such works as *The Ascension* (1955) being influenced by Roman Catholic mysticism. Others such as the *Turangalila* symphony (1949) are based on oriental music, or birdsong as in *Catalog of Birds* (1959).

MESSIAH (Hebrew: anointed one), according to Israelite prophets, especially ISAIAH, the ruler whom God would send to restore Israel and begin a glorious age of peace and righteousness (see ESCHATOLOGY). He would be a descendant of King DAVID. Christians recognize Jesus of Nazareth as the Messiah (or CHRIST); his role as "suffering servant" was alien to Jewish hopes of a political deliverer. The concept of a forthcoming divine redeemer is common to many religions.

MESSINA, historic seaport city in NE Sicily opposite mainland Italy. Sicily's third largest city and capital of Messina Province, Messina's industries include chemical and food manufacturing. It was founded as a Greek colony c700 BC. Pop 261500.

MESSINA, Strait of, 20mi long and 2–10mi wide channel separating Sicily from Italy. It contains dangerous rocks and whirlpools which in classical times gave rise to the myth of SCYLLA AND CHARYBDIS.

MESTA (Turkish: *Kara Su*, Greek: *Nestos*), river in SW Bulgaria and NE Greece. Rising in the W Rhodope Mts, it flows about 150mi SE to the N Aegean Sea.

MESTIZO (Spanish: mixture), person of mixed racial ancestry, especially one of mixed Spanish and Amerind parentage. Mestizos form a large percentage of the population in many Latin American countries.

MESTROVIĆ, Ivan (1883–1962), Yugoslav-born US sculptor. He studied at Vienna and Rome, and was influenced by classical Greek styles and RODIN. Professor of fine arts at Notre Dame U. from 1955, he executed mainly religious subjects and portraits.

METABOLISM, the sum total of all chemical reactions that occur in a living organism. It can be subdivided into **anabolism** which describes reactions which build up more complex substances from smaller ones, and **catabolism** which describes reactions which break down complex substances into simpler ones. Anabolic reactions require ENERGY while catabolic reactions liberate energy. Metabolic reactions are catalysed by ENZYMES in a highly integrated and finely controlled manner so that there is no overproduction or under utilization of the energy required to maintain life. All energy required to maintain life is ultimately derived from sunlight by PHOTOSYNTHESIS, and most organisms use the products of photosynthesis either directly or indirectly. The energy is stored in most living organisms in a specific chemical compound, adenosine triphosphate (ATP—see NUCLEOTIDES). ATP can transfer its energy to other molecules by a loss of phosphate, later regaining phosphate from catabolic reactions. (See also BASAL METABOLIC RATE.)

METAL, an element with high specific gravity; high opacity and reflectivity to light (giving a characteristic luster when polished); that can be hammered into thin sheets and drawn into wires (i.e., is malleable and ductile), and is a good conductor of heat and electricity, its electrical conductivity decreasing with temperature. Roughly 75% of the chemical elements are metals, but not all of them possess all the typical metallic properties. Most are found as ores and in the pure state are crystalline solids (mercury, liquid at room temperature, being a notable exception), their atoms readily losing electrons to become positive IONS. ALLOYS are easily formed because of the nonspecific nondirectional nature of the metallic bond.

METAL FATIGUE, deterioration and progressive cracking of metal parts caused by repeated and relatively low stresses. Imperfections in crystal grains, which often occur at notches, screw threads, welding defects etc., accumulate after numerous cycles in which a small inelastic strain is applied, often leading to eventual failure. Fatigue failure is guarded against by careful design.

METALLOID, or **semimetal**, an ELEMENT that has properties—physical and chemical—intermediate between those of METALS and those of NONMETALS. The metalloids—BORON, SILICON, GERMANIUM, ARSENIC, ANTIMONY, SELENIUM and TELLURIUM—form a diagonal band in the PERIODIC TABLE. They do not have high ELECTRONEGATIVITY or electropositivity, and form amphoteric OXIDES; they are SEMICONDUCTORS.

METALLURGY, the science and technology of METALS, concerned with their extraction from ores, the methods of refining, purifying and preparing them for use and the study of the structure and physical properties of metals and ALLOYS. A few unreactive metals such as silver and gold are found native (uncombined), but most metals occur naturally as MINERALS (i.e., in chemical combination with nonmetallic elements). Ores are mixtures of minerals from which metal extraction is commercially viable. Over 5000 years man has developed techniques for working ores and forming alloys, but only in the last two centuries have these methods been based on scientific theory. The production of metals from ores is known as process or extraction metallurgy; fabrication metallurgy concerns the conversion of raw metals into alloys, sheets, wires etc., while physical metallurgy covers the structure and properties of metals and alloys, including their mechanical working, heat treatment and testing. Process metallurgy begins with ore dressing, using physical methods such as crushing, grinding and gravity separation to split up the different minerals in an ore. The next stage involves chemical action to separate the metallic component of the mineral from the unwanted nonmetallic part. The actual method used depends on the chemical nature of the mineral compound (e.g., if it is an oxide or sulfide, its solubility in acids etc.) and its physical properties. Hydrometallurgy uses chemical reactions in aqueous solutions to extract metal from ore. ELECTROMETALLURGY uses electricity for firing a furnace or electrolytically reducing a metallic compound to a metal. Pyrometallurgy covers roasting, SMELTING and other high-temperature chemical reactions. It has the advantage of involving fast reactions and giving a molten or gaseous product which can easily be separated out. The extracted metal may need further refining or purifying: electrometallurgy and pyrometallurgy are again used at this stage. Molten metal may then simply be cast by pouring into a mold, giving, e.g., pig iron, or it may be formed into ingots which are then hot or cold worked, as with, e.g., wrought iron. Mechanical working, in the form of rolling, pressing or FORGING, improves the final structure and properties of most metals; it tends to break down and redistribute the impurities formed when a large mass of molten metal solidifies. Simple heat treatment such as ANNEALING also tends to remove some of the inherent brittleness of cast metals. (See also BLAST FURNACE; BRAZING; ROLLING MILLS; SINTERING; STEEL.)

METAMORPHIC ROCKS, one of the three main types of rocks of the earth's crust. They consist of rocks that have undergone change owing to heat, pressure or chemical action. SEDIMENTARY ROCKS undergo *prograde metamorphism*, by which they lose volatiles such as WATER and CARBON dioxide, under conditions of heat and pressure beneath the earth's surface. On exposure to the atmosphere this process may be reversed by weathering (see EROSION). LIMESTONE may be metamorphosed to give MARBLE, SHALE to give SLATE. IGNEOUS ROCKS and previous metamorphic rocks undergo *retrograde metamorphism*, absorbing volatiles, usually from nearby metamorphosing sediments. GRANITE, for example, may be metamorphosed to form a GNEISS.

METAMORPHOSIS, in animals (notably FROGS, TOADS and INSECTS), a marked and relatively rapid change in body form. This alteration in appearance is associated with a change in habits. Perhaps the best known example is the change which occurs when a tadpole becomes a frog.

METAPHOR, figure of speech in which something is described by words that are not strictly applicable. Metaphor, much used in poetry and deeply rooted in our language ("time flies") is akin to SIMILE: "He is a lion in battle" is metaphor; "He fights like a lion" is simile.

METAPHYSICAL POETS, early 17th-century English lyric poets characterized by an involved style relying on the metaphysical *conceit*, an elaborate metaphorical image. Most famous among them is John DONNE; others include Andrew MARVELL, George HERBERT, Richard CRASHAW, Henry VAUGHAN and Thomas CAREW. The Metaphysicals (a term first used by Samuel JOHNSON) extended the range of lyric poetry by writing about death, decay, immortality and faith. They declined in popularity after about 1660, but their complex intellectual content and rich exploration of feeling has made them a major influence on 20th-century poetry.

METAPHYSICS, the branch of philosophy concerned with the fundamentals of existence or reality. Although it takes its name merely from the title an early compiler gave a volume of ARISTOTLE's essays which he placed by "after the *Physics*" (*meta ta phusika*), many philosophers have assumed that the meta- of metaphysics has the sense of "beyond," thus regarding metaphysics as speculation concerning things that are beyond the scope of science. Positivists have thus denounced the study, not recognizing that their own principles were themselves strictly metaphysical. Indeed all philosophical controversies ultimately reduce to well-worn debates in metaphysics.

METAPHYTA, or **Embryophyta,** taxonomic term proposed to include plants that produce an embryo and multicellular sex organs and exhibit an ALTERNATION OF GENERATIONS. The Metaphyta is divided into two divisions: the BRYOPHYTA, including MOSSES, HORNWORTS and LIVERWORTS and the Tracheophyta (or VASCULAR PLANTS) including the CLUB MOSSES, HORSETAILS, FERNS, GYMNOSPERMS and ANGIOSPERMS. (See also EMBRYOPHYTES; PLANT KINGDOM.)

METAPSYCHOLOGY, FREUD's term for abstract consideration of psychological phenomena in terms of the *psychic apparatus*, which contains the EGO, SUPER-EGO and ID.

METASTASIO, Pietro (born Pietro Antonio Domenico Bonaventura Trapassi; 1698–1782), Italian poet and dramatist. He is best known for his melodramas used as opera librettos, including *Artaxerxes* and *La Clemenza di Tito*.

METAXAS, Ioannis (1871–1941), Greek general and from 1936 ultra-royalist premier and dictator of Greece. He made important social and economic reforms. He tried to maintain Greek neutrality in WWII, but after successfully resisting the Italian invasion in 1940 joined the Allied powers.

METAYAGE, system of landholding in France from the late Middle Ages to about 1800. The farmer was permanent tenant of the small plot of land he worked and paid annual rent in kind to the owner. Similar sharecropping systems have prevailed, or prevail in southern US, Italy, India and Japan.

METAZOA, all animals in which there is differentiation of cells to serve different functions, forming specialized tissues or organs. The term separates all other animals from the PROTOZOA and perhaps MESOZOA.

METCHNIKOFF, Élie (1845–1916), or **Ilya Mechnikov**, Russian biologist who shared with Paul EHRLICH the 1908 Nobel Prize for Physiology or Medicine for his discovery of phagocytes (in man called leukocytes) and their role in defending the body from, for example, bacteria. (See BLOOD.)

METEOR, the visible passage of a meteoroid (a small particle of interplanetary matter) into the earth's atmosphere. Owing to friction it burns up, showing a trail of fire in the night sky. The velocity on entry lies in the range 11–72km/s.

Meteoroids are believed to consist of asteroidal and cometary debris. Although stray meteoroids reach our atmosphere throughout the year, for short periods at certain times of year they arrive in profuse numbers, sharing a common direction and velocity. It was shown in 1866 by SCHIAPARELLI that the annual Perseid meteor shower was caused by meteoroids oribiting the sun in the same orbit as a comet observed some years before; moreover, since their period of orbit is unrelated to that of the earth, the meteoroids must form a fairly uniform "ring" around the sun for the shower to be annual. Other comet-shower relationships have been shown, implying that these streams of meteoroids are cometary debris.

Meteors may be seen by a nighttime observer on average five times per hour: these are known as sporadic meteors or shooting stars. Around twenty times a year, however, a meteor shower occurs and between 20 and 35000 meteors per hour may be observed. These annual showers are generally named for the constellations from which they appear to emanate: e.g., Perseids (PERSEUS), Leonids (LEO). Large meteors are called FIREBALLS, and those that explode are known as bolides.

Meteorites are larger than meteors, and are of special interest in that, should they enter the atmosphere, they at least partially survive the passage to the ground. Many have been examined. They fall into two main categories: "stones," whose composition is not unlike that of the earth's crust; and "irons," which contain about 80%–95% iron, 20%–5% nickel and traces of other elements. Intermediate types exist. Irons display a usually crystalline structure which implies that they were initially liquid, cooling over long periods of time. Sometimes large meteorites shatter on impact, producing large craters like those in Arizona and Siberia.

METEORITE. See METEOR.

METEOROLOGY, the study of the ATMOSPHERE and its phenomena, weather and climate. Based on atmospheric physics, it is primarily an observational science, whose main application is WEATHER FORECASTING AND CONTROL. The RAIN gauge and WIND vane were known in ancient times, and the other basic instruments—ANEMOMETER, BAROMETER, HYGROMETER and THERMOMETER—had all been invented by 1790. Thus accurate data could be collected; but simultaneous observations over a wide area were impracticable until the development of the telegraph. Since WWI observations of the upper atmosphere have been made, using airplanes, balloons, RADIOSONDE, and since WWII (when meteorology began to flourish) ROCKETS and artificial SATELLITES. RADAR has been much used. Meteorology may be classified by the type of phenomenon observed: CLOUDS, PRECIPITATION and HUMIDITY, WIND and air pressure, air temperature, and STORMS. More basic is the scale of the phenomena: the microscale deals with small, transient phenomena up to about 10km in size and lasting, say, 1h; the mesoscale, those up to 200km across and lasting a few hours; the synoptic scale is that of daily national and continental weather maps, while the macroscale treats of global, seasonal phenomena. The general circulation of the atmosphere is zonal by latitude (see JET STREAM; PREVAILING WESTERLIES; TRADE WINDS). Imposed on this are disturbances—chiefly CYCLONES and

Meteor Crater, near Winslow, Arizona. About 4000 ft in diameter, it should strictly be called a meteorite crater because it was formed by impact. Other, even larger, craters have been found in Canada and Siberia. In general the meteorites that make them break into small fragments on impact.

Metric system

Quantity	Unit	Symbol	Equivalent in other metric units	Approximate equivalent in US customary units
length	metre	m	—	1.093 613yd
area	are	a	$100m^2$	119.6sq yd
volume	stere	st	$1m^3$	1.308cu yd
capacity	litre	l	$0.001m^3$	1.057qt
mass	gram	g	—	0.035 274oz
mass	quintal	q	100kg	2.205 short cwt
mass	tonne	t	1000kg	1.102 short tons

anticyclones—due to imbalance of pressure and temperature. An air mass is a large region of air, roughly homogeneous horizontally, which forms by stagnant contact with a land or sea surface and which then moves elsewhere. When two air masses of different properties meet, a FRONT is formed. (See also ISOBAR; ISOTHERM.)

METHANE (CH_4), colorless, odorless gas; the simplest ALKANE. It is produced by decomposing organic matter in sewage and in marshes (hence the name *marsh gas*), and is the "firedamp" of coal mines (see DAMP). It is the chief constituent of NATURAL GAS, occurs in COAL GAS and WATER GAS, and is produced in PETROLEUM refining. Methane is used as a FUEL, for making carbon-black, and for chemical synthesis. MW 16.0, mp −183°C, bp −164°C.

METHANOL (CH_3OH), or methyl alcohol, or wood alcohol, colorless liquid, the simplest ALCOHOL. Formerly made by destructive distillation of wood, it is now almost all made by catalytic reaction of carbon monoxide and hydrogen. It is used to make FORMALDEHYDE and other industrial chemicals, in ANTIFREEZE, rocket fuels and as a solvent. Being highly toxic, it is used to make ETHANOL undrinkable ("denatured" or "methylated spirit"). MW 32.0, mp −94°C, bp 65°C.

METHEDRINE, i.e., methamphetamine, one of the AMPHETAMINES.

METHODISTS, members of Protestant churches that originated in the 18th-century EVANGELICAL REVIVAL led by John and Charles WESLEY. The name "Methodist" was used first in 1729 for members of the "Holy Club" of Oxford U., led by the Wesleys, who lived "by rule and method." Influenced by the MORAVIAN CHURCH, Methodism began as an evangelical movement in 1738 when the Wesleys and George WHITEFIELD began evangelistic preaching; banned from most Anglican pulpits, they preached in the open air and drew vast crowds. Converts were organized into class meetings and itinerant lay preachers appointed. Wesleyan Methodism was ARMINIAN; Whitefield's followers were CALVINIST but predominated only in Wales. After Wesley's death in 1791 the societies formally separated from the Church of England and became the Wesleyan Methodist Church. The American Methodist movement was established after 1771 by Francis ASBURY and Thomas Coke. Methodist polity in Britain is in effect presbyterian; in the US it is episcopal. Methodism traditionally stresses conversion, holiness and social welfare. In both the US and England Methodist groups have often seceded from the main church, but most have since reunited. Worldwide there are more than 43 million Methodists.

METHODIUS, Saint. See CYRIL AND METHODIUS.

METHUSELAH, in the Bible (Genesis 5), the longest-lived of the patriarchs before the Flood; died aged 969 years.

METHYL COMPOUNDS, organic compounds containing the methyl group, CH_3 (see ALKANES). The most important are: METHANOL, TOLUENE, methyl ethyl ketone (a solvent), and the methyl halides (see ALKYL HALIDES).

MÉTIS, Canadian people of mixed Indian and European stock, who lived in the Red River area of present Manitoba, and were important in the history of the Canadian West. In 1869 they rebelled and formed their own government. (See Louis RIEL.)

METRE (m), the SI base unit of length, defined as the length equal to 1 650 763.73 times the wavelength of radiation corresponding to the transition between the ENERGY LEVELS $2p_{10}$ and $5d_5$ of the krypton-86 atom (see SI UNITS). It was originally intended that the metre represent one ten millionth of the distance from the N Pole to the equator on the MERIDIAN passing through Paris. But the surveyors got their sums wrong and for 162 years (to 1960), the metre was defined as an arbitrary distance marked on a metal bar (from 1889–1960, the "international prototype metre," a bar of platinum-iridium which is still kept under controlled conditions near Paris).

METRIC SYSTEM, a decimal system of WEIGHTS AND MEASURES devised in Revolutionary France in 1791 and based on the METRE, a unit of LENGTH intended to equal a ten-millionth part of the distance from the equator to either geographic pole. The original unit of MASS was the GRAM, the mass of a cubic centimetre of water at 4°C, the TEMPERATURE of its greatest DENSITY. Auxiliary units were to be formed by adding Greek prefixes to the names of the base units for their decimal multiples and Latin prefixes for their decimal subdivisions. The metric system forms the basis of the physical units systems known as CGS UNITS and MKSA UNITS, the present International System of Units (SI UNITS) being a development of the latter. SI also provides the primary standards for the US Customary System of units. This means that exact interconversion can be easily accomplished.

METRONOME, electronic or mechanical instrument used, usually during practice sessions, to give a sense of musical tempo. Composers indicate the tempo by stating the number of metronome beats per minute and the note whose value equals one beat. "M.M." before the number is for "Mälzel's metronome," Johann Mälzel having made the first modern metronome in 1816.

METROPOLITAN, Christian bishop who has authority over other bishops in a given province. The title dates from before 325 AD. (See ARCHBISHOP.)

METROPOLITAN AREA, term for a major city, its suburbs and the area surrounding it, including other towns and cities, over which it has influence. Population figures of a city are often given for its metropolitan area.

METROPOLITAN MUSEUM OF ART, the world's largest and most comprehensive art museum. Founded in 1870 in New York City, its collections include art from ancient Egypt, Greece, Rome, Babylonia and Assyria and it has outstanding collections of musical instruments, prints, and of famous paintings and sculpture from all periods. Medieval art is housed in the Cloisters, constructed from actual medieval buildings.

METROPOLITAN OPERA, leading US and world opera company. The old Metropolitan Opera House was built in New York City in 1883 but in 1966 the company moved to the LINCOLN CENTER. "The Met" has been as famous for its singers as for its directors like Gatti-Casazza and Rudolf Bing, or for conductors like MAHLER and TOSCANINI.

METSU, Gabriel (1629–1667), Dutch painter famous for his pictures of markets and of well-to-do people. Influenced by DOU and VERMEER, he had a fine sense of tonality and coloring, as in *Vegetable Market at Amsterdam* (1660–65).

METTERNICH, Clemens Wenzel Nepomuk Lothar, Prince of (1773–1859), Austrian statesman. After a diplomatic career in Saxony, Prussia and France he became Austrian foreign minister in 1809. He gradually dissociated Austria from France and organized an alliance of Austria, Russia and Prussia against Napoleon. However at the CONGRESS OF VIENNA, 1814–15, he reestablished a system of power whereby Russia and Prussia were balanced by the combined power of Austria, France and England. Appointed state chancellor in 1821, his authority declined after 1826 and he was overthrown in 1848 (see REVOLUTIONS OF 1848). The period 1815–48 is often called the "Age of Metternich."

METUCHEN, historic borough in NE N.J. It produces electrical equipment, chemicals, tools and paper products. Pop 16 031.

METZ, city in NE France on the Moselle R, a center for iron and coal mining. Of pre-Roman origin, it became a bishopric and capital of AUSTRASIA. France annexed it in 1552 and Germany held it 1871–1918. Pop 166 000.

MEUSE RIVER, river in W Europe, rising in the Langres Plateau, France and flowing N for about 580mi across Belgium and the Netherlands into the North Sea. It is an important thoroughfare and line of defense for France and Belgium.

MEXICALI, town in NW Mexico, capital of Baja California state. Its economy is based on both tourism and cotton and cereal crops. Pop 390 411.

MEXICAN FOXGLOVE, a miniature plant of the genus *Allophyton*, closely related to the SNAPDRAGON, which produces small maroon-spotted, foxglove-like flowers. Indoors, it should be placed in a bright north-facing window or a short distance from a sunny window; it grows well at average house temperatures. The soil should be kept evenly moist, avoiding dryness. They are propagated from seeds or by separating offsets. Family: Scrophulariaceae.

MEXICAN HAIRLESS DOG, breed of toy dog, probably of Chinese origin and taken to Mexico in the late 16th century. It has no hair except on the top of its head and at the tip of its tail. Its skin is gray and it weighs about 10lb.

MEXICAN WAR (1846–1848), conflict between the US and Mexico. Its immediate cause was the question

The imposing facade of the main entrance to the Metropolitan Museum of Art, New York. Housing over a million items from all major cultures, the museum has regular touring exhibits and a special "junior museum"

of US annexation of Texas. In 1835 Americans in the Mexican state of Texas rebelled against SANTA ANNA's dictatorship. On his defeat Texas became an independent republic and the US annexed it in 1845. Mexico claimed that the Texas boundary was the Nueces R, and the US that it was the Rio Grande. President POLK sent John Slidell to negotiate this question and to discuss the purchase of California and New Mexico from Mexico. The Mexicans refused to negotiate and in March 1846 Gen. Zachary TAYLOR was sent with troops to the Rio Grande. A Mexican force met him, and Congress declared war in May. It has been debated whether Polk's motives in promoting hostilities were based on a sincere grievance or on his desire to annex California.

US strategy was to invade N.M. and Cal.; to advance along the Rio Grande; and to invade Mexico City from the N. The American forces were successful in all these campaigns and General Taylor defeated Santa Anna in Feb. 1847 at BUENA VISTA. General Winfield SCOTT landed troops at Veracruz, defeated the Mexicans at CERRO GORDO, CONTRERAS and CHURUBUSCO, and after the battle of CHAPULTEPEC captured Mexico City in Sept. 1847.

By the Treaty of GUADALUPE HIDALGO, Feb. 1848, Mexico ceded to the US the territory N of the line formed by the Rio Grande, the Gila R., and across the Colorado R to the Pacific. The US agreed to pay $15 million and settle all claims by US citizens against Mexico. Americans were divided over the war, mainly because the extension of territory involved the problem of extending slavery, and debates on this point brought to the forefront of political conflict issues which led to the Civil War.

MEXICO, officially the United Mexican States, covers 761 530sq mi in southernmost North America. Straddling the Central American isthmus, it is bounded on the N by the US, about two-thirds of the border following the Rio Grande (Rio Bravo in Mexico). In the S it borders on Guatemala and Belize. On the E lies the Gulf of Mexico and on the W, the Gulf of California, which separates Baja (Lower) California from the rest of Mexico and the Pacific Ocean.

Land. About 75% of Mexico is occupied by a central plateau with low hills, basins and mountains and bounded by the Sierra Madre Occidental and Sierra Madre Oriental. Its S edge is formed by volcanoes, some still active, including Popocatépetl (17 877ft), Iztaccíhuatl (17 343ft) and Citlaltépetl, or Orizba (18 700ft, highest peak in Mexico). S of the central plateau is another high and rugged region. On the E and W escarpments drop steeply to the coastal plains, the broader being the Gulf Coast plain extending from the Rio Bravo to the Yucatán peninsula and consisting mainly of swamps and lagoons. N Mexico is arid and has few rivers. Three main rivers drain the central plateau: the Santiago-Lerma, the Pánuco-Moctezuma and the upper Balsas R.

There are four climatic zones: *tierra caliente* (hot land) lying between sea level and 2 500ft and embracing the Yucatán, coastal lowlands and part of Baja California; *tierra templada* of the central plateau; and *tierra fria* (cold land, 6000–12 000ft). Above 12 000ft is *tierra helada* (frozen land). Rainfall, heaviest in the SE, decreases inland and to the N.

People. The population, estimated at over 54 million, continues to increase rapidly due to the high birthrate. About 50% live in the towns and cities, the largest being Mexico City, the capital. Guadalajara is the second largest city. Most Mexicans are mestizos (of mixed Indian and white stock) and most are Roman Catholics. Spanish is the official language, but there are many Indian dialects. Though education has progressed, more than 20% of the population are still illiterate.

The Economy has expanded since WWII, but though industrialization has made great progress, agriculture remains the most important sector. Less than 15% of the land surface is cultivable. Most cultivated land is on the central plateau. Since the revolution of 1910, most large estates have been expropriated and the land redistributed among the peasants, organized in landholding communities (*ejidos*). The chief subsistence crops are corn and

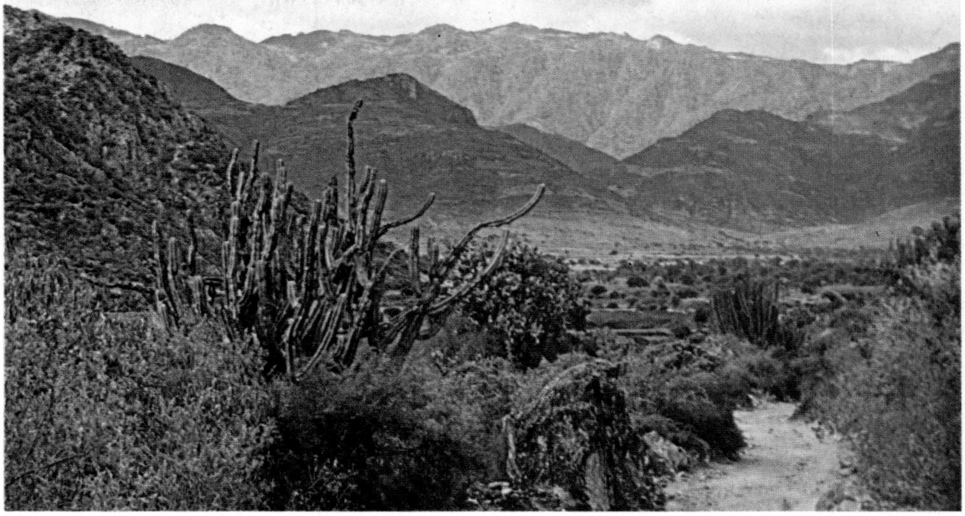

The Oaxaca valley in the Mexican highlands is an example of an area which has been consistently farmed over the centuries, in spite of the prevalent arid conditions.

Official name: The Mexican United States
Capital: Mexico City
Area: 761 530sq mi
Population: 54 530 000
Languages: Spanish
Religions: Roman Catholic
Monetary unit(s): 1 Mexican peso = 100 centavos

beans. The main commercial crops are wheat, corn, beans, cotton, coffee, sugarcane and sisal. Tropical crops are grown on the coastal lowlands. Irrigation projects have transformed parts of the arid N. Cattle are reared in the N and in the rugged region S of the central plateau. There are valuable forests (pine, mahogany, cedar) and fisheries (sardines, tuna, shrimps).

Mexico is rich in minerals, especially silver, zinc, lead, copper, coal, oil, natural gas and sulfur. Abundant reserves of iron ore and uranium await development. Large hydroelectric plants have been constructed on some rivers. Major industries include iron and steel (Monterrey, Monclova and the new, much larger Las Truchas project), and textiles (Mexico City and nearby Puebla and Toluca). Mexico also makes chemicals, electric goods, ceramics, paper, footwear, glass, processed foods and other products. Tourism is a major industry which has stimulated highway improvement and new resort centers.

History. People were living in Mexico by 10 000 BC and maize cultivation led to a farming culture (c1000 BC). Later advanced Indian civilizations developed (see AZTECS; MAYAS; MIXTECS; TOETIHUACAN; TOLTEC; ZAPOTEC). The arrival of Hernán CORTÉS (1519) and his destruction of Aztec power (1521) brought Mexico under Spanish rule, which was not challenged until 1810 by Father Miguel HIDALGO Y COSTILLA, but independence was not won until 1821 under the leadership of Agustin de ITURBIDE. The federal republic was created in 1824. Texas broke free of Mexico in 1836 and in the MEXICAN WAR, the republic lost NW territories to the US (1848). There followed a French attempt to make MAXIMILIAN of Austria puppet emperor of Mexico (1864–67), which was defeated by American pressure and the resistance movement of Benito JUÁREZ; the long reformist dictatorship of Porfiro DIÁZ (1876–80, 1884–1911) and the MADERO revolution of 1910. A liberal constitution was introduced by President CARRANZA (1917) and further reforms by later presidents, notably Lázaro CÁRDENAS (1934–40). The National Revolutionary Party, formed from all major political groups in 1929 and later renamed the Institutional Revolutionary Party (PRI), remains the effective political force and is still reformist in character.

MEXICO, state in S central Mexico. Much of the state is located 10 000ft above sea level. Cereal agriculture, coffee, mining and metal manufacturing are important economic products. The state capital is Toluca.

MEXICO, city in NE central Mo., seat of Audrain Co. The economy is based on the fire clay industry, agriculture and shoe-manufacture. Pop 11 807.

MEXICO, Gulf of. See GULF OF MEXICO.

MEXICO CITY, capital of Mexico. Located at an altitude of 7 347ft and at the S end of Mexico's central plateau, it is surrounded by the mountain ranges of Iztaccíhuatl and Popocatépetl. The climate is cool and dry, but the city, built on land reclaimed from Lake Texcoco, has often been damaged by local floods. Subsidence has caused heavy buildings to sink up to 12in in a year. Mexico City is on the site of the old AZTEC capital of TENOCHTITLAN founded in 1176. CORTES captured the city in 1521 and for the next 300 years it was the seat of the viceroyalty of New Spain and it consequently possesses some of the finest Spanish colonial architecture. Pop 3 025 564.

The old Basilica of Our Lady of Guadeloupe near Mexico City, built in 1709, now a museum. In 1976 a new basilica has been inaugurated on the square in front of it as the old one was sinking in the spongy soil.

MEYER, Adolf (1866–1950), Swiss-born US psychiatrist best known for his concept of *psychobiology*, the use in psychiatry of both psychological and biological processes together.

MEYER, Julius Lothar (1830–1895), German chemist who, independently from MENDELEYEV, drew up the PERIODIC TABLE, publishing his version in 1870. He showed the periodicity of atomic volume.

MEYERBEER, Giacomo (1791–1864), German composer, born Jakob Liebmann Meyer Beer. His work for the romantic and spectacular Paris operas with librettos by SCRIBE, set the vogue for French opera. Most famous are his operas *Robert le Diable* (1831), *Les Huguenots* (1836) and *L'Africaine* (1865.)

MEYERHOF, Otto (1884–1951), German physiologist who shared with A. V. HILL the 1922 Nobel Prize for Physiology or Medicine for their independent work on the biochemistry of MUSCLE action.

MEYERHOLD, Vsevolod Yemilyevich (1874–1942), Russian theatrical director and actor, whose work revolutionized the Russian theater. Rejecting stage illusionist conventions, he adopted abstract "constructivist" settings and advocated "biomechanics"—a system of acting methods and responses.

MEZUZAH, hollow container for a parchment scroll on which are inscribed verses from Deuteronomy 6:4–9, and 11:13–21. Jews fix a mezuzah to the right doorpost of the front door.

MEZZOTINT, a method of copper or steel engraving which gives tonal qualities and shading to a print. The surface of the plate is uniformly "burred" with a rocker, the burrs holding the ink; the plate is scraped and burnished where less absorption of ink by the paper is required. Invented in the 17th century in Holland, Mezzotint was prominent in the 18th and 19th centuries.

MHO, or reciprocal OHM, a unit of CONDUCTANCE.

MIAMI, second largest city in Fla., the seat of Dade Co., located at the mouth of the Miami R on Biscayne Bay. Its fine climate and beaches have made it a world famous resort center. Miami is also a major manufacturing center with a huge port and international airport. Pop 334 859.

MIAMI, city in NE Okla., seat of Ottawa Co. It is a trading and shipping center for a mining and agricultural region. Pop 13 880.

MIAMI BEACH, famous resort city in SE Fla., on an island in the Atlantic $2\frac{1}{2}$mi E of Miami. Its chief industry is tourism, with more than 3 million visitors annually. Pop 87 072.

MIAMI INDIANS, an ALGONQUIAN-speaking North American Indian group, of the Great Lakes region. They hunted buffalo and grew crops. In the 18th century they numbered not more than 1 750. They were allies of the French during the FRENCH AND INDIAN WARS and aided the British during the American Revolution.

MIAMI RIVER, or Great Miami, river in W Ohio, about 160mi long. It rises in Indian Lake, and flows S and SW into the Ohio R.

MIAMISBURG, city, SW Ohio, on Miami R, 10mi S of Dayton. It manufactures paper and metal products; many people are employed in the Atomic Energy Commission's research labs. Pop 14 797.

MIAMI SPRINGS, NW suburb of Miami, SE Fla. Miami International Airport is directly adjacent. Pop 13 279.

MICA, group of common SILICATE minerals composed of sheets of linked SiO_4 tetrahedra, with aluminum replacing silicon to some extent, and containing cations and hydroxyl groups between the layers. The three main types are BIOTITE, MUSCOVITE and PHLOGOPITE; others include CHLORITE and GLAUCONITE. Micas occur widespread in many igneous, metamorphic and sedimentary rocks, and weather to CLAY minerals. They show perfect basal cleavage, producing thin, flexible flakes which are used as electrical insulators and as the dielectric in CAPACITORS; ground mica is used in paints, inks, wallpaper, rubber and waterproof coatings.

MICAH, Book of, the sixth of the Old Testament MINOR PROPHETS, the oracles of the Judean prophet Micah (flourished late 8th century BC). Chapters 4 through 7 are thought to be later. Ethical in tenor, the book prophesies judgment for sin and restoration by the MESSIAH, centered on Zion.

MICHAEL, Saint, an ARCHANGEL, the princely guardian of Israel (Dan. 10:13, 21; 12:1). In Christian tradition he is the militant angel who triumphs over the devil. Many folk customs are observed on Michaelmas Day, Sept. 29.

MICHAEL VIII (c1224–1282), Byzantine emperor, 1261–82; first of the Palaeologus dynasty which ruled the BYZANTINE EMPIRE until 1453. He became sole ruler of Byzantium when his troops recovered the city from the Crusader Latins (1261). He engineered the SICILIAN VESPERS revolt(1282), which robbed Charles of Anjou of Sicily as a base for operations against the empire.

MICHAEL (1921–   ), king of Romania, 1927–30; 1940–47. During WWII Michael was a puppet of Rumania's pro-German dictator Ion ANTONESCU. In 1947 he led support for the Allies, but after the war was exiled from Rumania by the communists.

MICHAEL (1596–1645), first ROMANOV czar of Russia, 1613–45. During his rule, peace was made with Sweden and Poland, and some western ideas on army organization and industrial methods were introduced. However the peasants were forced further into serfdom.

MICHAEL CERULARIUS (c1000–1058), patriarch of Constantinople, 1043–58. His claim for autonomy and subsequent excommunication by LEO IX was a factor leading to the GREAT SCHISM between the Roman Catholic and the Eastern churches (1054).

MICHELANGELO (1475–1564), one of the world's most famous artists. Italian sculptor, painter, architect and poet, Michelangelo Buonarroti was probably the greatest artistic genius of the Renaissance. As a child he was apprenticed to the Florentine painter GHIRLANDAIO. He went to Rome in 1496 where his beautiful and poignant marble *Pietà*, 1498–99, established him as the foremost living sculptor. In Florence for 1501–05 he sculpted the magnificent *David*, 1501–04, the largest marble statue carved in Italy since the end of the Roman empire. In 1505 Michelangelo went to Rome to work on a gigantic tomb for Pope JULIUS II. In Rome he painted the ceiling of the SISTINE CHAPEL, and this work has been one of the most influential in the history of art. After living in Florence 1515–34 and building the New Sacristy and library for the MEDICI family, he moved permanently to Rome. He painted the *Last Judgment* in the Sistine Chapel, 1536–41, and his last very great work was rebuilding SAINT PETER'S BASILICA, 1546–64. His architectural designs were influential throughout Italy, and in France and England.

MICHELET, Jules (1798–1874), French historian, a professor of history and a director of the national archives (1830–51). Among his voluminous works is the monumental *Histoire de France* (1833–67), with its incomparable descriptions of Medieval times.

MICHELOZZO (Michelozzo di Bartolommeo Michelozzi; 1396–1472), Florentine sculptor and architect of the Early Renaissance. His architectural works include the Palazzo Medici-Riccardi in Florence (1444–59) which influenced later palace and town house architecture in Italy.

MICHELS, Robert (1876–1936), German political sociologist. He formulated the "iron law of OLIGARCHY" which postulated that political parties and organizations tend to elitist rule even in a democracy. His most famous work, *Political Parties* (1911), sets forth his ideas.

MICHELSON-MORLEY EXPERIMENT, important experiment whose results, by showing that the ETHER does not exist, substantially contributed to EINSTEIN's formulation of RELATIVITY theory. Its genesis was the development by **Albert Abraham Michelson** (1852–1931) of an INTERFEROMETER (1881) whereby a beam of light could be split into two parts sent at right angles to each other and then brought together again. Because of the earth's motion in space, the "drag" of the stationary ether should produce INTERFERENCE effects when the beams are brought together: his early experiments showed no such effects. With E. W. MORLEY he improved the sensitivity of his equipment, and by 1887 was able to show that there was no "drag," and therefore no ether. Michelson, awarded the Nobel Prize for Physics in 1908, was the first US Nobel prizewinner.

MICHENER, James Albert (1907–   ), US author. His Pulitzer prize-winning *Tales of the South Pacific* (1947), based on his US Navy experience in WWII, inspired the famous musical *South Pacific* (1949) by RODGERS and HAMMERSTEIN.

MICHIGAN, a leading US industrial state of the N Midwest. Michigan consists of two separate land areas, the Upper Peninsula and the mitten-shaped Lower Peninsula. The two are connected by the Mackinac Bridge. The W half of the Upper Peninsula is a part of the Superior upland regions, a rugged, forested area which possesses some of the nation's richest iron and copper deposits. It is a popular vacation land. The E half of the Upper Peninsula and the entire Lower Peninsula lie in the Great Lakes plain region. While winters in the Upper Peninsula may be extremely severe, the Lower Peninsula has a damp, relatively milder, climate, with hot summers and snowy winters. The Lower Peninsula contains most of the state's industry and fertile farmland.

People. About three-fourths of the population lives in urban areas, with over 95% in the Lower Peninsula. Detroit (pop about 1.5 million) is the state's largest city, famous as the "automobile capital of the world."

Economy. Michigan's economy is highly industrialized. The state's automobile industry produces about two-fifths of the total US output of motor vehicles and parts. Other leading products are breakfast cereals, machine tools, furniture, upholstery and sporting goods. The rich soil of the Lower Peninsula supports livestock and dairy farming. Corn, wheat, hay, dry beans and fruit are also important. Michigan provides about 15% of the nation's iron ore. Tourism is important to the state's economy.

History. The first settlements in what is now Michigan were French (late 17th century). In the middle of the 18th century the area came under British control. After the War of 1812 the Michigan area came permanently under the control of the US, and pioneers began to settle the Lower Peninsula in earnest. Michigan was admitted to the Union in 1837. The REPUBLICAN PARTY was organized at Jackson (1854). At the end of the 19th century Michigan's population was about 2.4 million, but the state was still primarily rural. This was changed by Henry Ford

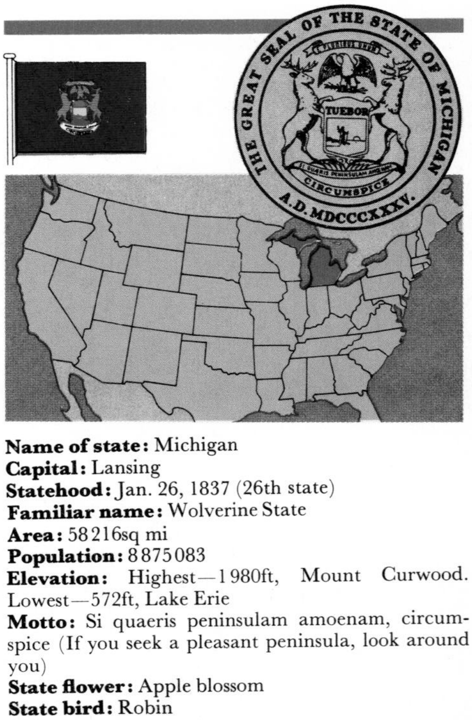

Name of state: Michigan
Capital: Lansing
Statehood: Jan. 26, 1837 (26th state)
Familiar name: Wolverine State
Area: 58 216sq mi
Population: 8 875 083
Elevation: Highest—1 980ft, Mount Curwood. Lowest—572ft, Lake Erie
Motto: Si quaeris peninsulam amoenam, circumspice (If you seek a pleasant peninsula, look around you)
State flower: Apple blossom
State bird: Robin
State tree: White pine
State song: "Michigan, My Michigan"

Ship passing through the Soo locks at Sault Ste Marie linking Lake Superior and Lake Huron. This important canal carries about 90 million tons of cargo each year.

and others who set up factories for mass-produced automobiles in the 1900s (Ford, Chrysler and General Motors). By 1920 the population had increased to almost 3.7 million. For three decades Michigan prospered, but the state was badly hit by the Depression. Today the auto industry, centered in Detroit, still dominates the state.

MICHIGAN, Lake, third largest of the GREAT LAKES, in North America. It is the largest freshwater lake wholly within the US, with an area of 22 178sq mi. In the N, Lake Michigan empties into Lake Huron by the Straits of Mackinac. It is connected to the Atlantic Ocean via the SAINT LAWRENCE SEAWAY, and there are also a series of connections linking it to the Mississippi R and the Gulf of Mexico. Important ports on the lake include Milwaukee, Wis., Chicago, Ill. and Gary, Ind.

MICHIGAN, University of, the first institution of higher education in the US to be governed by a board of elected regents. Founded in Detroit in 1817, the university moved to Ann Arbor in 1837. It has prominent schools of law, medicine, aeronautical engineering and astronomy.

MICHIGAN CITY, city in NW Ind., on Lake Michigan. It is an industrial manufacturing center as well as a popular lakeside resort. Pop 39 369.

MICHOACÁN, state, SW Mexico, with an area of 23 202sq mi., extending from the Pacific Ocean through an area of volcanic mountains and fertile valleys in the central Mexican plateau. It produces forest and agricultural products and a wide range of minerals.

MICHURIN, Ivan Vladimirovich (1855–1935), Russian horticulturalist whose theories of heredity, including the inheritance of ACQUIRED CHARACTERISTICS (see also LAMARCK), officially displaced GENETICS in Soviet science from 1948 until LYSENKO's fall from power in 1964.

MICMAC INDIANS, Canadian Indians of New France (Nova Scotia, New Brunswick, Prince Edward Island and coastal Quebec), of the ALGONQUIAN language group. They lived by hunting and fishing, using canoes for transportation, and numbered about 3 000 in the 17th and 18th centuries. They survive today as a tribal group engaged in guiding and farming.

MICROBIOLOGY, the study of microorganisms, including BACTERIA, VIRUSES, FUNGI and ALGAE. Departments of microbiology include the traditional divisions of ANATOMY, PHYSIOLOGY, GENETICS, TAXONOMY and ECOLOGY, together with various branches of MEDICINE, VETERINARY SCIENCES and PLANT PATHOLOGY, since many microorganisms are pathogenic by nature. Microbiologists also play an important role in the food industry, particularly in BAKING and BREWING. In the pharmaceutical industry, they supervise the production of ANTIBIOTICS.

MICROCHEMISTRY, branch of CHEMISTRY in which very small amounts (1μg to 1mg) are studied. Special techniques and apparatus have been developed for weighing and handling such minute quantities. Tracer methods, especially labeling with radioactive ISOTOPES, are useful, as are instrumental methods of ANALYSIS. Microanalysis is the chief part of microchemistry; another important aspect is the study of rare substances such as the TRANSURANIUM ELEMENTS.

MICROCLINE, common mineral in the FELDSPAR group, occurring in igneous rocks as vitreous crystals of various colors. It has the same chemical composition as ORTHOCLASE, and differs from it only in the arrangement of the silicon and aluminum atoms.

MICROECONOMICS, the study in economics of the basic constituent elements of an economy, the individual consumers (households) and producers (firms). By analyzing their behavior and interaction, microeconomics seeks to explain the relative prices of goods and the amount produced and demanded. (See also MACROECONOMICS.)

MICROENCAPSULATION, technique for enclosing minute portions of a substance (often a drug or a dye) in tiny capsules from which it is released when these are ruptured or dissolved. Its uses include NCR (no carbon required) copy paper, and the production of slow-release drugs and pesticides.

MICROFICHE; MICROFILM. See INFORMATION RETRIEVAL.

MICROMETER, instrument for measuring accurately dimensions or separations. Its basis is that when a screw is turned once, it advances or retreats a distance equal to its pitch (see BOLTS AND SCREWS). The hairlines in telescope and microscope eyepieces are adjusted by means of a precision micrometer screw to measure separations. The **micrometer caliper** has a G-shaped frame on whose "leg" is a scale; inside the leg runs a screw (of pitch usually 0.5mm) attached to a thimble, calibrated for fractions of a turn, which runs over the scale. An object is placed between the screw's sprindle and an anvil at the far side of the G's opening, and the screw turned until the object is just held. For greater accuracy (of the order of 1μm) a VERNIER SCALE may also be used.

MICRON (μ), unit of length in the CGS system (see CGS UNITS), equal to one millionth of a METRE. In SI UNITS it is replaced by the micrometre (μm).

MICRONESIA, a NW subdivision of the Pacific islands of OCEANIA, N of MELANESIA and divided from POLYNESIA by the international date line. The 2 250 small islands and atolls have a total land area of less than 1 500sq mi, and include the Caroline, Marshall, Marianas and Gilbert islands, Wake Island, Marcus Island and independent Nauru.

MICROPHONE, device for converting sound waves into electrical impulses. The **carbon microphone** used in TELEPHONE mouthpieces has a thin diaphragm behind which are packed tiny carbon granules. SOUND waves vibrate the diaphragm, exerting a variable pressure on the granules. This varies their RESISTANCE, so producing fluctuations in a DC current (see ELECTRICITY) passing through them. The **crystal microphone** incorporates a piezoelectric crystal in which pressure changes from the diaphragm produce an alternating voltage (see PIEZOELECTRICITY). In the **electrostatic microphone** the diaphragm acts as one plate of a CAPACITOR, vibration producing changes in capacitance. In the **moving-coil microphone** the diaphragm is attached to a coil located between the poles of a permanent magnet: movement induces a varying current in the coil (see INDUCTANCE). The **ribbon microphone** has, rather than a diaphragm, a metal ribbon held in a magnetic field; vibration of the ribbon induces an electric current in it.

MICROSCOPE, an instrument for producing enlarged images of small objects. The simple microscope or MAGNIFYING GLASS, comprising a single converging LENS, was known in ancient times, but the first compound microscope is thought to have been invented by the Dutch spectacle-maker Zacharias JANSSEN around 1590. However, because of the ABERRATION unavoidable in early lens systems, the simple microscope held its own for many years, Anton van LEEUWENHOEK constructing many fine examples using tiny near-spherical lenses. Compound microscopes incorporating ACHROMATIC LENSES became available from the mid 1840s.

In the compound microscope a magnified, inverted image of an object resting on the "stage" is produced by the objective lens (system). This image is viewed through the eyepiece (or ocular) lens (system) which acts as a simple microscope, giving a greatly magnified virtual image. In most biological microscopy the object is viewed by transmitted light, illumination being controlled by mirror, diaphragm and "substage condenser" lenses. The near-transparent objects are often stained to make them visible. As this usually proves fatal to the specimen, phase-contrast microscopy, in which a "phase plate" is used to produce a DIFFRACTION effect, can alternatively be employed. Objects which are just too small to be seen directly can be made visible in dark-field illumination. In this an opaque disk prevents direct illumination and the object is viewed in the light diffracted from the remaining oblique illumination. In mineralogical use objects are frequently viewed by reflected light.

Although there is no limit to the theoretical magnifying power of the optical microscope, magnifications greater than about 2 000× can offer no improvement in resolving power (see TELESCOPE) for light of visible wavelengths. The shorter wavelength of ULTRAVIOLET LIGHT allows better resolution and hence higher useful magnification. For yet finer resolution physicists turn to electron beams and electromagnetic focusing (see ELECTRON MICROSCOPE). The FIELD-ION MICROSCOPE, which offers the greatest magnifications, is a quite dissimilar instrument.

MICROTOME, device to prepare thin sections for the microscope. The specimen is embedded in a block of wax, then placed in the microtome. Turning a handle raises and lowers the block against a blade. At the top of its rise the block is advanced by a MICROMETER screw, which controls the thickness of the section cut on the descent.

MICROWAVES, ELECTROMAGNETIC RADIATIONS of wavelength between 1mm and 30cm; used in RADAR, telecommunications, SPECTROSCOPY and for cooking (microwave ovens). Their dimensions are such that it is easy to build ANTENNAS of great directional sensitivity and high-efficiency WAVEGUIDES for them.

MIDAS, in Greek mythology, king of Phrygia whose wish that everything he touched might turn into gold was granted by the god Dionysius. When even his food was so transformed, Midas asked the god to free him from the "golden touch."

MIDDLE AGES, the period in W European history between the fall of the Roman Empire and the dawn of the RENAISSANCE—roughly the 5th to the 15th centuries AD. The centuries preceding the 11th century are often called the DARK AGES. In the 5th century the W half of the Roman Empire broke up. Trade declined, cities shrank in size, law and order broke down. By the 10th century Europe was fragmented into numerous small kingdoms in which economic life for the masses of people was reduced to subsistence level.

Church, feudalism and society. The single unifying institution throughout the Middle Ages was the Christian Church. It provided some care for the poor and sick and its monasteries preserved the writings of the Greeks and Romans. But while the Church provided the spiritual foundations of the Middle Ages, society was ordered according to FEUDALISM. Its most important feature was the idea of service in return for land, protection and justice. At the top of the feudal pyramid was the Holy Roman Emperor (see HOLY ROMAN EMPIRE); then kings and princes, then warrior knights and at the bottom were the peasants. Each had a duty to pay homage to those above him and to provide military service when required to do so. In return each vassal was allowed by his suzerain or overlord to exercise control over his own domain and provided protection and justice for those below him.

Breakup of the old order. Around the 11th century the long phase of European decline was reversed and population began to grow again. Trade revived and cities grew (see GUILDS). During the 13th and 14th centuries the cities became powerful, and allied

The most magnificent and lasting achievements of European medieval architecture were the Gothic cathedrals and churches. This Flemish miniature, dating from 1460, depicts a number of such buildings in various stages of construction.

themselves with the emerging centralized monarchies against the Church and the feudal barons. New centers of learning, the universities, emerged. By the end of the 16th century LUTHER had set Europe aflame with his criticisms of the Catholic Church, GUTENBERG had invented the printing press and COLUMBUS had discovered a New World.

MIDDLE AMERICA, a current geographical term for the vast region of land and sea between the US and South America comprising MEXICO, CENTRAL AMERICA and the Caribbean islands (see WEST INDIES). The area's land features include the central plateau of Mexico and many rugged mountain chains and active volcanoes. The region is earthquake-prone. Though lying mainly in the tropics, it has a wide climatic range.

Middle America has a population of more than 89 000 000, of whom more than 66 000 000 live in Central America. The growth rate is such that the population may exceed 178 000 000 by the year 2000 AD. The main racial groups include *mestizo* (mixed Indian-Spanish), pure Indian and Negro.

Agriculture employs more than 66% of the work force. Plantation crops like coffee, bananas, sugar and cotton account for 90% of exports by value. Minerals are richest and industry is most advanced in Mexico, but regional development has been stimulated by the Central American common market. Recently, tourism has been expanding.

Middle America had important pre-Columbian civilizations like the Olmecs, the Teotihuacán culture, the Mayas, Toltecs and Aztecs (whose empire was destroyed by Hernán CORTÉS). Spanish rule profoundly affected the area's language, religion and culture. The British, French and Dutch had local influence, especially in the islands. (See also BELIZE; COSTA RICA; GUATEMALA; HONDURAS; NICARAGUA; PANAMA; EL SALVADOR.)

MIDDLEBORO, town in SE Mass. Its prime industry is the processing of cranberries. A prehistoric Indian site (c2500 BC) is nearby. Pop 13 607.

MIDDLEBURG HEIGHTS, village in N Ohio, a suburb S of Cleveland. Pop 12 367.

MIDDLE EAST, a large region, mostly in SW Asia but extending into SE Europe and NE Africa. Today the term usually includes the following countries: Bahrain, Cyprus, Egypt, the Lebanon, Libya, Syria, Iran, Iraq, Israel, Jordan, Kuwait, Turkey, Sudan, Saudi Arabia and the other countries of the Arabian peninsula. Politically, other countries of predominantly Islamic culture like Algeria, Morocco and Tunisia are sometimes included. The Middle EGYPT, ANCIENT; BABYLONIA AND ASSYRIA; MESO-civilizations, the Egyptian and Mesopotamian (see EGYPT, ANCIENT; BABYLONIA AND ASSYRIA; MESOPOTAMIA). The Middle East was also the birthplace of JUDAISM, CHRISTIANITY and ISLAM. It has been the seat of many great empires, including the OTTOMAN EMPIRE which survived into the present century.

MIDDLE RIVER, an industrial suburb in N Md., E of Baltimore, Pop 19935.

MIDDLESBOROUGH, city in SE Ky., near Cumberland Gap on the Ky.-Tenn.-Va. border. It is a manufacturing and coal mining center. Pop 11 878.

MIDDLESEX, borough, N central N.J., 6mi N of New Brunswick. Paint, chemicals and perfume are among its diversified products. Pop 15 038.

MIDDLETON, Thomas (c1580–1627), English dramatist. He wrote lively, natural comedies, the Lord Mayor of London's pageants and various masques, and two outstanding tragedies concerning human corruption: *The Changeling* (1653) and *Women beware Women* (1657). *A Game at Chess* (1624) was his satire on political marriages with Spain, suppressed under James I.

MIDDLETOWN, city in central Conn., seat of Middlesex Co., on the Connecticut R 14mi S of Hartford. It has light industry, is an agricultural commerce center, and is the home of Wesleyan U. Pop 36 924.

MIDDLETOWN, city in SE N.Y., on the Walkill R, 23mi W of Newburgh. It is a farming center and produces leather goods and clothing. Pop 22 607.

MIDDLETOWN, industrial city in SE Ohio, on the Miami R. Steel is its major industrial product. Pop 48 767.

MIDDLETOWN, town in SE R.I., on Narragansett Bay, 5mi N of Newport. It is a dairy farming area and a summer resort. Pop 29 290.

MIDDLE WEST, a term which usually refers to the following US states: Ohio, Ind., Ill., Mo., Mich., Ia., Wis., Minn., Kan., Neb., N.D. and S.D. The term is often shortened to Midwest. The region includes seven of the 10 leading agricultural states and six of the 10 leading manufacturing states. Although often scorned by Easterners as an area lacking in cultural amenities, Middle West cities have many great universities, museums and orchestras.

MIDIANITES, in the Bible, a wandering Bedouin tribe in and around N Arabia, encountered by the ancient Israelites. Moses married their priest's daughter. The Midianites were descendants of Abraham's son Midian by his second wife Keturah. (Gen. 25:2).

MIDLAND, city in central Mich., 18mi W of Bay City, seat of Midland Co. It is a leading US chemical-producing center. Pop 35 176.

MIDLAND, city in W Tex., seat of Midland Co. It is the center of a major oil-producing and cattle-raising region. Pop 59 463.

MIDLOTHIAN, town in NE Ill., 18mi S of Chicago. Pop 15 939.

MIDNIGHT SUN, phenomenon observed N of the Arctic Circle and S of the Antarctic Circle. Each summer the sun remains above the horizon for at least one 24-hour period (a corresponding period of darkness occurs in winter), owing to the tilt of the EARTH's equator to the ecliptic.

MID-OCEAN RIDGE. See OCEANS; PLATE TECTONICS.

MIDRASH, ancient rabbinical interpretations of Scripture. The Midrash Halachah includes legal works. But there is also the Midrash Haggadah, a series of non-legal biblical narratives and teachings, including Midrash Rabbah (5th century AD) and Midrash Tanchuma (9th century AD).

MIDWAY, Battle of, an air-sea battle of WWII, fought in early June, 1942. It began with an American attack on a hostile Japanese force approaching the American base on MIDWAY ISLAND in the Pacific. The battle was a decisive US naval victory, and marked the passing of the initiative in the Pacific to the Allies.

MIDWAY-HARDWICK, urban area in Baldwin Co., central Ga. Pop 14 047.

MIDWAY ISLAND, two islands in a 6mi-wide atoll, in the Pacific Ocean, about 1 300mi NW of Honolulu. It is an air and naval base, controlled by the US Navy.

MIDWEST CITY, suburb E of Oklahoma City, in central Okla. Pop 48 212.

MIDWIFE TOAD, *Alytes obstetricans*, a toad of W Europe in which the male collects the eggs as they are laid by the female and cares for them, periodically visiting water to keep them moist.

MIES VAN DER ROHE, Ludwig (1886–1969), German-American architect, famous for his functional but elegant buildings in the INTERNATIONAL STYLE, constructed of brick, steel and glass. His work includes the Illinois Institute of Technology campus in Chicago, and the Seagram Building (with Philip JOHNSON) in New York. Although he had no formal training, he was a director of the BAUHAUS and one of the 20th century's leading architects.

MIFFLIN, Thomas (1744–1800), American soldier and statesman. A member of the First Continental Congress, during the Revolutionary War he rose to the rank of quartermaster general. He was later a delegate to the Constitutional Convention (1787), and the first governor of Pa. (1790–99) during the WHISKEY REBELLION.

Typical farm of the America Middle West, at the heart of an enormous network of grain fields, on plains made fertile by a thick layer of glacial drift. The Middle West includes seven of the most agriculturally productive states, helping to make the US the world's largest grain producer.

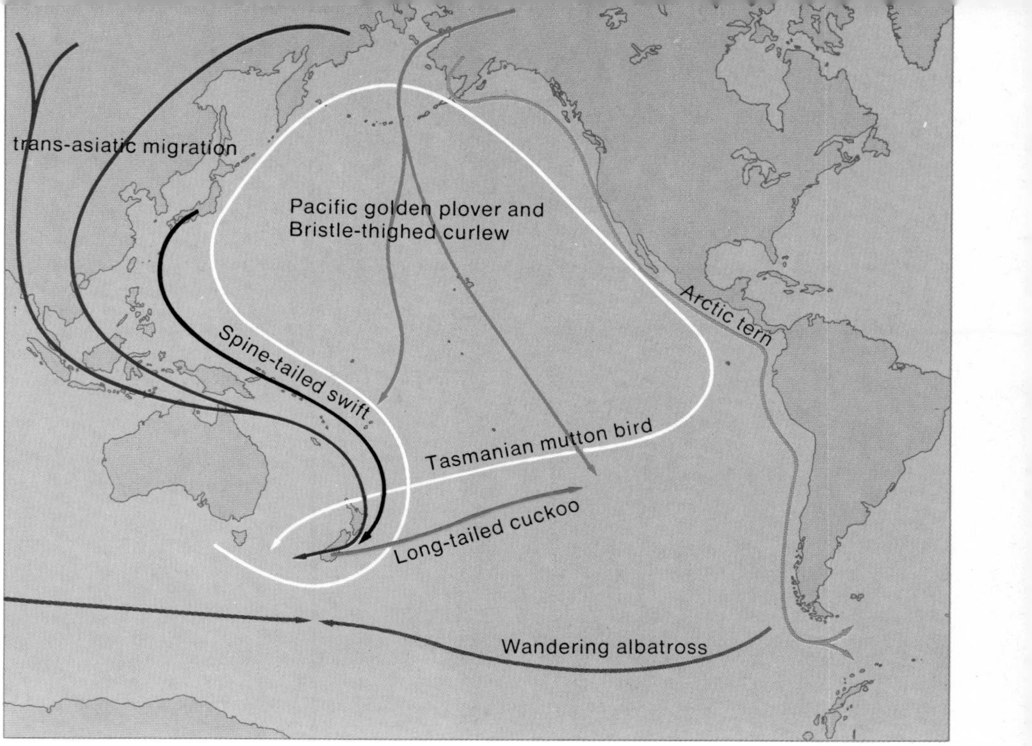

The main annual migration routes of Pacific birds migrating over the greatest distances. The Arctic tern makes the longest journey of all, traveling some 11 000mi from its nesting place within the Arctic Circle to the Antarctic.

MIGNONETTE, *Reseda odorata*, a popular garden plant of North America and Europe, with tiny yellow-white fragrant flowers. The name is derived from the French for "little darling." Family: Resedaceae.

MIGRAINE. See HEADACHE.

MIGRANT LABOR, workers who move from place to place, usually in search of seasonal agricultural employment. Although found elsewhere, migrant labor is primarily a US phenomenon, particularly in the W and SW. The workers, without fixed homes and unprotected by trade unions or governments, live in appalling conditions, such as those depicted in STEINBECK's *Grapes of Wrath.* Since 1970, however, Californian migrant workers under Cesar CHAVEZ have secured some improvement.

MIGRATION, long-distance mass movements made by animals of many different groups, both vertebrate and invertebrate, often at regular intervals. Generally animals move from a breeding area to a feeding place, returning as the breeding season approaches the following year. This is the pattern of annual movements of migratory birds and fishes. Migrations of this nature may be over great distances, up to 11 000km (7 000mi) in some birds. Navigation is extremely accurate: birds may return to the same nest site year after year; migratory fish return to the exact rivulet of their birth to spawn. In other cases, migrations may follow cycles of food abundance: Gnu in E Africa follow in the wake of the rains grazing on the new grass; CARIBOU in Canada show similar movements. Certain carnivore species may follow these migrations, others capitalize on a temporary abundance as the herds move through their ranges.

MIGRATIONS, mass movements of people which modify world population and culture patterns. Prehistoric hunter-gatherer tribes migrated in search of food following climatic changes as in the ICE AGES. Other migrations include those of the ancestral North American INDIANS from Asia, c25 000 years ago; of the CELTS across Europe in the 2nd millennium BC; of the Aryans into India c1500 BC; of the Germanic GOTHS driven by migrating HUNS into the ROMAN EMPIRE; of the ARAB peoples in the 7th century AD; of the Mongols in the 13th century (see MONGOL EMPIRE); of the TURKS into Anatolia in the 14th century. Since the 16th century colonial expansion, war, political and religious oppression, and poverty at home combined with the opportunity for exploitation abroad have led to massive migrations from Europe. More than 15 million have migrated to India, Africa and Oceania and some 65 million to North and South America. Pogroms in 19th-century Tsarist Russia drove thousands of Jews to W Europe and America, while millions of Jews and others were displaced by NAZISM in the 1930s. (See also NORMANS; VIKINGS; ANGLES; SAXONS; IMMIGRATION; REFUGEES.)

MIHAJLOVIĆ, Draža (1893–1946), Yugoslav partisan leader in WWII. A royalist and a Serbian nationalist, he sometimes collaborated with the Germans against TITO and the communists, who after the war accused him of treason and shot him.

MIKOYAN, Anastas Ivanovich (1895–), Soviet statesman, deputy premier under KHRUSHCHEV 1955–57, 1958–64, and chairman of the Presidium of the Supreme Soviet (i.e., head of state) 1964–65. From 1926 his career was largely in departments of trade. In 1956 he took a lead in denouncing STALIN's regime.

MIKI, Takeo (1907–), Japanese politician, prime minister from 1974. The ruling Liberal Democratic Party's compromise choice after the resignation of Kakuei TANAKA's scandal-ridden administration, he at once began a program of vigorous political reform.

MILAN, city in N Italy. An important European trade and transportation hub, it is Italy's major industrial and commercial center, producing automobiles, airplanes, textiles, chemicals, electrical equipment, machinery and books. Milan was a major late Roman city, and the principal city state of LOMBARDY under the Visconti (1277–1447) and SFORZA families. Spanish from 1535, it fell to Austria in 1713, and became a center of the 19th-century RISORGIMENTO. Artistic treasures include the cathedral, LEONARDO DA VINCI's *Last Supper*, the Brera palace and art gallery and LA SCALA opera house. Pop 1 724 173.

MILAN, Edict of, 313 AD, decree of the Roman emperors CONSTANTINE I and Licinius, which ensured toleration for Christianity in the Roman Empire.

MILAN DECREE, Dec. 1807, issued by Napoleon to tighten his blockade of British trade (see BERLIN DECREE; CONTINENTAL SYSTEM; NAPOLEONIC WARS). It declared that neutral shipping which entered British ports or acknowledged the Royal Navy's powers of search would be seized by France. Although the decree was not enforceable against British naval superiority, it damaged US trade and fueled the Anglo-American ill will that led to the WAR OF 1812.

MILDEW, general name for the superficial growth of many types of fungi often found on plants and material derived from plants. Powdery mildews are caused by fungi belonging to the Ascomycetes order Erysiphales, the powdery effect being due to the masses of spores. These fungi commonly infest roses, apples, phlox, melons etc. Downy mildews are caused by Phycomycetes. They commonly infest many vegetable crops. Both types of disease can be controlled by use of FUNGICIDES.

MILE, name of many units of length in different parts of the world. The statute mile (st mi) is 1 760 yards (exactly 1 609.344m); the international (US) nautical mile is 1.150 78st mi; the UK nautical mile, 1.151 51st mi. The name derives from the Roman (Latin) *milia passuum*, a thousand paces.

MILES, Nelson Appleton (1839–1925), US soldier, army commander in chief 1895–1903. A Union general in the CIVIL WAR, in the INDIAN WARS he campaigned against the Sioux and also accepted the surrenders of Chiefs JOSEPH (1877) and GERONIMO (1886). He also commanded in Puerto Rico (1898).

MILETUS, ancient IONIAN Greek city, on the W coast of Asia Minor. It fell under Persian rule in the late 6th century and led the Ionian revolt which involved Greece in the PERSIAN WARS. It was the home of the PRE-SOCRATIC philosophers THALES, ANAXIMANDER and ANAXIMENES.

MILFORD, city in SW Conn., on Long Island Sound. It is a fishing and resort center with some light industry. Pop 50 858.

MILFORD, town in S Mass. It has furniture and clothes industries, and pink granite is quarried nearby. Pop 19 352.

MILHAUD, Darius (1892–1974), French composer, one of Les SIX, noted for his polytonality (the simultaneous use of different keys). His vast output includes the jazz-influenced ballet, *Creation of the World* (1923), *Saudades do Brasil* (1921) for piano, symphonies, chamber music and operas, among them *Christophe Colombe* (1930).

MILITARY POLICE, an army division which serves as police to armed forces personnel. Its function is to maintain order among servicemen, investigate crime among the forces, and enforce military law.

MILITIA, a part-time army of volunteer or conscripted civilians, assembled in times of emergency. The citizen armies of ancient Greece are early examples. In England the first militia force was the Anglo-Saxon *fyrd*, and in Europe militias of different kinds were maintained until the 18th century. In modern times, Switzerland alone has a militia army. The US militia arose in late colonial times, and the Militia Act of 1792 made militia service obligatory. After the 1860s most state conscript militias were displaced by the volunteer NATIONAL GUARD.

MILK, a white liquid containing water, PROTEIN, FAT, SUGAR, VITAMINS and inorganic salts which is secreted by the mammary glands of female mammals. The secretion of milk (LACTATION) is initiated immediately after birth by the hormone PROLACTIN. The milks produced by different mammals all have the same basic constituents but the proportion of each ingredient differs from species to species and within species. In any species the milk produced is a complete food for the young until weaning. Milk is of high nutritional value and man has used the milk of other animals as a food for at least 5 000 years. Milk for use by man is produced in the largest volume by cows and water buffalo (especially in India); goat milk is also produced in some areas, particularly the Middle East. Milk is an extremely perishable liquid which must be cooled to 10°C within two hours of milking and maintained at that temperature until delivery. The storage life of milk is greatly improved by PASTEURIZATION. Because of the perishable nature of milk large quantities are processed to give a variety of products including BUTTER; CHEESE; cream; evaporated, condensed and dried milk; YOGHURT; milk protein (CASEIN) and LACTOSE.

MILKFISH, *Chanos chanos*, a marine and estuarine fish found throughout the tropical and subtropical Indo-Pacific. It feeds on diatoms and algae and may grow to 1.8m (6ft). It is an important food fish in SE Asia where it is actively farmed.

MILK OF MAGNESIA, emulsion of MAGNESIUM hydroxide, used for its properties both as an ANTACID in ULCER and HEARTBURN, and as a LAXATIVE.

MILK RIVER, about 625mi long, formed in Alberta, Canada, by the junction of two head streams that rise in NW Mont., US. After 100mi it reenters Mont. and flows E into the Missouri R. It is important for irrigation in Mont.

MILK SNAKE, or False coral snake, *Lampropeltis triangulum*, one of the KING SNAKES of North America. The name derives from an old myth that these snakes suck milk from cows. They prey in fact on small mammals, lizards and other snakes.

MILKWEED, popular name for plants that produce a milky sap, particularly those of the genus *Asclepias* which are native to Africa and North America. The name silkweed is also applied since the plants have silky seeds. Family: Asclepiadaceae.

MILKWORT, popular name for plants of the genus *Polygala*. They are so-named because of their alleged property to improve the milk yield of cows. Most species are native to North America, but a few occur in Europe. Family: Polygalaceae.

MILKY WAY, our GALAXY. It is a disk-shaped spiral galaxy containing some 100 billion stars, and has a radius of about 15kpc. Our SOLAR SYSTEM is in one of the spiral arms and is just over 9kpc from the galactic center, which lies in the direction of SAGITTARIUS. The galaxy slowly rotates about a roughly spherical nucleus (diameter about 1.5kpc), though not at uniform speed; the sun circles the galactic center about every 230 million years. The galaxy is surrounded by a spheroidal halo some 50kpc in diameter composed of gas, dust, occasional stars and GLOBULAR CLUSTERS. The Milky Way derives its name from our view of it as a hazy milk-like band of stars encircling the night sky. Irregular dark patches are caused by intervening clouds of gas and dust.

MILL, James (1773–1836) and **John Stuart** (1806–1873), distinguished British economists and philosophers. James Mill rose from humble origins to a senior position in the East India Company. He was an able apologist for the UTILITARIANISM of his friend Jeremy BENTHAM. A famous account of the education James imposed on his son John Stuart can be found in the latter's *Autobiography* (1873). The younger Mill is noted for his strictly empiricist *A System of Logic* (1843), his *Principles of Political Economy* (1848), and for his essay *On Liberty* (1854). J. S. Mill's circle included F. D. Maurice, Thomas CARLYLE and, later, Herbert SPENCER.

MILLAIS, Sir John Everett (1829–1896), English painter, a founder of the PRE-RAPHAELITE BROTHERHOOD (1848). His *Christ in the House of his Parents* (1850) caused a scandal by its realism; later works such as *The Blind Girl* (1856) and *Bubbles* (1886) became more sentimental.

MILLAY, Edna St. Vincent (1892–1950), US poet of bohemian rebellion. Her reputation was established with *A Few Figs from Thistles* (1920), and *The Harp Weaver* (1922) won a Pulitzer Prize. Other works include *Wine from these Grapes* (1934) and the verse drama *Aria da Capo* (1921).

MILLBRAE, residential city in W Cal., near San Francisco. Pop 20920.

MILLBURY, town in S central Mass. It has textile and metal industries. Pop 11987.

MILLE, Cecil B. de. See DE MILLE, CECIL BLOUNT.

MILLEDGEVILLE, city in central Ga., seat of Baldwin Co. From 1807 to 1868 it was the seat of state government. It has textile and other light industries. Pop 11601.

MILLENNIUM, in Christian ESCHATOLOGY, a 1000-year period in which Jesus Christ will reign gloriously. The doctrine, occurring in Revelation 20, ties in with Old Testament prophecies of the MESSIAH's reign. Millenarianism takes two forms: postmillennialists believe in a golden age of righteousness preceding Christ's SECOND COMING; premillennialists believe in a literal reign of Christ on earth after the Second Coming. Many in the early Church were millenarians (or chiliasts), but the idea was spiritualized by St. AUGUSTINE and recurred mainly in enthusiast Protestant sects, FUNDAMENTALISM and among ADVENTISTS.

MILLER, Arthur (1915–), US playwright. A committed liberal, he explores individual and social morality in such plays as *Death of a Salesman* (1949; Pulitzer Prize), *The Crucible* (1953) on the witch trials in SALEM, Mass., *A View from the Bridge* (1955; Pulitzer Prize), the partly autobiographical *After the Fall* (1964) and the screenplay *The Misfits* (1961), for his second wife Marilyn MONROE.

MILLER, Glen (1904–1944), US trombonist and band leader in the 1930s big band "swing" era. His blend of instrumental colors, the "Glen Miller sound," had immense success, notably with *Moonlight Serenade*. He died in a plane crash while touring troop bases in Europe in WWII, but his popularity continues.

MILLER, Henry (1891–), US writer, noted for his candid treatment of sex and his espousal of the "natural man." *Tropic of Cancer* (1934) and *Tropic of Capricorn* (1939), were banned as obscene in America until 1961. Other books include the trilogy *Rosy Crucifixion* (1949–60). He was a major influence on the BEAT GENERATION of writers.

MILLER, Joaquin, pen name of Cincinnatus Hiner Miller (c1839–1913), US poet. His flamboyant and romantic poems about frontier life include *Pacific Poems* (1871) and *Song of the Sierras* (1871).

MILLER, William (1782–1849), US religious leader who prophesied the second coming of Christ for 1843. His followers, called **Millerites** or Adventists, laid the foundations of modern ADVENTIST sects.

MILLES, Carl (1875–1955), Swedish-born US sculptor. He was early influenced by RODIN, but later work, including the monumental *Man and Nature* (1940) at the Rockefeller Center, New York, became more formal and classical.

MILLET, popular name for a large number of GRASSES that are cultivated throughout the world for their GRAIN, particularly in regions with hot, dry summers. Millets have been in cultivation in China since 2700 BC. The grain is used for both human and animal consumption and the remainder of the plant may be used locally as a poor quality forage or hay crop. Family: Graminae.

MILLET, Jean François (1814–1875), French painter, a leading member of the BARBIZON SCHOOL. His famous peasant subjects like *The Gleaners* (1857) and *The Angelus* (1859) are naturalistic in style if somewhat romanticized.

MILLIBAR (mbar or mb), CGS UNIT of PRESSURE. See BAR.

MILLIGAN, Ex parte, 1866, a US Supreme Court ruling defining the limits of military courts. The civilian Milligan had been condemned to death by a military tribunal in 1864 for pro-South COPPERHEAD agitation. The court ruled that a civilian cannot be tried by military courts, even in wartime, if the civil courts are functioning. Milligan was freed.

MILLIKAN, Robert Andrews (1868–1953), US physicist awarded the 1923 Nobel Prize for Physics for his determination of the charge on a single ELECTRON (the famous oil-drop experiment) and his work on the PHOTOELECTRIC EFFECT. He also studied and named COSMIC RAYS.

MILLINGTON, town in SW Tenn. It is a trading center for livestock and poultry, with a large Air Force base nearby. Pop 21177.

MILLIPEDES, slow-moving, usually elongated arthropods with a great many distinct segments and, typically, two pairs of legs per segment. They are well-armored, with a calcified cuticle, and when disturbed may curl up into a tight spiral, as in Snake millipedes, or into a ball, as in Pill millipedes. In temperate regions they are mostly nocturnal and secretive. In the tropics, in damp conditions, there are many brightly-colored diurnal species some of which reach great size.

MILLS, Charles Wright (1916–1962), US sociologist and penetrating critic of US capitalism and militarism. His books include *White Collar* (1951), *The Power Elite* (1956), *The Causes of World War Three* (1958) and *The Sociological Imagination* (1959), which argues that sociologists should not be passive observers but active agents of social change.

MILLS, Robert (1781–1855), US architect and engineer. From 1836 official architect of public buildings in Washington D.C., he aimed at an American neo-classical style. He designed the Washington Monument, the Treasury and the old Post Office building.

MILLS, Wilbur Daigh (1909–), US lawyer and Democratic politician. A Congressman from 1939 and chairman of the Committee of Ways and Means from 1958, he was an expert on tax and revenue and one of the most powerful men in Congress until scandal over his private life caused him a setback in 1974.

MILL SPRINGS, Battle of, Jan. 19, 1862, a Confederate defeat in the US Civil War. The Union forces' victory near the village of Mill Springs, S Ky., opened E Tenn. to them.

MILL VALLEY, city in W Cal. It is a residential suburb of San Francisco and a popular resort of artists. Pop 12942.

MILLVILLE, city in SW N.J., on the Maurice R. Neighboring silica deposits supply its glass industry; it also markets fish. Pop 21366.

MILNE, A. A. (Alan Alexander Milne; 1882–1956), English writer and dramatist, famous for the children's stories and poems he wrote for his son Christopher Robin. They were *Winnie-the-Pooh* (1926), *The House at Pooh Corner* (1928), *When We Were Very Young* (1924) and *Now We are Six* (1927).

MILTIADES (d. ?489 BC), Greek general who defeated the Persians at MARATHON (490 BC). Before this, he had served the Persian king DARIUS I against the Scythians.

MILTON, John (1608–1674), English poet whose blank-verse epic *Paradise Lost* (1667), retailing Lucifer's revolt against God and the fall of Adam and Eve in the Garden of Eden, is one of the masterpieces of English literature. His major early works are the ode *On The Morning of Christ's Nativity* (1629), *L'Allegro* and *Il Penseroso* (c1631), *Comus* (c1632) and *Lycidas* (1638). A Puritan supporter during the English Civil War, he wrote many political pamphlets and the famous prose piece in defense of freedom of the press, *Areopagitica* (1644). In retirement after the Restoration (1660), and now totally blind, he dictated his final great works: *Paradise Lost*, *Paradise Regained* (1671) and *Samson Agonistes* (1671).

MILWAUKEE, largest city in Wis., seat of Milwaukee Co. It is an industrial center notable for its breweries, and a leading Great Lakes port. The Milwaukee, Menomonee and Kinnickinnic rivers flow through it into SW Lake Michigan. Pop 717372.

MILWAUKIE, city in NW Ore., on the Willamette R. It has a large cherry-growing industry. Pop 16379.

MIME, the dramatic art of gesture and facial expression, also any silent acting. Mime was popular in classical times, often featuring topical or obscene subjects. It played an important part in the improvised Italian COMMEDIA DELL' ARTE of the 16th century.

MIMICO, town in SE Ontario, Canada. It is 6mi W of Toronto, on Lake Ontario. Pop 19341.

MIMICRY, the close resemblance of one organism to another which, because it is unpalatable and conspicuous, is avoided by certain predators. The mimic will thus gain a degree of protection on the strength of the predator's avoidance of the mimicked. Mimicry is well developed among insects. (See also BATES, HENRY W.)

MIMOSA, genus of tropical and subtropical herbs and trees that are mainly native to the Americas. They are also called "sensitive plants" because the leaves rapidly fold together when touched (see TROPISMS). Family: Leguminosae.

MIMS, Fort, stockade near the junction of the Alabama and Tombigbee rivers. It was the scene of a massacre of whites by Indians under William WEATHERFORD on Aug. 30, 1813.

MINARET, a tower of a MOSQUE. From its gallery Muslims are called to prayer by a *muezzin* (official caller). The original (7th century) low square minarets were gradually replaced by tall cylindrical or octagonal shapes.

MINAS BASIN, in central Nova Scotia, Canada. It is connected to the NE part of the Bay of Fundy by the Minas Channel.

MINAS GERAIS, state in E Brazil. Rich in mineral deposits (iron, manganese, bauxite, zinc, nickel) and agricultural products, it also has some heavy industry. Its capital is Belo Horizonte.

MIND, man's mental organ, with which he thinks, reasons, remembers and wills. The existence of the mind, as separate from the workings of the BRAIN, is denied in MATERIALISM, but affirmed in DUALISMS such as that taught by DESCARTES.

MINDANAO, island in the S Philippines, NE of Borneo. It produces coffee, rice, coconut, corn and abaca, and has some heavy industry.

MINDEN, city in NW La., seat of Webster parish. There are oil and gas reserves in the vicinity. Pop 13 996.

MIND READING, an aspect of telepathy. See ESP.

MINDSZENTY, József (1892–1975), Hungarian Roman Catholic cardinal who was sentenced (1949) to life imprisonment for his opposition to communism. Released in the uprising of 1956, he took refuge in the US Legation in Budapest. He refused to leave until the charges against him were withdrawn. This condition was met in 1971 by arrangement between the Vatican and the Hungarian government, and Mindszenty left for Rome.

MINE. See MINING.

MINEOLA, village in SE N.Y., seat of Nassau Co., and suburb of New York City. Pop 21 744.

MINERALS, naturally-occurring substances obtainable by MINING, including COAL, PETROLEUM and NATURAL GAS; more specifically in geology, substances of natural inorganic origin, of more or less definite chemical COMPOSITION, CRYSTAL structure and properties, of which the ROCKS of the earth's crust are composed. (See also GEMS; ORE.) Of the 3 000 minerals known, fewer than 100 are common. They may be identified by their color (though this often varies because of impurities), HARDNESS, luster, SPECIFIC GRAVITY, crystal forms and CLEAVAGE; or by chemical ANALYSIS and X-RAY DIFFRACTION. Minerals are generally classified by their ANIONS—in order of increasing complexity: elements, SULFIDES, OXIDES, HALIDES, CARBONATES, NITRATES, SULFATES, PHOSPHATES and SILICATES. Others are classed with those which they resemble chemically and structurally, e.g. arsenates with phosphates. A newer system classifies minerals by their topological structure (see TOPOLOGY).

MINERAL WELLS, health resort in N central Tex., close to the helicopter training school of Fort Wolters. Pop 18 411.

MINERVA, Roman goddess of arts and crafts, equivalent to the Greek ATHENA. Later she was also goddess of war.

MINES, concealed explosive devices placed to destroy enemy lives and equipment. They are often triggered by pressure or proximity. but some have a time mechanism and others are detonated by remote control. (See also BOMB; EXPLOSIVES.)

Landmines are of two main types, antivehicular and antipersonnel, differing in little more than sensitivity and in violence of explosion. They are buried just below ground and triggered by pressure or a tripwire. "Bouncing mines" have an auxiliary charge to throw them into the air, so that the explosion kills a maximum number of people.

Naval mines are of three main tyes, floating, moored and bottom. Moored mines, anchored to lie below the surface, may be triggered by contact, but more usually are attached to equipment that detects changes in the local magnetic field or water pressure, or the sound of engines. Bottom mines, usually set off by remote control, are placed on the sea bed in shallow coastal waters.

Southwestern minaret of the Great Mosque of Sultan Hassan in Cairo, dating from the 14th century. It is the only one of the mosque's original minarets to have survived.

MINESWEEPER, a naval vessel with special equipment for detecting and destroying MINES. Some tow *paravanes*, which cut the cables that keep floating mines below the surface; others generate a magnetic field to detonate magnetic mines safely.

MING DYNASTY, Chinese dynasty which ruled from 1368 to 1644, between the Mongol and the Manchu dynasties. The first Ming emperor was Chu Yüanchang. At its zenith, Ming rule extended from S Mongolia and Korea in the north to Burma in the south. Among the great cultural achievements of the era is the famous Ming porcelain.

MINGUS, Charlie (1922–), US jazz composer, bassist and one of the pioneers of BOP. Since the 1960s, he has attempted to widen further the scope of JAZZ with compositions of daring TONALITY.

MINIATURE PAINTING, small and detailed painting such as the illustrations in medieval manuscripts. There are fine miniatures in Indian, Persian and Turkish art. Portrait miniatures, of which the first European master was HOLBEIN the Younger, were common from the 16th to the 19th centuries.

MINIMUM WAGE, a basic wage which employers are obliged by law to pay employees. They may pay more than this bottom limit, but not less. It is designed to protect the lowest paid workers, who may not have powerful unions to act on their behalf. In 1974, the minimum wage in America stood at $2.30 per hour.

MINING, the means for extracting economically important MINERALS and ORES from the earth. Where the desired minerals lie near the surface, the most economic form of mine is the *open pit*. This usually consists of a series of terraces, which are worked back in parallel so that the mineral is always within convenient reach of the excavating machines. *Strip mining* refers to stripping off a layer of overburden to reach a usually thin mineral seam (often COAL). The excavating machines used in open-pit mining are frequently vast. Soft minerals such as KAOLIN can be recovered hydraulically—by directing heavy water jets at the pit face and pumping out the resulting slurry. Where a mineral is found in alluvial (river bed) deposits, bucket or suction dredgers may be used. But where minerals lie far below the surface, various deep mining techniques must be used. Sulfur is mined by pumping superheated water down boreholes into the mineral bed. This melts the sulfur which is then pumped to the surface (see FRASCH PROCESS). Water-soluble minerals such as SALT are often mined in a similar way (*solution mining*). But most often, deep minerals and ores must be won from underground mines. Access to the mineral-bearing strata is obtained via a vertical *shaft* or sloping *incline* driven from the surface, or via a horizontal *adit* driven into the side of a mountain. The geometry of the actual mining area is determined by the type of mineral and the strength of the surrounding material. All underground mines require adequate ventilation and lighting, facilities for pumping out any groundwater or toxic gases seeping into the workings, and means (railroad or conveyor) for removing the ore and waste to the surface. As in open-pit mining, the rock is broken mechanically or with explosives. However, particular care must be exercised when using explosives underground. Several occupational diseases (e.g., PNEUMOCONIOSIS) are associated with

The largest known deposits of iron ore in the United States are in Minnesota, where the mining industry has revived considerably as a result of new developments in mining techniques facilitating the conversion of low-grade taconite into iron ore suitable for blast furnaces.

mining and extraction metallurgy, particularly where high dust levels and toxic substances are involved. About 900 000 persons are employed in the mineral industries in the US.

MINISTRY, in the Christian Church, those ordained (see ORDINATION) to functions of leadership, preaching, administering the SACRAMENTS, pastoral care, etc. The Anglican churches recognize a "threefold ministry" of BISHOPS, PRIESTS (or presbyters) and DEACONS. The Roman Catholic and Eastern churches have recognized also subdeacons, and the "Minor Orders" of acolytes, readers, exorcists and porters; subdeacons and porters no longer exist in the Roman Catholic Church, and only subdeacons, readers and cantors are retained in the Eastern churches. Other churches usually recognize only pastors (or ministers), elders (or presbyters) and deacons.

MINIVETS, slender, arboreal birds of the tropics with brightly-colored plumage. Gregarious except when nesting, they move through treetops feeding on insects. Their distribution extends from China and Japan to Burma and India. Family: Campephagidae.

MINK, semiaquatic carnivores of the WEASEL family. There are two species, one (*Mustela lutreda*) of European distribution, the other (*M. vison*) originating in North America but now widely distributed throughout Europe where it has escaped from fur farms. Feeding on small fish, eggs, fledgeling birds and small mammals, they are fearless hunters, and often kill more than they can eat—creating havoc when they raid domestic chicken farms. Mink are extensively farmed for their prized fur.

MINNEAPOLIS, city in E Minn., the largest in the state, seat of Hennepin Co., on the Mississippi R. With its twin city, St. Paul, it is a trading and manufacturing center, notable for grain-processing and the production of electronic equipment. Pop 434 400.

MINNESINGER, minstrel-poet of medieval Germany who composed and sang songs of courtly love (*minne*). The Minnesingers, heirs to the Provençal TROUBADOURS, flourished from c1150 to c1350. They included WALTHER VON DER VOGELWEIDE and TANNHÄUSER.

MINNESOTA, largest of the midwestern states of the US. It is one of the most scenic regions of the nation, with about 15 000 lakes and extensive forests. Its vast wheat fields, flour mills and dairy products have given it the nickname "Bread and Butter State."

Land. The state lies within two major geographical regions: its NE part belongs to the Superior Upland (the S tip of the CANADIAN SHIELD); the remainder belongs to the Central Lowland Region of North America, mostly a treeless, gently rolling plain, where glaciers have deposited fertile topsoil. Three great river systems rise in Minnesota: the Mississippi, flowing SE from Lake Itasca and joined by the Minnesota R in St. Paul-Minneapolis; the Red R system flowing N into Hudson Bay; and the St. Louis R (an ultimate source of the St. Lawrence R) flowing into Lake Superior. Minnesota's climate varies from an average of about 8°F in January to an average of about 71°F in July.

People and Economy. Two thirds of the population live in urban areas. Extensive Scandinavian immigration in the late 19th century made a strong cultural impact. There are about 15 000 Indians. The largest religious groups are Lutherans and Roman Catholics. Schooling is compulsory between the ages of 7 and 16. There are 24 universities.

The manufacture of nonelectrical machinery is the largest single industry in the state, with food-processing coming second. Other leading industries include printing and publishing, pulp and paper products, chemicals and electrical machinery. Livestock and dairy products are prominent, and major crops are oats, corn, hay, rye, spring wheat, alfalfa, soybeans, sugar beet, potatoes and apples. Rich in natural resources, Minnesota provides about 60% of America's iron ore.

History. Penetrated by French trader-explorers in the 17th century, for over 100 years Minnesota was noted chiefly as a rich fur-trading area. Immigrant settlement began in the early 1800s and accelerated rapidly throughout the century as land was taken from the Indians. The state's prosperity rested on timber until well into the 20th century.

Name of state: Minnesota
Capital: St. Paul
Statehood: May 11, 1858 (32nd state)
Familiar name: Gopher State
Area: 84 068sq mi
Population: 3 805 069
Elevation: Highest—2 301ft, Eagle Mountain. Lowest—602ft, Lake Superior
Motto: L'Etoile du Nord (The Star of the North)
State flower: Pink and white lady's slipper
State bird: Common loon
State tree: Norway pine
State song: "Hail! Minnesota"

MINNESOTA RIVER, 322mi long river in S Minn., flowing E from Big Stone Lake to join the Mississippi at St. Paul.

MINNETONKA, suburb of Minneapolis in SE Minn; near Lake Minnetonka. Pop 35 737.

MINNOWS, a term used loosely in the US for any small carplike fishes, from over 40 genera. In Europe it is restricted to *Phoxinus phoxinus*, a small freshwater fish, common in rivers and streams with sandy or gravel bottoms. Although mainly known as the "tiddlers" caught by small boys, minnows play an important part in freshwater ECOLOGY, as food for KINGFISHERS, HERONS and larger fish.

MINOAN CIVILIZATION. See AEGEAN CIVILIZATION.

MINOAN LINEAR SCRIPTS, two written languages, samples of which, inscribed on clay tablets, were found in Crete by Sir Arthur EVANS (1900), and named Linear A and B. Linear B was deciphered (1952) by Michael Ventris (1922–1956) and shown to be very early Greek (from c1400 BC). Linear A is yet to be deciphered, though some symbols have been assigned phonetic values. (See also AEGEAN CIVILIZATION.)

MINO DA FIESOLE (1429–1484), Italian sculptor, one of the first of the RENAISSANCE to execute portrait busts. His work, chiefly to be found in Florence (where he lived) and in Rome, includes tombs and church sculptures such as the altar in Fiesole Cathedral.

MINOR, a person under the age of legal responsibility, usually 21 years. In some states of the US women reach majority at the age of 18. A minor cannot be bound by a contract made with an adult, but can be held responsible in certain circumstances. Laws vary as to whether children under 14 can be considered to be aware of the consequences of their actions.

MINORCA, or Menorca, second largest of the BALEARIC ISLANDS in the W Mediterranean, belonging to Spain. Its capital is Mahón.

MINOR PROPHETS, in the Old Testament, the 12 shorter books of the PROPHETS, often taken together (for list see BIBLE). The **Major Prophets**—the longer prophetic books—are Isaiah, Jeremiah and Ezekiel. No distinction of value is intended.

MINOS, legendary King of Crete for whom the MINOAN CIVILIZATION is named. He was the son of Zeus and Europa, and he married Pasiphaë, the mother of the MINOTAUR.

MINOT, town in NW N.D., seat of Ward Co. It is a trading center for farm produce, and has some heavy industry. Pop 32 390.

MINOT, George Richards (1885–1950), US physician who shared with W. MURPHY and G. WHIPPLE the 1934 Nobel Prize for Physiology or Medicine for his work with Murphy showing daily consumption of large quantities of raw liver to be an effective treatment for pernicious ANEMIA.

MINOTAUR, in Greek mythology, monster with a man's body and the head of a bull, to whom 14 young Athenians were sacrificed every year. Kept by King MINOS of Crete, it was eventually killed by THESEUS.

MINSK, capital of the Belorussian SSR, on the Svisloch R. Devastated in WWII, it recovered to become a major industrial and cultural center of the USSR. Pop 916 000.

MINSTREL, in medieval times, a wandering professional musician who composed and sang, often accompanying himself on a lute, harp or other instrument. Minstrels were among the earliest secular entertainers. (See also MINNESINGER; TROUBADOUR.)

MINSTREL SHOW, form of entertainment native to the US, in which white performers blacked their faces in imitation of Negroes and alternated jokes with Negro songs, many of which thus became well-known American folksongs. The entertainers, led by a "Mister Interlocutor," sat in a semicircle with the "end men" at each end.

MINT, strong-scented herbs of the genus *Mentha* and closely related species. The common mint or **spearmint** *(Mentha spicata)* is widely cultivated throughout the world for its leaves, which are used for culinary purposes. Family: Labiatae.

MINT, United States Bureau of the, a bureau of the Department of the Treasury responsible for the manufacture of domestic coins and for the handling of gold and silver bullion. The first US Mint was established at Philadelphia in 1792, and the present bureau in 1873.

MINUET, a French dance in three-quarter time with delicate mincing steps. It became very popular first at the court of Louis XIV and then throughout Europe in the 17th and 18th centuries. It also became a form of lively musical composition, particularly in the works of HAYDN and MOZART.

MINUIT, Peter (1580–1638), colonial administrator in North America. He was the first director-general of NEW NETHERLAND for the Dutch West India Company, and is remembered for buying Manhattan Island from the Indians for about $24 in trinkets in 1626. He founded New Amsterdam, now New York City, and later established NEW SWEDEN on the Delaware R for the Swedes.

MINUTEMAN. See MISSILE.

MINUTEMEN, volunteer militia in the American REVOLUTIONARY WAR, who were ready to take up arms "at a minute's notice." Mass. minutemen fought at the battles of LEXINGTON and CONCORD, Mass. (1775). Md., N. H. and Conn. also adopted the system.

MIOCENE, the penultimate epoch of the TERTIARY, which lasted from 25 to 10 million years ago. (See GEOLOGY.)

MIQUELON. See SAINT PIERRE AND MIQUELON.

MIRABEAU, Honoré Gabriel Victor Riqueti, Comte de (1749–1791), French Revolutionary leader. A powerful orator, he became an early moderate leader of the JACOBINS and represented the third estate (the commoners) in the STATES-GENERAL (the French parliament). He worked secretly to establish a constitutional monarchy, but was mistrusted by both revolutionaries and royalists. He was elected president of the National Assembly in 1791, but died a few months later.

MIRACLE, a wonderful event, transcending the known laws of nature, due to supernatural intervention. Belief in miracles is found in all religions; they are important not so much for their own sake as for their religious significance in revealing a god and his character or authenticating his agents. In theistic religions (see THEISM), only God has intrinsic power to work miracles (though he may delegate it). Miracles are immediate acts of God: normal events are ordered by God mediately through natural law. In the Bible, miracles occur in cycles associated with redemption, culminating in those wrought by Jesus Christ, and, above all, in his RESURRECTION. Roman Catholicism claims that miracles have continued in the Church, associated with saints, martyrs, their relics, and images; at least two authenticated posthumous miracles are required for CANONIZATION. Rationalist denial of miracles became important from the 18th century in PANTHEISM, DEISM and the skepticism of David HUME and others. Modern liberal Protestantism explains miracles as myths expressing a religious world-view.

MIRACLE PLAY. See MYSTERY PLAY.

MIRAGE, optical illusion arising from the REFRACTION of light as it passes through air layers of different densities. In *inferior mirages* distant objects appear to be reflected in water at their bases: this is because light rays traveling initially toward the ground have been bent upward by layers of hot air close to the surface. *In superior mirages* objects seem to float in the air: this occurs where warmer air overlies cooler, bending rays downward.

MIRAMAR, city in SE Fla., located S of Fort Lauderdale, near the Atlantic coast. Pop 23 973.

MIRANDA, Francisco de (1750–1816), Venezuelan patriot, who formed the idea of liberty for the entire Spanish-American continent. He fought in the American Revolutionary War and in the French and Spanish-American revolutions. With Simón BOLÍVAR he proclaimed the first South American republic in Caracas on July 5, 1811.

MIRÓ, Joan (1893–   ), Spanish abstract painter. A pioneer of SURREALISM, his imaginative works are freely drawn and are characterized by bright colors and clusters of symbolic forms. His work includes murals and large ceramic decorations for UNESCO in Paris.

MIRROR, a smooth reflecting surface in which sharp optical images can be formed. Ancient mirrors were usually made of polished bronze but glass mirrors backed with tin AMALGAM became the rule in the 17th century. Silvered-glass mirrors were first manufactured in 1840, five years after LIEBIG discovered that a silver mirror was formed on a glass surface when an ammoniacal solution of silver nitrate was reduced by an ALDEHYDE (now usually FORMALDEHYDE).

Undistorted but laterally reversed virtual IMAGES can be seen in plane (flat) mirrors. (Such images are "virtual" and not "real" because no light actually passes through the apparent position of the image.) Concave spherical mirrors form real inverted images of objects farther away than half the radius of curvature of the mirror and virtual images of closer objects. Concave mirrors (usually with an unglazed metallic surface) are used in astronomical TELESCOPES because of their freedom from many LENS defects. Parabolic concave mirrors, which focus a parallel beam of light in a single point, also find use as reflectors for solar furnaces and searchlights. Convex spherical mirrors always form distorted virtual images but offer a wider field of view than plane mirrors. Half-silvered glass mirrors are used in many optical instruments and can be used to give a one-way mirror effect between a well-lit and a dimly illuminated room. (See also LIGHT; REFLECTION.)

MISCARRIAGE, popular term for spontaneous ABORTION.

MISCH METAL, an ALLOY composed of 50% CERIUM, 25% LANTHANUM, 15% NEODYMIUM, 10% other RARE EARTHS, and iron. It is used to make "flints" for cigarette lighters and as a deoxidizer for vacuum tubes.

MISDEMEANOR, in US law a minor crime incurring a lesser penalty than a FELONY, generally a fine or jail sentence of less than one year. Very minor offenses such as parking violations are not classified even as misdemeanors in some states.

MISES, Ludwig Edler von (1881–1973), Austrian-born US economist. A professor at Vienna, 1913–38, and New York U., 1945–69, his most famous work is *The Anti-Capitalistic Mentality* (1956) on intellectual opposition to mass demand in a free market place.

MISHAWAKA, city in N Ind., lying on both banks of the St. Joseph R; near South Bend. It is an industrial city on the site of an old Indian village. Pop 35 517.

MISHIMA, Yukio (1925–1970), Japanese author, born Kimitake Hiraoka into a SAMURAI family. His writing is obsessed with the conflict between traditional and post-WWII Japan. He formed a private army devoted to ancient martial arts and committed HARA KIRI. His work includes the novels *The Temple of the Golden Pavilion* (1956), *Sun and Steel* (1970), *Sea of Fertility* (4 vols., 1970), *Patriotism* (1966), on ritual suicide, and modern Kabuki and Nō plays.

MISHNAH, the codification of Jewish laws from the biblical books of Exodus, Leviticus, Numbers and Deuteronomy, which with the GEMARA is one of the two main sections of the TALMUD. Compiled under the editorship of the scholar JUDAH-HA-NASI, it is divided into six orders or sections, and is a collection of civil, criminal, ceremonial, practical and religious laws and legal interpretations.

MISKOLC, city in NE Hungary, on the Sajó R. It is heavily industrialized and is Hungary's second biggest city. It produces iron, steel and automobiles. Pop 172 952.

MISSAL, in the Roman Catholic Church, a book containing LITURGY and ritual directions for celebration of the MASS. The Roman Missal was set forth in 1570 for use everywhere; the latest, thoroughly revised, version (1970) is in Latin and vernacular languages.

MISSILE, anything that can be thrown or projected. In modern usage the word most often describes the self-propelled weapons developed during and since WWII, properly called guided missiles.

The first rocket missiles were used by the Chinese in the 13th century, but the ancestors of the modern missile were the German V-1 and V-2 rockets used to bombard London in WWII. The V-2 could reach 3 500mph, and there was no defense against it. Captured V-2s gave Russia and the US the starting point for further ROCKET development culminating in intercontinental missiles capable of delivering nuclear warheads to any spot on the globe—and also of launching mankind into space.

Missiles can be classified according to their range, by the way they approach their target (guided, unguided or ballistic), by their use (surface-to-surface, surface-to-air and so on), or by their target (as with antitank missiles). The *Minuteman*, for example, is an intercontinental ballistic missile (ICBM), with a range of more than 7 000 miles and a ballistic arc trajectory, like a shell fired from a gun.

Missiles are normally propelled by solid-fueled rockets equipped with an oxidant that allows the fuel to burn outside the atmosphere. Liquid propellants are more volatile and not generally used. Larger missiles, such as the *Minuteman*, comprise several stages, generally mounted on one another, each with its own motor. This arrangement gives the missile increased speed, range and lifting capacity and so is generally also used in spacecraft-launching missiles such as *Atlas* or *Saturn*. A few missiles, such as the *Hound Dog* air-to-surface missile carried by the B-52 bomber, are powered by jets, while Britain's *Bloodhound* is driven by a ramjet (see JET PROPULSION).

Guidance systems vary from wire guidance for short-range missiles to elaborate homing systems which eliminate almost all possibility of escape. Some short-range missiles such as *Honest John* need no guidance at all, while those equipped with nuclear warheads cause such widespread destruction that pinpoint accuracy is not required. Wire guidance allows the operator to control the course of the missile through two fine wires paid out behind it. Other more complex systems use a radio beam directed at the target, or even a radar or laser-fed computer tracking and correcting the missile's course. Homing systems involve devices which detect waves emitted by or reflected from the target. Some home on heat in the form of infrared rays; others use radar. Many can be jammed electronically, but some are pre-set with a complete flight plan to guide the missile to a selected target, and to correct any deviation from course. Most long-range missiles have an INERTIAL GUIDANCE system to detect changes in course and velocity.

Missile launchers range from the simple tube of the BAZOOKA to the massive self-propelled mobile launcher/transporter used for *Honest John*. Larger missiles such as ICBMs require so much elaborate support equipment that they must be stored in heavily defended underground silos. Nuclear-powered missile submarines are more difficult to detect and destroy, and the US has over 40 of these, each carrying 16 POLARIS missiles. Surface vessels may also use missiles, gyro-stabilized to allow for the movement of the ship. Aircraft-launched missiles usually have a guidance system enabling the aircraft itself to remain a considerable distance from the target. The crippling expense and high risks involved in the uncontrolled development of nuclear missiles and antimissile systems has led to STRATEGIC ARMS LIMITATION TALKS between the US and Russia. (See also NUCLEAR WARFARE.)

MISSIONS, organizations for propagating a religious faith. Found from time to time in most religions, they are most characteristic of Christianity. The basis of Christian mission lies in the saving action of God to all men, found in Israelite prophetic writings and especially in the New Testament, and in Jesus' commission to his APOSTLES to "make disciples of all nations." Vigorous missionary activity, pioneered by St. PAUL, spread Christianity through the Roman Empire and beyond. From the 5th to the 10th centuries the rest of Europe was converted (sometimes by force), though N Africa was lost to ISLAM. There was then little missionary activity until after the Council of TRENT, when the Roman Catholic Church sent missionaries, especially JESUITS, to the Far East and the empires of Spain, Portugal and France; such work has been administered since 1622 by the Congregation for the Propagation of the Faith (see PROPAGANDA). Protestant missionary work began in the 17th century among the American Indians (see ELIOT, JOHN; BRAINERD, DAVID), but became a major enterprise only after the EVANGELICAL REVIVAL, when numerous missionary societies, denominational and voluntary, were formed, starting with the Baptist Missionary Society (1792). Today, missions operate in most countries of the world, aiming to help native churches and to do medical and educational work.

MISSISSAUGA, town, SE Ontario, Canada, on the W shore of Lake Ontario. It is a residential suburb of Toronto as well as a heavy industrial center and the site of Toronto International Airport. Pop 222 437.

MISSISSIPPI, a central US state which covers some 47 716sq mi and lies between Tenn. to the N, Ala. to the E and Ark. and La. across the Mississippi R to the W. On the S it borders on the Gulf of Mexico, and includes a chain of small islands separated from the mainland by the Mississippi Sound.

Land. The W edge of the state is in the fertile Mississippi alluvial plain known as the Delta, which has numerous streams, rivers and lakes. The rest of the state lies in the Gulf coastal plain. Pine forests cover much of the S area (about 55% of the state is commercial woodland), and the NE is hilly agricultural land. The general climate is subtropical with some 200 to 300 days of growing season and average rainfall of 50in per year.

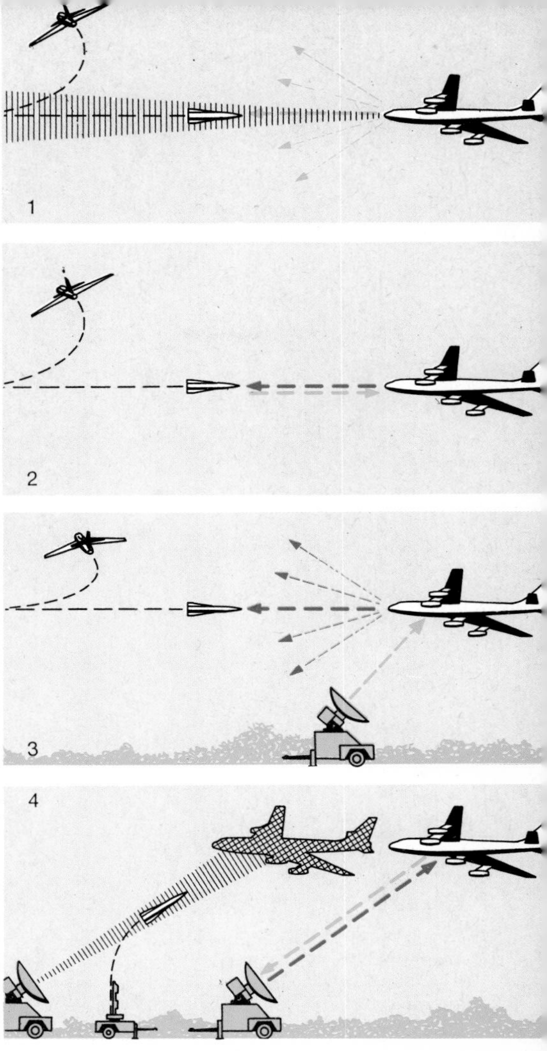

Methods of guiding missiles. (1) Passive target-seeking—the missile homes on heat or sound radiated by the target; (2) active seeking—the missile emits radar pulses (*green*) and homes on the reflections (*red*); (3) semi-active seeking—the missile homes on the reflections of radar from a ground transmitter; (4) beamriding—target radar (*right*) activates another transmitter (*left*) along whose beam the missile is directed. In daylight the beam can be directed from special binoculars.

Economy. In the 1960s for the first time Mississippi's income from agriculture came second to that from industry. Although cotton is no longer "king" in what was virtually a one-crop economy until the 1860s, it is produced in greater bulk than anywhere but Tex. Other important produce includes soybeans, pecans, sweet potatoes, rice, sugarcane, poultry, livestock and seafood from the Gulf. Petroleum and natural gas are the main natural resources besides timber. Major manufacturing is concerned with clothing and textiles, paper and wood products, food processing, chemicals and shipbuilding.

People. The present population is about 60% rural. The white population is more than 98% native-born of native stock with primarily British, Irish and N European ancestors, while the black population is also of old stock and almost wholly native-born.

History. Mississippi was discovered by Hernando DE SOTO in 1540. Part of the area was claimed by Britain after the French and Indian Wars and ceded after the

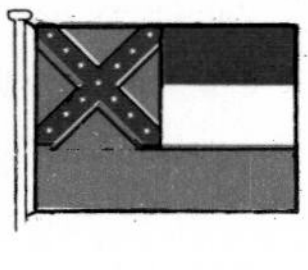

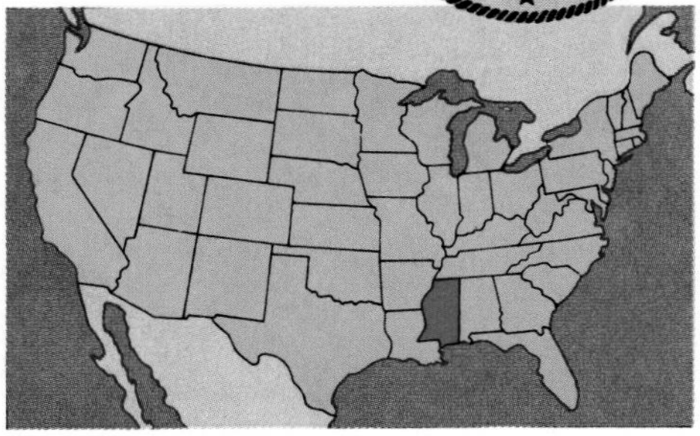

Name of state: Mississippi
Capital: Jackson
Statehood: Dec. 10, 1817 (20th state)
Familiar name: Magnolia State
Area: 47 716sq mi
Population: 2 216 912
Elevation: Highest—806ft, Woodall Mountain. Lowest—sea level, Gulf of Mexico
Motto: Virtute et Armis (By Valor and Arms)
State flower: Magnolia
State bird: Mockingbird
State tree: Magnolia
State song: "Go Mississippi"

American Revolution; Spanish claims in the S were not relinquished until 1798. Mississippi became a slave-based agricultural economy and was the second state to secede from the Union (Jan. 1861) before the CIVIL WAR. Subsequently the state suffered under RECONSTRUCTION and its aftermath has plagued Mississippians for 100 years. After WWII agriculture in the state was boosted with federal funds and farm programs. By the 1970s Mississippi had undergone a period of intense change which brought increasing industrial employment and also bitter protests over black civil rights. By the 1970s the state's economy was more prosperous than it had ever been and its racial problems were generally being confronted in a more balanced atmosphere.

MISSISSIPPIAN, the antepenultimate period of the PALEOZOIC, lasting from about 345 to 315 million years ago. (See also CARBONIFEROUS; GEOLOGY.)

MISSISSIPPI RIVER, the chief river of the North American continent and one of the world's great rivers. It divides the US from N to S between Lake Itasca in NW Minn. and the Gulf of Mexico below New Orleans, La. Known as the "father of waters," it drains an area of approximately 1 244 000sq mi. With the MISSOURI and OHIO rivers (its chief tributaries) and the Jefferson-Beaverhead-Red Rock system it forms the world's third longest river system (some 3 710mi). Its main course is some 2 348mi. It receives more than 250 tributaries. The Mississippi is noted for sudden changes of course; its length varies by 40–50mi per year. The river's average discharge is 700 000cu ft per sec, but in high water season this soars to some 2 300 000cu ft per sec. Flooding is a serious problem, but dikes and levees have been built to contain its periodic massive overflows. The river was historically a major transportation artery of the US and of fundamental importance in the development of the American continent. Although it no longer plays the same major role, its annual freight tonnage (with the Illinois, Missouri and Ohio rivers) was around 420 million tons in 1972.

MISSISSIPPI SCHEME, a commercial venture, also known as the "Mississippi Bubble," devised by Scotsman John LAW who founded the Compagnie d'Occident in 1717 for the colonization, under the French flag, of territories in the Mississippi R valley. Settlement of New Orleans was financed, but the company, now virtually a state bank, collapsed disastrously in 1720, ruining most of its shareholders.

MISSOULA, city in W Mont., seat of Missoula Co., on the Clark fork of the Columbia R. The US federal government maintains a forest fire fighting depot, laboratory and training center there. Pop 29 497.

MISSOURI, a W central US state, covering an area of 69 686sq mi, bounded by Ia. to the N, Ark. to the S, Kan., Neb. and Okla. to the W; on the E it is separated from Ill., Ky. and Tenn. by the Mississippi R. Its largest cities are St. Louis, Kansas City, Springfield and Independence, the home of former President Harry S. TRUMAN.

Land. The state's development has been shaped by its two principal rivers. The Missouri was an early

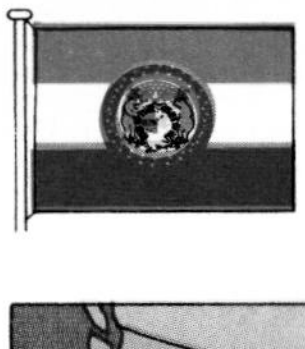

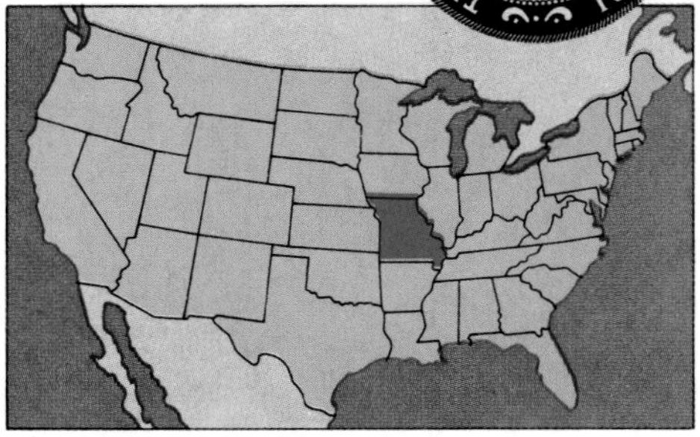

Name of state: Missouri
Capital: Jefferson City
Statehood: Aug. 10, 1821 (24th state)
Familiar name: Show Me State
Area: 69 686sq mi
Population: 4 677 399
Elevation: Highest—1 772ft, Taum Sauk Mountain. Lowest—230ft, St. Francis River in Dunklin County
Motto: Salus populi suprema lex esto (Let the welfare of the people be the supreme law)
State flower: Hawthorn
State bird: Bluebird
State tree: Flowering Dogwood
State song: "Missouri Waltz"

pioneering route to the West, while the Mississippi linked the state to the South. The N third of the state above the Missouri lies in the Midwest "corn belt," while the SE corner lies in the fertile Mississippi alluvial plain. In the central and S portion of the state is the forested Ozark plateau, which has poor, stony soil but great scenic beauty and is a popular tourist region.

People. Over 70% of the people now live in urban areas and the population continues to move from rural areas. In 1970 Negroes formed about 11% of the state's total population, many moving into the state from the South. Overall, Missouri is losing population rather than gaining it.

Economy. Agriculture has always been important in the state, which grows cotton, soybeans, melons and has large wheat farms. Livestock, including Missouri mules and poultry, are prime sources of income—the state ranks fourth in hog production, fifth in turkeys and sixth in cattle. Manufacturing is heavily concentrated around the St. Louis-Kansas City area which is a major mid-continental transportation crossroads and industrial center. Production of transportation equipment (automobile assembly, railroad cars, airplanes, rocket engines, space capsules and other aerospace technology) ranks first; the second-largest industry is food processing. Missouri is a leading iron ore and lead producer and also manufactures chemicals, clothing and machinery. Banking (with Federal Reserve banks in St. Louis and Kansas City) and other financial institutions are important.

History. Missouri was explored by the Spanish in the mid-16th century, but claimed for France by LA SALLE in 1682 and was subsequently developed by French fur traders. It was acquired by the US in the LOUISIANA PURCHASE (1803). Under the MISSOURI COMPROMISE, the state entered the Union as a slave state in 1821. Historically, the state was a central point of departure for traders, explorers and pioneers moving westward. It was also a border state between N and S, conservative in politics but generally northern in sympathies. During the Civil War many battles were fought on its territory, but afterwards industry expanded with the arrival of German, Irish, Polish and Jewish immigrants.

In 1839, the U. of Mo. was the first state university to be founded W of the Mississippi. Its world-famous School of Journalism (established 1908) was the first in the world. Since WWII technological industrialization has displaced agriculture in the economy and many new industries have created new jobs, but still the state's growth has fallen behind other states with similar natural resources and wealth.

MISSOURI COMPROMISE, a measure adopted by the US Congress in 1820, to resolve the issue of Missouri's admission to the Union as a slave state. At the time of Missouri's first petition (1819), there were 11 free and 11 slave states in the Union. The addition of Missouri would have changed the balance of power in the US Senate and reopened the bitterly contested issue between N and S as to whether slavery should be permitted and allowed to spread in the US. Action on Missouri's petition was delayed until Maine (formerly a part of Massachusetts) requested admission as a free state. A series of maneuvers led by Henry CLAY resulted in Missouri being admitted as a state in which slavery was legal, while Maine was admitted as a state in which it was not, with the added proviso that slavery would not be permitted in the rest of the territory of the LOUISIANA PURCHASE (of which Missouri had been part) N of 36° 30′. The compromise was later repealed in 1854 by the KANSAS-NEBRASKA ACT, which introduced the doctrine of popular sovereignty.

MISSOURI RIVER, longest river in the US (about 2 466mi) and the chief tributary of the MISSISSIPPI, with which it forms the major waterway of the US. Formed in SE Mont. by the Jefferson, Madison and Gallatin rivers in the Rocky Mts, it flows N and then E through Mont. and then enters N Dak. continuing generally SE to empty into the Mississippi R N of St. Louis. Its main tributaries along the way include the Cheyenne, Kansas, Osage, Platte and Yellowstone, James and Milk rivers. The Missouri was explored by JOLIET and MARQUETTE in 1673 and the LEWIS AND CLARK EXPEDITION in 1804–05. Like the Mississippi, it has been subject to disastrous flooding, which has been brought under control in the past three decades (see MISSOURI RIVER BASIN PROJECT).

MISSOURI RIVER BASIN PROJECT, a program first authorized by the US Congress in 1944 and expanded in the 1950s to harness and develop the waters and resources of the Missouri R, whose basin (stretching from SW Mont. to the Mississippi above St. Louis, Mo.) covers about one-sixth of the US. Flood control, improved navigation, irrigation and the provision of electric power are its main aims. The project, expected to extend over a 50-year period, involves the construction of over 130 dams and reservoirs, some already completed.

MISTI, El, a volcano, rising 19 031ft high in the Andes Mts, S Peru, near Arequipa. Its last eruption was in 1600. El Misti has been the source of many legends and played a part in the religion of the INCAS.

MISTLETOE, many species of evergreen plant parasites with small inconspicuous flowers, belonging to the family Loranthaceae. In Europe, the common mistletoe (*Viscum album*) commonly grows on apples, poplar, willow, linden and hawthorns, while the common mistletoes of the US (*Phoradendron spp* and *Arceuthobium spp*) occur on most deciduous trees and some conifers. Mistletoes derive some of their nutrients from the host plants, but being green produce some by PHOTOSYNTHESIS. Seed dispersal is achieved by fruit-eating birds that deposit the seeds on the bark of trees.

MISTRAL, cold wind blowing S from the Central Plateau of France to the NW Mediterranean. It occurs mainly in winter and speeds up to about 140km/h have been recorded. It is a hazard to air and surface transport, crops and buildings.

MISTRAL, Frédéric (1830–1914), French poet. He won the 1905 Nobel Prize for Literature and for his work as leader of a movement to restore the former glories of the Provençal language and culture. Among his works are the epic poems *Mirèio* (1859), *Calendau* (1867), *Nerto* (1884) and *Lou Pouèmo dóu Rose* (1897).

MISTRAL, Gabriela (1889–1957), pen name of Chilean poet, educator and diplomat, Lucila Godoy Alcayaga, awarded the Nobel Prize for Literature in 1945. Her simple, lyrical poems express a deep sympathy with nature and mankind. Her work includes *Desolation* (1922) and *Tenderness* (1924).

M.I.T. See MASSACHUSETTS INSTITUTE OF TECHNOLOGY.

MITCHELL, city in SE Dak., seat of Davison Co. It is located in an agricultural region of the James R valley. Pop 13425.

MITCHELL, John Newton (1913–), former US attorney general (1969–72) convicted for his part in WATERGATE. He managed Richard Nixon's presidential campaign in 1968 and was chairman of the Committee to Re-Elect the President (CREEP) in 1972.

MITCHELL, Margaret (1900–1949), US writer. Her best selling and only novel *Gone With the Wind* (1936) won the 1937 Pulitzer Prize and was made into a phenomenally successful film (1939).

MITCHELL, Maria (1818–1889), US astronomer, who discovered a comet in 1847. She was the first woman to be elected to the American Academy of Arts and Sciences (1848) and was professor of astronomy at Vassar College (1865–88).

MITCHELL, Wesley Clair (1874–1948), US economist and educator. He helped organize the National Bureau of Economic Research (1920) and was its research director, 1920–45. He served on many government boards and was the world's leading authority on business cycles.

MITCHELL, William ("Billy") Lendrum (1879–1936), US army officer and aviator. After leading US air services in WWI, he became an active champion for a strong air force independent of army or naval control. Court-martialed for insubordination, and suspended from duty for five years in 1925, he resigned from the army in 1926.

MITCHELL, Mount, US peak in the Black Mts, W N.C. It is the highest peak (6684ft) E of the Mississippi R.

MITES, small ARACHNIDA of the subclass Acari, frequently microscopic in size. Over 17000 species have been described and the mites are a diverse group. Many species are soil dwellers feeding on plant debris; mites in soil may number up to 100000 per square metre. Other species are predators on insect pests. A few species are important as parasites or agricultural pests, but these are a minority.

MITHRA, or Mithras, Indo-Iranian sun-god, also Mitra, one of the ethical lords or gods in ZOROASTRIANISM. By 400 BC, he was the chief Persian deity. His cult spread over most of Asia Minor and, according to Plutarch, reached Rome in 68 BC. Mithraism was especially popular among the Roman legions. Roman Mithraism, which amounted to a virtual parody of Christianity, declined after 200 AD and was officially suppressed in the 4th century.

MITHRADATES VI (c132–63 BC), king of Pontus, on the Black Sea, who fought three wars against the Roman state. In the first (88–84 BC), he overran Asia Minor and massacred its Roman citizens, but was subsequently forced to make peace. He won the second war (83–81 BC) but lost the third (74–63 BC) and fled to the Crimea, where he ordered a mercenary to kill him.

MITO, industrial and commercial city in Japan, 60mi NE of Tokyo. A branch of the TOKUGAWA family lived in Mito from 1606. Pop 173789.

MITOCHONDRIA. See CELL.

MITOSIS, the normal process by which a CELL divides into two. Initially the CHROMOSOMES become visible in the nucleus before longitudinally dividing into a pair of parallel *chromatids*. The chromosomes shorten and thicken and arrange themselves on a spindle across the equator of the cell. The cell then divides so that each daughter contains a full complement of chromosomes.

MITSCHER, Marc Andrew (1887–1947), US naval commander. In WWII, he commanded the carrier *Hornet* in the battles for Midway (1942) and the Solomon Islands (1943). He headed the massive Task Force 58, which took part in most of the large-scale Pacific air and sea battles during 1944–45. As admiral, he commanded the Atlantic fleet from 1945.

MIXED ECONOMY, an economy in which private and state enterprise coexist. It may also include enterprises which although privately owned are regulated by the state.

MIXTECS, or **Mixtecas,** Indian people occupying Guerrero, Puebla and Oaxaca states, in SW Mexico. They were one of the most important and culturally advanced pre-Columbian peoples in Mesoamerica. They eclipsed the ZAPOTEC INDIANS by the 14th century, but were themselves overshadowed by the AZTECS prior to the arrival of the Spanish who defeated the last Mixtec kingdom c1550. The Mixtec language is today spoken by some 300000 Mexican people.

MIYAZAKI, city in SE Kyushu, Japan. It has an important SHINTO shrine and is a tourist resort. Its products include chemical, charcoal and wood pulp. Pop 202859.

MKSA UNITS, or **Giorgi System,** a metric system of units based on the METRE (length), KILOGRAM (mass), SECOND (time) and AMPERE (electric current), forming the basis of the now internationally accepted SI UNITS. The system is "rationalized" in that, with the PERMEABILITY of free space set at $4\pi \times 10^{-7}$ henry/metre, equations contain factors reflecting the geometry of the situations they describe: 2π for cylindrical symmetries; 4π for spherical.

MNEMOSYNE, the Greek goddess of memory and mother (by Zeus) of the nine MUSES.

MOAB, ancient kingdom E of the Dead Sea, in what is now Jordan. The Moabites were a pastoral, Semitic people related to the Hebrews. Much of our knowledge of them comes from the MOABITE STONE and from biblical references in Deuteronomy, Kings and Numbers.

MOABITE STONE, a black basalt inscribed stone dating from c850 BC and recounting the victories of Mesha, king of MOAB. It bears 35 lines of writing in the Hebrew-related Moabite script. The stone was discovered in 1868 at Dhiban and is now in the Louvre, Paris.

MOAS, several species of extinct flightless birds of New Zealand related to the OSTRICH. Almost entirely herbivorous, moas flourished in the absence of significant competitors or predators. They had well-developed hind limbs and small heads. The largest moas measured 3m (10ft) or more in height.

MOBERLY, industrial city in N central Mo., seat of Randolph Co. Located in a dairy farming and coal-mining region, it manufactures auto brakes and footwear. Pop 12988.

MOBILE, industrial seaport in SW Ala., seat of Mobile Co., on the Mobile R. It is a shipbuilding and oil refinery center. Capital of French Louisiana 1710–19, it was an important Confederate naval base in the Civil War. Pop 190026.

MOBILE, a moving, three-dimensional abstract sculpture. The form was invented by Alexander CALDER c1930 and named by Marcel DUCHAMP. A mobile consists of a group of shapes connected together by rods or wires, and suspended to move freely in the air, changing the spatial relationships between each piece as they turn.

MOBILE BAY, Battle of, Civil War conflict on Aug. 5, 1864, in which Union admiral FARRAGUT's command broke through the Confederate defensive forts and torpedo lines and destroyed key units of the South's fleet. The battle formed part of the North's wider strategy to encircle the confederacy.

MÖBIUS STRIP, a topological space (see TOPOLOGY) formed by joining the two ends of a strip of paper or other material after having turned one of the ends through an ANGLE of 180°. It is of interest in that it has only one side: if a line is drawn from a point A on the surface parallel to the edges of the strip it will eventually pass through a point A′ directly through the paper from A. This closed curve is known as a nonbounding cycle since it does not bound an area of the surface. (See also KLEIN BOTTLE.)

MOBUTU SESE SEKO (1930–), born Joseph Désiré Mobutu, president of the Republic of Zaire (formerly the Belgian Congo) from 1965. He ousted President KASAVUBU.

MOCCASIN, *Agkistrodon piscivorus*, an amphibious, venomous snake of America, which feeds on fish, frogs and small mammals. Also called **Water moccasin** or **Cottonmouth** it is noted for its habit of opening wide its white-lined mouth.

MOCKINGBIRDS, a family, Mimidae, of songbirds of the Americas; or, certain species within that family. They are long-tailed birds with short, rounded wings and well-developed legs, which skulk in low scrub feeding on insects and fruit. Certain species may flick their wings when searching for food, perhaps to disturb insects that would otherwise remain undetected.

MOCK ORANGE. See SYRINGA.

MODE. See MEAN, MEDIAN AND MODE.

MODE, in music, the method of tone selection as a basis for melody and harmony. Starting on any "home" note to designate key, each mode follows a fixed progression of tones and semitones to form a SCALE. By about 1600 Western music retained only the Major and Minor modes of 14 that grew from the eight Plainsong modes of Medieval church music. The eight Greek modes, ancestors of these, were conceived from the top note down.

Modes in Music

T = tone S = semitone TS = 1½ tones

Usual Modern Modes

Major	Melodic Minor
T-T-S-T-T-T-S	T-S-T-T-T-T-S
Harmonic Minor	Natural (Aeolian) Minor
T-S-T-T-S-TS-S	T-S-T-T-S-T-T
Pentatonic	Whole-tone
T-TS-T-T-TS	T-T-T-T-T-T

Two Ancient Greek Modes

Dorian	Phrygian
T-S-T-T-T-S-T	S-T-T-T-S-T-T

MODEL CITIES, or Concentrated Community Development, a US government program which aims to plan new housing and redevelop cities. It was established by the Demonstration Cities and Metropolitan Development Act (1966). The US Department of Housing and Urban Development administers the program.

MODEL PARLIAMENT, an English parliament set up in 1295 by Edward I. The Model Parliament's wide representation of clergy, earls, barons, two knights from each county and two burgesses from each borough indicated Parliament's developing representational role, although these principles of membership were by no means strictly observed through much of the 14th century.

MODENA, historic Renaissance city in N central Italy, built on the site of an ancient Etruscan settlement, now an industrial center. Pop 171063.

MODERNISM, in Christian theology, a movement in the late 19th and early 20th centuries that aimed to reinterpret traditional doctrine to align it with modern trends in philosophy, history and the sciences. It espoused the liberal, critical view of the Bible, was skeptical about the historicity of Christian origins, and downgraded traditional credal dogma. Modernism became dominant in Protestantism (though opposed by FUNDAMENTALISM). The similar movement in Roman Catholicism was formally condemned by Pius X (1907) and largely disappeared.

MODESTO, agricultural trading city in central Cal., seat of Stanislaus Co. It has some of the world's largest wineries and canneries. Pop 61 712.

MODIGLIANI, Amedeo (1884–1920), Italian painter and sculptor. He is best known for studies of nudes and for portraits, works characterized by elongated forms and elegant draftsmanship. He was influenced by African sculpture and by BRANCUSI.

MODOC INDIANS, North American Indian tribe, who occupied parts of what is now Cal. and Ore. They are closely related to the KLAMATH INDIANS with whom, in 1864, they agreed to move to an Ore. reservation. In 1870, a Modoc group, led by Chief Kintpuash ("Captain Jack") fled back to N Cal. The group was attacked by a US army unit in 1872, bringing about the Modoc War (1872–73). Gen. Edward CANBY was killed during the peace negotiations, and the tribe subsequently returned to Ore.

MODULAR ARITHMETIC, an algebraic system of positive INTEGERS in which there is a maximum n such that any number, greater than n (the modulus) is expressed as the REMAINDER left after its DIVISION by n.

MODULATION. See RADIO.

MODULUS, a term with several meanings in mathematics. The modulus of a REAL NUMBER is its positive value, shown by placing the number between vertical lines: thus $|-2|=|+2|=2$. The modulus (or absolute value) of a complex number (see IMAGINARY NUMBERS) z, where $z=x+iy$, is defined as $\sqrt{(x^2+y^2)}$. If z is represented by a point on an ARGAND DIAGRAM, then its modulus, r, is the distance from the origin to that point. Again, the term modulus sometimes refers to a constant of proportionality (see PROPORTION). In LOGARITHMS, if $\log_a x = k \log_b x$, where a and b are different bases, k is known as the modulus. (See also MODULAR ARITHMETIC.)

MOFFAT TUNNEL, a 6mi railroad tunnel running through James Peak in N central Col., at a height of 9 094ft. The tunnel, built 1923–28, was named for David Halliday Moffat (1839–1911).

MOGADISHU, or Mogadiscio, capital and chief seaport of Somali republic on the Indian Ocean, NE Africa, an important trading center since the 12th century. Its harbor was modernized in the 1960s with American aid. Pop 200 000.

MOGOLLAN CULTURE, North American Indian culture of c200 BC–c1200 AD in what is now SW N.M. and SE Ariz., believed to have developed from the earlier Cochise culture. As Mogollan pottery, the first in the SW, was from the beginning very fine, it is thought that the art was imported from Mexico.

MOGUL EMPIRE, 16th and 17th century empire in India, founded by BABUR, who invaded India from Afghanistan in 1526. His son Humayun was defeated by the Afghan Sher Shah Sur, but Mogul power was restored by AKBAR (1556–1605). He established firm, centralized government throughout Afghanistan and N and central India. The Mogul "golden age" was in the reign of SHAH JEHAN (1628–58). During this time, the TAJ MAHAL, the Pearl Mosque of Agra and many of Delhi's finest buildings were erected. In the 1700s, the rising power of the MAHRATTAS weakened the empire. In 1803 the British occupied Delhi and in 1857 they deposed the last puppet Mogul emperor, Bahadur Shah II.

MOHAIR, the fleece of the Angora GOAT. The fibers are long, straight and lustrous, and when woven it behaves like WOOL. Highly durable, it is used in many textile fabrics.

MOHAMMED, or **Muhammad** or **Mahomet** (c570–632), "the Praised One," founder of ISLAM, the Muslim faith. He was born in Mecca and was a member of its ruling tribe. He became a merchant and his trade from Mecca brought him into contact with Judaism and Christianity. At the age of 40, he had a religious vision (a vision of the archangel Gabriel) which bade him go forth and preach. This, and subsequent visions, were recorded in the KORAN, the Muslim sacred book. Mohammed proclaimed himself God's messenger and called on the Meccans to accept Allah as the only god. At first, he made few converts. Among the earliest were his wife Khadija, his daughter FATIMA, her husband and his cousin, ALI and his friend ABU BAKR. As Mohammed's influence increased, the Meccans began to fear he might gain political control of the city. They persecuted his followers and plotted to murder him. In 622, he fled to Yathrib, which he subsequently renamed MEDINA, "City of the Prophet," with Abu Bakr and some followers. This event is known as the HEGIRA (departure). Muslim calendars are dated from the Hegira. In Medina, Mohammed formed an Islamic community based upon religious faith, rather than tribal or family loyalties. He rapidly extended his territory by conquest and conversion. In 630, after a long period of warfare with Mecca and winning the battles of Badr (624) and Uhud (625) he captured Mecca with little bloodshed, making it both the political and religious capital of Islam. He proclaimed the KAABA a mosque and laid down the ceremonies of the *Hajj* (pilgrimage) to Mecca.

MOHAMMED II (c1430–1481), Ottoman sultan from 1451 known as "the conqueror." His capture of Constantinople (1453) destroyed the BYZANTINE EMPIRE. He made the city his capital and went on to capture most of the Balkan Peninsula, Serbia, Croatia and Scutari (1478–79) and various Venetian and Genoese possessions.

MOHAMMED V (Sidi Mohammed ben Youssef; 1909–1961), first king of Morocco, 1957–61. He became sultan in 1927 and was exiled by the ruling French authorities, 1953–55.

MOHAMMED AHMED. See MAHDI.

MOHAMMED ALI. See MEHMET ALI.

MOHAMMED REZA PAHLAVI (1919–), shah of Iran, from 1941. After troubles with extreme nationalists in the early 1950s he established a program of social and economic reform, known as the "White Revolution." He has made Iran an important military power.

MOHAVE INDIANS, or **Mojave Indians,** North American tribe of the Hokan-Siouan linguistic family, who occupied parts of what is now Ariz. and Cal., chiefly the Colorado R valley. A semi-sedentary people, they lived mainly by agriculture. About 1000 Mohaves now live in the Colorado River and Fort Mohave School Reservations.

MOHAWK INDIANS, North American tribe of Indians, members of the IROQUOIS League. They aided the British in their victories at Lake George, 1755, and Fort Niagara, 1759, and during the Revolutionary War.

MOHAWK RIVER, river in N.Y., longest tributary (148mi) of the Hudson R, which it joins at Cohoes. From Rome to Cohoes the river forms part of the N.Y. State Barge Canal.

MOHAWK TRAIL, route through the Appalachians, following the Mohawk R, taken by early settlers on their way to the Midwest. Its importance waned after the opening of the Erie Canal in 1825.

MOHAWK VALLEY, fertile valley of the Mohawk R. It was the home of the IROQUOIS League and the site of various Revolutionary War skirmishes. The Revolutionary victory at Oriskany (1777) won the valley for the Americans.

MOHEGAN INDIANS. See MOHICAN INDIANS.

MOHENJO-DARO, large prehistoric city in S Sind, Pakistan, and a site of the INDUS VALLEY CIVILIZATION (c3000–1500 BC).

MOHICAN INDIANS, name of two related North American Indian tribes: the Mahican Indians of the upper Hudson R, and the Mohegan Indians of SW Conn. After the coming of the Dutch, the Mahicans dispersed westward. The Mohegans and the PEQUOT INDIANS were at this time living as one tribe. They enjoyed great power under Sassacus and UNCAS. Today there are about 35 Mohegans.

MOHL, Hugo von (1805–1872), German botanist who gave the name "PROTOPLASM" to the plastic material he found on the periphery of the CELL.

MOHO, abbreviation for MOHOROVIČIĆ DISCONTINUITY.

MOHOLY-NAGY, László (1895–1946), Hungarian painter, designer and member of the German Constructivist school. He was professor at the BAUHAUS 1923–28. He founded the Chicago Institute of Design in 1939 and was an important influence on US industrial design.

MOHOROVIČIĆ DISCONTINUITY, a layer of the earth originally regarded as marking the boundary between crust and mantle (see EARTH), evidenced by a change in the velocity of seismic waves (see EARTHQUAKE). It is now regarded as of little physical significance. The US project Mohole, designed to drill through the "Moho," was abandoned in 1966. More important are the discontinuities between the core and the mantle (Gutenberg or Oldham Discontinuity), with a radius of about 3 500km; and between the inner and outer cores, with a radius of about 1 200km to 1 650km.

MOHS' SCALE. See HARDNESS.

MOIRAI. See FATES.

MOIRÉ PATTERN, a family of CURVES formed by the INTERSECTIONS of one family of curves with another over which it has been superimposed. Moiré patterns may be seen by looking through the folds of a gauze or nylon curtain: motion of the curtain or observer will cause dramatic changes in the patterns observed. They are of particular note in color printing, where special techniques are employed to prevent their appearance in HALFTONES; and are used in industry to determine, for example, the degree of flatness of a surface. They are used also as MATHEMATICAL MODELS of physical phenomena, and occasionally in the solution of mathematical problems. Their disturbing optical properties are of interest in psychology.

MOISSAN, Ferdinand Frédéric Henri (1852–1907), French chemist awarded the 1906 Nobel Prize for Chemistry for isolating FLUORINE (1886) and for developing the electric arc furnace (see ELECTRIC FURNACE). He also claimed to have synthesized DIAMONDS (1893).

MOIVRE, Abraham de. See DE MOIVRE, ABRAHAM.

MOJAVE DESERT, or Mohave Desert, an area of barren mountains and desert valleys in S Cal. It is swept by strong winds; average annual rainfall is 5in. It includes DEATH VALLEY in the N, and the JOSHUA TREE NATIONAL MONUMENT in the S. It is a rich source of minerals.

MOKP'O, seaport city in South Korea, in an important rice growing region. Fishing and food processing are principal industries. Pop 177 801.

MOLASSES, yellow to dark brown syrup, usually obtained as a byproduct in the production of SUGAR from SUGARCANE juice. It was originally used for FERMENTATION of industrial ethyl alcohol, but is now mainly used in animal feeds, adhesives, fertilizers and the pharmaceutical industry.

MOLASSES ACT, prohibitive duties introduced by England in 1733 in an attempt to force the American colonies to import molasses, sugar, rum and other spirits exclusively from the British West Indies. Rendered ineffective through smuggling, it was replaced by the SUGAR ACT (1764).

MOLD, general name for a number of filamentous FUNGI that produce powdery or fluffy growths on fabrics, foods and decaying plant or animal remains. Best known is the blue bread mold caused by *Penicillium*, from which the ANTIBIOTIC, PENICILLIN, was first discovered.

MOLDAU RIVER. See VLTAVA.

MOLDAVIA, former principality lying between the Carpathian Mts and the Dniester R, including BESSARABIA and BUKOVINA. A fertile area of 14 690sq mi, it is now divided by the Prut R into the Moldavian SSR and the Moldavian region of ROMANIA. From the 16th century it was ruled by the Ottoman Turks, but fell gradually under the influence of Russia.

MOLE, pigmented spot or nevus in the SKIN, consisting of a localized group of special cells containing MELANIN. Change in a mole, such as increase in size, change of color and bleeding should lead to suspicion of MELANOMA.

MOLE (mol), the SI base unit of amount of substance, defined as the amount of substance of a system which contains as many elementary entities (of a specified kind) as there are atoms in 0.012kg of carbon-12 (i.e., the AVOGADRO Number). One mole of a compound is its MOLECULAR WEIGHT in grams. The

molarity of a solution is its concentration in moles per litre; a solution whose molarity is 1 is called molar. (See SI UNITS.)

MOLECULAR BIOLOGY, the study of the structure and function of the MOLECULES which make up living organisms. This includes the study of PROTEINS, ENZYMES, CARBOHYDRATES, FATS and NUCLEIC ACIDS. (See also BIOCHEMISTRY; BIOLOGY, BIOPHYSICS.)

MOLECULAR WEIGHT, the sum of the ATOMIC WEIGHTS of all the atoms in a MOLECULE. It is an integral multiple of the empirical FORMULA weight found by chemical ANALYSIS, and of the EQUIVALENT WEIGHT. Molecular weights may be found directly by MASS SPECTROSCOPY, or deduced from related physical properties including gas DENSITY; effusion; osmotic pressure (see OSMOSIS), and effects on solvents: lowering of VAPOR PRESSURE and freezing point, and raising of boiling point; for large molecules the ultracentrifuge is used. (See also MOLE.)

MOLECULE, entity composed of ATOMS linked by chemical BONDS and acting as a unit; the smallest particle of a chemical compound which retains the COMPOSITION and chemical properties of the compound. The composition of a molecule is represented by its molecular FORMULA. Elements may exist as molecules, e.g., oxygen O_2, phosphorus P_4. FREE RADICALS and IONS are merely types of molecules. Molecules range in size from single atoms to **macromolecules**—chiefly PROTEINS and POLYMERS—with MOLECULAR WEIGHTS of 10000 or more. The chief properties of molecules are their structure (bond lengths and angles)—determined by electron diffraction, X-RAY DIFFRACTION and SPECTROSCOPY—spectra, and DIPOLE MOMENTS. (See also ORBITAL; VAN DER WAALS.)

MOLES, small insectivores adapted to an underground digging existence, family Talpidae. The family includes a number of species of European and American distribution. All have large spade-shaped hands projecting sideways from the body and long, mobile muzzles. The eyes are small and there is no external ear. They are solitary animals and live in a complicated system of burrows feeding on soil invertebrates, largely earthworms. Parallel evolution has produced identical adaptations in Marsupial moles, and GOLDEN MOLES.

MOLEY, Raymond Charles (1886–1975), US expert on government and public law. He became a member of Roosevelt's BRAIN TRUST and was appointed assistant secretary of state in 1933. Resigning shortly after, he founded the magazine *Today* and became a critic of the NEW DEAL.

MOLIÈRE, stage name of Jean-Baptiste Poquelin (1622–1673), France's greatest comic dramatist, renowned for his satire on hypocrisy and his characters personifying particular vices and types. After touring the provinces as actor-manager and playwright for many years, he eventually became established in Paris with the success of *Les Précieuses ridicules* in 1659. Among his best-known works are *Tartuffe* (1664), *Le Misanthrope* (1666), *Le Bourgeois gentilhomme* (1670) and *Le Malade imaginaire* (1673).

MOLINA, Tirso de. See TIRSO DE MOLINA.

MOLINE, industrial city in NW Ill., on the Mississippi R. It is a major producer of farm machinery. Pop 46237.

MOLISE. See ABRUZZI E MOLISE.

MOLLET, Guy (1905–1975), French statesman, wartime resistance leader and secretary general of the French socialist party 1946–69. He was premier in the center-left government of Jan. 1956–May 1957, and minister of state under De Gaulle 1958–59.

MOLLUSKS, soft-bodied INVERTEBRATES, typically having a calcareous shell into which the body can withdraw. They include SLUGS and SNAILS, LIMPETS, winkles, CLAMS, MUSSELS and OYSTERS, as well as the apparently dissimilar OCTOPUSES and SQUIDS. Mollusks have adapted to an incredible variety of niches in the sea, in fresh water and on land. This has resulted in equal diversity of structure and habit. Major groups of mollusks include BIVALVES, CEPHALOPODA, CHITONS and GASTROPODA.

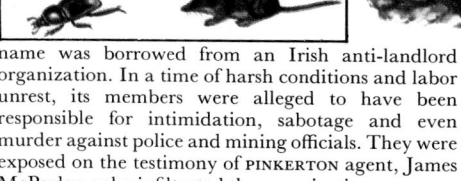

MOLLY MAGUIRES, Irish-American secret society in the Pa. anthracite mining area c1862–79, whose name was borrowed from an Irish anti-landlord organization. In a time of harsh conditions and labor unrest, its members were alleged to have been responsible for intimidation, sabotage and even murder against police and mining officials. They were exposed on the testimony of PINKERTON agent, James McParlan, who infiltrated the organization.

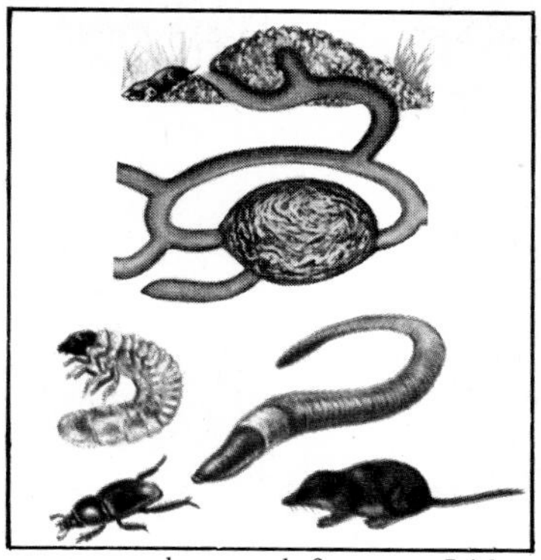

Above left: how the burrowing activity of moles results in the familiar molehills on the surface. Moles feed almost exclusively on soil fauna, especially earthworms, and so spend most of their lives tunneling. *Above right:* the Common mole, *Talpa europaea*.

MOLNÁR, Ferenc (1878–1952), Hungarian author and playwright, who lived in the US from 1940. His play *Liliom* (1909) was adapted as the musical *Carousel* (1945). He also wrote novels and short stories.

MOLOCH, or Molech, the Canaanite god of fire, to whom children were sacrificed, identified in the Old Testament as a god of the Ammonites. His worship, introduced by King Ahaz, was condemned by the prophets, and his sanctuary at Tophet near Jerusalem later became known as GEHENNA.

MOLOKAI, island in Hawaii state, between Oahu and Maui. A volcanic and mountainous area of 259sq mi, it supports cattle and pineapple plantations. The Kalaupapa leper colony lies on the N coast.

MOLOTOV, Vyacheslav Mikhailovich (1890–), born Vyacheslav Mikhailovich Skriabin, Russian statesman. He became a Bolshevik in 1906, and after the RUSSIAN REVOLUTION quickly rose to power in the Communist Party. He was Soviet premier 1930–41 under Stalin. As foreign minister 1939–49 and 1953–56, he negotiated the 1939 non-aggression pact with Germany and played an important role in the USSR's wartime and postwar relations with the West. Under Khruschev, he lost power and only held minor posts, and in 1964 it was revealed that he had been expelled from the Communist Party.

MOLTING, the shedding of the skin, fur or feathers by an animal. It may be a seasonal occurrence, as a periodic renewal of fur or plumage in mammals and birds, or it may be associated with GROWTH as in insects or crustaceans. In birds and mammals the molt is primarily to renew worn fur or feathers so that plumage or pelage is kept in good condition for waterproofing, insulation or flight. In addition it may serve to shed breeding plumage in birds, or to change between different summer and winter coats. In invertebrates the rigid external skeleton must be shed and replaced to allow growth within. In larval insects the final molts are involved in the METAMORPHOSIS to adult form.

MOLTKE, Helmuth Johannes Ludwig, Graf von (1848–1916), German chief of staff 1906–14, nephew of Helmuth Karl MOLTKE. Responsible for German strategy at the start of WWI, he was dismissed after the first battle of the MARNE.

MOLTKE, Helmuth Karl Bernhard, Graf von (1800–1891), Prussian and, later, German chief of staff 1858–88. A strategist of genius, he won victories against Denmark (1864), Austria (1866), and France (1870–71), greatly furthering German unification (1871).

MOLUCCAS, or **Maluku,** or **Spice Islands,** a group of fertile, volcanic islands in E Indonesia, between Celebes and New Guinea. Once the center of the world trade in nutmeg and cloves, the islands now export copra and forest products, as well as spices.

MOLYBDENITE (MoS_2), soft, gray SULFIDE mineral, the chief ore of MOLYBDENUM, mined mainly in Col. Purified molybdenite has properties very similar to those of GRAPHITE, and is used as a lubricant.

MOLYBDENUM (Mo), silvery-gray metal in Group VIB of the PERIODIC TABLE; a TRANSITION ELEMENT. It is obtained commercially by roasting MOLYBDENITE in air and reducing the oxide formed with carbon in an electric furnace or by the THERMITE process to give ferromolybdenum. Because of its high melting point, it is used to support the filament in electric lamps and for furnace heating elements. It also finds use in corrosion-resistant, high-temperature STEELS and ALLOYS. Molybdenum is unreactive, but forms various covalent compounds. Some are used as industrial CATALYSTS. Molybdenum is a vital trace element in plants and a catalyst in bacterial NITROGEN FIXATION. AW 95.9, mp 2610°C, bp 5560°C, sg 10.2 (20°C).

MOMBASA, capital of Coast Province, Kenya, on an island in an inlet of the Indian Ocean. It is an industrial center, major market and port for Kenyan agricultural produce. Pop 247073.

MOMENT, the product of a quantity and its distance from some specific point connected with it. Statical moments such as the moment of a force (measuring its turning effect on a body by multiplying the force's magnitude by its perpendicular distance from the rotation axis) enter equations of static equilibrium. The **moment of inertia**, I, of a rotating body (the analog of MASS in the dynamics of translation) is the sum of the products of its mass elements, m_i, with the squares of their distances, r_i, from the rotation axis.

$$I = \sum_i m_i r_i^2$$

MOMENTUM, the product of the MASS and linear VELOCITY of a body. Momentum is thus a VECTOR quantity. The linear momentum of a system of interacting particles is the sum of the momenta of its particles, and is constant if no external forces act. The rate of change of momentum with time in the direction of an applied force equals the force (Newton's second law of motion—see MECHANICS). In rotational motion, the analogous concept is **angular momentum**, the product of the moment of inertia and the angular velocity of a body relative to a given rotation axis. If no external forces act on a rotating system, the direction and magnitude of its angular momentum remain constant.

MOMMSEN, Theodor (1817–1903), German liberal classical scholar and historian, winner of the 1902 Nobel Prize for Literature. He was an authority on Roman law, and wrote a famous *History of Rome* (3 vols; 1854–56).

MONACO, independent principality on the Mediterranean near the French-Italian border, about 370 acres in area. It is a tourist center with a yachting harbor and a world-famous casino.

The reigning constitutional monarch, Prince Rainier III, succeeded to the throne in 1949 and married the US film actress Grace Kelly in 1956. In 1962, after a crisis with France over Monaco's tax free status, he proclaimed a new constitution, guaranteeing fundamental rights, giving the vote to women and abolishing the death penalty. The government consists of three councillors, headed by a minister of state who must be French. There is an 18-

member National Council elected for five-year terms by universal suffrage, which shares legislative powers with the Prince.

Monaco's towns are MONTE CARLO, Monaco-Ville (capital), La Condamine (commercial center) and Fontvieille (small industrial area).

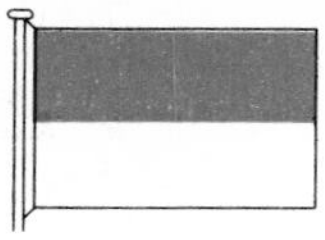

Official name: Principality of Monaco
Capital: Monte Carlo
Area: 0.7sq mi
Population: 23 400
Languages: French
Religions: Roman Catholic
Monetary unit(s): 1 French franc = 100 centimes

Impression: Fog (1872) by Monet, the painting for which the Impressionist movement is named. Monet was attempting to capture transient light effects in fog over Le Havre harbor.

MONAD, in the philosophy of LEIBNIZ, one of the individual substances which together constitute the universe—a sort of metaphysical atom, having properties but not composed of matter.

MONADNOCK, isolated hill formed of erosion-resistant bedrock in an area otherwise well eroded (see EROSION; PENEPLAIN); named for Mt Monadnock, Cheshire Co., N.H.

MONA PASSAGE, a channel about 80mi wide between Haiti and Puerto Rico, a main shipping route from the N Atlantic to the Panama Canal.

MONARCH BUTTERFLY, *Danaus plexippus*, an American BUTTERFLY remarkable not only for its size and coloration, but because it is one of those species of butterfly that undertake long MIGRATIONS. In spring they fly north to Canada, returning along exactly the same route in the fall. As an antipredator device, monarchs have an unpleasant taste; the coloration is mimicked for protection by other less distasteful species.

MONARCHY, form of government in which sovereignty is vested in one person, usually for life. The office may be elective but is usually hereditary. A monarch who has unlimited power is an *absolute monarch*; one whose power is limited by custom or constitution is a *constitutional monarch*. In modern parliamentary democracies a monarch is usually a non-party political figure and a symbol of national unity. (See also DIVINE RIGHT OF KINGS.)

MONASTICISM, way of life, usually communal and celibate, always ascetic, conducted according to a religious rule. It is found in all major religions. Christian monasticism aims at holiness by fulfilling vows of poverty, chastity and obedience. It was founded in Egypt by St. ANTONY OF THEBES, and spread rapidly. Most early monks were HERMITS or lived in small groups; later, CENOBITES predominated, engaging in prayer and manual work, and sometimes teaching and scholarship. In W Christianity, under the pervasive rule of St. BENEDICT OF NURSIA, communities were contemplative and "enclosed" (see BENEDICTINE ORDERS), as e.g. CISTERCIANS are today; but AUGUSTINIAN, DOMINICAN and FRANCISCAN friars abandoned enclosure in the 13th century. Important monastic centers included Mount ATHOS, CLUNY and MONTE CASSINO. Monasticism was abolished where the REFORMATION succeeded, but has revived and spread since the mid-19th century.

MONAZITE, PHOSPHATE mineral of widespread occurrence, mined in India, Brazil, the US and South Africa as an ore of the RARE EARTHS and THORIUM. It usually forms small brown prismatic crystals in the monoclinic system.

MONCK, Charles Stanley, 1st Baron (1819–1894), Irish peer and British Liberal MP. As governor general of British North America (1861–67), he promoted confederation of the Canadian provinces and became the first governor general of the Dominion of Canada (1867–68).

MONCK (or **Monk**), **George, 1st Duke of Albermarle** (1608–1670), English general and naval commander. At first supporting CHARLES I in the English CIVIL WAR, he later became CROMWELL'S commander-in-chief in Scotland (1650–52; 1654–60). After Cromwell's death he was the architect of the RESTORATION of Charles II. He was a successful commander of the fleet in the DUTCH WARS (1652–54; 1666).

MONCTON, city in SE New Brunswick, Canada. It is a port, transportation and manufacturing center on the Petitcodiac R. Pop 47 891.

MOND, Ludwig (1839–1909), German-born British industrial chemist whose discovery (1889) of nickel carbonyl (see TRANSITION ELEMENTS) led him to devise the Mond Process for refining NICKEL, and so to found the Mond Nickel Company.

MONDALE, Walter Frederick "Fritz" (1928–), 41st US vice-president from Nov. 1976, under James CARTER. As a senator from Minn. he was known as a liberal and populist reformer. His early career was furthered by Hubert HUMPHREY.

MONDAY, second day of the week, held sacred to the moon in pre-Christian societies. Its name derives from the Old English, *mōnandaeg* or moon day, which translates the Latin *lunae dies* (French *lundi*).

MONDRIAN, Piet (1872–1944), Dutch painter and theorist, a founder of the DE STIJL movement. At first a symbolist, he was influenced by CUBISM, and evolved a distinctive abstract style relating primary colors and black and white in grid-like arrangements.

MONEL METAL, strong, corrosion-resistant ALLOY composed of 68% nickel, 29% copper, 3% iron, manganese, silicon and carbon; used for turbine blades, propellers, etc. Originally made by smelting nickel/copper ore from Sudbury, Ontario.

MONERA, taxonomic term proposed by some authorities to include unicellular, prokaryotic organisms (see CELL) belonging to the PLANT KINGDOM. Included in the Monera is one division, the SCHIZOPHYTA, containing the BACTERIA (Schizomycetes) and BLUE-GREEN ALGAE (Schizophyceae).

MONESSEN, city in SW Pa., on the Monongahela R. It has a large steel industry. Pop 15 216.

MONET, Claude (1840–1926), French painter, leading exponent of IMPRESSIONISM, a term coined after his picture *Impression, Sunrise* (1872). He worked in and around Paris, in poverty in his early years. Always fascinated by varying light effects, around 1889 he began painting series of pictures of a subject at different times of day, such as those of *Rouen Cathedral* (1892–94). His last pictures of *Water Lilies* are virtually abstract.

MONEY, in any economic system, is a medium of exchange, of labor and products, or for payment of debts. In primitive societies, BARTER, direct physical exchange, was commonly used. The precise origin of money is unknown. It evolved gradually out of the needs of commerce and trade. A wide variety of objects have at one time or other been used as money: shells, nuts, beads, stones etc. Gradually, metal was adopted because of its easy handling, durability, divisibility, and—especially with gold or silver—for its own value. The oldest coinage dates back to about 700 BC, when COINS of gold and silver alloys were made in Lydia (Asia Minor). Paper money was known in China as early as the 9th century, but it did not develop in Europe until the 17th century. The banknote and the modern BANKING system evolved when goldsmiths began, for safekeeping, to store gold and coins for others. Money thus deposited or invested could be re-used by the borrower, who therefore paid INTEREST as a fee for its availability. The realization that available money could make more money overthrew the medieval Church's view that money was barren and usury wrong. An over-reaction led to MERCANTILISM, in which money was preferred to all other forms of wealth.

The stability and value of paper currency is usually guaranteed by government or banks (those invested with legal authority to issue currency) with some bullion holdings. However, it is tempting for governments to over-issue money as an easy way to pay their debts. This can lead to INFLATION and DEVALUATION of the currency. (See also FEDERAL RESERVE SYSTEM.)

In the last twenty or thirty years, there has emerged a school of economists who argue that monetary policies (controlling the volume of money in circulation) should be utilized to achieve MACROECONOMIC objectives, such as growth rates, employment levels and curbing inflation.

The monetary system of the US during most of the 19th century was based on BIMETALLISM, with the dollar defined as 371.25 grains of fine silver or 24.75 grains of fine gold. From 1900, the dollar was defined in terms of gold, with the passing of the GOLD STANDARD Act of 1900 and the Gold Reserve Act of 1934. However, in 1970 the dollar's dependency on gold was ended when the requirement set by the Treasury of 25% gold backing for all Federal Reserve rates was dropped. (See also FIAT MONEY.)

MONGOL EMPIRE, founded in the 1200s by GENGHIS KHAN who united the Mongol tribes of central Asia. Already superb horsemen and archers, the Mongols were united by Genghis Khan into a huge, well-disciplined, swiftly-moving army, which had conquered N China by 1215, and then swept W to engulf Bukhara, Samarkand, Gurgan and S Russia in a wave of terror and destruction. After his death, the bloody Mongol invasions were continued under his son Ogotai. During 1237–40, the Mongol general BATU KHAN, a grandson of Genghis Khan, crossed the Volga, crushed the Bulgars and Kumans, devastated central Russia and invaded Poland and Hungary. Further conquest was halted only by the death of Ogotai in 1241.

By about 1260 the Empire was organized into four Khanates: the Il Khanate (Persia); the Kipchak Khanate, founded by the GOLDEN HORDE (Russia); the Jagatai (Turkestan); and the Great Khanate (China). During KUBLAI KHAN's rule (1260–94) the Great Khanate became the YÜAN DYNASTY of China. The Empire stretched from the China Seas to the Danube R. After his death, it disintegrated. But the Mongol tradition of conquest was revived by TAMERLANE in the 1300s and BABUR in the 1500s.

MONGOLIA, Inner. See INNER MONGOLIA.

MONGOLIAN PEOPLE'S REPUBLIC, commonly known as Outer Mongolia, republic in Central Asia between China and the USSR, set up in 1921. The country is a steppe plateau fringed on the N and W by mountains. Much of the SE is part of the Gobi desert. The climate is dry, with harsh extremes of temperature, and the country is very thinly populated. There are forests in the mountainous north. Over 50% of the population live on state collective farms, and almost 25% in the capital, Ulan Bator.

The economy is based on livestock farming, principally of sheep and goats, but also of horses, cattle, yaks and (in the desert) camels. There is some agriculture, and hunting of sable and other wild animals for fur. Coal, iron ore, gold and other minerals are mined. Industry is developing at Choybalsan, Darkhan and Ulan Bator, but is limited to felts, furniture, and other consumer goods. Chief exports are of livestock, wool, hides, meat and ores. The Trans-Mongolian railroad links the country with the USSR (her chief trading partner) and China; roads and communications are poor.

Formerly the heartland of the MONGOL EMPIRE and a Chinese province since 1691, Mongolia declared itself independent in 1911, but was reoccupied by China in 1919. With Soviet support the country declared its independence again in 1921, and in 1924 adopted its present name. Its communist government has since maintained close links with the USSR.

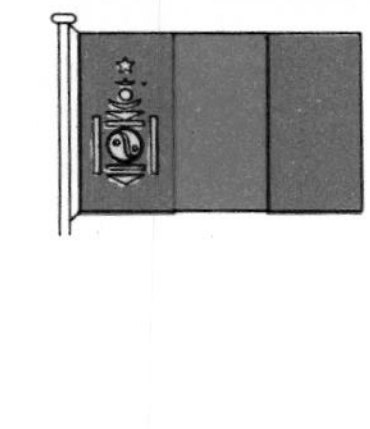

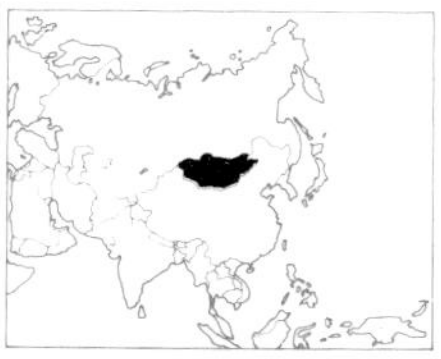

Official name: Mongolian People's Republic
Capital: Ulan Bator
Area: 604 095sq mi
Population: 1 300 000
Languages: Mongolian
Religions: No official religion
Monetary unit(s): 1 Togrog = 100 mongo

MONGOLISM, or Down's syndrome, a relatively common (1 in 600 births) congenital disorder due to a chromosomal abnormality, usually of CHROM OSOME 21. It causes characteristic facial appearance (resembling that of a Mongolian), HAND shape and SKIN patterns; floppiness in the baby; MENTAL RETARDATION, and delayed growth. Congenital diseases of the HEART and GASTROINTESTINAL TRACT are common, as is CATARACT. Mongols also have an increased incidence of LEUKEMIA. As the average age of parenthood advances, mongolism is becoming increasingly common.

MONGOLOID, one of the three racial divisions of man (see RACE). Mongoloids generally have straight black hair, little facial hair, yellow to brown skins and the distinctive epicanthic fold, a fold of skin over the eyes giving them a slanting appearance. The AMERINDS, Eskimos, Polynesians and Patagonians are Mongoloid peoples.

MONGOOSES, small carnivores of the Viverridae, with a reputation for killing snakes and stealing eggs. There are about 48 species occupying a variety of habitats around the Mediterranean, in Africa and southern Asia. Most of them are diurnal, feeding on lizards, snakes, eggs and small mammals. They are usually solitary although a few species form colonies, often in burrows in termite mounds. All mongooses have great immunity to snake venom. One of the best known species is the Common or Egyptian mongoose sometimes known as the ICHNEUMON.

MONICA, Saint (c332–387), mother of St. AUGUSTINE. She converted both Augustine and his father to Christianity, and is often the patron saint of Christian wives' and mothers' organizations.

MONISM, any philosophical system asserting the essential unity of things—that all things are material (see MATERIALISM), or mind (see IDEALISM), or of some other essence. Monism is contrasted with the various kinds of DUALISM or pluralism.

MONITOR AND MERRIMACK, two pioneer ironclad warships famous for the first battle fought by iron armored vessels during the US CIVIL WAR at Hampton Roads, Va., on March 9, 1862. The *U.S.S. Merrimack* was a scuttled Union steam frigate, salvaged by the Confederates, renamed the *C.S.S. Virginia* and reinforced with iron plate. The *U.S.S. Monitor* was designed by John ERICSSON and equipped with a revolving gun turret. The ships' battle had little real effect on the war except to boost morale on both sides.

MONITORS, lizards belonging to the genus *Varanus* found in Africa, S Asia, Australia and the islands of the East Indies. An example is the KOMODO DRAGON. Monitors are predators: the smaller species catch mainly insects; the larger ones eat small mammals, other lizards, eggs and carrion. They are snakelike with long necks and tails, and a long, forked tongue.

MONIZ, Antonio Caetano de Abreu Freire Egas (1874–1955), Portuguese brain surgeon awarded with W. R. HESS the 1949 Nobel Prize for Physiology or Medicine for his development of frontal LOBOTOMY as a treatment for mental disorders. The treatment is now little used (see PSYCHIATRY).

MONK, Thelonious Sphere (1920–   ), US jazz pianist and composer; with Dizzy GILLESPIE and Charlie PARKER, he was a leading innovator of modern jazz from the mid-1940s and 1950s. His jazz ballad *'Round Midnight* and compositions *Epistrophy, Straight No Chaser* and *Blue Monk* are standard in modern jazz repertoires.

MONKEY, a term used to describe any higher PRIMATE, suborder *Anthropoidea*, that is not an ape or a man. It includes both New World and Old World forms. There is thus little uniformity in the group; monkeys have adapted to a variety of modes of life. All have flattened faces, the Old and New World groups being distinguised by nose shape. New World, platyrrhine monkeys, family Cebidae, have broad, flat noses with the nostrils widely separated. Old World, catarrhines, family Cercopithecidae, have the nostrils separated by only a thin septum. Monkeys are normally restricted to tropical or subtropical areas of the world. Old World forms include LANGURS, Colobines, MACAQUES, GUENONS, MANGABEYS and BABOONS. Monkeys of the New World include Sakis, UAKARIS, HOWLERS, Douroucoulis, SQUIRREL MONKEYS and CAPUCHINS. (See also ANTHROPOID APES.)

MONKEY FLOWER, common name for plants of the genus *Mimulus*, which are native to North and South America, Africa and Asia and widely cultivated throughout the world. They are so-called because of the resemblance of the corolla to a monkey's face. Family: Scrophulariaceae.

MONKEY-POD TREE, or **rain tree,** *Lecythis ollaria*, tree, native to Brazil, which yields edible seeds known as Sapucaja nuts. These are generally collected from the wild and yield an oil used for lighting and soap manufacture. Family: Lecythidaceae.

MONKEY-PUZZLE TREE, *Auracaria araucana*, a tall coniferous tree native to Chile and grown widely as an ornamental. It is so-called because its branches form a complex network which baffles climbing animals. Family: Araucariaceae.

MON-KHMER LANGUAGES, a linguist subfamily and geographical language group of the so-called Austro-Asiatic or Southeast Asian language family, spoken by some 35 million to 45 million people. Khmer is spoken in Cambodia and Mon in Burma; related dialects are used in South Vietnam, the Malay peninsula, the Nicobar islands and India. (See also MALAYO-POLYNESIAN LANGUAGES.)

MONMOUTH, city, W Ill., seat of Warren Co., 15mi W of Galesburg. It is a market center for a farming area, with light industry. Pop 11 022.

MONMOUTH, Battle of, engagement in the REVOLUTIONARY WAR, June 28, 1778, near Monmouth Courthouse (now Freehold, N.J.). Gen. Charles LEE's treacherous orders to retreat led to Sir Henry CLINTON's march on New York City. Molly PITCHER was the legendary American heroine of the battle.

MONMOUTH, James Scott, Duke of (1649–1685), illegitimate son of Charles II of England, pretender to the English throne. He was involved in many plots to prevent the Roman Catholic James II from gaining and keeping the throne. In June 1685 he raised a force of troops but was defeated at Sedgemoor, and beheaded at Tower Hill, London.

MONNET, Jean (1888–   ), French economist and statesman; known as the architect of a united W Europe. He created the Monnet Plan (1947) to help France's economic recovery from WWII, planned and served as first president of the EUROPEAN COAL AND STEEL COMMUNITY (ECSC) and helped plan the COMMON MARKET.

MONOCOTYLEDON, name for flowering plants or ANGIOSPERMS that produce seeds with only one seed leaf (or COTYLEDON). Monocotyledons have parallel-veined leaves and the flowering parts are generally in threes or multiples of threes. (See also DICOTYLEDONS.)

MONOD, Jacques Lucien (1910–1976), French biochemist who, with F. JACOB and A. LWOFF, received the 1965 Nobel Prize for Physiology or Medicine for his work with Jacob on regulatory GENE action in BACTERIA.

MONOECIOUS PLANTS, ones where the male and female organs are borne on the same plant, but in separate flowers. Examples are OAK, CORN (*Zea mays*) and WALNUT. (See also DIOECIOUS PLANTS.)

MONOMIAL. See POLYNOMIAL.

MONONA, city in Wis., SE of Madison. Lake Monona, one of the connecting Four Lakes, is nearby. Pop 10 420.

MONONGAHELA, river in N W. Va. and the SW corner of Pa. It flows 128mi before it joins the Allegheny R, to form the Ohio R at Pittsburgh, Pa. It is navigable for most of its length.

MONONUCLEOSIS, Infectious, or **glandular fever,** common VIRUS infection of adolescence causing a variety of symptoms including severe sore throat, HEADACHE, FEVER, malaise and enlargement of LYMPH nodes and SPLEEN. Skin rashes, hepatitis (see LIVER) with JAUNDICE, pericarditis (see PERICARDIUM) and involvement of the NERVOUS SYSTEM may also be prominent. Atypical lymphocytes in the BLOOD and specific agglutination reactions (see ANTIBODIES AND ANTIGENS) are diagnostic. Severe cases may require STEROIDS and convalescence may be lengthy. It can be transmitted in SALIVA and has thus been nicknamed the "kissing disease."

MONOPHYSITE CHURCHES, branches of the EASTERN CHURCH formed in the 6th century by the schismatic adherents of MONOPHYSITISM: the ARMENIAN, COPTIC and JACOBITE CHURCHES. Their doctrine is now essentially orthodox.

MONOPHYSITISM (from Greek *monos*, one, and *physis*, nature), heretical doctrine that in the Person of Christ there is but one (divine) nature. It arose in opposition to the orthodox Council of CHALCEDON (451). A confused controversy resulted, and despite reconciliation attempts the schism hardened. (See also INCARNATION.)

MONOPOLY, an economic term describing significant control or ownership of a product or service (and thereby its price) because of command of the product's supply, legal privilege or concerted action. There are different kinds of monopoly. PATENTS and COPYRIGHTS are legal monopolies granted by a government to individuals or companies. A nationalized industry or service such as the US Post Office has a monopoly. A FRANCHISE granted by

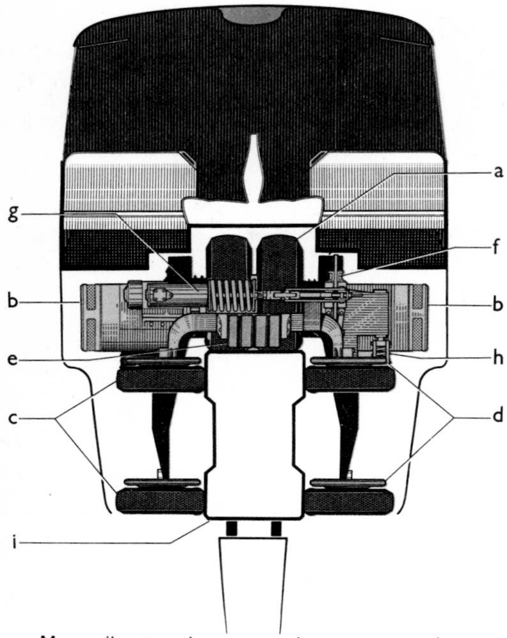

Monorail systems have many advantages over other forms of transport; in the right conditions they take up less room and are relatively cheap to build and run. Shown here is the popular Alweg system developed by Dr. Axel L. Wenner-Gren of Sweden.
(a) Driven supporting wheels
(b) Drive motor
(c) Freerunning guide and stabilizing wheels
(d) Safety wheels with solid rubber tires
(e) Solid rubber safety rollers
(f) Disc brakes for lower speeds
(g) Brake cylinder
(h) Bodywork coilspring suspension
(i) Monorail beam of reinforced concrete

government to a public company to run a public utility (such as an electrical company) creates a monopoly. Trading and industrial monopolies have the power to decide upon supply and price of goods. Sometimes labor unions act as monopolies in the supply of workers' services. In the case of national monopolies, it is considered that they can provide mass-produced goods or services at a lower price, or more efficiently, than could be provided in a competitive situation; in practice this is not always true. Business or manufacturing monopolies may often discourage competitors from entering the field of competition. There is legislation designed to control monopolies that conspire to restrain price or trade (see SHERMAN ANTITRUST ACT; CLAYTON ANTITRUST ACT; FEDERAL TRADE COMMISSION).

MONORAIL, railway with only one rail. The cars may hang beneath it, run on top of it (with a guide rail above or a GYROSCOPE to keep them upright), or straddle it. The first was built in London (1824), the cars being horse-drawn. The first successful system was the *Lartigue system*: the cars straddled the rail and had horizontal wheels that ran on guide rails beneath. The *SAFEGE system* has cars hung from a box girder, split at the bottom, inside which the driving and guide wheels run. In the *Alweg system* the cars straddle a broad rail, on either side of which horizontal wheels run to provide stability. Monorails have been proposed as replacements for city subways.

MONOSODIUM GLUTAMATE, white crystalline solid, the acid sodium salt of glutamic acid, an AMINO ACID. Obtained from GLUTEN or SOYBEAN protein, it is added to many foods to bring out their flavor.

MONOTHEISM, belief in one God, contrasted with POLYTHEISM, PANTHEISM or ATHEISM. Classical monotheism is held by Judaism, Christianity and Islam; some other religions, such as early Zoroastrianism and later Greek religion, are monotheistic to a lesser degree. In the theories of E. B. TYLOR, religions have evolved from animism through polytheism and **henotheism** (the worship of one god, ignoring others in practice) to monotheism. There is, however, evidence for residual monotheism (the "High God") in primitive religions.

MONOTHELITISM, (from Greek *monos*, one, and *thelema*, will), heretical doctrine that in the Person of Christ there is but one will. It was designed as a political compromise to reconcile the Monophysites (see MONOPHYSITISM) and so to strengthen the threatened Empire. With imperial advocacy it attracted much support, but was opposed by the papacy and condemned by the Third Council of Constantinople (680), which proclaimed that Christ has two wills, divine and human.

MONOTREMES, the order Monotrema of egg-laying MAMMALS, displaying also some reptilian (see REPTILES) characteristics. They are not viviparous; the hip girdles and limbs are reptilian, and the mammary glands do not have nipples. Living monotremes, the PLATYPUSES and ECHIDNAS, closely resemble the FOSSILS that exist, and both the living and fossil animals occur only in Oceania.

MONOTYPE, technique of letterpress printing in which each character is individual and fresh-cast out of molten type metal (see ALLOY). Keying by the operator encodes a ribbon with perforations that represent characters and spaces, with special codes punched after sets of characters that almost fill a line to instruct the machine to justify (align the right-hand margin). In response to the perforations, matrices (molds) are drawn from the matrix case, and from these the characters are cast. (See also LINOTYPE.)

MONROE, town in Conn., 10mi N of Bridgeport, on the Housatonic R. It is primarily residential with some light industry. Pop 12 047.

MONROE, city in La., seat of Ouachita parish on the Ouachita R. It produces natural gas, chemical and wood products. Pop 56 374.

MONROE, city in Mich., seat of Monroe Co., on Lake Erie at the mouth of the Raisin R. It is located in an agricultural area with large nurseries nearby. Pop 23 894.

MONROE, city in N.C., seat of Union Co. It produces agricultural goods, textiles and airplane parts. Pop 11 282.

MONROE, Harriet (1860–1936), US editor and poet; the founder of *Poetry* magazine (1912), which published many influential and important 20th century poets such as Ezra POUND, William Carlos WILLIAMS, Carl SANDBURG, Marianne MOORE, D. H. LAWRENCE and T. S. ELIOT.

MONROE, James (1758–1831), fifth president of the US, 1817–25, who promulgated the MONROE DOCTRINE, one of the most fundamental statements of foreign policy in the history of American diplomacy.

Monroe was born in Westmoreland Co., Va. He fought in the Revolution, was wounded at Trenton, commended for gallantry and became a lieutenant colonel. In 1780 he began to study law under Thomas JEFFERSON, and with his sponsorship was elected to the Virginia House of Delegates (1782), beginning a career of public service which would last over 40 years. He served in the Congress of the Confederation (1783–86) and began his law practice in 1788. Elected by Va. in 1790 for the US Senate, he joined Jefferson and James MADISON in forming the DEMOCRATIC-REPUBLICAN PARTY.

Monroe's first diplomatic foray as minister to France (1794) went badly when he criticized the JAY TREATY and was recalled. He withdrew into Virginia politics, becoming governor from 1799 to 1802. During Jefferson's presidency, he was envoy extraordinary to France (1803) where he and Robert LIVINGSTON arranged the terms of the LOUISIANA PURCHASE, but was less successful in Madrid with the Spaniards, who refused to consider American claims to W Fla. As minister to Great Britain (1806), he was unsatisfactory and an attempt to secure the presidential candidacy from Madison in 1808 was a failure. In 1811 he was once again elected governor of Va., and in the same year became Madison's secretary of state. After the British burned Washington, D.C., in the WAR OF 1812, he added the duties of secretary of war to those of secretary of state (1814). In 1816 he easily defeated his Federalist opponent for the presidency and was reelected unopposed four years later.

Monroe's administration years were called the "era of good feeling." The country prospered after the war and expanded westward. Monroe was a moderate man who believed in a decentralized federal government. During his presidency, Fla. was purchased from Spain (1819), Mo. was admitted to the Union (1821) under the MISSOURI COMPROMISE, the RUSH-BAGOT agreement was concluded with Great Britain, the 49th parallel was established as the US-Canadian boundary, the MONROE DOCTRINE guaranteed that European interference would not be tolerated in the Americas and the Santa Fe Trail to the SW was opened. Monroe retired after his presidency, but served as regent of the U. of Virginia and in 1829 presided over Va.'s constitutional convention.

James MONROE
5th US President

Born: April 28, 1758
Died: July 4, 1831
Term of office: March 4, 1817–March 3, 1825
Political party: Democratic-Republican

MONROE, Marilyn (1926–1962), US movie star, Norma Jean Baker, who became world-famous as a blond sex-symbol. A comic actress of considerable talent, her films include *Gentlemen Prefer Blondes* (1953), *The Seven-Year Itch* (1955), *Bus Stop* (1956) and *Some Like It Hot* (1959).

MONROE, Fort, historic six-sided US Army fortress surrounded by a moat, 11mi N of Norfolk, Va., at the entrance to Chesapeake Bay and Hampton Roads. The British introduced black slaves for the American colonies there in 1619 and after the CIVIL WAR Jefferson DAVIS was imprisoned there (1865–67). Since 1946 it has been the US Continental Army Command headquarters.

MONROE DOCTRINE, a declaration of American policy towards the newly independent states of Latin America, issued by President James MONROE before the US Congress on Dec. 2, 1823. It stated in effect that any attempt by European powers to interfere with their old colonies in the western hemisphere would not be tolerated by the US and that the Americas were "henceforth not to be considered as subjects for further colonization by any European powers." The declaration relied for its force on British reluctance, backed by her naval supremacy, to see her own New World position threatened by other European states. President Theodore Roosevelt's corollary to the doctrine (1904) asserted that the US had the power and the right to control any interference in the affairs of the hemisphere by outside governments, and to ensure that acceptable governments were maintained there (this became known as the "big stick" policy; it was repudiated in 1928 by the Clark memorandum). Although the doctrine was mostly ignored until the last decade of the 19th century, it has remained a fundamental policy of the US.

MONROEVILLE, suburban borough in Pa., about 12mi E of Pittsburgh. It has some industrial research plants. Pop 29 011.

MONROVIA, capital, chief port and largest city of Liberia, near the mouth of the St. Paul R on the Atlantic. It is a cultural and economic center of the country with large harbor facilities exporting iron ore and other products. Pop 96 200.

MONROVIA, city in Cal., 9mi E of Pasadena. It manufactures dairy products, aircraft parts and electrical goods. Pop 30 015.

MONSOON, wind system where the prevailing WIND direction reverses in the course of the seasons, occurring where large temperature (hence pressure) differences arise between oceans and large landmasses. Best known is that of SE Asia. In summer, moist winds, with associated HURRICANES, blow from the Indian Ocean into the low-pressure region of NW India that is caused by intense heating of the land. In winter, cold dry winds sweep S from the high-pressure region of S Siberia.

MONSTERA, a genus of evergreen climbers, of which *Monstera deliciosa* is widely grown as a house plant for its dark green, deeply notched leaves. Mature plants produce ARUM-like flowers. This species resembles the closely-related PHILODENDRONS, differing in its climbing habit. Family: Araceae.

MONTAGE, an art technique in which pictures or picture fragments, usually chosen for their subject matter or message, are mounted together. It is used in advertising, notably with photographs (photomontage), and also in motion-picture editing where contrasting film sequences are spliced together—a technique pioneered by EISENSTEIN in *The Battleship Potemkin* (1925).

MONTAGNA, Bartolomeo (c1450–1523), Italian early Renaissance painter. His stark, somber works were influenced by MANTEGNA and BELLINI and he founded a school of painting at Vicenza. His works include a *Madonna and Child* at the Venice Academy and an *Ecce Homo* in the Louvre, Paris.

MONTAGU, Elizabeth Robinson. See BLUESTOCKING.

MONTAGU, Lady Mary Wortley (1689–1762), English writer. She is noted for her so-called Embassy Letters, written from Turkey, and her society verse. Alexander POPE satirizes her under the name Sappho. She is also remembered as a pioneer in the use of smallpox inoculation, to which she submitted her children.

MONTAIGNE, Michel Eyquem, seigneur de (1533–1592), French writer, generally regarded as the originator of the personal essay. The first two books of his *Essays,* published in 1580, were written in an informal style and display an insatiable intellectual curiosity—his motto was always *Que sais-je?* (What do I know?). A third book of essays appeared in 1588, and the posthumous edition of 1595 includes his last reflections. He studied law, held various provincial political offices in Bordeaux and engaged in diplomacy during the French religious civil wars.

MONTANA, a US Rocky Mountain state, bounded on the N by Canada along the 49th parallel, on the E by N.D. and S.D., on the S by Wyo. and on the SW and W by Ida. The fourth largest state, it can be divided into two physiographic regions: the mountains to the W, rising to Granite Peak (12 799ft), which cover two-fifths of the state and the Great Plains to the E. The state's major rivers include the Missouri (its headwaters are in SW Mont.) and the Yellowstone, and the Clark Fork, Flathead and Kootenai in the W; there are many other rivers and lakes. About half the state is grassland, and about one-quarter is forest lands (22 400 000 acres). Climatic differences between E and W are marked, but the yearly average temperature ranges are 14°–70°F in the E and 20°–64°F in the W. Annual rainfall averages 15½in, while snow varies from 15in to 300in. The state has an abundance of wildlife and protected herds of buffalo.

People and Economy. About half the population live in farming areas; the largest cities are Billings and Great Falls. There are about 21 000 Indians (3% of the state population). The economy is dominated by agriculture; livestock brings in about half of the agriculture income, while the other half comes from crops, notably durum wheat, barley, hay, sugar beets, rye, oats and potatoes. Oil production is important, and Mont. is rich in mineral resources—petroleum, copper, gold, lead, zinc and silver. Numerous other minerals are also mined. Lumbering, food production and the smelting and refining of nonferrous metals are other major industries. Natural power resources are supplemented by large-scale hydroelectric power schemes. Tourism is also important throughout the state.

History. Under the LOUISIANA PURCHASE, E Mont. became a US territory (1803). The first recorded exploration was undertaken by the LEWIS AND CLARK EXPEDITION in 1805–06, but except for fur traders and missionaries to the Indians, settlement did not begin till the discovery of gold at Grasshopper Creek (1852). The resulting lawlessness led to the creation of the Montana Territory (1864). Escalating conflict between the settlers and the Indians culminated in the massacre of Gen. CUSTER and his troops by the Sioux at the Battle of the Little Bighorn (1876), but the Sioux surrendered by 1881. The NEZ PERCE INDIANS made a dramatic march to freedom across Mont., but surrendered before reaching Canada. In 1889 the territory became a state. At the end of the century there were feuds between mine-owners for control of the copper industry and of state politics. Agriculture prospered until the 1930s depression. After the depression, industry began to expand and natural resources were further developed with construction of large dams and many federal reclamation projects.

Name of state: Montana
Capital: Helena
Statehood: Nov. 8, 1889 (41st state)
Familiar name: Treasure State
Area: 147 138sq mi
Population: 694 409
Elevation: Highest—12 799ft, Granite Peak. Lowest—1 800ft, Kootenai River in Lincoln County
Motto: Oro y Plata (Gold and Silver)
State flower: Bitterroot
State bird: Western meadowlark
State tree: Ponderosa pine
State song: "Montana"

MONTANUS (flourished 2nd century AD), Phrygian founder of the heretical Christian sect of **Montanism**. Claiming direct inspiration by the Holy Spirit, he prophesied the fulfilment of PENTECOST and the MILLENNIUM. The sect had a strict ascetic discipline and ecstatic religious experience (including GLOSSOLALIA), and was puritan and anti-intellectual. It separated from the catholic Church and was denounced, but spread widely; TERTULLIAN was a member. Montanism largely died out in the 5th century.

MONTAUK POINT, the easternmost end of Montauk peninsula, Long Island, N.Y. A lighthouse stands on the point which is part of Montauk Point State Park.

MONT BLANC. See BLANC, MONT.

MONTCALM, Louis Joseph de (1712–1759), French general; military commander in Canada from 1756 during the FRENCH AND INDIAN WARS. He captured Fort Ontario (1756) and Fort William Henry (1757) and repulsed the British at Ticonderoga (1758). He was defeated and killed on the Plains of Abraham (Sept. 13, 1759) while defending Quebec against the British General James WOLFE, who was also killed.

The monastery of Monte Cassino dominates an Italian hillside. Used as a strongpoint by German forces in WWII, it held up the Allied advance for months; attempts to capture it cost enormous American casualties, and it eventually had to be razed by bombardment. In 1952 it was rebuilt, and is now a national monument and art museum.

MONTCLAIR, city in SE Cal. Primarily residential, it is in a citrus fruit producing area. Pop 22 546.

MONTCLAIR, town in NE N.J., 6mi NNW of Newark. It is a residential suburb of Newark and New York City with some light industry. Pop 44 043.

MONTEBELLO, residential and industrial city in S Cal., 9mi E of Los Angeles. It produces automobiles and rubber. Pop 42 807.

MONTE CARLO, town in the independent principality of MONACO, on the Mediterranean coast known as the French Riviera. It is an international resort with a gambling casino, a yacht harbor and an annual automobile rally and the Monaco Grand Prix car race. It is the home (and tax haven) of many international firms. Pop 9 948.

MONTE CASSINO, an Italian monastery founded by St. BENEDICT OF NURSIA c529 AD, which was the ruling house of the BENEDICTINE ORDERS and an influential cultural and religious center for centuries. Its buildings were destroyed for the fourth time in their history in WWII by bombardment but have since been rebuilt; the abbey is now a national monument.

MONTEGO BAY, city in NW Jamaica, West Indies, in St. James parish. It is a port, a commercial center and a popular Caribbean resort. Pop 42 800.

MONTENEGRO, the smallest of Yugoslavia's six constituent republics, at the S end of the Dinaric Alps on the Adriatic Sea. Its capital is Titograd. The area is mountainous with heavy forests. Mining and the raising of livestock are its chief occupations.

MONTEREY, city in W Cal., 120mi S of San Francisco, on S Monterey Bay. The old capital of Spanish Cal., the US flag was first raised over the Presidio (its old Spanish garrison) in 1846. The city is a popular historical tourist site. Pop 26 307.

MONTEREY PARK, city in S Cal., 5mi E of Los Angeles, of which it is both a residential and light industrial suburb. Pop 49 166.

MONTERÍA, capital and chief city of Córdoba department, NW Colombia. The surrounding area is an important cattle raising region. Pop 121 200.

MONTERREY, city in Mexico, capital of Nuevo León state, near the Tex. border. Founded by the Spanish in 1579, it is today the country's third largest city with a large industrial complex. Pop 858 107.

MONTESQUIEU, Charles Louis de Secondat, Baron de la Brède et de (1689–1755), French political philosopher who profoundly influenced 19th and 20th century political and social philosophy. His theory that governmental powers should be separated into legislative, executive and judicial bodies to safeguard personal liberty was developed in his most important work *The Spirit of the Laws* (1748), which influenced the US Constitution and others. A member of the French Academy (from 1728) his other notable writings include *Persian Letters* (1721), a satire on Parisian life, and *Reflections on the Rise and Fall of the Roman Empire* (1734–48).

MONTESSORI, Maria (1870–1952), Italian psychiatrist and educator. The first woman to gain a medical degree in Italy (1894), she developed a system of preschool teaching, the Montessori Method, in which children of 3 to 6 are given a wide range of materials and equipment which enable them to learn by themselves. There are about 600 schools in the US using this method which encourages individual initiative.

MONTEUX, Pierre (1875–1964), French-American conductor. He is remembered especially for his performance of the music of Stravinsky, Debussy and Ravel, as conductor of DIAGHILEV's Ballet Russe (1911–14). Later he was conductor of the Boston Symphony Orchestra (1919–24), the San Francisco Symphony (1935–52) and the London Symphony Orchestra (1960–64).

MONTEVERDI, Claudio (1567–1643), Italian composer. His innovative operas were the predecessors of modern opera, in which aria, recitative and orchestral accompaniment all enhance dramatic characterization. *Orfeo* (1607) is considered the first modern opera. His other compositions include the ornate *Vespers* (1610) and much other sacred music, the operas *The Return of Ulysses to his Country* (1641) and *The Coronation of Poppea* (1642), and many MADRIGALS.

MONTEVIDEO, capital and largest city of Uruguay and of Montevideo department, located in the S on the Rio de Plata. It is the industrial, cultural and transportation center for the country, as well as a seaport and popular resort. Pop 1 280000.

MONTEZ, Lola (c1818–1861), stage name of Marie Dolores Eliza Rosanna Gilbert, a notorious Irish adventuress who became famous in Europe, the US and Australia as a "Spanish" dancer. The mistress of Franz Liszt, Alexandre Dumas *père* and then Ludwig I of Bavaria, she gained powerful enemies because of her influence over the king and was forced to leave the country when revolution broke out in 1848.

MONTEZUMA, name of two Aztec rulers of Mexico before its conquest. **Montezuma I** (c1390–1469), was a successful conqueror who ruled from 1440. His descendant **Montezuma II** (1466–1520), was the last Aztec emperor (1502–20). When the Spanish conquistadors arrived, Montezuma failed to resist them because he believed CORTES to be the white god QUETZALCOATL, and he became a hostage. The Aztecs rebelled and Montezuma II was killed in the struggle.

MONTEZUMA CASTLE NATIONAL MONUMENT, site of pre-Columbian (c1100 AD) cliff dwellings of the PUEBLO INDIANS. The monument's 843 acres are in central Ariz. in the Verdi R valley. Established in 1906, it features a well-preserved five-story "castle" constructed in the shelter of limestone cliffs.

MONTFORT, Simon de, Earl of Leicester (c1208–1265), Anglo-French leader who mounted a revolt to limit Henry III's power by law. The BARONS' WAR followed which ended in the capture of the king (1264). The famous parliament of 1265, summoned by Montfort, was a landmark in English history with representatives from every shire, town and borough. In fighting that followed Montfort was killed at the Battle of Evesham.

MONTGOLFIER, Joseph Michel (1740–1810) and **Jacques Étienne** (1745–1799), French brothers noted for their invention of the first manned aircraft, the first practical (hot-air) BALLOON, which they flew in 1783. Later in the same year Jacques assisted Jacques CHARLES in the launching of the first gas (hydrogen) balloon.

MONTGOMERY, capital city of Ala., seat of Montgomery Co., about 90mi SE of Birmingham. It is the marketing center for a fertile blacksoil farm region and has a large livestock market, as well as diversified industry. It is known as the "Cradle of the Confederacy" because the CONFEDERATE STATES OF AMERICA was formed in the city in Feb., 1861. Pop 133 386.

The picturesque Flower Market in the Place Jacques Cartier of Old Montreal, with the City Hall in the background.

MONTGOMERY, Bernard Law, 1st Viscount Montgomery of Alamein (1887–1976), British army leader known as the commander who never lost a battle. He defeated ROMMEL at El Alamein (1942) driving the Germans out of N Africa. Promoted to field marshal, he commanded the British forces in the invasion of Normandy (1944) and later became deputy supreme commander of NATO, 1951–58.

MONTGOMERY, Richard (1738–1775), Irish-American army officer. He fought in the French and Indian Wars, and left Britain to settle in N.Y. in 1772. He became a delegate to the provincial congress (1775) and brigadier general in the colonial army. In the Canadian campaign he captured Montreal, but was killed in the attack on Quebec.

MONTH, name of several periods of time, mostly defined in terms of the motion of the MOON. The synodic month (lunar month or lunation) is the time between successive full moons; it is 29.531 DAYS. The sidereal month, the time taken by the moon to complete one revolution about the earth relative to the fixed stars, is 27.322 days. The anomalistic month, 27.555 days, is the time between successive passages of the moon through perigee (see ORBIT). The solar month, 30.439 days, is one twelfth of the solar YEAR. Civil or calendar months vary in length throughout the year, lasting from 28 to 31 days (see CALENDAR). In popular usage, the (lunar) month refers to 28 days.

MONTHERLANT, Henri-Marie Joseph Millon de (1896–1972), French novelist and playwright. His work stressed masculine as opposed to feminine virtues and his characters are heroic idealists. His many works include the novels *The Girls* (1936–39) and *Chaos and Night* (1963) and the plays *Malatesta* (1946) and *La guerre civile* (1965).

MONTICELLO, a 640-acre estate planned by Thomas JEFFERSON in Va., 3mi from Charlottesville. Construction of the neoclassical mansion atop a small mountain began in 1770; Jefferson moved in before it was completed and lived there for 56 years. His tomb is nearby and the house became a national shrine in 1926, and is open to the public.

MONTMAGNY, town in SE Quebec, Canada, on the St. Lawrence R, 34mi NE of Quebec city. Its products include textiles, furniture, stoves and pumps. Pop 12 432.

MONTMARTRE, the highest hill (432ft) in Paris, France, on the right bank of the Seine. Topped by the famous Sacré-Coeur church, the hill was celebrated as the bohemian haunt of artists and writers and for its night life.

MONTPELIER, capital of Vt. and the seat of Washington Co. Its industries include life insurance, granite quarrying and lumbering. It is a winter tourist resort. Pop 8 609.

MONTPELLIER, town in S France, capital of Hérault department, near the Mediterranean Sea. It is a commercial and industrial center with a 13th-century university and a noted botanical garden (established 1593). Pop 167 211.

MONTPENSIER, Anne Marie Louise d'Orléans, duchesse de (1627–1693), French princess, the daughter of LOUIS XIII's brother, known as "Mademoiselle." During the FRONDE of the Princes she aided CONDÉ and the rebels, relieving Orléans and opening the gates of Paris to them (1652). She was exiled from the court and later wrote her memoirs and two short novels.

MONTREAL, city in S Quebec, Canada, located on the island of Montreal at the confluence of the St. Lawrence and Ottawa rivers. It is a huge inland port, despite its distance of 1000mi from the sea, Canada's largest city and the second largest French-speaking city in the world. A French mission was built on the site in 1642 and then became an important fur trading center. Ceded to Britain in 1763, the city retained much of its French character. In the 19th century Montreal grew into an important transportation and industrial center aided by its many natural resources and abundance of hydroelectric power. It is the site of McGill U., the U. of Montreal and Sir George Williams U. Pop 1 214 352.

MONTREAL-NORD, town on Montreal island, S Quebec, Canada, bordering on NE Montreal on the Rivière des Prairies. It produces lumber products, electrical goods and transportation equipment. Pop 89 139.

MONTREUX CONVENTION, an international agreement, which gave Turkey military control of the DARDANELLES, signed in 1936. Ratified by Turkey, Great Britain, France, USSR, Germany, Greece, Bulgaria and Yugoslavia (and Japan, with reservations), it closed the straits to warships if Turkey was at war and allowed passage of merchant ships in peace and war (if the countries were neutral in respect of Turkey). The convention still stands.

MONT-ROYAL, high point reaching 763ft in the center of MONTREAL, Quebec, Canada. The city takes its name from this prominent landmark.

MONTS, Pierre de Guast, Sieur de (c1560–?1630), French colonizer. With Samuel de CHAMPLAIN he explored the area around the Bay of Fundy (1604) and founded Port Royal, Nova Scotia (1605). As governor of Acadia, he sent Champlain to explore Canada in 1608 and 1610.

MONT-SAINT-MICHEL, rocky island off the NW coast of France, about 1000yds in circumference and rising from the sea to a height of 260ft. It is crowned by a famous medieval Benedictine monastery, and is accessible from the mainland only by a causeway.

MONTSERRAT ("saw-toothed mountain"), mountain in Catalonia, NE Spain, rising from the plain NW of Barcelona to a height of 4 054ft. The Benedictine monastery there contains a celebrated wooden statue of the Virgin Mary.

MONTSERRAT, one of the LEEWARD ISLANDS in the West Indies. Discovered by Christopher Columbus in 1493, it has been a British colony since 1783. Its chief product is Sea Island cotton, marketed in the capital city, Plymouth.

MONTVILLE, town in SE Conn., NW of New London on the Thames R. Its products include paper goods and textiles. Pop 15 662.

MOODY, Dwight Lyman (1837–1899), US evangelist, who toured the US and Britain on missions with the hymn writer Ira D. SANKEY. He founded several schools and set up a Bible Institute in Chicago (1889) to promote religious learning.

MOON, a SATELLITE, in particular, the earth's largest

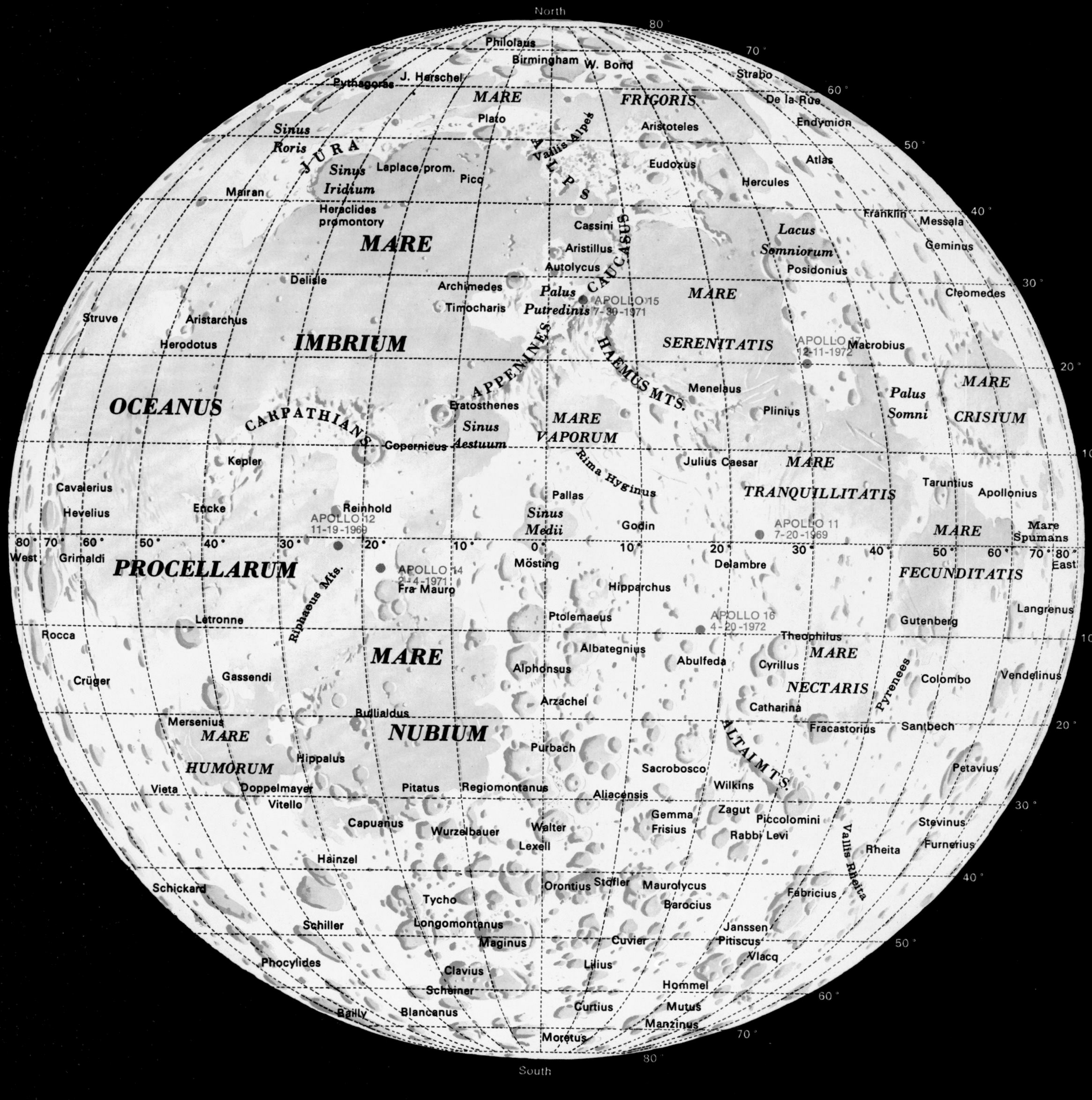

Map of the visible side of the moon, showing the *maria* ("seas"), major craters and mountain ranges. The sites of the Apollo program manned landings are shown in red, with dates. The names we find on the moon may seem odd today, but it was not illogical of the early astronomers to assume that there must be seas, bays and lakes on this other world, as in our own. Today these names remain to lend the lunar landscape an extra air of romance.

natural satellite. The moon is so large relative to the earth (it has a diameter two thirds that of MERCURY) that earth and moon are commonly regarded as a double planet. The moon has a diameter of 3476km and a mass 0.0123 that of the earth; its ESCAPE VELOCITY is around 2.4km/s. The orbit of the moon defines the several kinds of MONTH. The distance of the moon from the earth varies between 363Mm and 406Mm (perigee and apogee) with a mean of 384.4Mm. The moon rotates on its axis every 27.322 days, hence keeping the same face constantly toward the earth; however, in accordance with KEPLER's second law, the moon's orbital velocity is not constant and hence there is exhibited the phenomenon known as *libration*: to a particular observer on the earth, marginally different parts of the moon's disk are visible at different times. There is also a very small physical libration due to slight irregularities in its rotational velocity.

The moon is covered with craters, whose sizes range up to 200km diameter. These sometimes are seen in chains up to 1Mm in length. Other features include rilles, trenches a few kilometres wide and a few hundred kilometres long; the *maria* (Latin: seas) or great plains; the bright rays which emerge from the large craters, and the lunar mountains. There are also lunar hot spots, generally associated with those larger craters showing bright rays: these remain cooler than their surrounds during lunar daytime, warmer dur ing the lunar night. It has been shown, both by the

Astronaut Harrison H. Schmitt, first geologist to visit the Moon, photographed by fellow Apollo 17 crewman Eugene A. Cernan. The third, Ronald E. Evans, remained to pilot the orbiting command module while Evans and Schmitt spent a record 74h 59min on the lunar surface (December 1972).

samples brought back by the Apollo 11 (1969) and subsequent lunar expeditions (see SPACE EXPLORATION) and measurements of crater circularities carried out in 1968, that the smaller lunar craters are in general of meteoritic (see METEOR) origin, the larger of volcanic origin. It is believed that the earth and the moon formed simultaneously, the greater mass of the earth accounting for its higher proportion of metallic iron; the heat of the young earth's atmosphere, which evaporated silicates, accounting for their higher proportion on the moon.

MOONEY, Thomas J. (1883–1942), US labor activist. A key figure in labor's struggle for recognition on the West Coast, he was sentenced to death for his part in a bomb outrage in San Francisco, Cal., in 1916. He was widely believed to be innocent, and his sentence was commuted in 1918. He was pardoned in 1939.

MOONEYE, *Hiodon tergisus*, a freshwater fish of North America related to the Bony tongues. Fairly abundant in the lakes and rivers of the US, they feed on insects and worms. When breeding they migrate to shallow backwaters and lake feeder streams.

MOONFLOWER, common name for herbaceous vines of the genus *Calonyction* from the MORNING GLORY family (Convolvulaceae). They are native to tropical regions of the world and have white or purple flowers that open at night.

MOONSTONE, translucent variety of alkali (or plagioclase) FELDSPAR, showing opalescence due to unmixing of sodium and potassium; a GEM stone.

MOORE, city in central Okla., a suburb to the S of Oklahoma City. Its industries are food processing and aircraft maintenance. Pop 18 761.

MOORE, Clement Clarke (1779–1863), US educator and poet. He wrote the popular Christmas poem *A Visit from St. Nicholas*, which begins "'Twas the night before Christmas" (1823), and was a professor of Oriental and Greek literature at New York City's General Theological Seminary for 29 years.

MOORE, George Augustus (1852–1933), Irish writer. He spent his youth in Paris and came under the influence of BALZAC and ZOLA, returning to England to stir literary society with realistic novels such as *Esther Waters* (1894) and his masterpiece *Héloise and Abélard* (1921). He contributed much to the Irish literary revival and the ABBEY THEATRE's success.

MOORE, George Edward (1873–1958), English philosopher who led the 20th-century reaction against IDEALISM. His work, especially *Principia Ethica* (1903) influenced such philosophers as Bertrand RUSSELL.

MOORE, Henry (1898–), English sculptor and artist, one of the outstanding sculptors of the 20th century. His inspiration comes from natural forms such as stones, roots and bones and often expresses itself in curving abstract shapes perforated with large holes. His work, with repeated themes such as mother and child, is monumental and full of humanity and includes *Family Group* (1949) and *Reclining Figure* (1965).

MOORE, Marianne Craig (1887–1972), US poet, winner of the 1952 Pulitzer Prize for her *Collected Poems*. She edited the *Dial* magazine (1925–29) and translated Fontaine's *Fables*. Her subjects and themes are often taken from nature. Along with Emily DICKINSON, she is considered one of America's finest poets.

MOORE, Stanford (1913–), US biochemist who shared with C. B. ANFINSEN and W. H. STEIN the 1972 Nobel Prize for Chemistry for his part in determining the structure of the ENZYME ribonuclease (see also NUCLEIC ACIDS).

MOORE, Thomas (1779–1852), Irish poet. He is remembered for his *Irish Melodies* (1808–34), including "The Last Rose of Summer" and other lyrics. Extremely popular in his own day, he also wrote an oriental romance *Lalla Rookh* (1817) and lives of Sheridan (1825) and of Byron (1830).

MOORESTOWN, township in SW N.J., 9mi E of Camden. An industrial suburb of the greater Philadelphia area, it manufactures electronic chemicals and metal products. Pop 15 577.

MOORHEAD, city in NW Minn., the seat of Clay Co., on the Red R. It is a food processing and trading center for a rich farming region. Pop 29 687.

MOORS, Muslim Caucasoid people of N Africa primarily, originally of Berber-Arab stock but today also of Spanish, Jewish or Turkish ancestry. In the 8th century they conquered much of Spain, basing their rule on Cordoba and Granada, but were driven out by 1492.

MOOSE, *Alces alces*, a large long-legged DEER of cold climates, known as the ELK in N Europe and Asia, and Moose in North America. It is characterized by its large size, long legs and overshot muzzle. The males have large, palmate antlers, as much as 2m (6.6ft) across. Often living near water, the moose feeds on aquatic plants as well as browsing from bushes and mature trees.

MOOSE, Loyal Order of, a fraternal organization with a broad scope of community service activities, operating in the US, Canada and Great Britain. Founded in 1888, it has over 2 000 local lodges and a membership of over 1 million. The Moose are similar to the ELKS and other fraternal groups.

MOOSE FACTORY, a trading post in NE Ontario, Canada, on James Bay. Built by the Hudson's Bay Company as a fort (early 1670s) and rebuilt in 1730, it is still operating today.

MOOSE JAW, industrial city in S central Saskatchewan, Canada, 45mi W of Regina. Its industries include oil refining, food processing, and milling of various products. Pop 31 854.

MORAINE, accumulation of debris carried or dropped by a glacier. *Ground moraine* is DRIFT left in a sheet as the GLACIER retreats. *Terminal moraines* are ridges deposited when the ice is melting prior to the glacial retreat; a series of ridges may mark pauses in the retreat. *Lateral moraines* are formed of debris that falls onto the glacier: when two glaciers merge their lateral moraines may unite to form a *medial moraine*.

MORALITY PLAY, form of drama popular in the Middle Ages from about the 14th to the 16th centuries. It was intended to instruct watchers on the eternal struggle between good and evil for human souls. The characters were personifications of virtues and vices. The most noted English example is *Everyman* (from the 1500s) which is still sometimes performed. Morality plays grew out of earlier religious pageants and were an important step in the secularization of drama. (See also MYSTERY PLAY.)

MORAL REARMAMENT (MRA), movement emphasizing spiritual values in everyday life, founded in the 1920s by the American evangelist Frank BUCHMAN. Buchmanite groups, often called Oxford Groups, spread to countries throughout the world. Headquarters are in New York and Los Angeles.

MORAVIA, central region of Czechoslovakia, bounded on the W by the Bohemian highlands and on the E by the CARPATHIANS. Historically the homeland of the Moravian Empire, from 1029 Moravia was a province of Bohemia. In 1526 it passed under Hapsburg rule, and was part of Austria-Hungary until 1918. Moravia is a fertile and now highly-industrialized region. BRNO, the largest city, is notable for its manufacture of textiles.

MORAVIA, Alberto (1907–), Italian novelist, born Alberto Pincherle, whose detached and colloquial style lends realism to his theme of disaffection and aridity in modern life. His novels include *The Woman of Rome* (1947) and *Two Women* (1957).

MORAVIAN CHURCH, Protestant church known as the Church of the Brethren or *Unitas Fratrum*, formed (1457) by Bohemian followers of Jan HUS, believers in simple worship and strict Christian living, with the Bible as their rule of faith. They broke with Rome in 1467. During the THIRTY YEARS' WAR (1618–48), they were persecuted almost to extinction, but revived in Silesia and in 1732 began the missionary work for which they are still known. The first American settlements were in Pa. (1740) and N.C. (1753). In 1969 the Moravian Church had 353 228 members but its influence, especially in shaping modern Protestantism, has been far greater than its numbers suggest. (See also ZINZENDORF.)

MORDANTS, substances which fix DYES to fabrics by precipitating them in the fibers or by forming LIGAND complexes with them. Generally, metal salts and hydroxides (including ALUM), now chiefly CHROMIUM salts and dichromates, are used. They modify the hue and improve fastness.

MORE, Paul Elmer (1864–1937), US scholar and literary critic, an exponent (with Irving BABBITT) of the New Humanism. His works include *Shelburne Essays* (1904–21) and *The Greek Tradition* (1921–31).

MORE, Sir Thomas (1478–1535), English statesman, writer and saint who was executed for his refusal to take the oath of supremacy recognizing Henry VIII as head of the English Church. A man of brilliance, subtlety and wit, he was much favored by the king. When Cardinal WOLSEY fell in 1529 More was made lord chancellor. Probably because of Henry's determination to divorce Catherine of Aragon in defiance of the pope, More resigned only three years later. Considered dangerously influential even in silence and retirement, More was condemned for high treason. More's best-known work is *Utopia*, a description of an ideal society based on reason. Long recognized as a martyr by the Roman Catholic Church, More was canonized in 1935.

MOREAU, Gustave (1826–1898), French painter noted for his highly dramatic studies of mythological and supernatural scenes, such as *Oedipus and The Sphinx* (1864). As a teacher he greatly influenced MATISSE and ROUAULT.

MORELIA, city in Mexico, capital of Michoacán state, 130mi WNW of Mexico City. Food crops and cattle are processed there. Pop 209 507.

MORELOS, state in S central Mexico. Rich in agriculture, it produces rice, sugarcane, corn, fruits and vegetables. Its capital is CUERNAVACA.

MORGAGNI, Giovanni Battista (1682–1771), Italian anatomist whose *Of the Seats and Causes of Diseases as Investigated by Anatomy* (1761) established him as the father of morbid anatomy.

MORGAN, US banking family famous for its immense financial power and its philanthropic activities. The banking house of J. S. Morgan and Co. was founded by **Junius Spencer Morgan** (1813–1890), and built up into a vast financial and industrial empire (J. P. Morgan & Co.) by his son, **John Pierpoint Morgan** (1837–1913). Many of J. P. Morgan's commercial activities aroused controversy, and in 1904 his Northern Securities Company was dissolved as a violation of the SHERMAN ANTI-TRUST ACT. Notable philanthropic legacies include part of his art collection in the Metropolitan Museum of Art, and the Pierpont Morgan Library, which was endowed by his son. **John Pierpont Morgan, Jr.** (1867–1943) was American agent for the Allies during WWI, when he raised huge funds and organized contracts for military supplies. Most of the large postwar international loans were floated by the house of Morgan.

MORGAN, Daniel (1736–1802), American general in the REVOLUTIONARY WAR. He was captured in the attack on Quebec (1775). Later as brigadier-general he defeated the British in the battle of Cowpens (1781). He helped to put down the WHISKEY REBELLION (1794) and was a member of Congress (1797–1799).

MORGAN, Sir Henry (c1635–1688), notorious English adventurer and leader of the West Indies BUCCANEERS. The destruction (1671) of Panama City, his most daring exploit, took place after the signing of a treaty between England and Spain. Recalled under arrest, he was subsequently pardoned, knighted (1673) and made lieutenant governor of Jamaica.

MORGAN, John Hunt (1825–1864), Confederate general in the American Civil War, famous for his skilled and daring raids behind Union lines. His great raid (1863) through Kentucky, Indiana and Ohio ended in his capture, but he escaped to resume fighting until killed at Greenville, Tenn.

MORGAN, Lewis Henry (1818–1881), US ethnologist best known for his studies of kinship systems in his attempts to prove that the AMERINDS had migrated into North America, and to discover their place of origin. His techniques and apparently successful results have earned him regard as a father of the science of cultural ANTHROPOLOGY.

MORGAN, Thomas Hunt (1866–1945), US biologist who, through his experiments with the fruit fly *Drosophila*, established the relation between GENES and CHROMOSOMES and thus the mechanism of HEREDITY. For his work he received the 1933 Nobel Prize for Physiology or Medicine.

MORGANTON, town in west N.C., seat of Burke Co. A holiday resort of natural beauty, it has some light industry. Pop 13 625.

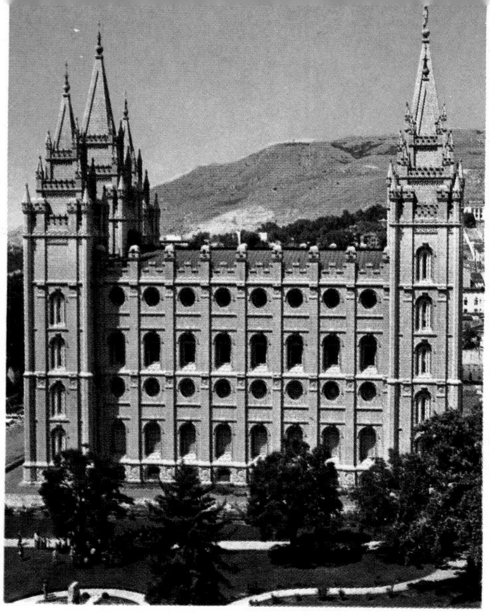

The Mormon Temple in Salt Lake City, Utah, completed in 1893 after thirty years abuilding, is a striking reminder of the important role played by the Mormons in the development of the state.

MORGANTOWN, city in W Va., seat of Monongalia Co. It is the center of a coal-mining area and manufactures glass and textiles. Pop 29 431.

MORGENTHAU, Henry Jr. (1891–1967), US agriculturist and secretary of the treasury (1934–45) whose WWII Victory Bonds campaign helped to finance the US defense program. He took part in the BRETTON WOODS CONFERENCE (1944), but his plans for controlling Germany by eliminating German heavy industry were rejected.

MÖRIKE, Eduard (1804–1875), major German lyric poet. His poetry, first collected in the volume *Gedichte* (1838), is small in quantity but richly varied in theme and technique. He also wrote a novel and some short stories.

MORIOKA, city in N Honshu, Japan, capital of Iwate Prefecture. It is a center for commerce and industry. Ironware is manufactured. Pop 196 036.

MORISON, Samuel Eliot (1887–1976), US historian who wrote the official 15-volume history (1947–62) of the US Navy during WWII. He also won Pulitzer Prizes for his *Admiral of the Ocean Sea* (1942), a life of Christopher Columbus, and *John Paul Jones* (1959).

MORLEY, Edward Williams (1838–1923), US chemist who worked on the relative densities of OXYGEN and HYDROGEN, but is best known for his role in the MICHELSON-MORLEY EXPERIMENT.

MORLEY, Thomas (c1557–?1603), English composer noted especially for his madrigals. A pupil of William BYRD and organist of St. Paul's Cathedral, he also wrote *A Plaine and Easie Introduction to Practicall Musicke*, an invaluable source of information on Elizabethan musical practice.

MORMON CRICKET, *Anabrus simplex*, a large wingless insect in the same family as KATYDIDS, Tettigoniidae. When abundant this is an important agricultural pest in the western US.

MORMONS, members of the Church of Jesus Christ of Latter-Day Saints founded (1830) by Joseph SMITH. Mormons accept Smith as having miraculously found and translated a divinely-inspired record of the early history and religion of America, the *Book of Mormon*. With Smith's own writings and the Bible, this forms the Mormon scriptures. Smith's teachings quickly gained a following, but the Mormons' attempts to settle met with recurrent persecution, culminating in the murder of Smith in 1844. It was Brigham YOUNG who led the Mormons in 1847 beyond the frontier to what is now Salt Lake City (still the location of their chief temple). In 1850 Congress granted them the Territory of Utah with Young as Governor. Hostility to the flourishing agricultural community which then developed focused on the Mormon sanction of polygamy and came to a climax with the "Utah War" (1857–58). In 1890 the Mormons abolished polygamy, and Utah was admitted to the Union in 1896. The Mormons have no professional priesthood, but a president and counselors. They stress repentance and believe in the afterlife and the Last Judgment. The Mormons are notably temperate and law-abiding; their religion is an integral part of their lives. They have a membership of over 3 million.

MORNING GLORY, annual and perennial vines of the genus *Ipomoea*, which are native to temperate and tropical regions of the world. They are widely cultivated for their large colorful trumpet-shaped flowers that open in the morning and close later in the day. Family: Convolvulaceae.

MORNING SICKNESS. See PREGNANCY.

MOROCCO, country is NW Africa, on the Mediterranean and the Atlantic, bordering Algeria (S and E) and the Spanish Sahara (S). Its topography varies from the fertile coastal region (which includes the RIF Mts along the Mediterranean) to barren desert, with the great ATLAS mountain chain enclosing extensive plains W to E across the center. N Morocco has a Mediterranean climate.

People. Most Moroccans are of Arab descent but about one third are BERBERS, and there are Jewish, French and Spanish communities. Less than a third of the people are town dwellers. The largest cities are CASABLANCA, MARRAKESH and RABAT (the capital).

Economy. About 30% of the Gross National Prod uct is provided by agriculture. Wheat, barley, corn, beans, dates, citrus and other fruits are grown. Timber, livestock and fishing are also sources of income, and tourism is increasingly important. The chief mineral is phosphate. Coal, manganese, iron ore, lead, cobalt, zinc, silver and some oil are also produced. There are leather, textile and cement industries. Traditional Moroccan handicrafts are world-famous.

History. The Arabs swept into N Africa from the east (c683 AD), converting the native Berbers to Islam and enlisting their aid in the 8th-century conquest of Spain, but lengthy Arab-Berber strife followed under a succession of dynasties. European (chiefly Portuguese) penetration of Morocco, beginning in 1415, was checked after the founding of the present in 1660, but resumed in the 19th and 20th centuries by France, Spain and Germany. Independent since 1956, Morocco is now ruled by King Hassan II. It is a member of the ARAB LEAGUE, the ORGANIZATION OF AFRICAN UNITY, and the United Nations.

Official name: Morocco
Capital: Rabat
Area: 166000 sq mi
Population: 15 379 259
Languages: Arabic. French, Spanish also spoken
Religion: Muslim
Monetary unit(s): 1 Dirham = 100 centimes

MORÓN, city in E Argentina, suburb of BUENOS AIRES. Industries include meat packing, dairying, and food canning. Pop 485 983.

MOROS, a group of Muslim people of the S Philippines and Borneo, largely of Malayan origin. Until the 19th century they waged constant war against the Christian Filipinos. An agricultural people noted also for their metal work, they now represent about 4.9% of Filipinos.

MORPHEME, any of the smallest meaningful elements of a language. A morpheme may be a whole word (e.g., "talk"), a syllable (e.g., the "ing" of "talking") or merely a letter (e.g., the "s" of "talks"). (See also PHONEME.)

MORPHEUS, Greek and Roman god of dreams who was one of the children of Hypnos, god of sleep. He assumed human form to bring his dreams. Morphine (from opium) is named for him.

MORPHINE, OPIUM derivative used as a NARCOTIC ANALGESIC and also commonly in DRUG ADDICTION. It depresses RESPIRATION and the COUGH reflex, induces sleep and may cause VOMITING and CONSTIPATION. It is valuable in HEART failure and as a premedication for ANESTHETICS; its properties are particularly valuable in terminal malignant DISEASE (see also HEROIN). Addiction and withdrawal syndromes are common.

MORRILL, Justin Smith (1810–1898), US Senator and Representative who helped organize the Republican party and spent 43 years in Congress. He was responsible for the Morrill Act (1862), which provided for federal grants of public land for educational purposes.

MORRIS, Gouverneur (1752–1816), American statesman responsible for planning the US decimal coinage system. He was a member of the New York provincial congress (1775–77). At the Constitutional Convention of 1787 he argued for a strong, property-based federal government, and was responsible, as a literary adviser, for much of the wording of the US Constitution. He was minister to France (1792–94) and later played a leading part in promoting the Erie Canal.

MORRIS, Robert (1734–1806), American financier who funded the American Revolution and was a signatory of the Declaration of Independence. As superintendant of finance (1781–84) he saved the nation from bankruptcy by raising money (chiefly from the French) to establish the Bank of North America.

MORRIS, William (1834–1896), English artist, poet and designer. One of the PRE-RAPHAELITE BROTHERHOOD, he sought to counteract the effects of industrialization by a return to the aesthetic standards and craftsmanship of the Middle Ages. In 1861 he set up Morris and Co. to design and make wallpaper, furniture, carpets and other home furnishings. Influenced by RUSKIN, he formed the Socialist League (1884). His founding (1890) of the Kelmscott Press had a primary impact on typographical and book design.

MORRIS DANCE, English folk dance associated with ancient ritual festivals such as May Day. Literary references to the Morris Dance occur from the 1400s, and it still survives today. The dancers performed in groups, often centered around a man symbolically disguised as an animal.

MORRIS JESUP, Cape, the world's most northern land point, in the Peary Land region of Greenland, 440mi from the North Pole.

MORRISTOWN, town in N.J., seat of Morris Co., 17mi WNW of Newark. It is mainly residential, but has varied light industry. Pop 17 662.

MORRISTOWN, city in NE Tenn., seat of Hambledon Co., 41mi NE of Knoxville. Metals, furniture and synthetic fabrics are manufactured there. Pop 20 318.

MORRISTOWN NATIONAL HISTORICAL PARK, Morristown, N.J., an area of 1 245 acres established in 1933. The site was Washington's headquarters in 1779–80.

MORRISVILLE, borough in SE Pa., on the Delaware R, across from Trenton, N.J. Industries include plastics and rubber products. Pop 11 309.

MORROW, Dwight Whitney (1873–1931), US diplomat and lawyer who helped to bring about many reforms in N.J. Appointed ambassador to Mexico (1927), he did much to improve US diplomatic relations there. In 1930 he was elected to the US Senate. His daughter Anne married Charles A. LINDBERGH.

MORSE, Samuel Finley Breese (1791–1872), US inventor of an electric TELEGRAPH. His first crude model was designed in 1832, and by 1835 he could demonstrate a working model. With the considerable help of Joseph HENRY (which later he refused to acknowledge) he developed by 1837 electromagnetic

US morse code		International morse code
·—	**A**	·—
—···	**B**	—···
·· ·	**C**	—·—·
—··	**D**	—··
·	**E**	·
·—·	**F**	··—·
——·	**G**	——·
····	**H**	····
··	**I**	··
—·—·	**J**	·———
—·—	**K**	—·—
⸺	**L**	·—··
——	**M**	——
—·	**N**	—·
· ·	**O**	———
·····	**P**	·——·
··—·	**Q**	——·—
· ··	**R**	·—·
···	**S**	···
—	**T**	—
··—	**U**	··—
···—	**V**	···—
·——	**W**	·——
·—··	**X**	—··—
·· ··	**Y**	—·——
··· ·	**Z**	——··
·——·	**1**	·————
··—··	**2**	··———
···—·	**3**	···——
····—	**4**	····—
———	**5**	·····
······	**6**	—····
——··	**7**	——···
—····	**8**	———··
—··—	**9**	————·
⸺	**0**	—————

relays to extend the range and capabilities of his system. WHEATSTONE's invention had preceded Morse's, so that he was unable to obtain an English patent, and in the US official support did not come until 1843. His famous message, "What hath God wrought!", was the first sent on his Washington-Baltimore line on May 24, 1844. For this he used MORSE CODE, devised in 1838. In early life, Morse was a noted portrait painter.

MORSE, Wayne Lyman (1900–1974), US congressman known for his work in labor relations and as an outspoken opponent of the war in Vietnam. He served as Senator for Oregon, 1945–68.

MORSE CODE, signal system devised (1838) by Samuel MORSE for use in the wire TELEGRAPH, now used in radiotelegraphy and elsewhere. Letters, numbers and punctuation are represented by combinations of dots (brief taps of the transmitting key) and dashes (three times the length of dots).

MORTAR, building material used to bind together stones, blocks or bricks. Early mortar was made from mud and straw. Today a mixture of CEMENT, sand and water is prepared immediately prior to being applied as a paste. When set, it is strong and water-resistant.

MORTAR, short-barreled gun which fires a shell in a high trajectory. Developed for trench warfare in WWI, it consists of a mounted tube into which the shell is dropped for firing. It has become a universally-used infantry weapon, and its lightness, simplicity and high trajectory make it suitable for GUERRILLA WARFARE in confined spaces and difficult terrain.

MORTGAGE, loan given on the security of the borrower's property. A mortgage is sometimes taken out on property already owned, but is more often used to help finance the purchase of property. If the loan is not repaid on time the mortgage may be foreclosed: that is, the person who loaned the money may obtain a court order to sell the property, and take what he is owed from the proceedings. Mortgages taken out for the purchase of a home usually run for 20 years or more. In the US, most mortgages are granted by banks or savings and loan societies. Mortgages are also issued for the purchase of machinery (especially farm machinery), when property other than real estate is often used as security.

MORTICIAN. See UNDERTAKER.

MORTMAIN (French: dead hand), in law, the state of property belonging to corporate entities such as churches. In the past mortmain was often the object of restrictive legislation because such property, being owned in perpetuity, did not change hands (it was held by a "dead hand"), and escaped certain kinds of taxation.

MORTON, village in central Ill., 10mi SE of Peoria, in a farming area noted for grain and livestock. Pop 10 419.

MORTON, Ferdinand "Jelly Roll" (1885–1941), US jazz composer, pianist and bandleader of the Red Hot Peppers, born Ferdinand Joseph La Menthe. He was a pioneer of the original New Orleans jazz style.

MORTON, Julius Sterling (1832–1902), US secretary of agriculture and advocate of scientific farming who originated ARBOR DAY in Neb. in 1872.

MORTON, Levi Parsons (1824–1920), US politician and financier whose company helped finance the Union in the Civil War. He was congressman (1879–81), minister to France (1881–85), vice-president (1889–93) and governor of New York (1895–96).

MORTON, Thomas (c1590–c1647), English adventurer and colorful leader (from 1626) of the Merry Mount settlement (now Quincy, Mass). His erection of a maypole, general merriment and commercial rivalry outraged his Puritan neighbors in Plymouth and Boston who imprisoned and expelled Morton several times. Morton satirized Puritan New England in his book *New English Canaan* (1637).

MORTON, William Thomas Green (1819–1868), US dentist who pioneered the use of diethyl ETHER as an ANESTHETIC (1844–46). In later years he engaged in bitter litigation over his refusal to recognize the contributions of former colleagues and especially C. W. LONG's prior use of ether in this way.

MORTON GROVE, village in NE Ill., 15mi N of Chicago, of which it is a residential suburb. It has large areas of forest preserves. Pop 26 369.

MOSAIC, general name for VIRUS DISEASES of plants such as tobacco, tomatoes, potatoes, soybeans and peas, which produce a characteristic leaf mottling and stunted growth. A number of viruses cause this type of disease, for example, tobacco mosaic virus. Transmission of the disease may be via aphids or by mechanical contact. Control may be achieved by use of INSECTICIDES and by careful cultivation techniques.

MOSAIC, ancient mode of decorating surfaces (mainly floors and walls) by inlaying small pieces of colored stone, marble, or glass, fitted together to form a design. Greek pebble mosaics survive from about 400 BC. There are fine Roman mosaics at Pompeii near Naples and outstanding Byzantine examples may be seen in Ravenna, Italy. American Indian stone mosaics have been found at Chichén Itza in Mexico.

MOSASAURS, an abundant group of marine lizards which developed during the upper Cretaceous in Europe and North America. They preyed on fish.

MOSBY, John Singleton (1833–1916), Confederate Civil War hero who led Mosby's Partisan Rangers, a cavalry troop known for their daring raids behind enemy lines in Md. and Union-occupied Va. After the war he became a Republican and entered government service.

MOSCA, Gaetano (1858–1941), Italian politician and jurist who held that all governments are run by entrenched elitist groups and that majority rule is therefore a myth. His ideas, set out in *The Ruling Class* (1896) and other writings, were distorted to suit apologists of FASCISM.

MOSCOW, city in NW Ida., seat of Latah Co., on the Wash. border. It is an agricultural trading center and has some light industry. Pop 14 146.

MOSCOW, capital of the Soviet Union (USSR) and of the Russian Soviet Federated Socialist Republic, administrative center of Moscow region, on both banks of the Moskva R. It is the USSR's largest city, and its political, cultural, commercial, industrial and communications center. Some leading industries are oil-refining, chemicals, textiles, wood products and a wide range of machinery including aircraft and automobiles. Moscow became the capital of all Russia under IVAN IV in the 16th century. Superseded by St.

Petersburg (now LENINGRAD) in 1713, it regained its former status in 1918, following the Russian Revolution. At the city's heart is the KREMLIN, location of the headquarters of government and containing notable architectural relics of tsarist Russia. Immediately east of the Kremlin, from which wide boulevards radiate in all directions, lies Red Square, the site of parades and celebrations, overlooked by the Lenin Mausoleum. Among outstanding cultural and educational institutions are the BOLSHOI THEATER, the MOSCOW ART THEATER, the Maly Theater, Moscow University, the Academy of Sciences, the Tchaikovsky Conservatory and the Lenin State Library. Pop 7 061 000.

MOSCOW ART THEATER, influential Russian repertory theater famed for its ensemble acting and its introduction of new techniques in stage realism. Founded in 1897 by Konstantin STANISLAVSKY and Vladimir NEMIROVICH-DANCHENKO, it introduced plays by such authors as CHEKHOV and GORKI.

MOSELEY, Henry Gwyn Jeffreys (1887–1915), British physicist who showed that an ELEMENT's properties depend on what he called its atomic number (see ATOM), equivalent to its nuclear charge.

MOSELLE RIVER, important waterway of W Europe, 320mi long. It rises in Vosges dept. in NE France and flows N to join the RHINE at Coblenz in West Germany.

MOSES (c13th century BC), Hebrew lawgiver and prophet who led the Israelites out of Egypt. According to the Bible, the infant Moses, hidden to save him from being killed, was found and raised by the pharaoh's daughter. After killing a tyrannical Egyptian, he fled to the desert. From a burning bush, God ordered him to return and demand the Israelites' freedom under threat of the PLAGUES. On PASSOVER night Moses led them out of Egypt (the "exodus"); the Red Sea was parted to let them cross. On Mt. Sinai he received the TEN COMMANDMENTS. After years of ruling the wandering Israelites in the wilderness, Moses died within sight of the promised land. Traditionally he was the author of the PENTATEUCH.

MOSES, Grandma (Anna Mary Robertson Moses; 1860–1961), US artist of the so-called primitive style. Self-taught, she began painting at age 76 and won wide popularity with her lively, unpretentious pictures of rural life.

MOSES, Robert (1888–), US administrator who helped plan the N.Y. state and city parks and parkways and the N.Y. World's Fair (1964–65). He also served as director of the Lincoln Center for the Performing Arts.

MOSES IN THE CRADLE, *Rhoeo discolor*, an evergreen perennial that produces strap-shaped, fleshy leaves that are dark green on the upper surface and rich purple beneath. The plant is so named because its small white flowers are produced in a cradle-shaped cup of olive-green bracts. It grows well at average house temperatures in sunny windows, although direct sunlight should be avoided in summer. The soil should be kept evenly moist, avoiding under- or over-watering which may cause the leaves to die at the tips. Propagation is by taking shoot cuttings or by removing offsets. Family: Commelinaceae.

MOSES LAKE, city in central Wash. on the E shore of the lake of that name. It produces sugar. Pop 10 310.

MOSLEM LEAGUE. See MUSLIM LEAGUE.

MOSLEMS. See MUSLIMS.

MOSLEY, Sir Oswald Ernald (1896–), British politician who formed (1932) the British Union of Fascists, popularly called the Blackshirts. He was interned during WWII. In 1948 he founded the extreme right-wing British Union Movement.

MOSQUE, Muslim place of worship. The name derives from the Arabic *masjid*, meaning "a place for prostration" (in prayer). Mosques are typically built with one or more MINARETS; a courtyard with fountains or wells for ceremonial washing; an area where the faithful assemble for prayers led by the *imam* (priest); a *mihrah* (niche) indicating the diretion (*qiblah*) of MECCA; a *mimbar* (pulpit) and sometimes, facing it, a *maqsurah* (enclosed area for important persons). Some mosques include a *madrash* (religious school). (See also ISLAM; ISLAMIC ART AND ARCHITECTURE.)

Left: the Cathedral of St. Basil in Red Square, Moscow, commissioned by Ivan the Terrible to commemorate his victory at Kazan. *Right:* sumptuous Kievskaya station on the famous Moscow subway.

MOSQUITO COAST, strip of land on the E coast of Nicaragua and Honduras, c300mi long and 40mi wide, named for the native Mosquito Indians. Briefly an autonomous region (1860–94), the area was long the subject of territorial disputes involving Nicaragua, Honduras, Britain and indirectly the US.

MOSQUITOES, two-winged flies of the family Culicidae, with penetrating, sucking mouthparts. The females of many species feed on vertebrate blood, using their needle-like stylets to puncture a blood capillary, but usually only when about to lay eggs. The males, and the females at other times, feed on sugary liquids such as nectar. Both the larvae and pupae are entirely aquatic, breathing through spiracles at the tip of the abdomen. In all but the Anopheline mosquitoes, the spiracles are at the tip of a tubular siphon, and the larva's body is suspended from this below the surface film. Mosquitoes are involved in the transmission of many diseases in man including YELLOW FEVER, FILARIASIS, and MALARIA.

MOSQUITO FISH, *Gambusia affinis*, a small freshwater fish of North America. It is a predator of MOSQUITO larvae, but also feeds on the eggs and young of other fishes. Thus, although it has been introduced in many areas to control mosquitoes, its introduction has serious side effects on local fish populations.

MOSSADEGH, Mohammed (c1880–1967), Iranian prime minister (1951–53) who nationalized Iran's British-controlled oil industry. A subsequent boycott by foreign consumers brought Iran near to economic disaster, and Mossadegh was forced out of office and imprisoned (1953–56).

MOSS ANIMALS. See BRYOZOA.

MÖSSBAUER EFFECT, the recoilless emission of GAMMA RAYS from certain CRYSTALS, discovered by Rudolf Ludwig Mössbauer (1929–) in 1957. When gamma rays are emitted from most nuclei, the latter recoil to a variable extent, giving the emitted PHOTONS a broad ENERGY spectrum. Mössbauer found that certain crystals, e.g. Fe^{57}, recoiled as a whole, i.e., their effective recoil was negligible. Gamma rays of closely specified frequency are thus produced and can be used for nuclear clocks and for testing RELATIVITY theory predictions.

MOSSES, large group of plants belonging to the class Musci, of the division BRYOPHYTA. Each moss plant consists of an erect "stem" to which primitive "leaves" are attached. The plants are anchored by root-like rhizoids. Mosses have worldwide distribution and are usually found in woods and other

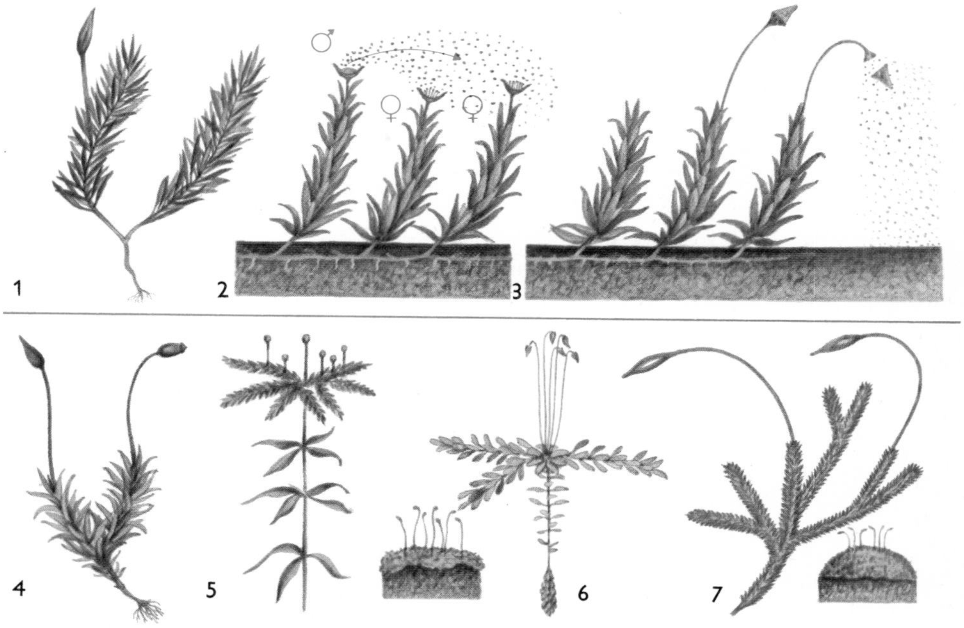

(1) Broom or cranesbill moss, *Dicranum scopanarium*, is much used in flower arrangement; (2) sexual stage of reproduction of broom moss, in which male and female cells combine to form a zygote; (3) the asexual stage begins with the formation of a spore-bearing capsule from the zygote. The spore germinates into a branching green thread, or *protonema*, from which buds develop that will eventually grow into new plants; (4) Haircap moss, *Polytrichum commine*, a tougher variety found in humid forests; (5) Peat moss, *Sphagnum cymbifolium*; (6) Star moss, *Mnium undulatum*; (7) Pillow moss, *Leucobryum glaucum*, is able to retain considerable amounts of moisture.

damp habitats. They are often early colonizers of bare soil and play an important role in preventing soil erosion. SPHAGNUM debris is an important constituent of PEAT. (See also ALTERNATION OF GENERATIONS; HORNWORTS; LIVERWORTS.)

MOSS PINK, *Phlox subulata*, or creeping phlox, a popular rock garden plant native to North America. It has a moss-like form and bears small pinkish flowers. Family: Polemoniaceae.

MOSS POINT, city in SE Miss., 20mi E of Biloxi. Its industries include lumber and shipbuilding. Pop 19321.

MOST, Johann Joseph (1846–1906), German-American anarchist, many times imprisoned (in Germany, England and the US) for publication of his views, such as his defense of the assassinations of Alexander II of Russia and America's William McKINLEY.

MOST-FAVORED-NATION, phrase referring to a trading agreement between international partners, by which benefits accorded to any one of the participating nations must be accorded to them all. This concept underlay, for example, the US Reciprocal Trade Agreements Act of 1934.

MOSUL, ancient city in N Iraq, the provincial capital, on the TIGRIS R, across from the ruins of NINEVEH, 220mi NNW of Baghdad. It is the center of an oil-producing region. Pop 243311.

MOTET, polyphonic vocal music, usually unaccompanied, which has occupied a place in sacred services, largely Roman Catholic, analogous to that of the Protestant ANTHEM. Like the MADRIGAL, its secular counterpart, the motet reached its zenith in the 16th and 17th centuries. Notable composers of motets include PALESTRINA and BACH.

MOTHER GOOSE, fictitious character to whose authorship many collections of fairy tales and nursery rhymes have been ascribed. The name seems to have been first associated with Charles PERRAULT's *Tales of Mother Goose* (1697).

MOTHER-OF-PEARL, or **nacre**, the iridescent substance of which PEARLS and the inner coating of bivalved mollusk shells are made. It consists of alternate thin layers of aragonite (CALCIUM carbonate) and conchiolin, a horny substance. Valued for its beauty, it is used in thin sheets for ornament, jewelry and for buttons.

MOTHER'S DAY, holiday observed in the US on the second Sunday in May to honor motherhood. It was officially recognized by Congress in 1914. Similar days of remembrance are observed in Canada, Australia and Britain.

MOTHERWELL, Robert (1915–   ), US painter and theoretician, a leading exponent of ABSTRACT EXPRESSIONISM. His work is characterized by restrained colors and large indefinite shapes.

MOTHS, insects which, together with the BUTTERFLIES, constitute the order LEPIDOPTERA. The differences between moths and butterflies are not clearly defined. Butterflies usually fly by day and rest with the wings raised over the back. Moths are mostly nocturnal and rest with the wings outspread. The antennae of butterflies are usually simple and end in a knob; this is rare in moths, where the antennae, at least in the males, are often feathery. This confers powerful long-range scent perception. In many species females produce "pheromones"—chemical sexual attractants. The males can detect even a single molecule of this, sensing females as far as 1.6km (1mi) away. In many species, melanistic forms (see MELANISM) have developed or increased in numbers in industrial areas. Darker coloration provides a better camouflage against birds on the blackened trees of these regions, an example of evolution in progress.

MOTION, change in the aspect of one body relative to another by translation, rotation or revolution, or by combinations of these. (See also MECHANICS; PERPETUAL MOTION; RELATIVITY; VELOCITY.)

MOTION PICTURES, a succession of photographs projected rapidly onto a screen to create the illusion of continuous movement. Modern "movies" project 24 frames per second. Film may be 8mm, 16mm, 35mm or 70mm wide and may have a sound track (see SOUND RECORDING).

Research into persistence of vision, using drawings, in the 19th century, and the development of photography, culminated in Thomas EDISON's Kinetoscope (1894), a peep-show version of the movies. Projection of motion pictures, using Edison's Vitascope (1896), was a success in vaudeville. Static camera work soon gave way to creative use of both camera and film-editing processes and in 1903 Edwin S. Porter exploited these in the one-reel narrative film, *The Great Train Robbery*. The success of this movie helped establish NICKELODEONS in the US, and this led in turn to the building of movie palaces. By 1913 the American film industry was established, aimed at satisfying a massive popular craving. Independent producers moved to Cal. to escape the power of distribution trusts. Cecil B. DE MILLE's *The Squaw Man* (1914) and Mack Sennett's comedies helped finance the establishment of the Hollywood studios. D. W. GRIFFITHS was the creative genius of the era. From 1908, he explored the possibilities of film and created "stars" to increase the appeal of his work. He made the first feature length films (1913), and his epics *The Birth of a Nation* (1915) and *Intolerance* (1917) are considered landmarks of cinema history. WWI had stopped film production in Europe, but afterwards German cinema attained influence with films such as *The Cabinet of Dr. Caligari* (1919), and the work of PABST and Fritz LANG. Russia's Sergei EISENSTEIN, the Scandinavians Carl Dreyer and Victor Sjöström were among those directors who achieved major reputations in a medium which, despite employment of many technicians, writers and actors, is ultimately controlled artistically by the director and film editor—except in the case of a few extraordinarily creative producers such as David O. SELZNICK and Irving Thalberg.

Elegy to the Spanish Republic XXXIV, painted in 1954 by the American abstract expressionist painter and theorist, Robert Motherwell.

Uses of motion pictures other than for narrative were established early. Newsreels were produced by Charles PATHÉ in Paris by 1909; Robert FLAHERTY's *Nanook of the North* (1922) consolidated the appeal of documentary films; cartoons became popular features of cinema programs, especially after Walt DISNEY created Mickey Mouse in the late 1920s.

The coming of sound in *The Jazz Singer*, 1927, briefly set film back as an art: the camera was immobilized, but regained its fluidity when sound techniques were improved and it was realized that sound was merely a useful adjunct. Color techniques were finally established with films such as *The Wizard of Oz* (1939) and the epic *Gone With the Wind* (1939), among the first in which color was an integral part of the effect and not a mere novelty. After WWII the industry experimented with Cinerama, Cinemascope, VistaVision and even 3-D, but the cinema still achieves the most powerful results with techniques of editing and photography based on the silent era.

The great age of Hollywood (1930–1950) occurred partly because of its ability to provide cheap entertainment during the Depression and because of the dominance of totalitarian censorship which crippled film making in much of Europe (Lang and von STERNBERG were among those who fled to America). The Western and the musical were recognized as uniquely successful North American film genres. The British film industry produced notable successes under Alexander Korda's production and Alfred HITCHCOCK's direction, while French directors René CLAIR and Jean RENOIR were among the most acclaimed of the era.

Since WWII the split has grown between "art" and popular cinema and the movies no longer hold their supremacy in mass entertainment. Television has drastically reduced audiences, and producers try to win them back by producing wide-screen spectaculars or specific-appeal films, whether the appeal is violence, sex or intellectual content. Yet film distribution has become more truly international. Directors such as FELLINI, DE SICA, Satyajit RAY, KUROSAWA, ROSSELLINI, BUÑUEL, Truffaut and Ingmar BERGMAN have made exciting contributions to cinematic art. Hollywood's dominance has been superseded by many independent productions worldwide, and the vigor and popularity of film, both as art and as entertainment, continues unabated.

MOTION SICKNESS, nausea and VOMITING caused by rhythmic movements of the body, particularly the head, set up in automobile, train, ship or airplane travel. In susceptible people, neither stimulation of the EAR labyrinths nor their action on the vomiting centers in the BRAIN stem are adequately suppressed. Hyoscine and phenothiazines can prevent it if taken before travel.

MOTLEY, John Lothrop (1814–1877), US historian known for his books on Dutch history, *The Rise of the Dutch Republic* (1856) and *History of the United Netherlands* (1860–67). He was also sent as a diplomat to Russia, Austria and England.

MOTMOTS, eight forest-dwelling species of birds, family Momotidae, of tropical regions of the New World. Greenish, olive or red-brown birds, they live in the depths of forests, feeding on insects and berries. The two central tail feathers are elongated and naked, except for a racquet-like tip.

MOTON, Robert Russa (1867–1940), US Negro educator, noted for his efforts to establish racial good will. In 1915 Moton conducted a survey of the conditions of Negro soldiers in the US army. He wrote *Racial Good Will* (1916) and *What the Negro Thinks* (1929).

MOTOR, Electric, a device converting electrical into mechanical energy. Traditional forms are based on the FORCE experienced by a current-carrying wire in a magnetic field (see ELECTROMAGNETISM). Motors can be, and sometimes are, run in reverse as GENERATORS.

Simple direct-current (see ELECTRICITY) motors consist of a magnet or ELECTROMAGNET (the *stator*) and a coil (the *rotor*) which turns when a current is passed through it because of the force between the current and the stator field. So that the force keeps the same sense as the rotor turns, the current to the rotor is supplied via a *commutator*—a slip ring broken into two semicircular parts, to each of which one end of the coil is connected, so that the current direction is reversed twice each revolution.

For use with alternating-current supplies, small DC motors are often still suitable, but **induction motors** are preferred for heavier duty. In the simplest of these, there is no electrical contact with the rotor, which consists of a cylindrical array of copper bars welded to end rings. The stator field, generated by more than one set of coils, is made to rotate at the supply frequency, inducing (see INDUCTION, ELECTROMAGNETIC) currents in the rotor when (under load) it rotates more slowly, these in turn producing a force accelerating the rotor. Greater control of the motor speed and torque can be obtained in "wound rotor" types in which the currents induced in coils wound on the rotor are controlled by external resistances connected via slip-ring contacts.

In applications such as electric clocks, **synchronous motors**, which rotate exactly in step with the supply frequency, are used. In these the rotor is usually a permanent magnet dragged round by the rotating stator field, the induction-motor principle being used to start the motor.

The above designs can all be opened out to form **linear motors** producing a lateral rather than rotational drive. The induction type is the most suitable, a plate analogous to the rotor being driven with respect to a stator generating a laterally moving field. Such motors have a wide range of possible applications, from operating sliding doors to driving trains, being much more robust than rotational drive systems, and offering no resistance to manual operation in the event of power cuts. A form of DC linear motor can be used to pump conducting liquids such as molten metals, the force being generated between a current passed through the liquid and a static magnetic field around it.

MOTORBOATING, the recreational or competitive sport of driving a motorboat. Motorboats are usually powered by one or more internal combustion engines, driving submerged propellers, and can travel up to 175mph. Smaller motorboats, between 10ft and 20ft long, are usually powered by outboard motors and are known as runabouts. They usually have "planing" or "gliding" hulls which enable the boat to skim across the water with its bow in the air, thus reducing water resistance and allowing high speeds to be achieved. Whereas runabouts only have seating facilities, the larger inboard cruisers, 20ft to 60ft long, are often fitted with luxurious cabins. Motorboat design first evolved in 1885 and in 1887 Gottlieb DAIMLER built a gasoline-powered motorboat. The highest speed ever attained by a jet-propelled motorboat was 328mph, by Donald CAMPBELL in 1967.

MOTORCYCLE, a motorized bicycle, first developed in 1885 by Gottlieb DAIMLER. The engine of a motorcycle may be either two-stroke or four-stroke and is usually air cooled. Chain drive is almost universal. In lightweight machines, ignition is often achieved by means of a MAGNETO inside the flywheel. Motorcycles were first widely used by despatch riders in WWI. Between the wars, the motorcycle industry was dominated by simple, heavy British designs. After WWII, Italy developed also the motor scooter, designed for convenience and economy, with 150cc two-stroke engines. In the 1960s the Japanese introduced a series of highly sophisticated, lightweight machines, which are now seen all over the world. (See IGNITION SYSTEM; INTERNAL COMBUSTION ENGINE.)

Motorcross, a popular form of motorcycle racing in the United States and elsewhere, severely tests the driver's skill in maneuvering over rough, often wet, terrain at high speeds. It requires a machine with a reinforced frame and special deep-tread tires.

MOTT, Lucretia Coffin (1793–1880), US reformer who was one of the first pioneers of women's rights. A Quaker by religion, she founded the Philadelphia Female Anti-Slavery Society (1833), and with Elizabeth STANTON organized the first women's rights convention at Seneca Falls, N.Y., in 1848.

MOTT, John Raleigh (1865–1955), US Christian social worker who shared the 1946 Nobel Peace Prize. He was a leader of the Young Men's Christian Association (YMCA), and for 1926–37 he was chairman of the World's Alliance of YMCAs.

MOTTELSON, Ben (1926–), US-born Danish physicist who shared the 1975 Nobel Prize for Physics with A. BOHR and L. J. RAINWATER for their work on the physics and structure of the atomic nucleus.

MO-TZU (c470–391 BC), Chinese philosopher who preached universal love, in opposition to CONFUCIANISM, and moderate social behavior. However, his movement, Mo-ism, died out shortly after his death.

MOUFLON, *Ovis musimon*, the smallest of the SHEEP family, a native of Corsica and Sardinia, distinguished from other species in having a distinct rump patch, out-curling horns and a white saddle on the back.

MOULTING. See MOLTING.

MOULTRIE, city in S Ga., seat of Colquitt Co. The city is primarily a center for livestock farming and textile industries. Pop 14400.

MOULTRIE, Fort, fort on Sullivan's Island 6mi from Charleston, S.C., named for William MOULTRIE. In the Civil War it was one of the strongest defenses of Charleston Harbor, held by the Confederates until Charleston was evacuated in Feb. 1865.

MOULTRIE, William (1730–1805), American Revolutionary general who repulsed a British fleet at Sullivan's Island, preventing the British from capturing Charleston (1776). He was twice governor of South Carolina (1785–87 and 1792–94).

MOUNDBIRDS, or **Incubator birds**, the family Megapodidae, 11 species of turkey-like ground birds of Malaysia and Australasia. In all species the eggs are incubated not by the bird itself, but by some form of natural heat: solar or volcanic heat or heat from composted vegetation. Some species build mounds in which the eggs are incubated. Their temperature is adjusted by the male, using the tongue as a thermometer.

MOUND CITY GROUP NATIONAL MONUMENT, monument in S Ohio, at the center of 24 mounds, burial shrines of Indians of the HOPEWELL CULTURE (500 BC–500 AD).

MOUNDS, artificial constructions of earth or, on occasion, piled stones built according to a predetermined plan, found in many areas of the eastern US. The largest known mound is one of the CAHOKIA MOUNDS and the oldest dates from c500 AD. Some mounds have been built in historic times. Dome-shaped burial mounds served the same purpose as BARROWS, while mounds in the form of truncated pyramids were used as bases for temples and other buildings. KITCHEN MIDDENS are sometimes erroneously termed mounds. Less common types of mounds are hill-top forts and mounds in effigy form.

MOUNDS VIEW, village in Minn., a suburb of Minneapolis. Pop 10641.

MOUNDSVILLE, city in W Va., seat of Marshall Co. Named for the prehistoric Indian Grave Creek Burial Mound. It has mining and lumber industries. Pop 13560.

MOUNTAIN, a landmass elevated substantially above its surroundings. The difference between a mountain and a hill is essentially one of size: the exact borderline is not clearly defined. Plateaus, or table-mountains, unlike most other mountains, have a large summit area as compared with that of their base. Most mountains occur in groups, ranges or chains (see also MASSIF). The processes involved in mountain building are termed orogenesis. OROGENIES can largely be explained in terms of the theory of PLATE TECTONICS. Thus the Andes have formed where the Nazca oceanic plate is being subducted beneath (forced under) the South American continental plate, and the Himalayas have arisen at the meeting of two continental plates.

Mountains are traditionally classified as Volcanic, Block or Folded. **Volcanic mountains** occur where LAVA and other debris (e.g., PYROCLASTIC ROCKS) build up a dome around the vent of a VOLCANO. They are found in certain well-defined belts around the world, marking plate margins. **Block mountains** occur where land has been uplifted between FAULTS in a way akin to that leading to the formation of RIFT VALLEYS (see also HORST). **Folded mountains** occur through deformations of the EARTH's crust (see FOLD), especially in geosynclinal areas (see GEOSYNCLINE), where vast quantities of sediments whose weight causes deformation, accumulate (see also SEDIMENTATION). EROSION eventually reduces all mountains to plains. But it may also play a part in the creation of mountains, as where most of an elevated stretch of land has been eroded away, leaving a few resistant outcrops of rock (see MONADNOCK).

Scene in the Rocky Mountains. Running the length of the western United States, the Rockies are part of the world's longest mountain chain, which includes the Sierra Madre Oriental of Mexico and the Andes of South America.

MOUNTAIN ASH, popular name for trees and shrubs of the genus *Sorbus*. The main North American species (*Sorbus americana*) grows to a height of 10m (33ft) and bears small yellowish flowers and reddish fruits. The main European species (*S. aucuparia*) is also known as the rowan. Family: Rosaceae.

MOUNTAIN BEAVER. See SEWELLEL.

MOUNTAIN BROOK, city in N central Ala., an E residential suburb of Birmingham. Pop 19509.

MOUNTAINEERING, the climbing of hills, cliffs and mountains for sport or exploration. Mountaineers almost always climb in a team, roped together for safety. The leader will hammer steel pegs called pitons into rock crevices, to act as anchor points for the climbing rope. In snow or ice climbing dark glasses are needed to avoid snow blindness, and steel-spiked crampons are fastened to the boots to ensure a good grip. On all but the shortest climbs, food, signaling devices, medical supplies and camping equipment are needed. At very high altitudes oxygen masks are used. The principal mountaineering club in the US is the American Alpine Club.

MOUNTAIN GOAT. See ROCKY MOUNTAIN GOAT.

MOUNTAIN LAUREL, *Kalmia latifolia*, an evergreen ornamental shrub with small pink flowers and leaves like those of the LAUREL. The mountain laurel is found over much of eastern North America and is the state flower of Pa. Family: Ericaceae.

MOUNTAIN LION. See PUMA.

MOUNTAIN MEN, pioneer fur trappers and traders in the Rockies in the 1820s and 1830s. Early mountain men included John COLTER, who stayed in the area after the LEWIS AND CLARK EXPEDITION of 1804–06, Thomas Fitzpatrick, Jedediah SMITH and W. S. WILLIAMS. Many mountain men, including James BRIDGER took part in William ASHLEY's expedition up the Missouri R in 1822. The mountain men were the first to begin opening up the Rockies and make the area's potential known. They were quickly followed by the big fur companies such as the Rocky Mountain Fur Company and the American Fur Company.

MOUNTAIN SHEEP. See BIGHORN.

MOUNTAIN SICKNESS. See ALTITUDE SICKNESS.

MOUNTAIN VIEW, city W Cal., on San Francisco Bay. It is an agricultural trading center and also has NASA laboratories. Pop 54206.

MOUNTBATTEN, Louis Francis Albert Victor Nicholas, 1st Earl Mountbatten of Burma (1901–), British admiral and administrator. In WWII he was supreme allied commander in SE Asia and liberated Burma from the Japanese. After WWII he was the last British viceroy of India, and led the negotiations for India's and Pakistan's independence.

MOUNT CLEMENS, city in SE Mich., seat of Macomb Co., on the Clinton R. It is a well known health resort, and has light industries. Pop 20 476.

MOUNT DESERT, resort island off SE Me. It was the site of a French Jesuit Mission (1613–1713), the first in America. It was badly damaged by forest fire in 1947.

MOUNT HOLLY, town in N.J., seat of Burlington Co., settled by the Quakers in 1676. It manufactures shoes, leather goods, textiles and clothing. Pop 12 713.

MOUNTIES. See ROYAL CANADIAN MOUNTED POLICE.

MOUNTLAKE TERRACE, city in NW Wash, a suburb of Seattle. Pop 16 600.

MOUNT PLEASANT, city in central Mich., seat of Isabella Co. Its economy rests on oil wells and refineries. Pop 20 504.

MOUNT PROSPECT, village in NE Ill., residential suburb 21mi NW of Chicago. Pop 34 995.

MOUNT VERNON, city in SE Ill., seat of Jefferson Co. It is an agricultural, industrial and mining center. Pop 16 382.

MOUNT VERNON, city in N.Y., residential suburb of New York City on the Bronx R. It has light industries, including automobile manufacturing. Pop 72 778.

MOUNT VERNON, city in central Ohio, seat of Knox Co. It has steel and heavy engineering industries and livestock farming. Pop 13 373.

MOUNT VERNON, the restored Georgian home (1747–99) of George WASHINGTON on the Potomac R in Va., S of Washington. The tomb of Washington and his wife Martha is nearby.

Mount Vernon, Washington's Virginia home, overlooking the Potomac River, was restored and is maintained as a national shrine by the Mount Vernon Ladies' Association of the Union. More than a million people visit it each year.

MOUNT WILSON OBSERVATORY. See HALE OBSERVATORIES.

MOURNING DOVE, a turtle-dove, *Zenaidura macroura*, of North America. Named for its mournful and repetitive call, it is a brown dove of woods and open country, distinguished by a pointed tail with a white border.

MOUSE, a term applied loosely to almost any small RODENT. The majority however fall into two groups: Old World mice, family Muridae, and New World mice of the family Cricetidae. Very active animals, often nocturnal, they are characteristically short-lived. Feeding on berries and grain, they are, in terms of biomass, extremely important herbivores, and in turn important as prey for many birds and mammals.

The Common house mouse, pictured here, originates from Asia and has spread all over the world, usually living in the nooks and crannies of buildings, and feeding on waste, scraps or any sort of food it can steal.

MOUSEBIRDS, a family, Coliidae, of long-tailed and crested arboreal birds found in open areas and the forest edge in Africa. They are extremely sociable birds usually living in small parties, huddling close together when resting or roosting. They feed on fruit, flowers and leaves.

MOZAMBIQUE, republic in SE Africa on the Indian Ocean between Tanzania and South Africa. A hot, humid coastal plain and low plateaux cover about two-thirds of the country, rising to mountainous regions in the N and W. Most of the coastal plain is infertile except in the Zambezi, Save, Limpopo and small river areas. The population is 95% African and comprises over 60 tribes; the rest are Europeans and Asians. The economy rests on subsistence agriculture, such as yams, cassava and corn. Cattle are reared in the S. Mozambique's exports include cashew nuts and cotton, but most of its revenue has come from providing Rhodesia and South Africa with outlets to the sea. The hydroelectric power from the Cabora-Bassa dam may expand industrialization. The first European to reach Mozambique was VASCO DA GAMA (1498). During the 1500s and 1600s the Portuguese set up small trading settlements. From the mid-18th until the early-19th century their great source of wealth was the black slave trade. Mozambique became a Portuguese colony in 1910 and Portugal placed controls on its economic growth and the Africans' social advancement. In 1962 the Mozambique nationalists formed the Mozambique Liberation Front (Frelimo) which engaged in fierce guerilla warfare with Portuguese troops for 1964–74. After the 1974 coup in Portugal negotiations led to the formation in June 1975 of an independent socialist republic in Mozambique. In 1976 after Rhodesian troops had attacked border villages in search of guerrillas, President Machel closed Mozambique's borders with Rhodesia and announced full economic sanctions, cutting off major railroad access to the sea.

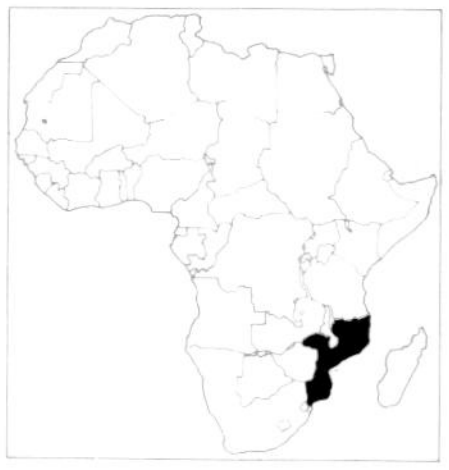

Official name: Mozambique
Capital: Maputo
Area: 303 070sq mi
Population: 8 100 000
Languages: Portuguese, Bantu languages
Religions: Muslim, Christian
Monetary unit(s): 1 Mozambique escudo = 100 centavos

MOZAMBIQUE CURRENT, warm ocean current of the Indian Ocean, moving W to the African coast, then S to feed the AGULHAS CURRENT.

MOZART, Wolfgang Amadeus (1756–1791), Austrian composer whose brief career produced some of the world's greatest music. He was a child prodigy of the harpsichord, violin and organ at the age of four and toured the European courts. He soon became a prodigious composer. Between 1771–81 he was concertmaster to the archbishop of Salzburg. Much of Mozart's early music is in a pure and elegant classical style, which is also extremely lively and spontaneous. In 1781 he moved to Vienna and became Court Composer to Joseph II, in 1787. He became a close friend of HAYDN and set DA PONTE's opera librettos *The Marriage of Figaro* (1786) and *Don Giovanni* (1787) to music. In a three-month period during 1788 he wrote three of his greatest symphonies, numbers 39–41. Mozart wrote over 600 works, including 50 symphonies, over 20 operas, nearly 30 piano concertos, 27 string quartets, about 40 violin sonatas and many other instrumental pieces. In all these genres his works have great expressive beauty and technical mastery, and he advanced the styles and musical forms of each.

MUCKRAKERS, term coined in 1906 by President Theodore Roosevelt to condemn journalists specializing in sensational exposés of corrupt businesses and political procedures. The name was adopted by a group of contemporary reformist writers and journalists. The "Muckrakers" included Lincoln STEFFENS who wrote about political corruption, Ida TARBELL who exposed the exploitative practices of an enormous oil company, and Upton SINCLAIR who uncovered deplorable conditions in the Chicago meat-packing industry.

MUCUS, viscid, aqueous solution of glycoproteins secreted by cells of the mucous membranes of the respiratory and gastrointestinal tracts, the salivary and other digestive system glands. It provides a nonliving protective layer which is constantly being renewed, allowing removal of any particulate matter absorbed onto it (in the BRONCHI) and lubrication of food and feces. It contains some GAMMA GLOBULIN, which may have a role in local IMMUNITY.

MUDD, Samuel Alexander (1833–1883), the doctor who set the leg of John Wilkes BOOTH after the assassination of President Lincoln in 1865. Mudd was unfairly sentenced to life imprisonment, but pardoned in 1869.

MUD DAUBERS, solitary tropical WASPS notable for the construction of nests made of clay or mud, attached to vegetation or plastered on the walls of buildings. The nests are provisioned with paralyzed insects and a single egg is deposited in each sealed cell.

MUDMINNOWS, several species of fish of the family Umbridae. Freshwater fishes of Europe and North America, they are related to the pike. The Alaska blackfish is the best-known member of the group.

MUDPUPPY, a name properly applied to *Necturus maculosus*, and by extension to other SALAMANDERS of that genus. Long-bodied animals, their most prominent feature is the retention of external gills into adult life. Technically, they never metamorphose to adults, but reproduce in larval form, a condition known as NEOTENY.

MUDSKIPPERS, a family, Gobiidae, of small goby-like fishes remarkable for their habit of leaving the water and skipping across exposed sand or mudflats. The pectoral fins are used for "walking" and leaps of 600mm (23.6in) are made by curling, then suddenly straightening the whole body. Mudskippers are found in brackish water in the Indo-Pacific region.

MUDSNAKE, a colubrid snake, *Farancia abacura*, of the US, often called Hoop snake because of the belief that they could hold the tail in the mouth and bowl along at great speed. A blue-black snake, it is marked with red spots on the flanks.

MUEZZIN, Muslim official who calls the faithful to prayer. He is the servant of a mosque, and at set times calls out the ritual formula from the door or minaret of his mosque.

MUFFLER, or **silencer**, device to reduce the exhaust noise of an INTERNAL COMBUSTION ENGINE. One effect is to cut down the velocity of the exhaust gases and so reduce the pressure waves they create (see SOUND). Some types have a central tube of perforated steel packed around with sound-absorbent fibrous material; in another, passage of the exhaust through different chambers reduces the noise by INTERFERENCE.

MUGGER, or **Marsh Crocodile**, a broad-nosed CROCODILE, *Crocodylus palustris*, of S Asia, similar to the Nile crocodile but considerably smaller.

MUGWUMPS, term for independent voters, or sometimes political fence straddlers. Particularly used for Republicans who voted for Democrat Grover CLEVELAND in 1884.

MUHAMMAD ALI. See ALI, MUHAMMAD.

MUHAMMED, Elija (1897–1975), US Black Muslim leader. In 1931 He met Wali "Prophet" Farad, founder of the first Temple of Islam in Detroit, Mich. Elijah became a prominent disciple and on Farad's disappearance (1934) became leader of the movement.

MUHLENBERG, US family of Lutheran leaders. **Henry Melchior Muhlenberg** (1711–1787), the German-born patriarch of Lutheranism in America. He organized the first American Lutheran synod (1748). **John Peter Gabriel Muhlenberg** (1746–1807), eldest son of the above, was a Lutheran minister, a major general in the Revolution and a US congressman. **Frederick August Conrad Muhlenberg** (1750–1801), another son, was a minister, member of the Continental Congress and first speaker of the US House of Representatives. His great nephew, **Frederick August Muhlenberg** (1818–1901), was a minister who established several colleges in Pa. and was the first president of Muhlenberg College at Allentown (1867).

MUIR, John (1838–1914), Scottish-American naturalist and writer, an advocate of US forest conservation. He described his walking journeys in the NW US and Alaska in many influential articles and books. Yosemite and Sequoia national parks and MUIR WOODS NATIONAL MONUMENT were established as a result of his efforts.

MUIR WOODS NATIONAL MONUMENT, a park of 503 acres 15mi NW of San Francisco, Cal., established in 1908 to preserve a large stand of virgin coastal redwoods (*Sequoia sempervirens*).

MUKDEN, now Shenyang, capital of Liaoning province, NE China, on the Hun R. An early capital of the MANCHUS, it was developed by the Russians and Japanese and is now an industrial, agricultural and shipping center for the NE (formerly Manchuria). Pop 3 000 000.

MULATTO, person with one Negro and one white parent; often used to describe a person of mixed Negro and Caucasian ancestry. A child of a true mulatto and a white was traditionally called a quadroon (one-quarter Negro ancestry).

MULBERRY, trees and shrubs of the genus *Morus* found growing in temperate regions of the N Hemisphere. They produce edible raspberry-like fruits and some are grown as ornamentals. The North American red mulberry (*Morus rubra*) produces dark red berries. The white mulberry (*M. alba*) produces white berries and in the Far East its leaves are used to feed SILKWORMS. Family: Moraceae.

MULCH, layer of usually organic material kept on the surface of SOIL in order to reduce surface EVAPORATION of moisture, to protect the soil from wind EROSION, or as a MANURE. Mulches may contain straw, PEAT or scattered topsoil.

MULE, a term now commonly used to describe infertile hybrids between various species. The name is properly restricted to the offspring of a male DONKEY and a mare. Mules have the shape and size of a HORSE, and the long ears and small hooves of a donkey. They are favored for their endurance and surefootedness as draft or pack animals. (See also HINNY.)

MULE DEER, *Odocoileus hemionus*, a long-eared DEER of western North America. Several subspecies are found in a variety of habitats. Mule deer are world-renowned to students of the factors controlling animal numbers, on account of their dramatic increase in numbers in ranges where wolves—their major predators—have been exterminated.

MÜLHEIM AN DER RUHR, city in North Rhine-Westphalia, West Germany, 7mi WSW of Essen. It is a leading commercial and industrial city in the Ruhr R valley. Pop 191 100.

MULLEIN, common name for biennial and perennial herbs of the genus *Verbascum* which are native to Europe, North America and Asia. The several hundred species vary enormously and include the long-stemmed and woolly *Verbascum thapsus*, a common yellow-flowered weed. Family: Scrophulariaceae.

MULLER, Hermann Joseph (1890–1967), US geneticist awarded the 1946 Nobel Prize for Physiology or Medicine for his work showing that X-RAYS greatly accelerate MUTATION processes.

MÜLLER, Paul Hermann (1899–1965), Swiss chemist awarded the 1948 Nobel Prize for Physiology or Medicine for his discovery of the effective insecticidal properties of DDT (1939), a major contribution to world health and food production.

MULLETS, a common name applied to two quite separate families of bony fishes, Red mullets, Mullidae, and Gray mullets, Mugilidae. Gray mullets are shoaling fishes of coastal waters with downward-oriented mouths, and which feed on algae on sand or rocks. Red mullets are also coastal fishes and have two barbels under the chin, used for "fingering" the sea bed in search of shrimps, worms and mollusks.

MULLIGAN, Gerry (Gerald Joseph Mulligan; 1927–), US jazz musician. Technically accomplished rather than just intuitive, he played baritone saxophone and piano for many leading JAZZ bands after WWII, formed a pianoless quartet in 1952 and arranged and composed pieces with a new tone color.

MULLIKEN, Robert Sanderson (1896–), US chemist and physicist awarded the 1966 Nobel Prize for chemistry for his work on the nature of chemical bonding and hence on the electronic structure of molecules (see BOND, CHEMICAL).

MULTAN, regional capital in the Punjab province, Pakistan, c200mi WSW of Lahore. An ancient settlement near HARAPPA, it is now an industrial center. Pop 544 000.

MULTIPLE BIRTH, the delivery of more than one child at the end of PREGNANCY. Twins, the commonest type of multiple BIRTH, are of two distinct varieties. Monozygotic or identical twins originate in a single fertilized egg (zygote) which divides, each half (containing identical genetic material) developing independently into EMBRYO and FETUS, although they may share a common PLACENTA. *Dizygotic* or non-identical twins originate in the release of two eggs at ovulation (see MENSTRUATION), each being fertilized, implanting (see implantation) and developing separately. There is no more relation between their GENES than between those of other siblings. Higher orders of multiple births (triplets, quadruplets, quintuplets, etc.) usually arise from multiple ovulation and are rare unless ovarian follicle stimulants (e.g., GONADOTROPHINS) have been used in the treatment of infertility; here the dosage is critical. Multiple pregnancy may run in families. Prematurity, toxemia, ANEMIA and other complications are more common in multiple pregnancy.

MULTIPLE SCLEROSIS, or **disseminated sclerosis**, a relatively common disease of the BRAIN and SPINAL CORD in which MYELIN is destroyed in plaques of INFLAMMATION. Its cause is unknown although slow VIRUSES, abnormal ALLERGY to viruses and abnormalities of FATS are suspected. It may affect any age group, but particularly young adults. Symptoms and signs indicating disease in widely separate parts of the NERVOUS SYSTEM are typical. They occur episodically, often with intervening recovery or improvement. Blurring of VISION, sometimes with EYE pain; double vision; VERTIGO; abnormal sensations in the limbs; PARALYSIS; ATAXIA, and BLADDER disturbance are often seen, although individually these can occur in other brain diseases. STEROIDS, certain DIETARY FOODS, and DRUGS acting on spasticity in muscles and the bladder are valuable in some cases. The course of the disease is extremely variable, some subjects having but a few mild attacks, while others progress rapidly to permanent disability and dependency.

MULTIPLICATION, a way of combining two numbers to obtain a third; symbolized by $\times$, ., or merely the juxtaposition of the numbers (where suitable). Where x and y are NATURAL NUMBERS, $x.y$ is commutative and defined by $x+x+\ ...\ +x$, the number x appearing y times (see ADDITION; SUM).

For multiplication of negative INTEGERS, such as $(-x)$ and $(-y)$, $(-x).y = x.(-y) = -(x.y)$; and $(-x).(-y) = x.y$. Multiplication of any number by 0 (see ZERO) is defined to give the PRODUCT 0. FRACTIONS may be multiplied by simple extension of the system. The INVERSE operation of multiplication is DIVISION, since $\frac{x}{y} = x.\frac{1}{y}$. In cases other than with REAL NUMBERS, multiplication must be independently defined (see IMAGINARY NUMBERS; VECTOR ANALYSIS).

MULTIPLIER, a factor in MACROECONOMICS which measures the extent to which, with a given level of SAVINGS and INVESTMENT in an economy, an increase in net investment can generate a larger increase in National INCOME. This happens because the extra money available is in part respent, generating more income. In turn, part of this is respent, and so on in an infinite series whose sum is the total increase in income. This may be expressed as a multiple of the increase in investment: the value of the multiple is called the multiplier.

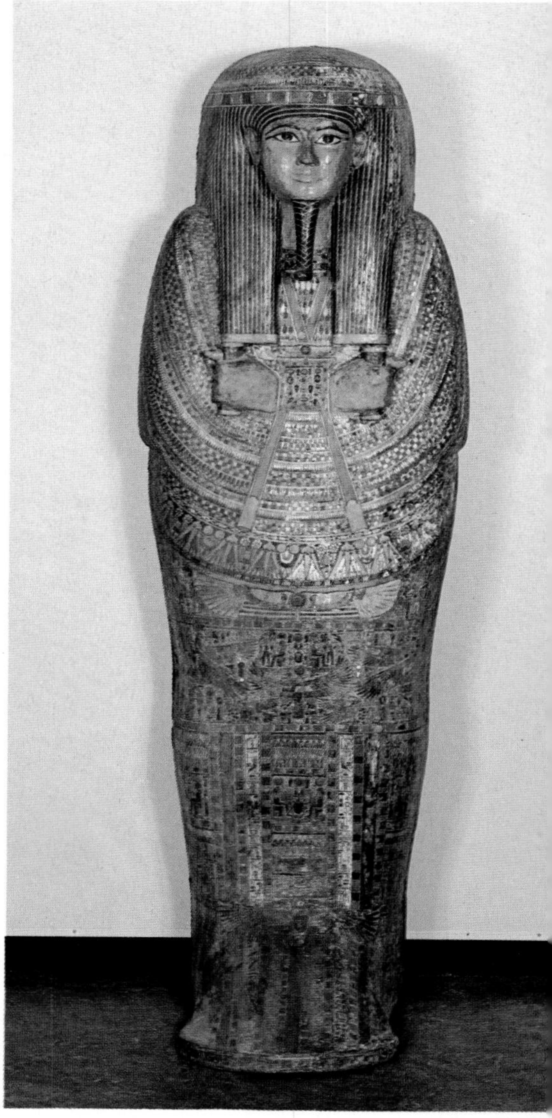

Late-period mummy case, richly decorated with spells and incantations designed to safeguard the occupant and assure his well-being in the afterlife. Often mummy cases were enormous, containing two or more inner coffins.

MULTNOMAH FALLS, waterfall on the Columbia R, NW Ore., 25mi E of Portland. The falls plunge 680ft in a series of cascades.

MUMFORD, Lewis (1895–), US social critic and historian, concerned with the relationship between man and his environment, especially in urban planning. His books include *The Brown Decades* (1931), *The Culture of Cities* (1934), *The City in History* (1961) and *The Pentagon of Power* (1971).

MUMMY, a corpse embalmed, particularly in ancient Egypt, in order to ensure its preservation for a protracted period after death. The earliest known attempts artificially to preserve bodies were about 2600 BC, though many bodies from earlier times were naturally preserved through the desiccating effect of the sand in which they were buried. (See EMBALMING.)

MUMPS, common VIRUS infection causing swelling of

the parotid salivary GLAND, and occasionally INFLAMMATION of the PANCREAS, an OVARY or a TESTIS. Mild FEVER, HEADACHE and malaise may precede the gland swelling. Rarely a viral MENINGITIS and less often ENCEPHALITIS complicates mumps. Very rarely a bilateral and severe testicular inflammation can cause STERILITY.

MÜNCH, Charles (1891–1968), French orchestra conductor. He conducted the Paris Conservatory orchestra 1936–46, the Boston (Mass.) Symphony Orchestra 1949–62, and was director of its Berkshire Music Center 1951–62.

MUNCH, Edvard (1863–1944), Norwegian painter and printmaker. His work foreshadowed EXPRESSIONISM and was influential in the development of modern art. His powerful, often neurotic pictures show his obsession with the themes of love and death.

MUNCHHAUSEN, Karl Friedeich Hieronymus, Freiherr von (1720–1797), German soldier and country gentleman. His exaggerated adventure tales were the basis of fantastic "tall tales" compiled by R. E. Raspe, published in London (1785). These stories became widely popular. The English *Adventures of Baron Munchhausen* (1793) is the standard edition.

MUNCIE, city in E central Ind., seat of Delaware Co., 50mi ENE of Indianapolis; an industrial center and the "typical American town" in the classic sociological study, *Middletown* (1929). Pop 69 082.

MUNDELEIN, village in NE Ill., 35mi NW of Chicago, a dairy center with light industry. Pop 16 128.

MUNHALL, borough in SW Pa., an industrial suburb 7mi SE of Pittsburgh, with steel works. Pop 16 574.

MUNICH, capital of Bavaria, West Germany, on the Isar R about 30mi N of the Alps. A cultural center with a cathedral and palace, it is also heavily industrialized (beer, textiles, publishing), and is Germany's third largest city. Founded in 1158 by Duke Henry the Lion, it was ruled 1255–1918 by the Wittelsbach family (dukes and kings). Munich was the birthplace and headquarters of NATIONAL SOCIALISM and the scene of Hitler's attempted "beer hall putsch" of 1923. Munich hosted the 1972 OLYMPIC GAMES. Pop 1 293 590.

MUNICH AGREEMENT, a pact, signed Sept. 30, 1938, prior to WWII, which forced Czechoslovakia to surrender its SUDETENLAND to Nazi Germany. The Sudetenland in W Czechoslovakia contained much of the nation's industry, about 700 000 Czechs as well as 3 million German-speaking citizens, the pretext for Hitler's demands for occupation. The agreement, which allowed an immediate German takeover, was signed by Adolph HITLER, Neville CHAMBERLAIN (Britain), Edouard DALADIER (France) and Benito MUSSOLINI (Italy). Neither the Czechs nor their Russian allies were consulted. The Allies hoped this would be Hitler's "last territorial claim," and that the pact would avert war, but in March 1939 he occupied the rest of Czechoslovakia.

MUNN v. ILLINOIS. See GRANGER CASES.

MUÑOZ MARÍN, Luis (1898–), Puerto Rican political leader, the first elected governor of the island (1948–64), founder of the Popular Democratic Party (1938). Elected to the legislature in 1932, he favored social reforms and ties with the US. He led the campaign for Puerto Rican self-government status, achieved in 1952.

MUNRO, Hector Hugh (pseudonym, Saki;

Mural painting flourished in the Renaissance, and among its highest achievements at this time were Michelangelo's frescoes in the Sistine Chapel. Shown here is the gigantic *Last Judgement* from the altar wall of the chapel, painted between 1536 and 1541. The vigor and intensity of the picture, emanating from the figure of Christ with his arm raised in wrath, remain enormously impressive even in reproduction.

1870–1916), British writer, known for his inventive, satirical and often fantastic short stories. Among his published works are stories collected in *Reginald* (1904) and *Beasts and Super-Beasts* (1914) and a novel, *The Unbearable Bassington* (1912).

MUNSEY, Frank Andrew (1854–1925), US newspaper publisher. *Munsey's Magazine* (founded 1889) pioneered cheap, illustrated mass circulation periodicals. He also built a profitable empire based on prominent New York City daily papers.

MÜNSTER, historic city in North Rhine-Westphalia, West Germany, 78mi NNE of Cologne. An industrial and commercial center, Münster was a prominent city of the HANSEATIC LEAGUE. The Peace of WESTPHALIA, which ended the THIRTY YEARS' WAR, was signed here (1648). Pop 204 600.

MUNSTER, residential town in NW Ind., 10mi S of Hammond and Lake Michigan. Pop 16 514.

MUNTJAC, *Muntiacus*, a small DEER widely distributed in Asia. The antlers are supported on skin-covered pedicles which continue on down the forehead in ridges. Well-developed canine teeth in the upper jaw are used for fighting. This deer is also called the Barking deer.

MUON. See SUBATOMIC PARTICLES.

MURAL PAINTING, any kind of painting executed on a wall. The earliest are the cave paintings of reindeer and bison at ALTAMIRA, Spain, and LASCAUX, France, which were probably a form of magic to Paleolithic man. Early Roman FRESCO murals were found in POMPEII. Wall paintings of sacred subjects were the chief form of religious instruction in the Byzantine Empire, medieval Europe and in Islamic and Indian civilizations. The fresco technique was adopted by Italian artists like GIOTTO at Padua and Assisi, MICHELANGELO for the ceiling of the SISTINE CHAPEL and TIEPOLO in N Italian palaces, and also by the 20th-century Mexican artist OROZCO.

MURANO, suburb of Venice, Italy, on five islets in the Venice Lagoon, 1mi N of the city. It is famous for Venetian glass. Pop 7 844.

MURASAKI, Shikibu (c978–1026?), Japanese court lady and author of *Genji Monogatari*, or the *Tale of Genji*, the greatest Japanese classic and probably the world's first novel.

MURAT, Joachim (1767–1815), French marshal under Napoleon Bonaparte and king of Naples 1808–15. Murat gained his reputation as a brilliant cavalry leader in the Italian and Egyptian campaigns, and contributed to French successes in the NAPOLEONIC WARS. He married Napoleon's sister Caroline. As king of Naples he fostered the beginnings of Italian nationalism. Although he joined the Allies in 1814, he supported Napoleon during the HUNDRED DAYS, but was executed after an attempt to recapture Naples.

MURCHISON FALLS, famous waterfall in the Victoria Nile R, 20mi E of Lake Albert, NW Uganda. It is 130ft high and is the central attraction of Kabarega National Park.

MURCIA, capital of Murcia province, SE Spain, on the Rio Segura, 47mi SW of Alicante. Settled before the 3rd century BC, the city has light industries and is a communications and agricultural marketing center. Pop 243 759.

MURDER, in US and UK law, the killing of another person with malice aforethought, distinguished from other types of HOMICIDE by the element of premeditation. In the US murder is graded in degrees of severity; only first degree murder can incur the death penalty, where that exists.

MURDOCH, (Jean) Iris (1919–), Irish-born British novelist. Her novels such as *Under the Net* (1954), *A Severed Head* (1961), *The Red and the Green* (1965), *A Fairly Honourable Defeat* (1970) and *Henry Cato* (1976) display wit and a gift for analyzing human relations.

MURFREESBORO, city in Tenn., seat of Rutherford Co., 29mi SE of Nashville, on the Stones R. It is a light manufacturing center. Pop 26 360.

MURFREESBORO, Battle of, (or **Stones River**), indecisive but bitter battle (Dec. 31, 1862–Jan. 2, 1863) in the American Civil War, fought near Murfreesboro, Tenn. The battle site is now the Stones River National Battlefield.

MURILLO, Bartolomé Estéban (1618–1682), Spanish BAROQUE painter, known as the "Raphael of Seville." The most famous painter of his time in Spain, Murillo produced religious narrative scenes expressing deep piety and gentleness, works of realism and fine portraits. Among his many famous paintings are the *Visions of St. Anthony*, the *Two Trinities* (known as the *Holy Family*) and *Beggar Boy*.

MURMANSK, capital of Murmansk region, on Kola Bay, 30mi from the Barents Sea. The largest city within the Arctic circle, it has an ice-free harbor and is the USSR's principal Arctic seaport. Pop 309 000.

MURNAU, Friedrich Wilhelm (1889–1931), German motion picture director, born Friedrich Wilhelm Plumpe. A pioneer in camera technique, he used close-ups to further action and to interpret mood and emotion. His films included *Nosferatu* (1922), *The Last Laugh* (1924) and *Tabu* (1931) with co-director Robert FLAHERTY.

MURORAN, city on SW Hokkaido island, Japan, at the entrance to Uchiura Bay. It is a naval base, seaport and industrial center. Pop 162 059.

MURPHY, Frank (1890–1949), US Supreme Court associate justice (1940–1949). As Attorney General he set up the civil rights division of the justice department. His Supreme Court dissent that internment of US Japanese residents in WWII was "legalization of racism" was eventually upheld.

MURPHY, John Benjamin (1857–1916), US surgeon who pioneered the use of immediate appendectomy (the surgical removal of the appendix) as a treatment for APPENDICITIS.

MURPHY, William Parry (1892–), US physician who shared the 1934 Nobel Prize for Physiology or Medicine with G. MINOT and G. WHIPPLE for his work with Minot showing that daily consumption of large quantities of raw liver is an effective treatment for pernicious ANEMIA.

MURPHYSBORO, city in SW Ill., seat of Jackson Co., 24mi W of Marion. It produces shoes, feed and fertilizer. Pop 10 013.

MURRAY, city in SW Ky., seat of Calloway Co. Its economy rests on agriculture, light industry and tourism. Pop 13 537.

MURRAY, city in Utah, 7mi S of Salt Lake City, on the Jordan R. An agricultural trading center and also a smelting center for lead mines. Pop 21 206.

MURRAY, George Gilbert Aimé (1866–1957), British classical scholar, best known for his translations of ancient Greek playwrights. He actively promoted the LEAGUE OF NATIONS.

MURRAY, James (1721–1794), British military and civilian governor of Quebec, Canada, 1759–68. He fought in WOLFE's expedition against Quebec, but as governor he was conciliatory toward the French-Canadians. He became governor of Minorca 1774.

MURRAY, Philip (1886–1952), Scottish-born US labor leader. President of the CONGRESS OF INDUSTRIAL ORGANIZATIONS (CIO) from 1940; prominent leader of the UNITED MINE WORKERS, 1912–42; organizer and head of the UNITED STEELWORKERS from 1942. In 1949–50 he helped rid the CIO of communist unions.

MURRAY RIVER, chief river of Australia; an important source of irrigation. It rises in the mountains of New South Wales and flows for 1 609mi, passing through Hume reservoir and Lake Victoria, on to Encounter Bay on the Indian Ocean.

MURRES, the American term for GUILLEMOTS of the genus *Uria*.

MURROW, Edward R. (Edward Egbert Roscoe Murrow; 1908–1965), US broadcaster. He was head of Columbia Broadcasting System's European bureau during WWII; from 1947–60 he produced many acclaimed radio and TV programs, including an exposé of Senator Joseph McCARTHY (1954). He directed the US INFORMATION AGENCY 1961–63.

MURRUMBIDGEE RIVER, tributary of the MURRAY R, Australia. Part of a major irrigation and hydroelectric scheme, it rises in the Australian Alps and flows 1 050mi through rich agricultural land.

MUSCAT, capital of the sultanate of OMAN, on the Gulf of Oman. It exports dates but is no longer Oman's chief port. Pop 18 000.

MUSCATINE, city in E Ia., seat of Muscatine Co., on the Mississippi R. An agricultural center, noted for melons and button making. Pop 22 405.

MUSCI. See MOSSES.

MUSCLE, the tissue whose contraction produces body movement. In man and other vertebrates there are three types of muscle. **Skeletal or striated muscle** is the type normally associated with the movement of the body. Its action can either be initiated voluntarily, through the central NERVOUS SYSTEM, or it can respond to REFLEX mechanisms. Under the microscope this muscle is seen to be striped or striated. It consists of cylinders of tissue 0.01mm in diameter, showing great variation in length (1–150mm) and containing many nuclei. Each cylinder consists of thousands of filaments, each bathed in cytoplasm (known as sarcoplasm) which is their source of nutrition. Energy for contraction is derived by the OXIDATION of GLUCOSE brought by the BLOOD and stored as granules of GLYCOGEN in the sarcoplasm. The oxidation and breakdown of the glucose takes place in the mitochondria (see CELL), the net result being the formation of adenosine triphosphate (ATP—see NUCLEOTIDES). This molecule provides a "high-energy" bond which enables actin and myosin, two proteins in the muscle filament, to slide into each other, an action which, repeated many times throughout the muscle, results in its contraction. The behavior of a particular fiber is governed by an "all-or-none" law, in that it will either contract completely or not at all. Therefore the extent to which a muscle contracts is dependent solely on the number of individual fibers contracting. If a muscle is starved of oxygen, a process termed GLYCOLYSIS provides the energy. However glycolysis involves LACTIC ACID production with the consequent risk of CRAMP. Skeletal muscle functions by being attached via TENDONS to two parts of the SKELETON which move relative to each other. The larger attachment is known as the muscle's origin. Contraction of the muscle attempts to draw together the two parts of the skeleton. Muscles are arranged in antagonistic groups so that all movements involve the contraction of some muscles at the same time as their antagonists relax. **Smooth or involuntary muscle** is under the control of the autonomic nervous system and we are rarely aware of its action. Smooth muscle fibers are constructed in sheets of cells, each with a single nucleus. They are situated in hollow structures such as the gut, BRONCHI, uterus and BLOOD vessels. Smooth muscle uses the property of "tone" (continual slight tension) to regulate the diameter of tubes such as blood vessels. Being responsive to HORMONES, notably ADRENALINE, it can thus decrease blood supply to nonessential organs during periods of stress. In the gut, the muscle also propels the contents along by contracting along its length in waves (PERISTALSIS). **Cardiac muscle**, found only in the HEART, has the property of never resting throughout life. It combines features of both skeletal and smooth muscle, for it is striped but yet involuntary. The fibers are not discrete but branching and interlinked, thus enabling it to act quickly and in unison when stimulated.

MUSCLE SHOALS, stretch of the Tennessee R, some 40mi long, NW Ala., formerly consisting of rocks and rapids. Three dams controlled by the TENNESSEE VALLEY AUTHORITY now generate hydroelectric power, control floods and have eliminated the navigation hazards.

MUSCOVITE, or **isinglass**, the commonest species of MICA, $KAl_2(Si_3Al)O_{10}(OH)_2$, chiefly obtained from pegmatite dikes in India and the US.

MUSCOVY DUCK, or **Barbary Duck**, *Cairina moschata*, a polygamous species of DUCK which originated in S America. It was later introduced to other parts of the world and domesticated. The wild muscovy is greenish-black with red wattles and a casque on the bill.

MUSCULAR DYSTROPHY, a group of inherited DISEASES in which MUSCLE fibers are abnormal and undergo ATROPHY. Most develop in early life or adolescence. *Duchenne dystrophy* occurs in males although the genes for it are carried by females. It starts in early life and some swelling (pseudohypertrophy) of calf and other muscles may be seen. A similar disease can affect females. Other types, described by muscles mainly affected, include *limb-girdle* and *facio-scapulo-humeral* dystrophies. There are many diverse variants, largely due to structural or biochemical abnormalities in muscle fibers. *Myotonic dystrophy* occurs in older men, causing BALDNESS, CATARACTS, TESTIS atrophy and a characteristic myotonus, in which contraction is involuntarily sustained. Muscular dystrophies usually cause weakness and wasting of muscles, particularly of those close to and in the trunk; a waddling gait and exaggerated curvature of the lower spine are typical. The muscles of RESPIRATION may be affected, with resulting PNEUMONIA and respiratory failure; HEART muscle, too, can also be affected. These two factors in particular may lead to early death in severe cases. Mechanical aids, including if necessary ARTIFICIAL RESPIRATION, may greatly improve well-being, mobility and life-span.

MUSES, in Greek mythology, nine patron goddesses of the arts, worshiped especially near Mt HELICON. Daughters of ZEUS and the goddess of memory (MNEMOSYNE), they were attendants of APOLLO, god of poetry. The chief muse was Calliope (epic poetry); the others were Clio (history), Euterpe (lyric poetry), Thalia (comedy, pastoral poetry), Melpomene (tragedy), Terpsichore (choral dancing), Erato (love poetry), Polyhymnia (sacred song) and Urania (astronomy).

MUSEUM, institution that collects, preserves and exhibits objects—natural or manmade—for cultural and educational purposes. A museum was originally a place sacred to the MUSES; the most famous ancient museum, at Alexandria, Egypt (founded c280 BC), was a center for Greek scholars. Public museums did not exist in the ancient world or in medieval Europe; they developed from private Renaissance collections. The royal collections of works of art at the LOUVRE in Paris were made public in 1793, and the English physician and naturalist Sir Hans SLOANE's widely varied collections were bought by the British government which then opened the BRITISH MUSEUM (1759). In the late 19th and 20th centuries numerous public museums were established, tending to specialize in particular subjects or time periods. Museums and their collections are of several kinds: general, art and picture galleries, historical, scientific, natural history, outdoors, specialized (industrial, commercial or professional) and regional or local.

MUSHIN, town in SW Nigeria; a SE suburb of Lagos with a large industrial area. Pop 180 949.

MUSHROOM, popular name given to many gill fungi or AGARICS. In general, mushrooms are considered to be edible, while poisonous or inedible agarics are called toadstools. The common field mushroom (*Agaricus campestris*) is the most frequent wild species eaten, while *Agaricus bisporus* is the cultivated mushroom. Some mushrooms are serious parasites of wood, plantation trees and garden plants. Although mainly eaten for their flavor, mushrooms are of some food value, containing 5% protein. (See also AMANITA; FUNGI.)

MUSIAL, Stanley Frank (1920–), known as "Stan the Man," famous US baseball player. He played for the St. Louis Cardinals in outfield and at first base 1941–63 with a career batting average of 0.331. He made 3 630 hits (475 home runs) and 1 951 runs batted in. He was elected the National League's most valuable player three times, was its batting champion seven times and entered the Baseball Hall of Fame in 1969.

MUSIC, the art of arranging sound. Music cannot be defined merely as the art of arranging pleasing sounds; discords (see DISSONANCE) have long been used, and many modern composers experiment with almost any kind of sound.

One of the most important elements of western music is HARMONY, the interaction of tones. An elaborate theory and technique of harmony has been evolved and can be used to great effect by a skilled composer. Eastern music, however, has largely developed without harmony and tends to rely more on complex melodic or rhythmic structures, as in the Indian *raga* or *tala*. Here the performer's ability to improvise within the traditional musical framework is important. Chinese musical theory depends on a single note, the *huang chung*, from which arises a series of twelve notes (*lue*), each of which is the basis of a pentatonic SCALE. RHYTHM is the one element common to music of all cultures. Music probably grew up as a rhythmical accompaniment to man's natural urge to dance.

Music has existed in every culture, and often seems to have developed in conjunction with religion. Music was used in Sumerian temple ceremonies c4000 BC. The ancient Greeks used music for religious and dramatic purposes. The Romans made much use of music for ceremonial occasions. The early history of western music is largely that of church music, with secular music taking a significant but secondary place until the Renaissance. Modern NOTATION was developed by the Benedictine monk GUIDO D'ARREZO in the 11th century, allowing a complex musical tradition to evolve. The current repertoire consists largely of music written after 1600, divided roughly into RENAISSANCE, BAROQUE, CLASSICAL, ROMANTIC and modern styles. Recently this has been extended to cover much earlier music, music of other cultures and less traditionally "serious" forms such as JAZZ and BLUES, POP MUSIC and FOLK MUSIC. The last has grown up as a separate tradition from formal music (though interacting with it) in almost all cultures, and has been transmitted orally from generation to generation.

Many people have tried to evolve a philosophy of music, but none has ever satisfactorily explained its power to heighten feeling and to communicate on a deeper level than language. What is certain is that a liking for music in one form or another is one of mankind's most natural and universal instincts. (See also ATONALITY; COUNTERPOINT; HOMOPHONY; POLYPHONY; SOUND; TONALITY.)

MUSICAL COMEDY, stage play, often witty and sentimental, using song, dance and dialogue. Related to OPERETTA, VAUDEVILLE and musical revues, the "musical" was developed mainly in the US after 1900. Integral use of ballet was pioneered by Agnes DE MILLE. Landmarks in musicals include *Oklahoma!* Jerome KERN's *Show Boat,* Irving BERLIN's *Annie Get Your Gun,* Leonard BERNSTEIN's *On the Town* and *West Side Story.* Notable book and music collaborators have included RODGERS and HART, Rodgers and HAMMERSTEIN, and LERNER and LOEWE. MOTION PICTURES have had great success adapting and creating musicals.

MUSIL, Robert (1880–1942), Austrian writer. He is known for *The Man without Qualities*, 3 vols., 1930–43, an encyclopedic novel about the ills of pre-war Austria.

MUSK, a strongly-scented substance used in the manufacture of perfume. The term is strictly applied to that obtained from the musk glands of the male MUSK DEER, but also covers other similar secretions, e.g., civet musk, badger musk.

MUSK DEER, three species of small deer, *Moschus*, of S Asia. Solitary animals, neither sex has antlers; instead, the males have upper canines up to 75mm (3in) long. They are hunted for their MUSK, a brownish wax secreted by the bucks from a gland on the abdomen.

MUSKEG, found in the far north, particularly in TUNDRA, a BOG or SWAMP almost completely filled with SPHAGNUM MOSS.

MUSKEGO, city in SE Wis., 16mi SW of Milwaukee. Pop 11 573.

MUSKEGON, city in W Mich., on Lake Michigan at the mouth of the Muskegon R; seat of Muskegon Co. An industrial city and Great Lakes port, it is linked with Milwaukee, Wis., by car ferry. Pop 44 631.

MUSKEGON HEIGHTS, city in W Mich., a S residential and industrial suburb of Muskegon. Pop 17 304.

MUSKEGON RIVER, river in W central Mich. Rising in Houghton Lake, it flows 227mi SW to the city of Muskegon, emptying into E Lake Michigan.

MUSKELLUNGE, or **Muskie**, a large game fish of North America, *Esox masquinongy*, related to the PIKES.

MUSKET, smoothbore, muzzle-loaded FIREARM developed by the Spanish in the early 16th century; a heavier HARQUEBUS. It was not very accurate and was at first fired from a forked rest by two men. Later muskets were lighter and more satisfactory, but they were superseded by the RIFLE.

MUSKIE, Edward Sixtus (1914–), US politician. He was governor of Maine (1954–58), then elected its first Democratic senator (1958–). On the Democratic ticket with Hubert HUMPHREY, he ran for vice-president 1968; in 1972 his bid for the Democratic presidential nomination failed.

MUSKOGEAN, one of the nine language families of the major North American Indian language group called Macro-Algonkian (see ALGONQUIAN). Muskogean has four languages. Today about 20 000 people speak the Choctaw, Chickasaw, Creek and Seminole dialects of Muskogean.

MUSKOGEE, city in E Okla., seat of Muskogee Co., 47mi SE of Tulsa. Its industries include heavy and light manufacturing; it is a new port (1971). Pop 37 331.

MUSKOKA LAKES, group of 800–1 000 lakes in SW Ontario, Canada, between Georgian Bay and the Ottawa R, drained by the Muskoka R. The Muskoka district is about 4 000sq mi in area: a major resort with extensive game-filled forests.

MUSK-OX, *Ovibos moschatus*, a heavily-built bovid from the Arctic of North America, not a true ox but related to sheep and goats. Musk-oxen have thick, shaggy coats and a pronounced hump over the shoulders. They are highly aggressive animals living in herds of up to 100. When threatened, herds form a circle of adults around the calves, with horns facing outward. Musk-oxen have always been hunted for their fur, but now they are also farmed commercially.

MUSKRAT, or **Musquash**, *Ondatra zibethica*, of North America, the largest of the VOLES, measuring up to 600mm (23.6in). It is an aquatic animal living in fresh water or salt marshes, feeding mainly on water plants. The feet are broad, the hindfeet being webbed, and the fur is thick and waterproof. Musk rats are frequently hunted for their fur.

MUSLIM LEAGUE, political group (originally the All-India Muslim League) founded in 1906 to protect the rights of MUSLIMS in India. From 1940 the league backed the idea of an independent Muslim state; PAKISTAN was formed (1947) and the league became its predominant political party until it split into factions in the 1960s.

MUSLIMS (Arabic: ones who submit), adherents of the religion of ISLAM. (See also ABBASIDS; ARAB; ARAB LEAGUE; CALIPHATE; CRUSADES; ISLAMIC ART AND ARCHITECTURE; OTTOMAN EMPIRE; SELJUKS.)

MUSSELS, bivalve MOLLUSKS of various families, mostly marine but with a few freshwater species. Their shells are olive or blue-black, in some species attached to the substrate by a series of threads, the byssal threads. Food is strained from a current of water drawn into the shell, by cilia on the gills.

MUSSET, Louis Charles Alfred de (1810–1857), French Romantic poet and playwright (see ROMANTICISM). After an affair with George SAND, he wrote "Les Nuits" (1835–37), some of the finest love poetry in French, and the autobiographical *Confession d'un enfant du siècle* (1836). His witty plays are often produced today.

MUSSOLINI, Benito (1883–1945) Italian founder of FASCISM, dictator of ITALY, 1924–43. Editor of the socialist party paper 1912–14, Mussolini split with them when he advocated Italy's joining the Allies in WWI. In 1919 he formed a Fascist group in Milan which, in that time of political unrest, attracted many Italians with its blend of nationalism and socialism. The Fascist Party was nationally organized 1921; in 1922 the Fascist militia conducted the march on Rome which led the king to make Mussolini premier. He consolidated his position, eliminated opponents, signed the LATERAN TREATY and began an aggressive foreign policy. He brutally conquered Ethiopia 1935–36 (see ITALO-ETHIOPIAN WAR), and annexed Albania 1939. He joined Hitler (see AXIS POWERS) and in 1940 declared war on the ALLIES. Italy suffered defeats in Greece, Africa and at home. Mussolini was captured by the Allies (1943). When rescued by the Germans he headed the fascist puppet regime in German-occupied N Italy; on its collapse he was shot by Italian PARTISANS. (See also CORPORATE STATE.)

MUSSORGSKY, Modest Petrovich, or Moussorgsky (1839–1881), major Russian composer. His *Boris Godunov* (1874) is one of the finest Russian operas.

He developed a highly original style around characteristically Russian idioms, as in the song cycle *Songs and Dances of Death* (1875–77) and the piano suite *Pictures from an Exhibition* (1874). An alcoholic, Mussorgsky left many unfinished works.

MUSTANG, small feral HORSE of the W US, descended from horses of N African stock brought over by the Spaniards. Well adapted to plains conditions, they were popular as cow ponies. A **bronco** is an untamed mustang.

MUSTARD, herbs of the genus *Sinapis*, which is part of the CABBAGE family, Cruciferae. White mustard (*Sinapis alba*) and black mustard (*S. nigra*), native to the Mediterranean region, are now widely cultivated for their seeds which are used as a condiment.

MUSTARD GAS, or dichlorodiethyl sulfide $(CH_2Cl\,CH_2)_2S$, a toxic vesicant gas made from ETHYLENE and sulfur(I) chloride. (See also CHEMICAL AND BIOLOGICAL WARFARE.)

MUTANCHIANG, city in SE Heilungkiang province, NE China, on the Mutan R; an industrial and administrative center. Pop 251 000.

MUTATION, a sudden and relatively permanent change in a GENE or CHROMOSOME set, the raw material for evolutionary change. Chemical or physical agents which cause mutations are known as *mutagens*. Mutations can occur in any type of CELL at any stage in the life of an organism but only changes present in the GAMETES are passed on to the offspring. A mutation may be dominant or recessive, viable or lethal. The majority are changes in individual genes (gene mutations) but in some cases changes in the structure or numbers of chromosomes may be seen. The formation of structural chromosome changes is used to test drugs for mutagenic activity. Mutation normally occurs very rarely but certain mutagens—X-RAYS, GAMMA RAYS, NEUTRONS and MUSTARD GAS—greatly accelerate mutation.

MUTE. See DUMBNESS.

MUTSUHITO (1852–1912), emperor of Japan from 1867, with regnal name **Meiji**. The long isolation of Japan under the SHOGUNS ended 1868 with the restoration of imperial power. Mutsuhito guided the transformation of Japan from a feudal empire into a modern nation. He established industries, promoted education, gave farmers titles to their land, and modernized the armed forces.

MUTUAL BROADCASTING SYSTEM. See BROADCASTING SYSTEMS, US.

MUTUAL FUNDS, investment companies which pool their shareholders' funds and invest them in a broad range of stocks and shares. This spreads the risks for a small investor, who receives dividends for his shares in the fund (rather than for individual company shares) and who can always sell his fund shares back to the company at net asset value (see also STOCKS AND STOCK MARKET).

MUTUALISM, a kind of SYMBIOSIS in which the organisms involved depend on each other for their continuing existence. An important example involves the RUMINANTS, which would be unable to digest the material they eat were it not for the cellulase-producing BACTERIA that live within their gut.

MUYBRIDGE, Eadweard (Edward James Muggeridge; 1830–1904), English-born US photographer. He pioneered studies of human and animal movement using a series of cameras with special shutters, and invented a precursor of the cinema projector to display his results, published in his *Animal Locomotion* portfolio (1887).

MYASTHENIA GRAVIS, a DISEASE of the junctions between the peripheral NERVOUS SYSTEM and the MUSCLES, probably due to abnormal IMMUNITY, and characterized by the fatigability of muscles. It commonly affects EYE muscles, leading to drooping lids and double VISION, but it may involve limb muscles. Weakness of the muscles of RESPIRATION, swallowing and coughing may lead to respiratory failure and aspiration or bacterial PNEUMONIA. Speech is nasal, regurgitation into the nose may occur and the FACE is weak, lending a characteristic snarl to the MOUTH. It is associated with disorders of THYMUS GLAND and THYROID GLAND. Treatment is with cholinesterase inhibitors; STEROIDS and thymus removal may control the causative immune mechanism.

View of the acropolis of Mycenae, showing houses of the 14th and 13th centuries BC and, in the right foreground, the royal tomb circle excavated by Schliemann in the late 19th century.

MYCENAE, city of ancient Greece and a late Bronze Age site, 7mi N of Argos in the NE Peloponnesus. The city of HOMER's King Agamemnon, it was destroyed by the Dorian invasion of 1100 BC. Historically the city is important as the center of Mycenaean civilization (see AEGEAN CIVILIZATION). The remains of the city include the Treasury of Atreus and other royal beehive and shaft tombs and the Lion Gate of the citadel wall. Heinrich SCHLIEMANN excavated the site (1876–78) and uncovered weapons, jewels, ornaments, gold and silverware.

MYCENAEAN CIVILIZATION. See AEGEAN CIVILIZATION.

MYCOLOGY, the scientific study of FUNGI.

MYCOPLASMAS, minute organisms intermediate in size between BACTERIA and VIRUSES. Structurally they consist of an outer three-layered pliable membrane surrounding proteinaceous cytoplasm that contains both RNA and DNA (see NUCLEIC ACIDS). Mycoplasmas cause diseases of man, animals and plants.

MYCORRHIZA, an association between the roots of vascular plants and a fungus. Mycorrhizas are found in many plant species, typically in forest trees, heath plants and ORCHIDS. Some plants grow very poorly in the absence of the fungus. The relationship appears to be symbiotic, that is, of benefit to both plant and fungus. There are two main types of mycorrhiza, the ectotrophic and endotrophic. In the ectotrophic association the fungus forms a sheath around the roots and in the endotrophic, the fungus penetrates the cells within the cortex of the roots. (See SYMBIOSIS.)

MYCOTA, a division of the PLANT KINGDOM that includes the SLIME MOLDS (Myxomycetes) and the true FUNGI.

MYELIN, specialized layering of the membranes of glial cells (in the BRAIN) and the Schwann cells (of the peripheral NERVOUS SYSTEM) which wrap around nerve fibers producing an electrically insulating sheath, interrupted at intervals, which facilitates rapid nerve impulse conduction. Its disorders include MULTIPLE SCLEROSIS, ENCEPHALITIS and NEURITIS.

MY LAI, a hamlet in South Vietnam where nearly 350 Vietnamese civilians were massacred by US soldiers in March 1968. Subsequent revelations (autumn, 1969) led to army and congressional investigations, courtmartial for some soldiers involved and great public controversy over the conduct of the VIETNAM WAR.

MYNA, Indian word for birds of the family Sturnidae, also known as starlings, occurring in India and the Orient. Best known are the Common myna and Hill myna: black birds with yellow bill and legs. They are successful mimics, widely kept as pets.

MYOCARDITIS, a rare INFLAMMATION of the HEART muscle caused by VIRUSES, BACTERIA, some metal poisons and drugs. It is a serious complication of acute RHEUMATIC FEVER. Treatment involves bed rest, but the heart may be permanently damaged.

MYOGLOBIN, molecule related to HEMOGLOBIN found in MUSCLE cells and which serves as a local store for OXYGEN. Its affinity for oxygen encourages the transfer of oxygen to it from the BLOOD.

MYOPIA, or near- or shortsightedness, a defect of VISION in which light entering the EYE from distant objects is brought to a focus in front of the retina. The condition may be corrected by use of a diverging spectacle LENS.

MYRDAL, Gunnar Karl (1898–), Swedish economist and politician, co-winner of the 1974 Nobel economics prize. He co-authored the influential sociological study *An American Dilemma: The Negro Problem and Modern Democracy* (1944). Myrdal was Sweden's minister of Commerce (1945–47) and was secretary of the UN Economic Commission for Europe (1947–57).

MYRIAPODA, obsolete name for a class of many-legged terrestrial arthropods now divided between the CENTIPEDES, MILLIPEDES, Symphyla and Pauropoda.

MYRMIDONS, in Greek mythology, inhabitants of Phthiotis in Thessaly, followers of Achilles in the TROJAN WAR. Their reputed ancestor king Myrmidon was the son of Eurymedusa, whom Zeus seduced in the form of an ant. The word Myrmidon (Greek *myrmex* meaning ant) is sometimes used to describe those who conduct themselves with supposedly antlike observance of routine and duty.

MYRON (5th century BC), Greek sculptor best-known for his DISCOBOLUS, a marble reconstruction of which is housed in Rome's National Museum. His work, almost exclusively in bronze, marks the apogee of early Classical art. It is predominantly concerned with the human figure at critical moments of poise and balance in the course of generally strenuous, often athletic actions.

MYRRH, the fragrant resin obtained from small thorny trees of the genus *Commiphora* from the family, Burseraceae. Myrrh has been used for embalming, in medicines and as incense and is now an important constituent of some PERFUMES.

MYRTLE, *Myrtus communis*, a fragrant evergreen shrub native to the Mediterranean regions. The white or pink flowers precede purple berries. The flowers, leaves and berries produce a fragrant oil that is used in perfumery. Both the plain green and variegated leaved varieties can be grown as house plants, and are often pruned into interesting shapes (topiary). They grow well at average house temperatures preferring a sunny position in the winter, although less sun is required in the summer. The soil should be kept evenly moist; propagation is by shoot-tip cuttings. Family: Myrtaceae.

MYSORE, city in S India in Karnataka (formerly Mysore) state, on the Deccan plateau S of the Cauvery R, 85mi SW of Bangalore. An ancient royal capital with many historic buildings, today it is a major industrial, marketing and transportation center. Pop 355 636.

MYSTERIES, secret religious rites of ancient Greece and Rome. Revealed only to initiated persons, they were called mysteries from the Greek word *mystes*, meaning an initiate. Disclosure of the secrets of the rites was punishable by death, hence the fragmentary nature of our knowledge of them. Of the Classical mysteries the most famous were the ELEUSINIAN MYSTERIES held at Eleusis and later in Athens. These were essentially ethonian and involved purification rites, dance, drama and the display of sacred objects such as an ear of corn. The Orphic mysteries were said to have been founded by ORPHEUS. Other mysteries were connected with nature deities and those of eastern cults such as CYBELE, ATTIS, ISIS, OSIRIS and MITHRA.

MYSTERY PLAY, medieval religious drama based on biblical themes, chiefly those concerning the Nativity, the Passion and the Resurrection. The form is closely related to that of the Miracle play, which is generally based on non-Biblical material, such as, for example, the saints' lives. The distinction between the two forms is not clearcut and some authorities refer to both as Miracle plays. Mystery plays, which are liturgical in origin, can be extraordinarily ambitious in scale, treating the whole of man's spiritual history from the Creation to judgment day in vast cycles which it required communal cooperation to perform. Important examples are the English York and Wakefield cycles, the French cycle *Miracle of Notre Dame* and the famous OBERAMMERGAU Passion, of Austria. (See also MORALITY PLAY.)

MYSTICISM, belief that man can experience a transcendental union with the divine in this life through meditation and other disciplines. It is at the core of most eastern religions, though it may be only loosely linked with them. The path to this union is usually seen as three stages: cleansing away of physical desires, purification of will and enlightenment of mind. Mysticism is important in most forms of Christianity. The goal is union and communion with God in love and by intuitive knowledge in prayer; mystical experience can be expressed only in metaphors, especially of love and marriage.

MYSTIC SEAPORT, a 20 acre village, at the mouth of the Mystic R, on Long Island Sound, part of Stonington, Conn. This popular tourist attraction is a recreated mid-19th century whaling port, with early American buildings, cobbled streets, old ships and marine and other museums.

MYTHOLOGY, a collection of traditional tales, usually of a particular people (such as the ancient Greeks, Indians or Norsemen), handed down orally through the generations. Most mythologies are of earlier date than the invention of writing in the cultures from which they spring. There are three main classes of myths: myths proper, which are imaginative and serious attempts to explain natural phenomena and are often concerned with gods and supernatural events occurring in a timeless past; folk tales, including fairy tales, which are narrative stories in historical time of social concerns; and sagas and legends, which recount embellished exploits of heroes of the past who may or may not have existed. Although most of the cultures of primitive men have mythologies, not all people do: one example is the Romans, who appear to have had very little in the way of oral tradition, but who borrowed and adapted Greek mythology. The term mythology is also applied to the study of such tales, from which past cultural exchanges can be inferred and historical archaeological sites can often be identified. The most famous such study was Sir James FRAZER's *The Golden Bough* (1890) which contains an extensive synthesis of many disparate myths and mythologies.

Mythology has greatly enriched the culture of and especially the literature of the world's peoples. Classical mythology became a theme for writers and artists during the RENAISSANCE. The mythology of Scandinavia, known through collections of early narrative verse, including the Icelandic poetic EDDA and the German epic poem NIBELUNGENLIED, made a significant contribution to European culture.

MYTILENE. See LESBOS.

MYXEDEMA, severe hypothyroidism. See THYROID GLAND.

MYXOPHYTA. See SLIME MOLDS.

The pantheons of some ancient mythologies

Pantheons of the Americas

Mythologies of the two Americas are based on TOTEMISM. Only in some of the more advanced civilizations did totemism become more complex and pantheons arise.

Name of god	*Description*
	Aztec
Huitzilopochtli	hummingbird of the south or he of the south; god of war and also a storm god
Tezcatlipoch	smoking mirror; the god of the sun
Quetzalcoatl	the snake bird; god of wind, master of life, creator, patron of every art
Tlaloc	pulp of the earth; god of the mountains, of rain, of freshwater springs
Coatlicoe	she whose garment is woven of snakes; mother of Huitzilopochtli
Chalchiuhtlicue	goddess of running water, springs and streams; wife of Tlaloc
Xiuhtectutli	god of fire
Tlazoleotl	goddess of guilty love or pleasure; goddess of filth
Chicomecoatl	goddess of rural plenty
Cihuatcoatl	goddess of childbirth
	Inca
Inti	also called Apu-Punchau, the head of the day; god of the sun
Mama Quilla	the moon, sister and wife of the sun (Inti); goddess who protects married women
Cuycha	the rainbow
Catequil	god of thunder and lightning
Chaca	the long-haired star (i.e. the planet Venus); protector of maidens and flowers
Pacha-mama	mother earth
Nina	fire
Vira Cocha	the foam or fat of the lake (lived in Lake Titicaca)
Pachacamac	he who animates the earth; the supreme god of the maritime Incas of Peru

Greece and Rome

Greek name	*Roman name*	*Description*
Aphrodite	Venus	goddess of love, beauty, fertility
Apollo	Apollo	god of light, male beauty, music and poetry, medicine
Ares	Mars	god of war
Artemis	Diana	virgin goddess of the moon, night, hunting, childbirth
Athena	Minerva	goddess of wisdom, the arts and handicrafts, war
Demeter	Ceres	god of earth, and agriculture, especially corn
Dionysus (Bacchus)	Liber	god of wine, vegetation, opposing spirit to Apollo in modern interpretations, god of revelry
Erinyes	Furiae	spirits of retribution and vengeance
Eros	Cupid	god of love, often represented as a blindfolded child
Hades (Pluto)	Dis	god of the underworld, of wealth
Hephaestus	Vulcan	god of fire, patron of crafts; the divine smith
Hera	Juno	goddess of marriage and maternity, sister and wife of Zeus/Jupiter; queen of all the gods
Hermes	Mercury	messenger of the gods and conductor of souls to the underworld
Hestia	Vesta	goddess of the hearth and of the home
Pan	Faunus	god of sheep and shepherds, fecundity and lust
Persephone	Proserpina	goddess of fertility of the death and rebirth of vegetation
Poseidon	Neptune	god of the sea, of earthquakes and of horses
Zeus	Jupiter	god of the sky and earth, weather, oaths; the supreme god

Egyptian

Name of god	*Description*
Amon (Ra/Re)	god of the sun and sky, the father of all things
Anubis	god of the dead and of embalming, conductor of the dead to the other world
Bes	goddess of marriage
Geb	god of earth, child of Shu and Tefnut
Hathor (Athyr)	goddess of the sky, love, beauty and joy
Horus	sky god in the form of a falcon-headed man, his eyes were the sun and the moon, the god of sun, light and goodness
Isis	powerful mother goddess, wife of Osiris and mother of Horus; goddess of fertility, nature and magic, the great enchantress of power surpassing all other deities
Nephthys	goddess of the dead
Nut	goddess of the sky, child of Shu and Tefnut
Osiris	god of fertility considered in later periods to be the personification of the dead king; husband of Isis, god of the sun, god of the Nile, judge of the underworld
Ptah (Phthah)	creator of the universe and patron of craftsmen, husband of Sekhmet and father of Nefertum; intermediary between men and the god was the sacred bull Apis
Sekhmet (Sekhet)	goddess of war; the eye of Re and destroyer of his enemies; consort of Ptah usually seen as a woman with a lion's head
Seth (Set, Setesh)	eventually god of evil and night, murderer of Osiris
Shu	god of light, air, support of the sky, twin and husband of Tefnut, personification of the divine intelligence
Tefnut	goddess of rain and dew
Thoth (Djhowtey)	early moon god, god of wisdom and learning, inventor of writing, creator of languages, adviser of the gods, often represented as human with an ibis head

N

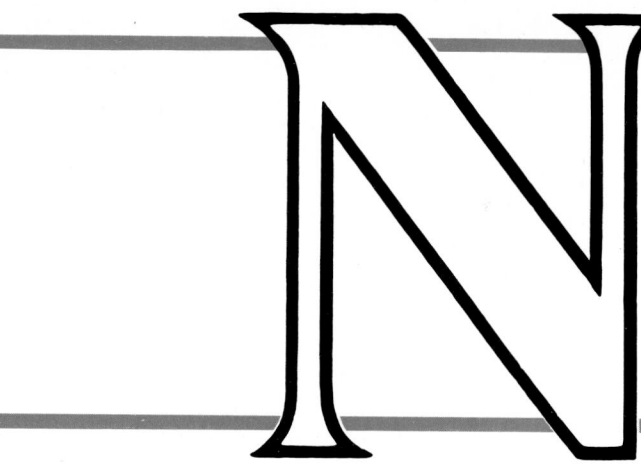

N, 14th letter of the English alphabet, corresponding with the 14th Semitic letter nūn and the Greek nū. N is the abbreviation for name, noun, neuter and north, among others. (See ALPHABET.)

NAACP. See NATIONAL ASSOCIATION FOR THE ADVANCEMENT OF COLORED PEOPLE.

NABATAEANS, ancient Arabs whose kingdom between the Euphrates R and the Red Sea prospered from the 4th century BC until Roman annexation (106 AD). PETRA, S of the Dead Sea, was the center of the Nabataean settlements which owed their wealth to control of caravan routes from Arabia to the Mediterranean coast.

NABIS (d. 192 BC), last ruler of independent Sparta (207–192 BC). An adroit leader, he fought with the Achaean League, gained Argos (197–95) and survived a defeat by Rome in 194. He was murdered by the Aetolians, who took Sparta.

NABLA. See DEL.

NABLUS (Nabulus), city 30mi N of Jerusalem, formerly in Jordan, now in the disputed West Bank area of Israel. It lies between Mts Ebal and Gerizem and was the ancient Hebrew Shechem of the Bible (or Schehem). It is now an industrial and agricultural center. Pop 44 200.

NABOKOV, Vladimir (1899–), Russian-US novelist and critic. Born in St. Petersburg (now Leningrad), he became a US citizen in 1945. Noted for his originality and satiric wit, he has published poetry, essays, short stories and novels in Russian and in English. His first English novel was *The Real Life of Sebastian Knight* (1938); he became famous for *Lolita* (1958), the story of a middle-aged man's passion for a young girl. His works include *Pnin* (1957), *Pale Fire* (1962), *Ada* (1969), and an English translation of *Eugene Onegin* (1963).

NABOPOLASSAR, first Chaldean king of Babylonia (626–605 BC); father of NEBUCHADNEZZAR II. With the Medes as allies he captured NINEVEH (612 BC), resulting in the destruction of the Assyrian Empire and the rise of the Neo-Babylonian Empire.

NACOGDOCHES, city in E Tex., seat of Nacogdoches Co., 20mi N of Lufkin. It has dairying, truck farming and lumber industries. It was the scene of the FREDONIAN REBELLION (1826). Pop. 22 544.

NACRE. See MOTHER OF PEARL.

NADAB (d. c909 BC), king of Israel. He succeeded his father, Jeroboam I, and was assassinated in the siege of Gibbethon.

NADER, Ralph (1934–), US consumer crusader and lawyer. The controversy which greeted his book *Unsafe at Any Speed* (1965), a criticism of safety standards in the auto industry, enabled him to gain widespread support for investigations into other areas of public interest, including chemical food additives, X-ray leakage and government agencies. His work has resulted in Congressional hearings and remedial legislation.

NADIR, the point on the CELESTIAL SPHERE directly opposite an observer's ZENITH.

NADIR SHAH (1688–1747), shah of Iran (1736–47), often called the "Napoleon of Iran." He created an Iranian empire reaching from the Indus R to the Caucasus Mts by ruthless military conquest, including the capture of Delhi (and its famous Koh-i-noor diamond and peacock throne).

NAGALAND, 6 366sq mi state in NE India, bordered by the states of Assam (N and W), Manipur (S) and Burma (E). The capital city is Kohima. It is a remote forested hill and mountain region. Hill rice is the chief crop. It was made a state (1961) following long struggles by Naga tribesmen.

NAGANO, capital of Nagano prefecture, Honshu, Japan, about 100mi NW of Tokyo. It is a commercial center producing textiles. Pop 285 355.

NAGAOKA, city in Niigata prefecture, NW Honshu, Japan, 35mi S of Niigata. It has oil refineries and produces chemicals. Pop 162 262.

NAGASAKI, capital of Nagasaki prefecture, Kyushu Island, Japan, a foreign trading center since 1571. In WWII about 40 000 residents were killed when the Americans dropped the second atomic bomb (Aug. 9, 1945). Today shipbuilding is the city's major industry. Pop 421 114.

NAGOYA, capital of Aichi prefecture, S Honshu, Japan, 75mi E of Kyoto. An industrial seaport, it produces textiles, cars, aircraft and chemicals. Pop 2 036 053.

NAGPUR, capital of Nagpur district, N Maharashtra state, India, 265mi N of Hyderabad. A commercial and industrial city, it is almost at the geographical center of India. Pop 866 144.

NAGUIB, Mohammed (1901–), Egyptian general and statesman, one of the Free Officers who overthrew King FAROUK and formed a republic in 1953. As president he favored a constitutional government, but was ousted by NASSER (1954).

NAGY, Imre (1896–1958) Hungarian communist leader and premier (1953–55). His criticism of Soviet influence led to his removal from office; but during the Oct. 1956 revolution he became premier again briefly. After Soviet troops crushed the uprising, the Russians tried and executed Nagy in secret.

NAHA, capital of Okinawa prefecture, SW OKINAWA, Ryukyu Islands, Japan. It is an industrial seaport and a post-WWII US military base. Pop 276 380.

NAHUATL, American Indian language spoken by ancient Aztecs and Toltecs, and by about 1 million people in Central America and S Mexico today.

NAHUM, Book of, the seventh of the Old Testament MINOR PROPHETS, the oracles of the prophet Nahum. It graphically relates the fall of Nineveh (612 BC) and is dated shortly before or after this.

NAIAD. See NYMPHS.

NAIL, metal shaft, pointed at one end and usually with a head at the other, that can be hammered into pieces of wood or other materials to fasten them together. In the making of common nails, steel wire is fed discontinuously between a pair of gripper DIES, which hold it while a hammer forms the head. The grippers part and the wire moves forward; nippers then shear the shaft and pliers form the point. Other forms are masonry nails, stamped from a plate, and U-shaped staples.

NAILS, a keratinous covering protecting the tips of the digits in VERTEBRATES. Primitively always present as claws, they are now modified as claws, true nails or, in UNGULATES, as HOOVES. (See also KERATIN.)

NAIROBI, capital of Kenya, E Africa, 330mi NW of Mombasa. A transport, trade and farming center, it processes and exports food products and has varied light manufacturing industries. Pop 509 286.

NAISMITH, James A. (1861–1939), Canadian–US physical education instructor who invented BASKETBALL (1891), and is credited with inventing the protective football helmet.

NAMANGAN, administrative city of Namangan oblast (region), NE Uzbek, USSR. It produces food and textiles. Pop 175 000.

NAMIBIA. See SOUTH WEST AFRICA.

NAMIER, Sir Lewis Bernstein (1888–1960), Polish-born British historian; professor at Manchester U. (1931–53). His controversial *The Structure of Politics at the Accession of George III* (1929) revolutionized English historiography.

NAMPA, city in SW Ida., 18mi W of Boise. A farming and railroad center, it produces refined sugar and vegetable seeds. Pop 20 768.

NANAIMO, city in SE Vancouver Island, British Columbia, Canada, 38mi W of Vancouver. Lumbering, fishing and agriculture are the chief industries. Pop 14 762.

NANCHANG, capital of Kiangsi province, on the Kan R, SE China. Heavily industrialized, it is an automotive manufacturing center. Pop 520 000.

NANCHUNG, city in central Szechwan province, China, about 95mi N of Chungking. It is a communications and agricultural market center, known for its silk production. Pop 206 000.

NANCY, capital of Meurthe-et-Moselle department, NE France, 175mi E of Paris; once the capital of the dukes of Lorraine. It produces coal, iron, salt and glass. Pop 123 428.

NANKING, capital of Kiangsu province, a port on the Yangtse R, E China. The present city was founded 1368 on an ancient site of the MING dynasty. It was twice capital of China (1928–37; 1946–49). It is a cultural, communications and major industrial center. Pop 1 700 000.

NANKING, Treaty of. See OPIUM WAR.

NANNING, city in Kwangsi Chuang region in SE China on the Yung Chiang R, 330mi W of Canton. It is a printing and paper manufacturing center. Pop 260 000.

NANNYBERRY, or sweet viburnum, *Viburnum cassinoides*, shrub native to North America producing dark blue berries in the fall. The fruits are eaten locally and the leaves are used to produce a tea substitute. Family: Caprifoliaceae.

NANSEN, Fridtjof (1861–1930), Norwegian explorer, scientist and humanitarian, awarded the 1922 Nobel Peace Prize, best known for his explorations of the Arctic. His most successful attempt at reaching the NORTH POLE was in 1895, when he achieved latitude 86° 14′, the farthest north then reached. He also designed the **Nansen Bottle**, a device for obtaining water samples at depth.

NANTES, capital of Loire-Atlantique department, NW France, at the head of the Loire estuary, 107mi W of Tours. An ancient Gallic capital and Roman commercial city, today it is an industrial, commercial and shipping center. Pop 269 400.

View of the tree-lined Via Orazio, Naples, and beyond it the cloud-shrouded volcano, Mount Vesuvius.

NANTES, Edict of, proclamation of religious toleration for French Protestants (HUGUENOTS) issued in the city by Henry IV in 1598. Protestants were granted civil rights and freedom of private and public worship in many parts of France (but not in Paris). In 1685 Catholic pressure brought Louis XIV to revoke the edict.

NANTICOKE, residential city in E Pa., 8mi W of Wilkes-Barre, on the Susquehanna R. It produces silk and rayon. Pop 14632.

NANTUCKET ISLAND, popular summer resort, 25mi S of Cape Cod, Mass., across Nantucket Sound. The 15mi-long island has a mild climate and 88mi of beaches. It was a world famous 18th-century whaling center. Pop 3774.

NANTUNG, seaport on the N side of the Yangtse estuary, SE Kiangsu province, E China, 65mi NW of Shanghai. Pop 240000.

NAPA, city in W central Cal., seat of Napa Co., 10mi N of San Pablo Bay. It is the center of the Napa valley wine producing area. Pop 35978.

NAPALM, a SOAP consisting of the aluminum salt of a mixture of CARBOXYLIC ACIDS, with aluminum hydroxide in excess. When about 10% is added to GASOLINE it forms a GEL, also called napalm, used in flame throwers and incendiary bombs; it burns hotly and relatively slowly, and sticks to its target. Developed in WWII, it was used in the Vietnam War and caused great havoc. (See also CHEMICAL AND BIOLOGICAL WARFARE.)

NAPERVILLE, city in NE Ill. 28mi W of Chicago. It manufactures furniture and electronic equipment. Pop 23885.

NAPHTALI, one of the 12 tribes of Israel, named for the younger son of Jacob and Bilhah (Rachel's handmaid). Conquered by Assyria (734 BC), the tribe became one of the "Ten Lost Tribes" of Israel.

NAPHTHA, volatile mixture of liquid HYDROCARBONS boiling in the range 80°C to 180°C, used as a solvent. It is obtained by distilling COAL TAR (yielding aromatic products) or shale oil, or from the refining and cracking of PETROLEUM.

NAPHTHALENE ($C_{10}H_8$), white crystalline solid, an AROMATIC HYDROCARBON consisting of two fused BENZENE rings, and more reactive than benzene. It is produced from COAL TAR, and is used to make phthalic anhydride (see ACID ANHYDRIDES), as an intermediate in DYE manufacture, and for mothballs. MW 128.2, mp 81°C, bp 218°C.

NAPIER, John (1550–1617), Scottish mathematician credited with the invention of LOGARITHMS (before 1614). Natural logarithms (to the base *e* (see EXPONENTIAL)) are often called **Napierian Logarithms** for him. He also developed the modern notation for the DECIMAL SYSTEM.

NAPIER, Robert Cornelis, 1st Baron Napier of Magdala (1810–1890), British field marshal and civil engineer; commander of Britain's successful Abyssinian Expedition (1868) and commander-in-chief in India (1870–76).

NAPLES, city in Italy, capital of Naples province and of the Campania region, on N shore of the Bay of Naples, 120mi SE of Rome. Founded by the Greeks (c600 BC), it was the capital of the Kingdom of NAPLES and later the TWO SICILIES. The historic city has a 13th-century cathedral and university (1224), and medieval castles and palaces. Nearby are the ruins of POMPEII. Naples is the financial and intellectual center of S Italy. A major seaport, its industries vary from heavy engineering and textiles to wine and glass manufacture. Pop 1258721.

NAPLES, city in Fla., seat of Collier Co., 35mi S of Fort Myers on the Gulf of Mexico. Close to the EVERGLADES, it is a tourist resort and shrimp fishing center. Pop 12042.

NAPLES, Kingdom of. It comprised all of Italy S of the Papal States, including Sicily. It emerged after the conquests of the Norman Robert Guiscard in the 1000s; his nephew Roger II took the title King of Sicily and Apulia (1130). Naples was ruled in turn by the HOHENSTAUFENS, the ANGEVINS, the Aragonese (see ARAGON) and the Spanish Crown. The Austrians conquered the kingdom in 1707, but it was taken by the Spanish BOURBON kings in 1734. NAPOLEON I annexed the kingdom to his empire and made his brother Joseph king (1806) followed by his brother-in-law MURAT. In 1815, after Napoleon's defeat, the Bourbon Ferdinand IV was restored; he reunited Naples and Sicily as the Kingdom of the TWO SICILIES. Bourbon rule collapsed before the advance of the revolutionary forces of GARIBALDI (1860). When VICTOR EMMANUEL was confirmed by the Italian parliament as king of all Italy (Feb. 1861), Naples became a part of the new Italian state, ending 700 years as an independent kingdom.

NAPOLEON I (1769–1821), general and emperor of the French (1804–14). Napoleon Bonaparte was born in Corsica, went to military schools in France and became a lieutenant in the artillery (1785). He associated with JACOBINS on the outbreak of the FRENCH REVOLUTION, drove the British from Toulon (1793), and dispersed a royalist rebellion in Paris (Oct. 1795). Soon after his marriage to Joséphine de BEAUHARNAIS, he defeated the Austro–Sardinian armies in Italy (1796–7) and signed the treaty of Campo Formio extending French territory. He returned to Paris a national hero. He then campaigned in Egypt and the Middle East, threatening Great Britain's position in India. Although he won land battles, the French fleet was destroyed in the Battle of the Nile (ABOUKIR) Aug. 1798. Napoleon later returned to Paris and helped to engineer the coup d'etat of Nov. 9, 1799, which established a CONSULATE with himself as First Consul and virtual dictator. He reorganized the government, established the Bank of France and the CODE NAPOLÉON, which is still the basis of French law.

Portrait by R. Le Fèvre of Napoleon I, Emperor of France, in 1810. Much less glorified and romanticized than other contemporary portraits, it nevertheless suggests the capacity for greatness that enabled him to rise from obscurity to become the most powerful man in Europe.

Continuing hostilities with Austria and Great Britain resulted in the Treaty of Lunéville, which recognized French dominance on the Continent. The Treaty of Amiens with Britain (March 1802) meant that Europe was at peace for the first time in ten years. Napoleon became first consul for life (1802) and crowned himself emperor (1804). In the NAPOLEONIC WARS he then won a series of great victories over the European alliance at Austerlitz (1805), Jena (1806) and Friedland (1807), dissolving the HOLY ROMAN EMPIRE (1806) and becoming ruler of almost the whole continent. After Jena he inaugurated the CONTINENTAL SYSTEM whereby he hoped to keep European ports closed to British trade, but the battle of TRAFALGAR (1805) established the dominance of Britain at sea.

In 1809 Napoleon divorced Joséphine and married MARIE LOUISE who bore him an heir, NAPOLEON II. The PENINSULAR WAR revealed growing French weakness, and in 1812 Napoleon began his disastrous campaign against Russia. A new alliance of European nations defeated the French at Leipzig (1813); in 1814 France was invaded, Napoleon abdicated and was exiled to the island of Elba. In March 1815 he escaped, returned to France and ruled for the HUNDRED DAYS, which ended in French defeat at WATERLOO (1815). Napoleon was then exiled to SAINT HELENA where he died in 1821. His remains were brought to Paris in 1840 and buried under the dome of Les Invalides.

NAPOLEON II (1811–1832), son of Napoleon and MARIE LOUISE, proclaimed king of Rome at birth. After his father's abdication (1814), he lived in Austria as Duke of Reichstadt. He died of tuberculosis.

NAPOLEON III (Louis Napoleon; 1808–1873), emperor of the French (1852–70); son of Louis Bonaparte, king of Holland, and nephew of Napoleon I. He attempted several coups against King LOUIS PHILIPPE, was jailed but escaped to England (1846). After the 1848 revolution, he was elected president of France; he dissolved the legislature and made himself emperor (1852). His regime promoted domestic prosperity but by the 1860s opposition to his repressive, corrupt government had grown. He joined in the CRIMEAN WAR (1854–56), but failed to make MAXIMILIAN emperor of Mexico. In 1870 his ill-judged war with Prussia ended in defeat, capture and the collapse of his empire; he died in exile in England.

NAPOLEONIC CODE. See CODE NAPOLÉON.

NAPOLEONIC WARS (1804–15), fought by France after NAPOLEON I became emperor. After the Peace of Amiens (1802) which had ended the FRENCH REVOLUTIONARY WARS (1792–1802), Britain declared war on France in May, 1803, maintaining that Napoleon was not keeping to the treaty. Napoleon planned to invade Britain but the British fleet proved too strong for him, especially after TRAFALGAR. The British, Austrians and Russians formed an alliance in July, 1805; Napoleon defeated the Austrians and Russians at Austerlitz (Dec. 1805); the Prussians at Jena (1806) and the Russians at Friedland (1807); the Peace of Tilsit (1807) left him nearly master of Europe. Meanwhile Britain had secured supremacy of the seas at the Battle of Trafalgar (1805). The CONTINENTAL SYSTEM begun after Jena was Napoleon's attempt to blockade British trade; on the pretext of enforcing it he invaded Portugal (1807) and Spain (1808). During the defeat of his armies by the British in the PENINSULAR WAR (1808–14), he signed the Peace of Schönbrunn (1809) with the defeated Austrians. In 1812 Napoleon invaded Russia with a grand army some 500000 strong. He barely won the Battle of Borodino (1812) and marched unchallenged to Moscow, but his troops suffered from lack of supplies and the cold weather. Their retreat from Moscow and Russia was horrifying; only about 30000 of Napoleon's soldiers returned. The French, by now drained of manpower and supplies, were decisively beaten at Leipzig (1813). Paris fell, and on April 6, 1814 Napoleon abdicated. The victorious allies signed the Treaty of Paris with the Bourbons. After Napoleon's escape from Elba and return (The HUNDRED DAYS) and his defeat at Waterloo (1815), the second Treaty of Paris was signed in 1815 (see PARIS, TREATIES OF).

NAPO RIVER, river in NW South America. It flows about 700mi from N central Ecuador E and SE over Peru's border to the Amazon R below Iquitos.

NARA, city in Japan, capital of Nara prefecture in W central Honshu. It was the country's first permanent capital (710–784) and was an early center for Buddhism. Today it is a major tourist attraction. Pop 208 257.

NARAYANGANJ, town in SE Bangladesh, on the Meghna R, 12mi E of Dacca. It is a river port and a market for jute and hides. Pop 326 500.

NARBONNE, city in SE France, 8mi from the Mediterranean and 31mi E of Carcassonne. It was the site of the first Roman colony in Gaul (118 BC). Pop 35 236.

NARCISSISM, exaggerated self-love, often at a sexual level, characteristic of early sexual development though sometimes retained. It may also develop through IDENTIFICATION with an object of desire as a DEFENSE MECHANISM against possible loss. (See also SEX.)

NARCISSUS, in Greek mythology, son of the river god Cephissus, who spurned the nymph ECHO's love. Punished by the gods, he fell in love with his own reflection in a pool and wasted away; a narcissus flower grew where he died.

NARCISSUS, a genus of bulbous perennial plants that produce white, yellow and orange trumpet-shaped flowers. Many horticultural varieties are in cultivation throughout the world. *Narcissus pseudo-narcissus* is known as the common trumpet narcissus or DAFFODIL. Many narcissi are also grown as house plants and can easily be induced to flower during the winter. Attractive exhibitions of flowers can be obtained by growing a number of bulbs together in a single bowl or pot. During the early stages of growth they should be placed in a cool, dark place and then be brought into the light once leaves start to emerge. Flowering occurs five to seven weeks after planting. They grow best at temperatures below 18°C (65°F). Propagation is achieved by removing the bulbs produced each season and growing these until they reach full size. Family: Amaryllidaceae.

NARCOLEPSY. See AMPHETAMINES.

NARCOTICS, DRUGS that induce sleep; specifically, the OPIUM-derived ANALGESICS. These affect the higher BRAIN centers causing mild euphoria and sleep (narcosis). They may act as HALLUCINOGENIC DRUGS and are abused in DRUG ADDICTION.

NARMADA RIVER (also Narbada), river in central India, sacred to the Hindus. It rises in the Maikala Hills, Madhya Pradesh, and flows 801mi W to the Gulf of Cambay.

NARODNIKI (Russian: populists), members of a socialist movement in 19th-century Russia. They ineffectually spread political propaganda among the peasants; failure and police repression turned them to terrorism, culminating in Tsar Alexander II's assassination (1881). They were succeeded by the Socialist Revolutionary Party (1901).

The Hermitage, former home of President Andrew Jackson in Nashville, Tenn., now preserved as his memorial. Nashville became the capital of Tennessee in 1843, during Jackson's presidency.

NARRAGANSETT BAY, inlet of the Atlantic Ocean extending 28mi inland, nearly dividing R.I. in two. An active shipping center since colonial days; Providence and Newport are its chief ports.

NARRAGANSETT INDIANS, North American tribe of the ALGONQUIAN linguistic family (numbering perhaps 5 000 before 1675) who inhabited most of Rhode Island. They were friendly to the colonists until KING PHILIP'S WAR (1675–76) resulted in their virtual annihilation.

NARROWS, The, strait between the W end of Long Island and Staten Island, SE N.Y., connecting Upper with Lower New York Bay. It is spanned by the Verrazano–Narrows bridge, the world's longest suspension bridge (4 260ft).

NARSES (d. 302 AD?), king of the SASSANIAN Empire in Persia from 293. He concluded a peace with Rome (296), on unfavorable terms, which lasted 40 years.

NARSES (c480–574), eunuch Byzantine general under Emperor JUSTINIAN I. After the recall of BELISARIUS, he conquered the OSTROGOTH kingdom in Italy (552) and was exarch there until 567.

NARTHEX, narrow enclosed portico or vestibule across the entire width of a Byzantine church at its entrance; an antechamber to the nave. In early Christianity, candidates for baptism were admitted only as far as the narthex.

NARVÁEZ, Pánfilo de (c1470–1528), Spanish conquistador. Under VELÁZQUEZ, he played a major role in subjecting Cuba to Spain. In 1520 Velázquez sent him on a punitive expedition against Hernán CORTÉS in Mexico which failed. He also led an unsuccessful expedition, on which he himself died, to subjugate and exploit Florida.

NARWHAL, *Monodon monoceros*, a "toothed whale" of the Arctic. The teeth are completely absent in both sexes except for a single spiral tusk in the male on the left-hand side of the jaw. This tusk may be up to 2.5m (8.2ft) long; its function is unknown. It is believed that narwhal tusks were once thought to be the horns of unicorns.

NASA. See NATIONAL AERONAUTICS AND SPACE ADMINISTRATION.

NASBY, Petroleum V. See LOCKE, DAVID ROSS.

NASH, John (1752–1835), British architect, famous for his development of Regent's Park and Regent St, London, begun 1811. He built the Royal Pavilion, Brighton, Sussex; redesigned St. James's Park, London; and began alterations to Buckingham Palace (1821). (See REGENCY STYLE.)

NASH, Ogden (1902–1971), US humorous poet with a witty, sometimes satirical style, punctuated by puns, asides, unconventional rhymes and unexpectedly long lines. He published 20 volumes of verse and wrote lyrics for musicals.

NASHE, Thomas (1567–1601?), English writer and satirical pamphleteer, whose *The unfortunate traveller, or, the life of Jacke Wilton* (1594) was the first English picaresque novel. He attacked the Puritans in the MARPRELATE controversy.

NASHUA, city in S N.H., seat of Hillsborough Co., on the Merrimack R. It produces paper products, shoes, electronic devices and chemicals. Pop 55 820.

NASHVILLE, capital city of Tenn., seat of Davidson Co., on the Cumberland R in N central Tenn. The last major battle of the Civil War was fought nearby (Dec. 1864). Nashville is a commercial, industrial and agricultural city; the center of the country music recording industry; and a religious educational and publishing center. Pop 448 003.

NASMYTH, James (1808–1890), Scottish engineer who invented many MACHINE TOOLS, including the steam hammer (1839).

NASSAU, capital city of the Bahama Islands, a port on NE New Providence Island. Long a pirate haunt, it is now a world-famous tourist resort. Pop 101 503.

NASSER, Gamal Abdel (1918–1970), Egyptian president and Arab leader. He led the military coup d'etat which overthrew King FAROUK I (1952), then ousted General NAGUIB and named himself prime minister (1954). He ended British military presence in Egypt (1954) and seized the SUEZ CANAL (1956). He was elected president of Egypt unopposed (1956), and was president of the UNITED ARAB REPUBLIC 1958–61. His "Arab socialism" policy brought new land ownership laws and agricultural policies, more schools, increased social services and widespread nationalization. He fought a brief war with Israel in 1956; after the disastrous 1967 "six-day war" with Israel, he resigned but resumed office by popular demand.

The narwhal's unique tusk may grow up to 2.5m (8.2ft) long. For centuries the tusk, thought to be unicorn's horn, was much valued as a medicine, and for making into drinking cups which were supposed to neutralize any poison.

NASSER, Lake, reservoir in Upper Egypt and N Sudan on the Nile R. Formed in the 1960s when the ASWAN HIGH DAM was built, its 1550sq mi submerged many historic sites.

NAST, Thomas (1840–1902), German-born US cartoonist, creator of the symbols for the Democratic Party (donkey) and the Republican Party (elephant). His attacks on the TAMMANY HALL political machine, symbolized as a tiger, contributed to its disintegration. Nast's drawings of SANTA CLAUS set a US popular image.

NASTURTIUM, general name for annual and perennial herbs of the genus *Tropaeolum* which are native to Mexico and temperate South America. The most widely cultivated species is *Tropaeolum majus*. Nasturtium leaves and stems have a pungent smell when crushed. Family: Tropaeolaceae.

NATAL, province of South Africa, on the Indian Ocean, 33 578sq mi in area, with capital Pietermaritzburg. It produces sugar, fruit, cereals and coal and manufactures fertilizers and textiles, mainly near

A commonly cultivated variety of the nasturtium (*Tropaeolum majus*).

Durban, the chief city. Natal was a British colony 1856–1910.

NATAL, capital city of Rio Grande do Norte State, NE Brazil. It is a seaport and a commercial and transportation center. Pop 270 124.

NATCHEZ, city in SW Miss., seat of Adams Co. The oldest city on the Mississippi R (established as a fort 1716), it was an important river port and cotton center. Today it retains antebellum character; major industries include lumber and petroleum. Pop 19 777.

NATCHEZ INDIANS, MUSKOGEAN-speaking tribe of SW Miss.; numbering about 6 000 in 1682. Primarily an agricultural people, they worshiped the sun and also maintained a rigid social caste system. They were driven from their villages near today's Natchez, Miss., after three wars with French settlers (1716, 1723, 1729), and mostly joined other tribes.

NATCHEZ TRACE, old road from Natchez, Miss., to Nashville, Tenn.; developed from Indian trails, it was of great importance c1780–1830. The **Natchez Trace National Parkway**, about 450mi long, follows the old route.

NATCHITOCHES, city in NW La., seat of Natchitoches Parish. It produces dairy and poultry products, cottonseed, oil and timber. Pop 15 974.

NATHAN, Israelite prophet who rebuked King David in a parable for seducing BATHSHEBA and having her husband Uriah killed. He secured the succession for Solomon.

NATHAN, George Jean (1882–1958), US editor and drama critic, author of numerous essays and of *The Theatre Book of the Year*, an annual 1943–51. With H. L. MENCKEN he edited *The Smart Set* and founded *American Mercury*.

NATHAN, Robert (1894–), US novelist and poet with a gently ironic style. Among his many novels, some fantasies, are *Peter Kindred* (1919), *One More Spring* (1933) and *Portrait of Jennie* (1940). His poetry collections include *The Green Leaf* (1950).

NATHANAEL, an early disciple of Jesus, mentioned only in John's Gospel, commonly identified with St. BARTHOLOMEW.

NATICK, residential town in NE Mass., 15mi WSW of Boston, with some light industry. Founded 1651 by John ELIOT for christianized Indians. Pop 31 057.

NATION, Carry Amelia (1846–1911), US temperance agitator. She began her campaign against liquor bars in the "dry" state of Kan. Formidable in size and appearance, from 1901 she smashed several saloons with a hatchet. Arrested on about 30 occasions, she paid fines by selling souvenir hatchets and lecturing. She was not supported by the national PROHIBITION movement.

NATIONAL ACADEMY OF DESIGN, US fine arts association, founded 1825. Membership is limited to 125 painters, 50 sculptors, 25 architects, 25 graphic artists and 25 aquarellists; associate membership is unlimited. It has a School of Fine Arts in New York City.

NATIONAL ACADEMY OF SCIENCES, private US organization of scientists and engineers, founded 1863. It officially advises the government on scientific questions, and coordinates major programs. Members are elected for distinguished research achievements.

NATIONAL AERONAUTICS AND SPACE ADMINISTRATION (NASA), US government agency responsible for nonmilitary SPACE EXPLORATION and related research. Founded by President Eisenhower (1958) as successor to the National Advisory Committee for Aeronautics (NACA), it has numerous research stations, laboratories and space flight launching centers, including Cape CANAVERAL and the Houston control center. Its headquarters are in Washington, D.C. The annual budget is about $3½ billion.

NATIONAL ANTHEM, official patriotic song or hymn of a nation, played or sung at state ceremonial occasions. The words of the US anthem, *The Star-Spangled Banner* (officially adopted 1916), were written in 1814 by Francis Scott KEY.

NATIONAL ARCHIVES AND RECORDS SERVICE. See ARCHIVES.

NATIONAL ASSOCIATION FOR THE ADVANCEMENT OF COLORED PEOPLE (NAACP), US voluntary interracial organization, founded in New York City (1909) to oppose RACISM and racial segregation and discrimination, and to ensure CIVIL RIGHTS AND LIBERTIES for black Americans. It works for the enactment and enforcement of civil rights laws, supports education programs and engages in direct action. An early success was the ending of LYNCHING. The NAACP Legal Defense and Education Fund was set up (1939) as its legal arm. NAACP's membership in the 1970s was about 450 000.

NATIONAL ASSOCIATION OF MANUFACTURERS (NAM), US organization of manufacturing companies, founded 1895 to coordinate their policies and represent them to the government and the public.

NATIONAL AUDUBON SOCIETY. See AUDUBON SOCIETY, NATIONAL.

NATIONAL BANK, a US commercial bank privately operated but chartered by the federal government. The First Bank (1791–1811) was proposed by Alexander HAMILTON; the Second Bank (1816–36) was attacked by President Jackson and its charter was not renewed. After a period of disorganized state banking, Acts of 1863 and 1864 authorized and regulated national banks, which issued national currency backed by federal bonds. From 1913 all national banks had to belong to the FEDERAL RESERVE SYSTEM.

NATIONAL BROADCASTING COMPANY (NBC). See BROADCASTING NETWORKS, US.

NATIONAL BUREAU OF STANDARDS (NBS), bureau of the US Department of Commerce, established 1901. It determines national WEIGHTS AND MEASURES, tests products and materials, and carries on research in science and technology. It also advises government agencies and industries on safety codes and technical specifications.

NATIONAL CAPITAL PARKS, system of parks, monuments and memorials in the area of Washington, D.C., the US capital, authorized by Congress in 1790. Its 7 024 acres contain 724 units in D.C., Md. and Va.

NATIONAL CITY, city in SW Cal. on San Diego Bay, 5mi S of San Diego. It is the Pacific Reserve Fleet headquarters and manufactures defense equipment. Pop 43 184.

NATIONAL COLLEGIATE ATHLETIC ASSOCIATION (NCAA), US advisory body founded 1906 to establish eligibility and competition rules for intercollegiate athletics. After 1921 most other college sports came under its jurisdiction. The NCAA compiles statistics on college sports and publishes rule books and guides. It has over 700 member institutions.

NATIONAL CONFERENCE OF CHRISTIANS AND JEWS, US organization founded 1928 to fight prejudice, intolerance and bigotry and to promote interfaith harmony. The conference sponsors BROTHERHOOD WEEK. It has about 260 000 members.

NATIONAL CONGRESS OF PARENTS AND TEACHERS. See PARENTS AND TEACHERS, NATIONAL CONGRESS OF.

NATIONAL COUNCIL OF THE CHURCHES OF CHRIST IN THE USA, organization of 33 Protestant and Eastern Orthodox churches (with combined membership 42 million), founded 1950 to promote interdenominational cooperation and understanding. It has educational, evangelistic, ecumenical, political and relief programs, and has allied itself with many other church bodies and missionary societies.

NATIONAL DEBT, the amount of money owed by a government, borrowed to pay expenses not covered by taxation revenue. The US national debt is now more than $400 billion. National debts are incurred to pay for wars, public construction programs etc. To obtain money, governments sell BONDS or short-term certificates to banks, other organizations and individuals. Some governments in crisis have defaulted or devalued the currency. The **public debt** includes not only the national debt but also debts of individual states, cities etc. (See also FUNDED DEBT.)

NATIONAL DEFENSE EDUCATION ACT (NDEA), US law passed 1958. It authorized massive federal aid to states and institutions to improve all areas of education, and set up low-interest loans to students. It prohibits federal control of educational programs or institutions.

NATIONAL EDUCATION ASSOCIATION OF THE UNITED STATES (NEA), organization of professional school teachers and administrators. Established 1857 to raise professional standards, it was chartered by Congress in 1907. The NEA works to improve education and to promote the welfare of its members.

NATIONAL FARMERS ORGANIZATION (NFO). See FARMERS ORGANIZATION, NATIONAL.

NATIONAL FARMERS UNION. See FARMERS UNION, NATIONAL.

NATIONAL FORESTS, US forests and grasslands under the management and protection of the FOREST SERVICE. They produce timber and provide recreation, grazing for livestock, and a protected environment for wildlife. The national forests include about 187 million acres in 44 states, Puerto Rico and the Virgin Islands.

NATIONAL GALLERY OF ART, US museum of nationally-owned works of art, opened 1941, in Washington, D.C. It is part of the SMITHSONIAN INSTITUTION. The initial collection was donated by Andrew MELLON (1937). The gallery possesses Jan van Eyck's *The Annunciation* and Raphael's *The Alba Madonna*; it has many works by Italian, French and American artists.

NATIONAL GEOGRAPHIC SOCIETY, nonprofit scientific and educational organization, established in Washington, D.C. (1888) "for the increase and diffusion of geographic knowledge." It publishes *National Geographic Magazine*, books, maps and school bulletins, and sponsors projects such as Admiral BYRD's polar expeditions, LEAKEY's anthropological research in Africa and the US expedition to Mt Everest (1963). It has a worldwide membership of more than 5 500 000.

NATIONAL GUARD, volunteer reserve groups of the US Army and Air Force, with a combined authorized strength of about 500 000, originating in the volunteer militia organized in 1792. Each state, territory, and the District of Columbia has its National Guard units, paid, equipped and supervised by the federal government since 1903 with partial state support. Army units are directed by the National Guard Bureau of the Department of the Army and air units by the Department of the Air Force. The National Defense Acts of 1920 and 1933 empower the president to call up units in time of national crisis. Governors may call up state units during strikes, riots, disasters and other emergencies—in recent years National Guard units have checked civil disturbances, often amid controversy. A guardsman takes a dual oath—to the federal government and to his state. In peacetime he attends 48 drill sessions and a two-week training camp annually.

NATIONAL INSTITUTES OF HEALTH (NIH), research agency of the US Public Health Service, Department of Health, Education and Welfare. It supports over one-third of the nation's medical research through nine institutes, a clinical center, fellowships and grants to medical and dental schools and universities. It also distributes biological and medical information.

NATIONALISM, political and social attitude of groups of people who share a common culture, language and territory as well as common aims and purposes, and thus feel a deep-seated loyalty to the group to which they belong, as opposed to other groups. Nationalism in the modern sense dates from the FRENCH REVOLUTION, but had its roots in the rise of strong centralized monarchies, in the economic doctrine of MERCANTILISM and the growth of a substantial middle class. Nationalism today is also associated with any drive for national unification or independence. It can represent a destructive force in multinational states.

NATIONALITY, in law, recognized membership of a particular country. Nations themselves determine who their nationals are. Two basic principles for deciding nationality are acknowledged by most countries: *jus sanguinis*, the right of blood, based on the nationality of a parent; and *jus soli*, the right of place of birth. (See also CITIZENSHIP; NATURALIZATION.)

Facsimile of a monolithic pre-Columbian head from Laventa, Mexico, in the hall of the National Geographic Society's headquarters in Washington, D.C.

NATIONALIZATION, transfer of ownership and control of an industrial or agricultural enterprise or other property from private individuals or corporations to the state. In law, governments usually possess the right to take over private property for public purposes; in modern times nationalization has often been used to implement socialist or communist theories of government.

NATIONAL LABOR RELATIONS ACT. See WAGNER ACT.

NATIONAL LABOR RELATIONS BOARD (NLRB), independent US government agency designed to prevent or correct unfair labor practices. Originally set up to administer the National Labor Relations Act of 1935 and protect fledgling unions from illegal interference, the board has since been granted power to police both illegal union and management practices. Its actions are subject, however, to approval by the federal courts.

NATIONAL MEDIATION BOARD, independent US federal agency which mediates and arbitrates in labor disputes threatening to disrupt interstate (airline and railroad) commerce. Its arbitration decisions are legally binding.

NATIONAL MONETARY COMMISSION. See ALDRICH, NELSON WILMARTH.

NATIONAL MOTTO. See E PLURIBUS UNUM.

NATIONAL OCEANIC AND ATMOSPHERIC ADMINISTRATION (NOAA), US government agency set up in 1970 to coordinate scientific research into atmosphere and oceans. Its specific aims are the monitoring and control of POLLUTION and the investigation of potential resources and weather-control techniques. The NOAA is responsible for the work of several formerly independent agencies including the Coast and Geodetic Survey (founded in 1807) and the Weather Bureau (founded in 1870).

NATIONAL PARK SYSTEM, system administered by the US National Park Service, a bureau of the Department of the Interior, whereby land of outstanding scenic or historical interest is protected "for the benefit and enjoyment of the people." The national park idea originated in the US; descriptions in 1870–71 of the wild country at the headwaters of the Yellowstone R in Wyo. led in 1872 to an Act of Congress creating Yellowstone National Park (2 221 733 acres). In Cal., Sequoia and Yosemite were declared parks in 1890, but few other sites were brought under protection until 1916, when President Woodrow Wilson instituted the Park Service. Today it administers more than 46 000sq mi of parkland, comprising about 300 protected areas—and the number is still growing. Of this land, 38 outstanding scenic areas are known simply as national parks. Another 82, combining scenery with precolonial history, natural or man-made objects, or geological, zoological or botanical phenomena, are called national monuments. The other 178 areas include battlefields (such as Gettysburg), forts and trading posts, pioneer trails, cemeteries, recreation areas, scenic lake shores and water-ways, important birthplaces (Washington's, Lincoln's), the National Scientific Reserve, the Statue of Liberty, memorials such as the Washington Monument and Mt Rushmore, and the White House. The service also protects shorelines in danger of erosion. (See also NATIONAL CAPITAL PARKS.)

NATIONAL RECOVERY ADMINISTRATION (NRA), principal government agency set up under the NEW DEAL by the National Industrial Recovery Act of 1933 to administer codes of fair practice for businesses and industries. Promise of higher prices and wages stimulated a minor boom which soon collapsed. By early 1934 the laboriously-negotiated codes had become intolerably cumbersome; and in May 1935 the Supreme Court ruled it unconstitutional. It was later abolished by the president.

NATIONAL REPUBLICAN PARTY, American political party formed when the Democratic-Republican Party split up in the 1828 presidential election. The party's candidate in 1832, Henry CLAY, was routed and during JACKSON's presidency, in 1836, the party merged with other political groups to form the WHIG party.

NATIONAL ROAD, famous old paved road for settlers emigrating to the West. It ran from Cumberland, Md., through Vandalia, Ill. to St. Louis, Mo. The first section, as far as Wheeling, W Va. (the Cumberland Road) was opened in 1818. Today's US Highway 40 closely follows the original route.

NATIONAL SCIENCE FOUNDATON (NSF), US federal agency set up in 1950. It promotes research, education and international exchange in the sciences and funds fellowships, projects such as the International Decade of Ocean Exploration, and several permanent observatories.

NATIONAL SECURITY COUNCIL (NSC), US defense council created by Congress in 1947 as part of the executive office of the president, to advise him on a wide range of matters relating to national security and defense policies. Chaired by the president, its permanent members include the vice-president, secretaries of state and defense and the directors of the office of mobilization and the foreign operations administration.

NATIONAL SOCIALISM. See NAZISM.

NATIONAL WAR COLLEGE, school for selected army, navy, air force, state department and other governmental personnel, established (1949) in Washington, D.C. and now under the authority of the JOINT CHIEFS OF STAFF.

NATIONAL WILDLIFE FEDERATION, US organization founded in 1936 to educate and interest the public in preservation of the country's wildlife and nature heritage. It issues relevant publications and helps finance local conservation projects and research. There are over 2 million members.

NATIONAL YOUTH ADMINISTRATION (NYA), US agency set up under the NEW DEAL in 1935 to provide job training for unemployed youths and to find part-time work for students. It was abolished in 1943.

NATIVISM, turning in of a country or society towards its own culture through movements rejecting foreign influences, ideas or immigrants; largely an anthropological term. Nativism is brought on by social stress or disintegration, as with primitive peoples faced by Western civilization. For notable examples of nativist movements in American history see KNOW-NOTHING; KU KLUX KLAN. (See also CHAUVINISM.)

NATO. See NORTH ATLANTIC TREATY ORGANIZATION.

NATTA, Giulio (1903–), Italian chemist awarded (with ZIEGLER) the 1963 Nobel Prize for Chemistry for his synthesis of POLYMERS of propene (one of the ALKENES). These have industrially desirable properties such as high melting point and strength.

NAT TURNER'S REBELLION, or the Southampton Insurrection, the largest slave uprising in US history, leading to harsher slave laws in the South and the eclipse of emancipation societies. On Aug. 21, 1831, Nat Turner, a Negro slave and Baptist preacher, believing himself called to free his fellow slaves, murdered his master, John Travis of Southampton Co., Va., and led a brief campaign in which 55 whites were killed. He was captured on Oct. 22, tried and hanged.

NATURAL BRIDGES NATIONAL MONUMENT, established 1908, an area of cliffs and box canyons (12sq mi) in SE Utah, 42mi W of Blanding. The largest of the three natural sandstone bridges, Sipapu, has a span of 268ft and rises to 220ft.

NATURAL GAS, mixture of gaseous HYDROCARBONS occurring in reservoirs of porous rock (commonly sand or sandstone) capped by impervious strata. It is often associated with PETROLEUM, with which it has a common origin in the decomposition of organic matter in sedimentary deposits. Natural gas consists largely of METHANE and ETHANE, with also propane and butane (separated for BOTTLED GAS), some higher ALKANES (used for GASOLINE), nitrogen, oxygen, carbon dioxide, hydrogen sulfide, and sometimes valuable HELIUM. It is used as an industrial and domestic FUEL, and also to make carbon-black and in chemical synthesis. Natural gas is transported by large pipelines or (as a liquid) in refrigerated tankers. Total world reserves are estimated at $54 \times 10^{12}m^3$, of which the USSR and the US together have about half; there are major fields also in the Netherlands, Algeria and the Middle East.

NATURALISM, attempt to apply the scientific view of the natural world to philosophy and the arts. There is nothing real beyond nature; man is thus a prisoner of his environment and heredity. This aesthetic movement, inspired by Émile ZOLA's argument for a scientific approach to literature in *The Experimental Novel* (1880), had a profound affect on the fine arts, literature and drama. Zola's ideas influenced many writers—Guy de MAUPASSANT, as well as Stephen CRANE and Theodore DREISER in the US; dramatists from Scandinavia's Henrik IBSEN and August STRINDBERG to Russia's Maxim GORKI and the modern American playwrights Arthur MILLER and Tennessee WILLIAMS; and painters such as COURBET, VAN GOGH, and the Impressionists.

NATURALIZATION, process whereby a resident alien obtains citizenship of a country. In the US, under the Immigration and Nationality Act of 1952, an alien is eligible for naturalization if he is over 18, entered the country legally and has resided there for at

Natural gas accounts for more than a fourth of the energy requirements of the United States. It is piped from the gasfields at high pressure through pipelines like the one under construction here.

least five years, is of "good moral character," names two referees who can vouch for his qualifications, can demonstrate familiarity with written and spoken English and American history and government, and is prepared to renounce all foreign allegiances and take an oath of loyalty and service to his new country. Citizenship may be granted on the recommendation of the immigration service after a court hearing. Alien wives of Americans may normally apply for naturalization after three years' residence. Naturalization of resident aliens in Canada proceeds on much the same lines as in the US, except that the minimum age is 21, and two court hearings are required before the citizenship oath is taken.

NATURAL LAW, the body of law supposed to be innate, discoverable by natural human reason, and common to all mankind. Under this philosophy, man-made or *positive* law, though changeable and culturally dependent, must—if truly just—be derived from the principles of natural law. The concept was rooted in Greek philosophy (see STOICISM) and Roman law, and particularly in the Christian philosophy of Thomas AQUINAS, where natural law—the sense of right and wrong implanted in men by God—is contrasted with revealed law (see REVELATION). It lay behind GROTIUS's ideas on international law (17th century). It was used as a basis for ethics, morality, and even for protests against tyranny by SPINOZA, LEIBNIZ, LOCKE, ROUSSEAU and many others, but with the development of scientific philosophies in the 19th century, natural law largely lost its influence.

NATURAL NUMBERS, the SET of all positive INTEGERS.

NATURAL RESOURCES, Conservation of. See CONSERVATION; RECYCLING.

NATURAL SELECTION, mechanism for the process of EVOLUTION discovered by Charles DARWIN in the late 1830s, but not made public until 1858. According to Darwin, evolution occurs when an organism is confronted by a changing environment. A degree of variety is always present in the members of an interbreeding population. Normally, the possession of a variant character by an individual confers no particular advantage on it, and the proportion of individuals in the population with a given variation remains constant. But if it ever arises in a changed environment that a given variation increases the chances of an individual's survival, then individuals possessing that character will be more liable to survive—and breed. The frequency with which the variant character occurs in future generations of the organism will thus increase, and, over a large number of generations, the general form of the population will change. The name "natural selection" derives from the analogy Darwin saw between this selection on the part of "Nature" and the "artificial selection" practiced by animal breeders.

NATURAL THEOLOGY, the knowledge of God and religious truth obtainable by natural human reason unaided by divine REVELATION. It includes the existence and attributes of GOD deduced from creation, the immortality of the soul, and NATURAL LAW. It was developed in medieval SCHOLASTICISM, but downgraded in REFORMATION theology and denied absolutely in NEO-ORTHODOXY.

NAUGATUCK, borough in SW Conn., 5mi S of Waterbury on the Naugatuck R. It has diversified industries. Pop 23 034.

NAURU, independent island republic (about 8sq mi) in the W Pacific Ocean, W of Gilbert Islands, 40mi S of the equator. The Polynesian population's revenue comes from phosphate rock covering the central plateau. A UN trusteeship from 1947, Nauru (formerly Pleasant Island) became independent in 1968 and joined the British Commonwealth in 1969.

NAUSICAÄ, in the ODYSSEY, daughter of Alcinous, king of Phaeacia. Finding the shipwrecked Odysseus, she led him to the palace, where he was feted before returning at last to Ithaca.

NAUTICAL MILE. See MILE.

NAUTILUS, or paper nautilus, a cephalopod mollusk with a pearly, gas-filled external shell. (See ARGONAUT.)

NAUTILUS, U.S.S., first nuclear-powered submarine, launched in Jan. 1955. Capable of submerged speed of over 20 knots, she made the first transpolar voyage passing beneath the North Pole on Aug. 3, 1958.

NAUVOO, city in W Ill., on the Mississippi R, 45mi N of Quincy. It was the home of the Mormons from 1839 to 1846 with a population of 20 000; later it was settled by Icarians (1849–56), socialists led by CABET. Pop 1 047.

NAVAHO INDIANS (or Navajo), migrants from the N who settled around 1000 AD in Ariz. and N.M.; cousins to the APACHE Indians. They learned agriculture, weaving and sand painting from the PUEBLO Indians. After the Spanish introduced sheep in the 1600s, they became pastoralists. Inveterate raiders of Spanish and American settlements in the SW, they were finally subdued (1864) by Kit CARSON and held at Fort Sumner, N.M. until their resettlement on a reservation in 1868. Today there are about 100 000 Navahos. The Navaho culture has an elaborate mythology and religion; their folk art includes painting, silver-working and the weaving of rugs and blankets.

NAVAJO NATIONAL MONUMENT, ruins of cliff dwellings, occupied by early Indians around the 13th century. Situated in NE Ariz. on a 360-acre site, it was established in 1909.

NAVAL OBSERVATORY, US, source of official standard time in the US. Founded in Washington D.C., in 1833, the observatory has moved several times to obtain better observing conditions. Since 1955 its main station has been in Flagstaff, Ariz.

NAVAL STORES, products derived from coniferous trees, especially the pine, such as PITCH, rosin (see RESIN), TAR and TURPENTINE. The name comes from the use of these (and other) materials in building and repairing wooden sailing ships.

NAVARINO, Battle of, naval action in the Greek War of Independence (Oct. 1827). It resulted in the destruction of an Egyptian fleet by a combined English–French–Russian fleet intervening on the side of Greece. This was the last major conflict between wooden sailing ships.

NAVARRE, BASQUE province in N Spain. Formerly an independent Basque kingdom, it was important in international politics as a buffer state between Spain and France because it controlled a principal mountain pass (RONCESVALLES) into Spain. Navarre was conquered in 1512 by Ferdinand of Aragon; it sank to provincial status in 1841. The northern part of Navarre remained independent until 1589, when Henry IV became ruler of France and Navarre. Today the area is part of the French department, Basses-Pyrénées.

NAVEL. See UMBILICAL CORD.

NAVIGATION, the art and science of directing a vessel from one place to another. Originally navigation applied only to marine vessels, but now air navigation and, increasingly, space navigation are also important. Although the techniques and applications of navigation have radically changed through time, the basic problems, and hence the principles, have remained much the same.

Marine Navigation. Primitive sailors could not venture out of sight of land without the risk of getting lost. But soon they learned to use sunset and sunrise, the prevailing winds, the POLE STAR and so forth as aids to direction. Early on, the first FATHOMETER, a weighted rope used to measure depth, was developed. Before the 10th century AD the magnetic COMPASS had appeared. But it was not until the 1730s that the inventions of the SEXTANT and CHRONOMETER heralded the dawn of accurate sea navigation. Both LATITUDE AND LONGITUDE could now be determined within reasonable tolerances. (See also ASTROLABE; GREENWICH OBSERVATORY.)

Modern navigation uses electronic aids such as LORAN and the radiocompass; celestial navigation, the determination of position by sightings of celestial bodies, and dead reckoning where, by knowing one's position at a particular past time, the time that has elapsed since, one's direction and speed (see LOG), one can tell one's present position. (See also DIRECTION FINDER; ECHO SOUNDER; MAP; SONAR; SUBMARINE.)

Air Navigation uses many of the principles of marine navigation. In addition, the pilot must work in a third dimension, must know his altitude (see ALTIMETER), and in bad visibility must use aids like the INSTRUMENT LANDING SYSTEM. RADAR is also used.

Space Navigation is a science in its infancy. Like air navigation, it works in three dimensions, but the problems are exacerbated by the motions both of one's source (the earth) and one's destination, as well as by the distances involved. But, prior to developments in new areas, it seems that SPACE EXPLORATION has inaugurated a new era in navigation by the stars. (See also CELESTIAL SPHERE; GYROCOMPASS; GYROPILOT; REMOTE CONTROL.)

NAVIGATION ACTS, laws regulating navigation at sea or in port, or restricting commercial shipping in the national interest. More specifically, regulations promulgated (from 1650) by the British during the American colonial period to try to insure that benefits of commerce would accrue to England (and to a lesser extent, the colonies) rather than to England's enemies. After 1763, strict enforcement of the acts caused friction between England and the American colonies and was a major factor leading to the outbreak of the REVOLUTIONARY WAR.

NAVY, a seaborne armed force maintained for national defense or attack. In ancient times, armed men usually put to sea to explore or raid distant territories. Assyria, Egypt and Phoenicia each deployed merchant fleets on military tasks. Among the first to create a permanent naval force were the Athenians. Their armed *triremes* (galleys with three tiers of oars) defeated the Persians at SALAMIS (480 BC) and were adopted by Carthage and later Rome, who, after the naval battle at ACTIUM in 31 BC, ruled the Mediterranean for 400 years. In Scandinavia, the VIKINGS created marauding fleets which ravaged the coasts of Europe from c800 AD for over 200 years. Only ALFRED THE GREAT withstood their raids by creating an English naval task force. Byzantium, Genoa, Venice and other Italian republics, the Arabs and Turks developed powerful navies in the Mediterranean. By the late 16th century most western European nations had acquired naval forces. Spain emerged as the leading naval power, but after her ARMADA was defeated by the English in 1588, England had mastery of the seas. Her naval supremacy was challenged by Holland (see DUTCH WARS) and France, but the Battle of TRAFALGAR in 1805 restored it for another 100 years. A powerful navy ensured that a country could maintain an overseas empire and world influence. Large armored BATTLESHIPS (called *dreadnoughts*) were built from before WWI, until they were outmoded in WWII. The submarine and the aircraft carrier then took over. In the postwar period, Britain was overshadowed as a leading naval power by the US and the USSR. The strike power of modern navies, capable of nuclear warfare, assures them a prominent place in the superpowers' armed forces in the future. (See also NAVY, UNITED STATES.)

NAVY, Department of the, one of three major divisions within the US Defense Department. Founded in 1798, it provides the administrative headquarters, in Washington, D.C., for the US Navy and Marine Corps, and in war, sometimes for the US Coastguard as well.

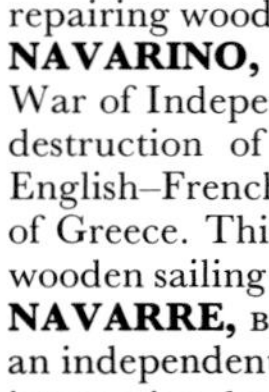

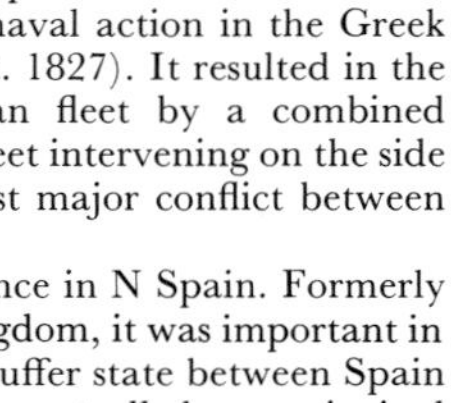

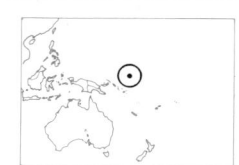

Official Name: Nauru
Capital: Nauru
Area: 8·2sq mi
Population: 6 768
Languages: Nauruan, English
Monetary Unit: Australian Dollar (A£) = 100 cents

Among the early devices used for navigation were the forestaff, the hourglass and the chip log. The fore staff (left) enabled a navigator to fix his position by moving the crosspieces along the staff in a line with the noonday sun or a polar star. The hourglass and chip log were used together to determine the speed of a ship. Weighted at the bottom and attached to a line, the chip log was thrown into the water, and the line was allowed to pay out. The length of line paid out in a time measured by the hourglass enabled the navigator to determine the speed of the ship.

NAVY, Royal Canadian, renamed (1968) under the Canadian Forces Reorganization Act as the Maritime Command, one of five commands under the Canadian Armed Forces. It was formed in 1910.

NAVY, United States, the branch of the US armed forces designed to maintain command of the sea, especially in regions considered vital to the defense of the US. It began in the American Revolution, when the Continental Congress voted (1775) the first naval budget to outfit ships designed to harry British naval ships. After the Revolution the US Navy was disbanded, but in 1794 Congress authorized six frigates to be built and used against the persistent attacks of pirates on American shipping off the North African coast. By 1798 the Navy Department was established. US navy ships helped suppress piracy and some slave trading, and were active in the MEXICAN WAR. In the American CIVIL WAR the Union navy was active in blockading Confederate ports. (See MONITOR AND MERRIMACK.) The outbreak of the SPANISH–AMERICAN WAR in 1898 brought the US to the forefront of the world's seapowers, second only to Great Britain. America entered WWII when much of the US Pacific fleet had been destroyed at PEARL HARBOR. The US Navy played a decisive role in halting the Japanese advance in the Pacific, in the Battle of the CORAL SEA and the Battle of MIDWAY (1942). Leading developments after the war were the nuclear-powered submarine (the US Navy commissioned the first, called *Nautilus*) and missiles (*Polaris* and *Poseidon*) carried on surface ships and submarines. By 1965, US fleets covered the oceans of the world. In 1976 the US Navy's fleet consisted of 479 combat and support ships and submarines—its smallest size since 1939; but its strength was expected to increase by about 4% per year for the following five years. (See NAVY; NAVY, DEPARTMENT OF THE; see also MARINE CORPS, UNITED STATES.)

The greatest single influence on naval development since WWII has been the introduction of nuclear power as both weapon and motive force, as in the US Navy's nuclear-powered guided missile frigates (*top*) and nuclear submarines (*bottom*); increased speed and mobility give them strike capacity out of proportion to their size.

NÁXOS, island in SE Greece, largest (165sq mi) of the CYCLADES in the Aegean Sea. It exports marble, granite, emery, wine and citrus fruits. An ancient Mycenaean settlement has been excavated there.

NAYARIT, state in W Mexico, on the central Pacific coast and rising into the Sierra–Madre Occidental, with an area of 10 664sq mi. Its capital is Tepic.

NAZARENE, Church of the. See CHURCH OF THE NAZARENES.

NAZARENES, group of German painters who founded the "Brotherhood of St. Luke" in 1809 with the aim of returning to the simplicity and piety of medieval art. They influenced the painters of the PRE-RAPHAELITE BROTHERHOOD.

NAZARETH, historic town in N Israel, lower Galilee, where Jesus Christ lived as a youth. A place of Christian pilgrimage, the town has many shrines and churches. It also has some light industry and is an agricultural market center. Pop 34 000.

NAZISM, or National Socialism, the creed of the National Socialist German Workers' Party (Nazi Party) led by Adolf HITLER from 1921 to 1945. The Nazi movement began (1918–19) when Germany was humiliated and impoverished by defeat in WWI and by the severe terms of the Treaty of VERSAILLES. There was growing economic, political and social chaos, and fear of increasing communist influence. The Nazi Party emerged as a political force during the worldwide GREAT DEPRESSION. From a membership of around 100 000 in 1928, the party increased in strength to 920 000 in 1932. Using Hitler's powerful talent for public oratory and propaganda, the Nazis set forth a program designed to appeal to the grievances of as wide a range of German society as possible. The ideas behind the program were rooted in nationalism, racism (especially ANTI-SEMITISM), authoritarianism and militarism. They were expressed by Hitler in *Mein Kampf* (*My Struggle*, 1923). Recovery of the German nation was to be accomplished by rearmament, territorial expansion to acquire *Lebensraum* (living space) for the Teutonic *Herrenrasse* (master race) and the restoration of self-respect under a unified military regime—*Ein Reich, Ein Volk, Ein Führer* (one state, one nation, one leader). The movement continued to grow, aided by publicity techniques, military pageantry and intimidation and terrorization of opponents by the party's brown-shirted militia, the *Sturm-Abteilung* (S.A.). In 1932 the Nazi party won more than one-third of the seats in the German parliament (*Reichstag*) and in Jan. 1933 politicians who hoped to be able to manipulate Hitler and use his political power base made him chancellor. In 1933–34 he reversed the situation by establishing a Nazi dictatorship. With the aid of the secret police (GESTAPO) and the S.A., Hitler began systematically to intern Jews, other non-Aryans and any opposing groups including labor unions and political parties in CONCENTRATION CAMPS. In the 1940s many of these were used for the systematic extermination of millions of Jews. Hitler's Nazi program of expansionism temporarily improved the German economic position, but led to WORLD WAR II, which resulted in the defeat of Germany and its allies and the end of the Nazi Party. (See also GERMANY; FASCISM.)

NCAA. See NATIONAL COLLEGIATE ATHLETIC ASSOCIATION.

NDJAMENA, formerly Fort-Lamy, largest city and capital of the Republic of Chad, on the Chari R. It is a transportation and commercial center. Pop 179 000.

The entrance to the Grotto of the Annunciation in the ancient town of Nazareth. It has long been venerated in the western Church as the place where the angel Gabriel announced to Mary that she was to become the mother of Christ.

NEANDERTHAL MAN. See PREHISTORIC MAN.
NEARCHUS (d. c312 BC), Cretan-born general under ALEXANDER THE GREAT. On Alexander's return from India Nearchus commanded the fleet which sailed down the Indus R and up the Persian coast.
NEARSIGHTEDNESS. See MYOPIA.
NEBO, Mount, 11 877ft high peak in Juab Co., W Ut. Also the Biblical name of the highest peak of a ridge of the Abarim Mts in Transjordan.
NEBRASKA, W central state of the US, bounded on the E by the Missouri R, on the S by Kan., on the SW and W by Col. and Wyo. and on the N by S.D.
Land. Nebraska is an undulating plain which slopes gradually from NW to SE. Over half of the state's 77 227sq mi are covered with fertile soil. Most of W Neb. consists of semiarid high plains, often broken by rugged hills called buttes. In the NW corner of the state lie 1 000sq mi of BADLANDS, used mostly for grazing. The state is crossed by many rivers (notably the Platte) which drain into the Missouri. There are over 2 000 lakes. The climate is unpredictable, marked by extremes of cold and heat.
People. Although Nebraska is primarily an agricultural state, just over half its people live in urban areas. About 97% of the population is native born. About one-third have German ancestors; other large groups which settled the state were the English and the Irish.
Economy. The state's chief field crop is corn, followed by wheat, hay, grain and sorghum. The production of beef cattle ranks just below Tex. and Ia. Food processing is the most important industry; other major industries are electrical machinery, chemicals, printing, metal products and transportation equipment.
History. In 1541 CORONADO's expedition reached the state, and in the 17th and 18th centuries the French established fur trading centers. Nebraska became part of the US with the LOUISIANA PURCHASE (1803), was set up as a territory under the KANSAS–NEBRASKA ACT (1854) and joined the Union in 1867. When the railroad crossed the state in that year, hordes of settlers began to move in. In the next two decades the pioneer farmers were active in the GRANGER and POPULIST movements. The state's prosperity depended upon agricultural productivity, and natural disasters and the Great Depression brought much hardship. After WWII increasing farm mechanization and new industries benefited the state's economy and steady growth.

Name of State: Nebraska
Capital: Lincoln
Statehood: March 1, 1867 (37th state)
Familiar Name: Cornhusker State, Beef State
Area: 77 227sq mi
Population: 1 483 791
Elevation: Highest—5 424ft, Kimball County
Lowest—840ft, Missouri River in Richardson County
Motto: Equality before the Law
State Flower: Goldenrod
State Bird: Western meadowlark
State Tree: American elm
State Song: "Beautiful Nebraska"

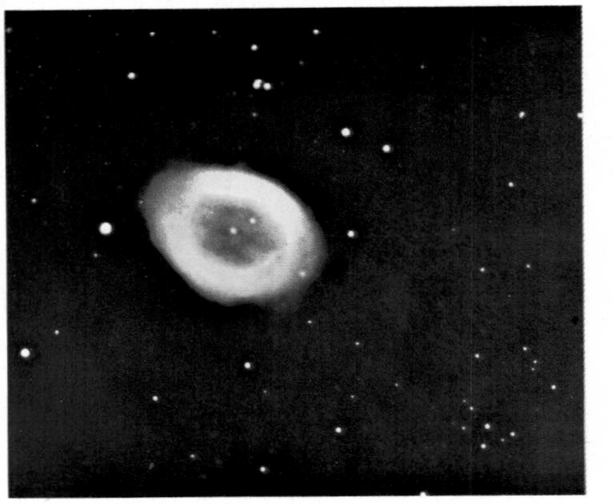

Nebulae are clouds of dust or gas floating in interstellar space. The Orion Nebula (*top*) is a bright nebula of particular interest because new stars appear to be forming within it. The Ring Nebula (*bottom*) in Lyra is a planetary nebula, a diffuse sphere of incandescent gases thrown off by the central star.

NEBUCHADNEZZAR, name of three kings of Babylonia. **Nebuchadnezzar I** (ruled c1124–1103 BC) conquered ELAM and extended Babylonian rule over most of ancient Mesopotamia. **Nebuchadnezzar II** (c630–562 BC) waged many military campaigns to consolidate the Neo-Babylonian or Chaldean Empire (see BABYLONIA AND ASSYRIA). He crushed the kingdom of Judah, destroyed Jerusalem (586), and took many captive Jews to Babylon. **Nebuchadnezzar III** (6th century BC), usurped the throne from DARIUS I for ten weeks before he was killed.
NEBULA, an interstellar cloud of gas or dust. The term is Latin, meaning "cloud," and was initially used to denote any fuzzy celestial object, including COMETS and external GALAXIES: this practice has now largely been abandoned. There are two main types of nebula. **Diffuse nebulae** are large, formless clouds of gas and dust and may be either bright or dark. *Bright nebulae*, such as the ORION Nebula, appear to shine due to the proximity or more usually presence within them of bright stars, whose light they either reflect (reflection nebula) or absorb and reemit (emission nebula). *Dark nebulae*, such as the Horsehead Nebula, are not close to, or do not contain, any bright stars, and hence appear as dark patches in the sky obscuring the light from stars beyond them. Study of diffuse nebulae is particularly important since it is generally accepted that they are in the process of condensing to form new STARS. **Planetary nebulae** are very much smaller, and are always connected with a star that has gone NOVA some time in the past. They are, in fact, the material that has been cast off by the star. They are usually symmetrical, forming an expanding shell around the central star, which is often still visible within. The Ring Nebula is an outstanding example.
NEBULAR HYPOTHESIS, theory accounting for the origin of the solar system put forward by LAPLACE. It suggested that a rotating NEBULA had formed gaseous rings which condensed into the planets and moons, the nebula's nucleus forming the sun.
NECESSITY, as contrasted with CONTINGENCY, in LOGIC, the property whereby a statement must be either true or false, this depending on the correct use of language in framing the statement. The statement "this leaf of paper has two sides" is a necessary truth since if it had either more or less than two sides it would not be a leaf according to the normal usage of the term.
NECESSITY, Fort, entrenchment built by George WASHINGTON in SW Pa. in July 1754, at Great Meadows. The clash with French troops which led to Washington's surrender on July 4 was one of the early battles in the last of the FRENCH AND INDIAN WARS.
NECESSITY AND SUFFICIENCY, in mathematical ANALYSIS, conditions which describe the validity of a statement. For example, for $4 < a < 10$ it is *necessary* that, say, $3 < a < 11$ since if this were not true then the original statement would not be true; and *sufficient* that $5 < a < 9$, since if this is true it implies the truth of the original statement. More generally, in LOGIC, a condition is necessary for the truth of a statement if the falsehood of the condition implies the falsehood of the statement, and sufficient if the truth of the condition implies the truth of the statement. (See also NECESSITY.)
NECHO II (d. c595 BC), Egyptian ruler of the XXVIth dynasty (c610–595 BC). He aided the Assyrians against the Neo-Babylonians but was defeated by NEBUCHADNEZZAR II at Carchemish in 605 BC. He sent an expedition that circumnavigated Africa, as recounted by HERODOTUS.
NECKAR RIVER, river in West Germany. It rises in the Black Forest and winds 228mi in a northerly direction to empty into the Rhine at Mannheim.
NECKER, Jacques (1732–1804), French banker; finance minister under LOUIS XVI. In 1777 he tried to raise money to support French involvement in the American Revolution. Later, before the States General, he proposed wide-sweeping public reforms, but opposition forced his resignation in 1790.
NECROMANCY, the belief that the future can be predicted by communication with the spirits of the dead. A common belief in ancient times, necromancy is condemned by the Christian church.
NECROPOLIS (Greek: city of the dead), a term applied to large cemeteries of ancient cities such as that found at MEMPHIS in Egypt.
NECROSIS, the death of body cells due to disease. (See DEATH.)
NECTAR, a sweet viscous secretion containing from 5% to 80% SUGAR, produced by the stems, leaves and flowers of higher plants. By attracting insects it facilitates POLLINATION. Nectars with over 15% sugar are used by honey BEES to make HONEY.
NECTAR, in Greek mythology, the drink of the gods. Together with ambrosia, their food, it brought youth and immortality.
NECTARINE. See PEACH.
NEDERLAND, city in SE Tex., in the Beaumont-Port Arthur area. It has oil refineries and manufactures related products. Pop 16 810.
NEEDHAM, town in E Mass., on the Charles R. It is a residential suburb of Boston with some light industry. Pop 29 748.
NEEDLEFISH. See GAR.
NEEDLEPOINT. See LACE.
NEEDLEWORK, work using a needle either for plain sewing like mending, darning, sewing seams or hemming, or for decorative embroidery such as smocking, needlepoint or canvas work (needlework on canvas backing), and drawnthread work. Quilting involves sewing together two layers of material with padding between; appliqué is attaching small pieces of material to a backing material. LACE may be made with a needle and thread, being then called needlepoint lace; TATTING employs shuttles, CROCHET employs a hook and KNITTING employs needles: all four are usually termed needlework. Samplers are traditional forms of recording various embroidery stitches and designs; one of the earliest, Jane Bostocke's (1598), includes satin, chain, ladder, buttonhole, arrowhead and cross stitches in metal thread and silk.
NÉEL, Louis Eugène Félix (1904–   ), French physicist awarded (with ALFVÉN) the 1970 Nobel Prize for Physics for his work on the magnetic properties of solids. His researches not only permitted

manufacture of products used in, e.g., computers, but also explained phenomena such as the recording by certain of the earth's rocks of past geomagnetic fields (see EARTH; PALEOMAGNETISM).

NEENAH, city in E central Wis., on Lake Winnebago. Menasha is its twin city on the N Fox R channel. Its main industry is papermaking. Pop 22 892.

NEFERTITI, or Nefretete (XVIII dynasty), queen of ancient Egypt, and subject of a famous painted limestone portrait bust now in the Berlin Museum. She was the wife of Pharaoh AKHENATON (reigned c1379–62 BC).

NEGEV, also Negeb, a triangular region of hills, plateaus and desert in S Israel, extending S from Beersheba to Eilat on the Gulf of Aqaba. It covers an area of around 5 000sq mi, over half of Israel. Although it is mainly an arid region, irrigation has made many areas fertile. It is rich in mineral and natural gas resources.

NEGLIGENCE, in law, inadvertent failure to act with the degree of care a situation demands. The degree may be determined by a contractual obligation or what the law defines as the standard of conduct of a "reasonable man." Conduct of an accident victim which contributed to his accident is contributory negligence, and may prevent him recovering compensation, or reduce the amount. Negligence is usually a civil offense, but may lead to a criminal charge such as MANSLAUGHTER.

NEGOTIABLE INSTRUMENTS, documents in the form of written contracts serving as substitutes for money, such as bills of exchange, drafts, promissory notes and checks. Transfer, often by endorsement (the signature of the original holder on the reverse of the document), allows the new holder the right to enforce payment against the maker of the instrument.

NEGRITOS, Spanish term applied to Negroid peoples of pygmy size living in various parts of the South Pacific. They include the Eta peoples of the Philippines.

NEGROES, American, descendants of Negro slaves brought from Africa to North America from the 16th to the 19th centuries. They belong to the Negroid race, although about one third of American Negroes possess some Caucasoid genes. Today there are about 24 million Negroes in the US, roughly the same number in South America and about 32 000 in Canada.

History. During the nearly 400 years of the slave trade, some 10–15 million slaves were brought to the Americas. The slaves were first brought over by the Spanish and Portuguese and then by the American colonists. The slave trade reached its height in the 18th century. After the Revolutionary War, however, it seemed for a time that slavery was dying out, with at least six states passing anti-slavery laws. This was all changed by Eli WHITNEY's invention of the cotton gin in 1793, for this made cotton a viable cash crop. The admission into the Union of the state of Louisiana (1812), quickly followed by Mississippi (1817) and Alabama (1819), opened up new lands for cotton and sugarcane. Although Congress prohibited the further importation of slaves (1808), the slave trade continued to flourish illegally, and by 1860 about half the population of the South were slaves. When the Civil War broke out there were nearly 4 million slaves in the US, plus about half a million freed slaves. However, the freed slaves never had a place in American society, and attempts were made to repatriate them to LIBERIA, on the W coast of Africa. The slavery issue was, of course, one of the main causes of the Civil War. While the slave-based cotton industry of the South had been booming, the North had been rejecting slavery. Of note are the founding of the American Anti-Slavery Society in 1833 (see ABOLITIONISM), and the publication in 1852 of Harriet Beecher STOWE's *Uncle Tom's Cabin*. The Civil War saw an end to slavery in the US, but it did little to improve the position of the freed Negro in American society. With the withdrawal of federal troops in 1877, the Negro in the South was soon reduced to a condition little better than that of slavery—it must be remembered that until the early 20th century, 90% of US Negroes lived in the South. Some Negro writers (e.g. Booker T. WASHINGTON) were willing to accept the position of the Negro as a second-class citizen, but others, including W. E. B. DU BOIS, the first Negro officer of the NATIONAL ASSOCIATION FOR THE ADVANCEMENT OF COLORED PEOPLE (founded in 1909), believed in fighting for Negro equality. But as is so often the case, economic change was a precursor to social and political change.

In the first half of the 20th century, some five million Negroes left the South for the overcrowded cities of the North. There the Negro could begin to have some political effect, and some individual Negroes were able to distinguish themselves professionally. However, it was not until the historic Supreme Court decision of May 17, 1954, ordering the integration of all schools, that the position of the Negro in American society began to change fundamentally. Under the leadership of Martin Luther KING, the civil rights movement spread all over the South, leading eventually to the voting rights Act of 1960, the anti-discrimination Act of 1964 and the Civil Rights Act of 1968. King, however, was out of touch with the problems of the Northern cities, which were more concerned with unemployment and poverty than the deliberate segregation by whites.

Between 1965 and 1967 many of the "Black ghettos" exploded into violence. The late 1960s saw the emergence of the BLACK POWER movement, with groups like the BLACK MUSLIMS and the BLACK PANTHERS. These groups rejected civil rights activity and wished to organize blacks into separate social and economic communities within a white America. By the mid-1970s, it seemed that while some of the more violent aspects of Black Power had dissipated themselves, American Negroes were asserting their own social and cultural identity. An indication of this was the rejection of the old term "Negro" in favor of "Black" or "Afro-American."

NEGROID, one of the racial divisions of man. The RACE is characterized by woolly hair and yellow, dark brown or black skin. Most negroid peoples originated in Africa, but Melanesians and Negritos are also negroid. (See also ANEMIA.)

NEHEMIAH (flourished 5th century BC), Jewish leader of the return from the BABYLONIAN CAPTIVITY. As described in the OLD TESTAMENT Book of Nehemiah (written with the Book of EZRA by the author of CHRONICLES), he rebuilt Jerusalem's walls and enforced moral and religious reforms.

NEHRU, Jawaharlal (1889–1964), first prime minister of independent India. An English-educated lawyer, he embraced the cause of India's freedom after the massacre at AMRITSAR (1919). In 1929 he became president of the Indian National Congress. He spent most of 1930–36 in prison for his part in civil disobedience campaigns. By 1939 his Marxist outlook had brought conflict to his long association with GANDHI, but during WWII the two leaders united in their opposition to aiding Britain unless India was freed. Released in 1945 after three years' imprisonment, Nehru began negotiations with Britain which culminated, in 1947, in the establishment of inde-

1

2
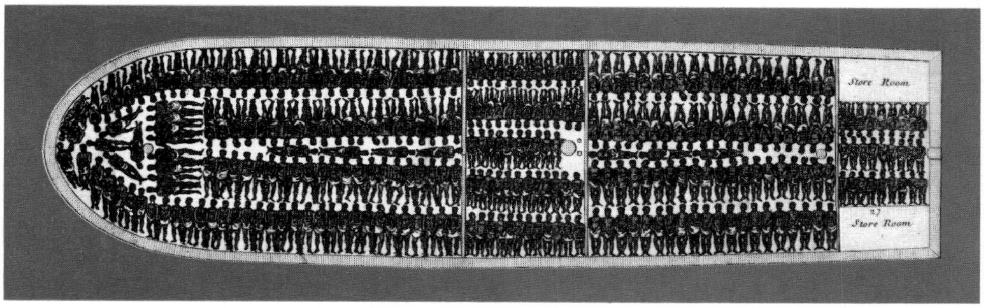

Between 10 and 15 million Negroes are thought to have been transported to the New World as victims of the slave trade. Negro slaves were traded as a valuable commodity, part of a three-cornered transaction in which West Indian sugar and molasses were taken to New England, made into rum and carried to Africa. *Top:* plate accompanying the published text of the last journals of the explorer and missionary David Livingstone. Any sick or injured captive rounded up for the slave trade was liable to meet a swift death. *Above:* diagram published in 1808 indicating the appalling method adopted by many slavers for stowing their human cargo. A 20% mortality figure on the Atlantic crossing was not uncommon.

pendent India. He was prime minister until his death, successfully guiding his country through the difficult early years of freedom. Although the eventual compromise of his neutralist and non-agressive policies evoked some criticism, he never lost the profound devotion of his countrymen.

NEICHIANG, city in S central China, in Szechwan province on the To R. It is a commercial and administrative center. Pop 240 000.

NEJD, or **Najd,** region in central Saudi Arabia; location of the country's capital, RIYADH. It was the first region ruled by Ibn Saud, the founder of modern Saudi Arabia.

NEKRASOV, Nikolai Aleksayevich (1821–1878), Russian poet, dissident author of *The Red-nosed Frost* (1863) and *Who Can Be Happy in Russia?* (1873). He was editor successively of the *Contemporary* and the *Annals of the Fatherland.*

NEKTON, the animals of the open sea: SQUIDS; CUTTLEFISHES; innumerable species of pelagic FISHES, and WHALES. The term is intended to complement PLANKTON, another pelagic assemblage, but of small animals with limited locomotor ability.

NELSON, Horatio, Admiral Lord Nelson (1758–1805), great British naval hero who defeated the French and Spanish Fleets at the Battle of TRAFALGAR. He entered the navy at age 12, was rapidly promoted, and given his first command in the French Revolutionary Wars. He was instrumental in defeating the Spanish fleet off Cape St. Vincent (1797). His destruction of the French fleet off Aboukir (1798) brought him fame and honors. Official disapproval caused by the scandal of his liaison with Emma, Lady HAMILTON, was dispelled by his defeat of the Danes at Copenhagen (1801). His pursuit of the French fleet on the renewal of the war in 1803 culminated in the Battle of Trafalgar, the occasion of his now-famous flag signal, "England expects that every man will do his duty." The victory cost Nelson his life, but ensured British naval supremacy for 100 years.

NELSON RIVER, the longest river in Manitoba, Canada. It flows NE for about 400mi from Lake Winnipeg to Hudson Bay at Port Nelson. Long a fur-trading route, it now provides hydroelectric power at Kelsey Rapids and other points.

NEMAN RIVER, German Memel, important river in W USSR, flowing about 580mi from its source near Minsk, W to Grodno, then NW through S Lithuania into the Baltic Sea.

NEMATODA. See ROUNDWORMS.

NEMEAN GAMES, ancient Greek festival of athletic and musical contests, held biennially in honor of Zeus at his temple in the valley of Nemea. From 573 BC it was Panhellenic. The victors were crowned with wild celery.

The Nemean games drew competitors from all over ancient Greece. Shown here at Nemea are the remains of the temple of Zeus, in whose honor the games were held.

NEMEAN LION, mythological beast, the terror of Nemea until HERCULES killed it in the first of his twelve labors. Thereafter he wore its skin.

NEMEROV, Howard (1920–), US poet and novelist noted for his satiric power. His *Blue Swallows* (1967) won the Theodore Roethke memorial prize for poetry. Among his novels are *The Melodramatists* (1949) and *The Homecoming Game* (1957).

NEMERTINEA. See RIBBON WORMS.

NEMESIS, in Greek mythology, the personification of divine retribution; later also the equalizer of good and ill fortune.

NEMIROVICH-DANCHENKO, Vladimir Ivanovich (1858–1943), Russian novelist, playwright and producer, cofounder, with Stanislavsky, of the MOSCOW ART THEATER. As a producer, Nemirovich-Danchenko was a great patron of the works of Ibsen and Chekhov.

NÉ-NÉ or **Hawaiian Goose,** *Branta sandvicensis*, an offshoot of the Canada goose stock, restricted to the Hawaiian archipelago. In the 1950s only 35 individuals remained in the wild. A few pairs were maintained in captivity and bred successfully. Release of birds from these collections back into Hawaii has increased the population there to about 1 000.

NEOCLASSICISM, in the visual arts and architecture, a movement, c1750–1850, to return to the style and spirit of classical times. A reaction against the BAROQUE, its ideals of simplicity and proportion were particularly successful in architecture. Leading figures included Thomas JEFFERSON in America, and Inigo JONES and Christopher WREN in England. In music, it was a movement from c1920 looking back to 18th-and 19th-century "classical" composers.

NEODYMIUM (Nd), one of the LANTHANUM SERIES. AW 144.2, mp 1021°C, bp 3068°C, sg 6.80 (20°C).

NEOLITHIC AGE. See PRIMITIVE MAN; STONE AGE.

NEON (Ne), one of the NOBLE GASES. It is used in discharge tubes, low-wattage glow lamps, SPARK CHAMBERS, and in helium-neon LASERS. Liquid neon is used as a refrigerant in the range 25–40K (see CRYOGENICS), and is added to liquid-hydrogen BUBBLE CHAMBERS to provide a better particle target. AW 20.2, mp −248.7°C, bp −246.0°C. Neon, the earliest of the noble gases to be employed in discharge tubes, glows orange when excited.

NEO-ORTHODOXY, a post-WWI movement in Protestant theology, so-called because its exponents adopted the language but not the literalism of Protestant orthodoxy. Led by Karl BARTH and Emil BRUNNER in Europe and Reinhold NIEBUHR in the US, it was concerned with contemporary society and its problems from a Christian viewpoint. Denying NATURAL THEOLOGY, it stressed God's transcendence and grace.

NEOPLASM. See CANCER, TUMOR.

NEOPLATONISM, a school of philosophy based on the work of Plato and dominant from the 3rd to the 6th centuries AD. It was developed by PLOTINUS and formulated in his *Enneads*. Neoplatonic philosophy set forth a systematized order which contained all levels and states of existence. From God, or the One, emanates the Divine Mind, from which the World Soul proceeds, and which in turn comprehends the visible world. Man's ideal is to rise upward toward union with the One. Neoplatonic philosophy greatly influenced early Christian theology through St. Augustine and others.

NEOPTOLEMUS, sometimes called Pyrrhus, in Greek mythology, the son of Achilles. He killed King Priam in the TROJAN WAR, and took as his slave Hector's wife Andromache, whom he later abandoned to marry Hermione. He was killed at Delphi.

NEOTENY, the retention of larval characters by an organism which has reached sexual maturity. Classically, neoteny is exhibited by certain salamanders (see AXOLOTL), but it also plays a part in the LIFE CYCLE of many invertebrates. Several times, the development of neotenic larvae may have been important in the course of EVOLUTION.

NEO-THOMISM. See THOMISM.

NEP. See NEW ECONOMIC POLICY.

NEPAL, independent kingdom of S Asia. It is a land of strongly contrasting climate and terrain, with the

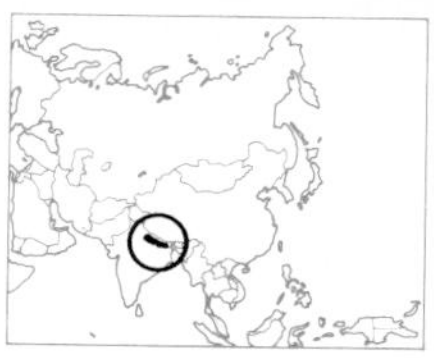

Official Name: Nepal
Capital: Katmandu
Area: 54 600sq mi
Population: 11 700 000
Languages: Nepali; Hindi, Tibeto–Burman dialects
Religions: Hindu, Buddhist
Monetary Unit(s): 1 Nepali rupee = 100 pice

Himalayas in the N, the temperate Valley of Nepal in the center, and the low-lying swamplands and forests of the Terai region in the S. Its major rivers rise in Tibet.

People. The population of Nepal is of mixed Mongolian and Indo–Aryan origin. Its main ethnic groups are the Newars, the Bhotias (who include the Sherpas) and the GURKHAS. Hinduism, numerically the dominant religion, has long coexisted with Buddhism. Tribal and caste distinctions retain considerable importance. In spite of rapid educational expansion since 1951, the illiteracy rate is still about 85%.

Economy. Nepal's economy is predominantly agricultural. Crops include rice, wheat, corn, oilseeds, potatoes, jute, tobacco, opium and cotton. Livestock is important. The forests of the Terai provide wood, and medicinal herbs are exported from the slopes of the Himalayas. Nepal's few industries, employing only about 1% of the labor force, rely chiefly on the processing of agricultural products, but include wood and metal handicrafts. Means of transportation, though still severely limited in the remoter areas, now include roads linking the Valley of Nepal with both Tibet and India, and an airport at Katmandu.

History. Nepal comprised numerous principalities until it was conquered by the Gurkhas in 1768. Political power was in the hands of the RANA family from 1846 to 1951, when it returned to the monarchy. The first democratically-elected government came to power in 1959, but a conflict resulted in 1962 in King Mahendra's banning all political parties. The present king, Birendra, came to the throne in 1972.

NEPER (Np), named for mathematician John NAPIER, unit used to express the ratio of quantities such as current or voltage. Thus the ratio $\mathcal{N}$, in nepers, of currents I_1 and I_2 is $\mathcal{N} = \ln(I_2/I_1)$. The neper is thus the natural logarithmic analogue of the DECIBEL. Power ratios, say of powers P_1 and P_2, can also be expressed in nepers; here $\mathcal{N} = \frac{1}{2}\ln(P_2/P_1)$, and 1 neper = 8.686dB.

NEPHRITE. See JADE.

NEPHRITIS, INFLAMMATION affecting the KIDNEYS. The term **glomerulonephritis** covers a variety of diseases, often involving disordered IMMUNITY, in which renal glomeruli are damaged by immune complex deposition (e.g., BRIGHT'S DISEASE); by direct autoimmune attack (Goodpasture's syndrome), or sometimes as a part of systemic disease (e.g., LUPUS, endocarditis, DIABETES or hypertension). Acute or chronic renal failure or nephrotic syndrome may result. The treatment is immunosuppressive or with STEROIDS. Acute **pyelonephritis** is bacterial infection of the kidney and renal pelvis, following SEPTICEMIA or lower urinary tract infection. Typically, this involves FEVER, loin pain and painful, frequent urination. The treatment requires ANTIBIOTICS. Chronic pyelonephritis includes recurrent kidney infection with permanent scarring and functional impairment.

NEPHRON. See KIDNEYS.

NEPHROSIS, or nephrotic syndrome, EDEMA associated with kidney disease (see NEPHRITIS).

NEPHTHYTIS, or arrowhead plant, a bushy climbing plant of the genus *Syngonium*, producing arrowhead-shaped leaves with silver, cream, white or yellow markings. It is frequently grown as a house plant, in which case it should be placed a short distance from a sunny window. It grows best at average house temperatures, failing to thrive below 13°C (55°F), and should be watered often enough to keep the soil evenly moist. The foliage should be misted often. Propagation is by taking shoot cuttings. Family: Araceae.

NEPTUNE, coastal town in E central N.J. It is chiefly a holiday resort. Pop 27 863.

NEPTUNE, the fourth largest planet in the SOLAR SYSTEM and the eighth in position from the sun, with a mean solar distance of 30.07AU. Neptune was first discovered in 1846 by J. G. Galle using computations by LEVERRIER based on the perturbations of URANUS' orbit. The calculation had been performed independently by John Couch ADAMS in England but vacillations on the part of the then Astronomer Royal had precluded a rigorous search for the planet. Neptune has two moons, Triton and Nereid, the former having a circular, retrograde orbit (see RETROGRADE MOTION), the latter having the most eccentric orbit of any moon in the Solar System. Neptune's "year" is 164.8 times that of the earth, its day being 15.8h. Its diameter is about 51Mm and its mass 17.45 times that of the earth. Its structure and constitution are believed to resemble those of JUPITER.

NEPTUNE, Roman god of the sea. Although originally god of fresh water, Neptune was identified with the Greek sea-god POSEIDON in the 4th century BC. Green arbors were erected at his feast, the Neptunalia (July 23). Horse races were held in his honor during the festivals of Consus, god of wise advice, also called the Equestrian Neptune.

NEPTUNISM, late 18th-century geological theory propagated by the school of A.G. WERNER in which it was claimed that the rocks originally forming the crust of the earth had been precipitated out of aqueous solution.

NEPTUNIUM (Np), the first TRANSURANIUM ELEMENT; one of the ACTINIDES. It is produced in breeder NUCLEAR REACTORS as a by-product of PLUTONIUM production by neutron irradiation of URANIUM (U^{238}). The stablest isotope is Np^{237} (half-life 2.2×10^{6}yr). Chemically neptunium resembles uranium. (For the **Neptunium Series** see RADIOACTIVITY.) mp 640°C, sg 20.45 (α).

NEREIDS, in Greek mythology, the 50 water-nymph daughters of NEREUS and Doris. They had the power of metamorphosis and of prophecy. They were friendly to sailors. Thetis, mother of Achilles, and Amphitrite, a consort of Poseidon, were nereids.

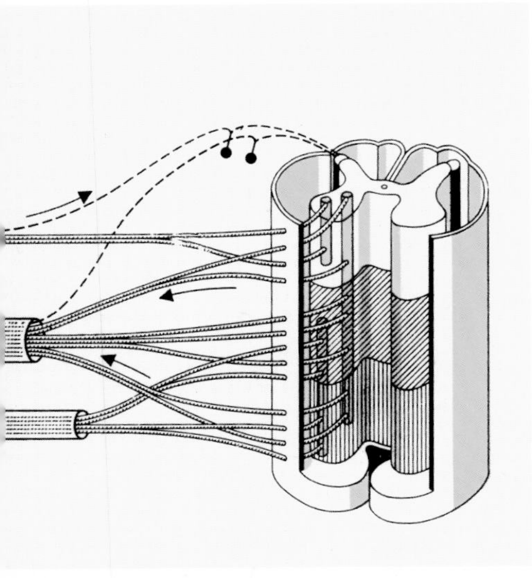

Diagram showing the basic structure of three nerves arising from roots in different segments of the spinal cord. The nerves can have motor fibers from more than one segment, and indeed, one segment of the spinal cord receives sensory fibers from many nerves. There are also nerves which have a purely motor or purely sensory function.

NEREUS, in Greek myth, a seagod. Wise and benevolent, he had the powers of prophecy and metamorphosis. He was the son of PONTUS and GAEA, and father of the NEREIDS by the nymph Doris.

NERI, Saint Phillip (Fillippo Neri; 1515–1595), a leading figure of the COUNTER-REFORMATION, and founder of the secular order of the Congregation of the Oratory which was devoted to care of the poor and sick. He was canonized in 1622.

NERNST, Walther Hermann (1864–1941), German physical chemist awarded the 1920 Nobel Prize for Chemistry for his discovery of the Third Law of THERMODYNAMICS.

NERO (37–68 AD), infamous Roman emperor. Born Lucius Domitius Ahenobarbus, he was adopted by his stepfather, emperor Claudius, whom he succeeded in 54 AD. Nero had Claudius' son Britannicus murdered in 55. In 59 he killed his mother Agrippina, and in 62 his wife Octavia, Claudius' daughter. The wise rule of SENECA and Burrus, to whom Nero had left affairs of state, ended in 62. Nero rebuilt Rome after the fire in 64 AD. Not himself responsible, he attributed the fire to the Christians, and the first Roman persecution followed. His cruelty, instability, and imposition of heavy taxes led to a revolt. Deserted by the PRAETORIAN GUARD, Nero committed suicide.

NERUDA, Pablo (1904–1973), born Neftalí Ricardo Reyes Basualto, influential Chilean poet and communist leader. He won the 1971 Nobel Prize for Literature. His verse collections, written in the surrealist vein, include *Twenty Love Poems and a Song of Despair* (1924) and the highly-regarded *Canto general* (1950).

NERVA, Marcus Cocceius (30–98 AD), Roman emperor. He was a consul in 71 and 90. In 96, after the assassination of Domitian, he was elected emperor by the senate. His was a benevolent, liberal but unimaginative rule. He was succeeded by his adopted son, Trajan.

NERVAL, Gérard de (1808–1855), born Gérard Labrunie, French romantic writer who anticipated the symbolist and surrealist movements in French Literature. His works include a collection of sonnets, *Les Chimères* (1854); some short stories, *Les Filles du Feu* (1854), and his autobiography, *Aurélia* (1853–54).

NERVE. See NERVOUS SYSTEM.

NERVE GAS. See CHEMICAL AND BIOLOGICAL WARFARE.

NERVI, Pier Luigi (1891–), Italian civil engineer and architect. In the 1940s he invented *ferrocemento*, a new form of reinforced concrete. Notable among his bold and imaginative designs are the Turin exposition hall, the railway station in Naples, the Olympic buildings in Rome, and (in collaboration) the Unesco headquarters in Paris.

NERVOUS BREAKDOWN, popular term used to describe various kinds of MENTAL ILLNESS, often associated with fatigue or emotional stress, which drastically impair a person's normal efficiency and disturb his social behavior.

NERVOUS SYSTEM, the system of tissues which coordinates an animal's various activities with each other and with external events by means of nervous impulses conducted rapidly from part to part via nerves. Its responses are generally rapid, whereas those of the endocrine system with which it shares its coordinating and integrating function are generally slow (see GLANDS, HORMONES).

The nervous system can be divided into two parts. The **central nervous system** (CNS), consisting of BRAIN and SPINAL CORD, stores and processes information and sends messages to muscles and glands. The **peripheral nervous system**, consisting of 12 pairs of cranial nerves arising in and near the medulla oblongata of the brain and 31 pairs of spinal nerves arising at intervals from the spinal cord, carries messages to and from the central nervous system.

A third system, the **autonomic nervous system**, normally considered part of the peripheral nervous system, controls involuntary actions such as heartbeat and digestion. It is divisible into two complementary parts: the *sympathetic system* prepares the body for "fight or flight," and the *parasympathetic system* controls the body's vegetative functions. Most internal organs are innervated by both parts.

The nervous system's basic anatomical and functional unit is the highly specialized nerve cell or NEURON, the shape of which varies greatly in different regions. It possesses two kinds of processes: *dendrites* which together with the cell body receive impulses from other neurons, and an *axon* which conducts impulses to other neurons. Axons vary greatly in length (up to a few metres) and speed of conduction (up to about 90m/s).

Sensory or *afferent neurons* carry information to the central nervous system from sensory receptors (such as skin receptors and muscle stretch receptors), whereas *efferent neurons* carry information away from it. Efferent neurons passing to muscle are called *motor neurons*.

Nerves are formed from many axons, both afferent and efferent, surrounded by their associated sheaths which insulate them from each other. Axons surrounded by a fat and protein sheath, called a MYELIN sheath, conduct fastest. Just prior to entering the spinal cord each spinal nerve divides into a *dorsal root* containing afferent axons only and a *ventral root* containing efferent axons only.

Adjacent neurons communicate through specialized contact points or *synapses* which are either excitatory or inhibitory. The elaborate neural circuitry arising from synaptic contact in the central nervous system is responsible for much of behavior, from simple reflex action to complex thought-communication patterns.

The nerve impulse, or action potential, is an electrical signal conducted at speeds far slower than ELECTRICITY. An electrical potential difference of about 70mV, called the resting potential, exists between the inside and outside of the neuron due to the ionic concentration imbalance between inside and outside, and a metabolic pump moving IONS across the cell membrane. If the resting potential is reduced below a certain threshold level, as may occur when impulses are received from other neurons, an impulse is initiated. Impulses are all the same strength ("all-or-none" law), and travel to the end of the axon to the synapse where a chemical transmitter substance (see ACETYLCHOLINE) is released which initiates a new electrical signal in the next neuron. (See also NEURALGIA; NEURITIS; NEUROLOGY.)

NESS, Loch, lake in Inverness Co., N central Scotland, about 23mi long, 1mi wide and 750ft deep. As yet there has been no conclusive evidence of the existence of the famous Loch Ness "Monster."

NESSUS, in Greek myth, the centaur who brought about the death of HERCULES. He was vengefully slain by Hercules after trying to seize his wife Deianira. The dying Nessus told Deianira to use blood from his wound as a love-charm. This she later did, and Hercules died in agony.

NEST, a structure prepared by many animals for the protection of their eggs and young, or for sleeping purposes. In social insects, the nest provides the home of the whole colony, and may have special structures for temperature control and ventilation. The sleeping nests of, for example, the great apes, are commonly no more than crudely woven hammocks of twigs and branches. The sleeping nests of other mammals (which may be used for hibernation) are as complex and woven as any breeding nest. Both these and the nests used by birds and mammals for breeding, must protect the animals within from both weather and predators. Nests can be built of mud, leaves, twigs, down, paper, and kinds of human garbage.

NESTOR, in Greek myth, king of PYLOS, aged hero of the TROJAN WAR, depicted by Homer as a seasoned counselor. He helped the Lapiths against the Centaurs, sailed with the Argonauts and helped hunt the Calydonian boar.

NESTORIANS, members of the heretical Christian sect named for Nestorius (Patriarch of Constantinople 428–431), who was condemned by the Council of Ephesus (431) for his rejection of the title "mother of God" for the Virgin MARY, and teaching the existence of two persons—divine and human—in Jesus Christ. The Nestorians expanded vigorously for 800 years, but were persecuted by the Mongols and—in recent times—by the Turks. The modern Nestorian (Assyrian) Church has about 100 000 members, mainly in Iraq, Iran, and Syria.

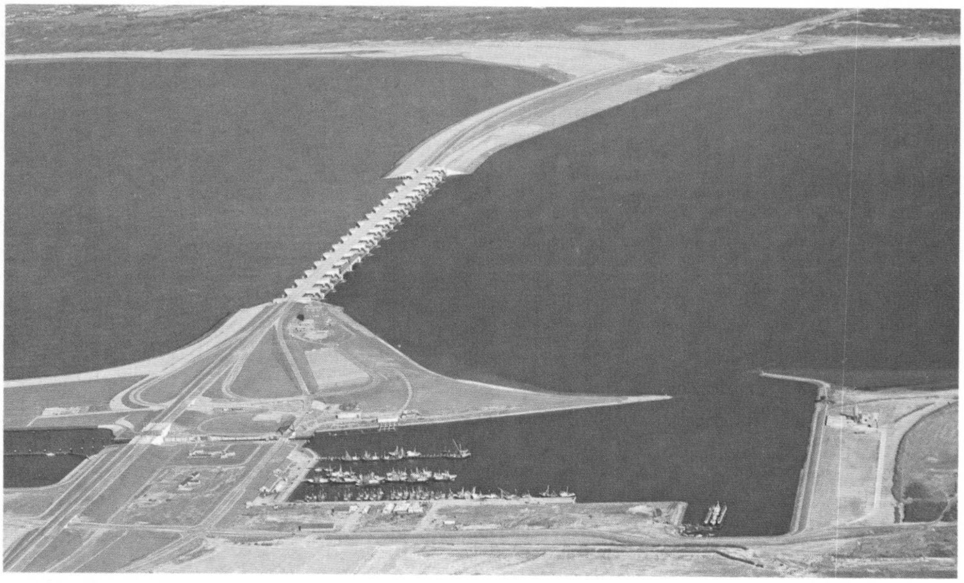

The Haringvliet dam, spanning a three-mile-wide channel, is part of a large network of dams and dikes that prevents major flooding occurring in the southwest of the Netherlands.

NETHERLANDS, The, kingdom in W Europe, commonly known as Holland. It has 11 provinces, subdivided into 957 municipalities. The land is mostly flat, and about 38% is below sea-level. It is protected from the sea by a narrow belt of dunes bordering the North Sea coast and a vast complex of dikes forming POLDERS. The major cities of the Netherlands are located in the polders region, which, with its rich clay soil, contains the finest agricultural land. The higher inland region has natural drainage but relatively poor, sandy soil, except where it is traversed by the Lower Rhine, Waal and Maas (Meuse) Rivers. The climate of the Netherlands is mild and damp.

People. The Netherlands is one of the world's most densely-populated countries. Nearly half the population lives close to the three largest cities—Amsterdam (the capital), The Hague (the seat of government) and Rotterdam. Schooling is compulsory for children between the ages of 6 and 15. The illiteracy rate (about 0.2%) is one of the lowest in the world. There are 12 universities, including the famous public universities at Leiden, Utrecht, Groningen, and Amsterdam. There is no official religion.

Economy. Industry now provides 40% of the Netherlands' GNP, and employs over a million people. There are reserves of oil, natural gas and coal, but most raw materials must be imported. Major industries include oil-refining, shipbuilding, iron, steel, textiles, machinery, electrical equipment and plastics. Dairy produce, the basis of Holland's intensive agriculture, sustains a large food-processing industry. Financial and transportation services contribute significantly. Tourism is also important. A highly-advanced transportation system includes about 4000mi of natural and artificial waterways. The Netherlands is a member of the COMMON MARKET.

History. The Low Countries' seven northern provinces (now the Netherlands) broke away from Spanish rule under William the Silent, Prince of Orange, to form the Union of Utrecht in 1579. Independence was declared in 1581 but not recognized by Spain until the Treaty of Westphalia (1648), which ended the THIRTY YEARS' WAR. The 17th century saw the golden age of the Netherlands: made prosperous by overseas trading and colonizing, it was also famed for its religious tolerance and cultural life (see REMBRANDT; VERMEER; SPINOZA). In the 18th century Holland was outrivalled by England and France. Popular sympathy with the French Revolution led (1795) to the establishment of the French-ruled Batavian Republic. After the defeat of Napoleon (1814), the United Kingdom of the Netherlands was formed, joining Holland with present-day Belgium. The latter broke away in 1830. Holland's subsequent history, under its constitutional monarchy, has been marked by a steady growth of prosperity and liberalism. Neutral in WWI, the Dutch recovered rapidly after the devastating German occupation in WWII. The present queen, Juliana, came to the throne in 1948.

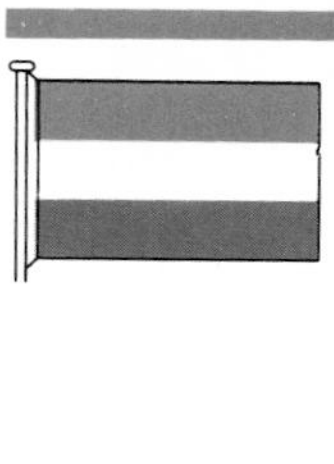

Official Name: Kingdom of the Netherlands
Capital: Amsterdam
Seat of Government: The Hague
Area: 15 785sq mi
Population: 13 387 623
Language: Dutch
Religions: Protestant, Roman Catholic
Monetary Unit(s): 1 Guilder = 100 cents

NETHERLANDS ANTILLES (the Dutch West Indies), two groups of islands in the Caribbean Sea. They are an autonomous part of the Netherlands. The S group comprises Curaçao (location of the capital, Willemstad), Aruba, and Bonaire, about 50mi off Venezuela. The N group, 500mi to the NE, comprises Saba, St. Eustacius, and the S half of St. Martin. The processing of petroleum from Venezuela accounts for 98% of exports. There is also some tourism. Pop 230 000.

NETHER PROVIDENCE, township in SE Pa., Delaware Co. Pop 13 644.

NETTLE, popular name for a number of plants with stinging hairs, particularly those belonging to the genus *Urtica*. The stinging or great nettle (*Urtica dioica*) is widely distributed in temperate regions and is frequently a troublesome weed. The "sting" of stinging nettles contains small quantities of FORMIC ACID. Family: Urticaceae.

NEUILLY, Treaty of (Nov. 27, 1919), post-WWI treaty between the Allies and Bulgaria, by which Bulgaria's W frontier was changed in favor of Yugoslavia and Greece. Bulgaria had also to pay reparations and to reduce its army.

NEUMANN, Johann Balthasar (1687–1753), leading German architect of the late BAROQUE style. He designed palaces, churches, houses, bridges and water systems. Especially notable are the church in Vierzehnheiligen and the Residenz at Würzburg.

NEURALGIA, pain originating in a nerve and characterized by sudden sharp, often electric shock-like pain or exacerbations of pain. Nerves commonly affected include the digital nerves of toes and intercostal nerves. Neuralgia may be due to INFLAMMATION or trauma.

NEURATH, Constantin, Baron von (1873–1956), German diplomat and statesman. He was foreign minister 1932–38. Considered over-lenient as "protector" of Bohemia and Moravia 1939–41, he was recalled by Hitler. He was sentenced to 15 years in prison at the NUREMBERG TRIALS.

NEURITIS, or peripheral neuropathy, any disorder of the peripheral NERVOUS SYSTEM which interferes with sensation, the nerve control of MUSCLE, or both. Its causes include DRUGS and heavy metals (e.g., gold); infection or allergic reaction to it (as with LEPROSY or DIPHTHERIA); inflammatory disease (rheumatoid ARTHRITIS); infiltration, systemic and metabolic disease (e.g., DIABETES or PORPHYRIA); VITAMIN deficiency (BERIBERI); organ failure (e.g., of the LIVER or KIDNEY); genetic disorders, and the nonmetastatic effects of distant CANCER. Numbness, tingling, weakness and PARALYSIS result, at first affecting the extremities. Diagnosis involves electrical studies of the nerves and nerve BIOPSY.

NEUROLOGY, branch of MEDICINE concerned with diseases of the BRAIN; SPINAL CORD, and peripheral NERVOUS SYSTEM. These include MULTIPLE SCLEROSIS, EPILEPSY, migraine (HEADACHE), STROKE, PARKINSON'S DISEASE, NEURITIS, ENCEPHALITIS, MENINGITIS, brain TUMORS (GLIOMAS), MUSCULAR DYSTROPHY and MYASTHENIA GRAVIS.

NEURON, or nerve cell, the basic unit of the NERVOUS SYSTEM (including the BRAIN and SPINAL CORD). Each has a long AXON, specialized for transmitting electrical impulses and releasing chemical transmitters that act on MUSCLE or effector cells or other neurons. Branched processes called dendrites integrate the input to neurons.

NEUROPTERA, an order of insects, including ALDERFLIES, LACEWINGS, DOBSON FLIES and ANT LIONS. The adults have biting mouthparts and usually membranous wings; the larvae, both aquatic and terrestrial forms, are always active and predaceous.

NEUROSIS, originally any NERVOUS SYSTEM activity; later, any disorder of the nervous system; though in PSYCHOANALYSIS, those mental disorders (e.g., HYSTERIA) unconnected with the nervous system. It is usually seen as based in UNCONSCIOUS conflict, with an unconscious attempt to conform to reality (not escape from it, as in PSYCHOSIS). **Actual neurosis** is based in disorders of current sexual behavior (see SEX); **psychoneurosis** is rooted in the past life; **anxiety neurosis** is characterized by exaggerated ANXIETY. (See OBSESSIONAL NEUROSIS.)

NEUROSURGERY. See SURGERY.

NEUSTRIA, W Frankish kingdom of the 6th–8th centuries, now NW France. It was defeated by and became united with its rival Austrasia (the E Frankish kingdom) in 687. Later, "Neustria" denoted the land between the Seine and the Loire, and by the 10th century it referred to Normandy.

NEUTRA, Richard Joseph (1892–1970), Austrian-born US architect who brought the International Style of architecture to the US. The Tremaine house (1947) in Santa Barbara, Cal., instances his skill in relating a building to its setting.

NEUTRALISM AND NONALIGNMENT, peacetime foreign policy such as that adopted after WWII by India, Burma, the United Arab Republic, Yugoslavia, and most of the new African and Asian states. These countries wished to preserve their independence by avoiding alignment with either the Communist or the Western power bloc, but, being active in the UN, were not isolationist.

NEUTRALITY, the status of a country which elects not to participate in a war between other countries. Under international law, a neutral state has the right to have its boundaries and territorial waters respected, and the obligation to remain impartial towards belligerents in its actions. The two World Wars, however, brought many violations of neutrality, e.g. Germany's invasion of Belgium in WWI. Before the US entered WWII, her neutrality was effectively nullified by her support of the Allies. With the need for would-be neutral countries to defend their status by aggression (as America in WWI), the viability of neutrality became questionable. Membership of the United Nations is not compatible with neutrality, since members may be called upon to act against aggressors.

NEUTRALITY ACTS, of 1935, 1936 and 1937, US legislation banning arms sales and loans to belligerent states. The acts were aimed at keeping America out of war. They were modified in 1939, and effectively replaced by the LEND LEASE Act of 1941, the purpose of which was to assist the Allies without direct participation in the war.

NEUTRALIZATION, a chemical reaction between two compounds of opposite chemical character, giving a relatively inactive product. Common examples include neutralization of an ACID by a BASE to give a SALT, and of an oxidizing agent by a reducing agent (see OXIDATION AND REDUCTION). (See also EQUIVALENT WEIGHT; TITRATION.)

NEUTRINO. See SUBATOMIC PARTICLES.

NEUTRON (n), uncharged SUBATOMIC PARTICLE with rest mass 1.6748×10^{-27}kg (slightly greater than that of the PROTON) and SPIN $\frac{1}{2}$. A free neutron is slightly unstable, decaying to a proton, an ELECTRON and an antineutrino with HALF-LIFE 680s:

$$n \rightarrow p^{+} + e^{-} + \bar{\nu}$$

But neutrons bound within the nucleus of an ATOM are stable. All nuclei save hydrogen contain neutrons, which contribute to the nuclear cohesive forces and separate the mutually repulsive protons. Free neutrons are produced in many nuclear reactions, including nuclear FISSION, and hence nuclear reactors and particle ACCELERATORS are used as sources. The neutron was discovered in 1932 by Sir James CHADWICK, who bombarded beryllium with ALPHA PARTICLES emitted by a radioisotope. Neutrons are highly penetrating, and are moderated (slowed down) by colliding with the nuclei of light atoms. They induce certain heavy atoms to undergo fission. Shielding requires thick concrete walls. Neutrons are detected by counting the ionizing particles or GAMMA RAYS produced when they react with nuclei. Neutrons have wave properties, and their DIFFRACTION is used to study crystal structures and magnetic properties. (See also CROSS-SECTION, NUCLEAR.)

NEUTRON BOMB, hypothetical "clean" variant of the HYDROGEN BOMB that would produce intense lethal neutron radiation but not much structural damage or radioactive fallout.

NEVADA, US western state, situated between the Rocky Mts and the Sierra Nevada. Most of the state lies in the Great Basin, an arid plateau at about 5 000ft above sea level which is broken by many short mountain ranges running from N to S. Nev.'s longest river is the Humboldt and the major lakes are the Mead (formed by the Hoover Dam), Tahoe, Pyramid and Walker. The state has the lowest average annual rainfall in the US, (7.4in), and because of its altitude, temperatures drop considerably at night. There are extremes of heat in summer and cold in winter. Much of Nev. is arid desert. Most of the population of Nev., which ranks 47th in state populations, is concentrated around Las Vegas and Reno. Over 90% of the population is white. the rest are Negro or Indian and there are a number of Indian reservations. Carson City is the smallest state capital in the US.

Economy. The Nev. economy depends heavily on tourism, which its liberal gambling and divorce laws attract; mining, especially of copper and iron ore, is also important. The manufacturing sector is gradually expanding, but agriculture plays a minor role, largely because of the arid climate.

History. Nev. may have been first explored by the Spanish in the 1770s. In 1827 Jedediah SMITH crossed Nev. towards Cal. In the 1840s John FRÉMONT explored it extensively. It first became a US possession by the treaty of GUADELOUPE-HIDALGO after the MEXICAN WAR. In 1859, with the discovery of the rich

Sheep ranching in the foothills of the White Pine Mountains in Nevada. Livestock ranching is Nevada's chief agricultural activity. Some irrigated crops are also cultivated, but agriculture plays only a minor role in the state economy.

COMSTOCK LODE, gold and silver veins attracted thousands of prospectors. In 1864 Nev. was made the 36th state, largely to secure its precious metal resources for the Union in the Civil War. In the late 19th century prosperity declined when the gold and silver mines were exhausted, but copper mining and tourism have brought new wealth to the state.

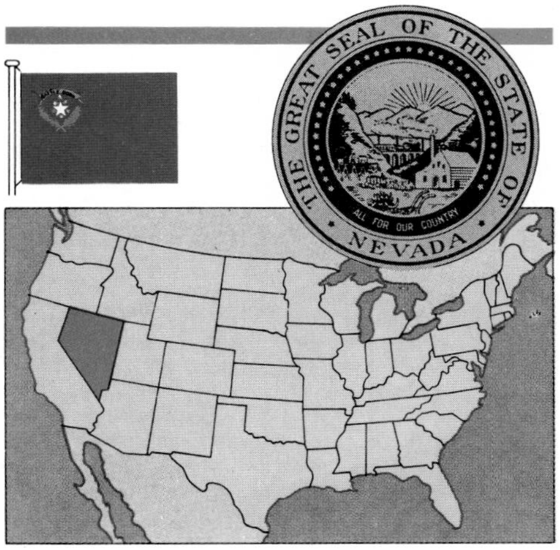

Name of State: Nevada
Capital: Carson City
Statehood: Oct. 31, 1864 (36th state)
Familiar Name: Silver State, Sagebrush State
Area: 110 540sq mi
Population: 488 738
Elevation: Highest—13 140ft, Boundary Peak
Lowest—470ft, Colorado River in Clark County
Motto: All for Our Country
State Flower: Sagebrush
State Bird: Mountain bluebird
State Tree: Single-leaf piñon
State Song: "Home Means Nevada"

NÉVÉ, compacted snow that lasts from year to year, representing one of the earliest stages in the development of a GLACIER. Further compaction, until there is no air left in the SNOW, results in the formation of *firn*.

NEVELSON, Louise (1900–), Russian-born US sculptor. She is famous for her intricate wooden constructions, which resemble vast ranges of box-like shelves with various objects on them.

NEVIN, Ethelbert Woodbridge (1862–1901), US composer and pianist. His compositions are in a simple, lyrical style. Nevin wrote many songs including *The Rosary* (1898) and the popular *Water Scenes* (1891), a cycle of piano pieces.

NEVINS, Allan (1890–1971), US historian, whose best known work is the Civil War series, *The Ordeal of the Union* (1947–60). Nevins received Pulitzer Prizes for his biographies, *Grover Cleveland* (1932) and *Hamilton Fish* (1936). His many other works include the biography *John D. Rockerfeller* (1953).

NEVIS. See SAINT KITTS-NEVIS-ANGUILLA.

NEVSKY, Alexander. See ALEXANDER NEVSKY.

NEVUS. See BIRTHMARK, FRECKLE, MOLE.

NEW ALBANY, manufacturing city in S Ind., on the Ohio R opposite Louisville, Ky., seat of Floyd Co. Industries include chemicals and machine parts. Pop 38 402.

NEWARK, city in W Cal., SE of San Francisco. Pop 27 153.

NEWARK, city in NW Del., the seat of Delaware U. Its industries include a large automobile plant, paper production and vegetable packing. Pop 21 078.

NEWARK, largest city and a port in N.J., seat of Essex Co., on the Passaic R. It is a commercial and industrial center of the Greater New York area. Its airport is one of New York's three major air terminals. Newark ranks as the third largest insurance center in the US. Pop 382 288.

NEWARK, village in W central N.Y., on the Barge Canal. It has many light industries including food processing and carton manufacturing. Pop 11 644.

NEWARK, industrial city in central Ohio, seat of Licking Co. A farm and livestock center, it is also a transportation hub. Pop 41 836.

NEW BEDFORD, city in SE Mass., seat of Bristol Co. In the 1850s it was one of the world's major whaling ports but now has important fishing industries and light manufacturing. Pop 101 777.

NEW BERLIN, city in SE Wis., a residential suburb of Milwaukee. Pop 26 910.

NEW BERN, city and port in N.C., on the Trent R, seat of Craven Co. New Bern was founded by Swiss and German settlers in 1710, and was a colonial capital of North Carolina. Pop 14 660.

NEW BRAUNFELS, city in central Tex., seat of Comal Co., settled in 1845 by German immigrants. The city is a manufacturing and shipping center. Pop 17 859.

NEW BRIGHTON, village in SE Minn. It is situated in an agricultural area known as the "squash center" of the state. Pop 19 507.

NEW BRITAIN, city in Conn., the state's leading manufacturer of building hardware, and known as "Hardware City." Pop 83 441.

NEW BRITAIN ISLAND, largest island (about 14 600sq mi) in the BISMARCK ARCHIPELAGO. Discovered in 1700, it has active volcanoes and rich mineral sources and is under Australian administration.

NEW BRUNSWICK, second largest of the Canadian Atlantic provinces, one of the Maritime Provinces. Its coast runs some 750mi along the Chaleur Bay, the Gulf of St. Lawrence, Northumberland Strait and the Bay of FUNDY.

Land and People. About 85% of the province is forested. The center is high land and there is a coastal plain in the NE. The province is well-drained by many swift-flowing rivers and streams. The fertile

View of St. John, the largest city in New Brunswick and its major port, being one of the only two sizable harbors on the Atlantic coast of Canada that remains ice free during the winter.

valley of the St. John R provides an excellent farming region. The climate is continental and ocean breezes moderate extremes along the coast. About half the population live in cities, the largest being Saint John, Moncton and the capital Fredericton. Over 50% of the population is of British origin, and 40% of French.

Economy. The economy is largely based on forest industries and on pulp and paper manufacturing. Copper, lead, silver and particularly zinc mining are being developed in the NE. Since WWII hydroelectric power has been exploited on an increasing scale.

History. Jacques CARTIER explored the region in 1534. Samuel de CHAMPLAIN established a settlement in 1604 in what became known as French ACADIA. Britain gained control of the region in 1713, but it was not until the arrival of Loyalists from the US after the Revolution that New Brunswick became a separate province (1784). The boundary with Maine was settled after the AROOSTOOK WAR by the WEBSTER–ASHBURTON TREATY of 1842. New Brunswick was one of the four original provinces to join the Dominion of Canada in 1867. The province developed slowly, inhabitants emigrated and it was an under-privileged area. However the discovery of mineral deposits, the growing importance of the port of Saint John and large federal financial support may lead to economic expansion.

Name of Province: New Brunswick
Joined Confederation: July 1, 1867
Capital: Fredericton
Area: 28 354sq mi
Population: 634 560

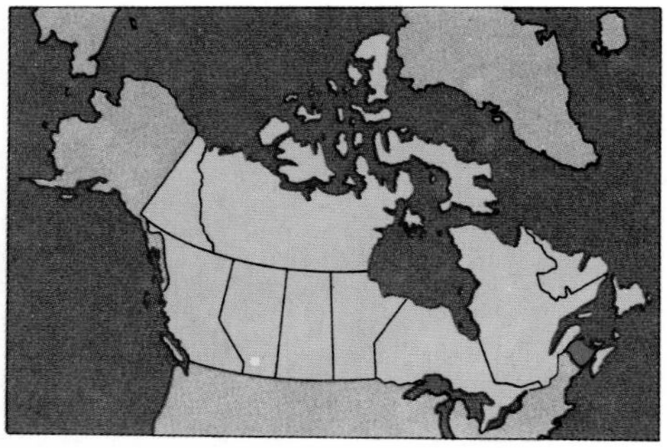

NEW BRUNSWICK, manufacturing city in N.J. on the Raritan R, seat of Middlesex Co. It has the largest medical supply houses in the US. Pop 41 885.

NEWBURGH, city in SE N.Y., on the Hudson R. WASHINGTON's headquarters, 1782–83, and once a whaling port, it now has textile industries. Pop 26 219.

NEWBURYPORT, city in NE Mass., seat of Essex Co. It has some fine 17th-century buildings, manufactures rum and silverware and specializes in clams. Pop 15 807.

NEW CALEDONIA, French overseas territory in the SW Pacific, formed by the islands of New Caledonia, Isle of Pines, LOYALTY ISLANDS and smaller groups, and covering 7 367sq mi. The economy rests on iron and nickel mining, coffee and copra. The capital, Noumea, is on the principal island, New Caledonia, which is 248mi by 31mi, mountainous, temperate but not widely fertile. It is rich in nickel, iron and chrome minerals. New Caledonia island was discovered by Captain COOK in 1774 and annexed by the French in 1853.

NEW CANAAN, a residential town in SW Conn. and a summer resort. It manufactures dairy and wood products and has large plant nurseries. Pop 17 455.

NEW CARROLLTON, city in W Md., a residential suburb of Washington, D.C. Pop 14 870.

NEWCASTLE, large Pacific port in New South Wales, Australia, set in a major coal mining region. Its main industries include shipbuilding and steel mills. Pop 145 718.

NEW CASTLE, historic colonial city in Del., on the Delaware R, founded by Peter STUYVESANT in 1651. In 1682 it fell into the control of William PENN. Pop 4 814.

NEW CASTLE, city in E Ind., seat of Henry Co. It is set in rich farming country and has famous rose nurseries, and manufactures automobile parts. Pop 21 215.

NEW CASTLE, city in W Pa., seat of Lawrence Co. It is a rich farm region and also has coal, iron and limestone mines. Pop 38 559.

NEWCASTLE UPON TYNE, industrial city and port on the NE coast of England. The site has been occupied since Roman times. Its industries include mining, shipbuilding and steel manufacture. Pop 222 153.

NEW CITY, village in SE N.Y., seat of Rockland Co., a residential suburb of New York City. Pop 27 344.

NEWCOMB, Simon (1835–1909), US astronomer. He computed new planetary tables whose data was so accurate that they remained in use for over half a century. Head of the *American Nautical Almanac* Office after 1877, he taught at Johns Hopkins U. 1884–94.

NEWCOMEN, Thomas (1663–1729), British inventor of the first practical STEAM ENGINE (before 1712). His device, employed mainly to pump water from mines, used steam pressure to raise the piston and, after condensation of the steam, atmospheric pressure to force it down again: it was thus called an "atmospheric" steam engine. (See also SAVERY, T.)

NEW DEAL, program adopted by President Franklin D. ROOSEVELT to alleviate the effects of the GREAT DEPRESSION. On his election in 1933, Roosevelt initiated a dramatic program of relief and reform, known as "the first hundred days." He called an immediate BANK HOLIDAY and restored confidence in those banks which were allowed to reopen by the EMERGENCY BANKING ACT. Bank funds and practices were overseen by the FEDERAL DEPOSIT INSURANCE CORPORATION and the FEDERAL RESERVE board. Measures were taken to control the Stock Exchange (see SECURITIES AND EXCHANGE COMMISSION).

Farm recovery was helped by the creation of credit facilities, subsidies, rural electrification programs and the resettlement of some farmers in more productive areas. The NATIONAL RECOVERY ADMINISTRATION (NRA) and the CIVILIAN CONSERVATION CORPS (CCC) were set up to boost business and create jobs, though many of the NRA's functions were later declared unconstitutional by the Supreme Court. Unions were protected by the Labor Relations Act (1935), and the FAIR LABOR STANDARDS ACT (1938) set a national MINIMUM WAGE. Measures were taken to relieve poverty and unemployment. The SOCIAL SECURITY system was established in 1935 and jobs were created by the WORKS PROJECTS ADMINISTRATION (WPA), including the massive TENNESSEE VALLEY AUTHORITY (TVA) project. The Home Loan Corporation and the FEDERAL HOUSING ADMINISTRATION (FHA) helped home owners and aided recovery in the construction industry.

After its initial popularity, the New Deal met increasing opposition in Congress and the Supreme Court. It ended in 1939 as the economy expanded to meet the demands of WWII. The question of its success remains controversial; many believe that only WWII finally ended the Great Depression. Its influence however was permanent; it changed the direction of social legislation, centralized control of the economy and altered the US public's attitude to the role of the Federal government.

NEW DELHI, capital of India. It was built by the British in 1912–29 to the S of Delhi, when the capital was transferred from Calcutta. New Delhi, a spacious city, was designed by the architect Sir Edwin Lutyens. Since independence new official buildings, shops and industrial quarters have been added to the city. Pop 292 857.

NEW DEMOCRATIC PARTY (NDP), Canadian moderate socialist political party, formed by the political alliance of the labor unions and the Co-operative Commonwealth Federation (CCF) in 1961. The CCF, founded in 1932, was popular in W Canada, advocating welfare measures, government economic planning and nationalization, but the NDP

The National Recovery Administration was set up in 1933 as part of President Roosevelt's "New Deal" to boost business and revitalize the American economy. Industries which observed the codes set up by the NRA were awarded the "Blue Eagle."

modified this program. In the 1972–74 parliamentary sessions it was the third largest party.

NEW ECONOMIC POLICY (NEP), economic policy adopted by Soviet Russia during 1921–28 to deal with the effects of the previous war years. The NEP made concessions to private enterprise in industry, trade and agriculture, and allowed the peasants to sell produce profitably. The NEP was very successful and by 1927 had restored the pre-war national income level.

NEW ENGLAND, Council for. See COUNCIL FOR NEW ENGLAND.

NEW ENGLAND CONFEDERATION, colonial alliance organized in 1643 by representatives from Massachusetts Bay, Plymouth, Connecticut and New Haven colonies. They formed "the United Colonies of New England" to settle boundary disputes and arrange defense. Inter-colonial rivalry hindered agreement and the confederation was dissolved in 1684.

NEWFOUNDLAND, largest Canadian Atlantic province, comprising Newfoundland Island and Labrador and their adjacent islands.

Land. Newfoundland Island has a long (6 000mi) indented coastline with many islands, which is most rugged in the S and E coast; the land rises from the E lowlands to a plateau and mountains, the highest being the Lewis Hills (2 672ft). The central plateau has many lakes and bogs. Avalon peninsula is the most densely populated part of the province, and contains the capital, St. John's. Labrador is a rugged, forested plateau (mountain peaks reaching 5 160ft) with a rocky coast and many fiords. Its climate is harsher than that of Newfoundland island; winters are severe throughout the whole province. More than 56% of Newfoundland province is forested.

People. The province is sparsely populated and most of the people live close to the sea. Only 3% live in Labrador, and 10% of these are of Indian or Eskimo descent.

Aerial photograph showing part of the coastal belt of Newfoundland, which is icebound and blanketed in snow throughout the winter months.

Economy. The economy is based on mining, forestry, fishing and manufacturing. There are very large iron-ore mines in Labrador; copper, gold, lead, silver and zinc are also mined. Fishing is Newfoundland's best-known industry. Fishermen from Europe and Japan are attracted to the famous GRAND BANKS, which abound in cod, haddock and other fish. Manufacturing accounts for some 44% of the economy; industries include paper, steel, textiles and clothing manufacture and food processing. Electricity is mostly provided by hydroelectric plants, the most recent being the gigantic Churchill Falls project (1972). The province's strategic position has made it important in transatlantic air travel; there are large air terminals at Gander and Goose Bay.

History. Remains of 10th-century Viking settlements have been found on Newfoundland Island. John CABOT rediscovered the island in 1497 and Sir Humphrey GILBERT claimed it for England in 1583. It was not until 1763, after the SEVEN YEARS' WAR, that England gained firm control although France retained the "French shore" on the W coast until 1904. Newfoundland gained fully responsible government in 1855, but Britain took control again in 1934 when the island's economy was hit by the Great Depression. Newfoundland chose to join the Dominion of Canada in 1949 and became Canada's tenth province. Since then federal aid and the boom in mining have dramatically raised the standard of living and reduced unemployment.

Name of Province: Newfoundland
Joined Confederation: March 31, 1949
Capital: St. John's
Area: 156 185sq mi
Population: 522 104

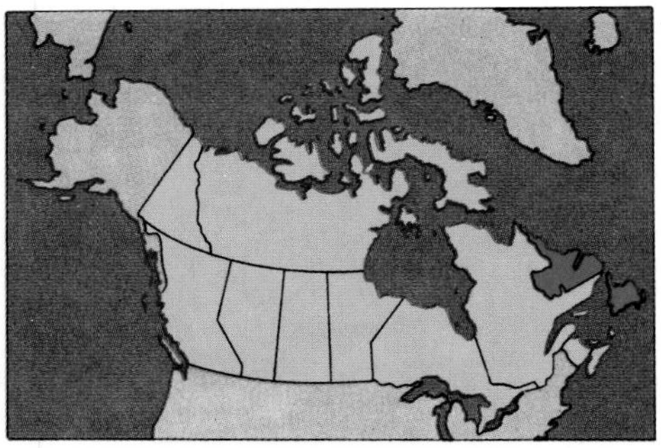

NEWFOUNDLAND DOG, a large water dog, probably originating from crossbreeding of native with European dogs. It has a broad head, stands about 28in high and has a dull jet black coat. The dog's webbed feet and oily coat make it a powerful swimmer.

NEW FRANCE, North American territories held by France from the 16th century to 1763 which extended W beyond the St. Lawrence to the Great Lakes and NE areas. France lost these territories in a series of colonial wars with Britain.

NEW FREEDOM, program adopted by President WILSON in 1912 which aimed to establish more political and economic opportunities in the US and to free the US economy from tariffs and other restrictions. He passed the UNDERWOOD TARIFF Act, the Federal Reserve Act (see FEDERAL RESERVE SYSTEM) and the Antitrust Act in 1913–17.

NEW GLASGOW, a manufacturing town in N Nova Scotia, Canada. It produces heavy machinery, steel, coal, paint, pulp and furniture. Pop 10 849.

NEW GRANADA, Spanish colony in NW South America which included present Colombia, Panama, Ecuador and Venezuela, established in the first half of the 16th century. It was named by Gonzalo JIMÉNEZ DE QUESADA in 1537 and attached to the vice-royalty of Peru until 1717 when it became a vice-royalty itself until independence in 1819.

NEW GUINEA, world's second largest island. It lies in the SW Pacific just S of the equator and is separated from N Australia by the Torres Strait and the Arafura and Coral Seas. The island covers an area of 319 713sq mi, and comprises a series of high central mountain ranges and densely-forested tropical lowlands. Djaja Peak is the highest mountain at 16 535ft. Politically, New Guinea is divided into two parts: WEST IRIAN, a province of Indonesia, and PAPUA NEW GUINEA, self-governing since 1973.

Melanesians and Papuans are the two largest population groups in New Guinea. In remote mountain areas there are primitive Negrito groups and Papuans some of whom are head-hunting tribes. Some animals such as the opossum are related to Australian species. There are more than 70 species of snakes, many species of butterflies and birds of paradise.

New Guinea was discovered by the Portuguese in the 16th century and named for Guinea, West Africa. It was colonized by the Dutch, Germans and British; after WWI, Australia gained the German sector. The island was bitterly contested by the Japanese and the Allies during WWII.

NEW HAMPSHIRE, the third-largest of the New England states and one of the original 13 colonies. Forests cover four-fifths of New Hampshire's surface, and it contains mountains, lakes and streams. Despite its rural appearance and fame as a tourist center it is also one of the most intensively industrialized states of the union.

New Hampshire can be divided into three main areas: the White Mountains in the N third of the state; the coastal lowlands in the extreme SE corner; and the New England Upland, a rolling plateau that covers the central and S portions of the state. Most of New Hampshire's people and industries are concentrated in the S, but the scenic beauty of the White Mountains attracts thousands of skiers, hikers, campers and sightseers. The 86-peak Presidential Range includes the highest point in New England, Mount Washington (6 288ft), and the Franconia Range includes Profile Mountain and the steep chasm of the Flume. The Merrimack R drains southward from the White Mountains, and most of the state's major cities, industries and farms are located along its hilly, uneven valley.

The first settlements were established along the coast in the 1620s, and in 1629 Capt. John MASON was granted the land between the Merrimack and Piscataqua rivers, which he named New Hampshire. Inland settlement was slow and began on a large scale only after the FRENCH AND INDIAN WARS. New Hampshire was the first colony to declare itself independent of British rule and to adopt a new constitution, 1776.

The original importance of agriculture, textiles and leather goods has declined, but under the far-sighted planning of the New Business Development Corporation, the development of new and more varied industries more than outweighs these losses. The population continues to rise at a faster rate than the national average.

Tourists flock to New Hampshire all year around, and the money they spend—whether in the ski resorts of the White Mountains (pictured here), or in the hotels on the beachfronts or on the banks of peaceful lakes—contributes a sizable proportion of the state's income.

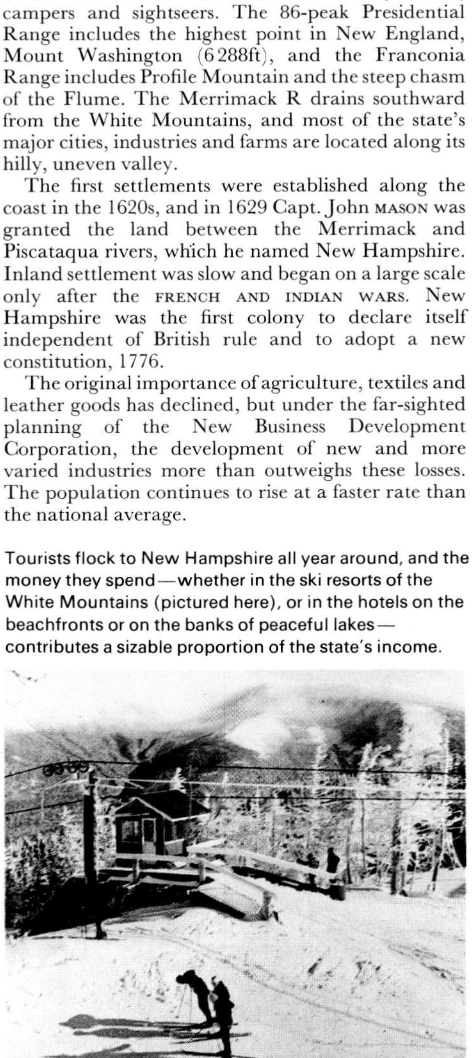

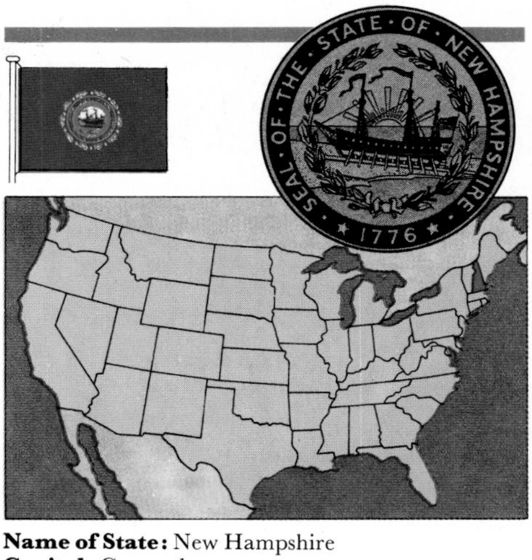

Name of State: New Hampshire
Capital: Concord
Statehood: June 21, 1788 (9th state)
Familiar Name: Granite State
Area: 9 304sq mi
Population: 737 681
Elevation: Highest—6 288ft, Mount Washington
Lowest—sea level, Atlantic Ocean
Motto: Live Free or Die
State Flower: Purple lilac
State Bird: Purple finch
State Tree: White birch
State Songs: "New Hampshire, My New Hampshire," "Old New Hampshire"

NEW HARMONY, town in SW Ind., the site of two cooperative communities in the early 1800s. "Harmonie" was settled in 1814 by George Rapp, leader of the HARMONY SOCIETY. In 1824 the colony was sold to Robert OWEN, and renamed New Harmony. The community, based on socialism and Owen's theories of human freedom, was a noted scientific and cultural center but broke up in 1828. Pop 971.

NEW HAVEN, third-largest city in Conn., its chief port, and famous as the seat of YALE UNIVERSITY. It is a noted cultural center and important for its varied industrial products. It was founded in 1638 by Puritans from Boston led by John DAVENPORT and Theophilus EATON. It was a flourishing port at the end of the 18th century, and only revived as such when a deep water channel was dredged in 1927. Pop 137 707.

NEW HEBRIDES, group of some 80 islands in the SW Pacific, about 500mi W of Fiji, and administered by France and Great Britain. In all they total about 5 700sq mi; the main islands include Espiritu Santo, Malekula and Efate on which stands the capital, Vila. The population is predominantly Melanesian and speaks Pidgin English. Copra, coffee and cocoa are the main export crops. Pop 86 000.

NEW HOPE, village in SE central Minn., a residential suburb of Minneapolis. Pop 23 180.

NEW HYDE PARK, village in SE N.Y., on Long Island. It is a residential area. Pop 10 116.

NEW IBERIA, city in S La., seat of Iberia parish. It is an industrial center for lumber, sugar, fishing and salt. Pop 30 147.

NE WIN (formerly Shu Maung; 1911–   ), Burmese general, political leader and president of Burma 1974–   . After being prime minister, 1958–60, he assumed power in 1962 in an army coup and has attempted to establish a form of socialist republic in Burma.

NEWINGTON, residential town in Central Conn., SW of Hartford, settled in 1670. Pop 26 037.

NEW IRELAND, narrow, volcanic island in the BISMARCK ARCHIPELAGO, part of PAPUA NEW GUINEA, about 3 340sq mi in area. When first sighted in 1616 it was thought to be part of NEW BRITAIN ISLAND.

NEW JERSEY, the smallest of the Middle Atlantic States, the nation's most highly urbanized and most densely populated state, and one of the original 13

Entrance to the Lincoln Tunnel in Union City, New Jersey, one of that state's successful traffic-flow developments. New Jersey was one of the first to introduce such advanced concepts in freeway design as clover-leaf junctions and viaducts.

colonies. New Jersey's importance is far greater than its size would indicate. It is one of the leading industrial states of America, a popular resort area and the home of small but highly efficient farms. Strategically located amid many rich markets, New Jersey has exceptional transport facilities and the most concentrated rail and road network in the nation.

The highly urbanized northeast corner of New Jersey, close to New York City, suffers from pollution, congestion and urban blight as serious as any in the US, yet two-thirds of the state is covered by farms and forests, and the Atlantic coast is dotted with well-known resorts such as Atlantic City and Asbury Park. Two great rivers, the Delaware and the Hudson, flow along its borders.

On a voyage for the Dutch East India Company, Henry HUDSON sailed up the Hudson River in 1609, and Dutch trading posts were soon established, but the first permanent settlement, Bergen, was not founded until 1660. In 1664 the Dutch possessions in North America were captured by the English (see NEW NETHERLAND), and New Jersey was divided and

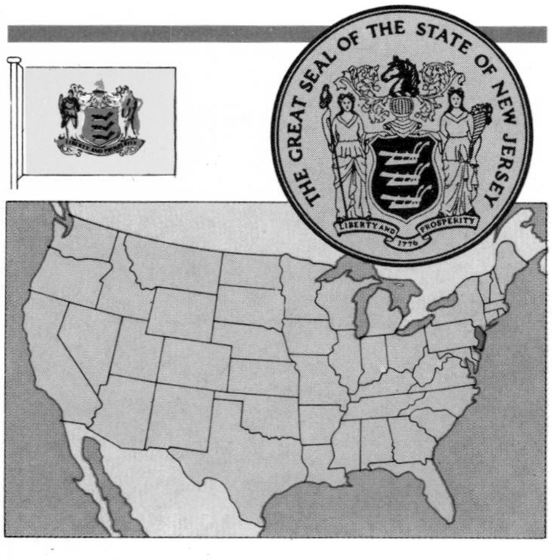

Name of State: New Jersey
Capital: Trenton
Statehood: Dec. 18, 1787 (3rd state)
Familiar Name: Garden State
Area: 7 532sq mi
Population: 7 168 164
Elevation: Highest—1 803ft, High Point
Lowest—sea level, Atlantic Ocean
Motto: Liberty and Prosperity
State Flower: Violet
State Bird: Eastern goldfinch
State Tree: Red oak
State Song: None

subdivided among various owners until 1702, when it became a single crown colony. After the British capture of New York in 1776, in which year New Jersey became a state, it became the "cockpit of the Revolution," as armies crossed and recrossed the state, fighting nearly 100 engagements.

New Jersey possesses 24 accredited four-year colleges and universities. Among the best-known are PRINCETON UNIVERSITY (fourth oldest in the US), with its famed INSTITUTE FOR ADVANCED STUDY; and Rutgers, the State University. After WWII a large number of industrial research centers were established, and these plants, now over 700 in number, play an important role in the state's industrial preeminence. The leading branch of manufacturing is the chemical industry, and its output ranks first in the nation. The second major industry is that of electrical machinery.

NEW JERUSALEM, Church of the. See SWEDENBORG, Emanuel.

NEW KENSINGTON, city in SW Pa., on the Allegheny R, in a coal-mining region. It is a major producer of aluminum. Pop 20 312.

NEWLANDS, Francis Griffith (1848–1917), US politician and lawyer. He represented Nev. in Congress, 1893–1903, and was a democratic senator 1903–1917. He wrote the Newlands Act (1913) which provided for mediation and conciliation in labor disputes, and was involved in federal trade and transportation affairs.

NEW LONDON, seaport city in SE Conn., near the mouth of the Thames R. Laid out in 1646, it became a famous whaling and shipbuilding port in the 19th century. Its industries include textiles and food-processing. Pop 31 630.

NEWMAN, John Henry (1801–1890), English clergyman and a founder of the OXFORD MOVEMENT in 1833. A Church of England vicar and tutor at Oxford University, he was converted to Roman Catholicism in 1845, becoming a cardinal in 1879. Much of his thought was controversial, opposed by Cardinal Henry MANNING and Charles KINGSLEY. He was a master stylist. His writings include *Apologia pro vita sua* (1864), a religious autobiography.

NEWMARKET, town in SE Ontario, Canada, 30mi N of Toronto, seat of York Co. It has various light industries. Pop 18 941.

NEW MEXICO, one of the states of the SW and the fifth largest of all the states; it is a mixture of three distinct cultures—Anglo-American, Spanish and Indian. Side by side with reminders of the old Indian and Spanish cultures are modern industries and research stations for atomic energy and space travel. The world's first atomic bomb, developed during WWII at the Los Alamos Laboratories north of Santa Fe, was exploded near Alamogordo in July 1945.

New Mexico's varied topography and geological history make the area of great interest to geologists. Innumerable fossils have been found in the various geological strata, including many extinct species of plants and animals. The state has an average elevation of about 5 700ft, the highest point being Wheeler Peak (13 160ft). New Mexico includes parts of four main regions: the Colorado Plateaus in the NW, the Rocky Mountain System in the N central area, the Great Plains in the E and the Basin and Range Region in the central and SW area of the state. The state is generally arid with limited water resources but it has two important rivers, the Rio Grande and the Pecos, both of which help to provide irrigation.

New Mexico is basically a mining state with rich deposits of many minerals, in particular, uranium. Atomic and space research is heavily funded by the federal government and is of great importance to the state's economy. Ranching is the state's most important agricultural activity, though there are other forms of farming including the growing of pecans.

There are about 55 000 Indians, many of whom live on reservations. Spanish-Americans constitute about 25% of the population, and Spanish influence is shown in architecture and place names as well as in the wide use of Spanish.

For about 20 000 years Indians have inhabited

Shiprock, New Mexico, is one of that state's most interesting rock formations; some of these may be up to 2 billion years old. Shiprock represents magma which solidified in the conduit of an ancient volcano; the volcano was then eroded away, leaving only the harder plug still standing.

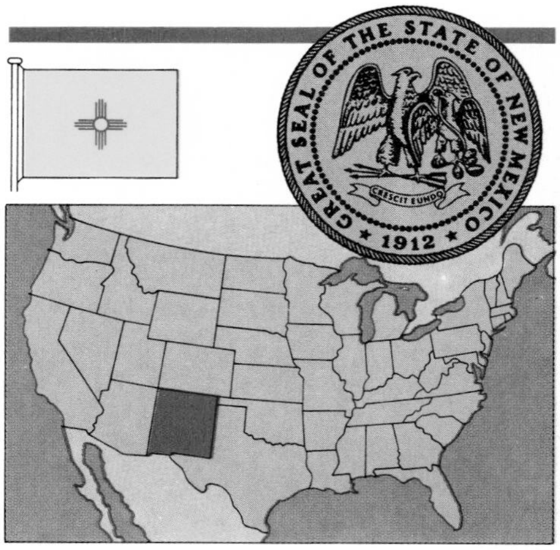

Name of State: New Mexico
Capital: Santa Fe
Statehood: Jan. 6, 1912 (47th state)
Familiar Name: Land of Enchantment
Area: 121 412sq mi
Population: 1 016 000
Elevation: Highest—13 160ft, Wheeler Peak
Lowest—2 817ft, Red Bluff Reservoir
Motto: Crescit eundo (It grows as it goes)
State Flower: Yucca Flower
State Bird: Roadrunner
State Tree: Piñon, or nut pine
State Song: "O, Fair New Mexico"

what is now New Mexico. They were conquered and colonized by the Spaniards from 1540 until in 1821 Mexico won independence from Spain and took over control of New Mexico, only to lose it to the US after the MEXICAN WAR (1846–48). Settlement continued and increased with the GADSDEN PURCHASE in 1853.

NEW MILFORD, town in W Conn., in an agricultural area, with light industries. It was the home of Roger SHERMAN. Pop 14 601.

NEW MILFORD, borough, in NE N.J., a residential suburb of New York City. French HUGUENOTS settled there in 1695. Pop 19 149.

NEWNAN, city in W Ga., seat of Coweta Co., formerly an agricultural center, it now has textile and metal industries. Pop 11 205.

NEW NATIONALISM, Theodore ROOSEVELT's political philosophy (about 1910) proclaimed in opposition to Woodrow WILSON's Democratic manifesto, the NEW FREEDOM. His ideas included increased federal intervention to regulate the economy and promote social justice, honest government and conservation of natural resources.

NEW NETHERLAND, Dutch colonial territory

extending roughly from Albany, New York to Manhattan island, and including parts of New Jersey, Connecticut and Delaware. It was granted in 1621 by the government of Holland to a group of merchants known as the DUTCH WEST INDIA COMPANY. In 1626 the company purchased Manhattan Island from the Indians and called it New Amsterdam. In 1664, under the British, New Amsterdam became New York City.

NEW ORLEANS, historic city in La., seat of Orleans parish, on the banks of the Mississippi R 107mi from the river's mouth. One of the world's great ports, New Orleans is the business and financial capital of the Deep South. Excellent transport facilities serve the port, which is also the main gateway for trade with Latin America. New Orleans is surrounded by oil and natural gas deposits. It is a center of huge aerospace, shipbuilding, oil and chemical industries, and has many manufacturing and processing plants. The city is famed for its picturesque French Quarter (*Vieux Carré*) and Mardi Gras Carnival, and as the birthplace of JAZZ. Its varied population includes French-speaking Creoles who are descended from early French and Spanish settlers (see LOUISIANA PURCHASE). The Creole cookery of New Orleans is famous. Pop 593 471.

NEW ORLEANS, Battle of, British attempt in 1815 to occupy New Orleans during the WAR OF 1812. The result was more of a massacre than a battle for the British, whom Andrew JACKSON repulsed in a terrible defeat. Jackson became a national hero for this, and eventually president.

NEW PHILADELPHIA, city in NE Ohio, seat of Tuscarawas Co. Located in a clay region, it manufactures ceramic machinery and pottery. Pop 15 184.

NEWPORT, city in N Ky., seat of Campbell Co., on the Ohio R. It has steel, clothing and lumber industries. Pop 25 998.

NEWPORT, historic resort city in SE R.I., seat of Newport Co., and an important naval base. Founded in 1639, it became a refuge from religious persecution for Quakers and Jews. It was a wealthy resort in the 19th century, and its jazz festivals in the 1950s were famous. Pop 34 562.

NEWPORT BEACH, residential city in SW Cal., on the Pacific Ocean. It is a beach resort and has mixed industries. Pop 49 422.

NEWPORT NEWS, port and city in SE Va., on HAMPTON ROADS. Settled in 1621 by Irish colonists, it developed rapidly in the 1880s with the growth of railroads. In 1862 the battle of the IRONCLADS, the *Monitor* and *Merrimack* occurred there. It is now a major port and shipbuilding center. Pop 138 177.

NEW PROVIDENCE, borough in NE N.J., 8mi SSE of Morristown. It has light industries and extensive horticultural nurseries. Pop 13 796.

NEW QUEBEC CRATER (formerly Chubb Crater), circular depression in N Quebec, possibly produced by a meteorite. It is 1 300ft deep and 2mi in diameter.

NEW ROCHELLE, residential city in SE N.Y., on Long Island Sound, purchased in 1688 by the HUGUENOTS. It also has light industries. Pop 75 385.

NEW SALEM, restored pioneer village in the New Salem State Park, central Ill., the home of Abraham LINCOLN 1831–37.

NEW SIBERIAN ISLANDS, Russian island group in the Arctic Ocean between the Laptev Sea and the East Siberian Sea. The chief islands are Kotelny, Faddeyevski and New Siberian Island. Meteorological stations have operated there since 1927.

NEW SMYRNA BEACH, resort city in E Fla., on the Atlantic Ocean, with citrus fruit, fishing and light manufacturing industries. Pop 10 580.

NEW SOUTH WALES, the fourth largest (309 433sq mi) of Australia's six states, situated in the SE. It is the most highly-developed industrial and agricultural state in Australia, steel, wheat, wool and meat being the principal products. The state has rich mining resources. Sydney is the state capital and chief port.

NEWSPAPER, daily or weekly publication of current domestic and foreign news. In addition newspapers often contain information, humor and advice on a great variety of subjects. In 59 BC Julius Caesar ordered the daily publication of a newssheet, the *Acta Diurna*, which was posted in public places. The first Chinese newspaper was published in the 8th century. Johann GUTENBERG's invention of movable type in the mid-15th century was an important step in the development of newspapers, and newspaper sheets appeared in Venice and Cologne in the 16th century. In 1620 fact-sheets printed in Amsterdam were sold in England. The *London Gazette* (1665) was the first paper issued regularly in a newspaper format. The first English daily, the *London Daily Courant*, appeared in England in 1702. The first regularly printed American paper was the *Boston Newsletter* (1704). Early newspapers were too expensive for the ordinary reader, but the gap was later filled by James Gordon BENNETT and Horace GREELEY publishing daily penny papers, such as *The New York Sun* (1833), the *New York Herald* (1835) and the *New York Tribune* (1841).

An era of fierce competitive journalism began with the end of the Civil War, when newspaper initiative took the form of stunts, crusades, scandal and increasing sensationalism. In the late 19th and early 20th centuries Joseph PULITZER, William Randolph HEARST, Colonel Robert McCORMICK and Joseph Medill Patterson, and Lords BEAVERBROOK and NORTHCLIFFE in England, were the tsars of vast newspaper empires, and an important force in national life and international politics. Newspapers have since toned down and have become in general a responsible medium for domestic and foreign news.

Radio, and later television, together with rising production costs, have forced many newspapers out of business in recent years.

NEW SWEDEN, Swedish colony on the Delaware R extending from the site of Trenton, N.J., to the mouth of the Delaware R. In 1633 the New Sweden Company was organized, and in 1638 two Swedish vessels arrived and Peter MINUIT founded Fort Christina (later Wilmington, Del.). The Dutch, led by Peter STUYVESANT, annexed the colony in 1655.

NEWT, term referring in the Old World to the genus *Triturus*; in the New World the word is less specific and includes other genera of the family Salamandridae. Newts are true amphibians, terrestrial during the greater part of the year, and aquatic during the breeding season. They feed on worms, slugs and insects on land, and aquatic larvae, crustaceans and mollusks when in the water.

NEW TESTAMENT, the part of the Bible which is distinctively Christian. In it are recorded the life and teachings of JESUS CHRIST and the beginnings of CHRISTIANITY. It comprises the four GOSPELS, the ACTS OF THE APOSTLES, the Epistles and the Book of REVELATION, numbering 27 books in all (for list see BIBLE). The Gospels (lives of Christ), are named for their traditional authors: Saints MATTHEW, MARK, LUKE and JOHN. The Epistles are early evangelical letters, written to local churches or individuals. Thirteen are ascribed to St. PAUL; the others (except the anonymous HEBREWS), are named for their traditional authors. The New Testament is written in everyday 1st-century Greek. The earliest copy fragments date from the early 2nd century. (See also CANON, BIBLICAL.)

NEW THOUGHT, a movement devoted to exploring the power of the mind, especially as a source of physical healing and well-being, spiritual guidance and human creativity. It comprises many different groups with similar aims.

NEWTON, city in S central Iowa, seat of Jasper Co., 30mi E of Des Moines. Industries include washing machines. Pop 15 619.

NEWTON, city in SE central Kansas, seat of Harvey Co., 35mi E of Hutchinson. It is a railroad center with railroad shops. Pop 15 439.

NEWTON, city in NE Mass., 7mi W of Boston, on the Charles R. It is a residential suburb composed of numerous distinct villages. Pop 91 263.

NEWTON, Sir Isaac (1642–1726), the most prestigious natural philosopher and mathematician of modern times, the discoverer of the CALCULUS and author of the theory of universal GRAVITATION. Newton went up to Trinity College, Cambridge, in 1661, retiring to Woolsthorp, Lincolnshire, during the Plague of 1665–66, but becoming a fellow in 1667 and succeeding Isaac BARROW in the Lucasian Chair of Mathematics in 1669. He was elected Fellow of the ROYAL SOCIETY in 1672, on the strength of his optical discoveries. In Cambridge, Newton spent much time in alchemical experiments, though, toward the end of the century, he tired of the academical life and accepted a position at the Royal Mint, becoming Master of the Mint in 1699. He resigned his chair and entered Parliament in 1701 and two years later began his presidency of the Royal Society, which he retained until his death. His whole life was one of ceaseless energy—investigating mathematics, optics, chronology, chemistry, theology, mechanics, dynamics and the occult—broken only by a period of mental illness about 1693. His achievements were legion: the method of FLUXIONS and fluents (calculus); the theory of universal gravitation and his derivation of KEPLER's LAWS; his formulation of the concept of FORCE as expressed in his three laws of motion (see MECHANICS); the corpuscular theory of LIGHT, and the BINOMIAL THEOREM, among many others. These were summed up in his two greatest works: *Philosophiae Naturalis Principia Mathematica* (1687)—the "Principia", which established the mathematical representation of nature as the paradigm of what counted as "science"—and the *Opticks* (1704). Newton's often bitter controversies with his fellow scientists (notably HOOKE and LEIBNIZ) are famous, but his influence is undoubted, even if, in the cases of optical theory and the Newtonian calculus notation, it retarded rather than accelerated the advance of British science.

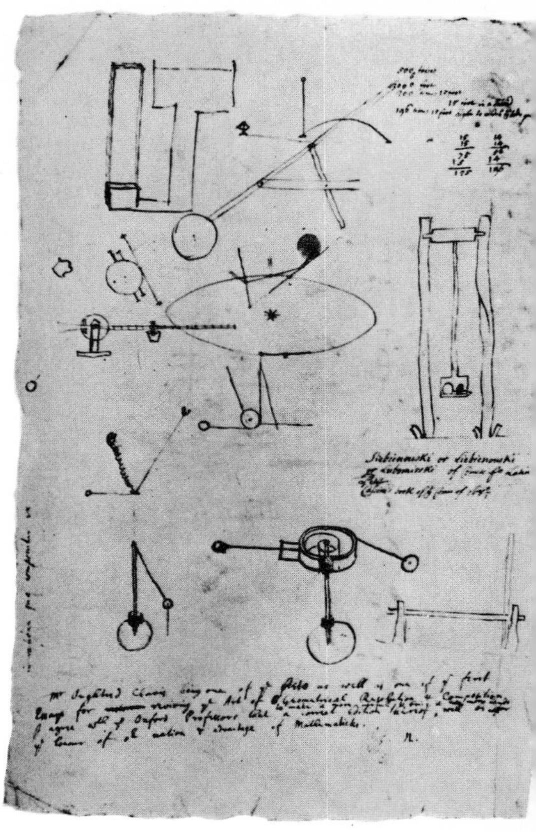

Isaac Newton left hundreds of pages of manuscript notes on alchemical, chronological, mathematical, physical and theological subjects—and many more were lost in a fire in the 1690s. Here is a rare page of pictorial sketches, possibly dating from about 1685. Various hydraulic, pendulum and centrifugal-force devices seem to be represented.

NEWTON'S RINGS. See INTERFERENCE.

NEWTOWN, town in SW Conn., in Fairfield Co. Mixed industries include plastic products. Pop 16 942.

NEW ULM, city in S Minn., seat of Brown Co., 24mi WNW of Mankato. It is the center of a farming region, with varied industry. Pop 13 051.

NEW WESTMINSTER, city in SW British Columbia, Canada, a suburb of Vancouver, on the

Fraser R. It has diversified industries. Pop 42 835.

NEW YEAR'S DAY, the first day of the year, the date of which varies according to which CALENDAR is being followed. In the Gregorian calendar it falls on Jan. 1. It is an ancient festival celebrated in most cultures, being particularly important among the Chinese.

NEW YORK, one of the Middle Atlantic states of the US, and one of the original 13 colonies, location of the nation's largest metropolis, NEW YORK CITY. It is bounded on the N by Canada and Lake Ontario, E by Vt., Mass., and Conn., S by Pa., N.J., and the Atlantic Ocean, and W by Pa., Lake Erie and Canada.

Land. The topography of N.Y. is rich in variety and scenic beauty. The Appalachian Plateau, its largest land region, slopes upward (NW to SE) from Niagara Falls to the Catskill Mts. In the NE is the Adirondack Upland. There are 1 637sq mi of inland waters in addition to those of the Great Lakes. The 300mi long Hudson R with its tributary the Mohawk, the St. Lawrence R and the Delaware R all form important transport routes.

People. Almost 90% of the population (including New York City) is urban. N.Y. has long been the immigration center of the nation. The numerically-dominant immigrant groups are from Italy, Germany, the Soviet Union, Poland, Ireland and Puerto Rico. N.Y. has the largest black population of any state in the US.

Shack in a clearing in the Catskill Mountains, in central New York State. Its wood comes from the forest around it; oak, beech and maple grow at lower elevations, spruce and fir on the higher crests.

Economy. New York is the nation's leading manufacturing and trading state. Major industries include printing and publishing, machinery, clothing and food products. N.Y.'s intensive agriculture contributes milk, grain, potatoes, apples and grapes. The state's varied natural resources are far from sufficient to supply manufacturing needs, but hydroelectricity is provided by the St. Lawrence and Niagara power plants. Being the only state to border on both the Atlantic and the Great Lakes, N.Y. has been a vital transport and shipping route throughout its history, and especially since the opening of the ERIE CANAL in 1825. The port of New York handles over 160 million tons of cargo a year.

History. Home of the IROQUOIS and ALGONQUIN INDIANS, the region of present-day N.Y. was established (1624) as the colony of NEW NETHERLAND by Dutch settlers. In 1664 Peter STUYVESANT, under whose administration the colony had flourished, was forced to surrender to British claims, when the state together with its capital New Amsterdam was renamed for the Duke of York (later James II of England). New York was a major battlefield during the FRENCH AND INDIAN WARS (1689–1763), and during the REVOLUTIONARY WAR was the scene of the decisive Battle of SARATOGA. The state contributed significantly to Union success during the CIVIL WAR.

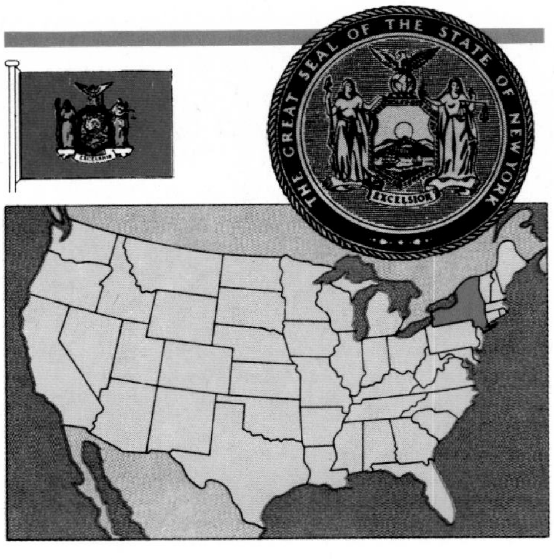

Name of State: New York
Capital: Albany
Statehood: July 26, 1788 (11th state)
Familiar Name: Empire State, Excelsior State
Area: 49 576sq mi
Population: 18 236 967
Elevation: Highest—5 344ft, Mount Marcy
Lowest—sea level, Atlantic Ocean
Motto: Excelsior (Ever Upward)
State Flower: Rose
State Bird: Bluebird
State Tree: Sugar maple
State Song: None

NEW YORK CITY, city in SE N.Y., the largest in the US and the Western Hemisphere. It is divided into five boroughs: Manhattan, the Bronx, Brooklyn, Queens and Richmond. The long, narrow island of Manhattan, upon which New York's complex network of bridges and tunnels all converge, is the city's economic and cultural heart. New York is the nation's richest port, and a world leader in trade and finance. It also leads in manufacturing (notably garments), communications (broadcasting, printing and publishing), and the arts.

In 1626, Dutch settlers of NEW NETHERLAND purchased Manhattan from the resident Indians, reputedly for $24 worth of goods, and it became the site of their major city, New Amsterdam. The city, which had flourished under the firm administration of its last Dutch governor, Peter STUYVESANT, was surrendered to the British in 1664, and renamed New York. Over the next hundred years it developed rapidly as a prosperous trade center. In the late Colonial period New Yorkers were among the most outspoken opponents of British rule, but after the defeat (1776) of George Washington at the Battle of Long Island (see LONG ISLAND, BATTLE OF) the city remained in the hands of English troops until the end of the REVOLUTIONARY WAR, after which it served briefly (1789–90) as the nation's capital. As early as the first census of 1790, New York was the largest city in the US, and by 1860 its population was almost a million. Already suffering from its rapid, unplanned growth, the city's population was doubled in the great wave of immigration between 1880 and 1900. Housing and transport problems caused by this influx were partly eased by the construction of the first elevated railway in 1867, Brooklyn Bridge in 1883, and the first subway system in 1904. Scarcity of land and subsequent high land prices produced a new architectural form—the skyscraper, which was to be for long the very symbol of modernity.

Map showing the administrative division of New York City into districts. The brown sections make up New York City proper: Manhattan (1); Bronx (2); Queens (3); Brooklyn (4); Richmond (5). The yellow sections make up the New York Metropolitan Region: Nassau (6); Suffolk (7); Rockland (8); Westchester (9); Hudson (10); Union (11); Essex (12); Bergen (13); Passaic (14); Morris (15); Somerset (16); Middlesex (17); Monmouth (18); Orange (19); Putnam (20); Dutchess (21); Fairfield (22).

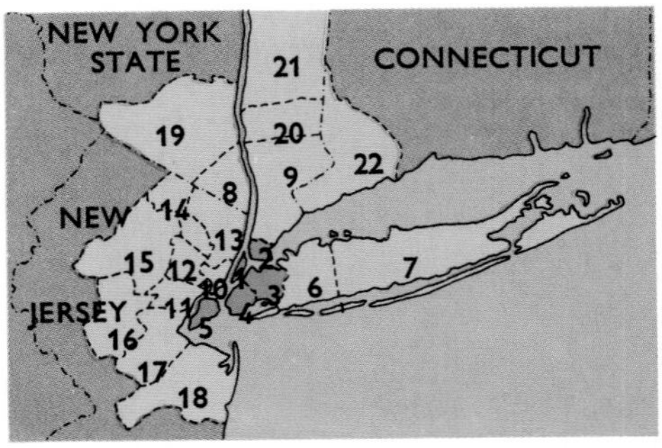

The familiar aspect of New York City. Visible to the east is the Queensboro Bridge across the East River.

Around the turn of the century bitter conflicts between labor and management resulted in highly progressive labor laws. New York's political leadership, at times notoriously corrupt, has included such notable reformers as Theodore ROOSEVELT, Fiorello LA GUARDIA and John LINDSAY.

New York has over 100 parks, some of them achieving a striking atmosphere of serenity within the often hectic bustle of activity which surrounds them. The city's cultural and sporting facilities offer an enormous range of interest and opportunity. Pop 7895563.

NEW YORK DRAFT RIOTS, in 1863, during the American Civil War, four days of rioting in protest against the Union draft law which allowed a man to buy his way out of the army for $300, thus forcing more poor people into the ranks. The riots caused high casualties and massive damage. Thirteen regiments were brought in to restore order.

NEW YORK STATE BARGE CANAL, inland waterway system which connects the Hudson R with the Great Lakes. It was completed in 1918. Its 524mi length includes the ERIE CANAL.

NEW ZEALAND, sovereign state within the British Commonwealth, 1200mi SE of Australia, in the S Pacific Ocean. The Country comprises North Island, South Island (the two principal islands), Stewart Island and the Chatham Islands, with other small outlying islands.

Land. Both major islands are mountainous, with fertile coastal plains. North Island has some volcanic ranges, a region of hot springs surrounding Lake Taupo in the center, and the country's major river, the Waikato. South Island includes large areas of forest, and many glaciers and lakes. Plants include subtropical species. There are hardly any native mammals, but many rare birds, such as the KIWI. The climate is temperate.

People. About 10% of New Zealand's population are MAORIS, and about 90% are descended from settlers who came from Britain. Over 40% of the population live in urban areas—notably Auckland, Christchurch, and the capital, Wellington.

Economy. Sheep and cattle are the main sources of income. Principal exports are frozen meat (mainly lamb), wool and dairy products. The country's varied light industry is dominated by food-processing. Some minerals are produced. New Zealand's beauty and diversity, and its famous fishing and winter sports attract growing numbers of tourists.

History. The chief Maori migrations (1200–1400) led to the eclipse of the earlier Moriori tribes in New Zealand. The islands were sighted by the Dutch seaman Abel TASMAN in 1642, and named for the Netherlands province of Zeeland. In the 1770s Captain James COOK visited New Zealand and claimed it for England. Missionaries became active in the early 19th century, and systematic colonization was begun by the New Zealand Company, founded in 1837. Maori chiefs acknowledged British sovereignty in exchange for recognition of their territorial rights at the Treaty of Waitangi (1840), but over the next 30 years the treaty was contravened by white settlers who fought Maoris for their land. As a colony, New Zealand was made independent from Australia in

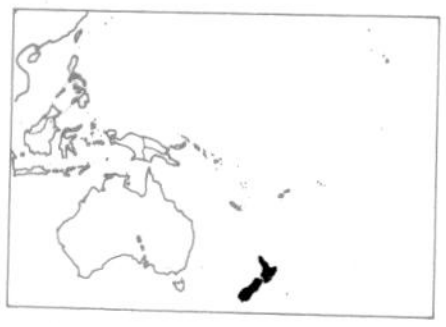

Official Name: New Zealand
Capital: Wellington
Area: 103736sq mi
Population: 2974659
Languages: English; Maori also spoken
Religions: Protestant, Roman Catholic
Monetary Unit(s): 1 New Zealand dollar = 100 cents

Sheep grazing on South Island, New Zealand, in the upland pastures of the New Zealand Alps, visible in the background. The abundance of good sheep grazing land has made wool and meat exports a mainstay of New Zealand's economy.

1841. It achieved self-government in 1852 and was made completely independent in 1931. A pioneer in social reform, New Zealand was the first country to give women the vote (1893) and inaugurated a progressive social security system in 1898. New Zealand fought with the Allies in WWI and WWII, and with the Americans in the Korean and Vietnam wars.

NEY, Michel (1769–1815), French Napoleonic marshal and military hero. His rear-guard defense during NAPOLEON I's retreat from Moscow (1812) was the most notable achievement of a brilliant career. Though he helped persuade Napoleon to abdicate, Ney's allegiance to the Bourbon Louis XVIII did not outlive Napoleon's return from exile. Ney fought with Napoleon at WATERLOO, and after it was condemned to death for treason by the British.

NEZ PERCÉ INDIANS (French: pierced nose), American Indian tribe of present-day central Idaho. Noted horse-breeders, they ceded (1855) much of their territory to the US. Fraudulently-enforced cession of a further 75% of their land (1863) and many land disputes led to the Nez Percé War of 1877, in which 300 Indians held out for five months against 5000 US troops before surrendering. In the mid-1970s, some 1500 Nez Percé Indians still remained in reservations.

NIACIN. See VITAMINS.

NIAGARA, Fort, National Monument in NW N.Y., a stone fortress built (1726) by the French at the mouth of the Niagara R. Captured in 1759 by the British, it was ceded to the US in 1796. During the War of 1812 it was briefly recaptured by the British.

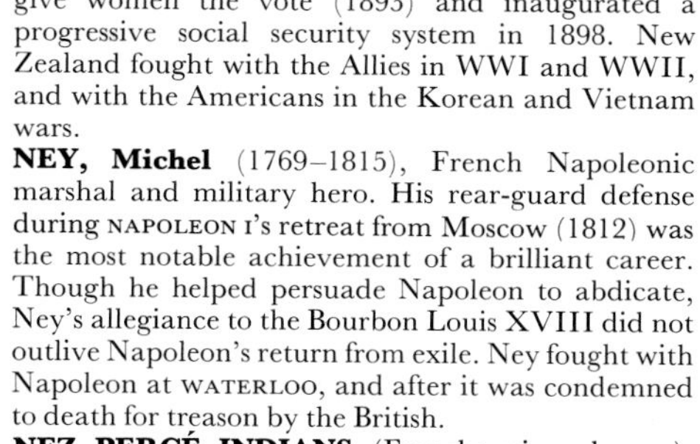

Aerial view of Niagara Falls, showing the graceful sweep of the Canadian, or Horseshoe, Falls.

NIAGARA FALLS, city in W N.Y., at the falls of the Niagara R. It is a major resort area and one of the nation's hydroelectric centers, with many varied industries. Pop 85615.

NIAGARA FALLS, city in SE Ontario, Canada, on the Niagara R just below the falls, linked by bridges to Niagara Falls, N.Y. It is a center of hydroelectric power, varied industries and tourism. Pop 67163.

NIAGARA FALLS, cataract in the Niagara R, between W N.Y. and S Ontario, Canada, world-famous spectacle and the continent's greatest natural source of waterpower. The river is divided into the American Falls (1060ft wide and 167ft high) and the Canadian, or Horseshoe Falls (2600ft wide and 158ft high) by Goat Island before plunging into the deep gorge with its Whirlpool Rapids. Some 200000cu ft of water per second pass over the Falls, which are gradually moving upstream as they erode the rock.

NIAGARA-ON-THE-LAKE, town in SE Ontario, Canada, on Lake Ontario at the mouth of the Niagara R. Pop 12552.

NIAGARA RIVER, 35mi long river in W N.Y., flowing N from Lake Erie to Lake Ontario (over Niagara Falls) and forming part of the US–Canada border.

NIAMEY, capital of the Niger Republic in West Africa, on the E bank of the Niger R, SW Niger. It is Niger's trade, transport and administrative center. Pop 102000.

NIBELUNGENLIED ("Song of the Nibelungs"), German epic written c1200 AD, partly based on Scandinavian myths. It tells how SIEGFRIED, who had gained the treasure of the Nibelungen dwarfs, is given Kriemhild in marriage as a reward for helping Gunther win BRUNHILD by trickery. Brunhild in revenge has Siegfried killed by Hagen, who hides the treasure in the Rhine. Kriemhild's subsequent vow to avenge Siegfried ends in a holocaust. The story inspired WAGNER's operatic tetralogy *The Ring of the Nibelungs*.

NICAEA, Councils of, the first and seventh ECUMENICAL COUNCILS. The first Nicaean Council, called in 325 AD by the Emperor CONSTANTINE, condemned ARIANISM, and drew up the NICENE CREED. The second Nicaean Council in 787 ruled in favor of the restoration of images in churches (see ICONOCLASTIC CONTROVERSY).

NICARAGUA, largest of the Central American republics, bounded on the N by Honduras, E by the Caribbean Sea, S by Costa Rica, and W by the Pacific Ocean. It is a country of volcanoes, lakes and forested plains. A prominent physical feature is the long, eastern lowland belt running diagonally across the country, which embraces two large lakes: Nicaragua and Managua. This lowland belt contains all the large towns and 90% of Nicaragua's relatively-sparse population. Earthquakes, such as the one which devastated the capital Managua in 1972, are not uncommon.

The people are predominantly (77%) of mixed Spanish-Indian descent, but include pure Spanish, pure Negroes and pure Indians.

Agriculture is the mainstay of the economy, though forestry and mining play an important part. The main exports are raw cotton, meat, coffee, gold, timber and rice.

Before the arrival of the Spanish conquistador Gil González de Ávila (1522) the country was inhabited by various Indian communities. Another Spanish expedition founded Leon and Granada in 1524. From 1570 the country was ruled as part of Guatemala. Nicaragua won independence from Spain in 1821, and was then annexed to Mexico, after which it became (1825) part of the Central American Federation. Independent from 1838, the country

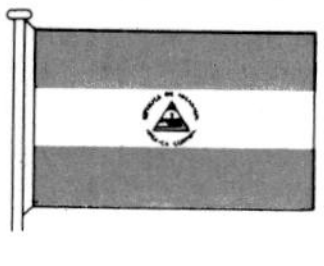

Official Name: Republic of Nicaragua
Capital: Managua
Area: 57143sq mi
Population: 2210000
Language: Spanish
Religion: Roman Catholic
Monetary Unit(s): 1 Cordoba = 100 centavos

The Conquistadors brought with them the Spanish style or architecture, seen clearly in the facades of buildings in Granada, the oldest town in the country, founded by Francisco Fernández de Córdoba in 1524 on the shores of Lake Nicaragua.

became convulsed by power struggles. In 1912 the US was asked for aid, and US Marines occupied the country almost continuously until 1933. Ostensibly a democracy, Nicaragua has been ruled by members of the powerful Somoza family since 1936.

NICARAGUA, Lake, in SW Nicaragua, the largest freshwater lake in Central America. It is 110ft above sea level, about 100mi long and up to 45mi wide. It is important for inland transport and for fishing.

NICCOLITE, coppery-red mineral consisting of nickel arsenide (NiAs); a minor NICKEL ore often found with PYRRHOTITE. It crystallizes in the hexagonal system.

NICE, seaport city in SE France, capital of the Alpes-Maritimes department, on the Mediterranean coast. It is the largest city on the French Riviera, and a major tourist resort and manufacturing center. Pop 338 300.

NICENE CREED, either of two early CREEDS. The first was issued by the first Council of Nicaea (325) to state orthodoxy against ARIANISM. The second was perhaps issued by the Council of Constantinople (381); much longer, it is used at Holy COMMUNION in both Eastern and Western Churches.

NICHE, the way of life adopted by an animal or plant by which it survives in a particular habitat. An organism requires space and food to live successfully, the description of its niche therefore involves consideration of these aspects of its habitat.

NICHOLAS, name of five Popes: **Nicholas I, Saint** (c825–867), reigned 858–867, a vigorous enforcer of papal authority, many of whose rulings set important precedents and were reflected in later canon law; **Nicholas II** (d. 1061), reigned 1059–61, established rules for the election of popes, confining the right to vote to cardinals (thus excluding the emperor and Roman nobles); **Nicholas III** (c1225–1280), reigned 1277–80, created a constitution for Rome which freed the city of foreign influence; **Nicholas IV** (1227–1292), reigned 1288–92; and **Nicholas V** (1397–1455), reigned 1447–55, a humanist scholar who founded the Vatican Library.

NICHOLAS, Saint, 4th-century patron saint of children, scholars, merchants and sailors and probably bishop of Myra in Lycia, Asia Minor. In many European countries he traditionally visits children and gives them gifts on his feast day (Dec. 6). The custom was brought to America by the Dutch, whose Sinter Klaas became the SANTA CLAUS of Christmas.

NICHOLAS, name of two Russian tsars: **Nicholas I** (1796–1855), emperor and tsar 1825–55, notorious for his despotic rule. His succession was challenged by a liberal revolt (see DECEMBRIST REVOLT) which was quickly crushed. A determined absolutist, he opposed all liberal reform or independence. He expanded Russian territory at the expense of Turkey and was only checked by the CRIMEAN WAR. **Nicholas II** (1868–1918), tsar 1894–1917, whose inflexibility and misgovernment helped bring about the RUSSIAN REVOLUTION and the overthrow of his dynasty. His wife, the empress ALEXANDRA, filled the court with irresponsible favorites of whom the monk RASPUTIN was the most influential. Russian defeats in the RUSSO-JAPANESE WAR (1904–05) led to a popular uprising and Nicholas granted limited civil rights and called the first representative DUMA (1905). The military defeats of WWI led to his abdication and eventual execution.

NICHOLAS OF CUSA (1401–1464), German cardinal best known for his advanced cosmological views: he held that the earth rotates on its axis, that space is infinite, and that the sun is a star like other stars (see also ASTRONOMY). He also suggested the use of concave lenses for the shortsighted (see GLASSES; LENS).

NICHOLSON, Ben (1894–   ), British abstract sculptor and painter of landscapes and still-lifes. His reliefs, like *White Relief*, 1939, are composed in an elegant pure linear style.

NICIAS (c470–413 BC), Greek general. Leader of a moderate party in Athens, he negotiated peace with Sparta in 421. With ALCIBIADES he commanded the naval expedition to Syracuse (415) and was executed by the Syracusans.

NICKEL (Ni), hard, gray-white, ferromagnetic (see MAGNETISM) metal in Group VIII of the PERIODIC TABLE; a TRANSITION ELEMENT. About half the total world output comes from deposits of PYRRHOTITE and PENTLANDITE at Sudbury, Ontario; garnierite in New Caledonia is also important. Roasting the ore gives crude nickel oxide, refined by electrolysis or by the Mond process (see MOND, LUDWIG). Nickel is widely used in ALLOYS, including MONEL METAL, INVAR and GERMAN SILVER. In many countries "silver" coins are made from cupronickel (an alloy of copper and nickel). Nickel-chromium alloys ("nichrome"), resistant to oxidation at high temperatures, are used as heating elements in electric fires, etc. Nickel is used for nickel plating and as a catalyst for HYDROGENATION. Chemically nickel resembles IRON and COBALT, being moderately reactive, and forming compounds in the +2 oxidation state; the +4 state is known in LIGAND complexes. AW 58.7, mp 1453°C, bp 2732°C, sg 8.902 (25°C).

NICKELODEON, early motion-picture theater. The first one opened in 1905 in McKeesport, Pa., and offered for five cents a screen program with piano accompaniment. It was so popular that there were 5 000 nickelodeons in the US by 1907. The name was subsequently applied to coin-operated, automatic phonographs.

NICKEL SILVER. See GERMAN SILVER.

NICKLAUS, Jack William (1940–   ), outstanding American golfer who turned professional after winning the US amateur title in 1961. He has won many golf tournaments, including the Masters five times and the US Open three times, and also over $2 million in prize money.

NICOBAR ISLANDS. See ANDAMAN AND NICOBAR ISLANDS.

NICOLAI, Carl Otto Ehrenfried (1810–1849), German composer. Of his many operas, the most famous is *The Merry Wives of Windsor*. He founded the Vienna Philharmonic concerts in 1842.

NICOLAY, John George (1832–1901), German-born US biographer. He was Abraham Lincoln's private secretary from 1860–65. He wrote (with John HAY) Lincoln's biography in 1890, and edited the *Complete Works of Abraham Lincoln*.

NICOLET, Jean (c1598–1642), French explorer who was probably the first European to visit the Lake Michigan area. In 1634 he set out by canoe through Lake Huron, entered Lake Michigan and explored Green Bay and the Fox River, making friendly contact with the WINNEBAGO INDIANS.

NICOLLE, Charles Jules Henri (1866–1936), French bacteriologist awarded the 1928 Nobel Prize for Physiology or Medicine for his discovery that the body louse is a carrier and a main transmitter of TYPHUS (1909). (See LICE.)

NICOLLS, Richard (1624–1672), the first British governor of New York. As governor he made the transition from Dutch to English government (1664–68) as gradual as possible, and treated the Dutch with "humanity and gentleness."

NICOL PRISM, optical device for producing a beam of plane POLARIZED LIGHT. Two pieces of CALCITE crystal are cemented together with CANADA BALSAM. Incident light is split into ordinary and extraordinary linearly polarized rays in the prism. The ordinary ray hits the balsam layer obliquely and is totally internally reflected; the other ray emerges plane polarized for a certain range of incidence angles.

NICOLSON, Sir Harold (1886–1968), British writer and diplomat. After 20 years' diplomatic service (1909–29), he became a member of Parliament (1935–45). He wrote biographies of Verlaine, Byron, Tennyson, Swinburne and King George V, and many reviews.

NICOSIA, capital and largest city of Cyprus. It has a long history of Lusignan, Venetian and Turkish rule and is now an agricultural and commercial center. Pop 117 000.

NICOTINE, colorless oily liquid, an ALKALOID occurring in tobacco leaves and extracted from tobacco refuse. It is used as an insecticide and to make nicotinic acid (see VITAMINS). Nicotine is one of the most toxic substances known; even the small dose ingested by SMOKING causes blood-vessel constriction, raised blood pressure, nausea, headache and impaired digestion.

NICOTINIC ACID. See VITAMINS.

NICTITATING MEMBRANE, or third eyelid, a membrane found in many vertebrates that can be drawn horizontally across the EYE. In birds it lubricates and cleans the eyeball without the necessity of blinking. It is present in a few mammals, and in man is represented by the pink triangle of flesh in the corner of the eye.

NIEBUHR, name of two American Protestant theologians, influenced by Karl BARTH. **Reinhold Niebuhr** (1892–1971), an active socialist in the early 1930s, turned back after WWII to traditional Protestant values, relating them to modern society in his "conservative realism." His *Nature and Destiny of Man* (1941–43) greatly influenced American theology. **Helmut Richard Niebuhr** (1894–1962), his brother, Yale professor of divinity, was concerned with historical revelation. His works include *The Kingdom of God in America* (1937).

NIEBUHR, Barthold Georg (1776–1831), Danish-born German historian and diplomat. In his *History of Rome*, 1811–32, he put forward a scientific method of historical explanation and demonstrated how different sources of material could be evaluated.

NIELLO, technique for decorating silver or gold ware, used by the Romans and in the Middle Ages, and still today, in the East. An engraved design is covered by a mixture of copper, silver, lead and sulfur with BORAX flux. After firing, the black alloy (containing sulfides) fills the lines of the design, and excess is scraped off.

NIELSEN, Carl August (1865–1931), Danish composer. His six symphonies are most notable for their original harmonic structure. He also wrote operas, concertos for flute, clarinet and violin and chamber music.

NIEMAN RIVER. See NEMAN RIVER.

NIEMEYER, Oscar (Oscar Niemeyer Soares Filho; 1907–   ), Brazilian architect whose outstanding work in Brazil culminated in BRASÍLIA, 1956–60. His most characteristic style is the curved, sculptural use of reinforced concrete.

NIEMÖLLER, Martin (1892–   ), German Lutheran pastor who opposed the Nazis and Adolf Hitler. He was confined in concentration camps (1937–1945). In 1945 he organized the "Declaration of Guilt" in which German Churches admitted their failure to resist the Nazis.

NIÉPCE, Joseph Nicéphore (1765–1833), French inventor who in 1826 made the first successful permanent photograph. The image, recorded in asphalt on a pewter plate, required an 8hr exposure in a camera obscura (see CAMERA LUCIDA AND CAMERA OBSCURA). The method used derived from heliography, Niépce's photoengraving process. In 1829 Niépce went into partnership with DAGUERRE.

NIETZSCHE, Friedrich (1844–1900), German philosopher, classical scholar and critic of

Christianity. In *Thus Spake Zarathustra* (1833–91) he introduced the concept of the "Superman," a great-souled hero who transcends the slavish morality of Christianity and whose motivating force is the supreme passion of "will to power," which is directed towards creativity. This passion distinguishes him from inferior human beings. Nietzsche's ideas have been much misrepresented, particularly by the Nazis who misappropriated the concept of the "Superman" to justify their own concepts of Aryan racial superiority.

NIFLHEIM, the name given in early Norse mythology to a region of endless darkness and cold, ruled by the goddess Hel. All who died of illness or age went there.

NIGER, the largest republic in West Africa. It is a landlocked country which has suffered from its remoteness. This, and its general aridity, helps explain its comparatively low population.

Land. Niger is bordered on the N by Algeria and Libya, on the S and SW by Nigeria and Dahomey. Most of the country is desert. The N is typically Saharan and the NE is virtually uninhabitable. The Air mountains are in N central Niger.

People. The people are divided into several different groups: the Hausa, who form over half the population, Djerma-Songhai and Beriberi-Manga in the S are mainly farmers; the Fulani, Tuareg and others in the N are nomadic pastoralists. The principal crops are millet, cassava, sorghum, groundnuts and rice. There are valuable but largely unexploited deposits of uranium ore in the N, and uranium, groundnuts, livestock and textiles are the main exports. A severe drought, which began in 1968, has destroyed much of the crop and livestock.

History. Niger became a French colony in 1922. In 1960 it achieved independence, and Hamani Diori, leader of the Niger Progressive party, became the first president until he was overthrown in a military coup in 1974.

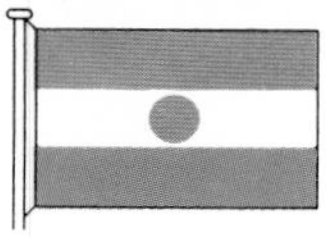

Official Name: Republic of Niger
Capital: Niamey
Area: 489 190sq mi
Population: 4 243 000
Languages: French; Hausa, Fulani
Religions: Muslim, Animist, Christian
Monetary Unit(s): 1 CFA franc = 100 centimes

NIGERIA, federal republic in West Africa, the most populous country in the African continent.

Land. Bordering on the Gulf of Guinea, it lies between Cameroon on the E and Dahomey on the W. Behind the coastal strip are lowlands which rise to the Jos Plateau and this falls away to the sandy high plains of Hausaland in the N. In the S Nigeria has a 475mi coastline of sandbars, mangroves and lagoons, with the great delta of the Niger R as the most prominent natural feature. The N is hot and dry; the S is more humid with the rainfall averaging more than 150in per year.

People. The population is almost entirely African and is concentrated mainly in the S, although the Kano area in the N is densely populated. There are over 250 ethnic groups and the principal tribes are the Hausa, the Fulani, the Yoruba and the Ibo. Nigeria is one of the most urbanized countries in Africa and the largest cities are Ibadan, Lagos, Ogbomosho, Kano and Oshogbo.

Economy. Crop and livestock agriculture is an important feature of the economy, employing 70% of

Kano, once an ancient walled settlement, has grown into one of Nigeria's major cities. Although traditional mud buildings still predominate in the inner city, there has been much modern development locally, and Kano is now served by one of the country's two international airports.

the working force. The valuable cash crops of peanuts, cotton and soybean are grown in the N, which also produces most of the livestock. Nigeria is a leading world producer of palm oil and cacao, which with rubber and timber are products of the S. The mining of the varied mineral deposits such as tin and coal, and the output of crude petroleum are rapidly increasing in importance. Industry, which is at present mostly light manufacturing, is also growing rapidly and will be speeded by the Kainji Dam project on the Niger R which will provide hydroelectricity.

History. The Nok culture of Negro settlers on the Jos Plateau, c800 BC–200 AD is the earliest known in Nigeria. Small trading city-states arose c1000 AD, especially in the N and by the 1300s became powerful empires such as the Kanem, Mali and the BENIN in the S. The Portuguese reached Nigeria in 1483. Their slave trade was taken over by the Dutch and then by the British in the 1700s. Britain annexed areas of Nigeria, partly to stop the slave trade, establishing it in 1914 as a colony and protectorate. In 1960 Nigeria became independent, and a republic in 1963. Political parties had long developed on regional lines, and after disputes over the 1964 election the collapse of law and order led to a series of military regimes until 1966,

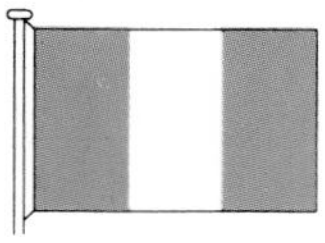

Official Name: Federal Republic of Nigeria
Capital: Lagos
Area: 356 669sq mi
Population: 65 000 000
Languages: English; Hausa, Ibo, Yoruba
Religions: Muslim, Christian, Animist
Monetary Unit(s): 1 Naira = 100 kobo

when General GOWON set up a military government. Gowon reorganized Nigeria into 12 states but the Ibo seceded to form the independent republic of BIAFRA. The Biafra civil war lasted until 1970. National and economic life gradually recovered and Gowon promised a return to civilian rule by 1976. In 1975 Gowon was deposed and exiled by a military coup led by Murtala Mohammed, who was assassinated in 1976 in an abortive coup. He was succeeded by Olusegun Obasanjo.

NIGER RIVER, the third longest river in Africa, 2600mi long. With its eastern branch, the Benue, it drains an area of more than 1 million sq mi. Rising in SW Guinea, it curves NE, E then SE into Nigeria and finally S towards the Gulf of Guinea where it forms a 14 000sq mi delta.

NIGHT BLINDNESS, or nyctalopia, inability to accommodate in or adapt to darkness. It may be a hereditary defect or an early symptom of VITAMIN A deficiency in adults. It is due to a defect in rod VISION.

NIGHTHAWKS, a subfamily, Chordeilinae, of the NIGHTJARS, restricted to the New World. The type species is the Common nighthawk, *Chordeiles minor*.

NIGHT HERONS, wading birds related to other HERONS. Typically squat, black-backed birds, distinguished by their short necks, they are gregarious, perching together in trees and flying down onto marshes at night to hunt fish, amphibians and small mammals.

NIGHTINGALE, *Luscinia megarhynchos*, bird of the thrush subfamily Turdinae, renowned for its beautiful song. A small brown bird, feeding on insects and other invertebrates, it lives in deciduous woodlands throughout most of Europe.

NIGHTINGALE, Florence (1820–1910), English founder of modern nursing, known as the "Lady with the Lamp" because she worked night and day during the Crimean War. She determined to make a career out of nursing the sick and traveled in Europe in the 1840s studying methods of nursing. In 1854 the British government asked her to tend the wounded of the CRIMEAN WAR. She sailed with 38 nurses to Scutari and established sanitary methods and discipline in the two huge army hospitals. In 1860 she set up a nurses' training school in London.

Period engraving of the Scutari Barracks Hospital near Istanbul, with Florence Nightingale on the left conferring with an officer. With saint-like fortitude, she reorganized the hospital to nurse casualties of the Crimean War in 1854, often working up to twenty hours a day to improve the appalling conditions she found on her arrival.

NIGHTJARS, some 67 species of the family Caprimulgidae, otherwise known as goatsuckers. They are normally nocturnal and insectivorous, hawking for insects on the wing. As an adaptation for this, the mouth has a very broad gape and is surrounded by stiff bristles to increase the catchment area. During the day they rest on the ground, and are difficult to see, because of effective camouflage.

NIGHT-JESSAMINE, *Cestrum nocturnum*, a shrub that is a popular house plant, grown mainly for its highly fragrant white flowers that open at night. The closely-related *C. diurnum* produces white flowers that open in daytime, while *C. purpureum* produces reddish-maroon flowers that remain open day and night. In winter they can be grown in full sun, but this is less desirable in summer. During the day the temperature should be about 21°C (70°F) dropping to about 17°C (63°F) at night. The soil should be kept evenly moist, above all avoiding extreme dryness. Propagation is by shoot tip cuttings. Family: Solanaceae.

NIGHTSHADE, popular name given to a number of plants of the genus *Solanum* and related species which produce small but distinctive tubular or flared flowers and rounded fruits. The nightshade family includes poisonous weeds (e.g., BELLADONNA) as well as valuable crops (e.g., POTATO). Family: Solanaceae.

NIHILISM, a doctrine that denies all values, questions all authority, and advocates the destruction of all social and economic institutions. The movement arose in 19th-century Russia in reaction against all authority, especially that of the tsar. It is romantic in origin and anarchist in outlook; its most noted exponent was KROPOTKIN.

NIIGATA, city and port in N Honshu, Japan on the Shinano R, with chemical industries and oil, machinery and textile trades. Pop 383 869.

NIIHAU, island off NW Hawaii. It is separated from Kauai Island by the Kaulakahi Channel and is used for cattle grazing.

NIJINSKY, Vaslav (1890–1950), famous Russian dancer whose outstanding technique and magnetic stage presence contributed greatly to the impact of Russian ballet on the West, when Sergei DIAGHILEV brought a company to Paris in 1909. With Diaghilev's encouragement, Nijinsky devised original choreography, based on Greek vase paintings, for DEBUSSY's *Afternoon of a Faun.* Mental illness ended his career in 1919.

NIJMEGEN, industrial city in E Netherlands on the Waal R, whose history dates from the Roman period. Pop 150 185.

NIKE. See MISSILE.

NIKE, Greek goddess of victory, patron of athletic and military contests. She is usually portrayed as winged, as in the famous Greek sculpture, the *Winged Victory of Samothrace*, in the Louvre, Paris.

NIKOLAYEV, important city in the Ukraine, USSR, at the confluence of the Bug R and Ingul R, with major shipbuilding, engineering and chemical industries. Pop 331 000.

NIKON (Nikita Minin; 1605–1681), Russian Patriarch who reformed the rites and discipline of the Russian Orthodox Church. However his reforms led to schisms in the church and the revolt of the OLD BELIEVERS. In 1658 he was banished and subsequently deposed.

NILE, Battle of the. See ABOUKIR.

NILE RIVER, the longest river in the world, flowing generally N about 4 150mi from central Africa to the Mediterranean coast of Lower EGYPT. Its remotest headstream is the Luvironza R in Burundi above Victoria Nyanza (Lake Victoria), from which flows the White Nile. The Blue Nile rises above Lake Tana in NW Ethiopia, and joins the White Nile at Khartoum, Sudan, to form the Nile proper. N of Cairo it fans out into a 115mi wide delta with principal outlets at Rosetta near Alexandria and Damietta near Port Said. Silt deposited by the Nile's annual overflow brought agricultural prosperity throughout Egypt's history. The river is now being harnessed, notably at the ASWAN HIGH DAM, to supply hydroelectricity as well as constant irrigation. The Nile is navigable the year round from its mouth to ASWAN, and in full spate is generally navigable as far south as Murchison Falls, Uganda.

NILES, village in NE Illinois, 14mi NW of Chicago. It is largely residential, with some light industry. Pop 31 432.

NILES, city in SW Michigan, 48mi SW of Kalamazoo. Varied industry includes paper, mushroom canning, and steel cables. Pop 12 988.

NILES, city in NE Ohio on the Mahoning R, 8mi NNW of Youngstown. Manufactures include varied steel products. Pop 21 581.

NILGAI, *Boselaphus tragocamelus*, an extremely large ANTELOPE of hilly grasslands in India, believed to be a relic of the group that gave rise to cattle and buffaloes. Nilgai are characterized in both sexes by a white ring above each hoof.

NILSSON, Birgit (1918–), Swedish soprano, widely regarded as the greatest Wagnerian soprano of her time; famed as Brünnhilde in *Der Ring des Nibelungen*, but known also for other roles, notably PUCCINI's Turandot and STRAUSS's Elektra.

NÎMES, city in S France, capital of Gard department, 64mi NW of Marseilles. It is a traditional center for trading and the manufacture of textiles and garments. Its notable Roman remains include a magnificent amphitheater. Pop 137 100.

NIMITZ, Chester William (1885–1966), US admiral who commanded naval operations in the Pacific after America entered WORD WAR II in 1941. Credited with originating the strategy of "island hopping," he had an outstandingly successful command. On Sept. 2, 1945, the Japanese surrender was signed aboard his flagship, U.S.S. *Missouri.*

NIMRUD, the ancient Calah, capital of Assyria until superseded by NINEVEH. It lay S of Nineveh on the Tigris R. It flourished in the 9th and 8th centuries BC. Ruins survive.

NINEVEH, capital of ASSYRIA in the 7th century BC, on the Tigris R, opposite modern Mosul, Iraq. Invaluable remains survive from its period of greatness under SENNACHERIB and ASHURBANIPAL. Its destruction by invaders in 612 BC ended the Assyrian Empire. (See also BABYLONIA AND ASSYRIA.)

NINGPO, city in China, NE Chekiang province, on the Yung R. Long an important port and cultural center, it now has large-scale industries. Pop 350 000.

NINIAN, or **Ringan, Saint** (d. c432 AD), first Christian missionary and bishop in Scotland. His church at Whithorn (founded c397) later became an important monastic center.

NIOBE, in Greek myth, archetype of the bereaved mother, daughter of TANTALUS and wife of Amphion, king of Thebes. By boasting of her fertility she insulted Leto, whose only two offspring APOLLO and ARTEMIS killed all 12 of Niobe's children in revenge. Zeus turned the weeping Niobe into a rock.

NIOBIUM (Nb), or **columbium,** soft silvery-white metal in Group VB of the PERIODIC TABLE; a TRANSITION ELEMENT. It occurs as COLUMBITE and pyrochlore. Niobium is unreactive and corrosion-resistant, and is used in STEELS, high-temperature ALLOYS and superconducting alloys (see SUPERCONDUCTIVITY). Being permeable to neutrons, it is also used in nuclear reactors. At high temperatures it reacts with nonmetals to give pentavalent covalent compounds. AW 92.9, mp 2468°C, bp 4927°C, sg 8.57 (20°C).

NIPIGON, Lake, in the Thunder Bay district of SW Ontario, Canada, from which Nipigon R flows about 40mi S to Lake Superior. Area 1 870sq mi.

NIPISSING, Lake, in the Nipissing district of SE Ontario, Canada, NE of Georgian Bay. It is drained by the French R flowing S to Georgian Bay.

NIPPUR, ancient Mesopotamian city which lay 100mi SE of BABYLON, a religious center sacred to the god En-Lil. Large numbers of SUMERIAN archives have been found there.

NIRENBERG, Marshall Warren (1927–), US biochemist who shared with HOLLEY and KHORANA the 1968 Nobel Prize for Physiology or Medicine for his major contributions toward the decipherment of the genetic code (see GENETICS).

NIRVANA, Sanskrit term used in Buddhism, Jainism and Hinduism to denote the highest state of existence, reached when all bodily desires have been quelled and the self is free to dissolve into the ocean of peace or God. It means literally "extinguished", denoting freedom from ego. Nirvana is the final escape from the cycle of rebirth (see TRANSMIGRATION OF SOULS).

NISEI (Japanese: second generation), those born of immigrant Japanese parents in the US. After the Japanese attack on PEARL HARBOR (1941), some 110 000 Americans of Japanese ancestry were forcibly evacuated from their homes on the West Coast and placed in detention centers, in most cases until WWII had ended.

NISHINOMIYA, city in Japan, in Hyogo prefecture, W Honshu, on the N shore of Osaka Bay. The chief manufacture is sake. Pop 377 043.

NISQUALLI INDIANS, a tribe of North American Indians of the Salishan branch of the ALGONQUIAN linguistic stock, noted for their wood-carving. The Medicine Creek Treaty (1854) settled them on a reservation in W central Washington, where they numbered about 200 in the early 1970s.

NITERÓI, city in SE Brazil, capital of Rio de Janeiro state, on Guanabara Bay, a residential and industrial suburb of Rio de Janeiro city. Pop 324 367.

NITRATES, salts of NITRIC ACID, containing the nitrate ion (NO_3^-). Almost all nitrates are soluble in water, and only SODIUM and POTASSIUM nitrate occur significantly in nature, others being made by the action of nitric acid on the metal or its salts. Nitrates are used in medicine, explosives, fertilizers and fireworks. (See also NITROGEN CYCLE; NITROGEN FIXATION.) ESTERS of nitric acid ($RONO_2$) are also called nitrates.

NITRATION, important process in ORGANIC CHEMISTRY, in which a nitro group ($-NO_2$) is introduced into a compound. AROMATIC COMPOUNDS are nitrated with a mixture of concentrated SULFURIC and NITRIC ACIDS, which contains the electrophile (see NUCLEOPHILES) NO_2^+; the production of TNT and nitrobenzene are important cases. "Nitration" is also used for the formation of NITRATE esters including NITROCELLULOSE and NITROGLYCERIN.

NITRIC ACID (HNO_3), strong mineral ACID, a colorless, fuming liquid when pure. Nitric acid is usually made by the OSTWALD PROCESS, the ELECTRIC-ARC PROCESS, or by the action of sulfuric acid on sodium nitrate. It is a powerful oxidizing agent, reacting with most metals to give NITRATES and oxides of NITROGEN; with many organic compounds NITRATION occurs. Nitric acid is used to make nitrates, plastics, explosives and dyes, and as a rocket fuel. mp −42°C, bp 83°C.

NITRILES, or organic CYANIDES, class of organic compounds of general formula RCN, named for the CARBOXYLIC ACID to which they can be hydrolyzed. The simplest is acetonitrile (or methyl cyanide), CH_3CN. Nitriles are prepared by dehydration of AMIDES or by reaction of sodium cyanide with ALKYL HALIDES or aryl SULFONATES. They may be catalytically hydrogenated to AMINES, and react with GRIGNARD REAGENTS to yield KETONES. Acrylonitrile is used to make POLYMERS; some other nitriles are used as softening agents for rubber etc.

NITROCELLULOSE, properly called cellulose nitrate, mixture of highly inflammable NITRATE esters of CELLULOSE made by NITRATION of cotton or wood pulp. The degree of nitration depends on the conditions used. Highly nitrated nitrocellulose—**guncotton**—was used as a high EXPLOSIVE and is still used as a propellant. Nitrocellulose with less than 12% nitrogen—**collodion**—is used in making propellants, DYNAMITE, lacquers and CELLULOID.

NITROGEN (N), nonmetal in Group VA of the PERIODIC TABLE; a colorless, odorless gas (N_2) comprising 78% of the ATMOSPHERE, prepared by fractional distillation of liquid air. Combined nitrogen occurs mainly as NITRATES. As a constituent of AMINO ACIDS, it is vital (see also NITROGEN CYCLE). Molecular nitrogen is inert because of the strong triple bond between the two atoms, but it will react with some elements, especially the ALKALINE-EARTH METALS, to give nitrides; with oxygen (see ELECTRIC ARC PROCESS); and with hydrogen (see HABER PROCESS); it also forms N_2 LIGAND complexes with Group VIII transition metals. Activated nitrogen, formed in an electric discharge, consists of nitrogen atoms and is much more reactive. Nitrogen is used in NITROGEN FIXATION and to provide an inert atmosphere; liquid nitrogen is a CRYOGENIC refrigerant. AW 14.0, mp −210°C, bp −196°C.

Nitrogen forms mainly trivalent and pentavalent compounds. **Nitric Oxide** (NO), is a colorless gas formed in the ELECTRIC-ARC PROCESS; it is readily oxidized further to nitrogen dioxide. The NO molecule is unusual in having an odd number of electrons, and so gives the nitrosyl ions NO^+ and NO^-. mp −164°C, bp −152°C. **Nitrites** are salts (or esters) of **Nitrous Acid** (HNO_2) and are mild reducing agents. **Nitrous Oxide** (N_2O), or laughing gas, is a colorless gas with a sweet odor, prepared by heating ammonium nitrate, and used as a weak anesthetic, sometimes producing mild hysteria, and also as an aerosol propellant. mp −91°C, bp −88°C. **Nitrogen Dioxide** (NO_2), a red-brown toxic gas in equilibrium with its colorless dimer (N_2O_4), is a constituent of automobile exhaust and smog. A powerful oxidizing agent, it is used in the manufacture of SULFURIC ACID and in rocket fuels. It is also an intermediate in the manufacture of NITRIC ACID. mp −11°C, bp 21°C. See also AMMONIA; OSTWALD PROCESS; CYANAMIDE PROCESS; HYDRAZINE.

NITROGEN CYCLE, the cycle of chemical changes exchanging NITROGEN between the air and the soil. NITROGEN FIXATION, industrial (producing FERTILIZERS) or by microorganisms, yields combined nitrogen as AMMONIA and NITRATES, which can be absorbed from the soil by plants, which use them to make protein. Animals ingest nitrogen by eating these plants. Excretion products and animal and plant remains return nitrogen to the soil as complex compounds which are converted by fungi and bacteria to ammonium salts, which may then be oxidized to nitrites (see NITROGEN) and nitrates by other bacteria. These are either reused by plants, or converted to nitrogen (by denitrifying bacteria) which returns to the air, thus completing the cycle. (See also ECOLOGY.)

NITROGEN FIXATION, conversion of NITROGEN gas into nitrogen compounds. Nitrogen usually reacts only at high temperatures and pressures. Industrially, it is fixed in the HABER PROCESS, the CYANAMIDE PROCESS and the ELECTRIC-ARC PROCESS.

Some bacteria (*Rhizobium*) in the root nodules of LEGUMINOUS PLANTS, and also some of those living free in the soil (e.g., *Azotobacter*), can fix nitrogen from the air as AMMONIA, NITRATES and nitrites (see NITROGEN). Some fungi and blue-green algae also fix nitrogen. (See also NITROGEN CYCLE.)

NITROGLYCERIN ($C_3H_5(ONO_2)_3$), properly called glyceryl trinitrate, the NITRATE ester of GLYCEROL, made by its NITRATION. Since it causes VASODILATION, it is used to relieve ANGINA PECTORIS. Its major use, however, is as a very powerful high EXPLOSIVE, though its sensitivity to shock renders it unsafe unless used in the form of DYNAMITE or blasting gelatin. It is a colorless, oily liquid. MW 227.1, mp 13°C.

NITROUS OXIDE. See NITROGEN.

NIUE, or **Savage Island,** a coral island in the SW Pacific Ocean, E of Tonga and 350mi SSE of Samoa, a territory of New Zealand.

NIXON, Richard Milhous (1913–   ), 37th president of the US (1969–74). Nixon was born of a Quaker family in Yorba Linda, Cal., and trained and practiced (1937–42) as a lawyer. An aviation ground officer in the navy in WWII, he began his political career with election to congress in 1946. As a congressman he became a prominent member of the House's anti-communist UN-AMERICAN ACTIVITIES COMMITTEE. In 1950 he was elected to the Senate, where his continued and aggressive anti-communist stance probably influenced Dwight D. Eisenhower's choice of Nixon as running-mate in 1952. As Eisenhower's vice-president (1952–60) Nixon was given an unusually prominent role both at home and abroad. In 1960 he was chosen as the Republican presidential nominee, but was narrowly defeated by John KENNEDY. After running unsuccessfully for the governorship of California in 1962, he announced his retirement to pursue his career in law. Reentering political life in 1964, however, Nixon gradually won wide backing and, with Spiro AGNEW as his running-mate, won the presidency in 1968. He was reelected in 1972 with a large majority.

Nixon had pledged withdrawal from the VIETNAM WAR, which had plagued the presidencies of his two predecessors. Although his actions did not always seem consistent with his electoral promise (notably his ordering of the invasions of Cambodia and Laos and of saturation bombing in North Vietnam), he began pulling US troops out of Vietnam almost at once. Eventually, with Secretary of State Henry KISSINGER as Nixon's chief negotiator, a cease-fire agreement was reached (1973). In the meantime COLD WAR tensions were eased by arms-limitation talks with the USSR in 1969, and again when Nixon visited Moscow (he was the first US president to do so) in 1972. This followed on his historic state visit to the People's Republic of China, which reopened contact with the mainland Chinese for the first time in 21 years. Nixon's domestic achievements were less notable. He scrapped many existing welfare policies and vetoed even congressionally-approved proposals for new welfare legislation. He did, however, succeed in imposing wage and price controls to help offset the nation's severe economic problems of recession and inflation.

Nixon's second term of office was overshadowed by the scandal of the WATERGATE affair, which led to revelations of widespread corruption, misinforming the public, and an unprecedented increase in the power of the White House at the expense of congress and the judiciary. Several of Nixon's top aides were tried and imprisoned, and a House judiciary committee recommended that Nixon be impeached. On August 9, 1974, Nixon resigned office, the first US president ever to do so.

Richard Milhous NIXON

37th US President

Born: January 9, 1913
Term of office: January 20, 1969–August 9, 1974
Political party: Republican

NIZA, Marcos de, ("Fray Marcos;" c1495–1558), Spanish Franciscan friar and explorer in the Americas, whose lavish account of the fabled Seven Cities of CIBOLA was rapidly discredited by CORONADO. Niza served as a missionary in Peru, Guatemala, and Mexico.

NIZHNI TAGIL, city in the USSR, W Sverdlovsk Oblast, on the Tagil R. It is a center of heavy industry within a metal-mining area. Pop 378 000.

NKRUMAH, Kwame (1901–1972), Ghanian who led his country to independence, and a champion of pan-Africanism. After the electoral victory (1951) of his Convention People's party, he became first prime minister of the then Gold Coast, in which role he established (1957) the independent Republic of Ghana. As president from 1960, his gradual assumption of dictatorial powers won him enemies, and his government was overthrown by a military coup in 1966.

NOAH, in the Bible (book of Genesis), progenitor of all humanity after the Flood. Because of Noah's righteousness, God warned him to build the Ark, in which he, together with his wife, sons, daughters-in-law, and a pair of every animal species, survived and came to rest on Mt ARARAT. The Flood also occurs in the Babylonian epic of GILGAMESH.

NOBEL, Alfred Bernhard (1833–1896), Swedish-born inventor of dynamite and other explosives. About 1863 he set up a factory to manufacture liquid NITROGLYCERIN, but when in 1864 this blew up, killing his younger brother, Nobel set out to find safe handling methods for the substance, so discovering DYNAMITE, patented 1867 (UK) and 1868 (US). Later he invented gelignite (patented 1876) and ballistite (1888). A lifelong pacifist, he wished his explosives to be used solely for peaceful purposes, and was much embittered by their military use. He left most of his fortune for the establishment of the Nobel Foundation and this fund has been used to award Nobel Prizes since 1901.

NOBELIUM (No), a TRANSURANIUM ELEMENT in the ACTINIDE series, prepared by bombardment of lighter actinides. The most stable isotope, No^{255}, has a HALF-LIFE of only 3min.

NOBEL PRIZES, annual awards given to individuals or institutions judged to confer "the greatest benefit on mankind" in any one of six fields: physics, chemistry, physiology or medicine, literature, peace and economics. Except for the prize in economics, instituted in 1969, the prizes have been awarded since 1901. The award of the peace prize, sometimes controversial, is made by a committee of five elected by the Norwegian parliament; the other prizes are awarded by the appropriate learned bodies in Sweden: the Royal Academy of Science, the Caroline Institute, and the Swedish Academy of Literature. The prize money comes from the foundation set up by Alfred NOBEL.

NOBILE, Umberto (1885–   ), Italian aeronautical engineer and Arctic explorer. He designed the airships *Norge, Roma* and *Italia*, and in 1926 flew over the North Pole in *Norge* with Roald AMUNDSEN and Lincoln ELLSWORTH.

NOBLE GASES, the elements in Group O of the PERIODIC TABLE, comprising HELIUM, NEON, ARGON, KRYPTON, XENON and RADON. They are colorless, odorless gases, prepared by fractional distillation of liquid air (see ATMOSPHERE), except helium and radon. Owing to their stable filled-shell electron configurations, the noble gases are chemically unreactive: only krypton, xenon and radon form isolable compounds. They glow brightly when an electric discharge is passed through them, and so are used in advertising signs: neon tubes glow red, xenon blue, and krypton bluish-white; argon tubes glow pale red at low pressures, blue at high pressures.

NOBLE METALS, the unreactive, corrosion-resistant precious metals comprising the PLATINUM GROUP, SILVER and GOLD, and sometimes including RHENIUM.

NOCK, Arthur Darby (1902–1963), US historian born in Portsmouth, England. He studied the history of Greek and Roman religions; in 1929 he became professor of history at Harvard U.

NODDIES, five species of birds of the subfamily Sterninae. They are small TERNS restricted to tropical seas. The Common noddy is one of the few seabirds to nest and molt at the same time.

NODE, in ANALYTIC GEOMETRY, a point of INTERSECTION of two or more parts of a single CURVE.

NOEL-BAKER, Philip John (1889–   ), British Labour politician who campaigned for international disarmament throughout a career which spanned the two World Wars. In 1958 he published *The Arms Race: A Programme for World Disarmament.* He was awarded the Nobel Prize for Peace the following year.

NOETIC SCIENCES, field of study embracing researches into ESP and PARAPSYCHOLOGY.

NOGUCHI, Hideyo (1876–1928), Japanese bacteriologist best known for his work on SYPHILIS and YELLOW FEVER.

NOGUCHI, Isamu (1904–   ), US abstract sculptor whose works, especially those created for specific architectural settings such as the Unesco building in Paris, have won international recognition. He was a student of BRANCUSI.

NOH, or **No,** the classical drama of Japan, developed under court patronage in the 14th century. Typically, a Noh play dramatizes the spiritual life of its central character, employing speech, singing, instrumental music, dancing and mime in a highly ritualized style. The performers are all male, and traditional wooden masks are used. Noh gave rise to the more popular KABUKI theater.

NOISE, unwanted SOUND. As far as man is concerned this is a subjective definition: people vary in their sensitivity to noise; many sounds are agreeable to some and noisy to others. Blasts or explosions can cause sudden damage to the ear and prolonged exposure to impulsive sounds such as a pneumatic drill may cause gradual HEARING impairment. In general, any sound that is annoying, interferes with speech, damages the hearing or reduces concentration or work efficiency may be considered as noise. From the physical view point, sound waves (either in air or vibrations in solid bodies) that mask required signals or cause fatigue and breakdown of equipment or structures are noise and should be minimized. In air, sound is radiated spherically from its source as a compressional wave, being partly reflected, absorbed or transmitted on hitting an obstacle. Noise is usually a nonperiodic sound wave, as opposed to a periodic pure musical tone or a sine-wave combination. It is characterized by its intensity (measured in DECIBELS or NEPERS), frequency and spatial variation; a sound level meter and frequency analyzer measure these properties. Noise may be controlled at source (e.g., by a MUFFLER), between it and the listener (e.g., by sound absorbing material) or at the listener (e.g., by wearing ear plugs).

NOISE, in electronics, any unwanted or interfering current or voltage in an electrical device or system. Its presence in the amplifying circuits of RADIOS, TELEVISION receivers etc. may mask or distort signals. Unpredictable random noise exists in any component with RESISTANCE because of the thermal motion of the current-carrying ELECTRONS, and in electron tubes due to random CATHODE emission. Thermal radiations and variations in the atmosphere also cause random noise. Nonrandom noise arises from spurious oscillations and unintended couplings between components.

NOLDE, Emil (1867–1956), born Emil Hansen, German expressionist, engraver and painter, notably of landscapes and figures, whose bold, visionary and highly emotional style is typified in his *Marsh Landscape* (1916). (See also EXPRESSIONISM.)

NOMAD, member of a tribe or community which moves from one place to another for subsistence. The nomadic way of life, though fast declining, is still to be found among herdsmen such as the BEDOUIN Arabs, and hunters such as some groups of Australian ABORIGINES. There are also semi-nomadic peoples, such as the LAPPS, who move from summer to winter pastures.

Tents of the Bedouin, one of the last thriving nomad cultures in the world. Their life style has changed little in thousands of years; such tents as these probably stood in the same area at the time of Christ.

NOME, city and port in W Alaska, on the S coast of the Seward Peninsula overlooking Norton Sound. Famous for the gold rush (1899–1903) upon which it was founded, it is now mainly a commercial and distributive center. Pop 2488.

NOMINALISM, in philosophy, usually as opposed to REALISM, the view that the names of abstract ideas (e.g., beauty) used in describing things (as in, a *beautiful* table) are merely conventions or conveniences, and should not be taken to imply the actual existence of universals corresponding to those names.

NONALIGNMENT. See NEUTRALISM AND NONALIGNMENT.

NONCONFORMISTS, or **Dissenters,** those who will not conform to the doctrine or practice of an established church; especially the Protestant dissenters from the Church of England (mainly PURITANS) expelled by the Act of Uniformity (1662). They now include Baptists, Brethren, Congregationalists, Methodists, Presbyterians and Quakers.

NON-EUCLIDEAN GEOMETRY, those branches of GEOMETRY that challenge EUCLIDEAN GEOMETRY's tenet that through any POINT A not on a LINE L there passes one and only one line parallel to L, but which accept in general all other Euclidean axioms with at most minor changes. The geometry based on the hypothesis that no lines pass through A parallel to L is RIEMANNIAN GEOMETRY; that based on the hypothesis that there is more than one such line is LOBACHEVSKIAN GEOMETRY. The first mathematician to open the doors for non-Euclidean geometry was GAUSS in the 19th century. He did not publish his work, however, and the fathers of non-Euclidean geometry are usually considered to be BOLYAI János and LOBACHEVSKY.

NONIMPORTATION ACT (1806), first of three attempted US embargoes on the entry of British goods, designed to force Britain to modify her drastic regulations on US imports. It was followed by the EMBARGO ACT and the NONINTERCOURSE ACT. (See also ORDERS IN COUNCIL.)

NONINTERCOURSE ACT (1809), US act permitting resumption of commerce between the US and all countries except Britain and France, superseding Jefferson's EMBARGO ACT (1807). (See also NONIMPORTATION ACT and ORDERS IN COUNCIL.)

NONMETAL, a substance—in particular, an ELEMENT—showing none of the properties characteristic of METALS. (See also METALLOID.) The 17 or so nonmetallic elements fill the top right-hand corner of the PERIODIC TABLE. Their atoms are in general relatively small, with nearly-filled electron shells, and have high IONIZATION POTENTIALS. They have high ELECTRONEGATIVITIES, and tend to form covalent BONDS with each other, and to form ANIONS.

NONO, Luigi (1924–), Italian composer of serial or TWELVE-TONE MUSIC. His choral and instrumental works, often political in content, include *Epitaffo per Federico García Lorca* (1952), *Il canto sospeso* (1956) and *Intolleranza* (1961).

NONPARTISAN LEAGUE, political association of farmers and farmworkers founded (1915) and centered in the Dakotas. Formed in response to the power of banking, grain and railroad bosses, the league campaigned for state-run elevators, mills, banks and insurance. Dominating N.D. government 1916–21, it realized most of its demands.

NONVIOLENT RESISTANCE. See CIVIL DISOBEDIENCE.

NOOTKA INDIANS. Of Wakashan linguistic stock, they lived on the W coast of Vancouver Island and in NW Wash. They hunted whales in 60ft seagoing canoes of cedar and lived in long wooden houses, several families to each house. The Nootka used *Dentalia* (tooth) shells for money and carved puppets and masks with moving parts.

NOOTKA SOUND, harbor on the W coast of Vancouver Island, British Columbia. After the Spaniards seized an English trading post there in 1789, war between Britain and Spain was only averted through lack of French support for Spain, which gave up its claim in the Nootka Convention of 1790. In 1846 the US resigned its claim to the area.

NORAD. See NORTH AMERICAN AIR DEFENSE COMMAND.

NORADRENALINE. See ADRENALINE.

NORDENSKJÖLD, Nils Adolf Eric, Baron (1832–1901), Finnish-born Swedish geologist, cartographer and explorer of Spitzbergen (reaching 81° 42′N in 1868) and of Greenland, where he studied inland ice. He was the first to navigate the NORTHEAST PASSAGE (1878–79).

NORDHOFF AND HALL, US novelists best known for *Mutiny on the Bounty* (1932). **Charles Bernard Nordhoff** (1887–1947) and **James Norman Hall** (1887–1951) met as pilots in WWI. Their first joint work was a history, *The Lafayette Flying Corps* (1920). The "Bounty" trilogy was completed by *Men Against the Sea* (1933) and *Pitcairn's Island* (1934). (See also BOUNTY, MUTINY ON THE.)

NORFOLK, city in NE Neb., 90mi NW of Omaha. It is the trade center for a fertile dairy and livestock area. Pop 16607.

NORFOLK, important city port of SE Va., founded in 1682 at the mouth of the Elizabeth R on HAMPTON ROADS. It is linked with the DELMARVA PENINSULA by the Chesapeake Bay Bridge-Tunnel. Coal, fertilizers, lumber and food products are exported. The main industries are shipbuilding, auto-assembly, and fertilizers. The US Naval Base, opened in 1817, has 38 commands, including NATO's Atlantic unit. Pop 307951.

NORFOLK ISLAND, a 13sq mi Australian territory in the S Pacific 930mi ENE of Sydney. Discovered by Cook in 1774, it was a British penal colony until PITCAIRN islanders settled in 1856. Citrus fruit is grown.

NORFOLK ISLAND PINE, *Araucaria excelsa*, an evergreen coniferous tree that is native to NORFOLK ISLAND where it can grow up to 60m (200ft) tall. However, it is also grown as a house plant since it is very slow-growing and produces attractive dense foliage. Plants over 1.2m (4ft) are best replaced. Indoors, it should be grown in a cool situation in bright indirect light. The soil must be kept evenly moist; needles and branches die in dry conditions and they are never replaced. Propagation is from seeds or by cutting off and rooting the tops of stems that have grown too tall. Family: Araucariaceae.

NORMAL, town in central Ill., 30mi E of Peoria. It grew up round Ill. State U. (1857) and lies in a dairy, fruit and livestock farm area. Pop 26396.

NORMAL DISTRIBUTION, in STATISTICS, an ideal distribution which is symmetrical (see SYMMETRY) about its mean (see MEAN, MEDIAN AND MODE). It can be written in the form

$$f(x) = \frac{1}{\sigma\sqrt{2\pi}} \quad e^{-\frac{1}{2}\left(\frac{x-\mu}{\sigma}\right)^2}$$

where $f(x)$ is the relative frequency, σ is the STANDARD DEVIATION, μ is the mean, and π (see PI) and e (see EXPONENTIAL) have their usual values. Note that in a normal distribution the mean, median and mode coincide. Many naturally-occurring distributions approximate to the normal. The typically bell-shaped curve shown when $f(x)$ is plotted against x is called the *normal curve*. The distribution is also named the "Gaussian distribution" for Karl GAUSS.

NORMALITY. See EQUIVALENT WEIGHT.

NORMAN, city in central Okla., seat of Cleveland Co. and of the U. of Oklahoma. Manufactures include airplanes and air conditioners. There are oil wells nearby. Pop 52117.

NORMAN ARCHITECTURE, style developed by the Normans of England, N France and elsewhere during the 11th and 12th centuries; a variation of the ROMANESQUE marked by bold, massive forms, round arches and zigzag (dog tooth) ornament. The N France style emphasized tower and spire elaboration and a round apse, the English the length of the church plan, and round pillars.

NORMAN CONQUEST, conquest of England by William, Duke of Normandy, following the Battle of HASTINGS (Oct 14, 1066) when William defeated and killed England's Saxon king, HAROLD. Although illegitimate, William claimed the English throne as EDWARD THE CONFESSOR's cousin and named successor. Crowned WILLIAM I in London, he quickly crushed revolts, building castles as he advanced. The land of the English nobles was distributed to NORMANS in return for their agreement to supply the king with mounted soldiers. The great DOMESDAY BOOK (1086) listed landholdings. The conquerers also brought to England the influence of their French language and innovatons in architecture and methods of warfare.

NORMANDY, region of NW France facing the English Channel, noted for dairy products, fruit, brandy, wheat and flax. Le Havre, Dieppe and Cherbourg are the main ports; Rouen and Caen are historic cathedral and university cities. Shipbuilding, steel, iron and textiles are the main industries. Home of the NORMANS, it was later much contested with

US troops coming ashore from a landing craft at Le Havre during the Normandy landings on and following D-Day in the summer of 1944.

England before finally going to France in 1450. In WWII it was chosen for the Allied landing, June 6, 1944.

NORMANS, inhabitants of NORMANDY, the former province of NW France. In 911 Rollo, leader of the VIKING raider-settlers, was recognized as duke of the area. Strong, warlike and excellent administrators, the Normans ("Northmen") became Christians in the 10th century and completed the NORMAN CONQUEST of England in the 11th. They were active in the CRUSADES, in the reconquest of Spain, in S Italy and Sicily.

NORNS, in Norse mythology, three women, Urd, Verdandi and Skuld, who controlled destiny, weaving the fates of men and gods alike into a great tapestry. They are very similar to the Greek FATES.

NORRIDGE, village in NE Ill., a residential and manufacturing suburb of W Chicago. Pop 17 020.

NORRIS, Frank (Benjamin Franklin Norris; 1870–1902), US novelist and newspaperman. His best-known novels are his first, naturalistic *McTeague* (1899) about life in San Francisco slums and his uncompleted trilogy *The Epic of Wheat* (*The Octopus*, 1901 and *The Pit*, 1903), in which he foreshadowed the MUCKRAKERS.

NORRIS, George William (1861–1944), noted US congressman (1902–42) and reformer. Elected to the House as a Republican from Neb., he led the fight which ousted Speaker Joseph CANNON. In 1912 he moved to the Senate. There his progressive, nonpartisan crusades embraced election reform, setting up the TENNESSEE VALLEY AUTHORITY, labor disputes (the Norris–La Guardia Act), farm relief, the 20th or LAME DUCK AMENDMENT which he authored, and POLL TAX abolition.

NORRISH, Ronald George Wreyford (1897–), British chemist awarded, with Manfred EIGEN and George PORTER, the 1967 Nobel Prize for Chemistry for studies of extremely fast chemical reactions, and, in particular, for the development of FLASH PHOTOLYSIS.

NORRISTOWN, borough in SE Pa., 17mi NW of Philadelphia, seat of Montgomery Co. Products include machinery, leather goods and chemicals. Pop 38 169.

NORSE. See SCANDINAVIAN LANGUAGES.

NORSEMEN. See VIKINGS.

NORTH, Frederick, Lord North, (later Earl of Guildford; 1732–1792), British Tory prime minister. His policies precipitated the break with the American colonies. A tool of George III, North answered the BOSTON TEA PARTY with the INTOLERABLE ACTS (1774), including the QUEBEC ACT which kept Canada loyal to Britain. He resigned in 1782, and in 1783 formed a brief coalition with Charles James FOX.

NORTH, Sir Thomas (1535–c1603), English translator (1579) of Plutarch's *Lives*, a source for many of Shakespeare's plays. A soldier in Ireland and the Low Countries, he was knighted and pensioned by Elizabeth I.

NORTH ADAMS, city in NW Mass. It makes electronic, rayon, chemical and paper products and is a Berkshire Hills resort. Pop 19 195.

NORTH AMERICA, third-largest continent, bounded in the N by the Arctic Ocean, in the S by South America, in the W by the Pacific and Bering Sea, and in the E by the Atlantic. It includes the US, Canada, Mexico, Central America, the Caribbean Islands and Greenland—one-sixth of the earth's land surface (9 361 791sq mi), with over 95 000mi of coastline.

Land. Its regions differ immensely: in the W Coastal Ranges from Alaska to the Gulf of California parallel to the Rocky Mts, the continent's backbone. Between lies the Intermountain Region, with the Great Basin and Mexican Plateau. E of the N Rockies is the bedrock of the Canadian Shield, then S the vast Interior Plain which includes the Great Plains, the Canadian Prairies, the US Midwest and the Great Lakes. This is separated from the Piedmont and Atlantic Coastal Plain by the Appalachian Mts. The CONTINENTAL DIVIDE, created by the Rockies, directs the main rivers: the Colorado, Columbia, Fraser and Yukon flow W to the Pacific; the Mackenzie St. Lawrence, Rio Grande, Missouri and Mississippi flow E to the Atlantic and Arctic oceans. The climate ranges from polar to tropical. Most of the interior has cold winters and hot summers; rainfall can reach 140in a year on the NW Pacific coast and in S Central America. Vegetation varies widely, with northern tundra in Greenland, Alaska and N Canada, desert in SW US and Mexico, and jungle in Central America. Wildlife is rich and diverse. North America has enormous mineral wealth and a large proportion of the land has a hospitable climate and fertile soils.

People. The continent ranks third in population, which is densest in the E US, SE Canada, the W coast of both, and in Mexico. The people, grouped into 15 independent nations, are mainly Caucasians of European descent, speaking English and French in the N, and Spanish in Mexico and Central America. Their ancestors emigrated following the first permanent European contacts made in the 1490s by Columbus in the Caribbean and the Cabots in Newfoundland. The settlers found Indians, descendants of the Mongoloid peoples who are thought to have moved E from Asia across the Bering Strait some 25 000 years ago (see ESKIMO; INDIANS, CENTRAL AND SOUTH AMERICAN; INDIANS, NORTH AMERICAN.) Negroes were brought in from Africa as slaves, and are now concentrated in the Caribbean and the US, where every European nation is represented and 10% of the population are NEGROES or MULATTOES. Of Mexicans 60% are MESTIZOS. Varied backgrounds have brought wide differences in culture, religion and standards of living (the world's highest is in the US and Canada). (See also CANADA; MEXICO; UNITED STATES and other countries.)

NORTH AMERICAN AIR DEFENSE COMMAND (NORAD), combined command for the air defense of North America, employing US and Canadian air force units and US army and navy air units. Set up in 1958, it chiefly comprises fighter-interceptor and long-range reconnaissance planes and radar.

NORTH AMERICAN BLACK BEAR, *Euarctos americanus*, smallest of the North American bears, reaching 150kg (330lb) and ranging in color from black and brown through white. The muzzle is often brown.

NORTHAMPTON, city in W Mass. on the Connecticut R, seat of Hampshire Co. and of Smith College, and home of Calvin COOLIDGE. The city makes cutlery, brushes and wire cable. Pop 29 664.

NORTH ANDOVER, town in NE Mass., on the Merrimack R, settled c1644. Products include chemicals, plastics and telephone equipment. Pop 16 284.

NORTH ARLINGTON, industrial and residential borough in N.J., a N suburb of Newark. Tools, dies, clothing and toys are produced. Pop 18 096.

NORTH ATLANTIC DRIFT, eastward-flowing continuation of the GULF STREAM, notable for its warming effect on the climates of W Europe.

NORTH ATLANTIC TREATY ORGANIZATION (NATO), defense organization of nations adhering to the North Atlantic Treaty. An extension of the 1948 Brussels Treaty for military cooperation between five European nations, the treaty is directed at the threat of armed communist attack in Europe or the N Atlantic or Mediterranean area. The new treaty was signed in April 1949 by Belgium, Canada, Denmark, France, Great Britain, Iceland, Italy, Luxembourg, the Netherlands, Norway, Portugal and the US, by Greece and Turkey in 1951 and by West Germany in 1954. Article 5 states that an armed attack on any one or two members will be taken as an attack on all; other clauses cover military, political and economic cooperation. The supreme body is the North Atlantic Council, backed up by committees. Headquarters are in Brussels, while the executive of the Military Committee is in Washington, D.C. NATO has three commands: Europe, the Atlantic, and the English Channel and North Sea. The Canada–United States Regional Planning Group coordinates North American defense with NATO. Friction among the members has grown as European tension and the COLD WAR have eased: France expelled NATO forces in 1966, the US resents her disproportionate share of cost and is accused of acting unilaterally in political matters, but the alliance holds through mutual self interest among the members.

NORTH ATTLEBORO, town in SE Mass., about 5mi E of the R.I. line. Manufactures include jewelry and brushes. Pop 18 665.

NORTH AUGUSTA, residential and manufacturing city of S.C., opposite Augusta, Ga. on the Savannah R. Pop 12 883.

NORTH BATTLEFORD, city in W Saskatchewan, Canada, distribution center for the region NW of Saskatoon. Pop 12 453.

NORTH BAY, city in SE Ontario, Canada, on Lake Nipissing. It is a summer resort and a transport center for dairy products and lumber, with nearby missile and jet bases. Pop 49 063.

NORTH BELLMORE, urban community in the SW of Long Island, N.Y., E of New York City. Pop 22 893.

NORTH BELMONT, urban area in SW N.C., due W of Charlotte, near the S.C. state line. Pop 10 759.

NORTH BORNEO. See SABAH.

NORTH BRADDOCK, borough in W Pa., a metalworking suburb E of Pittsburgh. Pop 10 838.

NORTH BRANFORD, residential town in S central Conn., with some light industry. Pop 10 778.

NORTHBRIDGE, town in S central Mass., 7mi SE of Worcester, on the Blackstone R. Pop 11 795.

NORTHBROOK, mainly residential village in NE Ill., a NW suburb of Chicago. Pop 27 297.

NORTH CANTON, village in NE Ohio, a suburb of Canton. Manufactures include bricks and vacuum cleaners. Pop 15 228.

NORTH CAPE, or **Nordkapp,** N Norway, point rising 1 007ft above the sea near the N end of Magerøy Island, at 71° 10′ 20″ N. It is popularly regarded as the most northerly point in Europe.

NORTH CAROLINA, Southern US state and one of the original 13 colonies.

Land. The Atlantic coastal plain of swamps and rich farmland, shielded in the N by a long chain of barrier islands, gives way to the rolling hills of the Piedmont, where industry has centered at Raleigh, the capital, the urban complex of Greensboro/Winston–Salem and Charlotte, the biggest city. To the W lie the BLUE RIDGE and GREAT SMOKY MOUNTAINS areas; Mt Mitchell (6 684ft) is the highest peak E of the Rockies. The many rivers mostly flow E, providing hydroelectric power. Forests cover over half of N.C. The mild climate has a mean annual temperature of 59°F and rainfall of about 50in.

People. Almost all the people are US-born; around 25% are black. Baptists are the largest religious group, followed by Methodists and Presbyterians.

Economy. Industry, intensified after WWII, now accounts for over 75% of N.C.'s income. N.C. is the leading US manufacturer of textiles, cigarettes and furniture. Chemicals, electrical machinery, food

NORTH AMERICA
vegetation
snow-and icecaps
tundras and high mountain flora
mixed forest and northern coniferous forest
tropical rain forest
monsoon forest and thorn scrub
steppe- and mountain grassland
desert and semi-desert
cultivated areas
irrigated areas
swamp
scale 1 : 40,000,000
0
500
1000 st. miles
North Pole
ARCTIC OCEAN
ASIA
BERING SEA
Arctic Circle
Wrangel Island
East Cape
Bering Strait
C. Lisburne
Nome
Yukon
Pt. Barrow
BROOKS RANGE
BEAUFORT SEA
ALASKA RANGE
Mt. Mc Kinley 20320
Anchorage
Kenai Peninsula
Alaska Peninsula
ALEUTIAN ISLANDS
Mt. Logan 19850
GULF OF ALASKA
ALEXANDER ARCHIPELAGO
QUEEN CHARLOTTE ISL.
MACKENZIE MOUNTAINS
Mackenzie
COAST RANGES
ROCKY MOUNTAINS
Great Bear Lake
Great Slave Lake
Peace River
Lake Athabasca
Athabasca
Reindeer Lake
Saskatchewan
Red Deer
Churchill
HUDSON BAY
Albany
Lake Winnipeg
Lake Manitoba
Winnipeg
13260 Mt. Waddington
Vancouver Island
Vancouver
Mt. Rainier 14410
Columbia
C. Blanco
C. Mendocino
Mt. Shasta 14162
San Francisco
SIERRA NEVADA
Mt. Whitney 14495
Los Angeles
Great Salt Lake
Great Basin
WASATCH RANGE
Mt. Elbert 14431
COLORADO PLATEAUS
Blanca Peak 14317
Snake
Yellowstone
Missouri
GREAT PLAINS
Platte
Colorado
Arkansas
Red River
Llano Estacado
Rio Grande
Kansas City
St Louis
Chicago
Central Plains
Mississippi
Ohio
Tennessee
Lake Superior
Lake Michigan
Lake Huron
Lake Ontario
Lake Erie
Detroit
New York
Long Island
Washington
ALLEGHENY MTS.
APPALACHIAN MTS.
Mt. Mitchell 6684
Piedmont Plains
C. Hatteras
C. Cod
C. Sable
Nova Scotia
Quebec
St. Lawrence
Anticosti I.
NEWFOUNDLAND
C. Race
Miquelon
St. Pierre
C. St. Charles
Lake Michikamau
LABRADOR
Hudson Strait
FOXE BASIN
Baffin Island
BAFFIN BAY
DAVIS STRAIT
SVERDRUP ISLANDS
C. Stallworthy
PARRY ISLANDS
Melville I.
Bathurst I.
Devon I.
Magnetic Pool
Banks I.
Prince of Wales I.
Somerset I.
Victoria I.
Ellesmere I.
Kane basin
Thule
C. Morris Jessup
C. Eiler Rasmussen
GREENLAND
Knud Rasmussens Land
Nansen Sound
King Frederik VI Coast
C. Farewell
DENMARK STRAIT
ICELAND
Jan Mayen
EUROPE
ATLANTIC OCEAN
BERMUDA ISLANDS
SARGASSO SEA
Gulf Coastal Plain
New Orleans
Florida
C. Canaveral
C. Sable
Straits of Florida
BAHAMA ISLANDS
GULF OF MEXICO
Havanna
CUBA
Yucatan Channel
Yucatan
GULF OF CAMPECHE
Mexico City
Popocatepetl 17887
Citlaltepetl 18696
SIERRA MADRE DEL SUR
Isthmus of Tehuantepec
SIERRA MADRE OCCIDENTAL
SIERRA MADRE ORIENTAL
Mexican Plateau
Rio Bravo del Norte
Lower California
GULF OF CALIFORNIA
Guadelupe
Eugena Pt
C. S. Lucas
Tropic of Cancer
REVILLAGIGEDO ISLANDS
PACIFIC OCEAN
GREATER ANTILLES
GRAND CAYMAN ISLANDS
JAMAICA
HISPANIOLA
PUERTO RICO
VIRGIN ISLANDS
St. Martin (Neth. Fr.)
Saba
Antigua
Guadeloupe
Dominica
Martinique
St. Lucia
St. Vincent
Barbados
Grenada
Trinidad
LESSER ANTILLES
ANTILLES (NETH.)
Aruba
Curaçao
Bonaire
Caracas
Orinoco
CARIBBEAN SEA
C. Gracias-a Dios
CENTRAL AMERICA
Lake Nicaragua
Chirripo 12861
Isthmus of Panama
Panama
Gulf of Panama
Magdalena
SOUTH AMERICA
Equator
Amazon
Guayaquil
GALÁPAGOS ISLANDS
110°
100°
90°
80°
70°
60°
170°
180°
160°
150°
140°
50°
40°
30°
20°
10°
0°

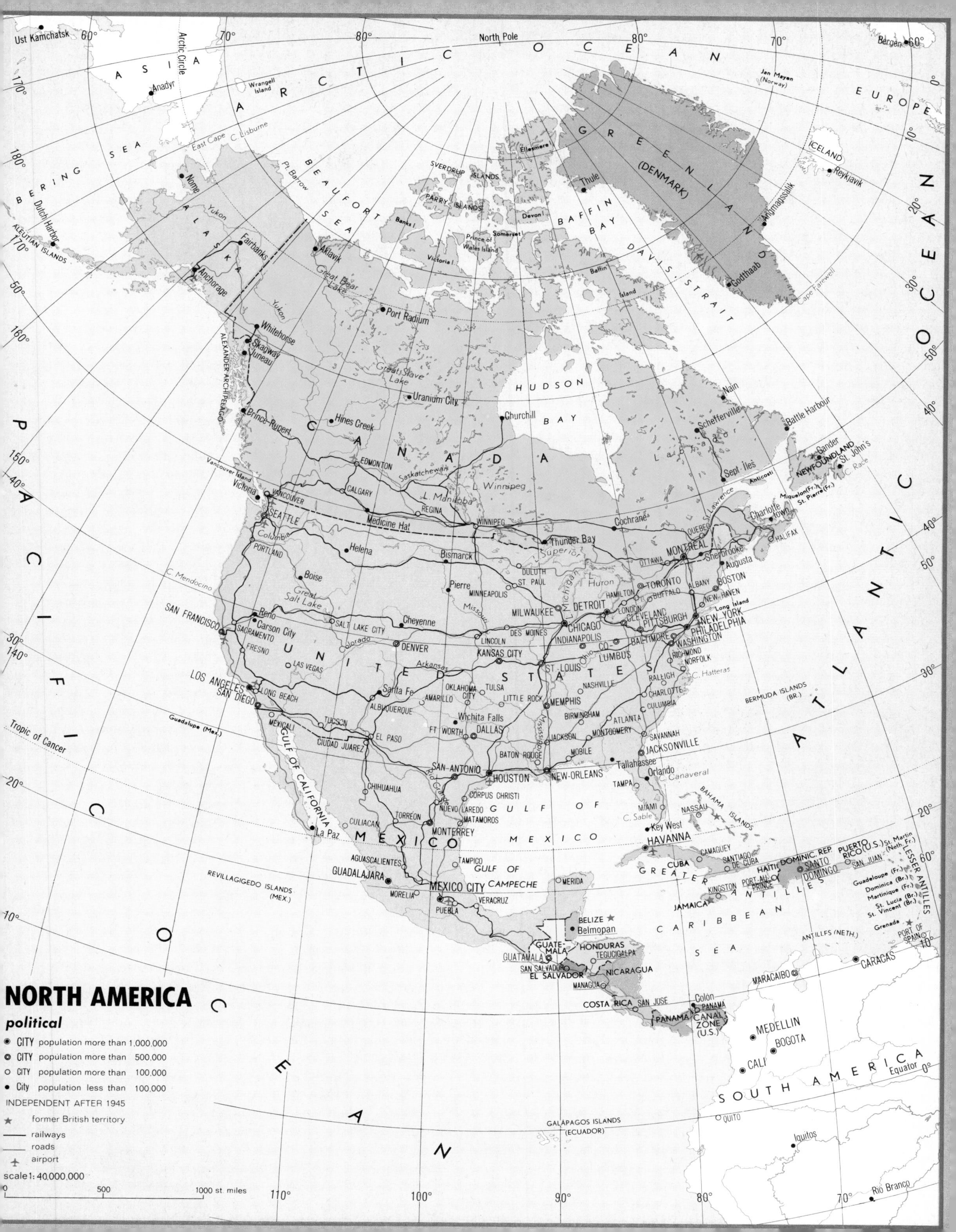
NORTH AMERICA
political
CITY population more than 1,000,000
CITY population more than 500,000
CITY population more than 100,000
City population less than 100,000
INDEPENDENT AFTER 1945
former British territory
railways
roads
airport
scale 1: 40,000,000
0
500
1000 st. miles
ARCTIC OCEAN
North Pole
ASIA
Ust Kamchatsk
Anadyr
Wrangell Island
Arctic Circle
BERING SEA
East Cape
C. Lisburne
Nome
Dutch Harbor
ALEUTIAN ISLANDS
ALASKA
Pt. Barrow
Yukon
Fairbanks
Anchorage
BEAUFORT SEA
Aklavik
Great Bear Lake
Port Radium
Whitehorse
Skagway
Juneau
ALEXANDER ARCHIPELAGO
Prince Rupert
SVERDRUP ISLANDS
PARRY ISLANDS
Banks I.
Prince of Wales Island
Victoria I.
Ellesmere
Devon I.
Somerset I.
Baffin Island
BAFFIN BAY
DAVIS STRAIT
GREENLAND (DENMARK)
Thule
Angmagssalik
Godthaab
Cape Farewell
Jan Mayen (Norway)
EUROPE
ICELAND
Reykjavik
Bergen
Great Slave Lake
Uranium City
Hines Creek
HUDSON BAY
Churchill
CANADA
EDMONTON
Saskatchewan
CALGARY
L. Winnipeg
L. Manitoba
REGINA
Vancouver Island
VANCOUVER
Victoria
SEATTLE
Medicine Hat
WINNIPEG
Thunder Bay
Cochrane
Labrador
Nain
Schefferville
Sept. Îles
Battle Harbour
Anticosti
NEWFOUNDLAND
Gander
St. John's
C. Race
Miquelon (Fr.)
St. Pierre (Fr.)
St. Lawrence
QUEBEC
Charlottetown
HALIFAX
MONTREAL
OTTAWA
Sherbrooke
Augusta
Columbia
PORTLAND
Helena
Bismarck
L. Superior
DULUTH
ST. PAUL
MINNEAPOLIS
L. Huron
L. Michigan
TORONTO
HAMILTON
BUFFALO
ALBANY
BOSTON
NEW HAVEN
Long Island
NEW YORK
C. Mendocino
Boise
Great Salt Lake
Pierre
Missouri
MILWAUKEE
DETROIT
LONDON
CLEVELAND
PITTSBURGH
PHILADELPHIA
SAN FRANCISCO
Reno
Carson City
SACRAMENTO
SALT LAKE CITY
Cheyenne
CHICAGO
DES MOINES
LINCOLN
INDIANAPOLIS
COLUMBUS
BALTIMORE
WASHINGTON
FRESNO
Colorado
DENVER
KANSAS CITY
Ohio
RICHMOND
NORFOLK
UNITED STATES
LAS VEGAS
Arkansas
ST. LOUIS
RALEIGH
C. Hatteras
LOS ANGELES
LONG BEACH
SAN DIEGO
Santa Fe
AMARILLO
OKLAHOMA CITY
TULSA
LITTLE ROCK
NASHVILLE
MEMPHIS
CHARLOTTE
COLUMBIA
BERMUDA ISLANDS (BR.)
ALBUQUERQUE
Wichita Falls
FT WORTH
DALLAS
BIRMINGHAM
ATLANTA
Guadalupe (Mex.)
Tropic of Cancer
MEXICALI
TUCSON
CIUDAD JUAREZ
EL PASO
JACKSON
MONTGOMERY
SAVANNAH
JACKSONVILLE
Mississippi
BATON ROUGE
MOBILE
Tallahassee
GULF OF CALIFORNIA
CHIHUAHUA
SAN ANTONIO
HOUSTON
NEW ORLEANS
Orlando
C. Canaveral
TAMPA
Rio Grande
CORPUS CHRISTI
NUEVO LAREDO
MATAMOROS
GULF OF MEXICO
MIAMI
C. Sable
Key West
BAHAMA ISLANDS
NASSAU
La Paz
CULIACAN
TORREON
MONTERREY
MEXICO
HAVANNA
CUBA
CAMAGUEY
SANTIAGO DE CUBA
AGUASCALIENTES
TAMPICO
GULF OF CAMPECHE
GUADALAJARA
MEXICO CITY
MORELIA
PUEBLA
VERACRUZ
MERIDA
REVILLAGIGEDO ISLANDS (MEX.)
GREATER ANTILLES
HAITI
PORT AU PRINCE
DOMINIC. REP.
SANTO DOMINGO
PUERTO RICO (U.S.)
SAN JUAN
St. Martin (Neth. Fr.)
LESSER ANTILLES
Guadeloupe (Fr.)
Dominica (Br.)
Martinique (Fr.)
St. Lucia (Br.)
St. Vincent (Br.)
Grenada
PORT OF SPAIN
KINGSTON
JAMAICA
BELIZE
Belmopan
CARIBBEAN SEA
ANTILLES (NETH.)
GUATEMALA
GUATAMALA
HONDURAS
TEGUCIGALPA
SAN SALVADOR
EL SALVADOR
NICARAGUA
MANAGUA
COSTA RICA
SAN JOSE
Colón
PANAMA
CANAL ZONE (U.S.)
CARACAS
MARACAIBO
MEDELLIN
BOGOTA
CALI
QUITO
SOUTH AMERICA
Equator
GALAPAGOS ISLANDS (ECUADOR)
Iquitos
Rio Branco
PACIFIC OCEAN
ATLANTIC OCEAN
110°
100°
90°
80°
70°
60°
50°
40°
30°
20°
10°
0°
180°
170°
160°
150°
140°

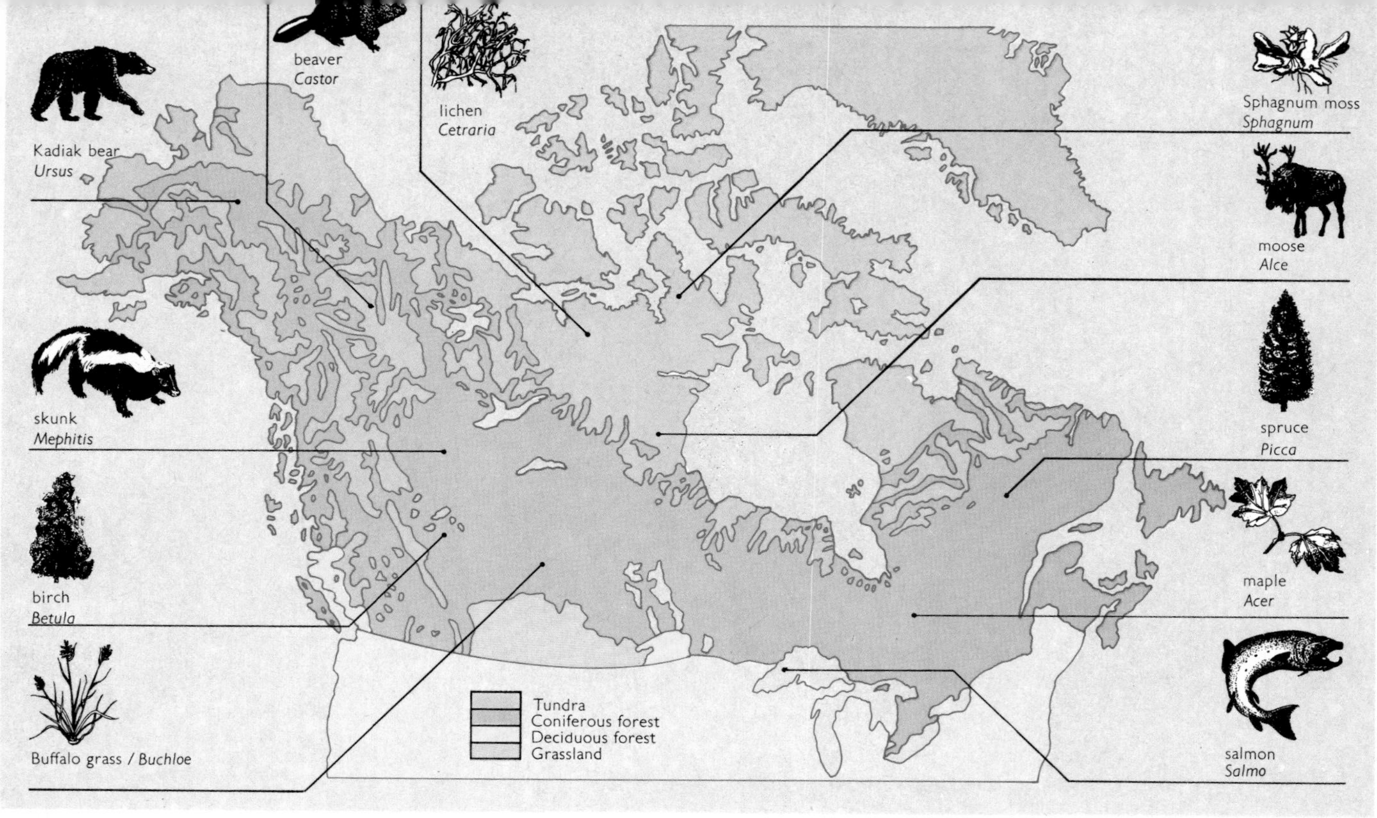

North American flora and fauna. The general distribution of natural vegetation, and indications of the kind of terrain typically associated with some main species of indigenous plants and animals, in Canada and Alaska (above) and in the United States (below).

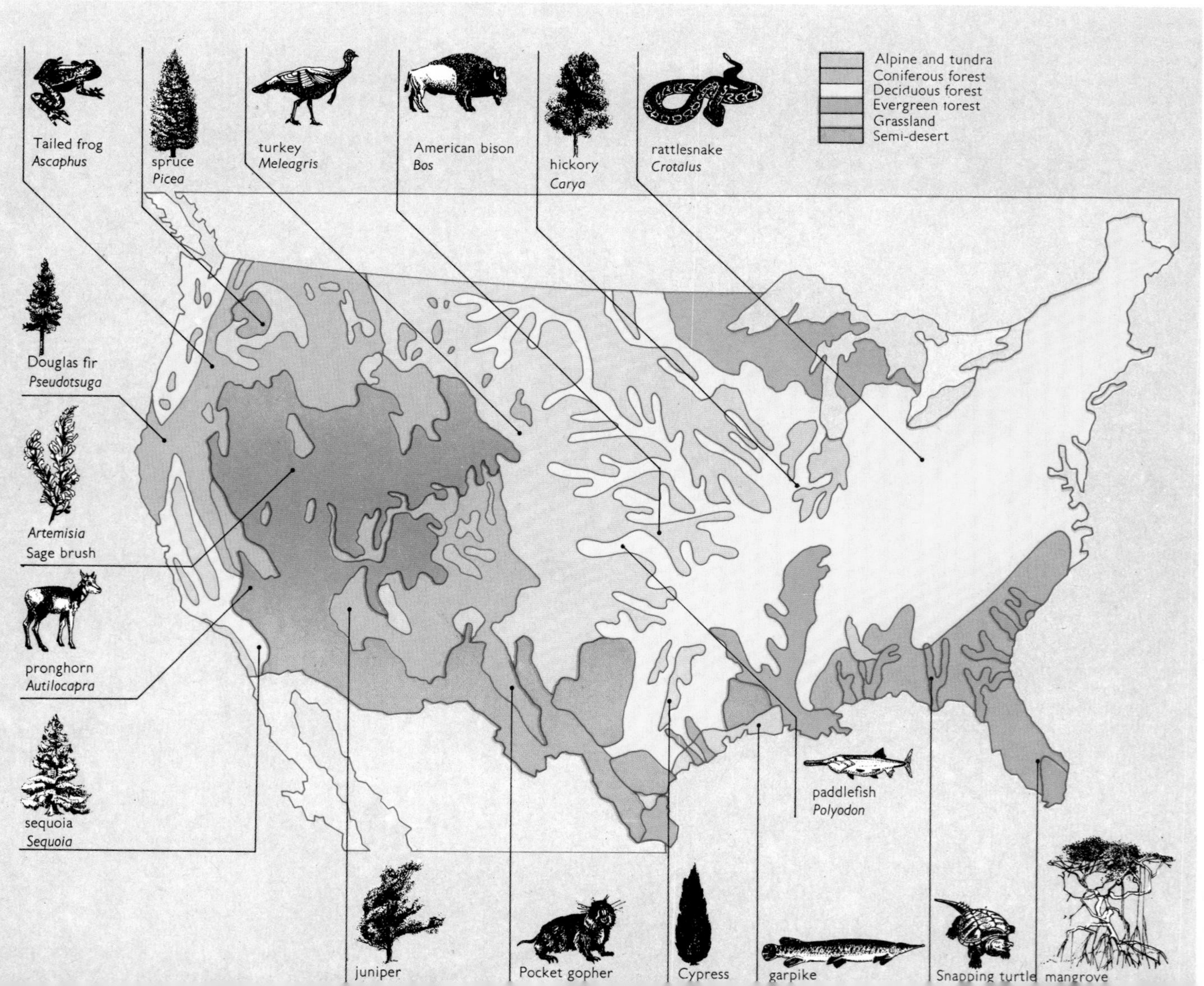

processing, pulp and paper are also important. In agriculture, tobacco leads, followed by soybeans, corn, peanuts and cotton. Tourism, supported by the scenic beauty in the W, five national forests and many historical sites, brings increasing revenue. Mining centers on construction materials, but N.C. is also the main source of felspar, lithium and mica in the US.

History. Sir Walter Raleigh failed twice in the 1580s to settle the area, inhabited by CATAWBA, CHEROKEE and TUSCARORA INDIANS (see LOST COLONY). Grants from Charles I (hence *Carolina*) and II were followed in 1677 by CULPEPER'S REBELLION by settlers. N.C. became a separate colony in 1712, a royal one in 1729. It was the first to instruct its delegates to vote for independence and in 1789 became the twelfth state of the US. It seceded in 1861 when it failed in efforts to preserve the Union. Development was spurred in the 1900s by a major expansion in education and after WWII by industrial diversification and provision of hydroelectric power. N.C. is now a pioneer in social legislation in the South.

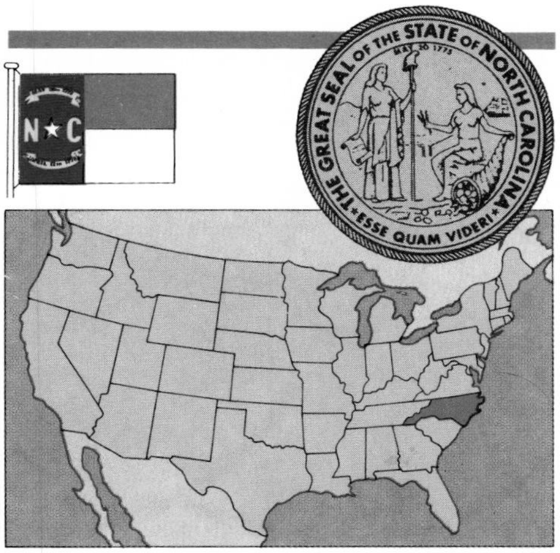

Name of State: North Carolina
Capital: Raleigh
Statehood: Nov. 21, 1789 (12th state)
Familiar Name: Tar Heel State
Area: 52 586sq mi
Population: 5 082 059
Elevation: Highest—6 684ft, Mount Mitchell
Lowest—sea level, Atlantic Ocean
Motto: Esse quam videri (To Be, Rather Than to Seem)
State Flower: Flowering Dogwood
State Bird: Cardinal
State Tree: Pine
State Song: "The Old North State"

NORTH CASCADES NATIONAL PARK, in NW Wash., opened in 1968, with an area of 505 000 acres. It lies E of Mt Baker, extending N to the Canadian border. It is a spectacular mountainous region with lakes, waterfalls, glaciers, forests and rich wildlife.

NORTH CHICAGO, city on Lake Michigan, Ill., 5mi S of Waukegan. It makes steel, generators, auto parts, chemicals and pharmaceuticals. Pop 47 275.

NORTHCLIFFE, Alfred Charles William Harmsworth, Viscount (1865–1922), creator of modern British journalism. On a basis of popular journals starting with *Answers* (1888), he built the world's biggest newspaper empire. He founded or bought the *London Evening News*, *Daily Mail*, *Sunday Dispatch*, *Daily Mirror*, *Observer* and the *Times*.

NORTH COLLEGE HILL, residential city in SW Ohio, a suburb 9mi N of Cinncinnati. Pop 12 363.

NORTH DAKOTA, N central US state, the most agricultural. It lies at the center of the North American land mass.

Land. The most populous part is the flat, fertile Red R valley in the E. The Red R of the North forms the E border with Minn. It drains E N.D. and flows N to Lake Winnipeg. The Drift Plains, with fertile glacial deposits and many lakes, roll W some 70mi in the S and 200mi in the N to the Missouri escarpment. Beyond, the Missouri Plateau, part of the Great Plains, covers the SW of the state. The Missouri R enters N.D. from Montana in the W and flows SE via the huge Garrison hydroelectric dam and reservoir to S.D. Near the W border lie the spectacularly eroded BADLANDS. The continental climate has temperatures averaging 70°F in the summer and 10°F in winter. The rain (only 20in in the E and 14in in the W), falls mostly in the growing season. Only 1% of the land is forested.

Cape Hatteras, off the northern coast of North Carolina, once known as the graveyard of the Atlantic because of the number of ships wrecked in its vicinity. Today its unspoiled beaches attract fishermen and bathers. Visible in the background is the famous Cape Hatteras lighthouse.

People. The people are nearly all native-born, of European descent; nearly two-thirds live in farm areas. Lutherans and Roman Catholics are the largest religious groups. Bismarck (the capital) and Minot in the center, Fargo and Grand Forks on the Red R are the main cities.

Economy. Over 75% of N.D.'s income is from agriculture. Wheat, grown in all 53 counties, is by far the most important crop, followed by flax, barley, rye, potatoes and oats. Earnings from livestock products of the W are second to those of wheat. Oil (discovered 1951 in the NW) and lignite (the US's largest deposits, in the SW) are the chief minerals exploited; there is also gas and uranium. Tourism and manufacturing (food processing and oil refining) roughly equal mineral exploitation in value.

History. The state was part of the 1803 LOUISIANA PURCHASE. After the 18th-century exploration of LA VÉRENDRYE and the LEWIS AND CLARK expedition, settlers were few until the arrival of railroads in 1871 and the 1881 defeat of the SIOUX chief SITTING BULL. Friction between farmers and grain monopolies led to the forming of the NONPARTISAN LEAGUE in 1915. WWII brought recovery from the drought, dust storms and depression of the 1930s, though the manufacturing sector remains modest.

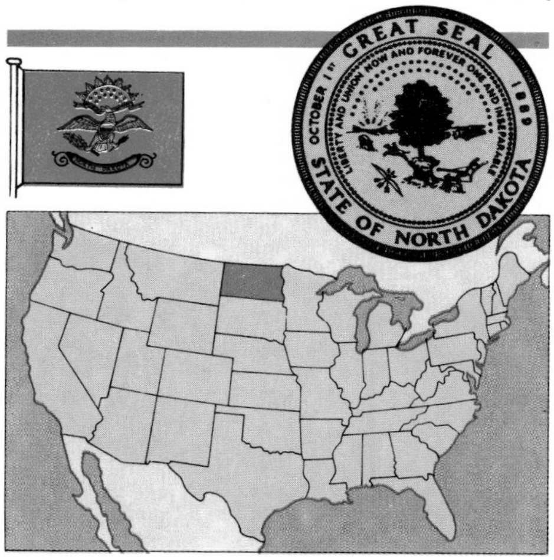

Name of State: North Dakota
Capital: Bismarck
Statehood: Nov. 2, 1889 (39th state)
Familiar Name: Flickertail State
Area: 69 273sq mi
Population: 617 761
Elevation: Highest—3 506ft, White Butte
Lowest—750ft, Red River in Pembina County
Motto: Liberty and Union, Now and Forever, One and Inseparable
State Flower: Wild prairie rose
State Bird: Western meadowlark
State Tree: American elm
State Song: "North Dakota Hymn"

The spectacular scenery of the Badlands of North Dakota, a popular tourist attraction. Part of the area is now protected as the Theodore Roosevelt National Memorial Park.

NORTHEAST PASSAGE, sea passage linking the Atlantic and Pacific oceans. It passes N of the Eurasian mainland along the Arctic coast of Norway and the USSR. Adolf Nordenskjöld, the Swedish explorer, was first to sail its length, 1878–79, although its exploration dates from the 15th century.

NORTHERN IRELAND. See IRELAND, NORTHERN.

NORTHERN LIGHTS. See AURORA.

NORTHERN RHODESIA. See ZAMBIA.

NORTHERN TERRITORY, N central area in Australia administered by the federal government. Sparsely populated (71 400 in 520 280sq mi), it produces beef cattle, gold, peanuts and pearls. Darwin is the chief port and administrative center, Alice Springs the main town inland. Its flat W coast has many bays and in the SE is the Simpson Desert. There are 15 Aboriginal reserves.

NORTHFIELD, city in S Minn., 50mi S of Minneapolis, a center for a dairy, poultry and stock farm area. There is some light industry. Pop 10 235.

NORTH GLENN, city in NE central Col. It is a residential suburb of Denver, the state capital. Pop 27 937.

NORTH HAVEN, town in S Conn., NNE of New Haven, on the Quinnipiac R., with light manufacturing industries. Pop 22 194.

NORTH HIGHLANDS, residential town in N central Cal., suburb of Sacramento. Pop 31 854.

NORTH KAMLOOPS, town in British Columbia, Canada, 15mi N of Kamloops. Its industries include mining and fruitgrowing. Pop 11 319.

NORTH KINGSTOWN, town in R.I., on Narragansett Bay, settled in 1641. A tourist center, it has light manufactures including machine tools. Pop 29 793.

NORTH KOREA. See KOREA.

NORTHLAKE, city in NE Ill., suburb of Chicago. Its industries include paper, food and electrical manufacturing. Pop 14 212.

NORTH LAS VEGAS, city SE Nev., a residential N suburb of Las Vegas. Its Garden of Cities attracts tourists. Pop 36 216.

NORTH LITTLE ROCK (formerly Argenta), industrial city in central Ark., on the Arkansas R

William Cody, "Buffalo Bill," outside his home near North Platte, Nebraska. The massive "Wild West Shows" he organized in his later life helped create the romantic popular view of the old West.

opposite Little Rock. Its industries include cotton and food products. Pop 60 040.

NORTH MERRICK, urban community in SE N.Y. on Long Island. Pop 13 650.

NORTH MIAMI, town in SE Fla., a residential suburb of Miami on Biscayne Bay and a tourist center. It manufactures aluminum and wood products. Pop 34 767.

NORTH MIAMI BEACH, residential city in SE Fla., N of Miami Beach and a tourist resort. Pop 30 723.

NORTH NEW HYDE PARK, town in SE N.Y. on Long Island. Pop 17 945.

NORTH OLMSTED, city in N Ohio, a residential suburb of Cleveland. It has a diversified industry. Pop 34 861.

NORTH PACIFIC CURRENT, ocean current, fed by the JAPAN CURRENT, heading E from the region of Japan to the US west coast, where it becomes the ALASKA CURRENT and CALIFORNIA CURRENT.

NORTH PLAINFIELD, residential borough in N central N.J., 9mi N of New Brunswick, site of a Revolutionary War cemetery. Pop 21 796.

NORTH PLATTE, city in central Neb., seat of Lincoln Co., where the North Platte and South Platte Rivers converge. It is a processing center for livestock and grain. Pop 19 447.

NORTH PLATTE RIVER, river, 680mi long, which rises in N Col., flows N into central Wyo., E and SE into W central Neb., uniting with the South Platte R in SW Neb. to become the Platte. The pioneer Overland Trail followed the river valley.

NORTH POLE, the point on the earth's surface some 750km N of Greenland through which passes the earth's axis of rotation. It does not coincide with the earth's N Magnetic Pole, which is over 1 000km away (see EARTH). The Pole lies roughly at the center of the Arctic Ocean, which there is permanently ice-covered, and experiences days and nights each of six months. It was first reached by Robert E. Peary (April 6, 1909). (See also CELESTIAL SPHERE; MAGNETISM; SOUTH POLE.)

NORTH PROVIDENCE, town in N R.I., a NW suburb of the city of Providence. Pop 24 337.

NORTH READING, residential town in NE Mass. 13mi ESE of Lowell, and an industrial and textile center. Pop 11 264.

NORTH RHINE-WESTPHALIA (German: *Nordrhein Westfalen*), industrial state in West Germany. Created in 1946 it produces a third of all the electricity, 90% of iron and steel and nearly all the coal of West Germany. Its transportation facilities include the Rhine, Ruhr, Wupper, Lippe and Ems Rivers. (See also RUHR.)

NORTH RICHLAND HILLS, residential town in N Tex., NE of Fort Worth of which it is a suburb. Pop 16 514.

NORTH RIDGEVILLE, residential village in N Ohio about 5mi NE of the industrial city of Elyria. Pop 13 152.

NORTHROP, John Howard (1891–), US biochemist who shared with W. M. STANLEY and J. B. SUMNER the 1946 Nobel Prize for Chemistry for his work crystallizing the ENZYMES pepsin (c1930), trypsin (c1932) and chymotrypsin (c1935). He was also the first to isolate a BACTERIOPHAGE (1938).

NORTH ROYALTON, city in N Ohio, a suburb 13mi S of Cleveland. It is a site of developing industries. Pop 12 807.

NORTH SAINT PAUL, village in E Minn., 7mi NE of St. Paul. Its industries include masonry products and conveyor systems. Pop 11 950.

NORTH SEA, arm of the Atlantic Ocean lying between Britain, Scandinavia and NW Europe, rich in fish, gas and oil. Almost 600mi long, it covers 222 125sq mi with an average depth of 300ft, falling to 2 400ft off Norway. Long a rich commercial fishing ground for flatfish and herring, the North Sea since the early 1960s has been prospected by more than 20 international companies for oil and gas. The first productive gas field was found in 1965, 42mi E of Britain's Humber Estuary. Since then, major gas and oil deposits have been found off the Dutch, Norwegian and Scottish coasts, with good yields expected by 1980.

NORTH STAR. See POLARIS.

NORTH TONAWANDA, city and port of entry in W N.Y., 10mi E of Niagara Falls, on the Niagara R and NEW YORK STATE BARGE CANAL. It makes dies, plastics, pumps, paints and furniture. Pop 36 012.

NORTHUMBERLAND STRAIT, channel between Prince Edward Island and E New Brunswick and Nova Scotia. It is almost 180mi long and between 13–30mi wide.

NORTHUMBRIA, English Anglo-Saxon kingdom of the 6th–9th centuries, extending from the Mersey and Humber Rivers on the S to the Firth of Forth in the N. It became the cultural center of England due to the civilizing work of monks (see BEDE, SAINT). The kingdom was overrun by the Danes, the N remnant becoming subject to Wessex.

NORTH VANCOUVER, residential city in British Columbia, Canada, on Burrard Inlet, opposite Vancouver. Its industries include sawmills and shipyards. Pop 31 847.

NORTH WEST COMPANY, organization founded in Montreal about 1784 by British traders to extend commerce, especially fur trading, W to the Pacific and into the Arctic. It set up 78 trading posts and competition with the older HUDSON'S BAY COMPANY was fierce, sometimes violent. The North West Company also clashed with the US fur traders as it occupied the Pacific coast from Alaska to the Columbia R. In 1821, it was merged with the Hudson's Bay Company.

NORTH-WEST MOUNTED POLICE. See ROYAL CANADIAN MOUNTED POLICE.

NORTHWEST ORDINANCE, ordinance adopted by Congress in 1787, which established the government of the NORTHWEST TERRITORY and provided a form for future territories to follow. It stated that Congress should appoint a territorial governor, a secretary and three judges. Once the territory had a voting population of 5 000 it could elect a legislature and send a non-voting representative to Congress. When the population reached 60 000, the territory could seek full admission to the Union. It barred slavery, guaranteed basic rights and encouraged education.

NORTHWEST PASSAGE, inland water route from the E coast of North America to the Pacific, and thus to the Orient. This was unsuccessfully sought for centuries. John CABOT explored the coast around Newfoundland in 1497 thinking it was China; Henry HUDSON sailed as far as Hudson Bay and beyond (1609–11); William BAFFIN and Robert Bylot found a way between Baffin Island and Greenland. Explorations opened up important new lands, but not until Robert MCCLURE's expedition of 1850–54 was the existence of a passage weaving among the Arctic islands proved. The first complete journey was made when Roald AMUNDSEN sailed W from Baffin Bay through Lancaster Sound, 1903–06. The entire Atlantic–Pacific crossing was not accomplished until the US Navy navigated the Northwest Passage by atomic submarine in 1958.

NORTHWEST REBELLIONS. See RIEL'S REBELLION.

NORTHWEST TERRITORIES, federally administered region of Canada comprising the mainland N of 60°N between Yukon Territory and Hudson Bay, the islands in Hudson, James and Ungava Bays and all islands N of the mainland. It is an immense, low-lying thinly-populated area: about half the region lies within the Arctic Circle. Two thirds of the mainland are covered by the Mackenzie R, its tributaries, and by lakes such as the Great Bear and Great Slave. The Mackenzie Mts to the W rise to 9000ft. There is permanent sea ice N of Melville Island where the winter temperature sinks to −40°F compared with −18°F in the Mackenzie delta. More than 60% of the population are Eskimos and Indians. Most of the Indians and whites are in the Mackenzie District, which is the most developed area and where the largest towns, Yellowknife, the capital, Fort Smith and Inuvik are. The principal industries are fishing, mining and trapping. The mineral potential of the Territories is enormous, the chief minerals being lead and zinc, followed by copper and gold and iron ore on Baffin Island. Farming in the region is still in an experimental stage. Early explorers include Sir Martin FROBISHER who reached Baffin Island in 1576, and the trader-explorers of the HUDSON'S BAY COMPANY. Sir Alexander MACKENZIE explored in the 1780s. The region was part of a larger area sold to Canada in 1870 by the Hudson's Bay Company. The Territories' boundaries were established in 1912.

Name of Territory: The Northwest Territories (Districts: Mackenzie, Keewatin, Franklin)
Joined Confederation: 1870 (as Rupert's Land, purchased by Canada from the Hudson's Bay Company; present boundaries set in 1912)
Capital: Yellowknife (since 1967; previously Ottawa)
Area: 1 304 903sq mi
Population (including districts): 34 807 (⅔ Eskimo and Indian)

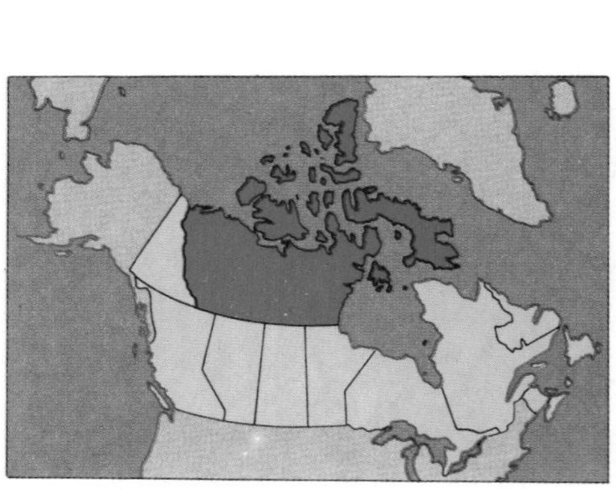

NORTHWEST TERRITORY, region between the Ohio and Mississippi Rivers, extending N around the Great Lakes. It was the first national territory of the US, eventually forming Ohio (1803), Ind. (1816), Ill. (1818), Mich. (1837), Wis. (1848) and part of Minn. Won by Britain from the French who explored it in the 1600s, it was ceded to the US by the Treaty of PARIS 1783, and its future determined by the Ordinance of 1787 (see NORTHWEST ORDINANCE). The first governor was Arthur St. Clair and settlement soon followed. Indians were defeated by General Anthony WAYNE at the battle of FALLEN TIMBERS and most of their lands taken by the Treaty of Greenville, 1795. Indiana, Michigan and Illinois became territories prior to statehood.

NORTON, residential city in NE Ohio, a suburb of Akron, on Little Cuyahoga R. Pop 12 308.

NORTON, Charles Eliot (1827–1908), US scholar and man of letters, known for his prose translation of Dante 1891–92. He was professor of the history of art at Harvard 1875–98.

NORTON SHORES, city in W Mich. on Lake Michigan, 7mi S of Muskegon. Pop 22 271.

NORWALK, city in Cal., SE of Los Angeles. It has light manufacturing industries. Pop 91 827.

NORWALK, city in SW Conn., on Long Island Sound, settled in 1650 and burned by the British in 1779. It manufactures office machines, electronic equipment and air compressors. Pop 79 113.

NORWALK, city in N Ohio, seat of Huron Co. It was founded by settlers from Norwalk, Conn. in 1816. It manufactures furniture, iron and steel. Pop 13 386.

Stave churches such as this one at Borgund, built c1150, are peculiar to Norway; some 24 survive today. Built entirely of wood, their construction resembles that of a ship; they are richly carved throughout with dragons and other mythological subjects, suggesting that they are copied from pagan temples.

NORWAY, European sovereign state in the W Scandanavian peninsula between the Atlantic, on the W, and Sweden. Finland and the USSR are to the NE. Norwegian territory also includes thousands of coastal islands.

Land. It is a rugged, mountainous land, famous for its beautiful fiords, with many deep lakes and swift rivers. The mountains, covering over half of Norway, extend nearly its whole length. It has the highest peak in Scandinavia (Galdhøpiggen, 8 098ft) and the largest ice field in mainland Europe, the Jostedalsbreen. Because of its maritime situation and on-shore winds, the climate is mild. Rainfall varies from 100in on the coast to 40in inland. Pine and spruce forests cover about a fourth of Norway.

People. The majority of the population are of the fair Nordic type, but there are some Lapps and Finns in the N. The S is the most heavily populated, the largest towns there being Oslo, the capital, Stavanger and Bergen and in the N, Trondheim. There are two official languages, Nynorsk and Bokmål, (see NORWEGIAN LANGUAGE) although the Lapps in the N use a Finno-Ugric speech.

Official Name: Norway
Capital: Oslo
Area: 125 020sq mi
Population: 3 948 235
Languages: Norwegian; Lappish, Finnish spoken in the North
Religion: Evangelical Lutheran
Monetary Unit(s): 1 Krone = 100 øre

Economy. Norway's natural resources are sparse: mineral deposits are minimal and about 3% of the land is under cultivation. Norway has developed a thriving economy since WWII by restricting imports and promoting industrialization, particularly in chemicals, textiles, machinery, paints and furniture. It is a world leader in aluminum production and shipbuilding. Agriculture, based on farms of 25 acres or less, gives high yields of oats, hay, barley, potatoes, fruits and vegetables, and livestock are raised in the mountains. Forestry and fishing, particularly of mackerel and cod, are very important industries.

History. Norway's separate history began about 800 AD when the VIKINGS began to raid European coastal towns. Until the 14th century there was a long series of civil wars. In 1397 Norway merged with Denmark (becoming a Danish province in 1536) and in 1814 with Sweden. In 1905 it became an independent constitutional monarchy under HAAKON VII. Germans occupied all of Norway 1940–45. Norway is a member of the NORTH ATLANTIC TREATY ORGANIZATION and of the EUROPEAN FREE TRADE ASSOCIATION, but refused by a 1972 referendum to join the COMMON MARKET.

NORWEGIAN CURRENT, or **Norway Current,** a continuation of the GULF STREAM passing NE along the NW Norwegian coast. (See also OCEAN CURRENTS.)

NORWEGIAN ELKHOUND, breed of dog, originally from Norway, used to hunt elk and herd flocks. It resembles a small spitz and has a short compact body, short pointed ears and a thick gray coat. In the US it is kept as a pet.

NORWEGIAN LANGUAGE, language of Norway, developed from the NORSE and influenced by union with Denmark 1397–1814. There are two official versions: *Nynorsk* or *Landsmål*, based on native dialects and *Bokmål* or *Riksmål*, a Dano-Norwegian used by writers and the press. Differences between them are growing less.

NORWICH, cathedral town of Norfolk, E England. It has been important since it was settled by the Saxons. It has over 30 medieval churches. It is an agricultural trade and industrial center and manufactures footwear. Pop 121 688.

NORWICH, city in Conn., seat of New London Co., on the Shetucket R, and the site of the great battle between the Mohican and Narragansett Indians in 1643. It has varied industries. Pop 41 739.

NORWICH TERRIER, English breed of small, short-legged terrier with a straight wiry red, gray or black-and-tan coat. Standing 10in at the shoulder, the neck is short and strong, the tail docked and the head has a foxy muzzle with ears pricked or dropped.

NORWOOD, residential town in E Mass., 13mi SW of Boston, founded in 1678. It has printing works and foundries. Pop 30 815.

NORWOOD, city in SW Ohio and suburb of Cinncinnati. It makes electric motors, machine tools and other light manufactures. Pop 30 420.

NOSE, the midline organ of the FACE, concerned with the perception of SMELL and the preparation of the air stream for RESPIRATION. It is a CARTILAGE extension of the facial bones with two external openings or nostrils. These pass into the nasal cavities, which are separated by a septum and contain turbinates which increase the mucous membrane surface and direct the air flow. The chemoreceptors for smell lie mainly in the roof of the nasal cavities, but fine nerve fibers throughout the nose contribute both to tactile sensation and smell. Nasal MUCUS protects the BRONCHI and LUNGS by removing dust particles, humidifying and warming inspired air. The COMMON COLD, RHINITIS and HAY FEVER are common afflictions of the nose.

NOSTRADAMUS (1503–1566), French astrologer, famed for his prophecies, published in verse and entitled *Centuries* (1555). His real name was Michel de Nostredame and he was court physician to Charles IX. His prediction of Henry II's death four years ahead made his name, though his prophecies were generally vague.

NOTARY PUBLIC, state-appointed official who certifies the authenticity of documents and takes oaths. His seal is affixed when he is sure the person signing is known to him and that the signature is genuine. Notarization is required for property deeds and marriage and birth certificates as a safeguard against forgery.

NOTATION, method of writing down music formalized between the 10th and 18th centuries into a system of stave notation, now in general use. It consists of five horizontal lines or staves as the framework on which eight notes are written—A, B, C, D, E, F, G (in ascending order of pitch) and thence to A again an octave higher (see also SCALE). Each note's special place on or between the lines depends on its pitch: in the base clef, if low, the treble clef if higher. A middle or alto clef is sometimes used. The KEY of the music is indicated by sharps and flats on the staves next to the clef sign at the beginning of the score. The length of the notes relative to each other is shown by their form. There are commonly seven forms of note from the longest held to the shortest. The beat of the music is shown by dividing the staves by vertical lines into *bars* and marking at the outset how many beats there are to each bar (see also RHYTHM). Other notations are the *tonic sol-fa* in which notes are related to each other, not to the established pitch of the written stave; and *tablature* in which a diagram indicates where to place the fingers on various instruments to obtain notes. New signs for use in ELECTRONIC MUSIC are being invented.

NOTOCACTUS, a genus of CACTI. They usually produce solitary, spherical stems and have attractively-colored spines and flowers. Many species, such as *Notocactus ottonis*, are popular house plants, and for best flowering they should be kept dry and cool—between 10°C and 16°C (50–60°F)—during the winter. Family: Cactaceae.

NOTOCHORD, the primitive longitudinal skeletal element characterizing the class Chordata, the first stage in the development of a flexible internal skeleton. All chordates possess a notochord at some time during life. Though replaced by cartilage or bone in the adult VERTEBRATE and absent in the adults of other chordate groups, e.g., TUNICATES, it is well developed in the embryos or larvae of all these groups, confirming evolutionary relationships within the class.

NOTORNIS, or Takahe, a large flightless bird of New Zealand, related to the Common GALLINULE. The size of a chicken, it has a heavy bill, a brilliant red frontal shield and purple plumage. Believed extinct since the 1850s it was rediscovered in 1948 in South Island.

NOTRE DAME DE PARIS, cathedral church of Paris, on the Ile de la Cité in the Seine R. Begun in 1163, it was finished in 1313 and is one of the finest examples of early Gothic architecture, especially for the ROSE WINDOW of the west facade and the sculptured portals. Some restoration was necessary after the French Revolution. (See also GOTHIC ART.)

NOTTINGHAM, city in the English Midlands on the Trent R, long famed for lace. A 9th-century Danish borough, it was the location of three parliaments, (1330–57). Charles I opened the Civil War here in 1642. Pop 299 758.

NOUAKCHOTT, capital of Mauritania, on the W

Atlantic coast of Africa and formerly a French colony. Since 1957 Nouakchott has become a bustling port city with light industries. Pop 37 000.

NOUMÉA, capital of French New Caledonia, on the SW coast of New Caledonia Island, SW Pacific. It has a large inland harbor and a trans-Pacific airfield. Pop 58 000.

NOVA, a star which over a short period (usually a few days) increases in brightness by 100 to 1 000 000 times. This is thought to be due to the star undergoing a partial explosion: that is to say, part of the star erupts, throwing out material at a speed greater than the ESCAPE VELOCITY of the star. The initial brightness fades quite rapidly though it is usually some years before the star returns to its previous luminosity, having lost about 0.0001 of its mass. At that time a rapidly expanding planetary NEBULA may be seen to surround the star. Recurrent novae are stars which go nova at irregular periods of a few decades. Dwarf novae are subdwarf stars which go nova every few weeks or months. Novae have been observed in other galaxies besides the MILKY WAY. (See also SUPERNOVA.)

NOVA IGUAÇU, city and major suburb of Rio de Janeiro, SE Brazil, about 50mi from the coast. It has varied light agricultural-related industry. Pop 331 457.

NOVALIS, the pen name of Friederich Leopold, Freiherr von Hardenberg (1772–1801), German poet. His works, notably the myth-romance *Heinrich von Ofterdingen* (1802), influenced later European exponents of ROMANTICISM. He attempted to unite poetry, philosophy and science into an allegory of the world.

NOVA SCOTIA, one of the four original provinces of the Dominion of Canada; it includes Cape Breton Island to the NE. It is also one of the MARITIME PROVINCES on the Atlantic seaboard. Linked to the mainland by the narrow Chignecto Isthmus, it is bounded on the N by New Brunswick and is separated from Prince Edward Island on the NW by Northumberland Strait; otherwise it is bounded by the Bay of Fundy and the Atlantic Ocean.

Land. Nova Scotia has an area of 21 425sq mi (1 023sq mi of inland water). There are many short rivers, the longest being the Mersey and St. Mary's (both run about 72mi). The Atlantic Upland is a distinctive feature of the landscape and is divided into five areas separated by fertile valleys and lowlands, notably the Annapolis Valley, famous for its apple orchards. The province generally has a cool climate, intensified by the cold Labrador Current; average temperatures are 24°F in Jan. with heavy snowfall and 65°F in July. Rainfall ranges from an average of 55in in the E to 40in in the W. Three-quarters of the province is forested; wildlife and birdlife are abundant.

People. Most Nova Scotians are of British or French ancestry, but important minority groups are descendants of Irish and German immigrants and of former West Indian slaves, and about 3 000 Micmac Indians live in the province. About 16% of the land is occupied by small farms averaging around 190 acres and while 6% of the people live on farms, 35% live in nonfarm rural areas. In coastal areas farming is combined with fishing and inland it is combined with dairying.

Economy. Lumbering is an important industry in the province, which has numerous other natural resources including coal, gypsum, barite and natural gas. There are rich fisheries and farmlands. Apples are the chief fruit crop; hay, oats, barley, wheat and vegetables are grown in substantial quantities. Manufacturing is diversified and chiefly concentrated around Halifax (which is also the main port), Sydney and Trenton and a few other small urban areas. Products range from iron and steel to chemicals, ships, automobiles, oil, sugar, plastics and clothing; meat packing and fish processing are important too. Tourism contributes to the provincial income; Nova Scotia is Canada's ocean playground with numerous wilderness areas.

History. Leif ERICSON may have visited Nova Scotia as early as 1 000 AD, but it is certain that John CABOT discovered Cape Breton Island in 1497. Canada's first permanent settlement was established in 1605 on the site of Annapolis Royal. In the 17th century the area was contested by the British and the French, but after the FRENCH AND INDIAN WARS it was gained by England. Nova Scotia became the first Canadian colony to gain responsible government in 1848 and in 1867 it formed the original Dominion with Quebec, Ontario and New Brunswick. Since then, Nova Scotia has been concerned with establishing its rightful place in the nation, alongside much larger and richer provinces. Much economic and social progress has been achieved, aided by large-scale industrial development around the Sydney area and construction of a deep-water port on the Strait of Canso.

Name of Province: Nova Scotia
Joined Confederation: July 1st, 1867
Capital: Halifax
Area: 21 425sq mi
Population: 794 000

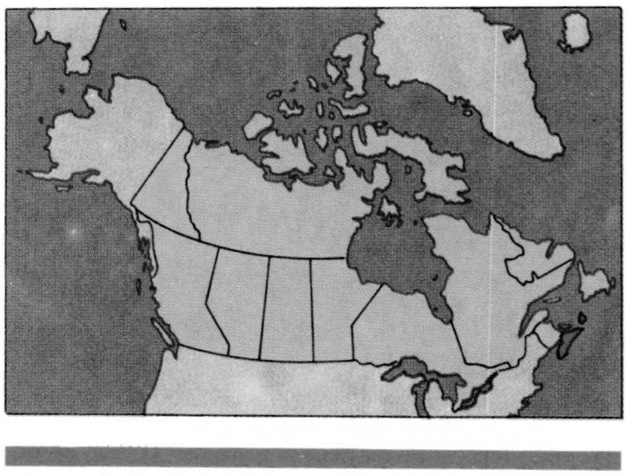

NOVAYA ZEMLYA, a group of islands (including two main ones) in NW USSR in the Arctic Ocean between the Barents Sea on the W and the Kara Sea on the E. Used as a Soviet nuclear testing site, the islands have a small native population which fishes and hunts in the S tundra areas.

NOVEL, a work of prose fiction (usually over 60 000 words long) generally portraying in one or more plot lines the interrelationship of a number of characters. Rudimentary forms of novel appear to have existed in ancient Egypt as long ago as 2000 BC; the Greek *Daphnis and Cloë* and the eclectic *The Golden Ass* by the Roman APULEIUS are the earliest known in the West. The Japanese *Tale of the Genji* (c1000) by Lady MURASAKI is a sophisticated and startlingly modern love novel. The modern European novel developed out of the Italian Renaissance *novella* form, typified by BOCACCIO's *Decameron.* RABELAIS' *Gargantua and Pantagruel* (1532–52) and CERVANTES' *Don Quixote* (1605–15) are prototypes of the European novel. In English literature the form was established in the works of DEFOE, and in the mid-18th century with the contrasting work of RICHARDSON and FIELDING. The 19th-century novel was a major form of mass entertainment throughout Europe and the Americas; it was also a forum for the discussion of politics and special problems, and so recorded them for posterity. The novels of GOETHE, Sir Walter SCOTT and others, inspired much Romantic drama and music. In France George SAND and Victor HUGO were among the first post-Revolutionary novelists of standing. In the US the novel contributed to the development of a national identity and the defining of a specifically American experience.

Giants of the form in both stature and output emerged in the 19th century such as BALZAC, DICKENS, George ELIOT, TOLSTOY, DOSTOYEVSKI and Herman MELVILLE who exploited the vast possibilities of the form. From the time of FLAUBERT there has been less emphasis on "story-telling"; the novel came to be seen as an intense psychological artefact with aesthetic aspirations akin to poetry. Henry JAMES, PROUST, James JOYCE, Virginia WOOLF and others have elaborated this emphasis, often at the expense of any easy accessibility. Writers such as Thomas HARDY and D. H. LAWRENCE, and HEMINGWAY and other US writers have, in their different styles, favored a more direct and passionate approach, while writers like ORWELL, KOESTLER and even SOLZHENITSYN emphasized political stance and almost documentary reportage. Despite contrary prophecies the novel's vitality appears to remain undiminished today.

NOVEMBER, the 11th month of the year, the ninth in the original Roman CALENDAR; its name derives from the Latin *novem*, nine. It now has 30 days, and the 4th Thurs. is THANKSGIVING DAY in the US.

NOVENA, in Roman Catholicism, prayers either in private or at public religious services on nine days, in petition for divine favor or intercession for a special event. The novena is often in a particular saint's honor. One famous public novena is that of the Feast of the IMMACULATE CONCEPTION (Nov. 30–Dec. 8). Novenas recall the nine days the apostles spent in prayer awaiting the gift of the Holy Spirit, and the practice was probably borrowed from pagan Rome where a nine-day mourning period was held after an emperor's death.

NOVGOROD, historic city and capital of Novgorod oblast, NW USSR. Located on the Volkhov R, it long formed a trade link between the Baltic and the Orient. The city was important as an ancient VARANGIAN capital, a cultural and a commercial center, and was later a trading center of the HANSEATIC LEAGUE. Pop. 128 000.

NOVOCAINE, alternative name for PROCAINE, a local anesthetic.

NOVOCHERKASSK, city in the SE USSR on a Don R tributary 25mi NE of Rostov-na-Donu, headquarters of the Don COSSACKS until 1920. It is a manufacturing city today. Pop 162 000.

NOVOKUZNETSK, city in S Siberian USSR, on the Tom R, formerly Stalinsk. Its industries include coal mining, iron, steel, aluminum and chemical production. Pop 499 000.

NOVOSIBIRSK, the largest city of Soviet Asia on the Ob R, USSR. It is Siberia's commercial, cultural and administrative center and is a major industrial complex of the USSR as well as being a hub of river, rail, air and road transport. Pop 1 161 000.

NOVOTNÝ, Antonín (1904–1975), Czechoslovakian Communist Party leader; president of Czechoslovakia, 1957–68. As a Stalinist and supporter of Moscow, Novotný fell from power in Jan. 1968 after years of economic stagnation and political unrest. He was succeeded by a liberal regime led by Alexander DUBČEK and others.

NOYES, Alfred (1880–1958), English poet, a traditionalist known for his popular, vigorous rhythmic ballads like *The Highwayman* and patriotic sea poems such as *Drake* (1908). His other works include the blank verse *Torch-Bearers* (1922–30) praising scientific progress, and *Collected Poems* (1947).

NOYES, John Humphrey (1811–1886), US religious reformer, founder of the ONEIDA COMMUNITY, 1848. He preached so-called "perfectionism" in his communities at Putney, Vt. and Oneida, N.Y., but "Bible Communism" and a form of polygamy aroused opposition and he fled to Canada in 1879.

NRA. See NATIONAL RECOVERY ADMINISTRATION.

NU, U (1907–), Burmese political leader, prime minister 1948–58 and 1960–62. A founder of the Anti-Fascist People's League after WWII, he was the first prime minister when Burma gained independence. Twice ousted from office by the army, he left Burma in 1969 but still supported minority rebel groups against the government until 1973.

NUBIA, ancient region of NE Africa, now mostly in the republic of Sudan, along both banks of the Nile R from Aswan nearly to Khartoum. Called CUSH by the Egyptians, its rulers overran Upper Egypt in 750 BC and Lower Egypt in 721 BC. The Assyrians drove the Cushites out about 667 BC. Around 200 AD the Nobatae, a Negro people, settled in Nubia and by 600 AD their powerful kingdom was Christianized, but eventually it disintegrated under Muslim pressure in the later 14th century.

NUCLEAR ENERGY, energy released from an atomic nucleus during a nuclear reaction in which the atomic number (see ATOM), MASS NUMBER or RADIOACTIVITY of the nucleus changes. The term atomic energy, also used for this energy, which is produced in large amounts by NUCLEAR REACTORS and NUCLEAR WEAPONS, is not strictly appropriate, since nuclear reactions do not involve the orbital ELECTRONS of the atom. Nuclear energy arises from the special forces (about a million times stronger than chemical bonds) that hold the PROTONS and NEUTRONS together in the small volume of the atomic nucleus (see NUCLEAR PHYSICS). Lighter nuclei have roughly equal numbers of protons and neutrons, but heavier elements are only stable with a neutron:proton ratio of about 1.5:1. If one could overcome the electrostatic repulsion between protons and assemble them with neutrons to form a stable nucleus, its mass would be less than that of the constituent particles by the *mass defect* Δm, of the nucleus, and the *binding energy*, BE, given by BE $= \Delta m c^2$ (where c is the electromagnetic constant), would be released. Because c is large, a vast amount of energy would be released, even for a very small value of the mass defect. The binding energy (equivalent to the work needed to split up the nucleus into separate protons and neutrons) is always positive—nuclei are always more stable than their separate nucleons (protons or neutrons)—but is greatest for nuclei of medium mass, decreasing slightly for lighter and heavier elements. The low binding energy of very light elements means that energy can be released by combining e.g., two DEUTERIUM nuclei to form a helium nucleus. This combination of two protons and two neutrons is particularly stable (see FUSION, NUCLEAR). For heavy elements the decrease in binding energy indicates that the more positively charged the nucleus becomes, the less stable it is, even though it contains more neutrons than protons. This sets a limit on the number of elements, and also explains why the nuclear-fission process, in which a heavy nucleus splits into two or more medium-mass nuclei with higher total binding energy, releases energy. The first nuclear reaction was performed experimentally in 1919 by RUTHERFORD who exposed NITROGEN to ALPHA PARTICLES (helium nuclei) from the radioactive element RADIUM, producing OXYGEN and HYDROGEN:

$$N^{14} + He^4 \rightarrow O^{17} + H^1$$

But, because nuclei are positively charged and repel each other, it was found difficult to bring them close enough together to react with each other. The discovery of the neutron in 1932 helped overcome this problem. Being uncharged and heavy (on the atomic scale), the neutron has high energy even when moving slowly and is good for initiating nuclear reactions. By 1939 many nuclear reactions had been studied, but none seemed feasible as an energy source. Although energy might be released in a reaction, more energy was expended in producing particles able to initiate the reaction than could be recovered from it. Moreover, only a small fraction of the reagent particles would react as desired and any product particles would have little chance of reacting again. The situation was like trying to set fire to a damp forest with a box of matches! A breakthrough came around 1939 when the violent reaction of the heavy element uranium on bombardment with slow nuetrons (first observed experimentally by Fermi in 1934) was successfully interpreted. It was realized that this was an example of nuclear fission, the slow neutrons delivering enough energy to the small proportion of U^{235} nuclei in natural uranium to split them into two parts. This split does not always occur in the same way, and many radioactive fission products are formed, but each fission is accompanied by the release of much energy and two or three neutrons (these because the lighter nuclei of the fission products have a lower neutron:proton ratio than uranium). These neutrons were the key to the large scale production of nuclear energy; they could make the uranium "burn" by setting up a chain reaction. Even allowing for the loss of some neutrons, sufficient are left to produce other fissions, each producing two or three more neutrons, and so on, leading to an explosive release of energy. The first controlled chain reaction took place in Chicago in 1942, using pure graphite as a moderator to slow down neutrons and natural uranium as fuel. Rods of neutron-absorbing material kept the reaction under control by limiting the number of neutrons available to cause fissions. The possibilities of nuclear energy as a weapon were exploited at once and WWII ended shortly after the United States dropped two ATOMIC BOMBS on Japan. Later, more powerful bombs exploiting nuclear fusion were developed. An increasing quantity of man's energy is produced in NUCLEAR REACTORS from nuclear fission, although the earth's natural supplies of fissionable material are surprisingly limited. Moreover, because the fission products from these reactors are radioactive with long HALF-LIVES, atomic waste disposal is a major environmental problem. At present the waste is stored in concrete vaults lined with stainless steel, though the possibilities of converting waste to an insoluble glass are being explored. Disposal in space, in geologically stable parts of the earth's crust or by chemical conversion to safer materials are ideas for the future. Nuclear fusion seems to offer much better long-term prospects for energy supply, although fusion reactors have not yet progressed beyond the research stage.

NUCLEAR PHYSICS, the study of the physical properties and mathematical treatment of the atomic nucleus and SUBATOMIC PARTICLES. The subject was born when RUTHERFORD postulated the existence of the nucleus in 1911. The nature of the short-range exchange forces which hold together the nucleus, acting between positively charged protons and neutral neutrons is still uncertain. Experimental data from MASS SPECTROSCOPY and scattering experiments have enabled various partially successful theoretical models to be devised. Despite the special techniques required to produce nuclear reactions, the subject has rapidly grown with the technical exploitation of NUCLEAR ENERGY.

NUCLEAR REACTOR, device containing sufficient fissionable material, arranged so that a controlled chain reaction may be started up and maintained in it. Many types of reactor exist: all produce NEUTRONS, GAMMA RAYS, radioactive fission products and HEAT, but normally use is made of only one of these. Neutrons may be used in nuclear research or for producing useful RADIOISOTOPES. Gamma rays are dangerous to man and must be shielded against, but have some uses (see IRRADIATION). The fragments produced by fission of a heavy nucleus have a large amount of energy and the heat they produce may be used for carrying out a variety of high-temperature processes or for heating a working fluid (such as steam) to operate a TURBINE and produce ELECTRICITY. This is the function of most commercial reactors, although a number are used to power ships and submarines, since a small amount of nuclear fuel gives these a very long range. In an electricity-generating reactor, the fuel is normally uranium pellets surrounded by a moderator and the cooling fluid heavy water or liquid sodium (which in turn heats the turbine fluid). There is much insulation and radiation shielding. The fuel is expensive, but produces several thousand times the heat of the same weight of coal. After some time it must be replaced (although only partly consumed) because of the build-up of neutron-absorbing fission products. This replacement, and the reprocessing of the radioactive products, needs costly remote handling equipment. New fast breeder reactors with no moderator avoid this problem, since as well as producing fission of U^{235}, they convert nonfissionable U^{238} to plutonium which also undergoes fission chain reactions—they effectively breed fuel! Research is continuing into more efficient reactors as power sources for the future.

NUCLEAR REGULATORY COMMISSION (NRC), independent US government agency set up in 1975 to take on all the licensing and regulatory functions formerly assigned to the Atomic Energy Commission. (See also ENERGY RESEARCH AND DEVELOPMENT ADMINISTRATION.)

NUCLEAR WARFARE, the use of nuclear weapons—the ATOMIC BOMB and the HYDROGEN BOMB—in warfare. The possible appalling consequences of large-scale nuclear warfare have overshadowed world politics since soon after WWII. Following FERMI's discovery of nuclear FISSION, preliminary experiments were done in the US starting in 1939, owing largely to fears of Germany's developing the atomic bomb first. With the US entry into the war, the MANHATTAN PROJECT was started, culminating in the atomic bombs dropped on Hiroshima and Nagasaki. The USSR tested its first such weapon in 1949; from then on an arms race between those two "great powers" escalated until the late 1960s. The US exploded its first hydrogen bomb in 1952: the USSR in 1953. The UK, France and China have also developed nuclear weapons; certain other countries may well have done so without testing them. Development and deployment of nuclear weapons has been dictated by the theory of the nuclear deterrent, the aim being the capability of "assured destruction" of the enemy nation, a stable strategic balance being achieved. Essential to this is the protection of a country's missiles against destruction in a "first strike," i.e., before any can be used in retaliation; thus the guided missiles are sited underground and in nuclear-powered SUBMARINES. The problem of radioactive FALLOUT pollution from nuclear tests led to the partial Nuclear Test-Ban Treaty, signed by the UK, US and USSR in 1963: this bans tests in space, in the atmosphere and underwater, but permits underground explosions that do not release fission products beyond national frontiers. Enforcement of the treaty requires explosions to be detected; this is done by detecting seismic or acoustic disturbances, radiation, or radioactive debris. Further disarmament negotiations led to the Treaty on the Non-Proliferation of Nuclear Weapons, ratified 1970 by 43 nations. There have also been attempts to limit delivery systems, especially intercontinental ballistic missiles (ICBMs), and defensive systems. Strategic arms limitation talks (SALT) began in 1969 and have achieved some limitation. Very stringent precautions are taken to prevent accidental or irresponsible use of nuclear weapons. Several persons validly authorized are required, and there is an electronic failsafe system. Military strategy in recent years has been directed toward limited nuclear warfare, using tactical nuclear weapons in the battle zone, and toward preventing middle-scale nuclear wars from escalating to a total nuclear holocaust.

NUCLEAR WEAPONS, those depending for their destructive capability on the energies released in nuclear fission (the ATOMIC BOMB) or in nuclear fusion (the HYDROGEN BOMB). (See also NUCLEAR ENERGY.)

NUCLEIC ACIDS, the vital chemical constituents of living things; a class of complex threadlike molecules comprising two main types: the deoxyribonucleic acids (DNA) and the ribonucleic acids (RNA). DNA is found almost exclusively in the nucleus of the living CELL, where it forms the chief material of the CHROMOSOMES. It is the DNA molecule's ability to duplicate itself (replicate) that makes cell reproduction possible; and it is DNA, by directing PROTEIN SYNTHESIS, that controls HEREDITY in all organisms other than certain VIRUSES which contain only RNA. RNA performs several important tasks connected with protein synthesis, and is found throughout the cell.

In both DNA and RNA the backbone of the molecule is a chain of alternate phosphate and sugar groups. To each sugar group is bonded one or other of four nitrogenous side groups, which are either purines or pyrimidines. Each unit consisting of a side group, a sugar and a phosphate is called a NUCLEOTIDE. DNA differs chemically from RNA in that its sugar group has one less oxygen atom (hence the prefix "deoxy-") and one of its side groups, thymine, is replaced in RNA by uracil. DNA molecules are usually very much longer than RNA and may contain a million or so phosphate-sugar links.

It is the sequence in which the side groups are arranged along the DNA molecule that constitutes stored genetic information and so makes the difference between one inherited characteristic and another. This information, in the form of coded instructions for the synthesis of particular protein molecules, is carried outside the cell nucleus by molecules of "messenger RNA," each incorporating a side-group sequence determined by DNA. Floating freely outside the nucleus are AMINO ACIDS, the "building blocks" of proteins, and molecules of another, smaller kind of RNA, "transfer RNA." Each of these RNA molecules is able to capture an amino acid molecule of a particular type and locate it in its proper place in a sequence dictated by messenger RNA.

The DNA molecule has not one but two sugar-phosphate chains twisted around each other to form a double helix. Linking the chains rather like the rungs of a ladder are the side groups, each interlocking with its appropriate opposite number, for a particular side group can be partnered by a side group of only one other kind. The molecule replicates by splitting down the middle, whereupon the side groups of each half bond with the appropriate side groups of free phosphate-sugar units to form a pair of identical DNA molecules. The elucidation of DNA structure, one of the greatest advances of 20th-century biology, is chiefly associated with the work of the Nobel prizewinners James WATSON, Francis CRICK and Maurice WILKINS.

NUCLEOPHILES, chemical species that donate ELECTRONS, or a share in electrons, to another molecule in a substitution reaction. They are thus in general BASES, especially ANIONS, which are attracted to partially positively-charged atoms in a molecule; examples are CYANIDE, HYDROXIDE, HALIDE and AMMONIA. **Electrophiles** are the exact opposite: species which receive electrons, or a share in electrons, from another molecule; in general ACIDS, especially CATIONS, attracted to partially negatively-charged atoms in a molecule; examples are HALOGENS, H^+ and NO_2^+.

NUCLEOTIDES, organic chemicals of central importance in the life chemistry of all plants and animals. Some nucleotides provide the basic molecular units for the synthesis of various more complex molecules, notably the NUCLEIC ACIDS—DNA and RNA; others— preeminently adenosine triphosphate (ATP)—provide a means of storing and releasing the ENERGY needed to drive biochemical processes.

The nucleotide molecule is a three-part structure, comprising a phosphate group linked to a 5-carbon sugar group (pentose) linked in turn to a nitrogenous side group (base). The five commonest bases are the purines adenine and guanine, and the pyrimidines cytosine, thymine and uracil. Adenine, guanine, cytosine and thymine serve in the DNA molecule as the four key "letters" of the genetic code. The nucleotide's pentose is either ribose or deoxyribose, the latter differing from the former only in having one less oxygen atom. The base-pentose component of a nucleotide is called a nucleoside.

The phosphate group consists of one or a combination of two or three phosphate units, and is accordingly termed a mono-, di- or triphosphate. The nucleotide adenosine triphosphate (ATP) is a nucleoside consisting of adenine and ribose bonded to a triphosphate group. The importance of ATP as an energy store depends on the third phosphate unit. When a third unit is added to adenosine diphosphate (ADP) to form ATP, an energy-rich chemical bond is formed; and it is this energy, released when ATP is converted back to ADP, that the CELL utilizes. (The human body daily builds up and breaks down approximately its own weight in ATP.) By releasing its energy, ATP activates or accelerates the action of ENZYMES, the catalysts of biochemical reactions, and so belongs to a class of substances called coenzymes. Most coenzymes are nucleotides.

NUCLEUS, Atomic. See ATOM; SUBATOMIC PARTICLES.

NUCLEUS, Cell. See CELL.

NUEVO LAREDO, city in NE Mexico on the Rio Grande R opposite Laredo, Tex. It is a major US–Mexico trade and distribution center. Pop 150 922.

NUEVO LEÓN, state in NE Mexico, 25 136sq mi, with its capital at Monterrey. It is a major industrial center, producing metals, cattle, cotton, iron, steel, glass and textiles. In the S and W are the Sierra Madre Mts which descend to a plateau in the E.

NUISANCE, in law, action taken by means of a court order or injunction to oblige a neighbor to stop interfering unreasonably with the plaintiff's comfort or convenience. Only a person owning a house or land can take legal action over a nuisance, and only has grounds for doing so if the neighbor fails to act reasonably. The injunction can require the nuisance to stop, or damages may be claimed.

NUKUALOFA, town on the N coast of Tongatabu Island, in the SW Pacific. It is the capital of TONGA and a commercial port. Pop 15 685.

NULLIFICATION, in US history, an act by which a state suspends a federal law within its borders. An extreme interpretation of STATES' RIGHTS, the tactic was particularly used by southern states to protect their minority status. First raised in the KENTUCKY AND VIRGINIA RESOLUTIONS of 1798, the doctrine was forcibly urged by John C. CALHOUN, whose *exposition* argued that the state of S.C. could nullify the so-called "Tariff of Abominations," passed in 1828. When another protective tariff passed in 1832, S.C. declared it null and void, threatening secession if coerced. President Jackson and Congress were ready to enforce the law by military action, but a compromise tariff was passed before the state's nullification order came into effect. The doctrine died when the south lost the Civil War. (See also HARTFORD CONVENTION; PROTECTIONISM; TARIFF.)

NULL SET. See SET THEORY.

NUMA POMPILIUS, the second of the seven traditional kings of Rome, probably 8th–7th centuries BC. He was credited with calendar reform and the reorganization, regulation and development of religious life, but no doubt only initiated practices and laws which evolved historically.

NUMAZU, city on the S coast of central Honshu, Japan, on the NE shore of Suruga Bay, about 76mi SW of Tokyo. It is a river port, the major agricultural market for Izu peninsula and a resort. Pop 189 038.

NUMBAT, or **Banded anteater,** *Myrmecobius fasciatus*, a pouchless termite-eating marsupial of Australia which lives in hollow fallen limbs of eucalyptus. It is the size of a rat, with reddish fur broken by six or seven white stripes across the back. Males are fertile only at certain times of the year.

NUMBER, an expression of quantity. In everyday terms, numbers are usually used with UNITS: e.g., "three metres" (or 3m); "6.589 3 kilograms" (or 6.589 3kg).

For ways of expressing numbers see CUBE; FRACTION; RECIPROCAL; ROOTS; SQUARE; SUM. For systems of expressing numbers see BINARY NUMBER SYSTEM; DECIMAL SYSTEM; DUODECIMAL SYSTEM. Types and systems of numbers include IMAGINARY NUMBERS; INTEGERS; IRRATIONAL NUMBERS; NATURAL NUMBERS; RATIONAL NUMBERS; REAL NUMBERS; TRANSCENDENTAL NUMBERS. (See also ALGEBRA; CARDINAL NUMBER; ORDINAL NUMBER; TRANSFINITE CARDINAL NUMBER and PERFECT NUMBER; PRIME NUMBER; ZERO.)

NUMBERS, the fourth book of the PENTATEUCH, so called because it records two censuses of the Israelites. It narrates their wanderings in the wilderness until they reached Canaan.

NUMERATOR, the DIVIDEND of a common FRACTION.

NUMIDIA, ancient country of N Africa, roughly the present-day Algeria. The famed Numidian cavalry took part in Hannibal's invasion of Italy in 218 BC (see PUNIC WARS). For supporting Rome, the E Numidian chief, Masinissa, was made king of all Numidia in 201 BC. The country was dominated by Rome after Julius Caesar's triumph in the Roman Civil war, 46 BC.

NUMISMATICS, the study of coins, including their origin, history, use, mythology and manufacture. A coin is a medium of exchange, usually made in metal and issued by government authority. In its widest sense, numismatics includes a study of medals, tokens, counters and earliest money forms as well as the coinage of all countries from earliest times to the present.

NUMMULITES, an extinct genus of bottom-living FORAMINIFERA, occurring in such numbers that their disk-shaped calcareous shells formed the major part of some limestone deposits, as for example, the Atlas mountains.

NUN, a woman member of a religious order who devotes her life to religious service. In Roman Catholic canon law, a nun is one who has taken solemn vows of poverty, chastity and obedience; some orders are devoted to prayer and contemplation. Nuns are called sisters and the term is specifically used of Roman Catholic nuns under "simple vows" (which allow retention of property).

NUNCIO, a permanent diplomatic representative of the Holy See to a nation or government, who acts as a link between the nation's church and papal headquarters in Rome. The post corresponds to and often has the same status as a secular ambassador.

NUREMBERG, historic city of Bavaria, S West Germany, located on the Pegnitz R, 92mi NNW of Munich. Founded in the 11th century, it became a cultural and trading center in the Middle Ages and was the first city to accept the Reformation. Here Hitler staged annual rallies in the 1930s and proclaimed anti-Jewish laws in 1934. Now a major manufacturing city, it was the scene of war crimes trials after WWII. Pop 473 555. (See also NUREMBERG TRIALS.)

NUREMBERG TRIALS, a series of WAR CRIMES trials held in Nuremberg, West Germany, 1945–1949, by the victors of WWII—the US, USSR, Great Britain and France. The accused, including von RIBBENTROP, GOERING, HESS and heads of the German armed forces, were tried for three kinds of crime: *Crimes Against Peace* (planning and waging aggressive war); *War Crimes* (murder or mistreatment of civilians or prisoners of war, killing of hostages, plunder of property, wanton destruction of communities, etc.); *Crimes Against Humanity* (extermination or enslavement of any civilian population before or during a war on political, racial or religious grounds; see GENOCIDE). The trials established new principles in the law of nations, above all that every person is responsible for his own acts.

NUREYEV, Rudolf (1938–), USSR virtuoso ballet dancer who sought asylum in the West when touring with the Kirov Ballet. As guest artist of the Royal Ballet, London, he became famed as a leading classical dancer and for his partnership with Margot FONTEYN.

NURMI, Paavo (1897–1973), Finnish track athlete. Between 1920 and 1932, he won nine individual and three team gold Olympic medals and also held 20 world running records. He was disqualified from amateur athletics in 1932 and became a sporting goods merchant.

NÜRNBERG. See NUREMBERG.

Defendants in the Nuremberg trials included (front row, left to right) Goering (hand over face), Hess, von Ribbentrop, Keitel, Kaltenbrunner, Rosenberg, Frank, Frick, Funk, Streicher, Schacht; (second row, left to right) Doenitz, Raeder, von Schirach, Sauckel, Jodl, von Papen, Seyss-Inquart, Speer, von Neurath and Fritsche.

NURSERY SCHOOLS, preschool care and early education for children from about three to five years old. Nursery schools developed from 19th-century infant-care programs for factory women's children, launched by Robert OWEN in Great Britain and copied in Europe as the Industrial Revolution spread. Johann PESTALOZZI (1746–1827), Friedrich FROEBEL (1782–1852) and Maria MONTESSORI (1870–1952) all pioneered preschool methods of nursery education. In the US the first nursery schools opened in the 1850s in large cities like New York and Philadelphia to release mothers for factory work. The first American effort to combine early care and educational projects began in 1915 at the U. of Chicago. Nursery schools today have developed programs in which the young learn by experience and through play to understand others, the world around them and themselves.

NURSING, care of the sick, injured or handicapped. Until the 19th century nursing was considered a charitable activity and was administered by religious bodies such as the Sisters of CHARITY (founded in 1634). In 1860 Florence NIGHTINGALE opened a school in London where experienced nurses and physicians gave instruction in nursing skills. This helped to establish nursing as a career rather than a religious vocation. In the US, nursing schools opened in New York City, Boston and New Haven, Conn. in the 1870s. Until then all nurses had been volunteers. Dorothea DIX was named by the US government as the first superintendent of nurses during the Civil War, after organizing 2 000 women into the Women's Central Association of Relief. By the 1970s there were about 1 350 schools of professional nursing in the US and an estimated 723 000 trained nurses employed. A nursing career today requires a high school education followed by a choice of three training programs: 1. a diploma after three years' training in hospitals and independent schools in the theory and practice of nursing and in the sciences; 2. a four year nursing course and general education from a university, leading to a bachelor's degree (B.Sc.); and 3. a similar but shorter two-year junior college course. After training a state licensing examination (each state sets its own standards) must be passed to obtain registration. "Practical nursing" after one year of study is becoming increasingly popular and valuable, relieving the registered nurse (R.N.), now in short supply, of routine chores. (See also HOSPITAL; MEDICINE.)

NUT, dry, indehiscent FRUIT with one seed, similar to an ACHENE, but having a hard outer shell or pericarp. Nuts are produced by, for example, HAZEL, OAK and CHESTNUT.

NUTATION, Astronomical, irregularities in the PRECESSION of the equinoxes owing to variations in the torque produced by the gravitational attractions of the sun and moon on the earth.

NUTATION, Mechanical, a "bobbing" superimposed on the PRECESSION of a rigid spinning body such as a GYROSCOPE. With increasing spin rate there is an increase in the frequency and decrease in the magnitude of the nutation.

NUTCRACKERS, two species of small, crow-like birds one of the Palearctic, the other of western North America. Nutcrackers are outstanding examples of birds that store food. Nuts and pine fruits are stored in the ground in the fall, and used throughout the winter. The birds appear never to forget a cache or to revisit an empty one. Genus: *Nucifraga.*

NUT GRASS, perennial grass-like herbs (*Cyperus rotundus* and *C. esculentus*) native to tropical Africa, which produce nut-shaped edible tubers that yield an oil used for cooking. Family: Cyperaceae.

NUTHATCHES, a genus, *Sitta,* of small, dumpy birds typically found foraging on tree trunks for insects and spiders, or using the heavy beak to hammer open seeds or fruits wedged into crevices in the bark. They are found throughout Asia, Europe and North America. Nuthatches both climb and descend trees head first.

NUTLEY, town in Essex Co., NE N.J., 6mi N of Newark of which it is a residential suburb. It produces chemicals, textiles and paper. Pop 31 913.

NUTMEG, a spice produced from the sun-dried seeds of various tree species of the genus *Myristica,* native to the Old World Tropics. *Myristica fragrans* is widely cultivated in the Tropics, but the bulk of world supplies still comes from the Moluccas.

Nutrition: daily intake figures for a healthy diet for moderately active young people of average height and weight.

Nutrient	Women	Men
Food energy (kcal)	2 200	3 000
Protein (g)	55	70
Calcium (mg)	800	800
Iron (mg)	12	10
Thiamine (vitamin B_1, mg)	0.9	1.2
Riboflavine (vitamin B_2, mg)	1.3	1.7
Niacin (mg equivalent)	15	18
Vitamin A (μg retinol equivalent)	750	750
Vitamin D (μg cholecalciferol)	2.5	2.5
Vitamin C (g)	30–60*	30–60*

* US authorities prefer the higher figure.

NUTRIA. See COYPU.

NUTRITION, the processes by which living organisms take in and utilize nutrients—the substances or foodstuffs required for GROWTH and the maintenance of LIFE. Vital substances that cannot be synthesized within the CELL and must be present in the food are termed "essential nutrients." Organisms such as green plants can derive ENERGY from sunlight and synthesize their nutritional requirements from simple inorganic chemicals present in the soil and air (see PLANT; PHOTOSYNTHESIS). Animals, on the other hand, depend largely on previously synthesized organic materials obtainable only by eating plants or other animals (see ANIMAL; DIGESTIVE SYSTEM; METABOLISM; ECOLOGY).

Human nutrition involves five main groups of nutrients: PROTEINS, FATS, CARBOHYDRATES, VITAMINS and minerals. Proteins, fats and carbohydrates are the body's sources of energy, and are required in relatively large amounts. They yield this energy by OXIDATION in the body cells, and nutritionists measure it in heat units called food CALORIES (properly called kilocalories, each equalling 1 000 gram calories). Carbohydrates (food STARCHES and SUGARS) normally form the most important energy source, contributing nearly half the calories in a well-balanced diet. Cereal products and potatoes are rich in starch; SUCROSE (table sugar) and LACTOSE (present in milk) are two common sugars. Fats, which provide about 40% of the calorie requirement, include butter, edible oils and shortening, and are present in such foods as eggs, fish, meat and nuts. Fats consist largely of fatty acids (see carboxylic acids), which divide into two main classes: saturated and unsaturated. Certain fatty acids are essential nutrients; but if there is too much saturated fatty acid in the diet, an excess of CHOLESTEROL may accumulate in the blood. Proteins supply the remaining energy needs, but their real importance lies in the fact that the body tissues, which are largely composed of protein, need certain essential AMINO ACIDS, found in protein foods, for growth and renewal. Protein-rich foods include meat, fish, eggs, cereals, peas and beans. Too little protein in the diet results in malnutritional diseases such as KWASHIORKOR.

Minerals (inorganic elements) and vitamins (certain complex organic molecules) provide no energy, but have numerous indispensable functions. Some minerals are components of body structures. Calcium and phosphorus, for example, are essential to BONES and TEETH. Iron in the BLOOD is vital for the transport of oxygen to the tissues: an iron deficiency results in ANEMIA. Milk and milk products are good sources of calcium and phosphorus; liver, red meat and egg yolk, of iron. Other important minerals, normally well supplied in the Western diet, include chlorine, iodine, magnesium, potassium, sodium and sulfur. Vitamins, which are present in small quantities in most foods, are intimately associated with the action of ENZYMES in the body cells, and particular vitamin deficiencies accordingly impair certain of the body's synthetic or metabolic processes. A chronic lack of vitamin A, for example, leads to a hardening and drying of the skin and can result in irreversible damage to the conjunctiva and cornea of the eye. BERIBERI is caused by a vitamin B_1 deficiency, SCURVY by a vitamin C deficiency, RICKETS by a lack of vitamin D.

Despite the fact that nutritionists now understand the basic requirements of a healthy diet, the difficulty of applying their knowledge world-wide is immense. About two-thirds of the world's population remains severely undernourished and subject to deficiency diseases. Even in the richer countries malnutrition occurs, but here it is likely to be due to an ill-chosen rather than impoverished diet. In the US, the Food and Nutrition Board of the United States Academy of Sciences National Research Council publishes a table of recommended daily nutrient allowances. (See also DIETETIC FOODS; DIETING; OBESITY.)

NUX VOMICA, seeds of *Strychnos nux-vomica,* a tree native to India and SE Asia. Nux vomica is the major commercial source of STRYCHNINE. Family: Strychnaceae.

NYALA, two species of *Tragelaphus,* ANTELOPES of Africa related to the KUDU.

NYASA, Lake, or **Lake Malawi,** third largest (about 360mi long) of the great lakes of the Rift Valley, East Africa, and at an altitude of 1 500ft. In the 1850s it was the center of the African slave trade.

NYASALAND. See MALAWI.

NYCTALOPIA. See NIGHT BLINDNESS.

NYCTINASTY, periodic response of plant organs to the alternation of day and night, such as the opening and closing of flowers. It is caused by changes in LIGHT intensity and TEMPERATURE. (See BIOLOGICAL CLOCKS.)

NYE, Bill (Edgar Wilson Nye; 1850–1896), US humorist, author of *Bill Nye's History of the United States* (1896). He also wrote with J. W. RILEY *Nye and Riley's Railway Guide* (1888).

NYE, Gerald Prentice (1892–1971), senator from N.D. (1925–45). He headed the senate committee investigating the huge profits of the munitions industry during WWI. He also sponsored the 1935 NEUTRALITY ACT.

NYERERE, Julius Kambarage (1921–), founder and first president of the East African state of Tanzania. He led Tanganyika to independence (1961) and united it with Zanzibar, forming Tanzania (1964). He supports nonalignment but has accepted aid from communist China. He believes in a one-party socialist democracy.

NYLON, group of POLYMERS containing AMIDE groups recurring in the chain. The commonest nylon is made by condensation of adipic acid and hexamethylene diamine. Nylon is chemically inert, heat-resistant, tough and very strong, and is extruded and drawn to make SYNTHETIC FIBERS, or cast and molded into bearings, gears, zippers etc.

NYMPH, a pre-adult stage in certain insects, strictly, used to contrast with LARVA. Nymphs typically resemble the adult in structure but are sexually immature and lack wings. Their METAMORPHOSIS is gradual and adult characters are developed progressively with each molt.

NYMPHS, Greek mythological maidens, associated with natural objects or places. Varieties of nymph include DRYADS and hamadryads (nymphs of trees and forests), naiads (streams, rivers and lakes), NEREIDS (Mediterranean Sea), oreads (mountains) and oceanids (the ocean). Many were daughters of ZEUS. Famous nymphs include ARETHUSA, CALYPSO, DAPHNE and ECHO.

NYSTAGMUS, oscillation of the EYES, usually with a relatively slow drift in one direction and a correcting flick in the other. Looking out of a moving vehicle at passing objects induces nystagmus. It can be caused by failure of VISION fixation, a hereditary defect; weakness of the eye muscles, or diseases of the EAR labyrinths, BRAIN stem or cerebellum.

O

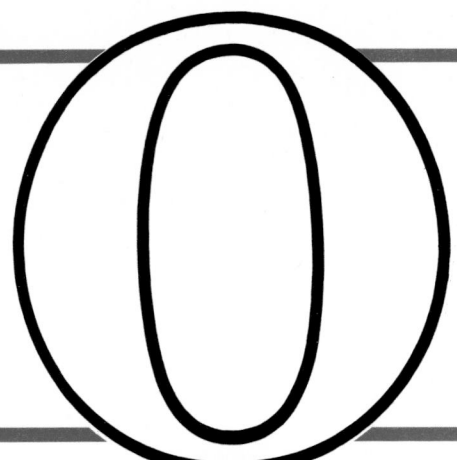

O, 15th letter and fourth vowel of the English ALPHABET. It began as the Semitic *'ayin* (eye), and the Greek *Omicron*, and became the 14th letter of the Roman alphabet. It also represents the number zero, and the element oxygen.

OAHE DAM, dam on the Missouri R near Pierre, S.D. Built as part of a power, irrigation and flood control project, it has created a 250mi reservoir along the river towards Bismarck.

OAHU, third-largest island (593sq mi) of Hawaii, containing Honolulu (the state capital), the naval base at Pearl Harbor and 80% of Hawaii's population. A fertile valley growing pineapples and sugarcane is flanked by coastal mountain ranges. Pop 629 145.

OAK CREEK, city in SE Wis., a suburb of Milwaukee. Its products include electronic components, machinery and concrete. Pop 13 928.

OAK FOREST, village in NE Ill., 20mi S of Chicago. It is mainly residential, with diversified agriculture in the area. Pop 17 870.

OAKLAND, city in W Cal., linked with San Francisco by the Bay Bridge. A port city, it is a major industrial and commercial center with shipbuilding, food processing, and chemical and oil refining industries. Pop 361 561.

OAKLAND, borough in NE N.J., Bergen Co. First settled by the Dutch in the 18th century, it is now largely residential. Pop 14 420.

OAKLAND PARK, city in SE Fla., lying N of Fort Lauderdale. It is a vegetable packing center. Pop 16 261.

OAK LAWN, residential village in NE Ill., 12mi SW of Chicago. Pop 60 305.

OAKLEY, Annie (1860–1926), US entertainer, born Phoebe Anne Oakley Mozee. Known as "Little Sure Shot" (she was only 5ft tall), she was a sharpshooter star of BUFFALO BILL's Wild West Show, together with her husband Frank Butler.

There are several different varieties of oat, among them *Avena orientalis* (1), *Avena sativa*, the common cultivated oat (2), and *Avena fatua*, a wild oat (3). The flower heads are enclosed in a protective covering, or hull, which is removed to expose the kernel, or groat.

OAK PARK, village in NE Ill., 10mi W of Chicago. A residential center, it is the birthplace of Ernest Hemingway. Pop 62 511.

OAK PARK, city in SE Mich., a mainly residential suburb of Detroit. Its light industry includes automobile parts. Pop 36 762.

OAK RIDGE, city in E Tenn., 17mi W of Knoxville. The site was chosen in 1942 as the WWII headquarters of the atomic energy program (the MANHATTAN PROJECT) because of its isolation and easy access to necessary resources. It is still a major research center, and houses the American Museum of Atomic Energy. Pop 28 319.

OAKS, trees and shrubs of the genus *Quercus*, which are native to the N Hemisphere. Oaks have cut or lobed leaves; some are evergreen, and the fruit is the acorn. Oaks produce valuable lumber which has great strength and durability. Important white oak species are *Quercus alba*, *Q. macrocarpa*, *Q. robur* and *Q. sessiliflora*; important red oaks are *Q. rubra*, *Q. velutina* and *Q. palustris*. The cork oak (*Q. suber*) is the source of CORK. Family: Fagaceae.

OAKUM, fibers of HEMP or FLAX used to make the seams of wooden ships watertight, a process known as "caulking." Oakum is made either from short flax fibers produced during LINEN manufacture or from old ropes picked apart and tarred.

OAKVILLE, town in SE Ont., Canada, on Lake Ontario 22mi SW of Toronto. A summer resort, it also produces automobiles, plastics and paper. Pop 61 483.

OAKWOOD, city in SW Ohio, 3mi S of Dayton, of which it is a residential suburb. Pop 10 095.

OARFISH, *Regalecus glesne*, a long, ribbon-like, marine fish, which may have been the source of legends of sea-serpents. The body, which may reach up to 6m (20ft) in length, is slender and silvery. When swimming the body undulates. The name oarfish derives from the shape of the scarlet pelvic fins which are thin and elongated, but expanded at the tip.

OAS. See ORGANIZATION OF AMERICAN STATES.

OASIS, a fertile area in the midst of a desert. The water source is generally a SPRING; though in the Sahara many oases have sprung up around WELLS. They may be hundreds of square kilometres in area, or merely a few trees clumped together. (See also DESERT; IRRIGATION.)

OATES, Titus (1649–1705), English conspirator who in 1678 claimed to have discovered a Roman Catholic plot against Charles II—known as the POPISH PLOT. No such plot existed, but his story set off a wave of persecution in which some 35 persons were executed. Exposed and imprisoned in 1685, he was freed and pensioned (1689) after the GLORIOUS REVOLUTION.

OATS, cereal plants from the genus *Avena*. Oats are cultivated in cool damp climates in the N Hemisphere. The grain is rich in starch and protein and is mainly used as a livestock feed, but some is processed for human consumption. Chief producers are the US, USSR and Canada, although production is declining. Family: Graminae.

OAXACA, city in S Mexico, capital of Oaxaca State, founded by the Aztecs in 1486. The home of Díaz and Juárez, it has many 16th century Spanish buildings, and a famous handicrafts market. Pop 99 509.

OAXACA, mountainous state in S Mexico, bordering the Gulf of Tehuantepec. Farming the fertile valleys is the most important activity, though silver and gold are mined. The inhabitants are mostly of Mixtec and Zapotec origin.

OBADIAH (or Abdias), Book of, shortest book of the Old Testament, fourth book of the MINOR PROPHETS. Probably written in the 6th century BC, its 21 verses foretell the triumph of Israel over its rival EDOM. Nothing is known of Obadiah himself.

OBBLIGATO (Italian: obligatory), term in music to denote a part in a score which is essential to the effect. In an aria accompaniment, for example, a violin or flute obbligato might well be as significant as the vocal part itself.

OBELISK, four-sided pillar tapering to a pyramidal top. Pairs of these, often as much as 105ft high, were erected in front of ancient Egyptian temples, carved with hieroglyphs for decorative, religious and commemorative purposes. CLEOPATRA'S NEEDLES are notable examples, dating from around 1500 BC. The WASHINGTON MONUMENT and others were inspired by Egyptian originals.

OBERAMMERGAU, village in the Bavarian Alps of West Germany, famous for its Passion Play. Every 10 years inhabitants of the village reenact the suffering, death and resurrection of Christ, in fulfillment of a vow made by the villagers in 1633 during a plague. Pop 4 603.

OBERHAUSEN, industrial city in the Ruhr region of West Germany. It is a canal port and rail and industrial center, with zinc refineries, foundries and chemical factories. Pop 246 736.

OBERTH, Hermann (1894–), pioneering German astrophysicist who established many of the basic principles of space-flight in his *Means of Space Travel* (1929), and *The Rocket into Interplanetary Space* (1934). He worked with Werner von BRAUN'S V-2 team during WWII, and on space research for the US Army 1955–58.

OBESITY, the condition of a subject's having excessive weight for his height, build and age. It is common in Western society, overfeeding in infancy being a possible cause. Excess ADIPOSE TISSUE is found in subcutaneous tissue and the ABDOMEN. Obesity predisposes to or is associated with numerous DISEASES including ARTERIOSCLEROSIS and high blood pressure; here premature DEATH is usual. Strict diet is essential for cure.

OBLATENESS, of a spheroid (see ELLIPSOID), the situation in which two of its axes of symmetry have an equal length greater than that of the third. The earth, in common with the other planets of the SOLAR SYSTEM, is oblate, its polar diameter being some 45km greater than that of its equator. A *prolate spheroid* is one with two axes of symmetry equal in length and shorter than the third.

OBOE, soprano WIND INSTRUMENT consisting of a double-reed mouthpiece at the end of a conically-bored tube. It is controlled by keys and finger holes. It was developed in 17th-century France, where it was called the *hautbois* (high wood), whence oboe. An orchestral instrument, it has also had important solo music written for it by composers from Purcell onwards.

OBREGÓN, Álvaro (1880–1928), President of Mexico from 1920 to 1924. A planter, he joined CARRANZA in overthrowing President HUERTA in 1913. He subsequently served in Carranza's government, but led the revolt against him in 1920. As president, Obregón promoted important economic and educational reforms. He was assassinated shortly after being reelected.

O'BRIEN, Flann (1911–1966), pseudonym of Brian O'Nolan, Irish novelist and dramatist. As Myles na gCopaleen he was also a well-known Dublin newspaper columnist. His comic and fantastic novel *At Swim-Two-Birds* (1939) was hailed as a masterpiece by James Joyce and others, but only achieved international fame when republished in 1960.

OB RIVER, river in the W Siberian USSR. Rising in the Altai Mts, it flows about 2 289mi mainly NW across the Siberian Plain to the Arctic Ocean, draining over 1 000 000sq mi. It is an important summer commercial waterway.

Obelisk at Karnak in Egypt. Carved from Aswan stone, it was erected about 3 400 years ago by Queen Hatshepsut. The top was originally covered in gold.

OBSCENITY. See PORNOGRAPHY.

OBSERVATORY, place from which a variety of astronomical observations are made. Ancient observatories such as STONEHENGE were used to predict SOLSTICES and EQUINOXES. With Tycho BRAHE (1546–1601) and the advent shortly after his death of the TELESCOPE, the modern observatory was born. Apart from the telescope, modern instruments used by observatories include the spectroscope (see SPECTROSCOPY), the transit instrument and the meridian circle (used to measure the right ascension and declination of stars: see CELESTIAL SPHERE), the coelostat and the coronagraph (for observing the sun), the PHOTOELECTRIC CELL (for measuring stellar brightnesses) and, in RADIO ASTRONOMY, the RADIO TELESCOPE.

OBSESSIONAL NEUROSIS, a NEUROSIS characterized by obsessions (inability to rid the CONSCIOUSNESS of certain ideas despite the individual's desire to do so and recognition of their abnormality) and COMPULSIONS.

OBSIDIAN, volcanic GLASS formed by rapid cooling of LAVA, usually with the composition of GRANITE. Commonly jet-black, but sometimes red, brown or variegated, it may be used as a GEM stone. There is a well-known occurrence at Yellowstone Park, Wyo. STONE AGE man used obsidian for implements.

OBSTETRICS, the care of women during PREGNANCY, delivery and the puerperium, a branch of MEDICINE and SURGERY usually linked with GYNECOLOGY. Antenatal care and the avoidance or control of risk factors for both mother and baby—ANEMIA, TOXEMIA, high blood pressure, DIABETES, VENEREAL DISEASE, frequent MISCARRIAGE, etc.—have greatly contributed to the reduction of maternal and fetal deaths. The monitoring and control of labor and BIRTH, with early recognition of complications; induction of labor and the prevention of post-partum HEMORRHAGE with OXYTOCIN; safe forceps delivery and CESARIAN SECTION, and improved ANESTHETICS are important factors in obstetric safety. ASEPSIS has made PUERPERAL FEVER a rarity.

OBTUSE, of an ANGLE, one between 90° and 180°.

OCALA, city in N central Fla., seat of Marion Co. It is a processing center for a fruit-growing and farming area. Pop 22 583.

OCARINA, small egg-shaped wind instrument, usually made of clay or plastic. Eight holes in the side are stopped with the fingers to vary the pitch.

O'CASEY, Sean (1880–1964), Irish playwright whose sardonic dramas depict the effects of poverty and war on the Irish. His early plays, such as *Juno and the Paycock* (1924), are the most highly-regarded. His later works were written in self-imposed exile due to hostility both from theater managements and from Irish nationalists who objected to his unglamorous portrayal of the independence movement.

OCCAM'S RAZOR. See OCKHAM, WILLIAM OF.

OCCLUSION, or occluded front. See FRONT.

OCCULT, body of knowledge pertaining to the supernatural, such as MAGIC, ALCHEMY, ASTROLOGY, FORTUNE-TELLING and NECROMANCY. The occult has also included EXTRA-SENSORY PERCEPTION, precognition and clairvoyance, which are now the subject of much serious research.

OCCULTATION, the ECLIPSE of one celestial body by another. The term is usually applied to eclipses of stars by planets and particularly eclipses of planets or stars by the moon.

OCCUPATIONAL THERAPY, the ancillary speciality to MEDICINE concerned with practical measures to circumvent or overcome disability due to DISEASE. It includes the design or modification of everyday items such as cutlery, dressing aids, bath and lavatory aids, and wheelchairs. Assessment and education in domestic skills and industrial retraining are also important. Diversional activities are arranged for long-stay patients.

OCEANARIUM, container in which living marine animals are exhibited or studied; also an establishment for the same purpose. Oceanarium tanks, much larger than aquarium tanks, can house a wide variety of fish and simulate ocean conditions.

OCEAN CITY, city in SE N.J. on the Atlantic coast 10mi SW of Atlantic City. It is primarily a seaside resort. Pop 10 575.

OCEAN CURRENTS, large-scale permanent or semipermanent movements of water at or beneath the surface of the OCEANS. Currents may be divided into those caused by winds and those caused by differences in DENSITY of seawater. In the former case, FRICTION between the prevailing wind and the water surface causes horizontal motion, and this motion is both modified by and in part transferred to deeper layers by further friction. Density variations may result from temperature differences, differing salinities, etc. The direction of flow of all currents is affected by the CORIOLIS EFFECT. Best known, perhaps, are the GULF STREAM and HUMBOLDT CURRENT. (See also EQUATORIAL CURRENT; TIDES; WHIRLPOOL.)

OCEANIA, vast section of the Pacific Ocean, stretching roughly from Hawaii to New Zealand and from New Guinea to Easter Island, divided into three broad cultural areas: MELANESIA in the SW, MICRONESIA in the NW and POLYNESIA in the E. The area has islands ranging from large masses of ancient rock to minute coral atolls—many of volcanic origin—and the vegetation varies from lush jungle to scanty palm trees. The Pacific Islands were probably peopled from SE Asia, though HEYERDAHL has shown the possibility of influences from South America. The native islanders live mainly by fishing and farming; their basic diet is vegetable, but some pigs and poultry are kept. First European contact was made by MAGELLAN in 1519, but the earliest comprehensive exploration of the area was that of Captain James COOK in the 18th century. Many of the islands were colonized, first by Britain and France and later by the US and Japan. They brought trade and missionaries, but also new diseases which wiped out thousands. The

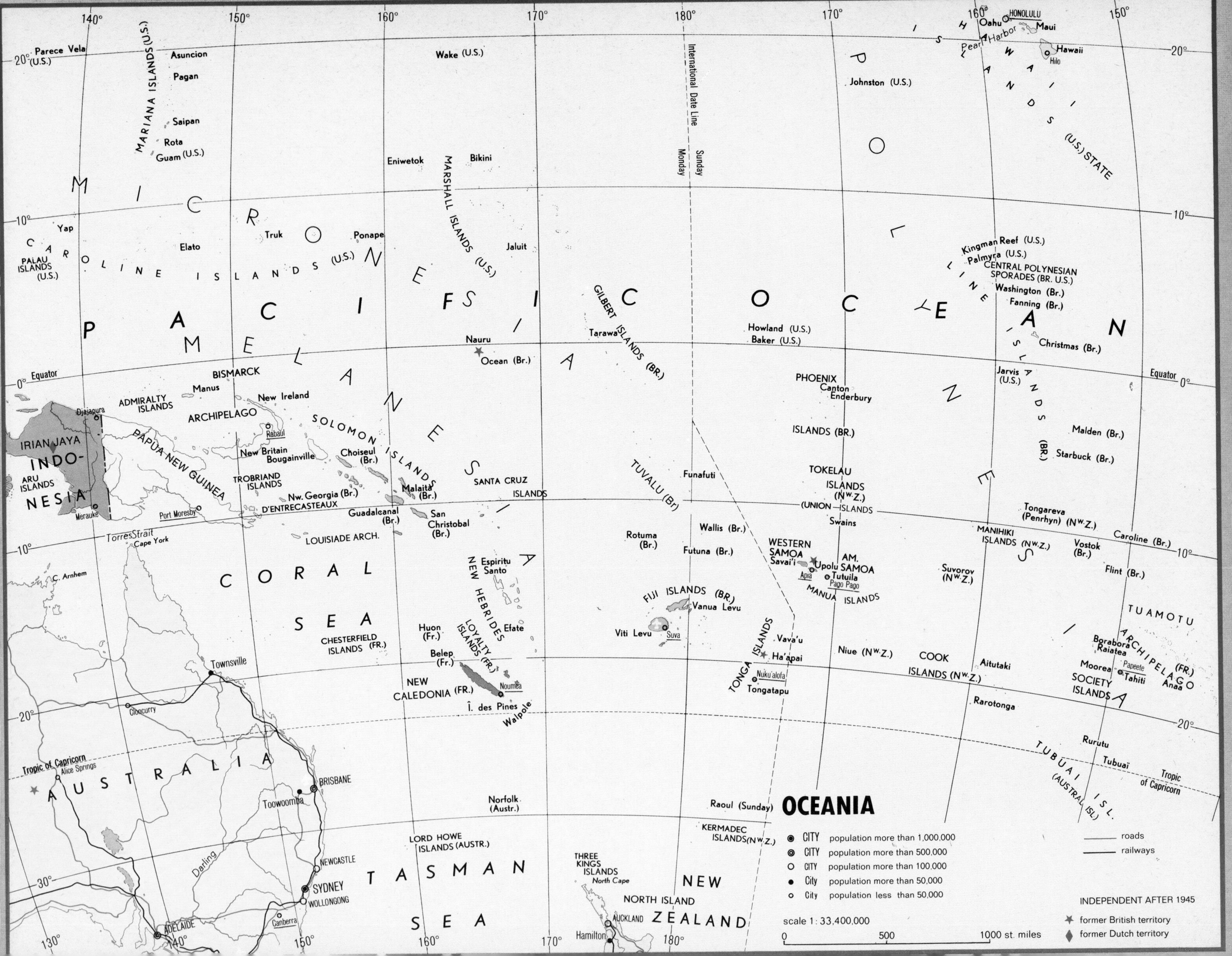
OCEANIA
PACIFIC OCEAN
MICRONESIA
MELANESIA
POLYNESIA
MARIANA ISLANDS (U.S.)
Parece Vela (U.S.)
Asuncion
Pagan
Saipan
Rota
Guam (U.S.)
Wake (U.S.)
Eniwetok
Bikini
MARSHALL ISLANDS (U.S.)
Jaluit
Johnston (U.S.)
International Date Line
Sunday
Monday
HAWAII ISLANDS (U.S.) STATE
Oahu
HONOLULU
Pearl Harbor
Maui
Hawaii
Hilo
Yap
PALAU ISLANDS (U.S.)
CAROLINE ISLANDS (U.S.)
Elato
Truk
Ponape
Kingman Reef (U.S.)
Palmyra (U.S.)
CENTRAL POLYNESIAN SPORADES (BR. U.S.)
LINE ISLANDS (BR.)
Washington (Br.)
Fanning (Br.)
Christmas (Br.)
Jarvis (U.S.)
Malden (Br.)
Starbuck (Br.)
GILBERT ISLANDS (BR.)
Tarawa
Nauru
Ocean (Br.)
Howland (U.S.)
Baker (U.S.)
PHOENIX
Canton
Enderbury
ISLANDS (BR.)
Equator
BISMARCK ARCHIPELAGO
Manus
ADMIRALTY ISLANDS
New Ireland
Djajapura
IRIAN JAYA
INDONESIA
ARU ISLANDS
Merauke
PAPUA NEW GUINEA
Rabaul
New Britain
Bougainville
SOLOMON ISLANDS
Choiseul (Br.)
Malaita (Br.)
TROBRIAND ISLANDS
Nw. Georgia (Br.)
D'ENTRECASTEAUX
Port Moresby
Guadalcanal (Br.)
San Cristobal (Br.)
SANTA CRUZ ISLANDS
TUVALU (Br)
Funafuti
TOKELAU ISLANDS (Nw Z.)
(UNION ISLANDS
Swains
Tongareva (Penrhyn) (Nw Z.)
MANIHIKI ISLANDS (Nw Z.)
Caroline (Br.)
Vostok (Br.)
Flint (Br.)
Torres Strait
Cape York
LOUISIADE ARCH.
C. Arnhem
CORAL SEA
Espiritu Santo
NEW HEBRIDES
Efate
Rotuma (Br.)
Wallis (Br.)
Futuna (Br.)
WESTERN SAMOA
Savai'i
Upolu
Apia
AM. SAMOA
Tutuila
Pago Pago
MANUA ISLANDS
Suvorov (Nw Z.)
FIJI ISLANDS (BR.)
Vanua Levu
Viti Levu
Suva
TUAMOTU ARCHIPELAGO (FR.)
CHESTERFIELD ISLANDS (FR.)
Huon (Fr.)
Belep (Fr.)
LOYALTY ISLANDS (FR.)
NEW CALEDONIA (FR.)
Nouméa
Î. des Pines
Walpole
TONGA ISLANDS
Vava'u
Ha'apai
Nuku'alofa
Tongatapu
Niue (Nw Z.)
COOK ISLANDS (Nw Z.)
Aitutaki
Rarotonga
Borabora
Raiatea
Moorea
Papeete
Tahiti
Anaa
SOCIETY ISLANDS
Townsville
Cloncurry
Tropic of Capricorn
Alice Springs
AUSTRALIA
BRISBANE
Toowoomba
Darling
NEWCASTLE
SYDNEY
WOLLONGONG
Canberra
ADELAIDE
Rurutu
Tubuaï
TUBUAI ISL. (AUSTRAL ISL.)
Norfolk (Austr.)
LORD HOWE ISLANDS (AUSTR.)
TASMAN SEA
Raoul (Sunday)
KERMADEC ISLANDS (Nw Z.)
THREE KINGS ISLANDS
North Cape
NEW ZEALAND
NORTH ISLAND
AUCKLAND
Hamilton
CITY population more than 1,000,000
CITY population more than 500,000
CITY population more than 100,000
City population more than 50,000
City population less than 50,000
scale 1: 33,400,000
0
500
1000 st. miles
roads
railways
INDEPENDENT AFTER 1945
former British territory
former Dutch territory
140°
150°
160°
170°
180°
170°
160°
150°
130°
20°
10°
0°
10°
20°
30°

influence of Western culture upon the fragile island societies was generally destructive.

OCEANIDS. See NYMPHS.

OCEANOGRAPHY, the study of all aspects of and phenomena associated with seas and OCEANS.

OCEANS. The oceans cover some 71% of the earth's surface and comprise about 97% of the water of the planet (see HYDROSPHERE). They provide man with food, chemicals, minerals and transportation; and, by acting as a reservoir of solar heat energy, they ameliorate the effects of seasonal and diurnal temperature extremes for much of the world. With the atmosphere, they largely determine the world's climate (see also HYDROLOGIC CYCLE).

Oceanography is the study of all aspects of, and phenomena associated with, the oceans and seas. Most modern maps of the seafloor are compiled by use of ECHO SOUNDERS (see also SONAR), the vessel's position at sea being accurately determined by RADAR or otherwise. Water sampling, in order to determine, for example, salinity and oxygen content, is also important. Sea-floor sampling, to determine the composition of the sea-floor, is carried out by use of dredges, grabs, etc. (see DREDGING), and especially by use of hollow DRILLS which bring up cores of rock. OCEAN CURRENTS can be studied by use of buoys, drift bottles, etc., and often simply by accurate determinations of the different positions of a ship allowed to drift. Further information about the sea bottom can be obtained by direct observation (see BATHYSCAPHE; BATHYSPHERE) or by study of the deflections of seismic waves (see EARTHQUAKE).

Oceanographers generally regard the world's oceans as a single, large ocean. Geographically, however, it is useful to divide this into smaller units: the Atlantic, Pacific, Indian, Arctic and Antarctic (or Southern) Oceans (though the Arctic is often considered as part of the Atlantic, the Antarctic as parts of the Atlantic, Pacific and Indian). Of these, the Pacific is by far the largest and, on average, the deepest. However, the Atlantic has by far the longest coastline: its many bays and inlets, ideal for natural harbors, have profoundly affected W civilization's history.

Ocean trenches are long, narrow depressions of V-shaped cross-section running, typically, roughly parallel to continental coastal MOUNTAIN ranges or volcanic island arcs (see VOLCANISM). **Midocean ridges** are submarine mountain belts: the first to be discovered was that running roughly N-S in the Atlantic. They are important sites of earthquakes and volcanic activity (see PLATE TECTONICS; SEA-FLOOR SPREADING).

(See also ABYSSAL PLAINS; FISHERIES; HYDROGRAPHY; HYDROLOGY; ICEBERG; MARINE BIOLOGY; OCEAN WAVES; OOZES; SUBMARINE CANYON; TIDES; TSUNAMI.)

OCEANSIDE, city in S Cal., on the Gulf of Santa Catalina. It has light industries, agricultural commerce and tourism. Pop 40494.

OCEAN SUNFISHES, large, disk-shaped fishes which have lost both tail and pelvic fins; the body ends abruptly and strikingly behind dorsal and anal fins. Sunfishes have thick skins, up to 75mm (3in) thick; the largest, the Ocean sunfish *Mola mola* can reach 3.5m (11.5ft) and weigh up to 1 tonne.

OCEANUS, in ancient Greek mythology, the endless river girdling the flat earth, personified as one of the TITANS, the son of Uranus (the Sky) and Gaea (the Earth).

OCEAN WAVES, undulations of the ocean surface, generally the result of the action of wind on the water surface. At sea, there is no overall translational movement of the water particles: they move up and forward with the crest, down and backward with the trough, describing a vertical circle. Near the shore, FRICTION with the bottom causes increased wave height, and the wave breaks against the land. Waves can thus cause substantial coastal EROSION. (See also TSUNAMI.)

OCELOT, *Panthera pardalis*, a South American cat related to the MARGAY. A small leopard-like cat, it has a beautifully marked coat. Ocelots feed on small birds and mammals, and are capable of bringing down prey the size of deer fauns.

OCHER, reddish-yellow IRON ore (oxides and silicates), ground and roasted for use as a PIGMENT; also, CLAY colored yellow by such iron ore.

OCHOA, Severo (1905–), Spanish-born US biochemist who shared with KORNBERG the 1959 Nobel Prize for Physiology or Medicine for his first synthesis of a NUCLEIC ACID (or RNA).

OCHS, Adolph Simon (1858–1935), US newspaper publisher largely responsible for creating the prestige of the *New York Times*. Born in Cincinnati, Ohio, he became the paper's manager in 1896, adopting the slogan "All the news that's fit to print."

OCKHAM (or Occam), William of (c1280–1349), English scholar who formulated the principle now known as **Occam's Razor:** "Entities must not unnecessarily be multiplied." This principle, interpreted roughly as "the simplest theory that fits the facts corresponds most closely to reality," has many applications throughout science.

OCMULGEE NATIONAL MONUMENT, area of 683 acres in central Georgia with ancient burial mounds. It was established in 1934.

O'CONNELL, Daniel (1775–1847), Irish statesman, called "the Liberator," who led the fight for Catholic emancipation. He founded the Catholic Association (1823) and his election (1828) to Parliament precipitated the CATHOLIC EMANCIPATION ACT. He contested the 1801 act uniting Ireland with Britain.

O'CONNOR, Feargus Edward (1794–1855), Irish radical, one of the leaders of CHARTISM. In 1837 he founded the *Northern Star*, soon the leading Chartist newspaper. Reelected to Parliament (1847), he presented a huge Chartist petition in 1848.

O'CONNOR, Flannery (May Flannery O'Connor; 1925–1964), US fiction writer noted for her brilliant style and her compelling vision of life in the South. Her novels include *Wise Blood* (1952).

OCOTILLO, or coach whip, *Fouquieria splendens*, a characteristic spiny plant from the deserts of the southwestern US and Mexico. The dry stems are burnt for firewood. Family: Fouquieriaceae.

OCTAGON. See POLYGON.

OCTAHEDRON. See POLYHEDRON.

OCTANE (C_8H_{18}), liquid ALKANE with 18 ISOMERS, constituents of GASOLINE. *Normal* octane occurs in PETROLEUM; the branched isomers, which have high antiknock values, are made by ALKYLATION. The **octane number** of a gasoline is the percentage of *iso*-octane (2,2,4-trimethylpentane) in the mixture of *iso*-octane with *n*-heptane which, in standard tests, knocks to the same degree as the gasoline. ANTIKNOCK ADDITIVES can raise the octane number above 100.

OCTAVE, in music, the interval between two pitches of which one has twice the frequency of the other. In the diatonic scale these are the first and the eighth tones. Because of its unique consonance, the octave gives an aural impression of a single tone duplicated.

OCTAVIA (d. 11 BC), wife of Mark ANTONY and sister of the Roman Emperor AUGUSTUS. Her marriage prevented civil war, but Mark Antony divorced her in 32 BC because of his love for CLEOPATRA.

OCTAVIA (42 AD–62 AD), daughter of Emperor Claudius I and wife of NERO (from 53 AD), who divorced and finally murdered her.

OCTAVIAN. See AUGUSTUS.

OCTOBER, the tenth month of the year. It contains 31 days. Its name comes from the Latin *octo* (eight), since it was the eighth month in the Roman calendar.

OCTOBER REVOLUTION. See RUSSIAN REVOLUTION.

OCTOBRISTS, Russian political party formed in 1905 by Alexander Ivanovich Guchkov (1862–1935). It was so called because its members (mainly moderates of the upper middle class) supported the new constitution established by the October Manifesto of that year, promising a wider franchise and a parliament with legislative power.

OCTOPUS, a cephalopod MOLLUSK whose most striking feature is the possession of eight tentacle-like "arms" which surround the mouth. Behind the beaked head is a sac-like body containing the viscera. Octopods can alter body form and outline, and also change color, and thus have excellent protective camouflage. In addition, a black pigment, SEPIA, can be ejected into the water from a special sac, forming a smoke screen which foils predators.

The Common octopus, rarely much larger than a human hand and hardly dangerous, although its bite may be poisonous. It is a popular delicacy in many parts of the world.

OCULIST, one who practices OPHTHALMOLOGY.

ODD FELLOWS, Independent Order of, a secret benevolent fraternity. Probably founded in 18th century England, it was first established in the US (Baltimore) in 1819. It has a world membership of over one million.

ODE, a stately lyric poem usually expressing praise. It is often addressed to the person, object or concept (such as "Joy" or "Autumn") being celebrated. It originated in the ancient Greek choral songs. PINDAR used a tripartite structure in his odes: strophe, antistrophe (both in the same meter) and epode (in a different meter). HORACE's odes were in stanzaic form. Poets of the 19th century such as KEATS and SHELLEY, wrote odes with irregular structures.

ODER, river in E central Europe rising in Moravia, Czechoslovakia, and flowing some 560mi NW through Poland to the Baltic Sea at Szczecin (formerly Stettin). Navigable for much of its length, it flows past such cities as Wroclaw, Poland, and Frankfurt an der Oder, East Germany. (See ODER-NEISSE LINE.)

ODER-NEISSE LINE, since 1945, the border between East Germany and Poland, formed by the ODER river and its tributary the Neisse.

ODENSE, city in S central Denmark. Of medieval origin, it is a major industrial and commercial center. Hans Christian ANDERSEN was born there. Pop 102 698.

ODESSA, city in W Texas, seat of Ector Co. Leading industries derive from major local oil deposits. Pop 78 380.

ODESSA, city and port in the Ukrainian SSR, USSR, on the Black Sea. It is a major transportation, industrial, commercial and cultural center. It was the scene of an abortive workers' revolt in 1905. Pop 892 000.

ODETS, Clifford (1906–1963), US playwright and screenwriter famous for his social-protest dramas about ordinary people caught in the Depression. He was a leading figure in the GROUP THEATER. His works include *Awake and Sing!* (1935), *Waiting for Lefty* (1935) and *Golden Boy* (1937).

ODIN, in Germanic mythology, the chief of the gods, also known as Wotan or Woden (whose name gave us Wednesday). He was the god of war, poetry, wisdom, learning and magic. He had a single all-seeing eye. He made the world from the body of the giant Ymir, man from an ash tree and woman from an elm.

ODOACER (c435–493), Germanic chief who overthrew the last of the West Roman emperors in 476 and was proclaimed king of Italy. The East Roman Emperor Zeno sent THEODORIC THE GREAT to depose him. After a long war, Odoacer was treacherously killed by Theodoric.

ODOMETER. See SPEEDOMETER.

ODONATA, the insect order containing the DRAGONFLIES—large insects with two pairs of membranous wings, which are strong fliers and active predators. The order is divided into two main groups: the DRAGONFLIES and the DAMSELFLIES.

ODYSSEUS, or Ulysses, legendary hero of ancient Greece, son and successor of King Laertes of Ithaca and husband of PENELOPE. He was the crafty counselor of the TROJAN WAR (described in Homer's ILIAD). After 10 years' adventures (subject of Homer's ODYSSEY) he returned home disguised as a beggar and, with his son TELEMACHUS, killed the suitors beleaguering his wife.

ODYSSEY, famous ancient Greek epic poem ascribed to HOMER, one of the masterpieces of world literature. Its 24 books relate the adventures of ODYSSEUS and his Greek friends after the TROJAN WAR. Rescued from the land of the Lotus-Eaters, they encountered the one-eyed cyclops POLYPHEMUS, the cannibal Laestrygonians and the sorceress CIRCE. They resisted the SIRENS and the perils of SCYLLA AND CHARYBDIS but Odysseus alone survived shipwreck at Trinacria. For seven years he lingered with the nymph CALYPSO before he finally reached his home, Ithaca, to be reunited with his wife PENELOPE.

OEDIPUS, in Greek legend, King of Thebes who was fated to kill his father King Laius and marry his mother Jocasta. Laius, warned by an oracle that he would be killed by his son, abandoned him to die. Oedipus survived and was adopted by the King of Corinth. As a young man he learned his fate from the oracle and fled Corinth, home of his supposed parents. On the road he killed Laius, an apparent stranger. Reaching Thebes, he solved the riddle of the SPHINX and was rewarded with the hand of the widowed Jocasta. He later discovered the truth and blinded himself. His story and that of his daughter ANTIGONE inspired tragedies by SOPHOCLES.

OEDIPUS COMPLEX, COMPLEX typical of INFANTILE SEXUALITY, sometimes retained in the adult, comprising mainly UNCONSCIOUS desires to exclude the parent of one's own SEX and possess the other. In boys, mother FIXATION and consequent father rivalry may lead to a CASTRATION COMPLEX.

OERSTED (Oe), the unit of MAGNETIC FIELD strength in CGS electromagnetic units (see ABAMPERE). It is defined as the field at the center of a single-turn circular coil of radius 1cm and carrying a current of $1/(2\pi)$ abamperes.

OERSTED, Hans Christian (1777–1851), Danish physicist whose discovery that a magnetized needle can be deflected by an electric current passing through a wire (1820) gave birth to the science of ELECTROMAGNETISM.

OFFA (d. 796), Anglo-Saxon king (from 757) who established the supremacy of Mercia and contributed to the unification of England. He made a commercial treaty with CHARLEMAGNE in 796, reorganized the Church and introduced silver pennies. He built the earthwork called *Offa's Dike* between his kingdom and Wales.

OFFENBACH, Jacques (1819–1880), French composer. He wrote over 100 operettas including the immensely popular *Orpheus in the Underworld* (1858), containing the famous can-can, and *La Belle Helène* (1864). His masterpiece is considered to be the more serious *Tales of Hoffman*, first produced in 1881.

OFFICE OF ECONOMIC OPPORTUNITY, US government agency which implements the Economic Opportunity Act (1964), designed to counteract underprivilege caused by poverty.

OFFICE OF MANAGEMENT AND BUDGET, US government agency founded to assist the president in preparing the budget and in managing the efficient expenditure of funds.

OFFICE OF PRICE ADMINISTRATION, a US government agency formed by President Roosevelt in 1941 to organize rationing and control prices and rents in WWII. It was dissolved in 1947.

OFFICE OF STRATEGIC SERVICES, US government agency formed in 1942 to collect and analyze strategic information during WWII. It was dissolved in 1945.

OFFSET LITHOGRAPHY. See PRINTING.

O'FLAHERTY, Liam (1897–), Irish novelist known for his realistic stories of ordinary people in trouble, such as *The Black Soul* (1924), *The Informer* (1925) and *The Assassins* (1928).

OGBOMOSHO, city in SW Nigeria. Founded in the 17th century, it is a center for commerce and crafts. Pop 387 000.

OGDEN, city in N Utah, seat of Weber Co. Industries are led by aircraft and food processing. Pop 69 478.

OGDEN, Charles Kay (1889–1957), English linguist who contributed to language learning. He founded (1912) *The Cambridge Magazine* and his works include *The Meaning of Meaning* (with I. A. Richards, 1923) and *The System of Basic English* (1934).

OGDEN, Peter Skene (1794–1854), Canadian fur trader who explored, among other regions, S Ore. and NE Cal. He discovered the Humboldt R in N Nev. in 1828.

OGDENSBURG, city in NE N.Y., on the St. Lawrence R. It is a transport and trading center with mixed light industry. Pop 14 544.

OGLETHORPE, James Edward (1696–1785), English philanthropist, general and member of parliament who obtained (1732) a charter to found the colony of Georgia. He settled the colony as a refuge for jailed debtors and was governor until he returned to England in 1743.

OGOTAI, or **Ogadai** (d. 1241), son and successor of GENGHIS KHAN. He continued the expansion of the MONGOL EMPIRE into northern China and Russia.

O'HARA, John Henry (1905–1970), US fiction writer known for his vigorous accounts of urban life in America. His novels include *Appointment in Samarra* (1934), *Butterfield 8* (1935) and *A Rage to Live* (1949).

O. HENRY. See HENRY, O.

O'HIGGINS, family famous in South American history. **Ambrosio O'Higgins** (c1720–1801), born in Ireland and educated in Spain, went to South America and rose to be governor of Chile (1789) and viceroy of Peru (1796). **Bernardo O'Higgins** (1778–1842), his natural son, liberated Chile from Spanish rule and became its dictator (1817). His reforms aroused such opposition that he was exiled to Peru in 1823.

OHIO, N central state of the US. It is bounded N by Mich. and Lake Erie, E by Pa. and W.Va., S by W.Va. and Ky., and W by Ind. The Ohio R forms the Ky. and W.Va. borders. Ohio has four land regions: the highland area of the Appalachian Plateau in the E; the narrow strip of Great Lakes Plains bordering Lake Erie; the Till Plains in the SW, the easternmost section of the great fertile Midwestern Corn Belt; and a small wedge of the Blue Grass region extending from Ky. into S Ohio. Excellent ports on Lake Erie have made the state a major transportation hub of the Midwest. Ohio's climate is humid continental with an average annual precipitation of 37in.

Economy. As an industrial state, Ohio is surpassed only by N.Y. and Cal. Widely varied manufactures include non-electrical machinery, primary metals, transportation equipment and fabricated metal products. Ohio leads the nation in tires, machine tools, playing cards, business machines, glassware and other products. Rubber, coal, and iron are important resources. Major agricultural products are livestock, cereal crops, fruit and dairy foods.

History. The Iroquois were the dominant Indian group in the area when La Salle investigated the Ohio valley in 1669. His voyage formed the basis for French claims to the entire Ohio valley, but English fur traders also frequented the region and Va. and other seaboard colonies had been granted parts of the Ohio country in their royal charters. Anglo-French rivalry culminated (1754) in the last of the FRENCH AND INDIAN WARS, as a result of which England was awarded the territory. After the Revolution the region was included by Congress (1787) in the NORTHWEST TERRITORY. The first permanent settlement was

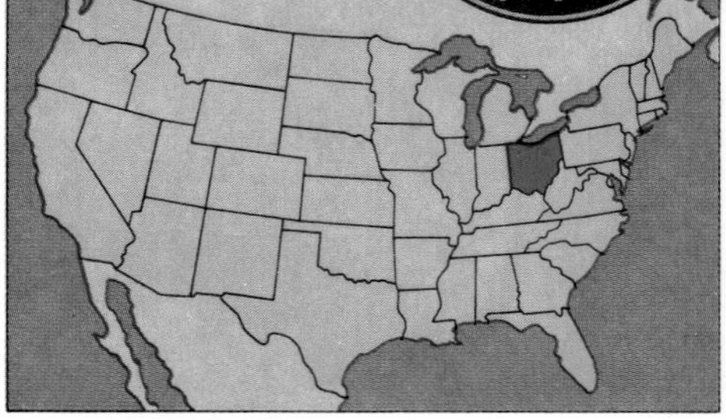

Name of state: Ohio
Capital: Columbus
Statehood: March 1, 1803 (17th state)
Familiar name: Buckeye State
Area: 41 222sq mi
Population: 10 652 017
Elevation: Highest—1 550ft, Campbell Hill in Logan County. Lowest—433 ft, Ohio River in Hamilton County
Motto: With God, All Things Are Possible
State flower: Scarlet carnation
State bird: Cardinal
State tree: Buckeye chestnut
State song: "Beautiful Ohio"

Severance Hall, Ohio, located in Cleveland's University Circle Cultural Area. Conductor George Szell first worked with the now world-famous Cleveland Orchestra here, now the orchestra's permanent home.

Marietta, founded in 1788. Ohio itself became a territory in 1799 and was the 17th state to enter the Union (1803). Rapid expansion in the 19th century was aided (1825) by the opening of the ERIE CANAL. In the period leading up to the Civil War Ohio had an active UNDERGROUND RAILROAD. Ohio has contributed seven presidents to the nation. The state's cultural and educational facilities are outstanding.

OHIO COMPANY, also called the Ohio Company of Virginia, land company formed in 1747 which obtained a grant to explore 200 000 acres west of the Allegheny Mountains. Its operations were ended by the American Revolution.

OHIO COMPANY OF ASSOCIATES, land company established in 1786 in Boston. It purchased 1 780 000 acres of land from Congress in present-day SE Ohio. Settlement began (1788) with the founding of Marietta.

OHIO RIVER, the main eastern tributary of the Mississippi River, which it joins at Cairo, Ill. It is formed at Pittsburgh, Pa., by the junction of the Allegheny and Monongahela rivers and flows generally southwest for about 980mi. Together with its main tributaries, it drains over 203 000sq mi and is navigable throughout.

OHM (Ω), the SI UNIT of electric RESISTANCE. A conductor has a resistance of one ohm when a potential difference of one VOLT across it gives rise to a current of one AMPERE.

OHM, Georg Simon (1789–1854), Bavarian-born German physicist who formulated OHM'S LAW. He also contributed to ACOUSTICS, recognizing the ability of the human ear to resolve mixed SOUND into its component pure (sinusoidal-wave) tones.

OHMMETER, instrument for providing a rapid, if approximate, value for the RESISTANCE of part of an electric circuit. It consists of an AMMETER (reverse calibrated in OHMS) in series with a fixed resistor and a BATTERY. A variable resistor connected across the ammeter is adjusted to zero the meter with the terminals of the instrument shorted. The test resistance is then introduced between these terminals. The reduction in the current so caused is a measure of the resistance.

OHM'S LAW, the statement due to G. S. OHM in 1827 that the electric POTENTIAL difference across a conductor is proportional to the current flowing through it, the constant of proportionality being known as the RESISTANCE of the conductor. It holds well for most materials and objects, including solutions, provided that the passage of the current does not heat the conductor, but ELECTRON TUBES and SEMICONDUCTOR devices show a much more complicated behavior.

OIL, any substance that is insoluble in water, soluble in ETHER and greasy to the touch. There are three main groups: mineral oils (see PETROLEUM); fixed vegetable and animal oils (see FATS; LIPIDS), and volatile vegetable oils (see ESSENTIAL OILS). Oils are classified as fixed or volatile according to the ease with which they vaporize when heated. Mineral oils include GASOLINE and many other fuel oils, heating oils and lubricants. Fixed vegetable oils are usually divided into three subgroups depending on the physical change that occurs when they absorb oxygen: oils such as linseed and tung, which form a hard film, are known as "drying oils"; "semidrying oils," such as cottonseed or soybean oil, thicken considerably but do not harden; "nondrying oils," such as castor and olive oil, thicken only slightly. Fixed animal oils include the "marine oils," such as cod-liver and whale oil. Fixed animal and vegetable fats, such as butterfat and palm oil are often also classified as oils. Examples of volatile vegetable oils, which usually have a very distinct odor and flavor, include such oils as bitter almond, peppermint and TURPENTINE. When dissolved in alcohol, they are called "essences."

OILBIRD, *Steatornis caripensis*, a large bird somewhat resembling a NIGHTJAR, with hooked beak, wide gape and bristles surrounding the gape. They feed mainly on fruit, living in colonies in mountain caves in South America, coming out to feed at night. Oilbirds cannot use their eyes in the depths of their caves; instead they orient by echolocation.

OIL CITY, city in NW Pa., S of Titusville, on the Allegheny R. It is the center of the state's oil industry with oilfields nearby. Pop 15 033.

OIL PALM, *Elaeis guineensis*, tree native to tropical W Africa and cultivated in Indonesia, Malaysia and parts of Middle and South America. The fruits yield PALM OIL and palm kernel oil, which are widely used in household and edible products. Family: Palmae. (See PALM.)

OIL REFINING. See PETROLEUM.

OILS, Natural. See FATS.

OIL SANDS, loose sand or sandstone containing viscous oil. Depending on the proportion of oil to sand, they may occur as ASPHALT lakes, such as those in Trinidad, or BITUMINOUS SANDS, such as the Athabaska tar sands (Alberta, Canada). Despite extraction problems, they are a potentially important OIL source.

OIL SHALE, a fine-grained, dark-colored sedimentary rock from which oil suitable for refining can be extracted. The rock contains an organic substance called kerogen, which may be distilled to yield OIL (see also DISTILLATION). It is nowadays an important oil source. (See also SEDIMENTARY ROCKS; SHALE.)

OIL WELL. See PETROLEUM.

OISE RIVER, a 188mi-long river rising in the Ardennes Mts in S Belgium and flowing to join the Seine R at Conflans, W of Paris, in France. It is navigable for about 80mi and connects with the Canal du Nord.

OISTRAKH, David Feodorovich (1908–1974), Russian violinist. His brilliant technique and strong emotional interpretation (especially of the romantic composers) brought him worldwide acclaim. PROKOFIEV and SHOSTAKOVICH wrote works for him. His son, Igor (1931–), is also a violinist and conductor of world renown.

OITA, city on NE Kyushu island, Japan, on Beppu Bay. It is the capital and industrial center of Oita prefecture. Pop 260 576.

OJIBWA INDIANS (or Chippewa), one of the largest ALGONQUIAN-speaking tribes of North America. They lived as small bands of hunter-gatherers, mainly in woodland areas around Lakes Superior and Huron, and to the west. They fought frequently with the SIOUX, but had little contact with early white settlers. LONGFELLOW's *The Song of Hiawatha* was based on a study of Ojibwa mythology. Today some 60 000 Ojibwas live on US and Canadian reservations.

OJOS DEL SALADO, the second highest mountain peak (22 539ft) in the Andean chain. It lies in the central ANDES, on the Chile-Argentina border.

OKA, a river, one of the chief W tributaries of the VOLGA R in Russia, serving an important farming and industrial area. Rising S of Orel, it flows some 948mi to Gorki; its 550mi below Kolomna are navigable for large vessels.

OKANOGAN INDIANS (or Okinagan), a North American confederation of hunter-gatherer Indian tribes of ALGONQUIAN linguistic stock. In the early 19th century they lived to the W of the Okanogan R, in Wash. state and in British Columbia. Today they live on reservations in the same area.

OKAPI, *Okapia johnstoni*, a close relative of the GIRAFFES, but with short legs and neck, found in dense rain forests of central Africa. It was unknown to zoologists until 1901. The okapi has a rich chocolate coat with white markings on the legs, thighs and throat.

OKAYAMA, city in SW Honshu, Japan, close to the Inland Sea. It is the capital and main industrial center of Okayama prefecture. Pop 375 106.

OKAZAKI, city in central S Honshu, Japan, on the Yahagi R, 20mi SE of Nagoya. It is an industrial city and manufactures textiles, food and other goods. Pop 210 515.

OKEECHOBEE, Lake, shallow lake on the N edge of the Fla. EVERGLADES. About 700sq mi in extent, it is the third largest freshwater lake located within the continental US.

O'KEEFFE, Georgia (1887–), US painter, noted for her delicate, abstract designs incorporating symbolic motifs drawn from observations of nature. She is also known for large symbolic flower paintings such as *Black Iris* (1926). Her paintings were first exhibited in 1916 by Alfred STIEGLITZ, whom she married in 1924.

OKEFENOKEE SWAMP, swamp and wildlife refuge in SE Ga. and NE Fla. Covering over 650sq mi, it is drained by the St. Marys and Suwannee rivers and has densely forested areas, grassy bog savannas, hummock islands, sand bars and large swamp areas of dark water overgrown by heavy brush and trees. The abundant wildlife includes alligators, deer, bears, raccoons and many species of birds and fish.

OKEGHEM, Jean d' (c1420–1495), Flemish Renaissance composer, whose work is noted for rich, sonorous vocal harmony and masterful contrapuntal technique. He was chaplain and composer to the French kings Charles VII, Louis XI and Charles VIII and the teacher of JOSQUIN DES PRÈS and Bunois. Among his surviving works are 14 masses, 10 motets and 20 chansons.

The broad Ohio River—navigable for virtually the whole of its length—was a key route to the Midwest during the early pioneering days, and is now one of the major industrial transportation arteries serving this same area.

OKHOTSK, Sea of, an arm of the Pacific ocean which lies between the Siberian mainland and the Kamchatka peninsula and is separated from the Pacific by the KURIL ISLANDS. Its 590 000sq mi are a jealously-guarded Russian fishing ground.

OKINAWA, largest (454sq mi) and most important of the Ryukyu Islands in the W Pacific, about 500mi SW of Japan. The island is part of Japan's Okinawa prefecture and Naha is its capital city. The island is mountainous and jungle-covered in the S, and hilly in the N. It is fertile—sugarcane, sweet potatoes and rice are grown, and there are good fisheries. Captured by the US during WWII, Okinawa was formally returned to Japan in 1972.

OKLAHOMA, a western S central US state lying immediately N of Tex. It is shaped somewhat like a saucepan, with a 34mi wide "panhandle" extending W 167mi. The state borders on Colo. and Kan. to the N, on Ark. and Mo. to the E and on Tex. and N. Mex. to the S and W.

Land. The state's 69 919sq mi show a wide variation of terrain. Plains in the W give way to rolling hills in the central region and mountain ranges in the E; scrubby sagebrush country contrasts with rich forestlands. The highest point in the state, Black Mesa (4 973ft), is in the far NW corner of the state. Over 65% of Okla. is in the Arkansas R basin and the rest is in the Red R drainage area. Numerous lakes, most of them man-made, provide sources of irrigation and hydroelectric power. All of the larger rivers drain into the Mississippi R. Rainfall is light in the W and heavy in the E. Extremes of temperature occur: the mid-summer average is about 83°F, but the overall state average is about 40°F. Timber is a major natural resource with forest and good stands of varied hard and softwood trees. Wild life is abundant.

Economy. Originally a farming state, Okla. now chiefly depends upon mineral production and manufacturing. It ranks third among the oil- and natural gas-producing states and also has large reserves of zinc, lead, granite, salt, gravel, gypsum and helium. Manufactures, which account for over 40% of the value of all goods produced, are based mainly on local agricultural and mineral production, but also include non-electrical machinery, transportation equipment, aircraft and fabricated metal, stone, glass and clay products. About 60% of agricultural income is based on livestock. Major crops are wheat, cotton, corn, beans, peanuts, oats, hay and barley.

People. The population is 90% white, 3% Indian—about one-third of the entire Indian population of the US ("Oklahoma" is Choctaw for "red people")—and 7% nonwhite. About 65% are urban dwellers, and many live in one of the state's three major cities: Oklahoma City, Tulsa and Lawton.

History. Okla. was acquired by the US as part of the LOUISIANA PURCHASE, and in 1834 the land was designated INDIAN TERRITORY and became a Federal dumping ground for many Indian tribes. Homesteading runs and "land lotteries" (1889–1910)

Oklahoma was once home of the Cherokee Indians, one of the few native American tribes to build permanent dwellings and rely more on agriculture than hunting to provide their food. The village of Tsa-La-Gi, pictured here, is a reconstruction based on an ancient Cherokee settlement at Tahlequah.

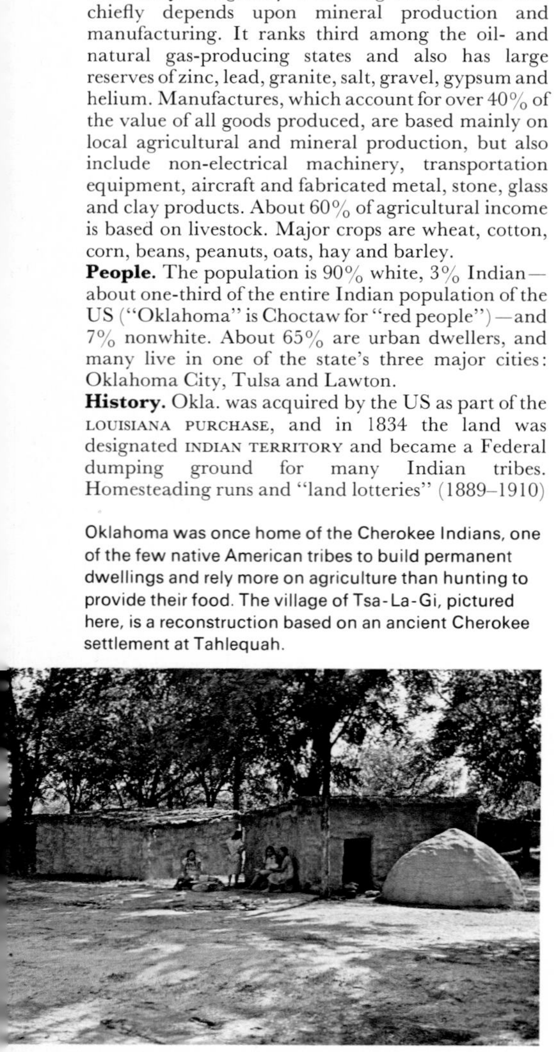

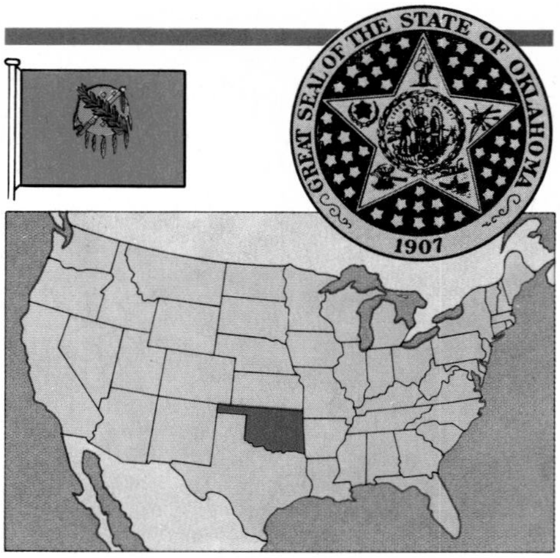

Name of state: Oklahoma
Capital: Oklahoma City
Statehood: Nov. 16, 1907 (46th state)
Familiar name: Sooner State
Area: 69 919sq mi
Population: 2 559 253
Elevation: Highest—4 973ft., Black Mesa in Cimarron County. Lowest—300ft, Red River in McCurtain County
Motto: Labor Omnia Vincit (Labor Conquers All Things)
State flower: Mistletoe
State bird: Scissor-tailed flycatcher
State tree: Redbud
State song: "Oklahoma"

brought a rush of settlers. The first major oilfield was opened in 1901; and on Nov. 16, 1907, after a constitution had been ratified by popular vote, Okla. was admitted to the Union. Unlike many other US states, Okla. maintains its particular Indian and pioneering heritage amidst a flourishing modern economy.

OKLAHOMA CITY, the capital city of Okla., centrally located on the North Canadian R. The second largest city in area in the US (650sq mi), it is a major processing and trading center for livestock and farm products and for petroleum and natural gas. It was founded on Apr. 22, 1889, the same day that the first portion of INDIAN TERRITORY was officially opened to pioneer settlement. Pop 368 856.

OKMULGEE, city and seat of Okmulgee Co., in E central Okla. It is the site of an old Creek Indian capital, in an oil area; it manufactures glass and processes foods. Pop 15 180.

OKRA, or **gumbo,** *Hibiscus esculentus,* a species of hibiscus plant belonging to the MALLOW family, Malvaceae, which is native to the Old World tropics. Its mucilaginous fruits are pickled or cooked as a vegetable or used to thicken and flavor broths. The seeds afford an oil and a coffee substitute.

ÖLAND, a Baltic island of 520sq mi, off SE Sweden, part of Sweden's Kalmar Co. Its chief town is Borgholm. It was the scene of many historic Scandinavian battles. The island's economy is based on agriculture, fishing, light industry and summer tourism.

OLATHE, city and seat of Johnson Co., NE Kan. A trading center on the old Santa Fe Trail, today its light industry manufactures aircraft equipment, machinery and plastics. Pop 17 917.

OLAV V (1903–   ), King of Norway from 1957. He was active in the fight for his country's liberation from the Germans in WWII and in 1944 took command of the Norwegian forces.

OLBERS, Heinrich Wilhelm Matthäus (1758–1840), German astronomer who discovered the ASTEROIDS Pallas (1802) and Vesta (1807), rediscovered Ceres (1802), and found five comets, one of which bears his name. He also formulated a method of calculating cometary orbits (1779); proposed that the pressure of light is responsible for COMETS' tails always pointing away from the sun (1811); and stated **Olbers' Paradox,** that, in an infinite, isotropic universe, the night sky should be uniformly illuminated, whereas in fact it is not. This he explained by suggesting the existence of clouds of INTERSTELLAR MATTER, later discovered; but the "paradox" was not fully resolved until HUBBLE showed that the UNIVERSE is expanding.

OLD AGE, strictly, a chronological division of human life; however, the term also suggests the manifestations and diseases associated with AGING. The SKIN becomes wrinkled and thins, largely due to the effect of ULTRAVIOLET RADIATION on COLLAGEN; HAIR production may be disordered, causing BALDNESS or graying. BONE alters (osteoporosis) with thinning of texture and susceptibility to FRACTURE, while the disks between the VERTEBRAE shrink with resulting loss of height. Wear and tear of the JOINTS frequently leads to osteoarthritis. ARTERIOSCLEROSIS, which starts in early life, becomes established in the elderly, resulting in STROKE, CORONARY THROMBOSIS and limb GANGRENE. Degenerative disease due to cell loss is especially important in the BRAIN. IMMUNITY may be less effective, leading to more frequent and serious infections (PNEUMONIA), and may account for the increased incidence of CANCER with age. VITAMIN deficiency diseases due to inadequate diet are common. Special social and psychiatric problems arise from the social isolation, decreased mobility and poor health associated with old age. (See also GERIATRICS; MEDICARE; SOCIAL SECURITY.) *Progeria* is a rare condition of children causing premature aging.

OLD BELIEVERS, seceders from the Russian ORTHODOX CHURCH who would not accept the liturgical reforms of Patriarch NIKON; excommunicated as schismatics 1667 and persecuted until the late 19th century. The major group depended on seceding priests until they could set up a hierarchy (1846); many small, extravagant lay sects also sprang up.

OLD CATHOLICS, group of churches which have seceded from the ROMAN CATHOLIC CHURCH. The Jansenist Church of Utrecht separated in 1724, followed after 1870 by churches in Germany, Austria and Switzerland, led by von DÖLLINGER, which would not accept the dogmas of papal infallibility and jurisdiction defined by the First VATICAN COUNCIL. Several smaller Slavic churches later separated. Virtually high Anglican in doctrine and practice, Old Catholics have been in full communion with the Church of England since 1932.

OLD CHURCH SLAVONIC, a language of the Slavic subfamily of the Indo-European family of languages, devised in the 9th century by the Greek scholars and saints CYRIL AND METHODIUS; presumed to be the first written Slavic language. Its descendant, Church Slavonic, was used as a literary language (from 1100 AD to c1700 AD) and is still the most widely used liturgical language in the Eastern Orthodox churches. (See also SLAVONIC LANGUAGES.)

OLDENBARNEVELDT, Johan van (1547–1619), Dutch statesman. As advocate of Holland (from 1586), he supported self-government for the burgher towns of the United Provinces, recently liberated from Spain, and encouraged commerce during the early years of the Dutch East India Co. He came into conflict with MAURICE OF NASSAU and the nobles over the role of the states-general and in the Calvinist-REMONSTRANTS controversy. Oldenbarneveldt was arrested on unfounded treason charges and executed.

OLD ENGLISH SHEEPDOG, a breed developed in England, probably about the 18th century, for driving cattle and sheep to market. Its squarish body, including its face, is covered with shaggy hair. Males stand about 22in at the shoulder.

OLD FAITHFUL, name given to an intermittent hot spring, or geyser, a tourist attraction at YELLOWSTONE NATIONAL PARK, Wyo., which at intervals of 66min erupts for about 5min up to heights of 150ft.

OLDFIELD, Barney (Berner Eli Oldfield; 1877–1946), pioneer US auto-racing driver. Victorious in Henry FORD's racing team driving the Ford-Cooper "999," he became the first mile-a-minute motorist (1903 at Indianapolis) and in 1910 set a world speed record of 131.724 mph.

OLD IRONSIDES. See CONSTITUTION, USS.

OLD-MAN CACTUS, *Cephalocereus senilis*, a cylindrically-shaped cactus popularly grown as a house plant for the showy long white hairs it produces. (See CACTI.)

OLD REGIME. See ANCIEN RÉGIME.

OLDS, Ransom Eli (1864–1950), pioneer US automobile engineer and manufacturer. He produced the Oldsmobile and Reo cars, and is generally considered the founder of the US automobile industry. His first powered vehicle was a steam-driven three-wheeler (1886). He established the Olds Motor Vehicle Company in 1899, marketed a 3hp Oldsmobile in 1901—the first commercially successful American car—and established the Reo Motor Car Company in 1904.

OLD TESTAMENT, or the Hebrew Bible, the first part of the Christian Bible (for list of books see BIBLE), describing God's covenant with Israel. The Jewish CANON was fixed by the 1st century AD and is followed by the Protestant churches; the Greek SEPTUAGINT version, containing also the APOCRYPHA, was followed by the VULGATE and hence by the Roman Catholic Church. The standard MASORETIC TEXT of the Hebrew Old Testament is now largely confirmed for most books by the DEAD SEA SCROLLS (almost 1000 years earlier). The Old Testament is traditionally divided into three parts: the Law (see PENTATEUCH), the Prophets—the Former Prophets being the earlier historical books, the Latter being the three Major Prophets and the MINOR PROPHETS—and the Writings, including the later historical books, Daniel and the poetic and "wisdom" books. Christianity regards the Old Testament as an inspired record of God's dealings with His people in preparation for the coming of Christ, containing in embryo much New Testament teaching.

OLDUVAI GORGE, a 300ft-deep canyon in N Tanzania, gouged through lake sediment, volcanic ash and other material deposited over the past few million years. In Bed I, the lowest of five layers into which the walls are divided, the anthropologists Louis and Mary LEAKEY found early fossil remains of PREHISTORIC MAN.

OLEAN, city in SW N.Y., 70mi SE of Buffalo, on the Allegheny R. It is located in the center of N.Y.'s oilfields and has oil refineries and varied manufacturing. Pop 19 169.

OLEANDER, *Nerium oleander*, and related species, a highly poisonous, ornamental evergreen shrub with red or white rose-like flowers, which is native to the eastern Mediterranean region. Family: Apocynaceae.

OLEASTER, *Elaeagnus angustifolia*, ornamental and hedge tree native to Eurasia. It resembles the OLIVE, the leaves having a silvery covering of hairs on their undersurface. They produce fragrant yellow flowers and egg-shaped fruits. Family: Elaeagnaceae.

OLEFINS. See ALKENES.

OLEG (d. c912 AD), leader of the VARANGIANS, who captured Kiev in 882 and made his capital there. He freed eastern Slavic tribes in Russia from KHAZAR rule; and made treaties with the Byzantines opening the trade route from Kiev to Constantinople which led subsequently to Greek Orthodox influence on Russia.

OLEIC ACID ($C_{17}H_{33}COOH$), an unsaturated CARBOXYLIC ACID used in lubricating oils and varnishes. Triolein, its ester with GLYCEROL is present in many natural oils and fats, helping to keep them liquid at room temperature. mp 16°C, bp 286°C.

OLEOMARGARINE, early name for MARGARINE.

OLFACTORY SYSTEM. See SMELL.

OLGA, Saint (d. 969?). Regent for her son SVIATOSLAV, grand prince of KIEV until c957, she managed the affairs of state when her son went on military expeditions. She was baptized a Christian at Constantinople, and her grandson VLADIMIR I became Kiev's first Christian ruler.

OLIGARCHY, a form of government rule, or control of a state or some other organization by a small elite group. The term often carries an implication that rule by an oligarchy is essentially interested. (See also GOVERNMENT.)

OLIGOCENE, the third epoch of the TERTIARY, of duration about 40–25 million years ago. (See also GEOLOGY.)

OLIGOCHAETES, a group of annelid worms which includes the EARTHWORMS and a number of smaller aquatic species. The chaetae, small bristles projecting from the body wall, are few in number and other appendages are absent. Oligochaetes are hermaphrodite. (See also ANNELIDA; POLYCHAETES.)

OLIGOPOLY, a market situation such as in the US steel and car industries where identical or very similar products are produced by a few firms. (See also MONOPOLY.)

OLIVARES, Gaspar de Guzmán, Conde-Duque de (1587–1645), Spanish statesman. A favorite of Philip IV, he ruled Spain, 1621–43, and attempted to abolish court corruption. He overrode the rights of autonomous regions, provoking revolts of the Portuguese and Catalans in 1640.

OLIVE, *Olea europaea*, an evergreen tree growing in Mediterranean climates and one of the world's oldest cultivated crops. Its unripe fruits are pickled, treated with lye solution to remove the bitter taste and stored in brine. When left to ripen they turn black and are pressed for their oil. Family: Oleaceae. (See OLIVE OIL.)

OLIVE OIL, edible OIL obtained from the fruit of the OLIVE tree. Oil is extracted at a number of stages during processing. The fruit is first pulped, and then pressed at least twice. Further extraction is achieved by using solvents such as hot water and carbon disulfide. Olive oil is used as salad oil, frying oil and in canning foods such as sardines. The lowest grades are used for making soap. Olive oil contains between 67% and 83% OLEIC ACID.

OLIVER, Isaac (d. 1617), French-born English miniature painter, a pupil of Nicholas HILLIARD. His portraits show his skillful effects of light and shade, as in *A Young Man, Said to be Sir Philip Sidney*.

OLIVER, Joseph "King" (1885–1938), American jazz musician. A leader of the New Orleans style of jazz, his band, the Creole Jazz Band, played blues pieces and tunes based on rags and marches. Oliver himself was a cornetist.

OLIVES, Mount of, ridge of hills E of Jerusalem. On the W slope is the Garden of GETHSEMANE where Jesus went with his disciples after the Last Supper. It is also the site of Christ's Ascension.

OLIVIER, Laurence Kerr, Baron Olivier of Brighton (1907–), English actor, producer and director. He is immensely versatile and brilliant in classical as well as modern roles, such as John OSBORNE's *The Entertainer*. His film of *Hamlet* (1948) won an Academy award. In 1962 he was appointed director of Britain's National Theatre.

OLIVINE, group of SILICATE minerals, orthosilicates of magnesium and iron ($(Mg,Fe)_2SiO_4$. It forms olive-green crystals in the orthorhombic system, and occurs commonly in IGNEOUS ROCKS, chiefly BASALT, GABBRO and PERIDOTITE. The transparent variety **peridot** is used as a GEM stone.

OLMEC INDIANS, a people of the SE coastal lowlands of ancient Mexico. Their culture, earliest of the major Mexican cultures, flourished from between 1000 BC and 500 BC until c1100 AD. They were skilled in artistic work with stone and produced huge sculptured basalt heads, beautiful jewelry, fine jade, white ware and mosaics. They knew how to record time and had a hieroglyphic form of writing. Their culture may have influenced the ZAPOTECS and TOLTECS.

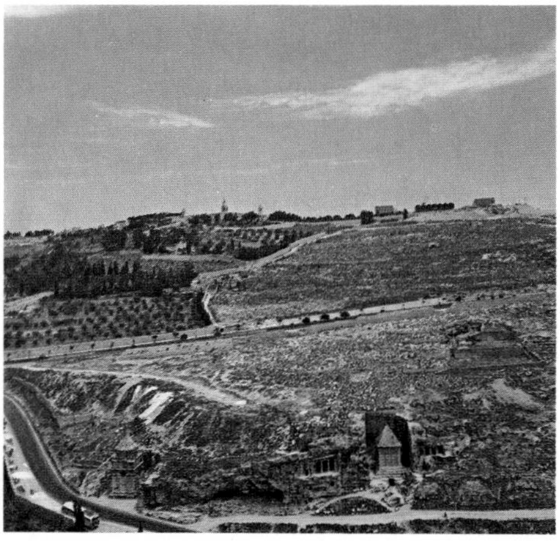

The Mount of Olives, traditional site of the Ascension.

Main stadium at the Montreal Olympic Games, 1976.

OLMSTEAD, Frederick Law (1822–1903), American landscape architect and writer. With Calvert Vaux he planned Central Park, New York, and himself designed other parks in Philadelphia, Brooklyn, Montreal and Chicago. In the 1850s he was well known for his perceptive travel books on the South.

OLNEY, Richard (1835–1917), US attorney general (1893–95) and secretary of state (1895–97) to President Cleveland. He is remembered for calling out troops to deal with workers involved in the PULLMAN STRIKE in 1894. He announced the controversial "Olney Corollary" to the Monroe Doctrine in 1895, declaring bluntly United States willingness to interfere in the internal affairs of South America.

OLSZTYN, or **Allerstein,** industrial city in NE Poland on the Lyna R. Founded by TEUTONIC KNIGHTS in the 14th century, it is the center of a lumbering and agricultural area. It was awarded to Germany in 1920, but reverted to Poland in 1946. Pop 94 100.

OLYMPIA, a small plain about 12mi E of Pirgos in SW Greece, famous in ancient times as a religious center and as the scene of the OLYMPIC GAMES. At the foot of Kronos Hill stood the temple of Zeus with its gold and ivory statue of Zeus by PHIDIAS that was one of the SEVEN WONDERS OF THE WORLD.

OLYMPIA, capital city of Wash., seat of Thurston Co., on the S side of Puget Sound. Its industries are shipbuilding, food-processing, lumbermilling and oyster culture. Pop 23 111.

OLYMPIAD, the period of four years between each celebration of the Olympic Games. The first year of the first Olympiad was 776 BC.

OLYMPIAS (d. 316 BC), wife of Philip II of Macedon and mother of ALEXANDER THE GREAT, whom she greatly influenced. After his death she contested power with CASSANDER, son of ANTIPATER, who had her killed.

OLYMPIC GAMES, the oldest international sporting contest traditionally for amateurs, held every four years. The games probably developed from the ancient Greek athletic contests in honor of a god or dead hero. Events such as boxing, wrestling, long jump, discus, javelin, distance running and chariot racing were added to the original sole event, a 210yd race, held in 776 BC at Olympia in honor of ZEUS. The games at Olympia lasted seven days. They lost popularity, largely through the growth of cheating, and were abolished by Emperor Theodosius I in 394 AD. In 1896 the first modern Olympic Games were held in Athens, organized by Pierre de COUBERTIN. Since then the games have been held in different cities, once every four years except 1916, 1940 and 1944. In 1924 the Winter Olympics were started at Chamonix, France. The 1972 games, with 8500 competitors from 124 countries in 195 events, were marred by the terrorist massacre of 11 Israelis. In 1976, 21 African countries withdrew, protesting New Zealand's rugby tour of South Africa.

OLYMPIC MOUNTAINS, part of the Pacific Coast Range, in NW Wash., W of Puget Sound and S of Juan de Fuca Strait. The highest points are Mt Olympus (7965ft) and Mt Constance (7777ft). On the W side the average annual rainfall is 130in. The region's wildlife includes elk, cougar, bear and black-tailed deer.

OLYMPIC NATIONAL PARK, scenic region established in 1938, which includes the Olympic Mts. There are glaciers, lakes, temperate rain forest, and wildlife sanctuaries.

OLYMPIO, Silvanus (1902–1963), African politician, first president of Togo 1961–63. He was prime minister from 1958 until independence from France was granted in 1960. His authoritarian regime brought about his assassination.

OLYMPUS, Mount, highest mountain in Greece, rises 9570ft at the E end of the 25mi range along the Thessaly-Macedonia border. The summit is snow-capped for most of the year. The Ancient Greeks believed it to be the home of Zeus and most other gods (the Olympians).

OM, Sanskrit sacred syllable (see MANTRA) signifying the primordial sound and divine energy; in HINDUISM it often represents the Trimunti, and in Buddhism the Absolute. It is commonly chanted repetitively to purify and concentrate the mind for meditation. LAMAISM often uses the mantra *om mani padme hum* (ah! the jewel is indeed in the lotus!).

OMAHA, city in E Neb., seat of Douglas Co., a port on the W bank of the Missouri R, largest city in the state and one of the world's great meat-packing and livestock markets and a transportation hub. Its industries include the manufacture of feed, farm machinery, fertilizers, food-processing and grain storage. It is also a well-known insurance center. Pop 346929.

OMAHA INDIANS, a Siouan-speaking North American tribe. They originally lived in the Ohio valley area, but moved with the PONCA INDIANS to the Missouri R region and then to what is now NE Neb. They were an agricultural and hunting tribe and lived mainly in earth lodges. Today 1000–1500 live on the Nebraska reservation.

OMAN (formerly Muscat and Oman), sultanate in SE Arabia, on the Arabian Sea. Much of Oman is barren, with little rainfall and temperatures reaching 130°F. There are dates in the Batinah coastal plain, NW of Muscat (the capital) and the Dhofar Province is noted for sugarcane and cattle. Grains and fruits are grown around Jebel Akhdar. Oil was found in 1963, and over 17 million tons are produced yearly. Closely associated with Britain (1798–1971), Oman's population is mostly Arab, but includes Negroes, Indians and Pakistanis. In 1970 the reformist Sultan Qabus bin Said ousted his father. Guerrilla warfare in the S was largely subdued by 1975.

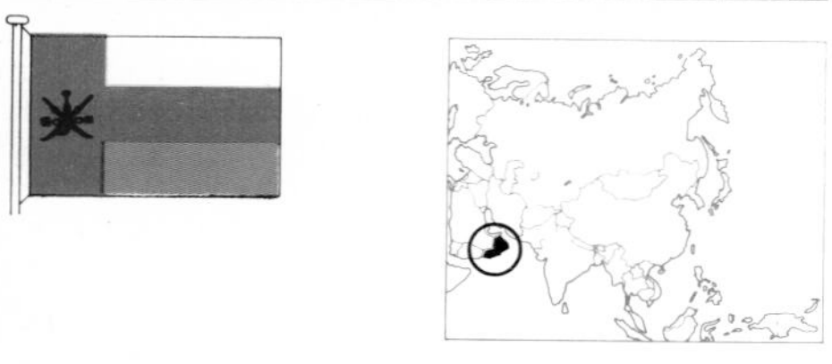

Official name: The Sultanate of Oman
Capital: Muscat
Area: 82000sq mi
Population: 750000
Languages: Arabic, English
Religions: Muslim
Monetary unit(s): 1 Rial Omani = 1000 baiza

OMAN, Gulf of, arm of the Arabian Sea between Oman and Iran. It is 350mi long and joins with the Persian Gulf through the Hormuz Strait.

OMAR II, or **Umar** (c581–644), 2nd caliph of Islam, 634–44, successor to ABU BAKR. In his reign Islam acquired an empire stretching to Egypt, Syria and the Persian Empire.

OMAR KHAYYAM, 11th century Persian poet, astronomer and mathematician. His epic poem *Rubaiyat*, dealing with nature and love, is known in the West through its translation by Edward FITZGERALD.

OMAYYADS (Umayyads), a dynasty of caliphs who ruled the Muslim empire from Damascus from 661 to 750 AD. They were essentially Arab in character and relied heavily upon the Syrian army. The Omayyad Caliphate is sometimes known as the Arab Kingdom. They were replaced by the ABBASIDS of Baghdad. The last Omayyad fled to Spain and set up the Caliphate of Cordoba in 756.

OMBUDSMAN, official appointed by the legislature to investigate complaints by citizens against government officials or agencies. The office originated in Sweden in 1809 and since 1955 has been adopted by Denmark, New Zealand and Britain. There is no federal ombudsman in the US.

OMDURMAN, largest city of the Sudan, and its chief commercial center, on the W bank of the Nile opposite Khartoum. From 1885 it was the Mahdist capital and burial place of the MAHDI, Mohammed Ahmed. In 1898 an Anglo-Indian army under Lord KITCHENER crushed the Mahdists. Pop 232000.

OMEGA-MINUS. See SUBATOMIC PARTICLES.

OMIYA, city in Japan, N of Tokyo on Honshu island, site of the 5th century BC Shinto Hikawa Shrine. It has vast railroad workshops. Pop 268777.

OMNIVORE, any animal that feeds on both plants and animals. (See also CARNIVORE; HERBIVORES.)

OMRI (9th century BC), king of ISRAEL; father of AHAB. He moved his capital to Samaria and conquered MOAB; of major international importance, he is remarked in the Bible for his ungodliness.

OMSK, city in W Siberia at the confluence of the Om and Irtysh Rivers. Its industries include agricultural machinery, textile plants, oil refining and flour milling. Pop 821000.

OMUTA, city and port in Japan, NW Kyushu, 22mi NW of Kumamoto. Its industries include coal mining and chemicals. Pop 175143.

ONAGER, *Equus hemionus onager*, a subspecies of the Asiatic wild ass, distributed from Iran to western India and the USSR. (See also DONKEY.)

ONASSIS, Aristotle Socrates (1906–1975), Turkish-born Greek shipowner and financier. In the 1920s he was a tobacco merchant in Buenos Aires. In 1925 he acquired Argentinian and Greek nationality. Buying his first ships in the early 1930s, he came to own many super-tankers. In 1968 he married Jacqueline Kennedy.

ONASSIS, Jacqueline Lee Bouvier Kennedy (1929–), US journalist who married first John F. KENNEDY (1953) and later Aristotle ONASSIS (1968). While first lady, she initiated and supervised the historical restoration of the White House.

OÑATE, Juan de (c1549–1628), Spanish explorer of the Southwest. He colonized what is now New Mexico. He led expeditions to the Wichita area of Kansas (1601) and to the Colorado R and Gulf of California (1605). Convicted of misconduct in 1614, he was pardoned in 1624.

ONCHOCHERCIASIS. See FILARIASIS.

ONEGA, Lake, the second largest lake in Europe, in Karelia, NE European USSR. It is about 150mi long by 60mi wide and up to 360ft deep. Petrozavodsk is the chief city on its shores.

ONEIDA, city in central N.Y., 13mi WSW of Rome. It produces silverware, plastic and paper products. Pop 11677.

ONEIDA COMMUNITY, a religious commune founded by J. H. NOYES in 1848 near Oneida, N.Y. The group shared both possessions and partners and thought of themselves as a "family" of God. They set up successful businesses in silver and steel products. The community social experiments broke down in c1881.

ONEIDA INDIANS, smallest of the original five nations of the IROQUOIS confederacy. They lived in present-day central N.Y. In the American Revolution they sided with the Colonists. About 3000 remain.

ONEIDA LAKE, lake in central N.Y., about 80sq mi in area. It is part of the NEW YORK STATE BARGE CANAL system.

O'NEILL, Eugene (Gladstone) (1888–1953), arguably the US's greatest playwright, winner of the 1936 Nobel Prize for Literature. Son of a popular actor, after trying the sea, journalism and gold prospecting he started to write plays during a convalescence from tuberculosis and was initially involved in early off-Broadway efforts to introduce European seriousness into American theater. Whether expressionistic (*The Emperor Jones*, 1920), naturalistic (*Anna Christie*, 1921), symbolist (*The Hairy Ape*, 1922) or updated Greek tragedy (*Mourning becomes Electra*, 1931), his large body of work was ambitious in scope and relentlessly tragic (except for the comedy *Ah, Wilderness!*, 1935), and culminated in masterpieces such as *The Iceman Cometh* (1946) and *Long Day's Journey Into Night* (1955).

O'NEILL, Margaret "Peggy" (1796–1879), the daughter of a tavern keeper and wife of John EATON, President JACKSON's secretary of war. The wives of the other cabinet ministers snubbed her socially, provoking a cabinet crisis in which VAN BUREN replaced CALHOUN as vice-president.

ONEONTA, city in E central N.Y. on the Susquehanna R. Its produce includes grain, and it manufactures electronic goods. Pop 16030.

ONION, *Allium sepa*, hardy biennial plant cultivated as an annual vegetable for its succulent and aromatic bulbs. Onions are used in salads, for flavoring and as pickles. Family: Alliaceae. (See also GARLIC; LEEK.)

ONION, Pregnant, *Ornithogalum caudatum*, an unusual plant named for the mass of bulbils (or babies) produced by the parent bulb. The plant produces narrow strap-shaped leaves and a spike of 100 or more white flowers, and is often grown indoors as an oddity. It should be grown at average house temperatures and placed in a sunny position. It should be well watered whenever the soil surface dries out. Propagation is by removing the bulbils and growing them to maturity. Family: Liliaceae.

ONITSHA, large port in Nigeria on the Niger R. Its principal industries are textiles and lumber products. Pop 189067.

ONNES, Heike Kamerlingh. See KAMERLINGH ONNES, HEIKE.

ONOMATOPOEIA, a word the sound of which corresponds to its meaning. Examples of onomatopoeic words include "bang," "click," "splash," "gurgle" and "slush."

ONONDAGA INDIANS, one of the original five nations of the IROQUOIS Confederacy, living in what is now N.Y. Because of their location they played an important role in the confederacy and provided the chairmen. In the 1700s their loyalties were divided between the French and British. About 1000 now remain in N.Y.

ONONDAGA LAKE, lake in central N.Y. 5mi long by 1mi wide, prominent in the 19th century for its salt factories.

ONSAGER, Lars (1903–1976), Norwegian-born US chemist awarded the 1968 Nobel Prize for Chemistry for his fundamental work on irreversible chemical and thermodynamic processes.

ONTARIO, the richest and most populous province of Canada.

Land. In the N part of Ontario lies the Hudson Bay Lowland, a poorly drained area covered by low forests, tundra and swamps, stretching 100mi to 200mi inland from the coast of Hudson Bay and James Bay. S of this is the CANADIAN SHIELD, covering half of Ontario's surface. Nickel, iron, platinum, copper, gold and uranium are among the valuable ores mined there. The Great Lakes Lowland, lying along Lakes Huron, Erie and Ontario, is the site of rich farmland as well as most of the province's industry. There are many rivers and 250000 lakes in Ontario, and Ontario has vast resources of hydroelectric power.

People. Nearly 90% of Ontarians live in the 10% of the province that lies S of the French River and Lake Nipissing, and 80% of the people live in towns. About three-fifths of the people are of British origin and the second largest ethnic group are the French Canadians. Since WWII over a million European immigrants, including British, Italians, Dutch, Germans and Poles have settled in Ontario.

Economy. Ontario is responsible for about half Canada's manufactured goods, a third of its agricultural wealth and a fourth of its mineral production. Metropolitan Toronto is the most important industrial center. There is car manufacturing in Oakville, Oshawa and Windsor, iron and steelmaking in Hamilton, nickel processing at Port Colborne and a petrochemical industry at Sarnia. The SW area of the Great Lakes Lowland is the main field crop region, where hay, tobacco, soyabeans, oats, tomatoes and corn are grown. Rich orchards and vineyards lie in the Niagara fruit belt. Beef and dairy cattle are reared in the NE of the Great Lakes Lowland. Ontario provides about 20% of Canada's commercial lumber.

History. In the early 17th century Ontario was explored by Étienne BRÛLÉ and Samuel de CHAMPLAIN. By 1671 the English Hudson Bay Company had set up a trading post at Moose Factory, and N Ontario became the scene of Anglo-French rivalry until 1763, at the end of the French and Indian Wars, when French North America was ceded to Britain. In the 1780s many American Loyalists settled in S Ontario. In 1791 Ontario broke from Quebec and became the colony of Upper Canada. After the rebellion of 1837–38, led by W. L. MACKENZIE, there were political reforms and in 1840 came reunion with Quebec. The Dominion of CANADA was established in 1867 with Ontario, Quebec, New Brunswick and Nova Scotia as original members. At the end of the 1800s many Ontarians left for richer agricultural lands westward and in the US. The coming of industry and the accessibility of rich mines and lumbering areas in the N led to rapidly increasing prosperity which was accelerated by the discovery of the world's largest uranium deposits at Elliot Lake in 1952.

Name of province: Ontario
Joined Confederation: July 1, 1867
Capital: Toronto
Area: 412 582sq mi
Population: 7 703 106

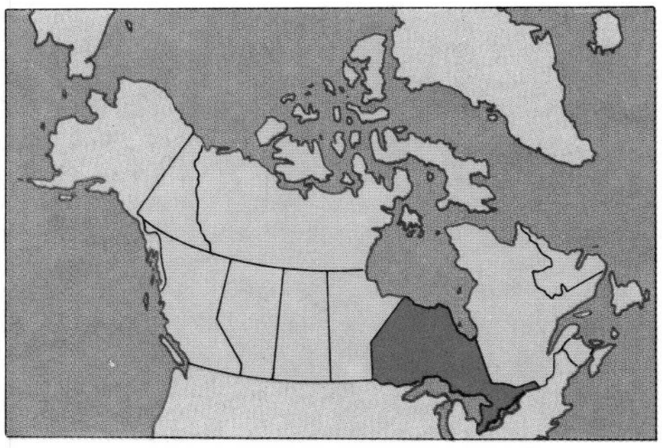

ONTARIO, city in SE Cal., 20mi W of San Bernardino. Its industries include wine, aircraft parts and various light manufacturing. Pop 64 118.

ONTARIO, Lake, the smallest (about 7 600sq mi) and farthest E of the five GREAT LAKES. The lake, bisected by the US-Canadian border, is about 193mi long and up to 53mi wide, with a maximum sounded depth of 802ft. A major link in the Great Lakes–SAINT LAWRENCE SEAWAY system, its cargo traffic includes coal, grain, lumber and iron ore. Principal ports are Toronto, Hamilton and Kingston (Ontario), and Oswego and Rochester (N.Y.).

ONTOGENY AND PHYLOGENY, terms respectively descriptive of the developmental (particularly embryonic) history of an individual organism and of the evolutionary history of its race. E. H. HAECKEL's "biogenetic law" proposed that "ontogeny recapitulates (repeats) phylogeny."

ONTOLOGY. See EPISTEMOLOGY.

ONYCHOPHORA, a small group of terrestrial animals related to the ARTHROPODA but with many worm-like features, such that they were at one time thought to represent a link between true annelids and arthropods. They have soft, cylindrical, segmented bodies with 14–44 pairs of short wide legs (depending on species).

Ontario's pioneer past is recalled by such buildings as this old watermill in Almonte, near Ottawa. It would have been used in milling corn.

ONYX, variety of CHALCEDONY with variegated bands, straight rather than curved as in AGATE. Sardonyx has white and brown bands; carnelian onyx white and red. It is used as a GEM stone, especially for CAMEOS and INTAGLIOS.

OOLITH, a more or less spherical particle of rock which has developed by the accretion of material about an initial nucleus. The accretion may be concentric (so that in cross-section circular bands of material may be seen) or radial, and combinations are known. Larger ooliths are termed *pisoliths.* Concentration of ooliths can form, for example, oolitic limestones, often called *oolites.*

OOMYCETES. See FUNGI.

OOSTENDE, town, fishing port and resort in NW Belgium. It dates from the 9th century, and now has shipbuilding industries. Pop 56 954.

OOZES, sediments on the deep-sea plains, consisting of PLANKTON remains, wind-borne volcanic dust, etc. Beneath about 5 000m no organic matter is present (*red clays*); between 5 000 and 3 900m RADIOCLARIANS predominate in the *siliceous oozes* (see also PROTOZOA); and between 3 900 and 2 000m FORAMINIFERA (especially GLOBIGERINA) are most common in the *calcareous oozes.*

O.P.A. See OFFICE OF PRICE ADMINISTRATION.

OPAH, *Lampris guttatus,* a large, deep-bodied ocean fish related to the OARFISH. Also called moonfish or kingfish, it is found in the warmer waters of the Atlantic and Pacific, reaching a length of nearly 2m (6.6ft). It feeds on cuttlefishes, crustaceans and possibly octopuses.

OPAL, cryptocrystalline variety of porous hydrated SILICA, deposited from aqueous solution in all kinds of rocks, and also formed by replacement of other minerals. Opals are variously colored; the best GEM varieties are translucent, with milky or pearly opalescence and iridescence due to light scattering and interference from internal cracks and cavities.

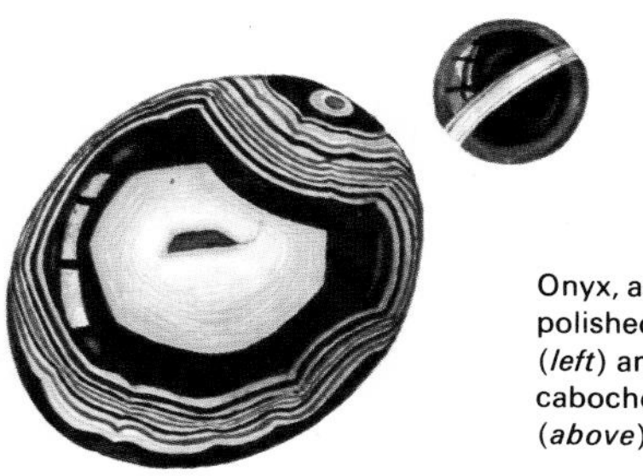

Onyx, as a polished stone (*left*) and as cut in cabochon form (*above*).

Common opal is used as an abrasive, filler and insulator.

OPA-LOCKA, city in SE Fla., residential suburb with some industry 10mi NE of Miami. Pop 11 902.

OP ART, abstract art style in which patterns and color values are composed to produce an illusion of movement on the picture-surface. The best-known artists in the style, which developed in the 1960s, are Victor Vasarely and Bridget Riley.

OPELIKA, city in E Ala., seat of Lee Co., 60mi NE of Montgomery, a trade and manufacturing center for the surrounding cotton and corn area. Pop 19 027.

OPELOUSAS, city in central S La., 22mi N of Lafayette, and seat of St. Landry parish. Industry centers on oil and agricultural products. Pop 20 387.

OPEN CLUSTERS. See GALACTIC CLUSTERS.

OPEN DOOR POLICY, policy of equal commercial rights for all nations involved in an area, usually referring to its enunciation in 1899 and during the BOXER REBELLION by US Secretary of State John Hay in notes to the main powers concerned with China. Its roots lay in the Nanking Treaty after the OPIUM WAR. It was confirmed 1921–22 (see WASHINGTON, TREATIES OF), and ended with the clash with Japan's "New Order" in the 1930s and with WWII.

Fall (1963), by Bridget Riley, perhaps the foremost of British Op art painters. The illusion of motion in the picture is produced by the eye's frustrated attempts to focus on the pattern.

OPEN-HEARTH PROCESS, technique which was, until recently, responsible for most of the world's STEEL production. It derives its alternative name, the Siemens-Martin Process, from the work of Sir William SIEMENS and Pierre Émile MARTIN in the 1850s and 1860s. The FURNACE has two ducts leading each to a chamber of brick checkerwork. In use, the hot exhaust fumes are passed out through one duct, heating the brick to high temperature, while air intake is through the other. Periodically the streams are reversed, so that the incoming air is preheated by the hot brick before passing the burners, thus greatly increasing the flame temperature. Some furnaces are liquid-fueled, but if the fuel is gaseous it may be fed in with the air. In the *basic process,* the charge is of IRON ore, scrap steel and LIMESTONE. The impurities in the ore combine with the limestone to form a basic SLAG. In the less important *acid process,* REFRACTORIES of SILICA result in an acid slag.

OPEN HOUSING, in the US, the sale and rental of residential units without discrimination on grounds of race, religion or nationality. The 1968 Civil Rights Act prohibits such discrimination in most housing, but in June, 1968, the Supreme Court ruled all such discrimination illegal. (See also CIVIL RIGHTS AND LIBERTIES.)

OPEN-PIT MINING. See MINING.

OPEN SHOP. See RIGHT-TO-WORK LAW.

OPERA, staged dramatic form in which the text is wholly or partly sung to an instrumental or orchestral accompaniment. It originated in 17th-century Italy, in an attempt to recreate Greek drama; this was combined with the popular semi-musical mystery plays and religious dramas into *dramma per musica* (drama through music), and spread through Europe. Much early opera was a mere excuse for spectacle, but works by MONTEVERDI, CAVALLI, LULLY, PURCELL and others greatly advanced the art and are again popular today. Dramatic standards had declined by the early 18th century (despite fine works by HANDEL), being caught up in stilted convention. GLUCK sought to avoid this by unifying plot, music and staging into a dramatic whole, while MOZART introduced greater depth of feeling into the music and realism of character on stage. The form was still further enriched by the Romantics, BEETHOVEN and WEBER in Germany and BERLIOZ and BIZET in France. The great Italians, BELLINI, DONIZETTI and ROSSINI developed the more stylized BEL CANTO form to which VERDI, in his later operas, gave greater depth and naturalism, a trend carried further in the seminal works and theories of Richard WAGNER. He sought to add a philosophical basis to Gluck's synthesis by creating *Gesamtkunstwerk*, the total work of art. He influenced many later composers such as Richard STRAUSS and DEBUSSY. The recent Italian *verismo* (naturalistic) school produced smaller scale, often sensational works: PUCCINI mastered both this and a more epic, fantastic style. Among the greatest 20th-century opera composers are JANAČEK, BERG and BRITTEN. (See also individual composers, especially BOITO; GOUNOD; MASCAGNI; MEYERBEER; MUSSORGSKY; TCHAIKOVSKY.)

OPERA BUFFA (Italian: comic opera), light operatic form, generally consisting of musical numbers linked by *recitativo secco*, a lightly-accompanied RECITATIVE more spoken than sung.

OPÉRA COMIQUE, French light opera of the 18th century, with spoken dialogue rather than recitative linking musical numbers. After c1800 the term was extended to cover any opera using spoken dialogue.

OPERA GLASSES. See BINOCULARS.

OPERATION. See SURGERY.

OPERATIONS RESEARCH, improvement of the efficiency of commercial, military and governmental organizations by techniques of numerical analysis. Its aims are to increase the result/effort ratio by either decreasing the effort required or increasing the result (or output) without increase in effort. (See also HUMAN ENGINEERING; LINEAR PROGRAMMING.)

OPERETTA, light opera with elements of romance and satire, such as the works of Johann STRAUSS, Franz LEHAR, Jacques OFFENBACH and in England W. S. GILBERT and Sir Arthur SULLIVAN. Operetta was one of the ancestors of 20th-century MUSICAL COMEDY.

OPHIR, a place often mentioned in the Old Testament as a source of gold and other valuables, particularly for Solomon's temple. Suggested sites include modern Somaliland, Yemen, Zimbabwe, N Africa and W India.

OPHTHALMIA, INFLAMMATION of the EYE. This may be CONJUNCTIVITIS, as in **neonatal ophthalmia** (often gonococcal—see VENEREAL DISEASE) or uveitis (or penophthalmitis) as in **sympathetic ophthalmia**. In this, an inflammatory reaction in both eyes follows injury to one. Infection may need ANTIBIOTICS, while sympathetic ophthalmia may benefit from STEROIDS.

OPHTHALMOLOGY, the branch of MEDICINE and SURGERY concerned with diseases of VISION and the EYE. In infancy, congenital BLINDNESS and STRABISMUS, and in adults, glaucoma, uveitis, CATARACT, retinal detachment and vascular diseases are common, as are ocular manifestations of systemic diseases— hypertension and DIABETES. Disorders of eye movement, lids and TEAR production; color vision; infection, and injury are also seen. Surgery to the lens, CORNEA (including corneal grafting), eye muscles and lids may be used, and cryosurgery (freezing) or coagulation employed in retinal disease.

OPHTHALMOSCOPE, instrument for examining the RETINA and structures of the inner EYE. A powerful light and lens system, combined with the CORNEA and lens of the eye allows the retina and eye blood vessels to be seen at high magnification. It is a valuable aid to diagnosis in OPHTHALMOLOGY and internal MEDICINE.

OPINION POLL. See POLL, PUBLIC OPINION.

OPIUM, NARCOTIC extract from the immature fruits of the opium poppy, *Papaver somniferum*, which is native to Greece and Asia Minor. The milky juice is refined to a powder which has a sharp, bitter taste. Drugs, some drugs of abuse (see DRUG ADDICTION), obtained from opium include the narcotic ANALGESICS, HEROIN, MORPHINE and CODEIN. (Synthetic analogues of these include methadone and pethidine.) Older opium preparations, now rarely used, include LAUDANUM and PAREGORIC. The extraction of opium outside the pharmaceutical industry is strictly controlled in the West.

OPIUM WAR (1839–42), fought in China by the British, the first in a series aimed at opening ports and gaining tariff concessions. The pretext was the burning of 20 000 chests of opium by the Chinese. China had banned the opium trade in 1799, but with the aid of corrupt Chinese officials British merchants still made enormous profits from it. British troops occupied Hong Kong in 1841, and the fall of Chinkiang in 1842 threatened Peking itself. The Treaty of Nanking ceded Hong Kong to Britain and granted British merchants full rights of residence in the ports of Amoy, Canton, Foochow, Ningpo and Shanghai; Britain was to receive over $50 million war indemnity. The US gained trade facilities by the 1844 Treaty of Wanghai. Further hostilities, in which French joined British troops (1856), led to more concessions, notably in the Treaties of Tientsin (1858) to which Britain, France, Russia and the US were parties and which legalized the opium trade, and in 1860, when Kowloon was ceded to Britain and part of Manchuria to Russia.

OPORTO, or Pôrto, second-largest city of Portugal, on the Douro R. Its seaport, Leixões, ships the world-renowned port wine, cork, fruits and olive oil. Chief manufactures are textiles, metal and leather goods. Pop 310 437.

OPOSSUMS, primitive arboreal MARSUPIALS of the Americas. The name has also been applied to Australian forms but these are now usually distinguished as POSSUMS. Opossums are carnivorous and usually have a prehensile tail. The pouch is developed only in some species, but all have an uneven number of teats, as many as 17 in the Virginian opossum. (The teats of all Australian marsupials are paired.) In size, opossums vary from mouse-like to forms about the size of a domestic cat. Family: Didelphidae.

OPOSSUM SHRIMPS, small, transparent marine crustaceans, mostly less than 25mm (1in) long, members of the Mysidae. Closely resembling small crayfish, the females carry their young in a pouch, or marsupium, from which habit their name derives.

OPPENHEIMER, Julius Robert (1904–1967), US physicist whose influence as an educator is still felt today and who headed the MANHATTAN PROJECT, which developed the ATOMIC BOMB. His main aim was the peaceful use of nuclear power (he fought against the construction of the HYDROGEN BOMB but was overruled by Truman in 1949); but, because of his left-wing friendships, was unable to pursue his researches in this direction after being labeled a security risk (1954). He also worked out much of the theory of BLACK HOLES.

OPPORTUNITY, urban community in NE Wash., an E suburb of Spokane. Pop 16 604.

OPPOSITION, in astronomy, the situation in which the earth lies directly between another planet (or the moon) and the sun.

OPTICAL ACTIVITY, the property, possessed by certain substances, of rotating the plane of polarization of plane-POLARIZED LIGHT passing through them. This optical rotation is measured by POLARIMETRY. Optical activity is shown by asymmetric CRYSTALS which have two mirror-image forms—the rotation being to the left or right respectively—and by compounds with asymmetric molecules showing optical STEREOISOMERISM.

OPTICAL ILLUSION. See ILLUSION.

OPTICIAN, one who practices OPTOMETRY.

OPTICS, the science of light and vision. Physical optics deal with the nature of LIGHT (see also COLOR; DIFFRACTION; INTERFERENCE; POLARIZED LIGHT; SPECTROSCOPY). Geometrical optics consider the behavior of light in optical instruments (see ABERRATION, OPTICAL; CAMERA; DISPERSION; LENS, OPTICAL; MICROSCOPE; MIRROR; PRISM; REFLECTION; REFRACTION; SPECTRUM; TELESCOPE). Physiological optics are concerned with vision (see EYE).

OPTOMETRY, measurement of the acuity of VISION and the degree of lens correction required to restore "normal vision" in subjects with refractive errors (MYOPIA, HYPEROPIA, ASTIGMATISM). Its principal instrument is a chart of letters which subtend specific angles to the EYE at a given distance; temporary lenses being used to correct each eye. (See GLASSES.)

ORACLE, in ancient times, the answer by a god or goddess to a human questioner, or the shrine at which the answer was given, usually through a priest or priestess (also called oracles). There were oracles in Egypt and Rome, but the greatest were in Greece: at Delphi, where Apollo spoke through a priestess, the Pythia, and Zeus' oracle at Dodona. Answers, often to important political questions, were obtained direct, or derived from dreams, from such signs as the rustling of leaves in a sacred tree, and from divination by lot.

ORAN, or Ouahran, Algeria's second city, a Mediterranean port about 210mi SW of Algiers. It is a commercial center, naval base and port exporting cereals, wine, wool, fruit, vegetables and iron ore. Pop 325 481.

The Virginia opossum, one of the few remaining North American marsupials, shown here carrying its young. If attacked an opossum may pretend to be dead in order to discourage predators—hence the expression "playing possum."

ORANGE, seat of Vaucluse department of SE France, 14mi N of Avignon in an agricultural area. It is notable for its Roman remains. It was the capital of the principality of Orange (see ORANGE, HOUSE OF). Pop 24 562.

ORANGE, city 3mi N of Santa Ana, SW Cal. Citrus fruit is canned, and manufactures include electronic, rubber and copper goods. Pop 77 365.

ORANGE, residential town 5mi W of New Haven, Conn., with some light industry. Pop 13 524.

ORANGE, town in N.J., a NW suburb of Newark, producing adding machines, pharmaceuticals, clothing and hats. Pop 32 566.

ORANGE, city and seat of Orange Co., SE Tex. A port on the Sabine R waterway, it has oil and gas wells, shipbuilding and petrochemical plants. Pop 24 459.

ORANGE, citrus fruit obtained from a number of trees and shrubs of the genus *Citrus*. Oranges have been in cultivation since ancient times, but probably originated in tropical regions of Asia. The sweet or China orange (*Citrus sinensis*) and the mandarin orange (*C. reticulata*) are the main species in cultivation; their main uses being as dessert fruit and for making orange drinks. The Seville or sour orange (*C. aurantium*) is mainly used in the preparation of marmalades. Family: Rutaceae.

ORANGE, House of, an important dynasty in the Netherlands since the 16th century. The line has included WILLIAM III of England and, since 1815, the monarchs of the Netherlands, including the present Queen JULIANA.

ORANGEBURG, city, seat of Orangeburg Co., S.C., 35mi S of Columbia. It is the commercial and industrial center of a farming area. Pop 13 252.

ORANGE FREE STATE, province of South Africa, covering 49 866sq mi of inland plateau between the Orange and Vaal rivers. Agriculture is based on livestock, cereals and fruit; gold, diamonds and coal are mined. The capital is Bloemfontein. (See also BOER WAR; SOUTH AFRICA.)

ORANGEMEN, or Loyal Orange Institution, a Protestant (chiefly Ulster), society, which since the first (1795) Lodge has identified with the Protestant ascendancy in Ireland and, more recently, union with Britain. The name is from William of Orange (see also BOYNE, BATTLE OF; WILLIAM III).

ORANGE RIVER, the longest river in South Africa (1 300mi). It flows W from NW Lesotho, through South Africa and along the South-West African border to the Atlantic at Oranjemund.

ORANG-UTAN, *Pongo pygmaeus*, a large, red, anthropoid ape of Sumatra and Borneo. Animals of thick rain forests, they are truly arboreal apes—walking quadrupedally along branches, or bipedally, with the arms holding on above. Occasionally the orang brachiates for short distances. They can move along the ground, but rarely descend from the trees. Orangs are vegetarians, feeding mainly on leaves, buds and fruit.

ORATORIANS, Roman Catholic congregation founded c1575 in Rome by St. Philip NERI. Members, organized in autonomous congregations, are secular priests who take no vows. NEWMAN founded oratories in Birmingham (1848) and London (1849). A separate society was founded in 1611 in Paris by Pierre de Bérulle.

ORATORIO, a musical composition for vocal soloists, chorus and orchestra, usually with a religious subject. The form evolved c1600 from medieval sacred drama. Early oratorio composers include SCARLATTI, J. S. BACH and HANDEL, whose *Messiah* is probably the most famous oratorio. Among later oratorio composers are BEETHOVEN, MENDELSSOHN and ELGAR. (See also PASSION.)

ORBIT, the path followed by one celestial body revolving under the influence of gravity (see GRAVITATION) about another. In the SOLAR SYSTEM, the planets orbit the sun, and the moons the planets, in elliptical paths, although Triton's orbit of NEPTUNE is as far as can be determined perfectly circular. The point in the planetary, asteroidal or cometary orbit closest to the sun is called its *perihelion*; the farthest point is termed *aphelion*. In the case of a moon or artificial satellite orbiting a planet or other moon, the corresponding terms are *perigee* and *apogee*. (See also APSIDES, LINE OF; KEPLER'S LAWS.) Celestial objects of similar masses may orbit each other, particularly DOUBLE STARS.

Right: an orange branch with unripe fruit (a); an orange flower (b) and its parts, including a bud (c), pistil (d), stamen (e), cross-section of the ovary (f) and longitudinal section of ovary (g). *Above:* the adult sweet orange, primarily for eating; in the United States oranges are grown mainly in Florida and California.

ORBITAL, in chemistry, the mathematical wave function (see QUANTUM MECHANICS) that describes the motion of an ELECTRON around the nucleus of an ATOM or several nuclei in a molecule. The orbital represents the probability distribution of the electron in space; in effect, for each point, the likelihood of finding the electron there. Orbitals are defined and characterized by three quantum numbers, representing the energy level (and hence the size), the angular momentum (and hence the shape), and the orientation. An orbital can be occupied by one or two electrons (of opposite spin), according to FERMI-DIRAC STATISTICS. The precise energy of each orbital depends on the local electromagnetic field, and is found by SPECTROSCOPY. In the formation of a covalent BOND, molecular orbitals are formed by linear combination of the outer atomic orbitals. (See also AROMATIC COMPOUNDS; RESONANCE.)

ORCAGNA, Andrea (c1308–1368), painter, sculptor and architect of Florence, Italy, leading artist in the Byzantine Gothic style. His work includes the Strozzi chapel altarpiece at S. Maria Novella and the Or San Michele tabernacle, Florence.

ORCHARD GRASS, or **cocks foot**, *Dactylis glomerata*, grass indigenous to Europe and cultivated over much of North America. It provides excellent pasture and hay for grazing animals. Family: Gramineae.

ORCHESTRA, the name given to most instrumental groups of more than a few players. The modern orchestra dates from the birth of OPERA c1600. The first great operatic composer, MONTEVERDI, wrote for orchestra, and for some time opera and orchestral music were closely linked. As the VIOLIN family replaced VIOLS, composers like VIVALDI, J. S. BACH and HANDEL began to write purely orchestral music. The SYMPHONY was developed around the same time (1700) from the operatic overture. In the 18th century HAYDN organized the orchestra into four groups: strings, woodwind, brass and percussion—a basic pattern that has not altered. With the great 18th and 19th century composers, the orchestra came to dominate the musical scene. New, and more numerous instruments were introduced, permanent orchestras established, and the art of conducting developed. The 20th century has seen a movement to return to smaller ensembles.

ORCHIDS, plants of the very large family Orchidaceae (15 000–30 000 species) which produce colorful and elaborate flowers. Some species are native to cold and temperate regions, but most occur in tropical, damp climates. Some grow as EPIPHYTES on forest trees. Orchid flowers are specially adapted to insect POLLINATION, some requiring a particular species of insect. Orchids produce minute seeds that are devoid of stored food and thus require the aid of fungi to supply the nourishment needed for germination (see MYCORRHIZA). Orchids are of little economic importance except as curious ornamental plants; cultivation has developed into an extensive hobby throughout the world. As house plants they should be grown in sunny windows at average house temperatures; they do well in fluorescent-light gardens. The soil should be drenched and then not watered again until almost dry. Propagation is by planting divisions.

ORCZY, Baroness Emmuska (1865–1947), English novelist famous for *The Scarlet Pimpernel* (1905), the first of a series of adventures with a background of the French Revolution.

ORDER. See TAXONOMY.

ORDER IN COUNCIL, in Great Britain, an order issued by the sovereign through the PRIVY COUNCIL. A series of such orders issued in 1807, in an attempt to blockade France, greatly annoyed the neutral US and was a major cause of the WAR OF 1812.

ORDERS, in architecture. See CLASSICAL ORDERS.

ORDINAL NUMBER, one that describes the order of an element in a SET. For example, in the phrase "my second and third candies," 2 and 3 are ordinal numbers. (See also CARDINAL NUMBER.)

ORDINANCE OF 1787. See NORTHWEST ORDINANCE.

ORDINATE, the perpendicular distance from the x-axis of a point in a system of CARTESIAN COORDINATES (see also ANALYTIC GEOMETRY); the y-coordinate of the point. (See also ABSCISSA.)

ORDINATION, in the Christian Church, the ceremonial appointment to one of the orders of MINISTRY. The ordination of BISHOPS is usually called consecration. Regarded by the Roman Catholic

Orchid with the conspicuous helmet- or pouch-shaped labellum characteristic of the genus *Paphiopedilum*.

Church as a SACRAMENT, ordination is performed in episcopal churches by a bishop (see also APOSTOLIC SUCCESSION), and in presbyterian churches by the presbytery. The rite includes prayer and the laying on of hands, traditionally in a eucharistic context.

ORDNANCE, a general term for weapons of war. It includes bombs, guns, missiles, ammunition, vehicles, manufacturing and servicing facilities, and stores. Weapons mounted on ships, planes and tanks are usually called armament.

ORDOVICIAN, the second period of the PALEOZOIC, which lasted from about 500 to 440 million years ago and immediately followed the CAMBRIAN. (See GEOLOGY.)

ORDZHONIKIDZE, industrial city of the Russian SFSR, USSR, capital of the North Ossetian ASSR, in the N Caucasus Mts. Pop 236 000.

ORE, aggregate of minerals and rocks from which it is commercially worthwhile to extract minerals (usually metals). An ore has three parts: the country rock in which the deposit is found; the gangue, the unwanted ROCKS and minerals of the deposit; and the desired MINERAL itself. Ore deposits may be, e.g., VEINS; infillings of breccia (consolidated TALUS); sedimentary formations, as of the EVAPORITES; certain DIKES; or, especially with the SULFIDES, hydrothermal replacement deposits (where hot or superheated water has dissolved existing rocks and deposited in their place minerals held in SOLUTION). MINING techniques depend greatly on the form and position of the deposit (see PLACER MINING; STRIP MINING).

OREADS. See NYMPHS.

OREGANO. See MARJORAM.

OREGON, a state of the Pacific Northwest, known to its millions of visitors for its lofty mountains, deep gorges and fine coastline. Oregon is divided in two by the Cascade Range of mountains which stretch north-south across the entire state. Between the Coastal Range and the Cascades lies Willamette Valley, which contains the state's most fertile land and most of its population and industries. This area has a mild and moist marine climate. Most of the land E of the Cascades is part of the Columbia Plateau, occupying two-thirds of Oregon. This area is drier and experiences a greater range of temperatures. Half of Oregon is forested and it represents one-fifth of US timber resources.

People. Two-thirds of Oregon's population live in or around Portland, Eugene and Salem in the Willamette Valley. Oregon's original constitution of 1859 is still in effect, with the amendments of 1902 providing for the initiative and referendum. These two measures, together with direct primaries and procedures for the recall of elected officials, became known as the "Oregon system" and were adopted by many states before WWI.

Economy. The most important manufactures are wood-processing and food-processing (especially fish canning). Other leading industries are machinery, transportation equipment, and metal processing, in which cheap hydroelectric power is used. Wheat, grown in E Oregon, is the most important crop. Livestock and turkey farming are also of importance. Oregon is the leading US producer of nickel.

History. The first American to visit the area (1792) was Captain Robert GRAY. The LEWIS AND CLARK EXPEDITION of 1805–06 to the mouth of the Columbia R reinforced American claims to the region. The state of Oregon was the 33rd to be admitted to the Union (1859). Although pioneers settled in Oregon from the 1840s (see OREGON TRAIL), development was slow until the coming of the railroad in the 1880s. The first two decades of this century saw the rapid development of the lumbering industry, and the post-WWII period has seen new developments in the metallurgical and electrochemical industries. Today the emphasis is also on the conservation of Oregon's natural resources.

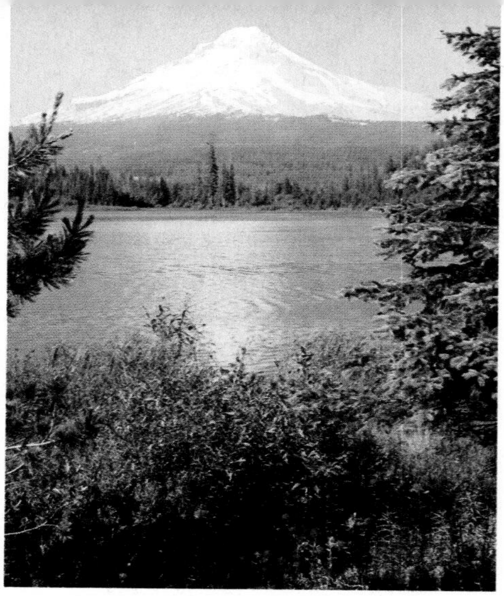

The highest point in Oregon, the towering pinnacle of Mount Hood (11 245ft). It forms the spectacular centerpiece of an extensive wooded region.

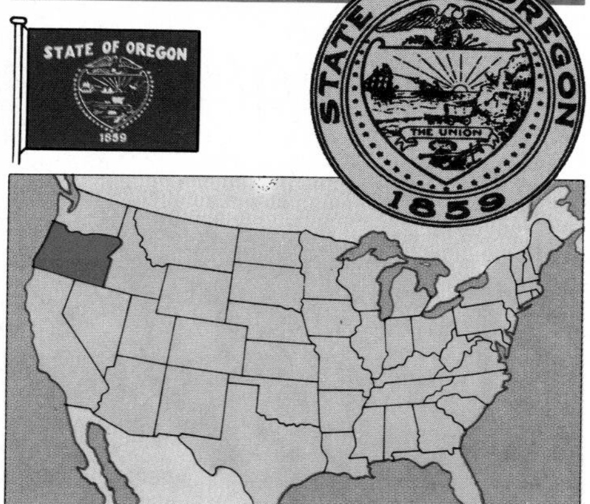

Name of state: Oregon
Capital: Salem
Statehood: Feb. 14, 1859 (33rd state)
Familiar name: Beaver State
Area: 96 981sq mi
Population: 2 091 385
Elevation: Highest—11 245ft, Mount Hood. Lowest—sea level, Pacific Ocean
Motto: The Union
State flower: Oregon grape
State bird: Western meadowlark
State tree: Douglas fir
State song: "Oregon, My Oregon"

OREGON, city in NW Ohio, E of Toledo, on Lake Erie. It includes a port and oil and chemical industries. Pop 16 563.

OREGON CAVES NATIONAL MONUMENT, in Josephine Co., SW Oregon, an area of 480 acres containing fine limestone caves and forests of Jeffrey pines.

OREGON CITY, city in NW Oregon, seat of Clackamas Co. Now an agricultural center, it was capital of Oregon Territory 1849–52. Pop 9 176.

OREGON GRAPE, *Mahonia aquifolium*, a North American evergreen shrub, found in the Pacific Northwest. It grows from 1m to 3m (3–10ft) high and produces bright yellow flowers and small blue berries. It is the state flower of Oregon. Family: Berberidaceae.

OREGON TRAIL, famous pioneer wagon route of 19th-century America between Independence, Mo., on the Missouri, and the Columbia R region of the Pacific Northwest. The 2000mi trail was most popular in the 1840s, before the beginning of the Californian GOLD RUSH. In that decade at least 10 000 pioneers made the arduous trek from NE Kansas, along the R Platte in Nebraska, to Fort Laramie, Wyoming. From there they crossed the Rockies at South Pass and passed through Snake River country to Fort Vancouver. The journey was recounted in Francis Parkman's classic, *The Oregon Trail* (1849).

OREL, capital of Orel oblast, Russian SFSR, USSR. An industrial city and agricultural trade center, Orel produces machinery and textiles. Pop 232 000.

ORELLANA, Francisco de (d. c1546), Spanish soldier and explorer. He left Gonzalo Pizarro's South American expedition (c1540) at the Napo R to explore the course of the Amazon R, reaching the Atlantic Ocean in 1541. The great river's name comes from his tales of Indian AMAZONS.

OREM, city in Utah, a N suburb of Provo, near Utah Lake. It processes truck farm produce and has a steel mill. Pop 25 729.

ORENBURG, capital of Orenburg oblast, Russian SFSR, USSR, on the Ural R. Engineering and clothing are the main industries. Pop 345 000.

ORESTES, in Greek mythology, son of AGAMEMNON and CLYTEMNESTRA. After Clytemnestra had killed Agamemnon, Orestes avenged his father by killing his mother and her lover, with the aid of his sister ELECTRA. Pursued by the FURIES, he stole the image of Artemis from Tauris to atone for his murders, helped this time by his sister IPHIGENIA.

ØRESUND, strait between Sjaelland Island, Denmark, and S Sweden. It is the deepest channel connecting the Kattegat with the Baltic Sea.

ORFF, Carl (1895–), German composer and music teacher. His works are marked by short melodic motifs and strong rhythms from a large and varied percussion section. The "scenic cantata" *Carmina Burana* (1937) is his most popular piece.

ORGAN, a musical instrument in which air is blown into pipes of different shape and size to produce a range of notes. Organ pipes are of two kinds: flue pipes which work like a flute or recorder, and reed pipes which operate on the same principle as a clarinet or oboe. Although organs go back to ancient times, the main developments in organ building took place between the 14th and the 18th centuries. Composers like SWEELINCK and BUXTEHUDE paved the way for J. S. BACH, the greatest of all composers for the organ. Bach and HANDEL wrote for the baroque organ, a relatively small instrument. In the 19th century many great organs were built, precursors of the huge electric-powered organs built in the 1920s and 1930s in cinemas and theaters. The modern Hammond organ produces its sound electronically. Small electronic organs are now frequently used by pop groups. (See also HARMONIUM.)

ORGAN, in biology, a functionally adapted part of an organism. Organs, such as the vermiform APPENDIX in man, which persist in a species although no longer of any use to it, are termed *vestigial organs*.

ORGANIC CHEMISTRY, major branch of CHEMISTRY comprising the study of CARBON compounds containing hydrogen (simple carbon compounds such as carbon dioxide being usually deemed inorganic). This apparently specialized field is in fact wide and varied, because of carbon's almost unique ability to form linked chains of atoms to any length and complexity; far more organic compounds are known than inorganic. Organic compounds form the basic stuff of living tissue (see also BIOCHEMISTRY), and until the mid-19th century, when organic syntheses were achieved, a "vital force" was thought necessary to make them. The 19th-century development of quantitative ANALYSIS by J. LIEBIG and J. B. A. DUMAS, and of structural theory by S. CANNIZZARO and F. A. KEKULÉ, laid the basis for modern organic chemistry. Organic compounds are classified as ALIPHATIC, ALICYCLIC, AROMATIC and HETEROCYCLIC COMPOUNDS, according to the structure of the skeleton of the molecule, and are further subdivided in terms of the FUNCTIONAL GROUPS present.

ORGANIZATION FOR ECONOMIC CO-OPERATION AND DEVELOPMENT (OECD), a consultative organization set up in 1961 to co-ordinate economic policies and encourage economic growth and world trade. The founder-states were 18 W European countries, the US and Canada. Japan, Finland and Australia are also members.

ORGANIZATION OF AFRICAN UNITY (OAU), an association of the independent African states (excluding South Africa and Rhodesia) which aims to promote unity and eradicate colonialism in Africa. Founded in 1963, the OAU has a permanent secretariat in Addis Ababa, Ethiopia and has had great influence at the United Nations.

ORGANIZATION OF AMERICAN STATES (OAS), an association of 24 republics of the Americas which aims to settle disputes peacefully, to create a collective security system, and to coordinate the work of other intra-American bodies. The OAS was founded in Bogotá, Colombia, in 1948 and has a permanent secretariat, the Pan American Union. Its activities have included support for the US blockade of Cuba in 1962, and mediation between Britain and Guatemala in 1972.

ORGANIZATION OF THE PETROLEUM EXPORTING COUNTRIES (OPEC), established 1960, coordinates the petroleum policies of Algeria, Ecuador, Gabon, Indonesia, Iran, Iraq, Kuwait, Libya, Nigeria, Qatar, Saudi Arabia, the United Arab Emirates and Venezuela. OPEC countries continue to deal jointly with oil companies despite the fall in world demand following their quadrupling of oil prices after the 1973 ARAB-ISRAELI WAR. Its headquarters are in Vienna.

ORGAN OF CORTI, the apparatus in the cochlea of the inner EAR, which, in hearing, converts pressure waves in the cochlear fluid into auditory nerve impulses.

ORGANOMETALLIC COMPOUNDS, class of compounds containing bonds from carbon atoms to metal (or metalloid) atoms, and thus at the crossroads of INORGANIC and ORGANIC CHEMISTRY. In the last 30 years the subject has expanded enormously, with the development of many medical, industrial and synthetic uses. There are three main types of organometallic compounds: (1) the alkyl derivatives of Group IA and IIA metals of the PERIODIC TABLE (including GRIGNARD REAGENTS), which have ionic BONDS, and are powerful BASES and reducing agents (see OXIDATION AND REDUCTION); (2) derivatives of other Main Group metals, which are volatile, covalently-bonded compounds; and (3) TRANSITION ELEMENT derivatives (including SANDWICH COMPOUNDS) with special *d*-ORBITAL bonding. Organometallic compounds are prepared by reacting a metal with an ALKYL HALIDE or a reactive HYDROCARBON, or by substitution.

ORGAN PIPE CACTUS, *Pachycereus marginatus*, a large cactus up to 6m (20ft) high, which grows in parts of the arid southwestern US and Mexico. Family: Cactaceae.

ORGAN PIPE CACTUS NATIONAL MONUMENT, an area of over 330 000 acres, located in S Arizona. Designated in 1937, it is famed for its magnificent cacti, particularly organ pipe cacti.

ORIGAMI, the Japanese art of paper folding. In Japan it is divided into two categories—the making of *no shi*, decorations attached to gifts, and the making of plant, animal and human figures. Origami has become popular in the West since WWII.

ORIGEN (c185–c254 AD), one of the foremost radical theologians of the early Christian Church. Born in Alexandria, Egypt, Origen tried to reconcile Greek philosophy with Christian theology in such works as his *De Principiis* and *Contra Celsum*.

ORIGINAL SIN, in Christian theology, the state of sinfulness in which all mankind is born, and which is the root cause of all actual SINS. According to St. PAUL, when Adam disobeyed God (the Fall), the whole human race fell in solidarity with him and inherited his sin and guilt, losing supernatural GRACE and communion with God, and our FREE WILL was made spiritually inoperative. In Catholic theology, original sin is washed away in BAPTISM.

ORIGIN OF SPECIES, short title of book (published 1859) by Charles DARWIN in which he set forth his theory of EVOLUTION by NATURAL SELECTION.

ORILLIA, town in SE Ontario, Canada. It is a resort on Lake Couchiching and manufactures mining machinery and other goods. Pop 24 040.

ORINOCO RIVER, great river of Venezuela, N South America, about 1 700mi long. It rises in the Parima highlands of SE Venezuela and eventually flows into the Atlantic Ocean through a 7 000sq mi delta. It is mostly navigable.

ORIOLES, a family, Oriolidae, of arboreal songbirds. In several species the males have bold yellow

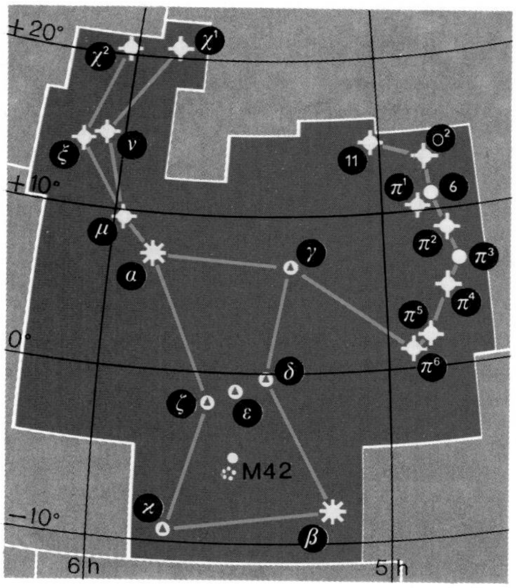

The constellation of Orion, the Hunter, in the Southern sky, visible in the North during winter. Orion's "sword" contains a gaseous nebula with some hot stars in it thought to be only a few thousand years old.

and black patterns. True orioles occur only in the Old World, but the name is sometimes given to some troupials, genus *Icterus*, in the Americas. Orioles are birds of the forest edge or forest, feeding in the tops of the trees on insects and fruit.

ORION (the Hunter), a large constellation on the celestial equator visible during winter in N skies, containing RIGEL, BETELGEUSE and the Orion NEBULA.

ORION, the great hunter of Greek mythology. In one legend, ARTEMIS was tricked by APOLLO into killing her lover Orion with an arrow. Grief-striken, Artemis placed Orion in the heavens as a constellation.

ORISKANY, Battle of, fought on Aug. 6, 1777, in central N.Y. during the REVOLUTIONARY WAR. The British and Indians ambushed the Americans, and there were severe losses on both sides.

ORIZABA, or Citlaltépetl, volcanic peak in central Veracruz state, Mexico. At 18 700ft, it is the highest point in Mexico.

ORIZABA, city in Veracruz state, E Mexico. It is an agricultural market town and tourist resort, with light textile industries. Pop 92 728.

ORKHAN (d. c1362), Ottoman sultan of Turkey from 1326. He conquered the W part of Asia Minor (1329–38), and captured Gallipoli in 1354, thus gaining a foothold for the Ottomans in Europe.

ORKNEY ISLANDS, group of about 70 islands north of Scotland, of which they are part. Their total area is 376sq mi but fewer than half are inhabited. The climate is mild and the soil fertile. Farming is the chief activity (grains, sheep, cattle, poultry), with some fishing.

ORLANDO, city in central Fla., seat of Orange Co. It is a fruit trading center, with aerospace and electronics industries. Pop 99 006.

ORLANDO, Vittorio Emanuele (1860–1952), Italian statesman, prime minister 1917–19. He led the Italian delegation at the VERSAILLES Peace Conference of 1919–20. Orlando retired from politics with the advent of fascism, but returned after the fall of Mussolini.

ORLÉANS, family name of two branches of the French royal line. The House of Valois-Orléans was founded by Louis, Duke of Orléans (1372–1407), whose grandson ascended the throne (1498) as LOUIS XII. The House of Bourbon-Orléans was founded by Philippe, Duke of Orléans (1640–1701), a brother of king LOUIS XIV. His son, Philippe (1674–1723), was regent of France 1715–23, and his great-grandson became king LOUIS XVI. LOUIS PHILIPPE was the sole member of the House to become king.

ORLÉANS, historic city of N central France on the Loire R, now an industrial city and the commercial center of a rich farming area. Pop 100 134.

ORLON, SYNTHETIC FIBER made by copolymerization of acrylonitrile with VINYL compounds.

ORMANDY, Eugene (1899–), Hungarian-born US conductor, a famous interpreter of Romantic works. Trained as a violinist, he became permanent conductor of the Philadelphia Orchestra in 1938.

ORMOLU, golden-colored BRASS used for furniture mountings, chiefly 18th century. It was cast, chased and often gilded by brushing with gold AMALGAM and firing.

ORMOND BEACH, residential city, E Fla., a resort on the Atlantic coast. Pop 14 063.

ORNITHOLOY, the scientific study of BIRDS. The observation of birds in their natural environment has a long history and is now so popular as to be the most widespread of zoological hobbies.

ORNITHOPTER, flying machine whose wings flap like those of a bird. Models date back as far as 400 BC, and LEONARDO DA VINCI made many designs and models. Though working models have been made, and toy ornithopters mass-produced, no larger, load-carrying design has yet been successful.

OROGENIES, periods of mountain building (orogenesis) in a particular area. They occur usually in geosynclinal regions (see GEOSYNCLINE). **Epeirogeny**, elevation or depression of large land masses, plays comparatively little part in MOUNTAIN building. (See PLATE TECTONICS.)

OROMOCTO, town in S central New Brunswick, Canada, near Gagetown, Canada's largest military camp. Pop 11 518.

ORONTES (Arabic name Nahr el 'Asi), a river rising in central Lebanon and flowing 250mi N through Syria and then W to enter the Mediterranean near Samandag in S Turkey.

OROZCO, José Clemente (1883–1949), major Mexican painter, who exploited the fresco technique in his large-scale murals, which express strong social convictions. His most famous works include the fresco *Prometheus* (1930) and a mural *Epic Culture in the New World* (1932–34).

ORPHEUS, in Greek mythology, famous musician of Thrace. Son of the Muse CALLIOPE, he could tame wild beasts with his lyre playing. After the death of his wife Eurydice, Orpheus sought her in HADES. He was allowed to lead her back to earth providing he did not

The Threats (1936), a mural by José Clemente Orozco at Jalisco, Mexico. Unlike his contemporary Diego Rivera his style owes little to the European mainstream, being a very personal development including the use of strong forms and vigorous colors.

look back, but he could not resist the temptation, and Eurydice vanished forever. He is said to have been killed by the women followers of DIONYSUS in Thrace. He was regarded as the founder of the Orphic MYSTERY cult.

ORPIMENT, soft, lemon-yellow SULFIDE mineral, arsenic(III) sulfide (As_2S_3), used as a pigment. It crystallizes in the monoclinic system, but is usually massive. It forms by deposition from GEYSERS or by alteration of REALGAR.

ORR, John Boyd Orr, 1st Baron. See BOYD-ORR, JOHN.

ORRERY, a mechanical model to show the motions of planets and/or their satellites, named for the 4th Earl of Orrery, patron of the probable inventor (c1710), George Graham (1673–1751). Time scales may be quite accurate, but size and distance proportions are of course wildly inaccurate.

ORRISROOT, the dried rhizomes of the IRISES, *Iris germanica*, *I. florentina* and *I. pallida*. Mainly produced in the Mediterranean region, orrisroot is used in perfumes, toothpastes and medicines. Family: Iridaceae.

ORSAINVILLE, town in S Quebec, Canada, 6m NW of Quebec. Pop 12 561.

ORSINI, powerful medieval family of Rome which provided soldiers, statesmen and three popes: CELESTINE III, NICHOLAS III, BENEDICT XIII. The family was devoted to the Guelph cause, and was known for its long feud with the Ghibelline Colonna family (see GUELPHS AND GHIBELLINES).

ORSK, city in the S Ural Mountains, USSR. It is a railroad center, with oil refining and heavy metallurgical industries. Pop 225 000.

ORTEGA Y GASSET, José (1883–1955), Spanish philosopher, whose best-known work, *The Revolt of the Masses* (1929), attributes Western decadence to the revolt of "mass man" against an intellectual elite. His philosophy attempts to reconcile reason with individual lives and needs. He founded the magazine *Revista de Occidente* (1923) and set up the Institute of Humanities in Madrid (1948).

ORTELIUS, Abraham (1527–1598), Flemish geographer who produced the *Theatrum Orbis Terrarum* (1570), the first modern atlas of the world.

ORTHOCLASE, common mineral in igneous rocks, consisting of potassium aluminum silicate ($KAlSi_3O_8$); vitreous crystals of various colors. It is one of the three end-members (pure compounds) of the FELDSPAR group. See also MICROLINE.

ORTHODONTICS. See DENTISTRY.

ORTHODOX CHURCHES, the family of Christian churches that developed out of the EASTERN CHURCH, remaining orthodox when the NESTORIANS and MONOPHYSITE CHURCHES separated. They finally broke with Rome in the GREAT SCHISM of 1054. Each church is independent, but all are in full communion and acknowledge the honorary primacy of the ecumenical patriarch of Constantinople; some are patriarchates, others are governed by SYNODS. The ancient patriarchates of Constantinople, Alexandria, Antioch and Jerusalem are dwarfed by the more recent churches of Russia, Serbia, Romania, Bulgaria, Georgia, Greece, Cyprus and others. There are now more than 123 million Orthodox worldwide, including 3 million in the US. Orthodoxy accepts the first seven ECUMENICAL COUNCILS, but often prefers not to define dogma very closely; it is characterized by MONASTICISM, veneration of ICONS and the importance of the laity. It rejects papal claims, the IMMACULATE CONCEPTION and PURGATORY, and does not require clerical celibacy.

Churches of the Orthodox Communion

The Four Ancient Patriarchates
Constantinople
Alexandria
Antioch
Jerusalem

The Five Patriarchates of more recent origin
Russia*
Serbia
Romania
Bulgaria
Georgia

Autonomous Churches governed by Synods
Cyprus
Greece
Czechoslovakia
Poland
Albania

Churches not fully independent though self-governing in most respects
Finland
China
Japan
The monastery of Sinai

*Expatriate Russians have three additional autonomous Church administrations.

ORTHOGENESIS, evolutionary change that appears to be directed over a long period of time. Orthogenesis is no longer regarded as an evolutionary mechanism but as the result of consistent selection for the same character in an animal.

ORTHOGRAPHIC PROJECTION. See DESCRIPTIVE GEOMETRY.

ORTHOPEDICS, speciality within SURGERY, dealing with BONE and soft-tissue disease, damage and deformity. Its name derives from 17th-century treatments designed to produce "straight children." Until the advent of anesthetics, ASEPSIS and X-RAYS, its methods were restricted to AMPUTATION and manipulation for dislocation, etc. Treatment of congenital deformity; FRACTURES and TUMORS of bone; OSTEOMYELITIS; ARTHRITIS, and JOINT dislocation are common in modern orthopedics. Methods range from the use of splints, PHYSIOTHERAPY and manipulation, to surgical correction of deformity, fixing of fractures and refashioning or replacement of joints. Suture or transposition of TENDONS, MUSCLES or nerves are performed.

ORTHOPTERA, an insect order which contains the GRASSHOPPERS, CRICKETS and KATYDIDS. All have simple chewing mouthparts, simple antennae and thick protective forewings. Most species jump strongly with powerful hindlegs, and can produce sounds by rasping the hind legs against the folded wings.

ORTOLAN, a name originally reserved for a small BUNTING of Europe and W Asia, *Emberiza hortulana*. This bird was formerly regarded as a gastronomic delicacy, and the name ortolan has been extended to cover all edible small birds.

ORVIETO, city in Umbria, central Italy. It is a tourist center and has a famous cathedral. Pop 23 158.

ORWELL, George (1903–1950), pen name of the English novelist Eric Arthur Blair, famous principally for *Animal Farm* (1945), a savage satire on communist revolution, and *Nineteen Eighty-Four* (1949), depicting a dehumanizing totalitarian society. Orwell was also a critic and essayist. Other works include the semi-autobiographical *The Road to Wigan Pier* (1937), and *Homage to Catalonia* (1938), an account of his experiences in the SPANISH CIVIL WAR.

ORYX, medium-sized ANTELOPE of the Afro-Asian desert, including the GEMSBOK. They are light-colored animals with black nose patch and eye stripes, and long, straight horns. Oryx live in small herds and are true desert animals, with many physiological adaptations to aridity. Indeed their relative independence of water has led to experiments to test the feasibility of ranching oryx as domestic stock in arid regions of Africa.

OSAGE INDIANS, Plains Indian tribe of the Siouan language group who lived in what is now W Mo. and Ark. in the late 17th century. In 1872 they were moved to a reservation in Okla., and became one of the richest communities in the world when oil was discovered on their reservation in the 19th century.

OSAGE ORANGE, *Maclura pomifera*, a spiny tree native to the south-central US. It produces inedible orange-like fruit. The trees are often trained to form hedges and the wood is used for making archery bows. Family: Moraceae.

OSAKA, second largest city in Japan, a major port on the S coast of Honshu. It is the center of the populous industrial area called the Kinki, and is one of Japan's most important commercial and industrial centers. Pop 2 980 409.

OSASCO, municipality in São Paulo state, SE Brazil, 9m NW of São Paulo. It has meat packing and some manufacturing industries. Pop 283 203.

OSAWATOMIE, city in E Kan., the site of a battle (1856) in which John BROWN and his abolitionist followers were routed by a party of Missourians. Pop 4 294.

OSBORNE, John (1929–), British dramatist whose *Look Back in Anger* (1956) made him the first ANGRY YOUNG MAN of the 1950s and established a new and vigorous realism in the theater. Later plays include *The Entertainer* (1957), *Luther* (1961) and *Inadmissible Evidence* (1964).

OSBORNE, Thomas Mott (1859–1926), controversial US prison reformer. He voluntarily served a term in prison, and as a prison governor introduced internal self-government and Mutual Welfare Leagues for the inmates. He became warden of New York's Sing Sing Prison (1914–16), and commander of the Portsmouth Naval Prison, N.H. (1917–20).

OSCAR, name of two kings of Sweden and Norway. **Oscar I** (1799–1859), king from 1854, was a liberal advocate of freedom of the press and penal reform, at a time of rapid social and economic progress. His younger son **Oscar II** (1829–1907), a great lover of literature and music, was king of Sweden from 1872, but was obliged to abdicate the Norwegian throne in 1905.

OSCARS. See ACADEMY AWARDS.

OSCEOLA (c1804–1838), Indian leader in the Second Seminole War against the US (1835–42), who used guerrilla tactics to resist a US plan to transport the Seminole Indians from Fla. to Okla. He was taken prisoner in 1837 and died in prison.

OSCILLATING UNIVERSE. See COSMOLOGY.

OSCILLATOR, a device converting direct to alternating current (see ELECTRICITY), used, for example, in generating RADIO waves. Most types are based on an electronic AMPLIFIER, a small portion of the output being returned via a FEEDBACK circuit to the input, so as to make the oscillation self-sustaining. The feedback signal must have the same PHASE as the input: by varying the components of the feedback circuit, the frequency for which this occurs can be varied, so that the oscillator is easily "tuned." "Crystal" oscillators incorporate a piezoelectric crystal (see PIEZOELECTRICITY) in the tuning circuit for stability; in "heterodyne" oscillators, the output is the beat frequency between two higher frequencies.

OSCILLOSCOPE, a device using a CATHODE RAY TUBE to produce line GRAPHS of rapidly varying electrical signals. Since nearly every physical effect can be converted into an electrical signal, the oscilloscope is very widely used. Typically, the signal controls the vertical deflection of the beam while the horizontal deflection increases steadily, producing a graph of the signal as a function of time. For periodic (repeating) signals, synchronization of the horizontal scan with the signal is achieved by allowing the attainment by the signal of some preset value to "trigger" a new scan after one is finished. Most models allow two signals to be displayed as functions of each other; dual-beam instruments can display two as a function of time. Oscilloscopes usually operate from DC to high frequencies, and will display signals as low as a few millivolts.

OSHAWA, industrial city on Lake Ontario, Canada. It is a center of the automobile and other manufacturing industries. Pop 91 587.

OSHKOSH, city in E Wis., seat of Winnebago Co. It is a summer resort with some manufacturing industry. Pop 53 221.

OSHOGBO, city in W Nigeria, about 50mi NE of Ibadan. It is a trading center, with dyeing, weaving and cotton industries. Pop 253 000.

OSIER, the popular name for species of WILLOW that are used for basket making and wickerwork. The common osier (*Salix viminalis*) grows in wet, alluvial soil in many parts of Europe. Family: Salicaceae.

OSIRIS, ancient Egyptian god, brother and husband of ISIS, and father of HORUS. He was killed by his evil brother SET, but restored to life by Isis. His cult was important in dynastic Egypt, and later became popular in the Roman Empire. A benefactor of mankind, Osiris was ruler of the underworld, and also a life-giving power, symbolizing the creative forces of nature.

OSKALOOSA, town in SE Ia., seat of Mahaska Co. An old coalmining town, it is now principally an agricultural center. Pop 11 224.

OSLER, Sir William (1849–1919), Canadian-born physician and educator best known for his work on platelets (see BLOOD) and for the informality of his educational techniques.

OSLO, capital, largest city and chief seaport of Norway. Foujded c1050, it was rebuilt after the great fire of 1624. Between 1625 and 1925 it was known as Christiania or Kristiania. Today it is Norway's chief commercial, industrial and cultural center. Oslo has many fine museums, castles and parks. Pop 481 548.

OSMAN, name of three sultans of Turkey. **Osman I** (1259–1326) is regarded as the founder of the Ottoman Empire. Succeeding his father as ruler of Sögüt, he asserted his independence of the overlord SELJUKS and conquered much of NW Asia Minor during a long campaign against the Byzantines. **Osman II** (1604–1622) ruled from 1618 until his assassination in 1622. **Osman III** (1699–1757) ruled 1754–57.

OSMIUM (Os), silvery-gray hard metal in the PLATINUM GROUP. It is slowly oxidized in air. AW 190.2, mp 3045°C, bp c5000°C, sg 22.48 (20°C). **Osmium (VIII) oxide** (OsO_4), a toxic oxidizing agent, is used to stain tissues for microscope slides.

OSMOSIS, the diffusion of a solvent through a SEMIPERMEABLE MEMBRANE that separates two solutions of different concentration, the movement being from the more dilute to the more concentrated solution, owing to the thermodynamic tendency to equalize the concentrations. The liquid flow may be opposed by applying pressure to the more concentrated solution: the pressure required to reduce the flow to zero from a pure solvent to a given solution is known as the *osmotic pressure of the solution.* Osmosis was studied by Thomas GRAHAM, who coined the term (1858); in 1886 VAN'T HOFF showed that, for dilute solutions (obeying Henry's Law), the osmotic pressure varies with temperature and concentration as if the solute were a GAS occupying the volume of the solution. This enables MOLECULAR WEIGHTS to be calculated from osmotic pressure measurements, and degrees of ionic DISSOCIATION to be estimated. Osmosis is important in DIALYSIS and in water transport in living tissue.

OSNABRÜCK, historic city in Lower Saxony, West Germany. Once a linen center and member of the HANSEATIC LEAGUE, it now has steelworks and engineering, chemical and textile industries. Pop 140 905.

OSPREY, *Pandion haliaetus*, a large fish-eating bird of prey, found throughout the world, except in South America. Also known as the **Fish hawk**, the osprey occupies both marine and freshwater areas, cruising above the water and plunging to take the fish in its talons. The future of the osprey is in some doubt in both Europe and North America, where it has suffered from increased use of persistent pesticides.

OSS. See OFFICE OF STRATEGIC SERVICES.

OSSIAN, legendary Gaelic bard who wrote of Finn Mac Cumhaill's heroic acts in S Ireland in about the 3rd century AD. James MACPHERSON's forgeries popularized the figure of Ossian in ROMANTICISM.

OSSICLES. See EAR.

OSSIETZKY, Carl von (1889–1938), German pacifist journalist, imprisoned by Hitler in a concentration camp (1933) for his articles on German rearmament. He was awarded the Nobel Peace Prize for 1935.

OSSIFICATION. See BONE.

OSSINING, village in SE N.Y. on the Hudson R, site of Sing Sing jail. Its chief manufacture is medical instruments. Pop 21 659.

OSTADE, Adriaen van (1610–1685), Dutch GENRE painter influenced by REMBRANDT and Jan STEEN. His scenes of bawdy peasant life include *Men and Women in an Inn* (1660) and *The Village Fiddler* (1673).

OSTEICHTHYES, the class of all bony FISHES. All have bony skeletons and gill arches, and paired fins. The class, also known as **Pisces**, is extremely diverse and contains all the higher fishes of both marine and fresh waters, indeed, all fishes but the jawless fishes, AGNATHA, and Cartilaginous fishes, SHARKS, RAYS and CHIMAERAS.

OSTEND. See OOSTENDE.

OSTEND MANIFESTO, agreement drawn up in Oostende (Ostend), Belgium in 1854 by three proslavery US diplomats, James BUCHANAN, John Y. MASON and Pierre SOULÉ. The manifesto implied that if Spain refused to sell Cuba the US would forcibly seize the island. The diplomats, who probably hoped to make Cuba a Union slave state, were denounced by all the political parties.

OSTEOLOGY, the study of the structure, function and diseases of BONE.

OSTEOMYELITIS, BACTERIAL infection of BONE, usually caused by STAPHYLOCOCCUS, STREPTOCOCCUS and SALMONELLA carried to the bone by the BLOOD, or gaining access through open FRACTURES. It commonly affects children, causing FEVER and local pain. If untreated or partially treated, it may become chronic with bone destruction and a discharging SINUS. ANTIBIOTICS and surgical drainage are frequently necessary.

OSTEOPATHY, system of treatment based on theory that DISEASE arises from the mechanical and structural disorder of the body skeleton. Prevention and treatment are practiced by manipulation, often of the spine. While it may have a role in treatment of chronic musculo-skeletal pain, its methods may be hazardous, especially to the SPINAL CORD. Furthermore, serious disease may be overlooked. Osteopathy is best regarded as an adjunct to, rather than a replacement for, orthodox medicine.

OSTIA, ancient town in Italy, a seaport for Rome at the mouth of the Tiber R. Founded in the 7th century BC, its greatest prosperity was in the 2nd century AD.

OSTRACISM, in ancient Greek times temporary banishment from Athens, decreed by popular vote. A man could be ostracized for up to ten years. The term comes from *ostrakon* (Greek: potsherd) on which a voter would write the name of the person whom he wished to be banished.

OSTRACODERMS, fossil members of the AGNATHA, or jawless fishes, named for the bony plates in the skin, particularly on the head. It was from this group that the jawed fishes arose, through modification of the first gill arches into true jaws.

OSTRACODS, or seed shrimps, a subclass of the CRUSTACEA, whose members are characterized by the possession of a bivalved shell enclosing the body. Occurring both in fresh water and in the sea, they have modified the crustacean form to an essentially molluscan way of life, using their limbs to draw a feeding current of water between the valves of the shell.

OSTRAVA, city in N central Czechoslovakia. At the center of a mining and industrial area, it has enormous chemical and steel industries. Pop 278 737.

OSTRICH, *Struthio camelus*, the largest living bird, at one time found throughout Africa and SW Asia, but now common in the wild only in E Africa. They are flightless birds, well adapted to a terrestrial life. They have long powerful legs, with two toes on each foot, an adaptation for running over dry grassland parallel to the reduction of digits in the horse's hoof (see HORSE). Ostriches are polygamous, living in groups of a single male and his harem.

OSTROGOTHS (East Goths), branch of the GOTHS, a Germanic people who originally occupied the lands to the N of the Black Sea. The accession of their king THEODORIC THE GREAT in 471 heralded an alliance with Zeno, Emperor of the East Roman Empire, who ordered him to invade Italy in 488. Theodoric reduced it to Ostrogothic rule in 493, ruling from Ravenna. The Byzantine general BELISARIUS destroyed Ostrogothic rule in the 530s; a subsequent Ostrogothic revolt was swiftly crushed in 552.

OSTROVSKY, Alexander Nikolayevich (1823–1886), Russian dramatist whose plays, usually about merchants and minor officials, are marked by powerful characterization and strong drama. His masterpiece is *The Storm* (1860), a domestic tragedy.

OSTWALD, Friedrich Wilhelm (1853–1932), Latvian-born German physical chemist regarded as a father of physical chemistry, and awarded the 1909 Nobel Prize for Chemistry for his work on CATALYSIS. He also developed the OSTWALD PROCESS.

OSTWALD PROCESS, process for manufacturing NITRIC ACID, developed by OSTWALD (1902). AMMONIA is oxidized by air to nitric oxide, at 900°C and 1–8atm using a platinum/rhodium catalyst. The nitric oxide is further oxidized to nitrogen dioxide, which is dissolved in water to give 60% nitric acid.

OSWALD, Saint (d. 641), king of NORTHUMBRIA, 633–41. He introduced Celtic missionaries from LINDISFARNE into his kingdom. Killed in battle by King Penda of Mercia, he was considered a Christian martyr.

OSWALD, Lee Harvey, the alleged assassin of President John F. KENNEDY in Dallas, Texas on Nov. 22, 1963, and of a local police officer. A former marine, he had lived in the USSR 1959–62. He was himself shot dead by Dallas nightclub owner Jack RUBY while being transferred from the city to the county jail on Nov. 24. The WARREN REPORT declared Oswald the sole assassin.

OSWEGO, industrial city in N.Y., seat of Oswego Co., now the largest US port on Lake Ontario, and an aluminum, paper and textile center. Pop 23 844.

OSWEGO, city and lake resort in NW Ore., on the Willamette R, 8mi S of Portland. Pop 14 573.

OSWEGO TEA, or bee balm, *Monardia didyma*, fragrant North American plant, widely cultivated as an ornamental. The leaves were once used as a tea substitute. Family: Labiatae.

ÓSWIECIM. See AUSCHWITZ.

OSWY (d. 670), king of Northumbria, ruling Bernicia 641–70, Deira 654–70 and Mercia 654–57. A leader of the Christian conversion of England, he called the Synod of WHITBY.

OTARU, city in Japan in SW Hokkaido, an import ant fishing and coal-exporting port. Pop 191 850.

OTHMAN. See OSMAN.

OTHO, Marcus Salvius (32–69 AD), Roman emperor, Jan–April 69 AD. He seized power after the murder of the emperor Galba and his heir Pisco, but was defeated by his rival, Vitellius, at Bedriacum and subsequently committed suicide.

OTIS, Elisha Graves (1811–1861), US inventor of the safety ELEVATOR (1852), first installed for passenger use in 1856, New York City.

OTIS, Harrison Gray (1765–1848), Mass. political leader and lawyer. He was a US Representative 1797–1801, and in 1814 was a prominent leader of the HARTFORD CONVENTION. He was a senator 1817–22.

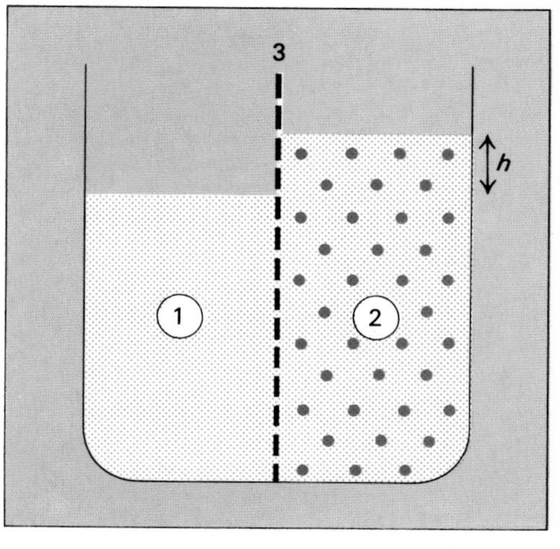

Schematic diagram of osmosis. Pure solvent (1) is separated from a solution (2) by a semipermeable membrane (3), through which the solvent molecules—but not the solute molecules—can freely pass. There is a tendency for solvent to diffuse into the solution and dilute it. Equilibrium is reached when this tendency (quantified as the *osmotic pressure*) is balanced by the hydrostatic pressure of the extra height *h* of the solution.

The Rideau Canal seen flowing through downtown Ottawa near where it joins the Ottawa R. The roofs and clocktower of Canada's parliament buildings can be seen in the background to the left.

OTIS, James (1725–1783), American colonial patriot and lawyer. He argued in 1761 that writs allowing customs officials to search colonial ships were against the rights of colonists as Englishmen, and that acts of Parliament authorizing the writs were void. He wrote many papers and pamphlets on the colonists' grievances. In 1769 he became insane after being struck on the head.

OTO INDIANS, North American tribe of the SIOUX INDIANS. They and the Missouri Indians left the WINNEBAGO INDIANS and moved SW from the Great Lakes. The Oto settled first in S Minnesota and then in Oklahoma c1882. They now number about 1000.

OTOSCLEROSIS. See DEAFNESS.

OTOSCOPE, instrument for examining the outer EAR and eardrum. It has a light, a lens and a conical earpiece.

OTRANTO, Strait of, sea passage between SE Italy and W Albania connecting the Adriatic Sea to the Ionian Sea. It is about 47mi wide.

OTTAWA, capital city of Canada, situated at the junction of Ottawa and Rideau Rivers, in SE Ontario. Ottawa is principally a government center; a major tourist attraction is the group of Parliament buildings, built in Victorian Gothic style. The city was built as a logging community, Bytown, in 1827, during the construction of the Rideau canal which divides the city. It became Ottawa (an anglicization of the local Outawouais Indians) in 1854, and capital in 1867. Pop 302 341.

OTTAWA, agricultural city in N Ill., seat of La Salle Co., where the first LINCOLN-DOUGLAS DEBATE took place. It is a major glass center. Pop 18 716.

OTTAWA, city in E Kan., seat of Franklin Co. It has varied light manufacturing and produces dairy products. Pop 11 036.

OTTAWA INDIANS, large North American tribe of the Algonquian family originally inhabiting, with the OJIBWA and POTAWATAMI INDIANS, the region N of the Great Lakes. The Ottawa later moved to Manitoulin Island. They were active traders and negotiated with the French.

OTTAWA RIVER, principal tributary of the St. Lawrence R. About 700mi long, it rises in SW Quebec province, flows W through a number of lakes as far as the Quebec-Ontario border, then SE past Ottawa to join the St. Lawrence near Montreal. Extensive hydroelectric power is developed in the lower reaches.

OTTERS, aquatic or semiaquatic carnivores of the weasel family, subfamily Lutrinae. There are five freshwater genera and one marine genus. The body is lithe and muscular, built for vigorous swimming, and covered with thick fur. The paws are generally webbed. The nostrils and eyes may be shut when swimming underwater. The prey consists of small fish, eels, crayfish and frogs. The Sea otter's diet is more specialized: sea otters have powerful rounded molars adapted for crushing sea urchins, abalones and mussels. A tool-using animal, it floats on its back, breaking open the urchin or mussel-shell on a stone anvil balanced on its chest. Unlike most other wild animals, otters remain playful as adults.

OTTERBEIN, Philip William (1726–1813), German-American missionary, influential in the German communities of Pa. and Md. In 1789 with Martin Boehm and six lay preachers he founded the United Brethren in Christ, which became the EVANGELICAL UNITED BRETHREN.

OTTERHOUND, large, powerful sporting dog closely resembling a bloodhound and originally bred in England to help in otter-hunting. An otterhound may attain a height of 25in, weighs 65–75lb and has a water-repellant coat.

OTTO, name of four Holy Roman Emperors: **Otto I the Great** (912–973), founder and first emperor of the Holy Roman Empire from 962. King of Saxony from 936, he invaded Italy and declared himself King of the Lombards (951). He subdued the Poles and Bohemians and routed the MAGYARS of Hungary (955). Otto was crowned Emperor in Rome (962) for helping Pope JOHN XII against Berengar II. **Otto II** (955–983), succeeded his father Otto I as emperor 973–83. He crushed the rebellion of Henry, Duke of Bavaria, defeated the Danes (974), but failed to extend his empire in Italy and was badly defeated by the Saracens in S Italy (982). **Otto III** (980–1002), succeeded his father Otto II as emperor 996–1002, after a regency. He lived in Rome and planned to make it the capital of a vast theocratic empire. **Otto IV** (c1174–1218), emperor 1198–1215. He was excommunicated by Pope INNOCENT II for attempting to master parts of Italy in 1210, and later deposed.

OTTO I (1815–1867), first king of Greece, 1832–62, appointed by a conference of European powers. He proved a weak and unconstitutional king and was deposed in 1862 by a military revolt.

OTTO, Nikolaus August (1832–1891), German engineer who built the first four-stroke INTERNAL-COMBUSTION ENGINE (1876), which rapidly replaced the STEAM ENGINE in many applications and facilitated the development of the AUTOMOBILE.

OTTOMAN EMPIRE, vast empire of the Ottoman Turks which at its height, during the reign of Sultan SULEIMAN I stretched from the far shore of the Black Sea and the Persian Gulf in the E to Budapest in the N and Algiers in the W. The Ottoman Turks, led by OSMAN I, entered Asia Minor in the late 1200s and, expanding rapidly, made Bursa their capital in 1326. They crossed to the Balkan Peninsula (1345) and in 1453 CONSTANTINOPLE fell to MOHAMMED II. The empire continued to expand in the 16th century under Selim I, the Terrible, 1512–20 and reached its zenith under Suleiman I. However, Suleiman I failed to capture Vienna (1529) and was driven back at Malta (1565). Directly after his death, the Ottoman fleet was annihilated at the naval battle of LEPANTO (1571). During the 1700s and 1800s the decaying empire fought against Russia and Greece won its independence. The reformist Young Turk movement led the empire into WWI on the German side, with disastrous results. Finally, the nationalists, led by ATATURK, deposed and exiled the last Sultan, Mohammed VI, and proclaimed the Turkish republic in 1922.

OTTUMWA, commercial and industrial city in SE Ia., seat of Wapello Co., located in a livestock-farming and coal region. Pop 29 610.

OTWAY, Thomas (1652–1685), English dramatist and poet. His two most outstanding tragedies, *The Orphan* (1680) and *Venice Preserved* (1682), are written in blank verse; they describe human passion in very moving yet simple terms.

OUACHITA MOUNTAINS, mountain range from Central Ark. to SE Okla., about 200mi in length. The highest peak is Magazine Mt (about 2 800ft).

OUACHITA RIVER, river rising in W Ark. It flows E and then S into N La., where it is joined by the Tensas R to form the Black R. Over half its length of 605mi is navigable. At Blakeley Mountain Dam there is a large hydroelectric plant.

OUAGADOUGOU, capital city of Upper Volta. Its economy rests on locally-grown peanuts, and on handicrafts. Pop 115 500.

OUAHRAN. See ORAN.

OUANANICHE, *Salmo ouananiche*, a small landlocked SALMON of SE Canada. Unlike other Atlantic salmon, it is nonmigratory.

OUIDA, pen name of Maria Louise de la Ramée (1839–1908), melodramatic English novelist. Among her works are *Under Two Flags* (1867), *A Dog of Flanders* (1872), and *Moths* (1880).

OUIJA BOARD, (from French *oui*: yes, and German *ja*: yes), device used in occultism consisting of a board on which letters of the alphabet are written. A smaller board moves over it under slight pressure and spells out a message.

OUNCE (oz), unit of WEIGHT in the apothecaries', avoirdupois and troy systems:
1oz ap = 1oz troy = 1.0971oz avoirdupois = 31.103g. (See APOTHECARIES' WEIGHT; TROY WEIGHT; WEIGHTS AND MEASURES.)

OUNCE, or **Snow Leopard,** *Uncia uncia*, a big cat of the Altai, Hindu Kush and Himalayas, which lives in coniferous scrub above 1 800m (6 000ft). About 600mm (2ft) at the shoulder, it has a long, thick fur of pale gray, marked with darker rosettes. It is nocturnal, feeding on wild sheep and mountain goats.

OUTBOARD MOTOR. See MOTORBOATING.

OUTCAULT, Richard Felton (1863–1928), US cartoonist who created the comic urchin "Yellow Kid" for the *New York World* 1896–97. His other famous strip was "Buster Brown," which was published in the *New York Herald* from 1902.

Portrait of the Ottoman emperor Mohammed II, who captured Constantinople in 1453. It was completed in 1480 by the Venetian painter Gentile Bellini and now hangs in the National Gallery in London.

OUTER BANKS, chain of sandy barrier islands off the N.C. coast. A few fishermen and farmers, "bankers," live on the banks, and the wildlife attracts sportsmen and vacationers.

OUTER MONGOLIA. See MONGOLIAN PEOPLE'S REPUBLIC.

OUTREMONT, residential city in S Quebec, Canada. It lies in the central part of Montreal Island and forms part of Greater Montreal. Pop 28402.

OVAMBO, Negroid BANTU people of northern SW Africa. Their tribes depend mostly on agriculture, living in villages of round, conical-roofed huts; some are nomadic cattle-rearers.

OVARY, the female reproductive organ. In plants it contains the ovules (see FLOWER); in humans, the FOLLICLES in which the eggs (*ova*) develop (see ESTROGEN; FERTILIZATION; GAMETE; PROGESTERONE; REPRODUCTION).

OVENBIRDS, a family, Furnariidae, of South American perching birds. Usually drab brown and typically insectivorous, many, though not all, of the 220 species build conspicuous domed nests resembling old-fashioned stone ovens, for which the group is named.

OVERBECK, Johann Friedrich (1789–1869), German romantic painter, a leader of the NAZARENES in Rome. A devout religious spirit pervades all his paintings, mainly of New Testament themes.

OVERLAND, city in E Mo., a residential suburb of St. Louis. Pop 24949.

OVERLAND MAIL COMPANY, US stage coach company. It was established under government contract in 1858 by John BUTTERFIELD; it provided a 25-day passenger and mail service between St. Louis and San Francisco. The company was acquired by Wells, Fargo and Company in 1866, and ceased operation with the completion of the transcontinental railroad.

OVERLAND PARK, city in NE Kan., a suburb of Kansas City. Pop 76034.

OVERLAND TRAIL, name of westward migration routes in the US, in particular for the S alternative route to the OREGON TRAIL, and for the route to the Cal. goldfields. This latter trail went from Fort Bridger to Sutter's Fort, Cal., and duplicated in part the Mormon Trail.

OVERLEA, town in N Md., a residential suburb to the NE of Baltimore. Pop 13086.

OVERTURE, orchestral piece played at the beginning of most operas, oratorios or plays with incidental music. Operatic overtures developed in the 17th century; GLUCK was one of the first composers to link the tunes of the overture with those of the subsequent opera. Self-contained works for the concert hall are also called overtures.

OVERWEIGHT. See DIETING; OBESITY.

OVID (Publius Ovidius Naso; 43 BC–18 AD), Latin poet. Popular in his time, he was exiled by the emperor Augustus to the Black Sea in 8 AD and died there; his *Sorrows* and *Letters from Pontus* are pleas for his return. He was a master of erotic poetry, as in his *Amores* and *Art of Love*, but his *Metamorphoses*, a collection of myths linked by their common theme of change, is generally considered to be his finest work.

OVIEDO, large industrial city in NW Spain. Founded in c760 AD, it became capital of ASTURIAS in 810 and has many ancient buildings. It is situated in an agricultural region with extensive iron and coal mining. Pop 154117.

OVIPAROUS ANIMALS, animals that reproduce by laying EGGS.

OVULATION. See MENSTRUATION.

OVULE. See FLOWER.

OVUM. See EGG.

OWATONNA, city in S Minn., seat of Steele Co. Agricultural machinery is manufactured here. Pop 15341.

OWEN, two industrialists and social reformers. **Robert Owen** (1771–1858), was a socialist and pioneer of the cooperative movement. He introduced better conditions in his cotton mills in Scotland and was active in the trade union movement in Britain. In the US Owen set up short-lived "villages of cooperation," such as that at NEW HARMONY, Ind. **Robert Dale Owen** (1801–1877), his son, campaigned in the US for birth control, women's property rights, state public schools and slave emancipation. He was a member of Congress from Ind. 1843–47.

Owls are found all over the world, in a wide variety of species. Among these are the Common Barn owl, *Tyto alba* (1); the Long-eared owl, *Asio otus* (2) and the Snowy owl, *Nyctea scandiaca* (3).

OWEN, Wilfrid (1893–1918), British poet who wrote movingly of the savagery and human sacrifice in WWI; he was deeply influenced by Siegfried SASSOON. Owen was killed in action a week before the end of WWI. Nine of his poems form the text of BRITTEN'S *War Requiem* (1962).

OWEN FALLS, waterfall, 100ft in height, in the Victoria Nile, Uganda, now submerged by the Owen Falls Dam, opened in 1954 to supply power to Uganda and Kenya.

OWEN GLENDOWER. See GLENDOWER, OWEN.

OWENS, Jesse (1913–), famous US Negro athlete. In 1935–36 he broke three world records at college athletics meets. By winning the 100 and 200 meters dash, the 400 meters relay and the broad jump at the 1936 Berlin Olympics, he shattered Hitler's attempt to demonstrate "Aryan superiority."

OWENSBORO, city in W Ky., seat of Daviess Co., on the Ohio R, at the center of a tobacco, farming, oil and industrial region. Pop 50329.

OWEN SOUND, port in SE Ontario, Canada, in an agricultural area. Its industries include printing. Pop 18469.

OWEN STANLEY MOUNTAINS, range in Papua New Guinea, 300mi in length. The highest peak is Mt Victoria (13363ft).

OWLS, soft-plumaged, nocturnal BIRDS OF PREY. Owls have large eyes, directed forward, and all have pronounced facial disks. Some species develop ear tufts and most have extremely sensitive hearing. Many species hunt primarily on auditory cues. The eyes are also extremely powerful: some 35–100 times more sensitive than our own. All owls are soft-feathered and their flight is completely silent. There are two main families, the Tytonidae, or Barn owls, with heart-shaped facial disks, and the Strigidae, which contain the orders Buboninae, to which the majority of species belong, and the Striginae.

OWOSSO, city in S central Mich. 26mi W of Flint, in a truck and livestock farm area. Manufactures include flour and electric motors. Pop 17179.

OX, term zoologically applied to many members of the BOVIDAE; also, in common usage, a castrated bull used for draft purposes or for its meat.

OXALIC ACID $(COOH)_2$, white crystalline solid, a toxic, dibasic CARBOXYLIC ACID occurring in many plants. It is made by heating sodium formate or by fusing sawdust with sodium hydroxide. Oxalic acid is a mild reducing agent used as a standard for VOLUMETRIC ANALYSIS, in the leather and dye industries, to remove ink and rust stains, and to dissolve radiator scale. MW 90.0, mp 189°C.

OXALIS, a large genus of mostly herbaceous plants, but including some shrubs. South Africa and South America are the main centers of distribution. The genus includes the common wood sorrel (*Oxalis acetosella*), but the genus is best known for its cultivated forms such as *O. siliquosa* (four-leaf clover), *O. hedysaroides rubra* (fire fern) and *O. rubra* which are popular house plants. They should be grown in a sunny window, avoiding more than two hours direct sun each day. Ideally the temperature should be kept at about 21°C (70°F) during the day, dropping to about 17°C (63°F) at night. The soil should be kept evenly moist, tuberous species being allowed to dry out for about two months yearly. Propagation is by plant divisions and taking shoot tip cuttings. Family: Oxalidaceae. (See also SHAMROCK; SORREL; WOOD SORREL.)

OXBOW LAKE, C-shaped lake formed when a river meanders almost in a full circle, the water cuts across the narrow neck, and deposits of SILT at the entrances to the original meander eventually cut it off from the main body of the river. (See also RIVERS AND LAKES.)

OXENSTIERNA, Axel Gustafsson, Count (1583–1654), Swedish statesman, chancellor 1612–54 and military adviser to King GUSTAVUS II during the THIRTY YEARS' WAR. On Gustavus's death in 1632, he became regent and virtual ruler of Sweden during Queen CHRISTINA'S childhood, introducing social and administrative reforms.

OXFORD, historic cathedral city in S central England, seat of OXFORD UNIVERSITY. In the CIVIL WAR it was the Royalist headquarters. Now an automobile manufacturing center, its beauty is largely retained by college architecture. Pop 108564.

OXFORD, residential and manufacturing town in central Mass., founded by French Protestants in 1687. Pop 10345.

OXFORD, city in N Miss., seat of Lafayette Co. There are sawmills and light manufacturing in the area. It is the seat of Mississippi U. Pop 13846.

OXFORD, residential village in SW Ohio. Located in an agricultural region, it is the seat of Miami U. Pop 15868.

OXFORD GROUP. See MORAL REARMAMENT.

OXFORD MOVEMENT, 19th-century religious movement aiming to revitalize the Church of England by reintroducing traditional Catholic practices and doctrines. It started in 1833 in Oxford; its leaders, John Keble, J. H. NEWMAN and, later, Edward PUSEY, wrote a series of *Tracts for the Times* to publish their opinions. They became known as the "Tractarians." Despite violent controversy over the Romeward tendency of some—culminating in Newman's

Of Oxford's many and varied colleges, Christ Church is among the largest and most splendid. Its central quadrangle is pictured here, with the statue of Mercury in the foreground, and behind it, over the college's main entrance, the famous tower built by Christopher Wren known as "Tom Tower."

conversion to Roman Catholicism (1845)—and over ritualism (from 1850), the movement has had great influence in the Anglican Church.

OXFORD UNIVERSITY, English university in Oxford comprising nearly 50 affiliated but autonomous colleges and halls, a great center of learning since its foundation in the 12th century. The oldest mens' college is University (1249) and the oldest womens' college Lady Margaret Hall (1879). The major university library is the famous BODLEIAN.

OXIDATION AND REDUCTION, or **redox reactions,** large class of chemical reactions, including many familiar processes such as COMBUSTION, CORROSION and RESPIRATION. Oxidation was originally defined simply as the combination of an element or compound with oxygen, or the removal of hydrogen from a compound; and reduction as combination with hydrogen or removal of oxygen. In the modern theory this has been generalized: oxidation is defined as loss of electrons, and reduction as gain of electrons. The two always go together: there is an oxidizing agent which is reduced, and a reducing agent which is oxidized. Thus, in the reaction

$$Fe^{3+} + I^- \rightarrow Fe^{2+} + \tfrac{1}{2}I_2$$

the iron (III) ion gains an electron and is reduced to iron (II), and the iodide ion loses an electron and is oxidized to iodine. The strength of a redox reagent, expressing its tendency to react, is measured by the electrode potential of the half-reaction (see ELECTROCHEMISTRY), and so redox reagents may be ranked in an extended ELECTROCHEMICAL SERIES. In a covalent compound or complex ion, each atom is assigned an *oxidation number* (O.N.), which is the charge it would have if all the BONDS were ionic—the electrons in a covalent bond between two atoms are assigned to the atom with the higher ELECTRONEGATIVITY. Thus the sulfur atom in sulfur dioxide has an O.N. of +4, and each of the two oxygen atoms has an O.N. of −2. When sulfur is oxidized by oxygen, $S + O_2 \rightarrow SO_2$, its O.N. increases from 0 (for elements, by definition) to +4, corresponding to a virtual loss of electrons. (See also INDICATOR.)

OXIDES, binary compounds of OXYGEN with the other elements (see also PEROXIDES). All the elements form oxides except helium, neon, argon and krypton. Metal oxides are typically ionic crystalline solids (containing the O^{2-} ion), and are generally BASES, though the less electropositive metals form amphoteric oxides with acidic and basic properties (e.g., ALUMINUM oxide). Nonmetal oxides are covalent and typically volatile, though a few are macromolecular refractory solids (e.g., SILICON dioxide); most are acidic (see ACIDS), some are neutral (e.g., CARBON monoxide), and WATER is amphoteric. Oxides may be prepared by direct synthesis, or by heating hydroxides, nitrates or carbonates. Many oxide minerals are known; simple oxides are binary metal oxides, complex oxides contain several cations, and SPINELS are intermediate between the two. Some metal oxides (e.g., TITANIUM (II) oxide) are nonstoichiometric (see COMPOSITION, CHEMICAL).

OXIMES, derivatives of ALDEHYDES or KETONES (termed aldoximes and ketoximes respectively) formed by condensation with hydroxylamine (NH_2OH), and containing the group C=N—OH. Being easily isolated and with characteristic melting points, they are used for identification. Ketoximes undergo the BECKMANN rearrangement.

OXNARD, industrial city in SW Cal., situated in an agricultural region on the Pacific coast. Pop 71 225.

OXPECKERS, two aberrant species of STARLINGS adapted for feeding on the hides of large grazing animals. They are found only in Africa, where they live and feed entirely on the backs of buffaloes, rhinos, giraffe, zebra and other UNGULATES. They live in small groups, scrambling over their "host," and feeding on blood-gorged ticks and flies on the animal's body.

OXUS. See AMU DARYA.

OXYACETYLENE. See ACETYLENE; WELDING.

OXY-ACIDS, those ACIDS that contain an acidic hydroxyl (see HYDROXIDES) group, i.e., whose acidic hydrogen is bound to oxygen. They include CARBOXYLIC ACIDS and PHENOLS, but are typically (e.g., sulfuric acid) the hydration products of acidic (nonmetal) OXIDES. Acids, such as hydrochloric acid, whose acidic hydrogen is bound to an element other than oxygen, are termed *hydracids*.

OXYGEN (O), gaseous nonmetal in Group VIA of the PERIODIC TABLE, comprising 21% by volume of the ATMOSPHERE and about 50% by weight of the earth's crust. It was first prepared by SCHEELE and PRIESTLEY, and named *oxygine* by LAVOISIER. Gaseous oxygen is colorless, odorless and tasteless; liquid oxygen is pale blue. Oxygen has two allotropes (see ALLOTROPY): OZONE (O_3), which is metastable; and normal oxygen (O_2), which shows PARAMAGNETISM because its diatomic molecule has two electrons with unpaired spins. Oxygen is prepared in the laboratory by heating mercuric oxide or potassium chlorate (with manganese dioxide catalyst). It is produced industrially by fractional distillation of liquid air. Oxygen is very reactive, yielding OXIDES with almost all other elements, and in some cases PEROXIDES. Almost all life depends on chemical reactions with oxygen to produce energy. Animals receive oxygen from the air, as do fish from the water (see RESPIRATION): it is circulated through the body in the blood stream. The amount of oxygen in the air, however, remains constant because of PHOTOSYNTHESIS in plants and the decomposition by the sun's ultraviolet rays of water vapor in the upper atmosphere.

Oxygen is used in vast quantities in metallurgy: smelting and refining, especially of iron and steel. Oxygen and ACETYLENE are used in oxyacetylene torches for cutting and WELDING metals. Liquid oxygen is used in rocket fuels. Oxygen has many medical applications (see OXYGEN TENT; ANESTHETICS) and is used in mixtures breathed by divers and high-altitude fliers. It is also widely used in chemical synthesis. AW 16.0, mp −218°C, bp—183°C.

OXYGEN TENT, enclosed space, often made of plastic, in which a patient may be nursed in an atmosphere enriched with OXYGEN. It is mainly used for small children with acute respiratory DISEASES, or in adults when the use of a face mask is impractical.

OXYHEMOGLOBIN. See HEMOGLOBIN.

OXYTOCIN, HORMONE secreted by the posterior PITUITARY GLAND (see also HYPOTHALAMUS). It causes WOMB contraction and is used in OBSTETRICS. It is also concerned with milk secretion by the BREAST.

OYSTERS, bivalve MOLLUSKS of shallow coastal waters. The edible oysters, as distinct from the Pearl oysters (see PEARL), belong to the family Ostreidae. While other bivalves are able to move by means of a muscular "foot," oysters have lost this foot and the animal lives cemented to the left valve of the shell to some hard substrate. Like all bivalves, oysters feed by removing suspended organic particles from a feeding current of water drawn into the shell. Food particles are trapped on highly filamentous gill plates. Oysters are extensively fished and cultivated all over the world.

A cluster of cultured pearls formed in an artificially stimulated oyster, on a Japanese oyster bed.

OYSTERCATCHERS, four species of wading birds of the sea shore. Some forms are completely black; most have a pied black and white plumage. All have stout, bright orange bills and orange legs. Oystercatchers are social birds which are adapted to feeding on marine shellfish and worms. Many are specialist feeders, with complex behaviors enabling them to feed on bivalve mollusks, particularly MUSSELS.

OYSTER PLANT, or **salsify,** *Tragopogon porrifolius*, a hardy biennial plant native to S Europe. It is cultivated as a vegetable for its fleshy tap root that has a flavor similar to oysters. Family: Compositae.

OZALID PROCESS, also known as the diazo or whiteprint process, a copying method in which paper coated with DIAZONIUM COMPOUNDS is exposed to ULTRAVIOLET LIGHT through a transparent original. Only the diazo in the shadows cast by the original survives to be developed with ammonia vapor to give a positive print.

OZARK, city in SE Ala., seat of Dale Co. It is a center for textile industries, and is set in an agricultural and farming region. Pop 13 555.

OZARK PLATEAU, mountainous tableland in the S central US, covering about 50 000sq mi from SW Mo. across NW Ark. into E Okla. Farming and lead and zinc mining are the chief economic activities; the forest scenery attracts tourism.

OZARKS, Lake of the, artificial reservoir lake in central Mo., created by the Bagnell dam on the Osage R. It is one of the world's largest artificial lakes, with an area of 93sq mi.

OZAWA, Seiji (1935–), Japanese conductor, best known for his fiery interpretations of Romantic and modern French composers. He is musical director of the San Francisco and Boston symphony orchestras, and of the Berkshire Music Festival.

OZONE (O_3), triatomic allotrope of OXYGEN (see ALLOTROPY); blue gas with a pungent odor. It is a very powerful oxdizing agent, and yields ozonides with OLEFINS. It decomposes rapidly above 100°C. The upper ATMOSPHERE contains a layer of ozone, formed when ULTRAVIOLET RADIATION acts on oxygen; this layer protects the earth from the sun's ultraviolet rays. Ozone is made by subjecting oxygen to a high-voltage electric discharge. It is used for killing germs, bleaching, removing unpleasant odors from food, sterilizing water and in the production of azelaic acid. mp −193°C, bp—112°C.

P-Q

P, the 16th letter of the English alphabet. It is descended from the Semitic *Pe*, the word for mouth. It then became the Greek *pi*, and was incorporated into Latin, and hence into English.

PABST, Georg Wilhelm (1885–1967), distinguished German film director noted for his imaginative treatment of realism in such films as *The Joyless Street* (1925), *Crisis* (1928), and *West Front 1918* (1931).

PACA, *Cuniculus paca*, a rodent of tropical America related to agoutis and acushis, but larger, up to 600mm (2ft) in length. Pacas are vegetarians. The skull is unique in that the cheekbones are enlarged and honey-combed, perhaps acting as resonance chambers.

PACARANA, *Dinomys branicki*, a South American rodent superficially resembling the PACA. Docile and slow-moving, it differs in appearance in the possession of a distinct tail, some 200mm (8in) long.

PACEMAKER. See PROSTHETICS.

PACIFIC, War of the. See WAR OF THE PACIFIC.

PACIFICA, residential city in W Cal. On the Pacific coast 12mi S of San Francisco, it is the site of a missile base. Pop 36 020.

PACIFIC GROVE, residential and resort city in W Cal., at the S end of Monterey Bay, famous for the migrations of MONARCH BUTTERFLIES. Pop 13 505.

PACIFIC ISLANDS. See OCEANIA.

PACIFIC ISLANDS, Trust Territory of the, US trust territory comprising some islands of MICRONESIA, the CAROLINE (with Palau), MARIANA (except Guam) and MARSHALL ISLANDS. There are 2 141 islands and atolls scattered over three million sq mi, but only 96 are inhabited. The population is Micronesian and the economy rests on agriculture, fishing and the export of copra. The formerly German islands were mandated to Japan in 1922 and after US occupation in WWII to the US. In 1970 the islanders rejected a proposal of self-government. Capital: Saipan. Pop 102 250.

PACIFIC OCEAN, world's largest and deepest ocean. Named by the 16th century navigator MAGELLAN, it extends from the Arctic to the Antarctic Ocean and from the coasts of the Americas to those of Asia. Its area of 70 million sq mi is one third of the earth's total surface. The equator divides the ocean into the North Pacific and the South Pacific. The average depth of the Pacific is about 14 000ft and the deepest point is 36 198ft in the Challenger Deep, Mariana Trench, SW of Guam. Plateaus, ridges, trenches (some over 6mi deep), sea mountains and GUYOTS make for many variations in depth. Japan, the Philippines, New Zealand and the thousands of OCEANIA islands lie on the connected series of ridges running from the Bering Straits to South China Sea, and the SE. Despite its name the ocean is not a calm area. In the tropical and subtropical zones over 130 cyclones occur per year. Many bring much-needed rain, but the winds of at least 150mph, the torrential rain and tempestuous seas of the HURRICANES in the NE, E and S, and the 400mph tidal wave, the TSUNAMI, are highly destructive. The first European to sight the Pacific was BALBOA in 1513 and the first to cross it was Magellan, 1520–21. It was explored by DRAKE, TASMAN, BOUGAINVILLE, BERING, Captain COOK and VANCOUVER. The ocean was the site of the WAR OF THE PACIFIC in WWII.

PACIFIC SCANDAL, corruption charges against the Canadian Premier John MACDONALD in 1872–73. In 1872 he awarded the contract to build the Canadian Pacific Railway to Sir Hugh ALLAN, who had financed his 1872 election campaign. Macdonald consequently resigned and the contract was cancelled.

PACIFISM, belief that violence is never justified, and hence that peaceful means should always be employed to settle disputes. A pacifist may not only refuse to use force himself, but also to abet its use, as by refusing to help produce weapons of war. Pacifists who refuse to serve in the armed forces are called CONSCIENTIOUS OBJECTORS. Supporters of nuclear DISARMAMENT or opponents of a specific war are not necessarily pacifist. Among the most successful pacifist statesmen was Mahatma GANDHI. (See also NEUTRALITY.)

PACK RATS, a genus, *Neotoma*, of rat-like animals found mainly in the western US. They have the habit of collecting bright objects with which to decorate their nests. The fact that they will frequently replace such objects with a pebble or piece of stick, earns them their other name: Trade rats.

PADÁNG, seaport town in West Sumatra, Indonesia. It is a major exporting center for coffee, rubber, cement, copra and spices. Pop 143 699.

PADDLEFISHES, primitive plankton-eating fishes, genus *Polyodon*, with a largely cartilaginous skeleton, related to the STURGEONS. There are two species, one in China, the other in the Mississippi basin. The snout is extended into a long flat paddle of unknown function.

PADDLETENNIS, form of tennis, with similar rules, first introduced in New York City playgrounds in the early 1920s. It is played on a smaller court than in lawn tennis, and players use a wooden bat, or paddle and a slow-bouncing sponge rubber ball.

PADEREWSKI, Ignace Jan (1860–1941), Polish statesman, composer and the most celebrated concert pianist of his time. He was the first prime minister of the Polish republic (1919) and in 1940–41 led the Polish government in exile.

PADRE ISLAND NATIONAL SEASHORE, barrier island, 113mi long and 3mi wide, off the Texas Gulf Coast, US, between Corpus Christi and Port Isabel. It is known for its great variety of marine and bird life.

PADUA, historic city in N Italy, a famous RENAISSANCE center and noted for its architecture. Its art treasures include works by GIOTTO, DONATELLO, MANTEGNA and TITIAN. GALILEO taught at its university. It is now an industrial, agricultural and commercial center. Pop 231 152.

PADUCAH, city in W Ky., seat of McCracken Co. on the Ohio R, a leading shipping center for farm produce and a tobacco marketing center. Pop 31 267.

PAESTUM, ancient city in S Italy, S of Salerno, founded by the Greeks in 600 BC. Part of MAGNA GRAECIA, it flourished in the 6th century BC, when two of its three superb Doric temples were built.

PAÉZ, José Antonio (1790–1873), Venezuelan soldier and president. He assisted BOLÍVAR in the Spanish defeats at Carabobo (1821) and Puerto Cabello (1823). He led the successful Venezuelan independence movement in 1829 and ruled Venezuela 1831–46 and 1861–63.

PAGANINI, Niccolo (1782–1840), Italian violinist, one of the greatest-ever virtuosos. By his use of adventurous techniques such as diverse tuning of strings and the exploitation of harmonics he extended the compass of the violin. His best-known compositions are his 24 *Caprices*.

PAGE, Walter Hines (1855–1918), US journalist and diplomat. He edited the *Atlantic Monthly* 1896–99 and founded and edited *The World's Book* 1900–13. As President WILSON's ambassador to Great Britain, 1913–18, he opposed US neutrality in WWI.

PAGODA, multistoried circular or polygonal tower of brick, wood or stone, with projecting roofs that may curve upward. Generally Buddhist shrines, they have been built in India and China since the 5th century, and have spread to Burma and Japan.

PAGO PAGO, village, port and capital of American Samoa. It is the site of an important US naval station. Pop 2 451.

PAHOEHOE, ropy lava. (See LAVA.)

PAIGE, "Satchel" (Leroy Robert Paige: 1906–), outstanding US baseball pitcher. Barred as a Negro from the major leagues until 1938, he played for the Cleveland Indians 1948–51 and the St Louis Browns from 1951 until his retirement in 1953.

PAIN, the detection by the nervous system of harmful stimuli. The function of pain is to warn the individual of imminent danger: even the most minor tissue damage will cause pain, so that avoiding action can be taken at a very early stage. The level at which pain can only just be felt is the *pain threshold*. This threshold level varies slightly between individuals, and can be raised by, for example, HYPNOSIS, ANESTHETICS, ANALGESICS and the drinking of alcohol. In some psychological illnesses, especially the NEUROSES, it is lowered. The receptors of pain are unencapsulated nerve endings (see NERVOUS SYSTEM), distributed variably about the body: the back of the knee has

Wood and thatch pagodas on the Indonesian island of Bali tower above the small shrines they contain.

about 230 per cm^2, the tip of the nose about 40. Deep pain, from the internal organs, may be felt as surface pain or in a different part of the body. This phenomenon, *referred pain*, is probably due to the closeness of the nerve tracts entering the SPINAL CORD. In psychoanalysis, "pain" refers to the distress felt when tension caused through frustration of INSTINCT goes unrelieved.

PAINE, Robert Treat (1731–1814), US lawyer, signatory of the DECLARATION OF INDEPENDENCE. He was a delegate to the first CONTINENTAL CONGRESS (1774–78), Mass., attorney general (1777–90) and state supreme court judge (1790–1804).

PAINE, Thomas (1737–1809), English-born writer and radical, a leading figure of the American Revolution. He emigrated to America in 1774; his highly influential pamphlet, *Common Sense*, 1776, urged the American colonies to declare independence. His patriotic pamphlets, *The Crisis* (1776–83) inspired the CONTINENTAL ARMY. He returned to England and wrote *The Rights of Man*, 1791–92, a defense of the FRENCH REVOLUTION and republicanism. Forced to flee to France, he was elected to the National Convention. His controversially deistic *The Age of Man* (1794–95) alienated his US support; he returned there in 1802, and died in obscurity.

PAINESVILLE, city in NE Ohio, seat of Lake Co. on the Grand R. It is a truck farming center and manufactures machinery and chemicals. Pop 16 536.

PAINT, a fluid applied to a surface in thin layers, forming a colored, solid coating for decoration, representation (see PAINTING) and protection (see also VARNISH). Paint consists of a PIGMENT dispersed in a "vehicle" or binder which adheres to the substrate and forms the solid film, and usually a solvent or thinner to control the consistency. Natural binders used, now or formerly, include GLUE, natural RESINS and OILS which dry by OXIDATION—linseed oil used to be the basis of the paint industry. These have been largely displaced by synthetic resins, latex and oils (to which drying agents are added). The solvents used are hydrocarbons or oils, except for the large class of water-thinned paints in which the binder forms an EMULSION or is dissolved in the water. Many specialized paints have been developed, e.g., to resist heat or corrosion. After applying a primer, the paint is brushed, rolled or sprayed on; dip coating and electrostatic attraction are more recent methods. (See also WHITEWASH.)

PAINTED DESERT, brightly-colored region (about 150mi long) of mesas and plateaux in N central Ariz., E of the Little Colorado R. Centuries of erosion have exposed red, brown and purple rock surfaces.

PAINTING, the depiction in terms of line and color of a representational or abstract subject on a two-dimensional surface. (For art preceding that of the RENAISSANCE see ALTAMIRA; LASCAUX CAVE; Ancient EGYPT; Ancient GREECE; ETRUSCANS; ROMAN ART; BYZANTINE ART; ROMANESQUE ART; GOTHIC ART. See also CHINESE ART; JAPANESE ART; ISLAMIC ART.)

Italian painting, 1300–1600. Giotto's FRESCO works broke away from Byzantine art by his realistic depiction of people and their emotions. His monumental, sculptural style was generally followed in 14th-century Florence. In Siena, the decorative linear style of DUCCIO and Simone MARTINI prevailed. The Florentine discovery of linear perspective was first employed by MASACCIO, and the tradition was continued by Fra ANGELICO, PIERO DELLA FRANCESCA and BOTTICELLI. This culminated in the High Renaissance style of LEONARDO DA VINCI, RAPHAEL and MICHELANGELO. MANNERISM, developed by GIULIO ROMANO and EL GRECO, was highly influential in Europe. From the mid-15th century a distinct Venetian style emerged, based on color. The most influential Venetian artists were Titian, Tintoretto and Veronese.

Painting outside Italy, 1400–1600. Flemish art was finely detailed, as in the work of Jan Van Eyck who, with his brother Hubert, is credited with innovating oil painting. A more emotional style was developed by Van der Weyden, while Bosch and Pieter Bruegel developed grotesque fantasy pictures. In the late-15th century, German art became influential with Durer's woodcuts and engravings, Grunewald's Isenheim altar and Hans Holbein's portraits.

Painting, 1600–1850. The prominent artists of the BAROQUE period were the Italian painter and architect Pietro da Cortona; the extraordinarily brilliant and imaginative Flemish painter, Rubens; Velazquez; two classical French painters, Poussin and Claude; and Rembrandt. Dutch painters like Steen and Vermeer specialized in GENRE scenes. The ROCOCO style was characterized by elegant, sensuous, often frivolous works by painters like Watteau and Boucher. English portraiture was developed by Reynolds and Gainsborough, influencing the first important American artists, Copley and Benjamin West. The Spanish Rococo painter, Goya, changed his style to depict the savagery of the Napoleonic wars. The first half of the 19th century in France was dominated by the CLASSICISM of Ingres and the ROMANTICISM of Delacroix.

Painting since 1850. Courbet promoted the importance of large-scale pictures of ordinary life and Manet influenced IMPRESSIONISM. Monet and Renoir pioneered painting out of doors. The painters of POST-IMPRESSIONISM, Gauguin and Van Gogh, became interested in the use of color and greatly influenced EXPRESSIONISM and FAUVISM. Cezanne's work was crucial to the development of CUBISM, which was largely invented by Picasso and Braque. Kandinsky and Malevich developed forms of ABSTRACT ART. SURREALISM used imagery taken from dreams, as in the works of Dali and Ernst. In the 1960s POP ART was developed by Jasper Johns, Robert Rauschenberg and Andy Warhol. Later in the decade, OP ART followed. (See also individual artists.)

PAIUTE INDIANS, several North American Indian tribes of the SHOSHONE INDIANS. They can be divided into the North Paiute of N Cal. and Nev. and the South Paiute (or Digger Indians) of Ariz. and S Nev. The Paiute GHOST DANCE religion, which began in 1870, led by WOVOKA, led to violent uprisings. Today about 4 000 Paiute live on reservations.

PAKENHAM, Sir Edward Michael (1778–1815), British commander whose forces were disastrously defeated at the Battle of NEW ORLEANS (1815) by Andrew JACKSON. Pakenham himself was killed in the action.

PAKISTAN (Urdu: land of the Pure), formerly West Pakistan, republic in the NW Indian subcontinent.

Land. Pakistan, on the Arabian Sea, between Afghanistan to the NW and India to the SE, with Jammu and KASHMIR to the NE, comprises the provinces of Punjab, Sind, Baluchistan and the North-West Frontier Province. High mountains dominate the N, and dry high plateaus and mountain ranges the W. The S includes part of the THAR DESERT and borders on the RANN OF KUTCH. Most of Pakistan is the huge INDUS alluvial plain, sloping to the Arabian Sea. Extensively irrigated by the Indus and the five rivers of the Punjab, it has high agricultural productivity. The climate has extremes of temperature and aridity and is modified by altitude. Summer temperatures reach 120°F in Sind.

People. Most of the population are relatively light-skinned Punjabis. Other groups include the tall, fairer and often blue-eyed Pathans, possibly of Semitic origin, and the Baluchi, of sturdy Iranian stock, an Aryan people; there are many tribal and linguistic differences. The literacy rate is about 16%. The majority of the population live in small, poor, virtually primitive villages. The largest cities are Karachi, Lahore, Lyallpur, Hyderabad and Rawalpindi.

Economy. Pakistan is among the world's poorest countries. It has few natural resources, lacks capital, trained personnel and modern equipment, and is dependent on its agriculture. Wheat is the main subsistence crop but fruit and livestock are important in the N. The limited mineral resources are still to be developed but low-grade coal and iron-ore, chromite, gypsum and limestone are being mined. Deposits of natural gas are large but of oil small. Pakistan exports wool and cotton textiles (some from cottage industries), and leather goods.

History. Demands for a Muslim state independent of Hindu India increased in the early 1900s. In 1906 the MUSLIM LEAGUE was founded and led from 1916 by Mohammed Ali JINNAH. He was first governor-general of the independent dominion of Pakistan, 1947, and Liaquat ALI KHAN prime minister. The new states of India and Pakistan fought bitterly, particularly over Kashmir. In the 1950s tension grew between Bengali East Pakistan and Punjabi West Pakistan which dominated the civil service and army. Pakistan was a republic from 1956, and General AYUB KHAN seized power in 1958. He introduced a new political system, "Basic Democracy," and land reforms. Political riots in 1969 and government policies led to the secession of East Pakistan as BANGLADESH, 1971, created a state after West Pakistan's defeat in the ensuing civil war. This halved Pakistan's population and meant the loss of the valuable jute crop. Pakistan and Bangladesh reached agreement in 1974, but political unrest continues.

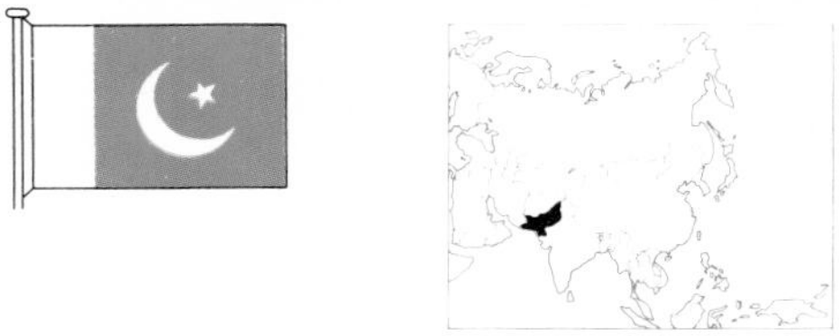

Official name: Islamic Republic of Pakistan
Capital: Islamabad
Area: 310 403sq mi
Population: 66 900 000
Languages: Urdu Bengali;
Sindhi, Punjabi, Pushtu, English
Religion: Muslim
Monetary unit(s): 1 Rupee = 100 paisa

PALADE, Georg Emil (1912–), Romanian-born US cell biologist awarded with A. CLAUDE and C. de DUVE the 1974 Nobel Prize for Physiology or Medicine for their researches into intercellular structures. Palade discovered the nature of what are now called RIBOSOMES.

PALATE, structure dividing the mouth from the NOSE and bounded by the upper gums and TEETH; it is made of BONE and covered by mucous membrane. At the back, it is a soft mobile connective-tissue structure which can close off the naso-PHARYNX during swallowing and speech.

PALATINATE, two historic states of Germany: the Lower or Rhine Palatinate on the Rhine R bordering France and the Saar, and the Upper Palatinate in NE Bavaria. The Countship Palatine of the former state was created by the Holy Roman Emperor Frederick I in 1156. The counts became electors of the Holy Roman Empire.

PALATINE, village in NE Ill., 28mi NE of Chicago. There is mixed light industry. Many inhabitants commute to Chicago to work. Pop 25 904.

PALATINE HILL. See SEVEN HILLS OF ROME.

PALEMBANG, city and major river port in Indonesia, capital of South Sumatra Province. It exports rubber and oil. Pop 583 000.

PALEOBOTANY. See PALEONTOLOGY.

PALEOCENE, the first epoch of the TERTIARY period, which extended between about 65 and 55 million years ago. (See also GEOLOGY.)

PALEOCLIMATOLOGY, the determination of climatic conditions of the geological past by study of the FOSSIL (*paleoecology*) and sedimentary (*sedimentology*) evidence.

PALEOGEOGRAPHY, the construction from geologic, paleontologic and other evidence of maps of parts or all of the earth's surface at specific times in the earth's past. Paleogeography has proved of considerable importance in CONTINENTAL DRIFT studies.

PALEOGRAPHY, the study of handwritten material from ancient and medieval times, excluding that on metal or stone (see EPIGRAPHY), for purposes of

Paleontology

Discovering a missing link

One of the most prolific animal groups living today is the class Mammalia which includes forms as diverse as cats, mice, elephants, horses, monkeys and man. All mammals share a number of anatomical features such as hair and milk secreting glands but, more importantly, they are capable of complex behavioral patterns that enable them to cope well with a variety of environmental situations and to display the high degree of parental care which has been largely responsible for their great success. Certainly the mammals are more successful than their closest relatives, the reptiles. Reptiles include lizards, snakes, turtles and crocodiles, which are almost entirely limited in their distribution to the warmer parts of the earth unlike the mammals which are ubiquitous.

It would be a mistake however to assume that, because mammals dominate over their scaly allies today, this has always been the case. It has not. Paleontologists, scientists who study the petrified remains of animals and plants preserved in the earth's sedimentary rocks, have known for over a century that the history of the reptiles extends back some 350 million years and that the mammals have their origins relatively recently—about 200 million years ago. Moreover, whereas the early mammals were small scuttling, mouse-like creatures, the reptiles were incredibly diverse and included, not only relatives of living forms, but groups such as the flying pterosaurs, marine ichthyosaurs and terrestrial dinosaurs which are now entirely extinct.

One of the great puzzles of paleontology is, from where did the mammals evolve? Darwin in his *Origin* showed how all living organisms change during long periods of geological time and that in the fossil record one might expect to find the ancestors of animals and plants living today. No such ancestor of the mammals has ever been discovered. Studies in comparative anatomy led zoologists to believe that the ancestor of mammals should be found among early reptiles, and the most likely group of such animals became known as the mammal-like reptiles. But there were several seemingly unsurmountable problems to this theory. Firstly, almost all mammal-like reptiles were large beasts not unlike the hippopotamus, and it appeared unlikely that such forms could have evolved into a mammal the size of a mouse. Other objections were more technical and only two need be mentioned here.

Reptiles are characterized by a lower jaw which is composed of a tooth bearing bone called the dentary behind which a number of smaller bones occur. One of these is called the articular and, as its name suggests, this bone articulates at the jaw joint with a bone which is attached to the lower part of the skull and which is called the quadrate. Another feature of all reptiles is found in the ear. Here, a single bone, the stapes, transmits vibrations from the eardrum to the so called inner-ear. These two characteristics differ markedly from the condition seen in mammals. In members of the Mammalia, the lower jaw is composed of a single dentary bone which articulates with a bone of the skull called the squamosal. Moreover, in the ear there are these bones which transmit vibrations from the ear drum: the stapes, which corresponds with the stapes in reptiles; and two new bones called the malleus and incus. How, if mammals evolved from reptiles, was the articular quadrate articulation replaced by the dentary squamosal articulation, and from where did the mammalian malleus and incus come from?

In 1964, an emeritus professor of zoology from the University of Harvard, called Alfred Sherwod Romer, mounted an expedition to Argentina to study rocks of the Triassic era. Throughout his long career as a paleontologist, Romer had studied mammal-like reptiles, notably those from the Texas Redbeds, and had made considerable contributions to our understanding of their early evolution. But he had failed, as had everyone before him, to find an animal that bridged the evolutionary gap between reptiles and mammals. He chose to go to Argentina because in the inhospitable western region of that country there occur thousands of feet of sedimentary rocks that were deposited in lakes and rivers 200 million years ago. In other words, these rocks were formed at a time when one might expect the elusive mammalian ancestor to have lived.

For two months Romer prospected these rocks with little success and, by Christmas 1964, he had consumed half his available time in the field and had met only with utter failure. Then, quite suddenly, there was a dramatic change of events. In a series of volcanic ash sediments he discovered a band of rock that contained numerous fossils. Over two hundred of these were collected and shipped back to the laboratory.

The preparation of fossil specimens is a painstaking process, and it requires great skill to remove the rock in which fossils are embedded without causing damage. Sometimes the paleontologist can dissolve the encapsulating rock in acid, leaving the more resistant fossil untouched, but in the case of the Argentinian specimens this was not possible and the rock was removed with the aid of dental drills and needles. Not surprisingly, over a year elapsed before the significance of some of the finds was realized. The wait was worthwhile however for, as well as large mammal-like reptiles that had been known from other parts of the world, the collection contained specimens of an animal later to become known as *Probainognathus jenseni*.

Probainognathus was a small animal about the size of a cat. It had a pointed snout and the shapes of its teeth show that it had carnivorous habits. But it was the nature of its jaw articulation that proved to be of such great significance. The lower jaw was composed of a large dentary bone behind which was situated an articular which articulated with the quadrate bone. However, alongside the articular there was a backward process of the dentary, and the end of this process articulated with the squamosal. Thus *Probainognathus* had a double jaw joint, an articular quadrate component which corresponded to the condition seen in reptiles, and a dentary squamosal component which corresponded to that seen in mammals. At last a link between the two groups had been discovered!

It is now possible to reconstruct the events which took place when the mammals originated. The old reptilian articular quadrate jaw joint became redundant in a group of mammal-like reptiles about 200 million years ago. Exactly why is not known, but it appears to have occurred in response to changes in the arrangement of the muscles which opened and closed the jaws. For whatever reasons, the dentary grew backwards until it met the squamosal and formed an articulation with that bone which became the mammalian jaw joint. *Probainognathus* represents a halfway stage in this evolutionary process.

It will be remembered that there are no articular or quadrate bones in mammals, and it would be reasonable to suppose that, having been relieved of their function, they would have become vestigial and eventually lost. The truth is for stranger than this simple explanation, for as the mammalian dentary extended backwards to meet the squamosal, it pushed the still articulated articular and quadrate bones backwards too. Even casual examination of a mammal such as a cat or dog reveals that the organ immediately behind the jaw joint is the ear. And it is in the ear that the articular and quadrate bones finished up. They were transformed into the malleus and incus and became associated with the stapes to assume the new task of transmitting vibrations. Nature, as Darwin frequently observed, is extremely parsimonious in her ways.

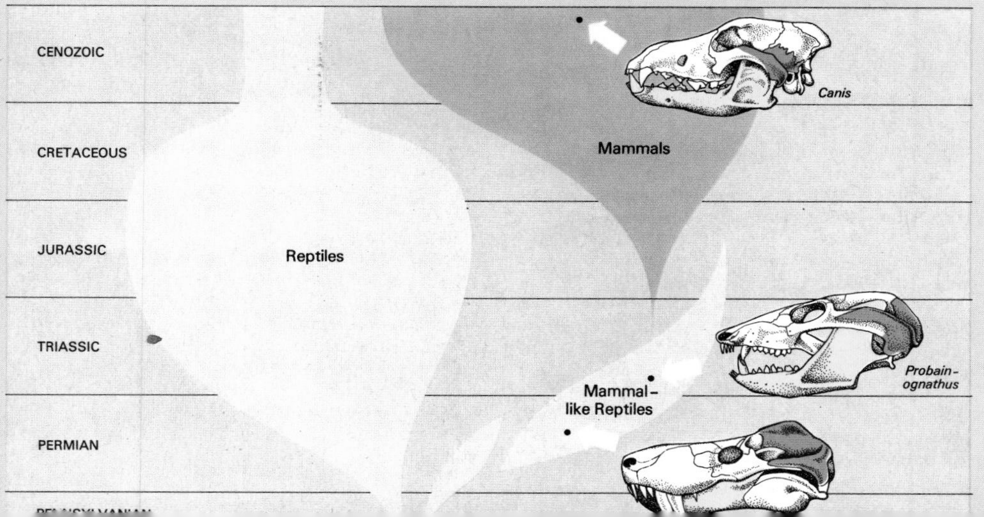

Chart showing the evolution of the mammal-like reptiles into true mammals, from the Pennsylvanian to the Cenozoic periods; during much of this time the world was effectively dominated by the great reptiles. As can be seen from the jaw structure and dentition of the skulls, *Probainognathus* represents a halfway stage between the still distinctly reptilian *Lycosuchus* and the modern *Canis*, the dog.

interpretation and the dating of events, and to trace the evolution of the written ALPHABET.

PALEOLITHIC AGE. See PRIMITIVE MAN; STONE AGE.

PALEOMAGNETISM, the study of past changes in the EARTH's magnetic field by examination of rocks containing certain iron-bearing minerals (e.g., HEMATITE, MAGNETITE). Reversals of the field and movements of the magnetic poles can be charted and information on CONTINENTAL DRIFT may be obtained. (See also SEA-FLOOR SPREADING.)

PALEONTOLOGY, or **paleobiology**, study of the remains of living organisms of past eras. The two branches are *paleobotany* and *paleozoology*, dealing with plants and animals respectively. Such studies are essential to STRATIGRAPHY, and provide important evidence for EVOLUTION and CONTINENTAL DRIFT theories. (See also FOSSILS; PALEOCLIMATOLOGY; RADIOCARBON DATING.)

PALEOZOIC, the earliest era of the PHANEROZOIC, comprising two sub-eras: the **Lower Paleozoic**, 570–400 million years ago, containing the CAMBRIAN, ORDOVICIAN and SILURIAN periods; and the **Upper Paleozoic**, 400–225 million years ago, containing the DEVONIAN, MISSISSIPPIAN, PENNSYLVANIAN and PERMIAN periods. (See GEOLOGY.)

PALERMO, capital of Sicily, its largest city and chief seaport, on the NW coast. Shipbuilding, textiles and chemicals are leading industries. Palermo was founded by Phoenicians in the 8th–6th centuries BC. Its notable medieval architecture has Byzantine, Norman and Muslim features. The SICILIAN VESPERS and other uprisings took place there. Pop 650 645.

PALESTINE, the biblical Holy Land, named for the PHILISTINES and also called CANAAN. Its boundaries, often imprecise, have varied widely. Palestine now usually refers to the region bounded W by the Mediterranean, E by the Jordan R and Dead Sea, N by Mt Herman on the Syria-Lebanon border and S by the Sinai Peninsula. It thus lies almost entirely within modern Israel, though extending into Jordan. There were Paleolithic and Mesolithic cultures in Palestine, and Neolithic JERICHO emerged by 7000 BC. SEMITES arrived c3000 BC and built a Bronze-Age civilization (3000–1500 BC). Soon after 2000 BC, Hebrew tribes under Abraham came from Mesopotamia (see JEWS). In 1479 BC Egyptians invaded, enslaving many Hebrews (or Israelites) in Egypt. Their descendants returned under MOSES c1200 BC. Successful wars against Canaanites and Philistines helped unite Hebrew tribes in one kingdom (c1020 BC), ruled by Saul, then David, then Solomon. After Solomon died the kingdom split into (N) Israel and (S) Judah (later JUDAEA), hence the term "Jew." Both kingdoms worshiped the One God, Yahweh (JEHOVAH), and Judaism developed under religious leaders called prophets. In 721 BC Assyrians overran Israel and in 587 BC Babylonians conquered Judah, deporting many Jews who only returned after Babylonia fell to Persia's CYRUS THE GREAT in 539 BC. Palestine was later controlled by Alexander the Great (332–323 BC), the Ptolemies of Egypt (323–198 BC) and the Seleucids of Syria (198–168 BC). Then JUDAS MACCABEUS began a national revolt which established the Jewish HASMONEAN dynasty (143–37 BC) in Judaea. Roman rule (63 BC–395 AD) saw the birth of Christianity, but also repression climaxed by the Roman destruction of Jerusalem (70 AD) followed by massive Jewish emigration. Control passed to the Byzantines (395–611 and 628–633 AD), Persians (611–628), and Arabs, whose conquest in the 630s began 1 300 years of Muslim rule, briefly disturbed by the CRUSADE. In 1918 the OTTOMAN EMPIRE collapsed and British rule followed. Jewish immigration had begun in the 1850s and increased rapidly after the British government's BALFOUR DECLARATION (1917) promising the Jews a national home in Palestine. Britain had also promised (1915–16) the Arabs an independent state in SE Asia. The British claim that Palestine was excluded from this promise has never been accepted by the Arabs. The appalling fate of the Jews in Europe after the rise of NAZISM brought widespread support for the creation of a Jewish state. In 1948 Jews, but not Arabs, accepted a UN recommendation to split Palestine into Jewish and Arab states. Jews proclaimed the state of Israel, and at the same time nearby Arab nations invaded the area, the first major step in an Arab-Israeli conflict which has continued into the 1970s. (See also ISRAEL; JORDAN; ARAB-ISRAELI WARS; PALESTINE LIBERATION ORGANIZATION.)

PALESTINE LIBERATION ORGANIZATION (PLO), coordinating body of Palestinian refugee groups, aiming to establish a Palestinian state on land regained from Israel; the ARAB LEAGUE recognizes it as the PALESTINE government. Led by Yassir ARAFAT, it conducts an armed campaign in the Middle East; its members are involved in world-wide terrorism.

PALESTRINA, Giovanni Pierluigi da (c1525–1594), Italian RENAISSANCE composer of unaccompanied choral church music. He wrote over 100 masses and is perhaps best known for his *Missa Papae Marcelli*. He was organist and choirmaster in several Roman churches.

PALEY, William (1743–1805), English theologian and utilitarian philosopher whose *Principles of Moral and Political Philosophy* (1785); *A View of the Evidences of Christianity* (1794), and *Natural Theology* (1802) featured largely in early 19th-century liberal education on both shores of the Atlantic.

PALIMPSEST, parchment or other writing material reused after previous writing has been erased. The high cost of parchments made palimpsests common in Greek and Roman times. Some old, erased texts have been deciphered.

PALISADES, basalt cliffs in SE N.Y. and NE N.J., on the W bank of the Hudson R. They form a wall of polygonal basalt columns 150–500ft high and 15mi long. The N section forms part of the Palisades Interstate Park.

PALISADES PARK, residential borough in NE N.J., 9mi N of Jersey City. Pop 13 351.

PALLADIO, Andrea (1508–1580), Italian architect, born Andrea di Pietro. He created the immensely influential Palladian style. His designs for villas, palaces and churches stressed harmonic proportions and classical symmetry. Palladio's *The Four Books of Architecture* (1570) helped to spread his style through Europe, notably (via Inigo JONES) to England.

PALLADIUM (Pd), white, soft, ductile metal in the PLATINUM GROUP. In addition to the general uses of these metals, palladium is used in dental and other ALLOYS. It absorbs 900 times its volume of hydrogen, forming a metallic HYDRIDE, and, being permeable to hydrogen at high temperatures, it is used in hydrogen purifiers. AW 106.4, m 1552°C, bp 2927°C, sg 11.97 (0°C).

PALLADIUM, in Greek myth, a sacred statue of Pallas ATHENA. Sent from heaven by Zeus, it was kept at Troy, which remained invincible until Odysseus and Diomedes removed the statue. Many Greek and Roman cities claimed to have acquired it thereafter.

PALLADIUS, Saint (d. 431 AD), British or Roman missionary who worked to crush PELAGIANISM in Britain and was the first bishop of Ireland. His stay in Ireland (431) was inconclusive.

PALLAS, Peter Simon (1741–1811), German naturalist best known for his *Travels through Various Provinces of the Russian Empire* (3 vols., 1771–76), an account of his 6-year expedition collecting extant and fossil plant and animal specimens.

PALM, any of over 3 000 species of trees and shrubs of the family Palmae, mainly native to tropical and subtropical regions. Palms are characterized by having an unbranched stem bearing at the tip a bunch of feather-like (pinnate) or fan-like (palmate) leaves. Flowers are greenish, borne in spikes, and the fruits are either dry or fleshy. Palm products are of great economic importance, both locally and in world trade. The COCONUT PALM and DATE PALM produce staple crops; wax is obtained from the CARNAUBA palm; the OIL PALM yields oils used in food, soap, toiletries and industrial processes (see also SAGO). Several palms make good house plants. Indoors, they grow well at average house temperatures and should be placed in a moderately sunny position. The soil should be kept wet to moist, though palms do not tolerate standing water. The foliage should be misted often. They can be propagated from seeds or by planting divisions.

PALMA, city in Spain, SW Majorca, capital of Majorca and of Baleares Province. It is a port and major tourist center. Pop 234 098.

PALM BEACH, town in SE Fla., on a sandbar between Lake Worth and the Atlantic. It was developed as a winter resort by H. M. FLAGLER. Pop 9 086.

PALMER, town in SW Mass., ENE of Springfield. Its industries include metal products, plastics and automobile parts. Pop 11 680.

PALMER, Alexander Mitchell (1872–1936), US attorney general (1919–21) notorious for the "Palmer Raids"—mass arrests of supposed subversives, many of whom were deported as aliens. A congressman 1909–15, he was US alien property custodian in WWI.

PALMER, Arnold (1929–   ), US golfer, the first to win the US Masters Tournament four times (1958, 1960, 1962, and 1964). He won the US Open in 1960 and the British Open in 1961 and 1962.

PALMER, Daniel David (1845–1913), Canadian-born US founder of CHIROPRACTIC (1895).

PALMER, Nathaniel Brown (1799–1877), US mariner and explorer, the reputed discoverer of the Antarctic continent. In 1820–21 he sighted Palmer Peninsula (now the Antarctic Peninsula) and discovered the South Orkney Islands.

PALMER, Samuel (1805–1881), English landscape painter and etcher, famous for his visionary, pastoral watercolors of Southern England. Prime exemplars of ROMANTICISM, his greatest works, those of the 1820s, were influenced by William BLAKE.

PALMERSTON, Henry John Temple, 3rd Viscount (1784–1865), British statesman remembered for his successful and often aggressive foreign policy. As foreign secretary 1830–34, 1835–41 and 1846–51, he was instrumental in securing Belgian independence (1830–31), in upholding the OTTOMAN EMPIRE (1839–41), and in maintaining peace in Europe during the REVOLUTIONS OF 1848. As prime minister 1855–58 and 1859–65, he led Britain to victory in the CRIMEAN WAR and kept out of the American Civil War, despite the TRENT AFFAIR.

PALMETTO, common name for about 20 species of PALMS of the genus *Sabal*, native to the Americas. They are characterized by large, fan-shaped leaves, small black berries and compound clusters of flowers. The terminal buds are eaten. Family: Palmae.

PALMISTRY, study of the characteristics of the hand for the purpose of DIVINATION. The various lines on the palm are held to indicate the individual's character and destiny. Over 4 000 years old, palmistry is still widely popular.

PALMITIC ACID ($C_{15}H_{31}COOH$), a FATTY ACID whose glyceryl ESTER is a major component of FATS. Palmitates are used in SOAPS.

PALM OIL, oil obtained from the fruit and seed kernel of the African OIL PALM. It is a rich source of VITAMIN A and is used in candles, cosmetics, oleomargarine, lubricants and soaps.

PALM SPRINGS, resort city in SE Cal., in the Coachella Valley, 44mi SE of San Bernardino. Pop 20 936.

PALM SUNDAY, the Sunday before EASTER and the first day of HOLY WEEK, commemorating Christ's triumphal entry into Jerusalem riding on an ass, when palm leaves were spread in his path. Palm leaves are blessed and carried in procession.

PALMYRA, ancient city in central Syria. Prominent as a trading center, Palmyra prospered under Roman rule and reached its height (3rd century AD) as an independent state under Queen ZENOBIA. In 273 it was largely destroyed by the Romans under Aurelian. Imposing ruins survive.

PALMYRA, village in W N.Y., 21mi E of Rochester. Nearby is Hill Cumorah, where Joseph SMITH said he found gold plates that became the basis of the Book of Mormon. Pop 3 776.

PALMYRA PALM, or deleb palm, *Borassus flabellifer*, a PALM found in India, Sri Lanka and tropical Africa. Its durable wood is used in construction work, its leaves for thatching and basketry, its sap to make arrack, jaggery and toddy drinks, and its seedlings to make a flour. Family: Palmae.

PALO ALTO, city in W Cal., 32mi SE of San Francisco. It makes electronic products and it neighbors the site of Stanford U. Pop 56 181.

PALO ALTO, Battle of, first battle of the MEXICAN WAR. On May 8, 1846, about 2 000 US troops under Gen. Zachary TAYLOR defeated about 6 000 Mexicans under Gen. Mariano Arista 12mi NE of Brownsville, S Tex.

PALOLO WORM, a polychaete worm, *Eunice viridis*, which lives in sand or in rock crevices on the sea bottom. At certain times of year the worms form swarms at the surface of the sea to breed. The rear half of the body, loaded with eggs or sperm breaks away and swims independently to the surface shedding its eggs and sperm into the water.

PALOMAR OBSERVATORY. See HALE OBSERVATORIES.

PALOVERDE, trees and shrubs of the genus *Cercidium*, native to arid areas of the southwestern US, Mexico, Middle America and Venezuela. They are leafless for most of the year, PHOTOSYNTHESIS being carried on within the bark. Family: Leguminosae.

PALYNOLOGY, the study of fossil pollen and spores. These are relatively resistant to decay and can be used both to index the dates of recent strata and reconstruct the flora and climate prevailing when they were laid down.

PAMIRS, mountainous region of central Asia. It forms a hub from which radiate the Hindu Kush, Karakorum, Kunlun and Tien Shan ranges. Most of it lies in the Tadzhik SSR, but parts are in Afghanistan, China and Kashmir. The highest peaks are Communism Peak (24 590ft) and Lenin Peak (23 508ft), both in the USSR.

PAMLICO SOUND, lagoon between the mainland of E N.C. and low, sandy offshore islands of the Atlantic. It is about 80mi long and up to 30mi wide.

PAMPA, city in NW Tex., seat of Gray Co. Mixed heavy industry is based on local oil. Pop 21 726.

PAMPAS, grassy plains of SE South America. They stretch about 300 000sq mi over Argentina and into Uruguay. The humid E Pampa bears some crops. The dry W Pampa supports livestock.

PAMPAS GRASS, *Cortaderia argentea*, a perennial grass native to Argentina and S Brazil. It grows in clumps and has leaves over 2m (6.6ft) long with the flowering stems up to 5m (16.4ft) high. It is frequently grown as an ornamental. Family: Graminae.

PAMPLONA, formerly Pampeluna, city in N Spain, capital of Navarre Province. It makes chemicals, processed foods and consumer goods, and has a university and cathedral. It was the capital of the old kingdom of Navarre. Pop 147 168.

PAN, in Greek myth, son of HERMES and god of pastoral fertility. He is usually represented with the head and torso of a man and the horns, ears and lower quarters of a goat. He roamed woods, led the satyrs and made love to nymphs. To escape his pursuit, the nymph Syrinx changed into a reed, from which Pan made the first panpipe.

The Panama Canal (blue) terminates on the Pacific coast 27mi *east* of its starting point on the Atlantic. Canal Zone borders are shown as red and railroads as black broken lines.

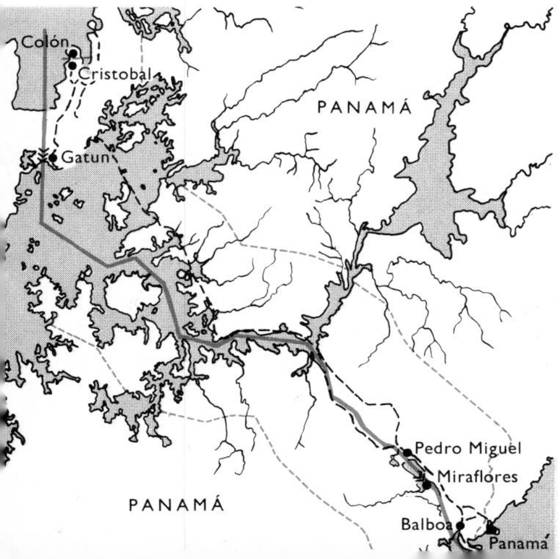

PANAMA, central American republic occupying the Isthmus of Panama (see PANAMA, ISTHMUS OF), and cut in half by the PANAMA CANAL ZONE. Panama is traversed by mountain ranges, flanked by well-watered valleys and plains. The climate is hot and rainy. Much of E Panama is dense tropical forest; the Pacific coast has savanna and forest.

People. The population is more than 70% mulatto, about 14% pure Negro and 12% European (mainly Spanish). There are about 60 000 Amerindians, mainly in E Panama and on the San Blas Islands off the Caribbean coast. Nearly one third of Panamanians live in Panama City or Colón, the largest centers. Most people are Roman Catholics. Education is free and compulsory (ages 7–15).

Economy. The canal provides 25% of the gross national product but the economy is basically agricultural. The farms, mostly under 25 acres, produce rice, corn, beans, bananas, cacao and coffee. Only half of all arable land is farmed, and Panama imports most of its food. Industry is chiefly consumer oriented. Major exports by value are bananas, shrimps, coffee, sugar, fishmeal and petroleum products. Food, industrial raw materials and manufactured goods largely account for Panama's huge trading deficit. There are about 1 000mi of surfaced road. The chief ports are Cristóbal and Balboa. In 1973 Panama had the world's eighth-largest merchant fleet by tonnage, foreign shipowners registering in Panama to profit from low fees and easy labor laws.

History. First sighted by Europeans in 1501, claimed by Spain and colonized under BALBOA and DÁVILA, Panama became a springboard for Spanish conquests in the Americas and a route for transshipping Peruvian gold to Spain. Panama lost importance in the 1700s, after buccaneer attacks forced treasure ships from Peru to sail around South America. In 1821 Panama broke free from Spain and became part of Colombia. In 1903, Panama gained independence with US support. The completion (1914) of the PANAMA CANAL brought some prosperity, but discontent with US control over the canal led to riots in 1959, 1962 and 1964. The mid-1970s saw continued negotiations to end US control over the canal. Gen. Omar Torrijos Herrera came to power after a military coup in 1968.

Official name: Republic of Panama
Capital: Panama
Area: 29 201sq mi
Population: 1 478 000
Language: Spanish
Religion: Roman Catholic
Monetary unit(s): 1 Balboa = 100 centesimos

PANAMA, Isthmus of, narrow neck of land linking North and South America, once called the isthmus of Darien. It also separates the Atlantic and Pacific oceans. The isthmus coincides with the republic of Panama and is cut by the Panama Canal.

PANAMA CANAL, ship canal which crosses the Isthmus of PANAMA to link the Atlantic and Pacific oceans. It runs 40mi SE from Colón on the Caribbean to Balboa on the Pacific. Ships are lifted to 85ft above sea level and lowered again by means of the Gatún, Pedro Miguel and Miraflores locks. Minimum depth is 41ft. Minimum width is 100ft. The Canal and flanking PANAMA CANAL ZONE are controlled by the US government. A French company led by de LESSEPS bought a Colombian canal-building concession, but after eight years' work in Panama (1881–89), labor problems and disease bankrupted the firm. A second French company bought the franchise in 1894, largely to keep it alive. The US negotiated the HAY-PAUNCEFOTE TREATY with Britain (1901) and aimed to build a canal through Nicaragua. The French offered the US the rights to the Panamanian project, but Colombia refused the US terms (see HAY-HERRAN TREATY, 1903). In 1903, a US warship and US troops helped Panama successfully revolt against Colombia and the ensuing HAY-BUNAU-VARILLA TREATY gave the US rights in perpetuity to a 10mi wide strip across the isthmus. The US completed the canal in 1914, due mainly to the work of the engineer G. W. GOETHALS and the government health officer Dr. W. C. GORGAS. After WWII there was US-Panamanian friction over canal sovereignty. In 1974 US and Panamanian representatives agreed to negotiate a new treaty handing eventual control to Panama.

PANAMA CANAL ZONE, strip of land extending 5mi on either side of the PANAMA CANAL. It is controlled by the US. The governor, normally a US army officer, is a presidential appointee. About 75% of the population are US citizens. Some 11 000 inhabitants are members of the US armed forces; the remainder are mostly government or Panama Canal Company employees. The administrative center is Balboa Heights.

PANAMA CITY, capital of Panama, on the Pacific Coast just E of the Canal Zone. It is Panama's largest city and chief business and transportation center. There are two universities. Panama City was founded in 1673 after Henry Morgan sacked the old city (founded 1519). Pop 420 000.

PANAMA CITY, seaport city in NW Fla., on the Gulf of Mexico, seat of Bay Co. It is an industrial, fishery and resort center. Pop 32 096.

PAN-AMERICAN GAMES, four-yearly amateur sports contest between nations of the Americas. The event is based on the OLYMPIC GAMES. It was proposed at the 1940 Pan-American Congress, but postponed by WWII and first held in 1951.

PAN-AMERICAN HIGHWAY, highway system linking Latin American countries with each other and with the Interstate Highway of the US. By the mid 1970s engineers in Panama and Colombia were closing the last big gap in the system. The highway was conceived at the Fifth International Conference of American States (1923).

PAN AMERICANISM, movement aimed at creating closer cultural, economic, political and social ties among the republics of the Western Hemisphere. It dates from 1826, when BOLÍVAR called a conference of Latin American states which agreed on a treaty of union and assistance. Further conferences followed. US involvement dates from the First International Conference of American States (1889–90) which founded the International Union of American Republics, reorganized in 1910 as the Pan American Union. Later landmarks in cooperation included the founding of the PAN-AMERICAN HIGHWAY, the PAN-AMERICAN GAMES and the ORGANIZATION OF AMERICAN STATES. The ALLIANCE FOR PROGRESS improved US relations with Latin America, but Pan Americanism is still an ideal rather than a reality.

PANCHEN LAMA, second-highest lama in Tibetan BUDDHISM (preceded only by the DALAI LAMA), revered as a reincarnation of Amitabha, the Buddha of Light. The then Panchen Lama nominally ruled TIBET 1959–64.

PANCREAS, organ consisting partly of exocrine GLAND tissue, secreting into the DUODENUM, and partly of ENDOCRINE GLAND tissue (the *islets of Langerhans*), whose principal HORMONES include INSULIN and GLUCAGON. The pancreas lies on the back wall of the upper ABDOMEN, much of it within the duodenal loop. Powerful digestive-system ENZYMES (pepsin, trypsin, lipase, amylase) are secreted into the gut; this secretion is in part controlled by intestinal hormones (SECRETIN) and in part by nerve REFLEXES. Insulin and glucagon have important roles in glucose and fat METABOLISM (see DIABETES); other pancreatic hormones affect GASTROINTESTINAL-TRACT secretion and activity. Acute INFLAMMATION of the pancreas due to VIRUS disease, ALCOHOLISM or duct obstruction by gallstones, may lead to severe abdominal pain with SHOCK and prostration caused by the release of digestive enzymes into the abdomen. Chronic pancreatitis leads to functional impairment and malabsorption. CANCER of the pancreas may cause JAUNDICE by obstructing the BILE duct.

PANDAS, two species of raccoon-like mammals of uncertain relation found in montane bamboo forests of Yunnan and Szechwan. Both have an unusual sixth digit, a modified wristbone which has evolved to thumb-like size and flexibility in the Giant panda, *Ailuropoda melanoleuca*, remaining vestigial in the Lesser or Red panda, *Ailurus fulgens*. Though they have evolved from carnivores, both pandas are vegetarians, their diet largely comprising bamboo shoots. The Giant panda has been adopted as the emblem of the World Wildlife Fund.

PANDEMIC. See EPIDEMIC.

PANDIT, Vijaya Läkshmi (1900–), Indian diplomat and politician, sister of NEHRU. She was active in the struggle for India's independence and helped implement India's postwar policy of nonalignment. Among many posts she was ambassador to the US 1949–51 and the first woman president of the UN General Assembly 1953–54.

PANDORA, in Greek myth, the first woman. Zeus ordered HEPHAESTUS to create her in retribution for PROMETHEUS' theft of fire, knowing that she would bring mankind evil. The gods gave Pandora a box, telling her never to open it. She did, and released all worldly ills.

PANGAEA, primeval supercontinent which, under plate tectonic action, split up to form Laurasia in the N and Gondwanaland in the S hemisphere (see GONDWANALAND; LAURASIA; PLATE TECTONICS). In turn these, too, split up to form our modern continents. (See also CONTINENTAL DRIFT.)

PANGOLINS, or **Scaly anteaters**, seven species of mammals of Asia and Africa whose bodies are covered with overlapping scales and thus resemble pine cones. They have short sturdy legs and powerful claws on the front paws for ripping open termite nests. Pangolins are strict insectivores; they have no teeth and the long sticky tongue is adapted for ant-eating.

PANKHURST, Emmeline (1858–1928), English suffragist. In 1903 she and her daughters **Christabel Pankhurst** (1880–1958) and **Sylvia Pankhurst** (1882–1960) founded the Woman's Social and Political Union, which soon became militant. She was constantly in prison and on hunger strike 1908–14. She died a month before women gained full voting equality with men. (See WOMEN'S RIGHTS.)

PANMUNJOM, village in N South Korea where the truce to end the Korean War was negotiated (1951–53) and signed (July 27, 1953).

PAN-SLAVISM, movement for the cultural and political solidarity of the SLAVS. It began in the 1830s. Pan-Slav Congresses were held in Prague (1848) and Moscow (1867). Pan-Slavism was a factor in the events leading to the Russo-Turkish War (1877–78), the Balkan Wars (1912, 1913) and WWI. Both pre- and post-communist Russia attempted to use Pan-Slavism as a cloak for Russian expansionism.

PANSY, or **heartsease**, annual and perennial plants of the genus *Viola*, which are commonly cultivated in gardens. Pansies are easy to grow and flower for a long time if well watered, shaded and deadheaded. Family: Violaceae. (See also VIOLET.)

PANTHEISM, religious or philosophical system in which God and the universe are identified, stressing God's IMMANENCE and denying his TRANSCENDENCE. Religious pantheists see finite beings as merely part of God; others deify the universe, nature being the supreme principle. Pantheism is found in HINDUISM, STOICISM, IDEALISM and notably in SPINOZA's thought; Christian MYSTICISM may tend to it.

PANTHEON, historically, a temple dedicated to the worship of all the gods. In modern times it refers to a structure where a nation's heroes are buried or honored. The most famous pantheon is an ancient circular temple (now a church) in Rome, built c120 AD and having a 142ft diameter dome.

PANTHER, a melanistic variety of the LEOPARD.

PANTOGRAPH, instrument for enlarging or reducing a geometric figure or motion. It consists of four hinged bars forming a parallelogram, one vertex being fixed. It is used in technical drawing and mapmaking. A spring-loaded pantograph linkage is used on electric locomotives to collect current from an overhead wire.

PANTOMIME, originally a drama performed entirely in MIME. Popular in Roman times, it was developed by the COMMEDIA DELL' ARTE and further adapted to become the traditional British Christmas pantomime (or "panto"), with its dialogue, song, spectacle and comedy loosely based on a well-known fairy story.

PANTOTHENIC ACID. See VITAMINS.

PAPACY, the office and institution of the pope. As bishop of Rome in succession to St. PETER, the first bishop of Rome, the pope claims to be Christ's representative, with supremacy over all other bishops. This claim is accepted only by Roman Catholics. The title pope, meaning father, was originally applied to all bishops. The authority of the pope at Rome was established in the West during the first five centuries AD but the refusal of the Eastern churches to accept it resulted (1054) in the first GREAT SCHISM. The papacy had strengthened its secular power in the West after LEO III crowned Charlemagne Holy Roman Emperor in 800. By 1200 the pope had more feudal vassals than any other power and CANON LAW was enforceable throughout Christian Europe. But growing secular forces weakened papal political authority by the late Middle Ages, and the second Great Schism (1378–1417) gravely divided the papacy. Renaissance popes worked to strengthen the PAPAL STATES and created a culturally brilliant papal court, but Church corruption led to demands for reform which culminated in the Protestant REFORMATION. The papacy reacted by founding the JESUITS (1540), reinforcing the INQUISITION (1542), and calling the reformist Council of TRENT. In the 17th and 18th centuries, the power of the papacy was weakened from within by disputes over JANSENISM and from without by increasing secularism and skepticism. In the 19th century the papacy recovered influence as a bulwark of tradition against revolution, and asserted its renewed confidence in such pronouncements as the doctrine of papal infallibility (1870), which held that the pope was infallible in matters of faith and morals when speaking as the vicar of Christ. The Papal States were lost in 1870 but the LATERAN TREATY of 1929 established the VATICAN CITY as an independent papal domain. In recent times popes such as JOHN XXIII and PAUL VI have opposed totalitarian rule, encouraged social justice and backed initiatives to renew the Church while maintaining its historic doctrines. (See also ROMAN CATHOLIC CHURCH; VATICAN COUNCILS.)

PAPADOPOULOS, George (1919–), Greek army officer, prime minister (1967–73) and president (June–Nov. 1973) of Greece under the military junta. In 1975, under civilian rule, he and others were tried and found guilty of crimes against the state.

PAPAGO INDIANS, North American Indian tribe of S Arizona and NW Sonora, Mexico, related to the PIMA INDIANS. They rebelled unsuccessfully against the Spanish (1695 and 1751) and in the 1860s joined the US government against the Apaches. Crops and cattle raising remain the primary economic activities.

PAPAL BULL, papal letter containing a weighty pronouncement and bearing a leaden seal (*bulla*). It may grant a favor, issue a reprimand, or proclaim the canonization of a saint. It is considered more important than an ENCYCLICAL.

PAPAL CONSISTORY, assembly of the college of cardinals to advise the pope. Today, consistories are generally ceremonial formalities.

PAPAL ENCYCLICAL. See ENCYCLICAL.

PAPAL INFALLIBILITY. See PAPACY; VATICAN COUNCILS.

PAPAL LEGATE. See LEGATE.

PAPAL NUNCIO. See NUNCIO.

PAPAL STATES, lands held by the popes as temporal rulers, 754–1870. The states date from PEPIN THE SHORT's donation of conquered Lombard lands to the papacy. Later gifts and conquests meant that by the early 1200s the states stretched from coast to coast across central Italy. VICTOR EMMANUEL II annexed the papal states, including, eventually, Rome itself (1870) during the RISORGIMENTO. The papacy refused to accept its loss of lands until the LATERAN TREATY (1929) created an independent VATICAN CITY.

PAPANICOLAOU, George Nicholas (1883–1962), Greek-born US anatomist largely responsible for the development of cytologic PATHOLOGY (see also CYTOLOGY). He devised the PAP SMEAR TEST, used to reveal early signs of CANCER.

PAPAW, or **paw paw**, *Asimina triloba*, small deciduous tree native to North America. The fruits of some varieties are edible with a flavor similar to that of the banana. Also, the PAPAYA is sometimes called a papaw. Family: Annonaceae.

PAPAYA, *Carica papaya*, small tropical fruit tree, widely cultivated for its large edible fruit. The juice of the stem, leaves and unripe fruit contain the protein-digesting enzyme papain. The papaya is sometimes called a PAPAW. Family: Caricaceae.

PAPEETE, seaport on the NW coast of TAHITI, its capital and the capital of FRENCH POLYNESIA. There is an international airport. Pop 24 000.

PAPEN, Franz von (1879–1969), German statesman. Lacking support as chancellor (June–Nov. 1932), he resigned and helped engineer the appointment of Hitler, supporting the Nazis as a bulwark against communism. He was Hitler's vice-chancellor 1933–34, and as German minister to Vienna (1934–38), he paved the way for German annexation of Austria.

PAPER, felted or matted sheets of CELLULOSE fibers, formed on a wire screen from a water suspension, and used for writing and printing on. Rags and cloth—still used for special high-grade papers—were the raw materials used until generally replaced by wood pulp processes developed in the mid-19th century. Logs are now pulped by three methods. Mechanical pulping normally uses a revolving grindstone. In full chemical pulping, wood chips are cooked under pressure in a solution that dissolves all but the cellulose: the kraft process uses alkaline sodium sulfide solution; the sulfite process uses various bisulfites with excess sulfur dioxide. Semichemical pulping employs mild chemical softening followed by mechanical grinding. The pulp is bleached, washed and refined—i.e., the fibers are crushed, frayed and cut by mechanical beaters. This increases their surface area and bonding power. At this stage various substances are added: fillers (mainly clay and chalk) to make the paper opaque, sizes (rosin and alum) for water resistance, and dyes and pigments as necessary. A dilute aqueous slurry of the pulp is fed to the paper machine, flowing onto a moving belt or cylindrical drum of fine wire mesh, most of the water being drained off by gravity and suction. The newly-formed continuous sheet is pressed between rollers, dried by evaporation, and subjected to CALENDERING. Some paper is coated to give a special surface.

PAPERFOLDING. See ORIGAMI.

PAPER NAUTILUS. See ARGONAUT.

PAPIER-MÂCHÉ, molding material of pulped paper mixed with flour paste, glue or resin. It is usually molded while wet but in some industrial processes is pressure-molded. The technique of making papier-mâché decorative objects began in the Orient, and reached Europe in the 18th century.

PAPILLON, breed of dog named for its wing-shaped ears (*papillon* is French for butterfly). A toy breed, it stands up to 11in at the shoulder and weighs up to 11lb. It has a long, silky coat and was once a popular lap dog.

PAPINEAU, Louis Joseph (1786–1871), Canadian politician, champion of French-Canadian rights in the English-dominated executive and legislature of Lower Canada (Quebec). He framed the Ninety-two Resolutions—a statement of French-Canadian grievances passed by the assembly in 1834. In 1837, a revolt broke out and Papineau fled to the US to avoid arrest. He settled back in Canada in 1845.

PAPRIKA. See PIMIENTO.

PAP SMEAR TEST, or Papanicolaou test, CANCER screening test in which cells scraped from the cervix of the WOMB are examined for abnormality under the microscope using the method of G. N. PAPANICOLAOU.

PAPUA NEW GUINEA, independent member of the Commonwealth since Sept. 16, 1975. The E half of NEW GUINEA Island, just N of Australia, comprises five-sixths of its territory. It includes the islands of BOUGAINVILLE, Buka and the Bismarck Archipelago to the NE and the smaller D'Entrecasteaux, Trobriand and Woodlark islands and Louisiade Archipelago to the SE. It is a mountainous, densely forested region with high temperature and rainfall and a rich variety of plant and animal life. The isolating nature of the environment has resulted in a great variety of racial groups and languages: Melanesian in the E and islands, Papuan and sporadic pygmy Negrito groups on the mainland. Most practice animism or tribal religions. In the interior some Stone Age cultures survive. Estate-farming replaces traditional subsistence agriculture in some areas. Exports include timber and coconut products, rubber, cocoa, tea, and coffee. Rich mineral deposits, largely unexploited, include oil, gas and copper. The N mainland and islands were part of German New Guinea 1884–1914. Seized by Australia in 1914, they later became the Trust Territory of New Guinea. The S area was British New Guinea 1884–1905, then, as the Territory of Papua, under Australian rule. The two areas were merged administratively in 1949.

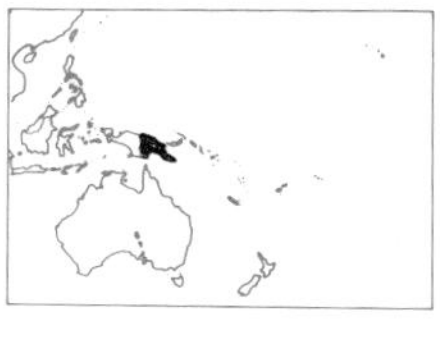

Official name: Papua New Guinea
Capital: Port Moresby
Area: 179 600sq mi
Population: 2 700 000
Language: English
Religions: Christian; tribal religions, animism
Monetary unit(s): 1 Kina = 100 toea

PAPYRUS, or paper reed, *Cyperus papyrus*, a stout, reed-like SEDGE, used in ancient civilizations as a writing material. It was also used for making sails, baskets and clothing, and the pith as food. Family: Cyperaceae.

PARÁ, sparsely-populated state in N Brazil. Its 481 869sq mi include much of the lower Amazon basin. The capital is Belém.

PARABOLA. See CONIC SECTIONS.

PARACEL ISLANDS, or Hsi-sha islands, a small group 175mi S of Hainan in the South China Sea, administered by China. There are oil deposits.

PARACELSUS, Philippus Aureolus (1493–1541), Swiss alchemist and physician who channeled the arts of ALCHEMY toward the preparation of medical remedies (see IATROCHEMISTRY). Born Theophrastus Bombast von Hohenheim, he adopted the name Paracelsus boasting that he was superior to CELSUS.

PARACHUTE, collapsible umbrella-like structure used to retard movement through the air. It was invented in the late-18th century, being used for descent from balloons, and made successively from canvas, silk and nylon. When opened—either manually by pulling a ripcord or by a line attached to the aircraft—the canopy fills with air, trapping a large air mass which, because of the parachute's movement, is at a higher pressure than that outside, producing a large retarding force. The canopy consists of numerous strong panels sewn together. Parachutes are used for safe descent of paratroops and others, for dropping airplanes or missiles, and returning space capsules. Sport parachuting, or SKYDIVING, has become popular.

PARADISE, urban community N of Sacramento, Cal. It lies in a fruit-growing region. Pop 14 539.

PARADISE, a term for HEAVEN, or a heaven-like state or condition on earth. The word (Old Persian: royal pleasure grounds) was adopted by the SEPTUAGINT translators of the Bible as synonymous with the Garden of EDEN. In medieval times, an "earthly paradise" was thought to exist in the East.

PARADISE FISH, *Macropodus opercularis*, a labyrinth fish of China and SE Asia. About 100mm (4in) long, it has a blue body marked with thin orange stripes. The tail fin is red and there is a red-edged spot on the gill-cover, or operculum.

PARADOX, commonly a literary or rhetorical device whereby a supposedly true statement is couched for effect in apparently contradictory terms: e.g., "The last shall be first." A "theoretical paradox" is the conclusion of an apparently convincing argument that is apparently inconsistent with a generally accepted body of theory.

PARAFFINS. See ALKANES.

PARAGUAY, landlocked republic of South America, bordered by Brazil, Argentina and Bolivia. The Paraguay R flows N-S and divides the country into two distinct regions. The sparsely populated W region known as the Chaco Boreal (part of the GRAN CHACO) is flat, scrubby country, increasingly arid to the W. The smaller but far richer E region is where most of the people live; it is itself divided into two distinct regions by a clifflike ridge running N from the Alto Paraná R near Encarnación. The sparsely populated and densely forested Paraná Plateau lies to the E. To the W, rolling country, rarely above 2 000ft, falls away to more populous low-lying terrain.

People and Economy. The majority of the people are mestizo, with Guaraní Indian stock predominating over Spanish influence. More than 65% of the working population is employed on the land, of which only about 3% is cultivated. Over a third of the gross national product, however, comes from agriculture. Products of ranch, farm (cotton, tobacco, coffee) and forest (timber, tannin, oils) are the chief exports. Industry is represented mainly by agricultural product processing. No commercially valuable minerals have been found, though oil deposits exist in the Chaco. Although over half the country is forested, even this resource is mainly unexploited.

History. Spanish exploration and settlement began in the 1500s. By the 1550s the region had become Spain's power base in SE South America. Jesuit influence 1609–1767 contributed significantly to the merging of Guaraní and Spanish cultures. During 1776–1811, Paraguay was part of the Spanish viceroyalty of La Plata. It gained independence in 1811 after a relatively peaceful revolt. Its third ruler, Francisco Lopez, led the disastrous War of the Triple Alliance against Brazil, Uruguay and Argentina (1865–70). Paraguay was laid waste and more than half the population died. Clashes with Bolivia over a border dispute led to the CHACO WAR (1932–35). Paraguay gained territory but was ruined economically. President Morínigo's comparatively stable and constructive rule (1940–48) ended in civil war. The incumbent president, Gen. Alfredo STROESSNER, seized power in 1954.

Official name: Republic of Paraguay
Capital: Asunción
Area: 157 042sq mi
Population: 2 328 780
Languages: Spanish, Guaraní spoken
Religion: Roman Catholic
Monetary unit(s): 1 Guarani = 100 centimos

Parachutist in training drifts to earth at the Naval Air Station in Lakehurst, New Jersey.

PARAGUAY RIVER, rises in Mato Grosso state, SW Brazil, and flows 1 584mi S to join the Paraná R in SW Paraguay. It is navigable for larger vessels up to Concepción. Asunción in Paraguay is the major port.

PARAÍBA RIVER, name of two Brazilian rivers which flow into the Atlantic. The 180mi long Paraíba do Norte lies in Paraíba state. The 600mi long Paraíba do Sul lies in E São Paulo and Rio de Janeiro states.

PARAKEETS, small or medium-sized PARROTS with long tails. They do not form a natural group, the name being given to species of many different genera. Most parakeets are brightly-colored, gregarious birds, feeding on fruits, buds and flowers in semiarid regions throughout the tropics.

PARALLAX, the difference in observed direction of an object due to a difference in position of the observer. Parallax in nearby objects may be observed by closing each eye in turn so that the more distant object appears to move relative to the closer. The brain normally assembles these two images to produce a stereoscopic effect (see BINOCULAR VISION). Should the length and direction of the line between the two points of observation be known, parallax may be used to calculate the distance of the object. In astronomy, the parallax of a star is defined as half the greatest parallactic displacement when viewed from earth at different times of the year (see PARSEC).

PARALLELEPIPED, a hexahedron (see POLYHEDRON) whose opposite faces are parallel, each side being a parallelogram (see QUADRILATERAL). Should the sides be rectangular, the figure is a cuboid; should they be square, the figure is a CUBE.

PARALLEL LINES, LINES which would have to be extended until they were of infinite length in order to intersect.

PARALLELOGRAM. See QUADRILATERAL.

PARALYSIS, temporary or permanent loss of MUSCLE power or control. It may consist of inability to move a limb or part of a limb or individual muscles, paralysis of the muscles of breathing, swallowing and VOICE production being especially serious. Paralysis may be due to disease of the BRAIN (e.g., STROKE; TUMOR); SPINAL CORD (POLIOMYELITIS); nerve roots (SLIPPED DISK); peripheral NERVOUS SYSTEM (NEURITIS); neuromuscular junction (MYASTHENIA GRAVIS), or muscle (MUSCULAR DYSTROPHY). Disturbance of blood POTASSIUM levels can also lead to paralysis.

PARAMAGNETISM, weak magnetization of a material in the same direction as an applied MAGNETIC FIELD. Normally stronger than DIAMAGNETISM, the effect varies inversely with TEMPERATURE, and involves the partial alignment of intrinsic or orbital ELECTRON dipoles.

PARAMARIBO, former (Dutch capital of Surinam Guiana), a port on the Surinam R, near the Atlantic. It is an important export center for bauxite products. Pop 102 297.

PARAMECIUM, one of the best-known genera of PROTOZOA. All are free-living in fresh or stagnant water, feeding on bacteria or particles of plant material. They are ovoid bodies, covered by cilia and, unlike many Protozoa, having a distinct mouth region.

PARAMETER, a VARIABLE whose value determines a distinct set (see SET THEORY) of cases in a mathematical statement. Parametric equations are those expressed in terms of parameters. For example,

$$f(x) = ax^2 + b$$

is the general equation (see ANALYTIC GEOMETRY) of a set of points corresponding to a parabola (see CONIC SECTIONS), expressed in terms of the parameters *a* and *b*. Substitutions of specific values of these defines a particular set. In STATISTICS, the parameters of a distribution are those elements of it which can be used to loosely define it. They may be location parameters, such as the MEAN, MEDIAN AND MODE, or parameters of dispersion, such as the STANDARD DEVIATION.

PARAMOUNT, suburban city of Los Angeles Co., SW Cal. Its products include metal and plastic goods and resin. Pop 34 734.

PARAMUS, residential borough in NE N.J. It is a major retail center for truck farms and produces building materials. Pop 28 381.

PARANÁ, state in S Brazil, 77 048sq mi in area. Mostly a series of generally fertile plateaus, it is a largely agricultural region. Its capital is Curitiba.

PARANÁ, river port city and capital of Entre Ríos province, E Argentina. It lies in a livestock and grain-farming region. Pop 107 551.

PARANAÍBA RIVER, formerly Paranahiba R, a 500mi long headstream of the Paraná R, Brazil. It rises in central Minas Gerais state.

PARANÁ RIVER, or **Alto Parannà** R, formed by the confluence of the Rio Grande and the Paranaíba R in S central Brazil. An important commercial artery, it flows 1 827mi S and SW to join the Paraguay R.

PARANOIA, a PSYCHOSIS characterized by delusions of persecution (hence the popular term, **persecution mania**) and grandeur, often accompanied by HALLUCINATIONS. The delusions may form a self-consistent system which replaces reality. (See also MENTAL ILLNESS; SCHIZOPHRENIA.)

PARANTHROPUS. See PREHISTORIC MAN.

PARAPLEGIA, PARALYSIS involving the lower part of the body, particularly the legs. Injury to the SPINAL CHORD is often the cause.

PARAPSYCHOLOGY, or **Psychic Research**, a field of study concerned with scientific evaluation of two distinct types of phenomena: those collectively termed ESP, and those concerned with life after death, reincarnation, etc., particularly including claims to communication with souls of the dead (spiritism or, incorrectly, spiritualism). Tests of the former have generally been inconclusive, of the latter almost exclusively negative. But in both cases many "believers" hold that such phenomena, being beyond the bounds of science, cannot be subjected to laboratory evaluation. In spiritism, the prime site of the alleged communication is the séance, in which one individual (the medium) goes into a trance before communicating with the souls of the dead, often through a spirit guide (a spirit associated particularly with the medium). The astonishing disparity between different accounts of the spirit world has led to the whole field being treated with skepticism.

PARÁ RIVER, in Brazil, the navigable E mouth of the Amazon R, 200mi long and 40mi wide at its mouth. It flows S and E of Marajó Island and receives the Tocantins R from the S.

PARASITE, an organism that is for some part of its life-history physiologically dependent on another, the host, from which it obtains nutrition and which may form its total environment. Nearly all the major groups of animals and plants from viruses to vertebrates and BACTERIA and angiosperms, have some parasitic members. The most important parasites, besides the viruses which are a wholly

The Île de la Cité, the heart of Paris. This island in the Seine, originally a settlement of the Gallic Parisii tribe, inspired the city's motto, *Fluctuat nec mergitur* (it floats but does not sink).

parasitic group, occur in the bacteria, Protozoa, Flatworms and Roundworms. Study of the parasitic worms, the platyhelminths, nematodes and acanthocephalans, is termed helminthology. Blood-sucking arthropods, such as mosquitoes, Tsetse flies and ticks, are also important because they transmit PARASITIC DISEASES and serve as vectors or transport-hosts for other parasites.

PARASITIC DISEASES, infestation or infection by PARASITES, usually referring to nonbacterial and nonviral agents (i.e., to PROTOZOA and helminths). MALARIA, LEISHMANIASIS, trypanosomiasis (see TRYPANOSOMES), CHAGAS' DISEASE, FILARIASIS, SCHISTOSOMIASIS, toxoplasmosis, amebiasis and TAPE WORM are common examples. Manifestations may depend on the life cycle of the parasite; animal or insect vectors are usual. CHEMOTHERAPY is often effective in treatment.

PARASOL ANTS. See LEAF-CUTTING ANTS.

PARASYMPATHETIC NERVOUS SYSTEM. See NERVOUS SYSTEM.

PARATHYROID GLANDS, a set of four small ENDOCRINE GLANDS lying behind the THYROID which regulate CALCIUM metabolism. Parathyroid hormone releases calcium from BONE and alters the intestinal absorption and KIDNEY excretion of calcium and phosphorus. Disease or loss of parathyroid glands may lead to TETANY, CATARACT or mental changes, and may be associated with disorders of IMMUNITY. Parathyroid overactivity or TUMORS cause raised blood calcium leading to bone disease, kidney disease (including stones) and mental abnormalities.

PARATYPHOID FEVER, BACTERIAL DISEASE similar to TYPHOID FEVER and caused by a related organism, causing FEVER, DIARRHEA, rash, SPLEEN and LYMPH node enlargement. Spread is by cases or carriers and contaminated food; ANTIBIOTICS may be helpful in treatment.

PARAZOA. See ANIMAL KINGDOM; METAZOA.

PARCHMENT, the skin of sheep, ewes or lambs, cleaned, polished, stretched and dried to make a material which can be written on, and also used to make drums and for bookbinding. Invented in the 2nd century BC as a substitute for PAPYRUS, it was widely used for manuscripts until superseded by paper in the 15th century, except for legal documents. **Vellum** is fine-quality parchment made from lamb, kid or calf skin. Both terms are now applied to high-quality paper. Vegetable parchment is paper immersed briefly in sulfuric acid and so made strong and parchment-like.

PARDON, in law, the official deletion of a conviction, usually by a country's chief executive. In US law the president can pardon any federal offense except IMPEACHMENT, and can pardon before conviction, or even indictment. State governors can pardon state offenses.

PARÉ, Ambroise (c1510–1590), French surgeon whose many achievements (e.g., adopting ligatures or liniments in place of CAUTERIZATION; introducing the use of artificial limbs and organs) have earned him regard as a father of modern SURGERY.

PAREGORIC, tincture of OPIUM, a NARCOTIC ANALGESIC.

PARENTS AND TEACHERS, National Congress of (PTA), voluntary US alliance which aims to further education and productive school-community relations. There are over 45 000 local units. The PTA grew from the National Congress of Mothers, founded 1897 by Alice McLellan Birney and Phoebe Apperson Hearst. The name was changed in 1924.

PARESIS, muscular weakness of a part, usually used in distinction from PARALYSIS, which implies complete loss of muscle power. It may be due to disease of the BRAIN, SPINAL CORD, peripheral NERVOUS SYSTEM or MUSCLES.

PARETO, Vilfredo (1848–1923), Italian economist and sociologist. He followed Walras in applying mathematics to economic theory. (See ECONOMICS.) His theories on elites, developed in *Mind and Society* (1916), influenced Mussolini's fascists.

PARICUTÍN, volcano 180mi W of Mexico City, the first to appear in the Western Hemisphere since 1770. It began to form on Feb. 20, 1943, and grew 1 500ft in a year, destroying nearby villages. The cone is 9 213ft above sea level. It has been inactive since 1952.

PARIS, capital and largest city of France. It is in the middle of the fertile ÎLE DE FRANCE region. The Seine R winds through Paris, spanned by 30 bridges, and flows 110mi NW to the English Channel. World-famous for its beauty, social and cultural life, Paris is an important port and France's chief manufacturing center. In the city itself, tourism, dressmaking and luxury trades predominate. Heavier industry (chiefly autos) is based further out in the metropolitan area. On the Left Banks of the Seine lies the SORBONNE in the Latin Quarter, associated with students and artists. Over 2 million tourists a year come to enjoy the EIFFEL TOWER, LOUVRE museum, NOTRE DAME cathedral, MONTMARTRE, the cafes, gardens, and nightlife.

The Parisii Gauls inhabited the Île de la Cité in the middle of the Seine when the Romans set up a colony at this important crossroads in 52 BC. In 507 AD King Clovis I of the Franks made Paris his capital, a status confirmed when Hugh Capet became King of France in 987 (see CAPETIANS). Growth increased in Philip II's reign (1180–1223) and was maintained even when Louis XIV moved the court to Versailles (1682). The rebuilding of Paris after the FRENCH REVOLUTION (1789) included Georges Haussman's great tree-lined boulevards. The work was interrupted 1870–71 by the FRANCO-PRUSSIAN WAR and by the PARIS COMMUNE. Pop 2 590 771.

PARIS, city in NE Tex., seat of Lamar Co. It is the commercial and market center for the surrounding agricultural region. Pop 23 441.

PARIS, or **Alexander,** in Greek myth, the son of King PRIAM and Queen HECUBA of Troy. Abandoned at birth on Mt Ida because of portents that he would ruin Troy, he was raised by shepherds. Zeus later ordered him to choose between the beauty of the goddesses Hera, Athena and Aphrodite. He chose the last. In reward, he was allowed to abduct HELEN, precipitating the TROJAN WAR and the fall of Troy.

PARIS, Pact of. See BRIAND PACT.

PARIS, Treaties of, name given to several treaties concluded at Paris. The **Treaty of Paris, 1763,** ended the SEVEN YEARS WAR including the FRENCH AND INDIAN WARS in America. France lost her military rights in E India (and thus any chance of ousting the British) and her American possessions. Britain gained Florida and parts of Louisiana, and Spain regained Cuba and the Philippines. Freed from the French threat, American colonists stepped up the struggle for independence, which was finally confirmed by the **Treaty of Paris, 1783,** ending the REVOLUTIONARY WAR. US boundaries were agreed as Canada in the N, the Mississippi in the W and Florida (regained by Spain) in the S, and the US won fishing rights off Newfoundland. The **Treaty of Paris, 1814,** attempted to end the NAPOLEONIC WARS after Napoleon's first abdication. France under the restored Bourbon monarchy was allowed to retain her 1792 boundaries and most of her colonies. The **Treaty of Paris, 1815,** signed after Napoleon's final defeat at WATERLOO, dealt with France more harshly. French boundaries were reduced to those of 1790 and France had to pay reparations and support an army of occupation for up to five years. The **Treaty of Paris, 1856,** ending the CRIMEAN WAR, was signed by Russia, Britain, France, Turkey and Sardinia. Designed largely to protect Turkey from Russia, it guaranteed Turkish independence, declared the Black Sea neutral, opened Danube navigation to all nations, and established MOLDAVIA and WALACHIA (later Romania) as independent states under Turkish suzerainty. The **Treaty of Paris, 1898,** ended the SPANISH-AMERICAN WAR and effectively ended the Spanish empire. Cuba became independent, and the US gained Puerto Rico, Guam and the Philippines. After WWI the treaties of NEUILLY, SAINT-GERMAIN, SÈVRES, TRIANON and VERSAILLES were concluded at the Paris Peace Conference. Treaties were also signed at Paris after WWII.

PARIS COMMUNE, insurrection of radical Parisians against the pro-royalist National Assembly, March–May 1871, following the humiliation of the FRANCO-PRUSSIAN WAR. The Communards drove the Assembly out of Paris, and elected their own Commune government, while similar movements broke out elsewhere. The Assembly sent in 130000 troops who crushed the movement in a week of bloody street fighting, killing some 20000 people.

PARIS GREEN, or **emerald green,** toxic, bright blue-green PIGMENT, copper acetoarsenate(III), $Cu_2(CH_3COO)AsO_3$; now used as a pesticide and wood preservative.

PARITY, physical property of a wave function (see WAVE MECHANICS) in QUANTUM MECHANICS specifying the function's behavior when its spatial coordinates are simultaneously reflected through the origin. If the parity is even, the wave function is unchanged by changing the sign of its coordinates; if it is odd, the wave function's sign changes. Parity has no significance in classical physics, but essentially arises from the symmetry of space. Strong nuclear and electromagnetic interactions conserve parity because they are governed by physical laws which do not distinguish between a right- or left-handed coordinate system (as in nature, where an object and its mirror image are equally realizable). Parity is not conserved in weak nuclear interactions.

PARITY, name for the government-supported farm prices in the US. The price of agricultural produce (mainly wheat, corn and cotton) is fixed in relation to other prices, and the equivalence, or parity, thus established is maintained by government aid if farm prices drop.

PARK, Mungo (1771–1806), Scottish explorer of W Africa. He made two exploratory journeys along the Gambia, upper Sénégal and Niger rivers, 1795–97 and 1805–06, publishing *Travels in the Interior Districts of Africa* in 1799. He was drowned at Bussa during attack by hostile Africans.

PARK CHUNG HEE, (1917–   ) president of South Korea since 1963. He served with the Japanese in WWII, became a general in the Korean army and took part in the 1961 military coup. Becoming progressively more dictatorial, in 1972 he assumed almost unlimited power.

PARKER, Alton Brooks (1852–1926), US jurist and Democratic presidential candidate. He was chief justice of the N.Y. court of appeals 1897–1904, and after losing to Theodore ROOSEVELT in 1904 returned to private practice.

PARKER, Charlie (Charles Christopher, 1920–1955), US jazz musician, known as "Bird." An outstanding improviser on the saxophone, he also composed, and was one of the creators of the 1940s jazz style known as BOP.

PARKER, Dorothy (1893–1967), US writer, critic and wit. She wrote short stories, satirical verse and newspaper columns, and was a celebrated conversationalist. Her tone is poignant, ironical and often cruelly witty and cynical.

PARKER, Theodore (1810–1860), US liberal preacher and social reformer. A Unitarian pastor in West Roxbury, Mass. (1837–46) and Boston (1846–59), he championed abolition of slavery, prison reform, temperance and education for women.

PARKERSBURG, city in W W.Va. on the Ohio R, seat of Wood Co. It is a river port and makes textiles, glass, and metal and plastic goods. Pop 44208.

PARK FOREST, village in NE Ill., 11mi S of Chicago. It was wholly planned and developed as a residential area for Chicago after WWII. Pop 30638.

PARKINSON'S DISEASE, a common disorder in the elderly, causing a characteristic mask-like facial appearance, shuffling gait, slowness to move, muscular rigidity and tremor at rest; mental ability is preserved except in those cases following ENCEPHALITIS lethargica. It is a disorder of the basal ganglia of the BRAIN and may be substantially helped by DRUGS (e.g., L-Dopa) that affect impulse transmission in these sites.

PARKLAND, town in W central Wash. It is a residential suburb 6mi S of Tacoma. Pop 21012.

PARKMAN, Francis (1823–1893), great US historian of the Frontier and of the Anglo-French struggle for North America. His chief work is the seven volumes collectively called *France and England in North America* (1865–92). Other works include his *History of the Conspiracy of Pontiac* (1851) and *The Oregon Trail* (1849), an enormously popular account of a journey made in 1846. He later became an expert horticulturalist.

PARK RIDGE, city in NE Ill. It is a residential suburb 13mi NW of Chicago. Pop 42614.

PARKS, areas of land set aside for public recreation. Urban parks gained importance as towns grew in the 19th century and are a distinctive feature of modern cities. Central Park in New York was laid out in 1857 by F. L. OLMSTED to produce the effect of countryside in the middle of a city. Such parks often imitated landscaped English parklands (see LANDSCAPE ARCHITECTURE) and featured ornamental lakes and artificial hills. In the 20th century the US NATIONAL PARK SYSTEM developed from the need to preserve large areas of countryside from being built on and to safeguard their wildlife. Since the creation of Yellowstone Park in 1872, about 46000sq mi of the US have been so protected.

PARKVILLE, unincorporated urban community in N Md., NE of Baltimore. It is a residential area. Pop 33897.

PARLEMENT, French high court of justice in Paris which operated from the Middle Ages until 1789. It had some political influence through its power of questioning the king's edicts. Membership became a hereditary privilege. There were also 12 provincial parlements. As bastions of reaction, they were swept away in the French Revolution.

PARLIAMENT, body of elected representatives responsible for a country's legislation and finance. The term parliamentary government is used to describe a system (distinct from the presidential system) in which the government's chief ministers, including the PRIME MINISTER, are elected members of parliament. This system operates in Britain, most Commonwealth countries and Scandinavia.

In a parliamentary system the head of state (a monarch or president) exists outside parliament and exercises only limited powers; real power rests with the prime minister, who leads the majority party or a coalition of parties. He rules with the help of a CABINET chosen from other elected members. The government in power has the right to dissolve parliament and call a new election before its term of office ends, but is obliged to resign if it fails to command a majority vote of members. All these features differ from presidential government as practiced in the US. The chief model for modern parliamentary government is the British Parliament, which began to take on its present form in the Middle Ages. (See also HOUSE OF COMMONS; HOUSE OF LORDS; LEGISLATURE; PRESIDENCY.)

PARMA, historic city in N Italy, an ancient Roman foundation and a center of learning in the Middle Ages. It is a rail and road center and makes machinery, fertilizer, footwear and glass. Parma ham and Parmesan cheese are famous. Pop 174655.

PARMA, city in NE Ohio, 8mi S of Cleveland. Mainly residential, it also manufactures automobile parts and has tool and die plants. Pop 100216.

PARMA HEIGHTS, residential city in NE Ohio. It is a SW suburb of Cleveland, adjoining Parma, from which it was settled in 1912. Pop 27192.

PARMENIDES (flourished c475 BC), Greek philosopher of Elea in southern Italy; foremost of the ELEATICS. His philosophy, anchored on the proposition "What is *is*," denied the reality of multiplicity and change. His uncompromising attempt to deduce the properties of the Real—a single eternal solid, all-embracing yet undifferentiated—marks the beginning of the Western tradition of philosophical reasoning. (See also PRE-SOCRATICS.)

PARNASSIANS, group of 19th-century French poets led by LECONTE DE LISLE. Influenced by GAUTIER's "art for art's sake" theories, they emphasized technical skill, restraint and objectivity.

PARNASSUS, mountain in central Greece, N of DELPHI and the Gulf of Corinth. It was once sacred to Dionysus and Apollo and celebrated as a home of the MUSES. It is 8061ft high.

PARNELL, Charles Stewart (1846–1891), Irish nationalist, leader of the Irish HOME RULE movement from within the British parliament from 1877. He obstructed parliamentary business and demanded Irish land reform, and his supporter's agitation persuaded GLADSTONE to adopt a home rule policy. His political career ended in 1890 when he was named corespondent in a divorce case.

PAROCHIAL SCHOOLS, in the US, elementary and high schools run by religious bodies. The Roman Catholic Church, the Lutheran system and the Jewish Day Schools between them cater for more than 10% of the nation's elementary and high-school pupils. Most parochial schools were set up in the 19th century. They expanded until the 1960s, but were then beset by financial problems, complicated by controversies over whether they should receive state and federal aid.

PAROLE, the system of releasing convicts from prison before the end of their sentences. Generally, parole is granted for good behavior in prison, if the parole board consider a prisoner psychologically and socially ready to readjust to the outside world. A parolee must usually observe certain standards of conduct, stay within certain areas, and report to a parole officer. (See also PRISONS; PROBATION.)

PAROTID GLANDS. See SALIVA.

PAROUSIA. See SECOND COMING.

Central Park's spacious and varied grounds offer recreational facilities to the citizens of New York City.

PARR, Catherine (1512–1548), sixth wife of King HENRY VIII of England (1543–47). Twice widowed before she married the king, she outlived him to marry again. She was a kindly influence at court and held some power in the reign of EDWARD VI.

PARRINGTON, Vernon Louis (1871–1929), US literary historian who stressed the influence of social and economic affairs upon American writers. His *Main Currents in American Thought* (1927–30) won a Pulitzer Prize.

PARRISH, Maxfield (1870–1966), US painter and illustrator with an elegant, richly decorative style. He is noted for murals, posters and book and magazine illustrations.

PARROTS, a family, Psittacidae, of about 320 species of birds distributed throughout the tropics. Most are brightly-colored birds with heavy, hooked bills, of which both mandibles articulate with the skull. Most are arboreal and diurnal, feeding on fruits, berries and leaves. There are four subfamilies: the Strigopinae (with only the KAKAPO of New Zealand), the Cacatuinae (the COCKATOOS) and the Lorinae (the LORIES and lorikeets, pygmy parrots and fig parrots). The fourth subfamily, the Psittacinae, contains some 200 species of "true" parrots, including the 130 species of American parrots.

PARROT FEVER. See PSITTACOSIS.

PARROT FISHES, a family, Scaridae, of colorful fishes of tropical seas. The upper jaw protrudes and the teeth in both jaws have become fused into a parrot-like beak. They live on coral reefs, feeding on the coral itself. Their droppings accumulate in specific sites as mounds of white, coral sand.

PARRY ISLANDS, group of Canadian islands in the Arctic Ocean N of Viscount Melville Sound, including Cornwallis Island, Melville Island and Prince Patrick Island.

PARSEC (pc), in astronomy, the distance at which 1 ASTRONOMICAL UNIT would subtend an angle of 1 second. Originally defined as the distance of a star with a PARALLAX of 1″ viewed from earth and sun, the parsec was introduced to replace the LIGHT YEAR. 1pc = 3.258ly = 206 265AU.

PARSEES, or Parsis, religious group who practice ZOROASTRIANISM. Their ancestors came from Persia in the 8th century to escape Muslim persecution. They now number about 120 000, mostly in NW India and Bombay. Many are traders, and the Parsees are among the wealthiest groups in India. They worship at fire temples and expose their dead.

PARSIFAL, knight of ARTHURIAN LEGEND, finder of the HOLY GRAIL. He appears (variously spelt) in works by CHRÉTIEN DE TROYES and WOLFRAM VON ESCHENBACH, and is the hero of WAGNER's *Parsifal*.

PARSIPPANY-TROY HILLS, urban township in NE N.J. It is a residential area, with some light industry, including drugs and cosmetics. Pop 55 112.

PARSLEY, *Carum petroselinium*, a hardy biennial herb, one variety of which is cultivated for use as a garnish and another as a root vegetable. Family: Umbelliferae.

PARSNIP, *Pastinaca sativa*, a carrot-like plant grown for its edible sweet-flavored yellowish-white root. They are easy to cultivate, but need a long growing season and are harvested in the fall and winter. Family: Umbelliferae.

PARSONS, city in SE Kan., 33mi W of Pittsburg. It is a shipping center for farm products and has some manufacturing industry. Pop 13 105.

PARSONS, Talcott (1902–   ), US sociologist, who taught at Harvard 1927–74. An inveterate theorizer, he advocated a "structural-functional" analysis of the units that make up a stable social system. Works include *The Structure of Social Action* (1937) and *The Social System* (1951).

PARSONS, Theophilus (1750–1813), US jurist. A member of the ESSEX JUNTO, he helped draft a new Mass. constitution in 1779, and was chief justice of the Mass. Supreme Court from 1806.

PARTHENOGENESIS, sometimes popularly termed virgin birth, the development into a new individual of an ovum that has not been fertilized by a sperm. It is usually regarded as an aberrant form of sexual reproduction.

PARTHENON, the most famous Greek temple, on

Above left: the Parthenon in Athens, arguably the most beautiful of all Greek temples, built at the instigation of Pericles. *Right:* replica in Nashville, Tennessee, completed in 1897.

the ACROPOLIS at Athens. Sacred to the city's patron goddess, Athena Parthenos (Athena the Virgin), it was built of marble 447–432 BC by ICTINUS and CALLICRATES, with PHIDIAS supervising the sculptures. It featured a roof on Doric columns, an inner room, and fine sculptures and friezes including the ELGIN MARBLES. The Parthenon remained well preserved until 1687 when a Venetian bombardment exploded a Turkish powder magazine inside it. (See also GREEK ART AND ARCHITECTURE.)

PARTHIA, ancient country SE of the Caspian Sea, where the ARSACID empire was founded c248 BC in revolt against the SELEUCIDS. It reached its zenith under Mithradates I (171–138 BC) and II (123–88 BC). Parthians conquered Persia and nearby lands, and their mounted archers continually withstood Roman aggression. A revolt established the SASSANIANS in power 224 AD. (See also PERSIA, ANCIENT.)

PARTICLES, Elementary. See SUBATOMIC PARTICLES.

PARTISANS, term usually used to describe the resistance movements in German-occupied territories in WWII. The original partisans were the communist supporters (*partizani*) of TITO in Yugoslavia. (See also GUERRILLA WARFARE; MAQUIS.)

PARTNERSHIP, business arrangement between two or more people combining labor, funds or property with a view to sharing profits. In law, partners are assumed to exercise joint control and can be held responsible for the liabilities of the partnership. The arrangement is common in professions such as law and accountancy and in small-scale service businesses. In limited partnerships a partner's liability is limited to his investment in the partnership.

PARTRIDGES, several genera of game birds distributed through Europe, Asia and Africa. Best known is the Gray or Common partridge, *Perdix perdix*, of Europe, with a chestnut horseshoe on the breast.

PARTY, Political. See POLITICAL PARTY.

PASADENA, city in S Cal., 10mi NE of Los Angeles, of which it is a wealthy suburb. It is a renowned cultural and educational center, and produces precision instruments, ceramics, plastics and chemicals. The California Institute of Technology is located here. Pop 112 981.

PASADENA, city in S Tex., 10mi SE of Houston. Its industry, mostly oil-based, includes chemicals, plastics and machinery. Pop 89 277.

PASANG, or **Bezoar**, *Capra hircus*, a wild GOAT best known as the source of the bezoar stone, reputed to be an antidote for all poisons. The stone is a concretion such as that found in the gut of most RUMINANTS, formed around some foreign material.

PASCAGOULA, city in SE Miss., on Mississippi Sound, seat of Jackson Co. It is a fishing and shipbuilding center and a resort. Pop 27 264.

PASCAL, Blaise (1623–1662), French mathematician, physicist and religious philosopher. Though not the first to study what is now called PASCAL'S TRIANGLE, he was first to use it in PROBABILITY studies, the mathematical treatment of which he and FERMAT evolved together, though in different ways. His studies of the CYCLOID inspired others to formulate the CALCULUS. His experiments (performed by his brother-in-law) observing the heights of the column of a BAROMETER at different altitudes on the mountain Puy-de-Dôme (1646) confirmed that the atmospheric air had weight. He also pioneered HYDRODYNAMICS and HYDROSTATICS, in doing so discovering PASCAL'S LAW, the basis of HYDRAULICS. His religious thought was dominated by his association with the Jansenist convent of Port Royal, and is expressed in his *Provincial Letters* (1656–57) and his posthumously published *Pensées* (1670 onward).

PASCAL (Pa), the SI UNIT of PRESSURE, being that due to a FORCE of one NEWTON acting per square metre.

PASCAL'S LAW, in HYDROSTATICS, states that the pressure in an enclosed body of fluid arising from forces applied to its boundaries is transmitted equally in all directions with unchanged intensity. This pressure acts at right angles to the surface of the fluid container.

PASCAL'S TRIANGLE, a tabular arrangement of the COEFFICIENTS of the terms in the expansion of a BINOMIAL raised to the POWERS 0 to n (see BINOMIAL THEOREM).

For $(a+b)^n$ where $n = 0, 1, 2, 3, \ldots$, the coefficients are

$(a+b)^0$	1
$(a+b)^1$	1 1
$(a+b)^2$	1 2 1
$(a+b)^3$	1 3 3 1
$(a+b)^4$	1 4 6 4 1
$(a+b)^5$	1 5 10 10 5 1
$(a+b)^6$	1 6 15 20 15 6 1

etc. The first and last figures in each row are 1; also, each figure is the SUM of the two to its right and left in the row above it. Moreover, the sum of each row is equal to the corresponding power of 2—$1+3+3+1=8=2^3$, etc.—and each row read across is numerically equal to the corresponding power of 11 ($1331=11^3$).

PASCHAL, name of two popes. **Saint Paschal I** (d. 824), a Roman, was pope from 817. He resisted the revival of ICONOCLASM in the East (see ICONOCLASTIC CONTROVERSY). **Paschal II** (d. 1118), born near Ravenna, became pope in 1099, and was involved in the INVESTITURE CONTROVERSY.

PASCHEN, Friedrich (1865–1947), German physicist and a pioneer of SPECTROSCOPY, best known for his experimental work on infrared spectra and for explaining the "Paschen-Back Effect"—which concerns the splitting of spectral lines in an intense MAGNETIC FIELD.

PASCO, city in SE Wash., seat of Franklin Co. It is an inland port and shipping center. Hanford Atomic Energy Works are nearby. Pop 13 920.

PASQUEFLOWER, common name for spring-flowering ANEMONES that are associated with Easter. The American pasqueflower (*Anemone patens*) is abundant in the prairies and the European pasqueflower (*A. pulsatilla*) grows in chalky pastures. Family: Ranunculaceae.

PASSACAGLIA, type of Spanish or Italian dance, better known as a musical form in slow triple time, similar to a CHACONNE, used among others by J. S. Bach and Brahms.

PASSAIC, city in NE N.J., 4mi SE of Paterson.

Settled by the Dutch in 1678, its industries now include electronics and rubber. Pop 55 124.

PASSENGER PIGEON, *Ectopistes migratorius*, extinct member of the PIGEON family Columbidae, extremely common until the 19th century over most of North America. They were highly gregarious and social birds migrating in huge flocks. They fed on invertebrates, fruits and grain, often doing extensive damage to crops. Hunted by man both as a pest and for food, they finally became extinct in 1914.

PASSERIFORMES, a single order of BIRDS which contains all the 5 000 plus species of perching birds and song birds. The order is incredibly diverse and its members have become adapted to an enormous variety of NICHES. All passerines are land birds with feet adapted for perching and walking. Passerine young are "nidicolous"—confined to a nest by their helplessness and cared for by the parents.

PASSION, musical setting of the Gospel texts describing the crucifixion. From early PLAINSONG developed medieval music-drama and Renaissance MOTET forms. Among the first works to use the name were those of SCHÜTZ, who influenced J. S. Bach, composer of the famous *St. John* and *St. Matthew* passions for soloists, chorus and orchestra.

PASSION, The, the sufferings of Jesus Christ for mankind (see ATONEMENT): the agony in the garden at GETHSEMANE, the trial and the crucifixion. **Passiontide**, in the CHURCH YEAR, is the last two weeks in LENT, from Passion Sunday until the Saturday of Holy Week.

PASSION FLOWERS, common name for over 400 tropical and subtropical American vines and shrubs of the genus *Passiflora*, most producing edible fruits. The name derives from religious symbolism which sees in the flower symbols of the Trinity and the crown of thorns. Family: Passifloraceae.

PASSION PLAY, dramatic presentation of Christ's suffering and death. It was one of the popular medieval MYSTERY PLAYS, performed by amateurs at religious festivals. The most famous passion play still performed is that at OBERAMMERGAU, staged every ten years since 1634.

PASSIVE RESISTANCE. See CIVIL DISOBEDIENCE; PACIFISM.

PASSOVER, ancient major Jewish festival held for eight days from 14th *Nisan* (March/April). It celebrates the Israelites' escape from Egyptian slavery, when each family slew a paschal lamb and sprinkled its blood on the doorposts, and the destroying angel passed over (see also PLAGUES OF EGYPT). At the *Seder* feast, on the evening of the first two days, special dishes symbolize the Israelites' hardships and the story of the Exodus is read from the HAGGADAH. During Passover unleavened bread (MATZAH) is eaten, and no LEAVEN may be used, a reminder of the hasty departure. (See also LAST SUPPER.)

PASSPORT, document issued by governments to citizens of their country, identifying and authorizing them to travel abroad and be readmitted to their homeland. Some countries also require a visitor to have a visa, issued by the consular authorities in his home country. In wartime passports may have restricted use.

PASTEL, drawing medium resembling a stick of colored chalk, and the pictures formed with it. The color is applied in broad areas and may be rubbed with the finger to form different tones. Usually it covers an entire surface, resembling painting rather than drawing. Masters of the art include J. B. S. CHARDIN and DEGAS.

PASTERNAK, Boris Leonidovich (1890–1960), Russian writer, best known for his only novel *Doctor Zhivago* (1958). He won the 1958 Nobel Prize for Literature but official pressure forced him to decline it. He was also a gifted translator of Shakespeare and Goethe, and the author of poems, short stories and an autobiography.

PASTEUR, Louis (1822–1895), French microbiologist and chemist. In his early pioneering studies in STEREOCHEMISTRY he discovered optical ISOMERISM. His attentions then centered around FERMENTATION, in which he demonstrated the role of microorganisms. He developed PASTEURIZATION as a way of stopping wine and beer from souring, and experimentally disproved the theory of SPONTANEOUS GENERATION. His "germ theory" of DISEASE proposed that diseases are spread by living germs (i.e., BACTERIA); and his consequent popularization of the STERILIZATION of medical equipment saved many lives. While studying ANTHRAX in cattle and sheep he developed a form of VACCINATION rather different from that of JENNER: he found inocculation with dead anthrax germs gave future IMMUNITY from the disease. Treating RABIES similarly, he concluded that it was caused by a germ too small to be seen—i.e., a VIRUS. The Pasteur Institute was founded in 1888 to lead the fight against rabies.

Mounted specimen of the Passenger pigeon, last relic of a species that once swarmed like locusts in the skies of North America. It is thought that when their numbers dropped below a certain level these gregarious birds lost the urge to breed.

PASTEURIZATION, a process for partially sterilizing MILK originally invented by L. PASTEUR for improving the storage qualities of wine and beer. Originally the milk was held at 63°C for 30min in a vat. But today the usual method is a continuous process whereby the milk is held at 72°–85°C for 16s. Disease-producing BACTERIA, particularly those causing TUBERCULOSIS, are thus destroyed with a minimum effect on the flavor of the product. Since the process also destroys a majority of the harmless bacteria which sour milk, its keeping properties are also improved.

PASTORAL LITERATURE, idealizes simple shepherd life, free from the corruption of the city. Typical forms are the verse elegy, prose romance and drama. Originating with THEOCRITUS in the 3rd century BC, the form was used by VERGIL, and later in England, after a Renaissance revival, by Shakespeare (in *As You Like It*), Sir Philip SIDNEY (in *Arcadia*) and MILTON (in *Comus*).

PATAGONIA, that part of South America S of the Rio Negro or, more usually, the dry tableland in this region between the Andes and Atlantic, including Tierra del Fuego. Both areas lie mainly in Argentina, partly in Chile. Sheep-raising is the main activity of the few inhabitants, and there are oil, iron ore and coal deposits.

PATAPSCO RIVER, rises in N Md. and flows 80mi SE into Chesapeake Bay. Baltimore lies on its estuary.

PATAS MONKEY, *Erythrocebus patas*, a GUENON of open country in W Africa. Patas are found in small, single-male troops; they are tall and rangy. The males are bright red and may weight up to 13kg (29lb).

PATCHOGUE, village in SE N.Y. on Long Island, 53mi E of New York City. It is a holiday resort noted for oysters from nearby Blue Point. Pop 11 582.

PATCHOULI, *Microtonea cymosa*, common name for an E Indian plant and the fragrant oil that is distilled from its leaves.

PATCH TEST, test used in investigation of skin and systemic ALLERGY, especially contact DERMATITIS. Patches of known or likely sensitizing substances are placed on the SKIN for a short period. Local ERYTHEMA or HIVES indicate allergy.

PATENT, a grant of certain specified rights by the government of a particular country, usually to a person whose claim to be the true and first inventor of a new invention (or the discoverer of a new process) is upheld. Criteria of the "novelty" of an invention are defined in law. The term derives from "letters patent"—the "open letters" by which a sovereign traditionally confers a special privilege or right on a subject. An inventor (or his assignee) who files an application for and is granted a patent is exclusively entitled to make, use or sell his invention for a limited period—17 years from the granting date, in the US and Canada. By granting the inventor a temporary monopoly, patent law aims to stimulate inventive activity and the rapid exploitation of new inventions for the public benefit.

PATERSON, city in N.J. and seat of Passaic Co., NW of New York City on the falls of the Passaic R. An industrial city since the American Revolution, home of the Colt revolver and once known as "Silk City," it now produces textiles, machinery, plastics, chemicals and electrical goods. Pop 144 824.

PATERSON, William (1745–1806), American statesman. Closely associated with N.J., he was author of the "New Jersey plan" at the Constitutional Convention (1787), a US senator 1789–90, governor of N.J. 1791–93, and from 1793 associate justice of the Supreme Court. Paterson, N.J. is named for him.

PATHÉ, Charles (1873–1957), French photographer and originator of the Pathé news, which he introduced as a regular feature c1909 in a Paris theater.

PATHET LAO, pro-communist nationalist movement long active in N and E Laos, now dominating the government. It comprises a Lao People's Party and a broader Lao Patriotic Front, whose chairman, Prince Souphanouvong, is now president of the new People's Republic of LAOS.

PATHOLOGY, study of the ANATOMY of DISEASE. Morbid anatomy, the dissection of bodies after DEATH with a view to discovering the cause of disease and the nature of its manifestations is complemented and extended by HISTOLOGY. In addition to AUTOPSY, BIOPSIES and surgical specimens are examined; these provide information that may guide treatment. It has been said that pathology is to MEDICINE what anatomy is to PHYSIOLOGY.

PATINA, the attractive thin film of CORROSION products formed on metals by weathering, especially the green tarnish on copper or BRONZE.

PATNA, capital of Bihar state, NE India, on the Ganges R 290mi NW of Calcutta, in a rice-growing region. It is the site of a university. Pop 474 349.

PATON, Alan Stewart (1903–   ), South African writer. His novel *Cry the Beloved Country* (1948), drawing on his experience as principal of a reform school for Africans, describes APARTHEID. In 1953 he became president of the Liberal Party, banned in 1968.

PATRAS, historic city and chief port of W Greece, 110mi W of Athens on the Gulf of Patras. It exports currants, tobacco, wine, olives and figs. Pop 111 238.

PATRIARCH, Old Testament title of the head of a family or tribe, especially the Israelite fathers, Abraham, Isaac, Jacob and Jacob's sons (see TWELVE TRIBES OF ISRAEL). The title was adopted by the early Christian bishops of Rome, Alexandria and Antioch, and now extends to certain other sees, especially of the ORTHODOX CHURCHES. It implies jurisdiction over other bishops.

PATRICIAN, in ancient Rome, an aristocrat by birth. In the early Republic the heads (Latin: *patres*) of the chief families dominated the Senate. They gradually lost power 500–250 BC to the PLEBEIANS, or common citizens, until *patrician* became a mere honorary title.

PATRICK, Saint, 5th-century missionary bishop, patron saint of Ireland. Controversy surrounds his identity, dates and works. In the popular and official version he was born in Britain c385, was captured by pagan Irish and was a slave six years. After training in Gaul he returned c432 to convert Ireland, with spectacular success in Ulster and at Tara. He founded his see at Armagh. Author of the autobiographical *Confessions*, he died c461. His feast day, an Irish festival the world over, is 17 March.

PATROONS, holders of huge estates in the Dutch colony of NEW NETHERLAND (now N.Y.). From 1629 patroonships, with tax exemptions, monopolies and feudal rights, were granted by the Dutch West India Company to sponsors of 50 or more settlers. The VAN RENSSELAER patroon excepted, the system did not encourage colonization, but vestiges remained until the ANTI-RENT WAR of 1839–46.

PATTERSON, Elizabeth (1785–1879), American wife of Jérôme BONAPARTE, whom he married in America in 1803. Napoleon rejected his brother's marriage, which was annulled in 1806.

PATTERSON, Floyd (1935–), US Negro boxer. He won an Olympic gold medal in 1952 and at 21 knocked out Archie Moore to become the youngest ever world heavyweight champion. Also the first to regain the title (from Ingemar Johansson in 1960), he lost it to Sonny Liston in 1962.

PATTON, George Smith, Jr (1885–1945), US general. His ruthlessness and tactical brilliance as a tank commander won him the nickname "Old Blood and Guts." Born of a military family, he graduated from West Point in 1909 and commanded a tank brigade in WWI. In WWII he was highly successful in N Africa and led the Third Army's rapid drive through France to SW Germany. He was killed in an automobile accident in Dec., 1945.

PAUL, Saint (d. c65 AD), APOSTLE to the Gentiles, major figure in the early Christian Church. His life is recorded in the ACTS OF THE APOSTLES. Son of a Roman citizen, he was a zealous Jew, active in the persecution of the Christians until a vision of Christ on the road to Damascus made him a fervent convert to the new faith. He went on extensive missionary journeys to Cyprus, Asia Minor and Greece. Returning to Jerusalem, he was violently attacked by the Jews and imprisoned for two years. An appeal to the Emperor brought a transfer (c60 AD) to Rome, where, according to tradition, he was executed after two years' house arrest. His epistles, some of which are preserved in the NEW TESTAMENT, have had an incalculable influence on Christian belief and practice.

PAUL, name of six popes. **Saint Paul I** (d. 767), pope from 757, succeeded his brother Stephen II. **Paul II** (1417–1471), pope from 1464, is chiefly remembered for his dissolution of the Roman Academy (1468), an act which gave much fuel for humanist writings against the papacy. **Paul III** (1468–1549), pope from 1534, encouraged the first major reforms of the COUNTER-REFORMATION, gave recognition to the Jesuit order, and convened the Council of TRENT (1545). **Paul IV** (1476–1559), reigned from 1555. He increased the powers of the Roman Inquisition, enforced segregation of the Jews in Rome and introduced strict censorship. His fanatical reformism proved self-defeating by creating widespread hostility. **Paul V** (1552–1621), pope from 1605, came into conflict with the Venetian Republic over papal jurisdiction. He became notorious for nepotism towards his family, the Borghese. **Paul VI** (1897–), was elected in 1963. He has continued the modernizing reforms of his predecessor, JOHN XXIII. His confirmation of the Roman Catholic Church's ban on contraception has caused much controversy.

PAUL I (Pavel Petrovich; 1754–1801), emperor of Russia from 1796. His despotism at home and erratic policies abroad caused widespread discontent. He was assassinated by army officers anxious to secure the succession of his son Alexander.

PAUL I (1901–1964), king of Greece from 1947, on the death of his brother George II. During his reign Greece was the recipient of US economic aid, and generally followed anti-communist policies.

PAUL BUNYAN. See BUNYAN, PAUL.

PAULDING, James Kirke (1778–1860), US writer and public official, who satirized British colonialism in such works as *John Bull in America* (1825), and did much to encourage the development of distinctively American literature. His five novels include *Westward Ho!* (1832).

PAULI, Wolfgang (1900–1958), Austrian-born physicist awarded the 1945 Nobel Prize for Physics for his discovery of the Pauli EXCLUSION PRINCIPLE, that no two fermions (see FERMI-DIRAC STATISTICS) in a system may have the same four quantum numbers. In terms of the ATOM, this means that at most two electrons may occupy the same ORBITAL (the two having opposite SPIN).

PAULING, Linus Carl (1901–), US chemist and pacifist awarded the 1954 Nobel Prize for Chemistry for his work on the chemical BOND (see also ELECTRONEGATIVITY) and the 1962 Nobel Peace Prize for his support of unilateral nuclear disarmament.

PAULIST FATHERS, officially the Society of Missionary Priests of St. Paul the Apostle, a missionary order of Roman Catholic priests in the US, founded by Isaac HECKER (1858).

PAUL OF THEBES, Saint (c230–c341). According to St. Jerome, his biographer, he fled Roman persecution to become the first Christian hermit, living in the Egyptian desert for nearly 100 years.

PAUL OF THE CROSS, Saint (1694–1775), Italian mystic who founded the PASSIONIST order of monks in 1720, and an order of the same name for nuns in 1770.

PAUNCEFOTE, Julian, 1st Baron Pauncefote of Preston (1828–1902), British diplomat, permanent undersecretary of foreign affairs (1882) and ambassador to the US (1893). The most significant contribution of a distinguished career was his negotiation of the HAY-PAUNCEFOTE TREATY (1901), which resolved US-British dispute over control of the projected Panama Canal.

PAVANE, a stately court dance of 16th and 17th century Europe, usually in duple time, performed by a procession of couples who circled the ballroom with a slow, swaying step.

PAVLOV, Ivan Petrovich (1849–1936), Russian physiologist best known for his work on the conditioned REFLEX. Regularly, over long periods, he rang a bell just before feeding dogs, and found that eventually they salivated on hearing the bell, even when there was no food forthcoming. He also studied the physiology of the DIGESTIVE SYSTEM, and for this received the 1904 Nobel Prize for Physiology or Medicine.

PAVLOVA, Anna Matveyevna (1882–1931), Russian ballerina, considered the greatest of her time. She formed her own company and was famed for her roles in *Giselle* and *The Dying Swan*.

PAWL. See RATCHET.

PAWNBROKING, the business activity of lending on the security of personal possessions, which are left with the pawnbroker in return for a sum of money (usually well below the value of the article). The borrower receives a ticket with which he can redeem his property within a certain time, after which it may be sold.

PAWNEE INDIANS, North American Indians of Caddoan linguistic stock who inhabited river valleys of Nebraska and Kansas from the 16th to the 19th century. They had an elaborate religion which for a time involved human sacrifice. They lived by farming and buffalo hunting, but by 1876 had ceded all of their land to the US government. They settled on a reservation in Oklahoma, where they numbered about 1 000 in the early 1970s.

Peace pipe of "Pehriska-Ruhpa," a famous Hidatsa Indian chief. Lithograph by Charles Bodmer (1839).

PAW PAW. See PAPAW.

PAWTUCKET, city in R.I., on the Blackstone R 4mi NE of Providence. Mixed industry includes electronic equipment and textiles. Pop 76 984.

PAYNE-ALDRICH TARIFF ACT, US statute passed in 1909, the first change in TARIFF law since 1897. As drafted by Representative Sereno E. Payne the act's intention was to reduce protectionist tariffs, but revision in the Senate, largely by Nelson ALDRICH, prevented substantial change.

PEA, herbaceous annual LEGUMINOUS PLANTS that are mainly cultivated for their edible seeds. They have alternate compound leaves, white or purple flowers and for fruit, a many-seeded pod or LEGUME. The garden pea (*Pisum sativum*) is native to Middle Asia and is now widely cultivated in North America, Europe and Asia. Family: Leguminosae.

PEABODY, city in NE Mass., a suburb of Boston, named for George PEABODY. Chief industries are leather, chemicals, metal and wood products. Pop 48 080.

PEABODY, Elizabeth Palmer (1804–1894), US educator, author and publisher who started the first US kindergarten and introduced FROEBEL's methods of education to the US. She wrote widely on educational theory, published early works of Nathaniel HAWTHORNE, and was an exponent of TRANSCENDENTALISM.

PEABODY, George (1795–1869), US financier and philanthropist. From 1837 he lived in London, where he set up an immensely prosperous investment banking house. His donations made possible such foundations as the Peabody Institute of Baltimore and the George Peabody College in Nashville, Tenn.

PEACE CORPS, agency of the US government established by President John F. KENNEDY in 1961. First envisaged by William JAMES in 1904, the aim of the Peace Corps is to help raise living standards in developing countries, and to promote international friendship and understanding. Peace Corps projects, ranging from farm assistance to nursing instruction, are established at the request of the host country. Its 14 000 volunteers normally serve for two years.

PEACE PIPE, or *calumet* (French: reed), a tobacco pipe, long-stemmed and elaborately decorated, smoked by most North American Indian peoples on ceremonial occasions such as the signing of peace treaties. The peace pipe was a symbol of its owners' power and honor, and as such was held sacred.

PEACE RIVER, in W Canada, the main branch of the Mackenzie R. Formed by the junction of the Finlay and Parsnip rivers in central British Columbia, it flows 1 065mi E into Alberta to join the Slave R near Lake Athabaska.

PEACH, popular name for *Prunus persica* and its rough-skinned fruit. Native to China, it is now cultivated in warmer regions throughout the world (notably in Calif.). There are several thousand varieties divided into freestone or clingstone types, according to the ease with which the flesh comes away from the stone. The **nectarine** is a variety of peach and has a smoother skin and a richer flavor. Family: Rosaceae.

PEACH TREE BORER, *Aegeria exitiosa*, a clearwing moth of North America whose naked larvae bore long galleries into the wood of PEACH trees. It can be a serious pest species when mass outbreaks occur.

PEACOCKS, properly **Peafowl**, large exotic ground birds of two genera, *Pavo* and *Afropavo*, well known as ornamental birds. The male, the peacock, has a train of up to 150 tail feathers, which can be erected in display to form a showy fan.

PEACOCK, Thomas Love (1785–1866), English novelist and poet, a brilliant satirist of contemporary intellectual trends. He was a close friend of SHELLEY and an able administrator in the East India Company. His best poetry is contained in his novels, which he described as comic romances. They include *Headlong Hall* (1816), *Nightmare Abbey* (1818) and *Crotchet Castle* (1831).

PEALE, an important family of early US painters. The prolific and versatile **Charles Willson Peale** (1741–1827) is best known for his portraits of Washington and other leading figures of the revolutionary period. He studied with Benjamin WEST in London, and in 1874 founded a museum in Philadelphia, later moved to Independence Hall, which housed a portrait gallery together with natural history and technology exhibits. His younger brother **James Peale** (1749–1831) was best known for his portrait miniatures. Charles' many sons included **Raphaelle Peale** (1774–1825), a pioneer of US still-life painting, and **Rembrandt Peale** (1778–1860), a portraitist and founder of the Peale Museum, Baltimore. His most famous work is a portrait of Thomas Jefferson (1805).

PEALE, Norman Vincent (1898–), US Protestant minister and author of best-selling books on the power of self-confidence and a positive outlook, such as *A Guide to Confident Living* (1948) and *The Power of Positive Thinking* (1952).

PEANO, Giuseppe (1858–1932), Italian mathematician whose ideas in mathematical LOGIC profoundly influenced those of A. N. WHITEHEAD and B. RUSSELL. He also devised the international language *Interlingua*, still occasionally used.

PEANUT, groundnut or **goober** (*Arachis hypogaea*), a low bushy LEGUMINOUS PLANT cultivated in tropical and subtropical regions. The "nut" is a fruit normally containing two seeds, which is produced when the yellow flowers grow down into the ground after pollination. Family: Leguminosae.

PEANUT WORMS, a common name for the phylum Sipunculoidea, a group of about 250 species of marine worms. All are bottom-dwellers, living in burrows in the sand or in empty snail shells or annelid tubes.

PEAR, *Pyrus communis* and related species, common name for these deciduous trees and their oval-shaped soft-fleshed fruit. There are hundreds of varieties of the fruit, the "Bartlett" pear being commonest in the US. Family: Rosaceae.

PEA RIDGE, Battle of, US CIVIL WAR battle in NW Ark. on March 7–8, 1862. Gen. Earl van Dorn led a Confederate attack on the Union army under General Samuel R. Curtis and was decisively defeated.

PEARL HARBOR, natural land-locked harbor on the island of Oahu in Hawaii, US. Of great strategic importance, it is best known as the scene of the Japanese bombing of the US Pacific fleet on Dec. 7, 1941. Most of the fleet was in harbor when Japanese carrier-based planes attacked without warning. Along with many smaller ships, eight battleships were damaged—three destroyed and another capsized; on the ground at Wheeler Field 188 planes were destroyed. The raid caused over 2 200 casualties with negligible losses to the Japanese. The attack brought the US into WWII.

PEARL RIVER (or Canton R), in S China, part of the Si R delta on the S China Sea coast, flowing E from Canton to its estuary between Hong Kong and Macao.

PEARL RIVER, 490mi long river which rises in E central Miss., flows generally S through Jackson into La., and empties into Mississippi Sound on the Gulf of Mexico.

PEARLS, white spherical gems produced by bivalve mollusks, particularly by Pearl oysters, *Pinctada*. In response to an irritation by foreign matter within the shell, the mantle secretes calcium carbonate in the form of NACRE (MOTHER OF PEARL) around the irritant body. Over several years, this encrustation forms the pearl. Cultured pearls may be obtained by "seeding" the oyster with an artificial irritant such as a small bead. Pearls are variable and may be black or pink as well as the usual white. Another bivalve group producing marketable pearls is the freshwater Pearl mussel, *Margaritifera margaritifera*.

PEARLY NAUTILUS, a shelled member of the cephalopod mollusks, with six species in the genus *Nautilus*, found in the southwestern Indo-Pacific. The shell is coiled and chambered. The growing animal lives always in the last chamber, the empty ones being gas-filled for flotation.

PEARSE, Patrick Henry (1879–1916), Irish educator, writer and patriot, a major figure in the Gaelic revival. He led the Irish Republican Brotherhood in the EASTER RISING of 1916. When it collapsed he was tried and executed.

PEARSON, Drew (1897–1969), pen name of Andrew Russell Pearson, US journalist who wrote the syndicated column *The Washington Merry-go-round* (begun 1932), which specialized in exposés of national politics and political figures.

PEARSON, Karl (1857–1936), British mathematician best known for his pioneering work on STATISTICS (e.g., devising the CHI-SQUARED TEST) and for his *The Grammar of Science* (1892), an important contribution to the philosophy of mathematics. He was also an early worker in the field of EUGENICS.

PEARSON, Lester Bowles (1897–1972), Canadian diplomat, prime minister (1963–68) and winner of the 1957 Peace Prize for his mediation in the Suez crisis (1956). In 1928 he joined the Department of External Affairs, becoming first secretary, and in 1945 he was appointed ambassador to the US. As secretary of state (1948–57) he made notable contributions to the UN and NATO. In 1958 he became the Liberal leader. After resigning as prime minister he headed the WORLD BANK commission which produced the Pearson Report on developing countries.

PEARY, Robert Edwin (1856–1920), US Arctic explorer who discovered the North Pole. He entered the US Navy in 1881, and first journeyed to the interior of Greenland in 1886. On leaves of absence from the navy, he led a series of exploratory

Courtship ritual of the peacock, displaying its magnificent fan of tail-feathers to the comparatively drab peahen. In Greek mythology the pattern on the tail feathers represents the eyes of Argus.

The peanut, which is a fruit pod rather than a true nut, develops underground. After pollination the yellow flower of the peanut drops, and from its base a stalk or *peg* grows down into the ground. The tip of the peg, which carries the fertilized ovules, then develops into the characteristic pod containing two seeds.

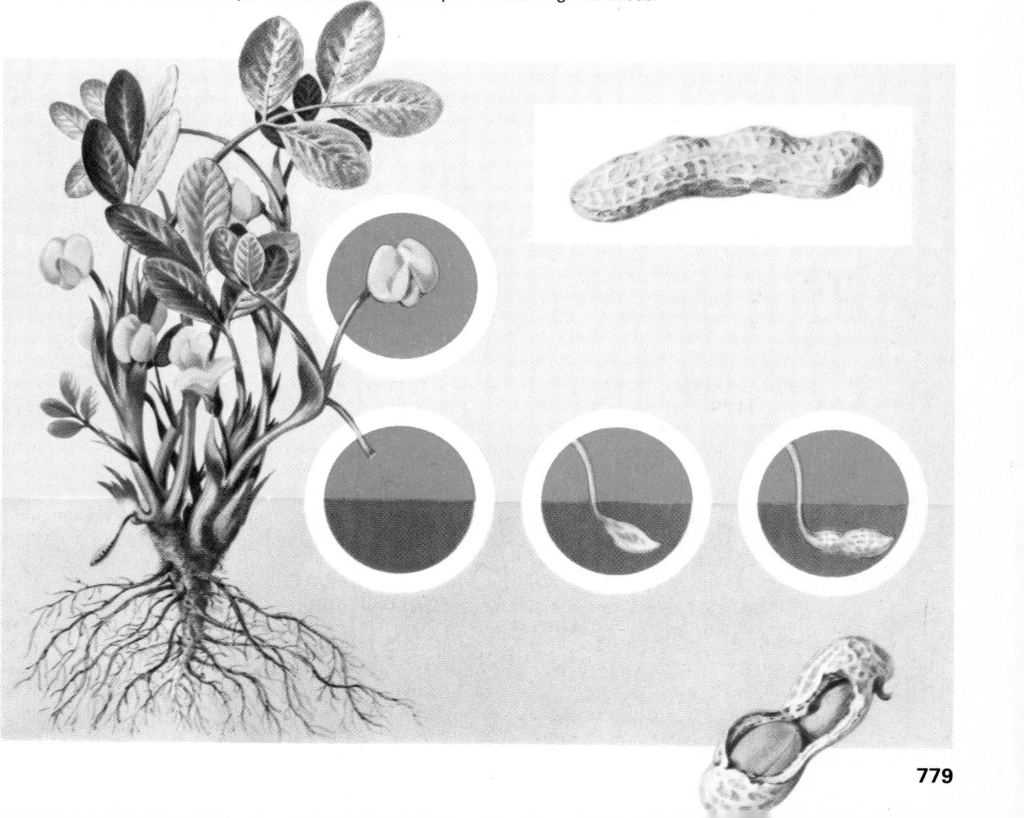

expeditions to Greenland which culminated in his reaching the North Pole on April 6, 1909. Peary's books, including *The North Pole* (1910) and *Secrets of Polar Travel* (1917), give an account of his journeys and an impression of his extraordinary stamina and courage.

PEARY LAND, in N Greenland, uninhabited mountainous peninsula, the most northerly point of land in the Arctic region, named for R. E. PEARY.

PEASANTS' WAR, popular revolt (1524–26), which began in SW Germany and spread to many parts of Germany and Austria. The social turmoil created by the REFORMATION and the decay of FEUDALISM seem to have been at the root of the discontent. The movement collapsed when LUTHER denounced the uprising and supported its ruthless suppression.

PEAT, partly decayed plant material found in layers, usually in marshy areas. It is composed mainly of the peat mosses SPHAGNUM and Hypnum, but also of sedges, trees, etc. Under the right geological conditions, peat forms COAL. It is used as a MULCH and burned for domestic heating.

PEAT MOSS. See SPHAGNUM.

PECAN, common name for varieties of the North American deciduous tree *Carya illinoensis* and the oily edible nut it produces. Family: Juglandaceae. (See also HICKORY.)

PECCARIES, pig-like mammals of the southwestern US and northern South America, inhabiting bushy thickets or forests. There are two species within the family Tayassuidae, the Collared peccary (*Pecari tajacu*) and White-lipped peccary (*Tayassu pecari*). Both are long-legged, with thick bristly hair and an erectile mane along the back.

PECK ORDER, the term given to a DOMINANCE HIERARCHY in BIRDS. The top bird can peck all others; the second can peck all but the top bird, and so on down to the bottom bird who is pecked by all but can peck none. Frenzied pecking soon decides the rank of any new bird introduced to the group.

PECOS, city in W Tex., seat of Reeves Co., an agricultural and oil center on the Pecos R. It has the world's first annual RODEO (from 1883). Pop 12 682.

PECOS RIVER, main tributary of the Rio Grande. It rises in N N.M. and flows 925mi SE into Tex. to join the Rio Grande NW of Del Rio. With several dams, it is important for irrigation.

PECTIN, a polysaccharide found in plant tissue, capable of forming thick GELS with strong, acid SUGAR solutions and extensively used in the food industry to set JELLIES AND JAMS. Commercial quantities are obtained from citrus and apple wastes after removal of the juice.

PEDIATRICS, branch of MEDICINE concerned with care of children. This starts with newborn, especially premature, babies in whom intensive care is required to protect the baby from and adapt it to the environment outside the WOMB. An important aspect is the recognition and treatment of congenital DISEASES in which structural or functional defects occur due to inherited disease (e.g., MONGOLISM) or disease acquired during development of EMBRYO or FETUS (e.g., SPINA BIFIDA). Otherwise, INFECTIOUS DISEASE, failure to grow or develop normally, MENTAL RETARDATION, DIABETES, ASTHMA and EPILEPSY form the bulk of pediatric practice.

PEDICEL. See FLOWER.

PEDRO, two emperors of Brazil. **Pedro I** (1798–1834) was the son of John VI of Portugal, who fled with his family to Brazil when Napoleon invaded his homeland in 1807. On his father's return to Portugal in 1821, Pedro remained in Brazil, declared Brazilian independence (1822) and was crowned emperor. His subsequent mismanagement led to his abdication (1831). He was succeeded by his son **Pedro II** (1825–1891), declared of age in 1940, who gave Brazil over half a century of stable government. But his liberal policies, especially his attempt to abolish slavery, alienated the Brazilian landowning classes. They organized a bloodless coup in 1889 and made Brazil a republic.

PEE DEE RIVER, name of the Yadkin R after it is joined by the Uharie R in S central N.C., flowing 230mi SE into Winyah Bay, S.C. Its hydroelectric plants are a major power source for the Carolinas.

PEEKSKILL, city in SE N.Y., on the Hudson R, 39mi N of New York city. It has varied light industry. Pop 19 283.

PEEL, Sir Robert (1788–1850), British statesman. As home secretary in the 1820s, Peel set up the British police force and sponsored the CATHOLIC EMANCIPATION ACT (1829). Though he opposed the REFORM BILL (1832), he became more progressive, and after a brief term (1834–35) as prime minister, he organized the new Conservative Party out of the old Tory Party, aided by young politicians such as DISRAELI and GLADSTONE. His second term in office (1841–46) saw the introduction of an income tax, banking controls and Irish land reforms, and the further removal of discriminatory laws against Roman Catholics. The repeal of the CORN LAWS (1846) led to an era of FREE TRADE but caused a party split which led to his resignation.

PEEPUL. See BO TREE.

PEGASUS, in Greek mythology, the winged horse that sprang from the blood of MEDUSA. He was ridden by BELLEROPHON in battle against the CHIMERA. A fountain of poetic inspiration sprang where his hoof struck Mt Helicon. He flew to heaven and served ZEUS as a constellation.

PEGASUS (the Winged Horse), a large N Hemisphere constellation noticeable for its Great Square, formed by four bright stars. Pegasus contains a GLOBULAR CLUSTER (M15).

PEGLER, James Westbrook (1894–1969), US journalist who won a Pulitzer Prize (1941) for his reporting. His column featured exposés, especially of labor racketeering, and was syndicated nationally 1944–62.

PEGMATITE, very coarse-grained IGNEOUS or METAMORPHIC ROCK formed by slow crystallization from a melt containing volatiles. They usually have the composition of GRANITE, but often contain unusual MINERALS, including GEMS, and rare elements.

PEI, Ieoh Ming (1917–), Chinese-born US architect of public buildings and urban complexes, e.g. the Mile High Center in Denver. They are noted for simplicity and environmental harmony.

PEIPING. See PEKING.

PEIPUS, Lake, or **Lake Chudskoye,** in the USSR, on the border of the RSFSR (Pskov oblast) and the Estonian SSR. ALEXANDER NEVSKI defeated the Teutonic Knights on the frozen lake in 1242.

PEIRCE, Charles Sanders (1839–1914), US philosopher, best known as a pioneer of PRAGMATISM. He also made important contributions to LOGIC and the philosophy of science, being also a noteworthy mathematician and experimental scientist.

PEKIN, city in central Ill., seat of Tazewell Co. A port on the Illinois R, it ships livestock, grain and coal. Pop 31 375.

PEKING, capital of the People's Republic of China, lying within Hopeh Province, but administratively independent. It is the political, commercial, cultural and communications center of the country, and embraces a massive industrial complex. The city's rectangular layout was the work of KUBLAI KHAN in the 13th century, and its splendors were described by Marco POLO. It became the capital of China in 1421. Its occupation by French and British troops from 1860 was a contributing cause of the BOXER REBELLION (1900). In 1928 Peking (renamed Peiping) was superseded by Nanking, but regained its capital status (1937) under Japanese occupation following the SINO-JAPANESE WAR. Its name was restored with the communist victory in 1949. Peking has two historic districts: the Inner City, enclosing the Imperial City and the Forbidden City; and the Outer City. Pop 8 000 000.

PEKINGESE, lap-dog, bred for centuries only in the Chinese court, now a popular pet. It stands only 6–9in high, is longhaired and has a flat skull.

PEKING MAN. See PREHISTORIC MAN.

PELAGIANISM, Christian heresy based on the teachings of the British theologian **Pelagius** (c353–c425); an ascetic movement chiefly of aristocratic laity. Pelagius held that men are not naturally sinful, and have FREE WILL to take the first steps to salvation by their own efforts. This challenged the basic Christian doctrines relating to GRACE, ORIGINAL SIN and Christ's ATONEMENT. Pelagianism was opposed by St. AUGUSTINE and condemned by the Council of Ephesus in 431. A middle position, **Semi-Pelagianism,** was dominant in Gaul until condemned by the Council of Orange (529).

PELAGIUS, name of two popes. **Pelagius I** (d. 561) reigned from 556. His early support of the NESTORIANS was retracted too late to prevent schism in the Italian church. He established papal political power, granted 554. **Pelagius II** (d. 590) reigned from 579. He was responsible for defending Rome against constant Lombard invasion.

PELÉE, Mount, active volcano on MARTINIQUE, in the French West Indies; 4 583ft high. Its eruption in 1902 destroyed the town of St. Pierre and killed some 40 000 people.

PELHAM, town in SE N.Y., a residential suburb 17mi NE of New York City. Pop 13 933.

PELIAS, in Greek mythology, usurper of the throne of Thessaly who sent JASON to win the Golden Fleece. MEDEA, hoping to make Jason king, later tricked Pelias' daughters into killing him.

PELICANS, large aquatic birds of the genus *Pelecanus*. The long bills are provided with an expansible pouch attached to the lower mandible, used, not for storage, but simply as a catching apparatus, a scoop-net. They are social birds, breeding in large colonies. Most species also fish in groups, swimming together, herding the fish in horseshoe formation. All are fine fliers.

PELICAN FLOWER, *Aristolochia grandiflora*, tropical vine that bears large, carrion-scented greenish-yellow flowers, the buds of which resemble a pelican. Family: Aristolochiaceae.

PELLAGRA, VITAMIN deficiency DISEASE (due to lack of niacin), often found in maize- or millet-dependent populations. A DERMATITIS, initially resembling sunburn, but followed by thickening, scaling and pigmentation, is characteristic; internal EPITHELIUM is affected (sore tongue, DIARRHEA). Confusion, DELIRIUM, hallucination and ultimately dementia may ensue. Niacin replacement is essential and food enrichment is an important preventative measure.

PELLIONIA, a genus of perennial plants of which *Pellionia daveauana* (brownish, purple-edged silvery leaves) and *P. pulchra* (gray-green leaves with dark-brown veins) are grown indoors, particularly for ground cover under shrubs and trees. They should be grown at average house temperatures, above 13°C (55°F), and placed in a moderately bright position, such as a north-facing window. The soil should be kept evenly moist. They are propagated by means of shoot tip cuttings. Family: Urticaceae.

PELOPIDAS (d. 364 BC), Theban general responsible with EPAMINONDAS for the brief dominance (371–362) of Thebes in ancient Greece. In 379 he freed Thebes from Spartan occupation and, leading the Sacred Band, defeated the Spartans in the battle of Leuctra (371). From 369 he fought Alexander, tyrant of Pherae, but was killed in the final victory. In 367 he had become ambassador to Artaxerxes.

PELOPONNESIAN WAR (431–404 BC), war between the rival Greek city-states of ATHENS and SPARTA which ended Athenian dominance and marked the beginning of the end of Greek civilization. The war was fought in two phases. The first (431–421) was inconclusive because Athenian sea power was matched by Spartan land power, and a stalemate was acknowledged by the Peace of NICIAS. Nicias had been the third Athenian leader in the war following PERICLES and CLEON, and his leadership was now challenged by ALCIBIADES, who initiated the second and decisive phase of the conflict (418–404). In an attack on Syracuse in 413, the Athenians suffered a major defeat. The Spartans, with Persian aid, built up a powerful fleet under the leadership of LYSANDER who blockaded Athens and forced her final surrender. (See also GREECE, ANCIENT.)

PELOPONNESUS, peninsula forming the S part of the Greek mainland, linked with the N by the Isthmus of Corinth. It is mostly mountainous but its fertile lowlands provide wheat, tobacco, and fruit crops. Its largest city and port is Patras. In ancient times it was the center of the MYCENAEAN CIVILIZATION and, later, was dominated by SPARTA in the SE.

PELOPS, in Greek mythology, founder of the Mycenaean Pelopid dynasty, son of TANTALUS (who served his flesh for the gods to eat) and father of ATREUS. The Peloponnesus is named for him.

PELOTA. See JAI ALAI.

PELOTAS, city and canal port in S Brazil, SE Rio Grande do Sul state. It is a major shipping and food processing center. Pop 208 017.

PELTIER EFFECT, the heating or cooling effect at a junction between two dissimilar METALS when an electric current is driven through a circuit containing the junction. The effect is named for **Jean Charles Athanase Peltier** (1785–1845), the French scientist who discovered it in 1834. (See also THERMOCOUPLE.)

PELVIS, lowest part of the trunk in animals, bounded by the pelvic BONES and in continuity with the ABDOMEN. The principal contents are the BLADDER and lower GASTROINTESTINAL TRACT (rectum) and reproductive organs, particularly in females—the WOMB, OVARIES, FALLOPIAN TUBES and vagina. The pelvic floor is a powerful muscular layer which supports the pelvic and abdominal contents and is important in urinary and fecal continence. The pelvic bones articulate with the LEGS at the hip JOINTS.

PELYCOSAURS, extinct reptiles of the CARBONIFEROUS and PERMIAN. They were up to 4m (13ft) long, and had massive jaws. A long spine on each vertebra, up to 1m (3.3ft) high probably supported a web of skin over the back, perhaps used in thermoregulation.

PEMBROKE, town in SE Ontario, Canada, seat of Renfrew Co., on the Ottawa R. It is a lumbering center, with some light industry. Pop 16 544.

PEMBROKE PINES, city in SE Fla., a residential suburb of Fort Lauderdale. Pop 15 520.

PEMMICAN, a concentrated food used by North American Indians on journeys. Dried meat was pounded to a paste and mixed with melted fat.

PEN, an instrument for writing with INK. The earliest pens were the Chinese brush and the Egyptian reed pen for use on PAPYRUS. Quill pens, usually made from goose feathers, were used until the mid-19th century, when steel pens largely replaced them. The modern fountain pen was invented in 1884; its nib is supplied with ink from a reservoir in the barrel by capillary action. The BALLPOINT PEN is now very popular.

P.E.N., acronym of the International Association of Poets, Playwrights, Editors, Essayists and Novelists. Founded in 1922, the association aims to promote international intercourse and cooperation between men of letters.

PENAL COLONY, overseas settlement in which convicts were isolated from society. The forced labor that was part of their punishment was often used for colonial development. All colonial powers had penal colonies, as had Russia in Siberia. Britain transported large numbers of convicts to the American colonies and to Australia. (See also DEVIL'S ISLAND.)

PENAL LAWS, in England and Ireland, a series of discriminatory laws against Roman Catholics after the REFORMATION. In the 16th and 17th centuries these laws deprived Roman Catholics of virtually all civil rights, and harshly penalized participation in Roman Catholic worship. Although enforcement lapsed, the laws were only gradually repealed in successive Acts of 1791, 1829 (see CATHOLIC EMANCIPATION ACT), 1832 and 1926.

PENANCE, a SACRAMENT of the Roman Catholic Church. A priest, after receiving the CONFESSION of a penitent, may (as the agent of God) grant ABSOLUTION, imposing a penance and requiring restitution for harm done to others. The penance—now usually prayers, though formerly a rigorous ascetic discipline—represents the temporal punishment for sin. (See also INDULGENCE.)

PENANG, a state of Malaysia. It comprises Province Wellesley, on the W coast of the Malay peninsula, and Penang Island. On the island is the capital, Penang (formerly George Town), Malaysia's chief port.

PENATES. See LARES AND PENATES.

PEN-CH'I, city in S Liaoning province, China. It has a large steel industry. Pop 750 000.

PENCIL, instrument for writing or drawing, usually consisting of a wooden rod with a core of mixed powdered GRAPHITE and CLAY. The mixture is extruded as a soft paste and placed in the grooves of two half-pencils, which are glued together and dried. The term "lead pencil" comes from an early view that graphite is a form of lead. Pencils vary in hardness, the hardest (10H) containing the most clay, the softest and blackest (8B), the least. HB and F are intermediate grades.

PENDERGAST, Thomas Joseph (1872–1945), US politician. He was the Democratic political boss of Kansas City and Mo. during the 1920s and 30s. Pendergast was convicted and imprisoned for evading income tax (1939).

PENDLETON, city in NE Ore., seat of Umatilla Co., on the Umatilla R. It is the commercial center of a large agricultural region. Pop 13 197.

PENDLETON, Edmund (1721–1803), American jurist and revolutionary statesman who became the first speaker of the Va. House of Delegates after independence. He helped revise the laws of Va., and in 1788 presided over the Va. convention which ratified the Federal Constitution.

PENDLETON ACT, US Federal law (1883) by which Federal employment was given on the basis of merit rather than political affiliation, thus establishing the modern CIVIL SERVICE. Sponsored by Senator Pendleton of Ohio after public disquiet at corruption, the law provided for selection by open competitive examination.

PEND OREILLE LAKE, lake in N Ida., 148sq mi in area, formed by the Clark Fork R and drained from its NW corner by the Pend Oreille R.

PENDULUM, a rigid body mounted on a fixed horizontal axis that is free to rotate under the influence of gravity. Many types of pendulum exist (e.g., Kater's and the FOUCAULT PENDULUM), the most common consisting of a large weight (the bob) supported at the end of a light string or bar. An idealized simple pendulum, with a string of negligible weight and length, l, the weight of its bob concentrated at a point and a small swing amplitude, executes SIMPLE HARMONIC MOTION. The time, T, for a complete swing (to and fro) is given by $T=2\pi\sqrt{l/g}$, depending only on the string length and the local value of the gravitational ACCELERATION, g. Actual physical or compound pendulums approximate this behavior if they have a small angle of swing. They are used for measuring absolute values of g or its variation with geographical position, and as control elements in CLOCKS.

PENELOPE, in Greek mythology, the wife of ODYSSEUS, and a paragon of virtue. During Odysseus's absence at the TROJAN WAR, she evaded her many suitors by promising to choose one when she had woven a shroud; each night she unraveled the day's work.

PENEPLAIN, the state that William Davis (1850–1934) proposed would result after millions of years of constant EROSION in an area: a featureless, perfectly horizontal plain at sea-level.

PENFIELD, town in W N.Y., about 7mi SE of Rochester. Pop 23 782.

PENGUINS, the most highly-specialized of all aquatic birds, with 17 species in the order Sphenisciformes, restricted to the S hemisphere. Completely flightless, the wings are reduced to flippers for "flying" through the water. Ungainly on land, penguins only leave the water to breed. The nest is usually a skimpy affair; Emperor and King penguins brood their single eggs on their feet covered by a flap of skin. Most species nest in colonies. Penguins are long-lived birds: the Yellow-eyed penguin may live for 20 years or more.

PENICILLIN, substance produced by a class of FUNGI which interferes with cell wall production by BACTERIA and which was one of the first, and remains among the most useful, ANTIBIOTICS. The property was noted by A. FLEMING in 1928 and production of penicillin for medical use was started by E. B. CHAIN and H. W. FLOREY in 1940. Since then numerous penicillin derivatives have been manufactured, extending the range of activity, overcoming resistance in some organisms and allowing some to be taken by mouth. STAPHYLCOCCUS, STREPTOCOCCUS and the bacteria causing the VENEREAL DISEASES of gonorrhea and syphilis are among the bacteria sensitive to natural penicillin, while bacilli negative to GRAM'S STAIN, which cause urinary-tract infection, SEPTICEMIA, etc., are destroyed by semisynthetic penicillins.

PENINSULAR CAMPAIGN, in the US CIVIL WAR, Union campaign against the Confederate capital of Richmond, Va., April to July 1862, led by George B. McCLELLAN across the peninsula between the James and York rivers. Although the Union troops, 100 000 strong, initially inflicted severe losses on the rebels, they were heavily defeated in the Seven Days' Battles (26 June–2 July), by Confederate forces under Robert E. LEE, and Richmond was saved from capture.

PENINSULAR WAR (1808–1814), part of the NAPOLEONIC WARS, in which the French, fighting against the British, Portuguese and Spanish, were driven out of the Iberian Peninsula. Anxious to increase his security in Europe, NAPOLEON sent General JUNOT to occupy Portugal (1807), and in 1808 despatched Murat to occupy Spain, although she was an ally. The Spanish and the Portuguese soon rebelled, and, with the aid of the British under Arthur Wellesley (later Duke of WELLINGTON), the French were driven out of Portugal (1809). In the long struggle that followed, the British—aided by Portuguese and Spanish guerrillas—gradually gained the upper hand, despite many reverses. By 1813 the French forces in Spain had been defeated, and Wellesley invaded S France. The war ended on Napoleon's abdication.

PENIS, male reproductive organ for introducing sperm and semen into the female vagina and WOMB; its urethra also carries URINE from the BLADDER. The penis is made of connective tissue and specialized blood vessels which become engorged with BLOOD in sexual arousal and which cause the penis to become stiff and erect; this facilitates the intromission of semen in sexual intercourse. A protective fold, the foreskin, covers the tip and is often removed for ethnic or medical reasons in circumcision.

PENITENTIARY. See PRISONS.

Emperor penguins, the tallest variety, seen at Cape Crozier, Ross Island, Antarctica.

PENN, William (1644–1718), English QUAKER, advocate of religious tolerance, and founder of PENNSYLVANIA. He wrote numerous tracts on Quaker beliefs and was several times imprisoned for his nonconformity. In 1675 he became involved in American colonization as a trustee for one of the proprietors of W N.J. (then West Jersey). In 1681, he and 11 others bought the rights to E N.J. (then East Jersey), and he received a vast province on the W bank of the Delaware R in settlement of a debt owed by Charles II to Penn's father. Thousands of European Quakers emigrated there in search of religious and political freedom. In 1682 Penn visited the colony and witnessed the fulfillment of his plans for the city of Philadelphia. He returned in 1699 to revise the constitution.

PENNAMITE WARS (1769–71, 1775–84), two major conflicts amid a series of clashes between Conn. and Pa. over their long-standing rivalry for the Wyoming Valley. Both wars ended with the Conn. settlers in possession of the valley, and the controversy ended only in 1799 when Conn. yielded to the claims of Pa., by then legally recognized. A compromise was reached, and the New England culture of the Conn. settlers became a major influence on the state.

PENNELL, Joseph (1857–1926), US etcher and writer, noted for his prolific and original book illustrations. He spent much of his life in London, but returned to the US in WWI. He wrote a biography (1908) of WHISTLER, by whom he was influenced.

PENN HILLS, urban township in SW Pa., an E suburb of Pittsburgh. Pop 62 886.

PENNSAUKEN, township in SW N.J., just E of Camden. Pop 36 394.

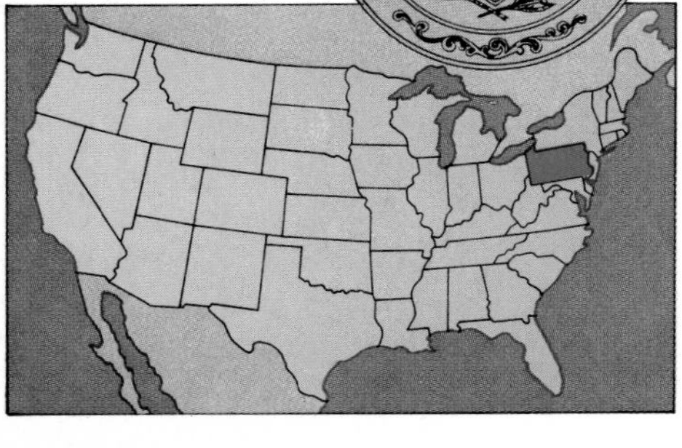

Name of state: Pennsylvania
Capital: Harrisburg
Statehood: Dec. 12, 1787 (2nd state)
Familiar name: Keystone State
Area: 45 333sq mi
Population: 11 793 909
Elevation: Highest—3213 ft. Mount Davis. Lowest—sea level Delaware River
Motto: Virtue, Liberty and Independence
State flower: Mountain laurel
State bird: Ruffed grouse
State tree: Hemlock
State song: None

PENNSYLVANIA, Middle Atlantic state of the US, one of the original 13 colonies. It is bounded on the N by Lake Erie and N.Y., E by N.Y. and N.J., S by Del., Md. and W. Va., and W by W. Va. and Ohio.

Land. The state embraces the vast ranges of the APPALACHIAN and ALLEGHENY Mts; its only lowlands are the coastal plains SE and NW. The main rivers are the Delaware and Susquehanna in the E and the Allegheny and Monongahela in the W. The state is still richly forested, and many of its spectacularly beautiful inland regions retain an air of wilderness. Pa. has a moist climate with pronounced seasonal variations.

People. Pennsylvania is the third-largest state in population terms. Over two-thirds of the people are urban. Religious freedom in colonial times attracted diverse groups of immigrants including QUAKERS and the PENNSYLVANIA DUTCH.

Economy. The state of Pa. ranks fifth in industrial importance. The pig-iron and steel industry, centered in Pittsburgh, produces a quarter of the national total. Other major manufactures include electrical and other machinery, food processing, metal products and clothing. Tourism, agriculture (mainly livestock) and coal mining are also of major importance. The outstanding communications and distribution facilities of Pa. include the two great ports of Philadelphia and Erie.

History. When Henry Hudson entered Delaware Bay in 1609, the region was inhabited by ALGONQUIAN and IROQUOIS Indians. The first permanent settlement was made by the Swedes in 1643. Swedish rule gave way to control by the Dutch in 1655, and in 1664 the region was captured by the English. It was granted (1681) to William PENN. Under Penn's guidance, the colony became a tolerant, peaceful and prosperous community, initially on good terms with the Indians. The peace was broken by the FRENCH AND INDIAN WARS (1754–63) and again by the REVOLUTIONARY WAR, in which the location and resources of Pa. were vital. The Declaration of Independence was signed in Philadelphia, the nation's capital from 1790 to 1800 and for long its foremost city. Pennsylvanian Quakers had been outspoken opponents of slavery, and the state entered the Civil War on the Union side. It was the scene of the crucial Battle of GETTYSBURG (1863). From the end of the war, the state's steady growth in prosperity was halted only by floods in 1889 and the Great Depression of the thirties.

PENNSYLVANIA DUTCH (from German *Deutsch*, meaning German), descendants of German-speaking immigrants who came to Pa. during the 17th and 18th centuries in search of religious freedom. They were mainly Lutheran and Reformed Protestants, but included such Pietist sects as the AMISH, DUNKERS, MENNONITES and MORAVIANS, who still retain their original culture.

PENNSYLVANIAN, the penultimate period of the PALEOZOIC, stretching between about 315 and 280 million years ago. (See CARBONIFEROUS; GEOLOGY.)

PENNYROYAL, European perennial herb (*Mentha pulegium*) with small, pungently aromatic leaves; also an erect hairy branching American herb (*Hedeoma puleigioides*). Extracts from both have been used in folk medicine. Family: Labiatae.

PENOBSCOT RIVER, longest river in Me. (350mi from the head of its longest branch). Rising near the Canadian border it flows E and S to Penobscot Bay on the Atlantic.

PENOLOGY. See PRISONS; PUNISHMENT.

PENSACOLA, seaport city in NW Fla., seat of Escambia Co., on Pensacola Bay. Industries include shipping, fishing, chemicals, lumber and tourism. It was founded in 1698 as a Spanish colony. The main Navy flight training school is here. Pop 59 507.

PENSION, regular payment made to people after they retire from employment because of age or disability, received from the government under SOCIAL SECURITY programs, or from private employers, or both. In the US, almost all large corporations provide pension plans for their employees, based on salary and length of service, and financed either by the company alone or jointly by company and employee (contributory plans). The most common forms are the trust fund, administered by a bank or trust company; the group annuity in which an insurance company collects payments from the corporation to build up the retirement fund; and profit-sharing plans, in which pension funds are accumulated annually as a percentage of company profits.

PENTADACTYL LIMB, the limb found in VERTEBRATES other than fish which primitively bears five digits (FINGERS or toes). It is variously modified: e.g., by loss of digits as in cursorial forms; by elongation of digits as in bats, and by forming a paddle or flipper as in aquatic forms.

PENTAGON. See POLYGON.

PENTAGON, The, five-sided building in Arlington, Va., which houses the US Department of Defense, built in 1941–43. The largest office building in the world, it consists of five concentric pentagons covering a total area of 34 acres.

Signpost on Pennsylvania's border with Virginia, extolling its proud role in the birth of the US.

PENTATEUCH (Greek: five books), the first five books of the OLD TESTAMENT: GENESIS, EXODUS, LEVITICUS, NUMBERS and DEUTERONOMY. They were traditionally assigned to MOSES, but are now regarded as a compilation of four or more documents (J, E, P and D) dating from the 9th to the 5th centuries BC and distinguished by style and theological bias. (See also TORAH.)

PENTATHLON. See TRACK AND FIELD.

PENTECOST (Greek: 50th), distinct Jewish and Christian festivals. The Jewish Pentecost, called SHAVUOT, celebrated on the 50th day after PASSOVER, is a harvest feast. The Christian Pentecost (Whitsunday)—the 50th day inclusively after Easter (see CHURCH YEAR)—commemorates the descent of the HOLY SPIRIT upon the Apostles, marking the birth of the Christian Church.

PENTECOSTAL CHURCHES, Protestant churches, fundamentalist (see FUNDAMENTALISM) and revivalist, that emphasize holiness and spiritual power as initiated by an experience ("baptism in the Spirit") in which the recipient "speaks in tongues" (see GLOSSOLALIA). They base their distinctive doctrines and practice of CHARISMATA on New Testament teaching and accounts of the bestowal of the Holy Spirit. Pentecostalism began c1906 and spread rapidly; it is now influential in most other major denominations. The largest Pentecostal churches in the US are the Assemblies of God and the United Pentecostal Church.

PENTLANDITE, bronze SULFIDE mineral with metallic luster, of composition $(Fe,Ni)_9S_8$; the chief ore of NICKEL. Usually found with PYRRHOTITE, its major occurrence is at Sudbury, Ontario.

PENTOTHAL SODIUM, or **thiopentone,** a BARBITURATE drug injected into a vein to produce brief general ANESTHESIA, also used in PSYCHIATRY as a relaxant to remove inhibitions (a so-called "truth drug").

PENUMBRA. See SHADOW.

PENZA, city in the USSR, W RSFSR, capital of Penza oblast, on the Sura R. Its major industries include machinery, paper and lumber. Pop 374 000.

PEONAGE, form of coercive servitude by which a laborer (peon) worked off his debts—often inescapable and lifelong—to his creditor-master. In Spanish America, where it was most prevalent, and in the Southern states of the US (in a modified form), peonage did not end until the 20th century.

PEONY, or paeony, popular name for plants of the genus *Paeonia*, which are widely cultivated for their large showy flowers. Most species are perennial herbs, but the tree peony has a woody trunk of up to 2m (6.6ft) high. Family: Ranunculaceae.

PEOPLE'S PARTY (in US history). See POPULISM.

PEORIA, city in N central Ill., seat of Peoria Co., on Lake Peoria. It is a marketing, industrial and distribution center. Pop 126 963.

PEPEROMIA, a genus of over 1 000 species of evergreen plants, tufted or climbing, many of which have attractive foliage, making them popular house plants. *Peperomia caperata* has heart-shaped corrugated dark-green leaves with a purple tinge, while in *P. obtusifolia* the leaves are more fleshy. They grow well in sunny east- or west-facing windows at average house temperatures. They should be well watered whenever the soil surface dries out. They are propagated from leaf and shoot tip cuttings or by division of the plants. Family: Piperaceae.

PEPIN OF HERISTAL (Pepin II; d. 714), Carolingian mayor of the palace of AUSTRASIA from 679, father of CHARLES MARTEL. He defeated the leaders of NEUSTRIA at the battle of Tertry (687) and became ruler of the Franks.

PEPIN THE SHORT (Pepin III; c714–768), first CAROLINGIAN king of the Franks, who succeeded on the deposition (751) of Childeric, the last of the MEROVINGIAN kings. He was the younger son of CHARLES MARTEL and father of CHARLEMAGNE. In return for papal recognition he helped to establish the temporal power of the papacy.

PEPPER, name for several unrelated plants from which pungent spices are obtained. Black and white pepper are the dried ground berries of a woody climbing vine (*Piper nigrum*) which grows in India and SE Asia, while long pepper is obtained from the related *P. longum*. Red, green and CHILI peppers and the PIMIENTO are the fruits of varieties of *Capsicum annuum*; the condiments paprika and cayenne pepper are produced from the pimento. Melegueta pepper is obtained from *Aframomum melegueta*. *C. annuum* is also sold as a house plant under the name **Christmas pepper**, its main attraction being the bright red fruits produced. It grows well at average house temperatures and requires a sunny position. The soil should be kept evenly moist and the foliage misted often. Christmas peppers are raised from seed.

PEPPERMINT, *Mentha piperita*, a wild herb whose leaves contain an oil widely used for flavoring. MENTHOL, a derivative, is used in medicines. Family: Labiatae. (See also MINT.)

PEPPERRELL, Sir William (1696–1759), American colonial leader and soldier who, backed by a British fleet, conquered (1745) the reputedly impregnable French fortress of LOUISBOURG on Cape Breton, Canada, during the FRENCH AND INDIAN WARS. He was the first American to be created baronet.

PEPSIN, an ENZYME which breaks down PROTEINS in the DIGESTIVE SYSTEM.

PEPTIDE, a compound containing two or more AMINO ACIDS linked through the amino group ($-NH_2$) of one acid and the carboxyl group (-COOH) of the other. The linkage -NH-CO- is termed a peptide bond. Peptides containing two amino acids are called dipeptides; with three, tripeptides, and so on; those with many acids are polypeptides.

PEPYS, Samuel (1633–1703), English diarist. Although he was a successful reforming naval administrator and president of the Royal Society (1684–85), it is his talent in recording contemporary affairs and his own private life for which he is famed today. His diary, written in cipher 1660–69, was not decoded and published until 1825.

PEQUOT INDIANS, North American Indians of the ALGONQUIAN language group, who lived in S New England. Their murder of a colonial trader by whom they had been mistreated led to the **Pequot War** (1637), the first major white massacre of Indians in North America, in which almost the entire tribe was slaughtered or enslaved. The Pequot were resettled (1655) on a Connecticut reservation, where they numbered about 30 in the early 1970s.

PERCENT (%—from Latin *per centum*, by one hundred), the expression of a RATIO or FRACTION by setting $a:b=p:100$, where $a:b$ is the original ratio, and p its expression as a percentage.

PERCEPTION, the recognition or identification of something. External perception relies on the SENSES, internal perception, which is introverted, relying on the CONSCIOUSNESS. Some psychologists hold that perception need not be CONSCIOUS: in particular, subliminal perception involves reaction of the UNCONSCIOUS to external stimuli and its subsequent influencing of the conscious (see also SUGGESTION).

PERCÉ ROCK, great arched rock off Gaspé peninsula in E Quebec, Canada. It is a great tourist attraction and a bird sanctuary with nesting places on its virtually inaccessible cliffs.

PERCHES, a family of spiny-finned fishes with protrusible upper jaw and sharp-edged scales. The true perches are all freshwater and belong to the family Percidae, but the name perch is often used for other perch-like fishes within the order Perciformes. True perches include both the European and the American perch, both predatory fishes.

PERCHING BIRDS. See PASSERIFORMES.

PERCUSSION INSTRUMENTS, musical instruments from which sound is produced by striking. These are divided into two main classes: **idiophones**, such as BELLS, CASTANETS, CYMBALS and GONGS, whose wood or metal substance vibrates to produce sound, and **membranophones**, chiefly DRUMS and TAMBOURINES, in which sound is produced by vibrating a stretched skin. Though the PIANO, CELESTA, TRIANGLE, XYLOPHONE and GLOCKENSPIEL can be classed as percussion, the term commonly denotes those instruments used chiefly for rhythmic effect. The TIMPANI can be tuned to different notes.

PÈRE DAVID'S DEER, *Elaphurus davidianus*, a Chinese red deer, some 1.2m (4ft) at the shoulder, a long tail, wide splayed hooves and strange-looking antlers. No one has ever seen it in the wild, the only remaining animals being those of a herd of about 300 at Woburn Park in England.

PEREGRINE, *Falco peregrinus*, one of the largest and most widespread of the FALCONS. They are found in mountainous areas or on sea cliffs, feeding on birds up to the size of a duck, caught in the air. Numbers are declining all over Europe and North America with the increased use of pesticides.

PEREIRA, city in W central Colombia, capital of Risaralda dept. It is a center for coffee and cattle, with varied light industry. Pop 249 500.

PERELMAN, Sidney Joseph (1904–), US humorous writer noted for his collaboration as screen writer on several MARX BROTHERS films, and for many articles which appeared in the *New Yorker*. He won an Academy Award in 1956.

PERENNIAL, any plant that continues to grow for more than two years. Trees and shrubs are examples of the perennials that have woody stems that thicken with age. The herbaceous perennials such as the PEONY and DAFFODIL have stems that die down each winter and regrow in the spring from underground perennating organs, such as TUBERS and BULBS. (See ANNUAL; BIENNIAL.)

PÉREZ JIMÉNEZ, Marcos (1914–), president of Venezuela 1952–58. One of a three-man junta from 1948, he seized sole power in 1952. Inadequate reforms and corrupt rule led to his overthrow and flight. Extradited and imprisoned 1963–68, he settled in Madrid.

PERFECT NUMBER, a NATURAL NUMBER equal to the SUM of its FACTORS. Two such numbers are 6 (divisible by 1, 2, 3, and $1+2+3=6$) and 28 (1, 2, 7, 4, 14). Only 23 perfect numbers are known.

PERFUME, a blend of substances made from plant oils and synthetic materials which produce a pleasant odor. Perfumes were used in ancient times as INCENSE in religious rites, in medicines and later for adornment. Today they are utilized in cosmetics, toilet waters, soaps and detergents, and polishes. A main source of perfumes are ESSENTIAL OILS extracted from different parts of plants, e.g., the flowers of the ROSE, the leaves of LAVENDER, CINNAMON from bark and PINE from wood. They are extracted by steam distillation; by using volatile solvents; by coating petals with fat, or by pressing. Animal products, such as AMBERGRIS from the sperm whale, are used as fixatives to preserve fragrance. The development of synthetic perfumes began in the 19th century. There are now a number of synthetic chemicals with flower-like fragrance, for example citronellol for rose and benzyl acetate for JASMINE.

PERGAMUM, ancient Greek city of NW Asia Minor, the modern Bergama in Turkey. In the 2nd and 3rd centuries BC it became a cultural center under the Attalid kings (see ATTALUS). It was famed for mosaics, sculptures and buildings, including a great library. Bequeathed to Rome by Attalus III, the city prospered as a Christian center.

PERGOLESI, Giovanni Battista (1710–1736), Italian opera composer famed for his comic intermezzo *The Maid as Mistress* (1733). He also composed serious opera and religious music, such as the *Mass in F* (1734) and *Stabat Mater* (1736).

PERI, Jacopo (1561–1633), Italian composer whose *Dafne* (1597) may have been the first opera. Only his opera *Euridice* (1600) and the sensitive madrigals of *Le varie musiche* (1609) survive.

PERIANTH. See FLOWER.

PERICARDIUM, two thin connective-tissue layers covering the HEART surface. It may become inflamed due to VIRUS or bacterial infection and in UREMIA.

PERICLES (c495–429 BC), Athenian general and statesman. A strong critic of the conservative AREOPAGUS council, he obtained (461) the OSTRACISM of Cimon and became supreme leader of the Athenian democracy. The years 462–454 BC saw the furthering of that democracy, with salaried state offices and supremacy of the assembly. Pericles' expansionist foreign policy led to defeat of Persia (449), a truce with Sparta (445) and the transformation of the DELIAN LEAGUE into an Athenian empire. The peace of 445–431 saw the height of Athenian culture under his rule. The PARTHENON and PROPYLAEA were both built at Pericles' request. One of the instigators of the PELOPONNESIAN WAR he was deposed but reelected in 429; his death in a plague soon after may have lost Athens the war.

PERIDOT. See OLIVINE.

PERIDOTITE, dark IGNEOUS ROCK consisting mainly of OLIVINE with some PYROXENE and HORNBLENDE but little FELDSPAR; it alters to SERPENTINE. Some varieties bear chromium ore, platinum or diamonds (see KIMBERLITE).

PERIGEE. See ORBIT.

PERIHELION. See ORBIT.

PERIODIC TABLE, a table of the ELEMENTS in order of atomic number (see ATOM), arranged in rows and columns to illustrate periodic similarities and trends in physical and chemical properties. Such classification of the elements began in the early 19th century, when Johann Wolfgang Döbereiner (1780–1849) discovered certain "triads" of similar elements (e.g. calcium, strontium, barium) whose atomic weights were in arithmetic progression. By the 1860s many more elements were known, and their atomic weights determined, and it was noted by John Alexander Reina Newlands (1837–1898) that similar elements recur at intervals of eight—his "law of octaves"—in a sequence in order of atomic weight. In 1869 MENDELEYEV published the first fairly complete periodic table, based on his discovery that the properties of the elements vary periodically with atomic weight. There were gaps in the table corresponding to elements then unknown, whose properties Mendeleyev predicted with remarkable accuracy. Modern understanding of atomic structure has shown that the numbers and arrangement of the electrons in the atom are responsible for the periodicity of properties; hence the atomic number, rather than the atomic weight, is the basis of ordering. Each row, or period, of the table corresponds to the filling of an electron "shell"; hence the numbers of elements in the periods is 2, 8, 8, 18, 18, 32, 32. (There are n^2 ORBITALS in the nth shell). The elements are arranged in vertical columns or groups containing those of similar atomic structure and properties, with regular gradation of properties down each group. The longer groups, with members in the first three (short) periods, are known as the Main Groups, usually numbered IA to VIIA, and 0 for the NOBLE GASES. The remaining groups, the TRANSITION ELEMENTS, are numbered IIIB to VIII (a triple group), IB and IIB. The characteristic VALENCE of each group is equal to

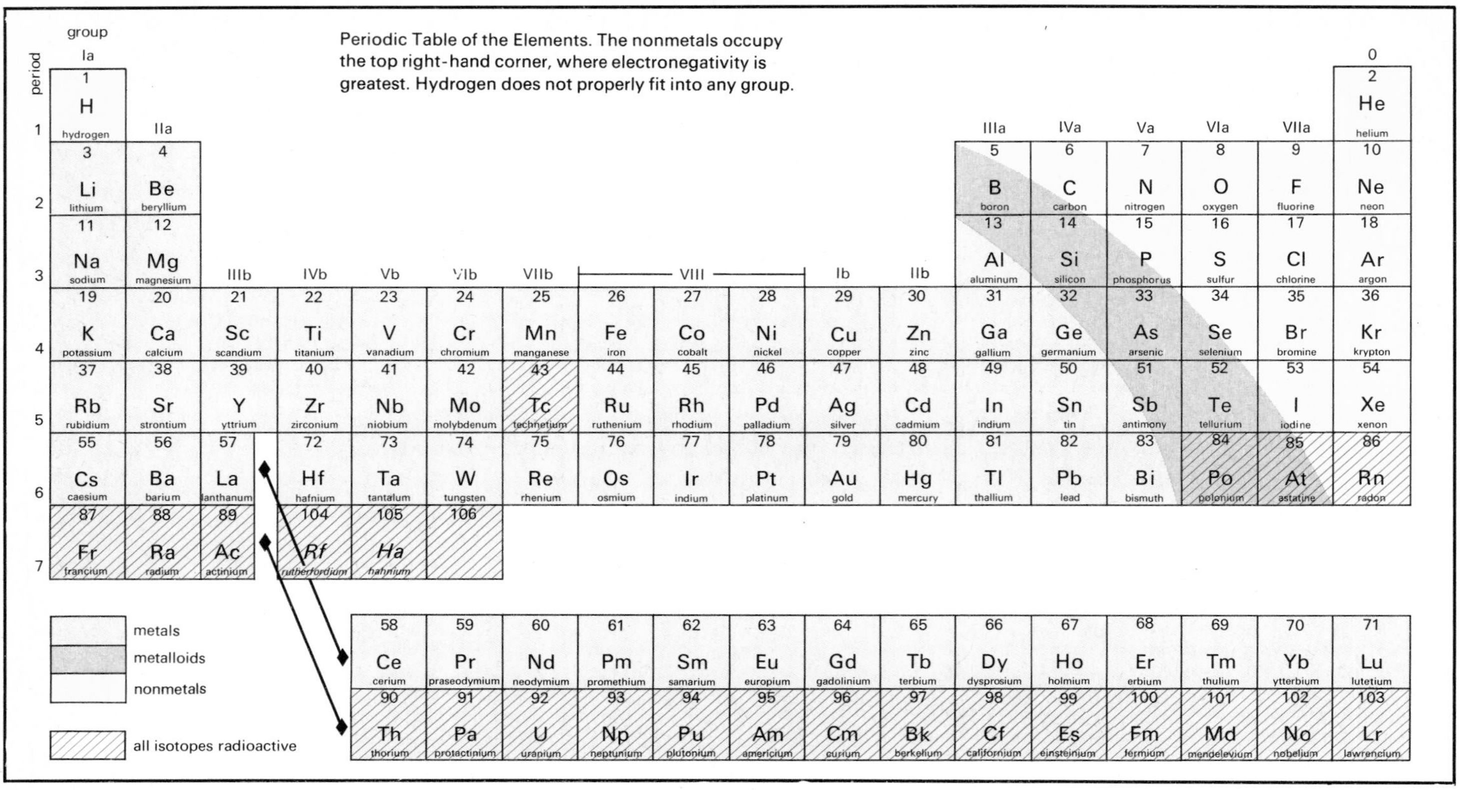
group
period
Ia
IIa
IIIb
IVb
Vb
VIb
VIIb
VIII
Ib
IIb
IIIa
IVa
Va
VIa
VIIa
0
1 H hydrogen
2 He helium
3 Li lithium
4 Be beryllium
5 B boron
6 C carbon
7 N nitrogen
8 O oxygen
9 F fluorine
10 Ne neon
11 Na sodium
12 Mg magnesium
13 Al aluminum
14 Si silicon
15 P phosphorus
16 S sulfur
17 Cl chlorine
18 Ar argon
19 K potassium
20 Ca calcium
21 Sc scandium
22 Ti titanium
23 V vanadium
24 Cr chromium
25 Mn manganese
26 Fe iron
27 Co cobalt
28 Ni nickel
29 Cu copper
30 Zn zinc
31 Ga gallium
32 Ge germanium
33 As arsenic
34 Se selenium
35 Br bromine
36 Kr krypton
37 Rb rubidium
38 Sr strontium
39 Y yttrium
40 Zr zirconium
41 Nb niobium
42 Mo molybdenum
43 Tc technetium
44 Ru ruthenium
45 Rh rhodium
46 Pd palladium
47 Ag silver
48 Cd cadmium
49 In indium
50 Sn tin
51 Sb antimony
52 Te tellurium
53 I iodine
54 Xe xenon
55 Cs caesium
56 Ba barium
57 La lanthanum
72 Hf hafnium
73 Ta tantalum
74 W tungsten
75 Re rhenium
76 Os osmium
77 Ir indium
78 Pt platinum
79 Au gold
80 Hg mercury
81 Tl thallium
82 Pb lead
83 Bi bismuth
84 Po polonium
85 At astatine
86 Rn radon
87 Fr francium
88 Ra radium
89 Ac actinium
104 Rf rutherfordium
105 Ha hahnium
106
58 Ce cerium
59 Pr praseodymium
60 Nd neodymium
61 Pm promethium
62 Sm samarium
63 Eu europium
64 Gd gadolinium
65 Tb terbium
66 Dy dysprosium
67 Ho holmium
68 Er erbium
69 Tm thulium
70 Yb ytterbium
71 Lu lutetium
90 Th thorium
91 Pa protactinium
92 U uranium
93 Np neptunium
94 Pu plutonium
95 Am americium
96 Cm curium
97 Bk berkelium
98 Cf californium
99 Es einsteinium
100 Fm fermium
101 Md mendelevium
102 No nobelium
103 Lr lawrencium
metals
metalloids
nonmetals
all isotopes radioactive

Periodic Table of the Elements. The nonmetals occupy the top right-hand corner, where electronegativity is greatest. Hydrogen does not properly fit into any group.

its number N, or to $(8-N)$ for some nonmetals. Two series of 14 elements each, the LANTHANIDES and ACTINIDES, form a hyper-transition block in which the inner *f* ORBITALS are being filled; their members have similar properties, and they are usually counted in Group IIIB. (See also TRANSURANIUM ELEMENTS.)

PERIODONTICS, branch of DENTISTRY concerned with the structures which fix the teeth in the jaw.

PERIPATETIC SCHOOL, in philosophy, the name given to the school of philosophy founded by ARISTOTLE and THEOPHRASTUS. The term derives from the covered arcade (*peripatos*) at the Lyceum where Aristotle taught in Athens.

PERIPATUS, the best-known genus of the ONYCHOPHORA, occurring in Australasia. They are nocturnal, carnivorous creatures, found under stones and in crevices in bark or soil in damp regions.

PERIPHERAL NERVOUS SYSTEM. See NERVOUS SYSTEM.

PERISCOPE, optical instrument that permits an observer to view his surroundings along a displaced axis, and hence from a concealed, protected or submerged position. The simplest periscope, used in tanks, has two parallel reflecting surfaces (prisms or mirrors). An auxiliary telescopic gunsight may be added. Submarine periscopes have a series of lenses within the tube to widen the field of view, crosswires and a range-finder, and can rotate and retract.

PERISSODACTYLA, the order of mammals containing the odd-toed ungulates, with two suborders: the Hippomorpha, the HORSE and its relatives, and the Tapiromorpha, the TAPIRS and RHINOCEROSES. The middle toe in each foot has become the main support for the body; during evolution the other toes have been reduced. The perissodactyls are nonruminant.

PERISTALSIS, the coordinated movements of hollow visceral organs, especially the GASTROINTESTINAL TRACT, which cause forward propulsion and mixing of the contents. It is effected by autonomic NERVOUS SYSTEM plexuses acting on visceral MUSCLE layers.

PERITONEUM, two thin layers of connective tissue lining the outer surface of the abdominal organs and the inner walls of the ABDOMEN. A small amount of fluid lies between them in an extensive potential space, allowing free movement of the organs over each other.

PERITONITIS, INFLAMMATION of PERITONEUM, usually caused by BACTERIAL INFECTION or chemical irritation of peritoneum when internal organs become diseased (as with APPENDICITIS) or when GASTROINTESTINAL TRACT contents escape (as with a perforated peptic ULCER). Characteristic pain, sometimes with SHOCK, FEVER, and temporary cessation of bowel activity (ileus), are common. Urgent treatment of the cause is required, often with SURGERY; ANTIBIOTICS may also be needed.

PERIWINKLE, the name given to several creeping plants of the genus *Vinca* which bear pink, blue or purple flowers. The ground-covering lesser-periwinkle (*Vinca minor*) is native to Europe and is naturalized in North America. Family: Apocynaceae.

PERIWINKLES, small marine snails, genus *Littorina*, living mainly in the shore zone, feeding on seaweeds which they rasp with their horny tongue, or radula. They show pronounced "zonation" with different species characteristic of different parts of the shore.

PERJURY, the making of a willfully false statement under oath (or affirmation) during legal proceedings. It is an offense punishable by a substantial fine or imprisonment, as is persuading others to lie under oath—subornation to perjury.

PERKIN, Sir William Henry (1838–1907), English chemist who, in 1856, while studying under von HOFMANN, discovered mauve, the first synthetic dye (see DYES AND DYEING). He manufactured this and other dyes until 1874, then devoted his remaining years to research. In 1868 he synthesized coumarin, the first synthetic PERFUME.

PERKINS, Frances (1882–1965), US secretary of Labor 1933–45, first US woman cabinet member. From 1910 she was active in N.Y. state factory and labor affairs. Appointed labor secretary by President F. D. ROOSEVELT, she administered NEW DEAL programs.

PERM, capital city of Perm oblast, USSR, in the E central Ural Mts. It is a major producer of machinery and chemicals. Pop 850 000.

PERMAFROST, permanently frozen ground, typical of the treeless plains of Siberia (see TUNDRA), though common throughout polar regions to depths of as much as 600m.

PERMALLOY, an ALLOY of iron and nickel, often with 5% molybdenum; it has a very high magnetic PERMEABILITY and is used in TRANSFORMERS.

PERMANENT COURT OF ARBITRATION. See HAGUE TRIBUNAL.

PERMANENT COURT OF INTERNATIONAL JUSTICE. See INTERNATIONAL COURT OF JUSTICE.

PERMEABILITY (μ), the ratio of the electromagnetic INDUCTION in a material to the MAGNETIC FIELD producing it. Materials showing DIAMAGNETISM and PARAMAGNETISM have permeabilities just below and above the free space value ($\mu_0 = 4\pi \times 10^{-7}$ H/m); ferromagnets have a permeability a thousand times greater.

PERMIAN, the last period of the PALEOZOIC, stretching between about 280 and 225 million years ago. (See also GEOLOGY.)

PERMITTIVITY (ε), a constant of proportionality between an electric charge and the ELECTRIC FIELD emanating from it. The factor by which it exceeds the free space value ($\varepsilon_0 = 8.85 \times 10^{-12}$F/m) in a given material is known as the *relative permittivity*, or DIELECTRIC constant for the material.

PERMUTATIONS AND COMBINATIONS, respectively, the different orders that can be given to the elements of a SET; and the different selections of elements that may be taken from the set, every selection being of the same size, no element being a member of more than one selection, and order within each selection being immaterial. For a set of n elements there are $n(n-1)(n-2)\ \dots\ 2.1$ $(=n!$—see FACTORIAL) permutations, taking the elements singly; and, taking the elements in *ordered* subsets each containing k elements, there are $n(n-1)(n-2)\ \dots\ (n-(k-1))$ $(=\frac{n!}{(n-k)!})$ permutations. For the same set, taking k elements in each *unordered* subset, there are $\frac{n!}{k!\,(n-k)!}$ combinations.

PERNAMBUCO, NE Atlantic state of Brazil. Its narrow coastal area rises in terraces to a broader inland plateau. The capital is Recife. Chief products in the largely agricultural economy are sugar, coffee, cotton and tobacco.

PERÓN, Isabel (Maria Estela Martínez de Perón; 1931–), president of Argentina 1974–76. Personal secretary to Juan PERÓN since 1956, she married him in 1961. She was elected vice-president in 1973 and became president on her husband's death. She was deposed by a military junta in 1976.

PERÓN, Juan Domingo (1895–1974), president of Argentina 1946–55, 1973–74. As head of an army clique, he helped overthrow Castillo in 1943. He won union loyalty as secretary of labor. Elected president (after police intervention), he began with his first wife Eva (1919–1952) a program of industrialization and social reform. Church and army opposition to corruption and repression forced him into exile. Peronist influence survived, however; he returned in 1972, and was reelected president in 1973.

PEROXIDES, compounds of OXYGEN containing the peroxy group (-O-O-). ALKALI METAL and ALKALINE-EARTH METAL peroxides, containing the peroxide ion O_2^{2-}, are formed by heating the metals or their OXIDES in excess air. Covalent peroxides include peracetic acid and peroxymonosulfuric acid ("Caro's acid"). They are powerful oxidizing agents, used in bleaching. (See also SUPEROXIDES.) **Hydrogen Peroxide** (H_2O_2) is a colorless liquid, usually produced as aqueous solutions by electrolytic or organic oxidation processes; a powerful oxidizing agent which readily decomposes into water and oxygen on heating or with various catalysts. It is used in bleaching, organic synthesis, medicine and in rocket fuels. mp −0.4°C, bp 150°C.

PERPENDICULAR, a LINE drawn through a fixed POINT P and cutting a fixed line L at right angles (see ANGLE). Should it cut L at L's center, it is termed a perpendicular bisector.

PERPENDICULAR STYLE, name given to the period of English Gothic architecture from the late 14th to the middle 16th century. It is characterized by the vertical tracery on windows and wall panels and by fan vaults. King's College chapel, Cambridge, is a famous example of the style.

PERPETUAL MOTION, an age-old goal of inventors: a machine which would work forever without external interference, or at least with 100% efficiency. No such machine has worked or can work, though many are plausible on paper. Perpetual motion machines of the *first kind* are those whose efficiency exceeds 100%—they do work without energy being supplied. They are disallowed by the First Law of THERMODYNAMICS. Those of the *second kind* are machines that take heat from a reservoir (such as the ocean) and convert it wholly into work. Although energy is conserved, they are disallowed by the Second Law of Thermodynamics. Those of the *third kind* are machines that do no work, but merely continue in motion forever. They are approachable but not actually achievable, because some energy is always dissipated as heat by friction etc. An example, however, of what is in a sense perpetual motion of the third kind is electric current flowing in a superconducting ring (see SUPERCONDUCTIVITY), which continues undiminished indefinitely.

PERRAULT, name of two eminent French brothers. **Charles Perrault** (1628–1703), poet, fairy-tale writer and man of letters, is best known for his *Contes de ma mère l'Oye* (*Tales of Mother Goose*; 1697) which include "Little Red Riding Hood," "Cinderella" and "Puss in Boots." **Claude Perrault** (1613–1688), architect, scientist and physician, is remembered for his buildings, notably the colonnade of the Louvre (1667–70), the Paris Observatory (1667–72) and for his translation of the works of VITRUVIUS (1673).

PERRIN, Jean Baptiste (1870–1942), French physical chemist awarded the 1926 Nobel Prize for Physics for his studies of BROWNIAN MOTION in which, by examining colloidal particles, he was able to arrive at a good value of the AVOGADRO NUMBER.

PERROT, Nicolas (1644–c1718), French explorer. Through work with the Jesuits, then as a fur trader, he gained influence with the Wisconsin Indians. He fought against the Iroquois and gained the upper Mississippi areas for New France (1689).

PERRY, two US brothers who became distinguished naval officers. **Matthew Calbraith Perry** (1794–1858) was instrumental in opening Japan to US and world trade. He commanded the first US steam warship, the *Fulton II* (1838) and led US naval forces suppressing the slave trade; he fought in the MEXICAN WAR. In 1853 Perry took four vessels into Tokyo Bay and remained there until a Japanese envoy agreed to receive President FILLMORE's request for a diplomatic and trade treaty. He returned in Feb. 1854 to conclude the treaty, which was a turning point in US-Japan relations. **Oliver Hazard Perry** (1785–1819), became a hero of the WAR OF 1812. After assembling a fleet of nine ships at Erie, Pa., he defeated six British warships on Sep. 10, 1813 off Put-in-Bay, Ohio, in the battle of Lake ERIE. He announced his victory in the famous message "We have met the enemy and they are ours."

PERRY'S VICTORY AND INTERNATIONAL PEACE MEMORIAL NATIONAL MONUMENT. See PUT-IN-BAY.

PERSE, St.-John (1887–1975), pen name of Alexis Saint-Léger, French poet and diplomat. He was secretary general of the French foreign office (1933–40). His poetry includes *Anabase* (1924), translated by T. S. ELIOT, and *Amers* (1957). In 1960 he was awarded the Nobel Prize for Literature.

PERSECUTION MANIA. See PARANOIA.

PERSEPHONE, in Greek mythology, the goddess of agriculture and queen of the underworld, daughter of ZEUS and DEMETER. Her abduction by Hades (PLUTO) so saddened Demeter that she neglected the fruitfulness of the earth. But Persephone returned each spring for two-thirds of the year. Thus winter is barren and growth begins in spring. (See ELEUSINIAN MYSTERIES.)

PERSEPOLIS, ancient ceremonial capital of the ACHAEMENIAN kings of Persia, lying 30mi NE of Shiraz, SW Iran. It flourished under DARIUS I (d. 486 BC) and his successors but was later destroyed by Alexander the Great in 330. In 1971 the 2500th anniversary of the Iranian monarchy was celebrated among the ruins of the city.

PERSEUS, in Greek myth the son of Danae by ZEUS, who visited her in a shower of gold. Told by an oracle that his grandson Perseus would kill him, Acrisius cast Perseus and Danae into the sea. They were rescued by Polydectes, who sent Perseus to slay MEDUSA the GORGON. Perseus also rescued ANDROMEDA. On his return he accidentally killed Acrisius during a discus-throwing contest.

PERSEUS, large N Hemisphere constellation containing the eclipsing binary (see DOUBLE STAR) ALGOL, two GALACTIC CLUSTERS, one of which is a double cluster, and the bright star Mirfak. It gives its name to the Perseid METEOR shower.

PERSHING, John Joseph (1860–1948), US general. After distinguished service in the Indian Wars (1886, 1890–91), the Spanish-American War (1898) and in the Philippines (1899–1903), he was promoted to brigadier general (1906). He led a punitive expedition to Mexico against VILLA (1916) and a year later became commander of the AMERICAN EXPEDITIONARY FORCE in Europe. Pershing insisted on independent authority over US forces. In 1919 he became general of the armies, and was chief of staff from 1921 until his retirement in 1924.

PERSIA. See IRAN.

PERSIA, Ancient, the high plateau of Iran, home of several great civilizations. In the 2nd millennium BC the literate civilization of ELAM developed in the SW of the plateau, with its capital at SUSA. Its W neighbors, BABYLONIA and ASSYRIA, had trading and political interests in the state and attempted takeovers. The civilization was ended in 639 BC by the invasion of Ashurbanipal of Assyria. Assyrian downfall followed in 612 after the sacking of NINEVEH by the Babylonians and the MEDES, an Aryan kingdom S of the Caspian Sea. The area of Parsumash to the S of the Medes was ruled by the ACHAEMENIANS. CYRUS THE GREAT expanded the Achaemenid empire and at his death (529) he controlled the Middle East from the Mediterranean to the Indus R. Under DARIUS I (522–486) PERSEPOLIS succeeded PASAGARDAE as capital; a road system linked the great empire, a canal linked the Nile and Red Sea. Flourishing trade, commerce and public works continued under XERXES I (586–465). Xerxes' murder by his son was followed by intrigues and rebellions that weakened the Achaemenians. In c330 the empire was conquered by ALEXANDER THE GREAT and at his death most of it became part of the brief empire of the SELEUCIDS, who were conquered by the Parthians from SW of the Caspian. The empire of PARTHIA (3rd century BC–3rd century AD) had its capital at CTESIPHON and halted the nomads in the NE and the Romans in the W, defeating CRASSUS in 53 BC and later Mark Anthony. In 224 AD, a successful revolt by Ardashir, ruler of the Fars (the S Persian homeland), established the vigorous SASSANIAN empire. Arts, architecture and religion (ZOROASTRIANISM) revived, the wars with Rome continued, and in 260 AD Shapur, the son of Ardashir, captured the Emperor Valerian. Later, after constant struggles with the Byzantines, the Sassanian empire was overwhelmed by the Arabs in 651.

PERSIAN, the language of Iran, where 12 million of its 15 million speakers live (the others are in Afghanistan). It is an INDO-EUROPEAN LANGUAGE. Modern Persian emerged after the Arab conquest in the 7th century. It has many borrowed Arabic words and a modified Arabic alphabet.

PERSIAN CAT, long-haired type of cat, first introduced into Europe from Turkey and Persia at the end of the 16th century; in the US the official name for the group of long-haired breeds with cobby bodies, short legs and round heads which may be a variety of colors in tabby, self-color, particolor or smoke. Breeders have developed cats with flowing and luxuriant silky coats which require daily grooming, for they cannot be kept in condition by the cat itself.

PERSIAN GULF, or **Arabian Gulf,** an arm of the Arabian Sea between Iran and Arabia. About 550mi long and 120mi wide, the gulf is entered from the Gulf of Oman by the Straits of Hormuz. The bordering regions of Iran, Kuwait, Saudi Arabia, Bahrain, Qatar and the United Arab Emirates contain more than half the world's oil and natural gas resources.

PERSIAN WARS (500–449 BC), wars between Greek states and the Persian empire. Athenian support of the revolt of Greek states within the empire precipitated Persian offensives in Greece. However, by 449 BC Greek strength had secured Europe from further Persian invasions. (See GREECE, ANCIENT.)

PERSIMMON, common name for trees and shrubs of the genus *Diospyros* related to EBONY, and their sweet globular fruit. Its 200 species are found throughout the N Hemisphere. The black heartwood is used for golf clubs. Family: Ebenaceae.

PERSONA, term used by JUNG to describe the individual's projection of himself; i.e., the role that he plays to conform with others' expectations of his personality. In particular, a man with a strong anima (see ANIMA AND ANIMUS) may project an especially strong male persona.

PERSONAL PROPERTY. See PROPERTY.

PERSPECTIVE, in DESCRIPTIVE GEOMETRY, the representation of a three-dimensional object on a PLANE surface by projection (see PROJECTIVE GEOMETRY) of the object onto the plane from a POINT. In PAINTING and SCULPTURE perspective is a method for representing spatial extension and depth on a flat surface or on a RELIEF. The effect is to give the illusion of three dimensions; foreshortening is used, parallel lines converging to a point.

PERSPEX. See LUCITE.

PERSPIRATION, or **sweat**, watery fluid secreted by the SKIN as a means of reducing body temperature. Sweating is common in hot climates, after EXERCISE and in the resolution of FEVER, where the secretion and subsequent evaporation of sweat allow the skin and thus the body to be cooled. Humid atmospheres and high secretion rates delay the evaporation, leaving perspiration on the surface. Excessive fluid loss in sweat, and of salt in the abnormal sweat of CYSTIC FIBROSIS, may lead to SUNSTROKE. Most sweating is regulated by the HYPOTHALAMUS and autonomic NERVOUS SYSTEM. But there is also a separate system of sweat glands, especially on the palms, which secretes at times of stress. *Hyperidrosis* is a condition of abnormally profuse sweating.

PERTH, capital city of Western Australia, on the Swan R estuary. In spite of its geographical isolation it is an administrative, commercial and industrial center, and a transportation hub. Pop 97 242.

PERTH AMBOY, city in N.J., 20mi SW of New York. It is a port of entry on the Raritan R, with metal-refining and other heavy industries. Pop 38 978.

PERTURBATION, in the elliptical orbit of one celestial body around another, an irregularity caused by the gravitational attraction of a third.

PERTUSSIS. See WHOOPING COUGH.

Official name: Republic of Peru
Capital: Lima
Area: 496 093sq mi
Population: 14 100 000
Languages: Spanish; Quechua, Aymara
Religion: Roman Catholic
Monetary unit(s): 1 Sol = 100 centavos

PERU, third-largest nation in South America. It has a mountainous backbone and a 1400mi coastline bordering the Pacific.

Land. Peru is divided into three geographical regions. The coastal zone, averaging 40mi in width, contains a third of the population and most of the large cities. It is mainly arid, but fertile where irrigated by rivers flowing down from the mountains. The mountainous region (the *Sierra*) of the Andes consists of parallel ranges, some with peaks over 20 000ft. Although conditions are harsh, over half the population live in the Sierra. The *Montaña*, consisting of the lower slopes of the E Andes and the E plains, forms part of the tropical forest of the Amazon basin. Rainfall is very low (less than 2in per year) in the coastal zone, moderate in the Sierra and heavy (100in or more) in the E.

People. Peru's population is composed of about 50% Amerindians, 37% *mestizos* (mixed white and Indian) and 13% whites. There is a great division between the poor, less-educated Indians and *mestizos*, and the wealthier, predominantly white Spanish-speakers. Forty percent of the adult population were illiterate in 1970.

Economy. Subsistence agriculture provides the means of livelihood for most of the population. Cotton, sugarcane, coffee and cacao are the chief export crops. Fishing is an important industry, the main catch being *anchovetas* which are processed into fishmeal, the country's chief export. Copper, iron, phosphates and other minerals are mined and exported, and manufacturing industry is developing. The high mountains make communications difficult, and transportation problems hinder economic growth. Principal cities are Lima (capital), Callao, Arequipa, Trujillo, Chimbote (fishing port), Cuzco (ancient INCA capital) and Iquitos on the Amazon.

History. The ancient Inca Empire in Peru was destroyed by the Spanish conquistador PIZARRO (1532). Spanish rule, based at Lima, lasted until the revolutions led by BOLÍVAR and SAN MARTÍN (1820–24). After independence power continued to be concentrated in the hands of a small number of wealthy landowners. This century has been characterized by unstable governments and military coups. In 1968 General Juan Velasco Alvarado instituted a leftist military regime, which began a program of social reform, suspended the constitution and seized US-owned companies. Alvarado was overthrown in a military coup in 1975 led by Francisco Morales Bermudez.

PERU, city in N Ill., 15mi W of Ottawa, a port on the Illinois R, with some light industry, including clockmaking. Pop 11 772.

PERU, city in N Ind. on the Wabash R, seat of Miami Co. It is a trading center for an agricultural region, and has some manufacturing industry. Pop 14 139.

PERU CURRENT. See HUMBOLDT CURRENT.

PERUGIA, historic city in Umbria, central Italy. Once an Etruscan city, the walled, hilltop town is renowned for its architecture, paintings and archeological museum. It has some light industry, principally chocolate and textiles. Pop 128 542.

PERUGINO (Pietro Vannucci, c1446–1523), Italian Renaissance painter, teacher of RAPHAEL. His frescoes in the Vatican SISTINE CHAPEL, including the *Delivery of the Keys to St. Peter* (1481), established his fame. He worked much in Florence, and later in his native Umbria.

PERUTZ, Max Ferdinand (1914–   ), Austrian-born British biochemist who shared with KENDREW the 1962 Nobel Prize for Chemistry for their research into the structure of HEMOGLOBIN and other globular PROTEINS.

PERUZZI, Baldassare (1481–1536), Italian High Renaissance architect and painter. In Rome he built the Villa Farnesina, which he decorated with illusionist paintings (1508–11), and the Mannerist Palazzo Massimo (1532–36).

PESCADORES, group of about 64 small islands, about 50sq mi of land area, belonging to Taiwan, in the Formosa strait. The chief occupations are fishing and farming. Pop 87 720.

PESHAWAR, capital of NW Frontier province, Pakistan, near the Khyber Pass. It is a trading center for handicrafts and farm produce. Pop 296 000.

PESTALOZZI, Johann Heinrich (1746–1827), famous Swiss educator. At his school at Yverdon he stressed the importance of the individual, and based his methods on the child's direct experience, rather than mechanical learning. His teacher-training methods also became renowned. *How Gertrude Teaches Her Children* (1801) was his most influential work.

PESTICIDE, any substance used to kill plants or animals responsible for economic damage to crops, either growing or under storage, or ornamental plants, or which prejudice the well-being of man and domestic or conserved wild animals. Pesticides are subdivided into INSECTICIDES (which kill insects); miticides (which kill mites); herbicides (which kill plants—see WEEDKILLER); FUNGICIDES (which kill fungi), and rodenticides (which kill rats and mice). Substances used in the treatment of infectious BACTERIAL DISEASES are not generally regarded as pesticides. The efficient control of pests is of enormous economic importance for man, particularly as farming becomes more intensive. A major question with all pesticides is the possibility of unfortunate environmental side effects (see ECOLOGY; POLLUTION).

PÉTAIN, Henri Philippe (1856–1951), French WWI hero who became chief of state in the collaborationist VICHY regime (1940). Famous for his defense of Verdun (1916), he was made chief-of-staff (1917), and subsequently held important military offices. In 1934 he served briefly as war minister. Recalled from his post as ambassador to Spain in June 1940, he became premier and negotiated an armistice with the Nazis. As head of the Vichy government, he aided the Nazis, and in 1945 was tried for treason and sentenced to life imprisonment.

PETAL. See FLOWER.

PETALUMA, city in W. Cal., on the Petaluma R. It is a dairy and poultry farming center, with some light industry. Pop 24 870.

PETER, Saint (Simon Peter; d. c64 AD), leader of the 12 APOSTLES, and regarded by Roman Catholics as the first pope. A Galilean fisherman when Jesus called him to be a disciple, he was a dominating but impulsive figure, and denied Jesus after his arrest. He played a leading role in the early Church, especially in Jerusalem, as related in Acts. By tradition, he died a martyr at Rome.

PETER, name of three tsars of Russia. **Peter I, the Great** (1672–1725) became joint tsar in 1682 and sole tsar in 1796. As a young man he traveled in W Europe (1797–98), learning techniques of war and industry and recruiting experts to bring back to Russia. His war against Turkey was intended to gain access to the Mediterranean, and the long conflict with Sweden (1700–21) led to Russian domination of the Baltic Sea. He established his new capital of St. Petersburg on the Baltic, as a symbol of his policy of westernization. Domestically, he introduced sweeping military, administrative and other reforms. A man of enormous size, strength and demonic energy, Peter was also savage in the exercise of power, and although he modernized, reformed and strengthened Russia, it was at great cost. **Peter II** (1715–1750) ruled from 1727. **Peter III** (1728–1762) ruled in 1762.

PETER I (1844–1921), king of Serbia. A Serbian prince, he spent years in exile, and joined the anti-Turkish Herzegovinian revolt in 1875. He became an honorary senator of Montenegro in 1883, and was elected king of Serbia in 1903.

PETER II (1923–1970), king of Yugoslavia. On the death of his father ALEXANDER I his cousin governed as regent (1934–41). Peter fled to London after the Nazi invasion (1941), and set up an exile government. In 1945 Yugoslavia became a republic, and Peter a pretender.

PETER, Epistles of, two New Testament letters, traditionally attributed to St. PETER. The first is written to encourage persecuted Christians in Asia Minor; the second closely parallels the Epistle of JUDE and refers to the Second Coming. The authorship is doubtful, particularly of the second, which some scholars date c150 AD and which was admitted late to the CANON.

PETERBOROUGH, city in SE Ontario, Canada. Connected with Lake Ontario by the Trent canal, it is an industrial center and a resort for the Kawartha Lakes region. Pop 58 111.

PETER CLAVER, Saint (1581–1654), "Apostle of the Negroes." A Spanish Jesuit, he went in 1610 to Cartagena, Colombia, and against official opposition he visited every slave ship that arrived at the port, nursing the sick and preaching.

PETER LOMBARD. See LOMBARD, PETER.

PETERLOO MASSACRE, name applied to the meeting held Aug. 16, 1819, in St. Peter's Fields, Manchester, England. When 60 000 radicals demonstrated peacefully to demand a reform of Parliament, the local magistrates, fearing a riot, ordered the militia to stop the meeting. Their cavalry support charged the crowd, killing 11 and wounding over 400.

PETERSBURG, historic city in SE Va., on the Appomattox R. Founded as Fort Henry (1646), it was occupied in the CIVIL WAR by Confederate forces under Gen. LEE, and successfully besieged by Gen. GRANT 1864–65. It is now an important tobacco center. Pop 36 103.

PETER THE HERMIT (c1050–1115), French monk who preached the First CRUSADE (1095). He led an army into Asia Minor which was annihilated, and later played an undistinguished part at Antioch and Jerusalem.

PETIPA, Marius (1819–1910), French dancer and choreographer who created the modern classical ballet. An outstanding dancer and mime, he joined the Russian ballet at St. Petersburg in 1847, becoming chief choreographer in 1869. There he created over 60 full-length ballets, including *The Nutcracker*, *Swan Lake* and *The Sleeping Beauty*.

PETIT, Alexis Thérèse (1791–1820), French physicist who worked with P. L. DULONG to discover Dulong and Petit's Law.

PETITION OF RIGHT, document presented to CHARLES I of England by Parliament (1628) in protest against his arbitrary fiscal methods. It asserted four principles: no taxation without parliamentary consent; no imprisonment of subjects without due legal cause; no billeting of soldiers in private houses without payment; no declaring of MARTIAL LAW in peacetime. Accepted but later disregarded by the king, it represents a landmark in English constitutional history.

PETIT MAL. See EPILEPSY.

PETLYURA, Simon (1879–1926), Ukrainian nationalist leader. In 1919 he became head of an independent Ukrainian republic, but when the Ukraine came under Soviet control in 1921, he went into exile, and was assassinated in Paris.

PETN, or **pentaerithrytol tetranitrate,** $C(CH_2ONO_2)_4$, colorless crystalline solid made by NITRATION of pentaerithrytol. It is a high EXPLOSIVE used in detonators and grenades.

PETRA, ancient ruined city in SW Jordan. Famous for its tombs and temples cut into sandstone cliffs, it was the capital of the NABATEANS, prospered under the Romans but lost its trade to Palmyra. Its decline continued under Muslim rule, and its ruins were discovered by BURCKHARDT in 1812.

PETRARCH (Francesco Petrarca; 1304–1374), Italian poet and early HUMANIST. Supported by influential patrons, he spent his life in study, travel and writing. He wrote poetry, epistles and other prose works in Latin, but also much in vernacular Italian, of which he is one of the earliest masters. He himself rated his Latin works highest, but his great fame now rests on the Italian *Canzoniere*, mostly sonnets inspired by his love for the enigmatic Laura, who died of plague in 1348.

PETRELS, seabirds of the tubenosed-bird order, Procellariiformes, particularly the typical petrels and shearwaters of the family Procellariidae. All have webbed feet and hooked bills, with nostrils opening through horny tubes on the upper mandible. They are marine birds which swim and fly expertly, feeding far from the shore on fish, squids and offal. Normally they go ashore only to breed.

PETRI DISH, shallow glass dish with a loose lid, used for growing CULTURES, named for Julius Petri (1852–1921), an assistant to R. KOCH.

PETRIE, Sir William Matthew Flinders (1853–1942), British archaeologist who devised a system of sequence dating. A relative CHRONOLOGY could thus be established between sites and dates attributed to the superimposed layers of a site.

PETRIFACTION. See FOSSILS.

PETRIFIED FOREST NATIONAL PARK, a park of 147sq mi in E Ariz. The fossil remains of a TRIASSIC forest are exposed on the surface, creating the largest display of petrified wood in the world.

PETROCHEMICALS, chemicals made from PETROLEUM and NATURAL GAS, i.e., all organic chemicals, plus the inorganic substances carbon black, sulfur, ammonia and hydrogen peroxide. Many petrochemicals are still made also from other raw materials, but the petrochemical industry has grown rapidly since about 1920. Polymers, detergents, solvents and nitrogen fertilizers are major products.

PETROGRAD. See LENINGRAD.

PETROLATUM, or **Petroleum Jelly.** See VASELINE.

PETROLEUM, naturally-occurring mixture of HYDROCARBONS, usually liquid "crude oil," but sometimes taken to include NATURAL GAS. (See also ASPHALT; BITUMEN.) Petroleum is believed to be formed from organic debris, chiefly of plankton and simple plants, which has been rapidly buried in fine-grained sediment under marine conditions unfavorable to oxidation. After some biodegradation, increasing temperature and pressure cause CRACKING, and oil is produced. As the source rock is compacted, oil and water are forced out, and slowly migrate to porous reservoir rocks, chiefly sandstone or limestone. Finally, secondary migration occurs within the reservoir as the oil coagulates to form a pool, generally capped by impervious strata, and often associated with natural gas. Some oil seeps to the earth's surface: this was used by the early Mesopotamian civilizations. The first oil well was drilled in western Pa. in 1859. The industry thus begun has grown so fast that it now supplies about half the world's energy, as well as the raw materials for PETROCHEMICALS. Modern technology has made possible oil-well drilling to a depth of 5km, and deep-sea wells in 150m of water. Rotary drilling is used, with pressurized mud to carry the rock to the surface and to prevent escape of oil. When the well is completed, the oil rises to the surface, usually under its own pressure, though pumping may be required. The chief world oil-producing regions are the Persian Gulf, the US (mainly Tex., La., Okla. and Cal.), the USSR, N and W Africa, and Venezuela. After removing salt and water, the petroleum is refined by fractional DISTILLATION producing the fractions GASOLINE, KEROSINE, diesel oil, fuel oil, lubricating oil, and ASPHALT. Undesirable compounds may be removed by solvent extraction, treatment with sulfuric acid, etc., and less valuable components converted into more valuable ones by CRACKING, reforming, ALKYLATION and polymerization. The chemical composition of crude petroleum is chiefly ALKANES, saturated ALICYCLIC COMPOUNDS, and AROMATIC COMPOUNDS, with some sulfur compounds, oxygen compounds (carboxylic acids and phenols), nitrogen and salt. (See also OIL SHALE.)

PETROLOGY, branch of geology concerned with the history, composition, occurrence, properties and classification of rocks. (See GEOLOGY; ROCKS.)

PETRONIUS ARBITER, Caius (d. 66 AD), Roman satirist. He became NERO's "Arbiter of Taste," but fell from favor and committed suicide. *Trimalchio's Dinner* is the best-known fragment of his *Satyricon*, a sensual, amoral and often obscene romance.

PETROV, Yevgeny (1903–1942), Russian journalist, born Yevgeny Petrovich Katayev, coauthor, with I. A. ILF, of popular satirical novels. Brother of V. P. KATAYEV, he was killed while a war correspondent in WWII.

PETTY, Sir William (1623–1687), British physician, statistician, anatomist, musician and economist best known for his *A Treatise of Taxes and Contributions* (1662).

PETUNIA, a genus of about 40 species of herbaceous plants, many hybrids of which, coming under the general name *Petunia hybrida*, are grown as garden ornamentals. Although they are mainly perennials most are grown as annuals, since they flower in the first year. Family: Solanaceae.

PEVSNER, Antoine (1886–1962), Russian-born sculptor who studied in Paris 1911–13 and settled there from 1922. In 1920 he launched CONSTRUCTIVISM with his brother NAUM GABO in Moscow. Light and space play important roles in his sculptures.

PEWEES, or **Wood pewees,** a genus, *Cantopus*, of tyrant-flycatchers (KINGBIRDS) of the New World. Also known as peewees, these birds feed on insects and sometimes fruits snapped up in flight.

PEWTER, class of ALLOYS consisting chiefly of TIN, now hardened with copper and antimony, and usually containing lead. Roman pewter was high in lead and darkened with age. Pewter has been used for bowls, drinking vessels and candlesticks.

PEYOTE, *Lophophora williamsii* and related cactus species, native to Texas and Mexico. The cut, dried tops are chewed by Indians to release the hallucinogenic drug MESCALINE. This habit was first described in 1560. Family: Cactaceae.

pH, measure of the acidity (see ACID) of an aqueous solution, defined as $pH = \log_{10}\{H^+\}$, where $\{H^+\}$, the thermodynamic activity of the hydrogen ions in the solution, approximates to their concentration in MOLES/litre for dilute solutions. Pure water has a pH of 7 (i.e., contains 10^{-7} mol/l H^+); acidic solutions have pH less than 7, basic ones greater than 7. (See also BUFFER.)

PHACOLITH. See LACCOLITH.

PHAECIA, in Greek myth, a hospitable island whose inhabitants entertained ODYSSEUS.

PHAEDRA, in Greek mythology, daughter of Minos and Pasiphae, wife of THESEUS of Athens. When her stepson Hippolytus rejected her advances, she killed herself, leaving a note accusing him of attempted rape. Hippolytus fled, but was killed by POSEIDON at Theseus' request.

PHAEOPHYTA, or brown algae. See ALGAE.

PHAETON, in Greek mythology, son of HELIOS the sun god. He attempted to drive the chariot of the sun for a day, but was unable to control the horses and began to scorch the earth. To save the world, Zeus struck him dead.

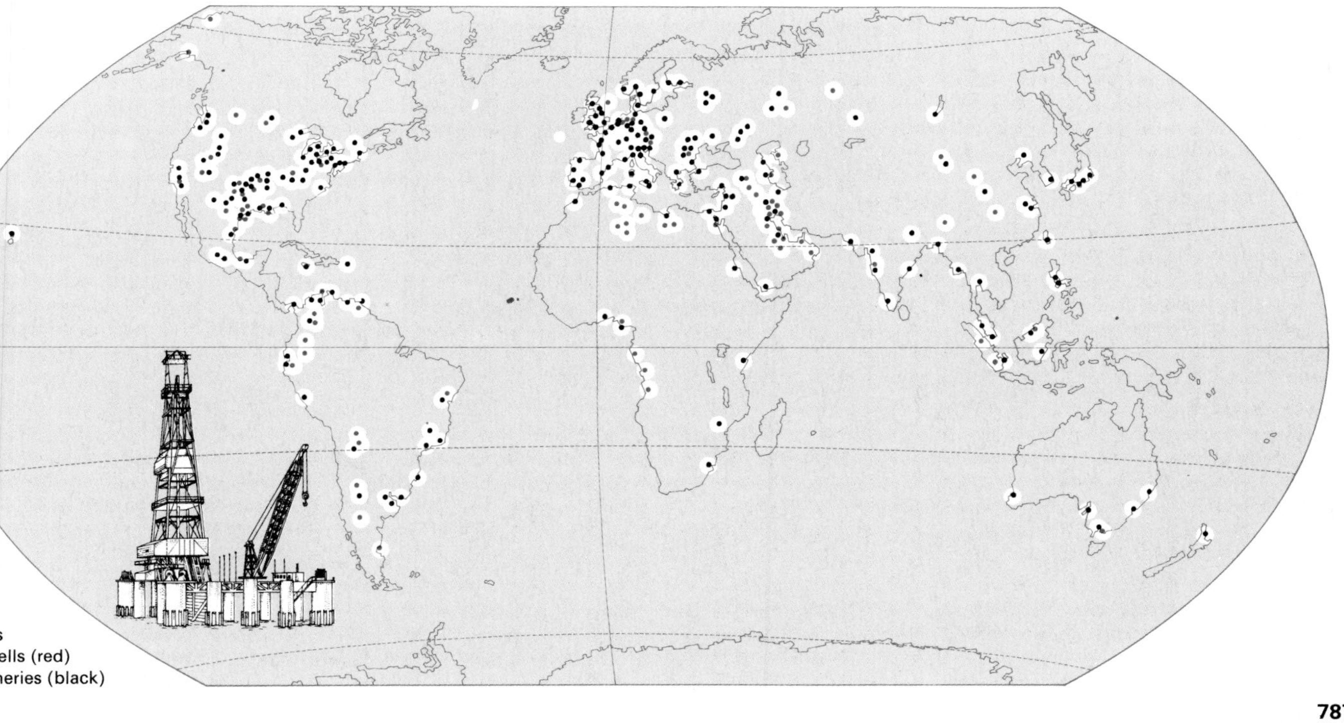

The world's major oil wells (red) and oil refineries (black)

PHAGE. See BACTERIOPHAGE.

PHAGOCYTE, any CELL, typically a BLOOD leukocyte, able to engulf and thus eliminate foreign bodies.

PHAISTOS, ancient city of the MINOAN CIVILIZATION in S Crete. Many remains have been excavated there, particularly of the great palace (dating from c2200 BC).

PHALANGERS, herbivorous marsupials of Australia. The family Phalangeridae includes Flying phalangers, Pygmy possums and POSSUMS. All feed on leaves, grass and herbs, and the most common species can do extensive damage to agriculture. Phalangers have long prehensile tails, usually furred.

PHALANX, ancient Greek infantry formation, consisting of rows of eight men, each heavily armed with an overlapping shield and long pike. PHILIP II of Macedon developed a phalanx 16 men deep, which his son ALEXANDER THE GREAT used in defeating the Persians. Only after defeat by Rome in 168 BC did the phalanx become outmoded.

PHALAROPES, three species of small semiaquatic wading birds, family Phalaropididae. They have long thin bills and feed on insects and crustaceans; when feeding they spin round and round in the water. In phalaropes the breeding roles of the sexes are reversed: the female develops breeding plumage and courts the drabber male, who has sole responsibility for incubation and care of the young.

PHANEROZOIC, the aeon of visible life, the period of time represented by rock strata in which FOSSILS appear, running from about 570 million years ago through to the present and containing the PALEOZOIC, MESOZOIC and CENOZOIC eras. (See also CRYPTOZOIC; GEOLOGY; PRECAMBRIAN.)

PHARAOH, Hebrew form of the title of the kings of ancient Egypt. The term (actually *per-'o*: great house) described his palace and, by association, the king. The Egyptians believed the pharaoh to be the personification of the gods HORUS and, later, AMON.

PHARISEES, an ancient Jewish sect devoted to strict observance of the Holy Law and strongly opposed to pagan practices absorbed by Judaism, and to the SADDUCEES. Their moral fervor and initially progressive nature made them an important political force. Tradition has made them synonymous with hypocrisy and self-righteousness, but Jesus only attacked the debasement of their ideals.

PHARMACOLOGY, the study of DRUGS, their chemistry, mode of action, routes of absorption, excretion and METABOLISM, drug interactions, toxicity and side-effects. New drugs, based on older drugs, traditional remedies, chance observations etc., are tested for safety and efficacy, and manufactured by the pharmaceutical industry. The dispensing of drugs is PHARMACY. Drug prescription is the cornerstone of the medical treatment of DISEASE.

PHARMACOPEIA, a text containing all available DRUGS and pharmacological preparations, providing a vital source for accurate prescribing in MEDICINE. It lists drugs; their properties and formulation; routes and doses of administration; mode of action, METABOLISM and excretion; known interaction with other drugs; contraindications and precautions in particular DISEASES; toxicity, and side-effects.

PHARMACY, the preparation or dispensing of DRUGS and pharmacological substances used in MEDICINE; also, the place where this is practiced. Most drugs are now formulated by drug companies and the pharmacist need only measure them out and instruct the patient in their use. In the past, however, the pharmacist mixed numerous basic substances to produce a variety of medicines, tonics, etc.

PHAROS, a peninsula near Alexandria, Egypt, whose lighthouse was one of the SEVEN WONDERS OF THE WORLD. The tower of white marble was completed about 280 BC. From pictures it seems to have been about 400ft high with a ramp leading to the top, where a beacon was kept burning day and night. It stood for some 1 600 years, until demolished by an earthquake in 1302.

PHARR, city in the S tip of Texas. Its leading industries are fruit and vegetable packing and shipping, and cotton production. Pop 15 829.

PHARSALUS, Battle of, the decisive struggle of the Roman civil war fought between POMPEY and Julius CAESAR in Epirus (48 BC). After being defeated by an army half the size of his own, Pompey fled to Egypt, where he was killed.

PHARYNX, the back of the throat where the mouth (oropharynx) and NOSE (nasopharynx) pass back into the ESOPHAGUS. It contains specialized MUSCLE for swallowing. The food and air channels are kept functionally separate so that swallowing does not interfere with breathing and speech.

PHASE, the proportion of a cycle already executed by an oscillating system, expressed as an angle (360° or 2π radians corresponding to a full cycle). Thus if an AC voltage is at its maximum value while the current is passing through zero, there is said to be a 90° ($\pi/2$) phase difference between them. In mathematics, the phase of a complex number is the angle between the real axis and a line from the number to the origin (see IMAGINARY NUMBERS).

PHASE EQUILIBRIA, in THERMODYNAMICS, EQUILIBRIA between substances in different phases (solid, liquid or gas). Phase diagrams, basic to engineering, eetallurgy and mineralogy, are empirical graphs showing what phases exist at different pressures and temperatures. The *phase rule*, deduced by J. W. GIBBS, states that, for a closed system, $F = C - P + 2$, where P is the number of phases, C the number of independent chemical components and F the number of degrees of freedom, i.e., the number of variables (pressure, temperature, composition) whose values must be specified to define the system.

PHEASANTS, game birds of the 16 genera of subfamily Phasianinae. They originated in Asia, but are now found all over the world. They are ground birds which scratch the earth for seeds and insects. When they fly they rise almost vertically on short broad wings. Males are usually brightly-colored, and many species are kept as ornamentals.

The Common pheasant, *Phasianus colchicus*, a popular sporting bird introduced into the US from Europe in the late 18th century.

PHEIDIPPIDES, Athenian courier who, after running four times to and from Sparta, ran to announce the victory at MARATHON; he died on arrival.

PHELPS, William Lyon (1865–1943), US literary critic and teacher of modern drama and fiction during his 41 years at Yale. He was a very popular lecturer and columnist.

PHENACETIN, mild ANALGESIC commonly used in mixed analgesic preparations. It causes KIDNEY disease if ingested in quantity for any period; its active component **paracetamol** is now used as a safer drug.

PHENIX CITY, city in E Ala., seat of Russell Co., on the Chattahoochee R. Its industries are based on cotton and lumber. Pop 25 281.

PHENOBARBITAL, or **phenobarbitone**. See BARBITURATES.

PHENOL (C_6H_5OH), or **carbolic acid**, the simplest of the PHENOLS, a white, hygroscopic crystalline solid, isolable from COAL TAR, but made by acid hydrolysis of cumene hydroperoxide, or by fusion of sodium benzenesulfonate (see SULFONIC ACIDS) with sodium hydroxide. Formerly used as an ANTISEPTIC, phenol is now used to make BAKELITE and many other resins, plastics, dyes, detergents, drugs etc. MW 94.1, mp 43°C, bp 182°C.

PHENOLS, class of AROMATIC COMPOUNDS in which a HYDROXIDE group is directly bonded to an aromatic ring system. They are very weak ACIDS, and, like ALCOHOLS, form ETHERS and ESTERS. They are very liable to undergo electrophilic substitution (see NUCLEOPHILES), and hence condense with formaldehyde to form resins. The main phenols are PHENOL itself, CRESOL, RESORCINOL, pyrogallol (see GALLIC ACID) and PICRIC ACID.

PHENOMENOLOGY, a school of philosophy based on a method of approach due to Edmund HUSSERL. Unlike the NATURALIST, who describes objects without reference to the subjectivity of the observer, the phenomenologist attempts to describe the "invariant essences" of objects as objects "intended" by consciousness. As a first step toward achieving this, he performs the "phenomenological reduction," which involves as far as possible a suspension of all preconceptions about experience.

PHENOTYPE, the appearance of, and characteristics actually present in an organism, as contrasted with its GENOTYPE (its genetic make-up). Heterozygotes and homozygotes with a dominant GENE have the same phenotype but differing genotypes. Organisms may also have an identical genotype but differing phenotype due to environmental influences.

PHENYLKETONURIA (PKU), inherited DISEASE in which phenylalanine METABOLISM is disordered due to lack of an ENZYME. It rapidly causes MENTAL RETARDATION, as well as irritability and vomiting, unless DIETARY FOODS low in phenylalanine are given from soon after birth and indefinitely. Screening of the newborn by urine tests (with confirmation by blood tests) facilitates prompt treatment.

PHI BETA KAPPA, the most prestigious US honor society for college and university students in the liberal arts and sciences, who are generally elected in their third or fourth year on the basis of academic achievements. The oldest Greek letter society in the US, the fraternity was founded at William and Mary College, Va. in 1776.

PHIDIAS (c500–c432 BC), perhaps the greatest Greek sculptor, whose work showed the human form idealized and with great nobility. As none of his works survive, his reputation rests on contemporary accounts, on Roman copies and on the PARTHENON statues made under his direction. Under Pericles he had artistic control over the ACROPOLIS.

PHILADELPHIA, historic city in SE Pa., the fourth largest in the US. It is a key shipping port with important metal, machinery, clothing, petrol, chemical and food industries. It has long been a center for publishing, education and the arts, and was one of the first planned cities. Its founder, William PENN, created his colony in 1682 as a "holy experiment" in which all sects could find freedom. Philadelphia (Greek: brotherly love) attracted immigrants and brought commerce that made it the largest and wealthiest of US cities. In the Old City, near the Delaware R, is the INDEPENDENCE NATIONAL PARK, whose buildings include INDEPENDENCE HALL, where both the Declaration of Independence and the Constitution were adopted. The city was US capital 1790–1800; subsequent corruption in government and growth of slums accompanied a decline. In the 1950s massive urban renewal projects were initiated. Today the city has the world's largest freshwater port, linked with the Atlantic by the Delaware R. Philadelphia is part of an urban complex stretching from Boston to Washington D.C. Pop 1 950 098.

Row of houses in Elfreth Alley, the oldest street in Philadelphia. The buildings date from about 1720.

PHILAE, an island in the Nile R 2mi above the 1902 Aswan Dam, SE Egypt. The Ptolemaic-Roman temples that mark this ancient site include a beautiful temple of ISIS, but they are submerged by dam-waters for most of the year.

PHILATELY. See STAMP COLLECTING.

PHILEMON. See BAUCIS AND PHILEMON.

PHILEMON, Epistle to, New Testament letter written c61 AD by St. PAUL to Philemon, a Colossian Christian, asking him to forgive his runaway slave Onesimus, who had become a Christian and who returned with the letter.

PHILIP, Saint, one of the 12 APOSTLES. Born in Bethsaida, he was according to legend martyred at Hierapolis in Phrygia.

PHILIP, six kings of France. **Philip I** (1052–1108), reigned from 1059. He enlarged his small territories and prevented union of England and Normandy. His practice of simony and his disputed second marriage led him into conflict with the papacy. **Philip II** (Philip Augustus; 1165–1223), reigned from 1179, established France as a European power. He joined the CRUSADES, only to quarrel with RICHARD the Lion Heart and seize his French territories. By 1204 he had added Normandy, Maine, Anjou, Touraine and Brittany to his domain, in which he set up new towns and a system of royal bailiffs. **Philip III** (the Bold; 1245–85), reigned from 1270, secured Auvergne, Poitou and Toulouse for France. **Philip IV** (the Fair; 1268–1314), reigned from 1285, added Navarre and Champagne to the kingdom, but attempts to overrun Flanders led to his defeat at Courtrai in 1302. He seized Pope BONIFACE VIII in a quarrel about taxation of clergy, obtained the election of CLEMENT V, a puppet pope residing at Avignon (see BABYLONIAN CAPTIVITY), and seized the land of the crusading order of the KNIGHTS TEMPLAR. **Philip V** (1294–1322), reigned from 1317, invoked the SALIC LAW of male succession and carried out reforms to strengthen royal power. The succession in 1328 of **Philip VI** (1293–1350) through the Salic Law was disputed and led to the HUNDRED YEARS' WAR against England.

PHILIP II (382–336 BC), king of Macedonia from c359 and father of ALEXANDER THE GREAT. His powerfully reorganized army (see PHALANX) conquered N Greece, acquiring the gold mines of Thrace and advancing S as far as Thermopylae, the key to central Greece. He defeated Athens and Thebes at Chaeronea (338) and became ruler of all Greece. His reign marked the end of the independent and warring city-states.

PHILIP, five kings of Spain. **Philip I** (1478–1506) was archduke of Austria, duke of Burgundy and inheritor of the Netherlands. He became first Hapsburg king of Castile in 1506, ruling jointly with his wife Joanna. **Philip II** (1527–1598), crowned in 1556, united the Iberian peninsula and ruled an empire which included Milan, Naples, Sicily, the Netherlands and vast tracts of the New World. Though son of the Holy Roman Emperor CHARLES V, he never became emperor. A fanatical Catholic, he married MARY I of England, supported the Inquisition and tried in vain to crush the Protestant Netherlands. He was recognized king (Philip I) of Portugal in 1580, but lost naval supremacy to England after the ARMADA (1588). His son **Philip III** (1578–1621), crowned in 1598, made peace with England and the Netherlands but was frustrated in Italy by the THIRTY YEARS' WAR. **Philip IV** (1605–1655), crowned in 1621, son of Philip III and last Hapsburg king of Spain, was the patron of VELÁZQUEZ. He attempted unsuccessfully to dominate Europe by fighting France, Germany and Holland in the THIRTY YEARS' WAR, but lost Portugal in the process (1640). **Philip V** (1683–1746), crowned in 1700, founder of the BOURBON line, restored influence but his accession in 1700 led to the war of the SPANISH SUCCESSION. By the Treaty of UTRECHT (1713) his title was recognized, though he ceded possessions in Italy and the Netherlands to Austria.

PHILIP, King. See KING PHILIP'S WAR.

PHILIP, Prince, Duke of Edinburgh (1921–), consort of Queen ELIZABETH II of England. The son of Prince Andrew of Greece and Princess Alice of Battenburg, he renounced his Greek title, became a British citizen and married the then Princess Elizabeth in 1947; he was created prince in 1957.

PHILIP NERI, Saint. See NERI, SAINT PHILIP.

PHILIPPI, ancient city of MACEDONIA, in present-day Greece, named for PHILIP II of Macedon. It was there Brutus and Cassius were defeated (42 BC) by Mark Antony and Octavian Augustus, and St. PAUL first preached the gospel in Europe.

PHILIPPIANS, Epistle to the, NEW TESTAMENT letter written by St. PAUL from prison in Rome (c62 AD) to the Christians at PHILIPPI, whom he himself had converted. He encourages them affectionately, and quotes an early hymn on Christ's humility.

PHILIPPINES, republic in the SW Pacific Ocean, between the equator and the Tropic of Cancer, comprising more than 7 000 islands. The islands range in size from tiny rocks to the biggest, LUZON (41 845sq mi). Only 730 of the islands are inhabited, and 11 of these account for most of the total land area and most of the population. All the larger islands are volcanic and mountainous. The climate in the lowlands is humid, with temperatures averaging 80°F.

People. The population is predominantly of Malay origin, but includes groups of Chinese, Indonesians, MOROS, Negritos (descendants of the earliest inhabitants) and people of mixed blood.

Economy. About 70% of Filipinos work on the land. The leading crops are rice, coconut, corn and sugar. Abaca (manilla hemp) and lumber are important exports, and the islands are rich in mineral resources. Manila, the largest city, is the main industrial center. Manufactures include wood products, processed foods, textiles, aluminum and tobacco.

History. The islands were first visited by Europeans on MAGELLAN's expedition (1521), and were later named in honor of the future Philip II of Spain. By the 1570s Spanish rule there was secure; it lasted until the end of the SPANISH-AMERICAN WAR (1898), when the Philippines were ceded to the US. A revolutionary nationalist movement had sprung up in the meantime, and, under the leadership of Emilio AGUINALDO, helped the US defeat Spain; the US then took control. The issue of independence loomed large in US politics until the establishment (1935) of the Commonwealth of the Philippines, with Manuel QUEZON as president. Occupied by the Japanese during WWII, the country was made an independent republic in 1946, with Manuel ROXAS and later Ramon MAGSAYSAY as presidents. Communist revolutionary movements have been active since 1949. The powers of the presidency were greatly increased (1973) with the introduction of martial law under President Marcos and his family.

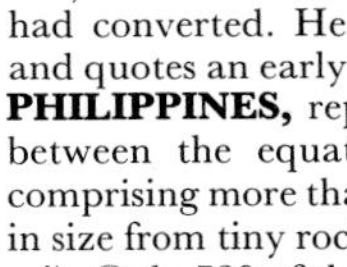

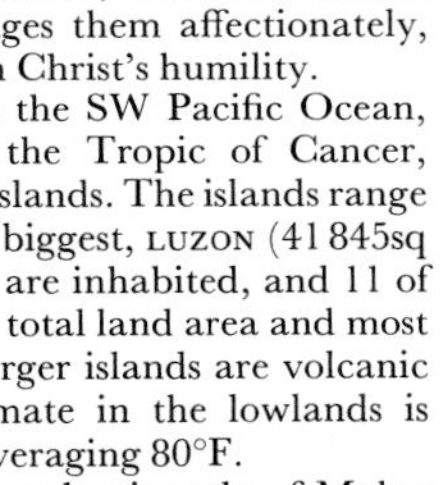

Official name: Republic of the Philippines
Capital: Quezon City
Area: 115 830sq mi
Population: 39 769 000
Languages: Tagalog; English, Spanish
Religions: Roman Catholic; Muslim. Protestant
Monetary Unit(s): 1 Philippine peso = 100 centavos

PHILIP THE BOLD (1342–1404), duke of Burgundy from 1364. In 1382 he put down a Flemish rebellion. He took over government of France when in 1392 his nephew Charles VI went insane.

PHILIP THE GOOD (1396–1467), duke of Burgundy from 1419. He was prominent in the complex politics of the HUNDRED YEARS' WAR by varying his alliances with CHARLES VII of France and the English King HENRY VI. During his reign Burgundy was briefly Europe's strongest state.

PHILISTINES, a non-Semitic people who lived in PALESTINE from the 12th century BC. They were hostile to the Israelites and for a time held considerable power. The term "philistine" may nowadays denote an uncultured person.

PHILLIPS, David Graham (1867–1911), US journalist and novelist, a MUCKRAKER famous for his magazine exposés of political corruption. His many novels include *The Great God Success* (1901).

PHILLIPS, Wendell (1811–1884), US orator and social reformer. He gave up law in 1835 to campaign for the abolition of slavery with W. L. GARRISON. After the Civil War he worked for Negroes' civil rights, women's suffrage and other reforms.

PHILLIPSBURG, town in NW N.J., on the Delaware R opposite Easton, Pa. Products include drills, boilers and chemicals. Pop 17 849.

PHILOCTETES, in Greek myth, inheritor of Hercules' bow and arrows, with which he killed Paris in the TROJAN WAR. Abandoned on the way to Troy because of a snakebite, he was rescued when a seer revealed that Troy could not be taken without the weapons of Hercules.

PHILODENDRON, a genus of South American evergreen plants frequently grown as greenhouse and house plants. Many are vigorous climbers and produce attractive foliage, but rarely flower in cultivation. The most popular climbing species are *Philodendron oxycardium* (heart-leaf philodendron), *P. sodiroi* (silver-leafed) and *P. panduraeforme* (fiddle leaf or horsehead), while *P. bipinnatifidum* and *P. selloum* are self-heading cut-leaved types, closely resembling MONSTERA except for their nonclimbing habit. (The closely related *Monstera deliciosa* is sometimes known as *P. pertusum.*) Philodendrons grow best in a bright north or sunny east window (or similar bright position) but the young plants in particular can tolerate less light. They grow well at average house temperatures, failing to thrive below 16°C (60°F). The soil should be kept evenly moist; the foliage benefits from frequent misting. Propagation is by shoot cuttings or air-layering. Family: Araceae.

PHILO JUDEAS (c20 BC–c50 AD), Alexandrine Jewish philosopher whose attempt to fuse Greek philosophical thought with Jewish Biblical religion had a profound influence on both Christian and Jewish theology.

PHILOLOGY, the study of literature and the language employed in it. The term is used also for those branches of LINGUISTICS concerned with the evolution of languages, especially those dealing with the interrelationships between different languages (comparative philology).

PHILOSOPHER'S STONE. See ALCHEMY.

PHILOSOPHES, 18th-century French school of thinkers, scientists and men of letters who believed that the methodology of science should be applied to contemporary social, economic and political problems. Inspired by DESCARTES and the school of SCEPTICISM, they included MONTESQUIEU, VOLTAIRE, DIDEROT and ROUSSEAU.

PHILOSOPHY (from *philosophos*, lover of wisdom), term applied to any body of doctrine or opinion as to the nature and ultimate significance of human experience considered as a whole. It is perhaps more properly applied to the critical evaluation of all claims to knowledge—including its own *and* anything that is presupposed about its own nature and task. In this latter respect, it is widely argued, philosophy differs fundamentally from all other disciplines. What philosophy "is" (what methods the philosopher should employ, what criteria he should appeal to, and what goals he should set himself) is as perennial a question for the philosopher as any other. Traditionally, philosophers have concerned themselves with four main topic areas: LOGIC, the study of the formal structure of valid arguments; METAPHYSICS, usually identified with ontology—the study of the nature of "Being" or ultimate reality; EPISTEMOLOGY, or theory of knowledge, sometimes treated as a branch of metaphysics; and axiology, or theory of value—including AESTHETICS, the philosophy of taste (especially as applied to the arts), ETHICS, or moral philosophy, and political philosophy (see POLITICAL SCIENCE). In modern times, as traditional philosophy has yielded up the subject matters of the natural sciences, of other descriptive studies such as PSYCHOLOGY and SOCIOLOGY, and of such formal studies as logic and mathematics, all once numbered among its legitimate concerns, philosophers have become increasingly conscious of their critical role. Most now tend to interest themselves in special philosophies, e.g., philosophy *of* logic, philosophy *of* science (see SCIENTIFIC METHOD) and philosophy *of* religion. The first attempts to answer distinctively philosophical questions were made from about 600 BC by certain Greek philosophers known collectively as the PRESOCRATICS; their intellectual heirs were SOCRATES, PLATO and ARISTOTLE, the three towering figures in ancient philosophy. Later ancient philosophies include EPICUREANISM, STOICISM and NEOPLATONISM. Foremost among medieval philosophers were St. AUGUSTINE and St. Thomas AQUINAS. (See also SCHOLASTICISM; THOMISM; NOMINALISM; REALISM.) Modern philosophy begins with René DESCARTES and a parallel development of RATIONALISM and EMPIRICISM culminating in the philosophy of Immanuel KANT. The IDEALISM of G. F. W. HEGEL and the POSITIVISM of Auguste COMTE were major forces in 19th-century philosophy. The DIALECTICAL MATERIALISM of Karl MARX had its roots in both. (See also MATERIALISM.) The philosophical orientations of most 20th-century philosophers are developments of MARXISM, NEOKANTIANISM, LOGICAL POSITIVISM, PRAGMATISM, PHENOMENOLOGY or EXISTENTIALISM.

PHIPS, Sir William (1651–1695), colonial governor (1692–94) of Mass. who led (1690) the troops that captured the French colony of Port Royal in the FRENCH AND INDIAN WARS.

PHLEBITIS, INFLAMMATION of the VEINS, usually causing THROMBOSIS (thrombophlebitis) and obstruction to BLOOD flow. It is common in the superficial veins of the legs, especially VARICOSE VEINS, and visceral veins close to inflamed organs or ABSCESSES. Phlebitis may complicate intravenous INJECTIONS of DRUGS or indwelling cannulae for intravenous fluids. Pain, swelling and ERYTHEMA over the vein are typical with it becoming a thick tender cord. Occasionally, phlebitis indicates systemic DISEASE (e.g., CANCER).

PHLOEM, or **bast,** a vascular tissue responsible for the transport of dissolved food substances through the roots, stems and leaves of higher PLANTS. Phloem mainly consists of elongated living sieve tubes, which have perforated end plates.

PHLOGISTON, the elementary principle postulated by G. H. STAHL to be lost from substances when they burn. The phlogiston concept provided 18th-century CHEMISTRY with its unifying principle. The phlogiston theory of COMBUSTION found general acceptance until displaced by its inverse—LAVOISIER's oxygen theory.

PHLOGOPITE, a range of magnesium-rich varieties of MICA, grading into BIOTITE.

PHLOX, generic and common names of a number of hardy perennial plants widely cultivated in gardens. The plants are either low-growing or upright and bear masses of tubular flowers that open to a flat whorl of petals. Family: Polemoniaceae.

PHNOM-PENH, capital and river port of CAMBODIA, on the Tônlé Sap R where it joins the Mekong. It is the country's administrative, commercial, communications and cultural center. It was the focus of a massive civil war campaign 1970–75. Pop 470 000.

PHOBIA, a NEUROSIS characterized by exaggerated ANXIETY on confrontation with a specific object or situation; or the anxiety itself. Phobia is sometimes linked with OBSESSIONAL NEUROSIS, sometimes with HYSTERIA; in each case the object of phobia is usually merely symbolic. Classic phobias are AGORAPHOBIA and CLAUSTROPHOBIA.

PHOBOS, the inner moon of MARS, diameter about 16km, orbiting in 7.65h at a distance of 9 370km. It has the lowest ALBEDO in the SOLAR SYSTEM.

PHOEBES, a name now applied to many small insectivorous birds in the US, but properly restricted to species of KINGBIRDS of the genus *Sayornis*.

PHOENICIA, ancient territory corresponding roughly to the coastal region of modern Lebanon, inhabited by the Phoenicians (originally called Canaanites) from c3000 BC. It included the city-states of SIDON and TYRE. Being on the trade route between Asia Minor, Mesopotamia and Egypt, Phoenicia became an important center of commerce. By 1200 BC, with the decline of Egyptian dominance, Phoenicians led the Mediterranean world in trading and seafaring. They colonized many Mediterranean areas which later became independent states, such as CARTHAGE and UTICA. From the 9th century BC Phoenicia was intermittently dominated by ASSYRIA, and in 538 came under Persian rule. By the time ALEXANDER THE GREAT conquered Tyre (332) Phoenician civilization had largely been eclipsed. The Greeks were the inheritors of their outstanding cultural legacy—most notably their alphabetic script, from which the modern Western alphabet is descended.

PHOENIX, largest city and capital of Ariz., seat of Maricopa Co. on the Salt R. It is a major center for agricultural marketing, electronics research and production, and manufactures such as aluminum products, aircraft, chemicals and textiles. Pop 581 562.

PHOENIX, symbol of rebirth, a mythical bird of ancient Egypt connected with the worship of the sun god Ra. It was said to immolate itself at the end of its 500-year life, and rise again out of its own ashes.

PHOENIX ISLANDS, group of eight coral atolls in the central Pacific Ocean, ESE of the Gilbert Islands. Part of the Gilbert and Ellice Island Colony but jointly controlled by the US, they have been uninhabited since a settlement failed in 1963.

PHOENIXVILLE, borough in SE Pa., 24mi NW of Philadelphia on the Schuykill R. Its major industries are iron and steel. Pop 14 823.

PHON, in ACOUSTICS, a unit of loudness. Loudness in phons is given by the number of DECIBELS above the reference level, 20 μPa, of a pure 1kHz-frequency SOUND which is judged by listeners to be of equal loudness with the original.

PHONEME, any of the smallest units of spoken language serving to differentiate between utterances: e.g., the "p" and "t" of "pin" and "tin." (See also MORPHEME.)

PHONETICS, the systematic examination of the sounds made in speech, concerned not only with the classification of these sounds but also with physical and physiological aspects of their production and transmission, and with their reception and interpretation by the listener. **Phonology**, the study of phonetic patterns in languages, is of importance in comparative LINGUISTICS. **Phonemics** is the study of PHONEMES.

PHONOGRAPH, or **record player**, instrument for reproducing sound recorded mechanically as modulations in a spiral groove (see SOUND REPRODUCTION). It was invented by Thomas EDISON (1877), whose first machine had a revolving grooved cylinder covered with tinfoil. Sound waves caused a diaphragm to vibrate and a stylus on the diaphragm made indentations in the foil. These could then be made to vibrate another stylus attached to a reproducing diaphragm. Wax discs and cylinders soon replaced tinfoil, then, when by etching or electroplating metal master discs could be made, copies were mass-produced in rubber, wax or plastic. The main parts of a phonograph are the turntable to rotate the disc at constant angular velocity; the stylus, which tracks the groove and vibrates with its modulations; the pickup or transducer that converts these movements piezoelectrically or electromagnetically into electrical signals; the AMPLIFIER, and the LOUDSPEAKER. (For high-quality reproduction, see HIGH-FIDELITY.)

PHONON, in SOLID STATE PHYSICS, the particle (quantum) counterpart of the SOUND wave or LATTICE vibration, considered to play an important role in the CONDUCTION of HEAT in electrical insulators.

PHORONIDS, or **Horseshoe worms,** marine animals of shallow water which live in chitinous tubes buried in sand or attached to rock. The head bears a lophophore, a crescent-shaped structure of ciliated tentacles used for feeding. This shows their relationship with BRACHIOPODS and BRYOZOA.

PHOSGENE, or **carbonyl chloride** ($COCl_2$), colorless, reactive gas, hydrolyzed by water, made by catalytic combination of CARBON monoxide and CHLORINE, and used to make RESINS and DYES. Highly toxic, it was a poison gas in WWI.

PHOSPHATES, derivatives of phosphoric acid (see PHOSPHORUS): either phosphate ESTERS, or salts containing the various phosphate ions. Like SILICATES, these are numerous and complex, the simplest being orthophosphate, PO_4^{3-}. Of many phosphate minerals, the most important is APATITE. This is treated with sulfuric acid or phosphoric acid to give calcium dihydrogenphosphate ($Ca[H_2PO_4]_2$), known as **superphosphate**—the major phosphate FERTILIZER. The alkaline trisodium phosphate (TSP) (Na_3PO_4) is used as a cleansing agent and water softener. Phosphates are used in making GLASS, SOAPS AND DETERGENTS.

PHOSPHOR, a substance exhibiting LUMINESCENCE, i.e., emitting LIGHT (or other ELECTROMAGNETIC RADIATION) on nonthermal stimulation. Important phosphors include those used in TELEVISION picture tubes (where stimulation is by ELECTRONS) and those coated on the inside wall of fluorescent lamp tubes to convert ULTRAVIOLET RADIATION into visible light.

PHOSPHORESCENCE, or **afterglow.** See LUMINESCENCE.

PHOSPHORUS (P), reactive nonmetal in Group VA of the PERIODIC TABLE, occurring naturally as APATITE. This is heated with silica and coke, and elementary phosphorus is produced. Phosphorus has three main allotropes (see ALLOTROPY): white phosphorus, a yellow waxy solid composed of P_4 molecules, spontaneously flammable in air, soluble in carbon disulfide, and very toxic; red phosphorus, a dark-red powder, formed by heating white phosphorus, less reactive, and insoluble in carbon disulfide; and black phosphorus, a flaky solid, resembling GRAPHITE, consisting of corrugated layers of atoms. Phosphorus burns in air to give the trioxide and the pentoxide, and also reacts with the halogens, sulfur and some metals. It is used in making matches, ammunition, pesticides, steels, phosphor bronze, phosphoric acid and phosphate fertilizers. Phosphorus is of great biological importance. AW 31.0, mp (wh) 44°C, bp (wh) 280°C, sg (wh) 1.82, (red) 2.20, (bl) 2.69. Phosphorus forms phosphorous (trivalent) and phosphoric (pentavalent) compounds. **Phosphine** (PH_3), is a colorless, flammable gas, highly toxic, and with an odor of garlic. It is a weak BASE, resembling AMMONIA, and forms phosphonium salts (PH_4^+). **Phosphoric acid** (H_3PO_4), is a colorless crystalline solid, forming a syrupy aqueous solution. It is used to flavor food, in dyeing, to clean metals, and to make PHOSPHATES. **Phosphorus Pentoxide** (P_4O_{10}), is a white powder made by burning phosphorus in excess air. It is very deliquescent (forming phosphoric acid), and is used as a dehydrating agent.

PHOTOCHEMISTRY, branch of PHYSICAL CHEMISTRY dealing with chemical reactions that produce LIGHT (see CHEMILUMINESCENCE; COMBUSTION), or that are initiated by light (visible or ultraviolet). Important examples include PHOTOSYNTHESIS, PHOTOGRAPHY and bleaching by sunlight. One PHOTON of light of suitable wavelength may be absorbed by a molecule, raising it to an electronically excited state. Re-emission may occur by fluorescence or phosphorescence (see LUMINESCENCE), the energy may be transferred to another molecule, or a reaction may occur, commonly DISSOCIATION to form FREE RADICALS. The *quantum yield*, or efficiency, of the reaction is the number of molecules of reactant used (or product formed) per photon absorbed; this may be very large for chain reactions. (See also FLASH PHOTOLYSIS; LASER; RADIATION CHEMISTRY.)

PHOTOCONDUCTIVE DETECTOR, an electrical component whose CONDUCTIVITY increases as more LIGHT falls on it. Used in light detectors, light-sensitive switches, light meters, and in the Vidicon television camera tube, most employ photoconductive SEMICONDUCTORS such as lead telluride or cadmium sulfide.

PHOTOCOPYING. See OZALID PROCESS; XEROGRAPHY.

PHOTOELECTRIC CELL, a device with electrical properties which vary according to the LIGHT falling on it. There are three types: PHOTOVOLTAIC CELLS; PHOTOCONDUCTIVE DETECTORS and phototubes (see PHOTOELECTRIC EFFECT).

PHOTOELECTRIC EFFECT, properly **photoemissive effect**, the emission of ELECTRONS from a surface when struck by ELECTROMAGNETIC RADIATION such as LIGHT. In 1905 EINSTEIN laid one of the twin foundations of QUANTUM THEORY by explaining photoemission in terms of the action of individual PHOTONS. The effect is used in phototubes (ELECTRON TUBES having a photoemissive cathode), often employed as "electric eye" switches. Special types are used in image intensifiers and in the Image Orthicon TELEVISION camera.

The Einstein photoelectric law:

$$E_k = h\nu - \omega$$

where: E_k is the maximum kinetic energy of emitted electrons,
h is Planck's constant,
ν is the frequency of the radiation,
ω is the surface work function for photoemission.

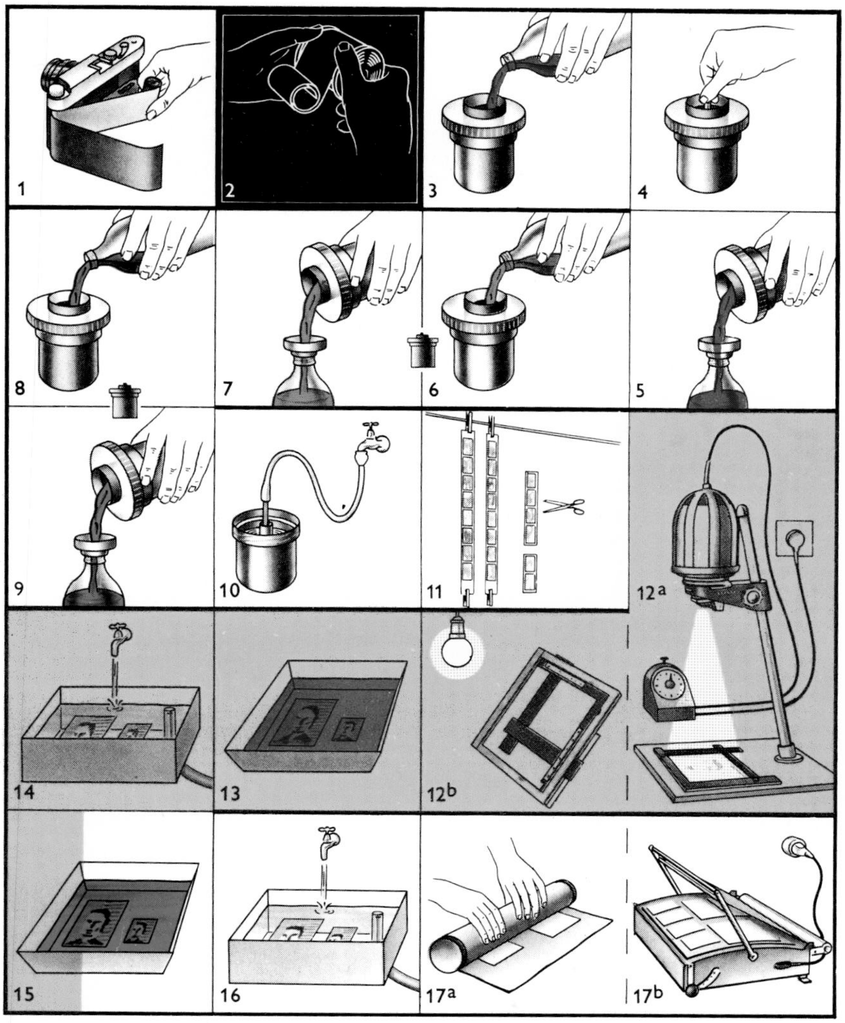

In photographic developing and printing, the exposed film is removed from the camera (1) and, in the darkroom, is wound on to a reel (2) that fits into a light-proof tank. Steps 3 through 11 may be carried out with the lights on. The tank is filled with developer (3) and agitated during development (4). After the proper time has elapsed, the developer is poured out (5) and the tank is filled with the stop bath (6) to halt development. The stop bath in turn is poured out (7), and the fixer is poured in (8) and removed after a specified time (9). The negative is then washed (10) and dried (11). To make enlargements, light is shone through the negative in the enlarger (12a) onto sensitive paper, which may be held in a frame (12b). Using red light, the photographer develops the prints (13), washes them (14)—sometimes after using a stop bath—and fixes them (15). The prints are then washed again (16) and dried by hand (17a) or in a dryer (17b).

PHOTOGRAMMETRY, the use of photographs in map-making. Series of overlapping air photographs are generally used. If exposed in stereo pairs at a known altitude, such photographs can be used to make detailed, accurate relief maps.

PHOTOGRAPHY, the use of light-sensitive materials to produce permanent visible images (photographs). The most familiar photographic processes depend on the light-sensitivity of the SILVER halides. A photographic emulsion is a preparation of tiny crystals of these salts suspended in a thin layer of gelatin coated on a glass, film or paper support. On brief exposure to light in a CAMERA or other apparatus, a latent image in activated silver salt is formed wherever light has fallen on the emulsion. This image is made visible in development, when the activated silver halide crystals (but not the unexposed ones) are reduced to metallic silver (black) using a weak organic reducing agent (the developer). The silver image is then made permanent by fixing, in the course of which it becomes possible to examine the image in the light for the first time. Fixing agents (fixers) work by dissolving out the silver halide crystals which were not activated on exposure. The image made in this way is densest in silver where the original subject was brightest and lightest where the original was darkest; it is thus a "negative" image. To produce a positive image, the negative (which is usually made on a film or glass (plate) support) is itself made the original in the above process, the result being a positive "print" usually on a paper carrier. An alternative method of producing a positive image is to bleach away the developed image on the original film or plate before fixing, and reexpose the unactivated halide in diffuse light. This forms a second latent image which on development produces a positive image of the original subject (reversal processing).

The history of photography from the earliest work of NIÉPCE, DAGUERRE and Fox TALBOT to the present has seen successive refinements in materials, techniques and equipment. Photography became a popular hobby after EASTMAN first marketed roll film in 1889. The silver halides themselves are sensitive to light only from the blue end of the SPECTRUM so that in the earliest photographs other colors appear dark. The color-sensitivity of emulsions was improved from the 1870s onward as small quantities of sensitizing dyes were incorporated. "Orthochromatic" plates became available after 1884 and "panchromatic" from 1906.

New sensitizing dyes also opened up the way to infrared and color photography. Modern "tripack" color films have three layers of emulsion, one each sensitive to blue, green and red light from the subject. Positive color transparencies are made using a reversal processing method in which the superposed, positive, silver images are replaced with yellow, magenta and cyan dyes respectively.

Motion-picture photography dates from 1890, when EDISON built a device to expose Eastman's roll film, and rapidly became an important art form (see MOTION PICTURES). Not all modern photographic methods employ the silver-halide process; XEROGRAPHY and the BLUEPRINT and OZALID processes work differently. FALSE-COLOR PHOTOGRAPHY and the diffusion process used in the POLAROID LAND CAMERA are both developments of the silver-halide process.

PHOTOMETRY, the science of the measurement of LIGHT, particularly as it affects illumination engineering. Because the brightness experienced when light strikes the human EYE depends not only on the POWER conveyed by the radiation but also on the wavelength of the light (the visual sensation for a given power reaching a maximum at 555nm), a special arbitrary set of units is used in photometric calculations. In SI UNITS, the photometric base quantity is luminous intensity which measures the intensity of light radiated from a small source. The base unit of luminous intensity is the CANDELA (cd). The luminous flux (the photometric equivalent of the power radiating) from a point source is measured in lumens where 1 lumen (lm) is the flux radiating from a 1 cd source through a solid angle of a steradian. The illuminance falling on a surface (formerly known as its illumination) is measured in luxes where 1 lux (lx) is the level of illuminance occurring when a luminous flux of 1 lm falls on each m² of the surface. Up to the 1970s considerable confusion reigned among scientists regarding the concepts and terminology best to be used in photometry and many alternative units—APOSTILBS, BLONDELS, FOOT-CANDLES and LAMBERTS—are still commonly encountered. (See also LUMINANCE.)

PHOTON, the quantum of electromagnetic energy (see QUANTUM THEORY), often thought of as the particle associated with LIGHT or other ELECTROMAGNETIC RADIATION. Its ENERGY is given by $h\nu$ where h is the PLANCK CONSTANT and ν the frequency of the radiation.

PHOTOSPHERE, a 125–190km-thick layer of gas on the sun, visible to us as the sun's apparent surface, emitting most of the sun's light. Its TEMPERATURE is estimated at 6000K.

PHOTOSYNTHESIS, the process by which green plants convert the ENERGY of sunlight into chemical energy which is then stored as CARBOHYDRATE. Overall, the process may be written as:

$$6CO_2+6H_2O \xrightarrow{light} C_6H_{12}O_6+6O_2$$

Although in detail photosynthesis is a complex sequence of reactions, two principal stages can be identified. In the "light reaction," CHLOROPHYLL (the key chemical in the whole process) is activated by absorbing a quantum of LIGHT, initiating a sequence of reactions in which the energy-rich compounds ATP (adenosine triphosphate—see NUCLEOTIDES) and TPNH (the reduced form of triphosphopyridine nucleotide—TPN) are made, water being decomposed to give free oxygen in the process. In the second stage, the "dark reaction," the ATP and TPNH provide the energy for the assimilation of carbon dioxide gas, yielding a variety of SUGARS from which other sugars and carbohydrates, including STARCH, can be built up.

PHOTOTROPISM. See TROPISMS.

PHOTOVOLTAIC CELL, a device for converting LIGHT radiation into ELECTRICITY, used in LIGHT METERS and for providing spacecraft power supplies. The photovoltage is usually developed in a layer of SEMICONDUCTOR (e.g., SELENIUM) sandwiched between a transparent electrode and one providing support.

PHRENOLOGY, study of the shape and detailed contours of the SKULL as indicators of personality, intelligence and individual characteristics. The method, developed by F. J. GALL and promoted in the UK and US by George Combe (1788–1858), had many 19th-century followers and led to the more enlightened treatment of offenders and the mentally ill.

PHRYGIA, ancient region and sometime kingdom (8th–6th centuries BC) in present-day central Turkey. Its early kings included MIDAS and Gordius. Excavation shows the Phrygians to have been highly cultured. The Phrygian worship of CYBELE was taken over by the Greeks. (See also GORDIAN KNOT.)

PHYFE, Duncan (c1768–1854), US cabinetmaker, designer of the most distinctive US neoclassical furniture. He came to the US from Scotland in 1784, and based his work on European styles such as the SHERATON and the EMPIRE STYLE.

PHYLACTERY, in Jewish religious practice, a small leather case containing extracts from EXODUS and DEUTERONOMY which is worn by men on the left arm and forehead during morning prayers (except on the Sabbath and festivals).

PHYLLOXERA, a genus of small APHIDS including *P. vitrifoliae*, a pest of European grapevines. It shows ALTERNATION OF GENERATIONS: one forms galls on grape leaves, the other in the roots.

Three Musicians, painted in 1921 by Pablo Picasso, one of the artist's many remarkable Cubist works. Unrivaled in his influence on the development of 20th-century art, Picasso displayed his own genius in a wide variety of art forms, as sculptor, printmaker, ceramist and stage designer as well as painter.

PHYLOGENY. See ONTOGENY AND PHYLOGENY.

PHYLUM. See TAXONOMY.

PHYSICAL CHEMISTRY, major branch of CHEMISTRY, in which the theories and methods of PHYSICS are applied to chemical systems. Physical chemistry underlies all the other branches of chemistry and includes theoretical chemistry. Its main divisions are the study of molecular structure; COLLOIDS; CRYSTALS; ELECTROCHEMISTRY; chemical EQUILIBRIUM; GAS laws; chemical KINETICS; MOLECULAR WEIGHT determination; PHOTOCHEMISTRY; SOLUTION; SPECTROSCOPY, and chemical THERMODYNAMICS.

PHYSICAL EDUCATION, instruction designed to further the health, growth and athletic capacity of the body. It may include GYMNASTICS, sports, and Oriental techniques such as YOGA. Culturally important in ancient China and ancient Greece, physical education later had a primarily military application until the 19th century, when it began to be incorporated into school programs in Europe and the US.

PHYSICAL THERAPY. See PHYSIOTHERAPY.

PHYSICIAN. See MEDICINE.

PHYSICS, originally, the knowledge of natural things (=natural science); now, the science dealing with the interaction of MATTER and ENERGY (but usually taken to exclude CHEMISTRY). Until the "scientific revolution" of the Renaissance, physics was a branch of PHILOSOPHY dealing with the natures of things. The physics of the heavens, for instance, was quite separate from (and often conflicted with) the descriptions of mathematical and positional ASTRONOMY. But from the time of GALILEO, and particularly through the efforts of HUYGENS and NEWTON, physics became identified with the mathematical description of nature; occult qualities were banished from physical science. Firm on its Newtonian foundation, classical physics gathered more and more phenomena under its wing until, by the late 19th century, comparatively few phenomena seemed to defy explanation. But the interpretation of these effects (notably BLACKBODY RADIATION and the PHOTOELECTRIC EFFECT) in terms of new concepts due to PLANCK and EINSTEIN involved the thoroughgoing reformulation of the fundamental principles of physical science (see QUANTUM THEORY; RELATIVITY). Physics today is divided into many specialisms, themselves subdivided manyfold. The principal of these are ACOUSTICS; ELECTRICITY and MAGNETISM; MECHANICS; NUCLEAR PHYSICS; OPTICS; QUANTUM THEORY; RELATIVITY, and THERMODYNAMICS.

PHYSIOCRATS, 18th-century French school of economists founded by Francois QUESNAY, who held that agriculture, rather than industry or commerce, was the basis of a nation's prosperity, and that land alone should be subject to tax. Their belief in a natural economic law, which merely required non-interference to be successful, is reflected in their famous formula *laissez faire* (let it be). The physiocrats influenced Adam SMITH.

PHYSIOLOGY, the study of function in living organisms. Based on knowledge of ANATOMY, physiology seeks to demonstrate the manner in which organs perform their tasks, and in which the body is organized and maintained in a state of HOMEOSTASIS. Normal responses to various stresses on the whole or on parts of an organism are studied. Important branches of physiology deal with RESPIRATION, BLOOD CIRCULATION, the NERVOUS SYSTEM, the DIGESTIVE SYSTEM, the KIDNEYS, the fluid and electrolyte balance, the ENDOCRINE GLANDS and METABOLISM. Methods of study include experimentation on anesthetized animals and on human volunteers. Knowledge and understanding of physiology is basic to MEDICINE and provides the physician with a perspective in which to view the body's disordered function in DISEASE.

PHYSIOTHERAPY, system of physical treatment for disease or disability. Active and passive muscle movement; electrical stimulation; balancing exercises; HEAT, ULTRAVIOLET or shortwave RADIATION, and manual vibration of the CHEST wall with postural drainage, are some of the techniques used. Rehabilitation after FRACTURE, SURGERY, STROKE or other neurological disease, and the treatment of LUNG infections (PNEUMONIA, BRONCHITIS), are among the aims.

PHYTOPLANKTON. See PLANKTON.

PHYTOSAURS, thecodont reptiles extremely abundant in Europe and North America during the TRIASSIC. They were very similar in both appearance and habits to modern CROCODILES, though not directly ancestral.

PI (Greek π), the ratio between the circumference of a CIRCLE and its diameter. π is an IRRATIONAL NUMBER whose value to five decimal places is 3.14159. Approximate values of π have been known to several ancient civilizations, such as Babylonia, where the accepted value was 3.0.

PIACENZA, town in N Italy, capital of Piacenza prov., on the Po R. An agricultural and trading center. Pop 106461.

PIAF, Edith (1915–1963), French singer of cabaret and music-hall. Born Edith Giovanna Gassion, she began singing for a living at 15 and won international fame with such songs as *Milord.*

PIAGET, Jean (1896–), Swiss psychologist whose theories of the mental development of children, though now often criticized, have been of paramount importance. His many books include *The Psychology of Intelligence* (1947).

PIANO, keyboard instrument in which depression of the keys causes the strings to be struck with hammers. These hammers rebound immediately after striking, so that the strings go on sounding their notes until the keys are released, when the strings' vibrations are stopped with dampers. Bartolommeo Cristofori made the first piano in 1709, and by 1800 it had overtaken the HARPSICHORD and the CLAVICHORD in popularity. Today the two basic types of piano are the upright piano with vertical strings, and the grand piano with horizontal strings, which has a range of seven octaves. Composers who have written for the piano include CLEMENTI, C. P. E. BACH, HAYDN, MOZART, BEETHOVEN and CHOPIN.

PIAZZI, Giuseppe (1746–1826), Italian astronomer who discovered Ceres, the first ASTEROID (1801). Through illness he lost it again, and it was rediscovered the following year by OLBERS.

PICARDY, pre-Revolutionary province of N France, on the English Channel, now a geographical region which includes the Somme, Oise and Aisne depts. Its principal city and former capital is Amiens.

PICARESQUE NOVEL, early type of the novel in which the episodic adventures of a roguish, anti-heroical character are narrated in the first person. Of 16th-century Spanish origin, the picaresque novel was popular until the mid-1700s, and included notable English examples such as Defoe's *Moll Flanders* (1722).

PICASSO, Pablo Ruiz y (1881–1973), Spanish-born French painter, sculptor, graphic artist and ceramist, greatest artist of the 20th century. An extraordinarily precocious painter, after his melancholy "Blue Period" and his lyrical "Rose Period" (1901–06) he was influenced by African and Primitive art as shown in *Les Demoiselles d'Avignon*, 1907. Together he and BRAQUE created CUBISM, 1907–14. His friends at this time included APOLLINAIRE, DIAGHILEV for whom he made stage designs, and Gertrude STEIN. In 1921 he painted both the Cubist *Three Musicians*, and the classical *Three Women at the Fountain*. In the 1930s he adopted the style of SURREALISM, using it horrifically in *Guernica*, 1937 (see GUERNICA). His later work employed Cubist and Surrealist forms and could be beautiful, tender or grotesque. His output was enormous and at the end of his life he produced a brilliant series of etchings.

PICAYUNE, city in S Miss., 35mi WNW of Gulfport. It is a food processing and distribution center with varied industry. Pop 10467.

PICCARD, name of the Swiss twin brothers **Auguste** (1884–1962), a physicist, and **Jean Félix** (1884–1963), a chemist. Both made famous high-altitude BALLOON ascents in order to study COSMIC RAYS with a minimum of atmospheric interference, Auguste in 1931 and 1932, and Jean in 1936. In 1948 Auguste successfully conducted an unpiloted trial dive of the BATHYSCAPHE, a deep-sea diving device built to his own design; the first piloted dive—in a new bathyscaphe—followed in 1953.

PICCOLO. See FLUTE.

PICKENS, Andrew (1739–1817), American Revolutionary commander who fought at the Battle of COWPENS (1781) and other notable victories. He reached the rank of brigadier general and served (1793–95) in Congress.

PICKENS, Fort, historical fortification in NW Fla., on Santa Rosa Island at the entrance to Pensacola Bay. It was held by Union troops throughout the Civil War.

PICKERELS, three small species of PIKE of North America. They have shorter snouts than other pike, and larger scales. All are freshwater predators.

PICKEREL WEED, *Potederia cordata*, a herb native to warm regions of America with edible fruits eaten in times of famine. Family: Pontederiaceae.

PICKERING, name of two US astronomers, **Edward Charles Pickering** (1846–1919) and his brother **William Henry Pickering** (1858–1938). Edward made important contributions to stellar PHOTOMETRY and was the inventor of the meridian photometer. William, in 1898, discovered Phoebe, the ninth moon of the planet SATURN.

PICKERING, Timothy (1745–1829), American statesman. After a distinguished military career in the Revolutionary War, he served as postmaster general (1791–95), secretary of state (1795–1800), senator (1803–11) and representative (1813–17).

PICKETING, the practice of patrolling a place of employment against which the employees have a grievance, in order to publicize the grievance, to discourage patronage of the place being picketed, or to prevent strike-breaking. It is also done for political reasons.

PICKETT, George Edward (1825–1875), Confederate general in the US CIVIL WAR who led the disastrous assault (July 3, 1863) on Cemetery Ridge in the Battle of GETTYSBURG. Of the 15000 Confederate troops who charged the Union line some 6000 were killed. Pickett later suffered a second major defeat at the Battle of FIVE FORKS (April 1, 1865).

PICKFORD, Mary (1893–), US movie actress, born Gladys Smith. Her roles in such films as *Daddy Long Legs*, under the direction of D. W. GRIFFITH, won her the title of "America's sweetheart." In 1919 she helped found United Artists.

PICKLE, food that has been preserved in VINEGAR or BRINE to prevent the development of putrefying BACTERIA. Spices are usually added for flavor. Cucumbers, onions, beets, tomatoes and cauliflowers are used to make popular pickles. Pigs' feet and corned beef are also sometimes pickled. (See FOOD PRESERVATION.)

PICO DELLA MIRANDOLA, Count Giovanni (1463–1494), Italian Renaissance philosopher and humanist who attempted to reconcile Christianity with NEOPLATONISM. He was a member of Lorenzo de MEDICI's Platonic Academy in Florence. Shortly before his death he became a follower of SAVONAROLA. (See also HUMANISM.)

PICO RIVERA, city in SW Cal., SE of Los Angeles. Varied industry includes plastics, cement, automobiles and chemicals. Pop 54170.

PICRIC ACID, or 2,4,6-trinitrophenol, yellow crystalline solid, made by NITRATION of PHENOL or its derivatives. A moderately strong ACID, it has been used as a DYE, as an ANTISEPTIC and ASTRINGENT for treating burns, and as a high EXPLOSIVE. MW 229.1, mp 122°C.

PICTOGRAPHY, WRITING system using pictures and drawings as vehicles of communication. A pictograph used to represent an idea is an IDEOGRAM; one that represents a word, a logogram.

PICTS, ancient inhabitants of Scotland whose forebears probably came from the European continent c1000 BC. By the 8th century AD their kingdom extended from Fife to Caithness. In 843 they united with the kingdom of the SCOTS, and were assimilated into the Scottish nation.

PICTUREPHONE, system of video TELEPHONE, introduced in 1971. The scanned TELEVISION picture, requiring a wide BANDWIDTH, is relayed along auxiliary telephone wires.

PIDGIN, a language of simplified grammar and vocabulary, most often based on a western European language. Pidgins originate as a means of communication (e.g. for trading purposes) between peoples with different mother tongues. Varieties of pidgin English were developed in China and elsewhere. (See also LINGUA FRANCA.)

PIECE OF EIGHT, Spanish silver coin (*peso*) of the 17th and 18th centuries. It was worth eight *reals* and was stamped with the numeral eight.

PIEDMONT, region of NW Italy in the upper valley of the Po R, bounded N and W by the Swiss and French Alps. Turin, its capital, is one of Italy's chief industrial centers.

PIEDMONT, plateau in the E US, part of the Atlantic plain. It lies E of the Blue Ridge and Appalachian Mts, and extends from the Hudson R to central Ala.

PIEDMONT, city in W Cal., a suburb of Oakland, 5mi E of San Francisco Bay. Pop 10917.

Franklin PIERCE

14th US President

Born: November 23, 1804
Died: October 8, 1869
Term of office: March 4, 1853–March 3, 1857
Political party: Democratic

PIERCE, Franklin (1804–1869), fourteenth president of the US (1853–57). The youngest president the nation had then known, Pierce was the inexperienced compromise candidate of a badly divided Democratic Party, and he was unable to cope with the sectional strife that heralded the Civil War. Born in New Hampshire, Pierce trained and practiced as a lawyer before entering politics. After rapid advancement he spent two terms (1833–37) as a Democratic member of the House of Representatives, and then became a member of the Senate. In 1842 he retired from national politics, but 10 years later, at a time when he was virtually unknown, he won the Democratic nomination after the four leading candidates had brought the Baltimore convention to deadlock. In the 1852 election Pierce easily defeated Winfield Scott, last national candidate of the declining Whig Party. As president, Pierce proved to be fatally pliable and vacillating. His initial concentration on fulfilling the electoral promise of an expansionist foreign policy led to such conspicuous failures as his attempt to procure Hawaii and Alaska for the US, and to annex Cuba from Spain (see OSTEND MANIFESTO). On the domestic scene, apart from the acquisition of the GADSDEN PURCHASE from Mexico, Pierce's administration proved equally inept. Pierce had pledged loyalty to the COMPROMISE OF 1850, but in 1854, yielding to pressure, he passed the KANSAS-NEBRASKA ACT. This repealed the MISSOURI COMPROMISE which had prohibited slavery in the Kansas region. The dormant slavery controversy was reopened and the Northern part of the Democratic Party split to form the new "Republicans." A wild rush of slavery and anti-slavery supporters poured into Kansas, leading to a local civil war. Pierce's mishandling of the crisis wrecked his administration and his chances of renomination. He left office a discredited figure, retired from public life and died in virtual obscurity.

PIERO DELLA FRANCESCA (c1420–1492), Italian painter, one of the greatest RENAISSANCE artists. His concern for the harmonious relationship of figures to their setting was expressed through simple, elegant forms, clear colors and tones, atmospheric light and perspective as is found in his FRESCO, *Legend of the True Cross*, 1452–59 in AREZZO.

PIERO DI COSIMO (1462–1521), Italian RENAISSANCE painter in Florence, remembered for his strange behavior and curious poetic pictures like *Death of Pocris; Venus, Cupid and Mars* and *Battle of the Centaurs and Lapiths* which is based on OVID.

PIERRE, capital of S.D. and seat of Hughes Co., on the Missouri R. It is the trade and shipping center of a large agricultural region. Pop 9 699.

PIERREFONDS, city in S Quebec, Canada, in Montreal and Jesus Islands Co. Pop 33 046.

PIETÀ, subject in art representing the Virgin Mary supporting the body of the dead Christ after the Deposition. It originated in N Europe in the 14th century and was popular in the Italian RENAISSANCE and carved three times by MICHELANGELO.

PIETERMARITZBURG, capital of Natal, E South Africa. It is an administrative center with mixed industries. Pop 112 666.

PIETISM, 17th-century evangelical revivalist movement in the German LUTHERAN CHURCH. It attacked the prevalent dead orthodoxy and stressed individual piety and devotion, but tended to MYSTICISM and anti-intellectualism. It influenced the Moravians, Methodists, and American Lutherans.

PIETRO DA CORTONA (1596–1669), Italian BAROQUE painter whose facade for *Santa Maria della Pace*, Rome, 1656–57, made him a leading architect of the period. Another masterpiece was the ceiling painting, *Divine Providence*, 1633–39, an allegory for the BARBERINI's fortunes.

PIEZOELECTRICITY, a reversible relationship between mechanical stress and electrostatic POTENTIAL exhibited by certain CRYSTALS with no center of symmetry, discovered in 1880 during investigations of *pyroelectric* crystals (these are also asymmetric and get oppositely charged faces when heated). When pressure is applied to a piezoelectric crystal such as QUARTZ, positive and negative electric charges appear on opposite crystal faces. Replacing the pressure by tension changes the sign of the charges. If, instead, an electric potential is applied across the crystal, its length changes; this effect is linear. A piezoelectric crystal placed in an alternating electric circuit will alternately expand and contract. Resonance occurs in the circuit when its FREQUENCY matches the natural vibration frequency of the crystal, this effect being applied in frequency controllers. This useful way of coupling electrical and mechanical effects is used in MICROPHONES, PHONOGRAPH pickups and ULTRASONIC generators.

PIG. See HOG.

PIGEONS, a family, Columbidae, of some 255 species of birds, with worldwide distribution. They are a diverse group, but the typical pigeon is a pastel gray, pink or brown bird with contrasting patches of brighter colors. The body is compact, the neck short and the head and bill fairly small. Most species are gregarious and many are seen in very large flocks. The food may be stored in a distensible crop.

PIGEON HAWK, or **Merlin,** *Falco columbarius*, not a hawk but a small FALCON of open country. Merlins have very long wings and hunt small birds—larks and pipits—on the wing.

PIGEON RIVER, river in NE Minn., 40mi long, flowing into N Lake Superior. It forms part of the US–Canada (Ontario) boundary.

PIGGYBACK PLANT, *Tolmiea menziesii*, an evergreen perennial plant grown as a house plant or outdoors for ground cover. It has hairy, maple-like, mid-green leaves, on the surface of which young plants are produced. Indoors, it should be grown in a bright north window or a short distance from other windows, avoiding direct sunlight. It requires average house temperatures. The soil should be kept wet to moist and the leaves misted often. Propagation is by rooting the young plants produced on the leaves. Family: Saxifragaceae.

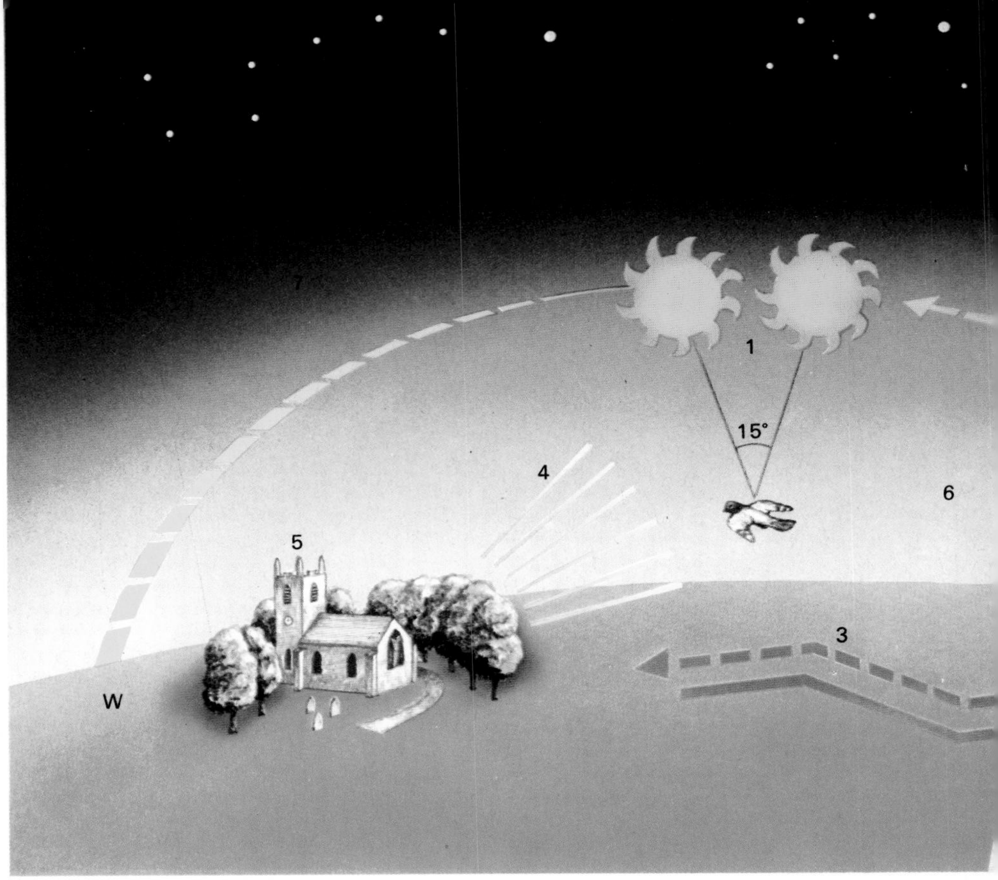

PIG IRON, crude CAST IRON produced in a BLAST FURNACE and cast into ingots or "pigs." It is used to make WROUGHT IRON and STEEL. (See also IRON.)

PIGMENTS, Natural, chemical substances imparting colors to animals and plants. In animals the most important examples include MELANIN (black), RHODOPSIN (purple) and the respiratory pigments, HEMOGLOBIN (red) and HEMOCYANIN (blue). (See also MIMICRY; PROTECTIVE COLORATION.) In plants, the CHLOROPHYLLS (green) are important as the key chemicals in PHOTOSYNTHESIS. Other plant pigments include the carotenes and xanthophylls (red-yellow), the anthocyanins (red-blue) and the anthoxanthins (yellow-orange). In nature, whiteness results from the absence of pigment (see ALBINO) and is comparatively uncommon.

PIGWEED. See GOOSEFOOT.

PIKA, a member of the LAGOMORPHA, resembling a small, short-eared, tailless rabbit, and also known as Calling hare, Mouse hare or CONEY. There is a single genus, *Ochotona,* distributed throughout the colder regions of the N hemisphere. They are colonial animals, living in rock crevices. Pikas do not hibernate, but hoard food against the winter.

PIKE, freshwater fishes of the N hemisphere. They are mottled fish with a long head and snout and large jaws. The fins are set well back on the body—a characteristic of predatory fishes that lie in wait for prey and make a sudden dash to catch it. The genus *Esox* includes the European or Northern pike, the MUSKELLUNGE, and the PICKERELS.

PIKE, Zebulon Montgomery (1779–1813), US general and explorer, best known as the man who discovered (1806) the Colorado mountain thereafter called PIKES PEAK.

PIKE PERCHES. See WALLEYE.

PIKES PEAK, mountain, 14 110ft, in E central Col., part of the Rocky Mts., near Colorado Springs, one of the most famous in the US. Its solitary position and commanding vistas make it a popular tourist attraction.

PIKESVILLE, city (unincorporated) in central Md., a NW residential suburb of Baltimore. Pop 25 395.

PILATE, Pontius, Roman procurator of Judea (26–36 AD) who ordered the crucifixion of Christ, afterwards washing his hands to disclaim responsibility. Hated by the Jews, he was recalled to Rome after his behavior had provoked a riot which had to be put down by troops.

PILCHARD, *Sardina pilchardus*, a member of the herring family of the eastern N Atlantic and the Mediterranean. Widely fished, it is known in its marketed form as both pilchard and SARDINE.

PILE, a heavy beam or column made of wood, steel or concrete, sunk into the ground to support a load. When they rest on bedrock they are known as end-bearing piles; when supported by the friction of the soil, friction piles. Some concrete piles are cast in place, but most are driven in by piledrivers, large hammers worked by gravity or by hydraulic or pneumatic power. Vibratory piledrivers are an efficient recent innovation.

PILE, Atomic. See NUCLEAR REACTOR.

PILEA, a genus of evergreen perennial plants, several of which are grown as house plants for their attractive foliage. Species and varieties commonly grown include *Pilea serpillacea, P. repens*, 'silver tree' and 'moon valley.' Indoors they should be grown at average house temperatures, not below 16°C (60°F), in a sunny east or west window or under fluorescent lighting. The soil should be kept evenly moist and the foliage misted often. Propagation is by taking shoot cuttings. Family: Urticaceae.

PILES. See HEMORRHOIDS.

PILGRIM FATHERS, 102 English emigrants on the MAYFLOWER, including 35 PURITAN separatists formerly settled in the Netherlands, who became the first English settlers in New England (1620). Their settlement was named PLYMOUTH COLONY. (See also ALDEN, JOHN; BRADFORD, WILLIAM; BREWSTER, WILLIAM; CARVER, JOHN; STANDISH, MILES.)

PILGRIMS, those who journey to a holy place for penance or to seek divine help. Pilgrimages today include those by Roman Catholics to ROME, LOURDES and FÁTIMA; by Hindus to VARANASI; by Muslims to MECCA, Shi'ites to KARBALA and by Buddhists to KANDY.

PILLARS OF HERCULES, the rocky summits on each side of the Strait of Gibraltar, in Greek myth set up by HERCULES, and held to mark the W limits of the seas he had made safe for sailing.

PILOT FISH, *Naucrates ductor*, a small fish found worldwide, habitually associated with SHARKS and larger fishes. They feed on scraps of food left by the

How do pigeons navigate? We cannot pretend to understand fully how the "homing" ability of the pigeon works but scientific studies of pigeons suggest that some or all of the "navigational aids" shown in this diagram play a part. The diagram shows a northern hemisphere location.
(1) The sun used as a compass to determine orientation in terms of north to south and east to west position. This hypothesis assumes that pigeons have some kind of internal clock to compensate for the changing position of the sun (15° per hour). Under cloudy conditions there is some evidence that sunlight reflected from a patch of blue sky can be used, even if the sun itself is obscured. This hypothesis assumes that the pigeon has an ability to detect planes of polarized light—a skill already shown to exist in honeybees.
(2) The earth's magnetic field used to determine position. This hypothesis assumes that the pigeon has an interpretative ability so far not found in other animals.
(3) Inertial guidance used. This hypothesis assumes the ability to remember changes of course during the outward journey and to repeat them in reverse during the homeward journey. There is little evidence to support this theory.
(4) Navigation by olfactory information. This hypothesis assumes that the pigeon has a sophisticated recognition of smells and smell gradients—as has been shown to exist in salmon. There is little evidence to support this theory.
(5) Recognition of landmarks to guide navigation There is little evidence to suggest that this comes into use except during the last few hundred yards of the journey.
(6) Pressure pattern used. This hypothesis assumes an ability to recognize small changes in barometric pressure. There is some evidence to suggest that pigeons are able to do this.
(7) Navigation by recognition of stellar positions. This hypothesis assumes that the pigeon has an internal clock and can correct visual information for celestial rotation.

host, and are supposed to have some immunity from being preyed on themselves, although this is probably due more to the pilot fish's ability to keep out of range.

PILOT WHALES, several species of large DOLPHINS, black, with a rounded forehead and narrow flippers. They are highly social, forming schools of several hundreds, and often swimming around and in front of ships.

PILSEN. See PLZEŇ.

PILSUDSKI, Józef (1867–1935), Polish general and statesman. Imprisoned several times for his nationalism, he led a private army against Russia in WWI and directed the RUSSO-POLISH WAR. From 1918 to 1922 he was president of the new Polish republic. After a coup d'etat in 1926 he became virtual dictator.

PILTDOWN MAN, *Eoanthropus dawsoni*. In 1908–15 were found under Piltdown Common, Sussex, UK, a skull with ape-like jaw but large, human cranium and teeth worn down in a way unlike those of any extant ape, surrounded by FOSSIL animals that indicated an early PLEISTOCENE date. Piltdown Man was held by many as an ancestor of *Homo Sapiens* until 1953, when the fraud was exposed: the skull was human but relatively recent; the even more recent jaw that of an orangutan; the teeth had been filed down by hand; and the fossil animals were not of British origin. The remains had been artificially stained to increase confusion.

Plaque commemorating the Pilgrim Fathers in Plymouth, England. The 52 names listed include those of the heads of families on board the *Mayflower*.

PIMA INDIANS, a North American Indian tribe living with MARICOPA INDIANS on the Gila R and Salt R reservations in S Ariz. A sedentary agricultural group, they are related to the PAPAGO INDIANS and descended from the HOHOKAM Peoples. They were noted for their domeshaped houses and basketry.

PIMENTO, Jamaican pepper, or ALLSPICE, the dried berry of the Jamaica tree *Pimenta officinalis* (also called *Eugenia pimenta*), which is used as an aromatic culinary spice. Family: Myrtaceae.

PIMIENTO, the fruit of *Capsicum annuum*, forms of which are used to make various PEPPER condiments, including **paprika** and CAYENNE PEPPER. Family: Solanaceae.

PIMPERNEL, delicate plants of the genus *Anagallis*. Best known is the Scarlet pimpernel (*Anagallis arvensis*), native to Europe, but widely naturalized in North America. It has scarlet, white or bluish flowers that close in rainy or cloudy weather. Family: Primulaceae.

PIN, peg used for fastening. In engineering the term is applied to a metal peg of any size used to join parts. In ordinary usage, a pin is a headed piece of wire, sharp at one end, used from earliest times to secure cloth to be sewn, clothing or the hair. Safety pins have a spring shield for the point.

PINCHOT, Gifford (1865–1946), US pioneer forester. He introduced systematic forestry to the US, and his ability and enthusiasm did much for the conservation movement. He helped found the PROGRESSIVE PARTY, and was governor of Pa. 1923–27, 1931–35.

PINCKNEY, a wealthy, influential S.C. family which produced a number of important figures in the early days of the Republic. **Elizabeth Lucas Pinckney** (1722–1793) was a successful planter, notably of INDIGO, as well as a leading patriot and champion of independence. Her son **Charles Cotesworth Pinckney** (1746–1825), was a soldier in the Revolutionary War and a member of the Constitutional Convention. He is best known for his part in the XYZ AFFAIR. **Thomas Pinckney** (1750–1828), soldier and statesman, arranged PINCKNEY'S TREATY with Spain in 1795. He served as governor of S.C. and was, like his brother, C. C. Pinckney, an unsuccessful FEDERALIST PARTY candidate for the vice-presidency. Their cousin **Charles Pinckney** (1757–1824) brought the "Pinckney Draft" to the Constitutional Convention of 1787. Most of its clauses were adopted. Three times governor of S.C., he became US minister to Spain (1801–05).

Because of their attractive plumage and the ease with which they are tamed, pigeons of many kinds are popular as pets in the United States. Illustrated above are the blue-winged red archangel, or peak crest (*top*), and the red-saddled fantail.

PINCKNEY'S TREATY, or **the Treaty of San Lorenzo el Real.** After years of US–Spanish dispute, in 1795 Thomas PINCKNEY negotiated a treaty which established trade arrangements, set the US boundary at the 31st parallel, and gave the Americans the right to navigate the entire Mississippi R and of tax-free deposit at the port of New Orleans.

PINDAR (c518–c438 BC), Theban noble and greatest of Greek lyric poets, perfector of the choral *epinician* ODE celebrating a victory in the national games. His odes combine lofty praise of athlete, patron and gods with extended mythical metaphor. From them was developed the Pindaric ode, consisting of a strophe, antistrophe and epode, chiefly used in 17th- and 18th-century English poetry.

PINE, general name for a large group of coniferous trees (see CONIFERS) that produce needle-like leaves in clusters of two to five. The Longleaf pine (*Pinus palustris*) has needles up to 460mm (18in) long. The Sugar pine (*P. lambertiana*) is the tallest pine, growing up to 80m (260ft). The term "pine" is generally confined to about 100 species that belong to the genus *Pinus*. In general, they are able to tolerate dry, harsh conditions and are of importance in providing wood, OILS and RESINS. Family: Pinaceae.

PINEAL BODY, or Pineal gland, a gland-like structure situated over the BRAIN stem and which appears to be a vestigial remnant of a functioning ENDOCRINE GLAND in other animals. It has no known function in man, although DESCARTES thought it to be the seat of the soul. It has a role in pigmentation in some species; calcium deposition in the pineal makes it a useful marker of midline in skull X-rays.

PINEAPPLE, *Ananas comosus*, short-stemmed plant with spiny leaves, native to tropical America, but now widely cultivated in warm climates. The dense head of flowers develops into a single sweet, juicy compound fruit. Family: Bromeliaceae.

PINE BLUFF, city in SE central Ark., seat of Jefferson Co., on the Arkansas R. A port, it has varied industry including lumber and cotton. Pine Bluff Arsenal to the N has laboratories for CHEMICAL AND BIOLOGICAL WARFARE. Pop 57 389.

PINEL, Philippe (1745–1826), French pioneer of the scientific study of MENTAL ILLNESS and the humane treatment of mental patients, whose remarkably modern ideas have earned him regard as a father of psychiatry.

PINELLAS PARK, residential city in W central Fla., 7mi NW of St. Petersburg. Manufactures include medical and electronic equipment. Pop 22 287.

PINE NUT. See PIÑON.

PINES, Isle of, Cuban island, 1 182sq mi in area, off the SW coast of Cuba, largely covered in pine forest. Its economy depends on fishing, farming and tourism.

PINE SISKIN, *Spinus pinus*, a small, heavily-streaked brown FINCH of coniferous forests in North America, distinguished by patches of yellow on wings and tail. It is a gregarious species, occasionally occurring in very large flocks.

PING-PONG. See TABLE TENNIS.

PINK BOLLWORM, *Pectinophora gossypiella*, a small moth whose larva is a worldwide pest of cotton bolls.

PINKERTON, Allan (1819–1884), Scottish-born founder of America's most famous pioneer detective agency. He organized a Civil War espionage network which became the Federal Secret Service. "Pinkerton Men" became famous; they were used to break the HOMESTEAD STRIKE in 1890 and were responsible for destroying the MOLLY MAGUIRES.

PINKEYE, common name for CONJUNCTIVITIS.

PINKNEY, William (1764–1822), US lawyer and politician. A specialist in constitutional, maritime and international law, he negotiated maritime claims with England and served as US minister there (1807–11) and to Russia (1816–18). He was US attorney general (1811–14) and an Md. congressman and senator.

PINK POLKADOT PLANT, or **freckleface,** a species of the genus *Hypoestes* which has olive-green leaves flecked with pink—a characteristic that makes them a curiosity. It grows best between 13°C (55°F) and 24°C (75°F) and should be placed in a sunny window in winter, but avoiding direct sun in summer. The soil should be kept evenly moist, avoiding dryness, which causes wilting and leaf drop. The foliage should be misted often. Propagation is by shoot tip cuttings. Family: Acanthaceae.

PINKS, plants of the genus *Dianthus*, cultivated varieties of which include the CARNATION and SWEET WILLIAM. Most wild species are native to the Mediterranean region. Family: Caryophyllaceae.

PINNACLES NATIONAL MONUMENT, in W central Cal., 35mi SE of Salinas, covers 14 498 acres. Its spires of eroded volcanic rock tower hundreds of feet above caves and canyons.

PINOCHLE, card game played mainly in the US, probably brought by German immigrants. It is played with a 48-card pack, containing two of each suit of ace, king, queen, jack, 10 and 9. Varieties include two-hand, partnership and, most popular, auction pinochle, which is a bidding game, like BRIDGE. Points are scored for card combinations declared by the winner of a trick.

PIÑON or **pine nut**, any of various low-growing PINE trees with large edible seeds, mainly native to the southwestern US. Family: Pinaceae.

PINSCHER, Miniature, scaled-down version of a smooth-coated German ratting dog which has become a popular pet. Alert and lively, with pricked-up ears, it stands 10–12in high, may be red, black or brown with tan markings, and makes a good watchdog.

PINT, name of various units of dry or liquid measure. See WEIGHTS AND MEASURES.

PINTAIL, *Anas acuta*, a slender, surface-feeding DUCK characterized by a pointed tail. The breeding male has a chocolate-colored head, white neck and gray body with a needle-like tail. The female is mottled brown. Pintail are shy duck of Eurasian distribution.

PINTER, Harold (1930–), English dramatist and director. His "comedies of menace" have ambiguous and deceptively casual dialogue, cat-and-mouse situations and a fine balance of humor and tension; notable are *The Caretaker* (1960), *The Homecoming* (1965) and *No Man's Land* (1974). He has written several successful screenplays.

PINTURICCHIO (Bernardino di Betto di Biagio; c1454–1513), Italian (Umbrian) Renaissance painter. A pupil of PERUGINO, he helped paint the SISTINE CHAPEL. His most important frescoes are in the Vatican and in the Siena cathedral library.

PINWORM, *Enterobius vermicularis*, a nematode parasite of the large intestine in humans, feeding from the gut wall. The gravid female migrates to the anus to deposit her eggs. Irritation of the anal region may cause scratching: reinfection is possible by ingestion of eggs from contaminated fingers.

PINZÓN, family of Spanish navigators (brothers) who took part with COLUMBUS in discovering America. **Martín Alonso** (c1441–1493) commanded the *Pinta*; he left Columbus after reaching Cuba and unsuccessfully tried to reach Spain first. **Francisco Martín** (c1441–1493?) served under him. **Vicente Yáñez** (c1460–1524?) commanded the *Niña* and stayed with Columbus; he went on to discover Brazil (1500) and to explore the coasts of Central and N South America.

PIONEER PROBES, US space probe series started in 1958. Pioneers 1–3 studied the VAN ALLEN RADIATION BELTS. Pioneers 5–8 were launched into solar orbit to study interplanetary space and the sun itself. Pioneers 10 and 11 were Jupiter "fly-by" probes.

PIPEFISHES, a family, Syngnathidae, of highly-elongated and specialized fishes related to the SEA HORSES. They are mainly marine, and have a long thin prehensile body completely encased in bony rings. The eggs are brooded in special structures on the males' bellies.

PIPES AND PIPELINES, tubes for conveying fluids—liquids, gases or slurries. Pipes vary in diameter considerably, according to the flow rate required and the pressure gradient: oil pipelines may be up to 1.2m in diameter. Materials used include steel, cast iron, other metals, reinforced concrete, fired clay, plastic, bitumenized-fiber cylinders, and wood. They are often coated inside and out with bitumen or concrete to prevent corrosion. Concrete, plastic and steel pipes can now be made and laid in one continuous process, but most pipes still need to be joined by means of welding, screw joints, clamped flange joints, couplings, or bell-and-spigot joints caulked with lead or cement. Pipelines, consisting of long lengths of pipe with valves and pumps at regular intervals (about 100km for oil pipelines), are used chiefly for transporting water, sewage, chemicals, foodstuffs, crude oil and natural gas.

PIPE SMOKING has been practiced since antiquity. In Africa and Asia, SMOKING (usually of MARIJUANA leaves) was a ritual, sometimes inducing trance. OPIUM was first smoked in the 1600s, when pipe smoking and TOBACCO were also brought to Europe from America, supposedly by Sir Walter RALEIGH, and spread to Africa and Asia. Pipes are made of briar wood, clay or MEERSCHAUM. (See also PEACE PIPE.)

PIPE SPRING NATIONAL MONUMENT, 40 acres in the Kaibab Indian reservation, NW Ariz., with a desert spring and a stone fort built by Mormon pioneers.

PIPESTONE NATIONAL MONUMENT, 283 acres in Pipestone city, SW Minn. It has quarries of red pipestone from which Indians made PEACE PIPES.

PIPETS, small somber insectivorous birds of open country related to WAGTAILS. They are generally brown, streaked with black above, and lighter below. They have a characteristic undulating flight.

PIPSISSEWA, *Chimaphila umbellata*, an evergreen shrub with thick shining leaves and white or pinkish flowers, which is native to Europe, Asia and North America. The astringent leaves were once used as a tonic and diuretic. Family: Pyrolaceae.

PIQUA, industrial city in W Ohio on the Miami R. It produces metal goods, paper, wood and textiles. Pop 20 741.

PIRACY, armed robbery on the high seas; the plundering of shipping by freebooters. It has existed since earliest times, though efficient navies and communications have virtually ended it today. Piracy was rife in the Mediterranean in ancient times. POMPEY suppressed it, but later the ruthless CORSAIRS, based on Algiers and TRIPOLI, were much feared PRIVATEERS (licensed by government). Piracy also flourished in northern seas and the HANSEATIC LEAGUE

Pines are common in the northern temperate zone, being well able to withstand relatively arid conditions. Shown here are (a) short-lived male cones growing on a leaved branch, (b) the young female cone before pollination, (c) the mature seed cone which has developed from the female cone, (d) a winged seed, and (e) a pollen grain with air bladders.

Tractors laying the giant Alaska pipeline. Connecting the rich oil wells of Alaska with the port of Anchorage brought enormous problems which stretched the resources of men and machines.

was formed partly to protect its member cities. New World shipping gave piracy a fresh impetus and BUCCANEERS seized much of the West Indies for England. Chinese pirates operated until WWII. (See also HIJACKING; BARBARY WARS; BLACKBEARD; DRAKE, SIR FRANCIS; KIDD, WILLIAM; LAFFITE, JEAN; MORGAN, SIR HENRY.)

PIRAEUS, chief port and third largest city of Greece, 6mi SW of Athens, whose ancient history it shares. It handles over half the country's seaborne trade. Its industries include shipbuilding, engineering and textiles. Pop 187458.

PIRANDELLO, Luigi (1867–1936), Italian dramatist and author of novels and short stories. A most influential writer, he won the Nobel Prize for Literature in 1934. He is noted for his grimly humorous treatment of psychological themes and of the reality of art compared with "real" life, as in his best-known play *Six Characters in Search of an Author* (1921).

PIRANESI, Giovanni Battista (1720–1778), Italian etcher, draftsman and architect, known for his prints of old and contemporary Roman buildings, *Views of Rome* (begun 1748), and for a series of fantastic *Imaginary Prisons* (c1745). They are notable for their grandeur and lighting contrasts.

PIRANHAS, or **Caribes**, small, but extremely ferocious, shoaling freshwater fishes from South America. The jaws are short but powerful, armed with sharp cutting teeth. They quickly strip the flesh from other fish and mammals and have even been known to attack humans on river crossings. Family: Characidae.

PISA, historic city of NW central Italy, on the Arno R in Tuscany. GALILEO was born at Pisa, which is famous for its marble campanile (see LEANING TOWER OF PISA) and rich in architecture and art. Pop 103677.

PISA, Council of (1409), uncanonical Roman Catholic ECUMENICAL COUNCIL of 500 prelates and delegates from all over Europe, met to try to heal the GREAT SCHISM. It deposed the rival popes of Rome and Avignon, and elected a third pope, Alexander V. This, however, merely created three separate parties.

PISANELLO (Antonio Pisano; c1395–c1455), Italian Renaissance painter and medalist, best known for his portrait medals, frescoes (including *St. George and the Princess*) in Verona, and a complete set of drawings now in the Louvre, Paris.

PISANO, two sculptors, father and son, of Pisa, Italy: **Nicolo Pisano** (c1220–1284?), who revived the art of sculpture in Italy; and **Giovanni Pisano** (c1250–after 1314). They combined classical and Gothic forms in works which include richly decorated pulpits at Pisa, Siena and Pistoia, a fountain at Perugia and the facade of Siena cathedral.

PISCATAWAY, township in central N.J., N of the Raritan R. Pop 36418.

PISCES (the Fishes), a large, faint constellation on the ECLIPTIC, the 12th sign of the ZODIAC. The vernal EQUINOX now lies in Pisces.

PISISTRATUS (c600–527 BC), "tyrant" of Athens, whose benign rule and fostering of commerce and the arts made Athens the foremost city in Greece. In 560 BC he seized power in a popular coup d'etat. Aristocrats, having returned from exile, ousted him in 552, but in 541 he established himself firmly. He enforced SOLON's laws, promoted public works, and was succeeded by his sons.

PISSARRO, Camille (1830–1903), leading French Impressionist painter. Born in the West Indies, he came to Paris in 1855. Influenced by the BARBIZON SCHOOL at first, he was with CÉZANNE, MONET and RENOIR a founder of IMPRESSIONISM. His works, most notably landscapes and street scenes, are famous for their freshness, vividness and luminous color.

PISTACHIO, *Pistacia vera*, a small tree native to the Mediterranean region and cultivated also in the US for its edible nuts, which are used for flavoring and in confectionery. Family: Anacardiaceae.

PISTIL. See FLOWER.

PISTOL, small FIREARM that can be conveniently held and operated in one hand. It developed in parallel with the shoulder weapon from the 14th century, first becoming really practical in the early 16th century with the invention of the wheel-lock firing mechanism, soon superseded by the FLINTLOCK. Modern rapid-fire pistols are usually either REVOLVERS or automatics. Automatic pistols, such as the Colt .45 Automatic, contain a magazine of cartridges in the butt and are automatically reloaded and cocked by the energy of recoil when a round is fired (see AMMUNITION).

PISTON, solid cylindrical piece that moves up and down inside a hollow cylinder in an ENGINE OF PUMP, being driven by, or driving, fluid under pressure. The piston is fitted with rings to fit the cylinder snugly. In the INTERNAL-COMBUSTION ENGINE (but not the FREE-PISTON ENGINE) it bears a connecting rod to transmit the power to the crankshaft.

PISTON, Walter (1894–   ), US neoclassical composer, professor of music at Harvard from 1944. His austere but dynamic music incorporates complex rhythms and harmonies in traditional forms. His *7th Symphony* (1961) won a Pulitzer Prize.

PITCAIRN ISLAND, small British colony (2sq mi) in the Pacific midway between New Zealand and Panama, famous as the uninhabited island settled by BOUNTY mutineers and Tahitian women (1790), from whom the present 90-odd English-speaking islanders are descended.

PITCH, black solid BITUMEN; the residue from distilling COAL TAR, wood tar or PETROLEUM, sometimes occurring naturally. It is used in roadmaking, for waterproofing and for caulking seams.

PITCH, Musical, refers to the FREQUENCY of the vibrations constituting a SOUND. The frequency associated with a given pitch name (e.g., Middle C) has varied considerably over the years. The present international standard sets Concert A at 440Hz.

PITCHBLENDE, or **Uraninite**, brown, black or greenish mineral, the most important source of URANIUM, RADIUM and POLONIUM. The composition varies between UO_2 and $UO_{2.6}$; thorium, radium, polonium, lead and helium are also present. Principal deposits are in Zaire, Bohemia, at Great Bear Lake, Canada, and in the Mountain States.

PITCHER, Molly (1754–1832), popular heroine of the American Revolution. Born Mary Ludwig, she earned her nickname by carrying water for the Continental soldiers during the battle of MONMOUTH. According to legends, she manned her husband's gun when he collapsed.

PITCHER PLANTS, insect-catching plants from several families, in which the leaves form a pot-shaped trap. Unwary insects make their way into the pitcher, are trapped and their bodies digested by ENZYMES secreted by the plant. Pitcher plants usually grow as EPIPHYTES or in boggy soil. (See also INSECTIVOROUS PLANTS.)

PITHECANTHROPUS ERECTUS. See PREHISTORIC MAN.

PITMAN, a residential borough 2mi N of Glassboro, SW N.J. It is a summer resort in a truck-farming area. Pop 10257.

PITMAN, Sir Isaac (1810–1897), English school teacher who invented a famous SHORTHAND based on phonetic principles, still one of the most widely used systems of stenography in English.

PITOT TUBE, device invented by **Henri Pitot** (1695–1771) in 1732 and widely used in fluid dynamics for measuring FLUID velocities. One open end of a cylindrical tube points directly into the flowing stream, and the other end is connected to a pressure-measuring device. This compares the pitot-tube pressure with the static stream pressure, the difference being a measure of the fluid velocity.

PITT, the name of two British statesmen. **William Pitt, Earl of Chatham** (1708–1778), known as "Pitt the Elder," was an outstanding war minister and empire builder during the SEVEN YEARS' WAR. He was also famous for his defense of the rights of the American colonists. By 1761 he had completely transformed Britain's position in Europe and throughout the world. He strengthened the British navy, and extended British control in Canada and India. **William Pitt** (1759–1806), second son of the Earl of Chatham, known as "Pitt the Younger." At 24 he became Britain's youngest prime minister, at the invitation of GEORGE III, and he dominated British politics until his death. In his 1783–1801 ministry he strengthened national finances but war with France and agitation at home forced him to shelve parliamentary reform measures. His 1804–06 ministry was marked by defeats on land but victory at sea in the NAPOLEONIC WARS.

PITTOSPORUM, a genus of tender and half-hardy evergreen flowering shrubs which have attractive green or gray-green leaves and sweet-scented, bell-shaped or tubular white flowers. As house plants they should be grown at temperatures between 13°C and 21°C (55°F and 70°F), and in winter placed in a sunny east or west window, or a short distance from a south window, avoiding direct sun in the summer. The soil should be kept moist most of the time, but allowing short periods of slight drying. The leaves benefit from frequent misting. Propagation is by shoot tip cuttings of half-ripened wood. Family: Pittosporaceae.

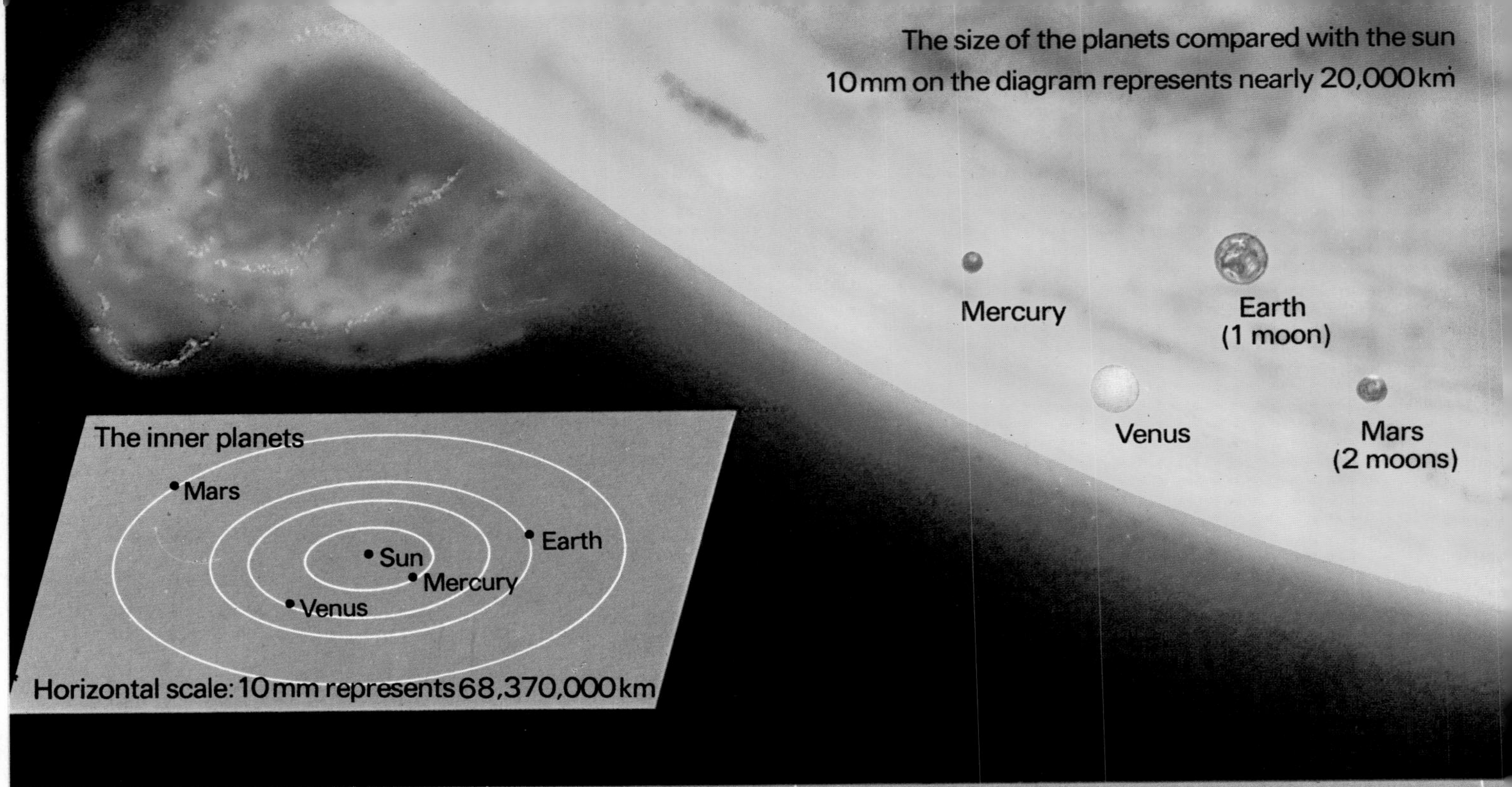

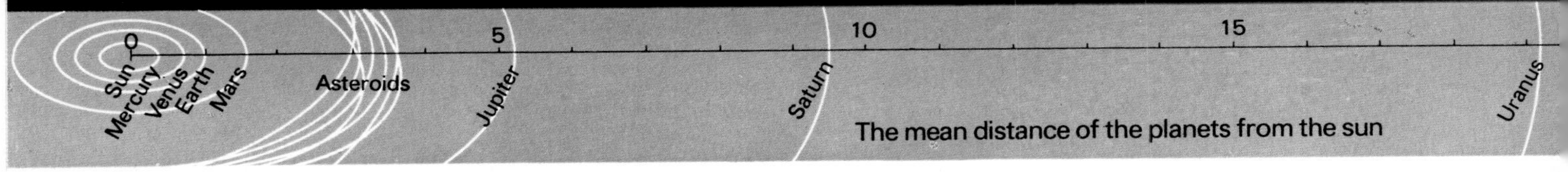

PITTSBURG, industrial city in W Cal. at the confluence of Sacramento and San Joaquin rivers. Steel and chemicals are principal products. Pop 20651.

PITTSBURG, city in SE Kan., a mining area with coal, zinc, lead, gas and oil resources. The town has aircraft and pipe factories. Pop 20171.

PITTSBURGH, steel-producing city in SW Penn., seat of Allegheny Co., and the state's second largest city. It occupies over 55sq mi around its business center, the "Golden Triangle" where the Allegheny and Monongahela rivers meet to form the Ohio. Its economic wealth is based on steel mills, coke from Allegheny coal, pig iron, glass and a variety of manufactured products. It has an impressive transport system and is the biggest inland river port in the US. Pittsburgh is rich in cultural institutions, with universities, a symphony orchestra, opera company, and many other amenities. Pop 520117.

PITTSFIELD, city in Mass., tourist center and seat of Berkshire Co. Its industries include paper, chemical and electrical goods. Pop 57020.

PITUITARY GLAND, major ENDOCRINE GLAND situated just below the BRAIN, under the control of the adjacent HYPOTHALAMUS and in its turn controlling other endocrine glands. The posterior pituitary is a direct extension of certain cells in the hypothalamus and secretes VASOPRESSIN and OXYTOCIN into the BLOOD stream. The anterior pituitary develops separately and consists of several cell types which secrete different HORMONES, including growth hormone, FOLLICLE STIMULATING HORMONE, LUTEINIZING HORMONE, PROLACTIN, thyrotrophic hormone (which stimulates thyroid gland) and adrenocorticotrophic hormone (ACTH). Growth hormone is concerned with skeletal growth and development as well as regulation of blood sugar (anti-INSULIN activity). The anterior pituitary hormones are controlled by releasing hormones secreted by the hypothalamus into local blood vessels; the higher centers of the brain and environmental influences act by this route. FEEDBACK from the organs controlled occurs at both the hypothalamic and pituitary levels. Pituitary TUMORS or loss of blood supply may cause loss of function, while some tumors may be functional and produce syndromes such as GIGANTISM or acromegaly (due to growth hormone imbalance). Pituitary tumors may also affect VISION by compressing the nearby optic nerves. Sophisticated tests of pituitary function are now available.

PIT VIPERS, an important group of highly venomous SNAKES, family Crotalidae, best known in the New World where they are represented by the RATTLESNAKES. They are named for a double pit in front of the eye which is used as a heat sensor for detecting prey.

PIUS, name of twelve popes. **Saint Pius I** reigned c140–c155. **Pius II** (1405–1464), a leading HUMANIST scholar, became pope in 1458. He attempted to organize a crusade against the Turks. **Pius III** (1439–1503), reigned barely a month before he died. **Pius IV** (1499–1565), pope from 1659, reconvened the Council of TRENT for its successful conclusion. **Saint Pius V** (1504–1572) succeeded in 1566. With some severity he restored a degree of discipline and morality to the papacy in the face of the Protestant challenge, and organized the Spanish-Venetian expedition which defeated the Turks at LEPANTO in 1571. **Pius VI** (1717–1799), elected in 1775, drained the Pontine marshes and completed St. Peter's. The French Revolution led to the occupation of the papal territories and Pius' death in captivity. **Pius VII** (1740–1823) succeeded him in 1800. Under an 1801 CONCORDAT French troops were withdrawn, but the PAPAL STATES were later annexed by Napoleon, whom he had consecrated emperor in 1804. **Pius VIII** (1761–1830) reigned just 20 months. **Pius IX** (1792–1878) began the longest papal reign in 1846 with liberal reforms, but became an extreme reactionary in both politics and dogma after the REVOLUTIONS OF 1848. The Immaculate Conception became an article of dogma (1854), and papal infallibility was proclaimed in 1870 by the first VATICAN COUNCIL (see ULTRAMONTANISM). In 1871 the new kingdom of Italy passed The Law of Guaranties, defining the relations between the state and the papacy, but Pius refused to accept the position. **Saint Pius X** (1835–1914), elected in 1903, condemned modernism in the Church. **Pius XI** (1857–1939), elected in 1922, concluded the LATERAN TREATY (1929). He issued encyclicals condemning communism, fascism and racism. **Pius XII** (1876–1958) who reigned from 1939 was an active diplomat in a difficult period and undertook a considerable amount of humanitarian work in WWII. His encyclical *Mediator Dei* led to changes in the Mass.

PIZARRO, Francisco (c1474–1541), Spanish conquistador who destroyed the INCA empire in the course of his conquest of PERU. He was with BALBOA when he discovered the Pacific (1513). In 1524 and 1526–27 Pizarro attempted to conquer Peru with Diego de ALMAGRO and Fernando de Luque. In 1531, with royal assent, he began a new campaign and found Peru in an unsettled state under the Inca emperor ATAHUALPA. At Cajamarca in the Andes Pizarro's small band, at first pretending friendship, kidnapped Atahualpa and massacred his unarmed followers; he forced the emperor to pay a massive ransom, then executed him. A vicious and greedy man, Pizarro cheated Almagro and eventually had him killed; he was himself assassinated by Almagro's followers.

PKU. See PHENYLKETONURIA.

PLACEBO, a tablet, syrup or other form of medication which is inactive and is prescribed in lieu of active preparations, e.g., in experimental studies of DRUG effectiveness.

PLACENTA, in PLACENTAL MAMMALS including MAN, specialized structure derived from the WOMB lining and part of the EMBRYO after IMPLANTATION; it separates and yet ensures a close and extensive contact between the maternal (uterine) and fetal (umbilical) BLOOD CIRCULATIONS. This allows nutrients and OXYGEN to pass from the mother to the FETUS, and waste products to pass in the reverse direction. The placenta thus enables the embryo and fetus to live as a PARASITE, dependent on the maternal organs. GONADOTROPHINS are produced by the placenta which prepares the maternal body for delivery and the BREASTS for LACTATION. The placenta is delivered after the child at BIRTH (the afterbirth) by separation of the blood vessel layers; placental disorders may cause ante- or post-partum HEMORRHAGE or fetal immaturity.

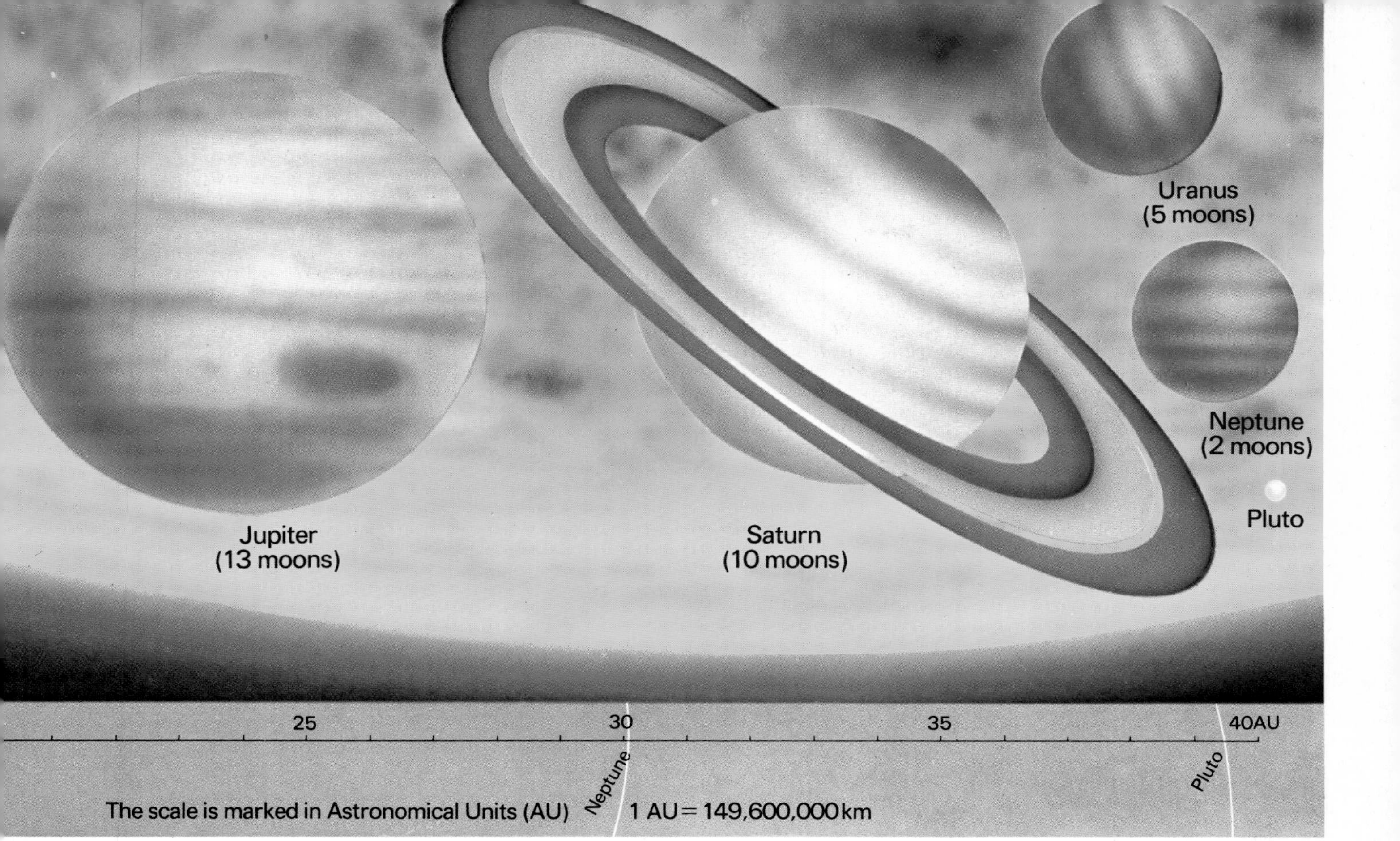

PLACENTAL MAMMALS, Eutheria, or True mammals, those mammals, distinct from MARSUPIALS and MONOTREMES, in which the FETUS is nourished in the womb attached to a highly organized PLACENTA until a comparatively late state in its development. By contrast, marsupials give birth to far less well developed young, further development occurring while the young is attached to the mother's teat. Other differences are in the structure of the reproductive system and in the BRAIN. Placental mammals have larger brains and possess a *corpus callosum*: threads of tissue connecting the two halves of the brain.

PLACENTIA, city in S Cal., 25mi SE of Los Angeles. It has some light industry but is mainly a residential center for industries in the area. Pop 21 948.

PLACER MINING, the extraction of minerals such as gold, platinum and diamonds from ORE that has accumulated through the processes of weathering or EROSION. The earliest and best known form of placer mining is gold panning.

PLACID, Lake, beautiful small lake (4.37sq mi) in the Adirondack Mts., in NW N.Y., 1 860ft above sea level. It is a year-round tourist attraction.

PLAGUE, a highly infectious disease due to a bacterium carried by rodent fleas. It causes greatly enlarged LYMPH nodes (buboes, hence bubonic plague), SEPTICEMIA with FEVER, prostration and COMA; plague PNEUMONIA is particularly severe. If untreated, DEATH is common and EPIDEMICS occur in areas of overcrowding and poverty. It still occurs on a small rural scale in the Far East; massive epidemics such as the **Black Death**, which perhaps halved the population of Europe in the mid-14th century, are rare. Rat and flea control, disinfection and ANTIBIOTICS are the mainstay of current prevention and treatment.

PLAGUES OF EGYPT, in the Book of EXODUS, the 10 disasters inflicted on Egypt by God when the pharaoh refused MOSES' demand that the Israelites be freed. They were: the rivers turned to blood, frogs, lice, flies, murrain, boils, hail, locusts, darkness, and finally the death of all firstborn. After the last plague, from which the Israelites were protected by the PASSOVER, they were allowed to leave.

PLAICE, *Pleuronectes platessa*, one of the most popular of the edible European flatfishes, with red spots on the upper surface. As in all true flatfishes, both eyes have migrated to the upper surface. Plaice are found mainly on sand or gravel.

PLAINFIELD, a textile town in E Conn., founded in 1689 on the Quinebaug R. Other products are metal, china and plastic goods. Pop 11 957.

PLAINFIELD, industrial city in NE N.J., 15mi SW of Newark. Diversified industries include machinery, chemicals and electronics. Pop 46 862.

PLAINS OF ABRAHAM. See ABRAHAM, PLAINS OF.

PLAINSONG, or **plainchant,** one of the earliest forms of music in Christian Europe, still used in the Roman Catholic Church. It is a sung version of the LITURGY in which an unaccompanied line of melody, at its simplest all on one note (psalmodic intonation), follows the rhythm of the words. The "Ambrosian chant" developed in Milan under St. AMBROSE (c340–397). Today's Gregorian chant was developed in Rome and codified in the time of Pope GREGORY I (c540–604), adapting Greek modes. (See MODE; NOTATION; POLYPHONY.)

PLAINVIEW, an unincorporated urban area in N.Y., in central Long Island. It is mainly residential, with some light industry. Pop 32 195.

PLAINVIEW, city and seat of Hale Co., NW Texas. It processes produce from the diversified farms of the Llano Estocado. Pop 19 076.

PLAINVILLE, an industrial town in Conn., 12mi SW of Hartford. Its varied manufactures include ballbearings and electrical equipment. Pop 16 733.

PLANARIANS, free-living flatworms which, with the Trematodes, or FLUKES, and Cestodes, TAPEWORMS, make up the phylum Platyhelminthes. Planarians (class Turbellaria) are free-living predators, and include freshwater, marine and terrestrial forms.

PLANCK, Max Karl Ernst Ludwig (1858–1947), German physicist whose QUANTUM THEORY, with the Theory of RELATIVITY, ushered physics into the modern era. Initially influenced by CLAUSIUS, he made fundamental researches in THERMODYNAMICS before turning to investigate BLACKBODY RADIATION. To describe the electromagnetic radiation emitted from a BLACK BODY he evolved the **Planck Radiation Formula**, which implied that ENERGY, like MATTER, is not infinitely subdivisible—that it can exist only as quanta (see PLANCK CONSTANT). Planck himself was unconvinced of this, even after EINSTEIN had applied the theory to the PHOTOELECTRIC EFFECT and BOHR in his model of the ATOM; but for his achievement he received the 1918 Nobel Prize for Physics.

PLANCK CONSTANT, h ($=6.6256\times10^{-34}$Js), a quantity fundamental to quantum physics, named for Max PLANCK, who in 1900 solved a long-standing problem in radiation physics with the hypothesis that the energy of a system vibrating with frequency ν had to be a whole-number multiple of $h\nu$. The Planck constant also governs the accuracy with which different properties can be measured simultaneously (see UNCERTAINTY PRINCIPLE) and the wavelength of the wave associated with a particle (see QUANTUM MECHANICS).

PLANE, a surface having two DIMENSIONS only, length and breadth, any two POINTS of which can be joined by a straight LINE composed entirely of points also in the plane. A plane may be determined by two intersecting or PARALLEL lines, by a line and a point that does not lie on the line, or by three points that do not lie in a straight line. The intersection of two planes is a straight line; the intersection of a plane and a line in a different plane is a point. An infinite number of planes may pass through a single point or line. A plane is parallel to another plane if all PERPENDICULARS drawn between them are of equal length.

PLANE OF SYMMETRY, a PLANE cutting a geometrical figure such that the parts of it lying on either side are symmetrical. (See also AXIS OF SYMMETRY; SYMMETRY.)

PLANET, in the SOLAR SYSTEM, one of the nine major celestial bodies orbiting the sun; by extension, a similar body circling any other star. In 1963 it was discovered that BARNARD's Star has at least one companion about 1.5 times the size of Jupiter, implying that planets are by no means unique to the sun.

PLANETARIUM, an instrument designed to represent the relative positions and motions of celestial objects. Originally a mechanical model of the

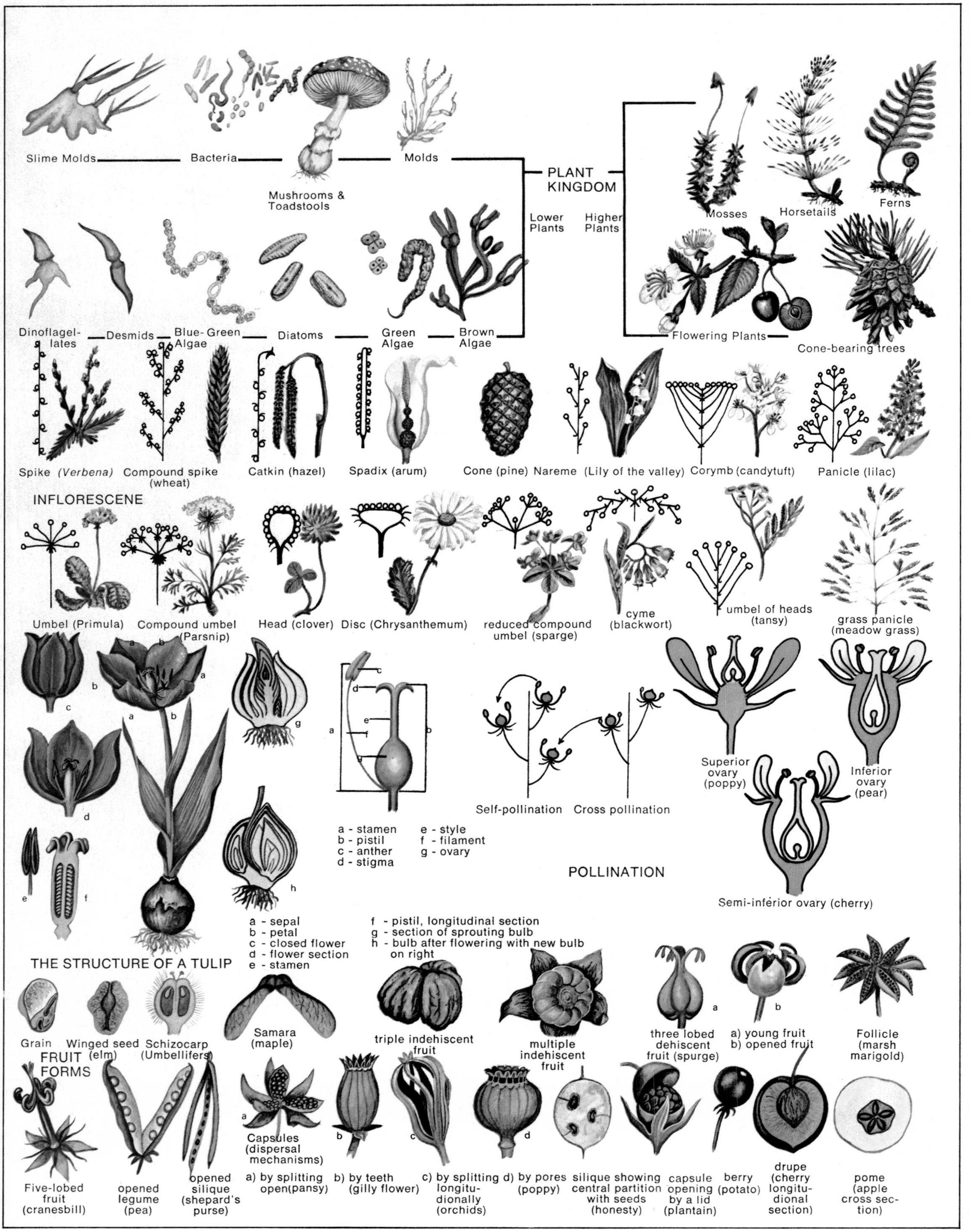
Slime Molds
Bacteria
Molds
Mushrooms & Toadstools
PLANT KINGDOM
Lower Plants
Higher Plants
Mosses
Horsetails
Ferns
Dinoflagel-lates
Desmids
Blue-Green Algae
Diatoms
Green Algae
Brown Algae
Flowering Plants
Cone-bearing trees
Spike (Verbena)
Compound spike (wheat)
Catkin (hazel)
Spadix (arum)
Cone (pine)
Nareme (Lily of the valley)
Corymb (candytuft)
Panicle (lilac)
INFLORESCENE
Umbel (Primula)
Compound umbel (Parsnip)
Head (clover)
Disc (Chrysanthemum)
reduced compound umbel (sparge)
cyme (blackwort)
umbel of heads (tansy)
grass panicle (meadow grass)
a - stamen
b - pistil
c - anther
d - stigma
e - style
f - filament
g - ovary
Self-pollination
Cross pollination
Superior ovary (poppy)
Inferior ovary (pear)
POLLINATION
Semi-inferior ovary (cherry)
a - sepal
b - petal
c - closed flower
d - flower section
e - stamen
f - pistil, longitudinal section
g - section of sprouting bulb
h - bulb after flowering with new bulb on right
THE STRUCTURE OF A TULIP
Grain
Winged seed (elm)
Schizocarp (Umbellifers)
Samara (maple)
triple indehiscent fruit
multiple indehiscent fruit
three lobed dehiscent fruit (spurge)
a) young fruit
b) opened fruit
Follicle (marsh marigold)
FRUIT FORMS
Capsules (dispersal mechanisms)
Five-lobed fruit (cranesbill)
opened legume (pea)
opened silique (shepard's purse)
a) by splitting open(pansy)
b) by teeth (gilly flower)
c) by splitting longitu-dionally (orchids)
d) by pores (poppy)
silique showing central partition with seeds (honesty)
capsule opening by a lid (plantain)
berry (potato)
drupe (cherry longitu-dional section)
pome (apple cross sec-tion)

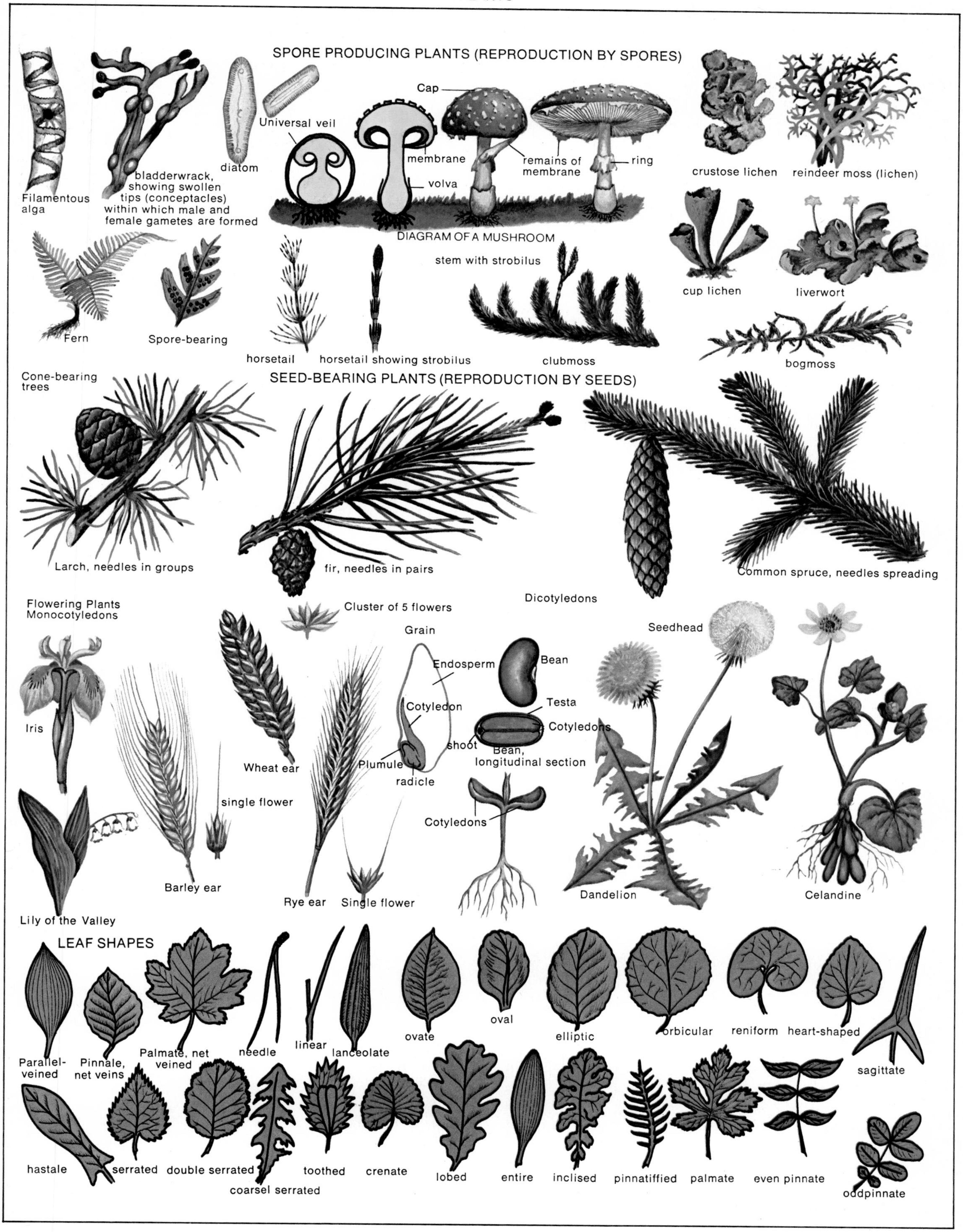
SPORE PRODUCING PLANTS (REPRODUCTION BY SPORES)
Filamentous alga
bladderwrack, showing swollen tips (conceptacles) within which male and female gametes are formed
diatom
Universal veil
Cap
membrane
volva
remains of membrane
ring
DIAGRAM OF A MUSHROOM
crustose lichen
reindeer moss (lichen)
cup lichen
liverwort
Fern
Spore-bearing
horsetail
horsetail showing strobilus
stem with strobilus
clubmoss
bogmoss
SEED-BEARING PLANTS (REPRODUCTION BY SEEDS)
Cone-bearing trees
Larch, needles in groups
fir, needles in pairs
Common spruce, needles spreading
Flowering Plants Monocotyledons
Cluster of 5 flowers
Dicotyledons
Iris
Wheat ear
Grain
Endosperm
Cotyledon
Plumule
radicle
Bean
Testa
Cotyledons
shoot
Bean, longitudinal section
Seedhead
single flower
Barley ear
Rye ear
Single flower
Cotyledons
Dandelion
Celandine
Lily of the Valley
LEAF SHAPES
Parallel-veined
Pinnale, net veins
Palmate, net veined
needle
linear
lanceolate
ovate
oval
elliptic
orbicular
reniform
heart-shaped
sagittate
hastale
serrated
double serrated
coarsel serrated
toothed
crenate
lobed
entire
inclised
pinnatiffied
palmate
even pinnate
oddpinnate

SOLAR SYSTEM (see ORRERY), the planetarium of today is an intricate optical device that projects disks and points of light representing sun, moon, planets and stars on to the interior of a fixed hemispherical dome. The various cyclic motions of these bodies as seen from a given latitude on earth can be simulated. Of great assistance to students of ASTRONOMY and celestial NAVIGATION, planetariums also attract large public audiences. The first modern planetarium, built in 1923 by the firm of Carl ZEISS, is still in use at the Deutsches Museum, Munich, West Germany.

PLANETESIMAL HYPOTHESIS, a discarded theory proposed by T. C. Chamberlin and F. R. Moulton to explain the formation of PLANETS. It states that a passing star drew matter out of the sun, some of which condensed to form small solid particles (planetesimals) which in turn coalesced to form planets.

PLANE TREE, *Platanus orientalis*, a relative of the SYCAMORE, native to Greece and W Asia. The seeds are borne in spiky balls. Planes are planted in cities because the bark flakes off, carrying away soot and dirt and leaving colorful underlayers. Family: Platanaceae.

PLANKTON, microscopic animals and plants that live in the sea. They drift under the influence of OCEAN CURRENTS and are vitally important links in the marine food chain (see ECOLOGY). A major part of plankton comprises minute plants (phytoplankton), which are mainly ALGAE, but include DINOFLAGELLATES and DIATOMS. Phytoplankton may be so numerous as to color the water and cause it to have a "bloom." They are eaten by animals (zooplankton), which comprise the eggs, larvae and adults of a vast array of animal types, from Protozoa to JELLYFISH. Zooplankton is an important food for large animals such as WHALES and countless fishes such as HERRING. Phytoplankton is confined to the upper layers of the sea where light can reach, but zooplankton has been found at great depths. (See also OCEANS.)

PLANNED PARENTHOOD—WORLD POPULATION (PPWP), the chief organization in the US for promoting FAMILY PLANNING, the use of BIRTH CONTROL methods and the availability of devices for CONTRACEPTION. Founded in 1914 by Margaret SANGER, its affiliates operate some 400 clinics in over 150 US cities. PPWP is funded by donations.

PLANO, city in Tex., 15mi N of Dallas. It has cotton and flour mills and light metal industries. Pop 17872.

PLANT, a living organism belonging to the PLANT KINGDOM. Green plants are unique in being able to synthesize their own organic molecules from carbon dioxide and water using light energy by the process known as PHOTOSYNTHESIS. Mineral nutrients are absorbed from the environment. Plants are the primary source of food for all other living organisms (see ECOLOGY). The possession of CHLOROPHYLL, the green photosynthetic pigment, is probably the most important distinction between plants and animals, but there are several other differences. Plants are stationary, have no nervous system and the cell wall contains large amounts of CELLULOSE. But there are exceptions. Some plants, such as ALGAE and BACTERIA, can move about, and others, including FUNGI, bacteria and some PARASITES do not contain chlorophyll and cannot synthesize their own organic molecules, but absorb them from their environment. Some INSECTIVOROUS PLANTS obtain their food by trapping insects.

Although the more primitive plants vary considerably in their overall structure, the higher plants (GYMNOSPERMS and ANGIOSPERMS) are much the same in their basic anatomy and morphology. In a typical angiosperm, four main regions can be recognized: ROOT, STEM, LEAF and FLOWER. Each region has one or more basic functions.

When examined under the microscope, a piece of plant tissue can be seen to consist of thousands of tiny CELLS, generally packed tightly together. The cells are not all alike and each one is adapted to do a certain job. All are derived, however, from a basic pattern. This basic plant cell tends to be rectangular and it has a tough wall of cellulose which gives it its shape, but the living boundary of the cell is the delicate cell membrane just inside the wall. Inside the membrane is the PROTOPLASM, which contains the nucleus, the CHLOROPLASTS and many other microscopic structures. In the center of the protoplasm there is a large sap-filled vacuole, which maintains the cell's shape and plays an important part in the working of the whole plant.

Both sexual and asexual REPRODUCTION are widespread throughout the plant kingdom. Many plants are capable of both forms and in some cases the life cycle of the plant may involve the two different forms (see ALTERNATION OF GENERATIONS). (See also BOTANY; FERTILIZATION; FRUIT; GERMINATION; GROWTH; OSMOSIS; PLANT DISEASES; POLLINATION; TRANSPIRATION.)

PLANTAGENETS, name given to the branch of the ANGEVIN dynasty descended from GEOFFREY PLANTAGENET which ruled England 1154–1485. From HENRY II until the deposition of RICHARD II in 1399 the succession was direct. Thereafter the crown passed to other branches of the family until the defeat of the Yorkist Plantagenet RICHARD III at the hands of Henry Tudor (HENRY VII), who had remote Plantagenet connections.

PLANTAIN, popular name for plants, from the genus *Plantago* and some of the genera *Alisma* and *Musa*. All produce a dense rosette of leaves. Many are persistent weeds that are difficult to eradicate. The tropical plantain fruit is produced by *Musa paradisiaca*, which is closely related to the BANANA.

PLANTATION, city in SE Fla. It is a residential suburb of Fort Lauderdale. Pop 23523.

PLANT CITY, city in W central Fla. It is a shipping and processing center for fruit and vegetables. Pop 15451.

PLANT DISEASES cause serious losses to crop production; they may kill plants completely, but more often they simply reduce the yield. Most plant diseases are caused by microorganisms which infect the tissues, the most important being FUNGI, including MILDEW, RUSTS and SMUTS. Control methods are based on FUNGICIDES. VIRUSES are the next most damaging group of plant pathogens. Most of them are carried by aphids and other sap-sucking insects and control is largely a matter of controlling these insect carriers. BACTERIA are less important, their main role being in secondary infection, causing the tissues to rot. Deficiency diseases are caused by a lack of available minerals in the soil. Insect pests, such as the BOLL WEEVIL on cotton, can also cause serious crop damage.

PLANTIN, Christophe (1514–1589), French printer who settled in Antwerp. He published books in many languages, distinguished for their fine typography and engravings and including a famous Polyglot Bible.

PLANT KINGDOM, the second great group of living organisms. The plant and ANIMAL KINGDOMS together embrace all living things except VIRUSES, and only overlap in the most primitive organisms. The plant kingdom is extremely diverse (over 400000 species are now known), and they are found in almost every conceivable habitat. They range in size from microscopic BACTERIA to 100m (330ft) SEQUOIAS. The plant kingdom can be arranged into an orderly hierarchical pattern of classification (see TAXONOMY) containing divisions, classes, orders, families, genera and species. Indeed, several systems have been evolved to do this. In the classical Eichler system there are four divisions: the THALLOPHYTA, including bacteria, SLIME MOULDS, ALGAE and FUNGI; the BRYOPHYTA, including LIVERWORTS, HORNWORTS and MOSSES; the PTERIDOPHYTA, including FERNS, CLUB MOSSES and HORSETAILS; and the SPERMATOPHYTA, including GYMNOSPERMS and ANGIOSPERMS, the latter being divided into DICOTYLEDONS and MONOCOTYLEDONS. However, this system has been replaced recently by a more natural arrangement of 11 divisions: Schizophyta, bacteria and blue-green algae; Euglenophyta, euglenoids; Chlorophyta, green algae; Xanthophyta, yellow-green algae; Chrysophyta, golden algae and DIATOMS; Phaeophyta, brown algae; Rhodophyta, red algae; Pyrrophyta, dinoflagellates and cryptomonads; Mycota, slime molds and fungi; Bryophyta, liverworts and mosses; and Tracheophyta, the vascular plants, including horsetails, ferns, gymnosperms and angiosperms. Under this system some authorities break the plant kingdom into three kingdoms: the Monera, including the division Schizophyta; the Metaphyta, including the Bryophyta and Tracheophyta; and the Protista, which includes all the other divisions.

PLANT LICE. See APHIDS.

PLASMA, almost completely ionized GAS, containing equal numbers of free ELECTRONS and positive IONS. Plasmas such as those forming stellar atmospheres (see STAR) or regions in an electron discharge tube are highly conducting but electrically neutral and many phenomena occur in them that are not seen in ordinary gases. The TEMPERATURE of a plasma is theoretically high enough to support a controlled nuclear FUSION reaction. Because of this, plasmas are being widely studied particularly in MAGNETOHYDRODYNAMICS research. Plasmas are formed by heating low-pressure gases until the ATOMS have sufficient energy to ionize each other. Unless the plasma can be successfully contained by electric or magnetic fields, rapid cooling and recombination occurs; indeed the high temperatures needed for thermonuclear reactions cannot as yet be maintained

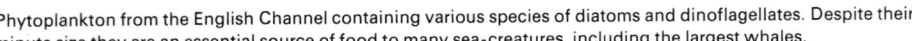

Phytoplankton from the English Channel containing various species of diatoms and dinoflagellates. Despite their minute size they are an essential source of food to many sea-creatures, including the largest whales.

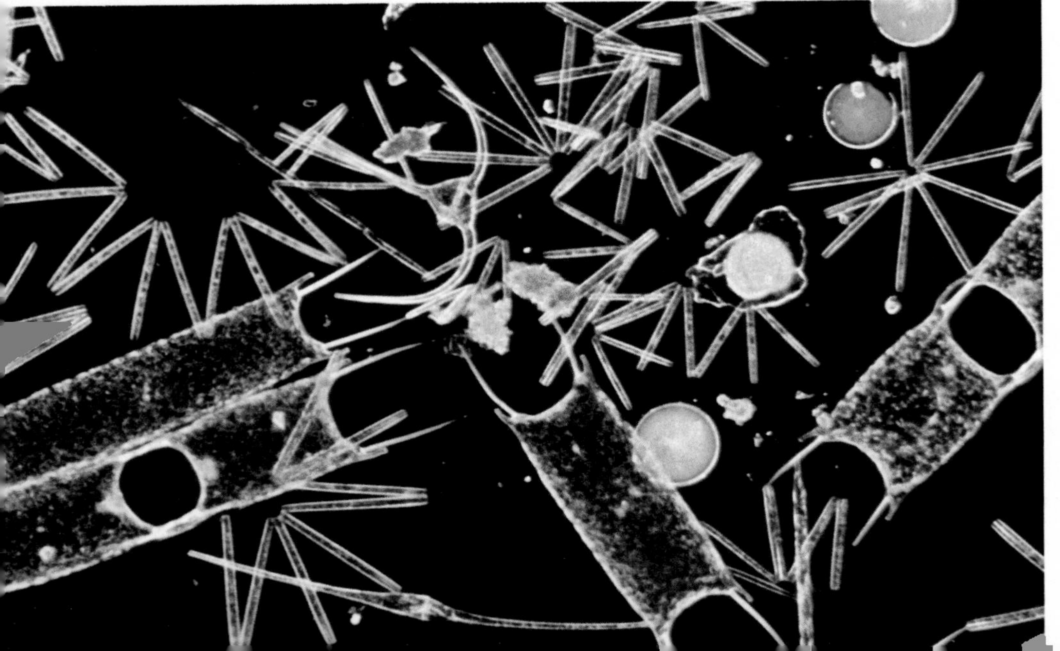

Plate Tectonics

Wandering continents

Men have speculated concerning the similarity between the shapes of the west coast of Africa and the eastern margin of South America since the 17th century. The hypothesis that the continents are continually wandering over the surface of the earth, although supported by much circumstantial evidence and particularly attractive to biologists seeking to trace the pathways of evolution, nevertheless failed to convince the majority of geoscientists before the discovery of a mass of new evidence in the 1960s. Alfred Wegener's famous theory of "continental drift" (1915) always suffered from its inability to explain how the continental land masses could travel through the seemingly solid material which formed the earth's crust at the bottom of the oceans.

The solution to these difficulties came with W. J. Morgan's proposal in 1967 of the theory of "plate tectonics." According to this model, the surface of the earth comprises a mosaic of distinct units called plates which, although themselves rigid, can move relative to each other. The continents, including the "continental shelf"—their submerged margins down to about 6000ft (2000m)—ride on the surface of these plates, being composed of lighter materials than the rest of their substance. The continents cannot move relative to the plates in which they are situated and can only move with them. The motion of the plates has two components—one simply the relative motion of adjoining plates but the other involving the continual creation and destruction of the earth's crust at the active edges of the plates.

Running down the middle of most oceans is a double ridge where there is much volcanic activity and a high local heat flow. Semi-molten basaltic material rises to the surface at these ridges and solidifies, forming new oceanic crust which is added to the plates meeting at the ridge. These plates are pushed slowly apart as they grow, allowing more plastic basalt to rise to the ocean floor.

Perhaps the most striking evidence in favor of the theory of plate tectonics came from the measurement of the magnetic "fingerprints" of the basalt rocks of the ocean bed. Most igneous rocks are magnetized in the direction of the earth's magnetic field prevailing at the time when they solidified from the plastic state. In the early 1960s it was discovered that the basalt of the Pacific floor was magnetized in alternating stripes of north-seeking and south-seeking polarity, arranged symmetrically on either side of the East Pacific Rise. It was known that the earth's magnetic field reverses its polarity roughly twice every million years and so the successive stripes were interpreted as crust formed at the ridge during the relevant periods. The symmetry of the pattern was seen to be strong evidence for the hypothesis of ocean-floor spreading.

Just as the oceanic plates are growing on their midocean margins, in other areas adjoining plates are converging with the resulting destruction of crustal material. Where two plates of oceanic material are converging, there is usually a deep ocean trench as one plate plunges beneath the other and remelts in the upper mantle. The descending portions of crust break up as they melt releasing elastic energy in the form of earthquake shockwaves. By tracing the centers from which these shockwaves originate, shallow near the surface trench, but successively deeper as they occur farther back under the over-riding plate, it is possible to follow the melting crust on its journey down, often to depths of 450mi (700km). Material melted from the descending plate rises through the upper plate causing the arc of volcanoes which fringes the majority of midocean trenches.

The rocks which form the continental masses are lighter than the basaltic material of the oceanic crust and thus ride on the surface of the basalt plates like parcels on a conveyor belt. When at length a continent is carried to the edge of a boundary where two plates are converging, it rides up on the descending plate forming high mountain ranges such as the South American Andes. Like the oceanic island arcs, such mountains are areas of great earthquake and volcanic activity.

By winding back the conveyor belts carrying the continents across the globe, it is possible to arrive at reconstructions of the face of the earth at successively earlier periods. This process must come to an end on reaching the world map of 200 million years ago because all the present continents are then found to be amalgamated in one large landmass known as Pangaea. But there are good reasons to suppose that plate-tectonic processes similar to those in action today operated for at least 400 million years before the formation of Pangaea and perhaps different plate processes began 1 400 million years before then. This takes us back to little short of the time when the shield regions at the heart of the major continents were formed. The Ural mountains were probably the result of the collision of two continents long before Pangaea came together, as was the Caledonian-Appalachian chain, now divided by the spreading of the North Atlantic ocean.

Some geologists have pointed to the implications of plate tectonics in the search for the earth's mineral resources. Conditions favorable to the trapping of oil and natural gas are expected to be found where there are beds of evaporites in continental-shelf regions close to the edges of expanding oceans, and much exploration is consequently planned in such regions. Similarly, metal ores are likely to be intruded into continental mountain blocks near zones of plate convergence, where molten minerals have risen from the distintegration of descending oceanic crust.

While the mechanism of the processes in the earth's mantle which power plate tectonics are still a matter for speculation among scientists, the pattern of developments on the surface of the earth can today be displayed in confident detail, a triumph for the defenders of a once-ridiculed idea.

in the laboratory for sufficiently long.

PLASMA, the part of the BLOOD remaining when all CELLS have been removed, and which includes CLOTTING factors. It may be used in resuscitation from SHOCK.

PLASMODIUM, genus of PROTOZOA responsible for MALARIA. Four main types are recognized: *P. falciparum*; *P. vivax*; *P. ovale*, and *P. malariae*, which cause variants of malaria and are endemic in different areas. *P. falciparum* causes cerebral malaria.

PLASTER OF PARIS, or calcium sulfate hemihydrate. See CALCIUM.

PLASTIC EXPLOSIVE, putty-like EXPLOSIVE made by mixing RDX with oil. Convenient and weather-resistant, it is used for demolition.

PLASTICS, materials that can be molded (at least in production) into desired shapes. A few natural plastics are known, e.g., BITUMEN, RESINS and RUBBER, but almost all are man-made, mainly from PETROCHEMICALS, and are available with a vast range of useful properties: hardness, elasticity, transparency, toughness, low density, insulating ability, inertness and corrosion resistance, etc. They are invariably high POLYMERS with carbon skeletons, each molecule being made up of thousands or even millions of atoms. Plastics fall into two classes: thermoplastic and thermosetting. **Thermoplastics** soften or melt reversibly on heating; they include celluloid and other cellulose plastics, LUCITE, NYLON, POLYETHYLENE, STYRENE polymers, VINYL polymers, polyformaldehyde and polycarbonates. **Thermosetting** plastics, although moldable when produced as simple polymers, are converted by heat and pressure, and sometimes by an admixed hardener, to a cross-linked, infusible form. These include bakelite and other phenol resins, EPOXY RESINS, polyesters, SILICONES, urea-formaldehyde and melamine-formaldehyde resins, and some polyurethanes. Most plastics are mixed with stabilizers, fillers, dyes or pigments and plasticizers if needed. There are several fabrication processes: making films by calendering (squeezing between rollers), casting or extrusion, and making objects by compression molding, injection molding (melting and forcing into a cooled mold) and casting. (See also LAMINATES; SYNTHETIC FIBERS.)

PLASTIC SURGERY, the branch of SURGERY devoted to reconstruction or repair of deformity, surgical defect or the results of injury. Using bone, cartilage, tendon, and skin from other parts of the body, or artificial substitutes, function and appearance may in many cases be restored. In skin grafting, the most common procedure, a piece of skin is cut, usually from the thigh, and stitched to the damaged area. Bone and cartilage (usually from the ribs or hips), or sometimes plastic, are used in cosmetic remodeling and facial reconstruction after injury. Congenital defects such as HARELIP and CLEFT PALATE can be treated in infancy. "Face lifting," the cosmetic removal of excess fat and tightening of the skin, is a delicate and often unsuccessful operation, carrying the added risk of infection.

PLASTIDS, variously shaped bodies found in the cytoplasm of plant CELLS, containing CHLOROPHYLL (chloroplasts), other PIGMENTS (chromoplasts) or unpigmented (leucoplasts).

PLATA, Río de la. See RÍO DE LA PLATA.

PLATAEA, Battle of (479 BC), in Boeotia, Greece. The Greek land forces under PAUSANIUS decisively repulsed the invading Persian army led by XERXES' General Mardonius (see PERSIAN WARS).

PLATELET. See BLOOD.

PLATERESQUE, ornate style of Spanish architecture in the early 16th century, showing Italian, Moorish and late Gothic influence in its elaborate decoration of simple forms. Fine examples are Granada cathedral and Seville town hall.

PLATE TECTONICS, Theory of, fundamental theory of modern geology, arising from studies of CONTINENTAL DRIFT, EARTHQUAKE and VOLCANO distributions, and sea-floor spreading, which phenomena it largely explains. The earth's crust is viewed as consisting of a number of semirigid plates in relative motion. Where plates meet, one edge is subducted beneath (forced under) the other: in midocean, this results in OCEAN trenches, deep seismic activity and arcs of volcanic ISLANDS; at continental margins, similar subduction of the oceanic plate results also in OROGENIES. Where lighter continental blocks are forced together, neither edge is subducted and more complex orogeny occurs. Belts of shallow earthquakes define the midocean ridges where new material is emerging from below. (See SEA-FLOOR SPREADING.)

PLATINUM (Pt), soft, silvery-white metal in the PLATINUM GROUP. In addition to the general uses of these metals, platinum is used as a catalyst for the CONTACT PROCESS and (alloyed with rhodium) for the OSTWALD PROCESS. AW 195.1, mp 1772°C, bp 4010°C, sg 21.45 (20°C).

PLATINUM GROUP, the six NOBLE METALS in Group VIII of the PERIODIC TABLE, i.e., RUTHENIUM, RHODIUM, PALLADIUM, OSMIUM, IRIDIUM and PLATINUM (see also TRANSITION ELEMENTS). They are found together in PYROXENE deposits in South Africa and in the copper and NICKEL ores of Canada and the USSR. All are highly inert and corrosion-resistant, though palladium, osmium and platinum dissolve in AQUA REGIA; the others can be dissolved by fused oxidizing alkalis. Palladium dissolves slowly in oxidizing acids. Ruthenium and osmium show chief oxidation states +3, 4, 6 and 8; the other metals seldom exceed +4. All six metals form numerous HALIDES and complex halogen ions, and many other LIGAND complexes, including carbonyls resembling those of iron, cobalt and NICKEL. The platinum group metals are used, usually as ALLOYS with each other, for jewelry, the tips of pen nibs, electrical contacts, THERMOCOUPLES, crucibles, surgical instruments, standard WEIGHTS AND MEASURES, and (finely divided) as catalysts (see CATALYSIS).

PLATO, Greek philosopher (c427–347 BC). A pupil of SOCRATES, c385 BC he founded the ACADEMY, where ARISTOTLE studied. His early dialogues present a portrait of Socrates as destructive arguer, but in the great middle dialogues he develops his own doctrines such as the Theory of Forms (*Republic*), the immortality of the soul (*Phaedo*), knowledge as recollection of the Forms by the soul (*Meno*), virtue as knowledge (*Protagoras*), and attacks hedonism and the idea that "might is right" (*Gorgias*). The *Symposium* and *Phaedrus* sublimate love into a beatific vision of the Forms of the Good and the Beautiful. The late dialogues (*Sophist, Theaetetus, Politicus, Philebus, Parmenides*) are difficult and technical; the *Timaeus* contains cosmological speculation. In the *Republic* Plato posits abstract Forms as the supreme reality. The highest function of the human soul is to achieve the vision of the Form of the Good. Drawing an analogy between the soul and the state, he presents his famous ideal state ruled by philosophers, who correspond to the rational part of the soul. In the late *Laws* Plato develops in detail his ideas of the state. His idealist philosophy, his insistence on order and harmony, his moral fervor and asceticism and his literary genius have made Plato a dominant figure in Western thought.

PLATT, Thomas Collier (1833–1910), US businessman and New York City political boss, a Republican senator in 1881 and 1897–1909. Hoping to weaken Theodore ROOSEVELT's power thereby securing his nomination as vice-president, he lost influence when Roosevelt became president.

PLATT AMENDMENT, a provision forced through Congress and into the Cuban constitution by Senator Orville Platt in 1901. Setting out conditions for US intervention, it virtually made Cuba a US protectorate. It was abrogated in 1934.

PLATTE RIVER, a W tributary of the Missouri R, flowing 310mi E through central Neb. to Plattsmouth.

PLATT NATIONAL PARK, in S Okla. near Sulphur. Established in 1906, it is 912 acres in area. It is known for its mineral and freshwater springs.

PLATTSBURGH, city in NE N.Y., seat of Clinton Co. on Lake Champlain. It is a resort center, with a lumber and paper-making industry. Pop 18 715.

PLATTSBURGH, Battle of (1814), the most important US naval victory of the WAR OF 1812. The US navy destroyed all the British ships on Lake Champlain, and without naval support the British land forces occupying Plattsburgh were forced to retreat to Canada.

PLATYHELMINTHES. See FLATWORMS.

The platypus, or duckbill, now protected, was once hunted for its fur. Among the many features it possesses that are unusual in mammals are the soft-skinned eggs it lays, the nippleless mammary glands in the female, and the poison spur on each hindfoot in the male.

PLATYPUS, or **Duck-billed platypus,** *Ornithorhynchus anatinus*, an amphibious MONOTREME (egg-laying mammal) found in Australia and Tasmania. They have webbed feet and thick fur (equipping them for an aquatic life); a short, thick tail, and a flat, toothless, bill-like mouth used for taking insects and crustaceans off the surface of the water. Like ECHIDNAS, the other monotreme group, they retain many reptilian characters. There is no scrotum; the TESTES are internal. The mammary glands are diffuse and lack distinct teats. Moreover, in the platypus, the right ovary and oviduct are nonfunctional.

PLAUTUS, Titus Maccius (c254–184 BC), Roman writer of comedies, 21 of which have survived. He based them on Greek New Comedy, especially MENANDER, but adapted them to Roman tastes and situations, and added his own brand of lively, bawdy humor. Popular in his time, he influenced SHAKESPEARE and MOLIÈRE among others.

PLAY, a distinctive type of behavior of both adult and juvenile animals, of unknown function and involving the incomplete, ritualized expression of normal adult behavior patterns. Movements are extravagant and exaggerated. Play occurs particularly in carnivores, primates and certain birds.

PLAYA, found in undrained areas in arid regions, a level tract formed of deposits from a temporary lake that has formed owing to flooding or heavy rainfall, and then evaporated. (See also ALKALI FLATS; EVAPORITES.)

PLAYER PIANO, a PIANO with a mechanism for playing automatically, first patented as the Pianola in 1897. A roll of paper is perforated with holes so placed that as it moves, air pumped through them strikes the hammers. Its popularity declined with the rise of the gramophone.

PLAYING CARDS, pieces of card with numerical and pictorial sequences marked on them, used in games of skill and chance. Probably originating in the Orient, they were known in Europe by the 14th century. Developed from the TAROT deck, the modern pack has 52 cards in four *suits* (Clubs, Diamonds, Hearts, Spades). In most card games players attempt to make winning combinations of cards following a particular set of rules. (See BLACKJACK; BRIDGE; CANASTA; PINOCHLE; POKER; RUMMY; WHIST.)

PLEASANT HILL, residential city in W Cal. Pop 24 610.

PLEASANT HILLS, borough in SW Pa., a residential suburb of Pittsburgh. Pop 10 409.

PLEASANTON, city in W Cal, in the Oakland-San Francisco urban complex. It is a center for wine and dairy produce. Pop 18 328.

PLEASANTVILLE, city in E N.J. On an arm of the sea W of Atlantic City, it is a resort and fishing center. Pop 13 778.

PLEASURE PRINCIPLE, a concept of FREUD, the avoidance of PAIN or unpleasantness, the sole influence on the mind before the EGO has developed. In later stages, it is modified by the **reality principle**, which recognizes physical and social constraints.

PLEASURE RIDGE PARK, unincorporated town in N Ky. It is a residential suburb of Louisville. Pop 28 566.

PLEBEIANS, the non-aristocratic classes in ancient Rome. In their continual rivalries with the ruling PATRICIAN aristocracy, they created their own assemblies and officers, and gained full political and civil rights by about 300 BC. (See TRIBUNE.)

PLEBISCITE, in Roman history, a law enacted by the plebeian *comitia*, or assembly of tribes. In modern times a plebiscite is a direct vote of the whole body of citizens on some specific issue (for instance, acceptance of a new constitution).

The Pleiades star cluster, 153 parsecs (about 500 light years) distant, seen here in a long-exposure photograph taken at the Mount Palomar Observatory, California. It shows parts of the surrounding nebula from which the stars are thought to have formed.

PLÉIADE, seven French poets of the 16th century, the chief being RONSARD and DU BELLAY. Named for an ancient Alexandrian school, they aimed to develop French as a literary language, while imitating classical and Italian forms.

PLEIADES, a GALACTIC CLUSTER in the constellation TAURUS. Seven of the stars can be seen by the naked eye, and these are named after the seven daughters of ATLAS. The Pleiades are about 153pc from the sun and are surrounded by a bright NEBULA.

PLEISTOCENE, the earlier epoch of the QUATERNARY, stretching from between about 4 million through 10000 years ago. (See also GEOLOGY; HOLOCENE.)

PLEKHANOV, Georgi Valentinovich (1857–1918), Russian Marxist thinker. Always opposed to political terror, he at first supported LENIN, but after 1903 espoused MENSHEVIK views, holding that the revolution must be supported by the majority of the population.

PLEOMELE, a genus of evergreen shrubs with attractive green or striped elongated leaves. They are often grown as house plants, surviving considerable neglect. Ideally the temperature should not drop below 13°C (55°F), and they should be placed in a bright window, avoiding hot direct sun. Occasional slight drying of the soil does no harm, but it should be kept moist for most of the time. The foliage benefits from misting. Propagation is by shoot tip cuttings or air-layering. Family: Liliaceae.

PLESIOSAURS, extinct marine reptiles of the late TRIASSIC to late CRETACEOUS. They had broad, flattened bodies with a short tail and four turtle-like flippers, long necks and small heads. The flippers were moved with a rowing action, and plesiosaurs probably seized their prey, fish and squid, with a darting movement of the head and neck.

PLESSY v. FERGUSON, important US Supreme Court ruling on segregation in 1896 which interpreted the 14th Amendment as having been fulfilled if segregated accommodations were "separate but equal." This decision was reversed in 1954 when the Supreme Court unanimously ruled against segregation in the case of Brown v. Board of Education. (See INTEGRATION.)

PLEURISY, INFLAMMATION of the pleura, the two thin connective tissue layers covering the outer LUNG surface and the inner CHEST wall. It causes a characteristic chest pain, which may be localized and is made worse by deep breathing and coughing. It may be caused by infection (e.g., PNEUMONIA, TUBERCULOSIS) or TUMORS and inflammatory disease.

PLEXIGLAS. See LUCITE.

PLIMSOLL MARK, a line on the side of a seagoing ship indicating the safe loading limit. Samuel Plimsoll (1824–1898) first secured its compulsory marking on British ships in 1876.

PLINY, name of two Roman authors. **Pliny the Elder** (c23–79 AD) is known for his *Natural History,* a vast compendium of ancient sciences, which though of little scientific merit was popular throughout antiquity and the Middle Ages. He died attempting to help the citizens of POMPEII in the eruption of Vesuvius. **Pliny the Younger** (c61–113 AD), a nephew of Pliny the Elder, was a lawyer, statesman and administrator, primarily known for his elegant *Letters,* which throw much light on the political, economic and social life of the Roman Empire.

PLIOCENE, the final period of the TERTIARY, immediately preceding the QUATERNARY, lasting from about 10 to 4 million years ago. (See also GEOLOGY.)

PLOTINUS (205–270 AD), Greco-Roman philosopher, founder of NEOPLATONISM. Probably born in Egypt, he became a teacher in Rome; his work, the *Enneads,* was edited by his pupil PORPHYRY. His complex philosophical cosmology involves a hierarchy of degrees of being, the highest being the ineffable One or Good which controls the rest, down to the lowest (the physical world), by a process of *emanations.* The human soul reaches its highest state in the mystical contemplation of the One.

PLOVDIV, second-largest city in Bulgaria, 80mi ESE of Sofia. An ancient Thracian city and a Roman provincial capital, it is now an industrial and market center. Pop 262000.

The Blacksmith plover (*Holopterus armatus*), of southern Africa, has a fighting spur on each wing.

PLOVERS, small or medium-sized wading birds of the family Charadriidae. The family contains the LAPWINGS and the true plovers. Fairly leggy birds, most plovers have an olive or brown back, with lighter underparts. Typically, they have a dark band across the belly and a white band on a black head. Plovers feed on insects or crustacea in mud and sand.

PLOW, an implement for tilling the soil, which breaks up the surface crust for sowing and turns under stubble and manure. Essentially it is a horizontal blade (*share*) to cut the furrow, and a projecting *moldboard* to turn the soil over. Plows have been used since the Bronze Age. Roman plows had an iron-shod share with a beam to draw it. Wheels were used in Saxon plows, and developments after 1600 led to the steel plow of the US engineer John DEERE (1837), *disk plows* with revolving concave disks instead of shares and moldboards, and tractor-drawn plows making multiple furrows.

PLUM, trees of the genus *Prunus,* which produce soft-fleshed fruits enclosing a single pit. The European plum (*Prunus domestica*) has been cultivated for 2000 years. Wild species of North American plum include the American plum, Chicksaw plum and Canada plum. Wild species have been crossed with the European plum to make hardy varieties. **Prunes** are plums that have been preserved by drying. Family: Rosaceae.

The Common European plum, *Prunus domestica*, originated in Asia Minor. The flowers, which often appear before the leaves, occur singly or in pairs (1). Longtitudinal section of the flower (2) shows the pistil (a), corolla (b), receptacle (c) and stamens (d). The fruit (3), seen here in longtitudinal section, has a single pit which contains the seed.

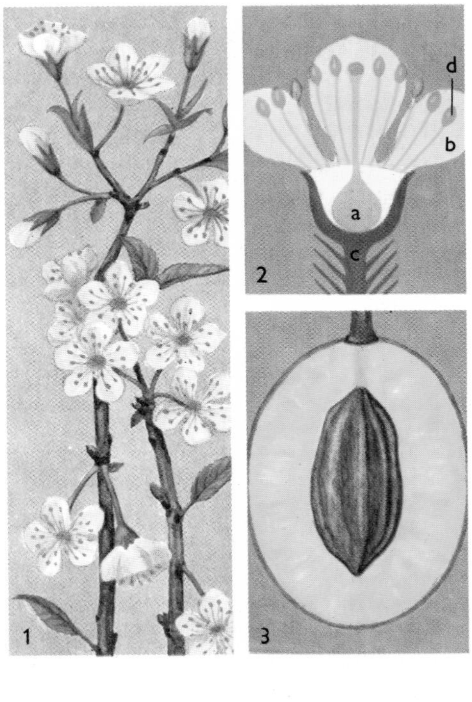

PLUMBING, the arrangement of pipes and related equipment which carries water to and around a building and carries dirty water and SEWAGE away from it. See also PIPES AND PIPELINES; PUBLIC HEALTH.

PLUNKET, Saint Oliver (1629–1681), Irish churchman, primate of all Ireland from 1669. Falsely accused by Titus OATES of planning a foreign invasion of Ireland, he became the last Roman Catholic martyr in England.

PLUTARCH (c46–c120 AD), Greek philosopher and biographer. A native of BOEOTIA, he visited Rome and lectured there, and was for 30 years a priest at DELPHI. His *Parallel Lives* of famous Greeks and Romans, grouped in pairs for comparison, exemplifies the private virtues or vices of great men and has had great influence on European literature, notably on SHAKESPEARE. His *Moralia* is a vast collection of philosophical essays.

PLUTO, the ancient Greek god of the underworld, also known as HADES.

Fortifications at the Cattewater in Plymouth, England, at the mouth of the River Plym. From this historic port in 1620 the Pilgrim Fathers set sail for America. Earlier, in 1588, the British fleet had sailed from Plymouth to attack the Spanish Armada.

PLUTO, the ninth planet of the SOLAR SYSTEM, orbiting the sun at a mean distance of 39.53AU in 248.4 years. Pluto was discovered in 1930 following observations of PERTURBATIONS in NEPTUNE's orbit. Because of its great distance from us, little is known of Pluto's composition, atmosphere, mass (probably less than 0.1 that of the earth) or diameter (probably 5000–6000km). Its orbit is very eccentric: indeed, for a period after 1987 it will be closer to the sun than is Neptune.

PLUTONISM, or **Vulcanism**, the geological theory, often associated with the followers of J. HUTTON, that the rocks of the earth were originally volcanic in origin. In the early 19th century, plutonism rivalled NEPTUNISM for acceptance as the fundamental geological principle.

PLUTONIUM (Pu), the most important TRANSURANIUM ELEMENT, used as fuel for NUCLEAR REACTORS and for the ATOMIC BOMB. It is one of the ACTINIDES and chemically resembles URANIUM. Pu^{239} is produced in BREEDER REACTORS by neutron irradiation of uranium (U^{238}); like U^{235}, it undergoes nuclear FISSION, and was used for the Nagasaki bomb in WWII. mp 640°C, bp 3235°C, sg 19.84 (α; 25°C).

PLYMOUTH, city in Devon county, England, on the Plymouth Sound, from which the MAYFLOWER sailed. It is now an important maritime center and naval base. Pop 239314.

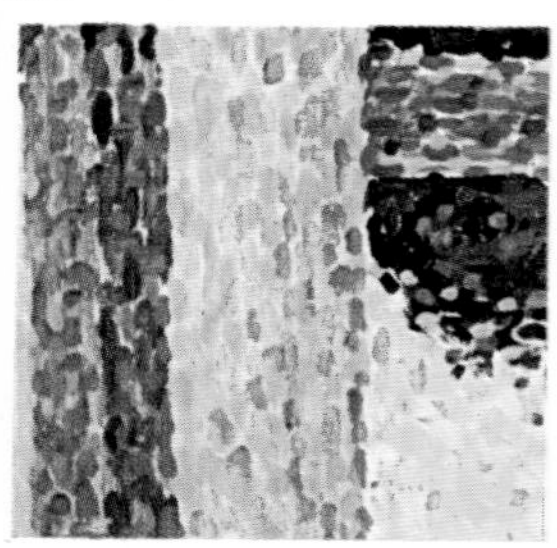

Cypresses by Paul Signac, one of the masters of pointillism. The detail illustrates the technique of this style, in which tiny dots of pure primary colors are juxtaposed to give an overall impression of grades and variants of color and shadow.

PLYMOUTH, town in W Conn. near the Nangatuck R, N of Waterbury. It manufactures metal products and has granite quarries. Pop 10 321.

PLYMOUTH, historic town in SE Mass., seat of Plymouth Co., where the PILGRIM FATHERS landed from the MAYFLOWER in 1620, and established PLYMOUTH COLONY. Its tourist features include PLYMOUTH ROCK and a reconstruction of the original settlement. Pop 18 606.

PLYMOUTH, city in SE Mich., on the Rouge R, 22mi W of Detroit. It has varied industries. Pop 11 758.

PLYMOUTH, village in SE Minn., a suburb of Minneapolis. It manufactures computer systems and metal products. Pop 18 077.

PLYMOUTH COLONY, first English settlement in what is now New England, and the second permanent English settlement in America, founded by the PILGRIM FATHERS in Dec., 1620. In 1691 it was merged with Massachusetts Bay Colony to form Massachusetts. The colony was founded by a group of Puritan Separatists from the Church of England, who were blown off their course to Virginia and agreed in the famous MAYFLOWER COMPACT to form a government where they landed. The settlers included John CARVER and William BRADFORD, the first two governors. Half the colony died during a bitter first winter, but the survivors were helped by the friendly Indian chief MASSASOIT, and by 1624 it was thriving.

PLYMOUTH COMPANY, speculative joint-stock company founded in 1606 by a group of English "merchant adventurers." Its purpose was to colonize the coast of North America and thus increase English wealth and trade. It had exclusive rights to the region between 45°N and 41°N. After the failure of its first and only colony on the Kennebec R in Me. (1607–08), it was reorganized in 1620 as the COUNCIL FOR NEW ENGLAND.

PLYMOUTH ROCK, a granite boulder on the shore at Plymouth, Mass., on which, according to tradition, the PILGRIM FATHERS first set foot in America in 1620. There is no documentary evidence confirming the legend.

PLYWOOD, strong, light wood composite made of layers of VENEER glued with their grain alternately at right angles. Thick plywood may have a central core of sawn lumber. It is made of an odd number of layers, and is termed 3-ply, 5-ply, etc. Being strong in both directions, and almost free from warping and splitting, it is used for construction of all kinds.

PLZEŇ, or **Pilsen,** historic city in Czechoslovakia, 52mi WSW of Prague, famous for Pilsner beer and the Skoda (now Lenin) works producing heavy machinery. It also has lumber and paper industries. Pop 148 032.

PNEUMATIC TOOLS, implements powered by compressed air. This, usually at a PRESSURE of about 6atm (90lb per sq in), is fed into an "air motor," which operates on either a reciprocating-piston or rotary-vane principle.

PNEUMOCONIOSIS, restrictive disease of the LUNGS caused by deposition of dusts in the lung substance, inhaled during years of exposure, often in extractive industries. SILICOSIS, anthracosis and asbestosis are the principal kinds, although aluminum, iron, tin and cotton fiber also cause pneumoconiosis. Characteristic X-RAY changes are seen in the lungs.

PNEUMONIA, INFLAMMATION and consolidation of LUNG tissue. It is usually caused by bacteria (pneumococcus, STAPHYLOCOCCUS, GRAM'S STAIN negative bacilli), but rarely results from pure VIRUS infection (INFLUENZA, MEASLES); other varieties occur if food, secretions or chemicals are aspirated or inhaled. The inflammatory response causes lung tissue to be filled with exudate and PUS, which may center on the bronchi (**bronchopneumonia**) or be restricted to a single lobe (**lobar pneumonia**). Cough with yellow or green sputum (sometimes containing BLOOD); FEVER; malaise, and breathlessness are common. The involvement of the pleural surfaces causes PLEURISY. ANTIBIOTICS and PHYSIOTHERAPY are essential in treatment.

PNEUMOTHORAX, presence of air in the pleural space between the LUNG and the CHEST wall. This may result from trauma, rupture of lung bullae in EMPHYSEMA or in ASTHMA, TUBERCULOSIS, PNEUMOCONIOSIS, CANCER etc., or, in tall thin athletic males, it may occur without obvious cause. Drainage of the air through a tube inserted in the chest wall allows lung re-expansion.

PNOM PENH. See PHNOM PENH.

PO, the longest river in Italy. Rising in the Cottain Alps near the French border, it winds E for 405mi through N Italy to the Adriatic Sea S of Venice. The Po drains almost all N Italy, and helps to make the plain of Lombardy Italy's richest agricultural region.

POCAHONTAS (c1595–1617), daughter of the North American Indian chief POWHATAN, who befriended the settlers at Jamestown, Virginia. According to Captain John SMITH, leader of the colony, Pocahontas saved his life when he had been captured by her father and was about to be executed. In 1614 she was christened, married John ROLFE and went to England, where she died of smallpox.

POCATELLO, city in SE Ida., seat of Bannock Co. It is a livestock and agricultural shipping-point, with phosphate mining and some manufacturing industry. Pop 40 036.

POCHARDS, a name given to most members of the Aythyini, or Diving DUCKS. Most are freshwater species of open lakes and lagoons. With often a sharp distinction between darker upper- and lighter underparts, pochards have dark breasts and heads.

POCKETBOOK PLANT, popular name for house plants of the genus CALCEOLARIA.

POCKET MOUSE, *Perognathus*, a genus of small nocturnal mice with long tails and fur-lined, external cheek-pouches, occurring in open areas throughout North America. They feed on seeds, amassing sizeable stores in their nests. (See also MOUSE.)

POCONO MOUNTAINS, mountain range in NE Pa., c2 000ft high, part of the Appalachian system and a popular resort area.

PODGORNY, Nikolai Viktorovich (1903–), Russian statesman and Communist Party leader, chairman of the Presidium of the Supreme Soviet (i.e., head of state) since 1965. He has made his name as an administrator.

PODIATRY, or **chiropody**, care of the FEET, concerned with the nails, CORNS AND CALLUSES, bunions and toe deformities. Care of the SKIN of the feet is especially important in the elderly and in diabetics.

PODOCARPUS, a genus of evergreen trees popular in outdoor gardens. Trees 1–1.5m (3.3–4.9ft) tall make attractive house plants. They grow best at temperatures between 13°C and 21°C (55°F to 70°F) and tolerate a wide range of light, from sunny east or west windows to bright north windows. The soil should be kept evenly moist, avoiding extremes of dryness, and the foliage should be misted often. Propagation is by shoot cuttings of half-ripened wood.

PODZOL or **podsol**, SOIL found in moist, cool climates under coniferous FORESTS, TUNDRA, etc. Podzol is unsuitable for agricultural purposes, having little HUMUS.

POE, Edgar Allan (1809–1849), US short-story writer, poet and critic, famous for his tales of mystery and the macabre, such as *The Murders in the Rue Morgue* (1841) and *The Purloined Letter* (1844), prototypes of the detective story, and *The Fall of the House of Usher* (1839). His poems, including "The Raven" (1845) and "Annabel Lee" (1849), are musical and striking in imagery. Poe discussed beauty and form in art in *The Philosophy of Composition* (1846), which influenced BAUDELAIRE and the French Symbolists.

POET LAUREATE, royal appointment held by a British poet. Traditionally he writes poems for state occasions, but the title is now largely honorific. DRYDEN first had the title in 1668, but the custom started when Ben JONSON received a royal pension in 1616. The present Laureate is Sir John BETJEMAN.

POETRY, meaningful arrangement of words into an imaginative or emotional discourse, always with a strong rhythmic pattern. The language, seeking to evoke image and idea, uses IMAGERY and METAPHORS. RHYME or alliteration may also be important elements. The length of poems may vary from brief LYRIC POETRY to long narrative poems such as COLERIDGE's *Ancient Mariner* or EPIC poetry with the length and scope of a novel, such as BYRON's *Don Juan*. The poet may choose BLANK VERSE or any simple or complex rhyme scheme as his medium. Traditional forms also exist; BALLADS are often rhymed in QUATRAINS. The poet has a number of devices available that would be obtrusive or pretentious in prose, such as alliteration or onomatopoeia. The kind of forms and devices used most often or most successfully in poetry depends on the language of the poet. Since the sense of poetry is so intimately tied to its sound it is extremely difficult to translate. The heightening of thought as well as of language, however, and the intensifying and concentration of emotion and observation have meant that the great poets of each country and time have become in some measure accessible to the world as a whole. In most cultures poetry, linked by its rhythmic elements to music and dance, develops before prose literature; the poetic form aids oral transmission. Eventually it is written down; a "higher" form then develops, poetry destined largely for the printed page, although a vital oral tradition may accompany it. Even such written poetry, however, must remain to some extent "musical"; this and its great association with the THEATER still remind one of poetry's origins. (See also articles on individual poets.)

POGONOPHORA, or **beardworms,** a complete phylum of over 100 species of gutless worm-like marine animals unclassified as such before 1950. They are almost exclusively sessile, deep-sea animals, which live in chitinous tubes probably fixed upright on the sea bottom.

POGROM, term (from the Russian for devastation or riot) for the officially condoned mob attacks on Jewish communities in Russia between 1881 and 1921. More generally, it is used to describe any massacre of a defenceless minority, particularly JEWS, such as those organized by the NAZIS. The pogroms were a major factor in the large-scale emigration of European Jews to the US.

POINCARÉ, Jules Henri (1854–1912), French mathematician, cosmologist and scientific philosopher, best known for his many contributions to pure and applied MATHEMATICS and celestial mechanics.

POINCARÉ, Raymond Nicholas Landry (1860–1934), French statesman, three times premier (1912, 1922–24, 1926–29) and president 1913–20. A strongly nationalist conservative, he ordered the French occupation of the RUHR (1923). His financial policies succeeded in stabilizing the currency (1928).

POINCIANA, a small genus of ornamental tropical and subtropical trees and shrubs that have bright red or orange flowers. The Barbados pride (*Poinciana pulcherrima*) and the Bird-of-paradise bush (*P. gilliesii*) are widely cultivated in warm climates. Family: Leguminosae.

POINSETT, Joel Roberts (1779–1851), US diplomat and statesman. He was minister to Mexico, 1925–29, introduced the POINSETTIA in the US and was VAN BUREN's secretary of war, 1837–41.

POINSETTIA, *Euphorbia pulcherrima*, a plant native to Mexico and Central America. In the wild they grow up to 3m (10ft) high; they are extensively cultivated as smaller plants for use as indoor ornamentals. The flowers are small, but the large red, yellow or white bracts (modified leaves) are very attractive. Poinsettias are popular house plants ideally suited to average house temperatures and sunny positions. The soil should be kept evenly moist. Propagation is by shoot tip cuttings taken in the spring.

POINT, in GEOMETRY, entity defined as having none of the DIMENSIONS length, breadth or depth. A point may also be defined as the INTERSECTION of two straight LINES or of a straight line and a PLANE.

POINT SET. See SET THEORY.

POINT BARROW. See BARROW, POINT.

POINTE-A-PITRE, city in SW Grande-Terre, Guadaloupe. It is the principal port of Guadaloupe and commercial center for coffee, sugar, rum and bananas. Pop 29 757.

POINTE-AUX-TREMBLES, city in Quebec province, Canada, on the E shore of Montreal Island on the St. Lawrence R. It manufactures paper. Pop 35 567.

POINTE-CLAIRE, city in Quebec province, Canada, on the S shore of Montreal Island. It is a residential and industrial suburb of Montreal. Pop 27 303.

POINTE-GATINEAU, town in Quebec province, Canada, at the confluence of the Ottawa and Gatineau rivers. It is a N suburb of Ottowa. Pop 15 607.

POINTER, sporting or gun dog bred in England. Standing 23–26in high at the shoulder, Pointers have a smooth coat, usually white with black or reddish-brown markings, and a long muzzle. Scenting out their quarry, they stiffen and point towards it.

POINT FOUR PROGRAM, technical assistance plan for underdeveloped nations proposed by President Harry TRUMAN in his Inaugural Address of Jan., 1949, so named because it was the fourth point in the speech. Launched in 1950 and now merged with other aid programs, it provided technical, educational and health assistance, and aimed to encourage private investment and increase US influence.

POINTILLISM, painting technique, in which tiny paint dots of color are juxtaposed on the canvas to build up the form. The dots of color are additively mixed by the eye of the observer. This method was developed by the impressionist painters, SEURAT and SIGNAC, to achieve more luminosity and greater control of tone.

POINT PELEE NATIONAL PARK, Canadian bird and wildlife sanctuary on W Lake Eyrie, S Ontario.

POINT PLEASANT, resort and residential borough in E N.J. It is in a truck farming area. Pop 15 968.

POINT REYES NATIONAL SEASHORE, peninsular in W Cal., at the head of Tomales Bay, comprising sand dunes, hills and forests. It was possibly visited by Sir Frances DRAKE in 1579.

POISON GAS. See CHEMICAL AND BIOLOGICAL WARFARE.

POISON IVY, POISON OAK, and POISON SUMAC, vines or shrubs of the genus *Rhus* native to North America. They contain a poisonous agent, urushiol, that causes itching or blisters, by contact or indirectly through contaminated clothes. Immediate washing with an alkaline soap may prevent the irritation. Family: Anacardiaceae.

POISONING, the taking, via ingestion or other routes, of substances which are liable to produce illness or DEATH. Poisoning may be accidental, homicidal, suicidal or as a suicidal gesture. DRUGS and medications are often involved, either taken by children in ignorance of their nature from accessible places, or by adults in suicide or attempted suicide. Easily available drugs such as ASPIRIN, paracetamol and mild SEDATIVES are often taken, though in serious suicidal attempts, BARBITURATES and ANTI-DEPRESSANTS are more common. Chemicals, such as disinfectants and weedkillers, cosmetics and paints are frequently swallowed as drinks by children, while poisonous berries may appear attractive. Poisoning by domestic gas or carbon monoxide has been used for suicide and homicide. Heavy metals (see LEAD POISONING, MERCURY POISONING, ARSENIC), INSECTICIDES and CYANIDES are common industrial poisons as well as being a risk in the community. Poisons may act by damaging body structures (e.g., weedkillers); preventing OXYGEN uptake by HEMOGLOBIN (carbon monoxide); acting on the NERVOUS SYSTEM (heavy metals); interfering with essential ENZYMES (cyanides, insecticides); with HEART action (antidepressants), or with the control of RESPIRATION (barbiturates). In some cases, antidotes are available which, if used early, can minimize poisoning, but in most cases, life is supported until the poison is eliminated.

POITIERS, Battle of, famous English victory in the HUNDRED YEARS' WAR, fought in 1356, near Poitiers in W central France. The English, led by EDWARD THE BLACK PRINCE, were outnumbered four to one by their French opponents, but won a brilliant victory over JOHN II and PHILIP THE BOLD.

POKER, a card game whose earliest forms date back to c1520 in Europe, developing into such bet-and-bluff games as *brag* in England, *pochen* ("bluff") in Germany and *poque* in France. *Poque* was taken by the French to America c1800, where it was developed and reexported to Europe as poker, c1870. It is now one of the world's top three card games. There are many variations, but basically five or seven cards are dealt and each player tries to make up a winning combination, on which he bets and bluffs in a contest of skill and nerves against the unknown combinations of his opponents.

POLAND, republic in central Europe on the Baltic Sea, lying between East Germany and the USSR and N of Czechoslovakia.

Land. Poland is very flat with about 90% of it under 1 000ft, though in the S are the peaks of the Silesian and Carpathian Mountains, forming a natural barrier between Poland and Czechoslovakia. The main rivers, the Vistula (which flows through Warsaw and Kraków), the Oder, Neisse, Bug and Warta, are important for transportation to the large Baltic ports. The principal cities are Warsaw, Lodz, Kraków, Wroclaw, Poznan and Gdánsk (Danzig). The climate is moderate in summer with temperatures averaging about 60°F. Winters are generally cold (32°F–24°F). About 50% of Poland comprises arable land and 25% forests.

People. Most of the population are of Polish descent. After WWI Poland had sizeable minorities of Ukrainians, Jews and Belorussians, comprising over 30% of its people. By the mid-1960s there were only small minority groups, and an estimated 10 million Poles living abroad.

Economy. Poland was an agricultural country until WWII since when it has been rapidly industrialized. State agricultural collectivization was resisted by the peasants and there are now very few state farms. The chief products are wheat, rye, barley, oats, potatoes and sugar beet. Industry is largely state-owned. Poland is a big producer of coal, zinc, steel, petroleum and iron-ore. Manufactures include machinery, textiles, cement and chemicals. There is a sizeable shipbuilding industry at Gdánsk. The principal exports are coal, ships, metal products and processed meat.

History. Poland's recorded history dates back to the 10th century, when Slavic tribes first united. Later Germans settled in Poland, particularly on the Baltic coast. After Swedish invasions in the 17th century, Poland was divided between Austria, Prussia and Russia in 1772. This lasted until 1918. In 1919 the Treaty of VERSAILLES established a new Poland, formed the POLISH CORRIDOR and made GDÁNSK a free city. In 1939 Germany invaded Poland, occupying the W region. The USSR occupied the E. The population was decimated by massacre, starvation or

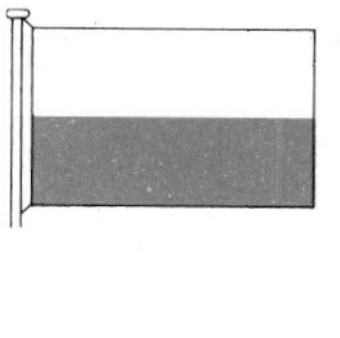

Official name: Polish People's Republic
Capital: Warsaw
Area: 120 633sq mi
Population: 3 202 000
Language: Polish
Religion: Roman Catholic
Monetary unit(s): 1 Zloty = 100 groszy

Polar Regions

Great contrasts and neglected importance

> Anything written on the Arctic comes out as a strange mixture of realism and fantasy.
>
> George W. Rogers

Whether one contemplates the mysterious pingos of Tuktoyaktuk in the Northwest Territories—those enormous, natural, earthcovered 200ft domes of ice (one is employed as the village walk-round freezer)—or, in Antarctica, the spectacular "dry valleys," surrounded by thousands of years of accumulated ice, Professor Rogers' comment does indeed seem an understatement.

There is a common tendency to regard the two polar regions as much alike, both being characterized by abundant cold and snow. In fact, though their similarities are numerous, their differences are impressive.

The Arctic (within the 50°F (10°C) July isotherm which follows the northern treeline) is mostly ocean, with the adjacent parts of the northern USSR, Norway, Iceland, Greenland and North America. The Antarctic is a continent, fifth largest and the world's tallest, bounded by sea. Its average height of 7 000ft is more than twice that of the next in altitude, Asia. Indeed, one may perceive this contrast in the two polar regions by imagining a saucer laid right way up into the upper axis of a globe of the earth while a similar saucer would be set so that its bottom protruded below the lower axis.

Antarctica contains more than 90% of the world's ice. Its depth ranges down to 14 000ft, while Arctic Ocean ice is an average 5–8ft thick. The range of temperatures is distinctive. The lowest temperature ever recorded on the earth was −126.9°F (−88.3°C) on August 24, 1960, at Vostok, the Soviet Antarctic station. The lowest Arctic temperature, recorded in NE Siberia, was −96°F (−71.1°C). The mean temperature of the North Pole in August is just about freezing point. Month for month, for comparable seasons, Antarctica is 30°F to 40°F colder than similar latitudes in the Arctic.

If the Arctic ice were to melt it would have relatively little effect on the level of the earth's oceans, though this would drastically affect the climate. Were all the Antarctic ice to melt, the oceans would rise from 150–200ft, thus inundating most of the world's great cities. Indeed, it probably will sometime melt, since it has not always been there. The Antarctic is the only continent which has never been a permanent home to man, while the Arctic regions are his most recently settled home.

The political and military significance of the Arctic becomes apparent if one looks down on a globe of the earth, with the North Pole at the center of the N hemisphere. It will be seen that most of the earth's land regions are in view. Ninety percent of all the earth's people live north of the equator; 43 of the world's largest 50 cities lie between the Arctic Circle and the Tropic of Cancer, where most oceanic traffic also occurs.

Lenin was the first national leader to understand the political and military significance of intensive research and exploration of the Arctic (although Lincoln's secretary of state William Seward wanted to buy Greenland and Iceland, and did buy Alaska).

Only as WWII approached did interest awaken in the US and Canada. So impressed was the WWII US Air Force commander, General Arnold, that he ventured the opinion that the strategic center of World War III would be the North Pole. One result was the construction after the war of the DEW line (Distant Early Warning) across upper North America to watch for Soviet air strikes. (The E–W distance between Moscow and San Francisco is 15 500mi, over the Arctic only 5000mi.) With the rapid advancement of radar technology the several DEW line stations were replaced by three powerful BMEWS (Ballistic Missile Early Warning System) stations. Also after WWII, the US and Canada began the semipermanent placement of research stations on floating ice islands (the USSR had first occupied such an island in 1937). While most Arctic ice is no more than 8ft thick, ice islands may be 75–100ft thick; they are actually the calvings of glaciers from the west coast of Ellesmere Island. As they circulate about the Antarctic guided by winds and currents they gradually melt, but may last for a century or more. These research stations have provided a vast amount of new information and experience, even including the problem of establishing the legal jurisdiction for a murder that took place on a US-occupied floating island. It is expected that in the future the US will place an immobile ship to float with the Arctic ice.

While the Arctic was becoming the focus of intensified military interest, the Antarctic may be said to have been contributing to détente or, to use the term of the time, peaceful coexistence. The US and USSR had conducted seemingly fruitless negotiations over the control of nuclear weapons for several years in the 1950s at Geneva. This experience and the successes of the International Geophysical Year (1957–58), led to the US proposal and the successful negotiation of the 12-nation Antarctic Treaty of 1959. A seminal document, the treaty was signed by the nations that historically had claimed Antarctic territories (several claims overlapped; the US and one other signatory nation had never made Antarctic claims). Its most significant provisions determined that there would be a 30-year moratorium on all territorial claims, that all national efforts would be devoted to research with no military presence, that free inspection and personnel exchange would take place, that flora and fauna would be protected, and that there would be no nuclear explosions or dumping of atomic wastes. Many now view this treaty, little noticed at the time, as the beginning of the end of the Cold War. Its signing also came shortly after the launching of Sputnik I and the treaty quite soon became a model for the entirely new realm of international space law which needed to be developed. There followed the nuclear and space treaties of the 1960s and 1970s.

It is common knowledge that the polar regions have a strong influence on weather and climate but despite more than three decades of research, the heat and water budgets of the polar regions are little understood. Only in 1957 was it determined that Antarctica held more ice than previously thought. Even now we are only nearing the final stages of mapping the entire continent.

Antarctic coal was discovered in 1928. Recently considerable evidence has been put forward to support the theory that Antarctica formed part of a supercontinent, Gondwanaland, which included all the present S-hemisphere continents before it drifted apart 125–75 million years ago in the late Mesozoic era. The theory of plate tectonics (the continuous moving of the earth's subsurface in the form of vast plates 60–90mi thick) is supported by finding similar plant and animal fossils on Antarctica and on the other continents of the S hemisphere, life which could not have survived transport by sea water. Antarctica has both saline lakes and steaming volcanoes, notably Mt Erebus, in the daily view of a major US station at McMurdo. It is thought that it was a land of forests and swamps 250 million years ago, and that the present stage of ice and glaciers began 20 million years ago. Now the mighty Beardmore glacier flows from the South Pole to the sea, and that portion of it that extends out over the sea before calving, the Ross Ice Shelf, is four-fifths the size of Texas.

Our rapidly growing knowledge of climatic change can now identify some change within millennia, indeed within centuries or less. The cultural, social, economic and political consequences of these changes can be imposing. It was recently suggested by a major foreign policy study group that most nations' foreign

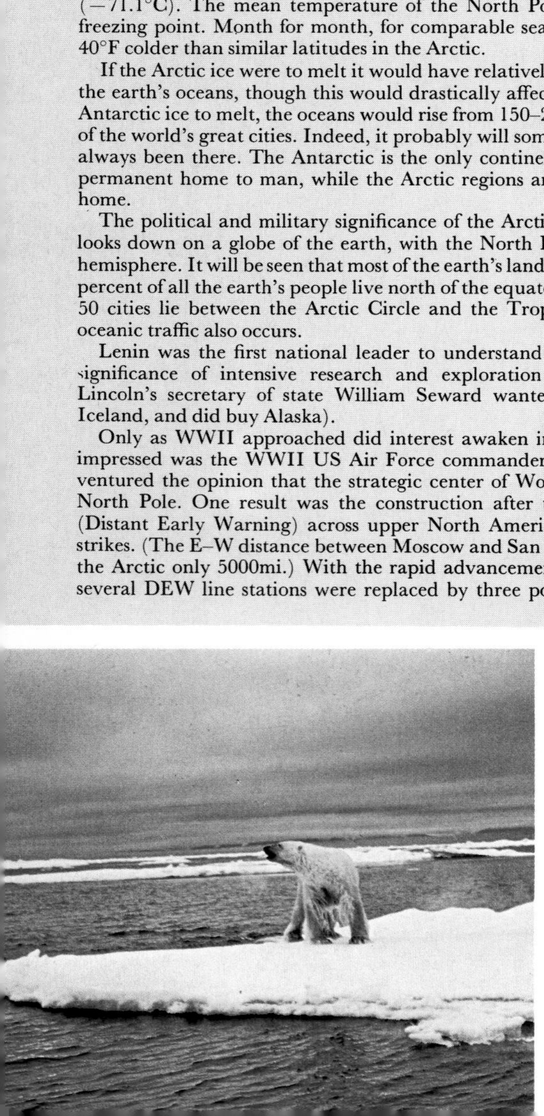

Polar bears are strong swimmers; here a large bear, between swims, rests on an Arctic ice floe.

imprisonment in concentration camps like AUSCHWITZ. The Germans were expelled in 1945 and a provisional government was set up under Soviet auspices. The communists dominated the 1947 elections, and the Russian ROKOSSOVSKY was made minister of defence (1949). The 1952 constitution was modeled on Russian lines. After STALIN's death, opposition to Soviet control led to widespread rioting in 1956, and GOMULKA became leader of the anti-Soviet revolt. He freed Cardinal WYSZYNSKI, and for several years there was considerable freedom in Poland. But by the early 1960s Gomulka was following Russian policies. In 1970 Edward GIEREK replaced Gomulka, and instituted many reforms and controled inflation. In 1972 Germany and Poland ratified the Oder-Neisse line as Poland's W boundary.

POLAR BEAR, *Thalarctos maritimus*, the most carnivorous of the BEARS. Essentially an aquatic and polar animal, rarely found south of 70°N, it can swim strongly and is also agile on land. It hunts seals, whale calves, fishes, and, on land, arctic foxes and even lemmings. A large bear, up to 750kg (1 650lb), it is well adapted to withstand cold conditions.

POLAR COORDINATES. See ANALYTIC GEOMETRY.

POLARIMETRY, measurement of OPTICAL ACTIVITY by means of a polarimeter or polariscope, an instrument having two NICOL PRISMS, one fixed (the polarizer) and one rotatable (the analyzer), with the sample between them (see POLARIZED LIGHT). It is used in chemical ANALYSIS (notably for measuring sugar concentrations) and to study molecular configurations. The polariscope is also used to study strain (see MATERIALS, STRENGTH OF) in materials showing DOUBLE REFRACTION.

policies, painfully developed over decades, would become irrelevant were the earth's mean temperature to drop but three degrees.

Beginning 1200 years ago, a dramatic change came to the prairie people of what is now the US. As Arctic air expanded and warm gulf winds decreased, a 200-year drought got under way. Tall grass became short grass, bison replaced deer as a staple food, forests disappeared and villages east of the Rockies were abandoned. The drought persisted until about 1400, when the Arctic warmed. Two hundred years later, and until our present century, the Arctic cooled again. Europe was colder, sea ice more prominent, there was famine in Iceland. But early in the 20th century temperatures began to rise. The normal midsummer frost in the middle of America ceased to be. Some research suggests we have experienced an anomaly of warmth. Knowing that a glacial period can dissipate within a century, some scientists are now investigating their theory that we may be beginning a new period of glaciation to be fully developed within a century. Since the time of WWII polar air has been more influential in middle latitudes, as in the periods 1200–1400 and 1600–1900. In the past 30 years, the mean temperature of the earth has declined as much as it rose in the previous 50 years. The growing season in Britain is now reduced by a fortnight. Thousands of square miles NW of Moscow have experienced repeated drought. The shifting monsoons have had devastating effects on the people of the Sahel.

How delicate and susceptible to man's manipulations are these crucial balances? One of America's leading climate and ice scientists suggested several years ago that with a 40-year-old DC3 airplane and a few tons of coal dust he could in three days, by flying predetermined patterns over a particular Arctic location and releasing the dust (which would contain rather than reflect solar heat) trigger the melting of the entire Arctic ice cap, some four million square miles. One consequence predicted was the rapid conversion to a desert of the triangle bounded by Boston, Cleveland, and Washington, D.C.

It is everyone's inclination to complain about or commend today's, or the hour's, weather. Weather is ever-present in our attention, but we generally perceive weather and climate as beyond our ken to do anything about. Mark Twain's plaint, "Everyone talks about the weather, but no one does anything about it," may be subject to re-examination by the 21st century.

Apart from coal, a variety of mineral deposits are known in the Antarctic. Their accessibility and economic value may now seem distinct, but the 12 signatory nations of the Antarctic Treaty are already holding secret meetings to determine their ultimate disposition. The economic role of the Arctic is today of greater, and rapidly increasing importance. The Arctic is generally mineral rich. The USSR produces nearly as much gold in the sub-Arctic as is produced in South Africa. Quebec iron ore registers 41%–61% on a dry basis, and Baffin Island ore, not yet mined, is a rare 67% pure. Coal has long been mined in Greenland and Spitzbergen and exists on half the Arctic islands. Other deposits being mined include nickelferrous ore, copper, lead, zinc, tungsten, uranium, platinum, diamonds and tin. Should these minerals near depletion in middle latitudes, their Arctic and sub-Arctic warehouses will become ever more attractive.

For North America, oil is the latest important Arctic discovery. By 1890 oil was known to exist on the North Slope of Alaska (the broad plain lying between Brooks Range and the Arctic Ocean), and the US Navy staked out its petroleum reserves in 1923. It was in 1968 that the first major commercial oil strike occurred on the North Slope. In less than a decade this has changed the economic, social and cultural life of Alaska and brought about the largest private engineering and construction project in the history of man, the Alaska pipeline.

The economics of the pipeline ($7.7 billion invested before one dollar of income can be realized) required that it be built fast, in 36 months. Construction of the 798-mile pipeline, which runs from its gathering pipes on the North Slope to the south-coast ice-free port of Valdez, first required a haul road where no road had ever existed. It is a gravel pad, 4–40ft deep, designed to protect the permafrost beneath. A parallel pad carries the pipeline where it must be above ground, sections of the hot oil line are externally refrigerated so as to prevent the melting of the surrounding permafrost. The pipe itself is the largest ever produced, each section being 48in in diameter and 60ft long. The line crosses seven geological faults and is designed, above ground at these locations, to move fully loaded with oil as much as 22ft horizontally and 8ft vertically, and to function safely in an earthquake of up to 7.2 on the Richter scale.

An icebreaker plowing its way through pack-ice in the Antarctic.

In places the pipeline is raised to accommodate the migration of caribou and other wildlife. In others, it detours known nestings of rare birds or a previously unobserved spawning stream only two feet wide. Probably no major construction project has been as sensitive to environmental quality as has the Alaska pipeline. However, though the original plan called for dismantling the pipeline, gravel pad and haul road to restore the tundra to its native state when all the oil is extracted in some 40 years, this now seems unlikely.

Some two years after the first flow of oil, scheduled for the third quarter of 1977, great quantities of gas will follow, probably by a similar route. Oil has recently been discovered in the far northern Canadian archipelago. Extensive discussions are under way considering a new pipeline from the mouth of the Mackenzie R, south to connect with existing pipelines in Alberta. There are also tentative plans to connect the Alaskan North Slope fields with the Mackenzie pipeline. Additional oil exploration is taking place in the Beaufort Sea, north of the North Slope, and will soon begin in the Alaskan Gulf.

Renewable resources are abundant in the Arctic. Alaska provides one-seventh of the fish consumed in the US and her waters are heavily (Alaskans believe excessively) fished by Japan and the USSR. Such intensive harvesting long ago ended whaling in these waters and threatens extinction of whales in Antarctica. The most valuable renewable resource are the boreal forests. The USSR has the world's greatest timber resources, which lie mainly in the Arctic territories; Canada ranks third in forest resources. Hunting and fur-trapping are significant to the native population. One Canadian island settlement of 40 enjoys an annual income averaging $35000 each by trapping the white fox.

There is a little-known project in Alaska to domesticate the musk-ox (a member of the sheep family). The hair of the musk-ox, known as kiviut, is half the diameter and twice the length of angora fiber. It is available only to the native population and a cottage industry has been established with the weaving of scarves and exquisite dresses weighing only an ounce or two. Young shepherds are trained to follow the musk-ox herd. A continuing problem for this locally significant industry is the failure of the US Department of Agriculture to declare the musk-ox a domestic, and thus a protected, animal.

Space exploration demands a high order of courage, but it is hugely expensive and depends on the reliability of high technology. It is strange that the polar regions remain so remote and relatively unimportant in the thought of most of mankind, for their exploration has also exacted supreme acts of courage. More important, the polar regions touch everyone's life every day and may hold in their secret places the key to the future course of civilizations. It seems likely that we shall come to want to know, and understand, these regions better than we do now.

POLARIS (Alpha Ursae Minoris), a CEPHEID VARIABLE star in the LITTLE DIPPER. Because of its close proximity to the N celestial pole (see CELESTIAL SPHERE), Polaris is also known as the Polestar or North Star, and has been used in navigation for centuries: owing to PRECESSION, Polaris is moving away from the N celestial pole.

POLARIS MISSILE, two-stage, solid-propellant guided MISSILE. It is 31ft long, has a 2875mi range and attains 7800mph. Developed from 1957, it is designed to be armed with a nuclear warhead and to be fired underwater from nuclear-powered submarines (see *illustr.*, p810). (See also ROCKET.)

POLARIZED LIGHT, LIGHT in which the orientation of the wave vibrations displays a definite pattern. In ordinary unpolarized light the wave vibrations (which occur at right-angles to the direction in which the radiation is propagated) are distributed randomly about the axis of propagation. In *plane-polarized light* (produced in reflection from a DIELECTRIC such as glass or by transmission through a NICOL PRISM or polarizing filter), the vibrations all occur in a single plane. Polaroid filters work by subtracting the components of light orientated in a particular plane; two filters in sequence with their transmission planes crossed transmit no light. In *elliptically polarized light* (produced when plane-polarized light is reflected from a polished metallic surface) and *circularly polarized light* (produced on transmission through certain CRYSTALS exhibiting double refraction), the electric vector of the radiation at any point describes an ellipse or a circle. Much of the light around us—that of the blue sky, or reflected from lakes, walls and highways—is partially polarized. Polarizing sunglasses reduce glare by eliminating the light polarized by reflection from horizontal surfaces. Polariscopes employing two polarizing filters have proved to be valuable tools in organic chemistry (see POLARIMETRY).

POLAROGRAPHY, chemical ANALYSIS, particularly for metals or organic groups, by measuring the saturation current and threshold voltage (see ELECTRICITY) for ELECTROLYSIS of a solution of the substance.

POLAROID LAND CAMERA, photographic CAMERA announced by LAND in 1947 which produces a finished print only seconds after exposure. The optical system is similar to that of other cameras but the film pack used contains positive paper and developing reagent as well as negative film. On advancing the film after exposure, it is pressed against the paper (which is not light-sensitive) and the contents of a reagent pod are spread between them. A positive print formed by a diffusion process on the paper can be stripped off seconds later.

POLAR REGIONS. See ANTARCTICA; ARCTIC REGIONS.

1. Propeller
2. Rudder
3. Rear diving plane
4. Condenser
5. Air purifier
6. Turbine
7. Rear escape hatch
8. Compressor
9. Carbon dioxide dispenser
10. Reactor
11. Steam line
12. Boiler
13. Gyroscope
14. Guided missile control room
15. Missile tubes
16. Snorkel

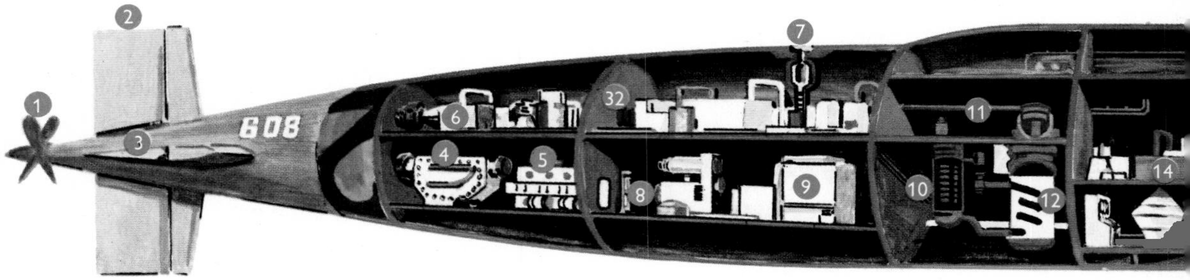

Cutaway drawing of a Polaris submarine, the *Ethan Allen.* Such vessels play a key role in modern military strategic planning. Their missiles can hit any place on earth.

POLDERS, name given in the Netherlands to areas of agricultural land reclaimed by constructing dikes and canals and draining swamps, lakes or shallows. Much of the land around IJSSELMEER consists of polders below sea level.

POLE. See NORTH POLE; SOUTH POLE.

POLECATS, members of the WEASEL family, best known for the pungent odor secreted by their anal glands. With thick, yellowish underfur and black or black-tipped guard hairs, they are lithe and loose-limbed giving an amazing impression of fluidity. A domestic strain used for flushing rabbits from burrows is the FERRET.

POLESTAR. See POLARIS.

POLE VAULT. See TRACK AND FIELD.

POLICE, civil body, part of the EXECUTIVE, charged with the maintenance of public order and the protection of persons and property from unlawful acts. While most civilizations have had some kind of law enforcement agency, most modern forces are descended from the Metropolitan Police established in London by Sir Robert PEEL in 1829; in the US, Boston introduced a similar force in 1838, and New York City soon afterwards. Today the US police force is made up of around 40 000 separate forces, consisting of local, district, county and state police and the sheriffs and deputies of around 35 000 towns and villages. There are also federal police agencies such as the FBI, the Bureau of Narcotics and Dangerous Drugs, the Border Patrol and the Internal Revenue Service, each responsible to its own civil governing authority. Uniformed police are largely responsible for the maintenance of public order, regulating traffic, highways and crowds, patrolling the streets and arresting lawbreakers in the course of these duties; in many countries they are also responsible for helping strangers, tracing runaway children and many other duties not involving crime. With the increasing complexity and sophistication of crime, however, most forces have introduced "plainclothes" branches, some specially to deal with homicide, robbery and burglary, vice and crime involving fraud, narcotics, computer fraud and fine art thefts, and forgery. There are also specialized services such as forensic science laboratories, information and statistics services. Police powers are in most countries strictly circumscribed by law and constitution. In the US and Great Britain they are obliged to inform an arrested person of his rights.

POLICE POWER, in US law, the inherent power of the state to regulate personal and property rights in the public interest. Although not provided for in the Constitution, the courts have held that it does not violate the 14th Amendment.

POLIOMYELITIS, or **infantile paralysis,** VIRAL DISEASE causing muscle PARALYSIS as a result of direct damage to motor nerve cells in the SPINAL CORD. The virus usually enters by the mouth or GASTROINTESTINAL TRACT and causes a mild feverish illness, after which PARESIS or paralysis begins, often affecting mainly those muscles that have been most used in preceding days. Treatment is with bed rest and avoidance or treatment of complications: contracture; bed sores; venous THROMBOSIS; secondary infection; MYOCARDITIS; respiratory failure, and swallowing difficulties. Current polio vaccine is a live attenuated strain taken by mouth which colonizes the gut and induces IMMUNITY. Poliomyelitis VACCINATION has been one of the most successful developments in preventive medicine.

POLISH, one of the W group of the Slavic languages. It is the official and literary language of Poland where it is spoken by more than 30 million people. In the US it is the language of over three million. Modern literary Polish, dating from the 16th century, was originally based on dialects in the vicinity of Poznań.

POLISH CORRIDOR, strip of Polish land about 25mi–65mi wide and 90mi long. Formerly German, it was granted to Poland in 1919 to give her access to the Baltic Sea. The predominantly German port of Danzig (now GDÁNSK) adjoining the Corridor was declared a free city. The separation of East Prussia from the rest of Germany by the Corridor precipitated the German invasion of Poland (1939).

POLISHING. See GRINDING AND POLISHING.

POLISH NATIONAL CATHOLIC CHURCH OF AMERICA, an OLD CATHOLIC church founded by immigrant US Polish Catholics in 1897. Its first synod was held in Scranton, Pa., in 1904, and the first bishop, Father Francis Hodur, was consecrated in 1907. There are now four bishops in the US and some 350 000 members.

POLITBURO, in the USSR, permanent secretariat of top political officials, first formed in 1917, which dominates the Central Committee of the Soviet Communist Party. It is the chief policy-making and governing body of the Communist Party and to a large extent of the USSR. It has about 11 full and nine alternative members. (See also PRESIDIUM; SUPREME SOVIET.)

POLITIAN. See POLIZIANO, ANGELO.

POLITICAL CONVENTION. See CONVENTION.

POLITICAL ECONOMY, a social science, equivalent to modern ECONOMICS, concerned with how a state raises, increases and uses its revenues. The study evolved with the 17th-century rise of MERCANTILISM and was developed by Adam SMITH, David RICARDO and John Stuart MILL, whose *Principles of Political Economy* (1848) is a classic statement. The term had fallen out of use by the 20th century.

POLITICAL PARTY, body or organization which puts forward candidates for public office and contends for power in elections. Parties pose alternative programs and candidates and provide a means by which voters can make their desires and opinions felt. Party connections and party loyalty help to coordinate the separate branches and levels of government necessary in the US system. Primarily, however, political parties institutionalize conflict and the struggle for power. The alternation of parties in office is a peaceful means of replacing those in power, thus ensuring change without revolution.

In some countries a **two-party system** exists whilst in others there is a multiplicity of parties. The US and many English-speaking powers are dominated by two major parties, and a third party may poll a significant number of votes overall without having a single representative elected. By contrast, in European legislatures, representatives are generally chosen under the system of **proportional representation** which allows the election of candidates from a number of parties in exact proportion to their popular strength. Often in such cases no one party may have a simple overall majority and a coalition will be necessary. Communist states and many newly independent states have a **single-party system**, and the political party is in effect part of the state apparatus. (See also DEMOCRATIC PARTY; REPUBLICAN PARTY; TORY; WHIG.)

POLITICAL SCIENCE, the study of government and political institutions and processes. It was initiated by PLATO's *Republic* and ARISTOTLE's *Politics*, and well-known political theories have included those of MACHIAVELLI, BODIN, HOBBES, LOCKE, MONTESQUIEU, BENTHAM, Jean Jacques ROUSSEAU and MARX. Traditionally, the study has been primarily concerned with the nature of the state, of SOVEREIGNTY and of government. Today greater emphasis is placed on the human associations, the behavior of interest groups and the decision-making processes. The basis of the study is human power over other humans. This leads to a study of social organization. Pertinent areas of inquiry concern the institutions that dispose of power, the systems through which they operate and the motives of those who run them. These questions are closely connected with the question of the morality of power and general theories of man and society. Past theories cannot provide for the complexity of modern society and a standard view today is to regard society as a set of interacting interdependent systems.

POLIZIANO, Angelo, or **Politian** (1454–1494), Italian poet, scholar and humanist. Perhaps the greatest RENAISSANCE classical scholar, he also wrote the first Italian play, *Orfeo* (1480), and the famous lyrical love poem *Stanze per la Giostra* (1475–78).

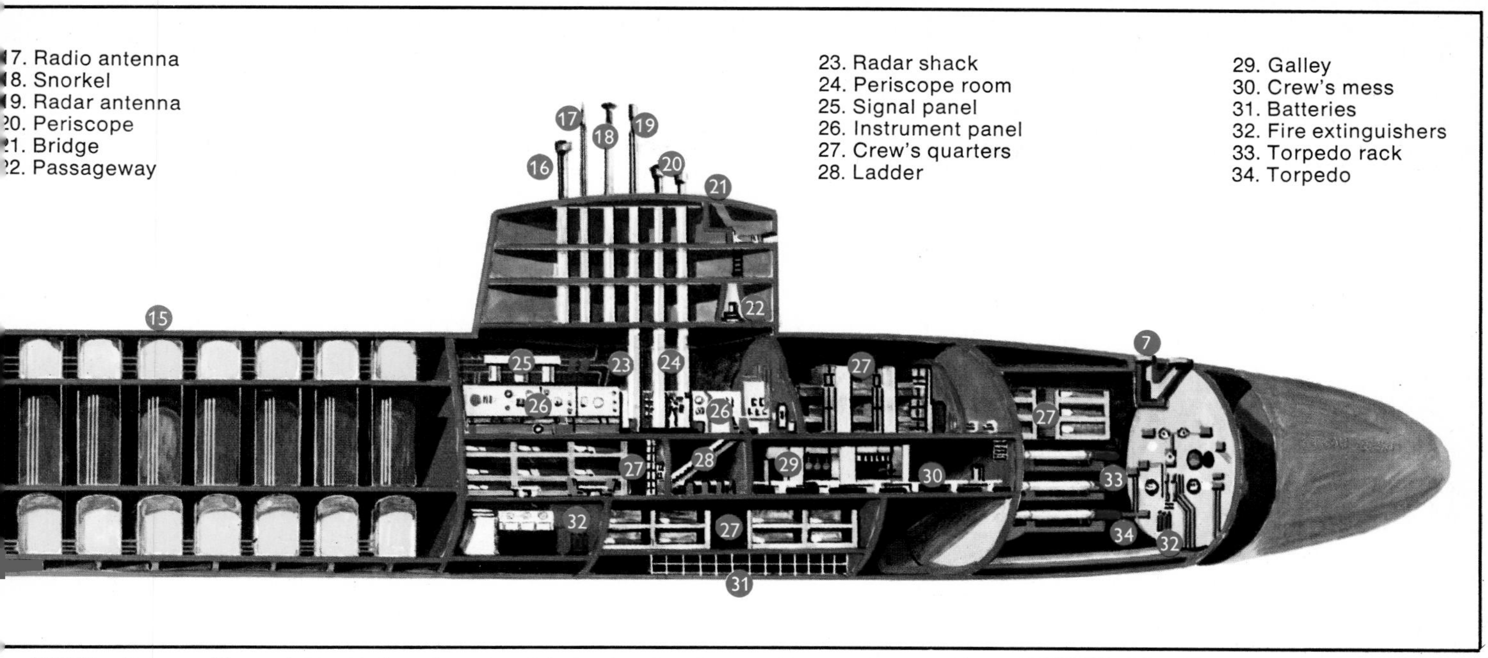

POLK, James Knox (1795–1849), eleventh President of the US, 1845–49, elected on a Democratic platform pledged to expand the existing territories of the nation according to the doctrine of MANIFEST DESTINY.

In 1825 Polk was elected to the US House of Representatives and during Andrew JACKSON's presidency he became the administration's leading spokesman in the House. After Jackson's reelection (1832) Polk became chairman of the Ways and Means Committee in 1833. He was speaker of the House 1835–39, and governor of Tennessee 1839–41. Chosen as a compromise candidate by the Democrats, Polk defeated Henry CLAY and was inaugurated as president on May 4, 1845, having campaigned on five main objectives, each of which he managed to achieve. The first, the annexation of Texas, was in fact achieved before Polk took up office, for the outgoing President, John TYLER, had already accepted the Democratic victory as a mandate and sanctioned the admission of Texas as a slave state of the Union (March, 1845). The second objective was to extend the boundary in Oregon Territory to a latitude of 54°40′. In the event, he compromised with Great Britain in the Oregon Treaty (1846) which established the boundary between the US and British America at the 49th parallel. The third objective, to acquire California from Mexico, involved the US in the MEXICAN WAR, 1846–48. By the Treaty of GUADALUPE HIDALGO (1848) Mexico ceded all her claims to the territory of California and New Mexico and recognized the border at the Rio Grande. The fourth objective, a promise to the South to lower the tariff, was enacted by the Walker Tariff (1846). Polk's final objective, to reestablish an INDEPENDENT TREASURY SYSTEM, was achieved by the Independent Treasury Act (1846) which survived with some modifications until 1913. Broken in health by overwork, he chose not to run for reelection and died shortly afterwards, having achieved impressive successes in fulfilling his aims.

James Knox POLK

11th US President

Born: November 2, 1795
Died: June 15, 1849
Term of office: March 4, 1845–March 3, 1849
Political party: Democratic

POLK, Leonidas (1806–1864), US clergyman, first bishop of Louisiana, 1841–61, and major-general who abandoned the ministry to fight in the Confederate army during the CIVIL WAR. He served in the Army of Tennessee and fought at Shiloh, Murfreesboro and Chickamauga, before being killed in action at Pine Mountain, Ga.

POLKA, dance with a basic 2/4 rhythm originating as a folk dance in Bohemia. It became fashionable in the 19th century.

POLL, Public Opinion, technique for measuring the range of opinions held by the general public or by specifically limited groups of people. It developed during the 1920s. Opinion polls rely on certain statistical laws which show that small carefully chosen samples of any group can accurately represent the range of opinions of the whole group or population. The population in question, known as the "universe," may be a general one (all voters in US) or a limited one (all car workers in Detroit). Accuracy depends on the care with which the sample is constructed and on the size of the sample. Since 1944 all polls have adopted the method of random selection pioneered by the US Census Bureau in which each member of the "universe" has an equal chance of being questioned.

POLLACK, *Pollachius pollachius*, a cod-like fish of the eastern Atlantic. It resembles the cod but lacks barbels on the chin. It may reach 11kg (24lb) and feeds on small fishes, worms and crustaceans. It is a food fish of moderate importance.

POLLAIUOLO, Antonio (c1431–1498), Florentine goldsmith and painter. Often collaborating with his brother **Piero**, his works include the *Martyrdom of St Sebastian* (1475), many portraits of women in profile and the tomb of Pope Innocent VIII in St. Peter's, Rome. His pictures are noted for their landscapes and their anatomical details.

POLLEN. See POLLINATION.

POLLEN COUNT, an estimate of atmospheric pollen each day during spring and summer, which gives a guide to the intensity of the stimulus to ASTHMA and HAY FEVER in subjects with pollen ALLERGY. It is affected by wind, rain and humidity.

POLLINATION, in plants, the transfer of the male GAMETES (*pollen*) from the anthers of a FLOWER to the stigma of the same or another flower, where subsequent growth of the pollen leads to the fertilization of the female gametes (or EGGS) contained in the ovules and the production of SEEDS and FRUIT. Wind-pollinated plants, such as grasses, produce inconspicuous flowers with large feathery stamens and stigmas and usually large quantities of pollen. Insect-pollinated flowers have large conspicuous and colorful flowers, produce NECTAR and have small stigmas. (See PLANT; REPRODUCTION.)

POLLOCK (Paul) Jackson (1912–1956), US painter, leader of ABSTRACT EXPRESSIONISM. Influenced by SURREALISM, he developed "action painting"—dripping paint on canvas placed flat on the floor, and forming marks in it with sticks, trowels, knives. His pictures, like *Number 32* (1950) and *Blue Poles* (1953) comprise intricate networks of lines.

POLL TAX, a tax levied equally on each individual in a community. In the US a special poll tax was levied on voters in elections, which effectively disenfranchised the blacks and poor whites. This was banned for federal elections by the 24th amendment to the Constitution (1964), and the ban was extended to local elections in 1966.

POLLUTION, the contamination of one substance by another so that the former is unfit for an intended use; or, more broadly, the addition to any natural environmental resource on which life or the quality of life depends or any substance or form of energy at a rate resulting in abnormal concentrations of what is then termed the "pollutant." Air (see AIR POLLUTION), water and soil are the natural resources chiefly affected. Some forms of pollution, such as urban sewage and garbage or inshore petroleum spillage, pose an immediate and obvious environmental threat; other forms, such as those involving potentially toxic substances found in industrial wastes and agricultural PESTICIDES, present a more insidious hazard: they may enter biological food chains and, by affecting the metabolism of organisms, create an ecological imbalance (see ECOLOGY). Populations of organisms thriving abnormally at the expense of other populations may themselves be regarded as pollutants. Forms of energy pollution include: NOISE, e.g., factory, airport and traffic noise; THERMAL POLLUTION, e.g., the excessive heating of lakes and rivers by industrial effluents; light pollution, e.g., the glare of city lights when it interferes with astronomical

Pollution

The dirtiest of animals

No keen observer of city, countryside or shore can have failed to notice that a direct consequence of man's increasingly reckless exploitation of the earth's natural resources is the contamination and destruction of the environment on which he depends to support his very existence.

Man is the dirtiest of animals. In the US the average person produces about 4.5lb (2kg) of trash every day. All over the world, cities from Sydney to Milan, New York or Los Angeles suffer from acute problems of air pollution caused by the burning of domestic and industrial waste, coal and heavy oils for heating, and light hydrocarbon fuels by airplanes and motor vehicles.

The home probably comes top of the league of earth-polluters. Sewage and trash—particularly the packaging materials in which all consumer products now seem to be double-wrapped—not only represent vast quantities of apparently useless waste materials but also a criminal misuse of the earth's precious and dwindling stock of natural resources. "Planned obsolescence" in domestic products, if, in the short run, commercially desirable and the seemingly unavoidable consequence of technological progress, also results in vast accumulations of untreated junk littering both townscape and countryside. Particularly great problems are posed by synthetic plastics which cannot be naturally broken down and reused in biological cycles. A great research effort is currently under way aimed at producing "biodegradeable" plastics which nevertheless are stable enough to be useful.

Industry produces its share of pollution—from the great spoil heaps associated with quarrying and mining to the air pollution issuing from chemical and metallurgical processes and from coal and oil-fired power plants.

A third more specialized type of pollution occurs when intensive agriculture employs herbicides, insecticides and inorganic fertilizers which break down to harmful residues. The natural concentration in the course of biological food-chains of the originally minute concentrations of these residues which enter rivers and thus the oceans, can result in sudden catastrophic drops in the fertility of the species at the ends of the chains.

The remedies for pollution are clear once its sources are identified. Air pollution results both from burning wastes from home and factory and fuels for heating and transportation and from certain industrial processes which release dust and dangerous chemicals into the atmosphere. The development of more efficient means of burning fuels (through carbon dioxide rather than the poisonous carbon monoxide) and processes for removing dust from factory flues (using electrostatic precipitators) offer partial solutions to air pollution.

The air is also the medium carrying noise pollution—from airplanes, traffic and industrial processes—which has so greatly increased during the 20th century. In modern cities complete silence is a most unusual experience. Solutions to noise pollution come from a combination of quietening the sources of noise and soundproofing homes and places of work.

Man uses more water than he does any other natural resource. Although supplies of water from precipitation are indefinitely renewable, in using them man contaminates the water with an increasing burden of dissolved and suspended refuse. As a result he not only drastically reduces the value of his water resources but eventally poisons the seas and oceans, destroying all marine life. The Mediterranean Sea already shows signs of becoming one vast basin of sewage and the many rivers which serve as the sewers of industry are lifeless, if watery, deserts. The solution to water pollution is clear; effluent water must be purified before it is discharged into rivers.

Conservation, the rational and well-managed exploitation of the earth's natural resources, is the other side of the pollution coin. The recycling of waste products, particularly of used paper and metallic products, not only reduces the problem of pollution but also conserves supplies of timber and metal ores. As the world runs short of energy-producing minerals and conservationists become increasingly concerned at the disturbing of the ecological balance in rivers into which water warm with the waste heat of industry is discharged, more efficient insulation of homes and the beneficial employment of thermal waste thus offer relief to problems both of thermal pollution and of energy conservation. With water itself becoming daily more precious, the elimination of pollution and the desirability of reuse come to be seen as identical causes.

Conservation of a second kind is concerned with the protection and preservation of as wide a range of living species as possible. Every animal and plant represents an irreplaceable reservoir of genetic material available to be used for the benefit of mankind; the extinction of any one of them would be a serious loss not only to science but also to the world at large. The very success of mankind has destroyed the natural habitats of many species and careful management of the local environment is necessary if such species are to be preserved.

A final division of the conservation movement, known as rural conservation, is concerned to prevent the continual encroachment by land-greedy cities upon the rural environment. The pleasure men feel when they visit or live in a relaxed country environment is at last recognized as being of as great value as benefits more easily evaluated financially.

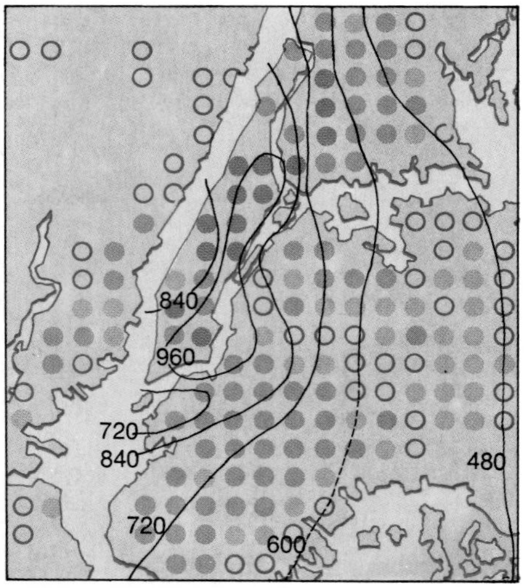

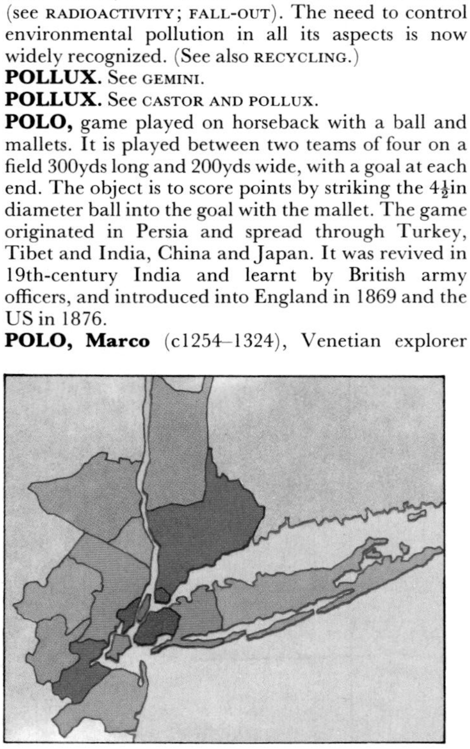

Pollution in New York. Sulfur dioxide and dust, for example, are seen on the map (*above*) to be heaviest in areas the map (*right*) shows to be most heavily populated—most notably Manhattan.

observations, and radiation from radioactive wastes (see RADIOACTIVITY; FALL-OUT). The need to control environmental pollution in all its aspects is now widely recognized. (See also RECYCLING.)

POLLUX. See GEMINI.

POLLUX. See CASTOR AND POLLUX.

POLO, game played on horseback with a ball and mallets. It is played between two teams of four on a field 300yds long and 200yds wide, with a goal at each end. The object is to score points by striking the 4½in diameter ball into the goal with the mallet. The game originated in Persia and spread through Turkey, Tibet and India, China and Japan. It was revived in 19th-century India and learnt by British army officers, and introduced into England in 1869 and the US in 1876.

POLO, Marco (c1254–1324), Venetian explorer famous for his overland journey to China, 1271–95. Reaching China in 1275 he served as an envoy to the ruler KUBLAI KHAN. He was appointed governor of Yangchow for three years and assisted in the capture of the city of Sainfu. He returned home to Venice (1295) laden with a treasure in precious stones. He commanded a galley against the Genoese at the battle of Curzola (1298) and was captured. In prison, he wrote an important account of his travels which later inspired explorers such as Christopher COLUMBUS to search for a sea passage to the East.

POLONAISE, slow Polish dance in 3–4 time, probably developed from the *promenade*. Polonaises were written by MOZART, BEETHOVEN, CHOPIN and many others.

POLONIUM (Po), soft, gray metal in Group VIA of the PERIODIC TABLE, occurring in PITCHBLENDE; usually produced by neutron bombardment of bismuth. All its isotopes are highly radioactive; the commonest, Po^{210}, emits ALPHA PARTICLES (half-life 138.4 days), and is used in NEUTRON sources. AW 210, mp 254°C, bp 962°C, sg 9.32 (α).

POLTAVA, Battle of, fought in 1709 near Poltava, in the Northern War between Russia under Tsar PETER I the Great, and the combined forces of CHARLES XII of Sweden and the Cossack chief MAZEPPA. It was a major Russian victory.

POLTERGEIST (German: noisy spirit), malicious spirit causing usually noisy and destructive phenomena. Such phenomena, whatever their cause, commonly occur around pubescent girls.

POLYCHAETES, marine worms forming one of the main classes of ANNELIDA. Segmented worms, they possess many bristle-like *chaetae* on each segment and distinct appendages or *parapodia*, used for walking. In tube-dwelling forms these may be reduced or modified. There are two main groups, the Errantia, with more motile forms such as the RAGWORMS, and the SEDENTARIA, tube-dwelling forms including the fanworms and peacock worms.

POLYCLITUS, 5th-century BC Greek sculptor, renowned for his bronze statues of athletes, of which numerous marble copies survive. His most famous statues were a colossal statue of Hera, now lost, and the *Doryphoros* or *Spear-Bearer*, which became the model for ideal proportion.

POLYCYTHEMIA, excessive number of ERYTHROCYTES in the BLOOD, which leads to plethora, itching and a tendency to THROMBOSIS. It may be primary or secondary to prolonged hypoxia (with LUNG disease) or certain TUMORS.

POLYETHYLENE, white, translucent RESIN, a POLYMER of ETHYLENE made catalytically at high pressure. Tough, elastic and inert, it is used to make plastic film, molded items, and SYNTHETIC FIBERS.

POLYGAMY, marriage in which husbands may have several wives at one time (*polygyny*), or wives several husbands (*polyandry*). It is still practised in parts of Asia and Africa; both the Muslim and Hindu religions permit polygyny. It was once also a custom of US MORMONS; always illegal, it is now forbidden.

POLYGON, a closed PLANE figure bounded by three or more straight lines. Polygons with three sides are called TRIANGLES; with four, QUADRILATERALS; with five, pentagons; with six, hexagons; with seven, heptagons; with eight, octagons; with twelve, dodecagons. Polygons may be either convex or concave (except triangles, which are always convex): convex polygons have INTERIOR ANGLES that are all acute or obtuse; in concave polygons one or more of these angles is reflex (see ANGLE). A polygon with equal angles and sides equal in length is called a regular polygon. A *spherical polygon* is a closed figure on the surface of a sphere bounded by arcs of great circles (see also SPHERICAL GEOMETRY). The sum of the interior angles of a plane polygon is given by: $s=(n\times 180°)-360°$, where s is the sum in degrees and n the number of sides of the polygon.

POLYGRAPH. See LIE DETECTOR.

POLYHEDRON, a three-dimensional figure bounded by four or more PLANE sides. There are only five types of convex polyhedron that can be regular (i.e., have faces that are equal regular POLYGONS, each face being at equal angles to those adjacent to it): these are the tetrahedron, the octahedron and the isocahedron, with 4, 8 and 20 faces respectively, each face being an equilateral TRIANGLE; the hexahedron, with 6 square faces (see CUBE); and the dodecahedron, with 12 pentagonal faces. Regular polyhedrons may be circumscribed about or inscribed in a SPHERE (see CIRCUMSCRIPTION; INSCRIPTION; PYRAMID).

POLYHYMNIA. See MUSES.

POLYMER, substance composed of very large MOLECULES (macromolecules) built up by repeated linking of small molecules (monomers). Many natural polymers exist, including PROTEINS, NUCLEIC ACIDS, polysaccharides (see CARBOHYDRATES), RESINS, RUBBER, and many minerals (e.g., quartz). The ability to make synthetic polymers to order lies at the heart of modern technology (see PLASTICS; SYNTHETIC FIBERS). Polymerization, which requires that each monomer has two or more FUNCTIONAL GROUPS capable of linkage, takes place by two processes: CONDENSATION with elimination of small molecules, or simple addition. CATALYSIS is usually required, or the use of an initiator to start a chain reaction of FREE RADICALS. If more than one kind of monomer is used, the result is a copolymer with the units arranged at random in the chain. Under special conditions it is possible to form stereoregular polymers, with the groups regularly oriented in space; these have useful properties. Linear polymers may form crystals in which the chains are folded sinuously, or they may form an amorphous tangle. Stretching may orient and extend the chains, giving increased tensile strength useful in synthetic fibers. Some cross-linking between the chains produces elasticity; a high degree of cross-linking yields a hard, infusible product (a thermosetting PLASTIC).

POLYMORPHISM, in zoology the existence of more than two forms or types of individual within the same species of animal. An example is seen in some social insects such as ants and bees in which many different types of worker are structurally adapted for different tasks within the colony.

POLYMORPHISM, in zoology, the existence of the existence of certain compounds in more than one crystalline form (see CRYSTAL). Usually the various forms are stable under different conditions. In some cases one is always stable, the others being metastable; thus CALCIUM carbonate has a stable hexagonal form CALCITE and a metastable orthorhombic form aragonite. (See also ALLOTROPY.)

POLYNESIA, archipelagos and islands in the central Pacific, part of Oceania. They include the Hawaiian, Cook, Phoenix, Ellice and Easter Islands, Samoa, French Polynesia, Tonga, and ethnologically if not geographically New Zealand. They are either of volcanic origin, or are atolls built up by coral reefs.

POLYNICES, in Greek myth son of OEDIPUS, leader of the Seven against Thebes. Slain by his brother Eteocles, he was denied burial rites, but ANTIGONE performed them.

POLYNOMIAL, an algebraic expression containing more than one term. $ax^5+bx^4+cx^3+dx^2+ex+f$, where a, b, c, d, e, f are CONSTANTS, is a polynomial of 6 terms in x (since $f=fx^0$). A polynomial with two terms is a binomial, with three a trinomial. Algebraic expressions with only one term (e.g., x^a) are called monomials.

POLYP, benign TUMOR of EPITHELIUM extending above the surface, usually on a stalk. Polyps may cause NASAL obstruction and some (as in the GASTROINTESTINAL TRACT) may have a tendency to become a CANCER.

POLYP, a column-shaped form of certain CNIDARIA typified in the CORALS and HYDRAS.

POLYPHEMUS, in the ODYSSEY, a man-eating CYCLOPS. He imprisoned ODYSSEUS, who freed himself and his friends by burning out Polyphemus' eye and escaping from the cyclops' cave among his sheep.

POLYPHONY (from Greek: many sounds), music made up of several independent but harmonically linked melodic lines. The name is usually applied to the sacred choral music of the late Renaissance, particularly that of PALESTRINA, LASSUS and William BYRD.

POLYSACCHARIDES. See CARBOHYDRATES.

POLYSCIAS, a genus of evergreen trees and shrubs, often grown indoors for their attractive foliage, which can be white, chartreuse or dark green in color. They respond to bonsai treatment, and thus can be kept relatively small. Indoors, polyscias should be grown in a sunny east or west window, but the older leaves tend to drop if the plants are moved from a bright position to a dimmer one. They grow well at average house temperatures. The soil should be kept evenly moist; the foliage benefits from frequent misting. Propagation is by shoot tip cuttings. Family: Araliaceae.

POLYSTYRENE, polymer of STYRENE ($C_6H_5CH{=}CH_2$) used as a rigid molded plastic and (for upholstery and thermal insulation) as a foam.

POLYTHEISM, belief in many gods, as opposed to MONOTHEISM or DUALISM; characteristic of most religions, notably HINDUISM and Greek and Roman religion. It may arise from the personification of forces worshiped at a more primitive level in ANIMISM. One god may dominate the others (e.g. ZEUS); sometimes a supreme Being is recognized, transcending the gods. (See also MYTHOLOGY.)

POLYWATER, or **"anomalous water,"** a liquid formerly supposed to be a polymeric form of WATER. First reported in 1962, it is made by condensing water in very fine glass or silica capillary tubes, and has unusual properties (mp −40°C, bp c500°C, sg 1.4). It is now thought to contain substances dissolved from the glass.

POME, a false fruit, the fleshy part of which is derived from the receptacle of the FLOWER, and not from the ovary. E.g., in the apple, only the core represents the ovary. (See FRUIT.)

POMEGRANATE, *Punica granatum*, a shrub or tree from Asia which bears orange-red flowers and orange-like fruits covered by a dry, yellow or reddish, leathery skin enclosing a soft reddish pulp with many seeds. Family: Punicaceae.

POMERANIA, former Prussian province, now mostly part of Poland. It lay S of the Baltic Sea, mainly between the Oder and Vistula rivers. After a history of Polish, Imperial, Brandenburg and Swedish rule the region was under Prussian rule from 1815 until 1919 when it was divided between Poland, East Germany, and GDÁNSK.

POMERANIAN, small dog with a pointed face and small pointed ears, related to sled-dogs. Varied in color, it stands 6–7in high.

POMO INDIANS, Hozan-speaking Indian tribe living in N Cal., famous for their intricate basket making. They were a wealthy tribe with many natural resources and used shells as currency.

POMONA, city in S Cal., a residential suburb of Los Angeles and a shipping point for fruit and vegetables. Pop 87 384.

POMPADOUR, Jeanne Antoinette Poisson, Marquise de (1721–1764), famous mistress of King LOUIS XV of France from 1745. She was a patroness of the arts and had much influence on the political and artistic life of France.

POMPANO, *Trachinotus carolinus*, a marine fish related to the Horse mackerels and PILOT FISH, of considerable economic importance in America.

POMPANO BEACH, resort city in SE Fla. It manufactures pleasure boats and plastic products. Pop 38 544.

POMPEII, ancient Roman city in S Italy, buried by an eruption of Mt VESUVIUS in 79 AD. It was rediscovered in 1748. Excavations have revealed a town preserved much as it was on the day of its destruction, even to several bodies. The site has yielded invaluable information of Roman urban life and beautiful examples of Roman art.

A process for the purification of water polluted by industrial effluents, an essential step in maintaining the usefulness of water bodies and the plant and animal life they support. Water from factories is neutralized with acid or alkali (1) and filtered to remove solids (2); the water is then reoxygenated (3) and mixed with bacteria (4), which are allowed to digest any remaining organic waste (5) before the water is pumped back into the river (6).

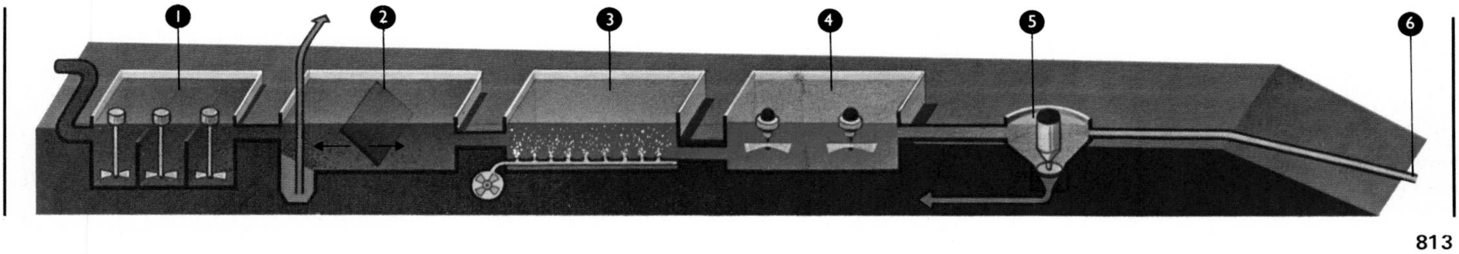

POMPEY (Gnaeus Pompeius Magnus; 106 BC–48 BC) known as the Great, Roman general and statesman. He crushed the rebellion in Spain (76 BC), defeated SPARTACUS (72 BC), and King MITHRIDATES (63 BC). In 61 BC he entered the First TRIUMVIRATE, becoming the colleague and later rival of Julius CAESAR. In the civil war following the latter's return from Gaul, Pompey was defeated at PHARSALUS in 48 BC and fled to Egypt, where he was assassinated.

POMPIDOU, Georges Jean Raymond (1911–1974), French statesman, president of France 1969–74. He joined the DE GAULLE government in 1944 and again in 1958. In 1961 he prepared the truce negotiation with the FLN, the Algerian nationalist organization. He was prime minister 1962–68, and succeeded De Gaulle as president in 1969. He died in office, of cancer.

POMPONAZZI, Pietro (1462–1525), Italian philosopher, author of *De Immortalitate Animae* (1516) and *De Incantationibus* (1520) which provoked controversy by proposing that, despite physical evidence, revealed truth transcended philosophical truth.

POMPTON LAKES, residential borough in NE N.J., with some light industry. It was settled in 1682. Pop 11 397.

PONCA CITY, manufacturing city in N Okla., with oil and gas wells. It is in a livestock and grain area. Pop 25 940.

PONCA INDIANS, North American Siouan-speaking Indian tribe. In the 17th century they settled in SW Minn. and the Black Hills of South Dakota, but were forced to move to Okla. in 1865. Finding conditions unacceptable they walked 600mi to Neb. to find shelter with the OMAHA. They were arrested and after a sensational trial were freed to settle in Neb. or Okla. Today about 1 000 remain.

PONCE, large city and port in S Puerto Rico, and one of the oldest cities in the Americas. Its varied manufacturing includes agricultural products. Pop 128 233.

PONCE DE LEON, Juan (c1460–1521), Spanish discoverer of Florida. He sailed with Christopher COLUMBUS in 1493, and in 1508 he conquered Puerto Rico and became its governor. Leading an expedition, possibly to find the mythical Fountain of Youth, he discovered and named Florida in 1513, but when he attempted to colonize it in 1521 he was driven off and mortally wounded by Indians.

PONCHIELLI, Amilcare (1834–1886), Italian opera composer. His best-known works are *I Promessi Sposi* (1856) and *La Gioconda* (1876), with its famous ballet, *Dance of the Hours*.

PONDEROSA PINE, or Western yellow pine, *Pinus ponderosa*, a tree with an attractive fissured bark native to the western US. Family: Pinaceae.

PONDWEED, freshwater plants of the genus *Potamogeton* that can clog streams and ponds, but which are an important food for wildlife. They produce leaves on or below the water surface and reproduce by the production of nutlets, tubers and "winter buds." Family: Potamogetonaceae.

PONTCHARTRAIN, Lake, shallow lake in SE La., 630sq mi in area. Discovered by Sieur d'IBERVILLE in 1699, it is now crossed by the world's longest highway built over water, and is connected to the Mississippi R and the Gulf of Mexico.

PONTIAC, city in central Ill., seat of Livingston Co. Its economy rests on agriculture and light industries. Pop 10 595.

PONTIAC, industrial city in SE Mich., seat of Oakland Co., on the Clinton R. It is a major center of the automobile industry. Pop 85 279.

PONTIAC (c1720–1769), chief of the Ottawa Indians. He opposed the English during the FRENCH AND INDIAN WARS, and was one of the leaders of an unsuccessful war against them, called **Pontiac's Rebellion** (1763–65), in which Pa., Va. and Md. were seriously threatened. He signed a peace treaty in 1766.

PONTIANUS, Saint (d. c236), pope 230–35, was exiled to Sardinia in 235 by Emperor Maximus at the beginning of his persecution of Christians.

PONTIFEX, high priest of ancient Rome, one of the 16 members of the Pontifical College presiding over the state religion. The highest religious authority was the *pontifex maximus* (supreme pontiff); this title was adopted by the emperors and later the popes.

PONTINE MARSHES, low-lying area in S Latium, central Italy. Fertile farmland in the Roman period, the area subsequently became a deserted malarial swamp. It was drained and repopulated in the 1930s.

PONTIUS PILATE. See PILATE, PONTIUS.

PONTUS, ancient kingdom in NE Asia Minor by the Black Sea. Dating from the 4th century BC, it reached its height under MITHRIDATES VI, but was annexed by the Roman Empire in 9 BC after it had challenged Roman power.

PONIES, small, sturdy HORSES, usually less than 15 hands (1.5m), hardy and able to live on small amounts of poor food. Races of pony include the Exmoor, Dartmoor, Welsh, Shetland, Iceland and Mongolian. All derive from a Celtic stock of prehistoric British and Scandinavian work horses.

PONY EXPRESS, famous relay mail service between St. Joseph, Mo., and Sacramento, Cal., from April 1860 to October 1861. It used horses, not ponies, with riders chosen for their small size. The route covered 1 966mi, with stations where the horses were changed at 10–15mi intervals. The goal of 10-day delivery was often met, and only one delivery was ever lost. It was superseded by the transcontinental telegraph.

PONYTAIL, or elephant-foot plant, *Beaucarnea recurvata*, a perennial house plant producing a rosette of lanceolate, grass-like leaves from an unusual bulb-like swollen stem that stores water. Large specimens grow up to 3m (10ft) tall. They grow well at average house temperatures, failing to thrive above 24°C (75°F), and are suited to sunny positions. They should be well watered whenever the soil surface dries out, although mature plants can tolerate longer periods of dryness. They are propagated by sowing seeds or by rooting offsets. Family: Liliaceae.

POODLE, thick-coated breed of dog originally bred in 16th-century Germany. There are three varieties, of differing height: the *toy* poodle is 10in or below, the *miniature* is between 10–15in, and the *standard* poodle is over 15in high.

POOL, game of BILLIARDS in which a player, using cue balls of different colors attempts to pocket the ball of an opponent. This is called taking a "life"; each player has three "lives." The last player with a "life" wins.

POONA, city in W central India, an industrial and commercial center famous for its 17th and 18th century architecture. Pop 853 226.

POOPO, Lake, salt lake in W Bolivia, 965sq mi in area, and at a height of 11 000ft. Its average depth is 10ft.

POOR CLARES, Franciscan closed order of nuns, founded by St. CLARE and St. FRANCIS OF ASSISSI in 1212. They are a mainly ascetic and contemplative order.

POOR LAWS, laws developed in England from the 16th century enforcing parish assistance to the aged, sick and poor. It was revised in 1834 to provide minimal relief for the able-bodied poor, and after WWI was replaced by a system of public welfare services under the social legislature.

POORWILL, *Phalaenoptilus nuttalli*, a small NIGHTJAR of North America. It is nocturnal and characteristic of sage-brush steppe, feeding on insects caught on the wing. It is apparently unique among birds in that in winter it exhibits a true HIBERNATION.

POP ART, modern art movement dating from the mid-1950s, based on images of advertising, commercial illustration and mass-produced objects. Developed in England and the US, it included artists like Richard Hamilton, David HOCKNEY, Andy WARHOL and Robert RAUSCHENBERG.

POPÉ (d. c1692), medicine man of the PUEBLO INDIANS who organized the so-called Pueblo Revolt in 1680 against the Spanish in New Mexico. He succeeded in driving them out of Sante Fe, and temporarily destroyed Spanish practices, restoring the Pueblos' ancient traditions.

POPE. See PAPACY.

POPE, Alexander (1688–1744), the greatest English poet and satirist of the AUGUSTAN AGE. Only 4ft 6in tall, he was partly crippled by tuberculosis. He first set out his literary ideals in his *Essay on Criticism* (1711), written in rhymed (heroic) couplets. His best-known works are the mock epic *The Rape of the Lock* (1712), his translations of the *Iliad* (1720) and the *Odyssey* (1726), *The Dunciad* (1728 and 1743), a satirical attack on literary critics, and his essays on moral philosophy, *An Essay on Man* (1733–34) and *Moral Essays* (1731–35).

POPE, John (1822–1892), US Union general. Born in Louisville, Ky, he commanded the newly-organized army of Va. in 1862. He was defeated at the second battle of BULL RUN, and was deprived of the command.

POPHAM, George (c1550–1608), early English colonist of America. With Raleigh Gilbert he founded Fort St. George (1607), the first New England colonial settlement, at the mouth of the Sagadahoc (now Kennebec) R. When he died there it was abandoned.

POPISH PLOT. See OATES, TITUS.

POPLAR, fast-growing hardy deciduous trees of the genus *Populus* which are native to the N Hemisphere. There are about 35 species, of which 15 are native to North America. Family: Salicaceae. (See also ASPEN; COTTONWOODS.)

POPLAR BLUFF, city on the Black R, SE Mo., seat of Butler Co. It is an agricultural marketing center, with some light industry. Pop 16 653.

POP MUSIC, the popular music of the latter half of the 20th century. Much of its vitality derives from the interaction of its diverse styles, all largely affected by commercial pressures. Most have their roots in American FOLK MUSIC, especially in the BLUES and its descendant, rhythm'n'blues. This latter led in the 1950s to rock'n'roll, a form based on electronic amplification and a simple, dominant beat. In the 1960s, British performers such as the BEATLES and the Rolling Stones experimented lyrically and musically with pop and traditional forms; while the US underwent a "folk revival" led by Bob DYLAN who, like Joe HILL and Woody GUTHRIE before him, adapted folk styles in pursuit of contemporary relevance, at first chiefly through quasipolitical protest. With increased lyrical sophistication came folk-rock; and its fusion with the "British" style, by

A landmark of Pop Art, *Campbell's Soup Can* by Andy Warhol (1962). It epitomizes the movement's concentration on "manufactured" subjects such as comic strips, flags, advertisements and packaging, in styles deriving from press and commercial illustration and the advertising industry. In its placing of an extreme emphasis on the immediacy and objectivity of everyday objects Pop Art represents a reaction to American Abstract Expressionist painting.

The dormant volcano Popocatépetl—in Aztec "smoking mountain"—lies about forty miles southeast of Mexico City. Mexico's second highest volcano, Popocatépetl is thought to have been first climbed by a European in 1519—by one of Cortes' men.

now adopted and adapted in the US, was responsible for much of the pop of the late 1960s and early 1970s. Indian (and later, African) music and JAZZ influenced form and instrumentation; technological advance stimulated closer ties with "serious" music; and a reaction from such complexities resulted in the resurgence of the unsophistication of rock'n'roll. (See also ROCK MUSIC.)

POPOCATÉPETL, dormant volcano, 17 887ft high, in central Mexico. The crater, about half a mile in diameter, contains vast sulfur deposits. It last erupted in 1702, but still occasionally emits smoke.

POPPAEA SABINA (d. 65 AD), mistress and then wife (62 AD) of the Roman emperor NERO. Exercising great influence over him, she is said to have persuaded him to murder his mother Agrippina and his wife Octavia.

POPPER, Sir Karl Raimund (1902–), Austrian-born British philosopher, best known for his theory of falsification in the philosophy of science. Popper contends that scientific theories are never more than provisionally adopted and remain acceptable only as long as scientists are devising new experiments to test (falsify) them.

POPPY, annual or herbaceous perennial plants of the genus *Papaver* and related genera. There are about 100 species in *Papaver*, which are mostly native to temperate and subtropical areas of Eurasia and N Africa. The flower bud is enclosed by two thick green sepals which drop off to allow the thin petals to unfold. The seeds are enclosed in a CAPSULE. The unripe capsules of the Opium poppy yield OPIUM. Family: Papaveraceae.

POPULAR FRONT, coalition of left-wing and center parties formed in the 1930s to present a united front against FASCISM. Reflecting a change in Soviet policy, the idea was proclaimed at the 1935 meeting of the Communist International, and communists cooperated with socialist and liberal parties in forming anti-Fascist governments. A Popular Front government led by BLUM ruled France 1936–37; the Spanish Popular Front, elected in 1936, was eventually overthrown by FRANCO.

POPULAR SOVEREIGNTY. See SQUATTER SOVEREIGNTY.

POPULATION. Population growth is a serious threat to modern society. Some 4 billions inhabit the earth today, compared with some 1.5 billions in 1900: there may be over 6 billions by 2000 AD. Some countries have taken steps (e.g., encouraging BIRTH CONTROL) to counter this trend, and some are even experiencing a population decrease. Four factors affect national populations: births, immigration; deaths, emigration. Ideally, these balance and population stays steady (zero population growth—"ZPG").

POPULISM, generally, a "grass roots" political movement which is basically agrarian, but which incorporates a farmer-labor coalition. Specifically, it refers to the doctrines of the US People's Party. This grew from the post-Civil War farm depression which created agrarian reform movements such as the GRANGE and the FARMERS' ALLIANCE. In 1891–92 delegates from the Farmers' Alliance and labor organizations set up the People's Party, which fielded J. B. WEAVER as presidential candidate in 1892 on a platform including an eight-hour day, government ownership of railroads, graduated income tax, government postal savings banks, direct election of Senators, increase of the money supply and FREE SILVER. Weaver gained over 1 000 000 votes, and the party gained support rapidly. In the 1896 presidential elections, however, the Democratic candidate, W. J. BRYAN, captured most of the populist vote by campaigning on the issue of free silver, and thereafter the People's Party declined. It failed because its money-supply and free silver theories did not present a sound economic analysis, and because it did not gain urban support.

The term populism can also describe any policies aimed to appeal to the "little man."

POPULISTS, in Russian history. See NARODNIKS.

PORBEAGLES, large sharks related to the MACKEREL SHARKS or Makos. Heavy-bodied fishes, distinguished by two keels on the body in front of the tail, they are found in temperate oceans.

PORCELAIN. See POTTERY AND PORCELAIN.

PORCUPINES, large spiny vegetarian rodents of two quite distinct families: one, Erithizontidae, confined to the Americas, the other, Hystricidae, to the tropics of the Old World. Old World forms include about a dozen species in Africa and S Asia. They are among the largest of rodents and the entire body is covered with spines. The American porcupines have an equal armory of spines, but when relaxed, these are concealed in a thick underfur.

PORCUPINE FISHES, a family, Didontidae, of tropical marine fishes related to the PUFFERS, which possess well-developed spines on the body. Like puffers, porcupine fishes can inflate the body with air or water, thus erecting the spines as an antipredator device.

PORCUPINE GRASS, *Stipa vaseyi*, a tufted perennial grass, native to the western US and Mexico, used locally to make brushes. At the base of the mature fruiting scale enclosing the grain there is a barbed point with stiff hairs which can injure animals. Family: Graminae.

PORCUPINE RIVER, tributary of the Yukon R, 448mi long. It rises in the NW Yukon Territory, Canada, and flows N then W into NE Alaska.

PORGIES, a family, Sparidae, of food fishes found in many parts of the world. Perchlike fishes, they have large scales and a spiny dorsal fin. In addition they have strong teeth, some species showing a differentiation between front and side teeth.

PORK BARREL, term for a US congressional appropriation for local improvements or public works, often unnecessary, supported by politicians for the patronage benefits accruing as a local spin-off; in other words, corruption. (See also LOG-ROLLING.)

PORNOGRAPHY AND OBSCENITY LAWS, in the US are held to exist for the protection of public morality. Pornography may be defined as material designed by its explicitness to appeal exclusively to a prurient interest in sex. The often explicit contents of genuine works of art and literature and medical texts are thus not pornographic, although in certain circumstances may be deemed obscene. Obscenity, like pornography, is not well defined in law, but may be said to be anything tending to corrupt public morals, generally in a sexual sense. Obscenity laws vary widely from country to country, and in the US from state to state, as does the degree of toleration extended by police and public. US Supreme Court decisions such as *US v Roth* (1957) tended to relax legal strictures, taking the standard as that of the "average reasonable adult" and laying down that a work must be judged as a whole. This made the law vaguer and hence hard to administer, and a great deal of "hard-core" pornography became freely available. Supreme Court decisions in the 1970s tended to reverse the

The North American porcupine (*Erethizon dorsatum*), best known of the New World species, is a good climber, unlike the terrestrial Old World species; also, its quills are almost entirely hidden by its long stiff fur. Despite its name, it is found as far south as Brazil.

trend, but it was uncertain how much public support they had.

PORPHYRIA, metabolic disease due to disordered HEMOGLOBIN synthesis. It runs in families and may cause episodic abdominal pain, skin changes, NEURITIS and mental changes. Certain DRUGS can precipitate acute attacks. Porphyria may have been the cause of the "madness" of George III of England.

PORPHYRINS, water-soluble nitrogen-containing pigments, consisting of four substituted pyrrole nuclei joined in a ring structure, occurring widely in nature. Combinations of porphyrins with metal ions include CHLOROPHYLL (containing MAGNESIUM) and heme (containing IRON); combinations of heme with proteins give HEMOGLOBIN and the CYTOCHROMES. The BILE pigments bilirubin and biliverdin are also related.

PORPHYRY (c233–c305 AD), Greek NEOPLATONIST philosopher and pupil of PLOTINUS, whose *Enneads* he edited. His *Introduction* (*Isagoge*), dealing with the concepts of genus, species, differentia, property and accident, became a standard medieval textbook. He wrote an anti-Christian polemic, and other philosophical and philological works.

PORPHYRY, an IGNEOUS ROCK having many large crystals (phenocrysts) set in a very fine-grained matrix, occurring in DIKES and SILLS. More generally, rocks are said to have porphyritic texture if they contain some phenocrysts in a finer-grained matrix (e.g., porphyritic granite).

PORPOISES, small Toothed whales, family Phocaenidae. Distinguished from DOLPHINS in being smaller, rather tubby and having a rounded head with no projecting beak-like mouth, they feed mainly on shoaling fishes. Unfortunately the name is now also loosely applied in the US to the various species of dolphin kept in captivity.

PORT, a sweet wine, usually red, fortified with brandy. It comes from grapes grown in the Douro valley, Portugal, and is shipped from Oporto, whence its name.

PORT. See HARBOR.

PORTAGE, city in NW Ind., on Lake Michigan. It has a new port and a steel industry. Pop 19 127.

PORTAGE, city in SW Mich., S of Kalamazoo. It produces paper products, plastics, machinery and pharmaceuticals. Pop 33 590.

PORTAGE LA PRAIRIE, city in S Manitoba, Canada. Originally a fur trading post, it is now principally an agricultural marketing center. Pop 12 950.

PORT ALBERNI, city on Vancouver Island, British Columbia, Canada. It is a fishing and lumbering center at the head of Barkley Sound. Pop 20 063.

PORTALES, city in E N.M., seat of Roosevelt Co. It lies in the state's major livestock region. Pop 10 554.

PORT ANGELES, city and port, NW Wash., seat of Clallam Co. It is a resort, with fishing and lumber industries. Pop 16 367.

PORT ARTHUR, Ontario. See THUNDER BAY.

PORT ARTHUR, city and deep-water port in SE Tex. It is a major world oil and petrochemical port. Pop 57 371.

PORT ARTHUR AND DAIREN, now **Lüshun** and **Lüda,** two ports at the southern end of the Liaotung peninsula, China, first developed under Russian (1898) and Japanese (1905) control. Port Arthur is a strategically important naval base, and Dairen a major commercial port and industrial city. Pop: Port Arthur 200 000; Dairen 1 500 000.

PORT-AU-PRINCE, capital, principal city and seaport of Haiti, at the head of the Gulf of Conaïves. Sugar and coffee are exported, and there are food-processing, rum-distilling and textile industries. Pop 493 932.

PORT CHESTER, village in SE N.Y., on the N shore of Long Island Sound. It is an industrial suburb of New York, with mixed light manufactures. Pop 25 803.

PORT COLBORNE, city in S Ontario, Canada. At the Lake Erie entrance to the WELLAND SHIP CANAL, it is a transshipment center, with some heavy industry. Pop 21 420.

PORT COQUITLAM, city in SW British Columbia, Canada, 15mi E of Vancouver. It has sand and gravel workings, and metallurgical and manufacturing industries. Pop 19 749.

PORT ELIZABETH, city in South Africa, SE Cape province. It is a major seaport, tourist center, and industrial city. Pop 386 577.

PORTER, Cole (1893–1964), US popular song composer. After WWI, he achieved great success as a sophisticated writer of songs and musical comedies. His prolific output included *Anything Goes* (1934), *Kiss Me, Kate* (1948), *Can-Can* (1953), the film score for *High Society* (1956) and many classic songs.

PORTER, David Dixon (1813–1891), US naval officer, distinguished in the CIVIL WAR. He served successfully in the New Orleans, Vicksburg, Red River and Fort Fisher campaigns, becoming rear admiral in 1863. In an administrative post 1865–69, he was made admiral in 1870.

PORTER, Sir George (1920–   ), British chemist awarded the 1967 Nobel Prize for Chemistry with Manfred EIGEN and Ronald NORRISH for their studies of extremely fast chemical reactions, and, in particular, for their development of FLASH PHOTOLYSIS.

PORTER, Katherine Anne (1890–   ), US short-story writer and novelist who won the 1966 Pulitzer Prize for her *Collected Short Stories* (1965). Her first collection of stories was *Flowering Judas* (1930), followed by *Pale Horse, Pale Rider* (1939). *Ship of Fools* (1962) is her only novel.

PORTER, Rodney Robert (1917–   ), British biochemist who shared with G. M. EDELMAN the 1972 Nobel Prize for Physiology or Medicine for his work on the molecular structure of ANTIBODIES.

PORTER, William Sidney. See HENRY, O.

PORTERVILLE, city in central Cal., on the Tule R. It is a residential town and trading center. Pop 12 602.

PORT HARCOURT, seaport in the Niger delta, SE Nigeria. It is an important export and industrial center. Pop 217 043.

PORT HUENEME, city in S Cal., on the Pacific coast. It has a deepsea harbor and is the site of the US naval construction-battalion, "Seabee." Pop 14 295.

PORT HURON, city in S Mich., seat of St. Clair Co., at the junction of Lake Huron and St. Clair R. It is a shipping and manufacturing city. Pop 35 794.

PORTLAND, city in SW Me., seat of Cumberland Co. It is a major oil port and the commercial and industrial center of SW Me. Pop 65 116.

PORTLAND, city and port in NW Ore., seat of Multnomah Co. It is the principal city of Ore., and an important trading, industrial, transportation and cultural center. Pop 380 555.

PORTLAND CEMENT, widely-used CEMENT made by calcining a mixture of lime and clays, reputedly named for the resemblance of the set cement mortar to limestone from the Isle of Portland, England.

PORT LAVACA, city on Lavaca Bay, S Tex., seat of Calhoun Co. It is an oil, gas, aluminum and fishing center. Pop 10 491.

PORT LOUIS, capital of Mauritius in the W Indian Ocean. It is a port and center of the island's international trade. Pop 141 125.

PORT MOODY, port and industrial city in SW British Columbia, 12mi E of Vancouver. Pop 10 780.

PORT MORESBY, capital city of Papua New Guinea. A modern city with a deepwater harbor, it is a trading, commercial and administrative center. Pop 66 244.

PORT NECHES, city in SE Tex. Near the mouth of Neches R, it is an oil-shipping port with rubber and petrochemical industries. Pop 10 894.

PORTO. See OPORTO.

PÔRTO ALEGRE, city in SE Brazil. It is a major port with industries mostly connected with processing food and farm products from the interior, and also an important commercial center. Pop 885 564.

PORT OF NEW YORK AUTHORITY, agency which administers and plans the development of New York's port facilities. Founded in 1921, it comprises six commissioners from N.Y. and six from N.J.

PORT OF SPAIN, capital of Trinidad and Tobago, on the W coast of Trinidad. It is a major Caribbean commercial and shipping center. Pop 67 867.

PORTOLÁ, Gaspar de (c1723–c1784), Spanish colonizer of California. In 1769, as governor of the Californias, he mounted an expedition from Mexico which founded San Diego and Monterey.

PORTO-NOVO, capital of Dahomey, W Africa. It is a seaport and commercial center, but does not have any major industry. Pop 84 000.

PORTO RICO. See PUERTO RICO.

PORT ROYAL, Nova Scotia. See ANNAPOLIS ROYAL.

PORT SAID, Egyptian port at the N end of the Suez Canal. Founded when the Suez Canal was built, it became the fuelling and service center for the canal, and Egypt's second-largest port. Pop 320 000.

PORTSMOUTH, naval base and seaside resort in the county of Hampshire, S England. It stands on Portsea Island and has a naturally protected harbor on the English Channel. The naval dockyard is the largest in the UK. Pop 196 973.

PORTSMOUTH, seaport and resort in SE N.H. The US naval shipyard is a major source of employment. Pop 25 717.

PORTSMOUTH, city in S Ohio, seat of Scioto Co. On the Ohio R, it is a transportation and industrial center. Pop 27 633.

PORTSMOUTH, town in SE R.I. It is a summer resort, with fishing and shipbuilding industries. Pop 12 521.

PORTSMOUTH, city in SE Va. The site of the largest US naval shipyard, it is also a commercial port with some manufacturing industry. Pop 110 963.

PORTSMOUTH, Treaty of, the treaty which ended the 1904–05 Russo-Japanese War. After mediation by President Roosevelt, it was signed Sept. 5, 1905, at Portsmouth Navy Yard, N.H. Russia conceded Japanese supremacy in Korea, and Manchuria was restored to China.

PORTUGAL, republic of the W Iberian Peninsula, between Spain and the Atlantic, and including the Azores and Madeira.

Land. The N half of Portugal consists of mountains and high plateaus, cut by deep valleys. The S is characterized by lower, rolling countryside and plains. Two large rivers, the Tagus and Douro, cut the country from E to W. The climate is mild and humid in winter and warm and dry in summer.

Economy. Portugal is one of Europe's poorer countries. It is basically agricultural, with most of the population living in villages and small towns. Most farms are very small and poor, although there are some large estates in the S. Grain, livestock, wine, olives, citrus fruits and almonds are the principal products. There are large forests in the mountainous areas, and Portugal is the world's biggest producer of cork. Fishing is important, the chief catches being sardines and tuna. Industries include food-processing, textiles, metals, mining and hydroelectricity. The principal cities are Lisbon, Oporto, Coimbra and Setúbal. Chief exports are cork, wine, sardines and fruit.

History. Portugal became an independent kingdom in 1143, under Alfonso I. In 1385, John I founded the Aviz dynasty. His reign started a period of colonial expansion, leading to an empire that by the second half of the sixteenth century included much of South

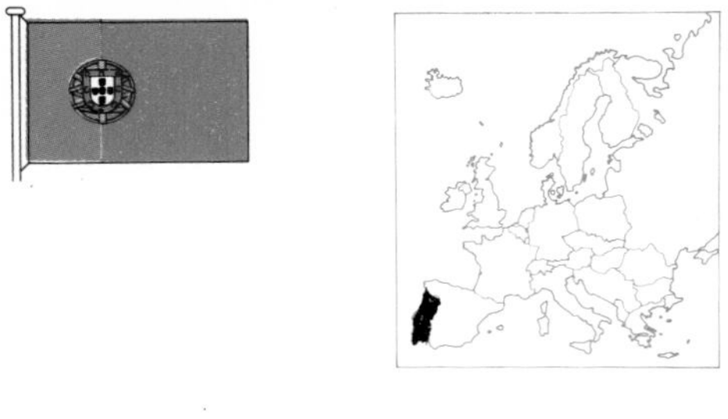

Official name: Republic of Portugal
Capital: Lisbon
Area: 35 510sq mi
Population: 9 668 000
Language: Portuguese
Religion: Roman Catholic
Monetary unit(s): 1 Escudo = 100 centavos

Sorting, cleaning and packaging sardines and tuna on a beach in the Algarve, home of Portugal's important fishing industry.

America, Africa and S and SE Asia. In 1580 King Philip II of Spain seized Portugal, and Spanish kings ruled until the successful revolt of 1640 which established the ruling house of Braganza. Portugal had already lost much of her power, especially in the Far East, and in the ensuing period of increasing absolutism never recovered it. During the NAPOLEONIC WARS she was invaded by the French and Spanish (see PENINSULA WAR). By 1825 Brazil was lost to the empire, and a period of conflict and unrest led to a republic being declared in 1910. In 1926 there was a military coup, after which Dr SALAZAR became virtual dictator until he was succeeded by Marcello CAETANO in 1968. In 1974 a military coup brought about a new government under General SPÍNOLA which restored freedom of political expression, and promised popular elections and independence for Portugal's overseas territories. In the struggle between leftist and rightist forces that followed, he was replaced in Sept. 1974 by General Costa Gomes. Continuing strife led to his resignation (1976) and the election of General Eanes for a five-year term. Of Portugal's overseas territories, GUINEA-BISSAU became independent in 1974, followed by ANGOLA, the CAPE VERDE ISLANDS, MOZAMBIQUE and SÃO TOME and PRINCIPE in 1975; in 1976 Portuguese TIMOR became part of Indonesia and MACAO gained greater autonomy.

PORTUGUESE, official language of Portugal and Brazil. It is one of the ROMANCE LANGUAGES and developed from the Latin spoken in Roman Iberia. Brazilian Portuguese has absorbed words and phrases from the languages of the Indian and African slave populations.

PORTUGUESE EAST AFRICA. See MOZAMBIQUE.

PORTUGUESE GUINEA. See GUINEA-BISSAU.

PORTUGUESE INDIA, name of former Portuguese possessions on the W coast of India. See GOA.

PORTUGUESE MAN-O'-WAR, *Physalia physalis*, a colorful jellyfish of the Siphonophora. A colonial Cnidarian, it consists of an assemblage of four kinds of POLYPS: the most obvious of which is a gas-filled bladder 300mm (1ft) long, which carries a high crest and is colored blue or purple. Below this float are supported other polyps including the long stinging tentacles used for catching prey. The sting can be painful to humans.

PORTUGUESE WEST AFRICA. See ANGOLA.

PORT WASHINGTON, unincorporated Long Island resort in SE N.Y. It is a yachting and boatbuilding center. Pop 15 923.

POSEIDON, Greek god of sea and water. He received the sea as his share when he and his brothers ZEUS and HADES overthrew their father CRONUS. Also associated with horses, he was father of PEGASUS. With his trident he raised storms and caused earthquakes.

POSHAN, city in Shantung province, NE China. In a coalmining area, it is an important center for heavy industry. Pop 1 200 000.

POSITIVISM, philosophical theory of knowledge associated with the 19th-century French philosopher Auguste COMTE. It holds that the observable, or "positive," data of sense experience constitute the sole basis for assertions about matters of fact; only the truths of logic and mathematics are additionally admitted. The speculative claims of theology and metaphysics, regarded as the primitive antecedents of "positive" or scientific thought, are discounted. (See also LOGICAL POSITIVISM.)

POSITRON, the antiparticle corresponding to the ELECTRON. (See ANTIMATTER.)

POSSUMS, Australian marsupial mammals, members of the Phalangeridae (see PHALANGERS). The term is also used, wrongly, for the OPOSSUMS of the New World.

POST, Emily (1873–1960), US writer who became an accepted authority on correct social behavior through her book *Etiquette* (1922). She broadcast regularly and her daily column was syndicated to over 200 newspapers.

POST, Wiley (1899–1935), US aviator, who made a record-breaking world flight in 1931 and repeated the performance solo in 1933. He and his passenger, humorist Will ROGERS, died in a plane crash.

POSTAL SERVICE, the collection, transmission and delivery of mail. Postal systems grew out of the military and administrative needs of the early empires. Communications were maintained by networks of runners or mounted couriers in Egypt by 2000 BC, in China by 1000 BC, and in the Persian Empire by CYRUS THE GREAT; in Europe the Roman Empire had a network whose efficiency was not matched again until the 19th century.

Modern postal services originated in the late Middle Ages. There was an international network in the Hapsburg empire in the 15th century, and CHARLES I of England and LOUIS XIV of France set up regular postal services in the 17th century. As the amount of traffic increased private enterprise gave way to government monopoly, and modern postal systems are all government controlled. First stagecoaches, then railroads and steamships, and finally airplanes have dramatically reduced delivery times, and a milestone in the organization of the post was the "penny post" (1840) in England, with prepaid adhesive stamps and a single rate (see HILL, ROWLAND.) International standardization of procedures was achieved in 1875 (see UNIVERSAL POSTAL UNION). The international postal system now handles enormous numbers of items every day, but is faced with great financial and administrative problems because the handling of mail cannot easily be tackled by mechanized processes, and costs rise while the letter faces competition from the telephone. (See also POST OFFICE, US.)

POSTAL UNION, Universal. See UNIVERSAL POSTAL UNION.

POSTER, printed placard, posted up to advertise an event, product or service, or for propaganda purposes. The invention of LITHOGRAPHY made it possible to produce brightly-colored posters cheaply and quickly. Famous artists who designed posters include Jules Chéret, TOULOUSE-LAUTREC and Aubrey BEARDSLEY.

POSTIMPRESSIONISM, term coined to refer to certain painters c1880–90 who developed from the IMPRESSIONISTS, notably GAUGUIN, SEURAT and VAN GOGH. The artists shared an interest in simplified technique and in symbolism.

POST MORTEM. See AUTOPSY.

POST OFFICE, US, formerly a US government department, since 1970 an independent agency. It administers the POSTAL SERVICE of the US, under the direction of the postmaster-general, formerly a cabinet member, but now appointed by a corporate board of governors. By far the largest in the world, the US Post Office employs 700 000 people and operates 33 000 post offices, handling around 100 000 000 000 items of mail every year.

POSTULATE. See AXIOM.

POTASH, or potassium carbonate. See POTASSIUM.

POTASSIUM (K), a soft, silvery-white, highly reactive ALKALI METAL. It is the seventh most abundant element, and is extensively found as SYLVITE, carnallite and other mixed salts; it is isolated by ELECTROLYSIS of fused potassium hydroxide. Potassium is chemically very like sodium, but even more reactive. It has one natural radioactive isotope, K^{40}, which has a half-life of 1.28 billion yr. K^{40} decays into Ar^{40}, an isotope of argon; the relative amounts of each are used to date ancient rocks. Potassium salts are essential to plant life (hence their use as fertilizers), and are important in animals for the transmission of impulses through the nervous system. AW 39.1, mp 64°C, bp 774°C, sg 0.862 (20°C).

Potassium carbonate (K_2CO_3), or **Potash**, is a hygroscopic colorless crystalline solid, made from potassium hydroxide and carbon dioxide, an ALKALI used for making glass.

Potassium chloride (KCl), is a colorless crystalline solid, found as SYLVITE. Used in fertilizers and as the raw material for other potassium compounds.

Potassium nitrate (KNO_3), or **Saltpeter**, is a colorless crystalline solid, soluble in water, which decomposes to give off oxygen when heated to 400°C. It is made from sodium nitrate and potassium chloride by fractional crystallization, and is used in GUNPOWDER, matches, fireworks, some rocket fuels, and as a fertilizer.

POTATO, *Solanum tuberosum*, herbaceous plant with an edible, fleshy tuberous underground stem, originating in the South American Andes. The tubers became a popular European foodstuff in the 18th century, the Irish in particular becoming dependent on the crop. Family: Solanaceae.

POTATO BUG. See COLORADO BEETLE.

POTATO FAMINE, in 19th-century Ireland, famine caused by potato blight. The 1845 and 1846 potato crops failed, and in the subsequent famine nearly a million people died and over a million emigrated, particularly to the US. Ireland's population fell from about 8 500 000 in 1845 to 6 550 000 in 1851.

POTAWATOMI INDIANS, a North American Indian tribe of the ALGONQUIAN language family. In the 18th century they lived around the S of Lake Michigan. They allied with the French colonists and joined chief PONTIAC in his rebellion (1763). They later supported the British in the Revolutionary War and in the War of 1812. Coming under pressure from settlers, they moved W, and in 1846 most of them were forced into a reservation in Kan. The Potawatomi in Kansas have preserved much of the aboriginal culture. Other groups live in Mich., Okla. and Wis.

POTEMKIN, Prince Grigori Aleksandrovich (1739–1791), Russian soldier, statesman and favorite of Catherine the Great. For the last 20 years of his life, he was the most powerful man in Russia. He enlarged the Russian army and navy, and annexed the Crimea in 1782.

POTENTIAL, Electric, the work done against ELECTRIC FIELDS in bringing a unit charge to a given point from some arbitrary reference point (usually earthed), measured in VOLTS (i.e., joules per coulomb). Charges will tend to flow from points at one potential to those at a lower potential, and potential difference, or **voltage**, thus plays the role of a driving force for electric current. In inductive circuits, the work done in bringing up the charge depends on the route taken, and potential ceases to be a useful concept.

POTENTIOMETER, a device for accurate measurement of electric POTENTIAL by comparison with a standard cell potential: numerous DC and AC variants exist, mostly depending on OHM'S LAW. Typically, a potential drop is established in a long wire by a BATTERY, and a sliding contact used to tap a variable proportion of this drop, the lengths needed to balance the standard and unknown potentials being noted in turn. The ratio of these lengths is the ratio of the potentials. The same arrangement is also used to vary an applied voltage, for example, in the thin-carbon-film "potentiometers" used as volume controls in transistor RADIOS.

POTHOS, or devil's-ivy, *Scindapsus aureus*, an evergreen climbing plant that in the juvenile phase produces aerial roots and ovate, pointed, bright-green leaves flecked with yellow. In the adult phase the leaves are heart-shaped, with perforated margins. Indoors, pothos tolerates relatively dim light, such as a north window or fluorescent lights, and grows well at average house temperatures. The soil should be kept evenly moist most of the time, but occasional drying out is beneficial. The foliage should be misted often. Propagation is by shoot tip cuttings. Family: Araceae.

POTLATCH, in many tribal cultures, especially among the Indians of the American NW coast, an elaborate ceremonial feast at which the host distributes or destroys wealth to gain status or office in his tribe. Wealthier guests are expected to match or exceed this in turn. Although banned for a while in Canada the potlatch is still an important tribal institution.

POTOMAC RIVER, US river flowing through Washington, D.C. Formed by the confluence of the 110mi long N Branch and the 140mi long S Branch, it flows 287mi into Chesapeake Bay. Navigation for large ships is prevented above Washington D.C., by the Great Falls. The river is noted for its scenic attraction.

Falls and rapids in the Potomac River, near Washington D.C. The Potomac forms part of the West Virginia-Maryland and Virginia-Maryland state lines.

POTSDAM, city in E Germany, near Berlin. In the 18th century it was chosen by FREDERICK II as his principal residence and became a center and symbol of Prussian militarism. Noted for its royal palaces, it is now also an industrial city. It was the site of the 1945 POTSDAM CONFERENCE. Pop 111 288.

POTSDAM CONFERENCE (July–Aug. 1945), a "summit" meeting at Potsdam, Germany, between STALIN, TRUMAN and, in succession, CHURCHILL and Clement ATTLEE. They agreed that a four-power Allied Control Council would rule defeated Germany, disarming it and fostering democratic government; Poland would gain part of E Germany; the German economy would be decentralized; Germans in Hungary, Poland and Czechoslovakia would be repatriated. The conference also discussed reparations payments and issued an ultimatum to Japan. The agreements were almost all breached as the COLD WAR hardened. (See also YALTA CONFERENCE.)

POTTER, Beatrix (1866–1943), British author of children's books. Her works, illustrated by herself, include *Peter Rabbit* (1902), *The Tailor of Gloucester* (1903), *Benjamin Bunny* (1904), *Mrs Tiggy-Winkle* (1905), *Jemima Puddle-Duck* (1908) and *Pigling Bland* (1913). Her books have become children's classics and remain widely popular.

POTTER, Paul (1625–1654), Dutch animal and landscape painter. Among his finest works is *Landscape with Cattle* (1647). He was also an accomplished etcher.

POTTERY AND PORCELAIN, CERAMIC articles, especially vessels, made of CLAY (generally KAOLIN) and hardened by firing. The simplest and oldest type of pottery, **earthenware** (nonvitreous), is soft, porous and opaque, usually glazed and used for common tableware. TERRA COTTA is a primitive unglazed kind. Earthenware is fired to about 1000°C. **Stoneware**, the first vitreous ware (of low porosity), was developed in China from the 5th to the 7th centuries AD. Fired to about 1200°C, it is a hard, strong, nonabsorbent ware, opaque and cream to brown in color. From stoneware evolved **porcelain** during the Sung dynasty (960–1279). This is a hard, nonporous vitreous ware, white and translucent. Made from flint, kaolin and feldspar, it is fired to about 1350°C.

In the manufacture of pottery the clay is made plastic by blending with water. The article is then shaped: traditionally by hand, by building up layers of strips (coiled pottery), by "throwing" on the potter's wheel or by molding; industrially by high-pressure molding or by a rotating template. The clay is fired in a kiln, slowly at first, then at higher temperatures to oxidize and consolidate it. The **glaze** (if desired) is then applied by spraying or dipping, and the article refired. Glazes are mixtures of fusible minerals and pigments, similar to those used for ENAMEL, powdered and mixed with water.

Among the most celebrated potters were the ancient Greeks (see GREEK ART) and the Chinese. Chinese porcelain had a profound influence on the ceramic arts of both Islam and W Europe. From the 9th century the Muslims used tin glaze to imitate Chinese ware, and this was in turn imitated in the European FAÏENCE and MAJOLICA wares. Porcelain was developed as a luxury ware in Europe in the 18th century, the greatest centers being Dresden (see DRESDEN CHINA) and SÈVRES. In England the great ceramics manufacturers were Josiah SPODE (see also BONE CHINA) and Josiah WEDGWOOD. (See also DELFT.)

POTTO, *Perodicticus potto*, a clumsy-looking nocturnal omnivorous LORIS of the rain forests of central Africa. It has forward-facing eyes and strong, grasping hands and feet. A striking offensive weapon is formed by spiny processes of certain vertebrae which are covered with a thin layer of skin and project from the back of the neck.

POTTSTOWN, borough in SE Pa., on the Schuylkill R. Site of the first cold-blast iron furnace in the US, it is now a trade and manufacturing center. Pop 25 355.

POTTSVILLE, city in central Pa., seat of Schuylkill Co. Once a mining city, it was a center for the MOLLY MAGUIRES. It now has varied manufactures. Pop 19 715.

POUGHKEEPSIE, city on the Hudson R, SE N.Y., seat of Dutchess Co. It has a wide range of manufacturing industries. Pop 32 029.

POULENC, Francis (1899–1963), French composer, member of the post-WWI group of composers called 'Les SIX." His music is light in texture, although serious. His best-known works include *Mouvements perpetuels* for piano (1918), the ballet *Les Biches* (1924) and the operas *Les Mamelles de Tirésias* and *Dialogue des Carmélites* (1957). He was also a notable songwriter.

POULTRY FARMING, the rearing of all types of domesticated farm fowls for eggs and flesh. The CHICKEN is by far the most popular bird, followed by the TURKEY, DUCK, GOOSE and other types. Important chicken breeds are the Leghorn and Rhode Island Red for eggs, and the Plymouth Rock and Cornish for meat. Modern scientific breeding programs aim at producing strains which will combine all the desirable qualities of the separate breeds. Before WWII, most flocks were kept on general farms. Today, nearly all economicaly valuable fowls live in controlled environments, with artificial lighting and heating, and small pens for individuals or groups. Chickens are hatched in incubators, reared in brooders and transferred to laying or fattening quarters. An annual output of 200–250 eggs per bird is essential for good profits. Marketing is organized through farmers' cooperatives and marketing boards. (See also AGRICULTURE.)

POUND (lb), the name of various units of weight (see WEIGHTS AND MEASURES). The pound avoirdupois is defined as being exactly 0.453 592 37kg. The "metric pound" commonly used in continental Europe is 500g.

POUND, Ezra Loomis (1885–1972), major 20th-century US poet, critic and translator. A gifted linguist, he came to Europe in 1908, and soon won recognition. His most important works are *Homage to Sextus Propertius* (1918), *Hugh Selwyn Mauberley* (1920) and the epic *Cantos* (1925–60). He championed the IMAGIST and VORTICIST movements, and influenced T. S. ELIOT, Robert FROST and W. B. YEATS, among others. He supported MUSSOLINI, and after broadcasting pro-fascist propaganda during WWII he was indicted for treason by the Americans, found unfit to plead, and confined to a mental institution until 1958.

POUND, Roscoe (1870–1964), US botanist, jurist and educator who championed flexibility in the law and efficiency in court administration. He was professor of law at Harvard 1910–37, and advocated a "sociological jurisprudence" that would adapt the law to changing social and economic conditions.

POUSSIN, Nicolas (1594–1665), the greatest 17th-century French BAROQUE painter. He worked mostly in Rome, and based his style on RAPHAEL and antiquities. His classical and religious subjects, such as *Shepherds of Arcadia* (c1629), *The Rape of the Sabine Women* (c1635) and *The Seven Sacraments* (1644–48) are rich in color, austere in handling, dramatic, and evocative in mood. He influenced Jacques DAVID, CÉZANNE and PICASSO.

POVERTY, a shortage of the income or resources considered necessary for a minimum standard of living in a particular society. Because of the differences between societies, it is impossible to define precisely; an American may be considered poor if he does not possess an automobile, while the poor in Africa, Asia or South America may be actually starving to death. The vast gap between rich and poor, and especially between rich and poor countries, is a major fact of the modern world. In the underdeveloped countries, whose populations are increasing fast, many people suffer from MALNUTRITION, and are poor by any standards. Despite aid from the rich and technologically advanced nations, the gap is increasing.

Awareness of poverty in the US was greatly increased when the 1960 census figures revealed that 20% of the population were living below the poverty level as defined by the SOCIAL SECURITY administration, and large-scale WELFARE programs were promoted under the HEALTH, EDUCATION AND WELFARE Department.

POWDERLY, Terence Vincent (1849–1924), US labor leader. A machinist, he became grand master workman (president) of the KNIGHTS OF LABOR (1879–93), was three times mayor of Scranton, Pa. (1878, 1880, 1882) and held high posts in the Bureau of Immigration.

POWDER RIVER, shallow stream which rises in the Big Horn Mts of Wyoming and flows 385mi N to join the Yellowstone R near Terry, E Mont.

POWELL, Adam Clayton Jr. (1908–1972), US politician. A clergyman, he was New York's first black councillor (1941). He founded *The People's Voice* (1942) and, as the flamboyant "Voice of Harlem," was a Democratic Representative 1945–70. Excluded from Congress for alleged misuse of funds (1967), he was reelected twice, but defeated in 1970.

POWELL, Anthony (Dymoke) (1905–), English novelist, best known for his contemporary comedy of manners *A Dance to the Music of Time*, a series which started with *A Question of Upbringing* (1951).

POWELL, Cecil Frank (1903–1969), British physicist and pacifist awarded the 1950 Nobel Prize for Physics for his development of a direct means of photographing the tracks of SUBATOMIC PARTICLES and subsequent discovery of the π-meson.

POWELL, John Wesley (1834–1902), US geologist and ethnologist best known for his geological and topographical surveys, and for his anthropological studies of the AMERINDS.

POWELL, Lake, formed by Glen Canyon dam across the Colorado R in Glen Canyon National Recreation Area, S Utah. It covers 252sq mi.

POWER, the rate at which WORK is performed, or ENERGY dissipated. Power is thus measured in units of work (energy) per unit time, the SI UNIT being the watt

(= the joule/second) and other units including the horsepower (= 745.70W) and the *cheval-vapeur* (= 735.5W). Frequently in engineering (and particularly in transportation) contexts, what matters is the power that a given machine can deliver or utilize—the rate at which it can handle energy—and not the absolute energies involved. A high-power machine is one which can convert or deliver energy quickly. While mechanical power may be derived as a product of a FORCE and a VELOCITY (linear or angular), the electrical power utilized in a circuit is a product of the potential drop and the current flowing in it (volts × amperes = watts). Where the electrical supply is alternating, the root-mean-square (rms) value of the voltage must be used.

POWER, the PRODUCT of a number used several times as a factor. Thus 2^4 ("two to the power four") is 16. By extension, 2^{-4} is $1/2^4 \equiv 1/16$; $2^{\frac{1}{4}}$ is $\sqrt[4]{2}$, and by definition $2^0 \equiv 1$.

POWER OF ATTORNEY, in US law, a legal document authorizing a person to act on behalf of the signatory, usually in business and financial matters. To be officially recorded, it must usually be certified by a notary public. A *general* power allows the agent to act for the signatory in all circumstances, while a *special* power covers only items listed.

POWERS, Hiram (1805–1873), US sculptor. Born in Woodstock, Vt., he worked in Florence from 1837. His work includes the famous neoclassic *Greek Slave* (1843) and busts of eminent Americans.

POWHATAN (c1550–1618), personal name Wahunsonacock, chief of the POWHATAN INDIANS and head of the Powhatan Confederacy of tribes which he enlarged until it covered most of the Virginia tidewater region and part of Maryland. He befriended the JAMESTOWN settlers under their leader John SMITH (1608). Later hostilities were settled when his daughter POCAHONTAS married John ROLFE (1614).

POWHATAN INDIANS, North American tribe in E Va., of ALGONQUIAN linguistic stock. They grew corn, hunted, fished and lived in villages with palisades. Under POWHATAN their confederacy dominated some 30 tribes. After his death (1618) violent clashes with encroaching settlers led to their defeat. Some 3 000 Powhatan live in E Va. today.

POWYS, John Cowper (1872–1963), English writer. His work included novels such as *Wolf Solent* (1929) and *A Glastonbury Romance* (1932), his *Autobiography* (1934), poems, essays and lectures.

POZNAŃ, historic city in W central Poland, on the Warta R. It has heavy industry and hosts an annual trade fair. Pop 469 085.

PRAETOR, in ancient Rome (from 366 BC), a magistrate elected annually to administer justice, second in rank to the CONSUL. By 197 BC there were six praetors, four of whom were responsible for provincial administration.

PRAETORIAN GUARD, the elite household troops of the Roman emperors, consisting of 9 (later 10) cohorts of 1 000 foot soldiers with higher rank and pay than ordinary troops. Instituted by Augustus in 2 BC, they assumed enough power to overthrow emperors. Constantine disbanded them in 312.

PRAETORIUS, Michael (German name Schultheiss; 1571–1621), prolific German composer of choral church music and dances, and author of *Syntagma musicum* (1614–20), a historically important treatise on theory and instruments.

PRAGMATIC SANCTION, an edict by a ruler pronouncing on an important matter of state, such as the succession. The most famous was issued by the Holy Roman Emperor Charles VI in 1713 (published 1718), declaring that his eldest daughter MARIA THERESA should inherit the throne in the absence of a male heir. This resulted in the War of the AUSTRIAN SUCCESSION.

PRAGMATISM, a philosophical theory of knowledge whose criterion of truth is relative to events and not, as in traditional philosophy, absolute and independent of human experience. A theory is pragmatically true if it "works"—if it has an intended or predicted effect. All human undertakings are viewed as attempts to solve problems in the world of action; if theories are not trial solutions capable of being tested, they are pointless. The philosophy of pragmatism was developed in reaction to late 19th-century IDEALISM mainly by the US philosophers C. S. PEIRCE, William JAMES and John DEWEY. (See also INSTRUMENTALISM.)

PRAGUE (Praha), capital of Czechoslovakia, on the Vltava R. One of Europe's great historic cities, it became prominent under Emperor Charles IV, who founded the university, the first in central Europe (1348). The Hapsburgs ruled Prague for nearly 300 years, until Czechoslovakia's independence after WWI. Prague was invaded by the Nazis in 1939 and by Warsaw Pact countries in 1968. The city has great cultural, commercial and industrial importance and is the center of the country's engineering industry. Pop 1 078 096.

PRAIRIE CHICKENS, two species of North American grouse, genus *Tympanuchus*, weighing about 1kg (2.2lb). Once widespread in grassland and prairies of North America, due to pressure on land for farming as well as over-hunting they are now extremely uncommon. The HEATH HEN, the type species, is already extinct.

PRAIRIE DOGS, GROUND SQUIRRELS of the genus *Cynomys*. Social animals of the open plains of North America, they live in large colonies in burrows. They are short-tailed marmot-like creatures, active by day, feeding, grooming or sunbathing near their burrows. They frequently raise themselves on their hindlegs to watch for danger. A sharp whistle, given as warning, sends the colony dashing into the burrows.

PRAIRE DU CHIEN, city in SW Wisc., seat of Crawford Co., a former frontier post on the Mississippi R, with varied light industry. Pop 5 540.

PRAIRIE PROVINCES, the popular name for the Canadian provinces of Manitoba, Saskatchewan and Alberta.

PRAIRIES, the rolling GRASSLANDS of North America. There are three types: tallgrass, midgrass (or mixed-grass) and shortgrass, which is found in the driest areas. Typical prairie animals are the coyote, badger, prairie dog and jackrabbit, and the now largely vanished bison and wolf. (See also STEPPES.)

PRAIRIE SCHOONER, the "ship of the plains," the typical canvas covered wagon used in migration to the West. It developed about 1820 from the CONESTOGA WAGON but was lighter and often drawn by oxen.

PRAIRIE VILLAGE, city in NE Kan., a S suburb of Kansas City. Pop 28 138.

PRASEODYMIUM (Pr), one of the LANTHANUM SERIES. AW 140.9, mp 931°C, bp 3512°C, sg 6.48 (20°C).

PRATTVILLE, city in central Ala., the seat of Autauga Co. It has textile, lumber and paper industries. Pop 13 116.

PRAWNS, zoologically, shrimp-like crustaceans of the suborder Natantia, specifically those groups which possess a pointed rostrum projecting between the eyes. In common language, the term is often used interchangeably with SHRIMP, and applied to any large shrimp.

PRAXITELES (active about 370–330 BC), greatest Greek sculptor of his time. Of his major works, which introduced a new delicacy, grace and sinuosity of line, only a marble statue of Hermes carrying the infant Dionysus survives. There are Roman copies of his *Aphrodite of Cnidus* and *Apollo Sauroctonus*. (See GREEK ART AND ARCHITECTURE.)

PRAYER, in all religions, communication with the sacred; the major element in most private and public worship, often associated with SACRIFICE. It includes adoration, praise, thanksgiving, confession of sin and intercession for others as well as asking for one's own material and spiritual needs. Prayer ranges from the ardent spiritual experience of the mystic (see MYSTICISM) to traditional formal LITURGY. In Islam a set prayer is recited five times daily towards Mecca. In Christianity prayer is made through Jesus Christ and on his authority; it is based on God's power and PROVIDENCE. (See also LORD'S PRAYER.) Praying to the SAINTS is practiced in the Roman Catholic and Orthodox Churches.

PRAYER PLANT, popular name for two species of foliage house plants, *Maranta leuconeura kerchoveana* and *Maranta leuconeura massangeana*. Family: Marantaceae. (See MARANTA.)

PRAYING MANTIS. See MANTISES.

PREBLE, Edward (1761–1807), American naval officer. He commanded the first American warship to go beyond the Cape of Good Hope (1799), and in 1804 led the unsuccessful assault on Tripoli (see BARBARY WARS).

PRECAMBRIAN, the whole of geological time from the formation of the planet earth to the start of the PHANEROZOIC (the aeon characterized by the appearance of FOSSILS in rock strata), and thus lasting from about 4 550 to 570 million years ago. (See also GEOLOGY.)

PRECESSION, the gyration of the rotational axis of a spinning body, such as a GYROSCOPE, describing a right circular CONE whose vertex lies at the center of the spinning body. Precession is caused by the action of a TORQUE on the body. **Precession of the equinoxes** occurs because the earth is not spherical, but bulges at the EQUATOR, which is at an angle of 23.5° to the ECLIPTIC. Because of the gravitational attraction of the sun, the earth is subject to a torque which attempts to pull the equatorial bulge into the same plane as the ecliptic, therefore causing the planet's poles, and hence the intersections of the equator and ecliptic (the equinoxes), to precess in a period of about 26 000 years. The moon (see NUTATION) and planets similarly affect the direction of the earth's rotational axis.

PRECIOUS STONES. See GEMS.

PRECIPITATION, in meteorology, all water particles that fall from CLOUDS to the ground; including RAIN and drizzle, SNOW, SLEET and HAIL. Precipitation is important in the HYDROLOGIC CYCLE.

PRE-COLUMBIAN ART, art of what is now Latin America prior to COLUMBUS' discovery of the Americas in 1492. The two main cultural areas were the central Andes (S Colombia, Ecuador, Peru, Bolivia, NW Argentina and N Chile) and Meso-America (Mexico and central America). In both areas artistic development took place after c3000 BC. Mono-

The Castillo, a Toltec-Maya temple at Chichen-Itza in Yucatan. In the foreground another example of Pre-Columbian art, is a Chacmool figure, a type of altar. Offerings were placed on the figure's belly.

Presidency

Changing times for the Presidency

The office of President of the United States has been construed differently by each of the 39 men who have held the post since the adoption of the Constitution in 1789. There has been considerable confusion and controversy about the proper role of the Presidency ever since the earliest days of the Republic. John Jay put the basic question to George Washington in 1787: "Shall we have a king?" The Constitution did not establish a kingship in name, but many have argued that in reality the US does indeed have a monarch. Henry Jones Ford declared in 1818 that "American democracy has revived the oldest political institution of the race: the elective kingship." Others have disagreed strongly with this characterization, including some previous occupants of the Oval Office. James K. Polk, President in the 1840s, insisted that "There (is) no King in this country, (only) a citizen chosen by the people to manage the government for a limited time." Perhaps a more balanced and objective view of the role of the President is provided by Harold J. Laski, one of the foremost US political scientists. He observed that "The President of the US is both more and less than a king; he is, also, both more and less than a prime minister. The more carefully his office is studied, the more does its unique character appear."

Despite variations which have occurred from time to time, scholars have identified two main approaches to the Presidency: leadership and stewardship. Theodore Roosevelt, President during most of the first decade of the twentieth century and one of the most active chief executives in history, asserted that the President's duty was "to do anything that the needs of the nation demand, unless such action is forbidden by the Constitution or the laws." Teddy Roosevelt, then, staunchly believed in the leadership approach to the Presidency, and clearly practiced what he preached while in office. Roosevelt's hand-picked successor, William Howard Taft, had other ideas, however. Taft cautioned that the President possessed "no undefined residium of power which he can exercise because it seems to him to be in the public interest." It is easy to see why Roosevelt became so disillusioned with the stewardship of William Howard Taft.

While some recent Presidents have been stronger than others, it is agreed by almost all political observers that the power and influence of the Presidency have expanded enormously in the last half-century. The nation is unlikely to see the likes of a Calvin Coolidge in the Oval Office again. Coolidge, president 1923–39, was known as "Silent Cal." A parsimonious New Englander cut from a coarse cloth, he slept ten to twelve hours a night and took a nap every afternoon. Coolidge's laissez-faire philosophy led inevitably to a minimization of the Presidency. At the end of his second term, Coolidge was strolling along Pennsylvania Avenue in Washington, D.C. with one of his party's senators. As they neared the White House, the senator asked the President facetiously, "I wonder who lives there?" Coolidge replied, "Nobody. They just come and go." Coolidge came and went with less notice than most.

One cannot imagine Franklin D. Roosevelt, Harry Truman, Dwight Eisenhower, John Kennedy, Lyndon Johnson, Richard Nixon, or Jimmy Carter making the same comment, if only in jest. Their inability to deny their own importance would stem from the clear and singular prominence of the modern Presidency in US life and government. Every President since Franklin D. Roosevelt has set the tone and mood for the country. The Presidents have initiated the bold and innovative programs, the Presidents have committed the country to wars, and orchestrated the peace to a much greater degree than ever before. So overwhelming had the power and the prestige of the Presidency become by the late 1960s that observers were warning of imminent danger to the system of checks and balances by a presidential dictatorship, in substance if not in name. Books and editorials by the hundreds were written denouncing the "imperial presidency." The Presidents themselves, by their actions, gave clear notice that such fears were not wholly unwarranted. The Watergate scandals and the wars in Indochina provided many examples of presidential abuse of power, often based on a quasi-regal assumption of absolute rule which also often manifested itself in subtler ways.

According to the original intention and plan of the Founding Fathers, the legislative branch should have served to check this massive power growth in the executive. There are many institutional reasons for Congress' failure to do so, but one sure explanation is the conscious desire and effort of the modern executive to dominate and subdue the legislative branch. Since the advent of the New Deal in 1933, the crucial test of a President's success and leadership has been the degree to which he has mastered Congress. This is not to say that Presidents have not been whipped on occasion by Congress. Every President has shared Theodore Roosevelt's fondest wish: "Oh if I could only be President and Congress, too, for just ten minutes!" Every President has shared Richard Nixon's frequent and private lament to his staff: "Why do they (Congress) do these things to us?" Yet every chief executive has also shared Franklin D. Roosevelt's overriding desire to let Congress know who was boss. "Give me a bill I can veto!" thundered Roosevelt.

Whereas the President's success is most dependent upon the positive and decisive actions which he takes, a congressman's success seems to be rooted in inaction, and deference to his seniors. An individual congressman does not rock the boat; he waits his turn. As former Speaker of the House of Representatives Sam Rayburn was fond of saying, "To get along, you got to go along." Realistically, this may be the only practical and efficient way to run a group of 535 potential prima donnas in a system where party plays such a minor role. Unlike the UK's strong and disciplined parties, the US political parties are both less ideological and less cohesive. Only a few attempts are made to force party loyalty in congressional votes, and fewer still are the penalties imposable on recalcitrant congressmen. Just as the party cannot effectively impose its views and positions on its elected officials, so too the congressman's constituency has a notoriously poor track record. Few constituencies are informed enough to make their representative accountable for his votes. Since the congressman knows his constituency, for the most part, isn't looking, he is rather free to go his own way. Without real constraints from either his party or his constituency, he is independent to a considerable degree. This tends to complicate the legislative process. As Lewis Dexter observed: "The complexity of the organization and procedures of Congress reduces the effect of external voices on it. Its social organization exerts constraints on what any single congressman can do. It also enables him to confuse the issue as to what he has in fact done and why he did it. Clearly, influencing Congress is more than a matter of pressuring individual congressmen. The job is to approach the *right* congressman at the *right* time and in the *right* way."

This system is frustrating to almost all new Representatives and Senators.

chrome-decorated pottery, female figurines and elaborately designed textiles have been discovered in Ecuador and Peru dating from 3000–2500 BC. The great Andean classical period noted for textiles, ceramics, gold and silver work, jewelry and stone masonry took place in 1000 BC–800 AD prior to the INCA kingdom. The great city buildings at CUZCU, MACHU PICCHU and TIAHUANACO are striking achievements. The Meso-Americans excelled in the graphic and plastic arts. From about 1000 AD the illuminated codex writings of the MAYAS, MIXTECS and AZTECS recorded mythological stories. Their temples, as at CHICHEN-ITZA, were decorated with elaborately carved stone sculptures and reliefs, with wall frescoes inside. The OLMECS made small jade carvings and colossal stone heads. In Colombia the CHIBCHA INDIANS were skilled in ceramics, textiles and jewelry.

PREDESTINATION, in theology, the decree made by God before the creation of the world, that certain persons (the elect) should infallibly be saved. Resting on God's PROVIDENCE and GRACE, it is taught throughout the Bible, especially by St. Paul, and was elaborated by St. AUGUSTINE in opposition to PELAGIANISM. CALVINISM taught also the predestination of the non-elect to damnation, and denied any power to FREE WILL, regarding saving grace as irresistible and wholly gratuitous. JANSENISM was a similar Roman Catholic movement. Islam likewise teaches absolute predestination. (See also ARMINIANS.)

PREEMPTION ACT, an act passed in 1841 by the US Congress, allowing Western settlers to claim up to 160 acres of virgin land after 14 months' residence, and to pay just $1.25 an acre. It was later exploited by speculators and repealed in 1891. (See also HOMESTEADING.)

PREGL, Fritz (1869–1930), Austrian chemist awarded the 1923 Nobel Prize for Chemistry for his pioneering work on the microanalysis of organic compounds (see ANALYSIS, CHEMICAL; MICROCHEMISTRY).

PREGNANCY, in humans the nine-month period from the fertilization and IMPLANTATION of an EGG, the development of EMBRYO and FETUS through the BIRTH of a child. Interruption of MENSTRUATION and change in the structure and shape of the BREASTS are early signs; morning sickness, which may be mild or incapacitating is a common symptom. Later an increase in abdominal size is seen and other abdominal organs are pushed up by the enlarging WOMB. LIGAMENTS and JOINTS become more flexible in preparation for delivery. MULTIPLE PREGNANCY, hydatidiform mole, spontaneous ABORTION, antepartum HEMORRHAGE, toxemia and premature labor are common disorders of pregnancy. The time following birth is known as the puerperium.

PREHISTORIC AND PRIMITIVE ART, the earliest forms of art. **Prehistoric art** is the art of the STONE AGE. The first known works of art date from c15000 BC when man was carving statuettes of "mother-goddesses," like the *Venus of Willendorf*, in ivory, bone and stone, and painting bison, deer and cattle on cave walls, as at ALTAMIRA and the LASCAUX CAVES. Such depiction possibly had a magical function, helping hunters to capture their prey. In the NW European Mesolithic period (c8000–3000 BC) Scandinavian and Spanish cave painters depicted inter-tribal wars, harvest scenes and hunts. Complex rock paintings in the central Sahara regions of Africa, at Tassili-n-Ajjer, date from the Neolithic period (8000–3000 BC).

Primitive art is that of primitive societies (but the term PRIMITIVES applies to pre-1500 Italian painters and the naive painters like Henri ROUSSEAU). Primitive societies are usually hunting or agricultural

Richard Nixon reflected on his years in both houses of the Congress: "You know, you come to Washington, you have great ideas, and there you are in the committees or on the floor of the House, and you have an inability to implement your ideas. . . You've got to learn how to play the game."

Playing the game is difficult for members of Congress, yet it is far more frustrating for the President, even when he has served in one or both houses of Congress. The friction between President and Congress often boils down to this: the President is active and the Congress is not. The temptation is great for the President to run roughshod over Congress. He can accomplish his objectives much more swiftly and completely by ignoring congressional prerogatives, and minimizing the role of Congress in setting governmental policy.

Again, the constitutional system of checks and balances was designed to prevent such an occurrence, but it works only to a limited degree. The Constitution is quite ambiguous in many respects. Some claim that the flexibility thus provided is its real genius, yet this vagueness ensures that time and circumstance, more than the basic document of state, will determine the precise operation of government.

For example, a severe dispute in constitutional interpretation of executive powers developed over the years. The *expressed* powers of the executive—those specifically mentioned in the Constitution's text—were easily understood. These included the pardoning power and the appointment of certain public officers. Trouble developed about *implied* powers, however, because of the phrase "The executive power shall be vested in a President of the United States." An expressed executive power is the receiving of foreign ambassadors. An implied presidential power is the recognizing of foreign governments. The second power does not necessarily follow from the first, but the force of precedent over the years has made it an accepted practice for Presidents. As William Howard Taft noted, "so strong is the influence of custom that it seems almost to amend the Constitution."

The extent of expressed executive power has become especially controversial in the legislative area. The President gradually usurped certain legislative functions. The Constitution provides that treaties shall be concluded by the President with the advice and consent of at least two-thirds of the Senate, yet Presidents managed to evade their constitutional partner through the use of "executive agreements." Between 1940 and 1970 only 310 treaties were submitted to the Senate. During the same period, 5653 executive agreements were concluded unilaterally by the Presidents—and some of those executive agreements were far more extensive than the submitted treaties. One must add to this the more than 50000 "executive orders" which have been issued from the office of the president since 1907, none of which are submitted to Congress. By a similar device, Theodore Roosevelt increased the country's national forestland by 43 million acres. And the President has been called "chief legislator" by many as well, since at least 50% of all bills introduced in Congress originate in the White House and other executive departments.

This executive usurpation came about through the resourcefulness of strong Presidents and the opportunities given by history. National emergencies thrust upon the President expansive powers which Congress gladly yielded. The Great Depression, World War II, Korea, the Cold War and many other crisis situations resulted in the ceding of vast new responsibilities to the Oval Office. The President, one man, is certainly more capable of swift action than Congress, 535 men. During the "hundred days" of FDR's administration in 1933, the Congress obediently passed thousands of measures without so much as a whimper, and granted broad, sweeping authority to Roosevelt. Dissenters in Congress were shouted down with cries of "Vote, vote!" as they tried to speak. One legislator urged on his fellows with the cry "The house is burning down and the President of the United States says this is the way to put out the fire."

There are other reasons for the growth of presidential power, such as the chief executive's continuity of experience and office. Each Presidency extends over several Congresses and is a full-time office, while Congress takes long breaks several times each year. The President is the recognized channel for almost all foreign communications. He provides a national representation while Congress is fragmented and seemingly parochial. As Harry Truman was fond of saying, "The President is the only lobbyist all the . . . people in this country have!" And until the early 1970s Congress did not have even a fraction of the facilities and staff of the executive department. Thus, fact-finding and coordination naturally lodged with the President and his branch of government.

The trend toward executive hegemony was a dangerous one. But like so many other dangers, it was not fully comprehended until the country was shaken by crises resulting from executive abuse of power. Indochina and Watergate shook both Congress and the US people out of their complacency. A veritable revolution in executive-legislative relations took place from 1969 to 1976, aided by the tension which naturally existed between a Republican President and a Democratic Congress. First, Congress reasserted itself in war policy, passing the Cooper-Church amendment to end the US incursion into Cambodia in 1970. Then, while a weakened President struggled under the growing weight of Watergate, a War Powers Act was drafted and passed. This act gave Congress a near-equal voice in war-making policy, forcing withdrawal of all US troops committed abroad by the President within 60 days, unless Congress by joint resolution extended the foreign involvement.

Even more important were the structural and procedural reforms which Congress forced upon itself and its hierarchy. Staff sizes were doubled, research arms of Congress were strengthened considerably, and computer technology was utilized to improve support services. Both houses of Congress established budget committees to regain legislative control over appropriations and finance. These committees have proven most effective, counterbalancing the executive budget office. Thanks to Watergate, the congressional organization and hierarchy was streamlined and democratized to a greater extent than ever before. The 90 freshmen elected to Congress in the wake of the Nixon scandals in 1974 forced reform of the seniority system, fairer allocation of committee seats, and better utilization of the talents of each congressman. Congress also repealed many of the emergency grants of executive power, initiated an attempt to require that all federal regulations be submitted to Congress for approval, and exercised long-dormant supervisory powers over the CIA and the FBI. Significant progress was made toward a healthier legislative-executive balance of power.

The key word is "balance." If presidential predominance is not ideal, neither surely is congressional. Thomas Jefferson warned more than once that "The tyranny of the legislature is really the danger most to be feared." And even a presidential critic as severe as Arthur Schlesinger, Jr., cautions: "In demythologizing the Presidency, we must be careful not to remythologize Congress."

The relationship between President and Congress is not supposed to be one of harmony, of sweetness and light. Rather, there must be creative tension and constructive friction between the two branches. Cooperation has to be won through conflict; the very best policy may well emerge when some tension exists. But it can exist only when President and Congress are near equals in power and prestige.

The two twin tragedies of Indochina and Watergate, then, contained a broad and priceless silver lining for the US—a reawakening of congressional responsibility and the chance of a return to a proper executive-legislative equilibrium. As former senator J. William Fulbright suggested, "The greatest single virtue of a strong legislature is not what it can *do*, but what it can *prevent*." Congress appears well-equipped to prevent executive abuse in the future. At the same time, strong presidential leadership is not precluded. Political scientists Rexford Tugwell and Thomas Cronin have insisted that "a strong Presidency . . . should be a lean and candid one." The climate of change now prevailing will be the test of this bold ideal.

groups. However unsophisticated their artistic materials and workmanship, their art tends to be functional, related to religion, magic and rituals. Ancestor worship and the power of dead spirits, and thus spirit masks, are very important, especially in SE Asia. Ornamental skulls—heads were thought to be the home of the spirit—are common in New Zealand and New Guinea, and the motif of the squatting figure found in South America, Indochina and Indonesia suggests contact between their primitive peoples at some time. Some of the finest primitive art works are the magnificent 14th-century bronze-cast heads produced by the African IFE and BENIN tribes. (See PRIMITIVE MAN.)

PREHISTORIC ANIMALS, those members of the ANIMAL KINGDOM such as DINOSAURS, which flourished, reached their prime and then became extinct before the present day. Many of them gave rise to more successful groups which eventually replaced them. A large number are preserved in the FOSSIL record and from such material their evolutionary position and relationships can be worked out. This in turn may provide clues as to the evolutionary history of modern forms.

PREHISTORIC MAN. Study of early man is hampered by the difficulty of distinguishing between what was to become *Homo sapiens* and the ancestors of our modern apes. The actual point of separation of the two strains is so long ago, probably before either bore any resemblance to their modern descendants, that it is unlikely ever to be discovered. The earliest known form of man is **Ramapithecus**, though there is still debate as to whether he should be classed as of the Hominidae (family of man) or of the Pongidae (anthropoid-ape family). Only small fragments of Ramapithecus fossil skeletons exist, the earliest of these dating from some 14 million years ago, the latest from some 10 million years ago. The next earliest human fossil dates from about 3 million years ago and is tentatively designated Ethiopian Man: once again only fragments remain. In 1972 Richard Leakey discovered a skull, known as **Skull 1470**, which dates from 2.6 million years ago and which shows strong resemblances to modern man. It is now thought that men of Skull 1470 type evolved over a period of more than 2 million years into our recent ancestors, Neanderthal Man and Cro-Magnon Man, although there is as yet no fossil evidence to show this evolution. Rather later than Skull 1470, and assumed to be examples of parallel evolution, are **Australopithecus**, containing such subdivisions as Paranthropus and Zinjanthropus, and **Homo habilis**, who may well be merely a variant of Australopithecus. Australopithecines had small brain capacities (300–600cm³) as compared with those of Skull 1470 (800 cm³) or modern man (c1300cm³) and had distinctly ape-like features. They existed from 2 to 1 million years ago. Descended possibly from the australopithecines, possibly from Skull 1470 men, are the various forms of **Pithecanthropus erectus**, including Peking Man and Java Man: the earliest fossil examples date from possibly as much as 1.9 million years ago, the most recent from as little as 200000 years ago. Their brain capacity was of the order of 1000cm³. The exact relation of Heidelberg Man, dated c400000 BC, to Pithecanthropus Erectus and to modern man is not known. **Homo sapiens** remains first appear from about 400000 years ago onward. The oldest known example is that from Vértesszöllős, with a brain capacity of 1400cm³. In more recent times, there were two distinct types of prehistoric man: Neanderthal and CRO-MAGNON MAN. **Neanderthal Man**, who was either absorbed or annihilated by invading Cro-Magnon men, did not have a fully erect posture but, despite this and his remarkably simian appearance, had an average brain capacity (1400cm^3) greater than that of modern man. It is thought that Neanderthal Man, who effectively became extinct during the STONE AGE, was probably an offshoot from the mainstream of human evolution. With his disappearance and the emergence of Cro-Magnon Man, the stage was set for the final evolution into the races of modern man. (See PRIMITIVE MAN.)

PRELOG, Vladimir (1906–), Yugoslav-born Swiss chemist who shared with CORNFORTH the 1975 Nobel Prize for Chemistry for his work on ENZYMES.

PRELUDE, an instrumental, usually keyboard, introduction to a musical work. It was employed by J. S. BACH to introduce FUGUES and SUITES. In later piano music it is often a self-contained composition, as in the *Preludes* of CHOPIN, SCRIABIN or DEBUSSY.

PREMIER. See PRIME MINISTER.

PREMINGER, Otto Ludwig (1906–), Austrian-born film director, who came to the US in 1936. His films include *Carmen Jones* (1954), *Anatomy of a Murder* (1959), *Exodus* (1960) and *The Man with the Golden Arm* (1955), the story of a heroin addict.

PRENDERGAST, Maurice Brazil (1859–1924), US painter influenced by POSTIMPRESSIONISM, a member of the EIGHT. His work includes *Umbrellas in the Rain* (1899) and *Central Park* (1901).

PRE-RAPHAELITE BROTHERHOOD, influential group of English artists formed in 1848 in reaction against the prevailing academic style. An allegorical subject, bright colors and minute naturalistic detail are typical of their work, as in *Christ in the House of his Parents* (1950) by MILLAIS or *The Scapegoat* (1854) by H. HUNT. A third founder member was D. G. ROSSETTI, and BURNE-JONES and William MORRIS were later followers. Critic John RUSKIN was an advocate of the Pre-Raphaelites.

PRESBYOPIA, a defect of VISION coming on with advancing age in which the LENS of the EYE hardens, causing loss of the ability to accommodate (focus) nearby and often distant objects. The condition is corrected by supplying two pairs of GLASSES (one for close work, the other for distant vision), though these may be combined in bifocal lenses.

PRESBYTER (from Greek *presbyteros*, elder), office of MINISTRY in the early Church. There were several presbyters in each congregation, ordained as leaders and teachers. At first identical with the "overseers" (or "bishops"), presbyters became by the 2nd century a distinct order of PRIESTS. (See also BISHOP; ELDER.)

PRESBYTERIANISM, form of church government by ELDERS. Midway between episcopacy and congregationalism, it was espoused at the Reformation by the REFORMED CHURCHES, who viewed it as a rediscovery of the apostolic practice of government by PRESBYTERS. There is a hierarchy of church courts: the *kirk-session*, the minister and elders elected by the local congregation; the *presbytery*, representative ministers and elders from a given area; the SYNOD, members chosen from several presbyteries; and the *general assembly*, the supreme body, consisting of ministers and elders from all the presbyteries. (Various names are used for these courts.) Presbyterian doctrine is biblical CALVINISM, usually with the WESTMINSTER CONFESSION as a subordinate standard. Worship is simple and dignified.

PRESCOTT, city in central Ariz., seat of Yavapai Co. First capital of the territory, it is now a resort and mining and livestock center. Pop 13 134.

PRESCOTT, Samuel (1751–c1777), American patriot who in a famous ride with Paul REVERE escaped to warn his home town CONCORD, Mass., of the British advance (1775). Later captured, he died in prison.

PRESCOTT, William (1726–1795), American Revolutionary colonel. He commanded the militia in the Battle of BUNKER HILL (1775) and took part in the Battles of LONG ISLAND (1776) and SARATOGA (1777).

PRESCOTT, William Hickling (1796–1859), US historian. Despite the handicap of near blindness he became an authority on Spain and the Spanish conquest of America. His *History of the Reign of Ferdinand and Isabella the Catholic* (1837), *History of the Conquest of Mexico* (1843) and *History of the Conquest of Peru* (1847) became classics, admired for their narrative skill as well as their historical rigor.

PRESERVES. See JELLY AND JAMS.

PRESIDENCY, in many countries the office of head of state and often of chief executive; also of the head of many business, educational and other organizations. The US president is both head of state and chief executive. The Founding Fathers intended the presidency to act as a point of unity for the separate states and provide a commander in chief for joint defense. The office has been molded by events and by the elected presidents themselves and has steadily grown in power and prestige. President and vice-president are the only elected US federal executives. A candidate for president must be over 35 years of age and be a "natural-born" US citizen resident for at least 14 years. By a majority vote the ELECTORAL COLLEGE chooses a president for a four-year term. A president may serve not more than two terms.

The Constitution empowers the president to appoint, with the advice and consent of the Senate, cabinet ministers, Supreme Court justices, ambassadors and other high officials. The president similarly appoints heads of boards, agencies and commissions set up by Congress. As commander in chief, the president represents the supremacy of civil authority over the military. He has powers under the Constitution and statutes to issue an EXECUTIVE ORDER in times of emergency; the TAFT–HARTLEY ACT gives powers to intervene in labor-management disputes. The president plays a customary role of great importance in foreign policy, owing to his ability to use speed, flexibility and secrecy in negotiations. This role is enhanced by his sole authority in determining the use of nuclear weapons. Although the president cannot declare war, he can create a condition of war by ordering up troops, as did Kennedy, Johnson and Nixon in Laos, Cambodia and Vietnam. Under the Constitution, the LEGISLATURE, like the JUDICIARY, is independent of the authority of the president, who is responsible for the execution of laws. But the president's ability to VETO legislation and to initiate it through his party, and his position as a patron and popular figurehead carry great weight in the lawmaking process.

The Executive Office of the President provides the agencies, bureaus and councils vital to the execution of presidential duties. The White House Office Staff includes the president's secretaries, military aides, advisors and his personal physician.

The office's great power of political leadership depends ultimately on the political skills of the president. His control of patronage and his ability to exert pressure on the legislative and judicial branches of government by appealing directly to the people are powerful weapons for the maintenance of presidential power. (See also CHECKS AND BALANCES; SEPARATION OF POWERS; CONGRESS OF THE UNITED STATES; UNITED STATES CONSTITUTION; WATERGATE.)

PRESIDENTIAL RANGE, a range of the White Mts, in N N.H. Mt Washington (6 288ft) is the highest of many peaks in this resort area named for US presidents, e.g. Mts Jefferson, Adams and Monroe.

PRESIDIUM, in the USSR, the supreme state authority between sessions of the SUPREME SOVIET, responsible for legislation. The Supreme Soviet elects its chairman, who is titular head of state, 15 vice-chairmen (one from each union republic), 20 members and secretary. At different times the POLITBURO has also been termed Presidium.

PRESLEY, Elvis (1935–), US singer, born at Tupelo, Miss. He came to fame as a Rock 'n' Roll singer in 1956, dominated ROCK MUSIC until the early 1960s and starred in many movies.

PRE-SOCRATIC PHILOSOPHY, term applied to the thought of the early Greek philosophers (c600–400 BC) whose work came before the influence of SOCRATES. Their works survive mostly in obscure fragments, but their fame and importance lie in their being the first to attempt rational explanations of the universe. They are grouped into the IONIAN school in Asia Minor (THALES, ANAXIMANDER, ANAXIMENES, XENOPHANES, HERACLITUS, ANAXAGORAS, and the ATOMISTS, LEUCIPPUS and DEMOCRITUS) and PYTHAGORAS and the ELEATICS (PARMENIDES, ZENO, EMPEDOCLES) in S Italy and Sicily. PROTAGORAS and the SOPHISTS are usually also included.

PRESQUE ISLE, city in NE Maine. It is a processing center for Aroostook Valley agricultural products and a tourist resort. Pop 11 452.

PRESS, Freedom of the. See FREEDOM OF THE PRESS.

PRESSBURG. See BRATISLAVA.

PRESSBURG, Treaty of (1805), between Napoleon and Holy Roman Emperor Francis II after Austria's defeat at AUSTERLITZ. Among other concessions, Austria lost her Italian possessions and recognized Napoleon as King of Italy. (See NAPOLEONIC WARS.)

PRESSURE, the FORCE per unit area acting on a surface. The SI UNIT of pressure is the PASCAL (Pa = newton/(metre)^2) but several other pressure units, including the atmosphere (101.325kPa), the bar (100kPa) and the millimetre of mercury (mmHg = 133.322Pa), are in common use. In the universe, the pressure varies from roughly zero in interstellar space to an atmospheric pressure of roughly 100kPa at the surface of the earth and much higher pressures within massive bodies and in STARS. According to the KINETIC THEORY of matter, the pressure in a closed container of GAS arises from the bombardment of the container walls by gas molecules: it is proportional to the temperature and inversely proportional to the volume of the gas. Pressure is a stress characterized by its uniformity in all directions and usually produces a decrease in volume. The value of the pressure affects most physical, chemical and biological processes. Consequently many different types of pressure gauges have been developed (see MANOMETER).

PRESSURE COOKER, small AUTOCLAVE used for domestic cooking. Water boils inside the vessel at a pressure greater than atmospheric (commonly 2atm), at which pressure its BOILING POINT is considerably higher than 100°C, so that the food cooks much more rapidly than if boiled normally. The pressure, regulated by a weighted or spring-loaded valve, is due to the steam produced by the boiling water.

PRESTER JOHN, legendary Christian priest-king. A purported letter from 'Presbyter John," probably of Western authorship, reached the papal court in 1165. It described a great Christian utopia in the "three Indies," identified in later legend as Ethiopia.

PRESTON, industrial town and health resort in SE Ontario, Canada. Flour milling and furniture making are the principal industries. Pop 16 530.

PRETORIA, administrative capital of South Africa and capital of the Transvaal. Named for PRETORIUS, it has fine government buildings, art galleries and museums. Its industries include iron, steel, chemicals, glassware, engineering and paint. Pop 543 950.

PRETORIUS, Andries Wilhelmus Jacobus (1799–1835), commandant of the BOERS and GREAT TREK leader. His defeat of the ZULUS at Blood R (1838) led to the founding of Natal. He led the 1848 trek into the Transvaal.

PREVAILING WESTERLIES, the predominant WINDS which blow between latitudes 30° and 60° both N and S of the equator. In the N Hemisphere they blow from the SW; in the S Hemisphere, from the NW.

PRÉVERT, Jacques (1900–), French writer. His popular poems, sometimes satirical, sometimes melancholy, include *Paroles* (1946). Among his screenplays is that for Carné's *Les Enfants du paradis* (1945).

PRÉVOST D'EXILES, Antoine François (Abbé Prévost) (1697–1763), French writer, priest and adventurer. *Manon Lescaut*, a love story, is the masterpiece among his many novels.

PRIAM, in Greek mythology, last king of TROY. Most of his 50 sons, including HECTOR and PARIS, were killed in the TROJAN WAR. Priam was slain by Pyrrhus (Neoptolemus) while taking refuge on the altar of Zeus after the sack of Troy. (See also ACHILLES; CASSANDRA; HECUBA; ILIAD.)

PRIAPULIDS, a class or phylum, depending on classification, of soft-bodied marine worms. They live burrowed in sand or mud in intertidal regions of colder seas. The front end of the body comprises an eversible proboscis; a short cylindrical trunk ends abruptly and, characteristically in the genus *Priapulus*, in a multibranched respiratory appendage.

PRIBILOF ISLANDS, a group of four small islands

of volcanic origin in the Bering Sea. They lie about 300mi SW of Alaska and were acquired by the US in 1867. The two largest are St. Paul and St. George. Every spring, about 80% of the world's fur seals visit the islands to breed. Since 1911 the seal herds have been protected and the US permits only 60 000, out of some 2 000 000, to be taken annually.

PRICE, the amount of money (or goods in a barter system) for which a commodity or service is exchanged. In theory, prices are set in a FREE ENTERPRISE SYSTEM by SUPPLY AND DEMAND, while in a planned economy (see SOCIALISM) the state decides prices centrally. (See also MONEY; WAGE AND PRICE CONTROL.)

PRICE, Leontyne (1927–), US soprano. Her first success was as Bess in Gershwin's *Porgy and Bess* (1952). Since then she has achieved international fame in such operatic roles as Verdi's *Aïda*, Puccini's *Tosca* and Bizet's *Carmen*.

PRICE CONTROL. See WAGE AND PRICE CONTROL.

PRICHARD, industrial city in SW Ala., a N suburb of Mobile. Its chief industries are cotton processing and chemicals. Pop 41 578.

PRICKLY ASH, *Zanthoxylum americanum*, a tree or shrub native to eastern North America, which produces spiny stems that form dense thickets. Prickly ash bark is used as a folk remedy for toothache and rheumatism. Family: Ritaceae.

PRICKLY HEAT, or heat rash, an uncomfortable itching sensation due to excessive sweating, mainly seen in Europeans visiting the tropics.

PRICKLY LETTUCE, *Lactuca scariola*, an annual or biennial herb, native to Europe and introduced to North America. Oil from the seeds is used in the preparation of foods. Family: COMPOSITAE.

PRICKLY PEAR, tree-like CACTI of the genus *Opuntia*, which have flat stems and yellow flowers. They are native to the southern US, but extend farther north than any other cacti. Prickly pears are troublesome weeds and, when introduced into Australia, could be controlled only by introducing a small moth whose caterpillars burrowed into the stems. Family: Cactaceae.

PRIDE'S PURGE. See RUMP PARLIAMENT.

PRIEST, in most religions, a cultic officer who mediates the sacred to the people; a spiritual leader, expert in ritual and generally the offerer of SACRIFICE. In the Old Testament an initial patriarchal priesthood was later restricted to the descendants of AARON, assisted by LEVITES (see also HIGH PRIEST). In the Christian Church PRESBYTERS came to be called priests—an order of the threefold MINISTRY—with powers of ABSOLUTION and to offer the sacrifice of the MASS. At the Reformation the priesthood of Christ, and in him that of all believers, were emphasized. (See also ORDINATION.)

PRIESTLEY, J. B. (John Boynton Priestley; 1894–), English man of letters. His writings include many plays but he is best known for such popular novels as *The Good Companions* (1929) and *Angel Pavement* (1930) and for his major critical work *Literature and Western Man* (1960).

PRIESTLEY, Joseph (1733–1804), British theologian and chemist. Encouraged and supported by Benjamin FRANKLIN, he wrote *The History and Present State of Electricity* (1767). His most important discovery was OXYGEN (1774; named later by LAVOISIER), whose properties he investigated. However, he never abandoned the PHLOGISTON theory of COMBUSTION. He later discovered many other gases—AMMONIA, CARBON monoxide, hydrogen SULFIDE—and found that green plants require sunlight and give off oxygen. He coined the name RUBBER. His association in the 1780s with the LUNAR SOCIETY brought him into contact with scientists such as James WATT and Erasmus DARWIN. His theological writings and activity were important in leading the English Presbyterians into Unitarianism; indeed he is regarded as a principal architect of the Unitarian Church. Hostile opinion over this and his support of the French Revolution led to his emigration to the US (1794).

PRIMARY ELECTION, in the US, an election in which party members elect candidates to run in a subsequent general election. Primary elections are used throughout the US for choosing candidates for

Primula vulgaris elatior, a cultivated variety of the wild yellow primrose, often sold under the common name polyanthus.

Congress, state offices and even local government posts. In most states the candidates are proposed by petition, after which an election determines which candidate is the ultimate party choice. In primary elections for national campaigns the candidates are always listed by party and most states operate "closed" primaries in which only registered party members vote. One third of the states hold primaries to nominate their delegates to the national party convention which chooses the presidential candidate. In presidential preference primaries the voter chooses the person he wants nominated by the convention (see ELECTION.)

PRIMATES, the order of MAMMALS containing MAN, the ANTHROPOID APES, MONKEYS, TARSIERS, POTTOS, BUSHBABIES and LEMURS. Compared with most mammal groups, primates are peculiarly unspecialized; the brain, however, is proportionately larger and more developed. The stages in the evolution of primates are mostly represented in extant forms. From tarsier-like forms evolved the lemurs and lorises; from the EOCENE Omomyidae arose the Anthropoidea; the Catarrhini, Platyrrhini and Hominoidea.

PRIME MINISTER, or premier, head of the executive in a parliamentary system. The prime minister appoints and directs his own CABINET, which is the source of all major legislation. He also has the power to make and dismiss ministers and to call an election before the full term of a government. The office developed in England at the time of Robert WALPOLE. Most parliamentary democracies distinguish between the head of state (a monarch or president) and the prime minister, who is head of the government. (See also PARLIAMENT.)

PRIME NUMBER, a NATURAL NUMBER which cannot be expressed as the PRODUCT of other natural numbers, e.g., 1, 2, 3, 5, 7, 11, 13, 17 and 19.

PRIME RATE, in the US, the rate of INTEREST on short-term loans charged to the major corporations by commercial banks. It governs the whole system of US commercial interest rates.

PRIMITIVE ART. See PREHISTORIC AND PRIMITIVE ART.

PRIMITIVE MAN, term for societies whose culture has reached a level little, if any, higher than the STONE AGE. Although technologically limited and economically unsophisticated, primitive societies may have extremely complex social structures with extensive rules directing behavior such as MARRIAGE, kinship and religion (see TABOOS). Most contemporary primitive societies are Neolithic; that is, they practice agriculture, make pots, weave textiles and work stone to make tools. A few, however, are of Paleolithic type, such as the AUSTRALIAN ABORIGINES and the recently extinguished TASMANIANS. PREHISTORIC MAN probably first formed primitive societies about 250 000 years ago.

PRIMITIVES, in art history, a term describing several groups of painters: the pre-1500 Netherlandish or Flemish school, including VAN EYCK; all Italian painters between GIOTTO and RAPHAEL; and more recent naive, untrained artists such as Henri ROUSSEAU, and the Americans Edward HICKS and Grandma MOSES.

PRIMO DE RIVERA, Miguel (1870–1930), Spanish general and politician. Supported by King Alfonso XIII, he overthrew the government in 1923 and became dictator. Popular discontent, economic failure and loss of army support forced him to resign in 1930. His son, **José Antonio Primo de Rivera**, founded the FALANGE and was executed by loyalists in 1936.

PRIMOGENITURE, law by which the eldest son inherits family lands. It originated in medieval Europe for the support of the son who gave military service to his king. Never widely established in the US, primogeniture is still customary in England.

PRIMROSE, low herbs of the genus *Primula*, native to the N Hemisphere, particularly in cooler regions. They produce clusters of leaves near the ground and colorful flowers growing either among the leaves or on long stems. The common primrose (*Primula vulgaris*) produces yellow flowers. Many *Primula* varieties are cultivated. Family: Primulaceae. The **Cape primrose** (species of the genus *Streptocarpus*) produces attractive mid-green foliage and numerous pink, purple or blue flowers, making it a popular house plant. It grows well at average house temperatures, and should be placed in a sunny east or west window. The soil should be kept evenly moist. Propagation is by leaf cuttings, offsets or from seeds. The Cape primrose is not related to the true primroses, but belongs to the family Gesnariaceae.

PRIMROSE, William (1904–), Scottish violist, US resident since 1937. He cofounded the Festival Quartet in 1956. Several composers, including Bartók, have written works especially for him.

PRINCE, royal title (Latin *princeps*: leader). It is given to the son of a monarch, the consort of a reigning queen or the head of a small state or principality. The male issue of a deposed royal family, such as the Bourbons, may retain the title, though it often simply denotes high birth or family headship as in the case of many Russian, Italian and French princes.

PRINCE ALBERT, city in central Saskatchewan, Canada. It is a resort and a manufacturing city with beer, flour, timber, dairy and oil products. Pop 27 613.

PRINCE ALBERT NATIONAL PARK, Canadian national park in central Saskatchewan. It is a forested resort region covering 1 496sq mi with many lakes and waterways.

PRINCE EDWARD ISLAND, Canadian maritime province. It is Canada's smallest province, both in area and in population, but it is the most densely

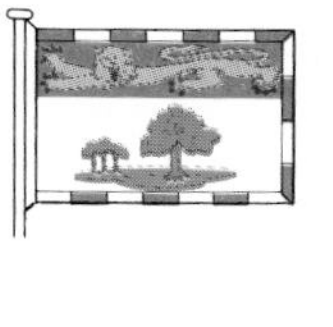

Name of province: Prince Edward Island
Joined Confederation: July 1, 1873
Capital: Charlottetown
Area: 2 184sq mi
Population: 111 641

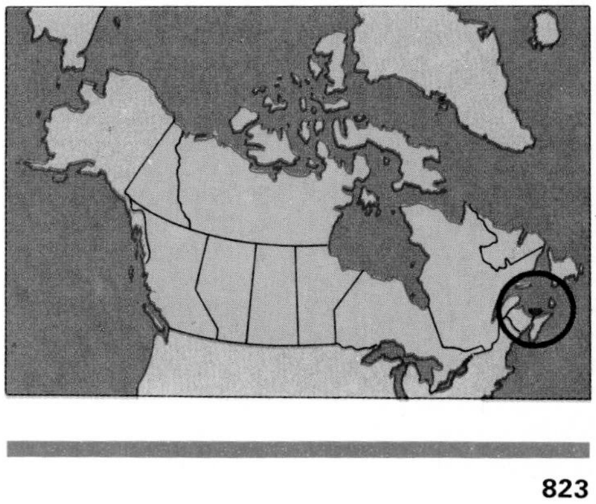

populated. The island lies in the Gulf of St. Lawrence and is separated from the mainland by the Northumberland Strait. Its length is about 145mi and greatest width 35mi. There are many tidal inlets, known as "rivers," and no point is more than 10mi from the sea. The surface is gently rolling with small hills in the center and SE; the highest point is 450ft above sea level. The climate is milder than on the mainland and often humid. Annual precipitation averages 40in and heavy snowfalls are common in winter.

Prince Edward Island's economy is based on farming, fishing, tourism and light industry. There are two ferryboat links to the mainland and an airline to Charlottetown, the capital, and Summerside. The population has remained at about 110 000 for many decades; emigration to the mainland has held down the growth rate. Some 80% of the population descends from British and 15% from original inhabitants of ACADIA. There are several hundred MICMAC INDIANS living on reservations.

Jacques CARTIER was the first European known to have explored the island and in 1603 CHAMPLAIN claimed it for France. Settled by the French in 1719, it became part of the British colony of Nova Scotia in 1763 and was named Prince Edward Island in 1799 for the future father of Queen Victoria. In 1851 the island won control of its own affairs and it hosted the Confederation Conference of 1864 which led to the foundation of the Dominion of Canada. Prince Edward Island joined the Dominion in 1873 and gained financial support for its depressed economy. It has remained basically rural but since WWII the central government has mounted large construction and aid programs for the islanders.

PRINCE EDWARD ISLAND NATIONAL PARK, a recreational area in Prince Edward Island, Canada. The park comprises a 25mi strip of cliffs, dunes and marshes on the N coast and has many fine beaches.

PRINCE GEORGE, city in central British Columbia, Canada. It is a summer resort and a center for the lumber industry. It also has an oil refinery and chemical plants. Pop 32 755.

PRINCE OF WALES. See WALES, PRINCE OF.

PRINCE OF WALES, Cape, cape on the W tip of Seward Peninsula, Alaska. It is the most westerly point on the mainland of North America.

PRINCE RUPERT, city and port in W British Columbia, Canada, on the Pacific Ocean, 10mi N of the Skeena R. It is a major distribution center. Pop 15 747.

PRINCETON, borough in N.J., 11mi NNE of Trenton. PRINCETON UNIVERSITY and other major educational establishments are located there. Pop 12 311.

PRINCETON, Battle of (Jan. 3, 1777), in the American REVOLUTIONARY WAR, battle fought in Princeton, N.J., in which the British under Cornwallis were defeated by George Washington in a surprise attack.

PRINCETON UNIVERSITY, private university in Princeton, N.J. Chartered as the College of New Jersey in 1746, it was renamed in 1896. One of the leading universities in the US, it includes world-famous graduate schools of engineering, architecture and scientific research. It has admitted women since 1969.

PRINCIP, Gavrilo (1895–1918), Serbian nationalist who assassinated Archduke Francis Ferdinand of Austria-Hungary on June 28, 1914 at SARAJEVO. The incident precipitated WWI.

PRINCIPATE, period in Roman history from 27 BC to 284 AD (the beginning of Augustus' reign to the beginning of Diocletian's) when the unofficial title of the emperors was *Princeps.* The term came to denote autocracy, and under Diocletian was replaced by the Dominate, from his assumption of the title *Dominus.*

PRINCIPE. See SAO TOME AND PRINCIPE.

PRINTED CIRCUIT. See ELECTRONICS.

PRINTING, the reproduction of words and pictures in ink on paper or other suitable media. Despite the advent of INFORMATION RETRIEVAL systems, the dissemination and storage of knowledge are still based primarily on the printed word. Modern printing begins with the work of Johann GUTENBERG, who probably invented movable type and type metal in the 15th century. Individual characters could be used several times. Little changed for 400 years until the invention of machines that could cast type as it was required (see LINOTYPE; MONOTYPE). Letterpress and lithography are today the two most used printing techniques. **Letterpress** uses raised type that is a mirror image of the printed impression. The type is inked and the paper pressed to it. A number of typeset pages (usually 8, 12, 16, 24 or 32) are tightly locked in a metal form such that, when a sheet of paper has been printed on both sides, it may be folded and trimmed to give a *signature* of up to 64 pages. The arrangement of the pages of type is the *imposition.* Most newspapers use **rotary letterpress**: the forms are not flat but curved backward, so that two may be clamped around a cylinder. Paper is fed between this cylinder and another, the impression cylinder. This technique is especially swift when the paper is fed in as a continuous sheet (a *web*). **Lithography** depends on the mutual repulsion of water and oil or grease. In the fine arts, a design is drawn with a grease crayon on the surface of a flat, porous stone, which is then wetted. The water is repelled by the greasy areas; but ink is repelled by the damp and adheres to the greasy regions. Modern mechanized processes use the same principle. Commonest is **photo-offset**, where the copy to be printed is photographed and the image transferred to a plate such that the part to be printed is oleophilic (oil-loving), the rest hydrophilic (water-loving). The plate is clamped around a cylinder and inked. The impression is made on an intermediate "blanket cylinder," which prints onto the paper. **Gravure** is another major printing technique. The plate is covered with a pattern of recessed cells in which the ink is held, greater depth of cell increasing printed intensity. Gravure is good for color and the plates long-lasting, but high initial plate-making costs render it suitable only for long runs. Little-used for books, it is much used in packaging as it also prints well on media other than paper. **Illustrations**, in letterpress, are reproduced using line or HALFTONE blocks (see also ETCHING). In photo-offset black and white illustrations are printed much as is text; and gravure is inherently suitable for printing tones. For COLOR, the illustration is photographed for each of the colors magenta, cyan, yellow and black, and separate plates or blocks made: the four images are superimposed in the printing to give a full-color effect. (See also INK PAPER; PHOTOGRAPHY.)

PRINTZ, Johan Björnsson (1592–1663), governor of NEW SWEDEN (1643–53), a Swedish colony on the Delaware R. He resigned because of popular dissatisfaction with his rule, and returned to Sweden.

PRISM, in GEOMETRY, a solid figure having two faces (the bases) which are parallel equal polygons and several others (the lateral faces) which are parallelograms. Prismatic pieces of transparent materials are much used in optical instruments. In spectroscopes (see SPECTROSCOPY) and devices for producing monochromatic LIGHT, prisms are used to produce DISPERSION effects, just as Newton first used a triangular prism to reveal that sunlight could be split up to give a SPECTRUM of colors. In BINOCULARS and single-lens reflex cameras reflecting prisms (employing total internal reflection—see REFRACTION) are used in preference to ordinary MIRRORS. The NICOL PRISM is used to produce POLARIZED LIGHT.

PRISONER OF WAR, in wartime, combatant who has been captured by or has surrendered to an enemy state. The Hague Convention of 1907 and the GENEVA CONVENTIONS of 1929 and 1949 established rules in international law for the protection of such prisoners, notably that they should not be maltreated nor required to give any information other than their name and rank, and that they should be repatriated upon cessation of hostilities.

PRISONS, institutions for confining people accused and/or convicted of breaking a law. There are three types of prisons in the US. Jails and lockups are run by city and county governments mainly for those awaiting trial, but also for some convicts serving short sentences. State prisons are operated by the individual states and contain the majority of those convicted of serious crimes. Federal prisons house those convicted of offenses relating to the drug and liquor laws, income tax or immigration laws, misuse of the mails, threats to national security and crimes carried out across the state borders.

By the early 1800s, most of the Western world had adopted imprisonment (rather than CORPORAL PUNISHMENT, CAPITAL PUNISHMENT, or exile to PENAL COLONIES) as the chief method of dealing with criminals. The purpose of prisons has long been to protect society, and to punish people for their crimes in a manner sufficiently unpleasant to act as a deterrent. More recently there has been a movement to shift the emphasis from punishment to reform and rehabilitation. The PAROLE system, developed in the 19th century, gives the convict an opportunity to re-adapt himself to society towards the end of his prison sentence. Twentieth-century innovations include open (i.e. unfortified and relatively unguarded) prisons, facilities to do useful work and to learn trades, and the provision of psychiatric care, but these reforms are not widespread.

PRIVACY, customary right of a citizen to maintain his private life without "undue" interference or publicity. In many countries, the right of privacy is written into the constitution. The concept represents a balance of interests between the individual and the state. In general, privacy may only be interfered with by constitutionally-approved means such as powers given to the police or other government bodies. In the US, a major threat to privacy arises from government and commercial organizations having acquired and computerized large bodies of information about individuals.

PRIVATEER, armed vessel which was privately owned, but commissioned by a government to prey upon enemy ships in wartime. Privateers thus often supplemented a nation's navy. The practice of privateering was outlawed (1856) by the Declaration of Paris.

PRIVET, Old World shrubs of the genus *Ligustrum* whose dense growth makes them popular for hedges. The California privet (*Ligustrum ovalifolium*), native to Japan, is popular in colder climates as it retains its leaves in freezing conditions. Family: Oleaceae.

PRIVILEGE, in law, immunity from a normal liability. Diplomatic privileges, for instance, exempt foreign diplomats from income-tax laws. Privileged communications are those, e.g. between husband and wife or attorney and client, that need not be disclosed in connection with legal prosecutions.

PRIVY COUNCIL, in British history, an advisory council to the monarch, by whom its members were chosen. Powerful in the 15th and 16th centuries, it declined thereafter with the ascendancy of Parliament.

PRIZE FIGHTING. See BOXING.

PROBABILITY, the statistical RATIO between the number n of particular outcomes and the number N of possible outcomes: n/N; where all of N are equally likely. For example, when throwing a die there is 1 way in which a six can turn up and 5 ways in which a "not six" can turn up. Thus $n = 1$ and $N = 5 + 1 = 6$, and the ratio $n/N = 1/6$. If two dice are thrown there are 6×6 ($= 36$) possible pairs of numbers that can turn up: the chance of throwing two sixes is 1/36. This does not mean that if a six has just been thrown there is only a 1/36 chance of throwing another: the two events are independent; the probability of their occurring *together* is 1/36.

Consider throwing a die six times with the aim of getting each of the six numbers exactly once. If you want to do this in order (a permutation), say from 1 to 6, working out the probability of your doing so is easy: you have 1/6 chance of throwing a one, 1/6 chance of throwing a two, and so on; so that the probability of a favorable result overall is $(1/6)^6 = 1/46\,656$. If you are not concerned with the order (combination) the situation is different: the probability of a favorable result on the first throw is 1 (any number is favorable), on the second 5/6, and so on, so the overall probability is

$$6/6 \times 5/6 \times 4/6 \times 3/6 \times 2/6 \times 1/6$$

or $6!/6^6$ (see FACTORIAL)—about 1/65. Clearly one is more likely to succeed with a desired combination

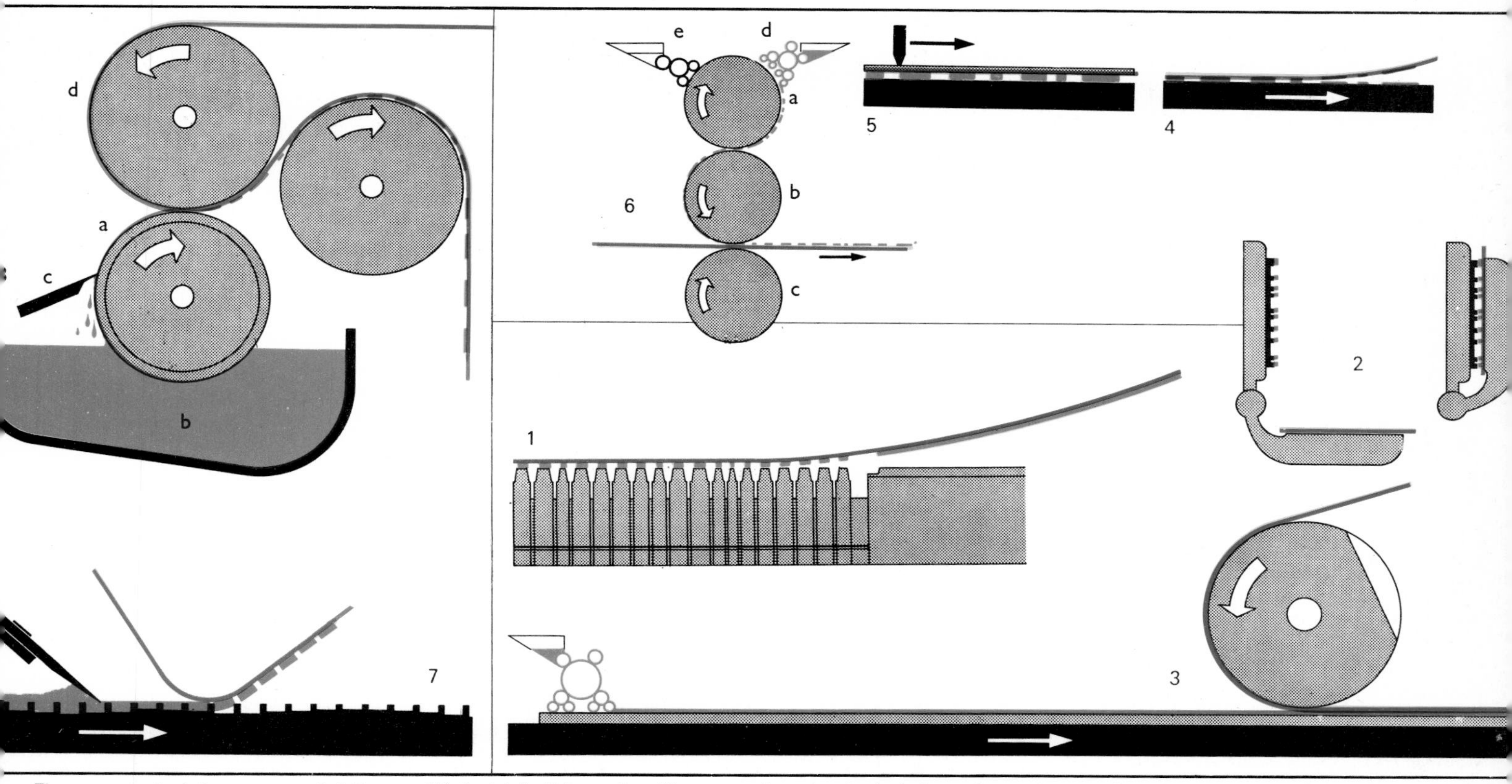

The commonest printing processes. In letterpress (1), the ink (red) is transferred by pressure from the raised printing surface to the paper (green). Pressure may be supplied by a platen (2) or by a cylinder in the flatbed cylinder technique (3). The latter speeds up printing by producing high pressures over the line of contact between cylinder and printing surface. In lithography (4), the printing surface is a flat stone or plate treated to repel ink in non-image areas and attract it in image areas. In offset lithography (6), the commonest modern method, the plate is wrapped around a cylinder (a)—fed by ink (d) and water (e) rollers—which transfers ("offsets") the inked image to an intermediate blanket cylinder (b) which prints it onto the paper fed between it and the pressure cylinder (c). In gravure (7) the printing surface is recessed in cells etched into a plate; the deeper the cells the deeper the image. In the rapid rotogravure process (8), a continuous web of paper is pressed over a gravure plate on a cylinder (a) by another cylinder (d); ink is fed from an ink reservoir (b), surplus ink being removed by a "doctor" blade (c).

than with a permutation. (See PERMUTATIONS AND COMBINATIONS.)

Probability theory is plainly intimately linked with STATISTICS. More advanced probability theory has contributed vital understandings in many fields of physics, as in THERMODYNAMICS, behavior of particles in a COLLOID (see BROWNIAN MOTION) or molecules in a GAS, and atomic physics (see ATOM; ELECTRON; BOSE–EINSTEIN STATISTICS).

PROBATE, the legal process of proving that a WILL is valid. Before a will can take effect, it must be shown that it is genuine, that it was the deceased's last will, that he signed it voluntarily and that he was of sound mind. Probate requires all possible heirs of the testator's property to be notified before a special hearing is held in a probate court, where objections can be lodged.

PROBATION, an alternative to prison, whereby convicted offenders are placed under the supervision of a probation officer, on condition that they maintain good behavior. The aim is to encourage reform, particularly for the young, when a spell in prison might simply reinforce criminal tendencies. (See also PAROLE; PUNISHMENT.)

PROBOSCIS MONKEY, a large LANGUR, *Nasalis larvatus*, remarkable for its nose, which in the male is extremely long and pendulous. Confined to Borneo, they live in mangrove swamps in troops of about 20.

PROCAINE, prototype local anesthetic agent related to COCAINE; used now mainly for surface ANESTHESIA. Its derivative procainamide is used in suppression of HEART arrhythmias. The hydrochloride of procaine is known as novocaine.

PROCESS PHILOSOPHY, a radical alternative to positivistic philosophies (see POSITIVISM), in which the physicists' "spatial" notion of TIME is rejected and interest centers in the developmental process. First propounded by Henri BERGSON, process philosophy influenced William JAMES, George SANTAYANA and Alfred North WHITEHEAD.

PROCLAMATION OF 1763, proclamation made by the British at the end of the FRENCH AND INDIAN WARS, establishing territorial rights for North American Indians. It aimed both to appease the Indians and to prevent land disputes, but it angered (and was in many respects disregarded by) the colonialists.

PROCONSUL, in ancient Rome, a CONSUL whose year of office was prolonged so that he could continue a military campaign. After the beginning of the Roman Empire in 27 BC it referred simply to the governor of a province.

PROCONSUL, an extinct ape represented by part of a skull found in Kenya in 1948. The smooth contour of the forehead and small brain show it to be more primitive than modern forms.

PROCRUSTES, in Greek legend, a notoriously cruel bandit whose victims were made to fit an iron bed by being stretched or by having their legs cut off.

PROCYON, Alpha Canis Minoris, a visual DOUBLE STAR, the brightest star in CANIS MINOR. It has absolute magnitude +2.7 and is 3.53pc distant.

PRODUCER GAS, fuel GAS made by partial combustion of coal or coke in mixed air and steam. It contains carbon monoxide, hydrogen, methane, and incombustible nitrogen and carbon dioxide. It has a low calorific value, 5 MJ/m³ (see FUEL), but being easy to make it is used in large furnaces.

PRODUCT, the result of MULTIPLICATION. Thus in $a.b=c$, the product is c.

PROFILE MOUNTAIN. See GREAT STONE FACE.

PROGESTERONE, female sex HORMONE produced by the corpus luteum under the influence of LUTEINIZING HORMONE. It prepares the WOMB lining for IMPLANTATION and other body organs for the changes of PREGNANCY. It is used in some oral CONTRACEPTIVES to suppress ovulation or implantation.

PROGRAMMED LEARNING, teaching method whereby matter to be learned is arranged in a coherent sequence of small clear steps (programmed) and presented in such a way that the student is able to instruct, test and, if necessary, correct himself at each step. The learning program is usually embodied in a book or booklet or adapted for use in conjunction with a TEACHING MACHINE. It enables the student to learn at his own pace, with a minimum of wasted effort. There are two basic kinds of program. The "linear program," based on the work of the Harvard psychologist B. F. SKINNER, obliges the student to compare his own response at each step with the correct response. The "intrinsic (or branching) program," originally developed for instructing US Air Force technicians, offers a limited choice of responses at each step. The correct response is immediately reinforced; an incorrect response obliges the student to follow a corrective subprogram leading back to the point at which the error occurred.

PROGRAMMING. See COMPUTER.

PROGRAM MUSIC, music with extra-musical meaning. It may describe an event, as in Byrd's *The Battell*, or a place, as in Vaughan Williams' *London Symphony*, or it may express specific feelings, as in Beethoven's *Pastoral Symphony*.

PROGRESSION, an ordered set of numbers; with the exception of the arithmetic, geometric and harmonic progressions, such sets are more usually termed SEQUENCES.

Arithmetic progression. A progression of the form $a, a+d, a+2d, \ldots, a+(n-1)d$, where a is the first term (x_1) and d is the common difference, $a+(n-1)d$ being the nth term (x_n). The sum to n terms, S_n, of an arithmetic progression is given by

$$S_n = n\left(a+\frac{n-1}{2}d\right).$$

The arithmetic mean of two terms, x_s and x_{s+2}, is given by $(x_s+x_{s+2})/2=x_{s+1}$.

Geometric progression. A progression of the form $a, ar, ar^2, ar^3, \ldots, ar^{n-1}$, where a is the first term and r the common ratio, ar^{n-1} being the nth term. The sum to n terms of a geometric progression is given by

$$S_n = a\frac{1-r^n}{1-r},$$

and the geometric mean of two terms, x_s and x_{s+2}, by $\sqrt{x_s . x_{s+2}} = x_{s+1}$. The geometric mean of any two different positive numbers is always less than their arithmetic mean.

Harmonic progression. A progression of the form

$$\frac{1}{a}, \frac{1}{a+d}, \frac{1}{a+2d}, \ldots, \frac{1}{a+(n-1)d},$$

the terms being the RECIPROCALS of those in an arithmetic progression. There is no simple expression for S_n in this case. The harmonic mean of two terms, x_s and x_{s+2}, is given by

$$\frac{2x_s x_{s+2}}{x_s + x_{s+2}} = x_{s+1}.$$

(See also MEAN, MEDIAN AND MODE.)

PROGRESSIVE CONSERVATIVE PARTY, one of Canada's two main political parties. Although on some issues it is more conservative in outlook than Canada's LIBERAL PARTY, the margin between the two is narrow. Called the Liberal-Conservative Party until 1942, it was formed in 1854 out of a coalition designed and led by J. A. MACDONALD (later first prime minister of Canada).

PROGRESSIVE EDUCATION, an educational reform movement which grew from the idea that schooling should cater for the emotional as well as the intellectual development of the child, and that the basis of learning should be the child's natural and individual curiosity, rather than an enforced discipline. In the US the movement, led by John DEWEY, was most active c1890–1950. (See also EDUCATION.)

PROGRESSIVE PARTY, the name of three American political organizations which fought in 20th-century presidential campaigns. Each was largely characterized by programs of social and economic reform. The Progressive Party of 1912 (better known by its nickname, the Bull Moose Party) chose ex-President Theodore Roosevelt as its nominee. It seceded from the Republican Party after the nomination of TAFT, but was reunited with it during the campaign of 1916.

The Progressive Party of 1924 was formed by farm and labor leaders dissatisfied with the conservatism of the Republican administration. Its position, like that of the Bull Moose Party, was that there should be government control of trusts, and it upheld the right of government intervention in private wealth. Its presidential nominee was Robert LA FOLLETTE. The Progressive Party of 1948 nominated former Democratic Vice-President H. A. WALLACE for the presidency. The party sought better relations with the USSR and an end to the Cold War. It had support from many left-wing groups but was labeled a "Communist front" organization. It polled little more than a million votes out of 48 000 000.

PROHIBITION, restriction or prevention of the manufacture and sale of alcoholic drinks. It refers in particular to the period from 1919 to 1933 when (by means of the 18th Amendment to the Constitution) there was a Federal prohibition law in the US. In spite of the intensive economic and group pressures which had brought it about, it soon became apparent that the law was too unpopular and too expensive to enforce. A now-notorious time of gangsterism followed, with a vast illegal liquor business (the activities involved were known as bootlegging) in the control of men such as Al CAPONE. Prohibition was repealed (1933) by the 21st Amendment. A few states in the US maintained local prohibition laws as late as 1966. See also VOLSTEAD ACT; NATION, CARRY; WOMEN'S CHRISTIAN TEMPERANCE UNION.)

PROJECTILES. See BALLISTICS.

PROJECTION, in PSYCHOLOGY and PSYCHIATRY, the treatment by an individual of mental activity as reality (see DREAMS; EIDETIC IMAGE; HALLUCINATION; ILLUSION). In PSYCHOANALYSIS, the term describes the interpretation of situations or the actions of others in such a way as to justify one's self-opinion or beliefs, as in PARANOIA and paranoid SCHIZOPHRENIA.

PROJECTION, of a POINT P onto a LINE L, the INTERSECTION of the line and the line drawn PERPENDICULAR to it passing through the point.

PROJECTION TEST, test whereby an individual's personality may be gauged by his completion of unfinished sentences, his interpretation of "pictures" from inkblots, etc.

PROJECTIVE GEOMETRY, that branch of GEOMETRY based on PERSPECTIVE. Consider the three-dimensional figure defined by a PLANE figure A and a point P not in that plane; this is a projection of A from P. Should the projection be cut by another plane, a plane figure A′ is formed: the relationship between A and A′ is termed a perspective transformation. If A′ is projected from a new point P′ onto a third plane, the figure A″, the result of two perspective transformations, is formed. The result of a sequence of perspective transformations is termed a *projective transformation*. Projective geometry may be viewed as the study of those of the figure's properties that are unchanged by projective transformation.

PROKARYOTE; PROKARYOTIC CELL. See CELL.

PROKHOROV, Aleksandr Mikhailovich (1916–), Soviet physicist awarded with N. G. BASOV and C. H. TOWNES the 1964 Nobel Prize for Physics for work with Basov leading to development of the MASER.

PROKOFIEV, Sergei (1891–1953), Russian composer. A student at the St. Petersburg Conservatory with RIMSKY-KORSAKOV, Prokofiev created a fierce, dynamic, unemotive style which later became somewhat softer and more eclectic. His works include the popular Classical Symphony, the opera *The Love for Three Oranges* (1921) and *Peter and the Wolf* (1936), a piece for narrator and orchestra.

PROLACTIN, or **luteotrophic hormone,** HORMONE secreted by the PITUITARY GLAND concerned with LACTATION after PREGNANCY.

PROLATENESS. See OBLATENESS.

PROLETARIAT, name given to industrial employees as a social and economic class. In Marxist theory, the proletariat is exploited by and inimical to the bourgeois class of employers and property owners.

PROMETHEUS, a demi-god of Greek mythology, one of the TITANS and a brother of ATLAS. He was sometimes said to have created humankind out of earth and water. In a widespread legend, Prometheus stole fire from the gods and brought it to man. ZEUS punished Prometheus by having him bound to a rock and sent evils among mankind by means of PANDORA's box.

PROMETHIUM (Pm), radioactive element (see RADIOACTIVITY) in the LANTHANUM SERIES. It has no naturally occurring isotopes, and is formed in nuclear reactors. It is used in miniature nuclear-powered batteries. AW 147, mp 1080°C.

PROMINENCE, Solar. See SUN.

PRONGHORN, *Antilocapra americana*, the only horned animal that sheds its horn sheath, and the only one with branched HORNS as distinct from ANTLERS. They live in groups in arid grasslands and semi-desert of western North America, feeding on forbs and browse plants. Conservation efforts have restored numbers from an estimated 30 000 in 1924 to a present 400 000.

PRONUNCIATION, the ways in which words, syllables and letters are spoken. Pronunciation varies from language to language, as well as within a language, different accents deriving from differing geographical locations or educational backgrounds. Studies of pronunciation in the past are assisted by both rhyming verse and the transliteration of words borrowed from other languages. The concept of a "correct" pronunciation is now largely obsolete. (See also PHONETICS.)

PROOF SPIRIT, term describing the proportion of alcohol (ETHANOL) in distilled liquor. In the US the proof value is twice the percentage of ethanol by volume. Thus 90 proof represents 45% ethanol. In the UK, proof spirit is somewhat stronger, containing 57.1% ethanol by volume.

PROPAGANDA, selected information, true or false, which has been promoted with the aim of persuading people to adopt a particular belief, attitude or course of action. During the 20th century all the major political ideologies have employed propaganda and made use of modern media to reach a mass audience. It has an important role in modern warfare and by WWII separate bureaux and ministries were established to promote morale and subvert the enemy. The 1972 budget of the US Information Agency was $192 819 000. In the West there has been an increase in professional propagandists such as people in public relations and in ADVERTISING. (See also GOEBBELS.)

PROPANE (C_3H_8), colorless gas, an ALKANE found in NATURAL GAS and light PETROLEUM. Mixed with butane, it is sold as BOTTLED GAS. It is also used to make ETHYLENE by CRACKING, and is oxidized to ACETALDEHYDE. MW 44.1, mp −190°C, bp −42°C.

PROPELLER, a mechanical device designed to impart forward motion usually to a SHIP or AIRPLANE, operating on the screw principle. It generally consists of two or more inclined blades (AIRFOILS) radiating from a hub, and the amount of THRUST it produces is proportional to the product of the mass of the fluid it acts on and the rate at which it accelerates the fluid. The inclination, or "pitch," of the propeller blades determines the theoretical distance moved forward with each revolution. A "variable-pitch propeller" can be adjusted while in motion, to maximize its efficiency under different operating conditions; it may also be possible to reverse the propeller's pitch, or to "feather" it—i.e., minimize its resistance when not rotating. John FITCH, in 1796, developed the first marine screw propeller; John ERICSSON perfected the first bladed propeller, in 1837. (See also CAVITATION.)

PROPER MOTION, the rate of motion at right angles to our line of sight of a star, measured in seconds of arc per year.

PROPERTIUS, Sextus (c50–c16 BC), Roman elegaic poet, whose poems center on his celebrated love-affair with his mistress Cynthia. Though often obscure, he is vivid, imaginative and powerful.

PROPERTY, social concept and legal term indicating the ownership of, or the right to enjoy, something of value; it may also be an interest in something owned by another. Under some systems such as FEUDALISM or COMMUNISM, ownership of some or all kinds of property is vested not in the individual but in the state or its head. The US Constitution establishes the individual's right to property. COMMON LAW distinguishes between *real property*, land and generally non-transportable goods such as houses and trees, and *personal property*, all other kinds; financial rights such as copyrights or patent holdings are personal. The law treats the two kinds differently in such areas as tax, debt, inheritance and other significant obligations and relationships. (See also DEED; ESTATE; MORTGAGE.)

PROPHETS, in the Old Testament, men who by special REVELATION proclaimed the word of God by oracles and symbolic actions; originally seers and ecstatics. Often a scourge of the establishment, they were religious and social reformers who called for righteousness and faithfulness to God, and pronounced judgment on the ungodly. (See also ESCHATOLOGY; MINOR PROPHETS; OLD TESTAMENT.) In the early Church prophecy was a recognized CHARISMA, but soon died out except in Montanism (see MONTANUS). It was revived among ANABAPTISTS, QUAKERS, MORMONS and PENTECOSTALS. In Islam Mohammed is the last and greatest prophet. Oracular prophets are found in many religions. (See also ORACLE; SHAMANISM.)

PROPORTION, a statement that two RATIOS are equivalent, written $a:b = c:d$, as in the statement $2:3 = 6:9$. Two FUNCTIONS are proportional if, for all x, $f(x) = kg(x)$, where k is the CONSTANT of proportionality. If the value of k is not known, the statement may be written $f(x) \propto g(x)$.

PROPORTIONAL REPRESENTATION. See ELECTION.

PROPRIETARY COLONIES, in US colonial history, English colonies granted by royal charter to an individual or small group, mostly in the period 1660–90. Large tracts of land in N.Y., N.J., Pa., N.C. and S.C. were allocated in this way. The proprietors had almost despotic power in theory, but in practice had to yield rights to the colonists, and the system was ended after the REVOLUTIONARY WAR.

PROPYLAEA, monumental entrance to the W end of the ACROPOLIS in Athens, still largely intact. Consisting of a large columned hall, it was built by the famous Greek architect Mnesicles c435 BC.

PROSERPINE. See PERSEPHONE.

PROSPECTING, the hunt for MINERALS economically worth exploiting. The simplest technique is direct observation of local surface features characteristically associated with specific mineral deposits. This is often done by prospectors on the ground, but increasingly aerial photography is employed (see PHOTOGRAMMETRY). Other techniques include examining the seismic waves caused by explosions—these supply information about the structures through which they have passed; testing local magnetic fields to detect magnetic metals or the metallic gangues associated with nonmagnetic minerals; and, especially for metallic sulfides, testing electric CONDUCTIVITY.

PROSTATE GLAND, male reproductive GLAND which surrounds the urethra at the base of the BLADDER and which secretes semen. This carries sperm made in the TESTES to the PENIS. Benign enlargement of prostate in old age is very common and may cause retention of the urine. CANCER of the prostate is also common in the elderly but responds to HORMONE treatment. Both conditions benefit from surgical removal.

PROSTHETICS, mechanical or electrical devices inserted into or onto the body to replace or supplement the function of defective or diseased organs. **Artificial limbs** designed for persons with AMPUTATIONS were among the first prosthetics; but metal or plastic JOINT replacements or BONE fixations for subjects with severe ARTHRITIS, FRACTURE or deformity are now also available. Replacement TEETH for those lost by CARIES or trauma are included in **prosthodontics** (see also DENTISTRY). The valves of the HEART may fail as a result of rheumatic or congenital heart disease or bacterial endocarditis, and may need replacement with mechanical valves (usually of ball-and-wire or flap types) sutured in place of the diseased valves under cardiorespiratory bypass. If the **pacemaker** of the heart fails, an electrical substitute can be implanted to stimulate the heart muscle at a set rate.

PROSTHODONTICS. See PROSTHETICS.

PROSTITUTION, exchange of sexual intercourse for money or gifts as a commercial transaction, usually by women. Despite condemnation through all ages, and often being officially illegal or restricted, prostitution has flourished in almost all societies, particularly in urban centers, where social pressures are less, anonymity can be maintained and many people lead transitory and lonely lives. Today it is generally regarded by governments as unavoidable, and legislation aims merely to "keep it off the streets" and to prevent criminal abuses, such as "protection" and procuring.

PROTACTINIUM (Pa), rare metal in the ACTINIDE series, found in URANIUM ores. More than 12 isotopes are known, all radioactive; Pa^{231} is the longest lived (half-life 34000yr). Protactinium is usually pentavalent, resembling NIOBIUM and TANTALUM. AW 231, mp $<$1600°C, sg 15.37 (calc.).

PROTAGORAS (c490–421 BC), most famous of the Greek SOPHISTS, remembered for the maxim "man is the measure of all things." A respected figure in Athens, where he spent most of his life, he taught RHETORIC and the proper conduct of life ("virtue"), and was appointed lawmaker to the Athenian colony of Thurii in 444 BC. Little is known of his teaching, but he is thought to have been a relativist concerning knowledge and a sceptic about the gods, although he upheld conventional morality.

PROTECTIONISM, in INTERNATIONAL TRADE, a policy by which a country seeks to protect its own industries by controling the import and export of goods. It generally takes the form of restrictive TARIFFS or QUOTAS on imported goods. The US has had a long tradition of protectionism, and still has a number of restrictive import quotas, in spite of the general world trend towards freer trade (see GENERAL AGREEMENT ON TARIFFS AND TRADE).

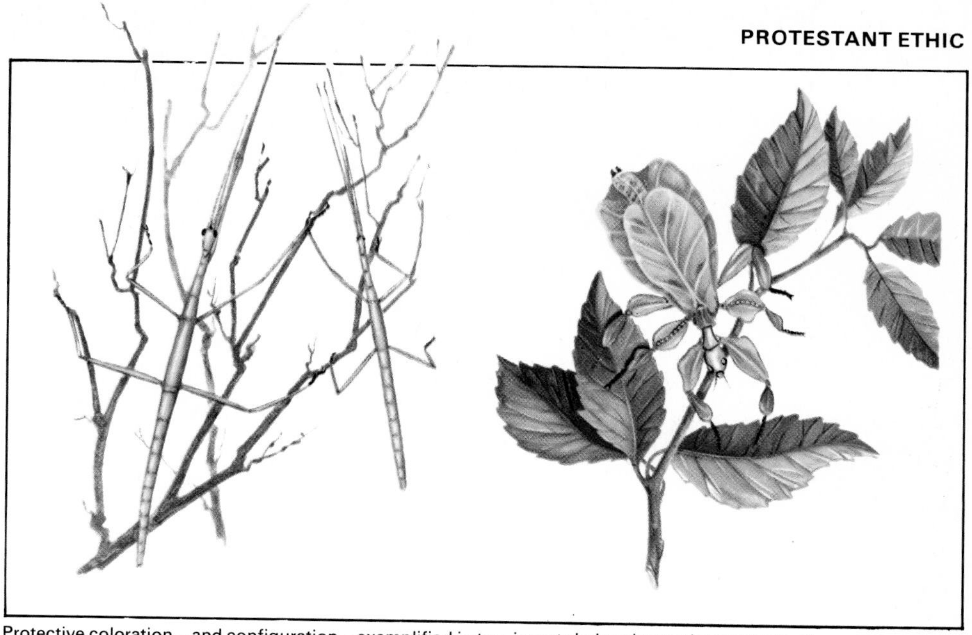

Protective coloration—and configuration—exemplified in two insects belonging to the mantis family.

PROTECTIVE COLORATION. Many animals have adapted their coloration as a means of defense against predators. Except where selection favors bright coloration for breeding or territorial display, most higher animals are colored in such a way that they blend in with their backgrounds—by pure coloration, by disruption of outline with bold lines or patches, or by a combination of the two. The most highly developed camouflage is found in ground-nesting birds, for example, NIGHTJARS, or insects, such as WALKING STICKS or LEAF INSECTS. Associated with this coloration must be special behavior patterns enabling the animal to seek out the correct background for its camouflage and to "freeze" against it. Certain animals can change the body texture and coloration to match different backgrounds: OCTOPUSES, CHAMELEONS, and some FLATFISHES. An alternative strategy adopted by some animals, particularly insects, is the use of shock-coloration. When approached by a predator these insects flick open dowdy wings to expose bright colors, often in the form of staring "eyes," to scare the predator.

PROTECTORATE, a country which is nominally independent, but surrenders part of its SOVEREIGNTY, such as control over foreign policy, in return for protection by a stronger state. The degree of control and dependency may vary. Many states in the European colonial empires were governed as protectorates.

PROTECTORATE, The, period of English history from 1653 to 1659 when the country was ruled by a Lord Protector, a Council of State, and Parliament. It was in effect, a dictatorship. Oliver CROMWELL was the first Lord Protector, succeeded in 1658 by his son Richard, who, unable to control army and Parliament, resigned in 1659, paving the way for the RESTORATION.

PROTEIN, a high-molecular-weight compound which yields AMINO ACIDS on HYDROLYSIS. Although hundreds of different amino acids are possible, only 20 are found in appreciable quantities in proteins, and these are all α-amino acids. Proteins are found throughout all living organisms. Muscle, the major structural material in animals, is mainly protein; the 20% of blood which is not water is mainly protein. ENZYMES may contain other components, but basically they too are protein. Approximately 700 different proteins are known. Of these 200–300 have been studied and over 150 obtained in crystalline form. Some proteins, such as those found in the hides of cattle and which can be converted to LEATHER, are very stable, while others are so delicate that even exposure to air will destroy their capability as enzymes. The most important and strongest bond in a protein is the PEPTIDE bond joining the amino acids in a chain. Other bonds hold the different chains together: HYDROGEN BONDING, together with strong disulfide bonds and secondary peptide links are important here. The three dimensional structure of proteins helps to determine their properties; X-RAY studies have shown that the amino acid chain is sometimes coiled in a spiral or helix. Although proteins are very large molecules (with molecular weights ranging from 12000 to over 1 million), many of them are partly ionized and hence are soluble in water. Such differences in size, solubility and electrical charge are exploited in methods of separating and purifying proteins. The separation of proteins in an electrical field (ELECTROPHORESIS) is widely applied to human serum in the diagnosis of certain diseases.

PROTEIN SYNTHESIS. All the PROTEIN in any living organism is undergoing a continual process of breakdown and resynthesis. The white rat replaces half its protein in 17 days; in man this requires 80 days. However not all proteins are broken down and resynthesized at the same rate: e.g., half the human blood-serum proteins are replaced in 10 days; liver protein requires 20–25 days, while replacement of bone protein is very slow. Protein synthesis is very rapid; within minutes of injecting an animal with a radiolabelled AMINO ACID, radiolabelled protein can be isolated. Protein synthesis takes place within the CELLS of an organism. The first step is the activation of an amino acid by reaction with ATP (see NUCLEOTIDES). This activated amino acid is then bound to a specific soluble form of RNA (see NUCLEIC ACIDS) known as transfer RNA. There are at least 20 different types of transfer RNA, one for each amino acid. The soluble RNA-amino acid complex then travels to the RIBOSOME where the amino acid is added to other amino acids to form a polypeptide (see PEPTIDE). The order in which the specific transfer RNAs bring each amino acid to the ribosome is determined by messenger RNA. The transfer RNA then returns to the CYTOPLASM to collect another molecule of its specific amino acid. Messenger RNA contains the code for a particular protein and is only used a few times before being destroyed. Messenger RNA from one organism can be used with transfer RNA and ribosome from another to synthesize a protein; this may explain how VIRUSES take over the synthetic systems of a cell.

PROTEROZOIC, the portion of the PRECAMBRIAN running from about 2390 to 570 million years ago, divided into three eras: **Aphebian**, 2390–1640; **Helikian**, 1640–880; and **Hadrynian**, 880–570. (See also ARCHEOZOIC; GEOLOGY.)

PROTESTANT EPISCOPAL CHURCH. See EPISCOPAL CHURCH, PROTESTANT.

PROTESTANT ETHIC, set of attitudes thought to be embodied in calvinistic PROTESTANTISM, especially the value placed on hard work, "for the greater glory of God." The term was introduced by M. WEBER in *The Protestant Ethic and the Spirit of Capitalism*

(1904–05), which argued that the Protestant ethic was responsible for the rise of capitalism.

PROTESTANTISM, the principles of the REFORMATION. The name derives from the *Protestatio* of the minority reforming delegates at the Diet of SPEYER (1529). Protestantism is characterized by subordinating TRADITION to the Bible as its basis for doctrine and practice, and stresses JUSTIFICATION BY FAITH, biblical preaching and a high personal morality (see also EVANGELICALISM). In reaction to Roman Catholicism it rejected papal claims, the MASS and the worship of the SAINTS. The main original branches were LUTHERANISM, CALVINISM, ANGLICANISM and Zwinglianism (see ZWINGLI, HULDREICH), with small ANABAPTIST sects on the left wing. Exercise of the right of private judgment in interpreting Scripture led to much fragmentation, a trend reversed in recent decades by the ECUMENICAL MOVEMENT. Protestant churches of later genesis include the CONGREGATIONAL CHURCHES, BAPTISTS, QUAKERS, METHODISTS, the MORAVIAN CHURCH, the SALVATION ARMY and the PENTECOSTAL CHURCHES. Initial rapid expansion (see REFORMATION), followed by consolidation and scholastic doctrinal orthodoxy (17th century), was succeeded by a period of liberalism influenced by romantic subjectivism (see SCHLEIERMACHER) and the ENLIGHTENMENT. From this sprang MODERNISM, opposed in different ways by FUNDAMENTALISM and NEO-ORTHODOXY. In some churches desire for détente with Rome has led to repudiation of the term "protestant."

PROTEUS, minor sea-god of Greek mythology, herdsman of the sea-creatures, and servant of POSEIDON. A prophet, he would change shape when asked questions (hence the word *protean*), but was forced to answer if he was held firmly.

PROTISTA, taxonomic term proposed by some authorities to include unicellular, colonial and filamentous forms of eukaryote (see CELL) organisms from both the ANIMAL KINGDOM and PLANT KINGDOM. Included in this group are ALGAE and FUNGI.

PROTON, stable elementary particle found in the nucleus of all ATOMS. It has a positive charge, equal in magnitude to that of the ELECTRON, and rest mass of $1.672\,52 \times 10^{-27}$kg (slightly less than the NEUTRON mass but 1836.1 times the electron mass). As the HYDROGEN ion, the proton is chemically important, particularly in aqueous solutions (see ACID), and is widely used in physics as a projectile for bombarding atoms and nuclei.

PROTOPLASM, the substance including and contained within the plasma membrane of animal CELLS but in plants forming only the cell's contents. It is usually differentiated into the nucleus and the cytoplasm. The latter is usually a transparent viscous fluid containing a number of specialized structures; it is the medium in which the main chemical reactions of the cell take place. The nucleus contains the cell's genetic material.

PROTOZOA, animals consisting of a single CELL, with all life functions carried on within that cell, distinct from the METAZOA, multicelled organisms in which cells are differentiated in function and are united into groups in ORGANS or TISSUES. Nearly 50 000 species of Protozoans have been described. They occur all over the world in every possible kind of habitat. They are divided into four classes: the Mastigophora, or flagellated Protozoa; the Sarcodina, which move using PSEUDOPODIA; the Sporozoa, nonmotile and parasitic, and the Ciliata, ciliated forms.

PROTRACTOR, an instrument for measuring ANGLES. Usually semicircular, it is marked off in degrees along the semicircular edge.

PROUDHON, Pierre Joseph (1809–1865), French social thinker, and a founder of modern ANARCHISM. From a poor family, he gained an education through scholarships, and also became a printer. He first gained notoriety with his book *What is Property?* (1840), to which his famous answer was "Property is theft." However, he was not a socialist, but believed in a society in which property would be distributed among free individuals who cooperated spontaneously without a framework of state authority—a philosophy he called *mutualism*. In 1847 he clashed with MARX, and started a struggle between libertarian and authoritarian views on socialism which continued long after his death. Proudhon spent his life propagating his ideas, writing much of his work in prison (1849–1852) and in exile (1858–1862). His influence can be traced in SYNDICALISM, and in French radicalism.

PROUST, Joseph Louis (1754–1826), French chemist who established the law of definite proportions, or Proust's Law (see COMPOSITION, CHEMICAL).

PROUST, Marcel (1871–1922), French novelist whose seven-part work *Remembrance of Things Past* is one of the greatest novels of the 20th century. It was written during the period 1907–19, after Proust, who suffered continually from asthma, had retired from Parisian high society and become virtually a recluse. A semi-autobiographical exploration of time, memory and consciousness, with an underlying theme of the transcendency of art over the futility of man's best efforts, it broke new ground in the art of the novel, and was enormously influential.

PROVENÇAL, or *langue d'oc*, a ROMANCE LANGUAGE developed from the Latin spoken in S France, principally Provence. During the Middle Ages, Provençal produced a notable literature which reached its highest point with the courtly love poetry of the TROUBADOURS.

PROVENCE, region and former province of France, embracing the lower Rhône R (including the CAMARGUE) and the French Riviera. The chief cities are Nice, Marseilles, Toulon, Avignon, Arles and Aix-en-Provence (the historic capital). It is a sunny and picturesque region, famous for historical associations and its fruit, vineyards and olives. It was the first transalpine Roman province (hence the name), and later it became an independent kingdom (879–933), finally passing to the French kings in 1486.

PROVERBS, Book of, book of the OLD TESTAMENT; an example of the "wisdom literature" popular in post-exilic Judaism. Its eight sections, attributed in their headings to various authors including SOLOMON, consist of numerous pithy proverbs, mostly unconnected moral maxims, probably dating between the 9th and 2nd centuries BC.

PROVIDENCE, state capital of R.I., at the head of Providence Bay. It is a busy port, and industries include textiles, jewelry, machinery and metal products. It is also an important educational center, and the home of the famous Rhode Island School of Design. Founded by Roger WILLIAMS in 1636, it is one of the oldest cities in the US. Pop 179 116.

PROVIDENCE, in THEISM, the government by God of the universe. By his almighty power, he infallibly determines and regulates all events—in general providence by means of natural laws: in special providence by MIRACLES or other direct actions. CALVINISM stresses the providential government of free human actions. (See also CREATION.)

PROVINCETOWN, town in SE Mass. on the tip of Cape Cod, the first landing place of the PILGRIM FATHERS (Nov. 20, 1620). It is now a popular summer resort and a fishing port. Pop 2911.

PROVO, city in N central Ut., seat of Utah Co. Settled by the MORMONS in 1849, it is now an iron and steel center with diverse manufacturing industries. Pop 53 131.

PROXIMA CENTAURI, the closest star to the sun (1.33pc distant), a red dwarf star orbiting ALPHA CENTAURI.

PRUDHOMME, René François Armand. See SULLY PRUDHOMME.

PRUD'HON, Pierre Paul (1758–1823), French painter. His best-known works are the portrait of the Empress Josephine (1805) and *Crime Pursued by Vengeance and Justice* (1808). His painting, influenced by CORREGGIO, is soft and sensual in character.

PRUNE. See PLUM.

PRUNING, practice of cutting off parts of cultivated plants to encourage growth in the rest of the plant. It is commonly used on rose, fruit and ornamental trees and shrubs to regulate growth and improve the quality of flowers and fruits. The timing and degree of pruning is usually critical.

PRUSSIA, militaristic state of N central Europe that dominated Germany until the rise of NAZISM. At the height of its strength it stretched from W of the Rhine to Poland and Russia. The Baltic territory later known as East Prussia was Germanized by the TEUTONIC KNIGHTS in the 1200s and later became the duchy of Prussia. In 1618 it came under the rule of the Electors of nearby Brandenburg, the Hohenzollerns, and FREDERICK I declared himself king of Prussia in 1701. Under his successors, particularly FREDERICK THE GREAT, the Prussian state expanded to become the strongest military power in N Europe. It received a setback in the NAPOLEONIC WARS, but recovered. In 1862 BISMARCK became premier, and as a result of a planned series of wars and skilful diplomacy conducted under his direction, King WILLIAM I of Prussia was declared Emperor of Germany in 1871. Prussia was the largest and most powerful of the states of the united Germany, and continued so until 1934, when by a decree of HITLER the separate German states ceased to exist as political entities. After WWII former Prussian territory was divided between East Germany, Poland and the USSR.

PRUSSIAN BLUE, or potassium ferric ferrocyanide ($KFe[Fe(CN)_6]$), deep-blue paint pigment made by reacting potassium ferrocyanide with any ferric salt.

PRUSSIC ACID, or hydrocyanic acid. See CYANIDES.

PRZEWALSKI'S HORSE, or Eastern Wild Horse, the last remaining race of true wild horses. Of the three subspecies of *Equus przewalskii*, two, the Steppe tarpan and Forest tarpan, were exterminated by the middle of the 19th century. Only Przewalski's horse remained, undiscovered until 1881. Ancestors of the domestic HORSES, they are about the size of a PONY, yellow to red-brown and with an erect mane. It is probable that they, too, are now extinct in the wild.

PSALMS, Book of, collection of 150 songs in the OLD TESTAMENT, used as the HYMN book of Judaism since the return from exile, and prominent in Christian LITURGY. Metrical psalms are sung in the REFORMED CHURCHES. Many psalms are traditionally ascribed to DAVID; modern scholars date them between the 10th and 2nd centuries BC. Their fine poetry embodies a rich variety of religious experience, both national and individual. (See also BAY PSALM BOOK.)

PSALTERY, musical instrument related to the dulcimer and consisting of strings stretched over a flat soundbox, and plucked. Of Near Eastern origin, it enjoyed great popularity in the West in the 13th–15th centuries. No medieval examples are extant.

PSEUDEPIGRAPHA (Greek: writings falsely ascribed), uncanonical books excluded from the APOCRYPHA and generally pseudonymous. Such Jewish works, written largely from c150 BC to c100 AD, include the *Book of Enoch*, *Assumption of Moses* and *Apocalypse of Baruch*. Christian pseudepigrapha, also called New Testament apocrypha, include numerous Gospels, Acts of most of the apostles, and spurious epistles; they are mostly fanciful and heretical.

PSEUDOHALOGENS, class of monovalent inorganic radicals which chemically resemble the HALIDES and HALOGENS. They include CYANIDE (CN^-) and CYANOGEN ($[CN]_2$), cyanate (OCN^-), thiocyanate (SCN^-), and azide (N_3^-).

PSEUDOPODIUM, the "false limb" by which certain PROTOZOA are able to move. The internal pressure of the CELL forces the elastic cell membrane out in a bulge; the cell contents flow behind into the new position. Pseudopodia can be formed at any position on the cell surface.

PSILOCYBIN, HALLUCINOGENIC DRUG derived from a Mexican fungus (*Psilocybe mexicanus*) and related to LSD.

PSITTACOSIS, or **Parrot fever**, LUNG disease with FEVER, cough and breathlessness caused by a bedsonia, an organism intermediate between BACTERIA and VIRUSES. It is carried by parrots, pigeons, domestic fowl and related birds. TETRACYCLINES provide effective treatment, but any infected birds must be destroyed.

PSKOV, city in the NW Russian SFSR, USSR, historic capital of Pskov oblast, on the Velikaya R SE of Lake Pskov. Its principal manufactures are linen and machinery. Pop 127 000.

PSORIASIS, common SKIN condition characterized by patches of red, thickened and scaling skin. It often affects the elbows, knees and scalp but may be found anywhere. Several forms are recognized and the manifestations may vary in each individual with time. Coal tar preparations are valuable in treatment but STEROID creams and cytotoxic CHEMOTHERAPY may be needed. There is also an associated ARTHRITIS.

PSYCHE, Greek word meaning soul. In the 5th century BC the soul was personified as a beautiful woman, whom the god of Love, Eros (CUPID), fell in love with and tormented.

PSYCHE, in psychology, the MIND.

PSYCHEDELIC DRUGS. See HALLUCINOGENIC DRUGS.

PSYCHIATRY, the branch of medicine concerned with the study and treatment of MENTAL ILLNESS. It has two major branches: one is PSYCHOTHERAPY, the application of psychological techniques to the treatment of mental illnesses where a physiological origin is either unknown or does not exist (see also PSYCHOANALYSIS); the other, medical therapy, where attack is made either on the organic source of the disease or, at least, on its physical or behavioral symptoms. (Psychotherapy and medical therapy are often used in tandem.) As a rule of thumb, the former deals with NEUROSES, the latter with PSYCHOSES. (See also PSYCHOLOGY.) DRUGS are perhaps the most widely used tools of psychiatry. Many emotional and other disturbances can be simply treated by the use of mild SEDATIVES OR TRANQUILLIZERS. A major area of success for drug therapy is ALCOHOLISM. Other major areas of success are in DRUG ADDICTION and the amelioration of the effects of EPILEPSY. (See also PSYCHOPHARMACOLOGY.) Drastic therapies include shock treatment and BRAIN surgery. The principal shock treatments are insulin shock and electroshock (electroconvulsive therapy—ECT). INSULIN, used primarily in cases of SCHIZOPHRENIA, may be given in increasingly large doses until shock level is achieved. In electroshock treatment, an electric current is passed through the brain, producing convulsions and, often, unconsciousness: it is used in cases of MANIC-DEPRESSIVE PSYCHOSIS. Both techniques are unpredictable in result. LOBOTOMY, a surgical operation which severs certain of the neural pathways, is now rarely used.

PSYCHICAL RESEARCH. See PARAPSYCHOLOGY.

PSYCHOANALYSIS, a system of psychology having as its base the theories of Sigmund FREUD; also, the psychotherapeutic technique based on that system. The distinct forms of psychoanalysis developed by JUNG and ADLER are more correctly termed respectively analytical psychology and individual psychology. Freud's initial interest was in the origins of the NEUROSES. On developing the technique of FREE ASSOCIATION to replace that of HYPNOSIS in his therapy, he observed that certain patients could in some cases associate freely only with difficulty. He decided that this was due to the memories of certain experiences being held back from the CONSCIOUS mind (see REPRESSION) and noted that the most sensitive areas were in connection with sexual experiences. He thus developed the concept of the UNCONSCIOUS (later to be called the ID), and suggested (for a while) that ANXIETY was the result of repression of the LIBIDO. He also defined "resistance" by the conscious to acceptance of ideas and impulses from the unconscious, and TRANSFERENCE, the idea that relationships with people or objects in the past affect the individual's relationships with people or objects in the present. (Other important psychoanalytic ideas include CENSORSHIP; DEFENSE MECHANISM; EGO; INHIBITION; PLEASURE PRINCIPLE; SUPEREGO. See also DREAMS; GROUP INSTINCT; LYCANTHROPY; METAPSYCHOLOGY; PROJECTION; SEX.)

PSYCHOLOGICAL TESTS, experiments devised to elicit information about the psychological characteristics of individuals. Such characteristics may relate to the INTELLIGENCE, vocation, personality or aptitudes of the individual. Tests must be both consistent and accurate so, if possible, a large sample is used. (See also GRAPHOLOGY; IQ; PROJECTION TEST; PSYCHOLOGY; STANFORD-BINET TEST.)

PSYCHOLOGICAL WARFARE, the use of psychological pressure to undermine an enemy's will to resist. It usually consists of printed or broadcast PROPAGANDA aimed at civilians or armed forces, and is often preceded or accompanied by supporting economic or military measures.

PSYCHOLOGY, originally the branch of philosophy dealing with the mind, then the science of mind, and now, considered in its more general context, the science of behavior, whether human or animal. It is intimately related with ANTHROPOLOGY (the science of man) and Somatology (the science of body). (See also ANIMAL BEHAVIOR.) Clearly, psychology is closely connected with, on one side, MEDICINE and, on the other, SOCIOLOGY. There are a number of closely interrelated branches of human psychology. **Experimental psychology** embraces all psychological investigations controlled by the psychologist. His experiments may center on the individual or GROUP, in which latter case STATISTICS will play a large part in the research. In particular, in **clinical psychology**, information is gained through the treatment of those suffering from MENTAL ILLNESS. **Social psychologists** use statistical and other methods to investigate the effect of the group on the behavior of the individual (see also CYBERNETICS; INDUSTRIAL PSYCHOLOGY). In **applied psychology**, the discoveries and theories of psychology are put to practical use. **Comparative psychology** deals with the different behavioral organizations of animals (including man). In this century, the most important offspring of psychology are PSYCHIATRY and PSYCHOANALYSIS. Both are concerned with the treatment of mental illness, but from radically different viewpoints (see also PSYCHOTHERAPY). The former, in particular, is helped by the discoveries of **physiological psychology**, which attempts to understand the NEUROLOGY and PHYSIOLOGY of behavior. Two rather different branches of psychology sprang originally from FREUD's psychoanalysis. They are **analytical psychology**, founded by Carl Gustav JUNG, and **individual psychology**, founded by Alfred ADLER. See also Alfred BINET; Francis GALTON; William JAMES; Wilhelm WUNDY; and BEHAVIORISM; GESTALT PSYCHOLOGY; IDEA; INTELLIGENCE; PARAPSYCHOLOGY; PSYCHOLOGICAL TESTS; PSYCHOPHARMACOLOGY.)

PSYCHOPATH, person emotionally disturbed to a degree approaching MANIA, but who suffers no specific MENTAL ILLNESS; or, loosely, person with psychopathic (see PSYCHOPATHY) symptoms.

PSYCHOPATHY, any specific MENTAL ILLNESS characterized by abnormal, antisocial behavior.

PSYCHOPHARMACOLOGY, the study of the effects of DRUGS on the mind, and particularly the development of drugs for treating MENTAL ILLNESS.

PSYCHOSIS, in contrast with NEUROSIS, any MENTAL ILLNESS, whether of neurological (see NEUROLOGY) or purely psychological origins, which renders the individual incapable of distinguishing reality from unreality or fantasy. If the loss of mental capacity is progressive, the illness is termed a deteriorative psychosis.

PSYCHOSOMATIC ILLNESS, any illness in which some mental activity, usually ANXIETY or the INHIBITION of the EMOTIONS (see also REPRESSION), causes physiological malfunction. There is debate as to which disorders are psychosomatic, but among the most likely candidates are gastric ULCERS, ulcerative COLITIS and certain types of ASTHMA.

PSYCHOTHERAPY, the application of the theories and discoveries of PSYCHOLOGY to the treatment of MENTAL ILLNESS. Psychotherapy does not usually involve physical techniques, such as the use of drugs or surgery (see PSYCHIATRY). The term is sometimes used misleadingly to distinguish other forms of therapy from PSYCHOANALYSIS.

PTA. See PARENTS AND TEACHERS, NATIONAL CONGRESS OF.

PT BOAT. See TORPEDO BOAT.

PTARMIGAN, several species of game birds of the GROUSE family, typically found in the Arctic and subarctic. The name is sometimes applied to other members of the grouse family, but true ptarmigans molt into a white winter plumage.

PTERANODON. See PTERODACTYL.

PTERIDOPHYTA, a traditional but artificial division of the PLANT KINGDOM which includes FERNS, HORSETAILS and CLUBMOSSES. Although all these plants contain vascular tissues and have a dominant SPOROPHYTE generation differentiated into ROOTS, STEMS and LEAVES, it is now clear that they are not closely related. (See ALTERNATION OF GENERATIONS; SPERMATOPHYTA.)

Przewalski's horse may now survive only in zoos.

PTERODACTYLS, a name which has come to be used for all Pterosaurs or flying reptiles, though originally reserved for a single genus. Pterosaurs were a large and diverse group of reptiles adapted for different kinds of flight. The wings consisted of a naked membrane supported by the fourth finger only. Pterosaurs were almost certainly warm-blooded and had a thick fur. *Pteranodon* was the most specialized, with a wing-span of 9m (29.5ft), adapted for soaring and gliding over sea-cliffs.

PTEROPSIDA, a subdivision of the PLANT KINGDOM which includes the FERNS, GYMNOSPERMS and ANGIOSPERMS (flowering plants).

PTOLEMY, name used by all 15 Egyptian kings of the Macedonian dynasty (323–30 BC). **Ptolemy I Soter** (c367–283 BC) was one of Alexander the Great's generals. He secured Egypt for himself after Alexander's death and defended it in a series of wars against the other DIADOCHI. He founded the library of Alexandria, which became a center of HELLENISTIC CULTURE. **Ptolemy II Philadelphus** (308–246 BC) succeeded in 285. Under him Alexandria reached its height; he completed the PHAROS and appointed CALLIMACHUS librarian. **Ptolemy III Euergetes** (c280–221 BC), succeeded in 246. He extended the empire to include most of Asia Minor, the E Mediterranean and Aegean Islands. After 221 the Ptolemaic empire entered a long period of decline, gradually losing its overseas possessions. **Ptolemy XV Caesarion** ("son of Caesar"; 47–30 BC) ruled from 44 BC jointly with his mother CLEOPATRA VII. On their defeat at the battle of Actium (31 BC), Egypt became a Roman province.

PTOLEMY, or **Claudius Ptolemaeus** (2nd century AD), Alexandrian astronomer, mathematician and geographer. Most important is his book on ASTRONOMY, now called *Almagest* ("the greatest"), a synthesis of Greek astronomical knowledge, especially that of HIPPARCHUS: his geocentric cosmology dominated Western scientific thought until the Copernican Revolution of the 16th century (see COPERNICUS, N.). His *Geography* confirmed Columbus' belief in the westward route to Asia. In his *Optics* he attempts to solve the astronomical problem of ATMOSPHERIC REFRACTION. (See also EPICYCLE.)

PTOMAINE POISONING, old name for FOOD POISONING.

PTYALIN, an ENZYME secreted by the salivary GLANDS of the DIGESTIVE SYSTEM, which has a minor role in STARCH breakdown.

PUBERTY, the time during the GROWTH of a person at which sexual development occurs, commonly associated with a growth spurt. Female puberty involves several stages—the acquisition of BREAST buds; of sexual hair, and the onset of MENSTRUATION—which may each begin at different times. Male puberty involves sexual-hair development; VOICE change, and growth of the TESTES and PENIS. Precocious puberty is when the pubertal features develop abnormally early (before 9 years in females). The average age at puberty has fallen in recent years.

PUBLIC BROADCASTING SYSTEM (PBS). See BROADCASTING NETWORKS, US.

PUBLIC DEFENDER, in US law, an official paid to defend in court those unable to afford to pay a lawyer. The defender is employed and compensated by the state, county or city authority.

PUBLIC DOMAIN, in US law, ownership of a property or resource by the people. In 1962 public domain or public land made up 34% of US land. Processes, plans and creative works not protected by PATENT or COPYRIGHT are said to be in the public domain.

PUBLIC HEALTH, the practice and organization of preventative MEDICINE within a community. Many threats to health are beyond individual control. DISEASE, EPIDEMICS, POLLUTION of the air and purity of WATER can only be effectively regulated by laws and health authorities. Among the strictest controls are those on SEWAGE and WASTE DISPOSAL. Most advanced countries have pure food laws controlling food purity, freshness and additives. In the US, these controls are the responsibility of the FOOD AND DRUG ADMINISTRATION. The work of individual countries in the public health field is coordinated by the WORLD HEALTH ORGANIZATION. Some countries have complete public health services which provide free or low-cost medical treatment of all kinds. (See also HEALTH, EDUCATION AND WELFARE; MEDICARE; JENNER, EDWARD; PASTEUR, LOUIS.)

PUBLIC HEALTH SERVICE (PHS), the chief US health agency, set up in 1870. In 1953, it became a division of the new Department of Health, Education, and Welfare.

PUBLIC OPINION POLL. See POLL, PUBLIC OPINION.

PUBLIC WORKS ADMINISTRATION (PWA), or Federal Emergency Administration of Public Works, a NEW DEAL agency set up in 1933 to stimulate employment and purchasing power. Under H. L. ICKES it made loans and grants, mainly to government bodies, for projects which included the GRAND COULEE and BONNEVILLE dams. The PWA was phased out from 1939.

PUCCINI, Giacomo (1858–1924), Italian operatic composer. His first international success, *Manon Lescaut* (1893), was followed by *La Bohème* (1896), *Tosca* (1900), *Madame Butterfly* (1904) and *Turandot* (uncompleted at Puccini's death). A lyric style and strong orchestration are characteristic of his operas, which have great dramatic and emotional power. Puccini's works are among the most popular in the operatic repertoire.

PUCK, in medieval English folklore, a malevolent imp. Later he is merely mischievous, as in Shakespeare's *A Midsummer Night's Dream.* He is identified with Robin Goodfellow and Hobgoblin.

PUDOVKIN, Vsevolod Ilarionovich (1893–1953), pioneer Russian film director. His silent movies include *The End of St. Petersburg* (1927), *Storm Over Asia* (1928) and *Mother* (1926).

PUDU, a genus of DEER living in the lower Andes in South America. The smallest of the deer, the pudu is only 370mm (14.6in) at the shoulder. Pudu bucks have small spiked antlers of 70–100mm (2.8–3.9in).

PUEBLA, mainly agricultural state in the E central Mexican interior. The land is mountainous with plains and fertile valleys. Principal crops are sugarcane, coffee, cotton and grains.

PUEBLA, or Puebla de Zaragoza, capital of PUEBLA state, Mexico. It lies on a 7000ft agricultural plain. Products include onyx, textiles, glassware, colored tiles. It has an outstanding cathedral begun in 1552 and historic theater (1790). Pop 521 885.

PUEBLO, city in S central Col., seat of Pueblo Co. It is a major industrial center, with giant steel mills. Pop 97 453.

PUEBLO INDIANS, several American Indian tribes living in SW US (Ariz. and N.M.) in permanent villages (*pueblos*). They have the oldest and most developed pre-Columbian civilization N of Mexico. The various tribes, which include the HOPI and ZUÑI, are descended from the BASKET MAKERS and CLIFF DWELLERS. Pueblo Indians are noted for their handiworks; their social system and religious practices remain largely intact today. (See also INDIANS, NORTH AMERICAN.)

PUEBLO REVOLT. See POPÉ.

PUERPERAL FEVER, disease occuring in puerperal women, usually a few days after the BIRTH of the child and caused by infection of the WOMB, often with STREPTOCOCCUS. It causes FEVER, abdominal pain and discharge of PUS from the womb. The introduction of ASEPSIS in OBSTETRICS by I. P. SEMMELWEISS greatly reduced its incidence. Today, ANTIBIOTICS are required if it develops.

PUERTO RICO, or **Porto Rico,** West Indian island, furthest E of the Greater Antilles. It is a selfgoverning commonwealth freely associated with the US.

Land and Climate. Roughly rectangular in shape, Puerto Rico extends 133mi E–W and 41mi N–S. The Cordillera Central, which rises to 4 398ft, gives way to foothills, valleys and a fertile coastal plain 1–12mi wide. The mild tropical climate, drier in the S, varies little apart from occasional storms July–Nov.

People. Puerto Ricans are US citizens but pay no federal taxes and may not vote in national elections. The Spanish element is predominant in the people's African and Spanish origins. The island is densely populated; two-thirds of the population is in San Juan, Ponce and Mayagüez. Unemployment has led many Puerto Ricans to migrate, mainly to New York.

Economy. Formerly a single-crop economy based on sugar, Puerto Rico now depends largely on manufacturing. From the 1940s "Operation Bootstrap" attracted investment. Today metals, chemicals, oil-refining, textiles and sugar products are the principal exports. The US is the main trading partner. Most of the remaining third of goods produced comprises sugarcane, coffee, tobacco and foods.

History. The island was discovered by Columbus in 1493. In 1508, Juan PONCE DE LEÓN founded a colony. The native ARAWAK INDIANS died out under Spanish rule and, from c1510, Negro slaves were imported to work on sugar plantations. Puerto Rico remained under Spanish rule until 1898 when, as a result of the SPANISH-AMERICAN WAR, the island was ceded to the US. In 1917, Puerto Ricans received US citizenship and the right to elect both houses of their legislature, but nationalism, active since the late 1800s, continued. In 1950, Puerto Rican extremists tried to assassinate President Truman. In 1952, the island became a free commonwealth with its own constitution, a status approved in a 1967 plebiscite.

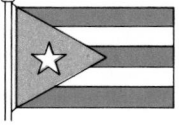

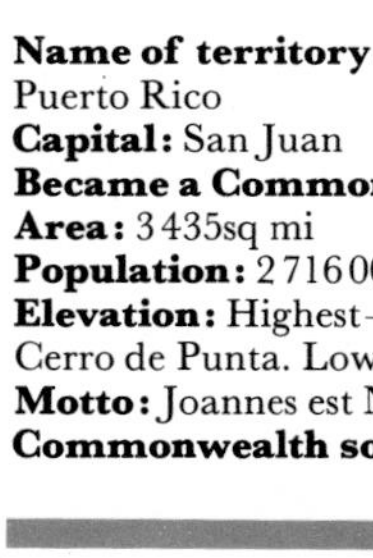

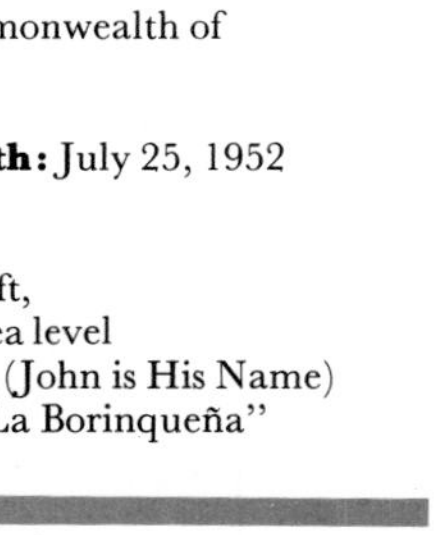

Name of territory: Commonwealth of Puerto Rico
Capital: San Juan
Became a Commonwealth: July 25, 1952
Area: 3 435sq mi
Population: 2 716 000
Elevation: Highest—4 389ft, Cerro de Punta. Lowest—sea level
Motto: Joannes est Nomen (John is His Name)
Commonwealth song: "La Borinqueña"

PUFENDORF, Samuel, Baron von (1632–1694), German jurist, philosopher and historian. In his great Latin work *On the Law of Nature and of Nations* (1672) he stressed NATURAL LAW as opposed to positive (man made) law in relations between states.

PUFFBALL, common name for fungi of the genus *Lycoperdon*. When mature, they have a white fleshy interior. This eventually breaks down to a mass of powdery spores which are expelled in clouds when the skin is pressed. Puffballs are commonly found in woods and fields.

PUFFERS, or Pufferfishes, fishes of tropical waters, related to PORCUPINE FISHES, and, like them, capable of inflating their bodies with air or water as a defense mechanism. Some are also poisonous. Unlike most fishes, puffers swim with the dorsal and pectoral fins only, using the tail purely as a rudder. Family: Tetradontidae. (See also GLOBEFISH.)

PUFFINS, stubby sea birds of the AUK family, Alcidae. Black or black-and-white birds, they are characterized by their large and laterally compressed bills, which, at the beginning of the breeding season, become still further enlarged and brightly patterned. Puffins live in colonies on sea cliffs, nesting in burrows.

PUG, small dog of Chinese origin with a short, deeply wrinkled face, and tail curled tightly over its back. The body is sturdy, 11in high and weighs 14–18lb. Its short smooth coat is usually fawn, but can be black.

PUGACHEV, Emelian Ivanovich (c1742–1775), Cossack leader of the great Urals peasant revolt (1773–74). Claiming to be PETER III, murdered husband of CATHERINE II of Russia, he declared serfdom abolished and led an army of serfs and Cossacks which seized several cities and killed thousands before he was captured and executed.

PUGET SOUND, irregular inlet of the Pacific in NW Wash. It extends S about 100mi to Olympia and is navigable by large ships (US navy yard at Bremerton). Seattle and Tacoma lie on its shores and the state's fish and lumber industries are centered in the area. It was first explored by George VANCOUVER in 1792.

PULASKI, industrial town in SW Va., seat of Pulaski Co. The town has textile and lumber mills. It lies in a farming region with coal, iron and zinc deposits. Pop 10 279.

PULASKI, Casimir, Count (1748–1779), Polish soldier, hero of the anti-Russian revolt of 1768 who, exiled from Poland, fought in the American Revolutionary War. He fought at the Battles of BRANDYWINE and GERMANTOWN. In 1778, he formed his own cavalry unit, the Pulaski Legion. He was mortally wounded at the siege of Savannah.

PULASKI, Fort. See FORT PULASKI NATIONAL MONUMENT.

PULI, best known of Hungarian sheep dogs. Of medium size, it stands about 17in at the shoulder and weighs 25–35lb. It has a soft undercoat and a long, coarser outercoat, giving a matted appearance. It is usually black, but may be gray or white.

PULITZER, Joseph (1847–1911), Hungarian-born US publisher who created the PULITZER PRIZES. In 1883, he bought the New York *World* and raised the circulation tenfold in seven years by aggressive reporting (the term "yellow journalism" was coined to describe its style). In the 1890s Pulitzer was involved in a circulation war with William Randolph HEARST's New York *Journal*. He consistently ran liberal crusades. He also endowed the school of journalism at Columbia U.

PULITZER PRIZES, awards for achievement in US journalism and letters, given every May since 1917 through a foundation created by the estate of Joseph PULITZER and administered by Columbia U. There are eight $1000 awards for journalism, five for literature ($500) and four $1500 traveling scholarships. An award for music ($500) was added in 1943.

PULLEY, grooved wheel mounted on a block and with a cord or belt passing over it. A pulley is a simple MACHINE applying the equilibrium of TORQUES to obtain a mechanical advantage. Thus, the block and tackle is a combination of ropes and pulleys used for hoisting heavy weights. A belt and pulley combination can transmit motion from one part of a machine to another. Variable speed can be obtained from a single-speed driving shaft by the use of stepped or cone-shaped pulleys with diameters that give the correct speed ratios and belt tensions. To help prevent excessive belt wear and slipping, the rim surface of a pulley is adapted to the material of the belt used.

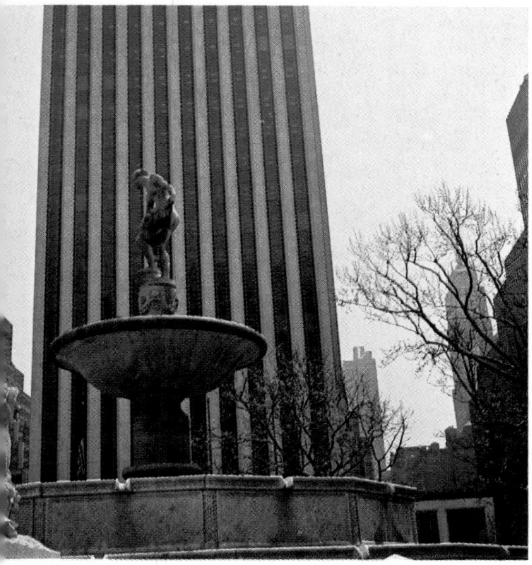

This fountain, dedicated to Joseph Pulitzer, stands in Grand Army Plaza, New York City. Pulitzer's will provided $2 million for the establishment of Columbia University's school of journalism.

PULLMAN, city in SE Wash., commercial center of a wheat, pea and dairy farm area and site of Washington State U. Pop 20 509.

PULLMAN, George Mortimer (1831–1897), US industrialist and inventor of the first modern railroad sleeping car—the "Pullman." In 1880, he built a model company town—Pullman, Ill. (now part of Chicago), later site of the PULLMAN STRIKE.

PULLMAN STRIKE, May–July 1894, famous boycott of rolling stock of the Pullman Palace Car Co., Pullman, Ill. by E. V. DEBS' American Railway Union to protest the company's wage cuts and victimization of union representatives. After the owners obtained a federal injunction the strike was broken by federal troops, and the US labor movement suffered a major setback.

PULP, or wood pulp. See PAPER.

PULQUE, or pulke, intoxicating Mexican national drink made from freshly fermented sap of several species of MAGUEY (AGAVE) plants. The alcoholic content is about 6%.

PULSAR, short for pulsating radio star, a celestial radio source emitting brief extremely regular pulses of ELECTROMAGNETIC RADIATION (with one exception, entirely radio-frequency). Each pulse lasts a few hundredths of a second and the period between pulses is of the order of one second or less. Though the pulse frequency varies from pulsar to pulsar, for each pulsar the period is as regular as man can measure. The first pulsar was discovered in 1967 by HEWISH and S. J. Bell. The fastest pulsar yet observed has a period of 0.033s, emitting pulses of the same frequency in the X-ray and visible regions of the spectrum. It is likely that there are some 10 000 pulsars in the MILKY WAY, though less than 50 have as yet been discovered. It is believed that pulsars are the neutron STAR remnants of SUPERNOVAE, rapidly spinning and radiating through loss of rotational energy.

PULSE, the palpable impulse conducted in the ARTERIES representing the transmitted beat of the HEART. A normal pulse rate is between 68 and 80, but athletes may have slower pulses. FEVER, heart disease, ANOXIA and ANXIETY increase the rate. The pulse character may suggest specific conditions, loss of pulse possibly indicating arterial block or cessation of the heart.

PULSES, the edible seeds produced by LEGUMINOUS PLANTS, such as PEAS and BEANS, and a general name for plants yielding such seeds.

PUMA, *Felis concolor*, the **Cougar** or **Mountain lion**, the most widespread of the big CATS of the Americas, occupying an amazing variety of habitats. Powerful cats, resembling a slender and sinuous lioness with a small head, they lead solitary lives preying on various species of deer. The lifespan of a puma in the wild is about 18 years. A puma can cover up to 6m (20ft) in a bound, and will regularly travel up to 80km (50mi) when hunting.

PUMICE, porous, frothy volcanic glass, usually silica-rich; formed by the sudden release of vapors as LAVA cools under low pressures. It is used as an ABRASIVE, an AGGREGATE and a railroad ballast.

PUMP, device for taking in and forcing out a fluid, thus giving it kinetic or potential ENERGY. The HEART is a pump for circulating blood around the body. Pumps are commonly used domestically and industrially to transport fluids, to raise liquids, to compress gases or to evacuate sealed containers. Their chief use is to force fluids along pipelines (see PIPES AND PIPELINES). The earliest pumps were waterwheels, endless chains of buckets, and the ARCHIMEDES screw. Piston pumps, known in classical times, were developed in the 16th and 17th centuries, the suction types (working by atmospheric pressure) being usual, though unable to raise water more than about 10.4m (34ft). The STEAM ENGINE was developed to power pumps for pumping out mines. Piston pumps—the simplest of which is the SYRINGE—are reciprocating **volume-displacement pumps**, as are diaphragm pumps, with a pulsating diaphragm instead of the piston. One-way inlet and outlet valves are fitted in the cylinder. Rotary volume-displacement pumps have rotating gear wheels or wheels with lobes or vanes. **Kinetic pumps**, or FANS, work by imparting momentum to the fluid by means of rotating curved vanes in a housing: centrifugal pumps expel the fluid radially outward, and propeller pumps axially forward. **Air compressors** use the TURBINE principle (see also JET PROPULSION). **Air pumps** use compressed air to raise liquids from the bottom of wells, displacing one fluid by another. If the fluid must not come into direct contact with the pump, as in a nuclear reactor, **electromagnetic pumps** are used: an electric current and a magnetic field at right angles induce the conducting fluid to flow at right angles to both (see MOTOR, ELECTRIC); or the principle of the linear INDUCTION MOTOR may be used. To achieve a very high vacuum, the **diffusion pump** is used, in which atoms of condensing mercury vapor entrain the remaining gas molecules.

PUMPKIN, *Cucurbita pepo* and *C. moschata*, vines producing yellow, bell-shaped flowers and soft-fleshed gourds weighing up to 70kg (154lb). The gourds are used either as a vegetable or as a fruit in pastries. Family: Cucurbitaceae. (See also SQUASH.)

PUNCH AND JUDY, leading handpuppet characters in a children's Punch and Judy show. Punch is descended from Pulcinella (Punchinello) of the COMMEDIA DELL'ARTE. He is a hooknosed, hunchbacked, wifebeating rogue who usually ends on the gallows or in a crocodile's mouth. He is accompanied by his shrewish wife Judy (originally called Joan) and their dog, Toby. The Devil, Baby, Hangman, Policeman and Doctor may also appear. (See also PUPPET.)

PUNCTUATION, those marks, distinct from letters and accents, which clarify the meaning of written language. Punctuation does not determine pronunciation, though it often reflects it. It is an important element of GRAMMAR.

PUNIC WARS, three wars between ancient Rome and CARTHAGE, each marking a crucial phase in the expansion of Roman empire in the western Mediterranean, the third culminating in the total destruction of Carthage itself. (The Carthaginians, PHOENICIAN by descent, were known to the Romans as *Poeni*; hence *Punic*.) The **First Punic War** (264–241 BC) turned on a struggle for the strategically important island of Sicily. The Carthaginians had some success on land, notably under Xanthippus and HAMILCAR BARCA, but were defeated at sea, the decisive battle being fought off the Aegadian Isles in 241. Rome's naval supremacy was thenceforth unchallenged. The **Second Punic War** (218–201 BC), provoked by Roman moves to check Carthaginian expansion in Spain, began with HANNIBAL's daring invasion of Italy via an overland route which obliged him to cross the Alps in winter. Despite several remarkable victories, including the virtual annihilation of a strong Roman army at CANNAE (216), his plan to isolate Rome from her Italian allies was ultimately frustrated. Roman counterattacks in Spain and then in Africa—at ZAMA (202), under SCIPIO Africanus—forced a Carthaginian surrender on terms which included the forfeiture of her Spanish empire and war fleet. Roman misgivings at the subsequent revival of Carthage as a mercantile power led to the **Third Punic War** (149–146 BC). After a two-year siege of Carthage, SCIPIO Aemilianus took the city and razed it to the ground. Carthaginian territory became the Roman province of "Africa."

PUNISHMENT, imposition of pain or suffering, deprivation or discomfort, on a person who has infringed the law, rule or custom of a community. The ancient individual exaction of "an eye for an eye" in retaliation or revenge has given way to socially imposed retribution. Supernatural or religious authority may be adduced, though this has yielded to arguments based on the wellbeing of a community. Today revenge is seen by most people as only one aspect of punishment. Another important aspect is to function as a deterrent, and in the 19th and 20th centuries, the work of reformers such as John HOWARD and Elizabeth FRY led to reform and rehabilitation being considered important factors. (See CRIMINAL

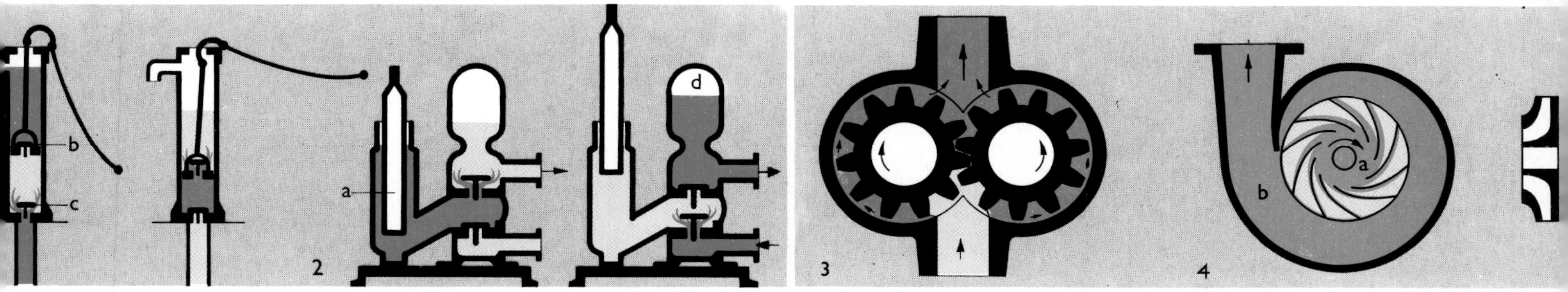

The three main types of pump include the reciprocating pump (1 and 2), the rotary pump (3) and the centrifugal pump (4). (1) In the simple lift pump, the piston (a) is raised to force the water in the cylinder out of the spout. At the same time, the upper valve (b) closes, while the lower valve (c) opens to admit more water into the cylinder. When the piston is lowered (*right*), the lower valve closes, the upper valve opens and the water is forced into the upper part of the cylinder. (2) In the force pump, the downstroke of the piston (a) forces water through the upper valve and toward the outlet. On the upstroke (*right*), the lower valve opens to admit more water. The air reservoir (d) forces a steady flow of water through the outlet. (3) A gear pump has two meshing gear wheels that rotate in opposite directions to set the fluid in motion. (4) In the centrifugal pump, a rotating impeller (a) forces fluid or gas through the outlet (b).

LAW; CAPITAL PUNISHMENT; CORPORAL PUNISHMENT; PRISONS.)

PUNJAB (Sanskrit: five rivers), large wheat-growing region in the NW of the Indian subcontinent, on the upper Indus R plain. Formerly the British Indian province of Punjab, it was divided in 1947 into what became known as **Punjab** (**Pakistan**)—79 704sq mi; pop 36 900 000; capital: LAHORE—and **Punjab** (**India**). In 1966 Punjab (India) was divided into two further provinces, with CHANDIGARH as their joint capital: **Punjab**—19 495sq mi; pop 13 729 951; Punjabi-speaking—and **Haryāna**—17 010sq mi; pop 9 971 165.

PUNTA ARENAS, or **Magallanes,** seaport city and naval base, capital of Magallanes province, S Chile. It exports wool and mutton. Pop 64 958.

PUNTA DEL ESTE, seaside resort town in SE Uruguay, 70mi E of Montevideo. Conferences here proclaimed the ALLIANCE FOR PROGRESS (1961) and suspended Cuba from the Organization of American States (1962).

PUPA, an immature stage in the development of those insects which have a LARVA completely different in structure from the adult, and in which "complete" METAMORPHOSIS occurs. The pupa is a resting stage in which the larval structure is reorganized to form the adult: all but the nervous system changes. Feeding and locomotion are meanwhile suspended.

PUPIN, Michael Idvorsky (1858–1935), Hungarian-born US inventor who made many contributions to TELEPHONE science, including a technique whereby longer-distance communication can be sustained.

PUPPET, figure of a person or animal manipulated in dramatic presentations. There are hand, or glove, and finger puppets; jointed *marionettes* or string-puppets controlled from above; and rod puppets, often used in shadow plays. Puppetry, with which VENTRILOQUISM is associated, is an ancient, flexible entertainment, popular in many countries. (See also PUNCH AND JUDY.)

PURCELL, Edward Mills (1912–), US physicist who shared with F. BLOCH the 1952 Nobel Prize for Physics for his independent work on nuclear magnetic moment, discovering nuclear magnetic resonance (NMR) in solids (see SPECTROSCOPY).

PURCELL, Henry (c1659–1695), English composer, the foremost of his time. A master of melody and counterpoint, he wrote in every form and style of the period: odes and anthems for royal occasions, many choral and instrumental works, and music for plays and masques, including his opera *Dido and Aeneas* (1689).

PURDAH (Hindi: screen, veil), mainly in India, the seclusion of Muslim and some Hindu women. The practice is now dying out (see HAREM).

PURE FOOD AND DRUG LAWS. See CONSUMER PROTECTION; FOOD AND DRUG ADMINISTRATION.

PURGATORY, in Roman Catholicism, the place where Christians after death undergo purifying punishment and expiate unforgiven venial sins, before admission to HEAVEN. INDULGENCES, MASSES and prayers for the dead are held to lighten their suffering.

PURI, town in Orissa state, NE India, visited each year by millions of Hindu pilgrims who come to worship at the famous 12th-century temple of Jagannātha (see JUGGERNAUT), a deity. Pop 72 712.

PURIM, the Feast of Lots, Jewish festival of the 14th day of Adar (Feb.–March), a joyful celebration of the deliverance from massacre of Persian Jews, through intervention by ESTHER and Mordecai. The story is told in the Book of Esther.

PURINE ($C_5H_4N_4$), the parent compound of a class of organic bases of major biochemical importance. The purines adenine and guanine are present in NUCLEIC ACIDS. A combination of a purine and a 5-carbon sugar is termed a nucleoside, which when phosphorylated gives a NUCLEOTIDE. Other important purine derivatives include CAFFEINE and theobromine. The end product of purine metabolism is URIC ACID which is excreted in the urine.

PURITANS, English reforming Protestants who aimed for a simpler form of worship expressly warranted by Scripture, devout personal and family life, and the abolition of clerical hierarchy. They stressed self-discipline, work as a vocation and the christianizing of all spheres of life. Most were strict Calvinists. The term "puritan" was first used in the 1560s of those dissatisfied with the compromise of the Elizabethan settlement of the CHURCH OF ENGLAND; under James I, after the unsuccessful HAMPTON COURT CONFERENCE, some separated from the Church of England. Archbishop LAUD set about systematic repression of puritanism, causing some to emigrate to America (see PILGRIM FATHERS). The English CIVIL WAR—known also as the Puritan Revolution—led to the establishment of PRESBYTERIANISM, but under Oliver CROMWELL puritan dominance was weakened by internal strife. Most puritans were forced to leave the Church after the Restoration (1660), becoming NONCONFORMISTS. Many New England settlers were puritan, and their influence on America was marked, especially their concern for education and church democracy. (See also COVENANTERS; HALF-WAY COVENANT.)

PURKINJE, Johannes Evangelista (1787–1869), Bohemian-born Czech physiologist and pioneer of HISTOLOGY, best known for his observations of nerve cells (see NERVOUS SYSTEM) and discovery of the Purkinje Effect, that at different overall light intensities the eye is more sensitive to different colors (see VISION).

PURPLE PASSION PLANT, *Gynura aurantiaca* and *G. sarmentosa*, evergreen perennial plants which are grown as house plants for their attractive dark-green leaves covered with purple hairs. They should be grown at average house temperatures and for the most brilliant display of color should be placed in a sunny window. The soil should be kept evenly moist and the foliage misted often. Propagation is by shoot tip cuttings. Family: COMPOSITAE.

PURSLANE, common name for very hardy small fleshy plants of the genus *Portulaca*, which are used in salads and as potherbs. The common purslane of Europe (*Portulaca oleracea*) is a widespread weed. Family: Portulacaceae.

PURUS RIVER, a principal branch of the Amazon R in South America, mostly navigable. Rising in the Andes in SE Peru, it meanders NE some 2 100mi through Brazil to join the Amazon above Manaus.

PUS, off-white or yellow liquid consisting of inflammatory exudate, the debris of white BLOOD cells and BACTERIA resulting from localized INFLAMMATION, especially ABSCESSES. Pus contained in cavities is relatively inaccessible to ANTIBIOTICS and may require drainage by SURGERY. Pus suggests but does not prove the presence of bacterial infection.

PUSAN, chief port and second largest city of South Korea, on the SE coast 200mi SSE of Seoul. Seat of S Kyŏngsang province, it has textile, metal, ship-building and fishing industries. Pop 1 880 710.

PUSEY, Edward Bouverie (1800–1882), English clergyman, professor of Hebrew at Oxford University (1828) and a leader of the OXFORD MOVEMENT. He preached the REAL PRESENCE, helped found the first Anglican sisterhood (1845) and established private confession as an Anglican practice.

PUSHKIN, Alexander (1799–1837), poet, widely recognized as the founder of modern Russian literature. A sympathizer of the DECEMBRIST REVOLT, he spent his adult life in exile or under police surveillance. His poetic range included the political, humorous, erotic, lyrical, epic, and verse tales or novels like *Ruslan and Ludmila* (1820), *The Prisoner of the Caucasus* (1822) and his masterpiece *Eugene Onegin* (1833). Other works are the great drama *Boris Godunov* (1831) and such prose works as *The Queen of Spades* (1834) and *The Captain's Daughter* (1836).

PUSHTU. See PASHTO.

PUSSY WILLOW, shrubs or small trees of the WILLOW genus *Salix*, which are native to the N temperate zones. They bear flowers in elongated clusters or catkins, which are first covered with grayish silky hairs and then, in male flowers, become a golden color when the bearing stamens become visible. Family: Salicaceae.

PUT-IN-BAY, South Bass Island, Lake Erie, NW Ohio, site of a National Park set up in 1936 to mark PERRY's victory over the British in 1813 (see ERIE, BATTLE OF LAKE) and the peace which followed.

PUTNAM, Israel (1718–1790), American patriot and general in the REVOLUTIONARY WAR. A veteran of the FRENCH AND INDIAN WARS, he was prominent in the Battle of BUNKER HILL, but had less success as commander of Continental forces at the Battle of LONG ISLAND.

PUTNAM, Rufus (1738–1824), American pioneer who served in the FRENCH AND INDIAN WARS and in many of the engagements of the REVOLUTIONARY WAR. He emerged a brigadier general and chief engineer of the army, and in 1786 helped organize the OHIO COMPANY OF ASSOCIATES. In 1788 he led the first settlers into Ohio and founded Marietta.

PUTREFACTION, the natural decomposition of dead organic matter, in particular the anaerobic decomposition of its PROTEIN by BACTERIA and FUNGI. This process produces foul-smelling substances such as AMMONIA, hydrogen SULFIDE and organic SULFUR compounds. The amino-acid nitrogen of the protein is recycled by incorporation in the bacteria and fungi.

PUYALLUP, city in W central Wash., 8mi SE of Tacoma, in a rich agricultural area, named for an Indian tribe of the Puyallup R valley. Pop 14 742.

P'U YI, Henry (also known as Hsüan-t'ung; 1906–1967), last Chinese Emperor of the CH'ING (Manchu) dynasty (1908–12) and Japan's puppet emperor of MANCHUKUO (MANCHURIA), 1934–45. He died in Peking.

PWA. See PUBLIC WORKS ADMINISTRATION.

PYGMALION, in Greek mythology, king of Cyprus who fell in love with and married a statue brought to life by Aphrodite. The story inspired G. B. SHAW's *Pygmalion*. In Virgil's *Aeneid* Pygmalion is the king of Tyre and brother of DIDO.

PYGMY, term used to denote those peoples whose adult males are on average less than 1.5m tall. Some Kalahari Desert Bushmen are of pygmy size, but the most notable pygmys are the Mbuti, or Bambuti, of the Ituri Forest, Zaire, who, through their different blood type, skin color and other characteristics, are regarded as distinct from the surrounding peoples and were probably the original inhabitants of the region. A Stone Age people, they are nomadic hunters, living in groups of 50 to 100. Asian pygmies are generally termed **Negritos**. Peoples rather larger than pygmies are described as pygmoid.

PYLE, Ernie (Ernest Taylor Pyle; 1900–1945), US journalist and war correspondent. He accompanied US troops to all the major fronts in Europe and N Africa, and his popular news column won a Pulitzer Prize in 1944. He was killed by Japanese machine-gun fire during the Okinawa campaign.

PYLE, Howard (1853–1911), US writer and illustrator of children's books such as *The Merry Adventures of Robin Hood* (1883) and *The Story of King Arthur and His Knights* (1903).

PYLOS (modern Greek Pílos, formerly Navarino), ancient port in the SW Peloponnese, Greece, site of a Mycenean palace of the 1200s BC associated with king NESTOR. (See also AEGEAN CIVILIZATION; NAVARINO, BATTLE OF.)

PYM, John (c1584–1643), English statesman. A PURITAN, he led parliamentary opposition to CHARLES I and organized the impeachment of the Duke of BUCKINGHAM (1626). Dominating the SHORT and LONG PARLIAMENTS, he narrowly escaped arrest by the king in 1642, and arranged an alliance with the COVENANTERS (1643).

P'YŎNGYANG, capital and largest city of North Korea. It lies on the Taedong R in an important coal-mining area and is a major industrial center producing iron, steel, machinery and textiles. Pop 1 364 000.

PYORRHEA, or flow of PUS, usually used to refer to the pus related to poor oral hygiene and exuding from the margins of the gums and TEETH; it causes loosening of the teeth and HALITOSIS.

PYRAMID, a POLYHEDRON whose base is a POLYGON and whose sides are TRIANGLES having a common VERTEX. A pyramid whose base is triangular is termed a tetrahedron (or triangular pyramid); one whose base is a regular polygon is termed regular; one with a square base, square; one with a rectangular base, rectangular.

PYRAMID, Lake, in W Nev., in Pyramid Lake

Indian Reservation. Now 30mi long and 5–12mi wide, it is the main remnant of the ancient and much larger Lake Lahontan.

PYRAMIDS, Battle of the (July 21, 1798), battle fought near Embabeh on the W bank of the Nile R, Egypt, in which NAPOLEON shattered the MAMELUKE army and gained access to Cairo and Egypt.

PYRAMUS AND THISBE, two lovers in Greek mythology. Awaiting Pyramus at a tryst, Thisbe had to flee a lion. Pyramus found her bloody veil, presumed her dead and killed himself, as did his lover on her return. Fruit on the nearby mulberry turned from white to red. The story, told by Ovid in *Metamorphoses*, is parodied in Shakespeare's *A Midsummer Night's Dream*.

PYRENEES, mountain range between France and Spain, stretching 270mi from the Bay of Biscay to the Mediterranean and rising to Pico de Aneto (11 168ft) in the central section. The average height is about 3 500ft and the maximum width about 50mi. There are extensive forests and pasture land. Mineral deposits include iron, zinc, bauxite and talc, and there are sports and health resorts and a growing tourist industry.

PYRENEES, Peace of the (Nov. 7, 1659), by which the Franco-Spanish war (1648–59) ended in French preeminence in Europe. France secured Roussillon, parts of Flanders, and a marriage contract between LOUIS XIV and Marie-Thérèse, daughter of PHILIP IV of Spain.

PYRETHRUM, a common name for several herbs of the genus *Chrysanthemum*. The perennial *Chrysanthemum coccineum* is the florist's pyrethrum, while several other species are the chief sources of the INSECTICIDE pyrethrum. Family: Compositae.

PYREX, a borosilicate GLASS used in chemical and industrial apparatus and in ovenware. It is inert, a good insulator and heat-resistant (having a low coefficient of expansion and a high softening temperature).

PYRIDINE (C_5H_5N), a colorless heterocyclic aromatic base with an unpleasant smell, found in bone oil and coal tar. It is used as a solvent and to denature grain alcohol (ETHANOL). Important derivatives are **pyridoxine** (VITAMIN B_6) and niacin.

PYRIMIDINE ($C_4H_4N_2$), HETEROCYCLIC COMPOUND with a 6-membered aromatic ring containing nitrogen atoms in the 1 and 3 positions. The nucleus occurs in many important PURINE compounds.

PYRITE, or iron pyrites (FeS_2, iron (II) disulfide), a hard, yellow SULFIDE mineral known as **fool's gold** from its resemblance to gold. Of worldwide occurrence, it is a major ore of SULFUR. It crystallizes in the isometric system, usually as cubes. It alters to GOETHITE and LIMONITE.

PYROCLASTIC ROCKS, rocks made up of particles thrown into the air by volcanic eruptions. (See also LAVA; VOLCANISM; VOLCANO.)

PYROELECTRICITY. See PIEZOELECTRICITY.

PYROLUSITE, soft, gray-black OXIDE mineral composed of manganese (IV) oxide (MnO_2); of widespread occurrence, it is the chief ore of MANGANESE. It is a secondary mineral of aqueous origin crystallizing in the tetragonal system.

PYROLYSIS, chemical DECOMPOSITION of a substance by heat. (See also CALCINATION; COMBUSTION.)

PYROMETER, a temperature measuring device used for high temperatures. Platinum resistance thermometers and pyrometers operating on the principle of the THERMOCOUPLE have the disadvantage that they must be in contact with the hot body, but optical and radiation pyrometers can be used at a distance. Optical pyrometers estimate temperature from the light intensity in a narrow band of the visible spectrum by optical comparison of a glowing filament with an image of the hot body. Radiation pyrometers focus the body's heat radiation on a responsive thermal element such as a thermocouple.

PYROXENES, major group of SILICATE minerals occurring in IGNEOUS ROCKS. They have a chain structure, with prismatic CLEAVAGE close to 90°, and are related to the AMPHIBOLES. They are monoclinic or orthorhombic. Jadeite (see JADE) and SPODUMENE are commercially important.

PYRRHO OF ELIS (c360–c270 BC), Greek philosopher, the founder of SKEPTICISM. He taught that, as nothing can be known with certainty, suspension of judgment and imperturbability of mind are the true wisdom and source of happiness.

PYRRHOTITE, bronze-brown iron SULFIDE mineral with the NICCOLITE structure, occurring in basic igneous rocks in Scandinavia and Ontario. It is nonstoichiometric (see COMPOSITION, CHEMICAL) with composition $Fe_{1-x}S$. Improved smelting techniques now make it possible to extract the iron.

PYRRHUS (c319–272 BC), king of Epirus, NW Greece. King at 12, he served with DEMETRIUS I of Macedonia in Asia Minor, was helped by PTOLEMY I of Egypt to regain his throne, and later won and lost Macedonia. His costly defeat of the Romans at Asculum (279), during an Italian campaign, gave rise to the term "Pyrrhic victory." Further campaigns in Macedonia and Sparta failed. He was killed in Argos.

PYRROPHYTA, or dinoflagellates and cryptomonads. See ALGAE.

PYTHAGORAS (c570–c500 BC), Greek philosopher who founded the Pythagorean school. Attributed to the school are: the proof of PYTHAGORAS' THEOREM; the suggestion that the earth travels around the sun, the sun in turn around a central fire; observation of the ratios between the lengths of vibrating strings that sound in mutual harmony, and ascription of such ratios to the distances of the planets, which sounded the "harmony of the spheres," and the proposition that all phenomena may be reduced to numerical relations.

PYTHAGORAS' THEOREM, or **Pythagorean Theorem**, the statement that, for any right-angled TRIANGLE, the SQUARE on the HYPOTENUSE is equal to the sum of the squares on the other two sides. The earliest known formal statement of the theorem is in the *Elements* of EUCLID, but it seems that the basis of it was known long before this time and, indeed, long before the time of PYTHAGORAS himself. (See also EUCLIDEAN GEOMETRY.)

PYTHEAS (flourished c300 BC), Greek navigator, the first of his countrymen to explore the Atlantic coast of Europe and visit the British Isles. According to the Greek historian POLYBIUS, he reported the existence of an inhabited island called Thule, six days' sail to the north of Britain—possibly Norway or Iceland.

PYTHIAN GAMES, one of four great festivals of ancient Greece, held at Delphi to celebrate Apollo's slaying of the PYTHON. Staged every eighth year, then after the Delphic AMPHICTYONY took control c582 BC every four years, they included dramatic, poetic, musical, athletic and equestrian contests and continued until at least 424 AD.

PYTHIAS. See DAMON AND PYTHIAS.

PYTHIAS, Knights of. See KNIGHTS OF PYTHIAS.

PYTHON, in Greek mythology, a great serpent which guarded the oracle at DELPHI until slain by the god APOLLO, who founded his own oracle there. The PYTHIAN GAMES were held to honor his victory.

PYTHONS, the Old World equivalent of the New World BOAS, like them SNAKES bearing small spurs as the vestiges of hindlimbs. These two groups are clearly the closest relatives of the ancestral snake type. Like boas, pythons are nonvenomous constrictors. They are found from Africa to Australia in a wide variety of habitats. All have bold color patterns in browns and yellows. The largest species, the Reticulate python of Asia, reaches 10m (33ft). Pythons feed on small mammals, birds, reptiles and frogs; the larger African species also take small antelope.

Q, the 17th letter of the alphabet, traceable to the Semitic letter *koph* and the archaic Greek letter *koppa*. Q is used to designate a hypothetical source of the SYNOPTIC GOSPELS; and "Q" was the pseudonym of the British writer Sir Arthur Thomas Quiller-Couch (1863–1944).

QADDAFI (or Gaddafi), Muammar al- (1938–), Libyan leader. One of a group of army officers who deposed King Idris in 1969, he became chairman of the ruling Revolutionary Command Council and commander-in-chief of the armed forces. (See LIBYA.)

QATAR, oil-rich state on a peninsula in the Persian Gulf on the coast of Saudi Arabia. Mainly desert, it is dominated by the oil industry, centered in the Dukhan oilfield in W Qatar, one of the richest in the Middle East. Formerly a British protectorate, the country became independent in 1971, and with the wealth from its oil revenues is undergoing rapid technological development.

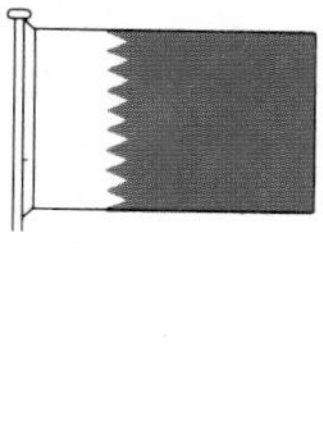

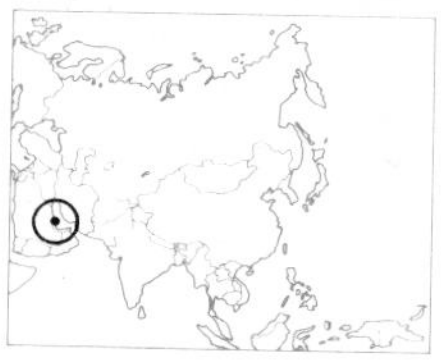

Official name: State of Qatar
Capital: Doha
Area: 4247sq mi
Population: 180 000
Language: Arabic; English for commercial use
Religion: Muslim
Monetary unit(s): 1 Qatar riyal = 100 dirhams

QATTARA DEPRESSION, barren low-lying area in NW Egypt, 130mi W of Cairo. Its area is about 7 000sq mi and at one point it is 436ft below sea level.

Q FEVER, or **query fever**, INFECTIOUS DISEASE due to *Coxiella*, an organism intermediate between BACTERIA and VIRUSES, causing FEVER, HEADACHE and often dry cough and chest pain. It is transmitted by ticks from various farm animals and is common among farm workers and veterinarians. Its course is benign but TETRACYCLINES may be used in treatment.

QUACK GRASS, or **couch grass,** *Agropyron repens*, a grass that is a problematical weed of cultivated fields. It is native to N Europe and North America and thrives in rich soil. The dried and roasted rhizome has been used as a coffee substitute. Family: Graminae.

QUAD CITIES, a collective name for the four industrial cities of Davenport, Moline, East Moline and Rock Island on the Ia.-Ill. border.

QUADRANGLE, in GEOMETRY, a QUADRILATERAL.

QUADRANT, in plane CARTESIAN COORDINATES, one of the four divisions of the PLANE made by the AXES. In SPHERICAL GEOMETRY, a quadrant is a spherical distance of $\pi/2$. A quadrant of a circle is a sector with a central ANGLE of $\pi/2$.

QUADRANT, a simple astronomical and navigational instrument used in early times to measure the altitudes of the sun and stars. It consisted typically of a pair of sights, a calibrated quadrant (quarter) of a circle, and a plumb line. (See also SEXTANT.)

QUADRAPHONIC SOUND. See HIGH FIDELITY.

QUADRILATERAL, in geometry, a PLANE four-sided POLYGON. Quadrilaterals with two pairs of sides parallel are called parallelograms; with one pair of sides parallel, trapezoids; with no two sides parallel, trapeziums (the word trapezium is often used as a synonym of trapezoid). Parallelograms whose sides are all of equal length are termed rhombuses. Each side of a parallelogram is equal in length to the side parallel to it; and each INTERIOR ANGLE is equal to the interior angle diametrically opposite it. A parallelogram whose interior angles are each 90° is a rectangle: a special case of this is the square, all of whose sides are equal. The sum of the interior angles of a quadrilateral is always 360°.

QUADRILLE, a type of dance, not unlike square dancing. Performed by four couples, it was very popular in the 18th and 19th centuries. A popular variation was known as the Lancers.

QUADRIVIUM. See SEVEN LIBERAL ARTS.

QUADROON. See MULATTO.

QUADRUPLE ALLIANCE, an alliance of four countries. Historically, the most famous are: (1) An alliance between England, France, Austria and the Netherlands formed in 1718 to prevent Spain from changing the terms of the Peace of UTRECHT. Spain later joined the alliance. (2) An alliance between

Britain, Austria, Russia and Prussia, signed in 1814 and renewed in 1815. Its purpose was to defeat Napoleon and after his defeat and first abdication to ensure that France abided by the terms of the 1815 Treaty of PARIS.

QUADRUPLETS. See MULTIPLE BIRTH.

QUAESTOR, or **questor,** an official in ancient Rome. In the early Republic quaestors acted as magistrates in criminal cases. They later took on financial responsibilities. The quaestorship commonly represented the first stage in a senator's political career.

QUAGGA, *Equus quagga quagga*, a type of ZEBRA striped on the front half only, thus seemingly half-zebra, half-ass, formerly abundant in South Africa but exterminated in the wild by 1860.

QUAHOG, *Venus mercenaria*, the American Hard-shelled clam, a bivalve MOLLUSK living close under the surface of sand or silt, with short breathing siphons. It is widely fished in Europe and the US.

QUAI D'ORSAY, a quay in Paris on the left bank of the Seine. It is the location of the French Foreign Office, and the ministry and its policies are often referred to by that name.

QUAILS, two distinct groups of game birds: Old World and New World quails. Small, rounded ground birds of open country, they feed on insects, grain and shoots. They rarely fly even when disturbed. The tiny Painted quail was carried by Chinese mandarins to warm the hands. Family: Phasianidae.

QUAKERS, or the Society of Friends, a church known for its pacifism, humanitarianism and emphasis on inner quiet. Founded in 17th-century England by George FOX, it was persecuted for its rejection of organized churches and of any dogmatic creed, and many Quakers emigrated to America, where in spite of early persecution they were prominent among the colonizers. In 1681 William PENN established his "Holy Experiment" in Pennsylvania, and from that point the church's main growth took place in America.

The early Quakers adopted a distinctive, simple style of dress and speech, and simplicity of manner is still a characteristic Quaker trait. They have no formal creed and no clergy, and put their trust in the "Inward Light" of God's guidance. Their meetings for worship, held in "Meeting Houses," follow a traditional pattern of beginning in silence, with no set service and no single speaker.

The Quakers have exercised a moral influence disproportionate to their numbers through actually practicing what they believe, particularly pacifism. In the US they were prominent abolitionists and have been among the pioneers of social reform. They today number about 126 000 in the US.

QUANTITY THEORY OF MONEY, theory relating changes in the level of prices to changes in the amount of MONEY in circulation; i.e., distinguishing between money, whose value may alter with price fluctuations, and true wealth. In the 19th century it was used to support FREE TRADE against protectionism. After the work of KEYNES in the 1930s it lost favor, but it regained popularity in the 1960s, when control of the money supply was seen as important in the fight against inflation.

QUANTRILL, William Clarke (1837–1865), Confederate guerrilla leader in the American CIVIL WAR. A criminal before the war, Quantrill was made a Confederate captain in 1862. On Aug. 21, 1863, with a force of 450 men he attacked the town of Lawrence, Kan., and slaughtered 150 civilians. He was killed while on a raid in Kentucky.

QUANTUM MECHANICS, fundamental theory of small-scale physical phenomena (such as the motions of ELECTRONS and nuclei within ATOMS), developed during the 20th century when it became clear that the existing laws of classical mechanics and electromagnetic theory were not successfully applicable to such systems. Because quantum mechanics treats physical events that we cannot directly perceive, it has many concepts unknown in everyday experience. DE BROGLIE struck out from the old QUANTUM THEORY when he suggested that particles have a wavelike nature, with a wavelength $\lambda = h/p$ (h being the Planck constant and p the particle momentum). This wavelike nature is significant only for very small particles such as electrons. These ideas were developed by SCHRÖDINGER and others into the branch of quantum mechanics known as WAVE MECHANICS. HEISENBERG worked along parallel lines with a theory incorporating only observable quantities such as ENERGY, using matrix algebra techniques. The UNCERTAINTY PRINCIPLE is fundamental to quantum mechanics, as is Pauli's EXCLUSION PRINCIPLE. DIRAC incorporated relativistic ideas into quantum mechanics.

The Quaker house in Philadelphia. It was in Philadelphia that Quakers were at last able to practice their religion freely.

QUANTUM THEORY, theory developed at the beginning of the 20th century to account for certain phenomena that could not be explained by classical PHYSICS. PLANCK described the previously unexplained distribution of radiation from a BLACK BODY by assuming that ELECTROMAGNETIC RADIATION exists in discrete bundles known as quanta, each with an ENERGY $E = h\nu$ (ν being the radiation frequency and h a universal constant—the PLANCK CONSTANT). EINSTEIN also used the idea of quanta to explain the PHOTOELECTRIC EFFECT, establishing that electromagnetic radiation has a dual nature, behaving sometimes as a WAVE MOTION and sometimes as a stream of particle-like quanta. Measurements of other physical quantities, such as the frequencies of lines in atomic spectra and the energy losses of electrons on colliding with atoms, showed that these quantities could not have a continuous range of values, discrete values only being possible. With RUTHERFORD's discovery in 1911 that ATOMS consist of a small positively charged nucleus surrounded by ELECTRONS, attempts were made to understand this atomic structure in the light of quantum ideas, since classically the electrons would radiate energy continuously and collapse into the nucleus. BOHR postulated that an atom only exists in certain stationary (i.e., nonradiating) states with definite energies and that quanta of radiation are emitted or absorbed in transitions between these states; he successfully calculated the stationary states of hydrogen. Some further progress was made along these lines by Bohr and others, but it became clear that the quantum theory was fundamentally weak in being unable to calculate intensities of spectral lines. The new QUANTUM MECHANICS was developed c1925 to take its place.

QUAPAW INDIANS, North American plains Indians of the Siouan language group. By the 17th century they had migrated from the Ohio valley to near the mouth of the Arkansas R. They conceded most of their lands to the US in 1818. About 750 remain, living on a reserve in Okla.

QUARANTINE, period during which a person or animal must be kept under observation in isolation from the community after having been in contact with an INFECTIOUS DISEASE. The duration of quarantine depends on the disease(s) concerned and their maximum length of INCUBATION. The term derives from the period of 40 days that ships from the Levant had to wait before their crews could disembark at medieval European ports, from fear of their carrying PLAGUE.

QUARK. See SUBATOMIC PARTICLES.

QUARRY, a large open excavation from which rock is extracted. Special drills, saws and chisels are used to extract valuable building or ornamental stone. Rock for cement-making, road-building and industrial uses is usually extracted by blasting and then processed by crushing machines. EXCAVATORS are used directly to extract sand, gravel and other materials from pits. (See also MINING.)

QUART, name of various units of liquid and dry measure. See WEIGHTS AND MEASURES.

QUARTERMASTER CORPS, the section of the US Army responsible for providing food, clothing, accommodation and equipment for the troops. Its functions were taken over in 1962 by the newly set up Army Materiel Command.

QUARTZ, rhombohedral form of SILICA, usually forming hexagonal prisms, colorless when pure ("rock crystal"). A common mineral, it is the chief constituent of SAND, SANDSTONE, QUARTZITE and FLINT, and also occurs as the GEMS: CHALCEDONY; AGATE; JASPER, and ONYX. Quartz is piezoelectric (see PIEZOELECTRICITY) and is used to make oscillators for clocks, radio and radar; and also to make windows for optical instruments. Crude quartz is used to make glass, glazes and abrasives, and as a flux.

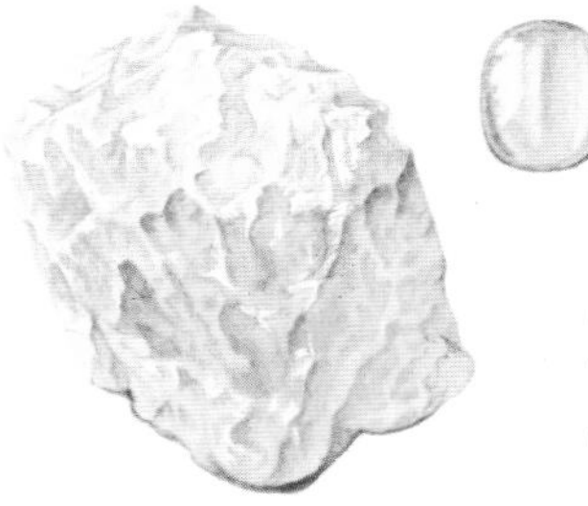

Rose quartz—as a raw mineral (*left*) and, cut and polished, as a cabochon.

QUARTZITE, common rock consisting of QUARTZ, formed by metamorphism of SANDSTONE. It is tough, resisting weathering, and is used as road metal.

QUASAR, or quasi-stellar object, a telescopically star-like celestial object whose SPECTRUM shows an abnormally large RED SHIFT. Quasars may be extremely distant objects, receding from us at high velocities, although some recent research has cast doubt upon this, since the spectra of quasars do not seem to have been affected by the interpolation of intergalactic gas. Quasars show variability in light and radio emission (although the first quasars were discovered by RADIO ASTRONOMY, not all are radio sources), which might indicate that they are comparatively small objects less than 0.3pc across, comparatively close to us (larger—and more distant—objects being unlikely to vary in this way). There are about 200 quasars in each square degree of the sky.

QUASIMODO, Salvatore (1901–1968), Italian poet and translator of poetry awarded the 1959 Nobel Prize for Literature. During and after WWII he turned (originally because of his opposition to Fascism) from a complex, introverted Hermetic style to social protest and examination of the plight of the individual, as in *Day after Day* (1947).

QUASSIA, a number of tropical trees, the wood of which yields principles used in medicines and in condition powders for domestic animals. *Quassia amara* is native to the W Indies and northeastern South America. Family: Simaroubaceae.

QUATERNARY, the period of the CENOZOIC whose beginning is marked by the advent of man. It has lasted about 4 million years, up to and including the present. (See also TERTIARY; GEOLOGY.)

QUATERNION, a type of complex number (see IMAGINARY NUMBERS) developed by W. R. Hamilton (1805–1865) to operate in three dimensions as ordinary complex numbers do in two.

QUATRAIN, a stanza or piece of verse of four lines, often with alternate rhyme (abab).

QUAY, Matthew Stanley (1833–1904), US politician. A lawyer, he fought in the Civil War and later became boss of the Republican Party machine in Pa., making skillful use of patronage. Elected US senator 1887, he was unseated in 1899 after corruption charges, but reelected 1901.

QUEBEC, the largest province in Canada, stretching from Hudson Bay to S of the St. Lawrence R.

Land. Over 90% of the province lies within the CANADIAN SHIELD, a great rocky plateau, much of it an uninhabited wilderness of forests, lakes and streams. South of the Shield are the agricultural St. Lawrence Lowlands containing most of the cities of Quebec. The third major region is the Appalachian Uplands in the SE. The St. Lawrence R, running through Quebec, has played a key role in its development. The province has severe winters and warm humid summers.

People. Quebec's population is concentrated in the S. About 75% are urban dwellers. French-Canadians, most of them descendants of 17th-and 18th-century settlers, constitute 80% of the population; over 60% speak French only, and there are separate English and French schools, radio and TV stations and newspapers. Roman Catholicism dominates the religious life of the province.

Economy. Quebec has vast resources of raw materials and almost limitless hydroelectric power. Industries include paper, aluminum processing, foodstuffs, textiles, chemicals and metal products. Montreal and Quebec City are the leading manufacturing centers. The chief mineral products are iron ore, asbestos and copper. Dairying is the most important branch of agriculture, and Quebec's forestry accounts for nearly half of Canada's wood and paper products.

History. The first permanent settlement in Quebec dates from 1608 when CHAMPLAIN built a trading post at the site of Quebec City. From then until defeat by the British in the FRENCH AND INDIAN WAR (1754–63), the French controlled the province. Since the advent of British rule in 1763, Quebec's history has been dominated by its effort to preserve its French identity, in which the QUEBEC ACT of 1774 played a significant part. In 1837 a revolt under PAPINEAU flared up. In 1867 Quebec became a founding province of the Dominion of Canada, with considerable autonomy. In the 1960s a French separatist movement emerged, and the Canadian government has since made several concessions in the field of education and has established French as the major language in Quebec. (See also CANADA.)

One of the best known sights in Quebec province, St. Joseph's Oratory on the slopes of Mont Royal attracts over 3 million pilgrims a year.

Name of Province: Quebec—Québec
Joined Confederation: July 1, 1867
Capital: Quebec City
Area: 594 860sq mi
Population: 6 027 764

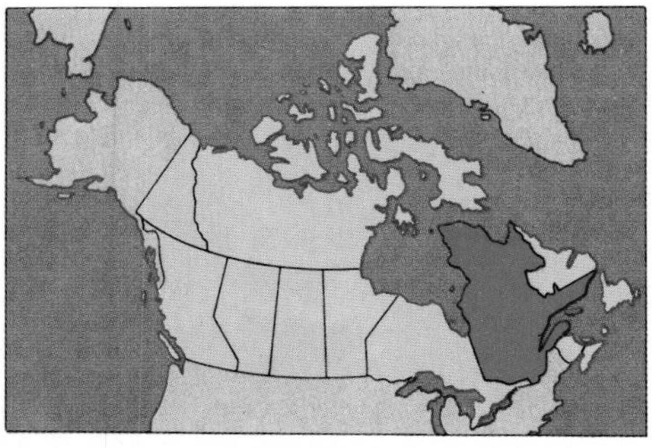

QUEBEC, the capital of QUEBEC province, situated on the St. Lawrence R. Founded in 1608 by CHAMPLAIN, it is Canada's oldest city. Quebec has remained essentially French, and more than 90% of its citizens claim French ancestry. Today it is a leading manufacturing center and transatlantic port. Industries include shipbuilding, paper milling, food processing, machinery and textiles. The city is a major tourist attraction. Pop 186 088.

QUEBEC, Battle of, the most important battle of the FRENCH AND INDIAN WAR, whose outcome transferred control of Canada from France to Britain. French troops under MONTCALM were defending Quebec City. On the night of Sept. 12, 1759, British troops under WOLFE silently scaled the cliffs W of the city to the Plains of Abraham. After a short, bloody battle the French fled. Both Wolfe and Montcalm were mortally wounded.

QUEBEC ACT, passed by the British Parliament in 1774, one of the INTOLERABLE ACTS. It guaranteed the use of the French civil code and established religious freedom for the Roman Catholic Church in Quebec, and extended Quebec's boundary to the Ohio and Mississippi rivers.

QUEBEC CONFERENCE, a conference in the city of Quebec, Oct. 1864, that laid the foundations of the Canadian Confederation. Representatives from the British provinces in North America produced a series of 72 resolutions outlining a centralized federal union. This became the basis of the BRITISH NORTH AMERICA ACT (1867) which created the Dominion of Canada.

QUEBEC CONFERENCES, two important conferences held in the city of Quebec during WWII. In Aug. 1943 ROOSEVELT and CHURCHILL met with the Canadian prime minister and the Chinese foreign minister to make arrangements for operations in the Far East and for the Allied invasion of Europe. In Sept. 1944 Roosevelt and Churchill met again to discuss broad military strategy.

QUEBRACHO, or **axebreaker,** a number of tropical trees found particularly in South America. They are valued for their extremely hard wood, which is used to make railroad sleepers and in general carpentry. Family: Anarcardiaceae.

QUECHUA, South American Indians, once part of the INCA empire and now living mostly as peasants in the Andean highlands from Colombia to N Chile. Quechua is also the name of the family to which the official language of the Incas belonged, and some 28 languages of the family are still spoken.

QUEEN, Ellery, pen-name and fictional hero of detective writers, Frederic Dannay (1905–) and Manfred B. Lee (1905–1972). Their successful *The Roman Hat Mystery* (1929), was followed by over 100 other novels characterized by complexity of plot. *Ellery Queen's Mystery Magazine* was founded in 1941.

QUEEN ANNE'S LACE, or wild carrot, *Daucus carota*, a North American weed that closely resembles the cultivated CARROT. It is cultivated for its lacy clusters of flowers. Family: Umbelliferae.

QUEEN ANNE'S WAR. See FRENCH AND INDIAN WARS.

QUEEN CHARLOTTE ISLANDS, archipelago off the coast of British Columbia, N of Vancouver Island, consisting of Graham, Moresby and many smaller islands. Its population is mostly HAIDA Indians. The economy rests on lumber and fishing.

QUEEN ELIZABETH ISLANDS, group of Canadian islands, part of the N Arctic Archipelago, named (1953) for Queen Elizabeth II. Including the Parry Islands, the largest are Ellesmere, Devon, Melville and Axel Heiberg. Oil is being drilled in the area.

QUEEN MARY COAST, or Queen Mary Land, part of Antarctica between Wilkes Land and Cape Filchner. The region is controlled by the UK.

QUEEN MAUD LAND, part of Antarctica between Enderby Land and Coats Land, discovered in 1930 and claimed by Norway in 1939.

QUEENS, largest borough, in area, of New York City, located at the W end of Long Island. It includes the industrial and commercial centers of Long Island City and Astoria, and residential neighborhoods such as Forest Hills. The site of John F. Kennedy Airport, it was the scene of the 1939–40 and 1964–65 World Fairs. Pop 1 973 708.

QUEENSBERRY RULES, the basic rules of modern BOXING, drawn up in 1865 under the auspices of the 8th Marquess of Queensberry, supplanting the old London prize-ring rules. Innovations included the use of padded gloves instead of bare fists, a 10-second count to determine a knockout, and the division of the bout into rounds with intermissions.

QUEENSLAND, state in NE Australia, 667 000sq mi in area. Tropical and eucalyptus forests in the rugged E contrast with pasture and desert on the vast W plain. It produces sheep, nearly half of Australia's cattle, and such crops as sugarcane, wheat, cotton and fruit. There are valuable oil and mineral deposits. Almost half the population, mainly of British descent, lives in BRISBANE, the state capital.

QUEENSTON HEIGHTS, Battle of, battle in the WAR OF 1812, at Queenston Heights, S Ontario, near Niagara Falls (Oct. 13, 1812). Though the British commander, Sir Isaac BROCK, was killed, the US invaders, led by VAN RENSSELAER, were successfully repulsed.

QUEIROZ, José Maria Eça. See EÇA DE QUEIROZ, JOSÉ MARIA.

QUELEA, *Quelea quelea*, one of the WEAVERBIRDS of drier parts of Africa, a small land bird notorious as a major agricultural pest. They are gregarious, and huge flocks may descend on fields of ripening grain, rapidly stripping them.

QUEMOY, small island in the Formosa Strait, close to mainland China. Ruled by Nationalist Chinese, the island was subjected to shelling from the Communist mainland in the 1950s and 1960s.

QUERCITRON BARK, the bark of the Black oak (*Quercus velutina*), indigenous to the US. It contains a yellow dye, quercitrin, which is commonly used for dyeing wool and as a basis for producing a red dye, quercetin. Family: Fagaceae.

QUERÉTARO, Central Mexican state noted for opals and mercury. Other deposits include silver, iron and copper. Its main crops are sugarcane, cotton and tobacco.

QUERÉTARO, capital city of Querétaro state, an important textile, pottery and cotton-milling center. Formerly an Aztec city, it was taken by the Spanish in 1531. Pop 140 379.

QUESADA, Gonzalo Jiménez de. See JIMÉNEZ DE QUESADA, GONZALO.

QUESNAY, François (1694–1774), French economist and a leader of the PHYSIOCRATS. Although trained in medicine—he was physician to Louis XV—his fame rests on his essays in political economy, which first began to appear in 1756 in DIDEROT's *Encyclopédie*, and on his *Economic Table* (1758), which influenced Adam SMITH.

QUETTA, city in W Pakistan near the Afghanistan

border, capital of Baluchistan province, commanding the ancient trade route of the Bolan Pass. It was hit by a major earthquake in 1935. Pop 140000.

QUETZAL, *Pharomachrus mocino*, a large bird of mountain forests in middle America, closely related to TROGONS. The male has a striking plumage of iridescent green upperparts and breast, with a bright crimson belly. In breeding condition four tail coverts grow into long shimmering display plumes.

QUETZALCOATL, the plumed serpent, ancient Mexican god identified with the morning and evening star. He is said to have ruled the pre-Aztec TOLTEC empire and to have invented books and the calendar. Whether he was an historical chieftain or merely mythological is not certain. MONTEZUMA II welcomed CORTEZ, believing him to be descended from the god.

QUEVEDO Y VILLEGAS, Francisco Gómez de (1580–1645), great Spanish satirist, poet and prose writer. Master of the *conceptismo* style of terse and arresting intellectual conceits, he is best known for *The Life of a Swindler* (1626), a parody of the PICARESQUE NOVEL, and *Visions* (1627), a bitter, fantastic view of the inhabitants of hell.

QUEZON, Manuel Luis (1878–1944), Filipino statesman who played a leading role in the Philippine independence movement before becoming the first president of the Philippine Commonwealth. His presidency, continued (after Japanese invasion) from 1942 in the US, was marked by efforts to improve conditions for the poor.

QUEZON CITY, capital city of the Philippines since 1948, on Luzon Island, 10mi NE of the former capital MANILA. A trading and transportation center, it was named for Manuel QUEZON. Pop 754452.

QUICHÉ INDIANS, largest Guatemalan Indian group, now numbering about 340000, found mainly in the W highlands. Of Mayan linguistic stock, they have, since their conquest in 1524 by the Spanish Pedro de ALVARADO, colorfully adapted many Western customs and religious traditions to their own.

QUICKSAND, sand saturated with water to form a sand-water SUSPENSION possessing the characteristics of a liquid. Quicksands may form at rivermouths or on sandflats, and are dangerous as they appear identical to adjacent SAND. In fact, the DENSITY of the suspension is less than that of the human body so that, if a person does not struggle, he may escape being engulfed.

QUICKSILVER. See MERCURY.

QUIDDE, Ludwig (1858–1941), German writer and pacifist politician who shared with Ferdinand BUISSON the 1927 Nobel Peace Prize.

QUIDS, early US political faction, led by John RANDOLPH, of extreme protagonists of states' rights. Convinced that Thomas JEFFERSON and James MADISON had become virtual nationalists, they attempted to block Madison's Democratic-Republican presidential nomination in 1808.

QUIETISM, mystical religious movement originated in 17th century Spain by Miguel de Molinos (1640–c1697), which later spread to France as the less extreme Semiquietism. Molinos advocated a wholly passive mysticism. After papal condemnations, Quietism (1687) and Semiquietism (1699) collapsed.

QUIMBY, Phineas Parkhurst (1802–1866), US pioneer of mental healing, an early user of SUGGESTION as a therapy. A strong influence on Mary Baker Eddy, he is held as a father of the New Thought movement.

QUINCE, an Asian tree (*Cydonia oblonga*) that bears small, yellow, pear-shaped fruits, mainly used in preserves and jellies. Family: Rosaceae.

QUINCY, city in W Ill., on the Mississippi R, seat of Adams Co., and an industrial, agricultural and distribution center. Pop 45288.

QUINCY, city in E Mass., situated on Boston Harbor, 8mi S of Boston, birthplace of presidents John ADAMS and John Quincy ADAMS. It is an industrial center. The Fore River shipyards are among the most important in the US. Pop 87966.

QUINCY, Josiah (1772–1864), US politician, educator and author. Elected to Congress in 1804, he resigned in 1813 after opposing the WAR OF 1812. He later distinguished himself as a reforming mayor of Boston (1823–28) and as president of HARVARD UNIVERSITY (1829–45).

QUINE, Willard Van Orman (1908–), US philosopher and logician, best known for his rejection of such longstanding philosophical claims as that analytic ("self-evident") statements are fundamentally distinguishable from synthetic (observational) statements, and that the concept of synonymy (sameness of meaning) can be exemplified.

QUININE, substance derived from CINCHONA bark from South America, for long used in treating a variety of ailments. It was preeminent in early treatment of MALARIA until the 1930s when ATABRINE was introduced; after this more suitable quinine derivatives such as CHLOROQUINE were synthesized. Quinine is also a mild ANALGESIC and may prevent CRAMPS and suppress HEART rhythm disorders. Now rarely used, its side effects include VOMITING, DEAFNESS, VERTIGO and VISION disturbance.

QUINOA, *Chenopodium quinoa* and *Amaranthus caudatus*, South American herbs of the GOOSEFOOT family, Chenopodiaceae. For centuries in Chile and Peru the seeds have afforded a staple food, being eaten like rice or in the form of porridge or cakes.

Carved serpent heads, representing the god Quetzalcoatl as a plumed serpent, adorn the staircase of a major temple devoted to him at Teotihuacan in central Mexico.

QUINQUAGESIMA. See CHURCH YEAR.

QUINSY, acute complication of TONSILLITIS in which ABSCESS formation causes spasm of the adjacent jaw muscles, FEVER and severe pain. Incision and drainage of the PUS produce rapid relief, though ANTIBIOTICS are helpful and the TONSILS should be excised later.

QUINTAL, Metric (q), unit of MASS equal to 100kg.

QUINTANA ROO, territory in SE Mexico occupying much of the E part of the YUCATÁN PENINSULA. Because of its dense natural cover and inhospitable climate it remains undeveloped. The people are primarily of Mayan descent.

QUINTILIAN (Marcus Fabius Quintilianus: c35 AD–c96 AD), Roman rhetoric teacher, whose famous 12-book *Institutio Oratoria*, covering rhetorical techniques, educational theory, literary criticism and morality, deeply influenced Renaissance culture.

QUINTUPLETS. See MULTIPLE BIRTH.

QUIRINAL HILL. See SEVEN HILLS OF ROME.

QUIRINO, Elpidio (1890–1956), Filipino statesman. Political aide to Manuel QUEZON for many years prior to WWII, he became an underground leader during the Japanese occupation. He was president of the Philippine republic 1948–54.

QUIRINUS, one of the state gods of ancient Rome, probably originally worshiped by the SABINES. Early rather similar to MARS, he came in the late Republic to be identified with ROMULUS.

QUISLING, Vidkun Abraham Lauritz (1887–1945), Norwegian fascist leader who assisted the German invasion of Norway (1940) and was afterward appointed by HITLER premier of Norway's puppet government (1942–45). He was executed for treason. His name has come to mean "traitor."

QUITO, capital and second largest city of Ecuador and oldest capital in South America, is located just S of the equator at the foot of the Pichincha volcano, at an altitude of 9350ft. Seized from the INCAS by a Spanish conquistador in 1534, it is famous for its Spanish colonial architecture. It has minor industries. Pop 575000.

QUITRENTS, system whereby an "incomplete sale" of land was concluded between tenant and landlord, the latter collecting annual rent in perpetuity and retaining the option to repurchase the land at 75% of the sale price. Prevalent in the US in the 17th and 18th centuries, the system largely disappeared in the mid-19th century.

QUIVIRA, name given to land sought and found by Francisco CORONADO in 1541, and generally identified with the Great Bend area, Kan. Later explorers thought of Quivira as an unexplored city of gold.

QUMRAN, village on the NW shore of the Dead Sea, Jordan, near the caves where the DEAD SEA SCROLLS were found (1947). Built by ESSENES (c130–c110 BC), it was destroyed by an earthquake (31 BC), rebuilt, and destroyed again by the Romans (68 AD).

QUODDY HEAD. See WEST QUODDY HEAD.

QUOITS, traditional English country game. Each player of each team throws in turn two quoits (iron or rubber rings) in an attempt to ring them over pins (hobs) set into the ground 54–72ft apart.

QUOKKA, *Setonix brachyurus*, a small herbivorous nocturnal WALLABY found in SW Australia.

QUORUM, the number or proportion of members who must be present before an organization or legislative body can legally or constitutionally transact business.

QUOTAS, limits imposed by governments on the number of immigrants or the quantity (sometimes the value) of goods that may be exported or imported. Tariff quotas allow a certain number of goods to be imported duty-free, quantities above the quota being subject to duty.

QUOTIENT, in the DIVISION of one positive INTEGER by another, the largest number of times (k) the DIVISOR (a) must be multiplied so that $0 \leqslant (b-ka) < a$, where b is the DIVIDEND and $(b-ka)$ the REMAINDER.

QUO WARRANTO, originally a writ under English law initiating a civil action to test "by what authority" an individual held title or office. In most states of the US it is still used, occasionally to test the authority of public or corporate bodies but more often that of individual franchisees or office holders.

R

R, the 18th letter of the alphabet, corresponding to Greek *rho* and Semitic *rēsh* ("head"). Its present capital form comes from classical Latin; the small letter derives from Carolingian script.

RA, or **Re,** sun god of ancient Egypt, one of the most important gods of the pantheon. From the 6th dynasty all pharaohs claimed descent from Ra. He was commonly represented as a falcon or falcon-headed figure with the solar disk on his head. The later cult of ATON was based on that of Ra.

RABAT, capital of Morocco, at the mouth of the Bou Regreg R. The city, which dates from the 12th century AD, produces textiles and carpets. Pop 325 000.

RABAUL, town on NEW BRITAIN. Once capital of the Territory of New Guinea (1920–41), it was totally rebuilt after WWII Allied bombing. Its main export is copra. Pop 21 400.

RABBI (Hebrew: my master, or my teacher), the leader of a Jewish religious congregation with the role of spiritual leader, scholar, teacher and interpreter of Jewish law. The term originated in Palestine, meaning merely religious teacher, after the return from exile and destruction of the hereditary priesthood, the more official role of a rabbi developing from the Middle Ages.

RABBIT FEVER. See TULAREMIA.

RABBITS, herbivorous members of the LAGOMORPHA, usually with long ears and a white scut for a tail. Best known is the European rabbit *Oryctolagus cuniculus.* These live in discrete social groups in colonial burrows. Territory is defended by all members of the group and within the group there is distinct dominance ranking. It attains maturity at three months and can breed every month thereafter. In many areas they have reached plague proportions. Numbers have been reduced in Australia and Europe by the introduction of a VIRUS disease, myxomatosis.

RABBIT-TRACK PLANT, popular name for the foliage house plant *Maranta leuconeura kerchoveana.* Family: Marantaceae. (See MARANTA.)

RABELAIS, François (1494?–1553), French monk, doctor and humanist author of *Gargantua and Pantagruel* (four books 1532–52, arguably a fifth 1564). This exuberant mixture of popular anecdote, bawdry and huge erudition with vastly inventive language and broad satire of tyrants and bigots, recounts two giants' quest for the secret of life.

RABI, Isidor Isaac (1898–   ), Austrian-born US physicist whose discovery of new ways of measuring the magnetic properties of ATOMS and MOLECULES both paved the way for the development of the MASER and the ATOMIC CLOCK and earned him the 1944 Nobel Prize for Physics.

RABIES, or **Hydrophobia,** fatal VIRUS disease resulting from the bite of an infected animal, usually a dog. HEADACHE, FEVER, and an overwhelming fear, especially of water, are early symptoms following an INCUBATION period of 3–6 weeks; PARALYSIS, spasm of muscles of swallowing, respiratory paralysis, DELIRIUM, CONVULSIONS and COMA due to an ENCEPHALITIS follow. Wound cleansing, antirabies vaccine and hyperimmune serum must be instituted early in confirmed cases to prevent the onset of these symptoms. Fluid replacement and respiratory support may help, but survival is rare if symptoms appear. Infected animals must be destroyed.

RABINOWITZ, Solomon. See SHOLEM ALEICHEM.

RACCOONS, probably the best known of the American mammals, stout, bear-like animals, 600mm to 1m (2.0–3.3ft) long with a distinctive black mask and five to eight black bands on the bushy tail. They live in trees, alone or in small family groups, descending at night to forage for crayfish, frogs and fish in shallow pools. Family: Procyonidae.

RACE, within a SPECIES, a subgroup most of whose members have sufficiently different physical characteristics from those exhibited by most members of another subgroup for it to be considered as a distinct entity. In particular the term is used with respect to the human species, *Homo sapiens,* the three most commonly distinguished races being CAUCASOID, MONGOLOID and NEGROID (see also AUSTRALOID). However, in practice it is impossible to make unambiguous distinctions between races: a classification by color would yield a quite different result to one by blood-group (see ANTHROPOMETRY). According to DARWIN's theories of EVOLUTION, races arise when different groups encounter different environmental situations. Over generations, their physical characteristics evolve until each group as a whole is physically quite different from its parent stock. Should the isolation of the group continue long enough, and the environment be different enough, the divergent race will eventually become a distinct species, unable to mate with the species from which it originally sprang. This has obviously not happened in the case of man, whose races may interbreed successfully and, in many cases, advantageously. It is not known when man became racially differentiated, but certainly it was at a very early stage in his evolution (see PREHISTORIC MAN): nowadays, with the rise of efficient transportation, racial convergence in man is accelerating and seems likely to result in complete racial fusion, in which individuals will nevertheless vary considerably.

RACE, Cape, the SE tip of the Avalon Peninsula in Newfoundland, Canada.

RACEME. See INFLORESCENCE.

RACERS. See WHIPSNAKES.

RACERUNNERS, a genus, *Cnemidophorus,* of active diurnal LIZARDS, ranging from the US to northern Argentina. They feed on insects and mollusks.

RACHEL, second of the four wives of JACOB, mother of JOSEPH and BENJAMIN, and sister of LEAH.

The European wild rabbit, *Oryctolagus cuniculus* (*below*), is now found not only throughout Europe but all over the world; it is the ancestor of nearly all domesticated rabbits.

In the US and Canada is found its counterpart (*above*), the American cottontail, *Sylvilagus floridanus.*

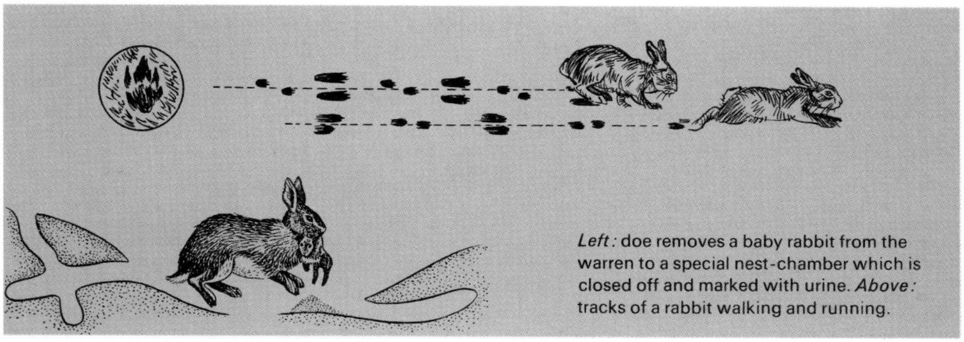

Left: doe removes a baby rabbit from the warren to a special nest-chamber which is closed off and marked with urine. *Above:* tracks of a rabbit walking and running.

Racial Minorities

A perspective on minority rights

The noticeable increase in tensions between groups in European countries in recent decades underscores the fact that minority problems in highly industrialized nations are not confined to societies with established racial systems, such as the United States and the Republic of South Africa. Since 1945, millions of immigrants from Asia, Africa, the West Indies and the less industrialized parts of Europe, such as Turkey, Greece, and Southern Italy, have arrived in Western Europe in search of higher-paying jobs and an improved standard of living. Because they lack industrial training and, in some instances, are unable to speak or understand the language when they arrive, the immigrants are overwhelmingly concentrated in menial and unskilled jobs. In France, Switzerland, and Germany, many immigrants find that their subordinate economic positions are reinforced by lack of citizenship, as restrictive laws and regulations impede their chances for occupational mobility. Although there are variations in the way the immigrants are perceived and treated, it is quite clear that the pattern of minority status and unequal racial access to rights and privileges, so characteristic of the more established racial orders, has been firmly reproduced in Western Europe. This brief essay aims to demonstrate the global significance of racial matters by comparing the experiences of blacks over the issue of minority rights in the United States with those of nonwhites in Great Britain and the Republic of South Africa.

Black Americans constitute roughly 11% of the total population in the United States, and by 1970 81% of blacks resided in urban areas. The growth of the black urban population coincided with industrial expansion in the United States, as millions of blacks, in search of a better life (in a movement quite similar to the trek of immigrants from less developed nations to Western Europe) migrated from the rural South to the industrial centers of the North and West throughout the first half of the 20th century. Although the city provided blacks with greater employment opportunities and a somewhat higher standard of living, they were nonetheless trapped in sprawling ghettoes and concentrated overwhelmingly in menial and low-paying jobs.

However, the increasing movement of blacks to the cities of the North significantly strengthened their political power. By 1948, it became clear that the black vote in certain pivotal northern states was large enough to determine close national elections. Indeed, Presidents Truman and Kennedy could not have defeated their Republican rivals in the 1948 and 1960 elections without the support of black voters. Moreover, many congressional, state, and municipal elections in the North during the 1950s and 1960s were decided by the preferences of black voters.

In addition to the increase of political resources, the concentration of blacks in urban areas contributed to the growth of a black middle class. More specifically, the expanding occupational opportunities in urban areas enabled a relatively small, but nonetheless significant, number of blacks to improve their standard of living by upgrading their jobs and enlarging their incomes. It is the middle-class segment of an oppressed minority group that is most likely to initiate and participate in a disciplined and sustained drive for social justice. As the status of individual minorities improves, expectations for a better life likewise increase and dissatisfaction with existing injustices multiplies. Thus, it was the black middle class that organized civil rights campaigns in the late 1950s and early 1960s. Moreover, it was the black middle class that recognized and clearly articulated the view that because of the growing black political resources, the pressures of black protest, and America's concern for world-wide opinion, the government was likely to respond to a disciplined nonviolent campaign for civil rights with the enactment of laws against racial bias. They were correct. The passage of the 1964 Civil Rights Bill (which outlawed, among other things, discrimination in employment, public accommodations and public facilities) clearly indicated the success of the nonviolent protests against racial injustice. This legislation and the subsequent voting rights bill of 1965 (which was designed to enforce the 15th Amendment to the United States Constitution) and the Civil Rights Bill of 1968 (which banned discrimination in the sale or rental of homes—except for single-family houses sold by the owner himself) allayed the concerns of the black middle class. However, they did not sufficiently tackle the unique problems of the black lower class.

It is true that the civil rights campaign also heightened the lower-class black awareness of racial inequality and thereby generated a militant racial mood in the ghetto. It is also true that these feelings were dramatically expressed in a proliferation of ghetto riots from 1964 to 1968. But a close examination of ghetto black discontent revealed issues that transcended the creation and implementation of civil rights laws, issues that had to do with de facto segregation and social class subordination, issues, in particular, that pertained to inferior ghetto schools, deteriorated housing, and, most important, unemployment and underemployment. Thus, in the late 1960s, some black leaders emphatically proclaimed that for lower-class ghetto blacks, the question of human rights is far more fundamental than the question of civil rights. From these points it is clear that even if all legal racial barriers are removed, ghetto blacks could hardly compete on equal terms with the rest of society because of an accumulation of disadvantages, created by previous periods of discrimination and prejudice, passed on from generation to generation. Furthermore, the situation for ghetto blacks is complicated by basic structural changes in our advanced industrial economy whereby adequate training and education are increasingly important for entry into the higher-paying and desirable jobs, and growing technology and automation have helped to create

RACHMANINOV, Sergei Vasilyevich (1873–1943), Russian composer and virtuoso pianist. After a successful career in Russia he left in 1917, settling in Switzerland (until 1935) and then the US. His extensive output of piano music, symphonies, songs and choral music includes such popular works as the Second Piano Concerto (1901).

RACINE, industrial city in SE Wis., seat of Racine Co., on Lake Michigan. An important shipping center, it manufactures heavy machinery and electrical equipment. Pop 95 162.

RACINE, Jean Baptiste (1639–1699), greatest of French tragic poets. After a JANSENIST education at PORT ROYAL schools, he surpassed his rival CORNEILLE with seven tragedies, from *Andromaque* (1667) and *Britannicus* (1669) to *Phèdre* (1677), possibly his masterpiece. His greatness lies in the beauty of his verse, expressing both powerful and subtle emotions, and the creation of tragic suspense in a classically restrained form.

RACING. See AUTOMOBILE RACING; HORSE RACING.

RACISM, the theory that some races are inherently superior to others. The concept of racism in the early 19th century was really an offshoot of NATIONALISM, and emphasis was placed on the development of individual cultures. But at the same time a systematic study of human types was revealing the existence of races distinguished by physical characteristics. Despite the theories of LINNAEUS and BLUMENBACH that environment rather than heredity molded intellectual development, many theorists associated culture with race, and assumed white superiority. Guided by such thinkers as GOBINEAU, a concept of "tribal nationalism" began to appear. It was used to justify IMPERIALISM, the imposition of colonial status on backward peoples, and finally the concept of the "master-race" fostered by the NAZIS. The mass-exterminations before and during WWII, together with advances in ANTHROPOLOGY, discredited racism as a tenable intellectual doctrine. (See also RACE.)

RACKHAM, Arthur (1867–1939), English artist best known for his fanciful, delicately-colored illustrations for children's books such as *Grimm's Fairy Tales* (1900), *Peter Pan* (1906) and *A Wonder Book* (1922).

RACQUETS, a game for two or four players, normally played in an enclosed court 60ft long and 30ft wide, with a front wall 30ft high and a back wall 15ft high. Rules are similar to those of SQUASH, but the ball is much harder and hence the game more dangerous.

RAD (rad, or rd where it might be confused with rad(ian)), a unit used for expressing absorbed dose of ionizing RADIATIONS. It represents the dosage absorbed when 1kg of matter absorbs 0.01 joules of energy.

RADAR (*ra*dio *d*etection *a*nd *r*anging), system that detects long-range objects and determines their positions by measuring the time taken for RADIO waves to travel to the objects, be reflected and return. Radar is used for NAVIGATION, air control, fire control, storm detection, in radar astronomy and for catching speeding drivers. It developed out of experiments in the 1920s measuring the distance of the IONOSPHERE by radio pulses. R. A. WATSON-WATT showed that the technique could be applied to detecting aircraft, and from 1935 Britain installed a series of radar stations which were a major factor in winning the Battle of Britain in WWII. From 1940 the UK and the US collaborated to develop radar. There are two main types of radar: **continuous-wave radar**, which transmits continuously, the frequency being varied sinusoidally, and detects the signals received by their instantaneously different frequency; and the more common **pulsed radar**. This latter has a highly directional antenna which scans the area systematically or tracks an object. A cavity magnetron or klystron emits pulses, typically 400 per second, $1\mu s$ across, and at a frequency of 3GHz. A duplexer switches the antenna automatically from transmitter to receiver and back as appropriate. The receiver converts the echo pulses to an intermediate frequency of about 30MHz, and they are then amplified, converted to a video signal, and displayed on a CATHODE-RAY TUBE. A synchronizer measures the time-lag between transmission and reception, and this is represented by the position of the pulse on the

The present distribution of races throughout the world reflects the former migrations of whole nations of people, the colonization by some people of large tracts of territory in parts of the world formerly inhabited by other races, and the forced movement of whole populations to work agricultural systems dependent on the institutions of slavery.

a surplus of untrained black workers.

In the opinion of some observers, therefore, there is little more that the government can do to ameliorate the problems of ghetto blacks and that since talented and educated blacks are making significant economic and social progress in the aftermath of the civil rights era, the issue is clearly no longer one of racial discrimination. Others, particularly black leaders, argue that drastic measures are necessary to erase the cycle of poverty, unemployment, and poor education; that, in the final analysis, the basic institutions of American society, including governmental institutions, have to design and carefully implement a program to deal with the fundamental economic class problems of millions of disadvantaged blacks.

The United States is not the sole country that has taken steps to protect the civil rights of nonwhites, only to be faced with more fundamental problems related to economic class disadvantages. In Great Britain, Parliament attempted to ease the difficulties experienced by nonwhite immigrants from other parts of the Commonwealth (India and Pakistan and parts of Africa and the West Indies) by passing the Race Relations Act of 1968. This Act, modeled after the 1964 Civil Rights Bill in the United States, made discrimination in housing, employment and public accommodation illegal in Great Britain. But despite this legislation, the racial problems in Great Britain may be becoming more explosive.

The nonwhite unemployment rate in Great Britain is about double the national average and the proportion of young nonwhites unemployed is near four times as great as the national average. Although there are no exclusively black ghettoes in Great Britain, there is an increasing tendency for immigrants to be concentrated in the most impoverished sections of large cities, sections that have a disproportionate number of inferior schools. Just as industrial technology, poor training and education have restricted the occupational chances for ghetto blacks in America, so too have these same factors circumscribed the mobility opportunities for nonwhites in Great Britain.

The responses of the British minorities to these patterns of subordination have become increasingly militant, particularly among younger blacks. Unlike the first-generation immigrants, who were born outside Great Britain and who readily accepted menial jobs such as dishwashers, hospital orderlies, and sanitation workers when they arrived in the country, the British-born second-generation nonwhites openly claim that they should have the same opportunities for economic and social advancement as their white counterparts. It is no doubt true that young blacks' expressions of discontent have been partly inspired by the black protest movement in America; expressions such as "Black Power" were not infrequently echoed in the immigrant quarters in recent years. However, except for periodic racial flareups, such as the riot that occurred in Notting Hill, London, in 1976, the growing black discontent has yet to produce the kind of sustained protest against racial inequality that occurred in the United States during the 1960s. Members of Parliament and other leaders in Great Britain are mindful of this fact and continue to debate the proper steps that should be taken to ease the threat of racial disturbances. Some feel that strict measures should be taken to end all immigration, others are calling for more stringent laws against racial discrimination, and still others, who feel that civil rights laws do not sufficiently address the problem, are advocating a comprehensive program to provide meaningful jobs that would generate minority hope for the future and a sense of pride and self-worth.

Whereas minority civil rights in the United States and Great Britain are protected by law, in the Republic of South Africa the law has been effectively used to reinforce the subordinate status of nonwhites. Whereas the United States and Great Britain adhere to the principle of a democratic society for all their citizens, South Africa has a "Herrenvolk democracy," that is a democracy only for the relatively small white population, as neither freedom of speech and behavior nor equality as an ideal value is institutionalized for nonwhites.

The white population in South Africa is represented by both the Afrikaners, descendants of the early Dutch settlers who arrived in South Africa in 1652, and the English-speaking group, whose ancestors came to South Africa when she was established as a British colony in the early nineteenth century after the Napoleonic Wars. And although whites control the social, political, and economic life of the country, they constitute only about 17% of the total population. Accordingly, whereas whites in the United States and Great Britain do not associate the granting of civil rights to minorities with the threat of a nonwhite takeover, South African whites firmly believe that their economic and political survival depends on effectively suppressing and controlling the larger nonwhite group. Thus they vehemently support a rigid policy of apartheid (which literally means racial separation) whereby nonwhites are required by law to live in separate areas, to attend separate schools, to work in only unskilled and some semiskilled jobs with considerably lower pay scales than whites, and to have neither voting rights nor the opportunity to run for elected office.

Nonwhites in South Africa have openly expressed their resentment against racial oppression in a series of protest demonstrations in recent decades. In the late 1950s the more educated South African blacks organized a campaign of nonviolent resistance. Encouraged by the growing criticism of apartheid around the world (for example, the threats of economic boycotts against South African products and the denunciations by the United Nations of South Africa's racial policies) they believed that the external pressures combined with the internal pressures of nonviolent protests would crumble the walls of apartheid. But unlike the nonviolent resistance campaign in the United States, the attempt in South Africa failed. The government ignored the worldwide criticisms and firmly repressed the demonstrators. Disillusioned blacks then turned to terrorist activities in the early 1960s, but such activities were also vigorously quashed by the government. In 1976 South Africa was in the throes of the most serious and violent racial protests in the nation's history. Whereas the previous racial demonstrations tended to be organized and were led and initiated by more educated and socially aware blacks, the recent incidents tended to be sporadic violent outbreaks and included many of the most impoverished blacks who, after years of apathy, have developed a heightened sensitivity to racial oppression.

Supporters of apartheid have reacted to the racial disturbances with the argument that policies of "separate development" of the races have enabled nonwhites in South Africa to enjoy one of the highest standards of living in all of Africa and that attempts to dismantle apartheid would only lead to economic and political chaos. Opponents of apartheid argue, on the other hand, that all citizens of South Africa should have the opportunity to compete freely and openly for rights and privileges, and that the deliberate policy of suppressing a substantial majority of the population will ultimately result in a massive race war that would destroy the very fabric of South African society and erase any possibilities for a racial reconciliation.

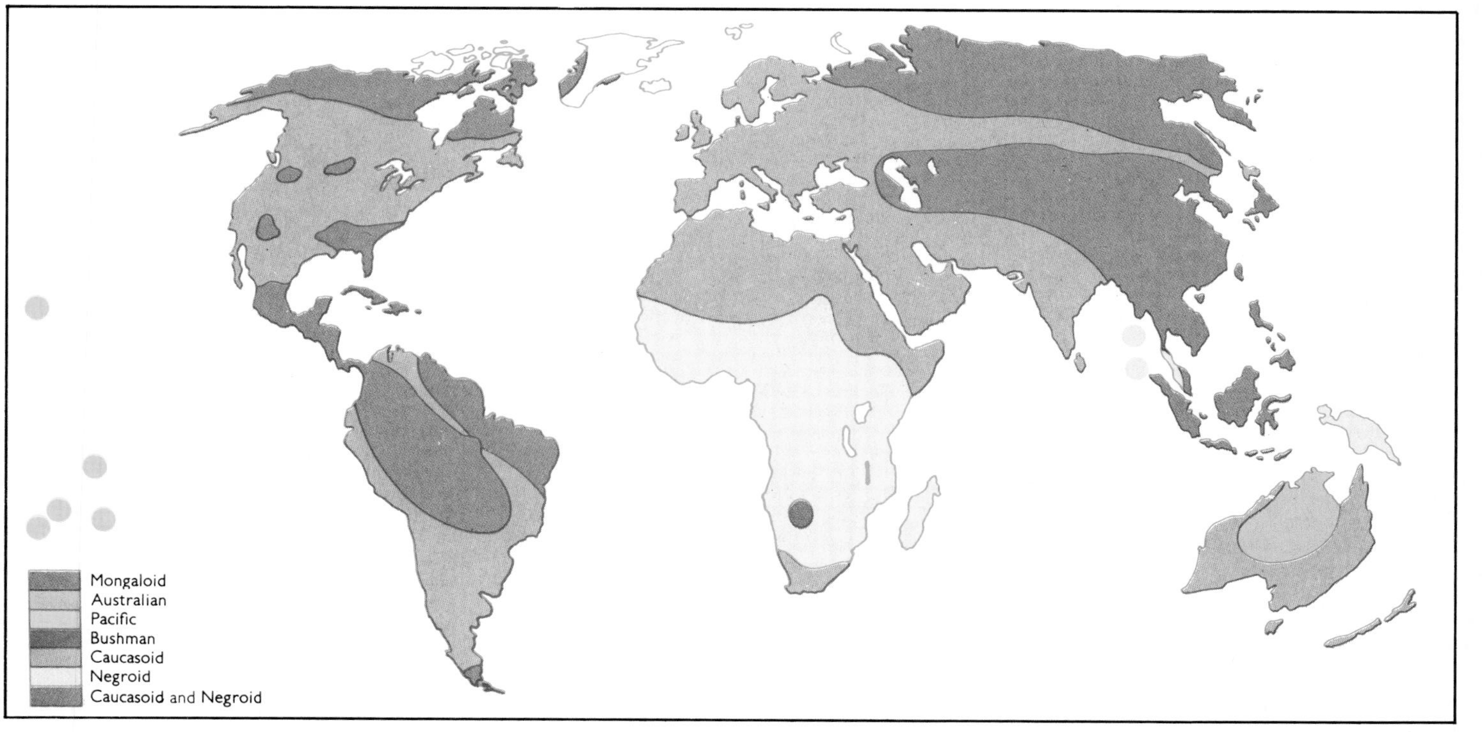

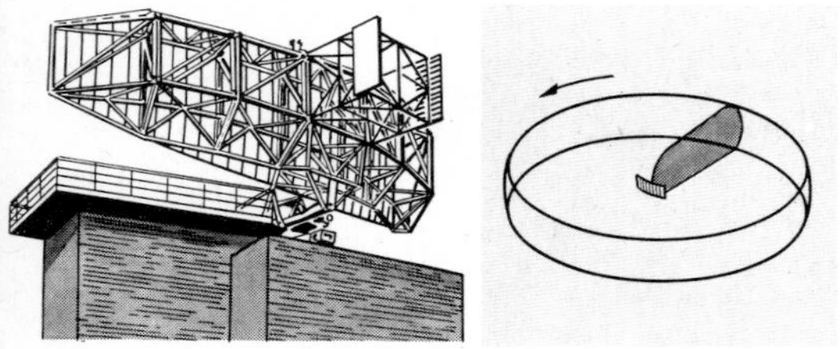

1

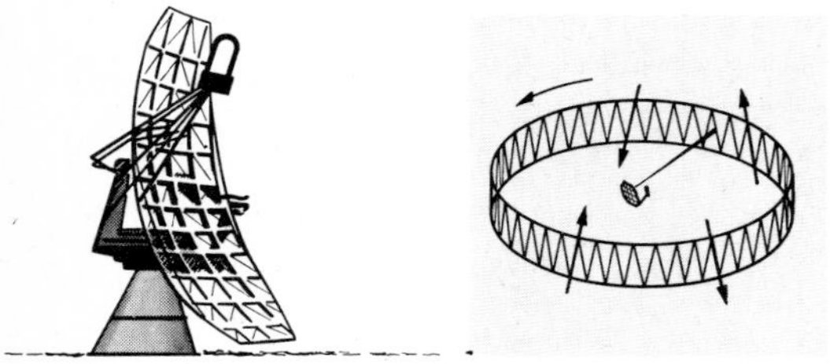

2

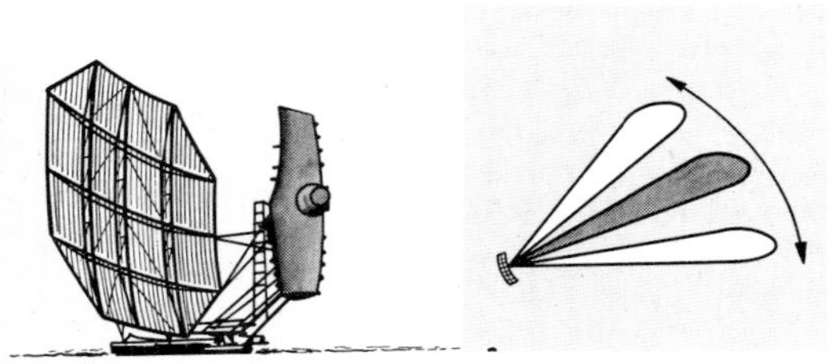

3

4

(1) The standard rotating radar has a constantly rotating antenna which sends and receives radiation in all directions. When a target reflects pulses, a "blip" appears on the radar screen. (2) By moving the radar beam up and down as it scans, one can determine the direction, range and height of a target such as an airplane. (3) A range height indicator (RHI) uses a flat radar beam moving in a vertical plane. It can determine the range and height of a target. (4) Tracking radar may send three or four beams in the direction of a moving object. When one beam strikes the target, the echo causes the radar set to "lock" on to the target.

screen. Various display modes are used: commonest is the plan-position indicator (PPI), showing horizontal position in polar coordinates. (See also LORAN.)

RADCLIFFE, Ann (born Ann Ward; 1764–1823), English novelist remembered for her GOTHIC NOVELS, notably *The Mysteries of Udolpho* (1794) and *The Italian* (1797).

RADCLIFFE-BROWN, Sir Alfred Reginald (1881–1955), British anthropologist whose comparative studies of social structures provided a firm basis for the development of social ANTHROPOLOGY.

RADEK, Karl Bernardovich (born Karl Sobelsohn: 1885–1939?), Russian communist politician close to LENIN during the 1917 revolution. Dismissed from the party as a TROTSKY supporter in 1927, readmitted 1930, he fell victim to STALIN's purges in 1937 and was sent to prison where, it is believed, he died.

RADFORD, independent city in Montgomery Co., SW Va., on the New R. As a division point of the Virginia and Tennessee Railroad, it was a site of fighting in the Civil War. Pop 11 596.

RADIAL SYMMETRY, symmetry about a single polar axis. It is a condition rare in nature though not infrequent among the unicellular PROTOZOA. Less than perfect radial symmetry is more common, five-fold symmetry being characteristic of ECHINODERMS.

RADIAL VELOCITY, the component of the motion of a celestial body in the direction of the line of sight; that is, toward or away from the observer.

RADIAN. See ANGLE.

RADIATION, the emission and propagation through space of ELECTROMAGNETIC RADIATION or SUBATOMIC PARTICLES. Exposure to X-RAYS and GAMMA RAYS is measured in RÖNTGEN units; absorbed dose of any high-energy radiation in RADS.

RADIATION BELTS. See VAN ALLEN RADIATION BELTS.

RADIATION CHEMISTRY, study of the chemical effects produced by interaction of RADIATION with matter. These include the effects of light (see PHOTOCHEMISTRY) but are in general more complex; IONS are often formed. It is important in infrared and X-ray PHOTOGRAPHY and the study of MUTATIONS and of the origin of LIFE.

RADIATION SICKNESS, malaise, nausea, loss of appetite and VOMITING occurring several hours after exposure to ionizing RADIATION in large doses. This occurs as an industrial or war hazard, or more commonly following RADIATION THERAPY for CANCER, LYMPHOMA OR LEUKEMIA. Large doses of radiation may cause BONE MARROW depression with ANEMIA, AGRANULOCYTOSIS and bleeding, or gastrointestinal disturbance with distension and bloody DIARRHEA. Skin ERYTHEMA and ulceration, LUNG fibrosis, NEPHRITIS and premature ARTERIOSCLEROSIS may follow radiation and there is a risk of malignancy developing.

RADIATION THERAPY, use of ionizing RADIATION, as rays from an outside source or from radium or other radioactive metal implants, in treatment of malignant DISEASE—CANCER, LYMPHOMA and LEUKEMIA. The principle is that rapidly dividing TUMOR cells are more sensitive to the destructive effects of radiation on NUCLEIC ACIDS and are therefore damaged by doses that are relatively harmless to normal tissues. Certain types of malignancy indeed respond to radiation therapy but RADIATION SICKNESS may also occur.

RADICAL, term formerly meaning FUNCTIONAL GROUP, now meaning FREE RADICAL.

RADICAL REPUBLICANS, a militant group of the Republican Party active after the US Civil War, putting pressure on LINCOLN and later Andrew JOHNSON to ensure full civil rights for the Southern blacks. Their most important achievement was the RECONSTRUCTION Act (1867).

RADIO, the communication of information between distant points using radio waves, ELECTROMAGNETIC RADIATION of wavelength between 1mm and 100km. Radio waves are also described in terms of their FREQUENCY—measured in HERTZ (Hz) and found by dividing the velocity of the waves (about 300Mm/s) by their wavelength. Radio communications systems link transmitting stations with receiving stations. In a transmitting station a piezoelectric OSCILLATOR is used to generate a steady radio-frequency (RF) "carrier" wave. This is amplified and "modulated" with a signal carrying the information (see INFORMATION THEORY) to be communicated. The simplest method of modulation is to pulse (switch on and off) the carrier with a signal in, say, MORSE CODE, but speech and music, entering the modulator as an audio-frequency (AF) signal from tape or a MICROPHONE, is made to interact with the carrier so that the shape of the audio wave determines either the amplitude of the carrier wave (amplitude modulation—AM) or its frequency within a small band on either side of the original carrier frequency (frequency modulation—FM). The modulated RF signal is then amplified (see AMPLIFIER) to a high power and radiated from an ANTENNA. At the receiving station, another antenna picks up a minute fraction of the energy radiated from the transmitter together with some background NOISE. This RF signal is amplified and the original audio signal is recovered (demodulation or detection). Detection and amplification often involve many stages including FEEDBACK and intermediate frequency (IF) circuits. A radio receiver must of course be able to discriminate between all the different signals acting at any one time on its antenna. This is accomplished with a tuning circuit which allows only the desired frequency to pass to the detector (see also ELECTRONICS). In point-to-point radio communications most stations can both transmit and receive messages but in **radio broadcasting** a central transmitter broadcasts program sequences to a multitude of individual receivers. Programs are often produced centrally and distributed to a "network" of local broadcasting stations by wire or MICROWAVE link. Because there are potentially so many users of radio communications—aircraft, ships, police and amateur "hams" as well as broadcasting services—the use of the RF portion of the electromagnetic SPECTRUM is strictly controlled to prevent unwanted INTERFERENCE between signals having adjacent carrier frequencies. The INTERNATIONAL TELECOMMUNICATION UNION (ITU) and national agencies such as the US FEDERAL COMMUNICATIONS COMMISSION (FCC) divide the RF spectrum into bands which it allocates to the various users. Public broadcasting in the US uses MF frequencies between 535kHz and 1605kHz (AM) and VHF bands between 88MHz and 108MHz (FM). VHF reception, though limited to line-of-sight transmissions, offers much higher fidelity of transmission (see HIGH-FIDELITY) and much greater freedom from interference. International broadcasting and local transmissions in other countries frequently use other frequencies in the LF, MF and HF (short wave) bands. (See the electromagnetic spectrum table at ELECTROMAGNETIC RADIATION.)

The Development of Radio. The existence of radio waves was first predicted by James Clerk MAXWELL in the 1860s but it was not until 1887 that Heinrich HERTZ succeeded in producing them experimentally. "Wireless" telegraphy was first demonstrated by Sir Oliver LODGE in 1894 and MARCONI made the first trans-Atlantic transmission in 1901. Voice transmission was first achieved in 1900 but transmitter and amplifier powers were restricted before the advent of Lee DE FOREST's triode ELECTRON TUBE in 1906. Only the development of the TRANSISTOR after 1948 has had as great an impact on radio technology. Commercial broadcasting began in the US in 1920.

RADIO, Amateur, a hobby practiced throughout the world by thousands of enthusiasts, or "hams," who communicate with one another on short-wave radio, by "phone" (voice) or by using International MORSE CODE. Permitted amateur bands include 160, 80, 40, 20, 15 and 10 metres. In the US, the various grades of license may be obtained by passing tests of progressively greater difficulty.

RADIOACTIVITY, the spontaneous disintegration of certain unstable nuclei, accompanied by the emission of ALPHA PARTICLES (weakly penetrating HELIUM nuclei), BETA RAYS (more penetrating streams of ELECTRONS) or GAMMA RAYS (ELECTROMAGNETIC RADIATION capable of penetrating up to 100mm of LEAD). In 1896, BECQUEREL noticed the spontaneous emission of ENERGY from URANIUM compounds (particularly PITCHBLENDE). The intensity of the effect depended on the amount of uranium present, suggesting that it involved individual atoms. The CURIES discovered further radioactive substances such as THORIUM and RADIUM, and about 40 natural radioactive substances are now known. Their rates of decay are unaffected by chemical changes, pressure, temperature or electromagnetic fields, and each nuclide (nucleus of a particular ISOTOPE) has a characteristic decay constant or HALF-LIFE. RUTHERFORD and SODDY suggested in 1902 that a radioactive nuclide decays to a further radioactive nuclide, a series of transformations taking place which ends with the formation of a stable "daughter" nucleus. It is now known that for radioactive elements of high ATOMIC WEIGHT, three decay series (the thorium, actinium and uranium series) exist. As well as the natural radioactive elements, a large number of induced radioactive nuclides have been formed by

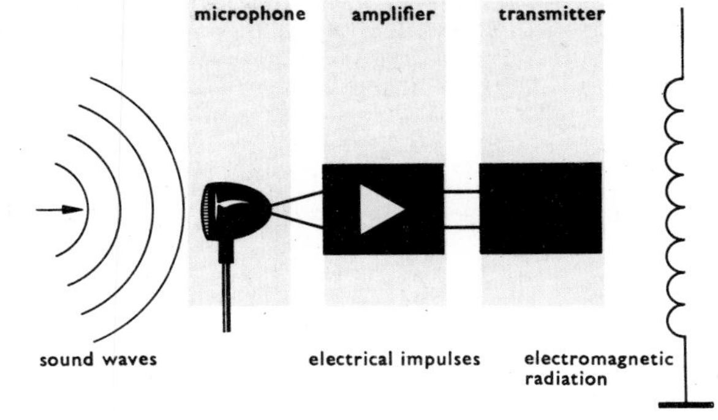

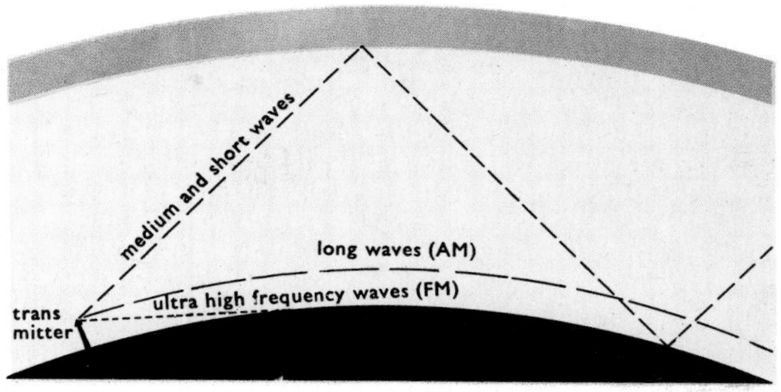

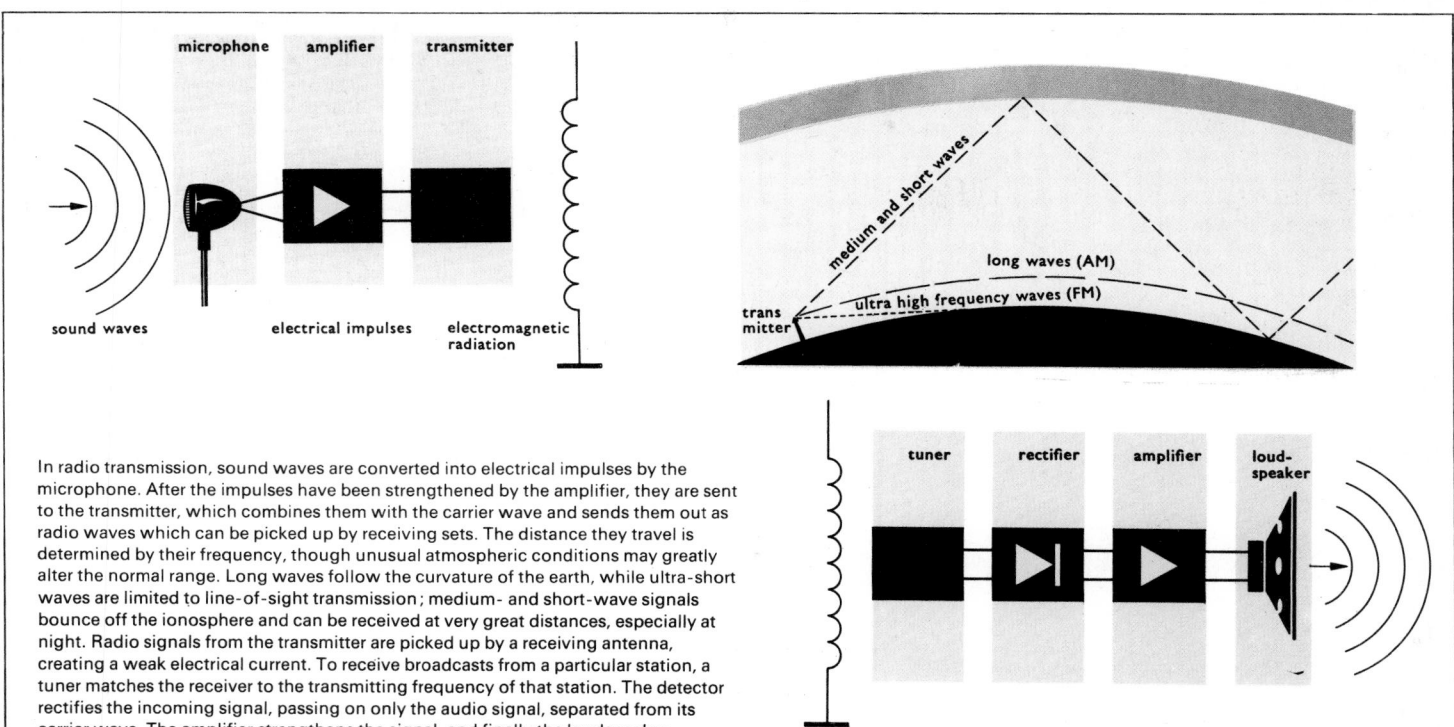

In radio transmission, sound waves are converted into electrical impulses by the microphone. After the impulses have been strengthened by the amplifier, they are sent to the transmitter, which combines them with the carrier wave and sends them out as radio waves which can be picked up by receiving sets. The distance they travel is determined by their frequency, though unusual atmospheric conditions may greatly alter the normal range. Long waves follow the curvature of the earth, while ultra-short waves are limited to line-of-sight transmission; medium- and short-wave signals bounce off the ionosphere and can be received at very great distances, especially at night. Radio signals from the transmitter are picked up by a receiving antenna, creating a weak electrical current. To receive broadcasts from a particular station, a tuner matches the receiver to the transmitting frequency of that station. The detector rectifies the incoming signal, passing on only the audio signal, separated from its carrier wave. The amplifier strengthens the signal, and finally the loudspeaker converts the electrical waves back into sound.

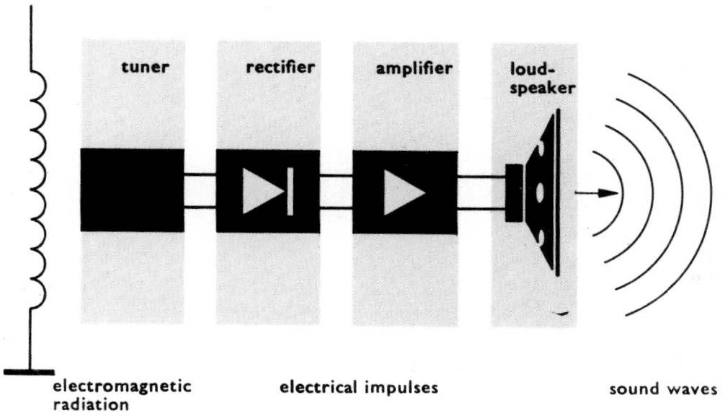

nuclear reactions taking place in ACCELERATORS or NUCLEAR REACTORS (see also IRRADIATION; RADIOISOTOPE). Some of these are members of the three natural radioactive series. Various types of radioactivity are known, but beta emission is the most common, normally caused by the decay of a NEUTRON, giving a PROTON, an electron and an antineutrino (see SUBATOMIC PARTICLES). This results in a unit change of atomic number (see ATOM) and no change in MASS NUMBER. Heavier nuclides often decay to a daughter nucleus with atomic number two less and mass number four less, emitting an alpha particle. If an excited daughter nucleus is formed, gamma-ray emission may accompany both alpha and beta decay. Because the ionizing radiations emitted by radioactive materials are physiologically harmful, special precautions must be taken in handling them.

RADIO ASTRONOMY, the study of the ELECTROMAGNETIC RADIATION emitted or reflected by celestial objects in the approximate wavelength range 1mm–30m, usually by use of a RADIO TELESCOPE. The science was initiated accidentally in 1932 by Karl Jansky who found an INTERFERENCE in a telephone system he was testing: the source proved to be the MILKY WAY. In 1937 an American, Grote Reber, built a 9.5m radio telescope in his back yard and scanned the sky at a wavelength around 2m. After WWII the science began in earnest. Investigation of the sky revealed that clouds of hydrogen gas in the Milky Way were radio sources, and mapping of these confirmed our galaxy's spiral form (see GALAXY).

The sky is very different for the radio astronomer than for the astronomer. Bright stars are not radio objects (our sun is one solely because it is so close), while many radio objects are optically undetectable. Radio objects include QUASARS, PULSARS, supernova remnants (e.g., the CRAB NEBULA) and other galaxies. The work of Martin RYLE in the 1960s and 1970s has enabled radio galaxies that are possibly at the farthest extremities of the universe to be mapped. The universe also has an inherent radio "background noise" (see COSMOLOGY).

RADIOCARBON DATING, a technique of dating organic material up to 70 000 years old. The radioactive carbon ISOTOPE C^{14} is produced naturally by the impact of COSMIC RAYS on NITROGEN atoms in the atmosphere, and, in the form of $C^{14}O_2$, enters the ecological CARBON CYCLE. Assuming that the amount of C^{14} produced in this way is constant, one may deduce that the proportion of C^{14} atoms present in living material is uniform throughout time. Knowing that C^{14} decays into N^{14} with a HALF-LIFE of 5730 ± 40 years, examination of the amount of C^{14} remaining in organic material provides a reasonably accurate method of dating. Recent advances in DENDROCHRONOLOGY have shown that production of C^{14} in the atmosphere is not constant, and corrections have accordingly been made to the radiocarbon system.

RADIOCHEMISTRY, the use of RADIOISOTOPES in chemistry, especially in studies involving chemical ANALYSIS, where radioisotopes provide a powerful and sensitive tool. Tracer techniques, in which a particular atom in a molecule is "labeled" by replacement with a radioisotope, are used to study reaction rates and mechanisms (see KINETICS, CHEMICAL). (See also RADIATION CHEMISTRY.)

RADIOCOMPASS. See COMPASS; DIRECTION FINDER.

RADIO CONTROL. See REMOTE CONTROL.

RADIOGRAPH, a photograph exposed with X-RAYS or GAMMA RAYS. Special plates having thick emulsions are used to increase sensitivity.

RADIOISOTOPE, radioactive ISOTOPE of an element. A few elements, such as RADIUM or URANIUM, have naturally occurring radioisotopes, but because of their usefulness in science and industry, a large number of radioisotopes are produced artificially. This is done by IRRADIATION of stable isotopes with PHOTONS, or with particles such as NEUTRONS in an ACCELERATOR or NUCLEAR REACTOR. Radioisotopes with a wide range of HALF-LIVES and activities are available by these means. Because radioisotopes behave chemically and biologically in a very similar way to stable isotopes, and their radiation can easily be monitored even in very small amounts, they are used to "label" particular atoms or groups in studying chemical reaction mechanisms and to "trace" the course of particular components in various physiological processes. The radiation emitted by radioisotopes may also be utilized directly for treating diseased areas of the body (see RADIATION THERAPY), sterilizing foodstuffs or controlling insect pests.

RADIOLARIANS, single-celled animals possessing an internal skeleton, usually siliceous but sometimes of strontium sulfate. Members of the Sarcodine class of PROTOZOA, all are marine and are abundant in PLANKTON. The skeletons sink after death and build up into thick sediments.

RADIOLOGY, the use of RADIOACTIVITY, GAMMA RAYS and X-RAYS in MEDICINE, particularly in diagnosis but also in treatment. (See also RADIATION THERAPY.)

RADIOMETER, instrument for measuring the intensity of radiant ENERGY. The term is usually applied to a simple vane type instrument (Crookes' radiometer) consisting of an evacuated glass bulb containing a pivot supporting vertical metal vanes blackened on one side. Incident radiation is more strongly absorbed by the blackened side of the vanes and the forces exerted on them by residual gas molecules initiate rotation proportional to the radiation intensity.

RADIOSONDE, meteorological instrument package attached to a small BALLOON capable of reaching the earth's upper ATMOSPHERE. The instruments measure the TEMPERATURE, PRESSURE and HUMIDITY of the atmosphere at various altitudes, the data being

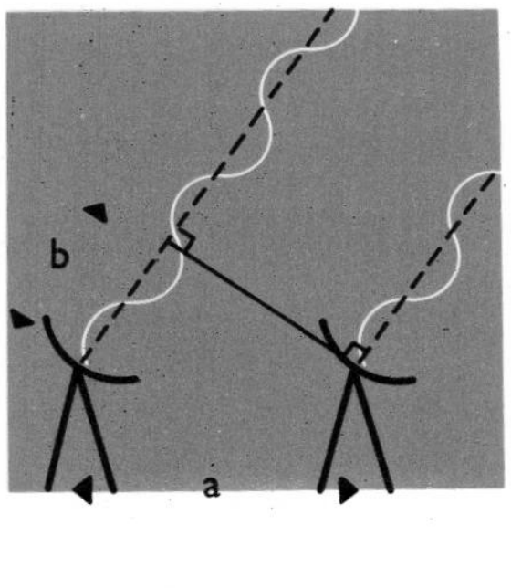

In radio astronomy, one of the chief instruments used to pinpoint and study celestial radio sources is the radio interferometer. This consists of two radio telescopes separated by long distance (a). When the phase difference (b) of the radio waves is an integral multiple of the wavelength, they most effectively reinforce each other; when the waves are half a wavelength out of phase, they cancel each other out. Because of the earth's rotation, the direction from which the waves come is constantly changing, and the phase relationship also changes. By measuring the precise times when reinforcement is greatest, it is possible to calculate the direction of the source. The greater the distance (a), the more exactly this can be done.

The radio telescope at Stanford University in California has a dish 150ft in diameter, the largest steerable parabolic dish in the United States.

relayed back to earth via a RADIO transmitter. Radiosondes provide a cheap and reliable method of getting information for WEATHER FORECASTING.

RADIO TELESCOPE, the basic instrument of RADIO ASTRONOMY. The receiving part of the equipment consists of a large parabola, the big dish, which operates on the same principle as the parabolic mirror of a reflecting TELESCOPE. The signals that it receives are then amplified and examined. In practice, it is possible to build radio telescopes effectively far larger than a single big dish could physically exist by using several connected dishes; this is known as an array.

RADIOTHERAPY. See RADIATION THERAPY.

RADISH, *Raphanus sativus*, a relative of MUSTARD, probably native to China but long naturalized in Europe. Its edible root has a burning flavor and is eaten raw. Radishes are the easiest of garden vegetables to grow. Family: Cruciferae.

RADISSON, Pierre Esprit (c1636–c1710), French fur trader who worked for both French and British in the exploration of parts of present-day Minn. and Wis. His reports of the wealth of furs obtainable prompted the creation of the HUDSON'S BAY COMPANY.

RADIUM (Ra), radioactive ALKALINE-EARTH METAL similar to BARIUM, isolated from PITCHBLENDE by Marie CURIE in 1898. It has white salts which turn black as the radium decays, and which emit a blue glow due to ionization of the air by radiation. It has four natural ISOTOPES, the commonest being Ra^{226} with HALF-LIFE 1622 years. Radium is used in industrial and medical radiography. AW 226.0, mp 700°C, bp 1140°C, sg 5.

RADIUS, the distance from the point of INTERSECTION of the axes of symmetry (see AXIS OF SYMMETRY) of a closed CURVE to a point on the curve. The term is usually applied to CIRCLES, ellipses (see CONIC SECTIONS) and SPHERES. All radii of a circle or sphere are equal; and it is generally profitable to consider only the longest and shortest radii (semi-major and semi-minor axes) of an ellipse. (See also CYLINDER; ELLIPSOID; MENSURATION.)

RADNOR, urban township in SE Pa., to the W of Philadelphia. Pop 28849.

RADOM, city in E central Poland, one of the earliest Polish settlements. Its industries include engineering, chemicals and glass. Pop 158640.

RADON (Rn), a radioactive NOBLE GAS formed in the radioactive decay of RADIUM, ACTINIUM or THORIUM. Found in some radioactive minerals, Rn^{222} has a HALF-LIFE of 3.8 days, making it suitable for use in RADIATION THERAPY. Other natural and synthetic ISOTOPES have shorter half-lives. Radon (II) fluoride (RnF_2) is the only radon compound known. AW 222, mp −71°C, bp −62°C.

RAEDER, Erich (1876–1960), German admiral, commander in chief of the German Navy from 1928–43. For his aggressive naval strategy, as in the invasions of Denmark and Norway, he was convicted as a war criminal in 1946 (released 1955).

RA EXPEDITIONS. See HEYERDAHL, THOR.

RAFFIA, a number of tropical African PALMS, including *Raphia gigantea* and *R. pedunculata*, the fibers from the tough leaves of which are used for basket making and as twine. Family: Palmae.

RAFFLES, Sir Thomas Stamford (1781–1826), British colonial administrator who founded Singapore (1819). He persuaded the British government to seize Jawa, which he governed from 1811 to 1815. His career was marked by his liberalism, especially in his opposition to slavery.

RAFFLESIA, a genus of parasitic Malayan and Indonesian plants, including *Rafflesia arnoldii*, the flowers of which are up to 1m (3.3ft) across. Family: Rafflesiaceae.

RAFINESQUE, Constantine Samuel (1783–1840), US naturalist, of French-German parentage, whose evolutionary theories predated those of DARWIN.

RAGLAN, Fitzroy James Henry Somerset, 1st Baron (1788–1855), commander of British forces in the CRIMEAN WAR. He was widely criticized for the failure of the siege of Sevastopol (1854–55) and for the Earl of CARDIGAN's disastrous Charge of the Light Brigade (1854).

RAGNAROK, in Scandinavian mythology, the end of the universe and the doom of the gods. After a battle between the gods and the forces of evil, in which all is destroyed by fire, the earth is reborn from the sea to be ruled by BALDER.

RAGTIME, a style of piano playing in which the left hand provides harmony and a firm beat, while the right hand plays the melody, usually syncopated. Famous exponents of the style, which was the immediate predecessor of JAZZ, are Scott JOPLIN and "Jelly-Roll" MORTON.

RAGUSA, Yugoslavia. See DUBROVNIK.

RAGWEED, common weeds belonging to the genus *Ambrosia*, including the Giant ragweed or Buffalo weed, which may reach 5m (16.4ft) in height. The seeds of *Ambrosia artemissiifolia* contain 19% potentially edible oil. Family: Compositae.

RAGWORMS, genus *Nereis*, the most widespread and familiar of POLYCHAETE worms. Segmented annelids with little differentiation between segments, they have well-developed walking appendages, or parapodia. Common on sandy beaches, they are frequently brightly-colored.

RAHMAN, Mujibur (called Sheikh Mujib; 1920–1975), first premier (1972–74) and then president (1974–75) of BANGLADESH. He was secretary and president of the Awami League, whose object was autonomy for E Pakistan. He rebuilt Bangladesh following the war of independence (1971), but was assassinated after assuming dictatorial powers.

RAHMAN, Tunku Abdul (1903–1973), first prime minister of the Federation of Malaya (1957–63) and then of the Federation of Malaysia (1963–70). He helped found the United Malay National Organization in 1945 and was its president 1952–55.

RAHWAY, industrial city in NE N.J., 10mi SW of Newark, producing pharmaceuticals, chemicals, vacuum cleaners and automobile parts. Pop 29114.

RAILS, certain species of water birds of the family Rallidae which also includes crakes, COOTS and GALLINULES. Rails are typically gray or brown, with short wings and tail and long legs, well adapted to wading at the water's edge or out on floating vegetation. They feed on insects and crustaceans.

RAILROAD, land transportation system in which cars with flanged steel wheels run on tracks of two parallel steel rails. From their beginning railroads provided reliable, economical transport for freight and passengers; they promoted the Industrial Revolution and have been vital to continued economic growth ever since, especially in developing countries. Railroads are intrinsically economical because the rolling friction of wheel on rail is very low, so that a LOCOMOTIVE of only 750W (1hp) per gross tonne pulled is needed—10% of that required for road transport. However, fixed costs of maintenance etc., are high, so high traffic volume is needed. This, together with rising competition and overmanning, has led to the closure of many minor lines in the US and Europe, though elsewhere many new lines are still being built. Maintenance, signalling and many other functions are now highly automated.

Railroads developed out of the small mining tracks or tramways built in the UK and Europe from the mid-16th century. They used gravity or horse power, and the cars generally ran on flanged rails or plateways. These were hard to switch, however, and the system of flanged wheels on plain rails eventually predominated. The first public freight railroad was the Surrey Iron Railway (1801). The modern era of mechanized traction began with TREVITHICK's steam locomotive "New Castle" (1804) (see also STEAM ENGINE). Early locomotives ran on toothed racks to prevent slipping, but in 1813 this was found to be

The railroad played a vital part in the settlement of the American West. Here, homesteaders await the opening of the famous Cherokee Outlet at noon on September 16, 1893. The Choctaw Coal and Railway Company, later part of the Rock Island system, laid on special trains to carry settlers into the new lands created out of Indian territory.

The first steam locomotives, such as that built by Blenkinsop in 1812 (1), did not run on smooth rails (which, it was thought, would not provide enough grip for the iron wheels) but used a toothed wheel fitting into a rack rail. (2) George Stephenson's *Rocket* (1829), however, successfully relied on friction between wheels and track, and traveled at a maximum speed of 30mph. It won a prize for the best traction design. (3) The principle of the steam engine. The steam is raised in the fire-tube boiler, passing through the superheater (a) so that the pressure of steam from the dome (b) is increased. The slide valve (c) is synchronized with the movement of the piston (f) by the link rod (d) and the flycrank (e) in such a way that the steam enters the inlet ports in the cylinder in the correct sequence (4). The piston powers the driving wheels via a driving rod and coupling rods. (5) In order to drive the locomotive in reverse, the lever (a) is pivoted by pulling the reversing rod, so that the movement of the slide valve is reversed.

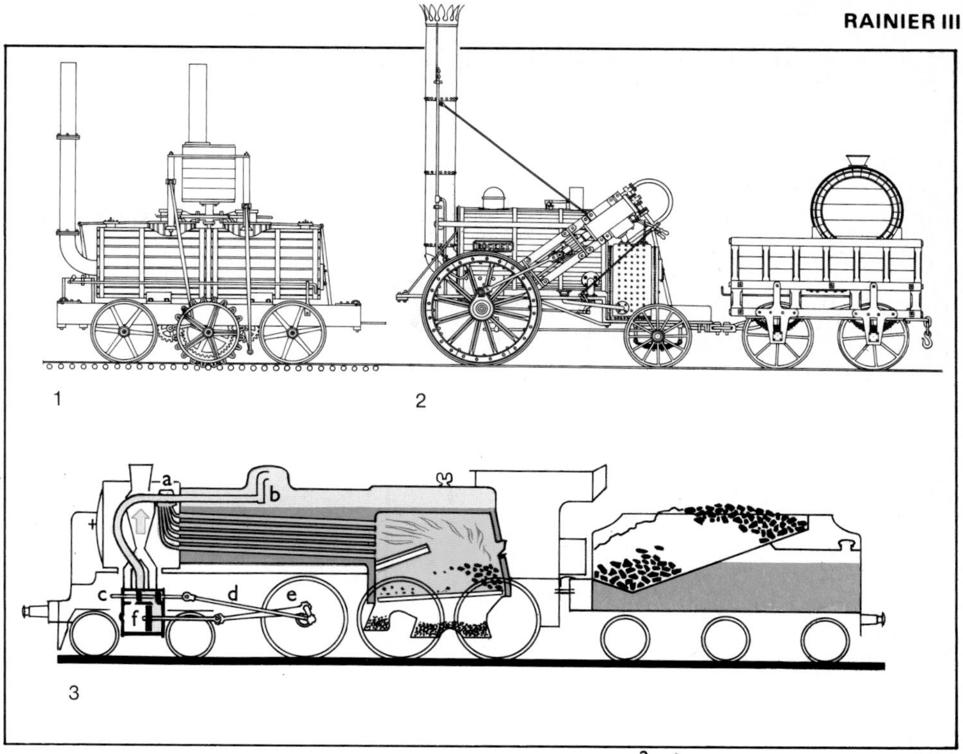

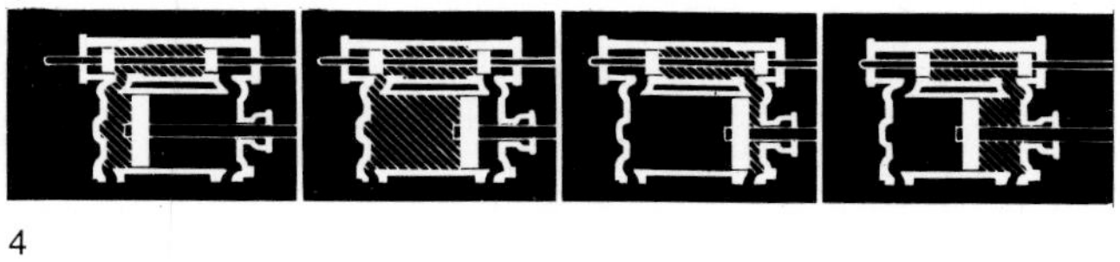

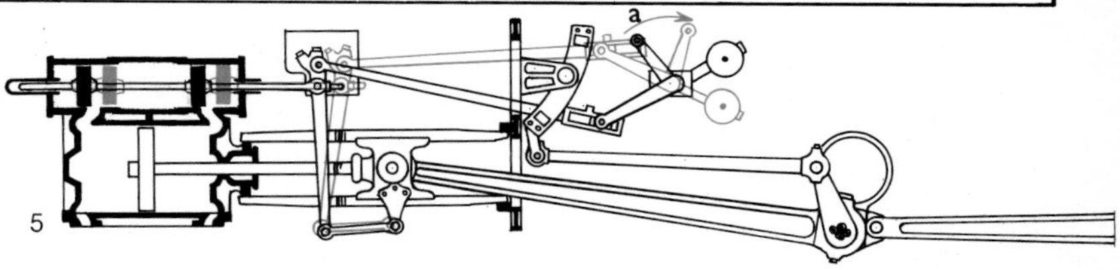

unnecessary. The first public railroad to use locomotives and to carry passengers was the Stockton and Darlington Railway (1825). The boom began when the Liverpool and Manchester Railway opened in 1830 using George STEPHENSON's "Rocket," a much superior and more reliable locomotive. Railroads spread rapidly in Britain, Europe and the US. The first US railroad was the Baltimore and Ohio (1830). The rails were laid on wooden (later also concrete) crossties or sleepers, and were joined by fishplates to allow for thermal expansion. Continuous welded rails are now generally used. Track gauges were at first very varied, but the "standard gauge" of 4ft 8½in (1.435m) soon predominated. Railroads must be built with shallow curves and gentle gradients, using bridges, embankments, cuttings and tunnels as necessary. (See also SUBWAY.)

Amtrak

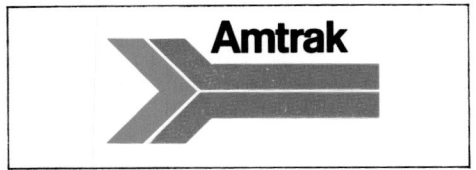

The symbol of the National Railroad Passenger Corporation, which in 1971 took over the operation of US intercity passenger railroad lines. "Amtrack" is a contraction of "American traveltrack."

RAILROAD WORM. See APPLE MAGGOT.

RAIN, water drops falling through the atmosphere; the chief form of PRECIPITATION. Raindrops range in size up to 4mm diameter; if they are smaller than 0.5mm the rain is called **drizzle**. The quantity of rainfall (independent of the drop size) is measured by a **rain gauge**, an open-top vessel which collects the rain, calibrated in millimetres or inches and so giving a reading independent of the area on which the rain falls. Light rain is less than 25mm/h, moderate rain 25 to 75mm/h, and heavy rain more than 75mm/h. Rain may result from the melting of SNOW or HAIL as it falls, but is commonly formed by direct condensation. When a parcel of warm air rises, it expands approximately adiabatically, cooling about 1K/100m. Thus its relative HUMIDITY rises until when it reaches saturation the water vapor begins to condense as droplets, forming CLOUDS. These droplets may coalesce into raindrops, chiefly through turbulence and nucleation by ice particles or by cloud seeding (see also WEATHER FORECASTING AND CONTROL). Moist air may be lifted by CONVECTION, producing **convective rainfall**; by forced ascent of air as it crosses a mountain range, producing **orographic rainfall**; and by the forces within CYCLONES, producing **cyclonic rainfall**. (See also GROUNDWATER; HYDROLOGIC CYCLE; METEOROLOGY; MONSOON.)

RAINBOW, arch of concentric spectrally colored rings seen in the sky by an observer looking at rain, mist or spray with his back to the sun. The colors are produced by sunlight's being refracted and totally internally reflected (see REFRACTION) by spherical droplets of water. The primary rainbow, with red on the outside and violet inside, results from one total internal reflection. Sometimes a dimmer secondary rainbow with reversed colors is seen, arising from a second total internal reflection.

RAINBOW BRIDGE NATIONAL MONUMENT, probably the largest natural bridge in the world, of pink sandstone, 278ft long and 309ft high, in S Utah near to Navajo Mt. Discovered in 1909, it was established as a national monument in 1910.

RAINBOW DIVISION, the 42nd US Army Infantry division, the first US combat division to fight in France in WWI. It was involved in the Saint-Mihiel campaign (Sept. 1918) and the attack on the Meuse-Argonne region (Oct./Nov. 1918).

RAIN FOREST. See FOREST.

RAINIER III, Louis Henri Maxence Bertrand (1923–), prince of MONACO since 1949. He married the US actress Grace KELLY in 1956.

The French T.G.V. (Très Grande Vitesse) 001 has reached speeds of up to 200mph during speed tests. This turbo-electric locomotive has 12 axles. Some new lines are being added to the network of French and Italian railroads to accommodate this super-express train.

White sunlight is split up into its component colors when it passes through a raindrop, since the shorter wavelengths (violet) are refracted to a greater extent than the longer wavelengths (red). When there is a single internal reflection in the raindrop the result is the primary rainbow arc at an angle of 42° from its center, subtended at the observer. If there is a double reflection, there is a secondary rainbow at an angle of 51°.

RAINIER, Mount, extinct volcano in the Cascade Range and highest peak in Wash., 14410ft high, lying 40mi SE of Tacoma in Mt Rainier National Park. The fine scenery and skiing slopes in the area attract many tourists.

RAIN SHADOW, area of low rainfall on the lee side of a mountain barrier, which shelters it from prevailing rainbearing winds. Rainfall on the corresponding windward side of the barrier is extremely high. (See also CLIMATE; RAIN.)

RAIN TREE. See MONKEY-POD TREE.

RAINWATER, Leo James (1917–), US physicist who shared the 1975 Nobel Prize for Physics with Aage BOHR and Ben MOTTELSON for their work on the physics and structure of the atomic nucleus.

RAINY LAKE, lake on the US–Canadian border between Minn. and Ontario. Its 350sq mi area is dotted with over 500 islands. It drains into Lake of the WOODS via the Rainy R.

RAIS, or **Retz, Gilles de** (1404–1440), baron and marshal of France, satanist, noted patron of the arts and soldier, who served with JOAN OF ARC at the relief of Orléans, 1429. He was executed for the abduction and murder of 140 children.

RAISIN RIVER, Battle of, engagement in 1813 during the WAR OF 1812, in which US troops under General James Winchester surrendered to a British and Indian Force near Frenchtown (Monroe, Mich.). The US wounded—though protection had been promised by the British—were massacred by the Indians.

RAJA, or **Rajah** (from Sanskrit *rājan*, king), an Indian or Malay prince (extended to other men of rank during British rule). Higher-ranking princes were styled *maharajas* (or maharajahs). A raja's wife is a *rani*.

RAJASTHAN, India's second largest state (132149 sq mi), in NW India. The capital is Jaipur. The W is sparsely populated, but agriculture is possible in the E. Mineral deposits and textiles are important to the economy.

RAJPUTS (Sanskrit: kings' sons), military and land-owning caste mostly of the Rajasthan (now Rajputana) region, India. Their origins date back nearly 1500 years, when successive pulses of invaders were absorbed into Indian society. Their influence in N and central India has waxed and waned, being at times considerable, and since INDIA's independence (1947) has steadily declined.

RÁKÓCZY, Francis II (1676–1735), prince of Transylvania who led a Hungarian rising against the Hapsburg Empire. Initially successful, he was elected prince in 1704, but after several crushing defeats he left the country in 1711 and died in exile in Turkey.

RALEIGH, state capital of N.C. and seat of Wake Co., named for Sir Walter RALEIGH; a center for the surrounding agricultural areas and for culture, education and science. Its light industries include chemicals, electronics and textiles. Pop 123793.

RALEIGH, or **Ralegh, Sir Walter** (1554?–1618), English adventurer and poet, a favorite of Queen Elizabeth I. His efforts to organize colonization of the New World resulted in the tragedy of the LOST COLONY. In 1589 he left court and consolidated his friendship with SPENSER, whose *Faerie Queene* was written partly under Raleigh's patronage. Returning, he distinguished himself in raids at Cadiz (1596) and the Azores (1597). James I imprisoned him in the Tower of London 1603–16, where he wrote poetry and his uncompleted *History of the World*. After two years' freedom he was executed.

RAM (the constellation). See ARIES.

RAMA, in N India, the most popular incarnation of the Hindu god VISHNU; he was the son of King Dasaratha of Ayodha, and his legend, narrated in the RAMAYANA, portrays an heroic figure, dedicated more to ridding the earth of evildoers than to conveying spiritual instruction.

RAMA, name of seven kings of Thailand (Siam), reigning consecutively since 1782. Their line was founded by the general Chao P'ya Chakri (reigned 1782–1809), who restored order after a Burmese invasion, took the name of the Hindu hero RAMA and established Bangkok as his capital. Following a coup d'etat in 1932, the monarchy became constitutional.

The head of Ramses II, part of one of the four vast statues of that monarch carved into the temple facade at Abu Simbel in Egypt. Three of the statues survive. The entire temple complex, built in the 13th century BC, during the second longest reign in Egyptian history, has been transferred to a higher level and so saved from inundation by the waters of the Aswan High Dam.

RAMADAN, ninth month of the Muslim calendar, during which the revelation of the KORAN to MOHAMMED is commemorated by abstention from food, drink and other bodily pleasures between sunrise and sunset.

RAMAKRISHNA PARAMAHANSA (1836–1886), Indian saint whose teachings, now carried all over the world by the Ramakrishna Mission (founded in Calcutta in 1897), emphasize the unity of all religions and place equal value on social service, worship and meditation. His followers consider him to have been an incarnation of God.

RAMAN, Sir Chandrasekhara Venkata (1888–1970), Indian physicist awarded the 1930 Nobel Prize for Physics for his discovery of the **Raman Effect**: when a medium is exposed to a beam of ELECTROMAGNETIC RADIATION, light scattered at right angles to the beam has a range of frequencies characteristic to the medium. This is the basis for Raman SPECTROSCOPY.

RAMAPITHECUS. See PREHISTORIC MAN.

RAMAYANA, major Hindu epic poem, composed in Sanskrit in about the 3rd century BC, concerning the war waged by RAMA against Ravān, the demon-king of Lanka, who was terrorizing the earth. Helped by Hanuman, king of the monkeys, Rama eventually rescues his wife, Sita, whom Ravān had abducted, and slays the demon, enabling the righteous once more to live in peace.

RAMBERT, Dame Marie (1888–), ballet producer, director and teacher who founded the **Ballet Rambert** (1935). Polish by birth, she became a British citizen in 1918, and exercised a major influence on British ballet. Among her pupils was Frederick ASHTON.

RAMEAU, Jean Philippe (1683–1764), French composer and one of the founders of modern harmonic theory. He achieved recognition with his *Treatise on Harmony* (1722), and in Paris became a celebrated teacher and composer of some 30 operas, *Hippolyte et Aricie* (1733) being the first.

RAMÉE, Marie Louise de la. See OUIDA.

RAMESES. See RAMSES.

RAMIE, *Boehmeria nivea*, a fiber-yielding plant of the nettle family, Urticaceae, native to E Asia. Although useful in making coarse textiles, ramie fiber is difficult to extract and weave.

RAMJET. See JET PROPULSION.

RAMÓN Y CAJAL, Santiago (1852–1934), Spanish neurohistologist who shared with GOLGI the 1906 Nobel Prize for Physiology or Medicine for his work showing the NEURON to be the fundamental "building block" of all nervous structures.

RAMPION, common name for a European bellflower, *Campanula rapunculus*, whose white tuberous roots are sometimes eaten in salads. The term is also used for several other blue-flowered members of the bellflower family, Campanulaceae.

RAMSAY, Sir William (1852–1916), British chemist awarded the 1904 Nobel Prize for Chemistry for his discovery, prompted by a suggestion from RAYLEIGH (1892), of all the NOBLE GASES, including (with SODDY) HELIUM, although it had been earlier detected in the solar spectrum (1868).

RAMSES II (reigned c1304–1237 BC), "Ramses the Great," Egyptian pharaoh who built hundreds of temples and monuments, probably including ABU SIMBEL and the columned hall at KARNAK. He campaigned against the HITTITES, and celebrated a battle at Kadesh (1300 BC) on many of his monuments, but was eventually obliged to make peace (c1283 BC). His long reign marked a high point in Egyptian prosperity.

RAMSEY, residential borough in N.J., 27mi N of New York, in a dairy-farming area. Pop 12571.

RANA, a family of Nepalese nobles who ruled the country from 1846 to 1951 by making the office of prime minister hereditary within the family. They were excluded from power in 1951 when anti-Rana forces, in alliance with the royal family and supported by the newly independent Indian government, set up a constitutional monarchy.

RANCÉ, Armand Jean Le Bouthillier de (1626–1700), French monk, Abbot of La Trappe,

Normandy (1664–95), who founded the TRAPPISTS, a reformed branch of the Roman Catholic Cistercian Order. He was an extreme ascetic, and his rule emphasized silence, prayer, fasting and manual labor.

RANCE, river entering the sea at St. Malo, on the N coast of France. The large estuary has a very high tidal range, and is the site of the world's first major electricity generating plant (1967) powered by the motion of flood and ebb tides.

RANCHO CORDOVA, town in Cal., 15mi SE of Sacramento. It provides housing for the nearby Mather Air Force Base. Pop 30451.

RAND, Ayn (1905–), Russian-born US writer. Her "objectivist" philosophy, individualistic, egoistic and capitalist in inspiration, is at the core of such successful novels as *The Fountainhead* (1943) and *Atlas Shrugged* (1957).

RAND, The. See WITWATERSRAND.

RANDOLPH, township in Mass. In the Boston metropolitan area, it is mainly residential with some light industry. Pop 27035.

RANDOLPH, name of a well-known Virginia family. **William Randolph** (c1651–1711), was born in England and became a successful planter and colonial administrator. He was attorney general for Virginia 1694–98, a post also held by his son **Sir John Randolph** (1693–1737), and his grandson **Peyton Randolph** (1721–1775). **Edmund Jennings Randolph** (1753–1813), a nephew of Peyton, was a lawyer who became attorney general (1776–86) and then governor (1786–88) of Virginia. At the Constitutional Convention (1787) he drafted the "Virginia Plan," calling for representation in Congress to be related to state population. He did not sign the Constitution, but later urged its ratification. He became the first US attorney general (1789–94) and secretary of state (1794–95). **John Randolph of Roanoke** (1773–1833), great-grandson of William Randolph, entered the US House of Representatives in 1799. A much-feared orator and champion of states' rights, he opposed many popular measures and led Southern opposition to the MISSOURI COMPROMISE in 1820. **George Wythe Randolph** (1818–1867), great-great-great grandson of William Randolph and grandson of Thomas Jefferson, became Confederate secretary of war in 1862.

RANDOLPH, Asa Philip (1889–), US Negro labor leader. He became an outspoken socialist during WWI and organized the Brotherhood of Sleeping Car Porters in 1925. His campaigning was instrumental in the setting up of the FAIR EMPLOYMENT PRACTICES COMMITTEE in 1941. In 1963 he directed the March on Washington for Jobs and Freedom.

RANDOLPH, Edward (1632?–1703), British colonial agent whose reports led to the Massachusetts charter being revoked in 1684. He was secretary and register of the Dominion of New England (1685–89), and in 1691 became surveyor general of customs for North America.

RANGE FINDER, instrument for remote measurement of distance. RADAR and SONAR provide nonoptical range finders. Optical range finders—used in CAMERAS for correct focusing, and in military applications—are of two types. **Coincidence range finders** measure the angles formed from each end of a base line to the object viewed, and calculate the distance by TRIGONOMETRY. The images from each optical path are made to coincide. **Stereoscopic range finders** use stereobinoculars which are adjusted until the stereo image formed by reticles in the eyepieces appears to be at the same distance as the object.

RANGERS, name given to special small military units that originated in America during the FRENCH AND INDIAN WAR (1754–63). Notable Ranger units include ROGERS' RANGERS, the Connecticut Rangers who fought in the REVOLUTIONARY WAR and the TEXAS RANGERS. The success of the six US ranger battalions during WWII led to the formation in 1950 of airborne ranger infantry within each US infantry division. Rangers were not maintained in separate units after 1952.

RANGOON, capital, largest city and chief port of Burma, on the Rangoon R. Capital since 1753, it was developed into a modern city from 1852 under British rule. It is now the country's commercial center, with textile, sawmilling, food-processing and petroleum industries. Its Shwe Dagon pagoda is the country's principal shrine. Pop 1844000.

RANI. See RAJA.

RANK, Otto (1884–1939), Austrian-born US psychoanalyst best known for his suggestion that the psychological TRAUMA of birth is the basis of later anxiety NEUROSIS; and for applying PSYCHOANALYSIS to artistic creativity.

RANKE, Leopold von (1795–1886), German historian, one of the founders of modern historical research methods. Professor of History at Berlin 1834–71, Ranke insisted on objectivity and the importance of original documents, and wrote a monumental series of works, including the *History of the Popes* (1834–36) and a *History of the Reformation in Germany* (1839–47).

RANKIN, Jeanette (1880–1973), pacifist, feminist, social reformer and first woman elected to the US Congress. She became Republican Congresswoman at large for Montana 1917–19, and returned to the House in 1941, when she cast the only vote against entering WWII. In the 1960s she reemerged as a leader of the campaign against the war in Vietnam.

RANKINE SCALE, scale expressing absolute TEMPERATURES in Fahrenheit degrees, devised by Scottish engineer William Rankine (1820–1872).

RANN OF KUTCH, extensive waste of mud and salt flats (area 9000sq mi) in the Kutch district, NW India, on the border with Pakistan. In 1965 and 1971 it saw border clashes between the two countries.

RANSOM, John Crowe (1888–1974), US poet and proponent of the New Criticism, which emphasized textual, rather than social or moral, analysis. Professor of Poetry at Kenyon College, Ohio, 1937–58, he founded and edited the *Kenyon Review* (1939–59). His poetry includes *Chills and Fever* (1924).

RANTOUL, village in Ill., 14mi ENE of Champaign. Chanute Air Force Base is nearby. Pop 25562.

RAOULT, François Marie (1830–1901), French physical chemist best known for his work on the theory of SOLUTIONS. **Raoult's Law**, in its most general form, states that the VAPOR PRESSURE above an ideal solution is given by the sum of the PRODUCTS of the vapor pressure of each component and its mole fraction (the number of MOLES of the component divided by the total number of moles of all the components). (See also DISTILLATION.)

RAPALLO, Treaty of, name of two separate treaties. One, between Italy and Yugoslavia, signed Nov. 12, 1920, temporarily established Fiume (RIJEKA) as a free state. The other, between Germany and the USSR, was signed April 16, 1922. The two countries reestablished diplomatic relations, renounced war debts and claims on one another and agreed on economic cooperation.

RAPA NUI, native name for EASTER ISLAND.

RAPE, *Brassica napus*, a cultivated plant from the MUSTARD family, Cruciferae. Seeds of annual varieties contain colza oil which is used for cooking, fuel and lubrication. The seed residue is used for animal feed. Biennial varieties are used as forage crops.

RAPHAEL, ARCHANGEL regarded in Jewish tradition as the third after MICHAEL and GABRIEL. He figures prominently in Enoch and Tobit. In Christian tradition he is associated with healing.

RAPHAEL (Raffaello Santi or Sanzio; 1483–1520), Italian High RENAISSANCE painter and architect. Born in URBINO, he was early influenced by PERUGINO, as in *Marriage of the Virgin* (1504). In Florence, 1504–08, he studied the work of MICHELANGELO and LEONARDO DA VINCI, being influenced especially by the latter, and painted his famous Madonnas. From 1508 he decorated the Vatican Rooms for JULIUS II: the library frescoes, masterly portrayals of symbolic themes, use Raphael's new knowledge of classical art. His SISTINE CHAPEL tapestries (1515–16) and his sympathetic portraits were much imitated. From 1514 he worked rebuilding SAINT PETER'S BASILICA.

RAPID CITY, city in S.D., seat of Pennington Co. Its economy is based on mining, lumbering and ranching, and it is also a tourist center for the Black Hills. Pop 43836.

RAPP, George (1757–1847), German-born ascetic who founded the Rappites, a PIETIST sect which emigrated to the US and formed several communes. The sect became known as the HARMONY SOCIETY.

RAPPAHANNOCK RIVER, river flowing 212mi SE from the Blue Ridge Mts, Va., to Chesapeake Bay. It is joined by its main tributary, the Rapidan, above Fredericksburg near the Salem Church Dam.

RARE EARTHS, the elements SCANDIUM, YTTRIUM and the LANTHANUM SERIES, in Group IIIB of the PERIODIC TABLE, occurring widespread in nature as MONAZITE and other ores. They are separated by CHROMATOGRAPHY and ION-EXCHANGE resins. Rare earths are used in ALLOYS, including MISCH METAL; and their compounds (mixed or separately) are used as ABRASIVES, for making glasses and ceramics, as "getters," as catalysts (see CATALYSIS) in the petroleum industry, and to make PHOSPHORS, LASERS and MICROWAVE devices.

RARE GASES, former name for the NOBLE GASES.

RARITAN RIVER, river in N.J. From the confluence of the North Branch and the South Branch it flows 75mi SE into Raritan Bay. Its lower reaches are navigable.

RASHI (acronym from Rabbi Shlomo Yitzhaqi; 1040–1105), medieval French commentator on the Bible and TALMUD. His classic commentaries on the Old Testament and especially the Talmud have exercised an enduring influence on Jewish scholarship.

RASMUSSEN, Knud Johan Victor (1879–1933), Danish Arctic explorer and ethnologist. From Thule, Greenland, he undertook many expeditions to study Eskimo culture, including the longest dog-sledge journey known, from Greenland to Alaska (1923–24), described in his *Across Arctic America* (1927).

RASPBERRY, fruit-bearing bushes of the genus *Rubus*, of which some 200 species are known. European cultivated red-fruited varieties are derived from *Rubus idaeus*, while North American varieties, including a number which are black-fruited, are derived from three species. Red raspberries are propagated by suckers and black raspberries by tipping, i.e., by burying a shoot tip in the ground which then roots and produces a new plant. Family: Rosaceae.

RASPE, Rudolph Erich (1737–1794), German scholar and thief best known for *The Adventures of Baron Münchhausen* (1785), a collection of tall stories.

RASPUTIN, Grigori Yefimovich (1872?–1916), Russian mystic, known as the "mad monk," who gained influence over the Tsarina ALEXANDRA FYODOROVNA after supposedly curing her son's hemophilia in 1905. The scandal of his debaucheries, as well as his interference in political affairs, contributed to the undermining of the imperial government in WWI. He was assassinated by a group of ultra-conservatives.

RASTRELLI, Bartolomeo Francesco (1700–1771), Italian architect who worked in St. Petersburg (Leningrad). Chief architect to the imperial court from 1736, he did much, through his several baroque and rococo palaces such as the Winter Palace (1754–62), to Europeanize Russian architecture.

RATCHET, a simple mechanical device consisting of a pivoted bar, or "pawl," resting on a toothed wheel or shaft designed so that the wheel can rotate in one direction only. If a second pawl is used an intermittent rotary motion can be transmitted.

RATEL, or **Honey badger,** *Mellivora capensis*, a heavyset powerful mammal of Africa and Asia. It is black on the limbs and ventral surface, with a gray or white cowl on the upper parts. It is omnivorous, but is best-known for its association with the HONEYGUIDE in opening bee nests and feeding on the combs and larvae.

RATFISHES. See CHIMAERAS.

RATHENAU, Walther (1867–1922), German industrialist, statesman and political philosopher. Heir to a vast electrical company, during WWI he organized raw material supply. A founder of the German Democratic Party, he became minister of reconstruction in the WEIMAR REPUBLIC (1921), and as foreign minister (1922) concluded the Treaty of RAPALLO. A Jew, he was assassinated by right-wing extremists.

RATIO, a numerical relationship between two quantities of the same kind. Ratios may be expressed in the form $a:b$; as FRACTIONS, a/b; or as percentages, $\frac{100a}{b}\%$ (see PERCENT). Ratios are usually reduced to their lowest terms: e.g., $15:3 \equiv 5:1$. (See also PROPORTION.)

RATIONALISM, a philosophical approach based on the view that reality has a logical structure accessible to deductive reasoning and proof, and holding, as against EMPIRICISM, that reason unsupported by sense experience is a source of "synthetic knowledge"—knowledge, primarily of certain fundamental concepts and principles in logic and mathematics, which, it is argued, cannot be denied without contradiction and yet cannot be dismissed as merely analytic (see LOGIC; UNIVERSALS; REALISM). Major rationalists in modern philosophy include DESCARTES, SPINOZA and LEIBNIZ.

RATIONAL NUMBERS, those numbers that can be expressed as the RATIO of two INTEGERS. They include all positive and negative integers as well as, clearly, any number that can be expressed as a FRACTION. The set (see SET THEORY) of all rational numbers is a very dense one, in that it can be proved that between any two rational numbers there is a third; but, despite this, there are infinitely many numbers that are not members of this set (see IRRATIONAL NUMBERS; REAL NUMBERS).

RATIONING, apportionment of scarce supplies on the basis of fairness or need, rather than ability to pay (i.e., higher PRICES). First employed on a national scale by Britain in WWI, it was used by most countries at war in WWII. President HOOVER's Food Administration controlled US sugar and wheat supplies in WWI; in WWII wider rationing was organized by the OFFICE OF PRICE ADMINISTRATION.

RAT ISLANDS, SW Alaska, in the W ALEUTIAN ISLANDS, mountainous group including Kiska, Amchitka, Rat and Semisopochnoi islands.

RATITES, a group of flightless birds lacking a keel on the sternum for the attachment of flight muscles. All have extremely powerful legs and feet. Living forms are confined to the S hemisphere and include CASSOWARIES, EMUS, KIWIS, OSTRICHES and RHEAS. They have not necessarily originated from the same ancestors, since they have lost the power of flight comparatively recently.

RATS, a vast number of species of RODENTS belonging to many different families, largely Muridae and Cricetidae. The name is given to any large mouse-like rodent. The best known rats are perhaps the Brown and Black rats, *Rattus norvegicus* and *R. rattus*, familiar farmyard and warehouse pests. A strong exploratory urge, with an ability to feed on almost anything, makes them persistent pests; in addition, they transmit a number of serious diseases such as TYPHUS and PLAGUE. These rats originated in Asia but are now widespread in Europe and America. The New World has its own, Cricetid, rats: the Wood rats or PACK RATS, *Neotoma*; the Cotton rats, *Sigmodon*, and the Rice rats, *Oryzomys*.

RATTAN, long thin many-jointed stems of a number of Malaysian climbing palms, especially those of the genera *Calamus* and *Daemonorops*. Rattan canes are used for walking sticks, light construction work and wickerwork.

The brown rat, *Rattus norvegicus*, probably originated in southern central Asia, but has now spread all over the world. Albino brown rats are widely used for laboratory research purposes.

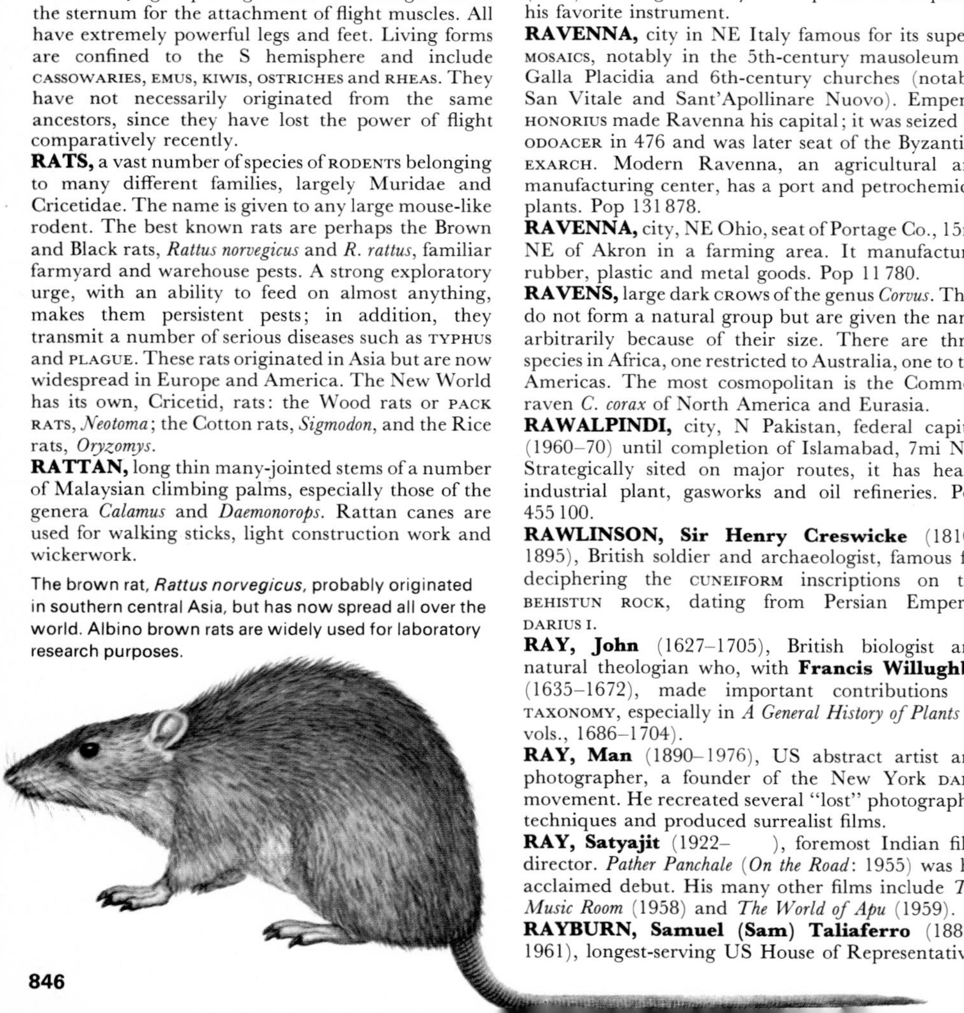

RATTIGAN, Sir Terence Mervyn (1911–), popular British playwright. He has turned from light comedies such as *French Without Tears* (1936) to the more serious, in *The Winslow Boy* (1946), *Ross* (1960) and *In Praise of Love* (1974).

RATTLESNAKES, two genera, *Crotalus* and *Sistrurus*, of PIT VIPERS of the Americas, named for a rattle on the tip of the tail. This rattle is composed of successive pieces of dead skin sloughed off the tail and is vibrated at great speed. Rattlers have moveable fangs which fold up into the roof of the mouth when not in use and are shed and replaced every three weeks. They are extremely venomous snakes, some quite ready to attack humans.

RATZEL, Friedrich (1844–1904), German geographer. With works such as *Anthropogeography* (1882–91), *Political Geography* (1897), *The History of Mankind* (1896–98) and *Lebensraum* (1901) he strongly influenced later German GEOPOLITICS.

RAUSCHENBERG, Robert (1925–), US artist, an initiator of the POP ART of the 1960s. His "combines" (collages) use brushwork with objects from everyday life such as pop bottles and news photos.

RAUSCHENBUSCH, Walter (1861–1918), US Baptist minister, reformer and theologican. A leader of the SOCIAL GOSPEL movement, he became a national spokesman for social evangelism with his *Christianity and the Social Crisis* (1907).

RAUWOLFIA SERPENTINA, tropical shrub from which **reserpine**, a drug used in hypertension and some mental illnesses, is extracted. The drug affects the HEART and NERVOUS SYSTEMS by reducing the supply of noradrenaline (see ADRENALINE).

RAVEL, Maurice Joseph (1875–1937), influential French composer, known for his adventurous harmonic style and the combination of delicacy and power in such orchestral works as *Rhapsodie Espagnole* (1908) and *Bolero* (1928), and the ballets *Daphnis and Chloé* (1912) and *La Valse* (1920). *Gaspard de la Nuit* (1908) is among his many masterpieces for the piano, his favorite instrument.

RAVENNA, city in NE Italy famous for its superb MOSAICS, notably in the 5th-century mausoleum of Galla Placidia and 6th-century churches (notably San Vitale and Sant'Apollinare Nuovo). Emperor HONORIUS made Ravenna his capital; it was seized by ODOACER in 476 and was later seat of the Byzantine EXARCH. Modern Ravenna, an agricultural and manufacturing center, has a port and petrochemical plants. Pop 131 878.

RAVENNA, city, NE Ohio, seat of Portage Co., 15mi NE of Akron in a farming area. It manufactures rubber, plastic and metal goods. Pop 11 780.

RAVENS, large dark CROWS of the genus *Corvus*. They do not form a natural group but are given the name arbitrarily because of their size. There are three species in Africa, one restricted to Australia, one to the Americas. The most cosmopolitan is the Common raven *C. corax* of North America and Eurasia.

RAWALPINDI, city, N Pakistan, federal capital (1960–70) until completion of Islamabad, 7mi NE. Strategically sited on major routes, it has heavy industrial plant, gasworks and oil refineries. Pop 455 100.

RAWLINSON, Sir Henry Creswicke (1810–1895), British soldier and archaeologist, famous for deciphering the CUNEIFORM inscriptions on the BEHISTUN ROCK, dating from Persian Emperor DARIUS I.

RAY, John (1627–1705), British biologist and natural theologian who, with **Francis Willughby** (1635–1672), made important contributions to TAXONOMY, especially in *A General History of Plants* (3 vols., 1686–1704).

RAY, Man (1890–1976), US abstract artist and photographer, a founder of the New York DADA movement. He recreated several "lost" photographic techniques and produced surrealist films.

RAY, Satyajit (1922–), foremost Indian film director. *Pather Panchale* (*On the Road*: 1955) was his acclaimed debut. His many other films include *The Music Room* (1958) and *The World of Apu* (1959).

RAYBURN, Samuel (Sam) Taliaferro (1882–1961), longest-serving US House of Representatives speaker (17 years from 1940) and congressman (1913–61). A dedicated Democrat, he helped build NEW DEAL policy and was uniquely esteemed for his political skills and experience.

Robert Rauschenberg is one of the most important pioneers of Pop art; his early work combines items from everyday life. Seen here is his *Black Market* (1961, Wallraf-Richartz Museum, Cologne).

RAYLEIGH, John William Strutt, Third Baron (1842–1919), British physicist awarded the 1904 Nobel Prize for Physics for his measurements of the DENSITY of the atmosphere and its component gases, work that led to his isolation of ARGON (see also RAMSAY, SIR WILLIAM). He worked in many other fields of physics, and is commemorated in the terms **Rayleigh scattering** (which describes the way that ELECTROMAGNETIC RADIATION is scattered by spherical particles of radius less than 10% of the wavelength of the radiation—see SCATTERING) and **Rayleigh waves** (see EARTHQUAKES).

RAYMOND, Henry Jarvis (1820–1869), founder-editor of the *New York Times* (1851) who took an active part in forming the REPUBLICAN PARTY. He was in the House of Representatives 1865–67, losing renomination over his moderate stand on RECONSTRUCTION.

RAYNAUD'S DISEASE, a condition in which the fingers (or toes) suddenly become white and numb, often on exposure to mild cold, and become in turn blue and then red and painful. It is caused by digital artery spasm. Raynaud's disease usually occurs in otherwise fit young women; Raynaud's syndrome is the same symptom as a manifestation of an underlying disease (e.g., LUPUS).

RAYON, name for various textile fibers made from regenerated CELLULOSE. (See also SYNTHETIC FIBERS.)

RAYS, a group of cartilaginous fishes whose pectoral fins are generally greatly expanded and wing-like. Rays swim by undulation of these "wings." The highly flattened body and large pectoral fins adapt them for a bottom-living existence. Rays are divided into six groups: SKATES; Rays; MANTA RAYS (which have abandoned bottom-living for a pelagic existence); Electric rays (in which blocks of muscle are adapted as electric batteries); SAWFISHES, and Guitarfishes.

RAYTOWN, residential and industrial city, suburb of Kansas City, W Mo., incorporated 1950 with only about 500 inhabitants. Pop 33 306.

RAZIN, Stenka (Stepan Timofeyevich; d. 1671), leader of a great but unsuccessful peasant uprising in 1670–71 in the Volga region against landlords and tsarist absolutism. After his torture and execution he became a Russian folk hero.

RAZORBILL, *Alca torda*, a black and white seabird of the N Atlantic related to the GUILLEMOTS. It breeds in colonies on cliffs, principally in the Old World, and feeds on fish which it catches under water with the razor-shaped bill.

RAZORSHELL CLAMS, or **Jack-knife clams,** bivalve MOLLUSKS with elongated razor-like shells and a large powerful foot specialized for deep burrowing in sand, found on sandy beaches throughout the world. They are commercially harvested for food in the US.

RDX, or cyclonite, or cyclotrimethylenetrinitramine, a high EXPLOSIVE made by NITRATION of the condensation product of FORMALDEHYDE and AMMONIA. First introduced in WWII, it is used in blasting caps and PLASTIC EXPLOSIVE.

RE. See RA.

REACTANCE, the ratio of an AC voltage applied to a single component of an electric circuit (particularly an inductor or CAPACITOR) to the current produced, the maximum values of each being taken irrespective of their relative PHASE. (See also IMPEDANCE.)

READ, Sir Herbert (1893–1968), British poet and critic, champion of art education, free verse and the English 19th-century Romantic writers. His best known works are *The Philosophy of Modern Art* (1952) and *The Tenth Muse* (1959). He edited the *Burlington Magazine* 1933–39.

READING, mainly residential town, NE Mass., 11mi N of Boston. It has diverse light industry, with nearby truck and dairy farms. Pop 22 539.

READING, city in SW Ohio, 9mi N of Cincinnati, with light manufacturing. Pop 14 303.

READING, industrial city, SE Pa., seat of Berkshire Co., on the Schuylkill R 50mi NW of Philadelphia. Famous for textiles, metal products and railroad shops, it also produces coal, bricks and chemicals. Pop 87 643.

READING, the process of assimilating language in the written form. Initial language development in children is largely as speech (see SPEECH AND SPEECH DISORDERS) and has a primarily auditory or phonetic component; the recognition of letters, words and sentences when written represents a transition from the auditory to the visual mode. The dependence of reading on previous linguistic development with spoken speech is seen in the impaired reading ability of deaf children. Normal reading depends on normal VISION and the ability to recognize the patterns of letter and word order and grammatical variations. In reading, vision is linked with the system controlling EYE movement, so that the page is scanned in an orderly fashion. Reading is represented in essentially the same areas of brain as are concerned with speech, and disorders of the two often occur together (e.g., DYSPHASIA). In DYSLEXIA, pattern recognition is impaired and a specific defect of reading and language development results. The ability to read and write, and thus to record events, ideas, etc., represented one of the most substantial advances in human civilization after the acquisition of speech itself.

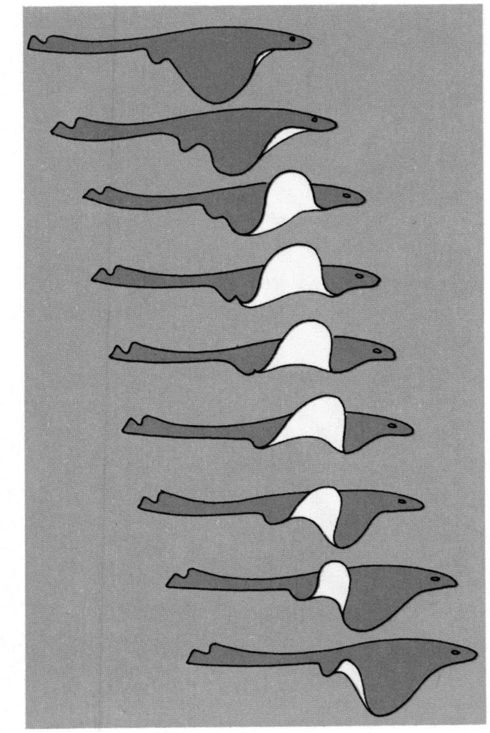

Rays swim by undulation of the pectoral fins.

The revolutionary reaper invented by Cyrus Hall McCormick (1831), shown in a contemporary print.

REAGAN, Ronald (1911–), governor of Cal. 1967–75. Born in Tampico, Ill., he became a film actor in 1937 and in 1947 was elected president of the Screen Actors Guild. He campaigned for GOLDWATER as a conservative Republican in 1964, twice won the Cal. governorship and made two unsuccessful bids for the presidential nomination in 1968 and 1976.

REALGAR, soft, bright-red SULFIDE mineral, arsenic disulfide (As_2S_2), an ore of ARSENIC associated with ORPIMENT and found in central Europe, Nev. and Ut. It forms monoclinic CRYSTALS.

REALISM, in art and literature, the faithful imitation of real life; more specifically, the artistic movement which started in France c1850 in reaction to the idealized representations of ROMANTICISM and NEOCLASSICISM, with a social dimension derived from scientific progress and the REVOLUTIONS OF 1848. In France the leading painters were COROT, COURBET, DAUMIER and MILLET, and its main literary expression was in the novels of BALZAC, FLAUBERT and ZOLA (see NATURALISM). In the US, EAKINS, Winslow HOMER and the ASHCAN SCHOOL were Realistic painters, and in literature Stephen CRANE, Theodore DREISER, William HOWELLS, Henry JAMES and Frank NORRIS led the movement.

REALISM, in philosophy, is a term with two main technical uses. Philosophers who believe, as PLATO did, that UNIVERSALS exist in their own right, and so independently of perceived objects, are traditionally labeled "realists." Realism in this sense is opposed to NOMINALISM. On the other hand, realism also describes the view that perceived objects exist independently of our perceptions of them. Realism in this sense is opposed to the extreme EMPIRICISM of such as BERKELEY and HUME.

REALITY PRINCIPLE. See PLEASURE PRINCIPLE.

REAL NUMBERS, those numbers that can be represented directly by lengths of LINES. The SET (see SET THEORY) of real numbers therefore includes ZERO and both positive and negative RATIONAL NUMBERS and IRRATIONAL NUMBERS. It does not include the IMAGINARY NUMBERS.

REALPOLITIK, policy based on practicalities and power rather than on doctrine or ethical objectives. Its famous exponent was BISMARCK, who as German chancellor eschewed ideology for national interest.

REAL PRESENCE, term designating those doctrines of Holy COMMUNION that stress the actual presence of Christ's body and blood in the sacrament—whether physically as in TRANSUBSTANTIATION, or in an undefined mode as in moderate ANGLICANISM—as opposed to the more extreme Protestant view that they are present only symbolically.

REAPER, a grain-cutting machine. The first simple reapers were invented in the UK and the US in the early 19th century. They increased in popularity as they were developed to include mechanical gathering and binding.

REAPPORTIONMENT. See APPORTIONMENT, LEGISLATIVE.

RÉAUMUR, René Antoine Ferchault de (1683–1757), French scientist whose most important work was in ENTOMOLOGY, but who is best remembered for devising the now little used **Réaumur temperature scale**, in which 0°R = 0°C and 80°R = 100°C.

REBATE, a refund to the purchaser of part of a price. In the US the Interstate Commerce Act (1887) banned rebates by railroad companies, but was largely ignored. The practice was ended by the Elkins Act (1903), making both shipper and carrier guilty.

REBEC, three-stringed bowed instrument, the precursor of the VIOLS, of Moorish origin. Popular in medieval Europe, it is now found in the folk music of the Balkans.

REBECCA, in the Old Testament, wife of ISAAC and mother of ESAU and JACOB.

REBELLION OF 1837–1838, two unsuccessful and parallel uprisings against British colonial rule in Canada, prompted by an economic depression and desire for local self-government. The first, led by Louis PAPINEAU in Lower Canada (roughly Quebec), collapsed swiftly: Papineau fled to the US. While troops were occupied here, colonists in Upper Canada (now Ontario) revolted in Toronto under William MACKENZIE. After defeat, he too fled to the US (see CAROLINE AFFAIR). Lord DURHAM's subsequent report, accepted in principle by the British government, urged the union of Upper and Lower Canada (which became law with the 1840 Act of Union).

REBUS, a riddle or pun in which names of objects depicted, numbers, etc., sound like the intended words: for example, IOU. The rebus is common in heraldry (e.g., a doe between three bells: arms of the Dobells).

RECALL. See INITIATIVE, REFERENDUM AND RECALL.

RECAPITULATION, in embryology. See ONTOGENY AND PHYLOGENY.

RECEIVER, in law, a person, bank or trust appointed by a court to take charge, for a fee, of a company's or person's assets, often in BANKRUPTCY cases. His first duty is to safeguard existing assets to

During Reconstruction a number of Negroes were elected to Congress. Shown here are Rep. Robert C. Delarge of South Carolina (left, standing) and Rep. Jefferson H. Long of Georgia (right, standing); and (left to right), Sen. Hiram R. Revels of Mississippi, Rep. Benjamin S. Turner of Alabama, Rep. Josiah T. Walls of Florida, Rep. Joseph H. Rainy of South Carolina and Rep. R. Brown Elliott of South Carolina.

meet creditors' claims, but he may also administer the business in the interim.

RECEPTACLE. See FLOWER.

RECIFE, seaport in E Brazil at the mouth of Capibaribe R, capital of Pernambuco state. The "Brazilian Venice" is an administrative, university and transport center, and exports sugar, cotton and textiles. Pop 1 078 819.

RECIPROCAL, of a number a, that number b such that $a.b = 1$. With REAL NUMBERS, the reciprocal of a is $1/a$ for all a except ZERO (1/0 has no meaning). With IMAGINARY NUMBERS this is true also: the reciprocal of i is $\frac{1}{i}$, which can be expressed as $\frac{i}{i^2}$ and hence as $-i$. (See also INVERSE.) **Reciprocal trigonometric functions,** the functions cosec, sec and cot of an ANGLE (see also TRIGONOMETRY). They are defined as cosec A = 1/sin A; sec A = 1/cos A; cot A = 1/tan A.

RECIPROCATING ENGINE, an ENGINE in which a PISTON oscillates in a cylinder, being driven by the pressure of the working fluid.

RECIPROCITY, in international trade, mutual concessions in tariff rates, quotas, etc., granted by treaties or agreements between two or more countries. Reciprocal agreements may also cover treatment of foreigners.

RECITATIVE, lightly accompanied narration or dialogue linking musical numbers in OPERA and ORATORIO. Originally more spoken than sung, it has become increasingly integrated into the musical framework.

RECLAMATION. See LAND RECLAMATION; RECYCLING.

RECLAMATION, US Bureau of, agency of the Department of the Interior, created to administer the Reclamation Act of 1902 for reclaiming arid land by irrigation in the 16 W states. Its responsibilities were later progressively expanded.

RECOGNITION, in diplomacy, procedure in international law by which a new independent state is formally accepted by other states or a new form of government in an existing state is accepted as the legal representative of that state.

RECOMBINATION, the presence in offspring of GENE combinations not found in either parent. Such new combinations may be formed by the crossing over of CHROMOSOMES in MEIOSIS, and, being thus present in either GAMETE, unite randomly at FERTILIZATION.

RECONSTRUCTION, period (1865–77) when Americans tried to rebuild a stable Union after the Civil War. The deadlock inherited by Andrew JOHNSON on Lincoln's death, over who should control Reconstruction, hardened with increasing congressional hostility towards restoring the South to its old position (see WADE-DAVIS BILL). Republicans wanted to press home the Union victory by following the 13th Amendment abolishing slavery (1865) with full civil rights for the Negro, including the vote. Instead, while Congress was not in session, Johnson implemented Lincoln's policy of lenience by giving amnesty in return for a loyalty oath. He also condoned BLACK CODES, which practically reintroduced slavery in another guise. Reconvening (1866) with a landslide victory, however, the radical Republicans took control. Their first Reconstruction Act of 1867 divided ten Southern states into five military areas with a major general for each. Under army scrutiny, black and white votes were registered, and constitutions and governments instituted. In 1868, six Southern states were readmitted to the Union, followed in 1870 by the other four. By ratifying the 14th Amendment (1868) on Negro civil rights, Tenn. escaped the military phase. There were no mass arrests, no indictments for treason and the few Confederate officials jailed were (except for Jefferson DAVIS) soon released. Apart from slaves, the property of the Confederate leaders was untouched, although no help was given to rescue the ruined economy. On readmission, the Southern governments were Republican, supported by enfranchised Negroes, SCALAWAGS (white Republicans) and CARPETBAGGERS (Northern profiteers). Constructive legislation was passed in every state for public schools, welfare taxation and government reform, although the governments were accused of corruption and incompetence. The FREEDMEN'S BUREAU only lasted four years, but it did help to found Atlanta, Howard and Fisk universities for Negroes. Southern conservatives, hostile to the radical Republican policies, turned to the Democrats; societies like the Ku Klux Klan emerged to crusade against Negroes and radicals. Full citizenship for Negroes, though legally assured by the 14th and 15th (1870) amendments, was denied by intimidation, literacy tests and POLL TAX. The Republican Party, secure again in the North, abandoned the Negro. In 1877, when federal troops withdrew (see HAYES, RUTHERFORD), the last GOP governments collapsed and Reconstruction was over.

RECONSTRUCTION FINANCE CORPORATION (RFC), US government agency set up (1932) under President Hoover to lend money and so stimulate the economy. In its 25-year life the RFC loaned some $50 billion.

RECORDER, wind instrument related to the FLUTE and held vertically, with a mouthpiece which channels the airstream, and no keys. Relatively easy to play, soft and sweet in tone, it was most popular about 1600–1700 and is again popular today (see DOLMETSCH, ARNOLD). There are soprano, alto, and (with some keys) tenor and bass recorders.

RECORD PLAYER. See PHONOGRAPH.

RECTANGLE. See QUADRILATERAL.

RECTIFIER, a device such as an ELECTRON TUBE or SEMICONDUCTOR junction which converts alternating electric current (AC—see ELECTRICITY) to direct current (DC) by allowing more current to flow through it in one direction than another. A **half-wave rectifier** transmits only one polarity of the alternating current, producing a pulsating direct current; two such devices are combined in full-wave rectification, giving a continuous pulse train which may be smoothed by a filter.

RECYCLING, the recovery and reuse of any waste material. Of obvious economic importance where reusable materials are available more cheaply than fresh supplies of the same materials, the recycling principle is finding ever wider application in the conservation of the world's natural resources and in solving the problems of environmental POLLUTION. The recycling of the wastes of a manufacturing process in the same process—e.g., the resmelting and recasting of metallic turnings and offcuts—is commonplace in industry. So also is the immediate use of wastes or by-products of one industrial process in another—e.g., the manufacture of cattle food from the grain-mash residues found in breweries and distilleries. These are often termed forms of "internal recycling," as opposed to "external recycling": the recovery and reprocessing for reuse of "discarded" materials, such as waste paper, scrap metal and used glass bottles. The burning of garbage to produce electricity and the extraction of pure water from sewage are other common examples of recycling.

RED BANK, resort borough, E N.J., on the Navesink R estuary 40mi SW of New York. It is a yachting center with light industry. Pop 12 847.

RED BANK, town in SE Tenn., residential suburb about 7mi N of Chattanooga, on the Tennessee R. Pop 12 715.

REDBIRD CACTUS, or **Devil's Backbone,** a shrubby, succulent plant of the genus *Pedilanthus*, sometimes grown as a house plant for its red, birdlike flowers and light, dark and gray-green leaves that have white and rose markings. To keep the foliage in good condition, plants should be grown in a sunny position at average house temperatures, and watered when the soil becomes nearly dry. To induce flowering, plants should be kept at 4.5°C–10°C (40°F to 50°F) without water for two months during the winter. Propagation is by shoot tip cuttings. Family: Euphorbiaceae.

RED BUD. See JUDAS TREE.

RED CLOUD (1822–1909), chief of the Oglala Sioux and leader of the Indian struggle against the opening of the Bozeman Trail (see BOZEMAN, JOHN M.). The trail was closed in 1868 following the FETTERMAN MASSACRE.

RED CORPUSCLES, or erythrocytes. See BLOOD.

RED CROSS, international agency for the relief of victims of war or disaster. Its two aims are to alleviate suffering and to maintain a rigid neutrality so that it may cross national borders to reach those otherwise unaidable. An international committee founded by J. H. DUNANT and four others from Geneva secured 12

Headquarters of the International Red Cross in Geneva. The Red Cross was originally founded to care for war-wounded and prisoners of war.

nations' signatures to the first of the GENEVA CONVENTIONS (1864) for the care of the wounded. Aid was given to both sides in the Danish-Prussian War the same year. During WWI and WWII, the Red Cross helped prisoners of war, inspecting camps and sending food and clothing parcels; it investigated about 5 million missing persons and distributed $200 000 000 in relief supplies to civilians. The International Red Cross won the Nobel Peace Prize in 1917 and 1944. It works through the International Committee (1880), made up of 25 Swiss citizens. Over 100 national Red Cross societies (Red Crescent in Moslem countries) carry out peacetime relief and public health work. The US Red Cross (1882) has some 3 300 chapters.

RED DEER, city in S Alberta, Canada on the Red Deer R 90mi N of Calgary, a dairy, poultry and grain center, with gas and oil refineries. Pop 27 674.

RED DEER, *Cervus elaphus*, a large, red-brown DEER of Europe, Asia and America. The six North American subspecies are referred to as WAPITIS. All are heavy deer, characteristic of poorer habitats. Stags develop large ANTLERS, shed and regrown annually, which are used for fighting during the rut.

REDDING, city in N Cal., seat of Shasta Co. at the head of Sacramento R valley. It is a resort, with sawmills, foundries and machine shops. Pop 16 659.

REDEMPTORISTS (Congregation of the Most Holy Redeemer), a religious order founded 1732 in Naples by St. ALPHONSUS LIGUORI to preach the Gospel to the poor and the abandoned. Now established in five continents, it entered the US in 1832.

REDFIELD, Robert (1897–1958), US cultural anthropologist best known for his comparative studies of primitive and highly civilized cultures, and for his active support of racial integration.

REDFISH. See ROSEFISH.

REDHEAD, *Aythya americana*, a member of a genus of diving DUCKS of fresh and coastal waters, that also includes the CANVASBACK, POCHARDS and the Ring-necked duck. The American Redhead, in color very like the European Pochard, is a favorite quarry of wildfowlers.

REDI, Francesco (1627–1697 or 1698), Italian biological scientist who demonstrated that maggots develop in decaying meat not through SPONTANEOUS GENERATION but from eggs laid there by flies.

RED JACKET (Sagoyewatha; c1758–1830), Seneca Indian chief named for the red coat he wore when an English ally in the Revolution. Later an ally of the US in the War of 1812, he strongly opposed white customs and Christianity for his people in N.Y.

REDLANDS, city in SE Cal., 8mi SE of San Bernardino. Manufactures include missiles, furniture and hosiery. It is the site of Redlands U. Pop 36 355.

RED LEAD. See LEAD.

REDMOND, John Edward (1856–1918), Irish nationalist. He succeeded PARNELL as Irish nationalist leader in parliament and secured the passage of the 1914 HOME RULE Bill. After the repression of the 1916 EASTER RISING he lost power to SINN FEIN.

REDON, Odilon (1840–1916), French painter and engraver associated with the Symbolists. His oils, usually of flowers and full of color and light, contrasted with bizarre lithographs such as *The Cyclops*, c1898.

REDONDO BEACH, residential and resort city in SW Cal., on the Pacific SE of Los Angeles. Pop 57 425.

REDPOLL, *Carduelis flammea*, a small, streaked, gray-brown finch with a bright red patch on the forehead and a black chin. They are sociable birds which may be distinguished by an undulating flight. They live in deciduous woodland, feeding mainly on seeds.

RED RIVER, 1 222mi-long river, which rises in N Tex. and flows SE to join the Mississippi R between Natchez and Baton Rouge. Named for its red sediment, it drains about 90 000sq mi and forms most of the Okla.-Tex. boundary.

RED RIVER, river in SE Asia, flowing about 500mi SE from Yunnan province, S China (where it is named Yüan Chiang R), across North Vietnam (as the Hong R), past Hanoi into the Gulf of Tonkin. Its wide fertile delta E of Hanoi is North Vietnam's economic center.

RED RIVER OF THE NORTH, about 540mi long, is formed at Wahpeton, N.D. by the junction of the Bois de Sioux and Otter Tail rivers. It flows N as the N.D.-Minn. boundary and enters Manitoba, Canada, emptying into Lake Winnipeg. It drains some 43 500sq mi of rich wheatlands.

RED RIVER REBELLION. See RIEL, LOUIS.

RED RIVER SETTLEMENT, Canadian community founded in 1811 by Lord SELKIRK at the junction of the Red and Assiniboine rivers in present-day S Manitoba, on land granted by the Hudson's Bay Co. Violent hostility from the North West Co. ended with the union of the two fur companies (1821).

RED SEA, sea separating the Arabian Peninsula from NE Africa. It extends some 1 300mi from the Bab al-Mandab strait by the Gulf of Aden in the S to the gulfs of Suez (with the Suez Canal) and Aqaba in the N. It is up to 250mi wide and up to 7 800ft deep.

REDSHANK, *Tringa totanus*, a common wading bird of Europe and Asia, named for its long red legs. It is a streaked gray bird of marshes and flood waters, wintering on estuaries and mudflats, probing in mud and silt for worms, insects and crustaceans.

RED SHIFT, an increase in wavelength of the light from an object, usually caused by its rapid recession (see DOPPLER EFFECT). The spectra of distant GALAXIES show marked red shifts and this is usually, though far from always, interpreted as implying that they are rapidly receding from us. (See also COSMOLOGY.)

RED SNAPPER, a perch-like fish of the genus *Lutjanus*, with large mouth and jaws. Valuable commercial fishes of the Indo-Pacific, they are active predators, feeding on other fishes and crustaceans.

RED SPIDER MITES, various prostigmatid MITES which infest a wide range of plant species in orchards and greenhouses. They habitually spin a fine web around the leaves on which they are feeding.

REDSTARTS, *Phoenicurus*, a genus of small perching birds of woods, heathland and rocky slopes of Asia and Europe. Both sexes have a constantly flicking red tail and rump. The unrelated American redstart, *Setophaga ruticilla*, is a North American member of the WOOD WARBLERS, Parulidae.

RED TIDE, effect caused by the release into sea water of a red pigment, toxic to fish, by certain DINOFLAGELLATES.

REDUCTION. See OXIDATION AND REDUCTION.

RED WING, city in SE Minn., seat of Goodhue Co., on the Mississippi R 40mi SE of St. Paul. Manufactures include footwear. Pop 10 441.

RED-WINGED BLACKBIRD, *Turdus musicus*, a small European THRUSH, with typical thrush coloration but distinguished by chestnut flanks particularly obvious in flight. The name is also locally used for another species of thrush, the North American *Agelaius phoeniceus*.

REDWOOD. See SEQUOIA.

REDWOOD CITY, city in W Cal., seat of San Mateo Co., on the bay 18mi SE of San Francisco. It is a center for electronics. Pop 55 686.

REDWOOD NATIONAL PARK, area in N Cal. of 57 094 acres, including 40mi of coastline, established in 1968 to preserve groves of ancient redwood trees, which include the world's tallest (367ft).

REED, John (1887–1920), US journalist and radical, author of the famous eye-witness *Ten Days That Shook The World* (1919) which recounts the Russian October Revolution.

REED, Stanley Forman (1884–   ), US jurist, associate justice (1938–57) of the US Supreme Court, where his moderate's vote was often decisive. As solicitor general under F. D. Roosevelt he argued important cases arising from NEW DEAL legislation.

REED, Thomas Brackett (1839–1902), US Republican speaker of the House of Representatives 1889–91 and 1895–99, called "Tsar Reed" for his strong control. His "Reed Rules" (1890) are still the basis for procedure in Congress. He supported high tariffs and opposed the Spanish-US war and the annexation of Hawaii.

REED, Walter (1851–1902), US Army pathologist and bacteriologist who, in 1900, demonstrated the role of the mosquito *Aëdes aegypti* as a carrier of YELLOW FEVER, so enabling the disease to be controlled.

REEDBUCK, small ANTELOPE related to the WATERBUCK. There are three species within the genus *Redunca*. Gray-fawn antelope, distributed throughout Africa, they are found in small groups in savanna areas, typically in more swampy regions.

REED INSTRUMENTS. See WIND INSTRUMENTS.

REEDS, cosmopolitan GRASSES inhabiting wet ground and shallow water. They grow from a tangle of rhizomes and have feathery flowers and hollow stems, which are used in thatching. Family: Graminae.

REEF, line or ridge of rocks just below the surface of the sea. See CORALS.

REEL, lively rustic dance in 4/4 time originating in Scotland about the 16th century. After 1770, the foursome reel dominated, the dancers alternating traveling steps with more elaborate ones in one place.

REEVE, Tapping (1744–1823), US jurist who started the movement to secure the legal right of married women to dispose of their property. He also founded a famous law school at Litchfield, Conn. (1784).

REFERENDUM. See INITIATIVE, REFERENDUM AND RECALL.

REFINING, the purification of crude substances, especially metals (see METALLURGY), ORES, PETROLEUM and SUCROSE. Methods used, include DISTILLATION, ELECTROLYSIS and FLOTATION.

REFLECTION, the bouncing back of energy waves (e.g., LIGHT radiation, SOUND or WATER waves) from a surface. If the surface is smooth, "regular" reflection takes place, the incident and reflected wave paths lying in the same plane as, and at opposed equal angles to, the normal (a line perpendicular to the surface) at the point of reflection. Rough surfaces reflect waves irregularly, so an optically rough surface appears matt or dull while an optically smooth surface looks shiny. Reflected sound waves are known as ECHOES. (See also MIRROR; PRISM; REFRACTION.)

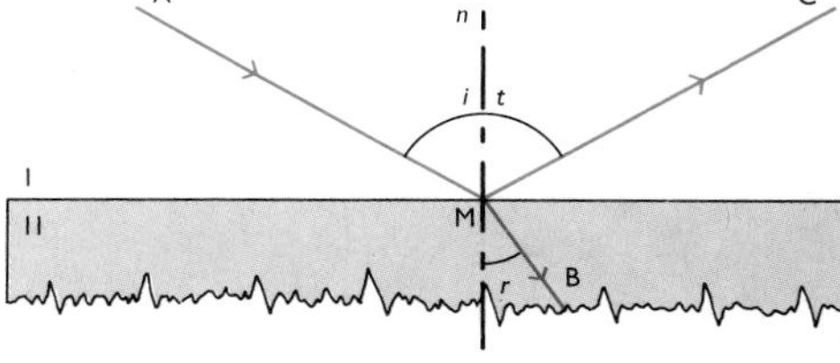

A ray coming from A and striking a surface at M is reflected along the line MC, and angle *i* (the angle of incidence) equals angle *t* (the angle of reflection). AM, MC and *n* (the normal) all lie in the same plane. In refraction, waves or rays are bent in passing from one substance to another. If a ray from A in medium I (air) passes at M into medium II (water), it will be refracted so as to follow the path MB. The angle of refraction is then *r*. By Snell's Law, $\sin i = \mu \sin r$ where μ is the refractive index of medium II.

REFLEX, MUSCLE contraction or secretion resulting from nerve stimulation by a pathway from a stimulus via the NERVOUS SYSTEM to the effector organ without the interference of volition. Basic primitive reflexes are stylized responses to stress of protective value to an infant. Stretch or tendon reflexes (e.g., knee-jerk) are muscle contractions in response to sudden stretching of their TENDONS. **Conditioned reflexes** are more complex responses described by PAVLOV that follow any stimulus which has been repeatedly linked with a stimulus of normal functional significance.

REFLEX, of an ANGLE, one between 180° and 360°.

REFORMATION, religious and political upheaval in W Europe in the 16th century. Primarily an attempt to reform the doctrines of the Roman Catholic Church, it led to the establishment of PROTESTANTISM. ANTICLERICALISM spread after the movements led by John WYCLIFFE and the LOLLARDS in 14th-century England and by John HUS in Bohemia in the 15th century. At the same time the PAPACY had lost prestige through its 70-year exile, the BABYLONIAN CAPTIVITY at AVIGNON and the 50-year GREAT SCHISM. RENAISSANCE thought, particularly HUMANISM, stimulated liberal views, spread by the invention of

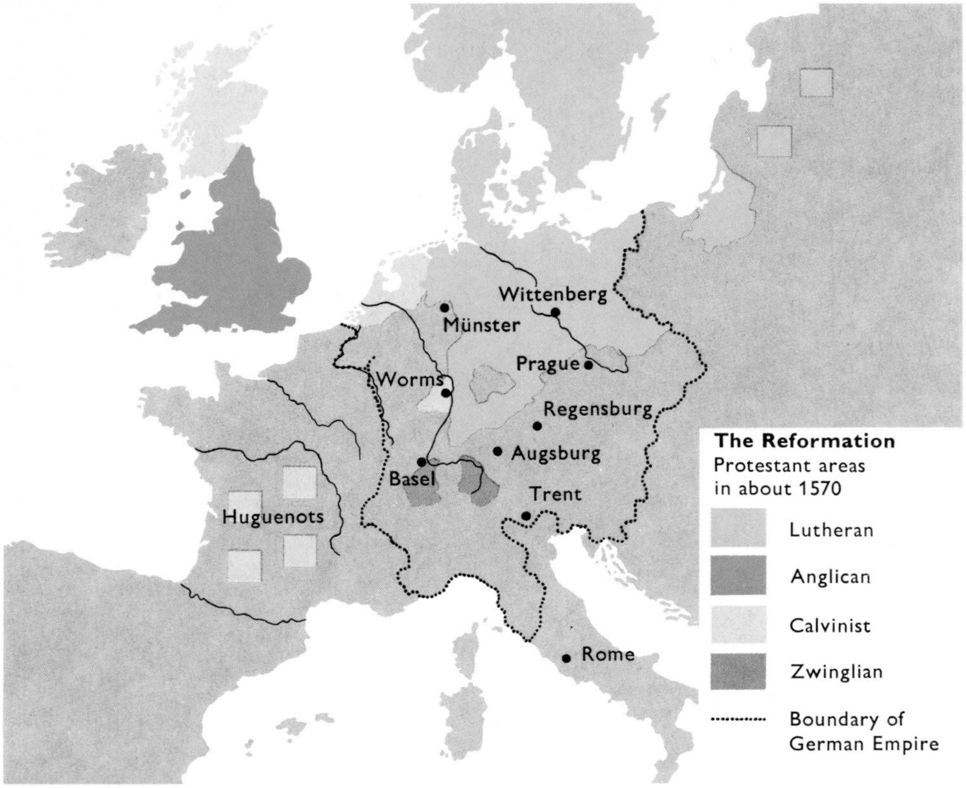

The progress of the Reformation in western Europe in its first 50 years. Significant minorities are indicated by small squares. In Switzerland, Calvinism—centered on Geneva—was displacing Zwinglianism as the basis of the Reformed churches; there were also important Reformed churches in Transylvania and other parts of southern central Europe. Ulster was beginning to acquire its Protestant (Anglican and Calvinist) color. In Bohemia the Brethren were as important as the Lutherans.

printing. There were many critics, like Martin LUTHER, of the low moral standards of Rome, and of the sale of INDULGENCES, distributed in Germany by TETZEL. Luther also challenged papal authority and the accepted Roman Catholic doctrines, such as TRANSUBSTANTIATION and CELIBACY, and argued strongly for JUSTIFICATION BY FAITH. Luther's ideas spread in Germany after the Diet of WORMS, 1521, and after the PEASANTS' WAR, when Luther won the support of many German princes and of Denmark and Sweden. The protest made by the Lutheran princes at the Diet of SPEYER (1529) provided the term "Protestant."

The Swiss divine Huldreich ZWINGLI won a large following in Switzerland and SW Germany. He carried out radical religious reforms in Zürich, abolishing the mass. After his death (1531), John CALVIN led the Swiss reform movement and set up a reformed church in Geneva. Calvin's *Institutes of the Christian Religion* (1536) had great influence, notably in Scotland where CALVINISM was led by John KNOX. In France Calvin's religious followers, the HUGUENOTS, were involved in the complex political struggles leading to the Wars of RELIGION, 1562–98. The Protestant movement in the Low Countries was linked with the national revolt which freed the Dutch from Roman Catholic Spain. The English Reformation was initiated by HENRY VIII, who denied papal authority, dissolved and seized the wealth of the monasteries, and made the CHURCH OF ENGLAND autonomous to increase the royal government's power. Henry VIII remained in doctrine a Catholic but the influence of Reformers such as RIDLEY and LATIMER established Protestantism under EDWARD VI, when Thomas CRANMER issued a new prayer book (1549). There was a Roman Catholic reaction under MARY I but in 1558 ELIZABETH I established moderate Protestantism as the basis of the English Church. The religious position of Europe as a whole, however, was not settled for another century.

REFORMATION, Catholic. See COUNTER-REFORMATION.

REFORM BILLS, three acts of Parliament passed in Britain during the 19th century to extend the franchise. The first (1832) abolished rotten boroughs (boroughs which returned two members to Parliament long after their populations disappeared), and enfranchised industrial cities like Birmingham and Manchester, and the propertied middle class. The second bill (1867) gave the vote to urban dwellers and the third (1884) extended it to agricultural workers.

REFORMED CHURCHES, the Protestant churches arising from the REFORMATION that adhere to CALVINISM doctrinally and to PRESBYTERIANISM in church polity, and thus distinct from the LUTHERAN CHURCHES and the CHURCH OF ENGLAND. They grew up especially in Switzerland, Germany, France (see HUGUENOTS), Holland (see DUTCH REFORMED CHURCH), Scotland (see CHURCH OF SCOTLAND), Hungary and what is now Czechoslovakia. Each had its own simple formal LITURGY, and all acknowledged the Reformed Confessions. There are several Reformed Churches in the US, the largest being the CHRISTIAN REFORMED CHURCH.

REFRACTION, the change in direction of energy waves on passing from one medium to another in which they have a different velocity. In the case of LIGHT radiation, refraction is associated with a change in the optical density of the medium. On passing into a denser medium the wave path is bent toward the normal (the line perpendicular to the surface at the point of incidence), the whole wave path and the normal lying in the same plane. The ratio of the sine of the angle of incidence (that between the incident wave path and the normal) to that of the angle of refraction (that between the normal and the refracted wave path) is a constant for a given interface (Snell's law). When measured for light passing from a vacuum into a denser medium, this ratio is known as the refractive index of the medium. Refractive index varies with wavelength (see DISPERSION). On passing into a less dense medium, light radiation is bent away from the normal but if the angle of incidence is so great that its sine equals or exceeds the index for refraction from the denser to the less dense medium, there is no refraction and total (internal) REFLECTION (applied in the reflecting PRISM) results. Refraction finds its principal application in the design of LENSES. (See also DOUBLE REFRACTION.)

REFRACTOMETER, an instrument measuring the refractive index (see REFRACTION) of liquids for a particular color of light: the index is often very sensitive to impurities besides allowing easy determination of the proportions present in two-component mixtures such as water/ethanol.

REFRACTORIES, substances able to resist high temperatures without melting, decomposing or reacting, and hence used for thermal INSULATION and to line FURNACES. Often made into FIREBRICKS, refractories are composed of various substances (mostly oxides), including the acidic FIRECLAY, SILICA and ZIRCON; the basic CHROMITE, DOLOMITE and MAGNESITE; and the neutral CARBORUNDUM, CORUNDUM and GRAPHITE. (See also CERAMICS.)

REFRIGERATION, removal of HEAT from an enclosure in order to lower its TEMPERATURE. It is used for freezing water or food, for FOOD PRESERVATION, for AIR CONDITIONING and for low-temperature chemical processes and CRYOGENICS studies and applications. The ancient Egyptians and Indians used the evaporation of water from porous vessels; and the Chinese, Greeks and Romans used natural ice, a method which became a major industry in the 19th-century US. Modern refrigerators are insulated cabinets containing the cooling elements of a HEAT PUMP. The pump may use mechanical compression of refrigerants such as AMMONIA or FREON, or may accomplish compression by absorbing the refrigerant in a secondary fluid such as water and pumping the solution through a heat exchanger to a generator where it is heated to drive off the refrigerant at high pressure. Other cycles, similar in principle, using steam or air, are also used. Refrigeration based on the PELTIER EFFECT is being developed but is not yet economically competitive.

REFUGEE, person fleeing from his native country to avoid a threat or restriction. In the 15th century MOORS and JEWS were expelled from Spain, and religious refugees fled to the New World in the 17th century. In the 20th century refugees have created a world problem. POGROMS forced Jews to leave Russia; in WWI Greeks and Armenians fled from Turkey and about 1.5 million Russians settled in Europe after the RUSSIAN REVOLUTION. In the 1930s Spaniards and Chinese left their respective homelands. The WWII legacy of about eight million refugees led to the UN Relief and Rehabilitation Administration, replaced in 1946 by the International Refugee Organization. Both resettled millions of homeless, from for example the KOREAN WAR. The many thousand Arabs displaced when Israel was created in 1948 are still in camps and are a serious political problem. The war of BANGLADESH produced over nine million refugees most of whom have subsequently settled in Bangladesh.

REFUSE DISPOSAL. See WASTE DISPOSAL.

REGELATION, the refreezing of ice that has melted under PRESSURE alone, once the pressure is released. Ice skating depends on regelation, but as ice melts readily under pressure only while its temperature is near its FREEZING POINT, skating may not be feasible in very cold weather.

REGENCY STYLE, English architectural and decorative style during the regency and reign of George IV (1811–30). It was characterized by extreme classical elegance, refinement and the use of classical Egyptian and Oriental forms. John NASH was the most noted architect of the period. The term may also be given to the elaborate and fantastic decorative style of the French Régence (1715–23) which developed into ROCOCO.

REGENERATION, the regrowing of a lost or damaged part of an organism. In PLANTS this includes the production of, e.g., dormant buds and adventitious organs. All ANIMALS possess some power to regenerate, but its extent varies from that in sponges, in which all the cells in a piece of the body can be almost completely separated and will yet come together again to build up new but smaller sponges, to that in the higher animals, in which regeneration is limited to the healing of wounds.

REGENERATION, the spiritual rebirth by which the Christian is given new life in Christ. In Catholic theology it is effected in BAPTISM: in Protestant theology it occurs at conversion.

REGENSBURG, (Ratisbon), historic city in Bavaria, W Germany on the Danube R. It is now an industrial center. Pop 129589.

REGER, Max (1873–1916), German composer and pianist best known for his organ music and orchestral works. His music is characterized by elaborately structured polyphonic forms.

REGGIO DI CALABRIA, city in Calabria, S Italy, an agricultural market and resort on the Strait of Messina. Founded by Greek colonists in the 8th century BC, its exports include fruit and tobacco. Pop 162888.

REGIMENT, large body of troops within an army with their own colors, headed by a colonel and divided into companies or battalions. In 1957, the US Army abolished the regiment as a tactical body, but regimental units, although attached to different divisions, continue to carry their colors and identify with their regiments.

REGINA, capital city of Saskatchewan, Canada, about 100mi from the US border. Founded in 1883 as capital of the Northwest Territories and named for Queen Victoria, its economy depends on wheat, meat packing and oil refining. Pop 139468.

REGIOMONTANUS (1436–1476), born **Johann Müller,** Prussian mathematician and astronomer whose *Five Books on all Types of Triangles* (1533) laid the foundations for modern TRIGONOMETRY.

REGNAULT, Henri Victor (1810–1878), German-born French chemist best known for work on the physical properties of gases (e.g., showing that BOYLE'S LAW works only for ideal gases), and for inventing an air THERMOMETER and a HYGROMETER.

REGRESSION, any return to an earlier stage of mental development or mode of behavior. In particular the term describes a (usually unsuccessful) DEFENSE MECHANISM whereby the individual avoids some ANXIETY situation by regressing to an earlier stage of LIBIDO development.

REGULATORS, movement formed in W North Carolina 1764–71, to resist the extortion and oppression of the colonial government officials. After failing to get reforms against excessive taxes, huge legal fees and multiple office holdings, they rose in revolt, but were defeated at Allemance Creek, 1771, by Governor Tryon, who hanged six leaders for treason.

REGULUS, Marcus Atilius (d. c249 BC), Roman general captured in the first PUNIC WAR (255 BC). He was sent to Rome to deliver Carthage's peace terms, under parole to return if they were rejected. He nevertheless urged their rejection, returned and was apparently tortured to death.

REGULUS, Alpha Leonis, the brightest star in LEO. Its apparent magnitude is +1.35 and its distance from the sun 25.75pc. It is a visual triple star.

REHABILITATION, means of enabling the handicapped to lead lives which are as normal as possible considering their disability. The term can cover social disability (treatment of prisoners) as well as physical or mental difficulty. Physical rehabilitation starts once immediate threat to life is absent and its success calls for the active participation of the patient. When the damage has been assessed, a program is designed to stop degeneration of the unaffected parts, to strengthen the injured area and to encourage the patient to accept his handicap realistically. Also efforts are made to remove external sources of anxiety. With the body so strengthened, the patient is prepared for reentry into daily life, through aids and equipment where appropriate, for example, wheelchairs, artificial limbs. Skills are taught, such as braille, and finally help given by social workers in job-finding. In mental disturbances, treatment tries to break down isolation and prevent self-withdrawal through interaction with others. In hospitals, rehabilitation aims to involve patients in social activities and then gradually to detach them from dependence on the center by trips outside until outpatients' visits only are necessary. The federal agency, the Vocational Rehabilitation Administration, makes grants to states to finance programs and encourage their expansion. It carries out research and advises the state agencies who must direct the actual program. Voluntary bodies, charitable foundations and industrial concerns supplement government provisions. (See also OCCUPATIONAL THERAPY.)

REHOBOAM, (c960 BC–c915 BC), last king of united Israel and first king of JUDAH, the S half of the kingdom of Israel. Son and successor of SOLOMON, he was rejected by the N under JEROBOAM.

REICH, Wilhelm (1897–1957), Austrian-born US psychoanalyst best known for his controversial theory that there exists a primal life-giving force, *orgone* energy, in living beings and in the atmosphere. He designed and sold orgone boxes, supposed to concentrate orgone energy in the person within. He died in prison after violating an injunction against selling these boxes.

REICHSTADT, Duke of. See NAPOLEON II.

REICHSTAG, imperial parliament (see DIET) of the Holy Roman Empire, and from 1871–1945 Germany's lower legislative house, the upper being called the Reichsrat. The ruling body of the WEIMAR REPUBLIC, it was a mere cipher under the NAZI regime. The Reichstag building was burnt down in Jan. 1933, probably as a Nazi propaganda trick.

REICHSTEIN, Tadeus (1897–), Polish-born Swiss chemist awarded (with E. C. KENDALL and P. S. HENCH) the 1950 Nobel Prize for Physiology or Medicine for his work, independent of Kendall's, on the corticoids and isolation of what is now known as cortisone (see STEROIDS).

REICHSWEHR, German army rebuilt after WWI, chiefly by Hans von SEECKT, who planned to make it the core of the national army and a mobile shock force.

REID, Thomas (1710–1796), Scottish philosopher who, through his investigations of and rejection of HUME'S skepticism, is regarded as a founder of the COMMON SENSE SCHOOL of philosophy.

REID, Whitelaw (1837–1912), US journalist, ambassador to Britain 1905–12. Editor of the New York *Tribune* 1872–1912, he was Republican vice-presidential candidate in 1892.

REIDSVILLE, city and port in N N.C. and a large tobacco center. Pop 13636.

REIGN OF TERROR, 1793–94, period in the FRENCH REVOLUTION when fanatical reformers of the JACOBINS including ROBESPIERRE, DANTON and Hébert, seized control from the GIRONDINS. They guillotined over 2600 "counterrevolutionaries" (including Danton and Hébert, eventually) in Paris and sanctioned "Terrors" elsewhere, notably in Nantes. The Terror ended with the guillotining of Robespierre himself in July 1794.

REIMARUS, Hermann Samuel (1694–1768), German philosopher admired by G. LESSING. He held that the truths of a natural religion, the existence of a wise God and the immortality of the soul, can be the basis of a universal religion, because they are discoverable by reason. Revealed religion, however, based on miracles and mysteries which can be denied, could not be accepted by all.

REIMS, city in N France, about 100mi E of Paris on the Besle R. Dating from Roman times, it is famed for its Gothic cathedral built 1211–1430. All but two French kings 1179–1825 were crowned in Reims. Center of champagne and woolen production, it also makes chemicals, machinery and paper. Pop 152967.

REINCARNATION. See TRANSMIGRATION OF SOULS.

REINDEER, *Rangifer tarandus*, a large ungainly-looking DEER widely distributed in Europe, Asia and North America, where they are referred to as CARIBOU.

REINDEER LAKE, lake in central Canada, on the Saskatchewan-Manitoba border. Its area is 2467sq mi.

REINDEER MOSS, *Cladonia rangifera*, a LICHEN abounding in N Europe (especially in Lapland), the Siberian tundra and Arctic America, giving winter food for REINDEER. An ESSENTIAL OIL distilled from it can be used in perfumery and the plant can be fermented to yield alcohol (ETHANOL).

REINER, Fritz (1888–1963), Hungarian-born US conductor, director of the orchestras of Cincinnati (1922–28), Pittsburgh (1938–48), Chicago (1953–62), and the Metropolitan Opera (1948–53).

REINHARDT, Django (Jean Baptiste Reinhardt; 1910–1953), Belgian gypsy guitarist who, despite losing the use of two fingers, excelled in the Quintet of the Hot Club of France (1934–39). He was the first foreign musician to influence US JAZZ.

REINHARDT, Max (1873–1943), Austrian theatrical director famous for his vast and spectacular productions—especially of *Oedipus Rex* and *Faust*—and for his elaborate and atmospheric use of stage machinery and management of crowds.

RELAPSING FEVER, INFECTIOUS DISEASE caused by a spirochetal bacterium carried by lice or ticks on rodents and causing episodic FEVER; it occurs in epidemics in areas of poverty and overpopulation. Rash, bleeding and respiratory symptoms are common and the central NERVOUS SYSTEM may be affected. TETRACYCLINES are usually effective in treatment.

RELATIVITY, a frequently referred to but less often understood theory of the nature of space, time and matter. EINSTEIN'S "special theory" of relativity (1905) is based on the premise that different observers moving at a constant speed with respect to each other find the laws of physics to be identical, and, in particular, find the speed of LIGHT waves to be the same (the "principle of relativity"). Among its consequences are that events occurring simultaneously according to one observer may happen at different times according to an observer moving past the first (although the order of two causally related events is never reversed); that a moving object is shortened in the direction of its motion; that time runs more slowly for a moving object; that the velocity of a projectile emitted from a moving body is less than the sum of the relative ejection velocity and the velocity of the body; that a body has a greater MASS when moving than when at rest, and that no body can travel as fast as, or faster than, the speed of light (2.998×10^8m/s—at this speed, a body would have zero length and infinite mass, while time would stand still on it).

These effects are too small to be noticed at normal velocities; they have nevertheless found ample experimental verification, and are commonplace considerations in many physical calculations. The relationship between the position and time of a given event according to different observers is known (for H. A. LORENTZ) as the Lorentz transformation. In this, time mixes on a similar footing with the three spatial dimensions, and it is in this sense that time has been called the "fourth dimension." The greater mass of a moving body implies a relationship between kinetic ENERGY and mass; Einstein made the bold additional hypothesis that *all* energy was equivalent to mass, according to the famous equation $E = mc^2$. The conversion of mass to energy is now the basis of NUCLEAR REACTORS, and is indeed the source of the energy of the sun itself.

Einstein's "general theory" (1916) is of importance chiefly to cosmologists. It asserts the equivalence of the effects of ACCELERATION and gravitational fields (see GRAVITATION), and that gravitational fields cause space to become "curved," so that light no longer travels in straight lines, while the wavelength of light

Regina, the capital city of Saskatchewan, is an oasis of modern bright lights in the midst of vast prairies—very different from its beginnings, when it was called Pile O' Bones.

falls as the light falls through a gravitational field. The direct verification of these last two predictions, among others, has helped deeply to entrench the theory of relativity in the language of physics.

RELIC, in the Roman Catholic Church, an object revered for its association with a holy person, especially a saint—usually all or part of the saint's body, or an article used by him.

RELIEF, form of sculpture in which the elements of the design, whether figures or ornament, project from the background. In **high relief** the elements stand out prominently and may even be undercut; in **low relief** they hardly emerge from the plane of the background. Fine examples of low relief are the PARTHENON friezes. (See also INTAGLIO.)

RELIEF. See WELFARE.

RELIGION, a system of belief to which a social group is committed, in which there is a supernatural object of awe, worship and service. It generally provides a system of ETHICS and a worldview that supply a stable context for each person to relate himself to others and to the world, and to understand his own significance. Religions are found in all societies, and are generally dominant (modern secularism being an exception). Some form of religion seems to fulfill a basic human need. Some features are common to most religions: the recognition of a sacred realm from which supernatural forces operate; a mediating priesthood; the use of ritual to establish a right relationship with the holy (though ritual used to manipulate the supernatural becomes MAGIC); and a sense of group community. It is uncertain by what stages religion evolved; a linear progression from ANIMISM through POLYTHEISM to MONOTHEISM is not now firmly held. (See also DUALISM; MYTHOLOGY; PANTHEISM; DEISM; THEISM.) Some religions have no deity as such, but are natural philosophies: see BUDDHISM; CONFUCIANISM; TAOISM. (See also ANCESTOR WORSHIP; MYTHOLOGY; LITURGY; SACRIFICE; TABOO; THEOLOGY.)

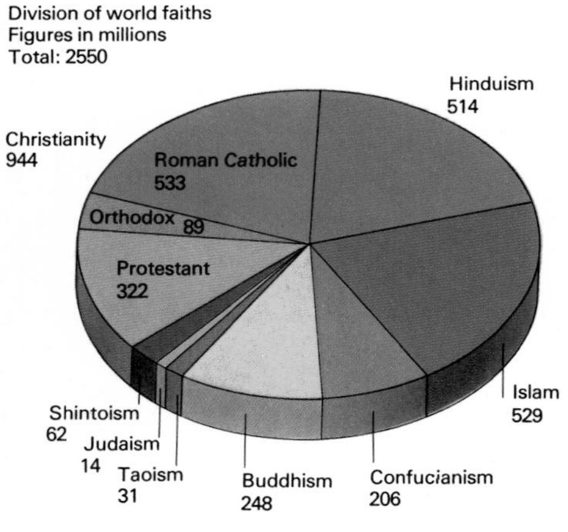

The adherents of the major world religions (figures in millions). The entire pie represents 2550 million people, about 66% of the total world population. The statistics are approximate, especially for the eastern religions; the definitions of an "adherent" may vary widely.

RELIGION, Wars of, French civil wars, 1562–98. They were caused partly by the REFORMATION conflict between the Roman Catholics and the Protestant HUGUENOTS, and partly by the rivalry between the French kings and such great nobles as the dukes of GUISE. The worst event was the SAINT BARTHOLOMEW'S DAY MASSACRE (1572). The Edict of NANTES (1598), established religious freedom and concluded the wars.

REMAGEN, bridge in a town of the same name in Rhineland-Palatinate, West Germany. It was here in March 1945 that US troops, advancing towards Berlin, first crossed the Rhine.

REMAINDER, in the DIVISION of an INTEGER a by another integer b, the least difference between a and a number less than it which is a multiple of b. Thus, dividing 7 by 2, the remainder is 1.

REMARQUE, Erich Maria (1898–1970), German novelist famous for his powerful anti-war *All Quiet on the Western Front* (1929), describing the horror of the trenches in WWI. In 1932 Remarque emigrated to Switzerland, later becoming a US citizen. Other works include *The Night in Lisbon* (1962).

REMBRANDT (Rembrandt Harmensz van Rijn; 1606–1669), greatest of Dutch painters. Born and trained in Leiden, he moved to Amsterdam in 1631 and achieved recognition with a group portrait, *The Anatomy Lesson* (1632). Adapting the styles of CARAVAGGIO, HALS and RUBENS, his painting became, during 1632–42, BAROQUE in style, as in *Saskia as Flora* (1634), *Blinding of Samson* (1636) and *Night Watch* (1642). The years 1643–56 were notable for his magnificent drawings and etchings, predominantly of New Testament themes, such as *The Three Crosses* (1653–61). From mid-1650s his painting was more solemn and spiritual in mood and richer in color as shown in portraits (*Jan Six* 1654, *The Syndics of the Amsterdam Cloth Hall*, 1662), a series of moving self-portraits, and religious paintings like *David and Saul* (c1658).

REMINGTON, Eliphalet (1793–1861), US FIREARMS developer and manufacturer. Under his eldest son, **Philo Remington** (1816–1889), the Remington companies for a time manufactured the Remington SEWING MACHINE (1870–82) and the Remington TYPEWRITER (1873–86).

REMINGTON, Frederic (1861–1909), US painter, sculptor and writer chiefly known for his portrayals of the Old West, where he traveled extensively. His paintings, usually of Indians, cowboys and horses, skillfully convey violent action and are notable for authenticity of detail.

REMONSTRANTS, Dutch ARMINIANS who in 1610 published a *Remonstrance* criticizing the doctrine of PREDESTINATION. The Synod of DORT (1618–19) rejected their views and they were persecuted until 1625. They became an independent church in 1795; a small group survives in the Netherlands.

REMORAS, or **Shark suckers,** curious fishes in which the first dorsal fin has become modified as a large sucking disk over the head, with which they attach themselves to SHARKS, TURTLES and other large marine animals. It is not certain what advantage the remora derives from such attachment, but some fishermen use tethered remoras to catch large fish and turtles.

REMOTE CONTROL, control of a mechanized

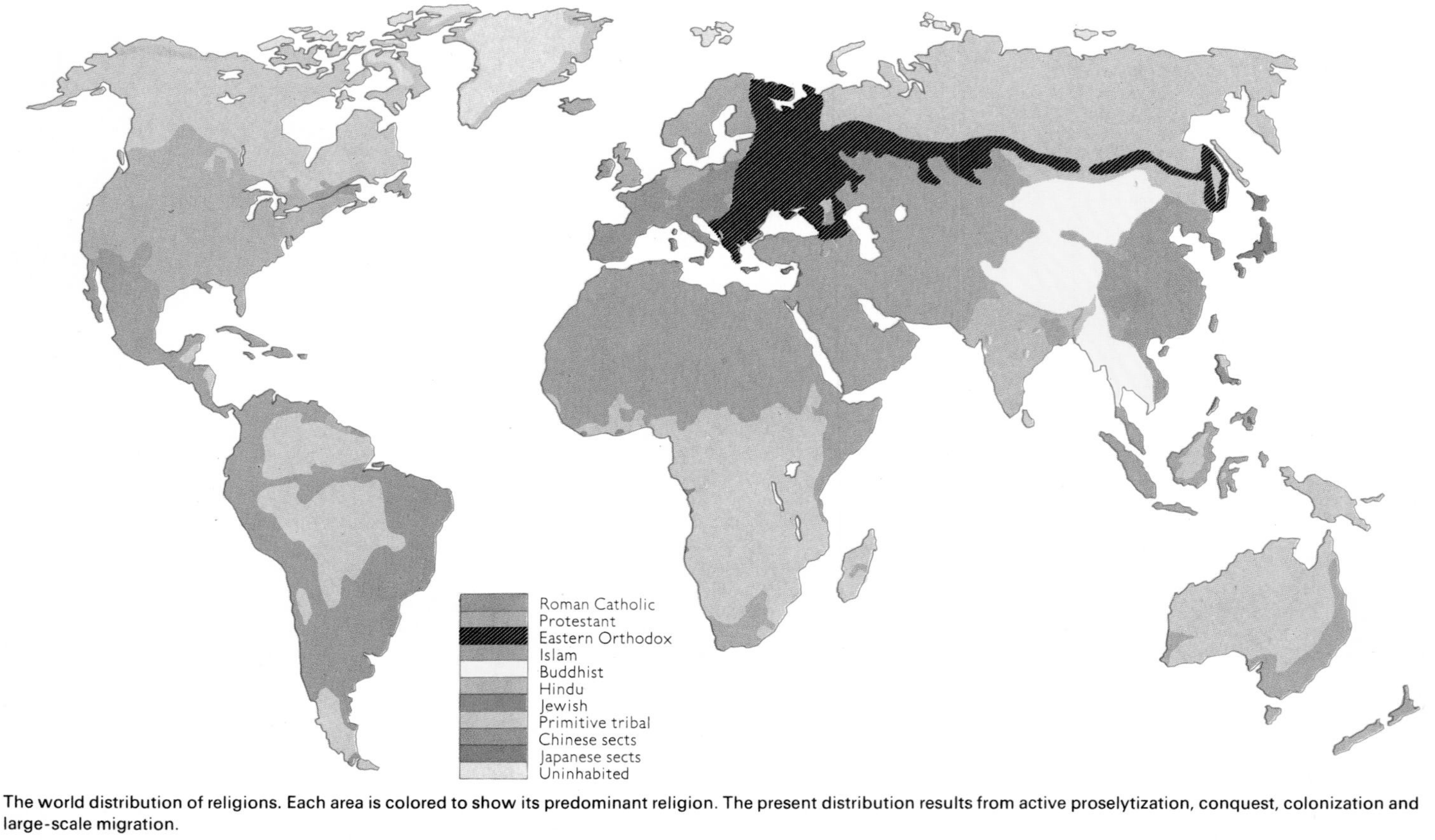

The world distribution of religions. Each area is colored to show its predominant religion. The present distribution results from active proselytization, conquest, colonization and large-scale migration.

The dignity, harmony and order of an ideal Renaissance city is seen in this painting by Piero della Francesca (c1472; Urbino), which also exemplifies his mastery of perspective, the theory of which he largely developed.

system from afar. Signals are sent from a control center by electrical circuits or radio to trigger or guide an operation elsewhere. There is usually FEEDBACK to the control center. (See also MECHANIZATION AND AUTOMATION.)

REMSEN, Ira (1846–1927), US chemist who, with his student **Constantin Fahlberg** (1850–1910), discovered SACCHARIN (1879).

REMUS. See ROMULUS AND REMUS.

REMUS, Uncle. See HARRIS, JOEL CHANDLER.

RENAISSANCE (French: rebirth or revival), the transitional period between the MIDDLE AGES and modern times, covering the years c1350–c1650. The term was first applied by the historian BURCKHARDT in 1860. The Renaissance was a period of deeply significant achievement and change. It saw the REFORMATION challenge the unity and supremacy of the Roman Catholic Church, along with the rise of HUMANISM, the growth of large nation-states with powerful kings, far-ranging voyages of exploration and a new emphasis on the importance of the individual. It was a period of extraordinary accomplishment in the arts, in scholarship and the sciences, typified in the universal genius of LEONARDO DA VINCI. The origins of the Renaissance are disputed, but its first flowering occurred in Italy. In the world of learning a new interest in secular Latin literature can be detected in the early 14th century, and by the middle of the century PETRARCH and BOCCACCIO were avidly searching for old texts and self-consciously cultivating a prose style modeled on CICERO. They inaugurated an age of research and discovery in which the humanists ransacked the monastic libraries of Europe for old manuscripts, and such scholars as FICINO, BESSARION, POLITIAN, VALLA and ERASMUS set new standards in learning and critical scholarship. Greek was also studied, particularly after the fall of Constantinople in 1453 drove many Greek scholars to the West. The invention of printing (c1440) and the discovery of the New World (1492) by COLUMBUS gave further impetus to the search for knowledge.

The Renaissance marked the end of FEUDALISM and the rise of national governments, in Spain under FERDINAND II of Aragon, in France under FRANCIS I, in England under HENRY VIII and ELIZABETH I, and in Holland. In Italy, however, independent city states—Ferrara, Florence, Mantua, Milan, Venice, papal Rome—engaged in fierce rivalry, providing MACHIAVELLI with his famous "ideal" of a Renaissance prince. Prosperous trading provided money for the arts, and princes like Cosimo de' MEDICI eagerly patronized artists, musicians and scholars. Renaissance PAINTING and SCULPTURE flourished in Florence and Rome with the works of BOTTICELLI, MICHELANGELO and RAPHAEL. Literary revivals occurred in England, France and Spain; SHAKESPEARE and SPENSER were prominent in Renaissance ENGLISH LITERATURE and some of the finest French writing came from RABELAIS and RONSARD. *Musica Reservata*, composed by JOSQUIN DES PRES and LASSUS, was among the styles of Renaissance music. In science the findings of the astronomers COPERNICUS and GALILEO were the basis of modern astronomy and marked a turning point in scientific and philosophical thought.

RENAN, Joseph Ernest (1823–1892), French historian and orientalist. Agnostic and subtly ironical, he wrote on the origins of Christianity, notably the *Life of Jesus* (1863). Among many other works is the *History of the People of Israel* (1887–93).

RENAULT, Louis (1843–1918), French jurist who was devoted to the advancement and practice of international law. He was professor at the University of Paris and served also on the HAGUE TRIBUNAL. In 1907 he shared the Nobel Peace Prize.

One of the best-known Renaissance portraits is Piero della Francesca's *Federigo da Montefeltro* (c1465; Uffizi, Florence). The court of Federigo, duke of Urbino, was an important cultural center.

RENÉ OF ANJOU (1409–1480), duke of Anjou and Provence. He inherited a claim to the kingdom of Naples (1435) but was defeated by ALFONSO V of Aragon in 1442. His daughter MARGARET OF ANJOU married HENRY VI of England. René's court at Angers in France was a brilliant cultural center.

RENI, Guido (1575–1642), Italian BAROQUE painter. After studying at the CARRACCI academy he developed an elegant classical style, using light tones, for religious and mythological themes, such as *Aurora* (1613–14) and *Baptism of Christ* (1623).

RENNER, Karl (1870–1950), Austrian socialist statesman. He was the Austrian Republic's first chancellor (1919–20), president of parliament (1931–33) and, after heading the provisional government, president of Austria, 1945–50.

RENNES, historic city in NW France. Once an important Gallo-Roman town, it is now a commercial, textile and leather center. Pop 197 500.

RENNET, a commercial preparation for curdling or junketing MILK. It is prepared from the ENZYME rennin. This solidifies milk in the stomach of young animals, increasing its retention time and thus improving the animal's digestive efficiency.

RENO, second-largest city in Nev., seat of Washoe Co. on the Truchee R. A major tourist resort, it fully

Frederic Remington's *Cavalry Charge on the Southern Plains*, typical of his vigorous and authentic portrayal of the old American West.

1

2

3

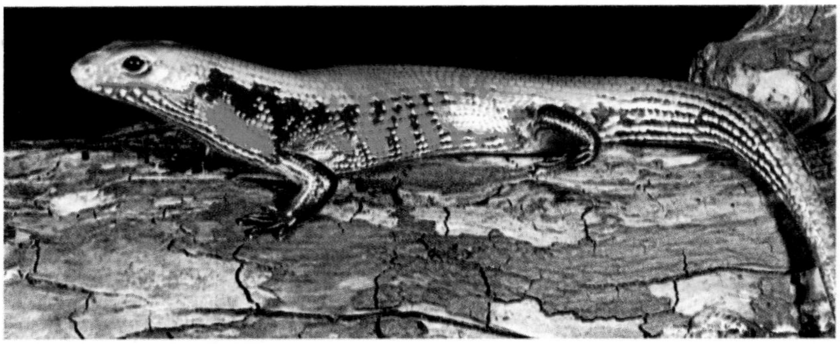
4

5

6

Some of the various kinds of reptiles. (1) Two young alligators; these feed mainly on insects, mice etc., while the adults feed on large prey and hence are dangerous to human beings. (2) The green iguana, a large herbivorous lizard found in the tropical rain forests of South America. (3) A python, one of the giant snakes. Note the mouth opening, through which the snake protrudes its tongue, which it uses as an organ of smell and touch. (4–5) Two of the many species of skink. Skinks are found in various habitats, from desert to rainforest. (6) The Greek tortoise.

exploits the state's liberal gambling and divorce laws. Pop 72 863.

RENOIR, Jean (1894–), French film director, son of Pierre Auguste RENOIR. His motion pictures are characterized by a sensitive feeling for atmosphere and a strong pictorial sense. *La grande illusion* (1937) and *The Rules of the Game* (1939) are his masterpieces.

RENOIR, Pierre Auguste (1841–1919), French Impressionist painter. He started painting—with MONET, PISSARRO and SISLEY—scenes of Parisian life, such as *La Grenouillère* (1869) and *The Swing* (1876), using vibrant luminous colors. After IMPRESSIONISM he became mostly interested in figure painting, and his later works are usually large female nudes set in rich landscapes.

RENSSELAER, commercial city in E N.Y., on the Hudson R. A 17th-century Dutch settlement, it now manufactures chemicals and concrete. Pop 10 136.

RENSSELAER, Stephen van. See VAN RENSSELAER, STEPHEN.

RENT, in law, the price a tenant pays for the use of another's property; and in economics, any income or yield from something capable of producing wealth. In general usage the term now covers the monetary return for the use of anything–whether it be real estate, cars or computers. From the 16th to the 18th centuries rent meant interest on a loan. Gradually, however, the term came to signify a fixed periodic return on land, and as such featured in the theories of the PHYSIOCRATS and of the classical economists, Adam SMITH and David RICARDO, as an important economic factor.

RENTON, industrial city in W Wash., suburb of Seattle, and port on Lake Washington. It manufactures steel and aircraft. Pop 26 648.

RENWICK, James (1818–1895), US architect who designed Grace Church (1843–46) and St. Patrick's Cathedral (dedicated 1879), New York, and other notable buildings, including the SMITHSONIAN INSTITUTION (1846) and Vassar College (1860).

REPARATIONS, term applied since WWI to monetary compensation demanded by victorious nations for material losses suffered in war. In 1919 Germany was committed to pay enormous reparations to the Allies (although the US subsequently waived all claim). Again, in 1945, reparations were exacted from Germany, and Japan was also assessed.

REPENTIGNY, town in S Quebec, Canada, a residential suburb of Montreal. Pop 19 441.

REPLICATION. See NUCLEIC ACIDS.

REPOUSSÉ, metalwork, usually of gold or silver, where the design, in relief, has been hammered out from a thin sheet. (See also EMBOSSING.)

REPRESENTATIVES, House of. See CONGRESS OF THE UNITED STATES.

REPRESSION, the DEFENSE MECHANISM whereby an impulse or idea is restricted by the EGO or SUPEREGO to the UNCONSCIOUS (primary repression), or in which derivatives of it are similarly restricted (secondary repression). FREUD considered primary repression essential to ego-development. (See also INHIBITION.)

REPRIEVE, in criminal law, the postponement of a sentence, usually a stay of execution of a death sentence. In the US the state governor or the president may grant a reprieve. (See also PARDON.)

REPRODUCTION, the process by which an organism produces offspring, an ability that is a unique characteristic of ANIMALS and PLANTS. There are two kinds of reproduction: asexual and sexual. In **asexual reproduction**, parts of an organism split off to form new individuals, a process found in some animals but which is more common in plants: e.g., the FISSION of single-celled plants; the budding of YEASTS; the fragmentation of filamentous ALGAE; SPORE production in BACTERIA, algae and FUNGI, and the production of vegetative organs in flowering plants (bulbs, rhizomes and tubers). In **sexual reproduction**, special (haploid) CELLS containing half the normal number of CHROMOSOMES, called gametes, are produced: in animals, sperm by males in the TESTES and ova by females in the OVARY; in plants, pollen by males in the stamens and ovules by females in the ovary. The joining of gametes (FERTILIZATION) produces a (diploid) cell with the normal number of chromosomes, the zygote, which grows to produce an individual with GENES inherited from both parents (see also HEREDITY). Fertilization may take place inside the female (internal fertilization) or outside (external fertilization). Internal fertilization demands that sperm be introduced into the female—insemination by copulation—and is advantageous because the young spend the most vulnerable early stages of their life-histories protected inside the mother.

At the molecular level, the most important aspect of reproduction is the ability of the chromosome to duplicate itself (see NUCLEIC ACIDS). The production of haploid cells is made possible by a process called MEIOSIS and is necessary to prevent doubling of the chromosome number with each generation in sexually reproducing individuals. The advantage of sexual reproduction is that the bringing together of genes derived from two individuals produces variation in each generation enabling populations to change and thus adapt themselves to changing environmental conditions (see also EVOLUTION; NATURAL SELECTION).

REPTILES, once one of the most numerous and diverse groups of animals, today reduced to four groups: the CROCODILES; the LIZARDS and SNAKES; the TORTOISES and TURTLES; and the TUATARA. Modern reptiles are characterized by a scaly skin, simple teeth in the jaw, and an undivided heart. They are cold-blooded, and sexual reproduction results in the laying of large yolky eggs. However, when fossil groups are considered the class is not so clearly defined, for the later reptiles merge with their avian and mammalian descendants. Many were fur-covered and warm-blooded and had developed other features of present-day birds and mammals. Some may even have been viviparous.

REPTON, Humphry (1752–1818), English landscape designer. Influenced by the Picturesque movement, his gardens aimed at a gradual transition between the house and its surroundings. (See LANDSCAPE ARCHITECTURE.)

REPUBLIC (from Latin *res publica*: the state), form of government in which the head of state is not a monarch, and today is usually a president. Popularly, the idea of a republic includes the notion of elected representation and democratic control by the people, but many modern republics do not fulfill this condition. *The Republic* is also the name of the famous dialogue in which PLATO outlined his ideal state.

REPUBLIC, Fund for the, US educational corporation set up in 1952 to defend and advance the principles of the UNITED STATES CONSTITUTION, the DECLARATION OF INDEPENDENCE and the BILL OF RIGHTS. Supported by the FORD FOUNDATION and other donors, it initiates political and ideological studies.

REPUBLICAN PARTY, one of the two major political parties of the US. It was founded in 1854 by dissidents of the WHIG, DEMOCRATIC and FREE SOIL parties to unify the growing anti-slavery forces. Its first national nominating convention was held in 1856; J. C. FRÉMONT was adopted as presidential candidate. Campaigning on the abolition of slavery and of polygamy in the territories, he captured 11 states. LINCOLN became the first Republican president, and in spite of the unpopularity of the subsequent RECONSTRUCTION policies and the secession of the LIBERAL REPUBLICAN PARTY in 1872, the Republicans remained dominant in US politics, winning 14 out of 18 presidential elections between 1860 and 1932. In an era of scandal, the Republicans consolidated a "pro-business" and "conservative" reputation with the nomination and election of William McKINLEY in 1896. His successor Theodore ROOSEVELT adopted a progressive stance; he defected to the Bull Moose party (see PROGRESSIVE PARTY) in 1912. In 1932 the Democrats swept to power, not to be dislodged until the election of the Republican president EISENHOWER in 1952. His successors KENNEDY and JOHNSON were Democrats. Barry GOLDWATER failed as presential candidate in 1960, but Richard NIXON's landslide victory in 1972 marked a zenith of party strength. WATERGATE shattered this, contributing to the defeat of Gerald FORD in the 1976 elections.

REPUBLICAN RIVER, a river, 422mi long, rising in E Col. and flowing through Neb. and Kan. It unites with Smoky Hill R to form the Kansas R.

REQUIEM, or **Requiem Mass,** a musical setting of the Roman Catholic MASS for the souls of the dead. The classic settings of the Requiem by MOZART and VERDI are generally performed as concert pieces.

REREDOS, an ornamental wall or screen behind the altar in a church. Originally a tapestry, it became a permanent architectural feature, usually of stone or wood and often containing sculpted figures in a richly decorated framework.

RESACA DE LA PALMA, Battle of, second battle of the MEXICAN WAR. On May 9, 1846, after the engagement at PALO ALTO the previous day, US forces under General Zachary TAYLOR pursued and routed the retreating Mexicans.

RESEARCH, the use of appropriate methods in attempting to discover new knowledge or to develop new applications of existing knowledge or to explore relationships between ideas or events. Scientific discoveries, technological achievements and scholarly publications are all the fruits of research. Every discipline develops research methods and tools appropriate to its subject matter; but whether undertaken by scholar, technologist or scientist, research always involves three basic steps: the formulation of a problem; the collection and analysis of relevant information, and a concerted attempt to discover a solution or otherwise resolve the problem in a manner dictated by the available evidence. Quite different kinds of initial problem may be formulated. In the field of science and technology, for example, fundamental (or properly scientific) research aims at enlarging man's understanding of observable phenomena; the search is for general explanatory principles. Unlike applied (or technological) research, fundamental research is not explicitly directed toward the solution of a practical problem, although its results may, and usually do, suggest new technological possibilities. Knowledge of atomic structure is a goal of fundamental research; possible applications of this knowledge—nuclear power plants and weapons—demand technological research and development. In practice, however, the distinction is less clear-cut: accidental scientific discoveries are often made by research workers pursuing a technological goal. (See also SCIENTIFIC METHOD.)

RESERPINE. See RAUWOLFIA SERPENTINA.

RESERVE CURRENCY, used in foreign trade by governments and others, and held in quantity in their reserves. The viability of the dollar and sterling as the West's two major reserve currencies has been undermined by BALANCE OF PAYMENTS deficits and DEVALUATION.

RESERVE OFFICER TRAINING CORPS (ROTC), US Army recruiting project that holds courses in military leadership in schools and colleges. It grew out of the Land Grant Act of 1862, and began operating full scale under the National Defense Act of 1916. It comprises two to four years of course work and drill plus six weeks of field training. The US Navy and Air Force have similar programs.

RESHEVSKY, Samuel (1911–), Polish-born US chess player. Formerly a child prodigy, he was US champion five times between 1936 and 1946, and one of the great modern masters of the game.

RESIDUE, in mathematics, see MODULUS.

RESIN, a high-molecular-weight substance characterized by its gummy or tacky consistency at certain temperatures. Naturally occurring resins include congo copal and BITUMEN (found as fossils), SHELLAC (from insects) and **rosin** (from pine trees). Synthetic resins include the wide variety of plastic materials available today and any distinction between PLASTICS and resins is at best arbitrary. The first partially synthetic resins were produced in 1862 using NITROCELLULOSE, vegetable OILS and CAMPHOR, and included Xylonite and later, in 1869, CELLULOID. The first totally synthetic resin was BAKELITE, which was produced by L. H. BAEKELAND in 1910 from PHENOL and FORMALDEHYDE. The work in the 1920s of H. STAUDINGER on the polymeric nature of natural RUBBER and STYRENE resin, which laid the theoretical basis for POLYMER science, was a major factor in stimulating the extremely rapid development of a wide range of synthetic plastics and resins.

RESISTANCE, the ratio of the voltage applied to a conductor to the current flowing through it (see ELECTRICITY; OHM'S LAW), measured in OHMS. It is characteristic of the material of which the conductor is made (the resistance presented by a unit cube of a material being called its **resistivity**) and of the physical dimensions of the conductor, increasing as the conductor becomes longer and/or thinner. Resistance rises with TEMPERATURE in METALS, but falls in SEMICONDUCTORS and SOLUTIONS. Its accurate measurement is performed by the WHEATSTONE BRIDGE method.

RESONANCE, the large response of an oscillatory mechanical, acoustical or electrical system driven near its natural FREQUENCY. The ENERGY dissipation (against FRICTION, etc.) of all practical systems is termed *damping*: the amount of damping controls both the size of the resonant response and the sharpness of the resonance as a function of frequency.

RESONANCE, in chemistry, theory of molecular structure in which the actual state of the bonding in a molecule is expressed as a "resonance hybrid" between two or more valence-bond structures (see BOND, CHEMICAL), and is intermediate between them, but of lower energy. There is no actual oscillation, and the model is equivalent to molecular ORBITAL theory. First proposed for BENZENE, resonance stabilizes AROMATIC COMPOUNDS and conjugated double-bond systems such as 1,3-BUTADIENE.

RESORCINOL (m-$C_6H_4(OH)_2$), one of the dihydric PHENOLS, a colorless crystalline solid made by sulfonation (see SULFONIC ACIDS) of benzene followed by fusion with sodium hydroxide. It is used to make adhesives, formaldehyde RESINS, DYES, EXPLOSIVES, photographic developers, and as an ANTISEPTIC. (See also FLUORESCEIN.) MW 110.1, mp 111°C, bp 281°C.

RESOURCE ALLOCATION, the apportionment of relatively scarce land and natural resources, labor and capital among different uses, by means ranging from LAISSEZ-FAIRE policies to economic planning. It is a major preoccupation of MICROECONOMICS.

RESPIGHI, Ottorino (1879–1936), Italian composer, director (1924–26) of the Accademia di Santa Cecilia in Rome. He is best known for such tone poems as *The Fountains of Rome* (1917) and *The Pines of Rome* (1924).

RESPIRATION, term applied to several activities and processes occurring in all ANIMALS and PLANTS: e.g., the breathing movements associated with the LUNGS, the uptake of OXYGEN and the release of CARBON dioxide, and the biochemical pathways by which the ENERGY locked in food materials is transferred to energy-rich organic molecules for utilization in the multitude of energy-requiring processes which occur in an organism. Breathing movements, if any, and the exchange of oxygen and carbon dioxide, may be called "external respiration," while the energy-releasing processes which utilize the oxygen and produce carbon dioxide are termed "internal respiration" or "tissue respiration." In man, external respiration is the process whereby air is breathed from the environment into the lungs to provide oxygen for internal respiration. Air, which contains about 20% oxygen, is drawn into the lungs via the NOSE or MOUTH, the PHARYNX, TRACHEA and

BRONCHI. This is achieved by muscular contraction of the intercostal muscles in the CHEST wall and of the DIAPHRAGM; their coordinated movement, controlled by a respiratory center in the BRAIN stem, causes expansion of the chest, and thus of the lung tissue, so that air is drawn in (inspiration). Expiration is usually a passive process of relaxation of the chest wall and diaphragm, allowing the release of the air, which is by now depleted of oxygen and enriched with carbon dioxide. Exchange of gases with the BLOOD circulating in the pulmonary capillaries occurs across the lung alveoli and follows simple diffusion gradients. Disorders of respiration include lung disease (e.g., EMPHYSEMA, PNEUMONIA and PNEUMOCONIOSIS); muscle and nerve disease (e.g., brain-stem STROKE, POLIOMYELITIS, MYASTHENIA GRAVIS and MUSCULAR DYSTROPHY); skeletal deformity; ASPHYXIA, and disorders secondary to metabolic and HEART disease. In man, tissue respiration involves the combination of oxygen with GLUCOSE or other nutrients to form high-energy compounds. This reaction also produces carbon dioxide and water.

RESPIRATION, Artificial. See ARTIFICIAL RESPIRATION.

RESPONSIBLE GOVERNMENT, a government whose executive is responsible to an elected legislature. An example is the British Cabinet, which is answerable to the elected House of Commons.

RESTIGOUCHE RIVER, 130mi-long river in New Brunswick, Canada. It is known for its trout and salmon fishing.

RESTON, James Barrett (1909–), Scottish-born US journalist who won Pulitzer Prizes in 1944 and 1957. He has been associated with the *New York Times* since 1939, being its vice-president 1969–74.

RESTORATION, name given to the return of CHARLES II as king of England in 1660, after the fall of the PROTECTORATE. Coinciding with a national mood of reaction against the PURITANS, the Restoration was widely popular. The Restoration period (1660 to the fall of JAMES II in 1688) was one of irreverent wit, licentiousness and scientific and literary achievement (see RESTORATION COMEDY). Politically, it was a period of uneasy relations between king and parliament, culminating in the GLORIOUS REVOLUTION.

RESTORATION COMEDY, name given to the witty, bawdy and often satirical comedies written after the reopening of the theaters at the RESTORATION. Masters of the genre include CONGREVE, ETHEREGE, FARQUAR, OTWAY, VANBRUGH and WYCHERLEY.

RESUMPTION ACT, 1875, US government act fixing Jan. 1, 1879, as the date on which payments in specie (i.e., coin) would be resumed. Resumption actually took place on Dec. 17, 1878.

RESURRECTION, the raising of a dead person to life. The resurrection of JESUS CHRIST on the third day from his death and burial is a basic Christian doctrine attested by earliest New Testament tradition. In recognizable but glorified bodily form he appeared to several groups of disciples; though skeptical, they became convinced that he had overcome death. Christians' eternal life is viewed as participation in Christ's resurrection life, culminating in the general bodily resurrection of the dead at the SECOND COMING (see also ESCHATOLOGY; IMMORTALITY).

RESURRECTION PLANTS, popular name for plants that roll up into balls when dry, but open up and become green when wet. Examples are the ROSE OF JERICHO, the moss-like *Selaginella lepidophylla* and the resurrection fern, *Polypodium polypodioides*.

RETICULO-ENDOTHELIAL SYSTEM, generic name for those CELLS in the body that take up dyes and other foreign material from the BLOOD stream and other body fluids; they are also known as **macrophages**. Blood monocytes are functionally part of the system as are macrophages in the LYMPH nodes, SPLEEN, BONE MARROW, LIVER (Kupffer cells) and LUNG alveoli. When foreign material (e.g., BACTERIA) is introduced into the blood stream, macrophages rapidly take it up and destroy it with intracellular ENZYMES. This constitutes a primary defence system and may play a role in establishing IMMUNITY. Similarly, particulate matter in the lungs or liver is cleared by local macrophages.

RETINA, part of the EYE responsible for conversion of LIGHT into nerve impulses; it contains nerve cells including the rod and cone receptors for light/dark and color VISION respectively.

RETINOL, or vitamin A. See VITAMINS.

RETROGRADE MOTION, the apparent backward (i.e. westward) motion of a PLANET due to the earth's own motion (see ORBIT); also, the motion of any SOLAR SYSTEM body rotating or orbiting in the opposite (clockwise as viewed from the N celestial pole) direction to the majority.

RETROLENTAL FIBROPLASIA, a form of BLINDNESS occurring in premature babies exposed to high OXYGEN concentrations during the treatment of respiratory distress syndrome. Moderation in the use of oxygen and prevention of prematurity have reduced its incidence.

RETTING, the decomposition of the organic tissues of plants by microorganisms, usually while immersed in water. Resistant components such as CELLULOSE fibers are left behind. Retting is used in the processing of FLAX, HEMP and JUTE.

RETZ, Gilles de. See RAIS, GILLES DE.

REUBEN, in the Old Testament, the eldest son of JACOB and Leah; saved his brother Joseph from being killed. A PATRIARCH, he was the progenitor of one of the TWELVE TRIBES OF ISRAEL.

RÉUNION, volcanic island (970sq mi) in the W Indian Ocean, an overseas department of France since 1947. The islanders, mostly of mixed descent, are nearly all Roman Catholic and speak a Creole patois. Its products include sugar, rum and vanilla. The capital is St. Denis. Pop 455 200.

REUTER, Ernst (1889–1953), German political leader. He became a communist in 1916 as a prisoner of war in Russia, but in 1922 rejoined the German Social Democratic Party. In exile 1935–46, he returned to become mayor of West Berlin from 1948.

REUTERS, an international news agency, based in Britain, which distributes information to local agencies, newspapers, television and radio around the world. Founded by P. J. von Reuter (1816–1899) in Germany in 1849, it moved to London 1851, and is today a trust owned mainly by the British press.

REUTHER, Walter Philip (1907–1970), US labor leader, president of the UNITED AUTOMOBILE WORKERS from 1946 until his death in a plane crash. He was president of the Congress of Industrial Organizations 1952–56, and one of the architects of its merger with the AMERICAN FEDERATION OF LABOR, becoming vice-president of the combined organization.

REVEL. See TALLINN.

REVELATION, the disclosure of truths by God, either directly to PROPHETS or by inspiring Scripture (see BIBLE; KORAN). Whether propositional or embodied in God's "mighty acts," it is the basis of **revealed theology** as opposed to NATURAL THEOLOGY. Protestants hold that revelation is sufficiently contained in the Bible; Roman Catholics and Orthodox regard TRADITION as revelatory.

REVELATION, Book of, or **Apocalypse,** the last book of the NEW TESTAMENT, traditionally ascribed to St. JOHN the Apostle but probably by another John, and dated probably c96. After seven letters to the Asia Minor churches, it is a series of apocalyptic visions in Old Testament imagery, giving a Christian philosophy of world history.

REVELS, Hiram Rhoades (1822–1901), pastor and educator, and first black US senator. Elected by the Republicans in Miss. for 1870–71, he was subsequently involved in state politics and became president of Alcorn College, Lorman, Miss.

REVELSTOKE, Mount, mountain, over 7000ft high, in the Mount Revelstoke National Park in SE British Columbia, Canada.

REVERBERATION. See ACOUSTICS.

REVERE, city in E Mass., named for Paul REVERE. It is a residential suburb of Boston with some light industry. Pop 43 159.

REVERE, Paul (1735–1818), American revolutionary hero, immortalized by LONGFELLOW for his ride from Boston to Lexington (April 18, 1775) to warn the Massachussetts minutemen that "the British are coming." A silversmith and engraver, he joined in the BOSTON TEA PARTY in 1773. During the REVOLUTIONARY WAR, he served the new government, designing and producing the first Continental money, casting official seals and supervising gunpowder and cannon manufacture. After the war he became a prosperous merchant, known for his copper and silver work and his bronze bells.

REVISIONISM, term originally applied to the theories of Eduard BERNSTEIN, who attempted to revise some of MARX's doctrines. It has become a term of abuse in communist polemics, signifying the alleged deviation from or betrayal of true Marxist principles.

REVIVALS, intense renewals of religious fervor, especially those of the EVANGELICAL REVIVAL. PENTECOST and the REFORMATION may be regarded as earlier revivals. In modern times "revival" has come to mean a popular, emotional campaign (see CAMP MEETINGS), usually led by professional evangelists such as Billy GRAHAM.

REVOLUTION, sudden, forced change of an established government, transforming the social and political order. There are cases of "bloodless" revolutions like the English GLORIOUS REVOLUTION (1688), but violence generally occurs when a ruling group is overthrown. Failed revolutions are often called "rebellions," "risings" or "insurrections." A violent change of government which replaces only the personnel in power, but leaves the political order as a whole unaltered, is usually termed a *coup d'état*. The term "revolution" is also applied to radical changes occurring over a period of time, like the INDUSTRIAL REVOLUTION. The idea of a proletarian revolution against capitalism is central to MARXISM.

REVOLUTIONARY WAR, American, in which Britain's 13 colonies gained their independence. It was a minor war with immense consequences—the founding of the US, and the forging of a new, dynamic democratic ideology in an age of absolutism. Despite elements of civil war and of revolution, the conflict was above all a political, constitutional struggle, and as such began many years before the actual fighting. While the expanding colonies were growing wealthy and independent, Britain adhered to the theory that they were supposed to exist solely for its own profit, and were to be tightly ruled by King and Parliament (see MERCANTILISM; NAVIGATION ACTS). Up to 1763, however, control was lax; but after France had been defeated in the New World (see FRENCH AND INDIAN WARS) Britain decided to restore control and tax the colonies to help pay for it. The Navigation Acts were strictly enforced (see SUGAR ACT), settlement beyond the Appalachian Mountains was forbidden, a standing army was to be sent to America and quartered at colonial expense, and in 1765 a stamp tax (see STAMP ACT) was imposed. The outraged colonists, near rebellion, drew upon liberal ideas from England and the continent (see ENGLIGHTENMENT) to assert the principle of no taxation without representation in the English Parliament. After duties levied by the TOWNSHEND ACTS (1767) resistance centered in Boston, leading to the BOSTON MASSACRE (1770) and the BOSTON TEA PARTY (1773). But after the INTOLERABLE ACTS (1774), aimed at Boston, patriot local assemblies took control in all colonies, and non-importation associations and COMMITTEES OF CORRESPONDENCE flourished, culminating in the First CONTINENTAL CONGRESS (1774). In April-June 1775 fighting flared around disaffected Boston (see battles of LEXINGTON; CONCORD; BUNKER HILL), and in July George WASHINGTON took command of the Continental Army. In March 1776 the British were forced to evacuate Boston, but an American attempt to conquer Canada (1775–76) failed. Meantime the Second CONTINENTAL CONGRESS, emboldened by Thomas PAINE's pamphlet *Common Sense*, declared for independence in July 1776. (See Special Article on DECLARATION OF INDEPENDENCE.)

Washington, with never more than 10–20000 regulars, plus state militia (see MINUTEMEN), fought a defensive war; the British, with regulars, Tories and mercenaries (see HESSIANS), suffered from confused strategy and extended supply lines across the ocean, and were hindered by the small US Navy and some 2000 privateers (see JONES, JOHN PAUL). After a brief strike at the South, the British took New York City in September 1776, forcing Washington to retreat into New Jersey. The small victories of TRENTON and

PRINCETON heartened the patriots, but Philadelphia fell in September 1777. Meantime General BURGOYNE, sweeping down into New York from Canada, was forced to surrender his troops at SARATOGA in October, an American triumph that brought France in as an ally of the US. But Washington, wintering at VALLEY FORGE, was barely able to keep his troops together.

Turning to the South, the British took Savannah (1778) and Charleston (1780), defeating GATES at CAMDEN, S.C. in August, 1780. But after the defeat of KINGS MOUNTAIN in October, the British gradually withdrew N into Va. In 1781 CORNWALLIS, bottled up in Yorktown, Va. by a French fleet and a Franco-American army under Washington, surrendered on October 19, virtually ending the war, though the Treaty of PARIS was not signed until September 3, 1783. The ideological struggle, which had found its best expression in the Declaration of Independence, came to a noble conclusion with the framing of the Constitution in 1787. (See also UNITED STATES CONSTITUTION.)

REVOLUTION OF 1688. See GLORIOUS REVOLUTION.

REVOLUTIONS OF 1848, series of unsuccessful revolutionary uprisings in France, Italy, the Austrian Empire and Germany in 1848. They were relatively spontaneous and self-contained, but had a number of common causes: the successful example of the FRENCH REVOLUTION of 1789, economic unrest due to bad harvests and unemployment, and a growing frustration, fired by nationalist fervor, about the repressive policies of conservative statesmen like METTERNICH and GUIZOT. In Feb. 1848, a major uprising in Paris overthrew King LOUIS PHILIPPE and Guizot, but it was suppressed and the Second Republic proclaimed. In Italy, during the RISORGIMENTO, short-lived republics were proclaimed, and there was agitation to secure independence from Austria, which was itself shaken by revolutions in Vienna, Prague and Hungary. The demand for a representative government led to an all-German Diet in Frankfurt, which failed in its efforts to unite Germany. In England there was working-class agitation (see CHARTISM), and other European countries were also affected.

REVOLVER, a small hand firearm, or PISTOL, incorporating an automatic loading mechanism in the form of a revolving cylinder. The cylinder contains usually five or six chambers into which cartridges are inserted, and activation of the trigger mechanism, in addition to firing a bullet, automatically aligns a fresh chamber with the breech of the barrel. The first practical revolver design was patented in 1836 by Samuel COLT.

REX CAT, curly-coated breed of cat, developed from accidental mutations, which lacks the guard hairs that form most of other cats' fur. Although of domestic-type stock, all Rex show a "foreign" body type.

REXROTH, Kenneth (1905–), US poet, translator, painter and journalist. He belonged to the BEAT GENERATION of the 1950s, and his works include *The Dragon and the Unicorn* (1952) and *In Defense of the Earth* (1956).

REYES, Point. See POINT REYES NATIONAL SEASHORE.

REYES, Rafael (1850–1921), president of Colombia 1904–09. After 10 years exploring the Amazon jungles, he fought in the civil wars 1885–95. Dictatorial as president, he resigned over his treaty with the US recognizing an independent Panama.

REYKJAVÍK, capital of Iceland and its chief port, commercial and industrial center, and home of its cod-fishing fleet. Its name means "smoking bay," from the nearby hot springs which provide the city with central heating. Pop 81 684.

REYNARD THE FOX, leading character in a popular medieval series of FABLES. Appearing first in the area between Flanders and Germany in the 10th century, the tales, with their cunning but sympathetic hero and biting satire, became popular in France, Germany and the Low Countries.

REYNAUD, Paul (1878–1966), Conservative French statesman. An opponent of the NAZIS, he became premier in 1940, but resigned and spent WWII in prison. Afterwards he returned to politics, held several posts and helped draft the constitution of the Fifth Republic (1958).

Revolutionary War: British general John Burgoyne surrenders to General Horatio Gates at Saratoga (1777).

REYNOLDS, Sir Joshua (1723–1792), perhaps the most famous English portrait painter. Ambitious and popular, he became first president of the ROYAL ACADEMY OF ARTS in 1768. He held that great art is based on the styles of earlier masters, and espoused the "Grand Style." He painted nearly all his notable contemporaries, including his friend Samuel JOHNSON (1772), and published influential *Discourses* (1769–90).

REYNOLDS, Osborne (1842–1912), British physicist best known for his important contributions in FLUID MECHANICS, in particular his derivation (1883–84) of the REYNOLDS NUMBER.

REYNOLDSBURG, city in central Ohio. It is a residential suburb of Columbus. Pop 13 921.

REYNOLDS NUMBER, important dimensionless parameter in FLUID MECHANICS, given by $R = \rho ul/\mu$, where ρ is the density, u the velocity, l the length and μ the viscosity of the fluid. The value of R allows for the effects of fluid viscosity on motion and determines whether a given fluid flow is steady or turbulent. It is useful for evaluating the behavior of scale models.

REZA SHAH PAHLEVI (1877–1944), Shah of Iran, 1925–41. An army officer, he led a coup in 1921, becoming prime minister and later (1925) founder of the Pahlevi dynasty. He made important military, administrative and economic reforms, but the Allies forced him to resign in WWII for attempting to keep Iran neutral.

RHADAMANTHUS, in Greek mythology, son of EUROPA and ZEUS, and brother of MINOS and Sarpedon. He and Minos were made judges of the dead in HADES.

RHAETO-ROMANIC, a group of minor ROMANCE LANGUAGES. They include *Romansh* (spoken in SE Switzerland), *Ladin* (the Italian Tyrol) and *Friulian* (NE Italy), all probably derived from Latin. (See also INDO-EUROPEAN LANGUAGES.)

RHAPSODY, a free musical composition, not written in a set form or style, and often a free or romantic treatment of one or more themes. Well-known examples are LISZT's *Hungarian Rhapsodies* and GERSHWIN's *Rhapsody in Blue*.

RHAZES, or abu Bakr Muhammad ibn Zakariyya **al-Razi** (c860–925), Persian physician and practical chemist, the author of the *Book of Secret of Secrets* and possibly the earliest to distinguish MEASLES from SMALLPOX.

RHEAS, two species of large flightless RATITE birds, the South American equivalent of the OSTRICH. Their legs are long and powerful, bearing three toes. Rheas are gregarious, living in flocks of 20–30 but breaking up into single male harems of 6–8 females for breeding. They live in grassland or open bush country.

RHEA, in Greek mythology, a TITAN, sister and wife of CRONUS, mother of ZEUS, POSEIDON, HADES, HERA, HESTIA and DEMETER. She was often identified with CYBELE.

RHEBOK, *Pelea capreolus*, a small South African ANTELOPE, the counterpart of the European CHAMOIS. They are dwarf antelope with soft, rabbit-like fur, living in family groups in areas above 1 200m (4 000ft). The males are extremely aggressive.

RHEE, Syngman (1875–1965), first president of South Korea 1948–60. An exile in the US from 1910 (president-in-exile of Korea from 1919), he returned under US auspices after WWII, and won the presidential election by strong-arm methods. His corrupt, tyrannical regime was deposed after a ballot-rigging scandal.

RHEIMS. See REIMS.

RHEIN. See RHINE RIVER.

RHENIUM (Re), very hard, silvery-white TRANSITION ELEMENT in Group VIIB of the PERIODIC TABLE. It is very rare, and is obtained as a by-product of MOLYBDENUM extraction. Analogous to MANGANESE, it forms compounds of all oxidation states between 0 and +7, those of the higher states being volatile and stable. Its uses are similar to those of the PLATINUM GROUP metals. AW 186.2, mp 3180°C, bp 5627°C, sg 20.5 (20°C).

RHEOLOGY, branch of physics concerned with the structure and behavior of flowing and deformed materials, such as the way the shape and size of a body alters with time when subjected to mechanical forces. Properties such as FRICTION, stickiness and roughness are treated, and the study finds application in many fields from engineering to plant physiology.

RHEOSTAT, a variable resistor used to control the current drawn by an electric MOTOR, to dim LIGHTING, etc. It may consist of a resistive wire, wound in a helix, with a sliding contact varying the effective length, or of a series of fixed resistors connected between a row of button contacts. Or, for heavy loads, ELECTRODES dipped in SOLUTIONS can be used, the RESISTANCE being controlled by the immersion depth and separation of the electrodes.

RHESUS FACTOR, or **Rh factor.** See BLOOD.

RHESUS MONKEY, *Macaca mulatta*, an omnivorous MACAQUE found in many parts of Asia.

RHETORIC, the art of speaking and writing with the purpose of persuading or influencing others. It was taught by the Greek SOPHISTS in the 5th century BC. The first systematic treatise on it is ARISTOTLE's *Rhetoric*. CICERO and QUINTILIAN wrote on it, and it was a major course at medieval universities as one of the SEVEN LIBERAL ARTS.

RHETT, Robert Barnwell (Robert Barnwell Smith; 1800–1876), US FIRE-EATER, representative (1837–49) and senator for S.C. (1850–52). A violent secessionist, he helped draft the Confederate Constitution in 1861.

The Marble House in Newport, Rhode Island. One of the many magnificent mansions along Newport's Cliff Walk, it was built for William K. Vanderbilt in 1892, when the town was America's most fashionable summer resort.

RHEUMATIC FEVER, feverish illness, following infection with STREPTOCOCCUS and caused by abnormal IMMUNITY to the bacteria, leading to systemic disease. SKIN RASH, subcutaneous nodules and a migrating ARTHRITIS are commonly seen. Involvement of the HEART may lead to palpitations, chest pain, cardiac failure, MYOCARDITIS and INFLAMMATION of the PERICARDIUM; murmurs may be heard and the ELECTROCARDIOGRAPH may show conduction abnormality. Sydenham's CHOREA may also be seen, with awkwardness, clumsiness and involuntary movements. Late effects include chronic valve disease of the heart leading to stenosis or incompetence, particularly of the mitral or aortic valves. Such valve disease presents in young to middle age and may require surgical correction. Treatment of acute rheumatic fever includes bed rest, ASPIRIN and STEROIDS. PENICILLIN treatment of streptococcal disease may prevent recurrence. Patients with valve damage require ANTIBIOTICS during operations, especially dental and urinary tract SURGERY, to prevent bacterial endocarditis.

RHEUMATISM, imprecise term describing various disorders of the JOINTS, including RHEUMATIC FEVER and rheumatoid ARTHRITIS.

RHINE, Confederation of the. See CONFEDERATION OF THE RHINE.

RHINE, Joseph Banks (1895–), US parapsychologist whose pioneering laboratory studies of ESP have demonstrated the possible occurrence of telepathy (see PARAPSYCHOLOGY).

RHINELAND-PALATINATE, or **Rheinland-Pfalz,** a West German state, to the W of the RHINE RIVER. Its capital is Mainz. Its most famous product is wine, but the majority of the population are employed in industry.

RHINE RIVER (German: *Rhein*), largest river in Western Europe, rising in Switzerland and flowing 820mi through Germany and the Netherlands into the North Sea near Rotterdam. It is of great historical and commercial significance, being navigable by seagoing ships up to Cologne, and by large barges as far as Basel. Canals link it to the Rhône, Marne, Ems, Weser, Elbe, Oder and Danube rivers. Some of its finest scenery is along the gorge between Bingen and Bonn, with terraced vineyards, ruined castles and famous landmarks like the LORELEI rock.

RHINITIS, INFLAMMATION of the mucous membranes of the NOSE causing runny nasal discharge, and seen in the COMMON COLD, INFLUENZA and HAY FEVER. Irritation in the nose and sneezing are common.

RHINOCEROS BEETLES, large Scarabeid BEETLES in which the males have conspicuous horns on the head, very similar in appearance to those of the related Hercules beetle of the US.

RHINOCEROSES, a family, Rhinocerotidae, of five species of heavy land animals characterized by a long nasal "horn" or "horns." They are bulky animals with thick, hairless skin, often falling in heavy loose folds. They live in transitional habitat between open grassland and high forest, grazing or browzing on the bushes or shrubs. All five species—the Square-lipped, or White, rhino; the Black rhino; the Great Indian; Sumatran, and Javan rhinos—are on the verge of extinction. The horn is not true horn but is formed of a mass of compacted hairs.

RHIPSALIDOPSIS, a genus of two species of CACTI which produce trumpet-shaped, pendulous flowers. Popular as a house plant, *Rhipsalidopsis gaertneri* is also known as the Easter cactus, since its flowers are produced in March and April.

RHIZOME, or **rootstock,** the swollen horizontal underground stem of certain PLANTS that acts as an organ of perennation and vegetative propagation. They last for several years and new shoots appear each spring from the axils of scale leaves.

RHODE ISLAND, a New England state in the NE US, the smallest state of the Union.

Land. Most of Rhode Island lies W of Narragansett Bay, which extends 28mi inland. There are two major regions: the Seaboard or Coastal Lowlands, the islands in Narragansett Bay and the land E of the bay; and the New England Upland to the W. About two-thirds of the state is forested. The climate ranges from about 28°F in winter to about 70°F in summer.

People. The population is heavily urban (87%), and the largest cities are Providence, Warwick, Pawtucket and Cranston. About 97% of the population are white, and over half are Roman Catholic.

Economy. The textile industry is still of prime importance, with tourism second and agriculture third. The chief farm products are milk, eggs, potatoes and hay. Apples are the principal fruit crop, and fish and shellfish also contribute to the economy. Manufactures include jewelry, electrical machinery, primary and fabricated metals, and plastic and rubber goods.

History. Da VERRAZANO probably reached Rhode Island in 1524, and in 1636 Roger WILLIAMS established the first settlement at Providence on land purchased from the NARRAGANSETT INDIANS. Charles II of England granted a charter in 1663. Religious and political freedom from the start formed part of the colony's traditions. In the 18th century Rhode Islanders resented British interference in their flourishing trade and Rhode Island was the first colony to declare independence from Britain in 1776

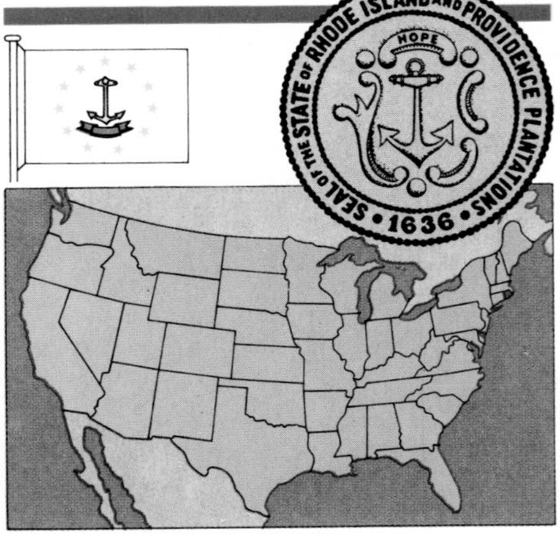

Name of State: Rhode Island (Officially: Rhode Island and Providence Plantations)
Capital: Providence
Statehood: May 29, 1790 (13th state)
Familiar Name: Little Rhody
Area: 1 214sq mi
Population: 949 723
Elevation: Highest—812ft, Jerimoth Hill
Lowest—sea level, Atlantic Ocean
Motto: Hope
State Flower: Violet
State Bird: Rhode Island Red
State Tree: Red maple
State Song: "Rhode Island"

but also the last of the original 13 colonies to ratify the US Constitution. A new liberal state constitution followed after DORR's rebellion in 1842. The fast-expanding textile industry attracted thousands of immigrants while the state became known as the summer home of wealthy industrialists. Since WWII varied industries have begun to replace the declining textile industry.

RHODES, Greek island (540sq mi) and its capital city off the SW coast of Turkey. Its exports include wine, fruit and olive oil. The city of Rhodes was a prosperous city-state in the 3rd century BC. At its harbor stood the COLOSSUS OF RHODES.

RHODES, Cecil John (1853–1902), British statesman and business magnate, who first opened up RHODESIA to European settlement. He founded the De Beers Mining Company in 1880 at Kimberly in South Africa, and in 1889 formed a company to develop the area that is now Rhodesia. Premier of the Cape Colony from 1890, he was forced to resign through his complicity in the JAMESON raid (1896). Much of his £6 000 000 fortune went to found the RHODES SCHOLARSHIPS.

RHODES, Colossus of. See COLOSSUS OF RHODES.

RHODES, Knights of. See KNIGHTS OF SAINT JOHN.

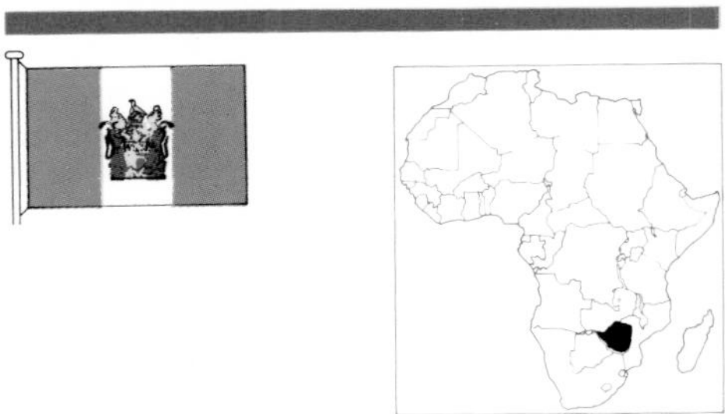

Official name: Rhodesia
Capital: Salisbury
Area: 150 820sq mi
Population: 5 890 000
Languages: English; Sindebele, Chishona
Religions: Christian; Animist
Monetary unit(s): 1 Rhodesian dollar = 100 cents

RHODESIA (African: *Zimbabwe*), landlocked selfgoverning British colony in southern Africa which illegally declared independence in 1965.

Country. Rhodesia's principal feature is the wide belt of savanna grassland, 3 000ft–5 000ft high, running NE-SW across the country—the Middle Veld and High Veld. Mt Inyangana in the E highlands rises to 8 503ft. The altitude makes the climate mild for the tropics; rainfall varies from about 20in per year in the S to about 70in in the highlands.

People. The white minority, constituting about 5% of the population, mostly live in Salisbury and Bulawayo; others own big farms. The black majority belong principally to the Bantu Ndebele and Shona groups, and have preserved their own languages and religion. Some 60% of the blacks are agriculturalists on tribal land.

Economy. Rhodesia is basically agricultural; the black population live by subsistence farming, growing maize, groundnuts, millet and sorghum and raising cattle. Important European-farmed crops are tobacco (Rhodesia's major export), cotton, sugar, citrus fruits and tea. Minerals are also important, including gold, asbestos, chrome, coal, iron and copper. Power is provided by the KARIBA DAM. Economic sanctions since 1965 have had a slight but appreciable effect on the economy.

History. Bantu tribes settled in the area c400 AD, and by 1000 AD the Shona civilization had developed at ZIMBABWE. European penetration began in the 19th century, and in 1889 Cecil RHODES (for whom the country is named) obtained a charter to promote trade and colonization. Southern Rhodesia became a self-governing colony in 1923. After the collapse of the Federation of RHODESIA AND NYASALAND, Rhodesia under Ian SMITH illegally declared independence in 1965, and proclaimed a republic in 1970. Since then a

UN economic embargo has failed to destroy the Smith regime; talks aimed at a constitutional settlement were revived by the mission of Henry KISSINGER in 1976. Terrorist activities have continued throughout the dispute.

RHODESIA AND NYASALAND, a federation of British colonies and protectorates 1953–63. The member states were Northern Rhodesia (now Zambia), Nyasaland (now Malawi) and Southern Rhodesia, Zimbabwe. Salisbury was the federal capital. Economic advantages of federation, such as the completion of the KARIBA DAM project, were not enough to outweigh African nationalist fears of perpetual white domination, and after a period of tension 1959–63 the federation was wound up.

RHODESIAN RIDGEBACK, or **African lion hound,** large hunting dog bred in South Africa. Tan in color and up to 27in at the shoulder, it has a ridge of forward-growing hair down its back.

RHODES SCHOLARSHIPS, instituted at OXFORD UNIVERSITY by the bequest of Cecil RHODES for students from the British Commonwealth, the US, South Africa and Western Germany. Elections are made on general grounds as well as on academic ability.

RHODIUM (Rh), moderately hard metal, the whitest of the PLATINUM GROUP. In addition to the general uses of these metals, rhodium is used for MIRROR surfaces, and a platinum-rhodium alloy is used as a catalyst in the OSTWALD PROCESS. AW 102.9, mp 1966°C, bp 3727°C, sg 12.4 (20°C).

RHODODENDRON, a genus of mostly evergreen shrubs that are mainly native to the forests of the E Himalayas. They bear leathery dark-green leaves and, in late spring, masses of fragrant blossom. There are many popular horticultural varieties in cultivation. AZALEAS are deciduous members of the same genus. Family: Ericaceae.

RHODOPHYTA, or **red algae.** See ALGAE.

RHODOPSIN, or visual purple, photosensitive pigment, derived from VITAMIN A, found in the RETINAS of many vertebrates, including man. Its bleaching by incident light is the basis of light-and-dark distinction in VISION.

RHOMBUS. See QUADRILATERAL.

RHÔNE RIVER, an important European river, 507mi long, rising in Switzerland and flowing through Lake Geneva and then SW and S through France into the Mediterranean Sea. With its tributaries, particularly the Isère and the Saône, it has a large flow of water, which has been harnessed in major hydroelectric schemes. Navigable in part, it is linked by canal to the CAMARGUE.

RHUBARB, or **Pieplant,** *Rheum rhaponticum*, was first cultivated in China for its purgative medicinal rootstock. As a vegetable the pink fleshy leaf-stalks, or petioles, are eaten stewed or in pies. The petioles sprout from underground rhizomes and bear large green leaves that can be poisonous. Family: Polygonaceae.

RHUMB LINE, or loxodrome, in NAVIGATION, line of constant compass direction, crossing all lines of LONGITUDE at the same angle, and represented by a straight line on the MERCATOR projection. It spirals toward the poles, and is not as short a distance between two points as the GREAT CIRCLE ROUTE.

RHYME, in poetry, the placing of words with identical or similar sounds in a regular pattern, usually at the ends of lines. Rhymes can be strong (*harp, sharp*), weak (*cotton, rotten*—accent not on last syllable) or imperfect in other ways. Rhyme has characterized much European poetry since the Middle Ages, and certain forms, for example the BALLAD or SONNET, have set rhyme-patterns.

RHYOLITE, light-colored volcanic IGNEOUS ROCK, of the same composition as GRANITE, and very common and widespread. Often banded from LAVA flow as it solidified, it is fine-grained and usually porphyritic (see PORPHYRY). (See also OBSIDIAN; PUMICE.)

RHYTHM, a regular pattern of stressed beats, especially characteristic of MUSIC and POETRY. In Western music the commonest rhythms are 2/4, 3/4, 4/4 and 6/8 (two, three, four and six beats in a bar). A typical 3/4 rhythm is the waltz. Broken rhythms are called SYNCOPATION. In poetry the term describes the pattern of stressed and unstressed words in a line of verse or a poem.

RHYTHMS, Biological. See BIOLOGICAL CLOCKS.

RIALTO, city in S Cal., a suburb of San Bernadino in a fruit-growing area. Pop 28 370.

RIAU ARCHIPELAGO, group of over 1000 islands in the Malacca Strait at the S end of the Malay peninsula, politically part of Indonesia. Bintan, the largest island, has bauxite deposits.

RIB. See SKELETON.

RIBAUT, Jean (or Ribault; c1520–1565), French mariner who colonized Fla. On present-day Parris Island, S.C., he set up a colony in 1562. He fled to England to escape persecution as a HUGUENOT, and in 1563 published *The Whole and True Discouerye of Terra Florida*. In 1565 he was shipwrecked off Fla., and killed by Spanish forces.

RIBBENTROP, Joachim von (1893–1946), German Nazi leader, ambassador to the UK 1936–38 and foreign minister 1938–45. He helped to negotiate the Rome–Berlin Axis in 1936 and the Russo–German non-aggression pact of 1939 and to plan the invasion of Poland, but wielded little influence in WWII. He was hanged for war crimes.

RIBBONFISHES, a general name for the family Trachipteridae, which includes the OARFISH. They are long, ribbon-like fishes of oceanic waters. All are recognizable by long silvery bodies and bright red fins.

RIBBON GRASS, or **Reed Canary Grass,** a grass native to Europe, but now widely cultivated both in the Old and New World for pasture and hay. An ornamental variety with striped leaves is grown in gardens. Family: Graminae.

RIBBON WORMS, elongate worm-like invertebrates also known as **Nemertineans**. There are nearly 600 species, mostly marine. They may be free-swimming or burrowing in habit; some are tube-dwellers. Their most distinctive feature is an eversible proboscis which is shot out to catch the prey: mainly annelids.

RIBERA, Jusepe de (1591–1652), Spanish painter who lived after 1616 in Naples. His work, influenced by CARAVAGGIO, is noted for its combination of naturalism and mysticism, as in the *Martyrdom of St. Sebastian* (1630) and *The Penitent Magdalen* (c1640).

RIBICOFF, Abraham Alexander (1910–   ), US statesman and senator, best known as a champion of consumer protection. He was Conn. congressman 1949–53, governor 1955–61 and senator since 1963. Under President KENNEDY he was secretary of health, education and welfare 1961–62.

RIBOFLAVIN, or vitamin B_2. See VITAMINS.

RIBONUCLEIC ACID (RNA). See NUCLEIC ACIDS.

RIBOSOMES, tiny granules, of diameter about 10nm, found in CELL cytoplasm. They are composed of PROTEIN and a special form of ribonucleic acid (see NUCLEIC ACIDS) known as ribosomal RNA. The ribosome is the site of PROTEIN SYNTHESIS.

RICARDO, David (1772–1823), English economist, founder with Adam SMITH of the "classical school." He made a fortune on the Stock Exchange, and then devoted his time to economics and politics, becoming a member of Parliament 1819–23. His main work is *Principles of Political Economy and Taxation* (1817), which pioneered the use of theoretical models in analysing the distribution of wealth. (See also ECONOMICS; RENT; VALUE.)

RICCI, Matteo (1552–1610), Italian Jesuit missionary to China. After teaching in Goa, he entered China in 1583, learned Chinese and eventually won acceptance, reaching Peking in 1601. He introduced Western mathematics, astronomy and geography to the Chinese, and in turn sent the first modern detailed reports of China back to the West.

RICCIO, David. See RIZZIO, DAVID.

RICE, *Oryza sativa*, a grain-yielding annual plant of the GRASS family, Graminae. It is grown chiefly in S and E Asia where it is the staple food of hundreds of millions of people. Rice needs hot moist conditions to grow, which historically made it highly dependent on MONSOON rainfall. But improved irrigation, fertilizers, pesticides and the development of the improved

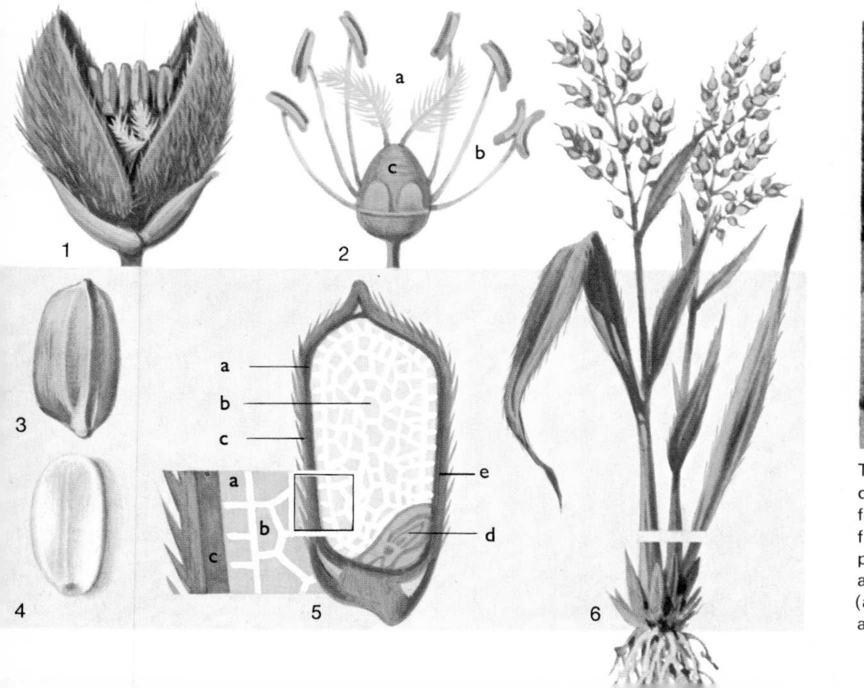

Terraced rice paddies, a common sight all over Asia. Rice requires a great deal of water , and so paddies are usually flooded to the depth of about a foot. (1) A rice-plant head, opened to show the flower. (2) The rice flower, or spikelet, showing stigmas (a), stamens (b) and ovary (c) ; after pollination the anthers take on an X-form. (3) A grain after harvesting, and (4) after milling. (5) Cross-section of a grain, showing the pericarp (a) and starch endosperm (b), lemma or hull (c), germ or embryo (d), and glume (e). (6) The complete rice plant.

varieties have enormously increased the yield. Machinery for planting and harvesting rice is used in the US and parts of South America, but in the Orient rice-farming methods are still primitive, using hand labor. Rice has a reasonable nutrient value, but when "polished" much of its VITAMIN B_1 content is lost, resulting in a high incidence of the deficiency disease, BERIBERI, wherever polished rice is staple.

RICE, Elmer (1892–1967), US dramatist. His plays on social themes include *The Adding Machine* (1923), an expressionist fantasy on mechanization, *Street Scene* (1929), a Pulitzer prize-winning portrait of life in a New York tenement, and the romantic comedy, *Dream Girl* (1945).

RICE, Grantland (1880–1954), US sporting journalist noted for his stories and syndicated column, "The Sportlight." His books include *Songs of the Open* (1924) and *Only the Brave* (1941).

RICE, Wild. See WILD RICE.

RICE PAPER, the edible pith from the stem of the rice paper tree (*Fatsia papyrifera*). Rice paper is used as a decoration on foods and in the Orient as artists' paper and for making artificial flowers. Family: Araliaceae.

RICHARD, name of three kings of England. **Richard I** (1157–1199), called *Coeur de Lion* (the Lion Heart) was the third son of Henry II, whom he succeeded in 1189. He spent all but six months of his reign out of England, mainly on the Third CRUSADE. After taking Cyprus and Acre in 1191 and recapturing Jaffa in 1192, he was captured returning to England and handed over to the Emperor HENRY VI who held him to ransom till 1194. After a brief spell in England he spent the rest of his life fighting against PHILIP II in France. **Richard II** (1367–1400), son of Edward the Black Prince, succeeded his grandfather EDWARD III in 1377. In his minority the country was governed by a group of nobles dominated by his uncle JOHN OF GAUNT. Richard quarreled with them but only began to assert himself after 1397; he executed his uncle the Duke of Gloucester and banished Henry Bolingbroke, Gaunt's son, and confiscated his estates. Bolingbroke returned in 1499 to depose Richard and imprison him in Pontefract castle, where he died. Bolingbroke succeeded as Henry IV. **Richard III** (1452–1485), third son of Richard Plantagenet, Duke of York, and the younger brother of EDWARD IV, usurped the throne in 1483. The traditional picture of him as a hunchbacked and cruel ruler who murdered his nephews in the Tower has little historical backing. He instituted many reforms and encouraged trade, but had little hope of defeating his many enemies gathering in France under Henry Tudor (later HENRY VII). They defeated and killed Richard at BOSWORTH.

RICHARDS, Dickinson Woodruff (1895–1973), US physiologist awarded with COURNAND and FORSSMANN the 1956 Nobel Prize for Physiology or Medicine for his work with Cournand using Forssman's CATHETER technique to probe the heart, pulmonary artery and lungs.

The Virginia state capitol building at Richmond, designed by Thomas Jefferson. Richmond has been the state capital since 1779.

RICHARDS, Ivor Armstrong (1893–   ), influential English literary critic and semanticist. He developed with C. K. OGDEN the concept of **Basic English**, a primary vocabulary of 850 words. His books include *The Meaning of Meaning* (with Ogden, 1923) and *Principles of Literary Criticism* (1924).

RICHARDS, Theodore William (1868–1928), US chemist awarded the 1914 Nobel Prize for Chemistry for his determination of the ATOMIC WEIGHTS of some 60 ELEMENTS. In particular, his accurate work showed the existence of ISOTOPES, predicted earlier by Frederick SODDY.

RICHARDSON, city in N Tex., a residential suburb of Dallas. Pop 48 582.

RICHARDSON, Elliot Lee (1920–   ), US lawyer and government official, assistant secretary of health, education and welfare 1957–59, then Mass. lieutenant governor (1965–67) and attorney general 1967–69. Secretary of health, education and welfare 1970–73, he was appointed attorney general 1973, but resigned over the WATERGATE SCANDAL. He was ambassador to the UK 1975–76, US secretary of commerce from 1976.

RICHARDSON, Henry Hobson (1838–1886), influential US architect who pioneered an American Romanesque style. Among his important buildings were the Trinity Church, Boston, and the Marshall Field Wholesale Store in Chicago.

RICHARDSON, Sir Owen Willans (1879–1959), British physicist awarded the 1928 Nobel Prize for Physics for his pioneering work on THERMIONIC EMISSION. The **Richardson equation** relates the rate of thermionic emission to the absolute TEMPERATURE of the heated metal.

RICHARDSON, Samuel (1689–1761), important English novelist, best known for his novels in epistolary form, especially *Pamela* (1740–41), the story of a servant girl's moral triumph over her lecherous master. *Clarissa* (1747–48), his tragic masterpiece, is also on the theme of seduction. *Sir Charles Grandison* (1753–54) portrays a virtuous hero, in contrast to the amoral hero of FIELDING's *Tom Jones*.

RICHARD THE LION HEART. See RICHARD I.

RICHELIEU, Armand Jean du Plessis, Duc de (1585–1642), French cardinal, statesman and chief minister to LOUIS XIII for 18 years. By a mixture of diplomacy and ruthlessness he helped make France the leading power in Europe with a monarchy secure against internal revolt. He destroyed HUGUENOT power by 1628, foiled an attempt by Maria de MÉDICIS to oust him in 1630, and suppressed the plots of the Duc de Montmorency in 1632 and of Cinq-Mars in 1642, at the same time reducing the power of the nobles. In foreign policy he opposed the Hapsburgs, intervening against them in the THIRTY YEARS' WAR. Richelieu strengthened the navy, encouraged colonial development and patronized the arts.

RICHELIEU RIVER, Canadian river flowing 75mi N from Lake Champlain through S Quebec to the St. Lawrence R. It is important for the lumber industry, with pulp and paper mills along its banks.

RICHET, Charles Robert (1850–1935), French physiologist awarded the 1913 Nobel Prize for Physiology or Medicine for his studies of ANAPHYLAXIS, which term he also coined.

RICHFIELD, city in SE Minn., S of Minneapolis, in a dairy and truck farming area. It makes metal and wood products. Pop 47 231.

RICHLAND, city in S Wash., in a rich farming area. It grew rapidly when it became headquarters of the Hanford atomic energy plant. Pop 26 290.

RICHMOND, city and port in W Cal., 16mi NE of San Francisco. Industries include petroleum refining, chemicals and food processing. Pop 79 043.

RICHMOND, city in E Ind., seat of Wayne Co. Founded by Quakers, it is now a center for manufacturing industry, including buses and trucks. Pop 34 999.

RICHMOND, city in central Ky., seat of Madison Co. It is a tobacco and livestock market in a cattle-raising area. Pop 12 168.

RICHMOND, state capital of Va. and from 1861 to 1865 capital of the Confederacy. Located at the navigation head of the James R, it is a port and a financial and distribution center, as well as being an important industrial city, with tobacco and food processing, chemicals, metals and wood products. It has many historic buildings and places of higher education. Pop 249 430.

RICHMOND, borough of New York City. See STATEN ISLAND.

RICHMOND HEIGHTS, city in E Mo., 7mi W of St. Louis, of which it is a residential suburb. Pop 13 802.

RICHMOND HILL, town in SE Ontario, Canada, 10mi N of Toronto. It is in an agricultural area and produces clothing and plastics. Pop 32 399.

RICHTER, Hans (1843–1916), Hungarian conductor who conducted the first performance of WAGNER's *Ring* cycle at BAYREUTH in 1876. A BRAHMS specialist also, he conducted in England for many years.

RICHTER, Johann Paul Friedrich (1763–1825), German humorous and sentimental novelist, who wrote as Jean Paul. His early works were satirical; but he achieved popularity with such works as *The Invisible Lodge* (1793), *The Life of Quintus Fixlein* (1796) and the four-volume *Titan* (1800–03).

RICHTER, Sviatoslav (1915–   ), Russian pianist, particularly renowned for his sensitive treatment of Beethoven, Schubert, Schumann, Debussy and Prokoviev.

RICHTER SCALE, scale devised by C. F. Richter (1900–   ), used to measure the magnitudes of EARTHQUAKES in terms of the amplitude and frequency of the surface waves. The scale runs from 0 to 10, about one quake a year registering over 8.

RICHTHOFEN, Manfred, Baron von (1892–1918), German WWI airman, nicknamed the "Red Baron." Known for the daring and chivalry with which he led his squadron, he shot down around 80 opponents and was himself killed in action.

RICKENBACKER, Edward Vernon (1890–1973), US air ace of WWI; he shot down 26 aircraft. In the 1920s he returned to automobile racing and later became an airline executive.

RICKETS, VITAMIN D deficiency disease in children causing disordered BONE growth at the EPIPHYSES, with growth retardation, defective mineralization of bone, epiphyseal irregularity on X-RAY, and pliability and tendency to FRACTURE of bones. It is common among the malnourished, especially in cool climates where vitamin D formation in the SKIN is minimal. Treatment is by vitamin D replacement.

RICKETTSIA, organisms partway between BACTERIA and VIRUSES that are obligatory intracellular organisms but have a more complex structure than viruses. They are responsible for a number of diseases (often borne by TICKS or LICE) including TYPHUS, SCRUB TYPHUS and ROCKY MOUNTAIN SPOTTED FEVER; related organisms cause Q FEVER and PSITTACOSIS. They are sensitive to TETRACYCLINES and cause characteristic serological reactions cross-specific to Proteus bacteria.

RICKEY, Branch Wesley (1881–1965), US baseball executive, nicknamed "The Mahatma." He had a particular gift for selecting and training talented young players.

RICKOVER, Hyman George (1900–   ), Russian-born US admiral who brought nuclear power to the US Navy. Head of the Navy's electrical division in WWII, he moved to the Atomic Energy Commission in 1947, and developed the first nuclear-powered submarine, the *Nautilus* (1954).

RIDEAU CANAL, canal in Canada connecting Kingston, Ontario, with Ottawa. It is 126mi long and includes the Rideau R and Rideau Lake. It was built 1926–32.

RIDGEFIELD, residential town in SE Conn. It has many colonial houses and was the site of a battle on April 27, 1777. Pop 18 188.

RIDGEFIELD, residential borough in NE N.J., 8mi N of Jersey City. Pop 11 308.

RIDGEFIELD PARK, village in NE N.J. It has some manufactures, including paper products. Pop 13 990.

RIDGEWOOD, residential village in NE N.J., 5mi

NNE of Paterson. It was the scene of fighting in 1780. Pop 27 547.

RIDGWAY, Matthew Bunker (1895–), US military leader. During WWII he led the first full-scale US air attack in the invasion of Sicily (1943) and took part in the invasion of France (1944). He became commander of the United Nations forces in Korea (1951), supreme commander of NATO Allied Forces in Europe (1952–53) and US army chief of staff 1953–55.

RIDING MOUNTAIN NATIONAL PARK, a forested highland area of 1 148sq mi in SW Manitoba, Canada. It was established in 1929 and has many lakes. It is a game preserve.

RIDLEY, Nicholas (c1500–1555), English Protestant martyr. Under CRANMER's patronage he became a chaplain to HENRY VIII and bishop of Rochester (1547) and London (1550). He helped compile the BOOK OF COMMON PRAYER. On the accession of the Roman Catholic MARY I (1553) he was imprisoned and burnt as a heretic with LATIMER at Oxford.

RIEGGER, Wallingford (1885–1961), US composer. In many of his works he used TWELVE-TONE techniques. He wrote ballet scores, symphonies and chamber works.

RIEL, Louis (1844–1885), Canadian *métis* (person of mixed Indian and French descent) and rebel leader. In 1869 he organized the *métis* of Red River, now in Manitoba, to oppose Canada's annexation of these territories. He fled to the US after government troops had moved in (1870). On his return to Canada (1873) he was elected to the House of Commons, but was expelled in 1874 and banished in 1875. In 1884 he led another Indian uprising in Saskatchewan, but was captured in May, 1885. His execution for treason became a cause of friction between English and French Canadians.

RIEMANN, Georg Friedrich Bernhard (1826–1866), German mathematician, the best known among whose contributions to diverse fields of mathematics is the initiation of studies of NON-EUCLIDEAN GEOMETRY. Elliptic geometry is often named RIEMANNIAN GEOMETRY for him.

RIEMANNIAN GEOMETRY, or elliptic geometry, the branch of NON-EUCLIDEAN GEOMETRY based on the hypothesis that for any point P not lying on a line L, no line can be drawn through P parallel to L.

RIEMENSCHNEIDER, Tilman (c1460–1531), German sculptor. He worked in Würzburg, where many of his works survive, and carved the marble tomb of Emperor Henry II and his wife in Bamberg Cathedral (1499–1513).

RIENZI, Cola di (c1313–1354), Italian popular leader. With papal support, he became "Tribune" of a popular republic in Rome (1347), but his plans for restoring the Roman Empire led to his overthrow by the nobles and exile. He returned triumphantly in 1354 but was killed in a riot.

RIESMAN, David (1909–), US sociologist whose best-known work, *The Lonely Crowd* (1950), explores the changing nature of the US social character in a highly industrialized urban society.

RIFLE, strictly any FIREARM with a "rifled" bore — i.e., with shallow helical grooves cut inside the barrel. These grooves, by causing the bullet to spin, steady it and increase its accuracy, velocity and range. The term "rifle" is more narrowly applied to the long-barreled hand weapon fired from the shoulder. Rifles are generally classified by caliber (see AMMUNITION) or decimal fractions or by mode of action. "Single-shot" rifles are manually reloaded after each discharge; "repeaters" are reloaded from a magazine by means of a hand-operated mechanism that ejects the spent cartridge case and drives a fresh cartridge into the breech. In semiautomatic rifles, these operations are powered by gas produced as the weapon is fired. Today, many rifles have an optional fully automatic action, a single squeeze of the trigger emptying the magazine in seconds.

RIFT VALLEY, or **graben,** a valley formed by the relative downthrow of land between two roughly parallel FAULTS. The best known are the Great Rift Valley of E Africa, and the Rheingraben.

RIGA, capital of the Latvian SSR. It is a major Baltic port, and a commercial, cultural and industrial center (machinery, ships, textiles, chemicals, paper). Pop 733 000.

RIGAUD, Hyacinthe (1659–1743), or **Hyacinthe Rigau y Ros,** French portrait painter in the style of VAN DYCK. His subjects included Louis XIV (1701), Louis XV (1715) and BOSSUET (1702).

RIGEL, Beta Orionis, the brightest star in ORION. A quadruple star consisting of a visual binary and a spectroscopic binary (see DOUBLE STAR), it is 276pc distant.

RIGHT ASCENSION. See CELESTIAL SPHERE.

RIGHT-HANDEDNESS. See HANDEDNESS.

RIGHT OF ASSEMBLY, the democratic right of citizens to assemble publicly for peaceable purposes, such as worship, debate or the expression of grievances. This basic freedom is written into the 1st Amendment (1791) to the UNITED STATES CONSTITUTION.

RIGHT OF PETITION, the democratic right of a citizen or group to petition or appeal to the government. This is written into the 1st Amendment (1791) to the UNITED STATES CONSTITUTION. In England the right is expressed in the MAGNA CARTA (1215) and the BILL OF RIGHTS (1689).

RIGHT OF SEARCH, in international law, the right of a nation at war to search merchant ships of neutral states to ensure that they are not being used in the service of a belligerent state. In peacetime it can be used to enforce revenue laws up to 3 or 12mi off a country's coast.

RIGHTS OF MAN, Declaration of the. See DECLARATION OF THE RIGHTS OF MAN.

RIGHT-TO-WORK LAW, laws enforced in 19 US states requiring industry to maintain an "open shop." This means that a person may not be prevented from working because he does not belong to a union, nor may he be forced to take up, or maintain, membership of a union.

RIGHT WHALES, baleen WHALES of the colder waters of the N Hemisphere which may grow up to 15m (49ft). They were extensively hunted both for oil and BALEEN, or whalebone. Being slow and relatively easy to catch, they are now extremely rare.

RIGOR MORTIS, stiffness of the body MUSCLES occurring some hours after DEATH and caused by biochemical alterations in muscle. The body is set in the position held at the onset of the changes.

RIG VEDA. See VEDA.

RIIS, Jacob August (1849–1914), Danish-born US journalist and social reformer whose book, *How the Other Half Lives* (1890), drew attention to slum conditions in New York City. He worked as a police reporter on the *New York Tribune* (1877–88) and the *New York Evening Sun* (1888–99).

RIJEKA (Italian: *Fiume*), a seaport in NW Yugoslavia, on the Gulf of Kvarner. Its industries include oil-refining, shipbuilding, chemical manufacturing and metal-working. It was ruled by Austria (1466–1723), Hungary (1779–1919) and then Italy (1924–45), having been seized by Gabriele D'ANNUNZIO in 1919. (See RAPALLO, TREATY OF.) Pop 132 933.

RILEY, James Whitcomb (1849–1916), US poet, known as the "Hoosier poet." *The Old Swimmin' Hole and 'Leven More Poems* (1883), was the first of many popular collections of humorous and sentimental dialect poems.

RILKE, Rainer Maria (1875–1926), German lyric poet. His complex and symbolic poems are preoccupied with spiritual questioning about God and death, as in the *Book of Hours* (1905) and *New Poems* (1907–08). His later *Duino Elegies* (1912–20; published 1923) and the *Sonnets to Orpheus* (1923) are richly mystical. Rilke is one of the great founding figures in modern literature.

RIMBAUD, Arthur (1854–1891), French poet. A precocious youth, he associated with VERLAINE, published *A Season in Hell* in 1873, and thereafter denounced his poetry, becoming an adventurer. His vivid imagery and his "disordering of consciousness," reflected in the fragmented technique of such poems as "The Drunken Boat," have had an enormous influence on modern poetry.

RIME. See FROST.

RIMINI, seaport in N Italy, on the Adriatic coast. An ancient Roman town, it is a popular tourist center, with wineries and flour mills. Pop 114 467.

RIMINI, Francesca da. See FRANCESCA DA RIMINI.

RIMOUSKI, city in Quebec province, Canada, on the St. Lawrence R. A tourist center, it produces lumber and dairy foods. Pop 26 546.

RIMSKY-KORSAKOV, Nikolai Andreyevich (1844–1908), Russian composer and a member of THE FIVE. While still a naval officer he started teaching composition at the St. Petersburg Conservatory (1871). He wrote scores for the operas *The Snow Maiden* (1882) and *The Golden Cockerel* (1907) and a colorful symphonic suite, *Scheherazade* (1888).

RINDERPEST, acute VIRUS disease of, particularly, cattle, common in N Africa and S Asia. Although there have been outbreaks in other parts of the world, North America has hitherto remained unaffected by this usually fatal disease.

RING, a circlet, often of precious metal, usually worn on the finger. Rings are also worn in the ears, the nose or around the neck in some societies. They may be worn for adornment, or may symbolize love pledges, authority or marital status.

RING, a set (see SET THEORY) with the following properties: it has two BINARY OPERATIONS, ADDITION and MULTIPLICATION ($+$ and $\times$); it is an ABELIAN GROUP under addition; multiplication is associative, and distributive over addition (see ALGEBRA); and if a and b are members of the set, $a \times b$ has a unique value c, also a member of the set. If there is a member n of the set such that $a \times n = a$ for every member a of the set, the ring is a "ring with unity." A ring in which multiplication is commutative is a "commutative ring."

RINGLING BROTHERS, five US brothers who created the world's largest circus. Led by **John Ringling** (1866–1936), they started with a one-wagon show and became BARNUM and BAILEY's chief rivals, buying them out in 1907. The circus was the world's largest by 1930, and remained in the family's hands until 1967.

RINGTAIL CAT. See CACOMISTLE.

RINGWOOD, borough in NE N.J., 17mi NNW of Paterson. Pop 10 393.

RINGWORM, common FUNGUS disease of the SKIN of man and animals which may also affect the HAIR or nails. Ringshaped raised lesions occur, often with central sparing; temporary BALDNESS is seen on hairy skin, together with the disintegration of the nails. ATHLETE'S FOOT is ringworm of the toes, while *tinea cruris* is a variety affecting the groin. Various fungi may be responsible, including *Trichophyton* and *Microspora*. Treatments include topical ointments (e.g., benzyl benzoate) or systemic antifungal ANTIBIOTICS such as Griseofulvin.

RIO DE JANEIRO, state in SE Brazil, total area 16 568sq mi. It encompasses Cuanabara state, which contains the city of Rio de Janeiro. The main agricultural products are coffee, sugarcane, rice and citrus fruits, and industries include textiles, metallurgy and foodstuffs.

RIO DE JANEIRO, second largest city of Brazil, on the Atlantic coast about 200mi W of São Paulo. It is a leading commercial center and port, and also an industrial center, manufacturing clothing, furniture, glassware and foodstuffs. The area was settled by the French (1555–67) and then by the Portuguese. It was the Brazilian capital from 1822 to 1960, when it was supplanted by Brazília. Pop 4 394 000.

RIO DE LA PLATA (English: Plate R), an estuary formed by the Paraná R and Uruguay R, separating Argentina to the S and Uruguay to the N. It flows 171mi SE into the Atlantic.

RIO GRANDE, one of the longest rivers in North America, known in Mexico as the Río Bravo del Norte. It rises in the San Juan Mts in SW Col. and flows 1 885mi SE and S to the Gulf of Mexico at Brownsville, Tex., and Matamoros, Mexico. From El Paso, Tex., to its mouth, it forms the US–Mexico border.

RIO GRANDE DO NORTE, state in NE Brazil, total area 20 469sq mi. Apart from the fertile coastal area the region is semiarid and devoted largely to livestock raising.

RIO GRANDE DO SUL, state in S Brazil, total area 108951sq mi. Its agriculture includes rice, corn and wheat and it is an important livestock raising area. Pop 6755000.
RÍO MUNI, former name of Mbini province of Equatorial Guinea in West Africa. Its seaport capital is Bata.
RIO NEGRO, chief tributary of the Amazon R. It rises as the Guainia and flows 1400mi SE through Amazonas state, Brazil, to join the Amazon above Manaus.
RIOT, in criminal law an offense against public order involving violence by a group of people. By definition a riot must be caused by three or more people coming together deliberately to commit some unlawful act, which must be at least partially achieved. Riots often grow out of some deep-seated social unrest, as with race riots in the US.
RIO TREATY, Inter-American Treaty of Reciprocal Assistance signed in 1947 by all states of the W hemisphere except Canada, Ecuador and Nicaragua. It binds the signatories not to use force on the American continent without the unanimous consent of the others, and regards an attack against one as an attack against all.
RIOUW ARCHIPELAGO. See RIAU ARCHIPELAGO.
RIPARIAN RIGHTS, or **water rights,** belonging to owners of land on the edge of streams, rivers and lakes. They allow a landowner to use the water for domestic, agricultural or commercial purposes, usually with the provision that such use should not infringe the rights of other riparian owners.
RIPLEY, George (1802–1880), US social reformer and literary critic. Beginning as a Unitarian pastor, he became a TRANSCENDENTALIST, founded and ran the BROOK FARM community, 1841–47. Later he became an influential literary critic with the *New York Tribune*.
RISORGIMENTO (Italian: resurgence), Italian 19th-century period of literary and political nationalism leading to a unified Italy in 1870. After 1815, various states, stirred by revolutionaries like MAZZINI, rose against their Austrian or papal rulers. Unification under VICTOR EMMANUEL II was achieved by CAVOUR, who involved the French and British in wars against Austria, and by the spectacular victories of GARIBALDI.
RITES OF PASSAGE, ceremonies within a community to mark the achievement by an individual of a new stage in his life cycle (e.g., birth, puberty, marriage) and his consequent change of role in the community.
RITTENHOUSE, David (1732–1796), American astronomer and mathematician, who invented the DIFFRACTION grating, built two famous ORRERIES, discovered the atmosphere of VENUS (1768) independently of LOMONOSOV (1761), and built what was probably the first American TELESCOPE.
RITTER, Johann Wilhelm (1776–1810), Silesian-born German physical chemist, a pioneer of ELECTROCHEMISTRY, who first positively identified ULTRAVIOLET RADIATION (1801).
RITTER, Karl (1779–1859), German geographer. Professor at Berlin from 1820, he was one of the founders of modern human and comparative geography. His great work, *Earth Science in Relation to Nature and the History of Man* (1822–59), stresses the influence of environment on man's development.
RIVERA, Diego (1886–1957), Mexican mural painter. He studied in Europe, returning to Mexico in 1921. He painted large murals of social life and political themes throughout Mexico and also in the US, where his Marxist views aroused controversy.
RIVERA, José Eustasio (1889–1928), Colombian novelist. He is famous for his novel *The Vortex* (1924) which tells of the exploitation of rubber gatherers in the dense, hostile rain forest.
RIVERA, Primo de. See PRIMO DE RIVERA, MIGUEL.
RIVER BRETHREN, Christian revivalist sect originating in 1770 among German settlers in Pennsylvania. They were probably called River Brethren because of their ritual of river baptism. Members reject war and worldly pleasures such as alcohol and tobacco, and wear plain dress.
RIVERDALE, village in NE Ill. It is a suburb of Chicago, and produces steel. Pop 15806.

Detail from *The Conquest* (1929–34) by Diego Rivera, a mural in the Palacio Nacional, Mexico City, typical of the artist's work.

RIVER EDGE, residential borough in NE N.J., on the Hackensack R. Pop 12850.
RIVER FOREST, village in NE Ill. It is a residential suburb of Chicago, noted for houses designed by Frank Lloyd WRIGHT. Pop 13402.
RIVER ROUGE, city in SE Mich., 6mi SW of Detroit. It has shipbuilding, steel, automobile and paper industries. Pop 15947.
RIVERS, Larry (1923–), US painter. He adapted the style of ABSTRACT EXPRESSIONISM to the popular imagery of well-known pictures or commercial advertisements, as in *Dutch Masters Series* (1963).
RIVERS, William Halse Rivers (1864–1922), British anthropologist and psychologist who initiated the study of experimental PSYCHOLOGY at the University of Cambridge (c1893).
RIVERS AND LAKES, bodies of inland water. Rivers flow in natural channels to the sea, lakes or, as tributaries, into other rivers. They are a fundamental component of the HYDROLOGIC CYCLE (see DRAINAGE). Lakes are land-locked stretches of water fed by rivers; though the term may be applied also to temporary widenings of a river's course or to almost-enclosed bays and LAGOONS. In many parts of the world rivers and lakes may exist only during certain seasons, drying up partially or entirely during DROUGHT (see also ARROYO; PLAYA; WADI).
Rivers. The main sources of rivers are SPRINGS, lakes and GLACIERS. Near the source a river flows swiftly, the rocks and other abrasive particles that it carries eroding a steep-sided V-shaped VALLEY (see EROSION). Variations in the hardness of the rocks over which it runs may result in WATERFALLS. In the middle part of its course the gradients become less steep, and lateral (sideways) erosion becomes more important than downcutting. The valley is broader, the flow less swift, and meandering more common. Toward the rivermouth, the flow becomes more sluggish and meandering prominent: the river may form OXBOW LAKES. Sediment may be deposited at the mouth to form a DELTA (see also ESTUARY). (See also CANYON; HYDROELECTRIC POWER.)
Lakes. Most lakes are the result of glacial erosion during the ICE AGES. Glaciers hollowed out deep basins, often depositing MORAINE to form natural dams. Most lakes have an outflowing stream: where there is great water loss through EVAPORATION there is no such stream and the lake water is extremely saline (see also EVAPORITES), as in the Dead Sea. Lakes are comparatively temporary features on the landscape as they are constantly being infilled by silt. (See also DIVIDE; FIRTH; FJORD; GROUNDWATER; RESERVOIR.)
RIVERSIDE, city in S Cal., seat of Riverside Co. Its economy depends largely on the orange industry. Manufactures include machinery and aircraft parts. Pop 140089.
RIVERSIDE, village in NE Ill. It was planned as a model suburb of Chicago by F. L. OLSTED and C. Vaux, with buildings by Frank Lloyd WRIGHT. Pop 10432.
RIVERVIEW, city in SE Mich., a suburb of Detroit, on the Detroit R. It manufactures steel and chemical products. Pop 11342.
RIVETING, the joining of machine or structural parts, usually plates, by rivets. These are headed bolts, usually steel, which are passed through the plates, a second head then being formed on the plain end by pressure, hammering or an explosive charge. Large rivets are heated for satisfactory closing. Although riveting can be automated, it is slowly being displaced by arc WELDING.
RIVIERA, coastal region of the Mediterranean Sea in SE France and NW Italy. It is a major tourist center, noted for its scenery and pleasant climate. The Riviera's fashionable resorts include Cannes, Nice and St. Tropez in France; Monte Carlo in Monaco; and Bordighera, Portofino, Rapallo and San Remo in Italy.
RIVIÈRE DU LOUP, city in E Quebec, Canada. It is an important lumbering and agricultural center and summer resort. Pop 12760.
RIYADH, capital of Saudi Arabia, about 240mi E of the Persian Gulf. It is an important commercial center and has rapidly expanded recently because of the oil trade. Pop 300000.

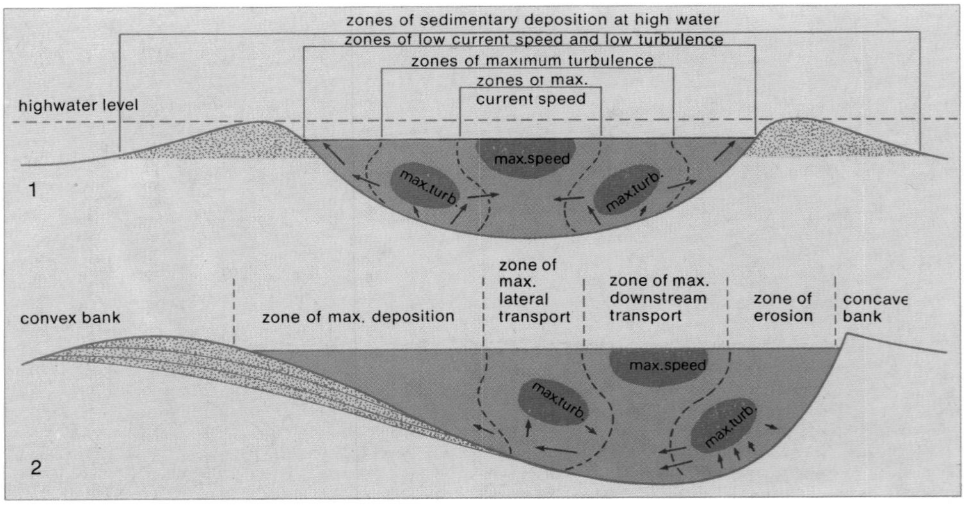

Diagram showing processes of change at work within a river. The material of the river-bed is being continually worn away, and transported and deposited elsewhere; how much and how far depends on the river's speed and turbulence. The movement of eroded material is indicated by arrows. (1) Straight river with a symmetrical bed; the eroded material is deposited on the banks when the water level is high. (2) Winding river with an asymmetrical bed; material is worn off the concave bank, usually the outer side of a curve, and deposited on the convex

RIZAL, José (1861–1896), Philippine writer and patriot. His novels, *The Lost Eden* (1886) and *The Subversive* (1891), denounced Spanish rule in the Philippines. His execution by the Spanish on false charges of instigating insurrection led to a full-scale rebellion.

RIZZIO, David (c1533–1566), favorite of MARY QUEEN OF SCOTS. An Italian musician, he became Mary's secretary in 1564. Scottish nobles, including Lord DARNLEY, Mary's husband, assassinated him.

RNA, ribonucleic acid. See NUCLEIC ACIDS.

ROACH, *Rutilus rutilus*, one of the common carp-like fishes of Europe, found in both lakes and rivers. A high-backed omnivorous fish, it may grow to 400mm (16in) and weigh 1.4kg (3lb).

ROACH. See COCKROACHES.

ROAD. See HIGHWAY.

ROADRUNNERS, two species, genus *Geococcyx*, of large slenderly-built, mainly terrestrial CUCKOOS of arid regions in central America. They fly weakly but have strong legs and run very rapidly, up to 24km/h (15mph), catching lizards and small rodents. Although they are cuckoos, roadrunners are not nest parasites.

ROAN ANTELOPE, *Hippotragus equinus*, a large African ANTELOPE related to the SABLE. They are gray-roan in color and both sexes have shortish horns used for fighting. They live in bush country.

ROANOKE ISLAND, island off the NE coast of N.C., 12mi by 3mi, site of the 16th-century LOST COLONY. Its economy depends on fishing and tourism.

ROANOKE RAPIDS, industrial city in N N.C. It manufactures cotton textiles and paper. Pop 13 508.

ROANOKE RIVER, river in S Va. and NE N.C. It flows for 410mi, of which 112mi are navigable, toward Albermarle Sound, N.C., and is a source of hydroelectric power.

ROBBE-GRILLET, Alain (1922–), French novelist, originator of the "new" or "anti-novel." In works such as *The Voyeur* (1955), *Jealousy* (1957) and the screen play for *Last Year at Marienbad* (1960), structure, objects and events displace character and story.

ROBBER FLIES, certain species of flies, family Asilidae, so called because the adults of both sexes feed exclusively by catching other insects in flight and sucking them dry. In the tropics some are huge: up to 75mm (3in) in length.

ROBBERY, the unlawful stealing of property by means of violence or threats. Armed robbery is a specific crime in US and English COMMON LAW.

ROBBIA, della, Italian Florentine family of sculptors who developed the art of glazed TERRACOTTA relief sculptures. **Luca** (c1399–1482), sculpted the famous marble "Singing Gallery" for Florence cathedral (1431–38) before turning to glazed relief work. The lunette *Madonna and Angels* (c1450) exemplifies the best of his style. His nephew and pupil **Andrea** (1435–1525) made roundels of *Infants in Swaddling Clothes* (1463) for the Hospital of the Innocents in Florence. Andrea's son, **Giovanni** (1469–1529), produced beautiful reliefs for the Church of St. Maria Novella, Florence; another son, **Girolamo** (1488–1566), worked for the French court.

ROBBINS, Frederick Chapman (1916–), US virologist who shared the 1954 Nobel Prize for Physiology or Medicine with J. F. ENDERS and T. H. WELLER for their cultivation of the POLIOMYELITIS virus in nonnerve tissues.

ROBBINS, Jerome (1918–), US choreographer and dancer. His first ballet was *Fancy Free* (1944). He was artistic director to the New York City Ballet 1949–63. He helped create *Fiddler on the Roof* (1964) and *West Side Story* (1957) for which he received an Academy Award.

ROBBINSDALE, city in SE central Minn. It is a residential suburb of Minneapolis. Pop 16 845.

ROBERT I, King of Scotland. See BRUCE, ROBERT.

ROBERTS, Sir Charles George Douglas (1860–1943), Canadian poet and writer. His simple descriptive poems of the Maritime provinces were an important contribution to the emerging Canadian consciousness. Among his best-known works are animal stories such as *Red Fox* (1905).

ROBERTS, Kenneth Lewis (1885–1957), US writer and *Saturday Evening Post* correspondent. He wrote a series of popular historical novels, including *Arundel* (1930) and *Northwest Passage* (1937), receiving a special Pulitzer Prize citation for them in 1957. He also wrote travel books.

ROBERTS, Owen Josephus (1875–1955), US associate justice of the Supreme Court, 1930–45. He was a prosecuting attorney in the TEAPOT DOME scandal 1924 and was involved in economic legislation in the Depression. He led the inquiry into the PEARL HARBOR disaster, 1941.

ROBERTSON, James (1742–1814), American frontier leader who brought settlers from North Carolina to Tennessee in 1771. He explored the Cumberland R area, founded Nashville (1780) and helped draft the Tennessee Constitution (1796).

ROBERTSON, "Big O" (Oscar Robertson: 1938–), US basketball player. He has played professionally with the Cincinnati Royals, 1960–70, and the Milwaukee Bucks from 1970. One of the all-time scorers, he has made over 9 000 scoring assists.

ROBESON, Paul (1898–1976), US singer and stage and film actor. A popular singer of Negro spirituals, his most famous song was "Ol' Man River" from the musical *Show Boat* (1928). Robeson starred in the play and film of *Emperor Jones* (1925; 1933) and in Shakespeare's *Othello*. Ostracized in the US for his communist beliefs, he lived in Europe 1958–63.

ROBESPIERRE, Maximilien François Marie Isidore de (1758–1794), fanatical idealist leader of the FRENCH REVOLUTION. An Arras lawyer, he was elected as being representative of the third estate in the STATES GENERAL in 1789 and rose to become leader of the radical JACOBINS in 1793. He liquidated the rival moderate GIRONDINS and as leader of the Committee of Public Safety he initiated the REIGN OF TERROR. He hoped to establish a "Reign of Virtue" by ridding France of all its internal enemies. However, the National Convention rose against him, alienated by his increasing power, by the mass executions and the threat of further purges, and by the new religious cult of the "Supreme Being." He was arrested, summarily tried and executed.

ROBIN, vernacular name for various unrelated species of small birds with red breasts, referring to different species in different countries. They include the European robin, *Erithacus rubecula*, American robin, *Turdus migratorius*, Pekin robin, *Leiothrix lutea*, and Indian robin, *Saxicoloides fulicata*. Most familiar are the European robin (Robin redbreast), an insectivorous thrush of woods and gardens, noted for its beautiful song, and the American robin, a common garden and woodland bird of the US.

ROBIN HOOD, legendary medieval English hero. He is usually depicted as an outlaw, living with his band of "merry men" including Little John, Friar Tuck and Maid Marian in Sherwood Forest in Nottinghamshire and robbing the Norman overlords to give to the poor.

ROBINSON, Edward G. (born Emmanuel Goldberg; 1893–1973), US actor, famous for portrayals of ruthless gangster characters in such films as *Little Caesar* (1931), and *Kid Galahad* (1937), and for his role in *Double Indemnity* (1948).

ROBINSON, Edwin Arlington (1869–1935), US poet, known for his series of terse, sometimes bitter verse characterizations of the inhabitants of the fictitious "Tilbury town." Two of his long narrative poems, *The Man Who Died Twice* (1924), and *Tristram* (1928), won Pulitzer prizes.

ROBINSON, Jack Roosevelt (1919–1972), the first black baseball player to be admitted to the major US leagues and a great baserunner. He joined the Brooklyn Dodgers in 1947 and maintained a batting average of 311 through 10 seasons.

ROBINSON, James Harvey (1863–1936), US historian. He was one of the founders of the "new history," studying the intellectual, social and scientific development of man rather than the narrow range of political events.

ROBINSON, John (c1576–1625), English pastor to the PILGRIM FATHERS in Holland. He moved to Leiden with a group of SEPARATISTS in 1609, founded a new church and actively encouraged the voyage of the Pilgrims to America. He wrote several tracts on the Separatist position.

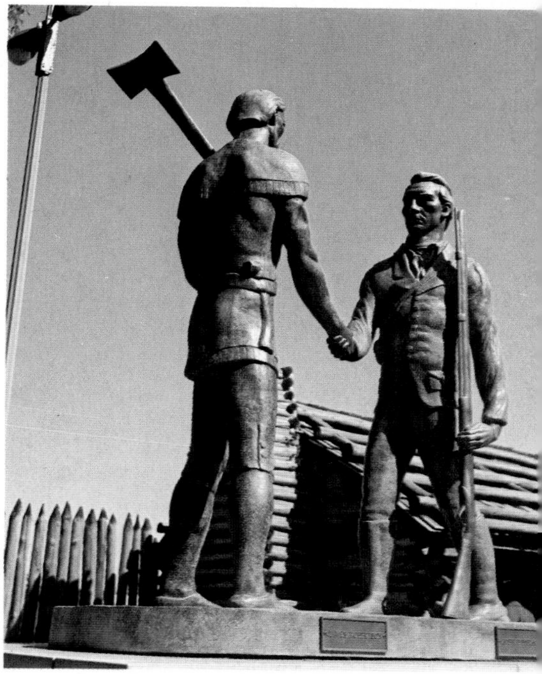

A statue of James Robertson stands outside Fort Nashborough, which he founded as the nucleus of Nashville, Tenn. He is depicted shaking hands with fellow pioneer Colonel John Donelson.

ROBINSON, "Sugar" Ray (born Walter Smith; 1921–), US boxer who won the world welterweight title in 1946 and the middleweight title in 1951. He retired in 1952, but returned in 1955 to regain it, becoming in 1958 the first boxer to win a divisional world championship five times.

ROBINSON, Sir Robert (1886–), British organic chemist awarded the 1947 Nobel Prize for Chemistry for his pioneering studies of the molecular structures of the ALKALOIDS and other vegetable-derived substances.

ROBINSON CRUSOE. See DEFOE, DANIEL; SELKIRK, ALEXANDER.

ROBOT (from Czech *robota*, work), or automaton, an automatic machine that does work, simulating and replacing human activity; known as an android if humanoid in form (which most are not). Robots have evolved out of simpler automatic devices, and many are now capable of decision-making, self-programming, and carrying out complex operations. Some have sensory devices. They are increasingly being used in industry and scientific research for tasks such as handling hot or radioactive materials. Science fiction from Čapek to Asimov and beyond has featured robots. (See also MECHANIZATION AND AUTOMATION; REMOTE CONTROL.)

ROB ROY (1671–1734), nickname of Scottish outlaw Robert MacGregor, romanticized in Sir Walter SCOTT's *Rob Roy*. He was evicted and outlawed for cattle theft in 1712 by the Duke of Montrose, whose tenants he then plundered. Hunted for many years he surrendered in 1722, but was pardoned in 1727.

ROBSON, Mount, peak in Mount Robson Park, E British Columbia, Canada, and highest Canadian peak of the Rocky Mts (12 972ft).

ROBSTOWN, city in S Tex., 15mi W of Corpus Christi. It is an oil, grain and cotton shipping center. Pop 11 217.

ROCHAMBEAU, Jean Baptiste Donatien de Vimeur, Comte de (1725–1807), French general who commanded French troops sent to help WASHINGTON in the American revolution. Involved in the French Revolution, he narrowly escaped execution in the Reign of Terror, and was later pensioned by NAPOLEON.

ROCHELLE SALT. See TARTARIC ACID.

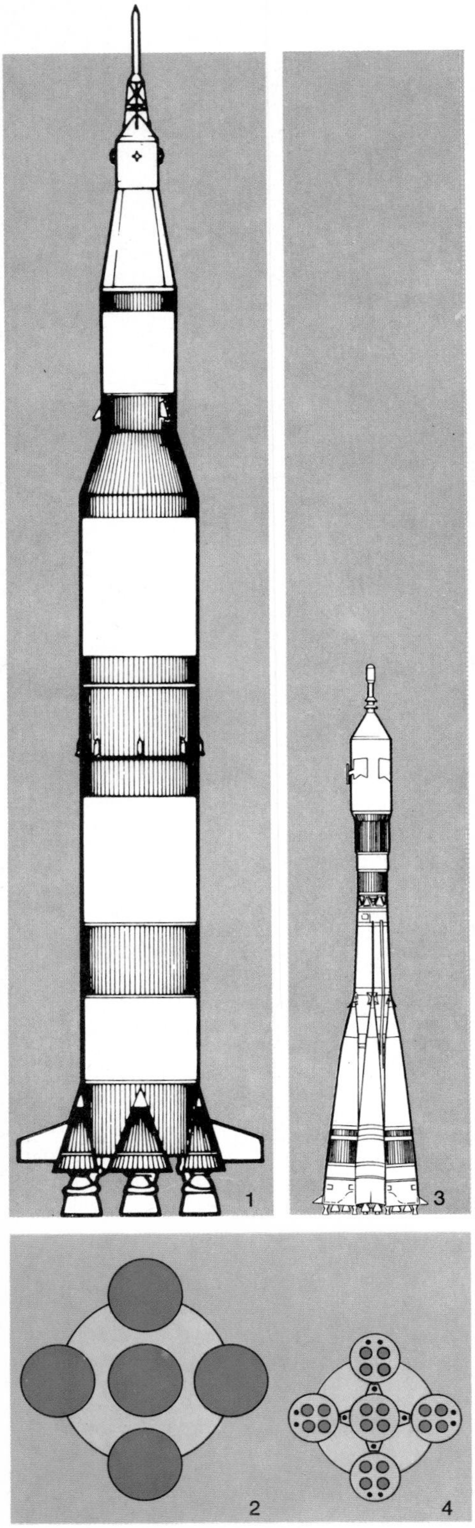

The space program led to great advances in rocket development in the 1950s and 1960s, especially in the use of multiple stages to lift larger payloads. Perhaps the most spectacular result of this was the gigantic Saturn V, used to launch the Apollo moon missions (1) The first stage alone *(below)* is 10m in diameter, and is driven by five F-1 rocket motors developing 3750 tonnes thrust, arranged in a four-pointed star (2). The USSR, lacking such powerful motors, used 32 smaller motors for their RNS rocket (3), arranged in a similar configuration (4). The RNS 49m is much shorter than the 110m Saturn, and has a proportionally much wider base.
(Right) a Thor-Delta rocket.

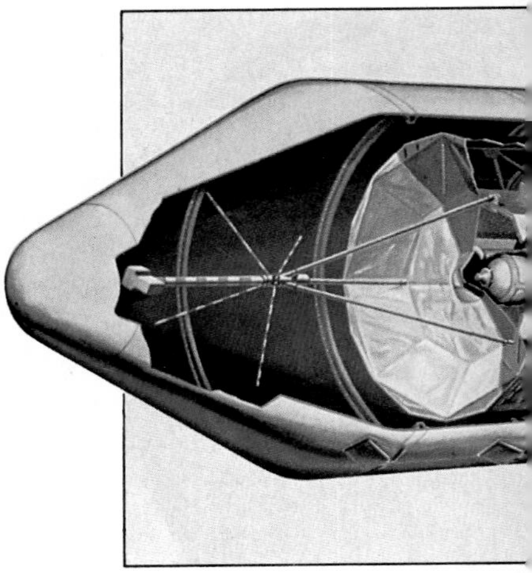

ROCHESTER, manufacturing city in SE Minn. Seat of Olmsted Co., it is an agricultural center and site of the MAYO CLINIC. Pop 53 776.

ROCHESTER, manufacturing city in SE N.H. Its chief industries are paper, and woolen and rayon textiles. It has fruit and dairy farming. Pop 17 938.

ROCHESTER, industrial city and port in N.Y., seat of Monroe Co. on the Genesee R. The city is known as a cultural center, and is the site of Rochester U. and other colleges. It has diverse industries. Pop 296 233.

ROCK BORERS, bivalve MOLLUSKS adapted for boring out galleries in rock in which to live. The serrated margins of the partially-opened valves of the shell are used to drill out the rock. The group includes the genera *Pholas, Hiatella* and *Barnea*.

ROCK CRYSTAL. See QUARTZ.

ROCKEFELLER, family of US financiers. **John Davison Rockefeller** (1839–1937), entered the infant oil industry at Cleveland, Ohio, at the age of 24, and ruthlessly unified the oil industry into the Standard Oil Trust. He devoted a large part of his later life to philanthropy, creating the ROCKEFELLER FOUNDATION. **John Davison Rockefeller, Jr.** (1874–1960), only son of John D. Rockefeller, followed his father's business and charitable interests. He donated the land for the UN headquarters and helped found the Rockefeller Center in New York. **Nelson Aldrich Rockefeller** (1908–   ), second son of John, Jr., governor of N.Y. 1959–73, was appointed US vice-president in 1974. He sought presidential nomination in 1960, 1964 and 1968. He expanded transportation, welfare, housing and other social services in N.Y. **Winthrop Rockefeller** (1912–1973), son of John, Jr., was Republican governor of Ark. (1967–1970). **David Rockefeller** (1915–   ), youngest son of John, Jr., is president of the Chase-Manhattan Bank and chairman of the Rockefeller University.

ROCKEFELLER FOUNDATION, second largest of US philanthropic foundations, with assets of nearly $1000 million. Founded in 1913 by John D. ROCKEFELLER, it supports research in three main areas: medical and natural sciences, agricultural sciences, and the humanities and social sciences.

ROCKET, form of JET-PROPULSION engine in which the substances (fuel and oxidizer) needed to produce the propellant gas jet are carried internally. Working by reaction, and being independent of atmospheric oxygen, rockets are used to power interplanetary space vehicles (see SPACE EXPLORATION). In addition to their chief use to power MISSILES, rockets are also used for supersonic and assisted-takeoff airplane propulsion, and sounding rockets are used for scientific investigation of the upper atmosphere. The first rockets—of the firework type, cardboard tubes containing GUNPOWDER—were made in 13th-century China, and the idea quickly spread to the West. Their military use was limited, guns being superior, until they were developed by William CONGREVE. Later Congreve rockets mounted the guide stick along the central axis; and William Hale eliminated it altogether, placing curved vanes in the exhaust stream, thus stabilizing the rocket's motion by causing it to rotate on its axis. The 20th century saw the introduction of new fuels and oxidants, e.g., a mixture of NITROCELLULOSE and NITROGLYCERIN for solid-fuel rockets, or ETHANOL and liquid oxygen for the more efficient liquid-fuel rockets. The first liquid-fuel rocket was made by R. H. GODDARD, who also invented the multistage rocket. In WWII Germany, and afterward in the US, Wernher von BRAUN made vast improvements in rocket design. Other propulsion methods, including the use of nuclear furnaces, electrically-accelerated PLASMAS and ION PROPULSION, are being developed.

ROCK FALLS, industrial city in NW Ill., 50mi SW of Rockford on the Rock R. It is set in an agricultural area. Pop 10 287.

ROCKFISHES, any of a great variety of fishes inhabiting rocky sea bottoms, particularly the genera *Pholis*, slender, eel-like rockfishes, and *Sebastodes*, viviparous fishes with armored heads including the bocacios and chilipeppers.

ROCKFORD, second largest city in Ill., seat of Winnebago Co. on the Rock R. A major industrial city, it is also an agricultural trade center. Pop 147 370.

ROCK HILL, city in N S.C. Its industries include textiles, plastics and farming. Pop 33 846.

ROCKINGHAM, Charles Watson-Wentworth, 2nd Marquess of (1730–1782), British statesman, prime minister 1765–66. He repealed the Stamp Act, 1765 and tried to conciliate the American colonies. During his second term as premier (1782) he urged peace with the US.

ROCK ISLAND, city in NW Ill., seat of Rock Island Co. on the Mississippi R. It has diverse manufacturing industries, including one of the world's largest manufacturing arsenals. Pop 50 166.

ROCKLAND, industrial town in E Mass. Its products include shoes and plastics. Pop 15 674.

ROCKLEDGE, city in E central Fla., on the Indian River lagoon, 4mi W of Cocoa. Pop 10 523.

ROCK MUSIC, popular music which derived its name from dancing known as Rock 'n' Roll. Introduced in the mid-1950s by performers such as Bill Haley and the Comets, famous for their "Rock around the Clock," and by Elvis PRESLEY, it used electronically amplified guitars and an emphatic rhythmic beat. In the 1960s, British groups like the BEATLES introduced new styles; Rock musicians also began to adopt jazz and classical elements. Rock operas and Rock oratorios have been produced; there is also "hard rock," which relies on sheer volume of sound.

ROCKNE, Knute Kenneth (1888–1931), Norweg-

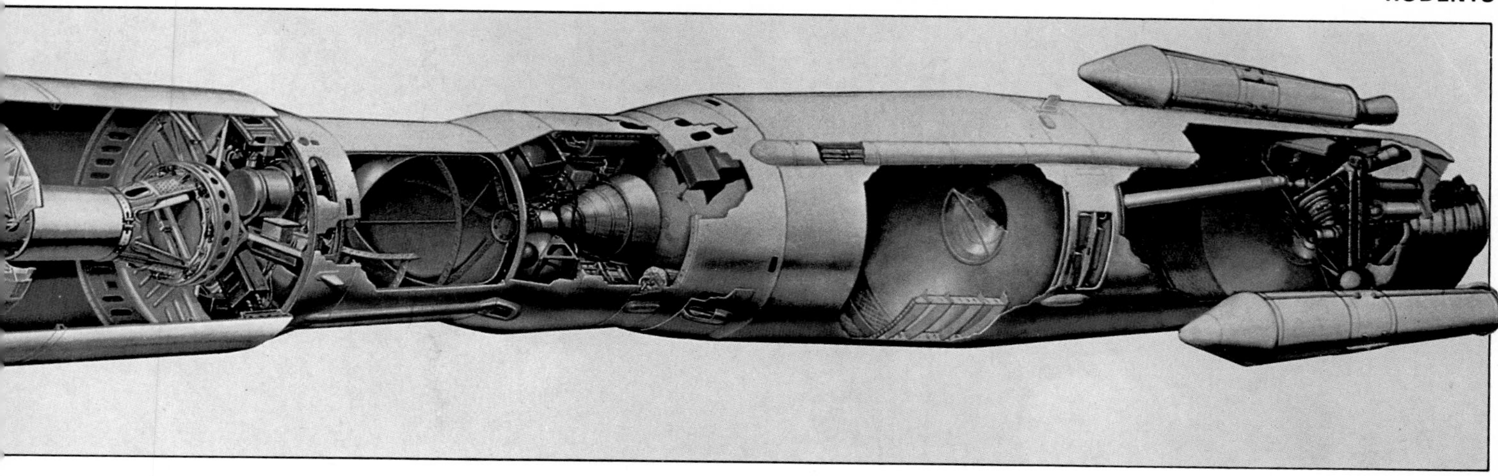

ian-born US football coach. He was head coach at Notre Dame, Chicago, where he played from his student days until his death. His revolutionary attacking tactics achieved for his teams 105 victories, five ties and only 12 defeats.

ROCK PIGEON, or **Rock Dove**, *Columba livia*, a species of PIGEON widely distributed throughout Europe, from which all domestic, and thus feral, pigeons derive. In the wild, the Rock dove is a small, cliff-nesting species, with gray plumage and green or brown neck.

ROCK RIVER, rises in SE Wis. and flows 285mi S and SW through NW Ill., meeting the Mississippi R at Rock Island.

ROCKS, the solid materials making up the earth's crust. They may be consolidated (e.g., sandstone) or unconsolidated (e.g., sand). The study of rocks is **petrology**. Strictly, the term applies only to those materials which, unlike MINERALS, are not homogeneous and have no definite chemical composition. The primary constituents of rocks are OXYGEN and SILICON, combined with each other to form SILICA (see QUARTZ) and with each other and further elements (e.g., aluminum, iron, calcium, potassium, sodium and magnesium) to form SILICATES. Together, silica and silicates make up about 95% of the earth's rocks. There are three main classes of rocks, igneous, sedimentary and metamorphic. IGNEOUS ROCKS form from the MAGMA, a molten, subsurface complex of silicates. They are the primary source of all the earth's rocks. SEDIMENTARY ROCKS are consolidated accumulations of fragmented inorganic and organic material. They are of three types: classic, formed of weathered (see EROSION) particles of other rocks (e.g., SANDSTONE); organic deposits (e.g., COAL, some LIMESTONES); and chemical precipitates (e.g., the EVAPORITES). (See also FOSSILS; STRATIGRAPHY.) METAMORPHIC ROCKS have undergone change within the earth under heat, pressure or chemical action. Sedimentary, igneous and even previously metamorphosed rocks may change structure or composition in this way. (See also EARTH; GEOLOGY.)

ROCK SALT, or **Halite**. See SALT.

ROCK SPRINGS, city in SW Wyo., site of coal and uranium mines and oil wells. It is a livestock shipping center. Pop 11 657.

ROCKVILLE, city in central Md., the seat of Montgomery Co., 15mi NNW of Washington. Pop 41 654.

ROCKVILLE CENTER, village in SE N.Y. It is a residential suburb of New York. Pop 27 444.

ROCKWEED, various species of coarse SEAWEED, particularly those of the genera *Fucus* and *Ascophyllum*, which are found on rocky coasts. They form a slippery, olive-green mass of vegetation.

ROCKWELL, Norman (1894–), US illustrator, known for his realistic and humorous scenes of US small town life. His work includes magazine covers for *The Saturday Evening Post* and a series of paintings of the FOUR FREEDOMS.

ROCKY HILL, town in N Conn., on the Connecticut R, first settled in 1650. It manufactures metal products and firearms. Pop 11 103.

ROCKY MOUNT, city in NE N.C. Besides being a large tobacco market, it produces cotton, corn, textiles and chemicals. Pop 34 284.

ROCKY MOUNTAIN GOAT, *Oreamnos americanus*, a goat-antelope of North America, distantly related to the European CHAMOIS. They are abundant on wet, cold mountain ranges, and are highly-adapted to living on steep, usually snow-covered slopes. Both sexes have thick white woolly coats and muscular legs with broad hooves.

ROCKY MOUNTAIN NATIONAL PARK, natural wild area in N central Col., in the heart of the Rocky Mts. Founded in 1915, the park is dominated by Longs Peak (14 255ft), third highest peak in North America. The park has many glaciers.

ROCKY MOUNTAINS, principal range of W North America. Extending from N Alaska for over 3 000mi to N.M., they form the continental divide; streams rising on the E slopes flow to the Arctic or Atlantic and on the W toward the Pacific. Rivers rising in the Rockies include the Missouri, Rio Grande, Colorado, Columbia and Arkansas. A relatively new system, the Rockies were formed by massive uplifting forces that began about 70 million years ago. The system can be divided into: the Southern Rocky Mts of S Wyo., Col., and N N.M.; the Central Rocky Mts between Mont. and N Ut.; the Northern Rocky Mts of Wash., Mont. and Ida.; the Canadian Rockies of British Columbia, Alberta and Yukon; and the Brooks Range of Alaska. The highes peak is Mt Elbert (14 431ft). National Parks in the Rockies include JASPER NATIONAL PARK, GLACIER NATIONAL PARK, YELLOWSTONE and GRAND TETON. The Rockies are one of the richest mineral deposits in North America, and a major tourist center.

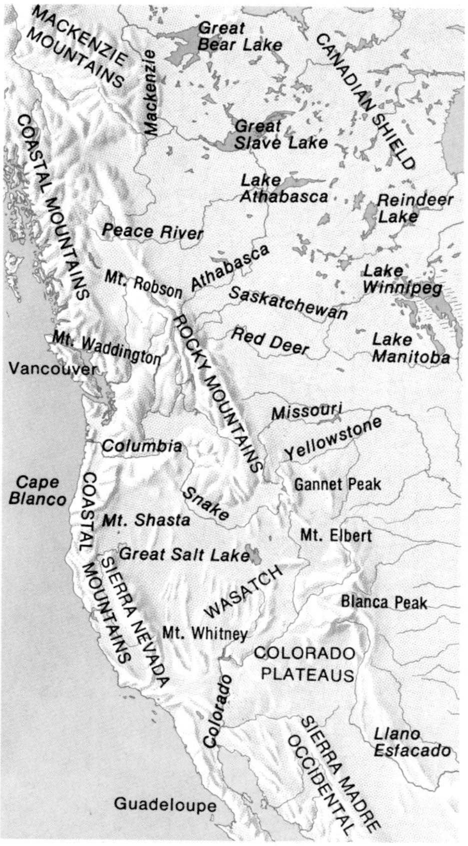

The extent of the enormous Rocky Mountain chain along the west of North America.

The Athabaska glacier flows around Mount Athabaska in the Canadian Rockies. The effect of the glacier on the rock of this relatively young chain can be clearly seen on the valley walls, eroded smooth.

ROCKY MOUNTAIN SHEEP. See BIGHORN.

ROCKY MOUNTAIN SPOTTED FEVER, tick-borne rickettsial disease (see RICKETTSIA) seen in much of the US, especially the Rocky mountain region. It causes FEVER, HEADACHE and a characteristic rash starting on the palms and soles, later spreading elsewhere. TETRACYCLINES are effective, though untreated cases may be fatal.

ROCKY RIVER, city in N Ohio, on Lake Erie, 8mi W of Cleveland, of which it is a residential suburb. Pop 22 958.

ROCOCO, 18th century European artistic and architectural style. The term derives from *rocaille* (French: grottowork), whose arabesque and ingenious forms are found in many Rococo works. The style, characterized by lightness and delicacy, emerged c1700 in France, finding expression in the works of BOUCHER, FRAGONARD and others. Some of the greatest achievements of Rococo sculpture and decoration are found in the palaces and pilgrimage churches of Austria and S Germany.

RODENTS, the largest order of MAMMALS including some 1 500 species of MICE, RATS, PORCUPINES and SQUIRRELS. Rodents are easily identified by the

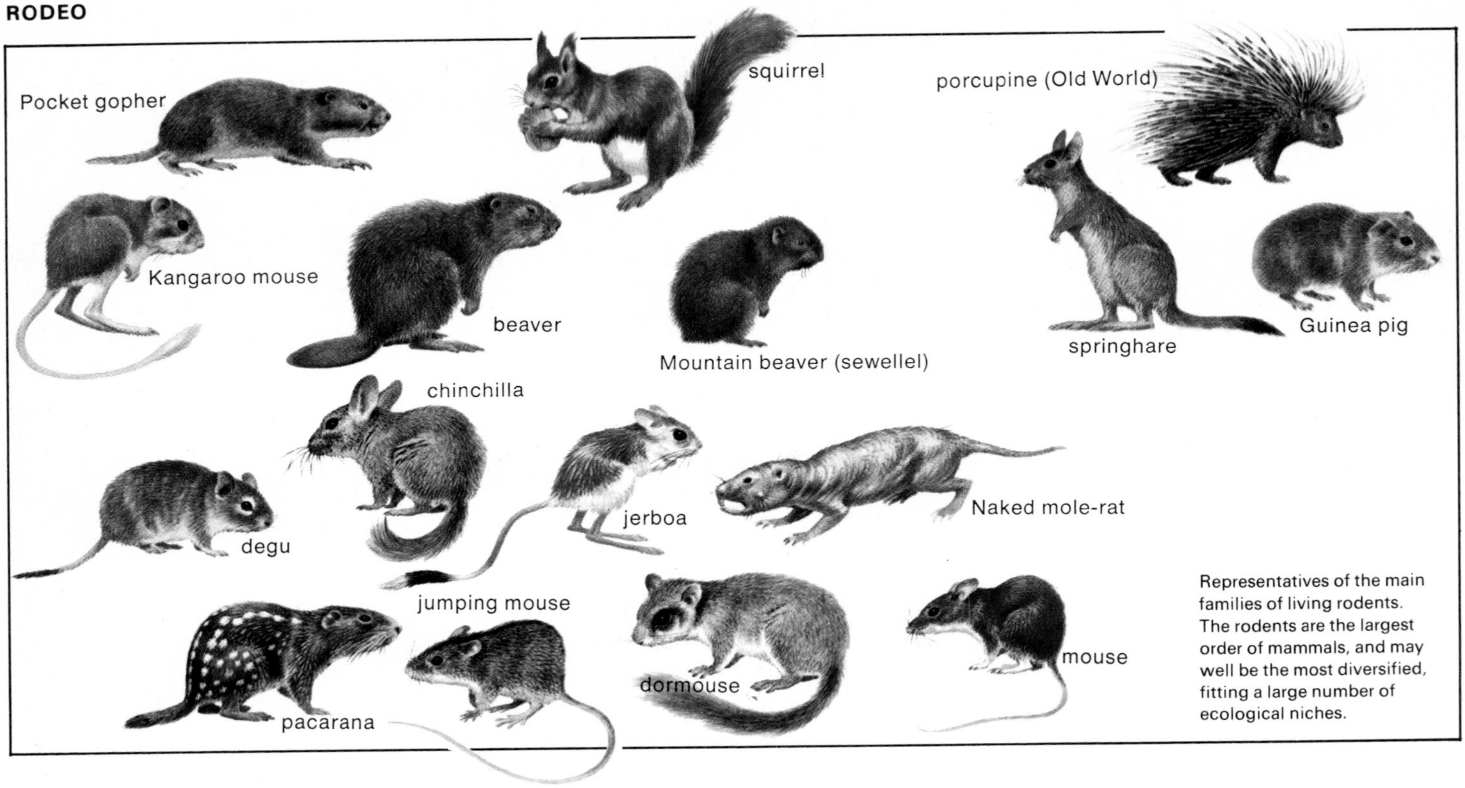

Representatives of the main families of living rodents. The rodents are the largest order of mammals, and may well be the most diversified, fitting a large number of ecological niches.

structure and arrangement of the TEETH. There is a single pair of incisors in the upper and lowe jaws which continue to grow throughout life. The wearing surface develops a chisel-like edge. Behind the incisors is a gap, or diastema, to allow recirculation of food in chewing. Furthermore, the cheek skin can be drawn across the diastema in front of the molars and premolars, leaving the incisors free for gnawing. Rodents are predominantly eaters of seeds, grain and other vegetation. Their adaptability in feeding on a variety of vegetable matter allows them to exploit a variety of NICHES.

RODEO, in the US and Canada, contest and entertainment based on ranching techniques; it derives from late 19th-century COWBOY meets when contests were held to celebrate the end of a cattle drive. It usually comprises five main events: *calf-roping*, in which a mounted cowboy must rope a calf, dismount, throw the calf and tie three of its legs together; *steer-wrestling*, in which the cowboy jumps from a galloping horse and wrestles a steer to the ground by its horns; *bareback riding*, on an unbroken horse for 8–10 secs; *saddle-bronc riding*, and *bull-riding*.

RODGERS, Richard Charles (1902–), US composer of musicals. He collaborated with librettist Lorenz HART on *A Connecticut Yankee* (1927), *Pal Joey* (1940) and many others, and with Oscar HAMMERSTEIN II on the Pulitzer prize-winning *Oklahoma* (1943), *South Pacific* (1949) and *The King and I* (1951).

RODIN, Auguste (1840–1917), major French sculptor. He rose to fame c1877, and in 1880 began the never-completed *Gate of Hell*, source of such well known pieces as *The Thinker* (1880) and *The Kiss* (1886). His works, in stone or bronze, were characterized by energy and emotional intensity, as in *The Burghers of Calais* (1884–86).

RODNEY, Caesar (1728–1784), American patriot and statesman who helped to bring Delaware into the Revolutionary War. He was Delaware's delegate to the Continental Congress, 1775–76, signed the Declaration of Independence and was president of Delaware, 1778–81.

RODNEY, George Brydges Rodney, 1st Baron (1719–1792), English admiral. His achievements include capturing Martinique (1762) in the SEVEN YEARS WAR, relieving Gibraltar from the Spanish in 1780, and defeating the French West Indies fleet in 1782.

RODS AND CONES. See VISION.

ROEBLING, John Augustus (1806–1869), German-born US bridge engineer who pioneered modern suspension bridge design. His most famous works are the Brooklyn Bridge in New York City, and the Niagara Falls Bridge (1885), using wire rope instead of chains. He died before the completion of the Brooklyn Bridge, finished by his son **Washington Augustus Roebling** (1837–1926).

ROEBUCK, John (1718–1794), British inventor of the LEAD CHAMBER PROCESS for making sulfuric acid (1746), and patron of James WATT.

ROE DEER, *Capreolus capreolus*, a medium-sized DEER distributed throughout Europe and Asia. A rich red coat of summer months is molted to a grayer pelage with a pronounced white rump patch in winter. Solitary deer, roe bucks have small ANTLERS of up to six points.

ROEHM, Ernst (1887–1934), German Nazi leader, organizer of the SA (see STORM TROOPS) and as such a serious rival to HITLER from the 1920s. A dissolute adventurer, he was executed in the June 1934 purge for plotting Hitler's overthrow.

ROEMER, Ole or **Olaus**. See RØMER, OLE OR OLAUS.

ROENTGEN (or **Röntgen**)**, Wilhelm Conrad** (1845–1923), German physicist, recipient in 1901 of the first Nobel Prize for Physics for his discovery of X RAYS. This discovery was made in 1895 when by chance he noticed that a PHOSPHOR screen nearby a vacuum tube through which he was passing an electric current fluoresced brightly, even when shielded by opaque cardboard. (See also RÖNTGEN (unit).)

Bronco-busting at a rodeo in Saskatchewan, Canada. The rodeo as such seems to have begun in North Platte, Nebraska, in 1882, when Buffalo Bill Cody decided to celebrate the Fourth of July with an "Old Glory Blowout."

ROETHKE, Theodore (1908–1963), US poet, influenced by T. S. ELIOT and YEATS, who won the 1954 Pulitzer Prize for *The Waking Poems* (1933–1953). Much of his imagery is drawn from nature.

ROGATION DAYS, in the CHURCH YEAR, April 25th and the three days preceding Ascension Day, days of intercession for harvests.

ROGERS, resort city in NW Ark., with meat-processing and electrical industries. Pop 11 050.

ROGERS, Carl Ransom (1902–), US psychotherapist who instituted the idea of the patient determining the extent and nature of his course of therapy, the therapist following the patient's lead.

ROGERS, Henry Huttleston (1840–1909), pioneering US oil magnate who developed refining techniques and invented oil pipeline transportation.

ROGERS, John (1829–1904), US sculptor known for realistic figural groups such as *The Slave Auction*. His extremely popular works were often mass-produced.

ROGERS, Robert (1731–1795), American frontiersman who led the famous British–American *Rogers' Rangers*, commandos who adopted Indian tactics, in the FRENCH AND INDIAN WARS. An associate of Jonathan CARVER, he was involved in various dubious enterprises and was a Loyalist during the Revolution.

ROGERS, William Penn Adair, "Will" (1879–1935), US humorist known for his homespun philosophy and mockery of politics and other subjects previously considered "untouchable." Part Irish and part Cherokee, he became famous in the Ziegfield Follies of 1916. He also contributed a syndicated column to 350 newspapers.

ROGERS, William Pierce (1913–), US lawyer and statesman, President NIXON's first secretary of state, 1969–73. He was US attorney general (1957–61) and set up the civil rights division of the Justice Department.

ROGERS' RANGERS. See ROGERS, ROBERT.

ROGET, Peter Mark (1779–1869), English scholar and physician, remembered for his definitive *Thesaurus of English Words and Phrases* (1852). He described it as a "dictionary in reverse"; if one has the general idea, the book will provide the precise word to convey it.

RÓHEIM, Géza (1891–1953), Hungarian-born US anthropologist best known for his application of the ideas of PSYCHOANALYSIS in ETHNOLOGY studies.

ROKOSSOVSKY, Konstantin Konstantinovich (1896–1968), Russian army commander who defended Moscow in 1941 and defeated the Germans at Stalingrad in 1943. He was deputy premier of Poland, 1952–56, and Russian deputy defense minister, 1956–58.

ROLAND, one of CHARLEMAGNE's commanders, hero of the CHANSON DE ROLAND. Ambushed by Basques at RONCESVALLES in 778, he and his men were massacred because he was too proud to summon help.

ROLAND DE LA PLATIÈRE, Jean Marie (1734–1793), French revolutionary, leader of the GIRONDINS in 1791 and minister of the interior 1792–93. He fled Paris in 1793, after trying to save LOUIS XVI. He committed suicide on hearing of the execution of his wife, Jeanne, whose salon had been an important Girondin intellectual gathering.

ROLFE, Frederick William (1860–1913), English novelist, also known as Baron Corvo. His works include *Hadrian the Seventh* (1904) and *The Desire and Pursuit of the Whole* (1934).

ROLFE, John (1585–1622), early English settler in Virginia who married the Indian princess POCAHONTAS in 1614. His methods of curing tobacco made it the basis of the colony's later prosperity. He was probably killed in an Indian massacre.

ROLLA, city in central Mo., seat of Phelps Co., located in a farming area of the Ozarks. Pop 13 245.

ROLLAND, Romain (1866–1944), French novelist and musicologist who won the 1915 Nobel Prize for Literature. He is best known for his biographies, including *Beethoven* (1909), his WWI pacifist articles *Above the Battle* (1915), and the 10-volume novel-cycle *Jean Christophe* (1904–1912), about the life of a musical genius.

ROLLER SKATING, popular sport and recreation, formerly a pastime of nearly every US child, but now increasingly enjoyed by adults in indoor rinks. Invented by an unknown Dutchman, the skates consist of four wheels with ball bearings, attached to a shoe or steel platform. The roller derby is a rough-and-tumble marathon race.

ROLLING MEADOWS, city in NE Ill., residential suburb of Chicago, with light manufacturing. Pop 19 178.

ROLLING MILLS, equipment—essentially sets of power-driven heavy steel rollers—used for flattening metal ingots and producing sheets, bars, rails etc. STEEL is usually rolled hot; nonferrous metals cold.

ROLLO, or **Hrolf** (c860–c932), Viking chieftain, first duke of Normandy. He was granted Normandy in 911 by the French crown when he adopted Christianity.

RØLVAAG, Ole Edvaart (1876–1931), Norwegian-born novelist, who came to the US in 1896 and wrote in Norwegian. His trilogy *Giants in the Earth* (1927–31) is the story of Norwegian settlers in the US Northwest.

ROMAINS, Jules, pen name of Louis Farigoule (1885–1972), distinguished French author and exponent of unanism, or the collective personality. He is known for his plays and his 27-volume cycle *Men of Good Will* (1932–46).

ROMAN ART AND ARCHITECTURE, art of the Roman republic and empire, derived from GREEK ART AND ARCHITECTURE and the art of the ETRUSCANS. In architecture, the Romans combined the arch and column and developed the structural function of vaults and buttresses. Triumphal arches were erected throughout the empire to commemorate important events; the Romans, using concrete instead of stone, excelled in building temples, forums, basilicas, baths, amphitheatres, bridges, aqueducts and sophisticated villas. In art they are known for their realistic portrait busts and carved reliefs on monuments and on triumphal arches. Some of the finest extant Roman painting is at POMPEII, applied to walls as interior decoration. Floor mosaics range from geometric configurations to stylized floral and figure compositions. In the minor arts, the skills of making medallions, coins and cameos, and of carving gems were highly developed.

ROMAN CATHOLIC CHURCH, major branch of the Christian Church, arising out of the WESTERN CHURCH, consisting of those Christians who are in communion with the pope (see PAPACY). It comprises especially the ecclesiastical organization that remained under papal obedience at the REFORMATION, consisting of a hierarchy of bishops and priests (see MINISTRY), with other officers such as CARDINALS. Roman Catholicism stresses the authority of tradition and of the Church (as capitulated in ECUMENICAL COUNCILS and the papacy) to formulate doctrine and regulate the life of the Church. Members participate in GRACE, mediated through the priesthood, by means of the seven SACRAMENTS: the MASS is central to Roman Catholic life and worship. In the Middle Ages the Church influenced all aspects of life in W Europe, and the prelates controlled vast estates. There was a constant struggle with kings and the emperor over the Church's political pretensions. The challenge of the Reformation was met by the Council of TRENT and by the COUNTER-REFORMATION, many abuses being remedied and large-scale MISSIONS begun. Doctrinally, Roman Catholic theologians since the Reformation have stressed and elaborated the role of the Virgin MARY and the authority and infallibility of the pope. Other distinctive doctrines include clerical celibacy, LIMBO and PURGATORY. Those held in common with the ORTHODOX CHURCHES (but rejected by Protestants) include invocation of SAINTS, veneration of images, the acceptance of the APOCRYPHA, the entire sacramental system, and MONASTICISM. Especially from the 18th century, ANTICLERICALISM weakened the Church's prevailing influence, and the loss of the PAPAL STATES was perhaps its political nadir. Since the Second VATICAN COUNCIL there has been a vigorous movement toward détente with the modern world, cautious dealings with the ECUMENICAL MOVEMENT and

Three massive arches are all that remain of the Basilica of Maxentius in the Forum Adjectum in Rome (*top*). Completed by Constantine the Great, it marks the decline of Roman art, since after his reign the cultural center of the empire shifted to Constantinople (Byzantium), which he made his eastern capital. *Below*: among the best preserved examples of Roman architecture outside Italy are these Roman baths at Bath in England.

Caricature of the great Romantic composer Berlioz conducting a bizarre orchestra, a satire on the use of new instruments in Romantic works.

encouragement of lay participation and vernacular LITURGY. There are now c600 million Roman Catholics, and the Church's economic and political influence remains moderately strong, especially in S Europe, South America and the Philippines. (See also CATHOLIC; CHRISTIANITY; CURIA; MODERNISM; OLD CATHOLICS; UNIATE CHURCHES.)

ROMANCE, work of fiction concerning romantic or chivalric adventures. It derived from the French medieval *roman*, sung or recited by TROUBADORS, and developed into the popular CHANSON DE GESTE.

ROMANCE LANGUAGES, one of the main groups of the INDO-EUROPEAN LANGUAGES. It comprises those languages derived from the vernacular Latin which was spread by Roman soldiers and colonists, and superseded local tongues. The languages include Italian, the Rhaeto-Romanic dialects of Alpine regions, Provençal, French, the Walloon dialect of S Belgium, Spanish, the Catalan dialect around Barcelona, Portuguese and Romanian. Although differentiated by dialects the languages share a similar vocabulary and grammatical development.

ROMAN CURIA. See CURIA.

ROMAN DE LA ROSE, Le, medieval French poem, an elaborate allegory of love in 22 000 lines, of which 4 058 were written by Guillaume de Lorris c1240. The rest, a meandering dissertation on Christian love, was composed by Jean de Meun, c1280.

ROMANESQUE ART AND ARCHITECTURE, artistic style prevalent in Western Christian Europe from c950 to c1200. Romanesque preceded GOTHIC ART AND ARCHITECTURE and is so called because its forms are derived from ROMAN ART AND ARCHITECTURE. The architecture, based on the round Roman arch and improvised systems of vaulting, produced a massive, simple and robust style with great vitality, particularly in the case of NORMAN ARCHITECTURE. Churches had immense towers; interiors were decorated by FRESCOES of biblical scenes. The sculptural style was very varied, vigorous and expressive, and there were carved, sculptured scenes on column capitals, and larger reliefs and figures on exterior portals and tympanums. The production of metalwork flourished, and many of the pilgrimage churches had elaborate reliquaries and valuable treasuries. There are many fine illuminated manuscripts. The Romanesque style was spread by traveling artists and craftsmen throughout Europe.

The apse and towers of the cathedral at Worms, one of the most impressive Romanesque churches in the Rhine Valley. Only part of the present structure belongs to the original church, consecrated in 1018; the remainder was built during the 12th-14th centuries. The round arch is a characteristic architectural feature of Romanesque buildings.

ROMAN EMPIRE. See ROME, ANCIENT.

ROMAN FORUM. See FORUM.

ROMANIA, or **Rumania,** republic in SE Europe on the Black Sea, lying between the USSR and Hungary to the N and Bulgaria and Yugoslavia to the S.

Land. In the N is the SE end of the Carpathian Mts, separating Moldavia in the E from Transylvania in the W. The Carpathians join the Transylvanian Alps running from E to W. The principal rivers are the Danube in the S and W and the Prut in the NE. The climate is continental, but with severe winters.

Official Name: Romanian Socialist Republic
Capital: Bucharest
Area: 91 699sq mi
Population: 20 660 000
Languages: Romanian
Religions: Romanian Orthodox, Roman Catholic
Monetary Unit(s): 1 Leu = 100 bani

People. Over 60% of the population is rural. About 85% are Romanians, with Hungarian and German minorities. Largest cities are Bucharest, the capital, Cluj, Timisoara, Iasi, Brasov and Galati.

Economy. Over 60% of the land area is agricultural, but Romania is just becoming industrialized. More than 90% of farmland is collectivized, grain being the most important crop. About 25% of Romania is forested, particularly by conifers. With large oil fields in the Prahova R valley, Romania is second largest producer of petroleum and natural gas in Europe. Copper, lead, coal and iron ore are mined; principal industries are iron and steel, machinery, textiles and chemicals, and main exports oil, cement and farm products.

History. Most of modern Romania was part of ancient DACIA, thoroughly imbued with Roman language and culture, which survived barbarian conquests. After the 13th century the two principalities of Moldavia and Walachia emerged, Turkish dependencies until 1829 and then Russian protectorates. United in 1861–2, Romania became independent in 1881. In the 1930s Fascists, especially the IRON GUARD, were dominant, and in 1941 dictator Ion ANTONESCU sided with the Axis powers. Overrun by the USSR in 1944, it became a satellite state, and a republic after King Michael's abdication in 1947. In the 1960s and 1970s Romania achieved greater independence under Nicolae CEAUCESCU, establishing relations with the West.

ROMAN NUMERALS, letters of the Roman ALPHABET used to represent numbers, the letters I, V, X, L, C, D and M standing for 1, 5, 10, 50, 100, 500 and 1000, respectively. All other numbers are represented by combinations of these letters according to certain rules of addition and subtraction; thus, for example, VIII is 8, XL is 40, MCD is 1400 and MCDXLVIII is 1448.

ROMANO, Giulio. See GIULIO ROMANO.

ROMANOV, ruling dynasty of Russia 1613–1917. The name was adopted by a Russian noble family in the 16th century; the first Romanov tsar was MICHAEL. The last of the direct Romanov line was PETER, but succeeding tsars retained the name of Romanov, down to NICHOLAS II (reigned 1894–1917).

ROMANS, Epistle to the, NEW TESTAMENT book written by St. PAUL to the Christians of Rome c58 AD. It presents his major statement of JUSTIFICATION BY FAITH, and the Christian's consequent freedom from condemnation, sin and the law. It stresses God's sovereignty and grace.

ROMANSH. See RHAETO-ROMANIC.

ROMANTICISM, 19th-century European artistic movement. Its values of emotion, intuition, imagination and individualism were in opposition to the ideals of restraint, reason and harmony of CLASSICISM. The word "Romantic" was first applied to art by Friedrich von SCHLEGEL in 1798, and later to works emphasizing the subjective, spiritual or fantastic, concerned with wild, uncultivated nature, or which seemed fundamentally modern rather than classical. The Middle Ages were thought to express Romantic values. The evocative qualities of nature inspired poets such as WORDSWORTH, COLERIDGE and LAMARTINE, and painters such as TURNER, PALMER and FRIEDRICH. BLAKE and GOETHE sought to develop new spiritual values; individualism concerned artists as disparate as Walt WHITMAN and GOYA. The lives of BYRON and CHOPIN seemed to act out the Romantic myth. Among the greatest Romantic composers were WEBER, BERLIOZ, MENDELSSOHN, LISZT and WAGNER.

ROMANY, a Dardic Indo-Iranian language, the tongue of GYPSIES, related to SANSKRIT. Gypsies migrated from central to NW India and then to Europe; the three main Romany dialects, Asiatic, Armenian and European, reflect the principal gypsy settlement areas. Romany has acquired much vocabulary from peoples among whom gypsies have traveled.

ROMBERG, Sigmund (1887–1951), Hungarian-born US composer. He settled in the US in 1909, and wrote over 70 operettas and musicals, including *The Student Prince* (1924) and *The Desert Song* (1926). He went on to write many film scores.

ROME, or **Roma,** capital and largest city of Italy, a center of Western civilization for over 2 000 years. "The Eternal City" was capital of the Roman Empire (see ROME, ANCIENT), and is of unique religious significance, with the headquarters of the Roman Catholic Church in the VATICAN CITY. Administration (of the Italian government as well as of Roma province and of the region of LATIUM), religion and tourism are the most important aspects of modern Rome, which is also a center for commerce, publishing, movies and fashion. The city is a great transportation hub, but has relatively little industry.

Rome covers 582sq mi, with a metropolitan area of 756sq mi. It is located on the rolling plain of the Roman Campagna in central Italy, 15mi from the Tyrrhenian Sea, the site of the ancient city being the SEVEN HILLS OF ROME. The Tiber R flows through the city from NE to SW. There are many important relics of classical Rome, such as the FORUM, the COLOSSEUM, the baths of CARACALLA and the PANTHEON. Rome is famous for its squares, Renaissance palaces, churches, basilicas (see SAINT PETER'S BASILICA), CATACOMBS and fountains, of which the best known is the Trevi fountain. There are also many fine museums, art collections and libraries, the Rome opera house, and the Sta. Cecilia music academy, the world's oldest (1584). The university, Italy's largest, was founded in 1303. Pop 2 799 836.

ROME, city in NW Ga., seat of Floyd Co. Industries include textiles and lumbering. Pop 30 759.

ROME, industrial city in E central N.Y., on the

Two of the best-preserved ancient temples in Rome, in the Forum Boarium (the cattle market). The one on the right, probably that of the harbor god Portunus, has the usual rectangular shape; the other, of uncertain dedication, is round, with Corinthian orders.

Mohawk R, noted for its copper and brass manufactures. Pop 50 148.

ROME, Ancient, initially a tiny city-state in central Italy that, over some six centuries, grew into an empire which at its greatest extent (c117 AD) comprised almost all of the Western world known at the time, including most of Europe, the Middle East, Egypt and N Africa.

According to legend, Rome was founded in 753 BC by ROMULUS AND REMUS, descendants of the Trojan prince AENEAS. Until c500 BC, when the Romans set up an independent republic, the area around the SEVEN HILLS OF ROME was controlled by the Etruscans. (See also ETRUSCAN CIVILIZATION; SABINES.) The Romans were a disciplined, thrifty and industrious people whose genius in organization, administration, building and warfare enabled them not only to create their vast empire, but also to make it one of the most enduring ever.

Throughout the period of the republic (c500–31 BC) warfare was almost continuous. Under government by CONSULS and SENATE, Rome became master of central and S Italy and defeated CARTHAGE (see PUNIC WARS). Expansion continued: Greece, Asia Minor, Syria, Palestine and Egypt were conquered between 250 and 30 BC; Gaul (58–51 BC) and England (after 43 AD) followed. From about 100 BC, Rome began to move steadily toward dictatorship. Civil wars arose from conflicts between senatorial factions, and between rich and poor, PATRICIAN and PLEBEIAN forces. (See GRACCHUS; MARIUS; SULLA; SPARTACUS.) The army leaders POMPEY and Julius CAESAR emerged to form the first TRIUMVIRATE with CRASSUS. After Caesar's assassination and the avenging of his death by Mark ANTONY, his nephew Octavian defeated Mark Antony and CLEOPATRA and became the first emperor, AUGUSTUS.

For more than 200 years (27 BC–180 AD) the Roman empire embodied peace and law (the *Pax Romana*) and provided an excellent road and communication system which facilitated the spread of trade and new ideas, particularly Christianity. Its culture sprang from late Hellenism, but Romans surpassed the Greeks in practical achievements such as law (laying the basis for modern CIVIL LAW), civil engineering, a standard coinage and a system of weights and measures (see also ROMAN ART AND ARCHITECTURE). In literature, poets such as CATULLUS, VERGIL and HORACE, and dramatists such as PLAUTUS and TERENCE followed Greek models. LIVY and TACITUS were important Roman historians, and CICERO Rome's greatest orator. After Augustus, major emperors were TIBERIUS, CLAUDIUS, NERO, VESPASIAN, DOMITIAN, TRAJAN, HADRIAN and MARCUS AURELIUS. The empire was at its largest under TRAJAN (emperor 98–117). But from about 200 a decline set in, with internal strife and barbarian raids, particularly by the GOTHS. DIOCLETIAN (joint emperor 284–305) restored order and revived trade. Under his successor CONSTANTINE I (emperor 306–337) the capital was moved to BYZANTIUM (renamed Constantinople after him) and Christianity officially recognized. THEODOSIUS (emperor 379–95) was the last ruler of the united empire; it was then divided into Eastern and Western. From 376, the VISIGOTHS attacked, sacking Rome in 410. The VANDALS followed. The last puppet Western emperor abdicated in 476, but the BYZANTINE EMPIRE lasted until 1453 (see also JUSTINIAN; BELISARIUS). The HOLY ROMAN EMPIRE was not established until 800.

ROME-BERLIN AXIS. See AXIS POWERS.

ROMEOVILLE, village in NE Ill., on Des Plaines R, with oil refineries and a power station. Pop 12 674.

RØMER, Ole or **Olaus** (1644–1710), Danish astronomer who first showed that light has a finite velocity. He noticed that JUPITER eclipsed its moons at times differing from those predicted and correctly concluded this was due to the finite nature of light's velocity, which he calculated as 227 000km/s (a modern value is about 299 800km/s).

ROMMEL, Erwin (1891–1944), German field marshal, named the "Desert Fox" for his tactical genius as commander of the *Afrika Korps* 1941–43. His E advance ended with the battle of EL ALAMEIN. He commanded Army Group B in N France when the Allies landed in Normandy (he had led an armored division into France, 1940). After being wounded, he was implicated in the July 1944 plot to assassinate Hitler. Given the choice of suicide or trial, he took poison.

ROMNEY, George (1734–1802), English portrait painter, rival of REYNOLDS in late 18th-century London. Influenced by classical sculpture (he spent two years in Italy), he tended to flatter his sitters, among whom was Lady HAMILTON.

ROMULO, Carlos Pena (1901–), Filipino journalist and statesman. His broadcasts during the Japanese occupation of the Philippines were known as "the Voice of Freedom." He won a 1941 Pulitzer Prize, and was ambassador to the US, president of the UN general assembly 1949–50, education secretary 1966–69, and foreign secretary from 1969.

ROMULUS AND REMUS, mythical founders of Rome (by tradition in 753 BC), twin sons of Rhea Silvia, descendant of AENEAS, by MARS. Abandoned as infants, they were suckled by a she-wolf until adopted by a herdsman. After long rivalry, Remus was killed by Romulus, who became the first king of Rome and was later worshiped as the god QUIRINUS.

ROMULUS AUGUSTULUS ("little Augustus"; b. c461), last Western Roman emperor (475–6), puppet of his father Orestes. The end of the Western Roman empire dates from his overthrow by ODOACER.

RONDO, musical composition, derived from the medieval verse *rondeau*, in which repeats of a refrain or theme alternate with other contrasting sections. It became the finale of 18th-century sonatas and symphonies.

RONDÔNIA, or Guaporé, federal territory of W Brazil, bordering Bolivia. Its capital Pôrto Velho, lies on the Madeira R. It exports rubber, Brazil nuts, diamonds, bauxite and gypsum.

RONSARD, Pierre de (1524–1585), 16th-century French "Prince of Poets," leader of the influential PLÉIADE. Best known as a lyric poet, as in *Sonnets for Hélène* (1578), he also wrote lofty *Hymnes* (1556) on more public subjects and an epic, *La Franciade* (1572).

RÖNTGEN (R), a unit of radiation exposure named for W. C. ROENTGEN. Its value in SI UNITS is such that exposure to 1 röntgen of X RAYS or GAMMA RAYS causes 0.000258 coulombs of ionization per kg of air.

ROOD (Old English: cross), crucifix supported by a rood-screen over the chancel or choir entrance, a feature of 14th- and 15th-century European churches. The screen sometimes supported a rood-loft, reached by stairs from the nave.

ROOK, *Corvus frugilegus*, a large CROW widespread in Europe and parts of Asia. Totally black, but for a bald patch of skin at the base of the bill, they are gregarious birds of farmland, feeding on insects, slugs and snails. They nest in colonies, or "rookeries," at the tops of tall trees.

ROON, Count Albrecht Theodor Emil von (1803–1879), Prussian soldier and statesman. His army reorganization, under BISMARCK, made success in the AUSTRO-PRUSSIAN and FRANCO-PRUSSIAN wars possible. War minister 1859–73, he was Prussian premier in 1872.

ROOSEVELT, unincorporated urban community on Long Island, SE N.Y. Pop 15 008.

ROOSEVELT, (Anna) Eleanor (1884–1962), US humanitarian, wife of Franklin Delano Roosevelt and niece of Theodore Roosevelt. Active in politics and social issues (notably for women and minority groups), she was a UN delegate (1945–53, 1961) and coauthored the Universal Declaration of Human Rights. Her many books included *This is My Story* (1937) and *On My Own* (1958).

ROOSEVELT, Franklin Delano (1882–1945), 32nd and longest-serving US president (1933–45). His twelve years of office included the Great Depression and a global war. Born of Dutch descent in Hyde Park, N.Y., on Jan. 30, 1882, and brought up in "aristocratic" surroundings, he graduated from Harvard and married his distant cousin, Eleanor Roosevelt, in 1905; they had six children. In 1910, after a spell at Columbia U. law school, he worked in a N.Y. law firm until elected as a Democrat to the N.Y. Senate. He established himself as a leading Democrat and opponent of TAMMANY HALL. In 1913 he became assistant secretary of the navy, and ran unsuccessfully in 1920 as Democratic vice-presidential candidate. He suffered a severe attack of polio in Aug. 1921, and became partially paralyzed. He returned to politics in 1924 and was elected governor of N.Y. in 1928 (reelected 1930) and finally US president in 1933, when he stood against Herbert HOOVER. The GREAT DEPRESSION had begun in 1929, and Roosevelt attempted to combat it with the NEW DEAL, beginning with the "Hundred Days" during which nearly all the preliminary New Deal legislation was passed. Everybody appeared to benefit, farmer, industrialist and worker. (See AGRICULTURAL ADJUSTMENT ADMINISTRATION; CIVILIAN CONSERVATION CORPS; NATIONAL RECOVERY ADMINISTRATION; TENNESSEE

Franklin Delano ROOSEVELT

32nd US President

Born: Jan. 30, 1882
Died: April 12, 1945
Term of Office: March 4, 1933–April 12, 1945
Political party: Democratic

VALLEY AUTHORITY.) In 1933 Roosevelt launched the GOOD NEIGHBOR POLICY in Latin America and recognized the Soviet government. After increasing criticism from both sides Roosevelt turned his administration in the second phase of the New Deal sharply to the left, introducing the WAGNER ACT of 1935, the massive relief program of the WORKS PROJECTS ADMINISTRATION, a tax reform bill, a social security act and a youth administration. He was reelected in 1936, but labor violence and his efforts to reform the Supreme Court and purge conservative Congressmen damaged his prestige. Reelected again after WWII had broken out, he tried to keep the US out of war, although aiding Britain (see ATLANTIC CHARTER; FOUR FREEDOMS; LEND-LEASE). But four days after the PEARL HARBOR attack, he declared war against Japan, Germany and Italy. He easily won reelection for a fourth term in 1944 on the slogan "don't change horses in mid-stream!" However, his health was failing, and he died suddenly on April 12, 1945, of a cerebral hemorrhage.

ROOSEVELT, Nicholas J. (1767–1854), US engineer who, at the request of Robert FULTON and Robert LIVINGSTON, built and operated the *New Orleans*, the first Mississippi paddle-wheel steamer (1811).

ROOSEVELT, Theodore (1858–1919), 26th US president (1901–09), affectionately known as "Teddy" or "T.R.," one of the most popular presidents as well as the youngest, at 42. He was at different times both a progressive and a conservative. His great energy took him outside politics on many hunting and exploring expeditions; he published over 2000 works on history, politics and his travels. Born in New York City into an established middle-class family, he graduated from Harvard and in 1880 married Alice Hathaway Lee, who died four years later leaving a daughter. He became a rancher in Dakota Territory. In 1886 he returned to New York City and married Edith Kermit Carow, by whom he had five children. He ran unsuccessfully as Republican candidate for mayor, but established a reputation as an efficient administrator and reformer, while a commissioner for the Civil Service and the New York City police. As assistant secretary of the navy (1897–98), he advocated the buildup of a strong fleet and when war broke out with Spain, he joined it in Cuba with his famous volunteer cavalry troop, the ROUGH RIDERS. He returned a national hero, and for two years served as governor of N.Y. He was persuaded to run with McKINLEY for vice-president in 1908 and took over the presidency when McKinley was assassinated on Sept. 6, 1901. He tried to regulate the evergrowing industrial and financial monopolies, using the 1890 SHERMAN ANTITRUST ACT. Despite his "trust-busting," he tried to give both labor and business a "square deal." Reelected in 1904, he secured passage of the Hepburn Act (1906) to prevent abuses in railroad shipping rates, and the Pure Food and Drug Act. He was proudest of his conservation program, which added over 250000000 acres to the national forests. His foreign policy was intent on expansion (see PANAMA CANAL), but he won the 1906 Nobel Peace Prize for mediating in the RUSSO-JAPANESE WAR (see GENTLEMAN'S AGREEMENT). He also proclaimed the so-called "Roosevelt Corollary" of the MONROE DOCTRINE, reserving the role of international policeman for the US. He withdrew from election in 1908, choosing W. H. TAFT as his successor; he contested the 1912 election for the PROGRESSIVE PARTY. When Woodrow WILSON was elected, he retired from politics to lead an expedition into South America. He died of a blood clot in 1919.

ROOSEVELT CAMPOBELLO INTERNATIONAL PARK, jointly administered by the US and Canada, covers 2722 acres on Campobello Island, SW New Brunswick, Canada, including the home of F. D. ROOSEVELT.

ROOT, in ALGEBRA, one of the equal FACTORS of a given number: if $x^n = c$ then x is the nth root of c, written $x = \sqrt[n]{c}$ (see EXPONENT; POWER). The 2nd and 3rd roots of a number are specially named the square and cube roots respectively. Of particular interest is i, the imaginary square root of -1 (see IMAGINARY NUMBERS).

ROOT, Elihu (1845–1937), US statesman. A successful corporation lawyer, he reorganized the command structure of the army as war secretary under President McKinley, and as Roosevelt's secretary of state developed a pattern of administration for the new possessions won from Spain. A champion of the League of Nations and the World Court, he won the 1912 Nobel Peace Prize for work as an international negotiator. He was also a N.Y. Republican senator 1909–15.

ROOTS, that part of a PLANT which absorbs water and nutrients from the soil and anchors the plant to the ground. Water and nutrients enter a root through minute root hairs sited at the tip of each root. Roots need oxygen to function and plants growing in swamps have special adaptations to supply it, like the "knees" of BALD CYPRESS trees and the aerial roots of MANGROVE. There are two main types of root systems: the taproot system, where there is a strong main root from which smaller secondary and tertiary roots branch out; and the fibrous root system where a mass of equal-sized roots are produced. In plants such as the SUGAR BEET, the taproot may become swollen with stored food material. Adventitious roots anchor the stems of climbing plants, such as IVY. Epiphytic plants such as ORCHIDS have roots that absorb moisture from the air (see EPIPHYTE). The roots of parasitic plants such as MISTLETOE and DODDER absorb food from other plants.

ROOTS OF AN EQUATION, the values of the VARIABLE for which an EQUATION in it holds. For example, the roots of a quadratic equation $f(x) = ax^2 + bx + c$ may be found by application of the formula (where $f(k) = 0$):

$$k = \frac{-b \pm \sqrt{b^2 - 4ac}}{2a}$$

where $b^2 - 4ac$ is the DISCRIMINANT.

ROOTSTOCK. See RHIZOME.

ROOT-TAKAHIRA AGREEMENT, signed between the US and Japan on Nov. 30, 1908, to maintain the status quo in the Pacific and the OPEN DOOR policy in China. War was averted and mutual trade encouraged.

ROPE, or cordage, a thick, strong cord made from twisted lengths of natural FIBER. It can be made from MANILA HEMP, HENEQUEN, SISAL, true HEMP, coir (COCONUT PALM fiber), FLAX, JUTE and COTTON. The last three are generally used for lighter ropes such as cords and twines. SYNTHETIC FIBERS, particularly NYLON and polyesters, are used for lighter and more durable rope. Other ropes are made from wire, for example, for suspension cables in bridge building. Rope-making resembles SPINNING.

Theodore ROOSEVELT

26th US President

Born: Oct. 27, 1858
Died: Jan. 6, 1919
Term of Office: Sept. 14, 1901–March 3, 1909
Political party: Republican

RORAIMA, federal territory, N Brazil, named for **Mt Roraima**, a plateau on the borders of Brazil, Guyana and Venezuela, about 9mi by 3mi with a maximum height of about 9200ft. It provided the inspiration for Conan DOYLE's *The Lost World* (1912).

RORQUALS, or **Fin whales**, baleen WHALES of the genus Balaenoptera. The group includes the BLUE WHALE, the largest of all whales. All rorquals make long migrations, moving toward warmer waters in the winter to breed, returning in the summer to the richer krill feeding grounds of the Arctic or Antarctic.

RORSCHACH, Hermann (1884–1922), Swiss psychoanalyst who devised the **Rorschach Test** (c1920), in which the subject looks at a series of ten symmetrical inkblots, and describes what he sees there. It is intended that, from his description, details of his personality can be deduced.

ROSA, Salvator, (1615–1673), Italian artist, poet and musician, famous for his wild landscapes and battle scenes, and regarded in the 19th century as the exemplar of a romantic artist.

ROSARIO, Argentina's second largest city, on the Paraná R 200mi NW of Buenos Aires. An important trading, shipping and manufacturing center for N and central provinces, it handles and processes grain and cattle. Pop 798292.

ROSARY, closed string of beads used as counters in reciting devotional prayers. The usual Roman Catholic rosary has 5 decades, each of 10 beads and each separated by a larger bead.

ROSARY VINE, *Ceropegia woodii*, a prostrate, wiry plant which has fleshy bulblets formed at intervals along the stem and produces flowers that resemble unopened parachutes. As a house plant it is particularly suited to display in a hanging basket or on a pedestal. It grows well at average house temperatures, failing to thrive below 13°C (55°F), and should be placed in a sunny window. The soil can be allowed nearly to dry out before watering, although extremes of dryness and wetness should be avoided. The plant is easily propagated by planting the bulblets or by taking shoot tip cuttings. Family: Asclepiadaceae.

ROSAS, Juan Manuel de (1793–1877), Argentine dictatorial governor of Buenos Aires province 1835–52, who built up his own private army of *gauchos* (cowboys). Bribery, force, expansionism and continuous revolt marked his rule, which nevertheless contributed to Argentine unification.

ROSCIUS, Quintus (Quintus Roscius Gallus; d. 62

BC), Roman actor of such renown that "Roscius" was long a compliment for actors.

ROSE, the popular name for various woody shrubs and vines of the genus *Rosa*, with tough thorns and colorful flowers. There are some 100 wild rose species native to the N Hemisphere, but only nine have been involved in the breeding of the hundreds of cultivated varieties now available. In many cultivated varieties the stamens become petaloid producing double flowers. The rose family, Rosaceae, contains many important cultivated plants including the APPLE, CHERRY, PLUM and STRAWBERRY.

ROSEBERY, Archibald Philip Primrose, 5th Earl of (1847–1929), British Liberal statesman, foreign secretary (1886, 1892–94) and successor as prime minister to GLADSTONE (1894–95). An opponent of Irish HOME RULE, he resigned because his imperialist views were rejected by his party.

ROSEBURG, city in SW Oregon, seat of Douglas Co., center of a lumber area with sheep, cattle and fruit farms and a nickel mine. Pop 14 461.

ROSE CHAFERS, a genus, *Macrodactylus*, of scarabeid BEETLES whose adults feed on the leaves of cultivated trees and shrubs, and whose larvae are root pests of crops and pasture.

ROSECRANS, William Starke (1819–1898), Union general in the American Civil War. After early successes in W Va. and Miss., he was given command of the Army of the Cumberland in 1862 but was heavily defeated at the Battle of CHICKAMAUGA in Sept., 1863, and relieved of command.

ROSEFISH, or **Redfish** or **Ocean Perch** or **Norway Haddock**, *Sebastes marinus*, a perch-like marine fish of the Arctic and western Atlantic. Found mainly on rocky ground at depths of 100–600m (330–1 970ft), they are important food fishes, especially in the US.

ROSELLE, residential borough, NE N.J., 2mi W of Elizabeth, site of EDISON's laboratory and first town with electric street lamps. Pop 22 585. **Roselle Park**, adjoining, was the site of MARCONI's plant during WWI. Pop 14 277.

ROSEMARY, *Rosmarinus officinalis*, evergreen shrub, native to the Mediterranean region and widely cultivated in the UK and the US. The leaves are used as a seasoning and yield an oil used in perfumes. Family: Labiatae.

ROSEMEAD, city in SW Cal., a suburb of Los Angeles. Pop 40 972.

ROSENBERG, city in SE Texas, on Brazos R 30mi SW of Houston. It lies in an agricultural (largely sugar) area, with oil and gas. Pop 12 098.

ROSENBERG, Alfred, (1893–1946), Nazi propagandist, early associate of HITLER. In his *Myth of the 20th Century* (1930). he outlined a theory of Nordic racial superiority, used to justify Nazi anti-Semitism and German world-conquest. After the NUREMBERG TRIALS he was executed for war crimes.

ROSENBERG, Julius (1918–1953) and **Ethel** (1915–1953), husband and wife, the only US citizens put to death in peacetime for espionage. Convicted (1951) for passing atomic secrets in WWII to the USSR, then a US ally, they were electrocuted on June 19, 1953. Despite worldwide protests, President Eisenhower twice refused pleas for clemency. Many still protest their innocence.

ROSENWALD, Julius (1862–1932), US businessman and philanthropist. He worked with Sears Roebuck and Co. for 35 years to make it the largest mail-order firm in the world, and gave some $63 million to charities, including the Julius Rosenwald Fund (1917–48) to provide educational facilities for Negroes.

ROSE OF JERICHO, or RESURRECTION PLANT, *Anastatica hierochuntica*, small herb native to the Middle East. During the dry season it forms a ball that blows with the wind, but when wetted it opens up again. Family: Cruciferae.

ROSE OF LIMA, Saint (1586–1617), born in Lima, Peru, first canonized saint in the New World and patron saint of South America. She was canonized by Pope Clement X in 1671.

ROSE OF SHARON, name of various plants cultivated as garden shrubs, including *Hibiscus syriacus*, a native of China now growing wild in the US, and *Hypericum calycinum*, native to S Europe and Asia Minor, including the Plain of Sharon, Israel.

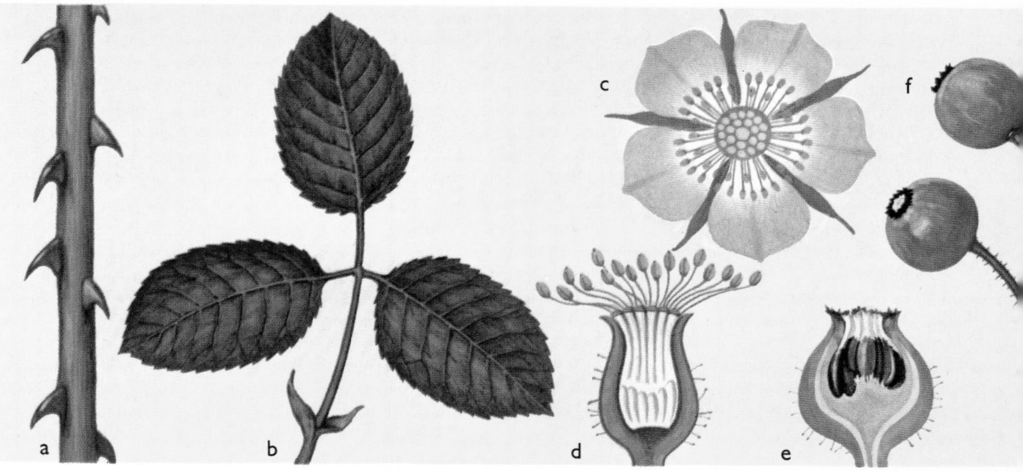

Main features of a typical rose plant. The stem (a) bears numerous thorns which can take many forms from delicate spines to stout curved hooks. The leaf (b) is formed of three leaflets with a pair of stipules at the base of the leaf stalk; the flowers (c), viewed from above, consists of five green sepals, five colored petals (often more in cultivated varieties), numerous stamens and numerous free carpels (female organs); the receptacle (d), shown here in longitudinal section, is cup-shaped and encloses the carpels; the fruit (e; f) is the familiar rose hip and consists of a number of achenes enclosed in the fleshy receptacle.

ROSES, Wars of the, intermittent struggle for the English throne between the noble houses of Lancaster (emblem, a red rose) and York (badge, a white rose). Dissatisfied by the weak government of the Lancastrian HENRY VI and the defeats of the English at the end of the HUNDRED YEARS' WAR, the Earl of WARWICK (the "king-maker"), using as figurehead Richard, Duke of York, captured Henry in 1455 and took control of government. MARGARET OF ANJOU, Henry's queen, fought to regain power (1459–64) and killed York but, as Warwick proclaimed York's son EDWARD IV, the attempt failed. A second Lancastrian attempt (1471), this time aided by LOUIS XI of France and the disaffected Warwick, also failed. With Warwick and Henry dead and Margaret captured, Edward reigned in peace until his death in 1483. His young son, EDWARD V, was supplanted by his uncle, RICHARD III. The final Lancastrian claim was made by Henry Tudor, who killed Richard at Bosworth (1485) and was crowned HENRY VII in 1485. He linked York and Lancaster by marrying Elizabeth, the daughter of Edward IV.

ROSETTA STONE, an inscribed basalt slab, discovered in 1799, which provided the key to the decipherment of Egyptian HIEROGLYPHICS. About 1.2m long and 0.75m wide, it is inscribed with identical texts in Greek, Egyptian demotic and Egyptian hieroglyphs. Decipherment was begun by Thomas YOUNG (c1818) and completed by Jean-François CHAMPOLLION (c1821–22). Found near Rosetta, Egypt, the stone is now in the British Museum.

ROSEVILLE, city in E Cal., 18mi NE of Sacramento. It has extensive rail yards and produces wine, formica and missile components. Pop 18 221.

ROSEVILLE, city in SE Mich., a residential suburb 13mi NE of Detroit. Pop 60 529.

ROSEVILLE, village in E Minn., suburb of St. Paul with computer and steel industries. Pop 34 518.

ROSE WINDOW, large circular window, often of stained glass, with stone tracery, particularly common in French Gothic cathedrals. The basic design with segments ending in a pointed arch (as at Notre Dame, Paris) developed more intricate curves in the FLAMBOYANT STYLE.

ROSEWOOD, *Dalbergia nigra*, a Brazilian tree, the deep red-brown wood of which is finely grained and was once extensively used for cabinetmaking. Rosewood is also obtained from a number of other tropical trees. Family: Leguminosae.

ROSH HASHANAH (Hebrew: head of the year), the Jewish New Year, observed on the first day of the seventh Jewish month, Tishri (usually in Sept.). It is revered as the Day of Judgment when each person's fate is inscribed in the Book of Life. The *shofar* (ram's horn) calls Jews to ten days of penitence which end on YOM KIPPUR.

ROSICRUCIANS, worldwide group of secret brotherhoods claiming esoteric wisdom, tinged with MYSTICISM, sometimes with MASONRY and the CABALA. The movement's stimulus was *Fama Fraternitatis* (1614), relating the purported travels of, and secrets learned by, Christian Rosenkreuz.

ROSIN. See RESIN; TURPENTINE.

ROSKILDE, historic city in Denmark at the head of Roskilde Fjord, W of Copenhagen, of which it is a residential suburb. It was the capital of Denmark until 1443. Pop 39 984.

The Rosetta Stone, now in the British Museum, London. The inscription is a decree of the pharaoh Ptolemy V (196 BC), in hieroglyphs, Demotic and Greek; it was his name that helped link the three inscriptions.

ROSS, urban township in SW Penn., to the N of Pittsburgh. Pop 32 982.
ROSS, Betsy (1752–1836), American seamstress who is said to have made, to George Washington's design, the first US flag (1776).
ROSS, Edward Alsworth (1866–1951), US sociologist and author of *Social Control* (1901) and *Social Psychology* (1908).
ROSS, Harold Wallace (1892–1951), founder and lifetime editor of the *New Yorker* magazine (1925). Originally conceived as basically by and for New Yorkers, the magazine won national prestige and has had an enduring effect on American journalism.
ROSS, Sir James Clark (1800–1862), British polar explorer who reached a point farther S (78°10′S) than any explorer until 1900. He made a number of Arctic expeditions, some with his uncle Sir John ROSS, and with William PARRY. He located the N Magnetic Pole in 1831. In the historic 1839–43 Antarctic expedition he discovered the ROSS SEA and VICTORIA ISLAND.
ROSS, John (1790–1866), of part Cherokee, part Scots parentage, CHEROKEE INDIAN chief and, from 1839, chief of the united Cherokee nations. He led opposition to the US government's attempt to move his people W of the Mississippi R, but in 1838 was forced to lead them to Okla.
ROSS, Sir John (1777–1856), British arctic explorer whose first, unsuccessful, expedition in search of the NORTHWEST PASSAGE was made in 1818 with James ROSS and William PARRY. In a return voyage (1829–33) he discovered and surveyed Boothia Peninsula, the Gulf of Boothia and King William Land.
ROSS, Robert (1766–1814), British soldier in the WAR OF 1812 who commanded a brigade which won the Battle of BLADENSBERG and the same evening burned Washington. Shortly after, he was mortally wounded when attacking Baltimore.
ROSS, Sir Ronald (1857–1932), British physician awarded the 1902 Nobel Prize for Physiology or Medicine for his investigations, prompted by Sir Patrick MANSON, of the *Anopheles* MOSQUITO in relation to the transmission of MALARIA, in course of which he isolated malarial cysts in the mosquito's intestinal tract, later correctly identifying these with cysts he found in the bloodstreams of diseased birds (1897–98).
ROSS DEPENDENCY, sector of Antarctica between 160°E and 150°W extending from the S pole to Cape Adare and Edward VII Peninsula, including the Ross Ice Shelf. Proclaimed a New Zealand territory in 1923, it covers about 165 000sq mi.
ROSSELLINI, Roberto (1906–   ), Italian film director. His *Open City* (1946), partly made up of footage of the Italian resistance during WWII, established him as a leader of the neorealist movement.
ROSSELINO, two Italian Renaissance sculptor-architects. **Bernardo** (1409–1464) made the tomb of Leonardo Bruni in Sta. Croce, Florence. He taught his brother **Antonio** (1427–1479), whose works in Florence and elsewhere include tombs, fine stone reliefs and incisive portraits.
ROSSETTI, name of two leading English Victorian artists. The poems of **Christina Georgina Rossetti** (1830–1894), a devout Anglican, ranged from fantasy (*Goblin Market*, 1862) to religious poetry. Her brother, **Dante Gabriel Rossetti** (1828–1882), was a founder of the PRE-RAPHAELITE BROTHERHOOD. His paintings, of languid, mystical beauty, have subjects from Dante and medieval romance. As a poet he excelled, notably in his exquisite love sonnets.
ROSSINI, Gioacchino Antonio (1792–1868), Italian composer best known for his comic operas, especially *The Barber of Seville* (1816). The dramatic grand opera *William Tell* (1829), with its famous overture, was his last opera; always lazy by nature, he then retired. He was admired by WAGNER and BEETHOVEN, among others.
ROSSO FIORENTINO (Giovanni Battista di Jacopo Rosso; 1495–1540), Italian painter. *The Deposition* (1521) exemplifies the elongated figures, hectic color and emotionalism of his paintings. He decorated the François I gallery at FONTAINEBLEAU and brought MANNERISM to France.
ROSS SEA, Antarctic inlet of the S Pacific Ocean, between Victoria Land and Edward VII Peninsula. Its S limit is the 400mi Ross Ice Shelf, and it contains Ross Island, with the 12 450ft Mt Erebus, the most southerly active volcano known.
ROSTAND, Edmond (1868–1918), French dramatist, famous for his play *Cyrano de Bergerac* (1897), which led a Romantic revival.
ROSTOCK, industrial city and chief seaport of East Germany, on the Baltic Sea. It was a member of the HANSEATIC LEAGUE. Badly damaged in WWII, it now has machine, chemical, shipbuilding and fishing industries. Pop 201 000.
ROSTOV-ON-DON, major industrial city of S USSR, 25mi from the Sea of Azov. It is a busy sea, river and canal port in a rich farming area. Industry (notably farm machinery) is based on the nearby Donets coalfield. Pop 789 000.
ROSTROPOVICH, Mstislav Leopoldovich (1927–   ), Soviet cellist. A celebrated musician, he has had works composed for him by PROKOFIEV, SHOSTAKOVICH, and some non-Soviet composers, such as BRITTEN. He also accompanies his wife Galina Vishnevskaya, a notable soprano, on the piano.
ROSWELL, city in SE N.M., seat of Chaves Co. It ships livestock, cotton, meat and fruit, is a winter resort and an oil center. Pop 33 908.
ROSZAK, Theodore (1907–   ), Polish-born US sculptor. Best known for his sinister, birdlike figures in steel and bronze, he also designed the 45ft spire of the Massachusetts Institute of Technology chapel.
ROT, name given to the symptoms produced by a number of FUNGI and BACTERIA that infect plants. (See also PLANT DISEASES.)
ROT, rotor or **rotation of a vector,** equivalent to CURL. (See also VECTOR ANALYSIS.)
ROTARY INTERNATIONAL, governing body of over 14 000 Rotary Clubs in 148 countries. Members, mostly professional and businessmen, aim to promote high standards of service in both work and welfare spheres. The first was started in 1905 by a Chicago lawyer, Paul Harris; meetings were held in members' offices in rotation.
ROTC. See RESERVE OFFICER TRAINING CORPS.
ROTENONE, insecticide derived from tropical woody vines of the genus *Derris* and related species. It is used as either a dust or spray. It is also used to stupefy fish, which can then be eaten, since rotenone has no harmful effects on warmblooded animals.
ROTH, Philip (1933–   ), leading US novelist and short story writer. His protagonists agonize between a traditional Jewish upbringing and modern urban society. His first novel was *Letting Go* (1962), and his best-known work is *Portnoy's Complaint* (1969), a hilarious, bitter account of sexual frustration.
ROTHKO, Mark (1903–1970), Russian-born US painter, a leader of New York ABSTRACT EXPRESSIONISM. On large canvases he used rich and somber colors to create designs of simple, lightly painted rectangular shapes.
ROTHSCHILD, family of European Jewish bankers who wielded great political influence for nearly two centuries. The founder of the house was **Mayer Anselm Rothschild** (1743–1812), who established banks at Frankfurt, Vienna, London, Naples and Paris, with his sons as managers. The financial genius who raised the business to dominance in Europe was his son **Nathan Mayer Rothschild** (1777–1836), who handled Allied loans for the campaign against Napoleon.
ROTIFERS, class of minute multicellular animals of marine and fresh waters, characterized by possession of a crown of cilia used as both a feeding and swimming organ. Rotifers are all less than 2mm (0.08in) in length. They are remarkable in that each organism contains a constant number of cells.
ROTTERDAM, commercial and industrial seaport in South Holland province, second largest city in the Netherlands. Site of the Rotterdam-Europort industrial and harbor complex, it lies at the center of an extensive canal system connecting with other parts of the Netherlands and the German Rhine ports and RUHR. Major industries include shipyards and oil refineries. Pop 654 024.
ROTTWEILER, German working dog sometimes used by police forces, by tradition originally bred from a Roman cattle dog left by the legions at Rottweil, Germany. It has a short black coat with brown markings.

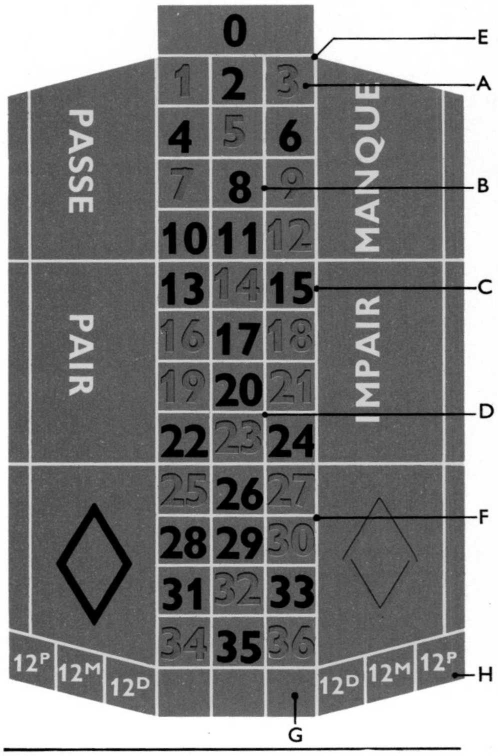

Various roulette bets and possible returns. (A) Plein (betting on one number) pays back 36 times the stake; (B) Cheval (betting on two numbers) pays back 18 times the stake; (C) Transversale pleine (betting on three numbers) pays back 12 times the stake; (D) Carré (betting on four numbers) pays back 9 times the stake; (E) first four numbers pays back 9 times the stake; (F) Transversale simple (betting on six numbers) pays back 6 times the stake; (G) betting on all twelve numbers in a column pays back 3 times the stake; (H) betting on the twelve first, middle or last numbers pays back 3 times the stake; red or black pays back 2 times the stake; odd or even pays back 2 times the stake; betting on 1–18 (manque) or 19–36 (passe) pays back 2 times the stake.

ROUAULT, Georges (1871–1958), French painter and graphic artist known especially for his intense religious paintings such as *The Three Judges* (1913). Influenced by medieval stained glass work, he developed a distinctive style with the use of thick black outlines.
ROUBILIAC, Louis François (c1702–1762), French sculptor. Influenced by BERNINI, he gained fame in England for his portrait busts and monuments such as *Monument to the Duke of Argyle* (1749).
ROUEN, major port on the Seine R, industrial and commercial city, capital of historic Normandy and today of Seine-Maritime department, NW France. JOAN OF ARC was burned here, and de CHAMPLAIN and de LA SALLE sailed from here. Pop 120 471.
ROUGET DE LISLE, Claude Joseph (1760–1836), French soldier who composed the MARSEILLAISE (1792).
ROUGH RIDERS (1st Regiment of US Cavalry Volunteers), a unit comprising cowboys and ranchers, organized by Theodore ROOSEVELT and Leonard WOOD at the outbreak of the SPANISH-AMERICAN WAR.
ROULETTE, popular game of chance. The roulette wheel is divided into a series of small compartments, alternatively black and red, numbered 1 to 36 with an additional zero (the US game sometimes has two zeros). A croupier spins the wheel and releases into it a small ivory ball. Players bet on where (usually which number or which color) the ball will settle.
ROUMANIA. See ROMANIA.
ROUND (in music). See CANON.

ROUNDERS, British game played with a stick and ball by two teams of nine. The game is very similar to, and may be an ancestor of, BASEBALL.

ROUNDHEADS, an originally derogatory name for Puritans in the Parliamentary forces in the English CIVIL WAR. Many wore their hair closely cropped, in sharp contrast to their royalist opponents.

ROUNDWORMS, the **Nematodes**, among the commonest and most widely distributed of invertebrates. Although best known as parasites of man and his domestic animals, the majority are free-living and there are terrestrial, freshwater and marine forms. All roundworms are long and thin, tapering at each end. The outside of the body is covered with a complex cuticle. The sexes are usually separate. The internal organs are suspended within a fluid-filled body cavity or pseudocoel. The free-living and plant-parasitic forms are usually microscopic, but animal-parasitic species may reach a considerable length— the Guinea worm, up to 1m (3.3ft). Nematodes are divided into the Adenophorea, containing the majority of free-living forms, and the Sercenentea, which contains the parasitic orders.

ROUS, Francis Peyton (1879–1970), US physician who shared (with C. B. HUGGINS) in the 1966 Nobel Prize for Physiology or Medicine for his discovery (c1910) of a VIRUS which causes TUMORS in chickens.

ROUSSEAU, Henri (1844–1910), known as *Le Douanier*, self-taught French "primitive" painter much admired by GAUGUIN, PICASSO and others. He is known mainly for his portraits, landscapes and jungle paintings, such as *Sleeping Gypsy* (1897) and *Virgin Forest at Sunset* (1907).

ROUSSEAU, Jean Jacques (1717–1778), Swiss-born French writer, philosopher and political theorist. He wrote for DIDEROT's *Encyclopédie* in Paris from 1745. Made famous by his essay on how arts and sciences corrupt human behaviour (1749) he argued in an essay on the *Origin of the Inequality of Man* (1755) that man's golden age was that of primitive communal living. *The Social Contract* (1762), influential in the FRENCH REVOLUTION, claimed that when men form a social contract to live in society they delegate sovereignty to a government; but that sovereignty resides ultimately with the people, who can withdraw it when necessary. His didactic novel *Émile* (1762) suggested that education should build on a child's natural interests and sympathies, gradually developing its potential. *Confessions* (1782) describe Rousseau's Romantic feelings of affinity with nature.

ROUSSEAU, (Pierre Etienne) Théodore (1812–1867), French landscape painter, a leader of the BARBIZON SCHOOL. His scenes of wooded landscapes at sunset include *Coming out of the Fontainebleau woods* (c1850).

ROUSSEL, Albert Charles Paul Marie (1869–1937), French composer. Although influenced by DEBUSSY, D'INDY and visits to the East, his music was based on contrapuntal rather than tonal construction, varying in style from *The Feast of the Spider* (1913) to *Padmavati* (1914–18).

ROUSSILLON, historic French region corresponding roughly to today's Pyrenées-Orientales department. Its ownership was disputed until the Spanish formally handed over the province in 1659.

ROUX, Pierre Paul Émile (1853–1933), French bacteriologist noted for his work with PASTEUR toward a successful ANTHRAX treatment, with METCHNIKOV on SYPHILIS, and with YERSIN on DIPHTHERIA. Using Roux' and Yersin's results, von BEHRING was able to develop the diphtheria ANTITOXIN.

ROUYN, city in SW Quebec, Canada, the center of a gold- and copper-mining region. Pop 17821.

ROWING, propelling a boat by means of oars. In sport there are two types: *sculling*, in which each oarsman uses two oars, and *sweep rowing*, in which each has one. For speed, the craft (shells) are long, narrow and light. The first recorded race was held on the Thames R, London (1716). The annual Oxford-Cambridge race began in 1829, and the Yale-Harvard race in 1852. The most famous international rowing event is England's annual Henley Royal Regatta (from 1839).

ROWLAND, Henry Augustus (1848–1901), US physicist and engineer who developed the concave DIFFRACTION grating, in which the lines are ruled directly onto a concave spherical surface, thus eliminating the need for additional MIRRORS and LENSES. (See also SPECTROSCOPY.)

ROWLANDSON, Thomas (1756–1827), English caricaturist, etcher and painter. His work is a valuable though satirical record of contemporary English life. His work includes *The English Dance of Death* (1815–16) and illustrating *The Tour of Dr Syntax in Search of the Picturesque* (1812).

ROXANA (d. 311 BC), daughter of a Bactrian ruler and wife of ALEXANDER THE GREAT. After his death, she and her son were involved in the DIADOCHI wars and murdered by order of CASSANDER.

ROXAS Y ACUÑA, Manuel (1894–1948), first president of the Philippine republic, 1946–48: earlier he had been a member of the Japanese-sponsored Philippine puppet government in WWII. His administration was marked by corruption.

ROY, residential city in NE Utah which was settled by Mormons in 1877. Pop 14356.

ROYAL ACADEMY OF ARTS, British institution founded 1768 by George III, first president being Joshua REYNOLDS. It has a president, 40 academicians (RA) and 30–35 associates. It maintains an art school and holds an open summer exhibition.

ROYAL CANADIAN MOUNTED POLICE, Canadian federal police force. It was formed 1873, as the North West Mounted Police, to bring law and order to the new Canadian territories. In 1874, the NWMP numbered 300 men and their persistence and determination became legendary: "the Mounties always get their man." In 1904 the force numbered 6000 and was given the prefix "Royal." In 1920 it absorbed the Dominion Police and received its present name and duties. Its 14000 members serve as a provincial police force in the nation's provinces (excluding Ontario and Quebec) and as an equivalent of the FBI.

ROYALE, Isle. See ISLE ROYALE NATIONAL PARK.

ROYAL GEOGRAPHICAL SOCIETY, British institution founded 1830 as the Geographical Society of London, taking its present name 1859. Its aims are to advance geographical exploration, research and education.

ROYAL GORGE, in the Grand Canyon of the Arkansas, S central Col., a 5mi-long scenic gorge with sheer walls rising over 1000ft. It is crossed by the Royal Gorge Suspension Bridge (1053ft high).

ROYAL INSTITUTION, an English scientific society, founded in 1799 by Benjamin Thompson (see Count RUMFORD) to encourage scientific study and the spread of scientific knowledge. It has associations with many eminent men of science, including Humphry DAVY and Michael FARADAY.

ROYAL JELLY. The social organization of a beehive consists of a queen—a sexually mature female—attended by drones—males—and supported by armies of worker bees—females whose sexual development has been suppressed. Both queen and workers come from the same larval stock. The sexual development of the few grubs chosen to replace the

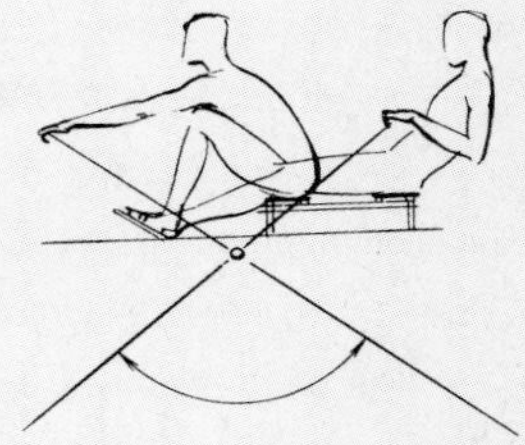

The sliding seat, introduced in 1857, enables the oarsman to use his body weight to maximum advantage.

Various craft propelled by oars. *Top:* the wherry, a popular pleasure boat on many rivers. *Above:* a "single scull." *Right:* an eight-oared racing shell, in which a ninth crew member, the coxswain, steers and calls the stroke. Strictly speaking, only an oarsman who grasps a single oar with both hands is rowing; an oarsman who grasps an oar with one hand only is said to be sculling.

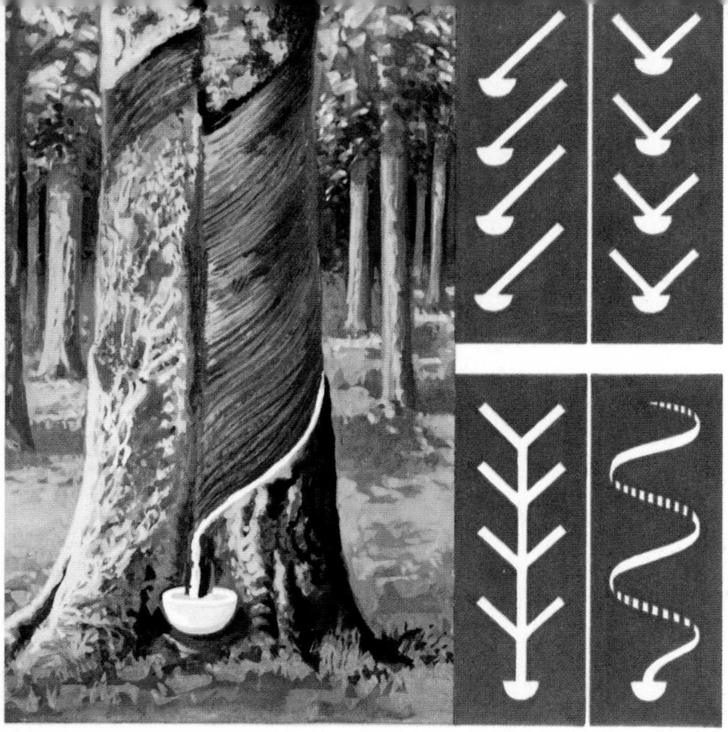

A typical rubber plantation, with young trees in the background and a mature tree that has been tapped many times in the foreground. Several methods have been used to tap the latex, but the one shown lower right is the correct method if tapping is to be maintained over a long period.

queen depends upon their being fed a "royal jelly" produced by special glands of the worker "nursemaids."

ROYAL OAK, commercial city, SE Mich., a residential suburb of Detroit. Pop 86 238.

ROYAL PALM, several species of feather-leaved PALM of the genus *Roystonea*, which are native to tropical America. They are popular ornamental plants throughout the tropics.

ROYAL SOCIETY OF LONDON FOR THE IMPROVEMENT OF NATURAL KNOWLEDGE, the premier English scientific society. Probably the most famous scientific society in the world, it also has a claim to be the oldest surviving. It had its origins in weekly meetings of scientists in London in the 1640s and was granted a royal charter by Charles II in 1660. Past presidents include Samuel PEPYS, Sir Isaac NEWTON and Lord RUTHERFORD.

ROYCE, Josiah (1855–1916), US philosopher, a major proponent of IDEALISM. Influenced by HEGEL, he postulated the existence of Absolute Truth. His contributions to varied fields of logic and philosophy, as expressed in his numerous books, were of considerable distinction.

RSFSR. See RUSSIAN SOVIET FEDERATED SOCIALIST REPUBLIC.

RUANDA-URUNDI, trust territory until 1962 of central Africa. It comprised Ruanda (now RWANDA) in the N and Urundi (now BURUNDI) in the S. Formerly part of German East Africa, it was mandated to Belgium 1919 by the League of Nations, and became a UN trust territory 1946.

RUBAIYAT. See FITZGERALD, EDWARD; OMAR KHAYYAM.

RUBBER, an elastic substance; that is, one which quickly restores itself to its original size after it has been stretched or compressed. Natural rubber is obtained from many plants, and commercially from *Hevea brasiliensis*, a tree native to South America and cultivated also in SE Asia and W Africa. A slanting cut is made in the bark, and the milky fluid latex, occurring in the inner bark, is tapped off. The **latex**—an aqueous COLLOID of rubber and other particles—is coagulated with dilute acid, and the rubber creped or sheeted and smoked. Natural rubber is a chain POLYMER of ISOPRENE, known as caoutchouc when pure; its elasticity is due to the chains being randomly coiled, but tending to straighten when the rubber is stretched. Known to have been used by the Aztecs since the 6th century AD, and first known in Europe in the 16th century, it was a mere curiosity until the pioneer work of Thomas Hancock (1786–1865) and Charles MACINTOSH. Synthetic rubbers have been produced since WWI, and the industry has developed greatly during and since WWII. They are long-chain polymers, elastomers; the main types are: copolymers of butadiene/styrene, butadiene/nitriles and ethylene/propylene; polymers of chloroprene (neoprene rubber), butadiene, isobutylene and SILICONES; and polyurethanes, polysulfide rubbers and chlorosulfonated polyethylenes. Some latex (natural or synthetic) is used as an adhesive and for making rubber coatings, rubber thread and foam rubber. Most, however, is coagulated, and the rubber is treated by VULCANIZATION and the addition of reinforcing and inert fillers and antioxidants, before being used in tires, shoes, rainwear, belts, hoses, insulation and many other applications.

RUBBER PLANT, or India rubber fig, *Ficus elastica*, a popular house plant, native to India and the E Indies. It was once grown for its gum, which was made into india-rubber erasers. Family: Moraceae.

RUBELLA. See GERMAN MEASLES.

RUBENS, Peter Paul (1577–1640), Flemish artist, one of the greatest BAROQUE painters. Influenced by TINTORETTO, TITIAN and VERONESE, he developed an exuberant style depending on a rich handling of color and sensuous effects. His works include portraits and mythological, allegorical and religious subjects such as *Raising of the Cross* (1610), *Descent from the Cross* (1612), *History of Marie de Médicis* (1622–25), *Judgment of Paris* (c1638) and portraits of his wife. His works influenced many artists, including VAN DYCK and RENOIR.

RUBICON, river in N central Italy which formed the boundary between Italy and Cisalpine Gaul during the Roman Republic. In 49 BC, Julius CAESAR led his army across the river into Italy, so committing himself to civil war against POMPEY. To "cross the Rubicon" means to take an irrevocable decision.

RUBIDIUM (Rb), a soft, silvery-white, highly reactive ALKALI METAL. It is fairly abundant, but is found only as a minor constituent of POTASSIUM and CESIUM minerals. It is more reactive than potassium, and reacts violently with water and ice. Metallic rubidium, prepared by ELECTROLYSIS of the chloride or reduction of the carbonate, is used in electron tubes, and its salts in making special glasses and ceramics. AW 85.5, mp 39°C, bp 688°C, sg 1.532 (20°C).

RUBINSTEIN, Anton Grigoryevich (1829–1894), Russian piano virtuoso and composer. In 1862 he founded the St Petersburg Conservatory, where he was director 1862–67 and 1887–91.

RUBINSTEIN, Arthur (1889–   ), born US pianist who has remained at the top of his profession for over 70 years. He is especially famous for his interpretations of CHOPIN.

RUBLEV, Andrei (c1370–c1430), Russian painter famous for his icon of the *Old Testament Trinity*, c1420. As he did not sign his works, it is often difficult to distinguish his style.

RUBY, deep-red GEM stone, a variety of CORUNDUM colored by a minute proportion of chromium ions. It is found significantly only in upper Burma, Thailand and Sri Lanka, and is more precious by far than diamond. The name has been used for other red stones, chiefly varieties of garnet and spinel. Rubies have been synthesized by the Verneuil flame-fusion process (1902). They are used to make ruby LASERS.

RUBY, Jack (1911–1967), nightclub owner who fatally shot Lee Harvey OSWALD, presumed assassin of President KENNEDY, on Nov. 24, 1963, before a "live" TV audience.

RUDDERFISHES, various perch-like fishes of tropical oceans deriving their common name from their habit of following ships, perhaps to scavenge scraps thrown overboard. Their main foods are small algae and seaweeds. Shoaling fishes, many are caught for food.

RUDE, François (1784–1855), French sculptor. His neoclassical works include the *Neapolitan Fisherboy* (1833), but most of his works, such as *Departure of the Volunteers of 1792* (1835–36), are dramatically realistic.

RUDOLF II (1552–1612), King of Bohemia and Hungary, succeeded his father Maximilian II as Holy Roman Emperor in 1576. He was a patron of BRAHE and KEPLER, but his religious persecutions and a Hungarian rebellion led to his progressive replacement by his brother Matthias.

RUDOLF I (1218–1291), German king, elected in 1273, who established the HAPSBURG dynasty by gaining control of Austria and Styria. The Diet of Augsburg (1282) invested his two sons with these duchies.

RUDOLF (1858–1889), archduke and crown prince of the Austro–Hungarian Empire. He and 17-year-old Baroness Mary Vetsera were found shot in the royal hunting lodge at Mayerling, apparent victims of a suicide pact. The exact circumstances of the deaths, which caused endless speculation, have never been clarified.

RUDOLF, Lake, in N Kenya, 10–20mi wide and 154mi long, lies N-S in the GREAT RIFT VALLEY. Its marshy N tip lies on the Ethiopian border. The lake has no outlet.

RUE, or herb of grace, *Ruta graveolens*, a hardy evergreen perennial plant native to Europe. It contains a volatile, acrid oil, which has been used as a stimulant. The leaves are used for a seasoning.

RUEF, Abraham (c1865–1936), US political boss who controlled San Francisco in exceptionally corrupt fashion 1901–06 through mayor E. F. Schmitz. He was indicted 1906 and imprisoned 1911–14 for bribery.

RUFF, *Philomachus pugnax*, a migrant wading bird of marshes and meadows in the Palearctic. The males are much larger than the females, which are called "reeves," and develop colored eartufts and a ruff of feathers around the neck in the breeding season. Polygamous birds, they have communal display grounds, or "leks."

RUFFED GROUSE, *Bonasa umbellus*, a chicken-like game bird of woodlands in America. Usually found in upland areas, it is a red-brown or gray-brown bird, sometimes locally known as the American partridge.

RUFFIN, Edmund (1794–1865), US planter, a strong supporter of slavery and secession said to have fired the first shot on Fort Sumter, S.C., at the outbreak of the Civil War. He committed suicide rather than submit to the US government. A noted agriculturalist, he pioneered crop rotation and founded the *Farmers' Register* (1833).

RUGBY, ball game possibly originated at Rugby school, England, during a SOCCER match (1823). Play is on a field 75yd wide by 110yd between goal lines. There are two 40min "halves." In Rugby Union there are 15 players per side, in Rugby League, 13. Each side attempts to ground the oval leather-covered ball beyond the opponents' goal: this, a try, is worth 4 points; place-kicking a goal after a try is 2 further points; and a goal from a free, or penalty kick, or from a drop-kick during play, 3. The game is similar to American FOOTBALL, but little protective equipment is worn and play is almost continuous.

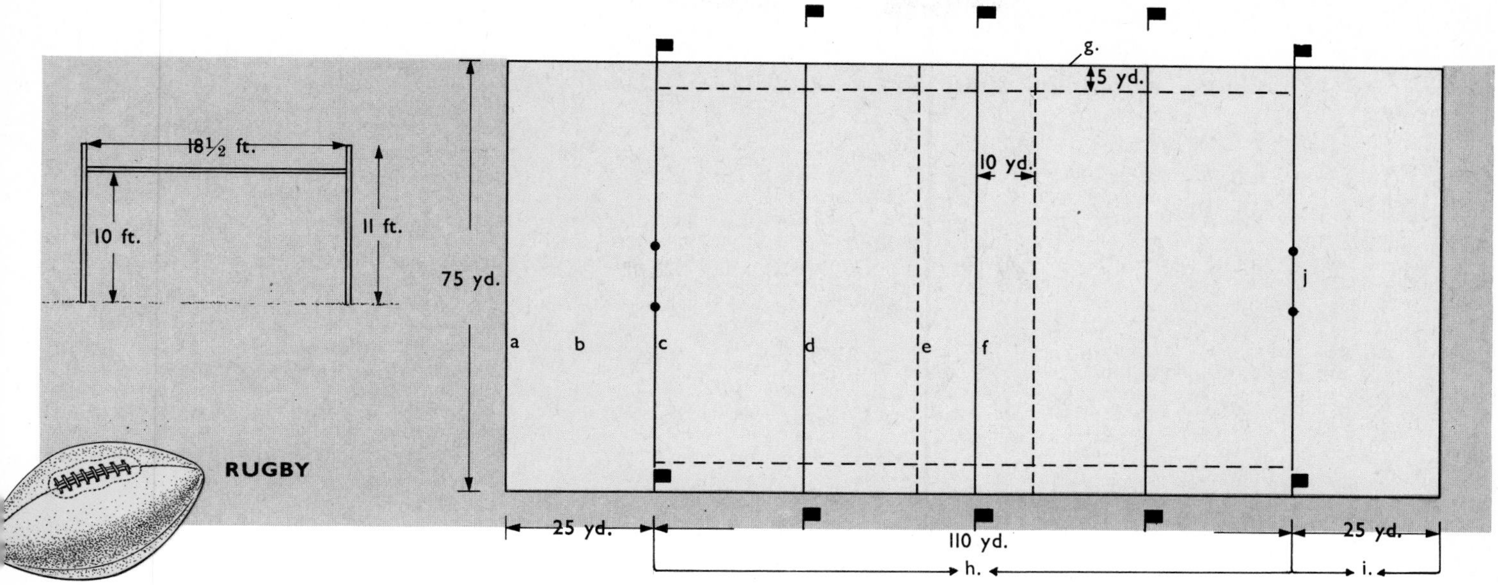

The rugby field, with the dead-ball line (a), in-goal area (b), goal line (c), 25-yd line (d), 10-yd line (e), halfway line (f), touch line (g), touch (h), touch-in-goal (i) and goal (j).

RUGGLES, Carl (1876–1971), controversial US composer. His often dissonant style may be heard in the symphonic poems *Men and Mountains* (1924) and *Sun-Treader* (1927–32). He also achieved recognition as a painter.

RUGS AND CARPETS. Reed mats date from at least 5000 BC, but carpet-weaving with sheep's wool was first highly developed in the Near East. Persian carpets were internationally famous by 600 AD. Their vivid, long-lasting dyes came from natural materials such as bark and roots. Persian designs influenced the 16th- and 17th-century carpets of India's Mogul courts, and the beautiful Chinese carpets produced from the 14th to 17th centuries. Carpet-weaving spread in the West, particularly in the 17th century, via France, Belgium and England.

Oriental carpets were woven on looms, still the basic technique of carpet-making. Foundation threads (the *warp*) are stretched on the loom; crosswise foundation threads are called the *weft*. The surface material (*pile*) is made by tying small tufts of fiber, usually wool, to the warp. Today, major types of the more expensive loom-made carpets and rugs are: *Axminster, chenille, velvet* and *Wilton*. *Tufted* carpets are made by machines which do the tufting with hundreds of needles onto a prewoven backing, attached to a latex rubber base. Knitted carpets use a combination of loom and tufting processes. (See also TAPESTRY; WEAVING.)

RUHR, great coal-mining and iron-and-steel industrial region in West Germany. It lies mainly E of the Rhine R, between the valleys of the Ruhr and Lippe rivers, and has more than 30 large cities and towns merged into one industrial megalopolis with a population of about 6 million. Chief cities include Düsseldorf, Essen and Dortmund. Materials are transported by the Rhine R, Dortmund-Ems Canal, Rhine-Herne Canal, and road and rail networks.

RUISDAEL, Jacob van (c1629–1682), greatest Dutch landscape painter of the 17th century. He favored a new heroic-romantic style in which small figures are dwarfed by forests, stormy seas and magnificent cloudscapes.

RUIZ CORTINES, Adolfo (1890–1973), Mexican president, 1952–58. During his presidency, corruption was curbed, the "march to the sea" to aid maritime industry initiated, the WETBACKS supported and women given the vote (1954).

RUIZ DE ALARCÓN, Juan. See ALARCÓN Y MENDOZA, JUAN RUIZ DE.

RUM, alcoholic liquor, usually produced by distilling fermented MOLASSES. It acquires a brown color from the wooden casks in which it is stored and from added CARAMEL or burnt sugar. It is made mainly in the West Indies. (See also ALCOHOLIC BEVERAGES.)

RUMANIA. See ROMANIA.

RUMANIAN, official language of ROMANIA. Descended from the Latin of DACIA province, it is a ROMANCE LANGUAGE with Greek, Hungarian, Slavic and Turkish influences. In the 18th century, the script changed from Cyrillic to the Latin alphabet.

RUMELIA, Balkan possessions of the OTTOMAN EMPIRE, including much of present-day N Greece, Yugoslavia, Bulgaria and Albania. E Rumelia became an autonomous province of Turkey by the treaty of Berlin (1878) and in 1885 became part of Bulgaria.

RUMFORD, Sir Benjamin Thompson, Count (1753–1814), American-born adventurer and scientist best known for his recognition of the relation between WORK and HEAT (inspired by observation of heat generated by FRICTION during the boring of cannon), which laid the foundations for JOULE's later work. He played a primary role in the founding of the ROYAL INSTITUTION (1799), to which he also introduced Humphry DAVY.

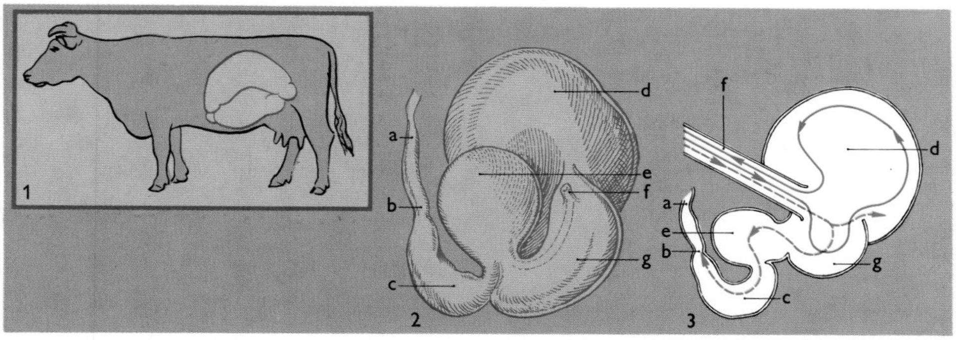

(1) Location and relative size of the stomach of a typical ruminant, the cow. (2) The compound stomach of a ruminant: (a) duodenum; (b) pylorus; (c) abomasum; (d) rumen; (e) psalterium; (f) esophagus; (g) reticulum. (3) The passage of food before rerumination (*in red*) and after regurgitation (*in green*).

RUMI, or **Jalal-ad-din Rumi** (1207–1273), great Sufi poet and mystic of Persia. His major work was the *Mathnawi*, a poetic exposition of Sufi wisdom in some 27 000 couplets.

RUMINANTS, animals that regurgitate and rechew their food once having swallowed it. They feed by filling one compartment of a three- or four-chambered stomach with unmasticated food, bringing it back up to the mouth again to be fully chewed and finally swallowed. It is an adaptation in many herbivores to increase the time available for the digestion of relatively indigestible vegetable matter.

RUMMY, any of a group of card games derived from Spanish conquian (with whom). In basic rummy, devised about 1895, the object is to lay down as many sets (*melds*) of cards as possible. Melds consist of three or four cards of the same value in different suits or sequences of three or four cards in the same suit. Melding an entire hand in one turn is a *rummy*. (See also CANASTA.)

RUMP PARLIAMENT, 60 remaining members of the British LONG PARLIAMENT after Col. Thomas Pride in "Pride's Purge" had ejected all opposition to Oliver CROMWELL's army (1648). They created a high court which tried CHARLES I and had him executed (1649), abolished the House of Lords and monarchy, and established a ruling Council of State. The attempt to pass a bill prolonging its life indefinitely led to the Rump's forcible dissolution by Cromwell (1653–59). Purged members returned in 1660, prior to the RESTORATION. (See CIVIL WAR, ENGLISH.)

RUNDSTEDT, Karl Rudolf Gerd von (1875–1953), German field marshal. In WWII he led army groups in Poland, France and Russia, was military ruler of France, and commander, W Europe, on D-DAY and during the Battle of the BULGE.

RUNES, characters of a pre-Christian writing system used by the Teutonic tribes of N Europe from as early as the 3rd century BC to as late as the 10th century AD, and sometimes after. The three distinct types are Early, Anglo-Saxon and Scandinavian. The Runic alphabet is sometimes known as **futhork** for its first six characters. (See also WRITING, HISTORY OF.)

RUNNEMEDE, residential borough, SW N.J., 7mi S of Camden, settled by Quakers in 1683. It has some light industry. Pop 10 475.

RUNNING, a sport since ancient times. There are three basic classes: sprints, middle-distance and long-distance. Varieties include relay racing, STEEPLECHASING and cross-country. (See also MARATHON; TRACK AND FIELD.)

RUNNYMEDE, meadow in Surrey, S England, on the bank of the Thames R. Here King John conceded the barons' demands embodied in the MAGNA CARTA (1215). There is a memorial to President John F. Kennedy (unveiled 1965).

RUNYON, Alfred Damon (1884–1946), US journalist and writer. His entertaining stories of tough-talking gangsters, Broadway actors and the sporting underworld were written in the colorful vernacular of New York City. *Guys and Dolls* (1932), the first of several collections, was the basis of a successful musical (1950).

RUPERT, Prince (1619–1682), count palatine of the Rhine and duke of Bavaria, brilliant royalist cavalry commander in the English CIVIL WAR. Dismissed by his uncle Charles I after surrendering Bristol to parliamentarians (1645), he commanded a fleet which harried Commonwealth shipping (1648–50). After the RESTORATION, he was first lord of the admiralty. He introduced MEZZOTINT to Britain and was a founder of the HUDSON'S BAY COMPANY.

RUPERT'S LAND, or **Prince Rupert's Land**, vast, mineral-rich region of NW Canada granted to the HUDSON'S BAY COMPANY in 1670 by Charles II. Named for PRINCE RUPERT, it comprised the basin of Hudson Bay. In 1818, the US acquired the portion S of the 49th parallel. In 1869, the remainder became part of the NORTHWEST TERRITORIES.

RUPTURE, common name for HERNIA.

RURAL ELECTRIFICATION ADMINISTRATION (REA), agency of the US Department of Agriculture (since 1939), formed 1935 to finance distribution of electricity by giving loans to cooperatives, private utilities, public power districts etc.

RURAL FREE DELIVERY (RFD), in the US postal service, begun 1896 in W Va. through pressure from the GRANGE. Now 35 000 rural carriers serve 35 million people.

RURIK, or **Ryurik** (d. 879), semi-legendary Viking founder of the Russian empire. Based in Novgorod, he ruled from c862. The Rurik dynasty gave way to the house of ROMANOV in the early 17th century.

RUSH, aquatic grass-like plants of marshes, lake edges, paths and ditches. Many rushes belong to the genus *Juncus*. They have cylindrical stalks and hollow stem-like leaves, which are used for chair seats, mats and basketwork. The pith of the stems is used as wicks for oil lamps and candles. Other important rushes belonging to the genera *Typha* (BULRUSHES), *Cyperus* and *Scirpus*.

RUSH, Benjamin (1746–1813), US physician, abolitionist and reformer. His greatest contribution to medical science was his conviction that insanity is a disease (see MENTAL ILLNESS): his *Medical Enquiries and Observations upon the Diseases of the Mind* (1812) was the first US book on PSYCHIATRY.

RUSH, Richard (1780–1859), US statesman, son of Benjamin Rush. Holder of many high US offices, he negotiated with Great Britain the RUSH-BAGOT CONVENTION and the 49th parallel between Canada and the US, prepared the way for the Monroe Doctrine and helped in founding the SMITHSONIAN INSTITUTION.

RUSH-BAGOT CONVENTION (1817), negotiations after the WAR OF 1812, between Richard RUSH and Sir Charles BAGOT, which agreed mutual US-British disarmament on the Great Lakes.

RUSHMORE, Mount, or **Mount Rushmore National Memorial,** rises to 5600ft in the Black Hills, W S.D. In the granite of the NE face, 60ft portraits of presidents Washington, Jefferson, Lincoln and (Theodore) Roosevelt were carved 1925–41 by Gutzon BORGLUM.

RUSK, (David) Dean (1909–), US secretary of state, 1961–69, in the Kennedy and Johnson administrations. Previously a university professor and WWII army colonel, he worked in the Department of State (1946–52) and was president of the Rockefeller Foundation (1952–60). He became President Johnson's main spokesman on Vietnam.

RUSKIN, John (1819–1900), English art critic, writer and reformer. The first volume of his *Modern Painters* (1843) championed J. M. W. TURNER. A major influence on the arts, he was behind the Victorian GOTHIC REVIVAL. *Unto This Last* (1862), first of his "letters" to workmen, attacked "laissez-faire" philosophy. An autobiography, *Praeterita* (1885–89), was unfinished.

RUSSELL, prominent family in British politics. The first member to gain national fame was **John Russell** (c1486–1555), created 1st earl of Bedford for helping Edward VI to quell a 1549 rebellion. The family fortune, including Woburn Abbey, Bedfordshire, was acquired during this period. **William, 5th earl** (1613–1700), was a parliamentary general in the Civil War. He was created 1st duke of Bedford in 1694, partly because of the fame, as a patriotic martyr, of his son Lord William RUSSELL (1639–1683), first notable WHIG in the family. The title of Lord John RUSSELL, 1st earl of Kingston Russell (1792–1878; third son of the 6th duke), was inherited by his grandson Bertrand RUSSELL.

RUSSELL, Bertrand Arthur William, 3rd Earl Russell (1872–1970), British philosopher, mathematician and man of letters. Initially subscribing to IDEALISM, he broke away in 1898 eventually to become an empiricist (see EMPIRICISM). His most important work was to relate LOGIC and MATHEMATICS. After having written to FREGE pointing out a paradox in Frege's attempt to reduce all mathematics to logical principles, Russell endeavored to perform this task himself. His results appeared in *The Principles of Mathematics* (1903) and, in collaboration with A. N. WHITEHEAD, *Principia Mathematica* (3 vols., 1910–13). Russell was a vehement pacifist for much of his life, his views twice earning him prison sentences (1918, 1961): during the former he wrote his *Introduction to Mathematical Philosophy* (1919). His other works include *Marriage and Morals* (1929), *Education and the Social Order* (1932), *An Inquiry into Meaning and Truth* (1940), *History of Western Philosophy* (1945) and popularizations such as *The ABC of Relativity* (1925), as well as his *Autobiography* (3 vols., 1967–69). He received the 1950 Nobel Prize for Literature; and founded the Bertrand Russell Peace Foundation in 1963.

RUSSELL, Bill (William Felton Russell; 1934–), US basketball player, in 1966 the first black coach of a major professional sports team. In his 13 years with the Boston Celtics (1956–69) the team won 11 NBA championships.

RUSSELL, Charles Marion (1864–1926), US cowboy painter, sculptor and author. His many canvases of frontier life, Indians, horses and cattle camps, usually set in Mont., were enormously popular.

RUSSELL, Charles Taze (1852–1916), US founder of the International Bible Students, forerunner of JEHOVAH'S WITNESSES. He prophesied the invisible return of Jesus and the MILLENNIUM.

RUSSELL, George William (1867–1935), Irish poet, nationalist, mystic and painter, known under the pseudonym "A.E." A theosophist, he was with W. B. YEATS a leader of the CELTIC RENAISSANCE and a cofounder of Dublin's ABBEY THEATRE.

RUSSELL, Henry Norris (1877–1957), US astronomer who, independently of HERTESPRUNG, showed the relation between a STAR's brightness and color: the resulting **Hertzsprung-Russell diagram** is important throughout astronomy and cosmology.

RUSSELL, Lord John, 1st Earl Russell (1792–1878), British Whig statesman and liberal reformer. A leading supporter of the CATHOLIC EMANCIPATION ACT (1830), he also fought for the 1832 REFORM BILL. Twice prime minister (1846–52, 1865–66), he was influential in maintaining British neutrality in the US Civil War.

RUSSELL, Lillian (1861–1922), US singer, actress, flamboyant beauty of the "Gay Nineties." Born Helen Louise Leonard, she became a star in the show *The Great Mogul* (1881). She married four times, but her affair with "Diamond Jim" BRADY spanned 40 years.

RUSSELL, Richard Brevard (1897–1971), influential US Democratic senator from Ga. from 1933. Governor of Ga. 1931–33, he was twice candidate for the presidential nomination.

RUSSELL, Lord William (1639–1683), English Whig statesman who during the Popish Plot led the attempts to bar the duke of York (later JAMES II) from the royal succession. Dubiously implicated in the RYE HOUSE PLOT, he was executed.

RUSSELL CAVE NATIONAL MONUMENT, established 1961 in NE Ala., an area of 310 acres including a cave which contains an archaeological record of its human inhabitants from about 6000 BC to 1650 AD.

RUSSELL SAGE FOUNDATION. See SAGE, RUSSELL.

RUSSELLVILLE, city in NW central Ark., seat of Pope Co. on the Arkansas R, in an area with coal, timber and mixed agriculture. Pop 11 750.

RUSSIA, or the **Union of Soviet Socialist Republics (USSR)** or **Soviet Union.** The largest country in the world, it encompasses 8 649 412sq mi of the Eurasian land mass. Its maximum W-E extent, E Europe to the Pacific, exceeds 6 500mi. It extends 1 800mi–3 000mi N-S from the Arctic to its frontiers with Turkey, Iran, Afghanistan, China and Mongolia.

This vast country, most of which lies in the high latitudes N of the 50th parallel, has a population of nearly 250 000 000, exceeded only in China and India. There are more than 100 ethnic groups, the three chief Slav groups—Russians, Ukrainians and Belorussians—making up more than 71% of the population. The Soviet Union comprises 15 federated republics, each of which is inhabited mainly, but not exclusively, by a major ethnic group. The Russian Soviet Federated Socialist Republic (RSFSR) is the largest and its capital, Moscow, is also the capital and largest city of the USSR. Several republics have subdivisions—autonomous republics, autonomous *oblasts* (regions) and national *okrugs* (districts)—reflecting minority ethnic groups.

The Land. W of the Yenisey R (about 90°E) are the vast W Siberian and E European plains, divided by the N-S Ural Mts (which also divide Asia from Europe). The W Siberian plain, never above 600ft and with large marshy areas, is drained to the N by the Ob and Irtysh rivers and to the S is separated by the Kazakh hills from the largely arid Aral-Caspian lowlands drained by the Amu and Syr rivers. The E European plain is drained N by the Dvina and Pechora rivers, and S by the Dnieper, Don and Volga rivers. E of the Yenisey are the Central Siberian plateau between the Yenisey and Lena rivers, and the Taimyr region along the Arctic, including the N Siberian lowland. Mountain regions include the Caucasus, NE Siberia and the Kamchatka peninsula (with its active volcanoes) and the Altai-Sayan region NW of Mongolia. Russia's highest peaks are in the Pamir ranges of central Asia near the Afghan-Tibetan border. More modest mountain areas are Baikalia, between Lake Baikal and the Amur R in the SE, and the Amur maritime region between that river and the Pacific Ocean.

Climate and Vegetation. Most of Russia has a continental climate marked by severe winters. The Arctic coast is icebound for most of the year and more than 50% of the country is snow-covered for about six months. But summers are usually warm; the Crimean coast enjoys mild winters and warm summers. The vegetation zones, N-S, comprise tundra, *taiga* (forest zone), the treeless grassland steppes, the semi-desert and desert zone and the subtropical vegetation zone bordering the Black Sea.

The People are unevenly distributed: over two-thirds live in the European plain, with heavy concentrations around Moscow and Leningrad, the only two cities with more than 2 million inhabitants. Although there has been some intermingling, the 100 or more ethnic groups are mainly territorially distinct.

Official name: Union of Soviet Socialist Republics
Capital: Moscow
Area: 8 649 412sq mi
Population: 248 600 000
Languages: Russian; numerous regional languages
Religions: No official religion; Russian Orthodox
Monetary unit(s): 1 Rouble = 100 kopeks

Russia

Politics and people

Constituent republics of Russia (USSR)
SSR = Soviet Socialist Republic.
SFSR = Soviet Federated Socialist Republic

Republic	Area sq mi	Population	Capital and population
Armenian SSR	11 506	2 730 000	Yerevan (870 000)
Azerbaijan SSR	33 436	5 519 000	Baku (1 359 000)
Belorussian SSR	80 154	9 261 000	Minsk (1 095 000)
Estonian SSR	17 413	1 418 000	Tallinn (392 000)
Georgian SSR	26 911	4 883 000	Tbilisi (984 000)
Kazakh SSR	1 048 300	13 924 000	Alma-Ata (813 000)
Kirgiz SSR	76 641	3 219 000	Frunze (474 000)
Latvian SSR	24 595	2 450 000	Riga (776 000)
Lithuanian SSR	25 174	3 257 000	Vilnius (420 000)
Moldavian SSR	13 012	3 733 000	Kishinev (432 000)
Russian SFSR	6 592 812	132 892 000	Moscow (7 528 000)
Tadzhik SSR	55 251	3 282 000	Dushanbe (422 000)
Turkmen SSR	188 455	2 428 000	Ashkhabad (279 000)
Ukrainian SSR	233 089	48 562 000	Kiev (1 887 000)
Uzbek SSR	173 591	13 276 000	Tashkent (1 552 000)

The Soviet System

The Soviet Union is a federal state and each of the 15 constituent (Union) republics has a constitutional right to secede. All republics are closely knit in a pyramidal system of soviets (councils) with the Supreme Soviet at its apex. According to the constitution, the Supreme Soviet is "the highest organ of state power in the USSR." It is the highest legislative body and appoints the Supreme Court and the Council of Ministers, and elects the Presidium. It comprises two houses, with equal legislative rights, elected for 4-year periods by all citizens over 18: the Soviet of the Union (one deputy for every 300 000 of population), and the Soviet of Nationalities (representatives of all constituent and autonomous republics, autonomous regions and national areas). The Supreme Soviet normally has two formal sessions yearly, each lasting only a few days. But at this and lower levels, much of the work continues in numerous standing committees, while individual deputies work among their own electorates.

Between sessions of the Supreme Soviet the highest state authority is the Presidium of 37 members elected at a joint session of both houses. It includes a chairman, who is also head of state (president) of the USSR, and 15 vice-chairmen, one from each constituent republic. But executive power is vested in the Council of Ministers. Its chairman is premier of the USSR, and its members, who normally include the 15 premiers of the constituent republics, are chosen by him (and approved by the Supreme Soviet). The Council of Ministers is empowered to legislate by decree.

The same structure exists at lower levels. Each republic has its own council of ministers and supreme soviet, and there are lesser soviets for local, urban and district government. In all there are about 50 000 soviets and other governing bodies, and these, along with other organizations such as the 300 000 standing committees, the cooperatives and street committees, give citizens ample opportunities for participating in government and administration, probably to a far greater extent than in many western democracies.

While the Soviet system has democratic institutions like universal suffrage and the secret ballot, it is utterly foreign to western-style democracy. There is only one permitted political party, the Communist Party of the Soviet Union (CPSU), which effectively controls political activity at all levels and in the armed forces, where every unit has its political commissar. The wider electorate has no real choice of candidates at elections: single candidates for the Supreme Soviet elections are selected at constituency conferences, where delegates from organizations which have nominated candidates discuss those who wish to stand. The name of the selected candidate, who may be a non-party citizen (like 28% of the Supreme Soviet elected in June 1970), appears on a ballot paper and voters can only register disapproval by striking out the name. The constitution ostensibly guarantees freedom of speech, of the press and of assembly, and the right to demonstrate freely. In practice these rights are reserved for the CPSU and approved organizations.

The Communist Party

Curiously the CPSU is mentioned only once in the Soviet constitution, where it is described as a voluntary organization of the "more advanced, politically more conscious section of the working class, collective-farm peasantry and intelligensia." Official figures show that, compared with the total population of the USSR, its membership is small but growing (14.5 million in 1971, 14.8 million in 1973). There are over 300 000 local party units in the Soviet Union. Young Soviet citizens may belong successively to the Little Octobrists (7–9), Young Pioneers (9–15) and the *Komsomol* or Young Communist League (15–28), before applying to join the Communist Party. The All-Union Party Congress does not meet as often (at least once every four years) as the CPSU's own rules stipulate, and its election of the party's Central Committee of about 350 regular and alternate members is largely a formal business. The election by the Central Committee of the two other top party bodies also contains a large element of self-selection. These bodies are the Politburo and, the apex of power, the Secretariat, whose first secretary (currently Leonid Brezhnev) is the most powerful man in both the party and the USSR.

Everyday Life and Expectations

What does the Soviet citizen expect from his loyalty to the system? Not least the assurance of a job: there is no unemployment in the USSR (though some observers believe there is underemployment). He can also look forward to not less than three weeks' annual vacation with pay and to comprehensive social services ranging from free medical and dental care to noncontributory old-age pensions. Because of the "Great Patriotic War" (WWII), in which some 20 million Soviet citizens died, the older generation includes many widows, and special payments are made to them and to fatherless families and the physically disabled. Since 1970 the average working week has been under 40 hours—less in industries like coal-mining, where conditions are hazardous or unhealthy. Rates of pay are based on the importance of the industry, the skills involved, working conditions and geographical location (wages in the remote north are often double those paid for similar work elsewhere).

In the Soviet Union's work force of about 100 million, over half are women, active in a wide range of jobs from street-cleansing and construction work to senior positions in education, the sciences, technology and administration. Most Soviet physicians are women. But even while holding down a job, women do most of the work in the house. The family, though traditionally viewed by the CPSU as a bourgeois institution, is valued as a stabilizing force in Soviet society. However, the divorce rate is high, especially in the cities.

The average Soviet citizen is reasonably content with living standards, even if they are still below the average in rich countries of the West. In 1971 Premier Kosygin, outlining the 9th Five-year Plan (1971–75), promised better times for all, and though the national income growth rate of 4% in 1972 was the lowest for 10 years, there have been increases in average wages and incomes, improvements in housing and more and better food and clothing. There has also been a marked increase in the output of consumer goods. In Moscow, for example, the number of privately-owned automobiles had risen to more than 250 000 by 1973—more than double the number in 1970. Perhaps the decades of sacrifice, when all had been subordinated to the development of heavy industry and postwar reconstruction, are about to pay off. However, the perennial problems of bureaucratic inefficiency and restraints upon personal expression and political discussion survive. From a young age Soviet citizens are instructed in Marxism–Leninism and taught to regard the USSR as its supreme practitioner. They are conditioned against unhealthy influences from the outside world, and brought up to fulfill a useful role in the service of people and state. Assured benefits await those who do not deviate from the system or question its fundamental principles as interpreted by the ruling hierarchy. Dire penalties await the dissenter. Among those harrassed by the KGB (Committee for State Security) and its agents have been the novelist Boris Pasternak, who was pressurized into refusing the 1958 Nobel Prize for Literature; the poet Andrey Sinyavsky, sent in 1966 to a labor camp; the novelist Alexander Solzhenitsyn, deprived of his Soviet citizenship and expelled from the USSR (1974); and leaders of the civil rights movement like the nuclear physicist Andrei Sakharov (1974). Some dissidents, like the mathematician Yury Shakhanovich, have been confined in mental hospitals; others, like the cellist Mstislav Rostropovich, have been prevented on occasion from travelling abroad. Spokesmen of Crimean Tatars and Germans deported in WWII have been imprisoned. Such persecution is not limited to those seeking greater intellectual and political freedom in the USSR, but is also inflicted on those wishing to emigrate, especially Soviet Jews. Only the pressure of public opinion in western countries won exit permits for the ballet-dancer Valery Panov and his wife Galina (1974). There is far less juvenile crime in the USSR than in the USA and other western countries. But some observers detect a certain restlessness in Soviet youth directed at the regimentation of the system, and a growing curiosity about the freedoms enjoyed in the West. Among some intellectuals, political dissidents, and dissatisfied national minorities, *samizdat* or underground literature circulates, and there are occasional strikes and demonstrations of workers. But there is little sign of mass pressure for reform, nor of a lifting of restrictions. The promise of the liberal changes when Khrushchev denounced Stalin's dictatorship (1956) now seems a thing of the past.

Slav groups (including Russians, who comprise 55% of USSR population) predominate in the European USSR, Siberia and the far E and non-Slav groups in the Caucasus and Soviet Central Asia. More than 100 languages are spoken along with Russian, the official and universal language. (See entries for each Soviet Socialist Republic.)

Economy. Russia has a planned socialist economy in which all resources and means of production belong to the state. An industrial superpower second only to the US, Russia is self-sufficient in most minerals and energy resources including coal (Donets and Kuznetsk basins, Karaganda and Pechora), oil and natural gas (Volga-Ural oil field, N Caucasus, Baku, W Siberia) and iron ore (Krivoi Rog, Urals, NW Kazakhstan and E Siberia). Industry is concentrated notably in the Urals and E Ukraine (iron, steel, heavy engineering) and manufacturing in cities like Moscow, Leningrad, Kiev, Kharkov, Minsk, Riga and Voronezh. About 10% of Russia's land is used for crops and about 25% for all farming, nearly all of which comes within the 15 500 state farms and 32 000 COLLECTIVE FARMS.

History. The SLAVS probably first entered Russia from the W in the 400s AD. In the 800s Scandinavian conquerors known as "Russes," led by RURIK, settled in Novgorod and Kiev, whose ruler, VLADIMIR, was converted to Christianity c989. After the 12th-century Tatar invasions (see MOGUL EMPIRE), Moscow rose to preeminence. Its Grand Prince IVAN IV (the Terrible) was the first to be crowned tsar (1547). The election of MICHAEL as tsar (1613) established the ROMANOV dynasty which ruled until the Russian Revolution. PETER the Great founded St. Petersburg (now Leningrad) and made it imperial capital (1721). His program of westernization and Russian expansion continued under CATHERINE the Great. Russia survived invasion by Napoleon (1812) but was in

Muscovites enjoying chess and checkers at tables set up in the open air in Gorky Park. Chess is not only a national pastime, but is taken as seriously as any sport involving national prestige.

decline during the 19th century (nevertheless the greatest period of Russian literature). Reforms, including liberation of the serfs (1861), failed to check internal unrest which culminated in the Russian Revolution. The throne was toppled and power seized from the moderates under KERENSKY by the BOLSHEVIKS led by LENIN. After civil war (1918–20) the USSR was proclaimed (1922). The power struggle following Lenin's death (1924) was won by Joseph STALIN, who led Russia to victory in WWII. After his death (1953), leadership eventually passed to Nikita KHRUSHCHEV, who denounced Stalin's tyrannies and inaugurated "peaceful co-existence" with the West. China then broke with the USSR; in the 1960s and 1970s the rift increased. Khrushchev was deposed in 1964 and succeeded by Aleksei KOSYGIN as premier and Leonid BREZHNEV as party leader.

RUSSIAN, native language of 130 million Russians, chief official language of the USSR. Most important of the E Slavic INDO-EUROPEAN LANGUAGES (Belorussian and Ukrainian diverged from c1300), Russian is written in the 33-character Cyrillic alphabet introduced in the 800s by Christian missionaries. A difficult language for English speakers, it has very different word-roots and is heavily inflected in nouns and verbs. By combining colloquialism with the formal Church Slavonic the poet PUSHKIN did much to shape modern literary Russian, which is based on the Moscow dialect.

RUSSIAN-AMERICAN COMPANY, chartered 1799 by the Russian government, monopoly controller of Russian settlements in North America until 1862. Its first manager, Aleksandr BARANOV, virtually governed Alaska and founded New Archangel (1799).

RUSSIAN BLUE, cat breed of "foreign" type with a soft blue coat and green, almond-shaped eyes. They have quiet voices and a reputation for shyness.

RUSSIAN REVOLUTION, momentous political upheaval which changed the course of world history. It destroyed the autocratic tsarist regime and culminated in the establishment of the world's first communist state, the Soviet Union (1922). Its roots lay in the political and economic backwardness of Russia and the chronic poverty of most of the people, expressed in rising discontent in the middle and lower classes since the late 1800s.

The Revolution of 1905 began on "Bloody Sunday," Jan. 22 (Jan. 9, old Russian calendar), when troops fired on a workers' demonstration in St. Petersburg. Widespread disorders followed, including mutiny on the battleship Potemkin and a national general strike organized by the St. Petersburg *soviet* (workers' council). These events, coupled with the

Above: one of Russia's major cultural institutions, the Bolshoi Theater in Moscow. It has its own internationally famous ballet and opera companies.

Left: the Church of the Resurrection in Leningrad, second largest city in the Soviet Union.

disastrous RUSSO-JAPANESE WAR, forced Tsar Nicholas II to grant civil rights and set up an elected *duma* (parliament) in his "October Manifesto." Under premier B. A. STOLYPIN repression continued until late WWI, in which Russia suffered severe reverses.

The February Revolution (1917). Food shortages and strikes provoked riots and mutiny (March 8–10). A provisional government under the progressive Prince Georgi LVOV was set up (later headed by Alexander KERENSKY) and Nicholas II abdicated (March 15). **The October Revolution (1917).** On Nov. 6 (Oct. 24), the Bolsheviks, led by V. E. LENIN, staged an armed coup. Moscow was seized and the remnants of the provisional government arrested; the constitutional assembly was dispersed by Bolshevik troops and the CHEKA set up. Next day a Council of People's Commissars was set up, headed by Lenin and including Leon TROTSKY and Joseph STALIN. In the civil war (1918–20), the anticommunist "Whites," commanded by A. I. DENIKIN, A. V. KOLCHAK and P. N. WRANGEL were defeated. Russian involvement in WWI ended with the Treaty of BREST-LITOVSK. The tsar and his family were murdered at Ekaterinburg (July, 1918), and the new Soviet constitution made Lenin and the Communist (formerly Bolshevik) Party all-powerful.

RUSSIAN SOVIET FEDERATED SOCIALIST REPUBLIC (RSFSR), largest of the USSR's constituent republics, one of the original four united in the Soviet Union (1922). It holds over 50% of the population, and over 76% of the land area, of the Soviet Union. Its W section is a great plain broken only by the N-S Ural Mts. E of the Yenisey R lie eroded plateaus and ridges, with high, folded mountains in the S. About 83% of the population are Russians and there are some 38 other ethnic groups. The capital and largest city is Moscow, the chief port Leningrad. With 90% of Russia's forests, rich mineral resources and abundant hydroelectric power, the RSFSR provides about 70% of Russia's total industrial and agricultural output.

RUSSIAN WOLFHOUND. See BORZOI.

RUSSO-FINNISH WARS, two conflicts during WWII. The first, the "Winter War" (1939–40), arose from rejection of Russian demands for military bases in Finland, territorial concessions and the dismantling of the MANNERHEIM line, Finland's defense system across the Karelian isthmus. When the Russians attacked (Nov. 30), the Finns unexpectedly threw them back. But in Feb., 1940 the Mannerheim line was broken and Finland signed the Peace of Moscow (March 12) surrendering about 10% of her territory, including much of KARELIA, Petsamo (now Pechenga) and Viipuri (Vyborg). In the "Continuation War"

(1941–44), Finland fought alongside Nazi Germany, and was forced to pay $300 million reparations to the USSR and to lease it the PORKKALA area (returned in 1956).

RUSSO-GERMAN PACT, nonaggression pact signed by MOLOTOV and RIBBENTROP on Aug. 23, 1939. It cleared the way for Hitler's invasion of Poland (Sept. 1) which precipitated WWII, and for the division of Poland between Nazi Germany and Russia (which invaded Sept. 17 from the E).

RUSSO-JAPANESE WAR, 1904–05, culmination of rivalry in the Far East, where both powers sought expansion at the expense of the decaying Chinese empire. Russia occupied Manchuria during the BOXER REBELLION and coveted Korea. On Feb. 8, 1904 the Japanese attacked the Russian naval base of PORT ARTHUR (now Lü-shun), which they captured in Jan., 1905. The Russians were also defeated at MUKDEN in Manchuria and their Baltic fleet, sent to retrieve the situation, was destroyed in the battle of TSUSHIMA (May 27, 1905). Mediation by US president Theodore Roosevelt ended the war in the Treaty of PORTSMOUTH (1905). Russia ceded the Liaotung peninsula and S Sakhalin to Japan, recognized Japan's dominance in Korea and returned Manchuria to China. Russia's disastrous defeat was an immediate cause of the 1905 RUSSIAN REVOLUTION and won Japan great power status.

RUSSO-POLISH WAR, 1919–20, started when newly-constituted Poland, under Józef PILSUDSKI, joined with Ukrainian nationalist Simon PETLYURA to invade the Ukraine. Driven back by Soviet forces almost to Warsaw, the Poles with French aid forced Russian retreat. By the treaty of Riga (March 18, 1921) the Poles regained parts of BYELORUSSIA and the UKRAINE.

RUSSO-TURKISH WARS, fought intermittently over three centuries, were caused by Russia's determination to absorb the Black Sea coast and Caucasus, dominate the Balkans and control the Bosporus and Dardanelles straits. The first major Russian success was the capture of Azov by Peter I (the Great) in 1696. In two wars against the Turks (1768–74, 1787–91), Catherine the Great, allied with Austria, gained the rest of the Ukraine, the Crimea, and an outlet to the Black Sea and the straits. Russia adopted the role of protecting Christians in the declining OTTOMAN EMPIRE. Russia won Bessarabia in the war of 1806–12 and made further gains in the war of 1828–29. When Russia next pressurized the Turks, France and Britain intervened, defeating Russia in the CRIMEAN WAR (1853–56). Russia regained territory in the last war of 1877–78, though the terms of the treaty of SAN STEFANO were modified by the congress of BERLIN (1878). Russia and Turkey were again opponents in WWI, and concluded a separate peace treaty (1921).

Poster produced in 1920, during the civil war that concluded the Russian Revolution. It urges workers to celebrate the national holiday on May 1 by increasing their work quotas.

RUSSWURM, John Brown (1799–1851), Jamaican-born US abolitionist who led a "back to Africa" movement in the 1820s and eventually settled in Liberia in 1829. He founded (1827) and edited *Freedom's Journal*, first black-owned US newspaper.

RUST, a large number of FUNGI which cause many PLANT DISEASES. They form red or orange spots, their spore-bearing organs, on the leaves of infected plants. Spores are carried by the wind to infect new plants. Some rusts are heteroecious: they alternate between two different host plants. The most important rust fungus is probably *Puccinia graminis* which causes black stem rust of wheat. (See also SMUT.)

RUST. See CORROSION.

RUSTICATION, in architecture (especially Classical and Renaissance), masonry in which the contact surfaces and edges of the stones are flat, leaving a rough and projecting exposed surface.

RUSTIN, Bayard (1910–   ), US civil rights activist, Quaker and pacifist. One of the original Freedom Riders (1947) for integration in the South, he helped found the SOUTHERN CHRISTIAN LEADERSHIP CONFERENCE and was chief organizer of the 1963 civil rights march on Washington.

RUSTON, industrial city in N La., seat of Lincoln parish. It lies in a major oil, gas and agricultural region. Pop 17 565.

RUTABAGA, Swede or **Swedish turnip,** *Brassica napo-brassica*, a biennial plant grown for its edible taproot. The root has firm yellow or white flesh and is used primarily as a vegetable and in stock feed. (See also TURNIP.)

RUTH, Moabite heroine of the Old Testament book bearing her name. Widowed during a famine in the time of the JUDGES, Ruth followed her Judahite mother-in-law, Naomi, to Bethlehem. She survived by gleaning barley from the fields of her husband's next-of-kin, Boaz, who eventually married her. Their great-grandson was DAVID.

RUTH, Babe (George Herman Ruth; 1895–1948), famous US baseball player. Sold to the New York Yankees in 1920 for the phenomenal sum of $125 000, he was largely responsible for building the team's prestige. In his 22 major league seasons, he hit 714 home runs and his lifetime batting average was .342. A flamboyant figure, he was elected to the Baseball Hall of Fame in 1936.

RUTHENIA, region SW of the Carpathian Mts. Formerly part of Hungary, then of Czechoslovakia (from 1919), it was ceded to the USSR (1945) and is now Transcarpathian *oblast*, the most westerly in the Ukrainian SSR. Uzhgorod is capital of this mountainous and densely forested region.

RUTHENIUM (Ru), hard metal in the PLATINUM GROUP. It is added to platinum or palladium to form hard ALLOYS. Ruthenium is a catalyst (see CATALYSIS) used in organic chemistry. AW 101.1, mp 2250°C bp 3900°C, sg 12.30(20°C).

RUTHERFORD, residential borough, NE N.J., 7mi SSE of Paterson on the Passaic R. Fairleigh Dickinson U. was founded here in 1942. Pop 20 802.

RUTHERFORD, Sir Ernest, 1st Baron Rutherford of Nelson (1871–1937), New Zealand born British physicist. His early work was with J. J. THOMSON on MAGNETISM and thus on RADIO waves. Following ROENTGEN's discovery of X-RAYS (1895), they studied the CONDUCTIVITY of air bombarded by these rays and the rate at which the IONS produced recombined. This led him to similar studies of the "rays" emitted by URANIUM (see RADIOACTIVITY). He found these were of two types, which he named alpha and beta (see ALPHA PARTICLES; BETA RAYS). As a result of their work on RADIUM, ACTINIUM and particularly THORIUM, he and Frederick SODDY were able in 1903 to put forward their theory of radioactivity. This suggested that the atoms of certain substances spontaneously emit alpha and beta rays, being thereby transformed into atoms of different, but still radioactive, ELEMENTS of lesser ATOMIC WEIGHT. He later showed alpha rays to be positively charged particles, in fact, HELIUM atoms stripped of two ELECTRONS. He was awarded the 1908 Nobel Prize for Chemistry. In 1911 he proposed his nuclear theory of the ATOM, on which BOHR based his celebrated theory two years later. In 1919 he announced the first artificial disintegration of an atom, NITROGEN being converted into OXYGEN and HYDROGEN by collision with an alpha particle. He was President of the ROYAL SOCIETY from 1925 to 1930. His work was commemorated (1969) by the naming of RUTHERFORDIUM.

RUTHERFORDIUM (Rf), a TRANSURANIUM ELEMENT in Group IVB of the PERIODIC TABLE; atomic number 104. Soviet scientists claimed to have synthesized this element, which they called **kurchatovium**, in 1964, but their results are unconfirmed. American scientists claimed synthesis of rutherfordium in 1969 by bombarding californium-249 with carbon ions.

RUTILE, red-to-black OXIDE mineral consisting of impure titanium (IV) oxide (TiO_2), a TITANIUM ore of widespread occurrence. It is used to color porcelain, and synthetic rutile is used for GEMS.

RUTLAND, industrial city in W Vt., seat of Rutland Co. It is a Green Mountains resort center with marble quarries nearby. Pop 19 293.

RUTLEDGE, Ann (c1816–1835), daughter of an innkeeper at New Salem, Ill., where Abraham Lincoln lived 1831–37. Her early death deeply grieved Lincoln, but stories of a romance or even engagement are probably apocryphal.

RUTLEDGE, John (1739–1800), US lawyer and statesman, champion of American independence. He was twice delegate to the CONTINENTAL CONGRESS. As a delegate to the 1787 Constitutional Convention, he was largely responsible for concessions to slaveholders. He helped frame S.C.'s constitution (1776) and was governor 1779–82. Washington's nomination of him for Chief Justice (1795) was not confirmed by the Senate. His brother **Edward Rutledge** (1749–1800) was delegate to the Continental Congress 1774–76, a signer of the Declaration of Independence, and S.C. governor, 1798–1800.

RUWENZORI RANGE, in central Africa, stretches 70mi between lakes Albert and Edward on the Uganda-Zaire border. Snow-capped Mt Stanley (Ngaliema) rises to 16 763ft. Nile headwaters form in the Ruwenzori (rainmaker) range, named "Mountains of the Moon" by the geographer PTOLEMY and rediscovered by Henry M. STANLEY in 1889.

RUYSBROECK, or **Ruusbroec, Jan van** (1293–1381), Dutch mystic. He founded the Augustinian abbey at Groenendaal. His *The Spiritual Espousals* (c1350), a guide for the soul in the quest for God, was influential in Germany, France, Spain and Italy.

RUYSDAEL, Jacob van. See RUISDAEL, JACOB VAN.

RUYTER, Michiel Adriaanszoon de (1607–1676), Dutch admiral who fought the English in the DUTCH WARS. After the first (1652), he became vice-admiral of Holland. In the 2nd, he defeated the English off Dunkirk (1666) and destroyed much of the English fleet in the Medway R (1667). In the 3rd, he prevented an Anglo-French invasion of Holland (1673).

RUZICKA, Leopold (1887–1976), Croatian-born Swiss chemist who shared with BUTENANDT the 1939 Nobel Prize for Chemistry for his work on the TERPENES and for his demonstration that the ring compounds muskone and civetone had respectively 16 and 17 carbon atoms in the ring (see ALICYCLIC COMPOUNDS): previously it had been thought that rings with more than 8 carbon atoms would be unstable.

RWANDA, formerly Ruanda, small, landlocked independent republic of E central Africa.

Land, economy, people. Bordered by Uganda, Tanzania, Burundi and Zaire, Rwanda mainly comprises highlands of the GREAT RIFT VALLEY sloping in ridges from Mt Karisimbi in the NW (14 787ft).

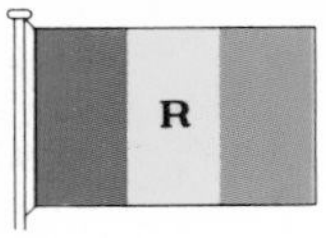

Official Name: Republic of Rwanda
Capital: Kigali
Area: 10 166sq mi
Population: 5 500 000
Languages: Kinyarwanda, French; Kiswahili
Religions: Roman Catholic, Animist, Muslim
Monetary Unit(s): 1 Rwanda franc = 100 centimes

Main street in the city of Kigali, capital of Rwanda.

Farming, the occupation of most Rwandese, is threatened by soil erosion due to LEACHING and heavy farming. Coffee is the main export, followed by tin and tungsten ore by four Belgium companies. Industry is limited, the population is 98% rural and illiteracy is about 90%. Some 90% of the people are Hutu (Bahutu) Bantu farmers; 9% Tutsi (Watutsi or Watusi) cattle-raisers, and 1% pygmy Twa hunters.
History. In the 1500s, the majority Hutu group were mastered by the taller Tutsi. From 1897, Rwanda was part of German East Africa and, after WWI, part of the Belgian trust territory, Ruanda-Urundi (administered with Belgian Congo 1925–60). In 1959 a bloody Hutu rising destroyed the Tutsi kingdom and ousted the *Mwami* (king), Kigeri V. About 120 000 Tutsi fled to Burundi. The Hutu party (Parmehutu) set up a republican regime. In 1962 Belgium granted full independence. In 1973 a coup established a military dictatorship.
RYAZAN, city, capital of Ryazan oblast, USSR, 120mi SE of Moscow in a mainly agricultural region. An historic city, it has important engineering, oil and chemical industries. Pop 357 000.

RYDER, Albert Pinkham (1847–1917), major US painter, noted for his darkly poetic landscapes, seascapes and allegorical scenes such as *Toilers of the Sea* (1884), *The Flying Dutchman* (c1890) and *The Race Track* (1895).
RYDER CUP, golf trophy awarded to winners of a biennial Anglo-US professional team match. The US has won 14½ to 4½ since 1927, when Samuel Ryder of St. Albans, England, presented the cup.
RYE, city in SE N.Y., on Long Island Sound. It is a residential suburb and resort area with several yacht and country clubs. Pop 15 869.
RYE, *Secale cereale*, hardiest of all CEREAL CROPS. It can grow in poor, sandy soils in cool and temperate climates. Most rye is used for human consumption, but rye grain and middlings (a byproduct of milling) are also fed to livestock. Rye malt is used to make rye whiskey. Rye is also used for cattle pasture. The leading producer of rye is the USSR. The ERGOT fungus disease of rye produces contaminated grains, which yield a drug that helps control bleeding and relieves MIGRAINE.
RYE GRASS, several annual and perennial Old World grasses that are used for pastures and lawns. Perennial rye grass (*Lolium perenne*) and Italian rye grass (*L. italicum*) are naturalized in North America. Darnel (*L. temulentum*) is an annual weed, the seeds of which contain an ALKALOID, temuline. Family: Graminae.
RYE HOUSE PLOT, radical Whig plot in 1683 to kill Charles II and the Duke of York (later JAMES II) at Rye House, Hertfordshire, and crown the Protestant Duke of MONMOUTH king. Among Whigs arrested on insubstantial evidence, the Earl of Essex apparently committed suicide, and Lord William RUSSELL and Algernon SIDNEY were executed.
RYKOV, Alexei Ivanovich (1881–1938), Russian communist leader. Active in the October Revolution (1917), he was Soviet premier 1924–30. An early supporter of STALIN against TROTSKY, he was himself executed after a show trial.
RYLE, Gilbert (1900–1976), English philosopher, a major figure at Oxford in the tradition of "ordinary language" philosophy, which views philosophical problems as conceptual confusions resulting from an unwary use of language. In his best-known work, *The Concept of Mind* (1949), he seeks to expose the legacy of such confusions bequeathed by the DUALISM of DESCARTES.
RYLE, Sir Martin (1918–), radio astronomer, corecipient with HEWISH of the 1974 Nobel physics prize. He was the first Professor of RADIO ASTRONOMY at Cambridge (1959), knighted in 1966, and became British Astronomer Royal in 1972.
RYSWICK, Treaty of, in 1697, ended the war in which the Great Alliance of the League of Augsburg, England and the Netherlands sought to block expansion of Louis XIV's France (see AUGSBURG, WAR OF THE LEAGUE OF). France gave up most territories won since 1678, but kept all but one of the Hudson's Bay Company forts seized in KING WILLIAM'S WAR. France also recognized William of Orange's right to the English throne, taken in the GLORIOUS REVOLUTION. The Dutch gained trade concessions and the right to garrison forts in the Spanish Netherlands.
RYUKYU ISLANDS, or **Riukiu Islands,** a chain forming a 650mi arc between Japan and Taiwan. Dividing the East China and Philippine seas, the 100-plus islands include the Osumi and Tokara (NE), the Amami and OKINAWA (center) and the Miyako and Yaeyama (SW). Many have coral reefs and some have active volcanoes. There are about 1 million islanders, mostly farmers and fishermen. Disputed with China, the Ryukyus became part of Japan in 1879. After WWII the US gave up the N islands in 1953, and the remainder in 1972, but maintains many bases.

Rye, the hardiest cereal, is a major food source in many countries. (1) Summer rye; (2) winter rye; and (3) a rye plant in bloom. (*Top*) Spikelets of summer (left) and winter varieties, each containing a seed.

S

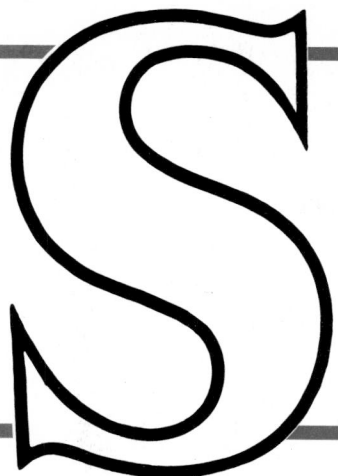

S, the 19th letter of the English alphabet. It derived from the Semitic language and progressed through Phoenician, Greek and Roman to its present form. It is an abbreviation for *south*, and in some languages (e.g. Italian) for *saint*.

SAADI or Sa'di (c1184–c1292), Persian lyric poet perhaps best known for two ethical works: a poem, the *Gulistan* (*The Rose Garden*, 1258) and the more popular prose and verse *Bustan* (*The Orchard*, 1257).

SAADIA BEN JOSEPH (882–942), leading figure in medieval JUDAISM. He was head of the academy at Sura, Babylonia, and orthodox champion against the KARAITES. He wrote a Hebrew grammar and lexicon, an Arabic translation of the Bible, and the *Book of Beliefs and Opinions* (933).

SAAR, or Saarland, a West German state of the W Rhineland, bordering France in the S and W. It is a major coal-mining and iron-and-steel region whose control has historically alternated between France and Germany. After WWI, it was administered by France under the League of Nations. It was reunited with Germany after a plebiscite (1935), occupied by France after WWII and became a German state in 1957.

SAARBRÜCKEN, industrial city and capital of Saar, West Germany. It lies on the Saar R at the Franco-German frontier. Pop 127 989.

SAARINEN, name of two modern architects, father and son. **Eliel Saarinen** (1873–1950), the leading Finnish architect of his day, designed the influential Helsinki railroad station (1905–14). In 1923, he emigrated to the US, where he designed numerous buildings in the Midwest. **Eero Saarinen** (1910–1961) collaborated with his father 1938–50. His spectacular work includes the General Motors Technical Center (1948–56), the TWA terminal at Kennedy Airport (1962) and Dulles Airport (1962).

SAAVEDRA LAMAS, Carlos (1878–1959), Argentinian lawyer and statesman. As Argentina's foreign minister (1932–38), he presided over the conference which ended the CHACO WAR (1935). He won the 1936 Nobel Peace Prize.

SABA, island of the Netherlands Antilles in the N Leeward Islands, NE West Indies. It is an extinct volcano, settled by the Dutch in 1632.

SABAEANS, ancient Semitic people who inhabited SW Arabia, in the area of modern Yemen. They are the Sheba of the Old Testament. The kingdom of Saba lasted from the 8th century BC to the 6th century AD. It was famous for its great wealth, in particular its incense, spices, precious stones and gold.

SABAH, or North Borneo, formerly British North Borneo, since 1963 a state of Malaysia. Rubber cultivation is the chief industry in this area.

SABATIER, Paul (1854–1941), French chemist who shared with GRIGNARD the 1912 Nobel Prize for Chemistry for his work on catalyst action in organic syntheses (see CATALYSIS), especially his discovery that finely divided nickel accelerates HYDROGENATION.

SABBATAI ZEVI (1626–1676), Jewish mystic born in Smyrna, who proclaimed himself the messiah in 1648 and attracted a large following. Arrested in Constantinople, he accepted Islam rather than risk the wrath of the sultan Mohammed IV (1666).

SABBATH, seventh day of the Hebrew week. The Jews observe it as the day of rest laid down in the fourth commandment to commemorate the Creation. It starts at sunset on Friday and ends at sunset on Saturday. Christians adopted Sunday as the Sabbath (Hebrew: rest) to commemorate the Resurrection. (See also BLUE LAW.)

SABBATICAL YEAR. Among ancient Jews every seventh year was a "year of rest" for the land, ordained by the law of Moses. Crops were to be unsown and unreaped, debtors were to be released. Today a professor's sabbatical is for rest or research.

SABER-TOOTHED TIGERS, two genera of extinct CATS of the CENOZOIC: *Smilodon* of North America and *Machairodus* of Europe and Asia. Slightly smaller than lions, but similar in build, saber-toothed tigers had enormous upper canines, up to 230mm (9in) long. They probably preyed on large, thick-skinned animals, using the canines as daggers to pierce the skin.

SABIN, Albert Bruce (1906–   ), US virologist best known for developing the oral POLIOMYELITIS vaccine, *Sabin* (1955). (See also SALK, J. E.).

SABINE RIVER, rises in NE Tex. and flows 360mi SE to form part of the border of Tex. and La. It empties through Sabine Lake into the Gulf of Mexico.

SABINES, tribe who lived NE of ancient Rome. The legend of the abduction of the Sabine women by the Romans is fictitious, but there were numerous Roman–Sabine wars. Sabines became Roman citizens c268 BC and disappeared as a separate group.

SABINIAN (d. 606), pope from 604, following Gregory the Great, under whom he was papal legate at Constantinople. Sabinian's meanness is apocryphal.

SABLE, *Martes zibellina*, a carnivorous fur-bearing mammal related to the MARTENS. The name is also used for the rich pelt. Sable are ground-living mustelids of coniferous forests, now restricted to parts of N Asia. About 500mm (20in) long, they prey on small rodents.

SABLE, Cape, southernmost tip of the Fla. peninsula and of the US mainland.

SABLE ANTELOPE, *Hippotragus niger*, a large, grazing ANTELOPE of open woodlands of Africa. Closely related to the ROAN ANTELOPE, Sable are distinguished by their long, strongly-curved horns, up to 1.8m (5.9ft) long. The males are glossy black, the females chestnut to black.

SABLE ISLAND, ridge of sand-dunes about 20mi long, off Nova Scotia, Canada. Site of many shipwrecks, it is known as the "graveyard of the Atlantic."

SAC. See STRATEGIC AIR COMMAND.

SACAJAWEA (c1784–1884?), Shoshone Indian guide with the LEWIS AND CLARK EXPEDITION. She was the wife of the interpreter, Toussaint Charbonneau and joined the expedition in 1805. Although not the expert guide that legend portrays, she was invaluable in the expedition's dealings with Indians.

SACCHARIDES. See CARBOHYDRATES.

SACCHARIN, or *o*-sulfobenzoic imide, a SWEETENING AGENT, 550 times sweeter than sucrose, normally used as its soluble sodium salt. Not absorbed by the body, it is used by diabetics and in low-calorie DIETETIC FOODS.

SACCO-VANZETTI CASE, famous legal battle which polarized opinion between US liberal-radicals and conservatives in the 1920s. In 1921, Nicola Sacco and Bartolomeo Vanzetti were found guilty of murdering a paymaster and factory guard. But it was claimed that there had been insufficient evidence, and that the trial had been unduly influenced by the fact that they were aliens and anarchists and had also been draft-evaders. The Supreme Court of Mass. declined to intervene. Eventually, Governor Fuller and an advisory board ruled the trial fair. The two were executed in 1927.

SACHS, Hans (1494–1576), the most popular German poet and dramatist of his time, one of the MEISTERSINGERS, and by trade a shoemaker. His prolific output included *The Nightingale of Wittenberg* (1523), a work in honor of Luther and the Reformation. He was the model for Wagner's *Die Meistersinger*.

SACHS, Julius von (1832–1897), German botanist regarded as the father of experimental plant physiology. Among his many contributions are his discovery of what are now called CHLOROPLASTS; the elucidation of the details of the GERMINATION process, and his studies of plant TROPISMS.

SACHS, Nelly (1891–1970), German-Jewish poet who fled to Sweden in 1940. Her poems deal with the sufferings and destiny of the Jewish people. She shared the 1966 Nobel literature prize.

SAC INDIANS. See SAUK INDIANS.

SACKETS HARBOR, village and summer resort in N N.Y. It lies on Lake Ontario and was an important US naval station in the War of 1812, attacked by the British. Pop 1 202.

SACKVILLE, Thomas, 1st Earl of Dorset (1536–1608), English statesman and poet. He was co-author of the first English blank-verse tragedy, *Gorboduc* (1561). He is also noted for his *Induction* and *Complaint of Buckingham* in the collection *A Mirror for Magistrates* (1563).

SACKVILLE-WEST, Victoria Mary (1892–1962), English poet, novelist and biographer, associated (like her husband Harold Nicolson) with the BLOOMSBURY GROUP. Her works include the poem *The Land* (1926) and her novels *The Edwardians* (1930) and *All Passion Spent* (1931).

SACO, residential city in SE Me. It lies opposite Biddeford on the Saco R, in a diversified farming region. It was settled in 1630. Pop 11 678.

SACRAMENT, in Christian theology, a visible sign and pledge of invisible GRACE, ordained by Christ. The traditional seven sacraments (first listed by Peter LOMBARD) are BAPTISM, Holy COMMUNION, CONFIRMATION, PENANCE, ORDINATION, MARRIAGE and EXTREME UNCTION, of which only the first two are accepted as sacraments by Protestants. In Roman Catholic theology the sacraments, if validly administered, convey grace objectively to the believing recipients; Protestants stress the joining of Word and sacrament, and the necessity of faith.

SACRAMENTALS, in the Roman Catholic Church, are not sacraments, but aids to devotion founded by

An Annamite pagoda in Saigon, Vietnam, a city once known as "the Pearl of the Far East."

the Church. They include PRAYER, CONFESSION, HOLY WATER and the ROSARY.

SACRAMENTO, capital city of Cal. and of Sacramento Co. It lies at the confluence of the Sacramento and American rivers, and is the industrial, transportation, market and commercial center for the important truck- and fruit-farming region of Central Valley. First settled 1839, it became state capital 1854. Pop 257 105.

SACRAMENTO RIVER, largest river in Cal. It rises in Siskiyou Co., NE Cal., and flows about 380mi into Suisun Bay, joining the San Joaquin S of Sacramento, to form the rich agricultural region of Central Valley.

SACRIFICE, a cultic act found in almost all religions, in which an object is consecrated and offered by a PRIEST in worship to a deity. It often involves the killing of an animal or human being and thus the offering up of its life; sometimes a communion meal follows. Sacrifice may also be seen as the expiation of sin, the sealing of a covenant or a gift to the god which invites blessing in return. Ancient Israel had an elaborate system of sacrifices (chief being the PASSOVER) which ceased when the Temple was destroyed (70 AD). In Christianity Christ's death is viewed as the one perfect and eternal sacrifice for sin (see ATONEMENT); the MASS is a dependent sacrifice. (See also ALTAR.)

SACROILIAC JOINT, the JOINT between the sacrum or lower part of the vertebral column and the iliac bones of the PELVIS. Little movement occurs about the joint but it may be affected by certain types of ARTHRITIS, such as ankylosing spondylitis.

SADAT, Anwar Al- (1918–), president of the United Arab Republic since 1970. He had been a comember with NASSER of the revolutionary society which seized power in 1952. (See also EGYPT.)

SADDLE, seat to support a rider on the back of an animal. Most horse saddles are leather and are held in place by a *girth* (strap) passing underneath the horse. Two *stirrup-leathers* (straps) support the *stirrups* in which the rider places his feet. The *English* saddle is light, almost flat, and used by jockeys and horse-show riders. The *Western* saddle is heavier, has a raised frontal horn to which a lariat may be attached, and is used by cowboys and rodeo riders.

SADDLE BROOK, residential urban township in NW N.J. There is some small-scale manufacturing. Pop 15 975.

SADDUCEES, aristocratic Jewish religious group in Roman Judea, opposed to the PHARISEES. They rejected the Pharisaic Oral Law and based their faith on the TORAH. Their great political influence ended with the destruction of the Temple at Jerusalem (70 AD).

SADE, Donatien Alphonse François, Comte de (1740–1814), usually known as the Marquis de Sade, French soldier and writer who gave his name to SADISM. He argued that since sexual deviation and criminal acts exist, they are natural. He escaped a death sentence for sodomy and poisoning and spent his last 11 years in Charenton lunatic asylum.

SA'DI. See SAADI.

SADISM, the derivation of erotic pleasure from inflicting PAIN on others; possibly a retention of INFANTILE SEXUALITY. (See also MASOCHISM.)

SAFAD, or Safed or Zefat, resort city of N Israel, near the Sea of Galilee. It is one of the four Jewish holy cities. It was an important center of medieval Jewish learning and mysticism. Pop 13 100.

SAFE. See LOCKS AND KEYS.

SAFETY GLASS, reinforced GLASS used chiefly in automobile windscreens, aircraft, and where bullet resistance is needed. Some safety glass is glass toughened by being heated almost to softening and then cooled; some has wire mesh embedded to guard against shattering; most is a LAMINATE with a thin layer of PLASTIC (polyvinyl butyral) between two glass layers, so that, if broken, the glass fragments adhere to the plastic.

SAFETY LAMP, lamp used to detect explosive "firedamp" (METHANE) in mines, invented in 1815 by the British chemist Sir Humphry DAVY to provide a safe form of lighting underground. A double layer of wire gauze surrounding the flame dissipated its heat, so preventing a methane atmosphere from reaching its ignition temperature, and yet allowed any methane present to cause a noticeable change in the flame's appearance. A safety lamp was also invented independently by George STEPHENSON.

SAFETY VALVE, a VALVE, sealed by a compressed spring or a weight, that opens to allow fluid above a preset pressure to escape. It is then held open until the pressure has fallen by a predetermined amount. They are used on all pressurized vessels (BOILERS, etc.) to prevent explosion.

SAFFLOWER, *Carthamus tinctorius*, thistle-like flower native to Asia. The dye produced from its bright reddish-orange flowers is used to color foods and in cosmetics. Safflower oil from the seeds is used in medicine and in varnish production. Family: Compositae.

SAFFRON, dye extracted from the stigmas and stamens of the Saffron crocus, *Crocus sativus*. Today, it is primarily used for coloring and flavoring foodstuffs. It is the most expensive of all spices.

SAGA, epic narrative, usually in prose, of 11th–14th century Scandinavian and Icelandic literature. Sagas often have historical settings, but their content is mainly fictional; their style is spare and understated, often bleak and grim. Probably the greatest saga author was SNORRI STURLUSON, whose *Heimskringla* (c1230) traced the history of the kings of Norway. Subjects of sagas range from odd incidents to histories of individuals, whole families or, as in *Njal's Saga*, of feuds.

SAGE, aromatic perennial plants of the genus *Salvia*, from the mint family, Labiatae, especially *Salvia officinalis*, the leaves of which are used for seasoning meat. There are several US species, including the Crimson and Purple sages of Cal. and the Lyre-leaved sage of New England.

SAGE, Russell (1816–1906), US financier who amassed a fortune from the wholesale grocery, railroad and other businesses. He left $70 million, part of which his widow used to establish the Russell Sage Foundation (1907), which aims to better US social conditions.

SAGEBRUSH, *Artemisia tridentata*, and related species, small aromatic shrubs with purple or yellow flowers, native to plains and mountains of western North America. Sagebrushes are so common in Nev. that it is nicknamed "the sagebrush state." Family: Compositae.

SAGINAW, city in central Mich., seat of Saginaw Co. It is a port of entry on the Saginaw R and is the manufacturing and commercial center of the surrounding agricultural region. Pop 91 849.

SAGITTARIUS (the Archer), a constellation on the ECLIPTIC lying in the direction of the galactic center (see MILKY WAY). Sagittarius is the ninth sign of the ZODIAC.

SAGO, the starchy food obtained from the pith of a number of PALMS, particularly *Metroxylon rumphii* and *M. sagu*, which are native to Indonesia. The trees take 15 years to mature, and when the flower spike is produced the pith becomes gorged with starch. Harvesting takes place at this time; if left until the fruits form, the starch is lost. The **sago palm** (*Cycas revoluta*) is not a true palm. It produces attractive, stiff dark-green fronds, making it a popular house plant. It grows best at temperatures between 13°C and 24°C (55°F and 75°F) and benefits from a few hours direct sun each day. It should be well watered whenever the soil surface dries out. It is difficult to propagate, but this can be achieved by removing the sparsely produced offsets.

SAGUARO, or desert sage, *Cerpus giganteus*, a North American desert cactus that grows up to 12m (39.4ft) high, with finger-like branches growing vertically alongside the main stem. Its white flowers are raided by bats, doves, hummingbirds and moths and its crimson fruits and seeds are eaten by rodents. It is the state flower of Ariz. Family: Cactaceae.

SAGUARO NATIONAL MONUMENT, established 1933, a forest of giant saguaro cacti, 15mi SE of Tucson, S Ariz. It covers 78 644 acres.

SAGUENAY RIVER, river of S Quebec, Canada. It flows 105mi E from Lake St. John to the St. Lawrence R at Tadoussac. It is navigable below Chicoutimi.

SAHARA DESERT, the world's largest DESERT, covering about 3 500 000sq mi. It stretches across N Africa from the Atlantic to the Red Sea. The terrain includes sand hills, rocky wastes, tracts of gravel and fertile oases. The central plateau, about 1000ft above sea level, has mountain groups rising well above 6 000ft. Rainfall ranges from under 5in to 15in annually and temperatures may soar above 120°F and plunge to under 50°F at night. Since WWII the Sahara has gained economic importance with the discovery of extensive oil, gas and iron-ore deposits.

SAHARANPUR, town in Uttar Pradesh, N India, 90mi NNE of Delhi. It has railroad workshops and produces sugar, cotton and paper. Pop 225 698.

SAHEL, semi-arid region S of the Sahara desert, with savanna-type grassland and scrub. Rainfall is 4–8in a year, mostly in June–August. There is some millet and groundnut cultivation. The term is also applied to the coastal region of N Africa.

SAIGA, a strange ANTELOPE of Asia. Although very sheep-like in appearance, it is in fact more closely related to GAZELLES. Saiga have curious, inflated noses: within each nostril is a large sac with mucous membranes, to warm and moisten inhaled air—an adaptation to fast running in a semidesert environment.

SAIGON, city in Vietnam, capital of South Vietnam 1954–75, 60mi from the South China Sea, on Saigon R. An industrial center and river port with a trade in rice and textiles, it suffered considerable damage during the VIETNAM WAR. Pop 1 804 880.

SAILFISH, *Istiophorus platypterus*, a large oceanic fish occurring in all tropical and subtropical seas. The upper jaw is extended into a bill or sword like that of the SWORDFISH. The dorsal fin is enormously extended forming a "sail" on the back, erected above the water surface. The fin is folded down when the fish is swimming at speed.

SAINT, term used in the New Testament to refer to all the faithful, and in the early Church to refer to the martyrs: it is now used to denote those who by the exceptional holiness of their lives are recognized by a Church as occupying an exalted position in heaven and being worthy of veneration (see CANONIZATION).

SAINT ALBANS, British market city, 20mi NW of London, site of Roman Verulamium. An important medieval monastic town and an early center of the printing industry, it is now principally a "dormitory" town for London. Pop 52 057.

SAINT ALBANS, city of NW Vt., 15mi S of the Canadian border, seat of Franklin Co. A tourist center, it produces chemicals and maple sugar. Pop 8 082.

SAINT ALBERT, agricultural town in Alberta, Canada, NW of Edmonton. Pop 11 800.

SAINT ANDREWS, university city and seaport in Fife, E Scotland. It is a tourist resort and famous golfing center. Pop 11 633.

SAINT ANN, suburb of St. Louis, E Missouri. Pop 18 215.

SAINT ANTHONY'S FIRE, name once given to ergotism (see ERGOT); also, the skin infection, ERYSIPELAS.

SAINT AUGUSTINE, Fla., oldest city (founded 1565) in the US, seat of St. John's Co., on the Atlantic coast 35mi SE of Jacksonville: it did not become part of the US until 1821. It is a tourist center with a fishing industry. Pop 12 352.

SAINT BARTHOLOMEW'S DAY, Massacre of, the killing of French HUGUENOTS which began in Paris on Aug. 24, 1572. Jealous of the influence of the Huguenot de COLIGNY on her son King CHARLES IX, Catherine de MÉDICIS plotted to assassinate him. When this failed Catherine, fearing Huguenot reaction, persuaded Charles to order the deaths of all leading Huguenots. On the morning of St. Bartholomew's Day thousands were slaughtered. Despite government orders to stop, the murders continued in the provinces until Oct.

SAINT BERNARD, a large mastiff dog with droopy ears and lips and a heavy coat, named for St. Bernard de Menthon, the monks of whose hospice in the Swiss Alps used them as guides and rescue dogs.

SAINT BERNARD PASSES, two passes over the Alps. The Great St. Bernard (8 100ft) links Martigny in Switzerland with Aosta in Italy. The Little St. Bernard (7 177ft) connects the Isère Valley in France with Aosta.

SAINT BONIFACE, industrial city in S Manitoba, Canada, on the Red R opposite Winnipeg. Industries include meat packing, flour milling and oil refining. Pop 46 714.

SAINT CATHARINES, Canadian city on the S shore of Lake Ontario, seat of Lincoln Co. Industries include fruit packing and processing and heavy engineering. Pop 109 722.

SAINT CHARLES, industrial and residential city of NE Ill., 37mi W of Chicago. It manufactures iron and steel goods. Pop 12 928.

SAINT CHARLES, city of E Mo., seat of St. Charles Co., on the Missouri R 20mi NW of St. Louis. It is an industrial and distribution center for the surrounding agricultural district. Pop 31 834.

ST. CLAIR, Arthur (1736–1818), US soldier and politician. He served in the REVOLUTIONARY WAR, and in 1787 became President of the Continental Congress, then Governor of the NORTHWEST TERRITORIES. His military career ended with defeat by the Indians in 1791. Unpopular as governor, he was removed from office in 1802.

SAINT CLAIR, Lake and River, forming part of the US/Canada border between LAKE HURON and LAKE ERIE. The river flows S from Lake Huron into the shallow St. Clair Lake. The river and lake are part of the SAINT LAWRENCE SEAWAY.

SAINT CLAIR SHORES, residential city of SE Mich., on the shores of Lake SAINT CLAIR, 13mi NE of Detroit. Pop 88 093.

SAINT CLOUD, industrial city of Minn., seat of Stearns Co., on the Mississippi R 58mi NW of Minneapolis. Pop 39 691.

SAINT CROIX, largest island of the US VIRGIN ISLANDS. A tourist center, it markets sugarcane and rum. Pop 31 892.

SAINT CROIX ISLAND NATIONAL MONUMENT, is on an island near the mouth of the SAINT CROIX RIVER. It covers the ruins of a French settlement (1604–05).

SAINT CROIX RIVER, forming the international boundary between Me., US, and New Brunswick, Canada, flows from the Chiputneticook lakes to Passamaquoddy Bay.

ST. DENIS, Ruth (Ruth Dennis; 1877?–1968), dancer, choreographer and teacher who made a major contribution to US dance. Greatly influenced by Hindu philosophy, she staged her first major success, *Radha, the Dance of the Senses*, in 1906.

SAINTE ANNE DE BEAUPRÉ, a village of Quebec, Canada, 20mi NE of Quebec city. It is the site of a 17th-century shrine and a Roman Catholic place of pilgrimage. Pop 1 797.

SAINTE-BEUVE, Charles Augustin (1804–1869), French writer and critic whose biographical approach revolutionized French literary criticism. His works include the collection of critical essays, *Causeries du Lundi* (1851–62).

SAINTE FOY, suburb of Quebec city. Pop 68 385.

SAINT ELIAS MOUNTAINS, a range of mountains c250mi long in SW Yukon, Canada, and SE Alaska. They reach a height of 19 850ft at Mt Logan, Canada's highest mountain.

SAINT ELMO'S FIRE, the glowing electrical discharge seen at the tips of tall, pointed objects—church spires, ships' masts, airplane wings, etc.—in stormy weather. The negative electric charge on the storm clouds induces a positive charge on the tall structure. The impressive display is named (corruptly) for St. Erasmus, patron of sailors.

SAINTE THÉRÈSE, city in S Quebec, Canada, NW of Montreal. Pop 17 175

SAINT-ÉTIENNE, industrial city of SE France, 36mi SW of Lyons, a center of the textile and steel industries. Pop 216 000.

SAINT EUSTASIUS, a Caribbean island of the Netherlands Antilles, 9mi NW of St. Kitts. It became a Dutch possession in 1632. Pop 1 341.

SAINT-EXUPÉRY, Antoine de (1900–1944), French aviator and writer who pioneered air routes over South America and NW Africa. In 1939 he became a military reconnaisance pilot, and was killed in action. His books include *Night Flight* (1932) and the children's classic tale, *The Little Prince* (1943).

SAINT FRANCIS, suburb of Milwaukee, SE Wis. Pop 10 489.

SAINT-GAUDENS, Augustus (1848–1907), US sculptor famed for his large public monuments. His works include the Adams Memorial (1891) in Rock Creek Cemetery, Washington D.C., and the Robert G. Shaw monument in Boston (1897).

SAINT GEORGE'S, chief town and administrative center of the island of Grenada in the West Indies. Pop 6 657.

SAINT GEORGE'S CHANNEL, the strait, about 100mi long and 50–95mi wide, linking the Irish Sea and the Atlantic Ocean.

SAINT-GERMAIN, Treaty of (1919), ended the war between Austria and the Allies in WWI. It reduced Austrian territory, made Austria liable for war reparations, and forbade any alliance with Germany. The treaty was not ratified by the US.

SAINT GOTTHARD PASS, in Switzerland, road and rail route through the Alps from central Europe to Italy. The rail tunnel beneath the pass is over 9mi long.

SAINT HELENA, British island in the S Atlantic Ocean. Its capital is Jamestown, where NAPOLEON I died in exile in 1821. The climate is temperate, and the island has a growing tourist industry. Pop 5 056.

SAINT HELIER, seaside resort and chief town of Jersey, Channel Islands, off the NW coast of France. It is a commercial center. Pop 28 135.

SAINT HUBERT, town in Quebec province, Canada, E of Montreal. It is residential, with some light industry. Pop 21 753.

SAINT HYACINTHE, city in S Quebec province, Canada, 30mi NE of Montreal. It is a commercial, cultural and administrative center. Pop 24 562.

SAINT JAMES, residential suburb of Winnipeg, Manitoba, Canada. Pop 41 731.

SAINT JAMES'S PALACE, London, England, situated in Pall Mall and once a royal residence (1698–1837). Royal gatherings are still held here and foreign ambassadors to Britain are received at the Court of St. James.

SAINT-JEAN, industrial city of Quebec, Canada, seat of Saint-Jean Co., 20mi SE of Montreal. Products include textiles and bricks. Pop 32 863.

SAINT JÉRÔME, industrial city of SW Quebec, Canada, 38mi NW of Montreal, seat of Stafford Co. It produces textiles, rubber, paper and other wood products. Pop 26 524

SAINT JOHN, city of New Brunswick, Canada, on the Bay of Fundy. It is an ice-free port with salmon fishing, paper-making, oil refining and food processing industries. Pop 105 227.

SAINT JOHN, smallest of the VIRGIN ISLANDS of the US. Chief economic activities are cattle raising, the production of bay leaves and tourism. Pop 1 729.

ST. JOHN, Henry. See BOLINGBROKE, HENRY ST. JOHN, 1ST VISCOUNT.

SAINT JOHN, Knights of. See KNIGHTS OF SAINT JOHN.

SAINT JOHN RIVER, largest river in New Brunswick, Canada, 418mi long, forming 80mi of the US/Canadian border between Me. and New Brunswick before turning SE to flow into the Bay of Fundy at ST. JOHN.

The St. Bernard was originally bred in Switzerland as a guard dog, but became famous as the rescue dogs of the hospice of St. Bernard de Menthon, where they are still kept.

SAINT JOHN'S, capital city of Newfoundland, Canada, on the SE Atlantic coast. It is a natural deep water harbor and fishing port, and the commercial and transportation center of the province. Pop 86 290.

SAINT JOHNS RIVER, a navigable river of E Fla. Rising N of Lake Okeechobee, it flows 285mi N into the Atlantic near Jacksonville.

SAINT JOHN'S WORT, small shrub-like plants of the genus *Hypericum*, usually with yellow flowers and leaves scattered with transparent glands. Over 300 species are found in temperate and tropical zones. Some are cultivated for their showy yellow blooms. Family: Hypericaceae.

SAINT JOSEPH, manufacturing city of SW Mich. It produces auto parts. Pop 11 042.

SAINT JOSEPH, city of NW Mo., seat of Buchanan Co., on the Missouri R 55mi NW of Kansas City. Important as a livestock and grain marketing center, it is famed as the starting station for the Pony Express (1860). Pop 86 915.

SAINT-JUST, Louis de (1767–1794), French revolutionary leader. He entered the National Convention 1792 and became president two years later. He supported ROBESPIERRE, helped engineer the downfall of DANTON, and was guillotined when Robespierre fell.

SAINT KITTS-NEVIS-ANGUILLA, three islands in the E Caribbean with a capital at Basseterre, St. Kitts. They became a self-governing state in 1967, although Anguilla later seceded. The islands produce and export sugar, molasses and cotton. Area 153sq mi, pop approx 51 500.

SAINT LAMBERT, residential suburb of Montreal, Canada. Pop 18 616.

SAINT LAURENT, manufacturing city 6mi W of Montreal, Quebec, Canada. Pop 62 955.

ST. LAURENT, Louis Stephen (1882–1973), Canadian Liberal Prime Minister 1948–57. He became federal minister of justice and attorney general in 1942, and in 1945 played an important role in the setting up of the UNITED NATIONS. As prime minister he strengthened Canada's position in the COMMONWEALTH and was instrumental in founding the NORTH ATLANTIC TREATY ORGANIZATION. Domestically, his greatest achievement was the incorporation of Newfoundland as a Canadian province in 1949.

SAINT LAWRENCE, Gulf of. See GULF OF SAINT LAWRENCE.

SAINT LAWRENCE ISLANDS NATIONAL PARK, S Ont., Canada consists of 17 of the THOUSAND ISLANDS. It comprises 260 acres of wooded park.

SAINT LAWRENCE RIVER, largest river in Canada, flowing 760mi NE from Lake Ontario to the Gulf of St. Lawrence. It forms 120mi of the US/Canadian border, and is a major inland waterway. See (SAINT LAWRENCE SEAWAY.)

SAINT LAWRENCE SEAWAY, the US/Canadian inland waterway for ocean-going vessels connecting the GREAT LAKES with the Atlantic Ocean, and comprising a 2342mi long system of natural waterways, canals, locks, dams and dredged channels (including the WELLAND SHIP CANAL). It was completed in 1959. The waterway, once restricted to small river vessels, has opened the industries and agriculture of the Great Lakes to international trade.

ST. LEGER, Barry (1737–1789), British officer in the American REVOLUTIONARY WAR, and founder of the famous horse race at Doncaster, England, which bears his name.

SAINT LEONARD, residential suburb of Montreal, Canada. Pop 52013.

SAINT LOUIS, on the Mississippi R, largest city of Mo. Founded as a fur-trading post by the French in 1763, it was ceded to Spain in 1770, and after reverting briefly to the French became part of the US under the LOUISIANA PURCHASE in 1803. The city expanded rapidly, and became a major inland port, transportation center and market for agricultural center. Pop 622236.

SAINT LOUIS PARK, city in SE Minn., suburb of Minneapolis. Its industries include machinery and electronic equipment manufacturing. Pop 48922.

SAINT LUCIA, island (238sq mi) of the WINDWARD ISLANDS. Possibly discovered by COLUMBUS, it achieved associate status with the UK in 1967.

SAINT MARK'S CATHEDRAL (San Marco), Venetian 11th-century church, outstanding example of BYZANTINE ARCHITECTURE, built in the form of a Greek cross surmounted by five large domes. The richly constructed and sculptured West Façade has Gothic additions. Its famous four bronze horses were brought from Constantinople in 1204.

SAINT MARTIN, island (37sq mi) of the LEEWARD ISLANDS. The N is part of French Guadeloupe and the S part of the Netherlands Antilles. It produces cotton, sugarcane and fruits.

SAINT MARYS RIVER, river about 68mi long, forming part of the boundary between US and Canada, flowing from Lake Superior to Lake Huron.

SAINT MATTHEWS, residential suburb of Louisville, Ky. Pop 13152.

SAINT-MIHIEL, town on NE France, famous for its Benedictine abbey founded in 709. Held by the Germans for most of WWI, it was recovered by the Allies in 1918. Pop 5262.

SAINT PATRICK'S DAY, March 17, anniversary of the death (c461 AD) of Saint PATRICK, Ireland's patron saint.

SAINT PAUL, city in E Minn. on the Mississippi R, state capital and seat of Ramsey Co. An enormous port and transportation center, its important industries are machinery, electronics equipment, motor vehicles, metal and petroleum products and abrasives. Printing and livestock sales are major activities. Pop 309828.

The magnificent Byzantine facade of Saint Mark's Cathedral, Venice. The main door is surmounted by the famous bronze horses.

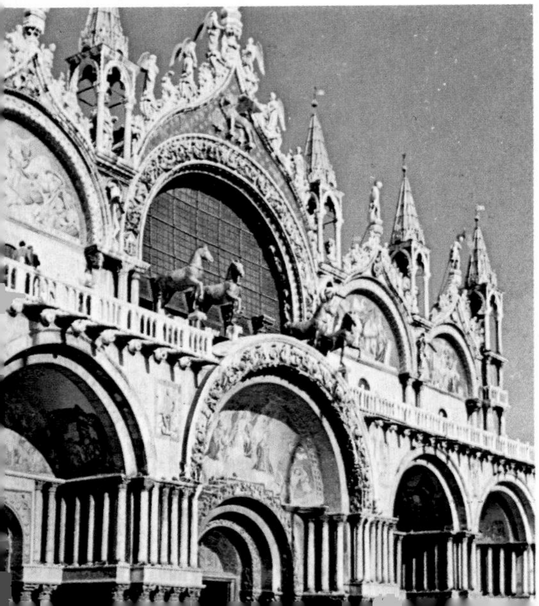

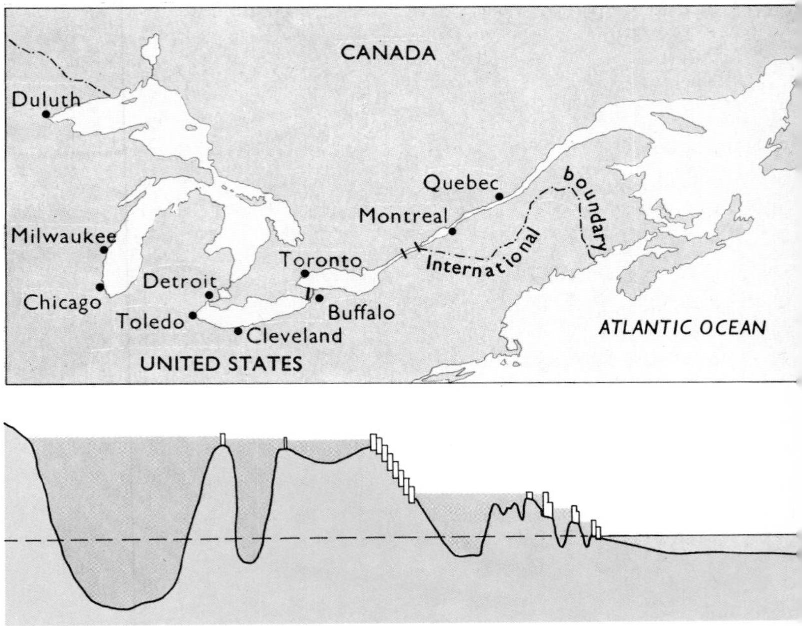

Cross-section of the Saint Lawrence Seaway, showing the massive lock complex that enables it to link the Atlantic Ocean with Lake Superior, over a distance of 2360mi and a difference in altitude of 600ft.

SAINT PETER'S BASILICA, Rome, the world's largest church, built on the supposed tomb of St. PETER between 1506 and 1667 by architects including BRAMANTE, RAPHAEL, SANGALLO, MICHELANGELO, Carlo MADERNO and BERNINI. It forms a huge Latin cross capped by a great dome. Gilt, mosaic, bronze and marble embellish the interior and an enormous canopy by Bernini encloses the main altar.

SAINT PETERSBURG, resort city in W Fla. at the S tip of Pinellas peninsula, known as "Sunshine City" because of its fine climate. It manufactures electronic and boating equipment. Pop 216232.

SAINT PETERSBURG. See LENINGRAD.

SAINT PIERRE AND MIQUELON, French islands in the Atlantic Ocean, S of Newfoundland. The capital is Saint Pierre. Chief occupations are cod-fishing, fox- and mink-farming and tourism. First visited in the 17th century by Breton and Basque fishermen, the islands were long disputed between France and Britain, finally becoming French in 1804, a French Overseas Territory in 1946 and French overseas departments in 1976.

SAINT-SAËNS, Charles Camille (1835–1921), French composer. He composed many large-scale symphonies, piano concertos, symphonic poems and operas like *Samson and Delilah* (1877), but today it is his lighter music which is best known, especially *Danse Macabre* (1874) and *Carnival of the Animals* (1886).

SAINT-SIMON, Claude Henri de Rouvroy, comte de (1760–1825), French protosocialist philosopher who advocated a state organized by scientists and industrialists. Especially concerned by working-class conditions, his teachings launched the **Saint-Simonism** movement, c1830, calling for meritocracy, female emancipation, nationalization and abolition of inherited wealth.

SAINT-SIMON, Louis de Rouvroy, duc de (1675–1755), French statesman and writer of *Mémoires* (1739–51), where he brilliantly criticized the court of King LOUIS XIV.

SAINT-SOPHIA. See HAGIA SOPHIA.

SAINT THOMAS, city, seat of Elgin Co., SE Ontario. Set in an agricultural region, its industries include automobiles and aircraft. Pop 25545.

SAINT THOMAS, island (32sq mi) of the US VIRGIN ISLANDS. Charlotte Amalie, its capital, is a fine harbor. The economy rests on tourism. Pop 28960.

SAINT VINCENT, island state (150sq mi) in the WINDWARD ISLANDS, comprising St. Vincent Island and the N Grenadines. Main products of these volcanic islands are bananas, arrowroot and sugarcane. Pop 90000.

SAINT VINCENT, Cape, SW point of Portugal, thought in ancient times to be the most W tip of Europe. Nearby, HENRY THE NAVIGATOR built his navigation school (c1425).

SAINT VITAL, residential suburb of Winnipeg, Manitoba. Pop 32963.

SAINT VITUS' DANCE, or Sydenham's chorea. See CHOREA.

SAIPAN, island (c48sq mi) of the MARIANA ISLANDS, and headquarters of the US Trust Territory of the Pacific Islands. It is mountainous and fertile, growing copra, bananas and breadfruit.

SAKAI, city in S Honshu, Japan. A major port in the 15th–17th centuries, it is now a center for engineering and chemicals. Pop 594369.

SAKE, or saki, an alcoholic drink made from fermented RICE. It is the national beverage of Japan and contains 14% to 15% by volume of ETHANOL.

SAKHALIN, long, narrow island in USSR (about 30000sq mi) off the E Siberian coast. It is mountainous, covered largely with tundra and forest: its resources include oil, coal, timber and fish. Its ownership has been much disputed by Japan.

SAKHAROV, Andrei Dimitrievich (1921–), Soviet physicist who played a prominent part in the development of the first Soviet HYDROGEN BOMB. He subsequently advocated worldwide nuclear disarmament (being awarded the 1975 Nobel Peace Prize) and became a leading Soviet dissident.

SAKI. See MUNRO, HECTOR HUGH.

SAKKARA, or **Saqqara**, village in Lower Egypt, near the necropolis of MEMPHIS, where IMHOTEP built the Step Pyramid for the 3rd-dynasty pharaoh, Djoser. There are also pyramids of later dynasties, and many MASTABAS.

SALADIN (Salah-ad-Din Yusuf ibn-Ayyub; 1138–1193), Muslim leader who crushed the crusaders in Palestine. Becoming Sultan of Egypt in 1174, he established there his own dynasty. He reclaimed Syria and most of Palestine including Jerusalem (1187) from the crusaders, and forced a stalemate on England's RICHARD I (1192) during the third CRUSADE, leaving the Muslims masters of Palestine. He was famed for his chivalry.

SALAMANCA, city in W central Spain, conquered by HANNIBAL c220 BC. Its medieval university (founded c1220) was renowned as a center of Arabic learning. Pop 125220.

SALAMANDER, general term for all tailed AMPHIBIA, comprising eight families. They are long-bodied and retain the tail throughout their life. Their limbs are usually small and are not used for locomotion to any great extent; most movement is achieved by wriggling, with the belly close to, or touching, the ground—effectively "swimming" on

land. Salamanders occupy a variety of aquatic, semiterrestrial and terrestrial habitats throughout the world. Most feed on insects and other invertebrates.
SALAMIS, mountainous and fertile Greek island (35sq mi), about 10mi W of Athens. Salamis, chief town and port, is at the W end. The famous naval battle (480 BC), when THEMISTOCLES destroyed the stronger Persian fleet, was fought in the straits to the E of the island.
SAL AMMONIAC, or ammonium chloride. See AMMONIA.
SALAZAR, António de Oliveira (1889–1970), dictator of PORTUGAL (1932–68). Although he reorganized public finances and achieved certain modernizations, education and living standards remained almost static and political freedom was restricted.
SALEM, city in SE India. Principal industries are weaving and machining. Pop 308 303.
SALEM, manufacturing city in NE Mass., a seat of Essex Co., NE of Boston. It was founded in 1626, and a number of 17th-century buildings are still standing. It is famous as the site of witchcraft trials (1692) in which 19 were hanged (see SEWALL, SAMUEL), and as the birthplace of Nathaniel HAWTHORNE. Pop 40 556.
SALEM, town in SE N.H. Settled 1652, incorporated 1750, it is known for its racecourse and archaeological site, Mystery Hill. Pop 20 142.
SALEM, city in NE Ohio, once center of the Western Anti-Slavery society and an important station of the UNDERGROUND RAILROAD. Its diverse industries include machining. Pop 14 186.
SALEM, state capital of OREGON, seat of Marion Co., founded in 1840 by Methodist missionaries. An agricultural center, it has food-processing plants. Pop 68 296.
SALEM, independent city in SW Va., seat of Roanoke Co., on the Roanoke R. Pop 21 982.
SALERNO, capital of Campania, S Italy. Founded by the Romans in 197 BC, it was occupied by ROBERT GUISCARD in 1076: its medical school was the earliest in medieval Europe (11th century). Pop 152 800.
SALES, Saint Francis de. See FRANCIS OF SALES, SAINT.
SALES TAX. See TAX.
SALIC LAW, law code drawn up by the Salian FRANKS. The unconnected **Salic Law of Succession** states that a woman, or one descended through the female line, cannot be heir. It was first cited in France in the early 14th century when PHILIP IV's last son (CHARLES IV) died without direct male heir: EDWARD III of England's consequent exclusion from inheriting France was a cause of the HUNDRED YEARS' WAR.
SALICYLIC ACID (o-$C_6H_4(OH)COOH$), white crystalline solid, made from PHENOL and CARBON dioxide; used in medicine against CALLUSES and WARTS, and to make ASPIRIN and DYES. Its sodium salt is an ANALGESIC and is used for rheumatism. MW 138.1, mp 159°C. **Methyl salicylate**, an ESTER, occurs in oil of WINTERGREEN, and is used as a liniment and a flavoring.
SALIERI, Antonio (1750–1825), Italian composer, for nearly 60 years court musician in Vienna, who taught SCHUBERT, BEETHOVEN and LISZT.
SALINA, city in central Kan., seat of Saline Co. It is a major grain and livestock production and shipping center. Pop 37 714.
SALINAS, city in W Cal., seat of Monterey Co., an agricultural center, and birthplace of John STEINBECK. Pop 58 896.
SALINGER, Jerome David (1919–), US author whose first novel *The Catcher in the Rye* (1951) became one of the most popular postwar books, its adolescent "hero" Holden Caulfield being presented as a spokesman of his generation. Salinger's short stories, many concerning the Glass family, include *For Esmé—With Love and Squalor* (1950).
SALISBURY, or **New Sarum**, city in Wiltshire, UK, near the site of Old Sarum, which dates back to the Iron Age. It is noted for its cathedral (c1220), which has the tallest spire in England (404ft). Pop 35 271.
SALISBURY, city in SE Md., seat of Wicomico Co. Its principal industries are poultry processing and light manufacturing. Pop 15 252.
SALISBURY, historic city in central N.C., seat of Rowan Co., site of a large Confederate Civil War prison camp. The principal products are textiles and lumber. Pop 22 515.
SALISBURY, capital and largest city of Rhodesia, in a gold-mining and corn- and tobacco-growing area. It is the commercial and transportation hub of the country. It was founded in 1890 by RHODES' Pioneer Column. Pop 501 930.
SALISBURY, Robert Arthur Talbot Gascoyne-Cecil, 3rd Marquess of (1830–1903), British statesman, entered parliament 1853. As Conservative prime minister (1885–86, 1886–92, 1895–1902), he opposed parliamentary reform and Irish HOME RULE, and acted as his own foreign minister. He maintained good relations in Europe, and successfully expanded the British Empire in Africa and Asia.
SALISBURY, Robert Cecil, 1st Earl of (1563–1612), English secretary of state under ELIZABETH I from 1596, chief minister from 1598. Before Elizabeth's death he negotiated with JAMES VI that monarch's accession to the English throne, and remained chief minister thereafter.
SALIVA, the watery secretion of the salivary GLANDS which lubricates the MOUTH and food boluses. It contains MUCUS, some gamma globulins and PTYALIN and is secreted in response to food in the mouth or by conditioned REFLEXES such as the smell or sight of food. Secretion is partly under the control of the parasympathetic autonomic NERVOUS SYSTEM. The various salivary glands—parotid, submandibular and sublingual—secrete slightly different types of saliva, varying in mucus and ENZYME content.
SALK, Jonas Edward (1914–), US virologist best known for developing the first POLIOMYELITIS vaccine, *Salk* (1952–54). (See also SABIN, A. B.)
SALLUST (Caius Sallustius Crispus; 86–c34 BC), Roman senator, and first Roman historian to interpret the events which he recorded and to describe limited historical periods, though his accounts are flawed by bias and inaccuracy. His major work is *Bellum Catilinarium*, on the CATILINE conspiracy.
SALMON, large, highly palatable fishes of two genera. The Atlantic salmon, *Salmo salar*, lives in the N Atlantic, while in the N Pacific, there are five species in the genus *Onchorhynchus*. All salmon return to freshwater to breed. While the Pacific salmon die on completion of their first spawning, Atlantic salmon return to the sea, and may come back to spawn a second time. Adult salmon return to their natal streams to breed; they spawn in "redds" in the sand or gravel of the stream bed. The young remain in freshwater until they are about 18 months old, then migrate down to the sea. Adults remain in the sea, feeding, for one to two years before returning to breed. (See also OUANANICHE.)
SALMONELLA, bacteria, some species of which cause FOOD POISONING or ENTERITIS; specific types cause TYPHOID and PARATYPHOID FEVER.
SALMON RIVER, river, about 425mi long, rising in the Sawtooth and Salmon River Mts in Ida., and emptying into the SNAKE RIVER.
SALOME (1st century AD), granddaughter of HEROD the Great. Her dancing so pleased her stepfather Herod Antipas that he promised her anything she wanted. Prompted by her mother Herodias, she asked for JOHN THE BAPTIST's head, which was presented to her on a platter.
SALOMON, Haym (1740–1785), Polish-born US patriot and financier prominent in the early days of the republic. After his death, the US government repeatedly refused to repay their vast debts to his descendants.
SALONIKA, or **Thessaloníki,** capital of Greek Macedonia, a major seaport and industrial center for manganese, textiles, tobacco, hides and shipbuilding. Pop 339 496.
SALSIFY. See OYSTER PLANT.
SALT, common name for **Sodium Chloride** (NaCl), found in seawater and also as the common mineral, rock salt or halite. Pure salt forms white cubic CRYSTALS. Some salt is obtained by solar evaporation from salt pans, shallow depressions periodically flooded with seawater; but most is obtained from underground mines. The most familiar use of salt is to flavor food. (Magnesium carbonate is added to table salt to keep it dry.) It is, however, used in much larger quantities to preserve hides in leather-making, in soap manufacture, as a food preservative and in keeping highways ice-free in winter. Rock salt is the main industrial source of chlorine and caustic soda. mp 801°C, bp 1413°C.
SALT, Chemical, an electrovalent compound (see BOND, CHEMICAL) formed by neutralization of an ACID and a BASE. The vast majority of MINERALS are salts, the best known being common SALT, sodium chloride. Salts are generally ionic solids which are good electrolytes (see ELECTROLYSIS); those of weak acids or bases undergo partial HYDROLYSIS in water. Salts may be classified as normal (fully neutralized), acid (containing some acidic hydrogen, e.g., BICARBONATES), or basic (containing hydroxide ions). They may alternatively be classified as simple salts, double salts (two simple salts combined by regular substitution in the crystal lattice) including ALUMS, and complex salts (containing complex ions: see LIGAND).
SALT DOME, a mass of EVAPORITE minerals which has pierced the strata above it and domed the strata near the surface. They often form natural traps for PETROLEUM, and occasionally penetrate to the surface to form *salt glaciers*.
SALTEN, Felix (1869–1945), pen name of Siegmund Salzmann, Austrian novelist and journalist whose books include *Bambi* (1923: filmed by Walt Disney 1942), the anthropomorphized life of a deer.
SALT FLAT, dried-up bed of an enclosed stretch of water that has evaporated, leaving the salts that it held in solution as a crust on the ground. Best known are the Lake Bonneville flats, near Salt Lake City, Ut. (See also EVAPORITES.)
SALTILLO, capital city of Coahuila state, Mexico. Its economy rests on agriculture, textiles and food processing. Pop 191 879.
SALT LAKE CITY, 15mi from the Great Salt Lake, capital and largest city in Utah and seat of Salt Lake Co. Founded in 1847 by Brigham YOUNG leading a band of Mormons from persecution, it is the world center of the Church of Jesus Christ of Latter-Day Saints: 65% of its residents are members. It is a commercial and industrial center for minerals, farming, oil refining and chemicals. Pop 175 885.
SALT LICK, any naturally occurring deposit of common SALT frequented by animals, who lick the salt. Most frequently, the deposit is associated with a salt spring.
SALTON SEA, large saline lake in SE Cal. Until flooded by the Colorado in 1905, it was a depression, "the Salton Sink," 280ft below sea level. It now covers 370sq mi and is 232ft below sea level.
SALTPETER, or potassium nitrate. See POTASSIUM.

Sea salt is produced by evaporating seawater, sometimes in open-air salt "pans" such as these, in Thailand, where newly formed salt crystals are being raked into neat heaps.

The salvage tug USS *Edenton*. The maintenance of such specialized vessels is justified by the enormous sums of money at stake in maritime salvage operations.

SALT RIVER, 200mi-long tributary of the Gila R flowing from E Ariz. to Phoenix. Irrigation from the Salt and its tributaries renders the region richly fertile.
SALT TALKS. See STRATEGIC ARMS LIMITATION TALKS.
SALT TAX. See GABELLE.
SALTYKOV, Mikhail Evgrafovich (1826–1889), known as Saltykov-Shchedrin, one of the finest Russian satirists. His *History of a Town* (1869–70), attacked Russian bureaucrats. His only novel is *The Golovyov Family* (1876), a story of declining gentry.
SALUKI, ancient breed of dog, usually 23–28in high at the shoulder and weighing 45–60lb. It has a short silky smooth coat. Colors may be white, tan, red or black.
SALVADOR, or **Bahia**, port on the Bay of All Saints, once Brazil's capital (1549–1763). It exports sugar, cotton, tobacco, leather and cacao. Pop 1 007 744.
SALVADOR, El. See EL SALVADOR.
SALVAGE, rescue or recovery of a ship or its cargo from disaster at sea. The salvager does not automatically gain possession of the property: the owner may claim it back on payment of "salvage money."
SALVARSAN, or **arsphenamine**, organic arsenical agent introduced by Paul EHRLICH for the CHEMOTHERAPY of syphilis (see VENEREAL DISEASES) and protozoal infection (e.g., TRYPANOSOMES). It has been superceded by PENICILLIN in syphilis and safer protozoal drugs.
SALVATION, a key religious concept: man's deliverance from the evils of life and of death. It is presupposed that man is in bondage to suffering, SIN, disease, death, decay etc., from which he may be rescued and restored to primordial blessedness. In DUALISM salvation is release of the soul from the corrupting prison of the body; in HINDUISM release from the cycle of rebirth (see TRANSMIGRATION OF SOULS). In Judaism, Christianity and Islam it is liberation from evil into communion with God, and hence deliverance from HELL, the RESURRECTION of the body and (in Christian eschatology) the regeneration of the entire universe. Judaism stresses ethnic salvation, as typified by the Exodus. In these W religions salvation is provided by the "mighty acts" of God, who is the savior (see also ATONEMENT; SACRIFICE); elsewhere salvation may be self-attained by ritual, acquisition of knowledge, asceticism, good deeds or martyrdom. Christianity sees all history as a divine plan of salvation, consequent on Adam's fall (see ORIGINAL SIN), achieved in the INCARNATION, death and resurrection of JESUS CHRIST, and consummated at the LAST JUDGMENT.

The lean lines of the saluki echo those of the gazelle, which it was originally bred to hunt.

SALVATION ARMY, Christian organization founded by William BOOTH (1865). In 1878 the mission became the Army, with Booth as General. Under strict quasimilitary discipline, the members seek to strengthen Christianity and help (also save) the poor and destitute. The Army now operates 8 000 centers in the US alone. Its official journal is *War Cry*.
SALVIA, an ASTRINGENT derived from certain plants (*Salvia*), formerly used for sore throat and ULCERS.
SAL VOLATILE, or ammonium carbonate, $(NH_4)_2CO_3$, colorless crystalline solid made by combining aqueous AMMONIA and CARBON dioxide, the main ingredient of SMELLING SALTS.
SALWEEN RIVER, great river of SE Asia. Rising in Tibet it flows 1 750mi SE through China and E Burma into the Gulf of Martaban.
SALZBURG, historic city in central Austria, world famous for its annual music festival (begun 1917). The birthplace of MOZART, it lies on the Salzbach R. Pop 128 800.
SAMAR, island of the Visayan group, third largest of the PHILIPPINES.
SAMARA, winged ACHENE produced by, for example, the MAPLE and SYCAMORE. (See FRUIT.)
SAMARIA (modern Sabastiyah), ancient city in Palestine, 35mi N of Jerusalem. Built by OMRI of Israel (c800 BC), destroyed in 722 BC and again in 108 BC, it was rebuilt by Herod the Great (c30 BC).
SAMARITANS, inhabitants of the ancient district of Samaria. Originally non-Jewish colonists from Assyria, they intermarried with the Israelites, and accepted the Jewish TORAH. However, they were not socially accepted—hence the significance of the Good Samaritan in Luke's Gospel.
SAMARIUM (Sm), one of the LANTHANUM SERIES. AW 150.4, mp 1 077°C, bp 1 791°C, sg 7.52 (α).
SAMARKAND, city in Uzbekistan, USSR, in the Zeravshan R valley. One of the world's oldest cities, it was built on the site of Afrosiab (3000 BC or earlier) and was the great conqueror TAMERLANE's capital. Pop 267 000.
SAMMARTINI, Giovanni Battista (1701–1775), Italian composer, influential as an early composer of the concert symphony. His pupils included GLUCK.
SAMNITES, ancient warlike tribes of mountainous S Italy. After three wars with Rome, the Samnites were finally crushed in 290 BC.
SAMOA, chain of 10 islands and several islets in the South Pacific, midway between Honolulu and Sydney. Volcanic and mountainous, their total area is about 1 200sq mi. The people are mostly Polynesians. The soil is fertile, producing cacao, coconuts and bananas, and the climate tropical. Savai'i (the largest), Upolu and the other W islands constitute independent WESTERN SAMOA. **American Samoa** consists of the E islands: Tutuila, the Manua group and the Rose and Swains Islands. Discovered by the Dutch in 1772, Samoa was claimed by Germany, Great Britain and the US in the mid-19th century, but in 1899 the US acquired sole rights to what is now American Samoa. Capital: Pago Pago. Pop 27 159
SAMOS (modern Sámos), Greek island (184sq mi) in the Aegean Sea near Turkey. It was a maritime and cultural power in the 7th–6th centuries BC. Its economy now rests on fruit.
SAMOTHRACE (modern Samothráki), Greek island (71sq mi) in the NE Aegean Sea, where the WINGED VICTORY OF SAMOTHRACE was found (1863).
SAMOYED, dog originally bred for reindeer herding and pulling sleds. They have a husky-like appearance, with a white, cream or biscuit-colored coat, and stand 18in–25in at the shoulder.
SAMOYEDS, Mongoloid peoples inhabiting parts of Arctic Siberia. They are hunters, fishermen and nomadic reindeer herdsmen.

Site of the ancient city of Samaria, in central Palestine. The original city, built by Omri, was destroyed by the Assyrians in 722 BC.

SAMPLING. See STATISTICS.
SAMPSON, William Thomas (1840–1902), US Admiral, commander of the North Atlantic squadron in the SPANISH–AMERICAN WAR.
SAMSON, Hebrew hero whose feats are recorded in the Book of JUDGES. Captured by the PHILISTINES, he burst his bonds and killed 1 000 with an ass's jawbone. The secret of his strength lay in his uncut hair: his mistress DELILAH cut it as he slept, and he was captured and blinded. When his hair grew again, he took revenge by destroying a great Philistine temple, killing himself and thousands of Philistines.
SAMUEL, two Old Testament books (known to Catholics as 1 and 2 KINGS) which tell of the statesman, general and prophet, Samuel (c11th century BC). He united the tribes under SAUL, and chose DAVID as Saul's successor.
SAMUELSON, Paul Anthony (1915–), US economist, advisor to Presidents KENNEDY and JOHNSON and winner of the 1970 Nobel economics prize.
SAMURAI, hereditary military class of Japan. From c1000 AD the Samurai dominated Japan, though after c1600 their activities were less military than cultural. Comprising 5% of Japanese, they exerted influence through BUSHIDO, a code which demanded feudal loyalty and placed honor above life. The class lost its power in the reforms of 1868.
SAN'Ā, capital and largest city of the Yemen Arab Republic, 90mi from the Red Sea. An ancient walled city, it is an agricultural trade center. Pop 125 100.
SAN ANDREAS FAULT, break in the earth's crust, running 600mi from Cape Mendocino, NW Cal., to the Colorado desert. It was the sudden movement of land along this FAULT that caused the San Francisco EARTHQUAKE, 1906. The fracture, and the motion responsible for this and other quakes, is a result of the abutment of the eastern Pacific and North American plates (see PLATE TECTONICS).
SAN ANGELO, city in W central Tex., seat of Tom Green Co., a cattle and sheep shipping point. Pop 63 884.
SAN ANSELMO, residential city in W Cal., 14mi NW of San Francisco. Pop 13 031.
SAN ANTONIO, city in S Tex., seat of Bexar Co., on the San Antonio R 150mi N of the Gulf of Mexico. Founded in 1718, it was the site of the ALAMO (1836). It is one of the largest military centers in the US. Pop 654 153.
SAN BENITO, city in S Tex., a shipping center for fruit and vegetables. It is a winter tourist resort. Pop 15 176.
SAN BERNARDINO, city in S Cal., seat of San Bernardino Co., an industrial and commercial center in a rich Cal. agricultural area. Pop 104 783.
SAN BERNARDINO MOUNTAINS, coastal range in S Cal., of which the highest peaks are Mt San Gorgonio (11 502ft) and San Bernardino Mt (10 630ft).
SAN BLAS INDIANS (Cuna or Kuna Indians), tribe of central Panama. Once an important group with an

elaborate social system, they are now subsistence farmers.

SAN BRUNO, residential city, W Cal., suburb of San Francisco. Pop 36254.

SAN CARLOS, residential city in W Cal. Its industries include the manufacture of communications and electronic equipment. Pop 25924.

SAN CLEMENTE, residential city, SW Cal., site of President NIXON's "Western White House." Pop 17063.

SANCTIONS, in international politics, methods such as BOYCOTTS, ECONOMIC SANCTIONS, EMBARGOES or military threat to enforce the decisions of one (or more) states concerning (usually) the social structure of another (or others). Provided for by the UN charter, they have been applied recently against Rhodesia and South Africa.

SAND, in geology, collection of rock particles with diameters in the range 0.125–2.0mm. It can be graded according to particle size: fine (0.125–0.25mm); medium (0.25–0.5mm); coarse (0.5–1.0mm); and very coarse (1–2mm). Sands result from EROSION by GLACIERS, winds, or ocean or other moving water. Their chief constituents are usually QUARTZ and FELDSPAR. (See also BEACH; DESERT; DUNE; SANDSTONE.)

SAND, George (1804–1876), pseudonym of the French novelist Amandine Aurore Lucile Dupin, baronne Dudevant. Her novels, at first romantic, later socially oriented, include *Indiana* (1832) and *The Haunted Pool* (1846). Her life-style—coupled with its partial source, her ardent feminism—caused much controversy, her lovers including CHOPIN and notably de MUSSET. Her memoirs, *Histoire de Ma Vie* (1854–55), provide a graceful justification of her views.

SANDALWOOD, a number of trees whose timber exudes a fragrant odor. The wood takes a fine finish. Sandalwood paste, from *Santalum album*, is used for Brahman caste marks in India and in Buddhist funeral rites. Family: Santalaceae.

SANDBLASTING. See ABRASIVE.

SANDBUR, several weeds with bur-like fruits. The common sandbur (*Solanum rostratum*) is native to the American plains. The name applies to several grasses of the genus *Cenchrus*, which are native to the eastern US. Family: Graminae.

SANDBURG, Carl (1878–1967), American poet and biographer who won Pulitzer prizes for *Abraham Lincoln: the War Years* in 1940 and *Complete Poems* in 1951. He left school at 13, and at 20 fought in the Spanish-American war. While a journalist in Chicago, he wrote vigorous, earthy, free verse, as in *Chicago Poems* (1916) and *Smoke and Steel* (1920). He was also a notable folksong anthologist.

SAND CREEK MASSACRE, unprovoked surprise attack by US soldiers led by Colonel John Chivington on CHEYENNE INDIANS in Col. in Nov. 1864. Indians had camped near Fort Lyon to negotiate peace and, although they raised the US and white flags, around 500 were slaughtered and savagely mutilated.

SAND DOLLARS, irregular, flattened SEA URCHINS, disk-like, with a fur-like covering of short spines like that of the HEART URCHINS. Like these, sand dollars are burrowing ECHINODERMS. Almost all species are restricted to America and Japan.

SANDERLING, *Crocethia alba*, a small, active, wading bird of shorelines, related to the SANDPIPERS. It breeds in the Arctic tundra, and winters on sandy beaches in N Europe.

SAND FLIES, small, two-winged, biting flies, strictly those of the genus *Phlebotomus*, but the name is also used for biting midges, and in Australia, for BLACK FLIES. The true sand flies are tiny blood-sucking flies of the tropical and subtropical dusk.

SAND GROUSE, plump, desert-living ground birds of Eurasia, India and Africa. Unlike other desert-living animals they have no behavioral adaptations to heat and regulate their temperature by evaporation of water from a special throat patch. They must therefore drink daily, and the parents bring their young water trapped in special breast feathers. Family: Pteroclidae.

SAN DIEGO, on the Pacific Coast close to the Mexican border, third-largest city of Cal. and seat of San Diego Co. Its natural harbor houses a great Navy base, a large fishing fleet, and lumber and shipbuilding yards. Its heavy industries include aircraft, missiles and electronics factories. Pop 697027.

SAN DIMAS, city in SW Cal., 25mi E of Los Angeles, a citrus fruit shipping center. Pop 15692.

SANDOW, Eugene (1867–1925), German world weightlifting champion (1891) who popularized bodybuilding and devised several bodybuilding techniques.

SANDPIPERS, small to medium-sized wading birds forming part of the family Scolopacidae. Most are slim birds, with long straight bills and inconspicuous cryptic plumage. The group includes the stints, knots and "shanks" as well as the true sandpipers, dividing into two major groups, the Calidritine and Tringine pipers.

SANDRACOTTUS. See CHANDRAGUPTA.

SAND SHARKS, members of a family, Odontaspidae, of large SHARKS of tropical and temperate seas. Considered in South Africa and Australia perhaps the most dangerous of sharks, they normally feed on shoaling fishes.

SAND SPRINGS, manufacturing city in NE Okla. by the Arkansas R. It produces glass and textiles and has oil and gas wells. Pop 10565.

SANDSTONE, a SEDIMENTARY ROCK consisting of consolidated SAND, generally cemented by a matrix of CLAY minerals, CALCITE or HEMATITE. The sand grains are chiefly QUARTZ and FELDSPAR. The chief varieties are QUARTZITE, rich in silica; arkose, feldspar-rich; graywacke, coarse-grained and of varied composition; and subgraywacke, with more rounded grains and less feldspar than graywacke. Sandstone grades into CONGLOMERATE and SHALE. Sandstone beds may bear NATURAL GAS or PETROLEUM, and are commonly AQUIFERS. Sandstone is quarried for building, and crushed for use as AGGLOMERATE.

SANDSTORM, or dust storm, windstorms in which clouds of SAND or DUST are driven across the land. Because of the high wind-velocity, sandstorms are powerful factors in SOIL EROSION. (See also DUST BOWL; EROSION.)

SANDUSKY, city in N central Ohio, seat of Erie Co. It is a lake resort, ships coal, and is a center for fishing and light manufacture. Pop 32674.

SAND VERBENA, *Abronia latifolia*, herbaceous perennial plant native to Cal., the roots of which are eaten locally. Family: Nyctaginaceae.

SANDWICH COMPOUNDS, ORGANOMETALLIC COMPOUNDS in which the metal atom is sandwiched between two aromatic-ring LIGANDS—the whole of the ring electron system (see AROMATIC COMPOUNDS) interacting with the metal ORBITALS, giving great stability. Ferrocene and dibenzene-chromium are examples.

SANDY HOOK, peninsula in N.J., site of the oldest lighthouse still in service in the US (1763).

SANDYS, Sir Edwin (1561–1629), English statesman and a founder of the colony of VIRGINIA. During his management of the LONDON COMPANY, a representative assembly met in Virginia, the first such in the North American colonies (1619).

SANFORD, city in central Fla., seat of Seminole Co., has light engineering, truck farming and orchards. Pop 17393.

SANFORD, industrial town in SW Me. Pop 15812.

SANFORD, city in central N.C., seat of Lee Co. Its tobacco market is important. Pop 11716.

SAN FRANCISCO, famous city and seaport on the Pacific coast, noted for its cosmopolitan charm. Its economy is based on shipping and shipbuilding, with exports of cotton, grain, lumber and petroleum products. It is also the financial, cultural and communications center for the NW Coast. Its many tourist attractions include Chinatown, the Latin Quarter and Golden Gate Park. There are several museums and art galleries and the famous opera house. Founded by the Spanish (as Yerba Buena) in 1776, the city passed into US hands in 1846 and was named San Francisco (1847). The GOLD RUSH soon attracted thousands of settlers to the area. Parts of the city were rebuilt after the earthquake of 1906 (see SAN ANDREAS FAULT). (See also ALCATRAZ; GOLDEN GATE.) Pop 715674.

SAN FRANCISCO BAY, the world's largest natural harbor, 50mi long and up to 12mi wide, spanned by the GOLDEN GATE and San Francisco–Oakland Bay bridges.

SAN FRANCISCO CONFERENCE, conference, attended by 50 nations, held April–June 1945 to set up the UNITED NATIONS.

SAN GABRIEL, residential city in S Cal., some 8mi from Los Angeles. Pop 29336.

SANGALLO, Antonio da (Antonio Cordiani; 1483–1546), Italian architect and military engineer, succeeded RAPHAEL as architect of SAINT PETER'S BASILICA.

SANGAMON RIVER, river (225mi long) in central Ill., tributary of the Illinois R.

SANGER, city in S central Cal., in the San Joaquin valley. Pop 10088.

SANGER, Frederick (1918–), British biochemist awarded the 1958 Nobel Prize for Chemistry for his work on the PROTEINS, particularly for first determining the complete structure of a protein, that of bovine INSULIN (1955).

SANGER, Margaret (1883–1966), US pioneer of BIRTH CONTROL and feminism who set up the first birth-control clinic in the US (1916), founded the National Birth Control League (1917), and helped organize the first international birth-control conference (1927).

SAN GIMIGNANO, town in Siena province, central Italy, a tourist center with many medieval buildings, notably the 14 towers. Pop (estimated) 8000.

SANGRE DE CRISTO MOUNTAINS, range of the Rocky Mts reaching from S central Col. to N central N.M. The highest peak is Blanca Peak (14317ft).

SANHEDRIN, ruling councils of the Jews in Roman-occupied Palestine. The Great Sanhedrin was made up of 71 SADDUCEES and PHARISEES, presided over by the high priest. It served as a civil and religious court and was thus responsible for the trials of Christ and several of the Apostles. Lesser sanhedrins, made up of 23 members, tried minor offences and criminal cases.

SAN ILDEFONSO, Treaty of, treaty in which Spain was allied to the French Republic (1796).

San Francisco's famous hills, while affording attractive views, created a transport problem—solved by the introduction of rail cars.

SAN ISIDRO, city in NE Buenos Aires province, E central Argentina. Pop 250 008.

SANITATION. See PUBLIC HEALTH; SEWAGE.

SAN JACINTO, Battle of, decisive engagement (April 21, 1836) in the war for Texan independence. It was won by General HOUSTON whose troops, though outnumbered, surprised and defeated the Mexicans under SANTA ANNA, thereby establishing TEXAS as an independent republic.

SAN JOAQUIN RIVER, river in central Cal., rising in the Sierra Nevada and flowing for 350mi SW and then NW to join the SACRAMENTO RIVER near Suisun Bay.

SAN JOSÉ, capital of COSTA RICA and a commercial and cultural center. It is noted for its urban architecture. Pop 198 523.

SAN JOSE, city in W central Cal., seat of Santa Clara Co. Founded in 1777, it is now a center for fruit processing and has aerospace and electronics firms. Pop 445 779.

SAN JOSÉ SCALE, *Quadraspidiotus perniciosus*, a diaspid SCALE INSECT infesting deciduous fruit trees in the US and Canada.

SAN JUAN, capital and port of PUERTO RICO on the NE coast of the island. Founded in 1521 by PONCE DE LEON's followers, it is now a trade center producing sugar, rum, metal products, textiles and furniture. Pop 452 749.

SAN JUAN HILL, Battle of, victory at SANTIAGO DE CUBA won by the ROUGH RIDERS on July 1, 1898, which with the EL CANEY battle led to CERVERA Y TOPETE's defeat in the SPANISH–AMERICAN WAR.

SAN JUAN ISLANDS, group of 172 islands in Puget Sound of NW Wash. They were the subject of a long dispute between the US and Britain over the US/Canada border. Both countries moved in troops in 1859: after arbitration, the German Emperor WILLIAM I awarded the islands to the US.

SANKEY, Ira David (1840–1908), US evangelist hymn singer. He toured the US and Britain with Dwight MOODY. (See also REVIVALS.)

SAN LEANDRO, residential city in W Cal., with varied light industries. Pop 68 698.

SAN LORENZO, city in W Cal., near San Francisco Bay. Pop 24 633.

SAN LUIS OBISPO, city in SW Cal., seat of San Luis Obispo Co. It makes building materials, electronics, furniture and food products. Pop 28 036.

SAN LUIS POTOSÍ, state (24 266sq mi) on the central plateau of Mexico. Agriculture, livestock-raising and silver-mining are important economic activities.

SAN LUIS POTOSÍ, capital of SAN LUIS POTOSÍ state, an agricultural, manufacturing and silver-mining center, founded 1583. Pop 274 320.

SAN MARCOS, city in S central Tex., seat of Hays Co., and an agricultural and tourist center. Pop 18 860.

SAN MARINO, world's smallest republic and possibly the oldest state in Europe, located in NE Italy. Built on the three peaks of Mt Titano, its townships include San Marino (the capital) and Serravalle. Tradition reports that San Marino was founded as a refuge for persecuted Christians in the 4th century AD. Many historic buildings remain, and the modern state lives mainly by tourism and the sale of postage stamps. The republic is ruled by two "captains-regent" assisted by a 60-member council of state.

Official name: Republic of San Marino
Capital: San Marino
Area: 24.1sq mi
Population: 19 000
Language: Italian
Religion: Roman Catholic
Monetary unit(s): 1 Lira = 100 centesimi

The Governor's Palace in San Marino, capital of the state of San Marino. Most of the city's historic buildings survive intact today; their character and charm have made them tourist attractions of great economic importance.

SAN MARINO, residential city in S Cal., near Pasadena, where H. E. HUNTINGTON set up his library and art gallery. Pop 14 177.

SAN MARTÍN, José de (1778–1850), Argentinian general who, with BOLÍVAR, liberated Chile and much of Peru from Spanish rule. Educated in Spain, he served in the Spanish army before returning to South America in 1812. In 1817 he led the Argentinian army over the Andes to Chile and victory against the Spanish: his friend Bernardo O'HIGGINS became ruler of an independent Chile. In 1821 he proclaimed Peru independent and became its protector. In 1822 he retired to France.

SAN MATEO, residential and commercial city in W Cal. Pop 78 991.

SAN MIGUEL DEL PADRÓN, suburb of Havana, W central Cuba. Pop 119 753.

SANNAZZARO, Jacopo (c1456–1530), Italian poet whose *Arcadia* (1504), the first lyric pastoral romance, initiated a genre that rapidly spread throughout Western Europe.

SAN PABLO, city in W Cal. about 14mi NE of San Francisco. The economy rests on bathroom fixtures. Pop 21 461.

SAN RAFAEL, residential city in W Cal., seat of Marin Co. It makes electrical and metal goods. Pop 38 977.

SAN SALVADOR, capital and largest city of EL SALVADOR. In a volcanic region, it has suffered many earthquakes. It is a trade center, producing textiles, tobacco, etc. Pop 358 900.

SAN SALVADOR ISLAND, name given by COLUMBUS to his first landfall in the New World, now generally accepted to be Watling Island (now called San Salvador: 60sq mi) in the BAHAMAS. Its original Indian name was Guanahani.

SANS-CULOTTES (French: without knee-breeches), in the FRENCH REVOLUTION, the Parisian lower classes, who wore long trousers rather than breeches: the term thus implies extreme radical.

SAN SEBASTIAN, fishing port and resort city in N Spain, on the Bay of Biscay, noted especially for its superb ecclesiastical architecture. Pop 165 829.

SANSEVIERIA, a genus of 60 species of evergreen perennials, several species of which are grown as house plants for their attractive and unusual foliage. *Sansevieria trifasciata* (Mother-in-law's tongue) produces erect sword-like leaves which in the "Laurentii" variety have cream-yellow margins. *S. grandis* (**Snake plant**) is a smaller plant producing clusters of dark-green leaves with snake-shaped markings. Sansevierias occasionally produce sprays of greenish-white, fragrant flowers. They grow under almost any reasonable light intensity and temperature. They should be well watered whenever the soil dries out. Propagation is by dividing the plants or removing offsets. Family: Liliaceae.

SANSKRIT, classical language of the Hindu peoples of India and the oldest literary language of the Indo-European Family. Some early texts date from c1500 BC, including the Vedic texts (see VEDA). Vedic Sanskrit was prevalent roughly 1500–150 BC, Classical Sanskrit roughly 500 BC–900 AD. Sanskrit gave rise to such modern Indian languages as HINDI and URDU, and is distantly related to the CELTIC LANGUAGES, ROMANCE LANGUAGES and SLAVONIC LANGUAGES.

SANSOVINO, Jacopo (Jacopo Tatti; 1486–1570), Italian sculptor and architect, highly influential in Venice where he designed in a classical style the Library of St. Mark's (1536–38) and sculptured *Mars and Neptune* (1554–56).

SANS SOUCI, ROCOCO palace near Potsdam built for FREDERICK II of Prussia in 1745–47, who lived there for 40 years, making it a magnificent cultural center for such notable guests as VOLTAIRE.

SAN STEFANO, Treaty of, peace treaty signed in 1878 between Russia and the Ottoman Empire. Its terms, including the cession of land and payment of a large indemnity, greatly increased Russia's power in SE Europe. The treaty was later revised at the Congress of BERLIN.

SANTA ANA, industrial city in S Cal., seat of Orange Co., is the commercial center of the fertile Santa Ana Valley. Pop 156 601.

SANTA ANNA, Antonio Lopez de (1794–1876), Mexican general and military dictator who tried to suppress the Texan revolution and fought US troops in the MEXICAN WAR. He helped establish Mexican independence in 1821–29 and became president in 1833. When the Texan settlers revolted against his tyranny (1836), he defeated them at the ALAMO but lost the battle of SAN JACINTO, being himself captured, and had to resign: he was to gain and lose the presidency three further times (1841–44, 1846–47, 1853–55). He spent most of his later years in exile.

SANTA BARBARA, resort city in SW Cal., seat of Santa Barbara Co. The site of a large Spanish mission, its industries include oil drilling and food processing. Pop 70 215.

SANTA BARBARA ISLANDS, chain of mountainous islands, discovered (1542) by Juan CABRILLO, off S Cal., largest being Santa Cruz (98sq mi). (See also CHANNEL ISLANDS NATIONAL MONUMENT.)

SANTA CATALINA, or Catalina Island, island resort (72sq mi), one of the SANTA BARBARA ISLANDS.

SANTA CATARINA, state in S Brazil between the Atlantic and Argentina. Its high terrain covers 37 060sq mi, and the climate is temperate. It is an important coal-producing region and also has food-processing industries.

SANTA CLARA, city in W Cal. producing fiberglass and electronic equipment. Pop 87 717.

SANTA CLAUS, Christmastide bearer of gifts to children. The jolly fat man transported by flying reindeer and dropping presents down chimneys is a comparatively recent (19th-century) legend derived from St. NICHOLAS (introduced as Sinter Klaas to the New World by Dutch settlers), whose feast day (Dec. 6) was a children's holiday.

SANTA CRUZ, resort city in W Cal., seat of Santa Cruz Co., on Monterey Bay. Since 1965 it has been the site of the U. of California in Santa Cruz. Pop 32 076.

SANTA CRUZ DE TENERIFE, capital of Santa Cruz de Tenerife province in the CANARY ISLANDS. A tourist center, it exports vegetables and tobacco. Pop 151 361.

SANTA FE, capital of NEW MEXICO on the Santa Fe R, a minor tributary of the nearby Rio Grande. Founded by the Spanish c1610, it is the oldest state capital, ceded to the US after the MEXICAN WAR. Its many Spanish colonial buildings attract large numbers of tourists. Pop 41 167.

SANTA FE SPRINGS, residential city in SW Cal., a suburb of Los Angeles. Pop 14 750.

SANTA FE TRAIL, overland trade route between W Mo. and Santa Fe, N.M., in use from its opening-up in

1821 until the coming of the Santa Fe railroad in 1880. Manufactured goods passed W, furs and bullion E.

SANTA ISABEL (or Malabo), capital, seaport and commercial center of EQUATORIAL GUINEA, on Macías Nguema (Fernando Po). Pop 37 152.

SANTA MARIA, city in S Cal., 50mi NW of Santa Barbara. Industries include oil, dairy farming and light manufacturing. Pop 32 749.

SANTA MONICA, resort and residential city in S Cal. on Santa Monica Bay, has important communications and aerospace industries. Pop 88 289.

SANTA PAULA, city in SW Cal., on the Santa Clara R, is mainly agriculturally oriented. Its industries include oil-refining. Pop 18 001.

SANTA ROSA, city in W Cal., seat of Sonoma Co., and the commercial center of the Sonoma Valley. Pop 50 006.

SANTAYANA, George (1863–1952), Spanish-born US philosopher, writer and critic. He was an influential writer on aesthetics in books such as *The Sense of Beauty* (1896). His philosophy was expressed in *The Life of Reason* (1905–06), where he emphasized the importance of reason in understanding the world but was skeptical of what one can really know. *Skepticism and Animal Faith* (1923) suggests a relationship between faith and knowledge.

SANTIAGO, capital and principal industrial, commercial and cultural city of Chile, on the Mapocho R. It was founded 1541 by VALDIVIA. Pop 2 661 920.

SANTIAGO DE COMPOSTELA, city in NW Spain, an important Christian pilgrimage center since the discovery in the 9th century of the supposed tomb of the apostle St. JAMES the greater. Pop 70 893.

SANTIAGO DE CUBA, city, seaport in SE Cuba, exporting farm produce and metal ores. In the SPANISH-AMERICAN WAR (1898) the Spanish fleet under CERVERA Y TOPETE was blockaded in its harbor and later destroyed by US ships.

SANTO ANDRÉ, city in S Brazil, suburb of São Paulo. Its varied industries include textiles and rubber and metal products. Pop 418 578.

SANTO DOMINGO, capital and chief port of the Dominican Republic, at the mouth of the Ozama R. Founded by COLUMBUS' brother Bartholomew in 1496, it is the oldest continuously inhabited European settlement in the W Hemisphere. Pop 671 402.

SANTORIN. See THERA.

SANTOS, seaport city in São Paulo state, Brazil, the world's greatest coffee port. It also ships cotton, fruit, sugar and some manufactures. Pop 341 317.

SANTOS-DUMONT, Alberto (1873–1932), Brazilian-born pioneer aviator who experimented with balloons and powered dirigibles before flying his successful box-kite airplane (1906) and "Grasshopper" monoplane with undercarriage (1909).

SÃO FRANCISCO RIVER, great river of E Brazil. Partly navigable, it runs 1 800mi N and E from S Minas Gerais state to the Atlantic S of Maceió.

SÃO GONÇALO, city in SE Brazil, across Guanabara Bay from Rio de Janeiro. Industry includes chemicals and cement. Pop 161 392.

SÃO JOÃO DE MERITI, city in SE Brazil, a NW suburb of Rio de Janeiro. Pop 163 934.

SÃO LUIS, seaport capital of Maranhão state, NE Brazil, on Maranhão Island. It ships and processes sugar, lumber, cotton, fruit and hides. Pop 167 529.

SAÔNE RIVER, important waterway in E France, rises in the S Vosges Mts and flows about 300mi SW to meet the Rhône at Lyons. Barges work the Saône to Corre, 233mi upstream.

SÃO PAULO, largest city and industrial center of Brazil. Capital of São Paulo state, it lies 225mi SW of Rio de Janeiro. It grew rapidly with the development of the coffee industry in the 1880s, and still sends coffee to SANTOS. Its other industries are diverse. It is the site of three universities and of the largest cathedral in South America. Pop 5 901 533.

SÃO PAULO, state in SE Brazil, the country's most populous and economically important region, with industry centered on SÃO PAULO, the state capital. Products from the interior (coffee, cotton and tobacco) are exported at SANTOS on the coast.

SÃO TOMÉ E PRÍNCIPE, republic comprising two islands in the Gulf of Guinea off the W coast of Africa. São Tomé (330sq mi) lies 190mi W of Libreville, Gabon. Its volcanic rock rises to a 6 640ft peak. The capital São Tomé and most of the people are in the more level NE. Príncipe lies 100mi NE. Cacao comprises 80% of exports from the former plantation economy. Copra, coconuts, palm oil and coffee are also produced. The islands achieved independence from Portugal on July 12, 1975.

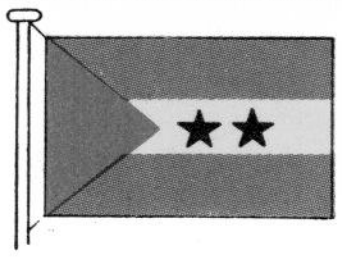

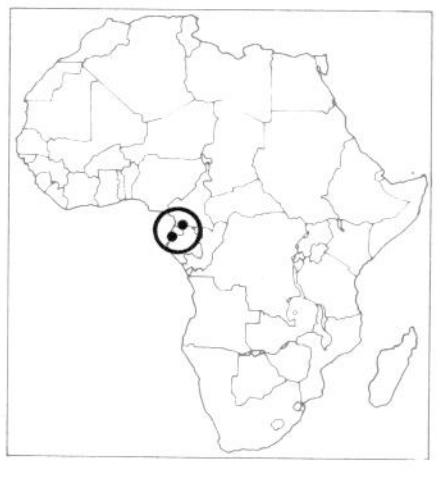

Official name: São Tomé e Príncipe
Capital: São Tomé
Area: 372sq mi
Population: 76 218
Languages: Portuguese
Religions: Roman Catholic
Monetary unit(s): 1 Escudo = 100 centavos

SAPIR, Edward (1884–1939), US anthropologist, poet and linguist whose most important work was on the relation between language and the culture of which it is a product, suggesting that one's perception of the world is dominated by the language with which one may express it.

SAPODILLA, *Acras sapota*, an evergreen tree which is native to tropical America and has been introduced to other parts of the world where the brown, pear-like fruits are eaten as food. The fruits and bark contain a milky latex which is collected in Middle America as CHICLE, the raw material for chewing gum. Family: Sapotaceae.

SAPONIFICATION. See SOAPS AND DETERGENTS.

SAPONINS, substances found in plants which form stable foams with water. They normally occur combined with a SUGAR in glycosides. The component STEROLS or triterpinoids are termed **sapogenins**. Many are of considerable value in medicine in spite of being highly poisonous. The HEART stimulant, DIGITALIS, is a saponin from the Purple foxglove. The sapogenin, diosegnin, from Mexican yams (*Dioscorea*) is a cheap precursor to the STEROID drugs.

SAPPHIRE, all GEM varieties of CORUNDUM except those which, being red, are called RUBY; blue sapphires are best-known, but most other colors are found. The best sapphires come from Kashmir, Burma, Thailand, Sri Lanka and Australia. Synthetic stones, made by flame-fusion, are used for jewel bearings, phonograph styluses, etc.

SAPPHO (6th century BC), Greek poet born in LESBOS. Surviving fragments of her work, mainly addressed to young girls, are among the finest classical love lyrics, combining passion with perfect control of many meters. The terms sapphism and lesbianism, meaning female HOMOSEXUALITY, derive from Sappho and Lesbos.

SAPPORO, university city, capital of Hokkaido island, N Japan. Industries include dairying, lumber, flour, beer and printing. Pop 1 010 123.

SAPROPHYTES, plants that absorb food from dead or decaying organic matter instead of carrying out PHOTOSYNTHESIS. The group includes most FUNGI, e.g., the YEASTS that ferment sugar and the MOLDS that decay fruit.

SAPSUCKERS, two species of WOODPECKERS of the genus *Sphyrapicus*, found in the western and central US. Although their main food is insects, sapsuckers also feed on the sap of trees, drilling rows of holes in the bark and lapping up the sap as it comes out.

SAPULPA, city in E Okla., seat of Creek Co., 15mi SW of Tulsa. In an oil and gas region, it makes glass, pottery and bricks. Pop 15 159.

SARABAND, wild dance of 16th-century Spain, refined in 17th-century France to a slow processional dance in triple rhythm. It is often a slow movement in the instrumental SUITE.

SARACENS, the name given by medieval Christians to the Arab and Turkish Muslims who conquered former Christian territory in SW Asia, N Africa, Spain and Sicily.

SARAGOSSA, or Zaragoza, provincial capital on the Ebro R, NE Spain, in a rich farm area. Products include machinery and chemicals. Its historic Gothic and Moorish buildings draw many tourists. Pop 479 845.

SARAH, wife of ABRAHAM and mother of ISAAC. Barren till her old age, Sarah bore her son as a gift of God.

SARAJEVO, capital of the republic of Bosnia and Herzegovina in Yugoslavia, on the Bosna R. Here, Austrian Archduke Francis Ferdinand and his wife were assassinated on June 28, 1914, the event which sparked off WWI. Pop 244 045.

SARANSK, capital of the Mordovinian Autonomous SSR, USSR, 330mi ESE of Moscow. Its manufactures include machinery, cable and electrical goods. Pop 190 000.

SARAPIS. See SERAPIS.

SARASATE, Pablo de (1844–1908), brilliant Spanish violinist for whom LALO, SAINT-SAËNS and others composed concertos.

SARASOTA, city on the W coast of Fla., seat of Sarasota Co. A tourist resort in truck farm country, it is famous for the Ringling museums. Pop 40 237.

SARATOGA, mainly residential city in W Cal., 8mi SW of San Jose. Industry includes wine making. Pop 27 110.

SARATOGA, Battles of, a key series of engagements in the American Revolution. On Sept. 17, 1777, a British force led by General John BURGOYNE attacked an American encampment around Bemis Heights, N.Y., defended by General Horatio GATES. Burgoyne's force, outnumbered, with heavy losses and without reinforcements was forced to retreat, and after further fighting eventually surrendered at Saratoga on Oct. 17. After this important victory, the French recognized American independence and allied themselves with the rebels. (See also REVOLUTIONARY WAR, AMERICAN.)

SARATOGA SPRINGS, city in E N.Y. in the foothills of the Adirondack Mts, famous for its medicinal springs and horse racing. Pop 18 845.

SARATOV, capital of Saratov oblast in the Russian SFSR, USSR, on the Volga R. It is a port with engineering, oil and natural gas industries. Pop 758 000.

SARAWAK, a state of the Malaysia federation. A former British colony, Sarawak comprises 48 000sq mi of mostly mountainous country on the NW coast of Borneo. Oil, bauxite, rice, rubber and sago are its principal products. The state capital is Kuching.

SARCODINA, a large assemblage of PROTOZOA containing those which possess PSEUDOPODIA. The class includes the AMOEBAS, FORAMINIFERA, Heliozoans and RADIOLARIANS. All have pseudopodia which are used for capturing prey as well as for locomotion. Most contain skeletal spicules of great complexity and beauty.

SARCOMA, a form of TUMOR derived from connective TISSUE, usually of mesodermal origin in EMBRYOLOGY. It is often distinguished from CANCER as its behavior and natural history may differ, although it is still a malignant tumor. It commonly arises from BONE (osteosarcoma), fibrous tissue (fibrosarcoma) or CARTILAGE (chondrosarcoma). Excision is required, though RADIATION THERAPY may be helpful.

SARD, a semiprecious stone, a brown variety of CHALCEDONY, closely related to CARNELIAN.

SARDINE, a small, herring-like fish, properly the young of the PILCHARD.

SARDINIA, Italian island in the Mediterranean 120mi to the W of mainland Italy and just S of CORSICA. It is a mountainous area of 9 301sq mi, with some agriculture on the coastal plains and upland valleys. Wheat, olives and vines are grown and sheep and goats raised: fish and cork are also exported. Many different ores are extracted from the ancient mines and tourism is growing in importance. The island is an autonomous region of Italy, with its capital at Caligari.

SARDINIA, Kingdom of, the European state that formed the nucleus of modern, united Italy. In 1720, Sardinia was ceded to Savoy and the duke of Savoy became first ruler of the new kingdom of Sardinia, made up of Savoy, Sardinia and Piedmont, N Italy. In the 19th century Sardinia championed political reform, national unification and independence from Austria. Through the diplomacy of CAVOUR, prime minister of Victor Emmanuel II, and the conquests of GARIBALDI, almost all of Italy was united under the house of Savoy in the period 1859–61, when Victor Emmanuel was proclaimed king of Italy. (See also RISORGIMENTO.)

SARDIS, about 50mi W of modern Izmir, Turkey, the ancient capital of LYDIA and a center of civilization from 650 BC until conquered by the Persians in c546 BC, being finally destroyed by TAMERLANE. (See also MIDAS.) Its ruins are Lydian, Roman and Byzantine.

SARDONYX. See ONYX.

SARGASSO SEA, oval area of the N Atlantic, of special interest as the spawning ground of American EELS, many of whose offspring drift across the Atlantic to form the European eel population. Bounded E by the CANARIES CURRENT, S by the N EQUATORIAL CURRENT, W and N by the GULF STREAM, it contains large masses of *Sargassum* weed.

SARGASSUM FISH, *Histrio histrio*, a small fish living among floating weeds in the SARGASSO SEA. Beautifully camouflaged to match the weeds in which it lives, it moves slowly amongst the fronds using a "fishing rod" modified from the first dorsal fin ray to attract its prey.

SARGENT, John Singer (1856–1925), US painter famous for his many portraits of high society figures in the US and UK. His most famous picture, *Madame X* (1884), showing the alluring Parisian Madame Gautreau, created a furore that hid the painting's brilliance.

SARGON, the name of two great rulers in ancient Mesopotamia. **Sargon of Akkad** (reigned c2335–2280 BC), founded the SEMITE Akkadian dynasty which displaced the SUMERIANS. He built an empire which covered all Mesopotamia and Syria and reached E to Persia, W to the Mediterranean and N to the Black Sea. **Sargon II of Assyria** (ruled 721–705 BC), consolidated the Assyrian empire. He concluded the siege of Samaria in Palestine and conquered Cyprus, Armenia and Babylonia. His method of retaining power was to deport hostile tribes.

SARK, one of the CHANNEL ISLANDS off NW France. It is the smallest self-governing unit of the UK (2sq mi; pop 590).

SARMATIANS, a central Asian people of Iranian stock who conquered the SCYTHIANS in SE Europe. They held S European Russia 400 BC–400 AD and raided in the Balkans.

SARMIENTO, Domingo Faustino (1811–1888), Argentine educator, writer and statesman, president 1868–74. He helped overthrow the dictator ROSAS (1852), and as president promoted education, commerce, immigration and communications.

SARNIA, city port in SE Ontario on St. Clair R, seat of Lambton Co. Important industries include an oil refinery and petrochemicals. Pop 56 727.

SARNOFF, David (1891–1971), Russian-born US radio and television pioneer. Starting his career as a telegraph messenger boy, he became president of RCA, and later founded NBC, the first commercial TV network (1926).

SAROYAN, William (1908–), US author. After short stories like *The Daring Young Man on the Flying Trapeze* (1934) came sketches reflecting his Armenian background (*My Name is Aram*, 1940) and colorful, optimistic accounts of Depression and war years, as in the play *The Time of Your Life* (1939) and the novel *The Human Comedy* (1943), both filmed.

SARRAUTE, Nathalie (1902–), Russian-born French writer, creator of the "antinovel." Her technique, in such accounts of bourgeois life and psychology as *Tropisms* (1939) and *Portrait of a Man Unknown* (1947), rejects that of Realist novelists.

SARSAPARILLA, substance found in the roots of certain vines of the genus *Smilax*, native to Middle and South America. It is used for flavoring carbonated drinks such as root beer, and to disguise the taste of some medicines.

SARSENS, large blocks of SANDSTONE found on the chalk downs of S England, used to construct STONEHENGE and other ancient monuments.

SARTO, Andrea del. See ANDREA DEL SARTO.

SARTRE, Jean Paul (1905–), French philosopher, novelist and playwright, famous exponent of EXISTENTIALISM. His works reflect his vision of man as master of his own fate, with his life defined by his actions: "existence precedes essence." Among his novels are *Nausea* (1938) and the trilogy *The Roads to Freedom* (1945–49). His drama includes *The Flies* (1943) and *In Camera* (1945). Sartre founded his review *Les temps modernes* in 1945. A close associate of Simone de BEAUVOIR and a communist who speaks eloquently for the left, his influence is international. In 1964 he refused the Nobel Prize for Literature.

SASANIANS, or **Sasanids.** See SASSANIANS.

SASEBO, city on the W coast of Kyūshū, SW Japan. Rebuilt after WWII bombing, it is a fishing and trading port with a US naval base. Pop 247 898.

Name of Province: Saskatchewan
Joined Confederation: Sept. 1, 1905
Capital: Regina
Area: 251 700sq mi
Population: 926 142

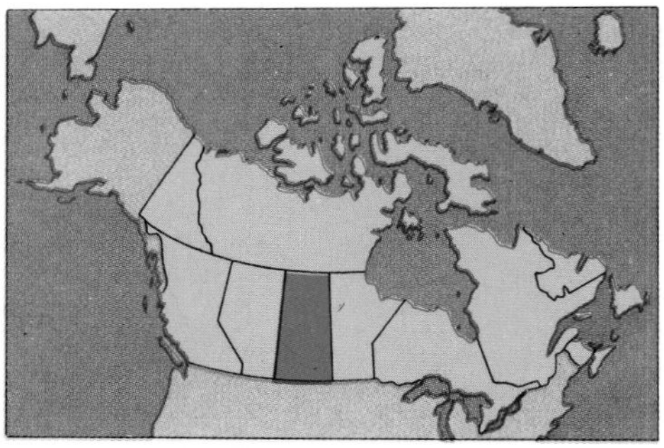

SASKATCHEWAN, inland prairie province of W Canada. Fifth largest of Canadian provinces, it is North America's most important wheat-growing region.

The land falls into two main divisions: the N third of the province is made up of the CANADIAN SHIELD, the S two-thirds of plains and lowlands. The N contains many forests, lakes, swamps and streams and is rich in mineral deposits including copper, zinc and uranium. The S has the best farming soil, and the majority of the population live there. The climate is continental with cold winters (average 15°F in the S and −20°F in the N) and summer temperatures averaging 57°–67°F.

The economy is heavily dependent on farming, with 60% of Canada's wheat grown in the area. Other crops are barley, rye and flax. Since WWII mining and manufacturing industries have grown fast in importance. Large quantities of potash, from the West's largest deposits, and petroleum are now produced. This has encouraged other industries such as the manufacture of chemicals, steel goods and cement.

People and History. Over 25% of the population lives in the two largest cities, Saskatoon and the capital, Regina. Some 40% are of British origin; other significant groups are of German, Ukrainian, Scandinavian and French-Canadian origin. White traders from the HUDSON'S BAY COMPANY first entered the area in 1690. The area was not properly explored until LA VÉRENDRYE visited it 40 years later. Farming settlements spread after the purchase in 1870 of the North West Territories by the new Dominion of Canada. Rapid growth followed after Saskatchewan became a province in 1905. The Depression and war years brought hardship and discontent and led to the

A typical prairie farm in Saskatchewan, Canada, ideal for the cultivation of cereal crops such as wheat and barley. Around 60% of Canada's total wheat production is contributed by Saskatchewan.

rise to power in 1944 of the Cooperative Commonwealth Federation, which remained in office till 1964. In the 1971 elections the NEW DEMOCRATIC PARTY defeated the LIBERAL PARTY.

SASKATCHEWAN REBELLION. See RIEL, LOUIS.

SASKATCHEWAN RIVER, flows E 340mi to Lake Winnipeg from the confluence of two branches in central Saskatchewan. The North Saskatchewan R rises 760mi W in the Columbian icefields. With its Bow R headwaters, the South Saskatchewan R flows 865mi E from the Rockies above Calgary.

SASKATOON, second largest city in SASKATCHEWAN and center for a rich grain, livestock and mining region. Pop 125 079.

SASSAFRAS, *Sassafras albidum*, an evergreen tree or shrub of the LAUREL family, Lauraceae, which is native to the eastern US. Its leaves are used to make sassafras tea and the aromatic oil of sassafras, extracted from its roots and bark, is used as a flavoring agent.

SASSANIANS, or Sasanids, the dynasty of rulers of the Persian empire founded by ARDASHIR I, c224 AD, and based on his capital at CTESIPHON. Named for Sasan, an ancestor of Ardashir, the dynasty included SHAPUR I and II and KHOSRU I and II. The empire was overrun by the Arabs in the 7th century. (See also PERSIA, ANCIENT.)

SASSETTA, or **Stefano di Giovanni** (c1400–1450), leading Italian painter of the Sienese school, and best known for his narrative altarpieces.

SASSOON, Siegfried (1886–1967), English poet and novelist. Decorated for bravery in WWI, he wrote bitterly satirical poetry such as *The Old Huntsman* (1917) and *Counterattack* (1918), which shocked the public with their graphic portrayal of trench warfare, their attacks on hypocritical patriotism and their pacifist conclusions. His novels include *Memoirs of a Fox-Hunting Man* (1928).

SATELLITE, in astronomy, a celestial object which revolves with or around a larger celestial object. In our SOLAR SYSTEM this includes PLANETS, COMETS, ASTEROIDS and meteoroids (see METEOR), as well as the moons of the planets; although the term is usually restricted to this last sense. Of the 32 known moons, the largest is Callisto (JUPITER IV), the smallest PHOBOS. The MOON is the largest known satellite relative to its parent planet; indeed, the earth-moon system is often considered a double planet.

SATELLITES, Artificial, man-made objects placed in orbit as SATELLITES. First seriously proposed in the 1920s, they were impracticable until large enough ROCKETS were developed. The first artificial satellite, Sputnik 1, was launched by the USSR in Oct. 1957, and was soon followed by a host of others, mainly from the USSR and the US, but also from the UK, France,

Canada, West Germany, Italy, Japan and China. They have many scientific, technological and military uses. Astronomical observations (notably X-RAY ASTRONOMY) can be made unobscured by the atmosphere. Studies can be made of the RADIATION and electromagnetic and gravitational fields in which the EARTH is bathed, and of the upper ATMOSPHERE. Experiments have been made on the functioning of animals and plants in space (with zero gravity and increased radiation). Artificial satellites are also used for reconnaissance, surveying, meteorological observation, as navigation aids (position references and signal relays), and in communications for relaying television and radio signals. Manned satellites, especially the historic Soyuz and Mercury series, have paved the way for **space stations**, which have provided opportunities for diverse research and for developing docking techniques; the USSR Salyut and US Skylab projects are notable. The basic requirements for satellite launching are determined by celestial mechanics. Launching at various velocities between that required for zero altitude and the escape velocity produces an elliptical orbit lying on a conic surface determined by the latitude and time of launch. To reach any other orbit requires considerable extra energy expenditure. Artificial satellites require: a power supply—SOLAR CELLS, BATTERIES, FUEL CELLS or nuclear devices; scientific INSTRUMENTS; a communications system to return encoded data to earth; and instruments and auxiliary rockets to monitor and correct the satellite's position. Most have COMPUTERS for control and data processing, thus reducing remote control to the minimum.

SATIE, Erik (1866–1925), French composer whose witty and highly original music was deliberately opposed to that of classic German composers. The word "surrealism" was first used in Apollinaire's notes to Satie's ballet music *Parade* (1917), scored for such instruments as typewriters and sirens.

SATINWOOD, trees and shrubs of the RUE family, Rutaceae, principally *Chloroxylon swietenia*, which is native to India and yields a deep yellow close-grained wood and *Zanthoxylum flavum*, which is native to Fla. and the W Indies and yields a golden yellow even-grained wood.

SATIRE, in literature or cartoons, on stage or screen, the use of broad humor, parody and irony to ridicule a subject. More serious than BURLESQUE, it contains moral or political criticism. In literature, classical satirists ARTISTOPHANES, HORACE and JUVENAL were followed by such writers as RABELAIS, DEFOE, SWIFT and VOLTAIRE.

SATO, Eisaku (1901–1975), prime minister of Japan 1964–72. A Liberal-Democrat, he presided over the reemergence of Japan as a major economic power and was active in foreign affairs. He won the 1974 Nobel Peace Prize.

SATRAP, governor of a satrapy, a province in the ancient Persian or ACHAEMENIAN empire. Satraps were usually members of the royal family or the nobility and headed the provincial administration and the judiciary.

SATURATION, term applied in many different fields to a state in which further increase in a variable above a critical value produces no increase in a resultant effect. A saturated SOLUTION is one which will dissolve no more solute, an EQUILIBRIUM having been reached; raising the temperature usually allows more to dissolve: cooling a saturated solution may produce **supersaturation**, a metastable state, in which sudden crystallization depositing the excess solute occurs if a seed crystal is added. In organic chemistry, a saturated molecule has no double or triple bonds and so does not undergo addition reactions.

SATURDAY, seventh day of the week, named for the Roman god SATURN. It is the SABBATH for Orthodox Jews and Seventh-day Adventists.

SATURN, in Roman mythology, an agricultural god, youngest son of Uranus (Heaven) and Gaea (Earth). Romans identified him with the Greek god CRONUS, and named SATURDAY for him (see also SATURNALIA).

SATURN, the second largest planet in the SOLAR SYSTEM and the sixth from the sun. Until the discovery of URANUS (1781) Saturn was the outermost planet known. It orbits the sun in 29.46 years at a mean distance of 9.54AU. Saturn does not rotate uniformly: its period of rotation at the equator is 10.23h, rather longer toward the poles. This rapid rotation causes a noticeable equatorial bulge: the equatorial diameter is 120.9Mm, the polar diameter 108.1Mm. Saturn has the lowest density of any planet in the Solar System, less than that of water, and may contain over 60% hydrogen by mass. Its total mass is about 95 times that of the earth. Saturn has ten moons; the largest, Titan, about the same size as MERCURY, is known to have an atmosphere. The most striking feature of Saturn is its ring system: three or more rings thought to be composed of countless tiny particles of ice. The rings are about 16km thick and the outermost has an external diameter of about 280Gm.

SATURNALIA, ancient Roman festival in honor of SATURN, god of the harvests. Schools and law courts were closed Dec. 17–23, work and commerce ceased, and both slaves and masters indulged in lavish feasting and the exchanging of gifts.

SATYAGRAHA, literally, "force born of truth," the philosophy and technique of nonviolent resistance developed by GANDHI.

SATYR, in Greek mythology, a male spirit of the forests and mountains, often shown as part man and part goat, with hooves, tail and pointed ears. Companions of DIONYSUS, satyrs played an important part in his orgiastic festivals.

SATYR PLAYS, plays that followed the three tragedies at the Dionysiac festivals of ancient Athens. In them, the chorus was dressed as satyrs. The purpose of the plays (as in Euripides' *Cyclops*) was to parody the heroic legends.

SAUD IV (1902–1969), king of Saudi Arabia 1953–64, son and successor of Ibn Saud. His reign saw the new oil revenues flow in but Saud was incompetent to manage state finance. He was forced to abdicate in favor of Faisal, his brother.

SAUDI ARABIA, kingdom covering most of the Arabian peninsula in SW Asia.

Land and Climate. Along the Red Sea in the W, the Hejaz and Asir mountains rise steeply from the coastal plain. In the center is the vast barren plateau of NEJD. The Rub al Khali (250 000sq mi) in the SE and the An Nafud (25 000sq mi) in the N are sand deserts. In the E are the oil-rich Hasa lowlands. Coastal areas are very humid. In the interior temperatures sometimes reach 120°F; yearly rainfall is generally less than 5in.

People. The population is almost entirely Arab. Riyadh, the capital, the Red Sea port of Jiddah and the holy cities of MECCA and Medina are the main centers. Despite the impact of oil, and the increase in educational and health facilities, 70% of the people live a traditional life in villages or as nomads.

Economy. Saudi Arabia is the fourth-largest oil-producer. The oil industry provides 60% of the gross national product. There are also iron, copper, phosphate, silver, gold, and gypsum deposits. Chief crops are sorghum, dates, wheat, barley, coffee, citrus fruits and millet. Livestock, raised mainly by nomadic Bedouin, includes camels, cattle, horses, donkeys, sheep and goats.

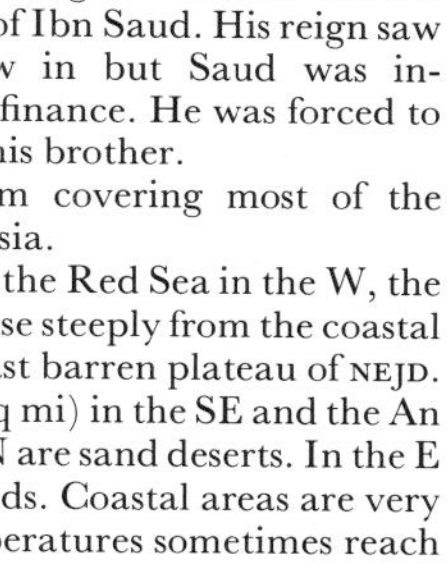

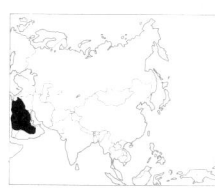

Official name: The Saudi Arabian Kingdom
Capital: Riyadh
Area: 927 000sq mi
Population: 7 965 000
Language: Arabic
Religion: Muslim
Monetary unit(s): 1 Saudi riyal = 20 qursh

History. From the 7th century Islam served to unify the nomadic and Semitic tribes of Saudi Arabia, but rival sheikdoms were later established. In the 1500s Arabia came under control of the OTTOMAN EMPIRE. The WAHABI sect, led by the Saudi rulers of Dariya, conquered most of the Arabian peninsula 1750–1800. Modern Saudi Arabia was founded by IBN SAUD (d. 1953), who conquered Nejd and the Hejaz, and joined them with Hasa and Asir. Succeeding rulers have been SAUD IV (deposed 1964), FAISAL (assassinated 1975) and Khaled. Saudi Arabia has supported Arab countries in conflict with Israel, and opposed, then recognized, the new republican regime in Yemen. It plays a major role in the ORGANIZATION OF PETROLEUM EXPORTING COUNTRIES.

SAUGUS, residential town, NE Mass., on the Saugus R 8mi NNE of Boston. It is the site of the Saugus Ironworks National Historic Site. Pop 25 110.

SAUK INDIANS, North American tribe of the ALGONQUIAN language group. Encountered by the French near Green Bay, Wisc. in 1667, they later lived along the Mississippi R hunting and farming. Many took part in the 1830s BLACK HAWK WAR rather than move W, but were eventually resettled in Okla. and Ia.

SAUL, first king of Israel, c1000 BC. The son of Kish of the tribe of Benjamin, he was anointed by SAMUEL after the tribes decided to unite under a king. His reign was generally successful, but he killed himself after a defeat by the Philistines. His rival DAVID succeeded him.

SAULT SAINTE MARIE, city in S Ontario, Canada, opposite Sault Sainte Marie, Mich. It is a port, with iron, steel, lumber and chemical industries. Pop 80 332.

SAULT SAINTE MARIE, city in N Mich., seat of Chippewa Co., on the St. Marys R across from Sault Sainte Marie, Ontario. It is a resort center. Pop 15 136.

SAULT SAINTE MARIE CANALS, three short canals on the St. Marys R, forming part of the SAINT LAWRENCE SEAWAY between Lake Superior and Lake Huron. Two of the canals (each 1.6mi) are in the US, and one (1.4mi) is in Canada. They are among the busiest in the world.

SAUROPTERYGIANS, an order of extinct aquatic reptiles common in the TRIASSIC and CRETACEOUS. They included the nothosaurs and PLESIOSAURS, and were characterized by having a series of intermeshed abdominal ribs. It is of this order that the famous Loch Ness Monster of Scotland is believed to be a remnant.

SAUSSURE, Ferdinand de (1857–1913), Swiss linguist whose contributions to structural linguistics (e.g., the idea that the structure of a language may be studied both as it changes with time and as it is in the present) have had a formative influence on 20th-century studies of GRAMMAR.

SAVANNA, tropical GRASSLANDS of South America and particularly Africa, lying between equatorial FORESTS and dry DESERTS.

SAVANNAH, city in SE Ga., its principal seaport, seat of Chatham Co., founded in 1733 by James OGLETHORPE. It is on the mouth of the SAVANNAH RIVER, 18mi from the Atlantic. Its produce includes paper, chemicals and fertilizer. It has shipyards and a cotton market. Pop 118 349.

SAVANNAH, first steamship to cross the Atlantic. A sailing packet on the New York-Le Havre route, she was fitted with engines which were used for 85hrs of the May–June 1819 voyage from Savannah, Ga. to Liverpool.

SAVANNAH RIVER, formed in NW S.C. where the Tugaloo and Seneca rivers join. It flows some 310mi SE to the Atlantic near Savannah and constitutes most of the S.C.-Ga. border.

SAVA RIVER, flows 585mi from the Italian-Yugoslav border through N Yugoslavia to the Danube at Belgrade. It is navigable for 360mi.

SAVATE, an old French sport, popular in the 1700s, of fighting with the feet rather than fists (*savate*: old shoe). A similar sport is popular in Thailand. In the 1800s, a fist-feet combination (*boxe française*) was briefly in vogue.

SAVERY, Thomas (c1650–1715), British inventor of an early form of STEAM ENGINE (patented 1698), used for pumping water. His patent covered NEWCOMEN's later invention (c1712), and for this reason the two entered partnership for the development of Newcomen's engine.

SAVIGNY, Friedrich Karl von (1779–1861), German jurist and legal historian, a founder of the historical school of jurisprudence. He believed that law develops gradually from the customs of society: the deliberate effort of the legislator is illusory, since he actually follows custom.

SAVINGS, in economics, that part of current INCOME not spent on consumption and retained after tax. Today, INTEREST-bearing accounts, and purchase of INSURANCE or a MORTGAGE have replaced the traditional mattress as a way of protecting savings. Savings may be channeled direct into INVESTMENT by buying STOCKS. In MACROECONOMICS, if the total amount invested in a country equals the amount saved, the economy will be in equilibrium. If savings exceed investment, production, income and employment will tend to fall. (See also MULTIPLIER.)

SAVONAROLA, Girolamo (1452–1498), Italian reformer. A Dominican friar, he campaigned boldly against the MEDICI in Florence. By 1494 the Medici had left and he had created a democratic republic in Florence. He was excommunicated by his opponent, Pope ALEXANDER VI (1495), but continued to preach until his enemies and the rival Franciscans had him hanged and burnt as a heretic.

SAVOY, former duchy in the W Alps, now comprising the departments of Haute-Savoie and Savoie, SE France. The ruling house, founded in 1026 by Count Humbert, played a leading role in uniting Italy (1859–70) and provided the kings of Italy from 1861 to 1946. The historical capital is Chambéry.

SAVOY, Eugene of. See EUGENE OF SAVOY.

SAW, cutting tool consisting of a flat blade or circular disk, having on its edge a row of sharp teeth of various designs, usually set alternately. Excepting jagged stone knives, the first saws (copper and bronze) were used in Egypt c4000 BC, but only with the use of steel did they become efficient. Hand saws include the crosscut saw for cutting wood to length, the backsaw for joints, the coping saw for shaping, and the hacksaw for cutting metal. Power saws include circular saws, band saws (with a flexible endless steel band running over pulleys) and chain saws.

SAWATCH MOUNTAINS, a range in the Rocky Mts, in central Col., with Mt Elbert (14433ft) its highest peak. It is a resort, dairying and ranching area.

SAWFISHES, a family, Pristidae, of flattened cartilaginous fishes with a greatly elongated snout bearing a series of 16–32 teeth on either side. The body is shark-like with small pectoral fins. Sawfishes are found in tropical seas, but also occur in some fresh waters. The function of the saw is uncertain, but may be for defense and for attacking prey.

SAWFLIES, primitive members of the HYMENOPTERA, including the horntails and woodwasps. The name sawfly derives from the serrated ovipositor of the female, adapted for sawing deep into wood or plant stems to deposit eggs. Unlike other Hymenoptera sawflies have fully-legged larvae very like butterfly or moth caterpillars. All are plant feeders and many are important pests of timber and agricultural crops.

SAW GRASS, *Cladium effusum*, a SEDGE native to the southern US, the leaves of which are sometimes used to make low quality paper. The closely related *C. mariscus*, native to Eurasia and Africa, is used for thatching. Family: Cyperaceae.

SAWTOOTH MOUNTAINS, a ridge in N central Wash., along the NE shore of Lake Chelan, forming the border between Okanogan and Chelan counties.

SAXE, Maurice, Comte de (1696–1750), illegitimate son of elector Frederick Augustus I of Saxony who became a brilliant general and marshal of France. (See AUSTRIAN SUCCESSION, WAR OF THE.) His greatest victory was over the English at Fontenoy (1745), during a successful Netherlands campaign.

SAXE-COBURG-GOTHA. See WINDSOR, HOUSE OF.

SAXHORNS, a family of brass wind instruments with valves and relatively wide bore, patented by the Belgian Adolphe Sax in 1845. It ranges from alto to countrabass horns. Saxhorns are used in military and brass bands in France, Britain and the US.

SAXIFRAGE, small rock plants of the genus *Saxifraga* with leaves growing in a rosette at the base of the stem and flowers growing in bunches at its tip. The family Saxifragaceae also includes CURRANTS and the GOOSEBERRY.

SAXO GRAMMATICUS (c1150–c1220), Danish historian who wrote *Gesta Danorum*, the first Danish history, covering the time from the legendary King Dan to the defeat of Pomerania in 1185 by Canute VI.

SAXONS, a Germanic people who with the ANGLES and the JUTES founded settlements in Britain from c450 AD, supplanting the CELTS (see also ANGLO-SAXONS). From modern Schleswig (N Germany) they also spread along the coast to N France before incorporation in CHARLEMAGNE's empire.

SAXONY (German: *Sachsen*, French: *Saxe*), region and former duchy, electorate, kingdom and state in E Germany, now part of the German Democratic Republic (districts of Leipzig, Dresden, and Karl-Marx-Stadt, formerly Chemnitz). Rich in minerals, the region has many industries and is noted for its textiles and Dresden china.

SAXOPHONE, a brass instrument, classed as woodwind since its sound is produced by blowing through a reed. Patented by the Belgian Adolphe Sax in 1846, the saxophone exists in soprano, alto, tenor, and baritone forms; the bass is rare. (See also WIND INSTRUMENTS.)

SAY, Jean-Baptiste (1767–1832), French economist, businessman and author of Say's Law, or the law of markets. This states that supply creates its own demand; hence there can be no overproduction or underproduction. This self-regulating nature of a capitalist economy was widely believed in until the depression of the 1930s.

SAYREVILLE, borough in central N.J., on Raritan Bay 5mi ESE of New Brunswick. Manufactures include bricks, chemicals and film. Pop 32508.

SAYVILLE, unincorporated community in N.Y., on Great South Bay, E Long Island. A residential part of Islip, it is a fishing and boating resort. Pop 11608.

SCABIES, infectious SKIN disease caused by a mite which burrows under the skin, often of hands or feet; it causes an intensely itchy skin condition which is partly due to ALLERGY to the mite. Rate of infection has a cyclical pattern. Treatment is with special ointments and should include contacts.

SCALAR, a quantity that can be described fully in terms of its magnitude, as contrasted with a VECTOR, which has both magnitude and direction.

SCALAWAG, in US history, a derisory term for Southern whites who cooperated with military and Republican RECONSTRUCTION governments after the Civil War. Mostly Republican Party members, they ranged from poor whites to rich planters and businessmen.

SCALDS. See BURNS AND SCALDS.

SCALE, in music, a term used for various sequences or progressions of notes, ascending or descending. The best-known scales are those of the 24 major and minor keys of conventional western harmony, but there are other types (see KEY). The *chromatic scale* progresses through all the notes of a piano keyboard, going up or down by half-tones. The six-note *whole-tone* scale goes up or down by a whole tone, starting from any note. The *pentatonic scale* has five notes, being the black notes on a piano keyboard or any equivalent sequence. The Greek and medieval MODES are another type of scale, and a new type is used in serial or TWELVE-TONE MUSIC.

SCALE, a flat, rigid or flexible plate forming a protective covering on some animals, notably fish. In plants, the term refers to a small, non-green leaf that protects a young bud.

SCALE INSECTS, plant-sucking HEMIPTERANS related to the mealy bugs. There are two major families, the Armored scales, Diaspididae, and Soft scales, Coccidae. Armored scales are minute insects characterized by a hard waxy scale covering the adult female formed from the first and second nymphal skins. Soft scales are covered with secreted wax. In both families the females are wingless and legless, the males minute and two-winged. Scales are among the most serious pests of shrubs and trees.

SCALLOPS, some 300 species of bivalve MOLLUSKS, family Pectinidae, distinguished by a characteristic shell: the valves being rounded, with a series of ribs radiating across the surface in relief. They have especially well developed eyes on the mantle rim. Unique among bivalves, scallops swim extremely well, propelled by jets of water expelled in snapping shut the shell.

SCALPING, removal of an enemy's scalp with hair attached. In North America, the practice, originally limited to the E, spread among Indians and frontiersmen largely as a result of Colonial governments' rewards.

SCALY ANTEATERS. See PANGOLINS.

SCAMMONY, a twining plant, *Convolvulus scammonia*, native to Asia Minor and Mediterranean regions. Its roots exude a RESIN that is used medicinally as a cathartic. Family: Convolvulaceae.

SCAMOZZI, Vincenzo (1552–1616), Italian architect of the late Renaissance. His work includes, in Venice, several palaces and the Procuratie Nuove and the Villa Pisani at Lonigo. His theoretical *Idea of Universal Architecture* (1615) became a classic.

SCANDERBEG. See SKANDERBEG.

SCANDINAVIA, region of NW Europe. Geographically it consists of the Scandinavian peninsula (about 300000sq mi) occupied by Norway, Sweden and NW Finland, but the term normally includes Denmark. Because of close historical development, Iceland and the Faroe Islands are also covered by the term in matters of language, culture, peoples and politics. Modern "Norden" is synonymous with this usage.

SCANDINAVIAN LANGUAGES, a Germanic group of Indo-European languages, comprising Danish, Faroese, Icelandic, Norwegian and Swedish. Icelandic preserves many features of OLD NORSE, the common tongue of Viking Scandinavia. The Scandinavian colonists who took their language W to N France, Ireland and England, S to Sicily and E to Kiev and Byzantium were later assimilated or died out.

SCANDIUM (Sc), silvery-white RARE-EARTH metal in Group IIIB of the PERIODIC TABLE; a TRANSITION ELEMENT. It is widely distributed in low concentrations, and is extracted from thortveitite or as a by-product of URANIUM extraction. Scandium forms trivalent ionic compounds and stable LIGAND complexes. The refractory scandium oxide (Sc_2O_3) is used in ceramics and as a catalyst; dilute scandium sulfate solution is used to improve germination of plant seeds. AW 45.0, mp 1541°C, bp 2831°C, sg 2.989 (25°C).

SCAPA FLOW, a large sea basin in the S Orkney Islands off the N coast of Scotland, the principal anchorage of the British navy in WWI and WWII. In 1919 the crews of the interned German fleet scuttled their ships here.

SCAPEGOAT. See AZAZEL.

SCAR, area of fibrous tissue which forms a bridge between areas of normal tissue as the end result of wound healing. The fibrous tissue lacks the normal properties of the healed tissue (e.g., it does not tan). The size of a scar depends on the closeness of the wound edges during healing; excess stretching forces and infection widen scars.

SCARABS, a family of BEETLES which includes the DUNG BEETLES, CHAFERS and Dor beetles. Most of the 20000 species are scavengers of decaying organic matter, especially dung, or feed on the foliage and roots of growing plants, as do the chafers, many of which may become agricultural pests.

SCARLATTI, Alessandro (1660–1725), Italian composer. A leading musical scholar and teacher, he composed hundreds of church masses, cantatas and oratorios, and over 100 operas. Few are now performed, but he is important for innovations in harmony, thematic development, and use of instruments. His son **Domenico Scarlatti** (1685–1757) also composed operas and church music, but is known for his many brilliant sonatas for harpsichord, which influenced Haydn and Mozart and are still widely played.

SCARLET FEVER, or scarletina, INFECTIOUS DISEASE caused by certain strains of *Streptococcus*. It is common

The Malaysian scarab, *Scarabaedae chalosoma*.

in children and causes sore throat with TONSILLITIS, a characteristic SKIN rash and mild systemic symptoms. PENICILLIN and symptomatic treatment is required. Scarlet fever occurs in EPIDEMICS; a few are followed by RHEUMATIC FEVER or NEPHRITIS.

SCARP, or **escarpment**, steep slope or inland cliff, most often that of a CUESTA. The term is sometimes applied to similar slopes resulting from EROSION or faulting (see FAULT).

SCARSDALE, residential town in SE N.Y., 20mi N of New York City. Pop 19 229.

SCATTERING, the deflection of moving particles and energy waves (such as ELECTRONS, PHOTONS or SOUND waves) through collisions with other particles. RAYLEIGH scattering of sunlight gives rise both to the blue color of the ATMOSPHERE when the sun is high in the sky and to the reds and yellows of the setting sun because the blue light is scattered more strongly than the red.

SCAUPS, *Aythya marila* (Greater scaup) and *A. affinis* (Lesser scaup), diving DUCKS related to the POCHARDS and GOLDENEYES. Sea ducks, though breeding inland on lake islands, the females are brown, while the males have a black head and chest, with pale gray back and flanks.

SCEPTICISM. See SKEPTICISM.

SCHACHT, Hjalmar Horace Greeley (1877–1970), German financier and banker. He helped halt post-WWI inflation and was finance minister (1934–37) and Reichsbank president (1933–39), but conflict with Goering and Hitler later led to imprisonment. He was acquitted at the NUREMBURG TRIALS.

SCHARNHORST, Gerhard Johann David von (1755–1813), Prussian general. After Napoleon's victory (1806) over an army in which he was serving, he reorganized the Prussian army. He laid the foundation of its general staff system and its reliance upon conscripted as opposed to professional men.

SCHAUMBURG, village in NE Ill., 25mi NW of Chicago, mainly residential, but with some light industry. Pop 18 730.

SCHECHTER, Solomon (1847–1915), Romanian-born Hebrew scholar. After teaching at Cambridge and London universities, he became president of the Jewish Theological Seminary in New York City (1902). He founded the conservative United Synagogue of America (1913).

SCHECHTER v US, important decision by the US Supreme Court in 1935 which ruled unconstitutional the 1933 New Deal National Industrial Recovery Act. The Schechter Poultry Co. had been convicted of breaking a NIRA code regulating interstate commerce. The Supreme Court ruled that the NIRA delegated too much legislative power to the US president.

SCHEELE, Karl (or **Carl**) **Wilhelm** (1742–1786), Swedish chemist who discovered OXYGEN (c1773), perhaps a year before Joseph PRIESTLEY's similar discovery. He also discovered CHLORINE (1774).

SCHEELITE, calcium tungstate ($CaWO_4$), a major ore of TUNGSTEN. It is of widespread occurrence, and forms tetragonal CRYSTALS of various colors.

SCHEER, Reinhard (1863–1928), German naval commander. Famous as a WWI submarine strategist, in 1916 he became commander of the high seas fleet which engaged in the indecisive Battle of JUTLAND.

SCHEFFLERA, or Queensland umbrella tree, *Brassaia actinophylla*, an evergreen house plant, grown for its shiny dark-green lanceolate leaves. Although it tolerates relatively dim light, it prefers a bright position. The temperature should not drop below 16°C (60°F), and the humidity should be kept above 30%. The soil should be well watered whenever the soil surface dries out. Scheffleras grow very rapidly and are easily propagated from shoot tip cuttings or by planting seeds. Family: Araliaceae.

SCHEHERAZADE. See ARABIAN NIGHTS.

SCHEIDT, Samuel (1587–1654), German composer. Famous, like SWEELINCK, for his organ music, he developed counterpoint, adopted Italian staff NOTATION, and also wrote sacred choral works.

SCHELDE RIVER, or Scheldt, important navigable waterway of NW Europe. Rising in Aisne department, NW France, it flows 270mi N and NE to Antwerp, Belgium, then NW, as the East and West Schelde rivers, through Holland to the North Sea. The Delta Plan has sealed off the East outlet (see NETHERLANDS). There are canal links to the Rhine and Meuse rivers.

SCHELLING, Friedrich Wilhelm Joseph von (1775–1854), German idealist philosopher of the Romantic period, a pioneer of speculative thought after KANT. A student contemporary of HEGEL, Schelling later turned to religious philosophy and mythology. Both EXISTENTIALISM and modern Protestant theology have been influenced by him.

SCHENCK v US, Supreme Court decision (1919) concerning free speech. C. T. Schenck, general secretary of the Socialist Party, was one of over 1 500 prosecuted under laws against espionage and sedition. Upholding the conviction, Justice Oliver Wendell HOLMES ruled that the test should be "clear and present danger" to life, property, state security or free speech laws.

SCHENECTADY, city in N.Y., seat of Schenectady Co., 13mi NW of Albany. Products include electrical goods, jet engines and locomotives. Knolls Atomic Power Laboratory is sited here. Pop 77 958.

SCHERZO (Italian: joke), in music, a quick movement developed by Haydn and Beethoven from the MINUET and trio. It may occur in a symphony, sonata or concerto, or as a separate piece.

SCHIAPARELLI, Giovanni Virginio (1835–1910), Italian astronomer who discovered the ASTEROID Hesperia (1861) and showed that METEOR showers represent the remnants of COMETS. He is best known for terming the surface markings of MARS *canali* (channels). This was wrongly translated as "canals," implying Martian builders: the resulting controversy lasted for nearly a century.

SCHICK, Béla (1877–1967), Hungarian-born US pediatrician who developed the Schick test to determine immunity to DIPHTHERIA (1913).

SCHIELE, Egon (1890–1918), Austrian expressionist painter. His work, influenced by the linear style of Gustav KLIMT, has great intensity, sometimes expressed in harsh color and brushwork. It includes nudes, portraits and landscapes.

SCHILLER, Johann Christoph Friedrich von (1759–1805), playwright, poet and essayist, a leading figure of German literature second only to his friend GOETHE. Human dignity and spiritual freedom are central to his work, which ranges from the poem "Ode to Joy" to the STURM UND DRANG drama *The Robbers* (1781) and the popular play *Wilhelm Tell* (1804). As professor of history at Jena he wrote on the THIRTY YEARS' WAR, later the setting of his great *Wallenstein* (1799).

SCHILLER PARK, village in NE Ill., a suburb 15mi NW of Chicago. Food is processed, and tools and electrical goods produced. Pop 12 712.

SCHIPPERKE, a Belgian watchdog bred for use on canalboats. It is small (12in, up to 18lb), stocky and tailless, with a pointed head. The black coat is thick, particularly about the neck.

SCHIRRA, Walter Marty, Jr. (1923–   ), US astronaut. He was one of the original seven astronauts selected in 1959. In 1962 he flew the Mercury capsule *Sigma 7*; in 1965 he commanded *Gemini 6* in its rendezvous with *Gemini 7* and in 1968 *Apollo 7*, the first manned *Apollo* flight.

SCHISM, Great. See GREAT SCHISM; PAPACY.

SCHIST, common group of METAMORPHIC ROCKS which have acquired a high degree of schistosity, i.e., the tendency to split into layers along perfect CLEAVAGE planes. Their major constituents are flaky or platy minerals, especially MICA, TALC, AMPHIBOLES and CHLORITE.

SCHISTOSOMIASIS, or **bilharzia**, a PARASITIC DISEASE caused by *Schistosoma* species of FLUKES. Infection is usually acquired by bathing in infected water, the different species of parasite causing different manifestations. Infection of the BLADDER causes constriction, calcification and secondary infection, and can predispose to bladder CANCER. Another form leads to GASTROINTESTINAL TRACT disease with LIVER involvement. ANTIMONY compounds are often effective in treatment.

SCHIZOMYCETES, a class of the PLANT KINGDOM that includes the BACTERIA. (See also MONERA; SCHIZOPHYTA.)

SCHIZOPHRENIA, formerly called **dementia praecox**, a number of PSYCHOSES characterized by confusion of IDENTITY, HALLUCINATIONS, AUTISM, delusion and illogical thought. The three main types of schizophrenia are CATATONIA; **paranoid schizophrenia**, which is similar to PARANOIA except that the intellect deteriorates, and **hebephrenia**, which is characterized by withdrawal from reality, bizarre or foolish behavior, delusions, hallucinations and self-neglect.

SCHIZOPHYCEAE, a class of the PLANT KINGDOM that includes the BLUE-GREEN ALGAE. (See also MONERA; SCHIZOPHYTA.)

SCHIZOPHYTA, a division of the PLANT KINGDOM that includes the BACTERIA and BLUE-GREEN ALGAE. (See also MONERA.)

SCHLEGEL, Friedrich von (1772–1829), German philosopher. His stress on the subjective and spiritual in art and his studies of world history and literature greatly influenced ROMANTICISM in Germany.

SCHLEICHER, Kurt von (1882–1934), German soldier and statesman. He held army commands from 1914 to 1931, and became minister of defense in 1932 and later in the same year chancellor. In 1933 he was succeeded by HITLER. He was murdered by the Nazis during the purge of June 30, 1934.

SCHLEIDEN, Matthias Jakob (1804–1881), German botanist who was among the first to recognize the CELL as the unit of structure and function in living things.

SCHLEIERMACHER, Friedrich Ernst Daniel (1768–1834), German Protestant theologian and philosopher. He became famous with *Speeches on Religion* (1799), arguing that religion exists independently of morality or science. His great *The Christian Faith* (1821–22) discussed the essence of religion and Christianity, and the role of doctrine and theology.

SCHLESINGER, name of two famous 20th-century US historians. **Arthur Meier Schlesinger** (1888–1965), best known for his *The Rise of the City, 1878–1898* (1933) in the series he edited, *A History of American Life*. He stressed the cultural, social and economic context of history. **Arthur Meier Schlesinger, Jr.** (1917–   ), his son, won Pulitzer prizes for both *The Age of Jackson* (1945) and *A Thousand Days* (1966), the latter written after a period as special assistant to President Kennedy.

SCHLESWIG-HOLSTEIN, state in N West Germany, 6 046sq mi, bordering Denmark. The capital Kiel lies at the E end of Kiel Canal, linking the North and Baltic seas. The main economic activities are dairy farming, fishing, shipbuilding and engineering. Prussia annexed these two Danish duchies in 1866. N Schleswig was reunited with Denmark after WWI.

SCHLEY, Winfield Scott (1839–1911), US naval officer who led an Arctic expedition which rescued A. W. GREELY in 1884. Credit for victory over the Spanish at SANTIAGO DE CUBA (1898) was disputed between him and Admiral SAMPSON.

SCHLICK, Moritz (1882–1936), German philosopher regarded as the founder of the Vienna Circle, an influential school of LOGICAL POSITIVISM.

SCHLIEFFEN, Alfred von (1833–1913), German general, later field marshal. He drew up the "Schlieffen Plan" (1905) to combat France and her

Science Fiction

Its cultural role

Science fiction originated as a literary response to a new and previously unprecedented human curiosity born of technological advance, and it is therefore the branch of literature most characteristic of our period and most relevant to it.

Technological advance has been characteristic of our species since early hominids began to chip pebbles into more useful shapes a couple of million years ago. What's more, technological advance has been by far the most significant cause of social change; some might argue the *only* significant cause. Consider how human life has changed as a result of the coming and going of rulers, or of victory or defeat in this battle or that, and compare that with changes brought about by the coming of fire, of agriculture, of metallurgy, of the magnetic compass, of gunpowder, of printing, of the steam engine.

Even where profound changes seem to have had nothing to do with technology, one can argue a hidden basis in technological change. One can tie in the success of the Protestant Reformation with Luther's use of the printing press; of the Crusades with the land hunger that followed the rise in population that in turn followed the introduction of the moldboard plow, the horseshoe and the horse-collar.

Nevertheless, although technological advance has had so important an effect on social change through almost all of human history, the connection went unnoticed. Technological advance was so slow, successive improvements in some technique came at such long intervals and radiated out from the point of origin with such deliberate speed, that to the average person in the course of his or her single short lifetime virtually no change was visible. Even historians, looking back on history through the swirling fog resulting from the lack of proper documentation, could make out hardly anything more than war and politics.

As a result, lack of change was assumed. In literature, until recently, tales of the past took no account of social change. The 13th-century tales of Arthur and his knights had those 6th-century heroes act in accord with 13th-century ways; medieval tales of the Trojan War turned Achilles and Hector into thirteenth-century knights as well.

There were, of course, stories of imaginary societies, deliberately made different from that of the writer and reader. These might involve talking animals, nonexistent animals, fabulous and superhuman intelligent beings. These are "fantasies," from a Greek word meaning "imagination," and these are still popular today. Examples of best-selling fantasies in this decade are J. R. R. Tolkien's *Lord of the Rings* and Richard Adams' *Watership Down*.

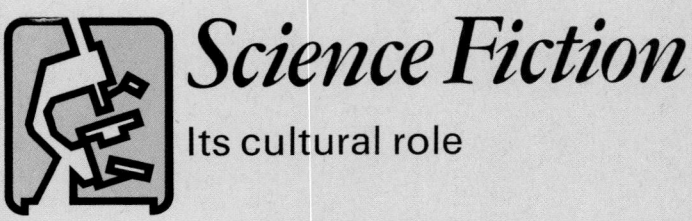

Included in the fantasies were travelers' tales that described distant lands and their strange marvels. These, like all fantasies in earlier times, were sometimes accepted as true by unsophisticated people. In reverse, some of the more cynical dismissed Marco Polo's mainly factual account of Asia in the 13th century as just another fantasy. Sometimes the distant land was the Moon, and because space travel became a staple of science fiction in modern times, these Moon stories are often considered early examples of the genre. It makes more sense, however, to consider them fantasies; all such imaginary societies of fantasy are permanently divorced from the real society we know. The fantasy worlds are not bound by the facts of the real world and by the laws of nature that constrain it. A jinn who can create a palace in the twinkling of an eye clearly disregards the laws of thermodynamics; since there is no way this can be done in the real world, the jinn and his works are and must remain fantasy, and nothing more.

Eventually, though, human beings came to recognize the existence of inevitable and continuing social change through technological advance and then a new kind of fantasy that wasn't quite fantasy became possible.

After all, though the rate of technological change through most of human history has been excessively slow, such change is cumulative. Technological change tends to make it possible for the population to grow and, in particular, for the number of technologically-trained to grow. With more and more people interested in technology and with a more and more extensive background of previous technological experience to draw on, the rate of technological advance might well be expected to accelerate throughout history—and so it has.

Clearly, then, the rate of change must eventually have accelerated to the point where social change would become noticeable to human beings within a single lifetime. This point was reached at about the year 1800 in those portions of the world in which the Industrial Revolution was beginning. The rate had by then become fast enough, you see, to cause apparent revolutions in the way of life.

Once individuals could see change—progressive and continuing change—there awoke a new curiosity. What would the future bring?

For the first time, the word "future" no longer meant merely a new king, or a new victory, or the rise of a new empire on the ruins of an old, or even the discovery of new lands. It meant new technological wonders and new ways of life. It meant flying through the air, not by wishes or by magic, but by balloon, or something more advanced. It meant the lightening of the human work-load, not by the enchantments of elves or jinni, but by ingenious man-made devices exploiting the laws of nature.

new ally Russia. The bulk of the German army would rapidly advance through Belgium and Holland to crush the French, before returning E to face the Russians. MOLTKE's modification of this plan failed in WWI.

SCHLIEMANN, Heinrich (1822–1890), German archaeologist, best known for his discoveries of Troy (1871–90) and Mycenae (1876–78). (See AEGEAN CIVILIZATION.)

SCHMALKALDIC LEAGUE, the association of German principalities and cities formed 1531, in the early REFORMATION, to defend the Protestant cause against the Holy Roman Emperor CHARLES V and his Catholic allies. Despite the League's defeat in 1547, Lutheranism was legalized under the Peace of AUGSBURG.

SCHMIDT, Bernhard Voldemar (1879–1935), Estonian-born German optician best known for developing the Schmidt TELESCOPE, today one of the most-used tools of ASTROPHOTOGRAPHY. Its special advantage is that it avoids LENS coma.

SCHNABEL, Artur (1882–1951), Austrian-US pianist. Best known for his reflective recordings of Beethoven's sonatas (which he edited), he was also a notable interpreter of Mozart and Schubert.

SCHNAUZER, name of three German breeds of dog: the more popular medium, or standard, schnauzer and its derivatives the giant and miniature. They have a blunt, heavily whiskered muzzle, squared body and wiry salt-and-pepper or black coat. The larger breeds serve as police dogs.

SCHNITZER, Eduard. See EMIN PASHA.

SCHNITZLER, Arthur (1862–1931), Austrian playwright; he wrote about love, lust and the personality basis of racism, particularly anti-Semitism, in the Vienna of Sigmund Freud. His work included *Anatol* (1893), *Playing with Love* (1896) and *Merry-go-Round* (1897).

SCHOENBERG, Arnold (1874–1951), German composer, theorist and teacher, who revolutionized music by introducing TWELVE-TONE MUSIC. His string sextet *Transfigured Night* (1899) with harmonic clashes was followed by the declaimed songs of *Pierrot Lunaire* (1912) and experiments in whole-tone and finally serial or 12-tone music culminating in his unfinished opera *Moses and Aaron* (1930–51). Schoenberg emigrated to the US in 1934. (See also ATONALITY; SCALE.)

SCHOFIELD, John McAllister (1831–1906), US Union general in the Civil War, from 1864 commander of its Army of the Ohio in the ATLANTA CAMPAIGN. Secretary of war 1868–69, he was commander of the US army 1888–95.

SCHOLASTICISM, the method of medieval Church teachers, or scholastics, who applied philosophic (primarily Aristotelian) ideas to Christian doctrine. They held that though reason was always subordinate to faith, it served to increase the believer's understanding of what he believed. Typical scholastic works are the *commentary* on an authoritative text and the *quaestio*. The latter is a stereotyped form in which the writer sets out opposing authorities and then reconciles them in answering a question. AQUINAS' *Summa Theologica* consists of a systematically constructed series of *quaestiones*. (See also ABELARD; ALBERTUS MAGNUS; BONAVENTURA; DUNS SCOTUS; WILLIAM OF OCKHAM.)

SCHONGAUER, Martin (or Martin Schön or Hübsch Martin; c1430–1491), German engraver and painter, born in Colmar, Alsace. His copper engravings of religious subjects had a profound influence on DÜRER and many others.

SCHOOLCRAFT, Henry Rowe (1793–1864), US ethnologist and explorer. Agent for the Lake Superior Indian tribes from 1822, he discovered the source of the Mississippi R in 1832 and published authoritative works on Indian culture and legends.

SCHOOLS. See EDUCATION.

SCHOPENHAUER, Arthur (1788–1860), German philosopher, noted for his doctrine of the will and systematic pessimism. In *The World as Will and Idea* (1819), his main work, he argued that will is the ultimate reality, but advocated the negation of will to avoid suffering, and the seeking of relief in philosophy and the arts. Schopenhauer's ideas influenced NIETZSCHE and modern EXISTENTIALISM.

SCHOTTISCHE, a lively dance for couples, in 2/4 or 4/4 time. Of Scottish (or possibly German) descent, it was popular in the 19th century.

SCHRIEFFER, John Robert (1931–), US physicist awarded with Leon COOPER and John BARDEEN the 1972 Nobel Prize for Physics for their work on SUPERCONDUCTIVITY.

SCHRÖDINGER, Erwin (1887–1961), Austrian-born Irish physicist and philosopher of science who shared with DIRAC the 1933 Nobel Prize for Physics for his elucidation of the **Schrödinger wave equation**, which is of fundamental importance in studies of QUANTUM MECHANICS (1926). It was later shown that his WAVE MECHANICS were equivalent to the matrix mechanics of HEISENBERG.

SCHUBERT, Franz Peter (1797–1828), Viennese composer. He wrote nine symphonies, of which the Fifth (1816), Eighth (1822) and Ninth (1828) are among the world's greatest. He is also famous for his piano pieces and chamber music (especially his string quartets), but above all his over 600 *lieder*, a form which he raised to unprecedented heights of

What, then, would the ways of the world be, this world you would not live to see?

It was to answer this curiosity that science fiction came to be written. Science fiction was a kind of fantasy since it imagined a society different from that of reality—but it differed from other fantasies in that it did not depict a society forever and eternally separated from ours by the difference between natural law and wishful chaos. Rather, the societies pictured in science fiction might conceivably be derived from our own by appropriate developments in science.

The British science fiction writer Brian Aldiss suggests that the first important science fiction story was *Frankenstein* by Mary Shelley, which was published in 1818. The suggestion fits. The story is based on the findings of the Italian anatomist, Luigi Galvani, who in 1771 first noticed that electric discharges could make freshly-dead frog muscles twitch as though they were alive. A quarter-century of controversy then ensued; many felt that electricity was somehow the stuff of life. It was a reasonable leap of the imagination to suppose that a further advance of scientific knowledge would reach the point where a dead man could be brought to life by the proper infusion of sufficient electricity, and in this way Frankenstein created his Monster.

From that point on, science fiction writers sought to keep one step ahead of the advance of science. Early attempts at building submarines inspired Jules Verne to imagine an advanced one, the *Nautilus*, in *Twenty Thousand Leagues Under the Sea* (1871). The growing importance of artillery in the American Civil War inspired the same author to imagine an American cannon powerful enough to fire a ship to the moon in *From the Earth to the Moon* (1865).

The English writer, H. G. Wells, took more daring steps. Controversy over the "canals" reported on Mars, and speculations that these might be products of an advanced civilization, allowed him to imagine an attempted Martian invasion of earth in *The War of the Worlds* (1898).

Wells also imagined advances that science then as now did not justify, such as time-travel in *The Time Machine* (1897) and anti-gravity in *First Men on the Moon* (1901). Modern scientific theory would make it appear that time-travel, anti-gravity, faster-than-light travel and other phenomena frequently found in science fiction stories are conceptually impossible. Such stories are consequently fantasies, in that the societies they describe cannot be reached from our own by any foreseeable change in science or technology. Nevertheless, a certain license is surely allowable—a science fiction writer may break a law of nature, if he or she understands that fact, and postulates, for the purposes of the story, some other law, made plausible by his or her art, in which he or she can seek refuge.

It is not surprising that a certain number of imagined advances in science and technology among the mass of science fiction stories have eventually come to pass. Television, giant planes, computers, atom bombs, spaceships and many other phenomena of today's real world were merely imagined phenomena in science fiction a generation ago. It is successful prophecy that has rescued science fiction (which entered a new phase in specialized magazines from 1926 on) from the contempt of the critics and has given it an air of almost frightening prescience.

This, of course, is almost entirely illusion. The percentage of successful prophecy in science fiction is very small. This small percentage gleams by contrast, however, since outside science fiction there has been, until very recently, virtually no attempt at futurism at all. Despite the actual experience of social change because of accelerated technological advance it seemed more comfortable for the general public and even for its leaders to form their decisions on the basis of past experience and to make no attempt to gauge, or even think about, possible additional change. But to continue to attempt to deal with the problems of the future on the basis of taking the past, or even the present, as the norm, could place humanity in extreme danger. The present is already uncomfortable because, in part, the changes the world has undergone in the past thirty years have been largely unforeseen.

Since World War II, the development of the transistor radio and of television has given the leaders of the non-industrialized portions of the world the ability to reach their people and to impose a successful nationalism never before felt. This has put an abrupt end to the European empires. The increasing use of oil and the increasing critical nature of that use in the last thirty years has given the Arab world a strength and power far out of proportion to its population or military capabilities. Did responsible national leaders foresee these changes and others at the time that WWII came to an end? Would we not have been better off if they had?

We may expect the changes of the next thirty years to be still more drastic. In that time, the world's population may nearly double, or may not double if the famines intervene. The development of satellites and optical fibers may introduce a new and an even more fundamental revolution in communication than any that have yet taken place. There is the possible continuing effect of computers, of the development of plans for space colonies, of the growing proportion of the aged, and the advancing role of women. All may have consequences that are very difficult to foresee in detail and yet must be taken into account if today's decisions are to have any meaning and are to help rescue civilization from the ever-present forces tending to dismantle it.

Can we find accurate predictions of those consequences in science fiction? Can science fiction serve as a blueprint of the future? Not very likely. Correct predictions may exist, yes, but they will be impossible to distinguish from the incorrect ones.

Science fiction, however, does predict change and does present change as inevitable: *that*, at least, is accurate. Science fiction readers come to expect change, therefore, and that way lies the beginning of wisdom. It should not be surprising, then, that in the course of the last thirty years, while the fortunes of fiction as a whole have been decaying, those of science fiction have been expanding and flourishing—especially among the young people who will have to face the future, whatever it is.

For the young, science fiction is relevant literature, for it is the only kind that tells them the world in which they now exist is not anything like the world they will be trying to guide when they are middle-aged. And if enough young people the world over begin assuming change to be inevitable, there may even be a chance of directing that change into the channels of salvation, instead of trusting to fickle circumstance.

expression and virtuosity. As well as individual lieder such as *The Erl King* and *The Trout* he wrote song cycles, among them *The Maid of the Mill* and *Winter's Journey*.

SCHULBERG, Budd (1914–), US novelist. He made his reputation with *What Makes Sammy Run?* (1941), a realistic novel about a self-made movie mogul. His best-known screen play, *On the Waterfront* (1954) won many awards.

SCHUMAN, Robert (1886–1963), French statesman. Prime minister 1947–48 and foreign minister 1948–52, he launched the "Schuman Plan" which resulted in the EUROPEAN COAL AND STEEL COMMUNITY, precursor of the COMMON MARKET.

SCHUMAN, William (1910–), US composer. His symphonies, chamber music, ballets and opera are known for their rhythmic vivacity and their debt to jazz. His 1942 cantata, *A Free Song*, won the first Pulitzer Prize for music.

SCHUMANN, Robert Alexander (1810–1856), major German composer whose compositions and music journal greatly influenced the music of his time. He did much to make known the early music of CHOPIN and BRAHMS. Though he wrote orchestral and chamber music, he best expressed his ardent Romanticism in his piano works and *lieder* (songs), most of the latter composed in 1840, when he married Clara Wieck, a leading pianist.

SCHUMPETER, Joseph Alois (1883–1950), Austrian-born Harvard economist. After studies of economic development and business cycles, he concluded that monopoly companies and government intervention would stifle the entrepreneur, the moving force of capitalism, and that socialism would result.

SCHUP, or **scup**, *Stenotomus chrysops*, marine fish of North America, occurring in schools. They are bottom-feeders, eating various invertebrates: worms, sand dollars and young squid.

SCHURZ, Carl (1829–1906), German-US statesman. Exiled after the German REVOLUTION of 1848, he supported Lincoln, who named him minister to Spain (1861). After Civil War service as a brigadier-general he was Republican senator for Mo., and an influential journalist, opposing President Grant's policies. He helped form the LIBERAL REPUBLICAN PARTY and was Hayes' secretary of the interior (1877–81).

SCHUSCHNIGG, Kurt von (1897–), Austrian politician. After Nazis murdered DOLLFUSS in 1934, he succeeded as chancellor, continued the authoritarian Christian Socialist government and tried in vain to preserve independence from Nazi Germany, which occupied Austria and imprisoned him 1938–45. He later taught 20 years in St. Louis.

SCHÜTZ, Heinrich (1585–1672), German composer. Apart from madrigals and *Dafne*, Germany's first opera, his works are vocal settings of sacred texts, in German, with or without instruments; his famous Passions influenced Bach.

SCHUYLER, Philip John (1733–1804), American soldier and statesman who served as major-general in the Continental army during the Revolutionary War. He served three terms in the N.Y. senate between 1780 and 1797, and was one of the first two US senators from N.Y. (1789–91 and 1797–98).

SCHUYLKILL RIVER, an important Penn. waterway and source of power, flowing 130mi SE from E central Penn. into the Delaware R at Philadelphia.

SCHWAB, Charles Michael (1862–1939), US industrialist. After helping to build and becoming president of the Carnegie Steel Co. (later J. Pierpoint Morgan's US Steel Corp.), he headed and expanded the rival Bethlehem Steel Corp. from 1903.

SCHWANN, Theodor (1810–1882), German biologist who proposed the CELL as the basic unit of animal, as well as of plant, structure (1839), thus laying the foundations of HISTOLOGY. He also discovered the ENZYME pepsin (1836).

SCHWARTZSCHILD RADIUS, the radius of the SPHERE into which a given body of known MASS must be compressed in order to become a BLACK HOLE.

SCHWARZKOPF, Elisabeth (1915–), German soprano, famous for operatic performances of Mozart, Strauss and Wagner in Vienna and London, and more recently for her expressive singing of German *lieder*.

SCHWARZWALD. See BLACK FOREST.

SCHWEITZER, Albert (1875–1965), German musician, philosopher, theologian, physician and missionary. An authority on Bach, and a noted performer of Bach's organ music, he abandoned an academic career in theology to study medicine and became (1913) a missionary doctor in French Equatorial Africa (now Gabon). He devoted his life to the hospital he founded there. His many writings include *The Quest of the Historical Jesus* (1906). Schweitzer won the 1952 Nobel Peace Prize for his inspiring humanitarian work.

SCHWINGER, Julian Seymour (1918–), US physicist who shared with FEYNMANN and TOMONAGA the 1965 Nobel Prize for Physics for his independent work in formulating the theory of quantum electrodynamics.

SCHWITTERS, Kurt (1887–1948), German artist and writer associated with DADAISM. He made collages and *"Merzbau,"* constructions of discarded objects, and poems of disparate print cuttings. He edited a Dadaist magazine, *Merz*, 1923–32.

SCIATICA, a characteristic pain in the distribution of the sciatic nerve in the LEG caused by compression or irritation of the nerve. The pain may resemble an electric shock and be associated with numbness and tingling in the skin area served by the nerve. One of the commonest causes is a SLIPPED DISK in the lower lumbar spine.

SCIENCE FICTION, literary genre which may loosely be defined as fantasy based upon speculation about scientific or social development. Probably the first true science fiction, or sf, work was *Frankenstein* (1818) by Mary SHELLEY; it developed a still popular theme, man's inability to control what his research may reveal. Only with the works of Jules VERNE and H. G. WELLS, however, did sf break away from supernatural fantasy. In the US in the 1920s "pulp" magazines popularized the form, but all too often debased it. John W. Campbell's magazine *Astounding* (founded 1937, now called *Analog*) revitalized the genre through its consistently high literary standard; it nurtured writers who today lead the field, among them Isaac ASIMOV, Robert HEINLEIN, Poul Anderson, Hal Clement, Eric Frank Russell and many others. Many sf writers, such as Asimov, Arthur C. CLARKE, Ray BRADBURY, Kurt VONNEGUT and John Wyndham have become household names; others, such as Fritz Leiber, Brian Aldiss, Robert Silverberg, Alfred Bester and Theodore Sturgeon, are less well known outside the field. The critical acclaim they and newer writers such as Larry Niven, Harlan Ellison and Ursula K. Le Guin receive indicates that the best science fiction may rank with the best contemporary general fiction.

SCIENTIFIC METHOD. Science (from Latin *scientia*, knowledge) is too diverse an undertaking to be constrained to follow any single method. Yet from the time of Lord BACON, well into the 20th century, the myth has persisted that true science follows a particular method—Bacon's celebrated "inductive method." This allegedly involved collecting a vast number of individual facts about a phenomenon, and then working out what general statements fitted those facts. After the 17th century nobody attempted to follow that program. In the 19th century, philosophers of science came to recognize the possible existence of the "hypothetico-deductive method." According to this model, the scientist studied the phenomena, dreamed up a hypothetical explanation, deduced some additional consequences of his explanation, and then devised experiments to see if these consequences were reflected in nature. If they were, he considered his theory (hypothesis) confirmed. But K. POPPER pointed to the logical fallacy in this last step—the theory had not been confirmed, but merely not falsified; it could, however, be worked with provisionally, so long as new tests did not discredit it. Philosophers of science now recognize that they cannot justly generalize about the psychology of scientific discovery; their role must be confined to the criticism of theories once they have been devised. Historians of science, meanwhile, have pointed to the importance in scientific discovery of "external factors" such as the contemporary intellectual context and the structures of the institutions of science. Once distinct terms—"theory," "model," "hypothesis," "explanation," "description," and "law"—are all now seen to represent different ways of looking at the same thing—the units in what constitutes scientific knowledge at any given time. Indeed there is still no general understanding of how scientists become dissatisfied with a once deeply-entrenched theory and come to replace it with what, for the moment, seems a better version.

SCILLA VIOLACEA, or **silver squill,** a bulbous, succulent plant which produces silver-spotted, olive-green foliage, with maroon coloration on the underside, and spikes of blue bell-shaped flowers. It is a popular house plant since it tolerates a wide range of light, heat, humidity and soil moisture. Propagation is achieved by dividing large plants. Family: Liliaceae.

SCILLY ISLANDS, group of rocky islets, 30mi W of the S tip of Cornwall, SW England. The population (2428) of the five inhabited islands (6sq mi) engage in tourism and flower growing. The capital, Hugh Town, is on St. Mary's Island.

SCINTILLATION COUNTER, instrument for detecting ionizing radiations. A brief localized light flash is produced in a PHOSPHOR when ionizing radiation such as X-rays or protons is incident on it. In early counters, the flashes were counted directly using a microscope, but now they are converted into electric impulses by a photomultiplier and counted electronically.

SCIOTO RIVER, rises in W Ohio and flows 237mi E and S to the Ohio R at Portsmouth, S Ohio.

SCIPIO, name of a patrician family of ancient Rome which became famous during the PUNIC WARS. **Publius Cornelius Scipio** (236–184 BC), called Africanus Major, conquered HANNIBAL in the second Punic War. He drove the Carthaginians from Spain, invaded Africa, and forced Hannibal to return from Italy to meet him. The resulting battle of Zama (202 BC) destroyed Carthaginian power. **Publius Cornelius Scipio Aemilianus** (185–129 BC), his adopted grandson, called Africanus Minor, commanded against Carthage in the third Punic War, capturing and destroying the city in 146 BC. He was an admirer of Greek culture, and his friends included TERENCE and POLYBIUS.

SCISSORTAIL, *Muscivora forficata*, a FLYCATCHER of the southern US and Mexico, characterized by an extremely long, forked tail.

SCITUATE, town in SE Mass. on the Atlantic 20mi SE of Boston. It is a summer resort, with some truck farming and fishing. Pop 16973.

SCLC. See SOUTHERN CHRISTIAN LEADERSHIP CONFERENCE.

SCOLIOSIS, a curvature of the spine to one side, with twisting. It occurs as a congenital defect or may be secondary to spinal diseases including neurofibromatosis. Severe scoliosis, often associated with kyphosis, causes HUNCHBACK deformity, loss of height and may restrict CARDIAC or LUNG function.

SCONE, Stone of, coronation seat of Scottish kings, removed to Westminster Abbey by Edward I in 1296. Scottish nationalists reclaimed it briefly 1950–51. Traditionally, Scone village, E Scotland, was the PICTS' capital.

SCOPES TRIAL, famous 1925 prosecution of a biology teacher for breaking a new Tenn. law forbidding the teaching of EVOLUTION in state-supported schools. Interwar religious fundamentalism secured such laws in several S states. For the defense Clarence DARROW unsuccessfully pitted himself against the orthodoxy of William BRYAN; the Tenn. supreme court reversed the conviction on a technicality. The defense had sought to challenge the law's constitutionality, but it was repealed only in 1967.

SCOPOLAMINE, or **hyoscine**, anticholinergic drug related to ATROPINE and used widely in premedication for ANESTHESIA. It tends to be a central-nervous-system DEPRESSANT but otherwise resembles atropine in reducing secretions, GASTROINTESTINAL TRACT activity and vagus effects on the HEART (causing increased PULSE rate) and in dilating the pupils of the EYES. It may cause confusion in the elderly. Other common uses include treatment of MOTION SICKNESS, use as a mild SEDATIVE and in PARKINSON'S DISEASE.

SCORE, in music. See NOTATION.

SCOREL, Jan van (1495–1562), Dutch painter. Many of his fine portraits survive. His religious works, largely destroyed by 16th-century Protestant iconoclasts, reflected his wide travels and helped introduce the Italian style to Holland.

SCORESBY SOUND, a large inlet on the E central coast of Greenland. It has fjords over 100mi long and islands. The Scoresbysund fishing and hunting settlement lies N of the entrance.

SCORIA, a vesicular form of LAVA, the vesicles having been formed by gases escaping from the lava while it was still hot.

SCORPIO (the Scorpion), a medium-sized constellation on the ECLIPTIC; the eighth sign of the ZODIAC. Scorpio contains the bright star ANTARES.

SCORPIONFISHES, a family, Scorpaenidae, of heavily-built fishes of temperate and tropical seas. They are bottom-livers with large mouths, and many species are ornamented with bony or fleshy spines or tubercles. Most species also have venom glands in these spines or poison spines in the fins and they are among the most poisonous of fishes.

SCORPION FLIES, an order, Mecoptera, of carnivorous flies, so called because adult males have the tip of the abdomen enlarged and curled upward. All have a characteristic elongated snout, or rostrum, which bears the biting mouthparts.

SCORPIONS, a homogeneous group of terrestrial arachnids (see ARACHNIDA) having two formidable palps (claws) held in front of the head and a stinging tail curled forward over the back. All scorpions have a poisonous sting but few are dangerous to man. The sting is usually used in defense, or with the palps in catching prey. Scorpions are restricted to dry, warm regions of the world and feed on grasshoppers, crickets, spiders and other arthropods.

SCOTCH. See WHISKEY.

SCOTCH-IRISH, the people of Scottish descent who emigrated to North America from Northern Ireland after 1713. They were largely descendants of the Scots who had colonized Northern Ireland.

SCOTCH PLAINS, mainly residential township in N.J., about 200mi SW of New York City. Pop 22279.

SCOTLAND, constituent kingdom of the UK (see GREAT BRITAIN). Covering N Britain and the HEBRIDES, ORKNEY and SHETLAND islands, it is 30414sq mi in area. Over 50% of the population is urban; major cities include Edinburgh, the capital and cultural center, Glasgow, the industrial center, Aberdeen and Dundee. English is spoken everywhere, but some 77000 Scots in the NW also speak GAELIC. Scotland was one of the first industrialized countries; its economy rests on iron and steel, aluminum, shipbuilding, chemicals, North Sea oil and the immensely lucrative whisky industry. Agriculture, mainly grain, sheep and cattle, and fishing are also important. Educational standards are among the world's highest, and cultural life flourishes. Scotland's original inhabitants were the PICTS, displaced by the Scots, Britons and Angles. United under KENNETH I MACALPIN, the country maintained an embattled independence from England, ensured by ROBERT THE BRUCE. A brief Renaissance flowering under JAMES IV ended in disaster at FLODDEN FIELD, and in the turmoil of the REFORMATION. James VI (JAMES I of England) united the crowns of Scotland and England, but union of government came only in 1707. It was widely resented, and England fueled this by attacking Scottish autonomy and prosperity; this helped incite the two JACOBITE rebellions (1715 and 1745). A great cultural rebirth followed, but also the hardships of the INDUSTRIAL REVOLUTION and Highland depopulation for sheep farming. Today Scotland, though closely linked to England, is tending to favor a greater degree of autonomy.

SCOTLAND, Church of. See CHURCH OF SCOTLAND.

SCOTLAND YARD, headquarters of the Criminal Investigation Department (C.I.D.) of the London Metropolitan Police. Its jurisdiction covers 786sq mi containing more than eight million people. It also coordinates police work throughout Britain and provides national and international criminal records.

SCOTS, English-based dialect of the Scottish Lowlands (not GAELIC, a different language). Its literary form flourished from the 13th to the mid-16th century, in the poetry of William DUNBAR and Gavin Douglas, and was revived by Allan RAMSAY and Robert BURNS in the 18th century.

SCOTT, urban township in SW Pa., SW of Pittsburgh. Pop 21856.

SCOTT, Dred. See DRED SCOTT DECISION.

SCOTT, Hugh Doggett, Jr. (1900–), US lawyer and politician, Republican senator for Pa. from 1958, and Republican minority leader from 1969.

SCOTT, Robert Falcon (1868–1912), British explorer remembered for his fatal attempt to be the first to reach the South Pole. In 1911 he led four men with sleds 950mi from the Ross Ice Shelf to the South Pole. They arrived on Jan. 18, 1912, only to discover that AMUNDSEN had reached the Pole a month before. Scurvy, frostbite, starvation and bitter weather hampered the grueling two-month return journey, and the last three survivors died in a blizzard, only 11mi from the next supply point.

SCOTT, Sir Walter (1771–1832), Scottish poet and the foremost Romantic novelist in the English language. Scott was the inventor of the historical novel, and his vivid recreations of Scotland's past were widely read throughout Europe. He started by writing popular narrative poems, including *The Lay of the Last Minstrel* (1805). After these successes he turned to fiction, and completed 28 novels and many nonfiction works. His novels included *Waverley* (1814), *The Heart of Midlothian* (1818) and *Ivanhoe* (1819).

SCOTT, Winfield (1786–1866), US political and military leader, known as "Old Fuss and Feathers" for his obsession with procedure and detail and for his elaborate uniforms. Scott became a hero for his part in the WAR OF 1812. He was active in the Indian wars and in 1846 was appointed a commander in the MEXICAN WAR, and captured Mexico City. In 1852 he was the unsuccessful Whig presidential candidate. He commanded the Union Army until 1861.

SCOTTISH DEERHOUND, breed of dog, 28in–32in high at the shoulder, with rough gray-blue or fawn coat. Noted for its great speed, it was bred in Scotland for hunting deer.

SCOTTISH FOLD, cat breed with drooping ears, produced from a mutation which appeared in Scotland in 1961.

SCOTTISH TERRIER, old Scottish breed of terrier now bred as a pet. It is 10in at the shoulder, has a large head, short legs, a deep broad chest and powerful shoulder muscles. It also has a very hard coat of wiry hair.

SCOTTSBLUFF, city in W Neb., on the North Platte R, on the OREGON TRAIL, now an agricultural processing and distribution center. Pop 14 507.

SCOTTS BLUFF NATIONAL MONUMENT, large promontory in W Neb. rising 800ft over the North Platte R, a landmark on the OREGON TRAIL and Mormon Trail.

SCOTTSDALE, residential city in central Ariz., site of Frank Lloyd WRIGHT's Taliesin West Architectural School. Pop 67 823.

SCRANTON, industrial and commercial city in NE Pa., seat of Lackawanna Co., at the heart of the Pa. anthracite coal region. It manufactures textiles and heavy machinery. Pop 103 564.

SCREAMERS, three species of South American birds of the family Anhimidae. Related to GEESE and SWANS, screamers differ in having unwebbed feet and longer legs. They are ground-living birds found near water or in marshes. Two spurs on the leading edge of the wings are used in fighting.

SCREE. See TALUS.

SCREW. See ARCHIMEDES; BOLTS AND SCREWS; MACHINE; PROPELLER.

SCREW PINE, trees and shrubs of the genus *Pandanus*. They have palm-like leathery leaves that are spirally arranged and are used for thatching, making mats, etc. They are native to the Old World tropics but have been introduced to temperate regions. Many varieties are cultivated for their ornamental foliage, growing well at average house temperatures and in a moderately sunny position. The soil should be kept evenly moist and the foliage misted often. Propagation is by planting the offsets produced. Family: Pandanaceae.

SCRIABIN, Alexander Nikolayevich (1872–1915), Russian composer and brilliant pianist, whose work was based on chords of fourths. He wanted performances of his *Prometheus* (1909–10) to be accompanied by a play of colored lights corresponding to the musical tones.

SCRIBE, professional copier of books by hand before the development of printing, found in royal courts. The name was earlier applied to the ancient Hebrew teachers of the Law, the *Sopherim*, the first of whom was EZRA (c400 BC). Sopherim revised and transmitted the text of the Old Testament, extending the basis of the Oral Law.

SCRIBE, Augustin Eugène (1791–1861), French playwright and librettist. Besides his libretto for VERDI's *The Sicilian Vespers* he also wrote librettos for AUBER and MEYERBEER.

SCRIPPS, Edward Wyllis (1854–1926), US newspaper publisher, founder of the first newspaper chain and of the wire service that eventually became United Press International. Beginning in the Midwest and West his chain eventually included 34 papers in 15 different states.

SCROFULA, TUBERCULOSIS of the LYMPH nodes of the neck, usually acquired by drinking MILK infected with bovine or atypical mycobacteria, and involving enlargement of the nodes with formation of a cold ABSCESS. The eradication of tuberculosis in cattle has substantially reduced the incidence. Treatment includes antituberculous CHEMOTHERAPY. It used to be called the **King's Evil** as the royal touch was believed to be curative.

SCRUB TYPHUS, or **Tsutsugamushi disease**, a disease caused by RICKETTSIA carried by mites, and leading to ulceration at the site of INOCULATION, followed by FEVER, headache, lymph node enlargement and generalized rash. COUGH and chest X-RAY abnormalities are common. ENCEPHALITIS and MYOCARDITIS may occur with fatal outcome. It occurs mainly in the Far East and Australia and is generally seen in people who work on scrubland. TETRACYCLINES eradicate the infection.

SCUBA. See AQUALUNG.

SCUBA DIVING. See DIVING; SKIN DIVING.

SCULPINS, the name given to marine relatives of BULLHEADS, family Cottidae. All are cryptically-colored, bottom-living fishes with large heads. They may grow to 600mm (2ft) in length.

SCULPTURE, the artistic creation of three-dimensional forms in materials such as stone, metal, wood, or even canvas or foam rubber. (This article deals mainly with Western sculpture. For other periods of sculpture see: AEGEAN CIVILIZATION; BYZANTINE ART AND ARCHITECTURE; CHINESE ART; EGYPTIAN ART AND ARCHITECTURE; JAPANESE ART AND ARCHITECTURE; PRE-COLUMBIAN ART; PREHISTORIC AND PRIMITIVE ART.)

High cost and durability tended to make ancient sculpture an official and conservative art form. This is evident in the style of the monumental sculpture of Egypt, which hardly changed in 2 000 years. Greek sculptors, who set enduring standards of taste and technique, aimed to portray beauty of soul as well as body, and idealized the human form. In the Archaic period (about 630–480 BC) Egyptian influence showed in their frontal, stylized figures, with little movement or emotion. Greater realism led to the classical perfection of PHIDIAS, and in the 4th century to PRAXITELES, with his more sensuous forms and wider range of expression. The HELLENISTIC AGE culture favored an exaggerated style of which the LAOCOÖN sculpture and the WINGED VICTORY OF SAMOTHRACE are fine examples. Roman sculpture was deeply indebted to Greek art, but was also under ETRUSCAN influence, and excelled at realistic portraiture.

The Western tradition revived c1000 AD with the elongated, stylized figures of ROMANESQUE, leading to the more graceful and expressive sculptures of GOTHIC ART. RENAISSANCE sculpture, starting about 1350, was dominated by the Italians. GHIBERTI and DONATELLO treated classical models in a new spirit, and MICHELANGELO gave to works such as his *David* an inner tension quite foreign to classicism. The elegant MANNERISM of Benvenuto CELLINI and the elaborate BAROQUE of BERNINI gave place about 1800 to the neo-classical reaction of HOUDON, CANOVA, FLAXMAN and THORVALDSEN. The greatest 19th-century sculptor, RODIN, created a style of partially unworked figures, such as his *Balzac*, influencing EPSTEIN. This century has seen the abstract art of BRANCUSI and ARP, while Henry MOORE and GIACOMETTI showed interest in the human form. Outstanding American sculptors are David SMITH and CALDER, who invented MOBILES.

SCURVY, or VITAMIN C deficiency, involving disease of the SKIN and mucous membranes, poor healing and ANEMIA; in infancy BONE growth is also impaired. It may develop over a few months of low dietary vitamin C, beginning with malaise and weakness. Skin bleeding around HAIR follicles is characteristic, as are swollen, bleeding gums. Treatment and prevention consist of adequate dietary vitamin C.

SCUTARI. See SHKODER (Albania); USKUDAR (Turkey).

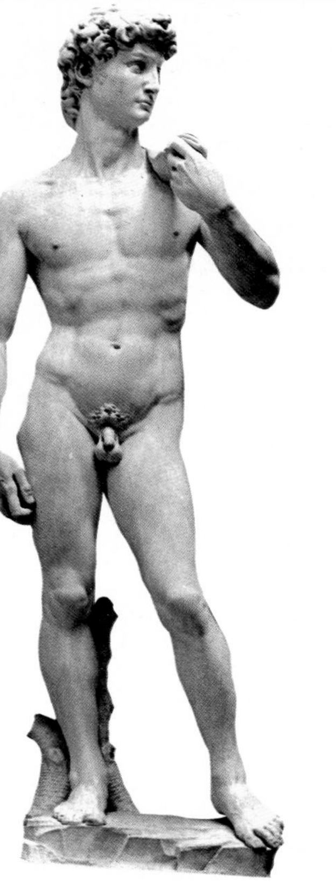

Michelangelo's colossal marble statue of *David* (1501–04), commemorating the restoration of republican rule in Florence.

SCYLLA AND CHARYBDIS, perils faced by ODYSSEUS, in the Straits of Messina. Scylla was a six-headed monster who ate all within reach, Charybdis a whirlpool. "Between Scylla and Charybdis" means a straight, narrow course between two dangers.

SCYTHIANS, ancient nomadic people from Central Asia or possibly W Siberia, one of the earliest peoples to learn horsemanship. After the 9th century BC they spread into E Europe and S Russia making raids into the settled Near East. Their power was curbed by the MEDES about 600 BC. The kingdom of the Royal Scyths, 9th–2nd century BC, was defeated by the SARMATIANS. The wealth of the Scythians was shown by their gold and silver objects and jewelry.

SEA. See OCEANS.

SEA ANEMONES, an order, Actiniaria, of solitary anthozoan CNIDARIA, familiar animals of rocky shores. Anemones are polypoid, the medusoid phase (see ALTERNATION OF GENERATIONS) of the life history of HYDROZOA and JELLYFISHES being absent. The polyp has a short, usually stubby, cylindrical body attached to the substrate by a basal disk. On the broad oral surface, numerous retractile tentacles are arranged in rings around the mouth. These and nematocysts, sting cells, are used for capturing prey.

SEABORG, Glenn Theodore (1912–   ), US physicist who shared the 1951 Nobel Prize for Physics with E. W. MCMILLAN for his work in discovering several ACTINIDES (see TRANSURANIUM ELEMENTS): in 1944 AMERICIUM and CURIUM, and in 1949 BERKELIUM and CALIFORNIUM. Later discoveries were EINSTEINIUM (1952), FERMIUM (1953), MENDELEVIUM (1955) and NOBELIUM (1957).

SEABURY, Samuel (1729–1796), American clergyman, first bishop of the Protestant EPISCOPAL CHURCH. His consecration, refused by the English bishops, was carried out by the Scottish Episcopal Church (1784) and confirmed by his own church in 1789.

SEA COWS, an order, Sirenia, of aquatic mammals. Probably evolved from a marsh-dwelling ancestor related to the elephants, all the Sirenia are completely aquatic and seal-like, with the forelimbs modified into flippers and the hindlimbs fused into the horizontal flukes of a whale-like tail.

SEA CUCUMBERS, a class, Holothuroidea, of ECHINODERMS found in seas worldwide. They are sausage-shaped with a mouth surrounded by a ring of

Cow of the Gray or Atlantic seal, a species common to both sides of the Atlantic.

tentacles at one end and an anus at the other. The body is covered with a thick, leathery skin containing spicules of CALCITE and is usually slimy. Most are bottom-dwelling forms. Sea cucumbers are eaten as bêche-de-mer.

SEA-FLOOR SPREADING, key phenomenon supporting the theory of PLATE TECTONICS. Along midocean ridges (see OCEANS) material emerges from the EARTH's mantle to form new oceanic crust. This material, primarily BASALT, spreads out to either side of the ridges at a rate of the order of 10–50mm/yr. New laid down basalt is able to "fossilize" the prevailing geomagnetism (see PALEOMAGNETISM): the main evidence for sea-floor spreading comes from the symmetric pattern of alternately magnetized strips of basalt on either side of the ridges.

SEAFORD, hamlet in SE N.Y. in S Long Island. Settled in 1643, it is now a residential suburb of New York City. Pop 17 379.

SEA GULLS. See GULLS.

SEA HORSES, small, highly-specialized fishes closely related to PIPEFISHES. Unique among fishes in that the head is set at right angles to the body, they swim with the body held vertically. The body is encased in bony rings or plates. There is no tailfin and the hind part of the body is prehensile and may anchor the fish in seaweed. Males brood the eggs in special pouches on the belly.

SEA ISLANDS, chain of more than 100 islands in the Atlantic off the coast of S.C., Ga., and Fla. Settled by the Spanish in the 16th century, the islands were in the early 19th century the first important North American cotton-growing region. Many are now resorts or wild-life sanctuaries.

SEAL BEACH, resort city in S Cal. on the Pacific Ocean, site of a US naval weapons station. Pop 24 441.

SEA LILIES, marine ECHINODERMS, order Articulata, which with the FEATHER STARS make up the class Crinoidea. This class comprises the remnants of a once abundant group of stalked echinoderms: sea lilies look much like BRITTLE STARS or feather stars on stems. The body, bearing long feathery food-gathering arms, is borne on a flexible stem of ossicles bonded together by ligaments, by which the lily is attached to the substratum. (See also CRINOIDS.)

SEA LIONS, family Otariidae, eared seals, differing from true SEALS in having external ears and an almost hairless body. These are the animals most commonly seen in circuses and zoos. They are large creatures—males may measure between 2–3m (6.6–9.8ft)—and are active marine carnivores, feeding on fishes, squids and other mollusks.

SEALS, members of the mammal order Pinnipedia, which includes both the SEALIONS, and the True seals of the family Phocidae. True seals have no external ears and have a thick coat of strong guard hairs. Seals are animals of the colder seas of both hemispheres. Northern species (subfamily Phocinae) include the Bearded seal, the Gray seal and the Common or Harbor seal. Southern species (subfamily Monachinae) include the Monk seals, ELEPHANT SEALS, Crabeater and Weddell seals. Most seals are gregarious; all are pelagic and many come ashore only to breed. A single, light-colored pup is born and further mating takes place immediately afterward. Males form harems of females on the breeding grounds. Many species are now uncommon, having been formerly extensively hunted for their skins and meat.

SEALYHAM TERRIER, Welsh breed of terrier, formerly used for hunting badgers, foxes and otters, but now pets. Standing 10in at the shoulder, the dogs are usually white, heavy-boned, with short legs.

SEA PENS, motile colonial forms of soft CORAL. The polyps are arranged on either side of a central axis arising as buds from the distal end of a primary polyp. The whole gives the appearance of an old-fashioned quill pen.

SEARCH, Right of. See RIGHT OF SEARCH.

SEARCH WARRANT, in law, a court order issued to give law officers the authority to enter and search private premises for evidence, persons, contraband goods, or illegal equipment such as counterfeiting-machinery. "Unreasonable searches and seizures" are forbidden in the Fourth Amendment to the US Constitution, and the scope of such a warrant is severely limited.

SEA ROBINS, American name for GURNARDS, a family of bottom-living marine fishes with armored heads. The name derives from the ability of many species to produce audible sounds.

SEARS TOWER, tallest inhabited building in the world (1 454ft), built in the mid-1970s, Chicago office building of Sears Roebuck. Prefabricated welded steel frames form a vertical core for the 110 floors.

SEASICKNESS. See MOTION SICKNESS.

SEASIDE, city in W Cal. on Monterey Bay. Its main industry is tourism. Pop 35 395.

SEA SNAKES, a family, Hydrophidae, of poisonous SNAKES that live permanently in the sea and are fully-adapted to an aquatic existence, swimming with a sculling action of the paddle-shaped tail. They are fully air-breathing but can submerge for long periods. They feed on small fishes, immobilizing them first with a potent, fast-acting venom.

SEASONS, divisions of the year, characterized by cyclical changes in the predominant weather pattern. In the temperate zones there are four seasons: spring, summer, autumn (fall) and winter. These result from the constant inclination of the earth's polar axis ($66\frac{1}{2}°$ from the ECLIPTIC) as the earth orbits the sun: during summer in the N Hemisphere the N Pole is tilted toward the sun, in winter—when the solar radiation strikes the hemisphere more obliquely—away from the sun. The summer and winter SOLSTICES (about June 21 and Dec. 22), popularly known as midsummer and midwinter, strictly speaking mark the beginnings of summer and winter, respectively. Thus spring begins on the day of the vernal EQUINOX (about Mar. 21) and autumn at the autumnal equinox (about Sept. 23).

SEA SQUIRTS, a class, Ascidiacea, of sedentary marine TUNICATES. They are flask-shaped, and at the end of the body not attached to the substrate are two siphons. Seawater, carrying particles of food, enters by one of these siphons, before the water, with the food strained from it, passes through slits in the gut wall and is exhaled through the other siphon. These curious animals are in fact CHORDATES, for while adults have adapted to a sessile life, the larvae show many unspecialized features comparable with the structure of the VERTEBRATES which have evolved from these, or related forms.

SEATO. See SOUTH EAST ASIA TREATY ORGANIZATION.

SEATTLE, largest city in Wash., the financial and commercial center and major port of the Pacific Northwest, seat of King Co. Seattle lies on Elliott Bay (Puget Sound), and its chief industries are aerospace production, steel, shipbuilding, food-processing and chemicals. Settled in 1852, Seattle rapidly expanded after the 1897 Alaska gold rush, and again following the boom created by WWII. Pop 530 831.

SEA URCHINS, spiny marine ECHINODERMS with spherical to somewhat flattened form, occurring worldwide. The basic structure is a sphere of 20 columns of calcareous plates. Within this "test," the internal structures: gut, gonads and water-vascular system, are looped around the inside wall. The center of the sphere is empty. The test bears tubercles and short spines, and also the pedicellaria: motile, pincer-like organs which clear the surface of detritus. Tube feet protrude through pores in the test, arranged in double rows down the sides.

SEAWEED, popular name for the ALGAE found around coasts from the shore to fairly deep water. Commonest are the brown algae or wracks. Some, such as bladderwrack, clothe the rocks between tides; others live up to 12m (39.4ft) deep. The large brown algae (KELPS) sometimes form thick beds of long, tangled fronds, with tough, well-anchored stems. GULFWEED is another widespread species. Delicate green and red seaweeds live mainly in rock pools. Seaweeds provide food and shelter to sea animals; many are used by man for food, fertilizer, iodine and gelatine.

SEBACEOUS GLANDS, small GLANDS in the SKIN which secrete *sebum*, a fatty substance that acts as a protective and water repellant layer on skin and allows the epidermis to retain its suppleness. Sebum secretion is fairly constant but varies from individual to individual. Obstructed sebaceous glands become BLACKHEADS which are the basis for ACNE.

SEBAGO SALMON, or Landlocked salmon. See OUANANICHE.

SEBASTIAN, Saint (d. c288), early Christian martyr. Legend relates that he was a captain under the Roman Emperor DIOCLETIAN, and was sentenced, as a Christian, to die by archery (a scene recorded in many Italian paintings). He survived but was finally clubbed to death in the Amphitheater.

SEBASTIAN (1554–1578), King of Portugal, successor (1557) to his grandfather JOHN III. A religious fanatic, he refused to marry but led a Crusade to Morocco, was defeated and killed in battle at ALCAZARQUIVIR. Rumors that he was alive led to persistent belief in his return to deliver Portugal from her 1580 defeat by Spain.

SEBASTIANO DEL PIOMBO (c1485–1547), Venetian painter. The warm colors of his early portraits and religious works show GIORGIONE's influence. He moved to Rome in his 20s and was associated with MICHELANGELO. His portrait of Columbus hangs in the Metropolitan Museum.

SEBASTOPOL. See SEVASTOPOL.

SEBORRHEA. See DANDRUFF.

SEC. See SECURITIES AND EXCHANGE COMMISSION.

SECANT. See CIRCLE; TRIGONOMETRY.

SECAUCUS, town in NE N.J., next to Jersey City on the Hackensack R. There are metal, chemical, clothing and food industries. Pop 13 228.

SECESSION, in US history, the withdrawal of the Southern states from the Federal Union, 1860–61. A right of secession, arising from a STATES' RIGHTS interpretation of the Constitution, was claimed in the early 1800s by the defeated Federalist Party in New England. The concept died in the US when the CIVIL WAR ended in the Southern states' defeat.

SECOND (s), in SI UNITS, the base unit of TIME, defined as the duration of 9 192 631 770 periods of the radiation corresponding to the transition between the two hyperfine levels of the ground state of the CESIUM-133 atom.

SECOND COMING, or **Parousia** (Greek: arrival), in Christian ESCHATOLOGY, the return of JESUS CHRIST in glory to end the present order, to raise the dead (see RESURRECTION) and to summon all to the LAST JUDGMENT. The Second Coming was prophesied by Christ himself and by St. Paul; the early Church, and many ADVENTIST groups since, regarded it as imminent; some cults such as the JEHOVAH'S WITNESSES have repeatedly forecast its date, predicting, among others, 1914 and 1975.

SECOND SIGHT, the power to "see" future or distant occurrences or objects. See CLAIRVOYANCE.

SECRETARY BIRD, *Sagittarius serpentarius*, a large long-legged, terrestrial bird of Africa, named for the untidy crest resembling quill pens tucked behind the ears. They are predators, the only terrestrial members of the order Falconiformes, feeding on rodents, insects and snakes in short grassland.

SECRETIN, a HORMONE of the GASTROINTESTINAL TRACT secreted by cells in the duodenum EPITHELIUM in response to the presence of food and increasing the secretion of pancreas ENZYMES and BILE.

SECRETION. See GLANDS.

SECRET POLICE, an organization, usually beyond democratic control, which aims its largely covert work at silencing political opposition or "threats to national security." Methods may range from surveillance to torture and murder. Notorious systems have been FOUCHÉ's in revolutionary France, the tsarist *Okhrana* and later the CHEKA, KGB and MVD in Russia, the German GESTAPO and the Italian Fascist *Ovra*.

SECRET SERVICE, UNITED STATES, a branch of the US TREASURY Department. Established 1865 to suppress counterfeiting of currency, it became responsible for protecting the president after the assassination of President William MCKINLEY (1901). It now also guards the vice-president, the president-elect and their families.

SECRET SOCIETIES, interest-groups with secret membership, initiation rituals and recognition signs. Most have specific aims: religious (ROSICRUCIANS; the MYSTERIES of ancient Greece); political (CAMORRA; CARBONARI; KU KLUX KLAN); social or benevolent (as in MASONRY and college fraternities); or criminal (MAFIA; MOLLY MAGUIRES).

SECURITIES AND EXCHANGE COMMISSION (SEC), an independent agency of the US government set up in 1934 to protect investors in securities (stocks and bonds). It requires disclosures of the structure of all public companies and registration of all securities exchanged. SEC hears complaints, initiates investigations, issues brokerage licenses, and has broad powers to penalize fraud. (See STOCKS AND STOCK MARKET.)

SEDALIA, city in W central Mo., seat of Pettis Co. Site of the state fair, it processes farm products and has diversified industry. Pop 22 847.

SEDAN, manufacturing city in NE France, on the Meuse R, Ardennes department, where the 1870 Franco-Prussian War ended with Napoleon III's defeat, and his surrender with 80 000 men. Pop 23 037.

SEDATIVES, DRUGS that reduce ANXIETY and induce relaxation without causing SLEEP; many are also hypnotics, drugs that in adequate doses may induce sleep. BARBITURATES were among the earlier drugs used in sedation, but they have fallen into disfavor because of addiction, side-effects, dangers of overdosage and the availability of safer alternatives. Benzodiazepines (e.g., Valium, Librium) are now the most often used and have proved safe and effective.

SEDER. See PASSOVER.

SEDGE, grass-like plants of the genus *Carex*, which grow in damp habitats. They have triangular, flattened or cylindrical stems and the leaves arise from sheaths that enclose the stem. Other common plants belonging to the sedge family (Cyperaceae) include BULRUSHES, COTTON GRASS and PAPYRUS.

SEDIMENTARY ROCKS, one of the three main ROCK types of the earth's crust. They consist of weathered (see EROSION) particles of igneous, metamorphic or even sedimentary rock transported, usually by water, and deposited in distinct strata. They may also be of organic origin, as in COAL, or of volcanic origin, as are PYROCLASTIC ROCKS. Most common are SHALE, SANDSTONE and LIMESTONE. Sedimentary rocks frequently contain FOSSILS, as well as most of the earth's MINERAL resources.

SEDIMENTATION, the processes whereby particles of solid material are transported and deposited elsewhere. The particles are the product of weathering (see EROSION); the transporting agent may be wind, water, GLACIERS or an AVALANCHE or landslide. Products of sedimentation thus include DRIFT, OOZES, TALUS and SEDIMENTARY ROCK.

SEDITION ACT (1798). See ALIEN AND SEDITION ACTS.

SEEBECK, Thomas Johann (1770–1831), German physicist who discovered but could not explain the Seebeck effect (1821). This was the first thermoelectric effect to be discovered (see THERMOCOUPLE).

SEECKT, Hans von (1866–1936), German general. After WWI he organized with some secrecy a highly efficient "nucleus" army despite VERSAILLES treaty restrictions, partly with Russian assistance.

SEED, the mature reproductive body of ANGIOSPERMS and GYMNOSPERMS. It also represents a resting stage which enables the PLANTS to survive through unfavorable conditions. The GERMINATION period varies widely from plant to plant. Seeds develop from the fertilized ovule. Each seed is covered with a tough coat called a testa and it contains a young plant or embryo. In most seeds three main regions of embryo can be recognized. A radicle, which gives rise to the root, a plumule which forms the shoot and one or two seed leaves or COTYLEDONS which may or may not be taken above ground during germination. Plants that produce one seed leaf are called MONOCOTYLEDONS and those that produce two, DICOTYLEDONS. The seed also contains enough stored food (often in the cotyledons) to support embryo growth during and after germination. It is this stored food which is of value to man. Flowering plants produce their seeds inside a FRUIT, but the seeds of conifers lie naked on the scales of the cone. Distribution of seeds is usually by wind, animals or water and the form of seeds is often adapted to a specific means of dispersal. (See also POLLINATION; REPRODUCTION.)

SEED SNIPE, four species of South American wading birds of the family Thinocoridae. Ground-nesting birds, which feed on seeds and leaves, they take their name from the strong behavioral resemblance to the SNIPE including an erratic zig-zag flight when disturbed.

SEEGER, Alan (1888–1916), US poet. He joined the French Foreign Legion at the outbreak of WWI and was killed in France. Among his *Collected Poems* (1916) is the famous "I Have a Rendezvous with Death."

SEEGER, Pete (1919–   ), US folk singer. A master of the 5-string banjo and 12-string guitar, he led the 1950s revival of folk with his group the Weavers. Many of his own freedom and pacifist songs have become classics of folk music.

SEEING EYE DOGS, dogs trained to guide the blind. The majority of US guide dogs are GERMAN SHEPHERDS, and are schooled by The Seeing Eye Inc., founded in 1929 by Dorothy Harrison Eustis.

SEEKONK, residential and light industrial town in SE Mass., 10mi NW of Fall River. Pop 11 116.

SEFERIS, George (1900–1971), Greek poet and diplomat. His lyrical, symbolic verse sets tragic modern events against the background of Greece's past. It includes *Turning Point* (1931) and *Poems* (1940). Seferis won the 1963 Nobel Prize for Literature.

SEGAL, George (1924–   ), US sculptor. Born in New York City, he is best known for his life-size white plaster casts of people, placed in such settings as a doorway or behind a steering wheel.

SEGESTA, ancient city of NW Sicily. It was an ally of Carthage but went over to Rome in the first of the PUNIC WARS. Its ruins (5th–1st century BC) include a theater, temples, baths and houses.

SEGHERS, Hercules (c1589–c1638), Dutch etcher and painter famous for his fantastic, forbidding landscapes. To convey light effects he used CHIAROSCURO and, in his masterly etchings, AQUATINT (the first to do so) and colored paper.

SEGMENT. See CIRCLE.

SEGMENTATION, the serial repetition of structures or organs along the long axis of the animal body. Segmentation is characteristic of many groups, notably the ANNELIDA.

SEGO LILY, *Calochortus nutalli* the state flower of Ut., a perennial plant found in western North America. It has bell-shaped flowers that are white, tinted with yellowish-green. The bulbs were once eaten locally. Family: Liliaceae.

SEGOVIA, historic provincial capital in central Spain, 40mi NNW of Madrid. Of minor industrial importance, it has a fortified palace (Alcázar), Gothic cathedral and great Roman aqueduct, still in use. Pop 41 880.

SEGOVIA, Andrés (1893–   ), Spanish guitarist, most celebrated of modern players. He has done much to revive serious interest in the guitar, transcribing many pieces for it. FALLA, VILLA-LOBOS and others have composed works for him.

SEGRÈ, Emilio Gino (1950–   ), Italian-born US nuclear physicist who shared with O. CHAMBERLAIN the 1959 Nobel Prize for Physics for their discovery (1955) of the antiproton (see ANTIMATTER). Earlier he had discovered TECHNETIUM, the first artificially produced ELEMENT (1937).

SEGREGATION. See INTEGRATION.

SEGREGATION, the process whereby a pair of GENES on a particular CHROMOSOME separate singly into different GAMETES during MEIOSIS. On fertilization either the original pair is reconstituted or a new pair is formed in the offspring. Segregation depends on the relative stability of genes.

The end of the battle of Sedan, a contemporary lithograph by Breidenbach. Napoleon III, emperor of France, is shown surrendering his sword to the king of Prussia, William I; to the right of the king is Crown Prince Friedrich and behind him Bismarck.

Propagation of various types of earthquake waves and characteristic seismograms for various distances. The distances along the earth's surface are measured in megameters (1 megameter = 1000 km or about 620 mi).

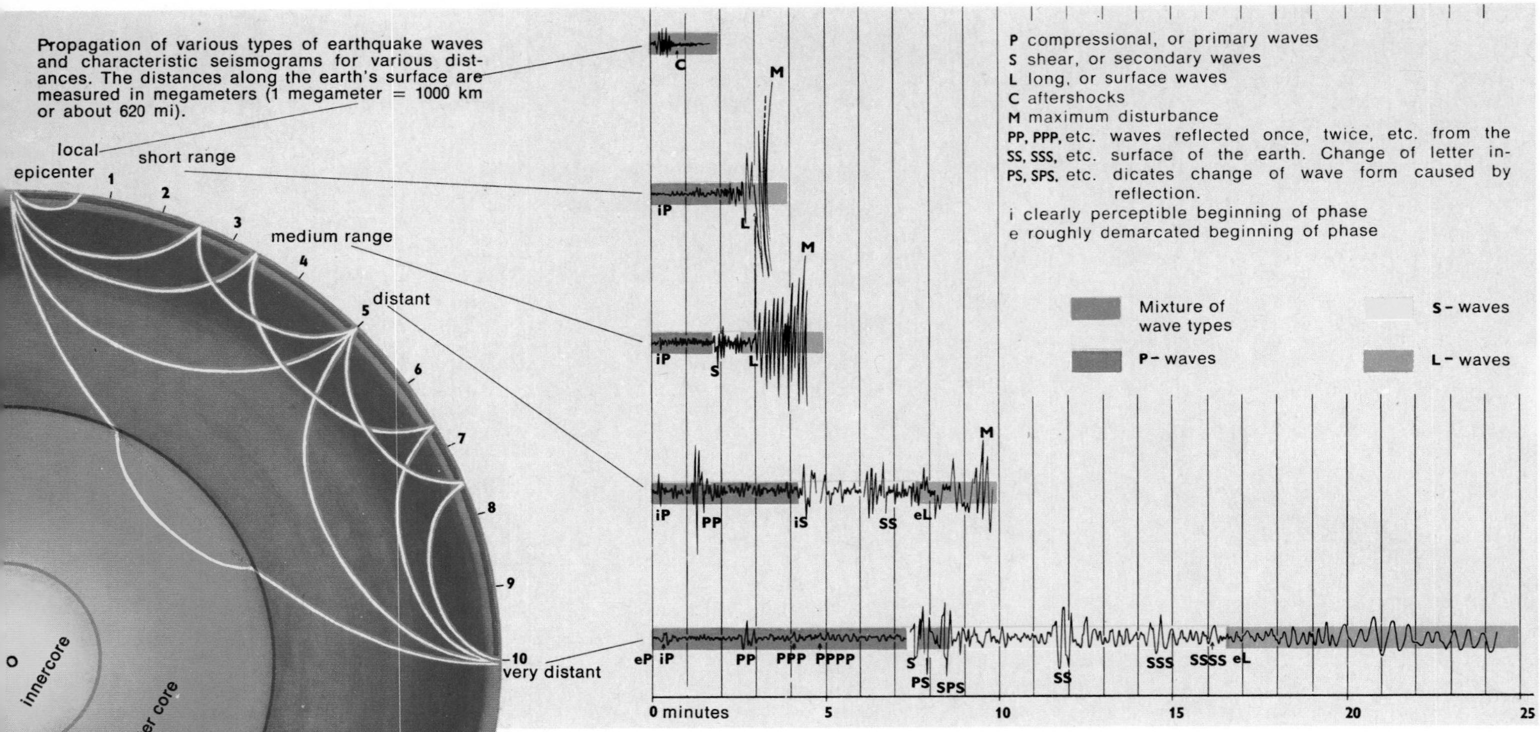

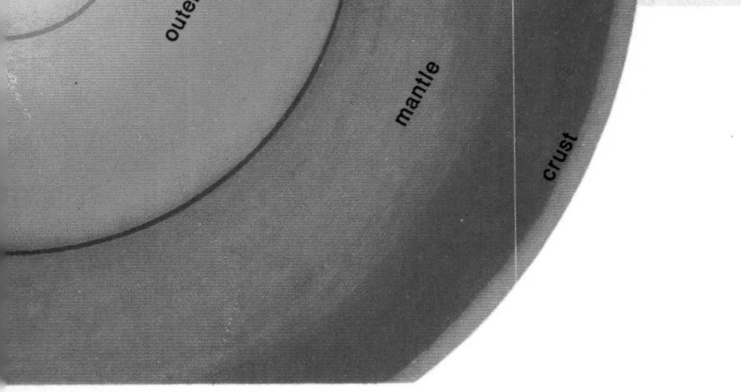

A seismograph records waves reaching it from an earth tremor that may have taken place thousands of miles away. By combining readings from several seismographs in different locations, one can determine the focus (point of origin) of an earthquake or an underground nuclear explosion. P (primary) and S (secondary) waves travel only *through* the earth, while L (long) waves travel only on the *surface* of the earth.

SEGUIN, city in S central Tex., seat of Guadalupe Co., in a farming and oil-producing region. Products include metal goods and fiberglass. Pop 15 934.

SEICHE, a standing wave system (see WAVE MOTION) occurring in a lake or bay, set up by a disturbance such as wind, ocean swell, an earth tremor or a sudden change in air pressure. The oscillation period depends on the size and shape of the basin.

SEINE RIVER, France's principal waterway. Rising on the Langres Plateau NW of Dijon, it winds 475mi NW to PARIS, where over 30 bridges span it, through Rouen and Normandy, to the English Channel. It is the main artery of a far-reaching river system converging on Paris. Canals link it to the Loire, Rhône, Rhine and Schelde rivers.

SEISMOGRAPH, instrument used to record seismic waves caused by EARTHQUAKES, nuclear explosions, etc.: the record it produces is a **seismogram**. The simplest seismograph has a horizontal bar, pivoted at one end and with a recording pen at the other. The bar, supported by a spring, bears a heavy weight. As the ground moves, the bar remains roughly stationary owing to the INERTIA of the weight, while the rest of the equipment moves. The pen traces the vibrations on a moving belt of paper. Seismographs are used in PROSPECTING.

SEISMOLOGY, the study of EARTHQUAKE phenomena.

SEKONDI-TAKORADI, city in SW Ghana, capital of the Western Region, a commercial and seaport city 110mi W of Accra. Pop 89 686.

SELAGINELLA, a genus of CLUB MOSSES, several species of which (e.g., *Selaginella emmeliana, S. kraussiana* and *S.k. brownii*) are grown as house plants, particularly in terrariums and bottle gardens since they require a moist draft-free environment. They grow well at temperatures between 13°C and 24°C (55°F and 75°F) in a bright north window or near a sunny window. The soil should be kept evenly moist and the foliage misted often. Propagation is by division or taking cuttings.

SELECTION. See NATURAL SELECTION; SEXUAL SELECTION.

SELECTION SERVICE. See DRAFT.

SELECTIVE PRESSURE, a measure of the forces acting on a population of organisms that stimulate evolutionary change. Selective pressure is proportional to the amount of genetic change produced. (See also EVOLUTION, NATURAL SELECTION.)

SELENE, an ancient Greek moon-goddess sometimes identified with ARTEMIS and HECATE. She was shown as a charioteer, the crescent moon on her head.

SELENITE, well-developed crystals of GYPSUM.

SELENIUM (Se), metalloid in Group VIA of the PERIODIC TABLE; it occurs as rare selenides with heavy-metal SULFIDES, and is obtained as a by-product of copper refining or the LEAD-CHAMBER PROCESS. Selenium has three allotropes (see ALLOTROPY), the most stable being the gray, metallic form. Its chemistry is analogous to that of SULFUR. It is used to make PHOTOELECTRIC CELLS, SOLAR CELLS, RECTIFIERS, in XEROGRAPHY and as a SEMICONDUCTOR; also to make ruby glass and to vulcanize rubber. AW 79.0, mp 217°C (gray), bp 685°C (gray), sg 4.79 (gray).

SELEUCIDS, a Hellenistic dynasty of Syria. It was founded in 312 BC by Seleucus I Nicator (d. 280 BC), a general of Alexander the Great and one of the DIADOCHI, who conquered lands from Thrace to India. Seleucid kings founded many Greek settlements and promoted commerce, but the empire dwindled through secession and revolt, until Syria fell to Rome in 64 BC. (See ANTIOCHUS III.)

SELF-DEFENSE, in law, a ground which may justify harm done to another. Inflicting injury, or even killing, may not be criminal if a person has reasonable cause to fear that otherwise he or someone in his care would suffer death or grave injury, provided he is not the aggressor.

SELF-DETERMINATION, in political theory, the right of a people to decide its political status (see PLEBISCITE; REFERENDUM) and its political, legal and economic systems.

SELF-INCRIMINATION, in law, the privilege of refusing to testify if giving evidence would tend to incriminate the witness. In US law as laid down in the Fifth Amendment, the witness may cite his privilege but the judge decides if he must testify, in which case he must answer all questions save those he thinks will incriminate him. (See PRIVILEGE.)

SELINUS, ancient Greek city near modern Castelvetrano, SW Sicily. Founded in the 600s BC, it was sacked by Carthaginians called in by rival SEGESTA (409 BC). The ruins include temples and an acropolis.

SELJUKS, the Turks who came from central Asia in the 11th century to found dynasties stretching from the borders of India to the Mediterranean Sea. They adopted Arabic culture and championed Islam, but soon fragmented into rival principalities weakened by Crusaders and by the Mongols to whom they fell in the 13th century. The OTTOMAN EMPIRE rebuilt Turkish power from the 1300s.

SELKIRK, Alexander (1676–1721), Scottish sailor whose life as a castaway inspired Daniel DEFOE's novel *Robinson Crusoe*. In Sept. 1704, after a quarrel with his privateer captain, Selkirk chose to be put ashore on one of the uninhabited Juan Fernández islands. He was rescued in 1709.

SELKIRK, Thomas Douglas, 5th Earl of (1771–1820), Scottish colonizer. He helped refugees from the Scottish highland clearances to settle in Prince Edward Island (1803) and founded the RED RIVER SETTLEMENT in 1811.

SELKIRK MOUNTAINS, a range in SE British Columbia, Canada, within the Big Bend of the Columbia R. The highest peak in its 200mi length is Mt Sir Sanford (11 590ft).

SELMA, industrial city in central Ala., seat of Dallas Co. It processes cotton, livestock and tobacco and manufactures farm machinery. Pop 27 379.

SELYE, Hans (1907–), Austrian-born Canadian physician best known for his work on the physiological effects of environmental stress, which he suggested might cause certain diseases (see PSYCHOSOMATIC ILLNESS).

SELZNICK, David Oliver (1902–1965), US motion picture producer. His many commercial and artistic successes included *Gone with the Wind* (1939) and *Rebecca* (1940).

SEMANTICS, semasiology or **semology**, the study of meaning, concerned both with the relationship of words and symbols to the ideas or objects that they represent, and with tracing the histories of meanings and changes that have taken place in them. Semantics is thus a branch both of LINGUISTICS and of LOGIC. **General semantics**, propounded primarily by Alfred KORZYBSKI, holds that habits of thought have lagged behind the language and logic of science: it attacks such Aristotelian logical proposals as that nothing can be both not-*x* and *x*, maintaining that these are simplifications no longer valid.

SEMAPHORE, system of visual signalling using movable arms, flags or lights to represent letters and numbers. The first such system was introduced by Claude Chappe (1763–1805): it used towers 8 to 16km apart. Semaphore is still used for signalling between ships and on some railroads.

SEMARANG, capital of Central Jawa province, Indonesia, a seaport and commercial center with textile, machine and shipbuilding industries. Pop 633 000.

SEMELE, in Greek mythology, daughter of King Cadmus of Thebes and mother by ZEUS of the god DIONYSUS. Her unborn child was rescued after she scorched to death before Zeus' full radiance.

SEMEN, fluid secreted by the TESTES containing SPERM. (See also REPRODUCTION.)

SEMICIRCULAR CANALS. See EAR.

SEMICONDUCTOR, a material whose electrical CONDUCTIVITY is intermediate between that of an insulator and conductor at room TEMPERATURE and increases with rising temperature and impurity concentration. Typical **intrinsic semiconductors** are single crystals of GERMANIUM or SILICON. At low temperatures their valence electron ENERGY LEVELS are filled and no ELECTRONS are free to conduct ELECTRICITY, but with increasing temperature, some electrons gain enough ENERGY to jump into the empty conduction band, leaving a **hole** behind in the valence band. Thus there are equal numbers of moving electrons and holes available for carrying electric current. Practical **extrinsic semiconductors** are made by adding a chosen concentration of a particular type of impurity atom to an intrinsic semiconductor (a process known as doping). If the impurity atom has more valence electrons than the semiconductor atom, it is known as a donor and provides spare conduction electrons, creating an **n-type semiconductor**. If the impurity atom has fewer valence electrons, it captures them from the other atoms and is known as an acceptor, leaving behind holes which act as moving positive charge carriers and enhance the conductivity of the **p-type semiconductor** that is formed. An n-and p-type semiconductor junction acts as a RECTIFIER; when it is forward biased, holes cross the junction to the negative end and electrons to the positive end, and current flows through it. If the voltage connections are reversed, the carriers will not cross the junction and no current flows. Semiconductor devices, such as the TRANSISTOR, based on the p-n junction have revolutionized ELECTRONICS since the late 1940s.

SEMIMETAL. See METALLOID.

SEMINOLE, the last Indian tribe to make peace with the US government. They formed in Fla. out of an alliance including refugee CREEK INDIANS (from Ga.), native APALACHEE INDIANS and runaway Negro slaves. They fought Andrew JACKSON's troops in 1817–18 while Fla. was still a Spanish territory. The major Seminole War began in 1835 when the US government ordered removal to W of the Mississippi. A fierce guerrilla war against overwhelming odds ended in 1842, after which most Seminole were moved to Okla. However, a small band held out in the Everglades until 1934, when they agreed to a settlement. (See also FIVE CIVILIZED TRIBES; OSCEOLA.)

SEMIOLOGY, or **semiotics**, the study of signs (including LANGUAGE), their uses, and the way in which they are used. Its branches are pragmatics (dealing with the relation between the signs and those using them), syntactics (the relation between different words and symbols) and SEMANTICS.

SEMIPALATINSK, industrial capital city of Semipalatinsk oblast, NE Kazakh SSR, USSR, on the Irtysh R in an agricultural and mining region. Pop 236 000.

SEMIPERMEABLE MEMBRANE, a MEMBRANE that allows certain substances, usually small molecules or ions, to pass through its pores, but which keeps back others. Examples are CELL membranes, PARCHMENT, cellophane, and copper(II) hexacyanoferrate(II). (See DIALYSIS; OSMOSIS.)

SEMIRAMIS, fabled queen of Assyria said to have built Babylon and conquered Persia and Egypt. The historical Semiramis was probably Queen Sammuramat of Assyria (regent c810–805 BC). Semiramis, often identified with ISHTAR, was worshiped for her beauty, valor and wisdom.

SEMITES, in the Old Testament, the "sons of Shem" (who was the son of NOAH). The term now generally applies to speakers of SEMITIC LANGUAGES including ancient Assyrians, Babylonians and Phoenicians, modern Arabs and most Ethiopians. (See also ANTISEMITISM.)

SEMITIC LANGUAGES, important group, found in the Near East and N Africa, of the Hamito-Semitic language family (see HAMITIC LANGUAGES). Most of the group are now extinct, extant members including Hebrew, Arabic and Maltese. A few were written in CUNEIFORM, but most used alphabets. The N Semitic alphabet, the first fully formed alphabetical WRITING system, is of particular importance to us as it is from here that most of the letters of our own ALPHABET have descended.

SEMLIKI RIVER, flows some 110mi from Lake Edward NE to Lake Albert along the W GREAT RIFT VALLEY, forming part of the Uganda-Zaire border.

SEMMELWEISS, Ignaz Philipp (1818–1865), Hungarian obstetrician who, through his discovery that PUERPERAL FEVER was transmitted by failure of obstetricians to thoroughly clean their hands between performing autopsies of mothers who had died of the disease and making examinations of living mothers, first practised ASEPSIS.

SEMMES, Raphael (1809–1877), American naval officer, commander of the Confederacy's first warship, the *Sumter*, and later the famous *Alabama*, which in two years accounted for some 70 Union ships before it was sunk. (See also ALABAMA CLAIMS.)

SEMYONOV, Nikolai Nikolaevich (1896–), Russian physical chemist who shared with HINSHELWOOD the 1956 Nobel Prize for Chemistry for his work on chemical KINETICS, especially concerning chemical chain and branched-chain reactions.

SENATE, Roman (Latin *senes*: elders), originally an advisory council to the kings of ancient Rome, in the later Roman republic the chief governing body as PLEBEIANS challenged the PATRICIAN nobility's monopoly of the 300 life appointments to the senate. Revolts led by the TRIBUNES and by military leaders (see GRACCHI; CINNA; MARIUS) preceded severe curtailment of the powers of the now corrupt Senate, which was thereafter dominated by the emperors.

SENATE, US. See CONGRESS OF THE UNITED STATES.

SENDAI, NE Honshū Island, N Japan's largest city, a manufacturing and cultural center, seat of Miyagi prefecture and of Tohoku U. Pop 545 065.

SENECA, Lucius Annaeus (c4 BC–65 AD), Roman statesman, philosopher and writer. The most important feature of his political life is the role he played in restraining the worst excesses of NERO. Writing in highly rhetorical, epigrammatic style, Seneca advocated STOICISM in his *Moral Letters*, essays, one masterly satire and nine bloody, intense tragedies. After implication in a conspiracy he was commanded to suicide.

SENECA FALLS CONVENTION, first women's rights convention in the US, organized by Lucretia MOTT and Elizabeth STANTON and held at Seneca Falls, W central N.Y., 1848. The convention's chief assertion was that women should be entitled to vote.

SENECA INDIANS, of W N.Y. and E Ohio, once the largest nation of the IROQUOIS League. The Seneca Nation, some 4 000 with four reservations, is now a republic. (See also CAYUGA INDIANS; HANDSOME LAKE.)

SENECA LAKE, one of the FINGER LAKES in central N.Y., about 35mi long and nearly 650ft deep. The canalized Seneca R links it to Cayuga Lake.

SENEGAL, republic in W Africa.

Land. The Senegal R with its fertile floodplain and its tributary the Falémé forms the N and E frontier with Mauritania and Mali. Guinea and Guiné-Bissau lie S. Other major rivers are the Gambia (along which for 200mi independent GAMBIA forms an enclave), the Casamance, Sine and Saloun. The low grassland plains rise, only slightly, in the center, E and SE.

Climate. Rainfall ranges from 60in in the SW Casamance to 10in in the N. Most of the year climate is pleasant along the coast, but hot inland.

People. Nearly all are Negro and 80% are Muslims. Tribal groups are important. About two-thirds of the population is rural, mostly along the Senegal R (Tukuler) and the 310mi coastline (Wolof and Serer) and S and E of Dakar. French is the official language. Illiteracy is still common, but there is a university at DAKAR. Kaolack, Thiès and St.-Louis are other important centers.

Economy. Peanuts and their products, phosphates and titanium are major exports. Crops include millet, rice, cotton and beans. There are rich coastal fisheries. Industry, centered on Dakar, includes food processing, fertilizers, cement, textiles and leather goods.

History. Parts of Senegal were within the medieval empires of Ghana, Mali and Songhai. Under French control from 1895, Senegal was part of the Federation of Mali 1959–60, but independent thereafter. SENGHOR has been president since 1960.

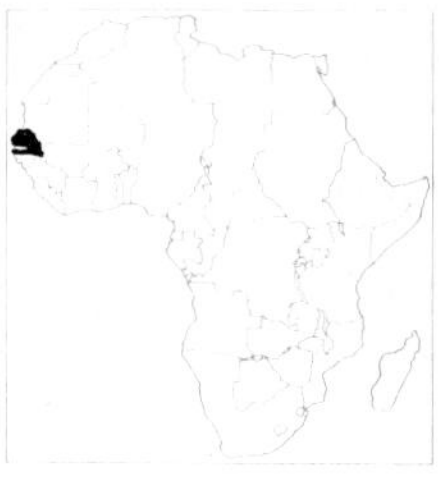

Official name: Republic of Senegal
Capital: Dakar
Area: 75 750sq mi
Population: 3 900 000
Languages: French; Wolof, Fulani. Mende spoken
Religions: Muslim, Christian
Monetary unit(s): 1 CFA franc = 100 centimes

SENEGAL RIVER, with its headwaters, flows 1 000mi N and NW from Guinea to St.-Louis, N Senegal, forming Senegal's border with Mauritania.

SENGHOR, Léopold-Sédar (1906–), Senegalese statesman and poet, Senegal's president since independence from France (1960). He is famous for his philosophy of *négritude*, a concept of socialism which incorporates black African values.

SENILITY, the state of OLD AGE, usually referring to the general mental and physical deterioration, often (but not always) seen in the elderly. Failure of recent MEMORY, dwelling on the past, episodic confusion and difficulty in absorbing new information are common. The degenerative changes in SKIN, BONE and connective TISSUE lead to the altered physical appearance characteristic of the elderly.

SENNA, dried leaves and pods of leguminous shrubs and trees of the genus *Cassia*, notably *C. acutifolia* and *C. angustifolia*, grown in the Sudan, Arabia and India. Introduced in Arabia during the 9th century, it is still used as a mild purgative.

SENNACHERIB (reigned 704–681 BC), one of the last great kings of Assyria. To maintain the great empire established by his father SARGON II, he put down rebellion in Syria and Palestine (but failed to capture Jerusalem) and conquered the Babylonians and Elamites, sacking Babylon as a lesson to his subjects. Finally he rebuilt NINEVEH and made it Assyria's capital.

SENNETT, Mack (1884–1960), Canadian-born US silent movie director-producer, the originator of "slapstick humor." After working with D. W. GRIFFITH he formed his own Keystone Co. and made over 1 000 "shorts" with his Keystone Cops, Bathing Belles and stars like CHAPLIN and W. C. FIELDS.

SENSATIONALISM, philosophical theory which in its most extreme forms (see CYRENAICS; CONDILLAC) holds that knowledge is composed wholly of sensations, the mind being regarded as a passive *tabula rasa* (clean slate).

SENSES, the media through which stimuli in the environment of an organism act on it (external senses); also, the internal senses which report on the internal state of the organism (through THIRST AND HUNGER; PAIN, etc.). The organs of sense, the eye, ear, skin etc., all contain specialized cells and nerve endings which communicate with centers in the NERVOUS SYSTEM. Sense organs may be stimulated by pressure (in TOUCH, hearing and balance—see EAR), chemical stimulation (SMELL; TASTE), or electromagnetic radiation (VISION; heat sensors).

SENSITIVE PLANT. See MIMOSA.

SENSORY DEPRIVATION, condition of perceptual isolation—which may result in HALLUCINATIONS, thought or emotional disorders or spatiotemporal disorientation—experienced by people confined in highly unstimulating environments, a subject of much recent research.

SENUSI, or Sanusiya, a missionary Muslim Sufi order founded in Mecca 1837 by al-Sanusi al-Kebir. It spread among the BEDOUIN of N Africa, and was opposed to Italian occupation. IDRIS, the founder's grandson, became first king of Libya.

SEOUL, capital, largest city and industrial and cultural center of South Korea, on the Han R, 25mi E of Inchon, its seaport. Seoul changed hands several times in the KOREAN WAR. Pop 5 536 337.

SEPAL, in plants, one of the outer rings of green leaf-like organs (together called the CALYX) which surrounds the petals of the FLOWER. In some plants the calyx is petal-like and colored.

SEPARATION, in law, an agreement between wife and husband to cease cohabitation. Separation often, though not necessarily, precedes DIVORCE. In most US states separation, either mutually agreed or in the form of DESERTION, constitutes grounds for divorce.

SEPARATION OF POWERS, political theory developed by MONTESQUIEU from his studies of the British constitution, arguing that the arbitrary exercise of government power should be avoided by dividing it between distinct departments, the EXECUTIVE, LEGISLATURE and JUDICIARY. This was a basic principle of the Founding Fathers in producing the US Constitution; legislative powers were vested in Congress, judicial powers in the Supreme and subsidiary courts and executive powers in the president and his governmental machinery. Each branch was to have its functions, duties and authority, and in theory no branch could encroach upon another. In practice there has always been a degree of necessary overlap. The legislature can oppose and impeach members of the executive, the president can veto legislation and the Supreme Court can adjudicate the actions of the other branches; its members, in turn, are presidential appointees subject to congressional approval. In US history one branch has always tended to dominate others for long periods, but this "checks and balances" effect has at least ensured that power can and does shift between them.

SEPARATISTS, those English religious congregations who sought independence from the state and established church, beginning in 1580 with the Norwich Brownists (see BROWNE, ROBERT). John ROBINSON led refugee Separatists in Leyden, Holland, who were later prominent among the PILGRIM FATHERS. (See also CONGREGATIONAL CHURCHES.)

SEPHARDIM, Spanish Jews who fled the INQUISITION (1480) for Portugal, N Africa, Italy, Holland (notably Amsterdam), the Balkans (Salonika), Near East and America. Sephardim had their own language, literature and ritual.

SEPIA, the "ink" of SQUIDS and OCTOPUSES which can be expelled into the sea to distract potential predators while the animal escapes. The word is taken up in the generic name of the European CUTTLEFISH. Sepia has been a popular drawing medium for 400 years.

SEPIK RIVER, New Guinea, flows some 700mi NW from the Victor Emmanual Mts., then E through sparsely populated swamp country, to the Bismarck Sea.

SEPIOLITE. See MEERSCHAUM.

SEPOY REBELLION, or **Indian Mutiny,** or the First War of Independence, a mutiny of Sepoys (Hindi: troops) in the Bengal Army of the EAST INDIA COMPANY. It began at Meerut, near Delhi, in May 1857 and spread over N India. The immediate cause was the issuing of cartridges greased with the fat of cows (sacred to Hindus) and pigs (unclean to Muslims), but years of increasing British domination led to a general revolt which was not suppressed until March 1858. As a result the British government took over the rule of India.

SEPSIS, the destructive invasion of TISSUES by BACTERIA. (See also ASEPSIS; SEPTICEMIA.)

SEPTEMBER, ninth month of the year, derived from Latin *septem*, seven, an indication of its old position on the pre-Julian Roman CALENDAR.

SEPTICEMIA, circulation of infective BACTERIA and the white BLOOD cells responding to them in the blood. Bacteria may transiently enter the blood normally but these are removed by the RETICULOENDOTHELIAL SYSTEM. If this system fails and bacteria continue to circulate, their products and those of the white cells initiate a series of reactions that lead to SHOCK, with warm extremities, FEVER or hypothermia. Septic EMBOLISM may occur causing widespread ABSCESSES. GRAN'S STAIN-negative bacteria (usually from urinary or GASTROINTESTINAL TRACT) and STAPHYLOCOCCUS cause severe septicemia. Treatment includes ANTIBIOTICS and resuscitative measures for shock.

SEPTIC TANK, large tank used for SEWAGE disposal from single residences not linked to the public sewer. The liquid part of the sewage drains off to a cesspool or distribution network in sandy soil. The sludge collects at the bottom of the tank and is largely decomposed by bacteria; it is pumped out every few years.

SEPT-ÎLES (or Seven Isles), port in E Quebec, handling much of the freight from the Quebec-Labrador iron fields. Pop 24 289.

SEPTIMIUS SEVERUS. See SEVERUS, LUCIUS SEPTIMIUS.

SEPTUAGESIMA. See CHURCH YEAR.

SEPTUAGINT, oldest Greek translation of the Hebrew OLD TESTAMENT, probably from an older source than any now extant. The PENTATEUCH was translated in Alexandria at the behest of PTOLEMY II (c250 BC), according to legend by 70 or 72 scholars (hence the name); completed, including the APOCRYPHA, c130 BC.

SEQUENCE, an ordered set of numbers (e.g., 2, 4, 6, 8, ... $2n$, ...) linked by a common mathematical formula. Most sequences are infinite, that is, they have an infinite number of terms, but there are some finite sequences, which end after a finite number of terms: finite sequences are generally of little importance. An infinite sequence may, however, be bounded. The terms of the sequence of typical term $1/n$ all lie between 0 and 1. As the successive terms tend toward 0, this is said to be the LIMIT of the sequence. A recursive series is one in which the value of each term depends on the value of the preceding terms.

SEQUOIA, genus including the two largest trees, the redwood *Sequoia sempervirens* and the Giant sequoia (*S. gigantea*), both found only in the Pacific northwest of the US. Furthermore, only the BRISTLECONE PINE lives longer. The tallest tree in the world is a redwood in Humboldt Co., Cal. which measures over 110m (360ft) high, and the largest living organism in the world is the General Sherman giant sequoia in SEQUOIA NATIONAL PARK which is over 82m (270ft) high with a circumference at the base of over 30m (100ft). Family: Taxodiaceae.

SEQUOIA NATIONAL PARK, 600sq mi park, S central Cal. (administered with the adjacent KINGS CANYON NATIONAL PARK), established 1890 to preserve the groves of giant SEQUOIA. Lying in the S Sierra Nevada, it includes Mt WHITNEY, highest US peak outside Alaska.

SEQUOYA (c1770–1843), Cherokee Indian silversmith who devised an alphabet whose 85 characters represented every sound in Cherokee language, so enabling thousands of Cherokees to read and write. The SEQUOIA tree is named for him.

SERAPIS, Greco-Egyptian deity established by PTOLEMY I c300 BC. Originally like OSIRIS Lord of the Dead, he became associated with the sun, healing, fertility and the sea.

SERBIA, historic Balkan kingdom, since WWII the easternmost of the six republics of YUGOSLAVIA. The Serbs were SLAVS who settled the Balkans from the 600s onward. Stephen Nemanja (ruled 1168–96) created the first united kingdom, which became a great empire under Stephen Dushan (1331–1355), but after the battle of Kosovo (1389) Serbia remained under Turkish rule until 1877. After WWI occupation by Austria, it became the core of the kingdom of Yugoslavia. Serbia (34 000sq mi) is mountainous and mainly agricultural. Its capital is BELGRADE.

SERBO-CROATIAN, the principal language of Yugoslavia. One of the SLAVONIC LANGUAGES, it is written in Cyrillic (by the majority Serbs) or Latin (by the Croats) characters.

SERE. See SUCCESSION.

SERF, a feudal peasant. Under FEUDALISM serfs were bound to the land they worked and had to give some of their labor or produce to an overlord. With the development of CAPITALISM, serfdom died out, although it survived into the 19th century in Russia and parts of E Europe.

SERGIPE, small Atlantic state of E Brazil, N of Bahia. The capital is Aracaju. Agriculture (sugar, coconuts, cotton) flourishes on the fertile land between the coast and the inland mountains.

SERGIUS, Saint (c1315–1392), Russian religious leader. His monastery at Radonezh (modern Zagorsk) near Moscow became a center for the moral and nationalist regeneration of Russia during Tatar oppression.

SERGIUS, the name of four popes, who all died in office. **Saint Sergius I** (reigned 687–701) opposed the influence of the Byzantine emperor JUSTINIAN II and healed the schism with AQUILEIA. **Sergius II** (reigned 844–47) crowned LOTHAIR'S son Louis king of Lombardy. Saracens raided Rome in 846. **Sergius III** (reigned 904–11), reputed lover of THEODORA and father of Pope JOHN XI, bloodily nullified FORMOSUS' pontificate, and restored the Lateran basilica. **Sergius IV** (reigned 1009–12), aided the poor but was powerless before the Roman nobles.

SERGIUS AND BACCHUS, Saints, two 4th-century Christian martyrs, Roman officers tortured and executed for refusing to sacrifice to Jupiter.

SERIAL MUSIC. See TWELVE-TONE MUSIC.

SERIEMAS, two species of South American birds resembling small brown cranes. Birds of open ground, occurring in pairs or small groups, they feed on seeds, berries, insects, reptiles and small rodents.

SERIES, the sum of the terms of a SEQUENCE. Most series are "infinite"—containing an infinite number of terms. Those which tend to a LIMIT are termed "converging," others being "diverging."

SERKIN, Rudolf (1903–), Bohemian-born US pianist. He studied with SCHOENBERG in Vienna, made his US debut in 1933 and joined the Curtis Institute of Music, Philadelphia, in 1939.

SERLIO, Sebastiano (1475–1554), Italian architect who worked at FONTAINEBLEAU. His *Architecture* (1537–51), first treatise to stress practice rather than theory, diffused MANNERISM and the style of BRAMANTE, RAPHAEL and PERUZZI.

SERMON ON THE MOUNT, Christ's most important discourse, described in Matthew 5–7. Encapsulating most of the principles of Christian ethics, stressing the power of love and God's role as a loving father, it contains also the BEATITUDES and the LORD'S PRAYER.

SEROTONIN, aromatic amine found in serum and other tissues that acts on BLOOD vessels; it is also involved in PERISTALSIS and in the central NERVOUS SYSTEM as a transmitter at SYNAPSES. It may be involved in ANAPHYLAXIS in some species; its action in increasing CAPILLARY permeability indicates its role in the reactions producing INFLAMMATION.

SERPENTINE, common magnesium SILICATE mineral, $Mg_3Si_2O_5(OH)_4$, whose structure resembles that of KAOLINITE. There are three varieties: CHRYSOTILE, antigorite and lizardite. Gray, green or yellow with an attractive texture and easily polished, serpentine is used as an ornamental stone.

SERRA, Junípero (1713–1784), Mallorcan Franciscan missionary. A famous preacher and professor, he went to Mexico in 1749 and worked among the Indians of the Sierra Gorda. Franciscans under his leadership established, from 1769 onward, nine missions in present-day Cal., including San Carlos at Monterey.

SERUM, the clear yellowish fluid that separates from BLOOD, LYMPH and other body fluids when they clot. It contains water, PROTEINS, fat, minerals, HORMONES and UREA. **Serum therapy** involves injecting (horse or human) serum containing ANTIBODIES (GLOBULINS), which can destroy particular pathogens. Occasionally injected serum gives rise to an allergic reaction known as serum sickness; a second injection of the same serum may induce ANAPHYLAXIS.

SERVAL, *Felis serval*, a slender long-legged CAT with large, erect ears. Confined to Africa, it is largely nocturnal, employing its sensitive hearing to capture Guinea fowl, francolins and small rodents.

SERVETUS, Michael (1511–1553), or **Miguel Serveto**, Spanish biologist and theologian. In *Christianity Restored* (1553) he mentioned in passing his discovery of the pulmonary circulation (see BLOOD CIRCULATION). For heretical views expressed in this book he was denounced by the Calvinists to the Catholic Inquisition: escaping, he foolishly visited Geneva where he was seized by the Protestants, tried for heresy and burned alive.

SERVICE, Robert William (1874–1958), Scottish-born Canadian writer. His enormously popular, often humorous ballads, starting with *Songs of a Sourdough* (1907), told of the rugged life and characters of the Yukon and of the KLONDIKE gold rush.

SERVICEBERRY, deciduous shrubs and small trees of the genus *Amelanchier*, mostly native to America. The berries are sometimes used to make jellies. Family: Rosaceae.

SERVIUS TULLIUS (reigned 578–534 BC), sixth king of ancient Rome. He made a treaty with the Latin League and built the first shrine of DIANA, before his son-in-law TARQUINIUS Superbus killed him.

SERVOMECHANISM, an automatic control device (see MECHANIZATION AND AUTOMATION) which controls the position, velocity or acceleration of a high-power output device by means of a command signal from a low-power reference device. By FEEDBACK, the error between the actual output state and the state commanded is measured, amplified and made to drive a servomotor which corrects the output. The drive may be electrical, hydraulic or pneumatic.

SESAME, *Sesamum indicum*, a tropical plant, cultivated mainly in China and India for its flat seeds. The seeds yield an oil which is used instead of olive oil as a salad or cooking oil and in margarine, cosmetics and ointments. The residue left after oil extraction is used as a cattle feed and fertilizer. Family: Pedaliaceae.

SESSILE ANIMALS, animals that spend part of their lives attached to the ground or sea bed. All sessile animals have, at some stage of their life-histories, a mobile phase facilitating dispersal.

SESSHU (1420–1506), Japanese master of ink painting. Influenced by Zen Buddhism, and by a visit to China, he painted sensitive but vigorous landscapes in both *shin* and *haboku* styles.

SESSIONS, Roger Huntington (1896–   ), US composer. He studied with Ernest BLOCH and has taught at leading US academic institutions. His orchestral, chamber and choral works are characterized by complexity, POLYPHONY, and rhythmic vitality.

SET, or Seth, an ancient Egyptian god of evil, represented with an ass's head and a pig's snout. Originally a royal deity, he came to personify evil as killer of OSIRIS, god of goodness. Osiris' son HORUS fought and killed Set.

SETI I (ruled c1318–1304 BC), king of Egypt, father of RAMSES II. He restored Egypt's lands and prestige and built the Hypostyle Hall, Karnak, and his own magnificent tomb at THEBES.

SETON, Elizabeth Ann or Mother Seton (née Bayley: 1774–1821), first native-born US saint. A devout Episcopalian, she was widowed at 28 with five children. In 1805, she converted to Catholicism. She opened an elementary school, now regarded as the basis of the US parochial school system, and in 1813 founded the first US religious society, the Sisters of Charity. She was canonized in 1975.

SETSQUARE, in classical GEOMETRY, an instrument used to draw right ANGLES and, with a straight edge particularly, PARALLEL LINES.

SET THEORY. A set is a collection of objects or quantities, symbolized by a capital letter. Thus

$$S = \{2, 4, 6, 8\}$$

means that S is the set of even numbers less than 10. A member of a set is called an element: symbolically, $2 \in S$ means that 2 is an element of S; $3 \notin S$ means that 3 is not an element of S. An ordered set is equivalent to a SEQUENCE. A set may be infinite, finite or empty: the set of all even numbers is infinite, that of all those less than 10 is finite, and that of all those less than 1 is empty. This empty or **null set** is symbolized ϕ or $\{\,\}$; and should not be confused with $\{0\}$, which is a set with one member, ZERO. If there is a one-to-one correspondence between the elements of two sets, then they are termed equivalent, and if the sets have identical elements they are equal:

$$S_1 = \{a, b, c, d\}$$
$$S_2 = \{e, f, g, h\}$$
$$S_3 = \{d, c, b, a\}$$

shows three equivalent sets; moreover $S_1 = S_3$. Two equivalent sets are written $S_1 \leftarrow S_2$.

If some elements of one set are also elements of another, then those elements are called the intersection of the two sets, symbolized $S_1 \cap S_2$. The set of all elements that are members of at least one of the two sets is their union, written $S_1 \cup S_2$. A set whose members are all members of another set is termed a subset. Thus, if,

$$S_1 = \{a, b, c, d, e\}$$
$$S_2 = \{b, d, f, g\},$$
$$\text{then } S_1 \cap S_2 = \{b, d\}$$
$$S_1 \cup S_2 = \{a, b, c, d, e, f, g\}.$$

Moreover, S_1 and S_2 are subsets of $S_1 \cup S_2$, written $S_1 \subset S_1 \cup S_2$ and $S_2 \subset S_1 \cup S_2$. The set of all elements of all the sets in a particular discussion is the universal set, or **domain**, symbolized by a capital U. The domain may contain elements in addition to all those under discussion.

Set theory is of importance throughout mathematics. In ANALYTIC GEOMETRY, for example, a CURVE may be considered as a set of points, or **point set**. For two FUNCTIONS $f(x)$ and $g(x)$, represented by the sets S_f and S_g, S_f fi S_g gives those points at which the curves intersect (see INTERSECTION). Sets can be represented pictorially by use of VENN DIAGRAMS. (See also FIELD; GROUP.)

SETTLEMENT, ACT OF. See ACT OF SETTLEMENT.

SETTLEMENT HOUSE. See SOCIAL SETTLEMENTS.

SEURAT, Georges (1859–1891), French painter, one of a small group representing Neoimpressionism or POSTIMPRESSIONISM. Interested in color from scientific and artistic points of view, he invented POINTILLISM. Best known of his paintings is probably *A Sunday afternoon on the Island of La Grande Jatte* (1884–86).

SEUSS, Dr. (1904–   ), pen name of Theodor Seuss Geisal, author-illustrator of many children's books. For 40 years, his imaginative verse tales and humorous fantasies have captivated the young.

SEVASTOPOL, Black Sea port of the CRIMEA peninsula, Ukrainian SSR, USSR. Now a major Soviet naval base, industrial city and railroad terminal, the city suffered long sieges in the CRIMEAN WAR (1854–55) and WWII (1941–42). Pop 229 000.

SEVEN CITIES OF CIBOLA. See CIBOLA, SEVEN CITIES OF.

SEVEN DAYS BATTLES (June 25–July 2, 1862), series of engagements in the US CIVIL WAR in which Robert E. LEE prevented a Unionist assault, led by George MCLELLAN, on Richmond, Va., the Confederate capital, so ending the PENINSULAR CAMPAIGN.

SEVEN HILLS, mainly residential city in N Ohio, a suburb 10mi S of Cleveland. Pop 12 700.

SEVEN HILLS OF ROME, on which the ancient city of ROME was built, probably chosen for their strategic position just E of the lowest crossing on the Tiber R. Traditionally, ROMULUS founded the city on the nearest hill, the Palatine, a settlement which soon linked with the neighboring Capitoline to the NW. By 378 BC the Servian Wall enclosed the other hills further out: the Aventine, Caelian, Esquiline, Viminal and Quirinal.

SEVEN LIBERAL ARTS, program of studies originating in ancient Greece which became the basis of elementary education in the Roman empire and medieval Europe. It consisted of a first stage, the *trivium*, embracing grammar, rhetoric and dialectic (elementary logic), and an advanced *quadrivium* of mathematical subjects, arithmetic, geometry, astronomy and music.

SEVEN PINES, BATTLE OF. See FAIR OAKS, BATTLE OF.

SEVEN SAGES, lawgivers of ancient Greece and Asia Minor (c600 BC), famous for such maxims as "know thyself" and "nothing in excess." The usual list is: Cleobulus of Rhodes, Periander of Corinth, Pittacus of Mitylene, Bias of Priene, THALES of Miletus, Chilon of Sparta and SOLON of Athens.

SEVEN SLEEPERS OF EPHESUS, legendary heroes of a famous resurrection. Seven Christians were immured in a cave during the persecutions of Decius (c250). They miraculously awoke, two centuries later, in the reign of Theodosius II.

SEVENTH-DAY ADVENTISTS. See ADVENTISTS.

SEVEN WEEKS' WAR. See AUSTRO-PRUSSIAN WAR.

SEVEN WONDERS OF THE WORLD, the seven greatest structures of the ancient world, as listed by Greek scholars. The oldest wonder (and only survivor) is the PYRAMIDS of Egypt: the others were the HANGING GARDENS OF BABYLON; the 30ft statue of Zeus at OLYMPIA; the great temple of ARTEMIS at EPHESUS; the MAUSOLEUM at Halicarnassus; the COLOSSUS OF RHODES; and the PHAROS of Alexandria.

SEVEN YEARS' WAR (1756–1763), a war between Austria, France, Russia, Saxony, Sweden (from 1757) and (after 1762) Spain on the one side; and Britain, Prussia and Hanover on the other. In America the struggle centered on colonial rivalry between Britain and France and formed part of the FRENCH AND INDIAN WARS. In Europe the main dispute was between Austria and Prussia for supremacy in Germany. Austria's MARIA THERESA aimed to recover recently-lost Silesia (see AUSTRIAN SUCCESSION, WAR OF THE). This provoked Prussia to attack Saxony and Bohemia. Although severely pressed, the Prussians avoided complete defeat. By the treaties of Hubertusberg and Paris (1763), Britain emerged as the leading colonial power and Prussia as a major European force.

SEVERN RIVER, Britain's longest river, 220mi long. It rises in E Wales and flows E and S into the Bristol Channel. A 3 240ft road suspension bridge crosses the estuary. The Severn BORE is famous.

SEVERSKY, ALEXANDER PROCOFIEFF DE. See DE SEVERSKY, ALEXANDER PROCOFIEFF.

SEVERUS, ALEXANDER. See ALEXANDER SEVERUS.

SEVERUS, LUCIUS SEPTIMUS (146–211 AD), Roman emperor 193–211. During his rule he suppressed opposition in Byzantium, Mesopotamia and Gaul. He died at York, while campaigning in Britain.

SEVIER, John (1745–1815), US pioneer and first governor of Tenn. He was prominent in the Carolina Campaign of the Revolutionary War and became head of the state of Franklin in 1783 (see FRANKLIN, STATE OF). Sevier was made governor of Tenn. in 1796, serving until 1801, and again 1803–09. He was also a congressman (1789–91 and 1811–15).

SEVILLE, or Sevilla, city of SW Spain, the capital of Seville province and an important industrial center and port on the Guadalquivir R. Seville is famous for its historic buildings and HOLY WEEK PROCESSIONS; it was the birthplace of VELÁZQUEZ and MURILLO. Pop 548 072.

SÈVRES, suburb 6mi SW of Paris, France. It gives its name to the famous Sèvres porcelain, manufactured in the town since 1756. There is a ceramics museum. Pop 20083. (See POTTERY AND PORCELAIN.)

SÈVRES, Treaty of (1920), post-WWI treaty between the Allies and Turkey, negotiated at SÈVRES. Never ratified by Turkey, it aimed to abolish the OTTOMAN EMPIRE and protect the independence of surrounding countries. The Turks gained better terms by the Treaty of LAUSANNE (1923).

SEWAGE, the liquid and semisolid wastes from dwellings and offices, industrial wastes, and surface and storm waters. Sewage systems collect the sewage, transport and treat it, then discharge it into rivers, lakes or the sea. Vaulted sewers were developed by the Romans but from the Middle Ages and until the mid-19th century sewage flowed through the open gutters of cities, constituting a major health hazard. Then sewage was discharged into storm-water drains which were developed into sewers. But the dumping of large amounts of untreated sewage into rivers led to serious water POLLUTION, and modern treatment methods arose, at least for major cities. An early solution (still sometimes practiced) was sewage farming, raw sewage being used as FERTILIZER. Chemically-aided precipitation was also tried, but neither proved adequate. Noting that natural watercourses can purify a moderate amount of sewage, sanitary engineers imitated natural conditions by allowing atmospheric oxidation of the organic matter, first by passing it intermittently through a shallow tank filled with large stones (the "trickling filter"), and later much more successfully by the **activated-sludge process**, in which compressed air is passed through a sewage tank, the sludge being decomposed by the many microorganisms that it contains. A by-product is sludge gas, chiefly methane, burned as fuel to help power the treatment plant. Sedimentation is carried out before and after decomposition; the filtered solids are buried, incinerated or dried for fertilizer. The sewer system is designed for fast flow (about 1m/s) to carry the solids; the sewers are provided with manholes, drainage inlets, regulators and, finally, outfalls. Dwellings not connected to the sewers have their own SEPTIC TANK.

SEWALL, Samuel (1652–1730), one of the judges in the SALEM witchcraft trials. The trials, as a result of which 19 accused were hanged, were born from malicious rumor and hysteria: Sewall made public apology in 1697 for his support of the sentencings. (See also MATHER, COTTON.) He also wrote the first American antislavery tract.

SEWARD, William Henry (1801–1872), US politician famous for his purchase of ALASKA from Russia in 1867. Seward served under Thurlow WEED in N.Y. and as a prominent antislavery senator was appointed secretary of state by President Lincoln in 1861. He did much to keep Britain out of the Civil War (see TRENT AFFAIR). Seward survived an assassination attempt by an accomplice of BOOTH and served as President Johnson's secretary of state.

SEWARD PENINSULA, in W Alaska, runs 180mi S from Kotzebue Sound to Norton Sound and is the most westerly point of North America.

SEWELLEL, or **Mountain Beaver**, *Aplodontia rufa*, a rather primitive form of burrowing RODENT. Stocky, with a blunt muzzle and short brown fur, it is restricted to western North America. It is unusual in that the cheek teeth grow throughout life.

SEWING MACHINE, machine for sewing cloth, leather or books: a major industrial and domestic labor-saving device. There are two main types: chain-stitch machines, using a needle and only one thread, with a hook that pulls each looped stitch through the next; and lock-stitch machines, using two threads, one through the needle eye and the other, which interlocks with the first in the material, from a bobbin/shuttle system (to-and-fro or rotary). Chain-stitch machines—the first to be invented, by Barthélemy Thimmonier (1793–1859)—are now used chiefly for sacks or bags. The lock-stitch machines now in general use are based on that invented by Elias HOWE (1846). Zigzag machines differ from ordinary straight-stitch machines in having variously-shaped cams that move the needle from side to side. Almost all US machines are electrically powered, but foot-treadle machines are common elsewhere.

Shakespeare in context

	Shakespeare's life and works (some dates are debated)	Parallel events (political events in brackets)
1558		(Accession of Elizabeth I.)
1561		Birth of Thomas Kyd, Robert Greene, Francis Bacon. Performance of Sackville and Norton's *Gorboduc*, earliest English blank-verse tragedy.
1564	Shakespeare born in Stratford, 23 April; son of John Shakespeare, glover, and his wife, Mary Arden.	Birth of Christopher Marlowe, Galileo Galilei. Death of Michelangelo.
1567		Birth of Richard Burbage.
1572		Birth of Ben Jonson, John Donne.
1576	James Burbage builds The Theatre, Shoreditch.	Death of Titian.
1579	Start of period of financial difficulties for the Shakespeare family.	Publication of North's translation of Plutarch.
1582	Marries Anne Hathaway.	
1583	Birth of a daughter, Susanna.	
1585	Birth of the twins, Hamnet and Judith. Shakespeare may have left Stratford in this year.	
1586	Conjectured to have embarked on a period as a teacher and/or traveling actor.	Death of Sir Philip Sidney. Birth of John Ford.
1587		(Execution of Mary, Queen of Scots.) (Sack of Cadiz by Sir Francis Drake.) Publication of Greene's *Euphues* and second edition of Holinshed's *Chronicles*.
1588	Probable date of Shakespeare's arrival in London.	(Defeat of Spanish Armada.) Birth of Thomas Hobbes.
1590	Working as an actor; *Henry VI* plays written.	Publication of Marlowe's *Tamburlaine* and books 1–3 of Spenser's *Faerie Queene*.
1591		Publication of Lyly's *Endymion* and Sidney's *Astrophel and Stella*.
1592	Writing *Richard III, Comedy of Errors*; has probably begun sonnets. Reference to Shakespeare in *Greenes groats-worth of witte*.	Plague kills 15000 in London. Philip Henslowe's theatrical diary begun.
1593	Publication of *Venus and Adonis*; writing of *Titus Andronicus* and *Taming of the Shrew*.	Closure of London theaters owing to plague. Christopher Marlowe killed.
1594	Publication of *Rape of Lucrece*; *Titus Andronicus* is first Shakespeare play to be printed. Becomes a charter member of the Lord Chamberlain's Men; working on *Two Gentlemen of Verona, Love's Labours Lost* and *Romeo and Juliet*.	London theaters reopened in May. Marlowe's *Edward II* acted and printed. Publication of Nashe's *Unfortunate Traveller*, first picaresque novel in English; and of Kyd's *Spanish Tragedy*. Death of Tintoretto, Palestrina, Kyd.
1595	Writes *Richard II, Midsummer Night's Dream*.	Publication of Spenser's *Epithalamion*.
1596	Writes *King John, Merchants of Venice*. Death of his son Hamnet. Coat of arms granted to Shakespeare family.	Publication of books 4–6 of Spenser's *Faerie Queene*. Opening of Blackfriars Theatre, London.

SEX, the totality of the differences between the male and female partners engaged in sexual REPRODUCTION. Examples of sex are found among all levels of life save the VIRUSES. In the higher orders, fertilization is brought about by the fusion of two GAMETES, the male SPERM conveying genetic information to the female EGG, or ovum (see HEREDITY). Many INVERTEBRATES, most PLANTS and some FISHES are HERMAPHRODITE; that is, individuals may possess functioning male *and* female organs. This is not the case with BIRDS and MAMMALS, though these on occasion display **intersexuality**, where an individual may possess a confusion of male and female characteristics. **Sexual behavior** is an important facet of animal behavior (see BREEDING BEHAVIOR; RITUALS): it may also be at the root of AGGRESSION and TERRITORIALITY. To the psychologist, "sex" and "sexual behavior" are used in connection with human drives linked to reproduction, and similarly fantasies, sensations, etc. To the psychoanalyst, sexual behavior has its roots in INFANTILE SEXUALITY as well as INSTINCT; and the term also covers a wide range of behavior derived from or analogous to sexuality and sexual drives. (See also HOMOSEXUALITY.)

SEXAGESIMA. See CHURCH YEAR.

SEX CHROMOSOMES. See X AND Y CHROMOSOMES.

SEX HORMONES. See ANDROGENS; ESTROGENS; GLANDS; HORMONES.

SEXTANT, instrument for NAVIGATION, invented in 1730 and superseding the ASTROLABE. A fixed telescope is pointed at the HORIZON, and a radial arm is moved against an arc graduated in degrees until a mirror which it bears reflects an image of a known star or the sun down the telescope to coincide with the image of the horizon. The angular elevation of the star, with the exact time (see CHRONOMETER), gives the LATITUDE. The **air sextant** is a similar instrument,

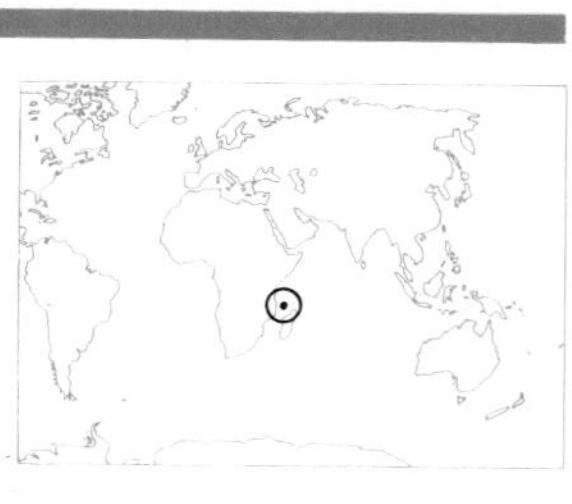

Official name: Seychelles
Capital: Victoria
Area: 107sq mi
Population: 56000
Languages: English, French; Creole patois spoken
Religion: Roman Catholic
Monetary unit(s): 1 Seychelle rupee = 100 cents

1597	Writes *Henry IV*, parts 1 and 2; *Henry V*. The Globe Theatre, Bankside, Southwark, is built with timbers from The Theatre and Shakespeare is made a shareholder with a tenth share.	Appearance of Chapman's translation of books 1–7 of Homer's *Iliad*. Jonson's *Every Man in His Humour* produced.
1599	Writes *Julius Caesar, As You Like It, Twelfth Night* in quick succession; begins *Hamlet*.	Death of Edmund Spenser. Birth of Oliver Cromwell. Jonson's *Every Man Out of His Humour* produced.
1600	Completion of *Hamlet*. *Merry Wives of Windsor* produced, probably at command of Elizabeth I.	Opening of the Fortune Theatre, London. Dekker's *Shoemaker's Holiday* produced.
1601	Writes *Troilus and Cressida*. Publication of *The Phoenix and the Turtle*. Shakespeare's father dies.	(Essex' rebellion against Elizabeth and execution of Essex; Elizabeth's last parliament held; the "Golden Speech" on November 20.)
1602	Writes *All's Well That Ends Well*.	
1603	Shakespeare's company becomes The King's Men and is allowed to wear king's livery.	(Death of Elizabeth I, accession of James VI & I.) Heywood's *A Woman Killed With Kindness* produced. Plague closes London's theaters again.
1604	*Measure for Measure* and *Othello* produced. Publication of the good quarto of *Hamlet*.	
1605	Completes *King Lear* and *Macbeth*.	(Discovery of the Gunpowder Plot.) Cervantes' *Don Quixote*, part 1, published in Spain.
1606	Writes *Antony and Cleopatra*.	Jonson's *Volpone* produced.
1607	Writes *Coriolanus* and *Timon of Athens*.	(Foundation of Jamestown, Va., by Captain John Smith.) Tourneur's *Revenger's Tragedy* produced. Beaumont's *The Knight of the Burning Pestle* produced.
1608	The King's Men play at Blackfriars. *Pericles* written, *Lear* and *Coriolanus* published.	Birth of Milton.
1609	Publication of the *Sonnets*. Original quartos of *Troilus* and *Pericles*. Writes *Cymbeline*.	Jonson's *Epicoene or the Silent Woman* produced.
1610	Writes *The Winter's Tale*.	Jonson's *The Alchemist* produced.
1611	Writes *The Tempest*. Retires and takes up virtually permanent residence at New Place.	Publication of the Authorized Version of the Holy Bible. Chapman's translation of Homer completed.
1612	Writes *Henry VIII*, probably with John Fletcher. Gives evidence in the Mountjoy lawsuit.	Webster's *White Devil* produced. (Dutch settlement of Manhattan Island; death of Robert Cecil.)
1613	Globe Theatre destroyed by fire during a performance of *Henry VIII*. Another probable Shakespeare–Fletcher collaboration, *The Two Noble Kinsmen*, produced.	(Francis Bacon made Attorney General of England.) Webster's *The Duchess of Malfi* produced.
1616	Death in Stratford on April 23	Jonson publishes a folio of his collected plays.
1623	John Heminges and Henry Condell publish the First Folio.	

Portrait engraving of William Shakespeare: the frontispiece of the First Folio, published in 1623.

usually periscopic, designed for use in aircraft, and has an artificial horizon, generally a bubble level.

SEXUAL SELECTION, the process whereby mates are chosen in sexually reproducing animal species. Competition for mates is thought to have been responsible for the EVOLUTION of secondary sexual characteristics.

SEYCHELLES, independent republic of some 85 islands (largest Mahé) in the Indian Ocean N and NE of the island of Madagascar. The climate is hot and often humid. Chief products are coconuts and spices, and fishing and tourism are important. A former British colony, it became independent in June 1976.

SEYMOUR, town in SW Conn., on the Naugatuck R, site of the first major US woolen mill. Modern manufactures include woolen goods and metal products. Pop 12 776.

SEYMOUR, city in S Ind., trade center for the surrounding farm region, with some light industry. Pop 13 352.

SEYMOUR, Horatio (1810–1886), US politician. As Democratic governor of New York (1862–64), he declared the EMANCIPATION PROCLAMATION unconstitutional and opposed national conscription, although encouraging voluntary enlistment. He was defeated by U. S. GRANT in the 1868 presidential election.

SEYMOUR, Lady Jane (c1509–1537), third wife of England's HENRY VIII (from 1536). She died after the birth of her son, EDWARD VI.

SEYSS-INQUART, Arthur (1892–1946), Austrian NAZI leader, governor of Austria (1938–39) and deputy governor of Poland (1939–40). As high commissioner for Holland (1940–45), his cruelty was notorious. He was executed for WAR CRIMES.

SFORZA, Ludovico (c1452–1508), *il Moro* (the Moor), ruler of Milan (1480–99) and patron of BRAMANTE and LEONARDO DA VINCI. Finally deposed by LOUIS XII, he spent his last years in a French prison.

S'GRAVENHAGE. See HAGUE, THE.

SHABA, formerly Katanga, a province of SE ZAIRE. The capital is Lumumbashi (formerly Elizabethville). It has fertile agricultural land, but its importance lies in its vast deposits of cobalt, copper and other minerals. With the Congo's independence (1960), Katanga proclaimed itself an independent republic under TSHOMBE; the secession was ended with UN help (1963).

SHACKAMAXON, Treaty of, or the Great Treaty (1683), treaty allegedly made between William PENN and the Delaware Indians. It is doubtful whether any treaty was signed.

SHACKLETON, Sir Ernest Henry (1874–1922), British Antarctic explorer. He was a member of SCOTT's 1901–04 expedition, and led his own parties in 1908–09 (when he located the S magnetic pole) and 1914–16. He died during a fourth expedition.

SHADS, marine herring-like fishes of the N Atlantic and Indo-Pacific. A food fish of economic importance, shads are caught in large quantities.

SHADOW, a nonilluminated region or area, shielded from receiving radiation from a light source by an extended object. A point source gives a sharply defined shadow, but an extended source gives rise to a region of full shadow (the umbra), surrounded by one of partial shadow (the penumbra).

SHAFTER, William Rufus (1835–1906), US soldier. In the SPANISH-AMERICAN WAR, he led the US expeditionary force which eventually gained the surrender of Santiago, Cuba (1898).

SHAFTESBURY, name of three important English earls. **Anthony Ashley Cooper** (1621–1683), 1st Earl, was a founder of the WHIG party and a staunch Protestant. After supporting both CROMWELL and the RESTORATION, he became lord chancellor in 1672, but was dismissed in 1673 for supporting the TEST ACT. He then built up the Whig opposition to CHARLES II, supporting MONMOUTH and opposing JAMES II's succession. He was acquitted of treason in 1681, but fled to Holland in 1682. **Anthony Ashley Cooper** (1671–1713), 3rd Earl, was a moral philosopher and pupil of John LOCKE. He aimed to found an ethical system based on an innate moral sense. **Anthony Ashley Cooper** (1801–1885), 7th Earl, was a statesman and leading evangelical Christian who promoted legislation to improve conditions in mines and factories and supported many movements for social improvement.

SHAH, Persian word meaning "king," borne as a title by the rulers of Middle Eastern and some Asian countries. It is used especially to refer to the ruler of Iran (Persia).

SHAH JAHAN (1592–1666), Mogul emperor of India (1628–58), famous for building the TAJ MAHAL. His reign saw the restoration of Islam as state religion, the conquest of S India and the golden age of Mogul art.

SHAHN, Ben (1898–1969), Lithuanian-born US artist. He used a realistic style to draw attention to social and political events. One of his best-known works is a series of paintings on the SACCO-VANZETTI CASE (1931–32).

SHAKER HEIGHTS, city in N Ohio, once a SHAKER colony, now a residential suburb of Cleveland. Pop 36 306.

SHAKERS, originally abusive term for the United Society of Believers in Christ's Second Appearing, a millenniastic sect who shook with ecstatic emotion in their worship. Originating among the QUAKERS of England, they were brought by "Mother" Ann Lee to the US in 1774, where they formed celibate communes which flourished until the mid-19th century.

SHAKESPEARE, William (1564–1616), English poet, playwright and actor-manager, one of the giants of world literature. Little certain is known of his early life. Son of a prosperous glover, he was born and educated at Stratford-upon-Avon in Warwickshire.

In 1582 he married Ann Hathaway, and they had three children. He moved to London c1589, probably as an actor at The Theatre, and by 1592 had made a name as a playwright. From 1594 he wrote and acted for the Lord Chamberlain's Men, and became a shareholding director of their new Globe Theatre in 1598. The theaters closed during the plague of 1592–94; during this time he wrote the two narrative poems *Venus and Adonis* and *The Rape of Lucrece*, and also the sonnets. The company survived the closure, rivalry and Puritan hostility to become the King's Men on the accession of James I in 1603, and in that year were able to buy the Blackfriars Theatre also. Shakespeare invested his money wisely, and so was able to retire to Stratford c1610, although he probably continued to write until 1613. Immensely successful in his time, Shakespeare stood out even against KYD, MARLOWE and Ben JONSON. He was recognized not only as the most richly endowed dramatist but as a poet of extraordinary sensibility and linguistic gifts.

Because his plays were generally not prepared for publication except to eclipse "pirated" versions, they have come down to us with many corruptions and variant readings. The chronology of the works is uncertain, and even the canon itself is disputed. For example, the *Henry VI* cycle is attributed to him alone, but may well have been a collaboration, as also *Henry VIII*. The first collected edition, known as the First Folio, was published in 1623. He probably revised many plays by others (*Pericles* may be one) and probably had a hand in other works, as in the anonymous plays known as the "Shakespeare Apocrypha." It seems certain, however, that it was Shakespeare and no other who wrote the plays that bear his name.

SHAKHTY, formerly Aleksandrovsk Grushevski, industrial city in the Donets Basin, European Russia, 40mi NE of Rostov-on-Don. It is an important anthracite-mining center. Pop 205 000.

SHAKTI, in Hinduism, the female generative principle, personified under many different names (e.g., KALI, LAKSHMI) corresponding to different aspects. Worship of Shakti as a mother goddess is prevalent in Bengal and Assam.

SHALE, fine-grained SEDIMENTARY ROCK formed by cementation of SILT particles usually also containing fragments of other minerals. Shales are rich in FOSSILS; and are laminated (they split readily into layers, or laminae). Their metamorphism (see METAMORPHIC ROCKS) produces SLATE. (See also OIL SHALE.)

SHALER, residential town in SW Pa., lying in the hills N of Pittsburgh. Pop 33 369.

SHALLOT, *Allium ascalonicum*, an onion-like plant that produces bunches of bulbs at ground level.

SHAMANISM, a primitive religious system centered around a shaman, or **medicine man**, who in trance state is believed to be possessed by spirits that speak and act through him. The shaman (from the language of the Tungus of Siberia) is expected to cure the sick, protect the tribe, foretell the future, etc. (See also MAGIC, PRIMITIVE.)

SHAMIL (c1797–1871), Muslim religious and political leader of the mountain peoples of Dagestan and Chechen in the N Caucasus. A leader of the Muridist religious sect, he established an independent state and withstood Russian attempts at conquest from 1834 to 1859.

SHAMMAI (c50 BC–c30 AD), Jewish scholar and, with HILLEL, the leading sage of his time. He founded the Bet Shammai school of Pharisaic philosophy, which was rigid in its interpretation of Jewish law, in opposition to Hillel's liberalism.

SHAMOKIN, city in E central Pa. Originally an anthracite-mining town, its various manufactures now include textiles and shoes. Pop 11 719.

SHAMROCK, popular name in Ireland for several LEGUMINOUS PLANTS, the trifoliate leaves of which were cited by St. Patrick as a symbol of the Christian Trinity. Among the plants called shamrock are the WOOD SORREL (*Oxalis acetosella*), white CLOVER (*Trifolium repens*) and black medic (*Medicago lupulina*).

SHANG DYNASTY, or Yin Dynasty, the first historic Chinese dynasty, traditionally said to have lasted c1766 BC–c1122 BC. The legendary founder was T'ang. The Shang civilization was agriculturally and technically advanced, and is famed for the artistic quality of its bronzes.

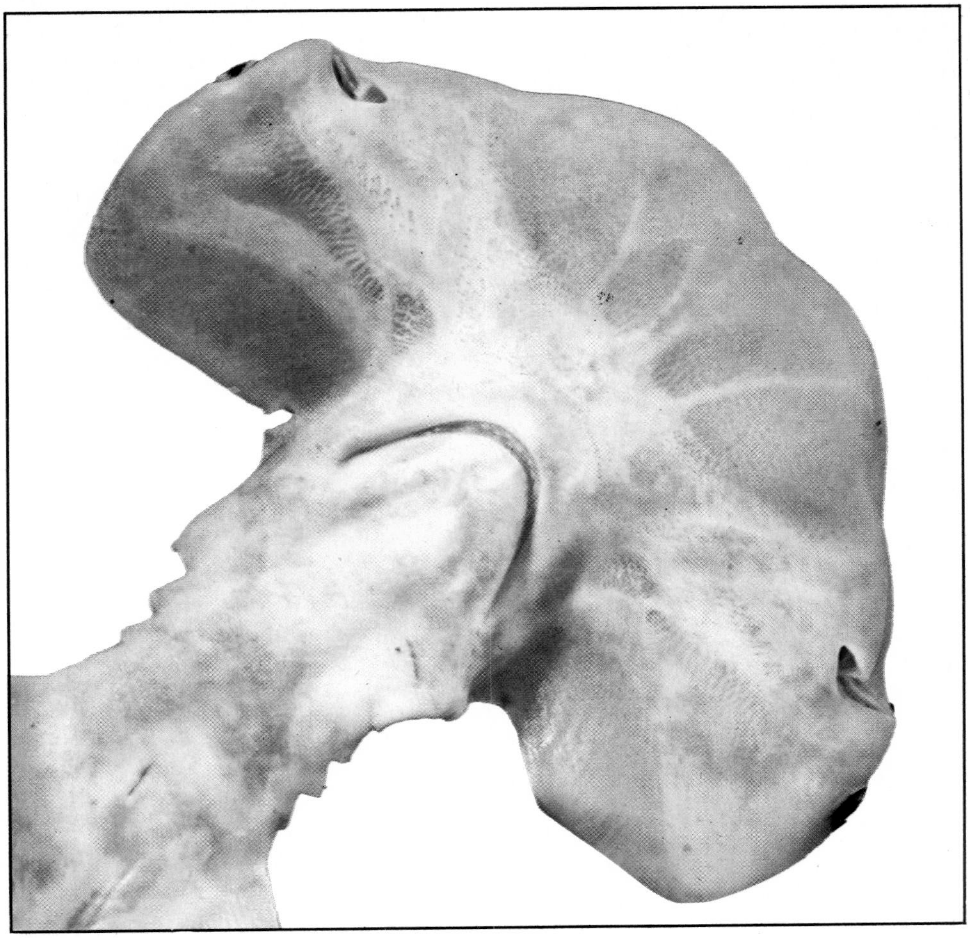

SHANGHAI, China's largest city, in SE Kiangsu province. It is a major seaport and a leading commercial and industrial center, producing textiles, iron and steel, ships, petroleum products and a wide range of manufactured goods. In 1842 it was the first Chinese port opened by treaty to foreign trade. Britain (1843), France (1849) and the US (1862) gained concessions to develop the city, and most of it remained under foreign control until WWII. The British and US concessions were renounced in 1943, France's in 1946. Pop 13 000 000.

SHANNON RIVER, chief river in Ireland and longest (240mi) in the British Isles. It rises in N Cavan and flows S and W through several loughs (lakes) into the Atlantic Ocean.

SHAO-HSING, or **Shaohing,** city in N Chekiang province, SE China, the commercial center of a silk, tea, rice and wine producing area. Pop 225 000.

SHAPLEY, Harlow (1885–1972), US astronomer who suggested that CEPHEID VARIABLES are not eclipsing binaries (see DOUBLE STAR) but pulsating stars. He was also the first to deduce the structure and approximate size of the MILKY WAY galaxy, and the position of the sun within it.

SHAPUR, or Sapor, name of two Persian kings of the Sassanian dynasty. **Shapur I** (d. 272 AD) was king c241–72. He expanded and consolidated his kingdom and decisively defeated the Romans under VALERIAN at Edessa. **Shapur II** (309–379) was proclaimed king at birth. A great general, he brought the Sassanian empire to the height of its power. Defeating and killing the Roman emperor JULIAN in battle, he imposed a humiliating peace on his successor JOVIAN and annexed Armenia.

SHARAKU TOSHUSAI (18th century), Japanese color-print artist. Himself a professional NOH dancer, in 1794–95 he produced over 136 striking prints of KABUKI theater performers.

SHARECROPPING, arrangement whereby a share of a tenant farmer's yearly land yield (usually 50%) went to the landowner in lieu of rent. The tenant provided the labor, while the landowner provided land, equipment and often loans to buy seed. The system was notorious for its abuses.

SHARE THE WEALTH MOVEMENTS, inflationary economic programs which arose in the US during the early 1930s, reflecting the anxieties of the Great Depression and hopes of a technological utopia. They sought to redistribute wealth and guarantee minimum incomes without destroying the capitalist system. Notable were the Townsend Plan for old-age pensions, the National Union for Social Justice and Huey LONG's Share-Our-Wealth clubs. They died out after the 1935 Social Security Act was passed.

SHARI'A, the Islamic sacred law. Based on divine revelation, it governs all human actions, which it classifies in five grades ranging from absolutely obligatory to absolutely prohibited. It still constitutes the civil law in Saudi Arabia, but other Muslim countries have modified it.

SHARIF, in the Islamic world, an honorific title usually reserved for descendants of Hasan, grandson of Muhammad. Traditionally, the most prominent sharif became ruler of Mecca and Medina.

SHARJAH, oil-producing emirate of the E Arabian Peninsula. Formerly British, since 1971 it has been a member of the UNITED ARAB EMIRATES. Capital: Sharjah. Area: 1 000sq mi. Pop 31 480.

SHARKS, an order, Pleurotremata, of about 250 species of CARTILAGINOUS FISHES of marine and fresh waters. Sharks, with the related RAYS and CHIMAERAS, have a skeleton formed entirely of CARTILAGE. Other distinguishing features are that the GILLS open externally through a series of gill-slits, rather than through a single operculum, and reproduction is by internal fertilization, unlike that of bony fishes. The body is fusiform and the upper lobe of the tail is usually better developed than the lower lobe. Sharks swim by sinuous movements of the whole body; there is no swimbladder (see AIRBLADDER) and they must swim constantly to avoid sinking. All are extremely

Left: various members of the shark family. (1) Mako, *Isurus oxyrinchus*, which may grow up to 10ft (3m) long; North Atlantic and Mediterranean. (2) Smooth hound, *Mustelus mustelus*; up to 3ft (1m) long; northwest Europe and Mediterranean. (3) Spurdog, *Squalus acanthias*; up to 3ft (1m) long; North Atlantic and Mediterranean. (4) Blue shark, *Prionace glauca*; up to 26ft (8m) long; all tropical and subtropical seas. (5) Spotted dogfish, *Scyliorhinus caniculus*; up to 2ft 6in (0.76m) long; northwest Europe and Mediterranean. (6) Basking shark, *Cetorhinus maximus*; up to 43ft (13m) long; North Atlantic and Mediterranean. (7) Hammerhead shark, *Sphyrna zygaena*; up to 13ft (4m) long; subtropical and tropical Atlantic and Mediterranean. *Opposite:* underside of the curiously-shaped head of a Bonnet shark, with the mouth, nostrils and eyes visible.

fast swimmers and active predators. Despite a universal reputation for unprovoked attack, only 27 out of the 250 known species have been definitely implicated in attacks on man.

SHARON, residential town in E Mass., 18mi SSW of Boston. Pop 12 367.

SHARON, industrial city in W Pa. Steel products and electrical equipment are manufactured. Pop 22 653.

SHARONVILLE, residential city in SW Ohio, 20mi NNE of Cincinnati. Pop 10 985.

SHARP, Granville (1735–1813), English abolitionist, philanthropist and biblical scholar. He obtained a ruling (1772) by which slavery was declared illegal in British possessions. A vigorous political and biblical pamphleteer, he founded the Association for the Abolition of Slavery (1787).

SHARPSBURG, Battle of, alternative name for the Battle of ANTIETAM.

SHARPS RIFLE, the first RIFLE with a really satisfactory breech-loading system, invented in Philadelphia in 1848 by Christian Sharps (1811–1874). The breechblock was raised and lowered in a vertical mortise by the action of a lever that also served as a trigger guard.

SHASTA, Mount, highest peak in the Cascade Range, N Cal. It is an extinct volcano 14 162ft high.

SHATT-AL-ARAB, river formed by the confluence of the Tigris R and Euphrates R in SE Iraq. It flows 120mi SE into the Persian Gulf, and forms part of the Iran–Iraq border.

SHAVUOT, Jewish festival celebrated on the sixth and seventh days of the month Sivan (usually May). Originally an agricultural festival, it commemorates the receiving of the TORAH on Mt Sinai.

SHAW, "Artie" (Arthur Arshewsky Shaw, 1910–), US jazz musician and bandleader. He was a brilliant clarinetist and, in the 1930s and 1940s, led several successful dance bands of the "Swing Era."

SHAW, George Bernard (1856–1950), British dramatist, critic and political propagandist whose witty plays contained serious philosophical and social ideas. Born in Dublin, he went to London (1876) and became a music and theater critic and a leader of the FABIAN SOCIETY. He began writing his brilliantly witty, ironical and polemical comedies in the 1890s. Success came with such plays as *Major Barbara* (1905), *Caesar and Cleopatra* (1906; written 1899), *Androcles and the Lion* (1912) and *Pygmalion* (1913; later adapted as a musical, *My Fair Lady*). He lost popularity for his opposition to WWI, but regained it with *Back to Methuselah* (1921); *St. Joan* (1923), his greatest success, was followed by the 1925 Nobel Prize in Literature. He continued to write up to his death.

SHAW, Henry Wheeler. See BILLINGS, JOSH.

SHAW, Lemuel (1781–1861), US judge. He was chief justice of the Mass. supreme court 1830–60, and many of his decisions influenced succeeding law.

SHAW, Robert Gould (1837–1863), US Unionist CIVIL WAR hero. Black himself, he led the first regiment of black troops to be raised in a free state. He was killed attacking Fort Wagner, S.C.

SHAWINIGAN, city in S Quebec, Canada. Its products include aluminum, paper, chemicals and abrasives. Pop 27 792.

SHAWM, double-reed woodwind instrument, a forerunner of the OBOE. Originating in the Near East, it was introduced to Europe at the time of the Crusades, and was in use up to the 18th century.

SHAWN, "Ted" (Edwin Myers Shawn, 1891–1972), US dancer, choreographer and teacher. With his wife, Ruth ST. DENIS, he founded the Denishawn school and company (1915–31), and developed an international dance center at Jacob's Pillow.

SHAWNEE, city in NE Kan. It is a residential suburb of Kansas City and a trade center for the surrounding agricultural area. Pop 20 482.

SHAWNEE, city in central Okla., seat of Pottawatomie Co. It is the center of a rich agricultural and oil-producing area. Pop 25 075.

SHAWNEE INDIANS, North American tribe of the ALGONQUIAN language group. They settled in the Ohio Valley during the 18th century, hunting and cultivating maize. In 1811, chief TECUMSEH attempted to unite the Indian tribes against the white man, but the Shawnee were defeated at the Battle of TIPPECANOE. They were eventually resettled in Okla., where about 2 250 still live.

SHAWNEE PROPHET. See TENSKWATAWA.

SHAYS' REBELLION, Aug. 1786–Feb. 1787, an armed uprising in Mass., led by Daniel Shays (c1747–1825) to protest high taxes and the severity of legal action against debtors during the postwar depression. The insurgents forced courts to drop actions against debtors, but were defeated attacking a federal arsenal. The uprising led to some reforms.

SHCHEDRIN, N. See SALTYKOV, MIKHAIL EVGRAFOVICH.

SHEARING, type of deformation in which parallel planes in an object tend to slide over one another. Shear forces are always present in beams and whenever an object is subjected to bending stresses.

SHEARWATERS, a group of some 15 species of seabirds of the family Procellariidae, which also includes the PETRELS. They are tube-nosed birds which have nostrils opening through horny tubes on the upper mandible. Quantities of oil are produced in the gut and are used variously in different species for waterproofing the plumage in preening, feeding to the young, or, vomited, as a defense mechanism. Shearwaters are oceanic birds except when they return to offshore islands to breed. They nest colonially in burrows.

SHEBA. See SABAEANS.

SHEBOYGAN, city in E Wis., on Lake Michigan, seat of Sheboygan Co. It is a port of entry with varied manufacturing industry. Pop 48 484.

SHEEN, Fulton John (1895–), US Roman Catholic archbishop, widely known in the US for his popular inspirational radio and television talks, and for his strong conservative stance on many issues.

Dramatist George Bernard Shaw in his 83rd year.

SHEEP, a diverse genus of mammals best known in the various races of the domestic sheep *Ovis aries* bred for both MEAT and WOOL. Wild sheep are a diverse group of mountain-dwelling forms with some 37 races alive today. They divide into two large groups: the Asiatic sheep, which include the MOUFLONS, urials and ARGALIS, and the American sheep, the Thinhorns and BIGHORNS. Asiatic sheep are long-legged, lightly-built animals which prefer a gentle rolling terrain. American-type sheep by comparison are heavy-set and barrel-chested, and characteristic of steep slopes and rocky areas, in part filling the role played in Europe and Asia by the IBEX. Sheep are social animals; males usually form bands following a dominant ram and females form separate parties following a mature ewe. The rams use their horns and the specially-thickened bone of their foreheads for combat, not only in the rut but also in dominance struggles.

SHEFFIELD, city in Yorkshire, England. It is famous for its cutlery and SHEFFIELD PLATE, and is a major heavy industrial center with steel, iron and brass foundries. Pop 519 703.

SHEFFIELD, industrial city in NW Ala. Power for its chemical and metallurgical industries comes from Wilson Dam. Pop 13 115.

SHEFFIELD PLATE, articles made from SILVER plated on copper by a method of FUSION involving heat and pressure, discovered about 1743 by a Sheffield cutler, Thomas Boulsover. This method was widely used before the advent of ELECTROPLATING.

SHEIKH, or Shaikh, or Shaykh, an Arabic title of respect applied to a worthy man over 50 years old, also to chiefs of families, villages and tribes, and to religious leaders.

SHELBY, city in SW N.C., seat of Cleveland Co. It lies in a rich cotton-growing area, and textiles form its main industry. Pop 16 328.

SHELBY, Isaac (1750–1826), US frontier leader who defeated the British at KING'S MOUNTAIN (1780) and planned the action at COWPENS (1781). He was the first governor of Kentucky, 1792–96. In the WAR OF 1812 he led volunteers who helped defeat the British at the Battle of the THAMES.

SHELBYVILLE, city in central Ind., seat of Shelby Co. It is the commercial center of a rich corn, dairy and livestock region. Pop 15 094.

SHELBYVILLE, city in central Tenn., seat of Bedford Co. It is noted for horse training and breeding, and has some light industry. Pop 12 262.

SHELDUCK, various species of DUCK related to the typical Dabbling ducks. There are two main genera, *Tadorna*, the typical shelducks of Europe, Africa and Asia, and *Clöephaga*, the sheldgeese of South America. Most are large piebald or parti-colored ducks of inland lakes and coastal waters.

SHELEKHOV, Grigori Ivanovich (1747–1795), Russian merchant who organized an expedition to Alaska (1783), and founded the first Russian colony there (1784). His company later developed into the Russian American Company (1799).

SHELL, any calcareous external covering secreted by an invertebrate, enclosing and protecting the body. The term is used particularly for the shells of MOLLUSKS, but also refers to those of FORAMINIFERANS, and may be used loosely to describe the CARAPACE or chitinous EXOSKELETON of CRUSTACEANS and INSECTS.

SHELLAC, brown, flaky RESIN secreted by the **lac insect**, *Laccifer lacca*, a SCALE INSECT. Naturally thermoplastic (see PLASTICS), it is used with fillers to make molded articles, and as an ingredient in paints, lacquers, polishes etc. A solution of shellac in ETHANOL is used as varnish.

SHELLEY, Mary Wollstonecraft (1797–1851), English writer, daughter of William GODWIN and Mary WOLLSTONECRAFT and wife of Percy Bysshe SHELLEY. Her best-known work is the Gothic horror-story *Frankenstein* (1818). She wrote several other novels and edited Shelley's poems.

SHELLEY, Percy Bysshe (1792–1822), English Romantic poet whose work reflects his revolutionary political idealism and his strong faith in the spiritual power of the imagination. It includes long narrative poems such as *Queen Mab* (1813), *The Revolt of Islam* (1818) and *Epipsychidion* (1821), the verse drama *Prometheus Unbound* (1820) and such famous lyrics as the "Ode to the West Wind." He was drowned in a boating accident in Italy, where he had settled with his second wife Mary.

SHELLFISH, any of a number of aquatic invertebrates. It has no taxonomic value but is commonly used for edible species of MOLLUSKS, SHRIMPS and PRAWNS.

SHELTER BELT, or **windbreak**, natural or specially planted barrier of vegetation arranged to protect crops and agricultural land from erosion by the wind. (See SOIL EROSION.)

SHELTON, city in SW Conn., on the Housatonic R. Manufactures include metal goods, textiles and furniture. Pop 27 165.

SHEM. See SEMITES.

SHENANDOAH NATIONAL PARK, in the Appalachian Mts, N Va. Covering about 300sq mi along the crest of the Blue Ridge Mts, it is heavily wooded and affords magnificent views along the Skyline Drive, which runs its whole length.

SHENANDOAH VALLEY, between the Allegheny and Blue Ridge Mts in NW Va. About 150mi long and up to 25mi wide, it is a rich farming area famed for its natural beauty. It was the scene of the CIVIL WAR Shenandoah Valley Campaigns (1862–64).

SHENYANG. See MUKDEN.

SHEPARD, Alan Bartlett Jr (1923–   ), first US astronaut (May 5, 1961). He was later grounded by a medical complaint, but overcame this to command the Apollo 14 moon-landing (Jan. 31, 1971).

Some varieties of domesticated sheep. (1) Rambouillet, a breed derived from the famous Merino, is kept for its fine wool; (2) the Southdown breed yields medium wool; (3) the Lincoln yields long coarse wool; (4) the Karakul breed, whose lambs give the so-called Astrakhan wool.

SHEPHERD'S PURSE, *Capsella bursa-pastoris*, common annual cruciferous herb that flowers the whole year round. It has been used for birdseed, in medicine and as an ingredient for salads.

SHERATON, Thomas (1751–1806), English furniture designer. His elegant style of furniture was popular around 1800, and his *Cabinet-Maker and Upholsterer's Drawing Book* (1791–94) was very influential.

SHERBROOKE, city in S Quebec, Canada. It is a trade center whose manufactures include textiles, machinery and rubber and leather goods. Pop 80 711.

SHERIDAN, city in N Wyo., seat of Sheridan Co. It is a resort, trade and transportation center in an agricultural and mining region. Pop 10 856.

SHERIDAN, "Little Phil" (Philip Henry Sheridan, 1831–1888), US general and Union CIVIL WAR hero. After successes in the Chattanooga and WILDERNESS campaigns, he commanded the army which defeated General EARLY and devastated the SHENANDOAH VALLEY (1864). In 1865 he won the Battle of FIVE FORKS and helped end the war by cutting off Robert E. LEE's line of retreat from APPOMATTOX. He became commander of the US army 1884.

SHERIDAN, Richard Brinsley (1751–1816), Irish-born English dramatist and politician famous for his witty comedies of manners, including *The Rivals* (1775), *The School for Scandal* (1777) and *The Critic* (1779). A Whig member of parliament (1780–1812), he played a leading part in the impeachment of Warren HASTINGS.

SHERIFF, chief law officer of US counties. The title derives from the chief administrator of the historic English shire (*shire reeve*). The modern sheriff is usually elected. Police-keeping functions vary according to local law, but duties generally include executing writs and guarding prisoners.

SHERLOCK HOLMES. See DOYLE, SIR ARTHUR CONAN.

SHERMAN, city in N Tex., seat of Grayson Co. It is a trading center for a farming region. Food-processing leads its industries. Pop 29 061.

SHERMAN, two brothers important in the CIVIL WAR era. **William Tecumseh Sherman** (1820–1891), was a Union commander, second in importance only to General Ulysses S. GRANT. He fought in the Battles of BULL RUN (1861), SHILOH (1862) and in the Vicksburg campaign (1862–63). He was given command of the Army of Tennessee and, with Grant, took part in the Chattanooga Campaign (1863). As supreme commander in the West (1864) he invaded Ga. capturing Atlanta and marching on Savannah. He then turned N, pushing General Joseph Johnson's army before him, and accepting its surrender at Durham, N.C., in April, 1865. The destruction he wrought in his attempt to destroy Confederate supplies and communications and break civilian morale made him a hero in the N and a villain in the S. He was US army commander 1869–84. **John Sherman** (1823–1900) was a founder member of the REPUBLICAN PARTY. A senator 1861–77 and 1881–97, and secretary of the treasury 1877–81, he introduced the SHERMAN ANTITRUST ACT and the SHERMAN SILVER PURCHASE ACT.

SHERMAN, James Schoolcraft (1855–1912), US Republican politician who was vice-president under W. H. Taft, 1909–12. He was a member of the House of Representatives 1887–91, 1893–1909.

SHERMAN, Roger (1721–1793), American patriot who helped draft, and signed, the Declaration of Independence. He was a member of the 1787 Constitutional Convention and, with Oliver ELLSWORTH, introduced the "Connecticut Compromise." (See UNITED STATES CONSTITUTION.) He was US Representative (1789–91) and senator (1791–93) for Conn.

SHERMAN ANTITRUST ACT (1890), first major federal action to curb the power of the giant business MONOPOLIES which grew up after the Civil War. Its failure to define key terms, such as *trust*, *combination* and *restraint of trade*, led to loopholes, and it was strengthened by the CLAYTON ANTITRUST ACT (1914).

SHERMAN SILVER PURCHASE ACT (1890), a compromise measure aiming to placate mineowners and the advocates of FREE SILVER, which required the

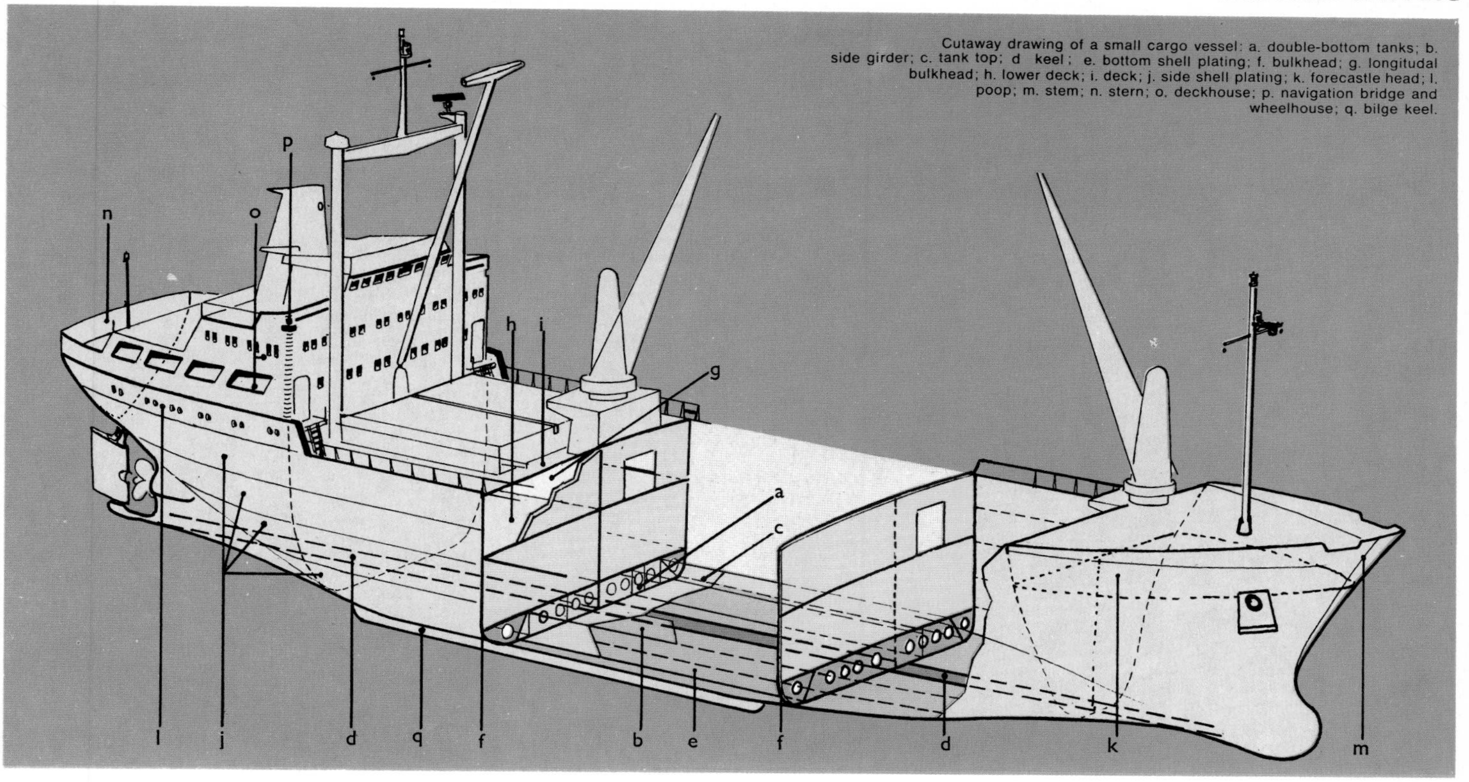

Cutaway drawing of a small cargo vessel: a. double-bottom tanks; b. side girder; c. tank top; d keel; e. bottom shell plating; f. bulkhead; g. longitudal bulkhead; h. lower deck; i. deck; j. side shell plating; k. forecastle head; l. poop; m. stem; n. stern; o. deckhouse; p. navigation bridge and wheelhouse; q. bilge keel.

US government to double its monthly silver purchases. It threatened to undermine gold reserves and was repealed when the panic of 1893 began.

SHERPA, Buddhist people of NE Nepal, famous as Himalayan porters. Of Tibetan origins and speaking a Tibetan language, they number some 85 000 and raise cattle, grow crops and spin wool in the high valleys of the Himalayas.

SHERRINGTON, Sir Charles Scott (1857–1952), British neurophysiologist who shared with E. D. ADRIAN the 1932 Nobel Prize for Physiology or Medicine for studies of the NERVOUS SYSTEM which form the basis of our modern understanding of its action.

SHERRY, an ALCOHOLIC BEVERAGE named for Jérez de la Frontera, Spain, where it originated. It is an aperitif wine, matured in wooden casks and fortified with brandy to bring the alcohol level to about 20% by volume.

SHERWOOD, Robert Emmet (1896–1955), US playwright who won four Pulitzer prizes: for *Idiot's Delight* (1936), *Abe Lincoln in Illinois* (1938), *There Shall Be No Night* (1940) and his biography *Roosevelt and Hopkins: An Intimate History* (1948).

SHETLAND ISLANDS, or Zetland, archipelago of some 100 islands off N Scotland, constituting its northernmost county. Less than a quarter are inhabited; Lerwick is the chief town and port. The main occupations are fishing and cattle and sheep raising. The Shetlands are famous for their knitted woolen goods and the SHETLAND PONY.

SHETLAND PONY, tiny and shaggy-haired, the smallest of the PONIES, probably a relict of prehistoric British and Scandinavian HORSES. Once restricted to the Shetland Isles, it has now been widely bred as a riding pony for children.

SHETLAND SHEEP DOG, breed of dog developed in the SHETLAND ISLANDS. It has a thick black, brown or blue-gray coat with white and tan markings and resembles a small COLLIE, standing about 15in at the shoulder.

SHIELD, a piece of ARMOR, usually carried on the left arm, whose purpose was to protect the body from an enemy's weapons. In the Middle Ages shields acquired a decorative and symbolic function (see HERALDRY). The introduction of firearms, requiring the use of both hands, rendered them obsolete.

SHIH-CHIA-CHUANG, city in NE China, capital of Hopeh province. It is a major transportation, commercial, and industrial center. Pop 1 500 000.

SHIH-HUANG-TI (259 BC–210 BC), "First Sovereign Emperor," title assumed in 221 BC by King Cheng of Ch'in (NW China) when he had created a unified Chinese empire and founded the CH'IN dynasty. He created the centralized government that was the model for all succeeding dynasties, and built the GREAT WALL OF CHINA.

SHIH TZU, a breed of toy dog originating in Tibet. Standing about 10in at the shoulder, it has a thick coat (in a variety of colors) which forms a beard and whiskers round its face. It is a popular pet.

SHI'ITES, members of an Islamic sect opposed to the orthodox SUNNITES. The Shi'ites reject the first three caliphs and recognize Ali (Mohammed's son-in-law) and his descendants as rightful successors to Mohammed. They number some 40 000 000, concentrated principally in Iran and Iraq.

SHIKOKU, smallest of the four principal islands (7 245sq mi in area) of Japan situated S of Honshu and E of Kyushu. With a subtropical climate, it produces tea, camphor, rice, fruit and tobacco.

SHILOH, Battle of, major conflict of the US CIVIL WAR, fought at Pittsburgh Landing, Tenn. (April 6–7, 1872). The Union Army under General Ulysses S. GRANT was forced back by a surprise onslaught of the 40 000 strong Confederate army under General A. S. JOHNSTON. The reinforced Union Army routed the Confederates in a counterattack the next day. Casualties were over 10 000 on each side.

SHIMIZU, city and seaport in Japan, in E central Honshu on Suruga Bay. It is a fishing center. Pop 234 966.

SHIMONOSEKI, historic seaport in Japan, situated in SW Honshu. It has large shipyards and heavy industrial plants. Pop 258 422.

SHIMONOSEKI, Treaty of, April 1895, treaty which ended the first SINO-JAPANESE WAR, 1894–95. China's defeat led to Korea's independence and Japan's acquisition of Taiwan and the Pescadores Islands.

SHINGLES, or **herpes zoster**, a VIRUS disorder characterized by development of pain, a vesicular rash and later scarring, often with persistent pain, over the SKIN of part of face or trunk. The virus seems to settle in or near nerve cells following CHICKENPOX, which is caused by the same virus, and then becomes activated, perhaps years later and sometimes by disease. It then leads to the acute skin eruption which is in the distribution of the nerve involved.

SHINN, Everett (1876–1953), US painter, member of "The Eight" or ASHCAN SCHOOL. He is best known for his pictures of the theater and music hall world, such as *Revue* (1908).

SHINTO ("way of the gods"), indigenous religion of Japan originally based on the belief that the royal family was descended from the sun-goddess Amaterasu Omikami. It later absorbed much Buddhist thought and practice. At its core is the idea that *kami* (divine power) is manifest at every moment in every thing; hence attention paid to each moment, however trivial, will lead to the realization of truth. Shinto shrines are plain wooden buildings in which priest and people perform simple rites; the imperial shrine is at Ise. Worship of the emperor and the ZEN influence on martial arts resulted in a close connection between Shinto and Japanese militarism. State Shinto ended after WWII.

SHIP MONEY, in English history, originally an emergency tax for naval defense in wartime. CHARLES I's attempt (1634–39) to establish it as a general and permanent tax was a cause of the English CIVIL WAR.

SHIPS AND SHIPPING, large seagoing vessels and their uses for transport and warfare. The first ships were probably developed from river craft by the Mesopotamians and Egyptians as early as the 4th millennium BC, and the Mediterranean became the home of the first sea-based civilizations (see MINOAN CIVILIZATION, MYCENAE, PHOENICIA). Early ships had a single sail on a fixed yard-arm, a stern oar for a rudder, and one or more banks of oars, a classic example being the Greek trireme. There is evidence that the Phoenicians ventured in such ships as far as Britain and round Africa before 600 BC. Under the Roman Empire the whole Mediterranean was controlled by a navy, and grain-carrying GALLEYS up to 180ft long were built.

In medieval Europe the VIKING longships developed into square-rigged GALLEONS, with fixed stern rudders. These were capable of long sea voyages, and the 15th and 16th centuries saw the great world explorations of Christopher COLUMBUS, Vasco da GAMA and Ferdinand MAGELLAN. In the age of colonial expansion, world trade and naval rivalry which followed, large navies and shipping fleets developed rapidly, and the great "men o' war" and the grain CLIPPERS represented the culmination of the age of sail.

A steamship first crossed the Atlantic in 1819, and the screw-driven GREAT EASTERN (1858) was the first large iron ship. By the early 20th century steel construction and steam turbines dominated, and passenger liners, warships and cargo ships increased spectacularly in size and power. Modern developments include SUBMARINES, AIRCRAFT CARRIERS, nuclear-powered vessels and supertankers of up to 500 000 tons. (See also BATTLESHIP; BOATS AND BOATING; JUNK; MERCHANT SHIPPING; NAVIGATION; NAVY; TRANSPORTATION; YACHTS AND YACHTING.)

SHIPWORM, despite its name, a bivalve MOLLUSK, *Teredo navalis*, notorious for burrowing into the timbers of piers and wooden ships. The body is long and wormlike, with the shell reduced to a tiny pair of abrasive plates at the head end. These are used for rasping into wood—at a rate sometimes exceeding 300mm (1ft) per month.

SHIRAZ, industrial and commercial city in SW central Iran. An important center since the 7th century, it is famous for its carpets and gold and silver work. More recent products include petrochemicals and cement. Pop 269 865.

SHIRE, river in SE Africa, flowing S for about 250mi from the S point of Lake Nyasa, Malawi, to the Zambezi R in central Mozambique.

SHIVA, important deity of HINDUISM, representing that aspect of the Godhead connected with the destruction necessary for renewal of life. He is sometimes depicted as an ascetic youth. In the role of recreator he is called the happy one. His phallic emblem is worshipped. (See also KALI.)

SHIVELEY, residential city in N central Ky. Liquor is distilled there. Pop 19 150.

SHIVERING, fine contractions of MUSCLES, causing slight repetitive movements, employed for increasing heat production by the body, thus raising body temperature in conditions of cold or when DISEASE induces FEVER. Uncontrollable shivering with gross movements of the whole body is a rigor only seen in some fevers.

SHIZUOKA, city and port in E Honshu, Japan, 55mi SW of Tokyo. Tea is a major export. Pop 416 379.

SHKODËR, or **Scutari**, city in NW Albania, possibly one-time capital of ILLYRIA. After Turkish rule, 1479–1913, it passed to Albania. It now has mixed industries including cement and textiles. Pop 55 300.

SHM. See SIMPLE HARMONIC MOTION.

SHOCK specifically refers to the development of low blood pressure, inadequate to sustain BLOOD CIRCULATION, usually causing cold, clammy, gray SKIN and extremities, faintness and mental confusion and decreased urine production. It is caused by acute blood loss; burns with PLASMA loss; acute HEART failure; massive pulmonary EMBOLISM, and SEPTICEMIA. If untreated, death ensues. Early replacement of plasma or BLOOD and administration of DRUGS to improve blood circulation are necessary to prevent permanent BRAIN damage and acute KIDNEY failure.

SHOCK, Electric. See ELECTRIC SHOCK.

SHOCKLEY, William Bradford (1910–   ), US physicist who shared with BARDEEN and BRATTAIN the 1956 Nobel Prize for Physics for their joint development of the TRANSISTOR.

SHOCK THERAPY, or electroconvulsive therapy (ECT), is a form of treatment used in MENTAL ILLNESS, particularly DEPRESSION, in which carefully regulated electric shocks are given to the BRAINS of anesthetized patients. (Muscular relaxants are used to prevent injury through forceful MUSCLE contractions.) The mode of action is unknown but rapid resolution of severe depression may be achieved.

SHOE, protective covering for the foot. The various types include the boot, whose upper extends above the ankle; the clog, a simple wooden-soled shoe; the moccasin, a hunting shoe whose sole extends around and over the foot; the sandal, an open shoe whose sole is secured to the foot by straps, and the slipper, a soft indoor shoe. Shoes have been made from earliest times, the type depending mainly on the climate; clogs, sandals and moccasins predominated until the early Middle Ages, since when boots and typical shoes in widely varying styles have been most popular. LEATHER has always been the main material used, shaped on a *last* of wood or metal, and hand-sewn, the sole being nailed to the upper. From the mid-19th century the SEWING MACHINE was adapted for sewing shoes, and nailing and gluing were also mechanized, allowing mass-production. Other materials have to some extent displaced leather—natural and synthetic RUBBER for the sole and heel, and various PLASTICS and synthetic fibers for the upper.

SHOEBILL, *Balaeniceps rex*, a heavily-built swamp bird of E Africa. Gray, and nearly 1.2m (3.9ft) high, they have a long neck, heavy head and massive bill almost as broad as it is long. They feed on fish, frogs and small turtles.

SHOEMAKER, "Willie" (William Lee Shoemaker, 1931–   ), US jockey who rode his 6 033rd winner in 1970, breaking all previous records. By 1972 he had won a record $50 000 000 in prize money.

SHOFAR, ram's horn used as a musical instrument on important Jewish ritual occasions such as ROSH HASHANAH and YOM KIPPUR.

SHOGUN, title of the hereditary military commanders of Japan who usurped the power of the Emperor in the 12th century and ruled the country for about 700 years. In 1867 the last TOKUGAWA Shogun was forced to resign and restore sovereignty to the Emperor.

SHOLAPUR, city in W central India, 170mi W of Hyderabad. It is an administrative center with important textile industries. Pop 398 122.

SHOLEM ALEICHEM (1859–1916), pseudonym of Solomon Rabinovitch, Russian-born YIDDISH humorous writer. He was an immensely prolific and popular author, and his novels, short stories and plays tell of the serious and absurd aspects of Jewish life in E Europe. His works include *The Old Country* and *Tevye's Daughters*.

SHOLES, Christopher Latham (1819–1890), US inventor (with some help from others) of the TYPEWRITER (patented 1868). He sold his patent rights to the REMINGTON Arms Company in 1873.

SHOLOKHOV, Mikhail Alexandrovich (1905–   ), Russian novelist, the first Soviet writer to be awarded the Nobel Prize in Literature (1965). He is best known for his stories about the Don Cossacks of S Russia. His greatest work is *Quiet Flows the Don* (1928–40).

SHOOTING. See TARGET SHOOTING; TRAPSHOOTING.

SHOOTING STAR. See METEOR.

SHOREVIEW, village in SE Minn., built around seven lakes, a residential suburb of St. Paul. It has ammunition industries. Pop 10 995.

SHOREWOOD, village in SE Wis., a residential suburb of Milwaukee. Pop 15 576.

SHORTHAND, or **stenography**, any writing system permitting the rapid transcription of speech. The three most used today are Isaac Pitman Shorthand, the first to be commercially developed (c1837), Gregg Shorthand, developed c1888 by John Robert Gregg, both of which are phonetic, using symbols to represent recurring sounds; and Speedwriting, which uses abbreviations. Shorthand is much used by secretaries, journalists, court reporters, etc. (See also STENOTYPE.)

SHORT PARLIAMENT, convened by the English king CHARLES I in April 1640 to finance the Scottish war. The House of Commons wanted first to settle major grievances, so the king dissolved Parliament in May. (See English CIVIL WAR.)

SHORTSIGHTEDNESS. See MYOPIA.

SHORT STORY, form of prose fiction, usually limited in character and situation, and between 500 and 20 000 words long. CHAUCER's *Canterbury Tales* and BOCCACCIO's *Decameron* are medieval collections of short stories. The artform was revived in the 19th century, and prominent short story writers have been POE, MAUPASSANT, CHEKHOV, O. HENRY, Henry JAMES, Katherine MANSFIELD, HEMINGWAY and O'HARA. (See also NOVEL.)

SHOSHONE INDIANS, group of North American Indians originally inhabiting the territory between SE Cal. and W Wyo. The Shoshoni of E Utah and Wyo. were typical buffalo hunting tribesmen of the plains. In the 18th century the COMANCHE INDIANS split off and moved S to modern Tex. There are about 8 000 Shoshoni on reservation lands today.

SHOSTAKOVICH, Dmitri (1906–1975), Russian composer. Some of his music is notably patriotic. His works include the opera *Lady Macbeth of the District of Mzensk* (1934) and 15 symphonies of which the most famous are the Fifth (1937), the Seventh, "the Leningrad," written during the seige of Leningrad (1941) and the Tenth (1953). His important works of chamber music include the *Piano Quintet* (1940).

SHOTGUN, smooth-bore FIREARM fired from the shoulder, designed to discharge a quantity of small lead pellets ("shot") in a diverging pattern, which increases the chances of hitting small fast-moving targets such as game-birds. Although repeating shotguns have been available since 1860, the double-barreled model has retained its popularity. One of the barrels usually has its bore "choked"—i.e., slightly tapered toward the muzzle to limit the pellet spread and increase the lethal range, which is usually about 50 yards.

SHOT PUT. See TRACK AND FIELD.

SHOULDER, JOINT between the upper ARM (humerus) and the upper trunk (scapula, COLLAR BONE and rib cage). It is an open ball-and-socket joint which is only stable by virtue of the numerous powerful MUSCLES around it; this leads to increased maneuverability.

SHRAPNEL, originally a projectile containing lead bullets, an explosive charge and a time fuze, invented by a British artillery officer, Henry Shrapnel (1761–1842). The term now refers to the fragmenting case of a high-explosive shell (see AMMUNITION).

SHREVEPORT, city in NW La., seat of Caddo parish, on the Red R. It is the commercial center of a large area producing lumber, oil (discovered 1906), natural gas and agricultural goods. It manufactures furniture and farm equipment. Pop 182 064.

SHREWS, small mouse-like insectivorous mammals with short legs and long pointed noses. They have narrow skulls and sharp, rather unspecialized teeth for feeding on insects, earthworms and small mammal carrion. They are highly active creatures. The somewhat indigestible nature of their food, combined with the high energy consumption of the constant activity, means that they may eat two to three times their own weight of food in a day. Having a pulse rate sometimes approaching 1 000 beats a minute, few shrews live longer than one year. Family: Soricidae.

SHREWSBURY, town in central Mass., birthplace of Artemas WARD. It manufactures plastic products. Pop 19 196.

SHRIKES, aggressive and predatory passerine birds of the family Laniidae, which kill insects, birds or small mammals (according to size) with their hooked bill. Because they store their victims impaled on thorns like the carcasses hung in a butcher's shop, they are often called butcherbirds. They have a worldwide distribution, living on the edges of woods and forests.

SHRIMPS, decapod CRUSTACEANS (suborder Natantia) which use their abdominal limbs to swim instead of crawling like LOBSTERS or CRABS. The body, more or less cylindrical and translucent, bears five pairs of walking legs and two pairs of very long antennae. The eyes are stalked. Shrimps are mostly scavengers or predators and may be found in the open ocean, inshore, in estuaries and even in freshwater. They are fished for food worldwide.

SHRIVER, Robert Sargent (1915–   ), first director of the PEACE CORPS under President Kennedy (1961–66) and director of the OFFICE OF ECONOMIC OPPORTUNITY under President Johnson (1964–68). He was ambassador to France (1968–70) and ran for the Vice-Presidency on the Democratic ticket with George McGovern in 1972.

SHROVE TUESDAY, the last day before Lent begins (see ASH WEDNESDAY). It is a traditional day for carnivals such as the New Orleans MARDI GRAS.

SHRUB, any small woody plant shorter than a TREE and with side shoots well developed.

SHUBRĀ AL-KHAYMAH, city in Egypt, N suburb of Cairo. Its products include textiles, glass and ceramics. Pop 252 500.

SHUBUN (flourished early 15th century), Japanese ink painter. His masterly works, many of them landscapes, led to the development of the distinctively Japanese style.

A Siamese cat of the Seal Point color variety.

SHUFFLEBOARD, game in which two or four players use cues to slide disks along a court (52ft by 6ft) which has a triangular scoring area at each end. The object is to knock the opponent's disks into the penalty section leaving one's own disks in one of the scoring positions on the triangle.

SHUTTLE DIPLOMACY, system of international negotiation, made possible by modern air travel, in which negotiators travel quickly to and fro—"shuttling"—between the countries involved. It was pioneered by US Secretary of State Henry KISSINGER.

SI, river. See SI-KIANG.

SIAL (*si*lica-*al*uminum), collective term for the rocks, lighter and more rigid than the SIMA and composed to a great extent of SILICA and ALUMINUM, that form the upper portion of the EARTH's crust. (See also ISOSTASY.)

SIALKOT, city in E Pakistan. It manufactures bicycles, ceramics, sports goods and surgical instruments. Pop 168 500.

SIAM. See THAILAND.

SIAMESE CAT, short-haired breed of eastern origin, although not proven to have originated in Thailand. Of svelte "foreign" type with a long, slim body, long tapering tail, wedge-shaped head, and large ears, it has a distinctive coat pattern of darker areas on face (mask), ears, tail and paws which are known as points. Its almond-shaped, slanting eyes are a deep blue. Color varieties are Seal Point (cream body color with seal brown points), Blue (white with blue-gray), Chocolate (ivory with milk chocolate) and Frost (or Lilac, magnolia with lilac). Many associations also recognize Red, Tortoiseshell, Tabby (Lynx) and Cream Points. All white or all lilac cats of Siamese type and with blue eyes are known as Foreign White and Foreign Lavender.

Siamese cats become closely involved with their owners and can frequently be taught to walk on a leash. They have rather loud voices and may be very talkative.

SIAMESE TWINS, twins (see MULTIPLE BIRTH) which are physically joined at some part of their anatomy due to a defect in early separation. A variable depth of fusion is seen, most commonly at the head or trunk. SURGERY may be used to separate the twins if no vital organs are shared.

SIAN, city in NE central China, ancient capital of the CH'IN and T'ANG DYNASTIES and scene of CHIANG KAI-SHEK's kidnapping in 1936. It has steel, chemical and textile industries. Pop 1 900 000.

SIBELIUS, Jean (1865–1957), Finnish composer. His most famous work is *Finlandia* (1900) which expressed his country's growing nationalist feeling. He composed a number of other tone poems such as *En Saga* (1892), which evokes the physical beauty and ancient legends of Finland. His works include many pieces for violin and for piano and seven symphonies.

SIBERIA, vast indefinite area of land (about 4 000 000sq mi) in N Asian USSR between the Ural Mts in the W and the Pacific Ocean in the E, forming most of the RSFSR. The landscape varies from the Arctic tundra to the great forest zone in the S and the steppes of the W. Summers are mild in most parts, winters extremely severe (as low as −90°F in some parts). Most of the people are Russian; Yakuts, Buryats and Tuvans form autonomous republics. The largest cities are Novosibirsk, Omsk, Krasnoyarsk, Irkutsk and Vladivostok. Siberia has rich natural resources—farmland, forests, fisheries and such minerals as coal, iron ore, tungsten, gold and natural gas. Industrial centers have developed in the regions of Krasnoyarsk and Lake Baikal (the world's deepest lake) and one of the world's largest hydroelectric plants is near Bratsk. Siberia was inhabited in prehistoric times. Russians conquered much of Siberia by 1598. Political prisoners were first sent to Siberia in 1710 and forced-labor camps still exist. The TRANS-SIBERIAN RAILROAD (1905) led to large-scale colonization and economic development.

SIBERIAN HUSKY, dog first bred in Siberia as a sled, guard and companion dog; taken to Alaska c1910 and used for dogsled races. The dog is colored black and white, tan, or gray, weighs 30–60lbs and is 20–25in high.

SIBYL, or **Sibylla,** in Greek mythology, a prophetess of APOLLO. Initially there was in the mythology only one Sibyl, but from the early 3rd century BC the name was generalized. The *sibylline oracles*, prophecies attributed to a sibyl, played a part in early Christian doctrine.

SICILIAN VESPERS, Sicilian revolt in 1282 against the Angevin French king of Naples and Sicily, CHARLES I. It led to his overthrow and Aragonese control of Sicily. After killing French soldiers at Vespers on Easter Monday in Palermo, Sicilians massacred 2 000 French inhabitants of the town.

SICILY, largest Mediterranean island (9 925sq mi); part of Italy, but with its own parliament at the capital, Palermo. Its most notable feature is the active volcano, Mt Etna (height varies around 10 900ft). Much of the island is mountainous, but there are lowlands along the coasts. About half the population live in the coastal towns Palermo, Catania, Messina and Syracuse. Agriculture is the mainstay of the economy, though hampered by the low rainfall and feudal land-tenure system. Wheat is the staple crop; grapes, citrus fruits and olives are also grown. Main exports, from Ragusa, are petroleum products. Sicily was the site of Greek, Phoenician and Roman colonies before conquest by the Arabs, who in turn were ousted by ROBERT GUISCARD. The SICILIAN VESPERS (1282) led to Spanish rule, ended by GARIBALDI (1860). In WWII, Sicily was conquered by the Allies (1943) and used as a base for attack on Italy.

SICKERT, Walter Richard (1860–1942), British painter. Trained by WHISTLER and DEGAS, he was from 1905 the main link between English and French art. His scenes of music halls and low-class life are in a rich and direct style.

SIDDHARTHA GAUTAMA. See BUDDHA.

SIDDONS, Sarah (*née* Kemble; 1755–1831), English actress who first appeared in London (without success) at the request of GARRICK (1775). She returned at the request of SHERIDAN (1782), and became the leading tragic actress of her day.

SIDEREAL TIME, time referred to the rotation of the earth with respect to the fixed stars. The sidereal DAY is about four minutes shorter than the solar day since the earth moves each day about 1/365 of its orbit about the sun. Sidereal time is used in astronomy when determining the locations of celestial bodies.

SIDERITE, brown or gray-green mineral consisting of iron(II) carbonate ($FeCO_3$), often with some magnesium, calcium and manganese. Of widespread occurrence in sedimentary or hydrothermal rocks, it is a major IRON ore. It has the CALCITE structure.

SIDEWINDERS, several species of snake, especially of the RATTLE-SNAKES, which exhibit a peculiar sideways looping motion when moving rapidly. The name is particularly applied to the Horned rattle-snake, *Crotalus cerastis*, of the southwestern US.

SIDNEY, city in W central Ohio, seat of Shelby Co. Located in an agricultural area, it manufactures machine tools and refrigerator parts. Pop 16 332.

SIDNEY, Algernon (1622–1683), English politician executed for his alleged part in the RYE HOUSE PLOT to overthrow CHARLES II. His *Discourses Concerning Government* (1698) contributed to the ideology of the American Revolution.

SIDNEY, Sir Philip (1554–1586), Elizabethan poet and courtier, a favorite with the queen and a model of RENAISSANCE chivalry. He had great influence on English poetry, both through his poems, of which the best known are *Arcadia* (c1580) and the love sonnets *Astrophel and Stella* (1591), and through his critical work, *The Defence of Poesie* (1595).

SIDON, now Saydā, great commercial city of ancient PHOENICIA, on the Lebanese coast. Founded in the 3rd millenium BC, it is mentioned in the Bible and in HOMER. It was famed for its purple dyes and glassware.

SIEGBAHN, Karl Manne Georg (1886–), Swedish physicist who was awarded the 1924 Nobel physics prize for his pioneer work in X-ray SPECTROSCOPY. He devised a way of measuring X-RAY wavelengths with great accuracy and developed an account of X-rays consistent with the BOHR theory of the ATOM.

SIEGFRIED, legendary figure of outstanding strength and courage. He appears in both the Icelandic EDDA and the 13th-century German NIBELUNGENLIED epic, and is the hero of WAGNER's operas *Siegfried* and *Götterdämmerung*.

SIEGFRIED LINE, defensive line built on the German W frontier in the 1930s which delayed the US advance in 1944–45.

SIEMENS, German family of technologists and industrialists. **Ernst Werner von Siemens** (1816–1892) invented, among other things, an ELECTROPLATING process (patented 1842), a differential GOVERNOR (c1844), and a regenerative STEAM ENGINE, the principle of which was developed by his brothers **Friedrich** (1826–1904) and then **Karl Wilhelm** (1823–1883), later **Sir (Charles) William Siemens**, to form the basis of the OPEN-HEARTH PROCESS. Ernst and Sir William both made many important contributions to TELEGRAPH science, culminating in the laying from the *Faraday*, a ship designed by William, of the ATLANTIC CABLE of 1874 by the company he owned.

SIEMENS-MARTIN PROCESS. See OPEN-HEARTH PROCESS.

SIENA, city in Tuscany, Italy, famous for its GOTHIC ARCHITECTURE and the RENAISSANCE art of DONATELLO, LORENZETTI and PISANO. Its main square is the scene of the historic and colorful *Palio* horse races every summer. Pop 65 661.

SIENKIEWICZ, Henryk (1846–1916), Polish novelist awarded the 1905 Nobel Prize in Literature. His greatest works are a trilogy about 17th-century Poland—*With Fire and Sword* (1884), *The Deluge* (1886) and *Pan Michael* (1888)—and the internationally famous *Quo Vadis?* (1896).

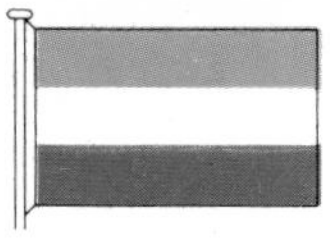

Official name: Republic of Sierre Leone
Capital: Freetown
Area: 27 925sq mi
Population: 2 600 000
Languages: English; Krio, Mende, Temne
Religions: Animist, Muslim, Christian
Monetary unit(s): 1 Leone = 100 cents.

SIERRA LEONE, republic in W Africa on the Atlantic Ocean, with Guinea to the N and E, Liberia to the S. Covering 27 699sq mi, it consists of a swampy coastal area, wooded inland plains crossed by several rivers and rising grassland in the N. The climate is tropical, with an average temperature of 79°F and annual rainfall of 90–150in. The population is almost entirely African, mostly belonging to the Mende, Temne, Limba and Kono tribes. About 30 000 Creoles, descendents of freed slaves, mainly from the Americas, live around Freetown, the capital and chief port. Bo, Kenema and Port Loko are important centers.

Economy. The economy is heavily dependent on subsistence farming, and 80% of the population live in rural areas. Rice is the staple crop, and the main export crops are palm kernels, cocoa beans, coffee and ginger. Cattle are raised in the N, pigs and poultry in the W. Diamonds account for 66% of the export market, and the industry is government controlled. Iron ore is exported to Japan. Bauxite and rutile are also mined.

History. Named by the Portuguese in 1460, the coastal area became the haunt of slavers: in 1787 Granville SHARP settled freed slaves there. In 1808 it became a British colony. Independent from 1961, Sierra Leone was declared a republic in 1971 under the presidency of Dr. Siaka Stevens.

SIERRA MADRE, great mountain system of Mexico. The E range (*Sierra Madre Oriental*) stretches 1 000mi S from the Rio Grande, forming the E edge of the central plateau and reaching 18 700ft in Orizaba (Citlaltépetl). The *Sierra Madre Occidental*, running SW from Ariz and N.M., borders the plateau on the W, rising to over 10 000ft. The *Sierra Madre de Sur* parallels the SW coast.

SIERRA MADRE, city in SW Cal., 15mi NE of Los Angeles. Mainly residential, it makes emergency oxygen equipment. Pop 12 140.

SIERRA MAESTRA, mountain range in SE Cuba. Its highest peak is Pico Turquino (6 560ft). There are valuable deposits of copper and manganese.

SIERRA NEVADA, mountain range in S Spain, about 60mi long, parallel to the Mediterranean Sea. In it is Spain's highest peak, Mulhacén (11 411ft).

SIERRA NEVADA, mountain range, 420mi long, in E Cal., including Mt Whitney (14 494ft), the highest mountain in the US outside Alaska. The spectacular scenery of the three national parks, Yosemite, King's Canyon and Sequoia, make the Sierra Nevada a popular vacation area.

SIEYÈS, Emmanuel Joseph (1748–1836), theorist of the FRENCH REVOLUTION. He advocated national sovereignty and organized the National Assembly. Joining the DIRECTORY in 1799 he took part in the coup of 18 BRUMAIRE with NAPOLEON I, who then ousted Sieyès from power.

SIGISMUND (1368–1437), Holy Roman Emperor from 1433 and king of Hungary from 1387, of Germany from 1410 and of Bohemia from 1419. He was involved in continual wars to maintain his power against other claimants, HUS's followers and the Turks.

SIGNAC, Paul (1863–1935), French painter, leading theorist of neoimpressionism. A friend of Georges SEURAT, he developed POINTILLISM, painting many views of ports, like *Port of St.-Tropez* (1894).

SIGN LANGUAGE, any system of communication using gesture (usually of the hand and arm) rather than speech. The most comprehensive sign language in modern use is that employed by the deaf and dumb, but sophisticated sign languages are also used by many primitive peoples to communicate with other tribes.

SIGNORELLI, Luca (c1440–1523), Italian RENAISSANCE painter. His greatest work, the FRESCO cycle at Orvieto Cathedral (1499–1502), reveals, as in *Resurrection of the Dead* and the *Last Judgement*, a masterly depiction of the nude, surpassed at the period only by MICHELANGELO.

SIHANOUK, Norodom (1922–), chief of state of CAMBODIA 1960–70 and 1975–76. King from 1941, he abdicated in 1955 to become premier. Deposed by a coup in 1970, he returned from exile in 1975 as figurehead of the communist victors. He resigned six months later.

SIKESTON, city in SE Mo., a cotton and soybean marketing and processing center. Pop 14 699.

SIKHS (from Hindi *sikh*, disciple), religious community of about nine million mostly in the PUNJAB, N India. Their religion, based on the sacred book Ādi Granth, combines elements of HINDUISM and BUDDHISM and was founded by the mystic Nānak, their first GURU, in the 16th century. There is no professional priesthood and officially no CASTE SYSTEM. In the 19th century, under RANJIT SINGH, the Sikhs developed a powerful military state before the British assumed control of India.

SI-KIANG, or **Hsi Chiang,** the longest river of S China. It flows E for 1 250mi from the highlands of Yunnan to the Canton River delta on the South China Sea. Much of it is navigable.

SIKKIM, Indian state (since 1975) in the E Himalayas, formerly a constitutional monarchy and protectorate of India. It lies between Tibet, Nepal, Bhutan and India, and covers 2 745sq mi, ranging from Kanchenjunga (28 146ft) to lush tropical forests barely 700ft above sea level. The economy rests on agriculture (rice, corn, millet, and fruits); and cardamon is the chief cash crop. Hydroelectricity and new roads are being developed.

SIKORSKI, Wladyslaw (1881–1843), Polish prime minister (1922–23), war minister (1923–25) and general. After the German invasion in 1939, he became leader of the Polish forces and government in exile.

SIKORSKY, Igor Ivanovich (1889–1972), Russian-born US aircraft designer best known for his invention of the first successful HELICOPTER (flown in 1939). He also designed several AIRPLANES, including the first to have more than one engine (1913).

SILAGE, or ensilage, winter cattle fodder made from grass, corn, legumes etc., by limited fermentation. The material is harvested when green, chopped and then stored in either a pit or a tower where air access can be carefully controlled. LACTIC ACID is formed from the CARBOHYDRATES while the loss of other nutrients is minimal.

SILENCER. See MUFFLER.

SILENUS, in Greek myth either one of several drunkards in the train of DIONYSUS; or the eldest of them, Silenus, who had educated the god in the joys of revelry.

SILESIA, region of E central Europe, extending from the Sudetes Mts and W Carpathians in the S up the Oder River valley. Mostly in Poland, it covers about 20 000sq mi and has fertile farmlands and forests and great mineral wealth. Upper Silesia is Poland's most important industrial region.

SILHOUETTE, style of art in which a dark monochrome image is set against a light ground, or vice versa. Its great vogue was in 1750–1850, particularly for quick profile portraits.

SILICA, or silicon dioxide (SiO_2), a very common mineral, having three crystalline forms, the most common being QUARTZ. Silica is refractory and inert, though it dissolves in hydrogen fluoride and reacts with bases to form SILICATES. It is used to make GLASS, CERAMICS, CONCRETE and CARBORUNDUM. (See also SILICON; KIESELGUHR.)

SILICA GEL, amorphous form of SILICA made by acidifying a SILICATE and dehydrating the silicic acid formed. It is widely used as an adsorbent (see ADSORPTION) and drying agent (see DEHYDRATION). (See also GEL.)

SILICATES, salts of silicic acids. Discrete silicate anions include orthosilicates (SiO_4^{4-}), metasilicates (SiO_3^{2-}), and groups of SiO_4 units linked by Si—O—Si bonds; such condensation also produces infinite anions in chains, layers or three-dimensional arrays. Silicates (including aluminosilicates) are the most important class of minerals, forming 90% of the earth's crust. (See also WATER GLASS.)

SILICON (Si), nonmetal in Group IVA of the PERIODIC TABLE; the second most abundant element (after oxygen), occurring as SILICA and SILICATES. It is made by reducing silica with coke at high temperatures. Silicon forms an amorphous brown powder, or gray semiconducting crystals, metallic in appearance. It oxidizes on heating, and reacts with the halogens, hydrogen fluoride, and alkalis. It is used in alloys, and to make TRANSISTORS and SEMICONDUCTORS. AW 28.1, mp 1410°C, bp 2355°C, sg 2.42 (20°C). Silicon is tetravalent in almost all its compounds, which resemble those of CARBON, except that it does not form multiple bonds, and that chains of silicon atoms are relatively unstable. **Silanes** are series of volatile silicon hydrides, analogous to PARAFFINS, spontaneously flammable in air and hydrolyzed by water. **Silicon tetrachloride** is a colorless fuming liquid, made by reacting chlorine with a mixture of silica and carbon, the starting material for preparing organosilicon compounds, including SILICONES. mp −70°C, bp 58°C. (For silicon carbide, see CARBORUNDUM; silicon dioxide, SILICA).

SILICONES, POLYMERS with alternate atoms of SILICON and oxygen, and organic groups attached to the silicon. They are resistant to water and oxidation, and are stable to heat. Liquid silicones are used for waterproofing, as polishes and anti-foam agents. Silicone greases are high- and low-temperature lubricants, and resins are used as electrical insulators. Silicone rubbers remain flexible at low temperatures.

SILICOSIS, a form of PNEUMOCONIOSIS, or fibrotic LUNG disease, in which long-standing inhalation of fine SILICA dusts in mining causes a progressive reduction in the functional capacity of the lungs. The normally thin-walled alveoli and small bronchioles become thickened with fibrous tissue and the lungs lose their elasticity. Characteristic X-RAY appearances and changes in lung function occur.

SILIQUE, dry, dehiscent FRUIT, similar to a CAPSULE, but formed from two carpels. When ripe, the carpels split apart leaving a thin septum between. They are formed by members of the CABBAGE family (Cruciferae).

SILK, natural FIBER produced by certain insects and spiders to make cocoons and webs, a glandular secretion extruded from the spinneret and hardened into a filament on exposure to air. Commercial textile silk comes from the various SILKWORMS. The cocooned pupae are killed by steam or hot air, and the cocoons are placed in hot water to soften the gum (sericin) that binds the silk. The filaments from several cocoons are then unwound together to form a single strand of "raw silk," which is reeled. Several strands are twisted together, or "thrown," to form yarn. At this stage, or after weaving, the sericin is washed away. The thickness of the yarn is measured in DENIER. About 70% of all raw silk is now produced in Japan.

SILK-SCREEN PRINTING, method of PRINTING derived from the stencil process (see also DUPLICATING MACHINE). A stencil is attached to a silk screen or fine wire mesh, or formed on it by a photographic process or by drawing the design in tusche (a greasy ink), sealing the screen with glue and washing out the tusche and its covering glue with an organic solvent. The framed screen is placed on the surface to be printed, and viscous ink is pressed through by a rubber squeegee. Each color requires a different screen. The process, which may be mechanized, is used for printing labels, posters, fabrics, and on bottles and other curved surfaces. Since 1938 it has been used by painters, who call it serigraphy.

SILKWORM, the caterpillar of a moth, *Bombyx mori*, which, like many other caterpillars, spins itself a cocoon of silk in which it pupates. The cocoon of *B. mori* is, however, especially thick and may be composed of a single thread commonly 900m (2 950ft) long. This is unraveled to provide commercial SILK. Originally a native of China, *B. mori* has been introduced to many countries. The caterpillar, which takes about a month to develop, feeds on the leaves of the MULBERRY tree.

SILKY TERRIER, first called Sydney Silky, a dog breed originally created by crossing Yorkshire and Australian Terriers. Its long (5–6in) and silky coat is blue-gray, with tan patches on muzzle, cheeks, around the ears, pasterns and the underside of the tail. It stands 9in on short legs.

SILL, tabular body of IGNEOUS ROCK, under 1cm to over 100m thick and perhaps hundreds of kilometres wide, lying parallel to the beds of surrounding rocks. It has been suggested that sills are an extreme form of LACCOLITH or phacolith.

SILLANPÄÄ, Frans Eemil (1888–1964), Finnish novelist awarded the 1939 Nobel Prize in Literature. His best known work is *The Maid Silja* (1931).

SILLERY, suburb 3mi SE of Quebec. Pop 13 950.

SILLIMAN, Benjamin (1779–1864), US chemist and geologist who founded *The American Journal of Science* (1819). The mineral **Sillimanite** (a form of aluminum SILICATE, Al_2SiO_5) is named for him.

SILO. See SILAGE.

SILONE, Ignazio (1900–), pseudonym of Secondo Tranquilli, Italian writer and social reformer. Opposed to fascism, he spent 1931–44 in exile in Switzerland. His novels include *Bread and Wine* (1937).

SILT, soil composed of particles whose diameters

range from 1/256 to 1/16mm. SOIL containing over 80% silt particles and less than 12% CLAY particles is often termed silt. In particular, **loess**, accumulations of wind-blown dust, has particles of silt-size in the range 1/32 to 1/16mm.

SILURIAN, the third period of the PALEOZOIC, which lasted between about 440 and 400 million years ago. (See also GEOLOGY.)

SILVER (Ag), soft, white NOBLE METAL in Group IB of the PERIODIC TABLE, a TRANSITION ELEMENT. Silver has been known and valued from earliest times and used for jewelry, ornaments and coinage since the 4th millennium BC. It occurs as the metal, notably in Norway; in COPPER, LEAD and ZINC sulfide ores; and in ARGENTITE and other silver ores. It is concentrated by various processes including cupellation and extraction with CYANIDE (see also GOLD), and is refined by electrolysis. Silver has the highest thermal and electrical conductivity of all metals, and is used for printed circuits and electrical contacts. Other modern uses include dental ALLOYS and AMALGAM, high-output storage batteries, and for monetary reserves. Although the most reactive of the noble metals, silver is not oxidized in air, nor dissolved by alkalis or nonoxidizing acids; it dissolves in nitric and concentrated sulfuric acid. Silver tarnishes by reaction with sulfur or hydrogen sulfide to form a dark silver-sulfide layer. Silver salts are normally monovalent. Ag^+ is readily reduced by mild reducing agents, depositing a silver MIRROR from solution. AW 107.9, mp 960.8°C, bp 2212°C, sg 10.5 (20°C). **Silver Halides** (AgX) are crystalline salts used in PHOTOGRAPHY. The chloride is white, the bromide pale yellow and the iodide yellow. On exposure to light, a crystal of silver halide becomes activated, and is preferentially reduced to silver by a mild reducing agent (the developer). **Silver Nitrate** ($AgNO_3$) is a transparent crystalline solid, used as an ANTISEPTIC and ASTRINGENT, especially for removing WARTS.

SILVER AGE. See AGES OF MAN.

SILVER CERTIFICATES, US certificates for 1, 5 and 10 dollars of silver value, first authorized in 1878 and issued until 1963. From then onwards, the US Department of the Treasury began withdrawing them in order to preserve silver for coinage.

SILVERFISH, *Lepisma saccharina*, an insect belonging to the group known as BRISTLETAILS or Thysanura. Scavengers of organic detritus, they are common in damp places in buildings all over the world.

SILVERIUS, Saint (d.537), Italian pope (536–37), deposed and exiled through the intrigues of Empress THEODORA. His feast day is June 20.

SILVERSIDES, small marine or freshwater fishes, family Atherinidae, related to FLYING FISHES. Distinguished by a bright silvery band down the flanks, they are almost worldwide in distribution. The eggs have long filaments sprouting from them by which they may be anchored to weeds. Some species (e.g., the GRUNION) have remarkable breeding habits.

SILVER SPRING, unincorporated community, central Md., a residential suburb of Washington D.C., with electronic and missile-research laboratories. Pop 77 496.

SILVER SPRINGS, one of the world's largest mineral springs, in N central Fla., with a basin 80ft deep and 300ft wide. The aquatic life in its crystal-clear waters is a tourist attraction.

SILVESTER. See SYLVESTER.

SIMA (*si*lica-*ma*gnesium), collective term for the rocks, denser and more plastic than the SIAL and composed to a great extent of SILICA and MAGNESIUM, that form the lower portion of the earth's crust. (See also ISOSTASY.)

SIMCOE, town seat of Norfolk Co., S Ontario, a canning and manufacturing center. Pop 10 793.

SIMCOE, John Graves (1752–1806), British soldier, the first lieutenant governor of Upper Canada, 1791–94. He developed agriculture and encouraged immigration of American loyalists.

SIMENON, Georges Joseph Christian (1903–), Belgian-born French author of over 200 novels and thousands of short stories. He is best known for his detective novels about Inspector Maigret, outstanding works of tightly plotted suspense and psychological insight.

SIMEON, in the Old Testament, son of JACOB and Leah, and progenitor of one of the 12 tribes of Israel.

SIMEON BEN YOHAI (2nd century AD), Palestinian rabbi and ascetic, allegedly author of the *Zohar*, a book on Hebrew mysticism.

SIMEON STYLITES, Saint (c390–c459) (from Greek *stylos*, pillar), Syrian ascetic and mystic who spent his last 40 years or so on top of a high column. His feast day is Jan. 5.

SIMFEROPOL, city in the Ukrainian SSR, USSR, on the Salgir R. A transporation hub, it is a commercial and food-processing center. Pop 250 000.

SIMHAT TORAH (Hebrew: rejoicing of the Law), Jewish festival marking the end of the annual reading of the TORAH in the synagogue. It is held on the ninth day of SUKKOT.

SIMI VALLEY, city in SW Cal. in an oil, farm and livestock region. It has mixed industries. Pop 56 464.

SIMLA, town in NW India, in the W Himalayas, established as a hill resort by the British in 1819 and summer capital of the British Raj. Pop 42 597.

SIMMS, William Gilmore (1806–1870), US author whose writings on the US South include historical novels, short stories, biographies and poetry. His most important work was *The Yemassee* (1835).

SIMON, Saint, one of the DISCIPLES OF CHRIST. His names of "the Canaanite" or "Zelotes" may suggest association with the ZEALOTS. His feast-day is Oct. 28.

SIMONE MARTINI. See MARTINI, Simone.

SIMONIDES OF CEOS (c556–469 BC), Greek lyric poet, famous for his epitaphs on the Greeks who fell at MARATHON and THERMOPYLAE. He was also well known for his elegies, odes and epigrams. Very little of his verse has survived.

SIMONS, Menno (c1496–1561), Frisian religious reformer and leader of the peaceful ANABAPTISTS in Holland and Germany. He was a Roman Catholic priest who converted to Anabaptism in 1536. The MENNONITES are named for him.

SIMONY, the buying and selling of sacred privileges. It is named for Simon Magus, a Samarian magician who tried to buy from St. Peter the power of transmitting the Holy Spirit.

SIMOOM, or **Simoon**, hot, dry wind or whirlwind occurring in the deserts of Arabia and N Africa. It usually carries much sand and greatly reduces visibility.

SIMPLE HARMONIC MOTION (SHM), a form of WAVE MOTION in which a moving particle traces a path symmetric (see SYMMETRY) about a midpoint or equilibrium position, through which it passes at regular intervals of time. The force responsible for the motion is always directed towards the midpoint, its magnitude proportional to the displacement of the particle. If the displacement of the particle is plotted as a FUNCTION of time the result is a sinusoidal CURVE,

$$y = A \sin 2\pi ft,$$

where A is the AMPLITUDE, f the FREQUENCY, y the displacement and t the time elapse from a particular zero-point. SHM derives its name from the fact that the vibrations produced by musical instruments (e.g., a string of a violin, the legs of a tuning fork), and hence the SOUND waves they propagate, approximate to it. In fact these, as all other vibrations and wave motions, may be treated as compounded of a number of SHMs.

SIMPLICIUS, Saint (d.483), pope from 468. The fall of the Western Roman Empire during his reign enhanced papal authority. Feast day, March 10.

SIMPLON PASS, 29mi long and 6590ft high, between Brig in Switzerland and Isella in Italy. NAPOLEON I built a road along it in 1800–06. In 1906 the Simplon Tunnel I, 12.5mi long, the world's longest railroad tunnel, was opened.

SIMPSON, Sir James Young (1811–1870), Scottish obstetrician who pioneered the use of CHLOROFORM as an anesthetic, especially for mothers during childbirth (see ANESTHESIA; BIRTH).

SIMSBURY, manufacturing town in N Conn., incorporated in 1670. The first colonial copper coins were minted here (1737). Pop 17475.

SIN, or transgression, an unethical act (see ETHICS) considered as disobedience to the revealed will of God. Sin may be viewed legally as crime —breaking God's commandments—and so deserving punishment (see HELL; PURGATORY), or as an offence that grieves God the loving Father, breaking communion with him. According to the Bible, sin entered the world in Adam's fall and all mankind became innately sinful (see ORIGINAL SIN). Both for this and for actual sins committed, man becomes guilty and in need of SALVATION. Since sin is rooted in character and will, each sinner bears personal responsibility; hence the need for repentance, CONFESSION and ABSOLUTION (see also PENANCE). Views as to what constitutes sin vary, being partly determined by church authority, social standards and one's own conscience. The traditional "seven deadly sins" are pride, covetousness, lust, envy, gluttony, anger and sloth. The Roman Catholic Church defines a mortal sin as a serious sin committed willingly and with clear knowledge of its guilt; a venial sin is less grave, does not wholly deprive of grace, and need not be individually confessed. (See also ATONEMENT; IMMACULATE CONCEPTION.)

SINAI PENINSULA, mountainous peninsula between the Gulf of Suez and the Gulf of Aqaba, the N arms of the Red Sea. It is thought that Mt Sinai, where MOSES received the TEN COMMANDMENTS, is one of the S peaks (Jebel Serbal or Jebel Musa).

SINALOA, state (22 500sq mi) in W Mexico, between the Sierra Madre Occidental and the Gulf of Cal. Important economic factors are rice, sugarcane, cotton and its rich mineral resources.

SINATRA, Frank "the Voice" (Francis Albert Sinatra: 1917–), US singer and film star. He began his career in radio in the 1930s: in the 1950s and 1960s he was the world's most popular singer.

SINCLAIR, Harry Ford (1876–1956), US oil producer in the Mammoth Oil Company who acquired, without competitive bidding, the TEAPOT DOME lease from A. FALL in 1922. He was later acquitted of fraud.

SINCLAIR, Upton Beall (1878–1968), novelist and social reformer. He is best known for *The Jungle* (1906), a novel exposing the horrors of the Chicago meat-packing industries; and for the 11 *World's End* novels centered on Lanny Budd, one of which (*Dragon's Teeth*, 1942) brought him the 1943 Pulitzer Prize.

SIND, province in SE Pakistan, 59 000sq mi in area, on the Arabian Sea. Its economy rests on agriculture, but its cotton and cement are nationally important. The INDUS VALLEY CIVILIZATION lay in Sind.

SINE. See TRIGONOMETRY.

SINE RULE, in any plane TRIANGLE with angles A,B,C and sides a,b,c,

$$\frac{a}{\sin A} = \frac{b}{\sin B} = \frac{c}{\sin C}$$

that is to say, the ratio between the length of a side and the sine of the ANGLE opposite it is equal for all three sides of the triangle. In SPHERICAL TRIGONOMETRY, the sine rule is

$$\frac{\sin a}{\sin A} = \frac{\sin b}{\sin B} = \frac{\sin c}{\sin C}$$

for a spherical triangle with angles A, B, C and sides a, b, c. (See also COSINE RULE.)

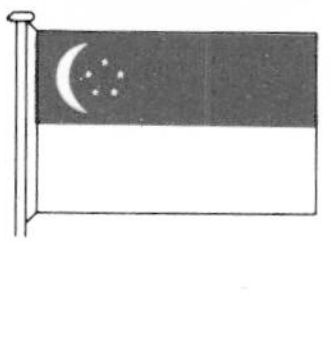

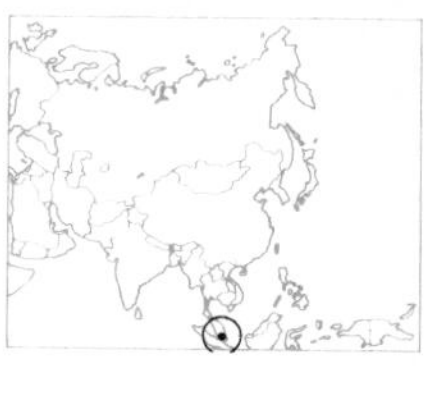

Official name: Republic of Singapore
Capital: Singapore
Area: 225.6sq mi
Population: 2 147 000
Languages: English, Mandarin, Malay, Tamil
Religions: Confucianist, Buddhist, Taoist, Muslim
Monetary unit(s): 1 Singapore dollar = 100 cents

SINGAPORE, republic in SE Asia, 225sq mi in area, at the S end of the Malay Peninsula, consisting of Singapore Island and 60 adjacent islets. Singapore

Island is largely low-lying and fringed by mango-swamps, its climate tropical: rainfall averages about 95in yearly. The population is predominantly Chinese, with large Malay and Indian minorities. The capital, Singapore city, is a fine natural harbor and SE Asia's foremost commercial and shipping center, conducting a flourishing international trade as a free port. It trades in textiles, rubber, petroleum, timber and tin, and produces electrical goods, and petroleum products. Shipbuilding and repair is an important new industry. Singapore was founded as a trading post by Sir Thomas RAFFLES in 1819. Self-governing from 1959, independent 1963, it joined MALAYSIA in 1963 but withdrew from the federation in 1965.

SINGER, Isaac Bashevis (1904–), Polish-born US YIDDISH novelist and short story writer, known for his portrayal of European Jewish life. His work includes *The Family Moskat* (1950), *The Magician of Lublin* (1960) and *The Estate* (1969).

SINGER, Isaac Merrit (1811–1875), US inventor of the first viable domestic SEWING MACHINE (patented 1851). Despite a legal battle with the earlier inventor Elias HOWE, the Singer sewing machine soon became the most popular in the world.

SINGLE TAX, proposed reform that tax on land value should be a government's sole revenue, stated by Henry GEORGE in *Progress and Poverty* (1879). He argued that economic rent of land results from the growth of an economy, not from an individual's effort; therefore governments are justified in appropriating all economic rents, thus eliminating the need for other taxes.

SINGSPIEL (German: song-play), OPERA, usually comic, with spoken dialogue, popular in Germany during the 18th century.

SINGULARITY, in mathematics a point at which a curve, function or property behaves unusually, e.g., by having a node, a cusp or an isolated point. In discussion of BLACK HOLES, singularity refers to the point or ring within which the gravitational field is of infinite strength.

SINH. See HYPERBOLIC FUNCTIONS.

SINHALESE, an INDO-ARYAN LANGUAGE, derived from SANSKRIT, spoken by two-thirds of the people of SRI LANKA. Most other Sinhalese people speak TAMIL.

SINK HOLE, doline or **swallow-hole**, well or funnel-shaped hole, typical of KARST landscapes, formed when GROUNDWATER dissolves an underground cavity in LIMESTONE, followed by slump of the surface.

SINKIANG, autonomous region in NW China between Mongolia and USSR. A predominantly agricultural area, it has very rich mineral resources and vast oil fields. Because of scant rainfall, Sinkiang has extensive irrigation systems. It is a strategic region of the defense of China.

SINN FEIN (Erse: we, ourselves), Irish nationalist movement which achieved independence for the Irish Free State in 1922. Formed by Arthur GRIFFITH in 1905, it was first widely supported in 1916 when most of the leaders of the EASTER RISING were martyred. Led by DE VALERA, it set up an Irish Parliament, the DAIL EIREANN, by 1919. (See also IRELAND; IRISH REPUBLICAN ARMY.)

SINO-JAPANESE WARS, two bitter conflicts between China and Japan. The first (1894–95) was precipitated by the rivalry of the two nations over Korea. China's navy was totally destroyed and its army routed by the Japanese. The Treaty of SHIMONOSEKI led to Japan becoming a great power. The second (1937–45) was the result of renewed Japanese expansionism in the Far East. Japan conquered Manchuria in 1931 and gradually penetrated into China. In 1937 Japan seized nearly all the coastal cities and industrial areas. The Chinese Nationalists and the communists united to fight the Japanese. After PEARL HARBOR the fighting became part of WWII.

SINTERING, the bonding together of compacted powder particles at temperatures below the melting point. The driving force is the decrease in surface energy that occurs as the particles merge and their total surface area lessens. The smaller the powder particles, the faster is the sintering. It is used to consolidate ORES, in powder METALLURGY, and in making CERAMICS and CERMETS.

SI Units

The International System of Units (SI units) is founded upon seven empirically defined *base units* (e.g., ampere), which can be combined, sometimes with the assistance of two geometric *supplementary units* (e.g., radian) to yield the *derived units* (e.g., cubic metre) which together with the base units constitute a coherent set of units capable of application to all measurable physical phenomena. Some of the derived units have special names (e.g., volt). For the sake of convenience smaller and larger units, the multiples and submultiples of the SI units, can be formed by adding certain prefixes (e.g., milli) to the names of the SI units. In any instance only one prefix can be added to the name of a unit (thus nanometre, not millimicrometre). Of the other units in common scientific use, it is recognized that several (e.g., hour) will continue to be used alongside the SI units, although combinations of these units with SI units (as in kilowatt hour) are discouraged. However, other units (e.g., angstrom unit) are redundant if the International System is fully utilized, and it is intended that these should drop out of use.

Base units

Quantity	Unit	Symbol
length	metre	m
mass	kilogram	kg
time	second	s
electric current	ampere	A
temperature	kelvin	K
luminous intensity	candela	cd
amount of substance	mole	mol

Supplementary units

Quantity	Name	Symbol
plane angle	radian	rad
solid angle	steradian	sr

Non-SI units in continuing use

(a) defined in terms of SI units

Quantity	Name	Symbol	Equivalent
plane angle	degree	$\circ$	$\pi/180$rad
plane angle	minute	$'$	$\frac{1}{60}^{\circ}$
plane angle	second	$''$	$\frac{1}{60}'$
time	minute	min	60s
time	hour	h	3 600s = 60min
time	day	d	86 400s = 24h
volume	litre	l	$10^{-3}m^3$
mass	tonne	t	10^3kg

(b) defined empirically

Quantity	Name	Symbol	Approximate value
energy	electronvolt	eV	1.602×10^{-19}J
mass	atomic mass unit	u	1.660531×10^{-27}kg
length	astronomical unit	AU	149600×10^6m
length	parsec	pc	30857×10^{12}m

Derived units with special names

Quantity	Name	Symbol	Equivalent in other units	As expressed in base units
frequency	hertz	Hz	—	s^{-1}
force	newton	N	—	$m.kg.s^{-2}$
work, energy	joule	J	N.m	$m^2.kg.s^{-2}$
power	watt	W	J/s	$m^2.kg.s^{-3}$
pressure	pascal	Pa	N/m^2	$m^{-1}.kg.s^{-2}$
quantity of electricity	coulomb	C	—	s.A
potential difference	volt	V	W/A	$m^2.kg.s^{-3}.A^{-1}$
electric resistance	ohm	Ω	V/A	$m^2.kg.s^{-3}.A^{-2}$
capacitance	farad	F	C/V	$m^{-2}.kg^{-1}.s^4.A^2$
conductance	siemens	S	A/V	$m^{-2}.kg^{-1}.s^3.A^2$
magnetic flux	weber	Wb	V.s	$m^2.kg.s^{-2}.A^{-1}$
flux density	tesla	T	Wb/m^2	$kg.s^{-2}.A^{-1}$
inductance	henry	H	Wb/A	$m^2.kg.s^{-2}.A^{-2}$
luminous flux	lumen	lm	—	cd.sr
illuminance	lux	lx	lm/m^2	$m^{-2}.cd.sr$

SI prefixes

Factor	Prefix	Symbol
10^{12}	tera	T
10^9	giga	G
10^6	mega	M
10^3	kilo	k
10^2	hecto	h
10^1	deka	da
10^{-1}	deci	d
10^{-2}	centi	c
10^{-3}	milli	m
10^{-6}	micro	μ
10^{-9}	nano	n
10^{-12}	pico	p
10^{-15}	femto	f
10^{-18}	atto	a

Temperature. The kelvin (K) as a unit of temperature difference is defined as 1/273.16 of the thermodynamic temperature of the triple point of water. It is thus identical to the old "centigrade degree" (C°). As an alternative to thermodynamic temperatures expressed in kelvins, it is often convenient to express commonly encountered temperatures using the Celsius temperature scale. Temperatures thus expressed in "degrees Celsius" (°C) are identical to thermodynamic temperatures given in kelvins (K) *less* 273.15K.

SINUS, large air space connected with the NOSE which may become infected and obstructed after upper respiratory infection and cause facial pain and fever (sinusitis). There are four major nasal sinuses: the maxillary, frontal, ethmoid and sphenoid. *Also,* a blind-ended channel which may discharge PUS or other material onto the skin or other surface. These may be EMBRYOLOGICAL remnants or arise from a foreign body or deep chronic infection (e.g., OSTEOMYELITIS). *Also,* a large venous channel, as in the LIVER and in the large vessels draining BLOOD from the BRAIN.

SIOUX CITY, city in NW Iowa, seat of Woodbury Co., an industrial and trade center for the surrounding livestock and agricultural area. Pop 85 925.

SIOUX FALLS, the largest city in S.D., seat of Minnehaha Co. Its industries are meat-packing, food processing and metal and wood products. Pop 72 488.

SIOUX INDIANS, the largest North American tribe of the Siouan language group. Also known as the *Dakota* ("allies"), they were originally a federation of seven tribes, most numerous being the Teton. After repeated revolt against white misrule and treachery, their final defeat was at WOUNDED KNEE (1890). Today about 35 000 live on reservations.

SIPHON, device, usually consisting of a bent tube with two legs of unequal length, which utilizes atmospheric pressure to transfer liquid over the edge of one container into another at a lower level. The flowing action depends on the difference in the pressures acting on the two liquid surfaces and stops when these coincide.

SIQUEIROS, David Alfaro (1898–), Mexican mural painter, best known for his murals in Mexico City on social subjects.

SIRACUSA (Italy). See SYRACUSE.

SIRENS, long-bodied, eel-like **salamanders**. Sirens are almost entirely aquatic; they have extremely small limbs and the hindlimbs are absent in some species. They swim by sinuous movements of the whole body. Sirens have external gills and exhibit NEOTENY.

SIRENS, in Greek mythology, nymphs with the bodies of birds and heads of women, who lured voyagers to death by their sweet songs. ODYSSEUS survived their singing by having himself lashed to the mast and his sailors' ears plugged with wax.

SIRHAN, Sirhan Bishara (1944–), Jordanian-born US assassin of Robert KENNEDY on June 5, 1968 in Los Angeles. He was sentenced to death, though this was later commuted to life imprisonment.

SIRICIUS, Saint (c334–399), pope from 384, and author of the first known papal decrees. His feast day is Nov. 26.

SIRIUS, Alpha Canis Majoris, the Dog Star, the brightest STAR in the night sky. 2.7pc distant, it is 20 times more luminous than the sun and has absolute magnitude +1.4. A DOUBLE STAR, its major component is twice the size of the sun; its minor component (the Pup), the first white dwarf star to be discovered, has a diameter only 50% greater than that of the earth, but is extremely dense, its mass being just less than that of the sun.

SIROCCO, in S Europe, warm, humid WIND from the S or SE, originating over the Sahara Desert and gaining humidity from the Mediterranean.

SISAL, or sisal hemp, *Agave sisalana*, a tropical American plant cultivated for its leaf fibers. It has a short stem and its sword-shaped leaves are cropped at intervals and their fibers extracted to make coarse ROPES and twine. In the plantations, flowering is prevented by removing the leaves so that each plant lives about 20 years. Family: Amaryllidaceae.

SISLEY, Alfred (1839–1899), Anglo-French painter, a founder of IMPRESSIONISM. His fine land-and snowscapes, painted in the 1870s, often show Paris, London and their neighborhoods. His work achieved wide recognition only after his death.

SISTERS OF CHARITY. See CHARITY, SISTERS OF.

SISTERS OF MERCY. See MERCY, SISTERS OF.

SISTINE CHAPEL, the papal chapel in the Vatican palace, Rome, renowned for its magnificent frescoes by MICHELANGELO and other Renaissance artists like PERUGINO, BOTTICELLI and PINTURICCHIO. It is named for Pope Sixtus IV, who began its construction in 1473, and is used by the College of Cardinals when it meets to elect a new pope.

SISYPHUS, in Greek myth, deceitful king of Corinth who cheated death and so was doomed to everlasting punishment in the Underworld. He had to push a boulder up a steep slope, watch it roll down, and then begin all over again.

SITAR, Indian stringed instrument with a long neck and smallish rounded soundbox. There are usually seven strings—five melody and two drone: these are plucked by a player seated on cushions or the floor.

SITKA, port and trading center in SE Alaska, W Baranof Island. Its chief industries are lumber, fishing and tourism. Founded as New Archangel (1799) it was headquarters of the RUSSIAN-AMERICAN COMPANY, and Alaska's capital 1884–1906. Pop 3 370.

SITKA NATIONAL MONUMENT, near SITKA, was established 1910. Its 54 acres mark the site of the TLINGIT INDIANS' last stand against the Russians (1804).

SITTER, Willem de (1872–1934), Dutch astronomer who helped to get EINSTEIN's theory of RELATIVITY widely known and who proposed a modification to it allowing for a gradual expansion of the universe.

SITTING BULL (c1831–1890), chief of the Teton SIOUX INDIANS who led the last major Indian resistance in the US. Born in S.D., he became head of the Sioux nation and inspired the 1876 campaign that resulted in the massacre at LITTLE BIGHORN. After the Sioux surrender (1881) he retired to Standing Rock reservation, N.D. During the GHOST DANCE Indian police killed him while attempting his arrest.

SITWELL, name of three distinguished English writers, children of Sir George Keresley Sitwell. **Dame Edith Sitwell** (1887–1964), leading poet and critic, helped launch *Wheels* (1916), a magazine of experimental poetry, wrote the satirical *Facade* (1922; music by William WALTON), and was a master technician of sound, rhythm and symbol. **Sir Osbert Sitwell** (1892–1969), satirist, novelist and short-story writer, is best known for his fantastic novel *The Man who Lost Himself* (1929) and his five-volume autobiography. **Sir Sacheverell Sitwell** (1897–), is a poet, art critic and traveler whose work includes *Southern Baroque Art* (1924), *All Summer in a Day* (1926) and *Mozart* (1932).

SI UNITS, the internationally adopted abbreviation for the *Système International d'Unités* (International System of Units), a modification of the system known as rationalized MKSA UNITS adopted by the 11th General Conference of Weights and Measures (CGPM) in 1960 and subsequently amended. SI Units are the legal standard in many countries and find almost universal use among scientists.

SIVA. See SHIVA.

SIWAH, or Amon, an oasis in NW Egypt. Siwa(h), the chief village, contains remains of a temple, site of the oracle of AMON. Pop 3 600.

SIX, Les, term coined in 1920 to group six French composers (Darius MILHAUD, Francis POULENC, Arthur HONEGGER, Georges AURIC, Louis Durey and Germaine Tailleferre) inspired by the work of Erik SATIE and Jean COCTEAU.

SIX-DAY WAR. See ARAB-ISRAELI WARS.

SIX NATIONS, the enlarged IROQUOIS League formed by the joining of the Tuscarora (1722).

SIXTUS, five popes, who all died in office. **Sixtus I, Saint** reigned c116–25: feast day April 6. **Sixtus II, Saint** (reigned 257–58) was martyred under VALERIAN: feast day Aug. 6. **Sixtus III, Saint** (reigned 432–40), a suspected former supporter of PELAGIANISM, opposed the Pelagians but reconciled CYRIL of Alexandria with John of Antioch: feast day Aug. 18. **Sixtus IV** (1414–1484; elected 1471) built the SISTINE CHAPEL. His reign was characterized by nepotism and SIMONY. **Sixtus V** (1521–90; elected 1585) brought the PAPAL STATES to order and made the pope one of Europe's richest princes. His reforms of church administration were part of the COUNTER-REFORMATION.

SKAGERRAK, arm of the North Sea some 140mi long and 80mi wide dividing Norway from Denmark and linking the North Sea with the Baltic Sea through the Kattegat.

SKAGWAY, town in SE Alaska, 70mi N of Juneau, a railroad terminus founded 1897 during the Klondike goldrush. Pop 675.

SKALDIC POETRY, in Old Norse literature, the poetry of the SAGA, recited by Scandinavian court poets (*skalds*) from about 800 onwards. It is noted for its syllabic metrical structure and elaborate metaphors (*kennings*).

SKANDERBEG, (George Kastrioti; c1405–1468), Albanian national hero. He organized the Albanian clans into a guerrilla force which for 25 years repelled the newly arrived Turkish invaders.

SKATES, a family, Rajidae, of flattened CARTILAGINOUS FISHES belonging to the order of RAYS, but differing from other rays in producing eggs and not giving birth to live young. The horny cases containing the eggs are known as Mermaid's purses.

SKATING. See ICE SKATING; ROLLER SKATING.

SKELETON, in VERTEBRATES, the framework of BONES that supports and protects the soft TISSUES and ORGANS of the body. (See also ENDOSKELETON; EXOSKELETON.) It acts as an attachment for the MUSCLES, especially those producing movement, and protects vital organs such as the BRAIN, HEART and LUNGS. It is also a store of calcium, magnesium, sodium, phosphorus and PROTEINS, while its bone marrow is the site of red BLOOD-corpuscle formation. In the adult human body, there are about 206 bones, to which more than 600 muscles are attached. The skeleton consists of two parts: the axial skeleton (the skull, backbone and rib-cage), and the appendicular skeleton (the limbs). The function of the **axial skeleton** is mainly protective. The SKULL consists of 29 bones, 8 being fused together to form the cranium, protecting the brain. The *vertebral column*, or backbone, consists of 33 small bones (or VERTEBRAE): the upper 25 are joined by LIGAMENTS and thick cartilaginous disks and the lower 9 are fused together. It supports the upper body and protects the SPINAL CORD which runs through it. The *rib-cage* consists of 12 pairs of ribs forming a protective cage around the heart and lungs and assists in breathing (see RESPIRATION). The **appendicular skeleton** is primarily concerned with LOCOMOTION and consists of the ARMS and pectoral girdle, and the LEGS and pelvic girdle. The limbs articulate with their girdles in ball and socket JOINTS which permit the shoulder and hip great freedom of movement but are prone to dislocation. In contrast the elbows and knees are hinge joints permitting movement in one plane only, but which are very strong.

The hanging of 38 Sioux at Mankato, Minnesota, in December 1862, following Indian massacres of white settlers; a lithograph made in 1883.

SKELTON, John (c1460–1529), English court poet and satirist; influential tutor to Henry VIII. His works include burlesques (*Philip Sparrow*, 1508), a morality play, *Magnificence* (1515), and satires directed against Cardinal WOLSEY such as *Colin Clout* (1522).

SKEPTICISM, philosophical attitude of doubting all claims to knowledge, chiefly on the ground that the adequacy of any proposed criterion is itself questionable. Examples of thoroughgoing skeptics, wary of dogmatism in whatever guise, were PYRRHO OF ELIS

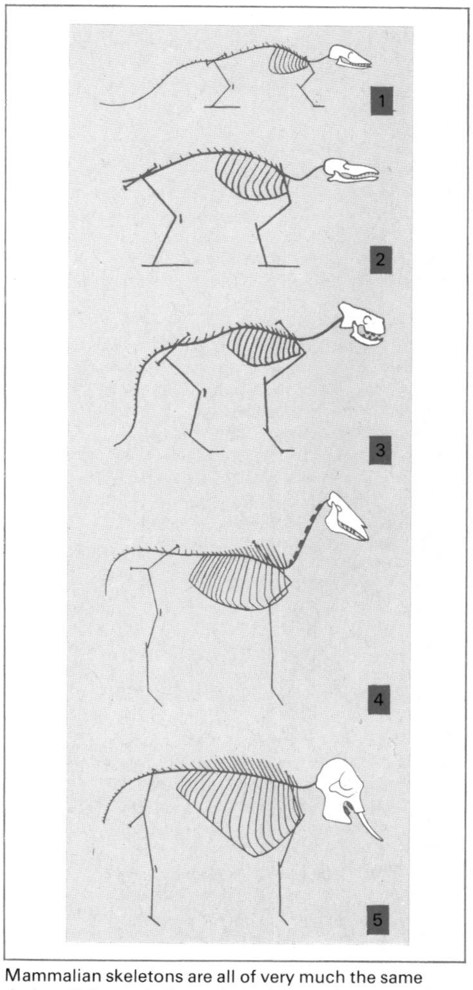

Mammalian skeletons are all of very much the same design, if size and minor adaptations are ignored. (1) Typical insectivore skeleton; (2) rodent skeleton; (3) carnivore; (4) horse; (5) elephant.

("Pyrrhonism" and "skepticism" are virtual synonyms) and HUME. Other thinkers, among them AUGUSTINE, ERASMUS, MONTAIGNE, PASCAL, BAYLE and KIERKEGAARD, sought to defend faith and religion by directing skeptical arguments against the EPISTEMOLOGICAL claims of RATIONALISM and EMPIRICISM. PRAGMATISM and KANT's critical philosophy represent two influential attempts to resolve skeptical dilemmas. (See also AGNOSTICISM.)

SKIING, the sport of gliding over snow on long, thin runners called skis. It began some 5 000 years ago in N Europe as a form of transport and became a sport in the 1800s. In 1924, the Fédération Internationale de Ski was formed and the first Winter Olympics held. Today, skiing is ever-increasing in popularity, as either Alpine downhill slalom or giant slalom obstacle courses, Nordic crosscountry skiing, or ski-jumping. Skis are generally made of laminated wood, fiberglass, plastic, metal or a combination of these. They have safety bindings attaching the boot firmly to the ski; ski poles are used for balance.

SKIMMERS, three species of gregarious tern-like birds of tropical rivers and shores which derive their name from their habit of skimming low over the water with bill open and the lower mandible slicing through the surface of the water to catch fish and small crustaceans. Family: Rhynchopidae.

SKIN, the TISSUE which forms a sensitive, elastic, protective and waterproof covering of the HUMAN BODY, together with its specializations (e.g., NAILS, HAIR). In the adult human, it weighs 2.75kg, covers an area of 1.7m² and varies in thickness from 1mm (in the eyelids) to 3mm (in the palms and soles). It consists of two layers: the outer, epidermis, and the inner, dermis, or true skin. The outermost part of the **epidermis**, the *stratum corneum*, contains a tough protein called KERATIN. Consequently it provides protection against mechanical trauma, a barrier against microorganisms, and waterproofing. The epidermis also contains cells which produce the MELANIN responsible for skin pigmentation and which provides protection against the sun's ultraviolet rays. The unique pattern of skin folding on the soles and palms provides a gripping surface, and is the basis of identification by FINGERPRINTS. The **dermis** is usually thicker than the epidermis and contains BLOOD vessels, nerves and sensory receptors, sweat glands, SEBACEOUS GLANDS, hair folicles, fat cells and fibers. Temperature regulation of the body is aided by the evaporative cooling of sweat (see PERSPIRATION); regulation of the skin blood flow, and the erection of hairs which trap an insulating layer of air next to the skin (see GOOSEFLESH). The rich nerve supply of the dermis is responsible for the reception of touch, pressure, pain and temperature stimuli. Leading into the hair follicles are sebaceous glands which produce the antibacterial sebum, a fluid which keeps the hairs oiled and the skin moist. The action of sunlight on the skin initiates the formation of VITAMIN D which helps prevent RICKETS.

SKINDIVING, underwater SWIMMING AND DIVING with or without selfcontained underwater breathing apparatus (SCUBA). The simplest apparatus is the SNORKEL, generally used with goggles, or mask, and flippers. An AQUALUNG consists of compressed air cylinders with an automatic demand regulator, which supplies air at the correct pressure according to the diver's depth. "Closed-circuit" SCUBA contains a chemical which absorbs carbon dioxide from exhaled air.

SKINKS, one of the two largest families of LIZARDS, the Scincidae. The most abundant lizards of Africa, the E Indies and Australia, they are smooth-scaled and cylindrical with short legs and a long protrusible tongue. Most are ground-dwellers or burrowers. Skinks are insectivorous or herbivorous.

SKINNER, Burrhus Frederic (1904–), US psychologist and author whose staunch advocacy of BEHAVIORISM has done much to gain it acceptance in 20th-century PSYCHOLOGY. His best known books are *Science and Human Behavior* (1953) and *Beyond Freedom and Dignity* (1971).

SKINNER, Cornelia Otis (1901–), US actress and author who wrote the autobiographical *Our Hearts Were Young and Gay* (1942; with E. Kimbrough). She is remembered for solo monologues often written by herself.

SKOKIE (until 1940 Niles Center), village in NE Ill., a NW suburb of Chicago producing chemicals, aluminum and plastic products. Pop 68 627.

SKOPJE, capital of Macedonia, S Yugoslavia. Virtually destroyed in a 1963 earthquake, it now has iron, steel, chemical and textile industries. Pop 312 091.

SKUAS, seabirds related to the GULLS, best known for their piratical attacks on other birds, forcing them to disgorge their food, which the skuas then eat. There are four species: Pomarine; Long-tailed; Arctic and the Great Skua, the first three known in the US as JAEGERS. The Great skua, *Catharacta skua*, differs widely from the others in appearance and habits.

SKULL, the bony structure of the head and face situated at the top of the vertebral column. It forms a thick bony protection for the BRAIN with small apertures for blood vessels, nerves, the SPINAL CORD etc., and the thinner framework of facial structure.

SKUNK CABBAGE, *Symplocarpus foetidus*, plant named for the vile odor it emits when crushed. It grows in damp woods and fields of the eastern US and its purple and green arum-like flowers appear in late winter. Family Araceae.

SKUNKS, carnivorous mammals of the WEASEL family, Mustelidae, renowned for the foul stink they produce when threatened. There are ten species distributed throughout the Americas. All are boldly-patterned in black and white. Most are nocturnal and feed on insects, mice and eggs. In defense a skunk can expel fine jets of foul-smelling liquid from scent glands under the tail. This can be shot out to a distance of 3m (10ft) with a remarkably accurate aim.

The Striped skunk (*Mephitis mephitis*), a member of the weasel family.

SKYDIVING, the sport of parachute jumping, developed since WWII. In competitions, points are awarded for acrobatic style in the maneuvers made during the free fall (the period before the parachute opens), and for accuracy in landing on target (the center of a 1,000ft circle). Parachutists generally drop from heights up to 13 000ft and open their parachutes at about 2 000ft.

SKYE, largest island of the Inner HEBRIDES off W Scotland. Cattle, sheep and tourism are the main sources of income.

SKYE TERRIER, an old, working breed originally from Skye. Its 5in-long coat covers the eyes and ranges from black to blond. About 10in high and about 20in long, it weighs some 25lb.

SKYLAB, US manned space station, launched May 25, 1973. First of its kind, it was converted from a Saturn IVB booster to serve as an orbital laboratory and earth resources monitor. The first of its three crews had to repair serious damage, but all set new endurance records in space.

SKYROS, or Skíros, largest of the Greek N SPORADES ISLANDS in the Aegean Sea. THESEUS (according to legend) and Rupert BROOKE died here.

SKYSCRAPER, a very tall building. From the mid-19th century the price of land in big cities made it worthwhile to build upward rather than outward, and this became practicable with the development of safe electric ELEVATORS. The first skyscraper was the 40m (130ft) high Equitable Life Assurance Society Building, New York (1870). A major design breakthrough was the use of a load-bearing skeletal iron frame, first used in the 10-story Home Insurance Company Building, Chicago (1885).

SLAG, waste formed as an upper, molten layer in the smelting of ores and refining of metals. It consists of impurities, oxides and ash, with a limestone FLUX, and serves to remove unwanted substances and to protect the metal from oxidation. Solidified slag is used as AGGREGATE, for road making, and as a phosphate FERTILIZER. (See also BLAST FURNACE; OPEN-HEARTH PROCESS.)

SLANDER, in law, spoken defamation, an untrue statement which injures another person's reputation. If circulated in writing, it is LIBEL. Slander may be subject to criminal action or a civil suit by the injured party.

SLANG, popular speech not acceptable in formal language. It may comprise new words, shortened forms, or new use of old words. Slang words may be shortlived, or become accepted. Jargon or argot is vocabulary restricted to a group, such as actors, criminals or social scientists.

SLATE, a dark gray, low-grade metamorphic rock. Because of the comparatively low temperatures and pressures under which it was formed, slate still retains the texture and cleavage properties of the SHALE from which it is derived. For this reason, it is widely used as a roofing material.

SLATER, Samuel (1768–1835), British-born founder of the US cotton textile industry. As an apprentice in England he memorized the principles of ARKWRIGHT's machinery. He set up his spinning mill (now a museum) in Pawtucket, R.I., in 1793.

SLAUGHTERHOUSE CASES, controversy following the granting (1869) by the La. legislature of a New Orleans monopoly in landing and slaughtering cattle to the Crescent City Live Stock Landing and Slaughterhouse Co. In 1873, the Supreme Court found, against other New Orleans butchers, that there was no infringement of the 14th Amendment.

SLAVE RIVER, or Great Slave River, part of the MACKENZIE RIVER system, Canada. It winds N 258mi from Lake Athabaska, Alberta, to GREAT SLAVE LAKE.

SLAVERY, a practice found at different times in most parts of the world, now condemned in the Universal Declaration of Human Rights.

Slavery generally means enforced servitude, along with society's recognition that the master has ownership rights over the slave and his labor. Some elements of slavery can be found in serfdom, as practiced during the Middle Ages and in Russia up to 1861; in debt bondage and PEONAGE, both forms of enforced labor for the payment of debts; and in forced labor itself, exacted for punishment or for political or military reasons, (examples being the "slave" labor used by the Nazis in WWII, and the Soviet labor camps). In some parts a form of slavery or bondage is still practiced today under the guise of exacting a bride price, or the "adoption" of poor children by wealthier families for labor purposes. While peonage is still rampant in South America, actual slavery is reputed to exist in Africa, the Arabian Peninsula, Tibet and elsewhere. Slavery in Saudi Arabia was officially abolished only in 1962.

Warfare was the main source of slaves in ancient times, along with enslavement for debt or as punishment, and the selling of children. But there was not necessarily a distinction in race or color between master and slave. Manumission (the granting of freedom) was commonplace, and in Greece and Rome many slaves or freedmen rose to influential posts: a slave dynasty, the Mamelukes, ruled Egypt from 1250 to 1517. In the West the Germans enslaved many Slavic people (hence "slave") in the Dark Ages. By the 13th century feudal serfdom was widespread in Europe (see SERF). Slavery increased again when the Portuguese, exploring the coast of Africa, began to import black slaves in 1433 to fill a manpower shortage at home. With the discovery of America and the development of plantations, the need for cheap, abundant labor encouraged almost 400 years of slave trade. See NEGROES, AMERICAN; ABOLITIONISM; MISSOURI COMPROMISE; COMPROMISE OF 1850; KANSAS-NEBRASKA ACT; DRED SCOTT CASE; EMANCIPATION PROCLAMATION; CIVIL WAR, AMERICAN; REPUBLICAN PARTY; RECONSTRUCTION; CIVIL RIGHTS AND LIBERTIES.

SLAVONIC LANGUAGES, a group of INDO-EUROPEAN LANGUAGES spoken by some 225 million people in central and E Europe and Siberia. There are

The Emancipation Proclamation of January 1, 1863, ending slavery throughout the United States, is read by a Union soldier to a group of slaves.

three groups: W Slavonic (Polish, Czech and Slovak), S Slavonic (Slovene, Serbo-Croatian, Macedonian and Bulgarian), and E Slavonic (Russian, Ukrainian and Belorussian). Byzantine missionaries in the 9th century first developed written Slavonic, using a modified Greek alphabet known as Cyrillic. Today, SLAVS converted by the Orthodox Church use Cyrillic characters and Slavs converted by the Roman Church use the Latin alphabet.

SLAVOPHILES AND WESTERNIZERS, two groups of 19th-century Russian intellectuals. The Slavophiles opposed the westernization of what they felt was a superior Russian or Slavic way of life. The Westernizers advocated the introduction of Western methods of capitalism, technology and liberalism.

SLAVS, largest European ethnic and language group, living today in central and E Europe and Siberia: all speak SLAVONIC LANGUAGES. About 4000 years ago they migrated to land N of the Black Sea and later split into three groups: the E Slavs, (Russians, Belorussians and Ukrainians), the W Slavs (Czechs, Slovaks and Poles) and the S Slavs (Serbs, Croats, Slovenes, Macedonians, Montenegrins and Bulgarians). Slavonic nations were formed from the 9th century but almost all were overwhelmed by Turkish or Mongol invaders. In the 15th century Russia gained national independence but it was not until WWI that the other Slav nations regained their national identities.

SLEEP, a state of relative unconsciousness and inactivity. The need for sleep recurs periodically in all animals. If deprived of sleep humans initially experience HALLUCINATIONS, acute ANXIETY, and become highly suggestible and eventually, COMA and sometimes DEATH result. During sleep, the body is relaxed and most bodily activity is reduced. Cortical, or higher, brain activity, as measured by the ELECTROENCEPHALOGRAPH; blood pressure; body TEMPERATURE; rate of heart beat and breathing are decreased. However, certain activities, such as gastric and alimentary activity, are increased. Sleep tends to occur in daily cycles which exhibit up to 5 or 6 periods of orthodox sleep—characterized by its deepness—alternating with periods of paradoxical, or rapid-eye-movement (REM), sleep—characterized by its restlessness and jerky movements of the eyes. Paradoxical sleep occurs only when we are dreaming and occupies about 20% of total sleeping time. Sleepwalking (SOMNAMBULISM) occurs only during orthodox sleep when we are not dreaming. Sleep-talking occurs mostly in orthodox sleep. Many theories have been proposed to explain sleep but none is completely satisfactory. Separate sleeping and waking centers in the HYPOTHALAMUS cooperate with other parts of the BRAIN in controlling sleep. Sleep as a whole, and particularly paradoxical sleep when dreaming occurs, is essential to health and life. Consequently the key to why animals sleep may reside in a need to DREAM. **Sleep learning** experiments have so far proved ineffective. A rested brain and concentration are probably the most effective basis for LEARNING.

SLEEPING PILLS. Drugs which induce SLEEP are properly termed hypnotics (see SEDATIVES). (See also ANESTHESIA; NARCOTICS.)

SLEEPING SICKNESS, INFECTIOUS DISEASE caused by TRYPANOSOMES occurring in Africa and carried by TSETSE FLIES. It initially causes FEVER, headache, often a sense of oppression and a rash; later the characteristic somnolence follows and the disease enters a chronic, often fatal stage. Treatment is most effective if started before the late stage of BRAIN involvement and uses arsenical compounds.

SLEEPWALKING. See SOMNAMBULISM.

SLEET, PRECIPITATION consisting of small ICE pellets (diameter 5mm or less) formed by the freezing of raindrops or of partially melted snowflakes. A mixture of rain and snow is often termed sleet. (See also HAIL).

SLIDELL, town in SE La., 30mi NE of New Orleans, primarily a dormitory community for the aerospace industry in the region. Pop 16101.

SLIDELL, John. See MASON AND SLIDELL.

SLIDE RULE, an instrument based on LOGARITHMS and used for rapid, though approximate, calculation. Two scales are calibrated identically so that, on each, the distance from the "1" point to any point on the scale is proportional to the logarithm of the number represented by that point. Since log $(a.b) = \log a + \log b$, the multiplication $a.b$ can be performed by setting the "1" point on scale (1) against a on scale (2), then reading off the number of scale (2) opposite b on scale (1). Division is performed by reversing the procedure. In practice, slide rules have several different scales for different kinds of calculation, and a runner (cursor) to permit more accurate readings.

SLIME MOLDS, organisms belonging to the class Myxophyta, regarded as FUNGI, but which at certain stages of their life cycle are free-living masses of naked PROTOPLASM that move by ameboid movement (see AMEBA). They are found in damp, dark woods and ingest solid food particles as they ooze over decaying leaves and wood. Slime molds reproduce by spores like other primitive plants, but lacking CHLOROPHYLL, they do not carry out PHOTOSYNTHESIS.

SLING, weapon for propelling missiles such as rocks, much used in ancient and medieval times. The simple sling was a leather strip, forming a pouch for the missile, with a cord at each end. The sling was whirled above the head, and one cord was loosed to dispatch the missile. The modern **slingshot**—a forked stick with an elastic band for shooting pebbles—is a descendant.

SLIPPED DISK, a common condition in which the intervertebral disks of the spinal column degenerate with extrusion of the central soft portion through the outer fibrous ring. The protruding material may cause back pain, or may press upon the spinal cord or on nerves as they leave the SPINAL CORD (causing SCIATICA). Prolonged bed rest is an effective treatment in many cases, but traction, manipulation or surgery may also be required particularly if there is PARALYSIS or nerve involvement.

SLOAN, Alfred Pritchard (1875–1966), US industrialist, president of General Motors from 1923 and chairman of the board for 1937–56. His Sloan Foundation (1934) finances social and cancer research.

SLOAN, John (1871–1951), US painter, a member of the ASHCAN SCHOOL and influential in the development of US modern art. He is famous for his paintings of nudes and of urban scenes, such as *McSorley's Bar* (1912) and *Wake of the Ferry* (1907).

SLOANE, Sir Hans, 1st Baronet (1660–1753), British physician and natural historian who served as President of the ROYAL SOCIETY (1727–41) after NEWTON. His collection of books and specimens, left to the nation (for a fee of £20000 to be paid to his family) formed the basis of the British Museum (founded 1759).

SLOE, or **Blackthorn,** *Prunus spinosa*, a Mediterranean tree, the fruit of which is too acid to eat but which is used to make a liqueur known as sloe gin. Family: Rosaceae.

SLOTH BEAR, or **Honey bear,** *Melursus ursinus*, an aberrant bear with narrow snout and long lips, adapted for feeding on insects. A pair of incisors is missing in both upper and lower jaws, and, after tearing open an ant- or termite-nest with its claws, it purses its lips and sucks the insects into its mouth.

SLOTHS, slow, tree-dwelling EDENTATE mammals. There are two genera of modern Tree sloths, the two-toed sloths (*Choloepus*) and three-toed sloths or **ai** (*Bradypus*), descending from the Giant GROUND SLOTHS, *Megatherium* of the PLEISTOCENE. The arms and legs are long, the digits are bound together by tissue and terminate in long, strong claws. With these the sloth can suspend the body from branches. All sloths are South American in origin and vegetarian, feeding on fruits, shoots and leaves.

SLOVAK, the official language of Slovakia. A W SLAVONIC LANGUAGE, it resembles Czech in dialect and is written in the Roman alphabet.

SLOVAKIA, E part of Czechoslovakia, 18922sq mi in area. It is mostly mountainous, but the mountains slope down to plains and the Danube R in the S and SW. Slovakia has rich farmlands and mineral deposits; shipbuilding and metal processing are also leading industries. The old capital, Bratislava, is an important port on the Danube. Slovakia was mainly under Hungarian rule from the early 900s to 1918. It was then part of Czechoslovakia until it became a German protectorate in 1939. After WWII it was reincorporated into Czechoslovakia.

SLOVENE, the language of Slovenia. It is an S SLAVONIC LANGUAGE, closely related to Serbo-Croatian, and has 46 individual dialects.

SLOVENIA, NW part of YUGOSLAVIA. It became independent of Austria in 1918 and a constituent republic of Yugoslavia in 1945. Its economy is based chiefly on agriculture and on iron, steel, and aluminum industries. The capital is Ljubljana.

SLOWWORM (*Anguis fragilis*). See ANGUID LIZARDS.

SLUGS, shell-less or nearly shell-less GASTROPOD mollusks living mainly in the soil. They have an elongated mucus-covered body with a loose mantle at the anterior end. They move by means of muscular waves passing over the mucus-lubricated foot. Slugs feed on vegetable matter, rasping material from plants with a toothed radula organ.

SLUM. See URBAN RENEWAL.

SLUTER, Claus (c1350–1406), Dutch sculptor famous for the portal, the tomb of PHILIP III of France, and a large crucifixion group, the *Well of Moses* at Chartreuse de Champmol, Dijon.

SMALLPOX, INFECTIOUS DISEASE, now restricted to a few areas, causing FEVER, headache and general malaise, followed by a rash. The rash characteristically affects face and limbs more than trunk and lesions start simultaneously. From a maculo-papular appearance, the rash passes into a pustular or vesicular stage and ends with scab formation; the lesions are deep and cause scarring. Major and minor forms of smallpox exist, with high fatality rate in major, often with extensive skin HEMORRHAGE. Transmission is from infected cases by secretions and the SKIN lesions; these are infectious for the duration of the rash. Immunization against smallpox was the earliest form practiced, initially through self-inoculation with the minor form. Later JENNER introduced VACCINATION with the related cowpox VIRUS (vaccinia is now used). QUARANTINE regulations and contact tracing are important in control of isolated outbreaks. It is important to confirm that apparent cases of CHICKENPOX are not indeed of smallpox.

SMART, Christopher (1722–1771), English poet. His masterpiece, *A Song to David* (1763), was written while he was confined in BEDLAM.

SMARTWEED, or water pepper, *Polygonum hydropiper*, an annual herb that grows in wet places and has lanceolate leaves and small flowers. The juice is acrid and can inflame tender skin.

SMELL, SENSE for detecting and recognizing substances at a distance and for assessing the quality of

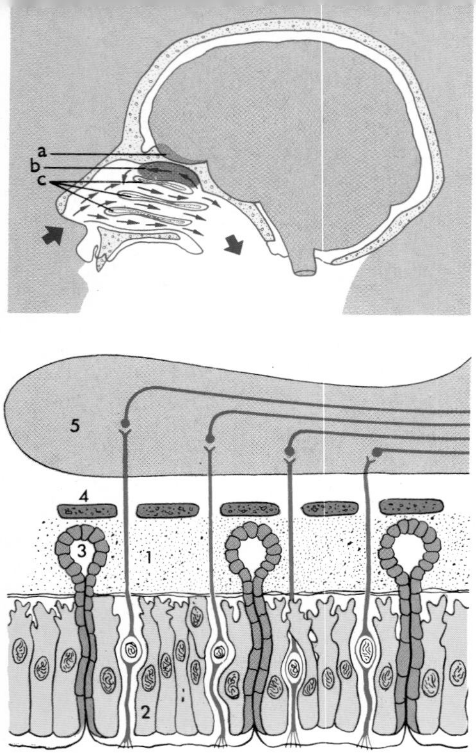

Schematic diagram of the operation of the sense of smell in human beings. *Top:* the olfactory system in the head. Bone is shown in yellow and nervous tissue in violet. The olfactory bulb of the brain (a) receives messages from the olfactory epithelium, or membrane (b); inhaled air does not reach this directly, but is passed through the nasal turbinals (c). *Above:* in the epithelium, sensory cells with long processes (1) are located between supporting cells (2). Below the epithelium some connective tissue is localized with secretory cells (3). Through the openings in the cribiform plate (bone; 4) the olfactory threads pass through to carry the messages from the sensory cells to the olfactory bulb of the brain (5).

food. One of the earliest senses to develop in EVOLUTION, it may have been based on the chemotaxis of lower forms. Recognition of environmental odors is of vital importance in recognizing edible substances, detecting other animals or objects of danger, and in sexual behavior and attraction. In recent years, particular odors called **pheromones** that have specific physiological functions in insect and mammal behavior have been recognized. Smell reception in insects is localized to the antennae and detection is by specialist (pheromone) receptors and generalist (other odor) receptors. In man and mammals, the NOSE is the organ of smell. Respiratory air is drawn into the nostrils and passes across a specialized receptor surface—the olfactory epithelium. Receptor cells detect the tiny concentrations of odors in the air stream and stimulate nerve impulses that pass to olfactory centers in the BRAIN for coding and perception. It is not possible to classify odors in the same way as the primary colors in VISION and it is probable that pattern recognition is more important. Certain animals depend mainly on the sense of smell, while man is predominantly a visual animal. But with training, he can achieve sensitive detection and discrimination of odors.

SMELLING SALTS, scented solution of SAL VOLATILE in alcohol or ammonia-water, used to revive the weak or faint.

SMELT, small estuarine fishes related to SALMON. Elongate fishes resembling small trout, they live in large shoals in estuaries and coastal waters of temperate regions of the N hemisphere. Like true salmon, smelt migrate up into fresher water to spawn. Smelt rarely grow to more than about 200mm (8in) but are considered a great delicacy.

SMELTING, in METALLURGY, process of extracting a metal from its ORE by heating the ore in a BLAST FURNACE or reverberatory furnace (one in which a shallow hearth is heated by radiation from a low roof heated by flames from the burning fuel). A reducing agent (see OXIDATION AND REDUCTION), usually COKE, is used, and a FLUX is added to remove impurities. Sulfide ores are generally roasted to convert them to oxides before smelting.

SMET, Pierre Jean de. See DE SMET, PIERRE JEAN.

SMETANA, Bedřich (1824–1884), Czech composer. Many of his compositions reflect Smetana's ardent Bohemian nationalism; most famous are the comic opera *The Bartered Bride* (1866) and the symphonic poems *Ma Vlast* ("My Country"; 1874–79).

SMIBERT, John (1688–1751), Scottish-born American portrait painter. He went to America in 1729 and settled in Boston, where he had a successful career.

SMILAX, a genus of tropical and subtropical lily-like vines and creepers. The rhizomes of *Smilax aristolochiaefolia* are a main source of SARSAPARILLA. Family: Smilacaceae.

SMILES, Samuel (1812–1904), Scottish writer and moralist. He wrote several didactic works based on the work ethic—*Self-Help* (1859), *Character* (1871), *Thrift* (1875) and *Duty* (1880).

SMITH, Adam (1723–1790), Scottish economist and philosopher. The free-market system he advocated in *The Wealth of Nations* (1776) came to be regarded as the classic system of economics. Smith drew on the ideas of TURGOT, Quesnay, MONTESQUIEU and his friend David HUME and argued that if market forces were allowed to operate without state intervention "an invisible hand" would guide self-interest for the well-being of all. His concept of the division of labor and the belief that value derives from productive labor were major insights. An earlier work, *Theory of Moral Sentiments* (1759) contrasts with *The Wealth of Nations* in its emphasis upon sympathy rather than self-interest as a basic force in human nature.

SMITH, Alfred Emanuel (1873–1944), US politician elected Governor of New York four times (1918, 1922, 1924, 1926), a TAMMANY HALL politician and a leading figure among the Democrats. Supported by F. D. ROOSEVELT in his bids for the presidency, he failed to gain nomination in 1924 and was beaten by HOOVER in 1928: when Roosevelt became president, Smith opposed the NEW DEAL.

SMITH, Bessie (c1898–1937), US jazz singer, perhaps the greatest BLUES singer. "The Empress of the Blues" came from a poor Tenn. home and first recorded in 1923; later she performed with many leading musicians, including Louis ARMSTRONG and Benny GOODMAN.

SMITH, David (1906–1965), US sculptor, famous for his constructions of wrought iron and cut steel. His late works, like *Cubi XVIII* (1964) comprised burnished or painted cubic forms dramatically welded together.

SMITH, Sir Donald Alexander. See STRATHCONA AND MOUNT ROYAL, 1ST BARON.

SMITH, Edmund Kirby. See KIRBY-SMITH, EDMUND.

SMITH, Frederick Edwin, 1st Earl of Birkenhead (1872–1930), British Conservative politician and jurist. He was against Irish HOME RULE and prosecuted CASEMENT. Lord Chancellor 1919–22, he served in BALFOUR's cabinet 1924–28 as secretary of state for India.

SMITH, Gerrit (1797–1874), US reformer. He financed many reforms with his large fortune and was a prominent abolitionist. He organized the LIBERTY PARTY and was a congressman 1853–54. He ran twice for the governorship of N.Y., in 1840 and 1858.

SMITH, Ian Douglas (1919–), Rhodesian politician, prime minister from 1965. As leader of a white minority government he declared unilateral independence from Britain in 1965, and made RHODESIA a republic in 1970.

SMITH, Jedediah Strong (1799–1831), US frontiersman and MOUNTAIN MAN who led fur-trapping expeditions to the Missouri R and to Wind R, and in 1824 discovered the South Pass route to the West. Smith was the first white man to cross the Sierra Nevada and to explore the Cal.-Ore. coast by land.

SMITH, John (c1580–1631), English explorer, soldier and writer who established the first permanent English colony in North America. He sailed to Virginia in 1607 and founded a settlement at JAMESTOWN. Smith claimed to have been captured by chief POWHATAN in 1607 and saved from death by the chief's daughter POCAHONTAS. Smith charted the coast of New England in 1614, publishing his findings in *A Description of New England* (1616).

SMITH, Joseph (1805–1844), founder of the Church of Jesus Christ of the Latter-Day Saints, based on the Bible and the Book of Mormon, which Smith claimed to have found (in the form of hieroglyphs on gold plates) and translated with the help of the angel Moroni. In 1844 he was accused of conspiracy and, while in prison, was murdered by a mob. (See MORMONS; NAUVOO.)

SMITH, Seba (1792–1868), US humorist famous for his series of satirical letters on politics written under the pen name Major Jack Downing in the Portland *Courier*.

SMITH, Sydney (1771–1845), English preacher, reformer and wit. In his sermons, his *Letters to Peter Plymley* (1807–08) and pieces in the *Edinburgh Review* (which he cofounded in 1802), he combined powerful arguments with biting satire of Protestant bigotry to press for Catholic emancipation.

SMITH, Walter Bedell (1895–1961), WWII US army chief of staff in Europe. He negotiated the surrenders of Italy (1943) and Germany (1945), was ambassador to the USSR 1946–49, CIA director 1950–53 and undersecretary of state 1953–54.

SMITH, William "Strata" (1769–1839), the "father of stratigraphy." He established that similar sedimentary rock strata in different places may be dated by identifying the fossils each level contains, and made the first geological map of England and Wales (1815).

SMITH ACT, or Alien Registration Act (1940), a federal US law making it a criminal offense to advocate the violent overthrow of the government or to belong to any group advocating this. Used to convict Communist Party leaders, the act also required registration and fingerprinting of aliens.

SMITHFIELD, town in N R.I., 10mi NW of Providence. Industry is based on textiles. Pop 13 468.

SMITH-HUGHES ACT, or Vocational Education Act (1917), federal US law setting up The Federal Board for Vocational Education and giving finance to approved state and local plans for adult training.

SMITH-LEVER ACT, or Cooperative Agricultural Extension Act (1914), federal US law providing for federal, state and county grants for education in agriculture and home economics.

SMITHSON, James (1765–1829), earlier known as James Lewis and Louis Macie, British chemist and mineralogist who left £100 000 (then about $500 000) for the foundation of the SMITHSONIAN INSTITUTION.

SMITHSONIAN INSTITUTION, US institution of scientific and artistic culture, located in Washington, D.C., and sponsored by the US Government. Founded with money left by James SMITHSON, it was established by Congress in 1846. It is governed by a

View of one of the newer buildings belonging to the complex of museums that house the historical, art and scientific collections of the Smithsonian Institution in Washington D.C.

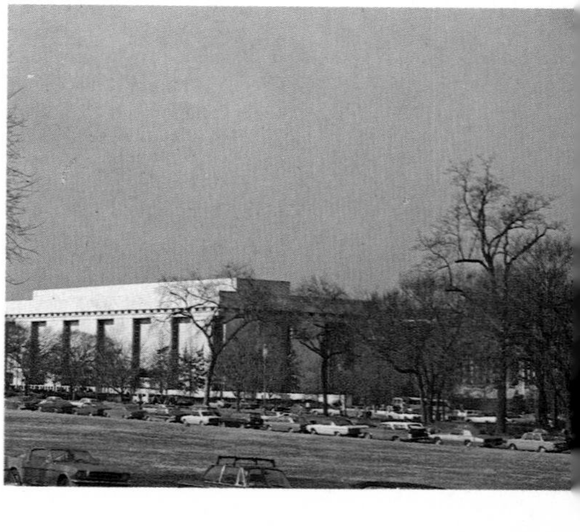

board of regents comprising the US Vice-President and Chief Justice, three Senators, three Representatives and six private citizens appointed by Congress. Although it undertakes considerable scientific research, it is best known as the largest US collection of museums, the "nation's attic:" these include the United States National Museum, the National Air and Space Museum, the National Gallery of Art, the Freer Gallery of Art, the National Portrait Gallery and the National Collection of Fine Arts.

SMITHSONITE, white, yellow or green mineral, formerly called CALAMINE, consisting of zinc carbonate ($ZnCO_3$). Smithsonite is of widespread occurrence, an ore of ZINC formed by alteration of other zinc minerals; it has the CALCITE structure. It was named for James SMITHSON.

SMOG. See FOG.

SMOKING, the habit of inhaling or taking into the mouth the smoke of dried tobacco or other leaves from a pipe or wrapped cylinder; it has been practised for many years in various communities, often using leaves of plant with hallucinogenic or other euphoriant properties. The modern habit of tobacco smoking derived from America and spread to Europe in the 16th century. Mass production of cigarettes began in the 19th century. Since the rise in cigarette consumption, epidemiology has demonstrated an unequivocal association with LUNG CANCER, chronic BRONCHITIS and EMPHYSEMA and with ARTERIOSCLEROSIS, leading to CORONARY THROMBOSIS and STROKE. Smoking appears to play a part in other forms of cancer and in other diseases such as peptic ULCER. It is not yet clear what part of smoke is responsible for disease. It is now known that nonsmokers may be affected by environmental smoke. A minor degree of physical and a large degree of psychological addiction occur.

SMOKY MOUNTAINS. See GREAT SMOKY MOUNTAINS.

SMOLENSK, historic city, capital of Smolensk oblast in the Russian SFSR, USSR, on the upper Dneiper R. It manufactures car bodies, textile machinery, bricks, footwear and glass. Pop 211 000.

SMOLLETT, Tobias George (1721–1771), British writer who developed the PICARESQUE NOVEL in his satires of 18th-century English society. They include *Roderick Random* (1748), *Peregrine Pickle* (1751) and his masterpiece, *Humphry Clinker* (1771), which is written in the letter form.

SMOOT-HAWLEY TARIFF, enacted by Congress in 1930, brought the US tariff to a very high level as a protectionist measure. It aggravated world depression: foreign countries replied with retaliatory measures and there was a steep decline in US foreign trade.

SMUGGLING, illegal import or export of goods or people, either to avoid customs duties or to effect transfers prohibited by law. In the US, smuggling of alcohol became so widespread in the 1920s and early 1930s that it helped force the repeal of PROHIBITION. (See also NAVIGATION LAWS.)

SMUT, parasitic FUNGI, so named for the masses of sooty spores formed on the surface of the host plant. Smuts require only one host plant to complete their life cycle, unlike RUSTS. *Ustilago maydis* is an important parasite of corn and *U. tritici* is the loose smut of wheat. (See also PLANT DISEASES.)

SMUTS, Jan Christiaan (1870–1950), South African lawyer, soldier and statesman. In the BOER WAR he led Boer guerrilla forces in Cape Colony. He worked with BOTHA to create the Union of South Africa (1910) and was in the WWI British war cabinet. He was South African prime minister 1919–24, and minister of justice 1933–39 in the coalition government led by HERTZOG, whom he succeeded as prime minister (1939–48) to bring South Africa into WWII on the British side.

SMYRNA, Turkey. See IZMIR.

SMYRNA, town in NW Ga., a residential suburb of Atlanta. Pop 19 157.

SNAILS, herbivorous GASTROPOD mollusks with, typically, a spirally coiled shell, found on land, in freshwater or in the sea. The shell is secreted by the underlying "mantle" and houses the internal organs.

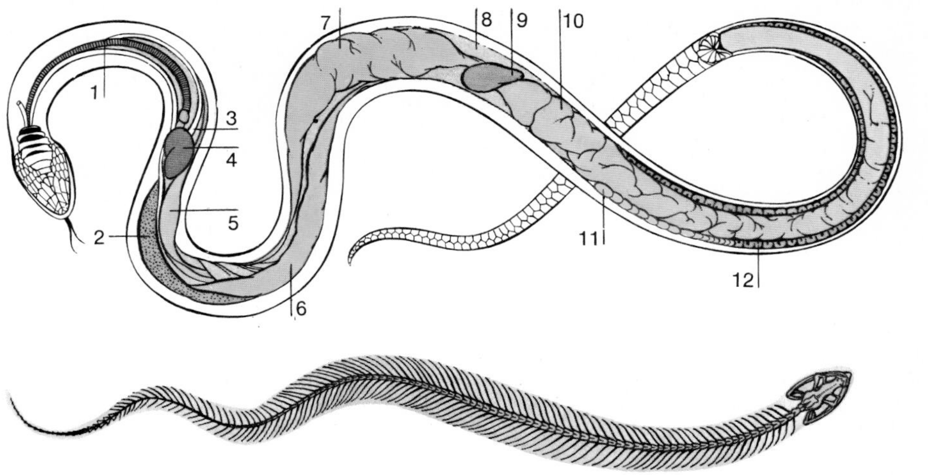

Anatomical drawing of a female Grass snake (*top*). (1) Windpipe; (2) lung; (3) left aorta; (4) heart; (5) gullet; (6) liver; (7) stomach; (8) fatty body; (9) gall bladder; (10) intestine; (11) ovary; (12) kidney. *Bottom*: skeleton of a Grass snake.

The internal structure is similar in all groups, though many land snails (Pulmonates) have their gills replaced with an air-breathing lung. Nonpulmonate snails are mostly unisexual while pulmonates are typically hermaphrodite.

SNAKEBIRD. See ANHINGA.

SNAKE BITE. A very small proportion of the world's snakes produce poisonous venom, and most of these live in the tropics. The venom may lead to HEMORRHAGE, PARALYSIS and central NERVOUS SYSTEM disorders as well as local symptoms of pain, EDEMA and ulceration. Treatment aims to minimize venom absorption, neutralize venom with antiserum, counteract the specific effects and support life until venom is eliminated. Antiserum should be used only for definite bites by identified snakes.

SNAKE FLIES, a family (Rhaphidiidae) of terrestrial insectivorous insects related to the ALDERFLIES. An extended THORAX forms a conspicuous "neck."

SNAKE PLANT. See SANSEVIERIA.

SNAKE RIVER, main tributary of the Columbia R, US. Rising in the Rockies of Yellowstone National Park, Wyo., it winds 1 038mi S, W, N and W through Ida. and Ore. to join the Columbia near Pasco, Wash. It is an important source of power and irrigation.

SNAKE ROOT, several plants supposed to contain remedies for snakebite or which are poisonous. Button snakeroot (*Liastris spicata*) and Black snakeroot (*Cimicifuga racemosa*) are North American herbs. White snakeroot (*Eupatorium aromaticum*) is a very dangerous plant causing milk sickness, a fatal disease of many early settlers, which was caused by consuming produce from cows that had eaten the plant.

SNAKES, an order, Squamata, of elongate legless reptiles. Snakes have a deeply-forked tongue covered with sense organs, which is flicked in and out of the mouth to test the surroundings. All snakes are carnivorous, feeding on insects, eggs, rodents and other larger mammals, depending on size. While those that feed on insects usually feed fairly regularly, snakes taking larger prey may feed only infrequently. To facilitate swallowing of large prey, upper and lower jaws may be dislocated and moved independently. All snakes swallow their prey whole without mastication. While many species have no accessories to assist them in the capture of prey, others are venomous, or subdue their prey by constriction before swallowing. Snakes may be aquatic terrestrial or arboreal.

SNAPDRAGON, or antirrhinum, popular garden plants of the genus *Antirrhinum* whose flowers have the upper and lower petals pressed together like animals' jaws. The common garden snapdragon (*Antirrhinum majus*) is native to the Mediterranean region. Family: Scrophulariaceae.

SNAPPERS, a family, Lutjanidae, of marine perch-like shore fishes occurring in warm waters. Many are deep-bodied fishes, generally banded or spotted in green or red, but the color pattern may change during growth. The larger species grow to about 1m (3.3ft) and are important food fishes in some areas.

SNAPPING TURTLE, Common (*Chelydra serpentina*), an edible freshwater TURTLE widespread in North and Central America, named for its aggressive disposition. Much smaller than the related ALLIGATOR SNAPPER, the common snapper rarely attains weights greater than 35kg (77lb). Family: Chelydridae.

SNCC. See STUDENT NATIONAL COORDINATING COMMITTEE.

SNEEZE, explosive expiration through the NOSE and MOUTH stimulated by irritation or INFLAMMATION in the nasal EPITHELIUM. It is a REFLEX attempt to remove the source of irritation.

SNEEZEWEED, *Helenium autumnale*, a yellow-flowered plant found in wet meadows throughout North America. Dried and powdered leaves cause violent sneezing. Family: Compositae.

SNELL'S LAW. See REFRACTION.

SNIPES, long-billed birds of the family Scolopacidae with flexible bill tips that can be opened below ground to grasp food items. Active mainly at dawn and dusk, snipe are dumpy birds of marshy areas or open moorland having large eyes set well back on the head. Extraordinarily well-camouflaged, if disturbed at close quarters they rise sharply and escape with an erratic zig-zag flight. In courtship many species produce loud whistling or drumming noises by vibration of the primaries or tail coverts in rapid dives.

SNOOK, a family, Centropomidae, of perch-like fishes of tropical seas, estuaries and fresh waters, including the giant Nile perch of Africa and the glassfish of India. The name is also used in Australia for the Narrow-barred mackerel, and in S Africa, for a fish resembling the Barracuda.

SNORING, stertorous respiration of certain persons during sleep, the noise being caused by vibration of the soft PALATE. It is predisposed to by the shape of the PHARYNX and by the sleeping position.

SNORKEL, breathing tube used by skin divers swimming near the surface, connecting the diver's mouth with the atmosphere. Also, a similar tube used by submarines in WWII to supply air to their engines without completely surfacing.

SNORRI STURLUSON (1179–1241), Icelandic poet and historian. The major figure in medieval Scandinavian literature, he wrote the still popular *Heimskringla* (*Orb of the World*), a vivid and eventful history of Norway's kings. He compiled the prose EDDA, a handbook of Norse mythology, poetic diction and meter.

SNOW, PRECIPITATION consisting of flakes or clumps of ICE crystals. The crystals are plane hexagonal, showing an infinite variety of beautiful branched forms; needles, columns and irregular forms are also found. Snow forms by direct vapor-to-ice condensation from humid air below 0°C. On reaching the ground, snow crystals lose their structure and become granular. Fresh snow is very light (sg about 0.1), and is a good insulator, protecting underlying plants from severe cold. In time, pressure, sublimation and melting and refreezing lead to compaction into NÉVÉ. The slow melting of mountain snow is important in natural irrigation.

SNOW, Charles Percy, Lord (1905–), English novelist. The 11 novels in his *Strangers and Brothers* series—including *Strangers and Brothers* (1940) itself, *The Masters* (1951) and *The New Men* (1954)—describe the dichotomy detailed in nonfiction form in *The Two Cultures and The Scientific Revolution* (1960).

SNOWBERRY, a number of plants which produce round white berries. The snowberry bush (*Symphoricarpus albus*) of North America is found in rocky habitats. The creeping snowberry (*Chiogenes hispidula*) is a trailing evergreen plant of the heath family.

SNOW BLINDNESS, temporary loss of VISION with severe pain, tears and EDEMA due to excessive ultraviolet light reflected from snow. Permanent damage is rare but protective POLAROID glasses should be used.

SNOW BUNTING, *Plectrophenax nivalis*, a small black and white BUNTING of the arctic tundra, which winters along sea shores and coasts of Europe. The winter plumage is almost pure white. They are gregarious birds often occurring in large flocks.

SNOWDROP, *Galanthus nivalis*, a Eurasian relative of the DAFFODIL which often produces white flowers while snow is about. Family: Amaryllidaceae.

SNOWFLAKE CURVE, a closed CURVE of infinite length derived by trisecting the sides of an equilateral TRIANGLE and constructing an equilateral triangle whose sides are one-third the length of those of the original on the center section of each side, indefinitely repeating the process for each side of the resultant polygon.

SNOW LEOPARD. See OUNCE.

SNOWMOBILE, or motor sled, motorized vehicle with two skis in front and propelled by an endless track, used for traveling over deep snow. First developed in the 1920s to replace dogsleds, they have become popular for recreation and racing since lightweight models were introduced (1959).

SNOWSHOE, light, broad footwear (about 1m × 0.4m) consisting of a wooden frame, laced with leather, strapped to the shod foot. Spreading the wearer's weight over a large area, they enable him to walk on deep, soft snow. Snowshoe racing is a popular sport, speeds of about 1km in 3min being attainable.

SNOWY MOUNTAINS, a range in the AUSTRALIAN ALPS, in E Victoria and SE New South Wales. The Snowy Mountain Scheme is a huge irrigation and hydroelectric project covering over 2 000sq mi.

SNUFF, powdered TOBACCO for inhaling through the nose. The practice of taking snuff crossed to Europe from America in the early 16th century.

SNYDER, seat of Scurry Co., Tex., 220mi W of Dallas, in an agricultural region with oil wells. Manufactures include chemicals. Pop 11 171.

SNYDERS, Frans (1579–1657), Flemish BAROQUE painter. A student of BRUEGEL the Younger and collaborator with RUBENS, Snyders painted scenes of hunting and of fighting beasts, and elaborate still lifes of fruit and game.

SOANE, Sir John (1753–1837), English architect. The severe linear style of his neoclassical Bank of England gave way to more picturesque eccentricity in Dulwich College gallery and his own London home in Lincoln's Inn Fields (now the Soane Museum).

SOAPS AND DETERGENTS, substances which, when dissolved in water, are cleansing agents. Soap has been known since 600 BC; it was used as a medicine until its use for washing was discovered in the 2nd century AD. Until about 1500 it was made by boiling animal fat with wood ashes (which contain the alkali potassium carbonate). Then caustic soda (see SODIUM), a more effective ALKALI, was used; vegetable FATS and oils were also introduced. **Saponification**, the chemical reaction in soap-making, is an alkaline HYDROLYSIS of the fat (an ESTER) to yield GLYCEROL and the sodium salt of a long-chain CARBOXYLIC ACID. The potassium salt is used for soft soap. In the modern process, the hydrolysis is effected by superheated water with a zinc catalyst, and the free acid produced is then neutralized. Synthetic detergents, introduced in WWI, generally consist of the sodium salts of various long-chain SULFONIC ACIDS, derived from oils and PETROLEUM products. The principle of soaps and detergents is the same: the hydrophobic long-chain hydrocarbon part of the molecule attaches itself to the grease and dirt particles, and the hydrophilic acid group makes the particles soluble in water, so that by agitation they are loosed from the fabric and dispersed. Detergents do not (unlike soaps) form scum in HARD WATER. Their persistence in rivers, however, causes pollution problems, and biodegradable detergents have been developed. Household detergents may contain several additives: bleaches, brighteners, and ENZYMES to digest protein stains (egg, blood, etc.).

SOAPBERRY, trees of the genus *Sapindus* which contain toxic SAPONINS. The fruits can be used as a substitute for soap. Family: Sapindaceae.

SOAPSTONE, or **steatite**, METAMORPHIC ROCK consisting of compacted TALC with SERPENTINE and carbonates, formed by alteration of PERIDOTITE. Soft and soapy to the touch, soapstone has been used from prehistoric times for carvings and vessels. When fired, it becomes hard and is used for insulators.

SOBIESKI, John. See JOHN III (king of Poland).

SOCAGE, an old English form of freeman's land tenure, the most common by which the king granted North American lands. Rent was paid in money or agricultural service. Tenure was inherited, on payment of a fixed sum.

SOCCER, most popular sport in the world, national sport of most European and Latin American countries and fast increasing in popularity in the US and among women. The pitch measures 115yd by 75yd, the netted goal is 8yd wide and 8ft high and the inflated leather ball 27–28in round. There are two 45min halves, one referee and two linesmen. The aim of each 11-man team is to score by kicking or heading the ball into the opponents' goal. To advance the ball, a player may *dribble* it (repeatedly kick it as he runs with it) or kick it to a teammate. The ball may not be touched with the hand or arm, except by the goalkeeper in the penalty area in front of his goal. Modern professional football began in the UK in 1885, in the US in 1967. (See also FOOTBALL.)

Soccer players (dots) lined up in two different formations. The players defending the goal at left are: goalkeeper (1); right fullback (2); left fullback (3); right halfback (4); center halfback (5); left halfback (6); outside right (7); inside right (8); center forward (9); inside left (10); outside left (11). The letters on the pitch refer to the corner (a), goal (b), goal line (c), goal area (d), penalty area (e), penalty spot (f), touch line (g), halfway line (h), kick-off circle (i).

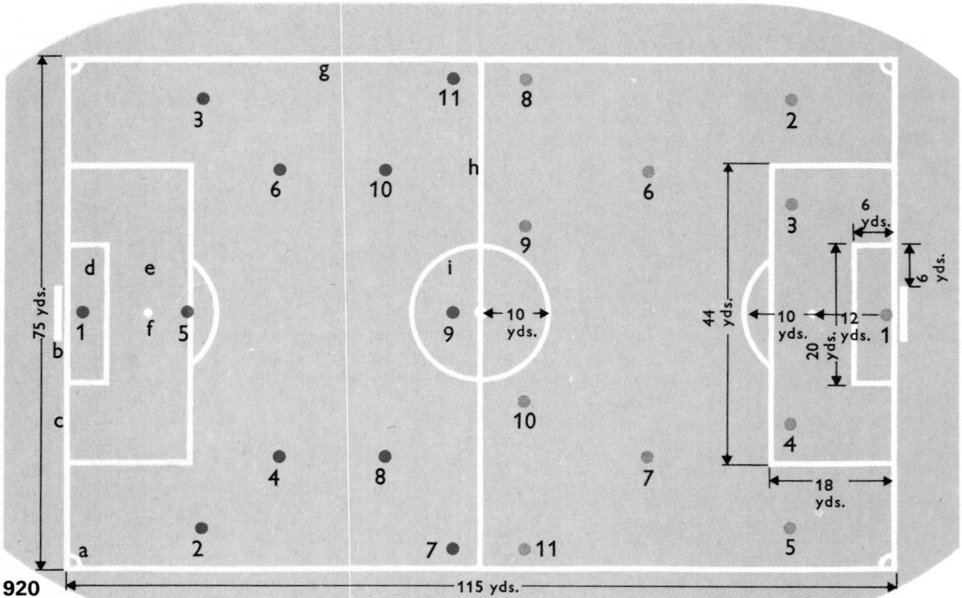

SOCHI, NE Black Sea port, in the Russian SFSR, USSR; a popular resort with long beaches and warm mineral springs. Pop 224 000.

SOCIAL CONTRACT, in political philosophy a concept of the formation of society, in which men agree to surrender part of their "natural" freedom to enjoy the security of the organized state. The idea, though of ancient origin, was first fully formulated in the 17th and 18th centuries by Thomas HOBBES (in *Leviathan*, 1651), LOCKE and ROUSSEAU, and was then controversial because it suggested that heads of state ruled only by their subjects' consent.

SOCIAL CREDIT PARTY, Canadian party formed (1935) by W. ABERHART. It aimed to implement C. Douglas' policy of avoiding economic depression by distributing surplus money as a "social dividend" to increase purchasing power. It failed in this but governed Alberta 1935–71 and British Columbia 1952–72.

SOCIAL DARWINISM, late 19th-century school of thought which held society to have evolved on DARWIN's biological model. Social inequalities were explained (and made to seem natural and inevitable) by the law of "SURVIVAL OF THE FITTEST." Its chief theorist was Herbert SPENCER.

SOCIAL DEMOCRATIC PARTIES, political parties found in many countries that seek socialism through constitutional reform, not revolution. They usually favor government intervention in the economy and nationalization of powerful industries. The Social Democratic Party of the US joined with the Socialist Labor Party in 1901 to form the SOCIALIST PARTY.

SOCIAL GOSPEL, a liberal Protestant social reform movement in the US c1870–1920. It promoted Christian ideas of love and justice in education and social and political service. Among its leaders were Horace BUSHNELL, Washington GLADDEN and Walter RAUSCHENBUSCH.

SOCIALISM, an economic philosophy and political movement which aims to achieve a just, classless society through public ownership and operation of the means of production and distribution of goods. Within this framework it has many forms, the principal two of which are, in common usage, social democratic ("reformist") and revolutionary.

Modern socialism arose in reaction to the hardships of the INDUSTRIAL REVOLUTION, its prevailing ideology of LAISSEZ-FAIRE liberalism and its economic system of CAPITALISM. The FRENCH REVOLUTION promoted hopes of a radically changed social order in the early 1800s. Early experimental cooperative communities in the US included BROOK FARM, NAUVOO and the ONEIDA COMMUNITY. In Europe, insurrectionary socialism in the tradition of the Frenchmen BABEUF and BLANQUI played an important role in the REVOLUTIONS OF 1848 and the PARIS COMMUNE (1871). The work of MARX and ENGELS helped build socialism into a potent force. Their COMMUNIST MANIFESTO (1848) is the best-known socialist document. MARXISM, and its principle of inevitable class conflict leading to the overthrow of capitalism, formed the theoretical basis of the RUSSIAN

REVOLUTION of 1917. The offshoots of ANARCHISM and SYNDICALISM developed in the years leading up to WWI; more important was the split between reformist social democrats like the FABIAN SOCIETY seeking gradual reform, and revolutionaries seeking working-class power through extra-legal means. (See LENIN; BOLSHEVISM).

Despite the efforts of such socialists as E. V. DEBS and Norman THOMAS, no strong socialist movement has emerged in the US. In W Europe, the SOCIAL DEMOCRATIC PARTIES have formed numerous governments. In "Third World" countries, socialism is often linked with independence movements.

SOCIALIST PARTY, US, formed in 1901 by E. V. DEBS and V. L. BERGER out of the Social Democratic Party and a split from the revolutionary Socialist Labor Party. It opposed US involvement in WWI. In 1919 many radicals left to join the COMMUNIST PARTY. In 1936 right-wing members separated to form the Social Democratic federation. In 1958 they rejoined and the party was readmitted to the Socialist International. It has continued to have some success in local and state elections.

SOCIALIST REALISM, USSR Communist Party artistic doctrine since the early 1930s, and the dominant philosophy and style in most communist countries. In order to serve the people and the revolution, artistic and literary works should be realistic (representational), yet portray, with "positive" heroes, the workers' progress towards socialism.

SOCIALIZATION, the indoctrination of an individual by a society resulting in his obeying the written and unwritten rules of conduct of that society. Socialization of an individual starts during childhood, the norms and basic tenets of parents and teachers generally being adopted, and continues throughout the individual's life.

SOCIALIZED MEDICINE, broad term comprising the various systems of free health care supported by the state from tax revenue. Specific groups of individuals may benefit as in the US VETERANS ADMINISTRATION or MEDICARE, or health care may be entirely state supported as in the UK National Health Service.

SOCIAL PSYCHOLOGY, term now used chiefly as a synonym for GROUP psychology.

SOCIAL SCIENCES, group of studies concerned with man in relation to his cultural, social and physical environment; one of the three main divisions of human knowledge, the other two being the natural sciences and the HUMANITIES. Although social scientists usually attempt to model their disciplines on the natural sciences, aspiring to achieve a similar level of consensus, their efforts in this direction continue to be frustrated by the crudeness of their conceptual tools in relation to the complexity of their subject matter and the limited scope afforded for controlled experiments. The social sciences are usually considered to include: ANTHROPOLOGY; ARCHAEOLOGY; CRIMINOLOGY; DEMOGRAPHY; ECONOMICS; EDUCATION; POLITICAL SCIENCE; PSYCHOLOGY; and SOCIOLOGY.

SOCIAL SECURITY, government programs for protecting people from hardship due to loss of income through old age, disability, unemployment, injury, sickness, etc. State social security systems developed in Europe after 1883, when Germany started a compulsory health insurance scheme. In 1911 Britain adopted an unemployment insurance program. In the US, in the GREAT DEPRESSION, the Social Security Act (1935) established a federal program of old-age insurance and a federal-state program of UNEMPLOYMENT INSURANCE. It also provided federal grants for public assistance, public health and child welfare services. The federal plan has become compulsory, except for railway and government workers, who have their own schemes, and special types of workers who are not regularly employed. The plan is financed by equal employer and employee contributions. Old-age and survivor benefits are paid to retired workers and their dependents or to survivors of workers who have died. The amount people receive is related to their average monthly earnings over a number of years. Disability benefits are paid to workers and dependents in the event of disability lasting over a year. Health Insurance for the Aged (see MEDICARE) was added in 1965. Those over 65 are automatically helped with payment for hospital and post-hospital care; a supplementary medical insurance scheme, at an extra voluntary premium, covers 80% of doctors' and some other bills. (See also WELFARE.) A claimant of unemployment insurance is usually eligible for about half his earnings. Public assistance, which in some states predates 1935, differs in being financed through federal grants (largely) and state revenues, rather than individual contributions. It goes to the care of the elderly, disabled, the blind and their dependents. WORKMEN'S COMPENSATION, dating from the early 1900s, and varying widely between states, aids those workers injured at work or with industrial disease. A few states run sickness insurance schemes. Government social insurance schemes are more comprehensive in most W European and communist countries. In the US private insurance companies play a more prominent role.

SOCIAL SETTLEMENTS, also known as settlement houses, centers of SOCIAL WORK in deprived areas of cities. The first, Toynbee Hall in London, was set up in 1884. In the US, in the late 1800s, many settlements were formed, often to help new immigrants. Their activities today include counselling, adult education, nurseries, sport and recreation.

SOCIAL WAR, 90–88 BC, conflict which arose when Rome's allies in central and S Italy demanded citizenship. It ended when Rome granted the demands so uniting under Rome all Italy S of the Po R. A war between the Athenians and Thebans (357–355 BC) is also called the Social War.

SOCIAL WORK, the activity of trained social workers which has as its aim the alleviation of social problems. Case work, group work and community organization are employed. Case work involves close cooperation with individuals or families who are under mental, physical or social handicaps. Group work developed from work in early SOCIAL SETTLEMENTS, and involves group education and recreational activities. Community organization involves the identification of community problems and the coordination of local welfare services, both public and private, in solving them. A social worker's training may include psychology, sociology, law, medicine and criminology. She or he might specialize in family serivce, child welfare, medical, psychiatric or correctional social work. (See also WELFARE.)

SOCIETY ISLANDS, a S Pacific group, in W FRENCH POLYNESIA. Named for Britain's Royal Society, the 14 islands have been French since 1843. Most of the population lives on the largest, TAHITI. Copra, sugar and tourism are important.

SOCIETY OF FRIENDS. See QUAKERS.

SOCIETY OF JESUS. See JESUITS.

SOCIETY OF THE CINCINNATI. See CINCINNATI, SOCIETY OF THE.

SOCINIANISM, a 16th-century humanistic religious doctrine developed in Poland by the Italians Laelius Socinus and his nephew Faustus. A forerunner of and profound influence on modern UNITARIANISM, it rejected the Trinity and the divinity of Jesus.

SOCIOLOGY, systematic study that seeks to describe and explain collective human behavior—as manifested in cultures, societies, communities and subgroups—by exploring the institutional relationships that hold between individuals and so sustain this behavior. Sociology shares its subject matter with ANTHROPOLOGY, which traditionally focuses on small, relatively isolated societies, and social PSYCHOLOGY, where the emphasis is on the study of subgroup behavior. The main emphasis in contemporary sociology is on the study of social structures and institutions and on the causes and effects of social change. This gives sociology a special relevance to issues in ECONOMICS and POLITICAL SCIENCE. Not yet a mature discipline, sociology still veers between the tradition of speculative enquiry out of which it arose and the attempt to model its investigations on those of the physical sciences. Mainly because of the complexity of its subject matter and the political implications of social change, questions as to its proper aims and methods remain far from settled. There can be little doubt, however, that pressing sociological problems do exist at all levels in all societies and that sociological concepts (e.g., "internalization"—the processes by which the values and norms of a particular society are learned by its members (see SOCIALIZATION)—and "institutionalization"—the processes by which norms are incorporated in a culture as binding rules of behavior) do often illuminate many of the issues involved. The two great pioneers of modern sociology were Émile DURKHEIM and Max WEBER. The anthropologists Bronislaw MALINOWSKI and Alfred RADCLIFFE-BROWN also exerted a profound influence on the development of the subject. Important US sociologists include the pioneers William SUMNER and George MEAD, and Talcott PARSONS, probably the most influential of postwar sociologists.

SOCIOMETRY, usually refers to techniques of measurement employed mainly by psychologists and sociologists in attempting to determine the relative strengths of interpersonal preferences and the relative status of individuals within groups. The term is sometimes applied to any attempt to quantify interpersonal relationships.

SOCRATES (c469–399 BC), Greek philosopher and mentor of PLATO. He wrote nothing, but much of his life and thought is vividly recorded in the DIALOGUES OF PLATO. The exact extent of Plato's indebtedness to Socrates is uncertain—e.g., it is still disputed whether the doctrine of the Forms (see REALISM; UNIVERSALS) is Socratic or Platonic; but Socrates made at least two fundamental contributions to Western philosophy: by shifting the focus of Greek philosophy from COSMOLOGY to ETHICS; and by developing the "Socratic method" of enquiry. He argued that the good life is the life illuminated by reason and strove to clarify the ideas of his interlocutors by leading them to detect the inconsistencies in their beliefs. His passion for self-consistency was evident even in his death: ultimately condemned for "impiety," he decided to accept the lawful sentence—and so remain true to his principles—rather than make good an easy escape.

SODA, or sodium carbonate. See SODIUM.

SODA WATER. See SOFT DRINKS.

SODDY, Frederick (1877–1956), British chemist awarded the 1921 Nobel Prize for Chemistry for his work with RUTHERFORD on radioactive decay and particularly for his formulation (1913) of the theory of ISOTOPES. He also worked with Sir William RAMSAY to discover HELIUM.

SÖDERBLOM, Nathan (1866–1931), Swedish Lutheran archbishop and student of comparative religion. For his work for church unity and world peace he received the 1930 Nobel Peace Prize.

SOD HOUSE, ancient N European type of house made from strips of turf. These were used like bricks, the roof being reinforced with wood. Sod houses were also built by early settlers on the Great Plains of the US and in W Canada.

SODIUM (Na), a soft, reactive, silvery-white ALKALI METAL. It is the sixth most common element, occurring naturally in common salt and many other important minerals such as cryolite and Chile saltpeter. It is very electropositive, and is produced by ELECTROLYSIS of fused sodium chloride (Downs process). Sodium rapidly oxidizes in air and reacts vigorously with water to give off hydrogen, so it is usually stored under kerosine. Most sodium compounds are highly ionic and soluble in water, their properties being mainly those of the anion. Sodium forms some organic compounds such as alkyls. It is used in making sodium cyanide, sodium hydride and the ANTIKNOCK ADDITIVE tetraethyl lead. Its high heat capacity and conductivity make molten sodium a useful coolant in some nuclear reactors. AW 23.0, mp 98°C, bp 883°C, sg 0.971 (20°C). **Sodium Bicarbonate** ($NaHCO_3$) is a white crystalline solid, made from sodium carbonate and carbon dioxide. It gives off carbon dioxide when heated to 270°C or when reacted with acids, and is used in BAKING POWDER, fire extinguishers and as an ANTACID. **Sodium Borates** are sodium salts of BORIC ACID, differing in their degree of condensation and hydration; BORAX is the most important. They are white crystalline solids, becoming glassy when heated,

The world's largest solar furnace, built at Odeillo in the Pyrenees in 1969. It consists of 63 mirrors on mountings which may be rotated to reflect solar radiation on to an enormous parabolic reflector made up of 9 000 smaller mirrors. This concentrates the solar radiation on a focal point at which temperatures of over 3 800 °C can be produced.

and used in the manufacture of detergents, water-softeners, fluxes, glass and ceramic glazes. **Sodium Carbonate** (Na_2CO_3), or (Washing) **Soda**, is a white crystalline solid, made by the SOLVAY PROCESS. It is used in making glass, other sodium compounds, soap and paper. The alkaline solution is used in disinfectants and water softeners. mp 851°C. **Sodium Hydroxide** (NaOH), or **Caustic Soda**, is a white deliquescent solid, usually obtained as pellets. It is a strong ALKALI, and absorbs carbon dioxide from the air. It is made by ELECTROLYSIS of sodium chloride solution or by adding calcium hydroxide to sodium carbonate solution. Caustic soda is used in the production of cellulose, plastics, soap, dyestuffs, paper and in oil refining. mp 318°C, bp 1390°C. **Sodium Nitrate** ($NaNO_3$), or **Soda Niter**, is a colorless crystalline solid, occurring naturally in CHILE SALTPETER. Its properties are similar to those of potassium nitrate (see POTASSIUM), but as it is hygroscopic it is unsuitable for gunpowder. mp 307°C. **Sodium Thiosulfate** ($Na_2S_2O_3$), or **Hypo**, is a colorless crystalline solid. It is a mild reducing agent, used to estimate iodine, and as a photographic fixer, dissolving the silver halides which have remained unaffected by light. (For sodium chloride, see SALT.)

SODIUM PENTOTHAL. See PENTOTHAL SODIUM.

SODOM AND GOMORRAH, in the Old Testament, two of the cities in the plain of Jordan which were destroyed by God (Genesis 19) for their wickedness. Only LOT and his family were spared. The cities were in the region of the Dead Sea.

SOFIA, capital and largest city of Bulgaria, its commercial and cultural center, between the Balkan Mts of the N and the Vitosha Mts in the S. Its industry, built up since WWII, includes machinery, textiles and electrical equipment. Pop 950 676.

SOFTBALL, type of BASEBALL played with a softer, larger ball (12in in circumference) and a thinner bat. The bases are 60ft apart and the pitcher stands 46ft from the home plate. The ball is pitched underhand and a game lasts only seven innings. Softball was developed in Chicago in 1888 by G. W. Hancock as an indoor form of baseball. Many countries, paricularly in the Americas, now compete in the annual amateur world championships.

SOFT-COATED WHEATEN TERRIER, old Irish breed of dog, short-bodied with small drop ears, standing 18in high and weighing 35lb. Its wheaten-colored coat is soft and wavy.

SOFT DRINKS, nonalcoholic beverages generally containing fruit acids, SWEETENING AGENTS, and natural or artificial flavorings and colorings. In the early 19th century, carbonated water ("soda water") was developed in imitation of effervescent spa water or mineral water; this was the antecedent of carbonated soft drinks, made by absorption of CARBON dioxide under pressure. The dissolved gas gives a pleasant, slightly acid taste, and acts as a preservative. Still drinks, without carbon dioxide, are frozen or subjected to PASTEURIZATION.

SOFTWARE, term used in the COMPUTER industry to refer to all the non-HARDWARE elements of a computer system, principally the programs.

SOFTWOOD, LUMBER produced from CONIFERS, accounting for about 80% of world production. The class includes woods that are physically both soft and hard. (See also FORESTRY; HARDWOOD; WOOD.)

SOIL, the uppermost surface layer of the earth, in which plants grow and on which, directly or indirectly, all life on earth depends. Soil consists, in the upper layers, of organic material mixed with inorganic matter resultant from weathering (see EROSION; HUMUS). Soil depth, where soil exists, may reach to many metres. Between the soil and the bedrock is a layer called the subsoil. Mature soil may be described in terms of four **soil horizons**: A, the uppermost layer, containing organic matter, though most of the soluble chemicals have been leached (washed out); B, strongly leached and with little or no organic matter (A and B together are often called the topsoil); C, the subsoil, a layer of weathered and shattered rock; and D, the bedrock. Three main types of soil are commonly distinguished: **pedalfers**, associated with temperate, humid climates, have a leached A-horizon but contain IRON and ALUMINUM salts with clay in the B-horizon; **pedocals**, associated with low-rainfall regions, contain soluble substances such as CALCIUM carbonate (soluble in rainwater, which contains CARBON dioxide) and other salts, and **laterites**, tropical red or yellow soils, heavily leached and rich in iron and aluminum. Soils may also be classified in terms of texture (see CLAY; SILT; SAND). LOAMS, with roughly equal proportions of sand, silt and clay, together with humus, are among the richest agricultural soils. (See also PERMAFROST; PODZOL.)

SOIL EROSION, the wearing away of soil, a primary cause of concern in agriculture. There are two types: **Geological erosion** denotes those naturally occurring EROSION processes that constantly affect the earth's surface features; it is usually a fairly slow process and naturally compensated for. **Accelerated erosion** describes erosion hastened by the intervention of man. **Sheet erosion** occurs usually on plowed fields. A fine sheet of rich topsoil (see SOIL) is removed by the action of RAIN water. Repetition over the years may render the soil unfit for cultivation. In **rill erosion**, heavy rains may run off the land in streamlets: sufficient water moving swiftly enough cuts shallow trenches that may be plowed over and forgotten until, after years, the soil is found poor. In **gully erosion**, deep trenches are cut by repeated or heavy flow of water. WIND erosion is of importance in exposed, arid areas. (See also CONSERVATION; LAND RECLAMATION.)

SOKA GAKKAI, or Value Creation Society, a Japanese lay Buddhist group which seeks to apply the 13th-century teachings of Nichiren to the modern world. Founded in 1930, it grew fast after WWII. By 1975 its political wing, the Komeito (Clean Government) party, was fourth largest in Japan.

SOKOL, a gymnastic organization noted for its mass displays, particularly in E Europe. It was founded 1862 in Prague to promote physical education and communal spirit. A US Sokol was founded in 1865.

SOKOTO, provincial capital in NW Nigeria, 230mi W of Kano. It was once seat of the FULANI empire. It has mixed light industries. Pop 108 565.

SOL, a COLLOID, usually in liquid form, in which the dispersed phase is initially a solid, the continuous phase initially a liquid. (See also GEL.)

SOLAR CELL, device for converting the ENERGY of the sun's radiation into electrical energy. The commonest form is a large array of SEMICONDUCTOR *p-n* junction devices in series and parallel. By the PHOTOELECTRIC EFFECT each junction produces a small voltage when illuminated. Solar cells are chiefly used to power artificial SATELLITES. Their low efficiency (about 12%) makes them uncompetitive on earth except for mobile or isolated devices.

SOLAR ENERGY, the ENERGY given off by the SUN as ELECTROMAGNETIC RADIATION. In one year the sun emits about 5.4×10^{33}J of energy, of which half of one-billionth (2.7×10^{24}J) reaches the earth. Of this, most is reflected away, only 35% being absorbed. The power reaching the ground is at most 1.2kW/m², and on average 0.8kW/m². Solar energy is naturally converted into WIND power and into the energy of the HYDROLOGIC CYCLE, increasingly exploited as HYDROELECTRIC POWER. Plants convert solar energy to chemical energy by PHOTOSYNTHESIS, normally at only 0.1% efficiency; the cultivation of ALGAE in ponds can be up to 0.6% efficient, and is being developed to provide food and fuel. Solar heat energy may be used directly in several ways. Solar evaporation is used to convert brine to SALT and distilled water. Flat-plate collectors—matt black absorbing plates with attached tubes through which a fluid flows to collect the heat—are beginning to be used for domestic water heating, space heating, and to run air-conditioning systems. Focusing collectors, using a parabolic mirror, are used in solar furnaces, which can give high power absorption at high temperatures. They are used for cooking, for high-temperature research, to power heat engines for generating electricity, and to produce electricity more directly by the SEEBECK effect. Solar energy may be directly converted to electrical energy by SOLAR CELLS.

SOLAR PLEXUS, the GANGLION of nerve cells and fibers situated at the back of the ABDOMEN which subserve autonomic NERVOUS SYSTEM function for much of the GASTROINTESTINAL TRACT. A sharp blow on the abdomen over the plexus causes visceral pain and "winding."

SOLAR SYSTEM, the sun and all the celestial objects that move in ORBITS around it, including the nine known planets (MERCURY; VENUS; EARTH; MARS; JUPITER; SATURN; URANUS; NEPTUNE; PLUTO), their 32 known moons, the ASTEROIDS, COMETS, meteoroids (see METEOR) and a large quantity of gas and dust. The planets all move in their orbits in the same direction, and, with the exceptions of Venus and Uranus, also rotate on their axes in this direction: this is known as direct motion. Most of the moons of the planets have direct orbits, with the exception of four of Jupiter's minor moons, the outermost moon of Saturn and the inner moon of Neptune, whose orbits are retrograde (see RETROGRADE MOTION). Most of the planets move in elliptical, near circular orbits, and roughly in the same plane. The origins of the solar system are not known, though various theories have been proposed (see NEBULAR HYPOTHESIS; PLANETESIMAL HYPOTHESIS). It would not appear to be unique among the stars (see PLANET).

SOLAR WIND, the electrically charged material thrown out by the sun at an average speed of 400km/s. The "quiet" component is a continuous stream to which is added an "active" component produced by bursts of activity on the sun's surface. The solar wind affects the magnetic fields of the earth and Jupiter, and causes the tails of COMETS.

SOLDERING, joining metal objects using a low-melting-point ALLOY, **solder**, as the ADHESIVE. Soft solder, commonly used in electronics to join wires and other components, is an alloy of mainly lead and tin. The parts to be joined are cleaned, and heated by applying a hot soldering iron (usually having a copper bit). A FLUX is used to dissolve oxides, protect the surfaces, and enable the solder to flow freely. The solder melts when applied, solidifying again to form a strong joint when the iron is withdrawn. Solder is often supplied as wire with a core of noncorrosive rosin flux. Soldering at higher temperatures is termed BRAZING.

SOLENODON, a genus of burrow-dwelling shrew-like insectivores about the size of a small cat. Two species, restricted to Haiti and Cuba, remain of what was once a large family. With many shrew-like features, particularly the long mobile nose, they are adapted to nocturnal foraging in soft soil and leaves.

SOLENOID, device, used in CIRCUIT BREAKERS, for producing a short lateral movement of a sliding iron core. This is attracted by the MAGNETIC FIELD produced when an electric current flows in one of the coils surrounding either end of the slider. *Also*, an elongated coil used to produce a region of uniform magnetic field.

SOLER, Antonio (1729–1783), Spanish composer noted for his instrumental church music. Organist at the ESCORIAL monastery from 1752, he was taught by Domenico SCARLATTI.

SOLES, a family, Soleidae, of rather elongate flatfishes of economic importance found in the N Hemisphere. Both eyes are on the left, upper surface; the mouth is small, and the snout projects well beyond the mouth.

SOLESMES, village in Sarthe department, central NW France, in which is situated the famous Benedictine abbey (founded 1010). Gregorian chant was revived here in the 19th century (see PLAINSONG).

SOLFERINO, Battle of, 1859, a costly victory for French and Sardinian over Austrian forces near Solferino, Lombardy. The subsequent agreement between NAPOLEON III and FRANCIS JOSEPH ceded Lombardy to Sardinia. DUNANT's presence on the battlefield led to the founding of the Red Cross.

SOLICITOR GENERAL, in the US, the Justice Department official responsible for the federal government case in litigation before the Supreme Court or other courts, as the ATTORNEY GENERAL directs.

SOLID, one of the three physical states of matter, characterized by the property of cohesion: solids retain their shape unless deformed by external forces. True solids have a definite melting point and are crystalline, their molecules being held together in a regular pattern by stronger intermolecular forces than exist in liquids or gases. Amorphous solids are not crystalline, melt over a wide temperature range and are effectively supercooled liquids. GLASS is a familiar amorphous solid.

SOLID ANGLE. See ANGLE.

SOLID STATE PHYSICS, branch of physics concerned with the nature and properties of solid materials, many of which arise from the association and regular arrangement of atoms or molecules in crystalline solids. The term is applied particularly to studies of SEMICONDUCTORS and solid-state electronic devices.

SOLINGEN, city in North Rhine-Westphalia, West Germany, 15mi ESE of Düsseldorf. It is noted for its cutlery and other metal products. Pop 176 420.

SOLIPSISM, extreme form of subjective IDEALISM based on an argument to the effect that since I can apprehend nothing that is not part of *my* experience, there can be no legitimate grounds for affirming the existence of an external world that is independent of my experience of it.

SOLOMON, second son of DAVID and BATHSHEBA who ruled ancient Israel about 970–933 BC at the height of its prosperity and gained a reputation for great wisdom. His success in establishing lucrative foreign trade and his introduction at home of taxation and forced labor enabled him to finance a massive building program which included a temple and royal palaces on an unprecedented scale of opulence. His story is told in 1 Kings 1–11 and 2 Chronicles 1–9 of the OLD TESTAMENT. Biblical writings later attributed to him include PROVERBS, ECCLESIASTES and the SONG OF SOLOMON.

SOLOMON ISLANDS, a chain of volcanic islands E of New Guinea, SW Pacific. The N Bougainville, Buka and Green islands are part of PAPUA-NEW GUINEA. The more numerous S islands form the British Solomon Islands Protectorate; its capital Honiara is on GUADALCANAL. Most of the protectorate's 173 000 inhabitants are Melanesians. Its economy depends largely on copra production.

SOLOMON'S SEAL, a number of lilies of the genus *Polygonatum*, native to N temperate regions; also, some species of *Smilacina* native to North America. Bell-shaped flowers are produced on slender drooping stems. The previous year's shoots leave seal-like scars on the underground rootstock. Family: Liliaceae.

SOLON (c639–559 BC), Athenian lawgiver and poet, one of the SEVEN SAGES. Elected *archon* (government leader) of Athens in 594 BC, he repealed the repressive laws of DRACO and freed those enslaved for debt. Dividing citizens into four income classes, he reformed the Greek oligarchy by allowing members of all four classes to sit in the assembly and the law courts. Later he resisted the tyrant PISISTRATUS.

SOLON, city in NE Ohio, a suburb 12mi SE of Cleveland, largely residential, with some light industry. Pop 11 519.

SOLSTICES, the two times each year when the sun is on the points of the ECLIPTIC farthest from the equator (see CELESTIAL SPHERE). At the summer solstice in late June the sun is directly overhead at noon on the TROPIC of Cancer; at winter solstice, in late December, it is overhead at noon on the Tropic of Capricorn.

SOLTI, Sir Georg (1912–   ), Hungarian-born British conductor. He is best known for his great recordings of Wagner and Richard Strauss, and as musical director of Covent Garden (1961–71) and, in the 1970s, of the Paris Opera and Chicago Symphony.

SOLUTION, a homogeneous molecular mixture of two or more substances, commonly of a solid and a liquid, though solid/solid solutions also exist. The liquid component is usually termed the SOLVENT, the other component, which is dissolved in it, the *solute*. The **solubility** of a solute in a given solvent at a particular temperature is usually stated as the mass which will dissolve in 100g of the solvent to give a saturated solution (see SATURATION). Solubility generally increases with temperature. For slightly soluble ionic compounds, the **solubility product**—the product of the individual ionic solubilities—is a constant at a given temperature. Most substances are solvated when dissolved: that is, their molecules become surrounded by solvent molecules acting as LIGANDS. Ionic crystals dissolve to give individual solvated ions, and some good solvents of high dielectric constant (such as water) cause certain covalent compounds to ionize, wholly or partly (see also ACID). Analogous to an ideal gas, the hypothetical **ideal solution** is one which is formed from its components without change in total volume or internal energy: it obeys RAOULT's law and its corollaries, so that the addition of solute produces a lowering of the freezing point, elevation of the boiling point and increase in osmotic pressure (see OSMOSIS), all proportional to the number of MOLES added. (See also DISSOCIATION; ELECTROLYSIS; EQUIVALENT WEIGHT.)

SOLVAY PROCESS, for the manufacture of sodium carbonate (see SODIUM). Salt, ammonia, carbon dioxide and water react to give precipitated sodium bicarbonate, which on heating gives sodium carbonate and carbon dioxide for RECYCLING.

SOLVENT, a liquid capable of dissolving a substance to form a SOLUTION. Generally "like dissolves like"; thus a nonpolar covalent solid such as naphthalene dissolves well in a hydrocarbon solvent. Overall, best solvents are those with polar molecules and high DIELECTRIC constant: WATER is the most effective known.

SOLZHENITSYN, Alexander Isayevich (1918–   ), Russian novelist. His own experience of Stalin's labor camps was described in *One Day in the Life of Ivan Denisovich* (1962), acclaimed in the USSR and abroad. But *The First Circle* and *Cancer Ward* (both 1968) were officially condemned. He accepted the 1970 Nobel Prize for Literature by letter. His expulsion in 1974 and his warnings on the moral and political fate of the West drew worldwide publicity. Solzhenitsyn's works include *August 1914* (1971) and *Gulag Archipelago* (1974 and 1976).

SOMALI CAT, breed developed from the Abyssinian cat but with long hair. Recognized in both Red and Ruddy varieties.

SOMALILAND, French. See FRENCH TERRITORY OF AFARS AND ISSAS.

SOMALI REPUBLIC, or Somalia, occupying the E "horn" of Africa, comprises two former colonies, British Somaliland and Italian Somaliland, which gained independence and united on July 1, 1960.

Land. A narrow, barren N coastal plain, hemmed in by high mountains, gives way to high plateaus, dry savanna plains and to the country's most fertile area, between the Shibeli and Juba rivers in the S. The climate is hot; yearly rainfall varies from about 3in in the N to 20in in the S. Wildlife includes big game and many species of antelope.

People and economy. The population consists mainly of Somalis belonging to northern nomadic or southern farming clans. Somali, the national language, lacks a written form. Arabic (widely spoken), Italian and English are the written languages. The literacy rate is about 15%. Most Somalis move from place to place with their herds and portable wood-frame huts; others live in small villages or trade centers built around a well. Camel milk, grains and mutton are the chief foods. The economy is mainly pastoral. Livestock, bananas, hides and skins are exported. Industry includes meat and fish processing and packing plants and a textile factory. Mineral deposits, which include iron ore and gypsum, have yet to be exploited.

History. Europeans colonized Somalia in the late 1800s. Independent Somalia continued its heavy dependence on US and Italian aid. In 1969 President Shermarke was assassinated and a revolutionary council headed by Maj. Gen. Mohammed Siyad took control. The Somali Democratic Republic was declared a socialist state and relations shifted towards communist-bloc countries.

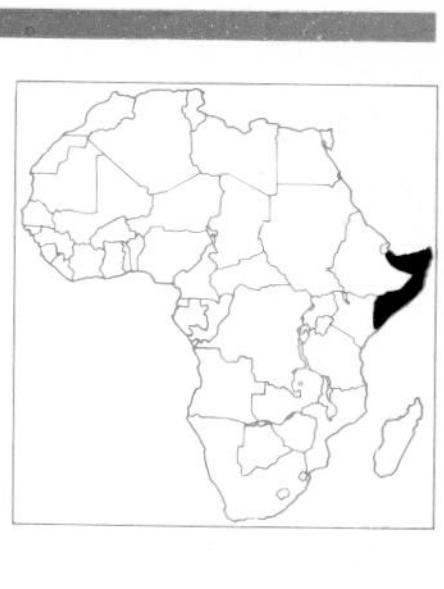

Official name: Somali Democratic Republic
Capital: Mogadishu
Area: 270 000sq mi
Population: 2 930 000
Languages: Somali; Arabic, English, Italian spoken
Religions: Muslim
Monetary unit(s): 1 Somali shilling = 100 centesimi

SOMATOTYPES, in ANTHROPOMETRY, descriptions of physique, sometimes supposedly also descriptive of temperament. The individual is classified by three digits representing the extent of his endomorphy (plumpness), mesomorphy (muscularity) and ectomorphy (slenderness), respectively.

SOMERSET, city in S Ky., NW of Lake Cumberland. Seat of Pulaski Co., a farming district, it has diversified light industries. Pop 10 436.

SOMERSET, town in SE Mass., on the Taunton R. Once famous for its clipper ships, it now manufactures varnish and paper products. Pop 18 088.

SOMERSET, Edward Seymour, 1st Duke of (c1500–1552), protector of England 1547–49 on the death of HENRY VIII and accession of EDWARD VI. He used his great power to repeal heresy and treason laws. Falsely accused of treason by his rivals, he was finally executed.

SOMERVILLE, city in E Mass. Settled in 1630 and prominent in the War of Independence, it is a residential and industrial N Boston suburb. Pop 88 779.

SOMERVILLE, borough in N central N.J., seat of Somerset Co. Washington lived here 1778–79. Its chief manufactures are electrical. Pop 13 652.

SOMME RIVER, in N France, rises near Saint-Quentin and flows W and NW some 150mi through

Amiens to its English Channel estuary at Saint-Valéry. Scene of the greatest WWI battle of attrition (July–Nov. 1916), it saw over a million casualties of all nations. On July 1 alone there were 57000 British casualties (19000 killed).

SOMNAMBULISM, or **sleepwalking**, state in which the body is able to walk and perform other automatic tasks while consciousness is diminished. Often seen in anxious children, it is said to be unwise to awaken them as intense fear may be felt.

SOMOZA, the name of a Nicaraguan family, three members of which have controlled Nicaragua since the 1930s. In 1936 **Anastasio Somoza Garcia** (1896–1956) deposed his uncle, President Sacasa, becoming president himself in 1937. Assassinated after 20 years of nepotistic dictatorship, he was succeeded by his son **Luis Somoza Debayle** (1922–1967), who held formal office until 1963. In 1967 Anastasio's second son **Anastasio Somoza Debayle** (1925–) was elected president. Replaced by a puppet triumvirate in 1972, he retained control of the army and was reelected president in 1974. (See NICARAGUA.)

SONAR, *s*ound *n*avigation *a*nd *r*anging, technique used at sea for detecting and determining the position of underwater objects (e.g. submarines; shoals of fish) and for finding the depth of water under a ship's keel (see ECHO SOUNDER). Sonar works on the principle of echolocation: high-frequency SOUND pulses are beamed from the ship and the direction of and time taken for any returning ECHOES are measured to give the direction and range of the reflecting objects.

Sonar can be used to locate and identify shoals of fish as well as to measure depth of water.

SONATA, in music, term used in the 17th and early 18th centuries to describe works for various small groups of instruments, as opposed to the CANTATA. Since the late 18th century, it has been restricted to works for piano or other solo instrument (the latter usually with keyboard accompaniment), generally in three movements. (See also SONATA FORM.)

SONATA FORM, term used to describe the structure of a piece of music in which the opening theme (*exposition*) is followed by an elaboration of its musical possibilities (*development*) and a conclusion restating the original theme (*recapitulation*). It is characteristic of the first movement of the SONATA, SYMPHONY and string quartet.

SONERILA, a genus of tropical flowering perennial plants, of which *Sonerila margaritacea* is grown as an ornamental house plant, particularly in terrariums and bottle gardens, for its ovate-lanceolate leaves; these are dark green marked with silvery-white spots. Sonerila requires only a few hours sunlight each day and grows well at average house temperatures, but fails to thrive at temperatures below 16°C (60°F). The soil should be well soaked whenever the soil surface dries out. Propagation is by shoot tip cuttings. Family: Melastomataceae.

SON ET LUMIÈRE (French: sound and light), an after-dark entertainment in which variations in the illumination of the façade of a building are synchronized with a narrative or dramatic sound-track. It was invented in 1952 in France.

SONG, a musical setting of words, usually a short poem, often with instrumental accompaniment. There are two basic kinds: songs in which each verse repeats the same tune, and songs with a continuous thematic development. The origins of the song are lost in the history of FOLK MUSIC and POETRY (poetry was originally sung); it became a mature art in Western cultures in OPERA arias, the German *lied*—those of SCHUBERT are supreme examples—and the French *chanson*. The song-forms that have most influenced 20th-century popular music are probably the BALLAD and the BLUES. (See also HYMN.)

SONGHAI, or Songhay, former West African empire, founded in the 8th century by a Berber farming and trading people around the middle Niger R. Converted to Islam in the 11th century, and adopting Gao as its capital, it expanded mainly at the expense of the MALI EMPIRE, and commanded trans-Saharan trade, reaching its greatest extent under Askia I, who ruled 1493–1528. Its breakup in the later 1500s was hastened by a Moroccan invasion (1591).

SONG OF ROLAND. See CHANSON DE ROLAND.

SONG OF SOLOMON, or **Song of Songs,** or **Canticles,** OLD TESTAMENT book traditionally ascribed to Solomon. A series of exquisite love poems, it has been interpreted by both Jews and Christians as an allegorical description of God's love for his people.

SONIC BOOM, loud noise generated in the form of a shockwave cone when an airplane traveling faster than the speed of sound overtakes the pressure waves it produces. Because of sonic boom damage, supersonic planes are confined to closely defined flight paths.

SONNET, a LYRIC poem of fourteen lines with traditional rules of structure and rhyme scheme. Devised in 13th-century Italy and perfected by PETRARCH, it entered English literature in the 16th century, and was adopted by such poets as SHAKESPEARE, MILTON, KEATS and WORDSWORTH as a vehicle for concentrated thought and feeling, very often of love.

SONOMA, city in Cal., 35mi N of San Francisco. In 1846 the shortlived BEAR FLAG REPUBLIC was proclaimed here by a band of Americans in revolt against Mexican rule. Pop 4112.

SONORA, state of NW Mexico, on the Gulf of California. It lies mainly in a region of mountain and desert, but river-fed irrigation schemes support local agriculture, principally cotton and wheat. Cattle raising, fishing and gold, silver and copper mining are also important. The capital is Hermosillo.

SONS OF LIBERTY, members of a patriotic society formed in the American colonies in 1765 to oppose the passage of the STAMP ACT. Their campaign of public protest eventually expanded into a general movement for American independence.

SOO CANALS. See SAULT SAINTE MARIE CANALS.

SOONERS, name given to the many Okla. homesteaders who entered the INDIAN TERRITORY in advance of the date of the first official "run"—April 22, 1889. Okla. is familiarly known to this day as the Sooner State.

SOONG, influential Chinese family of **Charles Jones Soong** (1866–1918), an American-educated Methodist minister and businessman in Shanghai. **Soong Ch'ing-ling** (1890–), married SUN YAT-SEN, and continued to play a leading role in the Chinese revolution after his death, becoming deputy head of state 1959. **Soong Tzu-wen** (T.V. Soong; 1894–1971), a wealthy financier and politician, held important posts in the Nationalist government (1925–47), but retired to the US in 1949. **Soong Mei-ling** (1897–), married CHIANG KAI-SHEK and, as Madame Chiang, became a well-known publicist for the Nationalist government.

SOOT, form of carbon black (see CARBON) formed by incomplete combustion of organic material.

SOPHISTS, "wise men," name given to certain teachers in Greece in the 5th and 4th centuries BC, the most famous of whom were GORGIAS and PROTAGORAS. They taught RHETORIC and the qualities needed for success in political life. PLATO attacked them for taking fees, teaching skepticism about law, morality and knowledge, and concentrating on how to win arguments regardless of truth—attacks still reflected in the modern word "sophistry."

SOPHOCLES (c495–406 BC), great Athenian dramatist, together with AESCHYLUS and EURIPIDES one of the founders of Greek tragedy. Only seven plays survive, the best-known being *Oedipus Rex, Oedipus Coloneus, Antigone* and *Electra*. They dwell on the tragic ironies of human existence, particularly on the role of fate. Heroic figures, tricked by fate into acts necessitating moral retribution, suffer in the event more harshly than they seem to deserve. The plays are highly dramatic (Sophocles regularly won first prize in the dramatic competitions), and contain much noble poetry.

SORBONNE, a college founded in Paris in 1253 by Robert de Sorbon. It was a famous medieval theological center, rebuilt in the 17th century by RICHELIEU and reestablished in 1808 after being closed in the French Revolution. Its name is often used to refer to the University of Paris, into which it was incorporated in the 19th century.

SORBS. See WENDS.

SOREL, city in S Quebec, Canada, on the St. Lawrence R. It is a grain-shipping center, with shipyards and iron, steel and textile industries. Pop 19347.

SOREL, Georges (1847–1922), French social theorist, philosopher of revolutionary SYNDICALISM and author of *Reflections on Violence* (1908). Despising democracy and the bourgeoisie, he believed in the moral regeneration of society through violence. He influenced both FASCISM and the far left.

SORGHUM, widely cultivated CEREAL CROP (*Sorghum vulgare*), the most important grown in Africa. It grows best in warm conditions and is most important as a drought-resistant crop. For human food, the grain is first ground into a meal and then made up into porridge, bread or cakes. The grain is also used as a cattle feed and the whole plants as forage. There are many types in cultivation including *durra* and KAFIR. Family: Graminae.

SOROKIN, Pitirim Alexandrovich (1889–1968), Russian-US sociologist. He distinguished between "sensate" (empirical, scientific) and "idiational" (mystical, authoritarian) societies, and wrote *Social and Cultural Dynamics* (1937–41).

SORREL, several herbs of the genus *Rumex* with acid-tasting leaves. The leaves of the garden sorrel (*Rumex acetosa*) can be used as a vegetable. Family: Polygonaceae. (See also DOCK; WOOD SORREL.)

SORREL TREE, or **sourwood**, *Oxydendrum arboreum*, deciduous tree native to the southern US. Its leaves have a sour taste and turn bright scarlet in the fall.

SORRENTO, historic town and tourist resort in S Italy, on the Sorrento Peninsula separating the Gulf of Salerno from the Bay of Naples. Pop 15133.

SOTER, Saint, an early pope (c166–c175 AD). He is known to have helped the Church of Corinth and to have fought against the Montanist heresy.

SOULÉ, Pierre (1801–1870), US politician and diplomat. He emigrated in 1825 from France to New Orleans, where he became a prominent Democrat. A US senator (1847; 1849–53) and minister to Spain (1853–54), he resigned after signing the OSTEND MANIFESTO.

SOUND, mechanical disturbance, such as a change of pressure, particle displacement or stress, propagated in an elastic medium (e.g. air or water), that can be detected by an instrument or by an observer who hears the auditory sensation it produces. Sound is a measurable physical phenomenon and an important stimulus to man. It forms a major means of communication in the form of spoken language, and both natural and manmade sounds (of traffic or machinery) contribute largely to our environment. The EAR is very sensitive and will tolerate a large range of sound energies, but enigmas remain as to exactly how it produces the sensation of hearing. The Greeks appreciated that sound was connected with air motion and that the PITCH of a musical sound produced by a vibrating source depended on the vibration FREQUENCY. Attempts to measure the velocity of sound in air date from the 17th century. Sound is carried as a longitudinal compressional wave in an elastic medium: part of the medium next to a sound source is compressed, but its elasticity makes it expand again, compressing the region next to it and so on. The velocity of such waves depends on the medium and the temperature, but is always much less than that of light. Sound waves are characterized by their wavelength and frequency. Humans cannot hear sounds of frequencies below 16Hz and above 20kHz, such sounds being known as infrasonic and ULTRASONIC respectively. The sound produced by a

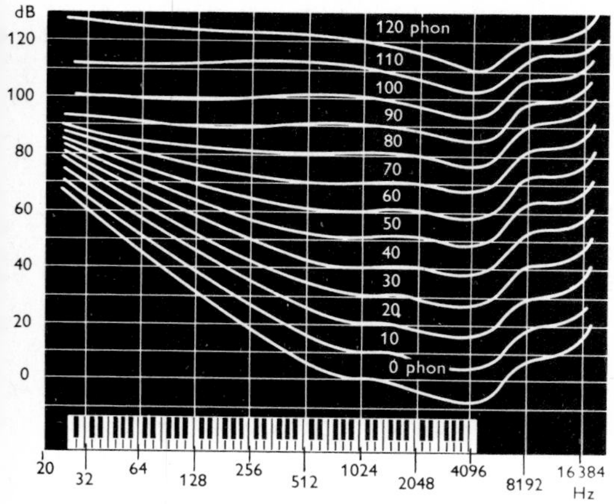

Diagram illustrating the relationship between the intensity of sound in decibels (dB—relative to the normal threshold level of human hearing), the frequency of sound in hertz (Hz), and its subjective loudness in phons. Each point on the diagram represents a note of a given frequency and intensity. The curves consist of points having the same loudness; thus the variation of intensity with pitch for sounds of each given loudness is clearly visible. At 1 000Hz the decibel and the phon are taken as equal and assigned the same numerical value. Above the frequency scale is shown a standard piano keyboard, illustrating the proportionality of frequency to pitch.

TUNING FORK has a definite frequency, but most sounds are a combination of frequencies. The amount of motion in a sound wave determines its loudness or softness and the intensity falls off with the square of distance from the source. Sound waves may be reflected from surfaces (as in an ECHO), refracted or diffracted, the last property enabling us to hear around corners. The intensity of a sound is commonly expressed in DECIBELS above an arbitrary reference level; its loudness is measured in PHONS.

SOUND BARRIER, term referring to the extra forces acting on an airplane when it goes SUPERSONIC.

SOUND RECORDING, the conversion of SOUND waves into a form in which they can be stored, the original sound being reproducible by use of playback equipment. The first sound recording was made by Thomas EDISON in 1877 (see PHONOGRAPH). In modern electronic recording of all kinds, the sound is first converted by one or more MICROPHONES into electrical signals. In the case of **mechanical recordings** (discs, or records), these signals—temporarily recorded on magnetic tape—are made to vibrate a stylus that cuts a spiral groove in a rotating disc covered with lacquer. The master disc is copied by ELECTROFORMING to produce stamper dies used to press the plastic copies. (See also HIGH-FIDELITY.) In **magnetic recording**, the microphone signals activate an ELECTROMAGNET which imposes a pattern of magnetization on moving magnetic wire, discs or tape with a ferromagnetic coating (see also MAGNETISM; TAPE RECORDER). **Optical recording**, used for many motion-picture sound tracks, converts the microphone signals into a photographic exposure on film using a light beam and a variable shutter. The sound is played back by shining a light beam through the track onto a PHOTOELECTRIC CELL. As with the playback equipment for the other recording methods, this reproduces electrical signals which are amplified and fed to a LOUDSPEAKER.

SOURWOOD. See SORREL TREE.

SOUSA, John Philip (1854–1932), US band master and composer. He wrote many light operas, but is remembered today for his military marches, including "The Stars and Stripes Forever" and "The Washington Post." Sousa was leader of the Marine Band in Washington before forming a world-touring band of his own.

SOUSAPHONE. See TUBA.

SOUTH AFRICA, independent republic occupying the southern tip of Africa. It is bounded N by SOUTH WEST AFRICA, which it rules, Botswana, Rhodesia, Mozambique and Swaziland, and it surrounds the republic of LESOTHO. It comprises four provinces: the Cape, Natal, Transvaal and the Orange Free State.

Land. A vast system of grassland plateaus is separated from narrow coastal plains by the ranges of the Great Escarpment, which reaches 11 000ft in the Drakensberg Mts in the E. The westward-flowing Orange R drains most of the interior plateau. The climate is mainly warm temperate. Much of the land in the W is arid or semiarid. Rainfall is greatest in the S and E.

People. The population is about 70% black African (mainly ZULU and XHOSA), 17.5% white, 9.5% of mixed descent and 3% Asiatic. Government is entirely in the hands of the white minority. About half the people are urban, the largest cities being Johannesburg, Durban, Cape Town, Pretoria and Port Elizabeth. The black Africans speak a variety of BANTU languages; many speak AFRIKAANS or English as well. Most of the population is Christian, belonging to a wide variety of churches.

Economy. South Africa produces most of the world's gem diamonds and gold, has large coal reserves and is also rich in uranium, iron ore, asbestos, copper,

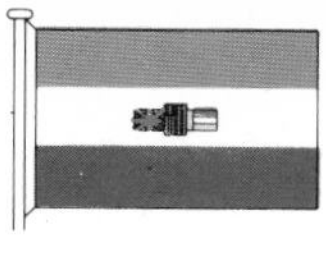

Official name: Republic of South Africa
Capital: Pretoria
Area: 472 359sq mi
Population: 21 448 169
Languages: Afrikaans, English
Religions: Christian, Bantu
Monetary unit(s): 1 Rand = 100 cents

manganese, nickel, chrome, titanium and phosphates. Mining, however, contributes only 12% of the Gross National Product, and agriculture 10%. The largest contributor is manufacturing, which includes food processing, iron, steel and oil-from-coal production, engineering and textiles. Industry and mining are concentrated in the S and E. The main farm product and a major export is wool. Corn is the chief crop; others include wheat, sugarcane, tobacco, potatoes, grapes and orchard and citrus fruits. Dairying also flourishes.

History. South Africa was already inhabited by BUSHMEN, HOTTENTOTS, and Bantu peoples from the N when white settlement began in 1652, with the Dutch establishing a colony at Cape Town. The main period of British rule (1806–1910) saw the GREAT TREK (1835–43), the founding of BOER (Dutch farmer) republics inland, and the BOER WAR (1899–1902). In 1910 the Union of South Africa was formed out of the various colonies (now the four provinces), and during WWI South West Africa was wrested from the Germans. Since 1948 South Africa has been ruled by the Afrikaner-led National Party, which has set up an efficient and repressive state apparatus to implement the policies of APARTHEID. In recent years several tribal and racial "homelands"—promised eventual "independence"—have been designated (see BANTUSTANS). In 1961 the country became a republic and left the Commonwealth.

SOUTH AFRICA WAR. See BOER WAR.

SOUTH AMERICA, the southern half of the American continent, linked with the north by the narrow land bridge of CENTRAL AMERICA. It comprises

Top left: the modern skyline of Santiago, capital of Chile, is a relatively recent development common to most major South American cities. *Below left:* the old market in Maracaibo, second largest city in Venezuela, provides a reminder of what the city looked like until the great oil boom. *Far left:* aerial view of the Essequibo river in Guyana, part of the continent that remains relatively untouched by modern developments; small settlements such as that visible in the background make little impact on this massive continent.

SOUTH AMERICA
political
CITY population more than 1,000,000
CITY population more than 500,000
CITY population more than 100,000
City population less than 100,000
railways
roads
airport
scale 1 : 35,000,000
0 250 500 750 st. miles
INDEPENDENT AFTER 1945
former British territory
former Dutch territory
ATLANTIC OCEAN
PACIFIC OCEAN
CARIBBEAN SEA
Drake Passage
Equator
Tropic of Capricorn
BRAZIL
ARGENTINA
CHILE
PERU
BOLIVIA
COLOMBIA
VENEZUELA
ECUADOR
PARAGUAY
URUGUAY
GUIANA
SURINAM
FR. GUIANA
SANTIAGO DE CUBA
KINGSTON
PORT-AU-PRINCE
SANTO DOMINGO
SAN JUAN
Belize
GUATEMALA
TEGUCIGALPA
SAN SALVADOR
MANAGUA
SAN JOSE
PANAMA
BARBADOS
Bridgetown
NETH. ANTILLES
Willemstad
Tobago
PORT-OF-SPAIN
TRINIDAD
I. Providencia (Col.)
Cayos de Albuquerque (Col.)
Malpelo (Col.)
GALAPAGOS ISLANDS (ECUADOR)
Desventurados Islands (Chile)
Juan Fernandez (Chile)
FALKLAND ISLANDS (BR)
Port Stanley
SOUTH GEORGIA (BR)
SOUTH SANDWICH ISLANDS (BR)
SOUTH ORKNEY ISLANDS (BR)
SOUTH SHETLAND ISLANDS (BR)
Fernando de Noronha (Braz.)
Trindade (Braz.)
Martim Vaz (Braz.)
BARRANQUILLA
CARTAGENA
SANTA MARTA
Riohacha
Pt Gallinas
MONTERÍA
MEDELLÍN
Quibdó
MANIZALES
PEREIRA
Tunja
BOGOTÁ
Villavicencio
BUENAVENTURA
CALI
IBAGUE
Popayán
Neiva
Florencia
Tumaco
PASTO
Mocoa
Mitú
CÚCUTA
SAN CRISTÓBAL
BUCARAMANGA
MARACAIBO
Coro
La Guaira
CARACAS
CUMANÁ
Maturín
VALENCIA
BARQUISIMETO
El Tigre
CIUDAD BOLÍVAR
Puerto Carreño
Esmeralda
Boa Vista
GEORGETOWN
PARAMARIBO
Cayenne
Macapá
Barcelos
MANAUS
Óbidos
Santarém
BELÉM
Bragança
SÃO LUIS
Parnaíba
FORTALEZA
Sobral
Caxias
TERESINA
Itaituba
Marabá
Porto Franco
Mossoró
Macau
Cape São Roque
NATAL
CAMPINA GRANDE
Crato
JOÃO PESSOA
OLINDA
RECIFE
Garanhuns
Juàzeiro
MACEIÓ
ARACAJU
SALVADOR
Pôrto Nacional
Peixe
Ilhéus
Diamantino
Mato Grosso
CUIABÁ
Goiás
BRASÍLIA
GOIÂNIA
Januária
Montes Claros
Caravelas
BELO HORIZONTE
Ouro Prêto
UBERABA
RIBEIRÃO PRÊTO
VITÓRIA
CAMPOS
JUIZ DE FORA
NOVA IGUAÇU
DUQUE DE CAXIAS
NITERÓI
RIO DE JANEIRO
CAMPO GRANDE
BAURU
CAMPINAS
SOROCABA
SANTOS
SÃO PAULO
PONTA GROSSA
CURITIBA
Paranaguá
Blumenau
FLORIANÓPOLIS
Passo Fundo
SANTA MARIA
PORTO ALEGRE
PELOTAS
RIO GRANDE
Livramento
Rivera
Corumbá
Pôrto Esperança
Pôrto Velho
Rio Branco
Riberalta
Leticia
Sapurara
Iquitos
QUITO
Ambato
Riobamba
GUAYAQUIL
Cuenca
Loja
Esmeraldas
Pt Pariñas
Paita
PIURA
CHICLAYO
Cajamarca
TRUJILLO
CHIMBOTE
Pucallpa
Huanuco
Cerro de Pasco
CALLAO
LIMA
Huancayo
Ayacucho
CUZCO
Sicuani
Pisco
Ica
AREQUIPA
Mollendo
Tacna
Arica
Trinidad
L. Titicaca
LA PAZ
COCHABAMBA
ORURO
Sucre
SANTA CRUZ
El Roboré
Potosí
Chocaya
Tarija
Iquique
Tocopilla
Chuquicamata
ANTOFAGASTA
Jujuy
SALTA
Caldera
Copiapó
Coquimbo
Ovalle
VIÑA DEL MAR
VALPARAÍSO
SANTIAGO
Rancagua
Talca
TALCAHUANO
Chillán
CONCEPCIÓN
Lota
TEMUCO
Valdivia
Osorno
Puerto Montt
Concepción
ASUNCIÓN
Villarrica
Formosa
RESISTENCIA
CORRIENTES
Encarnación
Posadas
SAN MIGUEL TUCUMÁN
SANTIAGO DEL ESTERO
Catamarca
La Rioja
CÓRDOBA
SANTA FE
SAN JUAN
MENDOZA
Rio Cuarto
ROSARIO
PARANÁ
Concórdia
Salto
Paysandú
San Nicolás
San Luis
BUENOS AIRES
LA PLATA
MONTEVIDEO
Rio de la Plata
Azul
Tandil
Santa Rosa
MAR DEL PLATA
Neuquén
Zapala
BAHIA BLANCA
Viedma
San Antonio Oeste
San Carlos de Bariloche
Rawson
Comodoro Rivadavia
Santa Cruz
Río Gallegos
Strait of Magellan
Punta Arenas
Tierra del Fuego
Ushuaia
Cape Horn
Amazon
Negro
Madeira
Orinoco
Magdalena
Marañón
Paraguay
Paraná
Araguaia
São Francisco

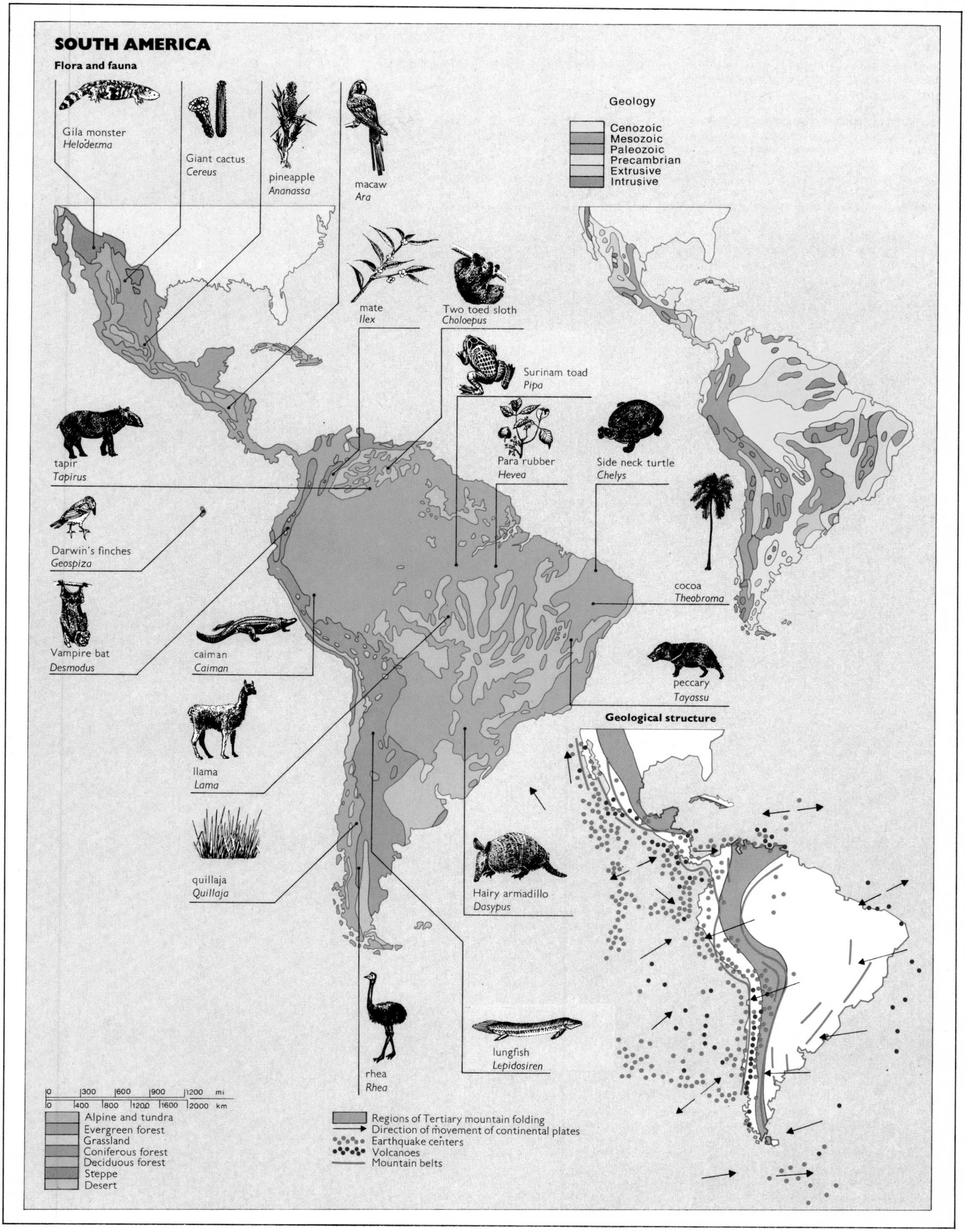
SOUTH AMERICA
Flora and fauna
Gila monster
Heloderma
Giant cactus
Cereus
pineapple
Ananassa
macaw
Ara
mate
Ilex
Two toed sloth
Choloepus
Surinam toad
Pipa
Para rubber
Hevea
Side neck turtle
Chelys
cocoa
Theobroma
peccary
Tayassu
tapir
Tapirus
Darwin's finches
Geospiza
Vampire bat
Desmodus
caiman
Caiman
llama
Lama
quillaja
Quillaja
Hairy armadillo
Dasypus
lungfish
Lepidosiren
rhea
Rhea
0 300 600 900 1200 mi
0 400 800 1200 1600 2000 km
Alpine and tundra
Evergreen forest
Grassland
Coniferous forest
Deciduous forest
Steppe
Desert
Geology
Cenozoic
Mesozoic
Paleozoic
Precambrian
Extrusive
Intrusive
Geological structure
Regions of Tertiary mountain folding
Direction of movement of continental plates
Earthquake centers
Volcanoes
Mountain belts

twelve independent republics: Argentina, Bolivia, Brazil, Chile, Colombia, Ecuador, Guyana, Paraguay, Peru, Surinam, Uruguay and Venezuela; and one European possession, French Guiana.

Land. The most prominent feature is the Andes mountain chain in the W, with over 50 peaks exceeding 20000ft. Other major features include the three river basins of the Amazon, Paraná and Orinoco, the Brazilian and Guiana highlands in the E and NE, the Pampas grassland and the Patagonian plateau of Argentina. The climate varies from the extreme cold of the high Andes to the tropical rain forests of the lowlands near the equator. Native plants include beans, pumpkins, squashes, tomatoes, peanuts, pineapples, red peppers, tapioca, rubber, tobacco and cocoa. Produce of the tropical forests, which cover about half the area of the continent, includes hardwoods, brazil and cashew nuts, quinine and quebracho bark, while sugarcane, coffee and oil palms are important imported crops. The many animal species include: hummingbirds, parrots and the condor; the llama and alpaca; anteaters, sloths, tapirs and armadillos; and piranhas and anacondas.

People. There are four main groups: the native Indians; white Europeans, mainly of Spanish or Portuguese descent; Negroes, who originally came as slaves; and the *mestizos*, of mixed Indian, Negro and European descent. The total population is about 200 million. The chief official languages are Spanish and Portuguese (the latter is spoken only in Brazil). Probably the most widely spoken Indian language is GUARANI. About 90% of the population is nominally Catholic.

Economy. Most South American economies depend on the exploitation of primary raw materials, notably such minerals as oil, copper, tin, lead, zinc, bauxite, antimony, tungsten, manganese and iron ore; and upon the export of one particular commodity to earn the foreign currency needed to pay for industrialization. Bolivia exports tin; Chile, copper; Guyana, bauxite; Venezuela, oil; Brazil and Colombia, coffee; Ecuador, bananas; Argentina, meat and wheat; Peru, fish products; and Uruguay, wool. Agriculture, which involves over 45% of the population, is generally primitive and inefficient. Industrial expansion is hampered by the difficulty of finding suitable export markets, the problem of attracting investment, the burdensome effects of foreign aid, and poor communications.

History. An Indian preserve until 1498, when COLUMBUS first sighted the mainland, South America was rapidly conquered by Spain and Portugal. Their rule lasted for just over three centuries. Between 1810 and 1825 most of the colonies, inspired by the leadership of BOLÍVAR and SAN MARTÍN, gained their independence. Political power and wealth, however, remained in the hands of tiny minorities, and have continued to do so. South American society has long been characterized by extremes of wealth and poverty, and political life by corruption and instability, with rapidly-changing dictatorships. (See also INDIANS, CENTRAL AND SOUTH AMERICAN.)

SOUTHAMPTON, city on the S coast of England, an important passenger and commercial port, with shipbuilding, marine engineering and light manufacturing industries, and a large oil refinery nearby. Pop 214826.

SOUTHAMPTON ISLAND, in NW Territories, Canada, at the entrance to Hudson Bay. Coral Harbour is the only trading post.

SOUTH ARABIA, Federation of, union of 17 small states in the S of the Arabian Peninsula, including the British Protectorate of Aden, built up between 1959 and 1965. The various regimes were overthrown in 1967 by the National Liberation Front, and an independent state was proclaimed (see YEMEN, PEOPLE'S DEMOCRATIC REPUBLIC OF).

SOUTH AUSTRALIA, state in S central Australia. The capital and chief port is Adelaide. Wheat, barley, wool and wine are produced in the fertile SE. Minerals include iron ore, opals, salt, gypsum and coal. Major industries, centered on Adelaide, include smelting, chemicals, fertilizers, engineering and automobiles.

SOUTH BEND, city in N Ind., seat of St. Joseph Co. Industries include automobile parts, farm and electrical machinery and metal goods. Pop 125580.

SOUTHBRIDGE, town in S central Mass. It produces optical and metal goods and textiles. Pop 17057.

SOUTH BURLINGTON, town in NW Vt., a residential community and resort. Pop 10032.

SOUTH CAROLINA, state of the SE US. Its three main regions are the Atlantic coastal plain, occupying the SE two-thirds of the state, the Piedmont plateau in the NW, and the Blue Ridge Mts in the extreme NW. It is drained by the SE-flowing Pee Dee, Santee, Edisto and Savannah river systems, which all produce hydroelectricity. Summers are hot (average daily temperature over 70°F) and winters mild. Rainfall averages 47in per year.

The population is about 55% rural, and mainly Protestant. Columbia, Charleston and Greenville are the major cities. Once overwhelmingly agricultural, the economy is now based principally on manufacturing. Textiles and clothing, employing 40% of the manufacturing workforce, are most important, followed by chemicals. Agricultural produce includes tobacco, soybeans, cotton and peaches. Livestock farming is on the increase, and the state's forests, covering two-thirds of its area, support growing lumber and paper industries.

South Carolina was first settled as a PROPRIETARY COLONY in 1670, but dissatisfaction with the proprietors led the colonists to revolt in 1719, and the province became a royal colony in 1729. During the REVOLUTIONARY WAR, victories at KING'S MOUNTAIN and COWPENS offset the fall of Charleston to the British in 1780. In 1786 the capital was moved to Columbia to help unify the two sections of the state, the rich planters of the lowlands and the poorer farmers of the Piedmont. In the NULLIFICATION and STATES' RIGHTS controversies preceding the CIVIL WAR, slave-owning South Carolina took the radical lead, and became the first state to secede from the Union. The first shots of the Civil War were fired at FORT SUMTER, and South Carolina experienced bitter fighting and an equally bitter Reconstruction period, followed by continuing agricultural depression and chronic political corruption. The black majority were effectively disenfranchised, and even in the 1960s, there was resistance to INTEGRATION. Blacks now number some 30% of the population. Since WWII an industrial and agricultural revival has assured the state's economic security.

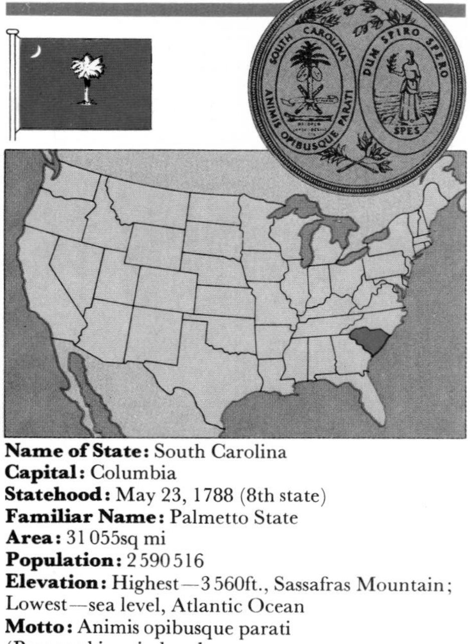

Name of State: South Carolina
Capital: Columbia
Statehood: May 23, 1788 (8th state)
Familiar Name: Palmetto State
Area: 31055sq mi
Population: 2590516
Elevation: Highest—3560ft., Sassafras Mountain; Lowest—sea level, Atlantic Ocean
Motto: Animis opibusque parati (Prepared in mind and resources); Dum spiro spero (While I breathe, I hope)
State flower: Carolina jessamine
State bird: Carolina wren
State tree: Palmetto
State song: "Carolina"

Former slave quarters at Boone Hall cotton plantation, near Charleston, South Carolina. Once supposed to be dependent on slave labor, such plantations continued to thrive without it.

SOUTH CHINA SEA, part of the Pacific Ocean, bounded by mainland Asia and Malaysia to the N and W, Borneo to the S, and the Philippines to the E. It is tropical, and subject to frequent typhoons.

SOUTH DAKOTA, a midwestern state of the US. It can be divided into the rugged Great Plains in the W and center, the more fertile Central Lowlands to the E, and the semi-arid BADLANDS and the Black Hills to the SW. The state is bisected by the Missouri R. Climate is continental, with low humidity and great seasonal temperature changes. Rainfall ranges from about 13in per year in the NW to 25in in the SE. Population is about 40% urban, and its density is the lowest in the US. The largest religious denomination is the Lutheran Church.

The barren but impressive landscape of the Badlands of southeastern South Dakota, much of which is now included in the Badlands National Monument.

Agriculture, particularly livestock and livestock produce, provides 80% of the total value of all goods produced in the state. Leading crops include wheat, corn, hay, flaxseed, rye and oats. Manufacturing is dominated by food processing. Gold is important and the Homestake Mine at Lead is the largest in the western hemisphere. Other minerals include sand, gravel, beryllium, clays and feldspar. The Black Hills and other areas attract millions of tourists.

Home of the ARIKARA, CHEYENNE and SIOUX Indians, South Dakota became part of the US with the LOUISIANA PURCHASE (1803) and was explored by LEWIS AND CLARK (1804–06). Settlement was first stimulated by the fur trade, but by the 1850s farmers had begun to move in. In 1861 South Dakota was included in the Dakota territory with its capital at Yankton. Increasing conflict with Indian tribes was settled by the Laramie Treaty (1868) which created the Great Sioux Reservation. General CUSTER violated the treaty in a search for gold in the Black Hills (1874), and soon the area was flooded with miners and prospectors; Indian resistance came to an end at WOUNDED KNEE (1890). New railroads brought more farmers, and the population tripled between 1880 and 1890. The boundary with North Dakota was drawn and both states entered the Union in 1889, but the boom was already almost over and the state suffered from successive droughts and depressions from which it did not recover until after WWII. Since then hydroelectric projects, farm mechanization, industrial expansion and tourism have marked a new prosperity.

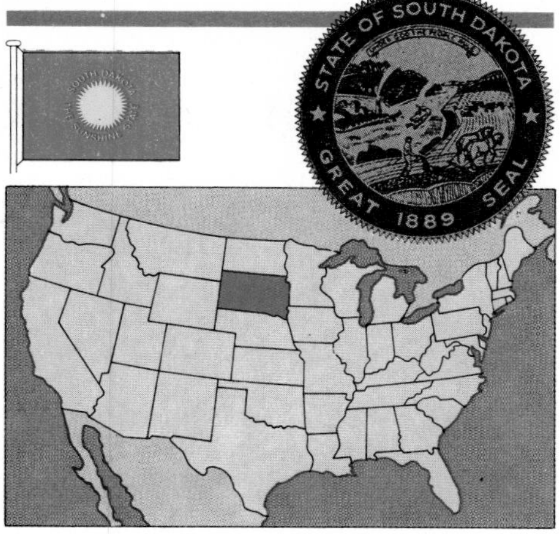

Name of State: South Dakota
Capital: Pierre
Statehood: Nov. 2, 1889 (40th state)
Familiar Name: Sunshine State, Coyote State
Area: 77 047sq mi
Population: 666 257
Elevation: Highest—7 242ft., Harney Peak; Lowest—962ft., Big Stone Lake
Motto: Under God the People Rule
State flower: American pasqueflower
State bird: Ring-necked pheasant
State tree: Black Hills spruce
State song: "Hail, South Dakota"

SOUTHEAST ASIA TREATY ORGANIZATION (SEATO), a defense treaty signed by Australia, France, UK, New Zealand, Pakistan, the Philippines, Thailand and the US after the French had withdrawn from Indochina in 1954. Its aim is to prevent communist expansion. There is a headquarters at Bangkok, Thailand, but no standing forces. The treaty was invoked by the US in the VIETNAM WAR. Pakistan withdrew in 1972.

SOUTH EL MONTE, city in Cal., 12mi E of Los Angeles. Mainly a residential community, it has some light industry. Pop 13 443.

SOUTHEND-ON-SEA, county borough on the Thames estuary 35mi E of London, England. It is mainly a residential town and seaside resort. Pop 162 326.

SOUTHERN ALPS, mountain range in the W of South Island, New Zealand, running about 200mi NE–SW. The highest peak is Mt. Cook (12 349ft).

SOUTHERN CHRISTIAN LEADERSHIP CONFERENCE (SCLC), a nonviolent CIVIL RIGHTS organization founded by Martin Luther KING, Jr, and others in 1957. It played a major part in the 1963 civil rights march on Washington and other anti-discrimination campaigns. After the assassination of King in 1968, leadership was taken by the Rev. Ralph ABERNATHY.

SOUTHERN CROSS, Crux, a small, bright constellation near the S celestial pole. The four bright stars forming the cross are Acrux (Alpha), Mimosa (Beta), Gacrux (Gamma) and Delta Crucis.

SOUTHERN LIGHTS. See AURORA.

SOUTHERN RHODESIA. See RHODESIA.

SOUTHERN YEMEN, former name for the People's Democratic Republic of YEMEN.

SOUTH EUCLID, city in NE Ohio, a residential suburb of Cleveland. Pop 29 759.

SOUTHEY, Robert (1774–1843), English Poet Laureate from 1813, a friend of WORDSWORTH and COLERIDGE. His large output includes long narrative poems, journalism, histories, biographies and verse collections. Famous in his day as a poet, he is now more admired as a prose writer, notably for his *Life of Nelson* (1813).

SOUTH FARMINGDALE, urban community on Long Island, SE N.Y., 20mi E of New York. Pop 20 464.

SOUTHFIELD, commercial and industrial city in SE Mich. A NE suburb of Detroit, it is the headquarters of many insurance companies. Pop 69 285.

SOUTH GATE, city in S Cal., an industrial suburb 7mi SE of Los Angeles, whose products include automobiles, aircraft parts, chemicals and glass. Pop 56 909.

SOUTH GEORGIA, a bleak, barren island (1 450sq mi) in the S Atlantic 1 100mi E of Cape Horn, a Falkland Islands dependency.

SOUTH HADLEY, town in S central Mass., N of Springfield. Manufactures include paper, electric equipment and metal goods. Pop 17 033.

SOUTH HOLLAND, village in Ill., a suburb 18mi S of Chicago. Pop 23 931.

SOUTH HOUSTON, town in Tex. just SE of Houston, of which it is a suburb. Pop 11 527.

SOUTHINGTON, industrial town in central Conn. Machine tools and other metal products are the principal manufactures. Pop 30 946.

SOUTH KINGSTOWN, town in S R.I., a summer resort with fishing and a woolen goods industry. Pop 16 913.

SOUTH KOREA. See KOREA.

SOUTH LAKE TAHOE, city in E Cal., 75mi E of Sacramento. It is a tourist resort. Pop 12 921.

SOUTH MIAMI, city in SE Fla., 8mi SW of Miami. It is residential, and also a packing and shipping center for fruit and vegetables. Pop 19 571.

SOUTH MILWAUKEE, industrial city in SE Wis. on Lake Michigan, a suburb of Milwaukee. Products include iron castings, excavating machinery and electronic equipment. Pop 23 297.

SOUTH ORANGE, village in NE N.J., a residential suburb for both Newark and New York. Pop 16 671.

SOUTH ORKNEY ISLANDS, barren and uninhabited group of islands, a dependency of the Falkland Is, about 450mi SE of Cape Horn in the S Atlantic.

SOUTH PASADENA, city in S Cal., a NE suburb of Los Angeles. It is residential, with some light industry, notably electronics. Pop 22 979.

SOUTH PLAINFIELD, borough in NE N.J. It is an industrial center producing steel, cement, chemicals and electrical goods. Pop 21 142.

SOUTH PLATTE RIVER, 440mi long, rises in central Col. and flows SE and then NE through Denver to join the North Platte R in W Neb.

SOUTH POLE, the point in Antarctica through which passes the earth's axis of rotation. It does not coincide with the earth's S Magnetic Pole (see EARTH). It was first reached by Roald Amundsen (Dec. 14, 1911). (See also CELESTIAL SPHERE; MAGNETISM; NORTH POLE.)

SOUTH RIVER, borough in E N.J. on South R 5mi SE of New Brunswick. Clothing and embroidery are the principal manufactures. Pop 15 428.

SOUTH SAINT PAUL, city in SE Minn. on the Mississippi R 5mi SSE of Saint Paul. It is a major marketing point for livestock. Pop 25 016.

SOUTH SAN FRANCISCO, city in W Cal., 9mi S of San Francisco. It is an industrial center producing steel, metal goods, chemicals and processed foods. Pop 46 646.

SOUTH SEA BUBBLE, popular name for speculation in the South Sea Company, created in England in 1711 to trade with Spanish America. In 1720 the company's proposal to take over the NATIONAL DEBT, aided by fraudulent promotions, pushed shares to fantastic prices. In the subsequent collapse many were ruined.

SOUTH SHETLAND ISLANDS, group of barren, uninhabited islands in the S Atlantic, part of British Antarctic Territory. They have been used as a base for sealing, whaling and scientific expeditions.

SOUTH VIETNAM. See VIETNAM.

SOUTHWELL, Robert (c1561–1595), English Jesuit, devotional poet and Roman Catholic martyr. He returned from Rome to England in 1586 as a missionary to the persecuted Catholics. Arrested in 1592, he was tortured and finally executed.

SOUTHWEST AFRICA, or **Namibia**, a territory in Africa bordered by the S Atlantic Ocean, Angola, Botswana and South Africa. It is ruled by South Africa. The land rises from the Namib, a desert coastal area some 60mi wide, to a plateau averaging 3 500ft above sea level covered in rough grass and scrub. In the E are the fringes of the Kalahari desert. There are few rivers, and the climate is hot and dry. The majority of the population are Bantu; whites constitute about 8%. Diamonds and other minerals are important products, and stockraising is the main agricultural pursuit. The country was annexed by Germany in 1884, and mandated to South Africa after WWI by the League of Nations (1920). After WWII South Africa refused to place it under the trusteeship of the UN, who in 1966 declared the original mandate terminated. In spite of a 1971 opinion of the International Court of Justice, South Africa denied the UN's authority, but in 1976 instituted a constitutional conference with a view to independence for Namibia. Capital: Windhoek. Area: 317 836sq mi. Pop 746 328.

SOUTH WESTBURY, urban community on Long Island, a suburb E of New York. Pop 10 978.

SOUTH WINDSOR, town in N Conn. on the Connecticut R 6mi NE of Hartford. It is a tobacco packing and shipping center. Pop 15 553.

SOUTINE, Chaim (1893–1943), Russian-born French expressionist painter. His style uses vivid primary colors and twisting, rhythmic forms, as in *Pastry Cook* (1922).

SOVEREIGNTY, supreme political power in a state. In political theory debates on sovereignty center on the role of the sovereign and on the nature of supreme power—by what rights, and by whom, it should be wielded. A *sovereign state* is one that is independent of control by other states (but see INTERNATIONAL LAW; UNITED NATIONS).

SOVIET, the basic political unit of socialist Russia (from *sovet*, a council). The soviets, ranging in importance from rural councils to the Supreme Soviet, the major legislative body of the Soviet Union, are elected policy-making and administrative units. The first soviets were the strike committees set up during the 1905 revolution.

SOVIET UNION. See RUSSIA.

SOVKHOZ, in the USSR, an agricultural estate operated by the state and organized in a similar fashion to factories for the purpose of large-scale industrial production.

SOWBUGS. See WOODLICE.

SOWTHISTLE, common name for *Sonchus oleraceus*, a weed of lawns and gardens, which is native to Europe, but introduced to North America. The leaves can be eaten as a vegetable. Family COMPOSITAE.

SOYBEAN, *Glycine max* or *G. soja*, a LEGUMINOUS PLANT native to E Asia providing food, animal feed and industrial raw material. It has been grown as a staple food in China for over 5 000 years. Richer in PROTEIN than most MEAT, it also contains calcium, VITAMINS, minerals, acids and lecithin. Soy flour is used to make artificial meats and is also an important food in times of famine. Soybean oil is used in the manufacture of margarine, paints, soap, linoleum, textiles, paper and agricultural sprays. Over half of the world's soybean crop is now grown in the US.

SPAAK, Paul Henri (1899–1972), Belgium's first Socialist premier (1938–39, 1947–49), and deputy premier 1961–65. He was foreign secretary several times between 1936 and 1966, and was president of the UNITED NATIONS General Assembly in 1946. He was influential in setting up the European COMMON MARKET and was secretary-general of the NORTH ATLANTIC TREATY ORGANIZATION 1957–61.

SPAATZ, Carl Andrew (1891–1974), US Air Force officer who fought in both world wars, taking a number of high command positions during WWII, and in 1945 directing the strategic bombing of Japan. He was Air Force Chief of Staff 1947–48.

SPACE, in MATHEMATICS, a bounded or unbounded extent. In GEOMETRY this extent may be in one, two or three DIMENSIONS, its nature being viewed differently in different geometries. According to EUCLIDEAN GEOMETRY space is uniform and infinite, so that we may talk of a LINE of infinite extent or a POLYGON of infinite AREA. In RIEMANNIAN GEOMETRY, however, all lines are of less than a certain, finite extent; and in LOBACHEVSKIAN GEOMETRY, there is a similar maximum of area. (See also VECTOR SPACE.)

SPACE EXPLORATION. At 10.56pm EDT on July 20, 1969, Neil ARMSTRONG became the first man to set foot on the MOON. This was the climax of an intensive US space program sparked off by the successful launch of the Russian artificial SATELLITE Sputnik 1 in 1957, and accelerated by Yuri GAGARIN's flight in Vostok 1, the first manned spacecraft, in 1961. Later that year Alan SHEPARD piloted the first American manned spacecraft, and President Kennedy set the goal of landing a man on the moon and returning him safely within the decade. On Feb. 20, 1962 John GLENN orbited the earth three times in the first MERCURY craft to be boosted by an Atlas rocket, but it was Valery Bykovsky who set the one-man endurance record with a 5-day mission in June 1963. The next Russian mission involved two craft, Vostoks 5 and 6, and made Valentina TERESHKOVA the first woman cosmonaut. Alexei Leonov completed the first space-walk in Oct. 1964: but then it was the turn of the GEMINI MISSIONS to break all records. Both countries lost men, on the ground and in space: among them V. I. GRISSOM, E. H. WHITE and R. B. Chaffee—in a fire on board Apollo during ground tests—and the crew of Soyuz 11, killed during reentry in 1971, though earlier Soyuz had docked successfully with the first space station and set new records. Unmanned probes such as Orbiter, Ranger and Surveyor were meanwhile searching out Apollo landing sites, while Russian Luna and Lunokhod craft were also studying the moon. In 1968 Apollo 7 carried out an 11-day earth-orbit flight, and at Christmas Apollo 8 made 10 lunar orbits. The lunar landing craft was tested on the Apollo 9 and Apollo 10 missions, leaving the way clear for the triumphant success of Apollo 11. Apollo 12 was equally successful, landing only 600 yards from the lunar probe Surveyor 3, but the Apollo 13 mission was a near disaster: an explosion damaged the craft on its way to the moon, and re-entry was achieved only with great difficulty. Apollo 14 had no such problems in visiting Fra Mauro, and on the Apollo 15 mission a Lunar Roving Vehicle allowed collection of a very wide range of samples. Apollo 16 brought back over 200lbs of moon rock, and in Dec. 1972 Apollo 17 made the last lunar landing. In 1973 the SKYLAB missions returned attention to the study of world resources from space, and movements toward cooperation in this field were demonstrated by the joint Apollo-Soyuz mission in 1975. Exploration of the planets has been carried out by unmanned probes: the MARINER series to Mars, Venus and Mercury; the PIONEER missions to the outer planets, and a number of Russian contributions, such as the Venera soft-landing missions to Venus, the Zond bypass probe and the Mars soft-landing craft. Results from the two American VIKING probes that soft-landed on Mars in 1976 did not reveal the existence of life there.

SPACE MEDICINE, the specialized branch of MEDICINE concerned with the special physical and psychological problems arising from space flight. In particular, the effects of prolonged weightlessness and isolation are studied, simulated space flight forming the basis for much of this work.

SPACE-TIME, a way of describing the geometry of the physical universe arising from EINSTEIN's special theory of RELATIVITY. Space and time are considered as a single 4-dimensional continuum rather than as a 3-dimensional space with a separate infinite 1-dimensional time. Time thus becomes the "fourth dimension." Events in space-time are analogous to points in space and invariant space-time intervals to distances in space.

SPADEFISHES, deep-bodied schooling fishes of the tropical Atlantic, family Ephippidae. The body is strongly compressed, almost oval, and the dorsal and anal fins are scythe-shaped.

SPAHN, Warren Edward (1921–), US baseball player who won 363 games, more than any other lefthanded pitcher. He pitched a lifetime total of 57 scoreless games. Spahn began his major league career with the Boston Braves in 1942, and retired in 1965.

SPAIN, a country occupying about four-fifths of the Iberian Peninsula S of the Pyrenees Mts in SW Europe. It includes the BALEARIC ISLANDS and the CANARY ISLANDS. The largely arid plateau of the Meseta forms most of the interior. The Andalusian or Baetic Mts near the Mediterranean coast include the SIERRA NEVADA, rising to Mulacen (11421ft), the highest peak in mainland Spain. The Guadalquivir R drains the fertile Andalusian plains, and narrow coastal plains lie along the E and SE coasts. The climate is mainly dry with cold winters and hot summers, more extreme on the Meseta. In N Spain the climate is equable, and the S and E coasts enjoy a Mediterranean climate.

People. About 41% of the population is urban. Regional differences are marked and the BASQUE provinces, GALICIA and CATALONIA have preserved their own languages.

Economy. Tourism makes the most important contribution to Spain's income, followed by industry and agriculture. Mineral wealth includes mercury, iron ore, coal, pyrites, potash and salt. Oil was found near Burgos in 1964. Manufacturing industries center on the N provinces, especially Catalonia, and include textiles, chemicals, iron and steel, paper, explosives and armaments. Agriculture is equally divided between crops and livestock. Oranges, olive oil and wine are exported. Fishing is important.

History. Spain was settled successively by Celts, Phoenicians, Greeks and Carthaginians (3rd century BC). A more enduring influence was that of the Romans, who conquered Spain during the second of the PUNIC WARS and remained dominant until the VANDALS and VISIGOTHS appeared in the 5th century AD. The last invaders were the MOORS (711 AD). The Christian kingdoms in the N achieved a gradual reconquest completed in the reign (1474–1504) of Ferdinand V (FERDINAND II of Aragon) and his wife ISABELLA of Castile. They introduced the INQUISITION and financed the voyages of COLUMBUS. Soon Spain had won a vast empire in the New World and N Africa, joined with the HAPSBURG lands by the election of Charles I as CHARLES V, Holy Roman Emperor. Under his son PHILIP II a period of outstanding cultural achievement unfolded with such figures as CERVANTES, Lope de VEGA, VELASQUEZ and El GRECO. At the same time Spain's political power declined. The Netherlands revolted in 1568, and the ARMADA was defeated in 1588. The War of the SPANISH SUCCESSION resulted in heavy losses. The French, invading in 1808, were driven out in the PENINSULAR WAR; but after the revolt of the Latin American colonies and the SPANISH-AMERICAN WAR the Empire was all but dead. After the SPANISH CIVIL WAR General FRANCO became dictator. On his death (1975) JUAN CARLOS succeeded, thus restoring the monarchy.

Official name: Spanish State
Capital: Madrid
Area: 194883sq mi
Population: 34443098
Languages: Spanish; Catalan, Galician, Basque
Religions: Roman Catholic
Monetary unit(s): 1 Peseta = 100 centimes

Commemorating the destruction of the Spanish fleet in Manila harbor, a week after the outbreak of the Spanish-American War: the front page of *The Chicago Daily Tribune* reproduced as a plaque.

SPALATO. See SPLIT.

SPALLANZANI, Lazzaro (1729–1799), Italian biologist who attacked the contemporary belief in the SPONTANEOUS GENERATION of life by demonstrating that organisms which usually appeared in vegetable infusions failed to do so if the infusions were boiled and kept from contact with the air.

SPANDAU, the chief industrial district of West Berlin. From 1946 its prison was used to house some Nazi war criminals, longest serving being Rudolf HESS.

SPANISH, a Romance language spoken by over 145000000 people in Spain and Latin America. Modern Spanish arose from the Castilian dialect centered on the town of Burgos in N central Spain.

SPANISH-AMERICAN WAR (1898), war fought between the US and Spain, initially over the conduct of Spanish colonial authorities in CUBA. Strong anti-Spanish feeling was fomented in the US by stories of the cruel treatment meted out to Cuban rebels, and the hardships suffered by American business interests. Though President Cleveland took no action, his successor, William McKINLEY, had promised to recognize Cuban independence. He succeeded in obtaining limited self-government for the Cubans, but an explosion aboard the US battleship *Maine* (1898), from which 260 died was blamed on the Spanish, and McKinley sent an ultimatum, some of whose terms were actually being implemented when Congress declared war on April 25. On May 1 George DEWEY destroyed the Spanish fleet in Manila harbor. What remained was trapped in Santiago harbor by Admiral W. T. SAMPSON, and destroyed on July 3 by American forces which had already shattered Spanish land forces. Santiago surrendered on July 17. General Nelson A. Miles occupied Puerto Rico, and on Aug. 13 troops occupied Manila. The Treaty of PARIS (Dec. 10 1898) ended Spanish rule in Cuba. The US gained the islands of GUAM, PUERTO RICO and the PHILIPPINES, thus acquiring an overseas empire with accompanying world military power and responsibilities.

SPANISH BAYONET, *Yucca aloifolia*, a shrubby plant with a stout woody trunk, sharp-pointed leaves and clusters of white flowers. It is native to sand dunes in SE US and is often grown as a house plant. Family: Liliaceae. (See also YUCCA.)

SPANISH CIVIL WAR (1936–39), major conflict between liberal and conservative forces in Spain. After the bloodless overthrow of the monarchy in 1931, the democratic republican government proposed far-reaching reforms which alienated conservatives. On the election (1936) of the POPULAR

FRONT, a left-wing coalition, the rightists under General FRANCO resorted to force. Supported by Hitler and Mussolini, Franco was on the verge of shattering the republicans when the Soviet Union began to send them aid. The West remained aloof. Madrid fell to Franco in 1938, Barcelona in 1939. Over 600 000, many of them foreign volunteers, died in the war, and the country suffered massive damage. The Luftwaffe's systematic destruction of GUERNICA, a preview of Hitler's *Blitzkrieg*, shocked the world.

SPANISH FLY, *Lytta vesicatoris*, a European beetle, family Meloidae, which is an important source of cantharidin, a crystalline drug used as an aphrodisiac, vesicant or diuretic.

SPANISH GUINEA. See EQUATORIAL GUINEA.

SPANISH MAIN, former name of the N coast of the South American mainland, now part of Colombia and Venezuela. It was the hunting ground of the English pirates and buccaneers who attacked the Spanish treasure fleets.

SPANISH MOSS, or Florida moss, *Tillandsia usneoides*, an EPIPHYTE that can be found festooning trees such as oaks and cypresses and even telephone poles and wires in the southeastern US. It absorbs water through scaly hairs on the leaves and stem. It is used as a substitute for horsehair stuffing and for insulation.

SPANISH SAHARA. See WESTERN SAHARA.

SPANISH SUCCESSION, War of the (1701–1714), conflict between France on the one hand and a Grand Alliance of England, Holland, Austria and the smaller states of the Holy Roman Empire on the other. The childless Charles II of Spain willed his kingdom and its empire to France on his deathbed. The Grand Alliance sought to prevent France from becoming the dominant European power. Though the decisive battles were fought in Europe, there were also engagements overseas, even in North America (see FRENCH AND INDIAN WARS). The Duke of Marlborough and Prince Eugene of Savoy won such remarkable victories as BLENHEIM (1704), Ramillies (1706) and Malplaquet (1709), but LOUIS XIV fought on. The accession of CHARLES VI as the new emperor removed obstacles to the recognition of Philip of Anjou as PHILIP V of Spain. England made a separate peace in 1712 and a general settlement of differences in the Peace of UTRECHT followed in 1713.

SPARK, momentary electric discharge in a gas.

SPARK, Muriel Sarah (1918–   ), Scottish writer best known for her witty, often satirical novels, including *Memento Mori* (1959), *The Prime of Miss Jean Brodie* (1961; later made into a play and a film) and *The Mandelbaum Gate* (1965).

SPARK CHAMBER, detector for visual investigation of SUBATOMIC PARTICLE paths in high-energy NUCLEAR PHYSICS. A large chamber filled with a NOBLE GAS contains a series of thin parallel metal plates 10–20mm apart. The entry of a particle into the chamber triggers a high voltage pulse (around 10kV) which is applied to the plates. An ELECTRON avalanche quickly builds up around the ionization produced along the particle's path. A bright and well-defined spark appears, which may be photographed, and cuts off the voltage pulse.

SPARK PLUG, an IGNITION SYSTEM fitted in the cylinder head of an INTERNAL-COMBUSTION ENGINE. It consists essentially of two electrodes separated by an air gap. When the fuel/air mixture is fully compressed, the DISTRIBUTOR connects a voltage of 20kV across the electrodes, producing a spark that ignites the mixture.

SPARKS, city in W Nev. 3mi E of Reno, a railroad division point. The area produces hay, potatoes and onions. Pop 24 187.

SPARKS, Jared (1789–1866), US historian best known for the 12-volume *Writings of George Washington* (1834–37). He edited the *North American Review* 1824–30, and was president of Harvard U. 1849–53.

SPARROWHAWKS, the name used both for the European sparrowhawk, *Accipiter nisus*, a true HAWK, very much like a smaller GOSHAWK, and the American sparrowhawk, *Falco sparverius*, which is more properly a FALCON, closely related to the European KESTREL.

SPARROWS, small gregarious seed-eating birds forming the subfamily Passerinae of the weaver-bird family Ploceidae. There are eight genera, five confined to Africa, the other three, the True sparrows, Rock sparrows and Snow finches, also found in the Palearctic. Of the true sparrows, one species, the House sparrow, *Passer domesticus*, has been successfully introduced to the Americas. Closely associated with human habitation, it is the only bird not known to occur at all in a "natural" habitat, but always with man.

SPARTA, or Lacedaemon, city of ancient Greece, the capital of Laconia in the Peloponnesus, on the Eurotas R. Its society was divided into three classes: the HELOTS, the free perioeci, and the Spartiates, whose rigorous military training became a byword. There were two hereditary kings, though real power resided with the five annually elected EPHORS. Founded in the 13th century BC, Sparta dominated the Peloponnesus by 550 BC. Despite alliance with Athens in the PERSIAN WARS, Sparta fought and won the PELOPONNESIAN WAR against Athens (431–404 BC) but a series of revolts and defeats destroyed Spartan power, and in 146 BC the city became subject to Roman rule.

SPARTACUS (d. 71 BC), leader of the Gladiators' War, a slave revolt against ancient Rome (73–71 BC). With an army of runaway slaves Spartacus heavily defeated forces sent against him and gained control of S Italy, but after his death in battle the revolt was quickly crushed, and 6 000 slaves were crucified along the Appian Way.

SPARTACUS LEAGUE, German revolutionary socialist group active after WWI and named for the slave leader SPARTACUS by its leaders, Karl LIEBKNECHT and Rosa LUXEMBURG. The league became the nub of the German Communist Party, but its attempt to seize power in Jan. 1919 was crushed by the government of Friedrich EBERT, and Liebknecht and Luxemburg were murdered while under arrest.

SPARTANBURG, city in S.C., seat of Spartanburg Co., 94mi W of Colombia. Its industry is dominated by textiles. Pop 44 546.

SPASTIC PARALYSIS, form of PARALYSIS due to DISEASE of BRAIN (e.g., STROKE) or SPINAL CORD (e.g., MULTIPLE SCLEROSIS), in which the involved MUSCLES are in a state of constantly increased tone (or resting contraction). Spasticity is a segmental motor phenomenon where muscle contraction occurs without voluntary control.

SPATHIPHYLLUM, peace-lily, or white flag, an evergreen perennial plant that produces attractive, shiny, dark-green, ovate-lanceolate leaves and graceful white flowers; it is often grown as a house plant. It should be placed in a bright north window or near a sunny window; it grows well at average house temperatures, failing to thrive below 13°C (55°F). The soil should be kept wet to moist. Propagation is achieved by planting root divisions. Family: Araceae.

SPEAKER. See LOUDSPEAKER.

SPEAKER, the officer presiding in the US House of Representatives. Formally elected by the whole House, the speaker is in fact selected from the majority party by its leaders, and holds powers of recognition, referral of bills to committee and control of debates. Other, wider powers were stripped from the speaker after the term of Joseph CANNON in 1910. (See also CONGRESS OF THE UNITED STATES.)

SPEAKER, Tristram E. (1888–1958), outstanding American League outfielder elected to the Baseball Hall of Fame in 1937. He compiled a lifetime batting average of .344 and set a standing major league doubles record (793).

SPEARFISHES, a name sometimes used for various groups of long-snouted fishes: MARLINS; SWORDFISHES; SAILFISHES and their relatives.

SPEARMINT. See MINT.

SPECIAL DRAWING RIGHTS (SDRS), the provisions by which member governments can draw on the INTERNATIONAL MONETARY FUND for monetary reserves which are in effect notes of credit guaranteed exchangeable for gold or the standard reserve currencies. Each government has a prearranged quota of Special Drawing Rights which it is not allowed to exceed.

SPECIAL FORCES, branch of the US Army trained for action behind enemy lines, including intelligence work and subversion. Created after the Korean War, the Special Forces troops were highly active in the VIETNAM WAR.

SPECIATION, the process by which new species originate. Speciation either involves change in an organism, or divergence of a population that results in the formation of two new species; both are the result of EVOLUTION.

SPECIE CIRCULAR, a treasury circular issued at the orders of President Andrew JACKSON in 1836, directing that only gold and silver be received in payment for public lands. It may have contributed considerably to the 1837 money crisis.

SPECIES. See TAXONOMY.

SPECIFIC GRAVITY (sg), or **relative density**, ratio of the density of a substance to that of a reference material at a specified temperature, usually water at 4°C. If the sg of an inert substance is less than unity (1), it will float in water at 4°C. The sg of liquids is measured with a HYDROMETER.

SPECIFIC HEAT, the HEAT required to raise the temperature of 1kg of a substance through one KELVIN; expressed in J/K.kg, and measured by CALORIMETRY. The concept was introduced by Joseph BLACK; DULONG and Petit showed that the specific heat of elements is approximately inversely proportional to their ATOMIC WEIGHTS, which could thus be roughly determined.

SPECTACLED BEAR, *Tremarctos ornatus*, the only South American BEAR. Small, and with a shaggy dark coat, they are herbivorous.

SPECTACLES. See GLASSES.

SPECTROHELIOGRAPH, a device used to obtain spectroheliograms, composite photographs of the SUN in LIGHT of a single wavelength. An optical IMAGE of the sun is scanned by a slit admitting light to a PRISM which forms a SPECTRUM. A second slit is used to select a particular wavelength and expose a photographic plate passing behind it at the same rate as the first slit is scanning the image.

SPECTROPHOTOMETRY, the measurement of the intensity of different colors (wavelengths) present in a beam of light, normally using a PRISM or DIFFRACTION grating, and a PHOTOELECTRIC CELL. It is used for COLOR comparison and in chemical ANALYSIS.

SPECTROSCOPY, the production, measurement and analysis of SPECTRA; an essential tool of astronomers, chemists and physicists. All spectra arise from transitions between discrete energy states of matter, as a result of which PHOTONS of corresponding energy (and hence characteristic FREQUENCY or wavelength) are absorbed or emitted. From the energy levels thus determined, atomic and molecular structure may be studied. Moreover, by using the observed spectra as "fingerprints," spectroscopy may be a sensitive method of chemical ANALYSIS. Most of the different kinds of spectroscopy, corresponding to the various regions of ELECTROMAGNETIC RADIATION, relate to particular kinds of energy-level transitions. **Gamma-ray spectra** arise from nuclear energy-level transitions; **X-ray spectra** from inner-electron transitions in atoms; **ultraviolet** and **visible spectra** from outer (bonding) electron transitions in molecules (or atoms); **infrared spectra** from molecular vibrations; and **microwave spectra** from molecular rotations. There are several more specialized kinds of spectroscopy. **Raman spectroscopy**, based on the effect discovered by C. V. RAMAN, scans the scattered light from an intense monochromatic beam. Some of the scattered light is at lower (and higher) frequencies than the incident light, corresponding to vibration/rotation transitions. The technique thus supplements infrared spectroscopy. **Mössbauer spectroscopy**, based on the MÖSSBAUER EFFECT, gives information on the electronic or chemical environments of nuclei; as does **nuclear magnetic resonance spectroscopy** (nmr), based on transitions between nuclear SPIN states in a strong magnetic field. **Electron spin resonance spectroscopy** (esr) is similarly based on electron spin transitions when there is an unpaired electron in an ORBITAL, and so is used to study FREE RADICALS. The intrument used is a **spectroscope**, called a *spectrograph* if the spectrum is recorded photographically all at once, or a *spectrometer* if it is scanned by wavelength and calibrated from the instrument.

Finishing straight of the Indianapolis Motor Speedway at Speedway, Indianapolis, where the world famous Indianapolis 500 takes place.

SPECTRUM, the array of colors produced on passing LIGHT through a PRISM; also, by extension, the range of a phenomenon displayed in terms of one of its properties. ELECTROMAGNETIC RADIATION arranged according to wavelength thus forms the electromagnetic spectrum, of which that of visible light is only a minute part. Similarly the mass spectrum of a particular collection of ions displays their relative numbers as a function of their masses. (See SPECTROSCOPY; MASS SPECTROSCOPY.)

SPECULATION, the carrying out of business transactions with the intention of making rapid profit from price fluctuations. A *bull* or *buying long* is a speculation based on an anticipated price rise. *Bears* or *selling short* involve speculation on an expected price fall. The term is also used for investment in a risky but potentially very profitable undertaking.

SPEECH, FREEDOM OF. See FREEDOM OF SPEECH.

SPEECH AND SPEECH DISORDERS. Speech may be subdivided into conception, or formulation, and production, or phonation and articulation, of speech (see VOICE). Speech development in children starts with associating sounds with persons and objects, comprehension usually predating vocalization by some months. Nouns are developed first, often with one or two syllables only; later acquisition of verbs, adjectives, etc. allows the construction of phrases and sentences. A phase of babbling speech, where the child toys with sounds resembling speech, is probably essential for development. READING is closely related to speech development, involving the association of auditory and visual symbols. Speech involves coordination of many aspects of BRAIN function (HEARING, VISION, etc.) but three areas particularly concerned with aspects of speech are located in the dominant hemisphere of right-handed persons and in either hemisphere of left-handed people (see HANDEDNESS). DISEASE of these parts of the brain leads to characteristic forms of dysphasia or APHASIA, ALEXIA, etc. Developmental DYSLEXIA is a childhood defect of visual pattern recognition. Stammering or stuttering, with repetition and hesitation over certain syllables, is a common disorder, in some cases representing frustrated left-handedness. Dysarthria is disordered voice production and is due to disease of the neuromuscular control of voice. In speech therapy, attempts are made to overcome or circumvent speech difficulties, this being particularly important in children (see also DEAFNESS).

SPEED. See VELOCITY; also AMPHETAMINES.

SPEEDBALL, team game combining elements of soccer, basketball and football invented by Elmer D. Mitchell in 1921. The field and goal posts are the same as for football, and the team has 11 players. A "fly" ball which has not touched the field since it was last played may be caught and thrown, but a ground ball must be dribbled as in soccer.

SPEEDOMETER, instrument for indicating the speed of a motor vehicle. The common type works by magnetic INDUCTION. A circular permanent magnet is rotated by a flexible cable geared to the transmission. The rotating magnetic field induces a magnetic field in an aluminum cup, so tending to turn it in the same direction as the magnet. This TORQUE, proportional to the speed of rotation, is opposed by a spiral spring. The angle through which the cup turns against the spring measures the speed. The speedometer is usually coupled with an **odometer**, a counting device geared to the magnet, which registers the distance traveled.

SPEEDWAY, town in Ind., a W suburb of Indianapolis, the site of the Indianapolis auto racetrack. Pop 15 056.

SPEER, Albert (1905–), German Nazi leader who was Hitler's architect and who organized slave labor for Germany during WWII. For this last the international tribunal at Nuremberg sentenced him to 20 years imprisonment in SPANDAU.

SPEKE, John Hanning (1827–1864), English explorer, the first European to reach Victoria Nyanza (Lake Victoria) in E Africa, a source of the Nile (1858). Speke and James Grant found the Nile exit (Ripon Falls) in 1862.

SPELEOLOGY, the scientific study of CAVES. The world's first speleological society was founded in France in 1895, and interest soon became worldwide. The US National Speleological Society was founded in 1939. Less academic cave exploration is called spelunking.

SPELLMAN, Francis Joseph (1889–1967), US Roman Catholic cardinal from 1946. Ordained in 1916, he was the first American to be attached to the secretariat of state in the Vatican (1925). He became Archbishop of New York in 1939.

SPELUNKING. See SPELEOLOGY.

SPEMANN, Hans (1869–1941), German embryologist awarded the 1935 Nobel Prize for Physiology or Medicine for his researches into the development of the EMBRYO, showing that specific CELLS adopted specific functions not through any predetermination of form but because of the action of local chemical "organizers" (in fact, HORMONES).

SPENARD, urban community in S central Alaska, S of Anchorage on Cook Inlet. Pop 18 809.

SPENCER, city in NW Iowa, seat of Clay Co., at the confluence of the Little Sioux R and the Ocheyadan R. It has mixed light industry. Pop 10 278.

SPENCER, Herbert (1820–1903), English philosopher, social theorist and early evolutionist. In his multivolume *System of Synthetic Philosophy* (1862–96), he expounded a world view based on a close study of physical, biological and social phenomena, arguing that species evolve by a process of differentiation from the simple to the complex. His political individualism deeply influenced US social thinking. (See also SURVIVAL OF THE FITTEST.)

SPENDER, Stephen Harold (1909–), English poet and critic, coeditor of the literary magazine *Encounter* 1953–65. His poetry collections include *Poems* (1933), *Ruins and Visions* (1942) and *The Generous Days* (1971).

SPENGLER, Oswald (1880–1936), German philosopher whose cyclic view of history is expressed in *The Decline of the West* (1918–22), a study of the rise and fall of civilizations. He believed that Western civilization was entering a period of decline, a view much favored between the wars.

SPENSER, Edmund (c1522–1599), English poet, best known for the six books of his unfinished epic poem *The Faerie Queene* (1590–96), an allegorical work celebrating the moral values of Christian chivalry. Steeped in English folklore, the poem displays the monumental scope of a Homer or Virgil. His other works include *The Shepheardes Calender* (1579) and *Epithalamion* (1595).

SPERM, the male GAMETE or sex cell in animals. Sperm are usually motile, having a single flagellum (see REPRODUCTION).

SPERMACETI. See SPERM WHALES.

SPERMATOPHYTA, traditional but artificial division of the PLANT KINGDOM which includes the GYMNOSPERMS and ANGIOSPERMS. Although these two groups are related, it is now clear that other groups such as the FERNS (set apart in the PTERIDOPHYTA) are also closely allied.

SPERM WHALES, or **Cachalots**, a family of Toothed Whales, with two species: the cachalot, *Physeter catodon*, and Pigmy Sperm whale, *Kogia breviceps*. They are among the best known of all WHALES because of the enormous, squared head. The front of the head contains a huge reservoir of **spermaceti** oil, perhaps used as a lens to focus the sounds produced by the whales in echolocation. Spermaceti solidifies in cool air to form a wax once used for candles and cosmetics. Sperm whales are also the source of AMBERGRIS, a secretion in the gut produced in response to irritation by the beaks of SQUIDS, an important prey item. Sperm whales are found in all oceans, migrating from the poles into warmer waters during the breeding season. It is a deep water whale, capable of diving to 500m (1 640ft) or more. Females and young form large schools of up to several hundred animals. Males tend to travel alone or in small groups.

SPERRY, Elmer Ambrose (1860–1930), US inventor of the GYROCOMPASS (first installed in a ship, 1911) and of a high-intensity arc searchlight (1918).

SPEYER, or Speier, city in SW West Germany, on the Rhine R. Long a cultural and historical center, it is now also important for industry. Pop 42 323.

SPEYER, Diet of (1529), an assembly summoned by Emperor CHARLES V to settle the relationship between Lutheranism and the Roman Catholic Church. Lutherans protested (hence "Protestant") against its decision to continue hampering Lutheranism.

SPHAGNUM, or **peat moss**, a large genus of MOSSES all of which have remarkable water absorptive powers. Sphagnum is used for packing bulbs and flowers, as compost and on some occasions for surgical dressings. Decomposed Sphagnum is an important consituent of PEAT.

SPHALERITE, or **Blende**, the low-temperature (β) form of zinc sulfide (ZnS); the chief ore of ZINC, occurring worldwide with GALENA. It forms lustrous crystals of the isometric system, white when pure, but usually brown to black with iron impurity. (See also WURTZITE.)

SPHENODON. See TUATARA.

SPHENOPSIDA. See HORSETAILS.

SPHERE, the surface produced by the rotation of a CIRCLE through 180° about one of its diameters. The intersection of a sphere and any plane is circular; should the plane pass through the center, the intersection is a great circle (see also SPHERICAL GEOMETRY). The surface AREA of a sphere is $4\pi r^2$, where r is the radius; its VOLUME $4\pi r^3/3$. If mutually perpendicular (see ANGLE) x-, y- and z-AXES are constructed such that they intersect at the center, the sphere's equation is $x^2+y^2+z^2=r^2$. (See also ELLIPSOID.)

SPHERICAL COORDINATES, a system in which a POINT P in SPACE is located by its position relative to three mutually perpendicular AXES (the x-, y- and z-axes) in terms of (1) its distance r from the origin, 0, (2) the ANGLE (θ) between the x-axis and the PROJECTION of OP onto the x-y PLANE, and (3) the angle (ϕ) between OP and the z-axis. The coordinates of P are thus expressed in the form (r,θ,ϕ). (See also ANALYTIC GEOMETRY.)

SPHERICAL GEOMETRY, the branch of GEOMETRY dealing with figures drawn on the surface of a SPHERE; sometimes considered as a special case of RIEMANNIAN GEOMETRY. A CIRCLE whose center coincides with that of the sphere is a great circle, other circles on the sphere's surface being small circles: since a great circle may be drawn through any two POINTS on the sphere's surface, one deals primarily with great circles only. The lengths of arcs of great circles are always given in terms of the radius of the sphere and the ANGLE subtended by the arc at the center; i.e., in the form $r\theta$, where r is the radius and θ the angle. It is usually convenient to consider the sphere as of unit radius, thus expressing the length of an arc as an angle. Problems concerning **spherical triangles** are solved using spherical trigonometry.

SPHERICAL TRIGONOMETRY, the branch of SPHERICAL GEOMETRY dealing with the ratios between the sides and ANGLES of spherical TRIANGLES. The sum of the angles of a spherical triangle is always between 180° and 540°, and the amount by which this sum exceeds 180° for a particular triangle is termed the excess; the area of the triangle is $\pi r^2E/180°$, where r is the radius of the sphere and E the triangle's excess.

The relations between the sides and angles of spherical triangles are governed by the COSINE RULE and the SINE RULE. **Spherical Astronomy**, of importance in positional ASTRONOMY and SPACE EXPLORATION, is the application of spherical trigonometry to determinations of stellar positions on the CELESTIAL SPHERE.

SPHEROID. See ELLIPSOID.

SPHINCTER, muscle, group of muscles or aggregation of smooth (visceral) muscle fibers, that can temporarily prevent movement of the contents of hollow viscera under autonomic or voluntary control.

SPHINX, mythical monster of the ancient Middle East, in Egypt portrayed as a lion with a human head and used as a symbol of the pharaoh. In Greek mythology the sphinx propounded a riddle to travelers on the road to Thebes: when OEDIPUS answered correctly the sphinx threw herself from her rocky perch.

SPHYGMOMANOMETER, instrument for measuring blood pressure by determining the pressure (with a MANOMETER) in a cuff attached around a limb needed to prevent blood flow. A stethoscope is used to hear the changing sounds over the ARTERY as the cuff deflates.

SPICE, a large number of aromatic plant products which have a distinctive flavor or aroma and are used to season food. Most spices are obtained from tropical plants and were once highly valued as a means of making poor quality food more palatable. (See also HERB.)

SPICE BUSH, *Lindera benzoin*, an aromatic shrub whose bark contains a fragrant oil. It is cultivated as a substitute for ALLSPICE. Found in damp areas of eastern North America, it bears yellow flowers in early spring. Family: Lauraceae.

SPICE ISLANDS, name once given to the MOLUCCAS.

SPIDER MONKEYS, *Ateles*, a genus of slender, fruit-eating MONKEYS of South and Middle America. Living in the high canopy, they sleep in groups of up to 100, breaking up into smaller feeding groups by day.

SPIDER PLANT, *Chlorophytum vittatum*, a popular evergreen house plant that produces narrow, linear green leaves that have white or cream longitudinal stripes. It produces small, insignificant flowers on long stems, but new plantlets develop directly from the flowers. They grow well at average house temperatures and require only a small amount of direct light. The soil should be kept evenly moist; the foliage benefits from misting. Propagation is by removing the plantlets or by dividing the plants. Family: Liliaceae.

SPIDERS, an order, Araneida, of the Arachnida, with the body divided into two parts, and with four pairs of walking legs. Unlike INSECTS, spiders have no antennae, have simple, not compound, EYES, and no larval or pupal stages. They are an incredibly diverse group of some 26 000 species. The evolution of spiders is closely linked with that of the insects on which they prey: as insects developed abilities of jumping, gliding and later flying, and evolved stings and other defenses, so the spiders developed so as still to be able to capture their changing prey. Thus from primitive running spiders have evolved such groups as the JUMPING SPIDERS; WOLF SPIDERS; Trapdoor spiders, and, of course, the Web-spinners.

SPIDERWORT, perennial herbs of the genus *Tradescantia*, native to tropical and temperate America, and cultivated as house plants. Their hairy stems produce a sticky substance which can be drawn out into fine threads. The three-petaled flowers occur in clusters which open and die within one day. Family: Commelinaceae. (See also WANDERING JEW.)

SPIEGELEISEN, an ALLOY based on PIG IRON, containing 5% carbon and 15%–30% MANGANESE. It is added during STEEL manufacture as a reducing agent and to supply manganese.

SPIKENARD, an aromatic ointment derived from an Indian plant (*Nardostachys jatamansi*). The name is also given to a herb (*Aralia racemosa*) growing in North America which has greenish flowers, red or purple berries and aromatic roots.

SPILLWAY. See DAM.

SPIN, intrinsic angular MOMENTUM of a nucleus or SUBATOMIC PARTICLE arising from its rotation about an axis within itself. Every particle has a definite spin, s, given by $nh/4\pi$, where n is an INTEGER and h is the PLANCK CONSTANT.

SPINA BIFIDA, congenital defect of the SPINAL CORD and spinal canal leading to a variable degree of leg PARALYSIS and loss of urine and feces SPHINCTER control; it may be associated with other malformation—particularly HYDROCEPHALUS. It is an embryological disorder due to failure of fusion of the neural tube. SURGERY has made it possible to treat mild cases by closure of the defect and ORTHOPEDIC procedures can be applied to balance muscle power. Also, any hydrocephalus must be shunted.

SPINACH, *Spinacia oleracea*, a leafy annual widely cultivated as a vegetable. Spinach leaves have a relatively high content of iron and VITAMINS A and C. Family: Chenopodiceae.

SPINAL COLUMN. See VERTEBRAE.

SPINAL CORD, the part of the central NERVOUS SYSTEM outside the SKULL. It joins the BRAIN at the base of the skull, forming the *medulla oblongata*, and extends downward in a bony canal enclosed in the VERTEBRAE. Between the bone and cord are three sheaths of connective TISSUE called the *meninges*. A section of the cord shows a central core of *gray matter* (containing the cell bodies of nerve fibers running either to the muscles or within the cord itself), completely surrounded by *white matter* (composed solely of nerve fibers). There is a central canal containing CEREBROSPINAL FLUID, which opens into the cavities of the brain.

SPINAL TAP, or **lumbar puncture**, procedure to remove CEREBROSPINAL FLUID (CSF) from the lumbar spinal canal using a fine needle. It is used in diagnosis of MENINGITIS, ENCEPHALITIS, MULTIPLE SCLEROSIS and TUMORS. In NEUROLOGY, it may be used in treatment, by reducing CSF pressure or allowing insertion of DRUGS.

SPINELLO ARETINO (c1346–1410), Italian painter of the late Gothic period whose most important works are two series of frescoes at the Campo Santo, Pisa and the Palazzo Pubblico, Siena.

SPINELS, group of OXIDE minerals of general formula $M_2^{III}M^{II}O_4$, formed in high-temperature IGNEOUS or METAMORPHIC ROCKS. The chief members are spinel itself, aluminum magnesium oxide, with some GEM varieties; CHROMITE; and MAGNETITE. Free substitution occurs. Synthetic spinels are used as refractories and in solid-state components.

SPINET, type of small HARPSICHORD which probably originated in 16th-century Italy. Inside the wing-shaped cabinet a single set of strings is set at an oblique angle to the keyboard. The name is also used for a small upright piano.

SPINNING, the ancient craft of twisting together FIBERS from a mass to form strong, continuous thread suitable for weaving. The earliest method was merely to roll the fibers between hand and thigh. Later two sticks were used: the distaff to hold the bundle of fibers, and a spindle to twist and wind the yarn. Mechanization began with the spinning wheel, invented in India and spreading to Europe by the 14th century. The wheel turned the spindle by means of a belt drive. In the 15th century the flyer was invented: a device on the spindle shaft that winds the yarn automatically on a spool. Improved WEAVING methods in the Industrial Revolution caused increased demand which provoked several inventions. The spinning jenny, invented by James HARGREAVES (c1767), spun as many as 16 threads at once, the spindles all being driven by the same wheel. Richard ARKWRIGHT's "water frame" (1769), so called from being water-powered, had rollers and produced strong thread. Then Samuel CROMPTON produced a hybrid of the two—his "mule"—which had a movable carriage, and was the forerunner of the modern machine. The other modern spinning machine is the ring-spinning frame (1828) in which the strands, drawn out by rollers, are twisted by a "traveler" that revolves on a ring around the bobbin on which they are wound.

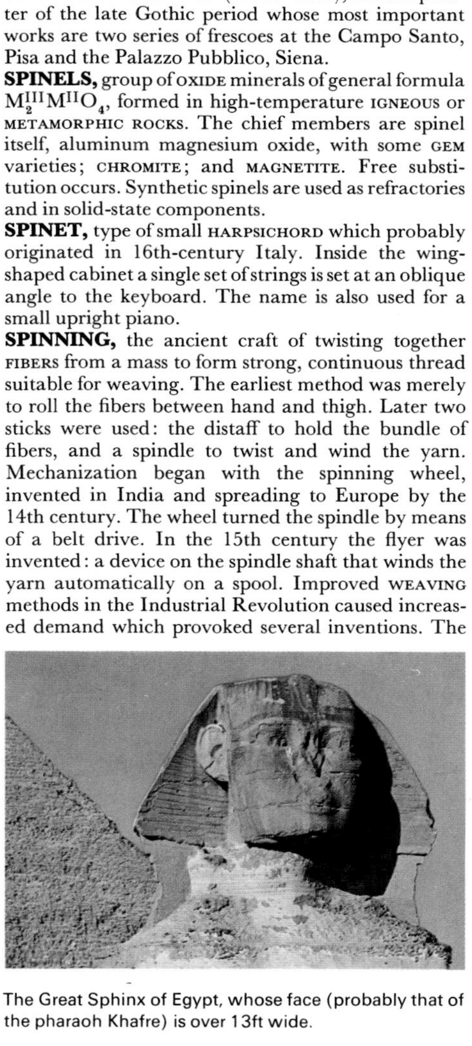

The Great Sphinx of Egypt, whose face (probably that of the pharaoh Khafre) is over 13ft wide.

SPÍNOLA, António Sebastião Ribeiro de (1910–), Portuguese army officer and political leader. Chief of staff in Portuguese Guinea 1968–72, in Mar. 1974 he was dismissed from the army for asserting in a book that Portuguese military victory in Africa was impossible. In April he led a military coup, and became provisional president until Sept. (See PORTUGAL.)

SPINOZA, Baruch or **Benedict de** (1632–1677), Dutch philosopher and rationalist (see RATIONALISM) who held that God is the totality of all things which exist, an interpretation which brought him expulsion from the Amsterdam Jewish community. Influenced by DESCARTES, he preached the right of all men to free speech and free thought. His most famous work is *Ethics* (1677). Organized "in the geometric style" like EUCLID's *Elements*, it contains the development of his mystical pantheism.

SPINY ANTEATER. See ECHIDNA.

SPIRAL, in plane ANALYTIC GEOMETRY, a CURVE traced by a POINT which either approaches or recedes from an origin while moving around it. The most frequently encountered is the Archimedean Spiral, whose equation in polar coordinates is $r = a\theta$ (see ARCHIMEDES). Others include the logarithmic spiral $r = e^{a\theta}$ (see EXPONENT; EXPONENTIAL) and the hyperbolic spiral $r = a/\theta$. Three-dimensional spirals such as the HELIX are traced by points moving about an axis.

SPIREA, a genus of N Hemisphere shrubs which bear tall clusters of pink or white flowers. Wild species include MEADOWSWEET, hardhack and queen-of-the-meadow. Family: Rosaceae.

SPIRILLUM, a type of BACTERIA, spiral in form.

SPIRIT LEVEL. See LEVEL.

SPIRITS, Distilled. See ALCOHOLIC BEVERAGES; DISTILLED LIQUOR.

SPIRITUAL, a form of religious folk song developed by the Negro slaves and their descendants in the southern US states. It usually consists of a number of verses for solo voice, with a rhythmic choral refrain.

SPIRITUALISM, religious movement believing in survival of the human personality after departure from this plane of being (i.e., "death"), and its ability to communicate with those left behind, usually through a medium. Spiritualist beliefs have had powerful effects, both for good and for bad, on the advance of psychic research (see PARAPSYCHOLOGY).

SPIROCHETE, spiral BACTERIA, species of which are responsible for RELAPSING FEVER, YAWS and syphilis (see VENEREAL DISEASES).

SPIROGYRA, filamentous green ALGAE consisting of long chains of CELLS. Free-floating, they often appear as a scum on still water.

SPITSBERGEN. See SVALBARD.

SPITTELER, Carl Friedrich Georg (1845–1924), Swiss poet, winner of the 1919 Nobel Prize for Literature. His heroic epics *Prometheus and Epimetheus* (1881) and *Olympic Spring* (1900–05; 1910) stressed spiritual nobility.

SPITTLE BUGS, Hemipteran insects of the family Cercopidae, also known as **Frog hoppers** or Cuckoo-spit insects. The name derives from the habit of nymphal stages, in the leaf stems of plants, of enveloping themselves in a frothy mass of bubbles, protecting the soft-bodied NYMPHS from direct exposure to the sun.

SPITZ, a general term for a group of stocky northern dogs including the chow chow, Samoyed and Pomeranian. They have a long, dense coat, tail curved over the back, and pointed, erect ears. The 25lb American spitz has a white coat.

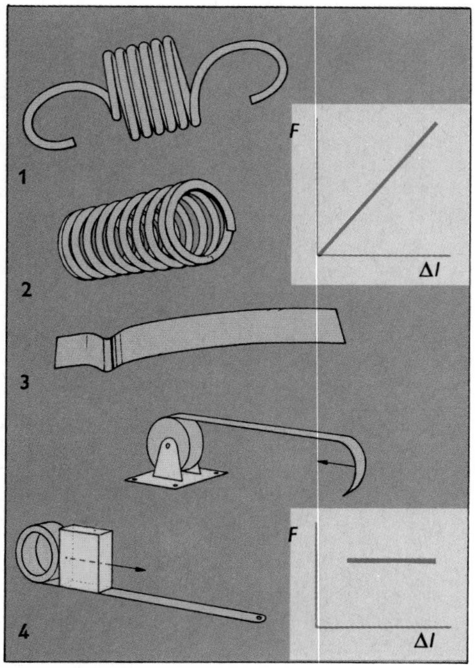

Some varieties of spring, and their specialized uses. On the graphs, F = force; Δl = displacement.
(1) Helical tension spring (steelyard or weighbeam).
(2) Helical compression spring (auto suspension).
(3) Flat bending spring (springboard).
(4) Constant-tension spiral spring (watch, clock).
In both types shown here, the inner end of the spiral spring is not anchored.

SPLEEN, spongy vascular lymphoid organ (see LYMPH) between the STOMACH and DIAPHRAGM on the left side of the ABDOMEN. A center for the RETICULOENDOTHELIAL SYSTEM, it also eliminates worn-out red BLOOD cells, recycling their iron. Most of its functions are duplicated by other organs. The spleen was classically the source of black bile, or melancholy (see HUMORS).

SPLENIC FEVER, name for ANTHRAX in animals.

SPLIT (formerly Spalato), seaport and commercial center on the Adriatic coast of S Croatia, Yugoslavia, noted for its Roman remains, especially the palace of DIOCLETIAN. Pop 151 875.

SPOCK, Benjamin McLane (1903–), known worldwide as "Dr. Spock," US pediatrician and pacifist best known for his *(Common Sense Book of) Baby and Child Care* (1946), which advocated a more liberal attitude on the part of parents, and *Bringing up Children in a Difficult Time* (1974).

SPODE, British family of pottery makers. **Josiah Spode** (1733–1797), founded the Spode works at Stoke-on-Trent and introduced transfer decoration and oriental motifs. **Josiah Spode** (1754–1827), developed stone china, porcelain and BONE CHINA. He popularized the willow pattern and gained royal patronage. (See also POTTERY AND PORCELAIN.)

SPODUMENE, a lithium-bearing PYROXENE, $LiAlSi_2O_6$; a major LITHIUM ore found in PEGMATITES, forming clear, monoclinic crystals, often large and when colored used as GEM stones.

SPOHR, Ludwig (Louis) (1784–1859), violinist, composer and conductor of the Romantic period. Among his extensive works are 9 symphonies and 11 operas, including *Faust* (1816) and *Jessonda* (1823).

SPOILS SYSTEM, the use of appointments to public offices to reward supporters of a victorious political party. With the growth of a two-party system in the US, political patronage increased. It was President Jackson's friend Senator William L. Marcy who said in 1832 that "to the victor belong the spoils," and the system soon operated on every political level. The PENDLETON ACT of 1883, introducing competitive entrance examinations for public employees, marked the gradual introduction of a merit system.

SPOKANE, second-largest city in Wash., on the Spokane R about 20mi W of the Ida. line. Manufactures include aluminum, foodstuffs, paper and wood products, cement, electronic equipment and rolling stock. It is an important cultural center. Pop 170 516.

SPONGES, primitive animals of both marine and fresh water, phylum Parazoa (Porifera). Sponges are true ANIMALS, although they have only a simple body wall and no specialized organ or tissue systems. They may be solitary or colonial. They are filter-feeders, straining tiny food particles out of water drawn in through pores all over the body surface, and expelled through one or more exhalant vents. The body wall is strengthened by spicules of CALCITE or SILICA, or by a meshwork of PROTEIN fibers: spongin. Sponges with spongin skeletons are fished for bath sponges. Sponges can exhibit REGENERATION to a remarkable degree. A sponge strained through silk to break it up into its component cells can reorganize itself into a functional sponge.

SPONTANEOUS COMBUSTION, COMBUSTION occurring without external ignition, caused by slow OXIDATION or FERMENTATION which (if heat cannot readily escape) raises the temperature to burning point. It may occur when hay or small coal is stored.

SPONTANEOUS GENERATION, or **abiogenesis**, theory, dating from the writings of ARISTOTLE, that living creatures can arise from nonliving matter. The idea remained current even after it had become clear that higher orders of life could not be created in this way; and it was only with the work of REDI, showing that maggots did not appear in decaying meat to which flies had been denied access, and PASTEUR, who proved that the equivalent was true of microorganisms (i.e., BACTERIA), that the theory was finally discarded.

SPOONBILLS, graceful, stork-like birds related to IBISES, with long straight bills broadening to spatulate tips. They feed by sweeping their bills from side to side in water and picking up anything edible they may encounter. There are four species in the Old World genus *Platalea*, which all have essentially white plumage. Their New World relative *Ajaia ajaja*, the Roseate spoonbill, has a rosy pink coloration.

SPORADES ISLANDS (Greek: scattered ones), two groups in the Aegean Sea, belonging to Greece. The N group includes Skopelos, Skiathos and Skyros. The S group includes Rhodes.

SPORE, minute single or multicelled body produced during the process of reproduction of many plants, particularly BACTERIA, ALGAE and FUNGI and in some PROTOZOA. The structure of spores varies greatly and depends upon the means of dissemination from the parent. Some, e.g., the zoospores of algae, are motile.

SPOROPHYTE, phase of the life-cycle of a plant representing the diploid generation. (See ALTERNATION OF GENERATIONS.)

SPOROZOANS, a group of parasitic PROTOZOANS of the groups Sporozoa and Cnidospora. All are parasitic and most have spore-like infective stages. They include the gregarines and coccidians, the latter including the organisms which cause MALARIA in humans.

SPOTSWOOD, Alexander (1676–1740), English lieutenant-governor and administrator of VIRGINIA colony, 1710–22. He promoted settlement to the W and fostered tobacco-growing and the iron industry.

SPOTSYLVANIA COURT HOUSE, Battle of (1864), in the American CIVIL WAR, bloody failure by General GRANT to dislodge Confederates blocking his way to their capital at Richmond, Va.

SPRAGUE, Frank Julian (1857–1934), US inventor of high-speed electric ELEVATORS and electric RAILROAD systems, including that now used in the New York SUBWAY.

SPRAIN. See LIGAMENT.

SPRAYING, in agriculture. See CROP DUSTING.

SPRECHSTIMME (German: speech-voice), in music, a mixture of speaking and singing. Though it had been used earlier, the first major use was in SCHOENBERG's *Pierrot Lunaire* (1912).

SPRING, a naturally occurring flow of water from the ground. This may be, for example, an outflow from an underground stream; but most often a spring occurs where an AQUIFER saturated with GROUNDWATER intersects with the earth's surface. Such an aquifer, if confined above and below by aquicludes, may travel for hundreds of kilometres underground before emerging to the surface, there, perhaps, in desert areas giving rise to OASES. Spring water is generally fairly clean, since it has been filtered through the permeable rocks; but all spring water contains some dissolved MINERALS. (See also GEYSER; HOT SPRINGS; WELL.)

SPRING, mechanical device that exhibits ELASTICITY according to HOOKE's Law. Most springs are made of steel, brass or bronze. The commonest type is the **helical spring**, a helical coil of stiff wire, loose-wound if to be compressed, tight-wound if to be extended under tension. They have many uses, including closing valves, spring BALANCES and ACCELEROMETERS. The **spiral spring** is a wire or strip coiled in one plane, responding to TORQUE applied at its inner end, and used to store energy, notably in CLOCKS AND WATCHES. The **leaf spring**, used in vehicle suspension systems, consists of several steel strips of different lengths clamped on top of each other at one end. When deformed, springs store potential ENERGY, and exert a restoring FORCE. Hydraulic and air springs work by compression of a fluid in a cylinder.

SPRING. See SEASONS.

SPRING BEAUTY, a number of early flowering wild plants of the genus *Claytonia* which are native to woodlands of eastern North America. They bear white, star-like flowers tinted with pink. Family: Portulacaceae.

SPRINGBOK, *Antidorcas marsupialis*, a colored GAZELLE once common throughout southern Africa, but now found mainly in the Kalahari desert. The Latin name refers to a large pouch on the back, everted as a warning signal to reveal a patch of white hair.

SPRINGER SPANIEL, English, all-round gundog with orange and white or liver and white coat. It points game instead of flushing it like the typical spaniel. Stands 21in tall, weighs about 40lb.

SPRINGER SPANIEL, Welsh, breed of sporting dog slightly smaller than its English counterpart and also distinguished by its dark red and white coloring. Stands 18–19in high and weighs 35–45lb.

SPRINGFIELD, capital of Ill., on the Sangamon R, central Ill. The city's economy is based on government, manufacturing and the marketing and processing of wheat and soybeans. Springfield became state capital in 1837 through the work of the "Long Nine" led by Abraham LINCOLN, whose home and tomb attract many visitors. Pop 91 753.

SPRINGFIELD, third-largest city of Mass., seat of Hampden Co., on the Connecticut R. Long famous for firearms, it is a major producer of machinery, chemicals and electrical equipment, and is noted for its museums and galleries. Pop 163 905.

SPRINGFIELD, city in SW Miss., seat of Greene Co., the manufacturing, distribution and processing center for a region of orchards, livestock and dairy farms and timberland. Pop 120 096.

SPRINGFIELD, residential town in NE N.J., just W of Newark, with light industry. Here General GREENE's Continentals forced a British retreat in June 1780. Pop 15 583.

SPRINGFIELD, city in W central Ohio, seat of Clark Co. on the Mad R. It produces a wide range of machinery. Pop 81 941.

SPRINGFIELD, city in W Ore. just E of Eugene on the Willamette R, the industrial center for a region of farmland and forests. Pop 27 047.

SPRINGFIELD, urban township, suburb of Philadelphia, SE Pa. Pop 22 394.

SPRINGFIELD, town in E Vt., on the Black R, an industrial center noted for machine tools. Pop 10 063.

SPRINGFIELD, unincorporated urban area, NE Va., 10mi S of the center of Washington D.C. Pop 11 613.

SPRINGFIELD RIFLE, breechloading rifle used as US army standard issue in WWI. From 1936 to 1960 the army used the M1 or Garand rifle, also made at Springfield, Mass.

SPRING GARDEN, urban township in S Pa., S of York. Pop 12 443.

SPRINGS, industrial city in the Transvaal, South Africa, 30mi E of Johannesburg, the center of a gold- and uranium-mining area. Pop 104090.

SPRINGTAILS, an order, Collembola, of small wingless insects occurring in extremely large numbers in the soil or at the soil surface. Unusual among insects in that there is no METAMORPHOSIS in the life history, Collembola also have anatomical peculiarities. Some of the legs of the ABDOMEN are retained, and the final pair is modified to form a powerful springing organ.

SPRING VALLEY, village in SE N.Y., a residential community and summer resort in a fruit-farming area. Pop 18112.

SPRUANCE, Raymond Ames (1886–1969), US admiral who commanded the cruiser force at the battle of MIDWAY in 1942, when four Japanese aircraft carriers were sunk. He was later chief of the Pacific Fleet.

SPRUCE, evergreen coniferous trees of the genus *Picea* with a conical form. There are some 40 species, all of which grow in the cooler regions of the N Hemisphere. Among the species found in the US are the Black (*Picea mariana*), Blue (*P. pungens*) and White (*P. glauca*) spruces. Spruce wood is used for pulp and general construction work and the whole trees as Christmas decorations. Family: Pinaceae.

SPURGE, common name for a number of species of plants from the genus *Euphorbia*, the stems of which contain a milky latex that is often used as a purgative. They range from water plants to desert succulents. Family: Euphorbiaceae.

SPUTNIK. See SATELLITES, ARTIFICIAL.

SPY. See ESPIONAGE; INTELLIGENCE SERVICE.

SPYRI, Johanna (née Heusser; 1829–1901), Swiss writer of children's books. *Heidi* (1880–81), set in the Swiss Alps, has become a worldwide classic.

SQUALL, a sudden increase in WIND speed of 8m/s or more, raising the wind speed to at least 11m/s and lasting for one minute or longer. Commonly associated with thunderstorms and heavy rain, squalls may do great damage. A **squall line** is a line of thunderstorms often hundreds of kilometres long with squalls along its advancing edge.

SQUANTO (d.1622), Pawtuxet Indian who befriended the newly arrived PILGRIMS, acting as their interpreter in dealings with MASSASOIT, and teaching them how to grow corn.

SQUARE, a regular QUADRILATERAL. In ALGEBRA, the square (x^2) of a number, x, is defined as $x \times x$: e.g., $10^2 = 10 \times 10 = 100$.

SQUARE DANCE, popular, lively American folk dance in which four couples formed in a square carry out steps and formations under the direction of a caller. It dates back to the quadrille dances of 15th-century Europe. (See also FOLK DANCING.)

SQUARE DEAL, policy of Theodore ROOSEVELT, when presidential candidate (1912), seeking to reconcile the demands of both workers and industrialists.

SQUARE ROOT. See ROOTS.

SQUASH, game similar to RACKETS but played with a softer, less bouncy ball. Singles squash is played on an indoor court 18½ft wide by 32ft long. Doubles squash requires a larger court. The ball may be hit against any of the four walls as long as it bounces on the front wall before striking the ground. The opponent must strike the ball before it bounces twice.

SQUASH, *Cucurbita maxima*, a gourd related to the PUMPKINS, native to tropical America. It is grown as a food and as cattle fodder. Winter squash varieties, which produce fruit weighing up to 45kg (100lb), are resistant to the cold. Family: Cucurbitaceae.

SQUATTER SOVEREIGNTY, or "popular sovereignty," a doctrine intended to end congressional controversy over the expansion of slavery just before the US Civil War. The inhabitants of a territory were to be allowed to decide for themselves whether or not to permit slavery. It was applied to Ut. and N.M. through the COMPROMISE OF 1850, and a popular sovereignty clause was included in the KANSAS-NEBRASKA ACT (1854) which repealed the MISSOURI COMPROMISE.

SQUAW VALLEY, in E Cal. in the Sierra Nevada, a skiing center, site of the 1960 Winter Olympics.

SQUETEAGUE. See WEAKFISH.

SQUIDS, shell-less CEPHALOPOD mollusks, order Teuthoidea. Although a few species live in coastal waters the majority are open ocean forms. Squids are streamlined animals with ten arms around the head, facing forward. The mantle at the rear of the body houses the gills and the openings of the excretory, sex and digestive organs. Sudden contraction of the whole mantle cavity sends out a blast of water that can be directed forward or backward by a movable funnel, providing the main means of propulsion. All squids can swim very rapidly and are active predators of fish, shooting out the long arms, provided with suckers and hooks, to grab their prey.

SQUILL, European herbs of the genus *Scilla* with attractive bell-shaped flowers and poisonous bulbs. Closely related, the Red squill (*Urginea maritima*) yields rat poison. Other species include the bluebell (*Scilla nonscripta*), common in British woodland clearings. Family: Liliaceae.

SQUINT. See STRABISMUS.

SQUIRREL FISHES, shallow-water tropical fishes of the family Holocentridae. Nocturnal fishes of coral reefs, they seem to be ancestral to the great modern group of perch-like fishes, Perciformes.

SQUIRREL MONKEY, *Saimiri sciurea*, one of the most abundant of the New World monkeys. Small monkeys of gallery forest and forest edge, they live in large troops, feeding on fruit and insects.

SQUIRRELS, one of the largest families, Sciuridae, of rodents. Commonly, the name refers only to Tree squirrels (see also GROUND SQUIRRELS). Tree squirrels are found in most forested parts of the world. Typically they have long bushy tails and short muzzles. They are diurnal, feeding on seeds, nuts and leaf buds, with some insect or other animal food. A number of temperate species, while not true hibernants, store food for the winter and enter deep torpor.

SQUIRRELTAIL GRASS, a species of wild BARLEY (*Hordeum jubatum*) which in North America often occurs as a troublesome weed in pastures and along roadside verges. Family: Gramineae.

SRI LANKA, formerly **Ceylon**, independent island republic within the British Commonwealth, separated from SE India by the Gulf of Mannar, Palk Strait and Adam's Bridge, a 30mi chain of shoals.

Land and Climate. Sri Lanka is about 270mi N–S and 140mi E–W. The mountainous central S area rises to Pidurutalagala (8281ft) and ADAM'S PEAK (7360ft); the major rivers, including the Mahaweli Ganga, rise here. Around the mountains stretches a coastal plain, up to 100mi wide in the N. Climate is tropical, but the island situation gives more equable temperatures than mainland India (around 81°F at Colombo). Rainfall ranges from 40in in the N to 200in in the SW mountains. In many areas the original tropical forest has been cleared for agriculture.

People. The few cities include the capital, COLOMBO on the W coast, JAFFNA in the N, KANDY in the S central mountains, Trincomalee on the E coast and Galle in the SW. Buddhist Sinhalese form 75% of the fast-growing population, and SINHALESE is the official language. Others include the Hindu Tamils, the forest Veddas (probably the aboriginal inhabitants), the Burghers (Christian descendants of Dutch-Sinhalese ancestors), the Moors and Malay Muslims.

Economy. Sri Lanka produces one third of the world's tea and over 100000 tons of rubber a year. Coconuts are commercially grown for their oil, but rice, the main food crop, has to be supplemented by imports. The country is the world's chief producer of high-grade graphite. Power is mainly hydroelectric. There is a good road and rail system.

History. The island was settled around 550 BC by Sinhalese who built ANURADHAPURA and made the island a center of Buddhist thought. From the 12th to the 16th century the Tamils held the N part. Europeans arrived in the 1500s, lured by the spice trade; they called the island Ceylon. Held by the Portuguese (landed 1505), the Dutch (after 1658) and finally the British (from 1796), the island attained independence in 1948 and became a republic in 1956. In 1972 Ceylon adopted a new constitution and the Sinhalese name Sri Lanka.

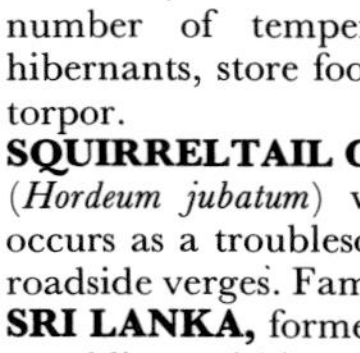

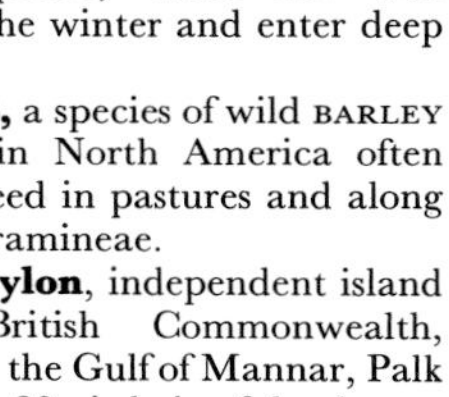

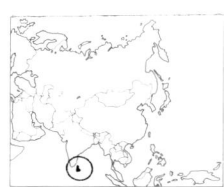

Official name: Republic of Sri Lanka
Capital: Colombo
Area: 25325sq mi
Population: 13000000
Languages: Sinhalese; English, Tamil
Religions: Buddhist, Hindu, Christian
Monetary unit(s): 1 Sri Lanka rupee = 100 cents

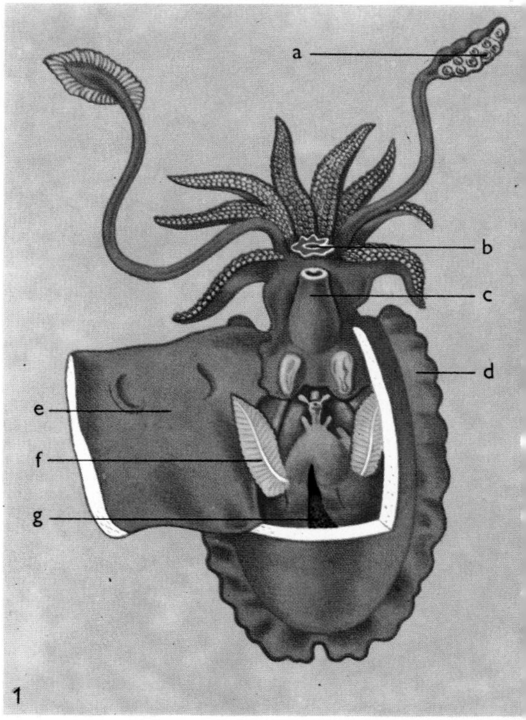

A typical squid, dissected to show the internal organs. (a) Tentacular sucker pads; (b) mouth; (c) siphon funnel, used for propulsion; (d) fin; (e) mantle wall; (f) gill; (g) ink sac.

SRINAGAR, summer capital of Jammu and KASHMIR state, India, on the JHELUM RIVER. It is a tourist center noted for its woolens, carpets and silks and for its waterways and Shalimar Gardens. Pop 403612.

SS (abbreviation of *Schutzstaffel*: defense echelons) or Blackshirts, dreaded elite corps of Nazi Germany, commanded by HIMMLER. It comprised the secret police (see GESTAPO), Hitler's personal bodyguard, the guards of the concentration and extermination camps, and some divisions of picked combat troops. (See NAZISM.)

SST (from *s*uper*s*onic *t*ransport), civil aircraft capable of supersonic speeds. The Soviet Tu-144 and British–French Concorde first flew in 1970 and are now in regular service. US plans for an SST were abandoned in 1971.

STABILIZER. See AIRPLANE; GYROSTABILIZER.

STADHOLDER, official title of provincial governors in the LOW COUNTRIES from the 16th century until 1795. The power of the princes of Orange depended on the Dutch stadholderates to which they were appointed or elected. (See ORANGE, HOUSE OF.)

STAËL, Anne Louise Germaine, Madame de (1766–1817), French-Swiss novelist and critic, celebrated personality and liberal opponent of Napoleon's regime, daughter of Jacques NECKER. A noted interpreter of German ROMANTICISM, she maintained brilliant salons in Paris and in exile near Geneva. She had liaisons with TALLEYRAND and CONSTANT.

STAFFORDSHIRE TERRIER, a bulldog/fox terrier cross specially bred in 19th-century England for dog fights, once known as the pit bull terrier. Standing about 18in tall and weighing 35–50lb, it is shortcoated, stocky and powerful.

STAFFORDSHIRE TERRIER, American, dog breed developed in the US. Standing 18–19in high and weighing 38lb, it is larger than the English Staffordshire Bull Terrier but, like that bull and bear-baiting breed, it is strong and courageous as its other names of Pit Dog and Bull Terrier suggest. Colors can be brindle, black, blue, red, fawn and white, or any of these with white.

STAG BEETLES, large BEETLES in which the males have enormous antler-like projections on the jaws. Many tropical species reach 100mm (4in) in length, with jaws equal in length to the rest of the body. The larvae feed on buried rotting wood.

STAGECOACH, closed coach, usually seating four to eight passengers and drawn by teams of two to six horses, traveling regularly between two stages. It was the principal means of public transportation in 18th- and 19th-century Europe and the US until superseded by railroads.

STAGE DESIGN. See THEATER.

STAGG, Amos Alonzo (1862–1965), US football coach. His career spanned 71 seasons, including 41 (1892–1932) with the University of Chicago. He was in the first All-American team (1889), developed many football formations and also promoted basketball.

STAHL, Georg Ernst (1660–1734), Bavarian-born German physician and chemist who developed the PHLOGISTON theory to explain combustion.

STAINED GLASS, pieces of colored glass held in place by a framework, usually of grooved lead strips (cames), to form patterns or pictures in a window. The earliest such windows date from the 11th century, but the art reached its highest development in the great period of GOTHIC ARCHITECTURE, c1150–1500: the series of windows made 1200–1240 for CHARTRES cathedral is perhaps the most famous example. Interest revived with the work of Edward BURNE-JONES and, in the US, the designs of Louis TIFFANY and John LA FARGE. Among recent masters of stained glass are the painters MATISSE, Fernand LÉGER, ROUAULT and CHAGALL. The glass is colored during manufacture, by mixing it with various metallic oxides; then cut according to the artist's full-scale cartoons. Details may be painted on to the glass with colored enamels, which fuse to the glass surface when it is heated.

Detail of one of the great stained glass windows in Chartres Cathedral, France, dating from the 13th century. Intricately designed and heavily leaded, it depicts Noah's Ark at the height of the Flood.

STAINLESS STEEL, corrosion-resistant STEEL containing more than 10% chromium, little carbon, and often nickel and other metals. Made in the ELECTRIC FURNACE, there are four main types: ferritic, martensitic, austenitic and precipitation-hardening. Stainless steel is used for cutlery and many industrial components.

STAKED PLAIN. See LLANO ESTACADO.

STALACTITES AND STALAGMITES, rocky structures found growing downward from the roof (stalactites) and upward from the floor (stalagmites) of CAVES formed in LIMESTONE. Rainwater percolates through the rocks above the cave and, as it contains atmospheric CARBON dioxide, can dissolve calcium carbonate en route. On reaching the cave, the water drips from the roof to the floor; as a drop hangs, some water evaporates, leaving a little calcium carbonate as CALCITE on the roof. Repetition forms a stalactite; and evaporation of the fallen water on the floor forms a stalagmite. On occasion, the rising stalagmite and descending stalactite fuse to form a pillar.

STALIN, Joseph (1879–1953), dictatorial ruler of the Soviet Union from 1929 until his death. Born Josif Vissarionovich Dzhugashvili, a Georgian village shoemaker's son intended for the priesthood, he joined the Georgian Social Democratic Party in 1901, becoming its Tiflis organizer in 1905. In 1912 LENIN coopted him onto the Bolshevik central committee, to which he was elected in 1917. After the RUSSIAN REVOLUTION he advanced rapidly. In 1922 he was elected general secretary of the Russian Communist Party. In the struggle for the leadership after Lenin's death (1924) he ousted from the Politburo first Trotsky (1925) then Kamenev and Zinoviev (1926). In 1928 he launched a vast development and industrialization program that involved the forced collectivization of agriculture and massive social redeployment. He also sought to "Russianize" the Soviet Union, attempting to eradicate by force the separate identities of minorities. Dissent was met with a powerful secret police, informers, mass deportations, executions and show trials. In 1935 Stalin initiated the first of the great "purges" which spared neither his family nor former political associates. Equally ruthless in foreign affairs, he partitioned Poland with Germany, and invaded Finland (1939) and imposed communist rule on the Baltic states (1940). The reversal of German fortunes on the WWII Eastern Front strengthened his hand. In 1945 at YALTA he sealed the postwar fate of East Europe to his satisfaction. Thereafter, he pursued COLD WAR policies abroad and supported rapid industrial recovery at home until his death from a brain hemorrhage. Almost immediately a process of "destalinization" began, culminating in KHRUSHCHEV's 1956 attack on the stalinist terror and personality cult.

STALINGRAD. See VOLGOGRAD.

STALINGRAD, Battle of, decisive engagement in WWII, fought in the vicinity of Stalingrad (now Volgograd) from Aug. 1942 to Feb. 1943. The 500 000-strong German 6th army under von Paulus surrounded the city on Sept. 14, 1942, but was itself encircled early in 1943 by a Russian army under ZHUKOV and forced to surrender. Not only was the German invasion halted, but the psychological initiative was wrested from the Nazis for the remainder of the war.

STALWARTS, US Republican Party faction that supported the SPOILS SYSTEM and opposed civil service reform by President HAYES and his "Half-breeds." Later "Stalwarts" campaigned for nomination of Ulysses S. GRANT in 1880 for a third presidential term.

STAMEN. See FLOWER.

STAMFORD, city in SW Conn., on Long Island Sound. A residential suburb of New York City, it is noted for its electronics and chemical industries. Pop 108 798.

STAMFORD BRIDGE, Battle of, victory in Yorkshire on Sept. 25, 1066, of newly crowned HAROLD II, last Anglo-Saxon king of England, over his brother Tostig and Harald Hardraade of Norway. (See HASTINGS, BATTLE OF.)

STAMITZ, Johann Wenzel Anton (1717–1757), Czech-born German composer and musician. As concertmaster of the court orchestra at Mannheim from 1745 and founder of the Mannheim school of symphonists, he had a profound influence on the work of Mozart.

STAMMER. See SPEECH AND SPEECH DISORDERS.

STAMP ACT (1765), the first direct tax imposed by the English Parliament on the 13 American colonies. All legal and commercial documents, pamphlets, playing cards and newspapers were to carry revenue stamps, which would help finance the British army quartered in America. The colonists balked at the idea of "taxation without representation," and delegates from nine colonies met in the Stamp Act Congress held in New York to protest against the law. A boycott of British goods finally led Parliament to repeal the Stamp Act in March 1766.

STAMP COLLECTING, or **philately.** The first postage stamps, the famous "Penny Blacks" and "Twopenny Blues," were issued in England on May 1, 1840: the first in the US appeared in 1847, and by 1860 most countries had adopted the prepaid postage stamp system. Today stamp catalogs list over 200 000 items. Serious collectors, who generally specialize in particular countries, periods or themes, make a close study of each stamp's paper, ink, printing method, perforations, cancellation (if used), design, information content and historical occasion. Stamps can also be a good investment: sums of up to $380 000 have been paid for rare specimens.

STANDARD DEVIATION, in STATISTICS, the positive square ROOT of the sample variance s^2, defined as the arithmetic mean (see MEAN, MEDIAN AND MODE) of the SQUARES of the deviations of the members of a sample from the arithmetic mean of the sample:

$$s^2 = \frac{1}{n}\sum_{i=1}^{n}(x_i - \mu)^2,$$

where n is the number of observations, μ the mean, and x_i the ith value. Here s is the *sample* standard deviation: the *population* standard deviation is given by the square root of the population VARIANCE. Standard deviations provide a measure of the dispersion of a distribution about its mean: for example, in a NORMAL DISTRIBUTION, about 68.3% of the population lies within one standard deviation of the mean. (See also CHI-SQUARED TEST.)

STANDARD TIME, the practice of defining the hour of the day throughout a specified geographical area (time zone) as being so many hours behind or ahead of an international standard, GREENWICH MEAN TIME (GMT). The US and Canada are covered by five such zones.

STANDISH, Miles (c1584–1656), Lancashire-born military adviser to the PILGRIMS and an important member of the PLYMOUTH COLONY, serving as its assistant governor and treasurer. About 1631 he helped found Duxbury, Mass. Longfellow's poem about him has no factual basis.

STANFIELD, Robert Lorne (1914–), Canadian politician, leader of the Progressive Conservative Party, the major opposition party, 1967–75. As premier of Nova Scotia (1956–67) he promoted industrial development. He resigned national leadership following the 1974 election defeat by TRUDEAU's Liberals.

STANFORD, Leland (1824–1893), US railroad pioneer and politician. Governor of Cal. (1861–63) and a Republican Cal. senator (1885–93), he also helped found and became president of the Central Pacific and Southern Pacific railroads and he established Stanford University (1885).

STANFORD-BINET TEST, an adaptation of the Binet-Simon test for INTELLIGENCE, introduced by TERMAN (1916, revised 1937), and used primarily to determine the IQs of children. (See also BINET.)

STANHOPE, Lady Hester Lucy (1776–1839), English traveler. She was secretary (1803–06) to her uncle William PITT the Younger. In 1814 she settled in Syria, and was venerated as a prophetess and ruler by the local Arab community.

STANISLAUS, Saint (1030–1079), patron saint of Poland. As Bishop of Kraków, he seems to have supported a plot against King Boleslaw II, who personally killed him.

STANISLAVSKI, Konstantin (1863–1938), Russian actor, director and producer. Born Konstantin Sergeyevich Alekseyev, he originated an influential approach, known as "the method," which involves subordination of personal style to an attempt to analyze, assimilate and live out the emotional content of the enacted role. In 1898 he founded the MOSCOW ART THEATER.

STANISLAW, name of two Polish kings. **Stanislaw I** (1677–1766), ruled from 1704 until 1709, when his patron Charles XII of Sweden was defeated by the Russians. Regaining the throne in 1733, he was immediately deposed by Russia and Austria. **Stanislaw II** (1732–1798) ruled 1764–95 as a pawn of Catherine II of Russia. Despite his efforts to preserve POLAND's identity, he was unable to prevent its partition.

STANLEY, family name of the US inventors and identical twins **Francis Edgar** (1849–1918) and **Freelon O.** (1849–1940). Their inventions included a dry photographic plate and a series of steam-powered automobiles—the famous Stanley steamers, the first of which appeared in 1897.

STANLEY, Sir Henry Morton (1841–1904), British explorer, soldier and journalist. Born John Rowlands, he took the name of a US merchant who adopted him. He fought in the US Civil War and in 1869 was sent to Africa by the *New York Herald* to find the missionary and explorer David LIVINGSTONE. Their famous meeting by Lake Tanganyika occurred in 1871. Stanley continued Livingstone's exploration (1874–77), crossing the continent E–W.

STANLEY, Wendell Meredith (1904–1971), US biochemist who shared with J. NORTHROP and J. SUMNER the 1946 Nobel Prize for Chemistry for his first crystallization of a VIRUS.

STANLEYVILLE. See KISANGANI.

STANTON, city in SW Cal., 20mi SE of Los Angeles. Its industry includes manufacture of concrete and metal goods. Pop 18 149.

STANTON, Edwin McMasters (1814–1869), US politician, an able Civil War secretary of war (1862–68) and important ally of the Radical Republicans during RECONSTRUCTION. As US attorney general in the last months of President BUCHANAN's cabinet, he stood against Southern secession. He resigned following President JOHNSON's narrow escape from impeachment (1868).

STANTON, Elizabeth Cady (1815–1902), US abolitionist and campaigner for women's rights. In 1848, with Mrs. Lucretia MOTT, she organized the first women's rights convention in the US, at Seneca Falls, N.Y., and in 1869 founded the Woman Suffrage Association with Susan B. ANTHONY.

STAPHYLOCOCCUS, BACTERIUM responsible for numerous SKIN, soft tissue and BONE infections, less often causing SEPTICEMIA, a cavitating PNEUMONIA, bacterial endocarditis and enterocolitis. BOILS, CARBUNCLES, IMPETIGO and OSTEOMYELITIS are commonly due to Staphylococci. Treatment usually requires drainage of PUS from ABSCESSES, and ANTIBIOTICS.

STAR, a large incandescent ball of gases held together by its own gravity. The SUN is a fairly normal star in its composition, parameters and color. The lifespan of a star depends upon its mass and luminosity: a very luminous star may have a life of only one million years, the sun a life of ten billion years, the faintest main sequence stars a life of ten thousand billion years. Stars are divided into two categories, Populations I and II. The stars in Population I are slower moving, generally to be found in the spiral arms of GALAXIES, and believed to be younger. Population II stars are generally brighter, faster moving and mainly to be found in the spheroidal halo of stars around a galaxy and in the GLOBULAR CLUSTERS. Many stars are DOUBLE STARS. It is believed that stars originate as condensations out of INTERSTELLAR MATTER. In certain circumstances a protostar will form, slowly contracting under its own gravity, part of the energy from this contraction being radiated, the remainder heating up the core: this stage may last several million years. At last the core becomes hot enough for thermonuclear reactions (see FUSION, NUCLEAR) to be sustained, and stops contracting. Eventually the star as a whole ceases contracting and radiates entirely by the thermonuclear conversion of hydrogen into helium: it is then said to be on the main sequence. When all the hydrogen in the core has been converted into helium, the now purely helium core begins to contract while the outer layers continue to "burn" hydrogen: this contraction heats up the core and forces the outer layers outward, so that the star as a whole expands for some 100–200 million years until it becomes a red **giant star**. Although the outer layers are comparatively cool, the core has become far hotter than before, and thermonuclear conversions of helium into carbon begin. The star contracts once more (though some expand still further to become **supergiants**) and ends its life as a white **dwarf star**. It is thought that more massive stars become **neutron stars**, whose matter is so dense that its PROTONS and ELECTRONS are packed together to form NEUTRONS; were the sun to become a neutron star, it would have a radius of less than 20km. Finally, when the star can no longer radiate through thermonuclear or gravitational means, it ceases to shine. Some stars may at this stage undergo ultimate gravitational collapse to form BLACK HOLES. (See also CARBON CYCLE; CEPHEID VARIABLES; CONSTELLATION; COSMOLOGY; GALACTIC CLUSTER; MAGELLANIC CLOUDS; MILKY WAY; NEBULA; NOVA; PULSAR; QUASAR; SOLAR SYSTEM; STAR CLUSTER; SUPERNOVA; UNIVERSE; VARIABLE STAR.)

STARCH, a CARBOHYDRATE consisting of chains of GLUCOSE arranged in one of two forms to give the polysaccharides amylose and amylopectin. Amylose consists of an unbranched chain of 200–500 glucose units, whereas amylopectin consists of chains of 20 glucose units joined by cross links to give a highly branched structure. Most natural starches are mixtures of amylose and amylopectin; e.g., potato and cereal starches are 20%–30% amylase and 70%–80% amylopectin. Starch is found in plants, occurring in grains scattered throughout the CYTOPLASM. The grains from any particular plant have a characteristic microscopic appearance and an expert can tell the source of a starch by its appearance under the microscope. Starches in the form of rice, potatoes and wheat or other cereal products supply about 70% of the world's food.

STAR CHAMBER, English law court, formally set up in 1487, abolished (1641) by the LONG PARLIAMENT. Operating outside COMMON LAW, with no jury, it was speedy and efficient, but also arbitrary and cruel, particularly under CHARLES I.

STAR CLUSTER, a cluster of stars sharing a common origin. There are two distinct types of star cluster: see GALACTIC CLUSTER; GLOBULAR CLUSTER.

STARETS (Old Slavic: elder), in the Eastern Orthodox Church, a revered monastic spiritual leader. The 14th-century St. SERGIUS of Radonezh was perhaps the most famous, but in the 18th–19th centuries *startsy* were again highly influential.

STARFISHES, a class, Asteroidea, of star-shaped marine ECHINODERMS, with five-fold symmetry. A starfish consists of a central disk surrounded by five or more radiating arms. There is a dermal skeleton of CALCITE plates and a water-vascular system gives rise to rows of tube feet on the lower surface by which the animal moves about. The mouth is on the lower surface. Most species are carnivorous or omnivorous scavengers. Starfishes can regenerate (see REGENERATION) lost or damaged parts.

STARK, Johannes (1874–1957), Bavarian-born German physicist awarded the 1919 Nobel Prize for Physics for discovering the **Stark effect** (1913), the splitting of degenerate spectral lines through the application of a powerful ELECTRIC FIELD. The explanation of this was an early triumph of QUANTUM THEORY. (See also ZEEMAN, P.)

STARK, John (1728–1822), American revolutionary soldier. After distinguishing himself at the battles of BUNKER HILL and Trenton he was made a brigadier general of New Hampshire militia. Stark won an important battle at BENNINGTON, Vt., and was instrumental in forcing final British surrender at SARATOGA. He was made a major general in 1783.

STARKVILLE, city in NE Miss., seat of Oktibbeha Co. A dairying center with some light industry, it is the site of Mississippi State University. Pop 11 369.

STARLING, Ernest Henry, British physiologist. See BAYLISS, SIR WILLIAM MADDOCK.

STARLINGS, a family, Sturnidae, of over 100 species of song birds. They have slender bills, an upright stance and smooth glossy plumage. Originally an Old World group, they are now found elsewhere. They feed on insects, other invertebrates and seeds, probing with the bill into turf or among leaves. They flock for feeding and roosting, with communal roosts of up to 500 000 birds.

The best-known member of the starling family, the common European starling, *Sturnus vulgaris*. Introduced into North America, among other places, it has become a serious pest in some areas.

STAR OF BETHLEHEM, name for the star which is said to have appeared in the East to guide the Wise Men (see MAGI) to the birthplace of JESUS. The story is related in the GOSPELS.

STAR OF BETHLEHEM, or Italian bellflower, a dwarf relative of the Canterbury bell, belonging to the genus *Campanula*. It is a popular house plant, producing blue or white, single or double, star-shaped flowers. Indoors, it grows well in a bright position and at average house temperatures, but it benefits from being placed outside in a shady position during the summer. The soil should be kept evenly moist during the spring and summer, but allowed to dry out more during the fall and winter. Propagation is by shoot tip cuttings taken in spring or early summer. Family: Campanulaceae.

STARR, Belle (c1848–1889), US outlaw. Her exploits with Jessie JAMES and Cole YOUNGER were made famous in *Bella Starr, the Bandit Queen; or the Female Jessie James* (1889) by Richard K. Fox. Her Okla. home became famous as an outlaw refuge.

STAR-SPANGLED BANNER, the US national anthem. The lyrics were drafted by Francis Scott Key in Sept. 1814, while he was held on a British ship during an attack on Fort McHenry, Md. The tune was a popular English song *To Anacreon in Heaven*. The *Star-Spangled Banner* was finally adopted as national anthem by Congress in 1931.

STASSEN, Harold Edward (1907–), US politician. He was governor of Minn. (1939–43) and a founder delegate to the UN. President of the University of Penn. 1948–53, he later held various posts in the Eisenhower administration and has made four unsuccessful bids for the Republican presidential nomination.

STATAMPERE, the unit of current in the CGS electrostatic system of units (esu—see CGS UNITS). Like

Stat-units

Quantity	CGS esu system	SI units
charge	1 statcoulomb =	3.336×10^{-10} coulomb
current	1 statampere =	3.336×10^{-10} ampere
potential	1 statvolt =	2.998×10^{2} volt
resistance	1 statohm =	8.987×10^{11} ohm
capacitance	1 statfarad =	1.113×10^{-12} farad
inductance	1 stathenry =	8.987×10^{11} henry

other **stat-units**, the statampere is used in computations in which the PERMITTIVITY of free space is set dimensionless (see DIMENSIONS) and equal to UNITY.

STATE, US Department of, oldest executive department of the US government. Originally in charge of domestic as well as foreign affairs, it now conducts US foreign policy. It collects and analyzes information from abroad, gives policy advice to the US president, negotiates treaties and agreements and maintains some 260 diplomatic and consular offices. The secretary of state, senior member of the president's cabinet, is assisted by undersecretaries, and assistant secretaries who run regional bureaus and bureaus dealing with international organizations, congressional relations, public, economic, educational and cultural intelligence, security and consular affairs.

STATE COLLEGE, residential borough in central Penn., 60mi NW of Harrisburg. It is the seat of Pennsylvania State University. Pop 33 778.

STATEN ISLAND, in New York harbor, coextensive with Richmond, one of NEW YORK CITY's five boroughs. It lies 5mi SW of Manhattan Island and is linked with Manhattan by ferry, with Brooklyn by the Verrazano-Narrows Bridge and with N.J. by several bridges. First settled in the 1660s, it became a N.Y. borough in 1898. It is now a residential suburb and growing industrial area. Pop 295 443.

STATESBORO, city in E Ga., the seat of Bulloch Co., 45mi NW of Savannah. It has cotton-, lumber- and peanut-processing industries. Pop 14 616.

STATES GENERAL, or **estates-general,** assemblies in European countries in the late Middle Ages which, in Germany, Poland, France and the Netherlands, evolved into modern parliaments. The "estates" were social classes, usually the clergy, the nobility and privileged commoners such as the new bourgeoisie of the towns. Though peasants were not represented, the estates spoke for the whole country, usually when summoned by the ruler to discuss a specific item. Their role was consultative rather than legislative.

STATES OF THE CHURCH. See PAPAL STATES.

STATES' RIGHTS, the rights of individual states in relation to the US federal government. The states' power, enshrined in the ARTICLES OF CONFEDERATION, was curtailed by the Constitution in the interests of federalism. Controversy soon arose over the relation between states' and federal rights: Thomas JEFFERSON opposed the federalists' advocacy of strong central government and declared with James MADISON, in the KENTUCKY AND VIRGINIA RESOLUTIONS (1798–99), that individual states could decide whether to enforce federal legislation or not. In the HARTFORD CONVENTION (1814–15), federalist New England expressed defiance of the Madison administration in the War of 1812, and in the 1850s several Northern states refused to implement the FUGITIVE SLAVE LAWS. The most extreme states' rights position was taken by John CALHOUN and set forth in N.C.'s NULLIFICATION ordinance (1832). Calhoun held that the Constitution in no way diminished state sovereignty; this view led logically to the doctrine of SECESSION. The Northern victory in the Civil War demolished the extreme states' rights position of nullification and secession, but states' rights has remained an important rallying cry, notably in the area of federal civil rights law.

STATESVILLE, industrial city in the Blue Ridge foothills, central N.C., seat of Iredell Co. Its manufactures include textiles and furniture. Pop 19 996.

STATIC, an accumulation of electric charge (see ELECTRICITY) responsible, e.g., for the attractive and repulsive properties produced in many plastics and fabrics by rubbing. It leaks away gradually through warm damp air, but otherwise may cause small sparks (and consequent RADIO interference) or violent discharges such as LIGHTNING.

STATICS, branch of MECHANICS dealing with systems in EQUILIBRIUM, i.e., in which all FORCES are balanced and there is no motion.

STATISTICS, the area of mathematics concerned with the manipulation of numerical information. The science has two branches: descriptive statistics, dealing with the classification and presentation of data, and inferential or analytical statistics, which studies ways of collecting data, its analysis and interpretation. Sampling is fundamental to statistics. Since it is usually impractical to treat of every element in a population (the group under consideration), a representative (often random) sample is instead examined, its properties being ascribed to the whole group. The data is analyzed in series of PARAMETERS such as the STANDARD DEVIATION and the MEAN of the data distribution. The distribution may be presented as a HISTOGRAM, a frequency polygon, or a frequency curve. Ideally, a statistician aims to devise a MATHEMATICAL MODEL of the distribution, especially if it approximates to normality (see NORMAL DISTRIBUTION); there are many tests which he can use to determine whether or not his model "fits" (see CHI-SQUARED TEST; STUDENT'S *t*-DISTRIBUTION). Statistics is used throughout science, wherever there is an element of PROBABILITY involved, and also in industry, politics, market analysis and traffic control. (See also DEGREES OF FREEDOM; STOCHASTIC PROCESS; VARIANCE.)

STATUE OF LIBERTY. See LIBERTY, STATUE OF.

STAT-UNITS. See STATAMPERE.

STATUTE OF LIMITATIONS. See LIMITATION, STATUTES OF.

STATUTE OF WESTMINSTER (1931). See WESTMINSTER, STATUTE OF.

STAUDINGER, Hermann (1881–1965), German chemist awarded the 1953 Nobel Prize for Chemistry for showing that the long chains of MOLECULES known as POLYMERS are really giant molecules held together by normal chemical BONDS.

STAUNTON, city in N Va., seat of Augusta Co. Woodrow Wilson's birthplace, it produces flour, textiles, furniture and metal goods. Pop 24 504.

STAVANGER, port on Stavanger Fjord, SW Norway, with shipbuilding, fishing and oil-refining industries. It has a fine 12th-century cathedral. Pop 82 079.

STAVE. See NOTATION.

STAVROPOL, capital of Stavropol territory, RSFSR, USSR, in the N Caucasus. It has food-processing, clothing and machinery industries. Pop 198 000.

STEADY STATE THEORY. See COSMOLOGY.

STEAM, the vapor formed from WATER at or above the boiling point (100°C). It is colorless, but appears white when it contains droplets of condensed water. Steam is used to make WATER GAS; it is a valuable industrial heat carrier because the LATENT HEAT of water is very high (40.65kJ/mol) and steam has a high SPECIFIC HEAT: it is thus used in central heating and in PRESSURE COOKERS. Because steam occupies about 1 700 times the volume of the water producing it, when water is heated in a boiler, pressure is built up, which is used to drive TURBINES and STEAM ENGINES. Steam occurs naturally in springs, geysers and volcanoes.

STEAM ENGINE, the first important heat ENGINE, supplying the power that made the Industrial Revolution possible, and the principal power source for industry and transport (notably railroad locomotives and steamships) until largely superseded in the 20th century by steam TURBINES and the various INTERNAL-COMBUSTION ENGINES. The steam engine is an external-combustion engine, the steam being raised in a BOILER heated by a furnace; it is also a RECIPROCATING ENGINE. There are two main types: condensing, in which the pressure drop is caused by cooling the steam and so condensing it back to water; and noncondensing, in which the steam is exhausted to the atmosphere. The first major precursor of the steam engine was Thomas SAVERY's steam pump (1698), worked by the partial vacuum created by condensing steam in closed chambers. It had no moving parts, however, and the first working reciprocating engine was that of Thomas NEWCOMEN (1712): steam was admitted to the cylinder as the piston moved up, and was condensed by a water spray inside the cylinder, whereupon the air pressure outside forced the piston down again. James WATT radically improved Newcomen's engine (1769) by condensing the steam outside the cylinder (thus no longer having to reheat the cylinder at each stroke) and by using the steam pressure to force the piston up. He later found that, if steam were admitted for only part of the stroke, its expansion would do a good deal of extra work. (The principles involved were later studied by CARNOT and became the basis of THERMODYNAMICS.) Watt also invented the double-action principle—both strokes being powered, by applying the steam alternately to each end of the piston—the flyball GOVERNOR, and the crank and "sun-and-planet" devices for converting the piston's linear motion to rotary motion. The compound engine (1781) makes more efficient use of the steam by using the exhaust steam from one cylinder to drive the piston of a second cylinder. Later developments included the use of high-pressure steam by Richard TREVITHICK and Oliver EVANS.

STEARIC ACID ($CH_3(CH_2)_{16}COOH$), white solid CARBOXYLIC ACID obtained from its ESTER, glyceryl tristearate (tristearin), which is found in many natural FATS and oils. Sodium stearate is a principal constituent of many SOAPS.

STEATITE. See SOAPSTONE.

STEATOPYGIA, excessive accumulation of fat in the buttocks, usually of females, common among the Hottentots and some other African peoples.

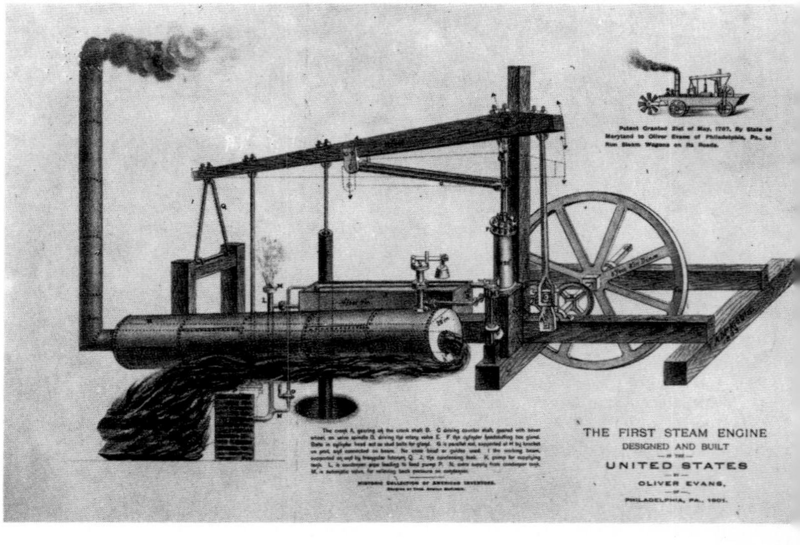

Lithograph of 1893, showing the first high-pressure steam engine designed and built in the United States, by Oliver Evans, in 1801.

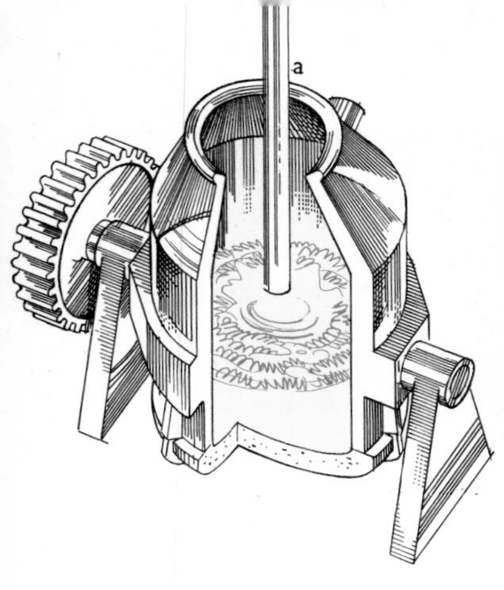

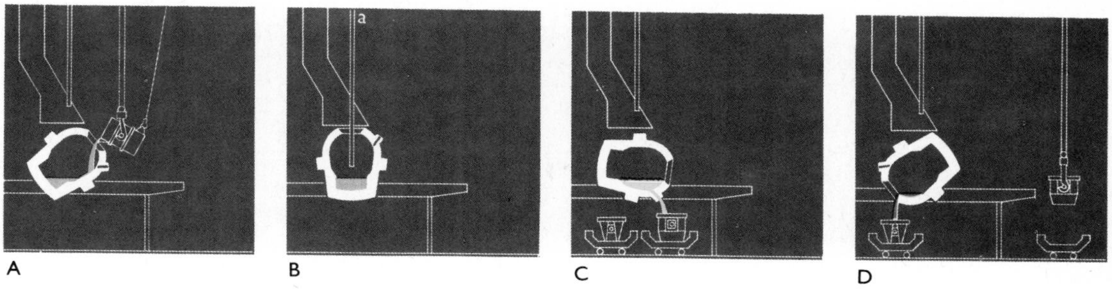

In the basic oxygen process for making steel, iron and scrap are mixed in the converter (A), and pure oxygen is blown through a tube (a) on to the surface of the molten metal (B). The steel is then poured off (C), and the slag is removed (D).

STEEL, an ALLOY of IRON and up to 1.7% carbon, with small amounts of manganese, phosphorus, sulfur and silicon. These are termed carbon steels; those with other metals are termed alloy steels; low-alloy steels if they have less than 5% of the alloying metal, high-alloy steels if more than 5%. Carbon steels are far stronger than iron, and their properties can be tailored to their uses by adjusting composition and treatment. Alloy steels—including STAINLESS STEEL—are used for their special properties. Steel was first mass-produced in the mid-19th century, and steel production is now one of the chief world industries, being basic to all industrial economies. The US, the USSR and Japan are the major producers. Steel's innumerable uses include automobile manufacture, shipbuilding, skyscraper frames, reinforced concrete and machinery of all kinds. All steelmaking processes remove the impurities in the raw materials—PIG IRON, scrap steel and reduced iron ore—by oxidizing them with an air or oxygen blast. Thus most of the carbon, silicon, manganese, phosphorus and sulfur are converted to their oxides and, together with added FLUX and other waste matter present, form the SLAG. The main processes are the BESSEMER PROCESS, the LINZ-DONAWITZ PROCESS and the similar electric-arc process used for highest-quality steel, and the OPEN-HEARTH PROCESS. Most modern processes use a basic slag and a basic refractory furnace lining: acidic processes are incapable of removing phosphorus. When the impurities have been removed, desired elements are added in calculated proportions. The molten steel is cast as ingots which are shaped while still red-hot in ROLLING MILLS, or it may be cast as a continuous bar ("strand casting"). The properties of medium-carbon (0.25% to 0.45% C) and high-carbon (up to 1.7% C) steels may be greatly improved by heat treatment: ANNEALING, CASEHARDENING and TEMPERING. Steel metallurgy is somewhat complex: unhardened steel may contain combinations of three phases—austenite, ferrite and cementite—differing in structure and carbon content; hardened steel contains martensite, which may be thought of as ferrite supersaturated with carbon.

STEELE, Sir Richard (1672–1729), English author and politician, best remembered for his wide-ranging essays in two periodicals founded with ADDISON, the *Tatler* (1709) and *Spectator* (1711). He was an active Whig member of Parliament, a journalist and a successful playwright, though his sentimental comedies are not now performed.

STEEN, Jan (1626–1679), Dutch genre painter, a master of color and facial expression. His 700 surviving works include jovial scenes of eating, drinking and revelry, portraits, landscapes and classical and biblical scenes.

STEEPLECHASING, horse-racing over a course with such obstacles as fences, hedges and water. It originated in England as a race from one church steeple to another. The world's most famous steeplechase is the English Grand National. US steeplechases are normally held at racing tracks or hunts. Steeplechases on foot are now an Olympic sport.

STEFAN-BOLTZMANN LAW. See BLACKBODY RADIATION.

STEFANSSON, Vilhjalmur (1879–1962), Canadian arctic explorer and author. He became an authority on Eskimo life and arctic survival. Stefansson also charted several islands in the W Canadian Arctic. He was a northern studies consultant at Dartmouth College, N.H., from 1947.

STEFFENS, Lincoln (1866–1936), US journalist. One of the MUCKRAKERS, he wrote for *McClure's Magazine* and the *American Magazine* and was famous for his exposés of corruption in politics and business. A selection of his articles was published in *The Shame of the Cities* (1904) and his autobiography (1931) is a classic of the muckraking era.

STEGOSAURUS, a genus of herbivorous DINOSAURS of the late JURASSIC, distinguished by a double row of plates and spines arrayed vertically along the back, perhaps as a defense against predators.

STEICHEN, Edward (1879–1973), pioneer US photographer. After Paris studies he worked in fashion, advertising and theater. At New York City's Museum of Modern Art he mounted the 1955 *Family of Man* exhibition.

STEIERMARK. See STYRIA.

STEIN, Gertrude (1874–1946), US author and celebrated personality who lived in Paris from 1903. Her first important work was the experimental *Three Lives* (1909). Stein is best known for her friendships with such figures as PICASSO, HEMINGWAY, MATISSE and GIDE. They are described in *The Autobiography of Alice B. Toklas* (1933).

STEIN, Heinrich Friedrich Karl, Baron vom und zum (1757–1831), Prussian statesman and reformer. He was minister of commerce (1804–07), and as chief minister (1807–08) after Prussia's defeat in the Napoleonic Wars he abolished serfdom and introduced many administrative and economic reforms, until he was dismissed by order of Napoleon.

STEIN, William Howard (1911–), US biochemist who shared with C. B. ANFINSEN and S. MOORE the 1972 Nobel Prize for Chemistry for his part in determining the structure of the ENZYME ribonuclease (see also NUCLEIC ACIDS).

STEINBECK, John (1902–1968), US author who came to the fore in the 1930s with his novels about poverty and social injustice. He won a Pulitzer Prize for *The Grapes of Wrath* (1939), about migrant farm workers in Cal., and the 1962 Nobel Prize for Literature. His other works include *Tortilla Flat* (1935), *Of Mice and Men* (1937), *Cannery Row* (1945), *East of Eden* (1952) and *The Winter of Our Discontent* (1961).

STEINBOK, *Raphicerus campestris*, a small GAZELLE of South and E Africa. Males have thick, smooth horns; females are hornless. There is a large, circular gland, surrounded by a bare patch, on the face.

STEINER, Rudolf (1861–1925), Austrian founder of ANTHROPOSOPHY, an attempt to recapture spiritual realities ignored by modern man. He founded the Waldorf School movement, and stressed music and drama as aids to self-discovery. Works include *The Philosophy of Spiritual Activity* (1922).

STEINMETZ, Charles Proteus (1865–1923), formerly **Karl August Rudolf Steinmetz**, German-born US electrical engineer who first worked out the theory of HYSTERESIS (c1892), but who is best remembered for working out the theory of ALTERNATING CURRENT (1893 onward), so making it possible for AC to be used rather than DC in most applications.

STEM, the part of the PLANT which supports the LEAVES, FLOWERS and FRUITS. It may be short or creeping in low-growing plants or tall as in TREES, or even underground (see RHIZOME). Stems also conduct nutrients, other substances and water between the various organs of the plant. Green stems carry out PHOTOSYNTHESIS.

STENCIL. See DUPLICATING MACHINE; SILK-SCREEN PRINTING.

STENDHAL (1783–1842), pen name of Marie-Henri Beyle, French pioneer of the psychological novel. *The Red and the Black* (1830) and *The Charterhouse of Parma* (1839) explore the search for happiness through love and political power, with minute analysis of the hero's feelings. His treatment of the figure of the "outsider," his social criticism and brilliant ironic prose style make him one of the greatest and most "modern" of French novelists.

STENGEL, Casey (1890–1975), US baseball manager. A popular and garrulous figure, he led the New York Yankees to seven world championships 1949–58, and managed the New York Mets 1962–68. He was elected to the Baseball Hall of Fame in 1966.

STEN GUN, simple type of submachine gun, used extensively in WWII by British airborne troops and supplied to partisans in occupied Europe, since it could use 9mm pistol ammunition.

STENNIS, John Cornelius (1901–), US politician. A Democrat, he was a Miss. circuit judge until elected US senator in 1947. As Armed Services Committee chairman he backed Vietnam involvement but called for limits to presidential powers to commit troops.

STENO, Nicolaus (1638–1686), or **Niels Stensen**, Danish geologist, anatomist and bishop. In 1669 he published the results of his geological studies: he recognized that many rocks are sedimentary (see SEDIMENTARY ROCKS); that FOSSILS are the remains of once-living creatures and that they can be used for DATING purposes, and established many of the tenets of modern crystallography.

STENOGRAPHY. See SHORTHAND.

STENOTYPE, system of machine SHORTHAND that uses a keyboard machine like a typewriter except that several keys may be depressed at once. Letter groups phonetically represent words. The machine, silent in operation, is capable of 250 words/min.

STENTOR, a large ciliate PROTOZOAN which may reach a length of 2mm (0.08in). Stentor are trumpet-shaped animals which are free-swimming, but attach themselves to the substrate by a holdfast when feeding. Rings of cilia around the mouth of the trumpet waft food particles toward the mouth region.

STEPHEN, Saint (d. c36 AD), first Christian martyr. Accused of blasphemy, he was stoned to death (Acts 6–8). His feast day is Dec. 26.

STEPHEN I, Saint (977–1038), first king of Hungary, often regarded as founder of the state. His formal coronation in 1000 marked Hungary's entry into Christian Europe. He established a strong church, and modeled his administration on German lines.

STEPHEN, name of nine popes. All died in office. The church today omits a tenth (formerly Stephen II, d. 752 before consecration) from its list. **Stephen I** (reigned 254–57), famous for his disputes with St. CYPRIAN of Carthage, whose rebaptism of heretics he denounced, died during Emperor Valerian's persecutions. **Stephen II** (reigned 752–57), was supported by PEPIN THE SHORT in his defeat of the Lombards. The PAPAL STATES were founded with land gifts from Pepin. Controversy over papal elections dominated the reign of **Stephen III** (768–72). **Stephen IV** (reigned 816–17), crowned LOUIS I emperor (establishing a prerogative of the papacy) and strengthened links with the Franks. **Stephen V** (reigned 885–91), survived opposition from Emperor Charles III and later crowned Guy of Spoleto emperor. **Stephen VI** (reigned 896–97), declared void the reign of his predecessor Formosus but was himself imprisoned and strangled. His rule marked the papacy's lowest point. **Stephen VII** (reigned 929–31) and **Stephen VIII** (939–42), were dominated by Roman noble families. **Stephen IX** (c1000–1058), reigned from 1057. He continued the reforms of LEO IX, enforcing priestly celibacy and attacking simony. But he failed to stop the rift between Eastern and Western churches.

STEPHEN (c1097–1154), king of England 1135–54. A nephew of Henry I, he was briefly supplanted (1141) by Matilda, Henry's daughter. Though a just and generous ruler, he was not strong enough to govern the warring factions of his realm.

STEPHEN, Sir Leslie (1832–1904), English man of letters. He edited (1882–91) *The Dictionary of National Biography*. A freethinker, he wrote major studies of 18th-century English literature and philosophy. Virginia WOOLF was his daughter.

STEPHEN BATHORY. See BATHORY.

STEPHENS, Alexander Hamilton (1812–1883), vice-president of the Confederate States of America 1861–65. A congressman from Ga. (1843–59), he opposed secession, but stayed loyal to his state in the Civil War. He led the delegation to the Hampton Roads peace conference (1865). Imprisoned for six months after the war, he returned to serve again in Congress (1873–82) and as governor of Ga. (1882–83).

STEPHENSON, British family of inventors and railroad engineers. **George Stephenson** (1781–1848) first worked on stationary STEAM ENGINES, reconstructing and modifying one by NEWCOMEN (c1812). His first LOCOMOTIVE, the *Blucher*, took to the rails in 1814: it traveled at 4mph (about 6.5km/h) hauling coal for the Killingworth colliery, and incorporated an important development, flanged wheels. About this time, independently of DAVY, he invented a SAFETY LAMP: this earned him £1 000 (then about $5 000), which helped finance further locomotive experiments. In 1821 he was appointed to survey and engineer a line from Darlington to Stockton: in 1825 his *Locomotion* carried 450 people along the line at a rate of 15mph (about 25km/h), and the modern RAILROAD was born. This was followed in 1829 by the success of the *Rocket*, which ran the 40mi (65km) of his new Manchester–Liverpool line at speeds up to 30mph (about 48km/h), the first main-line passenger rail journey. His only son **Robert Stephenson** (1803–1859) helped his father on both of these lines, and with the *Rocket*, but is best known as a BRIDGE builder, notably for the tubular bridges over the Menai Straits, North Wales (1850), and the St. Lawrence at Montreal (1859).

STEPINAC, Aloysius (1898–1960), Yugoslav Roman Catholic cardinal. Archbishop of Zagreb (1937), he denounced TITO's communism, was accused of Nazi collaboration, and imprisoned 1946–51. On his elevation to cardinal (1952) Yugoslavia broke off relations with the Vatican.

STEPPES, extensive level GRASSLANDS of Europe and Asia (equivalent to the North American prairies and South American pampas). They extend from SW Siberia to the lower reaches of the Danube R.

STERADIAN. See ANGLE.

STEREOCHEMISTRY, the study of the arrangement in space of atoms in molecules, and of the properties which depend on such arrangements. The two chief branches are the study of STEREOISOMERS and stereospecific reactions (which involve only one isomer); and CONFORMATIONAL ANALYSIS, including the study of steric effects on reaction rates and mechanisms.

STEREOISOMERS, ISOMERS having the same molecular structure, but differing in the spatial arrangement of their atoms. There are two main types. **Optical isomers** are asymmetric molecules—usually having an asymmetric carbon atom with four different groups bonded to it—which hence have two mirror-image forms (enantiomers) and show OPTICAL ACTIVITY. Absolute spatial configurations have now been found for many isomers, and may be represented by projection formulae. Resolution, i.e. separation of the two enantiomers, is achieved by combining them with a single optical isomer, thus producing a pair of diastereoisomers which, not being mirror-images, have different properties and are separable. Inversion of configuration often occurs in substitution reactions. **Geometrical isomers** contain groups which are differently oriented with respect to a double bond or ring where rotation is impossible; they have different properties.

STEREOPHONIC SOUND. See HIGH FIDELITY.

STEREOSCOPE, optical instrument that simulates BINOCULAR VISION by presenting slightly different pictures to the two eyes so that an apparently three-dimensional image is produced. The simplest stereoscope, invented in the 1830s, used a system of mirrors and prisms (later, converging lenses) to view the pictures. In the color separation method the left image is printed or projected in red and seen through a red filter, and likewise for the right image in blue. A similar method uses images projected by POLARIZED LIGHT and viewed through polarizing filters, the polarization axes being at right angles. The pictures are produced by a stereoscopic camera with two lenses a small distance apart. The stereoscope is useful in making relief maps by aerial photographic survey.

STEREOTYPE, in printing, a duplicate plate made by casting molten alloy in a papier mâché or plastic mold made from the original type. It has been largely superseded by electrotype (see ELECTROFORMING) except for newspaper printing.

STERILITY, the condition in which an organism is unable to produce offspring. Its many possible causes include failure by either sex to produce GAMETES; the production of abnormal gametes; the inability of the male to introduce sperm into the female, or inability of the embryo to develop normally. Sterility develops naturally in old age.

STERILIZATION, surgical procedure in which the FALLOPIAN TUBES are cut and tied to prevent eggs reaching the WOMB, thus providing permanent CONTRACEPTION. The procedure is essentially irreversible and should only be performed when a woman has completed her family. It may be done by a small abdominal operation, at CESARIAN SECTION or through an instrument, the laparoscope. (See also VASECTOMY.) *Also*, the treatment of medical equipment to ensure that it is not contaminated by BACTERIA and other microorganisms. Metal and linen objects are often sterilized by heat (in AUTOCLAVES). Chemical disinfection is also used and plastic equipment is exposed to GAMMA RAYS.

STERLING, city in NE Col., seat of Logan Co., on the South Platte R, trading center for a sugar beet, grain, cattle and oil-producing area. Pop 10 636.

STERLING, city in NW Ill., 110mi W of Chicago. It produces steel goods, wire, toys, builders' hardware and electrical appliances. Pop 16 113.

STERLITAMAK, city in S central Bashkir autonomous republic, RSFSR, USSR. It has petrochemical, machinery and food-processing industries. Pop 185 000.

STERN, Isaac (1920–), US violinist. Born in Kremenets, USSR, he studied and made his debut in San Francisco.

STERN, Otto (1888–1969), German-born US physicist awarded the 1943 Nobel Prize for Physics for his development of the molecular-beam method of studying the magnetic properties of ATOMS, and especially for measuring the magnetic moment of the PROTON.

STERNBERG, Joseph von (1891–1969), Viennese-born US film director. He won an Oscar for *The Last Command* (1928), but is most famous for the films he made with Marlene DIETRICH, of which the first was *The Blue Angel* (1930). Among other Dietrich films were *Morocco* (1930) and *Shanghai Express* (1932).

STERNE, Laurence (1713–1768), English novelist and clergyman, author of *The Life and Opinions of Tristram Shandy, Gentleman* (1760–67). One of the most widely read novels of its day, this whimsical work proceeds by association of ideas and conversation rather than by plot structure. *A Sentimental Journey* (1768) recounts travels in France and Italy.

STERN GANG, or Fighters for the Freedom of Israel, Jewish terrorist group in Palestine. Formed by Abraham Stern in 1940, it attacked transport networks and British personnel, killing Lord Moyne in 1944. After creation of Israel (1948) it was banned.

STEROIDS, HORMONES produced in the body from CHOLESTEROL, mainly by the ADRENAL GLANDS, and related to ESTROGENS and ANDROGENS. All have chemical structures based on that of the STEROLS. Cortisol is the main glucocorticoid (steroids that regulate GLUCOSE metabolism) and aldosterone the main mineralocorticoid (regulating SALT, POTASSIUM and WATER balance). Increased amounts of cortisol are secreted during times of stress, e.g., SHOCK, SURGERY and severe infection. Steroids, mainly of the glucocorticoid type, are also given in doses above normal hormone levels to obtain other effects, e.g., the suppression of INFLAMMATION, ALLERGY and IMMUNITY. Diseases that respond to this include ASTHMA, MULTIPLE SCLEROSIS, some forms of NEPHRITIS, inflammatory GASTROINTESTINAL TRACT disease and cerebral EDEMA; SKIN and EYE conditions may be treated with local steroids. High-dose systemic steroids may have adverse effects if used for long periods; they may cause ACNE, osteoporosis, hypertension, fluid retention, altered facial appearance and growth retardation in children.

STEROLS, naturally occurring secondary ALCOHOLS with a fused ring structure of three six-membered carbon rings and one five-membered carbon ring, all of which are hydrogenated and contain in total one or more double bonds. Sterols are generally colorless crystalline nonsaponifiable compounds. Important sterols include CHOLESTEROL, the major sterol found in most animals, and sitosterol, found in plants.

STETHOSCOPE, instrument devised by René T. H. Laënnec (1781–1826) for listening to sounds within the body, especially those from the HEART, LUNGS, ABDOMEN and blood vessels.

STETTIN. See SZCZECIN.

STETTINIUS, Edward Reilly, Jr. (1900–1949), US businessman and statesman. Chairman of United States Steel at 37, he administered the LEND-LEASE program (1941–43), was secretary of state 1944–45 and a founder delegate to the UN.

STEUBEN, Friedrich Wilhelm Augustin, Baron von (1730–1794), Prussian soldier who trained the CONTINENTAL ARMY. Arriving in America in 1777 with an introduction from Benjamin Franklin, he was appointed inspector general of the army by Congress in 1778. He organized Washington's troops in Valley Forge into an effective fighting force, seen at the battle of MONMOUTH (1778) and siege of YORKTOWN (1780).

STEUBENVILLE, city in E Ohio, seat of Jefferson Co. One of Ohio's earliest communities, it has steel, titanium and ferroalloy industries. Pop 30 771.

STEVENS, US family of inventors and engineers. **John Stevens** (1749–1838) made many contributions to steamboat development, including the first with a screw PROPELLER (1802) and the first seagoing steamboat (*Phoenix*, 1809). He also built (1825) the first US steam locomotive. His son **Robert Livingston Stevens** (1787–1856) assisted his father, and invented the inverted-T rail still used in modern RAILROADS (1830) as well as the technique of fastening them to wooden sleepers. **Edwin Augustus Stevens** (1795–1868), another son, also made contributions to railroad technology.

STEVENS, Thaddeus (1792–1868), controversial US politician. A staunch opponent of slavery, he wielded great power as a Vt. congressman and chairman of the US Senate Ways and Means Committee during the Civil War. He afterward dominated the joint committee on RECONSTRUCTION, leading the Radical Republicans with Senator SUMNER. He held that the defeated Southern states were "conquered provinces," subject to the will of

Congress. He proposed the 14th Amendment, fought for Negro suffrage, and led in the impeachment of President Johnson.

STEVENS, Wallace (1879–1955), US poet. He worked for a Connecticut insurance company and achieved wide literary recognition only with the 1955 Pulitzer Prize for his *Collected Poems*. Rich in imagery and vocabulary, his often difficult verse explores the use of imagination to ease tragic reality and give meaning to its confusion.

STEVENSON, Adlai Ewing, name of two US politicians. **Adlai Ewing Stevenson** (1835–1914), a lawyer and Democratic representative for Ill. (1875–76, 1879–80), was elected US vice-president in Cleveland's second term (1893–97). **Adlai Ewing Stevenson** (1900–1965), his grandson, also a lawyer, was special assistant to the secretary of the navy (1941–44) and a delegate to the UN (1946–47). In 1948 he was elected governor of Ill., where he backed reform. He was chosen as Democratic presidential candidate in 1952 and 1956 but lost to Eisenhower. His policies of halting the arms race and promoting the economies of Africa and Asia were unpopular at home. He lost the 1960 nomination to Kennedy. From 1961 to his death he was US ambassador to the UN.

STEVENSON, Robert Louis (1850–1894), Scottish author best known for such adventure stories as *Treasure Island* (1883) and *Kidnapped* (1886). He also wrote *Dr. Jekyll and Mr. Hyde* (1886), a horrific tale of inherent good and evil, and the sensitive verse of *A Child's Garden of Verses* (1885), as well as short stories, essays and travel books. A sufferer from tuberculosis, he sailed with his US wife to the South Pacific (1888) and settled in Samoa, where he continued to write and tell stories.

STEVENS POINT, city in central Wis., seat of Portage Co. Manufactures include paper products and furniture. Pop 23 479.

STEVINUS, Simon (1548–1620), or **Simon Stevin,** Dutch mathematician and engineer who made many contributions to HYDROSTATICS; disproved, before GALILEO, ARISTOTLE's theory that heavy bodies fall more swiftly than light ones; introduced the DECIMAL SYSTEM into popular use; and first used the triangle of forces in MECHANICS.

STEWART, Dugald (1753–1828), Scottish philosopher, a major member of the COMMON SENSE SCHOOL and a principal disciple of Thomas REID.

STEWART, Potter (1915–), associate justice of the US Supreme Court from 1958.

STIBNITE, soft, gray mineral, antimony(III) sulfide (Sb_2S_3), the chief ore of ANTIMONY, used in the manufacture of fireworks and matches; found in China, Czechoslovakia, Ida., Nev., and Cal.

STICK INSECTS. See WALKING STICKS.

STICKLEBACKS, a family, Gasterosteidae, of common marine and freshwater fishes, with a series of sharp spines in front of the dorsal fin. The most familiar species are the Three-spined and Ten-spined sticklebacks of Europe, Asia and North America.

STIEGEL, Henry William (1729–1785), German-born US iron and glass manufacturer. He emigrated to Philadelphia in 1750, made a fortune manufacturing iron stoves, and in 1760 founded Manheim, Pa., where he established a famous glass-factory. Extravagance led to bankruptcy in 1774.

STIEGLITZ, Alfred (1864–1946), US photographer who helped make photography a recognized art form; and who founded the gallery "291" in New York, where he put on pioneering exhibitions, including works by his wife, Georgia O'KEEFE.

STIFTER, Adalbert (1805–1868), Austrian writer noted for his fine descriptions of nature and his gentle praise of humble virtues. His works include *Colored Stones* (1853: a collection of short stories) and the novel *Indian Summer* (1857).

STIGMA. See FLOWER.

STIGMATA, apparent wounds on the hands, feet and side, similar to those of the crucified Christ. The earliest of over 300 recorded cases is that of FRANCIS OF ASSISI.

STIJL. See DE STIJL.

STIKINE RIVER, 335mi-long river flowing from N British Columbia W through the Coast Mountains across S Alaska to the Pacific, N of Wrangell.

STILB (sb), in PHOTOMETRY a unit of LUMINANCE, equal to 1 CANDELA per square centimetre.

STILICHO, Flavius (c365–408), greatest general of the late Roman Empire. Chief general under THEODOSIUS I and HONORIUS, he fought major campaigns against the barbarian invaders.

STILLWATER, city in E Minn., seat of Washington Co. Textiles, shoes and ventilating fans are among its manufactures. Pop 10 191.

STILLWATER, city in N central Okla., seat of Payne Co. Marketing and processing of farm produce is the principal industry. Pop 31 126.

STILTS, long-legged wading birds of the family Recurvirostridae. Black-and-white birds, distinguished by their extremely long legs and small heads, they are found in both salt and freshwater lagoons, feeding on crustaceans and other small invertebrates.

STILWELL, Joseph Warren (1883–1946), US commander of the Allied forces in the Far East in WWII. Driven back to India in 1942, he rebuilt his forces and counterattacked through Burma to China (1943–44). He was recalled in 1944 after disagreeing with CHIANG KAI-SHEK, under whom he was serving.

STIMSON, Henry Lewis (1867–1950), US lawyer and statesman, author of the "Stimson Doctrine." As secretary of state (1929–33), he declared at the time of Japan's invasion of Manchuria that the US would not recognize any territorial changes or treaties which impaired US treaty rights or were brought about by force. Recalled from retirement to become secretary of war (1940–45), he strongly advocated development and use of the atomic bomb.

STIMULANT, DRUG that stimulates an organ. NERVOUS SYSTEM stimulants range from ALCOHOL (an apparent stimulant only) and HALLUCINOGENIC DRUGS, to drugs liable to induce CONVULSIONS. CARDIAC stimulants include DIGITALIS and ADRENALINE and are used in cardiac failure and resuscitation respectively. Bowel stimulants have a LAXATIVE effect. WOMB stimulants (OXYTOCIN and ergometrine) are used in OBSTETRICS to induce labor and prevent postpartum HEMORRHAGE.

STINKBUGS, North American name for bugs of the family Pentatomidae. Moderately large bugs, they are mostly plant-feeders. They possess glands secreting waxy substances which are pungent-smelling in many species. A few (e.g., the HARLEQUIN BUG) are important plant pests.

STINKHORN, a number of foul-smelling FUNGI that send up from an underground egg-like structure a fruiting body which produces a sticky mass of spores with a nauseating odor that attracts flies.

STINNES, Hugo (1870–1924), German industrialist. Before, during and after WWI he built up a vast industrial empire. A founder of the right-wing National People's party, he served in the Reichstag (parliament) 1920–24.

STOA, in ancient Greece, a long, open building with a colonnade supporting the roof. Stoas were used as public meeting-places for business or pleasure.

STOAT, *Mustela erminea*, a small carnivore closely related to the WEASEL but slightly larger and distinguished by a black tip to the tail. The back is brown and the underside cream, but in northern parts of its range the stoat molts out to a pure white pelage in winter—keeping the black tailtip. In this phase it is known as ERMINE.

STOCHASTIC PROCESS, any process governed by the laws of PROBABILITY: for example, the BROWNIAN MOTION of the submicroscopic particles in a colloidal solution (see COLLOID). Most stochastics involve time: in the case of the particles, the state of the system at a time t is a random variable, $x(t)$. In mathematics, particularly STATISTICS, a stochastic is a family of random VARIABLES.

STOCKBREEDING. See BREEDING.

STOCKBRIDGE, town in W Mass., on the Housatonic R, where in 1734 John Sergeant set up a mission to the Indians later known as the Stockbridge Indians. Jonathan EDWARDS was pastor there 1751–57. It is now a summer and winter resort. Pop 2 312.

STOCKHAUSEN, Karlheinz (1928–), German composer and theorist, a pioneer of electronic music and new sound effects. A pupil of MESSIAEN, he has produced work like *Gruppen* (1959),

A replica of the stoa at Attalus, Greece, built on the site of the original by the American School of Archeology in 1956. Now a museum, it would once have served as a place of public business.

in which three orchestras play "groups" or blocks of sounds against each other, and the electronic *Kontakte* (1959–60).

STOCKHOLM, capital of Sweden, an architecturally fine city on a network of islands on the E coast. It is Sweden's major commercial, industrial, cultural and financial center, and an important port. Chief industries are machinery, paper and print, shipbuilding, chemicals and foodstuffs. Founded in the 13th century, it was long dominated by the HANSEATIC LEAGUE. Liberated in a national uprising in 1523, it became the capital in 1634. Pop 746 560.

STOCKS AND STOCK MARKET. Stocks represent shares of ownership in a corporation or public body. Issuing stocks provides a means for companies to raise CAPITAL (see INVESTMENT). Individuals buy stocks because they can easily be converted into cash and may gain in value. The initial par value of a stock is determined by the assets of the company, such as its plant, machinery, property. But par value has no bearing on the market value of a stock, which is the price people are willing to pay. If a company is seen to be doing well, the market value can soar above its original par value. This is one way an investor can make capital gains by owning stocks. A stockholder also expects to receive an annual dividend based on the profits of the company. Stocks can be divided into two categories, preferred and common. The preferred stockholder is entitled to a fixed percentage claim on profits prior to the common stockholder, who then gets the rest. Depending on profits, the common stockholder may either get no dividend, or get a much higher return than the preferred stockholder; common stocks are more speculative.

The stock market, or exchange, is the place where people who want to sell and buy stocks can get together. Most transactions are carried out by stockbrokers, who are paid a commission on each

One of the world centers of the stock market, the New York Stock Exchange on Wall Street. The frenetic activity may seem confusing to the outsider, but to the brokers it is just another day.

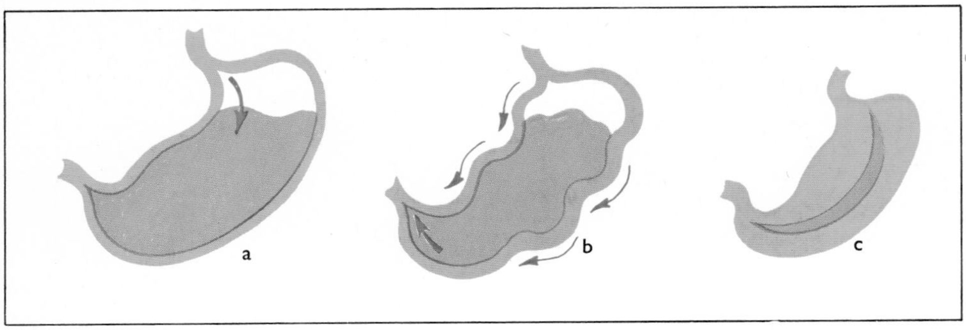

Action of the stomach. (a) After a meal the stomach wall (pink) is distended by food (green) entering from the esophagus; (b) between 1 and 2 hours afterwards peristaltic movements have shifted some of the partly digested food out through the pylorus into the small intestine; (c) the stomach is emptied, except for a residue of digestive fluid, and the walls contract. This may take anything between 3 and 10 hours, depending on the nature of the food and previous meals.

transaction. In the US, a customer may also buy stocks on credit, but he must pay an amount, or margin, specified by the Federal Reserve System, toward the transaction, with the balance advanced by the broker. All stock exchanges in the US are registered and regulated by the SECURITIES AND EXCHANGE COMMISSION.

STOCKTON, city in central Cal., seat of San Joaquin Co. It is a port and processing center for agricultural products, with some manufacturing industry, including farm machinery. Pop 109 963.

STOCKTON, Robert Field (1795–1866), US naval officer. In the MEXICAN WAR he captured Los Angeles and proclaimed himself governor of Cal. He was a US senator 1851–53, and played a major part in building and running the Delaware and Raritan canal (1828–38, 1853–66).

STOICISM, ancient Greek school of philosophy founded by ZENO OF CITIUM, who taught in a STOA in Athens c300 BC. Much influenced by the CYNICS, the stoics believed that man should live rationally and in harmony with nature, and that virtue is the only good. In performing his duty the virtuous man should be indifferent to pleasure, as well as to pain and misfortune, thus rising above the effects of chance and achieving spiritual freedom and conformity with the divine reason controlling all nature. Stoicism was influential for many centuries; among the most famous of the later Stoics were SENECA, EPICTETUS and MARCUS AURELIUS.

STOKE-ON-TRENT, city in W central England, known for its Staffordshire pottery and as the home of Josiah WEDGWOOD. It also has coalmining and brick, tile and chemical industries. Pop 265 153.

STOKER, Bram (Abraham Stoker; 1847–1912), British writer and theatrical manager best known for his *Dracula* (1897). In addition, he was manager to Henry IRVING 1878–1905.

STOKES (St), CGS VISCOSITY unit: 10^{-4} m^2/s.

STOKES, Carl Burton (1927–), US politician and lawyer, the first black mayor of a major American city (Cleveland, Ohio, 1967–71).

STOKOWSKI, Leopold (1882–), brilliant, flamboyant British-born US conductor. He gained his early reputation as musical director of the Philadelphia Orchestra (1912–36), and it was under his baton that they played the music for Disney's *Fantasia* (1940). He was noted especially for his modern repertoire and innovatory orchestration.

STOLYPIN, Pyotr Arkadevich (1862–1911), prime minister of imperial Russia 1906–11. Ruthless in suppressing unrest and opposition, he yet instituted land reforms aimed at creating a conservative land-owning peasantry, thereby making right-wing enemies. He was assassinated by a revolutionary who was also a police agent.

STOMACH, the large distensible hopper of the DIGESTIVE SYSTEM. It receives food boluses from the ESOPHAGUS and mixes them with hydrochloric acid and the stomach ENZYMES; fats are partially emulsified. After some time, the pyloric SPHINCTER relaxes and food enters the DUODENUM and the rest of the GASTROINTESTINAL TRACT. Diseases of the stomach include ULCER, CANCER and pyloric stenosis, causing pain, anorexia or VOMITING; these often require SURGERY.

STOMATA, tiny pores in the surface of leaves which are automatically opened and closed by a pair of guard cells. They allow exchange of gases and water vapor between the PLANT and the atmosphere.

STONE, former UK unit of weight (=14 pounds—see WEIGHTS AND MEASURES). ROCKS and minerals used in building are often called stone.

STONE, Edward Durell (1902–), US architect whose works include the US pavilion for the 1958 Brussels World Fair, the US embassy in Delhi (1958) and the J. F. Kennedy Center in Washington, D.C. (1971).

STONE, Harlan Fiske (1872–1946), appointed attorney general in 1924 to restore confidence in the scandal-ridden Justice Department, became associate justice (1925–41) and chief justice (1941–46) of the US Supreme Court. He was noted for his dissenting opinions, many upholding NEW DEAL legislation.

STONE, Isidor Feinstein "Izzy" (1907–), US crusading liberal journalist who founded and wrote *I. F. Stone's Weekly* (1953–71), which maintained a constant stream of criticism and comment on US politics, in particular attacking McCarthyism and the Vietnam War.

STONE, Lucy (1818–1893), US reformer and campaigner for women's rights. A fervent antislaver, she helped to found the American Woman Suffrage Association (1869) and edited its magazine *Woman's Journal* (1870–93).

STONE AGE, the stage in man's cultural development preceding the BRONZE AGE and the IRON AGE (see also PRIMITIVE MAN). It is characterized by man's use of exclusively stone tools and weapons, though some made of bone, wood, etc., may occur. It is split up into three periods: the **Paleolithic**, or Old Stone Age, began with the emergence of man-like creatures, the earliest stone tools being some 2.5 million years old and associated with the australopithecines (see PREHISTORIC MAN). Paleolithic tools, if worked at all, are made of chipped stone. The **Mesolithic**, or Middle Stone Age, was confined exclusively to NW Europe. Here, between c8000 and c3000 BC, various peoples enjoyed a culture showing similarities with both Paleolithic and Neolithic. In Europe, the **Neolithic**, or New Stone Age, began about 8000 BC, and was signaled by the development of agriculture, with consequent increase in stability of the population and hence elaboration of social structure. The tools of this period are of polished stone. Apart from farming, men also worked mines. The Neolithic merged slowly into the Early Bronze Age.

STONECROP, common name for a number of succulent plants of the genus *Sedum*, which inhabit rocks, walls and crevices. Several species, including the common yellow-flowering stonecrop (*Sedum acre*) are cultivated in rock gardens.

STONEFISH, *Synanceja verrucosa*, the most venomous of all the SCORPION FISHES. A bottom-living fish of the Indo-Pacific, it has poisonous dorsal spines quite capable of killing a man. The body is cryptic and covered by warts and flaps of skin that make it virtually invisible against its background.

STONEFLIES, an order of freshwater insects, the Plecoptera. Adults are stout-bodied insects found near water which do not fly well. The larvae, with two cerci at the tip of the ABDOMEN, live in streams beneath stones or in weeds.

STONEHAM, town in NE Mass., a residential suburb of Boston with an old-established shoemaking industry. Pop 20 275.

STONEHENGE, the ruins of a MEGALITHIC MONUMENT, dating from the STONE AGE and early BRONZE AGE, on Salisbury Plain, S England. Its most noticeable features are concentric rings of stones surrounding a horseshoe of upright stones, and a solitary vertical stone, the Heel Stone, some 100m to the NE. Stonehenge was built between c1900 BC and c1400 BC in three distinct phases. It appears to have been both a religious center and an observatory from which predictions of astronomical events could be made.

STONE MOUNTAIN, 650ft-high granite dome near Atlanta, Ga. A portion of the north face has been sculptured as a memorial to the heroes of the Confederacy, begun in 1928 by G. BORGLUM. It is part of the Stone Mountain Memorial Park, established in 1958.

STONES RIVER, Battle of. See MURFREESBORO, BATTLE OF.

STONEWARE. See POTTERY AND PORCELAIN.

STONINGTON, town in SE Conn., on Long Island Sound, a fishing center whose industry also includes boatbuilding, textiles and machinery. Pop 15 940.

STOPES, Marie Charlotte Carmichael (1880–1958), British pioneer of sex education and family planning. A professional paleobotanist, she wrote *Wise Parenthood* (1918) and set up (1921) the first UK birth-control clinic.

STORKS, large, heavily-built birds, family Ciconiidae, with long legs and necks, long, stout bills and commonly black and white plumage. The long legs and slightly webbed feet are adaptations for wading in shallow water, where they feed on freshwater animals and large insects. They tend to be gregarious and characteristic greeting ceremonies may be observed at nests and roosts. The family is largely of tropical distribution, the two temperate-breeding species undertaking long migrations to their breeding grounds.

STORM, a transient but often violent atmospheric disturbance with high WINDS, accompanied by SQUALLS, PRECIPITATION, and often thunder and lightning (see THUNDERSTORMS). Varying in type with latitude and season, storms are associated with CYCLONES. (See also HURRICANE; TORNADO.)

STORM AND STRESS. See STURM UND DRANG.

STORM TROOPERS (*Sturmabteilungen*, or SA), the strongarm gangs set up in Germany in 1921 by Ernst ROEHM to destroy resistance to the Nazis. They grew into a private army 2 000 000 strong, but were virtually disbanded after Hitler had Roehm killed in 1934.

STORY, Joseph (1779–1845), associate justice of the US Supreme Court from 1811, author of nine great legal commentaries and professor of law at Harvard from 1829. He participated in many historic decisions shaping federal law under Chief Justice MARSHALL, and exercised a great influence on US jurisprudence and legal education.

STOSS, Veit (c1447–1533), German sculptor of realistic and expressive carvings in wood. Major works include the altar (1477–89) in St. Mary's, Krakow, Poland, and the *Annunciation* (1517–19) in the church of St. Lorenz, Nuremburg.

STOUGHTON, town in E Mass. Manufactures include footwear, woolen goods and electric equipment. Pop 23 549.

STOW, city in NE Ohio, about 8mi NE of Akron. It is residential with some light industry. Pop 19 847.

STOW, John (c1525–1605), English self-taught scholar and antiquarian who edited medieval chronicles for Archbishop PARKER and is famous for his *Chronicles (Annales) of England* (1560–92) and *Survey of London* (1598).

STOWE, Harriet Elizabeth Beecher (1811–1896), US author famous for the antislavery novel *Uncle Tom's Cabin* (1852). Born into the BEECHER family, she moved to Cincinnati, Ohio, in 1832, and there learned about slavery in nearby Ky. Her other books include the documentary *The Key to Uncle Tom's Cabin* (1853), and the novels *Dred: A Tale of the Great Dismal Swamp* (1856) and *The Minister's Wooing* (1859).

STRABISMUS, cross-eye, or **squint,** a disorder of the EYES in which the alignment of the two ocular axes is not parallel, impairing binocular VISION; the eyes may diverge or converge. It is often congenital and may require SURGERY if orthoptics fail. Acquired squints are usually due to nerve or muscle disease and cause double vision.

STRABO (c63 BC–c23 AD), Greek geographer and historian. His *Historical Sketches* in 47 books are almost entirely lost, but the 17 books of his *Geography* have survived and are a principal source for our knowledge of ancient geography.

STRACHEY, Giles Lytton (1880–1932), English biographer and critic prominent in the BLOOMSBURY GROUP. His irreverent studies of the famous in *Eminent Victorians* (1918), and *Queen Victoria* (1921) caused a stir but suited the iconoclastic mood which followed WWI. They are still admired for their wit, irony and style. His last major work was *Elizabeth and Essex* (1928).

STRADELLA, Alessandro (c1642–1682), Italian composer of operas, oratorios, over 200 fine chamber cantatas and some notable orchestral music. Many legends surround his life and he is said to have been assassinated by a jealous nobleman.

STRADIVARI, or **Stradivarius, Antonio** (c1644–1737), Italian violin maker, most famous of a group of fine craftsmen who worked in Cremona (see also AMATI; GUANERI). Stradivarius violins, violas and cellos are today highly prized.

STRAFFORD, Thomas Wentworth, 1st Earl of (1593–1641), English statesman. From opposing CHARLES I's policies 1614–28, he changed sides and became a privy councillor 1629–32, lord deputy in Ireland 1633–39 and with LAUD an efficient and just but ruthless promoter of the king's absolutist ideals. He was executed to appease a hostile parliament.

STRAIN. See MATERIALS, STRENGTH OF.

STRAIT, a narrow strip of sea joining two large areas of sea, possibly the result of marine EROSION of an ISTHMUS. (See also FIRTH.)

STRANGENESS NUMBER, nonzero integral quantum number assigned to certain "strange" SUBATOMIC PARTICLES (K mesons and hyperons) because of their unusually long lifetimes. (Other particles have zero strangeness number.) Strangeness is conserved in strong nuclear interactions.

STRASBERG, Lee (1901–), Austrian-born US acting teacher and stage director, advocate of STANISLAVSKI's "method" acting. A founder and director of the Group Theatre (1930–37), he became director of the Actor's Studio in New York in 1948.

STRASBOURG, commercial and industrial city in NE France. A major river port linked with the Rhine and Rhône, it has metallurgical, petroleum, heavy machinery and food-processing industries. Seat of the Council of Europe, it was a free imperial city until French seizure in 1681. It was under German rule 1871–1919. Pop 260 300.

STRASSMANN, Fritz (1902–), German physicist who worked on uranium FISSION with Otto HAHN after Lise MEITNER had fled Germany (1938). All three shared the 1966 Fermi Award.

STRATEGIC AIR COMMAND (SAC), main US nuclear striking force, containing over 1 200 bombers and most of the US's strategic missiles. SAC is linked to US warning systems and is an independent command under the Defense Department.

STRATEGIC ARMS LIMITATION TALKS (SALT), talks entered into by the US and Russia in Dec. 1969 in Helsinki as both nations developed antiballistic-missile systems. The first phase of talks produced a treaty, ratified by the US Senate in 1972, limiting land and submarine-borne nuclear missile forces. In the second phase, resumed Nov. 1972, a standing consultative commission was set up.

STRATEGIC SERVICES, Office of. See OFFICE OF STRATEGIC SERVICES.

STRATEGY, the general design behind a war or military campaign. In a wider sense it involves "grand strategy": delineation of the broad political objectives determining military strategy. Strategy cannot be reduced to a set of general rules, but it always involves long-term planning; defining military objectives; analyzing one's own and the enemy's strength; understanding the geography of the land and planning moves accordingly; assessing options and preparing contingency plans; organizing transport, supplies and communications; anticipating enemy actions and determining when and where to fight. Among the great strategists in history are ALEXANDER THE GREAT, JULIUS CAESAR and NAPOLEON; among those of modern times are von CLAUSEWITZ, von MOLTKE, LIDDELL HART and Hugh TRENCHARD. Strategy and strategic theories are continually modified by technological, social and political changes. Since WWII, nuclear weapons at one extreme and GUERRILLA WARFARE at the other have made nonsense of conventional strategy, and it has become impossible to separate purely military strategy from wider political and economic objectives.

STRATFORD, city in S Ontario famed for its Shakespeare theater and festival. It has also engineering workshops and textile and furniture manufactures. Pop 24 508.

STRATFORD, town in SW Conn. on the Housatonic R. It has aeronautical and machine and hardware industries, and is the home of the US Shakespeare Festival. Pop 49 775.

STRATFORD-UPON-AVON, market town in W central England, home of SHAKESPEARE. A tourist mecca, it contains his birthplace (now a museum), his tomb in Holy Trinity church, and the riverside theater where the Royal Shakespeare Company perform. Anne Hathaway's cottage is nearby. The town also supports some light industry. Pop 19 449.

STRATHCONA AND MOUNT ROYAL, Donald Alexander Smith, 1st Baron (1820–1914), Canadian fur trader, financier, statesman and builder of the Canadian Pacific railroad (1885). Emigrating from Scotland in 1838, he joined the Hudson's Bay Company, eventually becoming governor in 1889. A member of the Canadian Parliament 1871–80, 1887–96, he was High Commissioner in London 1896–1914.

STRATIGRAPHY, the branch of GEOLOGY concerned with the chronological sequence and the correlation of rock strata in different districts. (See also PALEONTOLOGY; ROCKS; SEDIMENTARY ROCKS.)

STRATOSPHERE, the atmospheric zone immediately above the tropopause, including the OZONE layer. (See ATMOSPHERE.)

STRAUS, Oscar (1870–1954), Austrian composer, famous for *The Chocolate Soldier* (1908) and about 50 other operettas. He left Europe to escape the Nazis but later returned to Austria.

STRAUSS, David Friedrich (1808–1874), German theologian and philosopher whose *Life of Jesus* (1835–36) caused a storm by denying the historicity of supernatural elements in the Gospels and treating their accounts of Jesus as mythological.

STRAUSS, Franz Joseph (1915–), West German politician, leader of the conservative Bavarian Christian Social Union. As minister of defense (1956–62), he was an advocate of German rearmament. Criticized over the arrest of the editors of the left-wing magazine *Der Spiegel*, he lost his post, but returned as finance minister 1966–69.

STRAUSS, Johann, name of two famous Viennese composers of WALTZES. **Johann, the Elder** (1804–1849) achieved immense popularity and established the distinctive light style of the Viennese waltz. **Johann, the Younger** (1825–1899), wrote many favorites, including *The Blue Danube* (1866), *Tales from the Vienna Woods* (1868) and the opera *Die Fledermaus* (*The Bat*, 1873).

STRAUSS, Lewis Lichtenstein (1896–1974), US banker, member (1946–50) and chairman (1953–58) of the US Atomic Energy Commission, where he clashed with OPPENHEIMER over the development of the hydrogen bomb, which he supported. He became Secretary of Commerce 1958–59.

STRAUSS, Richard (1864–1949), German composer and conductor, the last of the great Romantic composers. He leapt to fame with the tone poem *Don Juan* (1888). Other symphonic poems include *Till Eulenspiegel* (1895), *Don Quixote* (1898) and *A Hero's Life* (1898). After 1900 he concentrated on vocal music, and with von HOFMANNSTHAL as librettist produced brilliantly scored and popular operas, including *Salome* (1905), *Elektra* (1909), *Der Rosenkavalier* (1911) and *Die Frau ohne Schatten* (1919). He is also famous for *Thus Spake Zarathustra* (1896).

STRAVINSKY, Igor Fyodorovich (1882–1971), one of the greatest modern composers, born in Russia. Taught by RIMSKY-KORSAKOV, he caused a sensation with his scores for DIAGHILEV's ballets: *The Firebird* (1910), *Petrouchka* (1911) and *The Rite of Spring* (1913). From 1920 he lived in France, adopting an austere neoclassical style, as in *Symphonies of Wind Instruments* (1920), the opera *Oedipus Rex* (1927) and *Symphony of Psalms* (1930). Emigrating to the US in 1939, he became a US citizen in 1945. Later works include *Symphony in Three Movements* (1942–45) and the opera *The Rake's Progress* (1951). He finally adopted TWELVE-TONE composition in works like *Agon* (1953–57) and *Threni* (1958).

Igor Stravinsky (right), with Pablo Picasso, in a famous sketch by Jean Cocteau.

STRAW, dried stalks of grasses, principally CEREAL CROPS. It has many farm uses: for litter or bedding; as livestock food (less nutritious than HAY), and as an ingredient of farmyard MANURE and composts for garden plants. Straw is used in the making of a thick low-quality cardboard (strawboard), straw hats and baskets, and in the thatching of houses.

STRAWBERRY, luscious fruit-bearing plants of the genus *Fragaria*, native to the Americas, Europe and Asia. Strawberries have been cultivated locally for many centuries though most modern varieties originated in crosses between New-World species. The FRUIT is in fact a swollen part of the flower stalk. Family: Rosaceae.

STRAWBERRY-GERANIUM, or strawberry-begonia, *Saxifraga stolonifera*, a low-growing creeper, producing rounded, geranium-shaped, silver-veined olive-green leaves, maroon on the underside, and strawberry-like runners. Some varieties have variegated leaves. They are popular house plants requiring a cool, moist atmosphere, with the soil kept on the dry side. Propagation is by rooting offsets. Family: Saxifragaceae.

STRAWFLOWER, best known of the "everlasting flowers," is an Australian species, *Helichrysum bracteatum*, which produces heads of yellow, red or white flowers. Tufted in growth, its large scale-like bracts preserve their appearance when dried. Family: Compositae.

STREAMLINING, the design of the shape of a body so as to minimize drag as it travels through a fluid; essential to the efficiency of aircraft, ships and submarines. At subsonic speeds turbulent flow is minimized by using a shape rounded in front, tapering to a point behind (see AERODYNAMICS; AIRFOIL; FLUID MECHANICS). At SUPERSONIC speeds a different shape is needed, thin and pointed at both ends, to minimize the shock waves.

STREAM OF CONSCIOUSNESS, a literary technique in which a character's thoughts are presented in the jumbled, inconsequential manner of real life, apparently without the author imposing any framework on them. Its best-known exponents are Marcel PROUST, James JOYCE and Virginia WOOLF.

STREAMWOOD, residential village in NE Ill., on the Fox R 30mi NW of Chicago. Pop 18176.

STREATOR, city in N central Ill., on Vermillion R. Local mineral deposits support brick, ceramic and glass industries. Pop 15600.

STREICHER, Julius (1885–1946), German Nazi journalist. In 1923 he founded *Der Stürmer*, a fanatical anti-Semitic periodical which he edited until 1945. He was tried at NUREMBERG and hanged.

STREPTOCOCCUS, BACTERIUM responsible for many common infections including sore throat, TONSILLITIS, SCARLET FEVER, IMPETIGO, cellulitis, ERYSIPELAS and PUERPERAL FEVER; a related organism is a common cause of PNEUMONIA and one type may cause endocarditis on damaged HEART valves. PENICILLIN is the ANTIBIOTIC of choice. RHEUMATIC FEVER and BRIGHT'S DISEASE are late immune responses to streptococcus.

STREPTOMYCIN, early ANTIBIOTIC (discovered by WAKSMAN) with wide spectrum antibacterial activity. For years it was the major drug for TUBERCULOSIS. Toxicity to HEARING and balance led to the use of the related gentamicin and kanamycin, and of rifampicin for tuberculosis.

STRESEMAN, Gustav (1878–1929), German statesman awarded the 1926 Nobel Peace Prize. He founded (1918) and led the conservative German People's Party, was chancellor of the Republic in 1923 and foreign minister 1923–29. He followed a program of moderation and reconciliation with Germany's former enemies, and as an author of the LOCARNO TREATIES (1925) took Germany into the League of Nations as an equal of the other powers.

STRESS. See MATERIALS, STRENGTH OF.

STRICKLAND, William (1787–1854), US architect and engineer, exponent of the classical style. He designed many public buildings in Philadelphia, including the Second Bank of the US (1819–24).

STRIKES AND LOCKOUTS. See UNIONS.

STRINDBERG, Johan August (1849–1912), Swedish playwright and novelist. His biting, pessimistic plays, *Mäster Olof* (1873), *The Father* (1887) and *Miss Julie* (1888), made a deep mark on modern drama; his novel *The Red Room* (1879) about injustice and hypocrisy won acclaim. Later plays such as *The Ghost Sonata* (1907) combine dream sequences with Swedenborgian religious mysticism.

STRINGED INSTRUMENTS, musical instruments whose sound is produced by vibrating strings or wires, the pitch being controlled by their length and tension. In the BALALAIKA, BANJO, GUITAR, HARP, LUTE, MANDOLIN, SITAR, UKULELE and ZITHER, the vibration is produced by plucking with the fingers or a plectrum. In the KEYBOARD INSTRUMENTS (CLAVICHORD, HARPSICHORD, PIANO, SPINET, VIRGINAL) the strings are either plucked or struck by hammers operated by depressing the keys. The VIOL and VIOLIN families are played with a horsehair bow, which is drawn across the string.

STRIP MINING, technique used where ORE deposits lie close enough to the surface to be uncovered merely by removal of the overlying material; most used for COAL. (See also MINING.)

STROBOSCOPE, instrument that produces regular brief flashes of intense light, used to study periodic motion, to test machinery and in high-speed photography. When the flash frequency exactly equals that of the rotation or vibration, the object is illuminated in the same position during each cycle, and appears stationary. A gas discharge lamp is used, with flash duration about 1 μs and frequency from 2 to 3000Hz.

STROESSNER, Alfredo, General (1912–   ), president of Paraguay since 1954. Army commander in 1951, he ousted his predecessor in a coup, and has created an efficient and stable totalitarian regime.

STROHEIM, Erich von (1885–1957), German-born US film director. Beginning under D. W. GRIFFITH, he became known for his realism, careful construction and attention to detail, as in *Greed* (1924) and *The Wedding March* (1928).

STROKE, or cerebrovascular accident, the sudden loss of some aspect of BRAIN function due to lack of BLOOD supply to a given area; control of limbs on one side of the body, APHASIA or dysphasia, loss of part of the visual field or disorders of higher function are common. Stroke may result from EMBOLISM, ARTERIOSCLEROSIS and THROMBOSIS, or HEMORRHAGE (then termed apoplexy). Areas with permanent loss of blood supply do not recover but other areas may take over their function.

STROMBOLI. See LIPARI ISLANDS.

STRONGSVILLE, city, a residential suburb of Cleveland, NE Ohio, with some light industry. Pop 15182.

STRONTIUM (Sr), reactive, silvery-white ALKALINE-EARTH METAL, occurring as strontianite ($SrCO_3$) and celestite ($SrSO_4$), found mainly in Scotland, Ark. and Ariz. Strontium is made by ELECTROLYSIS of the chloride or reduction of the oxide with aluminum. It resembles calcium physically and chemically. The radioactive isotope Sr^{90} is produced in nuclear FALLOUT, and is used in nuclear electric-power generators. Strontium compounds are used in fireworks (imparting a crimson color), and to refine sugar. AW 87.6, mp 769°C, bp 1384°C. sg 2.54.

STRUTHERS, city in NE Ohio on the Mahoning R, a suburb of Youngstown. It is an iron and steel producing center. Pop 15343.

STRUTT, John William. See RAYLEIGH, BARON.

STRUVE, Otto (1897–1963), Russian-born US astronomer known for work on stellar evolution (see STAR) and primarily for his contributions to astronomical SPECTROSCOPY, especially his discovery thereby of INTERSTELLAR MATTER (1938).

STRYCHNINE, poisonous ALKALOID from NUX VOMICA seeds causing excessive SPINAL CORD stimulation. Death results from spinal CONVULSIONS and ASPHYXIA.

STUART, Charles Edward. See CHARLES EDWARD STUART.

STUART, Gilbert (1755–1828), US portrait painter, creator of the famous portrait head of George Washington (1796). Praised for his color, technique and psychological insight, he painted nearly 1000 portraits and created a distinctive US portrait style.

STUART, Steuart or Stewart, House of, ruled Scotland 1371–1714 and Scotland and England 1603–1714. The first Stuart king, **Robert II** (reigned 1371–90) was a hereditary steward of Scotland whose father had married a daughter of Robert the BRUCE. A descendant, **James IV**, married Margaret, daughter of HENRY VII of England. Their grandson, **James VI**, became JAMES I of England in 1603. Between 1603 and 1714, six Stuarts ruled: James I, his son CHARLES I (1625–49), CHARLES II (1660–85), JAMES II (deposed 1688), MARY II (wife of WILLIAM III) and ANNE (1702–14). (For the Stuart pretenders descended from James II, see JACOBITES.)

STUART, James Ewell Brown (1833–1864), Confederate cavalry officer. Resigning from the US Army, he won command of a Confederacy brigade after the first Battle of BULL RUN (1861), and began his famous cavalry raids in 1862. Promoted to command all the cavalry in the N Va. Army, he was killed in the WILDERNESS campaign.

STUART, Mary. See MARY, QUEEN OF SCOTS.

STUBBS, George (1724–1806), English animal painter famous for his pictures of horses, such as *Mares and Foals* (c1760–70), and *Lion Devouring a Horse* (1769). The etchings of his *Anatomy of the Horse* (1766) came from years of anatomical study.

STUCCO, a fine, white MORTAR applied to interior walls and ceilings to form a smooth surface that may be painted (notably with frescoes), or to form modeled or molded relief decoration. In modern use, stucco is the common cement rendering applied to exterior walls.

STUDENT NATIONAL COORDINATING COMMITTEE (SNCC), leading nonviolent CIVIL RIGHTS organization of the 1960s, notably in the Southern integration and voter registration campaigns. Later, under the leadership of H. Rap Brown and Stokely CARMICHAEL, it promoted the idea of BLACK POWER.

STUDENTS FOR A DEMOCRATIC SOCIETY (SDS), US leftwing student organization founded in 1960. It spread through US universities and spearheaded opposition to the VIETNAM WAR. By 1970 it had split into many irreconcilable factions.

STUDENT'S *t*-DISTRIBUTION, in STATISTICS, a way of testing how closely a model of a population corresponds to the results of sampling. t is given by

$$t = \frac{\sqrt{n}(\bar{x} - \mu)}{s}$$

where n is the number of items in the sample, s the sample STANDARD DEVIATION, $\bar{x}$ the sample mean (see MEAN, MEDIAN AND MODE) and μ the mean of the NORMAL DISTRIBUTION which is one's model.

STUPA, Buddhist commemorative monument, also called a tope or dagoba. It is usually a solid masonry dome above a receptacle containing a sacred relic, and is surrounded by a railing.

STURBRIDGE, town in S central Mass. It is famous for "Old Sturbridge Village," a reconstruction of a 19th-century New England village. Pop 4878.

STURGEONS, primitive, often large, fishes from temperate waters of the N Hemisphere. Slow-moving and bottom-living, they feed on invertebrates, using the fleshy BARBELS around the mouth to detect prey. Many species migrate into fresh water to breed. They are important fishes commercially, prized for the eggs removed from the migrating females for CAVIAR. The flesh is also extremely good. (See also BELUGA.)

STURM UND DRANG (German: storm and stress), name given to a period of literary ferment in Germany c1770–84. Influenced by ROUSSEAU, its leading figures, HERDER, GOETHE and SCHILLER, espoused an anti-rationalist and rebellious individualism in opposition to the prevailing classicism.

STUTTER. See SPEECH AND SPEECH DISORDERS.

STUTTGART, industrial city in SW West Germany. It produces automobiles, machinery, electrical goods, precision instruments and textiles. Much of the historic city center has been rebuilt after destruction in WWII. Pop 633158.

STUTTGART, city in E central Ark., a seat of Arkansas Co. Industries include food processing (principally of rice) and footwear. Pop 10477.

STUYVESANT, Peter (c1610–1672), Dutch governor (1647) of NEW NETHERLAND. Autocratic and unpopular, he lost Dutch territory to Connecticut in 1650, conquered and annexed NEW SWEDEN in 1655, and finally surrendered New Netherland to England in 1664 after his citizens failed to support him against a surprise English attack. He retired to his farm "the Bouwerie," now New York's Bowery.

STY. See BOIL.

STYLE. See FLOWER.

STYMPHALIAN BIRDS, in Greek mythology, monstrous man-eating birds of the marshes near Lake Stymphalis in ARCADIA slain by HERCULES.

STYRENE, or vinylbenzene, colorless liquid, an AROMATIC COMPOUND found in COAL TAR and ESSENTIAL OILS, and made by dehydration of ethylbenzene. It is polymerized to make PLASTICS and RUBBERS; especially **polystyrene**, a molding plastic which (expanded to a solid foam) is used for heat insulation. MW 104.2, mp −31°C, bp 145°C.

STYRIA, or Steiermark, federal state of Austria, in the mountainous central and SE area, drained principally by the Mur R. Chief occupations are livestock raising, forestry and mining, and there are numerous ski resorts. The capital is Graz.

STYRON, William (1925–   ), US novelist and winner of the 1968 Pulitzer Prize for *The Confessions of Nat Turner* (1967), a controversial first-person account of an 1831 slave rebellion.

STYX, in Greek mythology, river in HADES across which the souls of the dead were ferried by CHARON. The most solemn, binding oaths of the gods were sworn by its name.

SUÁREZ, Francisco (1548–1617), Spanish Jesuit philosopher who represents a late flowering of SCHOLASTICISM. He was an important political and legal theorist, attacking the DIVINE RIGHT OF KINGS and arguing that international law is based on custom, not natural law.

SUBATOMIC PARTICLES, or **Elementary Particles**, small packets of matter-energy which are constituent of ATOMS or are produced in nuclear reactions or in interactions between other subatomic particles. The first such particle to be discovered was the (negative) ELECTRON (e^-), the constituent of CATHODE RAYS. Next, the **nucleons** were discovered; first the (positive) PROTON (p^+); then, in 1932, the (neutral) NEUTRON (n°). The same year saw the discovery of the first antiparticle, the positron (or antielectron, $\bar{e}^+$—see ANTIMATTER), and from that time the number of known subatomic particles, found in COSMIC RAYS or detected using particle ACCELERATORS, grew rapidly, until by the early 1970s about 100 were known or suspected. As yet no attempt to find theoretical order in this multitude of particles, many of which are highly unstable and have very short HALF-LIVES, has proved entirely successful. A first division of the particles classifies them according to whether they obey BOSE-EINSTEIN STATISTICS (bosons), or FERMI-DIRAC STATISTICS (fermions). Another division groups them into classons, leptons and hadrons. The **classons** are massless bosons which are associated with the fields known to classical physics: the familiar PHOTON associated with ELECTROMAGNETIC RADIATION and the as yet hypothetical graviton, the particle associated with GRAVITATION. The **leptons** are the electrons, the *neutrinos* and the *muons*. These fermions interact with the classical fields and the "weak force" involved in beta-decay. The neutrinos, of rest MASS zero, are products in various decay processes. The **hadrons**, including the mesons, nucleons and hyperons, interact additionally with the "strong force"—the intense force that holds the atomic nucleus together in spite of the mutual electric repulsion of its constituent protons. Boson hadrons are known as *mesons*; these were originally postulated as mediating the "strong force" in a similar way to that in which photons mediate the classical electromagnetic field. The mesons include the *pions* (pi mesons) and the heavier *kaons* (K-mesons). Fermion hadrons are known as *baryons*. These include the nucleons (protons and neutrons), and the heavier *hyperons*. The omega-minus particle (Ω^-) is a quasi-stable hyperon with a half-life of about 0.1ns. A recent attempt to explain the multiplicity of subatomic particles has involved postulating the existence of an order of yet smaller particles, called **quarks**, supposed to be constituent of all the conventional particles.

SUBCONSCIOUS, the area between CONSCIOUSNESS and UNCONSCIOUSNESS; in PSYCHOANALYSIS, a rarely used synonym for the UNCONSCIOUS.

SUBLETTE, William Lewis (c1799–1845), US fur trader and explorer in the West. Early associated with William ASHLEY and Jedediah SMITH, he made a fortune and became active in Miss. politics.

SUBLIMATION, in psychoanalysis, process whereby energies derived from instinctive DRIVES, particularly the sexual and aggressive (see SEX; AGGRESSION), are channelled into noninstinctive behavior, through INHIBITION or otherwise.

SUBLIMATION, transformation of a substance from the solid to the vapor state without its becoming liquid. All solids will sublime below their triple point (at which solid, liquid and vapor are all in EQUILIBRIUM), but in only a few cases—including DRY ICE, IODINE, NAPHTHALENE and SULFUR—is this at a high enough temperature and rate to be useful for purification. Freeze-drying (see DEHYDRATION) is by sublimation.

SUBLIMINAL PERCEPTION. See PERCEPTION; SUGGESTION.

SUBMARINE, a ship capable of underwater operation. The idea is an old one, but the first working craft was not built until 1620, by Cornelis Drebbel; it was a wooden frame covered with greased leather. The first submarine used in warfare was invented by David BUSHNELL (1776). It was a one-man, hand-powered, screw-driven vessel supposed to attach mines to enemy ships. In the Civil War the Confederate States produced several submarines. Propulsion, the major problem, was partly solved by the Rev. G. W. Garrett, who built a steam-powered submarine (1880). In the 1890s John P. HOLLAND and his rival Simon Lake designed vessels powered by gasoline engines on the surface and by electric motors when submerged, the forerunners of modern submarines. They were armed with TORPEDOES and guns. Great advances were made during WWI and WWII, which demonstrated the submarine's military effectiveness. The German U-boats were notably efficient, and introduced SNORKELS to hinder detection while recharging batteries. But none of these vessels could remain submerged for very long, and a true (long-term) submarine awaited the advent of nuclear power, independent of the oxygen of the air for propulsion. The first nuclear-powered submarine was the U.S.S. *Nautilus* (1955), which in 1958 made the first voyage under the polar ice-cap. The US, USSR, UK and France have nuclear submarine fleets fitted with ballistic missiles. Modern submarines are streamlined vessels, generally with a double hull, the inner being a pressure hull with fuel and ballast tanks between it and the outer hull. The submarine submerges by flooding its ballast tanks to reach neutral buoyancy, i.e., displacing its own weight of water (see ARCHIMEDES), and dives using its hydrofoil diving planes. Submarines are equipped with PERISCOPES and INERTIAL GUIDANCE systems. As well as their military uses, submarines are used for oceanographic research and exploration, salvage and rescue.

SUBMARINE CANYON, suboceanic canyon cutting across the CONTINENTAL SHELF, sometimes the continental slope. They are thought to be of comparatively recent origin.

SUBOTAI or Sabutai (1176?–1248?), Mongol general under GENGHIS KHAN and his successors. Having campaigned against Persia and Russia (1220–22) and China (c1230), he helped lead the GOLDEN HORDE into E Europe 1236–41.

SUBPOENA, legal order obliging a person to attend a court or official inquiry as a witness. A *subpoena duces tecum* obliges the person to produce documents relevant to the case. Failure to comply constitutes CONTEMPT OF COURT.

SUBTRACTION, the inverse operation of ADDITION. It can be seen as the solution of an EQUATION since the difference $(a-b)$ may be expressed as $b+x=a$. The subtraction of negative numbers is equivalent to addition, since $a-(-b) \equiv a+b$.

SUBTREASURY SYSTEM, part of the INDEPENDENT TREASURY SYSTEM set up in 1840 for holding and disposing of US government revenues. It was incorporated into the FEDERAL RESERVE SYSTEM in 1921.

SUBWAY, an underground railroad system designed for efficient urban and suburban passenger transport. The TUNNELS usually follow the lines of streets, for ease of construction by the cut-and-cover method in which an arched tunnel is built in an open trench, covered with earth and the street restored. Outlying parts of the system usually emerge to the surface. The first subway was built in London (1860–63) by the cut-and-cover method; it used steam trains and was a success despite fumes. A three-mile section of London subway was built (1886–90) using a shield developed by J. H. Greathead: this is a large cylindrical steel tube forced forward through the clay by hydraulic jacks; the clay is removed and the tunnel walls built. Deep tunnels are thus possible, and there is no surface disturbance. This London "tube" was the first to use electrically-powered trains, which soon replaced steam trains everywhere. Elevators were provided for the deep stations, later mostly replaced by escalators. Many cities throughout the world followed London's lead, notably Paris (the Métro, begun 1898) and New York (begun 1900). The New York subway, using the multiple-unit trains developed by Frank SPRAGUE, is now the largest in the world. The Moscow subway (begun 1931) is noted for its palatial marble stations. With increasing road traffic congestion in the 1960s, the value of subways was apparent, and many cities extended, improved and automated their systems; some introduced quieter rubber-tired trains running on concrete guideways.

SUCCESSION, the progressive change in a plant population during the development of vegetation, such as occurs in an abandoned field, which first becomes overgrown with weeds, then is progressively invaded by woody species until a climax vegetation of woodland develops; in all, this type of succession can take some 100 years. The term **sere** is often used to describe the sequence of plant communities; for example, lithosere describes the succession that starts on a bare rock, and hydrosere, one that starts with water.

SUCCOTH. See SUKKOTH.

SUCCULENTS, plants that have swollen leaves or stems and are thus adapted to living in arid regions. CACTI are the most familiar but representatives occur in other families, notably the Crassulaceae (STONECROPS and houseleeks) and Aizoaceae (LIVING STONES, mesembryanthemum). Many succulents have attractive foliage and colorful, though often short-lived, flowers.

SU-CHOU, or **Soochow**, historic city in E central China. Noted for its beauty and its ancient silk industry, it is also an industrial center, principally for textiles and steel. Pop 900 000.

SÜCHOW, or **Hsü-Chou**, city in E central China. It is a commercial and rail center in a coalmining area, and manufactures steel, textiles and machinery. Pop 800 000.

SUCKERS. See REMORAS.

SUCKLING, Sir John (1609–1642), English poet, wit, soldier and courtier, one of the CAVALIER POETS. He is remembered for his graceful love lyrics, collected after his death in *Fragmenta Aurea* (1646).

SUCRE, legal capital of BOLIVIA, some 8 500ft up in the Andes, about 250mi SE of La Paz, the administrative capital. It is a commercial and agricultural center. Pop 69 900.

SUCRE, Antonio José de (1795–1830), South American revolutionary leader, BOLÍVAR's chief aide

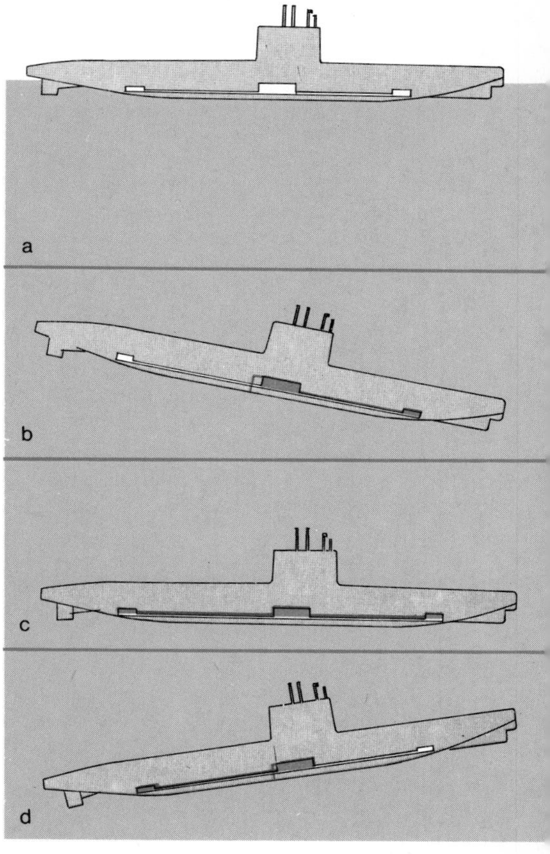

How a submarine submerges. (a) When the craft is on the surface all ballast tanks contain only air (*white*). (b) When about to submerge the central tank and fore trim tank are filled with seawater (*red*), pulling the submarine down nose first; vanes on the hull may assist and steady the dive. (c) To level off at a certain depth the water ballast is distributed throughout the tanks. (d) When resurfacing, the fore ballast tank is pumped out before the others, so that the submarine rises nose first.

and first president of Bolivia (1826–28). He liberated Colombia, Ecuador and Peru from Spanish rule, with a final victory at AYACUCHO (1824). He retired to Ecuador 1828, but returned to repel a Peruvian attack 1829. He was assassinated after presiding over a congress aimed at keeping Colombia and Venezuela united.

SUCROSE ($C_{12}H_{22}O_{11}$), or cane sugar, disaccharide CARBOHYDRATE, commercially obtained from SUGAR BEET, SUGARCANE and Sweet SORGHUM. As table sugar, sucrose is the most important of the SUGARS. It comprises a GLUCOSE unit joined to a FRUCTOSE unit. Sucrose, glucose and fructose all exhibit OPTICAL ACTIVITY and when sucrose is hydrolyzed the rotation changes from right to left. This is called inversion and an equimolar mixture of glucose and fructose is called invert sugar. The ENZYME which hydrolyzes sucrose to glucose and fructose is called invertase.

SUDAN, independent republic in NE Africa.

Land. Sudan has swamp and tropical rain forest in the S, savanna grassland in the center, desert and semidesert in the N and W. There are mountains in the NE, S, center and W. The country is bisected by the N-flowing Nile and its tributaries, along which the bulk of the population and almost all the towns are found. The climate is hot and rainfall ranges from almost nil in the N to almost 60in per year in the S.

People. There are two main groups: the Arab and Arabized Muslims of the N and W comprising about 70% of the population, and the black Negro and Nilotic tribes of the S. About 90% of the people are rural, and the illiteracy rate is high.

Economy. The Sudan is basically agricultural, and most people live by subsistence farming. The chief crops are cotton (the main export), millet, groundnuts, sesame, maize and dates. Livestock are raised in large numbers. Gum arabic is a major export, accounting for 90% of the world's supply. Manufacturing is limited to basic goods. The only port is Port Sudan on the Red Sea.

History. Called NUBIA in ancient times, N Sudan was colonized by Egypt c2000 BC. By 800 BC it had come under the CUSH kingdom, which had given way by 600 AD to independent Coptic Christian states. In the 13th–15th centuries these collapsed in the face of Muslim expansion, and the Muslim Funj state was established and lasted until Egypt invaded the Sudan in 1821. The nationalist MAHDI led a revolt in 1881, after which a series of campaigns resulted in joint Anglo-Egyptian rule in 1899. Since independence in 1956 the country has had two military governments (1958–64, 1969–) and continuing disputes between N and S, the latter resisting Muslim domination.

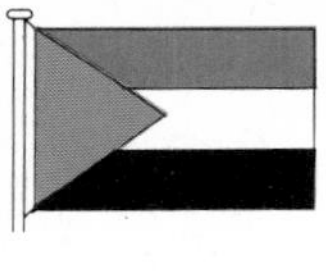

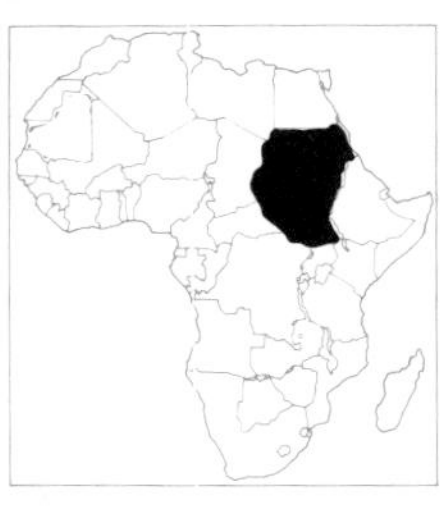

Official name: Democratic Republic of the Sudan
Capital: Khartoum
Area: 967 500sq mi
Population: 16 940 000
Languages: Arabic; English
Religions: Muslim, Animist, Christian
Monetary unit(s): 1 Sudanese pound = 100 piastres

SUDBURY, city in central Ontario, Canada, the center of the country's largest mining region, producing nearly half the world's nickel, and also copper, gold, silver, platinum and iron. Pop 90 535.

SUDBURY, town in E Mass., 18mi W of Boston. It is residential, with some light industry, including electronics. Pop 13 506.

SUDETENLAND, region of W Czechoslovakia. Originally it designated the area of the Sudetes Mts on the Bohemia-Silesia border, but came to apply to all the German-speaking Bohemian and Moravian borderlands incorporated into Czechoslovakia in 1919. The Sudetenland was ceded to Nazi Germany by the MUNICH AGREEMENT in 1938, and restored to Czechoslovakia in 1945.

The Suez Canal, a broad stretch of water traversing arid desert country. Opened in 1869, it was built almost entirely by manual labor.

SUE, Eugène (1804–1857), French novelist, best known for his sensational serialized tales of low-life Paris such as *The Mysteries of Paris* (1842–43) and *The Wandering Jew* (1844–45); they embraced his ideal of social reform.

SUEDE, LEATHER used with the buffed, napped surface outward for shoes and clothing.

SUETONIUS (c69–c140 AD), Roman biographer, author of *Lives of the Caesars*, 12 biographies from Julius Caesar to the emperor Domitian. They are full of entertaining scandal and are also valuable for their verbatim use of historical sources.

SUEZ, Egyptian port serving the S end of the SUEZ CANAL. It has oil refining and manufacturing industries. Pop 315 000.

SUEZ CANAL, ship canal in Egypt linking the Red Sea with the E Mediterranean; 101mi long, it cut over 4 000mi off the route from Britain to India and has been a major commercial waterway since its opening in 1869. In the 1960s it handled 15% of the world's sea traffic. Without locks, the canal runs N–S, passing through Lake Timsah and the Bitter Lakes. It has a minimum width of 179ft and a dredged depth of almost 40ft. Work began in 1859 under de LESSEPS, after the Ottoman khedive of Egypt had conceded a 99-year lease to the Suez Canal Company. The controlling interest was French, and in 1875 the khedive sold his 44% shareholding to the British government, which had initially been hostile. An international convention guaranteeing the canal's neutrality was signed in 1888. Egyptian interest increased after 1936 and culminated in 1956 when NASSER nationalized the canal, prompting an invasion by Britain and France. After UN intervention the canal reopened in 1957 under Egyptian control. It was closed again by the ARAB-ISRAELI WAR of 1967, but in 1974 agreement was reached, and after the canal had been cleared of wreckage it was reopened in 1975.

SUFFICIENCY. See NECESSITY AND SUFFICIENCY.

SUFFOCATION. See ASPHYXIA.

SUFISM, Muslim mystical philosophical and literary movement dating from the 10th and 11th centuries. Stressing personal communion with God, it has spread throughout Islam in a variety of forms.

SUGAR ACT (1764), in US colonial history, a British attempt to replace the unsuccessful MOLASSES ACT (1733). By selective duties it tried to create a monopoly for sugar grown in the British colonies and to raise revenue for colonial expenditure. Its harsh enforcement created great resentment.

SUGAR BEET, *Beta vulgaris*, a plant whose swollen root provides almost half the world's sugar. It was first extensively grown in Europe to replace cane sugar from the W Indies, supplies of which were cut off during the Napoleonic Wars. Careful breeding has improved the sugar yield. Sugar beet is grown in all temperate areas where cool summers ensure good sugar formation. Family: Chenopodiaceae.

SUGARCANE, grass of the genus *Saccharum*, from which the world obtains over half its sugar. Originally native to E Asia, it has been grown extensively in the West Indies and North and South America since the 18th century and now is cultivated in most warm humid areas. The fibrous material (bagasse) left after juice extraction is made into board. Family: Gramineae. (See also MOLASSES.)

SUGARS, sweet, soluble CARBOHYDRATES (of general formula $C_x(H_2O)_y$), comprising the monosaccharides and the disaccharides. **Monosaccharides** cannot be further degraded by HYDROLYSIS and contain a single chain of CARBON atoms. They normally have the suffix -ose and a prefix indicating the length of the carbon chain; thus trioses, tetroses, pentoses, hexoses and heptoses contain 3, 4, 5, 6 and 7 carbon atoms respectively. The most abundant natural monosaccharides are the hexoses, $C_6H_{12}O_6$ (including GLUCOSE), and the pentoses, $C_5H_{10}O_5$ (including xylose). Many different isomers of these sugars are possible and often have names reflecting their source, or a property, e.g., FRUCTOSE is found in fruit, arabinose in gum arabic and the pentose, xylose, in wool. **Disaccharides** contain two monosaccharide units joined by an oxygen bridge. Their chemical and physical properties are similar to those of monosaccharides. The most important disaccharides are SUCROSE (cane sugar), LACTOSE and MALTOSE. (Table sugar consists of sucrose.) The most characteristic property of sugars is their sweetness. If we accord sucrose an arbitrary sweetness of 100, then glucose scores 74, fructose 173, lactose 16, maltose 33, xylose 40 (compare SACCHARIN 55 000). The sweetness of sugars is correlated with their solubility.

SUGER (c1081–1151), French abbot of St.-Denis and counselor of Kings LOUIS VI and LOUIS VII. He rebuilt the famous abbey church, and was Louis VII's regent during the Second Crusade (1147–49).

SUGGESTION, process whereby an individual loses his critical faculties and thus accepts IDEAS and beliefs that may be contrary to his own. People under HYPNOSIS are particularly suggestible (see also BRAINWASHING), as are those in a state of exhaustion. **Heterosuggestion** (dependent on an exterior source) is usually verbally derived, but may involve any of the SENSES. **Autosuggestion** implies that the individual himself is the source. **Mass suggestion** is one of the main aims of advertising, whereby a mass of people may be influenced in favor of a certain product; it may employ **subliminal suggestion** (illegal in most countries), where the stimuli are so brief or faint that they are registered only by the UNCONSCIOUS.

SUHARTO (1921–), president of Indonesia from 1968. A veteran general, he opposed the corrupt SUKARNO regime and crushed the communist coup it sponsored in 1965; he has held effective power since, and has restored the country's prosperity.

SUICIDE, the act of voluntarily taking one's own life. In some societies (notably Japan: see HARA-KIRI) suicide is accepted or even expected in the face of disgrace. Judaism, Islam and Christianity, however, consider it a sin. Until 1961 the UK sought to discourage it by making it a crime, and it still is in some US states. Motivation varies enormously where there is no social sanction; a suicide attempt is often thought to be an implicit "plea" for help, and may result from extreme DEPRESSION.

SUITA, city in Honshu Island, Japan, a NE suburb of Osaka. It is a railway freight center, with metal, chemical and wood-pulp industries. Pop 259 619.

SUITE, musical form developed in Germany and France in the 17th and 18th centuries, consisting of a set of dance movements in the same or related keys. The regular combination was allemande, courante, sarabande, gigue; additional movements such as the minuet, gavotte or bourée could be added.

SUKARNO (1901–1970), first president of Indonesia 1945–67. A leader of the independence movement from 1927, he collaborated with the Japanese in WWII, and was instrumental in creating the republic in 1945. His flamboyant and corrupt rule became a dictatorship in 1959; he veered toward the communist bloc, while his policies ruined the economy. Implicated in an attempted communist coup (1965), he was gradually ousted by SUHARTO.

SUKKOTH, or Feast of Tabernacles, an autumn Jewish festival. It recalls the *sukkot* (huts) used in the wanderings in the wilderness and originally celebrated the end of the harvest. Symbolic *sukkot* are still made from branches.

SULAWESI (formerly Celebes), irregularly-shaped island in South East Asia, E of Borneo, politically part of Indonesia. It is mountainous and largely covered by tropical rain forest; the climate is hot and humid. Forest products are the main export.

SULEIMAN I (1494–1566), sultan of the Ottoman Empire 1520–66. He extended its borders W to Budapest and E to Persia and maintained a powerful Mediterranean fleet. Called the Magnificent by Europeans and *Kanuni* (lawgiver) by his subjects, he brought Turkish culture and statecraft to its zenith.

SULFA DRUGS, or **sulfonamides**, synthetic compounds (containing the $—SO_2NH_2$ group) that inhibit the multiplication of invading BACTERIA, thus allowing the body's cellular defense mechanisms to suppress infection. The first sulfa drug, sulfanilamide (Prontosil), was synthesized in 1908 and used widely as a dye, before, in 1935, DOMAGK reported its effectiveness against STREPTOCOCCI. Since then it has proved effective against several other bacteria including those causing SCARLET FEVER, certain VENERAL DISEASES and MENINGITIS. This and the many other sulfa drugs are now generally used in conjunction with ANTIBIOTICS.

SULFATES, salts of SULFURIC ACID, containing the sulfate ion (SO_4^{2-}); formed by reaction of the acid with metals, their oxides or carbonates, or by oxidation of SULFIDES or sulfites (see SULFUR). Most sulfates are soluble in water, the main exceptions being calcium, strontium, barium and lead sulfates. They decompose at high temperatures to give sulfur trioxide and dioxide. Sulfates form LIGAND complexes and double salts (see ALUM). Many sulfate minerals occur in nature, often as evaporites or from oxidation of SULFIDES (see ANHYDRITE; BARITE; EPSOM SALTS; GYPSUM). **Bisulfates** contain the ion HSO_4^-; they are acid, and are converted to pyrosulfates ($S_2O_7^{2-}$) on heating. ESTERS of sulfuric acid $(RO)_2SO_2$ are also called sulfates.

SULFIDES, binary compounds of SULFUR. For organic sulfides see THIOETHERS. Nonmetal sulfides, formed by direct synthesis, include CARBON disulfide and several sulfides of nitrogen and phosphorus. Metal sulfides (S^{2-}) are mostly insoluble (except those of the ALKALI METALS and ALKALINE-EARTH METALS), and are prepared by precipitation with hydrogen sulfide. Soluble sulfides are readily hydrolyzed to the soluble bisulfides (HS^-), and are used as reducing agents and in making dyes and pesticides. Many sulfide minerals are important ores: see ARGENTITE; ARSENOPYRITE; BORNITE; CHALCOCITE; CHALCOPYRITE; CINNABAR; REALGAR; SPHALERITE; STIBNITE; WURTZITE; BLENDE. **Hydrogen Sulfide** (H_2S), is a colorless, highly toxic gas with a foul odor of rotten eggs, occurring in volcanoes; a covalent HYDRIDE. It is obtained industrially as a by-product of petroleum refining, and prepared in the laboratory by reacting a sulfide with an acid. Hydrogen sulfide burns to give sulfur dioxide and water; in aqueous solution it is a very weak acid, forming sulfides with most metal salts. It is a good reducing agent. With sulfur, hydrogen sulfide gives hydrogen polysulfides (H_2S_n, $n = 2–9$), whose salts are also known. mp $-85.5°C$, bp $-61°C$.

SULFONAMIDES. See SULFA DRUGS.

SULFONIC ACIDS, organic compounds of general formula RSO_2OH; strong, water-soluble ACIDS often used as their sodium salts, sulfonates. AROMATIC sulfonic acids are made by **sulfonation** with fuming SULFURIC ACID. They are used to make detergents (see SOAPS AND DETERGENTS), DYES, SULFA DRUGS and ION-EXCHANGE resins. They are useful in synthesis, since the sulfonate group is readily replaced.

SULFUR (S), nonmetal in Group VIA of the PERIODIC TABLE. There are large deposits in Tex. and La., and in Japan, Sicily and Mexico; the American sulfur is extracted by the FRASCH PROCESS. It is also recovered from natural gas and petroleum. Combined sulfur occurs as SULFATES and SULFIDES. There are two main allotropes of sulfur (see ALLOTROPY): the yellow, brittle rhombic form is stable up to 95.6°C, above which monoclinic sulfur (almost colorless) is stable. Both forms are soluble in carbon disulfide; they consist of eight-membered rings S_8. Plastic sulphur is an amorphous form made by suddenly cooling boiling sulfur. Sulfur is reactive, combining with most other elements. It is used in gunpowder, matches, as a fungicide and insecticide, and to vulcanize rubber. AW 32.1, mp 113°C (rh), 119°C (mono), bp 445°C, sg 2.07 (rh, 20°C). **Sulfur dioxide** (SO_2) is a colorless, acrid gas, formed by combustion of sulfur. It is an oxidizing and reducing agent and is important as an intermediate in the manufacture of sulfur trioxide and SULFURIC ACID. It is also used in petroleum refining and as a refrigerant, disinfectant, preservative and bleach. It reacts with water to give sulfurous acid (H_2SO_3), which is corrosive. Thus sulfur dioxide in flue gases is a harmful cause of POLLUTION. mp $-73°C$, bp $-10°C$. **Sulfites** are salts containing the ion SO_3^{2-}, formed from sulfur dioxide and BASES; readily oxidized to SULFATES. Bisulfites are acid sulfites, containing the ion HSO_3^-. **Sulfur Trioxide** (SO_3) is a volatile liquid or solid formed by oxidation of sulfur dioxide (see CONTACT PROCESS). It reacts violently with water to give SULFURIC ACID. mp 17°C (α), bp 45°C (α). **Thiosulfates** are salts containing the ion $S_2O_3^{2-}$, usually prepared by dissolving sulfur in an aqueous sulfite solution. They are mild reducing agents, and form LIGAND complexes; in acid solution they decompose to give sulfur and sulfur dioxide. (For sodium thiosulfate, see SODIUM.)

SULFURIC ACID (H_2SO_4), an oily, colorless liquid, made in large quantities by the CONTACT PROCESS or the LEAD-CHAMBER PROCESS. It is an oxidizing agent, reacting with metals, sulfur and carbon on heating, and is a powerful dehydrating agent (see DEHYDRATION). In aqueous solution it is a strong ACID, and reacts with BASES and most metals to give SULFATES. Fuming sulfuric acid, or **oleum**, is 100% sulfuric acid containing dissolved sulfur trioxide; it is used to make SULFONIC ACIDS. Sulfuric acid is used to make fertilizers, paints, pigments, explosives, dyes and detergents, to refine petroleum and coal tar, and in lead-acid storage batteries. mp 10°C, bp 338°C (98%).

SULLA, Lucius Cornelius (138–78 BC), Roman general and dictator. Turning against his former commander MARIUS, he became the first Roman to lead an army against Rome (88 BC). He fought MITHRADATES in Asia Minor, 87–83 BC, and returned to defeat the Marians in a civil war. As dictator, 82–79 BC he massacred opponents for their property and restored the SENATE's power.

SULLIVAN, Anne (née Macy; 1866–1936), US teacher of Helen KELLER. Partially blind herself, in 1887 she taught Helen to read and communicate through the touch alphabet, and became her lifelong companion.

SULLIVAN, Sir Arthur Seymour (1842–1900), British composer best known for his partnership with W. S. GILBERT on their famous operettas. He also composed oratorios, grand operas and hymn tunes whose popularity has not endured to the same extent.

SULLIVAN, Harry Stack (1892–1949), US psychiatrist who made important contributions to SCHIZOPHRENIA studies and originated the idea that PSYCHIATRY depends on study of interpersonal relations (including that between therapist and patient).

SULLIVAN, John (1740–1795), US soldier and statesman. He distinguished himself in the REVOLUTIONARY WAR, and was N.H. delegate to the Continental Congress (1774–75, 1780–81) and three times president of N.H. (1786–89).

SULLIVAN, John Lawrence (1858–1918), US boxer, last world heavyweight champion 1882–89 under London Prize Ring (bareknuckle) rules. He lost his first defense of it under QUEENSBURY RULES in 1892 to "Gentleman" Jim Corbett after 21 rounds.

SULLIVAN, Louis Henry (1856–1924), US architect famous for his office buildings that pioneered modern design. He was a partner of Dankmar ADLER in Chicago (1881–95). His works include the Auditorium (1889) and the Carson Pirie Scott building (1899–1904) in Chicago, and the Guaranty Building in Buffalo (1894–95). His functionalism was expressed in his famous maxim "form follows function." Frank Lloyd WRIGHT was his pupil.

SULLY, Maximilien de Béthune, Duc de (1560–1641), French statesman. A Protestant protégé of King HENRY IV, he became superintendent of finances in 1598, and by capable management led the successful reorganization of France after the Wars of RELIGION. He retired after Henry's death in 1610.

SULLY, Thomas (1783–1872), English-born US portrait painter. He studied briefly under Gilbert STUART, and became popular and prolific. Queen Victoria (1839) and several US presidents sat for him.

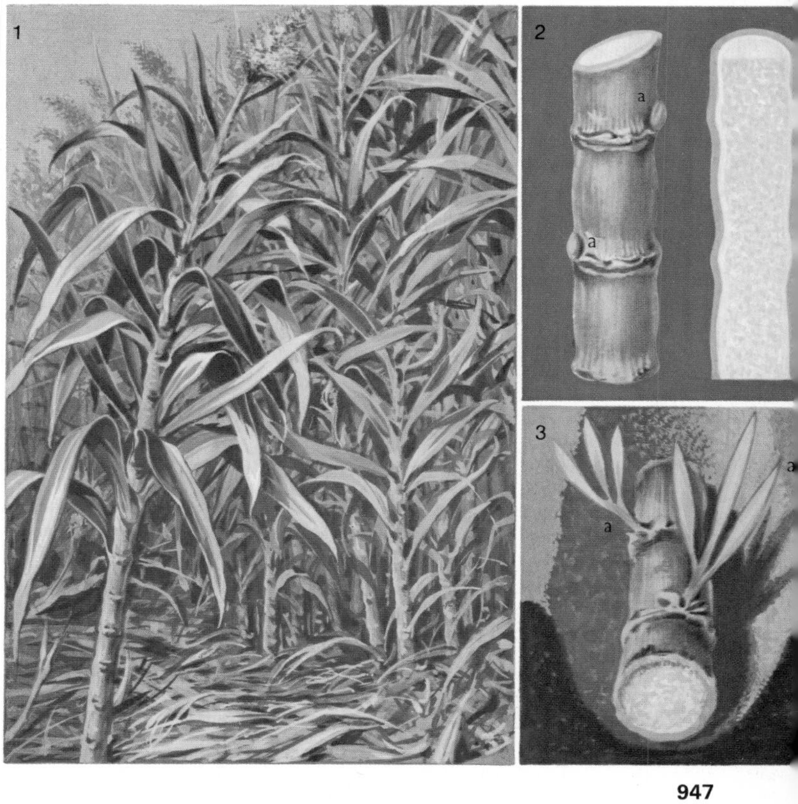

Sugarcane (1), the principal source of sugar, reaches a height of 6 to 12ft. Commercial sugarcane is grown from cuttings (2), each bud or "eye" of which (a) produces a plant. Within the stalk (cutaway view, 3) starch forms initially, followed by simple and then more complex sugars. The shoots (3a) grow into clumps of several stalks.

SULLY-PRUDHOMME, René Francois Armand (1839–1907), French PARNASSIAN poet, winner of Nobel Prize for Literature, 1901. He began writing melancholy and subjective poetry, but *La Justice* (1878) and *Le Bonheur* (*Happiness*; 1888) are philosophical.

SULPHUR, city in SW La. Center of a rice-growing and oil-producing region, it has petroleum and chemical industries. Pop 13551.

SULPHUR. See SULFUR.

SULPHUR SPRINGS, city in NE Tex., seat of Hopkins Co. It produces dairy goods, clothing and fertilizer. Pop 10642.

SULU ARCHIPELAGO, group of over 400 volcanic islands and coral islets in the SW Philippines. They are heavily forested. Marine products (fish, turtles, pearls, sea cucumbers) form the economic mainstay of the population of Muslim MOROS.

SULZBERGER, Arthur Hays (1891–1968), US newspaperman. As publisher of the *New York Times* 1935–61 he upheld the high journalistic standards of his predecessor Adolph Ochs. He joined the *Times* in 1918 and was chairman of the board 1957–68.

SUM, the result of ADDITION. If $a+b=c$, then c is the sum of a and b. The sum of two complex numbers (see IMAGINARY NUMBERS) $a+ib$ and $c+id$ is given by $(a+c)+i(b+d)$. (See also VECTOR ANALYSIS.)

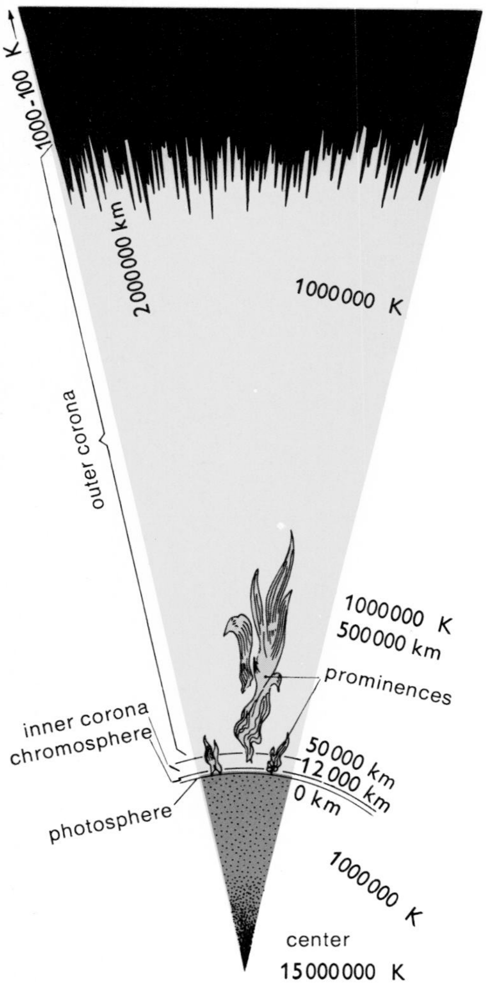

Sectional diagram showing the structure of the sun. The sun actually lacks a solid surface such as that of a planet, although the outer layer, or chromosphere, is much less dense than the inner layer, the photosphere. Under normal conditions only the photosphere is visible from earth, but during eclipses the chromosphere prominences may be seen. If observed with the naked eye a dark filter, much stronger than sunglasses, must be used or blindness may result. Ordinary telescopes and binoculars must never be used.

SUMAC, shrubs and small trees of the genus *Rhus*, which include POISON IVY, poison oak and poison sumac. Many of the species are used in TANNING. The fruits of the Staghorn sumac (*Rhus typhina*) are used to make a refreshing drink. Family: Anacardiaceae.

SUMATERA (formerly Sumatra), second-largest island of Indonesia. On the Equator, with a hot, wet climate, it is heavily forested and rich in oil, bauxite and coal, producing 70% of Indonesia's wealth. Export crops include rubber, coffee, pepper and tobacco. Medan and Palembang are the chief cities.

SUMER, S part of ancient MESOPOTAMIA in the fertile area at the head of the Persian Gulf in modern Iraq. It was the site of the SUMERIAN civilization.

SUMERIANS, inhabitants of S MESOPOTAMIA from earliest times, with a great civilization dating from c3300 BC. They established agriculture-based city-states such as ERECH, KISH, NIPPUR and UR, built irrigation canals, and achieved remarkable technical and artistic prowess, developing CUNEIFORM writing. Sumer fell to the AKKAD kingdom c2400 BC, and after a brief revival c2000 BC was absorbed into BABYLONIA.

SUMMATION, in mathematics, synonym for ADDITION or for the resulting SUM.

SUMMER. See SEASONS.

SUMMIT, village in NE Ill., 12mi W of Chicago. It is mainly residential, with some industry, including a large corn-processing plant. Pop 11569.

SUMMIT, city in NE N.J., 10mi W of Newark. A residential suburb of New York, it has some light industry, including pharmaceuticals. Pop 23620.

SUMMONS, legal order, served by an officer of a court, informing the person named in it that he or she must attend the court to answer a charge. A summons may also be issued by a committee of Congress or other government agencies.

SUMNER, Charles (1811–1874), US antislavery politician, senator from Mass. 1851–74. A law graduate (1833), he became an aggressive abolitionist and worked for world peace and prison and educational reform. Chairman of the Senate Foreign Relations Committee (1861–71), he was a prominent radical Republican during RECONSTRUCTION, and active in impeaching President Andrew JOHNSON.

SUMNER, James Batcheller (1887–1955), US biochemist who shared with J. H. NORTHROP and W. M. STANLEY the 1946 Nobel Prize for Chemistry for his first crystallization of an ENZYME (urease, 1926), showing it was a PROTEIN.

SUMNER, William Graham (1840–1910), US sociologist who expounded social Darwinism. This belief, based on DARWIN's theory of evolution, stated that social progress depends upon unrestrained competition, economic LAISSEZ-FAIRE and acceptance of inherent inequalities. He wrote *Folkways* (1907), examining the role of custom in society.

SUMO, type of Japanese wrestling in which great importance is put on size and weight, poundages up to 300 being not uncommon. The contests are usually brief.

SUMPTUARY LAWS, laws designed to restrict excessive consumption, especially of luxury items, in such areas as food, drink, clothing or ornament. Known since ancient times, sumptuary laws have usually been made on religious or moral grounds.

SUMTER, city in central S.C., seat of Sumter Co., 42mi E of Columbia. Manufactures include furniture and textiles. Local lumber is shipped. Pop 24555.

SUMTER, Thomas (1734–1832), partisan of the American Revolution who formed a guerrilla band and harrassed the British in the Carolina campaign (1780–81). He had notable successes at Hanging Rock, Fishdam Ford and Blackstock. Fort Sumter in Charleston harbor was named for him.

SUMTER, FORT. See FORT SUMTER NATIONAL MONUMENT.

SUN, the star about which the earth and the other planets of the SOLAR SYSTEM revolve. The sun is an incandescent ball of gases, by mass 69.5% hydrogen; 28% helium; 2.5% carbon, nitrogen, oxygen, sulfur, silicon, iron and magnesium altogether, and traces of other elements. It has a diameter of about 1393Mm, and rotates more rapidly at the equator (24.65 days) than at the poles (about 34 days). Although the sun is entirely gaseous, its distance creates the optical illusion that it has a surface: this visible edge is called the PHOTOSPHERE. It is at a temperature of about 6000K, cool compared to the center of the sun (20000000K) or the corona (1000000K); the photospheres of other stars may be at temperatures of less than 2000K or more than 500000K. Above the photosphere lies the **chromosphere**, an irregular layer of gases between 1.5Mm and 15Mm in depth. It is in the chromosphere that SUNSPOTS, FLARES and **prominences** occur: these last are great plumes of gas that surge out into the corona and occasionally off into space. The **corona** is the sparse outer atmosphere of the sun. During solar ECLIPSES it may be seen to extend several thousand megametres and as bright as the full moon, though in fact it extends to around the orbit of JUPITER. The earth lies within the corona, which at this distance from the sun is termed the SOLAR WIND. The sun is a very normal STAR, common in characteristics though rather smaller than average. It lies in one of the spiral arms of the MILKY WAY.

SUN BEAR, or **Malayan bear**, *Helarctus malayanus*, a small dark BEAR with chest and eye patches of light tan. Largely arboreal in habit, sleeping during the day in a rough tree nest, the Sun bear descends to the ground at night to feed on insects and fruit.

SUNBIRDS, tiny, brilliantly-colored birds of Old World tropics, of the Nectariniidae family, the equivalent of the American HUMMINGBIRDS. All are small with lightly-built bodies; fine, often decurved, bills, and tubular tongues as an adaptation to nectar-feeding.

SUNBURN, burning effect on the SKIN following prolonged exposure to ULTRAVIOLET RADIATION from the sun, common in travelers from temperate zones to hot climates. First-degree BURNS may occur but usually only a delayed ERYTHEMA is seen with extreme skin sensitivity. Systemic disturbance occurs in severe cases. Fair-skinned persons are most susceptible.

SUNBURY, city in E central Pa., seat of Northumberland Co., on the Susquehanna R. Industry includes textiles and processed foods. Pop 13025.

SUNDA ISLANDS, islands of the W Malay archipelago, lying between the S China Sea and the Indian Ocean. They comprise the Greater Sundas (notably JAWA, SUMATERA, BORNEO and SULAWESI), and the Lesser Sundas (notably BALI, Lombok, Alor and TIMOR).

SUN DANCE, religious ceremony observed by a number of Plains tribes of North American Indians during the 19th century, involving fasting, self-torture and the seeking of visions.

SUNDA STRAIT, channel between the islands of Sumatera and Jawa connecting the Java Sea with the Indian ocean. KRAKATOA is at its center.

SUNDAY, the first day of the week. Named for the sun, it is a day of worship for Christians, in remembrance of Christ's resurrection from the dead.

SUNDAY, Billy (1862–1935), US revivalist preacher noted for his flamboyance and his vivid version of fundamentalist theology. He claimed to have saved over a million souls and is thought to have collected over $1000000 in doing so. He was a professional baseball player before his conversion.

SUNDERLAND, seaport and borough in NE England. It is a center for shipping coal, with shipbuilding, engineering and fishing industries. Pop 216892.

SUNDEW, INSECTIVOROUS PLANTS of the genus *Drosera* which are found in boggy places throughout the world. The leaves bear sticky tentacles or hairs which hold any insect landing on them. Further hairs bend over until the insect is completely engulfed. It is then digested by ENZYMES secreted by the plant and the products of digestion are absorbed, supplying the plant with nutrients the soil lacks. Family: Droseraceae.

SUNDIAL, ancient type of CLOCK, still used (though rarely) in its original form. It consists of a style parallel to the earth's axis that casts a shadow on the calibrated dial plate, which may be horizontal or vertical. It assumes that the sun's apparent motion lies always on the celestial equator (see CELESTIAL SPHERE). Sundials usually show local TIME but may be calibrated to show standard time.

SUNFISHES, a family, Centrarchidae, of common freshwater perch-like fishes of North America including the CRAPPIES, Bluegills and Black basses. Popular sport and food fishes, the body is often deep and compressed.

SUNFLOWER, tall plants of the genus *Helianthus*, with large disk-shaped yellow and brown flowers which twist around to face the sun. Most of the 60 species are native to the US. The Common sunflower (*Helianthus annuus*) is cultivated in many parts of the world. The seeds yield an oil and the remainder becomes cattle feed. Family: Compositae.

SUNG, one of the strongest Chinese dynasties, founded in 960 AD by Chao K'uang-yin. It was swept away by the Mongols in the 1270s and replaced by the YUAN DYNASTY. The empire at its zenith reached from the GREAT WALL OF CHINA in the N to HAINAN in the S. The period was one of great economic and cultural advance.

SUNNITES, the orthodox majority of the followers of ISLAM, distinct from the SHI'ITES. The term refers to the traditional Way (*sunna*) of the Prophet MOHAMMED.

SUNNYVALE, city in W Cal., 8mi WNW of San Jose. Industries include food-processing and electronics. Pop 95408.

SUNSET CRATER NATIONAL MONUMENT, area of 5sq mi in N Arizona, E of San Francisco Peaks, containing a spectacular volcanic crater, ice caves and lava flows. It was established in 1930.

SUNSPOTS, apparently dark spots visible on the face of the SUN. Vortices of gas associated with strong electromagnetic activity, their dark appearance is merely one of contrast with the surrounding photosphere. Single spots are known, but mostly they form in groups or pairs. They are never seen at the sun's poles or equator. Their cause is not certainly known. Their prevalence reaches a maximum about every 11 years.

SUNSTROKE, or **heatstroke**, rise in body TEMPERATURE and failure of sweating in hot climates, often following exertion. DELIRIUM, COMA and CONVULSIONS may develop suddenly and rapid cooling should be effected.

SUN VALLEY, sports resort in S central Ida., in the Sawtooth Mts. Sun Valley Lodge was founded in 1936 as a skiing center. Pop 180.

SUN YAT-SEN (1866–1925), Chinese revolutionary, revered as the ideological father of modern China. Influenced by MARX and Henry GEORGE, he founded (1894) a movement against the MANCHUS. Exiled in 1895, he formulated the principles of *democracy*, *nationalism* and *socialism* underlying the KUOMINTANG, the party he founded and led. In 1911 the Manchus were overthrown and Sun returned to China. First president of the new republic, he soon resigned (1912) to YÜAN SHIH-KAI, whose rule became increasingly dictatorial. After a second exile (1913–17), in 1921 Sun led a rival "national" government at Canton. In the ensuing struggle against the rulers in Peking, he cooperated with the communists and organized a military academy under CHIANG KAI-SHEK who succeeded him on his death. (See also CHINA.)

SUPERCONDUCTIVITY, a condition occurring in many metals, alloys, etc., at low temperatures, involving zero electrical RESISTANCE and perfect DIAMAGNETISM. In such a material an electric current will persist indefinitely without any driving voltage and applied MAGNETIC FIELDS are exactly cancelled out by the magnetization they produce. In **type I superconductors**, both these properties disappear abruptly when the temperature or applied magnetic field exceed critical values (typically 5K and 10^4A/m), but in **type II superconductors** the diamagnetism decay is spread over a range of field values. Large ELECTROMAGNETS sometimes use superconducting coils which will carry large currents without overheating, and the exclusion of fields by superconducting materials can be exploited to screen or direct magnetic fields. Superconductivity was discovered by H. KAMERLINGH-ONNES in 1911, and is due to an indirect interaction of pairs of ELECTRONS via local elastic deformations of the metal CRYSTAL.

SUPERCOOLING AND SUPERHEATING. A liquid cooled below its FREEZING POINT without the solid phase separating out is in a metastable supercooled state. Addition of a small amount of solid or shaking may cause the liquid to freeze. A liquid heated above its BOILING POINT or a saturated vapor heated after all traces of liquid have evaporated is superheated. This state is also metastable.

SUPEREGO, according to FREUD's METAPSYCHOLOGY, the third and last part of the psychic apparatus to develop, a part of the EGO containing self-criticism, INHIBITIONS, etc. Unlike the conscience, its strictures may date from an earlier stage of the individual's development, even clashing with his current values.

SUPERFLUIDITY, the property whereby "superfluids" such as liquid HELIUM below 2.186K exhibit apparently frictionless flow. The effect requires QUANTUM MECHANICS for its explanation.

SUPERGIANT STAR. See STAR.

SUPERIOR, city in NW Wis., seat of Douglas Co., at the W end of Lake Superior. It is a major shipping and railroad center. Pop 32237.

SUPERIOR, Lake, largest of the North American GREAT LAKES, the world's largest freshwater lake. It is about 350mi long and 160mi wide, covering approximately 31800sq mi and having a maximum depth of over 1330ft. It is bounded E and N by Ontario, W by Minn., and S by Wis. and Mich. Some 200 rivers drain into it, the largest being the St. Louis. It connects with the ST. LAWRENCE SEAWAY, its principal port, Duluth-Superior, marking the W end of that system.

SUPERIORITY COMPLEX, overevaluation by an individual of his abilities, usually a DEFENSE MECHANISM countering an INFERIORITY COMPLEX.

SUPERNOVA, a NOVA which initially behaves like other novae but, after a few days at maximum brightness, increases to a far higher level of luminosity (a supernova in the ANDROMEDA galaxy, 1885, was one tenth as bright as the entire galaxy). It is thought that supernovae may be caused by the gravitational collapse of a star, or cloud of gas and dust, into a neutron STAR.

SUPEROXIDES, compounds of OXYGEN containing the ion O_2^-, resembling the PEROXIDES. Potassium superoxide is used in respirators. Rubidium and cesium superoxide are also known.

SUPERPHOSPHATE. See PHOSPHATES.

SUPERPOSITION, Principle of, law of STRATIGRAPHY first stated by William SMITH, that, when SEDIMENTARY ROCK strata are undisturbed, the younger ROCKS lie above the older.

SUPERSATURATION. See SATURATION.

SUPERSONICS, the study of fluid flow at velocities greater than that of SOUND, usually with reference to the supersonic flight of AIRPLANES and MISSILES when the relative velocity of the solid object and the air is greater than the local velocity of sound propagation.

SUPERSTITION, belief which predicts or explains events in terms of causes that have no rational connection with them, and assumes the existence of (often malign or arbitrary) supernatural forces. An example is the belief that putting on an article of clothing inside out will bring bad fortune. Any nonrational belief may also be described as superstition by those who do not hold it.

SUPPÉ, Franz von (1819–1895), Austrian composer of light music, especially light opera in the style of OFFENBACH. His works include *Poet and Peasant* (1846).

SUPPLY AND DEMAND, in economics, central concepts which seek to explain changes in prices, production and consumption of goods and services. Demand for a good depends largely on its price; usually, the higher the price, the less the quantity demanded. This relationship may be plotted as a demand curve. A supply curve may similarly be obtained showing that supply of a good is related to its price. The intersection of the two curves shows the equilibrium between the amount demanded and the amount supplied at a given price. Demand may also be explained by UTILITY, while supply can be explained by the producer's profit motive.

SUPRARENAL GLANDS. See ADRENAL GLANDS.

SUPREMATISM, art movement c1913–19 originated by the Russian-Polish painter Kasimir MALEVICH, establishing a system of non-representational composition in terms of pure geometric shapes and patterns. The movement's influence on graphic design and typography has been significant.

The massive neoclassical frontage of the United States Supreme Court building in Washington, D.C.

SUPREME COURT, highest court of the US, with the authority to adjudicate all cases arising under US law, including constitutional matters. The number of member justices is set by statute and so varies; presently the Court has a Chief Justice and eight other Associate Justices. The president appoints the justices as vacancies arise, but nominees must be confirmed by majority vote of the senate. Most nominees are easily confirmed, but the process is not perfunctory; Richard Nixon had two successive nominees rejected by the senate in 1970. Great care is taken in confirmation since justices serve "during good behavior" for life or until retirement. They can, however, be impeached and convicted for high crimes and misdemeanors. Although theoretically above politics the Court is vitally important to them, since it alone can determine the constitutionality of both state and federal laws. This power of "judicial review" is not explicitly stated in the Constitution, but is rather an operational precedent established by Chief Justice John MARSHALL in the cases of MARBURY V MADISON (1803) and MARTIN V HUNTERS LESSEE (1816). It may also overrule its own previous decisions, a provision that has kept it a living, vital body able to change with the times. A good example of this is the decision in *Brown v. Board of Education* (1954), forbidding racial segregation in education.

SUPREME SOVIET, in the USSR, the supreme state and legislative body. Its two chambers—the 767-member Soviet of the Union and the 750-member Soviet of Nationalities—have equal legislative rights, are elected to four-year terms and meet twice a year. Committees continue work between sessions. The Supreme Soviet elects its PRESIDIUM in joint session, appoints the Supreme Court and approves the Council of Ministers, the top executive and administrative body whose chairman heads the government.

SURABAJA, second-largest city in Indonesia, on the NE coast of Jawa. It is an important naval base and port with shipyards, oil refineries and chemical and textile plants. Pop 1273000.

SURAKARTA, city in Indonesia, S central Jawa, on the Solo R. It is a center for commerce with mixed manufactures and crafts. Pop 367626.

SURAT, city in W central India, capital of Surat district in Gujarat state. It produces textiles and handicrafts. Pop 471815.

SURDS, now little-used term for such irrational ROOTS as $\sqrt{3}$, $\sqrt{5}$, etc., or for their SUMS OR PRODUCTS; or for IRRATIONAL NUMBERS in general.

Surgery

Technology and the heart surgeon

Compared with many other branches of surgery, cardiac (heart) surgery has a very brief history. The remarkable "Edwin Smith Papyrus" (2nd millennium BC), perhaps the earliest scientific work yet discovered, is completely devoted to surgery yet makes no mention of heart surgery. Its unknown author describes about 50 cases of injuries of varying severity with his recommendations for treatment, but only three of these are chest injuries and none concern the heart. In fact he appears to have been very reluctant to treat those chest injuries he does describe.

This reluctance to treat the heart was an underlying theme in surgery until quite recently. In early classical times, in a world almost constantly at war, heart wounds were very common. But the ancients viewed the heart as the seat of the soul and of life, and dogmatically regarded all heart wounds as fatal. So cardiac surgery was completely neglected. Indeed Aristotle wrote "The heart alone among all the viscera cannot withstand injury."

It was not until the late 16th century that the authority of the ancient physicians was seriously questioned. When the practice of dissection was revived, examples of healed heart wounds were discovered and gradually the doctrine that all heart wounds were fatal disappeared. At this time, certain of the bolder surgeons began to operate on the heart. But they made very little progress. They could not keep the lungs from collapsing when the chest was opened to expose the heart. This formidable barrier to progress was finally overcome in 1904 when the German surgeon Ferdinand Sauerbruch (1875–1951) devised a special low-pressure chamber. When the chest was opened in this chamber, the lungs were prevented from collapsing and breathing could be artificially controlled.

The first successful heart operation was performed in 1896 by the German surgeon Ludwig Rehn (1849–1930) who successfully repaired a stab wound in the heart of a man who subsequently completely recovered. But despite Rehn's outstanding surgical achievement and Sauerbruch's chamber, progress remained slow. Adequate instruments did not exist; techniques were poor, and there was insufficient knowledge of blood typing and anesthetics to allow unhurried and safe operations. These problems have only been gradually solved. Indeed, it was only as recently as 1951 that cardiac surgery can be said to have come of age, with the introduction of the heart–lung machine which allowed unhurried open-heart surgery to be performed.

The Heart–Lung Machine and Open-heart Surgery

If the heart is stopped or opened for too long during surgery, without providing an alternative means for pumping the blood, the patient will die. When a heart–lung machine is used, blood from the veins entering the heart is diverted into the machine where it is oxygenated and pumped into the arteries which leave the heart. In this way the heart beat and respiratory movements can be stopped for sufficient time to enable the heart surgeon to perform heart operations carefully and with a high success rate.

The heart–lung machine was developed over many years by John Heysham Gibbon (1903–1973) of Philadelphia and was first used on humans in 1951. Prior to its introduction open-heart surgery was much more difficult, since even using the technique of cooling the whole body (hypothermia) to reduce its demand for oxygen only allowed the surgeon a few minutes time within the heart. Nowadays both the heart–lung machine and deep hypothermia are used together, thus allowing the surgeon several hours of operating time.

Why Operate?

A heart which pumps less blood to the body than the body needs is said to have failed. The symptoms of heart failure are many; the most notable are difficulty in breathing, chest pain and edema (swelling of the tissue through increase in its fluid content). These arise because the heart fails to meet the circulatory demands of the body. When a heart has failed or is failing due to damage, disease or deformity, it may be possible to restore normal function by operating upon it. This is the essential aim of cardiac surgery.

Heart Diseases

The heart is vulnerable to remarkably few disorders considering that it never rests from the time it starts beating (shortly after its formation) to the time its body dies.

Throughout life the heart must continue pumping and supplying the body tissues with oxygenated blood from the lungs, or the body will die. In order to keep beating the heart must itself be supplied with oxygen carried in the blood. The blood vessels supplying the heart with blood are called the coronary vessels and are an important site of heart disease. Indeed, coronary artery disease—where the coronary arteries become narrowed and unable to supply the heart with sufficient blood—is the most lethal type of heart disease.

The incidence of high blood pressure and coronary artery disease have greatly increased in the last 50 years. They occur most commonly in middle and old age, and more frequently in men than in women. But why this should be so is a matter for controversy.

In the case of coronary heart disease, links have been made with heredity, smoking, emotional stress, lack of exercise, overweight and diet. Some researchers have claimed that refined sugar is to blame; others, the excessive intake of saturated fats which are found in higher proportions in animal rather than vegetable fats and in battery-reared rather than free-range animals.

The symptoms of coronary heart disease are various. Gradual narrowing of the coronary arteries eventually produces severe chest pain (angina pectoris), whereas a sudden narrowing or blockage by, for example, a blood clot (thrombus) causes heart attack (coronary thrombosis).

The heart contains four chambers which contract or beat in a wavelike sequence. The "heart beat," which is a complete cycle of these contractions, originates with an electrical discharge from a small region (the sinoatrial node or cardiac pacemaker) in the wall of one of these chambers (the right atrium). This electrical signal spreads to the rest of the heart via the "cardiac conducting system," causing a wave of muscle contraction to spread throughout the heart.

There are many disorders of this rhythm; these can usually be effectively controlled by drugs but which occasionally require the additional use of pacemaker therapy. In this technique, electric shocks are applied to the heart at the normal rate, thus forcing the heart to beat rhythmically. The electrical leads for administering the shocks may be passed into the heart via a large vein or implanted directly (which necessitates opening the chest). Many irregularities of heart beat are caused by defects in the cardiac conduction system and can be analysed using the electrocardiograph.

SURFACE INTEGRAL, the DOUBLE INTEGRAL (see also CALCULUS) obtained through integration of a FUNCTION $f(x, y)$ over a surface S whose vertical projection on the xy-plane is the region R. The surface integral gives the VOLUME between the surface and the xy-plane and is written

$$\iint_R f(x,y)\,dx\,dy.$$

In vector notation (see VECTOR ANALYSIS), the surface integral is generally written

$$\iint_S \mathbf{V}\,.\,d\mathbf{S},$$

which is a SCALAR, $d\mathbf{S}$ being a surface element treated as the vector $d\mathbf{x} \times d\mathbf{y}$ and $\mathbf{V}$ being a vector function.

SURFACE TENSION, FORCE existing in any boundary surface of a liquid such that the surface tends to assume the minimum possible area. It is defined as the force perpendicular to a line of unit length drawn on the surface. Surface tension arises from the cohesive forces between liquid molecules and makes a liquid surface behave as if it had an elastic membrane stretched over it. Thus, the weight of a needle floated on water makes a depression in the surface. Surface tension governs the wetting properties of liquids, CAPILLARITY and detergent action.

SURFING, the sport of riding the surf on a surfboard. The surfer, facing the shore, is picked up by an incoming wave and rides on its crest, standing on the board. Surfing is thought to have originated in Hawaii, from where it spread (c1920) to the US. It is especially popular in Australia and S California.

SURGERY, the branch of MEDICINE chiefly concerned with manual operations to remove or repair diseased, damaged or deformed body tissues. With time surgery has become more complex and has split up into a number of specialities. In 1970 ten surgical speciality boards existed in the US and Canada: general surgery; OPHTHALMOLOGY; otolaryngology; OBSTETRICS and GYNECOLOGY; ORTHOPEDICS; colon and rectal surgery; urology; PLASTIC SURGERY; neurosurgery, and thoracic (chest) surgery. **Otolaryngology** deals with the EAR, LARYNX (voicebox) and upper respiratory tract: tonsillectomy is one of its most common operations. **Colon and rectal surgery** deals with the large intestine. **Urological surgery** deals with the urinary system (KIDNEYS, ureters, BLADDER, urethra) and male reproductive system. **Neurosurgery** deals with the NERVOUS SYSTEM (BRAIN, SPINAL CORD, nerves); common operations include the removal of TUMORS, the repair of damage caused by severe injury, and the cutting of dorsal roots (rhizotomy) and certain parts of the spinal cord (cordotomy) to relieve unmanageable pain. **Thoracic surgery** deals with structures within the chest cavity. There are also a number of sub-specialities; thus **cardiovascular surgery**, a sub-speciality of thoracic surgery, deals with the heart and major blood vessels.

SURINAM, republic on the NE coast of South America, bounded W by Guyana, S by Brazil and E by French Guiana. Agriculture is restricted to coastal areas, the interior being highlands and tropical forest. The population includes Creoles, Asian Indians, Jawanese, Negroes and Amerindians. Surinam is the world's third largest producer of bauxite. England gave Surinam to the Dutch (1667) in exchange for New Amsterdam (now New York City). It became a self-governing part of the Netherlands in 1954 and fully independent in 1975.

SURINAM TOAD, *Pipa pipa*, a curiously flattened tongueless frog living wholly in water in the Amazon

Congenital heart disease in which children are born with deformed or otherwise damaged hearts is the most common form of heart disease in young children. Typical abnormalities include deformed heart valves; coarctation (narrowing) of the aorta; patent ductus arteriosus (the failure of the blood vessel which bypasses the baby's lungs during pregnancy to close at birth), and septal defects (holes in the walls separating the chambers of the heart). Excellent results can be achieved in correcting these defects surgically.

Artificial Valves

The heart has four major valves—one situated at the outflow side of each chamber—which ensure that the blood flows in the right direction (from the veins to the arteries). Valvular diseases are the most common heart diseases and frequently occur as complications of rheumatic fever. Diseased heart valves may be narrowed (stenosed), so that blood does not flow freely through them, and/or incompetent, so that blood leaks through them in the wrong direction. Since the first workable artificial human valve was inserted by the US surgeon, Charles Anthony Hufnagel (1916–), in 1952, surgery to correct valvular disease has become highly successful. It has increasingly involved replacement of the diseased valve with an artificial valve made of plastic and/or metal.

Heart Transplants

In 1967 Christiaan Barnard of South Africa performed the first human heart transplant. In rapid succession many others were performed elsewhere, particularly in the US. These first heart transplants captured the public interest on account of the apparent power of the transplant surgeon to play God; associations of the heart as the seat of the soul and the emotions have not yet completely died. The ethical questions facing the physicians who were required to decide whether or not the potential heart donor could be revived, aroused public debate, although, in fact, physicians have had to make similar decisions for centuries.

So far the results of heart transplantation compare quite favorably with those of other organ transplants (e.g., kidney and liver transplants) at comparable stages in their development. There is every reason to believe that it may eventually become a useful procedure. However, difficulty in obtaining heart donors will probably ensure that the availability of the technique will remain limited. Also, if medicine achieves its ultimate goal of preventing disease, the extreme measure of heart transplantation will no longer be necessary.

Artificial Hearts

To overcome the problems of obtaining donor hearts for transplantation, it is necessary to develop artificial hearts. But there are formidable technical problems involved in finding a suitable design. The ideal artificial heart should be no larger than the natural one, and capable of beating continuously for many years. Also, the materials from which it is made should be strong and should not react with the body tissues. Many prototypes have been made but to date none has been completely successful. However, there is great promise in research projects devoted to building a completely implantable unit powered by nuclear energy.

The Future

In the near future the greatest impact will probably come from the continuing development of artificial devices—valves, blood vessels, pacemakers and hearts—since the long-term results of tissue grafts are generally unsatisfactory.

But in the distant future the need for much of cardiac surgery may be eliminated, with alteration of gene patterns to prevent congenital heart disease, changes in diet and the combating of bacterial and viral heart infections.

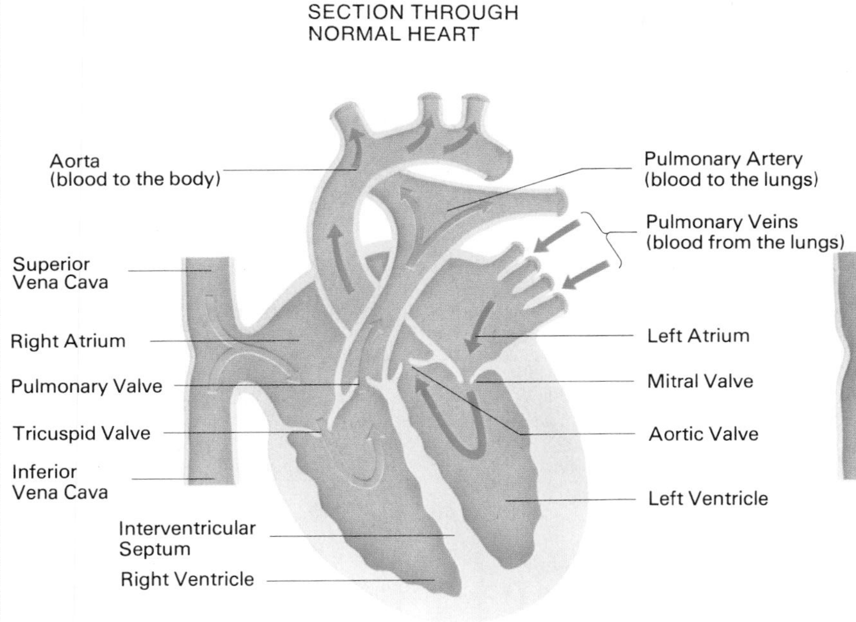

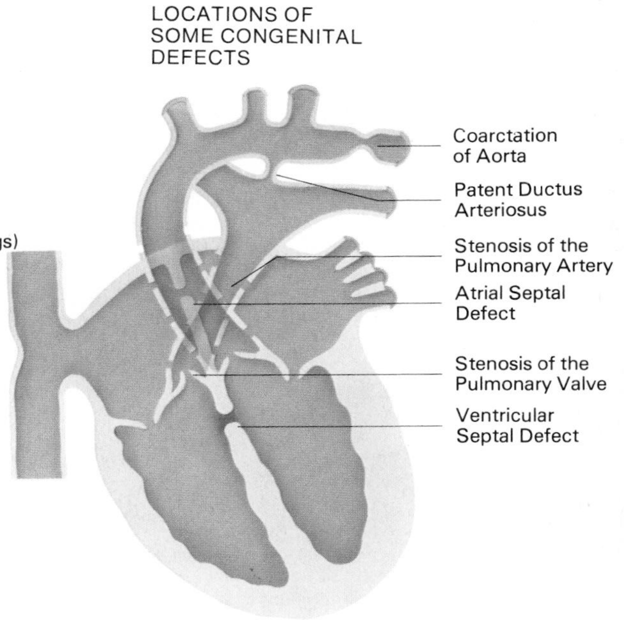

Official name: The Republic of Surinam
Capital: Paramaribo
Area: 55 000sq mi
Population: 384 900
Languages: Dutch, English, Hindi, Javanese, Chinese, "Surinamese" (lingua franca)
Religions: Hindu, Roman Catholic, Muslim, Protestant
Monetary unit(s): 1 Surinam guilder = 100 cents

and Orinoco basins. The eggs develop in small pits in the female's back, tadpoles or small froglets eventually escaping from these pockets.

SURPLUS VALUE, in Marxist economics, the difference between the value of goods or services produced by labor and the wages payed by the employer. Of the factors of production only labor produces surplus value. (See MARX, KARL; LABOR THEORY OF VALUE.)

SURRATT, Mary Eugenia (1820–1865), woman who was hanged for complicity in the assassination of Abraham LINCOLN, a crime of which she was accused because of her contact with the assassin John Wilkes BOOTH. It is now thought that her trial was flagrantly unjust, and she herself innocent.

SURREALISM, movement in literature and art which flourished between WWI and WWII, centered in Paris. Writers such as André BRETON and COCTEAU, and painters such as DALI, MIRÓ, MAGRITTE, TANGUY and ERNST were surrealists. They owed much to FREUD, emphasizing the world of dream and fantasy and believing that the unconscious mind reveals a truer reality than the natural world. In paintings, everyday objects were often placed in a dream-like setting and apparently unrelated objects were juxtaposed.

SURREY, Henry Howard, Earl of (c1517–1547), English poet who with his friend Thomas WYATT introduced the SONNET from Italy into England. In his translations from Vergil, Surrey was the first to employ blank verse in English.

SURTSEY, island, about 1sq mi, SW of the Westman Islands, off the S coast of Iceland. Formed by volcanic activity in 1963, it has been the subject of intensive and varied scientific research.

SURVEYING, the accurate measurement of distances and features on the earth's surface. The science began to attain modern accuracy in the 17th century with the introduction of Gunter's chain (1620)—66ft long and the standard for measuring distance until superseded by the steel or INVAR tape—and of the VERNIER SCALE, the telescopic sight and the spirit LEVEL. For making MAPS and charts, the LATITUDE and longitude of certain primary points are determined from astronomical observations. Geodetic surveying, for large areas, takes the earth's curvature into account (see GEODESY). After a base line of known length is established, the positions of other points are

The Trumpeter swan, once common in North America, has become increasingly rare. It is the heaviest flying bird in North America.

found by triangulation (measuring the angles of the point from each end of the base line) or by trilateration (measuring all the sides of the triangle formed by point and base line). Trigonometry, in particular the SINE RULE, yields the distances or angles not directly measured. A series of adjacent triangles is thus formed, each having one side in common with the next. Distances are measured by tape or electronically, sending a frequency-modulated light or microwave beam to the farther point and back, and measuring the phase shift. Angles are measured with the THEODOLITE or (vertically) the alidade. Vertical elevations are determined by LEVELS. Much modern surveying is done by PHOTOGRAMMETRY, using the STEREOSCOPE to determine contours. Surveying is important not only for mapmaking but also to chart land, to fix boundaries and to plan transportation routes, dams, etc.

SURVIVAL OF THE FITTEST, term first used by Herbert SPENCER in his *Principles of Biology* (1864) and adopted by Charles Darwin to describe his theory of EVOLUTION by NATURAL SELECTION.

SUSA, city of ancient Persia, the biblical Shushan. It was capital of ELAM and later a principal city of the ACHAEMENIANS. Its remains, including part of the palace of DARIUS I, stand in SW Iran. The famous legal code of HAMMURABI was found here in 1901.

SUSLOV, Mikhail Andreyevich (1902–), Soviet party official and editor of *Pravda* (1949–50). A member of the POLITBURO (1955) and one of its more conservative voices, he has been an influential theorist of party ideology.

SUSPENSION, system of macroscopic particles dispersed in a fluid in which settlement is hindered by intermolecular collisions and by the fluid's VISCOSITY. (See also COLLOID.)

SUSQUEHANNA RIVER, longest river in the eastern US. It rises in Otsego Lake in central N.Y. and flows 444mi through Pa. and Md. into Chesapeake Bay. It is not navigable. Disastrous flooding occurred in 1972.

SUSSEX SPANIEL, English breed of sporting dog, named for the county where it originated. Purposely bred low to the ground (16in tall) to work in bramble thickets, it weighs about 45lb. Its profuse, long coat lies close to the body and should be liver brown with a gold luster. It tends to give tongue when hunting.

SUTHERLAND, Earl Wilbur, Jr. (1915–1974), US physiologist awarded the 1971 Nobel Prize for Physiology or Medicine for demonstrating the role of cyclic adenosine 3′,5′-monophosphate in the way that HORMONES affect bodily organs.

SUTHERLAND, George (1862–1942), US statesman and lawyer. A Republican congressman (1901–02) and senator (1905–17), Sutherland was appointed Associate Justice of the Supreme Court in 1922, and retired in 1938. He was strongly conservative.

SUTHERLAND, Graham Vivian (1903–), English painter. His work includes landscapes and portraits, but he is best known for his post-WWII *Thorns* series, symbolic of Christ's Passion.

SUTHERLAND, Joan (1926–), Australian soprano, one of the foremost exponents of the art of BEL CANTO. She made her debut in Sydney in 1950 and has since become a leading international singer.

SUTLEJ RIVER, 900mi-long river of prime importance for irrigation in the PUNJAB. It rises in SW Tibet and flows through N India into Pakistan to help form the Panjnad R.

SUTRAS, precepts, treatises and commentaries in SANSKRIT literature. Principally written about 500–200 BC on religious and philosophical subjects, they are important in HINDUISM and BUDDHISM. They also include the *Kamasutra*, on love.

SUTTEE, Hindu custom compelling widows to throw themselves onto their husband's funeral pyre and burn to death with him. The practice was banned in India by the British in 1829.

SUTTER, John Augustus (1803–1880), Swiss-born pioneer of the US who founded a colony on the site of present-day Sacramento, Cal., and established a rich personal empire based on agriculture. His land was overrun and his property destroyed in the GOLD RUSH of 1848. He died bankrupt.

SUTTNER, Bertha von, Baroness (1843–1914), Austrian writer and pacifist whose novel *Lay Down Your Arms* (1892) was widely influential. She was the first woman to win the Nobel Peace Prize (1905).

SUVA, capital and chief port of FIJI and the largest town in the S Pacific. A trading and shipping center, it has light industry. Pop 63 200.

SUWANNEE RIVER, river which rises in SE Ga. and flows 250mi through N Fla. to the Gulf of Mexico. It is famous as the "Swanee River" of Stephen Foster's song.

SVALBARD, group of Arctic islands, including Spitzbergen, which belong to Norway. They cover about 24 000sq mi and are 700mi from the North Pole. They are rich in coal. Pop 4 225.

SVEDBERG, Theodor (1884–1971), Swedish chemist awarded the 1926 Nobel Prize for Chemistry for inventing the ultracentrifuge, important in studies of COLLOIDS and large MOLECULES. (See also CENTRIFUGE.)

SVERDLOVSK, city in the RSFSR, USSR, in the E foothills of the Ural Mts. It is a major producer of heavy machinery. The city was founded in 1723 and named Ekaterinburg for the future Empress CATHERINE I. Here Tsar NICHOLAS II and his family were shot by the Bolsheviks (1918). Pop 1 026 000.

SVERDRUP ISLANDS, group of islands in the Arctic archipelago, W of Ellesmere Island, Canada. The chief islands are Ellef Ringnes, Amund Ringnes, Isachsen and Axel Heiberg.

SVEVO, Italo (1861–1928), Italian fiction writer, born Ettore Schmitz. His masterpiece is the witty and perceptive psychological novel *Confessions of Zeno* (1923). He first became widely known through his friend and admirer James JOYCE.

SVIATOSLAV (d. 972), prince of Kiev (from 945) who waged expansionist wars against the Khazars, the Volga Bulgars and Byzantine possessions in the Balkans. The last pagan prince of Russia, he was defeated by a Byzantine force in 971.

SWABIA, historic region in Germany roughly corresponding to present-day S Baden-Württemberg and SW Bavaria, West Germany. In the 9th century it became a duchy but splintered in 1268 with the fall of the house of HOHENSTAUFEN. The Swabian League of 1488–1534, comprising the major Swabian cities, held considerable political power.

SWAHILI, a Bantu language (influenced by Arabic) which is the LINGUA FRANCA of much of E Africa, especially near the coast. The term also refers to some of the inhabitants of this area.

SWALLOWS, family, Hirundinidae, of some 78 species of birds. All have long sickle-shaped wings and long forked tails. The plumage is generally dark, often with a metallic sheen. Many species have lighter underparts. The legs and feet are small and weak: they can perch on wires or tree branches, but are adapted to spend most of their time on the wing, feeding on insects caught in flight. Many species are migratory. (See also MARTINS.)

SWAMMERDAM, Jan (1637–1680), Dutch microscopist whose precision enabled him to make many discoveries, including red BLOOD cells (before 1658).

SWAMP, a poorly drained, low-lying area of land permanently saturated with water. Swamps usually develop where the surface is flat enough for rainwater runoff to be very slow, or where a lake basin has become filled in; vegetation helps retain the swampiness. **Marshes** have standing surface water, and are usually only temporary. (See also BOG; MUSKEG.)

SWAMPSCOTT, town in NE Mass., on Massachusetts Bay, 11mi NE of Boston. It is residential, with fishing and tourist industries. Pop 13 578.

SWANEE RIVER. See SUWANNEE RIVER.

SWANS, a small group of large long-necked aquatic birds of the family Anatidae. There are eight species, seven within the genus *Cygnus*. Five of these are found in the N Hemisphere; all are white in adult plumage, but have different colored bills. These are the Trumpeter swan, Bewick's swan, Whooper, Whistling and Mute swans. The two remaining cygnids are the Black swan of Australia and the Black-necked swan of South America. Most feed on vegetation.

SWANSEA, city and seaport in S Wales on the mouth of the Tawe R. Steel and tin-plate dominate heavy industry. Pop 172 566.

SWANSEA, residential town in SE Mass., 3mi NW of Fall River. Pop 12 640.

SWASTIKA (Sanskrit: good fortune), ancient symbol of well-being and prosperity employed by such diverse peoples as Greeks, Celts, Amerindians and the Hindus of India, based on the form 卐. In the 20th century it gained notoriety as the hated symbol of NAZISM.

SWATOW, city and seaport in SE China, E Kwangtung Province. It is a major shipping and commercial center with growing industry. Pop 400 000.

SWAZILAND, independent kingdom in SE Africa, bounded N, W and S by the Republic of South Africa and E by Mozambique. It has three main regions: the mountainous High Veld in the W, the lower Middle Veld and the Low Veld rising in the E to the narrow Lebombo range. The four major rivers, running W–E, are being developed for irrigation and could provide abundant hydroelectricity. Temperatures average from 60°F in the W to 72°F in the E. The predominantly agricultural population is almost entirely Swazi, but about 45% of the land is European owned. Crops include sugar, rice, cotton, citrus fruits and corn. Livestock is important. There are large deposits of iron ore, asbestos, coal and other minerals, and the country is rich in timber. Settled in the early

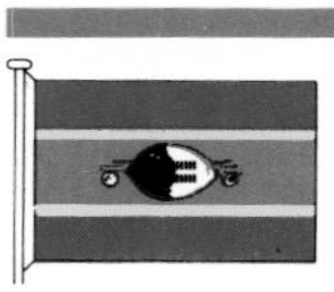

Official name: Swaziland
Capital: Mbabane
Area: 6 705sq mi
Population: 421 000
Languages: English, Siswati
Religions: Christian, Traditional beliefs
Monetary unit(s): 1 Lilangeni = 100 cents

1800s by the Swazis, a BANTU people, it became a British protectorate in 1907 and fully independent in 1968 under King Sobhuza II.

SWEAT. See PERSPIRATION.

SWEATSHOP, place of work with long hours, poor pay and bad conditions. Such places usually exploited those who found difficulty in obtaining employment, such as women, unskilled laborers, newly arrived immigrants and children. Sweatshops were curbed by the growth of organized labor (see UNIONS).

SWEDEN, Scandinavian kingdom of N Europe, bounded W by Norway, NE by Finland, E by the Gulf of Bothnia, SE by the Baltic Sea and SW by the North Sea.

Land. There are two main regions. Norrland ("the northland") occupies most of the country and slopes down from the Kölen Mts on the Norwegian border to the Gulf of Bothnia. Its northernmost parts lie within the Arctic Circle and include part of LAPLAND. Sparsely populated, Norrland contains most of the country's vast wealth of timber and its principal iron mines. To the south are the intensively cultivated lowlands where the major cities, including STOCKHOLM and GÖTEBORG, and the manufacturing industries are concentrated. In Feb., the coldest month, temperatures are below 32°F throughout Sweden but average 5°F and lower in the N. Summer temperatures average 60°F in the N and slightly higher in the S.

People. The population is almost entirely Swedish except for about 10 000 Lapps. More than 75% of the people are urban. Sweden enjoys one of the highest living standards in the world and an outstanding range of social services.

Economy. Sweden's forests cover about 55% of the country; it has rich deposits of iron ore, abundant hydroelectricity and enough good farmland to be almost self-sufficient in food. Metals and metal products dominate industry. Main exports are

Official name: Kingdom of Sweden
Capital: Stockholm
Area: 173 686sq mi
Population: 8 127 396
Languages: Swedish
Religions: Swedish Lutheran
Monetary unit(s): 1 Krona = 100 öre

machinery, iron, steel, paper, wood pulp, timber, foodstuffs and ships.

History. The Swedes were first recorded by the historian Tacitus in the 1st century AD. During the period of the VIKINGS they were known as Varangians in Russia where they pioneered a trade route as far as the Black Sea. Throughout the Middle Ages their history was tied to that of NORWAY and DENMARK. The Danes, dominant from the KALMAR UNION (1397), were driven out in 1523. In the 17th century GUSTAVUS II (Gustavus Adolphus) made Sweden a leading European power. In 1809 the monarchy became constitutional and remains so today. Sweden took no part in WWI and WWII. The Social Democrats, in power for 44 years, were defeated by the Center Party in 1976. The prime minister is Thorbjörn Fälldin.

SWEDENBORG, Emanuel (1688–1772), Swedish scientist, theologian and religious mystic. He had won recognition as a natural scientist when in 1745 he became the recipient of spiritual revelations. In his subsequent teachings he denied the Trinity, saying that Christ alone was God. He later claimed that Christ's second coming occurred in 1757. The Church of the New Jerusalem, founded (1788) after his death, embodies the theology set forth in his numerous works.

SWEDISH, one of the Germanic SCANDINAVIAN LANGUAGES, spoken by about 9 million people in Sweden, Finland, Estonia, the US and Canada. Old Swedish developed from Old Norse c800 AD and gave place to modern Swedish c1500 with the onset of standardization.

SWEDISH IVY, low-growing house plants with round, scalloped leaves that can be plain-green or white variegated (*Plectranthus australis*), or silver-olive above and burgundy below (*P. oertendahlii*). They are neither ivies nor native to Sweden. Indoors, they should receive several hours of direct sun each day; they grow well at average house temperatures. The soil should be kept evenly moist. Propagation is by shoot tip cuttings. Family: Labiatae.

SWEELINCK, Jan Pieterszoon (1562–1621), Dutch composer and organist who is known today for his development of organ techniques in his many compositions. He paved the way for J. S. BACH.

SWEEPSTAKE, form of lottery in which prizes of money are awarded for the winning ticket, usually on a horse race. The most famous is the Irish Hospitals Sweepstake, with up to 10 million ticket-holders. Banned in the US 1890–1963, sweepstakes are now run by many states.

SWEET ALYSSUM, *Lobularia maritima*, white-or violet-flowered half-hardy perennial plant, widely cultivated as an edging plant and for ground cover. Some varieties have white-edged leaves and some double flowers. Family: Cruciferae.

SWEETBREADS, the pancreatic tissue (see PANCREAS) or THYMUS GLANDS of various animals sold as MEAT.

SWEET BRIAR, or **eglantine**, *Rosa eglanteria*, branched hardy European rose with pink single or double flowers and sweet-smelling leaves that has been introduced into North America. Family: Rosaceae.

SWEET CLOVER, LEGUMINOUS PLANTS of the genus *Melilotus*, which are native to S Europe and Asia Minor. Several species are cultivated for forage, soil improvement and as bee plants and some are widely naturalized in the US.

SWEETENING AGENTS, substances used to sweeten food and drink (see TASTE). The commonest are the SUGARS, especially SUCROSE (table sugar) and GLUCOSE, which are themselves FOODS. Artificial sweeteners, with no food value and up to several thousand times sweeter than sugar, are used by diabetics and in DIETETIC FOODS, toothpaste, etc. They include CYCLAMATE and SACCHARIN. Some have been banned because of possible harmful effects.

SWEET GUM, *Liquidambar styracifula*, a deciduous tree native to the southern US and Middle America, with star-shaped leaves which turn brilliant scarlet in the fall. The sap yields a gum called storax which is used in medicines, perfumes and toiletries. Family: Hamamelidaceae.

SWEET PEA, *Lathyrus odoratus*, a climbing plant cultivated for its profusion of fragrant delicately colored flowers. Native to Italy, hundreds of varieties are now in cultivation, including many dwarf, nonclimbing forms. Family: Leguminosae.

SWEET POTATO, *Ipomoea batatas*, a trailing creeper, native to tropical America and producing a tuberous root which is sweet-tasting when cooked. In North America an orange variety is grown, with roots rich in carotene. Family: Leguminosae.

SWEETSOP, or sugar apple, *Annona squamosa*, small tree producing sweet yellow-green fruit resembling a stumpy pine cone. It is native to the West Indies and South America. Family: Annonaceae.

SWEETWATER, city of NW Tex., seat of Nolan Co. It ships and processes grain, wool, cotton and meat and has an oil refinery. Pop 12 020.

SWEET WILLIAM, *Dianthus barbatus*, a garden plant related to the CARNATION, producing clusters of white, red and purple flowers. Most varieties are cultivated as biennials although some strains can be treated as annuals. Family: Caryophyllaceae.

SWIFT, Gustavus Franklin (1839–1903), US butcher and businessman. First (1875) to slaughter cattle in Chicago for shipment E, he introduced refrigerated railroad cars, founded the giant Swift & Co., and pioneered manufacture of by-products.

SWIFT, Jonathan (1667–1745), Anglo-Irish writer, a journalist, poet and outstanding prose satirist. Born in Ireland, he was ordained in 1694, and in 1704 two of his satires were published: *The Battle of the Books* and *The Tale of a Tub*. He became a Tory in 1710, taking over *The Examiner*, the Tory journal. From 1714, he lived in Ireland, as Dean of St. Patrick's, Dublin. He deplored the plight of the Irish poor in the *Drapier's Letters* (1724). His masterpiece is *Gulliver's Travels* (1726), a children's fantasy as well as a political and social satire.

SWIFT CURRENT, city in SW Saskatchewan, Canada. It is the trading center of a wheat region, with some light industry. Pop 15 048.

SWIFTS, small, fast-flying insectivorous birds, very like SWALLOWS but placed with the HUMMINGBIRDS in the order Apodiformes. Both swifts and hummingbirds have very small feet and extremely short arm bones, the major flight feathers being attached to the extended hand bones. Entirely aerial, most species feed and even sleep on the wing.

SWIFTS, lizards of the genus *Sceloporus*, small, active lizards of arid regions throughout North America.

SWIM BLADDER. See AIR BLADDER.

SWIMMING AND DIVING, most popular of water sports. Common swimming styles include *side stroke*, a simple sidewise propulsion for distance swimming and lifesaving; *breaststroke*, a froglike arm-and-leg thrust which is probably the oldest stroke; *backstroke*, overarm or, for distance endurance, an inverted breaststroke; and *crawl*, the most common freestyle form, using an overarm pull and a flutter kick rather than the thrusting propulsion in most other strokes. The *butterfly*, a modified breaststroke which thrusts the head and arms up from the water and incorporates a dolphin kick, has become a popular competitive style. Synchronized swimming, or water ballet, is popular among US women. Fancy diving dates back to 17th-century Sweden and Germany. Competitions include forward, backward, reverse, inward, twisting and armstand dives in layout (extended), tuck (rolled in a ball), pike (bent at waist, legs straight) and free positions, from a platform or springboard. (See also DROWNING; LIFESAVING; ARTIFICIAL RESPIRATION.)

SWINBURNE, Algernon Charles (1837–1909), English lyric poet and critic. A friend of the PRE-RAPHAELITES, he led a dissolute life, ending in 30 years' seclusion. He won success with *Atalanta in Calydon* (1865), a poetic drama. *Poems and Ballads* (1866, 1878, 1889) dealt with the psychology of sexual passion. They shocked contemporaries but are now widely appreciated for their resonant language and powerful rhythms.

SWINE FEVER, a BACTERIAL DISEASE of hogs causing FEVER, immobility and failure of appetite.

SWING. See JAZZ.

SWISS CHARD, or chard, a kind of BEET (*Beta vulgaris*) which does not produce a swollen root but has edible leaves, rich in VITAMINS A and C. Family: Chenopodiaceae.

SWISS GUARDS, Swiss mercenary soldiers who served in various European armies, most notably as bodyguards to the French monarchs 1497–1792 and 1814–30. The colorfully uniformed Papal Swiss Guard at the Vatican Palace in Rome dates back to the late 1400s.

SWITHIN, or **Swithun, Saint** (c800–862), Anglo-Saxon bishop of Winchester and chaplain to EGBERT. Tradition says that St. Swithin's Day (July 15) determines the weather for the next 40 days.

SWITZERLAND, a landlocked central European confederation.

Land. The country borders Germany, Austria, Liechtenstein, Italy and France. In the far NW the JURA MOUNTAINS extend into France. The hills and plains of the Swiss Plateau, a SW–NE band in the NW, contain rich farming land, many lakes (lakes GENEVA and LUCERNE the largest) and 66% of the people (including Geneva, Lausanne, Bern and Zürich). The Swiss ALPS in the S and SE are little populated but attract many tourists. Climate varies

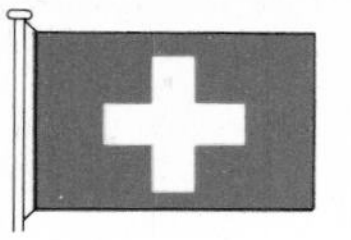

Official name: Swiss Confederation
Capital: Bern
Area: 15 941sq mi
Population: 6 311 000
Languages: German, French, Italian; Romansh
Religions: Roman Catholic, Protestant
Monetary unit(s): 1 Swiss franc = 100 rappen (German) or centimes (French)

greatly: temperature decreases and precipitation increases the higher the altitude. Sheltered S valleys have hot summers and mild winters, but elsewhere winters are cold, with heavy snowfalls.

People. The four official language groups are German (70%), French (19%), Italian (10%) and ROMANSH (1%). The population is divided almost equally between Protestant and Roman Catholic. There are some 1 000 000 foreign, mainly S European, workers. The 22 cantons (states) retain much autonomy and choose a 44-member Council of States, which with the directly elected 200-member National Council elects a 7-member executive Federal Council every 4 years. A president and vice-president are similarly elected each year. Women obtained the vote in 1971.

Economy. Highly industrialized, and with plentiful hydroelectric power, Switzerland exports watches, jewelry, precision tools and instruments, textiles and chemicals. Dairy cattle are raised. Cheese and chocolate are important exports, and tourism and international banking major industries.

History. Rome conquered the HELVETII in 58 BC. The area came under the ALMANNI, the BURGUNDIANS, the FRANKS, and the HOLY ROMAN EMPIRE (962). HAPSBURG oppression led to the Perpetual Covenant between Uri, Schwyz and Unterwald (1291), the traditional beginning of the Swiss Confederation. Wars against Austria resulted in virtual independence in 1499. Religious civil wars divided the country in the REFORMATION (see CALVIN, JOHN; ZWINGLI, HULDREICH) but it stayed neutral in the Thirty Years' War and independence was formally recognized by the 1648 Peace of WESTPHALIA. French revolutionary armies imposed a centralized Helvetic Republic 1798–1803. The 1815 Congress of VIENNA restored the Confederation. After a three-week civil war a federal democracy was set up in 1848. Switzerland remained neutral in both world wars and is still outside the UN.

SWORD, ancient principal form of hand weapon, its metal blade longer than a dagger. Leaf-shaped Bronze Age swords gave way to short flat blades in Rome, and longer laminated iron (in Damascus) and tempered steel (notably in Toledo) weapons. Asian curved cutting blades (the Turkish *scimitar*) inspired the cavalry *saber*. Japanese SAMURAI used a longer two-handed version. The thrust-and-parry *rapier* became the weapon of the DUEL and FENCING.

SWORDFISHES, a family of perch-like fishes, Xephiidae, with the snout prolonged into a powerful, flattened sword. Swordfishes are found worldwide, mainly in tropical oceans. The sword is reputed to be used to thrash among shoals of fish, the swordfish feeding at leisure on the injured fish. They are solitary animals which may weigh up to 680kg (1 500lb).

SWORDTAIL, *Xiphophorus helleri*, a live-bearing fish of Mexico and Guatemala, in which the lower caudal fin rays in the male are prolonged into a "sword" used in sexual display. A sex change is sometimes observed from female to male.

SYBARIS, ancient Greek city on the Gulf of Tarentum, S Italy, c720–510 BC. Its fabled wealth and luxurious self-indulgence gave rise to the word "sybaritic."

SYCAMORE, popular name for a number of deciduous trees. In North America the name is applied to a PLANE tree (*Platanus occidentalis*), the bark of which flakes off. In Europe, the sycamore is a MAPLE (*Acer pseudoplatanus*). The sycamore of ancient times is a FIG (*Ficus occidentalis*) which is now seldom cultivated.

SYDENHAM, Charles Poulett Thomson, 1st Baron (1799–1841), British merchant and statesman, Liberal member of Parliament 1826–39, governor general of Canada 1839–41. He effected the 1840 union of Upper and Lower Canada (today Ontario and Quebec).

SYDENHAM, Thomas (1624–1689), "the English Hippocrates," who pioneered the use of QUININE for treating MALARIA and of LAUDANUM as an ANESTHETIC, wrote an important treatise on GOUT, and first described Sydenham's CHOREA (St. Vitus' Dance).

SYDNEY, oldest and largest city in Australia, capital of New South Wales. Famous for its natural harbor, Harbor Bridge and opera house, Sydney was founded as a penal colony in 1788. Sydney ships wool, wheat and meat and is a major commercial, industrial, shipping, cultural and recreational center. Pop 61 940 (metropolitan area, 2 717 069).

SYDNEY, city and port in E Nova Scotia, Canada, on Cape Breton Island. It produces steel, chemicals and wood and food products. Pop 32 459.

SYLLABARY, a set of written characters which represent the syllables of a language, rather than the PHONEMES (as do letters) or complete ideas or words (see IDEOGRAM). Wholly or partly syllabary scripts include the MINOAN LINEAR SCRIPTS, Japanese, and some CUNEIFORM scripts.

SYLLOGISM, the logical form of an argument consisting of three statements: two premises and a conclusion. The conclusion of a valid syllogism follows logically from the premises and is true if the premises are true. (See also LOGIC.)

SYLVANIA, village in N Ohio, NW of Toledo on the Mich. border. It produces cement. Pop 12 031.

SYLVESTER, name of two popes. **Sylvester I, Saint** (d. 335), reigned 314–35. He sent legates to the 325 Council of NICAEA. An influential though spurious tradition relates that CONSTANTINE I, healed and baptized by Sylvester, gave him Rome and the Western empire (the Donation of Constantine). **Sylvester II** (c945–1003), reigned 999–1003. The first French pope and a reformer, he was renowned for his learning.

SYLVITE, HALIDE mineral consisting of POTASSIUM chloride (KCl); white, cubic crystals. Occurs in West Germany and N.M. in EVAPORITE deposits.

SYMBIOSIS, the relationship between two organisms of different species in which mutual benefit is derived by both participants. The main types of symbiotic relationship are commensalism and mutualism. **Commensalism** implies eating at the same table, e.g., the Sea anemone that lives on the shell occupied by the Hermit crab: the anemone hides the crab but feeds on food scattered by the crab. **Mutualism** is more intimate, there being close physiological dependence between participants. An example is seen in bacteria that live in the gut of herbivorous mammals. Here the bacteria aid digestion of plant material.

SYMBOLISM, a literary movement begun by a group of French poets in the late 19th century including Laforgue, MALLARMÉ, VALÉRY and VERLAINE. Influenced by BAUDELAIRE, SWEDENBORG and WAGNER, the symbolists aimed to create poetic images, or symbols, which would be apprehended by the senses and reach the preconscious world of the spirit. Though shortlived, symbolism influenced such great writers as JOYCE, PROUST, RILKE and YEATS.

SYMMACHUS, Saint (d. 514), pope during whose disputed reign (498–514) the view that no man may judge the pope was first formulated.

SYMMETRY. A geometrical figure is symmetrical about a POINT (CENTER OF SYMMETRY), LINE (AXIS OF SYMMETRY) or PLANE (PLANE OF SYMMETRY) if, respectively, the point lies at the midpoint of any line drawn through it that cuts the figure in two places; any line drawn PERPENDICULAR to the axis of symmetry cuts the figure at equal distances on either side, or any line drawn perpendicular to the plane intersects (see INTERSECTION) the figure at equal distances on either side. Figures may be symmetrical about combinations or pluralities of centers, axes and planes. **Crystal Symmetry.** If a plane can be drawn through a CRYSTAL such that the halves of the crystal on either side of it are exact mirror images of each other, the plane is a plane of symmetry, denoted *m*. If an axis can be drawn through it such that, when the crystal is rotated through a certain ANGLE (60°, 90°, 120°, 180° or 360°) about the axis, it fills exactly the same space, the axis is a (rotation) axis of symmetry, denoted 6, 4, 3, 2 or 1 (called hexad, tetrad, triad, diad or identity axes respectively) depending on how many times the "symmetry operation" must be repeated to bring the crystal back to its original orientation. (All crystals have an infinite number of identity axes.) The crystal may also have an inversion axis of symmetry about which, after inversion, the crystal may be rotated through a certain angle to occupy exactly the original space. Inversion axes are denoted $\bar{6}$, $\bar{4}$, $\bar{3}$ and $\bar{2}$ (a $\bar{2}$ axis is equivalent to a plane of symmetry and this notation is thus not generally used); a $\bar{1}$ axis implies that the crystal may be inverted through the center to occupy the same space. Crystals are usually classified according to the symmetry which they display.

SYMPHONIC POEM, or tone poem, a form of orchestral music in one movement, popular about 1850–1900, which describes a story or a scene. LISZT originated the form, but Richard STRAUSS is the most noted composer in the field.

SYMPHONY, the major form of music for ORCHESTRA. Developed from the OVERTURE, by 1800 it had four movements: a fairly quick movement in SONATA FORM; a slow movement; a MINUET and trio; and a quick RONDO. HAYDN and MOZART played a central role in developing the classical symphony. BEETHOVEN introduced the SCHERZO and a new range of emotion. Major symphonic composers include in the 1800s SCHUBERT, BERLIOZ, MENDELSSOHN, BRAHMS, BRUCKNER, DVOŘÁK and MAHLER, and in the 1900s STRAVINSKY, PROKOFIEV, SHOSTAKOVICH, VAUGHAN WILLIAMS, ELGAR, SIBELIUS and NIELSEN.

SYMPLEGADES, clashing rocks guarding the entrance to the Black Sea, successfully negotiated by the ARGONAUTS on their way to COLCHIS in quest of the GOLDEN FLEECE.

SYNAGOGUE (Greek: house of assembly), Jewish place of worship. The synagogue became the center of communal and religious life after destruction of the Temple in Jerusalem (70 AD) and dispersal of the Jews. Most synagogues have an ark containing the TORAH, an "eternal light," two candelabra, pews and a platform (*bimah*) for readings and conduct of services. Some strict Orthodox synagogues still segregate women. (See JUDAISM.)

SYNAPSE, the point of connection between two nerves or between nerve and muscle. An electrical nerve impulse releases a chemical transmitter (often ACETYLCHOLINE) which crosses a small gap and initiates electrical excitation (or inhibition) of the succeeding nerve or muscle. (See NERVOUS SYSTEM.)

SYNCHROCYCLOTRON, type of CYCLOTRON with one dee-shaped electrode where the accelerating electric field is frequency-modulated to give charged particles, such as PROTONS, high energies while their relativistic mass is large. Pulses of particles start at the center of the accelerator and move in circles of increasing radius, being accelerated as they enter and leave the dee.

SYNCHROTRON, particle accelerator for accelerating pulses of PROTONS, deuterons or ELECTRONS to high energies. The particles move in a circular path of almost constant radius, while the particles are accelerated by an alternating electric field. The path radius is kept constant by increasing the magnetic field while each pulse is accelerated.

SYNCLINE. See FOLD; GEOSYNCLINE.

SYNCOPATION, in music, the conscious contradiction of regular rhythm by stressing a normally unstressed beat, or eliminating the expected beat by a rest or tied note. It is a feature of JAZZ and the music of many modern composers.

SYNCOPE. See FAINTING.

SYNDICALISM (French *syndicat*: labor union), a revolutionary labor movement aiming at seizing control of industry through strikes, sabotage, even violence, and, as its ultimate weapon, the general strike. It originated in late 19th-century France, from the theories of PROUDHON and G. SOREL. Syndicalists agree with Marxist class analysis (see MARXISM) but like anarchists reject any state organization (see ANARCHISM). Syndicalism was strong in France and Italy in the early 1900s and found US expression in the industrial unionism of the INDUSTRIAL WORKERS OF THE WORLD. WWI and the advance of communism overtook the syndicalists; their influence lasted longest in Spain, but was finally destroyed in the civil war 1936–39.

SYNERGISM, the working together of two or more agencies (e.g., synergistic MUSCLES, or a chemical with a mechanical phenomenon, or even a chemist with a physicist) to greater effect than both would have working independently.

SYNGE, John Millington (1871–1909), Irish dramatist. Influenced by the CELTIC RENAISSANCE, he studied Irish peasant life and dramatized his view of Irish myth and character in his plays *In the Shadow of the Glen* (1903), *Riders to the Sea* (1904), *The Tinker's Wedding* (1908), and his most famous work, *The Playboy of the Western World* (1907). He was encouraged by W. B. YEATS and with him helped organize the Abbey Theatre in Dublin.

SYNGE, Richard Laurence Millington (1914–), awarded the 1952 Nobel Prize for Chemistry with A. J. P. MARTIN for developing paper CHROMATOGRAPHY, a tool of great biochemical importance.

SYNOD, a Christian ecclesiastical assembly, usually of both lay and clerical representatives from a limited area. Synods decide organizational, doctrinal and other questions. They are particularly important in the ORTHODOX, LUTHERAN and REFORMED CHURCHES.

SYNOPTIC GOSPELS, the three GOSPELS (Matthew, Mark and Luke) which—unlike the Gospel of JOHN—have a large degree of subject-matter and phraseology in common. Modern scholars commonly regard Mark as prior and suppose that Matthew and Luke also used Q, a lost source containing the non-Marcan material common to them, and other sources peculiar to each.

SYNOVIAL FLUID, the small amount of fluid which lubricates JOINTS and the synovial sheaths of TENDONS. It contains hyaluronic acid which contributes to its lubricating properties.

SYNTAX. See GRAMMAR.

SYNTHETIC FIBER, man-made textile FIBER derived from artificial POLYMERS, as opposed to regenerated fibers (such as rayon) made from natural substances, or to natural fibers. Almost all types of long-chain polymer may be used: NYLON, the first to be discovered, is a polyamide; **Dacron** is a polyester, useful for nonstretch clothing. Other widely-used synthetic fibers include ORLON, POLYETHYLENE and FIBERGLASS. Polyurethane fibers are ELASTOMERS, used in stretch fabrics. To make the fibers, the polymer is usually converted to a liquid by melting or dissolving it; this is extruded through a spinneret with minute holes, and forms a filament as the solvent evaporates (dry spinning) or as it passes into a suitable chemical bath (wet spinning). The filaments are drawn (stretched) to increase strength by aligning the polymer molecules. They may then be used as such, or cut into short lengths which are twisted together, forming yarn.

SYPHILIS. See VENEREAL DISEASES.

SYRACUSE, or Siracusa, city in SE Sicily. Founded by Corinthians c734 BC, it became a brilliant center of Greek culture, notably under HIERO I and DIONYSIUS THE ELDER. Syracuse was defeated in the PUNIC WARS by Rome (211 BC). Later conquerors were the Arabs (878) and Normans (1085). The modern provincial capital, a port and tourist center, has many ancient monuments. Pop 108 685.

SYRACUSE, important industrial and commercial city in central N.Y., seat of Onondaga Co. Most notable of its many manufacturing industries is electronics. Syracuse University was founded 1870. Pop 197 297.

SYR DARYA, 1 370mi-long river in the USSR. Rising in the Tien Shan Mts, it flows SW and NW through Kirgiz, Uzbek and Kazakh SSRs to the NE Aral Sea. It is important for irrigation but not navigable.

SYRIA, republic in SW Asia bordered by Turkey, Iraq, Jordan, Israel, Lebanon and the Mediterranean.

Land. The Euphrates R flows SE through Syria. To the N lie rolling plains, to the S and W the Syrian desert, ending in the SW with the Jebel Druz plateau and fertile Hauran plains. Further W lie the Anti-Lebanon Mts with Mt Hermon (9 232ft) in the S, and the Ansariya range with the cultivated coastal plain beyond it in the N. The warm Mediterranean climate gives way inland to a more extreme temperature range. Annual rainfall (Oct.–May) is heaviest (about 50in) on the W Ansariya slopes, while the desert has less than 5in.

People. After Damascus the largest cities are Aleppo, Homs and Hama (all in fertile zones E of the mountains) and the seaport of Latakia. Over 80% of the people are Arab-speaking Muslims, mostly SUNNITE, but there are nomadic BEDOUIN, and Kurdish, Turkish and Armenian minorities. Christian Orthodox churches claim some 500 000 members. There are about 120 000 DRUZES. Government programs have reduced illiteracy to some 50%. There are universities at Damascus and Aleppo.

Economy. About half the people work in agriculture. Cotton and some grain and tobacco are exported. Large estates have been expropriated and redistributed, and attempts are being made to increase yields through modern methods and irrigation. Manufacturing exports include textiles, petroleum and handicrafts. Though oil is drilled in the NE, most oil revenue derives from pipelines crossing the country.

History. Part of the ancient HITTITE empire, Syria was conquered by Assyrians, Babylonians, Persians and Greeks. Under the SELEUCIDS after the death of ALEXANDER THE GREAT, it was later incorporated into the Roman empire by POMPEY. The Arabs conquered Syria in the 600s (see MAMELUKES; OMAYYADS; SALADIN; SELJUKS). Part of the OTTOMAN EMPIRE from 1516, Syria was mandated to the French after WWI and became independent in 1944. It joined with Egypt in the UNITED ARAB REPUBLIC 1958–61. From the late 1950s, emphasis in trade shifted toward the USSR and E European countries. The ruling BAATHIST movement favors socialism and pan-Arab nationalism. Since 1967 Israel has occupied the Golan Heights in the SW.

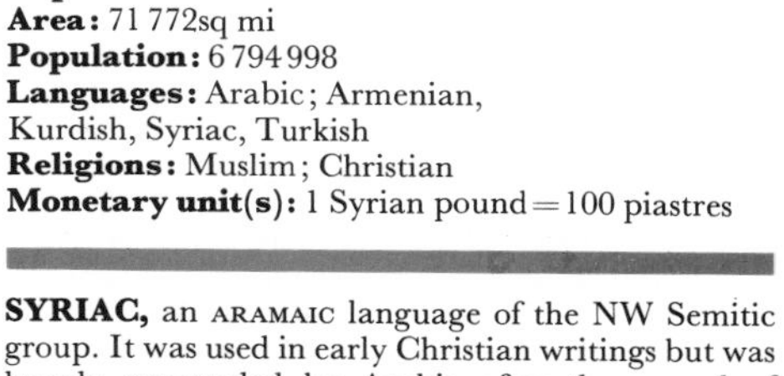

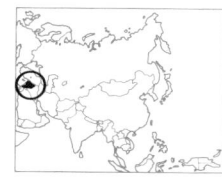

Official name: The Syrian Arab Republic
Capital: Damascus
Area: 71 772sq mi
Population: 6 794 998
Languages: Arabic; Armenian, Kurdish, Syriac, Turkish
Religions: Muslim; Christian
Monetary unit(s): 1 Syrian pound = 100 piastres

SYRIAC, an ARAMAIC language of the NW Semitic group. It was used in early Christian writings but was largely superseded by Arabic after the spread of Islam. Closely related to Hebrew, Syriac is still spoken by small groups in the Middle East.

SYRINGA, the scientific name for the LILAC genus (family: Oleaceae), which are shrubs originally native to Asia. It is not to be confused with the Mock orange or Wild syringa (*Philadelphus*), a white-flowered shrub of North America and Asia which belongs to the SAXIFRAGE family.

Synagogue entrance on lower Park Avenue, New York.

SYRINGE, a simple PUMP for drawing in and ejecting liquids. The ear syringe is merely a tapering tube with a rubber bulb at one end. The hypodermic syringe, used to give INJECTIONS, has a cylindrical barrel containing a PISTON and with an attached hollow needle.

SYRINX, a Greek nymph whose legend was narrated in Ovid's *Metamorphoses*. Pursued by PAN into a reed bed, she changed into a reed, from which he made the first pipe. In Greek the word means panpipes.

SYSTEMS ANALYSIS, management technique for determining the optional paths to a complex objective and evaluating the relative effectiveness and probable cost of each; or, the study of the general properties of controllable behavioral systems or, more broadly, of any system.

SYZRAN, city in SW Kuibyshev oblast, Russian SFSR, USSR, on the Volga R. It is an important river port, oil-refining and engineering center. Pop 174 000.

SZCZECIN, seaport in NW Poland, on the Oder R. It has major shipbuilding, chemical and metallurgical industries. Germany ceded Szczecin (Stettin) to Poland after WWII. Pop 337 200.

SZECHWAN, province of SW China, the country's most populous. Mountains rise to 24 000ft in the W. In the E the Red Basin produces rich crops. Coal, iron, salt, gold and other minerals are mined. The main cities are CHUNGKING and Ch'eng-tu, the capital.

SZEGED, city in S Hungary, capital of Csongrad Co. near the Yugoslav border. It is a port, food-processing and manufacturing center on the Tisza R. Pop 118 490.

SZELL, Georg (1897–1970), Hungarian-born US conductor. He established his reputation in Germany but emigrated to the US when the Nazis rose to power. Szell's many recordings with the Cleveland Orchestra have gained international acclaim.

SZENT-GYÖRGYI VON NAGYRAPOLT, Albert (1893–), Hungarian-born US biochemist awarded the 1937 Nobel Prize for Physiology or Medicine for work on biological COMBUSTION processes, especially in relation to VITAMIN C.

SZIGETI, Joseph (1892–1973), US violinist. Born in Hungary, he emigrated to the US in the 1920s. Szigeti is particularly famous for his performances of virtuoso contemporary works.

SZILARD, Leo (1898–1964), Hungarian-born US physicist largely responsible, with FERMI, for the development of the US atom bomb (see MANHATTAN PROJECT). In 1945 he was a leader of the movement against using it. Later he made contributions in the field of molecular biology.

SZOLD, Henrietta (1860–1945), founder in 1912 of the Women's Zionist Organization of America (Hadassah). Baltimore born, she moved to Palestine in 1920, and directed medical and rehabilitation work, particularly for children.

SZYMANOWSKI, Karol Maciej (1882–1937), Polish composer, leader of the Polish musical revival. His work includes three symphonies, two violin concertos, two operas, piano pieces and chamber music.

T

T, the 20th letter of our alphabet. Last letter of the ancient North Semitic alphabet, it became the 19th letter of the Greek (as *tau*) and Roman alphabets. The small t developed in 6th-century Roman script.
TABASCO, hot red pepper, a variety of capsicum, from which a pungent sauce is made.
TABBY CAT, breed with a striped or blotched coat like the pattern of taffeta (from *Attabiy*, the quarter of Baghdad where watered silk was originally made). Many household pets show a similar pattern, but very exact standards are laid down for the pedigree type. Brown, Blue, Red, Silver and Cream colors of either pattern are recognized in American Short-haired and Persian cats, and the tabby pattern has also been introduced into the points of the Lynx Point Siamese.
TABERNACLE, a portable temple carried by the Israelites during their nomadic period. According to Exodus its design was given to Moses on Mt. Sinai. The inner chamber contained the Ark of the Covenant, which held the Ten Commandments.
TABERNACLES, Feast of. See SUKKOT.
TABES DORSALIS, form of tertiary syphilis (see VENEREAL DISEASES) in which certain tracts in the SPINAL CORD—particularly those concerned with position sense—degenerate, leading to a characteristic high-stepping gait, sensory abnormalities and sometimes disorganization of JOINTS. Attacks of abdominal pain and abnormal pupil reactions are typical.
TABLE TENNIS, or **ping pong**, indoor game similar to a small-scale version of TENNIS. It is played by two or four players on a table divided by a 6-in high net into two 5ft × 4½ft courts. The players use wooden rackets to strike a hollow celluloid ball over the net into the opposite court. The game is administered by the International Table Tennis Federation and biennial world tournaments are held.
TABOO, tabu, tapu or kapu, Polynesian words meaning that which is forbidden. Negative taboos arise from fear of possible ill effects (e.g., incest); positive taboos from awe or reverence (e.g., approaching a god). In tribal society the TOTEM of each CLAN is often subject to taboo.
TABRIZ, city in NW Iran, capital of East Azerbaijan province. It is a center of road and rail communications, with industries including textiles, leather goods and carpets. Pop 420 000.
TABULA RASA (Latin: scraped tablet), philosophical term referring to the condition of the mind before it is modified by experience; often used by empiricists (see EMPIRICISM) to emphasize the dependency of knowledge on the senses.
TACHÉ, Sir Étienne Paschal (1795–1865), Canadian politician, premier 1856–57 and 1864–65 of the province of Canada. He presided over the historic Quebec Convention (1865) leading to federation of British North American colonies.
TACHINA FLIES, family, Tachinidae, of small dipteran flies in which the larva is parasitic on the larvae of other insects. They are used for the biological control of insect pests.
TACHOMETER, instrument for measuring the angular VELOCITY of a rotating shaft. The simplest is a timed revolution counter. Other mechanical tachometers include the centrifugal tachometer, similar to the flyball GOVERNOR; the vibrating-reed tachometer, a group of reeds of different lengths which is held against the shaft housing so that the reed whose natural vibration frequency equals the rotation frequency of the shaft vibrates by resonance; and the velocity-head tachometer, in which a pump or fan on the shaft produces a measured air pressure. Electrical tachometers are usually electric GENERATORS or electric impulse counters. The eddy-current tachometer is used as a SPEEDOMETER.
TACHYCARDIA. See HEART.
TACITUS, Cornelius (c55–c120 AD), Roman historian. His most famous works are critical studies of the 1st-century empire, the *Histories* and *Annals*. A son-in-law of AGRICOLA, of whom he wrote a biography, he rose to consul (97), and proconsul of Asia (112). His *Germania* is the earliest study of the Germanic tribes.
TACNA-ARICA DISPUTE, between Peru and Chile, fought over two provinces provisionally ceded by Peru to Chile in 1883 after the WAR OF THE PACIFIC. US arbitration settled the dispute in 1929; Tacna went to Peru and Arica to Chile.
TACOMA, port and industrial city on Puget Sound, SW Wash., seat of Pierce Co. Tacoma's industries include shipbuilding, chemicals, clothing, and metal and wood products. Its port can handle oceangoing ships. There are two universities. Pop 154 581.
TACONIC MOUNTAINS, a range of the Appalachian system running some 150mi along the Mass./N.Y. boundary into Vt. Highest peak is Mt. Equinox (3 816ft).
TACONITE, an unleached, low-grade IRON ore. It consists of fine-grained FLINT containing HEMATITE, MAGNETITE and several silicates. Taconite must be concentrated by leaching or magnetic processes before smelting. The US has large quantities, including a huge deposit near Lake Superior.
TADPOLES, the larvae of FROGS and TOADS. An aquatic larva is characteristic of all the AMPHIBIA but in SALAMANDERS and NEWTS it is similar in appearance to the adult. In frogs and toads, the tadpole is globular with a long muscular tail. A full METAMORPHOSIS must be undergone to reach adult form.
TADZHIKISTAN, or Tadzhik SSR, a central Asian republic of USSR. Its 55 247sq mi (including Communism Peak, 24 590ft) border Afghanistan and China. Most of the majority Tadzhiks, in a population of some 3 000 000, are Sunnite Muslims. DUSHANBE is the capital. Agriculture includes cotton, cereals, fruit and stockraising. There are important mineral deposits; and textile, engineering and other industries.
TAEGU, historic city in South Korea, capital of North Kyŏngsang province. Textile and machine industries predominate. Apples from the Taegu area are famed. Pop 1 082 750.
TAEJŎN, city in South Korea, a railroad, textile and food-processing center, and capital of South Ch'ungch'ŏng province. Pop 414 598.
TAFT, Lorado (1860–1936), US sculptor, author of a pioneering *History of American Sculpture* (1903). Typical of his allegorical monuments (often fountains) is *The Fountain of the Great Lakes* in Chicago. He taught at Chicago Art Institute from 1886.
TAFT, Robert Alphonso (1889–1953), US senator from Ohio, 1938–53. Eldest son of W. H. TAFT, he studied law, served in the Ohio legislature, and became a leading conservative Republican. Taft was a fiscal conservative, an opponent of the NEW DEAL and an isolationist. His most famous congressional achievement was the TAFT-HARTLEY ACT.
TAFT, William Howard (1857–1930), 27th president of the US. An enormous, self-effacing man, he had the misfortune to succeed Theodore ROOSEVELT and suffered in comparison. He never wanted to be president and was politically inept; yet the achievements of his administration were substantial.

After a promising legal career, in which he served as state judge, US solicitor general and federal judge, Taft became first civil governor of the Philippines (1901). In 1904 he became Roosevelt's secretary of war and his concerns included the reorganization of the PANAMA CANAL project and the settlement of the RUSSO-JAPANESE WAR. In 1908 Roosevelt named him his successor, and Taft easily defeated William Jennings Bryan.

The new president's policies were based largely on those of Roosevelt. He increased prosecutions under the SHERMAN ANTITRUST ACT and introduced controls on government expenditure. His domestic reforms included a bill requiring disclosure of campaign funds in federal elections. In foreign affairs his efforts at international peace-keeping failed through poor management, and his "dollar diplomacy" poisoned relations with Latin America. Taft's inability to

William Howard TAFT

27th US President

Born: September 15, 1857
Died: March 8, 1930
Term of office: March 4, 1909–March 3, 1913
Political party: Republican

reduce tariffs effectively, his failure to curb the powers of Speaker CANNON, and his dismissal of chief forester Gifford PINCHOT alienated progressive Republicans. With progressive support Roosevelt began to attack Taft and ran against him in the 1912 election on a BULL MOOSE ticket. The split allowed the Democrat Woodrow WILSON to sweep into power.

Taft's defeat allowed him to return to his legal career and in 1921 he achieved a lifelong ambition when he was appointed chief justice of the Supreme Court, thus becoming the only man to serve as both chief justice and president.

TAFT-HARTLEY ACT, the Labor-Management Relations Act of 1947, sponsored by Robert A. TAFT and Fred Hartley. It was passed over the veto of President TRUMAN and amended the WAGNER ACT. The act defined "unfair labor practices," and banned boycotts, sympathy strikes and strikes in interunion disputes. A federal arbitration service was set up and states were empowered to prohibit union shop agreements. A further controversial provision was presidential power to seek an 80-day injunction against a strike in cases of "national emergency." (See also LANDRUM-GRIFFIN ACT.)

TAGALOG, a people who comprise over 20% of the population of the Philippines. Their majority in Manila gives them preeminence in business, administration and the arts. Since 1937 Tagalog (or Pilipino) has been the national language.

TAGANROG, seaport city in Rostov oblast, SW Russian SFSR, USSR, on the Azov Sea. Its heavy industry includes shipbuilding, steel and machinery. Pop 254 000.

TAGORE, Sir Rabindranath (1861–1941), Bengali Indian poet, painter, musician and mystic who founded what is now Visva-Bharati U. to blend the best in Indian and Western culture. His literary work includes many songs, poems, plays, novels, short stories and essays. He received the 1913 Nobel Prize for Literature.

TAGUS RIVER, or Tajo, longest river in the Iberian peninsula. It flows W 556mi from the Montes Universales in central Spain to the Atlantic coast of Portugal at LISBON.

TAHITI, largest of the Society Islands in the S Pacific, the center of FRENCH POLYNESIA. Its 400sq mi are mountainous and rich in tropical vegetation. The 85 000 people are Polynesians, with some French and Chinese. PAPEETE is the capital. Tahiti, claimed for France by BOUGAINVILLE in 1768, was visited by James COOK and William BLIGH. Its beauty inspired GAUGUIN.

TAHITIAN BRIDAL VEIL, an ornamental plant of the genus *Gibasis*, which produces long thin stems with small olive-green leaves, blushed maroon on the underside, and masses of tiny, delicate white flowers. Indoors, they grow well at average house temperatures and should be placed in a sunny window. The soil should be kept evenly moist, and the foliage misted daily. Propagation is by stem cuttings taken at any season. Family: Commelinaceae.

TAHOE, Lake, a lake in the Sierra Nevada on the Cal./Nev. border about 6 230ft above sea level, 22mi N–S and 12mi E–W. Discovered in 1844 by John C. FRÉMONT, it is now a tourist resort.

TAHR, a group of mountain-dwelling mammals, genus *Hemitragus*, closely related to GOATS, with no beard and short horns. They are of Asian origin.

TAIGA, Siberian forest region lying between the TUNDRA and the STEPPES. Conifers predominate, though birches are occasionally found. Much of the ground is swampy. The term is applied also to other, similar, N-Hemisphere FORESTS.

TAILORBIRDS, two genera of warblers named for their method of nest-building: they stitch leaves together with fibers to form a pouch. *Orthotomus* is found in S Asia, *Cisticola* in Australia.

T'AI-NAN, coastal city in SW Taiwan. One of the island's oldest cities and a *quondam* capital (1683–1891), it has textile, rubber, metal, electrical, salt and fishing industries. Pop 479 353.

TAINE, Hippolyte Adolphe (1828–1893), French critic and historian who devised a "scientific" method of criticism based on study of an author's environment and historical situation. The implications of his determinism greatly influenced the growth of literary NATURALISM. His most famous work is *History of English Literature* (1864).

TAIPEI, or **T'ai-pei,** capital and largest city of TAIWAN, lying to the N on the Tanshui R. A major industrial city, with steel plants, oil refineries and glass factories, Taipei is also the cultural and educational center of Taiwan. Pop 1 742 626.

TAIPING REBELLION (1851–64), great Chinese peasant rising. Agrarian discontent was channeled into a mass movement by the mystic leader Hung Hsiu-ch'üan, who claimed to be the brother of Christ. His regime in Kwangsi province survived 10 years but was finally crushed with the help of Charles GORDON and his 3 000 mercenaries. The rebellion seriously weakened the Manchu dynasty.

TAIWAN, or Formosa, an island off SE mainland China, the Formosa Strait (about 120mi wide) intervening. It is the only province of China controlled by the (Nationalist) Republic of CHINA and includes the PESCADORES, QUEMOY and Lan Hsü islands.

Land. Forested and mountainous (Yü Shan, 13 113ft), with extensive plains in the W, Taiwan has a monsoon climate, tropical in the S, subtropical in the N, which permits two rice harvests.

People. Most people are of Chinese, largely Fukien province, origin. Taiwan is densely populated: the influx of 2 000 000 mainland Chinese helped double the population 1946–66. Most Taiwanese are Buddhists or Taoists. The 200 000 Malay-Polynesian aborigines live mainly in the E.

Economy. Taiwan's well-developed economy is largely agricultural. Irrigation is vital in growing rice, sweet potatoes, soybeans, sugar, "oolong" tea, fruits and cotton. There are rich fisheries and abundant timber. Minerals include coal, natural gas and some oil, gold, copper and silver. Industry includes steel, aluminum, textiles, petrochemicals, wood and food-processing, and a wide range of manufactured goods. Exports include textiles, metals, machinery, chemicals, sugar and tea.

History. Named Formosa ("beautiful") by the Portuguese, and from 1624 under Dutch control, Taiwan fell to a Ming general in 1662 and then to the Manchus (1683). Ceded to Japan in 1895, it was taken over by CHIANG KAI-SHEK in 1949 when Mao Tse-tung ousted the Nationalists from mainland China. From 1951 to 1965 the US gave $1.5 billion economic aid and $2.5 billion military aid. Though Taiwan (Republic of China) was expelled from the UN in 1971, it continued to enjoy US protection under the Mutual Defense Treaty of 1954.

T'AI-YÜAN, capital of Shansi province, NE China. It has large iron and steel, coal, engineering and chemical industries. Pop 2 725 000.

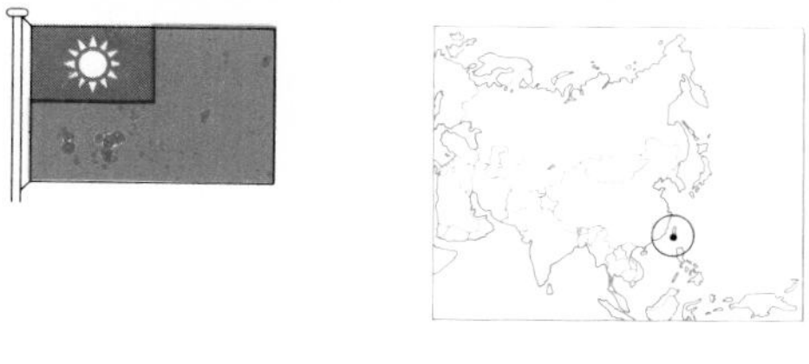

Official name: Taiwan
Capital: Taipei
Area: 13 892sq mi
Population: 15 290 000
Languages: Mandarin Chinese; Amoy, Hakka dialects
Religions: Buddhism, Taoism; Christian, Muslim
Monetary unit(s): 1 New Taiwan dollar = 100 cents

TAJ MAHAL, a MAUSOLEUM built by the Mogul emperor Shah Jahan for his wife Mumtaz-i-Mahal at Agra in N India. Faced in white marble, the central domed tomb stands on a square plinth with a minaret at each corner, surrounded by water gardens, gateways and walks. It took some 20 000 workmen over 20 years to complete (1632–54).

TAKAMATSU, seaport, NE Shikoku Island, Japan, capital of Kagawa prefecture, the island's main trading and travel outlet to Honshu island. Pop 274 367.

TAKLA MAKAN (Chinese: *T'a-k'o-la-ma-kan Shamo*), desert occupying most of the Tarim Basin, NW China. Its 125 000sq mi comprise shifting sands broken by patches of clay.

TAKOMA PARK, city in Md., a suburb of Washington D.C., home of Columbia Union College. Pop 18 455.

TALBOT, William Henry Fox (1800–1877), English scientist and inventor of the Calotype (Talbotype) method of PHOTOGRAPHY. In Calotype a latent image in silver iodide is developed in gallic acid and fixed in sodium thiosulfate giving a paper "negative." Thus, for the first time, any number of positive prints could be made from a single exposure by contact printing from the negative.

TALC, basic magnesium SILICATE mineral $Mg_3Si_4O_{10}(OH)_2$, occurring in METAMORPHIC ROCKS, chiefly in the US, USSR, France and Japan. It has a layer structure resembling that of MICA, and is extremely soft (see HARDNESS). Talc is used in ceramics, roof insulation, cosmetics, as an insecticide carrier and as a filler in paints, paper and rubber. Compacted talc forms SOAPSTONE.

TALIEN. See PORT ARTHUR AND DAIREN.

TALISMAN. See AMULET.

TALLADEGA, a manufacturing city in E Ala., seat of Talladega Co. The city's industries include quarrying and cottonseed oil. Pop 17 662.

TALLAHASSEE, state capital of Fla., seat of Leon Co. Famous for its gardens, the city is the commercial center of NW Fla. and has light industry and two state universities. Pop 71 897.

TALLCHIEF, Maria (1925–), US ballerina. She has played many roles for the New York City Ballet, notably those created for her by George BALANCHINE.

TALLEYRAND (Charles-Maurice de Talleyrand-Périgord; 1754–1838), French statesman. He was a member of the National Assembly during the FRENCH REVOLUTION, helped Napoleon found the First Empire (1804), assisted the restoration of the Bourbon kings (1814), then helped oust them in favor of a constitutional monarchy (1830). Talleyrand is best remembered for his brilliant diplomacy at the Congress of Vienna (see VIENNA, CONGRESS OF) and in the negotiations (1830–31) between France and Britain which set up the state of Belgium.

TALLINN, formerly Revel, capital of the Estonian SSR, USSR, a major port on the Gulf of Finland, with shipbuilding, textile and engineering industries and many educational institutions. Pop 363 000.

TALLIS, Thomas (c1505–1585), English composer and organist. He was a close associate of William BYRD, with whom he shared a state monopoly in the printing of music. Tallis is famous for his solemn, elaborately constructed choral church music and for his development of COUNTERPOINT.

TALLIT, a Jewish prayer shawl. Its fringe has symbolic knots at the corners. Covering the upper part of the body, the tallit, used by men only, is worn at prayer by Orthodox Jews and some Conservative Jews.

TALLOW TREE, *Sapium sebiferum*, a small tree native to China but cultivated in other warm regions. Its seed yields a white, greasy substance which is used to make candles and soap in the Orient. Family: Euphorbiaceae.

TALMADGE, name of two Ga. politicians. **Eugene Talmadge** (1884–1946) was governor of Ga. three times between 1933 and 1943. He supported segregation and opposed Roosevelt's New Deal programs and federal social security legislation. His son, **Herman Eugene Talmadge** (1913–), was governor 1948–55 and entered the US Senate in 1956.

TALMUD (Hebrew: teaching), ancient compilation of Jewish oral law and rabbinical teaching, begun 5th century AD. There are two versions: Babylonian and Palestinian. It has two parts: the MISHNAH and the GEMARA. These contain a wealth of traditional wisdom, legends and stories, comment on the Old Testament and record early legal decisions. The

Talmud is second only to the Bible in prestige, and its study has been the core of Jewish education for over 1000 years.

TALUS, or **scree**, accumulation of rocky debris at the base of a cliff or steep mountain slope, the result of mechanical weathering (see EROSION) of the rocks above. A **breccia** is a SEDIMENTARY ROCK formation of consolidated talus.

TAMANDUA, *Tamandua tetradactyla,* a South American ANTEATER with a characteristic snout, no teeth, a long extensible tongue for poking into rotten logs and termite nests, and a long prehensile tail. The powerful front limbs are armed with claws.

TAMARAU, *Bubalus mindorensis*, species of small BUFFALO from the Philippine island of Mindoro. Related to the water buffalo, it is smaller—1m (39in) high—and more robust, with short thick horns.

TAMARIND, *Tamarindus indica*, a tropical African tree, which is cultivated throughout the world for its fruits that are made into preserves and laxative drinks. Family: Leguminosae.

TAMARISK, evergreen shrubs of the genus *Tamarix*, which are adapted for life in salty or alkaline soils. Galls produced on some species are used for tanning. Native to Europe and Asia, tamarisks are planted as windbreaks and to improve poor soils. Family: Tamaricaceae.

TAMAULIPAS, NE Mexico state bordering Tex. Its 30822sq mi comprise a plain rising gently from the Gulf of Mexico to a cooler mountainous interior. Chief products are sugar, cotton, beef and oil (near TAMPICO). Ciudad Victoria is the capital.

TAMAYO, Rufino (1899–), Mexican painter. He combines the strength and color of native and pre-Columbian art with Expressionist and Surrealist styles. He has painted several frescoes but is best known for his small paintings of Indian figures.

TAMBOURINE, a PERCUSSION INSTRUMENT comprising a skin stretched across a hoop fitted with bells or "jingles" which rattle as it is tapped or shaken. Originating in the Middle East, it is used in folk music and in some orchestral scores.

TAMERLANE (c1336–1405), or Timur the Lame, Mongol conqueror. Claiming descent from GENGHIS KHAN, by 1370 he controlled from his capital SAMARKAND what is now Soviet Turkmenistan. He conquered Persia (1387), the Caucasus (1392), Syria (1400) and the Ottoman Turks (1402) in the W, and invaded India and sacked Delhi (1398). He died planning to invade China. The empire rapidly disintegrated.

TAMIL, a DRAVIDIAN language spoken by some 40 million, principally in SE India and NE Ceylon. It is the main language of Tamil Nadu (formerly Madras) state. Tamil has its own script, and a rich ancient literature.

TAMM, Igor Yevgenevich (1895–1971), Soviet physicist awarded, with P. A. CHERENKOV and I. M. FRANK, the 1958 Nobel Prize for Physics for work with Frank interpreting the Cerenkov effect (1937).

TAMMANY HALL, nickname from the 1800s for the corrupt New York Democratic Party machine, also the name of its Madison Avenue offices. The patriotic society of Tammany (a wise Delaware Indian chief) was founded in 1789, with a ritual based on Indian custom. It became a Democratic machine, dominating the city after c1830, with corruption common under "bosses" like William TWEED. Its influence spread beyond New York, but the reforms of LA GUARDIA (mayor, 1933–45) led to its decline.

TAMPA, city in W Fla., seat of Hillsborough Co. It is Fla.'s chief port, a tourist, university, fishing and manufacturing center processing citrus fruit, lumber, phosphates and tobacco. Pop 277 767.

TAMPERE, Finland's second city and chief industrial center, 125mi NW of Helsinki. It has important textile and machinery industries. Pop 157 697.

TAMPICO, seaport, resort and commercial center of NE Mexico, near the mouth of the Pánuco R on the Gulf of Mexico. It processes and exports oil, cattle and agricultural products. Pop 196 147.

TANA LAKE, N Ethiopia, the country's largest lake (about 1 100sq mi) and the source of the Blue Nile.

TANAGERS, small colorful forest birds, with 200 species in the family Thraupidae, all confined to the New World. All are fruit-eaters though many species also take insects.

TANAGRA, ancient town in E Boeotia, E Greece, where Spartans defeated the Athenians in 457 BC. Graceful terracotta figurines (4th and 3rd centuries BC) were excavated from its graves.

TANAKA, Kakuei (1918–), Japanese politician, prime minister 1972–74. He built up a construction business, headed the Liberal Democratic Party from 1965 and held cabinet posts from 1968. Acquitted in 1949 on bribery charges, he was arrested in the 1976 Lockheed bribery scandal.

TANANARIVE, capital and largest city of Madagascar, on the central plateau. It is its commercial, manufacturing (food products, textiles) and educational center. Pop 343 670.

TANANA RIVER, chief S tributary of the Yukon R, E and central Alaska. It flows about 475mi NW from the NE Wrangell Mts. The Alaska Highway runs alongside.

TANCRED (c1076–1112), a Sicilian Norman leader of the First CRUSADE (1096–99). He helped take Nicaea (1097), Antioch (1098) and Jerusalem (1099). Becoming regent of Antioch (1100) and Edessa (1104), he fought Turks and Byzantines and conquered N Syria.

TANEY, Roger Brooke (1777–1864), chief justice of the US (1836–64) whose DRED SCOTT CASE decision helped bring on the Civil War. As President Jackson's secretary of the treasury (1833–35), he crushed the Second BANK OF THE UNITED STATES. As chief justice, he steered a middle course on STATES' RIGHTS, and continued John MARSHALL's liberal interpretation of the Constitution. (See also SUPREME COURT OF THE UNITED STATES.)

TANGANYIKA. See TANZANIA.

TANGANYIKA, Lake, in W Tanzania and E Zaire, in the Great Rift Valley. Africa's second-largest lake, it is 420mi N–S, 30–45mi E–W and up to 4 710ft deep. It has important fisheries.

T'ANG DYNASTY (618–906), a "golden age" in Chinese history. Cofounded by the aristocrat Li Yüan and his son T'ai Tsung (ruled 627–49), the dynasty sent armies W to Central Asia and made China a cosmopolitan empire enjoying a cultural renaissance at its peak under Hsüan Tsung (reigned 712–56). There were remarkable advances in science, technology, printing, the arts and literature, with outstanding lyric verse by LI PO and Tu Fu.

TANGELO, a fruit tree formed by crossing a TANGERINE with a GRAPEFRUIT. The fruits are similar to the ORANGE. Family: Rutaceae.

TANGENT. See TRIGONOMETRY.

TANGENT OF A CURVE, a LINE touching, but not intersecting (see INTERSECTION), a CURVE. The GRADIENT of the tangent is equal to the instantaneous gradient of the curve at the POINT of contact (see CALCULUS). (See also CIRCLE.)

TANGERINE, a small, thin-skinned, easily peeled fruit produced by a variety of mandarin ORANGE. Family: Rutaceae.

TANGIER, seaport and residential and commercial city of Morocco, facing the Strait of Gibraltar. From 1923 to 1956 it was part of an international zone under French, Spanish and British administrators. Pop 187 894.

TANGO, Latin American dance, with long, gliding steps, deep bendings of the knees and syncopated music. It was a popular ballroom dance after WWII.

T'ANG-SHAN, city in NE China, 100mi ESE of Peking. It is a center for heavy industry, hit by a devastating earthquake in 1976. Pop 1 200 000.

TANGUY, Yves (1900–1955), French Surrealist painter, who lived in the US from 1939. Influenced by CHIRICO, he painted a dream-like world of strange inhuman shapes inhabiting a lunar landscape. (See SURREALISM.)

TANH. See HYPERBOLIC FUNCTIONS.

TANK, armored combat vehicle, armed with guns or missiles, and self-propelled on caterpillar treads; the chief modern conventional ground assault weapon. Tanks were first built in 1915 by Britain and used from 1916 against Germany in WWI. These early tanks were very slow, and development between the wars greatly improved speed and firepower. The Spanish civil war and WWII showed the effectiveness of concentrated tank attacks. Amphibious and airborne tanks were developed. Heavy tanks proved cumbersome, and were generally abandoned in favor of the more maneuverable (though more vulnerable) light and medium tanks. Improved models are now used where heavy guns are needed. Light tanks (less than 25 tonnes) are used mainly for infantry support.

TANKER, ship designed to carry liquid cargo in bulk, notably crude oil, gasoline or natural gas. The first tanker (1886), a 300ft vessel, carried 3 000 tons of oil. Some tankers today hold 100 times as much: a 483 939-ton vessel (the *Globtik London*, 1975) has been built in Japan. Ships this size greatly reduce per-ton transport costs, but cannot enter many ports; some large tankers transfer their cargo to smaller tankers offshore. In gross tonnage tankers account for over a third of all MERCHANT SHIPPING.

TANNENBERG (Polish: Stebark), village in N Poland, 15mi SE of Ostróda, site of two important battles. In 1410, the TEUTONIC KNIGHTS were defeated by the Lithuanians and Poles, and in WWI (August, 1914), the Germans severely defeated the Russians. Up to 1945 Tannenberg was in Germany.

TANNHÄUSER (c.1200–c1270), German MINNESINGER whose legend inspired Wagner's opera *Tannhäuser*. Seduced by Venus, he sought the pope's absolution, was rejected, returned to Venus and later disappeared forever.

TANNING, the conversion of animal hide into LEATHER. After cleaning and soaking, a tanning agent is applied that converts the GELATIN of the hide into an insoluble material which cements the PROTEIN fibers together and makes them incorruptible. Until the end of the 19th century vegetable extracts containing TANNINS were used; then the process was greatly shortened by using CHROMIUM salts, and also FORMALDEHYDE and FORMIC ACID.

TANNINS, or **tannic acid**, a group of complex organic substances occurring in many plants, especially oak gallnuts, tea, and the bark of oak, mangrove and sumac, from which they are extracted by boiling in water. Tannins may be classified as hydrolyzable (yielding GALLIC ACID) or condensed. They are used for TANNING, for making DYES and INKS, and in medicine as an ASTRINGENT.

TANSY, or bitter buttons, *Tanacetum vulgare* and related species, a European herb with button-like clusters of scented yellow flowers. Preparations of the foliage are used in seasoning and to destroy intestinal worms. Family: COMPOSITAE.

TANTALUM (Ta), hard, silvery-gray metal in Group VB of the PERIODIC TABLE; a TRANSITION ELEMENT. It is found in COLUMBITE with NIOBIUM, which it resembles closely. Tantalum oxide is separated by solvent extraction and reduced to the metal. It is highly inert, and is used in laboratory ware, capacitors, surgical instruments and as a "getter." AW 180.9, mp 2996°C, bp 5425°C, sg 16.6 (20°C).

TANTALUS, in Greek myth, son of ZEUS, source of the word "tantalize." For serving up his son PELOPS for the gods to eat (or for stealing their nectar and ambrosia) he had to stand with water and fruit just out of reach.

TANTRAS, the texts of Tantrism, a system of esoteric Hindu and Buddhist practices. Tantras are often dialogues between the male and female aspects (in Hinduism SHIVA and SHAKTI) of a supreme deity. They instruct in meditation and YOGA (including ritual sex) as a means of reaching ultimate truth through mind and body. They date from c500 AD.

TAN-TUNG. See ANTUNG.

TANZANIA, republic in E Africa, on the Indian Ocean. It was formed (1964) by the union of Tanganyika with ZANZIBAR and became a socialist state dominated by its first president Julius NYERERE.

Land. Tanzania is a beautiful country, with plateaus, mountain ranges, Africa's highest peak (Mt. Kilimanjaro), Rift Valley lakes and the S part of Lake Victoria. Inland the climate is hot and dry with some rain Dec.–May. Coral reefs and mangrove swamps line the coast. Grasslands and open woods dominate the extensive plains, famous for their wildlife.

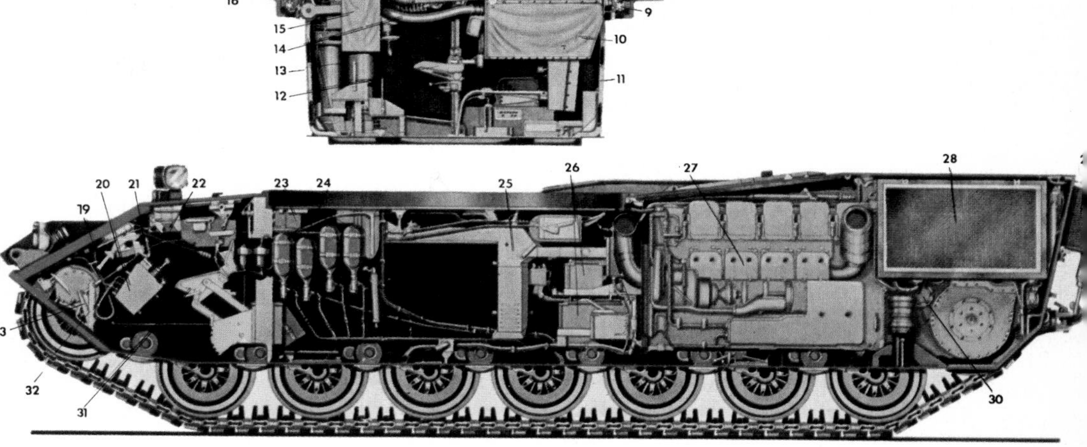

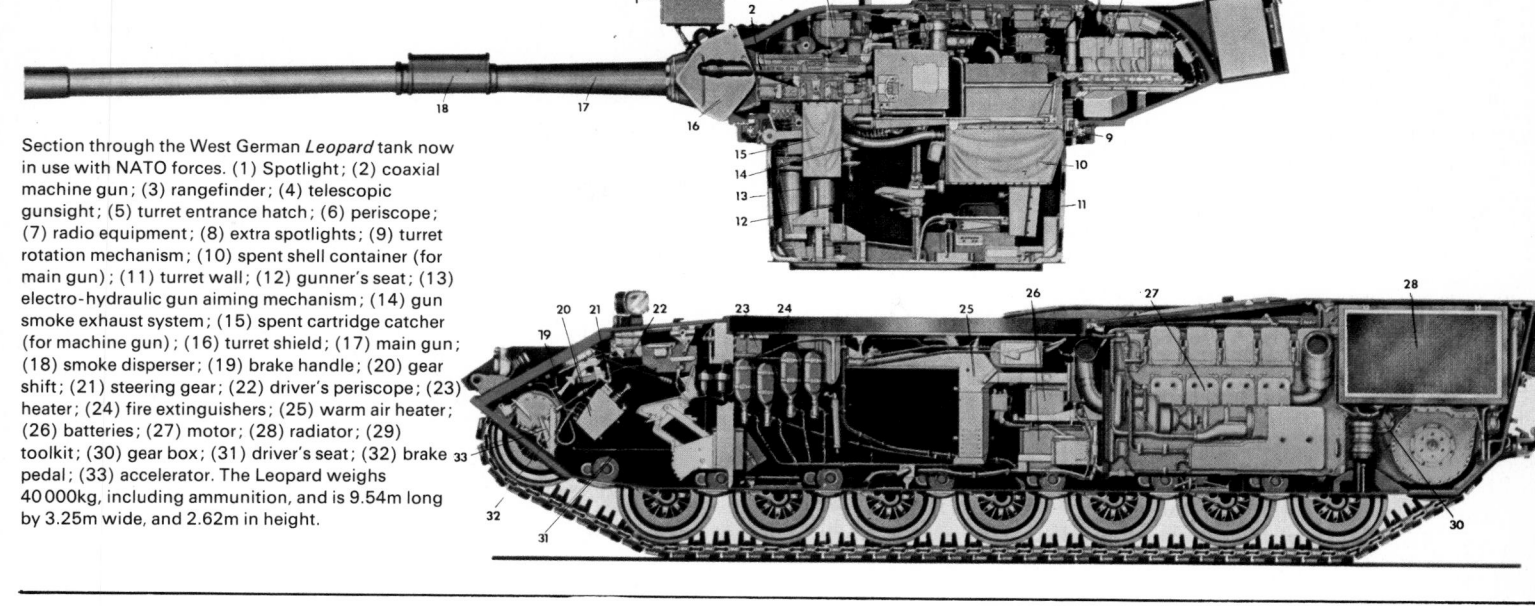

Section through the West German *Leopard* tank now in use with NATO forces. (1) Spotlight; (2) coaxial machine gun; (3) rangefinder; (4) telescopic gunsight; (5) turret entrance hatch; (6) periscope; (7) radio equipment; (8) extra spotlights; (9) turret rotation mechanism; (10) spent shell container (for main gun); (11) turret wall; (12) gunner's seat; (13) electro-hydraulic gun aiming mechanism; (14) gun smoke exhaust system; (15) spent cartridge catcher (for machine gun); (16) turret shield; (17) main gun; (18) smoke disperser; (19) brake handle; (20) gear shift; (21) steering gear; (22) driver's periscope; (23) heater; (24) fire extinguishers; (25) warm air heater; (26) batteries; (27) motor; (28) radiator; (29) toolkit; (30) gear box; (31) driver's seat; (32) brake pedal; (33) accelerator. The Leopard weighs 40 000kg, including ammunition, and is 9.54m long by 3.25m wide, and 2.62m in height.

People. The vast majority (94%) are rural. There are over 100 BANTU tribes, each with distinctive speech and customs, but the towns have many people of Indian descent, and there are Arab and European minorities. The illiteracy rate is high. The chief towns are DAR ES SALAAM, Zanzibar, Mwanza and Arusha.
Economy. Farming provides more than 60% of the gross national product and more than 80% of exports. These include coffee, cotton, sisal, cloves, diamonds, gold, salt and tin. Secondary manufacture is expanding. Railroads include the Chinese-built Tanzam Railroad (completed 1975) linking Dar es Salaam with Zambia.
History. OLDUVAI GORGE in N Tanzania has the world's earliest known human and pre-human remains. In historical times, the coast and Zanzibar came under Arab control from the 700s AD. Germany established a mainland protectorate (1891), but after WWI the region passed to Britain by League of Nations mandate. Tanganyika gained independence in 1961, Zanzibar in 1964. In 1967, Tanzania nationalized all banks and many industries.

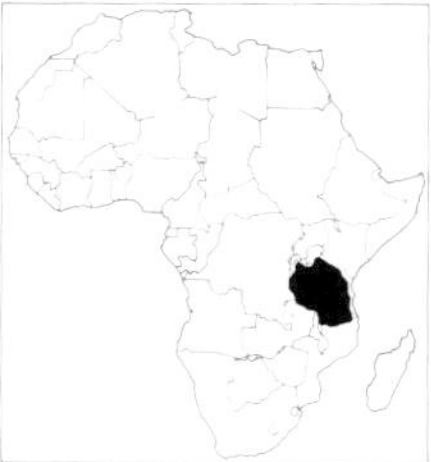

Official name: United Republic of Tanzania
Capital: Dar es Salaam
Area: 362 821sq mi
Population: 13 750 000
Languages: Swahili, English; Bantu dialects
Religions: Animist, Muslim, Christian
Monetary unit(s): 1 Tanzanian shilling = 100 cents

TAOISM, ancient Chinese philosophy, in influence second only to CONFUCIANISM, derived chiefly from the book *Tao-te Ching* (3rd century BC) attributed to LAO-TSE. It advocated a contemplative life in accord with nature, unspoiled by intellectual evaluations. Tao ("The Way") was considered impossible to describe save in cryptic imagery. Taoism later became a polytheistic religion.

TAOS, historic town in N central N.M., seat of Taos Co., at the foot of Sangre de Cristo Mts. It is famous for its writers and artists, and its picturesque Indian village (Taos Pueblo) and old Spanish farming community. Pop 2 475.

TAPAJÓS RIVER, S tributary of the Amazon, in N central Brazil. Formed by the junction of Juruena and Teles Pires rivers, it flows about 500mi NE to Santarém.

TAP DANCE, an exhibition dance in which the toes and heels are tapped rapidly against a hard surface. Metal-tipped shoes clarify the complicated rhythms. Tap dancing developed in US VAUDEVILLE. It reached a peak with such dancers as Fred ASTAIRE.

TAPE RECORDER, instrument for SOUND RECORDING on magnetic tape, and subsequent playback. The tape, consisting of small magnetic particles of iron oxides on a thin plastic film base, is wound from the supply reel to the take-up reel by a rotating capstan which controls the speed. The tape passes in turn the erase head, which by applying an alternating field reduces the overall magnetization to zero; the recording head, and the playback head. Standard tape speeds are $1\frac{7}{8}$, $3\frac{3}{4}$, $7\frac{1}{2}$, 15 or 30in/s, the higher speeds being used for HIGH-FIDELITY reproduction. **Cassettes** contain thin tape handily packaged, running at $1\frac{7}{8}$in/s. The somewhat larger **cartridges** contain an endless loop of tape on a single reel. Most recorders use two, four or even more tracks side by side on the tape.

TAPESTRY, a fabric woven with colored threads to form a design and used to cover walls and furniture. Warp threads are stretched on a loom, and colored threads, or wefts, are woven over and under them and then compacted (see also WEAVING). Tapestries were known in ancient Egypt, Syria, Persia and China. N Europe's great era of tapestry-making began in the 1300s, notably at ARRAS in Flanders. It reached a peak in the GOBELIN tapestries of the 1600s. Great painters who have made tapestry designs include Raphael and Rubens. The BAYEUX TAPESTRY is in fact embroidery.

TAPEWORMS, intestinal parasites, so named because they are long and flat, forming the class Cestoda of the FLATWORM phylum Platyhelminthes. A scolex, or head, only 1.5–2mm (about 0.06in) in diameter is attached to the gut and behind this the body consists of a ribbon of identical flat segments, or proglottids, each containing reproductive organs. These proglottids are budded off from behind the scolex. Mature proglottids containing eggs pass out with the feces where larval stages can infect intermediate hosts.

TAPIOCA. See CASSAVA.

TAPIRS, a family, Tapiridae, of large brown or black and white UNGULATES related to RHINOCEROSES. They are plump, thick-skinned vegetarian animals characterized by a short mobile nasal "trunk" and with four toes on the front feet and three on the hind feet. Of four living species, the largest, *Tapirus indicus* occurs in Malaya, the others being South American.

TAPPAN, Arthur (1786–1865) and **Lewis** (1788–1873), US silk merchants, abolitionists and philanthropists. They cofounded the American Anti-Slavery Society (1833), and formed a rival group in 1840. Arthur helped establish Kenyon and Oberlin Colleges. In 1841 Lewis founded the first US commercial credit-rating agency.

TAR, dark, odorous liquid obtained by destructive distillation of coal (see COAL TAR) or wood, especially from conifers. (See also CREOSOTE; PITCH.)

TARA, parish in Co. Meath, Ireland, 22mi NW of Dublin, site of 507ft Tara Hill, a sacred place from c2100 BC. The high kings of Ireland were crowned and had their seat there until c560 AD.

TARANTELLA, lively Italian dance with six beats to the bar. It is linked with tarantism, hysterical dancing once common near Taranto. The dance supposedly cured the bite of a tarantula spider.

TARANTO, seaport and industrial city in SE Italy, capital of Taranto province. It has shipyards, steel, chemical and fishing industries. Founded as a Greek colony c708 BC, it became the important Roman town of Tarentum. Pop 222 826.

TARANTULA, popular name, originally of the large WOLF SPIDER *Lycosa tarantula*, but now used for various unrelated giant SPIDERS throughout the world. All are long and hairy and eat large insects or small vertebrates. Their venom seldom has serious effects on humans.

TARASCAN INDIANS, a chiefly peasant-artisan group in Michoacán state, central Mexico. In 1522, the Tarascan state, having resisted the culturally similar AZTECS to the E, surrendered to Spain.

TARAWA, atoll in the W central Pacific, capital of the GILBERT AND ELLICE ISLANDS. It is the chief port and commercial center. Occupied by Japan in 1942, it was taken by US Marines in 1943. Pop 14 462.

TARBELA DAM, rock-filled dam on the Indus R, W Pakistan, 35mi NW of Islamabad. Completed 1975, it is the world's largest earth-fill dam. With the Mangla Dam it forms part of the Indus Basin Project.

TARBELL, Ida Minerva (1857–1944), US journalist, a leader of the MUCKRAKERS. Her exposure of malpractice in *The History of the Standard Oil Company* (1904) led to successful prosecution of the company in 1911.

TARGET SHOOTING, competitive shooting with a firearm at a target, usually a cardboard square with a central black bullseye surrounded by concentric circles. The closer a hit to the bullseye, the more it scores. The sport became popular in the 19th century; it has been an event of the Olympic Games since 1896.

TARGUM, an Aramaic translation or paraphrase of the Hebrew scriptures, or Old Testament, usually with a commentary. Some Targums date from c200 BC, when ARAMAIC was replacing Hebrew as an everyday language among many Jews.

TARIFFS, customs duties on exports or, more commonly, imports. The aim is generally to protect home industries from foreign competition, though it may be merely to provide revenue. During the 17th and 18th centuries the European powers created tariff systems that gave their colonies preferential treatment, but Britain's tariffs, by limiting North America's trade, helped provoke the Revolutionary War. In the early 1800s the FREE TRADE movement, bolstered by the economic philosophy of LAISSEZ-FAIRE, helped limit the spread of tariffs. However, US federal tariffs imposed to aid Northern industry damaged the South and contributed to the Civil War. US and European tariffs were moderate in the early 1900s but, after the Great Depression, both the US and UK adopted high tariffs, with a consequent decline in INTERNATIONAL TRADE. In 1947 the US and 22 other nations signed the GENERAL AGREEMENT ON TARIFFS AND TRADE (GATT) aimed at reducing trade discrimination. GATT has only partly achieved this, notably in the "Kennedy Round" (1964–67), involving over 50 nations and a broad range of commodities. In the mid-1970s, high EUROPEAN ECONOMIC COMMUNITY (EEC) tariffs against food imports and a general trade recession roused fears of revived PROTECTIONISM. (See also ECONOMICS; EUROPEAN FREE TRADE ASSOCIATION.)

TARKINGTON, Newton Booth (1869–1946), US writer famous for his novels reflecting Midwestern life and character, as in his *Penrod* (1914). He worked for *The Saturday Evening Post*, was an Ind. representative (1902–03), and won two Pulitzer prizes (1919, 1922) for *The Magnificent Ambersons* (1918) and *Alice Adams* (1921).

TARLETON, Sir Banastre (1754–1833), English cavalry soldier, commander of the British Legion in the REVOLUTIONARY WAR. Noted for cruelty, he was successful (1799–80) at Charleston, Waxhaws, CAMDEN and Fishing Creek but lost to General Charles MORGAN at COWPENS.

TARNISHING. See CORROSION.

TARO, plants (*Calocasia antiquorum* and *C. esculenta*), whose tubers provide a STARCH food for millions in eastern Asia and the Pacific. The tubers are eaten boiled to avoid the bitter flavor of calcium oxalate in the raw tubers. Family: Araceae.

TAROT, pack of 78 PLAYING CARDS used for fortune telling or for the card game *tarok* (tarot or tarocchi). There are four suits each of 14 cards (cups, pentacles, swords and wands) and a major arcana of 22 cards (also called tarots) which in the card game operate as permanent trumps.

TARPAN, a wild HORSE of Russia and Eastern Europe, ancestral to the modern horse. Of the three subspecies, two, the Forest tarpan and the Steppe tarpan, are now extinct. The third subspecies, PRZEWALSKI'S HORSE, may also have died out.

TARPONS, powerful, silvery fishes renowned for their fighting powers when hooked as game fishes. There are two species, primarily marine, the Indo-Pacific tarpon, *Megalops cyprinoides*, and the Atlantic tarpon *Tarpon atlanticus*, which may grow to 2.5m (8ft) and weigh 130kg (287lb).

TARPON SPRINGS, city in W Fla., 28mi N of St. Petersburg. It is a resort and a major producer of natural sponges.

TARQUINIA, ancient town in central Italy, 45mi NW of Rome. It has medieval fortifications and is the site of Tarquinii, the chief Etruscan city, with a famous burial ground containing fine tomb paintings (see ETRUSCAN CIVILIZATION). Pop 12 200.

TARQUINIUS, name of the 5th and of the last of Rome's seven semilegendary kings. **Lucius Tarquinius Priscus** (reigned 616–579 BC), built the Temple of Jupiter, Circus Maximus and Cloaca Maxima, crushed Latium and fought the Sabines. He was assassinated. His despotic son or grandson **Lucius Tarquinius Superbus** (reigned 534–510 BC), murdered his father-in-law SERVIUS TULLIUS and was expelled by popular revolt after his son's rape of LUCRETIA (see ROME, ANCIENT).

TARRYTOWN, residential village, SE N.Y., a suburb 24mi N of New York City. It is a resort and makes clothing and automobiles. Pop 11 115.

TARSIERS, three species of nocturnal Malayan mammals related to LEMURS, very similar in appearance to BUSHBABIES. True PRIMATES, they have large, forward-pointing eyes and a relatively large brain. They are insectivorous or fruit-eating, and move in a series of jumps with the body held vertically.

TARSUS, commercial town in S Turkey, birthplace of St. PAUL. Ancient Tarsus, chief city of CILICIA, was a great trading and cultural center in Roman and Byzantine times. Pop 57 737.

TARTAGLIA, Niccolò (1499–1557), Italian Renaissance mathematician who discovered a method of solving cubic EQUATIONS. He is also known for an encyclopedic work on elementary mathematics and for his contributions to BALLISTICS.

TARTAN, the checkered fabric of Scotland's native dress. Each clan is ascribed a particular tartan, though often in more than one variety—the hunting tartans are usually somber blues and greens, while reds generally predominate in the dress tartans. The authenticity of ascriptions to clans is questioned, and some tartans are of comparatively recent origin.

TARTARIC ACID, or dihydroxybutanedioic acid (HOOC.CHOH.CHOH.COOH), a CARBOXYLIC ACID having three STEREOISOMERS, used in foods and SOFT DRINKS, as a metal cleaner, and in dyeing and photography. It is obtained from the lees of wine fermentation, in which it occurs as potassium hydrogen tartrate, known as **argol**, or **cream of tartar** when pure, used in BAKING POWDER and in ELECTROPLATING. From argol are made **Rochelle salt**, potassium sodium tartrate, used in making processed cheese, mirrors and cathartics; and **tartar emetic**, antimony potassium tartrate, used as an emetic, insecticide, and mordant in dyeing.

TARTARS. See TATARS.

TARTARUS, in Greek myth, a dark abyss below HADES. In PLATO and VERGIL it is where the worst sinners are punished.

TARTINI, Giuseppe (1692–1770), Italian composer and violinist. He founded (1728) a school of violin playing at Padua, improved the violin and playing techniques, and contributed to musical theory. His works include some 200 concertos and 200 violin sonatas, notably *The Devil's Trill.*

TASHKENT, capital of Uzbek SSR, USSR. The largest city in Soviet central Asia, it is a major industrial center and has a university and academy of sciences. Pop 1 385 000.

TASMAN, Abel Janszoon (c1603–1659), Dutch sailor and S Pacific explorer. Sailing from Jawa in Dutch East India Company service (1642–43, 1644), he discovered Tasmania and New Zealand (1642), which he thought were parts of Australia, then Tonga and Fiji (1643).

TASMANIA, smallest Australian state (26 383sq mi, pop 392 500). The 150mi Bass Strait separates Tasmania from the SE mainland. It includes King, Flinders and Macquarie islands, as well as the main island (christened by TASMAN Van Diemen's Land). Tasmania's forests contain the unique TASMANIAN DEVIL and THYLACINE. Chief cities are HOBART (the capital), Launceston, Burnie and Devonport. Important industries are livestock (dairying, wool), horticulture, lumber and newsprint, mining and mineral processing (zinc, copper, lead). (See also TASMANIANS.)

TASMANIAN DEVIL, *Sarcophilus harrisii*, a dog-sized marsupial, now confined to Tasmania. It is a solitary, nocturnal animal which feeds on mammals, birds, invertebrates and carrion.

TASMANIANS, now extinct native population of TASMANIA, perhaps once the native race of Australia and physically and culturally quite unlike the AUSTRALIAN ABORIGINES. The pure stock were extinguished 1804–1876, although a few halfbreeds still exist.

TASMANIAN WOLF. See THYLACINE.

TASMAN SEA, part of the South Pacific Ocean, about 1 300mi across, between SE Australia and New Zealand.

TASS (Telegraph Agency of the Soviet Union), the state monopoly news agency of the USSR. Founded in 1925, it is managed by the Propaganda Department of the Communist Party's Central Committee.

TASSO, Torquato (1544–1595), Italy's major late Renaissance poet, a master of lyrical, sensuous, often mournful verse. His works include the pastoral drama *Aminta* (1573) and his masterpiece *Jerusalem Delivered* (completed 1575), an epic based on the First Crusade.

TASTE, special SENSE concerned with the differentiation of basic modalities of food or other substances in the mouth; receptors are distributed over the surface of the TONGUE and are able to distinguish salt, sweet, sour, bitter and possibly water as primary tastes. Much of what is colloquially termed taste is actually SMELL perception of odors reaching the olfactory EPITHELIUM via the naso-PHARYNX. Receptors for sweet are concentrated at the tip of the tongue, for salt and sour along the sides, with bitter mainly at the back. Taste nerve impulses pass via the BRAIN stem to the cortex.

TATARS, or **Tartars**, Turkic-speaking people of the USSR, where some 4 500 000 live in the Tatar Autonomous SSR, along the Volga R, in the Ural Mts. and the Uzbek and Kazakh SSRs. Most are Sunnite Muslims. Tatar also describes the E Mongolian tribes, part of the GOLDEN HORDE, which seized much of Russia in the 1200s (see MONGOL EMPIRE).

TATE, John Orley Allen (1899–), distinguished US writer, critic and teacher. Born in Ky., he helped found the FUGITIVES and advocated the "new criticism," with its stress on a work's intrinsic qualities. His own work includes several collections of his poetry and essays, biographies and a novel.

TATLIN, Vladimir (1885–1953), Russian painter and sculptor, leader of CONSTRUCTIVISM. Influenced by PICASSO's Cubist reliefs, he made in 1913 abstract reliefs of tin, wood, glass and plaster and *Corner-reliefs* (1915) suspended on wire. In 1920 he planned a symbolic monument to the Third INTERNATIONAL.

TATRAS, mountain range on the Polish–Czechoslovak border, highest range in the central CARPATHIANS. It is a resort area, with Gerlachovka (8 711ft) the highest peak.

TATTING, craft using thread and a shuttle to produce a lace-like fabric. Long popular in Italy, France and the East, it was widely practiced in the courts of 18th-century Europe.

TATTOOING, decorating the body by injecting colored pigment beneath the surface of the skin, a method of personal adornment used throughout history. Doctors now discourage tattooing except for specialist medical applications.

TATUM, Arthur "Art" (1910–1956), brilliant self-taught US jazz pianist. His command of jazz styles was comprehensive and influenced jazz and non-jazz musicians alike.

TATUM, Edward Lawrie (1909–1975), US biochemist awarded the 1958 Nobel Prize for Physiology or Medicine with G. W. BEADLE and J. LEDERBERG for work with Beadle showing that individual GENES control production of particular ENZYMES (1937–40).

TAUNTON, city in SE Mass. on the Taunton R, a seat of Bristol Co. It makes electric parts, engines, plastics, jewelry and silver. Pop 43 756.

TAURUS (the Bull), a large constellation on the ECLIPTIC; the second sign of the ZODIAC. It contains the CRAB NEBULA, the GALACTIC CLUSTERS the Hyades and PLEIADES, and the bright star Aldebaran.

TAURUS MOUNTAINS, a range in S Turkey, parallel with the Mediterranean coast and extending NE as the Anti-Taurus. They have many peaks of 10 000ft to 12 000ft. The range is well wooded and has various mineral deposits.

TAUTOMERISM, the existence of two interconvertible ISOMERS of a compound, usually in labile EQUILIBRIUM, though in some cases isolable. It may be demonstrated by spectroscopy or by the exhibition of properties characteristic of both tautomers. Most tautomerism is by hydrogen transfer, as with carbonyl compounds, in which the keto form (—CH—C=O) is in equilibrium with the enol form (—C=C—OH). SUGARS display tautomerism between cyclic and straight-chain forms.

TAVERNER, John (c1495–1545), English composer whose ornate masses and motets are among the finest early Tudor music. After 1530 he turned from music to suppressing monasteries as an agent of Thomas Cromwell.

TAWNEY, Richard Henry (1880–1962), British historian and social theorist. His best known book *Religion and the Rise of Capitalism* (1926), connects the hard work and individualism of the Protestants of N Europe in the 16th and 17th centuries with the growth of capitalism there.

TAXATION, the raising of revenue to pay for government expenditure. Broadly speaking a tax can be described as direct or indirect: income tax is paid directly to the government, but sales taxes are collected indirectly through government charges on goods or services. A tax is also progressive or regressive: income tax is usually progressive (its rate rises as the taxable sum increases); sales taxes tend to be regressive (their burden decreases as the taxpayer's income increases).

Modern taxation serves three purposes. It meets government expenditure on public services, administration and defense. Social justice is promoted by the redistribution of income: the rich are taxed at higher rates than the poor, who may receive grants from revenue. Control of the economy is achieved by adjusting direct or indirect taxes to curb consumption or encourage investment. It is often difficult to achieve all three objectives equally effectively.

In the US the Constitution at first required that taxes be levied in proportion to the population, and that indirect taxes must be uniform throughout all states. INCOME TAX, which does not meet these requirements, was permitted by the 16th Amendment in 1913, and came to replace TARIFFS and EXCISES as a principal source of revenue. During and after WWI, the federal government developed its individual and corporation income taxes, expanded excises, and introduced an estate INHERITANCE TAX and a social security payroll levy. By WWII federal taxes had reached new peaks and become important in regulating the economy, being used to curb inflation and prevent profiteering. The major form of state and local taxation is now the *property tax*; states also tax gasoline, retail sales and automobiles, and many states and cities tax income.

TAXATION WITHOUT REPRESENTATION, in US history, a cause of the REVOLUTIONARY WAR. In 1765 the British Parliament passed the STAMP ACT, obliging colonists to buy revenue stamps for documents and newspapers. This provoked the slogan "taxation without representation is tyranny," and a colonial congress in New York rejected as unconstitutional taxes imposed without the people's consent.

TAX COURT, US federal tribunal established in 1924 to rule on disputes between taxpayers and the INTERNAL REVENUE SERVICE. Most decisions may be appealed to the US Court of Appeals.

TAXIDERMY, stuffing animal skins to make lifelike replicas. Taxidermy is now practiced mainly in large museums, though it originated in the production of hunting trophies; nowadays, rather than stuffing, the animal's form is duplicated and the skin stretched over.

TAXONOMY, the science of classifying PLANTS and ANIMALS. The theory of EVOLUTION states that organisms come into being as a result of gradual change and that closely related organisms are descended from a relatively recent common ancestor. One of the main aims of taxonomy is to reflect such changes in a classification of groups, or taxa, which are arranged in a hierarchy such that small taxa contain organisms that are closely related and larger taxa contain organisms that are more distantly related. Taxa commonly employed are (in their conventional typography and starting with the largest): Kingdom, Phylum, Class, Order, Family, *Genus* and *species*.

TAYLOR, city in SE Mich., 20mi SW of Detroit. It makes machinery, cement, wood and glass products. Pop 70 020.

TAYLOR, Edward (c1642–1729), American Puritan clergyman, arguably North America's foremost colonial poet. His devotional verse combines homely diction with the striking imagery of the METAPHYSICAL POETS. His works were rediscovered only in 1937 (*Poetical Works*, 1939).

TAYLOR, Elizabeth (1932–   ), film actress. After *Lassie Come Home* (1943) and *National Velvet* (1944), her adult successes included *Cat on a Hot Tin Roof* (1958), *Butterfield 8* (1960) and, with Richard BURTON, with whom she had a highly publicized romance and marriage, *Cleopatra* (1963), *Who's Afraid of Virginia Woolf?* (1966), *The Taming of the Shrew* (1967).

TAYLOR, Frederick Winslow (1856–1915), US mechanical engineer who pioneered the principles of scientific management. He introduced TIME-AND-MOTION STUDY and held that careful analysis of every factory operation by man and machine alike was necessary for operational efficiency. These theories came to be known as **Taylorism**.

TAYLOR, Jeremy (1613–1667), English cleric and writer, known for the beauty of his prose. Chaplain to Archbishop Laud and King Charles I, he retired to Wales after the defeat of the Royalists and wrote pious works, including *Holy Living* (1650) and *Holy Dying* (1651).

TAYLOR, John (1753–1824), US political theorist and agricultural reformer, known as "John Taylor of Caroline." An early exponent of STATES RIGHTS, he was thrice elected US senator from Va. (1792, 1803, 1822).

TAYLOR, Maxwell Davenport (1901–   ), US Army general who largely organized the US army's first airborne units in WWII. He commanded the Eighth Army in Korea 1953–55, headed the US and UN Far East commands 1954–55, was US army chief of staff 1955–59 and ambassador to Vietnam 1964–65.

TAYLOR, Zachary (1784–1850), 12th US president. Known as "Old Rough and Ready" to his soldiers, Taylor was a bold and resourceful general in the Mexican War and one of the most popular presidents of his period. Nevertheless, his brief term in the White House—he died after only 16 months in office—has been all but forgotten, though he did take a bold stand against the extension of slavery, the one burning issue of his term. Three things shaped his life: he was 40 years a soldier (doing much to open the West to settlement); his parents belonged to the wealthy planting aristocracy of old Va.; and he himself was brought up in Ky., on the frontiers of an expanding nation. He fought in the WAR OF 1812 and the BLACK HAWK WAR (1832), and subdued the SEMINOLE Indians in Fla.; his defeat of General SANTA ANNA's forces in the MEXICAN WAR made him a national hero.

Standing as a Whig, he became president in 1849; his term was marked by the CLAYTON-BUTLER TREATY. More important, the acquisition of vast new territories threatened to upset the precarious balance between slave states and free (15 of each) established by the MISSOURI COMPROMISE of 1820. Determined to prevent expansion of slavery even though it might preserve the Union, and undoubtedly influenced by such advisors as William H. SEWARD, Taylor refused to compromise, even if it meant war. His sudden death in 1850 postponed the issue.

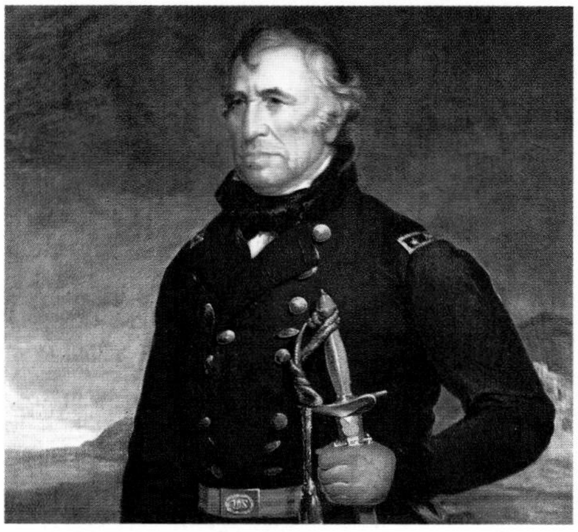

Zachary TAYLOR

12th US President

Born: November 24, 1784
Died: July 9, 1850
Term of office: March 4, 1849–July 9, 1850
Political party: Whig

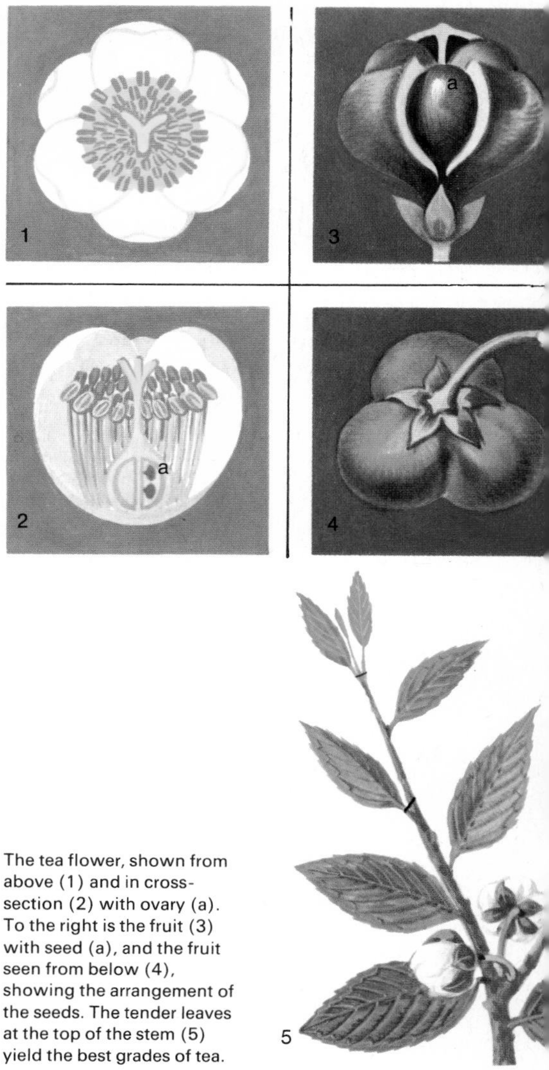

The tea flower, shown from above (1) and in cross-section (2) with ovary (a). To the right is the fruit (3) with seed (a), and the fruit seen from below (4), showing the arrangement of the seeds. The tender leaves at the top of the stem (5) yield the best grades of tea.

TAYRA, *Eira barbara*, carnivorous South American, forest-dwelling member of the WEASEL family, Mustelidae. Light brown and about 1m (3.3ft) long, they have relatively long legs and tails and are extremely agile—equally at home on the ground or in trees.

TBILISI, or **Tiflis,** capital of the Georgian SSR, SW USSR, on the Kura R. Tbilisi dates from c450 AD and is a major manufacturing, cultural and educational center and transportation hub. Pop 889 000.

TCHAIKOVSKY, Peter Ilich (1840–1893), Russian composer. He studied with Anton RUBINSTEIN, became professor at Moscow Conservatory and gave concerts of his own music in Europe and the US. His gift for melody and brilliant orchestration, plus the drama, excitement and emotional intensity of his music, makes him the most popular of all composers. Works such as the 1st Piano Concerto (1875), the Violin Concerto (1878) and *Pathétique* Symphony (No. 6; 1893) are known and loved by millions, and ballet owes much of its popularity to his *Swan Lake* (1876), *Sleeping Beauty* (1889) and *Nutcracker* (1892).

TCHELITCHEW, Pavel (1898–1957), Russian-born US painter. He designed ballets, notably for DIAGHILEV, but is best known for such studies of perspective and metamorphosis as *Hide-and-Seek* (1941).

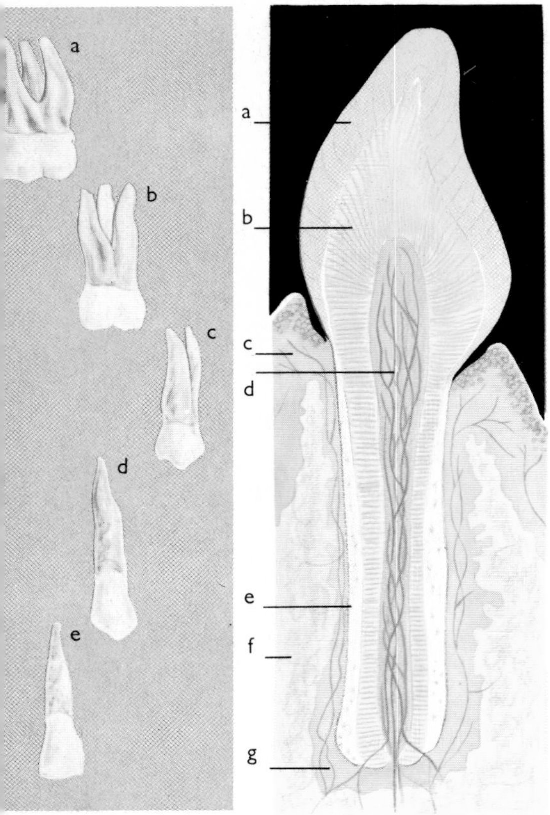

Left: varieties of human teeth: (a) wisdom teeth; (b) molars; (c) premolars; (d) canines; (e) incisors. *Right:* cross-section of a human incisor. (a) Enamel; (b) dentin; (c) gum; (d) pulp; (e) cementum; (f) socket; (g) periodontal membrane.

***t*-DISTRIBUTION.** See STUDENT'S *t*-DISTRIBUTION.

TEA, the cured and dried young leaves and tips of the tea plant (*Thea sinensis*) which are made into a drink popular throughout the world. Tea has been drunk in China since early times, but it was not until the early 1600s that the Dutch introduced it into Europe. Although expensive, it soon became fashionable. In the UK and the British colonies, the East India Company enjoyed a monopoly of the China tea trade until 1833; it was the attempt of the British government to levy a tax on tea imports into the American colonies that led to the BOSTON TEA PARTY of 1773. Today, the chief producers are India and Sri Lanka (Ceylon). Tea contains the stimulant CAFFEINE. The term tea is also used to describe many other local drinks produced from the leaves of a vast array of plants. Family: Theaceae. (See *illust.*, p961.)

TEACH, Edward. See BLACKBEARD.

TEACHING. In simple communities the parents and elders are the instructors in the tribal lore and skills which go with initiation into adult life. More complex societies and specialized skills require a more formal system, which in Western societies became linked with the Christian Church, priests having both learning and leisure. This reinforced the ethical content of teaching and gave the Church a near monopoly of education which lasted until the 19th century, when formal teacher-training first began (with a few earlier exceptions, such as the JESUITS). Today, courses in the theory and practice of teaching take several years.

Teaching now centers on the child's needs and interests as well as those of his future adult life, and on participation and teamwork. This shift owes much to the work of PESTALOZZI, FROEBEL, DEWEY and MONTESSORI. In the US, minority-group needs have led to such schemes as HEADSTART AND FOLLOW THROUGH. In the US there are now over 3 000 000 teachers. (See EDUCATION.)

TEACHING MACHINE, device whereby a student is presented with a series of problems; should he answer one correctly, the next is more difficult; whereas incorrect answers are followed by questions of at most comparable difficulty. This permits the student to proceed at his own pace. (See also PROGRAMMED LEARNING.)

TEAGARDEN, Weldon John "Jack" (1905–1964), US trombonist and jazz singer, one of the first (artistically) successful white jazzmen. He played with Paul WHITEMAN and after WWII with Louis ARMSTRONG. He led his own bands 1939–47 and 1951–57.

TEAK, a deciduous tree (*Tectona grandis*) whose wood is one of the most valuable in the world. Teaks grow in tropical climates from E India to Malaysia. The hard, oily wood is used for house construction, furniture, railroad sleepers etc. Several other trees produce a similar hardwood also called teak. Family: Verbenaceae.

TEAL, a group of mallard-like Dabbling DUCKS distinguished by a bright green speculum on the wings of both sexes. They are among the smallest of the ducks. Three species are common in North America: the Baikal, Blue-winged and Green-winged teals.

TEAMSTERS (International Brotherhood of Teamsters, Chauffeurs, Warehousemen and Helpers of America), largest US labor union. Formed by an amalgamation in 1903, it expanded to its present 2 000 000 membership, largely in trucking and warehousing, under presidents Daniel Tobin (1907–52), Dave Beck (1952–57) and Jimmy HOFFA (1957–71). The two latter were jailed for corruption. The Teamsters were in 1957 expelled from AFL-CIO.

TEANECK, a township in NE N.J., near the Hudson R 4mi NW of George Washington Bridge. Mainly residential, it has some light industry. Pop 42 355.

TEAPOT DOME, scandal over government malpractice under President HARDING. The naval oil reserve at Teapot Dome, Wyo., was leased in 1922 by agreement of secretary of the interior Albert FALL to the Mammoth Oil Co. with no competitive bidding. A Senate investigation followed and the lease was canceled. Fall was later convicted of receiving another bribe in a similar transaction.

TEAR GAS, volatile substance that incapacitates for a time by powerfully irritating the eyes, provoking tears. Various halogenated organic compounds are used, including α-chloroacetophenone (**Mace gas** or CN), and the even more potent CS gas. They are packed in grenades and used for riot control. (See also CHEMICAL AND BIOLOGICAL WARFARE.)

TEARS, watery secretions of the lacrymal GLANDS situated over the EYES which provide continuous lubrication and protection of cornea and sclera. A constant flow runs across the surface of the eye to the nasolacrymal duct at the inner corner, where tears drain into the NOSE. Excess tears produced in states of high emotion and conjunctival or corneal irritation overflow over the lower eyelid.

TEASEL, *Dipsacus fullonum*, a European plant that is naturalized in North America. The small blue flowers grow in a conical head which persists as a prickly head after they die. Teasels were once grown as a crop, the dead heads being used to raise a nap on cloth. Family: Dipsacaceae.

TEBALDI, Renata (1922–   ), Italian soprano. Her famous roles have included Mimi in *La Bohème*, Desdemona in *Otello*, Aïda and Tosca.

TECHNETIUM (Tc), radioactive metal (see RADIOACTIVITY) in Group VIIB of the PERIODIC TABLE; a TRANSITION ELEMENT. It does not occur naturally, but was discovered in 1937 by Emilio SEGRÈ and Carlo Perrier in bombarded molybdenum—the first element to be made artificially. It is now recovered from the fission products of nuclear reactors. Technetium is chemically very like RHENIUM. AW 99, mp 2172°C, bp 4877°C, sg 11.5 (20°C).

TECHNOCRACY, government by scientists and technologists who recognize only the dictates of technology. Arising from the ideas of Thorstein VEBLEN and engineer Howard Scott, a radical Technocracy movement roused wide discussion in the early 1930s in the US.

TECUMSEH (c1768–1813), great SHAWNEE INDIAN chief, warrior and orator who sought after the Revolution to unite Midwestern tribes against encroachment of their homelands. Despite British and widespread Indian support the effort failed with defeat of his brother TENSKWATAWA at the battle of TIPPECANOE (1811). Tecumseh died fighting for the British at the battle of the THAMES.

TEETH, the specialized hard structures used for biting and chewing food. Their numbers vary in different species and at different ages, but in most cases an immature set of teeth (milk teeth) is replaced during growth by a permanent set. In man the latter consists of 32 teeth comprising 8 incisors, 4 canines, 8 premolars and 12 molars, of which the rearmost are the late-erupting wisdom teeth. ("Dentition" refers to the numbers and arrangement of the teeth in a species.) Each tooth consists of a crown, or part above the gum line, and a root, or insertion into the BONE of the jaw. The outer surface of the crowns are covered by a thin layer of enamel, the hardest animal tissue. This overlies the dentine, a substance similar to bone, and in the center of each tooth is the pulp which contains blood vessels and nerves. The **incisors** are developed for biting off food with a scissor action, while the **canines** are particularly developed in some species for maintaining a hold on an object. The **molars** and **premolars** are adapted for chewing and macerating food, which partly involves side-to-side movement of one jaw over the other. Maldevelopment and CARIES of teeth are the commonest problems encountered in DENTISTRY.

TEFILLIN. See PHYLACTERIES.

TEFLON, or polytetrafluoroethene (PTFE), a FLUOROCARBON plastic, inert and heat-resistant, used as a nonstick coating for cooking utensils, and for making chemical and electrical components.

TEGEA (modern Piali), ancient Greek city in SE ARCADIA. It was involved with SPARTA, in alliance or revolt, in the 6th–4th centuries BC.

TEGU, *Tupinambis nigropunctatus*, a large teiid lizard of South America. About 1m (3.3ft) long, they are terrestrial, feeding on frogs, other lizards, insects, eggs and small birds.

TEGUCIGALPA, capital of HONDURAS. Center of a populous farming and mining region, it lies on a 3 000ft plateau, on the Chluteca R. Pop 218 510.

TEHERAN, or Tehran, capital and largest city of Iran, lies S of the Elburz Mts at about 3 800ft. Dating from the 1100s and Mogul destruction of nearby Ray (1220), it became capital in 1788. Modern Teheran is a manufacturing, transportation, cultural and tourist center. Pop 3 400 000.

TEHERAN CONFERENCE, inter-allied conference of WWII, held in Teheran Nov.–Dec. 1943 and attended by Stalin, Roosevelt and Churchill. Important items were coordination of landings in France with a Soviet offensive against Germany from the E, future Russian entry into the war against Japan, and agreement on Iran's future independence.

TEILHARD DE CHARDIN, Pierre (1881–1955), French Jesuit, philosopher and paleontologist. He was in China 1923–46, where he studied Peking Man (see PREHISTORIC MAN). *The Phenomenon of Man* (1938–40) attempted to reconcile Christianity and science with a theory of man's evolution toward final spiritual unity. His superiors held his views to be unorthodox and warned against them; fame came to him and his ideas only posthumously.

TEKTITES, glassy objects, usually of less than 100mm diameter, found only in certain parts of the world. Most are rich in SILICA: they resemble OBSIDIAN, though have less water. Despite suggestions that they are of extraterrestrial, particularly lunar, origin, it seems most likely that they have resulted from meteoritic impacts in SEDIMENTARY ROCK in the remote past.

TEL AVIV-JAFFA or -Yafo, largest city in Israel, on the Mediterranean coast NW of Jerusalem. It is a modern city-port and Israel's chief manufacturing center as well as a tourist resort. Tel Aviv was Israel's first capital, from 1948 to 1950 (when JAFFA was incorporated). Pop 384 000.

TELEGRAPH, electrical apparatus for sending coded messages. The term was first applied to Claude Chappe's SEMAPHORE. Experiments began on electric telegraphs after the discovery (1819) that a magnetic needle was deflected by a current in a nearby wire. In 1837 W. F. Cooke and Charles WHEATSTONE patented a system using six wires and five pointers which moved in pairs to indicate letters in a diamond-shaped array. It was used on English railroads. In the same year Samuel Morse, in partnership with Alfred Vail, and helped by Joseph Henry, patented a telegraph system using Morse code in the US. The first intercity line was inaugurated in 1844. At first the receiver embossed or printed the code symbols but this was soon replaced by a sounding device. In 1858 Wheatstone invented a high-speed automatic Morse telegraph, using punched paper tape in transmission. The telex system, using teletypewriters, is now most popular. In 1872 Jean-Maurice-Émile Baudot invented a multiplexing system for sharing the time on each transmission line between several operators. Telegraph signals are now transmitted not only by wires and land lines but also by submarine cables and radio.

TELEMACHUS, in Greek myth, son of Odysseus and Penelope. He went in search of his father, long absent after the Trojan War, and when Odysseus finally returned, helped him to destroy Penelope's suitors. He later married Circe.

TELEMANN, Georg Philipp (1681–1767), versatile and prolific German composer, a master of all the musical forms of his day. His oratorios and other sacred music, over 40 operas and many instrumental works are noted for their liveliness of rhythm and tunefulness.

TELEMETRY, the transmission of data from distant automatic monitoring stations to a recording station for analysis. It is of immense importance in space exploration. (See also radio.)

TELEOLOGY (from Greek *telos*, end), the study of an action, event, idea or thing with reference to its purpose or end. Aristotle argued that to have a complete understanding of anything its "final cause," its purpose in existing, had to be taken into account. Many modern scientists have questioned this notion, preferring to consider biological processes purely in mechanistic terms. The teleological argument for God's existence is that from design.

TELEPATHY. See esp.

TELEPHONE, apparatus for transmission and reproduction of sound by means of frequency electric waves. Precursors in telecommunication included the megaphone, the speaking tube and the string telephone—all of which transmitted sound as such—and the telegraph, working by electrical impulses. Although the principles on which it is based had been known 40 years earlier, the telephone was not invented until 1876, when Alexander Graham Bell obtained his patent. Bell's transmitter worked by the voltage induced in a coil by a piece of iron attached to a vibrating diaphragm. The same apparatus, working in reverse, was used as a receiver. Modern receivers use the same principle, but it was soon found that a more sensitive transmitter was needed, and by 1878 the carbon microphone (invented by Thomas Edison) was used. A battery-powered DC circuit connected microphone and receiver. In 1878 the first commercial exchange was opened in New Haven, Conn., and local telephone networks spread rapidly in the US and elsewhere. Technical improvements made for longer-distance transmission included the use of hard-drawn copper wire, underground dry-core cable, and two-wire circuits to avoid the cross-talk that occurred when the circuit was completed via ground. Distortion in long circuits was overcome by introducing loading coils at intervals to increase the inductance. The introduction also of repeaters, or amplifiers, made long-distance telephone calls possible. Today, microwave and radio links, and telecommunications satellites are used. Telephone subscribers are connected to a local exchange, these in turn being linked by trunk lines connecting a hierarchy of switching centers so that alternative routes may be used. When a call is dialed, each digit is coded as pulses or pairs of tones which work electromechanical or electronic switches. (See also picturephone.)

TELEPHOTO, or **wirephoto**, an apparatus for facsimile transmission of news photographs, weather maps etc. over electric telecommunication channels. Photographic scanning is used, and the data, transmitted over intercity networks, are photographically reproduced, usually in halftone.

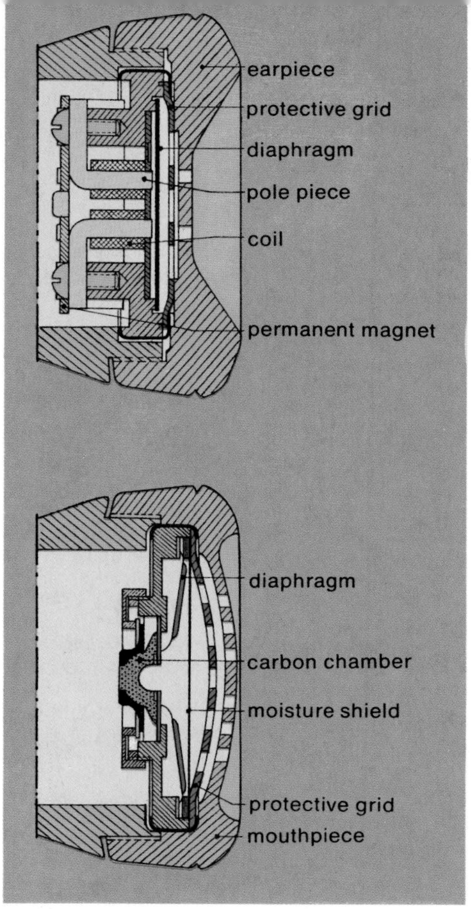

Section through the ear- and mouthpieces of a typical telephone handset.

TELESCOPE, Optical, instrument used to detect or examine distant objects. It consists of a series of lenses and mirrors capable of producing a magnified image and of collecting more light than the unaided eye. The refracting telescope essentially consists of a tube with a lens system at each end. Light from a distant object first strikes the objective lens which produces an inverted image at its focal point. In the terrestrial telescope the second lens system, the eyepiece, produces a magnified, erect image of the focal image, but in instruments for astronomical use, where the image is usually recorded photographically, the image is not reinverted, thus reducing light losses. The reflecting telescope uses a concave mirror to gather and focus the incoming light, the focal image being viewed using many different combinations of lenses and mirrors in the various types of instrument, each seeking to reduce different optical aberrations. The size of a telescope is measured in terms of the diameter of its objective. Up to about 30cm diameter the resolving power (the ability to distinguish finely separated points) increases with size but for larger objectives the only gain is in light gathering. A 500cm telescope can thus detect much fainter sources but resolve no better than a 30cm instrument. Because mirrors can be supported more easily than large lenses, the largest astronomical telescopes are all reflectors. (See also astronomy; astrophotography; binoculars; Clark, Alvan; Galileo; observatory; radio telescope; Schmidt.)

TELESPHORUS, Saint, eighth pope (reigned c125–c136). A Calabrian Greek, he was martyred in Emperor Hadrian's persecutions. His feast day is Jan. 2 or 5.

TELEVISION, the communication of moving pictures between distant points using wire or radio transmissions. In television broadcasting, centrally prepared programs are transmitted to a multitude of individual receivers, though closed-circuit industrial and education applications are of increasing importance. Often, a sound signal is transmitted together with the picture information. In outline, a television camera is used to form an optical image of the scene to be transmitted and convert it into electrical signals. These are amplified and transmitted, either directly by cable (closed-circuit) or as radio waves, to a receiver where the scene is reconstituted as an optical image on the screen of a cathode-ray tube. Today most television cameras are of the image orthicon or vidicon types, these having largely replaced the earlier iconoscope and orthicon designs. Since it is impossible to transmit a whole image at once, the image formed by the optical lens system of the camera is scanned as a sequence of 525 horizontal lines, the varying light value along each being converted into a fluctuating electrical signal and the whole scan being repeated 30 times a second to allow an impression of motion to be conveyed without noticeable flicker. The viewer sees

The control room of a modern television studio. Pictures from cameras, film scanners and other sources are simultaneously displayed on a bank of screens; the producer and his assistants, seated at the control desk, can select and switch from one to another in assembling a programme.

the image as a whole because of the persistence of VISION effect. In **color television**, the light entering the camera is analyzed into red, green and blue components—corresponding to the three primary COLORS of light—and electrical information concerning the saturation of each is superimposed on the ordinary luminance (brightness) monochrome signal. In the color receiver this information is recovered and used to control the three electron beams which, projected through a shadow mask (a screen containing some 200 000 minute, precisely positioned holes), excite the mosaic of red, green and blue PHOSPHOR dots which reproduce the color image. All three color television systems in use around the world allow monochrome receivers to work normally from the color transmissions.

Development of television. Early hopes of practical television date back to the early days of the electric TELEGRAPH, but their realization had to await several key developments. First was the discovery of the photoconductive properties of selenium (see PHOTOCONDUCTIVE DETECTOR), followed by the development of the cathode-ray tube (1897) and the ELECTRON TUBE (1904). The first practical television system, demonstrated in London in 1926 by J. L. BAIRD, used a mechanical scanning method devised by Paul Nipkow in 1884. Electronic scanning dates from 1923 when ZWORYKIN filed a patent for his iconoscope camera tube. Television broadcasting began in London in 1936 using a 405-line standard. In the US public broadcasting began in 1941, with regular color broadcasting in 1954. US television broadcasts are made in the VHF (Channels 2–13) and the UHF (Channels 14–83) regions of the RF spectrum (see RADIO). (See also ELECTRONICS; PICTUREPHONE; VIDEOTAPE.)

TELFORD, Thomas (1757–1834), Scottish civil engineer responsible for many British roads, harbors, canals and bridges. He is best known for his suspension BRIDGE over the Menai Straits, North Wales (1819–26); the construction of the Caledonian Canal, Scotland (1804–22); the Göta Canal, Sweden (1808–10), and for several Scottish harbors.

TELL, William, legendary 14th-century Swiss hero. Ordered by the Austrian bailiff Gessler to bow to a hat on a pole as a symbol of Austrian supremacy, he refused and was forced to shoot an apple from his son's head with a crossbow: in this almost impossible task he succeeded. Later he killed Gessler.

TELL EL-AMARNA, site of Akhetaton, capital of the Egyptian pharaoh AKHENATON. It lies on the E bank of the Nile R 60mi N of Asyut. Excavation of this short-lived city revealed naturalistic paintings and reliefs and, in 1887, a famous series of about 300 CUNEIFORM tablets.

TELLER, Edward (1908–), Hungarian-born US nuclear physicist who worked with FERMI on nuclear FISSION at the start of the MANHATTAN PROJECT, but who is best known for his fundamental work on, and advocacy of, the HYDROGEN BOMB.

TELLER, Henry Moore (1830–1914), US politician. A Col. senator for five terms and secretary of the interior 1882–85, he left the Republican Party (1896) in order to continue urging free coinage of silver, a major Col. product. His 1898 Teller Amendment pledged the US to an independent Cuba.

TELLURIUM (Te), silvery-white metalloid in Group VIA of the PERIODIC TABLE, occurring as heavy-metal tellurides, and extracted as a by-product of copper refining. Tellurium resembles SELENIUM in its chemistry, but is rather more metallic; tellurium (IV) compounds resemble PLATINUM (IV). It is added to metals to make them easier to machine and to lead for greater corrosion resistance; bismuth telluride is used in thermoelectric devices. AW 127.6, mp 450°C, bp 1390°C, sg 6.24 (20°C).

TELSTAR, US artificial SATELLITE, launched July 10, 1962, the first to relay TELEVISION signals across the Atlantic. It weighed 170lb. Broadcasts ended (Feb. 1963) after Van Allen belt radiation damaged some of the 1000 transistors.

TELUGU, a DRAVIDIAN language of S India. There are some 40 million Andhras (Telugu speakers), mainly in ANDHRA PRADESH. The extensive literature is written in a script derived from SANSKRIT.

TEMIN, Howard Martin (1934–), US virologist who shared with R. DULESCO and D. BALTIMORE the 1975 Nobel Prize for Physiology or Medicine for their work on cancer-forming VIRUSES.

TEMPE, city in S Ariz. about 10mi E of Phoenix. It has electronic and steel industries and is the site of Ariz. State U. Pop 63 550.

TEMPERA, painting technique in which dry pigments are "tempered" or bound with egg yolks and water. Applied to a panel coated with GESSO, in thin, drying layers, it produces a luminous mat surface. Especially popular 1200–1500 in Italy, it has been revived by modern artists.

TEMPERAMENT, in the tuning of keyboard musical instruments, the slight changing of intervals in an acoustically correct scale to produce 12 equally spaced semitones (equal temperament). This slightly incorrect but musically acceptable tuning, general in Europe since the 1700s, allows a piano to be played in all keys. (See SCALE; HARMONY.)

TEMPERATURE, the degree of hotness or coldness of a body, as measured quantitatively by THERMOMETERS. The various practical scales used are arbitrary: the FAHRENHEIT scale was originally based on the values 0°F for an equal ice-salt mixture, 32°F for the freezing point of water and 96°F for normal human body temperature. (See also CELSIUS, ANDERS.) Thermometer readings are arbitrary also because they depend on the particular physical properties of the thermometric fluid etc. There are now certain primary calibration points corresponding to the triple points, boiling points or freezing points of particular substances, whose values are fixed by convention. The thermodynamic, or ABSOLUTE, temperature scale, is not arbitrary; starting at ABSOLUTE ZERO and graduated in KELVINS, it is defined with respect to an ideal reversible heat engine working on a CARNOT cycle between two temperatures T_1 and T_2. If Q_1 is the heat received at the higher temperature T_1, and Q_2 the heat lost at the lower temperature T_2, then T_1/T_2 is defined equal to Q_1/Q_2. Such absolute temperature is independent of the properties of particular substances, and is a basic THERMODYNAMIC function, arising out of the zeroth law. It is an intensive property, unlike HEAT, which is an extensive property—that is, the temperature of a body is independent of its mass or nature; it is thus only indirectly related to the heat content (internal energy) of the body. Heat flows always from a higher temperature to a lower. On the molecular scale, temperature may be defined in terms of the statistical distribution of the kinetic energy of the molecules.

TEMPERATURE, Body. Animals fall into two classes: COLD-BLOODED ANIMALS, which have the same temperature as their surroundings, and WARM-BLOODED ANIMALS, which have an approximately constant temperature maintained by a "thermostat" in the brain. The normal temperature for most such animals lies between 95°F (35°C) and 104°F (40°C); it is greatly reduced during HIBERNATION. For man, the normal mouth temperature usually lies between 97°F (36°C) and 99°F (37.2°C), the average being about 98.6°F (37.0°C). It fluctuates daily, and in women monthly. The temperature setting is higher than normal in FEVER. When the body is too hot, the blood vessels near the skin expand to carry more blood and to lose heat by radiation and convection, and the sweat glands produce PERSPIRATION which cools by evaporation. When the body is too cold, the blood vessels near the skin contract, the metabolic rate increases and SHIVERING occurs to produce more heat. Fat under the skin, and body hair (FUR in other animals), help to keep heat in. If these defenses against cold prove inadequate, **hypothermia** results: body temperature falls, functions become sluggish, and death may result. Controlled cooling may be used in surgery to reduce the need for oxygen.

TEMPERATURE HUMIDITY INDEX (THI), formerly **discomfort index**, an empirical measure of the discomfort experienced in various warm weather conditions, and used to predict how much power will be needed to run air-conditioning systems. It is given by

$$\mathrm{THI} = 0.4(T_1 + T_2) + 15$$

where T_1 is the dry-bulb temperature and T_2 the wet-bulb temperature in degrees Fahrenheit (see HYGROMETER). When the index is 70 almost everyone feels comfortable; at 80 or more, no one.

TEMPERATURE INVERSION. See INVERSION.

TEMPERING, heat-treatment process in METALLURGY, used to toughen an ALLOY, notably STEEL. The metal is heated slowly to the desired temperature, held there while stresses are relieved and excess solution precipitates out from the supersaturated solid solution, and then cooled, usually by rapid quenching. The temperature determines the properties produced, and may be chosen to retain hardness.

TEMPLARS. See KNIGHTS TEMPLARS.

TEMPLE, city in central Tex., 35mi S of Waco in a cotton and grain area. It has railroad shops and metal and machinery industries. Pop 33 431.

TEMPLE, a (usually large) building for religious worship. The Jewish temple, a successor to the TABERNACLE, was envisaged by King DAVID and built by SOLOMON at Jerusalem, becoming the central shrine where alone SACRIFICE could legally be offered. This First Temple was destroyed by the Babylonian invasion in 586 BC. The Second Temple was built in 520 BC and was used until HEROD the Great built the most splendid and last temple, destroyed by the Romans in 70 AD.

TEMPLE, Shirley Jane (1928–), US child filmstar and later a politician. She made her movie debut at three and retired from films in 1949. After working on television in the 1950s Shirley Temple Black (her married name) took up Republican politics. She became a US delegate to the UN in 1969, ambassador to Ghana in 1975, and US Chief of Protocol 1976.

TEMPLE CITY, a city in SW Cal., a residential suburb of Los Angeles. Pop 31 040.

TEMPO (Italian: time), in MUSIC, speed at which a piece should be played, usually shown (*lento, allegro*, etc.) at the beginning of the score.

TENAFLY, a residential borough with some light industry, in NE N.J., near Englewood. Pop 14 827.

TENANT FARMING, system whereby a tenant works a farm and gives a share of the crops or proceeds to the owner. Either party provides management and equipment. Efficient in the UK and US Midwest, tenant farming is easily abused (see SHARECROPPING).

TEN COMMANDMENTS, or the Decalogue, the moral laws delivered by God to Moses on Mt. Sinai, as recorded in the Bible (Exodus 20:2–17; Deuteronomy 5:6–21). They provide the foundation for Jewish and Christian teaching.

TENDON, fibrous structure formed at the ends of most MUSCLES, which transmits the force of contraction to the point of action (usually a BONE). They facilitate mechanical advantage and allow bulky power muscles to be situated away from small bones concerned with fine movements, as in the HANDS.

TENERIFE, largest of the Spanish CANARY ISLANDS off NW Africa. The 500 000 people on its 795sq mi (Pico de Teide, 12 198ft) engage in farming and tourism. SANTA CRUZ DE TENERIFE is the capital.

TENIERS, David, the Younger (1610–1690), Flemish painter. A master colorist, he studied under his father, and became one of the most famous, sought-after and prolific painters of his time. His over 2 000 surviving works mainly comprise genre scenes of peasant life, still lifes and landscapes.

TENNENT, Gilbert (1703–1764), American Presbyterian clergyman, a leader of the GREAT AWAKENING. He attacked his more conservative colleagues as religious formalists with such vigor and disregard for authority that the Presbyterian Church became divided for 17 years (1741–58).

TENNESSEE, a central southern state of the US. It forms a narrow parallelogram extending from the Mississippi R in the W to the Blue Ridge region (with the GREAT SMOKY MOUNTAINS and Clingmans Dome, 6 642ft). The Appalachian ridge-and-valley farming region and coal-rich Cumberland Plateau give way W to the fertile central Nashville Basin bounded by a broad Highland Rim. Further W the N Gulf Coastal Plain slopes down to the alluvial Mississippi Bottoms. Dams on the Tennessee and Cumberland rivers have formed many lakes (including Kentucky Lake, 247sq

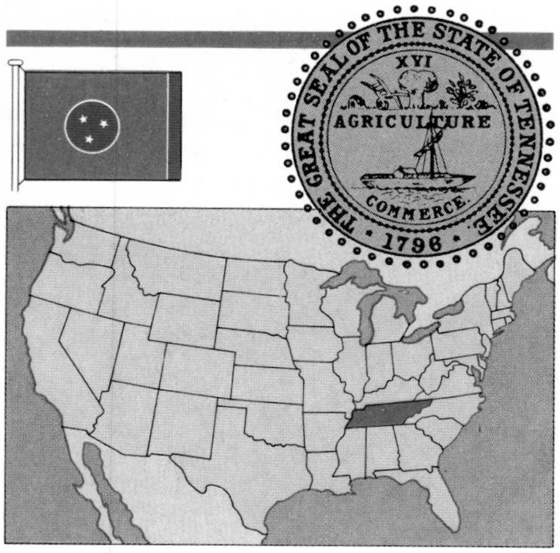

Name of state: Tennessee
Capital: Nashville
Statehood: June 1, 1796 (16th state)
Familiar name: Volunteer State, Big Bend State
Area: 42 244sq mi
Population: 3 923 687
Elevation: Highest—6 642ft., Clingmans Dome. Lowest— 182ft., Mississippi River
Motto: Agriculture and Commerce
State flower: Iris
State bird: Mockingbird
State tree: Tulip poplar
State song: "The Tennessee Waltz," "When It's Iris Time in Tennessee," "My Tennessee."

mi). The climate is humid (average 50in annual precipitation) and temperate.

Over half the population now lives in the metropolitan areas of MEMPHIS, NASHVILLE, CHATTANOOGA and KNOXVILLE, whose industries produce chemicals, foodstuffs, electrical machinery and metal, stone, clay and glass products. Research centers include OAK RIDGE (atomic energy) and Arnold Engineering Development Center (rockets).

The TENNESSEE VALLEY AUTHORITY speeded changeover from a primary-products to a manufacturing economy. Mining (stone, zinc, phosphate, coal), livestock (notably cattle and thoroughbred horses), tobacco, cotton and corn are important.

History. Among Indians encountered by DE SOTO and later white explorers were the CHEROKEE, CHICKASAW and SHAWNEE. The region was ceded to England by the Treaty of PARIS (1763). Settlers drew up North America's first written constitution, the WATAUGA ASSOCIATION, in 1772 and formed the independent state of FRANKLIN (1784–88). Bitterly divided over slavery, Tenn., the last Southern state to join the Confederates and the first to rejoin the Union, was the site of major Civil War battles. It has provided three US presidents: Andrew JACKSON, James K. POLK and Andrew JOHNSON. Normally Democratic, Tenn. voted heavily Republican in 1972.

TENNESSEE RIVER, principal tributary of the Ohio R. Formed by the junction of Helston and French Broad rivers near Knoxville, Tenn., it flows SW into Ala., then NW and N back across Tenn. and into Ky. It drains some 40 000sq mi. On its 652mi length are many dams and power facilities under the control of the TENNESSEE VALLEY AUTHORITY.

TENNESSEE VALLEY AUTHORITY (TVA), US federal agency responsible for developing the water and other resources of the Tennessee R Valley, established (1933) as one of the early measures of Roosevelt's NEW DEAL. The Authority has 26 major dams on the Tennessee R and its tributaries. The dams and reservoirs have made it possible to eliminate major flooding. Locks make the Tennessee navigable throughout, and TVA hydroelectric and steam plants provide most of the region's electricity. TVA projects have involved also conservation, agriculture and forestry.

TENNIEL, Sir John (1820–1914), English artist noted for his illustrations for Lewis CARROLL's *Alice's Adventures in Wonderland* and *Through the Looking-Glass*, and for hundreds of political cartoons for the English satirical magazine, *Punch* (1850–1901).

TENNIS, racket game played on a rectangular court by two or four players. The court, divided by painted lines into sections, is bisected by a net 3–3½ft high; the object is to hit the hollow ball (of cloth-covered rubber, about 2½in in diameter and 2oz in weight) over the net into the opposite court such that the opposing player is unable to return it. The racket has a metal or laminated wood frame with gut or nylon strings forming an oval "head," is about 27in long and weighs 12oz–1lb. Tennis originated in 15th-century France as indoor *court* tennis, and took its present form, *lawn* tennis, in 1870. It was first played in the US 1874. In 1877 England held the first Wimbledon Championship. Dwight DAVIS donated the Davis Cup in 1900. The International Lawn Tennis Federation regulates rules and play in over 80 countries.

TENNYSON, Alfred, 1st Baron Tennyson (1809–1892), English poet. His *Poems* (1842) established him as a great poet. His well-known philosophic elegy *In Memoriam* (1850) became the favorite of Queen Victoria, who appointed him POET LAUREATE. "Official" work included *The Charge of the Light Brigade* (1855). *Idylls of the King* (1842–1885) are based on the legends of King Arthur. His mastery of sound and rhythm, both vigorous and delicate, is perhaps best seen in such haunting lyrics as "The Lotus Eaters" and "The Lady of Shalott."

TENOCHTITLÁN, capital of the AZTECS, now in Mexico City center. Founded c1325 on an island in Lake Texcoco, connected to the mainland by causeways, it was a rich city of brick houses, palaces, canals, aqueducts and a great square of temple-topped pyramids. It was destroyed by CORTÉS in 1521.

TENRECS, primitive members of the Insectivora, related to MOLES and SHREWS. Once living in mainland Africa, they are now confined to Madagascar. Terrestrial animals, many species have spiny coats like those of HEDGEHOGS. The skull is long and narrow. They feed mainly on ground-dwelling invertebrates about dawn and at dusk.

TENSILE STRENGTH, the resistance of a material to tensile stresses (those which tend to lengthen it). The tensile strength of a substance is the tensile force per unit area of cross-section which must be applied to break it.

TENSKWATAWA (c1768–1834), or "Shawnee Prophet," Shawnee Indian who aimed with his twin TECUMSEH for a Northwest Indian confederacy. Famous for his "messages from God" and prediction of an eclipse, he urged rejection of the white man. He rashly engaged in the disastrous battle of TIPPECANOE (1811).

TENSOR, an abstract quantity expressed in terms of definite components within a coordinate system, and whose components obey certain transformation laws when the tensor is considered in relation to a different coordinate system. **Tensor Analysis** has as its chief aim the inspection and mathematical formulation of laws whose validity is unaffected by transfer from one coordinate system to any other. (See also VECTOR.)

TENT CATERPILLARS, name given to several species of gregarious CATERPILLARS which construct large, communal webs into which they can retreat to rest. The name is used more especially for the larvae of *Malacosoma americana*, a North American species which feeds on wild cherry and other fruit trees.

TENURE OF OFFICE ACT (1867), requiring US Senate consent to the president's dismissal of civil servants or members of the cabinet, was defied by President Andrew Johnson who dismissed (1867–68) secretary of war E. M. STANTON. The Act was repealed in 1887 and declared unconstitutional in 1926.

TEOTIHUACÁN, pre-TOLTEC metropolis of central America, c400 BC–c700 AD. Lying 30mi NE of Mexico City, it is laid out in grid pattern along the 1½mi Street of the Dead. Monuments include the Temple of Quetzalcoatl, Pyramid of the Moon and the huge Pyramid of the Sun.

TEPEE, or **tipi**, conical tentlike shelter used by the Plains Indians. Portable (unlike the WIGWAM), it has a covering of skins, mats, bark or cloth supported by poles.

TEQUILA, a type of Mexican brandy or mescal that is produced by the fermentation of the stems and leaf bases of a number of AGAVE species, particularly *Agave tecquilana*.

TERBIUM (Tb), one of the LANTHANUM SERIES. AW 158.9, mp 1360°C, bp 3041°C, sg 8.229 (25°C).

TER BORCH, Gerard (1617–1681), Dutch painter. Much traveled (Italy, France, England, Westphalia, Spain), he painted small, delicate portraits and dignified interior genre scenes. His group portrait *The Peace of Münster* (1648) is of historical note.

TERENCE (Publius Terentius Afer; c185–159 BC), Roman playwright. All his comedies (most based on MENANDER) survive: *The Woman from Andros, The Mother-in-Law, The Self-Tormentor, The Eunuch, Phormio* and *The Brothers*. Their refined realism, humor and language later influenced development of the COMEDY OF MANNERS.

TERESA OF ÁVILA, Saint (1515–1582), Spanish nun and mystic who reformed the CARMELITES; a patron saint of Spain. Canonized in 1622, she was proclaimed a "Doctor of the Roman Catholic Church" in 1970. Her *Interior Castle* (1588), *Life*

The tennis court, with the base line (a), singles side line (b), doubles side line (c), service line (d), left service court (e), right service court (f), net (g) and center service line (h).

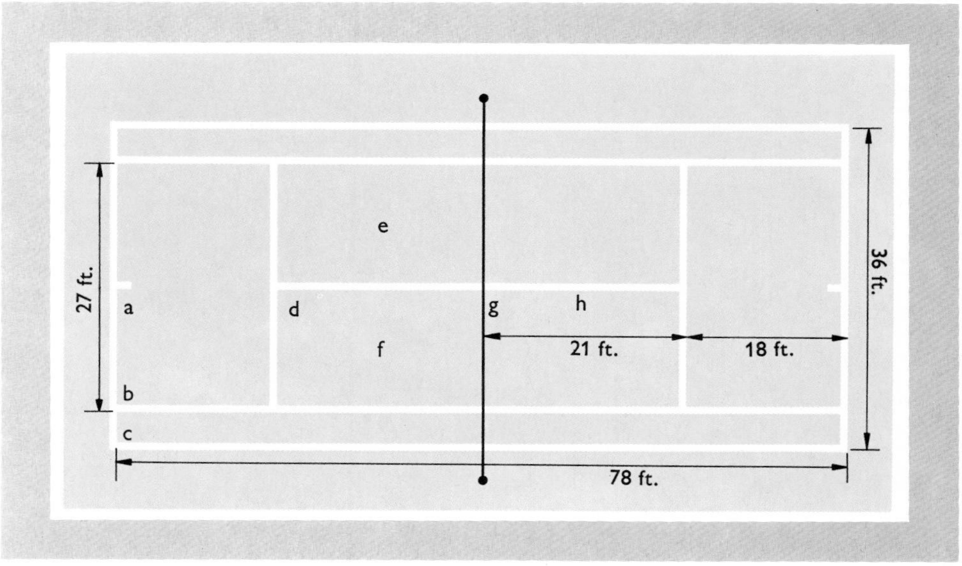

(1611) and other writings are classics of spiritual literature.

TERESHKOVA, Valentina Vladimirovna (1937–), Soviet cosmonaut, the first woman to fly in space. In 1963 she made a three-day flight in the capsule Vostok 6, completing 48 orbits of the earth.

TERESINA, capital of Piauí state, NE Brazil, near the confluence of the Parnaíba and Poti rivers. It ships livestock, rice and cotton, and produces textiles, sugar and rum. Pop 220 000.

TERMAN, Lewis Madison (1877–1956), US psychologist best known for developing the STANFORD-BINET TEST.

TERMITES, or **white ants**, primitive insects closely related to COCKROACHES, found in all warm regions. They have a complicated social system and live in well-regulated communities with different castes taking distinct roles. They build large nests of soil mixed with saliva, in which the colony of king, queen, workers, soldiers and juveniles live. Soldiers and workers are sterile individuals whose development has been arrested at an early stage. Termites feed on wood and vegetation, digesting the food with the aid of symbiotic PROTOZOA or BACTERIA in the gut.

TERNS, a subfamily, Sterninae, of the GULL family. All have long, pointed wings and deeply-forked tails while most are white with gray back and black head cap in the breeding season. Terns plunge into the sea to catch fish. The Arctic tern, *Sterna paradisaea*, yearly migrates from the Arctic to the Antarctic and back again.

TERPENES, HYDROCARBONS that are oligomers or POLYMERS of ISOPRENE, and their derivatives. Most are odorous liquids, reactive and unstable, and are found in ESSENTIAL OILS, especially TURPENTINE. They contain double bonds and usually one or more rings. They include CAMPHOR, CAROTENOIDS, MENTHOL and VITAMIN A. Latex is a polyterpene.

TERPSICHORE. See MUSES.

TERRA COTTA (Italian: baked earth), any fired earthenware product, especially one made from coarse, porous CLAY, red-brown in color and unglazed. Being cheap, hard and durable, it has been used from ancient times for building and roofing, and for molded architectural ornament and statuettes. Its use for sculpture and plaques was revived in the Renaissance and in the 18th century. (See also POTTERY AND PORCELAIN.)

TERRAMYCIN, or oxytetracycline. See TETRACYCLINES.

TERRA NOVA NATIONAL PARK, in Newfoundland, Canada, on Bonavista Bay. Its 153sq mi of varied scenery are popular among campers and fishermen.

TERRAPINS, the name given to seven geographical races of *Malaclemys terrapin*. They are moderate-sized TURTLES, up to 250mm (10in) long, living in coastal waters of eastern North America.

TERRE HAUTE, city of W Ind., seat of Vigo Co., on the Wabash, R 70mi SW of Indianapolis. It manufactures metal, chemicals and plastics. E. V. DEBS and Theodore DREISER were born here. Pop 70 335.

TERRELL, a city of NE Tex., 30mi E of Dallas. It processes cotton, grain and livestock and manufactures clothing, shoes and metal goods. Pop 14 182.

TERRELL, Mary Church (1863–1954), US champion of equal rights for women and blacks, notably in her home town of Washington. She cofounded the National Association of Colored Women (1896).

TERRITORIALITY, a behavioral drive causing animals to set up distinct territories defended against other members of the same species (conspecifics) for the purposes of establishing a breeding site, home range or feeding area. It is an important factor in the spacing out of animal populations. Territoriality is shown by animals of all kinds: birds, mammals, fishes and insects, and may involve displays or the scent-marking of boundaries. A territory may be held by individuals, pairs or even family groups.

TERRITORIAL WATERS, in international law, the belt of sea adjacent to a country and under its territorial jurisdiction. Important for control of shipping, seabeds and fisheries, such limits used to extend 3mi, and more recently 12mi, from low-water mark. A 200mi limit is gaining acceptance.

TERRITORY, in politics, an area under a government's control. Named territories have lower status than the mother country. All but 19 US states were once territories; Alaska and Hawaii were the last incorporated territories (with full Constitutional rights) to gain statehood. US territories include the Virgin Islands and Guam. The US administers the UN TRUST TERRITORY of the Pacific Islands.

TERROR, Reign of. See REIGN OF TERROR.

TERRY, Dame Alice Ellen (1847–1928), English actress. In her partnership with Henry IRVING at the London Lyceum (1878–1902) she became famous in roles from Shakespeare, traditional and modern dramatists.

TERTIARY, the period of the CENOZOIC before the advent of man, lasting from about 65 to 4 million years ago. Sometimes the Tertiary is regarded as synonymous with the Cenozoic, the QUATERNARY being merely a subperiod. (See also GEOLOGY.)

TERTULLIAN (Quintus Septimius Florens Tertullianus; c160–c225), early Christian Latin writer, born Carthage. Converted on return to Carthage from Rome, he wrote apologetics, polemics and ascetic works in which, aided by his law training, he denounced paganism, heresies and licentiousness.

TERVUREN, Belgian breed of sheepdog with a rich fawn coat, tipped with black, and a black mask, ears and tail tip. It stands 26in high and apart from color is like the BELGIAN SHEEPDOG to which it is closely related.

TESLA, Nikola (1856–1943), Croatian-born US electrical engineer whose discovery of the rotating magnetic field permitted his construction of the first AC INDUCTION MOTOR (c1888). Since it is easier to transmit AC than DC over long distances, this invention was of great importance.

TEST ACT (1673), an English law making profession of the Church of England faith a condition of holding public office. The test, which affected both Roman Catholics and Nonconformists, ended in 1828–29.

TESTES, pair of male GONADS, which in humans lie in the scrotum suspended from the perineum below the PENIS. This position allows a lower temperature than in the ABDOMEN, thus favoring SPERM production, the principal function of the testes. ANDROGEN hormones (mainly TESTOSTERONE) are also secreted by the testes under the control of HYPOTHALAMUS and PITUITARY GLAND. The testes develop at the back of the abdomen and descend in the FETUS and infant. Failure to descend in childhood may require surgical correction.

TESTOSTERONE, ANDROGEN STEROID produced by the interstitial cells of the TESTES, and to a lesser extent by the ADRENAL GLAND cortex, under the control of LUTEINIZING HORMONE. It is responsible for most male sexual characteristics—VOICE change, HAIR distribution and sex-organ development.

TETANUS, or **lockjaw**, BACTERIAL DISEASE in which a TOXIN produced by anaerobic tetanus bacilli growing in contaminated wounds causes MUSCLE spasm due to nerve toxicity. Minor cuts may be infected with the bacteria which are common in soil. The first symptom may often be painful contraction of jaw and neck muscles; trunk muscles including those of RESPIRATION and muscles close to the site of injury are also frequently involved. Untreated, many cases are fatal, but ARTIFICIAL RESPIRATION, antiserum and PENICILLIN have improved the outlook. Regular VACCINATION and adequate wound cleansing are important in prevention.

TETANY, involuntary MUSCLE contractions, with excessive muscular irritability due to lack of ionic CALCIUM in the BLOOD and tissues. True hypocalcemia may be due to PARATHYROID GLAND insufficiency or pancreatitis, while ALKALOSIS (e.g., from over-breathing) may transiently reduce ionization of calcium compounds.

TETE, Zambezi R port and district capital, NW Mozambique. Pop 38 962.

TETHYS, primeval sea that lay between the supercontinents GONDWANALAND and LAURASIA, separating what is now Africa from what is now S Eurasia. As the continents evolved toward their present form, the Tethys narrowed, leaving only the present Mediterranean. The sediments of the Tethys GEOSYNCLINE are to be found in folded MOUNTAIN ranges such as the Himalayas. (See also PLATE TECTONICS.)

TETON RANGE, a Rocky Mountain group in NW Wyo. It extends 40mi and lies mostly within GRAND TETON NATIONAL PARK.

TETRAS, any of a number of brightly-colored fishes native to Middle and South America. They represent 40 to 45 genera in the family Characinidae and show remarkable diversity of form and habit. They are popular aquarium fishes.

TETRACYCLINES, broad-spectrum ANTIBIOTICS (including Aureomycin and Terramycin) which may be given by mouth. While useful in BRONCHITIS and other minor infections, they are especially valuable in disease due to RICKETTSIA and related organisms; they can also be used in ACNE. Staining of TEETH in children and deterioration in KIDNEY failure cases are important side effects.

TETRAETHYL LEAD. See LEAD.

TETRAHEDRON. See POLYHEDRON.

TETRAZZINI, Eva (1862–1938) and **Luisa** (1871–1940), successful Italian operatic sopranos. Luisa, the younger sister, toured Russia, South America, Europe and the US and was renowned for her brilliant voice and coloratura technique.

TETZEL, Johann (1465–1519), German Dominican monk, appointed (1516) to sell indulgences to raise money for SAINT PETER'S BASILICA, Rome. His preaching near Wittenberg (1517) provoked LUTHER'S 95 theses, chiefly against indulgences. (See also REFORMATION.)

TEUTOBURG FOREST, Battle of (9 AD), the successful ambush of three Roman legions under Varus by Arminius, leader of the Cherusci Germans, which prevented Roman domination of Germany.

TEUTONIC KNIGHTS, religious military order established (1198) in Palestine. It successfully invaded, Germanized and Christianized Prussia in the 1200s. It declined after defeat by a Polish-Lithuanian army at TANNENBERG (1410). Its last branch, in central and S Germany, was dissolved by Napoleon (1805).

TEUTONS, originally a German tribe, defeated by the Romans in Gaul (102 BC). "Teutons" became

The jagged peaks of the Tetons, a mountain chain in the Rockies, lying south of Yellowstone lake in Idaho and Wyoming, first discovered by white settlers in the 1800s. The highest peak is Grand Teton (13 747ft), the focal point of the Grand Teton National Park.

synonymous with JUTES, ANGLES and SAXONS, then with "North Germans" in general; "teutonic" came to describe the languages of Scandinavia, Germany, Belgium and Holland.

TEVERE RIVER. See TIBER RIVER.

TEWKSBURY, town in NE Mass., 20mi NW of Boston, residential with light industry. Pop 22 755.

TEXARKANA, twin cities on the Ark.–Tex. border 170mi ENE of Dallas. Texarkana, NE Tex. (pop 30 497), and its twin city in SW Ark. (seat of Miller Co.; pop 21 682) manufacture rocket parts, railroad cars, building materials and lumber.

TEXAS, second-largest US state, bordered by Mexico, N.M., Okla., Ark., La., and the Gulf of Mexico.

The fertile West Gulf Coastal Plain extends inland 150–300mi to the Balcones escarpment. Divided by the Brazos R, the North-Central Plains contain the state's richest soils. The Texas Great Plains (W half of the Panhandle and along the Pecos R) reach W to N.M. In the extreme W the Basin and Range (Trans-Pecos) region is crossed by the Rocky Mts. Lake Texoma (225sq mi), shared with Okla., is the largest of many man-made lakes. Mean annual temperature ranges from 55°F in the Panhandle to 74°F along the lower Rio Grande in the S. Annual rainfall is 55in in the E but only 10in in the W.

The economy is based on minerals, agriculture and manufacturing. Texas is the leading state for cotton, beef-cattle and sheep. Important minerals are oil and natural gas, sulfur, salt, uranium, lime, granite, gravel and asphalt. Major crops include sorghums, rice, wheat, pecans and peanuts. Large chemical industries are concentrated along the Gulf. Food-processing and manufacture of transportation equipment, machinery, metals and textiles are important. NASA's Manned Spacecraft Center has since 1964 stimulated manufacture of scientific and electronic equipment. It lies near HOUSTON, third-largest US port and the Southwest's major industrial center. Other major cities are DALLAS, SAN ANTONIO, FORT WORTH, EL PASO and AUSTIN.

History. The subject of French, Spanish and US (1803) claims, Texas became part of independent Mexico 1821. After defeat at the ALAMO, victory for US settlers at SAN JACINTO preceded the independent republic (1836–45) and entrance into the US. The MEXICAN WAR ended Mexican claims (1848). Despite the views of governor Sam HOUSTON, Texas joined the Confederates (1861); it was readmitted to the Union in 1870. Railroads (later 1800s), discovery of oil (1901) and WWII helped economic development.

Texas is governed under its 5th (1876) constitution; its 31 senators serve four-year terms, its 150 representatives two years.

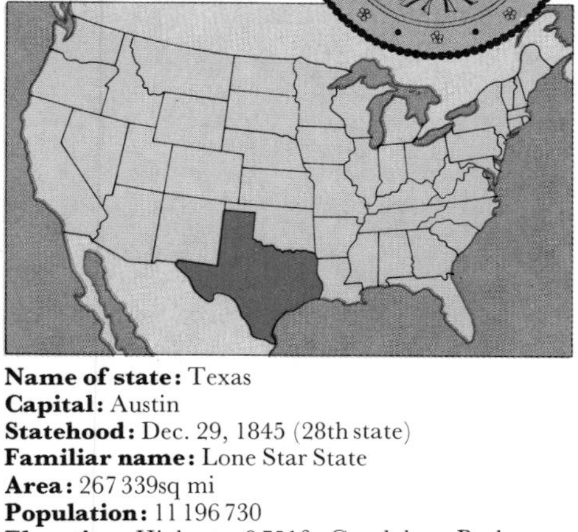

Name of state: Texas
Capital: Austin
Statehood: Dec. 29, 1845 (28th state)
Familiar name: Lone Star State
Area: 267 339sq mi
Population: 11 196 730
Elevation: Highest—8 751ft., Guadalupe Peak. Lowest—sea level, Gulf of Mexico
Motto: Friendship
State flower: Bluebonnet
State bird: Mockingbird
State tree: Pecan
State song: "Texas, Our Texas"

TEXAS CITY, industrial city, railroad center and port on Galveston Bay, SE Tex. It also has important oil refineries. Pop 38 908.

TEXAS FEVER, tick-borne disease of cattle caused by the protozoan *Babesia bigemina*.

TEXAS RANGERS, a law enforcement body, part of the Texas department of public safety. The first were ten men employed (1823) by S. F. AUSTIN to protect settlers from Indian and Mexican raiders. In 1935 the Rangers were merged with the state highway patrol.

TEXCOCO, Lake, a now almost dry lake in central Mexico, E of Mexico City. On an island (now further W) the Aztec capital, TENOCHTITLÁN, was built.

TEXTILES, fabrics made from natural FIBERS or SYNTHETIC FIBERS, whether knitted, woven, bonded or felted. The fibers are prepared (WOOL preparation being typical) and spun (see SPINNING) into yarn. This is then formed into fabric by WEAVING or other methods. Finishing processes include BLEACHING; CALENDERING; MERCERIZING; dyeing (see DYES AND DYEING), brushing, sizing, fulling and tentering. Chemical processes are used to impart crease-resistance, fireproofing, stain-resistance, waterproofing, or nonshrink properties.

THACKERAY, William Makepeace (1811–1863), English novelist, essayist and illustrator. He did much to shape *Punch*, and was first editor of *The Cornhill Magazine* (1860). His best known (and best) novel is *Vanity Fair* (1848), a gentle satire of the early 19th-century middle classes; its central character is the sly but goodnatured Becky Sharp. His other novels include *Barry Lyndon* (1844), *Pendennis* (1850) and *Henry Esmond* (1852).

THAILAND (formerly Siam), monarchy in SE Asia. The N part borders Cambodia, Laos and Burma; the S extends between the Gulf of Siam and Bay of Bengal down the Malay Peninsula to Malaysia.

Land. The densely wooded N–S hill ranges of the N, rich in teak, extend into Burma. The populous central region comprises the rice-producing alluvial plain of the Chao Phraya R. The drier NE Khorat Plateau drains E to the Mekong R. The narrow S region is mostly mountainous and forested, with some rice plains and many islands off the W coast. Rainfall ranges from an average 80in in the S and W to 40in in the E.

People. The Thais are of Mongol descent; most are Theravada Buddhists. Thai language is of the Sino-Tibetan family and written in script of Sanskrit origin. Chinese form an important urban minority; there are hill peoples in the N and Malays in the S.

Economy. Rice is the chief crop in an agricultural economy, with sugarcane, cotton, corn, coconuts, rubber and tobacco. Draft water buffalos are the principal livestock, though there are timber elephants. Fishing and forestry (teak, oils, resins, bamboo) are important. Textiles (including famous Thai silks) in BANGKOK and THON BURI are among the few manufactures. Thailand exports rice, corn, rubber and teak, and trades mainly with the West.

History. The Thais came from China about 1000 AD. Their center moved S under the Sukhothai (c1220–1350), Ayuthia (1350–1778) and Chakri (1782–) dynasties. Siam lost influence in the 1800s to the British (in Burma and Malaya) and French (in Laos and Cambodia) but kept her independence. Invaded by Japan in WWII, Thailand sent troops to Korea, joined the SOUTHEAST ASIA TREATY ORGANIZATION (HQ in Bangkok) and supported the US in Vietnam. The overthrow of Marshal Thanom Kittikachorn (1973) coincided with increased militancy among workers, peasants and students. Communist guerrilla activity continued in the NE, N and S and withdrawal of US troops began in 1975 (see MAYAGÜEZ INCIDENT). However, after a bloody confrontation with leftists, a military government was re-established.

THALAMUS, two nuclei of the upper BRAIN stem involved in transmission of impulses to and from the cerebral cortex, especially in sensory pathways.

The arid but fascinating scenery of Big Bend National Park, Texas, a largely desert area pierced by the rugged Chisos Mountains. It is named for the great curve in the Rio Grande, which has left the land almost waterless.

THALES (early 6th century BC), ancient Greek PRESOCRATIC philosopher, one of the SEVEN SAGES. He is reputed to have invented geometry and to have attempted the first rational account of the universe, claiming that it originated from water.

THALIA, muse of comedy. See MUSES.

THALIDOMIDE, mild SEDATIVE introduced in the late 1950s and withdrawn a few years later on finding that it was responsible for congenital deformities in children born to mothers who took the DRUG. This was due to an effect on the EMBRYO in early PREGNANCY, in particular causing defective limb bud formation.

THALLIUM (Tl), soft, bluish-gray metal in Group IIIA of the PERIODIC TABLE, resembling LEAD. Its extraction is the same as INDIUM's. It forms monovalent (thallous) compounds which may be oxidized to the less stable trivalent (thallic) compounds. Thallous sulfide is used in photocells, and mixed crystals of the bromide and iodide in infrared detectors. Thallium compounds are dangerously toxic. AW 204.4, mp 303.5°C, bp 1457°C, sg 11.85 (20°C).

THALLOPHYTA, a traditional but artificial division of the PLANT KINGDOM, which includes ALGAE and FUNGI. The thallophyta represents plants that lack specialized conducting tissues and which are not differentiated into true ROOTS, STEMS and LEAVES. However, since both the constituent groups are so diverse, it is clear they should be placed in separate divisions.

THAMES, Battle of the (1813), victory of the US troops of William H. HARRISON over British and Indian (under TECUMSEH) forces in Ontario in the WAR OF 1812. Following the battle of Lake ERIE, it consolidated US control of the Northwest.

THAMES RIVER, England's chief waterway, winds E 210mi from the Cotswolds to its North Sea estuary. On its banks lie OXFORD, READING, ETON, WINDSOR CASTLE, RUNNYMEDE, HAMPTON COURT PALACE and GREENWICH. Canals link it to the West and Midlands. Above LONDON it displays fine, gentle scenery; below London it is of considerable importance for shipping. It is tidal up to Teddington (10mi W of London).

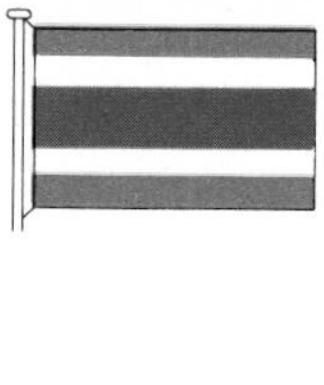

Official name: Thailand
Capital: Bangkok
Area: 198 456sq mi
Population: 34 200 000
Languages: Thai; English, Chinese, Malay, tribal languages
Religions: Buddhist; Muslim, Christian, Animist
Monetary unit(s): 1 Baht = 100 satangs

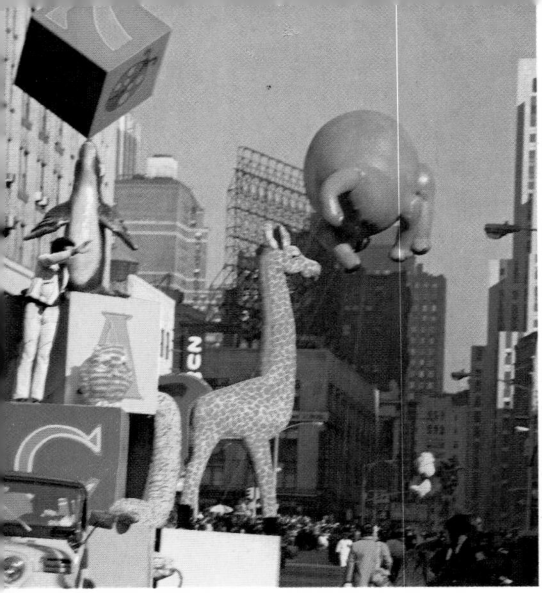

New York's famous annual Thanksgiving Day parade goes down Broadway from Central Park to Macy's department store, which organizes it.

THANATOS (Greek: death), in Greek mythology, the personfication of death and son of Nyx (night). He lived with his brother Hypnos (sleep) in HADES. He is usually represented either as a black-robed figure or as a winged spirit.

THANKSGIVING DAY, since 1863, an annual US national holiday to give thanks for blessings received during the year. It is celebrated on the fourth Thursday in November with feasting and prayers. The tradition was begun by the colonists of Plymouth, Mass., in 1621, and can be traced back to the English harvest festivals. In Canada, it is celebrated on the second Monday in October.

THANT, U (1909–1974), Burmese diplomat, UNITED NATIONS secretary-general 1961–71. A cautious and unassertive negotiator, he was involved in the Cuban Missile Crisis (1962), and in peace negotiations in Indonesia (1962), Congo (1963), Cyprus (1964) and the India-Pakistan war (1965).

THAR DESERT, or Great Indian Desert, in NW India and SE Pakistan. Rainfall of less than 10in per year supports only subsistence pastoralism, but irrigation projects are transforming some areas.

THAYER, Sylvanus (1785–1872), US military engineer and educator. Superintendent of West Point 1817–33, he was largely responsible for creating its world-wide reputation, and earned the title "father of the Military Academy."

THEATER, building in which plays are performed; also used as a term to refer to drama as an art form.

According to Aristotle, the drama of ancient Greece, the ancestor of modern European drama, grew out of the DITHYRAMB. The invention of TRAGEDY is accredited to THESPIS and the form was refined successively by AESCHYLUS, SOPHOCLES and EURIPIDES. COMEDY was a separate and later development of Greek theater. The plays of ARISTOPHANES are the only remains of Greek Old Comedy (5th century BC), a period when comedy was extremely licentious and still close to its ritual origins. Middle and New Comedy (4th and 3rd centuries BC respectively) became increasingly sentimental; only the New Comedy plays of MENANDER remain from these periods. Greek drama was performed as part of religious festivals in outdoor AMPHITHEATERS built into hillsides; one is still used at EPIDAURUS each summer. The Roman plays of PLAUTUS, TERENCE and SENECA show their Greek antecedents, but MIME and PANTOMIME were the popular theatrical forms in the Roman Empire and, through the COMMEDIA DELL'ARTE, provide the only direct link between ancient and medieval European drama.

Medieval drama evolved in the Church from musical elaborations of the service. Eventually these developed into MYSTERY PLAYS and were moved out of doors onto play wagons. Miracle Plays, based on lives of saints and on scripture, also developed; whole cycles of plays were performed at religious festivals. MORALITY PLAYS (such as EVERYMAN) and INTERLUDES appeared in the 15th century. During the RENAISSANCE the rediscovery of Greek and Roman dramatic texts led directly to the growth of secular drama. Buildings for the performance of plays were erected in Elizabethan times, one of the most famous being The Globe, associated with SHAKESPEARE. By the end of his career a roofed building inside which the audience ranged around an open stage came into use. The modern form of the stage, with painted scenery and a *proscenium arch* across which a curtain falls between acts, was established by the 17th century.

In England the drama went through distinct phases associated with the Renaissance, the RESTORATION and NEOCLASSICISM before settling into a long period of MELODRAMA and sentimentality. On the Continent, classical and neoclassical drama, represented supremely by CORNEILLE and RACINE in France, gave way to a period of ROMANTICISM during which SCHILLER and GOETHE in Germany, and later HUGO in France and PUSHKIN in Russia, made lasting contributions.

Drama of the modern era began with efforts by IBSEN, STRINDBERG, CHEKOV, ZOLA and George Bernard SHAW to reintroduce realism, honest character portrayal and serious social and political debate into the theater. Many experiments with dramatic form (EXPRESSIONISM, SURREALISM, NATURALISM) and language characterize this phase in the theater. This century has produced dramatists of considerable merit such as O'NEILL, BRECHT, LORCA, BECKETT, PINTER, ALBEE, Tennessee WILLIAMS and IONESCO. In recent times Western audiences have also become interested in Oriental theater, especially Japanese NOH and KABUKI drama. The term theater comprehends also such forms as MUSICAL COMEDY, VAUDEVILLE and OPERA as well as plays.

The ancestors of modern theater buildings. The Greek theater (1) was originally no more than a round acting area surrounded by spectators, but at its height the audience space was diminished by a *skene*, or scene-building, behind the acting area (*orchestra*) and space for the chorus at the sides. The Roman theater (2), although modeled on the Greek, increased the size of the acting area; audience space was reduced to a semicircle. When building the Teatro Olimpico (1580–85) at Vicenza, Italy (3), the architect Palladio adopted the Roman style; as can be seen from the floorplan here, he increased the depth of the stage to accommodate scene machinery, and added a surrounding building. This fusion of the modern and the classical became the model for theaters up to this century, when experimentation revived the pure classical styles and the three-sided English Elizabethan stage.

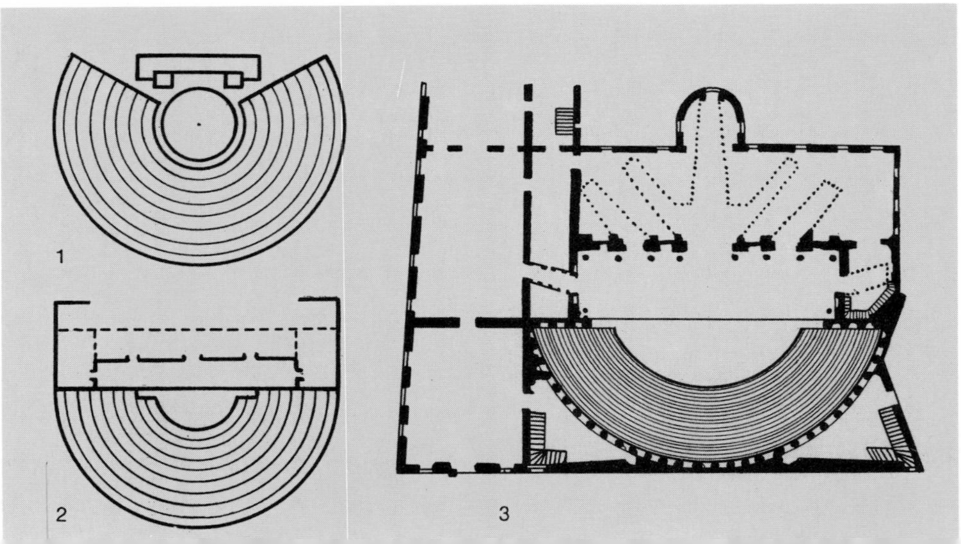

THEBES, ancient Egyptian city, 419mi S of Cairo, famous for its temples to AMON and its tombs of the pharaohs, capital of Egypt from c2100 BC, reaching its peak under the 17th and 18th dynasties (c1600 BC–1306 BC; see AMENHOTEP; KARNAK; LUXOR; TUTANKHAMEN). Already in decline by 1100 BC, it was sacked by the Assyrians in 661 BC and finally destroyed by the Romans in 29 BC.

THEBES, chief city in Boeotia, ancient Greece, founded by CADMUS. It was rich in legend (see ANTIGONE; OEDIPUS; POLYNICES). Hostile to Athens, Thebes supported Persia in the PERSIAN WARS, and later Sparta in the PELOPONNESIAN WAR. In 394 BC she turned against Sparta, and after early defeats dominated Greece (371–362 BC) under EPAMINONDAS. The city was destroyed by Alexander the Great in 336 BC.

THE DALLES, city in N Ore., seat of Wasco Co. An inland port on the Columbia R, it is a shipping and processing center for farm produce. Pop 10423.

THEFT, general term in US law covering the related offenses of ROBBERY, BURGLARY and LARCENY, for the taking of another's property without his consent and with intent to steal.

THEILER, Max (1899–1972), South-African-born US microbiologist awarded the 1951 Nobel Prize for Physiology or Medicine for his discovery that an attenuated strain of YELLOW FEVER could be prepared by infecting mice, so making possible the first yellow fever vaccine.

THEISM, a philosophical system, as distinguished from DEISM and PANTHEISM, that professes the existence of a personal, transcendent God who created, preserves and governs the world. Orthodox Christian philosophy is a developed form of theism. (See also MONOTHEISM; PROVIDENCE.)

THEMISTOCLES (c525 BC–c460 BC), Athenian statesman and naval strategist. During the PERSIAN WARS, he foresaw that the Persians would return, and persuaded the Athenians to build the fleet with which he won the battle of SALAMIS (480 BC). As ARCHON from 493 BC, he built up the fortifications of Athens. ARISTIDES and other rivals were exiled by OSTRACISM, and in 471 BC he was ostracized himself by his aristocratic enemies, eventually retiring to Persia.

THEOCRITUS (c300–c250 BC), Alexandrian Greek poet of the HELLENISTIC AGE, whose polished, artificial *Idylls* created the genre of the PASTORAL. He was imitated by VERGIL and many later poets.

THEODICY (from Greek *theos*, god; *dikē*, justice), that part of natural THEOLOGY concerned to justify God's goodness and omnipotence in the face of evil and suffering. The term was coined by LEIBNIZ, whose *Theodicy* on this theme appeared in 1710.

THEODOLITE, surveying instrument comprising a sighting TELESCOPE whose orientation with respect to two graduated angular scales, one horizontal, the other vertical, can be determined. It represents a development of the *transit*, which traditionally included only the horizontal scale.

THEODORA (c504–548), wife of Byzantine emperor JUSTINIAN I. Formerly an actress and dancer, she became a MONOPHYSITE Christian. Highly intelligent, she exercised enormous political influence, once saving the dynasty by persuading Justinian to remain in Constantinople during the Nika riots (532).

THEODORE, name of two popes. **Theodore I** (d. 649), was pope from 642. He devoted his energy to combating MONOTHELITISM. **Theodore II** (d. 897), was pope for 20 days before he died, possibly murdered. In a period of intrigue and corruption, he reinstated his predecessor FORMOSUS.

THEODORIC THE GREAT (c454–526 AD), king of the OSTROGOTHS (471) and conqueror of Italy. Alternately opposing and allying with the BYZANTINE EMPIRE, he became consul under the emperor Zeno (484), who sent him to invade Italy (489). Having defeated and murdered ODOACER (493), he set up an Italian kingdom, ruling with justice and toleration.

THEODOSIUS, name of two Roman emperors. **Theodosius I, the Great** (346–395), was a general's son who was chosen by the emperor Gratian to rule the East (379). In 388 he invaded Italy, defeated the usurper Maximus and restored VALENTINIAN II to power, becoming emperor himself in 392. He was an important opponent of ARIANISM. After his death, the Empire was divided between his sons ARCADIUS (East) and HONORIUS (West). **Theodosius II** (401–450), Arcadius' son, became emperor in 408, but his sister, his wife and various ministers held effective power. His *Theodosian Code* (438) is the first collection of imperial legislation.

THEOLOGY, the science of religious knowledge; the formal analysis of what is believed by adherents of a religion, making its doctrine coherent, elucidating it logically and relating it to secular disciplines. Its themes, therefore, are universal: GOD, man, the world, the Scriptures, SALVATION, ETHICS, the cultus, and ESCHATOLOGY. However, most religions have no well-developed theology. The concept arose in Greek thought, but its elaboration took place only in Christianity. The early Church Fathers and Doctors formulated doctrine in contemporary philosophical terms, and major advances were made by resolving controversies. In the Middle Ages SCHOLASTICISM developed, partly in reaction to the influence of NEOPLATONISM, and divided theology into NATURAL THEOLOGY and revealed theology (see REVELATION). From the Reformation each branch of PROTESTANTISM began to develop its own distinctive theology. From the Enlightenment rationalist theology became dominant, leading to MODERNISM and the modern critical view of the Bible. Partly in reaction arose NEO-ORTHODOXY, and the existentialist theology of NIEBUHR and TILLICH. The chief divisions of theology are: Biblical studies (including linguistic and other auxiliary disciplines), leading to the interpretation of Scripture; Biblical theology (the development of ideas in the Biblical writings); historical theology; systematic theology, and apologetics.

THEOPHRASTUS (c370–c285 BC), Greek philosopher of the Peripatetic School, a pupil of both PLATO and ARISTOTLE, generally considered the father of modern BOTANY. His *Enquiry into Plants* deals with description and classification, his *Plant Etiology* with physiology and structure. But he is best known for *Characters*, a collection of 30 brief character sketches, often satirical.

THEORELL, Axel Hugo Teodor (1903–), Swedish biochemist awarded the 1955 Nobel Prize for Physiology or Medicine for his studies of ENZYME action, specifically the roles of enzymes in biological OXIDATION AND REDUCTION processes.

THEOREM, any statement logically implied by a set of postulates, or AXIOMS. Once its dependence on the axioms is proved, a newly discovered theorem becomes a potential stepping-stone to the discovery and proof of other, similarly dependent, theorems.

THEOSOPHY (literally, divine wisdom), a mystical system of religious philosophy claiming direct insight into the divine nature. The speculations of such philosophers as PLOTINUS, Jakob BÖHME and SWEDENBORG are often called theosophical, as are many Eastern philosophies. The Theosophical Society was founded 1875 by Madame BLAVATSKY.

THERA, Greek island in the Aegean; it exports wine and pumice. Archeologists have unearthed a rich Minoan settlement there, destroyed by a volcanic eruption c1500 BC which may have ended the Cretan Minoan civilization (see AEGEAN CIVILIZATION).

THERAPSIDS, a group of extinct reptiles of the Permian and Triassic periods, 280–190 million years ago. Their skulls show some features similar to those of mammals suggesting that they may have been ancestral to one or more of the mammalian lines.

THÉRÈSE OF LISIEUX, Saint (1873–1897), the "Little Flower of Jesus," a French Carmelite nun who practiced the "little way"—achieving sanctity in performing the humblest tasks. Her spiritual autobiography was published posthumously.

THERMAL ANALYSIS, or **thermoanalysis**, group of methods for detecting and studying physical and chemical changes in substances heated at a standard rate through a temperature range; sometimes used for chemical ANALYSIS. In **thermogravimetric analysis** (TGA), the sample is weighed in a thermobalance—a sensitive BALANCE with the sample pan inside a furnace—and its weight is plotted against temperature. Weight loss is due to giving off gases or vapors; weight gain to reaction with the atmosphere. In **differential thermal analysis** (DTA), the sample is heated simultaneously with an inert reference substance (usually aluminum oxide), and the temperature difference between them is plotted against temperature. This deviates from zero in one direction when an exothermic reaction occurs, and in the other direction when an endothermic reaction occurs (see THERMOCHEMISTRY).

THERMAL POLLUTION, the release of excessive waste heat into the environment, notably by pumping warm water from power plant cooling towers into rivers and lakes. This may kill off some living species, decrease the oxygen supply, and adversely affect reproduction.

THERMIDOR, 11th month of the new calendar adopted in the FRENCH REVOLUTION, in force 1793–1805. It covered the period July–August (the name signifies heat). The coup marking the downfall of ROBESPIERRE (July 27, 1794) is called the coup of 9 Thermidor.

THERMIONIC EMISSION, spontaneous emission of ELECTRONS from metal or oxide-coated metal surfaces at temperatures between 1000K and 3000K. It supplies the electrons in electron- and cathode-ray tubes.

THERMISTOR, a SEMICONDUCTOR device the electrical RESISTANCE of which falls rapidly as its TEMPERATURE rises. It is used as a sensor in electronic circuits measuring or regulating temperature and also in time-delay circuits.

THERMITE, mixture of powdered ALUMINUM and IRON oxide (Fe_3O_4) in equivalent amounts, used in WELDING and INCENDIARY BOMBS. On ignition with a barium peroxide or magnesium fuze, a violently exothermic OXIDATION reaction occurs, producing molten iron at 2500°C and alumina slag. It thus supplies both the heat and the metal for welding, and can be used to join large parts in a preheated refractory mold.

THERMOCHEMISTRY, branch of PHYSICAL CHEMISTRY that deals with HEAT changes accompanying chemical reactions. Practical thermochemistry is mainly by CALORIMETRY, which yields standard heats of reaction or enthalpy values ($\Delta H°$) (see THERMODYNAMICS). If this is negative, the reaction is termed *exothermic* (heat-producing); if positive, *endothermic* (heat-absorbing). **Hess' law**, or the law of constant heat summation, a corollary of the first law of THERMODYNAMICS, states that the overall heat change in a chemical reaction is the same whether it takes place in one or several steps. Thus, by algebraic addition of chemical equations and their $\Delta H°$ values, inaccessible heats of reaction may be calculated, including the **heat of formation** of a compound, which is the heat change when one mole of the compound is formed from its constituent elements in their standard states.

THERMOCOUPLE, an electric circuit involving two junctions between different METALS or SEMICONDUCTORS; if these are at different temperatures, a small ELECTROMOTIVE FORCE is generated in the circuit (Seebeck effect). Measurement of this emf provides a sensitive, if approximate THERMOMETER, typically for the range 70K–1000K, one junction being held at a fixed temperature and the other providing a compact and robust probe. Semiconductor thermocouples in particular can be run in reverse as small refrigerators. A number of thermocouples connected in series with one set of junctions blackened form a **thermopile**, measuring incident radiation through its heating effect on the blackened surface. **Thermoelectricity** embraces the Seebeck and other effects relating heat transfer, thermal gradients, ELECTRIC FIELDS and currents.

THERMODYNAMICS, division of PHYSICS concerned with the interconversion of HEAT, WORK and other forms of ENERGY, and with the states of physical systems. Being concerned only with bulk matter and energy, **classical thermodynamics** is independent of theories of their microscopic nature; its axioms are sturdily empirical, and from them theorems are derived with mathematical rigor. It is basic to ENGINEERING, parts of GEOLOGY, METALLURGY and PHYSICAL CHEMISTRY. Building on earlier studies of the thermodynamic functions TEMPERATURE and heat, Sadi CARNOT pioneered the science by his investigations of the cyclic heat ENGINE (1824), and in 1850 CLAUSIUS stated the first two laws. Thermodynamics was further developed by J. W. GIBBS, H. L. F. von HELMHOLTZ, Lord KELVIN and J. C. MAXWELL.

In thermodynamics, a *system* is any defined collection of matter: a *closed system* is one that cannot exchange matter with its surroundings; an *isolated system* can exchange neither matter nor energy. The *state* of a system is specified by determining all its properties such as pressure, volume, etc. A system in stable EQUILIBRIUM is said to be in an equilibrium state, and has an equation of state (e.g., the general GAS law) relating its properties. (See also PHASE EQUILIBRIA.) A *process* is a change from one state A to another B, the path being specified by all the intermediate states. A *state function* is a property or FUNCTION of properties which depends only on the state and not on the path by which the state was reached; a differential dX of a function X (not necessarily a state function) is termed a *perfect differential* if it can be integrated between two states to give a value $X_{AB} = \int_A^B dX$ which is independent of the path from A to B. If this holds for all A and B, X must be a state function.

There are four basic laws of thermodynamics, all having many different formulations that can be shown to be equivalent. The **zeroth law** states that, if two systems are each in thermal equilibrium with a third system, then they are in thermal equilibrium with each other. This underlies the concept of temperature. The **first law** states that for any process the difference of the heat Q supplied to the system and the work W done by the system equals the change in the internal energy U: $\Delta U = Q - W$. U is a state function, though neither Q nor W separately is. Corollaries of the first law include the law of conservation of ENERGY, Hess' law (see THERMOCHEMISTRY), and the impossibility of PERPETUAL MOTION machines of the first kind. The **second law** (in Clausius' formulation) states that heat cannot be transferred from a colder to a hotter body without some other effect, i.e., without work being done. Corollaries include the impossibility of converting heat entirely into work without some other effect, and the impossibility of PERPETUAL MOTION machines of the second kind. It can be shown that there is a state function ENTROPY, S, defined by

$$\Delta S = \int dQ/T, \text{ where } T \text{ is the absolute temperature.}$$

The entropy change ΔS in an isolated system is zero for a reversible process and positive for all irreversible processes. Thus entropy tends to a maximum (see HEAT DEATH). It also follows that a heat ENGINE is most efficient when it works on a reversible CARNOT cycle between two temperatures T_1 (the heat source) and T_2 (the heat sink), the EFFICIENCY being $(T_1 - T_2)/T_2$. The **third law** states that the entropy of any finite system in an equilibrium state tends to a finite value (defined to be zero) as the temperature of the system tends to absolute zero. The equivalent NERNST heat theorem states that the entropy change for any reversible isothermal process tends to zero as the temperature tends to zero. Hence absolute entropies can be calculated from specific heat data. Other thermodynamic functions, useful for calculating equilibrium conditions under various constraints, are: **enthalpy** (or heat content) $H = U + pV$; the

Helmholtz free energy $A = U - TS$; and the **Gibbs free energy** $G = H - TS$. The free energy represents the capacity of the system to perform useful work. **Quantum statistical thermodynamics**, based on QUANTUM MECHANICS, has arisen in the 20th century. It treats a system as an assembly of particles in quantum states. The entropy is given by $S = k \ln P$ where k is the BOLTZMANN constant and P the statistical probability of the state of the system. Thus entropy is a measure of the disorder of the system.

THERMOELECTRICITY. See THERMOCOUPLE.

THERMOGRAPH, any type of THERMOMETER that is self-registering, recording variations of temperature with time on a graph. A bimetallic strip is often used as the temperature-sensitive element, its deflection being recorded on a rotating drum via a system of levers. Thermographs are widely used in meteorology and atmospheric investigations.

THERMOLUMINESCENCE, emission of light from a steadily heated material that has previously been excited by exposure to radiation. It is a type of LUMINESCENCE and arises from electron displacements within the material's crystal lattice. A long time delay may elapse between excitation and subsequent light emission; this is utilized in thermoluminescent dating in archaeology.

THERMOMETER, instrument for measuring the relative degree of hotness of a substance (its TEMPERATURE) on some reproducible scale. Its operation depends upon a regular relationship between temperature and the change in size of a substance (as in the mercury-in-glass thermometer) or in some other physical property (as in the platinum resistance thermometer). The type of instrument used in a given application depends on the temperature range and accuracy required.

THERMONUCLEAR REACTIONS, the reactions used in nuclear FUSION devices such as the HYDROGEN BOMB.

THERMOPHILE, any plant that either requires a high temperature for growth or can tolerate high temperatures. Thermophilic BACTERIA require temperatures between 45°C and 65°C for optimum growth.

THERMOPILE. See THERMOCOUPLE.

THERMOPYLAE, Battle of (480 BC), famous battle in which a small Greek force under LEONIDAS held up the invading Persian army for three days (see PERSIAN WARS). Thermopylae, a narrow pass in E central Greece, was on the principal route from the N. The battle has become celebrated as an example of heroic resistance.

THERMOS BOTTLE, trade name for VACUUM BOTTLE.

THERMOSTAT, device for maintaining a material or enclosure at a constant temperature by automatically regulating its HEAT supply. This is cut off if the TEMPERATURE rises and reconnected if it falls below that required. A thermostat comprises a sensor whose dimensions or physical properties change with temperature and a relay device which controls a switch or valve accordingly. **Bimetallic strips** are widely used in thermostats; they consist of two metals with widely different linear thermal coefficients fused together. As the temperature rises, the strip bends away from the side with the larger coefficient. This motion may be sufficient to control a heater directly.

THESEUS, in Greek mythology, king of Athens, son of AEGEUS (in some versions, POSEIDON). In Crete, he slew the MINOTAUR, and returned with ARIADNE, abandoning her at Naxos. He fought against the CENTAURS and repulsed an Amazon invasion. Hippolytus was his son by Antiope (see PHAEDRA).

THESPIS (6th century BC), Greek poet credited with inventing TRAGEDY by introducing a second character to exchange dialogue with the leader of the DITHYRAMB.

THESSALONIANS, Epistles to the, two NEW TESTAMENT books written c51 AD by St. PAUL to the Christians in Salonika, Macedonia. They contain an early expression of Paul's theological ideas, particularly about Christ's second coming.

THESSALONIKI. See SALONIKA.

THESSALY, fertile region of N central Greece famous in legend as home of ACHILLES and JASON. It was rarely united and, despite its fine cavalry, was militarily weak. From the 4th to 2nd centuries BC it was subject to Macedonia, later passing to Rome, the Byzantines and Turkey. It became Greek in 1881.

THETFORD MINES, industrial city in S Quebec. It has one of the world's largest asbestos mines. Pop 22003.

THETIS, in Greek mythology, one of the NEREIDS, mother of ACHILLES.

THE VILLAGE, city in central Okla., a residential suburb of Oklahoma City. Pop 13695.

THIAMINE, or aneurin, alternative name for VITAMIN B_1.

THIBODAUX, city in SE La., seat of Lafourche parish. Nearby are oil and gas wells, and truck and dairy farms. Sugar refining is important. Pop 15028.

THIERS, Louis Adolphe (1797–1877), French statesman, first president (1871–73) of the Third Republic. An influential journalist and popular historian of the French Revolution, he supported LOUIS PHILIPPE (1830) and held ministerial posts under him; opposed NAPOLEON III (1851) and was briefly exiled; negotiated the FRANCO-PRUSSIAN WAR's peace treaty and crushed the PARIS COMMUNE (1871).

THIEU, Nguyen van (1923–), president of South Vietnam, 1967–75. An army officer, he helped overthrow DIEM (1963), becoming premier in 1965 and president after KY's fall. He was reelected (1971) in elections widely thought to be rigged, but after US troops had withdrawn his dictatorial regime gradually collapsed, and he resigned in April, 1975.

THIMBU, or Thimphu, or Ta-shi Chho Dzong, capital of BHUTAN since 1962. It has fine traditional architecture and a hydroelectric plant. Pop 60000.

THIOETHERS, organic compounds structurally similar to ETHERS but in which sulfur substitutes for the oxygen bridging the two alkyl groups.

THIOSULFATES. See SULFUR.

THIRD WORLD, 1960s term for the poorer nations of Africa, Latin America and Asia (including China) as opposed to "Western" or communist countries.

THIRST AND HUNGER, complex specific sensations or desires for water and food respectively, which have a role in regulating their intake. Thirst is the end result of a mixture of physical and psychological effects including dry mouth, altered BLOOD mineral content, and the sight and sound of water; hunger, those of STOMACH contractions, low blood sugar levels, HABIT, and the SMELL and sight of food. Repleteness with either inhibits the sensation. Food and water intake are regulated by the HYPOTHALAMUS, and are closely related to the control of HORMONE secretion and other vegetative functions, being part of the system preserving the HOMEOSTASIS (constancy) of the body's internal environment. DRUGS, SMOKING, systemic disease and local BRAIN damage are among the many factors influencing thirst and hunger. Excessive thirst may be a symptom of DIABETES or KIDNEY failure (UREMIA), but organic excessive hunger is rare.

THIRTY-NINE ARTICLES, set of doctrinal statements, issued in 1571, outlining the position of the CHURCH OF ENGLAND on theological and civil matters. Formal assent to the articles was required of all Anglican clergy until 1865, when a less rigorous requirement of general approval was substituted.

THIRTY TYRANTS, a group of extreme oligarchs who set up a reign of terror in Athens (404–403 BC) after her defeat in the PELOPONNESIAN WAR. They were deposed by THRASYBULUS.

THIRTY YEARS' WAR, a series of European wars, 1618–1648. Partly a Catholic-Protestant religious conflict, they were also a political and territorial struggle by different European powers, particularly France, against its greatest rivals the HAPSBURGS, rulers of the HOLY ROMAN EMPIRE. War began when BOHEMIAN Protestants revolted. They were defeated by TILLY (1620), who went on to subjugate the PALATINATE (1623). In 1625 Denmark, fearing Hapsburg power, invaded N Germany, but was defeated in 1629, when the emperor FERDINAND II issued the Edict of Restitution, restoring lands to the Roman Catholic Church. In 1630 the Swedish king GUSTAVUS ADOLPHUS led the Protestant German princes against Ferdinand. He was killed at LÜTZEN (1632), and by 1635 the Swedes had lost support in Germany, and the German states concluded the Peace of Prague. But now France, under RICHELIEU, intervened. Further wars ensued, with France, Sweden and the German Protestant states fighting in the Low Countries, Scandinavia, France, Germany, Spain and Italy against the Holy Roman Empire, Spain (another Hapsburg power) and Denmark. Peace negotiations, begun in 1640, were completed with the Peace of WESTPHALIA (1648).

THISBE. See PYRAMUS AND THISBE.

THISTLE, common name for many prickly, herbaceous plants of the family COMPOSITAE. They normally have purple or yellow flowers. When the seeds are ripe, they are dispersed as fluffy "thistledown." Thistles normally produce a thick taproot which can be eaten or used as a coffee substitute.

THO, Le Duc (1911–), member of the North Vietnamese Politburo who, with Henry KISSINGER, was awarded the Nobel Peace Prize in 1975 for negotiating the ceasefire (1973) ending the VIETNAM WAR. He refused the prize on the ground that peace in Vietnam had not in fact been achieved.

THOMAS, Saint, or Didymus (Greek: twin), one of the 12 APOSTLES, known as "Doubting Thomas" because he would not believe Christ's resurrection until he put his fingers in Christ's wounds. His subsequent career, and martyrdom at Madras, are recounted in the apocryphal *Acts of Thomas*.

THOMAS, (Charles Louis) Ambroise (1811–1896), French composer remembered chiefly for his operas *Mignon* (1866) and *Hamlet* (1868). He also wrote several cantatas, chamber music and choral works.

THOMAS, Dylan Marlais (1914–1953), Welsh poet who first achieved recognition with *Eighteen Poems* (1934). His prose includes the quasi-autobiographical *Portrait of the Artist as a Young Dog* (1940) and *Adventures in the Skin Trade* (1955); his poetry *Deaths and Entrances* (1946) and *Collected Poems* (1952). Perhaps his most famous work is *Under Milk Wood* (1954), originally a radio play.

THOMAS, George Henry (1816–1870), US Union general victorious at MILL SPRINGS (1862) and dubbed the "Rock of Chickamauga" for his stand at that battle (1863). His Army of the Cumberland destroyed HOOD's army at Nashville, Tenn. (1864).

THOMAS, Norman Mattoon (1884–1968), US socialist leader who ran six times for the presidency as a Socialist Party candidate. He helped found the American Civil Liberties Union (1920) and the League for Industrial Democracy (1922). An ardent pacifist, he tried to keep the US out of WWII. Many of his radical proposals eventually became law.

THOMAS, Seth (1785–1859), US pioneer of mass production of clocks. He built his first factory (1812) at Plymouth, Conn., in a district later named Thomaston.

THOMAS À BECKET, Saint. See BECKET, THOMAS À, SAINT.

THOMAS À KEMPIS (Thomas Hemerken von Kempen; c1380–1471), German religious writer and Augustinian friar at Zwolle in the Netherlands. He is famous as the probable author of *On The Imitation of Christ* which, for its gentle humanity, has had an influence among Roman Catholics second only to the Bible.

THOMAS AQUINAS, Saint. See AQUINAS, SAINT THOMAS.

THOMASTON, city of W central Ga., seat of Upson Co. It lies in an area of mixed agriculture. The chief manufacture is textiles. Pop 10024.

THOMASVILLE, city in S Ga., seat of Thomas Co. It is a marketing and processing center for a livestock, lumber and farming area. Pop 18155.

THOMASVILLE, city of W central N.C., 20mi SW of Greensboro, in a tobacco, corn and wheat area. Products include furniture, textiles and plastics. Pop 15230.

THOMISM, philosophical system of Thomas AQUINAS and his commentators, a synthesis of the thinking of ARISTOTLE and such early Church Fathers as AUGUSTINE. Long the official philosophical doctrine of the Roman Catholic Church, it has had a revival

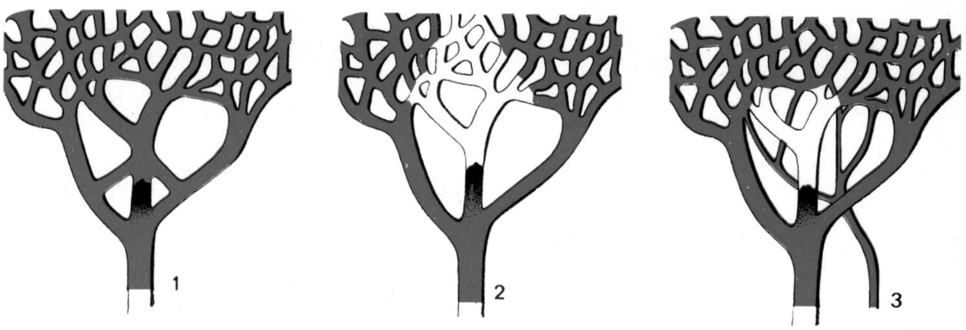

Thrombosis occurs when a bloodvessel, or the heart, is blocked by a blood clot. (1) A clot may not be immediately dangerous if the blood can easily pass through other vessels to supply tissue. (2) The tissue will die if the clot stops blood reaching it except through capillaries. (3) If the tissue is supplied by two arterial systems it will not necessarily die if one becomes blocked.

since the 1800s (as neo-Thomism). A central theme is the distinction between areas in which faith and reason should operate.

THOMPSON, town, N Manitoba, 130mi N of Lake Winnipeg. Founded in 1956, it has an integrated nickel mining-smelting-refining plant. Pop 19 000.

THOMPSON, Benjamin. See RUMFORD, COUNT.

THOMPSON, David (1770–1857), British fur-trader, explorer and geographer who headed (1816–26) a commission to survey the Canadian/US boundary. He worked for HUDSON'S BAY COMPANY 1784–97, then with the rival NORTH WEST COMPANY. He discovered (1798) Turtle Lake, a source of the Mississippi R and was first to travel the entire Columbia R (1811).

THOMPSON, Sir John Sparrow David (1844–1894), Canadian jurist and statesman. He was Nova Scotia's premier in 1882, federal minister of justice from 1885 and prime minister of Canada 1892–94.

THOMPSON, William Hale "Big Bill" (1869–1944), US politician noted for his anti-British tirades. As mayor of Chicago 1915–23 and 1927–31, he failed to take action to control Chicago's gangsters.

THOMSEN, Christian Jürgensen (1788–1865), Danish archaeologist who devised a three-part classification of prehistoric technologies (since applied also to contemporary primitive cultures): STONE AGE; BRONZE AGE, and IRON AGE.

THOMSON, Sir Charles Wyville. See CHALLENGER EXPEDITION.

THOMSON, Sir George Paget (1892–1975), British physicist awarded with C. DAVISSON the 1937 Nobel Prize for Physics for showing that ELECTRONS can be diffracted, thus demonstrating their wave nature.

THOMSON, James (1700–1748), British poet who wrote *Rule Britannia* (1740). He is otherwise best known for his blank-verse *The Seasons* (1726–30), a celebration of Nature.

THOMSON, Sir Joseph John (1856–1940), British physicist generally regarded as the discoverer of the ELECTRON. It had already been shown that CATHODE RAYS could be deflected by a MAGNETIC FIELD; in 1897 Thomson showed that they could also be deflected by an ELECTRIC FIELD, and could thus be regarded as a stream of negatively charged particles. He showed their mass to be much smaller than that of the HYDROGEN atom—this was the first discovery of a SUBATOMIC PARTICLE. His model of the ATOM, though imperfect, provided a good basis for RUTHERFORD'S more satisfactory later attempt. Thomson was awarded the 1906 Nobel Prize for Physics.

THOMSON, Virgil (1896–   ), US composer and music critic. Influenced by the SIX in Paris, he became a leading "Americanist." His works include operas, symphonies and instrumental, chamber and film music. He won a 1949 Pulitzer Prize for his *Louisiana Story* score.

THOMSON, William. See KELVIN, BARON.

THON BURI, part of BANGKOK–Thon Buri metropolis, Thailand, lies on the W bank of the Chao Phraya R. It was capital of Siam 1767–82. Pop 695 253.

THOR, Norse god, great god of thunder and provider of rain, subsidiary only to ODIN. The EDDAS recount his feats with Mjolnir, his magic hammer. Our name Thursday comes from "Thor's Day."

THORAX, the middle part of the body in INSECTS, lying between the head and the ABDOMEN and bearing the wings and legs. It houses many of the viscera and is equivalent to the mammalian CHEST region.

THOREAU, Henry David (1817–1862), US writer, philosopher and naturalist. He was taught TRANSCENDENTALISM by Ralph Waldo EMERSON. *Walden* (1854) records his life in harmony with nature at WALDEN POND, near Concord, Mass. A fierce opponent of slavery, Thoreau withheld poll tax in 1845 in protest, and defended the HARPERS FERRY raid in *A Plea for John Brown* (1859). His essay *Civil Disobedience* (1849) has influenced GANDHI, TOLSTOY and modern civil rights leaders with its defense of CIVIL DISOBEDIENCE against an unjust state.

THORFINN KARLSEFNI (11th century), Icelandic explorer who colonized North America. He sailed to Greenland, then (c1004) followed the route of Leif ERICSON to VINLAND, where he and 160 others attempted for two to three years to set up colonies.

THORIUM (Th), silvery-white radioactive metal, one of the ACTINIDES. Its chief ore is MONAZITE. Thorium is tetravalent, resembling ZIRCONIUM and HAFNIUM. The metal is used in magnesium ALLOYS and to produce uranium-233 for atomic fuel. The refractory thorium (IV) oxide was used to make incandescent gas mantles; it is added in small amounts to the tungsten filaments in electric lamps. AW 232.0, mp c1700°C, bp c4000°C, sg 11.66 (17°C).

THORNDIKE, Edward Lee (1874–1949), US psychologist whose system of psychology, **connectionism**, had a profound influence on US school education techniques, especially his discovery that the learning of one skill only slightly assists in the learning of another, even if related.

THORNTON, residential city of NE central Col. It is a N suburb of Denver. Pop 13 326.

THORNTON, William (1759–1828), US architect and inventor. Though without formal training, he won (1793) the competition to design the Capitol, Washington, D.C. His revised designs (1795) were used for the exteriors of the N and S wings.

THOROLD, industrial town of SE Ontario, Canada, on the Welland Ship Canal. Papermaking is the chief industry. Pop 15 052.

THOROUGH BASS. See FIGURED BASS.

THORPE, James Francis "Jim" (1888–1953), US all-around athlete, first man to win both decathlon and pentathlon at the Olympic Games (1912). He was named greatest US athlete and football player since 1900 in a 1950 Associated Press poll.

THORVALDSEN, Bertel (1768/1770–1844), Danish sculptor, an apostle of NEOCLASSICISM, and one of the most successful sculptors of the 19th century. The Thorvaldsen Museum, Copenhagen, houses many of his works.

THOTH, ancient Egyptian moon god, inventor of writing and patron of the arts and sciences. He was shown as, or with the head of, an ibis or baboon. The Greeks identified him with HERMES and hence with HERMES TRISMEGISTUS.

THOUSAND ISLANDS, group of over 1 500 islands, some Canadian, some US, in St. Lawrence R at the outlet of Lake Ontario. ST. LAWRENCE ISLANDS NATIONAL PARK includes 13 of them. Thousand Islands International Bridge (actually five bridges) is 8½mi long and carries traffic across the river.

THOUSAND OAKS, city in SW Cal., 30mi W of Los Angeles. It developed fast in the 1950s as a center of the aerospace industry. Pop 35 873.

THRACE, ancient region in the E Balkan Peninsula, SE Europe, bordering the Black and Aegean seas. It included modern NE Greece, S Bulgaria and European Turkey. The modern Thrace, an administrative region of Greece, comprises the SW parts of the old; while E Thrace constitutes European Turkey.

THRASHERS, medium-sized thrush-like birds of the Americas. Brown or gray-brown above and white below, with a long, often curved bill, thrashers are a subgroup of the MOCKINGBIRD family, Mimidae. They are ground-dwelling birds living in dense scrub in arid or semidesert regions.

THRASYBULUS (d. after 390 BC), a general of ancient Athens. He put down the Samos rising (411 BC) in the PELOPONNESIAN WAR. He was banished (404 BC) by the THIRTY TYRANTS, but returned (403 BC) and overthrew them, restoring democracy to Athens.

THREE KINGS. See MAGI.

THRESHER SHARKS, three large shark-like fishes of tropical and temperate seas, family Alopiidae, characterized by the enormous upper lobe of the tail which may be as long as the rest of the body. They thrash the water with this tail to concentrate shoals of fish before attacking them.

THRIPS, minute, slender-bodied insects of the order Thysanoptera. Most species are plant-feeders, often abundant inside flowers. Many are notorious pests including the Onion thrips and Grain thrips, *Thrips tabaci* and *Limothrips cerealium*.

THROMBIN, and **thromboplastin.** See CLOTTING.

THROMBOSIS, the formation of clot (thrombus) in the HEART OR BLOOD vessels. It commonly occurs in the legs and is associated with VARICOSE VEINS but is more serious if it occurs in the heart or in the brain arteries. Detachments from a thrombus in the legs may be carried to the lungs as an embolus (see EMBOLISM); this may have a fatal outcome if large vessels are occluded. The treatment includes ANTICOAGULANTS.

THRUSH, or **monilia** or **candidiasis,** mucous membrane infection with the fungus *Candida*, seen as multiple white spots, most often affecting the mouth or vagina. Patients with DIABETES OR KIDNEY failure and those on STEROIDS and/or ANTIBIOTICS are particularly at risk. Antifungal antibiotics are required.

THRUSHES, slender-billed song-birds of the subfamily Turdinae. The plumage is often gray or red-brown and many species have speckled or striated breasts. The tail is usually rounded or square and is held erect in some species. Birds of worldwide distribution, they feed largely on insects, worms and snails, but many species also take fruit and berries.

THRUST, in aerodynamics, the FORCE that propels an airplane or missile. The chemical energy converted in a rocket or jet engine exhausts a high-velocity gas stream whose MOMENTUM, according to Newton's third law of motion, produces the thrust force.

THUCYDIDES (c460–c400 BC), greatest Greek historian and first to probe the relationship between historical cause and effect. An Athenian naval commander exiled for his incompetence over the siege of Amphipolis (424 BC), he spent the rest of his life traveling, interviewing soldiers and writing his *History of the Peloponnesian War*, in which he stressed accuracy, objectivity and analysis of individual motivation.

THUGS, secret society of ritual murderers in India, dating back to the 1600s. Devotees of Kali, Hindu goddess of destruction, they traveled in gangs, strangling and robbing their victims. The last known Thug was hanged by the British in 1882.

THULE, in classical times, the northernmost land, perhaps Iceland. It is now the name of a settlement on Baffin Bay, NW Greenland, with a USAF base; and of a pre-European Eskimo culture.

THULIUM (Tm), least abundant of the RARE EARTHS; one of the LANTHANUM SERIES. AW 168.9, mp 1545°C, bp 1727°C, sg 9.321 (25°C).

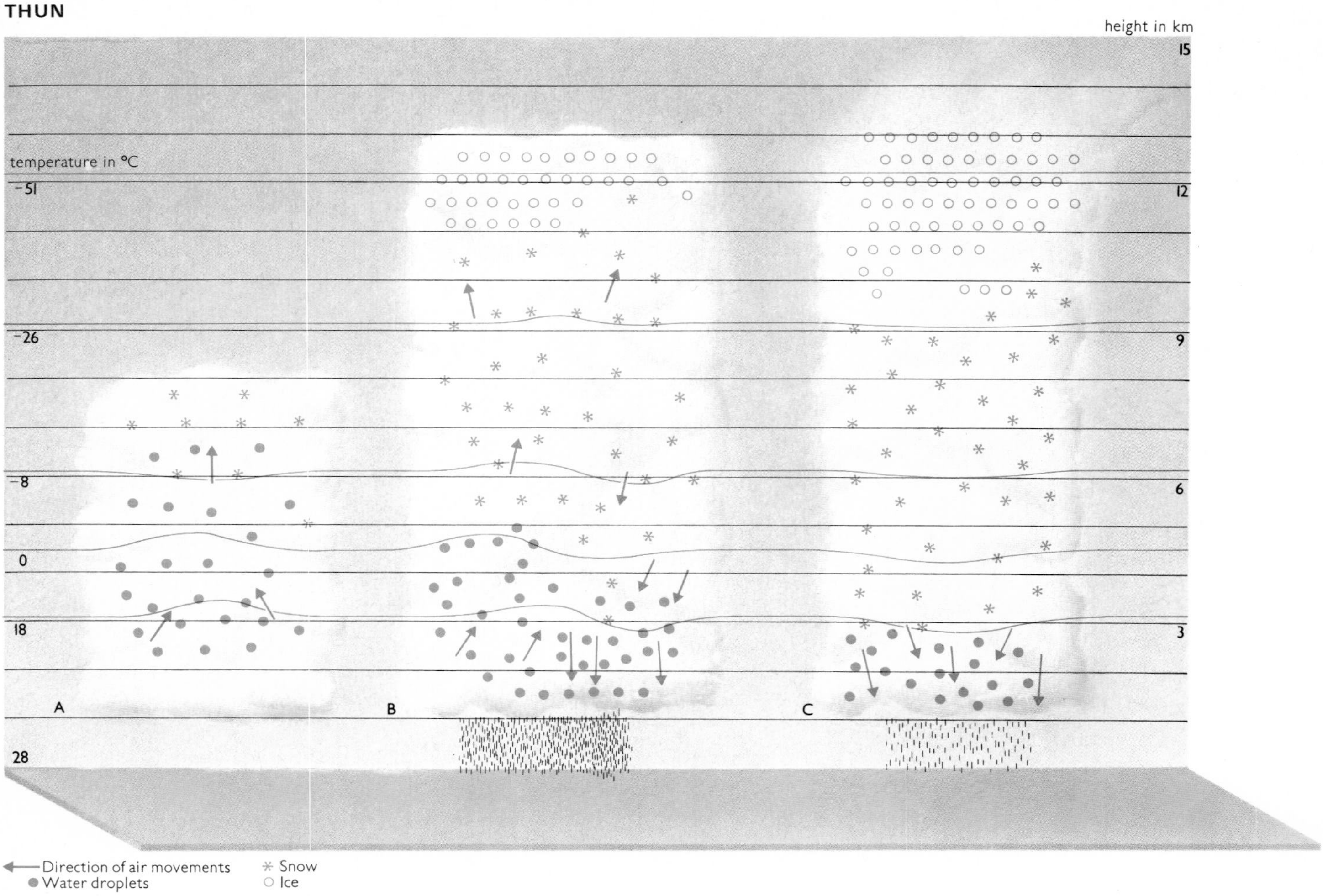

The development of a thunderstorm. (A) An updraft causes water droplets to be forced to heights of over 6mi (10km) resulting in the formation of ice and snow (B). Meanwhile compensating downdrafts force water droplets down to the surface as heavy rain. At a later stage (C), the cloud begins to dissipate as cool downdrafts produce light rain.

THUN, Lake of, in the Bernese Alps, central Switzerland, formed by the Aare R. Thun commune (pop 36 523), at the Aare's exit, is a tourist center.

THUNDER, the acoustic shock wave caused by the sudden expansion of air heated by a LIGHTNING discharge. Thunder may be a sudden clap, or a rumble lasting several seconds if the lightning path is long and thus varies in distance from the hearer. It is audible up to about 15km away; the distance in kilometres can be roughly estimated as one-third the time in seconds between the lightning and thunder.

THUNDER BAY, major port, city and seat of Thunder Bay district, Ontario, on the NW shore of Lake Superior. Created 1970 by merging Fort William and Port Arthur, it ships grain, minerals and lumber. Pop 108 411.

THUNDERSTORM, a STORM accompanied by THUNDER and LIGHTNING, heavy PRECIPITATION and SQUALLS. Usually short-lived, thunderstorms are generally associated with cumulonimbus CLOUDS.

THURBER, James Grover (1894–1961), US humorist and cartoonist. The sophisticated humor of his writing contrasts with the simplicity of his line drawings. Several stories, such as *The Secret Life of Walter Mitty* (1942), were filmed. He contributed to the *New Yorker* from 1927. His collections include *My Life and Hard Times* (1933) and *The Thurber Carnival* (1945).

THURMOND, (James) Strom (1902–), US politician, senator from S.C. since 1954. A hardline supporter of states' rights, he has opposed federal civil rights legislation and federal welfare schemes. He was S.C. governor 1947–51 and the 1948 States' Rights Democratic presidential candidate.

THURSDAY, fifth day of the week, named for THOR.

THURSTONE, Louis Leon (1887–1955), US psychologist whose application of the techniques of STATISTICS to the results of PSYCHOLOGICAL TESTS permitted their more accurate interpretation and demonstrated that a plurality of factors contributed to an individual's score.

THUTMOSE, name of four 18th-dynasty Egyptian pharaohs. **Thutmose I** (ruled c1525–1510 BC), enlarged the empire S into gold-rich Nubia and N to the Euphrates R. His was the first tomb built in the Valley of the Kings. **Thutmose II** (ruled c1510–c1490 BC), crushed a rebellion in Nubia. **Thutmose III** (ruled c1468–c1436 BC), was overshadowed by his father's wife HATSHEPSUT for 22 years until her death. A great soldier, he made Syria secure and extended Egypt's power in Asia. His many monuments (notably at KARNAK and HELIOPOLIS) include "Cleopatra's needles" (one now in New York, the other in London). **Thutmose IV** (ruled c1412–c1400 BC), made peace with the MITANNI in Syria and quelled a Nubian revolt. (See also EGYPT, ANCIENT.)

THYATIRA, ancient Greek city noted for purple dye, later one of the Seven Churches of Asia Minor. The Turkish town Akhisar occupies the site.

THYLACINE, *Thylacinus cynocephalus*, the Tasmanian or Marsupial Wolf, largest of the carnivorous marsupials. A tawny animal, about 1.7m (5.6ft) long, with 16–18 dark bars across its back, it is confined to Tasmania and may already be extinct.

THYME, perennial herbs of the genus *Thymus*, the aromatic leaves of which are used for seasoning and flavoring. Family: Labiatae.

THYMINE. See NUCLEIC ACIDS; NUCLEOTIDES.

THYMUS, a ductless two-lobed gland lying just behind the breast bone and mainly composed of lymphoid cells (see LYMPH). It plays a part in setting up the body's IMMUNITY system. Autoimmunity is thought to result from its pathological activity. After PUBERTY it declines in size.

THYROID GLAND, a ductless two-lobed gland lying in front of the trachea in the neck. The principal HORMONES secreted by the thyroid are thyroxine and triiodothyroxine; these play a crucial role in regulating the rate at which cells oxidize fuels to release ENERGY, and strongly influence growth. The release of thyroid hormones is controlled by thyroid stimulating hormone (TSH) released by the PITUITARY GLAND when blood thyroid-hormone levels are low. Deficiency of thyroid hormones (hypothyroidism) in adults leads to **myxedema**, with mental dullness and cool, dry and puffy skin. Oversecretion of thyroid hormones (hyperthyroidism or thyrotoxicosis) produces nervousness, weight loss and increased heart rate. GOITER, an enlargement of the gland, may result when the diet is deficient in iodine. (See also CRETINISM.)

TIAHUANACO, prehistoric empire of Peru and Bolivia in the pre-Incan period. Tiahuanaco ruins near the SE end of Lake Titicaca include monolithic statues, stylized carvings and a Temple of the Sun, dating from c1000 AD.

TIBER, river in central Italy, flowing 252mi from the Appenines S through Umbria and Latium and SW through Rome to the Tyrrhenian Sea near Ostia. Ancient ROME was built on its E bank.

TIBERIAS, Lake. See GALILEE, SEA OF.

TIBERIUS (42 BC–37 AD), or Tiberius Claudius Nero, second Roman emperor (from 14 AD). A general, he was adopted heir by AUGUSTUS. His reign, although generally peaceful, was often tyrannical, resulting in unrest in Rome.

TIBESTI MOUNTAINS, NW Chad, Africa, in the central Sahara region. The range is 300mi long. Emi Koussi (11 204ft) is the highest peak.

TIBET, autonomous region of China in central Asia, bordering Sinkiang Uighur; Tsinghai, Szechwan and Yunnan provinces; Burma; India; Nepal; Bhutan; and Sikkim. The 471 660sq mi of Tibet ("The Roof of the World") averages 16000ft in altitude. The Kunlun Mts. in the N are almost as high as the Himalayas, across the great Ch'iang T'ang plateau to the S. The Brahmaputra, Indus, Mekong and Yangtze rivers rise in Tibet.

Until the Chinese invasion (1950), Tibetans followed Buddhist LAMAISM, headed by the DALAI LAMA and the PANCHEN LAMA. There were many monasteries and 20% of the population were monks. The Chinese expropriated large estates and have greatly decreased emphasis on religion. The pastoral, livestock-based economy has been affected by roadbuilding and new cement, chemical, paper, textile and other industries. Tibet has deposits of coal and iron (exploited in the NE) and other minerals.

In 1956, China prepared to make Tibet an autonomous region. Rioting followed and, in 1959, a revolt which was suppressed. The Dalai Lama fled from the capital LHASA to India. Tibet became an autonomous region in 1965. There are thought to be some 500000 Chinese in the country in addition to some 1500000 Tibetans.

TIBETAN TERRIER, Tibetan herding dog, not in fact a terrier, looking rather like a miniature Old English Sheepdog. Height 15in and weight 30lb. It makes a good house and watchdog.

TIC, a stereotyped movement, habit spasm or vocalization which occurs irregularly, but often more under stress, and which is outside voluntary control. Its cause is unknown. **Tic dolouroux** is a condition in which part of the FACE is abnormally sensitive, any TOUCH provoking intense PAIN.

TICKS, a group of parasitic arthropods, with the MITES members of the order Acarina. Unlike most other arthropods, there is no head and the THORAX and ABDOMEN are fused. All ticks are blood-sucking external parasites of vertebrates. They are divided into two main families: the soft ticks, Argasidae, and hard ticks, Ixodidae. Ticks transmit more diseases to man and domestic animals than any other arthropod group except the mosquitoes.

TICONDEROGA, by Lake George, NE N.Y., village and site of Fort Ticonderoga, which commanded the route between Canada and the Hudson R valley. Taken (1759) by the British in the FRENCH AND INDIAN WARS, it fell (1775) in the Revolutionary War to the GREEN MOUNTAIN BOYS led by Ethan ALLEN and Benedict ARNOLD. It was recaptured (1777) by General BURGOYNE. The fort is now a museum.

TIDAL POWER, form of HYDROELECTRICITY produced by harnessing the ebb and flow of the TIDES. Barriers containing reversible TURBINES are built across an estuary or gulf where the tidal range is great. The Rance power plant in the Gulf of St. Malo, Brittany, the first to be built (1961–67), produces 240MW power, mostly at ebb tide.

TIDAL WAVE, obsolete term for TSUNAMI.

TIDES, the periodic rise and fall of land and water on the earth. Tidal motions are primarily exhibited by water: the motion of the land is barely detectable. As the earth-moon system rotates about its center of gravity, which is within the earth, the earth bulges in the direction of the moon and in the exactly opposite direction, owing to the resultant of the moon's gravitational attraction and the centrifugal forces resulting from the system's revolution. Toward the moon, the lunar attraction is added to a comparatively small centrifugal force; in the opposite direction it is subtracted from a much larger centrifugal force. As the moon orbits the earth in the same direction as the earth rotates, the bulge "travels" round the earth each lunar day (24.83h); hence most points on the earth have a high tide every 12.42h. The sun produces a similar though smaller tidal effect. Exceptionally high high tides occur at full and new moon (spring tides), particularly if the moon is at perigee (see ORBIT); exceptionally low high tides (neap tides) at first and third quarter. The friction of the tides causes the DAY to lengthen 0.001s per century.

TIDEWATER, the Atlantic coastal plain in E Va. It is crossed by several rivers. Here in the 1600s and 1700s large tobacco and later cotton plantations were established in what became the heart of "aristocratic" antebellum Virginia.

TIEN SHAN, great mountain system of Soviet central Asia and W China. It curves E from the NE PAMIRS for 1500mi and covers some 70000sq mi. Pobeda Peak (24406ft) is the range's highest.

TIENTSIN, capital of Hopei province, N China, on the Hai R 80mi SE of Peking. It is a great industrial center and sea, river and canal port with major steel, chemical and textile industries. There are three universities. Pop 4500000.

TIEPOLO, Giovanni Battista (1696–1770), great Venetian painter. Influenced initially by VERONESE, he developed his own colorful, airy but exuberant style in frescoes and ceilings in N Italy, Würzburg palace (Germany) and the royal palace in Madrid.

TIERRA DEL FUEGO, island group off S South America. Discovered (1520) by MAGELLAN and now divided between Chile and Argentina, its sparsely populated 28000sq mi comprise one large and many small islands. Sheep and oil are the economic mainstays.

TIFFANY, Louis Comfort (1848–1933), US artist and designer, a leader of ART NOUVEAU. Son of jeweler Charles Tiffany, he created decorative objects of iridescent "favrile" or Tiffany glass.

TIFFIN, city of N Ohio, seat of Seneca Co., on the Sandusky R. Its manufactures include machinery, wire and pottery. Pop 21596.

TIFLIS. See TBILISI.

TIFTON, city in S Ga., seat of Tift Co. 40mi ESE of Albany. It is an agricultural trading center with light industries. Pop 12179.

TIGER, *Panthera tigris*, the major CAT of Asia, with distinct races in different parts of that continent. Closely related to LIONS, they are the largest of all the cats, with a tawny coat broken with dark, vertical stripes providing excellent camouflage against natural patterns of light and shade. Tigers do not chase after food but prefer to stalk and spring. For the most part they are solitary animals, hunting in the cool of the day and otherwise lying up in the shade to rest.

TIGLATH-PILESER, three kings of Assyria. **Tiglath-Pileser I** (reigned 1116–1078 BC), extended Assyrian territory into Phoenicia, Anatolia and modern Syria and captured Babylon. Little is known of **Tiglath-Pileser II** (956–934 BC). **Tiglath-Pileser III** (reigned 745–727 BC), reversed the decline of Assyrian power by administrative reform and by conquering Israel and the Philistines, Gaza, Damascus and Babylon, where he proclaimed himself King Pulu. (See BABYLONIA AND ASSYRIA.)

TIGRIS RIVER, easternmost of the two great rivers of ancient Mesopotamia. The Tigris-Euphrates valley was the cradle of Middle-East civilizations (see BABYLONIA; NINEVEH; SUMER). Baghdad, city of the ABBASIDS, now capital of Iraq, stands on its banks. It rises in the Taurus Mts. in Turkey and flows 1150mi SE through Iraq to the Euphrates at Al Qurnah.

TIJUANA, city in Baja California state, NW Mexico, entry point and resort for US tourists. It has electronics and textiles industries. Pop 354805.

TIKAL, largest Mayan city, in the Petén jungle, NW Guatemala. The ruined plazas, pyramids, palaces and steles indicate its great cultural and ceremonial importance. Tikal flourished about 300 BC–800 AD and was at its greatest in the 600s.

TILDEN, Samuel Jones (1814–1886), US lawyer and politician. An early leader of the BARNBURNERS and FREE SOIL movements, he proved corruption among New York City politicians led by William TWEED. Governor of N.Y. 1875–76, he lost the hotly contested 1876 presidential election to Republican Rutherford B. HAYES by one electoral vote.

TILDEN, William (Bill) Tatem, II (1893–1953), US tennis champion. From 1920 to 1930 he was the top-ranked US player, winning US, Wimbledon singles (first American to do so) and Davis Cup titles. He turned professional in 1931.

TILE, thin slab of TERRA COTTA or other kinds of POTTERY AND PORCELAIN, used in building to cover surfaces. Roof tiles are commonly unglazed and functional; they are either flat, hooked over roof battens, or curved (often S-shaped) and cemented. Floor and structural tiles are hard and vitreous. Wall tiles, used from ancient times, are often decorated with bas-relief molding, painting and glazing. Seventeenth-century Delft tiles are famous. Plain glazed wall tiles are now commonly used in bathrooms etc. By analogy, squares of linoleum, vinyl polymers and cork are also called tiles.

TILEFISH, *Lopholatilus chamaelonticeps*, a large slender fish related to Sea PERCHES, first discovered in 1879 in the GULF STREAM waters of New England. Three years later the course of the Gulf Stream altered in gales and an influx of colder waters killed off the tilefishes in their millions. They are now believed to be building up their numbers again.

TILL, or **boulder clay**, the unsorted material left behind on the land after the retreat of a GLACIER. (See also DRIFT; DRUMLIN; MORAINE.)

TILLICH, Paul Johannes (1886–1965), German-born theologian and teacher. He attempted to synthesize Christianity and classical and modern existentialist philosophy in such works as *Systematic Theology* (1951–63) and the shorter, more popular *The Shaking of the Foundations* (1948) and *The Courage to Be*

Detail of a ceiling fresco by Tiepolo. Executed in the Residenz (palace of the Prince-Bishop) at Würzburg 1750–53, the fresco allegorically represents the continents of Europe (shown here), Asia, Africa and America. The use of color and lack of deep shadow are typical of the artist's style.

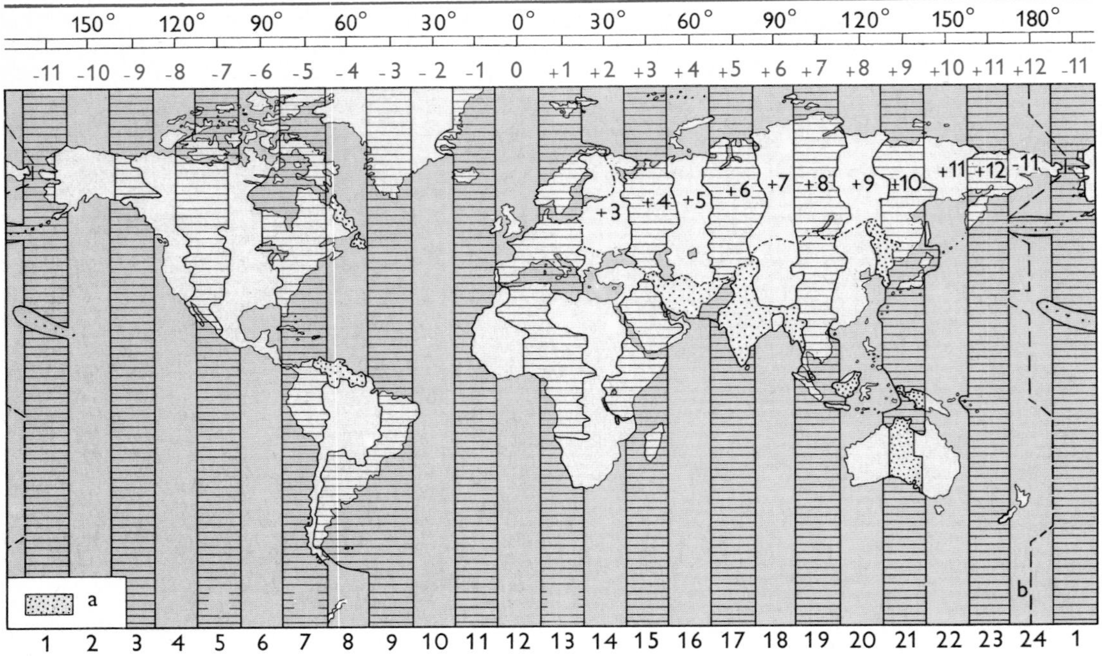

The time zones of the world, with degrees of longitude at top. The second line of numbers indicates the number of hours a given time zone is ahead of (+) or behind (−) Greenwich Mean Time (G.M.T.). In the Soviet Union local time is one hour later than sun time. Also shown are countries with local times differing by half an hour from sun time (*dotted areas, a*), and the International Dateline (*broken line, b*).

(1952). Dismissed from Frankfurt U. by the Nazis, he taught at New York, Harvard and Chicago.

TILLITE. See CONGLOMERATE.

TILLMAN, Benjamin Ryan (1847–1918), US politician, spokesman of the white rural South. "Pitchfork Ben" was S.C. governor (1890–94) and senator (1895–1918). He helped agrarians gain control of the Democratic Party (1896) but accomplished little for the Southern farmer.

TILLY, Johann Tserclaes, Count of (1559–1632), Bavarian general, commander (from 1618) of the Catholic League and (from 1630) of Imperial forces in the THIRTY YEARS' WAR. After several victories over the Protestants, he was defeated at Breitenfeld, Saxony (1631).

TIMBER. See FORESTRY; LUMBER.

TIMBUKTU, or Tombouctou, trading town and ancient city in central Mali, W Africa, near the Niger R. It was a wealthy trading and Muslim cultural center in the MALI EMPIRE (1300s) and under the SONGHAI (1400–1500s). Pop 10445.

TIME, a concept dealing with the order and duration of events. If two events occur nonsimultaneously at a point, they occur in a definite order with a time lapse between them. Two intervals of time are equal if a body in equilibrium moves over equal distances in each of them; such a body constitutes a clock. The sun provided man's earliest clock, the natural time interval being that between successive passages of the sun over the local meridian—the solar DAY. For many centuries the rotation of the earth provided a standard for time measurements, but in 1967 the SI UNIT of time, the SECOND was redefined in terms of the frequency associated with a cesium energy-level transition. In everyday life, we can still think of time in the way Newton did, ascribing a single universal time-order to events. We can neglect the very short time needed for light signals to reach us, and believe that all events have a unique chronological order. But when velocities close to that of light are involved, relativistic principles become important; simultaneity is no longer universal and the time scale in a moving framework is "dilated" with respect to one at rest—moving clocks appear to run slow (see RELATIVITY).

TIME-AND-MOTION STUDY, analysis of how a worker performs a given task, by study of his movements, methods and equipment. Changes can be made by laying out the job differently or adding labor-saving tools. F. W. TAYLOR was a pioneer in time-and-motion study. (See HUMAN ENGINEERING; LINEAR PROGRAMMING.)

TIMGAD (ancient Thamugadi), Roman city in NE Algeria 17mi SE of Batna, founded (100 AD) by Trajan, sacked by Berbers in 534. The extensive ruins include a triumphal arch and baths with mosaics.

TIMMINS, town in E Ontario. Center of a formerly gold-rich region, it has zinc-mining, lumber, brewing and tourist industries. Pop 28252.

TIMOR, largest and easternmost of the Lesser SUNDA ISLANDS, 400mi NW of Australia. Since Dec. 1975, when the former Portugese (eastern) Timor was occupied by Indonesian troops, the whole island has been under Indonesian control.

TIMOTHY, Saint, one of St. PAUL's companions, said to have been bishop of Ephesus after Paul. He was recipient of two of Paul's epistles (1 and 2 Timothy), which emphasize moral discipline and obedience to civil and religious authority.

TIMPANI, kettledrums, first used in orchestral music in the 1600s, having a calfskin head over a hollow brass or copper hemisphere. A set of timpani has usually three drums. Pitch is governed by the tension of the head; tone by the type of stick and by the region of the head struck.

TIMPANOGOS CAVE NATIONAL MONUMENT, 250-acre monument established 1922 in N central Utah, 25mi SW of Salt Lake City. Its limestone caves contain hundreds of colorful stalactites and stalagmites.

TIN (Sn), silvery-white metal in Group IVA of the PERIODIC TABLE, occurring as CASSITERITE in SE Asia, Bolivia, Zaire and Nigeria. The ore is reduced by smelting with coal. Tin exhibits ALLOTROPY: white (β) tin, the normal form, changes below 13.2°C to gray (α) tin, a powdery metalloid form resembling GERMANIUM, and known as "tin pest." Tin is unreactive, but dissolves in concentrated acids and alkalis, and is attacked by HALOGENS. It is used as a protective coating for steel, and in alloys including solder (see SOLDERING), BRONZE, PEWTER, BABBITT METAL and type metal. AW 118.7, mp 232°C, bp 2270°C, sg (β) 7.31. Tin forms organotin compounds, used as biocides, and also inorganic compounds: tin (II) and tin (IV) salts. **Tin (IV) Oxide** (SnO_2), white powder prepared by calcining CASSITERITE or burning finely divided tin; used in glazes and as an abrasive. subl 1800°C. **Tin (II) Chloride** ($SnCl_2$), white crystalline solid, prepared by dissolving tin in hydrochloric acid, used as a reducing agent, in tin-plating, and as a mordant for dyes. mp 246°C, bp 652°C.

TINAMOUS, 50 species of running birds of tropical South America. The body is compact and guineafowl-like. They fly weakly, preferring to run on their strong legs. They feed on organic material picked off the ground, using their long decurved bill.

TINBERGEN, Jan (1903–), Dutch economist who shared the first (1969) Nobel economics prize with Ragnar FRISCH for work in developing dynamic models (see ECONOMETRICS).

TINBERGEN, Nikolaas (1907–), Dutch ethologist awarded with K. LORENZ and K. von FRISCH the 1973 Nobel Prize for Physiology or Medicine for their individual, major contributions to the science of ANIMAL BEHAVIOR.

TINGUELY, Jean (1925–), Swiss sculptor best known for his *métamécaniques*, machine-like forms of KINETIC ART. Some themselves produce paintings.

TINIAN, one of the S MARIANA ISLANDS in the W Pacific Ocean N of Guam.

TINLEY PARK, village in NE Ill., a suburb of Chicago. Pop 12382.

TINTORETTO (Jacopo Robusti; 1518–1594), Venetian MANNERIST painter. His paintings and FRESCOES are characterized by free brushwork, dramatic viewpoint, movement, monumental figures and rich colors. He sought to express drama through color and light, as in the Scuola di S. Rocco *Life of Christ* (1564–87).

TIPPECANOE, Battle of (Nov. 7, 1811), between TECUMSEH's Shawnees, led by TENSKWATAWA, and US troops led by William HARRISON, near the Tippecanoe R, Ind. There were heavy casualties on both sides, but the "great victory" helped Harrison to the presidency in 1840. (See INDIAN WARS.)

TIRANË, or Tirana, capital of Albania, on a fertile plain 20mi E of Durrës, its port. Founded in the 1600s, it has a 75% Muslim population and is Albania's cultural and economic center. Pop 169300.

TIRE, ring-shaped cushion fitted onto a wheel rim as a shock absorber and to provide traction. The pneumatic tire (filled with compressed air) was patented in 1845 by R. W. Thomson, an English engineer, who used a leather tread and a rubber inner tube. Solid rubber tires were more popular, however, until the pneumatic tire was reinvented by John Boyd DUNLOP (1888), whose outer tube was of canvas covered by vulcanized rubber. The modern tubeless tire (without inner tube) dates from the 1950s. The basic structure of a tire comprises layers (plies) of rubberized fabric (usually polyester cord). The plies are combined with "beads"—inner circular wire reinforcements—and the outer tread and sidewalls on a tire-building drum. The tire is then shaped and vulcanized (see VULCANIZATION) in a heated mold under pressure, acquiring its tread design. Three types of tire are made: the bias-ply tire has the plies with cords running diagonally, alternately in opposite directions; the bias-belted tire is similar, with fiberglass belts between plies and tread; the radial-ply tire has the cords running parallel to the axle, and steel-mesh belts.

TIRESIAS, legendary prophet of Thebes, punished with blindness by the gods, but compensated with the gift of prophecy and long life.

TIROL, a state in W Austria. Over half its original area was ceded to Italy in 1919 (see ALTO–ADIGE). The Tirol is a beautiful mountainous land and contains Austria's highest peak, Grossglockner (12 461ft). Farming, lumber and tourism are its main activities. The capital is Innsbruck.

TIRPITZ, Alfred von (1849–1930), German admiral. As navy secretary (1897–1916) he built up the battle fleet to rival the British navy, precipitating an Anglo-German arms race. In WWI his fleet proved to be relatively useless.

TIRSO DE MOLINA (Gabriel Téllez; c1584–1648), Spanish dramatist and friar. His historical, cloak-and-sword and religious works are notable for insight into character. His *Seducer of Seville* (1630) introduced DON JUAN to the stage.

TIRUCHCHIRAPPALLI, industrial city in Tamil Nadu state, S India, 200mi SSW of Madras. Pop 306 247.

TIRYNS, prehistoric Greek city, on the Gulf of Argos, E Peloponnesus. Founded c3000 BC, it was a center of late Helladic or Mycenean civilization until destroyed by neighboring ARGOS (c468 BC). The massive citadel gave CYCLOPEAN ARCHITECTURE its name. (See AEGEAN CIVILIZATION.)

TISELIUS, Arne Wilhelm Kaurin (1902–1971), Swedish chemist awarded the 1948 Nobel Prize for Chemistry for his development of new techniques and equipment in order to apply ELECTROPHORESIS to the study of PROTEINS, notably those of the BLOOD.

TISHAH BE-AV, Jewish fast day, the ninth day of the month of Av, marking destruction of the first (587 BC) and second (70 AD) TEMPLES of Jerusalem.

TISSUES, similar CELLS grouped together in certain areas of the body of multicellular ANIMALS and PLANTS. These cells are usually specialized for a single function; thus MUSCLE cells contract but do not secrete; nerve cells conduct impulses but have little or no powers of contraction. The cells are held together by intercellular material such as COLLAGEN. Having become specialized for a single or at most a very narrow range of functions, they are dependent upon other parts of the organism for items such as food or oxygen. Groups of tissues, each with its own functions, make up ORGANS. **Connective tissue** refers to the material in which all the specialized body organs are embedded and supported. It includes ADIPOSE TISSUE and the material of LIGAMENTS and TENDONS. (See also HISTOLOGY.)

TITANIC, 46 328-ton British liner which sank in 1912 after hitting an iceberg on her maiden voyage to New York. At least 1 500 of the 2 200 aboard drowned. After the disaster (caused mainly by excessive speed), lifeboat, radio watch and ice patrol provisions were improved.

TITANIUM (Ti), silvery gray metal in Group IVB of the PERIODIC TABLE; a TRANSITION ELEMENT. Titanium occurs in RUTILE and in ILMENITE, from which it is extracted by conversion to titanium (IV) chloride and reduction by magnesium. The metal and its alloys are strong, light, and corrosion- and temperature-resistant, and, although expensive, are used for construction in the aerospace industry. Titanium is moderately reactive, forming tetravalent compounds, including titanates (TiO_3^{2-}), and less stable di- and trivalent compounds. **Titanium (IV) oxide** (TiO_2) is used as a white pigment in paints, ceramics, etc. **Titanium (IV) chloride** ($TiCl_4$) finds use as a catalyst. AW 47.9, mp 1660°C, bp 3287°C, sg 4.54.

TITANOTHERES, an extinct group of North American mammals closely related to HORSES and derived from forms related to Hyracotherium, the ancestor of modern horses. Animals of the Eocene, they were of great size, up to 2.5m (8.2ft) at the shoulder, many later forms bearing large horns or antlers on the forehead.

TITANS, in Greek myth, the children of URANUS (Heaven) and GAEA (Earth), including CRONUS, Coeus, HYPERION, OCEANUS and IAPETUS, all of great strength and height. Cronus overthrew Uranus and swallowed his own children—one, ZEUS, escaped. He and the other Olympians rebelled and defeated the Titans.

TITCHENER, Edward Bradford (1867–1927), British-born US psychologist, a disciple of WUNDT, who played a large part in establishing experimental PSYCHOLOGY in the US, especially through his *Experimental Psychology* (4 vols., 1901–05).

TITHE (Anglo-Saxon: tenth part), a church tax of one tenth of income or annual produce. Tithes, mentioned in the Bible, were adopted by the Western Church from the 6th century as a means of supporting priests, poor and churches.

TITIAN (c1480/90–1576), Venetian painter, leading Renaissance artist. Born Tiziano Vecellio, he worked for BELLINI and GIORGIONE, who influenced his early work. He became Venice's official painter 1516. His perceptive portraits, monumental altarpieces, historical and mythological scenes, are famous for their energetic composition, use of rich color and original technique.

TITICACA, Lake, on the Peru-Bolivia border in the Andes Mts. About 120mi long, it is the largest lake in South America (3 200sq mi) and the world's highest navigable lake (12 500ft). It was the center of the TIAHUANACO civilization.

TITMICE, or **Tits**, small insectivorous birds of the family Paridae, distributed throughout North America, Europe, Asia and Africa. All are small, weighing less than 20g (0.7oz). (See also CHICKADEES.)

TITO (Josip Broz; 1892–   ), communist president of YUGOSLAVIA (1953–   ), founder of the post-WWII republic. He became a communist while a WWI prisoner of war in Russia and later spent several years in Yugoslav jails. General secretary of the Communist Party from 1937, Tito organized partisan resistance to the Nazis in WWII, eclipsing the CHETNIKS, and after the war established a socialist republic. Tito broke with STALIN in 1948. He suppressed home opposition, while working for workers' self-management and reconciliation of national minorities. Recent years have seen a substantial liberalization of his policies.

TITRATION, common technique of VOLUMETRIC ANALYSIS in which a standard solution of one reagent is added little by little from a BURETTE to a second reagent whose amount is to be determined. The end point, at which an exactly equivalent amount of reagent has been added, may be determined by using an INDICATOR, or by measurements of color, resistance, current flow or potential, whose variation with added reagent changes abruptly when the end point is reached.

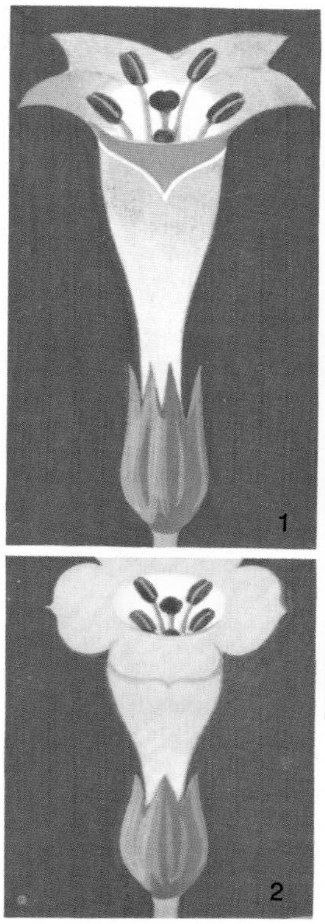

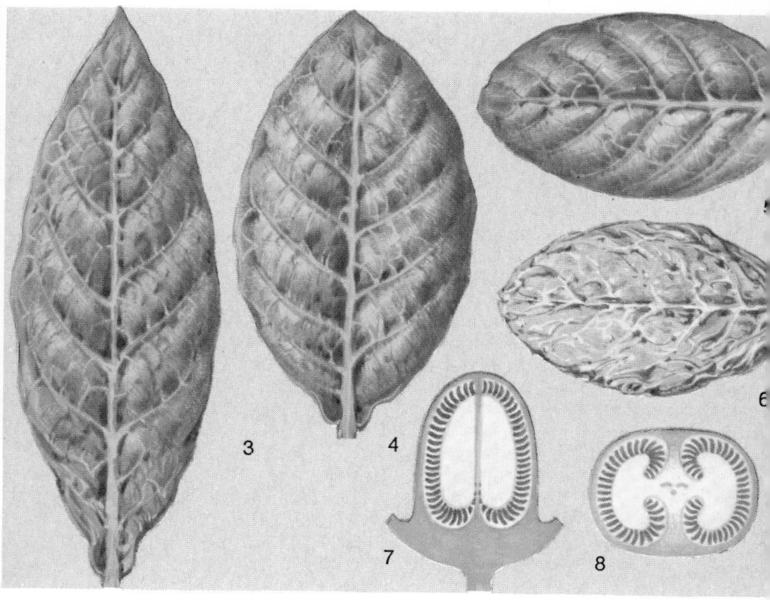

The dried and cured leaves of the tobacco plant, *Nicotiana tabacum* are used in snuff and smoking or chewing tobacco. Shown here are the flower of the Virginia variety (1); the flower of wild tobacco, *Nicotiana rustica* (2); a Virginia leaf (3); a *rustica* leaf (4); a leaf of Turkish tobacco (5); the same leaf after sun-curing (6); a vertical section of the fruit (7); and a horizontal section, showing the seed arrangement (8).

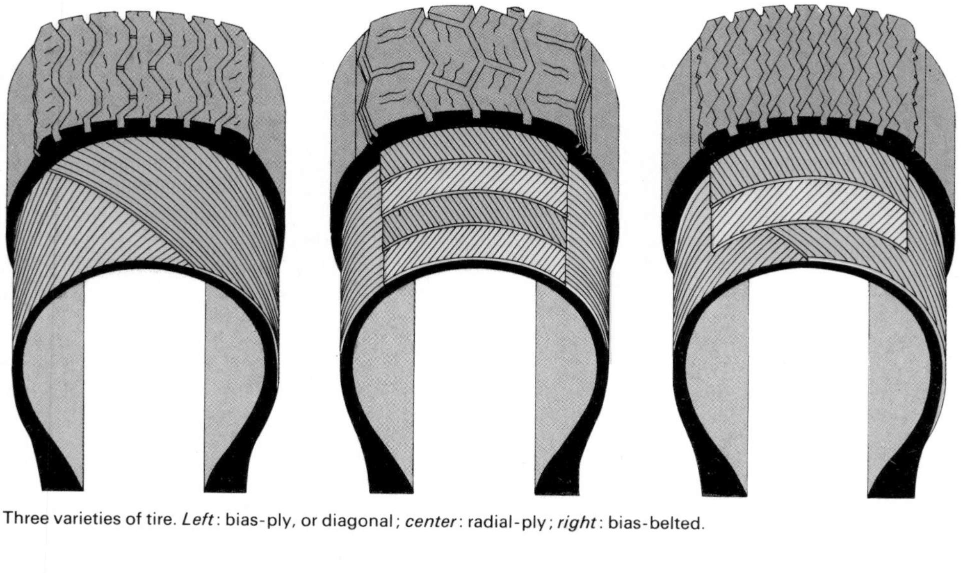

Three varieties of tire. *Left*: bias-ply, or diagonal; *center*: radial-ply; *right*: bias-belted.

TITUS, Saint, early Christian missionary, traditionally first bishop of Crete. He was St. PAUL's envoy to Corinth and Crete, and the recipient of St. Paul's *Epistle to Titus*, which describes the duties of elders and others.

TITUS (Flavius Sabinus Vespasianus) (39–81 AD), Roman emperor, successor (79) to his father VESPASIANUS. A successful soldier, he captured (70) Jerusalem in the Jewish revolt (66–70). Berenice, sister of HEROD Agrippa II, became his mistress. He was popular for lavish entertaining, and aid to victims of VESUVIUS (79) and of the fire at Rome (80).

TITUSVILLE, city in E Fla., seat of Brevaro Co. A citrus fruit shipping and tourist center, it also services Kennedy Space Center. Pop 30 515.

TITUSVILLE, industrial city in NW Penn., 40mi SE of Erie, where the world's first working oilwell was drilled (1859) by E. L. DRAKE. Pop 7 331.

TIVERTON, town in SE R.I. near the Sakonnet R, in a farm and resort region. Pop 12 559.

TIW (Norse: Tyr), ancient Germanic god associated with war, later identified with MARS, Roman god of war. The Roman Mars' day became in Germanic languages Tiw's day, or Tuesday.

TLAXCALA, smallest state of Mexico, with an economy based on cereals and the weaving of wool. Tlaxcala Indians aided CORTÉS, who established (1521) the Americas' oldest church in the capital, Tlaxcala.

TLINGIT INDIANS, largest group of North American INDIANS of the NW coast, now living in SE Alaska and numbering about 7 000. They belong to the Koluschan linguistic family and resemble HAIDA Indians in their complex social organization. Many still live by fishing, woodcarving, basketry and weaving. (See also ALASKA.)

TNT, or **trinitrotoluene**, pale yellow crystalline solid made by NITRATION of TOLUENE. It is the most extensively used high EXPLOSIVE, being relatively insensitive to shock, especially when melted by steam heating and cast. MW 227.1, mp 82°C.

TOADFISHES, sluggish, heavily-built, bottom-living fishes of tropical seas, family Batrachidae. They have broad, slightly flattened heads and their skin is virtually scale-less. Many have poisonous spines on the gill cover and in the dorsal fin.

TOADS, name strictly referring only to members of the family Bufonidae, but as the terms "frog" and "toad" are the only common names available for all the 2 000 species of tailless amphibians, "frog" is used for those which have smooth skins and live in or near water, and "toad" for all those with warty skins and living in drier areas. Toads are independent of water except for breeding, the larvae—TADPOLES—being purely aquatic. Most toads feed nocturnally on small animals.

TOBACCO, dried and cured leaves of varieties of the tobacco plant (*Nicotiana tabacum*), used for smoking, chewing and as SNUFF. Native to America, tobacco was introduced to Europe by the Spanish in the 16th century and from there spread to Asia and Africa. Today the US remains the world's largest producer, followed by China, India and the USSR. Consumption is increasing despite the health hazards of SMOKING. Tobacco is grown in alluvial or sandy soils and may be harvested in about four months. Cultivation is dependant on hand labor. Family: Solanaceae.

TOBACCO MOSAIC, VIRUS disease of plants, strains of which affect TOBACCO, TOMATOES, beans and many decorative plants. It restricts growth and causes the leaves to develop a mottled or mosaic pattern. Apart from avoiding infection, no cure has been found for this the most studied of all viruses, having been the first virus to be isolated and the first to be purified. (See also PLANT DISEASES.)

TOBAGO. See TRINIDAD AND TOBAGO.

TOBEY, Mark (1890–1976), US painter, strongly influenced by Chinese calligraphy and Zen Buddhism. He developed his "white writing" style in the 1930s in small abstracts representing street scenes. His later, delicately colored abstracts have more intricate linear rhythms.

TOBIT (Tobias), Book of, in the APOCRYPHA, recounts how Tobias, son of the devout but blinded Jew Tobit, (or Tobias), successfully undertakes a dangerous journey, helped by Angel RAPHAEL, to exorcise a demon from, and marry, Sara. He then helps Tobit regain his sight.

TOBOGGANING, winter sport of riding flat runnerless sleds (toboggans) with curved endpieces down slopes at up to 60mph. Toboggans are of American Indian origin. Today they are 4–9ft long by 18in wide, made of wood or metal. (See also BOBSLED.)

TOBRUK, or Tubruq, Mediterranean city-port, E Libya. Developed as a naval base by the Italians, it was captured (1941) in WWII by British forces, fell to ROMMEL (1942) and was retaken the same year. Pop 28 000.

TOCANINS RIVER, rises in S central Goiás, E central Brazil, and flows N, 1 680mi into the Pará R, 60mi SW of Bolém.

TOCCATA (Italian *toccare*: touch), composition for keyboard instrument, in which fast *toccata* runs alternate with full chords, often with a FUGUE section. Composers using the form, which originated in the 1500s, include BUXTEHUDE and J. S. BACH.

TOCOPHEROL, or Vitamin E. See VITAMINS.

TOCQUEVILLE, Alexis (Charles Henri Clérel) de (1805–1859), French historian famous for his analysis of the strengths and drawbacks of democracy. He discussed his observations in the US in *Democracy in America* (1835–40). He was impressed but foresaw a threat to individual liberty in the "tyranny of the majority," a theme developed in *The Old Regime and the French Revolution* (1856). A moderate liberal politician, he was French foreign minister in 1849.

TODD, Alexander Robertus, Baron Todd of Trumpington (1907–   ), British organic chemist awarded the 1957 Nobel Prize for Chemistry for his work on the structure and synthesis of NUCLEOTIDES.

TOGA, outer garment of freeborn citizens of ancient Rome, wrapped twice around the body and falling in folds. The adult male toga was plain white; boys and, later, magistrates wore one with a purple border; the emperor and triumphant generals wore an embroidered purple toga.

TOGLIATTI, Palmiro (1893–1964), Italian Communist Party leader (1926–64). He cofounded the party, now West Europe's largest, in 1921, became COMINTERN secretary (1935) and returned from exile (1944) to serve in several governments.

TOGO, West African republic, a 70mi-wide strip extending 340mi N from the Gulf of Guinea between Ghana and Dahomey. From the central Togo Mts. a grassy plateau slopes E to the Mono R and S to the sandy coastal plain. The N is savanna country. The climate is hot and humid, averaging 81°F, with yearly rainfall of 40–70in. The economy is agricultural: chief exports are cacao and coffee, but cassava, corn and cotton are also important. Large phosphate deposits are worked NE of the seaport capital LOMÉ. Over 90% of the people live in rural areas, mostly in the S. The population is made up almost entirely of African Negroes from the Ewe, Ouatchi, Mina, Kabre and other ethnic groups. French is the official language, Ewe the most widely used.

Official name: Republic of Togo
Capital: Lomé
Area: 21 853sq mi
Population: 2 022 000
Languages: French; tribal languages
Religions: Animist; Christian, Muslim
Monetary unit(s): 1 CFA franc = 100 centimes

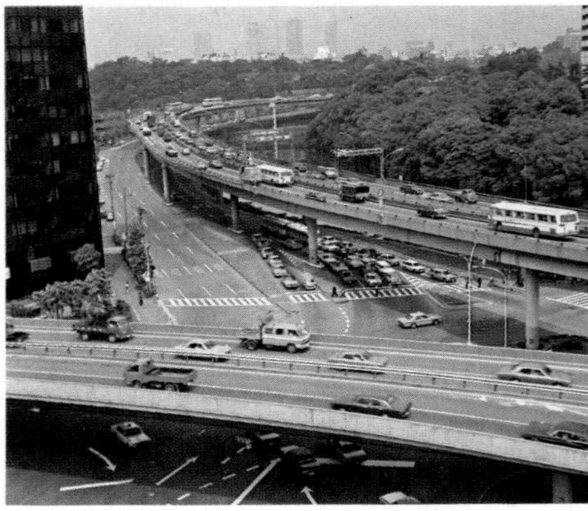

Intersection in Tokyo, during a comparatively quiet period. The influence of the West upon Japan is apparent in the city's congested traffic.

Formerly the E part of the German protectorate of Togoland, the area was administered by France after WWI and became independent in 1960. Since a military coup in 1967 it has been ruled by Étienne Eyadéma, who suspended the constitution and dissolved the legislative body.

TOGO, Heihachiro, Marquis (1847–1934), Japanese admiral and commander in chief of the Japanese navy in the RUSSO-JAPANESE WAR (1904–05). His ships successfully bombarded Port Arthur and destroyed the Russian fleet at TSUSHIMA (1905).

TOIT, Alexander Logie du (1878–1948), South African geologist, a disciple of WEGENER, whose work did much to validate Wegener's CONTINENTAL DRIFT theories and was to a great extent responsible for their eventual acceptance.

TOJO, Hideki (1884–1948), Japanese general and militarist statesman, prime minister and virtual dictator (1941–44) who ordered the attack on Pearl Harbor. A professional soldier, he was chief of staff of the army in China (1937), and minister of war from 1940. He was forced to resign when the US took Saipan (1944). Convicted of war crimes, he was hanged.

TOKELAU ISLANDS, or Union Islands, three atolls (Atafu, Nukunonu, Fakaofu) in the S Pacific 300mi N of Samoa, part of New Zealand since 1949. Copra is the chief export.

TOKUGAWA, dynasty of SHOGUNS (military governors) of Japan 1603–1867. Tokugawa Ieyasu (1542–1616), first of 15, ruthlessly unified Japan under his rule after the battle of Sekigahara (1600) and established his capital at Edo (Tokyo). The regime was a centralized feudalism with strict control over the barons. It fell in a revolution precipitated partly by the presence of Westerners.

TOKUSHIMA, seaport capital of Tokushima prefecture, E Shikoku island, Japan. Its manufactures include textiles and furniture. Pop 223 451.

TOKYO, capital of Japan. It lies at the head of Tokyo Bay on the SE coast of Honshu and contains over 10% of Japan's population. As Edo, it became capital of the TOKUGAWA shoguns in 1603; it was renamed and made imperial capital in 1868. Reconstruction after earthquake and fire (1923) and the air raids of WWII transformed much of Tokyo. It is today a center of government, industry, finance and education: the National Diet (parliament) meets here; most of Japan's great corporations have their head office in Maurunochi district; Tokyo University (founded 1877) is one of hundreds of educational institutions. Tokyo has many parks, museums and temples, the Imperial Palace and the Kabukiza theater (see KABUKI). Industries (with large complexes to the W) include printing, shipbuilding, metal manufactures, automobiles, chemicals and textiles. The harbor and airport are Japan's busiest. Pop (city) 8 787 249; (metropolis) 11 408 071.

TOLEDO, city in central Spain 40mi SW of Madrid, seat of Toledo province, former Roman and Visigoth capital, famous for sword blades since prosperous Moorish rule (712–1085). Landmarks are the Alcázar (citadel), Gothic cathedral (the archbishop is Spain's primate) and EL GRECO's house. Pop 44 382.

TOLEDO, city in NW Ohio, seat of Lucas Co., on Lake Erie. The world's busiest coalshipping port and famous for automobiles and glass, it also has oil refineries and shipyards. Pop 383 818.

TOLKIEN, John Ronald Reuel (1892–1973), British author and scholar, celebrated for his tales *The Hobbit* (1937) and the trilogy *The Lord of the Rings* (1954–55), which present a mythical world of elves and dwarfs, partly based on Anglo-Saxon and Norse folklore. Tolkien was professor of Anglo-Saxon, then of English language and literature, at Oxford University.

TOLSTOY, Leo Nikoleyevich, Count (1828–1910), Russian novelist. Educated at Kazan University, he served in the army, married in 1862 and spent the next 15 years on his estate at Yasnaya Polyana near Moscow. In this happy period he produced his masterpieces: *War and Peace* (1865–69), an epic of vast imaginative scope and variety of character, tells the story of five families against the background of the Napoleonic invasion of Russia. *Anna Karenina* (1875–77), the tragic story of an adulterous affair, is remarkable more for its psychological portrayal. In later years Tolstoy experienced a spiritual crisis, recounted in his *Confession* (1882), and embraced an ascetic philosophy of Christian anarchism. His other works include *Childhood* (1852), *The Cossacks* (1863) and *Resurrection* (1899).

Tomato plants grown in open ground often have to be staked (1), but those grown in greenhouses are tied to strings. (2) The side shoots of the plant are cut off to leave a single stem bearing flowers and fruits. (3) Parts of the tomato plant: (a) leaf; (b) flower, seen from above (top) and side (bottom left) with closeup of stamen duster from above (bottom right); (c) diagram of flower just after the fruit has set; (d) diagram of corolla opened out to show stamens attached.

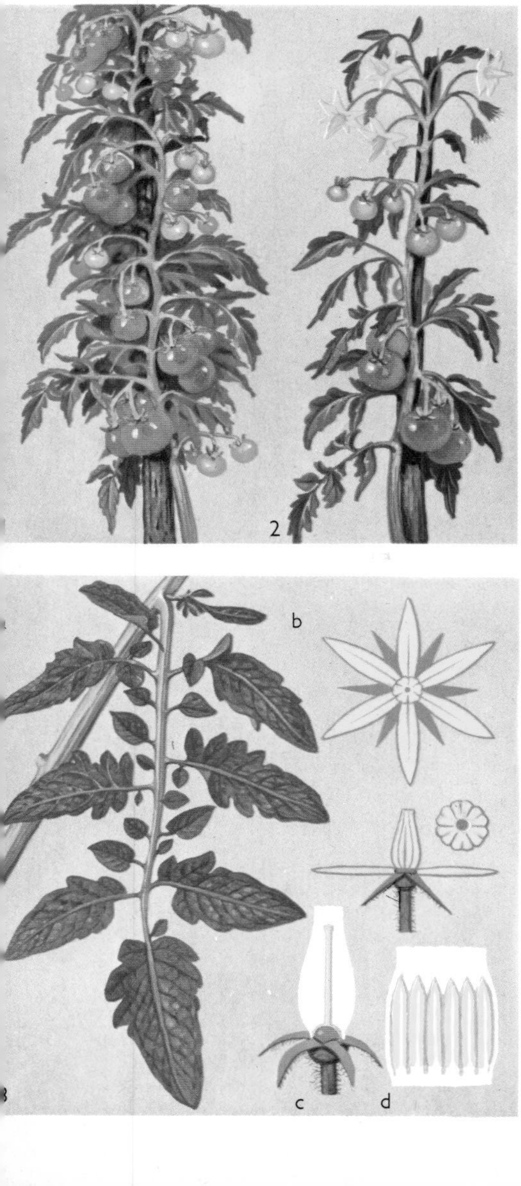

TOLTEC, Indian civilization dominant in the central Mexican highlands between the 900s and 1100s. The Toltec god was QUETZALCOATL. The Toltecs, sophisticated builders and craftsmen, erected their capital at Tollán (ruins near modern *Tula*, 60mi N of Mexico City). The dominant group were Nahua-speakers. AZTECS and others overran the area and adopted various aspects of Toltec culture.

TOLUCA, capital of Mexico state, Mexico, 40mi SW of Mexico City. It has food-processing, textile and handicraft industries. Pop 114 079.

TOLUENE, or methylbenzene ($C_6H_5CH_3$), colorless liquid HYDROCARBON, an AROMATIC COMPOUND produced from COAL TAR and by catalytic reforming of PETROLEUM hydrocarbons. It is used as a solvent, in GASOLINE, and for making TNT, BENZALDEHYDE, BENZOIC ACID etc. MW 92.2, mp −95°C, bp 111°C.

TOMAHAWK, light hatchet or war club of certain North American Indians. Originally a chip of stone fixed to a stick, it gained an iron ax head through trade with Europeans. Often incorporating a pipe bowl and stem, it had ceremonial value and was usually buried at the end of hostilities.

TOMATO, *Lycopersicon esculentum*, herbaceous plant, native to South America, but introduced to Europe in the 16th century and now cultivated worldwide. Most of the crop is canned or processed to make prepared foods, a relatively small proportion being grown for salad use. In northern latitudes, tomatoes are grown under glass, but the bulk is grown as a field crop. Italy, Spain, Brazil and Japan are among the leading producers. Family: Solanaceae.

TOMBAUGH, Clyde William (1906–), US astronomer who discovered the planet PLUTO (1930).

TOMBIGBEE RIVER, formed by confluence of East and West forks near Amory, NE Miss. It flows 409mi SSE through Ala. to the Alabama R N of Mobile. It is navigable for 350mi.

TOMBSTONE, tourist town in SE Ariz., 20mi NNW of Bisbee. Founded by a prospector who found silver in 1877, it was the scene of the Earp-Clanton shootout at the OK Corral. Pop 1 241.

TOMONAGA, Shinichiro (1906–), Japanese physicist who shared with FEYNMAN and SCHWINGER the 1965 Nobel Prize for Physics for their independent work on quantum electrodynamics.

TOMPKINS, Daniel D. (1774–1825), US vice-president under MONROE (1817–25). Of reforming views, he was N.Y. governor (1807–17), ran the state militia in the WAR OF 1812 and later disproved charges against him of misappropriation of state funds.

TOM THUMB, General (1838–1883), pseudonym for the US midget Charles Sherwood Stratton, who toured Europe and the US with the entertainer P. T. BARNUM. His adult height was only 40in.

TON, name of various actual or nominal units of WEIGHT. The short ton commonly used in the US is 2 000lb, the long ton 2 240lb. The metric ton or **tonne (t)** is 1 000kg (2 204.62lb). The ton used for measuring ships' cargoes is 40cu ft in the US, 42cu ft in the UK. The register ton used for describing the capacity of merchant ships is 100cu ft; the displacement ton used for describing warships (equivalent to 35cu ft of sea water) refers to the weight of water displaced by the ship—and hence to the actual weight of the ship.

TONALITY, the quality of music based on the tonic, or principal note of a particular KEY, as in most classical music; such music is tonal. Tonality compares with polytonality, the simultaneous use of many keys, and ATONALITY, the use of none.

TONAWANDA, city in NW N.Y., 10mi N of Buffalo, on the N.Y. State Barge Canal. It makes plastics, paper and metal products. Pop 21 898. Unincorporated Tonawanda town lies S (pop 107 282).

TONE, (Theobald) Wolfe (1763–1798), Irish nationalist. A cofounder (1791) of the Society of United Irishmen, he was forced to leave Ireland in 1794. Leading a French force to support the rebellion in W Ireland (1798), he was captured and condemned to hang, but committed suicide in prison.

Toltec pyramid complex at Tula in central Mexico, site of their ancient capital of Tollán.

TONE POEM. See SYMPHONIC POEM.

TONGA, or Friendly Islands, constitutional monarchy in the S Pacific comprising 150 islands (270sq mi) of which the chief groups are Tongatapu, Haapai and Vavau. The capital is Nukualofa on Tongatapu. Principal exports of the mainly Polynesian population of some 90 000 are copra and bananas. The present kingdom, founded in 1845 by George Tupu I, became a British protectorate in 1900 and achieved independence in 1970.

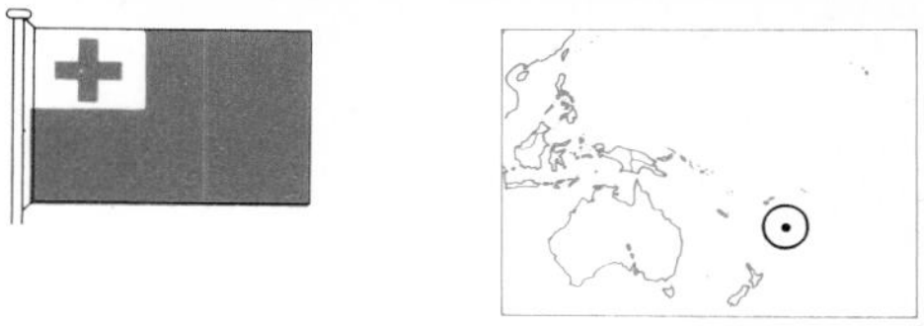

Official name: Kingdom of Tonga
Capital: Nukualofa
Area: 270sq mi
Population: 92 360
Languages: Tongan, English
Religions: Christian
Monetary unit(s): 1 Pa'anga = 100 seniti

TONGUE, muscular organ in the floor of the mouth which is concerned with the formation of food boluses and self-cleansing of the mouth, TASTE sensation and VOICE production. Its mobility allows it to move substances around the mouth and to modulate sound production in speech. In certain animals, the tongue is extremely protrusile and is used to draw food into the mouth from a distance.

TONGUES, Gift of. See GLOSSOLALIA.

TONKIN, or Tongking, historic region of SE Asia, now comprising most of northern VIETNAM. It was the European name for the region around the Red R delta, which became a French protectorate in 1883, part of French INDOCHINA.

TONNE (t), 1 000kg, the metric TON.

TONNIES, Ferdinand Julius (1855–1936), German sociologist noted for his distinction between rural communities governed by traditions rooted in the family and urban groupings based on rational self-interest and economic and legal interdependence. His theories are expressed in *Community and Society* (1887).

TONSILLITIS, INFLAMMATION of the TONSILS due to VIRUS or BACTERIAL infection. It may follow sore throat or other pharyngeal disease or it may be a primary tonsil disease. Sore throat and red swollen tonsils, which may exude PUS or cause swallowing difficulty, are common; LYMPH nodes at the angle of the jaw are usually tender and swollen. QUINSY is a rare complication. ANTIBIOTIC treatment for the bacterial cause usually leads to a resolution but removal of the tonsils is needed in a few cases.

TONSILS, areas of LYMPH tissue aggregated at the sides of the PHARYNX. They provide a basic site of body defense against infection via the mouth or NOSE and are thus particularly susceptible to primary infection (TONSILLITIS). As with the ADENOIDS, they are particularly important in children first encountering infectious microorganisms in the environment.

TONTI, Henri de (c1650–1704), French explorer and founder of Ill. In 1681–83 he built Fort St. Louis on the Illinois R with LA SALLE and brought settlers from Canada. By 1700 the colony was trading actively with the English in Carolina.

TONTO NATIONAL MONUMENT, covers 1 120 acres in S central Ariz. Founded in 1907, it contains Salada Indian cliff-dwellings, dating from c1350.

TOOELE, city in NW Utah, seat of Tooele Co., 25mi SW of Salt Lake City. Settled by Mormons in 1849, it has smelting industries. Pop 12 539.

TOOMBS, Robert (1810–1885), US statesman and Confederate leader. A US representative, then senator, he led the 1860 secession of Ga., and fought as a brigadier general, being wounded at ANTIETAM. After the Civil War he fled to Europe, returning unrepentant in 1867 to take up law and politics again.

TOOTH. See TEETH.

TOPAZ, aluminum SILICATE mineral of composition $Al_2SiO_4(F,OH)_2$, forming prismatic crystals (orthorhombic) which are variable and unstable in color, and valued as GEM stones. The best topazes come from Brazil, Siberia and the US.

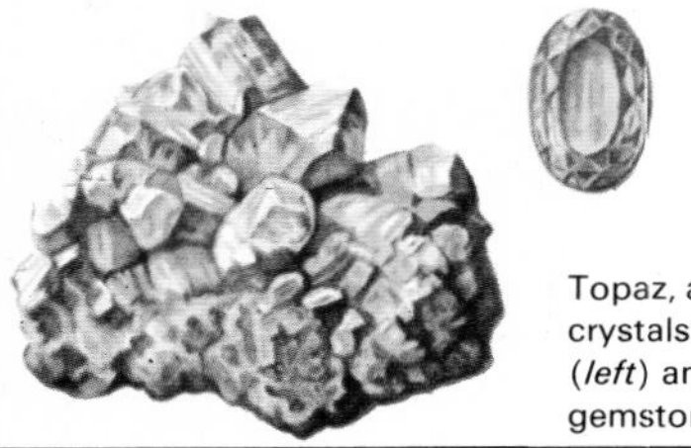

Topaz, as rough crystals in pegmatite (*left*) and cut as a gemstone.

TOPEKA, capital of Kan., seat of Shawnee Co., on the Kansas R 55mi W of Kansas City. It is a railroad center, processes grain and meat, and makes iron and steel products and automobile tires. The MENNINGER Foundation is here. Pop 125 011.

TOPOLOGY, a branch of mathematics related to GEOMETRY and dealing with the positions and relative positions of features of a geometric figure. Topologists are primarily concerned with pattern; that is, those features which are not affected by changes of size, angle, etc. (See also FOUR-COLOR PROBLEM; KLEIN BOTTLE; MÖBIUS STRIP.)

TOPSOIL. See SOIL.

TORAH (Hebrew: law, teaching), the PENTATEUCH (first five books of the Bible) kept in the Ark of every SYNAGOGUE. In a wider sense it is the whole body of oral and written teaching central to JUDAISM, and includes the rest of the Hebrew Bible, Rabbinic Codes, the TALMUD and MIDRASH.

TORDESILLAS, Treaty of, between Spain and Portugal in 1494, specifying where each might make colonial explorations. A papal bull of 1493 had allocated the New World to Spain and Africa and India to Portugal. The treaty shifted the demarcation W, enabling the Portuguese to claim E Brazil.

TORINO. See TURIN.

TORNADO, the most violent kind of STORM; an intense WHIRLWIND of small diameter, extending downward from a convective cloud in a severe THUNDERSTORM, and generally funnel-shaped. Air rises rapidly in the outer region of the funnel, but descends in its core, which is at very low pressure. The funnel is visible owing to the formation of cloud droplets by expansional cooling in this low pressure region. Very high winds spiral in toward the core. These, and explosions due to the low pressure, account for the almost total devastation and loss of life in the path of a tornado—which itself may move at up to 200m/s. Though generally rare, tornadoes occur worldwide, especially in the US and Australia in spring and early summer. (See also WATERSPOUT.)

TORONTO, capital of Ontario province and York Co., second-largest city in Canada (after Montreal), on the NW shore of Lake Ontario. It is a major port as well as a commercial, manufacturing and educational center and the cultural focus of English-speaking Canada. Its products include chemicals, machinery, electrical goods and clothing. The French Fort Rouillé (c1750) was replaced by the English York (1793) which was sacked in the War of 1812, renamed in 1834 and was Canada's capital 1849–51 and 1855–59. Pop (city) 712 786; metropolitan area (including York, East York, North York, Scarborough and Etobicoke boroughs) 2 628 043.

TORPEDO, self-propelled streamlined missile that travels underwater, its explosive warhead detonating when it nears or strikes its target. The torpedo was invented by Robert Whitehead, a British engineer, in 1866. Modern torpedoes are launched by dropping from airplanes or by firing from ships or submarines. They are electrically driven by propellers and guided by rudders controlled by a GYROPILOT. Many can be set to home in acoustically on their target. Rocket-propelled torpedoes are fired as guided missiles, and convert into torpedoes when they enter the water near their target. Torpedoes are now chiefly antisubmarine weapons.

TORPEDO BOAT, small, fast warship armed with torpedoes. The first torpedo boat was the *Lightning*, built in 1877 in R.I. for the British navy. The fast, armored destroyer was developed to counter its threat. The WWII torpedo boat measured 70–90ft and was capable of 50 knots. US navy PT (patrol torpedo) boats destroyed 250 000 tons of Japanese shipping in the Pacific. Since WWII, use of the PTs has declined, owing to high fuel consumption and instability in rough weather. The US navy now has a number of PTFs (patrol torpedo boats, fast).

TORQUE, a measure of the effectiveness of a FORCE or MOMENT in setting a body in rotation. In mechanics, a torque is a twisting moment or couple which tends to twist a fixed object such as a shaft about a rotation axis. If the shaft starts to rotate, the POWER it transmits is given by the product of the rotational speed and the torque.

TORQUEMADA, Tomás de (1420–1498), Spanish Dominican prior, fanatical general of Spain appointed by Ferdinand and Isabella in 1483. Using the INQUISITION to enforce religious and political unity, he was responsible for expelling 200 000 Jews from Spain and burning over 2 000 heretics.

TORRANCE, city in SW Cal., 15mi S of Los Angeles. It has oil wells, missile, electronics, steel and plastics industries. Pop 134 584.

TORRENS, Lake, shallow salt lake in E South Australia, N of Spencer Gulf. It is 130mi long and 30mi wide but it often dries to a marsh.

TORREÓN, city in Coahuila state, NE Mexico, in a farm region. It is a railway junction with cotton, flour, metal and chemical industries. Pop 257 045.

TORRES STRAIT, between Cape York Peninsula, NW Australia and New Guinea, joining the Coral and Arafura seas. Its 80mi width is dangerous to shipping because of its many reefs and islands.

TORREYA, a genus of evergreen trees related to the YEW which are native to North America and Asia. The stinking cedar (so-called for the smell of its bruised needles) found in Fla. and the Californian nutmeg have limited use for lumber. Family: Taxaceae.

TORRICELLI, Evangelista (1608–1647), Italian physicist and mathematician, a one-time assistant of GALILEO, who improved the telescope and microscope and invented the (mercury) BAROMETER (1643).

TORRINGTON, city, industrial and commercial center of NW Conn., 25mi W of Hartford. Its products include machinery and metal goods. Pop 31 952.

TORSION, strain produced by a twisting motion about an axis (a *torque*), such as a couple applied perpendicular to a cylinder axis. The resistance of a bar of given material to torsion is a measure of its rigidity and elasticity.

TORT (French: wrong), in law, a wrongful act against a person or his property for which that person can claim damages as compensation. It is distinguished from a crime, which the state will prosecute; it is up to the injured party to sue for redress of a tort. The same wrongful act, an ASSAULT for example, may be both actionable as a tort and prosecuted as a crime. Torts range from personal injury to SLANDER OR LIBEL; they include TRESPASS and damage or injury arising through NEGLIGENCE. Wrongful breach of an agreement, however, is covered by the law of CONTRACT.

TORTOISES, slow-moving, heavily-armored terres-terrestrial reptiles of the tropics, subtropics and warmer temperate regions. The body is enclosed in a box-like shell into which the head and limbs can be withdrawn. The shell is covered with horny plates or scutes. Toothless, the jaws are covered to form a sharp, horny beak. All tortoises move slowly, feeding on vegetable matter. There are many species, ranging from the familiar Garden tortoises to the 1.4m (4.6ft) Giant tortoises of the Galapagos and Seychelles.

TORTURE, deliberate infliction of extreme pain. It has been used for centuries as punishment or to extract information or confessions from prisoners, for religious (as in the INQUISITION) and, more often, purely political reasons. Banned by England's 1689 Bill of Rights, by the US Constitution's 8th Amendment and by the GENEVA CONVENTIONS, it was widely practiced by Axis countries in WWII, and still survives, even with refinements like electric shocks. Some consider BRAINWASHING to be mental torture.

TORUS, or **anchor ring**, doughnut-shaped topological space formed by rotating a CIRCLE about a straight LINE which lies in the same PLANE as the circle but nowhere intersects it. It has a VOLUME of π^2r^2d and a surface AREA of $4\pi^2rd$, where r is the radius of the circle and d the distance of its center from the line.

TORY, popular name of the Conservative and Unionist Party, one of Britain's two chief parties. The term (originally describing Irish highwaymen) was applied in 1679 to supporters of the future JAMES II of England. In the main, Tories became staunch church and king men, and "Tory" was applied to loyalist colonists in the American Revolution.

TOSCANINI, Arturo (1867–1957), Italian conductor, perhaps the greatest of his time, famous for dedication to each composer's intentions. He became musical director of LA SCALA in Milan (1898) and went on to conduct the New York Metropolitan (1908–14) and Philharmonic orchestras (1926–36). The NBC Symphony Orchestra was created for him in 1937.

TOTALITARIANISM, total state control over the individual. In common parlance, a totalitarian state has one party, often led by a dictator, and an ideology, spread through education and mass media, which penetrates all public and private life; dissent is suppressed. Nazi Germany and Soviet Russia are cited as examples.

TOTEM, an object, animal or plant toward which a TRIBE, CLAN or other group feels a special affinity, often considering it as a mythical ancestor. Killing of the totemic animal or animals by members of the group is TABOO, except, with some peoples, ritually during religious ceremonies. **Totem poles**, on which are carved human and animal shapes representing the particular warrior's heritage, were at one time common among the AMERINDS.

TOTOWA, residential and manufacturing borough in NE N.J., 3mi W of Paterson. Washington encamped here during the Revolution. Pop 11 580.

TOUCANS, a family, Ramphastidae, of about 37 species of South American birds with heavy bodies and long, bulky bills. Large birds with a bold plumage of black and yellow, orange or red, they inhabit woodland and forest. All are primarily fruit-eaters and, despite the huge, gaudily-colored bill, pick off individual berries with great delicacy.

TOUCH, the sensory system concerned with surface sensation, found in all external body surfaces including the SKIN and some mucous membranes. Touch sensation is crucial in the detection and recognition of objects at the body surface, including those explored by the limbs, and also in the protection of these surfaces from injury. Functional categories of touch sensation include light touch (including movement of HAIRS), heat, cold, pressure and pain sensation. These are to some degree physiologically distinct. Receptors for all the SENSES are particularly concentrated and developed over the FACE and HANDS. When the various types of skin receptor are stimulated, they activate nerve impulses in cutaneous nerves; these impulses pass via the SPINAL CORD and brain stem to the BRAIN, where coding and perception occur. With painful stimuli, REFLEX withdrawal movements may be induced at the segmental level.

TOULON, Mediterranean port in SE France. France's chief naval base, it has shipyards, oil refining, fishing and chemical industries. In WWII most of the French navy was scuttled here. Pop 174 746.

TOULOUSE, chief city of SW France, seat of Haute-Garonne department. A commercial and industrial center, it produces aircraft (including Concorde) and plastics and has an old university (1229). Pop 370 796.

TOULOUSE-LAUTREC, Henri de (1864–1901), French painter and lithographer who portrayed Parisian nightlife. Of an old aristocratic family, he was crippled at 15, studied art in Paris and settled in MONTMARTRE to paint the entertainers who lived there, such as Jane Avril and Aristide Bruant. Influenced by DEGAS and by Japanese prints, his work did much to popularize the lithographic poster.

TOURÉ, Sékou (1922–   ), president of the Republic of Guinea since he led it to independence in 1958. A labor leader in French colonial times, Touré is a Marxist, a political writer and winner of the 1960 Lenin Peace Prize.

TOURMALINE, borosilicate mineral of variable composition (in general $XY_3Al_6(BO_3)_3Si_6O_{18}(OH)_4$

Indian totem pole from the Alexander Archipelago in southeastern Alaska.

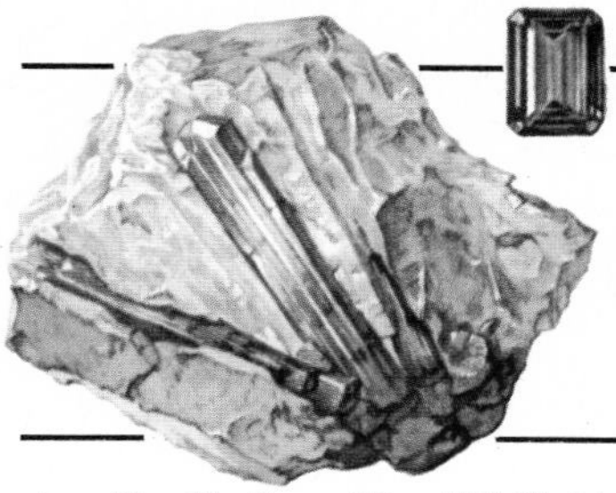

Tourmaline as crystals embedded in rock (*left*) and as a polished gemstone.

where X = Na,Ca and Y = Al,Fe^{III}, Li, Mg), found in PEGMATITES as trigonal/hexagonal crystals used as GEM stones. Tourmaline crystals exhibit DOUBLE REFRACTION and PIEZOELECTRICITY, and hence are used in polarizers and pressure-sensing devices.

TOURNAMENT, a series of games, originally a combat between armored knights, usually on horseback. Popular in Europe in the Middle Ages, it provided both entertainment and training for war. In the 13th century the dangerous *melée* was replaced by the *joust* contest between only two knights who tried to unhorse each other with lance, mace and sword.

TOURNEUR, Cyril (c1575–1626), English dramatist, supposed author of *The Revenger's Tragedy* (1607) and *The Atheist's Tragedy* (1611). These two revenge tragedies are powerful, violent and pessimistic.

TOURS, city in W central France, capital of Indre-et-Loire department, on the Loire R. A farm market and transportation center, it has metal, electrical and pharmaceutical industries. It has a famous Gothic cathedral and a university. The advance of the Moors was halted here in 732 AD. Pop 128 120.

TOUSSAINT L'OUVERTURE, Pierre François Dominique (c1743–1803), Haitian Negro patriot and general. A freed slave of French St.-Domingue, W Hispaniola (Haiti), he headed the 1791 slave revolt and through military success and diplomacy took all Haiti amid French, Spanish, British and mulatto resistance. Despite capture (1802) and his death in France, Haiti became independent in 1804.

TOWER OF LONDON, ancient fortress on the Thames R in E London. Built 1078–1300, mainly by WILLIAM I the Conqueror and HENRY III, its massive stone buildings are enclosed by high walls and a moat. It has been palace, prison, arsenal and mint. Today it houses the crown jewels and an armor museum. Here Thomas MORE, Anne BOLEYN and Roger CASEMENT were executed. Rudolf HESS was its last prisoner.

TOWHEES, a number of American finches placed either in the family Fringillidae or in the Emberizidae, with dark head and back and contrasting underparts. Common American species are the Greentailed towhee, Abert's towhee and the Eastern towhee or chewink.

TOWNES, Charles Hard (1915–   ), US physicist awarded the 1964 Nobel Prize for Physics with N. BASOV and A. PROKHOROV for independently working out the theory of the MASER and, later, the LASER. He built the first maser in 1951.

TOWN MEETING, a directly democratic form of local government, mainly in New England (Mass., N.H. and Vt.). In colonial days, all enfranchised citizens met to choose officials, decide taxes and discuss affairs. In the 1800s meetings became an annual event called by warrant. Today, most town meetings are attended only by officials and elected representatives.

TOWNSEND, Francis Everett (1867–1960), US reformer, author of the Townsend Plan (1933), a SHARE THE WEALTH program by which citizens over 60 were to receive $200 a month, the money to be raised by a federal tax. Claimed supporters of the plan numbered 5 000 000, but Congress rejected it.

TOWNSHEND, Charles (1725–1767), English statesman who in 1767 as chancellor of the exchequer originated the politically disastrous TOWNSHEND ACTS. He joined William PITT's cabinet in 1766, and exercised great influence, due partly to Pitt's illness.

TOWNSHEND ACTS (1767), four British parliament acts, initiated by Charles TOWNSHEND, which suspended the Massachusetts Assembly and imposed duties on lead, glass, paint, paper and tea imports to America. They proved hugely unpopular. The BOSTON MASSACRE and repeal of all but the tea tax took place on the same day in 1770. (See also BOSTON TEA PARTY.)

TOWSON, unincorporated area, seat of Baltimore Co., N Md. It is a N residential and manufacturing suburb of Baltimore. Pop 77 809.

TOXIN, a poisonous substance produced by a living organism. Many microorganisms, animals and plants produce chemical substances which are poisonous to some other organism; the toxin may be released continuously into the immediate environment or released only when danger is imminent. Examples include FUNGI which secrete substances which destroy BACTERIA (as ANTIBIOTICS these are of great value to man) and poisonous spiders and snakes which deliver their toxin via fangs. In some organisms, the function of toxins is obscure, but in many others they play an important role in defense and in killing prey. The symptoms of many INFECTIOUS DISEASES in man (e.g., CHOLERA; DIPHTHERIA; TETANUS) are due to the release of toxins by the bacteria concerned. (See also ANTITOXINS.)

TOXOID. See ANTITOXINS.

TOYNBEE, Arnold Joseph (1889–1975), English historian whose principal work, *A Study of History* (12 vols., 1934–61) divides the history of the world into 26 civilizations and analyzes their rise and fall according to a cycle of "challenge and response."

TOYON, or Christmas berry, *Heteromeles arbutifolia*, evergreen shrub with reddish orange fruits. Native to hilly areas of Calif., it is used decoratively in lieu of HOLLY. Family: Rosaceae.

TOYONAKA, city in SW Honshu, Japan. It is a residential suburb of Osaka, with machine, textile and petroleum industries. Pop 368 498.

TOYS, play-objects, principally for children. Some toys, such as balls, marbles, tops, rattles, whistles, pull-along toys, DOLLS, PUPPETS and miniature animals, have been universally popular throughout the ages. Mechanical toys, construction kits and working models of machinery are more recent innovations, as is the famous "Teddy Bear," named for Theodore ("Teddy") Roosevelt, who once refused to shoot a bear cub while out hunting. Educationalists such as FROEBEL and MONTESSORI have stressed the creative role of play in children's development, and toys and "play materials" are now an essential part of the modern educational curriculum.

TOY SPANIEL, English, known in Britain as the King Charles Spaniel, this diminutive Spaniel with a pug nose was a favorite breed of King Charles II. Weighing not more than 14lb, it has four color varieties: black and tan (King Charles proper), white, black and tan (Prince Charles), dark red (Ruby), and white with chestnut patches (Blenheim).

TRABZON. See TREBIZOND.

TRACE ELEMENTS, minerals required in minute quantities in an adequate human diet (see NUTRITION) or for the optimum growth and yield of plants (see FERTILIZERS).

TRACER, Radioactive. See RADIOCHEMISTRY; RADIOISOTOPE.

TRACHEA, the route by which air reaches the LUNGS from the PHARYNX. Air is drawn in through the mouth or NOSE and passes via the LARYNX into the trachea, which then divides into the major BRONCHI. It may be seen below the Adam's apple. In tracheostomy, it is incised to bypass any obstruction to RESPIRATION.

TRACHEAE, respiratory pathways permeating the insect body, branching from surface spiracles.

TRACHEOPHYTA. See VASCULAR PLANTS.

TRACHOMA, INFECTIOUS DISEASE due to an organism (bedsonia) intermediate in size between BACTERIA and VIRUSES, the commonest cause of BLINDNESS in the world. It causes acute or chronic CONJUNCTIVITIS and corneal INFLAMMATION with secondary blood-vessel extension over the cornea resulting in loss of translucency. Eyelid deformity with secondary corneal damage is also common. It is transmitted by direct contact; early treatment with SULFA DRUGS or TETRACYCLINE may prevent permanent corneal damage.

TRACK AND FIELD, athletic sports including running, walking, hurdling, jumping for distance or height and throwing various objects. In modern times organized athletic contests developed rapidly from

The pole vault, arguably the most spectacular and demanding of field events. Great pole-vaulting requires exceptional sprinting speed, considerable shoulder strength, the timing and balance of an acrobat, and a head for heights: vaults of over 18ft are nowadays not uncommon.

the 1860s onwards. The revival of the OLYMPIC GAMES in 1896 gave international and national competition an enormous boost, and in 1913 the International Amateur Athletics Federation was set up. Track and field events now constitute a popular sport throughout the world, and the training of champions is a serious business, backed up by government-sponsored programs, particularly in communist countries. The Olympic Games have developed into a quadrennial world championship, conducted in an atmosphere of intense rivalry, and politics has overtaken professionalism as the major problem confronting the organizers.
Track events. Distances raced vary from the 100 metres sprint to the marathon (26mi 385yds). Hurdlers and steeplechasers have to clear a set number of obstacles. In relay races a baton is passed from one runner to the next. **Field events.** In high jump and pole vault the contestant who clears the greatest height with the least number of attempts wins. A long jump or triple jump (hop, step and jump) competitor is permitted six jumps. Throwing events also permit six throws. The javelin is a spear thrown by running up to a line and releasing. The shot, a solid iron ball, is "put" from the shoulder. The discus is a circular plate, released with a sweeping sidearm action. The hammer throw consists of throwing an iron ball attached to a handle by a wire. All-around events include the 10-event decathlon and the 5-event pentathlon.

TRACTARIANS. See OXFORD MOVEMENT.

TRACTOR, self-propelled motor vehicle similar in principle to the AUTOMOBILE, but designed for high power and low speed. Used in agriculture, construction etc., tractors may pull other vehicles or implements, and may carry bulldozer and digging attachments. In the early 20th century the tractor, powered by the internal-combustion engine, largely superseded the steam traction engine and stationary farm-machinery engines. Many tractors have four-wheel drive or endless crawler tracks.

TRACTRIX, the CURVE to which a straight line AB, of length a, is always a TANGENT at A as B moves along the *x*-axis from $-\infty$ to $+\infty$. The term is sometimes loosely used to describe the solid formed by rotation of the curve about the *x*-axis.

TRACY, city in central Cal. 18mi SSW of Stockton, a fruit and vegetable packing center. Pop 14 724.

TRADE, International. See INTERNATIONAL TRADE.

TRADE CYCLE. See BUSINESS CYCLE.

TRADEMARK, device used by manufacturers to distinguish their products. It may be a design conjuring up an image of the product, a symbol, a "brand name" or a phrase. Trademarks are registered with the US Patent Office and their use is legally protected.

TRADESCANTIA, a genus of trailing, tender, perennial foliage house plants, one species of which is commonly called WANDERING JEW. Family: Commelinaceae. (See also SPIDERWORT.)

TRADE UNIONS. See UNIONS.

TRADE WINDS, persistent warm moist WINDS that blow westward from the high-pressure zones at about 30°N and S latitude toward the DOLDRUMS (intertropical convergence zone) at the equator. They are thus northeasterlies in the N Hemisphere and southeasterlies in the S Hemisphere. They are stronger and displaced toward the equator in winter.

TRADITION, in the Christian Church, the accumulated teachings and practices of the Church, handed down from one age to the next, by which Scripture and early Christian doctrine are elucidated and developed. It is embodied in the CREEDS, the decisions of ECUMENICAL COUNCILS and the writings of the Church Fathers and Doctors. The Roman Catholic Church recognizes tradition as authoritative because the Church is guided by the Holy Spirit; Protestants subordinate it to REVELATION and reason.

TRAFALGAR, Battle of, decisive naval engagement of the NAPOLEONIC WARS fought on Oct. 21, 1805. The British fleet of 27 warships under NELSON met a combined French and Spanish fleet of 33 ships off Cape Trafalgar (SW Spain). By attacking in an unorthodox formation Nelson surprised the enemy, sinking or capturing 20 vessels without loss, but was himself killed.

TRAGEDY, form of serious drama originating in ancient Greece, in which exceptional characters are led, by fate and by the very qualities that make them great, to suffer calamity and often death. ARISTOTLE, in his famous definition, spoke of purification (*catharsis*) through the rousing of the emotions of pity and fear. The great classical tragedians were AESCHYLUS, SOPHOCLES and EURIPIDES. Supreme in modern times is SHAKESPEARE. Great tragedians include Lope de VEGA, CALDERÓN DE LA BARCA, CORNEILLE, RACINE, GOETHE and SCHILLER. In the 19th and 20th centuries, whose drama usually shuns the heroic dimension of tragedy, the greatest exponent is probably IBSEN. (See also THEATER.)

TRAGOPANS, or Horned pheasants, five species of Asian game birds of the family Phasianidae. They are large and colorful birds of montane forest, found at altitudes of up to 3 600m (12 000ft).

TRAHERNE, Thomas (c1637–1674), English religious poet and prose writer. His work, often naive and even childlike in expression, conveys his ardent love of God and a mystical sense of his presence.

TRAIL, city in SE British Columbia, Canada. It is a mining and smelting center for lead, zinc, silver, gold and other metals. Pop 11 149.

TRAJAN (Marius Ulpius Trajanus; c53–117 AD), famous Roman emperor responsible for great extensions of the empire and vast building programs. He conquered Dacia (Romania) and much of PARTHIA, and rebuilt the Roman FORUM. Adopted heir by NERVA in 97 AD, he became emperor in 98. He was known as a capable administrator and a humane and tolerant ruler.

TRAKL, Georg (1887–1914) Austrian EXPRESSIONIST poet. His intense lyrics, with their haunting imagery, reveal a preoccupation with death and decay. An addict, he died of an overdose of cocaine while serving in the army.

TRAMPOLINE, elastic mat of net or canvas used for competitive gymnastics or recreation. The mat is anchored to a metal frame by springs, and athletes perform by bouncing up and down on it, performing various maneuvers in the air.

TRANQUILIZERS, agents which induce a state of quietude in anxious or disturbed patients. Minor tranquilizers are SEDATIVES (e.g., benzodiazepines) valuable in the anxious. In psychosis (see MENTAL ILLNESS), especially schizophrenia and (hypo-)mania, major tranquillizers are required to suppress abnormal mental activity as well as to sedate; phenothiazines (e.g., chlorpromazine) are often used.

TRANS-CANADA HIGHWAY, all-weather, high-standard 4 860mi-long highway crossing Canada from Victoria, British Columbia, to St. John's (Newfoundland). The world's longest national highway, it was originally planned in 1948, and completed in 1965.

TRANSCENDENCE, in theology, the existence of God above and beyond the universe. Being transcendent, he is ineffable except by analogy and surpasses creaturely understanding. (See also IMMANENCE.)

TRANSCENDENTALISM, an idealistic philosophical and literary movement which flourished in New England c1835–60. Regarding rationalist UNITARIANISM and utilitarian philosophy as morally bankrupt and shallow, the Transcendentalists took their inspiration from the German idealists, notably KANT, from COLERIDGE and from Eastern mystical philosophies. They believed in the divinity and unity of man and nature and the supremacy of intuition over sense-perception and reason as a source of knowledge. The major figures were Ralph Waldo EMERSON and Margaret FULLER, who edited *The Dial* (1840–44), Henry David THOREAU and Amos Bronson ALCOTT. The movement had considerable influence on US literature (HAWTHORNE; MELVILLE; WHITMAN) and politics (ABOLITIONISM; WOMEN'S RIGHTS; BROOK FARM).

TRANSCENDENTAL NUMBERS, those numbers that cannot be expressed as the ROOTS of a polynomial EQUATION whose coefficients are INTEGERS. Such numbers are not RATIONAL NUMBERS; they are irrational, though not all IRRATIONAL NUMBERS are transcendental. The two best-known such numbers are e (see EXPONENTIAL) and π (see PI).

TRANSCONA, industrial city in S Manitoba, Canada, an E suburb of Winnipeg. It has railroad workshops and some manufacturing industry. Pop 22 490.

TRANSDUCERS, devices which convert power levels or signals carried in one energy mode to equivalent signals in another mode; e.g., electric MOTORS; MICROPHONES; LOUDSPEAKERS; TURBINES.

TRANSDUCTION, a special type of RECOMBINATION of genetic material which involves an infectious process rather than the fusion of GAMETES. It occurs in microorganisms where DNA from a particular strain of BACTERIA can transform some of the genetic characteristics of a second strain. Resistance to ANTIBIOTICS can be passed from one bacterium to another by transduction.

TRANSFERENCE, the coloration of an individual's observation of a person (or object) by his ASSOCIATION of that person with another. In PSYCHOANALYSIS, the term means solely the effects of this process on a patient's attitudes toward his analyst.

TRANSFER-RNA. See NUCLEIC ACIDS.

TRANSFIGURATION, in Christianity, an event in the life of Jesus, when he appeared on a mountain bathed in a shining light and accompanied by Moses and Elijah. This manifestation of Christ's glory, witnessed by the disciples Peter, James and John, is recorded in the SYNOPTIC GOSPELS.

TRANSFINITE CARDINAL NUMBER, in SET THEORY, the number of elements of an infinite set. Though apparently meaningless, the concept of transfinite cardinal numbers is of use in the comparison of the number of elements in *different* infinite sets. For example, that of the set of all INTEGERS, aleph null ($\aleph_0$), is smaller than that of the set of POINTS on a straight LINE since, however the points are numbered, it is always possible to construct further points between them. (See INFINITY.)

TRANSFORMATION, term synonymous with MAPPING.

TRANSFORMER, a device for altering the voltage of an AC supply (see ELECTRICITY), used chiefly for converting the high voltage at which power is transmitted over distribution systems to the normal domestic supply voltage, and for obtaining from the latter voltages suitable for electronic equipment. It is based on INDUCTION: the "primary" voltage applied to a coil wound on a closed loop of a ferromagnetic core creates a strong oscillating MAGNETIC FIELD which in turn induces in a "secondary" coil wound on the same core an AC voltage proportional to the number of turns in the secondary coil. The core is laminated to prevent the flow of "eddy" currents which would otherwise also be induced by the magnetic field and would waste some ENERGY as HEAT.

TRANSFUSION, Blood, means of BLOOD replacement in ANEMIA, SHOCK or HEMORRHAGE by intravenous infusion of blood from donors. It is the simplest and most important form of transplant, though, while of enormous value, it carries certain risks. Blood group compatibility based on ANTIBODY AND ANTIGEN reactions is of critical importance as incompatible transfusion may lead to life-threatening shock and KIDNEY failure. Infection (e.g., HEPATITIS) may be transmitted by blood, and FEVER or ALLERGY are common.

TRANSHUMANCE, the practice of some farming peoples, especially of mountainous areas, of moving their herds from one region to another to allow for different climatic conditions through the year: e.g., from mountain to valley in winter and the reverse in summer.

TRANSISTOR, electronic device made of semiconducting materials used in a circuit as an AMPLIFIER, RECTIFIER, detector or switch. Its functions are similar to those of an ELECTRON TUBE, but it has the advantage of being smaller, more durable and consuming less power. The early and somewhat unsuccessful point-contact transistor has been superseded by the junction transistor, invented in 1948 by BARDEEN, BRATTAIN and SHOCKLEY. The junction transistor is a layered device consisting of two p-n junctions (see SEMICONDUCTOR) joined back to back to give either a p-n-p or n-p-n transistor. The three layers are formed by controlled addition of impurities to a semiconductor crystal, usually SILICON or GERMANIUM. The thin central region (p-type in an n-p-n transistor and n-type in a p-n-p one) is known as the *base*, and the two outer regions (n-type semiconductor in an n-p-n transistor) are the *emitter* and *collector*, depending on the way an external voltage is connected. To act as an amplifier in a circuit, an n-p-n transistor needs a negative voltage to the collector and base. If the base is sufficiently thin, it attracts ELECTRONS from the emitter which then pass through it to the positively charged collector. By altering the bias applied to the base (which need only be a few volts), large changes in the current from the collector can be obtained and the device amplifies. A collector current up to a hundred times the base current can be obtained. This type of transistor is analogous to a TRIODE, the emitter and collector being equivalent to the CATHODE and ANODE respectively and the base to the control grid. The functioning of a p-n-p transistor is similar to the n-p-n type described, but the collector current is mainly holes rather than electrons. Transistors revolutionized the construction of electronic circuits, but are being replaced by INTEGRATED CIRCUITS in which they and other components are produced in a single semiconductor wafer.

TRANSIT, the passage of a star across an observer's meridian (the great circle on the CELESTIAL SPHERE passing through his ZENITH and the north point of his horizon). The term is also applied to the passage of the inferior planets, Mercury and Venus, across the disk of the sun.

TRANSITION ELEMENTS, the elements occupying the short groups in the PERIODIC TABLE— i.e., Groups IIIB to VIII, IB and IIB—in which the *d*-ORBITALS are being filled. The transition elements are all metals, and include most of the technologically important ones. In general they are dense, hard and of high melting point. Their electronic structures, with many loosely-bound unpaired *d*-electrons, account for their properties: they exhibit many different VALENCE states, form stable LIGAND complexes, mostly colored and paramagnetic, and are generally good catalysts. They form many stable ORGANOMETALLIC COMPOUNDS and carbonyls (compounds in which carbon monoxide, CO, acts as a ligand) with specially stable "push-pull" bonding. The second and third row transition elements are less reactive than the first row, and stable in higher valence states.

TRANSJORDAN. See JORDAN.

TRANSKEI, former region and first BANTUSTAN (1963) of South Africa, proclaimed an independent state (1976), but not internationally recognized. The legislature is controlled by hereditary chiefs headed by Prime Minister Chief Kaiser Matanzima, and the economy is based on subsistence farming and migratory labor. Capital: Umtata.

TRANSMIGRATION OF SOULS, the belief that on death the souls of men and animals pass into new bodies of the same or different species as punishment or reward for previous actions. Central to Buddhist and Hindu thought (see also KARMA; NIRVANA), the doctrine is part of much mystical philosophy, and is often found in mystery cults and theosophical speculations (see MYSTERIES; THEOSOPHY).

TRANSMISSION, in engineering, a device for transmitting and adapting power from its source to its point of application. Most act by changing the angular velocity of the power shaft, either by step-variable means—GEARS, as in automobiles, or CHAINS, as in bicycles—with fixed ratios and no slip, or by stepless means—belt-and-pulley systems or traction drives employing adjustable rolling contact—with continuously variable ratios but liable to slip. In an AUTOMOBILE with manual transmission, the flywheel on the engine crankshaft is connected to the gearbox via the **clutch**, two plates that are normally held tightly together by springs so that through friction they rotate together. When the clutch pedal is depressed, the plates are forced apart so that the engine is disengaged from the rest of the transmission. This is necessary when changing gear: sliding different sets of gears into engagement by means of a manual lever. Modern gearboxes have **syncromesh** in all forward gears: a coned clutch device that synchronizes the rotation of the gears before meshing. The gearbox is coupled to the final drive by a drive shaft with universal joints. A crown wheel and pinion, connected to the half-shafts of each drive wheel via a DIFFERENTIAL, complete the system. In **automatic transmission** there is no clutch pedal or gear lever; a fluid clutch (see FLUID COUPLING), combined with sets of epicyclic gears selected by a GOVERNOR according to the program set by the driver, provides a continuously variable torque ratio for maximum efficiency at all speeds.

TRANSPIRATION, the loss of water by EVAPORATION from the aerial parts of PLANTS. Considerable quantities of water are lost in this way, far more than is needed for the upward movement of solutes and for the internal metabolism of the plant alone. Transpiration is a necessary corollary of PHOTOSYNTHESIS, in that in order to obtain sufficient CARBON dioxide from the air, considerable areas of wet surface, from which high loss of water by evaporation is inevitable, have to be exposed. Plants have many means for reducing water loss, STOMATA playing an important part. XEROPHYTES in particular are adapted for minimizing transpiration. (See also WILTING.)

TRANSPLANTS, organs that are removed from one person and surgically implanted in another to replace lost or diseased organs. Autotransplantation is the moving of an organ from one place to another within a person where the original site has been affected by local disease (e.g., skin grafting—see PLASTIC SURGERY). Blood TRANSFUSION was the first practical form of transplant. Here BLOOD cells and other components are transferred from one person to another. The nature of BLOOD allows free transfusion between those with compatible blood groups. The next, most important, and now most successful of organ transplants, was that of the KIDNEY. Here a single kidney is transplanted from a live donor who is a close relative or from a person who has recently suffered sudden DEATH (e.g., by traffic accident or irreversible BRAIN damage), into a person who suffers from chronic renal failure. The kidney is placed beneath the skin of the abdominal wall and plumbed into the major ARTERIES and VEINS in the PELVIS and into the BLADDER. High doses of STEROIDS and IMMUNITY suppressants are used to minimize the body's tendency to reject the foreign tissue of the graft. These doses are gradually reduced to lower maintenance levels, but may need to be increased again if rejection threatens. Here, tissue typing methods are used additionally to blood grouping to minimize rejection. HEART transplantation has been much publicized, but is limited to a few centers, many problems remaining. LIVER and LUNG transplants have also been attempted although here too the difficulties are legion. Corneal grafting is a more widespread technique in which the cornea of the EYE of a recently dead person replaces that of a person with irreversible corneal damage leading to BLINDNESS. The lack of blood vessels in the cornea reduces the problem of rejection. Grafts from nonhuman animals are occasionally used (e.g., pig SKIN as temporary cover in extensive BURNS). Both animal and human heart valves are used in cardiac surgery.

TRANSPORTATION. See AIR TRANSPORTATION (special feature); AUTOMOBILE; CANALS; HIGHWAY; MERCHANT SHIPPING; PIPES AND PIPELINES; RAILROAD; SUBWAY; TRUCK; TUNNEL.

TRANSPORTATION, US Department of, responsible for the development and coordination of national transport policies and agencies. Set up in 1966, it reports to Congress on the optimum use of federal transportation funds and runs bureaus of Research and Technology, Public Affairs, Policy and International Affairs, Environment and Urban Systems, and Administration. It also supervises the federal Aviation, Highway, Railroad and Urban Mass Transportation administrations, the US COAST GUARD, the SAINT LAWRENCE SEAWAY Development Corporation and the National Transportation Safety Board.

TRANS-SIBERIAN RAILROAD, in the USSR, longest railroad in the world, stretching 5 787mi from Moscow to Vladivostock on the Sea of Japan, a journey which takes eight days. Its construction (1891–1916) had a dramatic effect on the development of Siberia.

TRANSUBSTANTIATION, Roman Catholic doctrine that in Holy COMMUNION the substance of the bread and wine is changed into that of the body and blood of Christ. It affirms belief in the REAL PRESENCE. (See also CONSUBSTANTIATION.)

TRANSURANIUM ELEMENTS, the elements with atomic numbers greater than that of URANIUM (92—see PERIODIC TABLE; ATOM). None occurs naturally: they are prepared by bombardment (usually with NEUTRONS or ALPHA PARTICLES) of suitably-chosen lighter ISOTOPES. All are radioactive (see RADIOACTIVITY), and those of higher atomic number tend to be less stable. Those so far discovered are the ACTINIDES from neptunium through lawrencium, RUTHERFORDIUM and HAHNIUM. Only neptunium and plutonium have been synthesized in large quantity; most of the others have been produced in weighable amounts, but some with very short HALF-LIVES can be studied only by special tracer methods.

TRANSVAAL, second-largest province in the Republic of South Africa, between the Vaal and Limpopo rivers in the NE. It is mainly high VELD 3 000–6 000ft above sea level. The capital is PRETORIA and the largest city is JOHANNESBURG. Mineral wealth includes gold, silver, diamonds, coal, iron ore, platinum, asbestos and chrome. Its farmlands are noted for their cattle, corn and tobacco. (See also BOER WAR; SOUTH AFRICA.)

TRANSSYLVANIA, historic region of NW and

central Romania. It is a plateau separated from the rest of Romania by the Transylvanian Alps to the S and the Carpathian Mts. to the E and N. It has been under Ottoman, Austrian and Hungarian control. There are rich mineral deposits, large areas of forest and fertile plains. The chief center is Cluj.

TRAPEZIUM, and **trapezoid**. See QUADRILATERAL.

TRAPPISTS, popular name for Cistercians of the Reformed, or Strict, Observance, a Roman Catholic monastic order founded by de RANCÉ, abbot of La Trappe in Normandy, France 1664–1700, who instituted a rigorous discipline of silence, prayer and work. There are 12 US abbeys. The abbot general lives in Rome.

TRAPSHOOTING, sport of shooting with a shotgun at clay discs or "pigeons" sprung into the air from a "trap." It developed in England in the 19th century originally as a means of target practice for sportsmen. In the US today there are more than 100 000 trap-shooting enthusiasts.

TRASIMENO, Lake, shallow lake in central Italy, 10mi W of Perugia. It was the scene of HANNIBAL's famous victory over the Romans (217 BC).

TRAUMA, any sudden wound to the body or mind, often closely followed by SHOCK. In PSYCHOANALYSIS, a trauma is viewed as an immediate cause of ANXIETY which may develop into NEUROSIS. An *infantile trauma* is one that occurred in childhood but which affects the adult.

TRAVERSE CITY, city in NW Mich., seat of Grand Traverse Co. It is a resort and the biggest cherry-processing center in the US. Pop 18 048.

TRAVERTINE, compact, banded LIMESTONE, usually light-colored, evaporated or deposited from hot springs; sometimes applied also to STALACTITES AND STALAGMITES. Taking a high polish, it is used for interior decoration. **Tufa**, or calcareous sinter, is a porous equivalent.

TRAVIS, William Barret (1809–1836), US lawyer and hero of the ALAMO. As commander of the garrison at the Alamo which was wiped out by the Mexican army, he became a national hero for his bravery.

TREADMILL, vertically-mounted wheel turned by a man treading on pedals fixed to its rim, or a hollow cylinder turned by an animal walking along its internal circumference; an early power source, widely used for raising water and operating mills.

TREASON, behavior by a subject or citizen which could harm his sovereign or state. In many countries, including England before the 19th century, treason has been loosely defined and used as a political weapon. The US Constitution, however, states that treason consists only in levying war against the US or in adhering to its enemies, "giving them Aid and Comfort," and evidence of two witnesses or a confession in open court is necessary to secure a conviction.

TREASURY, US Department of, executive department of the US government, established in 1789 and responsible for federal taxes, customs and expenditure. It also plays a major role in national and international financial and monetary policies. Its head, the secretary of the treasury, the second-ranking member of the President's cabinet, is an *ex officio* governor of the INTERNATIONAL MONETARY FUND. The department's other responsibilities include the US SECRET SERVICE, and the bureaus of Customs, MINT, Engraving and Printing, Internal Revenue and Narcotics.

TREATY, an agreement in writing between two or more states. Treaties are bilateral (between two states) or multilateral (between several states), and cover matters such as trade, tariffs, taxation, economic and technical cooperation, diplomatic relations, international boundaries, extradition of criminals, defense and control of arms and aggression—anything on which international agreement is needed. Historically the most famous treaties have been those ending wars, such as the treaties of PARIS, VERSAILLES, WESTPHALIA. Some treaties, for example the NORTH ATLANTIC TREATY ORGANIZATION, are military; others set up international organizations: examples are the UNITED NATIONS; the COMMON MARKET (set up by the Treaty of Rome); the FOOD AND AGRICULTURE ORGANIZATION; the INTERNATIONAL TELECOMMUNICATIONS UNION. These have become an important part of modern INTERNATIONAL RELATIONS. (See also INTERNATIONAL LAW.)

TREATY PORTS, ports, notably in China and Japan, opened by treaty to foreign trade and whose foreign residents enjoyed EXTRATERRITORIALITY. In China 69 ports were opened—the first five to the British in 1842 after the OPIUM WAR. The system in Japan lasted 1854–99 but in China continued until WWII.

TREBIZOND, or Trabzon, seaport in NE Turkey on the Black Sea. An early Greek city founded c756 BC, it became the capital of a powerful trade-based empire, 1204–1461 AD, ruled by the former Byzantine imperial family. Byzantine churches and much of the medieval city still remain. Pop 81 528.

TREE, woody perennial PLANT with a well defined main stem, or trunk, which either dominates the form throughout the life cycle (giving a pyramidal shape) or is dominant only in the early stages later forking to form a number of equally important branches (giving a rounded or flattened form to the tree). It is often difficult to distinguish between a small tree and a SHRUB, but the former has a single trunk rising some distance from the ground before it branches while the latter produces several stems at, or close to, ground level. The trunk of a tree consists almost wholly of thick-walled water-conducting cells (xylem) which are renewed every year (see WOOD), giving rise to the familiar ANNUAL RINGS. The older wood in the center of the tree (the heartwood) is much denser and harder than the younger, outer sapwood. The outer skin or the BARK, insulates and protects the trunk and often shows characteristic cracks, or falls off leaving a smooth skin. Trees belong to the two most advanced groups of plants, the GYMNOSPERMS and the ANGIOSPERMS (the flowering plants). The former include the cone-bearing trees such as the PINE, SPRUCE and CEDAR; they are nearly all evergreens and mostly live in the cooler regions of the world. The angiosperms have broader leaves and much harder wood; in tropical climates they are mostly EVERGREEN, but in temperate regions they are DECIDUOUS. (See also FORESTRY; FORESTS.)

TREE FERN, a number of large FERNS with a tree-like growth habit that are native to humid regions of Middle and South America, Australasia and Hawaii. They grow up to 25m (82ft) high, with feathery fronds springing from slender trunks and propagate by spores. Family: Cyatheaceae.

TREE FROGS, strictly, FROGS of the family Hylidae, although frogs of other groups have secondarily taken on a tree-living habit. The Hylidae is a large family of 34 genera, 32 confined to the New World. Almost all are small and adapted to tree-living by having sticky disks at the tip of each finger and toe. Most must return to water to breed.

TREEHOPPERS, leaf-sucking insects related to SPITTLE BUGS, CICADAS and LEAFHOPPERS. Powerful jumpers, both nymphs and adults feed on juices sucked from the cells of tree leaves.

TREE OF LIFE. See ARBORVITAE.

TREE SHREWS, family Tupaiidae, small squirrel-like mammals of SE Asia with narrow shrew-like heads and bushy tails. Believed to represent an intermediate stage between the INSECTIVORA and the PRIMATES, most tree shrews feed on fruit and insects, a diet reflected in the unspecialized dentition of small pointed teeth.

TREFOIL, a number of LEGUMINOUS PLANTS with leaves divided into three leaflets, including species of the genus *Trifolium* (CLOVER), *Medicago* (Yellow trefoil), *Lotus* (Bird's-foot trefoil) and *Desmodium* (Tick trefoils). Family: Leguminosae.

TREMATODES, former name for certain FLUKES.

TRENCHARD, Hugh Montague Trenchard, 1st Viscount (1873–1956), first British air marshal. As first British chief of air staff (1918, 1919–29), he helped create the Royal Air Force, developing its offensive strategy and training facilities.

TRENCH FOOT. See IMMERSION FOOT.

TRENCH MOUTH, WWI name for VINCENT's ANGINA.

TRENT (Trento), industrial and tourist city in NE Italy, capital of Trentino-ALTO ADIGE, with textile, leather and printing industries. It was ruled by prince-bishops, 1027–1802. Pop 91 767.

TRENT, third-longest river (170mi) in Great Britain. It rises in Staffordshire and flows NE through central England to join the Ouse to form the Humber estuary on the E coast.

TRENT, Council of (1545–1563), the 19th ECUMENICAL COUNCIL of the Roman Catholic Church, at Trent, N Italy. In response to the REFORMATION, the council, first summoned by Pope PAUL III, formally redefined the Church's doctrines and banned many abuses. The council's reforms and doctrinal canons were the basis of the COUNTERREFORMATION and became definitive statements of Catholic belief.

TRENT AFFAIR, naval incident in the US CIVIL WAR that nearly brought Britain to military support of the South. In Nov. 1861, Charles WILKES, commanding *San Jacinto*, stopped the British ship *Trent* and seized the two Southern agents MASON AND SLIDELL. Britain demanded an apology for this violation of the freedom of the sea and ordered 8 000 troops to Canada. The men were freed in December.

TRENT CANAL, waterway in SE Ontario, Canada, linking the Bay of Quinte, Lake Ontario, to Lake Huron. Only 33mi of its 224mi length are man-made. It is now used for pleasure craft and hydroelectric power.

TRENTON, industrial town in SE Ontario, Canada, the S terminus of the TRENT CANAL. It produces steel, textiles and electronic components. Pop 14 589.

TRENTON, industrial city in SE Mich., SW of Detroit. It produces steel, plastics, chemicals, boats and automobile engines. Pop 24 127.

TRENTON, city in N.J., state capital and seat of Mercer Co., on the Delaware R. Settled by Quakers in 1679, it is now a major industrial center, producing steel cable, pottery, plastics, metal goods and textiles. Pop 104 638.

TRENTON, Battle of, American victory in the REVOLUTIONARY WAR, fought on Dec. 26, 1776. To forestall a British attack on Philadelphia, George WASHINGTON crossed the Delaware R at night and surprised a British force of 1 500 HESSIANS at Trenton, N.J. The battle was won in 45 minutes, rallying Washington's army and the American cause.

TREPHINE, surgical instrument used for trepanning—making a circular hole in an internal organ in order to drain fluid, PUS, BLOOD or air. Trepanning the SKULL was successfully practiced in ancient times.

TRESPASS, in law, a TORT involving unlawful entrance onto or presence in another's property, or unlawful injury to another's person. This may include assault of various kinds (which may also be crimes) or nonviolent offenses such as false imprisonment.

TREVITHICK, Richard (1771–1833), British mining engineer and inventor primarily remembered for his work improving the STEAM ENGINE and for building the first railroad LOCOMOTIVE (c1804).

TRIAL, judicial examination and determination of criminal prosecutions and law suits. In the US the right of an accused person to a speedy and public trial by a jury of his peers is guaranteed in the Constitution. Trials in COMMON LAW countries such as the UK and US are "adversary" proceedings, in which the court impartially decides between the evidence of two parties; under CIVIL LAW systems trials tend to be more "inquisitorial," allowing more scope for pre-trial investigation and the court itself a greater role in the gathering of evidence. Under both systems the judge ensures that procedure is followed and that rules of evidence are observed, and determines the guilty offender's sentence; in common law systems he decides questions of law. Questions of fact are left to a JURY, if there is one; jury trial is more expensive and time-consuming, and so is reserved for more serious offences. Although the US trial system today is designed to be as fair as possible, complexity, delay and expense create many serious flaws.

TRIANGLE, a three-sided POLYGON. There are three main types of plane triangle: scalene, in which no side is equal in length to another; isosceles, in which two of the sides are equal in length; and equilateral, in which all three sides are equal in length. A right (or right-angled) triangle has one INTERIOR ANGLE equal to 90°,

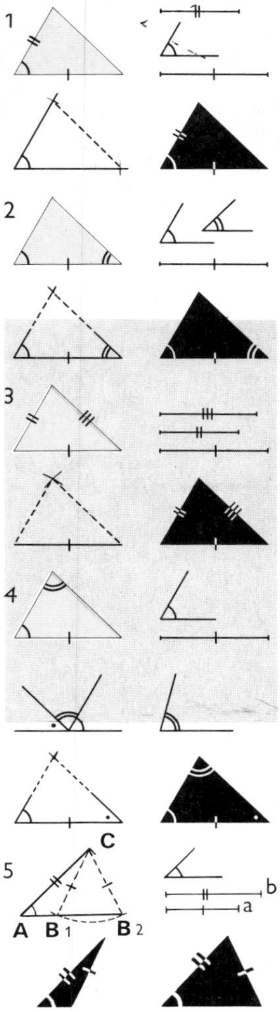

If certain elements of a triangle are known, another triangle may be constructed congruent with it; three elements are generally sufficient. (1) Two sides and the included angle (SAS); (2) One side and the angles at its ends (ASA); (3) Three sides (SSS); (4) One side, angle at one end of it and the facing angle (SAA) allow the third angle to be deduced, providing ASA as in (2), since angles in a triangle must total 180°; (5) Two sides and the angle opposite one (SSA) allow two triangles to be constructed.

and may be either scalene or isosceles (see PYTHAGORAS' THEOREM). The "corners" of a triangle are termed vertices (singular, vertex). The sum of the angles of a plane triangle is 180°. A **spherical triangle** is an area, bounded by arcs of three great circles (see SPHERICAL GEOMETRY), of the surface of a SPHERE, each arc being less than 180°, each side and interior angle being termed an element. The sum of the three sides is never greater than 360°, the sum of the three angles always in the range 180°–540°. (See also COSINE RULE; SINE RULE.)

TRIANGLE, one of the musical PERCUSSION INSTRUMENTS. It consists of a steel or iron rod, bent into a triangle with one corner open. It is suspended from the player's hand and struck with a metal rod.

TRIANGULAR TRADE, trading system in the 18th century. Rum and trinkets from New England were traded for West African slaves and ivory; these were taken to the West Indies and traded for tobacco and molasses, which were carried to New England. The MOLASSES ACT (1733) and the SUGAR ACT (1764) were British attempts to gain revenue from this trade.

TRIANON, Treaty of, WWI peace settlement between the Allies and Hungary, signed in 1920. Hungary ceded two-thirds of her territory and population to neighboring states, became liable for reparations, and had her army limited to 35 000 men.

TRIASSIC, the first period of the MESOZOIC era, which lasted from about 225 to 190 million years ago. (See also GEOLOGY.)

TRIBE (from Latin *tribus*, a third, referring to the three peoples who founded Rome), a people with a common territory, customs and, usually, language or dialect. Tribes may be merely a few families or great in numbers; social structures and customs vary from one tribe to another.

TRIBONIAN (d. 545 AD), Roman jurist and minister of the Byzantine emperor JUSTINIAN I. During 530–32 and 534–45 he was chief compiler of the codification of Roman law into the CORPUS IURIS CIVILIS.

TRIBUNE, an official in ancient Rome representing the PLEBIANS. By 449 BC, 10 tribunes were elected by the people. They could veto the SENATE's actions and introduce resolutions (*plebiscita*). After 287 BC, *plebiscita* had the force of law, and tribunes became powerful as both initiators and obstructors of legislation. Famous reforming tribunes were the GRACCHI. By 27 BC tribunes had lost their power. There were also military and financial tribunes.

TRICEPS, the major ARM muscle concerned with straightening the elbow. It has three heads or bellies at its upper end that have separate insertions.

TRICERATOPS, the best known of the horned DINOSAURS. It was about 6m (19.7ft) in length with a skull 2m (6.6ft) long bearing a short horn on the snout and a larger horn over each eye. The skull continued as a bony ruff around the neck.

TRICHINOSIS, infestation with the larva of a worm (*Trichinella*), contracted from eating uncooked pork etc., causing a feverish illness. EDEMA around the eyes, MUSCLE pains and DIARRHEA occur early; later the LUNGS, HEART and BRAIN may be involved. It is avoided by the adequate cooking of pork. CHEMOTHERAPY may be helpful in severe cases.

TRIESTE, city-seaport in NE Italy at the head of the Adriatic Sea, with steel, oil and shipbuilding industries. A busy port in Roman times, it was part of Austria, 1382–1919, and then of Italy. Claimed by Yugoslavia in 1945, it was made a Free Territory 1947–54, then restored to Italy. Pop 269 819.

TRIGGERFISHES, marine fishes of warm seas related to PUFFERS. The name derives from the action of the enlarged first dorsal spine which can be locked upright, making the fish difficult to remove from rock crevices and difficult for a predator to swallow. There are about 30 species, all brightly-colored.

TRIGONOMETRY, the branch of GEOMETRY that deals with the ratios of the sides of right-angled TRIANGLES, and the applications of these ratios. The principal ratios, when considering ANGLE A of triangle ABC whose sides are a, b and c, where b is the HYPOTENUSE, are:

name	*abbreviation*	*ratio*
tangent	tan A	$\frac{a}{c}$
sine	sin A	$\frac{a}{b}$
cosine	cos A	$\frac{c}{b}$
cotangent	cot A	$\frac{c}{a}$
cosecant	cosec A	$\frac{b}{a}$
secant	sec A	$\frac{b}{c}$

As can be seen, the cotangent is the RECIPROCAL of the tangent, the cosecant that of the sine, and the secant that of the cosine. (See COSINE RULE; SINE RULE.)

From these ratios are derived the **trigonometric functions**, setting y equal to tan x, sin x, etc. These FUNCTIONS are termed transcendental (nonalgebraic). Of particular importance is the sine wave, in terms of which many naturally-occurring WAVE MOTIONS, such as SOUND and LIGHT, are studied. (See also CALCULUS, SPHERICAL TRIGONOMETRY.)

TRIHEDRON, in DIFFERENTIAL GEOMETRY, a set of three mutually perpendicular (see ANGLE) VECTORS directed from a single point. If one considers a trihedron moving from point to point along, say, a CURVE, one has a handy coordinate system, using the three vectors as AXES, for study of the curve. This is termed a moving trihedron.

TRILLING, Lionel (1905–1975), US literary critic and author. *The Liberal Imagination* (1950), and studies of Matthew Arnold (1939), E. M. Forster (1943) and Freud (1955) are informed by psychological, philosophical and sociological insights and methods.

TRILLIUM, genus of woodland and cultivated plants, native to North America and Asia, which are spring-flowering. The leaves are in whorls of three surrounding white, pink or purple flowers, which have floral parts in threes. Family: Liliaceae.

TRILOBITES, an extinct group of bottom-dwelling arthropods of shallow seas. At least 10 000 species are known. They somewhat resembled modern crustaceans, having a flattened form, an upper surface covered by a thick chitinous EXOSKELETON, with soft chitin covering the underparts.

TRINIDAD AND TOBAGO, independent state in the West Indies consisting of the islands Trinidad (1 864sq mi) and Tobago (116sq mi) off the coast of Venezuela. Trinidad is very fertile and mainly flat, rising to about 3 000ft in the N, and Tobago has a mountain ridge 1 800ft high and is densely forested. The climate is tropical, with a rainfall range of 50–100in. The population is mostly Negro and East Indian (36%), and the largest city and chief port is Port-of-Spain, the capital. The country is rich in oil, natural gas and asphalt— Trinidad is famous for the large pitch lake near La Brea—and produces sugarcane, cocoa and fruit, but has to import many foodstuffs. Tourism is a growing industry. Trinidad was discovered by COLUMBUS in 1498 and settled by the Spaniards, but British rule was established in 1802. Trinidad and Tobago joined the West Indies Federation in 1958 but left in 1962 to become independent. Eric Williams has been premier since 1962.

Official name: Trinidad and Tobago
Capital: Port-of-Spain
Area: 1 980sq mi
Population: 1 026 750
Language: English
Religions: Christian, Hindu, Muslim
Monetary unit(s): 1 T and T dollar = 100 cents

TRINITROTOLUENE. See TNT.

TRINITY, river in E Tex. Formed by the junction of the Clear, Elm and West Forks, it flows 455mi SE into Trinity Bay. Its valley is the most heavily industrialized river basin in Tex.

TRINITY, the central doctrine of Christian theology, that there is one GOD who exists in three Persons and one Substance. The definition of the doctrine, implicit in the New Testament, by the early ECUMENICAL COUNCILS (notably NICAEA and Constantinople) was the product of violent controversy with such heresies as ARIANISM, MONOPHYSITISM, NESTORIANISM and

A steel band, the folk music of Trinidad. Its instruments, although made from trash cans and oil drums, produce a rich and mellow sound.

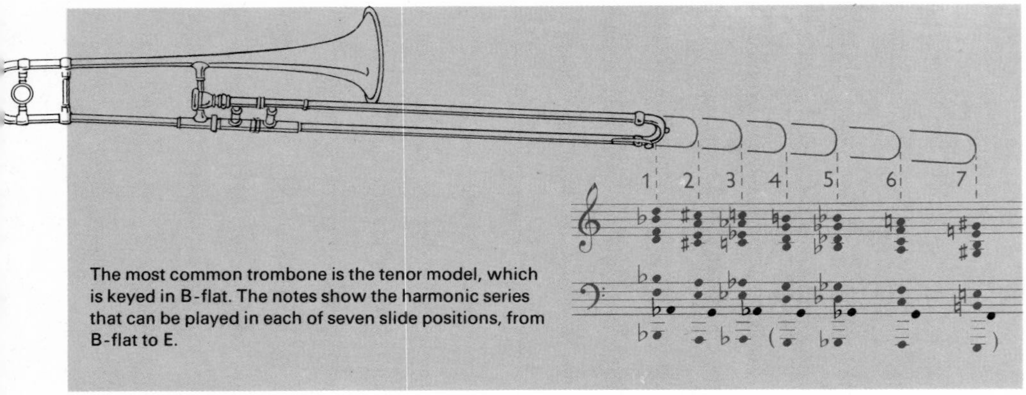

The most common trombone is the tenor model, which is keyed in B-flat. The notes show the harmonic series that can be played in each of seven slide positions, from B-flat to E.

Monarchianism. It is classically summed up in the ATHANASIAN CREED. The three Persons—the Father, the Son (see INCARNATION; JESUS CHRIST) and the HOLY SPIRIT—are each fully God: coequal, coeternal and consubstantial, yet are distinct. The Son is "eternally begotten" by the Father; the Holy Spirit "proceeds" from the Father and (in Western theology) from the Son. The doctrine is a mystery, being known by REVELATION and being above reason (though not unreasonable). Hence it has been challenged by rationalists (see DEISM; SOCINIANISM; UNITARIANISM) and by such sects as the JEHOVAH'S WITNESSES and MORMONS.

TRIODE, ELECTRON TUBE with positive ANODE, electron-emitting CATHODE and negatively biased control grid, used as an electronic AMPLIFIER or OSCILLATOR.

TRIPLE ALLIANCE, name of several European alliances: between England, Sweden and the Netherlands against France (1668); between England, France and the Netherlands (1717; see also QUADRUPLE ALLIANCE); between Germany, Austria-Hungary and Italy (1882).

TRIPLE ENTENTE, informal diplomatic understanding between Britain, France and Russia which acted as a counterweight to the TRIPLE ALLIANCE of 1882. It lasted 1907–17. After the outbreak of WWI, it became a military alliance. (See also ENTENTE CORDIALE.)

TRIPLETS. See MULTIPLE BIRTHS.

TRIPOLI, city and major port of NW Lebanon. An ancient PHOENICIAN city, it is now a pipeline terminal and refining center for Iraq oil, and exports citrus fruits. Pop 175 000.

TRIPOLI, seaport and capital of Libya, North Africa, founded by the PHOENICIANS. It is an important industrial and commercial center. Pop 162 200.

TRIPOLITANIA, historic region of W Libya, mostly desert. Inhabited originally by BERBERS, it was colonized by the PHOENICIANS, and later by the Romans and Arabs. It was under Turkish rule, 1553–1912. The coastal area and oases support agriculture.

TRIPOLITAN WAR. See BARBARY WARS.

TRISECTION OF AN ANGLE, the division of an ANGLE into three equal parts. Impossible using only straight edge and COMPASSES, it was one of the famous construction problems of classical GEOMETRY.

TRISTAN DA CUNHA, isolated British colony of volcanic islands in the S Atlantic. Tristan, the only inhabited island, is agricultural. When its volcano erupted in 1961 all the population were temporarily evacuated to Britain. Pop 280.

TRITIUM (T or $_1H^3$), the heaviest ISOTOPE of HYDROGEN, whose nucleus has one PROTON and two NEUTRONS, produced by neutron irradiation of lithium (Li^6). Tritium is weakly radioactive and emits BETA RAYS. It is used for tracer studies, in luminous paints, and (together with DEUTERIUM) in HYDROGEN BOMBS. (See also FUSION, NUCLEAR). AW 3.0, mp −252.5°C, bp −248.1°C.

TRITON, in Greek myth, a demigod of the sea, son of POSEIDON and Amphitrite. He was represented as a man with the tail of a dolphin or a fish, who blew a conch shell to raise or calm seas. Many stories speak of numerous tritons.

TRIUMVIRATE, in ancient Rome, a group of three leaders sharing office or supreme power. The First Triumvirate (60–53 BC) was formed by Julius CAESAR, POMPEY and CRASSUS. The Second Triumvirate (43–36 BC) consisted of Octavian (later the Emperor AUGUSTUS), Marcus LEPIDUS and Mark ANTONY.

TRIVANDRUM, seaport and commercial city in SW India, capital of Kerala state. It is renowned for its 18th-century Padmanabha Temple. Pop 409 761.

TRIVIUM. See SEVEN LIBERAL ARTS.

TROBRIAND ISLANDS, small group of coral islands in the Solomon Sea, SW Pacific Ocean, part of Papua New Guinea. Losuia is the principal settlement and stands on the largest island, Kiriwina. The islands are famous through the work of the anthropologist, Bronislaw MALINOWSKI.

TROGONS, a family, Trogonidae, of brightly-colored, tropical, forest-living birds. They are stout and heavy-bodied with long broad tails. They have small weak legs and feet and feed by darting from a perch to snatch insects, tree frogs and fruit.

TROIS-RIVIÈRES, or Three Rivers, city in S Quebec, Canada, on the St. Lawrence R. It is a major pulp and newsprint producer, and has iron and textile industries. Pop 55 869.

TROJAN WAR, conflict between Greece and Troy, made famous by HOMER'S *Iliad*. PARIS, son of PRIAM of Troy, carried off HELEN, wife of Menelaus of Sparta, and took her to Troy. The Greeks, led by AGAMEMNON, MENELAUS, ODYSSEUS, ACHILLES and other heroes, swore to take revenge. They besieged Troy for 10 years, then pretended to sail away, leaving a huge wooden horse outside the city, with Greek soldiers concealed in its belly. The Trojans dragged it into the city, and that night the soldiers opened the city gates to the Greek army. Most of the Trojans were killed and the city was burnt. The legend is thought to have been based on an actual conflict of c1250 BC (see TROY).

TROLLOPE, Anthony (1815–1882), English novelist, famous for his six *Barsetshire* novels about middle-class life in an imaginary cathedral town, including *The Warden* (1855) and *Barchester Towers* (1857). He was a sharp but sympathetic observer of social and political behavior, as revealed in his political *Palliser* novels, such as *Phineas Finn* (1869) and *The Prime Minister* (1876).

TROMBONE, musical instrument, one of the brass WIND INSTRUMENTS. It has a slide mechanism to alter the length of the playing tube and increase the note range. Developed from the sackbut, it was first used in a symphony orchestra by BEETHOVEN in 1808.

TROMP, Maarten Harpertszoon (1597–1653), Dutch admiral. He twice crushed the Spanish fleet in 1639 in the English Channel. In the first DUTCH WAR his defeat of the English admiral Robert BLAKE (1652) led to Dutch control of the Channel. After setbacks in 1653 Tromp was killed in battle.

TRONDHEIM, or Nidaros, port and industrial center in central Norway, Norway's second-largest city. It was capital 997–1380, and its cathedral is one of the finest Scandinavian Gothic buildings. Pop 127 699.

TROPICAL MEDICINE, branch of MEDICINE concerned with the particular diseases encountered in and sometimes imported from the tropics. These largely comprise INFECTIOUS DISEASES due to VIRUSES (e.g., YELLOW FEVER, SMALLPOX, lassa fever), BACTERIA (e.g., CHOLERA), protozoa (e.g., MALARIA, TRYPANOSOME diseases) and worms (e.g., FILARIASIS) which are generally restricted to tropical zones. The ANTIBIOTIC treatment and CHEMOTHERAPY of bacterial and PARASITIC DISEASES and their prevention with prophylactic DRUGS and by control of insect or other vectors are important aspects of this speciality. The diseases of MALNUTRITION—KWASHIORKOR, marasmus and the VITAMIN deficiency diseases of BERI-BERI, PELLAGRA etc.—often fall in the province of tropical disease as do SUNSTROKE and SNAKE BITES.

TROPICBIRDS, a genus, *Phaethon*, of large white seabirds of the order Pelicaniformes, sharing many features with the TERNS. The three species are very similar, with white plumage, long wings and tail streamers up to double the length of the bird.

TROPICS, the lines of latitude lying about $23\frac{1}{2}°$ N (**Tropic of Cancer**) and S (**Tropic of Capricorn**) representing the farthest northerly and southerly latitudes where the sun is, at one time of the year, directly overhead at noon. This occurs at the time of summer SOLSTICE in each hemisphere. The term is used also of the area between the two tropics.

TROPISMS, movements of PLANTS in response to external directional stimuli. If a plant is laid on its side, the stem will soon start to bend upward again. This movement (geotropism) is a response to the force of gravity. The stem is said to be negatively geotropic. Roots are generally positively geotropic and grow downward. Phototropisms are bending movements in response to the direction of illumination. Stems are generally positively phototropic (bend toward the light). Most roots are negatively phototropic, although some appear unaffected by light. Some roots exhibit positive hydrotropism: they bend toward moisture. This response is more powerful than the response to gravity; roots can be deflected from their downward course if the plants are watered only on one side. Tropisms are controlled by differences in concentration of growth HORMONES. (See also AUXINS.)

TROPOSPHERE, the innermost zone of the earth's ATMOSPHERE, extending from the surface up to the tropopause.

TROTSKY, Leon (Lev Davidovich Bronstein; 1879–1940), Russian revolutionary communist, a founder of the USSR. President of the Petrograd (Leningrad) soviet in the 1905 revolution, he escaped from prison to France, Spain and New York. In 1917 he returned, went over to BOLSHEVISM and led the Bolshevik seizure of power in the October RUSSIAN REVOLUTION. As commissar of foreign affairs (1917–18) he resigned over the treaty of BREST-LITOVSK and became commissar of war (1918–25), organizing the Red Army into an effective force. After LENIN'S death (1924) he lost power to STALIN and was deported (1929). Bitterly opposed to Stalin's "socialism in one country," he continued to advocate international revolution, founded the Fourth INTERNATIONAL and attacked Stalinism in *The Revolution Betrayed* (1937). He was murdered in Mexico City by a stalinist agent.

TROUBADOURS, courtly poet-musicians of Provence, S France, c1100–c1300. Their poems, written in PROVENÇAL, mostly on the theme of love, were sung. Troubadours developed the conventions of courtly love, and influenced poetry and music in Germany (see MINNESINGER), Italy, Spain and England.

TROUT, members of the SALMON family found in fresh waters of the N hemisphere, best known from the Brown trout, *Salmo trutta*, of Europe and the Rainbow trout, *S. gairdneri*, of the US. They are solid, powerful, active, usually spotted fishes that favor highly-oxygenated and cool waters. Most species have a variety of forms, some of which spend part of their time in the sea, migrating into fresh water to breed (e.g., the Sea trout, a race of *S. trutta*).

TROUT PERCHES, freshwater fishes of North America with a superficial resemblance to both TROUT and PERCHES, having a trout-like adipose fin and a spiny dorsal fin like that of a perch. Order: Percopsiformes.

TROY, city of ancient NW Asia Minor, near the

Dardanelles, described in HOMER's *Iliad* and rediscovered by SCHLIEMANN in 1870. The earliest site (Troy I) dates from c3000 BC. Troy II contained an imposing fortress and had wide trade contacts. Its famous treasure of gold, copper and bronze indicates a wealthy community. Troy VI, c2000–1300 BC, had a citadel surrounded by huge limestone walls, and large houses built on terraces. It was destroyed by earthquake. The rebuilt Troy VIIa was probably Homer's Troy. It was looted and destroyed by fire c1250 BC. Troy VIII was a small Greek village. Troy IX, the top layer, was the Greek and Roman city of Ilium.

TROY, commercial and industrial city in SE Ala., seat of Pike Co. It lies in a timber and farming region. Pop 11 482.

TROY, city in SE Mich., a suburb of Detroit. It has automobile and electronic parts industries. Pop 39 149.

TROY, city in E N.Y., seat of Rensselaer Co., on the Hudson R. It manufactures shirts, metal goods and instruments. Pop 62 918.

TROY, industrial city in W Ohio, seat of Miami Co., on the Great Miami R. Farm equipment, paper and tools are manufactured. Pop 17 186.

TROYES, Treaty of, 1420, agreement between CHARLES VI of France and HENRY V of England, recognizing Henry as heir to the French throne. The disinherited dauphin later repudiated the treaty, becoming CHARLES VII of France.

TROY WEIGHT, a system of weights used for precious metals and stones, named for the French town of Troyes, famed for its medieval trade fairs. Today the price of GOLD is still quoted in dollars per Troy ounce. The troy ounce, equivalent to 1.0971 ounces avoirdupois, is equal to the apothecaries' ounce. (See also APOTHECARIES' WEIGHTS; WEIGHTS AND MEASURES.)

TRUCIAL STATES. See UNITED ARAB EMIRATES.

TRUCK, automotive vehicle used for transporting freight by road. The typical long-distance truck is an articulated vehicle comprising a two- or three-axled "truck tractor" coupled to a two-axled "semitrailer." A two- or three-axled "full trailer" may in addition be coupled to the semitrailer. Most trucks are powered by a DIESEL ENGINE, have a manual TRANSMISSION with perhaps as many as 16 forward gears, and have AIR BRAKES. In the US, trucks carry about 40% of all intercity freight (compared with the railroads' 30%); the industry is organized under a trade association, American Trucking Associations Inc., while the American Association of State Highway Officials regulates truck sizes and weights. Overall supervision of trucking is undertaken by the INTERSTATE COMMERCE COMMISSION.

TRUCK FARMING, large-scale commercial production of fresh vegetables and fruits for local or distant markets. Modern truck farming has been revolutionized by mechanical harvesting and handling and by modern methods of preserving and transporting fresh produce. The principal US farming regions are in Cal., Fla., Tex., the Atlantic Coastal Plain and the Great Lakes area.

(1) The standard modern trumpet, ordinarily built in B flat, although other keys are often used. The characteristic coiled shape was introduced as early as the 15th century to make the length of tubing needed for an adequate range more manageable. (2) The *cornet à pistons* resembles a trumpet but has a shorter tube and a less bright sound.

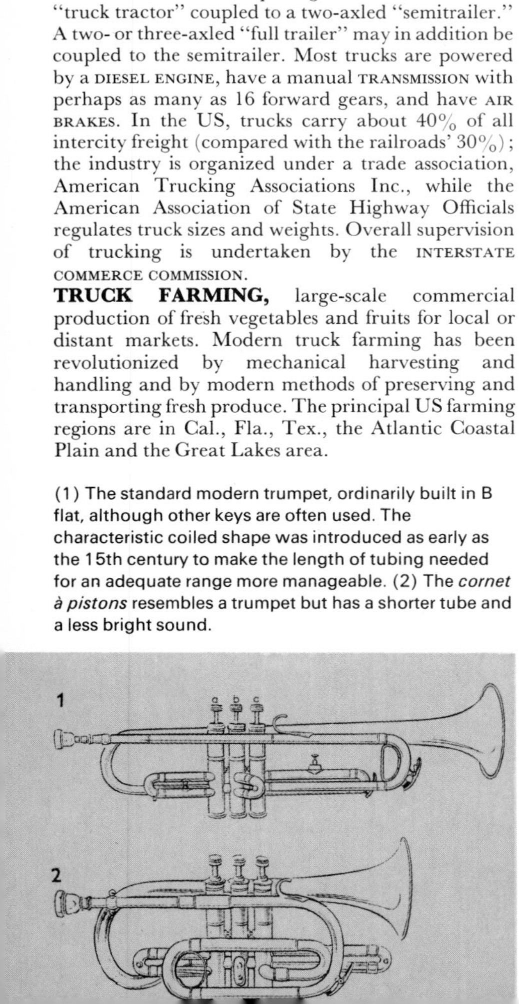

TRUDEAU, Pierre Elliott (1919–), Canadian politician. A liberal law professor, he entered parliament in 1965, became minister of justice in 1967 and succeeded Lester PEARSON as premier and Liberal Party leader (1968). He has sought to promote a dialogue between the provincial and federal governments and to contain the Quebec separatist movement, giving the French language equal status with English, but temporarily instituting martial law against terrorism. In 1970 he recognized the People's Republic of China.

TRUFFLE, underground fungi of the genus *Tuber* that have long been regarded as a delicacy. Pigs and dogs are trained to find them by scent. Some grow up to 1kg (2.2lb) and resemble potatoes; most are much smaller.

TRUJILLO MOLINA, Rafael Leonidas (1891–1961), Dominican dictator 1930–61, and president 1930–38, 1942–52. He introduced much material progress, but savagely suppressed political opposition and feuded with neighboring countries. He was assassinated.

TRUK ISLANDS, or Hogoleu Islands, group of about 55 volcanic islands (39sq mi) surrounded by a reef, part of the CAROLINE Islands, W Pacific Ocean. They were a Japanese WWII naval base.

TRUMAN, Harry S. (1884–1972), 33rd president of the US. Inexperienced and virtually unknown, he became president after F. D. ROOSEVELT's sudden death, and in the difficult post-WWII years attempted to contain communist expansion and to continue the NEW DEAL reforms. Truman entered politics in 1919 with help from the Democrat T. J. PENDERGAST who in 1934 backed his election as a Mo. senator. In 1940 he gained prominence as head of a committee investigating corruption in the Defense industries, and in 1944 was chosen as a compromise vice-president for Roosevelt. On becoming president Truman accepted the German surrender, was involved in the establishment of the UNITED NATIONS, attended the POTSDAM CONFERENCE and took the controversial decision to use the atom bomb against Japan, thus ending the war. He took a tough line over Russia's attempted annexation of Poland. At home, amid economic difficulties and labor unrest, a hostile Congress blocked most of his FAIR DEAL program, and passed the TAFT-HARTLEY ACT over Truman's veto. As the COLD WAR hardened, he regarded communist expansion as the major threat, and formulated the TRUMAN DOCTRINE and the MARSHALL PLAN, followed by the POINT FOUR PROGRAM and the setting-up of the NORTH ATLANTIC TREATY ORGANIZATION. (See also BERLIN AIRLIFT.) Truman's unpopularity at home made his decision to run again in 1948 seem hopeless, but despite all predictions he won. During his second term Truman again had his Fair Deal measures vetoed, except for a Housing Act (1949), was embroiled in the anti-communist hysteria generated by MCCARTHY, and had his seizure of the steel industry during a strike declared unconstitutional. He sent troops to fight the KOREAN WAR, and amidst controversy over US Far East policy, sacked General MACARTHUR for insubordination.

TRUMAN DOCTRINE, US declaration (1947), aimed to combat communist expansion, particularly in Greece and Turkey, stating the US would "support free peoples who are resisting attempted subjugation by armed minorities or by outside pressures."

TRUMBULL, town in SW Conn. situated in an agricultural community. It is residential, and has some light industry. Pop 31 394.

TRUMBULL, John (1750–1831), US poet and judge. A leader of the HARTFORD WITS, he is best known for *The Progress of Dulness* (1772–73) and *M'Fingal* (1775–82), a mock-epic based on Samuel BUTLER's *Hudibras*, satirizing the British Tories.

TRUMBULL, John (1756–1843), US painter. He studied with Benjamin WEST in London where he started *The Battle of Bunker's Hill* (1786). He made 36 life portrait studies for his best-known work, *The Declaration of Independence* (1786–94). In 1817–24 he painted four monumental pictures on revolutionary themes for the US Capitol rotunda.

TRUMPET, musical instrument, one of the brass WIND INSTRUMENTS. The modern trumpet comprises a cylindrical tube in a curved oblong form which flares out into a bell. Three piston valves, first introduced c1815, regulate pitch. The standard orchestral trumpet is generally in B Flat. The trumpet is a popular dance and jazz band instrument.

Harry S. TRUMAN

33rd US President

Born: May 8, 1884
Died: December 26, 1972
Term of office: April 12, 1945–January 19, 1953
Political party: Democratic

TRUMPETERS, a family, Psophiidae, of three species of chicken-sized birds of tropical forests of South America. Mainly black and with rather long legs, they live in flocks on the forest floor, feeding on insects and fruit.

TRURO, town in central Nova Scotia, Canada. Its industries include lumbering, printing, textiles and dairy processing. Pop 13 047.

TRUST, in law, a legal relationship in which property is administered by a **trustee**, who has some of the powers of an owner, for the benefit of a beneficiary; the trustee is obliged to act only in the beneficiary's best interest, and can derive no advantage except an agreed fee. His powers are limited to those specified or implied in the document establishing the trust. The trustee may be an individual, perhaps looking after the property of a child until he comes of age, or a corporate body; banks and trust corporations often act as trustees of larger properties. Trusts are a major feature of EQUITY law. Certain categories of trust, generally those with some charitable or other aim beneficial to the public, may be given tax relief. A specialized form, the corporation trust, gave a company's board of trustees the right to invest stockholders' money in a variety of enterprises which would normally have been in competition; this enabled the Standard Oil Co. and others to set up price-fixing CARTELS. These were attacked by the SHERMAN ANTITRUST ACT (1890), but remained current until the 1900s, when Theodore ROOSEVELT's opposition led to their decline. Except for a brief relaxation during the NEW DEAL, ANTITRUST LEGISLATION has since been vigorously enforced.

TRUSTEE. See TRUST.

TRUST TERRITORY, dependent territory administered under UNITED NATIONS supervision. A trustee nation is responsible for developing the trust territory and assisting it to independence. The Trusteeship Council helps the General Assembly and Security Council supervise trust territories. Of the 11 Trust Territories (mostly former MANDATES of the LEAGUE OF NATIONS)—British Cameroons, French Cameroons, Ruanda-Urundi, Italian Somaliland, Tanganyika, British Togoland, French Togoland, Nauru, Pacific Islands, New Guinea and Western Samoa—only the US-administered Pacific Islands have not yet gained independence.

TRUTH, philosophical concept deriving from the everyday notion of "telling the truth" as opposed to telling a deliberate falsehood. "Correspondence" theories of truth hold that a statement is true if it corresponds to the "facts" of experience. "Coherence" theories of truth contend, however, that facts are themselves statements of a kind whose truth cannot be tested by looking for further correspondences, but only by considering their logical coherence with other statements about supposed reality. "Pragmatic" theories of truth stress that the only usefully testable "truths" are those that enable us to anticipate or control the course of events. (See also EMPIRICISM; RATIONALISM; PRAGMATISM.)

TRUTH, Sojourner (c1797–1883), US abolitionist. A slave until 1827, originally called Isabella, she traveled the North from 1843 preaching Negro emancipation and women's rights. In the mid-1860s in Washington D.C. she worked to resettle ex-slaves.

TRUTH SERUM. See PENTOTHAL SODIUM.

TRUTH TABLE, in LOGIC, a convenient way of displaying the range of "truth values" (truth or falsity) of a compound statement as determined by the truth values of its simple component statements. For example, if the simple statements *p* and *q* are both true, then the compound statement *p and q* is true (1); but if either *p* or *q* or both *p* and *q* are false, then *p and q* is false (0). This is usually displayed in tabular form thus:

p	*q*	*p.q*
1	1	1
1	0	0
0	1	0
0	0	0

The table can be extended to show the range of truth values for other combinations of *p* and *q*.

TRYON, William (1729–1788), British governor of N.C. (1765–71). In 1771, after harshly crushing the revolt of the REGULATORS at the battle of ALAMANCE, he was appointed governor of New York.

TRYPANOSOMES, PROTOZOA responsible for trypanosomiasis of the African (SLEEPING SICKNESS) and South American (CHAGAS' DISEASE) varieties, carried by the tsetse fly and certain bugs respectively. They are relatively insensitive to CHEMOTHERAPY in established cases; prevention is therefore important.

TRYPSIN, ENZYME catalyzing the breakdown of PROTEINS in the vertebrate DIGESTIVE SYSTEM.

TSAR, or Czar (from Latin, *Caesar*), title used by Russian emperors. First adopted by IVAN IV, who in 1547 was crowned "tsar of all Russia," the title continued until 1918 when the last tsar, NICHOLAS II, was murdered.

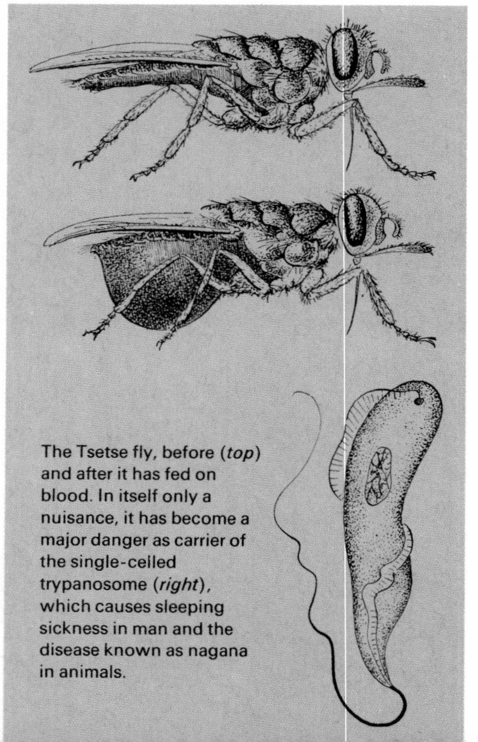

The Tsetse fly, before (*top*) and after it has fed on blood. In itself only a nuisance, it has become a major danger as carrier of the single-celled trypanosome (*right*), which causes sleeping sickness in man and the disease known as nagana in animals.

TSETSE FLIES, 20 species of muscoid flies of the genus *Glossina*. They are true winged flies very like HOUSEFLIES except that the mouthparts are adapted for piercing the skin of mammals and sucking blood. Widespread in tropical Africa, their significance lies in that some species act as vectors of the TRYPANOSOMES which cause SLEEPING SICKNESS in humans.

TSHOMBE, Moise Kapenda (1919–1969), president 1960–63 of the Congolese breakaway state of Katanga. Backed by Belgian interests, he opposed LUMUMBA and the UN. He returned from exile to be premier (1964–65) of the Congo (ZAIRE). Dismissed, he was sentenced to death, and died in prison in Algeria.

TSIMSHIAN INDIANS, or Chimmesyan Indians, a NW coast tribe of British Columbia and Alaska, dependent largely on fishing. They are famous for their carved and painted totem poles. About 6000 now live in reservations.

TSINAN, or Chinan, capital of Shantung province, NE China, with large automotive, iron, steel and chemical industries. It was a city in the 8th century BC. Pop 1 500 000.

TSINGTAO, or Ch'ing-Taó, major Yellow Sea port, E China, a textile, food, steel and engineering center. Germany, Japan, then the US had bases here 1898–1949. Pop 1 900 000.

TSIOLKOVSKY, Konstantin Eduardovich (1857–1935), Russian physicist who pioneered ROCKET science, but who is perhaps most important for his role in educating the Soviet government and people into acceptance of the future potential of SPACE EXPLORATION. He also built one of the first WIND TUNNELS (c1892). A large crater on the far side of the MOON is named for him; and the timing of Sputnik I's launch commemorated the 100th anniversary of his birth.

TSUNAMI, formerly called **tidal wave**, fast-moving ocean wave caused by submarine EARTHQUAKES, volcanic eruptions, etc., found mainly in the Pacific, and often taking a high toll of lives in affected coastal areas. In midocean, the wave height is usually under 1m, the distance between succeeding crests of the order of 200km, and the velocity about 750km/h. Near the coast, FRICTION with the sea bottom slows the wave, so that the distance between crests decreases, the wave height increasing to about 25m or more.

TSUSHIMA, Battle of, decisive sea battle of May 1905 which effectively ended the RUSSO-JAPANESE WAR. Japanese Admiral Heihachiro TOGO's fleet destroyed or captured almost all the Russian Baltic Fleet under Admiral Rozhdestvenski. The battle took place near Tsushima Island, between Japan and Korea.

TSVETAYEVA, Marina Ivanova (1892–1941), Russian modernist poet. Her lyrical poetry, such as *King-Maiden* (1922) is noted for its concise style and variety of rhythms. Away from Russia 1922–39, she returned home, later committing suicide.

TUAMOTU ISLANDS, or Dangerous Islands, archipelago, about 330sq mi in area, of some 80 small islands in FRENCH POLYNESIA, S Pacific. The main islands are Rangiroa and Fakarava. The Kon-Tiki raft ended its Pacific voyage at Raroia Island.

TUAREGS, a BERBER tribe in the Sahara, about 300 000 in number. Its people are fair-skinned; the social system comprises noble families, a large number of vassal tribes, and Negro slaves. Adult men, but not women, wear a blue veil. Tuareg script is like that of the ancient Libyans.

TUATARA, *Sphenodon punctatus*, an iguana-like animal belonging to the otherwise extinct reptilian order Rhynchocephalia—reptiles with a beak-like upper jaw and teeth fused to the jawbones, not set in sockets. Male tuataras are also unusual in having no copulatory organ; mating is accomplished by cloacal apposition. Tuataras are long-lived animals: estimates of life span vary from 100–300 years. The species is now restricted to small islands off the New Zealand coast.

TUBA, low-pitched brass musical WIND INSTRUMENT with three to five valves. It is held vertically. There are tenor, baritone, euphonium, bass and contrabass tubas—the CC contrabass being popular in orchestras, the BB contrabass in bands.

TUBER, swollen underground stems and roots which are organs of perennation and vegetative propagation and contain stored food material. The potato is a stem tuber. It swells at the tip of a slender underground stem (or stolon) and gives rise to a new plant the following year. Dahlia tubers are swollen roots.

TUBERCULIN, PROTEIN derivative of the mycobacteria responsible for TUBERCULOSIS. This may be used in tests of cell-mediated IMMUNITY to tuberculosis, providing evidence of previous disease (often subclinical) or immunization (BCG). The substance was originally isolated by KOCH.

TUBERCULOSIS (TB), a group of INFECTIOUS DISEASES caused by the BACILLUS *Mycobacterium tuberculosis*, which kills some 3 million people every year throughout the world. TB may invade any organ but most commonly affects the respiratory system where it has been called consumption or phthisis (see also LUPUS VULGARIS and SCROFULA). In 1906 it killed 1 in every 500 persons in the US, but today it leads to only 1 in 30 000 deaths, because of effective drugs and better living conditions. The disease is spread in three ways: inoculation via cuts, etc.; inhalation of infected sputum, and ingestion of infected food. In pulmonary TB there are two stages of infection. In primary infection there are usually no significant symptoms: dormant small hard masses called tubercles are formed by the body's defenses. In postprimary infection the dormant BACTERIA are reactivated due to weakening of the body's defenses and clinical symptoms become evident. Symptoms include fatigue, weight loss, persistent cough with green or yellow sputum and possibly blood. Treatment nowadays is mainly by triple drug therapy with streptomycin, para-aminosalicylic acid (PAS) and isoniazid, together with rest. Recovery takes about 2 years.

The TUBERCULIN skin test can show whether a person has some IMMUNITY to the disease, though the detection of the disease in its early stages, when it is readily curable, is difficult. Control of the disease is accomplished by preventive measures such as X-RAY screening, BCG vaccination, isolation of infectious people and food sterilization.

TUBEROSE, *Polianthes tuberosa*, a relative of the DAFFODIL which grows wild in Mexico and has single or double white flowers. It is a popular garden flower. Family: Amaryllidaceae.

TUBMAN, Harriet Ross (c1820–1913), US fugitive slave and abolitionist. She was active in the UNDERGROUND RAILROAD after 1850. Nicknamed "Moses," she helped over 300 slaves to freedom. In the Civil War she was a Union spy and scout.

TUBMAN, William Vacanarat Shadrach (1895–1971), president of Liberia (1944–71). He made extensive economic, social and educational reforms and extended the rights of tribespeople and women.

TUCO-TUCO, a genus, *Ctenomys*, of nocturnal vegetarian rodents of South America. From 230 to 330mm (9–13in) long, they live in colonies, excavating extensive burrows.

TUCSON, city in SE Ariz., seat of Pima Co. in Santa Cruz valley, whose climate attracts tourists. Dating from a Spanish military camp (1776), it has electronic, optic and aircraft industries and is a mining, cotton and livestock center. Pop 262 933.

TUDOR, Antony (1909–), English choreographer who introduced dramatic, emotional themes into US ballet. His most notable interpretations include *Lilac Garden* (1936) and *Pillar of Fire* (1942).

TUDOR, House of, reigning dynasty of England, 1485–1603. Of Welsh descent, Henry Tudor, Earl of Richmond and heir to the House of LANCASTER, ended the WARS OF THE ROSES by defeating Richard III in 1485 and became HENRY VII, first Tudor king. After him came HENRY VIII (reigned 1509–47), EDWARD VI (1547–53), MARY I (1553–58) and ELIZABETH I (1558–1603). Under the Tudors England became a major power and enjoyed a flowering of the arts.

TUDOR STYLE, English art and architecture from Henry VII to Mary I, 1484–1558. The architecture is characterized by the increasing application of RENAISSANCE details to the late GOTHIC Perpendicular style, and doors, windows, fireplaces and wood paneling have four-centered arches. Italian craftsmen and foreign artists, including the HOLBEINS, worked at the courts, such as HAMPTON COURT PALACE.

TUESDAY, third day of the week, named for TIW, the Germanic war-god. The French for Tuesday is *mardi*, for the Roman war-god Mars. MARDI-GRAS, or SHROVE TUESDAY, is the day before LENT begins.

TUFA. See TRAVERTINE.

TU FU (712–770), one of the greatest Chinese poets. His concise and evocative style, typical of the T'ANG period, expresses the tragic conditions of his life and that of the poor. He spent much of his life traveling in China.

TULA, city in W RSFSR, USSR, a transportation and iron-mining center, with arms and machine industries, site of Russia's first arms factory (1712). Pop 462 000.

TULARE, city in S central Cal., a processing center for cotton, dairy and other farm products. Pop 16 235.

TULAREMIA, or **Rabbit Fever**, INFECTIOUS DISEASE due to BACTERIA, causing FEVER, ulceration, LYMPH node enlargement and sometimes PNEUMONIA. It is carried by wild animals, particularly rabbits, and insects. ANTIBIOTICS are fully effective in treatment.

TULIP, bulbous plants of the genus *Tulipa*, which are native to Europe and Asia. Cultivated tulips were introduced to Europe via Holland in the 16th century and have become popular spring-flowering garden and pot plants. They have deep, cup-shaped flowers and new varieties are continually being bred. Family: Liliaceae.

TULIP TREE, popular name for *Liriodendron tulipifera*, a fast growing, stately tree of North America, which bears yellow and orange tulip-like flowers in early summer. It is frequently grown as an ornamental. Family: Magnoliaceae.

TULL, Jethro (1674–1741), British agricultural scientist who invented a horse-drawn hoe for cultivating the ground between the rows (after 1715).

TULLAHOMA, city in central Tenn. It makes clothes and sports gear. Nearby is the aeronautical Arnold Engineering and Development Center. Pop 15 311.

TULSA, manufacturing center and second city of Okla., seat of Tulsa Co., in NE Okla. Since the discovery of oil (1901) it has become a national center for the oil industry. Pop 330 350.

TUMACACORI NATIONAL MONUMENT, site of a mission in S Ariz., near the Mexican border, first built by Father KINO in 1696 and briefly reestablished by the Franciscans in 1822.

TUMBLEBUGS, alternative name for DUNG BEETLES.

TUMBLEWEED, common name for several plants native to North America that grow in clumps on waste land and dry into loose balls. These break from the soil and are blown by the wind, scattering seeds. Examples are the Russian thistle (*Salsola kali*) and *Amaranthus albus*.

TUMOR, strictly, any swelling on or in the body, but more usually used to refer only to an abnormal overgrowth of tissue (or **neoplasm**). These may be benign proliferations such as fibroids of the WOMB, or they may be forms of CANCER, LYMPHOMA OR SARCOMA, which are generally malignant. The rate of growth, the tendency to spread locally and to distant sites via the BLOOD vessels and LYMPH system, and systemic effects determine the degree of malignancy of a given tumor. Tumors may present as a lump, by local compression effects (especially with BRAIN tumors), by bleeding (GASTROINTESTINAL TRACT tumors) or by systemic effects including ANEMIA, weight loss, false HORMONE actions, NEURITIS etc. Treatments include surgery, RADIATION THERAPY and CHEMOTHERAPY.

TUNA, or tunny, large oceanic members of the MACKEREL family. They are powerful, torpedo-shaped fishes, the dorsal and pectoral fins folding away into grooves to reduce drag in rapid swimming. Active carnivores, feeding especially on squid, all are important sport and food fishes.

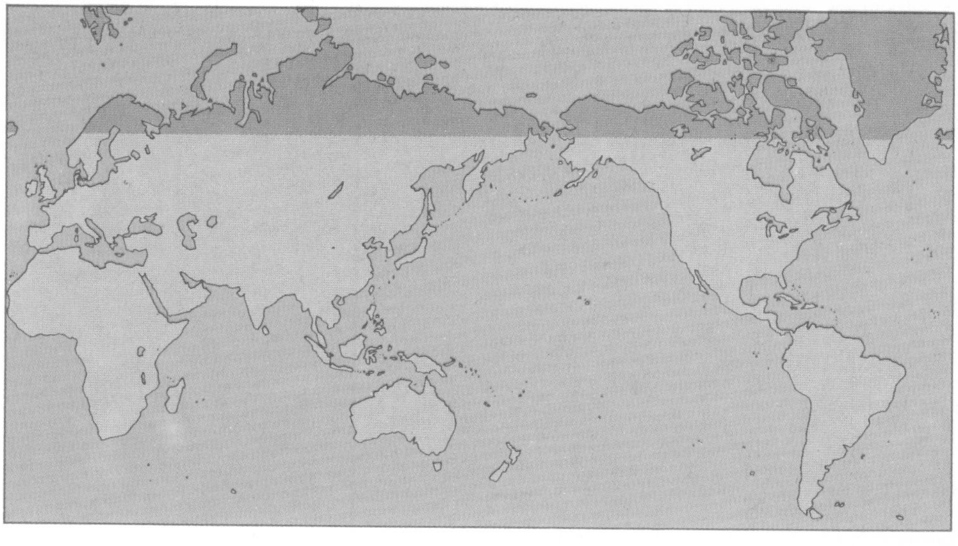

Map showing the distribution and extent of the Arctic tundra lands (darker area).

TUNDRA, the treeless plains of the Arctic Circle. For most of the year the temperature is less than 0°C, and even during the short summer it never rises above 10°C. The soil is a thin coating over PERMAFROST. Tundra vegetation includes lichens, mosses and stunted shrubs. Similar regions on high mountains (but generally without permafrost) are **alpine tundra**.

TUNG OIL, or China wood oil, important drying OIL and ingredient of many PAINTS and VARNISHES. It dries very rapidly, to form an intact and durable coating. Poisonous, it is extracted from the seeds of the tung oil tree (*Aleurites fordii*) and related species. Family: Euphorbiaceae.

TUNGSTEN (W), or **wolfram**, hard, silvery-gray metal in Group VIB of the PERIODIC TABLE; a TRANSITION ELEMENT. Its chief ores are SCHEELITE and WOLFRAMITE. The metal is produced by reduction of heated tungsten dioxide with hydrogen. Its main uses are in tungsten steel ALLOYS for high-temperature applications, and for the filaments of incandescent lamps. It is relatively inert, and resembles MOLYBDENUM. Cemented **tungsten carbide** (WC) is used in cutting tools. AW 183.9, mp 3410°C, bp 5660°C, sg 19.3 (20°C).

TUNGUS, an ALTAIC LANGUAGE people of subarctic E Siberia, related to the MANCHUS. They comprise two groups. The Evenki live E of the Yenisey R to the Pacific and from the Amur R to the Arctic, while the Lamuti live on the Sea of Okhotsk coast.

TUNICATES, a subphylum, Urochordata, of the CHORDATES, containing three classes of marine invertebrates, most notably the SEA SQUIRTS.

TUNING FORK, simple two-pronged instrument that emits a pure tone of fixed PITCH when struck. Made within a FREQUENCY range of 20 to 20 000Hz, they are used as acoustical frequency standards.

TUNIS, commercial and industrial city and capital of Tunisia, in NE Tunisia. It produces carpets, textiles and olive oil. Nearby are the ruins of ancient CARTHAGE. Pop 468 997.

TUNISIA, North African republic on the Mediterranean Sea, with Algeria to the W and Libya to the SE.

Land. The 639mi coastline has several good harbors. In the NW the Atlas mountains form a high wooded plateau and rise to 5 000ft in the W. The Medjerda R is the only permanent river; it irrigates a major wheat-producing area. In the S beyond Chott Djerid and other salt lakes lies the Sahara Desert. The summers are hot and dry, the winters mild and wet. Annual rainfall varies from 30in in the N to 4in in the S.

People. Tunisia is the most densely populated of North African countries. Most people live in the fertile N. The population is predominantly BERBER and Arab. The largest cities are Tunis, Sfax, Sousse, Bizerta and Kairouan, and 40% of the population live in towns.

Economy. The economy is agricultural; the main crops are wheat, barley, wine, citrus fruits, olives and dates. A large fishing industry is based on Sousse and Sfax. Tunisia is a major producer of phosphates, and mines iron ore. Oil production is increasing rapidly. Industries include sugar refining, chemicals, cellulose and tourism. The main exports are phosphates, olive oil, wine, citrus fruits and iron ore.

History. Formerly a Phoenician colony, Tunisia was conquered in 146 BC by the Romans, in 439 AD by the VANDALS, in 533 by the Byzantines, in 670 by the Arabs, in 1574 by Turkish pirates and in 1881 by the French who made it a protectorate. Habib BOURGUIBA founded the nationalist Neo-Destour Party in 1934 and after Tunisia's independence (1956) became president of the Tunisian republic in 1957. Still in power, he has largely created modern Tunisia.

Official name: Republic of Tunisia
Capital: Tunis
Area: 63 362sq mi
Population: 5 250 000
Languages: Arabic; French
Religions: Muslim
Monetary unit(s): 1 Tunisian dollar = 1 000 millimes

The town of Foum-Tatahouine, in southern Tunisia, is an important trade center, caravan base and military post on the edge of the Sahara.

TUNNEL, underground passageway, usually designed to carry a highway or railroad, to serve as a conduit for water or sewage, or to provide access to an underground working face (see MINING). Although tunnels have been built since prehistoric times, tunneling methods remained primitive and hazardous until the 19th century. Modern soft-ground tunneling was pioneered by Marc BRUNEL, who in 1824 invented the "tunneling shield"—a device subsequently improved (1869–86) by James Greathead. The Greathead shield is basically a large steel cylinder with a sharp cutting edge driven forward by hydraulic rams. Used in conjunction with a compressed-air atmosphere, it protects excavating workmen against cave-ins and water seepage. Tunneling through hard rock is facilitated by an array of pneumatic drills mounted on a "jumbo" carriage running on rails. Explosives are inserted in a pattern of holes drilled in the rock face and then detonated. Increasingly used today, however, are automatic tunneling machines called "moles," with cutting heads consisting of a rotating or oscillating wheel that digs, grinds or chisels away the working face. Another common tunnel-building method—used in constructing the New York SUBWAY—is "cut-and-cover," which involves excavating a trench, building the tunnel-lining and then covering it. The world's longest vehicular or railroad tunnel is the 19.8km (12.3mi) Simplon II in the Alps, completed in 1922.

TUNNEL DIODE, SEMICONDUCTOR device with a high impurity concentration and negative RESISTANCE over part of its operating range, used in amplifying, oscillating and switching circuits. Its operation depends on quantum-mechanical tunneling of charges through a narrow p-n junction at zero voltage which ceases at increased forward voltages.

TUNNEY, Gene (James Joseph; 1897–), US world heavyweight boxing champion, 1926–28. In 1926 he beat Jack DEMPSEY in the controversial fight of the "long count." He retired undefeated in 1928, having lost only one of his professional bouts.

TUPELO, city in NE Miss., seat of Lee Co., a livestock and cotton trading and processing center. In 1864 the Unionists fought off General FORREST's troops here. Pop 20471.

TUPELO, deciduous trees of the genus *Nyssa* which are native to eastern North America and Asia and cultivated as ornamentals for their attractive autumn foliage and cherry-like fruits. Tupelo wood has an interlocked grain which resists splintering under heavy wear. Family: Nyssaceae.

TUPOLEV, Andrei Nikolayevich (1888–1972), Russian aircraft designer. He was responsible for more than 100 designs, including the Tu-20 Bear turboprop bomber (1955) and the world's first supersonic passenger airliner, the Tu-144 (1969).

TUPPER, Sir Charles (1821–1915), Canadian statesman. As premier of Nova Scotia (1864–67), he led that province into the Dominion of Canada. He held several posts 1870–73, 1878–84 in the Conservative government, served as high commissioner in London (1884–96) and was briefly Canada's premier (1896).

TURACOS, or Plantain-eaters or louries, a family, Musophagidae, of 20 species of active arboreal birds of Africa. Related to cuckoos, all are large, often crested, brightly-colored birds which run and leap through tree branches with great agility.

TURBINE, machine for directly converting the kinetic and/or thermal ENERGY of a flowing FLUID into useful rotational energy. The working fluid may be air, hot gas, steam or water. This either pushes against a set of blades mounted on the drive shaft (impulse turbines) or turns the shaft by reaction when the fluid is expelled from nozzles (or nozzle-shaped vanes) around its circumference (reaction turbines). Water turbines were the first to be developed. They now include the vast inward-flow reaction turbines used in the generation of HYDROELECTRICITY and the smaller-scale tangential-flow "Pelton wheel" impulse types used when exploiting a very great "head" of water. In the 1880s, Charles Algernon Parsons (1854–1931), a British engineer, designed the first successful steam turbines, having realized that the efficient use of high-pressure steam demanded that its energy be extracted in a multitude of small stages. Steam turbines thus consist of a series of vanes mounted on a rotating drum with stator vanes redirecting the steam in between the moving ones. They are commonly used as marine engines and in thermal and nuclear power plants. GAS TURBINES are not as yet widely used except in airplanes (see JET PROPULSION) and for peak-load electricity generation.

TURBOJET. See JET PROPULSION.

TURBOT, *Scophthalmus maximus*, a large FLATFISH from shallow waters of the N Atlantic and European coasts. They are fine food fishes, growing to over 18kg (40lb). The body is not scaled, but is covered on the eyed, left, side with warty tubercles.

TURBULENCE, type of irregular flow of FLUIDS in which the motion at any point varies rapidly in magnitude and direction. The value of REYNOLDS NUMBER determines whether fluid flow is laminar (smooth and well-defined), or turbulent. Most natural fluid motion is turbulent.

TURENNE, Henri de la Tour d'Auvergne, Vicomte de (1611–1675), French military commander. During the THIRTY YEARS' WAR, his brilliant campaigns of 1644–47 helped secure the Peace of WESTPHALIA (1648). He supported first CONDÉ then LOUIS XIV in the FRONDE civil war (1648–50), fought against the Spanish (1654–59) and was killed in the third DUTCH WAR of 1672–78.

TURGENEV, Ivan Sergeyevich (1818–1883), great Russian writer. A liberal and pro-Western opponent of serfdom, he wrote of peasant and country life, at the same time embracing social and political themes. After criticism of his greatest novel, *Fathers and Sons* (1862), he lived mostly abroad. His plays include *A Month in the Country* (1850). Short stories such as *Torrents of Spring* (1872) are among his finest works.

TURGOT, Anne-Robert-Jacques (1727–1781), French economist and reformer. One of the PHYSIOCRATS, he favored free trade and a land tax and anticipated the Law of DIMINISHING RETURNS. He lost his post (1776) as comptroller general of finances when he pressed for an end to compulsory labor.

TURIN, city in NW Italy. It is a major industrial center, with automobiles (Fiat, Lancia), machinery, chemical and electrical industries. It was the capital of the Kingdom of SARDINIA (1720–1861) and the first capital of united Italy (1861–64). Pop 1 177 939.

TURINA, Joaquín (1882–1949), Spanish composer. His output, which includes colorful orchestral works, songs, piano pieces and two operas, was important in promoting a national Spanish style of music.

TURKESTAN, or Turkistan, historic region in central Asia, extending from the Caspian Sea to the Mongolian desert. It consists today of the S Kazakh, Kirgiz, Tadzhik, Turkmen and Uzbek SSRs in the USSR, Chinese Turkestan and part of NE Afghanistan. It has been the home of TURKIC-speaking peoples since c500 AD and was important for its great trade routes linking Europe with the Far East. The chief city is SAMARKAND.

TURKEY, a republic in extreme SE Europe and Asia Minor, bounded by the Black Sea, USSR, Iran, Iraq, Syria, the Mediterranean, Greece and Bulgaria.

Land. Turkey is mountainous, with an extensive semiarid plateau in Asia Minor; the highest peak is Mt. ARARAT (16945ft). The Euphrates and the Tigris rivers rise in the E; other rivers include the Kizil Irmak, Sakarya and Büyük Menderes. The strategic BOSPORUS and DARDANELLES separate European from Asian Turkey. Earthquakes occur frequently. The climate is Mediterranean around the coastal lowlands, but more extreme and drier inland, with harsh winters toward the NE.

People. The TURKISH-speaking population descends largely from the TATARS, who entered Asia Minor in the 1000s AD. There are small Kurdish and Arab minorities. Some 60% live in rural areas. Illiteracy is about 40%.

Economy. Agriculture is the basis of the economy. The chief crops are grains, cotton, fruits and tobacco. Cattle are reared on the Anatolian plateau. Turkish industry has been developed greatly since WWII and includes steel, iron and textile manufacture. There are large deposits of coal, iron and other metals, and some oil.

Official name: Republic of Turkey
Capital: Ankara
Area: 301 302sq mi
Population: 35 666 549
Languages: Turkish; Kurdish, Arabic spoken
Religions: Muslim; Jewish, Christian
Monetary unit(s): 1 Turkish Lira (or pound) = 100 kuruş (or piastres)

History. Formerly part of the HITTITE, PERSIAN, ROMAN, BYZANTINE, SELJUK and OTTOMAN empires, Turkey became a republic in 1923 under ATATURK, who initiated a vast program of reform and modernization aiming at establishing Turkey as a modern democratic state on European lines. Neutral for most of WWII, Turkey afterwards aligned herself with the West, joining the NORTH ATLANTIC TREATY ORGANIZATION and accepting substantial US aid. Democratic rule was shaken by an army coup in 1960, since when military intervention in government has continued, amid increasing economic difficulties, civil unrest and political instability. Tension with Greece has almost led to war on several occasions. In 1974 Turkey invaded and occupied part of Cyprus.

TURKEYS, two species of large New World game birds in their own family, Meleagrididae. The Common turkey, *Meleagris gallopavo*, occurs in open woodland and scrub of North America and is the ancestor of the domestic turkey. The head and neck of both species are naked and with wattles; a fleshy caruncle overhangs the bill. The naked skin in the Common turkey is red; in the Ocellated turkey, blue.

TURKIC LANGUAGES, a group of ALTAIC LANGUAGES spoken by the TURKS in Turkey, E Europe and central and N Asia. They include Turkish, Azerbaijani, Turkoman, Uzbek, Kirghiz, Tatar, Kazakh and Chuvash. Vowel harmony and wide use of suffixes are characteristic. Latin or Cyrillic have replaced Arabic script since the 1920s–30s.

TURKISH, a TURKIC language, official language of Turkey, also spoken by minorities in E Europe and SW Asia. Evolved during the OTTOMAN EMPIRE, it was written in Arabic script until ATATURK introduced a modified Latin alphabet in 1928.

TURKMENISTAN, a constituent republic of the USSR, in central Asia, bordering on Iran and Afghanistan. It is 90% desert, and farming is based on irrigation; cotton and grains are the leading crops. Turkomans also produce the famous ASTRAKHAN fur from KARAKUL sheep. There are large mineral deposits, including oil, and textile, chemical, and food-processing industries. The capital is Ashkhabad.

TURKS, a family of TURKIC-speaking, chiefly Muslim peoples extending from Sinkiang (W China) and Siberia to Turkey, Iran and E European USSR. They include the Tatars, Kazakhs, Uzbeks, Kirghiz, Turkmens, Vighurs, Azerbaijanis and many others. The Turks spread through Asia from the 6th century onwards, were converted to Islam in the 10th century. In the W they controlled vast lands under the SELJUKS (1000s–1200s) and OTTOMAN EMPIRE (1300s–1923).

TURKS AND CAICOS ISLANDS, a British colony comprising two island groups SE of the Bahamas, West Indies. There are six inhabited and over 30 smaller islands. The chief industries are sponge and shellfish collection and salt production. Pop 5675.

TURKU, city in SW Finland, a major Baltic seaport, cultural and industrial center, with shipyard, steel and textile industries and two universities. It was Finland's capital until 1812. Pop 155069.

TURLOCK, city in central Cal., 38mi SE of Stockton. Its economy is based on processing agricultural products. Pop 13992.

TURMERIC, *Curcuma longa*, an oriental herb that is cultivated for its rhizome which is a source of yellow dye used for coloring cloth and a condiment used in curries. Family: Zingiberaceae.

TURNER, Frederick Jackson (1861–1932), US historian. A Harvard professor (1910–24), he propounded an influential thesis about the American frontier and its role in shaping US individualism and democracy. *The Frontier in American History* (1920) reprinted earlier papers. He won a Pulitzer Prize for his study of sectionalism in the US (1932).

TURNER, Joseph Mallord William (1775–1851), outstanding Romantic landscape painter, perhaps the greatest British painter. His work is famous for its rich treatment of light and atmosphere, in oil, watercolor or engraving. His paintings include *The Fighting Téméraire* (1839) and *Rain, Steam and Speed* (1844). He left some 20000 works to the nation. (See also ROMANTICISM.)

TURNER, Nat. See NAT TURNER'S REBELLION.

TURNIP, *Brassica rapa*, a biennial plant, probably native to Asia, which is cultivated for its large, creamy colored taproot that is rich in STARCH and is used for feeding both cattle and humans. Family: Cruciferae. The Prairie turnip (*Psoralea esculenta*) is a LEGUMINOUS PLANT the roots of which are used as a vegetable. The Indian turnip is also known as JACK-IN-THE-PULPIT.

TURNSTONES, small wading birds found on rocky shores of the N hemisphere. Dumpy and short-billed, they potter along the shoreline turning over stones and shells to search for insects and marine worms.

TURNVEREIN (German: gymnastic club), an athletic, social and patriotic society set up in early 19th-century Prussia by Friedrich Ludwig JAHN. Though discouraged by German governments for their liberalism, the Turnvereins inspired several similar organizations in other countries.

TURPENTINE, exudate obtained from injured PINE trees. This is distilled to give the RESIN, rosin, and the ESSENTIAL OIL, oil of turpentine (also known as turpentine). The chief constituent of oil of turpentine, used as a solvent and thinner for PAINTS and VARNISHES, is pinene.

TURQUOISE, hydrated copper aluminum PHOSPHATE mineral, $CuAl_6(PO_4)_4(OH)_8 \cdot 4H_2O$; used as a semiprecious GEM stone, blue in color. Deposited from water, it occurs in veinlets and as masses. The finest turquoise comes from Iran.

TURTLES, aquatic relatives of TORTOISES, divisible into freshwater and marine groups. Like the tortoises, the body is encased in a horny shell. There are no teeth in the gums and the mouth has become adapted to form a sharp horny bill. Turtles are largely vegetarians. In freshwater forms the limbs normally retain free fingers and toes; in marine turtles they are modified into flat flippers, increasing their swimming ability. The amount of time spent in the water by the various species varies enormously: many of the freshwater species go for more or less extensive walks on land: others, like the marine turtles, leave the water only to lay their eggs. These are laid in scrapes in sand or soil on beaches and are left to incubate themselves. The young turtles make straight for the water on hatching.

Ariccia Sunset (1828), painted by the English artist Turner during his second visit to Italy, embodies the rich use of light that dominates his later works, foreshadowing Impressionism.

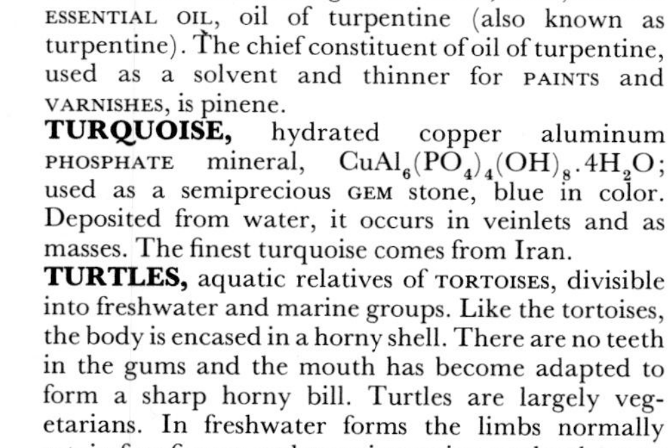

The Hawksbill sea turtle, *Eretmochelys imbricata*, is found in all tropical and some subtropical seas, such as the Mediterranean. It can be eaten only in some areas, such as the Caribbean; in others its flesh is known to be highly poisonous. It is hunted, sometimes to the point of local extinction, for its shell, the source of commercial "tortoiseshell."

TUSCALOOSA, city in W central Ala., seat of Tuscaloosa Co. It manufactures tires, chemicals, paper and cottonseed oil. State capital 1826–46, it is the home of Alabama U. Pop 65773.

TUSCANY, region in W central Italy, extending from the Apennine Mts. to the W coast. It is mostly mountainous, with fertile river valleys and coastal strip. Agricultural products include cereals, olive oil and Chianti wine. Iron and other minerals are mined; the chief manufactures are textiles, chemicals and machinery. Center of the ancient ETRUSCAN civilization, Tuscany has many famous cities such as Florence, Lucca, Pisa and Siena.

TUSCARORA INDIANS, tribe of North American Indians. They were driven from their lands in N.C. by white settlers and joined the IROQUOIS League in 1722. Some hundreds now live in N.Y. and Ontario.

TUSKEGEE, city in SE Ala., seat of Macon Co. and of TUSKEGEE INSTITUTE. Its chief industries are milling and cottonseed oil production. Pop 11028.

TUSKEGEE INSTITUTE, private college in Tuskegee, Ala. Founded by Booker T. WASHINGTON in 1881, it was one of the first colleges to educate freed slaves. The institute trained black school teachers and supported the work of George W. CARVER. Today it offers a wide range of subjects and has a fine library of American black history.

TUSK SHELLS, a class of MOLLUSKS, Scaphopoda, which live buried in sand on the sea bed and have a slightly curved, tapering, tubular white shell resembling a small tusk. A muscular foot is used for burrowing and a bunch of tentacles surrounding the head are used to transfer food to the mouth.

TUSSAUD, Marie Grosholtz (1760–1850), Swiss wax modeler. Forced to make death masks of guillotined aristocrats in the French Revolution, she left Paris to found (1802) her famous London waxworks exhibition. Today the waxworks contain tableaus and hundreds of models of well-known people.

TUSTIN, residential city in SW Cal. It is a processing center for citrus fruits and has some light manufactures. Pop 21178.

TUTANKHAMEN (reigned c1350 BC), Egyptian pharoah. He died at 18 but is famous for his tomb, discovered in THEBES by Howard CARTER in 1922 with its treasures intact. His solid gold coffin, gold portrait mask and other treasures are in the Cairo museum.

TUTSI. See WATUTSI.

TUTUILA, largest island (52sq mi) of US SAMOA in the Pacific Ocean. It is mountainous, with fertile valleys. The capital is Pago Pago. Canned fish and copra are exported. Pop 24548.

TUVALU, name of the nine Ellice Islands after the administrative separation of the GILBERT AND ELLICE ISLANDS.

TUZIGOOT NATIONAL MONUMENT, in central Ariz., covering about 43 acres, was established in 1939 and contains the ruins of a Pre-Columbian Indian pueblo (village).

TVA. See TENNESSEE VALLEY AUTHORITY.

TWAIN, Mark (1835–1910), pen name of Samuel Langhorne Clemens, US author and popular humorist and lecturer. After being a printer's apprentice (1848–53), he led a wandering life, becoming a Mississippi river pilot (1857–61) and then a journalist, establishing a reputation with his humorous sketches. In 1869 he produced his first bestseller, *The Innocents Abroad*, followed by *The Adventures of Tom Sawyer* (1876), *The Prince and the Pauper* (1882), his masterpiece *Huckleberry Finn* (1884) and the satirical *A Connecticut Yankee in King Arthur's Court* (1889). *Huckleberry Finn*, the story of a raft trip down the Mississippi, exemplifies Twain's gift of blending humor with realism. In later life, Twain lost most of his money through speculation and suffered the loss of his wife and daughters. His works became increasingly pessimistic and bitingly satirical, as in *The Tragedy of Pudd'nhead Wilson* (1894) and *The Man who Corrupted Hadleyburg* (1899).

TWEED, William Marcy (1823–1878), New York City politician. He became boss of TAMMANY HALL in 1868 and with the help of his cronies, known as the Tweed Ring, exercised corrupt control over the Democratic Party machine running New York. Tweed defrauded the city of over 30 million dollars, but was eventually convicted and died in jail.

TWEED RIVER, a 97mi-long river forming part of the Scotland to England border. It flows E from Peebles Co., Scotland, to the North Sea at Berwick.

TWEEDSMUIR, John Buchan, 1st Baron. See BUCHAN, JOHN.

TWELVE TABLES, Law of the, the earliest Roman code of laws. Written on tablets c450 BC, they were displayed in the FORUM. They contained civil, criminal and sacred legal precepts and became

John TYLER
10th US President

Born: March 29, 1790
Died: January 18, 1862
Term of office: April 6, 1841–March 3, 1845
Political party: Whig

revered as a prime source of law. Only fragments survive.

TWELVE-TONE MUSIC, or serial music, a type of music, developed in the 1920s, which rejects TONALITY as the basis for composition. Its most famous exponent, SCHOENBERG, laid down a method of composition which attempted to free music from the 8-note OCTAVE and its associated conventions. Twelve-tone compositions are constructed around a specific series of the twelve notes of the CHROMATIC SCALE. Later 20th-century composers have used the principles of twelve-tone composition with greater freedom. (See ATONALITY.) Later composers of twelve-tone music include STRAVINSKY, SESSIONS, PISTON, KRENEK, HENZE, DALLAPICCOLA, SHOSTAKOVICH and Schoenberg's pupils WEBERN and BERG.

TWELVE TRIBES OF ISRAEL, the twelve family groups into which the ancient Hebrews were divided. According to the Bible they were descended from and named for ten sons of JACOB and two sons of JOSEPH. Those descended from Jacob's sons were ASHER, BENJAMIN, DAN, GAD, Issachar, JUDAH, NAPHTALI, REUBEN, SIMEON, ZEBULUN; the two from Joseph's sons were EPHRAIM and MANASSEH. When the Jews finally reached the Promised Land they divided the country between these twelve family groups. A thirteenth tribe, LEVI, had no portion of land set aside for it. (See also JEWS.)

TWIN FALLS, city in S Ida., seat of Twin Falls Co. It is a manufacturing and processing center for the surrounding farming region. Pop 21 914.

TWINFLOWER, or Deer Vine, *Linnaea borealis*, evergreen creeper native to temperate regions, with sweet-scented bell-shaped flowers that hang from the stems in pairs. Family: Caprifoliaceae.

TWINING, Nathan Farragut (1897–), US Air Force commander. In WWII he commanded the 13th Air Force in the S Pacific and the 15th Air Force in Europe. He was US Air Force chief of staff 1953–57 and chairman of the Joint Chiefs of Staff 1957–60.

TWINS. See MULTIPLE BIRTHS; SIAMESE TWINS.

TWO RIVERS, city in E Wis., on Lake Michigan. Its manufacturing industries include metal goods, furniture and knitwear. Pop 13 533.

TWO SICILIES, Kingdom of the, a kingdom uniting SICILY and S Italy (see NAPLES). Originally founded by Normans in the 1000s, it was reunited by ALFONSO V of Aragon in 1442. A branch of the BOURBON family succeeded to the kingdom in 1759 and held it until the proclamation of a united Italy in 1861.

TYLER, city in E Tex., seat of Smith Co. It is a shipping and commercial center for the region's oil and rose-growing industries. Pop 57 700.

TYLER, John (1790–1862), tenth US president (1841–45). A Va. aristocrat, he studied law and was elected to the Va. legislature (1811–16, 1823–25, 1839), and served in Congress (1817–21). He became governor of Va. (1825–27), and then a US senator (1827–36). A conservative, he believed in STATES' RIGHTS and the restriction of federal power, opposing the MISSOURI COMPROMISE and the bill authorizing President JACKSON to use force against S.C. during the NULLIFICATION crisis. He broke with the Democrats and was chosen by the WHIGS to run for vice-president with William Henry HARRISON, who became president in 1841 but died within a month of his inauguration.

Tyler was the first vice-president to succeed a president in office and he chose to sit out the full term, although the Constitution was not clear on this issue. He alienated the Whigs by vetoing the nationalist program they presented under the leadership of Senator CLAY, and his entire cabinet, except Daniel WEBSTER, resigned. Nevertheless Tyler continued to veto nationalist bills and Congress responded by refusing to vote money for the upkeep of the White House. He was expelled from the Whig party and threatened with impeachment.

In foreign affairs Tyler was more successful; his major achievement was the conclusion of the WEBSTER-ASHBURTON TREATY (1843). Internally he encouraged settlement in the West, backed MORSE's telegraph system and reorganized the navy. In 1845 he brought Texas and Florida into the Union, despite Democratic opposition. After leaving office (1845), Tyler retired to Va. In 1861 he presided at a peace conference in Washington, hoping to avert civil war. When the southerners' terms were rejected, he voted for Va.'s secession and was elected to the Confederate House of Representatives, but died before he could take his seat.

TYLER, Royall (1757–1826), US jurist and writer. He served as chief justice of the Supreme Court of Vermont 1807–1813, but is chiefly remembered for his plays, including the first American comedy, *The Contrast* (1787).

TYLER, Wat (d. 1381), leader of the English Peasants' Revolt (1381), England's first popular rebellion, protesting high taxation after the BLACK DEATH. Tyler and his Kentish followers captured Canterbury, then took the TOWER OF LONDON. RICHARD II promised abolition of serfdom and feudal service. At a second meeting with the king, Tyler was stabbed and the revolt was brutally crushed.

TYLOR, Sir Edward Burnett (1832–1917), British anthropologist whose work, culminating in *Primitive Culture* (1871), established him as a father of cultural ANTHROPOLOGY. In 1896 he was appointed the first Professor of Anthropology in the University of Oxford.

TYNDALE, William (c1494–1536), English Bible translator, theologian and Protestant martyr. His New Testament, printed in Germany (1526), was suppressed in England. He lived abroad in hiding, translating the PENTATEUCH (1529–30) and Book of Jonah (1531). In 1535 he was captured in Antwerp, tried and burned for heresy. (See also BIBLE.)

TYNDALL, John (1820–1893), British physicist who, through his studies of the scattering of light by colloidal particles or large molecules in SUSPENSION (the **Tyndall effect**), showed that the daytime sky is blue because of the Rayleigh SCATTERING of impingent sunlight by dust and other colloidal particles in the air (see COLLIOD).

TYPE. See PRINTING.

TYPE METAL, various ALLOYS of lead, antimony and tin, easily cast to make printing type because they expand on solidifying.

TYPESETTING. See LINOTYPE; MONOTYPE; PRINTING.

TYPEWRITER, writing machine activated manually or electrically by means of a keyboard. Normally, when a key is depressed, a pivoted bar bearing a type character strikes an inked ribbon against a sheet of paper carried on a cylindrical rubber "platen," and the platen carriage automatically moves a space to the left. In some electric models all the type is carried on a single rotatable sphere that moves from left to right and strikes a fixed platen. The first efficient typewriter was developed in 1868 by C. L. SHOLES. (See also BUSINESS MACHINES.)

TYPHOID FEVER, INFECTIOUS DISEASE due to a SALMONELLA species causing FEVER, a characteristic rash, LYMPH node and SPLEEN enlargement, GASTROINTESTINAL TRACT disturbance with bleeding and ulceration, and usually marked malaise or prostration. It is contracted from other cases or from disease carriers, the latter often harboring asymptomatic infection in the GALL-BLADDER or urine, with contaminated food and water as major vectors. Carriers must be treated with ANTIBIOTICS (and have their gall-bladder removed if this site is the source); they must also stop handling food until they are free of the bacteria. VACCINATION may help protect high risk persons; antibiotics—chloramphenicol or cotrimoxazole—form the treatment of choice.

TYPHOON. See HURRICANE.

TYPHUS, INFECTIOUS DISEASE caused by RICKETTSIA and carried by LICE, leading to a feverish illness with a rash. Severe HEADACHE typically precedes the rash, which may be erythematous or may progress to skin HEMORRHAGE; mild respiratory symptoms of cough and breathlessness are common. Death ensues in a high proportion of untreated adults, usually with profound SHOCK and KIDNEY failure. Recurrences may occur in untreated patients who recover from their first attack, often after many years (Brill-Zinsser disease). A similar disease due to a different but related organism is carried by fleas (Murine typhus). Chloramphenicol or TETRACYCLINES provide suitable ANTIBIOTIC therapy.

TYPOGRAPHY, the design and layout of printed type. The object of typography is to enhance the legibility of a printed page, or, as in advertising and display, to attract the reader's attention. Early typefaces were derived from medieval Gothic and Renaissance humanistic scripts. A typeface usually consists of a set or *font* of capital and lower-case letters in three styles, roman, *italic* and **bold**, each cut in a range of sizes (measured in *points*). Famous typefaces include those produced by BASKERVILLE, BODONI, GARAMOND and Eric GILL. This page is printed in 8-point Baskerville. Good typography calls for intelligent positioning of word patterns set in types of appropriate face and size (see PRINTING).

TYRANNOSAURUS, the largest of the carnivorous DINOSAURS—bipedal and measuring up to 5.8m (19ft) in walking pose, with powerful hindlimbs and feet, enormous head and massive jaws but tiny forelimbs. They lived during the late CRETACEOUS.

TYRANT, a dictator in ancient Greece. With the growth of democracy in 5th-century BC Athens the word took on its present pejorative sense though in fact many tyrants were able and popular rulers. Some of the most famous were DIONYSIUS I and II, HIERO I and II and PISISTRATUS.

TYRE, town, and ancient PHOENICIAN city-port on the coast of Lebanon. After 1400 BC it began to dominate Mediterranean trade, and established colonies in Spain and CARTHAGE. Frequently mentioned in the Bible and famed for its silks and dyes, it was sacked by ALEXANDER THE GREAT (322) but recovered under the ROMAN EMPIRE. It was finally destroyed by the MAMELUKES in 1291. Today the small town of Sur occupies the site.

TYROL, see TIROL.

TYRRHENIAN SEA, part of the Mediterranean Sea bounded by the W coast of Italy, Corsica, Sardinia and Sicily. The strait of Messina in the S connects with the Ionian Sea. Its ports include Naples and Palermo.

TZARA, Tristan (1896–1963), Romanian-born French poet, founder of the DADA movement. In Paris he published the *Seven Dada Manifestos* (1924), working with André BRETON to destroy conventional values and language. He moved toward SURREALISM, and his mature lyrical poetry is more humanistic.

TZ'U-HSI (1835–1908), Chinese Dowager Empress. She was regent for her son and later her nephew, and finally ruled directly, dominating Chinese affairs for nearly 50 years. Her corrupt rule through a clique of conservative officials contributed to China's defeat in the SINO-JAPANESE WAR (1895) and to the BOXER REBELLION. Three years after her death the CH'ING dynasty was overthrown.

U

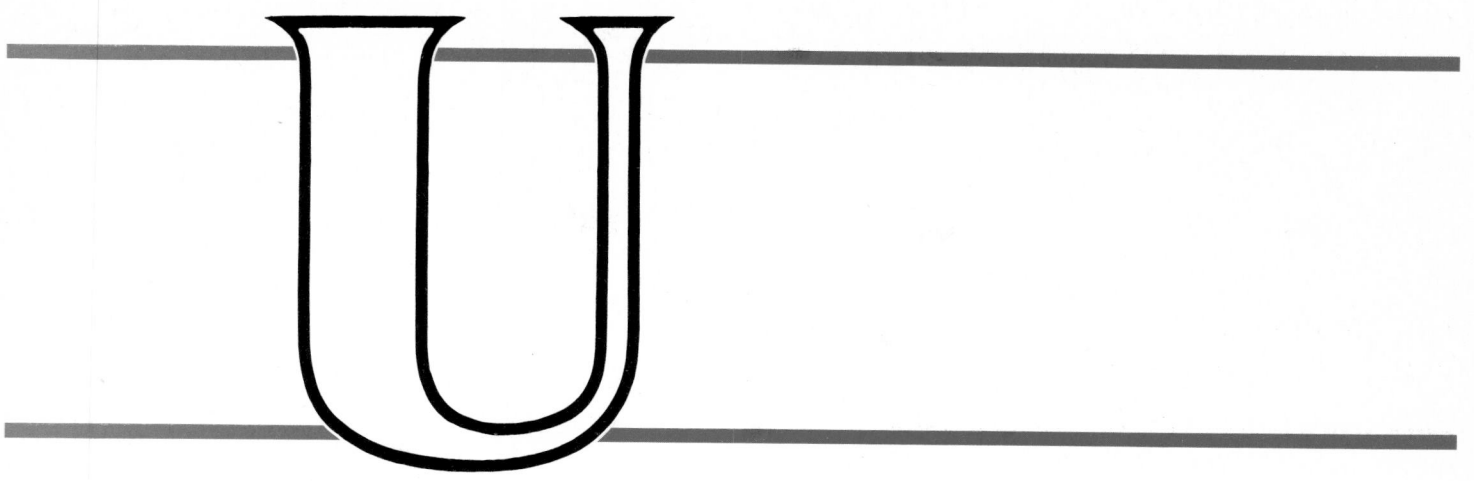

U, 21st letter of the English alphabet, derived from the Semitic *waw* via the Greek *upsilon.* In the Roman alphabet, *V* (lower-case *u*) was both vowel and consonant, and the modern *u* and *v* date from the 16th century. U is a Burmese honorific title.

U-2, US high-altitude reconnaissance jet plane. In 1960, a U-2 piloted by Francis Gary Powers on a CIA mission was forced down in the USSR. A summit meeting in Paris was cancelled following Premier KHRUSCHEV's protest.

UAKARI, two species of agile, shaggy-haired monkeys of South America, related to sakis. The more familiar species, the Bald uakari *Cacajao calvus,* has a naked head.

UBANGI RIVER, chief N tributary of the Congo R, central Africa. Formed by the junction of the Bomu and Uele rivers, it flows 700mi W and S, forming part of Zaire's NW frontier.

UBE, industrial seaport in the Yamaguchi prefecture, SW Honshu, Japan. It has chemical industries and nearby coalmines. Pop 152935.

UCAYALI RIVER, N Peru, chief headstream of the Amazon. Formed by the junction of the Urubamba and Apurímac rivers, central Peru, it flows 1000mi N to the MARAÑÓN RIVER, SW of Iquitos.

UCCELLO, Paolo (1397–1475), Florentine early RENAISSANCE painter, noted for his use of perspective. His best-known works are the *Creation* and *Noah* scenes (c1431–50) in Santa Maria Novella, Florence, and the three richly decorative panels of *The Battle of San Romano* (c1455–60).

UDALL, Nicholas (c1505–1556), English schoolmaster, scholar and playwright. Headmaster of ETON (1534–41) and Westminster (1554–56), he wrote the first known English comedy, *Ralph Roister Doister* (c1553).

UFA, capital of Bashkir Autonomous Soviet Socialist Republic, SW of the Ural Mts. in the RSFSR, USSR. It has oil, chemical, engineering and lumber industries. Pop 771000.

UFFIZI, 16th-century palace in Florence, Italy, built to designs by VASARI for Cosimo I de' MEDICI. It houses one of the world's finest art collections, rich in classical, Dutch, Flemish and, notably, Italian Renaissance paintings and sculptures.

UGANDA, landlocked E central African republic, bordering Kenya, Sudan, Zaire, Rwanda and Tanzania.

Land. Lying on the equator, Uganda has an average elevation of 4000ft. The fertile plateau is bounded by the Great Rift Valley and Ruwenzori Mts to the W and high mountains to the E. The Nile R, leaving Lake Victoria in the SE, is harnessed for electricity at Owen Falls dam. Annual rainfall is about 40in, and temperatures rarely exceed 85°F or fall below 60°F.

People. Bantu-speakers, two-thirds of the total, include the Baganda in the S, the largest and most prosperous group, Banyoro and Banyankole. Ethnic groups in the N include the Lango, Acholi and Iteso. Kampala, Jinja, Mbale and Entebbe are the chief centers. English is the official language, but Bantu, Swahili and other languages are commonly spoken.

Economy. The economy is agricultural and most farms are small, growing subsistence crops and raising livestock. Fishing and hardwoods are important. Copper, tin and iron ore and other minerals are extracted. Manufactures include textiles, cement, fertilizers and metal products. Coffee, cotton, copper, tea and tobacco are exported via the Kenyan port of Mombasa.

History. The Buganda kingdom, which had succeeded the Bunyoro kingdom by c1800, became a British protectorate in 1894, and the protectorate was extended to other kingdoms until by 1914 the present boundaries of Uganda became fixed. Uganda became independent in 1962, with Lango leader Milton Obote as premier, and formed the East Africa (economic) Community with Kenya and Tanzania (1967). Major General Idi AMIN headed a 1971 military coup, expelled 60000 Asians (1972) and took dictatorial control.

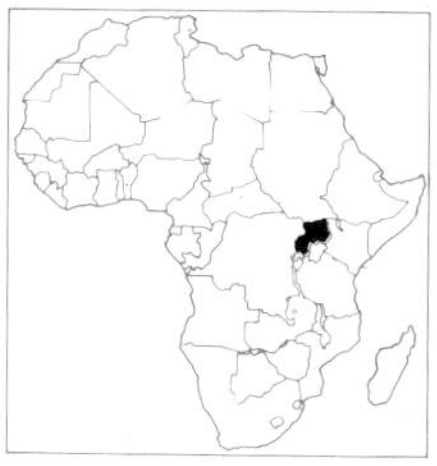

Official name: Republic of Uganda
Capital: Kampala
Area: 91134sq mi
Population: 11171900
Languages: English; Bantu languages, Swahili
Religions: Christian, Muslim; tribal religions
Monetary unit(s): 1 Uganda shilling = 100 cents

UGARIT, ancient city discovered in 1929 at Ras Shamra, NW Syria. Settled since the 5th millennium BC, it flourished c1400 BC. Numerous CUNEIFORM tablets have revealed much about Semitic culture and language, important for Old Testament studies.

UGRO-FINNIC LANGUAGES, the more important of the branches of the Uralic language family (see URAL-ALTAIC LANGUAGES). The Finnic division includes Finnish and Estonian; the Ugric, Hungarian.

UINTA MOUNTAINS, part of the Rockies, extend 120mi E from NE Ut. into SW Wyo. They contain Kings Peak, at 13528ft the highest point in Ut.

UJJAIN, city in W Madhya Pradesh, central India, once the center of SANSKRIT culture, and an ancient capital. It is one of seven Hindu holy cities. Pop 159024.

UKIAH, city in W Cal., seat of Mendocino Co. It processes fruit, makes wine and is the site of an International Latitude Observatory. Pop 10095.

UKRAINE, constituent Soviet Socialist Republic in the W USSR, third largest in area and second only to the RSFSR in population and economic importance. Mostly steppes, the Ukraine extends from the Carpathian Mts E to the Donets Ridge and Sea of Azov, and from the Black Sea N to Belorussia. The Dnieper R flows N dividing the Ukraine. In the NW lie the Polesye (Pripyat, Pripet) marshes; in the S, a fertile CHERNOZEM region.

The "breadbasket of Russia" supplies about a quarter of the USSR's food (wheat and other grains, root crops and flax) and 30% of the heavy industrial output. It is rich in oil, gas, coal, hydroelectricity, iron and salt. Major centers are KIEV (the capital), DNEPROPETROVSK, DONETSK (and the DONETS BASIN), KHARKOV and ODESSA. Culturally distinct UKRAINIAN speakers comprise over 75% of the people. The COSSACKS ("outlaws") arose in opposition to Polish and, later, Russian rule. The Ukraine was briefly independent, 1918–20, and nationalism remains.

UKRAINIAN, or Ruthenian, East Slavic SLAVONIC LANGUAGE. Distinguished from RUSSIAN since c1200 and written in a modified CYRILLIC alphabet, it emerged as a literary language in the 18th century. It is the official language of the Ukraine, with some 41000000 speakers.

UKULELE, or ukelele, small guitar from Hawaii, where the Portuguese had introduced a prototype. It has four strings which are strummed or plucked, and became popular for dance music in the US and Europe in the 1920s.

ULAN BATOR, formerly Urga, industrial city, capital of the Mongolian People's Republic, on the Tola R, N of the Gobi desert. Pop 282000.

ULANOVA, Galina (1910–), Russian prima ballerina of the BOLSHOI THEATER, Moscow, from 1944. She excelled as a dramatic and lyric dancer, notably in *Swan Lake* and Prokofiev's *Romeo and Juliet.*

ULAN-UDE, seat of Buryat autonomous SSR, E RSFSR, Siberian USSR, SE of Lake Baikal. Locomotives and machinery are built, lumber, food and wool processed. Pop 254000.

ULBRICHT, Walter (1893–1973), leader of post-WWII East Germany. A founder member (1918) of the German Communist Party, he became first deputy premier (1949) and head of state (1960–73) of the German Democratic Republic. An uncompromising Stalinist, he headed the Socialist Unity Party from 1950 until replaced (1971) by Erich HONECKER. He built the BERLIN WALL (1961), and in 1968 sent troops to Czechoslovakia.

ULCER, pathological defect in SKIN or other EPITHELIUM, caused by INFLAMMATION secondary to infection, loss of BLOOD supply, failure of venous return or CANCER. Various skin lesions can cause ulcers, including infection, arterial disease, VARICOSE VEINS and skin cancer. Aphthous ulcers in the MOUTH are painful epithelial ulcers of unknown origin. Peptic ulcers include gastric and duodenal ulcers, although the two have different causes; they may cause characteristic pain, acute HEMORRHAGE, or lead to perforation and PERITONITIS. Severe scarring or EDEMA around the pylorus may cause stenosis with VOMITING and STOMACH distension. ANTACIDS, rest, stopping SMOKING, and licorice derivatives may help peptic ulcer but surgery may also be needed.

ULSTER, historic province split since 1920 into the

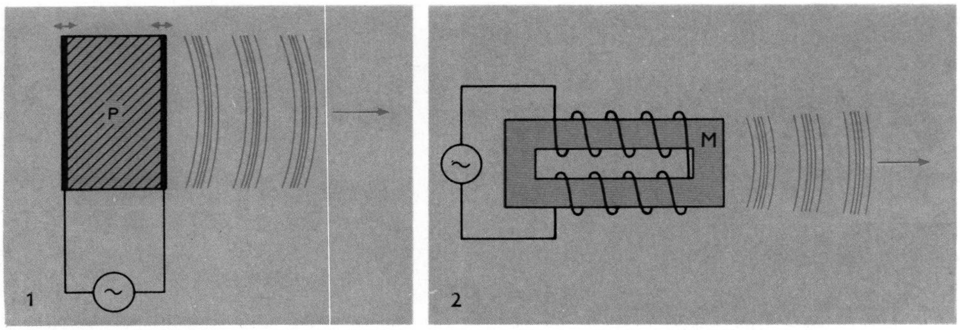

Two ways of generating ultrasonic waves: (1) as the dielectric between the two plates of a condenser, the piezoelectric material P converts a high-frequency electrical oscillation into a mechanical one; (2) a rapidly oscillating magnetic field produces ultrasonic vibrations in the magnetostrictive material M.

three-county Ulster province of IRELAND and six-county Northern Ireland (see IRELAND, NORTHERN).

ULTRACENTRIFUGE. See CENTRIFUGE.

ULTRA-HIGH-FREQUENCY WAVES (UHF). See ELECTROMAGNETIC RADIATION; RADIO.

ULTRAMICROSCOPE, a MICROSCOPE for studying liquid suspensions of particles too small for direct microscopy (10nm–1 μm), using light scattered by the particles at right angles. It allows their number and position to be determined, their motion to be followed, and their size to be estimated, though no structural detail can be discerned.

ULTRAMONTANISM, in Roman Catholicism, the movement to strengthen the authority of the pope and CURIA. It arose in reaction to Gallicanism (the 16th- to 18th-century movement for autonomy of the French church), JANSENISM and liberal tendencies, and finally triumphed at the First VATICAN COUNCIL (1870), which defined papal infallibility and universal jurisdiction. Some of its opponents seceded as OLD CATHOLICS.

ULTRASONICS, science of SOUND waves with frequencies above those that humans can hear (>20 kHz). With modern piezoelectric techniques, ultrasonic waves having frequencies above 24 kHz can readily be generated with high efficiency and intensity in solids and liquids, and exhibit the normal wave properties of REFLECTION, REFRACTION and DIFFRACTION. They can thus be used as investigative tools or for concentrating large amounts of mechanical energy. Low-power waves are used in thickness gauging and HOLOGRAPHY, high-power waves in surgery and for industrial homogenization, cleaning and machining.

ULTRAVIOLET RADIATION, ELECTROMAGNETIC RADIATION of wavelength between 0.1nm and 380nm, produced using gas discharge tubes. Although it constitutes 5% of the energy radiated by the sun, most falling on the earth is filtered out by atmospheric OXYGEN and OZONE, thus protecting life on the surface from destruction by the solar ultraviolet light. This also means that air must be excluded from optical apparatus designed for ultraviolet light, similar strong absorbtion by glass necessitating that lenses and prisms be made of QUARTZ or FLUORITE. Detection is photographic or by using fluorescent screens. The principal use is in fluorescent tubes (see LIGHTING) but important medical applications include germicidal lamps, the treatment of RICKETS and some skin diseases and the VITAMIN-D enrichment of milk and eggs.

ULYANOV, Vladimir Ilyich. See LENIN, V. I.

ULYANOVSK, capital of Ulyanovsk oblast, RSFSR, USSR. It is a port and industrial center on the Volga R, and birthplace of LENIN. Pop 351 000.

ULYSSES, Latin name for ODYSSEUS.

UMAYYADS. See OMAYYADS.

UMBILICAL CORD, long structure linking the developing EMBRYO or FETUS to the PLACENTA through most of PREGNANCY. It consists of BLOOD vessels taking blood to and from the placenta, and a gelatinous matrix. At BIRTH the cord is clamped to prevent blood loss and is used to assist delivery of the placenta. It undergoes ATROPHY and becomes the **navel**.

UMBRA. See SHADOW; ECLIPSE.

UMBRELLA BIRDS, crow-sized birds of the forests of South America, belonging to the genus *Cephalopterus*. They are black, with a large tuft of feathers on the head (which "umbrella" the male raises in display) and a large pendant lappet of feathers on the throat.

UMBRELLA PLANT, *Cyperus diffusus* and *C. alternifolius*, tender evergreen species producing clumps of dark-green leafless stems which are crowned by a ring of green leaf-like bracts arranged like the ribs of an umbrella. They are popular house plants, growing best at temperatures between 16°C and 21°C (60°F and 70°F) in a bright north window or near a sunny window. The soil should be kept wet or moist and the foliage misted often. Propagation is by planting rooted divisions. Family: Cyperaceae.

UMBRELLA TREE, *Magnolia tripetala*, a small MAGNOLIA tree with large showy white flowers. It grows in damp habitats in North America.

UMBRIA, ancient region in the Apennine Mts., central Italy. It is chiefly agricultural, with expanding industry based on hydroelectricity, notably at Terni. The capital is Perugia, center of the medieval Umbrian painters.

UMM AL-QAIWAIN, 300sq-mi sheikhdom in the UNITED ARAB EMIRATES. Activity among its 3 740 people includes oil production, farming and fishing.

UNALASKA, second-largest of the ALEUTIAN ISLANDS, SW Alaska, including Unalaska city (pop 180), the US navy base at Dutch Harbor and Makuskin volcano (6 678ft).

UN-AMERICAN ACTIVITIES COMMITTEE, renamed Committee on Internal Security in 1969, US House of Representatives body formed in 1938 to investigate subversive activities in the US. HUAC won notoriety after WWII for its investigation of alleged communist influence in government, unions, education and the film industry. Richard M. NIXON played a key role in its investigations leading to conviction of Alger HISS (1950). Its activities were paralleled in the 1950s by Joseph McCARTHY's anti-communist witch-hunts.

UNAMUNO, Miguel de (1864–1936), leading Spanish philosopher and writer, rector of Salamanca University from 1900. Influenced by KIERKEGAARD, he explored the faith-reason conflict and man's desire for immortality in *The Tragic Sense of Life* (1913), and in essays and novels such as *Mist* (1914). *The Christ of Velázquez* (1920) is his finest poem. Politically outspoken, he was exiled 1924–30.

UNCAS (c1588–c1683), chief of the MOHICAN INDIANS of Connecticut, celebrated in J. F. COOPER's *The Last of the Mohicans* (1826). He supported the colonists in the 1637 war against the related PEQUOT INDIANS. The English forced him to be neutral in KING PHILIP's WAR (1675).

UNCERTAINTY PRINCIPLE, or **indeterminacy principle,** a restriction, first enunciated by W. K. HEISENBERG in 1927, on the accuracy with which the position and MOMENTUM of an object can be established simultaneously: the product of the accuracies attainable in each cannot be less than the PLANCK CONSTANT. Relevant only near the atomic level, the principle arises from the wave nature of matter: a particle consists of a superposition of waves with slightly different speeds producing a localized disturbance of which neither the position nor the speed is precisely defined.

UNCIALS, compact, cursive capital letters developed from the 200s AD by Greek and Roman calligraphers and used for some 500 years. Half (lower-case) uncials developed later, notably in the British Isles.

UNCLE REMUS. See HARRIS, JOEL CHANDLER.

UNCLE SAM, popular figure officially adopted as a US national symbol in 1961. He is portrayed as a white-haired and bearded, angular gentleman dressed in the Stars and Stripes. The image was developed by 19th-century cartoonists. The name possibly derives from "Uncle Sam" Wilson, a War of 1812 beef supplier to the US army, from Troy, N.Y.

UNCONFORMITY, a surface between two contiguous rock strata representing a break in the normal succession; usually owing to EROSION having removed layers of rock before the deposition of the younger stratum. They may be parallel (strata parallel), angular (strata not parallel), heterolithic (sediment over intruded IGNEOUS ROCKS) or nondepositional (a genuine break in the deposition pattern). (See also SEDIMENTARY ROCKS.)

UNCONSCIOUS, that part of the mind in which take place events of which the individual is unaware; i.e., the part of the mind that is not the CONSCIOUS. Unconscious processes can, however, alter the behavior of the individual (see also DREAMS; INSTINCT). FREUD renamed the unconscious the ID. (See also COLLECTIVE UNCONSCIOUS.)

UNCONSCIOUSNESS, lack of awareness, the commonest example of which is sleep; or the lack of self-awareness displayed by most, if not all, animals (see CONSCIOUSNESS). (See also COMA.)

UNCTAD. See UNITED NATIONS CONFERENCE ON TRADE AND DEVELOPMENT.

UNDERGROUND RAILROAD, secret network which helped slaves to escape from the US South to the Northern States and Canada before the Civil War. Neither underground nor a railroad, it was named for its necessary secrecy and for the railroad terms used to refer to its operation. Most of the "conductors" were themselves slaves, Harriet TUBMAN being the best known. Other abolitionists, notably Quakers such as Levi COFFIN, ran "stations" providing food and shelter along the way. Some 40 000–100 000 slaves escaped this way. (See also ABOLITIONISM.)

UNDERWOOD TARIFF, enacted in 1913, the first important reduction in US TARIFFS since 1857. Sponsored by Ala. Democrat Oscar W. Underwood as part of President Woodrow WILSON's move away from PROTECTIONISM, it was effectively nullified by WWI.

UNDERWRITING, insuring against risk. Originally, as at LLOYD's OF LONDON, underwriters indicated readiness to share risk by signing insurance contracts. In INSURANCE, an underwriter (often an ACTUARY) assesses risk and sets premiums. In finance, underwriting is an agreement to buy STOCKS.

Uncle Sam shown in Thomas Nast's 1872 cartoon receiving from John Bull (Great Britain) the $15,500,000 compensation awarded by arbitrators settling the Alabama Claims dispute. The claims arose from damage caused in the Civil War by the *Alabama* and other Confederate warships built and fitted out in England, in conflict with Britain's neutrality.

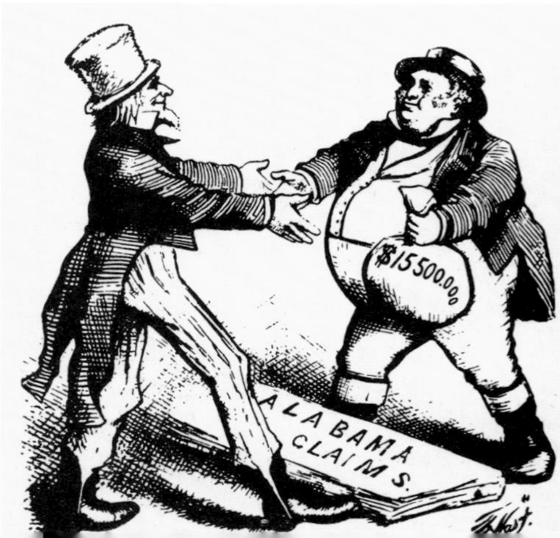

UNDSET, Sigrid (1882–1949), Norwegian novelist. For her epic trilogy set in medieval Norway, *Kristin Lavransdatter* (1920–22), she won the 1928 Nobel literature prize. Her contemporary novels dealt with modern woman and Roman Catholicism.

UNDULANT FEVER. See BRUCELLOSIS.

UNEARNED INCREMENT, an increase in property value not due to the owner's efforts. Arguing that the whole community contributed to such increases, Henry GEORGE proposed his SINGLE TAX on land. Many countries now have a CAPITAL GAINS TAX.

UNEMPLOYMENT, a situation where people who are normally members of the labor force, and are willing and able to work, cannot find employment. Large-scale unemployment can itself pose or exacerbate serious social problems. It can be caused by numerous factors, often beyond the control of the individual worker. Seasonal layoffs occur because certain jobs, for example in agriculture, are not available all year around. Cyclical unemployment occurs during an economic DEPRESSION or recession, when production declines along with reduced demand. Increased mechanization and automation in industries could in the long run create jobs for a small number of skilled workers, but in the short term usually create unemployment by displacing large numbers of manual workers. Structural unemployment is caused by shifts in a nation's demand pattern. Some declining industries, such as coalmining, may have to lay off workers; without proper retraining, it will be difficult for them to find other jobs. Keynesian economists seek to solve the unemployment problem by government intervention, maintaining that increased government spending and expansion of credit can stimulate the economy and thus reduce unemployment (see KEYNES, JOHN MAYNARD). But other economists argue that full employment is incompatible with low INFLATION and a stable BALANCE OF PAYMENTS.

UNEMPLOYMENT INSURANCE, a type of SOCIAL SECURITY providing income to people involuntarily unemployed. Most modern industrial nations have programs of this kind, financed by the government, employers, employees, or a combination of these.

In the 1800s some labor unions initiated unemployment benefits for out-of-work members. France introduced a voluntary national scheme in 1905, and Britain the first compulsory insurance program in 1911. In the US the first unemployment insurance law was passed in Wis. in 1932; three years later the Social Security Act established a federal–state program, now administered by the Department of LABOR.

UNESCO. See UNITED NATIONS EDUCATIONAL, SCIENTIFIC AND CULTURAL ORGANIZATION.

UNGARETTI, Giuseppe (1888–1970), Italian poet. Influenced by the poets of French SYMBOLISM, his evocative verse, in a condensed, purified language, marked a new direction in Italian poetry.

UNGAVA, a large peninsula NE of Hudson Bay, Canada. Most of its sparsely populated but mineral-rich 350 000sq mi comprises New Quebec. The E part lies in Labrador.

UNGUENTINE PLANT, *Aloe vera*, a perennial succulent plant producing rosettes of thick, tapering leaves with soft spines. It is frequently grown as a greenhouse or house plant, growing well at average house temperatures in sunny windows. Aloes should be well watered whenever the soil surface dries out. Propagation is by planting offsets. Family: Liliaceae.

UNGULATES, general name for all hoofed MAMMALS, including both the odd-toed and even-toed groups: PERISSODACTYLA and ARTIODACTYLA respectively.

UNIATE CHURCHES, those Eastern churches which accept the pope's authority and Roman Catholic doctrines, but retain their own languages, rites and canon laws allowing administration of both bread and wine in COMMUNION, baptism by immersion and marriage of clergy. An example is the MARONITE church. (See also JACOBITE CHURCH.)

UNICEF. See UNITED NATIONS CHILDREN'S FUND.

UNICORN, mythical creature with the body of a white horse and one straight horn on its forehead. It has appeared in the art and legends of India, China, Islam, and medieval Europe, where it was associated with virginity, and with Christ.

UNIDENTIFIED FLYING OBJECT (UFO). See FLYING SAUCER.

UNIFIED FIELD THEORY, theory which tries to incorporate electromagnetic together with the strong and weak nuclear forces into the general theory of RELATIVITY. If successful, one set of equations would describe these fundamental force fields, including gravity, in terms of the geometry of space-time. Einstein made the first attempt to produce such a theory; he wanted to represent physical reality entirely in terms of fields, yet, in his general theory of relativity, particles still exist as SINGULARITIES—regions where field equations break down.

UNIFORM CODE OF MILITARY JUSTICE, the law governing all members of the US armed forces. It sets out procedures for COURT-MARTIAL and military justice. Enacted in 1950, it unified the codes and laws of the Army, Navy, Air Force and Coast Guard.

UNIFORMITARIANISM, the principle, due to J. HUTTON and C. LYELL, that the same agencies are at work in nature today, operating at the same intensities, as they have always done throughout geologic time. It was originally opposed to CATASTROPHISM.

UNIMAK, largest of the ALEUTIAN ISLANDS and nearest to SW Alaska, in the Fox Islands group. 70mi long, it includes Shishaldin volcano (9 978ft).

UNION, township in NE N.J., site of a 1780 Revolutionary battle (Connecticut Farms). It produces paint, steel and metal goods. Pop 52 878.

UNION, city in N S.C., seat of Union Co. It produces textiles, metal goods and fertilizer. Pop 10 775.

UNION. See SET THEORY.

UNION, Act of, in British history. See ACT OF UNION.

UNION, Fort. See FORT UNION NATIONAL MONUMENT.

UNION CITY, city in W Cal., SE of Oakland. It makes metal products, aluminum and sugar. Pop 14 724.

UNION CITY, city in NE N.J., a N suburb of Jersey City. Light industries include toiletries, light bulbs and embroidery. Pop 58 537.

UNION CITY, city in NW Tenn., seat of Obion Co. and site of three Civil War battles. It produces shoes, automobile parts and textiles. Pop 11 925.

UNIONDALE, an urban community in N.Y., just W of Hempstead on SW Long Island. Pop 22 077.

UNION ISLANDS. See TOKELAU ISLANDS.

UNION LEAGUE, organization started in 1862 to promote loyalty to the Union in the Civil War. Working through Union League clubs, it raised money and recruits, and opposed the antiwar COPPERHEADS. During RECONSTRUCTION it built up Republican organization in the South.

UNION OF SOUTH AFRICA. See SOUTH AFRICA.

UNION OF SOVIET SOCIALIST REPUBLICS. See RUSSIA.

UNIONS, workers' organizations formed to improve pay, working conditions and benefits. There were medieval craft GUILDS in Europe, but modern labor unions arose out of the new concentrations of workers in the INDUSTRIAL REVOLUTION. A craft (horizontal) union organizes workers with a particular skill, an industrial (vertical) union includes all workers in an industry. Employer-controlled company unions are unaffiliated to labor groupings.

Unions negotiate contracts with employers by COLLECTIVE BARGAINING. A CLOSED SHOP or UNION SHOP increases bargaining strength but may be barred by RIGHT-TO-WORK LAWS. A dispute may be referred to ARBITRATION or members may resort to strike action, go-slow or featherbedding, PICKETING, BOYCOTT, and, rarely, sit-down or work-in.

In the US, local craft unions existed from the late 1700s. The influence of the socialistic KNIGHTS OF LABOR (1869–1917) gave way to that of the craft unions of the American Federation of Labor (founded 1886). In the early 1900s a revolutionary upsurge was expressed through the INDUSTRIAL WORKERS OF THE WORLD, but the Protocol of Peace ending the 1910 strike by the International Ladies' Garment Workers' Union set a pattern for union-management cooperation that accelerated in WWI. The industrial union-based Congress of Industrial Organizations was formed in the 1930s, a time of NEW DEAL legislation to improve industrial relations (see WAGNER ACT). Some of the 1947 TAFT-HARTLEY ACT restrictions were lifted by the LANDRUM-GRIFFIN ACT (1959).

The AMERICAN FEDERATION OF LABOR AND CONGRESS OF INDUSTRIAL ORGANIZATIONS merger occurred in 1955. Britain has one Trades Union Congress, but many countries have rival Christian and socialist bodies. Internationally, the Christian World Confederation of Labor claims 12 million members, the communist-led World Federation of Trade Unions 150 million, and the International Confederation of Free Trade Unions (the 1949 AFL-CIO-backed breakaway from the WFTU) 50 million.

UNION SHOP, industrial situation where all new employees at a workplace must join a particular union. (See also CLOSED SHOP.)

UNION TERRITORY OF GOA, DAMAN AND DIU. See GOA.

UNIONTOWN, city in SW Penn., seat of Fayette Co. Its traditional coal and coke industry has given way to metal goods, tires, glassware and lumber products. Pop 16 282.

UNITARIANISM, unorthodox Protestant faith that rejects the TRINITY and Christ's deity and asserts the unipersonality of God. It developed out of SOCINIANISM; and many 18th-century English Presbyterians became unitarian. Joseph PRIESTLEY gave it a great impetus in the US, where liberal, rationalist unitarianism preaching toleration and universal salvation was developing in CONGREGATIONAL CHURCHES. The American Unitarian Association, led by William CHANNING, was founded in 1825. Theodore PARKER and Ralph Waldo EMERSON were notable Unitarians.

UNITARIAN UNIVERSALIST ASSOCIATION, US Protestant church formed (1961) by merger of the Universalist Church of America and the American Unitarian Association. The Association brings together over 240 000 members from two churches with similar histories and views (see UNITARIANISM; UNIVERSALISM).

UNITAS, John (1933–   ), great quarterback in American football. He joined the Baltimore Colts in 1956 and led them to three championships (1958, 1959 and 1968). He holds the record for completed passes and yards gained passing.

UNITED ARAB EMIRATES, formerly Trucial States, oil-rich federation of emirates in the E Arabian Peninsula, on the Persian Gulf and Gulf of Oman. It comprises Abu Dhabi, Ajman, Dubai, Fujairah, Ras al-Khaimah, Sharjah and Umm al-Qaiwain. From 1820 truces linked the sheikhs with Britain. The independent federation was formed in 1971, neighboring BAHRAIN and QATAR opting for separate statehood.

Land and People. The country has a 400mi coastline and is mostly desert, with oases and, in the S, mountains allowing some cultivation (dates, grains, tobacco). Herding, fishing and pearling are traditional occupations and Dubai has long been a

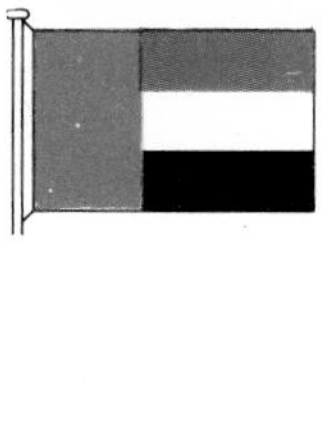

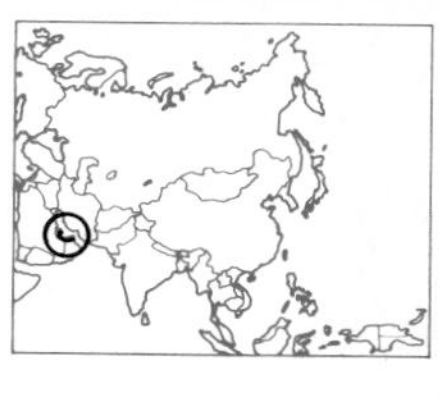

Official name: United Arab Emirates
Capital: Abu Dhabi
Area: 32 000sq mi
Population: 200 000
Languages: Arabic; English
Religions: Muslim
Monetary unit(s): 1 Bahrain Dinar = 1000 fils (Abu Dhabi)
1 Qatar riyal = 100 dirhams (elsewhere)

United Nations

Towards a world community

In the introduction to his 1974 report, Kurt Waldheim, Secretary General of the UN, stated that the UN had become "a very different organization from the one envisaged at San Francisco" (1945). It had, he claimed, developed its capacity as a peacekeeping organization and become an influential factor "in power relationships among the nations" and in economic, social and humanitarian matters. It had become "an agent for peaceful change, a channel for cooperative activity and a coordinating point for large humanitarian programs. . . . It has branched out into special activities far beyond the expectations of its founders."

Its critics, however, see the UN in a harsher light. Changed it certainly has, in character as well as size. Its balance has shifted from the US and other Western powers to the newly independent Afro-Asian countries, which now dominate the General Assembly. The editor of *National Review* and US delegate to the 29th session of the UN General Assembly, William F. Buckley Jr, claimed recently that the original values and high ideals of the UN have been abandoned by all but a few member countries. "The aim of the United Nations," he says, "is to make the world safe for revolution and unsafe for counterrevolution' (*United Nations Journal*, 1974). Other critics, while recognizing the valuable work done by its specialized agencies, seize upon the UN's failure in its peacekeeping and peacemaking operations. Third World countries point to the UN's failure to adjust the imbalance of power and wealth among the peoples of the world.

The UN Charter states that all peace-loving nations can be members of the organization provided they accept its basic purposes and principles. The main purposes of the UN are to maintain world peace and security; to promote just behavior between nations and international cooperation in solving problems; and to act as an agency for the realization of these aims. The principles require that all members respect the Charter; that all members enjoy equal rights whether they be large or small nations; and that all seek to settle disputes peacefully, resorting to force only in self-defense. Members must also support UN decisions and actions in implementing the Charter. The UN does not interfere in the internal policies or actions of any member-country unless they adversely affect another country. Nonmember countries are expected to cooperate in the preservation of world peace and security. Any member-country which violates the Charter is liable to suspension or expulsion.

The term "United Nations" was coined in 1941 by President Roosevelt to describe the Allies fighting the Axis powers. On Jan. 1, 1942, 26 nations including the US, Great Britain, USSR and China pledged adherence to the US–Great Britain Atlantic Charter (later the United Nations Declaration). The major Allied powers recognized the need for an international organization to replace the League of Nations in the Moscow Declaration (1943), at Teheran (1943), and at the Dumbarton Oaks Conference (1944). At Yalta (1945) the "Big Three" (US, USSR and Great Britain) prepared the San Francisco Conference (1945), where all 50 nations represented signed the UN Charter (Poland, the 51st Charter member, signed later). The Charter became operative on Oct. 24, 1945, now United Nations Day.

In the following 30 years the UN has become a vast and complex organization. It embraces many organizations, operational programs and specialized agencies, numerous special funds and semiautonomous bodies, and literally hundreds of intergovernmental committees, coordinating bodies and ad hoc groups.

The chief organs of the UN bear some resemblance to those of its predecessor, the League of Nations. There are six in all: the General Assembly; the Security Council; the Economic and Social Council; the Trusteeship Council; the International Court of Justice; and the Secretariat.

The **General Assembly** is the only major organ in which all members of the UN are represented. Each member may send not more than five representatives to the Assembly, but each member has only one vote. The Assembly approves applications for membership of the UN. Decisions on other than routine issues require a two-thirds majority. But the decisions of the Assembly are only recommendations; they have no legal force except in matters concerning the UN budget. Since 1950, when the "Uniting for Peace" resolution was adopted, the Assembly has had the power to act positively to maintain world peace whenever the Security Council reaches a deadlock or otherwise fails to act. In 1956, for example, it was an Assembly decision that led to the dispatch of a UN peacekeeping force to Egypt where Israeli, French and British troops were battling with the Egyptians.

The General Assembly's annual regular session starts in September and lasts some three months, but special meetings can also be held. Its work is divided between six main committees—political and security; economic and financial; social, humanitarian and cultural; trusteeship and non-selfgoverning territories; administrative and budgetary; and legal. There is also a Special Political (or Seventh) Committee. Every member has the right to be represented by one delegate on each of these committees.

The **Security Council** comprises 15 members, of which five have permanent seats (China—the People's Republic replaced the Republic in 1971—France, Great Britain, the USSR and the US). The other members are elected for two-year periods by the General Assembly in such a way that Africa, Asia, Latin America, E and W Europe are always represented. Nonpermanent members are not eligible for immediate reelection. The Council is primarily concerned with maintaining world peace and security and all UN members are supposed to bring disputes before the Council before resorting to force, though few in fact do. The Council has wide powers to deal with any situation endangering world peace and

center of Middle East trade. Most of the people are Sunnite Muslim Arabs of whom about 60% are farmers or nomads. The population has recently increased rapidly; there are Persian, Indian, Pakistani and European minorities.

Oil. In 1958 oil was discovered in Abu Dhabi, the largest state. Its per capita income is now one of the world's highest. In Jan. 1975 only Saudi Arabia, Libya and Kuwait produced more oil among members of the ORGANIZATION OF PETROLEUM EXPORTING COUNTRIES. Oil is also exported by Dubai.

UNITED ARAB REPUBLIC, union of Egypt and Syria proclaimed in 1958, as a step toward pan-Arab union. Cairo was capital, and NASSER president. The UAR formed with Yemen the nominal United Arab States (1958–61). Resenting Egyptian dominance, Syria seceded in 1961. A 1963 attempt to unite Egypt, Syria and Iraq failed. Egypt was named the UAR until 1971, when a loose Federation of Arab Republics (Egypt, Syria and Libya) was formed.

UNITED AUTOMOBILE WORKERS (UAW), powerful US industrial labor union, with local unions in Canada. Founded in 1935, it won recognition at General Motors, Chrysler and Ford (1937–41). Its 1 394 000 members (1974) are in automobile, space, aviation and metal industries. The UAW cofounded the CIO, but left the AFL-CIO in 1968. Walter REUTHER was president 1946–70. UAW headquarters are in Detroit.

UNITED CHURCH OF CANADA, Canadian Protestant church formed 1925 by union of the Methodist and most Presbyterian and Congregationalist churches. Ecumenical, national and missionary, it has a PRESBYTERIAN form of organization, stresses the rights of congregations, and has men and women ministers. It was joined in 1968 by Canada's Evangelical United Brethren Church and has over a million adult communicants.

UNITED CHURCH OF CHRIST, a US Protestant body set up by the 1957 union (with its 1961 constitution) of the Congregational Christian Churches and the Evangelical and Reformed Church. It gives strong local autonomy combined with national services and organization, and has over 2 000 000 members.

UNITED EMPIRE LOYALISTS, people of the original 13 colonies who remained loyal to Britain during the American Revolution and emigrated to Canada. The largest group, some 50 000 left New York City in 1783, and established New Brunswick (1784) and Upper Canada (now Ontario; 1791).

UNITED IRISHMEN, Society of, political group formed by Wolfe TONE and others in 1791 for the emancipation of Irish Catholics, parliamentary reform and, when forced underground (1794), Irish independence. The British arrested its leaders, intercepted French support, and broke the Irish revolt (1798).

UNITED KINGDOM OF GREAT BRITAIN AND NORTHERN IRELAND, consists of England, Scotland, Wales and Northern Ireland. Wales was conquered in 1282 and joined to England by the 1536 ACT OF UNION. James VI of Scotland became JAMES I of England in 1603 and Scotland was united with England by the 1707 Act. Ireland was united with Great Britain by the 1800 Act of Union. Only the six NE counties remained within the UK after most of Ireland gained independence in 1921. (See ENGLAND; GREAT BRITAIN; IRELAND, NORTHERN; SCOTLAND; WALES.)

UNITED MINEWORKERS OF AMERICA (UMW), US industrial union formed in 1890. Under John L. LEWIS (president 1920–60), it took militant stands on pay, safety, and political questions. A cofounder of the CIO in 1935 (now unaffiliated), it had 213 000 members in 1974. Ex-president Tony Boyle was convicted (1974) of murdering his left-wing rival Joseph Yablonski.

UNITED NATIONS, international organization of the world's states which aims to promote peace and international cooperation. Successor to the LEAGUE OF NATIONS, it was founded at the 1945 SAN FRANCISCO CONFERENCE prepared by the "Big Three" Allied Powers of WWII; 51 states signed the charter. Membership had grown to 117 in 1955, and to 144 by 1976. The headquarters are in New York.

The UN has six major organs. The *General Assembly*, composed of delegates from all member states, meets once a year and provides a general forum, but has little power of action. The *Security Council* has five permanent members each with a veto (China, France, Great Britain, the US and the USSR) and ten elected members. Intended to be a permanent peacekeeping all UN members are required to honor its decisions. All decisions require an affirmative vote of nine which on nonprocedural issues must include the votes of all permanent members. The negative vote of any of the "Big Five" effectively vetoes any proposal. The USSR has used the "veto" more than 100 times; its temporary withdrawal from the Council in 1950, protesting Nationalist China's membership, enabled the Council, under US leadership, to give UN support to South Korea in the Korean War.

The Security Council functions continuously and is assisted in its work by various committees, including a committee of "Experts," a Military Staff Committee and a committee on admission of new members. The Council must approve all applications for UN membership. The Council also selects a candidate for secretary general.

The **Economic and Social Council** has 27 member nations elected by the General Assembly for three-year terms of office and eligible for immediate reelection. It works to coordinate and improve economic, social, cultural, educational, health and related activities, through the UN specialized agencies and other bodies such as the Red Cross. Its various functional commissions cover social development, human rights, statistics, population, narcotics and the status of women. The Council also has regional economic commissions (Europe, Asia and the Far East, Latin America, Africa and Western Asia). The Council usually meets twice yearly, in New York City and Geneva.

The **Trusteeship Council**, formed to oversee administration of former Italian, German and Japanese territories, now has two responsibilities, the US-governed Trust Territory of the Pacific Islands, which is moving towards independence, and Namibia, or South West Africa, a former German colony mandated to South Africa by the League of Nations after WWI. South Africa refused to surrender its mandate to the UN after WWII. In 1967 the UN set up a special Council for Namibia. South Africa's mandate was terminated in 1969 and her occupation of the territory declared illegal by the International Court of Justice in 1971. South Africa continues with her own plans for Namibia.

The **International Court of Justice** at The Hague is the chief judicial organ of the UN. Its 15 judges are elected for nine-year terms by the Security Council and the General Assembly. Nine judges constitute a quorum and no two judges may be nationals of the same country. The court gives majority opinions and judgments on matters or disputes involving members of the UN and on international treaties and law. Any nation seeking a ruling must accept the Court's decision, but this does not always happen. In the Iceland–Great Britain fishing limits dispute, for example, the court's 1974 ruling in Great Britain's favor was rejected by Iceland.

The **Secretariat**, with a staff of about 10000 (half in New York), is the administrative organ of the UN. It is headed by the Secretary General, the most powerful official in the UN. According to the UN Charter, he is the only individual who can bring any situation threatening world peace to the attention of the Security Council. Many countries seek his advice and influence. The Secretary General is nominated by the Security Council with the support of all permanent members, and is then appointed by the General Assembly. Since Jan. 1, 1972, the Secretary General has been Kurt Waldheim (Austria), who was appointed for an initial five-year term.

The Specialized or Intergovernmental Agencies affiliated to the UN (the most important are listed in the separate text article) are to differing degrees autonomous—many of them in fact predated the UN. They operate on the basis that intergovernmental action in technical areas itself promotes peace and is better removed from direct political control. In addition, growing demand from "Third World" members for more than technical assistance led to the formation of formalized "pressure groups" within the UN, the United Nations Conference on Trade and Development (UNCTAD) in 1964 and United Nations Industrial Development Organization (UNIDO) in 1967, both organs of the General Assembly. However, these bodies still depend for funds on voluntary contributions from the richer member-nations.

The UN budget voted by the General Assembly was $745813800 for 1976–77. In 1974–75 the leading contributors were the US (25%), USSR (12.97%), Japan (7.15%) and West Germany (7.10%). France contributed 5.86%, China 5.50% and Great Britain 5.31%.

The impact of the UN organization on the world economic and social scene is far greater than many people realize. About 80% of UN expenditure is devoted to economic and social activities, and to this must be added the loans granted to member countries by the World Bank and International Monetary Fund. Member-countries have also benefited immeasurably from the work of the specialized agencies in health, agriculture, education and many other fields, and from the global conferences under UN auspices on the environment, population, food, trade and other topics.

Current examples of these activities include the continuing conference on the Law of the Sea dealing with such matters as territorial waters, fisheries, pollution and jurisdiction over the ocean bed; the World Population Conference of 1974, at which 137 countries and four liberation movements were represented; and the continuing work of UNIDO and UNCTAD. A declaration on the elimination of discrimination against women was unanimously adopted by the General Assembly in 1967, and the year 1975 was proclaimed International Women's Year.

The wide scope and ceaseless activity of the UN organization seem all the more remarkable when it is remembered that *total* UN expenditure since 1945 amounts to only 0.4% of the total gross national product of member-countries for the *single* year 1974. Annual current expenditure is barely equal to the amount spent on armaments by member countries in a mere 36 hours.

A fundamental Charter rule, without which the UN could not exist, states that "nothing in this charter is to authorize the United Nations to intervene in matters which are essentially within the domestic jurisdiction of any state." Partly because of this rule, but more often because UN intervention would have risked war when government policies of member-countries overrode commitment to UN principles, the UN has on occasion been unable to enforce General Assembly resolutions. Thus it did not act when Russia invaded Hungary in 1956. Nor has the UN been able to enforce General Assembly resolutions relating to the Arab–Israeli Wars.

It is the easiest thing in the world to criticize the UN, but it can never be any better than its members chose to make it. And it can be argued that even its less successful peacekeeping operations—in Cyprus, the Middle East and elsewhere—have at least had some effect: things would have been far worse without UN intervention. Furthermore, as a meeting place for all the peoples of the world it is far more representative than any predecessor. The changes in membership have given new expression to underlying world tensions, but as Winston Churchill said, "Jaw jaw is better than war war."

body with emergency executive powers, it has often been hamstrung by the Soviet veto. The *Economic and Social Council*, with 27 elected members, deals with "nonpolitical" matters, coordinating the work of the specialist agencies and operating important commissions of its own, such as those on children, refugees and human rights. The *Trusteeship Council* is responsible for UN TRUST TERRITORIES. The INTERNATIONAL COURT OF JUSTICE is the UN's principal organ for INTERNATIONAL LAW. The *Secretariat* is the administrative body headed by the Secretary General, who is an important figure with considerable executive power and political influence (see LIE, TRYGVE; HAMMARSKJÖLD, DAG; THANT, U; WALDHEIM, KURT). Other organs are the UNITED NATIONS CONFERENCE ON TRADE AND DEVELOPMENT, the Office of the UNITED NATIONS HIGH COMMISSIONER FOR REFUGEES, and the UNITED NATIONS CHILDREN'S FUND.

Major specialized agencies affiliated to the UN include the FOOD AND AGRICULTURE ORGANIZATION, GENERAL AGREEMENT ON TARIFFS AND TRADE, INTERNATIONAL ATOMIC ENERGY AGENCY (UN-sponsored), INTERNATIONAL CIVIL AVIATION ORGANIZATION, INTERNATIONAL LABOR ORGANIZATION, INTERNATIONAL MONETARY FUND, INTERNATIONAL TELECOMMUNICATION UNION, UNITED NATIONS EDUCATIONAL, SCIENTIFIC AND CULTURAL ORGANIZATION, UNIVERSAL POSTAL UNION, WORLD BANK, WORLD HEALTH ORGANIZATION, and WORLD METEOROLOGICAL ORGANIZATION.

UNITED NATIONS CHILDREN'S FUND (UNICEF), UN organization formed 1946 as the UN International Children's Emergency Fund to help in countries devastated in WWII. It became a permanent body in 1953, retaining the UNICEF acronym and specializing in child welfare, family planning and nutrition programs in disaster areas and in many poorer countries. It is financed voluntarily. In 1965 UNICEF was awarded the Nobel Peace Prize.

UNITED NATIONS CONFERENCE ON TRADE AND DEVELOPMENT (UNCTAD), a 1964 conference and now a permanent organ of the UN General Assembly, with a 55-member Trade and Development Board based in Geneva which meets twice a year or more. It designs the UN's trade policies and promotes trade agreements to assist developing countries. The UN's Development Program (1965) and Industrial Development Organization (1968) aim to increase technical and economic assistance.

UNITED NATIONS EDUCATIONAL, SCIENTIFIC AND CULTURAL ORGANIZATION (UNESCO), a UN agency established 1946 to promote international collaboration through science, education and cultural activities, thus advancing the human rights and freedoms laid down in the UN charter. Its policy-making general conference meets biennially at the Paris headquarters. UNESCO has helped develop education in poorer countries and arranges scientific and cultural exchanges.

UNITED NATIONS HIGH COMMISSIONER FOR REFUGEES, Office of the, UN agency, the 1951 successor to the International Refugee Organization. It has cared for refugees from many countries, and supports their right to be free from arbitrary expulsion, to work and be educated in their new homes. It received the 1954 Nobel Peace Prize. The separate UN Relief and Works Agency for Palestine Refugees (established 1949) is based in Beirut.

UNITED NATIONS RELIEF AND REHABILITATION ADMINISTRATION (UNRRA), body set up (1943) by WWII Allied Powers to help newly liberated regions. It provided emergency supplies and refugee camps and repatriated 7000000 refugees, mainly in China and E and S Europe. Its successors were the International Refugee Organization (1946–52) and the Office of the UNITED NATIONS HIGH COMMISSIONER FOR REFUGEES.

UNITED PRESBYTERIAN CHURCH IN THE USA, created in 1958 through merger of the Presbyterian Church in the USA and the United Presbyterian Church of North America. It is the largest Presbyterian body in the US, representing over 9000 churches with more than 3000000 members. It has many overseas missionaries, and is concerned with Christian social action. (See PRESBYTERIANISM; REFORMED CHURCHES.)

UNITED PRESS INTERNATIONAL (UPI), world's largest independent news agency, created by the 1958 merger of United Press (formed by Edward W. SCRIPPS) and William R. HEARST's International News Service. Its 200 bureaus (half in the US) send

United States

The second American Revolution

Americans celebrated their 200th anniversary of nationhood in 1976 in a spirit of renewal. But as the old virtues were reaffirmed a new and revolutionary relationship between the units of American government was emerging. The long-term trend toward greater power for the federal government in Washington, D.C., has been altered—even reversed. This revolution in "federalism" could result in as significant a change as any before it in the Republic's history.

Federalism, of course, is the structure of government mandated by the United States Constitution. Government exists at local, state and national levels, and each component of the "layer cake" has certain responsibilities and duties. While the interactions between the units of government have never been as orderly as this description—some have compared it to a "marble cake" rather than a "layer cake"—few would deny that the national government has become increasingly strong over the course of American history.

The states, on the other hand, have become more subservient. The New Deal of President Franklin Roosevelt and the massive social programs of Roosevelt's successors shifted virtually all attention to the national level. Most decisions which affected the daily lives of Americans were made in Washington. Many political observers began to write obituaries for the states—and with good reason. As Robert S. Allen contended in his book, *Our Sovereign State*, in 1949: "State government is the tawdriest, most incompetent, and most stultifying unit of the nation's political structure. In state government are to be found in their most extreme and vicious forms all the worst evils of misrule in the country."

Allen's indictment was not too harsh. For in the state governments could be found corruption in a thousand forms, absolute incompetence, ignorance of pressing social problems, repeated violations of basic constitutional rights, the crippling of the cities by refusals to meet their needs, and unjust, disproportionate representation in the legislatures which heavily favored rural areas. A modern and progressive Governor, Terry Sanford of North Carolina, characterized the "state of the states" in the early 1960s not too differently:

The states are indecisive.
The states are antiquated.
The states are timid and ineffective.
The states are not willing to face their problems.
The states are not responsive.
The states are not interested in cities.
These half-dozen charges are true about all of the states some of the time and some of the states all of the time.

It is fair to say that the states were more responsible than the federal government for the latter's assumption of authority. For the states had been the pillars of government in the Republic's early life. As James Madison stated in *The Federalist # 46* (1788): "The first and most natural attachments of the people will be to the governments of their respective states." This loyalty could only be transferred to the national government "from such manifest and irresistible proofs of a better administration, as will overcome all their antecedent propensities." Unfortunately for the states, the "irresistible proofs" were more than apparent to their citizens. President Eisenhower, speaking to the assembled Governors in 1957, identified clearly the main reason for the expansion of the federal government: "Every State failure to meet a pressing public need has created the opportunity, developed the excuse, and fed the temptation for the national government to poach on the states' preserves." Their predictable abdication of responsibility made the states a repository for conservative "states' rights" advocates, and few matters of importance were delegated to them. As Adlai Stevenson once remarked, "There would be less talk about states' rights if there had been fewer states' wrongs."

The national government attracted most of the bright young men and women interested in government service; the national government was the object of the hopes and fears of America. State governments were consigned to minor service functions and became the objects of mistrust and ridicule. Progressive Governor Tom McCall of Oregon recalled one incident illustrative of the attitudes so many held: "I debated the Mayor of San Juan on the relative roles of the state and local governments, and he was so critical of state governments. I said, 'Well, what do you think the state governments ought to do?', and he snapped at me, 'Roads and agriculture, period!' "

It is a mark of the rapidly changing character of American society that within little more than a single decade, the situation was reversed. By 1976 the Harris poll found "a dramatic shift in public confidence away from the federal government." By almost a 3 to 1 margin state government could be trusted more than the national government, and by a 6 to 1 margin state government was judged to be "closer to the people." Even more surprisingly, Washington was felt overwhelmingly to be more corrupt and wasteful than state government.

These impressions are grounded, at least in part, in fact. The Watergate scandals alone, while they account for much of the shift *from* the federal government, are harly responsible for such a significant shift *to* the states. Rather, it is the decisive actions of the states themselves which have, in good measure, restored them to a position of power and trust. Even a cursory view of the agenda covered by the governors and state legislatures of most states in the early 1970s gives and indication: campaign finance reform, consumer protection, "no-fault" auto insurance, crime prevention and penal reform, the enviroment, mass transportation, a wide range of social welfare, health, and education matters, urban relief and renewal legislation and rural development. The states have outstripped the federal government in many of these areas.

An even more significant indication of the new-found creativity and energy of state governments across the nation can be found in an examination of the hundreds of innovative programs and experiments which states have enacted and are conducting of late. Here are just a few which were compiled and studied by the Council of State Governments:

- Rural areas are no longer deprived of adequate health care under a North Carolina program which provides state funds to match local money for health construction and uses specially trained nurses for rural health care.
- Industries can escape some of the red tape in Washington by opting for a coordinated state review of their development proposals. The procedure coordinates various enviromental and land use permits required by state agencies.
- Whether or not a utility needs a rate increase can be determined without relying solely on the utility's own figures; the Public Service Commission in New York has independent audit facilities to evaluate their performance.
- Keeping state prisons from becoming overcrowded and encouraging community corrections are among the goals of a Minnesota program which provides state block grants to counties which agree not to commit offenders to state prisons.
- Economic development is the goal of a Rhode Island corporation with power to grant loans and venture capital, and to authorize land and plant transactions.
- Medical care to the poor is made less costly by an Oregon program which pools federal, state, and local health care funds.

How state governments have changed since Robert Allen described them and how wrong was the political scientist who predicted that the states might well "be left hollow shells, operating primarily as the field districts of federal departments"!

The turnaround of the states is one of the most important developments in American government in this century, and it is especially surprising that it occurred within such a short time. Two developments at the federal level helped to create a national mood which permitted the states to recoup. Firstly the promise of President Lyndon Johnson's Great Society was not fulfilled. Poverty was not eradicated, slums did not disappear, and urban minorities were not mollified. Instead, America saw the federal bureaucracy and budget both mushroom

news and pictures to some 6000 clients. (See also REUTERS; TASS.)

UNITED SERVICE ORGANIZATIONS (USO), independent, nonprofit grouping of organizations formed 1941 to provide recreational, entertainment, religious and social facilities for the US armed forces. It is recognized by the US Department of Defense. Affiliates include the YMCA, YWCA and Salvation Army.

UNITED STATES. For all US government departments and organizations (except USIA), see alphabetically under identifying name: AGRICULTURE, US DEPARTMENT OF; AIR FORCE ACADEMY, US; CONGRESS OF THE UNITED STATES, etc.

UNITED STATES CONSTITUTION, the supreme law of the nation. Written in Philadelphia in the summer of 1787, the Constitution was approved by the 55 delegates representing the 13 original states and went into effect on March 4, 1789 after ratification by the required nine states. The document was the sum of the young nation's experience to that point. The actions of the virtually autonomous states and the failure of the country's first constitution, the ARTICLES OF CONFEDERATION, convinced the Founding Fathers that a strong executive and a powerful federal government were needed if the US were to survive as a cohesive entity. Many compromises were necessary before final agreement was reached. The conflicting desires of large and small states resulted in a bicameral legislature, one house based on population size, the other house with an equal number of seats for each state (see CONGRESS). North and South compromised on including slaves in population totals. Most important, though, was the eventual, if begrudging, recognition by all states that a strong central government would be needed if the US was to be more than just a loose confederation. The states allayed their fears by constructing a SEPARATION OF POWERS to limit governmental power (see STATES' RIGHTS; EXECUTIVE; JUDICIARY; LEGISLATURE). A BILL OF RIGHTS to guarantee personal freedoms was also added as the first ten amendments to the Constitution. The document has proven adaptable and flexible; its timelessness is indicated by the addition of only 16 amendments since 1791. (See also PRESIDENCY, US;

United States of America: regional state groups (excluding Alaska and Hawaii). New England (I); Middle Atlantic (II); the South (III); Middle West (IV); Mountain States (V); Pacific States or Far West (VI).

because of policies which seemed to throw billions of dollars at problems without results. The resulting disillusionment with the promise of national government was transformed to disgust by the deceit and trickery which characterized both the conduct of the Vietnam War and the revelations of the Watergate scandals. To the American people, their government in Washington appeared distant, removed, and very out-of-touch with their standards and beliefs. To many, the federal government no longer merited their hopes and their trust.

Thus an opening was present for the resurgence of state government. But if the states had not undertaken to reform themselves, little would or could have been made of the opportunity. Not that the states changed willingly at first; "coercive" court decisions and Congressional actions provided the impetus. The abolition of the poll tax in the South in 1964 and the passage of the Voting Rights Act of 1965 enfranchised millions of citizens, both black and white, who were a catalyst for change in their states' politics. Even more crucial nationwide were the Supreme Court's reapportionment decisions, beginning with *Baker v. Carr* in 1962. With the mandate of "One man, one vote," legislatures were forced to reapportion themselves to "represent people, not trees or acres." The awakened and invigorated legislatures combined with a new breed of governors voted into office by a broadened, more urban electorate. Together they proceeded to restructure state government from top to bottom—reorganizing, computerizing, and staffing their governments to meet the challenges of the modern era.

At the same time as the states were flexing their long-atrophied muscles, the federal government was beginning to realize that its goals may have been too ambitious. In overreaching itself and attempting to control too many details at state and local levels, the federal government was ensuring failure for the programs it most desired to see succeed. With the help of a four-year lobbying effort by governors and mayors, the Congress passed and the President signed the Federal Revenue-Sharing Act in 1972. This Act, the largest domestic aid bill ever passed, provided $30.1 billion over a four-year period for state and local governments from the federal treasury—and all of it with few strings attached. Revenue-sharing was renewed in 1976 and appears to be becoming a permanent fixture in the federal budget. This aid has been supplemented by another multi-billion dollar revenue program called "block grants." Under this program states receive money for use in very broad subject areas (like health, community development, or transportation). With all of this recent activity and funding at the state level, it is little wonder that state governments are growing considerably faster than their counterparts at the national and local levels.

Perhaps the culmination of government's new state-oriented trend can be seen best in the quest for the presidency. For decades before 1976 state governors had been eclipsed by US senators and vice-presidents in the race for party presidential nominations. But in 1976 former Governor Ronald Reagan of California almost grabbed the Republican nomination away from incumbent President Gerald R. Ford. And on the Democratic side former Governor Jimmy Carter of Georgia captured his party's nomination in a crowded field of well-known contenders. In fact, of all the principal candidates, only Gerald Ford, a former congressman, was *not* a governor. And he was a candidate only by virtue of his unelected incumbency, obtained through appointment to the vice-presidency by President Richard Nixon and succession to the presidency when Nixon resigned in August, 1974.

No other development speaks more forcefully for the states, underlining the shift of power away from the national government. With new revenue sources, strengthened governors, more representative legislatures, reorganized governments, and the confidence of their citizenry, states have become full partners once again in the government of the United States. They are now equipped to be, as it was intended for them at the founding of the Republic, the "laboratories of democracy."

ELECTORAL COLLEGE; CONSTITUTIONAL LAW.)

UNITED STATES INFORMATION AGENCY (USIA), federal US agency established 1953 to convince peoples of other countries "that the objectives and policies of the US are in harmony with and will advance their legitimate aspirations for freedom, progress, and peace." US Information Service (USIS) offices in some 100 countries work through press, TV and radio (see VOICE OF AMERICA) and provide information pamphlets and English classes.

UNITED STATES OF AMERICA (USA or US), world's fourth-largest country after the USSR, Canada and China. The 48 conterminous states span North America from coast to coast. With Alaska, separated from them by Canada, they form the continental US. The 50th state is Hawaii. The federal capital is Washington, D.C. (District of Columbia). Overseas territories include Puerto Rico, the American Virgin Islands, Guam, American Samoa and the Trust Territory of the Pacific Islands. Other dependencies include Johnson, Midway, Wake and other Pacific islands. The US also controls the Panama Canal Zone.

Land. The conterminous US can be divided into six natural regions: the *Atlantic and Gulf Coastal Lowlands* stretching S from Long Island to Florida and then W to Mexico, averaging 200mi wide, with many lagoons and sandbars and, on the Gulf Coast, the Mississippi R delta; the *Appalachians*, running NE-SW from Nova Scotia (Canada), a low mountain chain that includes the White Mts of N.H. (Mt Washington, 6288ft), the Great Smoky Mts (Clingmans Dome, 6643ft), the Black Mts of N.C. (Mt Mitchell, 6684ft) and, to the W, the ridge and valley belt and the Allegheny Plateau; the *Central* or *Interior Plains*, stretching W to the Rocky Mts, a region drained chiefly by the Mississippi-Missouri river system and its branches and containing various uplands such as the Black Hills of Dakota, and the Ozarks; the *Rocky Mts*, with peaks exceeding 14000ft, glacial features and many national parks; the *Western Plateau and Basin* or *Intermontane Region*, separated from the Pacific coastlands by the Cascade and Sierra Nevada ranges and containing such features as the Grand Canyon

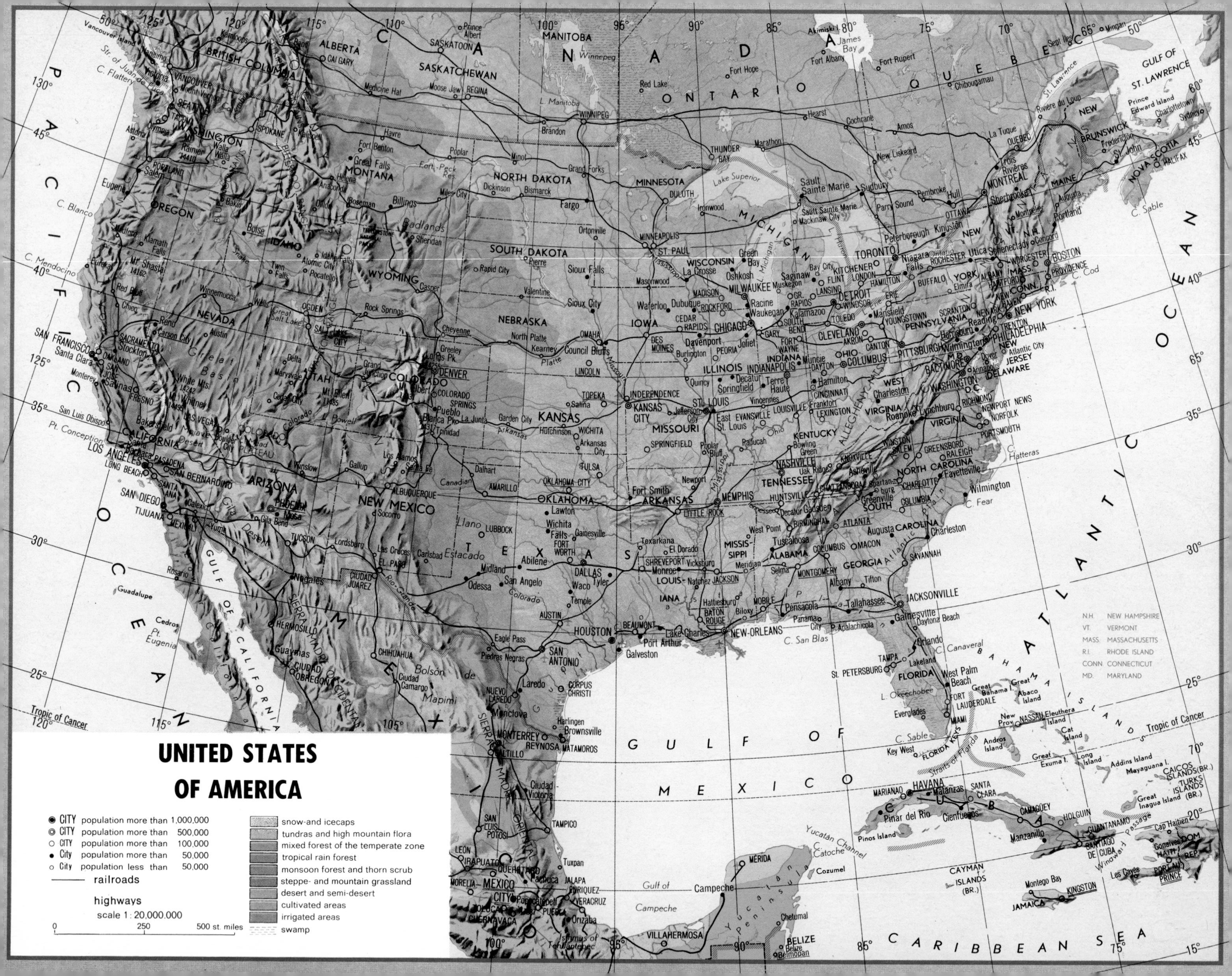
UNITED STATES
OF AMERICA
CITY population more than 1,000,000
CITY population more than 500,000
CITY population more than 100,000
City population more than 50,000
City population less than 50,000
railroads
highways
scale 1: 20,000,000
0 250 500 st. miles
snow-and icecaps
tundras and high mountain flora
mixed forest of the temperate zone
tropical rain forest
monsoon forest and thorn scrub
steppe- and mountain grassland
desert and semi-desert
cultivated areas
irrigated areas
swamp
N.H. NEW HAMPSHIRE
VT. VERMONT
MASS. MASSACHUSETTS
R.I. RHODE ISLAND
CONN. CONNECTICUT
MD. MARYLAND
PACIFIC OCEAN
ATLANTIC OCEAN
GULF OF MEXICO
CARIBBEAN SEA
CANADA
MEXICO
Tropic of Cancer

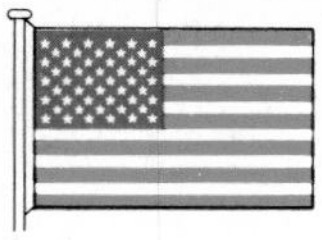

Official Name: United States of America
Capital: Washington, D.C.
Area: 3 536 855sq mi
Population: 204 765 770
Languages: English
Religions: Protestant, Roman Catholic, Jewish
Monetary unit(s): 1 US Dollar = 100 cents

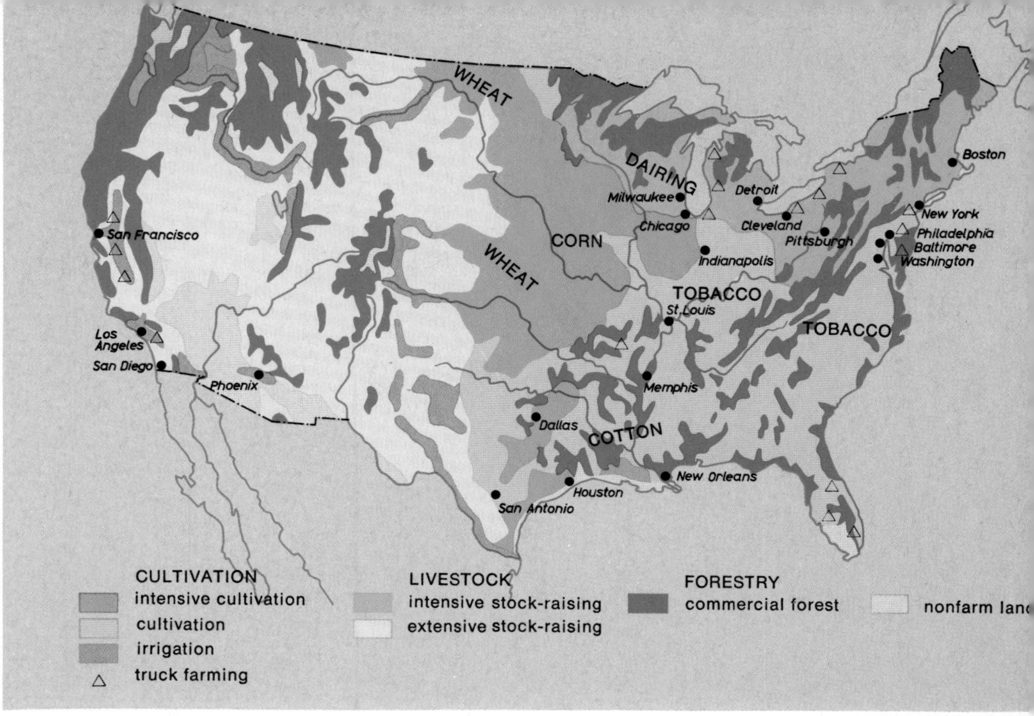

United States of America: agriculture.

and the Great Salt Lake; and the *Pacific Coastlands*, extending S from Puget Sound to the long Central Valley of California.

Climate is greatly influenced by the geographic position of the conterminous US between large oceans on the E and W, with a warm and shallow sea to the S and the Canadian landmass to the N. The W winds from the Pacific bring heavy rainfall to the NW coast in winter and the fall, but rainfall decreases rapidly E of the Western Cordillera. Winter temperatures vary greatly, being relatively high along the sheltered Pacific coast, but often extremely low in the interior and the E. Snowfall can be heavy in the N. Summer temperatures are mainly high, averaging over 75°F in most areas. The SE becomes subtropical and humid. Tornadoes can occur in spring, especially in the Mississippi valley, and summer thunderstorms and hurricanes are frequent along the S Gulf and Atlantic coasts.

Vegetation ranges from the mixed forests of the Appalachians to the grasslands of the Great Plains, and from the conifers of the Rocky Mts and NW states to the splendid redwoods of California, the cacti and mesquite of the SW deserts, and the tropical palms and mangroves of the Gulf.

People. The US is the world's fourth-largest nation by population after China, India and the USSR. Until 1840 immigrants came mostly from England and Scotland, but thereafter increasingly from other, mainly European, lands including Ireland, Germany, Scandinavia and, from the 1860s, Italy and the Slavic countries. Since 1820 more than 46 million immigrants are estimated to have been admitted, but since 1921 a quota system has been in force, annual admissions since 1968 being limited to 120 000 from the W Hemisphere and 170 000 from the E. Assimilation of European migrants has usually been rapid. The first Negroes came as slaves (from 1619). Today there are some 23 million black Americans, of whom about 50% still live in the South and most of the others in large cities like Washington, D.C., New York and Chicago. Indians, the original inhabitants, are found in all states with major concentrations in the Great Plains and the West. Other significant national groups include Spanish-Americans (Mexicans and Puerto Ricans), Chinese and Japanese. About 75% of Americans are urban-dwelling and more than 16% of the total population live in the Boston to Washington, D.C. stretch of the Atlantic coastal belt which contains the two most densely populated states, New Jersey and Rhode Island. During the 1960s California overtook New York to become the most populous state in the Union. The US has many religious groups, the strongest being the Protestants (71 000 000, chiefly Baptists, Methodists, Lutherans and Presbyterians) and Roman Catholics (48 000 000). Of the sizable Jewish community (over 6 000 000) some 1 800 000 live in New York City. There is a nationwide system of public education and only 2% of the population ar illiterate.

Economy. In 1975 the Gross National Product of the US was $1 499 000 million, about twice that of the USSR, her nearest rival as the world's leading economic nation. The American economy is predominantly free-enterprise. The US can grow nearly all temperate and subtropical crops and is self-sufficient in essential foods. About half the land surface is occupied by farms, with dairying important in the N and NE, livestock and feed grains in the Midwest (the Corn Belt), wheat on the plains, livestock on the High Plains and the intermontane areas of the W, and also in the S (along with dairying and various crops). Texas, Arizona, New Mexico and

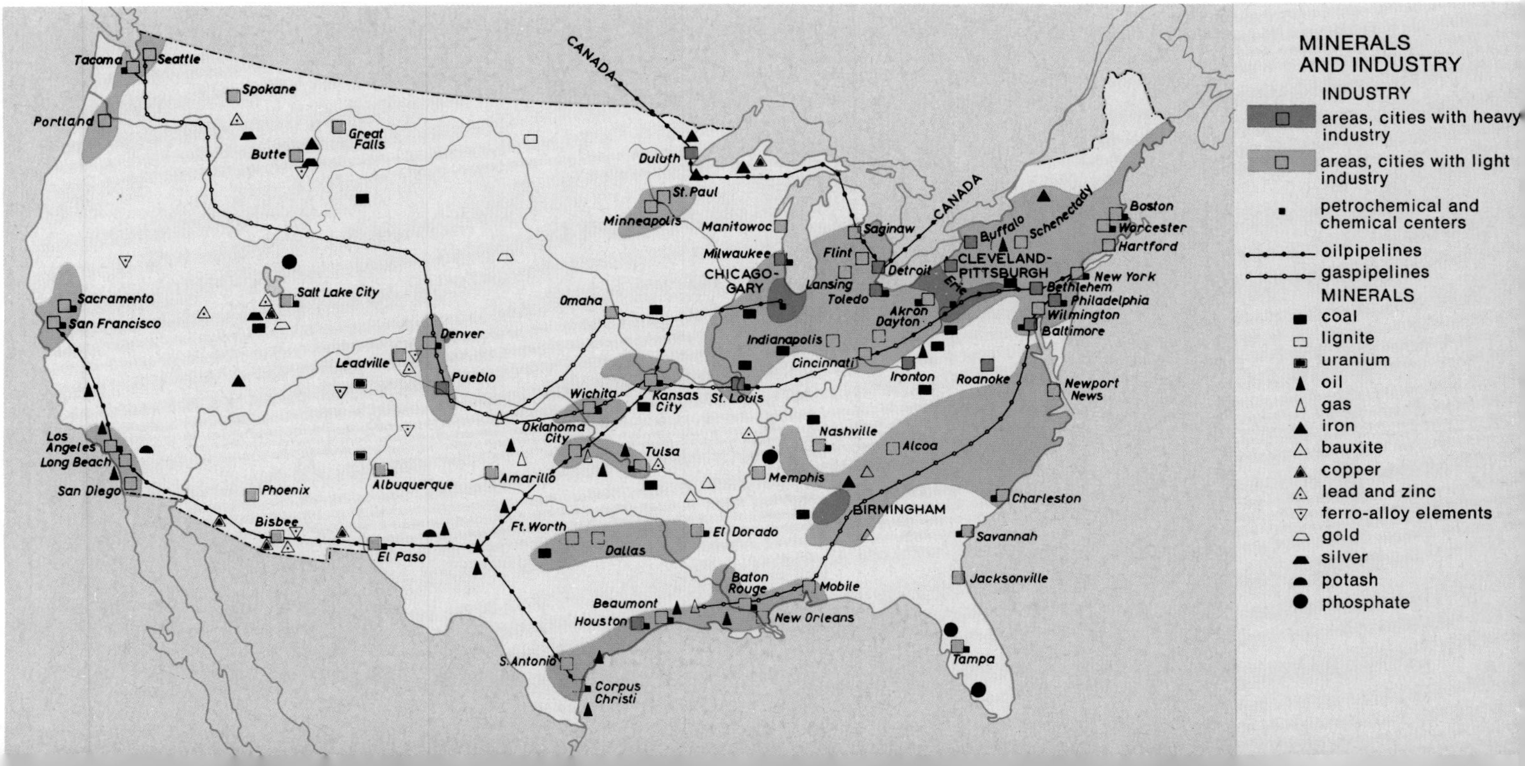

California lead in cotton and there are various speciality crops like fruit, rice, citrus fruits and sugarcane in the S. There are valuable forests and fisheries. The rich mineral resources include coal (Appalachians, Indiana-Illinois, Alabama), iron ore (near Lake Superior), petroleum and natural gas (Texas, Louisiana, the Great Plains and Alaska) and other vital minerals. But reserves of some minerals are declining and the US has increasingly become an importer of ores and oil. Major products include steel (Pittsburgh, Chicago-Gary and elsewhere), automobiles (Detroit), aircraft and aerospace products (the West and on the Great Plains), electric and electronic equipment (New England), textiles (North and South Carolina, Georgia) and most kinds of consumer goods. Some consumer goods industries, like tobacco and meat-packing, are located near their raw materials, others are widely scattered to meet their markets.

History. For an account of the original inhabitants of America and their dispossession, see INDIANS, NORTH AMERICAN; INDIAN WARS. The first permanent European settlement was Spanish (St. Augustine, Florida, 1565). Early English settlements were in Virginia (Jamestown, 1607), Massachusetts (Plymouth, 1620), Maryland (1634) and Pennsylvania (1681). From these and from French, Dutch and Swedish settlements came the original 13 colonies. Later opposition to Britain's colonial policy led to the REVOLUTIONARY WAR (1775–83) and independence as a federal republic with George WASHINGTON as first President (1789). Expansion westward followed. The area of the US was doubled by the LOUISIANA PURCHASE (1803) and later Florida was purchased from Spain (1819). Meanwhile the US had fought Britain in the WAR OF 1812. Texas was annexed in 1845 and other territories gained by the Treaty of Guadalupe Hidalgo ending the MEXICAN WAR (1848). The GADSDEN PURCHASE (1853) brought Arizona into the Union, and Alaska was purchased from Russia in 1867. Meanwhile rivalry between North and South had culminated in the CIVIL WAR (1861–65). There followed a period of RECONSTRUCTION (1865–77) and rapid development during which the Union Pacific, the first transcontinental railroad, was completed (1869). Hawaii was annexed in 1898, in which year certain overseas territories came under US rule as a result of the SPANISH–AMERICAN WAR. The US entered WORLD WAR I in 1917, but the prosperity which followed the war was ended by the GREAT DEPRESSION (1929). Economic decline was halted under Franklin D. ROOSEVELT and his NEW DEAL. The Japanese attack on PEARL HARBOR (1941) brought the US into WORLD WAR II. The Union emerged from that war as leader of the West and a "superpower" engaged in worldwide rivalry with the communist bloc (see COLD WAR), which led to her engagement in the KOREAN WAR (1950–53) and the VIETNAM WAR (1961–73). In spite of a business recession, inflation, racial strife violence, and exposure of corruption (see WATERGATE), the US remains economically immensely powerful and a major force in world affairs.

UNITED STEELWORKERS OF AMERICA, third largest US union (1974: 1 400 000 members). Superseding the Amalgamated Association of Iron, Steel and Tin Workers, the CIO's Steel Workers' Organizing Committee, recognized by the US Steel Corporation in 1937, took its present name in 1942.

UNIT RULE, voting rule used by US Democrats from 1860 to 1968. It allowed state delegations to a presidential CONVENTION to vote as a unit for the candidate endorsed by the majority of the delegation.

UNITS. See CGS UNITS; METRIC SYSTEM; MKSA UNITS; SI UNITS; STATAMPERE; WEIGHTS AND MEASURES.

UNITY, mathematical term for the number one.

UNIVERSAL, philosophical term referring to any possible attribute of more than one particular. Redness, for example, is the universal common to all red things. The question arises whether the general term naming a universal refers to an entity that exists independently of thought or is merely a principle of classification. (See also IDEALISM; REALISM; CONCEPTUALISM; NOMINALISM.)

UNIVERSALISM, heretical Christian doctrine that everyone will ultimately be saved (see SALVATION). HELL is denied. The Universalist Church in the US was formed by Hosea BALLOU and other New England nonconformists. Liberal and syncretist, in 1961 it joined the Unitarians to form the UNITARIAN UNIVERSALIST ASSOCIATION.

UNIVERSAL POSTAL UNION (UPU), a UN agency (since 1947) that determines procedures for the reciprocal flow of foreign mail. Its operations are based on the first (1875) Universal Postal Convention. The Universal Postal Congress meets every five years. Headquarters are in Bern, Switzerland. (See also POSTAL SERVICES.)

UNIVERSE, the closed system of all that exists or happens (see also HEAT DEATH). In COSMOLOGY, the term is applied to our universe, i.e., all that we can observe and the presumably homogeneous and isotropic extension thereof, since it is conceived that there may have been prior universes and that there may be subsequent universes.

UNIVERSITY CITY, city in E Mo., a residential suburb 8mi WNW of St. Louis. Pop 46 309.

UNIVERSITY HEIGHTS, a residential city in N Ohio, 8mi E of Cleveland. It is the site of John Carroll University. Pop 17 055.

UNKNOWN SOLDIER, in the US and some European countries after WWI, the unidentified body of a soldier killed in action, whose tomb is a national symbol honoring those killed in the war. The first US Unknown Soldier was buried in ARLINGTON NATIONAL CEMETRY, Va., on Nov. 11, 1921.

UNLEAVENED BREAD. See MATZAH.

UNTERMEYER, Louis (1885–), US poet and anthologist known particularly for his parodies and for popular anthologies such as *Modern American Poetry* (1919) and *Modern British Poetry* (1920).

UPANISHADS, ancient Indian Hindu scriptures (c1000 BC–600 BC) attached to the latter half of each VEDA and containing secret or mystical doctrine. They are of lesser authority than the *Aranyakes* and *Brahmanas* (expository texts), being intended more for the philosophical inquirer.

UPAS, *Antiaris toxicaria*, a large Asiatic tree belonging to the mulberry family, Moraceae. Its poisonous milky sap has long been used to tip arrows. Tradition declares it to have evil powers; nothing can live in its shadow.

UPDIKE, John Hoyer (1932–), US novelist, short-story writer and poet. With precise craftsmanship, he dissects contemporary US life in such novels as *Rabbit, Run* (1960), *The Centaur* (1963), *Couples* (1968), *Bech: A Book* (1970) and *Rabbit Redux* (1971), and short-story collections like *The Music School* (1966).

UPHOLSTERY. See CHAIR.

UPJOHN, Richard (1802–1878), British-born US architect, famous for his Gothic Revival churches, such as Trinity Church, New York City (1846). He was president of the American Institute of Architects 1857–76.

UPLAND, city in S Cal., 34mi E of Los Angeles. A citrus-fruit packing center, it also has some light industry. Pop 32 551.

Official name: Republic of Upper Volta
Capital: Ouagadougou
Area: 105 838sq mi
Population: 5 485 971
Languages: French; Mossi spoken
Religions: Animist; Muslim; Christian
Monetary unit(s): 1 CFA franc = 100 centimes

UPLAND PLOVER, *Bartramia longicauda*, an uncommon North American SANDPIPER, with long neck and small head. It is found locally in grassland.

UPOLU, largest island (430sq mi) of WESTERN SAMOA, S Pacific Ocean. Fertile and well watered, it produces copra, cocoa, coffee and bananas.

UPPER ARLINGTON, city in central Ohio, a NW residential suburb of Columbus. Pop 38 630.

UPPER DARBY, urban township in SE Pa. It is a residential suburb W of Philadelphia, with some light industry. Pop 45 000.

UPPER MORELAND, urban township in SE Pa. It is a N suburb of Philadelphia. Pop 24 866.

UPPER VOLTA, a landlocked West African republic, N of Ghana. With few natural resources, it is one of Africa's poorest countries.

Land. The country is a dry plateau drained by the upper streams of the Volta R. Rainfall averages 10–45in yearly, but is not retained by the thin soil, which supports little more than poor savanna; the N and NE is semidesert (see SAHEL). Temperatures range between 68°F and 95°F. The wet season lasts from June to October.

People. The largest ethnic group is the Voltaic Mossi (48%); other Voltaic groups are the Bobo (7%), Lobi (7%) and Gurunsi (6%). There are also Mande (7%) and Senufo groups, and Fulani and Tuareg nomads (11%). The population is 95% rural and concentrated in the S and E. The illiteracy rate is about 90%.

Economy. Subsistence agriculture supports about 95% of the population. Chief crops are millet, sorghum, maize, groundnuts, yams, rice and cotton. Livestock are raised, and cattle, groundnuts and cotton exported. About 500 000 Voltaians are migrant laborers in the Ivory Coast and Ghana. Manganese is mined.

History. Part of the powerful Mossi empire since c1000 AD, the region of Upper Volta was annexed by the French in 1896 and became a full French colony in 1919. It became independent in 1960, and in 1966 General Sangoulé Lamizana seized power.

UR, or "Ur of the Chaldees," ancient city of S MESOPOTAMIA. A center of the SUMERIAN civilization from c3000 BC, it was conquered by the Akkadian SARGON c2340 BC. A new dynasty arose c2060 BC under UR-NAMMU, who built the famous ZIGGURAT. After c1950 BC the city came under ELAM and BABYLON. Destroyed and rebuilt several times, it was finally revived by NEBUCHADNEZZAR II (c600 BC), but then declined and was abandoned by 300 BC, isolated by the Euphrates R changing its course. Ur was excavated by Leonard WOOLLEY.

URACIL. See NUCLEIC ACIDS; NUCLEOTIDES.

URAL-ALTAIC LANGUAGES, collective term for the Uralic language family and the ALTAIC LANGUAGES. The 20 or so languages of the Uralic family (best known being Finnish and Hungarian) are in two branches, the UGRO-FINNIC LANGUAGES and the relatively unimportant Samoyedic languages.

URAL MOUNTAINS, 1 500mi-long mountain system in W USSR. Running N–S from the Kara Sea into Kazakhstan N of the Aral Sea, they are the traditional boundary between Europe and Asia. Mt Narodnaya (6 214ft), in the N section, is the highest peak. The Urals are heavily forested and rich in minerals.

URAL RIVER, in the USSR, rises in the S Ural Mts, and flows 1 575mi S, W and S to the Caspian Sea. It has salmon and sturgeon fisheries.

URANIA. See MUSES.

URANINITE. See PITCHBLENDE.

URANIUM (U), soft, silvery-white radioactive metal in the ACTINIDE series; the heaviest natural element. Uranium occurs widespread as PITCHBLENDE (uraninite), CARNOTITE and other ores, which are concentrated and converted to uranium (IV) fluoride, from which uranium is isolated by electrolysis or reduction with calcium or magnesium. The metal is reactive and electropositive, reacting with hot water and dissolving in acids. Its chief oxidation states are +4 and +6, and the uranyl (UO_2^{2+}) compounds are common. Uranium has three naturally-occurring ISOTOPES: U^{238} (HALF-LIFE 4.5×10^9yr), U^{235} (half-life 7.1×10^8yr) and U^{234} (half-life 2.5×10^5yr). More than 99% of natural uranium is U^{238}. The isotopes may be separated by fractional DIFFUSION of the volatile uranium (VI) fluoride. Neutron capture by U^{235} leads to nuclear FISSION, and a chain reaction can occur which is the basis of NUCLEAR REACTORS and of the ATOMIC BOMB. U^{238} also absorbs neutrons and is converted to an isotope of PLUTONIUM (Pu^{239}) which (like U^{235}) can be used as a nuclear fuel. Uranium is the starting material for the synthesis of the TRANSURANIUM ELEMENTS. Some of its compounds are used to color ceramics. AW 238.0, mp 1132°C, bp 3818°C, sg 19.05 (α).

URANUS, in Greek mythology, the personification of sky or heaven. With GAEA (Earth), who had borne him, he fathered the TITANS—among them CRONUS, who castrated him. In one legend, the FURIES were born from Uranus' blood and APHRODITE from his severed genitals, which fell in the sea.

URANUS, the third largest planet in the SOLAR SYSTEM and the seventh from the sun. Physically very similar to NEPTUNE, but rather larger (53 Mm ± 5% equatorial radius), it orbits the sun every 84.02 years at a mean distance of 19.2AU, rotating in 10.75h. The plane of its equator is tilted 98° to the plane of its orbit, such that the rotation of the planet and the revolution of its five moons, which orbit closely parallel to the equator, are retrograde (see RETROGRADE MOTION).

URARTU (Biblical Ararat), ancient Armenian kingdom which flourished around Lake Van in E Turkey c1300–600 BC. At its height (8th century) it ruled N Syria. Technologically and culturally advanced, it was gradually destroyed by the Assyrians, CIMMERIANS, SCYTHIANS and BABYLONIANS.

URBAN, name of eight popes. **Saint Urban I** (reigned 222–30), is said to have been martyred. **Urban II** (reigned 1088–99) continued the reforms and the struggle against the emperor HENRY IV begun by his great predecessor GREGORY VII. At the Council of Clermont (1095) he initiated the CRUSADES. **Urban III** (reigned 1185–87) was absorbed in a struggle with emperor FREDERICK I Barbarossa and his son HENRY VI. **Urban IV** (reigned 1261–64) continued the struggle against the HOHENSTAUFEN emperors and gave the crown of Naples and Sicily to CHARLES I. The learned and pious **Saint Urban V** (reigned 1362–70) attempted to return the papacy to Rome from Avignon and to effect a reconciliation wth the Eastern Church (1267–70; see PAPACY). **Urban VI** (reigned 1378–89) was involved in disputes with his cardinals which precipitated the GREAT SCHISM. **Urban VII** (reigned 1590) died only 12 days after his election. **Urban VIII** (reigned 1623–44) played an ambiguous role in the THIRTY YEARS' WAR through political opposition to the Roman Catholic HAPSBURGS. An energetic administrator, he tried to increase the temporal power of the papacy.

URBANA, city in E central Ill., seat of Champaign Co. It is a trade center and principal home of the University of Illinois. Pop 32 800.

URBANA, city in W central Ohio, seat of Champaign Co. It manufactures plastics, airplane parts and metal goods. Pop 11 237.

URBANDALE, town in central Iowa, a suburb to the W of Des Moines with some light industry. Pop 14 434.

URBAN LEAGUE, National, philanthropic US interracial agency founded in 1910 to end segregation and promote the economic and social welfare of disadvantaged groups. It has been particularly effective in the area of equal job opportunities, and pursues programs in such fields as housing, education, health and welfare.

URBAN RENEWAL, name applied to city programs designed to eliminate slums and replace them with improved housing and amenities. See CITY PLANNING; HOUSING AND URBAN DEVELOPMENT, US DEPARTMENT OF; MODEL CITIES.

URBINO, city and today a tourist center in central Italy. In the 15th century it was a great artistic center under the 2nd duke of Urbino, whose palace is now a museum. Pop 16 234.

URDU, Indic language of the Indo-European family, a form of HINDUSTANI (see also HINDI). It has borrowed heavily from Arabic and Persian. Spoken by some 20 million people, it is an official language of India and Pakistan.

UREA, or carbamide, $CO(NH_2)_2$, the AMIDE of carbonic acid, a white crystalline solid, the end-product of protein METABOLISM in many animals, excreted in the URINE. Virtually the first organic compound to be synthesized—by Wöhler in 1828 from ammonium cyanate—it is now prepared by heating AMMONIA and CARBON dioxide under pressure. Urea's major uses are as a nitrogenous FERTILIZER, to make urea-formaldehyde resins (see PLASTICS), and to make BARBITURATES. MW 60.1, mp 135°C.

UREMIA, the syndrome of symptoms and biochemical disorders seen in KIDNEY failure, associated with a rise in blood UREA and other nitrogenous waste products of PROTEIN metabolism. Nausea, VOMITING, malaise, itching, pigmentation, ANEMIA and acute disorders of fluid and mineral balance are common presentations, but the manifestations depend on the type of disease, rate of waste buildup, etc. DIETARY FOODS may reduce uremic symptoms in chronic renal failure but dialysis or TRANSPLANTATION may be needed.

UREY, Harold Clayton (1893–), US chemist awarded the 1935 Nobel Prize for Chemistry for his discovery of DEUTERIUM, an isotope of HYDROGEN having one proton and one neutron in its nucleus, and who played a major role in the MANHATTAN PROJECT. He is also important as a cosmologist: his researches into geological dating using oxygen ISOTOPES enabled him to produce a model of the atmosphere of the primordial planet earth; and hence to formulate a theory of the planets' having originated as a gaseous disk about the sun (see SOLAR SYSTEM).

URIC ACID, or 2,6,8-trihydroxypurine, the end-product of protein METABOLISM in birds, invertebrates and snakes, and of PURINE metabolism in many insects, reptiles, birds, primates (including man) and the Dalmatian dog. Sufferers from GOUT have a high blood level of uric acid.

URINE, waste product comprising a dilute solution of excess salts and unwanted nitrogenous material, such as UREA and deaminated PROTEIN, excreted by many animals. The wastes are filtered from the BLOOD in the KIDNEYS or equivalent structures and stored in the BLADDER till excreted. The passage of urine serves not only to eliminate wastes, but also provides a mechanism for maintaining the water and salt concentrations and pH of the blood. While all MAMMALS excrete their nitrogenous wastes in urine, other groups—birds, insects and fishes—excrete them as AMMONIA or in solid crystals as URIC ACID.

UR-NAMMU (c2060 BC), ruler of the ancient city of UR and founder of a new SUMERIAN dynasty. He built the ZIGGURAT, and his code of law—promulgated some 300 years before that of HAMMURABI—is the oldest in recorded history.

URSA MAJOR. See GREAT BEAR.

URSA MINOR. See LITTLE DIPPER.

URSULA, Saint, legendary 4th-century Christian martyr. According to legend, she and 11 000 British maidens returning from a pilgrimage to Rome were martyred by HUNS at Cologne. She is no longer officially recognized by the Roman Catholic Church.

URSULINES, Roman Catholic religious order of women, the first to be devoted exclusively to the education of girls. The order was founded in Brescia, Italy, in 1535 by St. Angela Merici, with St. URSULA as patron saint.

URTICARIA. See HIVES.

URUGUAY, the smallest republic in South America, bordered by Argentina (W), Brazil (N and E), the Atlantic and the Río de la Plata in the S.

Land. A narrow coastal strip rises to low ridges (highest point 1 644ft), grassland plains and wooded valleys. The climate is temperate and rainfall (average 35in) is spread throughout the year. The Negro is the chief river.

People. The people are mostly of Spanish and Italian descent, and 80% urban. About two-fifths of the population live in Montevideo. There are some 300 000 MESTIZOS, mainly in the N.

Economy. The economy is based on cattle and sheep; meat, wool and hides provide 80% of the country's exports. Wheat, oats, flax, oilseeds, grapes, fruit and sugarbeet are grown. Meat-packing and tanning are the chief industries, and textiles, chemicals, plastics, electrical and other goods are manufactured. There are important fisheries, but few mineral resources.

Official name: Republic of Uruguay
Capital: Montevideo
Area: 721 172sq mi
Population: 2 921 000
Languages: Spanish
Religions: Roman Catholic
Monetary unit(s): 1 Uruguayan peso = 100 centesimos

History. The region was visited (1516) and settled (1624) by the Spanish, who resisted Portuguese incursions and founded Montevideo c1726. José ARTIGAS led the independence movement 1810–20, and Uruguay became independent in 1828. Civil strife continued into the 1900s, but from c1911 considerable economic and social progress was achieved. In 1951 a nine-man National Council replaced the presidency. Democratic in aim, this led to inefficient bureaucracy, which combined with high inflation and declining exports to produce growing social unrest, culminating in the guerrilla activities of the Marxist Tupamaros. Since the National Council was abolished in 1967 governments have become increasingly repressive.

URUGUAY RIVER, rises in S Brazil and flows W, then S for some 980mi to the RÍO DE LA PLATA estuary. It forms the Uruguay–Argentina boundary.

URUK. See ERECH.

URUMCHI, capital city of Sinkiang province, NW China, in the DZUNGARIA. It has iron, steel and chemical works and tanneries. Pop c500 000.

USHUAIA, port and capital of TIERRA DEL FUEGO territory, S Argentina. The world's southernmost city, it is a lumber and fishing center. Pop 5 677.

USIA. See UNITED STATES INFORMATION AGENCY.

USKUDAR, or Scutari, urban district of Istanbul, Turkey, on the E shore of the Bosporus. Florence NIGHTINGALE worked there during the CRIMEAN WAR. Pop 143 938.

USO. See UNITED SERVICE ORGANIZATIONS.

USSURI RIVER, river in E USSR, flowing 365mi from N of Vladivostock to the Amur R. Part of the China–USSR boundary, it is important for fishing and transporting timber.

USTINOV, Peter Alexander (1921–), English actor and playwright, also a famous raconteur and mimic. He has appeared in many movies and has often acted in his own plays, *Romanoff and Juliet* (1956) being probably the best-known.

UST-KAMENOGORSK, city in E Kazakhstan SSR, USSR, on the Irtysh R. It is a river port and metal-smelting center. Pop 230 000.

USURY, charging an exorbitant rate of INTEREST, usually to persons in financial distress; more strictly, the charging of interest at a higher rate than legally allowed. Before the Middle Ages, the charging of *any* interest was called usury and condemned by the Church, so that rich non-Christians, especially Jews, were forced by the nobility to become moneylenders.

UTAH, a Rocky Mountain state of the US.

Land. Utah falls into three regions: the ROCKY MOUNTAINS in the NE, the COLORADO PLATEAU in the S and E and the GREAT BASIN in the W. The NW is dominated by the GREAT SALT LAKE and desert. The

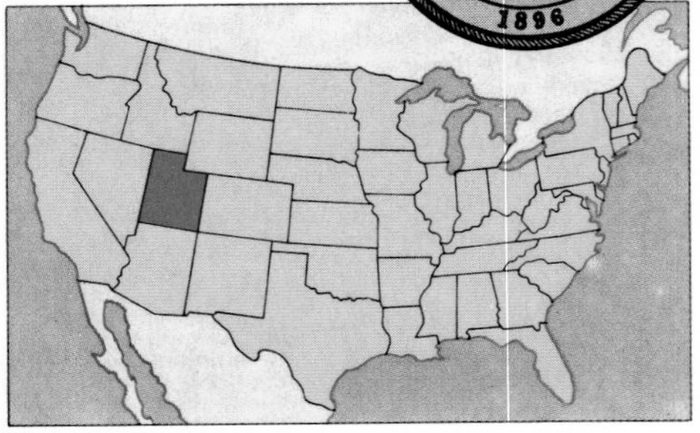

Name of State: Utah
Capital: Salt Lake City
Statehood: Jan. 4, 1896 (45th state)
Familiar Name: Beehive State
Area: 84 916sq mi
Population: 1 059 273
Elevation: Highest—13 498ft, Kings Peak
Lowest—2 000ft, Beaverdam Creek
Motto: Industry
State Flower: Sego lily
State Bird: Sea gull
State Tree: Blue spruce
State Song: "Utah, We Love Thee"

highest point is Kings Peak (13 498ft). The Colorado and its tributary the Green drain the E half. Average temperatures vary from 84°F in July in the SW to 20°F in January in the NE. Much of Utah is semiarid; annual rainfall varies from less than 5in to 50in (in the Wasatch Mts).

People. Over two-thirds of the population are MORMONS, whose headquarters are at Salt Lake City. Roman Catholics constitute the second-largest denomination. The population is 98% white; Indians number about 11 000. Salt Lake City, the state capital, is by far the largest city, followed by Ogden and Provo.

Economy. Since WWII manufacturing and mining have overtaken farming as the mainstays of the state economy. Large industries produce primary metals, transportation equipment, missiles and aerospace components, and foodstuffs including beet sugar, dairy products, flour and meat. Utah possesses large deposits of copper, oil, bituminous coal, uranium, iron and other metals. Extensive irrigation projects have opened up new farm land. The principal crops are hay, wheat, barley and sugar beet. Livestock-raising (cattle, sheep and poultry) is also important. Tourism is a fast-expanding industry.

History. Visited by Spanish missionaries in 1776 and later exploited by traders, Utah was first settled by the persecuted Mormons in 1847. It became part of the US in 1848, but did not become a state until 1896, after decades of strife with the federal government and warfare with the UTE INDIANS (for whom the state is named). The original 1895 constitution has remained in force.

UTAMARO, Kitagawa (1753–1806), Japanese artist famous for his elegant color prints of women. Highly popular in Japan, they were also admired by the French Impressionists.

UTE INDIANS, a North American tribe of the California-Intermountain group which once roamed parts of Ut., Col. and N.M. Originally peaceful hunter-gatherers, they became marauders and buffalo-hunters after obtaining Spanish horses in the 1800s. Some 4 000 now live in Col. and Ut.

UTERUS. See WOMB.

U THANT. See THANT, U.

UTICA, ancient PHOENICIAN city in N Africa, on the Medjerda R, 25mi NW of CARTHAGE. After siding with the Romans in the Third PUNIC WAR (149–146 BC) it became the Roman capital of Africa. It was destroyed c700 AD by the Arabs.

UTICA, city in central N.Y., seat of Oneida Co. Situated on the Mohawk R and the State Barge Canal, it is an important industrial center, turning out electronic and aviation equipment, textiles, tools, firearms and metal products. Pop 91 611.

UTILITARIANISM, a theory of ETHICS that the rightness or wrongness of an action is determined by the amount of happiness its consequences produce for the greatest number of people. Although the good action is that which brings about the greatest amount of happiness, it is not dependent on motive: an agent's bad motive may lead to others' happiness. The theory dates from the 18th-century thinker Jeremy BENTHAM who believed that actions were motivated by pleasure and pain and that happiness can be assessed by the quantity of pleasure; but J. S. MILL's *Utilitarianism* (1863) argued that some pleasures should be sought for their intrinsic quality.

UTILITY, in classical economics, defines the psychological satisfaction of consuming a given quantity of a particular good or service. It is an important concept in explaining demand. Goods with higher utility may be in greater demand and command a higher PRICE (see SUPPLY AND DEMAND). The concept underlies the law of MARGINAL UTILITY.

UTOPIA, term now used to denote any imaginary ideal state. Based on Greek words meaning "no place," it was coined by Sir Thomas MORE as the title of his *Utopia* (1516), in which he described a just society free of internal strife. Blueprints for such a society have been offered by many other authors, ranging from PLATO to MARX. Utopian thinking in 19th-century America was largely influenced by the theories of FOURIER; the best-known example is Edward BELLAMY's *Looking Backward* (1888). Aldous HUXLEY's *Brave New World* (1932) is a satirical Utopia.

UTRECHT, historic city in the Netherlands, 21mi SE of Amsterdam. Capital of Utrecht province, it is an important transportation and industrial center (chemicals, metal products, textiles). Pop 278 417.

UTRECHT, Peace of (1713–14), a series of treaties between England, France, the Netherlands, Portugal, Prussia, Spain and the Holy Roman Empire which concluded the War of the SPANISH SUCCESSION (see also FRENCH AND INDIAN WARS). It marked the end of a period of French expansion and the beginnings of the British Empire. Britain gained Newfoundland, Acadia (Nova Scotia) and the Hudson Bay territory from France, which retained New France (Quebec), recognized the Protestant succession in England and renounced PHILIP V of Spain's claim to the French throne. From Spain Britain gained Gibraltar and Minorca and a monopoly over the slave trade. Austria gained Milan, Naples, Sardinia and the Catholic Netherlands.

UTRILLO, Maurice (1883–1955), French painter best known for his Paris street scenes. His finest works, painted between about 1908 and 1914, capture the atmosphere of old Montmartre.

UTSUNOMIYA, city in central Honshū, Japan, capital of Tochigi prefecture. Food and tobacco are processed, and machinery and textiles manufactured. Pop 301 231.

UVALDE, city in SW Tex., seat of Uvalde Co. It is a processing center for agricultural produce. Pop 10 764.

UVULA, soft central portion of the soft PALATE which hangs at the back of the PHARYNX and forms part of the occluding mechanism which can functionally separate the nasopharynx from the oropharynx.

UXMAL, ruined city in Yucatán, Mexico. Built by the MAYAS, it flourished c600–900 AD and has some fine examples of the late-classical Puuc style of architecture. It was finally abandoned c1450 AD.

UZBEKISTAN, or Uzbek Soviet Socialist Republic, a republic of the USSR, bordering on Afghanistan. Much of it is desert but irrigated agriculture flourishes in the SE. The major cities are TASHKENT and SAMARKAND. It is Russia's chief cotton-producer and is also noted for its fruits, silk, rice, wheat, corn, grapes and sheep. There are rich deposits of coal, oil, natural gas and copper, and many industries.

UZZIAH, king of JUDAH c783–742 BC, whose reign marked the height of Judah's prosperity. According to the Old Testament, he became proud and died of leprosy.

The Temple of the Magician dominates the ruins of the ancient Mayan city of Uxmal, southwest Yucatán, Mexico. Its majestic pyramid is 80ft high and 240ft by 180ft at the base.

V

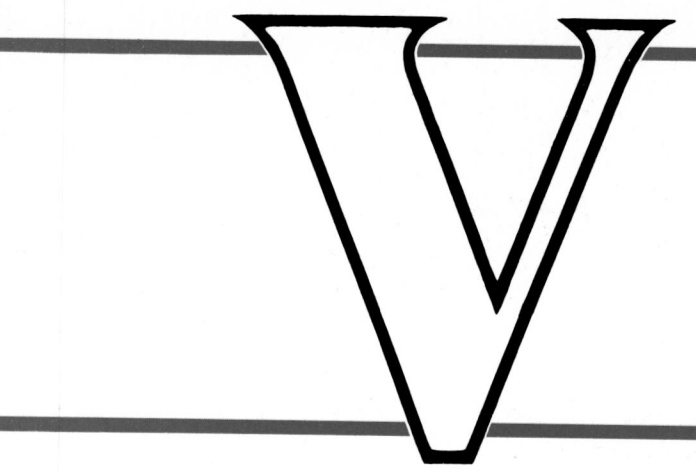

V, the 22nd letter of the English alphabet. Its origins are the same as those of the letter U, out of which it developed. In English the use of "v" for the consonantal sound was firmly established by the 17th century. "V" stands for five in Roman numerals.

V-1, or "flying-bomb," small pilotless airplane, with a ramjet engine, used by Germany during WWII against Britain and Belgium. It flew at about 360mph, carried a 2000lb bomb and had a range of about 150mi.

V-2, German WWII ballistic MISSILE which was the basis of modern US and Russian long-range missiles and space-exploration vehicles. It flew at about 3500mph and used ETHANOL and liquid oxygen fuel. Its range was about 220mi.

VAAL, river in South Africa, flowing about 750mi SW from SE Transvaal to the Orange R. It forms the Transvaal-Orange Free State boundary and is used for irrigation and Witwatersrand industry.

VACAVILLE, city in central Cal., 33mi WSW of Sacramento, with food-processing industries. Pop 21690.

VACCINATION, method of inducing IMMUNITY to INFECTIOUS DISEASE due to BACTERIA OR VIRUSES. Based on the knowledge that second attacks of diseases such as SMALLPOX were uncommon, early methods of protection consisted in inducing immunity by deliberate inoculation of material from a mild case. Starting from the observation that farm workers who had accidentally acquired cowpox by milking infected cows were resistant to smallpox, JENNER in the 1790s inoculated cowpox material into nonimmune persons who then showed resistance to smallpox. PASTEUR extended this work to experimental chicken CHOLERA, human ANTHRAX and RABIES. The term vaccination became general for all methods of inducing immunity by inoculation of products of the infectious organism. ANTITOXINS were soon developed in which specific immunity to disease TOXINS was induced. Vaccination leads to the formation of antibodies and the ability to produce large quantities rapidly at a later date (see ANTIBODIES AND ANTIGENS); this gives protection equivalent to that induced by an attack of the disease. It is occasionally followed by a reaction resembling a mild form of the disease, but rarely by the serious manifestations. Patients on STEROIDS, with immunity disorders or ECZEMA may suffer severe reactions and should not generally receive vaccinations.

VACUUM, any region of space devoid of ATOMS and MOLECULES. Such a region will neither conduct HEAT nor transmit SOUND waves. Because all materials which surround a space have a definite VAPOR PRESSURE, a perfect vacuum is an impossibility and the term is usually used to denote merely a space containing air or other gas at very low PRESSURE. Pressures less than 0.1μPa occur naturally about 800km above the earth's surface, though pressures as low as 0.01nPa can be attained in the laboratory. The low pressures required for many physics experiments are obtained using various designs of vacuum PUMP.

VACUUM BOTTLE, double-walled glass container designed by DEWAR in the late 19th century for storing liquified gases at low temperatures, but equally effective for storing hot substances. Heat transfer from the surroundings is minimized by silvering the glass walls to cut down heat RADIATION and evacuating the space between them to reduce the CONDUCTION of heat through them. A protective casing usually surrounds the glass walls.

VACUUM TUBE, an evacuated ELECTRON TUBE.

VADUZ, capital of Liechtenstein, on the Rhine R. Its museums and 16th-century buildings and castle make it a tourist center. Pop 3921.

VALDIVIA, Pedro de (c1498–1554), Spanish conquistador, one of PIZARRO's officers. He conquered Chile (1540–46) from the ARAUCANIAN INDIANS and founded Santiago, Valparaiso and Concepción. He was killed while attempting to suppress an Indian rebellion.

VAL D'OR, town in SW Quebec, Canada, a center for lumber and mining of gold, copper, lead, zinc and molybdenum. Pop 17421.

VALDOSTA, city in S Ga., seat of Lowndes Co., a processing and distribution center for lumber, tobacco, cotton, watermelon and livestock. Pop 32303.

VALENCE, or **valency**, the combining power of an ELEMENT, expressed as the number of chemical BONDS which one atom of the element forms in a given compound. In general, the characteristic valence of an element in Group N of the PERIODIC TABLE is N or $(8-N)$. (For **Oxidation Number**, see OXIDATION AND REDUCTION.)

VALENCIA, third-largest Spanish city in E Spain on the Turia R. A Roman settlement (138 BC), it came under the Moors c750–1238. Today it is a commercial center with shipyards and textile, chemical, metal and tile industries. Pop 653690.

VALENCIA, city in NW Venezuela. An industrial center in a fertile agricultural area, it produces cattle feed, foods, chemicals and textiles. Pop 366154.

VALENS (c328–378 AD), Roman emperor of the East 364–78, brother of VALENTINIAN I. He defeated the VISIGOTHS (369) and fought agains Persia (372–76). The Visigoths, admitted into the Empire in 377, revolted and defeated him at ADRIANOPLE.

VALENTINE, Saint, a Christian priest in Rome who was martyred c270 AD. His traditional association with love probably reflects the near-coincidence of his feast-day (Feb. 14) with the ancient Roman fertility festival of LUPERCALIA (held Feb. 15). The practice of sending Valentine cards dates from the 19th century.

VALENTINIAN, name of three Roman emperors of the West. **Valentinian I** (321–375) reigned from 364 and made his brother, VALENS, emperor of the East. He successfully secured the Western Empire's borders against Barbarian attacks. **Valentinian II** (371–392), his son, was nominally emperor from 375. His brother Gratian held power till 383, when Maximus took control of most of the West. Valentinian fled in 387, but was restored by THEODOSIUS I in 388. He was later murdered. GALLA PLACIDIA was regent for her son, **Valentinian III** (419–455), emperor from 425. His reign was disturbed by HUN and VANDAL invasions. In 454 he murdered AETIUS (virtual ruler of the empire from 433), whose followers then killed him.

VALENTINO, Rudolph (1895–1926), Italian-born US silent movie actor, known as "the great lover." The greatest romantic male star of the silent film era, Valentino's credits included *The Four Horsemen of the Apocalypse* (1921), *The Sheik* (1921) and *Blood and Sand* (1922).

VALENTINUS, (died c160 AD), Egyptian-born theologian and founder of the Gnostic sect of the Valentinians. See GNOSTICISM.

VALERIAN (c190–c260), Roman emperor (253–60). In 257 he campaigned against the Persians in the East but in 260 he was defeated and captured by the Persian emperor, SHAPUR I, and died in captivity.

VALÉRY, Paul (1871–1945), French poet, essayist and critic. His early verse, *Album de vers anciens* (1920), was influenced by MALLARMÉ; his best-known works are *La Jeune Parque* (1917) and *Le Cimetière marin* (1920). He wrote on poetry in *Monsieur Teste* (1896), and on philosophical and critical themes.

VALHALLA, in Norse mythology, the vast splendid "hall of the slain" in ASGARD where warriors killed in battle were entertained by ODIN. On RAGNAROK, the day of doom, they were to march out with Odin to battle with the giants.

VALKYRIES ("choosers of the slain"), ODIN's battle maidens in Norse myth, who transported the souls of the warriors they had chosen in battle to VALHALLA. (See also BRUNHILD.)

VALLA, Lorenzo (1407–1457), Italian humanist and pioneer of critical scholarship. He exposed the DONATION OF CONSTANTINE (1440), attacked SCHOLASTICISM and criticized the VULGATE. His influential *Elegantiae* (1435–44) helped establish classical (as opposed to medieval) Latin as a RENAISSANCE ideal.

VALLADOLID, historic city in NW Spain, on the Pisuerga R, 15th-and 16th-century Spanish capital. It is now an industrial and agricultural center, with textile, food, chemical, leather and metal industries. Pop 236341.

VALLANDIGHAM, Clement Laird (1820–1871), US Representative from Ohio (1858–63), leader of the pro-South COPPERHEADS during the Civil War, and a KNIGHTS OF THE GOLDEN CIRCLE commander. Court-martialed for "treasonable" sympathies (1863) he was "exiled" to the Confederacy. He returned to Ohio in 1864, politically influential but without office.

VALLE D'AOSTA, autonomous region in NW Italy, 1260sq mi in area, bounded by the Alps on the N, W and S. Ruled by the Romans, Burgundians and House of Savoy it became autonomous (1945) for its French cultural and linguistic connections.

VALLEJO, city and port in W Cal., on the Napa R, an agricultural processing and trade center. Pop 71710.

VALLETTA, seaport capital of Malta, in the NE of the island, built in 1565 by the KNIGHTS OF SAINT JOHN after the great siege of Malta. The huge dockyard, formerly a British Navy base, has been converted to commercial use. Pop 15547.

VALLEY, long narrow depression in the earth's surface, usually formed by GLACIER or river EROSION. Young valleys are narrow, steep-sided and V-shaped; mature valleys, broader, with gentler slopes. Some, RIFT VALLEYS, are the result of collapse between

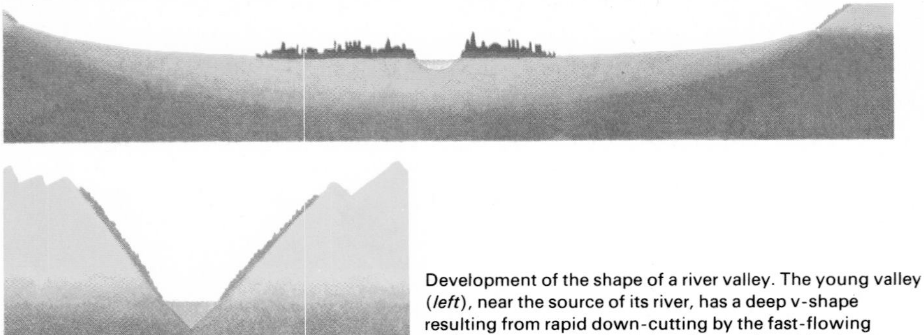

Development of the shape of a river valley. The young valley (*left*), near the source of its river, has a deep v-shape resulting from rapid down-cutting by the fast-flowing water. The mature valley (*above*), near the outlet, has been eroded into a wider, flatter form by the slower flow, and the river now cuts a curved channel in the center of this.

FAULTS. **Hanging valleys**, of glacial origin, are side valleys whose floor is considerably higher than that of the main valley.

VALLEYFIELD, city and port in S Quebec, Canada, on the S shore of Lake St. Francis. It has cotton, textile and chemical industries. Pop 30 173.

VALLEY FORGE, Revolutionary War encampment of Washington's CONTINENTAL ARMY on the Schuykill R, 22mi NW of Philadelphia, Pa., for Dec. 1777–June 1778. The army of 11 000 men was nearly destroyed by a harsh winter and lack of supplies. Hundreds of soldiers died, and mutiny was feared. But morale was restored, and the Prussian Baron von STEUBEN introduced efficient drilling.

VALLEY STATION, unincorporated town in N central Ky., on the Ohio R S of Louisville. Pop 24 471.

VALLEY STREAM, residential village in SE N.Y., on Long Island, a suburb of New York City. Pop 40 413.

VALMY, Battle of, victory during the FRENCH REVOLUTIONARY WARS of the French Revolutionary army, under Charles DUMOURIEZ, over the invading Austro–Prussian forces at Valmy, NE France, in Sept. 1792. It saved Paris and the FRENCH REVOLUTION.

VALOIS, Dame Ninette de. See DE VALOIS, DAME NINETTE.

VALOIS, House of, French royal dynasty, 1328–1589. Starting with PHILIP VI (1328–50) the direct line ended with Charles VIII, who was followed by LOUIS XII (1498–1515) of the ORLÉANS branch. The Angoulême branch succeeded, ending in HENRY III (1574–89).

VALPARAÍSO, Chile's second-largest city and chief port, on the Pacific about 75mi NW of Santiago. Founded in 1536, it is now an important industrial center for textiles, chemicals, paint and food and leather products. Pop 251 459.

VALPARAISO, city in NW Ind., seat of Porter Co. It has many light industries. Pop 20 020.

VALUE, in classical economics, the quality of a good or service that yields UTILITY when consumed. If a good with use-value can be exchanged for other goods or money, it has exchange-value as well. This is the more common sense of the term. Value theory therefore often coincides with PRICE theory. For SMITH, RICARDO and MARX, the basic measure of value was labor (see LABOR THEORY OF VALUE).

VALVE, mechanical device which, by opening and closing, enables the flow of fluid in a pipe or other vessel to be controlled. Common valve types are generally named after the shape or mode of operation of the movable element, e.g., cone, or needle, valve; gate valve; globe valve; poppet valve; and rotary plug cock. In the butterfly valve a disk pivots on one of its diameters. Self-acting valves include: safety valves, usually spring-loaded and designed to open at a predetermined pressure; nonreturn valves, which permit flow in one direction only; and float-operated valves, set to shut off a feeder pipe before a container overflows.

VALVE, Electronic. See ELECTRON TUBE.

VAMPIRE, in folklore, a spirit of the dead, which left its grave at night to suck the blood of living persons. Victims who died would be decapitated or buried with a stake through their hearts, to prevent them from also becoming vampires. (See DRACULA.)

VAMPIRE BATS, BATS which feed on the blood of larger mammals and birds; the only parasitic mammals. A slit is cut with the teeth and blood lapped from the wound, anticoagulants in the saliva ensuring a constant flow. They occur in South and Middle America and contribute to the debilitation of agricultural workers. They can transmit RABIES.

VAN, Lake, salt lake in E Turkey, Turkey's largest lake. About 1 450sq mi in area and at a height of 5 643ft, it has no apparent outlet.

VANADIUM (V), silvery-white, soft metal in Group VB of the PERIODIC TABLE; a TRANSITION ELEMENT. It is widespread, the most important ores being CARNOTITE and roscoelite; it is isolated by reduction of vanadium (V) oxide with calcium. Most is used in ALLOYS to make hard and wear-resistant STEELS. Vanadium is fairly unreactive. It forms compounds in oxidation states +2, +3, +4 and +5. Vanadium (V) oxide is used in ceramics and as a catalyst in the CONTACT PROCESS. AW 50.9, mp 1890°C, bp 3380°C, sg 5.96 (20°C).

VAN ALLEN, James Alfred (1914–   ), US physicist responsible for the discovery of the VAN ALLEN RADIATION BELTS (1958).

VAN ALLEN RADIATION BELTS, the belts of high-energy charged particles, mainly PROTONS and ELECTRONS, surrounding the earth, named for VAN ALLEN, who discovered them in 1958. They extend from a few hundred to about 50 000km above the earth's surface, and radiate intensely enough that astronauts must be specially protected from them. The mechanisms responsible for their existence are similar to those involved in the production of the AURORA.

VANBRUGH, Sir John (1664–1726), English dramatist and BAROQUE architect. His comedies include *The Relapse* (1696) and *The Provoked Wife* (1697). With HAWKSMOOR he built several grand houses, such as Blenheim Palace and Castle Howard, noted for the interplay of architectural masses.

VAN BUREN, Martin (1782–1862), eighth US president (1837–41), political heir to JACKSON. A consummate politician, he was called "the little magician" for his political maneuvering, use of patronage and power over the press.

Of Dutch descent and born in N.Y., the son of a farmer and tavern keeper, he studied law locally and was admitted to the bar (1803). He entered politics, was elected to the N.Y. senate (1813–20), became prominent among the Democrats and rivaled De Witt CLINTON for control of N.Y. Elected to the US senate for 1821–28 he maintained his power through TAMMANY HALL and his creation of the ALBANY REGENCY. As a Jeffersonian Van Buren stood for STATES' RIGHTS and opposed internal improvements. After unsuccessfully promoting W. H. CRAWFORD in 1824, he supported General Jackson for president in 1828. Briefly N.Y. governor for 1828–29, he became Jackson's secretary of state. One of the most powerful men in Washington, he developed the SPOILS SYSTEM. His resignation in 1831 assisted Jackson in removing the followers of vice-president CALHOUN from the government. Van Buren was Jackson's vice-president 1832–36, and in 1836 won the presidency for the Democrats. Shortly after his inauguration the financial panic broke out, bringing Van Buren great unpopularity. One crisis remedy was the INDEPENDENT TREASURY SYSTEM, passed by Congress in 1840. Van Buren also settled the CAROLINE AFFAIR and the AROOSTOOK WAR. Presidential candidate again in 1840 he was defeated by William HARRISON's "log cabin and hard cider" campaign in which Harrison's frontier background was contrasted with Van Buren's alleged luxurious tastes. In 1844 Van Buren failed to receive the Democratic nomination because he opposed the annexation of Texas. He ran in 1848 for the anti-slavery FREE SOIL PARTY, splitting the Democrats and contributing to Zachary TAYLOR's victory. At the outbreak of the Civil War he supported Lincoln.

Martin VAN BUREN
8th US President

Born: December 5, 1782
Died: July 24, 1862
Term of Office: March 4, 1837–March 3, 1841
Political Party: Democratic

VANCOUVER, largest city in British Columbia, on the Burrard Inlet, Strait of Georgia, and third-largest in Canada. It is an important Pacific port and a major manufacturing center for wood, paper, iron, steel and chemical products. Other industries are shipbuilding, oil refining and fish processing. After becoming the terminus of the trans-Canada railroad (1886) it rapidly expanded. Pop 426 256.

VANCOUVER, city and port in SW Wash., seat of Clark Co., on the Columbia R. It has aluminum, lumber, and paper industries and ships grain. Pop 42 493.

VANCOUVER, George (1757–1798), English

The Van Allen radiation belts surround the earth like a large doughnut (*below*). Protons, which are of prime significance in the inner belt, are almost absent from the outer belt, which principally comprises electrons. The doughnut is centered on the earth's magnetic rather than rotation axis (*right*).

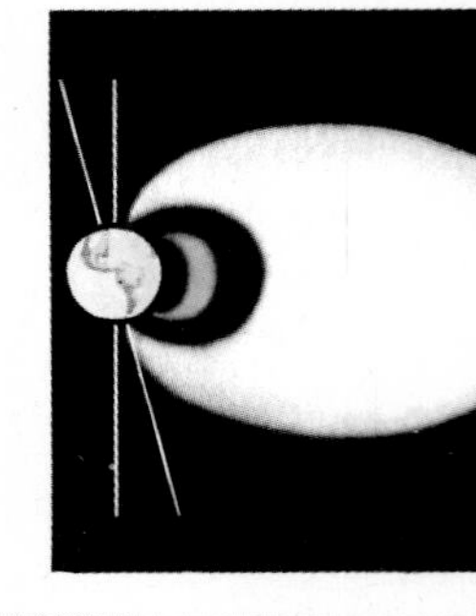

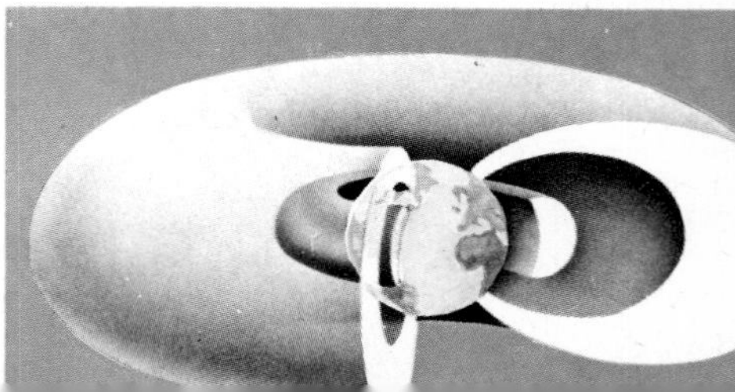

explorer. He took part in Captain COOK's voyages (1772–80) and in 1791–94 led an expedition which explored the Pacific and surveyed the American coast from San Luis Obispo, Cal., to British Columbia. He made surveys of Vancouver Island and the Strait of Georgia, visited Cook's Inlet, Alaska, and failed to find a NORTHWEST PASSAGE.

VANCOUVER ISLAND, largest island on the North American Pacific coast, separated from British Columbia, Canada, by the Strait of Georgia. About 285mi long and 30–80mi wide it is mountainous and heavily wooded, with fjords in the W. The chief city is Victoria, capital of British Columbia. The main economic activities are lumbering, mining (coal, iron, copper and gold), fishing and agriculture.

VANDALIA, city in SW Ohio, N of Dayton. There are truck farms and automobile-part industries. Pop 10 756.

VANDALS, ancient Germanic people. They gradually migrated from S of the Baltic to Pannonia and Dacia. In the 5th century they invaded the Roman Empire, ravaging Gaul and Spain. Under GENSERIC they established a strong Vandal kingdom in North Africa (429) which extended to Sicily, and in 455 they sacked Rome. The Vandals were finally defeated by the Byzantine BELISARIUS, after which they disappeared as a unified people.

VAN DE GRAAFF GENERATOR. See ELECTROSTATIC GENERATOR.

VANDENBERG, Arthur Hendrick (1884–1951), US Republican politician and senator from Mich. (1928–51). A leading isolationist until PEARL HARBOR, he was an important architect of the post-WWII bipartisan foreign policy, supporting NATO and the MARSHAL PLAN (1949).

VANDERBILT, wealthy American family whose fortune was built on steamship and railroad empires. **Cornelius Vanderbilt** (1794–1877), known as "Commodore," began with a ferry service which grew into an international steamship business. In the 1860s, he purchased a number of small E railroads. His group dominated the NE by the 1870s and controlled the New York-Chicago route. He established Vanderbilt University at Nashville, Tenn. His son, **William Henry Vanderbilt** (1821–1885), was chief of the New York Central Railroad, and his eldest son, **Cornelius Vanderbilt II** (1843–1899), next controlled the rail empire and amassed another fortune. Another son, **George Washington Vanderbilt** (1862–1914), established the 100000 acre Biltmore estate near Asheville, N.C. **Harold Sterling Vanderbilt** (1884–1970) won the AMERICA'S CUP three times and invented contract BRIDGE.

VAN DER GOES, Hugo (c1440–1482), Flemish painter. The sophisticated symbolism, naturalist details and oil paint technique of his major work, the Portinari altarpiece *Adoration of the Shepherds* (c1475), greatly influenced Italian RENAISSANCE art.

VAN DER WAALS, Johannes Diderik (1837–1923), Dutch physicist who investigated the properties of real GASES. Noting that the KINETIC THEORY of gases assumed that the molecules had neither size nor interactive forces between them, in 1873 he proposed **Van der Waals' Equation**: $(P+a/V^2)(V-b)=RT$, (where P, V and T are pressure, volume and absolute temperature, R is the universal GAS constant, and a and b are constants whose values depend on the particular gas in question) in which allowance is made for both these factors. The weak attractive forces between molecules are therefore named **Van der Waals forces**. He received the 1910 Nobel Prize for Physics.

VAN DER WEYDEN, Rogier. See WEYDEN, ROGIER VAN DER.

VAN DEVANTER, Willis (1859–1941), US jurist and US Supreme Court associate justice (1911–37). He was a conservative and opposed most of the legislation for the NEW DEAL.

VAN DE VELDE, Henri Clemens. See VELDE, HENRI CLEMENS VAN DE.

VAN DOREN, name of two US men of letters. **Carl Clinton Van Doren** (1885–1950), critic and biographer, famous for his work on the history of American literature. His biography *Benjamin Franklin* won a 1939 Pulitzer Prize. His brother **Mark Albert Van Doren** (1894–1972) wrote poetry, novels, short stories and criticism of English and American literature. His *Collected Poems 1922–1938* won a 1940 Pulitzer Prize.

VAN DRUTEN, John William (1901–1957), English dramatist whose plays include *Bell, Book and Candle* (1950), and *I Am a Camera* (1951) based on Christopher ISHERWOOD's *Goodbye to Berlin* (1939).

VAN DYCK, Sir Anthony (1599–1641), Flemish BAROQUE portrait and religious painter. He was a pupil of RUBENS and his portrait style, influenced by his study of Venetian art, was one of elegantly posed figures and rich but refined color and handling, particularly of materials. He painted Italian and English nobility and was court painter from 1632 to CHARLES I of England, who knighted him. He had great influence on the development of English art.

VANERN, lake in SW Sweden, 2 156sq mi in area, the largest in Sweden and third largest in Europe. Great forests and pulp and paper mills line the shore.

VAN EYCK, Jan (c1390–1441), Flemish painter, the leading early Netherlandish artist. His most famous work is the "Ghent altarpiece," *The Mystic Lamb* (1426–32), comprising over 250 figures in 20 panels and, like his other important works *Virgin of Autun* (1433–34) and *Arnolfini Wedding Portrait* (1434), remarkable for realistic, closely-observed details. He was the first painter to develop effects of richness, brilliance and intensity in oil paint.

VAN FLEET, James Alward (1892–), US general. He led the 8th Infantry Regiment (4th Division) on D-DAY (1944). During the Greek Civil War, he led the US military mission (1948–50); and, in the Korean War, the US 8th Army (1951–53).

VAN GOGH, Vincent Willem (1853–1890), Dutch painter and POSTIMPRESSIONIST. His early work in Holland was of dark-toned peasant life. Going to Paris 1886 he met GAUGUIN and SEURAT. In 1888 he moved to Arles, S France, and painted *Sunflowers* in a direct style, and the symbolic *The Night Cafe* using color suggestively. After a fit of insanity, in which he cut off his left ear (1889), he painted at the asylums of St. Rémy and Auvers. In *Portrait of Dr. Gachet* (1890) he attempted to express ideas and emotion in and through paint. He committed suicide.

VAN HISE, Charles Richard (1857–1918), US geologist best known for his studying the PRECAMBRIAN rock formations in the Lake Superior region, with particular regard to their iron ore deposits.

VANIER (until 1969, Eastview), industrial town in SE Ontario, Canada, on the Ottawa R, a suburb of Ottawa. Pop 22 477.

VANIER, Georges Philias (1888–1967), governor general of Canada from 1959, the second native Canadian (after Vincent MASSEY) to hold the office, and the first of French origin.

VANILLA, genus of climbing ORCHIDS which are native to tropical Asia and America. Since pre-Columbian times, **vanillin** has been extracted from the fleshy pods or "beans" by fermenting them in the sun. Most natural vanillin is obtained from *Vanilla planifolia*, which is native to SE Mexico, but cultivated elsewhere. Today, much commercial vanillin is synthetic.

VAN RENSSELAER, Stephen (1764–1839), US politician, soldier and landowner, called the PATROON. He was lieutenant governor of N.Y. 1795–1801 and its congressman 1822–29. During the WAR OF 1812 his attack on QUEENSTON HEIGHTS, Canada, was fiercely repelled. He was a member of the ERIE CANAL commission from 1810 and its president from 1825.

VAN'T HOFF, Jacobus Henricus (1852–1911), Dutch physical chemist awarded in 1901 the first Nobel Prize for Chemistry for his work laying the foundations of STEREOCHEMISTRY. (See also OSMOSIS.)

VAN VECHTEN, Carl (1880–1964), US music critic, novelist and photographer. He wrote *The Music of Spain* (1918), novels such as *Peter Whiffle* (1922) and *Nigger Heaven* (1926), and an autobiography, *Sacred and Profane Memories* (1932). Subsequently he took up photography and promoted Negro culture at Yale U.

VAN WERT, city in NW Ohio, seat of Van Wert Co., set in a grain-farming region. Its varied industries include electronic and metal equipment. Pop 11 320.

VAPOR, the gaseous state of a substance (usually one that is solid or liquid at room temperature). An isothermal increase in pressure can convert a vapor to a liquid. To convert a solid or liquid to vapor, heat is needed to overcome the cohesive forces between molecules and allow them to escape.

VAPOR LAMPS. See LIGHTING.

VAPOR PRESSURE, the pressure exerted by a VAPOR in EQUILIBRIUM with its liquid or solid. In an enclosed space this occurs when equal numbers of MOLECULES are entering and leaving the vapor, which is then saturated. For a pure substance, the saturated vapor pressure (SVP) depends on the temperature. The BOILING POINT of a liquid is reached when the SVP equals the external pressure.

VARANASI, or Benares, commercial city in N central India, on the Ganges R. It is very ancient and is the most holy Hindu city (known in this context as Kasi). It has more than 1500 temples. *Ghats* (steps) lead down to the river where pilgrims bathe in the waters. Pop 560 296.

VARANGIANS, name given by the Slavs and Byzantine Greeks to the VIKINGS who threatened

The Potato Eaters, by Vincent Van Gogh, is one of his best-known early works. These mostly depicted the everyday life of Dutch peasants in a realistic and compassionate style.

Constantinople in the 9th and 10th centuries. They were part of the Byzantine imperial guard from the late 10th century until 1453. In 862, the Rus tribe, under RURIK, established itself at Novgorod, founding the Russian state.

VARÈSE, Edgard (born Edgar; 1883–1965), French-born US composer. Trained under ROUSSEL and D'INDY, he went to the US in 1919. He explored new rhythms, harmonies and effects of dissonance. From the 1950s his compositions used electronic equipment.

VARGAS, Getúlio Dornelles (1883–1954), Brazilian statesman, president of Brazil 1930–45 and 1951–54. He set up a "New State" (1937), and a strongly-centralized government promoted industrial, economic and social development. Opposition during his second term led him to commit suicide.

VARIABLE, in mathematics, the algebraic (see ALGEBRA) quantity whose numerical value may change. The most-used symbols in elementary algebra are x and y. If one variable is a FUNCTION of the other, as in the EQUATION $y = ax^2 + bx + c$, where a, b, c are CONSTANTS, then y is termed the **dependent variable**, since its value depends on the value of the **independent variable** x. (See also PARAMETER.)

VARIABLE STARS, stars that vary in brightness. There are two main categories. **Extrinsic variables** are those whose variation in apparent brightness is caused by an external condition, as in the case of eclipsing binaries (see DOUBLE STAR). **Intrinsic variables** vary in absolute brightness owing to physical changes within them. They may vary either regularly or irregularly: NOVAE and SUPERNOVAE are irregular intrinsic variables, though some novae erupt in an approximate cycle. Pulsating variables, which vary in size, are the most common type of variable star: they include the RR Lyrae stars, with periods from 1.5h to little over a day, W Virginis stars and RV Tauri stars (all three types appearing principally in GLOBULAR CLUSTERS); long period and semiregular variables, which are red giants; and, possibly erroneously, the CEPHEID VARIABLES. Types of variable stars whose periods are known to have a relationship to their absolute brightness are especially important in that they can be used to determine large astronomical distances.

VARIANCE, in a sample (see STATISTICS) of items from a population, the average of the squares of the individual deviations of the items from the mean (see MEAN, MEDIAN AND MODE). The sample variance is usually denoted by s^2, the variance of the whole population by σ^2 (see also STANDARD DEVIATION).

VARIATION, diversity found in all natural populations of organisms. Variation is the result of differing effects of environmental factors and of differences in the genetic constitution of each individual. Genetic diversity is important because it provides variants, some of which may be more suited to prevailing conditions than others, which provide raw material for NATURAL SELECTION. (See also EVOLUTION.)

VARICELLA. See CHICKENPOX.

VARICOSE VEINS, enlarged or tortuous VEINS in the legs resulting from incompetent or damaged valves in the veins, with the pressure of the venous BLOOD causing venous distension and subsequent changes in the vein wall. Although unpleasant in appearance, they are more important for causing venous stagnation, with skin ECZEMA and ULCERS on the inside of the ankle, HEMORRHAGE and EDEMA. Treatment is by stripping or sclerosing injections.

VARNA, industrial city and port in E Bulgaria, on the Black Sea, where the Turks defeated the Hungarian crusader forces in 1444. Pop 230475.

VARNISH, solution of RESIN which dries to form a hard transparent film; widely applied to wood, metal and masonry to improve surface properties without changing appearance. There are two main types: "spirit varnishes," consisting of natural or synthetic resins dissolved in a volatile solvent such as alcohol; and "oleoresinous varnishes"—more resistant to heat and weather—which are mixtures of resins and drying oils dissolved in TURPENTINE or a petroleum oil. Lacquer, the original wood varnish, is the sap of the VARNISH TREE.

VARNISH TREE, several species of evergreen tree, found in the Far East, West Indies and Australia, yielding a sap or secretion from which lacquer and VARNISH are made. Most is obtained from *Taxicodendron verniciflurum*, a relative of POISON IVY.

VARRO, Marcus Terentius (116–27 BC), greatest scholar of ancient Rome, a prolific writer on a great variety of subjects. Of his many books only *On Farming* and *On the Latin Language* have substantially survived.

VARUS, Publius Quintilius (d. 9 AD), Roman general whose army of three legions was slaughtered in 9 AD in the Teutoburg Forest by ARMINIUS' German forces. Varus committed suicide. The Roman troops consequently withdrew W to the Rhine R.

VARVE, the layer of sediment deposited in the course of a single year, specifically in a lake formed of glacial meltwater. Characteristically, a varve has a SILT layer overlying a SAND layer. Study of varves is of great use in geological dating. (See also GLACIER; SEDIMENTATION.)

VASARI, Giorgio (1511–1574), Italian MANNERIST painter, architect and writer. His *Lives of the Most Eminent Italian Architects, Painters & Sculptors* (1550), a major source of knowledge of the Italian RENAISSANCE, is about the progress of art in Italy in the 13th–16th centuries.

VASCULAR PLANTS, members of the division **Tracheophyta** of the PLANT KINGDOM in which the SPOROPHYTE is dominant and the GAMETOPHYTE is inconspicuous and dependent on the sporophyte. Vascular tissues, such as XYLEM and PHLOEM are present and the plants are differentiated into ROOTS, STEMS and LEAVES. Vascular plants include the CLUB MOSSES, HORSETAILS, FERNS, GYMNOSPERMS and ANGIOSPERMS.

VASCULAR SYSTEM, the BLOOD CIRCULATION system, comprising BLOOD, ARTERIES, CAPILLARIES, VEINS and the HEART; the LYMPH vessels form a further subdivision. Its function is to deliver nutrients (including OXYGEN) to, and remove wastes from all organs, and to transport HORMONES and the agents of body defense.

VASECTOMY, form of FAMILY PLANNING in males in which the *vas deferens* on each side is ligated and cut to prevent SPERM from reaching the seminal vesicles and hence the urethra of the PENIS. It does not affect ejaculation but causes permanent STERILIZATION.

VASELINE, or **petrolatum,** high-boiling HYDROCARBON residue from the distillation of PETROLEUM; a jelly used for LUBRICATION and as an emollient.

VASOCONSTRICTION, narrowing of BLOOD vessels, facilitating control of blood pressure and body TEMPERATURE.

VASODILATION, or vasodilatation, widening of BLOOD vessels, facilitating control of blood pressure and body TEMPERATURE.

VASOPRESSIN, or antidiuretic hormone (ADH), HORMONE produced by the HYPOTHALAMUS and posterior PITUITARY GLAND, which is a mild vasoconstrictor, but primarily inhibits diuresis or loss of water in URINE. It is a vital link in the system for preserving the HOMEOSTATIS or constancy of body fluids.

VASSA, Gustavus (born Olaudah Equiano; 1745–1801), African slave in North America. After receiving his freedom he settled in England. His *The Interesting Narrative of the Life of Olaudah Equiano or Gustavus Vassa, The African* (1789) influenced the US antislavery movement.

VATICAN CITY, the world's smallest independent state, in Rome, Italy, ruled by the Pope, and the spiritual and administrative center of the ROMAN CATHOLIC CHURCH. The city is dominated by SAINT PETER'S BASILICA and by the Vatican Palace, the largest residential palace in the world. The city has many art treasures in the SISTINE CHAPEL, the Vatican Museum, and the Vatican Archive and Library which contain many priceless manuscripts. The Vatican has its own currency, postage stamps, broadcasting station, bank, railroad station, newspaper (*L'Osservatore Romano*) and army of SWISS GUARDS. The city does not have income tax and there is no restriction on the import or export of funds. It maintains diplomatic relations with other countries through ambassadorial legates and sends apostolic delegates to some countries, including the US and Canada, for religious matters. The official independence of the Vatican City from Italy was established in 1929 in the LATERAN TREATY between the PAPACY and the Italian government.

Official name: Vatican City State
Area: 0.15sq mi
Population: 1000
Languages: Italian; Latin (administrative and legislative)
Religions: Roman Catholic
Monetary unit(s): 1 Lira = 100 centesimi

VATICAN COUNCILS, the two most recent Roman Catholic ECUMENICAL COUNCILS, held at the Vatican. The **First Vatican Council** (1869–70), summoned by Pius IX, was ULTRAMONTANISM'S triumph. It restated traditional dogma against materialism, rationalism and liberalism. On the papal primacy, it defined the pope's jurisdiction to be universal and immediate; it also declared the pope to be infallible when, speaking *ex cathedra*, he defines a doctrine of faith or morals. Some dissenters seceded as OLD CATHOLICS. The **Second Vatican Council** (1962–65), summoned by John XXIII, aimed at renewal of the Church, updating its organization and attitude to the modern world, and ultimate reunion (see ECUMENICAL MOVEMENT). Protestant and Orthodox observers attended. Its decrees included reform of the MINISTRY and LITURGY, stressing lay participation and allowing vernacular languages; that the bishops with the pope form a body ("collegiality"); that the Virgin MARY is "Mother of the Church;" and statements on many other subjects such as missions and non-Christian religions.

VATTEL, Emerich de (1714–1767), Swiss jurist. His treatise, *The Law of Nations*, based on Christian von Wolff's *Jus Gentium* (1749), claimed that international law should be based on natural laws. His theory of liberty had great influence in the US.

VAUBAN, Sébastien Le Prestre, Marquis de (1633–1707), French military engineer, known for his siege tactics and defense fortifications. In 1673 he dug parallel and concentric trenches around Maastricht and in 1688 introduced ricochet gunfire and socket bayonets.

VAUDEVILLE, term for variety shows, deriving from *Vau de Vire*, a French valley and source of 15th-century songs, or from *Voix de Ville*, French street songs. It was applied from the 1880s to US shows with musical, comic, dramatic, acrobatic and juggling acts. Noted artists included Eddie CANTOR, Will ROGERS and W. C. FIELDS. Vaudeville declined in the 1930s.

VAUGHAN, Henry (1622–1695), Welsh poet. Some of his best religious and mystical verse, such as "The Retreate," "The Sap" or "I walkt the other day," influenced by the METAPHYSICAL POET, George HERBERT, appeared in his *Silex Scintillans* (1651–55).

VAUGHAN WILLIAMS, Ralph (1872–1958), English composer. He was influenced by secular and religious Tudor music and thus acquired methods of expression which differed from traditional classical music. His works, many drawing from English folk music, include *Norfolk Rhapsodies* (1906–07), *Fantasia on a Theme of Tallis* (1909), nine symphonies and five operas.

VEAL, pale, fine-textured, mild-flavored meat from

calves (young cattle) slaughtered when less than 14 weeks old, generally factory-farmed and fed a high-protein, iron-deficient diet.

VEBLEN, Oswald (1880–1960), US mathematician best known for his contributions to projective and differential GEOMETRY and especially for his pioneering role in the development of TOPOLOGY, set out in *Analysis Situ* (1922).

VEBLEN, Thorstein Bunde (1857–1929), influential US economist and social theorist. In *Theory of the Leisure Class* (1899) he used the satirical concept of "conspicuous consumption" (that people acquire goods for their status, rather than for their utility, value). *The Theory of Business Enterprise* (1904) attacked the capitalist system, and *The Engineers and the Price System* (1921) foreshadowed TECHNOCRACY.

VECTOR, a quantity having both magnitude and direction, unlike a SCALAR, which has only magnitude. One example of a vector quantity is VELOCITY. (See VECTOR ANALYSIS.)

VECTOR ANALYSIS, the application of the techniques of ANALYSIS and ALGEBRA to the study of VECTORS. Since vector quantities have both magnitude and direction, they may be represented geometrically by LINES with specified directions, whose lengths represent the magnitudes of the vectors concerned; the magnitude of a vector $\mathbf{V}$ is written V. The dot (or scalar) PRODUCT of two vectors $\mathbf{A}$ and $\mathbf{B}$ inclined at an angle c to each other is defined as $\mathbf{A}.\mathbf{B} = AB\cos c$. The cross (or vector) product of two vectors $\mathbf{A}$ and $\mathbf{B}$ inclined at an angle c to each other is defined as $\mathbf{A}\times\mathbf{B} = (AB\sin c)\,\mathbf{n}$ where $\mathbf{n}$ is a unit vector whose direction is PERPENDICULAR to the plane of $\mathbf{A}$ and $\mathbf{B}$ such that, looking along the direction of $\mathbf{n}$, a clockwise turn of less than 180° is required to bring $\mathbf{A}$ into $\mathbf{B}$.

VECTOR FIELD, a set of VECTORS such that every POINT in a particular region of space R is associated with a single vector; e.g., a MAGNETIC FIELD.

VECTOR SPACE, a set (see SET THEORY) of VECTORS together with a FIELD of SCALARS such that: the sum of any two members of the set is a vector also in the set, and multiplication of a member of the set by a member of the field produces a vector also in the set.

VEDA (Sanskrit: knowledge), most ancient of Indian scriptures, believed to have been inspired by God, and basic to HINDUISM. There are four *Samhitas* or collections of MANTRAS—the Rig, Yajur, Sama and Atharva-Veda. The oldest may date from 1500 BC. Vedic literature consists of the Veda itself, the *Brahmanas* and *Aranyakas* (later expository supplements), and the UPANISHADS.

VEDANTA (Sanskrit: end of knowledge), system of Hindu philosophy, based at first on the UPANISHADS (the final part of the VEDA), and later on the *Brahma-Sutras*, commentaries on the Upanishads, which date from the 1st century AD. The Vedanta concern the relation of the individual (*atman*) to the Absolute (*Brahman*).

VEERY, or Wilson's Thrush, *Hylocichla fuscescens*, a red-brown THRUSH with buff underparts common in overgrown woodlands of the northeastern US.

VEGA, Alpha Lyrae, the fourth brightest star in the night sky (absolute magnitude +0.5). It is 8pc distant, and 40 times as bright as the sun.

VEGA, Lope de (1562–1635), poet and Spain's first great dramatist. He created the *comedia*, a drama with comic, tragic, learned and popular elements. Vitality, wit and intricate plot typify *Peribáñez, Fuenteovejuna* and *The Knight of Olmedo*. Lope's 500 surviving works also include lyrical verse, the autobiographical *La Dorotea* (1632), religious and light "cloak-and-sword" plays.

VEGETABLES, general term for plants whose leaves, flowers, roots, stems or fruits are edible. "Vegetable" is used for those plants that are eaten in main courses of meals, usually after cooking, while the general term "fruit" refers to plants used as appetizers or desserts, or eaten out of the hand. Thus, botanically a tomato is a fruit, but it is popularly considered a vegetable.

VEGETATION, characteristic plant life of a region. There are four basic types: DESERT; FOREST; GRASSLAND, and TUNDRA. (See also CLIMATE.)

VEIN, a mineral formation of far greater extent in two dimensions than in the third. Sheetlike **fissure veins** occur where fissures formed in the rock become filled with MINERAL. **Ladder veins** form in series of fractures in, e.g., DIKES. **Saddle-veins** are lens-shaped, concave below and convex above. Veins that contain economically important ORES are often termed **lodes**.

VEINS, thin-walled collapsible vessels which return BLOOD to the HEART from the tissue CAPILLARIES and provide a variable-sized pool of blood. They contain valves which prevent back-flow—especially in the legs. Blood drains from the major veins into the inferior or superior VENA CAVA. Blood in veins is at low pressure and depends for its return to the heart on intermittent muscle compression, combined with valve action.

VELÁZQUEZ, Diego Rodríguez de Silva y (1599–1660), great Spanish painter. In 1623, he became court painter to King Philip IV of Spain. His style was influenced strongly by his Flemish contemporary RUBENS and also by Italian artists of the High RENAISSANCE. His masterpieces include *The Drunkards, Christ on the Cross* and *Maids of Honor*.

VELD, or **veldt,** open GRASSLAND of South Africa, divided into three types: High Veld, around 1500m above sea level, which is similar to the PRAIRIES; Cape Middle Veld, somewhat lower, covered with scrub and occasional low ridges of hills; and Low Veld, under about 750m above sea level.

VELDE, Henri Clemens van de (1863–1957), Belgian ART NOUVEAU architect and designer, interested in the idea of pure form in architecture. He founded (1906) and taught at the Weimar School of Applied Art which became the BAUHAUS in 1919.

VELLUM. See PARCHMENT.

VELOCITY, the rate at which the position of a body changes, expressed with respect to a given direction. Velocity is thus a VECTOR quantity, of which the corresponding scalar is **speed**: the rate of change in the position of a body without respect to direction. Translational velocity, usually expressed in calculus as

$$\mathbf{v} = \frac{d\mathbf{s}}{dt},$$

refers to movement through space; angular or rotational velocity,

$$\omega = \frac{d\theta}{dt},$$

to rotation about a given axis. (See also ACCELERATION.)

VENA CAVA. The *superior vena cava* is a VEIN collecting BLOOD from the head, neck and arms, and delivering it to the right side of the HEART. The *inferior vena cava* performs the same function with blood from the legs and abdomen.

VENDÉE, maritime department of W France, in Poitou, on the Atlantic. It was the scene of the peasants' counterrevolutionary **War of the Vendée** (1793–96), which threatened the new republican state. Savagely crushed at the outset, the peasants continued to resist and eventually achieved their aims of freedom of worship and freedom from conscription.

VENEER, thin slice of wood applied to the faces of cheap and unattractive wood. Low quality veneers are used for PLYWOOD, but normally high quality veneer, such as MAHOGANY or WALNUT, is used to improve the finish of furniture.

VENEREAL DISEASES, those INFECTIOUS DISEASES transmitted mainly or exclusively by sexual contact, usually because the organism responsible is unable to survive outside the body and the close contact of genitalia provides the only means for transmitting viable organisms. **Gonorrhea** is an acute BACTERIAL DISEASE which is frequently asymptomatic in females who therefore act as carriers, although they may suffer mild cervicitis or urethritis. In males it causes a painful urethritis with urethral discharge of PUS. ARTHRITIS, SEPTICEMIA and other systemic manifestations may also occur, and urethral stricture follow. Infection of an infant's eyes by mothers carrying the gonococcus causes neonatal OPTHALMIA, previously a common cause of childhood BLINDNESS. Gonorrhea is best treated with PENICILLIN. **Syphilis,** due to *Treponema pallidum*, a SPIROCHETE, is a disease with three stages. A painless genital ULCER or chancre—a highly infective lesion—develops in the weeks after contact; this is usually associated with LYMPH node enlargement. Secondary syphilis, starting weeks or months after infection, involves systemic disease with FEVER, malaise and a characteristic rash, mucous membrane lesions and occasionally MENINGITIS, HEPATITIS or other organ disease. If the disease is treated with a full course of penicillin in the early stages, its progression is prevented. Tertiary syphilis takes several forms; e.g., gummas—chronic granulomas affecting SKIN, EPITHELIUM, BONE or internal organs—may develop. Largely a disease of blood vessels, tertiary syphilis causes disease of the AORTA with aneurysm and aortic valve disease of the HEART, with incompetence. Syphilis of the NERVOUS SYSTEM may cause TABES DORSALIS, primary EYE disease, chronic meningitis, multifocal vascular disease resembling STROKE or general PARESIS with mental disturbance, personality change, failure of judgment and muscular weakness. Penicillin may only partially reverse late syphilis. Congenital syphilis is disease transmitted to the FETUS during PREGNANCY and leads to deformity and visceral disease. Other venereal diseases include Reiter's disease with arthritis, CONJUNCTIVITIS and urethritis (in males only); genital trichomonas; THRUSH; *Herpes simplex* virus, and "nonspecific urethritis." Tropical venereal diseases include chancroid; lymphogranuloma venereum, and granuloma inguinale.

VENEZUELA, republic of N South America, bounded N by the Caribbean Sea, E by Guyana, S by Brazil and W by Colombia. Its four main regions are the Venezuelan Highlands (W and N), an extension of the Andes; the oil-producing Maracaibo Lowlands, almost completely enclosed by mountains; the great central grassland plain of the Orinoco (the LLANOS); and the mineral-rich Guiana Highlands, S of the Orinoco R, very sparsely populated but covering about half the country.

People. The population is mainly MESTIZO. Of the rest, about 20% are of European stock (mainly Spanish), 7% Negroes and 6% Indians. The population is over 70% urban.

Economy. Venezuela produces about 10% of the world's output of oil. It also produces natural gas and iron ore. Chief agricultural products are coffee, rice and cocoa. Industry is expanding.

History. Venezuela was discovered by COLUMBUS, but may have been named by VESPUCCI. When the first Spanish settlement was founded (at Cumana, 1520) the country was inhabited by Arawaks and Caribs. Their fierce resistance did not prevent Spanish penetration. Venezuelan independence, unsuccessfully attempted by Francisco de MIRANDA (1806), was proclaimed by a national congress in 1811. Miranda became dictator in 1812, but was imprisoned by the Spanish. Simón BOLÍVAR led the independence struggle and triumphed in 1821. The country became

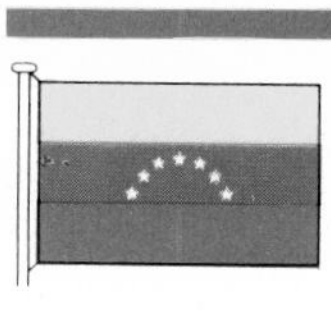

Official name: Republic of Venezuela
Capital: Caracas
Area: 352 143sq mi
Population: 10 721 522
Languages: Spanish
Religions: Roman Catholic
Monetary unit(s): 1 Bolivar = 100 centimes

The famous Rialto bridge over the Grand Canal in Venice. Built 1588–92 by the architect Da Ponte, it is 53yd long and over 24yd wide.

part of Greater Colombia, but broke free as an independent republic in 1830. Dictatorships and revolts followed. General Juan Vicente Gómez (president 1908–35) granted oil concessions to foreign companies until 1983. In 1958, the corrupt Marcos Pérez Jiménez dictatorship was overthrown by Rómulo BÉTANCOURT, and democracy restored. In 1975 legislation was passed to facilitate nationalization of the oil industry.

VENEZUELA BOUNDARY DISPUTE, chiefly from 1841, an Anglo-Venezuelan dispute over the location of the British Guiana–Venezuela border. In 1895 US president Grover Cleveland, invoking the MONROE DOCTRINE, demanded arbitration supervised by the US. This initially strained Anglo-US relations almost to the point of war, but Britain submitted to arbitration and a boundary was agreed in 1899.

VENICE, city in NE Italy, seaport capital of the Veneto region and Venezia province. It comprises 118 islands in the Lagoon of Venice at the head of the Adriatic Sea. Transport is mainly by motorboat and gondola. Venice is built on piles sunk deep into the mud and is linked by a causeway to the mainland. The first DOGE (duke or ruler) was elected in 697. Venice rose to control trade between Europe and the East. At its height (15th century), Venice ruled the E Mediterranean, the Aegean and parts of the Black Sea. Its power weakened during the long struggle with the Ottoman Empire (c1453–c1718). Venice is now a major tourist resort, boasting unique beauty and a magnificent cultural heritage. Pop 364 063.

VENIZELOS, Eleutherios (1864–1936), Greek statesman, premier of Greece (1910–15; 1916–20; 1928–32; 1933). He promoted the alliance which defeated Turkey in the first of the BALKAN WARS (1912–13) and, after CONSTANTINE I's abdication (1917), brought Greece into WWI on the Allied side.

VENN DIAGRAMS, a graphical way of representing concepts and relations occurring in SET THEORY.

Seen from earth, Venus appears to have phases like those of the moon. At its full phase (1, top left) the planet is at its farthest from earth, and so seems small. It appears larger as it approaches, but the area illuminated by the sun is increasingly that turned away from us, and so we see a diminishing crescent. At its closest we see only a bright thin sickle shape (2, right).

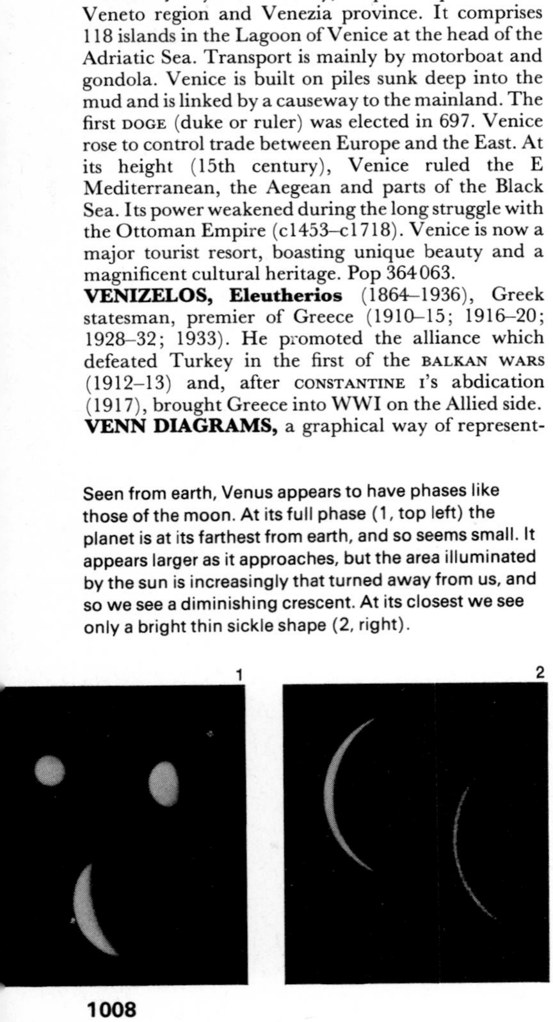

VENOM. See SNAKE; SNAKE BITE.

VENTNOR, or Ventnor City, city and seaside resort in SE N.J. It lies on Absecon Island, near Atlantic City. Pop 10 385.

VENTRILOQUISM, way of speaking to make the voice seem to come from a source other than the speaker's mouth. An ancient art, ventriloquism is still a popular form of entertainment, the ventriloquist usually having a dummy with whom he appears to converse.

VENTRIS, Michael George Francis (1922–1956), English linguist who deciphered one of the MINOAN LINEAR SCRIPTS (Linear B).

VENTURA, seaport city in SW Cal., seat of Ventura Co. It is an oil-producing center in an agricultural area. Pop 47 964.

VENTURI TUBE, short open-ended pipe with a central constriction used for measuring the flow rate of a FLUID. The fluid velocity increases and its pressure drops in the constriction. The fluid velocity is calculated from the pressure difference between the center and ends of the tube.

VENUS, in Roman mythology, the counterpart of APHRODITE, Greek goddess of love.

VENUS, the planet second from the sun, about the same size as the earth. Its face is completely obscured by dense clouds containing sulfuric acid, though the USSR's Venera-9 and Venera-10 (Oct. 1975) landers have provided photographs of the planet's rocky surface. Venus revolves about the sun at a mean distance of 0.72AU in 225 days, rotating on its axis in a retrograde direction (see RETROGRADE MOTION) in 243 days. Its diameter is 12.1Mm. Its atmosphere is 97% carbon dioxide. Its surface temperature is about 750K. Venus has no moons, and almost certainly does not support life.

VENUS DE MILO, famous statue of the Greek goddess APHRODITE. It was carved in marble c150 BC and was discovered 1820 on the island of Melos. It is now in the Louvre in Paris.

VENUS' FLYTRAP, *Dionaea muscipula*, INSECTIVOROUS PLANT native to the sandy country of the Carolinas. The outer part of each leaf forms a pad, hinged in the middle and edged with stiff teeth. Sensitive hairs protrude from the pad's center. When an insect brushes the hairs, the pad rapidly folds, catching the insect behind the teeth. Special secretions digest the soft parts of the insect's body. Family: Droseraceae.

VERACRUZ, industrial city in E Mexico, Veracruz state, on the gulf of Mexico. It is the country's leading port of entry. Pop 242 351.

VERACRUZ, state of E Mexico, on the Gulf of Mexico. It is the country's leading oil-producing state and a major commercial and industrial region.

VERB, a part of speech whose function differs from language to language. In English it expresses either action or a state of being (see also INFINITIVE). There are three verb types, transitive, which link subject and object ("*I* hit *him*"); intransitive, which have only subject ("*I fly*"); and auxiliary, used to indicate the tenses and moods of other verbs ("*I* must *fly*"). Tenses may be shown also by INFLECTION. (See also GRAMMAR.)

VERBENA, the type genus of the family Verbenaceae, this including tropical and subtropical herbs, shrubs and trees (e.g., TEAK). Several species of *Verbena* are cultivated as garden ornamentals, producing clusters of purple or blue flowers. SAND VERBENAS belong to a different family, the Nyctaginaceae.

VERCINGETORIX (d. 46 BC), chieftain of the Arveni tribe of Gaul who rebelled against Roman rule in 52 BC. He repelled Julius Caesar's forces at Gergovia, but was captured after the siege of Alesia and executed in Rome.

VERD ANTIQUE, green mottled form of SERPENTINE used for indoor decoration; also a dark green PORPHYRY containing FELDSPAR. **Verde antico** is the green PATINA formed on bronze.

VERDE, Cape. See CAPE VERDE.

VERDI, Giuseppe (1813–1901), Italian opera composer He rose to fame during the struggle for Italian unification and independence; early operas such as *Nabucco* (1842) express these political ideals. By the time of *Rigoletto* (1851), *Il Trovatore* (1853) and *La Traviata* (1853) he had developed his powerful individual style well beyond the conventions inherited from ROSSINI, DONIZETTI and BELLINI. *Don Carlos* (1867), *Aida* (1871) and the *Requiem* honoring MANZONI (1874) are works of his maturity. The two great Shakespearian operas of Verdi's old age, *Otello* (1887) and *Falstaff* (1893) were written to libretti by BOITO.

VERDIGRIS, blue-green powder, a basic copper (II) acetate, made by pickling copper in acetic acid and used as a PIGMENT and a mordant in dyeing.

VERDUN, residential city on Montreal Island, S Quebec, Canada. It is a suburb of Montreal on the St. Lawrence R. Pop 74 520.

VERDUN, manufacturing city of Meuse department, NE France, on the Meuse R, strategically placed between the Rhineland and Paris. Pop 24 716.

VERDUN, Battle of (Feb.–Dec. 1916), major WORLD WAR I engagement. The Germans launched a concentrated offensive against the fortified salient of VERDUN. The French dared not abandon this position and the Germans hoped to compel them to exhaust their forces in its defense. Total casualties were well over 700 000. No significant advantage was gained by either side.

VERDUN, Treaty of (843 AD), treaty concluding the civil war between the heirs of LOUIS I, by which CHARLEMAGNE's empire was divided between his three grandchildren (Louis' sons). LOTHAIR I kept the title emperor and received Italy and a narrow strip of land from Provence to Friesland. Louis the German received the lands between the Rhine and Elbe. Charles the Bald held the area W of the Rhine.

VÉRENDRYE, Pierre Gaultier de Varennes, Sieur de la. See LA VÉRENDRYE.

VERGA, Giovanni (1840–1922), Italian novelist and short-story writer whose work had a strong influence on modern Italian neorealist fiction. His story *Cavalleria Rusticana* (1880) was the basis for his own play and Pietro Mascagni's opera.

VERGENNES, Charles Gravier, Comte de (1717–1787), French statesman. As foreign minister 1774–87, he supported the American colonies in the Revolutionary War and joined them in a military alliance (1778). He negotiated the Treaty of PARIS (1783).

VERGIL, or **Virgil** (Publius Vergilius Maro; 70–19 BC), Roman poet, one of the greatest writers of EPIC. Born at Mantua, he studied at Cremona, Milan and finally Rome, where MAECENAS became his patron and Octavian (later the emperor AUGUSTUS) his friend. He won recognition with his *Eclogues* or *Bucolics*, PASTORAL poems reflecting the events of his own day. The *Georgics*, a didactic poem on farming, uses the world of the farmer as a model for the world at large. His last ten years were spent on his epic masterpiece, the *Aeneid*, about the wanderings of AENEAS and his struggle to found ROME.

VERLAINE, Paul Marie (1844–1896), French poet, an early and influential exponent of SYMBOLISM. While imprisoned 1873–75 for shooting and wounding his friend and lover Arthur RIMBAUD, he wrote *Romances sans Paroles* (1874), one of his finest volumes. After a period of religious piety he returned to his life of Bohemian dissipation and died in poverty.

VERMEER, Jan (1632–1675), Dutch painter in Delft. His interior scenes are noted for superb control of light, precise tonality, cool harmonious coloring and classical composition. Of the fewer than 40 works attributed to him his masterpieces include *Woman Reading a Letter* and *Head of a Girl* (both c1665).

VERMONT, state of the NE US, in New England, bounded N by Quebec, W by N.Y., S by Mass. and E by N.H. The Green Mts form the major geographical region, comprising several virtually continuous ranges running N–S through Vt.'s center. Most fertile are the broad Connecticut R Valley in the E and the Champlain Valley in the NW. The climate is cool, with long, cold winters.

Economy. The chief source of income is manufacturing, much of it based on the state's marble and granite quarries. However, with 60% of the population living in rural areas, agriculture—mainly dairy products—makes a significant contribution. Tourism is important, skiing in the Green Mts being a major attraction.

History. Vt. was one of three states (with Hawaii and Texas) recognized by the US government as independent republics before they joined the Union. When the French explorer de CHAMPLAIN arrived in 1609, the region was inhabited by Iroquois Indians from N.Y., who had driven out the original Algonquins. Champlain aided the Algonquins in their defeat of the Iroquois and claimed the region for France. In 1763, England gained Vt. as a result of the treaty ending the FRENCH AND INDIAN WARS. In 1770, Ethan ALLEN organized the GREEN MOUNTAIN BOYS to resist N.Y. claims to Vt. lands and to drive out N.Y. settlers. When the Revolutionary War broke out, the Green Mountain Boys joined other patriots to fight the British. The state's 1777 constitution prohibited slavery and was the first to provide for universal male suffrage. Vt. remained an independent republic until 1791, when it became the 14th state.

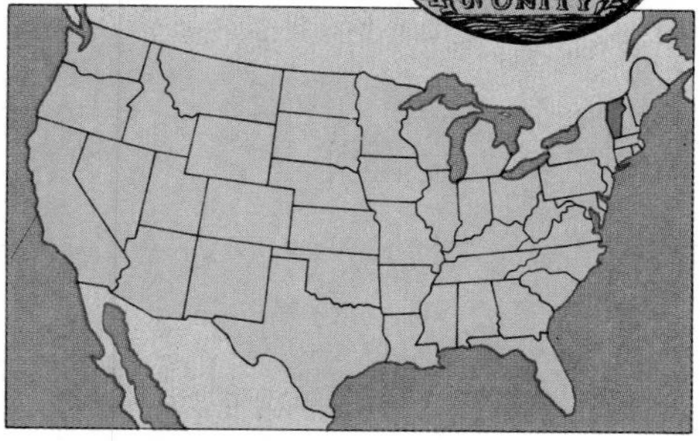

Name of State: Vermont
Capital: Montpelier
Statehood: March 4, 1791 (14th state)
Familiar Name: Green Mountain State
Area: 9 609sq mi
Population: 462 000
Elevation: Highest—4 393ft, Mount Mansfield
Lowest—95ft, Lake Champlain
Motto: Vermont, Freedom and Unity
State Flower: Red clover
State Bird: Hermit thrush
State Tree: Sugar maple
State Song: "Hail, Vermont!"

VERMOUTH, ALCOHOLIC BEVERAGE made from fortified (usually white) wine, various herbs and flavorings. The alcohol content is 10–20%. "French" (pale and dry) and "Italian" (sweet and dark) vermouths are now produced in many countries.

VERNAL EQUINOX. See EQUINOXES.

VERNE, Jules (1828–1905), popular French novelist and a father of the modern genre of SCIENCE FICTION. He often incorporated genuine scientific principles in his imaginative adventure fantasies, and anticipated the airplane, submarine, television, space travel, etc. His most famous novels include *Journey to the Center of the Earth* (1864), *Twenty Thousand Leagues Under the Sea* (1870) and *Around the World in Eighty Days* (1873).

VERNIER SCALE, an auxiliary scale used in conjunction with the main scale on many instruments (in particular the vernier caliper), allowing greater precision of reading. The vernier scale is graduated such that nine graduations on the vernier scale equal ten on the main scale. By observing which vernier graduation nearest the zero on the vernier scale coincides with a graduation on the main scale, the precision with which a reading can be made is improved by a factor of 10.

The Milkmaid (1658), by Jan Vermeer. One of his genre paintings, it is a superb example of his use of light (as on the wall behind the girl's head), muted color and rich textures, as in the still-life on the table, to achieve an almost mystical tranquility.

VERNON, city in S British Columbia, Canada. It is a lumber and fruit-processing center. Pop 13 283.

VERNON, town in N Conn., producing electronic parts, chemicals and textiles. Pop 27 237.

VERNON, city in N Tex., seat of Wilbarger Co. It is a processing center for farm products, with some light industry. Pop 11 454.

VERO BEACH, city in E Fla., seat of Indian River Co., a tourist and fishing resort with a citrus fruit-packing industry. Pop 11 908.

VERONA, ancient city in N Italy. It has many Roman and medieval landmarks, including an amphitheater from the 1st century AD. Manufactures include chemicals, textiles, food products and paper. Pop 263 589.

VERONA, borough in NE N.J. It is chiefly residential, with some light industry. Pop 15 067.

VERONESE, Paolo (Paolo Caliari; 1528–1588), Venetian painter of rich, brilliantly-colored religious, historical and mythological pictures. Works such as *Triumph of Venice* (post 1577) have crowds of people in splendid costumes and settings. The Inquisition admonished him for details in *Feast in the House of Levi* (1573).

VERRAZANO, Giovanni da (c1485–c1528), Italian navigator who discovered New York and Narragansett bays while exploring the North American coast in 1524. Some time after 1526, he set out for Central America and never returned.

VERRAZANO-NARROWS BRIDGE, suspension bridge across the narrows at the entrance to New York Harbor, completed 1964. It has a main span of 4 260ft, the world's longest.

VERROCCHIO, Andrea del (c1435–1488), Italian RENAISSANCE sculptor and painter. In pictures such as *Madonna and Child* (1468–70) he treated figures and landscape sculpturally. His greatest work, finished by Leopardi, the bronze *Monument to Bartolommeo Colleoni* (1483–96), shows his mastery of composition, technique and rich detailing.

VERRUCA. See WART.

VERSAILLES, French city, 12mi SW of Paris. It is world-famous for its magnificent Palace of Versailles, built for King LOUIS XIV in the mid-1600s. The seat of the French court for over 100 years, it was made a national museum in 1837, and the palace and its formal gardens are one of France's greatest tourist attractions. The modern city is principally a residential suburb of Paris. Pop 94 915.

VERSAILLES, Treaty of, agreement ending WORLD

An illustration from Jules Verne's *From the Earth to the Moon* (1865), in which he envisaged the first manned moonshot—literally, because the capsule was to be fired from a cannon. This is now known to be impossible—the rate of acceleration would crush passengers—but on several points his ideas were oddly accurate. His capsule was the same size as the Apollo capsule, was launched from Florida, was steered by rockets and splashed down in the sea on its return.

WAR I, imposed on Germany by the Allies on June 28, 1919. It also set up the LEAGUE OF NATIONS. Under the treaty, Germany lost all her colonies, Lorraine was given to France, Eupen-Malmédy to Belgium, Posen and West Prussia to Poland, and Memel (Klaipeda) to the Allies. GDAŃSK became a free city, the Saar (with its coalfields) was to be under international administration for 15 years, the Rhineland was to be demilitarized and occupied by the Allies for 15 years at German cost. Heavy REPARATIONS were imposed, and Germany's armed forces drastically reduced. German resentment of the treaty's harshness was a factor in the rise of NAZISM and the eventual outbreak of WWII.

VERSE, language with the regular rhythm characteristic of POETRY. Verse may be used as a general term for all such language (as opposed to prose), or to describe a single line of poetry or a QUATRAIN or stanza of a ballad or hymn. Verse generally has RHYME. The pattern of stressed beats in a line of verse is called the *meter*, and the study of the various types of meter and rhyme in poetry is called *prosody*, which employs a technical language to analyse the rhythmic units (called *feet*) making up the different styles of verse. (See also BLANK VERSE; FREE VERSE.)

VERS LIBRE. See FREE VERSE.

VERTEBRAE, BONES forming the backbone or **spinal column**, which is the central pillar of the SKELETON of the group of animals, including man, called VERTEBRATES. Vertebrae exist for each segmental level of the body and are specialized to provide the trunk with both flexibility and strength. In the neck, cervical vertebrae are small and their JOINTS allow free movement to the head. The thoracic vertebrae provide the bases for the ribs. The lumbar spine consists of large vertebrae with long transverse processes that form the back of the ABDOMEN; the sacral and coccygeal vertebrae, which are fused in man, link the spine with the bony PELVIS. Within the vertebrae there is a continuous canal through which passes the SPINAL CORD; between them run the segmental nerves. Around the spinal column are the powerful spinal muscles and ligaments.

VERTEBRATES, subphylum of the CHORDATES, containing all those classes of animals which possess a backbone—a spinal column made up of bony or cartilaginous VERTEBRAE.

VERTEX. See ANGLE; CONE; TRIANGLE.

VERTICAL TAKEOFF AND LANDING AIRPLANE (VTOL), AIRPLANE that can lift-off and land vertically, such as a HELICOPTER; now chiefly associated with "jump-jet" systems in which the exhaust gases of horizontally-mounted jet engines can be deflected downward. The British Hawker "Harrier" military strike airplane, capable of supersonic speeds in level flight, is the best-known example.

VERTIGO, sensation of rotation in space resulting from functional (spinning of head with sudden stop) or organic disorders of the balance system of the EAR or its central mechanisms. It commonly induces nausea or VOMITING and may be suppressed by DRUGS.

VERWOERD, Hendrik Frensch (1901–1966), Dutch-born South African politician, premier 1958–66. A professor of psychology from 1927, he became editor of the Afrikaans nationalist newspaper *Die Transvaler* (1937). A senator from 1948, he was appointed minister of native affairs (1950), and enforced APARTHEID rigorously, stressing "separate development" and creating the BANTUSTANS. He was assassinated.

VERY HIGH FREQUENCY (VHF). See ELECTROMAGNETIC RADIATION; RADIO.

VESALIUS, Andreas (1514–1564), Flemish biologist regarded as a father of modern ANATOMY. Initially a Galenist he became, after considerable experience of dissection, one of the leading figures in the revolt against GALEN. In his most important work, *On the Structure of the Human Body* (1543), he described several organs for the first time.

VESEY, Denmark (c1767–1822), self-educated US Negro who bought his freedom in 1800, acquired great wealth and influence and organized in Charleston the biggest slave revolt in US history (1822). The plot was discovered and prevented; Vesey and 34 others were hanged.

VESPASIAN (Titus Flavius Vespasianus; 9–79 AD), Roman emperor from 69. The son of a tax collector, he rose in the army under NERO and was sent in 66 to suppress a rebellion in Judaea. His reign began an era of order and prosperity. He began the building of the COLOSSEUM.

VESPERS, the principal evening service of the WESTERN CHURCH. An ancient monastic service, its main elements are the singing of psalms and the MAGNIFICAT. The Anglican Evensong is based on Vespers.

VESPUCCI, Amerigo (1454–1512), Italian navigator for whom America was named. In two voyages (1499–1500, 1501–02) he explored the coast of South America, and deduced that the "New World" must be a continent and not part of Asia. The name "America" first appeared on a map published in 1507.

VESTA, Roman virgin goddess of the domestic hearth, identified with the Greek goddess Hestia. In her sanctuary in Rome, a perpetual flame was tended by six VESTAL VIRGINS.

VESTAL VIRGINS, in ancient Rome, priestesses chosen very young, who had to serve the shrine of VESTA for 30 years. Punishment for breaking their vow of chastity was burial alive. Their chief responsibility was to tend the sacred flame in Vesta's temple.

VESTIGIAL ORGAN, an anatomical structure which is nonfunctional and frequently underdeveloped in a modern species but which represents the remnant of an organ which in the remote past was fully functional in an ancestor species; e.g., the vermiform APPENDIX in man.

VESUVIUS, Mount, the only volcano on mainland Europe, in S Italy near Naples. Its height, c4000ft, varies with each eruption. Capped by a plume of smoke, it is a famous landmark. Its lower slopes are extremely fertile. In 79 AD it destroyed the cities of POMPEII and HERCULANEUM. Recent eruptions occurred in 1906, 1929 and 1944.

VETCH, general name for about 150 species of leguminous plants from the genus *Vicia* and a few related genera. Vetches are found throughout North America and Eurasia and several are grown as forage and silage crops, e.g. *Vicia sativa* (common or spring vetch) and *V. villosa* (winter vetch). Family: Leguminosae.

VETERANS ADMINISTRATION, US federal agency established in 1930, responsible for administering all laws authorizing benefits for ex-servicemen and their dependents or beneficiaries. The present comprehensive program of medical care, pensions, housing, educational and other assistance was set up by the Serviceman's Readjustment Act of 1944, popularly known as the G.I. BILL OF RIGHTS.

VETERANS DAY, a US national holiday, celebrated on the 4th Monday in November, to honor American servicemen, past and present. Originally known as Armistice Day, it was first designated by Woodrow WILSON to commemorate the end of WWI.

VETERANS OF FOREIGN WARS, organization for all veterans of all US wars since the Civil War. Known as the VFW, it was founded in 1899 by veterans of the Spanish–American War. It helps rehabilitate ex-servicemen and aims to promote patriotism and a community spirit.

VETERINARY MEDICINE, the medical care of sick animals, sometimes including the delivery of their young. It is practiced separately from human MEDICINE since animal diseases differ largely from those affecting humans. Veterinarians treat domestic, farm, sport and zoo animals. Sometimes diseases can be controlled only through the slaughter of known or suspected carriers.

VETO, in politics, the power of the executive to reject legislation. It is a Latin word meaning "I forbid," pronounced by the Roman TRIBUNES when they exercised their right to block laws passed by the SENATE. Under the US Constitution (Article I, Section 7), the President can veto any bill passed by Congress, but this can be overridden by a two-thirds majority in both houses. In the Security Council of the UNITED NATIONS, the five permanent members (China, France, Great Britain, the US and USSR) each possess a veto over proceedings.

VIATICUM (Latin: provision for a journey), in the Roman Catholic Church, COMMUNION administered to a person in danger of dying.

VIBRAPHONE, musical instrument of the PERCUSSION group. A modern version of the XYLOPHONE, it has tuned metal bars struck by a hammer. Beneath each bar is an electrically operated resonator to give the distinctive vibrating sound.

VIBRATION, periodic motion, such as that of a swinging PENDULUM or a struck TUNING FORK. The simplest and most regular type of vibration is SIMPLE HARMONIC MOTION. ENERGY from a vibration is propagated as a WAVE MOTION. Excess mechanical vibration, as with noise pollution, can do considerable damage to buildings.

VIBURNUM, genus of white-flowering shrubs of the HONEYSUCKLE family mainly native to temperate and subtropical Asia and North America. They include the WAYFARING TREE and the cranberry tree (*Viburnum opulus*) which are naturalized in the US and the NANNYBERRY native to North America.

VICENTE, Gil (c1470–c1536), major Portuguese poet and dramatist. Between 1502 and 1536 he produced some 44 plays for the Portuguese court. Full of verve and satire, and with many exquisite songs, they include comedies, farces, morality plays and tragi-comedies.

VICENTE LÓPEZ, city in E central Argentina. Part of Greater Buenos Aires, it is a residential beach resort. Pop 247 656.

VICENZA, city in NE Italy. A commercial and industrial center, it produces machinery, chemicals and processed foods. It has much fine medieval architecture, and several famous buildings designed by PALLADIO, including the Teatro Olimpico (1580–84). Pop 115 747.

VICE-PRESIDENT, the second-highest elected official of the US. Constitutionally and politically this office does not carry great power, and its holder must rely on the confidence and discretion of the President for any power he wields. The Vice-President was originally intended to perform two roles: that of a neutral presiding officer in the Senate, and that of a constitutional successor on the death or resignation of a President. Eight Vice-Presidents have succeeded on the death of their predecessors. Traditionally the Vice-President has been a nonentity chosen for party political reasons rather than for ability (though several have become excellent Presidents), but the increase in presidential duties with WWII has been partly responsible for giving him a greater share in political and legislative matters, in particular as a member of the National Security Council.

VICEROY BUTTERFLY, *Limenitis archippus*, a deep orange-colored butterfly of North America with black and white wing markings. Its coloration mimics that of the MONARCH BUTTERFLY. Since the Monarch is distasteful, Batesian MIMICRY helps protect the Viceroy.

VICHY, health resort in S central France, famous for its mineral springs. Its chief industry is bottling Vichy water. In WWII it was the seat of the "Vichy government" of Marshal Henri PÉTAIN, which was set up in unoccupied France in 1940 and under LAVAL continued to collaborate with the Nazis after the whole of France was occupied in 1942. Pop 33 898.

VICKSBURG, city in W Miss., seat of Warren Co. and site of an important campaign in the US CIVIL WAR. A busy Mississippi R port, it produces chemicals, machinery and metal, lumber and food products. Built on the site of a Spanish outpost in 1791, its strategic position made it a key Confederate bastion, until it was taken by Union forces under GRANT in 1863 after a 14-month siege. Pop 25 478.

VICO, Giambattista (1668–1744), Italian philosopher of history whose ideas, embodied in *The New Science* (1725), greatly influenced 19th-and 20th-century social thought. A professor of rhetoric at Naples, he saw history as the study of human institutions and developed a cyclical theory of their rise and fall.

VICTOR, name of three popes. **Saint Victor I**, (reigned c189–99) asserted Rome's authority and imposed the Roman date of Easter on the East. **Victor II** (reigned 1055–57) forbade marriage and simony (sale of office) among the clergy and was politically active in the HOLY ROMAN EMPIRE. **Saint Victor III** (reigned 1086–87) was a famous abbot of MONTECASSINO. He excommunicated the antipope CLEMENT III.

VICTOR EMMANUEL, name of three Italian kings. **Victor Emmanuel I** (1759–1824) was king of SARDINIA 1802–21. He recovered his mainland possessions after NAPOLEON's fall (1814), but his harsh rule provoked a revolt in Piedmont led by the CARBONARI, and he abdicated. **Victor Emmanuel II** (1820–1878) was king of Sardinia 1849–61 and first king of united Italy 1861–78. With CAVOUR and GARIBALDI he played a major part in Italy's unification. **Victor Emmanuel III** (1869–1947) was king of Italy 1900–46, emperor of Ethiopia 1936–43 and king of Albania 1939–43. He appointed MUSSOLINI premier in 1922, and became a mere figurehead. His unpopular association with fascism ultimately obliged him to abdicate.

VICTORIA, state in SE Australia, the smallest and most densely populated in the country. It is divided E–W by an extension of the Australian Alps, with lowlands, hills and valleys in the S and low plains N and W. The climate is temperate. Agriculture is important: wheat, oats, barley and grapes are grown, and cattle and sheep raised. Automobiles, textiles and processed foods are produced and coal and some gold are mined. Victoria is the capital, Melbourne the largest city.

VICTORIA, city and port on Vancouver Island, Canada, capital of British Columbia. A commercial and administrative center, it has lumber, fishing, fish-canning and shipbuilding industries. Pop (city) 67 761; (metropolitan area) 195 800.

VICTORIA, or Hong Kong, seaport capital of HONG KONG colony, in the NW of Hong Kong Island. A center of world trade and site of Hong Kong U., it also has many light industries. Pop 521 612.

VICTORIA, city in S Tex., seat of Victoria Co. It produces aluminum, petrochemicals, machinery and processed foods. Pop 41 349.

VICTORIA (1819–1901), Queen of Great Britain and Ireland from 1837 and Empress of India from 1876. As a young queen she depended heavily on the counsel of Lord MELBOURNE. Her life was transformed by marriage in 1840 to Prince ALBERT, who became the greatest influence of her life. A devoted wife and mother (she bore nine children), she mourned for the rest of her life after his death in 1861. She had strong opinions and believed in playing an active role in government, and her relations with a succession of ministers colored the political life of her reign. Her dislike of PALMERSTON and GLADSTONE and fondness for DISRAELI, for example, were notorious. In old age she became immensely popular and a symbol of Britain's imperial greatness.

VICTORIA, Lake, or Victoria Nyanza, lies in the Great RIFT VALLEY of East Africa, bordered by Tanzania, Uganda and Kenya. It is the second-largest freshwater lake in the world, c200mi long and c150mi wide.

VICTORIA, Tomás Luis de (c1548–1611), Spanish composer. A priest in Rome, he was influenced by PALESTRINA, and composed some of the finest religious choral music of the Renaissance. Returning to Spain in 1594, he wrote his great *Requiem* in 1605.

VICTORIA FALLS, one of Africa's most spectacular sights, on the Zambesi R in S-central Africa between Rhodesia and Zambia, where the mile-wide river plunges c400ft into a narrow fissure. They were named for Britain's Queen Victoria by LIVINGSTONE in 1855.

VICTORIA ISLAND, third-largest island of the Arctic Archipelago in the Northwest Territories, Canada. There is a US–Canadian weather station in Cambridge Bay.

VICTORIA LAND, formerly South Victoria Land, a section of Antarctica, on the W shore of the Ross Sea S of New Zealand. Mostly in New Zealand's Ross Dependency, it rises to an ice-covered plateau 9 000ft high.

VICTORIAVILLE, town in S Quebec, Canada, 36mi SE of Trois Rivières. It produces furniture, clothing and agricultural machinery. Pop 22 047.

VICTORVILLE, city in S Cal., N of San Bernadino. Its chief industries are limestone quarrying, cement production and tourism. Pop 10 845.

VICUÑA, *Lama vicugna*, a member of the CAMEL family living in the western High Andes at up to 5 000m (16 400ft). They are believed to be the original of the domesticated ALPACAS. Vicuñas are graceful animals living in family groups of a stallion and up to 20 mares, occupying a fixed territory.

VIDAL, Gore (1925–), US novelist and playwright. Novels such as *Washington D.C.* (1967), *Myra Breckenridge* (1968), *Burr* (1973) and *1876* (1976) provide an urbane, satirical view of a corrupt society. His historical novel, *Julian* (1964), is also of note. Plays include *Visit to a Small Planet* (1956) and *The Best Man* (1960).

VIDEOTAPE, magnetic tape used to record TELEVISION programs. In order to record the vast amounts of information necessary to reconstruct a television picture, 2in-wide tape must be run through the tape heads at 15in/s. (See also TAPE RECORDER; SOUND RECORDING.)

VIENNA (Wien), capital of Austria, on the Danube R, one of the world's great cities. Associated with HAYDN, MOZART, BEETHOVEN and the STRAUSS family, it is a celebrated musical, theatrical and cultural center, and has many famous buildings and museums. A Roman town, it became the residence of the HAPSBURGS in 1282. It was besieged by the Turks in 1529 and 1683. A great period of prosperity and building began in the 18th century, and Vienna was capital of the Austro–Hungarian empire until 1918, when modern Austria was formed. In WWII it was occupied by the Nazis and over 100 000 of the Jewish population were killed. The modern city is also a commercial and industrial center, producing machinery, metals, textiles, chemicals, furniture, handicrafts and food products. Pop 1 614 841.

VIENNA, town in NE Va. It is a residential suburb W of Washington, D.C. Pop 17 152.

VIENNA, city in W W.Va., on the Ohio R. It manufactures glass. Pop 11 549.

VIENNA, Congress of, assembly held in Vienna, 1814–15, to reorganize Europe after the NAPOLEONIC WARS. Effective decision-making was carried out by METTERNICH of Austria, Tsar ALEXANDER I of Russia, CASTLEREAGH and WELLINGTON of Britain, von HUMBOLDT of Prussia and TALLEYRAND of France. Among other territorial adjustments, the Congress established the German Confederation and the kingdoms of the Netherlands and Poland (under Russian rule), and restored the PAPAL STATES and the kingdoms of SARDINIA and NAPLES. Austria gained parts of Italy, Prussia gained parts of Austria, and Britain gained overseas territories. The major powers thus distributed territories to achieve a new balance of power, ignoring the nationalist aspirations of the people concerned. (See also PARIS, TREATY OF; TRIPLE ALLIANCE; QUADRUPLE ALLIANCE.)

VIENTIANE, administrative capital and largest city of Laos. On the Mekong R near the Thailand border, it is a commercial center with small-scale industries. Pop 152 000.

VIETNAM, republic in SE Asia, united in 1976 after nearly 35 years of war.

Land. Narrow and S-shaped, Vietnam is a 1000mi-long strip bordered by Cambodia, Laos and China W and N and the Gulf of Tonkin, the South China Sea and the Gulf of Siam E and S. A heavily forested mountainous backbone and a narrow coastal strip link the Red R and Mekong deltas in the N and S. Vietnam has a tropical monsoon climate, with high humidity and rainfall.

People. About 80% of the people are Vietnamese, concentrated in the two great deltas. There are urban Chinese minorities, and several highland tribal peoples, such as the MEO, who preserve their own cultures. Hanoi (the capital), Saigon, Hue, Da Nang and Haiphong are the chief cities.

Economy. This is based principally on rice-growing in the Mekong and Red R deltas. Other crops include corn, cotton, hemp, sugarcane, rubber, coffee and tea. Fishing and forestry are important. Minerals, including coal, iron, tin, zinc, lead and phosphates, are found mainly in the N, where industry, chiefly iron and steel, chemicals and textiles, is concentrated. There is also some manufacturing industry around Saigon.

History. Established as a distinct people by the 2nd century BC, the Vietnamese occupy the historic regions of TONKIN (N), ANNAM (center) and COCHIN CHINA (S). Tonkin and Annam were conquered by China in 111 BC. In the 2nd century AD the CHAMPA kingdom emerged in central Vietnam. The Chinese were driven out in 939, and the Annam empire grew, defeating the Champas (1471) and expanding S into Cochin China. European traders and missionaries began to arrive in the 1500s. The French captured Saigon in 1859 and in 1862 annexed Cochin China, which was later merged into French INDOCHINA. After Japanese occupation in WWII, a republic was proclaimed under HO CHI MINH (1945). The French attempt to reassert their authority (1946–54) ended in defeat at DIEN BIEN PHU. At the GENEVA CONFERENCE (1954) the country was divided, pending free elections, into communist North Vietnam and non-communist South Vietnam. With US backing the regime of Ngo Dinh DIEM declared an independent republic in the South (1955) and refused to hold free elections (1956). The resulting VIETNAM WAR finally ended in 1975. The unified Socialist Republic of Vietnam was proclaimed in 1976.

Official name: Socialist Republic of Vietnam
Capital: Hanoi
Area: 128 401sq mi
Population: 46 000 000
Languages: Vietnamese
Religions: Buddhist, Taoist
Monetary unit(s): 1 Dông = 100 sau

VIETNAM WAR, conflict in South Vietnam between successive South Vietnamese governments, backed by the US, and communist guerrilla insurgents, the Vietcong, backed by North Vietnam. Its origins were in 1941, when the Vietminh guerrilla force was formed under HO CHI MINH to fight the Japanese. After 1946 it fought the French colonial government, defeating them at DIEN BIEN PHU. The GENEVA CONFERENCE then temporarily divided Vietnam at the 17th parallel between the Communists (North) and the Nationalists (South). Ngo Dinh DIEM, the South Vietnamese premier, cancelled national elections and declared the South independent in 1956. The *Viet Nam Cong San* (Vietnamese Communists), or Vietcong, was then formed to oppose his increasingly corrupt regime. The Vietcong were equipped and trained by North Vietnam, with Chinese backing, and included North Vietnamese troops especially in the later stages of the war. The Vietcong fought a ferocious guerrilla campaign that led Diem to call in US forces under a defense treaty in 1961. In 1963 he was overthrown by his officers; after a period of turmoil Nguyen van THIEU became president in 1967. In 1965 the US had begun bombing the North in retaliation for the use of Northern troops in the South; large numbers of US combat troops were brought in, amounting to 545,000 in 1968. The large-scale US campaign proved unable to do more than hold back the well-entrenched Vietcong; Vietnamese civilians suffered terribly at the hands of both sides. The use of napalm and defoliants, in a vain attempt to reduce the jungle that gave the Vietcong a great advantage in cover and mobility, provoked international controversy, as did the great publicity given to atrocities committed by US troops. This feeling, and the mounting toll of life and resources, roused world opposition to the war. Fruitless peace talks began in Paris (1968) and in 1969 President NIXON announced the handover of the war to South Vietnamese forces. The war had spread to Cambodia and Laos before a ceasefire in Jan. 1973, the prelude to the final withdrawal of US troops a few months later. The South was then overrun; the war effectively ended with the fall of Saigon in May 1975.

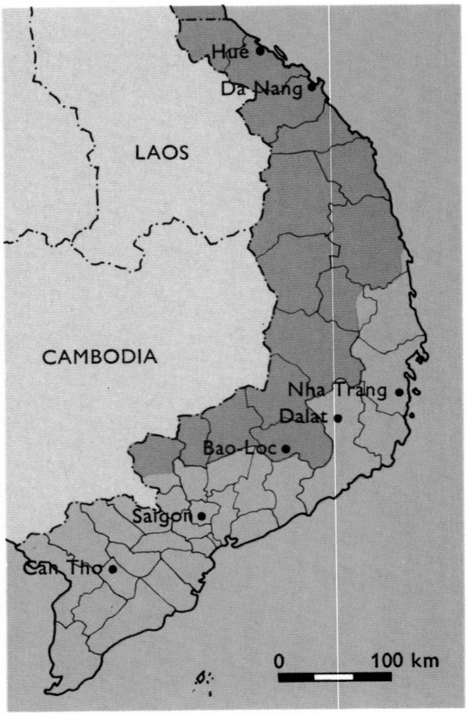

The last days of South Vietnam, a map showing the military situation there at the end of March 1975. After an unsuccessful "strategic retreat" by Saigon troops in mid-March, the Vietcong seized about two-thirds of the country (*dark brown*). They subsequently moved eastwards across high country and southwards over Highway 1, taking one coastal town after another.

Defoliated area of the nominally demilitarized zone between North and South Vietnam. The thick jungle in the zone was used by the North to cover supply and troop movements, and so US aircraft used mass defoliants in an attempt to create a clear strip. This strategy was only temporarily successful.

VIGILANTES, individuals who band together to punish summarily those they consider offenders. They were a feature of American frontier life, where frequent lawlessness drove citizens to form their own *vigilance committees*. They had no legal authority. (See also LYNCHING.)

VIGILIUS (c500–555), pope from 537. The emperor JUSTINIAN, hoping to appease MONOPHYSITISM, coerced him into accepting the condemnation of certain articles. His action aroused bitter opposition in the West.

VIGNEAUD, Vincent du. See DU VIGNEAUD, VINCENT.

VIGNOLA, Giacomo da (1507–1573), Italian architect, painter and sculptor. He designed the Villa Giulia in Rome (1550–55) and the Villa Farnese at Caprarola (1559–73). His designs for the Jesuit church Il Gesù and his *Rules of the Five Orders of Architecture* (1562) helped create the BAROQUE style.

VIGNY, Alfred Victor, comte de (1797–1863), French Romantic poet, novelist and playwright. His pessimistic works deal with solitude, alienation and spiritual conflict. The posthumous collection *Les Destinées* (1864) contains his most famous poems.

VIGO, city in NW Spain. A port, naval base and fishing center, it has shipyards, canneries, food processing and light manufacturing. Pop 197 144.

VIKING PROGRAM, series of US unmanned space probes designed to land on and study Mars. Viking 1 landed on July 20, 1976, sending back TV pictures; its soil-analysis experiments yielded results which suggest the presence of life, but may represent only unusual chemical reactions. Viking 2 landed Sept. 3, 1976.

VIKINGS, or "Norsemen," the Norwegian, Swedish and Danish seafarers who harassed Europe from the 9th to the 11th centuries. Expert shipbuilders and navigators, they were capable of long sea voyages, and their ferocity made them the terror of Europe. The Norwegians raided Scotland, Ireland and France, and colonized the Hebrides, Orkneys, the Faroes, Iceland and Greenland. They may also have discovered America (see VINLAND). The Danes raided England, France, the Netherlands, Spain and Italy. The Swedes went down the E shores of the Baltic, through what is now W Russia, and reached the Bosporus and Byzantium. In addition to being raiders the Vikings also traded and created permanent settlements. They united the Hebrides and the Isle of Man into a kingdom. The Shetlands, the Orkneys and Caithness became an earldom. Kingdoms were also set up in Ireland and Russia (see VARANGIANS). In 878 the Danish founded the DANELAW in NE England. In N France the Viking ROLLO was granted a dukedom in 911, which was the origin of the NORMAN kingdom. Remarkable for their restless energy, the Vikings exerted a considerable influence on European history.

VILLA, Francisco, known as **Pancho Villa** (1877–1923), Mexican bandit, revolutionary leader and popular hero. In 1909–11 he helped MADERO to power. He then supported CARRANZA (1913–14), but fell out with him. Villa and ZAPATA captured Mexico City but were defeated in 1915. In 1916 he raided US territory, and evaded capture by a US punitive force for 11 months. An outlaw until 1920, he was assassinated on his ranch.

VILLA-LOBOS, Heitor (1887–1959), Brazilian composer. Director of national musical education from 1932, he created a synthesis of classical and Brazilian folk music in numerous works, including *Chôros* (1920–29) and *Bachianas Brasileiras* (1930–44).

VILLANOVANS, early IRON AGE culture named for Villanova, Italy. They arrived in Italy from E Europe in the 10th–9th centuries BC, worked Tuscan iron and copper mines and were fine metalworkers.

VILLA PARK, village in NE Ill. It is a residential community 25mi W of Chicago. Pop 25 891.

VILLARD, Henry (1835–1900), German-born US journalist and financier. Correspondent for the *New York Herald* and *New York Tribune* in the Civil War, he later (1881) acquired the New York *Evening Post* and *The Nation*. Entering the railroad business in 1873, he created the Oregon Railway and Navigation Co. (1879), and became president of the Northern Pacific (1881–84, 1888–93). In 1890 he formed the Edison General Electric Co.

VILLEHARDOUIN, Geoffroi de (c1150–c1212), French nobleman, historian and crusader. His account of the years 1199–1207, covering the Fourth CRUSADE and its sack of Constantinople (1204), was the first major French prose work. He was given the title Marshal of Romania and a fief in Thrace (1205).

VILLEIN, type of agrarian peasant in medieval Europe. Like the SERFS, English villeins were unfree, but elsewhere they were free. Villeins were tied to the land by their feudal obligations (see FEUDAL SYSTEM).

VILLIERS, George. See BUCKINGHAM, 1ST DUKE OF.

VILLON, François (1431– after 1463), French poet who led a wandering, criminal life. In his coarse and cynical *Lais* ("Legacy") and *Testament*, which contain some celebrated lyrics, he both relishes and regrets his misspent life and expresses his horror of death.

VILNIUS (Russian, *Vilna*; Polish, *Wilno*), capital of the Lithuanian SSR, USSR. A transportation, commercial and cultural center, it produces agricultural machinery, electrical equipment, machine tools, foodstuffs and textiles. Pop 372 000.

VIMINAL HILL. See SEVEN HILLS OF ROME.

VIMY RIDGE, a 475ft high ridge in N France, 10mi N of Arras, scene of a WWI Allied attack, Apr. 9–14, 1917. The Canadian Corps took the ridge, but the offensive as a whole failed.

VINCENNES, city in SW Ind., seat of Knox Co. The oldest town in Ind., it now produces paper, glass, batteries and steel products. Pop 19 867.

VINCENT, John Heyl (1832–1920), US Episcopal Methodist clergyman and Sunday-school reformer. He founded the influential monthly *Sunday School Teacher* (1865), and in 1874 started the CHAUTAUQUA MOVEMENT.

VINCENT DE PAUL, Saint (c1580–1660), Roman Catholic priest who pioneered charities in France. In 1625 he founded the Congregation of the Mission (Lazarists), an order of secular priests devoted to rural missionary work. Later (1633) he founded the Daughters of Charity to help the poor in towns.

VINCENT'S ANGINA, sore throat due to infection of the PHARYNX with a pair of BACTERIA, commonly seen in undernourished or debilitated persons. Only ANTIBIOTICS and local measures are required.

VINCI, Leonardo da. See LEONARDO DA VINCI.

VINCULUM (from Latin *vincire*, to bind), symbol used in mathematics to indicate that two or more terms are to be treated as one: e.g., $a-\overline{b+c}$ meaning $a-(b+c)$. It is most commonly used with the ROOT symbol:

$$\sqrt[4]{6+10}=\sqrt[4]{16}=2.$$

VINE, any plant with a climbing or trailing stem that cannot grow upright without support. Some have tendrils (SWEET PEA, GRAPE and CUCUMBER) and others have adhesive disks (VIRGINIA CREEPER) or small roots (IVY) to anchor them to their supports. The HOP twines its stem around supports.

VINEGAR, a sour liquid used to flavor and preserve food. The taste comes from ACETIC ACID, which forms at least 4% of the total volume. Vinegar is made by FERMENTATION of wine, cider or any other alcohol solutions; BACTERIA (*Acetobacter* and *Acetomonas*) oxidize the alcohol (ETHANOL) to acetic acid. Malt vinegar is produced from alcohol fermented from potatoes or cereals.

VINELAND, city of S N.J., in a diversified farming area. It has glass, clothing, chemical and food-processing industries. Pop 47 399.

VINLAND, a region of E North America discovered c1000 AD by VIKING explorers, probably led by Leif ERICSON, and briefly settled c1004 by THORFINN KARLSEFNI. Some scholars believe it was in New England, others favor Newfoundland (where Viking remains have been found). The Norse sagas describe the discovery of a fertile region where grapes grew, hence "Vin(e)land." (See also KENSINGTON RUNE STONE.)

VINNITSA, capital of Vinnitsa oblast in the Ukrainian SSR, USSR, 130mi SW of Kiev. Industry includes sugar refining and machinery. Pop 212 000.

VINSON, Frederick Moore (1890–1953), Chief Justice of the US 1946–53. A Ky. Democrat, he was a member of the House of Representatives 1923–29,

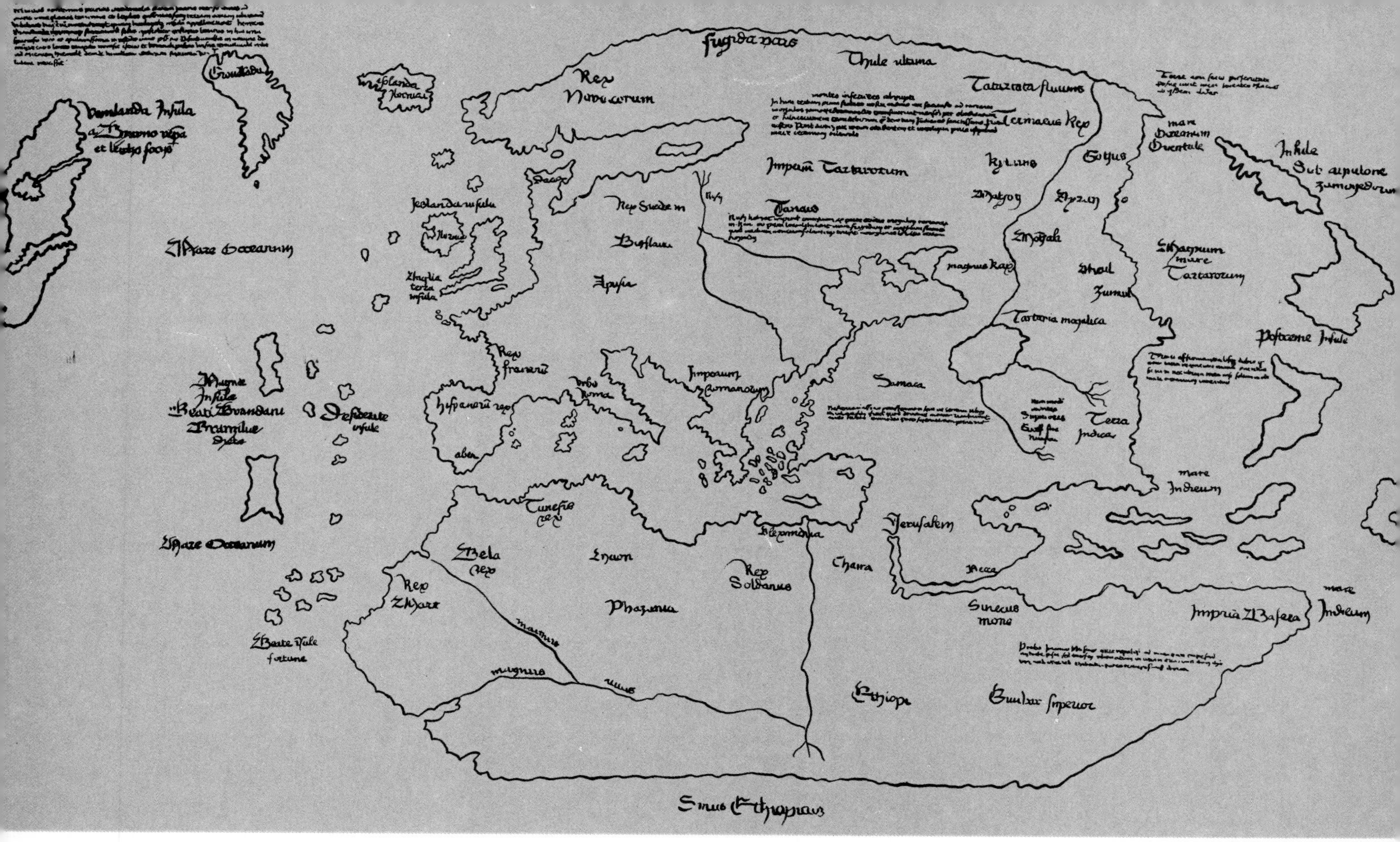

The so-called Vinland Map, supposedly a world map dating from about 1440, is often cited as additional evidence that the Vikings reached North America. An island whose east coast is evidently that of North America is marked "Vinland," the name of the Viking settlement there. Recent scientific study suggests the map is a modern forgery, but this does not cast doubt on the Vikings' achievement.

1931–38. While he was chief justice, the Supreme Court made important civil-liberty rulings.

VINYL COMPOUNDS, compounds containing the vinyl group, $CH_2{=}CH{-}$, formally derived from ethylene, but generally produced from ACETYLENE. They are polymerized (see POLYMERS) to form PLASTICS and RUBBERS. (See also ORLON.)

VIOL, the 15th–17th century forerunner of the VIOLIN. Viols have sloping shoulders, frets, a low bridge and a soft, mellow tone. The six strings are tuned in fourths. The treble, alto, tenor and bass (*viola da gamba*) viols are all held upright, as was the double-bass *violone*, which became today's DOUBLE-BASS. Interest in the viol has revived in the 20th century.

VIOLA, stringed musical instrument a little larger than the similar VIOLIN and tuned a fifth lower, with a range from C below middle C upward for over three octaves. From the 1700s part of the ORCHESTRA, it gained importance in the classical period and is now sometimes used a a solo instrument.

VIOLA DA GAMBA. See VIOL.

VIOLET, low herbaceous plants of the genus *Viola* that produce characteristically shaped flowers on slender stalks. Most species occur in the Andes, but many are found in North America and Europe. Several species, including the PANSY, are cultivated as garden ornamentals. They grow mainly in moist woods. Family: Violaceae.

VIOLIN, smallest, most versatile and leading member of the bowed, four-stringed violin family (violin, VIOLA, CELLO, DOUBLE-BASS). Violins succeeded the VIOL in the 1600s, differing in their flexibility, range of tone and pitch, arched bridge, squarer shoulders, narrower body and lack of frets. The violin proper, derived from the 16th-century arm viol, is tuned in fifths and ranges over 4½ octaves above G below middle C. Perfected by the craftsmen of CREMONA, it became a major solo instrument. The principal violinist leads the ORCHESTRA, violins forming most of the string section. Classical string quartets have two violins.

Members of the violin family: (a) violin; (b) viola; (c) cello, or violoncello; (d) double bass, which retains something of the appearance of the old viola da gamba, such as the high "shoulders." The stave behind shows the tuning of each instrument. *Bottom left*: parts of the violin. (a) Belly; (b) back; (c) f-hole; (d) purfling; (e) fingerboard; (f) strings; (g) head; (h) pegs; (i) tailpiece; (j) bridge; (k) soundpost; (l) bass bar; (m) chin rest.

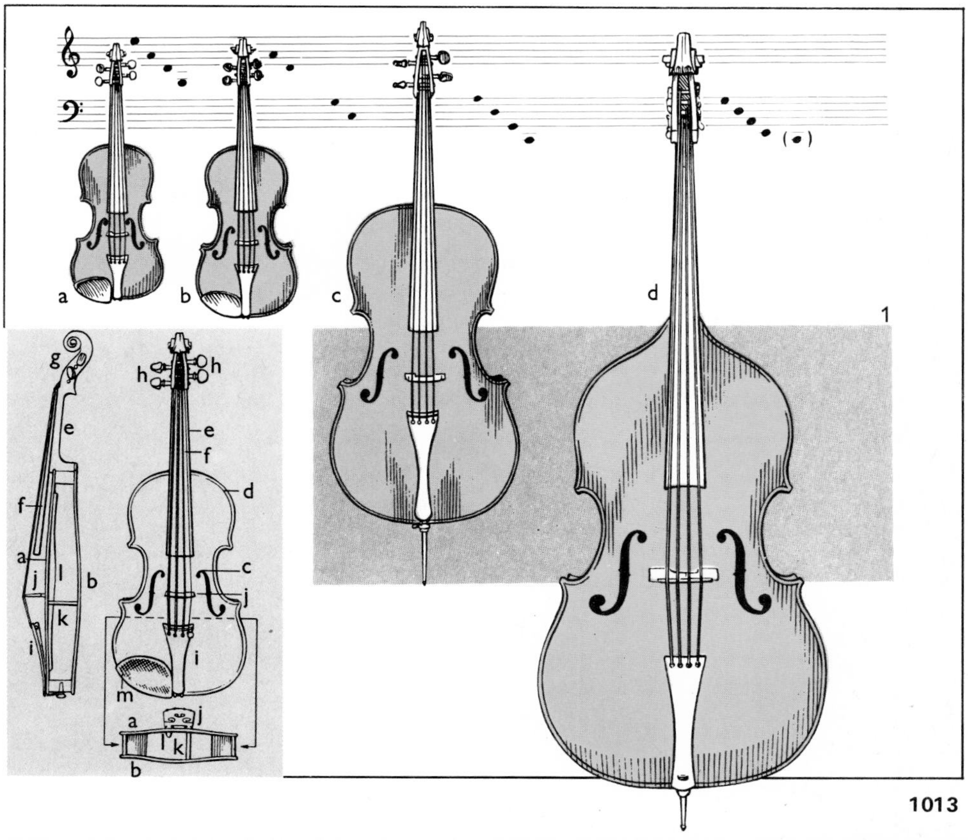

Viruses

The frontier between life and lifelessness

The word "virus" (from Latin, literally a slimy liquid or poison) for centuries was used to mean a venom produced by living things that caused infectious disease. The great French chemist and microbiologist Louis Pasteur (1822–1895) was the first to use the word in the modern sense of an infectious agent which is not a bacterium, but nevertheless associated with disease.

In 1935 the virus took on a still more profound meaning when the American biochemist Wendell M. Stanley discovered something that shook the scientific world. Everyone had always assumed that the ability to form crystals was a property of inanimate matter and not of living material. He showed that a virus could be purified as an apparently lifeless crystal. Here was a property unheard of before in a living organism; suddenly the frontier between life and lifelessness had blurred. Stanley also showed that the virus crystals could be dissolved and recrystallized as often as one pleased without affecting their infectiousness. A heated debate raged in the scientific community. Were they truly alive or lifeless?

Outside a cell, viruses are as lifeless as any other packets of nucleic acid and protein: they can even be crystallized. Yet within a cell (the host cell) they show some of the properties of life. In particular, they can reproduce themselves, but by a process of replication, the assembling of exact copies, thus contrasting with other living organisms in which a process of growth and division occurs. Viruses therefore have properties both of life and lifelessness and are probably best thought of as midway between the simplest living things (such as unicellular amoeba) and large molecules (such as proteins).

During the latter part of the last century many diseases of plants and animals had been shown to be caused by bacteria through the work of Louis Pasteur, Robert Koch and their followers, who firmly believed that bacteria were responsible for all diseases. Along with this bacterial theory of infection they accepted the ancient doctrine of specificity, which had been inherent in the Assyro-Babylonian concept of disease-demons: each disease was caused by one specific agent.

Bacteria were supposed to be the smallest particles of living matter capable of functioning as individual organisms, just as atoms were supposed to be the smallest division of inanimate matter. To isolate bacteria, these early microbiologists filtered the fluids collected from their diseased plants and animals through fine clay filters, which had been shown by Pasteur and others to prevent bacteria passing through. In this way they discovered many bacteria and explained many diseases. But there were still some very puzzling problems. The agents causing many diseases such as rabies, mumps, measles, influenza, the common cold, smallpox and yellow fever could not be found. Why were these germs so elusive? And why couldn't they be grown in a culture or in a flask like other bacteria?

In 1892, exactly ten years after Koch had discovered the bacterium causing tuberculosis, a Russian biologist Dmitry Iosifovich Ivanovski had been studying the mosaic disease which caused great destruction of tobacco, potato and tomato crops. The most powerful microscopes of the day had failed to reveal the microorganisms causing the disease. Ivanovski devised an experiment that was to signal the start of the history of virus research. He prepared a liquid from the sap of the infected tobacco plants and passed it through the finest clay filter available—one that would certainly trap all the bacteria. However, the filtered liquid was as infectious as ever—when it was dabbed on a healthy tobacco plant, that plant died, as well as all its neighbors. So clearly the agent causing the disease was much smaller than bacteria.

But for a time it was thought that these filterable agents or "filterable viruses" might only cause disease in plants. Then in 1898 the agent causing hoof-and-mouth disease in cattle was shown to be filterable in the same way. In rapid succession a large number of filterable viruses was isolated, among them African horse sickness (1900), yellow fever (1901), cattle plague (1902), trachoma (1908), typhus fever (1910), and measles (1911).

However, since no one had actually seen a virus, arguments raged for some 30 years over whether such diseases were caused by the filtered fluid itself or by microorganisms smaller than bacteria suspended in the fluid. Then in 1927 an American, Ernest W. Goodpasture, actually saw a virus. He had been studying tiny particles in chickens suffering from fowl-pox and was trying a special dye on his microscope slides to see what it would show up. On applying the dye he noted to his astonishment that it caused the particles to break up into thousands of much smaller particles, which he could just see with his most powerful light microscope. Perhaps these smaller particles were viruses. To test this he placed one of the large particles (actually about one ten-thousandth of an inch across) under the skin of a healthy chicken. The chicken developed the disease. So the smaller particles which he had just been able to see were probably viruses.

However, the ability to see viruses highly magnified, which has produced the great progress in virology of the last 30 years, is due to the invention of the electron microscope (commercially available in the US from 1940). A major impetus to the development of this device was appropriately enough the viruses themselves: specifically, the need to prevent further terrible viral epidemics such as the great influenza pandemic of 1918–19 which spread throughout most of the world and killed an estimated 21 000 000 people (about 2 000 000 in Europe alone).

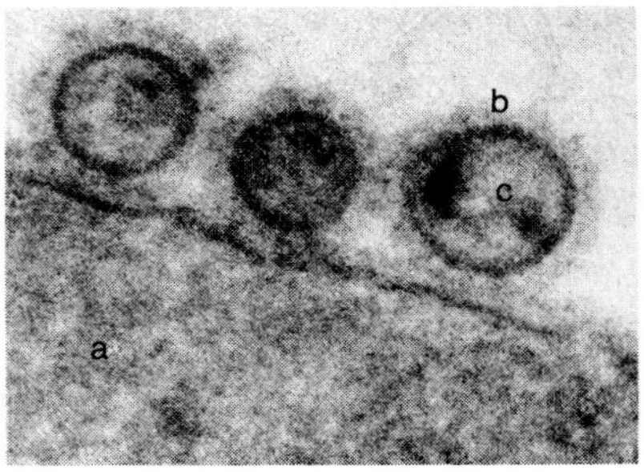

Microscopic section showing three influenza viruses on the outer membrane of red blood cell (a). Also visible are the protein shell of the virus (b) and its nucleus (c).

The discovery that bacteria also have virus diseases has greatly helped the study of viruses. In 1915, a University of London microbiologist, Frederick W. Twort, while studying bacterial colonies noticed that one had a few clear areas on its surface. Puzzled by this finding, he examined these clear areas (plaques) under the microscope and found that they contained disintegrated bacteria. Transferring a few drops of liquid to a normal colony from the colony with plaques caused the normal colony also to develop plaques. As his predecessors had done, he showed that the infectious agent was a virus by filtering it through a filter impermeable to bacteria. These bacterial viruses were called bacteriophages (or phages).

Many phages have been discovered, but the phages of the bacterium *E. Coli* (which inhabits the digestive tract) have been most extensively studied. The way in which the T phages infect *E. Coli* is one of the most remarkable mechanisms in all biology. T phages are basically tadpole shaped. The "head" is hexagonal in outline and contains genetic material, in this case DNA (some viruses contain RNA). The "tail" is a cylindrical sheath surrounding a hollow "needle" extending from the head to a hexagonal baseplate at its far end from which six tall fibers arise. At the start of infection the phage attaches itself to the host cell's wall by its tail fibers. The tail fibers become sharply bent bringing the base plate close to the cell wall. The tail sheath then contracts driving the needle through the cell wall. The phage's genetic material then flows into the host cell and brings about an extraordinary event: the normal functions of the cell are shut off and it is put to work making the materials required for replication of the phage. The phage's genetic material then controls the assembly of new phage particles and eventually the host cell bursts (lysis) and dies, releasing several hundred new phage particles, able to infect other cells. A phage which destroys its host cell in this way is called a "virulent" phage.

However there is another type (temperate phage) which does not usually cause lysis of its host cell. In 1953 a French research team discovered that the genetic material of temperate phages becomes incorporated into the chromosome of its host cell (lysogeny) and behaves exactly as if it were a normal part of the bacterial chromosome. This discovery gives us a clue as to how viruses may have originated—a problem which has caused much speculation ever since the position of viruses at the frontiers of life was recognized. Perhaps they are detached portions of the chromosomes of bacteria, or other cells, which have escaped, but under some circumstances can be reincorporated into their parent chromosome. Alternatively, they may have evolved from very simple cells such as Rickettsia (nonfilterable microorganisms between bacteria and viruses in size) or large molecules. More complex suggestions have been proposed but at present it is impossible to decide which alternative, if any, is correct.

In December 1967, at Stanford University in California, a group of scientists under the direction of Nobel Prize winner Arthur Kornberg succeeded in synthesizing some DNA outside a cell which, when injected into susceptible bacterial cells, resulted in the replication of normal phage particles and host cell lysis in the usual fashion. Some newspapers went so far as to proclaim that life had been artifically created in California. However, Kornberg had used a small amount of DNA from the bacterium *E. Coli* as a priming agent for the formation of his synthetic DNA. So the creation of life even at the frontier between life and lifelessness remains to be achieved at a future date if at all.

The hereditary material of viruses, bacteria and certain cells in culture can now be altered by the relatively simple technique of genetic surgery though it is not yet possible to control very closely which genes are operated upon. Genetic surgery raises a number of interesting possibilities. Among these are the artificial creation of potentially dangerous new viruses and bacteria, and perhaps eventually the replacement of human genes, thus making human beings to order with almost any set of predetermined characteristics. Thus man may be in the awesome position to control his own evolution, shaping it to suit his every desire, good or evil. If this becomes fact it will be largely due to the experience and understanding acquired at the frontier between life and lifelessness in the study of the lowly virus.

VIOLONCELLO. See CELLO.

VIPERS, a family of SNAKES with highly-developed venom apparatus, found in Europe, Africa and Asia. Vipers are short, stoutly-built and typically terrestrial. They lie in wait for their prey—lizards or small mammals—strike, injecting venom from modified salivary glands through the hollow poison fangs, and then wait for a while before tracking down their victim. One of the best known species is the ADDER.

VIRAL DISEASES, generally INFECTIOUS DISEASES due to VIRUSES. The COMMON COLD, INFLUENZA, CHICKENPOX, MEASLES and GERMAN MEASLES are common in childhood, while SMALLPOX and YELLOW FEVER are important tropical virus diseases. Viruses may also cause specific organ disease such as HEPATITIS, MENINGITIS, ENCEPHALITIS, MYOCARDITIS and PERICARDITIS. Most virus diseases are self-limited and mild, but there are few specific drugs effective in cases of severe illness. Prevention by VACCINATION is therefore crucial.

VIRCHOW, Rudolf (1821–1902), Pomeranian-born German pathologist whose most important work was to apply knowledge concerning the CELL to PATHOLOGY, in course of which he was the first to document LEUKEMIA and EMBOLISM. He was also distinguished as an anthropologist and archaeologist.

VIREOS, 20 species of small, insectivorous, perching birds with heavy, slightly-hooked bills. Most are forest, shrub-dwelling birds, widespread in Middle and North America. The closely related greenlets of South America belong to the same subfamily Vireoninae.

VIRGIL. See VERGIL.

VIRGINAL, type of small HARPSICHORD, its strings parallel to the single keyboard. There is one wire per note. Encased in a small rectangular box, the virginal was popular c1550–1650.

VIRGIN BIRTH, Christian doctrine that JESUS CHRIST was conceived by the Virgin MARY through the Holy Spirit's power, without a human father. Though stated in the GOSPELS of Matthew and Luke and embodied in the CREEDS, it has been criticized in the past 100 years as a legendary tradition endangering Jesus' full humanity. (See also INCARNATION.)

VIRGINIA, Southern state of the US, the largest and oldest of the original 13 colonies.

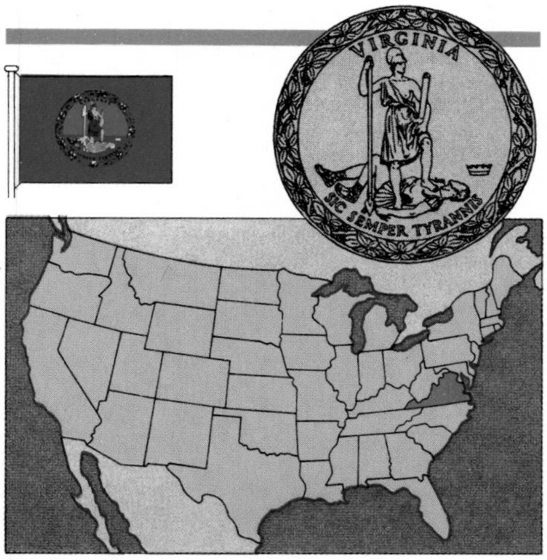

Name of State: Virginia
Capital: Richmond
Statehood: June 25, 1788 (10th state)
Familiar Name: Old Dominion
Area: 40 817sq mi
Population: 4 648 484
Elevation: Highest—5 729ft, Mount Rogers
Lowest—sea level, Atlantic Ocean
Motto: Sic Semper Tyrannis
(Thus Always To Tyrants)
State Flower: Flowering dogwood
State Bird: Cardinal
State Tree: None
State Song: "Carry Me Back to Old Virginia"

Land. The major regions are: the TIDEWATER coastal plain, extending about 100mi inland; the Piedmont, a rolling plateau rising to 2 000ft where it meets the Blue Ridge Mts., and the broad Appalachian Ridge and Valley Region in the W. There are many rivers, most of which run SE to Chesapeake Bay. The Potomac R forms most of the Va.–Md. boundary. Nearly two-thirds of Va. is forest. The climate is mild.

Economy. Va.'s strong economy is based on manufacturing (notably chemicals, tobacco, textiles, shipbuilding and foodstuffs) and agriculture (primarily tobacco and livestock). Tourism is a major addition to the economy. There are large coal deposits.

History. After Sir Walter RALEIGH's expedition to North America in the late 16th century, the name "Virginia" (for Elizabeth I, the "Virgin Queen") was applied to all of North America not claimed by Spain or France. In May 1607, colonists sent out by one of the VIRGINIA COMPANIES established the first permanent English settlement in the New World at JAMESTOWN.

In 1612 John ROLFE began to raise tobacco, which was to be for long the basis of Va.'s economy. In 1619 the first Negroes came to Va., as indentured servants, and by 1715 constituted about 25% of the population. Intermittent conflicts with the POWHATAN INDIANS reached a peak in 1622 when the Indians killed some 350 colonists in a single attack, reducing the colony by a third. In 1619 the first house of burgesses met at Jamestown, and the settlers' participation in their own governmental affairs continued after Va. became a royal colony in 1624. The British government of the RESTORATION attempted strict enforcement of the NAVIGATION ACTS limiting colonial trade to England. This was a contributing cause of BACON'S REBELLION in 1676.

Va. took a leading role in the REVOLUTIONARY WAR and events leading to it. Her distinguished patriots included Patrick HENRY, Thomas JEFFERSON, and George WASHINGTON. In May 1776, the fifth Virginia Convention declared the colony an independent commonwealth and the following month it became the first American colony to adopt a constitution and a declaration of rights. Va.'s Robert E. LEE led the South during the CIVIL WAR. In 1863 the W counties of Va. which had refused to secede formed the new state of WEST VIRGINIA. Most historic of states, Va. was the scene of the British surrender at YORKTOWN (1781) and the Confederate surrender at APPOMATTOX, and has provided eight US presidents.

VIRGINIA, city in NE Minn. 20mi E of Hibbing. It is a resort city with textile and dairy industries and iron mines. Pop 12 540.

VIRGINIA BEACH, independent coastal resort city in SE Va. Industries include tourism, truck farming, livestock and dairying. Pop 172 106.

VIRGINIA CITY, famous "ghost town," a village in W Nev., about 20mi S of Reno. Founded (1859) on discovery of the fabled COMSTOCK LODE, it was the major US silver-producing center until the 1880s, and is now a tourist attraction. Pop c700.

VIRGINIA COMPANIES, two companies of merchant-adventurers granted patents by the English crown in 1606 for colonizing America. The LONDON COMPANY, authorized to settle anywhere from present-day S.C. to N.Y., founded JAMESTOWN in 1607 (see also VIRGINIA). The PLYMOUTH COMPANY, granted rights from present-day Va. to Me., fared badly. It was reorganized (1620) into the COUNCIL FOR NEW ENGLAND, which made the original grant to the PILGRIM FATHERS and PURITAN settlers.

VIRGINIA CREEPER, woodbine or American ivy, *Parthenocissus quinquefolia*, a vine with five leaflets to each leaf and small clusters of green flowers that give rise to blue berries. The foliage turns red in the fall. It has slender tendrils tipped with disks that attach to walls and fences.

VIRGINIA DEER, a subspecies of the WHITE-TAILED DEER.

VIRGINIA RESOLUTION. See KENTUCKY AND VIRGINIA RESOLUTIONS.

VIRGIN ISLANDS, westernmost group of the Lesser Antilles in the WEST INDIES, E of Puerto Rico. The W islands belong to the US and the E group to Britain.

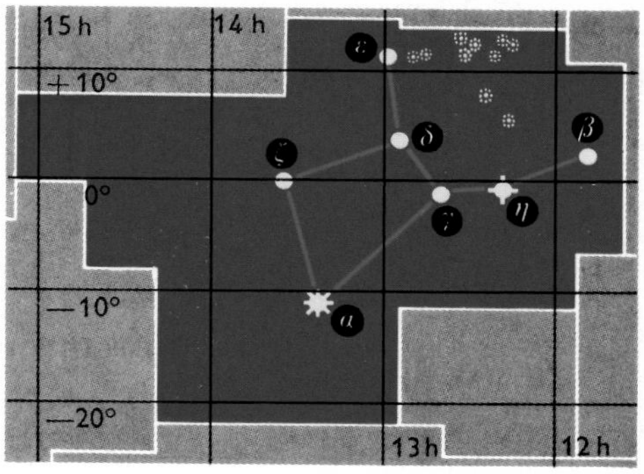

The constellation Virgo, sixth sign of the Zodiac, lies in the northern hemisphere of the sky.

Discovered and claimed for Spain by Christopher COLUMBUS (1493), the Virgin Islands were settled chiefly by English and Danes in the 1600s. England secured the British Virgin Islands in 1666. The Danish West Indies were acquired by the US for strategic reasons in 1917 and became the US Virgin Islands. The economy of both groups now depends on tourism but farming (food crops, livestock) and fishing are important. **The Virgin Islands of the US,** a US territory covering 133sq mi, comprise St. Thomas, St. John, St. Croix and some 65 islets. Charlotte Amalie, the capital and only city, stands on St. Thomas. Pop 62 468. **The British Virgin Islands** are separated from the American islands by a strait called The Narrows. Covering 59sq mi, the group consists of about 30 mainly uninhabited islands. The largest is Tortola, which has the capital and chief port, Road Town. Pop 10 484.

VIRGIN ISLANDS NATIONAL PARK, established 1956 on most of St. John (19sq mi), VIRGIN ISLANDS of the US, comprises 14 419 acres with interesting marine flora, fauna, and ruins of the Danish colony.

VIRGINIUS AFFAIR (1873), incident that nearly provoked war between the US and Spain. The *Virginius*, fraudulently registered as a US vessel and running arms to Cuban rebels against Spain, was seized by a Spanish man-of-war. Over 50 crew and passengers, including some Americans, were executed. Secretary of State Hamilton FISH issued an ultimatum, but a compromise was reached.

VIRGIN MARY. See MARY, THE BLESSED VIRGIN.

VIRGO (the Virgin), a large constellation on the ECLIPTIC; the sixth sign of the ZODIAC. It contains the bright spectroscopic binary (see DOUBLE STAR) Spica and a cluster of galaxies.

VIRTANEN, Artturi Ilmari (1895–1973), Finnish biochemist awarded the 1945 Nobel Prize for Chemistry for his work on winter SILAGE. He showed that keeping the silage acid ($pH<4$) stopped the FERMENTATION that would otherwise destroy it, without reducing its nutritive value or its palatability to animals (see pH).

VIRUS, submicroscopic parasitic microorganism comprising a PROTEIN or protein/lipid sheath containing nucleic acid (DNA or RNA). Viruses are inert outside living cells, but within appropriate cells they can replicate (using raw material parasitized from the cell) and give rise to the manifestations of the associated VIRAL DISEASE in the host organism. Various viruses infect animals, plants and BACTERIA (in which case they are BACTERIOPHAGES). Few drugs act specifically against viruses, although IMMUNITY can be induced in susceptible cells against particular viruses. Various pathogenic organisms formerly regarded as large viruses are now distinguished as *bedsonia*.

VISALIA, city in S Cal., in the San Joaquin Valley, seat of Tulare Co. It processes dairy products, cans fruit and makes electronic goods. Pop 27 268.

VISAYAN ISLANDS, large group around the Visayan Sea, central Philippines, about a quarter of the republic in area and population. It includes Panay, Negros, Cebu, Leyte, Bohol, Samar and Masbate.

VISCHACHAS, vegetarian South American rodents closely related to CHINCHILLAS. The Plains vischacha is large and heavily-built, with an enormous head. Like the more agile Mountain vischachas, they are colonial, living in extensive burrow networks.

VISCONTI, Luchino (1906–1976), Italian director in film and theater (notably operas for Maria CALLAS). His films include the neorealist *Ossessione* (1942), *Rocco and his Brothers* (1960), studies of decadence in times past (*The Leopard*, 1964; *Death in Venice*, 1971) and *Conversation Piece* (1975).

VISCOSITY, the property of a FLUID by which it resists shape change or relative motion within itself. All fluids are viscous, their viscosity arising from internal FRICTION between molecules which tends to oppose the development of velocity differences. The viscosity of liquids decreases as they are heated, but that of gases increases.

VISCOUNT MELVILLE SOUND, formerly Melville Sound, in the North West Territories, N Canada, a 100mi-wide section of the NORTHWEST PASSAGE between Melville and the Victoria islands.

VISHAKHAPATNAM, city in NE Andhra Pradesh, E India, on the Bay of Bengal, an important harbor with shipbuilding and oil refineries. Pop 182 000.

VISHINSKY, Andrei Yanuarievich (1883–1954), Russian statesman and jurist. Chief state prosecutor in the purge trials of 1936–38, he was deputy commissar (1940–49) and commissar (1949–53) for foreign affairs, and the USSR's chief UN delegate.

VISHNU, second deity in the Trimurti (see HINDUISM), representing the preserving and protecting aspect of the godhead. The ancient *Vishnu Purana* text describes him as the primal god, as do his followers (Vaishnavas) who also worship his many AVATARS such as RAMA, BUDDHA, and KRISHNA. Vishnu is often represented dark blue in color, holding in his four hands a lotus, mace, discus and conch. His consort is LAKSHMI.

VISIGOTHS (West Goths), Germanic people who in the 200s AD invaded Roman DACIA, under FRITIGERN defeated the Romans at Adrianople (378) and, led by ALARIC I, invaded Thrace and N Italy and sacked Rome (410). They founded (419) a kingdom in S Gaul and Spain, but ALARIC II lost (507) the N lands to CLOVIS, king of the Franks. Roderick, last Gothic king of Spain, lost his throne to the Moors 711. (See also GOTHS; OSTROGOTHS.)

VISION, the special sense concerned with reception and interpretation of LIGHT stimuli reaching the EYE; the principal sense in man. Light reaches the CORNEA and then passes through this, the AQUEOUS HUMOR, the lens and the VITREOUS HUMOR before impinging on the RETINA. Here there are two basic types of receptor: **rods** concerned with light and dark distinction, and **cones**, with three subtypes corresponding to three primary visual COLORS: red, green and blue. Much of vision and most of the cones are located in the central area, the macula, of which the FOVEA is the central portion; gaze directed at objects brings their images into this area. When receptor cells are stimulated, impulses pass through two nerve cell relays in the retina before passing back toward the BRAIN in the optic nerve. Behind the eyes, information derived from left and right visual fields of either eye is collected together and passes back to the opposite cerebral hemisphere, which it reaches after one further relay. In the cortex are several areas concerned with visual perception and related phenomena. The basic receptor information is coded by nerve interconnections at the various relays in such a way that information about spatial interrelationships is derived with increasing specificity as higher levels are reached. Interference with any of the levels of the visual pathway may lead to visual symptoms and potentially to BLINDNESS.

VISTA, unincorporated urban community in SW Cal., in a truck farm and resort area. Pop 24 688.

VISTULA RIVER, chief river of Poland. Rising in the Carpathians in the SW, it flows 675mi N past Kraków and Warsaw and into the Baltic Sea near Gdańsk.

VITALIAN, Saint, pope 657–672, at a time of conflict over MONOTHELETISM. In 668 he made Theodore of Tarsus archbishop of Canterbury.

VITALISM, the theory, dating from ARISTOTLE, that there is a distinguishing vital principle ("life force") in living organisms that is absent from nonliving objects.

VITAMINS, specific nutrient compounds which are essential for body growth or METABOLISM and which should be supplied by normal DIETARY FOODS. They are denoted by letters and are often divided into fat-soluble (A, D, E and K) and water-soluble (B and C) groups. **Vitamin A** , or **retinol**, is essential for the integrity of EPITHELIUM and its deficiency causes SKIN, EYE and mucous membrane lesions; it is also the precursor for RHODOPSIN, the retinal pigment. Vitamin-A excess causes an acute encephalopathy or chronic multisystem disease. Important members of the **vitamin B** group include thiamine (B_1), riboflavin (B_2), Niacin, Pyridoxine (B_6), Folic acid and cyanocobalamin (B_{12}). **Thiamine** acts as a coenzyme in CARBOHYDRATE metabolism and its deficiency, seen in rice-eating populations and alcoholics, causes BERIBERI and a characteristic encephalopathy. **Riboflavin** is also a coenzyme, active in oxidation reactions; its deficiency causes epithelial lesions. **Niacin** is a general term for nicotinic acid and nicotinamide, which are coenzymes in carbohydrate metabolism; their deficiency occurs in millet- or maize-dependent populations and leads to PELLAGRA. **Pyridoxine** provides an enzyme important in energy storage and its deficiency may cause nonspecific disease or ANEMIA. **Folic acid** is an essential cofactor in NUCLEIC ACID metabolism and its deficiency, which is not uncommon in PREGNANCY and with certain DRUGS, causes a characteristic anemia. **Cyanocobalamin** is essential for all cells, but the development of BLOOD cells and GASTROINTESTINAL-TRACT epithelium and NERVOUS SYSTEM function are particularly affected by its deficiency, which occurs in pernicious ANEMIA and in extreme vegetarians. Pantothenic acid, Biotin, Choline, Inositol and Para-aminobenzoic acid are other members of the B group. **Vitamin C**, or **ascorbic acid**, is involved in many metabolic pathways and has an important role in healing, blood cell formation and bone and tissue growth; SCURVY is its deficiency disease. **Vitamin D**, or **calciferol**, is a crucial factor in CALCIUM metabolism, including the growth and structural maintenance of BONE; lack causes RICKETS, while overdosage also causes disease. **Vitamin E**, or **tocopherol**, appears to play a role in blood cell and nervous system tissues, but its deficiency is uncommon and its beneficial properties have probably been overstated. **Vitamin K** provides essential cofactors for production of certain CLOTTING factors in the LIVER; it is used to treat some clotting disorders, including that seen in premature infants. Vitamin A is derived from both animal and vegetable tissue and most B vitamins are found in green vegetables. though B_{12} is found only in animal food (e.g., liver). Citrus fruit are rich in vitamin C. Vitamin D is found in animal tissues, COD LIVER OIL providing a rich source. Vitamins E and K are found in most biological material.

VITREOUS HUMOR, the jelly-like substance forming much of the inner substrate of the EYE, through which light is transmitted from the lens to the RETINA.

VITRIOL, Oil of, obsolete term for SULFURIC ACID.

VITRUVIUS POLLIO, Marcus (1st century BC), Roman architect, military engineer and author of *On Architecture*, dedicated to AUGUSTUS. This sole surviving Roman work on the subject had an enormous influence on RENAISSANCE architects.

VITTORINO DA FELTRE, real name Vittorino Ramboldini (1378–1446), Italian educator of the early Renaissance. At his boarding school at Mantua, established 1423 on humanist principles, he taught sons of poor as well as of famous rich citizens.

VIVALDI, Antonio (c1680–1741), Venetian composer, notably for the violin. He wrote vocal music, sonatas, some 450 concertos for violin and other instruments (helping establish the three-movement form: see CONCERTO), and *concerti grossi* including the famous *Four Seasons*. His work has a sparkling clarity, strong rhythms, and a wealth of melody.

VIVISECTION, strictly, the dissection of living animals, usually in the course of physiological or pathological research; however, the use of the term is often extended to cover all animal experimentation. Although the practice remains the subject of considerable popular controversy, it is doubtful whether research, particularly medical, can be effectively carried on without a measure of vivisection.

VIZCAYA or Biscaya (Biscay), BASQUE province of N Spain. It is Spain's second-smallest province (853sq mi), but the richest in minerals (iron, copper, marble). Industry, farming, fishing and tourism are important. BILBAO is the seaport capital.

VIZIER (Arabic: *wazir*), title of the chief adviser in the Muslim Abbasid Empire (750–1258), later the title of heads of government departments in the Ottoman Empire.

VIZSLA, or Hungarian pointer, a pointer-like Hungarian sporting dog, graceful but powerful, with a short, smooth rusty gold or yellowish coat. It weighs 40–60lb, stands 19–24in high, and usually has a docked tail.

VLADIMIR, capital of Vladimir oblast, Russian SFSR, USSR, 110mi E of Moscow. Once capital of a principality, it has machinery, textile, and plastics industries, and many historical buildings. Pop 234 000.

VLADIMIR, Saint, or Vladimir I (c956–1015), Russian grand duke of KIEV (c980–1015) who, after successful wars against Bulgars, Byzantines and Lithuanians, became a Christian c988, married Anna, sister of Byzantine Emperor BASIL II, and began the mass conversion of his people to Eastern Orthodox Christianity.

VLADIVOSTOK, capital of Primorski krai, E Russian SFSR, USSR, chief Pacific naval port of Russia, on Peter the Great Bay near North Korea. Founded in 1860, it has shipbuilding, engineering, chemical and fish-canning industries. Pop 442 000.

VLAMINCK, Maurice de (1876–1958), French painter. An admirer of VAN GOGH and a leader of FAUVISM, he evolved an expressionistic style in thickly painted often somber but brilliantly lit landscapes.

VLTAVA RIVER (German, *Moldau*), Czechoslovakia's longest river (267mi). It rises in the SW and flows SE, then N through Prague to the Elbe (Labe) R.

VODKA, a colorless and odorless ALCOHOLIC BEVERAGE made by distilling fermented grain or potatoes. It is a traditional drink in Russia, Poland, and the Baltic. (See DISTILLED LIQUOR.)

VOGT, William (1902–1968), US ecologist and ornithologist. He became (1951) US director of the Planned Parenthood Federation. Among his population and resource studies was *Road to Survival* (1948).

VOICE, the sound emitted in speech (see SPEECH AND SPEECH DISORDERS), the method of communication exclusive to *Homo sapiens*. It is dependent for its generation upon the passage of air from the LUNGS through the TRACHEA, LARYNX, PHARYNX and MOUTH and its quality in each individual is largely determined by the shape and size of these structures and the resonance of the NOSE and nasal SINUSES. Phonation is the sounding of the elements of speech by the action of several small muscles on the vocal cords of the larynx; these regulate the air passing through and vibrate when tensed against this air stream. Articulation consists in the modulation of these sounds by the use of the TONGUE, TEETH and lips in different combinations. Vowels are produced mainly by phonation while consonants derive their characteristics principally from articulation.

VOICE OF AMERICA, the radio division of the United States Information Agency, established 1942 to explain the US role in WWII. Its network now broadcasts, in English and other languages, a favorable view of life in the US to many (chiefly communist) countries.

VOLCANISM, or **vulcanicity**, the processes whereby MAGMA, a complex of molten silicates containing water and other volatiles in solution, rises toward the earth's surface, there forming IGNEOUS ROCKS. These may be extruded on the earth's surface (see LAVA; VOLCANO) or intruded into subsurface rock

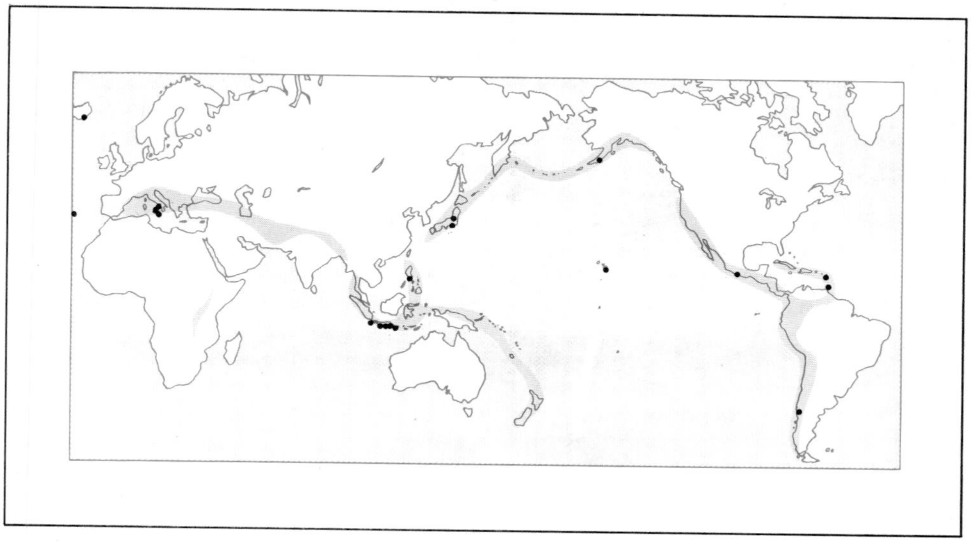

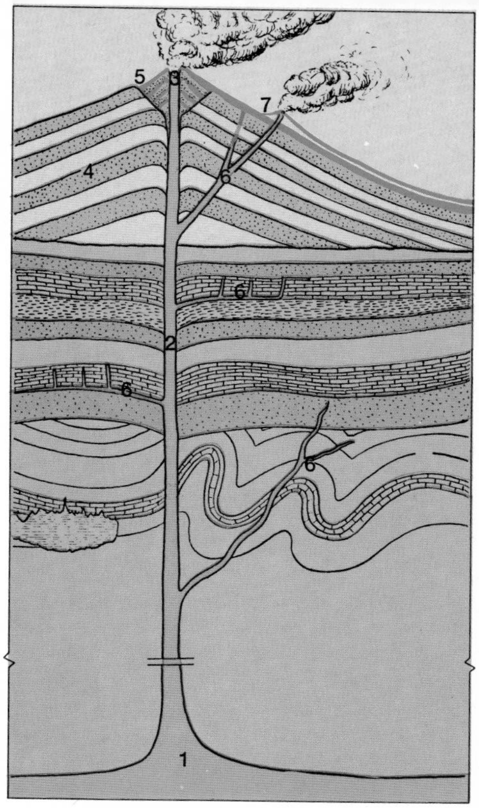

Above: map showing the distribution of the world's major volcanoes in relation to plate margins.

Right: cross section of a stratovolcano. (1) magma; (2) main conduit; (3) main outlet; (4) layers of ash and lava from previous eruptions; (5) large explosion crater, or caldera, partially filled with new volcanic matter; (6) branches of the main conduit; (7) parasitic cone formed by one of these.

Left: inflammable gases gush from a volcanic vent at Pozzuoli, near Naples (and Mount Vesuvius), Italy.

layers as, for example, DIKES, SILLS and LACCOLITHS. (See also FUMAROLE; GEYSER; HOT SPRINGS.)

VOLCANO, fissure or vent in the earth's crust through which MAGMA and associated material may be extruded onto the surface. This may occur with explosive force. The extruded magma, or LAVA, solidifies in various forms soon after exposure to the atmosphere. In particular it does so around the vent, building up the characteristic volcanic cone, at the top of which is a crater containing the main vent. There may be subsidiary vents forming "parasitic cones" in the slopes of the main cone. If the volcano is dormant or extinct the vents may be blocked with a *plug* (or *neck*) of solidified lava. On occasion these are left standing after the original cone has been eroded away. Volcanoes may be classified according to the violence of their eruptions. In order of increasing violence the main types are: Hawaiian, Strombolian, Vulcanian, Vesuvian, Peléan. Volcanoes are generally restricted to belts of seismic activity, particularly active plate margins (see PLATE TECTONICS). At mid-ocean ridges magma rises from deep in the mantle and is added to the receding edges of the plates (see SEA-FLOOR SPREADING). In MOUNTAIN regions, where plates are in collision, volatile matter ascends from the subducted edge of a plate, perhaps many km below the surface, bursting through the overlying plate in a series of volcanoes. (See also EARTHQUAKES.)

VOLCANO ISLANDS, also Kazan Retto or Iwo Retto, the islands IWO JIMA, Kita Iwo and Minami Iwo in the W Pacific S of Bonin Island, part of Japan. They were US-administered 1945–68.

VOLES, mostly small, mouse-like rodents with short tails, which, with the LEMMINGS, constitute the subfamily Microtinae. They are one of the dominant groups of herbivorous mammals in the N Hemisphere. The group includes the Bank voles and Red-backed voles of Eurasia and America, the Field voles, and the Water vole, a large semiaquatic Eurasian species.

VOLGA-BALTIC WATERWAY, in the USSR, 700mi link between the Baltic Sea, via Lakes Ladoga and Onega and Rybinsk reservoir, and the VOLGA RIVER N of Moscow. It is the N part of the world's greatest navigable waterway system.

VOLGA-DON CANAL, a 63mi link between the lower VOLGA RIVER and the Don. It opens up the Volga-Kama-Caspian Sea waterways.

VOLGA RIVER, chief river of Russia and the longest in Europe. It rises in the Valdai Hills NW of Moscow and flows 2293mi through Gorki, Kazan, Kuybyshev, Saratov, Volgograd and Astrakhan to its Caspian Sea delta. Draining an area of some 530000sq mi, it is the main artery of the world's greatest network of commercial waterways linking the White, Baltic, Caspian, Azov and Black seas.

VOLGOGRAD, or (1925–51) Stalingrad or (to 1925) Tsaritsyn, important industrial city on the Volga R, S Russian SFSR, USSR. It was the site of heroic resistance to the Germans in WWII (see STALINGRAD, BATTLE OF). It has iron-and-steel, engineering, chemical, textile and hydroelectricity plants. Pop 818000.

VOLLEYBALL, a popular game for two teams of six, who volley (using any part of the body above the waist) a large inflated ball across a high net, conceding points by failing to return the ball or by hitting it out of court. Invented at the Holyoake (Mass.) YMCA in 1895 by W. G. Morgan, it became an Olympic event at Tokyo (1964).

VOLSTEAD ACT, the United States National Prohibition Act, introduced by Minn. Representative Andrew J. Volstead. Passed in 1919, over the veto of President Wilson, it provided for enforcement of the 18th Amendment prohibiting the sale, manufacture or transportation in the US of intoxicating liquors. It proved unenforceable, and was modified, then repealed, in 1933. (See PROHIBITION).

VÖLSUNGA SAGA, late-13th-century Icelandic prose heroic saga, based partly on heroic lays in the Poetic EDDA. Like the Germanic NIBELUNGENLIED, it recounts the exploits of Sigurd (SIEGFRIED) and the Völsungs. This legendary material inspired WAGNER.

VOLT (V), the SI UNIT of electric POTENTIAL, potential difference, ELECTROMOTIVE FORCE, etc., defined such that ENERGY is dissipated at the rate of one WATT when a one-AMPERE current drops through a potential difference of one volt.

VOLTA, Alessandro Giuseppe Antonio Anastasio (1745–1827), French physicist who invented the voltaic pile (the first BATTERY) and thus provided science with its earliest continuous electric-current source. Volta's invention (c1800) demonstrated that "animal electricity" could be produced using solely inanimate materials, thus ending a long dispute with the supporters of GALVANI's view that it was a special property of animal matter.

(1) The ball, inflated to a diameter of about 27in and weighing 9–10oz, is made of leather with a rubber inner. (2) A full-sized volleyball court, about 60ft long by 30ft wide, is surrounded by a free area of about 6ft. Players' positions are shown in blue and red. (a) Service area (about 10ft wide); (b) back line; (c) attacking line; (d) center line. (3) The 3ft net is 9ft high for men, 7.5ft for women and 7ft or 6.5ft for children, and is 2ft wider than the court at 32ft.

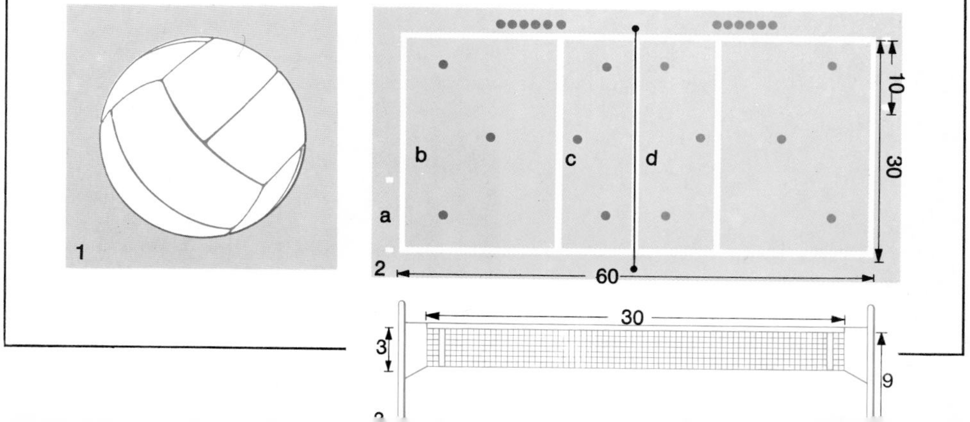

VOLTAIRE (1694–1778), pen name of François-Marie Arouet, French satirist, polemicist, poet, dramatist, novelist, historian and letter-writer, one of the PHILOSOPHES and a genius of the ENLIGHTENMENT. An enemy of tyrants everywhere, he spent much of his life in exile, including 23 years at his property on the Swiss border. His *Letters Concerning the English Nation* (1733) extolled religious and political toleration and the ideas of NEWTON and LOCKE. The famous tale *Candide* (1759), a rational skeptic's attack on the optimism of LEIBNIZ, shows Voltaire's astringent style at its best. A friend of FREDERICK II of Prussia, Voltaire contributed to DIDEROT's *Encyclopedia* and wrote his own *Philosophical Dictionary* (1764).

VOLTA RIVER, chief river system of Ghana, now dammed to form Lake Volta. From the (submerged) junction of the 840mi Black and 450mi White Volta rivers, it flows 290mi S to the Gulf of Guinea.

VOLTMETER, an instrument used to estimate the difference in electrical POTENTIAL between different points in a circuit. Most consist of an AMMETER connected in series with a high RESISTANCE and calibrated in VOLTS. By OHM'S LAW the current flowing is proportional to the potential difference, though the instrument itself inevitably reduces the potential under test. Accurate determinations of potential difference must employ a POTENTIOMETER.

VOLUME, the amount of SPACE occupied by a three-dimensional object. (See MENSURATION.)

VOLUMETRIC ANALYSIS, method of quantitative chemical ANALYSIS in which quantities are measured in terms of volumes, either of solutions or of gases, using apparatus such as the BURETTE, the pipette (a calibrated tube, filled by suction, capable of delivering a known volume of liquid), and the volumetric (calibrated) flask. The chief technique of volumetric analysis is TITRATION; also important is the measurement in a gas burette of the gas produced in a reaction, the weight of one reactant being known.

VOLUNTEERS OF AMERICA, a voluntary philanthropic society founded in New York City (1896) by Ballington and Maud BOOTH after a split with the Salvation Army. Nondenominational, it aims to win converts to Christianity and provides many social services. Though it retains military forms and titles, it is run democratically.

VOMITING, the return of food or other substance (e.g., blood) from the STOMACH. It occurs by reverse PERISTALSIS after closure of the pyloric SPHINCTER and opening of the esophago-gastric junction. It may be induced by DRUGS, MOTION SICKNESS, GASTROENTERITIS or other infection, UREMIA, stomach or pyloric disorders. Morning vomiting may be a feature of early PREGNANCY. Drugs may be needed to control vomiting, and fluid and nutrient replacement may be needed.

VON BÉKÉSY, Georg. See BÉKÉSY, GEORG VON.

VON BRAUN, Wernher. See BRAUN, WERNHER VON.

VONDEL, Joost van den (1587–1679), Dutch national poet. His sonorous verse celebrated the successes of the United Provinces. He translated French, Latin and Greek authors. His dramas, on political, national and religious themes, include *Palamedes* (1625), *Gijsbrecht van Aemstel* (1637) and *Lucifer* (1654).

VONNEGUT, Kurt, Jr. (1922–   ), US novelist noted for his satire and "black humor," with science, religion and war among his targets. His novels, most of which are rooted in science fiction, include *Player Piano* (1951), *The Sirens of Titan* (1959), *God Bless You, Mr. Rosewater* (1965) and the famous *Slaughterhouse-Five* (1969).

VON NEUMANN, John (1903–1957), Hungarian-born US mathematician who contributed to QUANTUM MECHANICS, showing the equivalence of HEISENBERG's matrix mechanics and SCHRÖDINGER's wave mechanics. But his most important work was to formulate GAME THEORY, especially the minimax theorem. He also devised high-speed computers which contributed to the US development of the HYDROGEN BOMB.

VOODOO, a folk religion, chiefly of Haiti, with West African and added Roman Catholic and native West Indian elements. It involves worship of the spirits of saints and ancestors who may "possess" participants. Prayers, drumming, dancing and feasts are part of the ritual. A cult group's priest or priestess is believed to act as a medium, work charms, lay curses and recall zombies (the "living dead").

VOORTREKKERS. See GREAT TREK.

VORARLBERG, westernmost state of Austria, noted for its Alpine scenery and its cotton and lace. Most of the land is pasture and forest. Hydroelectricity powers its many industries. The capital is Bregen.

VORONEZH, seat of Voronezh oblast, Russian SFSR, USSR. It has machine, chemical, radio-TV and nuclear-power plants. Pop 666 000.

VOROSHILOV, Kliment Yefremovich (1881–1969), Ukrainian Russian army and political leader. An early Bolshevik and associate of STALIN (whom he succeeded as head of state, 1953–60), he maintained high rank despite such failures as his WWII Baltic campaign.

VOROSHILOVGRAD, formerly Lugansk, capital of Voroshilovgrad oblast, E Ukrainian SSR, USSR, an industrial city and a center for the DONETS BASIN. Pop 384 000.

VORSTER, Balthazar Johannes (John) (1915–   ), prime minister of South Africa since succeeding VERWOERD in 1966. On the right of the Nationalist Party, he was in charge of education (1958–61), and as minister of justice (1961–66) responsible for some of the most repressive APARTHEID laws. He now seeks to improve relations with Black Africa.

VORTEX, a whirling mass of FLUID such as seen in a TORNADO, a WHIRLPOOL, a smoke ring or water running out of a bath. The term is used in HYDRODYNAMICS for a portion of fluid in which the individual particles have circular motions. A vortex may be produced when two adjacent fluid streams have different velocities or when a solid body moves through a fluid and vortex lines cannot begin or end inside the fluid.

VORTICELLA, a common and conspicuous freshwater ciliate PROTOZOAN, consisting of an inverted bell attached to water plants by a contractile stalk. The mouth of the bell is surrounded by a triple ring of cilia which create a vortex into which food particles are drawn, passing to the mouth region.

VORTICISM, English modern art movement (1914–15) which aimed to produce an energetic and abstract art form. It was led by P. Wyndham LEWIS, editor of *Blast*, and influenced by FUTURISM. Associated were artists GAUDIER-BRZESKA and EPSTEIN and writers Ezra POUND and T. S. ELIOT.

VORTIGERN, 5th-century British king who, according to BEDE, invited HENGIST AND HORSA, leaders of the JUTES, to help subdue the PICTS. After a disagreement the Jutes overran Kent, SE England.

VOSGES MOUNTAINS, low range in E France, running some 130mi N–S to the W of the Rhine R. The rounded hills are mostly forested, with some vineyards.

VOTING, formal collective expression of approval or rejection of a candidate for office or of a course of action. The ELECTION of officers is a basic feature of DEMOCRACY, but universal adult suffrage is recent: US women obtained the vote only in 1920. Sometimes voting is compulsory, as in Australia and in communist states.

In the US, voting originally followed English parliamentary practice, with the addition of the New England TOWN MEETING. Ballot papers first appeared in Mass. in 1634. Most US states now use voting machines to ensure secrecy, speed and accuracy. Voting through INITIATIVE, REFERENDUM AND RECALL is allowed for in many states. (See also POLL, PUBLIC OPINION; PLEBISCITE.)

VOWEL, speech element in whose production breath passes through the mouth with little or no restriction. The mouth, acting as a resonance chamber, alters configuration to form different vowel sounds, assisted by the tongue. In our alphabet there are five vowels (*a*, *e*, *i*, *o*, *u*, with, sometimes, *y*) but these, often compounded, may be used to represent many different vowel sounds.

VOYAGEURS NATIONAL PARK, authorized in 1971, a scenic 219 431-acre park in N Minn., with lakes, forests and interesting glacial features.

VRIES, Hugo de (1848–1935), Dutch botanist who rediscovered the Mendelian laws of inheritance (see HEREDITY) and applied them to C. DARWIN's theory of EVOLUTION in his *Mutation Theory* (1900–1903).

VTOL. See VERTICAL TAKEOFF AND LANDING AIRPLANE.

VUILLARD, Jean Édouard (1868–1940), French painter known particularly for his intimate and richly decorative interior domestic scenes. He was influenced by Japanese art and was a member of the NABIS group in Paris at the turn of the century.

VULCAN, Roman counterpart of HEPHAESTUS, Greek god of fire.

VULCANIZATION, the compounding of raw RUBBER with SULFUR so that it retains its shape and strength over a wide range of temperatures.

VULCANO. See LIPARI ISLANDS.

VULGATE, the Latin version of the BIBLE, so-called because it became the most widespread (Latin, *vulgata*) in use. Largely the work of St. JEROME, who revised earlier Old Latin translations, it was collected together in the 6th century and universally established by 800. In 1546 the Council of TRENT confirmed the Vulgate as the sole official version of the Roman Catholic Church.

VULTURES, two groups of large, soaring, diurnal BIRDS OF PREY. The New World vultures are a primitive family, Cathartidae; the Old World vultures are a branch of the Accipitridae, being most closely related to certain EAGLES. All vultures are adapted to feed on animal carrion. Their heads and necks are wholly or partially naked; several have specialized tongues to feed rapidly on liquid flesh or bone marrow.

(1) The Egyptian vulture, *Neophron percnopterus*, is one of the best-known Old World varieties. (2) The California condor, *Gymnogyps californianus*, one of the larger New World vultures.

W

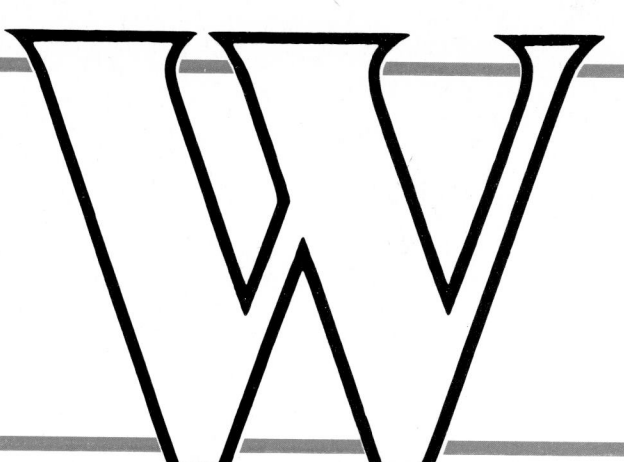

W, the 23rd letter of the English alphabet, originally (as the name indicates) a "double U." The form "uu," appearing in the earliest Old English texts, was replaced by the letter *wen* (ƿ) in the 700s, but reinstated by French-speaking scribes after the NORMAN CONQUEST (1066).

WAALS, Johannes Diderik Van der. See VAN DER WAALS, JOHANNES DIDERIK.

WABASH, city in N Ind., seat of Wabash Co. In an agricultural area, it has electrical and other light industries. Pop 13379.

WABASH, chief river of Ind., a tributary of the Ohio. Rising in Grand Lake, W Ohio, it runs 475mi through Ind., the last 200mi forming the state boundary with Ill.

WABASH CASE (Wabash, St. Louis and Pacific Railroad Co. *v.* Illinois, 1886), case in which the US Supreme Court ruled that states have no power to regulate interstate railroad traffic because the Constitution reserved control of INTER-STATE COMMERCE to Congress.

WAC. See WOMEN'S ARMY CORPS.

WACO, city in E Tex., seat of McLennan Co. on the Brazos R. A major commercial and industrial center, it has many attractive areas. Pop 95326.

WADDINGTON, Conrad Hall (1905–1975), British biologist and philosopher of science. His most important work was in embryology and genetics, and as a popular writer of books such as *Evolution of an Evolutionist* (1975).

WADE, Benjamin Franklin (1800–1878), US lawyer and senator from Ohio 1851–69, chairman of the committee on the conduct of the war during the Civil War. An ardent advocate of RECONSTRUCTION, he was co-author of the WADE-DAVIS BILL and Manifesto (1864).

WADE-DAVIS BILL, plan for RECONSTRUCTION produced by the Congressional committee on the conduct of the Civil War in 1864, named for senators B. F. WADE and H. W. DAVIS. President LINCOLN vetoed it.

WADI, or **arroyo,** stream-bed through which water flows only occasionally, found mainly in semiarid areas. Such **ephemeral streams** can swiftly erode quite deep, flat-bottomed gullies (see EROSION).

WADSWORTH, industrial city in NE Ohio, a suburb of Akron. Pop 13142.

WAF. See WOMEN IN THE AIR FORCE.

WAGE AND PRICE CONTROL, in economics, policy of countering INFLATION by government controls on the separate but interdependent movements of PRICES and wages. The policy may contain percentage or flat-rate limits on increases, and is sometimes preceded by a "freeze" or standstill period. The policy may be legally binding, or voluntary with back-up powers of government intervention. It usually entails a system of notification of price or wage increases. Its use has increased in Western countries since the 1960s.

WAGE-FUND THEORY, in classical economics, theory developed by Adam SMITH, following the PHYSIOCRATS, which tried to show that where wages were advanced to workers at the beginning of the production process, wages could be increased only when capital is increased, with capital in turn dependent on the level of SAVINGS.

WAGES AND HOURS ACT (1938). See FAIR LABOR STANDARDS ACT.

WAGNER, Honus (John Peter Wagner; 1874–1955), US baseball player, one of the greatest shortstops. He played for the Pittsburgh Pirates for 21 years and was their coach for another 19. He was elected to the Baseball Hall of Fame in 1936.

WAGNER, Richard (1813–1883), major German opera composer. His adventurous and influential works mark the high point of Romanticism in music. A conductor in provincial opera houses, he achieved his first success with *Rienzi* (1840). *The Flying Dutchman* (1841), *Tannhäuser* (1844) and *Lohengrin* (1848) pioneered his new ideas in music and drama (see OPERA); these were fulfilled in the myth-cycle *The Ring of the Nibelung*, consisting of *The Rhinegold* (1854), *The Valkyrie* (1856), *Siegfried* (1956–69) and *The Twilight of the Gods* (1874). Involved in the 1848 Dresden revolution, Wagner fled to Switzerland, where he wrote *Tristan and Isolde* (1859) and the comedy *The Mastersingers of Nuremberg* (1867). Ludwig II of Bavaria helped him found the BAYREUTH Festival. *Parsifal* (1882) was his last opera. In private life Wagner was often self-centered and bigoted.

WAGNER, Robert Ferdinand (1877–1953), German-born US reforming politician. After serving as a N.Y. senator (1910–18) and justice (1919–26), he became a Democratic US senator (1927–49), and helped create the NEW DEAL program, particularly in labor, social security and housing (see WAGNER ACT).

WAGNER, Robert Ferdinand, Jr. (1910–), US politician and administrator. Son of R. F. WAGNER, he held posts in New York (1938–41, 1946–53), and served three terms as mayor (1954–65), introducing controversial reforms in housing, education and civil rights. He was US ambassador to Spain 1968–69.

WAGNER ACT, popular name for the National Labor Relations Act, a key part of the NEW DEAL legislation, enacted in July, 1935. Sponsored by R. F. WAGNER, it guaranteed workers the right to organize and bargain collectively, and defined some unfair labor practices. It also set up the NATIONAL LABOR RELATIONS BOARD.

WAGNER VON JAUREGG (or Wagner-Jauregg), Julius (1857–1940), Austrian psychologist and neurologist awarded the 1927 Nobel Prize for Physiology or Medicine for his discovery that innoculation with MALARIA markedly improved the condition of sufferers from general PARESIS, hitherto fatal.

WAGRAM, Battle of, fought near Vienna between the Austrians and the French on July 5–6, 1809, during the NAPOLEONIC WARS. NAPOLEON was victorious and forced Austria to sign an armistice.

WAGTAILS, small birds, family Motacillidae, deriving their name from their habit of flicking their long tails up and down as they stand or walk. They are generally found near water.

WAHABI, a Muslim reform movement begun in 18th-century Arabia. It aimed to restore ISLAM to its primitive simplicity, and its influence spread as far as Africa and Sumatra. In Arabia the movement followed the fortunes of the royal family, becoming firmly established under IBN SAUD.

WAHIAWA, city on Oahu Island, Hawaii. It is a pineapple-shipping center, with a US Air Force base nearby. Pop 17598.

WAHOO, or Peto, *Acanthocybium solandri*, a fast-swimming oceanic fish related to TUNA. A stream-lined fish with a cigar-shaped body up to 55kg (121lb) in weight, the wahoo is a tropical species feeding on squids and other fishes.

WAIKIKI BEACH, seaside resort area on Oahu Island, Hawaii. It is lined with luxury hotels and famous for its surfing.

WAILING WALL, part of the western wall of the ancient Temple in Jerusalem, destroyed by the Romans in 70 AD. It is held sacred by the Jews, who gather there to pray and bewail their sufferings. Until the 1967 Arab-Israeli War, it was in Jordanian territory.

Jews praying at the Wailing Wall, Jerusalem.

WAINWRIGHT, Jonathan Mayhew (1883–1953), US general, veteran of WWI and hero of BATAAN and CORREGIDOR in the defense of the Philippines during WWII. Despite great courage in a hopeless situation, he had to surrender to the Japanese in 1942. A prisoner of war until 1945, he was awarded the Congressional Medal of Honor on his return.

WAIPAHU, city on S Oahu Island, Hawaii, on the NW shore of PEARL HARBOR. Pop 24150.

WAITE, Morrison Remick (1816–1888), US lawyer, chief justice of the US Supreme Court 1874–88. He first gained prominence in the ALABAMA CLAIMS dispute (1871–72). His most influential opinions concerned STATES' RIGHTS and the interpretation of the Fourteenth Amendment.

WAKAYAMA, city in S Honshū, Japan, 35mi SW of Osaka. Capital of Wakayama prefecture, it has textile and lacquerware industries. Pop 365267.

WAKEFIELD, town in NE Mass. It is a residential suburb of Boston, with some light industry, including footwear. Pop 25402.

WAKE ISLAND, atoll in the central Pacific Ocean, an unincorporated territory of the US. An important commercial and military airbase, it consists of three islets (Wake, Wilkes and Peale), a total of 3sq mi, around a shallow lagoon. It was occupied by Japan 1941–45.

WAKSMAN, Selman Abraham (1888–1973), Russian-born US biochemist, microbiologist and soil scientist. His isolation of STREPTOMYCIN, the first specific antibiotic (a term he coined) against TUBERCULOSIS, won him the 1952 Nobel Prize for Physiology or Medicine.

WALACHIA, or Wallachia, most prosperous region of Romania, between the Danube and the Transylvanian Alps, with rich agriculture, oilfields and industry centered on Bucharest. Formerly independent, it was united 1861–62 with MOLDAVIA to form modern Romania.

WALCOTT, Jersey Joe (1914–), US boxer who was the oldest fighter in modern times to win the world heavyweight championship when he knocked out Ezzard Charles in 1951. He lost the title in 1952 to Rocky MARCIANO.

WALD, George (1906–), US chemist and prominent pacifist whose work on the chemistry of VISION brought him a share, with HARTLINE and GRANIT, of the 1967 Nobel Prize for Physiology or Medicine.

WALD, Lillian D. (1867–1940), US nurse and social worker who pioneered public health nursing. In 1893 she founded the famous Henry Street Settlement in New York, and in 1902 began the city's public school nursing. She also helped establish the Federal Children's Bureau in 1912.

WALDEN POND, small pond near Concord, NE Mass., made famous by Henry THOREAU, who lived on its shore 1845–47.

WALDENSES, a reforming Christian sect founded in Lyons, France, in the 12th century. They preached poverty, rejected the PAPACY and took the Bible as their sole authority, for which they were excommunicated (1184) and persecuted. The survivors united with the Protestants in the REFORMATION. The Waldensian Church still exists, with several offshoots in the US.

WALDHEIM, Kurt (1918–), Austrian diplomat and minister of foreign affairs (1968–70), from 1972 secretary general of the UNITED NATIONS. He worked especially to strengthen the UN's peacekeeping role and increase aid to poor countries.

WALDSEEMÜLLER, Martin (c1470–1518), German cartographer who in 1507 published the first map showing the New World as a separate continent. He named it "America" in honor of Amerigo VESPUCCI, on whose discoveries the map was based.

WALDWICK, borough in NE N.J., 7mi N of Paterson. It is a residential suburb of New York. Pop 12,313.

WALES, historic principality of GREAT BRITAIN, politically united with England since 1536. It is a large roughly rectangular peninsula projecting into the Irish Sea W of England. Covering 8 016sq mi, it is dominated by the Cambrian Mts (Snowdon, 3 560ft). Rivers include the Severn, Wye, Usk, Taff and Teifi. The climate is mild and wet. The population (2 729 596) live mainly in the S near the rich coalfields. About 20% speak both WELSH and English. The largest cities are Cardiff, the capital, and Swansea. Major industries, including coalmining, steel, oil-refining, man-made fibers and electronics, are concentrated in the S. Agriculture, mostly cattle and sheep raising, predominates elsewhere. Limited independence has been proposed to meet the demands of the Welsh nationalist movement (Plaid Cymru).

WALES, Prince of, the title bestowed on the eldest son of the British sovereign. It was first used by EDWARD I (1301), after he had killed the last Welsh prince, for his newborn son. Prince Charles holds the title at present.

WALKER, city in W Mich., 6mi W of Grand Rapids. It is primarily residential. Pop 11 492.

WALKER, Francis Amasa (1840–1897), US economist and statistician. He directed the 1870 and 1880 US censuses and was president of Massachusetts Institute of Technology 1881–97. He wrote *The Wages Question* (1876) and advocated BIMETALLISM.

WALKER, James John (1881–1946), New York politician. A member (1915–20) and minority leader (1921–25) of the state Senate, he became Democratic mayor of New York (1926–32), instituting popular reforms. He resigned in a corruption scandal.

WALKER, Joseph Reddeford (1798–1876), US trapper and guide. He explored the Rockies with BONNEVILLE (1832) and guided expeditions to California (1845–46, 1849, 1861–62). Walker Lake and Pass are named for him.

WALKER, Mary Edwards (1832–1919), US surgeon and feminist, the first woman to be commissioned a surgeon in the Union army (1864). Later she practiced in Washington D.C. and campaigned for women's rights.

WALKER, Robert John (1801–1869), US politician. Senator for Miss. 1836–45, he became an able secretary of the treasury (1845–49) and US financial agent in Europe (1863–64). An ardent expansionist, he was governor of Kan. 1857–58.

WALKER, William (1824–1860), US adventurer. He tried to create a republic out of Lower Cal. and Sonora, Mexico (1853–54), then joined a revolution in Nicaragua, becoming president 1856–57. Ousted partly by VANDERBILT interests, but regarded by many as a hero, he was captured by the British and shot in attempting to regain Nicaragua.

WALKER LAKE, salt lake in W central Nev., covering c105sq mi. Part of Lake LAHONTAN, it has no outlet.

WALKIE-TALKIE, portable two-way RADIO frequently used by policemen, sportsmen and others on the move to communicate over distances up to a few km. In the US, walkie-talkies operate on one or more of 23 channels lying between 26.960 and 27.255MHz.

WALKING PURCHASE, fraud perpetrated by William PENN's son Thomas on the Delaware Indians in 1737. Claiming that in 1686 the Indians had agreed to sell as much land as a man could walk in 1½ days, he employed champion runners who covered 66½ miles and gained him ½ million acres. William Penn's 1682 walking purchase is a fiction.

WALKING STICKS, or **Stick Insects,** a group of insects related to the LEAF INSECTS, and sharing with them specialized camouflage. Sticks take their name from the long, slender body, green or brown in color, which resembles a knotted twig. The legs are very long and thin and are folded motionless against the body when the insect is disturbed.

WALLABIES, a large and diverse assemblage of kangaroo-like MARSUPIALS, generally smaller than true KANGAROOS, but like them in having large strong hindfeet and limbs and a long tail. They are herbivorous animals of Australia, Tasmania and New Guinea. All wallabies produce a single young, suckling it in the marsupium or pouch.

WALLACE, Alfred Russel (1823–1913), British socialist naturalist regarded as the father of ZOOGEOGRAPHY. His most striking work was his formulation, independently of C. DARWIN, of the theory of NATURAL SELECTION as a mechanism for the origin of species (see EVOLUTION). He and Darwin presented their results in a joint paper in 1858 before the Linnean Society.

WALLACE, George Corley (1919–), US politician and segregationist governor of Ala. 1963–67, 1971– . He served in the state legislature 1946–58, and achieved notoriety in 1963 by his stand against racial integration at the University of Alabama. He ran for president as an independent in 1968, and was paralyzed in an attempted assassination while campaigning for the Democratic nomination in 1972. His 1976 campaign came to little owing to Jimmy CARTER's successes in the South.

WALLACE, Henry Agard (1888–1965), 33rd Vice-President of the US (1941–45). A distinguished agricultural economist and plant geneticist, he was appointed secretary of agriculture in 1933. His success with NEW DEAL farm programs led to the vice-presidency. He became secretary of commerce (1945), but was dismissed in 1946 for criticizing TRUMAN. He stood in 1948 as candidate for the PROGRESSIVE PARTY.

WALLACE, Lew (1827–1905), US author, soldier and diplomat, known for his best-selling novel *Ben Hur* (1880). He served in the Mexican and Civil Wars, became Governor of N.M. (1878–81) and minister to Turkey (1881–85).

Statue of George Washington, on Wall Street, New York, erected on the spot where he was inaugurated as president in 1789, looks over to the neo-classical facade of the New York Stock Exchange, heart of this world-famous street.

WALLACE, Sir William (c1272–1305), Scottish national hero who led the rebellion against the English King EDWARD I. Victor at Stirling Bridge (1297), he was defeated at Falkirk (1298) and fled to Europe to rally support for the Scottish cause. Back in Scotland by 1304, he was captured in 1305 and executed for treason.

WALLACH, Otto (1847–1931), Russian-born German experimental organic chemist awarded the 1910 Nobel Prize for Chemistry for his analysis of the structures of the TERPENES.

WALLACHIA. See WALACHIA.

WALLAROOS, or Hill kangaroos, a number of species, or races, of KANGAROOS, distinguished from the remainder in having no hair between the nostrils.

WALLA WALLA, city in SE Wash., seat of Walla Walla Co. Center of an agricultural region, it produces processed foods and paper. Pop 23 619.

WALLENSTEIN, Albrecht Wenzel Eusebius von (1583–1634), general in the THIRTY YEARS' WAR. He rose to supreme command under FERDINAND II (1625) and achieved spectacular military success until the German princes, jealous of his power and ambition, forced his dismissal in 1630. Reinstated in 1632 but defeated at LÜTZEN, he intrigued secretly and was murdered as a traitor.

WALLER, Edmund (1606–1687), English poet and politician. His polished love poems and his panegyrics on both Cromwell and Charles II helped establish the heroic couplet as a standard poetic form.

WALLER, Thomas "Fats" (1904–1943), US jazz pianist and composer. Original and influential, he made hundreds of popular recordings and wrote such songs as *Ain't Misbehavin'* and *Honeysuckle Rose*.

WALLEYE, a pike perch, *Stizostedion vitreum*, of the US and Canada, taking its name from the blind, opaque appearance of its eyes. Like most other pike perches, it is a freshwater fish—a true PERCH though resembling the PIKES in appearance.

WALLFLOWER, *Cheiranthus cheiri*, a popular spring-flowering garden plant, native to S Europe, normally grown as a biennial, but in favorable conditions a perennial. Family: Cruciferae.

WALLINGFORD, town in S Conn. Well known for its silverware, it also produces steel, plastics, precision instruments and clothing. Pop 35 714.

WALLINGTON, borough in NE N.J., on the Passaic R. Its manufactures include paints, chemicals and textiles. Pop 10 284.

WALLIS, Sir Barnes Neville (1887–), British aeronautics engineer who designed the Wellington bomber and the skipping bomb used by the Dam Busters in WWII. He later devised the swing-wing principle used in some supersonic military airplanes.

WALLIS, John (1616–1703), British mathematician and cryptographer whose *Arithmetica infinitorum* (Arithmetic of Infinities, 1655) laid the foundations for much of modern algebra, introducing the concept of the LIMIT and the symbol ∞ for INFINITY. From this work were later developed CALCULUS and the BINOMIAL THEOREM.

WALLIS AND FUTUNA ISLANDS, French territory (64sq mi) in the SW Pacific Ocean, about

250mi W of Samoa, comprising three islands and numerous islets. The economy depends on taro, yams, fish and the export of copra and timber. Pop 8 546.

WALLOONS, the French-speakers of the S half of BELGIUM. There has long been friction between them and the Flemish-speaking majority, who have resented French political and cultural domination. Separate regional administrations were set up in 1974.

WALLOPS ISLAND, 6sq mi island in the Atlantic off the Va. coast, used as a rocket-launching base.

WALL STREET, the financial center of the US, in Lower Manhattan, New York, the home of the New York Stock Exchange, many other commodity exchanges and head offices of banks, insurance and brokerage firms.

WALNUT, trees of the genus *Juglans*, prized for the wood and nuts. In the US, the black walnut (*Juglans nigra*) grows to 45m (150ft), its wood being used for high-class furniture and gun stocks. The English walnut (*J. regia*), providing edible walnuts, is naturalized throughout the world. Family: Juglandaceae.

WALNUT CANYON NATIONAL MONUMENT, covering 1 879 acres in N central Ariz. It contains over 400 cliff-dwellings of the Sinagua Indians dating from 1000–1200 AD.

WALNUT CREEK, city in W Cal. It processes foods, including walnuts, and has electronics and industrial research establishments. Pop 39 844.

WALPOLE, industrial town in E Mass. Manufactures include paper and textiles. Pop 18 149.

WALPOLE, Horace, 4th Earl of Orford (1717–1797), son of Sir Robert, English novelist, letter-writer and connoisseur. His *Castle of Otranto* (1765) was the first GOTHIC NOVEL; and his famous villa, Strawberry Hill, helped stimulate the GOTHIC REVIVAL. Over 3 000 of his letters survive.

WALPOLE, Sir Robert (1676–1745), English statesman often described as Britain's first prime minister. A WHIG, he held ministerial posts 1708–17. Recalled after the SOUTH SEA BUBBLE to be first lord of the Treasury and chancellor of the Exchequer (1721), he dominated Parliament, creating political and financial stability. Facing opposition and unpopularity as Britain became involved in European wars from 1739, he resigned in 1742, becoming 1st Earl of Orford.

WALPURGIS NIGHT, the night of Apr. 30/May 1 when, according to central European legend, witches assembled on mountaintops to consort with the devil. Of ancient pagan origin, it has been mistakenly associated with 8th-century German St. Walburga.

WALRUSES, two subspecies of seal-like marine mammals, *Odobenus rosmarus*, distinguished by having the upper canines extended into long tusks which in a mature adult may reach 1m (3.3ft). Walruses are found in shallow water around Arctic coasts, often hauling out onto rocks or ice floes to bask. They feed almost exclusively on mollusks.

WALSH, Thomas James (1859–1933), US politician. Democratic senator from Mont., he advocated arms limitation, fought against child labor and exposed the ELK HILLS and TEAPOT DOME scandals. He died before taking office as attorney general.

WALSINGHAM, Sir Francis (c1530–1590), English statesman, ELIZABETH I's secretary of state 1573–90. A skillful diplomat, he created an intelligence system which exposed several plots against Elizabeth, secured MARY QUEEN OF SCOTS' downfall and gained advance knowledge of the ARMADA.

WALTER, Bruno (Bruno Walter Schlesinger; 1876–1962), German-born US conductor. A protegé of Gustav MAHLER's, his career in Europe was cut short by the Nazis, and he lived in the US from 1939. He was renowned for his interpretations of Mahler, Wagner, Beethoven and Brahms.

WALTER, Thomas Ustick (1804–1887), US architect, known for his pure classical style. He designed Girand College, Philadelphia (1833–47), and as government architect (1851–65) he added the dome and wings to the Capitol in Washington, D.C.

WALTHAM, city in E Mass., a suburb of Boston. Known as a watchmaking center from 1854, it now manufactures electronic components and precision instruments. Pop 61 582.

WALTHER VON DER VOGELWEIDE (c1170–c1230), most famous of the German MINNESINGERS. He wandered from court to court, until granted a fief by Emperor FREDERICK II. Apart from love poems, he composed political and religious poetry.

WALTON, Ernest Thomas Sinton (1903–), Irish nuclear physicist who shared with COCKCROFT the 1951 Nobel Prize for Physics for their development of the first particle ACCELERATOR, using which they initiated the first nuclear FISSION reaction using nonradioactive substances.

WALTON, Izaak (1593–1683), English writer remembered for *The Compleat Angler* (1653), a series of dialogues on the art of fishing which also praise the peaceful and simple life. He wrote biographies of friends he admired, like John DONNE.

WALTON, Sir William Turner (1902–), English composer. His music for Edith SITWELL's *Façade* (1923) shot him to fame. Other works include the oratorio *Belshazzar's Feast* (1931), film scores, notably for Shakespeare films, and the opera *Troilus and Cressida* (1954).

WALTZ, dance with three beats to the bar, originating from the LÄNDLER. Its popularity in the 19th century was due largely to the music of the STRAUSS family.

WALVIS BAY, bay in South West Africa; also the name of the town and surrounding territory (434sq mi), an exclave of South Africa. It is a fishing center and chief port for South West Africa.

WAMPANOAG INDIANS, North American Indians of the ALGONQUIAN language family, who lived E of Narragansett Bay. Their chief, MASSASOIT, made friends with the Pilgrim Fathers (1620). His son was the leader during KING PHILIP's WAR (1675), after which the tribe was virtually exterminated.

WAMPUM, strings of shell beads prized by North American Indians, who used them as money in trading. The early white settlers also accepted them as currency, but the production of counterfeit glass beads undermined their value in the early 18th century.

WANAMAKER, John (1838–1922), US businessman whose department stores pioneered advertising techniques and staff welfare and training schemes. He was postmaster general 1889–93.

WANDERING JEW, according to a legend first recorded in the 13th century, a Jew who taunted Jesus on the way to Calvary and who was doomed to wander the world until Jesus returned.

WANDERING JEW, or striped inch plant, several trailing plants that are grown indoors for their flowers and foliage. *Tradescantia fluminensis variegata* has green leaves, irregularly striped with white; *Callisia elegans* has green leaves with white pinstripes, and *Zebrina pendula* has purple, green and silver striped leaves. They grow best in sunny windows, and the growing tips should be pinched out to maintain bushy growth. The soil should be kept evenly moist. They survive temperatures as low as 13°C (55°F). They are extremely easy to propagate by taking cuttings and rooting them in water and wet sand. Family: Commelinaceae. (See also SPIDERWORT.)

WANG WEI (699–759), Chinese painter and poet. He is traditionally the originator of the monochrome ink-wash technique and founder of the renowned "Southern" School of landscape painting. His poetry and painting are imbued with a personal feeling for the beauty of nature.

WANKEL ENGINE, INTERNAL COMBUSTION ENGINE that produces rotary motion directly. Invented by the German engineer Felix Wankel (1902–), who completed his first design in 1954, it is now widely used in automobiles and airplanes. A triangular rotor with spring-loaded sealing plates at its apexes rotates eccentrically inside a cylinder, while the three combustion chambers formed between the sides of the rotor and the walls of the cylinder successively draw in, compress and ignite a fuel-and-air mixture. The Wankel engine is simpler in principle, more efficient and more powerful weight for weight, but more difficult to cool, than a conventional reciprocating engine.

WANTAGH, unincorporated urban community in SE N.J., on the S shore of Long Island. It is mainly residential. Pop 21 873.

WAPITI, the North American subspecies of the RED DEER, *Cervus elephas*. It differs from the typical European red deer in being larger and in that the terminal points to the antlers are in the same plane as the beam and do not form a "crown." Wapiti, once the most abundant deer in North America, are now severely reduced in numbers and range.

WAPPINGER CONFEDERACY, union of ALGONQUIN INDIANS, who occupied the area between the lower Connecticut and Hudson rivers. They included the Wappinger, Siwanoy, Tankiteke and Weckquaesgeek groups. Their power was destroyed by the Dutch (1640–45).

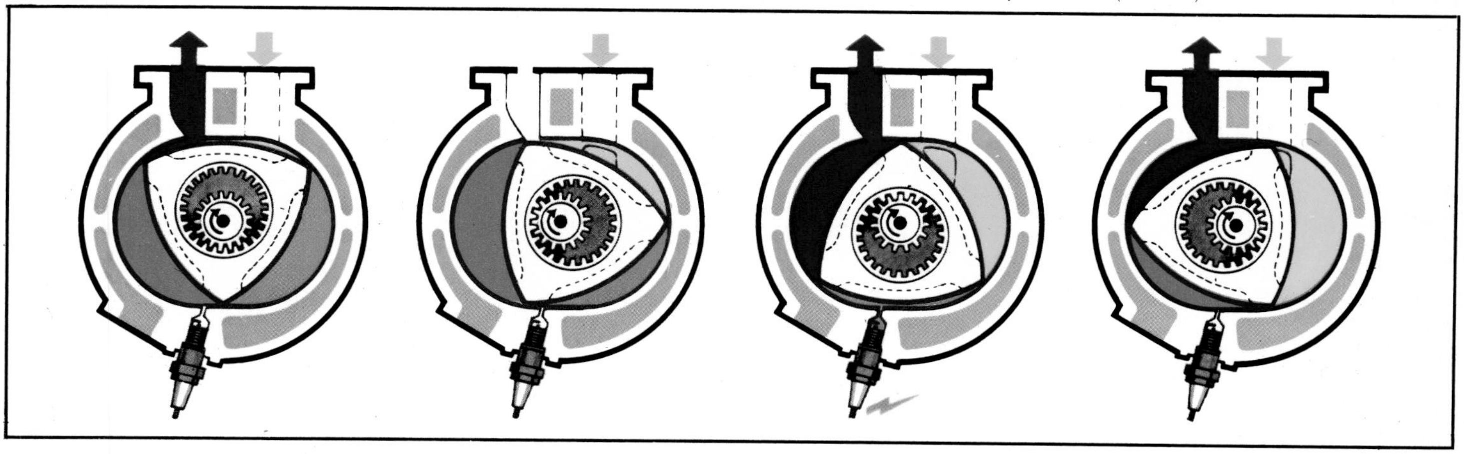

The Wankel engine cycle: suction (yellow), compression (orange), power (red), and exhaust (brown) phases in the four-stroke cycle. The phases occur simultaneously as the size of the three chambers is increased and decreased by the action of the triangular rotor on the walls of the cylinder.

WAR, organized armed conflict between groups of people or states. War is not found elsewhere in the animal kingdom. Since recorded history began, man has been involved in hostility, for different aims: power, territory, wealth, ideological domination, security, independence. Until modern times, most wars were fought with limited means for limited aims, but the modern weapons of mass destruction and total warfare can eliminate whole populations and endanger the survival of the human race. (See AIR FORCE; ARMY; GENEVA CONVENTIONS; GUERRILLA WARFARE; NAVY; NUCLEAR WARFARE; STRATEGY; WAR CRIMES.)

WARANGAL, city in S central India, an administrative and commercial center with textile and carpet industries. Pop 207 130.

WARBECK, Perkin (c1474–1499), Flemish-born pretender to the throne of England who, with Yorkist support, claimed to be a son of EDWARD IV (see ROSES, WARS OF THE). After a second attempt to invade England (1497), he was captured and imprisoned in the Tower of London. In 1498 he escaped but was recaptured and hanged (1499).

WAR BETWEEN THE STATES. See CIVIL WAR, AMERICAN.

WARBLE FLIES, or Gadflies, a family, Oestridae, of two-winged FLIES, resembling small bumblebees, which lay their eggs in the skin of cattle. The larvae, developing under the skin, form infected cysts and make the hide useless for LEATHER manufacture.

WARBLERS, small perching birds related to THRUSHES and FLYCATCHERS. Almost all have thin, pointed bills and they are mainly insectivorous. While some, tropical, species are brightly-colored, most are olive or brown. The common name refers to the melodious songs produced by many of the species.

WARBURG, Otto Heinrich (1883–1970), German biochemist awarded the 1931 Nobel Prize for Physiology or Medicine for his work elucidating the chemistry of cell RESPIRATION.

WAR CRIMES, in INTERNATIONAL LAW, the violation of the laws and rules of WAR. The first systematic attempt to frame laws for warfare was by GROTIUS (1625). Since 1864 various agreements have laid down principles for the treatment of combatants and civilians, and attempted to outlaw certain weapons (see GENEVA CONVENTIONS; HAGUE PEACE CONFERENCES; KELLOGG-BRIAND PACT).

Few have been convicted of war crimes. A Confederate officer, Henry WIRZ, was executed in 1865. An attempt was made to try the Kaiser after WWI, and some German officers were tried (mostly acquitted) by a German court. The only major war-crimes trial has been the NUREMBERG TRIALS. Here three categories of war crime were defined: crimes against peace (planning and waging aggressive war); "conventional" war crimes (murder of civilians or prisoners of war, plunder etc.); and crimes against humanity (murder, enslavement or deportation of whole populations). The principle of individual responsibility was also established. (See also MY LAI.)

WARD, an electoral and administrative unit in urban areas. In the US, most cities are divided into wards often subdivided into precincts. Each ward elects a representative to the city government.

WARD, Aaron Montgomery (1843–1913), US businessman. In 1872, with a capital of $2400, he started up the mail-order firm which became the vast house of Montgomery Ward & Co.

WARD, Artemas (1727–1800), American leader in the REVOLUTIONARY WAR. As governor of Massachusetts (1774–75), he besieged Boston until WASHINGTON arrived, and was second in command of the Continental Army 1775–76. He served in Congress 1791–95.

WARD, Artemus (1834–1867), pen-name of Charles Farrar Browne, US journalist and humorist. The character of Artemus Ward, an irreverent traveling showman, became a household name for his pungent and comically ungrammatical comments. Browne also became a popular lecturer.

WARD, Lester Frank (1831–1913), US sociologist and paleontologist. A fervent evolutionist, he pioneered US sociology with such works as *Dynamic Sociology* (1883), *The Psychic Factors of Civilization* (1893) and *Glimpses of the Cosmos* (6 vols., 1913–1918).

WARD, Nathaniel (c1578–1652), English Puritan clergyman who came to Mass. in 1634 and helped draft New England's first law code, the Body of Liberties (1641). Returning to England (1646), he published a satire, *The Simple Cobbler of Aggawam* (1647).

WAR DEBTS. See REPARATIONS.

WAR DEPARTMENT, former executive department of the US government, reconstituted in 1947 as the Department of the Army, a branch of the US Department of DEFENSE. It was first set up in 1789 to supervise the nation's military establishment, and also ran the Navy until 1798. It was headed by a civilian secretary who was automatically a member of the president's cabinet. After 1947, the secretary of war lost his cabinet post and became secretary of the army, responsible to the new secretary of defense.

WAREHAM, town in SE Mass., a summer seaside resort and shipping center for shellfish and cranberries. Pop 11 492.

WARFARIN, a derivative of coumarin used as an ANTICOAGULANT and hence also to kill rodents by causing internal bleeding. However, warfarin-resistant races of rodents have developed in some areas.

WAR HAWKS, group of expansionist US Congressmen who in 1810–12 helped precipitate the WAR OF 1812. Mostly Southerners and Westerners, they hoped to remove British hindrance to expansion in the Northwest and gain Florida from Spain, Britain's ally.

WARHOL, Andy (1930?–), US artist and filmmaker, famous for his POP ART paintings. His highly innovative, often erotic and often lengthy films include *Chelsea Girls* (1966) and *Lonesome Cowboys* (1969).

WARM-BLOODED ANIMALS, or Homoiotherms, animals whose body TEMPERATURE is not dependent on external temperature but is maintained at a constant level by internally-generated metabolic heat. This constant temperature enables the chemical processes of the body, many of them temperature-dependent, to be more efficient. Modern animals which have developed this homoiothermy are the MAMMALS and BIRDS, and it is now believed that PTERODACTYLS, THERAPSIDS, and many other extinct REPTILES may also have been warm-blooded.

WARM SPRINGS, health resort in W Ga., the site of the Warm Springs Foundation, established by F. D. ROOSEVELT in 1927 for the treatment of poliomyelitis sufferers. Pop 523.

WARNER, Charles Dudley (1829–1900), US journalist and author, known for his collections of essays and travel pieces, and for his collaboration with Mark TWAIN, *The Gilded Age* (1873).

WARNER, Glenn Scobey (1871-1954), known as "Pop Warner," US law graduate and famous college football coach, credited with perfecting the single and double wing formations and several other offensive moves.

WARNER, Seth (1743–1784), a hero of the American REVOLUTIONARY WAR and a leader of the GREEN MOUNTAIN BOYS. He helped capture Fort TICONDEROGA, took CROWN POINT (1775) and was largely responsible for the American victory at BENNINGTON (1777).

WARNER ROBINS, city in central Ga. It has grown since the establishment (1943) of Robins Air Force Base nearby. Pop 33 491.

WAR OF 1812, conflict between the US and Great Britain, 1812–15. It originated in the maritime policies of Britain and France in the NAPOLEONIC WARS. In 1806 Napoleon tried to prevent neutrals from trading with Britain (see CONTINENTAL SYSTEM; BERLIN DECREE; MILAN DECREE). Britain retaliated with ORDERS IN COUNCIL to prevent neutrals from trading with France. US trade slumped, and after the CHESAPEAKE incident she responded with the EMBARGO ACT (1807) and the NONINTERFERENCE ACT (1809), banning trade with the belligerents. However, the chief sufferer from the ban was the US. MACON'S BILL No. 2 (1810) lifted the ban, with certain provisions, but after agreement with Napoleon the US reimposed sanctions against Britain. Anti-British feeling, fed by WAR HAWKS and by the conviction that British support of the Indians (see TIPPECANOE, BATTLE OF) was hindering US expansion, led to war being declared on June 18, 1812.

The US was unprepared and in internal conflict over the war, and her attempted invasion of Canada (1812) was a failure. (See Sir Isaac BROCK.) Early naval successes led to a retaliatory British blockade. US successes came in 1813 with the Battles of Lake ERIE and the THAMES. In 1814 US troops held their own at Chippawa and LUNDY'S LANE, and by a victory at PLATTSBURGH halted a British advance on the Hudson Valley. In Chesapeake Bay a British force that had sacked Washington was repelled in its attempt to take Baltimore. There was military stalemate, and peace negotiations started in June, 1814. The Peace of GHENT, signed on Dec. 22, 1814, was essentially a return to the status quo before the war. A fortnight later, Andrew JACKSON, unaware of the peace, defeated the British at the Battle of NEW ORLEANS. The war had several far-reaching effects on the US: the military victories promoted national confidence and encouraged expansionism, while the trade embargo encouraged home manufactures.

WAR OF INDEPENDENCE. See REVOLUTIONARY WAR.

WAR OF THE PACIFIC (1879–1884), war fought by Chile against Bolivia and Peru over control of the nitrate-rich Atacama Desert in Bolivia (now N Chile's Antofagasta Province), bordering the Pacific. Chile conquered and annexed the desert and parts of Peru. (See also TACNA-ARICA DISPUTE.)

WARRANT, judicial order (signed usually by a judge or court clerk) authorizing arrest of a suspect or search of premises. Strict procedures govern the issuing of a warrant. There are also tax warrants and warrants of attorney and of attachment.

WARREN, city in SE Mich., a NE suburb of Detroit. It contains major steel and automobile plants. Pop 179 260.

WARREN, city in NE Ohio, seat of Trumbull Co. It has important iron-and-steel, automobile and electrical industries. Pop 63 494.

WARREN, city in NW Pa., seat of Warren Co., on the Allegheny R. It makes metal and electrical goods and has oil refineries. Pop 12 998.

WARREN, Earl (1891–1974), US Chief Justice 1953–69. Attorney general (1939–43) and governor (1943–53) of Cal., he was Republican vice-presidential candidate in 1948. Appointed to the Supreme Court by Eisenhower, he led it to a number of liberal judgements, notably the one in Brown *v.* Board of Education of Topeka, Kan. (1954) declaring racial segregation in schools unconstitutional. See also WARREN REPORT.

WARREN, Joseph (1741–1775), US physician and patriot. He joined in Massachusetts Whig opposition to the STAMP ACT of 1765 and to British reprisals after the BOSTON TEA PARTY. Elected president of the provincial assembly in 1775, he was killed at the battle of BUNKER HILL on June 14.

WARREN, Josiah (1798–1874), US anarchist. He advocated "sovereignty of the individual" in place of Robert OWEN'S socialism in *True Civilization* (1863), and founded a utopian colony, Modern Times (Brentwood), N.Y., and "equity stores" for exchange of goods and labor.

WARREN, Robert Penn (1907–), US novelist, poet, critic, and university teacher. He was a member of the FUGITIVES. Most of his poetry and popular novels have a Southern setting and political and moral themes. His three Pulitzer prizes include one for *All the King's Men* (1946).

WARREN REPORT, report of the commission set up by Lyndon JOHNSON to investigate the assassination of President John KENNEDY. It comprised Earl WARREN, US representatives Hale Boggs and Gerald FORD, US senators Richard RUSSELL and John S. Cooper, Allen DULLES and John J. McCloy, attorney and ex-president, World Bank. The report, released in Sept. 1964, concluded that neither putative assassin Lee OSWALD nor his killer Jack RUBY was part of a conspiracy. It criticized the FBI and Secret Service and recommended reforms in presidential security.

WARRENSBURG, city in W Mo., seat of Johnson Co., a coalmine, stock and dairy farm area. Products include clothing and metal goods. Pop 13 125.

WARRENSVILLE HEIGHTS, city in NE Ohio, a suburb of Cleveland. Chiefly residential, it has machinery and automobile-part plants. Pop 18 925.

WARRINGTON, unincorporated, chiefly residential, urban community in NW Fla. on Pensacola Bay, with some shipping industry. Pop 15 848.

WARSAW (Warszawa), largest city and capital of Poland and of Warsaw province, on the Vistula R. It is a commercial, industrial, cultural and educational center and transportation hub. Chief products are machinery, precision instruments, motor vehicles, electrical equipment, textiles and chemicals. Warsaw replaced Kraków as capital in 1596 and has frequently fallen into Swedish, Russian, Prussian or German hands. Much of it was razed in WWII and has been carefully reconstructed. Pop 1 308 112.

WARSAW PACT, or Warsaw Treaty Organization, mutual defense pact signed 1955 in Warsaw by the USSR and its W communist neighbors Albania, Bulgaria, Czechoslovakia, East Germany, Hungary, Poland and Romania, after formation of the NORTH ATLANTIC TREATY ORGANIZATION (NATO). Its unified command has headquarters in Moscow. In 1968 (when Albania formally withdrew), Pact forces invaded Czechoslovakia.

WARS OF RELIGION. See RELIGION, WARS OF.

WARS OF THE ROSES. See ROSES, WARS OF THE.

WART, scaly excrescence on the SKIN caused by a VIRUS which may arise without warning and disappear equally suddenly. Numerous remedies have been suggested but local freezing or CAUTERIZATION are often effective. **Verrucas** are warts pushed into the soles of the feet by the weight of the body.

WARTBURG, castle overlooking EISENACH, SW East Germany; rebuilt, and made a center of music and poetry, by Hermann I of Thuringia (d. 1217)—a setting used in WAGNER's *Tannhäuser*. St. ELIZABETH OF HUNGARY lived there and later Martin LUTHER.

WARTHOG, *Phacochoerus aethiopicus*, a large African HOG with warty lumps on the face. The lower canines are developed to form tusks curving out to the top of the snout. Found all over Africa, warthogs live in family parties in savanna or on the forest edge.

WARWICK, city in central R.I., a summer resort on Narragansett Bay. First settled 1643, it now manufactures aluminum and electronic products and clothing. Pop 83 694.

WARWICK, Richard Neville, Earl of (1428–1471), "The Kingmaker," most powerful English noble of his time. A Yorkist (see ROSES, WARS OF THE), he drove out HENRY VI and installed Edward of York as EDWARD IV (1461). He virtually ruled England, but lost royal favor, rose against Edward and reinstated Henry (1471). Warwick was defeated by Edward and killed at the battle of Barnet. He featured in Lytton's *The Last of the Barons* (1843).

WASATCH RANGE, part of the ROCKY MOUNTAINS, extending some 250mi S from SE Ida. to central Ut. along the E edge of the Great Basin. The highest point is Mt. TIMPANOGOS (12 008ft).

WASHINGTON, a NW Pacific state of the US bordering Ida., Ore., and British Columbia, Canada. Named for George Washington, the state is divided by the N–S CASCADE RANGE, which reaches 14 410ft (Mt RAINIER). The W half of the state is largely fertile lowland, deeply penetrated by Puget Sound. The E is mostly semiarid plateau intersected by deep canyons, the largest of which is dammed by the GRAND COULEE DAM on the COLUMBIA RIVER. The Columbia and its tributary Pend Oreille and the Snake and Yakima rivers provide irrigation just E of the Cascades, and a large amount of hydroelectricity. The climate is mild and damp (up to 150in rain per year) in the W, drier and more extreme to the E.

Apart from SPOKANE, VANCOUVER and WALLA WALLA, the chief towns are on Puget Sound (SEATTLE, TACOMA, EVERETT and OLYMPIA.) The economy depends primarily on manufactures, notably aircraft, food-processing, timber products, aluminum and chemicals. Agriculture (apples, cherries, wheat, livestock, and dairying), fishing, mining, lumber (half of Wash. is forest) and tourism are also important.

Under its 1889 constitution the governor, eight-member executive, senate, house of representatives, supreme court and court of appeals are all popularly

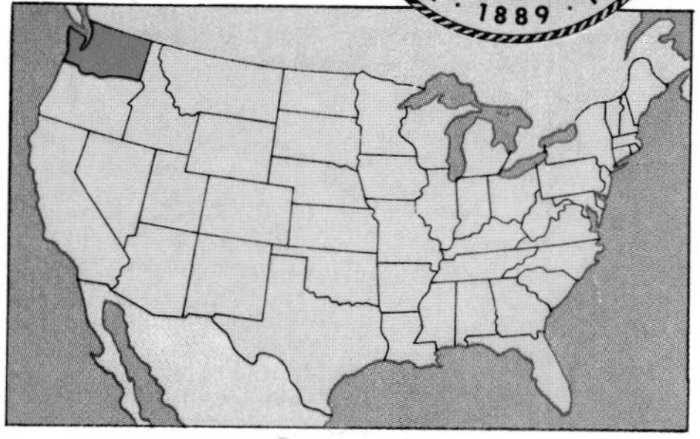

Name of State: Washington
Capital: Olympia
Statehood: Nov. 11, 1889 (42nd state)
Familiar Name: Evergreen State
Area: 68 192sq mi
Population: 3 409 169
Elevation: Highest—14 410ft, Mount Rainier
Lowest—sea level, Pacific Ocean
Motto: Alki (Bye and Bye)
State Flower: Coast rhododendron
State Bird: Willow goldfinch
State Tree: Western hemlock
State Song: "Washington, My Home"

elected. There are 16 accredited universities and senior colleges.

History. The first recorded landing on the Wash. coast was made by Spaniards in 1775, and James COOK and George VANCOUVER soon followed. The LEWIS AND CLARK EXPEDITION descended the Columbia R in 1805, and fur traders gradually moved in. In 1846 the 49th-parallel boundary with Canada was fixed. The area was included in the Oregon Territory (1848); Washington Territory, set up in 1853, lost part of W Ida. in 1863, and achieved statehood in 1889. The opening of the railroad in 1883 and the Alaska and Klondike gold rush in the 1890s boosted population, while labor conflicts gave Wash. a radical name. Though WWI brought a stimulus to the economy (especially shipbuilding), a collapse followed, and the situation worsened in the Great Depression. However, industries set up in WWII, postwar hydroelectric schemes, the expanding aerospace industry and diversification have brought increasing prosperity.

WASHINGTON, D.C., capital of the US, coextensive with the federal District of Columbia. It covers 69.2sq mi on the E bank of the Potomac R, but the metropolitan area now includes parts of Md. and

Looking toward the Potomac from the terrace of the Capitol, Washington, D.C., one can see (left to right) the towers of the Smithsonian Institution, the Washington Monument and Lincoln Memorial, the domed Museum of Natural History and National Gallery of Art, and the apex of the "Federal Triangle" which contains the main buildings of federal departments.

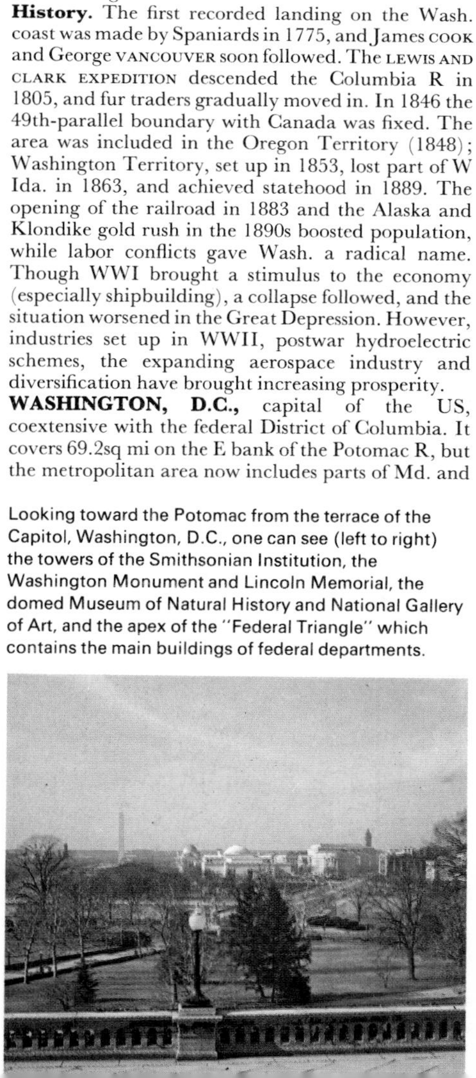

Va. The focal point is the domed CAPITOL, home of the CONGRESS OF THE US. To the NW lies the WHITE HOUSE. Other important buildings are the headquarters of numerous government departments and agencies, the SUPREME COURT, PENTAGON (in Va.), FEDERAL BUREAU OF INVESTIGATION and LIBRARY OF CONGRESS. Also a cultural and educational center, Washington is the site of the SMITHSONIAN INSTITUTION, the NATIONAL GALLERY OF ART and the new John F. Kennedy Center for the Performing Arts. There are many parks and famous memorials: the WASHINGTON MONUMENT, the LINCOLN MEMORIAL, and the JEFFERSON MEMORIAL. There is little industry, but many large corporations and other organizations have their offices there, including the FEDERAL RESERVE SYSTEM.

History. In 1783, the CONTINENTAL CONGRESS voted for a federal city. President Washington chose the present site in 1790 as a compromise between North and South, and the capital was built at its center. In 1800 Congress moved from Philadelphia. During the WAR OF 1812, the government buildings were burned down (1814) by British troops, and new and more splendid plans were made. Since then the population has risen steadily. Washington, long a gateway for blacks emigrating N (over half the people are Negro, many living in poverty), is a focus for demonstrations as well as government. There is an elected mayor but Congress retains the right to review the city's budget and legislation. There will be a subway by 1978. Pop 756 510.

WASHINGTON, industrial city in SW Ind., seat of Daviess Co. It has railroad shops and lies in a coal-mining and fertile farm area. Pop 11 358.

WASHINGTON, or Washington Court House, manufacturing city in SW Ohio, seat of Fayette Co., a dairy, poultry and grain farm area. Pop 12 495.

WASHINGTON, industrial city in SW Pa., seat of Washington Co., a region with coal and gas deposits. Products include steel, chemicals and glass. Pop 19 827.

WASHINGTON, Booker Taliaferro (1856–1915), black US educator. Born of a Va. slave family, he was chosen 1881 to head a new school for Blacks, the TUSKEGEE INSTITUTE, Ala. This he built up from two unequipped buildings to a complex with over 100 buildings and 1 500 students. Washington urged industrial education as the way to economic independence, favoring racial cooperation rather than political action. His extensive writings included an autobiography, *Up From Slavery* (1901).

Statue of George Washington in front of Independence Hall, Philadelphia, where in 1775 Washington accepted his appointment as commander-in-chief of the Continental Army.

WASHINGTON, George (1732–1799), first president of the US (1789–97). Born into a wealthy Va. family, he showed an early aptitude for surveying, in 1839 becoming surveyor of Culpeper Co. He first attracted notice with a report (1753) on the French threat in the Ohio Valley, and became commander in chief of the Va. militia (1755–58) after distinguishing himself in the mission of Edward BRADDOCK (see FRENCH AND INDIAN WARS). Returning to MOUNT

George WASHINGTON

1st US President

Born: February 22, 1732
Died: December 14, 1799
Term of office: April 30, 1789–March 3, 1797
Political party: Unopposed

VERNON, the estate he inherited in 1760, he married (1759) and became a member of the Va. house of burgesses (1759–74) and a justice of the peace (1760–74). His anti-British feelings were exacerbated by British taxes (see STAMP ACT; TOWNSHEND ACTS). He became a delegate to the CONTINENTAL CONGRESS (1774–75) and was appointed commander in chief of the Continental Army in 1775 (see REVOLUTIONARY WAR). From ill-trained and ill-equipped troops, he created a disciplined army, secured the fall of Boston (1776) but narrowly extricated himself after defeat at LONG ISLAND.

After successes at Trenton and Princeton, 1777 marked a low point in the war. Washington survived an attempt to displace him and wintered 1777–78 in VALLEY FORGE. Alliances with France (1778) and Spain (1779) changed the course of the war. Victory was secured by the capture of YORKTOWN (1781), and after peace had been reached (1783) Washington resigned and returned to Mount Vernon.

Dissatisfied with the 1781 ARTICLES OF CONFEDERATION, Washington played a major role in securing the adoption of the UNITED STATES CONSTITUTION, and was unanimously elected president in 1789. Believing in a strong central government, he created a federal judiciary (1789) and a national bank (1791), and put through other far-reaching financial measures. These led to party conflict centering round Thomas JEFFERSON and Alexander HAMILTON. His second term of office was marked by controversy over foreign affairs, as with the JAY TREATY and his efforts to keep the US neutral in Britain's war with France (1793). There were also Indian insurrections (see FALLEN TIMBERS, BATTLE OF) and internal dissension (see WHISKEY REBELLION). He refused a third term of office. His integrity, patience and high sense of duty and justice made him a great leader and won him the title of "Father of His Country."

The Washington Monument seen across the Tidal Basin of the Potomac, with the southern portico of the White House in the background.

WASHINGTON, Lake, 20mi-long lake in W central Wash. which forms the E waterfront of Seattle. It has the largest pontoon bridge in the world.

WASHINGTON, Martha Custis (1731–1802), wife of George Washington and first First Lady of the US. At 17 she married a wealthy planter, Daniel Parke Custis, who died in 1757. She married George Washington in 1759 and moved with her two surviving children to MOUNT VERNON, which she supervised during Washington's absences.

WASHINGTON, Mount, highest peak of the PRESIDENTIAL RANGE, in the White Mts., N.H. At the summit (6288ft) are an hotel, an observatory and a television transmitter.

WASHINGTON, Treaty of, 1871, agreement by the US and Britain, signed in Washington, D.C., to arbitration over such controversies as the ALABAMA CLAIMS, and boundary and fishing disputes. It was largely brought about by Hamilton FISH.

WASHINGTON CONFERENCE, post-WWI meetings convened by US President HARDING and held in Washington, D.C., 1921–22. The US, Britain, Japan, France and Italy agreed to limit their capital ships in the ratio $5:5:3:1\frac{2}{3}:1\frac{2}{3}$ respectively, to restrictions on submarine warfare and a ban on use of poison gas. France, Japan, Britain and the US agreed to respect each other's Pacific territories. A nine-power treaty with the additional signatures of Belgium, China, the Netherlands and Portugal guaranteed China's territorial integrity.

WASHINGTON MONUMENT, stone obelisk in Washington, D.C., honoring George WASHINGTON. Begun 1848, it was completed in 1884. Faced with white marble, it is 555ft high. Visitors may go to the top by elevator, or by climbing 898 steps.

WASHINGTON'S BIRTHDAY, a legal holiday in most states, celebrated on the third Monday in February in honor of George Washington. He was born Feb. 11, 1732, but the 1752 calendar reform made it Feb. 22.

WASHITA, Battle of the, 1868, massacre which ended hostilities by the CHEYENNE INDIANS. The 7th Cavalry, under General CUSTER, surprised and destroyed the camp of Chief Black Kettle on the banks of the Washita R, near Cheyenne, W Okla.

WASPS, stinging insects, banded black and yellow, related to BEES and ANTS in the order Hymenoptera. There are a number of families; most are solitary, but members of the Vespoidea are social, forming true colonies with workers, drones and queen(s). Most of the solitary species are hunting wasps. These make nest cells in soil or decaying wood, in which they place one or more paralyzed insects before the egg is laid, to act as a living larder for the larva when it hatches. Social wasps congregate to form a permanent colony with both adults and young. The nest is usually constructed of "wasp paper," a thick pulp of wood fibers and saliva. The adults feed the developing larvae on dead insects which have been killed by biting in the neck; the sting, which in solitary wasps is used to paralyze the prey, is reserved for defense. Adult wasps feed on carbohydrate: NECTAR, aphid honeydew or jam.

WASSERMAN, Jakob (1873–1934), German writer popular in the 1920s and 1930s for his novels of intense social criticism, powerful characterization, and mystical longing, especially for *The Mauritzius Case* (1928). He is sometimes compared with Dostoyevsky.

WASSERMANN TEST, screening test for syphilis (see VENEREAL DISEASES) based on a nonspecific serological reaction which is seen not only in syphilis but also in YAWS and diseases associated with immune disorders. More specific tests are available to discriminate between these.

WASTE DISPOSAL, disposal of such matter as animal excreta and the waste products of agricultural, industrial and domestic processes, where an unacceptable level of environmental POLLUTION would otherwise result. Where an ecological balance exists (see ECOLOGY), wastes are recycled naturally or by technological means (see RECYCLING) before accumulations affect the quality of life or disrupt the ecosystem. The most satisfactory waste-disposal methods are therefore probably those that involve recycling, as in manuring fields with dung, reclaiming metals from scrap or pulping waste paper for remanufacture. Recycling, however, may be inconvenient, uneconomic or not yet technologically feasible. Many popular waste-disposal methods consequently represent either an exchange of one form of environmental pollution for another less troublesome, at least in the short term—e.g., the dumping or burying of non-degradable garbage or toxic wastes—or a reducing of the rate at which pollutants accumulate—e.g., by compacting or incinerating bulk wastes before dumping. Urban wastes are generally disposed of by means of dumping, sanitary landfill, incineration and SEWAGE processing. Agricultural, mining and mineral-processing operations generate most solid wastes—and some of the most intractable waste-disposal problems: e.g., the "factory" farmer's problem of disposing of surplus organic wastes economically without resorting to incineration or dumping in rivers; the problems created by large mine dumps and open-cast excavations; and the culm-dumps that result from the processing of anthracite COAL. Another increasingly pressing waste-disposal problem is presented by radioactive wastes. Those with a "low level" of RADIOACTIVITY can be safely packaged and buried; but "high-level" wastes, produced in the course of reprocessing the fuel elements of NUCLEAR REACTORS, constitute a permanent hazard. Even the practice of encasing these wastes in thick concrete and dumping them on the ocean bottom is considered by many environmentalists to be an inadequate long-term solution (see also NUCLEAR ENERGY).

WATAUGA ASSOCIATION, 1772–75, government set up in land leased from the Cherokee along the Watauga R, present Washington Co., E Tenn. The settlers, from Va. and (after suppression of the REGULATORS) N.C., became part of the State of FRANKLIN in 1788.

WATCH. See CLOCKS AND WATCHES.

WATER (H_2O), pale-blue odorless liquid which, including that trapped as ICE in icecaps and glaciers, covers about 74% of the earth's surface. Water is essential to LIFE, which began in the watery OCEANS; because of its unique chemical properties, it provides the medium for the reactions of the living CELL. Water is also man's most precious natural resource, which he must conserve and protect from POLLUTION (see also WATER SUPPLY.) Chemically, water can be viewed variously as a covalent HYDRIDE, an OXIDE, or a HYDROXIDE. It is a good solvent for many substances, especially ionic and polar compounds; it is ionizing and itself ionizes to give a low concentration of hydroxide and hydrogen ions (see pH). It is thus both a weak ACID and a weak BASE, and conducts electricity. It is a good, though labile, LIGAND, forming HYDRATES. Water is a polar molecule, and shows anomalies due to HYDROGEN BONDING, including contraction when heated from 0°C to 4°C. Formed when hydrogen or volatile hydrides are burned in oxygen, water oxidizes reactive metals to their ions, and reduces fluorine and chlorine. It converts basic oxides to hydroxides, and acidic oxides to OXY-ACIDS. (See also DEHYDRATION; HARD WATER; HEAVY WATER; HYDROLYSIS; POLYWATER; STEAM.) mp 0°C, bp 100°C, triple point 0.01°C, sg 1.0.

WATER BEETLES, BEETLES exploiting an aquatic environment, the majority belonging to the families Hydrophilidae and Dytiscidae. Both are freshwater groups. Dytiscids are strong swimmers and active carnivores, while hydrophilids are herbivorous. The larvae are fierce predators.

WATER BOATMEN, aquatic, hemipteran BUGS. There are two families, Notonectidae, the fast-swimming, carnivorous insects known as BACKSWIMMERS, and the herbivorous Corixidae.

WATERBUCK, a large African ANTELOPE, *Kobus ellipsiprymnus*. There are a number of distinct races of these heavy-set, deer-like animals which have a thick gray coat and live in wooded grasslands near permanent water.

WATER BUFFALO. See BUFFALO; CARABAO.

WATER BUGS, any of a number of hemipteran insects found in ponds or streams, such as the Giant water bug *Bonacus grisseus*. The word Waterbug is also used for a croton bug or COCKROACH *Blattela germanica*.

WATERBURY, industrial city in W Conn. on the Naugatuck R. Long a center of the brass industry, it also produces clocks, instruments, electronic parts, tools and plastics. Pop 108 033.

WATER CHESTNUT, small aquatic herbs of the genus *Trapa*, with floating leaves, small white flowers and edible nut-like fruit. Mostly native to Asia and Europe, some species are naturalized in the US. Family: Hydrocaryaceae.

WATER CLOCK. See CLEPSYDRA.

WATERCOLOR, painting technique in which the pigment is mixed with water before application, more particularly the aquarelle technique of thin washes, mastered by such English artists as COTMAN and J. M. W. TURNER around 1800. Infelicities cannot be painted over, but watercolor permits powerful effects of transparency, brilliance and delicacy. Famous US watercolorists include Winslow HOMER and John MARIN. (See also FRESCO; GOUACHE; TEMPERA.)

WATERCRESS. See CRESS.

WATER CYCLE. See HYDROLOGIC CYCLE.

WATERFALL, a vertical fall of water where a river flows from hard rock to one more easily eroded (see EROSION), or where there has been a rise of the land relative to sea level or blockage of a river by a landslide. Largest in the world is one of the Angel Falls. Venezuela (815m).

WATER FLEA. See DAPHNIA.

WATERFORD, seaport capital of Co. Waterford, SE Ireland, on the Suir R. Famous for its cut glass, Waterford ships meat, dairy products and fish, and makes footwear and electrical goods. Pop 31 692.

WATERFORD, town in SE Conn. on Long Island Sound W of New London. Mainly residential, it has light industries. Millstone granite quarry is nearby. Pop 17 227.

WATER GAP, a short, narrow gorge cut through a ridge or region of high ground by a stream or river (see EROSION). If the river no longer passes through it, the gorge is termed a **wind gap**.

WATER GAS, or blue gas (because of its blue flame), a FUEL GAS consisting of HYDROGEN and CARBON monoxide, made by blowing steam (alternately with air) over red-hot coke. Enriched with petroleum hydrocarbons, it becomes carbureted water gas.

WATERGATE, series of scandals which brought down President NIXON's administration. On June 17, 1972, five men were arrested carrying electronic eavesdropping equipment in the Watergate office building headquarters of the Democratic Party national committee, Washington, D.C. Investigations opened a trail which led to Nixon's inner councils. Nixon easily won reelection in Nov. 1972; but his public support eroded after a televised US Senate investigation, newspaper revelations (notably by Carl Bernstein and Bob Woodward in the *Washington Post*) and testimony of Republican Party and former governmental officials clearly implicated him and his senior aides in massive abuse of power and obstruction of justice involving campaign contributions, the CIA, the FBI, the Internal Revenue Service, and other agencies. The House of Representatives Judiciary Committee voted to impeach Nixon in July 1974, and his ouster from office became inevitable; he resigned on Aug. 9, 1974. One month later he was granted a full pardon by Gerald FORD. Almost three score individuals, including former US attorney general John MITCHELL and senior White House staff were convicted of Watergate crimes, about half serving jail sentences.

WATER GLASS, aqueous solution of sodium SILICATE (Na_2SiO_3)—concentrated, syrupy and alkaline—made by fusing sodium carbonate with silica. It is used to preserve eggs, as a cement, in ore flotation, and for water- and fireproofing.

WATER HYACINTH, *Eichhornia crassipes*, an aquatic herb that floats on air-filled bladders and has trailing roots. It is native to Brazil, but has been introduced to other countries, including the southern US, and has become a troublesome weed in waterways. Family: Pontederiaceae.

WATER LILIES, aquatic plants of the genus *Nymphaea* (unrelated to true LILIES). They grow in calm shallow fresh water, with stems rooted in the mud and floating leaves. Many hybrids are used as ornamentals in water gardens. Family: Nymphaeaceae.

WATERLOO, manufacturing city in SE Ontario, a suburb of Kitchener. Products include farm machinery and furniture. It is the site of Waterloo U. Pop 36 677.

WATERLOO, city in NE Ia., seat of Black Hawk Co. It processes meat and makes farm machinery. The National Dairy Cattle Congress meets here. Pop 75 533.

WATERLOO, Battle of (June 18, 1815), the final engagement of the NAPOLEONIC WARS. Having escaped from exile on Elba and reinstated himself with a new army, NAPOLEON I faced a coalition of Austria, Britain, Prussia and Russia. He decided to attack, advancing into Belgium to prevent an Anglo-Dutch army under WELLINGTON from uniting with the Prussians. After separate battles with the British and Prussians on June 16, the French army, led by Marshall NEY, attacked Wellington's strongly defended position at Waterloo, S of Brussels. The intervention of a Prussian force under BLÜCHER allowed Wellington to take the offensive. The French were routed, losing some 25 000 men. Napoleon abdicated four days later.

WATERMELON. See MELON.

WATER MOCCASIN. See MOCCASIN.

WATER OPOSSUM. See YAPOK.

WATER OUZEL, alternative name for the DIPPERS.

WATER POLLUTION. See POLLUTION; WATER; WATER SUPPLY.

WATER POLO, ball game for two teams of seven played in a pool 19–30yd long, up to 20yd wide and at least 3ft deep. The goals at each end are 10ft wide, their cross-bars 3ft above water. The 26–27in-round ball may be moved on the surface by one hand, passed or dribbled in front of the body. Devised in England in the 1870s, the game became an Olympic event in 1900.

WATER POWER. See HYDROELECTRICITY; TURBINE.

WATERPROOFING, any method of making an absorbent material, such as cloth, paper, leather, wood or masonry, resist penetration by water. Waterproofing is usually effected by the application of such agents as hardened oils, greases, waxes, plastics or rubber. Waterproofed TEXTILES are of two main kinds. Those that are said to be "impervious" to water are protected by a solid film which sheds water completely, but as they are also impervious to air they are uncomfortable to wear. "Water-repellent" fabrics, sometimes termed "showerproof," admit air but will stand up to exposure to water for a limited period only.

WATER RIGHTS. See RIPARIAN RIGHTS.

WATERS, Ethel (1900–   ), US actress and singer. Her stage successes include *Mamba's Daughters* (1939), *The Member of the Wedding* (1950) and the stage and screen musical *Cabin in the Sky* (1940).

WATER SCORPIONS, genus *Nepa*, aquatic BUGS with the front pair of legs modified for seizing prey, and thus somewhat resembling scorpions. A slender "tail," in fact a breathing tube pushed up through the water's surface film, faintly resembles a scorpion's sting.

WATERSHED, a catchment basin (see DRAINAGE); or a DIVIDE.

WATER SKIING, sport in which a motorboat tows the skier along the surface of the water at the end of a line. Originating in S France and the US in the 1920s, it is now a popular recreation. National and international competitions include slalom races, trick riding and distance jumping. Jumps of 150ft and speeds of over 100mph have been achieved.

WATER SNAKES, nearly 80 species of the genus *Natrix*, which also includes the European Grass snake. They are non-venomous snakes living on fish and amphibians. The Eurasian water snakes lay eggs, while the two New-World species are viviparous.

WATER SOFTENING. See HARD WATER.

WATER SPANIEL, American, sporting dog developed in the US, standing 18in high and weighing 45lb. It is excellent for both flushing and retrieving game, although its curly waterproof coat can be a hindrance in some cover. The coat may be liver or dark chocolate, with white on toes and breast permissible.

WATERSPOUT, effect of a rotating column of air, or TORNADO, as it passes over water. A funnel-like CLOUD of condensed water vapor extends from a parent cumulonimbus cloud to the water surface, where it is surrounded by a sheath of spray.

WATER STRIDERS, or Pond Skaters, aquatic BUGS of the family Gerridae, which skate on long legs on the surface film of water. The front legs are very short and it is only the rear two pairs which are used to support and propel the insect.

WATER SUPPLY, available WATER resources and the means by which sufficient water of a suitable quality is supplied for agricultural, industrial, domestic and other purposes. Water precipitated over land (see HYDROLOGIC CYCLE) is available either as "surface water," in the form of rivers and lakes, usually supplemented by reservoirs, or as GROUND WATER, held underground—typically in an AQUIFER underlaid by impermeable rock—and brought to the surface by pumping or else rising as a spring or ARTESIAN WELL. Water may also be extracted from SEWAGE, purified and recycled (see RECYCLING).

WATER TABLE. See GROUNDWATER.

WATERTON, Charles (1782–1865), English naturalist and eccentric who published an account of his travels in the Americas. He made his mansion, Walton Hall, Yorkshire, a bird sanctuary.

WATERTON LAKES NATIONAL PARK, 203sq mi park in SW Alberta, since 1932 part of Waterton-Glacier International Peace Park (with GLACIER NATIONAL PARK, NW Mont.). It rises to Mt Blakiston (9 600ft) and has many lakes, glaciers, trails and wildlife species.

WATERTOWN, town in W Conn. Long a center of the silk industry, it now makes synthetic fibers, plastics, silk and metal goods. Pop 18 610.

WATERTOWN, town in NE Mass. on the Charles R, a W industrial suburb of Boston. It produces rubber goods, clothing, and machinery. Pop 39 309.

WATERTOWN, city in N N.Y., seat of Jefferson Co. on the Black R, whose falls power papermaking and many smaller industries. Pop 30 707.

WATERTOWN, city in NE S.D., seat of Codington Co. on Big Sioux R. It ships and processes farm produce and is a recreation center. Pop 13 388.

WATERTOWN, city in SE Wis. on Rock R. A farming center, it also manufactures paper and rubber products. Pop 15 683.

WATER TURKEY, another name for the ANHINGA.

WATERVILLE, city in SW Me., on the Kennebec

The Watergate office and apartment complex in Washington, D.C., where five men were arrested as they broke into the Democratic Party National Committee's offices during the 1972 presidential election campaign.

R. It has railroad shops and manufactures clothing, paper and wood products. Pop 18 192.

WATERVLIET, city in E N.Y. on the Hudson R opposite Troy. It has a US arsenal and makes steel products, textiles, and abrasives. It was the home of Philip SCHUYLER and of Ann LEE. Pop 12 404.

WATLING ISLAND. See SAN SALVADOR ISLAND.

WATSON, James Dewey (1928–), US biochemist who shared with F. H. C. CRICK and M. H. F. WILKINS the 1962 Nobel Prize for Physiology or Medicine for his work with Crick establishing the "double helix" molecular model of DNA. His personalized account of the research, *The Double Helix* (1968), became a best-seller.

WATSON, John Broadus (1878–1958), US psychologist who founded BEHAVIORISM, a dominant school of US psychology from the 1920s to 1940s, and whose influence is still strong today.

WATSON, Thomas Edward (1856–1922), US author and political leader from Ga. He attacked Blacks, socialists, Catholics and Jews. A FARMER'S ALLIANCE (1891–93) and Democratic (from 1920) Congressman, and POPULIST vice-presidential and presidential candidate (1896, 1904), he became a champion of the KU KLUX KLAN.

WATSONVILLE, city in W Cal., 15mi SE of Santa Cruz. It ships and processes fruit and vegetables and makes textiles and electronic equipment. Pop 14 569.

WATSON-WATT, Sir Robert Alexander (1892–), British physicist largely responsible for the development of RADAR, patenting his first "radiolocator" in 1919. He perfected his equipment and techniques from 1935 through the years of WWII, his radar being largely responsible for the British victory of the BATTLE OF BRITAIN.

WATT (W), the unit of POWER in SI UNITS, defined as the power dissipated when ENERGY is utilized at a rate of one JOULE per second.

WATT, James (1736–1819), Scottish engineer and inventor. His first major invention was a STEAM ENGINE with a separate CONDENSER and thus far greater efficiency. For the manufacture of such engines he entered partnership with John ROEBUCK and later (1775), more successfully, with Matthew BOULTON. Between 1775 and 1800 he invented the sun-and-planet gear wheel, the double-acting engine, a throttle valve, a pressure gauge and the centrifugal governor—as well as taking the first steps toward determining the chemical structure of water. He also coined the term HORSEPOWER and was a founder member of the LUNAR SOCIETY.

WATTEAU, (Jean) Antoine (1684–1721), French (of Flemish descent) draftsman and painter, strongly influenced by RUBENS. His gay, sensuous paintings have a melancholy quality. They include theater scenes, *fêtes galantes*, *The Embarkation for Cythera* (1717) and *Gilles* (c1718).

WATTERSON, Henry (1840–1921), US journalist-politician. A US Congressman 1876–77, he backed TILDEN. His Louisville, Ky., *Courier-Journal* editorials (1868–1919) urged Negro rights and Southern home rule. His editorials favoring US war on Germany won him a 1917 Pulitzer Prize.

WATTLE, Australian name for an ACACIA tree.

WATTLEBIRDS, a family, Callaeidae, of crow-like forest birds of New Zealand, characterized by brightly-colored, fleshy wattles at the corners of their bills. The family includes the huia, kokako and tieke or saddleback. All are extremely rare and localized.

WATTS, George Frederic (1817–1904), English Victorian artist noted for his allegorical paintings, including *Hope* (1886). He married Ellen TERRY.

WATTS, Isaac (1674–1748), English Dissenting theologian, author of numerous fine hymns (many, like "O God, our help in ages past," still sung today) and philosophical writings.

WAT TYLER'S REBELLION. See TYLER, WAT.

WATUSI (English version of Swahili *Watutsi*), the Tutsi people of BURUNDI and RWANDA in Central Africa (formerly Ruanda-Urundi). In the 1400s and 1500s the invading Watusi imposed a feudal system on the native Hutu, who revolted in 1959 and drove out their rulers. The Tutsi king of Burundi was deposed in 1966. The Watusi differ ethnically from other African peoples. Many attain a height of 7ft.

WAUBESHIEK (c1794–c1841), North American Indian prophet. Also called White Cloud, he advised Chief Black Hawk that victory would be his, and so perhaps prolonged the BLACK HAWK WAR.

WAUGH, three English writers, the descendants of journalist and publisher Arthur Waugh (1886–1943). **Alexander Raban (Alec) Waugh** (1898–) is the author of over 40 novels and travel books including *Loom of Youth* (1918) and *Island in the Sun* (1956). **Evelyn Arthur St. John Waugh** (1903–1966) wrote mainly satire, both elegant and biting. His conversion to Roman Catholicism in 1930 had a deep effect on his work. His novels include *Decline and Fall* (1928), *Vile Bodies* (1930), *Scoop* (1938), *Put out More Flags* (1942), *Brideshead Revisited* (1945) and his WWII trilogy *The Sword of Honour* (1952–61). Evelyn's son **Auberon Alexander Waugh** (1939–) is a novelist and miscellaneous writer: his novels include *Bed of Flowers* (1972).

WAUKEGAN, city in NE Ill., seat of Lake Co. A Lake Michigan port, it is part of the Milwaukee–Chicago urban-industrial complex. Pop 65 269.

WAUKESHA, city in SE Wis., seat of Waukesha Co. It produces limestone, engines, aluminum and electrical, wood and food products. Pop 40 258.

WAUSAU, city in N central Wis., seat of Marathon Co. It makes paper, machinery, plastics and dairy products. Pop 32 806.

WAUWATOSA, city in SE Wis., a W residential and industrial suburb of Milwaukee. Pop 58 676.

WAVEGUIDE, means for channeling high-frequency ELECTROMAGNETIC RADIATION by confining it within a tube whose walls are made of a conducting material (typically metal). Waveguides find their greatest use in MICROWAVE technology.

WAVELL, Archibald Percival Wavell, 1st Earl (1883–1950), British field marshal. He served in WWI, and was WWII British commander-in-chief, Middle East, defeating the Italians in N Africa 1940, and in India (from 1941), and viceroy and governor general of India in the years before independence (1943–47).

WAVE MECHANICS, branch of QUANTUM MECHANICS developed by SCHRÖDINGER which considers MATTER rather in terms of its wavelike properties (see WAVE MOTION) than as systems of particles. Thus an orbital ELECTRON is treated as a 3-dimensional system of standing waves represented by a *wave function*. In accordance with the UNCERTAINTY PRINCIPLE, it is not possible to pinpoint both the instantaneous position and velocity of the electron; however, the square of the wave function yields a measure of the probability that the electron is at any given point in space-time. The pattern of such probabilities provides a model for the "shape" of the electron ORBITAL involved. Given wave functions can be obtained from the Schrödinger wave equation. Usually, and not unsurprisingly, this can only be solved for particular values of the ENERGY of the system concerned.

WAVE MOTION, a collective motion of a material or extended object, in which each part of the material oscillates about its undisturbed position, but the oscillations at different places are so timed as to create an illusion of crests and troughs running right through the material. Familiar examples are furnished by surface waves on water, or transverse waves on a stretched rope; SOUND is carried through air by a wave motion in which the air molecules oscillate parallel to the direction of propagation, and LIGHT or RADIO waves involve ELECTROMAGNETIC FIELDS oscillating perpendicular to it. The maximum displacement of the material from the undisturbed position is the *amplitude* of the wave, the separation of successive crests, the *wavelength*, and the number of crests passing a given place each second, the *frequency*. The product of the wavelength and the frequency gives the *velocity of propagation*. According to the direction and form of the local oscillations of the medium, different *polarizations* of the wave are distinguished (see POLARIZED LIGHT). *Standing waves* (apparently stationary waves, where the nodes and antinodes—points of zero and maximum amplitude—appear not to move) arise where identical waves traveling in opposite directions superpose. The characteristic properties of waves include propagation in straight lines; REFLECTION at plane surfaces; REFRACTION—a change in direction of a wave transmitted across a plane interface between two media; DIFFRACTION—diffuse SCATTERING by impenetrable objects of a size comparable with the wavelength; and INTERFERENCE—the cancellation of one wave by another wave half a wavelength out of step (or *phase*) so that the crests of one wave fall on the troughs of the other. If the *wave velocity* is the same for all wavelengths, then quite arbitrary forms of disturbance will travel as waves, and not simply regular successions of crests and troughs. When this is not the case, the wave is said to be *dispersive* and localized disturbances move at a speed (the *group velocity*) quite different from that of the individual crests, which can often be seen moving faster or slower within the disturbance "envelope," which becomes progressively broader as it moves. Waves carry ENERGY and MOMENTUM with them just like solid objects; the identity of the apparently irreconcilable wave and particle concepts of matter is a basic tenet of QUANTUM MECHANICS.

WAVES (Women Accepted for Voluntary Emergency Service), women of the US navy (excluding nurses); originally meaning those recruited from Aug. 1942 for the WWII US Navy Women's Reserve. Some 7 000 now serve all over the world in supply, air and sea communications, traffic control and clerical posts.

WAX, moldable water-repellent solid. There are several entirely different kinds. **Animal waxes** were the first known: *wool wax* when purified yields LANOLIN; *beeswax*, from the honeycomb, is used for some candles and as a sculpture medium (by carving or casting); *spermaceti wax*, from the sperm whale, is used in ointments and cosmetics. **Vegetable waxes**, like animal waxes, are mixtures of ESTERS of long-chain ALCOHOLS and CARBOXYLIC ACIDS. *Carnauba wax*, from the leaves of a Brazilian palm tree, is hard and lustrous, and is used to make polishes; *candelilla wax*, from a wild Mexican rush, is similar but more resinous; *Japan wax*, the coating of sumac berries, is fatty and soft but tough and kneadable. **Mineral waxes** include *montan wax*, extracted from lignite (see COAL), bituminous and resinous; *ozokerite*, an absorbent hydrocarbon wax obtained from wax shales, and *paraffin wax* or petroleum wax, the most important wax commercially: it is obtained from the residues of PETROLEUM refining by solvent extraction, and is used to make candles, to coat paper products, in the electrical industry, to waterproof leather and textiles, etc. Various **synthetic waxes** are made for special uses.

WAXAHACHIE, city in N Tex., seat of Ellis Co. A prairie market center (chiefly for cattle), it has some light industry. Pop 13 452.

WAXBILLS, a family, Estrildidae, of small seed-eating birds, named for the bright scarlet bill found in many species. They include the waxbills of Africa and Arabia, the mannikins of Africa and Asia and the Grass finches of Australasia.

WAX FLOWER, or wax plant, trailing evergreen plants of the genus *Hoya*, popular as house plants for their plain green or variegated foliage and clusters of fragrant, waxy, five-pointed star-like flowers, with white to pink petals and rosy-pink to maroon centers. Indoors, they grow well at average house temperatures and should be placed in a sunny window. They should be well watered whenever the soil surface dries out, and the leaves misted often, especially in the case of the miniature wax plant (*Hoya bella*). Propagation is by leaf or stem cuttings. Family: Asclepiadaceae.

WAX MYRTLE, *Myrica carolinensis*, a shrub or small tree native to the US and grown as an ornamental plant. Its fruit masses are covered with a pale blue or grayish aromatic wax. Family: Myricaceae. (See also BAYBERRY.)

WAXWINGS, three species (genus *Bombycilla*) of small birds of N forests. The name refers to the shafts of the secondary wing feathers which are prolonged into red drop-shaped tips like blobs of sealing wax. They have brown back-swept crests and feed on insects in summer, fruits and berries in winter.

WAYCROSS, city in SE Ga., seat of Ware Co, with an economy based on tobacco, lumber, livestock and light industry. Pop 18 996.

WAYFARING TREE, *Viburnum lantana*, a tree native to Europe and N Africa, naturalized in the US and widely grown as an ornamental. Family: Caprifoliaceae. (See VIBURNUM.)

WAYLAND, town in E Mass., on the Sudbury R, W of Boston. It has chemical and electronic research laboratories. Pop 13 461.

WAYNE, city in SE Mich. on the Lower Rouge R, 17mi W of Detroit, producing automobiles and heavy machinery. Pop 21 054.

WAYNE, township in N N.J., named for Anthony WAYNE, first settled in 1695. It is mainly residential with some light industry. Pop 49 141.

WAYNE, Anthony (1745–1796), American Revolutionary general whose daring tactics earned him the name "mad Anthony." In 1779 he executed the brilliant victory of Stony Point over the British, and he was with Lafayette at the seige of YORKTOWN (1781). After defeating the Indians at FALLEN TIMBERS in 1794, he negotiated the Treaty of GREENVILLE (1795), in which the Indians ceded most of Ohio.

WAYNESBORO, borough in S Pa., the marketing center for a large dairy and fruit-growing region. There is some light industry. Pop 10 011.

WAYNESBORO, city in central Va., site of General EARLY's defeat by General SHERIDAN (1865), and now a manufacturing center. Pop 16 707.

WAYS AND MEANS COMMITTEE, US House of Representatives second-most important standing committee, responsible for assessing all tax and public finance bills, and the main source of revenue legislation. The Democrats of its 25 members also determine all committee assignments for Democrats in the House.

WEAKFISH, or **squeteague,** a marine food and sport fish of the genus *Cynoscion*, related to the drums and occurring off the Gulf Coast.

WEASEL, *Mustela nivalis*, a small carnivorous mammal very like the STOAT but smaller and lacking the black tail tip. A slender lithe red-brown creature, which often kills prey many times its own size, it measures only up to 280mm (11in) in the male, 200mm (7.9in) in the female. The normal diet is mice, voles and fledgling birds, though rabbits may be taken. The many races of weasel are distributed throughout Europe, Africa and North America.

WEATHERFORD, city in N central Tex., seat of Parker Co, with agriculture and oilfield-and electrical-equipment industries. Pop 11 750.

WEATHERFORD, William (c1780–1824), North American Indian chief who fought the Americans in the WAR OF 1812. He led the Creek Indians, roused by TECUMSEH at the battle of HORSESHOE BEND. He was defeated but pardoned by General Andrew JACKSON.

WEATHER, the hour-by-hour variations in the atmospheric conditions experienced at a given place. (See ATMOSPHERE; METEOROLOGY; WEATHER FORECASTING AND CONTROL.)

WEATHER FORECASTING AND CONTROL, the practical application of the knowledge gained through the study of METEOROLOGY. **Weather forecasting**, organized nationally by government agencies such as the US National Weather Service, is coordinated internationally by the WORLD METEOROLOGICAL ORGANIZATION (WMO). There are three basic stages: observation; analysis, and forecasting. Observation involves round-the-clock weather watching and the gathering of meteorological data by land stations, weather ships, and by using RADIOSONDES and weather SATELLITES. In analysis, this information is coordinated at national centers, and plotted in terms of ISOBARS, FRONTS, etc., on synoptic charts (weather maps). Then, in forecasting, predictions of the future weather pattern are made by the "synoptic method" (in which the forecaster applies his experience of the evolution of past weather patterns to the current situation) and by "numerical forecasting" (which treats the ATMOSPHERE as a fluid of variable density and seeks to use hydrodynamic equations to determine its future parameters). These methods yield short- and medium-term forecasts—up to four days ahead. Long-range forecasting, a recent development, depends additionally on the statistical analysis of past weather records in attempting to discern the future weather trends over the next month or season. **Weather control**, or weather modification, is an altogether less reliable technology. Indeed, the natural variability of weather phenomena makes it difficult to assess the success of experimental procedures. To date, the best results have been obtained in the fields of CLOUD seeding and the dispersal of supercooled FOGS.

WEATHERING. See EROSION.

WEATHER SERVICE, National, a part of the Environmental Science Services Administration (ESSA), in the US Department of Commerce. Its head office in Washington, D.C., near the National Meteorological Center, is where data from 300 weather stations in the US and from many other sources including aircraft, satellites, and balloons are coordinated and incorporated into charts for distribution to the 30 forecast centers across the country. Here long-and short-range forecasts are prepared, and warnings of hurricanes, flooding and other weather hazards given. Research to improve forecasting accuracy is also undertaken. (See also METEOROLOGY; WEATHER FORECASTING.)

WEAVER, James Baird (1833–1912), US politician. Elected to the House of Representatives (1879–80, 1885–88) on the GREENBACK PARTY ticket, he was the party's presidential candidate in 1880. He organized the People's Party and as their presidential candidate (1892) won over a million popular and 22 electoral votes. His career declined with the demise of POPULISM.

WEAVER, Robert Clifton (1907–), US economist and secretary of the Department of HOUSING AND URBAN DEVELOPMENT (1966–69), first black member of the US cabinet. He was the administrator of the N.Y. Rent Commission (1955–59) and led the federal Housing and Home Finance Agency (1961–66).

WEAVERBIRDS, a large family, Ploceidae of Old-World (particularly African) seed-eating birds. They are gregarious sparrow-like birds best known for their nests which hang from the tips of twigs and are enclosed structures, usually with a descending entrance tube.

WEAVING, making a fabric by interlacing two or more sets of threads. In "plain" weave, one set of threads—the *warp*—extends along the length of the fabric; the other set—the *woof*, or *weft*—is at right angles to the warp and passes alternately over and under it. Other common weaves include "twill," "satin" and "pile." In basic twill, woof threads, stepped one warp thread further on with each line, pass over two warp threads, under one, then over two again, producing diagonal ridges, or wales, as in denim, flannel and gaberdine. In satin weave, a development of twill, long "float" threads passing under four warp threads give the fabric its characteristically smooth appearance. Pile fabrics, such as corduroy and velvet, have extra warp or weft threads woven into a ground weave in a series of loops that are then cut to produce the pile. Weaving is usually accomplished by means of a hand- or power-operated machine called a loom. Warp threads are stretched on a frame and passed through eyelets in vertical wires (heddles) supported on a frame (the harness). A space (the shed) between sets of warp threads is made by moving the heddles up or down, and a shuttle containing the woof thread is passed through the shed. A special comb (the reed) then pushes home the newly woven line. (See also TEXTILES; RUGS AND CARPETS; BASKET WEAVING.)

WEBB, name of two English social reformers and economists. **Beatrice Webb** (née Potter, 1858–1943) studied working life for her *Life and Labour of the People in London* (1891–1903). Her husband, **Sidney James Webb, 1st Baron Passfield** (1859–1947), was a Labour Member of Parliament (1922–29) and held several Cabinet posts. The couple were leading intellectuals of the Labour movement and wrote together a *History of Trade Unionism* (1894). They were FABIANS and helped found the London School of Economics in 1895, and the left-wing journal *The New Statesman* in 1913.

A Maya Indian girl weaving on a simple hand loom.

WEBER (Wb), the unit of magnetic flux in SI UNITS, defined such that an ELECTROMOTIVE FORCE of one VOLT is induced in a single coil when the flux changes in the coil at the rate of one weber per second. (See INDUCTION, ELECTROMAGNETIC.)

WEBER, Carl Maria Friedrich Ernst von (1786–1826), German composer, pianist and conductor who established Romantic opera and paved the way in Germany for WAGNER, with the operas *Der Freischütz* (*The Marksman*; 1821), *Euryanthe* (1823) and *Oberon* (1826). He wrote a number of orchestral and chamber works, notably for the piano.

WEBER, Max (1864–1920), German economist and sociologist. In *The Protestant Ethic and the Spirit of Capitalism* (1904–05) he argued that the Calvinist emphasis on hard work helped develop business enterprise. He believed that many causes such as law, religion and politics combined with economics to determine the course of history. He defined a methodology for sociology.

WEBER, Max (1881–1961), Russian-born US painter who developed his style from primitive art and Jewish folklore. He studied in Europe (1905–09) but was in general outside the mainstream of modern art.

WEBER, Wilhelm Eduard (1804–1891), German physicist best known for his work with GAUSS on GEOMAGNETISM.

WEBERN, Anton von (1883–1945), Austrian composer who studied with SCHOENBERG and developed his TWELVE-TONE MUSIC form into a concentrated and individual style. His works include *Five Pieces for Orchestra* (1911–13), two symphonies, three string quartets and a number of songs.

WEBSTER, Daniel (1782–1852), US statesman, lawyer and orator whose advocacy of strong central government earned him the name of "defender of the Constitution." Early in his career, nonetheless, he defended STATES' RIGHTS and championed New England interests as N.H. member of the House of Representatives (1813–17) and Mass. representative (1823–27) and Senator (1827–41). As New England interests changed from shipping to industry, Webster became nationalist, and supported protective tariffs despite his earlier castigation of trade restrictions. His battle against NULLIFICATION began in 1830, and continued throughout the crisis of 1832–33; in his efforts to preserve the Union he supported the COMPROMISE OF 1850. He was twice Secretary of State. (See also WEBSTER-ASHBURTON TREATY.)

WEBSTER, John (c1580–c1625), English Jacobean playwright best remembered for his two powerful revenge tragedies, *The White Devil* (c1610) and *The*

Duchess of Malfi (c1615). Both are set in Renaissance Italy. Webster sometimes collaborated with other playwrights, notably John FORD and Thomas DEKKER.

WEBSTER, Noah (1758–1843), US lexicographer whose works such as *The Elementary Spelling Book*, called the "Blue-Backed Speller" (1829; earlier versions 1783–87), helped standardize American spelling. He compiled a grammar (1784) and a reader (1785). Working on dictionaries from 1803 he published *An American Dictionary of the English Language* (1828), with 70 000 entries and 12 000 new definitions.

WEBSTER-ASHBURTON TREATY (1842), agreement between the US and Great Britain settling the line of the NE border of the US between Me. and New Brunswick. Signed by Daniel WEBSTER for the US and Lord Ashburton for Great Britain, the treaty also agreed on joint suppression of the slave trade.

WEBSTER GROVES, city in E Mo., a mainly residential suburb of St. Louis. Some petroleum by-products are processed. Pop 27 455.

WEDDELL SEA, arm of the S Atlantic Ocean in Antarctica between Palmer Land and Coats Land. At its S end are the Ronne and Filchner Ice Shelves.

WEDEKIND, Frank (1864–1918), German playwright who attacked the hypocrisy and sexual mores of his times, notably in *Spring Awakening* (1891). His "Lulu plays," *Earth-Spirit* (1895) and *Pandora's Box* (1903), center on Lulu, a personification of natural sensuality, and inspired an opera by BERG. Many of his techniques foreshadowed EXPRESSIONISM.

WEDEMEYER, Albert Coady (1897–), US general, given the Distinguished Service Medal for his work as chief of the strategy section in WWII. He commanded US troops in China (1944–46) and the US 6th Army (1949–51).

WEDGE. See MACHINE.

WEDGWOOD, Josiah (1730–1795), outstanding English potter, inventor of Wedgwood ware. He patented his cream Queen's Ware in 1765; for the designs on his blue and white Jasper Ware he frequently employed John FLAXMAN. Wedgwood introduced new materials and machinery; his factory at Etruria, Staffordshire, was the first to acquire steam engines.

WEDNESDAY, fourth day of the week, named for the Germanic god ODIN or Woden. The French *mercredi* derives from the Roman god MERCURY.

WEED, Thurlow (1797–1882), US journalist and Whig political leader. He used his *Albany Evening Journal* to promote the ANTIMASONIC PARTY. He supported the presidential campaigns of William HARRISON and Zachary TAYLOR and the career of his friend, W. H. SEWARD. He joined the Republicans in 1855 and under LINCOLN was a special agent to England.

WEEDKILLERS, or **herbicides**, chemical compounds used to kill weeds (plants growing where they are unwanted). Originally general herbicides were used—diesel oil, sulfuric acid, sodium arsenite, sodium chlorate, etc.—but these dangerous substances have been largely superseded since WWII by a vast host of selective weedkillers, complex organic compounds (also dangerous) which at a suitable dosage are much more toxic to the prevailing weeds than to the crop. Contact herbicides, including paraquat, kill only the parts of the plants on which they are sprayed. The use of weedkillers complements good agricultural management, mechanical destruction of weeds and biological control.

WEEHAWKEN, township in NE N.J. on the Hudson R, an industrial port and railroad center. Settled by the Dutch (c1647), it was scene of the dual between BURR and HAMILTON.

WEEK, an arbitrary division of time, through most of the Christian era, of duration seven days. In most European languages, the days of the week are named for the planets or deities which were considered to preside over them.

WEEMS, Mason Locke (1759–1825), clergyman and (from 1794) traveling book agent who invented the story of George Washington and the cherry tree in the fifth edition of his *The Life and Memorable Actions of George Washington* (1800).

WEEVILS, the largest animal family, Curculionidae, 35 000 species of oval or pear-shaped BEETLES having a greatly drawn out head or snout bearing strong chewing mouthparts. They feed on hard vegetable matter, seeds and wood; the larvae, developing within seeds, are legless. Weevils are important economic pests of cotton and grain crops; also of stored peas, beans and flour.

WEGENER, Alfred Lothar (1880–1930), German meteorologist, explorer and geologist. His *The Origin of Continents and Oceans* (1915) set forth "Wegener's hypothesis," the theory of CONTINENTAL DRIFT, whose developments were in succeeding decades to revolutionize man's view of the planet he lives on (see also PLATE TECTONICS).

WEIDENREICH, Franz (1873–1948), German-born US physical anthropologist and anatomist best known for his work on fossil remains of *Sinanthropus*, *Pithecanthropus* and *Meganthropus* (see PREHISTORIC MAN), and for his chronological arrangement of the various stages in man's evolution.

WEIGHT, the attractive FORCE experienced by an object in the presence of another massive body in accordance with the law of universal GRAVITATION. The weight of a body (measured in newtons) is given by the product of its MASS and the local ACCELERATION due to gravity (g). Weight differs from mass in being a VECTOR quantity.

WEIGHTLIFTING, competitive sport. Long popular in Turkey, Egypt, Japan and Europe it has been a regular event in the Olympic Games since 1920. There are three basic lifts: the snatch (from the floor to over the head in a single motion); the clean and jerk (two movements—first to the chest and then over the head); and the military or two-hand press (similar to the clean and jerk, but retaining a "military" stance).

WEIGHTS AND MEASURES, units of WEIGHT, LENGTH, AREA and VOLUME commonly used in the home, in commerce and in industry. Although like other early peoples the Hebrews used measures such as the foot, the cubit (the length of the human forearm) and the span, which could easily be realized in practice using parts of the body, in commerce they also used standard containers and weights. Later, weights were based on the quantity of precious metal in coins. During and after the Middle Ages, each region evolved its own system of weights and measures. In the 19th century these were standardized on a national basis, these national standards in turn being superseded by those of the METRIC SYSTEM. In the western world, only the British Empire and the US retained their own systems (the Imperial System and the US Customary System) into the mid-20th century. With the UK's adoption of the International System of Units (SI UNITS), the US has found itself alone in not using metric units, although, as has been the case since 1959, the US customary units are now defined in terms of their metric counterparts and not on the basis of independent standards. In the US the administration of weights and measures is coordinated by the National Bureau of Standards (NBS) who also publish the version of the International System used in this volume. (See also APOTHECARIES' WEIGHTS; TROY WEIGHT.)

WEIL, Simone (1909–1943), French philosopher, religious mystic and left-wing intellectual. She was active in the Spanish Civil war and the French Resistance in WWII. She converted from Judaism to Christianity c1940. Her books include *Oppression and Liberty* (1955).

WEILL, Kurt (1900–1950), German-US composer. His most original music is for the two satirical operas on which he collaborated with BRECHT, *The Threepenny Opera* (1928) and *The Rise and Fall of the City of Mahagonny* (1930). He went to the US in 1935, and became a successful Broadway composer.

WEIMAR, city in SW East Germany, on the Ilm R, manufacturing agricultural machinery, electrical equipment and chemicals. It was capital of the Saxe-Weimar duchy from 1547, and its court became the German cultural and intellectual center in the 18th and 19th centuries, attracting BACH, GOETHE, SCHILLER, HERDER, LISZT and NIETSCHE. It was site of the BAUHAUS. BUCHENWALD concentration camp was nearby. Pop 63 689.

WEIMARANER, breed of sporting dog developed in Germany in the 19th century to hunt big game, now used as a bird dog and retriever. It stands 23–27in, weighs 55–85lb and has a gray coat and long ears.

WEIMAR REPUBLIC, German government (1919–33) based on the democratic republican constitution adopted at Weimar in 1919. Its presidents were EBERT and then von HINDENBURG who made HITLER chancellor in 1933; Hitler suspended the constitution the same year.

WEIRTON, industrial city in NW W.Va. on the Ohio R, with steel and coalmining industries. Pop 27 131.

WEISMANN, August (1834–1914), German biologist regarded as a father of modern GENETICS for his demolition of the theory that ACQUIRED CHARACTERISTICS could be inherited, and proposal that CHROMOSOMES are the basis of HEREDITY. He coupled this proposal with his belief in NATURAL SELECTION as the mechanism for EVOLUTION.

WEIZMANN, Chaim (1874–1952), Polish-born Zionist leader, first president of Israel from 1949. He emigrated to England in 1904 and became an eminent biochemist and director of the British Admiralty laboratories in 1916. He helped secure the BALFOUR DECLARATION (1917), which promised a Jewish state in Palestine. He was head of the World Zionist Organization (1920–29) and of the JEWISH AGENCY (1929–31, 1935–46). (See ZIONISM.)

WELCH, Joseph Nye (1890–1960), US lawyer, counsel for the US Army during the Senate Committee hearings on Government Operations conducted by Senator Joseph McCARTHY in 1954, and author of *The Constitution* (1956).

WELCH, William Henry (1850–1934), US pathologist and bacteriologist whose most significant achievements were in the field of medical education, playing a large part in the founding (1893) and development of the Johns Hopkins Medical School.

WELD, Theodore Dwight (1803–1895), US abolitionist, a founder of the American Antislavery Society (1833–34). He organized 70 agents to campaign in the North, edited the *Emancipator*, lobbied Congress and wrote the influential *American Slavery As It Is* (1839), a basis for H. B. STOWE's *Uncle Tom's Cabin*.

WELDING, bringing two pieces of metal together under conditions of heat or pressure or both, until they coalesce at the joint. The oldest method is forge welding, in which the surfaces to be joined are heated to welding temperature and then hammered together on an anvil. The most widely used method today is metal-arc welding: an ELECTRIC ARC is struck between an ELECTRODE and the workpieces to be joined, and molten metal from a "filler rod"—usually the electrode itself—is added. Gas welding, now largely displaced by metal-arc welding, is usually accomplished by means of an oxyacetylene torch, which delivers the necessary heat by burning ACETYLENE in a pure OXYGEN atmosphere. Sources of heat in other forms of welding include the electrical RESISTANCE of the joint (resistance welding), an electric arc at the joint (flash welding), a focused beam of ELECTRONS (electronbeam welding), pressure alone, usually well in excess of 1 400 000kPa (cold welding), and friction (friction welding). Some more recently applied heat sources include hot PLASMAS, LASERS, ULTRASONIC vibrations and explosive impacts.

WELFARE, direct government aid to the needy. In the US various programs, operated by the SOCIAL SECURITY office and state and local government, provide aid to the handicapped, aged, poor (see POVERTY) and unemployed. Benefits to the aged are nationally more-or-less standardized, but the form of, amount and qualifications for other benefits differ from state to state. Benefits fall under many programs, such as veterans' aid and WORKMEN'S COMPENSATION. All welfare programs are linked to programs which do not give direct financial assistance—housing, food stamps, MEDICARE and Medicaid. This patchwork of programs causes inequalities and hardships, which President NIXON hoped to resolve by his unsuccessful minimum family income plan (1971).

WELL, man-made hole in the ground used to tap water, gas or minerals from the earth. Most modern wells are drilled and fitted with a lining, usually of

Weights and Measures (a) US Customary System

Quantity	Unit	Symbol	Equivalent in same system	Approximate SI equivalent
weight (avoirdupois)	ton (short)	—	20 hundredweight (short)	0.907 tonne
	hundredweight	cwt	100 pounds	45.359 kg
	pound	lb (lb av)	16 ounces (7 000 grains)	*0.453 592 37 kg
	ounce	oz (oz av)	16 drams	28.350 g
	dram	dr (dr av)	27.344 grains	1.772 g
	grain	gr	—	*64.798 91 mg
length	mile	mi	1 760 yards	*1.609 344 km
	yard	yd	3 feet	*0.914 4 m
	foot	ft	12 inches	*0.304 8 m
	inch	in	—	*25.4 mm
area	square mile	sq mi (mi^2)	640 acres	2.589 99 km^2
	acre	—	4 840 sq yards	0.404 69 ha
	square yard	sq yd (yd^2)	9 sq feet	0.836 13 m^2
	square foot	sq ft (ft^2)	144 sq inches	0.092 90 m^2
	square inch	sq in (in^2)	—	*645.16 mm^2
volume	cubic yard	cu yd (yd^3)	27 cu feet	0.764 555 m^3
	cubic foot	cu ft (ft^3)	1 728 cu inches	0.028 317 m^3
	cubic inch	cu in (in^3)	—	*16 387.064 mm^3
capacity (liquid measure)	gall	gal	4 quarts	3.785 4 l
	quart	qt	2 pints	0.946 3 l
	pint	pt	4 gills	0.473 2 l
	gill	gi	4 fluidounces	0.118 3 l
	fluidounce	fl oz	8 fluidrams	29.573 ml
	fluidram	fl dr	60 minims	3.697 ml
	minim	min	—	0.061 610 ml
capacity (dry measure)	bushel	bu	4 pecks	35.238 l
	peck	pk	8 quarts	8.810 l
	quart	qt	2 pints	1.101 l
	pint	pt	—	0.551 l

(b) British Imperial System (where different from US Customary System)

Quantity	Unit	Symbol	Equivalent in same system	Approximate SI and US equivalents
weight (avoirdupois)	ton (long)	—	20 hundredweight (long)	1.016 tonne 1.12 short tons
	hundredweight (long)	cwt	112 pounds	50.802 kg 1.12 short cwt
liquid and dry measure	bushel	bu	4 pecks	36.369 l
	peck	pk	2 gallons	9.092 l
	gallon	gal	4 quarts	4.546 l 1.201 US gal
	quart	qt	2 pints	1.137 l
	pint	pt	4 gills	568.260 ml
	gill	gi	5 fluidounces	142.065 ml
	fluidounce	fl oz	8 fluidrams	28.413 ml 0.961 US fl oz
	fluidram	fl dr	60 minims	3.551 6 ml
	minim	min	—	0.059 194 ml

*exact equivalent.

steel, to forestall collapse. Though wells are sunk for NATURAL GAS and PETROLEUM oil, the commonest type yields water. Such wells may be horizontal or vertical, but all have their innermost end below the water table (see GROUNDWATER). If it should be below the permanent water table (the lowest annual level of the water table) the well will yield water throughout the year. Most wells require to be pumped, but some operate under natural pressure (see ARTESIAN WELL).

WELLAND, city in SE Ontario, Canada, on the WELLAND SHIP CANAL, an industrial center for textiles and steel and a fruit-trading center. Pop 44 397.

WELLAND SHIP CANAL, Canadian waterway running 27.6mi from Port Colborne on Lake Erie to Port Weller on Lake Ontario to form a major link of the SAINT LAWRENCE SEAWAY. The canal was built 1912–32 and has a minimum depth of about 30ft. It has eight locks to overcome the 326ft difference in height between lakes Erie and Ontario.

WELLER, Thomas Huckle (1915–   ), US bacteriologist and virologist who shared with J. F. ENDERS and F. C. ROBBINS the 1954 Nobel Prize for Physiology or Medicine for their cultivation of POLIOMYELITIS virus in non-nerve tissues.

WELLES, Gideon (1802–1878), US politician who helped organize the Republican party. Made secretary of the navy (1861–69) by Lincoln, during the CIVIL WAR he blockaded the Confederate coast and built up a powerful Union fleet of IRONCLADS.

WELLES, (George) Orson (1915–   ), US actor, director and producer. In 1938 his Mercury Theater's realistic radio production of H. G. WELLS' *War of the Worlds* made thousands of listeners panic. His film *Citizen Kane* (1941), was modeled on the life of newspaper magnate, W. R. HEARST. In films such as *The Magnificent Ambersons* (1942) and *Lady from Shanghai* (1947) innovative camera work and film editing continue to characterize his work.

WELLESLEY, residential town in E Mass., a suburb of Boston, site of Wellesley College for women (1870). Pop 28 051.

WELLESLEY, Richard Colley Wellesley, Marquess, 2nd Earl of Mornington (1760–1842), British statesman in India. As governor general of Bengal and governor of Madras (1797–1805) he greatly extended British authority in India. When lord lieutenant of Ireland (1821–28, 1833–34) he favored CATHOLIC EMANCIPATION.

WELLINGTON, founded 1840, capital city of New Zealand since 1865, at the S of North Island. It is an important trading port and transportation center with textile, food and mechanical industries and cultural amenities. Pop 135 677.

WELLINGTON, Arthur Wellesley, 1st Duke of (1792–1852), British general and statesman, "the Iron Duke," who defeated NAPOLEON I at the battle of WATERLOO. After distinguished military service in India (1796–1805), he drove the French from Spain and Portugal in the PENINSULAR WARS and entered France in 1813. After being created duke, he led the victorious forces at Waterloo (1815). Serving the Tory government for 1819–27, he became prime minister (1828–30), passed the CATHOLIC EMANCIPATION BILL but opposed Parliamentary reform. In 1842 he became commander-in-chief for life.

WELLS, Henry (1805–1878). US pioneer expressman. Associated with W. FARGO from 1844, he founded Wells, Fargo and Co. (1852) to supply express mail to Cal. and the West. By acquiring the OVERLAND MAIL COMPANY (1866) he owned the greatest US stagecoach network.

WELLS, H. G. (Herbert George; 1866–1946), British writer and social reformer. After being a draper's apprentice he studied science and taught. After such early science-fiction as *The Time Machine* (1895) and *The War of the Worlds* (1898), he wrote novels on the lower middle class, including *Kipps* (1905) and *The History of Mr Polly* (1910). A founder of the FABIAN SOCIETY, he was a social prophet (*A Modern Utopia*; 1905). After WWI he popularized knowledge in *Outline of History* (1920) and *The Science of Life* (1931).

WELLS, Horace (1815–1848), US dentist and pioneer of surgical ANESTHESIA, using (largely without success) nitrous oxide (see NITROGEN).

WELSBACH, Carl Auer von, Baron (1858–1929), Austrian chemist who invented the incandescent gas mantle (patented 1885) and the ALLOY, Auer metal, used to make lighter flints.

WELSH, or Cymraeg, one of the Brythonic group of CELTIC LANGUAGES, still widely spoken in Wales. There is a rich literature, particularly of poetry.

WELSH TERRIER, breed of dog developed in Wales to hunt foxes, badgers and otters. It is about 15in high and about 20lbs in weight, and has a wiry black-and-tan coat.

WELTY, Eudora (1909–   ), US novelist and short-story writer, known for sensitive tales of Miss. life. She superbly depicted atmosphere and characters in *The Wide Net* (1943), *The Ponder Heart* (1954), *The Optimist's Daughter* (1972; Pulitzer Prize) and others.

WEN, or sebaceous CYST, blocked SEBACEOUS GLAND, often over the scalp or forehead, which forms a cyst containing old sebum under the SKIN. It may become infected. Its excision is a simple procedure.

WENATCHEE, city in Wash. on the Columbia R, seat of Chelan Co., a commercial, fruit and industrial center and a resort. Pop 16 912.

WENCESLAUS, Saint (c907–929), Duke of Bohemia, famous for his efforts to Christianize his people. On him the song *Good King Wenceslaus* was based.

WENCESLAUS (1361–1419), Holy Roman Emperor, king of Germany (1378–1400) and of Bohemia (1378–1419). Often drunk and indolent, he failed to prevent wars among German princes, cities and nobility. Deposed as German king and emperor, he also lost effective power in Bohemia.

WENCHOU, or **Wenchow,** city in E China, a former TREATY PORT for tea, now a shipping center for lumber and bamboo. Pop 250 000.

WENDS, or Sorbs, Slavic people who by the 5th century settled between the Elbe and Oder rivers, Germany. German conquest of the Wends lasted from the 6th to the 12th century, by which date many Wends were Christianized. Today Wends are found in Lusatia.

WENTWORTH, Thomas. See STRAFFORD, THOMAS WENTWORTH, 1ST EARL OF.

WEREWOLF (Old English: man-wolf), in superstition, a man who can supernaturally turn into a wolf and devour humans. The belief dates from Greek legend and was widespread in medieval Europe and in the 19th-century Balkans. (See also LYCANTHROPY.)

WERFEL, Franz (1890–1945), Austrian novelist, poet and playwright, whose early plays and poetry such as *Der Spiegelmensch* (1920) were important works of German EXPRESSIONISM. His novels include *Embezzled Heaven* (1939) and *The Song of Bernadette* (1941).

WERNER, Abraham Gottlob (1750–1817), Silesian-born mineralogist who taught for over 40 years at the Freiberg Mining Academy, disseminating the doctrines of NEPTUNISM.

WERNER, Alfred (1866–1919), French-born Swiss chemist awarded the 1913 Nobel Prize for Chemistry for his theory of coordination complexes. (See BOND, CHEMICAL; LIGANDS.)

WERTHEIMER, Max (1880–1943), Czechoslovakian-born US founder, with KOFFKA and KÖHLER, of the school of GESTALT PSYCHOLOGY.

WESER, river in West Germany, formed at Münden by the junction of the Fulda and Werra rivers, which flows about 273mi N to the North Sea.

WESKER, Arnold (1932–   ), English playwright whose trilogy, *Chicken Soup with Barley* (1958), *Roots* (1959) and *I'm Talking About Jerusalem* (1960), is written from a socialist, working-class viewpoint. His best known play is *Chips With Everything* (1962).

WESLACO, city in S Tex., named for the W. E. Stewart Land Company. It has canning and fruit-and vegetable-processing industries. Pop 15 313.

WESLEY, name of two evangelistic preachers who with George WHITEFIELD founded METHODISM. **John Wesley** (1703–1791), ordained 1725, and his brother **Charles** (1707–1788), ordained 1735, formed an Oxford "Holy Club" of scholarly Christians, known as "Methodists" for their "rule and methods." In 1738 the brothers were profoundly influenced by the MORAVIAN CHURCH and John particularly by LUTHER's *Preface to the Epistle to the Romans*. Aiming to promote "vital, practical religion" the Wesleys took up evangelistic work by field or open-air preaching. Rejected by the church, they were enthusiastically received by the people, and they organized conferences of itinerant lay preachers. Charles composed more than 5 500 hymns. His grandson, **Samuel Sebastian Wesley** (1810–1876), was a noted composer of church music for both choir and organ.

WESSEX, Anglo-Saxon kingdom in S England, roughly comprising modern Somerset, Dorset, Wiltshire and Hampshire. Probably first settled by the SAXON Cedric in 495, it was at its largest under EGBERT (802–39). ALFRED THE GREAT (871–99) checked the Danish invasions and by 927 ETHELSTAN overturned DANELAW and controlled all England. Thomas HARDY revived the name in his novels.

WEST, Benjamin (1738–1820), American-born painter. After studying in Rome he settled in London (1763), becoming official history painter to King George III and a founder of the ROYAL ACADEMY OF ARTS. His best-known works are *The Death of General Wolfe* (1771) and *Penn's Treaty with the Indians* (1776).

WEST, Nathanael (1903–1940), pseudonym of Nathan Weinstein, US novelist. His satiric novels, *Miss Lonelyhearts* (1933), the story of an agony columnist, and *Day of the Locust* (1939) are bitter and disturbing, with sudden flashes of humor.

WEST, Dame Rebecca (Cicily Isabel Fairfield; 1892–   ), British novelist, critic and journalist. *Black Lamb and Grey Falcon: A Journey through Yugoslavia* (1941) is perhaps her finest work. Her novels include *Birds Fall Down* (1966).

WEST ALLIS, city in Wis., an industrial suburb of Milwaukee, manufacturing electronic equipment and heavy machinery. Pop 71 649.

WEST BEND, city in E Wis. on the Milwaukee R, seat of Washington Co. It has diverse light industry. Pop 16 555.

WEST BERLIN. See BERLIN.

WESTBOROUGH, residential town in E central Mass. on the Assabet R, with light industries. Pop 12 594.

WESTBROOKE, city in SW Me., an industrial suburb of Portland, manufacturing wood and paper products and shoes. Pop 14 444.

WESTBURY, residential village in SE N.Y. on Long Island, settled in 1650. Pop 15 362.

WEST CALDWELL, residential borough in NE N.J., suburb of New York City and Newark, with light industry. Pop 11 887.

WEST CARROLTON, city in SW Ohio on the Miami R, a suburb of Dayton. Pop 10 748.

WESTCHESTER, village in NW Ill., a suburb W of Chicago. Pop 20 033.

WEST CHESTER, residential borough in SE Pa., the seat of Chester Co., an agricultural processing and trade center, with light industry. Pop 19 301.

WEST CHICAGO, city in NE Ill., 30mi W of Chicago. Pop 10 111.

WEST COVINA, residential city in SW Cal., W of Los Angeles, formerly an agricultural community. Pop 68 034.

WEST DES MOINES (formerly Valley Junction), city in S central Ia., a suburb of Des Moines, manufacturing cement and foundry products. Pop 16 441.

WESTERLIES. See PREVAILING WESTERLIES.

WESTERLY, town in SW R.I., settled 1648 and incorporated 1669. Formerly a shipbuilding center it now has textile and varied industries. Pop 17 248.

WESTERN AUSTRALIA, largest Australian state (975 920sq mi), first settled 1826–29, covering the W third of the country. Beyond the narrow coastal strip and fertile SW, it is mostly dry plateau with vast desert wastes. Major products are wool, wheat and lumber; chief minerals are gold (80% of the national output), coal and iron. Its capital is Perth.

WESTERN CHURCH, one of the two great branches of the Christian Church (see EASTERN CHURCH). The Latin-speaking church of the western Roman empire, it was increasingly dominated by Roman usage and by the papacy, whose claims of supremacy grew and were enforced. It thus developed into the ROMAN CATHOLIC CHURCH, though the Protestant churches formed at the Reformation share the common western tradition. (See also CHRISTIANITY; GREAT SCHISM.)

WESTERN EUROPEAN UNION (WEU), defensive economic, social and cultural alliance (1955) of Belgium, France, Great Britain, Italy, Luxembourg, the Netherlands and West Germany. It supervised German rearmament. The Council of Europe took over economic and cultural activities (1960).

WESTERN FEDERATION OF MINERS (WFM), radical US miners' union (1893) of the W states. It clashed with federal, state and company forces. In 1905 WFM leader W. D. HAYWOOD, falsely charged, was acquitted of a former governor's murder. The WFM cofounded the INDUSTRIAL WORKERS OF THE WORLD (1905), seceded to rejoin the AMERICAN FEDERATION OF LABOR and became the International Union of Mine, Mill and Smelter Workers (1916).

WESTERN RESERVE, NE region of Ohio on the S shore of Lake Erie. In 1786, Conn. refused to cede this area to the NORTHWEST TERRITORY. In 1792, 500 000 acres were granted to Conn. citizens whose land was destroyed during the Revolution. The remaining land was sold to a land company which built Cleveland. The region joined the Northwest Territory 1800.

WESTERN SAHARA, former Spanish province in NW Africa, comprising 102 680sq mi of, mainly, desert on the Atlantic coast, rich in phosphate deposits. Despite active independence movements among native Arabs and Berbers, it was formally divided between neighboring Morocco and Mauritania in 1975. By supporting the Saharan guerrilla force Polisaro, Algeria created increasingly tense relations with Morocco in 1976.

WESTERN SAMOA, independent state in the SW Pacific Ocean, 1 097sq mi in land area, comprising two large islands, Savai'i and UPOLU, the much smaller islands of Apolima, Fanuatapa, Manono, Namua, Nuula, Nuusafee, Nuutele and coral formations. Most of the islands are mountainous, volcanic, forested and fertile. The climate is rainy and tropical. The people are Polynesian and the majority live in Upolu, where Apia, the capital and chief port, stands. Samoans speak probably the oldest Polynesian language in use. The economy is agricultural, the main exports, being copra, bananas and cacao. Tourism is important. The current development program, backed by foreign aid, aims to expand agriculture and encourage modest industrialization (e.g., soap, lumber).

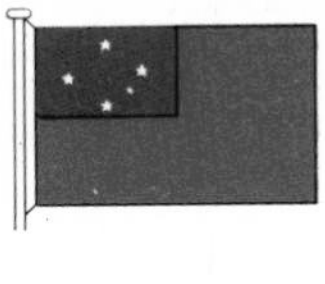

Official name: The Independent State of Western Samoa
Capital: Apia
Area: 1 097sq mi
Population: 146 635
Languages: Samoan; English
Religion: Christian
Monetary unit(s): 1 Western Samoa talā = 100 cents

History. The islands were probably discovered by the Dutch explorer, Jacob Roggeveen (1722). A British mission was founded on Savai'i in 1830. Germany, Great Britain and the US agreed in 1899 that SAMOA should be divided between the US and Germany. In 1914 New Zealand seized German Samoa, later administering it by League of Nations mandate, and as a UN trust territory. It became independent as Western Samoa in 1962.

WESTERN SCHISM. See GREAT SCHISM.

WESTERN SPRINGS, village in NE Ill., a suburb of Chicago, named in 1886 for local mineral springs. It has seed nurseries. Pop 12 147.

WESTERVILLE, city in central Ohio, 12mi N of Columbus, with varied manufacturing and dairy industries. Pop 12 530.

WESTFIELD, city in SW Mass., a suburb of Springfield. It manufactures paper, machinery and bicycles. Pop 31 433.

WESTFIELD, residential town in NE N.J., settled in 1700. Pop 33 720.

WESTFORD, town in NE Mass. in a granite-quarrying and fruit-farming region. It manufactures textile machinery. Pop 10 368.

WEST HARTFORD, town in central Conn., a suburb of Hartford. It manufactures machinery and metal products. Pop 68 031.

WEST HAVEN, residential town in S Conn., a suburb of New Haven. It has diversified industries. Pop 52 851.

WEST HELENA, city in E Ark., near the Mississippi R. It manufactures wood products. Pop 11 007.

WEST HEMPSTEAD-LAKEVIEW, residential city in SE N.Y., on Long Island. Pop 20 375.

WEST HIGHLAND WHITE TERRIER, jaunty little breed of dog, an offshoot of the CAIRN TERRIER, standing 11in high, weighing 18lb. A hardy and affectionate pet, its short, all-white coat needs little trimming and is easy to keep clean.

WEST HOLLYWOOD, urban region in SW Cal., NE of Beverly Hills. Pop 29 448.

WEST INDIES, chain of islands extending from Fla. to the N coast of South America, separating the Caribbean Sea and the Gulf of Mexico from the Atlantic Ocean. An alternative name (excluding the Bahamas) is the Antilles. The West Indies comprises three main groups: the BAHAMAS to the NE of Cuba and Hispaniola; the Greater Antilles (Cuba—the largest island in the West Indies, Hispaniola (HAITI and DOMINICAN REPUBLIC), Jamaica and Puerto Rico); and the Lesser Antilles (LEEWARD and WINDWARD ISLANDS, Trinidad and Tobago and Barbados); together with the NETHERLANDS ANTILLES and other islands off the Venezuelan coast. Many of the islands are mountainous and volcanic with lagoons and mangrove swamps on their coastlines. The climate is warm but there are frequent hurricanes. The principal crop is sugarcane. Tourism is an important industry. After COLUMBUS reached the West Indies (1492) they were settled by the Spanish followed by the English, French and Dutch who

exploited the spices and sugar using African slaves. The political status of the islands varies widely.

WEST INDIES ASSOCIATED STATES, island states in the Caribbean Sea, individually associated with the UK which, although each island is selfgoverning, is responsible for foreign relations and defense. The original (1967) five states—Antigua, Dominica, Grenada, St. Kitts-Nevis-Anguilla and St. Lucia—were joined by St. Vincent in 1969. Formerly British colonies, the states were part of the West Indies Federation 1958–62. In 1972, together with the Bahamas, British Honduras, Guyana, Jamaica, Montserrat and Trinidad and Tobago, they declared their intention to form a Caribbean Common Market.

WESTINGHOUSE, George (1846–1914), US engineer, inventor and businessman who pioneered the use of high-voltage AC electricity. In 1869 he founded the Westinghouse Air Brake Company to develop the air BRAKES he had invented for RAILROAD use. From 1883 he did pioneering work on the safe transmission of NATURAL GAS. In 1886 he founded the Westinghouse Electric Company, employing notably TESLA, to develop AC INDUCTION MOTORS and transmission equipment: this company was largely responsible for the acceptance of AC in preference to DC for most applications—in spite of opposition from the influential EDISON.

WEST IRIAN, or Irian Barat, renamed Irian Joya (1973), province, the W half of NEW GUINEA. It is mountainous and thickly forested. It is organized into hundreds of tribes, some of which still practice headhunting and cannibalism. Agriculture is at subsistence level and crops include sago, sweet potato, taro, bananas and rice. The chief export is crude oil. After centuries of Dutch rule the area was transferred to the UN in 1962 and came under Indonesian rule in 1963.

WEST LAFAYETTE, city in W central Ind., suburb of Lafayette, on Wabash R. near the site of the TIPPECANOE battle (1811). Pop 19 157.

WESTLAKE, (formerly Dover), light industrial city in N Ohio, a suburb of Cleveland, manufacturing ink and plastics. Pop 15 689.

WESTLAND, city in SE Mich., 20mi W of Detroit. Pop 86 749.

WEST MEMPHIS, city in E Ark., a shipping and industrial center on the Mississippi R. Pop 26 070.

WEST MIFFLIN, industrial borough in SW Pa., a suburb of Pittsburgh with steel and household appliance industries. Pop 28 070.

WESTMINSTER, residential city in SW Cal., SE of Long Beach, founded as a Presbyterian temperance colony. Pop 59 874.

WESTMINSTER, residential city in NE central Col., a suburb of Denver. Its economy is based on varied industries. Pop 19 432.

WESTMINSTER, Statute of (1931), British parliamentary act abolishing Britain's power to legislate for its dominions. It gave the dominions complete independence in the COMMONWEALTH OF NATIONS although they owed common allegiance to the British crown.

WESTMINSTER ABBEY, great English Gothic church in London, traditional scene of English coronations since that of WILLIAM the Conqueror, and a burial place for English monarchs and famous subjects. The present building, started in 1245, is on the site of a church (1065) built by EDWARD THE CONFESSOR.

WESTMINSTER CONFESSION, Reformation confession of faith (see CREED) forming the subordinate doctrinal standard of most REFORMED CHURCHES. A detailed statement of CALVINISM, it was produced 1643–46 by the Westminster Assembly, a synod called by the LONG PARLIAMENT to reform the Church of England. The assembly also issued the two Westminster Catechisms. (See also PURITANS.)

WEST MONROE, city in N La., on the Ouachita R opposite Monroe, in an agriculture and lumber region. Pop 14 868.

WESTMORELAND, William Childs (1914–), US general, US Army chief of staff 1968–72. He was superintendent of WEST POINT 1960–63 and the US commander in Vietnam 1964–68.

WESTMOUNT, residential city of S Quebec, Canada, a suburb of Montreal on Montreal Island. Pop 23 606.

WEST NEW YORK, residential town, NE N.J., on the Hudson R opposite New York City, of whose port it is part. It has embroidery industries. Pop 40 627.

WESTON, residential town in NE Mass., 12mi W of Boston, settled in 1642. Pop 10 870.

WESTON, Edward (1886–1958), US photographer, one of the most influential of the 20th century. He aimed for clarity of detail (using large-view cameras and small apertures) and composition, and seldom cropped, enlarged or touched-up. His best work is of still-lifes, nudes and sand dunes.

WEST ORANGE, residential town of NE N.J., a suburb of Newark. It manufactures electrical equipment. Pop 43 715.

WEST PALM BEACH, city in SE Fla., seat of Palm Beach Co., on Lake Worth opposite Palm Beach. It is a port and a tourist, commercial and industrial center. Pop 57 375.

WEST PATERSON, borough in N N.J., a suburb of Paterson with light manufacturing. Pop 11 692.

WESTPHALIA, part of the West German state of NORTH RHINE-WESTPHALIA, a former Prussian Province. It lies on the North German Plain between the Rhine and Weser valleys.

WESTPHALIA, Peace of, treaties signed by Sweden, France, Spain, the Holy Roman Empire and the Netherlands concluding the THIRTY YEARS' WAR in 1648. The treaties recognized the sovereignty of the German states of the Holy Roman Empire; declared the Netherlands and Switzerland independent republics; and granted religious freedom to Calvinists and Lutherans in Germany. Sweden acquired W Pomerania and Stettin; France Alsace, Metz, Toul and Verdun; and Brandenburg E Pomerania.

WEST POINT, site of, and common name for, the US Military Academy in SE N.Y., an institute of higher education which trains officers for the regular army. Established by Act of Congress in 1802, its training methods and traditions were set down by Colonel Sylvanus THAYER, superintendent of the academy 1817–33. Candidates for entry (since 1976 of either sex) to the academy must be unmarried US citizens aged 17–22 and must meet minimum academic requirements. Cadets are enlisted in the regular army on entrance. Graduates are awarded a BSc and a commission as 2nd lieutenant, and are expected to serve in the army for at least four years.

WESTPORT, residential town in SW Conn., a summer resort on Long Island Sound, at the mouth of the Saugatuck R. Pop 27 414.

WEST QUODDY HEAD, cape in NE Me., projecting into the Atlantic Ocean, easternmost point of the US, at the S entrance to Passamaquoddy Bay.

WEST SAINT PAUL, city in SE Minn., a suburb of St. Paul, manufacturing clothing, textiles and plastics. Pop 18 799.

WEST SPRINGFIELD, industrial town in SW Mass., on the Connecticut R, settled in 1654. It has varied manufacturing. Pop 28 461.

WEST UNIVERSITY PLACE, residential city in SE Tex., a suburb of Houston. Pop 13 317.

Officer cadets on parade at the United States Military Academy at West Point.

Name of State: West Virginia
Capital: Charleston
Statehood: June 20, 1863 (35th state)
Familiar Name: Mountain State
Area: 24 181sq mi
Population: 1 744 237
Elevation: Highest—4 862ft, Spruce Knob
Lowest—247ft, Potomac River
Motto: Montani Semper Liberi (Mountaineers are always free)
State Flower: Rhododendron
State Bird: Cardinal
State Tree: Sugar maple
State Songs: "The West Virginia Hills", "This is My West Virginia", "West Virginia, My Home Sweet Home"

WEST VIRGINIA, state in E central US.

Land. Most of West Virginia lies in the Appalachian Plateau, whose E edge is formed by the hills of Allegheny Front (over 4 500ft), the state's highest area. In the NE the Blue Ridge Mountains region is an area of fertile slopes and river valleys. The state's rugged terrain has the highest average elevation (over 1 500ft) E of the Mississippi. The chief rivers are the Ohio, on the NW border, the Potomac and the Kanawtha. The climate is mild, the annual temperature-range 34–70°F, and the annual rainfall about 45in.

Population. West Virginia is 60% rural. Most urban dwellers live in the industrial centers along the river valleys. Charleston and Huntingdon are the largest cities; there are no cities of over 100 000 people. Over 95% of the people are white.

Economy. The state is the leading US coal producer. Its prosperity has long been dependent on its bituminous COAL industry, but today other minerals such as natural gas, petroleum, stone and sand are exploited. The coal industry's decline in the 1950s prompted federal aid to expand industry and tourism; leading industries produce chemicals, iron, steel. Lumber is a significant resource. Farming is largely confined to the fertile river valleys.

History. West Virginia's history until 1861 is essentially that of VIRGINIA, although West Virginia was distinguished by its isolation from the state capital, the fact that few West Virginians owned slaves, and its economy—small-scale farming and industries based on mineral resources. In 1861 the West Virginians refused to secede from the Union with Va. They declared their independence, adopted a constitution (1862) and became 35th state of the Union in 1863. The state's rapid expansion in the coal, gas and steel industries was accompanied by severe labor-management conflicts and by riots, notably in the mines, which were resolved only by the NEW DEAL measures.

WEST WARWICK, town in central R.I. on the Pawtuxet R, dependent on agriculture and textile industries. Pop 24 323.

WESTWEGO, city in SE La., a suburb of New Orleans. Pop 11 402.

WESTWOOD, residential town in E Mass., SW of Boston. Pop 12 750.

The distinctive spouts of (left to right) the Sperm, Blue and Right whales.

WESTWOOD, residential borough in NE N.J., 9mi NE of Paterson. Pop 11 105.

WESTWOOD LAKES, village in SE Fla., a residential suburb of Miami. Pop 12 811.

WETBACKS, slang term for illegal Mexican immigrants in the US, which derives from how some immigrants avoided immigration control points—by swimming the Rio Grande.

WETHERSFIELD, residential town in central Conn., on the Connecticut R, the oldest permanent English settlement in Conn. (1634). It manufactures machinery and aircraft parts. Pop 26 662.

WEYDEN, Rogier Van der (c1400–1464), Flemish painter, the most influential painter of his period. Trained by CAPIN and influenced by VAN EYCK, he is noted for his tragic and emotional depiction of the scenes of the Passion such as *Descent from the Cross* (c1435) and *Calvary Triptych* (c1440–45). His portraits have the same intensity.

WEYLAND, Maxime (1867–1965), French general. He defended Warsaw (1920) in the RUSSO-POLISH WAR. As commander in chief in France he recommended the Franco-German armistice (1940). A member of the VICHY government, he was exonerated of German collaboration (1948).

WEYL, Hermann (1885–1955), German mathematician and mathematical physicist noted for his contributions to the theories of RELATIVITY and QUANTUM MECHANICS.

WEYLER Y NICOLAU, Valeriano, Marqués de Tenerife (1838–1930), Spanish soldier, governor and military commander of Cuba 1896–97, whose ruthless handling of the Cuban rebellion outraged US public opinion; he was recalled to Spain.

WEYMOUTH, residential town in E Mass., SE of Boston, the second oldest community in Mass. (1622), incorporated in 1635. Pop 54 610.

WEYPRECHT, Karl (1838–1881), German arctic explorer, whose advocacy of internationally coordinated polar exploration led to the first International Polar Year (1882–83). His 1872–74 expedition with Julius von Payer discovered FRANZ JOSEF LAND.

WHALES, an order, Cetacea, of large wholly-aquatic mammals. All are highly-adapted for life in water, with a torpedo-shaped body, front limbs reduced and modified as steering paddles, and hind limbs absent. They have a tail of two transverse flukes and swim by up-and-down movements of this tail. Most species have a fleshy dorsal fin which acts as a stabilizer. The neck is short, the head flowing directly into the trunk. The body is hairless and the smooth skin lies over a thick layer of BLUBBER which has an insulating function but also acts to smooth out the passage of water over the body in rapid swimming. The nose, or blowhole, is at the top of the head, allowing the animal to breathe as soon as it breaks the surface of the water. Modern whales divide into two suborders, the Mysticeti, or Whalebone Whales, and the Odontoceti, or Toothed whales. Whalebone whales feed on PLANKTON straining the enormous quantities they require from the water with special plates of whalebone, or BALEEN, developed from the mucus membrane of the upper jaw. Whalebone whales, the RIGHT WHALES, RORQUALS and Gray whales, are usually large and slow-moving. The group includes the BLUE WHALE, the largest animal of all time. Toothed whales, equipped with conical teeth, feed on fishes and squids. With the SPERM WHALE and NARWHAL, the group also includes the DOLPHINS and PORPOISES.

WHALE SHARK, *Rhincodon typus*, the largest of all fishes, of up to 13.5m (45ft) and weighing 13 tonnes. They are true SHARKS. Found in warmer waters, they are completely harmless to humans, despite their huge size.

WHALING, the hunting of WHALES, originally for oil, meat and BALEEN, practiced since the 900s if not earlier. The Basques and Dutch hunted from land and pioneered methods of flensing and boiling whale meat. American whaling started in the 1600s, and whaling ports such as Nantucket and New Bedford grew to great size in the 1700s. Whaling became safer after the invention (1856) of harpoons with explosive heads which caused instantaneous death and avoided the dangerous pursuit of a wounded whale. From the 1800s, whalers moved S in pursuit of the SPERM WHALE. Development of factory ships which processed the catch on board facilitated longer expeditions. In the 1900s whaling has centered on Antarctic waters. Reconaissance aircraft and electronic aids are now used. Whale products include oils, AMBERGRIS, spermaceti, meat and bone meal. Despite the (voluntary) restrictions of the International Whaling Convention, whales are still overfished, and many species face extinction.

WHARTON, Edith (1862–1937), US novelist, poet, and short-story writer, a friend of Henry JAMES. She wrote subtle and acerbic accounts of society in New York, New England and Europe, including *The House of Mirth* (1905), *Ethan Frome* (1911) and *The Age of Innocence* (1920, Pulitzer Prize).

WHEAT, *Triticum aestivum*, the world's main CEREAL CROP; about 300 million tonnes are produced every year, mostly used to make flour for bread and pasta. Wheat has been in cultivation since at least 7000BC and grows best in temperate regions of Europe, America, China and Australia. The USSR is the largest producer, followed by the US and Canada. There are many varieties of wheat and different parts of the grain are used to produce the various types of flour. Grains comprise an outer husk called the bran and a central starchy germ (which is embedded in a PROTEIN known as GLUTEN. Wheat is graded as hard or soft depending on how easily the flour can be separated from the bran. Wheat for bread is hard wheat and contains a lot of gluten. Soft wheat flours containing more STARCH and less protein are used for pastries. There are two main types of wheat; these are sown either in the fall (winter wheat), or in the spring (spring wheat). Harvesting is carried out by COMBINE HARVESTERS which cut and thresh the crop in one operation. Wheat is vulnerable to several diseases including SMUT, RUST, ARMY WORM and HESSIAN FLY. Family: Graminae.

WHEATLEY, Phillis (c1753–1784), early US black poet. Born in Africa, she was sold to John Wheatley of Boston, who educated her. Her *Poems on Various Subjects, Religious and Moral* were published in London 1773. She died in poverty.

WHEATON, city in NE Ill., seat of Du Page Co., a mainly residential suburb 25mi W of Chicago. Wheaton College is here. Pop 31 138.

WHEATON, unincorporated urban community in central Md., a residential suburb N of Washington, D.C. Pop 66 247.

WHEAT RIDGE, city in N central Col., a W residential suburb of Denver. Pop 29 795.

WHEATSTONE, Sir Charles (1802–1875), British physicist and inventor who popularized the WHEATSTONE BRIDGE; and invented the electric TELEGRAPH (with the help of Joseph HENRY) before MORSE (1837), the STEREOSCOPE (1838) and the concertina (1829).

WHEATSTONE BRIDGE, an electric circuit used for comparing or measuring RESISTANCE. Four resistors, including the unknown one, are connected in a square, with a BATTERY between one pair of diagonally opposite corners and a sensitive GALVANOMETER between the other. When no current flows through the meter, the products of opposite pairs of resistances are equal. Similar bridge circuits are used for IMPEDANCE measurement.

WHEEL, disk-like mechanical device mediating between rotary and linear motion, widely used to transmit POWER, store ENERGY (see FLYWHEEL) and to facilitate the movement of heavy objects. Wheels may be solid or spoked, flanged or unflanged, with or without TIRES. Most usefully, they are attached to an axle through the center. Indeed, the **wheel and axle** is one of the classic simple MACHINES, exemplified in the capstan, the WINCH and TRANSMISSION gears.

WHEELER, Burton Kendall (1882–1975), US

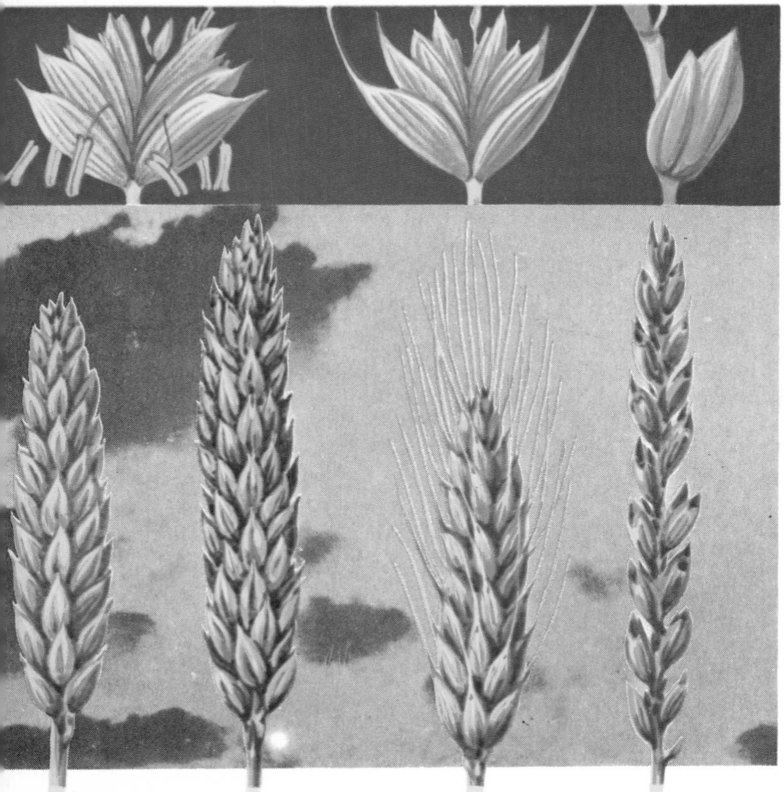

Grain clusters (*top*) and ears of (left to right): spring and winter varieties of common bread wheat (*Triticum aestivum*); durum wheat (*T. durum*), a hard wheat used in pasta; and the hardy spelt (*T. spelta*) with its two-grain spikelets.

senator for Mont. 1923–47. A Democrat, he stood in 1924 as vice-presidential candidate for the Progressive Party. In WWII he advocated isolationism.

WHEELER, Earle Gilmore (1908–), US general. He served in Europe in WWII and in 1962 was appointed army chief of staff. He was chairman of the Joint Chiefs of Staff 1964–70.

WHEELER, Joseph (1836–1906), US Confederate cavalry general. He fought, often brilliantly, in the Kentucky, Chatanooga and Atlanta Civil War campaigns. He held commands 1898–1900 in the Spanish-American War (in Cuba) and in the Philippines.

WHEELER, William Almon (1819–1887), US Vice-President 1877–81. A Republican N.Y. senator (1858–59) and congressman (1861–63, 1869–77), he was elected with Rutherford HAYES. His "Wheeler compromise" (1874) settled a disputed La. election.

WHEELING, village in NE Ill., a N suburb of Chicago adjacent to Highland Park. Pop 14476.

WHEELING, city in N W.Va., seat of Ohio Co. Coal and gas deposits fuel its iron-and-steel, textile, chemical and pottery industries. It was first capital of W.Va. (1863–70, 1875–85). Pop 48188.

WHEELOCK, Eleazar (1711–1779), American educator, Congregationalist preacher and founder of DARTMOUTH COLLEGE. He ran a free school for Indians at Lebanon, Conn. (1854–67) and founded Dartmouth College and the town of Hanover, N.H., in 1770.

WHELKS, common name given many marine GASTROPODS. Most have a spirally-coiled shell with a canal or "spout" at the mouth which holds the inhalant siphon for drawing water over the gills. They feed on living BIVALVES, wedging the shells open with their shell "spout" and feeding on the soft tissues inside with a long extensile proboscis.

WHEWELL, William (1794–1866), English philosopher and Master of Trinity College, Cambridge (1841–66), renowned as the last polymath. His interests ranged from mineralogy to moral philosophy, but he is chiefly remembered for his *Philosophy of the Inductive Sciences* (1840), which reflected his study of KANT and led to a famous controversy with J. S. MILL.

WHIG, an English and a US political party. In England, the term was applied in 1679 to Protestant opponents of the English Crown led by SHAFTESBURY (see GLORIOUS REVOLUTION). The Whigs enjoyed a period of dominance c1714–60, notably under Robert WALPOLE. Largely out of office under Charles FOX, they were increasingly associated with Non-conformism, mercantile, industrial and reforming interests. After the Whig ministries of 2nd Earl GREY and Lord MELBOURNE, the Whigs helped form the LIBERAL PARTY in the mid 1800s.

The US Whig Party was formed c1836 from diverse opponents, including the NATIONAL REPUBLICANS, of Andrew JACKSON and the Democrats. Its leaders were Henry CLAY and Daniel WEBSTER, and a national economic policy was its principal platform. Whig President W. H. HARRISON died in office and was succeeded 1841 by John TYLER, who was disowned by the Whigs when he vetoed their tariff and banking bills. Clay, the next Whig candidate, lost the 1844 election. During the second Whig presidency (1849–53; Zachary TAYLOR and Millard FILLMORE), the party was already divided by the issues of slavery and national expansion; the COMPROMISE OF 1850 did not last and Winfield SCOTT was heavily defeated in the 1852 election. The party never recovered, and many Whigs joined the new REPUBLICAN PARTY.

WHIP, in US and British politics, party member of a legislative body chosen to enforce party discipline in voting and attendance. The first US whip, Republican congressman James E. Watson, was appointed in 1899.

WHIPPET, English sporting and racing dog, derived from an 18th-century cross between greyhound and terrier. It is slender and light (10–28lb), stands 18–22in high and can run at up to 35mph. Its smooth-haired coat is usually white, tan, or gray.

WHIPPLE, Abraham (1733–1819), American naval officer noted for his successes in the Revolutionary War. In 1779 he captured 11 ships of the British Jamaica fleet. In 1780 he defended Charleston, S.C., but was captured when the city fell.

WHIPPLE, George Hoyt (1878–), US pathologist awarded the 1934 Nobel Prize for Physiology or Medicine for his discovery that feeding raw liver to anemic dogs improved their condition: the successful work of G. MINOT and W. MURPHY (who shared the award with him) in finding a treatment for pernicious ANEMIA sprang directly from this.

WHIPPOORWILL, *Caprimulgus vociferus*, a NIGHTJAR of North and Middle America, named for its characteristic call.

WHIP SCORPIONS, two groups of terrestrial ARACHNIDS with the first pair of walking legs elongated and whip-like. The Uropygi resemble small scorpions with a pair of stout appendages flanking the mouth and a slender, stingless, tail at the tip of the abdomen. The Amblypygi are tailless.

WHIP SNAKES, *Masticophis*, a genus of slender, non-poisonous snakes of the Americas, which, with the related **racers** (*Coluber*), are among the fastest snakes in the world, reaching a speed of 5.5km/h (3.4mph).

WHIRLPOOL, a rotary current in water. Permanent whirlpools may arise in the ocean from the interactions of the TIDES (see OCEAN CURRENTS). They occur also in streams or rivers where two currents meet or the shape of the channel dictates. Short-lived whirlpools may be created by wind. (See also VORTEX; WHIRLWIND.)

WHIRLWIND, rotating column of air caused by a pocket of low atmospheric pressure formed—unlike a TORNADO—near ground level by surface heating. They are far less violent than tornadoes. Whirlwinds passing over dry dusty country are sometimes called "dust devils."

WHISKEY, strong spirituous DISTILLED LIQUOR, drunk mixed or neat, made from grain. When from Scotland or Canada, whisky is spelt without an "e". The ingredients and preparation vary. In the US corn and rye are commonly used: 51% corn for *bourbon whiskey* and 51% rye for *rye whiskey*. A grain mash is allowed to ferment, then distilled, diluted and left to age. Bourbon and rye whiskey stand in oak barrels for four years. *Canadian whisky* is made from corn, rye and malted (germinated) barley and aged for 4–12 years. *Irish whiskey* uses barley, wheat, oats and rye, and vessels called potstills for the distilling process. *Scotch whisky* is the finest form: the best types are pure barley malt or grain whiskies, but blended varieties are cheaper. The secret of its flavor is supposed to be the peat-flavored water of certain Scottish streams. Whiskey is one of the most popular of ALCOHOLIC BEVERAGES. In the US an average of 16 bottles per person are drunk every year.

WHISKEY REBELLION, 1794, uprising of W. Pa., mainly Scotch-Irish farmer settlers against the federal excise tax imposed on whiskey by secretary of the treasury HAMILTON in 1791. Federal officers were attacked, some were tarred and feathered and one had his house burnt down. Resistance increased when official measures were taken to obtain the tax. At Hamilton's insistence, President Washington sent in 13000 militiamen to suppress the insurgents. They met no resistance, and Washington pardoned two ringleaders convicted of treason. Federalists claimed a victory—the federal government had demonstrated the power to enforce its law.

WHISKEY RING, US scandal exposed in 1875. Distillers in St. Louis, Chicago, Milwaukee and elsewhere had evaded tax through payments to Republican Party funds and individuals. The investigations of treasury secretary BRISTOW led to 237 indictments (including the chief treasury clerk and the president's private secretary) and 110 convictions. President Grant was cleared personally, but his party damaged.

WHIST, four-player card game. A 52-card pack is evenly dealt and the last card exposed to show trumps. Partners (facing players) aim to win tricks. Played in 17th-century England, it became popular and fashionable in the 1800s and 1900s. Solo whist and BRIDGE were 19th-century developments.

WHISTLER, James Abbott McNeill (1834–1903), US painter, etcher, and wit who lived in Paris and London. He advocated "art for art's sake," and stressed simplicity of color and design, as in the portrait of his mother, *Arrangement in Gray and Black* (1872) and *Falling Rocket: Nocturne in Black and Gold* (1874; over which Whistler sued the contemptuous John RUSKIN in 1878, receiving damages of one farthing).

WHITBY, Synod of, held 663 or 664 in the kingdom of Northumbria, England, to decide between Celtic and Roman church usage. King OSWY chose Roman practice, thus affecting not only the reckoning of Easter but linking the English church more closely with that of the rest of Europe.

WHITE, Andrew Dickson (1832–1918), US educator and diplomat, first president (1867–85) of Cornell U., founded as a nonsectarian university based on his liberal principles. He was a N.Y. senator 1864–67, US ambassador to Germany 1897–1903 and led the US delegation to the 1899 Hague peace conference.

WHITE, Byron Raymond (1917–), US jurist. Once famous as a professional football player, he was a J. F. Kennedy appointee as US deputy attorney general (1961) and associate justice of the Supreme Court (1962–).

WHITE, Edward Douglass (1845–1921), US jurist. A judge of the La. supreme court 1879–80, US senator 1890–94 and associate justice of the US Supreme Court from 1894, he was appointed chief justice by Taft in 1910. Generally a conservative, he wrote the "rule of reason" into antitrust law.

WHITE, Edward Higgins II (1930–1967), first US astronaut to walk in space. He stayed outside *Gemini 4* for 21 min on June 3, 1965. With GRISSOM and Chaffee, White was killed in a fire during tests of Project Apollo spacecraft.

WHITE, E(lwyn) B(rooks) (1899–), US writer, author of "Notes and Comments" (*New Yorker*), "One Man's Meat" (*Harper's*), poems, *Is Sex Necessary?* (1929, with THURBER), and such fantasies as *Stuart Little* (1945).

WHITE, Gilbert (1720–1793), English naturalist, author of *The Natural History and Antiquities of Selbourne* (1788), a finely written early classic of precise observation of a Hampshire village, in the form of delightful letters to two friends.

WHITE, Patrick (1912–), Australian novelist, winner of the 1973 Nobel Prize for Literature. His long novels, set mostly in Australia, include *The Tree of Man* (1955), *Voss* (1957), *Riders in the Chariot* (1961), *The Vivisector* (1970), and *The Eye of the Storm* (1974).

WHITE, Paul Dudley (1886–1972), US physician regarded from the 1940s to 1960s as the world's leading cardiologist.

WHITE, Pearl (1889–1939), popular US actress in early silent movies, heroine of such serials as *The Perils of Pauline*, noted for the cliff-hanging ending to each short episode.

WHITE, Peregrine (1620–1704), first New-England-born child of English parentage. Born Nov. 20 aboard the *Mayflower* in Cape Cod Bay, he settled in Marshfield, Mass.

WHITE, Stanford (1853–1906), US architect, noted for interior and decorative work. He cofounded (1879) the famous firm MCKIM, Mead, and White. Their work developed from domestic Shingle Style to "Beaux Arts" classical-Renaissance, as in the 1890 Madison Square Garden and the Century Club, New York. He was shot dead by the husband of his mistress Evelyn Nesbit Thaw.

WHITE, T(erence) H(anbury) (1906–1964), English novelist, noted for *The Once and Future King* (four books, 1938–58), a retelling of the legends of King Arthur (adapted for the musical *Camelot*) and *The Goshawk* (1951).

WHITE, Walter Francis (1893-1955), US Negro leader, from 1931 secretary of the National Association for the Advancement of Colored People. His works include his autobiography, *A Man Called White* (1948).

WHITE, William (1748–1836), American clergyman who led the foundation of the Protestant Episcopal Church of the US. Elected bishop of Penn. 1786, and consecrated by English bishops 1787, he drafted the Church's constitution and revised the Book of Common Prayer.

The White House: Hoban's 1824 south portico, the family dining room (*left*) and the East Room (*right*).

WHITE, William Allen (1868–1944), US journalist and author. A small-town liberal Republican, White became famous for his editorials in his own Emporia (Ken.) *Gazette* (1923 Pulitzer Prize). His posthumous autobiography won a 1946 Pulitzer Prize.

WHITE ANTS. See TERMITES.

WHITEBAIT, the fry of HERRINGS and sprats, which congregate in large shoals in coastal waters—a popular European food item when deep-fried.

WHITE BEAR LAKE, residential and resort city in SE Minn., 11mi NE of St. Paul on a scenic lake. It has boatyards and trout farms. Pop 23 313.

WHITEBOYS, members of small illegal (mainly Roman Catholic) peasant groups in 18th-century Ireland. Protesting against harsh landlords, enclosure of common lands and tithes, they conducted harrassing night raids in white disguise.

WHITE CORPUSCLES. See BLOOD.

WHITE-EYES, tiny thin-billed active arboreal birds of Africa and Australasia, characterized by a ring of white around each eye. The 87 species are very hard to tell apart. Family: Zosteropidae.

WHITEFIELD, George (1714–1770), English evangelist, founder of Calvinist Methodism. He joined the Methodists led by WESLEY, whom he followed (1738) to Ga., the first of seven missions to America (see GREAT AWAKENING). Adopting Calvinist views on predestination, he led the Calvinist Methodists from 1741.

WHITEFISH, silvery, salmon-like fishes of the genus *Coregonus*, confined to colder parts of the N hemisphere. There are about six species in Europe, 20 in America. They live in rivers and deep cold lakes, feeding on insect larvae, shellfish and crustaceans.

WHITEFISH BAY, village in SE Wis., a residential suburb on Lake Michigan, 5mi N of Milwaukee. Pop 17 402.

WHITEFLIES, small plant-sucking four-winged insects with a white, powdery wax covering the wings and body. Whiteflies are crop pests and vectors of virus diseases of cotton, tobacco and tomatoes.

WHITE-FOOTED MICE. See DEER MICE.

WHITE GOLD, an ALLOY of GOLD with nickel and sometimes other NOBLE METALS, used in dentistry.

WHITEHALL, city in central Ohio. It is an E suburb of Columbus, with some light industry. Pop 25 623.

WHITEHALL, borough in SW Pa., a residential suburb S of Pittsburg. Pop 16 551.

WHITEHEAD, Alfred North (1861–1947), English mathematician and philosopher. He was co-author with Bertrand RUSSELL of *Principia Mathematica* (1910–13), a major landmark in the philosophy of mathematics; and while teaching at Harvard University (from 1924) he developed a monumental system of metaphysics, most comprehensively expounded in his *Process and Reality* (1929).

WHITEHORSE, capital and largest city of Yukon Territory, Canada, on the Yukon R, 110mi N of Skagway, Alaska. It is an important shipping center for minerals, lumber and furs. Pop 11 217.

WHITE HOUSE, official home of the President of the US, in Washington, D.C. It was designed in the manner of an 18th-century English gentleman's country house by James HOBAN (1792). It was severely damaged by the British in 1814, but rebuilt and extended (and painted white) by 1818. In 1824 Hoban added the semicircular south portico. The grounds were landscaped in 1850 by Andrew DOWNING. Major renovations, including the addition of the executive office building, were carried out in the early 20th century by the architectural firm of MCKIM, Mead and White. From 1948 onward the building was extensively rebuilt.

WHITE HUNS, Asiatic tribe that invaded Persia and India in the 5th and 6th centuries AD, thought to have been of Tibetan or Turkish stock. In 484 they killed the Persian king Firuz, but were driven out of India by 528 and Persia by 557.

WHITE LEAD. See CERUSSITE.

WHITEMAN, Paul (1891–1967), US bandleader of the 1920s and 1930s. He is remembered for his collaboration with GERSHWIN and for his elaborate arrangements of jazz and dance music.

WHITE MOUNTAIN, Battle of the, the first major engagement of the THIRTY YEARS' WAR, Nov. 8, 1620. The Protestants of BOHEMIA, who had revolted, were defeated by TILLY, leading the forces of the German Catholic League and of the emperor FERDINAND II, and Bohemia's independence was destroyed.

WHITE MOUNTAINS, a section of the APPALACHIAN MOUNTAINS covering c1 200sq mi in W Me. and N.H. It includes the Presidential, Sandwich and Franconia ranges. The highest peak, Mt. Washington (6 288ft), is in the Presidential Range. Deep canyons, called "notches," have been carved out by glaciers. The area is noted for scenic beauty.

WHITE OAK, unincorporated community in central Md., a suburb of Washington, D.C. It is the site of a naval ordnance laboratory. Pop 19 769.

WHITE PLAINS, city in SE N.Y., a residential suburb of New York City, with some light industry. On July 9, 1776, the Provincial Congress ratified the DECLARATION OF INDEPENDENCE here, and a battle was fought on Oct. 28, 1776. Pop 50 346.

WHITEPRINT PROCESS. See OZALID PROCESS.

WHITE RUSSIANS, an alternative name for the Belorussians, an East SLAV people who live mostly in the BELORUSSIAN SOVIET SOCIALIST REPUBLIC in W USSR. The name "White Russian" has also been used for the anti-communist groups who fought the BOLSHEVIKS in the RUSSIAN REVOLUTION and Civil War (1917–20).

WHITE SANDS NATIONAL MONUMENT, an area of almost pure gypsum sand dunes in the Tularosa Basin, S central N.M., covering 146 535 acres.

WHITE SEA, almost landlocked arm of the Arctic Ocean covering 36 000sq mi and extending into NW USSR. It receives the Dvina, Mezen and Onega rivers, and freezes from Nov. to May. Its chief port is ARKHANGELSK.

WHITE SETTLEMENT, town in NE Tex., a W suburb of Fort Worth. Pop 13 449.

WHITE-TAILED DEER, *Odocoileus virginianus*, the most widespread of all the American DEER, named for its longish, white tail, raised erect as a danger signal when the deer is alarmed. It ranges from Canada to northern South America.

WHITEWASH, cheap nondurable PAINT composed of CHALK, a glue or casein binder, and water; the dry form is called **calcimine**.

WHITEWATER, city in SE Wis. It has food-processing and other light industries. Pop 20 038.

WHITE WHALE. See BELUGA.

WHITING, name given various fishes, including CROAKERS of the genus *Menticirrhus*; also *Merlangius merlangus*, a food fish related to the COD found in the eastern North Atlantic.

WHITMAN, town in SE Mass., 4 mi E of Brockton. It produces footware, plastics and metal products. Pop 13 059.

WHITMAN, Marcus (1802–1847), US physician, pioneer and missionary. He and his wife Narcissa journeyed W in 1836 and helped set up missions to the Indians at Waiilatpu near Walla Walla, Wash., and at Lapwai, Ida. In 1842–43 he made a famous 3 000mi journey E to persuade the Missionary Board not to disband the missions. The Whitmans and 11 others were killed by Indians who blamed them for a measles epidemic.

WHITMAN, Walter "Walt" (1819–1892), major US poet. Born in Long Island, N.Y., he became a printer and journalist. His *Leaves of Grass* (1855; expanded in successive editions) was praised by EMERSON and THOREAU but did not at first achieve popular recognition. Other works include the Civil War poems, *Drum Taps* (1865); *Democratic Vistas* (1871), studies of American democracy; and the autobiographical *Specimen Days* (1882–83). He rejected regular meter and rhyme in favor of flowing FREE VERSE, and celebrated erotic love, rugged individualism, democracy and equality, and expressed an almost mystical identification with America. (See also AMERICAN LITERATURE.)

WHITNEY, Eli (1765–1825), US inventor of the COTTON GIN (1793), from which he earned little because of patent infringements, and pioneer of MASS PRODUCTION. In 1798 he contracted with the US Government to make 10 000 muskets: he took 8 years to fulfil the 2-year contract, but showed that with unskilled labor muskets could be put together using parts that were precision-made and thus interchangeable, a benefit not only during production but also in later maintenance.

WHITNEY, Mount, a mountain in the Sierra Nevada range of E central Cal., at 14 494ft the highest in the US outside Alaska. It was named for the geologist Josiah Dwight Whitney (1819–1896), and first climbed in 1873.

WHITSUNDAY. See PENTECOST.

WHITTAKER, Charles Evans (1901–1973), US lawyer and judge. A prominent Kansas City lawyer, he became a District and Appeal Court judge (1954–57) and associate justice of the Supreme Court (1957–61).

WHITTIER, city in S Cal. A residential suburb of Los Angeles, it also has light industry producing machinery and metal products. Pop 72 863.

WHITTIER, John Greenleaf (1807–1892), US

Quaker poet and abolitionist. From 1833 to 1865 he was a campaigning journalist, and he published the antislavery poems, *Voices of Freedom* (1846). He later returned to New England themes in his "Yankee pastorals." The autobiographical *Snow-Bound* (1866) and *The Tent on the Beach* (1867) are among his best-known works.

WHITTINGTON, Richard (c1358–1423), English merchant and lord mayor of London, made famous in legend as the poor Dick Whittington with his cat, but in fact the son of a wealthy knight. He was mayor 1397–98, 1407–08 and 1419–20, and bequeathed his considerable fortune to charitable and public purposes.

WHITTLE, Air Commodore Sir Frank (1907–), British aeronautical engineer who invented the first aircraft JET PROPULSION unit (patented 1937, first used in flight 1941).

WHITWORTH, Sir Joseph, Baronet (1803–1887), British engineer, metallurgist and philanthropist who brought radically improved accuracy to the manufacture of MACHINE TOOLS and who invented the Whitworth rifle, used by the British Army in the late 1860s and 1870s, which had a hexagonal barrel.

WHOOPING COUGH, or **pertussis**, BACTERIAL DISEASE of children causing upper respiratory symptoms with a characteristic whoop or inspiratory noise due to INFLAMMATION of the LARYNX. It is usually a relatively mild illness, except in the very young, but VACCINATION is widely practiced to prevent it.

WHOOPING CRANE, *Grus americana*, a tall white wading bird with a red cap on the head. Once widespread through North America, they have for several decades been close to extinction and have been preserved only by determined conservation measures.

WHORF, Benjamin Lee (1897–1941), US linguist best known for proposing the theory that a language's structure determines the thought processes of its speakers. (See also LINGUISTICS.)

WHYMPER, Edward (1840–1911), British mountaineer and artist, first man to climb the MATTERHORN (1865). He later climbed in Greenland and South America. His illustrated books include *Scrambles amongst the Alps* (1871).

WICHITA, largest city of Kan., seat of Sedgewick Co., on the Arkansas R. It is an important marketing and processing center for livestock and grain. Manufactures include aircraft, heavy machinery and domestic appliances. Pop 276 554.

WICHITA FALLS, city in N Tex., seat of Wichita Co. It is the manufacturing and service center of a large oil and natural gas region. Pop 96 265.

WICHITA MOUNTAINS, mountain range in SW Okl. Its highest peak is Mt Scott, 2 464ft.

WICKIUP, American Indian hut, consisting of a conical framework of poles covered by either brushwood or mats. Wickiups were used as temporary homes by the Indians of the W and SW US.

WICKLIFFE, city in NE Ohio, on Lake Erie, a NE suburb of Cleveland. Mainly residential, it has also some light manufacturing industry. Pop 21 354.

WIDGEON, *Anas penelope*, a small DUCK of coasts and fresh water. The male is distinguished by a chestnut head, pinkish breast and gray back, with a yellow stripe on the crown. They are popular quarry of wildfowlers in Europe.

WIDOR, Charles Marie (1844–1937), French organist and composer, professor at the Paris Conservatoire 1891–1934. As well as 10 organ symphonies he wrote concertos and ballet, opera and chamber music.

WIELAND, Christoph Martin (1733–1813), German poet and novelist. His urbane and satirical works include the verse romance *Oberon* (1780), the psychological novel *Agathon* (1773) and the satire *The Abderites* (1774). He translated much of Shakespeare (1762–66).

WIELAND, Heinrich Otto (1877–1957), German organic chemist noted for his work on STEROIDS, especially his research on the BILE acids, which brought him the 1927 Nobel Prize for Chemistry.

WIEN. See VIENNA.

WIEN, Wilhelm (1864–1928), Prussian-born German physicist best known for his work on BLACKBODY RADIATION, work which was later to be a foundation stone for Planck's QUANTUM THEORY.

WIENER, Norbert (1894–1964), US mathematician who created the discipline CYBERNETICS. His major book is *Cybernetics: Or Control and Communication in the Animal and the Machine* (1948).

WIESBADEN, city in West Germany, on the Rhine R, 20m W of Frankfurt-am-Main. A famous spa since Roman times, it is a market center for Rhine wines. Industries include metal goods, chemicals, pharmaceuticals and textiles. Pop 250 122.

WIG, a covering for the head of real or artificial hair, worn as a cosmetic device, as a mark of rank or office, as a disguise or for theatrical portrayals. Known since ancient times, wigs became fashionable in 17th-and 18th-century Europe, when elaborate headpieces for women and full, curled wigs for men came into wide use. The latter are still worn in British lawcourts. In the 1960s wigs came back into fashion for women, and the toupee to conceal baldness became acceptable for men.

WIGGLESWORTH, Michael (1631–1705), English-born American Puritan poet, pastor at Malden, Mass., from 1656. His *Day of Doom* (1662) was extremely popular. He also wrote *Meat out of the Eater* (1669), on the moral benefits of affliction.

WIGHT, Isle of, diamond-shaped island, 147sq mi, off the S coast of England. Its scenery and mild climate make it a popular resort area. Cowes, the chief port, is a well-known yachting center.

WIGNER, Eugene Paul (1902–), Hungarian-born US physicist who shared with J. H. D. JENSEN and M. G. MAYER the 1963 Nobel Prize for Physics for his work in the field of nuclear physics. He also worked with FERMI on the MANHATTAN PROJECT, and received the 1960 Atoms for Peace Award.

WIGWAM, Abnaki Indian word for dwelling, especially the oval or round bark-covered homes used by the tribes in E North America. The English used the term to describe any Indian home, including the conical TEPEE and WICKIUP.

WILBERFORCE, William (1759–1833), English philanthropist and antislavery campaigner. A member of Parliament (1780–1825), he secured the abolition in the British Empire of the slave trade (1807) and of slavery itself (1833). A leader of the CLAPHAM SECT, he supported missionary work and devoted most of his fortune to evangelical and charitable purposes.

WILBRAHAM, town in S central Mass. It is a residential suburb 8 mi E of Springfield. Pop 11 948.

WILBUR, Richard (1921–), US poet and critic who won a Pulitzer Prize for *Things of this World* (1956). Using a formal structure and a witty style, he incorporated philosophy and myth into poems about ordinary life.

WILD CARROT. See QUEEN ANNE'S LACE.

WILDCATS, various species of small CATS distributed throughout the world. The name often refers specifically to the European wildcat, *Felis sylvestris*, a heavier version of the domestic cat, living in crevices in rock and preying mainly on mice and voles. It is extremely fierce and intractable.

WILDCAT BANKS, name for numerous unsound state-chartered US banks, c1830–63, which issued paper money (wildcat currency) without having adequate assets. They proliferated after President JACKSON dismantled the BANK OF THE UNITED STATES, and many collapsed in the 1837 financial panic. By 1863 most were brought under federal control.

WILDE, Oscar Fingal O'Flahertie Wills (1854–1900), Irish wit and playwright. A dandy and aesthete, believing in "art for art's sake," he achieved celebrity with the novel *The Picture of Dorian Gray* (1891) and witty society comedies such as *Lady Windermere's Fan* (1892), *An Ideal Husband* (1895) and *The Importance of Being Earnest* (1895), and the biblical *Salome* (written in French; 1893). His career was shattered by his imprisonment for homosexuality (1895–97), which prompted his best known poem, *The Ballad of Reading Gaol* (1898).

WILDEBEEST. See GNUS.

WILDER, Billy (1906–), Austrian-born US film director, known for his keen satire and realistic observation. After years as a screenwriter, he directed such films as *Sunset Boulevard* (1950), *Some Like it Hot* (1959) and *The Apartment* (1960).

WILDER, Thornton Niven (1897–1975), US novelist and playwright. Novels include *The Bridge of San Luis Rey* (1927; Pulitzer Prize) and *The Ides of March* (1948). Plays such as *Our Town* (1938), *The Skin of Our Teeth* (1942) and *The Matchmaker* (1954) experiment with stylized techniques.

WILDERNESS, Battle of the, the opening engagement, fought on May 5–6, 1864, in central Va. 10mi W of Fredericksburg, of the "Wilderness Campaign" in the US CIVIL WAR. Ulysses GRANT's 118 000-strong Army of the Potomac, advancing to annihilate the Confederate army in open battle, was met and held in heavily wooded country by 60 000 men under Robert E. LEE. Both sides suffered heavy losses. Grant then turned to attack SPOTSYLVANIA COURTHOUSE (May 8–19). Fighting continued in the Wilderness until early June.

WILDERNESS ROAD, an early American pioneer route. It ran from Va. through the Cumberland Gap into the Ohio Valley. Laid out in 1775 by Daniel BOONE, it was the main route W until c1840.

WILD RICE, *Zizania aquatica*, close relative of cultivated RICE, native to the lakes and streams of North America. The grain has long been eaten by Indians and settlers and is now planted to feed wildfowl. Family: Graminae.

WILEY, Harvey Washington (1844–1930), US chemist whose main achievements were in promoting pure food laws, being largely responsible for instituting the Pure Food and Drugs Act (1906).

WILHELM. See WILLIAM (German emperors).

WILHELMINA (1880–1962), Queen of the Netherlands from 1890 to 1948 (her mother was regent until 1898). She was primarily responsible for Dutch neutrality during WWI. After her Golden Jubilee in 1948, she abdicated in favor of JULIANA, her daughter.

WILKES, Charles (1789–1877), US naval officer and explorer. Head of the US navy department of charts and instruments (1833), he explored the Pacific, ANTARCTICA and the NW coast of America (1838–42), and was the first to designate Antarctica a separate continent. In 1861 he precipitated the TRENT AFFAIR.

WILKES, John (1727–1797), English politician and champion of liberty. Expelled from Parliament 1764, reelected and expelled again four times 1768–69, he became a popular champion of electors' rights, individual liberty and freedom of the press. Lord mayor of London (1774), he returned to Parliament (1774–90), where he supported parliamentary reform and opposed the war with America.

WILKES-BARRE, city in E Pa., seat of Luzerne Co., on the Susquehanna R. Manufactures include footwear, pencils, tires, electronic components and power tools. Pop 58 856.

WILKES LAND, coastal area of Antarctica facing the Indian Ocean, latitude 66° to 70°S and longitude 102° to 142°E.

WILKINS, Sir George Hubert (1888–1958), Australian polar explorer and pioneer aviator. In 1928 he was the first to fly W to E over the Arctic, from Alaska to Spitzbergen. He managed Lincoln ELLSWORTH's Antarctic expedition (1933–39) and later advised the US armed services.

WILKINS, Maurice Hugh Frederick (1916–), British biophysicist who shared with F. H. CRICK and J. D. WATSON the 1962 Nobel Prize for Physiology or Medicine for his X-RAY DIFFRACTION studies of DNA, work that was vital to the determination by Crick and Watson of DNA's molecular structure.

WILKINS, Roy (1901–), US CIVIL RIGHTS leader and executive secretary (director) of the NATIONAL ASSOCIATION FOR THE ADVANCEMENT OF COLORED PEOPLE since 1955. He was assistant secretary from 1931 and edited the journal, *Crisis* (1934–49). Dedicated to nonviolence, he has come under attack from militants since the 1960s.

WILKINSBURG, residential borough, SW Pa., 7mi E of Pittsburgh, producing machine tools. Pop 26 780.

WILKINSON, Geoffrey (1921–), British inorganic chemist awarded with Ernst Otto FISCHER

the 1973 Nobel Prize for Chemistry for their work on ORGANOMETALLIC COMPOUNDS.
WILKINSON, James (1757–1825), US army officer and adventurer. Involved in the CONWAY CABAL, he resigned as secretary to the Board of War 1778. In 1787 he intrigued with the Spanish to create a pro-Spanish republic in the SW. Governor of La. 1805–06, he was involved with Aaron BURR, but turned chief witness against him. He resumed an unsuccessful army career 1811–15.
WILL, legal document by which a person (the testator) gives instructions concerning the disposal of his or her PROPERTY after death. Under most jurisdictions a will must be attested in order to be legally valid: independent witnesses, who have nothing to gain under the will, must attest that the signature on the will is in fact that of the testator who has signed in their presence. Wills may be revoked during the life of the testator or altered by codicils. Wills generally appoint executors to administer the estate of the deceased and carry out his or her instructions. When a person dies intestate (without making a will), the property is normally divided among relatives.
WILLAERT, Adrian (c1490–1562) Flemish composer, choirmaster of St. Mark's, Venice (1527–62), and a major influence in developing the MADRIGAL. His works include madrigals, masses, motets, songs and settings of the psalms.
WILLAMETTE RIVER, flowing about 300mi N through NW Ore. into the Columbia R near Portland. Its fertile valley is important for agriculture.
WILLARD, Emma Hart (1787–1870), US campaigner for women's education. In 1821 she founded Troy Female Seminary, later renamed for her, which pioneered collegiate courses for women. She retired in 1838, but continued her educational work.
WILLARD, Frances Elizabeth Caroline (1839–1898), US temperance leader and reformer, president of the WOMAN'S CHRISTIAN TEMPERANCE UNION from 1879. A brilliant speaker and capable organizer, she also worked for women's suffrage and social reforms.
WILLARD, Jess (1883–1968), US heavyweight boxing champion of the world. He won the title by beating Jack JOHNSON in 1915, and lost it in 1919 to Jack DEMPSEY.
WILLEMSTAD, capital of the Netherlands Antilles, in S Curaçao. It is a free port and tourist center, with major oil refineries. Pop 43 547.
WILLET, *Catoptrophorus semipalmatus*, a large gray and white bird of North and South America, related to the SANDPIPERS and found in marshland and along the shoreline.
WILLIAM (German Wilhelm), name of two German emperors. **William I** (1797–1888), became king of Prussia in 1861. Conservative, autocratic and militaristic, under BISMARCK's guidance he organized the unification of Germany, largely through the AUSTRO-PRUSSIAN WAR (1866) and the FRANCO-PRUSSIAN WAR (1870–71), from which Prussia emerged as the leading German power. He was proclaimed emperor at Versailles in 1871. **William II** (1859–1941), grandson of William I and also of Queen VICTORIA, succeeded in 1888. Impulsive and with a passion for military affairs, he dismissed Bismark (1890), reinforced the TRIPLE ALLIANCE and promoted the nationalistic imperialism that was a factor leading to WWI. In 1918 he was forced to abdicate, and found asylum in Holland.
WILLIAM, name of four kings of England. **William I, the Conqueror** (1027–1087), duke of Normandy from 1035, became king in 1066 by defeating HAROLD at HASTINGS (see NORMAN CONQUEST), and had suppressed all opposition by 1071. He was a harsh but capable ruler, reorganizing England's military and landholding systems, building many castles and creating a strong feudal government (see FEUDALISM). The DOMESDAY BOOK was compiled by his order. His son, **William II "Rufus"** (the Red; c1056–1100), succeeded in 1087. Autocratic and brutal, he spent much time fighting, in England (against his own barons, 1088), France (1091, 1094, 1097–99), Scotland (1091–92) and Wales (1096–97), and quarreled with St. ANSELM over the independence of the Church. He was killed (probably deliberately) by an arrow while hunting in the New Forest. **William III, Prince of Orange** (1650–1702), was *stadtholder* (ruler) of Holland. His marriage in 1677 to MARY, Protestant daughter of JAMES II, resulted in Parliament inviting him to accept the crown jointly with his wife after the GLORIOUS REVOLUTION (1688). He subdued JACOBITE resistance in Ireland (see BOYNE, BATTLE OF THE) and Scotland, and ruled alone after Mary's death (1694). **William IV** (1765–1837) succeeded his brother GEORGE IV in 1830. He exercised little political influence, and was succeeded by his niece, VICTORIA.
WILLIAM, name of three kings of the Netherlands. **William I** (1772–1843), son of William V, Prince of Orange, was proclaimed king of the new kingdom of the Netherlands created at the Congress of VIENNA (1815). Unable to prevent the secession of Belgium (1830–39) and opposed to liberalizing the constitution, he abdicated (1840) in favor of his son, **William II** (1792–1849), who conceded a fully parliamentary constitution in 1848. A soldier, William II had fought with WELLINGTON at WATERLOO. His son, **William III** (1817–1890), succeeded in 1849 and reigned as a constitutional monarch. He was succeeded by his daughter WILHELMINA.
WILLIAM OF ORANGE. See WILLIAM III (king of England).
WILLIAM RUFUS. See WILLIAM II (king of England).
WILLIAMS, Daniel Hale (1858–1931), US surgeon who carried out the first repair operation on the damaged outer surface of a human heart (1893).
WILLIAMS, Ralph Vaughan. See VAUGHAN WILLIAMS, RALPH.
WILLIAMS, Roger (c1603–1683), British-born pastor, founder of RHODE ISLAND. A firm believer in religious freedom, he emigrated to Massachusetts Bay Colony in 1631. He became a pastor at Salem, but was banished for criticizing the expropriation of Indian lands and the enforcement of religious principles by civil power. In 1636 he founded PROVIDENCE on Rhode Island and obtained a charter for the colony (1644). Its constitution exemplified his principles of religious freedom, separation of church and state, democracy and local autonomy, all of which were influential in shaping US traditions.
WILLIAMS, Ted (1918–), US baseball player who achieved a major league batting average of .344 and aggregated 521 home runs. He joined the Boston Red Sox in 1939 and won six American batting championships before retiring in 1960.
WILLIAMS, Tennessee (1911–), US playwright whose emotionally intense plays deal with the warping effects on sensitive characters of failure, loneliness and futile obsessions. His first success, *The Glass Menagerie* (1945), was followed by *A Streetcar Named Desire* (1947) and *Cat on a Hot Tin Roof* (1955), both of which received Pulitzer Prizes. Other plays include *Sweet Bird of Youth* (1959) and *Night of the Iguana* (1961).
WILLIAMS, William Carlos (1883–1963), US poet. A doctor, he wrote about ordinary life in N.J., especially in the long reflective poem *Paterson* (1946–58). *Pictures from Breughel* (1963) won a Pulitzer Prize. He also wrote plays, fiction and essays, including *In the American Grain* (1925), a study of the American character.
WILLIAMS, William Sherley (1787–1849), US trapper and explorer known as "Old Bill," one of the MOUNTAIN MEN. He ranged over the territories of Cal., Col., Ut. and Ore., and was killed on T. C. FRÉMONT's disastrous Rio Grande expedition (1848–49).
WILLIAMSBURG, restored colonial town in SE Va., on the James R. The city (colonial capital of Virginia until 1780) contains over 500 original or reconstructed 18th-century buildings, including the Governor's Palace and the Capitol in which the Virginia Assembly met. Much of the restoration work was undertaken by John D. Rockefeller, Jr. Pop 9069.
WILLIAMSPORT, city in central Pa., seat of Lycoming Co., on the Susquehanna R. Manufactures include aircraft engines, metal products, textiles and leather goods. Pop 37 918.
WILLIAM THE CONQUEROR. See WILLIAM I (king of England).
WILLIAM THE LION (1143–1214), king of Scotland from 1165. He secured Scotland's ecclesiastical and political independence (1188–89), and began her historic friendship with France (1168).
WILLIAM THE SILENT (1533–1584), founder of Dutch independence. Son of the count of Nassau, he became Prince of Orange (1544) and *stadholder* (ruler) of Holland, Zeeland and Utrecht (1559). Resisting PHILIP II of Spain's oppressive anti-Protestantism, he had his estates confiscated (1567) and fled to Germany. He became a Protestant and led the revolt against Spanish rule, becoming first *stadholder* of the independent united Northern Provinces in 1579.
WILLIMANTIC, city in NE Conn., at the junction of the Natchaug R. and Willimantic R. It produces textiles, metal goods and instruments. Pop 14 402.
WILLINGBORO, township in S central N.J. It was built from 1958 as a planned residential community, with a light industrial zone. Pop 43 386.
WILLISTON, city in NW N.D., seat of William Co., on the Missouri R. It processes dairy products and has coalmines and oil wells nearby. Pop 11 280.
WILLKIE, Wendell Lewis (1892–1944), US businessman and politician. A lawyer and Democrat (1914–33), he became president of a giant utility company and led business opposition to the NEW DEAL. Joining the Republicans, he was presidential candidate in 1940, gaining a large popular vote. *One World* (1943) was a plea for international cooperation.
WILLMAR, city in central Minn., seat of Kandiyohi Co. It processes poultry and dairy products and has light engineering industries. Pop 12 869.
WILL-O'-THE WISP, or **Jack O'Lantern,** or **Ignis Fatuus** (Latin: foolish fire), light seen at night over marshes, caused by SPONTANEOUS COMBUSTION of METHANE produced by putrefying matter. Luring travelers into danger, it was popularly regarded as a wandering damned spirit bearing its own hell-fire.
WILLOUGHBY, city in NE Ohio, near Lake Erie. Its manufactures include rubber goods, metal products and clothing. Pop 18 634.
WILLOW, common name for about 300 species of trees of the genus *Salix*, which occur from the tropics to the Arctic. The leaves are generally sword-like and male and female catkins are borne on separate plants. The willows of the temperate zone are large but the dwarf willow found beyond the tree line of the Arctic only grows to about 150mm (6in). The long, pliable

The goat willow (*Salix caprea*) grows to a height of 10–30 feet and blossoms early, sometimes as early as in February, before the leaves have unfurled. The female (a) and male (b) flowers or "catkins" occur on separate plants. The broad leaves (c) are dark and smooth above and downy-gray below.

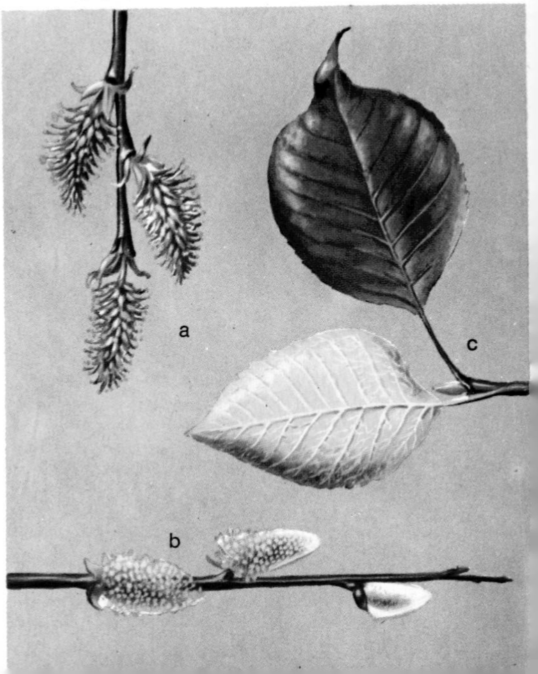

twigs of some species (OSIERS) are cut regularly for use in making wicker baskets and furniture. Other species are used for TANNINS or the light and durable wood. The ornamental Weeping willow is a native of China and SW Asia. Family: Salicaceae.

WILLOW GROVE, locality in SE Penn., 13mi N of Philadelphia. Center of a dairy and truck farming area, it has a machine-tool industry. Pop 16494.

WILLOWICK, city in NE Ohio, near Lake Erie, a residential suburb NE of Cleveland. Pop 21237.

WILLS, Helen Newington (1906–), US tennis star. Between 1923 and 1938 she won seven US singles titles and eight Wimbledon championships.

WILLSTÄTTER, Richard (1872–1942), German chemist awarded the 1915 Nobel Prize for Chemistry for his studies of the structure of CHLOROPHYLL.

WILMETTE, village in NE Ill., a residential suburb 15mi N of Chicago. Pop 32134.

WILMINGTON, city in NE Del., seat of New Castle Co., a port on the Delaware R. It has a major chemical industry producing chemicals, plastics, explosives, synthetic fibers and dyes. It also has shipyards and manufactures leather, rubber goods, textiles and machinery. Pop 80386.

WILMINGTON, town in NE Mass., a NW suburb of Boston. Its manufactures include aircraft and missile parts, plastics and electronics. Pop 17102.

WILMINGTON, city in SE N.C., seat of New Hanover Co. The state's largest port and a sport-fishing center, it produces textiles and clothing, wool products, boilers and fertilizer. Pop 46169.

WILMINGTON, city in SW Ohio, seat of Clinton Co. It manufactures tools, castings, automobile parts and air compressors. Pop 10051.

WILMOT PROVISO, an attempt by Democratic representative David Wilmot in 1846–47 to outlaw slavery in new US territories. A $2-million appropriation for a territorial settlement to the MEXICAN WAR had been proposed in Congress; Wilmot's amendment would have banned slavery in any territory purchased. Twice passed by the House but dropped by the Senate, the Proviso made slavery an explosive issue and led to bitter controversy.

WILSON, city in E N.C., seat of Wilson Co. It has a tobacco market and food-processing plants, and manufactures metal and wood products. Pop 29347.

WILSON, Alexander (1766–1813), Scottish-American poet and ornithologist. Author of dialect folk poems, he came to the US (1794), became a teacher, and took up ornithology in 1802, publishing the classic *American Ornithology* (1807–14).

WILSON, Angus (1913–), English novelist and short story writer who satirizes English class attitudes and social life. His novels include *Hemlock and After* (1952), *Anglo-Saxon Attitudes* (1956) and *No Laughing Matter* (1967).

WILSON, Charles Thomson Rees (1869–1959), British physicist awarded with A. H. COMPTON the 1927 Nobel Prize for Physics for his invention of the CLOUD CHAMBER (1911).

WILSON, Edmund (1895–1972), US critic and writer who investigated the historical, sociological and psychological background to literature. His prolific imaginative and critical output includes *Axel's Castle* (1931), a study of SYMBOLISM; *To the Finland Station* (1940) on the intellectual sources of the Russian Revolution; *The Wound and the Bow* (1941) on neurosis and literature; the explosive novel *Memoirs of Hecate County* (1949); and *Patriotic Gore* (1962), a study of Civil War literature.

WILSON, (James) Harold (1916–), British statesman. An Oxford economist, he entered Parliament (1945), became president of the Board of Trade (1947–51), leader of the Labour Party (1963) and prime minister 1964–70 and 1974–76. Identified initially with the left wing and known for his tactical skill, he preserved party unity during a period of economic crisis and division over the COMMON MARKET.

WILSON, Henry (1812–1875), US antislavery politician and vice-president 1873–75. Born Jeremiah Jones Colbath, he was a founder of the FREE SOIL PARTY (1848), senator from Mass. (1855–72) and a leading Radical Republican during RECONSTRUCTION.

WILSON, James (1742–1798), American jurist and signer of the Declaration of Independence, who played an important role in the 1787 Constitutional Convention. He became associate justice of the US Supreme Court from 1789 and first law professor at the University of Pa. from 1790.

WILSON, William Lyne (1843–1900), US educator and politician. He taught Latin (1865–71), practiced law (1871–82) and became president of W. Va. University (1882–83), Democratic representive (1883–95) and postmaster general (1895–97)

WILSON, Woodrow (1856–1924), 28th president of the US, 1913–21. Of Presbyterian stock, Wilson inherited a moral fervor and an impatient idealism which influenced his political life and contributed to the personal tragedy of his last years. After growing up in Ga. and S.C., he entered Princeton (1875) and Johns Hopkins (1883) to study history and political science. Teaching followed at Bryn Mawr (1885–88), Wesleyan University (1888–90) and Princeton (1890), where in 1902 he was elected president. His innovations strengthened the university but his attempt to abolish the aristocratic "eating clubs" aroused bitter controversy. Encouraged by N.J. Democratic political bosses, Wilson in 1910 ran for governor and, on being elected, energetically pushed through ambitious reforms which drew national attention. He captured the 1912 Democratic presidential nomination after 46 ballots and won the ensuing election. Assuming legislative leadership, and with a Democratic majority in Congress, Wilson achieved much, including the UNDERWOOD TARIFF (1913), which also provided for graduated income tax; the FEDERAL RESERVE SYSTEM (1913); the FEDERAL TRADE COMMISSION and CLAYTON ANTITRUST ACT (1914); the Federal Child Labor law, the Federal Farm Loans Act and an eight-hour day for railroad employees (1916). The constitutional amendments establishing PROHIBITION, women's votes and direct election of senators were also passed. In foreign affairs Wilson was led to intervene in Haiti, Nicaragua, the Dominican Republic and Mexico. In Europe, he struggled to maintain US neutrality in WWI, before finally declaring war on Germany in 1917. He mobilized the US behind him and urged a peace of reconciliation based on his famous FOURTEEN POINTS (1918). Wilson headed the US delegation at VERSAILLES (1919). Compromises were forced on him there, but he salvaged the LEAGUE OF NATIONS. In 1919, the Treaty signed, Wilson sought ratification of the League from a Republican-controlled Congress which demanded "reservations" protecting US sovereignty. He refused compromise and went on a countrywide speaking tour to gain support, but collapsed from the strain and suffered a stroke (Oct. 2, 1919). For the remaining 17 months of his term, the government was run informally by the cabinet, aided by his wife. Ratification failed, and although he was awarded the Nobel Peace Prize in 1920, Wilson retired a sick and disappointed man.

Woodrow WILSON
28th US President

Born: December 29, 1856
Died: February 3, 1924
Term of office: March 4, 1913–March 3, 1921
Political party: Democratic

WILT, condition where plants droop and wither due to a lack of water in their CELLS. This can be caused by lack of available moisture, physiological disorders, or FUNGI or BACTERIA damaging water conducting tissues inside roots or stems.

WILTON, town in SW Conn. It is a residential center in an agricultural area. Pop 13572.

WILTON MANORS, city in SE Fla., N of Fort Lauderdale. It is a residential community. Pop 10948.

WIMBLEDON CHAMPIONSHIPS. See TENNIS.

WINCH, device facilitating the hoisting or hauling of loads. It comprises a rotatable drum around which is wound a rope or cable attached to the load. The drum is turned by means of a hand-operated crank or a motor. (See also CRANE; WINDLASS.)

WINCHESTER, residential city in S England 65mi SW of London. Capital of the Anglo-Saxon kingdom of Wessex, it has a famous cathedral and a well known boys' school, Winchester College, founded in 1382 by William of Wykeham. Pop 31041.

WINCHESTER, town in NW Conn., which includes the city of Winsted. Light industries include electrical appliances and fishing tackle. Pop 11106.

WINCHESTER, city in E central Ky., seat of Clark Co. A tobacco and livestock center, it has some light industry. Pop 13402.

WINCHESTER, town in NE Mass. It is a residential suburb 8mi NW of Boston. Pop 22269.

WINCHESTER, city in N Va., in the Shenandoah valley, seat of Frederick Co. It produces cider, plastics, woolens and tin cans. Pop 14463.

WINCKELMANN, Johann Joachim (1717–1768), German archaeologist and art theorist. His *Thoughts on the Imitation of Greek Works in Painting and Sculpture* (1755) and *History of Ancient Art* (1764) created the Greek Revival in art and building.

WIND, body of air moving relative to the earth's surface. The world's major wind systems, or general winds, are set up to counter the equal heating of the earth's surface and modified by the rotation of the earth. Surface heating, at its greatest near the equator, creates an equatorial belt of low pressure (see DOLDRUMS) and a system of CONVECTION currents transporting heat toward the Poles (see HORSE LATITUDES). The earth's rotation deflects the currents of the N Hemisphere to the right and those of the S Hemisphere to the left of the directions in which they would otherwise blow, producing the NE and SE TRADE WINDS, the PREVAILING WESTERLIES and the Polar Easterlies. Other factors influencing general wind patterns are the different rates of heating and cooling of land and sea and the seasonal variations in surface heating. Mixing of air along the boundary between the Westerlies and the Polar Easterlies—the polar front—causes depressions in which winds follow circular paths, counterclockwise in the N Hemisphere and clockwise in the S Hemisphere (see CYCLONE). Superimposed on the general wind systems are local winds—winds, such as the CHINOOKS, caused by temperature differentials associated with local topographical features such as mountains and coastal belts, or winds associated with certain CLOUD systems. (See also ATMOSPHERE; BEAUFORT SCALE; HURRICANE; JET STREAM; MONSOON; TORNADO; WEATHER FORECASTING; WHIRLWIND.)

WINDAUS, Adolf (1876–1959), German organic chemist awarded the 1928 Nobel Prize for Chemistry for his work on the STEROLS, in course of which he determined the structure of CHOLESTEROL and showed that ULTRAVIOLET RADIATION transforms ergosterol into VITAMIN D_2.

WIND CAVE NATIONAL PARK, an area of 28059 acres in the BLACK HILLS, SW S.D. Established in 1903, it surrounds a cavern with alternating air currents and unusual crystal formations.

WINDERMERE, lake and town in the LAKE DISTRICT, NW England. The lake, 10½mi long and 1mi wide, is the largest in England and a popular tourist resort.

WIND GAP. See WATER GAP.

Wine

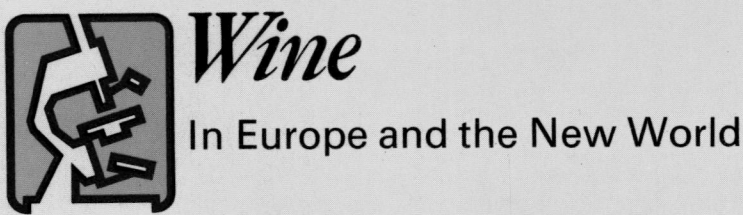

In Europe and the New World

Wine, the spontaneously-occurring product of ripe fruit, and especially of ripe grapes, has been the heart's delight of civilized man for thousands of years. One of the first plants to be domesticated, the grapevine has come to have a symbolic significance associated with the life-spirit in every culture where wine is drunk.

The Neolithic revolution of some ten thousand years ago signaled the beginning of horticulture. The subhuman predecessors of Neolithic man must have been attracted to the striking appearance, fragrance and sweetness of many wild fruits and berries, but it was probably no later than 6000 BC, in a small preagricultural community, that it happened that the only available liquid to quench a thirst was some leftover grape juice—left perhaps in a clay vessel, out in the sun. Such a suggestion as to the circumstances which brought about the discovery of wine is, of course, speculative; the behavior of this primitive drinker is not. It may well have caused his or her companions to suspect some kind of supernatural possession, but the drinker will have experienced, and possibly found great joy in, the sense of liberation which wine assuredly produces.

When man turned his attention to the cultivation of the vine, he found a remarkable plant—one speedily responsive to environment, adaptive, within wide limits, to new conditions, and unusually prone to the phenomenon of bud mutation, from which new varieties derive. These qualities alone were surely enough to earn the respect of anyone with green fingers.

Mesopotamia is often considered to be the source of viticulture, as it is of many of our Western arts and crafts, and from there the spread was rapid. Egypt's viticulture was quite well-advanced by 3000 BC, and the poets of Greece were praising their own wine a thousand years later. With the expansion of the Greek Empire, viticulture was introduced into Italy—called by its conquerors "the Land of the Vines." Contemporary depictions of Dionysus, the Greek wine-god, show a graceful and beautiful young man; somehow, by Roman times, he had degenerated into a plump little fellow, often shown tippling from a huge pot. At this period, we cannot consider the quality of wine drunk to be very high, even though, with the barrel, as opposed to the Greek amphora, the Romans had the technology necessary for the ageing of their wine. Like that of the modern Italians, the Roman wine was probably roughly-made and extrovert, to be appreciated in the context of a meal, rather than on its own.

In their turn, the Romans carried the art of wine-making to Gaul, and by the time of their withdrawal in the 5th century AD, the foundations had been laid for what is now France to become the world's most respected producer of wine. At the collapse of the Roman Empire, viticulture was established in every land which had known the tramp of the legionnaries' feet.

In the Middle Ages we find wine occupying a unique place in the developing European civilization, due in part to its significance in the Judaeo-Christian religious observances, but also to the fact that, during the Dark Ages, the Church was the one institution to act as retainer of Classical skills and knowledge. As a wealthy and expansionist church emerged as one of the most powerful agencies of Europe, so wine became associated, not only with the blood of Christ, but increasingly with a terrestrial domain of luxury and power. For centuries the Church owned most of the European vineyards, and it was within this freshly-established tradition that viticulture flourished, and particular regions slowly developed their own styles.

It was not until the 17th century that a technological discovery was made that eventually elevated wine-making from being an aspect of husbandry to a science, and added aesthetic delight to the wine-drinker's pursuit of comfort. This was the cork. At the time, wine was served from the barrel in broad-based bottles similar to modern carafes. It became apparent that wine stored in well-stopped bottles lasted much longer than wine in a barrel, which would go off sooner or later once it had been broached. Bottled wine aged differently, it was found; in fact, it often *improved* with age. Within a century, bottles were being used for storage. Their design was altered to the now-familiar slim shape which allows bottles to be stored lying flat, and thus has the wine keeping the cork moist and fully-expanded.

The benefits of bottle-age were soon appreciated all over Europe, and as particular regions developed their own unique styles and earned reputations, the European upper classes, in particular, found further reason to worship the vine and her produce.

In America, viticulture arrived with the very first colonists, who found many different varieties of native vine already growing. This profusion is undoubtedly why Leif Ericsson had called his discovery in 1000 AD "Vinland"—just as the Greeks had earlier named Italy. For the Catholic Europeans who traveled with Hernando Cortes wine was of the first importance for the celebration of the Mass. Even before the conquest of Mexico was complete, regulations were in force to guarantee importation of European vine-cuttings. These were then grafted onto native vine-stock as a means of increasing the new vineyards as quickly as possible. Thus, as the mission fathers traveled north into California, the vine went with them, often not in organized vineyards, but simply trailing over the mission-house itself.

North of Arizona and east of the Rockies, the early colonists were mostly English and French. They too brought European vine-cuttings across, and planted them. To their dismay they failed to flourish. Soil and climate were blamed, but the real

WINDHAM, town in NE Conn. It includes the industrial city of Willimantic. Pop 19 626.

WINDHOEK, capital of Southwest Africa, 180mi E of Walvis Bay. It is a trade center for karakul wool and has textile and food-processing industries. Pop 61 260.

WIND INSTRUMENTS, musical instruments whose sound is produced by blowing air into a tube, causing a vibration within it.

In *woodwind* instruments the vibration is made either by blowing across or into a specially shaped mouthpiece, as with the FLUTE, PICCOLO, RECORDER and its relative the flageolet; or by blowing such that a single or double reed vibrates, as in the CLARINET, SAXOPHONE, OBOE, COR ANGLAIS and BASSOON. The pitch is altered by opening and closing holes set into the tube.

In *brass* instruments, the vibration is made by the player's lips on the mouthpiece. The BUGLE and various types of posthorn have a single unbroken tube. The CORNET, FRENCH HORN, TRUMPET and TUBA have valves to vary the effective tube length and increase the range of notes; the TROMBONE has a slide mechanism for the same purpose.

WINDLASS, simple WINCH once widely used to draw water from wells. A load-bearing rope passes around a small-diameter drum which is turned by a hand-operated crank. A ship's capstan uses the same principle.

WINDMILL, machine that performs WORK by harnessing wind power. In the traditional windmill, the power applied to a horizontal shaft by four large radiating sails was transmitted to milling or pumping machinery housed in a sizable supporting structure. The windmill's modern cousin is the wind turbine, often seen in remote rural areas. Here a multibladed turbine wheel mounted on a steel derrick or mast and pointed into the wind by a "fantail" drives a pump or electric generator.

WINDPIPE, common name for the TRACHEA.

WIND RIVER RANGE, section of the Rocky Mts running 120mi SE through W central Wyo. It includes Gannett Peak (13 785ft). South Pass (7 550ft) carried the OREGON TRAIL over the Rockies.

WINDSOR, city in SE Ontario, Canada, on the Detroit R opposite Detroit. A port and transportation center, it produces automobiles, chemicals, machine tools and beer Pop 203 300.

WINDSOR, oldest town in Conn., N of Hartford on the Connecticut R. It is residential with some industry, including machinery and machine parts. Pop 22 502.

WINDSOR, Duke of. See EDWARD VIII (king of England.)

WINDSOR, House of, name of the ruling dynasty of the United Kingdom of Great Britain and Northern Ireland, adopted by King GEORGE V in 1917 to replace Saxe-Coburg-Gotha (from Albert, Queen VICTORIA's husband) when anti-German feeling was high.

WINDSOR CASTLE, principal residence of British sovereigns since the 11th century. Begun by WILLIAM I, it stands about 20mi W of London. The Round Tower, built in 1180, is the castle's center, and St. George's Chapel (1528) is a fine example of English Perpendicular architecture.

WINDSOR LOCKS, town in N Conn., on the Connecticut R. Aircraft components and paper are manufactured. Pop 15 080.

WIND TUNNEL, tunnel in which a controlled stream of air is produced in order to observe the effect on scale models or full-size components of airplanes, missiles, automobiles or such structures as bridges and skyscrapers. An important research tool in AERODYNAMICS, the wind tunnel enables a design to be accurately tested without the risks attached to full-scale trials. "Hypersonic" wind tunnels, operating on an impulse principle, can simulate the frictional effects of flight at over five times the speed of sound.

WINDWARD ISLANDS, group of islands in the Lesser Antilles, WEST INDIES, stretching toward Venezuela. They include Dominica, St. Lucia, St. Vincent and Grenada (see WEST INDIES ASSOCIATED STATES), the Grenadines and Martinique. The area is about 950sq mi and the people mainly Negro, producing bananas, cacao, limes, nutmeg and cotton. The tourist industry is growing.

WINDWARD PASSAGE, channel between the E end of Cuba and the NW tip of Hispaniola (Haiti). It links the Caribbean Sea with the Atlantic.

WINE, an ALCOHOLIC BEVERAGE made from fermented grape juice; wines made from other fruits are always named accordingly. **Table wines** are red, rosé or "white" in color; red wines are made from dark grapes, the skins being left in the fermenting mixture; white wines may be made from dark or pale grapes, the skins being removed. The grapes—normally varieties of *Vitis vinifera*—are allowed to ripen until they attain suitable sugar content—18% or more—and acidity (in cool years or northern areas sugar may have to be added). After crushing, they undergo FERMENTATION in large tanks, a small amount of sulfur dioxide being added to inhibit growth of wild yeasts and bacteria; the wine yeast used, *Saccharomyces*